W9-CBL-347

The New Encyclopædia Britannica

Volume 24

MACROPÆDIA

Knowledge in Depth

FOUNDED 1768
15 TH EDITION

Encyclopædia Britannica, Inc.
Robert P. Gwinn, Chairman, Board of Directors
Peter B. Norton, President
Philip W. Goetz, Editor in Chief

Chicago
Auckland/Geneva/London/Madrid/Manila/Paris
Rome/Seoul/Sydney/Tokyo/Toronto

THE UNIVERSITY OF CHICAGO

"Let knowledge grow from more to more
and thus be human life enriched."

The *Encyclopædia Britannica* is published with the editorial advice of the faculties of the University of Chicago.

Additional advice is given by committees of members drawn from the faculties of the Australian National University, the universities of British Columbia (Can.), Cambridge (Eng.), Copenhagen (Den.), Edinburgh (Scot.), Florence (Italy), Leiden (Neth.), London (Eng.), Marburg (Ger.), Montreal (Can.), Oxford (Eng.), the Ruhr (Ger.), Sussex (Eng.), Toronto (Can.), Victoria (Can.), and Waterloo (Can.); the Complutensian University of Madrid (Spain); the Max Planck Institute for Biophysical Chemistry (Ger.); the New University of Lisbon (Port.); the School of Higher Studies in Social Sciences (Fr.); Simon Fraser University (Can.); and York University (Can.).

First Edition	1768–1771
Second Edition	1777–1784
Third Edition	1788–1797
Supplement	1801
Fourth Edition	1801–1809
Fifth Edition	1815
Sixth Edition	1820–1823
Supplement	1815–1824
Seventh Edition	1830–1842
Eighth Edition	1852–1860
Ninth Edition	1875–1889
Tenth Edition	1902–1903

Printed in U.S.A.

Library of Congress Catalog Card Number: 89-81675
International Standard Book Number: 0-85229-529-4

CONTENTS

Metaphysics

Metaphysics is the philosophical study whose object is to determine the real nature of things—to determine the meaning, structure, and principles of whatever is insofar as it is. Although this study is popularly conceived as referring to anything excessively subtle and highly theoretical and although it has been subjected to many criticisms, it is presented by metaphysicians as the most fundamental and most comprehensive of inquiries, inasmuch as it is concerned with reality as a whole.

This article is divided into the following sections:

Nature and scope of metaphysics

ORIGIN OF THE TERM

Etymologically the term *metaphysics* is unenlightening. It means "what comes after physics"; it was the phrase used by early students of Aristotle to refer to the contents of Aristotle's treatise on what he himself called "first philosophy," and was used as the title of this treatise by Andronicus of Rhodes, one of the first of Aristotle's editors. Aristotle had distinguished two tasks for the philosopher: first, to investigate the nature and properties of what exists in the natural, or sensible, world, and second, to explore the characteristics of "Being as such" and to inquire into the character of "the substance that is free from movement," or the most real of all things, the intelligible reality on which everything in the world of nature was thought to be causally dependent. The first constituted "second philosophy" and was carried out primarily in the Aristotelian treatise now known as the *Physica;* the second, which Aristotle had also referred to as "theology" (because God was the unmoved mover in his system), is roughly the subject matter of his *Metaphysica.* Modern readers of Aristotle are inclined to take both the *Physica* and the *Metaphysica* as philosophical treatises; the distinction their titles suggest between an empirical and a conceptual inquiry has little foundation. Aristotle was not indifferent to factual material either in natural or in metaphysical philosophy, but equally he was not concerned in either case to frame theories for empirical testing. It seems clear, nevertheless, that if the two works had to be distinguished, the *Physica* would have to be described as the more empirical, just because it deals with things that are objects of the senses, what Aristotle himself called "sensible substance"; the subject matter of the *Metaphysica,* "that which is eternal, free of movement, and separately existent," is on any account more remote. It is also evident that the connection marked in the original titles is a genuine one: the inquiries about nature carried out in the *Physica* lead on naturally to the more fundamental inquiries about Being as such that are taken up in the *Metaphysica* and indeed go along with the latter to make up a single philosophical discipline.

The background to Aristotle's divisions is to be found in the thought of Plato, with whom Aristotle had many disagreements but whose basic ideas provided a framework within which much of his own thinking was conducted. Plato, following the early Greek philosopher Parmenides, who is known as the father of metaphysics, had sought to distinguish opinion, or belief, from knowledge and to assign distinct objects to each. Opinion, for Plato, was a form of apprehension that was shifting and unclear, similar to seeing things in a dream or only through their shadows; its objects were correspondingly unstable. Knowledge, by contrast, was wholly lucid; it carried its own guarantee against error, and the objects with which it was concerned were eternally what they were, and so were exempt from change and the deceptive power to appear to be what they were not. Plato called the objects of opinion phenomena, or appearances; he referred to the objects of knowledge as noumena (objects of the intelligence) or quite simply as realities. Much of the burden of his philosophical message was to call men's attentions to these contrasts and to impress them with the necessity to turn away from concern with mere phenomena to the investigation of true reality. The education of the Platonic philosopher consisted precisely in effecting this transition: he was taught to recognize the contradictions involved in appearances and to fix his gaze on the realities that lay behind them, the realities that Plato himself called Forms, or Ideas. Philosophy for Plato was thus a call to recognize the existence and overwhelming importance of a set of higher realities that ordinary men—even those, like the Sophists of the time, who professed to be enlightened—entirely ignored. That there were such realities, or at least that there was a serious case for thinking that there were, was a fundamental tenet in the discipline that later became known as metaphysics. Conversely, much of the subsequent controversy about the very possibility of metaphysics has turned on the acceptability of this tenet and on whether, if it is rejected, some alternative foundation can be discovered on which the metaphysician can stand.

Appearances and realities for Plato

CHARACTERIZATIONS OF METAPHYSICS

Before considering any such question, however, it is necessary to examine, without particular historical references, some ways in which actual metaphysicians have attempted to characterize their enterprise, noticing in each case the problems they have in drawing a clear line between their aims and those of the practitioners of the exact and empirical sciences. Four views will be briefly considered; they present metaphysics as: (1) an inquiry into what exists, or what really exists; (2) the science of reality, as opposed to appearance; (3) the study of the world as a whole; (4) a theory of first principles. Reflection on what is said under the different heads will quickly establish that they are not sharply separate from one another, and, indeed, individual metaphysical writers sometimes invoke more than one of these phrases when asked to say what metaphysics is—as, for example, the British Idealist F.H. Bradley does in the opening pages of his work *Appearance and Reality* (1893).

An inquiry into what exists. A common set of claims on behalf of metaphysics is that it is an inquiry into what exists; its business is to subject common opinion on this matter to critical scrutiny and in so doing to determine what is truly real.

Unreliability of common opinion

It can be asserted with some confidence that common opinion is certainly an unreliable guide about what exists, if indeed it can be induced to pronounce on this matter at all. Are dream objects real, in the way in which palpable realities such as chairs and trees are? Are numbers real, or should they be described as no more than abstractions? Is the height of a man a reality in the same sense in which he is a reality, or is it just an aspect of something more concrete, a mere quality that has derivative rather than substantial being and could not exist except as attributed to something else? It is easy enough to confuse the common man with questions like these and to show that any answers he gives to them tend to be ill thought-out. It is equally difficult, however, for the metaphysician to come up with more satisfactory answers of his own. Many metaphysicians have relied, in this connection, on the internally related notions of substance, quality, and relation; they have argued that only what is substantial truly exists, although every substance has qualities and stands in relation to other substances. Thus, this tree is tall and deciduous and is precisely 50 yards north of that fence. Difficulties begin, however, as soon as examples like these are taken seriously. Assume for the moment that an individual tree—what might be called a concrete existent—qualifies for the title of substance; it is just the sort of thing that has qualities and stands in relations. Unless there were substances in this sense, no qualities could be real: the tallness of the tree would not exist unless the tree existed. The question can now be raised what the tree would be if it were deprived of all its qualities and stood in no relations. The notion of a substance in this type of metaphysics is that of a thing that exists by itself, apart from any attributes it may happen to possess; the difficulty with this notion is to know how to apply it. Any concrete thing one selects to exemplify the notion of substance turns out in practice to answer a certain description; this means in effect that it cannot be spoken of apart from its attributes. It thus emerges that substances are no more primary beings than are qualities and relations; without the former one could not have the latter, but equally without the latter one could not have the former.

There are other difficulties about substance that cannot be explored here—*e.g.,* whether a fence is a substance or simply wood and metal shaped in a certain way. Enough has already been said, however, to indicate the problems involved in defining the tasks of metaphysics along these lines. There is, nevertheless, an alternative way of understanding the notion of substance: not as that which is the ultimate subject of predicates but as what persists through change. The question "What is ultimately real?" is, thus, a question about the ultimate stuff of which the universe is made up. Although this second conception of substance is both clearer and more readily applicable than its predecessor, the difficulty about it from the metaphysician's point of view is that it sets him in direct rivalry with the scientist. When the early Greek philosopher Thales inquired as to what is ultimately real and came up with the surprising news that all is water, he might be taken as advancing a scientific rather than a philosophical hypothesis. Although it is true that later writers, such as Gottfried Wilhelm Leibniz, a German Rationalist philosopher and mathematician, were fully aware of the force of scientific claims in this area and, nevertheless, rejected them as metaphysically unacceptable, the fact remains that the nonphilosopher finds it difficult to understand the basis on which a Leibniz rests his case. When Leibniz said that it is monads (*i.e.,* elementary, unextended, indivisible, spiritual substances that enter into composites) that are the true atoms of nature and not, for example, material particles, the objection can be raised as to what right he has to advance this opinion. Has he done any scientific work to justify him in setting scientific results aside with such confidence? And if he has not, why should he be taken seriously at all?

The ultimate stuff of the universe

The science of ultimate reality. To answer these questions, another description of metaphysics has been proposed: that it is the science that seeks to define what is ultimately real as opposed to what is merely apparent.

The contrast between appearance and reality, however, is by no means peculiar to metaphysics. In everyday life people distinguish between the real size of the Sun and its apparent size, or again between the real colour of an object (when seen in standard conditions) and its apparent colour (nonstandard conditions). A cloud appears to consist of some white, fleecy substance, although in reality it is a concentration of drops of water. In general, men are often (though not invariably) inclined to allow that the scientist knows the real constitution of things as opposed to the surface aspects with which ordinary men are familiar. It will not suffice to define metaphysics as knowledge of reality as opposed to appearance; scientists, too, claim to know reality as opposed to appearance, and there is a general tendency to concede their claim.

Components in the metaphysical conception of reality

It seems that there are at least three components in the metaphysical conception of reality. One characteristic, which has already been illustrated by Plato, is that reality is genuine as opposed to deceptive. The ultimate realities that the metaphysician seeks to know are precisely things as they are—simple and not variegated, exempt from change and therefore stable objects of knowledge. Plato's own assumption of this position perhaps reflects certain confusions about the knowability of things that change; one should not, however, on that ground exclude this aspect of the concept of reality from metaphysical thought in general. Ultimate reality, whatever else it is, is genuine as opposed to sham. Second, reality is original in contrast to derivative, self-dependent rather than dependent on the existence of something else. When Aristotle sought to inquire into the most real of all things, or when medieval philosophers attempted to establish the characteristics of what they called the *ens realissimum* ("the most real being"), or the original and perfect being, they were looking for something that, in contrast to the everyday things of this world, was truly self-contained and could accordingly be looked upon as self-caused. Likewise, the 17th-century Rationalists defined substance as that which can be explained through itself alone. Writers like René Descartes and Benedict de Spinoza were convinced that it was the task of the metaphysician to seek for and characterize substance understood in this sense; the more mundane substances with which physical scientists were concerned were, in their opinion, only marginally relevant in this inquiry. Third, and perhaps most important, reality for the metaphysician is intelligible as opposed to opaque. Appearances are not only deceptive and derivative, they also make no sense when taken at their own level. To arrive at what is ultimately real is to produce an account of the facts that does them full justice. The assumption is, of course, that one cannot explain things satisfactorily if one remains within the world of common sense, or even if one advances from that world to embrace the concepts of science. One or the other of these levels of explanation may suffice to produce a sort of local sense that is enough for practical purposes or that forms an adequate basis on which to make predictions. Practical reliability of this kind, however, is very different from theoretical satisfaction; the task of the metaphysician is to challenge all assumptions and finally arrive at an account of the nature of things that is fully coherent and fully thought-out.

The task of the metaphysician

It should be obvious that, to establish his right to pronounce on what is ultimately real in the sense analyzed, the metaphysician has a tremendous amount to do. He must begin by giving colour to his claim that everyday ways of thinking will not suffice for a full and coherent description of what falls within experience, thus arguing that appearances are unreal—although not therefore nonexistent—because they are unstable and unintelligible. This involves a challenge to the final acceptability of such well-worn ideas as time and space, thing and attribute, change and process—a challenge that metaphysicians have not hesitated to make, even though it has been treated with skepticism both by ordinary men and by some of their fellow philosophers (*e.g.,* G.E. Moore, a 20th-century British thinker who has greatly influenced modern Analytic philosophy). Second, granted that there are contradictions or incoherences in the thought of common sense, the metaphysician must go on to maintain that they cannot be resolved by deserting common sense for science. He will not deny that the concepts of science are in many respects different from those of everyday thought; to take one aspect only, they are altogether more precise and sharply defined. They permit the scientist to introduce into his descriptions a theoretical content that is lacking at the everyday level and in so doing to unify and render intelligible aspects of the world that seem opaque when considered singly. The metaphysician will argue, however, that this desirable result is purchased at a certain price: by ignoring certain appearances altogether. The scientist, in this way of thinking, does not offer a truer description of the phenomena of which ordinary thought could make no sense but merely gives a connected description of a selected set of phenomena. The world of the scientist, restricted as it is to what can be dealt with in quantitative terms, is a poor thing in comparison with the rich if untidy world of everyday life. Alternatively, the metaphysician must try to show that scientific concepts are like the concepts of common sense in being ultimately incoherent. The premises or presuppositions that the scientist accepts contain unclarities that cannot be resolved, although they are not so serious as to prevent his achieving results that are practically dependable. Many ingenious arguments on these lines have been produced by philosophers, by no means all of whom could be said to be incapable of a true understanding of the theories they were criticizing. (Leibniz, for example, was a physicist of distinction as well as a mathematician of genius; G.W.F. Hegel, a 19th-century German Idealist, had an unusual knowledge of contemporary scientific work; and Alfred North Whitehead, a pioneer of 20th-century metaphysics in the Anglo-Saxon world, was a professor of applied mathematics, and his system developed from physics and contained a wealth of biological ideas.) The fact remains, nevertheless, that few if any practicing scientists have been seriously troubled by such arguments.

Even if the metaphysician were thus able to make good the negative side of his case, he would still face the formidable difficulty of establishing that there is something answering to his conception of what is ultimately real and of identifying it. The notion of an original being, totally self-contained and totally self-intelligible, may not itself be coherent, as the 18th-century British philosopher David Hume and others have argued; alternatively, there may be special difficulties in saying to what it applies. The fact that different metaphysicians have given widely different accounts of what is ultimately real is certainly suspicious. Some have wanted to say that there is a plurality of ultimately real things, others that there is only one; some have argued that what is truly real must be utterly transcendent of the things of this world and occupy a supersensible realm accessible only to the pure intellect, while others have thought of ultimate reality as immanent in experience (the Hegelian Absolute, for example, is not a special sort of existent, but the world as a whole understood in a certain way). That metaphysical inquiry should issue in definitive doctrine, as so many of those who engaged in it said that it would, is in these circumstances altogether too much to hope for.

The science of the world as a whole. Another way in which metaphysicians have sought to define their discipline is by saying that it has to do with the world as a whole.

The implications of this phrase are not immediately obvious. Clearly, a contrast is intended in the first place with the various departmental sciences, each of which selects a portion or aspect of reality for study and confines itself to that. No geologist or mathematician would claim that his study is absolutely comprehensive; each would concede that there are many aspects of the world that he leaves out, even though he covers everything that is relevant to his special point of view. By contrast, it might be supposed that the metaphysician is merely to coordinate the results of the special sciences. There is clearly a need for the coordination of scientific results because scientific research has become increasingly specialized and departmentalized; individual scientific workers need to be made aware of what is going on in other fields, sometimes because these fields impinge on their own, sometimes because results obtained there have wider implications of which they need to take account. One can scarcely see metaphysicians, however, or indeed philosophers generally, performing this function of intellectual contact man in a satisfactory fashion. It might then be supposed that their concern with the world as a whole is to be interpreted as a summing up and synthesizing of the results of the particular sciences. Plato spoke of the philosopher as taking a synoptic view, and there is often talk about the need to see things in the round and avoid the narrowness of the average specialist, who, it is said, knows more and more about less and less. If, however, it is a question of looking at scientific results from a wider point of view and so of producing what might be called a scientific picture of the world, the person best qualified for the job is not any philosopher but rather a scientist of large mind and wide interests. Metaphysics cannot be satisfactorily understood as an account of the world as a whole if that description suggests that the metaphysician is a sort of superscientist, unlimited in his curiosity and gifted with a capacity for putting together other people's findings with a skill and imagination that none of them individually commands. Only a scientist could hope to become such a superscientist.

Metaphysics as a unified account of the world

More hope for the metaphysician can be found, perhaps, along the following lines. People want to know not only what the scientist makes of the world but also what significance to assign to his account. People experience the world at different levels and in different capacities: they are not only investigators but also agents; they have a moral and a legal, an aesthetic and a religious life in addition to their scientific life. Man is a many-sided being; he needs to understand the universe in the light of his different activities and experiences. There are philosophers who appear to find no problem here; they argue that there can be no possibility of, say, a moral or a religious vision of the world that rivals the scientific vision. In this view, morals and religion are matters of practice, not of theory; they do not rival science but only complement it. This neutralist attitude, however, finds little general favour; for most thinking people find it necessary to choose whether to go all the way with science, at the cost of abandoning religion and even morals, or to stick to a religious or moral world outlook even if it means treating scientific claims with some reserve. The practice of the moral life is often believed to proceed on assumptions that can hardly be accepted if science is taken to have the last word about what is true. Accordingly, it becomes necessary to produce some rational assessment of the truth claims of the different forms of experience, to try to think out a scheme in which justice is done to them all. Many familiar systems of metaphysics profess to do just that; among others there are Materialism, which favours the claims of science; Idealism, which sees deeper truth in religion and the moral life; and the peculiar dualism of the 18th-century German philosopher Immanuel Kant, which holds that science gives the truth about phenomena, while reserving a noumenal, or supersensible, sphere for moral agency.

This conception of metaphysics as offering an account of the world or, as is more often said, of experience as a whole, accords more obviously with the position of those who see ultimate reality as immanent, or inherent in what is immediately known, than of those who take it to be transcendent, or beyond the limits of ordinary experience. It is possible, in fact, to subscribe to the legitimacy of metaphysics as so understood without postulating the existence of any special entities known only to the metaphysician—a claim that plain men have often taken to connect metaphysics with the occult. This is not to say, of course, that metaphysical problems admit of easy solutions when understood along these lines. There is a variety of widely different ways of taking the world as a whole: depending on which aspect or aspects of experience the individual metaphysician finds especially significant; each claims to be comprehensive and to confute the claims of its rivals, yet none has succeeded in establishing itself as the obviously correct account. Even systems that are widely condemned as impossible, such as Materialism, turn out in practice to command constantly renewed support as new discoveries in the sciences suggest new ways of dealing with old difficulties. A cynic might take such facts as meaning that people subscribe to theories of this sort more as a matter of emotional than of rational conviction; metaphysics, as Bradley remarked with surprising frankness, consists in the finding of bad reasons for what one believes upon instinct.

The science of first principles. Another phrase used by Bradley in his preliminary discussion of metaphysics is "the study of first principles," or ultimate, irrefutable truths.

First principles as basic truths

Metaphysics could be said to provide a theory of first principles if it furnished men with a set of concepts in the light of which they could arrive at the connected account of experience as a whole just spoken of, and the two descriptions of the subject would thus be two sides of a single coin. The idea that metaphysics has to do with first principles, however, has wider implications.

The term "first principles" is a translation of the Greek word *archai.* An arche is something from which an argument proceeds—it can be either a primary premise or an ultimate presupposition. Plato, in a famous passage in *Politeia* (*The Republic*), contrasted two different attitudes to archai: namely that of the mathematician, who lays down or hypothesizes certain things as being true and then proceeds to deduce their consequences without further examining their validity; and that of the dialectician, who proceeds backward, not forward, from his primary premises and then seeks to ground them in an arche that is not hypothesized at all. Unfortunately, no concrete details exist of the way in which Plato himself thought this program could be carried out; instead he spoke of it only in the most general terms. The suggestion, nevertheless, that metaphysics is superior to any other intellectual discipline in having a fully critical attitude toward its first principles is one that still continues to be made, and it needs some examination.

As regards mathematics, for example, it might be said that mathematicians could be uncritical about the first principles of their science in the following ways: (1) They might take as self-evidently true or universally applicable some axiom or primary premise that turned out later not to possess this property. (2) They might assume among their first principles certain propositions about existence—to the effect that only certain kinds of things could be proper objects of mathematical inquiry (rational as opposed to irrational numbers, for example)—and time might indeed reveal that the assumption was inappropriate. The remedy for both sorts of error, however, is to be found within the realm of mathematics itself; the development of the discipline has consisted precisely in eliminating mistakes of this kind. It is not clear even that the discovery and removal of antinomies in the foundations of mathematics is work for the metaphysician, although philosophically minded persons like Gottlob Frege, a German mathematician and logician, and Bertrand Russell, perhaps the best known English philosopher of the 20th century, have been much concerned with them. The situation is not fundamentally different when the empirical sciences are considered. Admittedly, the exponents of these sciences give more hostages to fortune insofar as they have to assume from the first the general correctness of the results of other disciplines; there can be no question of their checking on these for themselves. Mathematicians, too, begin by assuming the validity of common argument forms without making any serious attempt to validate them, and there is nothing seriously wrong with their proceeding in this manner. If confidence in bad logic has sometimes been responsible for holding up mathematical advance, bolder mathematicians have always known in practice that the right thing to do is to let the argument take them wherever it will on strictly mathematical lines, leaving it to logicians to recognize the fact and adjust their theory at their convenience.

It thus seems that the assertion that a special science like mathematics is uncritical about its archai is false; there is a sense in which mathematicians are constantly strengthening their basic premises. As regards the corresponding claim about metaphysics, it has at one time or another been widely believed (1) that it is the business of metaphysics to justify the ultimate assumptions of the sciences, and (2) that in metaphysics alone there are no unjustified assumptions. Concerning (1), the question that needs to be asked is how the justification is supposed to take place. It has been argued that the metaphysician might, on one interpretation of his function, be said to offer some defense of science generally by placing it in relation to other forms of experience. To do this, however, is not to justify any particular scientific assumptions. In point of fact, particular scientific assumptions get their justification, if anywhere, when a move is made from a narrower to a more comprehensive science; what is assumed in geology, for example, may be proved in physics. But this, of course, has nothing to do with metaphysics. The difficulty with (2) is that of knowing how any intellectual activity, however carefully conducted, could be free of basic assumptions. Some metaphysicians (such as Bradley and his Scottish predecessor J.F. Ferrier) have claimed that there is a difference between their discipline and others insofar as metaphysical propositions alone are self-reinstating. For example, the Cartesian proposition *cogito, ergo sum* ("I think, therefore I am") is self-reinstating: deny that you think, and in so doing you think; deny that you exist, and the very fact gives proof of your existence. Even if it could be made out that propositions of this kind are peculiar to metaphysics, however, it would not follow that everything in metaphysics has this character. The truth is, rather, that no paradox is involved in denying most fundamental metaphysical claims, such as the assertion of the Materialist that there is nothing that cannot be satisfactorily explained in material terms or the corresponding principle of Aristotle that there is nothing that does not serve some purpose.

Metaphysicians as self-critical

The view that metaphysics, or indeed philosophy generally, is uniquely self-critical is among the myths of modern thought. Philosophers rely on the results of other disciplines just as other people do; they do not pause to demonstrate the legitimacy of the principles of simple arithmetic before entering on calculations in the course of their work, nor do they refrain from employing the reductio ad absurdum type of refutation (*i.e.,* showing an absurdity to which a proposition leads when carried to its logical conclusion) until they have assured themselves that this is a valid way of confuting an opponent. Even in their own field they tend, like painters, to work within traditions set by great masters rather than to think everything out from scratch for themselves. That philosophy in practice is not the fully self-critical activity its exponents claim it to be is shown nowhere more clearly than in the reception that philosophers give to theories that are unfashionable; they more often subject them to conventional abuse than to patient critical examination. It is, nevertheless, from the conviction that philosophy, and especially metaphysical philosophy, operates without unjustified assumptions that current claims about the superiority of this branch of thinking derive their force. This conviction connects with the views already mentioned, that metaphysics is the science of first principles and that the principles in question are ineluctable in the sense that they are operative in their own denial.

METAPHYSICS AND OTHER BRANCHES OF PHILOSOPHY

It may be useful at this point to consider the relations of metaphysics to other parts of philosophy. A strong tradition, derided by Kant, asserted that metaphysics was the queen of the sciences, including the philosophical sciences. The idea presumably was that those who worked within fields such as logic and ethics, as well as physicists and biologists, proceeded on assumptions that in the last resort had to be approved or corrected by the metaphysician. Logic could be conceived as a special study complete in itself only if the logician were allowed to postulate a correspondence between the neat and tidy world of propositions, which was the immediate object

The view of metaphysics as the queen of the sciences

of his study, and the world existing in fact; metaphysics might and sometimes did challenge the propriety of this postulate. Similarly, ethics, like law, could get nowhere without the assumption that the individual agent is a self-contained unit answerable in general terms for what he does; metaphysics had the duty of subjecting this assumption to critical examination. As a result of such claims it was widely believed that any results obtained by logicians or ethicists must at best be treated as provisional; followers of Hegel, who advanced these claims with passionate conviction, were inclined in consequence to regard logic and ethics alike as minor branches of philosophy. It has been a feature of 20th-century philosophical thought, especially in Britain and the United States, to dispute these Hegelian contentions and argue for the autonomy of ethics and logic; that is, for their independence of metaphysics. Thus, formal logicians of the school of Frege and Russell were apt to claim that the principles of logic applied unequivocally to all thinking whatsoever; there could be no question of their having to await confirmation, still less correction, from the metaphysician. If metaphysical arguments suggested that fundamental laws of logic such as the principle of noncontradiction—that a statement and its contradictory cannot both be true—might not be in order, the only conclusion to draw was that such arguments must be confused: without observation of the laws of logic there could be no coherent thinking of any sort.

Similarly, G.E. Moore, in a celebrated section of his *Principia Ethica* (1903), tried to show that statements like "This is good" are *sui generis* and cannot be reduced to statements of either natural or metaphysical fact; the Idealist belief that ethics ultimately depends on metaphysics rested on a delusion. Moore perhaps failed to see the force of the Idealist challenge to the individualist assumptions on which much ethical thinking proceeds, and he did not note that, in one respect at least, ethical results can be dependent on those of metaphysics: if metaphysics shows that the world is other than it is initially taken to be, conclusions about what to do must be altered accordingly. Again, the reaction among logicians to Hegelian attempts to merge logic into metaphysics certainly went too far. There is a genuine philosophical problem about the relation between the world of logic and the world of fact, and it cannot be solved by simply repeating that logic is an autonomous discipline whose principles deserve respect in themselves. None of this, however, shows that metaphysics is the fundamental philosophical discipline, the branch of philosophy that has the last word about what goes on in all other parts of the subject.

METAPHYSICS AND ANALYSIS

Modern British and American philosophers commonly describe themselves as engaged in philosophical analysis, as opposed to metaphysics. The interests of a metaphysician, according to this view, are predominantly speculative; he wants to reveal hitherto unknown facts about the world and on that basis to construct a theory about the world as a whole. In so doing he is necessarily engaged in activities that rival those of the scientist, with the important difference that scientific theories can be brought to the test of experience, whereas metaphysical theories cannot. Eschewing this conception of philosophy as impossible, the critic of metaphysics believes that philosophy should confine itself to the analysis of concepts, which is a strictly second-order activity independent of science and which need involve no metaphysical commitment.

Analysis in philosophy

The notion of analysis in philosophy is far from clear. Analysis on any account is meant to result in clarification, but it is not evident how this result is to be achieved. For some, analysis involves the substitution for the concept under examination of some other concept that is recognizably like it (as Gilbert Ryle, an English Analyst, elucidated the concept of mind by replacing it with the notion of "a person behaving"); for others, analysis involves the substitution of synonym for synonym. If the latter understanding of analysis is required, as in Moore's classic example of the analysis of brother as male sibling, not much enlightenment is likely to ensue. If, however, the philosopher is permitted to engage in what is sometimes pejoratively described as "reductive analysis," he will produce interest at the cost of reintroducing speculation. Ryle's *Concept of Mind* (1949) is a challenging book just because it advances a thesis of real metaphysical importance—that one can say everything one needs to say about minds without postulating mental substance.

A further aspect of the situation that deserves mention is this. If it is the case, as is often claimed, that analysis can be practiced properly only when the analyst has no metaphysical presuppositions, by what means does he select concepts for analysis? Would it not be appropriate for him, in these circumstances, to take any concept of reasonable generality as a suitable subject on which to practice his art? It turns out, in fact, however, that the range of concepts commonly recognized as philosophical is more limited than that, and that those concepts to which Analytic philosophers give their attention are chosen because of their wider philosophical bearings. Thus, recent philosophers have paid particular attention to the concept of knowledge not just because it is a notion whose analysis has long proved difficult but also because on one account at least it involves an immediately experienced mental act—something that many Analysts would like to proscribe as mythical. Similarly, the celebrated analysis of the idea of causality put forward by David Hume was not undertaken out of idle curiosity but with a wider purpose in mind: to undermine both the Aristotelian and the Cartesian views of the world and to substitute for them an atomism of immediate appearances in which all objects were "loose and separate"—that is, logically independent one of another. The insight into the constitution of nature promised in different ways by Aristotle and Descartes was an illusion, the truth being that scientific advance serves only to "stave off our ignorance a little." What Hume said about causation connects internally with his views about what exists. Despite his polemic against books of "divinity and school metaphysics," he had a metaphysics of his own to recommend.

Historical use of analysis by metaphysicians

The truth is that metaphysics and analysis are not separate in the way modern Analytic philosophers pretend. The speculative philosophers of the past were certainly not averse to analysis: witness the splendid discussion of the concept of knowledge in Plato's *Theaetetus,* or, for a more recent example, Bradley's account of the meanings of "self." The legend that a metaphysical philosopher has his eye so firmly set on higher things that he is entirely careless of the conceptual structure he seeks to recommend is absolutely without foundation. A metaphysical philosopher is a philosopher after all: argument and the passion for clarification are in his blood. Although some contemporary philosophers profess to undertake analysis entirely for its own sake and without explicit metaphysical motivation, it may be doubted if their claim is capable of being sustained. The "logical analysis" practiced by Russell in the early part of the 20th century was not metaphysically neutral, nor was the analysis of the Logical Positivists, who recommended a strongly scientific view of the world. Some current analytic work is motivated less by the desire to forward an overall theory than by a wish to destroy a prevailing or previously held theory that is considered objectionable. To seek to overthrow a metaphysical theory, however, is itself to engage in metaphysics—not very interesting metaphysics, perhaps, but metaphysics all the same.

It may be added, as a historical note, that the Rationalist philosophers of the 17th and 18th centuries, who emphasized the predominant role of reason in the construction of a system of knowledge, believed that the philosopher's task fell into two parts. He must first break down complex concepts into their simple parts; this was a matter of analysis. Then he must proceed to show how knowledge of these simples would serve to explain the detailed constitution of things; this would involve synthesis. That there are deep obscurities in this program—*e.g.,* whether it is a matter of analyzing concepts or getting down to the simplest elements of things—is less important in the present context than that analysis and synthesis were thus taken to be complementary. The classical statement of this point of view is to be found in Descartes's *Discours de la méthode* (1637; *Discourse on Method*), with the corresponding passages in the *Regulae ad Directionem Ingenii* (published posthumously 1701; *Rules for the Direction of the Mind*). That the idea persisted well into the 18th century is evidenced by the remarks made by Kant in his essay *Untersuchung über die Deutlichkeit der Grundsätze der natürlichen Theologie und der Moral* (1764; *Inquiry into the Distinctness of the Principles of Natural Theology and Morals*), in which he said that metaphysics was not yet in a position to pass beyond the stage of analysis to that of synthesis. He did not mean that for the time being philosophy must remain entirely nonmetaphysical, in the way some moderns suppose it can, but rather that it needs to go on elaborating a conceptual scheme, which, however, cannot be used constructively until it is complete. Actually, Kant belied his own professions at the time insofar as he thought himself in possession of a definitive proof of God's existence, which he explained in his essay *Der einzig mögliche Beweisgrund zu einer Demonstration des Daseyns Gottes* (1763; "The Only Possible Ground for a Demonstration of the Existence of God"). This, however, only illustrates the not very surprising fact that philosophers are often less clear about the nature of their own activities than they think.

Problems in metaphysics

To give a comprehensive account of the main problems of metaphysics in the space of a few pages is clearly quite impossible. What follows is necessarily highly selective and to that extent misleading; it, nevertheless, attempts to offer an introduction to metaphysical thinking itself rather than reflection on the nature of metaphysics.

THE EXISTENCE OF FORMS, CATEGORIES, AND PARTICULARS

Forms. The early Greek philosophers asked the question *ti to on*, "What is existent?" or "What is really there?" They originally interpreted this as a question about the stuff out of which things were ultimately made, but a new twist was given to the inquiry when Pythagoras, in the late 6th century BC, arrived at the answer that what was really there was number. Pythagoras conceived what is there in terms not of matter but of intelligible structure; it was the latter that gave each type of thing its distinctive character and made it what it was. The idea that structure could be understood in numerical terms was probably suggested to Pythagoras by his discovery that there are exact correlations between the lengths of the strings of a lyre and the notes they produce. By a bold extrapolation he seems to have surmised that what held in this case must hold in all cases.

Platonic theory

The Pythagorean theory that what is really there is number is the direct ancestor of the Platonic theory that what is really there is Forms, or Ideas (*eidē*, or *ideai*). Plato's Forms were also intelligible structures and not material elements, but they differed from Pythagorean numbers by being conceived of as separately existent. There was, as Plato put it, a "place accessible to the intelligence," which was the place, or realm, of Forms. Each Form was a genuine existent, in the sense of being precisely what it pretended to be; the Form of Beauty, for example, was beautiful through and through. By contrast, the many particular things that partook of or resembled what was truly beautiful were one and all defective. However beautiful any one of them might be, it was also in another respect lacking in beauty. It turned out to possess contradictory characteristics, and as such could never be identified with true reality.

Plato had taken over from his predecessor Heracleitus, who flourished at about the beginning of the 5th century BC, the doctrine that the world of sensible things is a world of things in constant flux; as he put it in the *Theaetetus*, nothing *is* in this world because everything is in a state of becoming something else. Forms were needed to provide stable objects for knowledge as well as to answer the question of what is ultimately real. Although Plato played down the reality of sensible things, making them mere objects of opinion and describing them as falling between what is and what is not, he did not deny their existence. It was not his thesis that Forms alone exist. On the contrary, he appears to have held that God (who was certainly not a Form) had somehow fashioned the physical world on the model of the Forms, using space as his material. This is the description that is given in the *Timaeus*, in a passage that Plato perhaps meant his readers not to take quite literally but that stated his view as plainly as he thought it could be stated. In this passage God appears in the guise of the "Demiurge," although he is referred to freely in other Platonic dialogues. Souls were also distinct from Forms in Plato's thought.

In the discussions that developed around the theory of Forms, many difficulties were revealed, most of them familiar to Plato himself. The question of how the one Form was supposed to relate to the many particulars that participated in or resembled it was nowhere satisfactorily answered. The difficulty turned on how the Form was to be thought of at once as an existent and as a structure. Plato seemed on occasion to think of it as a structure hypostatized, or given real existence. This thesis led to the antinomies exposed in the "third man" argument. According to this theory, particular men were alleged to be human because of their relationship to "Man himself"; *i.e.*, the Form of man. But whence did the latter derive its nature? Must there not be a second Form to explain what the first Form and its particulars have in common, and will not this generate an infinite regress? Again, the problem of the precise population of the world of Forms never got a definitive solution, perhaps because the theory of Forms was put to more than one purpose. Sometimes it was said that there is a Form corresponding to every general word, but elsewhere the theory was that what is merely negative (*e.g.*, lifeless) has no need of a special Form, nor does what is manufactured. There is even a question as to whether trivial everyday things such as mud and hair and dirt have Forms, though it is agreed that there is a Form of man.

The problems just referred to were stated trenchantly in Plato's dialogue the *Parmenides*; the discussion there ends with the statement that the Forms must be retained if an account of intelligible discourse is to be given, but no indication is offered as to how the theory is to be refurbished. Some Platonic scholars have inferred that Plato virtually gave it up, but such evidence as there is suggests that he only transformed it into a theory of Form-numbers, more openly Pythagorean than the earlier version. There are many references in Aristotle to this theory of Form-numbers, but no writing of Plato's own on the subject has survived, and it is virtually impossible at this late stage to say what this theory really comprised.

One further feature of the theory of Forms must be mentioned here: the view that there is a supremely important Form, the Form of goodness, or of the Good, which somehow determines the contents of the world of Forms and brings order into it. In a celebrated but brief and tantalizing passage in *Politeia*, the Form of the Good is spoken of as being to the intelligible realm what the sun is to the visible realm; just as the sun makes living things grow and renders them visible, so the Good is responsible for the existence and intelligibility of Forms, though it is itself "on the other side of Being." This passage had a tremendous historical influence on the Neoplatonists, who saw it as anticipating the ultimate ineffable reality—the One, from which everything describable was in some way an emanation—in which they came to believe. It seems possible, however, that Plato had no such mystical thoughts in mind but simply wanted to say that the world of Forms is ordered through and through, everything in it being there for a purpose. The Form of Good is, in fact, the counterpart of the nous (Mind) of Anaxagoras, another of Plato's predecessors, which was supposed to arrange everything for the best.

Aristotelian doctrine

Categories and universals. The most famous critic of Plato's theory of Forms was Aristotle, who devised his doctrine of categories largely to counter it. According to this doctrine, "being is spoken of in many ways": one can say that there are such things as individual horses, but one can also say that there is such a thing as being a horse, or as being upside down. Expressions can be classified under various heads: predicates signify substances (*e.g.,* "man" or "horse"), qualities (*e.g.,* "white"), relations (*e.g.,* "greater"), quantities (*e.g.,* "three yards long"), time (*e.g.,* "last year"), and so on—sometimes Aristotle listed ten categories, sometimes only eight. The kind of being that any predicate possesses, however, is derivative in comparison with the being of an individual substance, a particular man or a particular horse. It is such things that exist in the primary sense, and it is upon their existence that the existence of other types of being depends. Or, to put the point in not quite Aristotelian terms, primary substances are the only concrete existents; Socrates, the bearer of a proper name, exists in a way in which humanity or whiteness or being greater do not. The latter are really no more than abstractions, and nothing but confusion can arise from neglecting that fact.

Mention has already been made of the difficulties into which this doctrine led when it came to describing primary substances; it appeared that these entities could not be characterized but only named or pointed to, a conclusion accepted much later by Ludwig Wittgenstein, a 20th-century philosopher, in his *Tractatus Logico-Philosophicus* and by Russell in his lectures on logical atomism. These difficulties, however, were not seen at the time the theory was promulgated, and it is more important now to emphasize the fact that it undermined any doctrine of the Platonic type. To argue that Forms, or numbers, alone are real is to argue for the reality of abstractions; to put the point succinctly, beauty exists only so long as something is beautiful, and that something must be a concrete individual. Or if this is not quite true (for, after all, it could be said that there is such a thing as having a million sides even if nothing in fact has a million sides), concrete existence must precede abstract existence in some cases at least: the "x" in "x is red" must sometimes be replaceable by an actual rather than a merely possible entity.

The problem of universals

A prominent subject of philosophical discussion in the Middle Ages was what came to be known as the problem of universals, which concerned the ontological status, or type of existence, to be assigned to the referents of general words. One of Plato's critics had said, "I see particular horses, but not horseness"; and Plato had answered, "That is because you have eyes but no intelligence." There can be no doubt that Plato thought that horseness, the Form of horse or Horse itself, to use his own expression, was something that existed separately; it could be discerned not by the bodily eyes but by the eye of the soul. The view that besides individual horses there also exists the Form of horse was known in the Middle Ages as Realism. Aristotle was also alleged to be a Realist, because he too thought that Forms were really there, although only as embodied in particular instances. More skeptical philosophers denied the reality of universals altogether, some identifying them with thoughts (conceptualists), others with mere names (nominalists).

The dispute about universals was in fact very confused. At least two quite separate issues were involved. First of all, there was the question about the status to be assigned to whatever it was that predicates referred to; this question seemed urgent just because, for example, geometricians were able to discuss the properties of the triangle or the circle. What and where were the triangle and the circle? In fact, the Aristotelian doctrine of categories had already indicated that the being of any predicate was necessarily different from that of primary substances; the circle did not and could not exist as this man or this horse did. When Aristotle is described as a Realist in the dispute about universals, the description is very misleading. In one sense he did not believe that universals are real at all; in another sense, however, he did, and this is where the second issue arose. Some people who denied the reality of universals wanted to say that all classification is artificial; the descriptions men give of things depend upon their interests as much as upon what is really there. Aristotle, by contrast, believed in a doctrine of natural kinds; he thought that every particular horse embodied the form or objective essence of horse, which was accordingly a genuine, if abstract, constituent of the world. The question of the extent to which classification is artificial is clearly quite different from that of the status of universals; it remains to be solved even if the latter problem is dismissed, as it is by modern philosophers who say that only proper names and individuating phrases have referents; general words do not. These differences, however, were not clearly seen either in the Middle Ages or during the 17th century, when the whole question was discussed at length by philosophers like Thomas Hobbes and John Locke. (For the problem of natural versus artificial classification, see CLASSIFICATION THEORY.)

Basic particulars. In discussions of the problem of universals it was often claimed, especially by nominalists, that only particulars exist. The notion of a particular is in many respects unclear. Strictly, the terms particular and universal are correlatives; a particular is an instance of universal (*e.g.,* this pain, that noise). It would seem from this that particulars and individuals should be the same, but there are writers who distinguish them. Bradley, in his *Principles of Logic* (1883), treated particulars as mere momentary instantiations of universals and contrasted them with individuals as continuants possessing internal diversity. An individual cannot merely be identified but re-identified; because it lasts through time, it may possess incompatible attributes at different periods of its history. A particular, however, is nothing but an instantiation of an attribute and as such must possess that attribute if it is to be anything. Similarly, a particular can be met with once, but not again; as time moves on, it passes out of existence and is replaced by another particular that may resemble it but is not literally identical with it.

If particulars and individuals are thus distinguished, it is by no means clear that only particulars exist, or indeed that they exist at all; it could be that they are no more than abstract aspects of genuinely concrete entities such as persons or material things. But there are arguments on the other side, advanced in a variety of forms by David Hume and Bertrand Russell.

Hume's theory of particulars

Hume believed that the ultimate constituents of the world were either impressions or their fainter copies, ideas; both were species of perceptions. Impressions he defined as "internal and perishing existences"; they were of various kinds, embracing feelings as well as such things as experienced colours and smells, but all were at best extremely short-lived. Impressions arose in human consciousness from unknown causes; their existence could not, however, be denied. By contrast, the existence of continuing amd independent material objects and of continuing minds was extremely precarious; analysis showed both to be no more than bundles of perceptions, united by certain relations, and Hume more than once referred to them as "fictions," although it turned out on examination that they were not fictions in the way ghosts are. Hume's reasons for advancing these views were primarily epistemological; he thought that statements about continuants were all open to doubt, although statements about the contents of immediate experience could not be challenged. When it was a question of what really existed, the only sure answer was items in consciousness—namely, impressions and ideas.

Russell's theory of particulars

Russell, who was generally sympathetic to this answer, added another argument derived from logic: proper names, he said, were names of particulars, which must accordingly exist. Ordinary proper names (such as "Socrates") had other functions than to denote, but logically proper names ("this" was Russell's example) served simply to pick out objects of immediate acquaintance. Russell was apparently unabashed by the consequence that such objects would be both private to the experience of particular persons and of very brief duration; he thought his doctrine of "logical constructions," which allowed for "inferred entities" on the basis of what is immediately certain, would provide the publicity and continuity necessary to do justice to actual experience. These assumptions, however, have met with serious criticism. P.F. Strawson, a British philosopher whose thought centres on the analysis of the structure of ordinary language, especially in his *Individuals: An Essay in Descriptive Metaphysics* (1959), not only attacked Russell's account of proper names but argued that experience demands a framework of basic particulars that are not Russell's momentary private objects but continuing public existents—in fact, individuals in the terminology explained above. If experience consisted of nothing but sounds, the minimum prerequisite of intelligibility would be that there should be a continuing master sound, an analogue in this medium of continuing material substance in the material order. Without such basic particulars as continuing material things, identification and reidentification would be impossible. Strawson conceded that persons as well as things were genuine continuants, but maintained all the same that the hypothesis that reality might consist of nothing but minds was quite untenable. Minds are no more than aspects of persons, and persons have bodies as well as minds. Strawson agreed that disembodied existence was logically possible, but added that such existence would make no sense except as a survival of embodied existence in a common public world.

If this is correct, what exists cannot consist, as Hume supposed, of momentary items but must rather take the form of substances in the Aristotelian sense. These act as basic particulars in the actual intellectual scheme men adopt. Strawson, however, was not content merely to assert this fact; he wanted to argue that things must be like this if reference and description in their familiar form are to be possible at all. His main theory, which plainly owes a debt to Kant as well as to Wittgenstein, was worked out with primary reference to the physical world. It would be interesting to know if an examination of social reality would yield comparable results: whether individual persons or something larger—continuing societies or institutions—should be taken as basic particulars in that sphere. Many philosophers assert dogmatically that a society is nothing but an aggregate of its individual members. Nevertheless, men are members of society in virtue of their performance of a number of social roles, and role itself is a concept that makes sense only if the notion of society is presupposed. In one sense, a society is nothing apart from its members; remove them, and it would disappear. Equally, however, the members themselves are what they are because of their various roles; it is arguable that they would be nothing apart from their social relations. Hence, the force of Bradley's remark is evident, namely, that "the 'individual' apart from the community is not anything real."

It remains to add here that a number of philosophers have tried to argue that the basic items in reality should be described not as substances but in some other terms. Russell at one stage in his career spoke of the world as consisting of events; his former colleague A.N. Whitehead made the notion of process central in his metaphysics. Developments in modern physics undoubtedly lend a certain plausibility to these and similar views. Yet it remains difficult to understand what an event could be in which nothing was concerned, or how there could be a process in which nothing was in process. Event and process, in fact, are expressions that belong to derivative categories in the general Aristotelian scheme; like all other categories, they depend on the category of substance. If the latter is removed, as these metaphysicians propose to remove it, it is hard to know what is left.

THE EXISTENCE OF GOD

Proofs of the existence of God

Perhaps the most celebrated issue in classical metaphysics concerned the existence of God. God in this connection is the name of "the perfect Being" or "the most real of all things"; the question is whether it is necessary to recognize the existence of such a being as well as of things that either are or might be objects of everyday experience. A number of famous arguments have been advanced from the time of the Greeks in favour of the thesis that such a recognition is necessary. The neatest and most ingenious was the a priori argument of St. Anselm in the 11th century, who said that "that than which nothing greater can be conceived" must exist in fact as well as in thought, for if it existed only in thought and not in fact, something greater than it could be conceived, namely the same thing existing in fact. God necessarily exists, because the idea of God is the idea of that than which nothing greater can be conceived. This is the argument later known as the ontological proof. Relatively few philosophical theologians, either in the Middle Ages or later, could bring themselves to accept this bold piece of reasoning (although Descartes, Spinoza, Leibniz, and Hegel all accepted it in principle); most preferred to ground their case for God's existence on premises that claimed to be empirical. Thus, St. Thomas Aquinas, perhaps the most influential Scholastic philosopher, in the 13th century argued that to explain the fact of motion in the world, the existence of a prime mover must be presupposed; that to account for contingent or dependent being the existence of something that is necessary or self-contained must be presumed; that to see why the world is orderly and why the different things in it fit together harmoniously, a situation that might not have obtained, a Creator who fashioned it on these lines must be postulated—adding in each case "and this all men call 'God'." These are versions of the first cause argument and the argument from design, which were to figure prominently in the thinking of later theistically inclined metaphysicians.

The first cause argument should, perhaps, be examined in somewhat greater detail, because it both has an immediate plausibility and lies at the basis of many different kinds of metaphysical systems (that of Hegel, for example, as well as that of Aquinas). The argument begins with the innocent-looking statement that something contingent exists; it may be some particular thing, such as oneself, or it may be the world in general (thus, the description of the proof as being *a contingentia mundi,* or "from the contingency of the world"). In describing oneself or the world as contingent, one means only that the thing in question does not exist through itself alone; it owes its being to the activity of some other thing, as a person owes his being to his parents. Contingent things are not self-complete; they each demand the existence of something else if they are to be explained. Thus, the move is made from contingent to necessary being; it is felt that contingent things, of whatever order, cannot be endlessly dependent on other contingent things but must presuppose a first cause that is self-complete and so exists necessarily. In Hegel the necessary being is not a separate existent but, as it were, an order of things; the loose facts of everyday life and even of science are said to point to a system that is all-embracing and in which everything is necessarily what it is. The principle of the argument, however, is unchanged despite the change in the conclusion.

Criticisms of proofs

Damaging criticism was brought against all the traditional arguments for God's existence by Hume and Kant in the 18th century. The ontological proof was undermined by the contention that "being is not a real predicate"; existence is not part of the concept of God in the way in which, for example, being all-powerful is. To say that something exists is not to specify a concept further but to claim that it has an instance; it cannot be discovered whether a concept has an instance by merely inspecting it. The first cause argument, it was contended, suffers from two fatal weaknesses. Even if it is correct in its assertion that contingent being presupposes necessary being, it cannot identify the necessary being in question with God (as happened in each of the Thomistic proofs) without resurrecting the ontological argument. If it is true, as supporters of the causal proof suppose, that God alone can answer the description of a necessary being, then whatever exists necessarily is God and whatever is God exists necessarily. Modern supporters of the causal proof have tried to meet this objection by saying that the equivalence is one of concepts, not of concept and existent; the existence of a necessary being is already established in the first part of the argument, and the equivalence in the second part of the argument is between the concept of necessary being and the concept of God. In other words, they distinguish between existence and essence. In the first part of the argument, the existence of a necessary being is proved; in the second part of the argument, the essence of that necessary being is identified with what men call God. Beyond this first contended weakness, however, there are grave difficulties in the move from contingent to necessary existence. Things in the experienced world are causally related, and some account of this relationship can be given in terms of the temporal relations of events; causal relations hold primarily between kinds of events, and a cause is, at least, a regular antecedent of a specific kind of effect. But when an attempt is made to extend the notion of causality from a relationship that holds within experience to one that connects the experienced world as a whole to something that falls wholly outside it, there is no longer anything firm on which to hold. The activities of God cannot precede happenings in the world because God is, by definition, not in time; and how the relationship is to be understood in these circumstances becomes highly problematic. Some metaphysicians, like some recent theologians, seek to evade the difficulty by saying that God is not the cause of the world but its ground, or again by distinguishing causes of becoming, which are temporal, from a cause of being, which is not. It is doubtful whether these moves do more than restate the problem in different terms.

The argument from design is itself a form of causal argument and accordingly suffers from all the difficulties mentioned above, together with some of its own, as Hume and Kant both point out. Even on its own terms it is wrong to conclude the existence of a Creator rather than an architect. Furthermore, it infers that the being in question has unlimited powers, when all that the evidence seems to warrant is that its powers are very great. The argument lost much of its force by the publication of the English naturalist Charles Darwin's theory of natural selection. The unbroken reign of law throughout natural evolution is impressive, but as a line of reasoning it does not seem to bear close examination.

The metaphysical problem of God's existence is more of an issue today than the problem of universals; there are still thinkers who hope to restate the old proofs in more convincing ways. The ontological proof, in particular, has won renewed attention from thinkers such as Norman Malcolm, a philosopher strongly influenced by Wittgenstein, and Charles Hartshorne, an American Realist whose form of theism is called panentheism (the doctrine of a God who has an unchanging essence but who completes himself in an advancing experience). Increasingly, however, philosophers of religion are preoccupied not with these metaphysical abstractions but with the status and force of actual religious claims. "The most real of all things" is no longer at the centre of their attention: they seek to investigate God as a suitable object for worship.

THE SOUL, MIND, AND BODY

Platonic and Aristotelian theories of the soul

The soul–body relationship. As well as believing in the reality of Forms, Plato believed in the immortality of the human soul. The soul was, he thought, an entity that was fundamentally distinct from the body although it could be and often was affected by its association with the body, being dragged down by what he called in one passage "the leaden weights of becoming." The soul was simple, not composite, and thus not liable to dissolution as were material things; further, it had the power of self-movement, again in contrast to material things. Ideally the soul should rule and guide the body, and it could ensure that this situation persisted by seeing that the bodily appetites were indulged to the minimum extent necessary for the continuance of life. The true philosopher, as Plato put it in the *Phaedo,* made his life a practice for death because he knew that after death the soul would be free of bodily ties and would return to its native element. He also thought that the soul was "akin" to the Forms; it was through the intellect, the purest element in the soul, that the Forms were discovered.

Plato mentioned and attempted to refute alternative accounts of the relationship of soul and body, including a Pythagorean view that described the soul as an "attunement" of the body and thus tried to explicate it as a form or structure rather than an independently existing thing. A theory of this kind was worked out but not taken to its logical conclusion by Aristotle in his treatise *De anima* (*On the Soul*). Aristotle defined soul in terms of functions. The soul of a plant was concerned with nutrition and reproduction, that of an animal with these and with sensation and independent movement, that of a man with all these and with rational activity. The soul was, in each case, the form of some body, and the clear implication of this was that it would disappear as the body in question dissolved. To be more accurate, the soul was the principle of life in something material; it needed the material element to exist, although it was not itself either material or immaterial but, to put it crudely, an abstraction. Even though Aristotle was clearly committed by everything he said in the earlier parts of the *De anima* to the view that the soul is not anything substantial, he nevertheless distinguished toward the end of this work between what he called the active and the passive intellects and spoke of the former in Platonic terms. The active intellect was, it appears, separate from the rest of the soul; it came "from outside" and was in fact immortal. It was, moreover, essential to the soul considered as rational, for "without this nothing thinks." Aristotle thus showed the Platonic side of his thought in the very act of trying to emancipate himself from this aspect of Platonism.

The mind–body relationship. In more recent metaphysics less has been heard of the soul and more of the mind; the old problem of the relationship of soul and body is now that of the relationship of mind and body. Most, if not all, subsequent discussion of this subject has been affected by the thinking of Descartes. In his *Meditationes de Prima Philosophia* (1641; *Meditations on First Philosophy*), he argued that there was a total and absolute distinction between mental and material substance. The defining characteristic of matter was to occupy space; the defining characteristic of mind was to be conscious or, in a broad sense of the term, to think. Material substance was, so to speak, all one, although packets of it were more or less persistent; mental substance existed in the form of individual minds, with God as the supreme example. The mental and the material orders were each complete in themselves, under God; it was this fact that made it appropriate for him to use the technical term substance in this context: mental substance and material substance. The logical consequence of this view, drawn by some later Cartesians, was that there can be no interaction between mind and body; all causality is immanent, within one order or the other, and any appearance of mind affecting body or of body affecting mind must be explained as the result of a special intervention by God, who, on the occasion of changes in one substance, brings it about that there are corresponding changes in the other. Descartes himself, however, had no sympathy with this view, which was called occasionalism. On the contrary, he stated explicitly that he was not in his body as a pilot is in a ship but was "more intimately" bound up with it. Mind could affect body and vice versa because mind and body had a specially close relationship, which was particularly evident in the aspects of conscious life that have to do with sensation, imagination, and emotion as opposed to pure thought.

Cartesian theory

Descartes's conviction that, despite their intimate union in this life, mind is really distinct from body sprang from his confidence in the cogito argument. It was possible, he believed, to doubt the existence of his body (what was certain was only that he had the experience of having a body, and this might be illusory) but not the existence of his mind, for the very act of doubting was itself mental. That mind existed was evident from the immediate testimony of consciousness; that body existed was something that needed an elaborate proof, involving his doctrine of clear and distinct ideas and his attempt to establish the existence of a God who is no deceiver. Apart from this, Descartes appealed to arguments of a broadly Platonic type to bring out what was truly distinctive about mind. He admitted that sensation and imagination could be understood only if referred to the mind–body complex but contended that acts of the pure intellect and of will (here his thought was influenced by that of St. Augustine, the great 5th-century Christian thinker) belonged to the mind as it was in itself. Descartes did not claim to have a philosophical proof of the immortality of the soul—that, in his view, required the assurance of revelation—but he did think that his theory prepared the way for that doctrine by establishing the separate existence of mind.

The Cartesian account of mind and body had many critics even in Descartes's own day. Hobbes argued that nothing existed but matter in motion; there was no such thing as mental substance, only material substance. Materialism of a sort was also supported by Descartes's correspondent Pierre Gassendi, a scientist and Epicurean philosopher.

Theory of Spinoza

A generation later Spinoza was to refashion the whole Cartesian metaphysics on bold lines. In place of the two distinct substances, each complete in itself yet each liable to external interference should God will it, Spinoza posited a single substance, God or Nature, possessed of infinite attributes, of which the mental and the material alone are known to men. The "modes," or manifestations, of this substance were what they were as a result of the necessities of its nature; arbitrary will neither did nor could play any part in its activities. Whatever manifested itself under one attribute had its counterpart in all the others. It followed from this that to every mental event there was a precisely corresponding physical event, and vice versa. A man was thus not a mysterious union of two different elements but a part of the one substance that, like all other parts, manifested itself in different ways under different attributes. Spinoza did not explain why it was that physical events could be correlated with mental events in the case of a human being but not in that of, for example, a stone. His theory of psycho-physical parallelism, however, has persisted independently of his general metaphysics and has found supporters even in modern times.

One way in which Spinoza threw fresh light on the mind–body problem was in calling attention to the influence of the body on the mind and in taking seriously the suggestion that they be treated as a single unit. In this respect, his work on the subject was far in advance of the Empiricist philosophers of the next century. Hume notoriously dismissed Cartesian substance as a "chimera" and argued that minds and bodies alike were nothing but "bundles of perceptions," interaction between which was always possible in principle; in practice, however, he stuck to the old-fashioned view that mind is one thing and body another and did nothing to explore their actual relationships. Empiricist philosophy of mind, both in Hume and in his successors, such as James Mill, was generally crude; it consisted largely in an attempt to explain the entire life of the mind in terms of Hume's ontology of impressions and ideas. Nor did Kant make much, if any, advance in this particular direction, convinced as he was of the necessity of accepting an empirical dualism of mind and body. It was left to Hegel and the Idealists to look at the problem afresh and to bring out the way in which mental life and bodily life are intimately bound together. The accounts of action and cognition given by T.H. Green and Bradley, and more recently by R.G. Collingwood, are altogether more enlightening than those of Empiricist contemporaries just because they rest on a less dogmatic basis and a closer inspection of fact.

Modern theories

No metaphysical problem is discussed today more vigorously than that of mind and body. Three main positions are held. First, there are still writers (*e.g.,* H.D. Lewis in his work *The Elusive Mind* [1969]) who think that Descartes was substantially right: mind and body are distinct, and the "I" that thinks is a separate thing from the "I" that weighs 170 pounds. The testimony of consciousness is invoked as the main support of this conclusion; it is alleged that all men know themselves to be what they are, or at least who they are, apart from their bodily lives; it is alleged again that their bodily lives present themselves as experiences—*i.e.,* as something mental. The existence of mind, as Descartes claimed, is certain, that of body dubious and perhaps not strictly provable. Second, there are writers such as Gilbert Ryle who would like to take the Aristotelian theory to its logical conclusion and argue that mind is nothing but the form of the body. Mind is not, as Descartes supposed, something accessible only to its owner; it is rather something that is obvious in whatever a person does. To put it crudely, mind is simply behaviour. Finally, there are many philosophers who, although more generally sympathetic to the second solution than to the first, wish to provide for an "inner life" in a way in which Behaviourism does not; P.F. Strawson is a typical example. To this end they try to assert that the true unit is neither mind nor body but the person. A person is something that is capable of possessing physical and mental predicates alike. This is, of course, to say that the "I" that knows simple arithmetic and the "I" that has lost weight recently are the same. How they can be the same, however, has not so far been explained by supporters of this view.

Aside from these main positions, an interesting development is the stress laid by writers—such as Stuart Hampshire, an "ordinary language" philosopher—on self-activity as the distinguishing characteristic of mind. According to this view, a human being is a body among bodies but is, as Plato said, self-moving as material things are not. That this should be so—that human beings are possessed of wills and can in favourable circumstances act freely—is taken as an ultimate fact neither requiring nor capable of explanation. It is often denied that any scientific discovery could give rational grounds for questioning this fact. It is also stressed that the causality of a human being is fundamentally different from that of a natural subject, intentional action being quite other than mere behaviour determined from without.

The problem of differentiating men and machines

Connected with these topics is the problem, much discussed in recent philosophy as a result of the rise of cybernetics, of what differentiates men from machines. Two answers used to be given: the power to think and consciousness. Now, however, there exist machines whose calculating abilities far surpass those of any human being; such machines may not literally think, but they certainly arrive at conclusions. Furthermore, it is not true that their operations are of a purely routine nature: there is a sense in which they can improve their performance in the light of their "experiences." They even have an analogue of consciousness in the sensitivity they show to external stimuli. These facts suggest that the gap between minds and machines is less wide than it has often been thought to be; they do not, however, destroy it altogether. Human beings possess powers of creative thought unlike anything found in machines; as Noam Chomsky, an American linguistics scholar, has stressed (and as Descartes urged in his *Discours de la méthode*), the ability of human beings to handle language in such a way that they comprehend any one of an infinite number of possible expressions is something that cannot be explained in mechanical terms. Again, as J.R. Lucas, a British philosopher, has argued, human beings have the ability to diagnose and correct their own limitations in a way to which there is no parallel in machines. As some older philosophers put it, man is a being with the power of self-transcendence; he can work within a system, but he can also move to another level and so see the shortcomings of the system. A machine can only work within a system; it operates according to rules but cannot change them of its own accord.

Finally, mention should be made of an extreme Materialist solution to the mind–body problem: this solution holds that states of mind are in fact states of the brain. Supporters of this theory agree that the two are separate in idea but argue that physiology shows that despite this they are contingently identical. What seems to be a state of mind, above all to its possessor, is really a state of the brain, and mind is thus reduced to matter after all. It is not clear, however, why physiologists should be granted the last word on a topic like this, and, even if it were agreed that they should be, the correlations so far established between mental occurrences and states of the brain are at best sketchy and incomplete. Central-state Materialism, as this theory is called, professes to have the weight of contemporary science behind it, but it turns out in fact to have drawn to a remarkable degree on what it thinks will be the science of tomorrow.

NATURE AND THE EXTERNAL WORLD

The problem of the existence of material things, first propounded by Descartes and repeatedly discussed by subsequent philosophers, particularly those working within the Empiricist tradition, belongs to epistemology, or the science of knowledge, rather than metaphysics; it concerns the question of how it can be known whether there is a reality independent of mind. There are, however, problems about nature and the external world that are genuinely metaphysical.

The reality of material things. There is first of all

the question of the status, or standing, of material things, the kind of being they possess. It has been repeatedly suggested by metaphysical philosophers that the external world is in some way defective in reality, that it is a mere phenomenon, something that seems to be what it is not. Plato, as has already been pointed out, held that objects of the senses generally answered this description; they each appeared to possess characteristics that they could not in fact have (water could not be at once hot and cold) and were to that extent delusive rather than real. There was no stability in the world of phenomena and therefore no true reality. In taking this view, Plato drew no contrast between the world of nature and the world of man, although he undoubtedly believed that souls had a superior status. Leibniz, a later philosopher who also followed this general line of thought, began by explicitly opposing souls to material things. To speak precisely, nothing truly existed except monads, and monads were souls, or spiritual beings: all had perceptions, although these varied enormously in degree of clarity (the perceptions of the monads constituting what is commonly called a stone were singularly faint). Although the final description of the world must thus be given in mental terms, it did not follow that nature as normally perceived is a total illusion. Men perceive as well as think, and, although perception is in fact simply a confused form of thought, it is not for that reason to be set aside altogether. The world of nature, the world of things in space and time, is, as Leibniz put it, a "well-founded phenomenon"; it is what all men must judge to be there, given that they are not pure intellects but necessarily remain to some extent prisoners of their senses.

The external world as defective in reality

A theory on somewhat similar lines was worked out by Kant in the *Kritik der reinen Vernunft* (1781; *Critique of Pure Reason*), despite Kant's explicit dissent from Leibniz' account of perception as confused thinking. Kant contrasted a realm of things as they are in themselves, or noumena, with a realm of appearances, or phenomena. The former are unknown, and indeed unknowable, though it seems clear that Kant tended to think of them on lines like those of Leibniz; phenomena do not exist independently but are dependent on consciousness, though not on any one person's consciousness. Kant expressed this position by saying that things phenomenal are empirically real but transcendentally ideal; he meant that they are undoubtedly there for the individual subject, though when examined from the point of view of critical philosophy, they turn out to be conditioned by the mind through the forms of sensibility and understanding imposed upon them. Kant's most striking argument for this conclusion was that space and time are neither, as the English physicist Sir Isaac Newton supposed, vast containers inside which everything empirical is situated nor, as Leibniz had suggested, relations between things confusedly apprehended but are rather what he mysteriously called "pure intuitions," factors inherent in the sensibilities of observers. Without observers space and time disappear along with their contents; but once the human point of view is assumed, in the form of percipients who are directly aware of the world through their senses, space and time become as real as anything—indeed, more real because of their pervasive character. There is nothing that falls within experience that does not have temporal relations, and all the data of the senses have spatial relations as well.

Kant's arguments in support of his revolutionary thesis about space and time unfortunately depend to a large extent on his mistaken philosophy of mathematics, and they have accordingly been discounted by later philosophers. In modern philosophy the issues raised in these discussions survive only in the form of an inquiry into the status of nature as investigated by the natural scientist. Descartes already pointed out that material things in fact have properties different from those they seem to have; they appear to possess secondary qualities such as colour or smell but turn out when thought about strictly to be colourless and odourless lumps of matter occupying and moving about in space. Locke endorsed this distinction between primary qualities (such as extension, motion, figure, and solidity) and secondary qualities; but George Berkeley, a major British Empiricist of the early 18th century, criticized it sharply as absurd: to imagine something that has primary but no secondary qualities is psychologically impossible. For Berkeley the world of the scientist was a fiction and perhaps not even a necessary fiction at that. It seems clear, however, that Berkeley's arguments do not undermine the important distinction between primary and secondary qualities, where the former are treated as fundamental and the latter as derivative; they are valid only against Locke's mistaken claim that primary qualities are objective and secondary qualities subjective. Whatever the explanation, the fact remains that the scientist often knows why the phenomena are as they are, in contrast to the plain man; to that extent nature as he understands it is truer, if not more real, than nature as it is taken to be in everyday experience. Why this should be is not satisfactorily explained by philosophers who follow Berkeley's lead on this question. Nor has either party to the controversy noted sufficiently the extent to which nature as commonly thought of is conceived as penetrated by mind, both when it is taken as intelligible and, still more interestingly, when poets ascribe to it moods or treat it as kindly or hostile. There is analytic work to be done here to which critical philosophers have still to address themselves.

Primary and secondary qualities of material things

The organizing principles of nature. Connected with the questions just discussed are problems about the organizing principles of nature; *i.e.,* about natural causality. It has been said that the Greeks thought of the world as a vast animal (indeed, the conceptual scheme that Aristotle devised for dealing with nature makes sense only if something like this is presupposed). Nature is the sphere in which different kinds of things are all striving to realize their characteristic form; purpose, though not perhaps explicit purpose, governs it throughout. Aristotle was not entirely insensitive to what are now known as the physical and chemical aspects of the universe, but he treated them as subordinate to the biological aspect in a way modern thinkers find surprising. Even the four elements—earth, air, fire, and water—were seen by him as each seeking its natural place in the cosmos. The contrast between this view and that favoured by Descartes could hardly be sharper. According to Descartes nature is not an organism but a mechanism; everything in it, including animal and human bodies, although not including the human mind, must be understood on mechanical principles. In taking this line, Descartes was endorsing a way of thinking that was central in the new physical science developed by Galileo at the beginning of the 17th century and that was to remain central in the thought of Newton. Descartes himself was not a pure mechanist because he believed that mind was governed by principles of its own; his work, however, undoubtedly encouraged the thought, frequently debated at the time of the Enlightenment, that mental life equally with the physical world must be explicable in mechanical terms. This was a position whose validity at the theoretical level Kant reluctantly admitted, only to try to turn its edge by his dichotomy of theory and practice. Everything in nature, including human behaviour, was subject to causal determination. The dignity and uniqueness of man, however, could be preserved because of the fact that in moral action man raised himself above the sphere of nature by thinking of himself as part of a world of free spirits.

Nature as mechanical or teleological

Kant also produced interesting thoughts on the subject of living phenomena. Reflection on the concept of an organism had convinced him that a being of this sort could never be accounted for satisfactorily in mechanical terms; it was futile to hope that someday in the future there would appear a Newton of biology capable of explaining mechanically the generation of even so apparently simple a thing as a blade of grass. To judge or speak of organic phenomena demanded a special principle that was teleological (*i.e.,* related to design or purpose) rather than mechanical. Kant, however, refused to allow that this principle had constitutive force. It belonged, he said, only to "reflective judgment" and thus did not rank alongside the principles of understanding that were so important in physical science. Men must have recourse to a principle of purposiveness in order to speak of living things, but they must not imagine that such recourse would enable them to explain their existence and behaviour in any strict sense of the term. They have insight only into what they can produce, and what they can produce are machines, not organisms. Many of Kant's detailed remarks on this subject seem outmoded in the light of subsequent scientific developments; nevertheless, the problem he raised is still the subject of vigorous debate among philosophically minded biologists. His emphasis on the uniqueness of the concept of an organism, which he says is only imperfectly explicated in the language of ends and purposes, is particularly valuable.

It remains to mention the seemingly eccentric view of nature taken by Hegel, who regarded it as at once the antithesis to and a prefiguration of the world of spirit. Nature had to exist to provide material for spirit to overcome, although it was a gross mistake to think of it as essentially a lifeless mechanism. Instead of reducing the organic to the inorganic, men should see the latter as pointing forward to the former, which in turn offered a foretaste of the rational structure exhibited by the world of mind. Hegel's disdain for scientists of proved ability, such as Newton and John Dalton, and his endorsement against them of amateur scientists such as the German writer Goethe, make it hard to take his philosophy of nature seriously. It contains, even so, some interesting points, not least the demonstration that in finding nature to be throughout subject to law the scientist is presupposing that it is thoroughly penetrated by mind. To understand these views properly, however, it is necessary to understand Hegel's system as a whole.

SPACE AND TIME

Many metaphysicians have argued that neither time nor space can be ultimately real. Temporal and spatial predicates apply only to appearances; reality, or what is real, does not endure through time, nor is it subject to the conditions of space. The roots of this view are to be found in Plato and beyond him in the thought of the Eleatic philosophers Parmenides and Zeno, the propounder of several paradoxes about motion. Plato conceived his Forms as eternal objects whose true location was nowhere. Similarly, Christian philosophers conceived of God as existing from everlasting to everlasting and as present in all parts of the universe. God was not so much in space and time as the source of space and time. Whatever falls within space and time is thereby limited, for one space excludes another and no two times can be simultaneous. God, however, is by definition an infinite being and so must exist timelessly and apart from space.

Theories of Kant and Bradley

Reference has already been made to the way in which Kant argued for an intimate connection between time and space and human sensibility: that human beings experience things as being temporally and spatially situated is to be connected with the nature of their minds, and particularly with their sensory equipment. Kant was entirely correct to describe space and time as "intuitions," by which he meant that they are peculiar sorts of particulars; he was right again to insist on the centrality in sensing of the notions of here and now, which can be indicated but not reduced to conceptual terms. It is highly doubtful, however, whether he had sufficient grounds for claiming a priori insight into the nature of space and still more that of time; his case for thinking that space and time are "pure" intuitions was palpably inadequate. The lesson to draw from his careful discussion of this subject might well be not that there must be a form of reality lying beyond space and time but rather that nothing can be real that does not conform to spatial and temporal requirements. Space and time are bound up with particularity, and only what is particular can be real.

It was only in a weak sense that Kant denied the reality of time and space. Other philosophers have certainly been bolder, though generally on the basis of a less solid grasp than Kant possessed of what it is to experience temporally and spatially. Thus, Bradley argued against the view that space and time are "principles of individuation" by alleging that no specification of spatial or temporal position, whether in terms of here and now or by the use of spatial coordinates or dating systems, could achieve uniqueness. Any descriptions such as "at 12 o'clock precisely on January 4, 1962" or "just 75 yards due north of this spot" might apply to infinitely many times or places in the universe, for there was nothing to prevent there being infinitely many temporal and spatial orders. Bradley forgot that the whole meaning of a spatial or temporal description is not exhausted when attention is given to the connotations of the terms used; what has to be considered is the words as used in their context, which is that of a person who can indicate his position in space and time because of the fact that he is himself situated in space and time. One cannot express uniqueness in words as such, but he can use words to express uniqueness. Bradley's suggestion that it is possible to conceive of many temporal and spatial orders is by no means free from controversy. In general, men think of all events as happening before, simultaneously with, or after the moment that is called "now," all spatial positions as relating in some way or other to the point that is called "here." In circumstances where this cannot be done, as with events or places in a dream, men dismiss them as quite unreal. That there might be events or places with no relation to their own now and here is something they often refuse to take seriously, though there are theories in modern science that suggest that they are wrong to do so.

It was pointed out earlier that to say that something is unreal in a metaphysical context is often to say that it is unintelligible, and it is not surprising to find that arguments about the unreality of space and time have often turned on conceptual considerations. Thus, it is alleged that there is an incoherency in the notion of space because it claims to be a whole that is logically prior to its parts, and nevertheless turns out in practice to be merely an indefinitely extensible aggregate. Everything that occupies space falls within a wider spatial context; the thought of space as such is, as Kant saw, involved in any spatial description. Yet space as such is something that constantly eludes man's grasp; space, as man knows it, is just one spatial situation after another.

Theory of Bergson

The difficulties found in the notion of time turn on the combination in it of the idea that time is continuous and the idea that it is made up of discrete parts. Henri Bergson, a French philosopher who was concerned with the notions of duration and movement, said that time was experienced as continuous; it was only the "spatialized" time measured by clocks that was taken to have separable parts (minutes, hours, weeks, and so on), and this "public" time was merely conventional. This, however, seems altogether too easy a solution of the problem, for privately experienced time also goes by (one stretch of it follows another), and the thesis that public time is merely conventional is at best highly controversial. It must be allowed that time is commonly thought of as at once flowing and, as it were, subject to arrest. Whether this is, in fact, openly inconsistent may be doubted, but it is on points like this that the metaphysical case in question rests.

Few British or American philosophers discuss these questions now, largely because they have been persuaded by Moore that any attack on such central notions in men's thought as these must be mistaken in principle. As a result, little attention is given to a question that deserves investigation; namely, what is to take the place of space and time in metaphysical thought. Idealist writers constantly said that space and time qualified appearances, and that nothing that did so could fail to be taken up in the higher experience that was experience of reality. But how is this supposed to be done? Time is perhaps cancelled and yet preserved in the idea of eternity, space in the thought of something that is at once omnipresent yet not in any particular place. But what is there that is positive about these notions? The eternal, it is sometimes said, is not to be identified with what lasts through all time; it is, strictly, outside time altogether. But what does it mean to say this? When it is said, for example, that numbers or truths are eternal, the proper inference is that they have nothing to do with time; to inquire when they came into or will go out of existence is to ask a question that is ill posed. When God, however, is said to be eternal, the impression is often given that he has temporal characteristics, although in some higher form. What this higher form is deserves careful consideration, the result of which might be that it is not the conception of time that is incoherent but the conception of God.

THE CONCEPTION OF SPIRIT

As well as arguing for the separate existence of mental substance, metaphysicians have claimed that mind is, as it were, the key to the understanding of the universe. What exists is spirit, or at least is penetrated by spirit. This is the thesis of Idealism, a type of philosophy that is often derided but that, like its rival Materialism, has a constantly fresh appeal. This view is worth examining in more detail than has so far been possible.

It is best to begin by distinguishing the thesis of Idealism proper from some others with which it is readily confused. Leibniz said that the true atoms of nature were monads or souls; at bottom nothing existed except minds. Berkeley claimed that sensible things have no existence without the mind; there are spirits that experience, including an infinite spirit, and there are the contents of their experiences, but there is no independently existing world of matter. For the philosophers who followed Hegel, both Leibniz and Berkeley were "subjective" Idealists: they conceived of reality in terms of the experiences of individual minds.

Theory of Hegel

Hegel's view, by contrast, was that what exists is not so much pure mind as mind writ large; *i.e.,* the universe is penetrated by mind and exists for the sake of mind, and it cannot be understood unless this fact is grasped. Hegel was thus not committed to denying that there is an independent world of nature but, on the contrary, openly proclaimed it. Nature was there for mind to master it and in so doing to discover itself.

The field in which Hegel first worked out this theory was that of human affairs. The human world may be said to be mind made objective because it consists of a series of structures—examples would be a language, a set of moral or political procedures, a science, a practical art such as medicine—that constitute mental achievements. The mind involved in structures of this kind, however, is collective rather than personal. An art such as medicine or a science such as mathematics is not the invention of any particular individual; and although individuals have contributed and are contributing to the advancement of each structure, they do so not in their personal capacity but as embodying impersonal intelligence.

Because the human world thus embodies mind, or spirit, it needs to be understood in a special way—in terms of what Hegel called "concrete universals." Concepts of this kind are in order when it is a question of grasping a particular sort of subject matter—one in which there are intimate connections between the data under consideration. Connections in nature are, on the surface at any rate, of a purely external character; striking a match, for example, has nothing internally to do with producing a flame. When, however, a historian considers the different stages of some movement or process, or when an anthropologist studies the various aspects of the life of a society, the material they confront is internally related just because it represents the work of mind—not, of course, of mind working in a vacuum but of mind facing and reacting with greater or less intelligence to particular situations. It is not surprising in these circumstances to find that the conceptual structure employed by the student of human affairs is, in important respects, profoundly different from that employed by the student of nature. In the latter, what are in question are constant conjunctions, observed but not understood; in the former, men have insight into what happens or obtains because they can reenact in their own minds the thought behind the material they study.

All this is, or should be, comparatively uncontroversial; it represents the truth behind the claim of Wilhelm Dilthey, a German philosopher and historian of ideas, that human affairs can be understood, as it were, from within, by means of what he called *Verstehen* ("understanding"). But of course it is one thing to say this and another altogether to argue that the universe at large should be construed as if it were mind writ large. What makes Hegelianism intriguing to some and totally implausible to others is precisely that it makes this extravagant claim. As has already been mentioned, the world of nature for Hegel is in one way independent of mind: its being is certainly not its being perceived. It is, nevertheless, relevant to mind in all sorts of important ways: in providing a setting in which mind can act, in constituting an obstacle that mind can overcome, in presenting mind with something seemingly alien in which it can nevertheless find itself insofar as it discovers nature to be intelligible. If Hegel were asked why there was a world of nature at all, his answer would be "for the sake of mind." Just as man's social environment affords opportunities to the individual to come to full knowledge of himself by realizing his differences from and dependence upon others, so the world of nature affords similar opportunities. By transforming the natural scene, men make it their own. In so doing they come to know what they can do, and thus what they are.

All reality as spirit

There is, perhaps, more to this doctrine than appears at first sight. It is, however, easier to assent to it in general terms than to follow Hegel over it in detail. According to the Idealist account, there is in the end only one true description of the universe, namely that which is couched in terms of the concrete universal. Reality is a single self-differentiating system, all the parts of which are intimately connected; it is spirit that expresses itself in the natural and human worlds and comes to consciousness of itself in so doing. Any other account of the matter—for example, that given by the scientist in terms of experienced uniformities—must be dismissed as inadequate. To Hume's objection that there is an absolute logical difference between propositions expressing matters of fact and existence and propositions expressing relations of ideas, Hegel replies brusquely that the distinction is untenable. At a certain level, perhaps, facts are taken as "brute." Even the scientist, however, never abandons his aspiration to understand them—it is only provisionally that he talks in terms of "ultimate inexplicabilities"—and the philosopher knows that the demand to incorporate all knowledge in a single system is not to be denied. It is a demand that, as Hegelians are willing to admit, can in practice never be met but that, nonetheless, ceaselessly makes itself felt. That such is the case is shown by the extraordinary fascination exercised by this strange but remarkable type of philosophy.

To try to understand the universe in terms of spirit is characteristic of philosophers whose main extra-philosophical interests are in the humanities, particularly in historical studies. Relatively few scientifically minded thinkers have followed this line of thought, and many Idealists of repute, including Bradley and Benedetto Croce (an Italian philosopher and literary critic whose major philosophical work was published in four volumes between 1902 and 1917 under the general title *La filosofia dello spirito* ("The Philosophy of the Spirit"), have been least convincing when writing about science. Hegel himself, perhaps, had less sympathy with scientific than with historical aspirations; this is not to say, however, that he was ill-informed about contemporary science. He knew what was going on, but he saw it all from his own point of view, the point of view of one who was entirely convinced that science could not produce any ultimate answers. He valued science but rejected the scientific view of the world.

Types of metaphysical theory

To complement and, in a way, to correct this brief survey of the problems of metaphysics it will be useful at this point to insert a short summary of a number of overall metaphysical positions. Metaphysics, as already noted, professes to deal with "the world as a whole"; the thoughts of a metaphysician, if they are to make any impact at all, must be connected in a system. The object in what follows will be to present in outline metaphysical systems that have exercised and, indeed, continue to exercise a strong intellectual appeal. In all cases but one, these systems were given classical shape by particular philosophers of genius. Relatively little attention, however, will be paid to this fact here because the present concern is with types of view rather than with views actually held. Thus, reference will be made to Platonism instead of to the philosophy of Plato, and so on in other cases.

PLATONISM

Distinction between the world of appearances and the world of realities

The essence of Platonism lies in a distinction between two worlds, the familiar world of everyday life, which is the object of the senses, and an unseen world of true realities, which can be the object of the intellect. The ordinary man recognizes the existence of the former and ignores that of the latter; he fails to appreciate the extent to which his beliefs both about fact and about values are arbitrarily assumed and involve internal contradictions. The philosopher is in a position to show him how insubstantial is the foundation on which he takes his stand. The philosopher can demonstrate how little thought there is in popular conceptions of good and evil, and he can show that the very concept of sense knowledge involves difficulties because knowledge presupposes a stable object, and the objects of sense are constantly changing. The claim, however, is that he can do more than this. Because of the presence in him of something like a divine spark, he can, after suitable preparation, fix his intellectual gaze on the realities of the unseen world and, in the light of them, know both what is true and how to behave. He will not attain this result easily—to get to it will involve not only immense intellectual effort, including the repeated challenging of assumptions, but also turning his back on everything in life that is merely sensual or animal. Yet, despite this, the end is attainable in principle, and the man who arrives at it will exercise the most important part of himself in the best way that is open to him.

That this type of view has an immediate appeal to persons of a certain kind goes without saying. There is ample evidence in poetry and elsewhere of the frequently experienced sense of the unreality of familiar things and the presence behind them of another order altogether. Platonism may be said to build on "intuitions" of this kind; as a metaphysics, its job is to give them intellectual expression, to transfer them from the level of sentiment to that of theory. It is important, however, to notice that Platonism is not just the intellectualizing of a mood; it is an attempt to solve specific problems in a specific way. In Plato's own case, the problems were set by loss of confidence in traditional morality and the emergence of the doctrine that "man is the measure of all things." Plato thought he could counter this doctrine by appeal to another contemporary fact, the rise of science as shown in the development of mathematical knowledge. Mathematics, as he saw it, offered certain truth, although not about the familiar world; the triangle whose properties were investigated by the geometrician was not any particular triangle but the prototype that all particular triangles presuppose. *The* triangle and *the* circle belonged not to the world of the senses but to the world of the intelligence; they were Forms. If this could be said of the objects of mathematical discourse, the same should also be true of the objects of morality. True justice and true goodness were not to be found in popular opinions or human institutions but should be seen as unchanging Forms, eternally existing in a world apart.

Modern philosophers have found much to criticize in this system: as indicated already, they have objected that Forms are not so much existents as abstractions, and they have found the argument from science to morality quite inconclusive because of what they allege to be an absolute dichotomy between fact and value. It may be that nobody today can subscribe to Platonism in precisely the form given it by Plato himself. The general idea, however, has certainly not lost its hold, nor have the moral perplexities to which Plato hoped to find an answer been dissipated by further thought.

ARISTOTELIANISM

Making sense of the here and now

For many people, Plato is the type of an other-worldly, Aristotle of a this-worldly philosopher. Plato found reality to lie in things wholly remote from sense; Aristotle took form to be typically embodied in matter and thought it his job as a philosopher to make sense of the here and now. The contrast is to some extent overdrawn for Aristotle, too, believed in pure form (God and the astral intelligences—the intelligent movers of the planets—were supposed to satisfy this description), and Plato was sufficiently concerned with the here and now to want to change human society radically. It remains true, nevertheless, that Aristotelianism is in essentials a form of immanent metaphysics, a theory that instructs men on how to take the world they know rather than one that gives them news of an altogether different world.

The key concepts in Aristotelianism are substance, form and matter, potentiality and actuality, and cause. Whatever happens involves some substance or substances; unless there were substances, in the sense of concrete existents, nothing could be real whatsoever. Substances, however, are not, as the name might suggest, mere parcels of matter; they are intelligible structures, or forms, embodied in matter. That a thing is of a certain kind means that it has a certain form or structure. But the structure as conceived in Aristotelianism is not merely static. Every substance, in this view, not only has a form but is, as it were, striving to attain its natural form; it is seeking to be in actuality what it is potentially, which is in effect to be a proper specimen of its kind. Because this is so, explanation in this system must be given in teleological rather than mechanical terms. For Aristotle, form is the determining element in the universe, but it operates by drawing things on, so that they become what they have it in themselves to be rather than by acting as a constant efficient cause (*i.e.,* the agent that initiates the process of change). The notion of an efficient cause has a role in Aristotelianism—as Aristotle put it, it takes a man, a developed specimen of his kind, to beget a man; it is, however, a subordinate role and yields pride of place to a different idea, namely, form considered as purpose.

For reasons connected with his astronomy, Aristotle postulated a God. His God, however, had nothing to do with the universe; it was not his creation, and he was, of necessity, indifferent to its vicissitudes (he could not otherwise have been an unmoved mover). It is a mistake to imagine that everything in the Aristotelian universe is trying to fulfill a purpose that God has ordained for it. On the contrary, the teleology of which use is here made is unconscious; although things all tend to an end, they do not in general consciously seek that end. They are like organs in a living body that fulfill a function and yet seemingly have not been put there for that purpose.

As this last remark will suggest, an important source of Aristotelian thought is reflection on natural growth and decay. Aristotle, who was the son of a doctor, was himself a pioneer in natural history, and it is not surprising that he thought in biological terms. What is surprising, and gives his system a continuing interest, is the extent to which he succeeded in applying ideas in fields that are remote from their origin. He was without doubt more successful in some fields than in others: in dealing with the phenomena of social life, for instance, as opposed to those of physical reality. His results overall, however, were impressive enough for his system not only to dominate men's minds for many centuries but to constitute a challenge even today. Men still, on occasions, think like Aristotle, and, as long as that is so, Aristotelianism will remain a live metaphysical option.

THOMISM

Christian metaphysics

The advent of Christianity had important effects in philosophy as in other aspects of human life. Initially Christians were opposed to philosophical claims of any kind; they saw philosophy as an essentially pagan phenomenon and refused to allow the propriety of subjecting Christian dogma to philosophical scrutiny. Christian truth rested on revelation and did not need any certificate of authenticity from mere reason. Later, however, attempts were made to produce a specifically Christian metaphysics, to think out a view of the universe and of man's place in it that did justice to the Christian revelation and nevertheless rested on arguments that might be expected to convince Christians and non-Christians alike. St. Thomas Aquinas was only one of a number of important thinkers in medieval times who produced Christian philosophies; others—such as the philosophers John Duns Scotus in the late 13th century and William of Ockham in the first half of the 14th century—took significantly different views. In selecting the system of Aquinas for summary here, the factor that has weighed most has been its persistent influence, particularly in postmedieval times. Aquinas was not the only medieval philosopher of distinction, but Thomism is alive as other medieval systems are not.

The central claim of Thomism is that reflection on everyday things and the everyday world reveals it as pointing beyond itself to God as its sustaining cause. Ordinary existents, such as human beings, are in process of constant change. The change, however, is not normally the result of their own efforts, and even when it is, it does not depend on them exclusively. No object in the familiar world can fully account for its own *esse* (*i.e.,* its own act of existing), nor is it wholly self-sufficient; all are affected from without, or at least operate in an environment that is not of their own making. To say this is to say that they are one and all finite. Although finite things can be, and commonly are, stimulated to activity or kept in activity by other finite things, it does not follow that there might be finite things and nothing else. On the contrary, the finite necessarily points beyond itself to the infinite; the system of limited beings, each dependent for its activity on something else of the same kind, demands for its completion the existence of an unlimited being, one that is the source of change in other things but is not subject to change itself. Such a being would be not a cause like any other but a first or ultimate cause; it would be the unconditioned condition of the existence of all other things. Aquinas believed that human reason can produce definitive proofs of the existence of an infinite or perfect being, and he had no hesitation in identifying that being with the Christian God. Because, however, the movement of his thought was from finite to infinite, he claimed to possess only so much philosophical knowledge of the Creator as could be arrived at from study of his creation. Positive knowledge of the divine nature was not available; apart from revelation, man could only say what God is not, or conceive of his attributes by the imperfect method of analogy.

Aquinas worked out his ideas at a time when the philosophy of Aristotle was again becoming familiar in western Europe after a period of being largely forgotten, and many of his detailed theories show Aristotelian influence. He assumed the general truth of the Aristotelian picture of the natural world and the general correctness of Aristotle's way of interpreting natural phenomena. He also took over many of Aristotle's ideas in the fields of ethics and politics. He gave the latter, however, a distinctively different twist by making the final end of man not philosophical contemplation but the attainment of the beatific vision of God; it was Christian rather than Greek ideas that finally shaped his view of the *summum bonum* ("greatest good"). Similarly, his celebrated proofs of God's existence proceeded against a background that is obviously Aristotelian but that need not be presupposed for their central thought to have validity. Thomism can certainly be seen, and historically must be seen, as the system of Aristotle adapted to Christian purposes. It is important, however, to stress that the adaptation resulted in something new, a distinctive way of looking at the world that still has its adherents and still commands the respect of philosophers.

CARTESIANISM

Increased understanding of the physical world

René Descartes worked out his metaphysics at a time of rapid advance in human understanding of the physical world. He adopted from Galileo the view that physical things are not what they are commonly taken to be on the strength of sense experience—namely, possessors of "secondary" properties such as colour, smell, and feel—but are rather objects characterized only by the "primary" qualities of shape, size, mass, and mobility. To understand why a constituent of the physical world behaves as it does, what should be asked is where it is, how large it is, in what direction it is moving, and at what speed; once these questions are answered, its further properties will become intelligible. Descartes held further that all change and movement in the physical world is to be explained in purely mechanical terms. God was needed to give initial impetus to the physical system as a whole, but once it had got going it proceeded of its own accord. To pretend, as the Aristotelians had, to discern purposes in nature was to make the impious claim to insight into God's mind. Descartes applied this theory to the movements of animals as much as to those of inanimate bodies; he thought of both as mere automatons, pushed and pulled about by forces over which they had no control.

Although Descartes thus acquiesced in, indeed emphasized, the mechanistic tendencies of contemporary science, he was far from being a Materialist. Besides material substance there was also thinking substance, and this was in fact wholly different from matter both in kind and in operation. Bodies had as their essence to occupy space; minds were not in space at all. Bodies, again, were determined in their movements; minds were in some sense free, because they possessed will as well as intelligence. Descartes was less explicit on this point than he might have been; the principles on which mental substance is supposed to operate are not made clear, with the result that critics have said that Descartes thought of mental activities in para-mechanical terms. Whether this is true or not, however, there was no reason for Descartes to be in any special difficulty over this point. All he needed to urge was that minds act in the strict sense of the term, which is to say that they take cognizance of their situation and respond more or less intelligently to it. That they can do this differentiates them fundamentally from material things, which are caused to do what they do and are entirely unaffected by rational considerations.

The main crux in Descartes's metaphysics was the difficulty of bringing together the two orders of being, once they were separated. Mention has already been made of the expedient to which later Cartesians were driven in trying to solve this difficulty: in effect, they made the unity of the universe a continuing miracle, dependent upon the grace of God. It is worth mentioning here another move in the same area that many have found instructive. Kant, who was in some respects both a latterday Cartesian and a latter-day Platonist, argued that human activities could be looked at from two points of view. From the theoretical standpoint they were simply a set of happenings, brought about by antecedent events in precisely the same way as occurrences in the natural world. From the standpoint of the agent, however, they must be conceived as the product of rational decision, as acts proper for which the agent could be held responsible. The moment he began to act, a man transferred himself in thought from the phenomenal world of science to an intelligible world of pure spirit; he necessarily acted as if he were not determined by natural forces. The transference, however, was a transference in thought only (to claim any knowledge of the intelligible world was quite unjustified), and because of this the problem of the unity of the universe was dissolved. There was no contradiction in a man's thinking of himself both as a subject for science and as a free originator of action. Contradiction would appear only if he were present in both respects in an identical capacity. But appeal to the doctrine of the two standpoints was thought by Kant to rule this out.

Kantian development

It is only with some hesitation that one can speak of Kant as having put forward a metaphysics. He was in general highly suspicious of claims to metaphysical knowledge, and a principal aim of his philosophy was to expose the confusions into which professing metaphysicians had fallen. Nevertheless, it is clear that Kant had metaphysical convictions, for all his denial of the possibility of metaphysical knowledge; he was committed to the view that men can conceive a non-natural as well as a natural order and must necessarily take the former to be real when they act. The language he used—particularly his talk about man as phenomenon and man as noumenon—is not to the taste of present-day philosophers, but the thought behind it certainly survives. It is in this form, indeed, that Cartesianism may still be said to present a serious intellectual challenge.

IDEALISM

Descartes and Kant were both adherents of metaphysical dualism, though they worked out their dualisms in interestingly different ways. Many thinkers, however, find dualism unsatisfactory in itself; they look for a single principle by which to compass whatever exists. There are two broad steps that are open to the person who confronts a dualism of mind and matter and finds it unsatisfactory: he can either try to show that matter is in some sense reducible to mind, or conversely seek to reduce mind to matter. The first is the solution of Idealism, the second that of Materialism. Idealism has already been treated at length, and it will not be necessary to go into it again here. Only one point about it needs emphasis. As was pointed out, there are various forms of Idealism. In one version, this philosophy maintains that there literally is no such thing as matter; what the common man takes to be material things are, upon closer consideration, nothing but experiences in minds. Nothing exists but minds and their contents; an independently existing material world is strictly no more than an illusion. This was the view taken by Berkeley. In the more sophisticated Idealism of Hegel, however, it is not maintained that mind alone exists; material things are, in one way, taken to be as real as minds. The thesis advanced is rather that the universe must be seen as penetrated by mind, indeed as constituted by it. Spirit, to use Hegel's own word, is the fundamental reality, and everything that exists must accordingly be understood by reference to it, either as being directly explicable in spiritual terms or as prefiguring or pointing forward to spirit. Whatever the merits of this thesis, it is clear that it differs radically from that maintained by Berkeley. Idealism in the form espoused by Berkeley relies largely on arguments drawn from epistemology, though formally its conclusions are ontological, because they take the form of assertions or denials of existence. Hegel, however, had little or nothing to say about epistemology and was not even concerned to put forward an ontology. What he wanted to urge was a doctrine of first principles, a thesis about the terms in which to understand the world. The Hegelian "reduction" of matter to mind was thus reduction in a somewhat attenuated sense. It is important to get this point clear, if only because it has its parallel in the rival doctrine of Materialism.

Two solutions to the Cartesian dualism

MATERIALISM

The simplest form of Materialism is found in the claim that only matter exists. Stated thus baldly the claim is absurd, because it is clear that all sorts of things exist that are not of the nature of matter: thoughts and numbers and human institutions would be instances. In the light of these facts, the claim has to be revised to say that matter is the only substantial existent, with appeal being made to distinctions first worked out in Aristotle's doctrine of categories. According to this explanation, many things besides matter exist, but all of them are explicable (or so it is said) as modifications of matter. Thus, human institutions consist in patterns of movement among specific groups of human beings, and human beings in turn are nothing but highly complicated material bodies.

Matter as the only substantial existent

It is clear from these instances that Materialism is a controversial doctrine; it is also clear that its key word, modification, requires further explanation. When, for example, minds are said to be modifications of an underlying material substance, what is meant? A first and relatively easy point is that, like qualities and quantities, they could not exist separately. Unless there were material bodies, there could not be minds, because minds are—to put it crudely—states found in some material bodies. Minds are here equated with mentality, and mentality is clearly an abstraction. To say this, however, is not to remove the whole difficulty. When it is said that mentality is a state of some material body or bodies, is that meant literally or metaphorically? Bodies can often be described from the physical point of view as being in a certain state—for example, as being in a state of internal equilibrium. What is meant here is that the different particles of matter concerned stand in a certain relationship and as a consequence develop certain physical properties. But is mentality to be conceived as a physical property? It sounds extravagant to say so. Yet some such doctrine must be defended if Materialism is to be advanced as a form of ontology with a serious claim for attention. It is interesting in this connection to notice the arguments advanced by scholars like J.J.C. Smart, which purport to identify states of mind with states of the brain. If the two are identical—literally the same thing described from two points of view—thoughts may really be modifications of matter, and Materialism may be tenable in a strong form. If, however, the identity cannot be made out—and very few philosophers are in fact ready to accept it—Materialism can be true at most in a modified form.

This modified form of Materialism is perhaps better described as naturalism. Naturalism holds not that all things consist of matter or its modifications but that whatever exists can be satisfactorily explained in natural terms. To explain something in natural terms is to explain it on scientific lines; naturalism is in fact a proclamation of the omnicompetence, or final competence, of science. It is not essential to this type of view to argue that phenomena can be spoken of in one way only; on this point, as on the point about ontological reducibility, the theory can afford to be liberal. It is, however, vital to make out that the scientific account of a set of happenings takes precedence over any other. Thus, the language in which men commonly speak of action and decision, which may be called for short the language of reasons, must be held to be secondary to the language in which scientists might speak of the same facts. Scientific language is basically causal, and the thesis of this form of Materialism is that causal explanations are fundamental. Naturalism is thus the obverse of Hegelianism; it is a theory of first principles, and it draws its principles from science.

Naturalism

If the question is raised why anyone should take this form of Materialism seriously, the answer lies in a number of significant facts. Physiologists have established correlations between general states of mind and general states of brain activity; their hope is to extend this to the point where particular thoughts and feelings can be shown to have their physiological counterpart. Cyberneticists have produced artifacts that exhibit mindlike behaviour to a remarkable degree; the inference that man is no more than a complicated machine is certainly strengthened by their achievements. Sociologists have shown that, whatever the explicit reasons men give for their beliefs, these are often intelligible in the light of factors of which they themselves take little or no account. The old assumption that human judgments are typically grounded in reason rather than merely caused, is called in question by the results of such investigations, which gain support from findings both in Freudian and in orthodox psychology. None of this evidence is decisive by itself; there are ways in every case of blocking the conclusions that Materialists tend to draw from it. Yet it remains true that, cumulatively, the evidence is impressive. It certainly has enough force to make it necessary to take this type of theory with the greatest seriousness. Metaphysical disputes in the modern world are fundamentally arguments for or against Materialism, and the other types of theory here explored are all seen as alternatives to this compelling, if often unwelcome, view.

Argument, assertion, and method in metaphysics

Attention is now turned from description of the content of particular metaphysical views to more general treatment of the nature of metaphysical claims. The questions that will arise in this section concern such things as the nature and basis of metaphysical assertions, the character of metaphysical arguments and of what are taken to be metaphysical proofs, and the parts played in metaphysical thinking by insight and argument, respectively. They come together in the inquiry as to whether metaphysics can be said to be a science and, if so, what sort of a science it is.

METAPHYSICS AS A SCIENCE

Nature of an a priori science. Sciences are broadly of two kinds, a priori and empirical. In an a priori science such as geometry, a start is made from propositions that are generally taken to be true, and the procedure is to demonstrate with rigorous logic what follows if they are indeed true. It is not necessary that the primary premises of an a priori science should in fact be truths; for the

Hypothetical nature of a priori sciences

purposes of the system they need only be taken as true, or postulated as such. The main interest is not so much in the premises as in their consequences, which the investigator has to set out in due order. The primary premises must, of course, be consistent one with another, and they may be chosen, as in fact happened with Euclidean geometry, because they are thought to have evident application in the real world. This second condition, however, need not be fulfilled; a science of this kind can be and commonly is entirely hypothetical. Its force consists in the demonstration that commitment to the premises necessitates commitment to the conclusions: the first cannot be true if the second are false.

This point about the hypothetical character of a priori sciences has not always been appreciated. In many classical discussions of the subject, the assumption was made that a system of this kind will start from as well as terminate in truths and that necessity will attach to premises and conclusions alike. Aristotle and Descartes both spoke as if this must be the case. It is clear, however, that in this they were mistaken. The form of a typical argument in this field is as follows: (1) p is taken as true or given as true; (2) it is seen that if p, then q; (3) q is deduced as true, given the truth of p. There is no need here for p to be a necessary or self-guaranteeing truth; p can be any proposition whatsoever, provided its truth is granted. The only necessity that needs to be present is that which characterizes the argument form, "If p is true, and p implies q, then q is true," that is $[p \cdot (p \supset q)] \supset q$, in which $\cdot$ symbolizes "and," and $\supset$ means "implies"; and this is a formula that belongs to logic. It is this fact that makes philosophers say, misleadingly, that a priori sciences are one and all analytic. They are not because their premises need not answer this description. They, nevertheless, draw their lifeblood from analytic principles.

Metaphysics as an a priori science. It is clear that metaphysical philosophers have sometimes aspired to present their results in the form of a deductive system, to make metaphysics an a priori science. For this purpose they have taken a deductive system to require not just that the premises entail the conclusions but further that they themselves be necessarily true. Spinoza thus began the first book of his *Ethics* by laying down eight definitions and seven axioms whose truth he took to be self-evident and then proceeding in the body of the text to deduce, as he thought with strict logic, 36 propositions that follow in order from them. He repeated the procedure in the rest of his work. That philosophical conclusions should thus be capable of being set out "in the geometrical manner" was something that Spinoza took as axiomatic; to be worthy of attention at all, philosophy must issue in knowledge as opposed to mere opinion, and knowledge proper had to be exempt from the possibility of doubt, which meant that it must either be intuitively evident or deducible from what was intuitively evident. Spinoza took this conception of knowledge from Descartes, who had himself toyed with the idea of presenting metaphysical arguments in the geometrical manner. Descartes, however, pointed out that, although there was no difficulty in getting agreement to the first principles of geometry, "nothing in metaphysics causes more trouble than the making the perception of its primary notions clear and distinct"; the whole trouble with this discipline is that its students fail to see that they must start from what are in fact the basic truths. Descartes himself spoke as if the problem were no more than pedagogical; it was a question of making people see as self-evident what is in itself self-evident. His own "analytic" approach in the *Meditationes* was chosen to overcome these difficulties; it was, he said, "the best and truest method of teaching." But it may well be that this account is too optimistic. The difficulty with a system such as those of Descartes and Spinoza is that there are persons who cannot be brought to see that the primary propositions of the system are self-evidently true, and this not because they are lacking in attention or insight but because they see the world in a different way. This suggests that in any such system there will necessarily be an element that is arbitrary, or at least noncompulsive. However cogent the links that bind premises to conclusions, the premises themselves will lack a firm foundation. If they do, the interest of the system as a whole must be greatly diminished; it can be admired as an exercise in logic but not valued for more than that.

Deductive systems of Spinoza and Descartes

To avoid this unpalatable conclusion, two expedients are possible. The first is to say that the first premises of a metaphysical system must be not merely self-evident but also self-guaranteeing; they must be such that any attempt to deny them can only result in their reaffirmation. Descartes believed that he could satisfy this requirement by grounding his system in the cogito, though strictly this was the primary truth only from the point of view of subjective exposition and not according to the objective order of things. Aristotle somewhat similarly had argued that the logical principle of noncontradiction, which he took to express a highly general truth about the world, must be accepted as axiomatic on the ground that its correctness is presupposed in any argument directed against it.

Even the Idealists Bradley and Bernard Bosanquet at times spoke as if the first principles of their system were in some way logically compulsive; as Bosanquet put it, one had either to accept them or recognize that one could know nothing. Whatever the position may be about particular metaphysical propositions, however, it seems clear that not all truths that are taken as basic in metaphysics have the characteristic of being self-guaranteeing. A Materialist takes it as fundamental that whatever occurs happens as a result of the operation of natural causes; a theist sees things in the world as finite and thus as pointing beyond themselves to the infinite being who is their ground. No contradiction is involved in denying these positions, though of course for those who accept them the denial necessarily involves commitment to falsehood. It is, however, one thing for a proposition or set of propositions to be false, another altogether for it to be necessarily false. If the first principles of metaphysics were really self-guaranteeing, only one system of metaphysics could be coherent, and it would be true just because it was coherent. The very fact that there is an apparent choice between competing metaphysical systems, which may differ in plausibility but agree in being each internally self-consistent, rules this possibility out.

The alternative is to argue that fundamental metaphysical propositions, though not self-guaranteeing, are nevertheless not arbitrary; they have or, to be more cautious, can have a firm foundation in fact. Metaphysical speculation is not, as some opponents of metaphysics have suggested, essentially idle—that is, the mere working out of the logical consequences of premises that the metaphysician chooses to take as true. Or, rather, it does not necessarily answer this description because a metaphysician can have insight into the true nature of things and can ground his system on that. This second position in fact involves arguing that metaphysics is not an a priori but an empirical science.

Metaphysics as an empirical science. If metaphysics is an empirical science, the question of whether or not to accept a metaphysical theory must be answerable, in part at any rate, by reference to experience. It will not depend on experience alone, any more than does the acceptability of a scientific theory, because here, as in the scientific case, thinking comes into the reckoning too. A metaphysician can be mistaken in his deductions, just as a scientist can. But even if these are impeccable, he will not necessarily succeed on this view of his undertaking. It may be that he argues correctly from premises that are unacceptable—unacceptable because they lack the necessary foundation in fact. He will then be like a scientist who puts forward a hypothesis and deduces its consequences without mistake only to find that experience fails to confirm the supposition on which he is working.

Reference to experience

Scientific hypotheses are refuted, or at least called seriously into question, when predictions based on them fail to come true. As Karl Popper—who has emphasized that there is a unity of method in all generalizing or theoretical sciences—has insisted, every scientific hypothesis must be testable, and the way to test it is to look for circumstances in which it does not hold. To content oneself with favourable evidence is not enough; one must be searching all the time for unfavourable evidence. Further, it must be possible, if the hypothesis is genuinely scientific, to specify in advance what would count as unfavourable evidence; the circumstances in which the hypothesis needs to be abandoned, or at least modified, must be indicated precisely. In ideal conditions it is possible to devise a crucial experiment that will test a hypothesis definitively; the Michelson–Morely experiment, which disposed of the theory of the luminiferous ether, was such an experiment.

It can be asked, however, what parallels there are to this in metaphysics. The difficulty with testing a metaphysical thesis is twofold. First, metaphysical theories tend to be extremely general and as such highly unspecific. They announce, for example, that every event has some cause or other, or that every change is part of a process that serves some purpose. To find counterexamples to theses of such generality is on any account exceedingly difficult: how can one be sure that all the possibilities have been explored? There is, however, another and still more serious difficulty. The scientist, once he has laid down the conditions that would have to obtain for his hypothesis to prove false, makes no bones about their occurrence; it is, typically, a matter of whether or not a certain pointer reading is registered, and this is a simple question of ascertainable fact. Fact for the metaphysician, however, is altogether more slippery. Different metaphysicians see the world each in his separate way; what they take to be the case is coloured by their metaphysical conceptions. There is no neutral body of facts to which appeal can be made to show that a metaphysical theory falls down, and this being so, the attempt to assimilate metaphysics to science must fail.

That this should be the case is perhaps not surprising. Scientific thinking proceeds within a framework of presuppositions that it is the business of the scientist to use, not to argue for and still less to challenge—presuppositions to the effect, for example, that every change has a natural explanation. No doubt scientists can change their presuppositions, but they seldom do so consciously; their usual practice is to take them for granted. Metaphysicians, however, necessarily take a very different attitude toward presuppositions. It is their business to tell men how to understand the world, and this means that they must, among other things, put forward and argue for a set of interpretative principles. Metaphysicians differ radically in the interpretative principles they accept, and it is this that explains their failure to agree upon what to take as fact. It is naive to suppose that the points at issue between, for example, a Thomist and a Materialist can be settled by observation or even by experiment; the facts to which one might appeal in support of his theory may be seen in a very different light by the other, or perhaps be dismissed as simple illusion. Reflection on the phenomenon of religious experience will illustrate what is meant here. That men undergoing this experience are affected mentally and physically in certain specific ways is perhaps common to both Thomist and Materialist. But the further description of their state is entirely controversial and owes its controversial character to the varying preconceptions that the disputants bring to their task.

INITIAL METAPHYSICAL INSIGHTS

Origin. If metaphysics is far from being a simple empirical discipline, however, it does not follow that it is wholly without foundation in fact. The true situation can perhaps be put as follows. Every metaphysic consists in an imaginative view of the world elaborated into a conceptual system. Metaphysics, like poetry, begins by being a matter of vision; a metaphysician sees the scheme of all things in a certain light; for example, as nothing more than a vast mechanism or as God's creation. As a metaphysician, however, he cannot be content to rest in a vision of this sort, as for example the Romantic poet William Wordsworth does in his "Intimations of Immortality." He needs to think out terms in which whatever exists can be described so as to accord with his primary insight; he needs to produce and apply a conceptual system and to argue against possible alternatives. Whatever its origins, metaphysics is strictly intellectual in its development. When the question is raised of the source from which metaphysicians gain their initial insights, the answer that occurs most readily is that they are derived from reflection on certain evident facts. Thus, the source of the Materialist view of the world is undoubtedly the practice of science; the Materialist proposes to give unrestricted validity to ways of thinking that scientists have found effective in a certain restricted sphere. The source of Idealist thought is to be found in the practice of history, or more generally in the interpersonal relations of beings who are at once rational and sensitive; the Idealist philosopher takes concepts that are appropriate in these limited areas to apply to the whole of reality. Every system of metaphysics is grounded in some real experience and owes its initial appeal to that fact. This is not to say, however, that the metaphysician builds on experience as does his scientific colleague. To think that is to take altogether too simple a view of the whole question.

Metaphysics as a matter of vision

Tests of validity. A question of immense importance is whether there are any means of comparing the validity of initial metaphysical insights. If it has to be answered negatively—if it has to be allowed that, as it were, all candidates in this field start and finish on an equal footing—the argument that each of them has a foundation in fact will be entirely discounted. Whatever respectability their concepts possess in their original homes will be lost once they fall into the hands of the metaphysician, because the procedure of the latter in taking them up and extending them is essentially arbitrary. For example, that one sees the sum of things as a vast machine may be suggested by what goes on in science, but this view can neither claim scientific warrant itself nor draw on scientific prestige, because it seems to spring from nothing better than mere whim. There are, however, two reasons for thinking that initial metaphysical insights are based not on mere whim but on valid grounds.

Insights as limited in number and subject to experience

First, the number of what may be called viable metaphysical insights is in practice limited: there are varying ways of taking the world as a whole, but not an infinite variety. In the outline account of metaphysical theories given above, six different kinds of view were distinguished, each of which may be said to be grounded in one or more areas of experience. It would be possible to extend the list, but probably not very far; further candidates might well turn out to be no more than variations on themes already considered. Thus, Leibniz might be seen as a latter-day Platonist, and Spinoza as offering a different version of the dualism of Descartes, one that is more sympathetic to Materialism than was Descartes himself. If these claims are true, they are certainly important; for the facts here adduced suggest that the experiences or visions on which different metaphysicians build are not peculiar to individual minds but occur commonly and regularly. They are not the product of passing moods, seized on and exploited for no good reason, but connect with thoughts that recur repeatedly in sensitive and intelligent reflection.

Second, there is a sense in which, despite everything said above, metaphysical theories are subject to the test of experience. That metaphysics aspires to give an account of the world as a whole means that each metaphysician claims that his fundamental insight illuminates every department of life. It may be that there are no neutral facts to which a metaphysician can appeal to show the shortcomings of his opponents; metaphysicians pronounce on what is to count as fact, and this puts them in the happy position of being judges in their own case. It remains true, however, that everyone who engages in that type of philosophy has the formal task of accounting for all the facts that he recognizes, and this is something that can be done more or less well. The value of different metaphysical insights is sometimes shown in the success with which they are applied. Furthermore, it is not quite true that the metaphysician need consult no opinion but his own when it comes to working out his views. What might be called public opinion has a part to play as well, though it has no absolute right to a hearing. A metaphysician who chooses to dismiss areas of experience or ways of thinking that are commonly accepted as being in order does so at his peril; he reduces the initial plausibility of his own theories the oftener he finds himself in this position. He could, of course, be right and common opinion wrong; no genuine metaphysician is put off by the thought of such a conflict. Though he is not put off, however, he has to be wary all the same. He may be able to say what in the end is to count as fact, but if this involves him in dismissing as illusory what instructed opinion generally takes to be real, his triumph may be hollow. Whether he likes it or not, he has to frame a theory that will carry conviction with experts in the different fields concerned, or, if that is going too far, one that will strike them as not wholly implausible. A metaphysician who exercises his veto past that point is simply failing to do his job.

The test of self-consistency of theory

It must be admitted that the tests one can apply to determine the value of a metaphysical theory are at best unsatisfactory. Often one is driven back onto the expedient of asking if the theory is internally self-consistent; a surprisingly large number of philosophical theories are not. To confute a philosopher out of his own mouth is, perhaps, the most effective form of confutation. If this expedient will not apply, however, the questioner is not quite helpless. Whatever the explanation, it is a well-known fact that a philosopher can purchase consistency at the expense of plausibility; he can put forward theories that evade difficulties by simply declaring them nonexistent. In so doing, he turns his back on what instructed opinion generally takes to be fact. His hope is, of course, to persuade others to see the situation as he does, and there is always the possibility that he will succeed. If, however, after a suitable interval he has not, that must surely count against him. It is by this test that one decides, for example, that the metaphysics of Hobbes is not worth prolonged study, despite the enormous ingenuity of its author; there is too much in this system that seems to be sheerly arbitrary. The same comment could be made of certain forms of Idealism, which are so intent on the omnipresence of spirit that they neglect the materiality of the material order. Admittedly, the test is harder to apply when attention is transferred to the major theories in their most persuasive form, because here the question concerns views that have stood the test of time. It is not, however, entirely inapplicable even there. An individual, at least, may feel that this or that view will not do precisely because it achieves comprehensiveness by turning its back on fact; and, though it is unsatisfactory to fall back on personal judgment in this way, there is perhaps no other alternative in this difficult area.

Role of personal or social factors. Some writers on the philosophy of philosophy, such as Dilthey, have suggested that the persistence of a plurality of metaphysical systems is to be explained in terms of personal or social factors. Certain kinds of metaphysical outlook appeal to certain types of human being, or gain currency in social circumstances of this kind or that; to understand why they are accepted, recourse must be had to psychology or sociology or both. In the above account, stress has been laid on the historical background against which a number of famous metaphysical theories got their classical formulations; it is idle to deny that each was originally designed to solve a problem deemed to be urgent at the time. Nevertheless, the problem was, of course, an intellectual problem, and the solution offered claimed to be true, not simply comforting. No doubt wishful thinking is as rife in the field of metaphysics as anywhere; it is all too easy here to confuse what men ought to believe with what they want to believe. Philosophies reveal something about their authors and even about their historical age, as works of literature do; they constitute historical evidence as books on mathematics, perhaps, do not. Yet all this can be admitted without agreeing that metaphysics is merely of psychological or historical importance. Science does not cease to be true because it is shown to be useful. Nor is it true that metaphysical theories always in fact give comfort; there are cases in which men find themselves returning over and over again to possibilities that they would very much like to believe were not realized. A philosopher can commit himself to a view of the world that is not at all to his taste, simply because it seems to him on due consideration that this is how things are. That philosophers are godlike beings able to rise entirely above the limitations of their age seems unlikely. It is equally unlikely, however, that their opinions are determined throughout by nonrational factors, and thus that their thinking can lay no claim to truth.

METAPHYSICAL ARGUMENTS

Classes of metaphysical statements

Logical character of metaphysical statements. Metaphysical statements fall into two main classes: statements about what exists and prescriptions about how to take or understand what exists. It might seem obvious that the first is the more important; the metaphysician first lays down what he takes to exist, and then tells how to interpret it. This would be correct if metaphysics were a departmental inquiry like, for example, botany; but, of course, it is not. Metaphysicians possess no special resources for the detection of unfamiliar entities, and in consequence the realities they accept must all be argued for. The fundamental items that fill the metaphysical world are one and all theoretical; they are not so much palpable realities as artificial constructs. That being so, there is less of a gulf between the two types of metaphysical pronouncement than might at first appear. It could indeed be argued that the two go closely together to constitute what may be called a metaphysical point of view, a standpoint whose primary purpose is to provide understanding. In a metaphysical context, to say what exists is itself a step on the way to understanding; it is not something that antedates theory, but part of a theory itself.

It may be asked whether metaphysical pronouncements are empirical or a priori and, if the latter, whether they are analytic or synthetic. They are certainly not straightforwardly empirical, for reasons just set out, and cannot be merely analytic (*i.e.,* true in virtue of the definitions of their terms and of the laws of logic) if metaphysics is to retain any significance. The conclusion that they must be synthetic a priori (*i.e.,* such that, unlike analytic propositions, they convey new knowledge and yet claim complete universality and necessity) seems to follow, and it is just what the opponent of metaphysics wants the metaphysician to adopt. Metaphysics, as he sees it, is a wholly unwarranted attempt to say what the world must be like on the strength of pure thinking, an attempt that is doomed to failure from the start. Before this condemnation is accepted, however, the function that the metaphysician assigns to his principles should be considered. When this is done, it becomes plain that the charge that he claims factual knowledge of a nonempirical sort is false; in one way he recognizes exactly the same facts as anyone else. Where he claims superiority is in knowing how to take facts, and the burden of his message consists in the advocacy of principles that, he alleges, will provide overall understanding. One can describe these principles as synthetic a priori if one chooses. It is probably best, however, to avoid this misleading term and simply say that they are thought of by the metaphysician as applying unequivocally to whatever falls within experience. These metaphysical principles are instructive at least in the sense of having alternatives, and they are certainly treated as being necessary. It is not true, however, that they take the form of statements of fact, even highly general statements of fact; nor is their necessity the same as that which characterizes logical truths. The principles are prescriptions rather than statements, and their necessity arises from the role they play in the constitution of experiential knowledge. It is a necessity that is in one way absolute: nothing that can claim to be real can escape their jurisdiction, because they tell how to take whatever occurs. Nevertheless, in another way the necessity of the principles is merely conditional, for other ways of interpreting the same data can be conceived, and it is admitted that there are circumstances, however hard to specify exactly, in which it would have to be agreed that they do not apply.

Deductive and inductive arguments

Logical form of metaphysical arguments. There is also the question whether metaphysical arguments are inductive or deductive or whether they have some logical form peculiar to themselves. It is obvious that much metaphysical reasoning is, or purports to be, reasoning in the strict sense, which is to say that its form is deductive. Arguments like the first cause argument for God's existence claim to be demonstrations; their exponents believe that anyone who commits himself to the truth of the premises stands logically committed to the truth of the conclusions. This claim can stand, even if it turns out that the project to set out metaphysical results in the geometrical manner is a mistake. It may be impossible to model metaphysics on mathematics, but that does not make particular metaphysical arguments any less deductive.

As regards inductive arguments, it would be odd to find a metaphysician contending, as, for example, historians regularly do, that *p* is true and *q* is true and therefore it is reasonable to conclude that *r* is true. To assess probabilities in the light of established facts is too cautious for the average metaphysical mind. Yet it would be wrong to deny that metaphysicians are preoccupied with facts. Their objective is to give a reasoned account of what exists or obtains, and for this purpose attention to fact is of course indispensable. It figures in metaphysical thinking at two stages. First, at the beginning, when the metaphysician is concerned to formulate his main thesis; here there is a move from what holds in a restricted sphere (the sphere of physics, for example) to what is supposed to hold generally, a move that is possible only if the theorist concerned has an interest in the sphere in question. To arrive at his own position the metaphysician must extrapolate from what goes on outside metaphysics, and this means that he must be sensitive to significant developments in at least some of the main fields of learning and areas of practical activity. But he needs this extra-philosophical knowledge for a second purpose too: in estimating the success of his own theories. In principle he must show that his interpretation of experience covers the facts in an adequate way, and for this purpose what experts in the different spheres take to be established is of crucial importance. Metaphysics is not an empirical science—the element of speculation it includes is too strong for that—but the metaphysician can no more ride roughshod over facts than the scientist can. At the least he must explain away phenomena that seem to count against his thesis, or indicate how they might be explained away. Whether he explains or explains away, he needs to know what the main phenomena are.

Transcendental argument

Finally, it is sometimes said that metaphysics can make use of a form of argument that is neither deductive nor inductive but transcendental; a transcendental argument is supposed to proceed from a fact to its sole possible condition. A transcendental argument is simply a form of deduction, with the typical pattern: only if *p* then *q*; *q* is true; therefore, *p* is true. As this form of argument appears in philosophy, the interest, and the difficulty, reside not in the movement from premises to conclusions, which is absolutely routine, but in the setting up of the major premises—in the kinds of things that are taken as starting points. In Kant's case, it was such things as the possibility of pure mathematical knowledge, the possibility of making objectively true statements, the fact that there is a unitary system of time. Kant purported to prove a number of surprising propositions by the use of transcendental arguments; he tried to commend major premises such as his arguments about causality and substance by showing what would result if the protasis (*i.e., p*) did not hold. What he had to say under this head has attracted particular interest in recent years. It seems clear, however, that from the logical point of view no special significance attaches to this form of argument. Although Kant had been successful in demonstrating that a sufficient is also a necessary condition, he did not make clear why it should be taken as the sole such condition. There is an important gap in his reasoning here, as there is in that of other metaphysical writers.

Criticisms of metaphysics

Metaphysics has many detractors. The man who aspires "to know reality as against mere appearance," to use Bradley's description, is commonly taken to be a dreamer, a dupe, or a charlatan. Reality in this context is, by the metaphysician's own admission, something that is inaccessible to sense; as Plato explained, it can be discovered only by the pure intelligence, and only if the latter can shake itself free of bodily encumbrances. The inference that the metaphysical world is secret and mysterious is natural enough. Metaphysics in this view unlocks the mysteries and lets the ordinary man into the secrets. It is, not to put too fine a point on it, a study of the occult.

Metaphysics as a study of the occult

METAPHYSICS AS KNOWLEDGE OF THE SUPERSENSIBLE

That there are aspects of metaphysics that lend colour to this caricature can scarcely be denied. The language of Plato, in particular, suggests an absolute distinction between the deceitful world of appearances, which can never be an object of knowledge, and the unseen world of Forms, each of which is precisely what it appears to be. Plato urged his readers not to take seriously the things of sense; he told them that everything having to do with the senses, including the natural appetites and the life of the body, is unreal and unimportant. The philosopher, in his view, needs to live an ascetic life, the chief object of which is to cultivate his soul. Only if he does this, and follows a rigorous intellectual training, has he any hope of getting the eye of his soul fixed on true reality and so of understanding why things are what they are.

Yet even this program admits of an innocuous, or relatively innocuous, interpretation. The "dialectician," as Plato called his metaphysical philosopher, is said in one place to be concerned to "give an account," and the only things of which he can give an account are phenomena. Plato's interest, despite first appearances, was not in the unseen for its own sake; he proposed to go behind things visible in order to explain them. He was not so much disdainful of facts as critical of accepted opinions; his attack on the acquiescence in "appearances" was an attack on conventional wisdom. That this was so comes out nowhere more clearly than in the fact that his targets included not just beliefs about what there is but also beliefs about what is good. It is the opinions of the many that need correction and that can happen only if men penetrate behind appearances and lay hold on reality.

Plato is often presented as an enemy of science on the ground that he was bitterly opposed to Empiricism and because he said that, if there was ever to be progress in astronomy, the actual appearances of the starry heavens must be disregarded. He understood by Empiricism, however, the uncritical acceptance of apparent facts, with the attempt to trace regularities in them; it is an attitude that, in his view, is marked by the absence of thought. As for the starry heavens, it is certainly difficult to take Plato quite literally when he compares their function in astronomy to that of a well-drawn diagram in geometry. Yet he was not wrong to suggest that no progress could be made in astronomical inquiries until appearances were seen to be what they were and not taken for absolute realities. The subsequent progress of astronomy has shown this view to be entirely correct.

There are respects in which Plato's attitude to phenomena was precisely the same as that of the modern scientist. The fact remains, nevertheless, that he believed in a realm of unseen realities, and he is of course far from being the only metaphysician to do so. Many, if not quite all, metaphysicians are committed to claiming knowledge of the supersensible, in some degree at least; even Materialists are alleged to make this claim when they say that behind the familiar world of everyday experience there lies material substance that is not accessible to the senses. It has been a commonplace among critics of metaphysics since the early 18th century that no such claims can be justified; the supersensible cannot be known about, or even known of, whether directly or by inference.

SPECIFIC CRITICISMS

Hume. An early but powerful statement of these criticisms is to be found in the writings of David Hume, *A Treatise of Human Nature* (1739–40) and *An Enquiry Concerning Human Understanding* (1748). Hume argued first that every simple idea was derived from some simple impression and that every complex idea was made up of simple ideas; innate ideas, supposed to be native to the mind, were nonexistent. There were eccentricities in Hume's conception of idea (and for that matter in his conception of impression), but these did not destroy the force of his argument that the senses provide the materials

Necessity of sense experience

from which basic concepts are abstracted. A being that lacked sense experience could not have concepts in the normal sense of the term. Next, Hume proceeded to make a sharp distinction between two types of proposition, one knowable by the pure intellect, the other dependent on the occurrence of sense experiences. Propositions concerning matters of fact and existence answer the latter description; they either record what is immediately experienced through the senses or state what is taken to be the case on the basis of such immediate experiences. Such statements about matters of fact and existence are one and all contingent; their contradictories might have been true, though, as a matter of fact, they are not. By contrast, propositions of Hume's other type, which concern relations of ideas, are one and all necessary; reflection on the concepts they contain is enough to show that they must, in logic, be true. Though, in a sense, knowledge of these propositions is arrived at by the exercise of pure reason, no real significance attaches to this fact. It is not the case of some special insight into the nature of things; the truth is rather that these propositions simply make explicit what is implicit in the definitions of the terms they contain. They are thus what Kant was to call analytic propositions, and it is an important part of Hume's case that the only truths to which pure reason can attain are truths of this nature.

Finally, Hume sought to block the argument that, even if the supersensible could not be known directly, or through pure intellectual concepts, its characteristics could, nevertheless, be inferred. His analysis of causality had this as one of its aims. According to Hume, the only means by which men can go beyond the impressions of the memory and the senses and know what lies outside their immediate experience is by employing causal reasoning. Examination of the causal relation, however, shows that it is, among other things, always a relation of types of events in time, one of which invariably precedes the other. Causality is not, as Descartes and others supposed, an intelligible relation involving an internal tie between cause and effect; it is a matter of purely factual connection and reduces on its objective side to nothing more than regular precedence and succession. The importance of this for the present inquiry lies in the consequence that causal relations can hold only between items, or possible items, of experience. According to Hume, if the temporal element is removed from causality, nothing concrete is left; if it is kept, it becomes impossible to argue that one can proceed by causal reasoning from the sensible to the supersensible. Yet it was precisely this that Aristotle, Thomas Aquinas, and Locke had all attempted.

Hume's own explicit pronouncements about metaphysics are ambivalent. There is a famous passage in which he urged men to consign volumes of divinity and "school metaphysics" to the flames, "as containing nothing but sophistry and illusion," but in at least one other place he spoke of the need to "cultivate true metaphysics with some care, in order to destroy the false and adulterate." "True metaphysics," in this connection, meant critical philosophical reflection.

Critical philosophical reflection

Kant. Hume's successor Kant made a sharper distinction between metaphysics and critical philosophy. Much of Kant's philosophical effort was devoted to arguing that metaphysics, understood as knowledge of things supersensible, is an impossibility. Yet metaphysics, as a study of the presuppositions of experience, could be put on "the sure path of science"; it was also possible, and indeed necessary, to hold certain beliefs about God, freedom, and immortality. But however well founded these beliefs might be, they in no sense amounted to knowledge: to know about the intelligible world was entirely beyond human capacity. Kant employed substantially the same arguments as had Hume in seeking to demonstrate this conclusion but introduced interesting variations of his own. One point in his case that is especially important is his distinction between sensibility as a faculty of intuitions and understanding as a faculty of concepts. According to Kant, knowledge demanded both that there be acquaintance with particulars and that these be brought under general descriptions. Acquaintance with particulars was always a matter of the exercise of the senses; only the senses could supply intuitions. Intuitions without concepts, nevertheless, were blind; one could make nothing of particulars unless one could say what they were, and this involved the exercise of a very different faculty, the understanding. Equally, however, the concepts of the understanding were empty when considered in themselves; they were mere forms waiting to be brought to bear on particulars. Kant emphasized that this result held even for what he called "pure" concepts such as cause and substance; the fact that these had a different role in the search for knowledge from the concepts discovered in experience did not give them any intuitive content. In their case, as in that of all other concepts, there could be no valid inference from universal to particulars; to know what particulars there were in the world, it was necessary to do something other than think. Thus is revealed the futility of trying to say what there is on the basis of pure reason alone.

Differences between Hume's and Kant's criticisms

Kant's distinction between analytic and synthetic propositions has peculiarities of its own, but for present purposes it may be treated as substantially identical with Hume's distinction set out above. Similarly, the important differences between Kant and Hume about causality may be ignored, seeing that they agreed on the central point that the concept can be properly applied only within possible experience. If it is asked whether there are substantial differences between the two as critics of metaphysics, the answer must be that there are but that these turn more on temperament and attitude than on explicit doctrine. Hume was more of a genuine iconoclast; he was ready to set aside old beliefs without regret. For Kant, however, the siren song of metaphysics had not lost its charm, despite the harsh words he sometimes permitted himself on the subject. Kant approached philosophy as a strong believer in the powers of reason; he never abandoned his conviction that some of man's concepts are a priori, and he argued at length that the idea of the unconditioned, though lacking constitutive force, had an all-important part to play in regulating the operations of the understanding. His distinction between phenomena and noumena, objects of the senses and objects of the intelligence, is in theory a matter of conceptual possibilities only; he said that, just as one comes to think of things sensible as phenomena, so one can form the idea of a world that is not the object of any kind of sense experience. It seems clear, however, that he went beyond this in his private thinking; the noumenal realm, so far from being a bare possibility invoked as a contrast with the realm that is actually known, was there thought of as a genuine reality that had its effects in the sense world, in the shape of moral scruples and feelings. A comparison of what was said in Kant's early essay *Träume eines Geistersehers erläutert durch Träume der Metaphysik* (1766; *Dreams of a Spirit-Seer*), with the arguments developed in the last part of his *Grundlegung zur Metaphysik der Sitten* (1785; *Fundamental Principles of the Metaphysic of Morals*), would seem to put this judgment beyond serious doubt.

Though Kant remained convinced of the existence of things supersensible, he, nonetheless, maintained throughout his critical writings that there can be no knowledge of them. There can be no science of metaphysics because, to be true to fact, thinking must be grounded in acquaintance with particulars, and the only particulars with which human beings are acquainted are those given in sense. Nor was this all. Attempts to construct metaphysical systems were constantly being made; philosophers repeatedly offered arguments to show that there must be a first cause, that the world must consist of simple parts, that it must have a limit in space, and so on. Kant thought that all such attempts could be ruled out of court once and for all by the simple expedient of showing that for every such proof there was an equally plausible counterproof; each metaphysical thesis, at least in the sphere of cosmology—*i.e.,* the branch of metaphysics that deals with the universe as an orderly system—could be matched with a precise antithesis whose grounds seemed just as secure, thus giving rise to a condition that he called "the antinomy of pure reason." Kant said of this antinomy that "nature itself seems to have arranged it to make reason stop short in its bold pretensions and to compel it to self-examination."

Admittedly, the self-examination led to more than one result: it showed on the one hand that there could be no knowledge of the unconditioned and demonstrated on the other that the familiar world of things in space and time is a mere phenomenon, thus—to Kant—clearing the way to a doctrine of moral belief. Though this doctrine could not be expunged from Kant's philosophy without destroying it altogether, it is quite wrong to present it, as some modern German writers do, as amounting to the advocacy of an alternative metaphysics. What Kant was concerned with here is what must be thought, not what can be known.

Logical Positivists. Despite what has just been said, it must be admitted that Kant's constant talk about the supersensible makes many critics of metaphysics regard him as a dubious ally. This was certainly true in the case of the Logical Positivists, the philosophical school that has attacked metaphysical speculation most sharply in the 20th century. The Positivists derived their name from the "positive" philosophy of Auguste Comte, a 19th-century Frenchman who had represented metaphysical thought as a necessary but now superseded stage in the progression of the human mind from primitive superstition to modern science. Like Comte, the Logical Positivists thought of themselves as advocates of the cause of science; unlike Comte, they took up an attitude toward metaphysics that was uniformly hostile. The external reason for this was to be found in the philosophical atmosphere in the German-speaking world in the years following World War I, an atmosphere that seemed to a group of thinkers known as the Vienna Circle to favour obscurantism and impede rational thought. But there were, of course, internal reasons as well.

According to the Positivists, meaningful statements can be divided into two kinds, those that are analytically true or false and those that express or purport to express matters of material fact. The propositions of logic and mathematics exemplify the first class, those of history and the natural and social sciences the second. To decide whether a sentence that purports to state a fact is meaningful, one must ask what would count for or against its truth; if the answer is "nothing," it cannot have meaning, or at least not in that way. Thus, they adopted the slogan that the meaning of a (nonanalytic) statement is the method of its verification. It was this verification principle that the Positivists used as their main weapon in their attacks on metaphysics. Taking as their examples statements from actual metaphysical texts—statements such as "The Absolute has no history" and "God exists"—they asked first if they were supposed to be analytically or synthetically true, and then, after dismissing the first alternative, asked what could be adduced as evidence in their favour or against them. Many metaphysicians, of course, claimed that there was empirical support for their speculative conclusions; thus, as even Hume said, "the order of the universe proves an omnipotent mind." The very same writers, however, proved strangely reluctant to withdraw their claims in the face of unfavourable evidence; they behaved as if no fact of any kind could count against their contentions. It followed, said the Positivists, that the theses in which they were interested were compatible with any facts whatsoever and thus were entirely lacking in significance. An analytic proposition, such as "It either will or will not rain tomorrow," tells nothing, though there may be a point in giving voice to it. A metaphysical proposition claims to be very different; it purports to reveal an all-important truth about the world. But it is no more informative than a bare tautology, and, if there is a point in putting it forward, it has to do with the emotions rather than the understanding.

The verification principle

In point of fact, the Positivists experienced great difficulty in devising a satisfactory formulation of their verification principle, to say nothing of a satisfactory account of the principle's own status. In the early days of the movement the demand for verifiability was interpreted strictly: only what could be conclusively verified could be significant. This had the effect of showing that statements about the past and propositions of unrestricted generality, to take only two instances, must be without meaning. Later a move was made toward understanding verifiability in a weak sense: a statement was meaningful if any observations bore on its truth. According to A.J. Ayer, an English disciple of the Vienna Circle, writing in 1936,

> It is the mark of a genuine factual proposition, not that it should be equivalent to an experiential proposition, or any finite number of experiential propositions, but simply that some experiential propositions can be deduced from it in conjunction with certain other premises without being deducible from those other premises alone.

As Ayer admitted in his second edition, however, this formulation lets in too much, including the propositions of metaphysics. From "The Absolute has no history" and "If the Absolute has no history, this is red," it follows that "This is red," which is certainly an experiential proposition. Nor were subsequent attempts, by Ayer and others, to tighten up the formulation generally accepted as successful, for in every case it was possible to produce objections of a more or less persuasive kind.

This result may seem paradoxical, for at first glance the Positivist case is extremely impressive. It certainly sounds odd to say that metaphysical sentences are literally without meaning, seeing that, for example, they can be replaced by equivalent sentences in the same or another language. But if the term meaning is taken here in a broad sense and understood to cover significance generally, the contention is by no means implausible. What is now being said is that metaphysical systems have internal meaning only; the terms of which they consist may be interdefinable but perhaps do not relate to anything outside the system. If that were so, metaphysics would in a way make sense but for all that would be essentially idle; it would be a game that might amuse but could hardly instruct. The Positivists confront the metaphysician with the task of showing that this criticism is not correct. Whatever difficulties are involved in formulating a principle of verifiability, the challenge can hardly be ignored.

Moore and Wittgenstein. The Positivists were not the only modern critics of metaphysics. G.E. Moore never argued against metaphysics as such, but nevertheless he produced criticisms of particular metaphysical theses that, if accepted, would make metaphysical speculation difficult, if not impossible. It was characteristic of a certain type of philosopher, according to Moore, to advance claims of a highly paradoxical nature—to say, for instance, that "Time is not real" or that "There are no such things as physical objects." Moore's case for rejecting such claims was that they go against the most central convictions of common sense, convictions that people accept unhesitatingly when they are not doing philosophy. Men constantly say that they did this before that, that things are better or worse than they were; from time to time they put off things until later or remark that tomorrow will be another day. Moore took these facts as definitive proof of the reality of time and definitive disproof of any metaphysical theory that denied it. Supporters of Bradley, the philosopher here criticized, replied that Moore had missed the point. Bradley never denied the truth of temporal propositions as used in the description of appearances; what he questioned was the coherence and ultimate tenability of the whole temporal way of thinking. As Rudolf Carnap, a Logical Positivist, was to put it, he raised an external question and was given an internal answer by Moore. It was an answer, however, that carried considerable conviction. The simple denial of what seem to be obvious facts had always been part of the stock-in-trade of metaphysicians; they make much of the distinction between appearance and reality. Moore may not have demonstrated the impropriety of this insistence, but at least he made it necessary for the metaphysician to be more circumspect, to explain explicitly what he was denying and what he was ready to accept, and so to make his own case sharper and thus easier to confirm or reject.

Common-sense criticisms

Moore's implied criticisms of metaphysics lead on naturally to those of Wittgenstein. Moore took his stand on common sense, whereas Wittgenstein based his on living language. Arguing that men are each involved in a multitude of language games or autonomous linguistic activities, insofar as they are scientific investigators, moral agents, litigants, religious worshipers, and so on, Wittgenstein asked in what language game the claims and questionings of philosophers arose. He replied that there was no genuine

Language criticisms

linguistic context to which they belonged; philosophical puzzlement was essentially idle. Philosophers were preoccupied with highly general questions; they aspired to solve *the* problem of meaning or *the* problem of reality. Against that Wittgenstein argued that words and sentences have meaning as used in particular contexts; there is no single set of conditions that has to be fulfilled if they are to be thought meaningful. Equally, there is no single set of criteria that has to be satisfied by everything one takes to be real. Sticks and stones and men are taken as real in everyday discourse, but so are numbers in the discourse of mathematicians, and so is God in the discourse of religious men. There is simply no warrant for preferring one of these above the others—for saying, for example, with persons of an Empiricist turn of mind, that nothing can be real that does not have existence in space and time.

Wittgenstein's antipathy to metaphysical philosophy was in part based on self-criticism; in his early work the *Tractatus Logico-Philosophicus,* published in 1922, he had himself tried to give a general account of meaning. At least one doctrine of that enigmatic book survived in his later thought: the distinction between saying and showing. Wittgenstein in the *Tractatus* sought to pronounce on "what can be said" and came to the conclusion that only "propositions of natural science" can be. Though at this stage he spoke as if metaphysical statements were senseless, his motives for doing so were very different from those of the Positivists. The latter saw metaphysics as an enemy of science; in their view there was only one way to understand the world, and that was in scientific terms. But Wittgenstein, though agreeing that science alone can be clear, held that scientific thought has its limitations. There are things that cannot be said but can, nonetheless, be shown; the sphere of the mystical is perhaps a case in point. Unlike his Viennese contemporaries, Wittgenstein had no wish to rule out of court the thought that there are more things in heaven and earth than can be compassed in the language of science; writers whom he admired—such as Blaise Pascal, a 17th-century French scientist and writer on religious subjects, and Søren Kierkegaard, a Danish philosopher and theologian who is regarded as the founder of modern Existentialism—had discoursed of such matters in a way that was highly illuminating. They had made clear, however, that, just as one here went beyond the province of science, so also one went beyond that of philosophy. For them the idea that the metaphysician is privy to the most important of all things is absurd. There may be a sense in which men transcend everyday experience in moments of religious feeling or artistic insight, but there is no justification for thinking that when they do they arrive at the metaphysician's Absolute. As Kierkegaard said, the man who looks for speculative proofs in the sphere of religion shows that he does not understand that sphere at all.

Religious philosophers. It is important, in considering current criticisms of metaphysics, to appreciate that this discipline is now under double attack. In the first place, it must face the assault of those who regard it as a rival to science; it is against this assault that sympathizers like R.G. Collingwood, a British philosopher, historian, and archaeologist, seek to defend it. But metaphysics is also in disfavour among many religious philosophers. In earlier days, partisans of religion, and more generally believers in a spiritual order, looked to metaphysics to vindicate their claims against skeptical attack; now they are altogether more reluctant to do so. The continuing controversy about metaphysics has no doubt influenced this development; it scarcely seems sensible to take refuge in a fortress whose walls are so frequently breached. There is, however, another motive that operates here: the feeling that metaphysics is not only dubious but, worse, unnecessary. In an age whose tendencies are antiphilosophical rather than philosophical, there is widespread acceptance of the view that religion and morals, and for that matter science and history, are their own justification; none of them stands in need of a certificate of respectability from philosophy, and any pretense by metaphysicians to supply or refuse such a certificate must be without foundation. Though this view is widespread, it is even so not unchallenged; there are persons who find the fragmentation it involves—belief in God on Sundays, belief in science for the rest of the week—intolerable. For such persons, at least, the search for metaphysical truth and metaphysical answers must retain its fascination. (W.H.W.)

Tendencies in contemporary metaphysics

Background: the thought of Kant and Hegel

Kant's efforts to limit metaphysics opened new lines for its development. He had thought that reason is established by being limited and that some truths are certain independent of anything that can happen in experience because experience is structured by the interpretive categories reflected in these truths. Thus, it is possible to be certain of the world in its general structure but only insofar as it is an experienced, or phenomenal, world—that is, a world known by man, not a world as it is in itself. Hegel, however, argued persistently that knowledge of a thing unknowable in itself is a contradiction and that reason can know all that is real if the mind first accepts the given thing as "always already within experience as other." The mutual implication of knowing mind and reality known is accepted, and a science of self-consciousness that relates all categories and all reality to the knowing subject is envisaged. Thus, Kant's mutual implication of knowing subject and phenomenal thing was given ultimate metaphysical validity by Hegel, and Kant's reformulations of traditional dualisms—*e.g.,* subject–object, appearance–reality, perceptual–categorial, immanent–transcendent, regulative–constitutive—became momentous for metaphysics.

TENDENCIES IN THE UNITED STATES

John Dewey. In this milieu, John Dewey, an American educational reformer and pragmatic philosopher, published his "Kant and Philosophic Method" in 1884 in the journal of a group known as the St. Louis Hegelians. Although Dewey later rejected the full-scale Hegelianism expressed in the article, he did so only after gathering up in a partial synthesis the thought of both Kant and Hegel. In this he sounded the thematic notes of much contemporary American and continental metaphysics. Whether or not this metaphysics is explicitly termed transcendental (that is, concerned with experience as determined by the mind's conceptual and categorial makeup), it does two things: (1) it affirms Kant's insight that physical particulars cannot first be identified and later interrelated by means of the categories, but, to be identified at all, they must be assumed to be already categorized, and reasoning must proceed to expose those categorial structures that make the actuality of knowledge possible; (2) it agrees with Hegel's critique at least to the extent that Kant's idea that the source of sensations is external to the mind in a noumenon is regarded as a transgression of Kant's own doctrine that the categories, particularly that of causation, can be applied only within phenomenal experience. Dewey thought that Kant confused the empirical and transcendental standpoints by mixing analysis of the organism as sensationally responsive with analysis of mind. Kant forgot that it is only because the knowing subject already grasps the world through its categories that it can self-deceivingly regard its sensations as subjective and as caused by something not known. Thus, for Dewey, "The relation between subject and object is not an external one; it is one in a higher unity that is itself constituted by this relation."

In Dewey's extended later thought, metaphysics became the study of "the generic traits of existence." Concern with God and immortality slips nearly from view, and this is typical of much contemporary philosophy. Even so, Dewey's rethinking of the subject–object relation engenders a concept of a democratic and scientific community of persons, bound to each other through common ideals, which has religious overtones. Vague and ambivalent as this concept may be, it helps undermine the whole contrast between immanent and transcendent and leads metaphysics on new paths.

Location of the role of science in knowledge

William James. The work of William James, a leader of the Pragmatic movement, was typical of many contemporary tendencies, one of which was the attempt to locate the role of science in knowledge and culture. Trained in medicine, James hoped to protect the autonomy of psychology as a science by adopting a dualistic view of mind and matter. He "supposes two elements, mind knowing and thing known, and treats them as irreducible. Neither gets out of itself or into the other, neither in any way is the other." He presumed that mental states could be identified independent of a commitment to the metaphysical status of the things known by them and that they could then be correlated to the brain. Ironically, his attempts to identify mental states involved him in commitments to the nature of the world as presented to mind. The only meaning that can be given things is in terms of the anticipated consequences of one's actions upon these things in the world; this anticipation also supplies the meaningfulness of thoughts. This is the basis of the "instrumental" view of thoughts—*i.e.,* reflecting upon thoughts as "tools," or as "plans of action," tells one something about the things known by them, the "tooled"; the converse also occurs.

Each realm of the world is experienced in terms of temporal standards of thought natural to that realm; *e.g.,* standards of mathematics are peculiar because of their ideal, changeless objects. These criteria are not derived from mind alone or from things alone but from their relationship in what is termed experience. This is a "double-barreled" term—that is, an experiencing of experienced things. The mind cannot be specified independent of things that appear to the mind, and things cannot be specified independent of their modes of appearing to the mind. Phenomena regarded abstractly as singular, or "pure," are neutral between mind and matter, which are different contexts of the very same pure experiences—contexts that comprise a single world.

James would not claim that his method is transcendental. Yet the fact remains that for him subject and object cannot be specified independent of each other, and James undercuts dualism and moves toward a transcendental explanation of the conditions of knowledge.

James tried to avoid what can be called logicism, physicalism, and psychologism. The last claimed that, because knowing is a psychical act, all that is known about must be subject to psychological laws. James replied that the known-about, the experienced, has its own autonomy, either as pure experience, a "specific nature" studied by philosophy, as a physical context studied by physics, or, finally, as a psychical context, a human history, studied by psychology. The latter two are both dependent, at least for their ultimate meaningfulness, upon the first. Physicalism attempts to infer the nature of the psychical directly from the physical, thus reducing it to the physical. Most logicisms claimed that pure reason can grasp the real in itself. James agreed that reason entertains ideal objects, the relations between which are fixed independent of the sequence of sensory experience, but he asserted that this experience must decide which necessary truths apply to the world. Although some always do apply, the ascertainment of what is categorial for the world is always incomplete. Just when the world "plays into the hands of logic" is decided in that endless interaction of "worlds" or "orders of experience"—such as the perceptual, the imaginary, the mathematical—occasioned by a thing experienced sifting through the orders trying to find one that can contain it without contradiction; Pegasus, for example, is a mythical creature just because it cannot find a place in the world of real horses. The world of perceptual things, experienced as experienceable by all and as existing simultaneously, serves as a paradigm of reality even though other orders of experience are not reducible to it. Existence is an unusual predicate for James; it means that practical relationship of doing and concern within which things must be able to stand to men if they are to be counted as fundamentally real. James was not giving a subjectivistic account of reality, however, because he included in the fundamentally real all that can be related spatially and temporally to what can stand over against men's bodily selves. This was commonly forgotten by critics of James's popularized theory of truth, Pragmatism, which was thus systematically misunderstood.

James's contemporaries Charles Sanders Peirce and Josiah Royce stood in close dialectical exchange with him on these themes. Differences between them concerned the scope and conditions to be assigned experience. In general, Peirce argued that experience is to be construed more narrowly, in terms of mathematical logic and physics, whereas Royce argued that the understanding of truth, error, and meaning requires the assumption of an absolute knower or experiencer. Peirce was a seminal thinker whose thoughts were often beginnings in the more systematically developed philosophies of the other Americans.

TENDENCIES IN CONTINENTAL EUROPE

Edmund Husserl and Phenomenology. Edmund Husserl, the German philosopher, used the term Phenomenology to name a whole philosophy. In order to rid his transcendental investigation of empirical prejudgments and to discover connections of meaning that are necessary truths underlying both physical and psychological sciences, Husserl bracketed and suspended all judgments of existence and empirical causation. He did not deny them; rather, he no longer simply asserted them. He reflected upon their intended meaning. In reflection he claimed to see that things have meaning in terms of how they appear to men in their pre-reflective life and that awareness is in terms of this "how." In pre-reflective life, however, men are not aware of the "how" as such. By exposing this basic meaning through which men refer to things, he can free their eyes of the "cataracts" of the stereotyped and the obvious and can summon them "back to the things themselves."

Reflection on pre-reflective life

Husserl took traditional metaphysics to be infested with precritical commitments to existence, either physicalistic, psychologistic, or logistic. He used the term ontology, however, to apply to his study of objects of consciousness and even appropriated the Aristotelian term first philosophy. The world appears within the reflective bracket as existentially neutral (that is, as regards whether things have existence in themselves or exist for men) but ontologically ordered because, if various orders of beings exist, then what they are can be nothing but what they are intended to be. And what they are cannot be known until all they are intended to be is known.

Husserl distinguished two types of ontologies: formal ontologies, which are the domain of meanings, or essences, such as "one," "many," "whole," or "part," that are articulated by formal logic and which Husserl referred to as empty; and material ontologies, which discover and map the meaning and structure of sensory experience through transcendental investigation. In material ontology, for example, the essence of any physical thing is discovered by varying in the imagination the object that is given within its strictly correlative mode of perceptual consciousness; the essence is that identical something that continuously maintains itself during the process of variation. It is intuited that the perceived thing cannot vary in the imagination beyond the point of something given perspectively and incompletely to any given perceiving glance; hence, this is the essence of any physical thing. This is a truth of eidetic necessity and comprises a first principle in Husserl's projected philosophical science; *e.g.,* numbers are what they are because of the ways in which they are not like things.

The Existentialists. Husserl had early distinguished the primary task of description of "morphological essences" (those with "floating" spheres of application in the sensory life) from description of essences like those in geometry, which described closed, or definite, manifolds; but the question of the theoretical status of the ordinary perceptual world, or lived world (*Lebenswelt*), became increasingly disputed among Existentialists. They asked whether there can be a philosophical science that has made all its presuppositions transparent to itself. If transcendental elucidation of the *Lebenswelt,* with its historically established sediments of meaning, is really essential to show how theoretical sciences are grounded, then one may reasonably ask how Phenomenology can be sure it has accomplished the elucidation completely because it is itself a theory. The question gained urgency by Husserl's nearly imperceptible slide into what appeared to be an Idealist position regarding the source of all meaning, a commitment to an absolute ego. If this ego is regarded as individual in any way, the problem arises of how any other individual can be as other because it is constituted in this primal ego.

Husserl's theory of the ego was rejected by French Existentialists such as Jean-Paul Sartre and Maurice Merleau-Ponty. For the latter, the bracketing of meanings can never be completed, for consciousness is not an enclosed individual that could grasp through reflection all its possible motivations to experience and give meaning to a world. Knowers are subjects with bodies, whose perceptual life is articulated only incompletely and discloses the world in progressively surprising ways. More meaning is found in existence than can at any moment be expressed, and even the meaning of existence is not reducible to any definable set of meanings.

Husserl's approach was not nearly radical enough for Martin Heidegger, a German thinker sometimes called an Existentialist. In thinking that he could prescind so neatly from facts and retain the essence of facts, Husserl was still involved to some extent in the prejudgments—the psychologistic, physicalistic, and logistic dualisms—that he inveighed against. For Heidegger there is no realm of consciousness that constitutes meaning, and he does not think that some sharp but harmless line could be drawn between essence and fact. The ambiguity in Husserl's thought between "object" as sense of the particular and as the encountered particular in its bodily presence is not harmless. It is unjustifiable to think that consciousness can finally demarcate the essential sense of a thing. Thus, Heidegger discarded the very concept of consciousness and proposed a "fundamental ontology" of human being (*Dasein*). Man as a subject in the world cannot be made the object of sophisticated theoretical conceptions such as "substance" or "cause"; man, furthermore, finds himself already involved in an ongoing world that cannot as a whole be made the object of such conceptions; yet the structure of this involvement is the transcendental condition of any science of objects. For example, a man can band with other men in philosophical groups and can think about the metaphysical status of other men only because he is already essentially with others. He cannot hope to so purify his own thinking that it becomes that of an impersonal thinker, an absolute ego.

Ontology of *Dasein*

According to Heidegger, to rethink the problem of reality at its roots, it is necessary to rethink the fundamentally temporal, already-given structures of human involvement. Prejudice in the West, which construes reality, or being, on the basis of beings (that is, being as the most general feature of beings), must be overturned, and the problem of the real, the "transcendent," must be rethought on a ground on which distinctions between immanent and transcendent and between perceptual and categorial have been reconstructed. The being of the world transcends any constitution of the meaning of the world and is a condition of experience. Thus, a sense is required of being not as object but as the underlying condition for the reality of the being of all objects.

Heidegger wanted to propose a genuine phenomenology, a study that would presuppose nothing of the traditionally formulated distinctions such as subjective–objective or phenomenal–real. The transcendence of the world can be understood only as it appears; *i.e.,* when they are encountered openly, things appear as appearing in part, as both revealing and concealing themselves. If to the uneducated eye the Sun appears to be smaller than it is, the naive inference can be corrected only by educating the person to interpret appearances—to calculate, for example, the speed and direction of light. The real is given in and through its appearances.

THE THOUGHT OF WHITEHEAD

The thought of Alfred North Whitehead is a distinctive variation on these contemporary themes. Dualisms are undermined by a phenomenology that does not bracket factual assertions. Logical and mathematical deductive schemes must be able to be interpreted in relationships crudely observable in experience, and abstractions of physics and common sense parading as realism (*e.g.,* that things exist separately within their own surfaces) must be revealed for what they are, namely, abstractions. The basic units of reality are organismic unities, "actual occasions," which are spatial and temporal extensions that cannot be exhaustively expressed in terms of distributions of matter at an instant. Their unity is constituted in a perception-like responsiveness to the universe that, though usually lacking consciousness or apprehension, is an appropriation to and for itself of the whole. This appropriation cannot be exhaustively expressed by point-instant mechanics (mechanics that is worked out in connection with the physics of relativity and thus measures not only the distance but also the time intervals between points) but is minimally a "prehension" (a term proper to Whitehead indicating the point-transcending function of perception and consciousness).

Organismic unities

Each enduring object of ordinary perception—tables, chairs, animals—is, for Whitehead, a "society" of actual occasions inheriting, through a process of appropriation and reenactment in a predictable way, characteristics of its predecessors. Human perception is understood as a special case of prehension, in which qualities of the environment are mediated and projected on the basis of organic and affective experience of the perceiver's body, but in such a way that some of this process can be acknowledged by the percipient upon reflection. Because human consciousness is regarded as only a special case of prehensive relations, and because vacuous realisms and notions of transcendence are regarded as "fallacies of misplaced concreteness and simple location," mind–body dualisms are rejected.

Whitehead thought of "the primordial nature of God" as a general ordering of the process of the world, the ultimate basis of all induction and assertion of law, a "conceptual prehension" that functions in the selection of those "eternal objects," or repeatable patterns that are enacted in the world. God, however, does not create actual entities. He provides them with initial impetus, in the form of their subjective aim, to self-creation. Even God is the outcome of creativity, the process by which the events of the world are synthesized into new unities. It is the creative, not fully predictable, advance into novelty of a pluralistic process. The freedom of man and the determinism of nature were regarded by Whitehead as another artificial dualism.

The future of metaphysics is uncertain, not mainly because of 20th-century critics, the Logical Positivists, but because of its own not fully predictable nor controllable dynamisms. (B.W.W.)

BIBLIOGRAPHY. These works deal mainly with the nature and possibility of metaphysics.

For a discussion of the apparently conflicting views of Plato and Aristotle, see the commentary in ARISTOTLE, *Metaphysics,* ed. by W.D. ROSS, rev. ed., 2 vol. (1924, reissued 1966); and WERNER JAEGER, *Aristotle: Fundamentals of the History of His Development,* 2nd ed. (1948, reprinted 1968; originally published in German, 1923). Modern discussions of the methods of metaphysics are found in RENÉ DESCARTES, *The Philosophical Works of Descartes,* trans. by ELIZABETH S. HALDANE and G.R.T. ROSS, 2 vol. (1911–12, reprinted with corrections, 1981), and *Philosophical Letters,* trans. from the French and ed. by ANTHONY KENNY (1970). On the geometrical form of metaphysics, see the essay by BENEDICT SPINOZA, "Ethica, more geometrico demonstratis," available in a translation by W. HALE WHITE and rev. by AMELIA H. STIRLING, *Ethic: Demonstrated in Geometrical Order. . . ,* 4th ed. rev. (1927, reprinted 1930). CHRISTIAN WOLFF combined both the practice and theory of metaphysics in his voluminous metaphysical writings: *Vernünfftige* [sic] *Gedanken von Gott, der Welt und der Seele der Menschen,* new enlarged ed. (1751, reprinted 1983), *Philosophia Prima Sive Ontologia,* 2nd ed. (1736, reprinted 1962), *Cosmologia Generalis,* rev. ed. (1737, reprinted 1964), *Psychologia Rationalis,* rev. ed. (1740, reprinted 1972), and *Theologia Naturalis,* rev. ed., 2 vol. (1739–41, reprinted 2 vol. in 3, 1978–81). ALEXANDER GOTTLIEB BAUMGARTEN, *Metaphysica,* 7th ed. (1779, reprinted 1963), was in effect a digest of these last four works. The problem of the origin of ideas was first posed in JOHN LOCKE, *An Essay Concerning Humane* [sic] *Understanding* (1690, reissued 1979), on which G.W. LEIBNIZ wrote a critical commentary, *Nouveaux essais sur l'entendement humain* (1765), available also in an English translation ed. by PETER REMNANT and JONATHAN BENNETT, *New Essays on Human Understanding* (1981). GEORGE BERKELEY criticized Materialism in his *Treatise Concerning the Principles of Human Knowledge* (1710, reissued 1983), available also in a contemporary edition ed. by COLIN M. TURBAYNE. DAVID HUME applied Empiricist principles with complete generality in *A Treatise of Human Nature,* 3 vol. (1739–40, reprinted in 1 vol., 1975), and *An Enquiry Concerning Human Understanding* (1748, reissued 1977).

IMMANUEL KANT first discussed metaphysical method in his essay "Inquiry into the Distinctness of the Principles of Natural Theology and Morals," available in a translation by LEWIS WHITE BECK, *Critique of Practical Reason and Other Writings in Moral Philosophy* (1949); and Kant examined the whole question of the possibility of metaphysical knowledge in *Critique of Pure Reason* (1982; originally published in German, 4th ed., 1794), and *Prolegomena to Any Future Metaphysics That Will Be Able to Come Forward as Science,* trans. by PAUL CARUS (1902, rev. ed. 1977). For a sustained criticism of Kant's critical point of view, see the writings of G.W.F. HEGEL, especially *The Phenomenology of Mind,* 2nd ed. (1931, reissued 1977; originally published in German, 1807), *The Logic of Hegel,* trans. from the German by WILLIAM WALLACE (1873, reprinted with the title *Hegel's Logic,* 1975), *Hegel's Philosophy of Nature,* 3 vol., ed. and trans. from the German by M.J. PETRY (1970), and *Hegel's Philosophy of Mind,* trans. from the German by WILLIAM WALLACE, enlarged ed. (1971). These last three are translations from various editions of Hegel's *Encycklopädie der philosophischen Wissenschaften,* first published in 1817.

Only a few 19th-century philosophers added to the fundamental criticisms of metaphysics developed by earlier writers. See, for example, AUGUSTE COMTE, *Cours de philosophie positive,* 6 vol. (1830–42), available also in an edition of selections, ed. by STANISLAV ANDRESKI, *The Essential Comte* (1974); and JOHN STUART MILL, *System of Logic,* 2 vol. (1843, reissued 1978). Mill was sharply criticized by THOMAS HILL GREEN, *Prolegomena to Ethics,* 5th ed. (1907, reprinted 1969); and F.H. BRADLEY, *The Principles of Logic,* 2nd ed. rev. (1922, reissued 1963).

For American metaphysical thought of the same period, see CHARLES SANDERS PEIRCE, *Collected Papers of Charles Sanders Peirce,* ed. by CHARLES HARTSHORNE, PAUL WEISS, and A.W. BURKS, 8 vol. (1931–58, reissued in 4 vol., 1974–79); and WILLIAM JAMES, *A Pluralistic Universe* (1909, reprinted 1979).

There are interesting remarks on the philosophy of philosophy in the works of WILHELM DILTHEY, especially vol. 5 of his *Gesammelte Schriften,* 5th ed., 12 vol. (1962). Twentieth-century criticisms of metaphysics derive mainly from the work of the Vienna Circle; see VIKTOR KRAFT, *The Vienna Circle: The Origin of Neo-Positivism* (1953, reissued 1969; originally published in German, 1950). LUDWIG WITTGENSTEIN, *Tractatus Logico-Philosophicus* (1922, reissued 1983), was read as an improved version of Empiricism. Among the authors who influenced the Logical Positivists were ERNST MACH, *The Science of Mechanics: A Critical and Historical Accident of Its Development,* 6th ed. (1974; originally published in German, 9th ed., 1933); ALFRED NORTH WHITEHEAD and BERTRAND RUSSELL, *Principia Mathematica,* 2nd ed., 3 vol. (1925–27, reprinted 1968–73); and BERTRAND RUSSELL, *Our Knowledge of the External World as a Field for Scientific Method in Philosophy,* rev. ed. (1926, reprinted 1972). A.J. AYER (ed.), *Logical Positivism* (1959, reprinted 1978), anthologizes in translation some of the most famous papers from the Vienna Circle's periodical *Erkenntnis.* Ayer's own book, *Language, Truth and Logic,* 2nd ed. rev. (1946, reprinted 1970), was extremely successful in spreading Positivist ideas in America and Britain, where the work of GEORGE EDWARD MOORE, especially "Defence of Common Sense," in his *Philosophical Papers,* pp. 32–59 (1959, reprinted 1977), had created an atmosphere in which metaphysical claims were viewed with suspicion. Another influential book along the same lines as Ayer's was HANS REICHENBACH, *The Rise of Scientific Philosophy* (1951, reprinted 1968); see also MORRIS LAZEROWITZ, *The Structure of Metaphysics* (1955, reprinted 1968), which attempts to explain the activities of metaphysicians in terms of psychoanalysis. For criticism of Positivist ideas, see WINSTON H.F. BARNES, *The Philosophical Predicament* (1950); D.F. PEARS (ed.), *The Nature of Metaphysics* (1957, reprinted 1970); and KARL R. POPPER, *Conjectures and Refutations: The Growth of Scientific Knowledge,* 4th ed. rev. (1974). R.G. COLLINGWOOD, *An Essay on Metaphysics* (1940, reprinted 1979), purports to answer Ayer but instead contains an unconventional view of metaphysics as historical analysis. A division of metaphysical systems into "descriptive" and "revisionary" is proposed in P.F. STRAWSON, *Individuals: An Essay in Descriptive Metaphysics* (1959, reprinted 1964). For further discussions, see W.H. WALSH, *Metaphysics* (1963, reprinted 1966); A.J. AYER, *Metaphysics and Common Sense* (1969, reprinted 1973); ANTHONY QUINTON, *The Nature of Things* (1973, reprinted 1978); STEPHAN KÖRNER, *Metaphysics, Its Structure and Function* (1984); and D.W. HAMLYN, *Metaphysics* (1984). For a very different approach, compare MARTIN HEIDEGGER, *An Introduction to Metaphysics* (1959, reissued 1961; originally published in German, 1953).

Recent European thought is summarized in RÜDIGER BUBNER, *Modern German Philosophy* (1981), trans. by ERIC MATTHEW from an unpublished manuscript, which provides a critical survey of recent philosophy in Germany and compares it to philosophical work in the English-speaking world; VINCENT DESCOMBES, *Modern French Philosophy* (1980; originally published in French, 1979), a survey of contemporary philosophy in France; and ALAN MONTEFIORI (ed.), *Philosophy in France Today* (1983), a collection of essays by French philosophers describing their own work and interests. ANDRÉ DE MURALT, *The Idea of Phenomenology: Husserlian Exemplarism* (1974; originally published in French, 1958), studies the main themes in phenomenological philosophy. A useful introductory guide with an extensive bibliography is DAVID STEWARD and ALGIS MICKUNAS, *Exploring Phenomenology: A Guide to the Field and Its Literature* (1974). HERBERT SPIEGELBERG, *The Phenomenological Movement: A Historical Introduction,* 3rd rev. ed. (1982), discusses central themes in Phenomenology; and in *The Context of the Phenomenological Movement* (1981), he explains the background to that movement.

KARL-OTTO APEL, *Towards a Transformation of Philosophy* (1980; originally published in German, 1972), is an influential study of objectivity, subjectivity, and interpretation. JÜRGEN HABERMAS, *Knowledge and Human Interests,* 2nd ed. (1978; originally published in German, 1968), is a critique of Positivism. HANS-GEORG GADAMER, *Truth and Method* (1975, reissued 1982; originally published in German, 2nd ed., 1965), gives a Heideggerian account of the interpretation of experience. Another influential contribution to recent philosophy is EMMANUEL LÉVINAS, *Totality and Infinity: An Essay on Exteriority* (1969, reissued 1979; originally published in French, 1961).

Works that analyze the thought of specific philosophers include: R.E. AQUILA, "Two Problems of Being and Nonbeing in Sartre's Being and Nothingness," *Philosophy and Phenomenological Research,* 28(2):167–186 (December 1977); SUZANNE BACHELARD, *A Study of Husserl's "Formal and Transcendental Logic"* (1968; originally published in French, 1957); JOHN D. CAPUTO, *The Mystical Elements in Heidegger's Thought* (1978); JACQUES DERRIDA, *Edmund Husserl's "Origin of Geometry": An Introduction* (1978; originally published in French, 2nd rev. ed., 1974); JOSEPH P. FELL, *Heidegger and Sartre* (1979); WOLFGANG WALTER FUCHS, *Phenomenology and the Metaphysics of Presence: An Essay in the Philosophy of Edmund Husserl* (1976); AGNES HELLER (ed.), *Lukács Reappraised* (1983; U.K. title, *Lukács Revalued*); SANG-KI KIM, *The Problem of the Contingency of the World in Husserl's Phenomenology* (1977); A.M. MIRVISH, "Merleau-Ponty and the Nature of Philosophy," *Philosophy and Phenomenological Research,* 43(4):449–476 (June 1983); MARIE-LUISE SCHUBERT KALSI, *Alexius Meinong on Objects of Higher Order and Husserl's Phenomenology* (1978); and ANTHONY THISELTON, *The Two Horizons: New Testament Hermeneutics and Philosophical Description with Special Reference to Heidegger, Bultmann, Gadamer, and Wittgenstein* (1980).

(W.H.W./A.C.G.)

Mexico

Mexico, or the United Mexican States (Spanish: Estados Unidos Mexicanos), is a federal republic located in North America. Sharing a common border throughout its northern extent with the United States, the country is bounded on the west and south by the Pacific Ocean, to the east by the Gulf of Mexico and the Caribbean Sea, and on the southeast by Guatemala and Belize. Roughly triangular in shape, Mexico covers an area of 756,066 square miles (1,958,201 square kilometres). While it is more than 1,850 miles (3,000 kilometres) across the country from northwest to southeast, the width varies from less than 135 miles at the Isthmus of Tehuantepec to more than 1,200 miles in the north.

Mexico has a vast wealth of mineral resources, a limited amount of agricultural land, and a rapidly growing population. More than half of the people live in the central core, while vast areas of the arid north and the tropical south are sparsely settled. The long-held stereotype of Mexico as a country where life is slow-paced and the population consists mostly of subsistence farmers has little truth. Petroleum and tourism have come to dominate the economy, and industrialization is increasing in many parts of the country. Internal migration has caused urban centres to grow dramatically, and more than two-thirds of Mexicans now live in cities; in population, Mexico City, the capital, is the largest city in the world (though the Mexico City metropolitan area ranks third in population when compared to other metropolitan areas). Despite impressive social and economic gains made during the 1960s and '70s, most Mexicans remain poor. Beginning in the 1980s the country was wracked by severe inflation and an enormous foreign debt.

These growing pains of modernization are in sharp counterpoint to the traditional life-styles that prevail in the more isolated rural areas. Small communal villages remain, where Indian peasants live much as did their ancestors. The cultural remnants of great Indian civilizations, such as those at Chichén Itzá or Tulum, provide a contrast to colonial towns like Taxco or Querétaro. In turn, these towns appear as historical relics when compared to the modern metropolis of Mexico City. It is this tremendous cultural and economic diversity, distributed over an enormously complex and varied physical environment, that gives Mexico its character.

This article is divided into the following sections:

Physical and human geography

THE LAND

Relief. Mexico is located in one of the Earth's most dynamic tectonic areas. It is a part of the circum-Pacific "Ring of Fire," a region of active volcanism and frequent seismic activity. Towering peaks, such as Citlaltépetl (also called Orizaba; 18,701 feet [5,700 metres]) and Popocatépetl (17,883 feet [5,452 metres]), are extremely young in geologic terms (late Tertiary) and are examples of the volcanic forces that built much of the central and southern parts of the country. Mexico is situated on the western, or leading, edge of the huge North American Plate, whose interaction with the Pacific, Cocos, and Caribbean plates has, over geologic time, given rise to the earth-building processes of the area. The complexity found in southern Mexico's physiography is due to the interaction among these tectonic plates, which produces numerous and severe earth movements. It is in this dynamical but often unstable physical environment that the Mexican people have built their nation.

On the basis of geologic history and surface configuration, Mexico can be divided into eight major landform regions. The largest, and most important for human habitation, is the Mexican Plateau. Extending from the Isthmus of Tehuantepec northward to the U.S. border, this region consists of a central plateau and its dissected borders. The central plateau tilts gently upward from the north toward the south. At its northern end the plateau is about 4,000 feet above sea level, and it rises to more than 8,000

The Mexican Plateau

MAP INDEX

Political subdivisions

Aguascalientes . . 22 00 N 102 30 W
Baja California Norte . . . 30 00 N 115 00 W
Baja California Sur . . . 25 50 N 111 50 W
Campeche . . . 19 00 N 90 30 W
Chiapas . . . 16 30 N 92 30 W
Chihuahua . . . 28 30 N 106 00 W
Coahuila . . . 27 20 N 102 00 W
Colima . . . 19 10 N 104 00 W
Distrito Federal . . 19 15 N 99 10 W
Durango . . . 24 50 N 104 50 W
Guanajuato . . . 21 00 N 101 00 W
Guerrero . . . 17 40 N 100 00 W
Hidalgo . . . 20 30 N 99 00 W
Jalisco . . . 20 20 N 103 40 W
México . . . 19 20 N 99 30 W
Michoacán . . . 19 10 N 101 50 W
Morelos . . . 18 45 N 99 00 W
Nayarit . . . 22 00 N 105 00 W
Nuevo León . . . 25 40 N 100 00 W
Oaxaca . . . 17 00 N 96 30 W
Puebla . . . 18 50 N 98 00 W
Querétaro . . . 21 00 N 99 55 W
Quintana Roo . . . 19 40 N 88 30 W
San Luis Potosí . . 22 30 N 100 30 W
Sinaloa . . . 25 00 N 107 30 W
Sonora . . . 29 20 N 110 40 W
Tabasco . . . 18 00 N 92 40 W
Tamaulipas . . . 24 00 N 98 45 W
Tlaxcala . . . 19 25 N 98 10 W
Veracruz . . . 19 20 N 96 40 W
Yucatán . . . 20 50 N 89 00 W
Zacatecas . . . 23 00 N 103 00 W

Cities and towns

Acámbaro . . . 20 02 N 100 44 W
Acapulco . . . 16 51 N 99 55 W
Aguascalientes . . 21 53 N 102 18 W
Apatzingán . . . 19 05 N 102 21 W
Arriaga . . . 16 14 N 93 54 W
Autlán . . . 19 46 N 104 22 W
Caborca . . . 30 37 N 112 06 W
Campeche . . . 19 51 N 90 32 W
Cananea . . . 30 57 N 110 18 W
Cancún . . . 21 05 N 86 46 W
Carmen . . . 18 38 N 91 50 W
Casas Grandes . . 30 22 N 107 57 W
Celaya . . . 20 31 N 100 49 W
Cerro Azul . . . 21 12 N 97 44 W
Chetumal . . . 18 30 N 88 18 W
Chihuahua . . . 28 38 N 106 05 W
Chilpancingo . . . 17 33 N 99 30 W
Ciudad Acuña (Las Vacas) . . . 29 18 N 100 55 W
Ciudad de Mexico, see Mexico City
Ciudad Delicias . . 28 13 N 105 28 W
Ciudad Guzmán . 19 41 N 103 29 W
Ciudad Hidalgo . . 19 41 N 100 34 W
Ciudad Juárez . . . 31 44 N 106 29 W
Ciudad Mante . . . 22 44 N 98 57 W
Ciudad Obregón . . . 27 29 N 109 56 W
Ciudad Pemex . . 17 54 N 92 30 W
Ciudad Victoria . . 23 44 N 99 08 W
Coatzacoalcos . . 18 09 N 94 25 W
Colima . . . 19 14 N 103 43 W
Comitán . . . 16 15 N 92 08 W
Cosamaloapan . . 18 22 N 95 48 W
Cozumel . . . 20 31 N 86 55 W
Cuauhtémoc . . . 28 25 N 106 52 W
Cuernavaca . . . 18 55 N 99 15 W
Culiacán . . . 24 48 N 107 24 W
Díaz Gutiérrez . . . 22 12 N 100 57 W
Durango . . . 24 02 N 104 40 W
El Dorado . . . 24 17 N 107 21 W
Ensenada . . . 31 52 N 116 37 W
Escuinapa . . . 22 51 N 105 48 W
Fresnillo . . . 23 10 N 102 53 W
Gómez Palacio . . 25 34 N 103 30 W
Guadalajara . . . 20 40 N 103 20 W
Guadalupe . . . 25 41 N 100 15 W
Guadalupe Victoria . . . 24 27 N 104 07 W
Guanajuato . . . 21 01 N 101 15 W
Guasave . . . 25 34 N 108 27 W
Guaymas . . . 27 56 N 110 54 W
Hermosillo . . . 29 04 N 110 58 W
Heroica Nogales . 31 20 N 110 56 W
Hidalgo del Parral (Parral) . . 26 56 N 105 40 W
Iguala de la Independencia . . 18 21 N 99 32 W
Irapuato . . . 20 41 N 101 21 W
Jalapa . . . 19 32 N 96 55 W
Jerez de García Salinas . . . 22 39 N 103 00 W
Jiménez . . . 27 08 N 104 55 W
Juchitán . . . 16 26 N 95 01 W
La Paz . . . 24 10 N 110 18 W
La Piedad Cavadas . . . 20 21 N 102 00 W
Las Penas, see Puerto Vallarta
Las Vacas, see Ciudad Acuña
León . . . 21 07 N 101 40 W
Linares . . . 24 52 N 99 34 W
Los Mochis . . . 25 45 N 108 57 W
Los Tuxtlas, see San Andres Tuxtla
Macuspana . . . 17 46 N 92 36 W
Manzanillo . . . 19 03 N 104 20 W
Matamoros . . . 18 36 N 98 28 W
Matamoros . . . 25 53 N 97 30 W
Matehuala . . . 23 39 N 100 39 W
Mazatlán . . . 23 13 N 106 25 W
Mérida . . . 20 58 N 89 37 W
Mexicali . . . 32 40 N 115 29 W
Mexico City (Ciudad de Mexico) . . . 19 24 N 99 09 W
Mezquital . . . 23 29 N 104 23 W
Minatitlán . . . 17 59 N 94 31 W
Monclova . . . 26 54 N 101 25 W
Monterrey . . . 25 40 N 100 19 W
Morelia . . . 19 42 N 101 07 W
Mulejé . . . 26 53 N 112 01 W
Navojoa . . . 27 06 N 109 26 W
Nueva Rosita . . . 27 57 N 101 13 W
Nuevo Laredo . . . 27 30 N 99 31 W
Oaxaca . . . 17 03 N 96 43 W
Orizaba . . . 18 51 N 97 06 W
Pachuca . . . 20 07 N 98 44 W
Papantla . . . 20 27 N 97 19 W
Parral, see Hidalgo del Parral
Piedras Negras . . 28 42 N 100 31 W
Poza Rica . . . 20 33 N 97 27 W
Progreso . . . 21 17 N 89 40 W
Puebla . . . 19 03 N 98 12 W
Puerto Escondido . . . 25 48 N 111 20 W
Puerto Vallarta (Las Penas) . . . 20 37 N 105 15 W
Querétaro . . . 20 36 N 100 23 W
Reynosa . . . 26 07 N 98 18 W
Río Bravo . . . 25 59 N 98 06 W
Sabinas . . . 27 51 N 101 07 W
Salamanca . . . 20 34 N 101 12 W
Saltillo . . . 25 25 N 101 00 W
San Andrés Tuxtla (Los Tuxtlas) . . . 18 27 N 95 13 W
San Cristóbal de las Casas . . . 16 45 N 92 38 W
San Felipe . . . 31 00 N 114 52 W
San Francisco del Rincón . . . 21 01 N 101 51 W
San Ignacio . . . 27 27 N 112 51 W
San Lucas . . . 22 53 N 109 54 W
San Luis . . . 32 29 N 114 48 W
San Luis Potosí . . 22 09 N 100 59 W
San Miguel de Allende . . . 20 55 N 100 45 W
San Pedro . . . 25 45 N 102 59 W
Santa Bárbara . . . 26 48 N 105 49 W
Santa Catarina . . 25 41 N 100 28 W
Santiago Papasquiaro . . . 25 03 N 105 25 W
Silao . . . 20 56 N 101 26 W
Tampico . . . 22 13 N 97 51 W
Tapachula . . . 14 54 N 92 17 W
Taxco . . . 18 33 N 99 36 W
Tecomán . . . 18 55 N 103 53 W
Tecpan . . . 17 15 N 100 41 W
Tehuacán . . . 18 27 N 97 23 W
Tepic . . . 21 30 N 104 54 W
Tequila . . . 20 54 N 103 47 W
Tierra Blanca . . . 18 27 N 96 21 W
Tijuana . . . 32 32 N 117 01 W
Tizimín . . . 21 09 N 88 09 W
Tlaquepaque . . . 20 39 N 103 19 W
Tlaxcala . . . 19 19 N 98 14 W
Toluca . . . 19 17 N 99 40 W
Torreón . . . 25 33 N 103 26 W
Tula . . . 23 00 N 99 43 W
Tuxpan . . . 20 57 N 97 24 W
Tuxpan . . . 21 57 N 105 18 W
Tuxtla . . . 16 45 N 93 07 W
Uruapan . . . 19 25 N 102 04 W
Valles . . . 21 59 N 99 01 W
Veracruz . . . 19 12 N 96 08 W
Villahermosa . . . 17 59 N 92 55 W
Zacapú . . . 19 50 N 101 43 W
Zacatecas . . . 22 47 N 102 35 W
Zamora de Hidalgo . . . 19 59 N 102 16 W
Zapopan . . . 20 43 N 103 24 W

Physical features and points of interest

Ángel de la Guarda Island . . 29 20 N 113 25 W
Baja California (Lower California), *peninsula* . . . 28 00 N 113 30 W
Balsas, *river* . . . 17 55 N 102 10 W
Basaseachic Cascades National Park . . . 28 15 N 108 02 W
California, Gulf of (Cortes, Sea of) . . . 28 00 N 112 00 W
Campeche, Bay of . . . 20 00 N 94 00 W
Catoche, Cape . . . 21 35 N 87 05 W
Cedros Island . . . 28 12 N 115 15 W
Cedros Island Wildlife Reserve . . . 28 12 N 115 15 W
Chapala, Lake . . . 20 15 N 103 00 W
Chiapas, Cordillera de, see Soconusco, Sierra de
Chichén Itzá, *historical site* . . . 20 40 N 88 34 W
Citlaltépetl Volcano (Orizaba, Pico de) . . . 19 01 N 97 16 W
Conchos, *river* . . . 29 35 N 104 25 W
Corrientes, Cape . . . 20 25 N 105 42 W
Cortes, Sea of, see California, Gulf of
Costera Nororiental Plain (Gulf Coastal Plain), *region* . . 26 00 N 98 00 W
Cozumel Island . . 20 25 N 86 55 W
Fuerte, *river* . . . 25 54 N 109 22 W
Gran Desierto (Sonoran Desert) . . . 32 15 N 114 30 W
Grande de Santiago (Santiago), *river* . . . 21 36 N 105 26 W
Grijalva, *river* . . . 18 36 N 92 39 W
Gulf Coastal Plain, see Costera Nororiental Plain
Isabela Island National Park . . . 21 51 N 105 55 W
Juárez, Sierra de . . . 32 00 N 115 50 W
La Venta, *historical site* . . . 17 58 N 94 15 W
Lagunas de Montebello National Park . . . 16 03 N 91 45 W
Lerma, *river* . . . 20 13 N 102 46 W
Lower California, see Baja California
Madre, Laguna . . . 25 00 N 97 40 W
Madre Occidental, Sierra . . . 25 00 N 105 00 W
Madre Oriental, Sierra . . . 22 00 N 99 30 W
Madre del Sur, Sierra . . . 17 00 N 100 00 W
Magdalena Bay . . 24 35 N 112 00 W
Mapimí Basin, *desert* . . . 27 30 N 103 30 W
Marías Islands . . . 21 25 N 106 28 W
Mayo, *river* . . . 26 45 N 109 47 W
Mexican Plateau . . . 24 00 N 102 00 W
Mexico, Gulf of . . 25 00 N 91 00 W
Miguel Alemán Reservoir . . . 18 15 N 96 30 W
Moctezuma, *river* . . . 21 59 N 98 34 W
Monte Alban, *historical site* . . . 17 00 N 96 43 W
Nazas, *river* . . . 25 45 N 102 50 W
Norte, Mesa del . . 27 00 N 104 00 W
Oaxaca Valley . . . 17 00 N 97 00 W
Orizaba, Pico de, see Citlaltépetl Volcano
Pacific Coastal Lowlands . . . 26 00 N 108 00 W
Pacific Ocean . . . 18 00 N 110 00 W
Palenque, *historical site* . . . 17 31 N 91 58 W
Pánuco, *river* . . . 22 16 N 97 47 W
Paricutín Volcano . . . 19 28 N 102 15 W
Popocatépetl Volcano . . . 19 02 N 98 38 W
Revillagigedo Islands . . . 19 00 N 111 30 W
Rio Grande (Río Bravo) . . . 25 55 N 97 09 W
Salado, *river* . . . 26 52 N 99 19 W
San Lucas, Cape . . . 22 52 N 109 53 W
San Pedro Martír, Sierra . . . 30 45 N 115 13 W
Santiago, see Grande de Santiago
Sebastián Vizcaíno Bay . . . 28 00 N 114 30 W
Soconusco, Sierra de (Chiapas Cordillera) . . . 15 30 N 92 35 W
Sonora, *river* . . . 28 48 N 111 49 W
Sonoran Desert, see Gran Desierto
Southern Highlands . . . 18 00 N 100 00 W
Tamiahua, Laguna de . . . 21 35 N 97 35 W
Tehuantepec, Gulf of . . . 16 00 N 94 50 W
Tehuantepec, Isthmus of . . . 17 00 N 95 00 W
Términos, Laguna de . . . 18 37 N 91 33 W
Tiburón Island . . . 29 00 N 112 25 W
Toluca, Mount . . . 19 08 N 99 44 W
Tula, *historical site* . . . 20 03 N 99 21 W
Tuxpan, *river* . . . 20 59 N 97 18 W
Usumacinta, *river* . . . 18 24 N 92 38 W
Uxmal, *historical site* . . . 20 22 N 89 46 W
Vicente Guerrero Reservoir . . . 23 55 N 98 44 W
Yaqui, *river* . . . 27 37 N 110 39 W
Yucatán Peninsula . . . 19 30 N 89 00 W

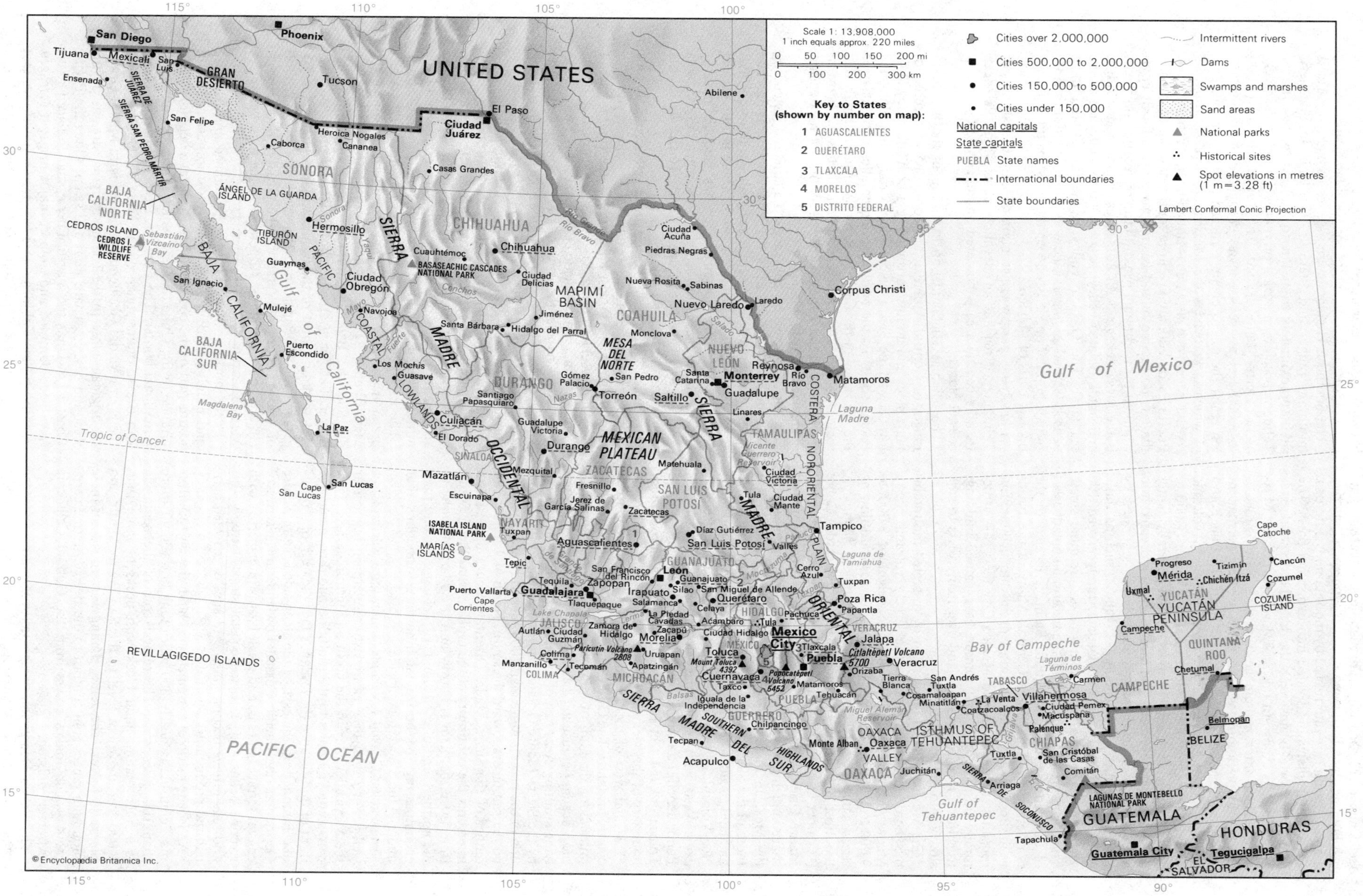
Scale 1: 13,908,000
1 inch equals approx. 220 miles
0 50 100 150 200 mi
0 100 200 300 km
Key to States (shown by number on map):
1 AGUASCALIENTES
2 QUERÉTARO
3 TLAXCALA
4 MORELOS
5 DISTRITO FEDERAL
Cities over 2,000,000
Cities 500,000 to 2,000,000
Cities 150,000 to 500,000
Cities under 150,000
National capitals
State capitals
PUEBLA State names
International boundaries
State boundaries
Intermittent rivers
Dams
Swamps and marshes
Sand areas
National parks
Historical sites
Spot elevations in metres (1 m = 3.28 ft)
Lambert Conformal Conic Projection
UNITED STATES
Gulf of Mexico
Gulf of California
PACIFIC OCEAN
Bay of Campeche
Gulf of Tehuantepec
SIERRA MADRE OCCIDENTAL
SIERRA MADRE ORIENTAL
SIERRA MADRE DEL SUR
MEXICAN PLATEAU
MESA DEL NORTE
MAPIMÍ BASIN
YUCATÁN PENINSULA
ISTHMUS OF TEHUANTEPEC
BAJA CALIFORNIA
GRAN DESIERTO
PACIFIC COASTAL LOWLANDS
NORORIENTAL COSTERA PLAIN
SOUTHERN HIGHLANDS
OAXACA VALLEY
REVILLAGIGEDO ISLANDS
MARÍAS ISLANDS
ISABELA ISLAND NATIONAL PARK
BASASEACHIC CASCADES NATIONAL PARK
LAGUNAS DE MONTEBELLO NATIONAL PARK
CEDROS ISLAND
CEDROS I. WILDLIFE RESERVE
TIBURÓN ISLAND
ÁNGEL DE LA GUARDA ISLAND
COZUMEL ISLAND
Tropic of Cancer
GUATEMALA
BELIZE
HONDURAS
EL SALVADOR
Mexico City
Guadalajara
Monterrey
Puebla
León
Ciudad Juárez
Tijuana
Mexicali
Chihuahua
Hermosillo
Culiacán
Mazatlán
Torreón
Durango
Acapulco
Veracruz
Mérida
Tampico
Matamoros
Nuevo Laredo
Reynosa
Saltillo
San Luis Potosí
Aguascalientes
Zacatecas
Querétaro
Morelia
Toluca
Cuernavaca
Oaxaca
Villahermosa
Campeche
Chetumal
Cancún
Tuxtla
Tapachula
San Diego
Phoenix
Tucson
El Paso
Abilene
Laredo
Corpus Christi
Guatemala City
Tegucigalpa
Belmopan
© Encyclopædia Britannica Inc.

feet south of Mexico City. Throughout the plateau, flattish intermontane basins and *bolsones* (ephemeral interior drainage basins) are interrupted by mountainous outcrops.

The central plateau is divided into two major parts. The Mesa del Norte begins near the U.S. border and ends near San Luis Potosí. In this arid, lower part of the Mexican Plateau, interior drainage (that is, without outlet to the ocean) predominates, and there are few permanent streams. The Mesa Central stretches from San Luis Potosí to just south of Mexico City. Formed largely by volcanic action, the surface of the Mesa Central is higher (7,000 to 9,000 feet above sea level), moister, and generally flatter than the Mesa del Norte. The Mesa Central is divided into a series of fairly level intermontane basins separated by eroded volcanic peaks. The largest valleys, such as those of Mexico, Puebla, and Guadalajara, rarely exceed 100 square miles in area, while many others are quite small. The basins are generally fertile; the traditional breadbasket of the country, the Guanajuato Basin, is located in the northern part of the Mesa Central. Many of the basins were sites of major lakes that were drained to facilitate European settlement. Around Mexico City the weak, structurally unstable soils that remain have caused buildings to shift on their foundations and over many years to sink slowly into the ground.

The Mexican Plateau is flanked by dissected mountainous borders. To the west is the largely volcanic Sierra Madre Occidental, with an average height of 8,000 to 9,000 feet. It has been highly incised by westward-flowing streams that eroded a series of deep canyons, or *barrancas,* the most spectacular of which is the Barranca del Cobre ("Copper Canyon"), Mexico's Grand Canyon. The Sierra Madre Oriental, a range of folded mountains formed of shales and limestones, is situated on the eastern side of the Mexican Plateau. With average elevations similar to those of the Sierra Madre Occidental, this highly dissected highland region has peaks exceeding 12,000 feet. The Neo-Volcánica Cordillera (also called the Transverse Volcanic Axis), with spectacular snow-capped peaks such as Popocatépetl, Ixtacíhuatl (17,342 feet [5,286 metres]), and Toluca (14,954 feet [4,558 metres]), forms the southern boundary of the Mexican Plateau.

Coastal lowlands

East and west of the Mexican Plateau lie the country's coastal lowlands. The Gulf Coastal Plain extends some 900 miles along the Gulf of Mexico from the Texas border to the Yucatán Peninsula. Characterized by lagoons and low-lying swampy areas east of the abrupt escarpment formed by the Sierra Madre Oriental, the triangular northern portion of the plain is more than 100 miles wide near the U.S. border but tapers toward the south. North of Tampico, an outlier of the Sierra Madre Oriental reaches the sea and interrupts the continuity of the Gulf Coastal Plain. South from there the plain is narrow and irregular, widening at the northern end of the Isthmus of Tehuantepec and then encompassing the horizontal limestone formations that underlie the Yucatán Peninsula.

The Pacific Coastal Lowlands, much narrower and less well defined than their east coast counterpart, begin near the Mexicali Valley in the north and terminate near Tuxpan, some 900 miles to the south; despite their name, for most of this distance the lowlands face the Gulf of California. Bounded on the east by the steep-sided Sierra Madre Occidental, the Pacific Coastal Lowlands are a series of coastal terraces, mesas, and small basins interspersed with riverine deltas and restricted coastal strips. Parts of this arid region have become important sites of irrigated agricultural production.

Baja California

An isolated strip of extremely arid land, the Baja California Peninsula is nearly 800 miles long but seldom more than 100 miles wide. The central core of the peninsula is a huge granitic fault block with peaks of more than 9,000 feet above sea level in the San Pedro Martír and Sierra de Juárez. The gently sloping western side of these mountain ranges is in contrast to the steep eastern escarpment, which makes access from the Gulf of California extremely difficult.

The Balsas Depression, which takes its name from the major river draining the region, lies immediately south of the Mexican Plateau. The depression is formed of small, irregular basins interrupted by hilly outcrops, which gives this hot, dry area a distinctive physical landscape.

The Southern Highlands are a series of highly dissected mountain ranges and plateaus. On their southwestern side, approximately from Puerto Vallarta to the Gulf of Tehuantepec, are a series of ranges known collectively as the Sierra Madre del Sur. These relatively low (7,000 to 8,000 feet above sea level) crystalline mountains often reach the sea to create a rugged coastal margin, part of which is known as the Mexican Riviera. Picturesque coastal sites, such as Ixtapa-Zihuatanejo, Acapulco, and Puerto Escondido, are favourite tourist destinations, while the less hospitable inland basins provide a difficult environment for traditional peasant farmers. Farther northeast is the Mesa del Sur, with numerous stream-eroded ridges and small, isolated valleys some 4,000 to 5,000 feet above sea level. The Oaxaca Valley is the largest and most densely settled of these valleys. With its predominantly Indian population, it is one of the most picturesque yet poorest parts of Mexico.

A low-lying, narrow constriction of land, the Isthmus of Tehuantepec reaches an elevation of less than 900 feet. Its hilly central area is bordered on either side by narrow coastal plains.

The Chiapas Highlands, an extension of the mountain ranges of Central America, are composed of a series of fault block mountains surrounding a high rift valley. The low, crystalline Sierra de Soconusco range lies along the Pacific coast. To the northwest and paralleling the coast is the rift valley of the Grijalva River. A group of highly dissected, folded, and faulted mountains is located between the valley and the Tabasco Plain, a southeastern extension of the Gulf Coastal Plain.

To the northeast of the Tabasco Plain and extending into the Gulf of Mexico is the Yucatán Peninsula. The peninsula's limestone terrain is generally flat to rolling and seldom exceeds 500 feet in elevation. There is little surface drainage, and subterranean erosion has produced caverns and sinkholes, the latter being formed when cavern roofs collapse. The islands of Cozumel and Mujeres lie off the peninsula's northeastern tip.

Drainage. Because of its climatic characteristics and arrangement of landforms, Mexico has few major rivers or natural lakes. The largest are found in the central part of the country. The Lerma River has its headwaters in the Toluca Basin, west of Mexico City, and flows westward to form Lake Chapala, the country's largest natural lake. The Santiago River then flows out of the lake to the northwest, crossing the Sierra Madre Occidental on its way to the Pacific. The eastward-flowing Moctezuma-Pánuco river system, which drains much of the eastern portion of the Mesa Central, has carved gorges through the Sierra Madre Oriental to reach the Gulf of Mexico. Lakes Pátzcuaro and Cuitzeo, west of Mexico City, are remnants of the numerous lakes that once were found in the Mesa Central.

The Balsas River and its tributaries drain the Balsas Depression as well as much of the southern portion of the Mesa Central. Dammed where it crosses the Sierra Madre del Sur, the Balsas is a major source of hydroelectric power. Farther southeast, the Grijalva-Usumacinta river system drains most of the humid Chiapas Highlands. Together with the Papaloapan River, which enters the Gulf of Mexico south of Veracruz, the Grijalva and Usumacinta account for about 40 percent of the total volume of Mexico's rivers.

In the north aridity and interior drainage limit the size and number of rivers. By far the most important stream in this part of the country is the Río Bravo del Norte (Rio Grande in the United States), which forms part of the international border. The Conchos River, a tributary of the Río Bravo, drains much of the Mesa del Norte. Because the Sierra Madre Occidental and the Sierra Madre Oriental originate close to the coastal margins, streams on the west and east coasts are short and steep. Along the Pacific Coastal Lowlands the Yaqui, Fuerte, and Culiacán rivers have been dammed and support major irrigated acreages. Aridity in Baja California and the porous limestones that underlie the Yucatán Peninsula cause these regions to be virtually devoid of permanent surface streams.

Soils. In the tropical areas of southern Mexico, lateritic soils predominate. Throughout southeastern Mexico, leaching produces infertile reddish or yellow soils high in iron oxides and aluminum hydroxides. The richest soils in the country are the chenozem-like volcanic soils found in the Mesa Central. Deep, easily crumbled, and rich in base minerals, these dark soils have been, in some areas, farmed continuously for several centuries. Because of their excellent drainage and good structural properties, they can be used for crops even on extremely steep slopes, but overuse has caused serious sheet erosion and exposure of tepetate (a lime hardpan) in many areas. In the arid north, gray-brown desert soils occupy the largest expanses. High in lime and soluble salts, these soils can be extremely productive when irrigated, but salt buildup is sometimes a serious problem.

Volcanic soils

Climate. Because of its topographic diversity and latitudinal range, Mexico has a wide array of climatic conditions, often occurring over short distances. More than half of the country lies south of the Tropic of Cancer. In these areas, tropical maritime air masses from the Gulf of Mexico, the Caribbean, and the Pacific, which are attracted by the relatively low pressures that occur over the land, are the main sources of precipitation that is heaviest during the period from May through August. Tropical hurricanes, which are spawned in oceans on both sides of the country, are common in the coastal lowland areas during the months of August through October. The climates in northern Mexico, situated latitudinally within one of the world's great desert regions, are strongly influenced by the semipermanent Pacific subtropical anticyclone, which minimizes precipitation.

Within the tropics temperature variations from season to season are small, often only about 10° F (5° C) between the warmest and coldest months. In these areas winter is defined as the rainy rather than the cold season. Because elevation rather than latitude is the primary climatic influence in southern Mexico, several vertical climatic zones are recognized. In the Mexican tropics, from sea level to just over 3,000 feet, is the *tierra caliente* ("hot land"), with uniformly high temperatures. Veracruz, located on the Gulf of Mexico, for example, has an average daily temperature of approximately 77° F (25° C). The *tierra templada* ("temperate land") extends to about 6,000 feet. Located at an elevation of more than 4,600 feet, Jalapa has an average daily temperature of 66° F (19° C). *Tierra fria* ("cold land") extends as high as 11,000 feet. Pachuca, at just under 8,000 feet, has an average annual temperature of 59° F (15° C). Above the *tierra fria* are the *paramos,* or alpine pastures, while the *tierra helada* ("frozen land"), or permanent snow line, in central Mexico is found between 13,000 and 14,000 feet.

North of the tropics, temperature ranges increase substantially and are greatest in the north central portion of the Mesa del Norte. In the northern interior, summer and winter temperatures are extreme. The highest temperatures in the country, exceeding 110° F (43° C), occur in July and August in central Baja California and in the northern Sonoran and Chihuahuan deserts. Outside of the high mountainous areas of northern Mexico and the north central portion of the Mesa del Norte, the lowest temperatures normally do not descend below 32° F (0° C).

Rainfall

Most of Mexico lacks adequate precipitation at least during a part of the year. With the exception of the highland areas of the Sierra Madre Occidental, the Sierra Madre Oriental, and the Gulf Coastal Plain, all of the area north of the Tropic of Cancer generally receives less than 20 inches (500 millimetres) of precipitation annually and is classified climatically as either tropical desert or tropical steppe. Nearly all of Baja California, much of Sonora state, and large parts of Chihuahua state receive less than 10 inches of rainfall yearly. Much of central and southern Mexico receives less than 40 inches of precipitation annually, most from May through August, and is classified as having tropical savanna or highland savanna climates. Only the Gulf Coastal Plain and the adjacent mountains, from roughly Tampico southward to Villahermosa, the Chiapas Highlands, and the southern part of the Yucatán Peninsula receive abundant rainfall year-round. In combination with uniformly high temperatures, this creates a tropical rain forest climate in these areas.

Plant and animal life. The tropical deserts of Baja California, Sonora, and north central Mexico are characterized by sparse desert scrub vegetation. On the higher portions of the Sonoran and Chihuahuan steppes, as well as in much of Coahuila and Tamulipas, there have evolved distinctive ecosystems composed of short grasses, scattered shrubs, and a variety of cacti and other succulents. Sonora and Chihuahua are the archetypes for flora groups that bear their names. The boojum tree is unique to a limited portion of Sonora and central Baja California.

Most of the Sierra Madre Occidental and large parts of the Mesa Central, including its dissected borders, originally were covered by forests of coniferous, evergreen deciduous, and deciduous trees. Similar forests extended southward into the Southern Highlands. Long periods of human occupation in these regions have decimated most of the natural vegetation. Major areas of coniferous forests are found at higher elevations in the Sierra Madre Occidental. The semiarid Balsas Depression has a tropical scrub vegetation composed of shrubs, low deciduous trees, and scattered cacti.

The high-precipitation zones of the Gulf Coastal Plain, the adjacent east-facing mountain slopes, the Chiapas Highlands, and the southern part of the Yucatán Peninsula are dominated by tropical rain forest, or selva, vegetation. These dense stands of broadleaf evergreen trees of varying heights are among the most luxuriant and diversified in the world. Valuable tropical hardwoods, as well as ferns, epiphytes, and a variety of palms, make these selva areas of particular interest. A large portion of the Pacific coastal area, from Mazatlán to the Guatemalan border, is covered by tropical deciduous or semi-deciduous forests, which lack the variety and density of tropical rain forests.

Mexico sits astride the commonly accepted boundary dividing North and Middle American animal species and, therefore, has a diverse array of fauna, especially in the selva regions of the south. The rain forests of the Gulf Coast and Chiapas Highlands and the semi-deciduous forests of the Pacific coast still provide a largely undisturbed habitat for monkeys, parrots, jaguars, tapirs, anteaters, and other tropical species. In contrast, the natural wildlife of northern Mexico was severely affected by the introduction of European grazing animals more than 400 years ago. While rabbits, snakes, and armadillos abound in the deserts and steppes, larger animals such as deer, pumas, and coyotes are found mainly in isolated or mountainous areas. Countless ducks and geese migrate into the northern part of the Sierra Madre Occidental to winter. A millennium of human habitation has brought about the decimation of natural fauna throughout much of the Mesa Central and parts of the Southern Highlands, especially in the Oaxaca Valley.

Settlement patterns. *Traditional regions.* Because of distinctive differences in physical environment, ethnic and racial characteristics, and settlement histories, specific cultural areas have evolved. Mexico traditionally has been divided between the Spanish-mestizo north and the Indian-mestizo south. This corresponds roughly to the pre-Columbian boundary that separated the highly developed Indian cultures of the Mesa Central and the south from the more primitive groups to the north.

Northern Mexico is a sparsely populated area with isolated clusters of settlement; it can be divided into four separate cultural regions. The largest region is the North, which closely corresponds in area to the Mesa del Norte. Mining and ranching were introduced there by the Spanish in the 16th and 18th centuries, respectively, and these industries have continued to characterize the region, though modern irrigation projects and industrialization programs along the border with the United States have diversified the economy.

The Northeast stretches from Tampico to the U.S. border and inland to the Sierra Madre Oriental. The Indian population of the area was eliminated by early European settlers, who established farms and ranches in the area. Although it was long one of the country's poorest regions, the emerging petroleum and steel industries and the develop-

Volcanic peak of Ixtacíhuatl overlooking a field of corn shocks in the agricultural region of Puebla state in the Mesa Central of Mexico.
Chip and Rosa Maria de la Cueva Peterson

ment of irrigation projects along the Río Bravo del Norte have greatly improved the region's economic condition.

The Northwest is an extensive region lying west of the crest of the Sierra Madre Occidental and stretching southward from the U.S. border to northern Nayarit state. This physiographically complex area had a substantial Indian population before the Spanish conquest, and the Tarahumara and Seri are among the Indian peoples still found in isolated parts of the region. As in the North, mineral resources originally attracted the Spanish, but agriculture, especially ranching, now characterizes the region.

Baja California, historically one of the more isolated parts of Mexico, is largely a desert, with major concentrations of settlement in urban areas at both ends of the peninsula. The original Indian population, scattered and culturally poorly developed, was decimated by diseases introduced by missionaries in the late 18th century. Europeans and mestizos established themselves in farming communities at oases, originally at sites such as San Ignacio and Mulejé.

Southern Mexico was much more strongly influenced by its Indian heritage than was the northern part of the country. The cultural core of the nation has been the Central region, which includes the central and eastern portions of the Mesa Central and its surrounding highlands. This was the centre of the Aztec Empire as well as numerous other Indian homelands. It became the core of New Spain and the political and economic capital of Mexico. In addition to being the primary centre of urbanization, this is also one of the nation's most important agricultural areas. Numerous basins, such as those of Mexico, Toluca, Puebla, and Morelos, are densely settled. Racial mixing has been intense in this region, but Indian groups are still found in the more isolated portions of Michoacán, Mezquital, Puebla, and Toluca. Nowhere is the contrast between modern urban Mexico and traditional rural Indian life-styles sharper than in this region.

The Central region

The West region is centred on the city of Guadalajara and encompasses the state of Jalisco along with portions of Colima, Nayarit, Aguascalientes, Zacatecas, and Guanajuato states. With its relatively high rural population, fertile basins, and access to the Pacific, it was historically the most important agricultural region in the nation. The Guanajuato Basin has long been called the "breadbasket of Mexico." Despite its agricultural prominence, a large number of small urban centres, such as Querétaro, Salamanca, Irapuato, and León, are developing industrially while Manzanillo has become the most important port on the Pacific. Many of the things often thought of as distinctively Mexican—such as tequila, mariachi music, and the ornate embroidered sombrero and charro costume—originated in the West.

The Balsas cultural region, which closely corresponds to the physiographic area of the same name, is arid, hot, and sparsely settled. Cattle ranching has been the mainstay of the economy, although subsistence-level slash-and-burn agriculture is widely practiced by impoverished peasant farmers.

The Southern Highlands, encompassing much of the states of Michoacán, Guerrero, and Oaxaca, is poverty-stricken. This region has the highest concentration of Indians in the country; and the Zapotec, Mixtec, and other Indian groups farm *minifundia* (small plots of land), using traditional methods. The picturesque, "crazy-quilt" landscape that results belies the widespread poverty. Modern coastal tourist centres, such as Acapulco and the more recently developed Puerto Escondido, are a marked contrast to the traditional rural life-styles of the region.

The Gulf Coast region includes the coastal zones of Veracruz and Tabasco as well as the adjacent east-facing slopes of the Sierra Madre Oriental. The population of the coastal area is overwhelmingly mestizo, but Indian groups are found in the mountains north of Veracruz. Veracruz, the cultural centre of this region, has long been the country's major non-petroleum port. Cattle ranching and commercial agriculture are important components of the rural economy. The southern parts of the region were disease-infested, swampy, and nearly devoid of settlement until the Papaloapan and Grijalva-Usumacinta river projects allowed commercial exploitation of the rich alluvial soils.

Most of the Chiapas region is relatively isolated from the rest of Mexico. Commercial agriculture, particularly cotton production, is practiced on the Soconusco (Pacific) coast, while livestock grazing and subsistence agriculture are important elsewhere. Indian peoples are the majority in the northern highlands around San Cristóbal de las Casas, but mestizos are the dominant population in the southern half of the region.

The Yucatán

The centre of the lowland Maya civilization, the Yucatán has a predominantly Indian rural population. This low-lying area is known for its archaeological sites, such as Chichén Itzá, Uxmal, and Tulum. Mérida, the only major city in the region, was the centre for the production of henequen (a type of *Agave*), which led to a regional economic boom in the late 1800s. In the tropical rain forests to the south, the sparse population depends on subsistence agriculture or hunting and gathering.

Rural settlement. Before the arrival of Europeans, the indigenous population was highly concentrated in the Central, West, and Southern Highland regions. The Spanish settled in existing Indian communities in order to exploit their labour in agriculture and mining. As a result, these areas have remained the most densely populated throughout Mexico's history.

Away from this central core, settlement was sparse and was attracted to specific opportunities, such as mines, mission sites, or military outposts. Mining had the largest impact on population redistribution. Silver-mining towns, such as Durango, San Luis Potosí, Aguascalientes, Pachuca, and Zacatecas, were founded in the middle to late 1500s and represented the first settlements outside the central core. By contrast, it was not until the mid-1800s that large-scale ranching was introduced into northern Mexico. This clustered pattern of settlement, with large areas effectively devoid of population, has characterized the nation's rural settlement pattern.

Urban settlement. Urbanization is taking place at a rapid pace in Mexico. While the largest urban places are growing the most rapidly in absolute numbers, small- and intermediate-sized cities have the highest percentage increases. By the mid-1980s the country had more than 100 urban centres with 50,000 or more people. The major axis of urbanization stretches as a narrow band across central Mexico from Puebla to Guadalajara, but the growth of the northern border cities has been the most spectacular.

Major cities

Within the hierarchy of Mexican urban places, Mexico City is the undisputed primary city. It is the political, economic, social, educational, and industrial capital of the nation. With a population of almost 10,000,000 in the mid-1980s, it is the largest city in the world (see MEXICO CITY).

Guadalajara is the nation's second largest urban area. It is a much more traditional city in structure and appearance than is Mexico City. As the regional capital of Jalisco and much of the West, Guadalajara is a major market centre and has developed a substantial industrial base. With a well-respected university and medical school, it is also a major educational and cultural centre.

Monterrey developed as the iron and steel centre of the nation. Because the modern city dates only to the beginning of the 20th century, and because much of its growth is recent, it is singularly unremarkable in appearance, and the arid Mesa del Norte provides a stark, somewhat barren setting. High-grade coal from the nearby Sabinas fields was a major consideration in siting the steel industry in Monterrey. A number of heavy industries also have been located in the urban area. As the centre of the National Action Party (PAN), Monterrey is a stronghold of political conservatism.

THE PEOPLE

Ethnic composition. Mexico's population is composed of many ethnic groups. At the time of European arrival in the early 1500s, the country was inhabited by people who are thought to have migrated into the New World from Asia some 40,000 to 60,000 years ago by crossing a former land bridge in the Bering Strait. After their arrival into what is now Mexico, centuries of isolation allowed the evolution of unique cultural traits among the many separate clusters. Highly organized civilizations occupied various regions for at least 2,000 years before European discovery.

By far the greatest number of people lived in the Mesa Central. At the time of European arrival, most lived under the general rule of the Aztec Empire, but many separate cultural groups thrived in this region, among them speakers of the Tarastec, Otomi, and Nahuatl languages. Outside of the Mesa Central were numerous other cultural groups, such as the Maya of the Yucatán and the Mixtec and Zapotec of Oaxaca. The splendid Aztec cities of the Mesa Central were marvels of architectural design, irrigation technology, and social organization. Spectacular Mayan ruins in the Yucatán give evidence of widespread urbanization and intense agricultural productivity dating back to well before the birth of Christ. In many ways the Indian civilizations of Mexico were more advanced than their Spanish conquerors.

With the advent of Europeans, racial mixing became commonplace and a new people, mestizos, were created.

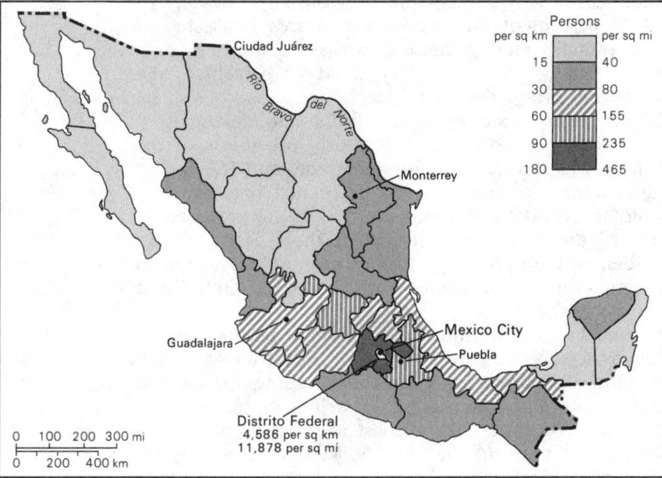

Population density of Mexico.

Over the past four centuries mestizos have become the dominant racial group in Mexico, accounting for at least half of the total population. Northern Mexico is overwhelmingly mestizo in both urban and rural areas. Because the number of Europeans in the total population has been small, the Indian contribution to the mestizo racial group has been relatively large. Indian racial characteristics therefore predominate in many Mexican mestizos. Europeans, including those who immigrated during the 20th century, account for about 15 percent of the population and are largely concentrated in urban areas, especially Mexico City, and in the West.

Although mestizos form the bulk of the population throughout the country, there are several areas where Indian speakers still represent the dominant population group. Maya speakers are the majority ethnic group in the rural Yucatán and the Chiapas Highlands. In the Southern Highlands, especially the Oaxaca Valley and remoter parts of the Sierra Madre del Sur, Indian (primarily Zapotec) communities abound. Despite their decreasing numbers, enclaves of Indians are still significant in isolated mountain areas on the eastern margin of the Mesa Central.

Linguistic composition. Spanish, which is the official national language and the language of instruction in schools, is spoken by more than 95 percent of the population. Although Indians are thought to represent about a quarter of the population, less than 10 percent of them speak an Indian language. There are, however, more than 50 Indian languages spoken by more than 100,000 people, including Maya in the Yucatán; Huastec in northern Veracruz; Nahuatl, Tarastec, Totonac, Otomi, and Mazahua mainly on the Mesa Central; Zapotec, Mixtec, and Mazatec in Oaxaca; and Tzeltal and Tzotzil in Chiapas.

Religion. There is no official religion in Mexico, as the constitution guarantees separation of church and state. However, Roman Catholicism is practiced by more than 95 percent of the population. The shrine of the Virgin of Guadalupe, the nation's patron saint, is located in Mexico City and is the site of annual pilgrimage for hundreds of thousands of people, many of them peasants. A significant proportion of Indians retain traditional religious beliefs and practices, despite their adherence to Roman Catholicism. Protestant missionaries are active in the country and have been especially successful in converting the urban poor.

Demographic trends. One of the most important characteristics of Mexico's population since 1940 has been the rapid rate of natural increase. Even though the rate slowed during the 1980s, the population is still growing about 50 percent faster than the world average and three times as rapidly as that of the United States. This growth rate is a reflection of the improved health care standards that were introduced beginning in 1940. There have been drastic declines in the death rate, and infant mortality, although still quite high in comparison to more developed countries, has been significantly reduced. The crude death rate, a gross measure of deaths within the population, has declined by as much as 50 percent since 1960.

Given the rapid growth, the population is disproportionately young; about 40 percent of the population is under 15 years of age. Life expectancy at birth has nearly doubled since 1930 and, at 70 years, is close to that in more developed countries.

The total population has increased more than 500 percent since 1915. Such growth has severely taxed the ability of the Mexican government to provide basic social services and economic opportunities for the people. Although the government traditionally has opposed limiting population growth, the position was modified in the late 1970s because of recurring economic difficulties.

Internal migration has altered the distribution of the population. Large numbers of peasants from rural areas and small towns have moved to cities since mid-century. An estimated 70 percent of Mexicans live in cities, 50 percent in cities of more than 50,000. This represents a substantial proportional decline in rural population, which accounted for half of all residents in 1960, although their absolute numbers have remained fairly constant. A lack of agricultural land, limited job opportunities, and the availability of few social amenities push people from the rural areas. The perception of increased chances for social and economic mobility as well as the dynamic character of urban places attracts rural people to the cities. Many internal migrants go to large regional centres such as Guadalajara, Puebla, and Monterrey, but Mexico City is the principal destination. Because of favourable employment prospects, increasing numbers of migrants have moved to cities on the U.S. border. As a result, Ciudad Juárez, Mexicali, and Tijuana are among the fastest growing cities in the nation.

Emigration

In addition to internal migration, the number of people who have emigrated from Mexico to the United States has grown sharply since the late 1970s. Estimates are highly inaccurate and vary drastically, but it is believed that somewhere between 4,000,000 and 8,000,000 Mexicans relocated illegally to the United States between 1970 and 1985. While a large proportion of these emigrants have low educational levels and limited technical skills, an increasing number of highly qualified technicians and professionals have found their way north, causing a "brain drain" for the country.

Illegal migration has acted as a safety valve in that it eases the social and economic problems associated with overly rapid population growth. The nation's resources would be stressed even further if large-scale emigration had not occurred. Remission of income earned outside of the country also represents a significant part of the nation's economy.

THE ECONOMY

Since the Revolution of 1910, Mexico's most notable economic achievement has been the sharp reduction of foreign ownership of the means of production while maintaining overall national growth. The economy is a combination of private, state, and mixed-capital enterprises.

State regulation of commerce

The state regulates the operation of private concerns in a number of ways, including the issuance of import licenses, the establishment of production quotas, and the control of prices on some products. In addition, private capital is barred from investment in certain activities. Private capital interests, with a majority of shares owned by Mexican nationals, control most industrial manufacturing activities, while semiautonomous state corporations operate the petroleum industry, generate and distribute electricity, run the banks, and oversee the telephone and telegraph systems. The government also controls foreign capital investment, usually by prohibiting it from certain industries, such as insurance, petroleum, and forestry, or by limiting it to a minority interest in others, such as mining, transportation, broadcasting, and soft-drink production.

Mexico is a developing nation economically. Nonetheless, in constant pesos, the gross domestic product per capita increased more than one and a half times between 1960 and 1980. Given very rapid population growth during the same period, the nation's economic growth has been impressive, with an average annual rate of nearly 7 percent. Services account for almost 50 percent of the total gross domestic product, manufacturing about 25 percent, and agriculture about 10 percent.

The nation's active labour force is equivalent to about one-third of the total population. The service sector accounts for the largest proportion of workers, about 30 percent. Slightly more than 25 percent of workers are employed in agriculture and about 12 percent in manufacturing. Nearly half of the nonagricultural labour force is unionized. The largest and most powerful union, the Confederation of Mexican Workers, is closely related to the ruling political party, the Institutional Revolutionary Party.

The economic boom that began in the 1970s was sustained by petroleum exports and spurred substantial capital investment from both the public and private sectors. The increase in capital created jobs and expanded the market for goods and services. Much of this development, however, was financed through loans from private banks and international lending institutions. The resulting debt, coupled with plummeting petroleum prices on the world market in the early 1980s, precipitated an economic crisis unparalleled in Mexico's history.

Resources. *Mineral resources.* Minerals have been an important part of the economy throughout Mexico's history, and some 40 are now extracted in commercial quantities. Silver was long the most valuable product mined in the country, and Mexico continues to be the world's leading producer of that commodity. The major mining area during the colonial period was the so-called Silver Belt, a region that extended from Guanajuato and Zacatecas in the Mesa Central to Chihuahua in the Mesa del Norte, with outposts such as San Luis Potosí farther east.

The Silver Belt

The Silver Belt is still the primary region of nonfuel mineral production in the country, although now both industrial and precious minerals are sought. Silver is still taken from the older centres of Guanajuato, Pachuca, and Zacatecas, but zinc, lead, gold, mercury, cadmium, and such trace minerals as antimony and manganese are more important in total value. Iron ore deposits have been worked near Durango since the early 1900s and have provided the raw materials used in iron and steel production at Monterrey. Coking-quality coal is mined at the Sabinas fields to the north of Monterrey. Rich copper deposits were discovered in the late 1800s near Santa Rosalía in Baja California, but these deposits have been largely depleted. The country's largest deposits of copper are located at Cananea and La Caridad in northern Sonora state.

Petroleum products

Since the mid-1970s, petroleum products have been Mexico's primary economic asset. Nearly 70 percent of the nation's foreign exchange earnings is derived from the sale of oil, the overwhelming majority of which is exported to the United States. The country's first commercially productive oil fields were discovered about 1900 off of Tampico on the Gulf Coast. Shortly thereafter additional producing zones were found farther south, near the Isthmus of Tehuantepec. Foreign capital was invested in the exploitation of petroleum, and most oil was exported until the industry was nationalized in 1938 with the creation of Petróleos Mexicanos (Pemex), a semiautonomous governmental agency charged with the exploration, production, and marketing of oil and natural gas.

Several major oil-producing fields are now in operation in the Gulf of Mexico and along its coast; the main fields include the Poza Rica (near Tuxpan), the Tampico-Misantla basin, and the Chiapas-Tabasco sites. Major natural gas fields are located near Reynosa in northeastern Mexico and near Veracruz and in the Chiapas-Tabasco region of the Gulf of Mexico coast. The country has huge proven and potential reserves of petroleum and substantial reserves of natural gas.

Biologic resources. Largely because of the diversity of its physical environment, Mexico produces a wide array of agricultural products in different areas. Despite the fact that farming and ranching have been the basic economic activities throughout its history, Mexico has a limited amount of good agricultural land. Much of the country is too arid or too mountainous for crops or grazing. Irrigation is required in many areas to bring the land into production. It is estimated that no more than 20 percent of the nation is potentially arable. Normally, between 10 and 12 percent of the country's total area is planted to crops annually, and, because of weather conditions, only half of that is harvested. Only about 20 percent of the cropland in production is irrigated.

Slightly more than one-fifth of the national territory is forested. It is estimated that nearly two-thirds of the country was covered by forests in the mid-1500s, but indiscriminate exploitation has decimated this resource. While conservation methods are now being practiced in some of the pine forests in the northern Sierra Madre Occidental, the uprooting of rain forest for conversion to grassland for rearing cattle continues in the Gulf Coast region and elsewhere.

Mexico has a bountiful supply of marine resources, although they do not form a major part of the national diet. The Gulf of California is known for its game fish, such as black marlin and other billfish, as well as its shrimp. Farther south along the Pacific coast tuna are commercially plentiful. In parts of the Gulf of Mexico, especially off the eastern coast of the Yucatán Peninsula, clean, clear waters teem with tropical fish. Large shrimping grounds are found in the northern part of the Gulf of Mexico as well as in the south near Campeche.

Hydroelectric resources. Oil and natural gas account for more than three-fourths of the fuels used by Mexican industry, but this represents a recent change brought about by abundant new supplies. In the 1940s and '50s hydroelectric power was seen as vital for the nation. Because of their proximity to major population clusters, most of the early projects were located on the streams exiting the eastern and southern escarpments of the Mesa Central. Better transmission technologies have permitted newer projects to be located farther away, such as the Malpaso Project on the Grijalva River on the margins of the Chiapas Highlands.

Agriculture, forestry, and fishing. *Agriculture.* About one-tenth of the gross domestic product is derived from agriculture, which employs one-fourth of the total work force. A significant proportion of Mexican agriculture still relies on traditional farming methods, especially in the regions having predominantly Indian populations. In these areas intensive subsistence agriculture based on corn (maize), beans, and squash is practiced on small plots of land, often as parts of communal village holdings. The system is highly labour-intensive and has low per capita productivity, which limits the opportunities for economic advancement.

The ejido system

While not its major objective, one of the legacies of the Revolution of 1910 was land reform, which produced the ejido system. At the time of the revolution, the rural peasantry was virtually landless and worked under a debt peonage system on haciendas (large estates). The Constitution of 1917 contained a statute limiting the amount of land that a person could own and, through the concept of social utility, legalized the federal government's expropriation and redistribution of land. Initially, small parcels were granted to communal groups whose members worked holdings individually (usually cropland) or in common (usually pasture or woodland). Later modifications brought about cooperative ejidos. By the end of the 1930s haciendas had all but disappeared from the Mesa Central, Balsas Depression, and Southern Highlands. Land redistribution produced a large number of small holdings, from 10 to 20 acres (four to eight hectares) in size. These small farms are barely viable as economic units, but although much of what is grown is used for subsistence, a considerable proportion of what they produce enters into commercial markets to supply the towns and cities of central and southern Mexico. Corn is the staple crop in most areas, but many crops and animal products are produced.

Commercial agricultural products come from three major regions of the country—the tropical regions of the Gulf Coast and Chiapas Highlands, the irrigated lands of the North and Northwest, and the Guanajuato Basin in the Mesa Central. Tropical crops have been grown on the Gulf Coastal Plain and its adjacent highlands since the early colonial period. Production now extends southeastward from near Tampico to the Chiapas Highlands and inland to the eastern slopes of the Sierra Madre Oriental. Coffee and sugarcane are the most important crops in value and acreage. They are produced in quantities sufficient to meet the country's internal demands as well as to provide sizable amounts for export. Coffee is Mexico's most valuable export crop. Increased local demand for sugar, however, has caused exports of that commodity to drop since the late 1970s. Bananas, pineapples, papayas, mangos, cacao, and rice are grown primarily for the domestic market. Mexico is one of the world's leading producers of vanilla, which is also grown in these areas. Smaller areas of cacao, coffee, and sugar production are found in western Chiapas. Cotton has become a major crop along the Pacific Coastal Plain near the Guatemalan border.

Irrigation projects

Irrigated agriculture has brought large-scale commercial production to the North and Northwest. Cotton has become the major crop in the areas developed by irrigation projects since the 1930s. The Laguna Project near Torreón was the nation's first attempt at providing water to the arid North, and huge cooperative ejidos were formed to farm cotton using modern mechanized methods. This was followed by the Las Delicias Project near Chihuahua, which also featured cotton but later brought substantial acreages of wheat into production. Much of the region's wheat is grown from drought-resistant hybrids. Despite its new producing areas, rapid population growth has made Mexico a net importer of grain since 1980.

Several new areas in the Northwest have been brought into production since the 1940s. The largest of the saline land reclamation projects are in the Fuerte and Yaqui river valleys, but a series of projects extends from Hermosillo in the north to Culiacán in the south. Much of the land is worked by cooperative ejidos, though significant areas of private land are also farmed there. Wheat, especially north of Sinaloa, is the most important crop in the region, which is now the country's centre of grain production. Cotton, vegetables, and oilseeds also make important contributions to the area's agricultural economy. Winter vegetables, especially tomatoes and lettuce, are grown mainly for markets in the United States. Cotton is the major crop of the Mexicali Valley.

Within the Mesa Central, the Guanajuato Basin traditionally has been considered the "breadbasket" of Mexico. Wheat, corn, vegetables, peanuts (groundnuts), strawberries, and beans are produced on small holdings. While still a major producing region with the advantage of proximity to major urban markets, the Guanajuato Basin has been eclipsed in agricultural preeminence by the Northwest.

Livestock ranching has been concentrated in the North since Mexico gained independence. Open-range cattle operations, frequently exceeding 250,000 acres in size, were created in the 1800s, and a number of large holdings persist despite agrarian reform. Because of the arid conditions and limited natural vegetation, the region's capacity for grazing animals is low. Nonetheless, a significant proportion of livestock is raised on relatively small ranches. In combination, these ranches have provided meat for the domestic market as well as substantial quantities for export.

Since the 1960s major improvements have been made in the ranching industry in the North. Many of the criollo cattle, descendants of stock introduced from Spain in the 1500s, have been replaced by Herefords, Brahman, and other breeds, while open-range methods are giving way to rotational grazing systems. Some natural pastures are being improved by means of irrigation, top-seeding, and fertilization. Supplemental feeding of stock has also become more common.

Cattle are also raised commercially for the domestic market in tropical areas, mainly in the Northeast, Gulf Coast, and Chiapas regions. In these areas Brahman, or Zebu, cattle are favoured because of their tolerance of heat and high humidity. Luxuriant vegetation and ample moisture make the animal-carrying capacity of the land much higher than in the North. Rain forests are being cleared and planted with imported African grasses to facilitate grazing.

Mexico produces two specialized crops that are rarely grown elsewhere. Henequen, a member of the genus *Agave,* yields a fibre used in furniture manufacturing and cordage. The plant was introduced into the northern Yucatán in the 1880s, and for many years this area was the sole source of henequen. Extensive plantations survived until the mid-1930s, when land reform led to their demise. Still an important export crop for the region, henequen is now grown on small farms and by cooperatives.

Maguey, also of the genus *Agave,* is planted in many parts of the Mesa Central. Originally used in making pulque, an inexpensive alcoholic beverage, maguey was a crop grown by many small farmers because it could be planted on infertile, rocky soils. Tequila, Mexico's national liquor, also is derived from maguey. Tequila takes its name from the town of Tequila in the state of Jalisco, the centre for its production and distilling. Yet another alcoholic drink derived from an agave is mescal, which is produced primarily in Oaxaca.

Forestry. By far the largest part of the forest area is located in the tropical east and south of the country. These tropical forests yield a wide variety of valuable products, including hardwoods, such as oaks and mahogany, and an assortment of fragrant woods, such as cedar and rosewood. In addition, the rain forests of Chiapas and the southern

Yucatán contain sapodilla trees, which are the principal source for chicle, the latex used in the manufacture of chewing gum. Softwoods are found in the Sierra Madre Oriental and the Sierra Madre Occidental above 6,000 feet. Stands of ponderosa, lodgepole, and other pines are especially well developed in the Sierra Madre Occidental, especially in the states of Chihuahua and Durango.

Fishing. Two shrimping areas of the Gulf Coast, from Tampico north to the U.S. border and from Veracruz south to Campeche, have been fished commercially since the 1940s. The Gulf of California shrimping grounds, first exploited on a large scale in the late 1950s, are now the most important in the nation. Deepwater fish abound off the Pacific coast of Baja California. Since the formation of a commercial fishing fleet in the 1960s, this area has become the country's main fishing ground, producing most of the total commercial catch. Sardines, anchovies, and tuna are the leading species taken. In the near-shore zone of the Pacific coast of Baja California, lobster and abalone are captured in commercial quantities. The rest of the commercial marine catch comes from the Gulf of Mexico, especially off the Campeche Bank north of the Yucatán Peninsula.

Industry. Mexico is one of the most industrialized countries in Latin America. Industry accounts for one-fourth of the gross domestic product and provides jobs for one-tenth of the total work force. A disproportionate share of manufacturing is located in the Mexico City metropolitan area, largely because of its huge market and superior infrastructure. An impressive array of industries has located there, including agricultural processing, automotive assembly, electronics manufacturing, iron and steel production, and the manufacture of a wide variety of consumer goods. The efforts of the federal government to disperse industry to sites outside the capital have had only modest success. In fact, much of the industrialization so dispersed has been to neighbouring cities of the Central region. One exception has been the growth in important border cities, spurred by the *maquiladora,* or "twin plant," program. This arrangement allows duty-free importation and exportation between the United States and Mexico of raw materials or parts made within a narrow border zone. The overwhelming majority of the plants are foreign-owned and have been located in Mexico to take advantage of low labour costs.

Mineral production and processing

Most of the mining of metals, industrial raw materials, and coal is found in the North, while oil and natural gas production is concentrated in the Northeast and Gulf Coast regions. Open-pit mining is used for extracting copper at Cananea and La Caridad, coal at Sabinas, and iron ore at Las Truchas and Monclova. The government-operated steel mills north of Mexico City were shut down in the late 1980s.

Pemex, Latin America's largest oil company, produces several hundred billion barrels of oil annually. A system of oil and gas pipelines has been constructed to move these products to major cities in the Mesa Central and to the U.S. border, where they formerly linked up with pipelines in the United States. Large, new oil refineries have been built near the Gulf of Mexico at Minatitlán and Reynosa to augment the older productive capacity of those at Ciudad Madero near Tampico. Additional refineries are located at Salamanca, Tula and Atzcapotzalco near Mexico City, Poza Rica, and Salina Cruz. Sulfur is found in conjunction with petroleum in many of the Gulf fields and is used in the manufacture of a wide variety of products. Petrochemical plants have been built in Veracruz state at Coatzacoalcos, the major export centre for sulfur products, and at Ciudad Pemex in Tabasco. Both are located in formerly unpopulated rain forest regions. A number of petrochemical sites are also found near refineries in the Mesa Central.

Manufacturing

The mechanical engineering sector is engaged in the production of automobiles and trucks. Auto assembly plants have been established in Puebla, Toluca, and Hermosillo in the Northwest. Textile production was traditionally more dispersed, with older centres located in Puebla and Guadalajara and newer ones in Torreón and Ciudad Juárez. The border industrialization program has seen a growing concentration of "high-tech" industries such as electronics assembly, including television and computer components, and other manufacturing in cities such as Tijuana and Ciudad Juárez.

Before the economic slowdown of the early 1980s, public-works projects such as housing and transportation infrastructure accounted for as much as half of the construction activity in the nation. Such programs were subsequently reduced, and privately financed construction was essentially curtailed because of high interest and inflation rates. A massive rebuilding program is needed to repair damage caused by the 1985 Mexico City earthquake.

The Federal Commission of Electricity operates the electrical power network for the country. Thermal generation, using oil and natural gas, has replaced hydroelectric power as the main source of electricity.

Tourism

Tourism is a major growth industry and Mexico's second largest economic asset after petroleum. Tourists once traveled mainly to Mexico City and the surrounding colonial towns of the Mesa Central or to the Mayan ruins of the Yucatán. More recently, tourists have discovered the country's beaches, and the government has invested heavily in this sector. The world-famous resorts of Acapulco, Puerto Vallarta, Ixtapa-Zihuatanejo, Cancún, Cozumel, Mazatlán, and Cabo San Lucas have been developed or significantly improved since the 1960s through the construction of new hotels, airports, and other tourist facilities. Given an exotic cultural diversity, tropical settings, relatively low prices, and easy accessibility, Mexico exerts a strong attraction on American tourists, who now represent most of its visitors.

Foreign debt

Finance. Mexico accumulated more than two-thirds of its foreign debt after the mid-1970s, largely in conjunction with the decline in international prices for petroleum. The country had to renegotiate its obligations to foreign lenders in the 1980s in order to meet debt service payments, and additional loans were secured to pay interest on the debt as well as to restructure payments. Many of the nation's most basic economic dilemmas stemmed from the foreign debt problem. To solve this problem the government embarked upon an austerity program, which included limiting federal spending and controlling prices and wages.

As a result of internal financial problems, there was a major outflow of capital to money markets in other countries, especially the United States. A general lack of confidence in the government's ability to overcome the debt problem stymied economic recovery, and foreign investment, except in *maquiladora* operations, was drastically reduced.

Banking structure

Until 1982 Mexico had a dual banking structure consisting of governmental financial institutions and private banks that were owned by commercial and industrial groups. The private banking sector was nationalized in an effort to reduce the perceived manipulation and exploitation of the financial markets by private capital. The Bank of Mexico has the sole right to issue bank notes; it also enforces credit controls, fixes reserve requirements, and sells gold to the public. There are other state financial institutions, the most important being the National Development Bank. It is one of the primary financial institutions through which foreign funds are channeled into industrial development projects.

The nation's stock exchange plays only a minor role in providing capital. Most funds are secured through government bonds or bank securities.

Trade. Mexican imports increased rapidly in the 1970s, especially capital goods and agricultural products. The value of exports during this time also increased substantially because of high petroleum prices on the world market. Since the early 1980s, however, the value of oil exports has been substantially reduced.

The United States is Mexico's major trading partner. Almost two-thirds of all exports go to the United States, mainly in the form of petroleum, while more than two-thirds of all imports are from the United States.

Transportation. Because of its physical diversity and developing economy, Mexico has had a difficult time creating an integrated transportation network. It was one of the first countries in Latin America to promote railway development, but the extensive state-owned railway system remains inefficient. Major rail routes extend outward from Mexico City northwestward along the Pacific coast to Mexicali, northward through the Central Plateau to El Paso and Laredo, Texas, eastward via the Gulf Coastal Plain to the Yucatán Peninsula, and southeastward to Oaxaca. Rail traffic, for both passengers and freight, is slow and unreliable.

As a result, highways are the major mode of transporting passengers and goods. Cross-country trucking accounts for most freight movement within the nation, and interstate buses carry most of the passengers. While they have been improved tremendously over the last two decades, Mexico's highways are barely adequate to serve the national need. As with rails, all major roads lead to Mexico City. Four major two-lane highways link northern border cities to the capital. Similar highways connect the Yucatán Peninsula and the Guatemalan border with the Mesa Central. The 1,250-mile Pan-American Highway runs from Ciudad Cuauhtémoc, on the border with Guatemala, to Nuevo Laredo, on the border with the United States, passing through Mexico City. Several parts of the country lack good rail and road connections, especially from east to west across northern Mexico. In addition, away from the main highways there are few feeder roads.

Air travel has become a major mode of transportation within Mexico. Largely in response to the needs of tourism, new airports have been built throughout the nation. Two national airlines, Aeroméxico and Mexicana, serve all tourist locations and medium-sized urban centres within the country as well as many international destinations.

ADMINISTRATION AND SOCIAL CONDITIONS

Government. Mexico is a federal republic composed of 31 states and the Federal District. Governmental powers are divided between executive, legislative, and judicial branches, but in practice the president has strong control. The Constitution of 1917 guarantees personal freedoms and civil liberties and also establishes economic and political principles for the country. Suffrage is universal for those over 18 years of age, and voting is mandatory.

The legislative branch has a Senate of 64 members, two from each state and the Federal District, as well as a Chamber of Deputies with one representative for each 250,000 people. Senators serve six-year terms and deputies three-year terms; members of the legislature cannot be reelected for the immediately succeeding term. Three-fourths of the deputies are elected directly by popular vote while the remainder are selected in proportion to the votes received by each political party. The legislature ratifies elections and thus has been able to declare candidates elected, regardless of vote totals. Although it has the right to verify presidential elections, pass the budget, and initiate tax bills, the legislature seldom does so and thus has lost much of its power and prestige.

The president is popularly elected and can serve only one six-year term. He is empowered to select a Cabinet as well as the governor of the Federal District, the attorney general, diplomats, high-ranking military officers, and supreme court justices, who serve life terms. As the leader of the Institutional Revolutionary Party (Partido Revolucionario Institucional; PRI), the president selects the candidate to succeed him. Because the PRI is the dominant political party and has never lost a major election, the president in effect chooses his successor. It is also common for him to approve legislative and state gubernatorial candidates. The president also has the right to issue *reglamentos,* or basic rules that have the effect of law.

In practice, because the PRI is firmly entrenched, Mexico is a one-party democracy. The main opposition party is the National Action Party (Partido Acción Nacional; PAN), but others, such as the Socialist Peoples and Communist parties, represent small minorities.

At the state and local levels, governors, unicameral legislatures, and mayors are elected by popular vote. Governors serve for six years, deputies for three. States can levy taxes and have all powers not delegated to the federal government, but in fact they have relatively little revenue-generating potential or political power.

The courts are responsible for the administration of justice. The Supreme Court of Justice is the highest tribunal, and there are state superior courts as well as civil and criminal courts. The constitution protects the rights of the accused and guarantees a free trial with due process.

The military has long been an apolitical force in the country, but its high-ranking officers are appointed by the president and serve at his pleasure. Conscripts serve a year's compulsory service. The military's primary role is maintenance of internal order, and for this reason about three-fourths of military personnel are in the army.

Education. Mexico has made great efforts to improve educational opportunities for its people. It is the goal of the federal government to eradicate illiteracy and to assure at least a primary education for all citizens. Attendance is required for those age six to 14. In addition to increasing the number of schools for children, adult literacy programs have been promoted vigorously since the 1970s. By the mid-1980s Mexico's literacy rate was estimated to be approximately 85 percent, up nearly 15 percent since 1970.

Public schools in Mexico are funded by the federal government. Although nearly three-fourths of all primary public schools are located in rural areas, such schools are the least well-developed in the nation and often do not cover the primary cycle. Many internal migrants move to cities because of the availability of better schools for their children and the social opportunities that derive from an education. In rural areas, as well as many low-income urban areas, teachers need only a secondary education to be certified to teach. Despite increases in the numbers of schoolrooms, teachers, and educational supplies, nearly 15 percent of all school-age children do not attend school.

Secondary schools are virtually nonexistent in rural areas, and universities are found only in the largest cities. As with primary education, private secondary schools are considered vastly superior to public ones, and families who can afford it send their children to private schools. This helps to maintain the socioeconomic imbalance in educational levels that greatly favours the middle and upper classes.

Of the more than 50 universities in the country, one-fifth are located in Mexico City, and a high percentage of all university students study there. The National Autonomous University of Mexico, the College of Mexico, and the Monterrey Institute of Technology and Higher Education are among the most prestigious institutions of higher education in the country. A college degree is a passport to social mobility in Mexico.

Health and welfare. The federal government plays a major role in providing health care. Subsidized medical and hospital care is available to all Mexican citizens. Several government institutions, including the Mexican Social Security Institute and the Security and Social Services Institute for Government Workers, operate hospitals. Public medicine, like public education, is considered inferior to private care, however, and those who can afford it avail themselves of private physicians and hospitals.

In rural areas basic medical treatment has been widely disseminated since 1970. Clinics, though sometimes attended only by a nurse, are found throughout the country. Anything more than the most basic medical needs, however, must be handled in the cities. The quality of medical service varies throughout the country, with Mexico City by far the principal centre for specialized treatment. The overall quality of medical care in Mexico lags behind that available in the United States and Europe, and many Mexicans travel outside the country for more sophisticated surgical procedures or treatments.

There are strong differences in health conditions from region to region within Mexico. In general, rural areas have much higher mortality and morbidity levels than do urban areas. Regions with large Indian populations, such as Chiapas, Oaxaca, and portions of Guerrero, as well as isolated mountainous sections of the Mesa Central, have especially low health standards and high death rates. There also are great differences in health conditions among social classes in cities.

Housing. A lack of adequate housing is one of Mexico's most serious problems. Although substandard housing is more visible in urban areas, living conditions are probably worse in rural areas. Within the cities, the federal government has built multiunit housing projects. The problem has increased more rapidly than new units can be constructed, however, and economic difficulties have reduced the funds available for new construction.

Economic and social divisions. Mexican society is sharply divided by income and educational level. Although a middle class is developing in the cities, the principal division is between the wealthy, well-educated elite and the urban and rural poor.

Widespread rural poverty is a serious problem. Agrarian reform in the central and southern parts of the country has institutionalized much of the rural peasantry, *ejidatarios* and *minifundistas,* into barely more than subsistence agriculturalists, with limited opportunities for economic or social advancement. An increasing proportion of the rural population is landless and depends on day labour, often at less than minimum wages, for survival. In many areas, but particularly in the northern half of the country, large landholders form an agricultural elite. Controlling extensive holdings and often using modern mechanized farming methods, they control nearly half of the income generated by agriculture. A rural middle class has evolved, but it represents only a small percentage of total agriculturalists.

By far the largest segment of the urban population is in the lowest socioeconomic class. It is estimated that at least 40 percent of city dwellers have incomes below the official poverty level, including a significant percentage of workers who are government employees. Extensive squatter settlements, often lacking basic services, are a common element of all Mexican cities. As an example, Nezahualcóyotl, on the eastern side of Mexico City, has more than 1,000,000 residents living in substandard housing and unsanitary conditions. In contrast, the relatively affluent middle- and upper-income groups enjoy the amenities of urban life and control most of the social, political, and economic activity of the country.

Wages and cost of living. Minimum wage laws have been in effect since 1934. Wages are determined by the type of work and the cost of living in specific regions. Urban job classifications pay higher minimum wages than rural categories, and the highest minimum wages are paid in Mexico City and the border cities of Tijuana, Mexicali, and Ciudad Juárez. Wage rates are theoretically adjusted every two years, but they have been changed more frequently since the 1970s.

Until about 1980 Mexico's inflation rate was relatively modest for a developing nation. The cost of living rose by less than 3 percent annually between 1960 and 1970, increasing to between 10 and 20 percent in the 1970s. Inflation rose to triple digits during the late 1980s.

CULTURAL LIFE

Because of its ethnic and regional diversity, as well as the socioeconomic divisions within the population, Mexico is culturally heterogeneous. Among rural peoples there are strong regional affinities and allegiances, often referred to as *patria chica* ("small homeland"), which help to perpetuate cultural diversity. The large number of Indian languages and customs still extant, especially in the south, also accentuate cultural differences. In an attempt to unite the nation culturally by identifying a uniquely Mexican culture, the government has supported indigenous folk arts and crafts as well as the European-inspired classical arts. Since the 1930s, *indigenismo,* or pride in the Indian heritage, has been a major unifying theme of the country.

The arts. Mexican writers and artists have received worldwide acclaim for their creativity and innovativeness. Within their work both a folk and classical tradition have been strong.

The country's best-known writers have gained their reputations by dealing with questions of universal significance, as did Samuel Ramos, whose philosophical speculations on man and culture in Mexico influenced post-1945 writers in several genres. The prolific critic and cultural analyst Octavio Paz is considered by many to be the foremost poet of Latin America. The novels of Carlos Fuentes are honoured throughout the world, Gustavo Sainz is a leader in Spanish-language literature, and Juan José Arreola's fantasies are widely admired. Among dramatists, Rodolfo Usigli has been extremely influential, and Luisa Josefina Hernández and Emilio Carballido have made important contributions.

Perhaps the most widely recognized Mexican art form is the mural, and the Mexican Muralist school counted among its members the most powerful figures of the genre. The murals created by Diego Rivera and David Alfaro Siqueiros, depicting aspects of the Mexican Revolution, the nation's modernization, and class struggle, have become legendary, and, among others, Rufino Tamayo and Juan Soriano have achieved stature. Perhaps the most popular of Mexico's folk artists is José Clemente Orozco, whose animated plaster-of-paris skeleton characters are both satirical and lifelike.

Mexican popular music, especially ranchero and mariachi music, has attracted a wide following throughout the Spanish-speaking world, and Mexico City has become one of the major recording centres for the Americas. The country's motion-picture and television industries are among the largest in Latin America, producing films and programs that circulate throughout the region.

Cultural institutions. To encourage and help disseminate Mexican art in all its forms, the federal government sponsors the National Institute of Fine Arts. Under its auspices are the programs of the National Symphony Orchestra, the Ballet Folklorico, and the Modern and Classical Ballet, all of which perform nationally and internationally to promote Mexican culture. Folk and popular culture also receive support through government bodies, among them the Native Institute, which seeks to preserve and stimulate traditional craftsmanship.

A number of internationally acclaimed museums, including the National Museum of Anthropology and the Museum of Folk Art, are supported by the Secretariat of Public Education. The National Autonomous University of Mexico, College of Mexico, and Cultural Seminary are important institutions contributing to the arts and humanities.

Recreation. Bullfighting is the country's national sport, and the Plaza México in Mexico City is one of the great venues for this spectacle. Soccer is still the most popular participatory sport, but baseball has attracted increasing numbers of spectators and players at both the professional and the amateur level. Mexico has produced a number of world champions in the lighter weight classes in professional boxing.

Press and broadcasting. Mexico City has a large number of daily newspapers, some of which are respected for their objectivity and relative independence. Although newspapers are guaranteed freedom of the press under the constitution and there is no official censorship, nearly all are muted in their criticism of the president and his policies. There are regional tabloids outside the capital, but they have little national impact. In publishing, Mexico City is now one of the leading centres for Spanish-language books and magazines.

For statistical data on the land and people of Mexico, see the *Britannica World Data* section in the BRITANNICA WORLD DATA ANNUAL. (E.C.G.)

History

PRE-COLUMBIAN MEXICO

Early Hunting Period. It is assumed that the first inhabitants of Middle America were early American Indians, of Asian and Mongoloid derivation, who migrated into the area at some time during the final stage of the Pleistocene Epoch. The date of their arrival in central Mexico remains speculative. The assertions of some archaeologists that early man resided in Mexico 30,000 to 40,000 years ago, before developing technology for big-game hunting, are rejected by most scholars. More generally accepted claims for early man in Mexico pertain to a somewhat later period and to hunters of large herd animals such as the mammoth. Human artifacts and mammoth bones dated to approximately 9000 BC have been found together in the same geologic strata in the Valley of Mexico at Santa Isabel Ixtapan.

Food-Collecting and Incipient Cultivation Period. With the increased dryness and change of fauna following the glacial retreat of the last Wisconsin substage (approximately 7500 BC), the inhabitants of Middle America were forced to turn from big-game hunting to other means of subsistence. These were the hunting of small game and the collecting of wild food plants. This mode of existence is best seen in the archaeological discoveries made in the Tehuacán Valley of Puebla.

In the earlier El Riego (7000–5000 BC) and Coxcatlán (5000–3400 BC) phases of this sequence the inhabitants of the Tehuacán Valley were seasonal nomads who divided their time between small hunting encampments and larger temporary villages, which were used as bases for collecting plants such as various grasses and maguey and cactus fruits. Maize (*Zea mays*), a wild grass, first came under cultivation in this time, probably as early as 5000 BC. Avocados, chili peppers, amaranth, zapotes, tepary beans, and squashes were also primitive cultigens. During the Abejas phase (3400–2300 BC) use of cultivated plants increased at the expense of wild plants and, probably, at the expense of hunting. A hybrid maize, crossed with the wild grass teosinte, appeared for the first time, and pumpkins and the common bean were introduced. Toward the end of the phase, settlement assumed a more permanent form in what appear to have been year-round pit-house villages. In the Purron phase (2300–1500 BC) the first pottery was produced in vessel forms that duplicate earlier stone vessels.

Cultivation of maize

Early Formative Period. By 2000 BC some village communities in Middle America were sustained largely or wholly by agriculture. Because these villages are located largely in southern Mesoamerica, it is likely that agriculture originated there. It soon spread to other areas. During the Early Formative Period the Middle American agricultural plant complex was assembled and improved by hybridization and more sophisticated cultivation techniques.

Middle Formative Period. The Middle Formative Period was a time of transition from the simple agricultural village to more complex societies organized around politico-religious capitals or nuclei. This trend had probably begun in the latter part of the Early Formative, but the first large ceremonial centres and the first monumental stone sculpture occur at about 1000 BC in southern Veracruz and Tabasco. The sites in question, San Lorenzo and La Venta, are locations of characteristic Olmec art. This art is amazingly sophisticated, with consummate control of both full round and bas-relief forms. The human theme predominates, although humans are frequently depicted with jaguar mouths and nostrils. The Olmec artists made great stone heads, altars, and stelae, and they also worked as lapidaries in exquisite jade figurines and other small objects. Olmec stylistic influence reached to Oaxaca, Chiapas, Guatemala, El Salvador, and the Valley of Mexico.

Olmec art

Late Formative Period. The Late Formative Period saw the spread of complex societies throughout much of Middle America. Hieroglyphics and complex calendrical calculations appeared. These elements of civilization are first noted in association with the Tres Zapotes, Izapan, and early Oaxacan art styles. The true city or urban centre also came into being during this period. One of the earliest manifestations of densely settled city life occurred in the Valley of Mexico at Teotihuacán, where the Late Formative urban zone covered some two square kilometres.

Classic Period. The characteristic Middle American aesthetic and religious patterns that began in the Late Formative crystallized in the Classic Period. In the Maya Lowlands polychrome ceramics, the use of the corbeled vault in temple construction, the foreshadowings of typical Maya art, and the probable beginnings of Initial Series calendrics all belong to the end of the Late Formative Period (100 BC–AD 300). The full Maya artistic, architectural, and calendric-hieroglyphic traditions were then ushered in during an Early Classic sub-period (AD 300–600). Tikal, Uaxactún, and Copán all attained their first glories in these centuries. In the Late Classic sub-period, between AD 600 and 900, ceremonial centres in the Maya Lowlands proliferated in number, as did the carving and erection of the inscribed and dated stelae and monuments.

The breakdown of the Classic Period civilizations began with the destruction of the city of Teotihuacán in about AD 700. This commercial, political, and religious metropolis appears to have fallen before the warlike Toltec, peoples of Uto-Aztecan speech who invaded central Mexico from the north and who established their capital at Tula.

Postclassic Period. Four trends characterized the Postclassic Period. First, there was a completion of the breakup of the old regional Classic Period cultures, with their distinctive art and architectural styles and religious traditions. Second, the new Postclassic cultures displayed more secular orientation. Third, fortifications and an increase of warlike themes in art bespoke a more militaristic attitude throughout much of Middle America. Fourth, the urban-type community, which first appeared in the Late Formative and was known through the Classic Period, was emphasized even more than previously.

In the later Postclassic Period Tenochtitlán, the Aztec capital, located where Mexico City now stands, became the dominant force in Middle America. An Aztec empire reached from coast to coast through central and southern Mexico; however, many tributary nations were held by the Aztecs in rather loose bonds, and when Cortés marched from Veracruz to Tenochtitlán he was aided by tribes anxious to free themselves from the Aztec yoke. In the Maya Lowlands the Toltec-controlled centre of Chichén Itzá lost its position of leadership in about AD 1200. Thereafter, there seems to have been something of a Maya resurgence, with the Yucatecan capital being eventually established at the walled city of Mayapán. (G.R.W./M.C.M.)

The Aztecs. The word Azteca is derived from Aztlán ("White Land"), where, according to Aztec tradition, their tribe originated. Aztlán probably is merely a general reference to the northwestern region of Mexico. The Aztecs are also known as Tenochca, a name derived from a legendary patriarch called Tenoch. Tenoch, or Tenochca, gave the name to Tenochtitlán ("Stone Rising in the Water"), a city founded by the Aztecs on an island in Lake Texcoco, in the Valley of Mexico. The Aztecs were also known as Mexica. The name Mexica came to be applied not only to the ancient city of Tenochtitlán but also to the modern Mexican nation and its inhabitants (Mexico, Mexicans).

The language of the Aztecs was Nahuatl, part of the Uto-Aztecan linguistic family which, at the time of the early explorations of America by Europeans, was making its influence felt intermittently in western North America from the Yellowstone River to Panama. Once the Aztecs achieved political ascendancy, their language gained currency in an area almost as large as present-day Mexico.

The Nahuatl language

The empire the Aztecs established was equaled in the New World only by that of the Incas of Peru, and the brilliance of their civilization is comparable to that of other great ancient cultures of America and the Old World. From their legendary land of Aztlán, the Aztecs came into contact with the highly developed Toltec civilization located in central Mexico and having as its capital the city of Tula. The appearance of the Aztecs is linked, however, not to the splendour of Tula and of the Toltec but to their decline. For reasons not fully known but having to do with internal social, political, and religious conflicts, a tremendous cultural catastrophe, which has been compared to the fall of the Roman Empire, occurred at the beginning of the 12th century AD. The city of Tula was attacked and destroyed, as were other important Toltec centres. Tribes of less-developed cultures—hunters and gatherers—took advantage of the situation and added to the chaos, traveling from the arid plateau of northern Mexico toward the fertile, civilized central zone. In their legends the Aztecs portray themselves as part of that wave of barbarian invaders known by the general term Chichimec ("Sons of the Dog").

The decline of the Toltec

From the beginning of the 12th century to the beginning of the 13th, the Aztecs wandered in search of a new place to settle. During that time a group of Chichimec, under the leadership of Xólotl, succeeded in gaining power in the Valley of Mexico, establishing their centre first in Tenayuca and later in Texcoco. Xólotl's Chichimec joined forces with the remaining Toltec, who were firmly entrenched in Culhuacán. The combination of strong

Chichimec power in rapid process of assimilating a higher culture and the restoration of Toltec power in Culhuacán led to a period of relative peace and cultural progress in the Valley of Mexico. The stabilization of this new situation attracted immigrants from all parts of the disturbed country, among them the Aztecs, who by then had established a precarious home near the ruins of Tula.

During their stay in Tula the Aztecs perfected their technological knowledge, especially with regard to agriculture. According to their traditions, it was there that they undertook irrigation cultivation and built *chinampas* (the famous, but misnamed, "floating gardens"). Aztec religion took definite form, centring on the god Huitzilopochtli ("Hummingbird-on-the-Left"), sun worship, and human sacrifice. Aztec tradition has it that Huitzilopochtli ordered them to take leave again in search of a permanent home.

Their long pilgrimage ended in the year of "two house," according to their calendar (AD 1325), when the wanderers found the land spoken of in their prophecies. On a small island in Lake Texcoco, the elder members of the tribe spotted an eagle, symbol of the sun and of Huitzilopochtli, resting on a nopal cactus. There they built the temple of their tribal god and, around it, the first dwellings of what was to become the powerful city of Tenochtitlán, the capital of the Aztec empire, of the viceroyalty of New Spain, and of the modern Mexican nation.

The founding of Tenochtitlán

The swamp-surrounded island on which the Aztecs were forced to take refuge was so uninviting that none of the powers in the Valley of Mexico had claimed it. Tenochtitlán was thus located at the edge of the lands occupied by the valley's three powers: the Chichimec of Texcoco, the Toltec of Culhuacán, and the Tepanec of Atzcapotzalco. It was not long before the Aztecs used their strategic position to advantage, placing their military forces at the service of the Tepanec, who were waging war against the Toltec and the Chichimec. It was in this capacity that the Aztecs began to form their notions about empire building. Under a succession of ambitious kings they established a dominion that eventually stretched over most of present-day Mexico.

The task of attempting to organize the empire along lines other than mere Aztec military strength was left to Montezuma II, the ninth Aztec king (1502–20). It was Montezuma's reign that produced the codices in which Aztec officials recorded the organization of the empire into provinces and the payment of tribute according to the production of each region. A gigantic political, military, and religious bureaucracy was built up, with governors, tax collectors, courts of justice, military garrisons, mail and messenger services, and other civil offices. Despite their feverish efforts at political organization, the Aztecs still had the strength to subjugate their allies, Texcoco and Tacuba, and to undertake new campaigns. It is probable that in this period Aztec troops pushed as far south as Central America.

The demise of Aztec hegemony

But the days of the Aztecs' greatest glory were also their last. Since 1517, Spanish expeditions led by Francisco Hernández de Córdoba, Juan de Grijalva, and Hernán Cortés had been exploring the coasts along the Gulf of Mexico. Rumours of ships as large as houses reached Tenochtitlán, and to them were added prophecies of the imminent return of the benign deity and cultural hero Quetzalcóatl; they could mean only disaster for the Aztecs and their god Huitzilopochtli. Cortés' bold march against Tenochtitlán set the stage for the final scene of the Aztec Empire. Spanish might, combined with a general revolt of the peoples under Tenochtitlán domination, proved superior to the Aztecs' strength. Under the last two Aztec kings, Cuitláhuac and Cuauhtémoc, Tenochtitlán was besieged and destroyed after a heroic Aztec defense. Over the still-smoldering ruins of Tenochtitlán a new city began to rise. Symbolizing the future Mexico, a Christian cathedral was erected on the stones of Huitzilopochtli's temple.

The almost incredible story of a small wandering tribe that was able to build an empire in one century (from the beginning of the 14th century to the beginning of the 15th) can be largely explained by three main factors: Aztec religion, the economy of the Valley of Mexico, and Aztec sociopolitical organization.

Aztec religion centred around the cult of Huitzilopochtli, a young warrior and symbol of the sun who died every evening to be born anew the following day. At dawn Huitzilopochtli began his daily struggle against the stars and the moon, driving them away with a shaft of light. At sunset he died and returned to the bosom of the earth, his mother (Coatlicue), where he renewed his strength in order to take up the fight against darkness. In order to guarantee human existence, Huitzilopochtli had to be well-nourished; his sustenance was human blood. The Aztecs were people of the sun, chosen by Huitzilopochtli to provide him nourishment. War was, therefore, not only their favourite occupation but also, more importantly, a religious obligation in which captured enemies were sacrificed to the sun. As Aztec power grew, the number of human sacrifices increased. Prisoners from all parts of the country were put to death in Tenochtitlán so that the universe and man might survive.

The economic basis of the Aztec hegemony was the Valley of Mexico's agriculture, characterized by *chinampas* and irrigation systems. It was mainly from the Toltec that the Aztecs had learned these techniques. Nevertheless, these methods date even further back in Mexican history; almost certainly they were in existence in the 6th century BC. The high productivity of the systems resulted in a heavy density of population in the Valley of Mexico and the development of large urban centres. In the early 16th century the population of the valley fluctuated around 2,000,000, with some cities approaching or exceeding 100,000. Because of this enormous concentration of population and economic resources, the Valley of Mexico became the pivotal key to power in the central part of the country. The group successful in uniting the valley under a single authority could go on to conquer the neighbouring valleys of Morelos, Mexico, Puebla, and Hidalgo, and, thence, the rest of the country.

From very early times, another factor contributed to the strategic importance of the Valley of Mexico: a system of lakes (Texcoco, Chalco, Xochimilco, Xaltoca, and Zumpango) that were connected naturally and by means of artificial canals. Extensive water transportation on the lakes compensated for the lack of the wheel and of domesticated animals and, in no small measure, furthered the early economic and political unification of the valley.

All these factors served as powerful stimuli to trade. Probably in keeping with an ancient tradition, the merchants (*pochteca*) of Aztec society were organized in powerful guilds, which even started wars on their own and sent trading expeditions to remote places. It was on the basis of the geographic data collected by their merchants that the Aztecs drew up maps not only of what is now Mexico but also of Central America. It is virtually impossible to separate the Aztecs' trade policy from their military and expansionist policy.

The third essential factor in Aztec imperialism was the sociopolitical organization of the tribe. Aztec society in the early 16th century displayed many features described as "primitive," together with manifestations of a highly advanced civilization. For example, the division of the tribe into *calpulli* ("big houses"), pseudo-family units established in Tenochtitlán, has sometimes been interpreted as proof of an egalitarian organization. Yet, evidence of social stratification is indisputable.

Aztec society has also been interpreted as "feudal." This assertion is based on the existence of an Aztec hereditary "nobility," behind which was a group of knighted commoners with access to land rights. Nevertheless, the relation of these noble groups to the Aztec kings, to the rest of society, and to land ownership cannot be compared with Old World feudalism. At the time it came into contact with the Spaniards, Aztec society was characterized by an Oriental-type political organization, in which the king was absolute. Particularly during the reign of Montezuma II, Aztec society and the empire itself were vigorously reorganized. A gigantic bureaucracy, completely dominated by the king, was charged with administering the immense empire and gradually absorbed the old social groups of nobles, knights, and merchants. (An.Pa./M.C.M.)

For fuller treatment of Maya, Aztec, and other Middle American civilizations, see the article PRE-COLUMBIAN CIVILIZATIONS.

CONQUEST OF MEXICO

Diego Velázquez, governor of Cuba, laid the foundation for the conquest of Mexico. In 1517 and 1518 Velázquez sent out expeditions headed by Francisco Hernández de Córdoba and Juan de Grijalva that explored the coasts of Yucatán and the Mexican Gulf. Velázquez commissioned Hernán Cortés to outfit an expedition to investigate their tales of great wealth in the area. Spending his own fortune and a goodly portion of Velázquez', Cortés left Havana in November 1518, following a break in relations with Velázquez. Cortés landed in Mexico and then freed himself from Velázquez' overlordship by founding the city of Veracruz and establishing a town council (*cabildo*) that in turn empowered him to conquer Mexico in the name of Charles I of Spain. Divining that Mexico was a fabulously wealthy realm held together by sheer force and that the Aztec ruler Montezuma held him in superstitious awe, Cortés pushed into central Mexico with only about 500 Europeans and several thousand Indian allies. In an incredible campaign lasting two years, Cortés took the capital city of Tenochtitlán on Aug. 13, 1521. His success was the result of a combination of factors: the hatred of the conquered tribes for the Aztec overlords; Montezuma's belief that Cortés was a returning god; Cortés' personal qualities of leadership and diplomacy; European arms—crossbows, muskets, and steel swords—and horses; disease; and the aid of Cortés' interpreter-mistress, Malinche.

EXPANSION OF SPANISH RULE

After taking possession of the Aztec Empire, the Spaniards quickly subjugated most of the other Indian tribes in southern Mexico, and by 1525 Spanish rule had been extended as far south as Guatemala and Honduras. The only area of southern Mexico where effective Indian resistance was encountered was Yucatán, inhabited by the Maya tribes. Francisco de Montejo undertook the conquest of this region in 1526, but, because Maya bands were so dispersed, it was nearly 20 years before the Spaniards won control of the northern end of the peninsula. Some of the Indians in the interior retained their independence for another century and a half.

The occupation of northern Mexico, which was thinly populated and largely arid, proceeded more slowly than did that of central and southern Mexico. Spanish expansion in this area was motivated chiefly by the hope of discovering precious metals, the need for defense against nomadic Indian raiders, and the desire to forestall incursions by the British and French.

Between 1530 and 1536 Jalisco and other Pacific coast regions were conquered by Nuño de Guzmán. The Indians of Jalisco rebelled in 1541 but were suppressed after hard fighting; this episode became known as the Mixton War. In order to complete the subjugation of the Indians, the Spaniards began to move into Zacatecas, where in 1546 they discovered immensely valuable silver mines. This was quickly followed by similar discoveries in Guanajuato and San Luis Potosí and by the occupation of most of this north central region. Meanwhile Álvar Núñez Cabeza de Vaca, shipwrecked on the coast of Texas in 1528, had spent eight years making his way across northern Mexico before reaching a Spanish settlement on the Pacific coast and had brought back stories of rich Indian civilizations that supposedly existed somewhere in the north. During the years 1540–42 Francisco Vázquez de Coronado led an expedition northward to search for these mythical kingdoms, exploring as far as Kansas before turning back in disappointment. The effective occupation of northern Mexico occurred later in the century and involved prolonged fighting with nomadic Indian tribes. Throughout much of the north the first Spanish settlers were Franciscans and Jesuits who established Indian missions. At the same time that exploration and settlement were bringing new areas under effective control, an administrative bureaucracy was being put into place. New Spain was organized as a viceroyalty governed by a viceroy appointed by the king.

Near the end of the 16th century the northern frontier of New Spain in most areas was close to the present Mexican–U.S. boundary line. Within the area that is now the United States a settlement had been made in Florida in 1565. In 1598 Juan de Oñate began the conquest of New Mexico, though the Indians of the region rebelled in 1680 and were not reconquered until 1694. Later northern expansion was undertaken mainly to check rival European powers. After the French had established colonies in Louisiana, Spanish settlements were made in Texas in 1716, while on the Pacific coast the threat of Russian expansion caused the Spaniards in 1769 to begin the occupation of Upper California. Throughout the 18th century there were incessant boundary disputes between Spain, Britain, France, and subsequently the United States, and some territories changed hands several times. Florida was ceded to Britain in 1763, restored to Spain in 1783, and sold to the United States in 1819. Louisiana became Spanish in 1763 but was regained by France in 1800 and sold to the United States three years later. The northern boundary of New Spain remained largely indeterminate until the Adams–Onís Treaty of 1819, by which the United States acquired Florida but recognized Spanish sovereignty over Texas, New Mexico, and California. (H.B.P./J.J.Jo./M.C.M.)

COLONIAL PERIOD, 1701–1821

A fundamental shift in the governance of New Spain occurred as a result of the War of the Spanish Succession (1701–13), when Bourbons replaced Habsburgs on the Spanish throne. Ruling by divine right, the Bourbon kings were enlightened despots whose major interests lay in increasing the economic returns from the Spanish Empire; they introduced many French practices and ideas into overseas administration.

Among the notable administrative reforms undertaken by Charles III in 1784 was the creation of 18 intendancies. In place of the numerous *alcaldías mayores* and *corregimientos,* which were abolished, *partidos* of about the same size were created within each intendancy. Headed by the intendancy of Mexico, each intendant was given considerable autonomy in increasing economic production within his sphere, developing useful arts and sciences, and bettering education and social conditions, all of the latter less for altruistic than for economic reasons.

Fed by currents of rationalism from England and Europe, the Enlightenment in Spain and Mexico spurred the spread of new scientific knowledge and, especially, its application to mining and agriculture. Political liberalism became a factor when the American and French revolutions called into question the divine right of kings. A later development was the proliferation of the military establishment under the impact of British and Russian pressures on the frontiers of New Spain. Having strung a series of mission-forts across northern Mexico, authorities in Madrid and Mexico augmented the few regular Spanish troops that could be spared from the peninsula by fostering a local militia with special exemptions (*fueros*) granted to Creole (Mexican-born) officers. Thus, an explosive combination resulted from the almost simultaneous appearances of new ideas, guns, and administrative confusion between the old Habsburg and the new Bourbon administrative systems.

The turmoil of Napoleonic Europe was the immediate background of the move for Mexican independence. Napoleon Bonaparte occupied Spain in 1808, imprisoned King Ferdinand VII, and attempted unsuccessfully to impose his brother Joseph Bonaparte as monarch. Rebelling, the Spanish resurrected their long-defunct Cortes (representative assembly) to govern as regent in the absence of the legitimate king, and, with representation from the overseas realms, the Cortes in 1812 promulgated a liberal constitution in the King's name. The document provided for a constitutional monarch, popular suffrage, a representative government, and other features taken from the French and U.S. constitutions. Continental events stimulated rivalries in Mexico as contradictory commands were being received from the mother country. The viceregal establishment put down sporadic rebellions by those who professed loyalty to the imprisoned king but who demanded some form of self-government.

Factionalism and rebellion

The most important local revolt was sparked by Miguel Hidalgo y Costilla, a parish priest in Dolores. On Sept. 16, 1810, Hidalgo issued the "Grito de Dolores" ("Cry of Dolores"), calling for the end of rule by Spanish peninsulars, for equality of races, and for redistribution of land. Mexican Independence Day commemorates this event.

Warning that the Spaniards would deliver Mexico to the godless French, Hidalgo exhorted his followers to fight and die for the Mexican Virgin, Our Lady of Guadalupe. When Hidalgo left his tiny village, he marched with his followers into Guanajuato, a major colonial mining centre peopled by Spaniards and Creoles. There the leading citizens barricaded themselves in a warehouse. Hidalgo captured the warehouse on September 28, but he quickly lost control of his rebel army. Most of the Creole elite were massacred, and the town was pillaged.

The Guanajuato massacre swung moderate and undecided support behind the viceroy's efforts to crush the Hidalgo rebellion, lest a full-scale caste war ensue. Royalist forces defeated Hidalgo at the Bridge of Calderón on Jan. 18, 1811. On March 19 he was captured along with other major insurgent leaders. On July 31 Hidalgo was executed, ending the first of the political civil wars that were to wrack Mexico for three-quarters of a century.

The Hidalgo cause was taken up by his associate José María Morelos y Pavón, another parish priest, who won control of substantial sections of southern Mexico. The constituent congresses, which Morelos called at Chilpancingo in 1813, issued at Apatzingán in 1814 formal declarations of independence and drafted republican constitutions for the areas under his military control.

At about the same time Napoleonic troops were withdrawing from Spain, and in 1814 Ferdinand VII returned from involuntary exile. One of his first acts was to nullify Spain's liberal 1812 constitution drawn up by the Cortes. The departure of the French freed Spanish troops needed to crush the Morelos revolution. Captured and defrocked, Morelos was shot as a heretic and revolutionary on Dec. 22, 1815. Scattered but dwindling guerrilla bands kept alive the populist, republican, nationalist tradition of Hidalgo and Morelos.

Mexican independence came about almost by accident when constitutionalists in Spain led a rebellion that, in 1820, forced Ferdinand VII to reinstate the liberal constitution of 1812. Conservatives in Mexico, alarmed that anticlerical liberals would threaten their religious, economic, and social privileges, saw independence from Spain as a method of sparing New Spain from such changes. They found a spokesman and able leader in Agustín de Iturbide, a first-generation Creole. Iturbide, who had served as a loyal royalist officer against Hidalgo and others, had been given command of royal troops with which he was to snuff out remnants of the republican movement, then headed by the future president Vicente Guerrero.

While ostensibly fighting Guerrero, however, Iturbide was in fact negotiating with him to join a new independence movement. In 1821 they issued the so-called Plan de Iguala, a conservative document that declared that the Mexican nation was to be independent, that its religion was to be Roman Catholicism, and that its inhabitants were to be united, without distinction between Mexican and European. It stipulated further that Mexico would become a constitutional monarchy under Ferdinand VII, that he or some Spanish prince would occupy the throne in Mexico City, and that an interim junta would draw up regulations for the election of deputies to a congress, which would write a constitution for the monarchy.

The Plan de Iguala

United as the Army of the Three Guarantees (independence, union, preservation of Roman Catholicism), the combined troops of Iturbide and Guerrero gained control of most of Mexico by the time Juan O'Donojú, appointed Spanish captain general, arrived in the viceregal capital. Without money, provisions, or troops, O'Donojú felt himself compelled to sign the Treaty of Córdoba on Aug. 24, 1821, thus officially ending New Spain's dependence on Old Spain. The convention provided that the Mexican nation, thenceforth to be styled the Mexican Empire, was to be recognized as independent. Under the treaty, the new empire's congress was to elect an emperor if no suitable European prince could be found. In one of the ironies of history a conservative Mexico had gained independence from a temporarily liberal Spain.

INDEPENDENCE

Although Spain at first disavowed O'Donojú's recognition of Mexican independence, the date now recognized as that of separation of New Spain from Old Spain is in fact Aug. 24, 1821.

The Mexican Empire, 1821–23. The first Mexican Empire spanned only a short transitional period from colony to republic. Independence had been the point on which republicans and conservatives alike could agree. The new constitutional monarchy shielded the conservatives from a Spanish government that had suppressed religious orders, tried clerical cases in civil courts, and decreed that the church could not acquire real property. Such a government was also palatable to the insurgents, whose major objective was independence.

Iturbide became president of a council of regents, which convoked a Sovereign Constituent Congress. Deputies to the congress represented the intendancies, the name they retained during the empire. When representatives from the Central American intendancies, part of the old viceroyalty of New Spain, decided that their areas did not wish to remain part of the Mexican Empire, they were allowed to withdraw and to organize their own independent governments.

On the evening of May 18, 1822, military groups proclaimed Iturbide Emperor Agustín I, and on the next day a majority in congress ratified the "people's choice" and recommended that the monarchy be hereditary, not elective. Agustín I was crowned in a long ceremony on July 21. The empire was recognized by the United States on Dec. 12, 1822, when the Mexican minister was officially received in Washington, D.C. But even then Agustín's power and prestige were already ebbing, and conflict soon developed between the military hero Iturbide and the primarily civilian congress. On Oct. 31, 1822, the Emperor dismissed congress and ruled through an appointed 45-man junta. The act, which was condemned by many as arbitrary, provided discontented military men with a pretext to revolt. Among their leaders was General Antonio López de Santa Anna, whom Agustín had first promoted for services in the Army of the Three Guarantees. In Veracruz, Santa Anna proclaimed a Mexican Republic on Dec. 2, 1823, and was supported by old guerrillas. Other military men had similar plans. Agustín was forced to reconvene congress and to abdicate. In 1824 he returned from European exile but was arrested and shot. This first epoch of independent Mexican national life thus foreshadowed many problems of the succeeding republic.

The early republic. When a republican constitution was adopted in 1824, the Mexican people had had little or no previous experience in self-government. Their economy was precarious; mining, a mainstay in colonial times, had declined during the many years of fighting, and widespread anti-Spanish feelings had caused an exodus of Spaniards, depleting both the nation's capital reserves and its pool of trained people. Political instability made borrowing abroad expensive, and nearly all public revenues had to come from customs receipts, which were pledged well in advance. As Mexico's national debt mounted, so did its problems. A vicious, seemingly unbreakable cycle marked the first half century of Mexican national life. Whenever public monies were insufficient to pay the army, its officers revolted, captured the government, and negotiated international loans. The high interest payments on such loans reduced available funds for education and other social and cultural improvements, which many Mexican leaders thought were urgent requirements.

Troubles of the new republic

The constitution of 1824 provided for a federal republic, consisting of 19 states, four territories, and a federal district; it also set a number of goals, toward which the nation subsequently inched its way. Although the monarchical idea survived for nearly half a century more, Mexico remained a republic. The constitution abolished slavery, which was never a major issue, and enfranchised all male inhabitants; Indians thus lost their special colonial status, and accompanying protections, as wards of the government. In many ways they were worse off during the 19th century than they had been under the paternalism of the Spanish crown. Restrictive state legislation excluded the great mass of peasantry from the political process.

Under various labels, two factions contended for control. Generally conservative, the Centralists favoured a strong central government in the viceregal tradition, a paid national army, and Roman Catholicism as the exclusive religion. Opposed to them were the Federalists, who favoured limited central government, local militia, and nearly autonomous states; they tended to be anticlerical and opposed the continuance of colonial *fueros,* which gave special status to ecclesiastics and the military and exempted them from various civil obligations.

The pendulum of power swung back and forth between the two groups. In 1824 Guadalupe Victoria, a Federalist and a leader in the independence movement, was elected president. Centralists replaced Federalists in 1828. A Federalist revolt in 1829 put Vicente Guerrero in the presidential chair, but he was soon overthrown by the Centralists, who held power until 1832. In 1833 another change placed Federalists in power until 1836, when Centralists again regained control and held it for nearly a decade.

The age of Santa Anna: Texas and the Mexican War. After the downfall of Iturbide, Mexican politics revolved for some time about the enigmatic personality of Antonio López de Santa Anna, a charismatic general with seemingly few fixed ideological or political beliefs. Allied with the Federalists, Santa Anna was first chosen president in 1833, but, rather than serve, he placed the liberal vice president Valentín Gómez Farías at the head of the government until Farías and his group in 1834 attacked the privileges of the clergy. Then Santa Anna assumed his presidential post and nullified the anticlerical legislation.

Problems over Texas

Santa Anna was president when difficulties over Texas first began to mount. Under favourable terms, some 30,000 U.S. immigrants had populated that previously desolate area. Fearful that their growing numbers posed a threat, the Mexican government in 1830 closed the border to further immigration and imposed on the Texans oppressive restrictions that contravened the Mexican constitution. When Santa Anna adopted a new constitution in 1836, and in the process eliminated all vestiges of states' rights, Texas declared itself an independent republic. Santa Anna quickly gathered an army to crush the revolt. He met with initial success when he trapped a small Texas garrison at the Alamo and totally eliminated it, but he was defeated and captured by Texas forces in April 1836 and subsequently freed. Though Mexico made no further efforts to reconquer Texas, it refused to recognize its independence.

At that time a doctrine now known as Manifest Destiny was at its height in the United States. It expressed a belief that it was the destiny of the United States to occupy all the North American continent and perhaps all of Mexico. The United States annexed the Republic of Texas in 1845, a move that caused the Mexican government to break off diplomatic relations. Santa Anna was overthrown for his apparent willingness to negotiate with the United States.

Although the United States claimed that the southern boundary of Texas was the Rio Grande, the boundary had always been the Nueces River. Shortly after his election in March 1845, U.S. President James K. Polk tried to secure an agreement on the Rio Grande boundary and to purchase California, but the Mexican government refused to discuss either matter. Polk ordered U.S. troops to occupy the disputed territory between the rivers. When Mexican and U.S. patrols clashed in April 1846, Polk asserted that American blood had been shed on American soil—an outrage that required action. Less warlike politicians, such as the Illinois congressman Abraham Lincoln, to no avail submitted resolutions asking Polk to point out the precise location of this outrage. Polk's congressional majority formally declared war on Mexico in April.

War with the United States

Without major difficulty, U.S. troops captured New Mexico and Upper California (now the state of California). General Zachary Taylor led the main U.S. force to quick victories in northeastern Mexico. At that juncture the government of Mexican president Mariano Paredes y Arrillaga was overthrown, and Santa Anna reemerged as president in September 1846. Almost immediately, Santa Anna mobilized Mexican forces and marched northward, boasting that the superior numbers and courage of his men meant that he would sign a peace treaty in Washington. Although Taylor and Santa Anna fought a close battle at Buena Vista, Santa Anna was beaten and forced to retreat on Feb. 23, 1847. Both sides sustained heavy losses.

A change in U.S. strategy left Taylor holding ground in northern Mexico; it was decided that Mexico could be beaten only by capturing Mexico City, via Veracruz. General Winfield Scott was given command of the expedition. On April 18, 1847, he defeated Santa Anna in the critical battle at Cerro Gordo. Though Mexican resistance continued to be formidable, Scott captured Mexico City on Sept. 14, 1847. Santa Anna went into voluntary exile while a new Mexican government negotiated peace.

Dated Feb. 2, 1848, the Treaty of Guadalupe Hidalgo terminated the war. Under its terms Mexico ceded all territory north of an irregular line of the Rio Grande and the Gila River across the Colorado to the Pacific. The United States paid Mexico $15,000,000 and assumed $3,250,000 in claims held by U.S. citizens against Mexico.

After the war Santa Anna figured in one more major episode before the political scene changed. In 1853 conservatives seized power and invited him to become dictator. Among other things, on Dec. 16, 1853, Santa Anna decreed that the dictatorship should be prolonged indefinitely and that he should be addressed as "His Most Serene Highness." To raise funds for an expanded army, he sold territory south of the Gila River to the United States for $10,000,000; this Gadsden Purchase, as it is now called, was the last significant boundary change of the Mexican Republic.

The Reform. Since independence a new generation of Mexicans had been born; appalled at the easy victory the United States had won, the more thoughtful among them felt that Mexico's survival as an independent nation depended on fundamental reform. Among the new faces was Benito Juárez, a Zapotec Indian educated as a middle-class liberal, who had moved to New Orleans and had discussed and planned Mexico's future with fellow expatriates. With no military force to implement their plans, they bided time until their opportunity came, in 1854, when Juan Álvarez, a surviving hero of independence, and Ignacio Comonfort, a political moderate, proclaimed a liberal rebellion against Santa Anna and forced him out of the presidency.

Neither Álvarez, who served a short term as president, nor Comonfort, who succeeded him, had any clearly defined program. The role of the returned expatriates was to act as a brain trust to carry out La Reforma ("The Reform"). Its aims were to abolish remnants of colonialism by removing special ecclesiastical and military privileges; to separate church and state by secularizing education, marriages, and burials; to reduce the economic power of the church by forcing it to sell its properties; to foster an economic development that envisaged Mexico as a country of yeoman farmers and small industrialists; and, above all, to establish a single standard of legal justice.

Juárez was made minister of justice. Among his first reforms was the so-called Ley Juárez (Nov. 23, 1855), which abolished *fueros* and the use of special military and ecclesiastical courts in civil cases. The minister of finance, Miguel Lerdo de Tejada, sponsored the Ley Lerdo (June 25, 1856), which restricted the right of ecclesiastical and civil corporations to own lands by decreeing that church lands not directly used for religious purposes must be sold and lands held in common by Indian communities (*ejidos*) be distributed to individual villagers.

Constitution of 1857

The reformers called a convention to draft a new constitution, which would provide a legal base for the reform. It was promulgated on Feb. 12, 1857, but did not become effective until the following September 16, the 47th anniversary of the "Grito de Dolores." The Constitution of 1857 prohibited slavery and abridgments of freedom of speech or press; it abolished special courts and prohibited civil and ecclesiastical corporations from owning property, except buildings in use; it eliminated monopolies; it prescribed that Mexico was to be a representative, democratic, republican nation; and it defined the states and their responsibilities. This constitution, which remained in force until it was modified in 1917, increased the power of the central executive.

Neither the religious community nor the military accepted the 1857 constitution, and both inveighed against the reform, calling for retention of "religion and *fueros*." The church excommunicated all civil officials who swore to support the constitution. When civil war erupted, Comonfort went into exile after his efforts at compromise had failed; Juárez automatically succeeded him as constitutional president. The conservatives captured Mexico City and set up a competing regime. Juárez and his government moved to Veracruz, where they controlled the customs receipts.

Foreign powers became involved in the Mexican struggle. On April 6, 1859, the United States recognized the Juárez government; President James Buchanan permitted war matériel to be shipped to Juárez' forces. Americans were encouraged to serve the liberal cause as volunteers; Spain and France generally favoured the conservatives, as did Great Britain.

In July 1859 Juárez issued a series of decrees: all church property except buildings used for worship was to be confiscated without compensation; all marriages apart from civil were declared annulled; the formal separation of church and state was proclaimed; cemeteries were declared public property, and burial fees were abolished. Moneys from the sale of confiscated church property, though less than anticipated, speeded the end of the civil war. On Dec. 22, 1860, the liberals won a critical battle, and, when the conservative president, Miguel Miramón, fled, the conservative cause collapsed. The victorious liberal army of about 25,000 men entered Mexico City on New Year's Day, 1861. On his return (January 11) Juárez was greeted by an enthusiastic populace who welcomed the end of the long and devastating civil war and the reestablishment of government under the constitution of 1857.

Ambitions of Napoleon III

French intervention. Exiled Mexican conservatives, who continued to intrigue, enlisted the help of a powerful ally, the French ruler Napoleon III, who wanted to create a Latin league that would include the Mediterranean lands and the former possessions of Spain and Portugal in the New World as well. (The term Latin America dates from this time and concept.) With its strategic position and its economic potential, Mexico seemed especially attractive to the Napoleonic imperial scheme. A French bastion in Mexico would check the Manifest Destiny of the United States and provide a base from which Central and South American protectorates could be added. The fact that the United States was engaged in a civil war (1861–65) was a determining element. In 1861 Napoleon III was willing to believe the Mexican conservatives' assertions that the masses of Mexican people would support his intervention to restore religion and set up a monarchy.

Mexico's chaotic economic situation afforded Napoleon III the perfect opportunity to implement his scheme. The government of Benito Juárez had a huge foreign debt, and in 1861 the Mexican government suspended all payments to Spain, Britain, and France. The three European powers prepared to send a punitive expedition to Mexico. The intervention was spearheaded by Spain, the forces of which landed at Veracruz on Dec. 14, 1861, and were followed soon after by French and British contingents. When the allies fell into dispute over the $15,000,000 French claim for payment of certain questionable bonds, both Spain and Great Britain disengaged from the joint venture.

The French expeditionary force began its march toward Mexico City. When the Mexican army made a stand at Puebla on May 5, 1862, the French retreated to await reinforcements. Napoleon dispatched 30,000 more troops under the command of the French general Élie-Frédéric Forey. The Mexicans could not withstand French might, and on June 10, 1863, Forey rode as conqueror into Mexico City. The French rapidly secured much of central Mexico, forcing Juárez and his government to keep constantly on the move in the north.

Napoleon III had already identified a pair of puppets to place on the Mexican throne: Maximilian of the House of Habsburg and his wife, Charlotte (Carlota), daughter of the King of Belgium. Assured of Napoleon's continued military support and the economic backing of the British, Maximilian and Charlotte arrived in Veracruz on May 28, 1864, having passed through Rome to confer with the Pope before they embarked. On June 12 Emperor Maximilian was welcomed in Mexico City.

Emperor Maximilian

Maximilian attempted to follow a policy of national conciliation, hoping to unite Mexican factions and interests. But he proved too much a Habsburg to be an effective tool of Napoleon's schemes, too much a liberal to please the conservatives who had engineered his coronation, and too tainted by conservative sponsorship to win republican support.

Maximilian was perhaps less naive than he has been pictured. Not fully convinced that a majority of Mexicans welcomed him as emperor nor sure that he should place full reliance on French troops, he tried to create a Mexican rural guard and a separate imperial army around a nucleus of Austrian and Belgian volunteers. His proposal to reduce the number of regular Mexican army generals to 18 brought early disillusionment to the army, a mainstay of conservatism, which had expected Maximilian to be a puppet. The Mexican officers became further irritated when, with Maximilian's approval, French officers outranked them. At this time the Habsburg emperor and the French commander, Achille-François Bazaine, were following conflicting army policies, Napoleon having ordered Bazaine to Mexicanize the army to cut time and costs of occupation.

At the same time, clerical groups, eager to reap rewards for their efforts on the Emperor's behalf, pressed him to reverse the Reform. A papal nuncio from Rome arrived with a message asking that Maximilian revoke the anticlerical laws, establish Roman Catholicism as the exclusive religion, restore the religious orders, remove the church from its dependence on civil authorities, turn education over to ecclesiastics, and return properties confiscated and sold by the republicans. Replying that he, not outsiders, would decide such matters, Maximilian issued decrees establishing religious toleration, with Roman Catholicism favoured but still dependent on the state. He confirmed that the previous sales of church property under the Reform laws were legal and that revenues the church had received from property Juárez had nationalized were to be ceded to the state. Thus, Maximilian's conservative support further dwindled because the clergy and their followers felt betrayed.

In September 1864 Maximilian took what amounted to a guided tour of the cities that supported his empire. The warm welcomes he received from the people led him to conclude that a majority of Mexicans wanted peace and justice, which the activities of the republican guerrillas threatened. He therefore decreed on November 4 that, thenceforth, republicans would be considered bandits and brigands, subject to extreme penalties; this negated Maximilian's attempts to woo their supporters by inviting them into his council of state.

In 1865 French troops chased Juárez to, but not over, the U.S. border. Believing that the Mexican president had left national territory and that republicanism had therefore collapsed, Maximilian on October 2 issued a strong decree, ordering that all guerrillas be court-martialed and shot within 24 hours; the same penalties were to apply to persons who hid, aided, or otherwise helped them. Juárez had earlier issued a parallel decree (January 1862) against those who aided the French interventionists and imperialists.

Withdrawal of foreign troops

French troops, though they were effective in keeping republicans on the outskirts of major productive areas, were also costly. Napoleon's Mexican adventure came under heavy press and parliamentary fire in France as costs in men and money mounted without economic or political advantages to compensate for the expenditures. There was criticism from overseas as well; with its civil war ended, the United States turned to the international scene. William H. Seward, the U.S. secretary of state, brought mounting diplomatic pressure on Napoleon to withdraw

French troops; in February 1866 Napoleon agreed to clear foreign troops from Mexico by November 1867. A U.S. request to the Austrian government to stop enrollment of volunteers for the Mexican imperial army also brought an affirmative response.

In liquidating his Mexican venture, Napoleon said that, since Maximilian had not carried out his part of the pact to bring peace and orderly government to Mexico, the French were relieved of their obligations for military and financial support. Stunned, Maximilian sought to have the decision reversed. The empress Charlotte tried without success to persuade the French ruler to honour his solemn pledge. From Paris she traveled to Rome to plead with the Pope; there she went mad and was taken to Belgium, where she lingered insane until her death in 1927. Bazaine, ordered to withdraw all French troops immediately, auctioned off military material not worth shipping to France—including horses and saddles—and destroyed large supplies of powder and projectiles rather than turn them over to Maximilian. In February 1867 Bazaine left Mexico City, and by March 12 all 28,690 men had embarked. Napoleon made Bazaine the scapegoat of the Mexican fiasco, blaming its high costs and lack of results on his mismanagement, and implied personal dishonesty.

As French power withdrew, republican forces reconquered Mexico, and Maximilian was left with only a regiment of Austrian hussars, a battalion of infantry, and a small army of relatively untrained Mexican draftees. After first considering abdication, Maximilian decided to defend his imperial status and his honour as a Habsburg by making as strong a stand as possible, though planning, in the event of defeat, to negotiate an honourable exile. With these resolves he concentrated most of his troops—9,000 men—at Querétaro, a city loyal to the imperial cause. On May 5, 1867, the republican forces laid siege, initially with 32,000 men, later with an additional 10,000. By May 14 the starving imperialist force, reduced to about 5,000, had decided to withdraw and take a stand in the mountains. A disaffected imperial officer, in return for a promise that Maximilian be spared, placed republican soldiers, whom he passed off as relief troops, at strategic places in Querétaro. The siege ended the next day when Maximilian and his generals surrendered.

Under Juárez' decrees of 1862, Maximilian and his two leading generals were court-martialed and sentenced to death by firing squad. President Juárez refused to be swayed by the petitions for mercy that poured in from foreign governments. He wanted to demonstrate that Mexico could act independently; that, as the Reform contended, all men were equal under law; that foreign monarchical adventures in Mexico were futile; and that the honour of the Mexican dead would be redeemed. Maximilian and the generals were executed on June 19, 1867, terminating a bizarre interlude of Mexican history.

The restored republic. At least 50,000 persons lost their lives in the struggles between republic and empire, and when Juárez reentered Mexico City on July 15, 1867, his immediate task was to abate the rancors of civil war. The vindicated Juárez regime took few major reprisals—principal imperialists were fined, some were imprisoned for short terms, and a few were exiled. One of Juárez' first acts was to start rebuilding the shattered economy. In an era of goodwill engendered by the sympathy and aid the United States had extended to the Mexican cause, the claims of the two countries against each other were settled by peaceful arbitration. Diplomatic relations were gradually reestablished with Europe.

Rebuilding the republic

In December 1867 Juárez was reelected president. Apart from trying to foster political tranquillity, his main aims were to improve public education and to put the economy on a sound footing. To avoid the problems of dogma and religious opinion that had divided Mexicans, Juárez entrusted the development of a national educational system to Gabino Barreda, a follower of the French thinker Auguste Comte, who had said that the human mind and society passed through three successive stages—religious, metaphysical, and positive. Known as positivists, Barreda and his followers contended that the Reform, by displacing the church and militarism, had done away with the earlier two stages and that Mexico was in the third, or positivist, stage. The public-education law for the Federal District, which was to serve as the national model, stressed the secular state as the inculcator of scientific ethical norms, with "Liberty, Order, and Progress" as the means, base, and product of the system.

The chief architect of economic rehabilitation was Matías Romero, who had been Juárez' minister in Washington and who believed that Mexico's development was dependent on three basic elements: immigration, communication networks, and the exploitation of natural resources. In 1867 and '68 the government renewed concessions to British capitalists for the completion of the Veracruz–Mexico City railway and issued concessions for others; it authorized the opening of new roads and the extension of the telegraph system. Work was begun on reforming the tax systems and tariff schedules.

The reelection of Juárez in 1871 was contested more heatedly than that of 1867 had been. Thereafter, despite formidable opposition in congress, tariff reform was approved, as was Mexico's adoption of the metric system, which ended the chaotic colonial system of weights and measures.

After a short illness, Juárez died suddenly on July 18, 1872, his death closing one era and opening another. Behind him lay Mexico's long colonial history and its partial survivals through the early 19th century. The notion of a Mexican monarchy had been forever buried with Maximilian. Under Juárez, Mexicans had begun to modernize the economy and some of the social institutions, to expand rail, road, and telegraph networks, and to develop secular education.

Juárez' death also brought temporary political peace. Without incident, Sebastián Lerdo de Tejada, the president of the supreme court, and next in line of succession, was sworn in as acting president on July 19. Congress immediately began to lavish posthumous honours on Juárez, who by his innate abilities and great strength of character had led his people through unprecedented travail. He remains a major figure in the history of Mexico.

Temporary political peace

A national election placed Lerdo in the presidential chair in his own right on Nov. 16, 1872. The course Juárez had charted remained unchanged. On New Year's Day, 1873, the Veracruz–Mexico City railway was inaugurated. Other works were commissioned. Congress and the executive branch of government continued to dole out railway and telegraph concessions. To safeguard the nation against future bloodshed, congress on May 31 added specific reform laws to the constitution of 1857—church and state were explicitly declared independent of one another; freedom of religion was proclaimed; church acquisition of real estate was abolished; religious oaths were banned in civil courts; forced labour was forbidden; and liberty of man in respect to labour, education, and religion was declared inviolable. The degree to which the Reform had triumphed was evidenced by the fact that no national movement developed against these additions to the organic laws. The Lerdo government in 1874 renewed diplomatic relations with France, Spain, and Prussia.

The age of Porfirio Díaz. From 35 years, from 1876 until a political revolution unseated him in 1911, the personality of Porfirio Díaz dominated the history of his country. Like Juárez, Díaz was a poor Indian from Oaxaca but of Mixtec rather than Zapotec heritage. Educated locally, he had chosen a military career and had become an outstanding general in the republican cause against the French intervention and empire. Although he vied for the presidency against Juárez in 1867 and again in 1871, their ideological differences were not great. When in 1875 Lerdo ran for reelection, Díaz led a successful revolt and assumed the presidency in November 1876.

Díaz took the blueprint for Mexico's future that Juárez and Lerdo had elaborated and implemented it. While clearing out pockets of political resistance, he turned the presidency over to Manuel González, a companion in arms. Díaz won the election again in 1884 and was regularly returned to that office through 1908. During his long regime he scrupulously kept democratic and constitutional forms intact, partly in the conviction that it was the president's duty to train the unready Mexican people to use them properly.

The *científicos*

Around him Díaz gathered many intellectuals (the *científicos*). They were positivists who stressed the need for rational planning and development. The emphasis was on economic development to assure social progress. How such development was to be achieved was translated into one of Díaz' political slogans, "*pan o palo*" ("bread or the club"), meaning that acquiescence to official policies would ensure livelihood, even wealth, but failure to agree would bring sure reprisals—harassment, imprisonment, death. Another slogan was "few politics, much administration." Liberty was dropped from the earlier positivist triad of liberty, order, and progress. It was the price the Mexican people were expected to pay for the benefits the *científicos* policies would provide.

Capital, though badly needed, could not be attracted until Mexico had tidied up its international and national fiscal affairs. Mexican finances were placed on a solid base, and a stable currency was established. With guarantees of political and social tranquillity, foreign investment was encouraged and obtained. European and U.S. funds built some 15,000 miles of railways, provided electricity and streetcars for the cities, created industrial complexes, rehabilitated port facilities, and developed the mining of industrial metals. Early petroleum concessions to foreigners laid the groundwork for serious problems later, when world navies shifted from coal to oil and when automobiles were mass-produced.

The Porfiriato

A complex mechanism in which all major and most minor decisions rested in the hands of the president evolved during the first two decades of the Díaz regime, or Porfiriato. The success of the practice rested on self-interest; Díaz made it worthwhile for everyone to support the system. For the most part, the small body of intellectuals was absorbed into the expanding bureaucracy or the subsidized press. The army and the church were made handmaidens of the regime rather than its adversaries; generals were encouraged to become entrepreneurs. While retaining the Reform laws on the books, Díaz was purposely conciliatory toward the church and allowed it to regain some of its former economic power without letting it develop significant political influence.

The regime also perfected instruments of repression and control, though for many years it used them sparingly. Forced military conscription lay in the hands of the president's appointees. Troublesome elements such as the Yaqui Indians were inducted en masse and shipped as cheap labour to the sisal plantations of Yucatán or the tobacco fields of Oaxaca. Governors were personal appointees of the president. Their actions were monitored by *jefes políticos* ("political chiefs"), who reported directly to the president and on his authorization intervened in municipal and state affairs. An elite constabulary, the *rurales,* like the Texas Rangers and Canadian Mounted Police, created a myth of ubiquity that eliminated the brigandage and banditry characteristic of earlier 19th-century Mexican countrysides.

In an era in which material success was highly regarded, Díaz' accomplishments were praised, but his popularity began to decline, perhaps about 1895. Prosperity had been preempted by a relatively small group, many of whom were foreigners. The Mexican economic and social elite self-consciously aped European (especially French) modes of dress, education, and even language. Between the affluent and the growing urban and rural proletariat there was an expanding middle-class body. Meanwhile, a new generation, which could recall none of the chaos of the days before Porfirio Díaz took charge, began to question the system. As criticism increased, so did repression. It was from this interaction that the Mexican Revolution resulted.

PRECURSORS OF THE REVOLUTION

The Regeneration group

Shortly after 1900 many Mexicans began to question the nation's apathetic acceptance of the Porfirian peace. The earliest and most vocal critics were Mexican radical groups, perhaps the most important of which called itself Regeneration. Its members were anarchists who adapted their dogmas to the Mexican scene. While always small in numbers and often ineffective in actions, this group had great influence. Many of the reforms and programs it advocated were embodied in the Mexican constitution of 1917.

The leader of the Regeneration group was Ricardo Flores Magón, who had been born in Oaxaca of an Indian mother and a mestizo father and had been sent for further education to Mexico City, where he had turned to idealistic student activism. For leading a small demonstration against the reelection of Porfirio Díaz in 1892, he was jailed for the first of many times. The group's movement took form in 1900, when Camilo Arriaga, a well-to-do engineer in San Luis Potosí, organized first a club and then a small party to restore the liberalism of Juárez. Arriaga called a national meeting of liberal clubs in 1901, and a short time later most of the small band were jailed, and their newspaper, *Regeneracion,* which Flores Magón edited, was suppressed. After they had served their prison sentences the young radicals fled north to the United States and Canada, settling for a while in St. Louis, Mo., where they formally organized the Mexican Liberal Party. Although its name suggests the earlier Reform, in fact it was anarcho-syndicalist, dedicated to the overthrow of the Mexican government and the total renovation of Mexican society.

In 1906 the Regeneration group published a comprehensive program in the form of a manifesto that had wide, if clandestine, circulation in Mexico. It advocated a one-term presidency, guarantees of civil liberties, breaking the hold of the Roman Catholic Church, vast expansion of free public education, and land reform. It asked that Mexican citizenship be a prerequisite to property ownership and that unused land be distributed to the landless. The manifesto proposed confiscation of the wealth that Díaz and the *científicos* had illegally acquired, the abolition of child labour, guaranteed minimum wages, and bettered working conditions for workers. In muted tones it criticized capitalism as a system of exploitation. The Regeneration group drew its main lines of thought from Mikhail Bakunin, a Russian revolutionary writer who believed that the power of any institution, including government, that exercised controls over individuals should be reduced.

Many charges by the Regeneration and similar groups were borne out when the Díaz troops, in bloody fashion, broke strikes in the textile region of Veracruz and the copper-mining regions of the northwest state of Sonora. Several of these strikes had been fomented by Regeneration organizers at the same time that U.S. muckrakers were exposing the evils of corrupt government, big business, and other aspects of life in the United States and abroad. Possibly to refute their unfavourable reports, Díaz gave an interview in 1908 to an American reporter, James Creelman, that became a milestone in prerevolutionary history. To blunt charges of one-man rule, Díaz very carefully but clearly said that in his view the time had come for Mexico to advance toward democracy, that he would welcome an opposition party in the 1910 presidential election, that he would be most happy to sustain and guide the opposition party, and that to inaugurate a democratic government in Mexico he would forget himself. This fell like a bombshell in Mexico, where most readers failed to note that he had not specified a time. It was widely believed that this implied he would not run for the presidency in 1910. Mexican newspapers not only reprinted the interview but also began openly to discuss Mexican political questions, long forbidden by the regime. Pamphlets and then books added to the political rumblings.

Political opposition to Díaz

Two main opposition groups soon emerged. One backed General Bernardo Reyes as vice presidential candidate over Díaz' handpicked candidate. Reyes forthrightly opposed *científico* theories and practices and, as governor of the progressive northern state of Nuevo León, had initiated a state workman's compensation law.

The other main party, anti-reelectionist, had been created largely through the efforts of Francisco I. Madero, then a political unknown, whose efforts elevated him to the highest place in the revolutionary pantheon as the "Apostle of Democracy." Born into one of the 10 richest families in Mexico, whose agricultural enterprises spread over much of northern Mexico, Madero was educated in the United States and France. In his own right he became an enlightened entrepreneur and amassed a considerable personal fortune.

Madero became concerned with how badly Mexico was faring in comparison to the rest of the world. Mexican food prices were rising, and rural and urban standards of living were dropping. He attributed Mexico's retrograde position to the prolonged political dictatorship. He helped journalists to expose these matters and provided considerable early financial support to the Regeneration group, but he disassociated from them after about 1907, when it became clearer that they intended to destroy, not reform, the system.

Madero, setting about to organize a national party to compete in the 1910 elections, published *La sucesión presidencial en 1910* ("The Presidential Succession in 1910") as a campaign document, two-thirds of which dealt with the history of Mexico and the corrupting influences of absolute power and the rest with his program to revive the democratic usages that had atrophied for so long. The initial aim was to win the vice presidency.

Despite harassment, Madero carried on a vigorous and wearying campaign in the summer of 1909. During an interview with Díaz, he was surprised by the dictator's advanced old age and his remoteness from current issues. Díaz' condition and the enthusiasm of Madero's crowds led the anti-reelectionists to modify their goals. Rather than accept Díaz as the inevitable president in 1910, they decided to try for the presidency themselves.

On June 14 Madero was arrested and jailed and thus became the martyr and victim of the system he was trying peacefully to change. Since it was perfectly clear that Díaz was not going to permit free and honest elections, Madero and his followers decided that the only hope of improving Mexico was through armed revolt. On Oct. 4, 1910, the Chamber of Deputies, which had assembled as the electoral college, declared that Díaz had been reelected. On October 5 Madero managed to escape from the San Luis Potosí jail. He arrived on October 7 in San Antonio, Texas, where with aides he prepared and issued, as of the day of his escape, the Plan of San Luis Potosí, which proclaimed the principles of "effective suffrage, no reelection." Madero declared that Díaz was illegally president of Mexico. Designating Sunday, November 20, as the day when citizens should take up arms against the government of Porfirio Díaz, he promised that a successful revolution would institute political reforms.

The Plan of San Luis Potosí

But on November 20, the official birthday of the Mexican Revolution, no mass uprisings took place. Small bands of guerrillas, most of them in northern Mexico, kept the rebellion alive while Madero used his family fortune to supply them with arms from Texas. Under the leadership of Pascual Orozco and Pancho Villa, the northern rebels began to defeat Federalist forces, who held most of the strategic rail lines, especially those emanating from Ciudad Juárez, on the U.S. border, where the Federalist troops had consolidated. Until the revolutionists laid siege to that city, no more than 2,500 armed men were engaged in the Madero revolution.

THE MEXICAN REVOLUTION AND ITS AFTERMATH, 1910–40

When armed outbreaks initiated the Mexican Revolution in 1910, the immediate object was to replace Díaz as president. What began as a relatively simple political movement broadened into a major economic and social upheaval that gave Mexico many unique characteristics. During the long struggle, the Mexican people developed a sense of identity and purpose, unmatched by any Latin-American republic. Many reforms had been established by 1940, when the goals of the revolution were institutionalized as guidelines for future Mexican policies.

The military revolution. On Feb. 14, 1911, Madero crossed into Mexico near Ciudad Juárez to head his forces. In the next few months the rebels learned how debilitated the Díaz army had become; led by aged generals, the Federalist troops lacked discipline, cohesion, unity of command, and effectiveness. Under these circumstances, the revolution gained ground and momentum. On May 10 the Federal commander surrendered at Ciudad Juárez, which marked the beginning of the end. An agreement negotiated with the Díaz regime provided that Díaz would resign, that an interim president, Francisco León de la Barra, would call general elections, and that revolutionary forces would be discharged. On May 25 Díaz resigned and sailed for Paris. Several revolutionary bands, including that of Emiliano Zapata, resisted being disarmed by the Federal army.

In the heated political atmosphere, congress on November 2 declared that Madero had won the presidency in an election held the previous month. The new government was able to withstand constant attacks from the right and left for only 15 months. A series of unsuccessful counterrevolutionary revolts culminated in a successful plot in February 1913. Following 10 days of cannonading the heart of Mexico City, with high civilian casualties, Victoriano Huerta, commandant of government forces, betrayed Madero and arranged for his arrest and that of his vice president, José María Pino Suárez, so that Huerta could assume the presidency himself. These plans were made with the knowledge, if not the connivance, of the U.S. ambassador, Henry Lane Wilson, who was thus defying President William H. Taft's instructions to remain aloof from domestic Mexican politics.

Shortly thereafter, presumably on Huerta's orders, Madero and Pino Suárez were shot while being transferred from one prison to another. Their deaths rekindled revolutionary fires. In northern Mexico, Venustiano Carranza, refusing to recognize Huerta as president, demanded that the office be elective, as specified in the constitution. He called his new movement the Constitutionalist Revolution. Former chieftains such as Pancho Villa made loose alliances with Carranza. The revived revolution took on highly local and regional aspects.

The new president of the United States, Woodrow Wilson, was determined to oust Huerta and, on flimsy pretexts, landed U.S. troops at Veracruz and occupied it. All of the revolutionary leaders except Villa rejected this external intervention in a national struggle. The combined revolutionary forces unseated Huerta in 1914 but then split over who was to exercise presidential power. Zapata in Morelos and Villa in the north joined to fight the revolutionary groups under Carranza, the most important of which was headed by General Álvaro Obregón. Obregón won a decisive victory over Villa at Celaya in April 1915 but failed to bring the civil war to an immediate end. Sporadic fighting continued for the next five years.

Split among revolutionary groups

The constitution of 1917. With most of central and southern Mexico under constitutionalist control, Carranza in 1916 convoked a constituent congress in Querétaro to revise and update the constitution of 1857. In the course of fighting, the economic and social demands of the radical precursors had become common slogans as contending revolutionary bands bid for popular support. The constitution of 1917 incorporated the aspirations of those groups involved in the revolution. A major concern of Zapata's followers was land reform. Carranza's advisers had prepared a draft document that included not only most of the revolutionary decrees about land reform but also the most advanced European social legislation.

The constitution of 1917 specifically incorporated the major features of the 1824 and 1857 charters regarding territorial organization, civil liberties, democratic forms, and anticlerical and antimonopoly clauses. The constitution completely reversed the concept widely held in Mexico that government should take only a limited, passive role. Its philosophy was that the national government had an obligation to take an active role in promoting the social, economic, and cultural well-being of its citizens. Article 3 sketched a vast plan of secular, free, compulsory public education. Article 14 reaffirmed the sanctity of private property and contracts, but article 27 interjected concepts of social utility and national benefit to limit the untrammeled use of private property. The most important new concepts came in Articles 27 and 123. The former reasserted national ownership of subsoil resources and outlined alternative land-reform and agrarian programs.

The latter, the magna carta of labour and social welfare, was set apart to highlight its importance; in addition to guaranteeing minimum wages and the right to organize and strike, it gave labour social status and destroyed the concept of it as an economic commodity to be bought at the lowest rates to maximize profits. Article 123 also outlined a comprehensive system of social security, including public health and welfare programs. Reflecting the nationalistic feelings of the revolutionaries, foreigners and foreign interests were placed under limitations. Article 33, for instance, permitted the president to deport foreigners at will.

The constitution of 1917 set the goals toward which presidents were to work. As expected, Carranza was elected president and given de jure recognition by the United States. When Zapata was betrayed and killed in 1919, the last organized opposition to the Carranza-Obregón reorganization dissolved. Pancho Villa retired from active campaigning after his raids across the border, especially one in Columbus, N.M. (March 9, 1916), had failed to embroil the United States in conflict with Carranza. Villa was ambushed and shot by political enemies in 1923.

The northern dynasty: Obregón and Calles. When Carranza failed to move toward immediate social reforms, General Obregón enlisted two other powerful north Mexican chieftains, Plutarco Elías Calles and Adolfo de La Huerta, to join him in an almost bloodless coup; together they formed the northern dynasty. Carranza was killed as he fled from Mexico City, and Obregón took office as president Dec. 1, 1920. The dynasty agreed that peace was needed to rehabilitate Mexico from the devastations of nearly a decade of civil upheaval. Using a combination of force and political incentives, Obregón placated many ambitious military leaders.

Overthrow of Carranza

Obregón began to implement the ideals set forth in the constitution. Administrative machinery was set up to distribute land to the landless and to restore communal holdings (ejidos) to villages. The government supported the Regional Confederation of Mexican Labour (Confederación Regional de Obreros Mexicanos; CROM). José Vasconcelos, who was named minister of education, was to implement the program of rural education. He sponsored a cultural program that brought Mexico worldwide fame and importance. Radical mural painters such as Rivera, Orozco, and Siqueiros, who were commissioned to portray Mexican and especially revolutionary history on public buildings, exalted the Indian past, as did creative writers.

At the end of his term, Obregón stepped aside for Calles. Calles' presidency followed the same general lines as had Obregón's. Land distribution was stepped up, an irrigation program was begun, and in 1925 renewed pressure was put on the petroleum companies to exchange for leases the titles they had obtained from Díaz. Problems with the church developed when Calles instituted vigorously anticlerical measures; in retaliation, the church suspended all religious ceremonies and approved and possibly sponsored a rebellion in western Mexico known as the Cristeros. Mediation of the church–state controversy was unofficially accomplished by Dwight W. Morrow, the U.S. ambassador to Mexico, whose sympathetic and skillful diplomacy also eased tensions between the two countries.

In 1928 the presidential term was extended from four to six years, and the doctrine of "no reelection" was modified to mean "no successive reelection." Obregón was the successful presidential candidate, but, before he could take office, he was assassinated by José de León Toral, a religious fanatic. With Calles unable to succeed himself, a peculiarly Mexican single-party system came into being.

Single-party system

Calles formed the National Revolutionary Party, a coalition of regional and local military bosses and labour and peasant leaders. To safeguard the gains of the revolution, he excluded the church and other possible reactionary elements. With Calles as chief, the official party governed in the name of the revolution. A congress, drawn from party ranks, named successive, short-term presidents to fill out the Obregón term.

In the period 1928–34 a worldwide depression and increasing personal vested interests caused many of the older, now conservative revolutionaries, including Calles, to go slowly in implementing the reform mandates of the constitution. The ruling clique continued to be militantly anticlerical, but government support was withdrawn from CROM, which disintegrated. Land distribution slowed down, and educational programs were curtailed. On the positive side, the Calles years saw the beginnings of an irrigation and road-building program.

Resurgence under Cárdenas. Within the revolutionary family, General Lázaro Cárdenas was a respected if not outstanding revolutionary. Having quietly and faithfully worked his way up the ladder of politico-military power during the Obregón and Calles years, he seemed a safe candidate in the 1934 elections. He was also acceptable to a powerful group within the party, which drafted a six-year plan incorporating extended revolutionary reforms.

With his election to the presidency for a six-year term beginning in 1934, Cárdenas strengthened the labour movement and took other steps that defied Calles. When the inevitable test of power came, Cárdenas won, and Calles fled into temporary exile, after which Cárdenas renamed and reorganized the party on a functional national basis—the agrarians formed one sector; labour another; the military yet another; and bureaucrats, teachers, and miscellaneous groups made up the popular sector. The four sectors agreed to support the slate of candidates the party designated. The local, state, and national representatives made party policy and ratified the president's choice of candidates.

With massive popular support and with the power elites under control, Cárdenas tirelessly pushed toward revolutionary goals. He and his advisers elaborated the land-reform programs; using land expropriated from private owners, they created communal cooperatives and gave them ejido status. By the end of his term about 40 percent of the rural working force was under the ejido program. Cárdenas also nationalized railways and placed them under the management of labour.

Perhaps Cárdenas' single most spectacular action was the expropriation of foreign petroleum companies following a labour dispute in which unions demanded not only wage increases but also participation in what management considered its exclusive role. A series of court cases and special boards found in favour of the workers. When the companies refused to accept the decisions, Cárdenas on March 18, 1938, decreed expropriation of their holdings, thus nationalizing the petroleum industry. Petróleos Mexicanos (Pemex), then a small agency, was designated to administer the industry for the nation. The British government, whose nationals had a far larger stake than U.S. firms, immediately broke diplomatic relations. After a short delay U.S. President Franklin D. Roosevelt indicated that, if Mexico would make prompt and fair payments, he would not intervene diplomatically on behalf of the oil companies. This sympathetic reaction was based largely on the advice of the U.S. ambassador, Josephus Daniels, who as secretary of the navy had ordered the occupation of Veracruz in 1914 but who over the years had become a warm friend of the Mexican people.

Expropriation of foreign petroleum companies

Mexicans consider March 18, 1938, as the anniversary of Mexican economic independence. Cárdenas had not only restored an important resource to national patrimony but also showed that national honour and dignity could not be flouted by foreign entrepreneurs, however powerful. After engaging in propaganda campaigns, boycotts, blacklists, and other forms of economic warfare, the oil companies eventually were forced to settle their claims on essentially Mexican terms.

Once the initial bungling was over, Pemex developed the capacity to fuel the industrial revolution that marked Mexico's next epoch. No one realized at the time how important petroleum would become on the world political and economic scene in the decades ahead.

General Manuel Ávila Camacho, whom Cárdenas supported, and General Juan Andreu Almazán fought a close and bitter contest for the presidency in 1940. When Almazán lost, he sought U.S. support for a revolution. But to emphasize the U.S. position toward Ávila Camacho and Mexico, Roosevelt sent Vice President Henry A. Wallace to attend the inauguration. When Cárdenas left the presidency in November 1940, a major chapter of the Mexican Revolution had closed.

Ávila Camacho's domestic policy was conciliatory. While retaining earlier forms, he placated Roman Catholic groups by announcing, "I am a believer." These words had political importance that transcended their immediate religious significance. In the larger sense they meant that the social programs of the Mexican Revolution would slow down after 1940. The overriding issues of the day, however, were diplomatic and economic; the Cárdenas resurgence had increased Mexico's self-respect but had left its economy in a depressed state. The economy would be severely tested during World War II.

WORLD WAR II, 1941–45

Industrialization

World War II brought profound changes to Mexico. Its basic economic structure was transformed, as to a lesser degree were its political, social, and cultural institutions. To offset wartime shortages industrialization and urbanization were accelerated to meet local needs.

Even before Mexico entered the war as a belligerent it supplied many necessary raw materials to the United States. For their mutual benefit, Mexico and the United States in November 1941 signed a General Agreement that resolved most outstanding quarrels between the two countries. The old problem of U.S. agrarian claims was settled, a reciprocal-trade treaty was outlined, and the Mexican peso was stabilized and supported to maintain a constant dollar ratio. The United States agreed to continue silver purchases at world prices and to provide long-term loans to buttress Mexico's economy. Separate agreements were reached on military aid, primarily to professionalize the Mexican Army and its small air force. As a step in that direction, the military sector was dropped from the official party, eliminating the army as a separate bloc in politics. Henceforth, officers and men were represented through the diversified popular sector.

The United States declared war on the Axis powers in December 1941. Mexico also became an active belligerent a few months later after Germany had sunk two of its tankers. The Mexican foreign secretary, Ezequiel Padilla, took the lead in urging other Latin-American countries to support the Allies as well. A Mexican–North American joint defense committee planned cooperative operations to be carried out in case the Japanese attacked Mexico's west coast. Former president Lázaro Cárdenas served on the committee and became minister of defense when that post was created in 1944. A small Mexican air unit operated with the United States in the Philippines. But Mexico's major contribution to the war effort was the steady supply of raw materials for U.S. industry.

If Mexico had only a minor impact on the outcome of the war, the war exerted a major impact on Mexico. With most of the free world producing war matériel, traditional Mexican imports became scarce or were unavailable. To fill this vacuum, Mexican light industry developed, almost exclusively with Mexican capital. By the end of the war the industrial goal was not simply to make Mexico self-sufficient but also to produce a surplus for export.

MEXICO SINCE 1945

A new kind of revolution

Mexico's population exploded at the end of World War II. The industrialism spawned by the war became a major element in the economy. The military increasingly faded into the background as arbiters of national policy, and Mexico had an unbroken line of civilian presidents, beginning with the election of Miguel Alemán in 1946. With him the emphasis shifted from the Cárdenas approach—dividing Mexico's small agricultural land area among many persons—to the development of new resources. Massive hydraulic projects were undertaken to furnish electric power, open new lands, provide flood control, and become the nuclei of regional agricultural–industrial complexes. The nationalized oil industry became a major producer of natural gas and petrochemicals in an effort to meet burgeoning domestic needs. Economic integration was accomplished by the extension of railroad, highway, and airline networks to nearly all regions. As the population increased, the domestic market expanded.

Civilian presidents

Postwar Mexico was marked by a continuity of basic policies unprecedented in Mexican history and by the peaceful constitutional transfer of presidential power from one civilian regime to the next. President Alemán was the chief architect of new departures in the official party. The name was changed from the Party of the Mexican Revolution to the Institutional Revolutionary Party (Partido Revolucionario Institucional; PRI). Suffrage in Mexico doubled when President Adolfo Ruiz Cortines enfranchised women, who first voted in 1958. Electoral reform laws broadened the political base, but opposition parties grew slowly as the PRI dominated the political power mechanisms of the state. By the 1980s only the conservative National Action Party (PAN) constituted any kind of a threat to the PRI. It was only a minor threat, however, with strength limited to a few northern states.

Economic crisis

For 35 years following World War II Mexico experienced unprecedented prosperity. Mexico's economic growth in the 1970s was financed with international loans totaling almost $80,000,000,000. Government planners calculated easy repayment from projected oil revenues, including income from the huge reserves discovered in 1976 in Tabasco and Chiapas states. They were unable, however, to predict the world oil glut of the early 1980s and the sharp fall in oil prices. As the infusions of "petrodollars" declined, Mexico found it increasingly difficult to pay even the interest on its huge foreign debt.

Other structural problems that beset the economy included high unemployment and underemployment, an unfavourable balance of trade, and an alarming inflation rate. A lack of confidence in the economy prompted wealthy Mexicans to reinvest their assets abroad, mainly in the United States. The Mexican peso, meanwhile, declined rapidly in foreign-exchange markets. President José López Portillo, elected in 1976, nationalized the country's banks and imposed strict foreign-currency controls in an effort to achieve some economic stability. Miguel de la Madrid Hurtado, who was elected to succeed López Portillo in 1982, established a program of economic austerity, but his policies brought little relief from the problems that had beset the country.

In the meantime, relations with the United States grew increasingly strained as the heavy flow of narcotics and immigrants across the border brought U.S. moves to tighten border control and to restrict immigration. The country's problems were complicated in September 1985 when an earthquake devastated Mexico City, killing an estimated 7,000 people and destroying or damaging hundreds of buildings. Slow recovery from the disaster brought strong criticism of the de la Madrid government, which was already being denounced for the depressed economy and alleged vote fraud in the 1985 local elections.

For later developments in the history of Mexico, see the *Britannica Book of the Year* section in the BRITANNICA WORLD DATA ANNUAL.

For coverage of related topics in the *Macropædia* and *Micropædia*, see the *Propædia*, sections 952, 966, and 974.

(H.F.C./M.C.M.)

BIBLIOGRAPHY

General works: Comprehensive works discussing political, economic, cultural, and social characteristics of the country include JAMES D. RUDOLPH (ed.), *Mexico, a Country Study*, 3rd ed. (1985); ROBERT C. WEST and JOHN P. AUGELLI, *Middle America, Its Lands and Peoples*, 2nd ed. (1976); and ALAN RIDING, *Distant Neighbors: A Portrait of the Mexicans* (1985). Guidebooks include YVETTE CAMP and ANDRÉ CAMP, *Mexico*, 2nd rev. ed. (1986; originally published in French, 1973); and ANDREW E. BERESKY (ed.), *Fodor's Mexico 1988* (1987). *Diccionario Porrúa de historia, biografía y geografía de México*, 5th rev. ed., 3 vol. (1986), is an encyclopaedic reference source.

Geography: Information on the geography of the country is provided in JORGE L. TAMAYO, *Geografía moderna de México*, 9th rev. ed. (1980). Natural resources and physical geography are examined in ANGEL BASSOLS BATALLA, *Recursos naturales de México, teoría, conocimiento y uso*, 16th ed. (1984); PRESTON E. JAMES and C.W. MINKEL, *Latin America*, 5th ed. (1986); DONALD D. BRAND, *Mexico, Land of Sunshine and Shadow* (1966); and HANS G. GIERLOFF-EMDEN, *Mexico: Eine Landeskunde* (1970). IAN SCOTT, *Urban and Spatial Development in Mexico* (1982), focuses on policies pursued in the traditional regions.

People: For demographic information, see FRANCISCO ALBA, *The Population of Mexico: Trends, Issues, and Policies* (1982; originally published in Spanish, 1976); COLEGIO DE MÉXICO, CENTRO DE ESTUDIOS ECONÓMICOS Y DEMOGRÁFICOS, *Dinámica de la poblacíon de México,* 2nd ed. (1981); and WOUTER VAN GINNEKEN, *Socio-Economic Groups and Income Distribution in Mexico* (1980). Social conditions are examined in RAMÓN E. RUIZ, *Mexico: The Challenge of Poverty and Illiteracy* (1963); SUSAN ECKSTEIN, *The Poverty of Revolution: The State and the Urban Poor in Mexico* (1977); and WAYNE A. CORNELIUS, *Politics and the Migrant Poor in Mexico City* (1975). Education and the intelligentsia are discussed in MARY KAY VAUGHAN, *The State, Education, and Social Class in Mexico, 1880–1928* (1982); CHARLES N. MYERS, *Education and National Development in Mexico* (1965); DANIEL C. LEVY, *University and Government in Mexico: Autonomy in an Authoritarian System* (1980); and RODERIC A. CAMP, *Intellectuals and the State in Twentieth-Century Mexico* (1985).

Economy: The history of the economy is discussed in D.A. BRADING, *Miners and Merchants in Bourbon Mexico, 1763–1810* (1971); ROBERT A. POTASH, *Mexican Government and Industrial Development in the Early Republic,* rev. ed. (1983); NORA HAMILTON, *The Limits of State Autonomy: Post-Revolutionary Mexico* (1982); MORRIS SINGER, *Growth, Equality, and the Mexican Experience* (1969); and CLARK W. REYNOLDS, *The Mexican Economy: Twentieth-Century Structure and Growth* (1970). CLAUDIO STERN, *Las regiones de México y sus niveles de desarrollo socioeconómico* (1973), studies regional disparities in economic conditions. Economic relations in the 1970s and '80s are analyzed in ROBERT E. LOONEY, *Mexico's Economy: A Policy Analysis with Forecasts to 1990* (1978); JOHN K. THOMPSON, *Inflation, Financial Markets, and Economic Development: The Experience of Mexico* (1979); JORGE I. DOMÍNGUEZ (ed.), *Mexico's Political Economy* (1982); CARLOS TELLO, *La política económica en México. 1970–1976,* 5th ed. (1982); and DONALD L. WYMAN (ed.), *Mexico's Economic Crisis* (1983).

The problems of the state versus private economy are explored in RAYMOND VERNON, *The Dilemma of Mexico's Development: The Roles of the Private and Public Sectors* (1963); ROGER D. HANSEN, *The Politics of Mexican Development* (1971); and SYLVIA MAXFIELD and RICARDO ANZALDÚA MONTOYA, *Government and Private Sector in Contemporary Mexico* (1987). Mexico's petroleum industry is examined in EDWARD J. WILLIAMS, *The Rebirth of the Mexican Petroleum Industry* (1979); GEORGE W. GRAYSON, *The Politics of Mexican Oil* (1980); and JUDITH GENTLEMAN, *Mexican Oil and Dependent Development* (1984). Other industries are surveyed in WILLIAM E. COLE, *Steel and Economic Growth in Mexico* (1967); MANUEL A. MACHADO, JR., *The North Mexican Cattle Industry, 1910–1975* (1981); and DOUGLAS C. BENNETT and KENNETH E. SHARPE, *Transnational Corporations Versus the State: The Political Economy of the Mexican Auto Industry* (1985).

The social and economic impact of relations with the United States is studied in MARK T. GILDERHUS, *Diplomacy and Revolution: U.S.-Mexican Relations Under Wilson and Carranza* (1977); BINATIONAL AMERICAN ASSEMBLY ON MEXICAN-AMERICAN RELATIONS, *Mexico and the United States* (1981); GEORGE W. GRAYSON, *The United States and Mexico: Patterns of Influence* (1984); LAWRENCE A. CARDOSO, *Mexican Emigration to the United States, 1897–1931: Socioeconomic Patterns* (1980); WAYNE A. CORNELIUS and RICARDO ANZALDÚA MONTOYA (eds.), *America's New Immigration Law: Origins, Rationales, and Potential Consequences* (1983); CARLOS VÁSQUEZ and MANUEL GARCÍA Y GRIEGO (eds.), *Mexican-U.S. Relations: Conflict and Convergence* (1983); JERRY R. LADMAN, DEBORAH J. BALDWIN, and ELIHU BERGMAN (eds.), *U.S.-Mexican Energy Relationships: Realities and Prospects* (1981); PEGGY B. MUSGRAVE (ed.), *Mexico and the United States: Studies in Economic Interaction* (1985); and CASSIO LUISELLI FERNANDEZ, *The Route to Food Self-Sufficiency in Mexico: Interactions with the U.S. Food System* (1985).

Agrarian developments and rural conditions are the subject of PAUL FRIEDRICH, *Agrarian Revolt in a Mexican Village* (1970; reprinted 1977 with an updated bibliography); MERILEE SERRILL GRINDLE, *Bureaucrats, Politicians, and Peasants in Mexico* (1977); MANUEL L. CARLOS, *Politics and Development in Rural Mexico: A Study of Socioeconomic Modernization* (1974); GEORGE A. COLLIER, *Fields of the Tzotzil: The Ecological Bases of Tradition in Highland Chiapas* (1975); STEVEN E. SANDERSON, *Agrarian Populism and the Mexican State: The Struggle for Land in Sonora* (1981); BILLIE R. DEWALT, *Modernization in a Mexican Ejido: A Study in Economic Adaptation* (1979); and P. LAMARTINE YATES, *Mexico's Agricultural Dilemma* (1981; originally published in Spanish, 1978).

Government: A broad survey of administrative and political conditions is provided in PABLO GONZÁLEZ CASANOVA, *Democracy in Mexico* (1970; originally published in Spanish, 1965; 16th Spanish ed., 1985); KENNETH F. JOHNSON, *Mexican Democracy: A Critical View,* 3rd ed. (1984); L. VINCENT PADGETT, *The Mexican Political System,* 2nd ed. (1976); JOSÉ LUIS REYNA and RICHARD S. WEINERT, *Authoritarianism in Mexico* (1977); JUDITH ADLER HELLMAN, *Mexico in Crisis,* 2nd ed. (1983); MARTIN C. NEEDLER, *Mexican Politics: The Containment of Conflict* (1982); DANIEL C. LEVY and GABRIEL SZÉKELY, *Mexico: Paradoxes of Stability and Change,* 2nd rev. ed. (1987); and JUDITH GENTLEMAN (ed.), *Mexican Politics in Transition* (1987). Modern political leadership is analyzed in RODERIC A. CAMP, *Mexico's Leaders, Their Education & Recruitment* (1980), and *Mexican Political Biographies, 1935–1981,* 2nd rev. ed. (1982). The development of the Mexican army is studied in JORGE ALBERTO LOZOYA, *El ejército mexicano,* 3rd ed. (1984); and DAVID RONFELDT (ed.), *The Modern Mexican Military, a Reassessment* (1984).

Art and culture: For the role of Mexican thought in Spanish-American culture, see LEOPOLDO ZEA, *América en la historia* (1957; reissued 1970), and *América como conciencia,* 2nd ed. (1972); and SOLOMON LIPP, *Leopoldo Zea: From Mexicanidad to a Philosophy of History* (1980). ANTHONY JOHN CAMPOS (ed. and trans.), *Mexican Folk Tales* (1977), provides insight into the folk tradition. See also CARLOS ESPEJEL, *Mexican Folk Ceramics,* trans. from Spanish (1975), and *Mexican Folk Crafts* (1978; originally published in Spanish, 1977); and JOSÉ MORENO VILLA, *Lo Mexicano en las artes plásticas* (1948, reissued 1986). A comprehensive survey of the visual arts is provided in JUSTINO FERNÁNDEZ, *A Guide to Mexican Art: From Its Beginning to the Present* (1969; originally published in Spanish, 2nd ed., 1961). For more detailed accounts, see SHIFRA M. GOLDMAN, *Contemporary Mexican Painting in a Time of Change* (1981). WALTER M. LANGFORD, *The Mexican Novel Comes of Age* (1971), reviews fiction. For other sources on literature, see DAVID WILLIAM FOSTER, *Mexican Literature: A Bibliography of Secondary Sources* (1981). RODOLFO USIGLI, *Mexico in the Theater* (1976; originally published in Spanish, 1932), covers pre-Columbian times to the 1920s. See also CARL J. MORA, *Mexican Cinema: Reflections of a Society, 1896–1980* (1982).

History: PEGGY K. LISS, *Mexico Under Spain, 1521–1556: Society and the Origins of Nationality* (1975, reprinted 1984), studies the first 35 years of Spanish rule; other studies of the colonial period and the struggle for independence include BRIAN R. HAMNETT, *Roots of Insurgency: Mexican Regions, 1750–1824* (1986); HUGH M. HAMILL, JR., *The Hidalgo Revolt: Prelude to Mexican Independence* (1966, reprinted 1981); and TIMOTHY E. ANNA, *The Fall of the Royal Government in Mexico City* (1978). DAVID J. WEBER, *The Mexican Frontier, 1821–1846* (1982), is a discussion of northern Mexico before the war with the United States in 1846. The Juárez era is covered in WALTER V. SCHOLES, *Mexican Politics During the Juárez Regime, 1855–1872* (1957, reprinted 1969). The late Juárez and Porfirian years are explored in DANIEL COSÍO VILLEGAS, *Historia moderna de México,* 8 vol. in 9 (1955–74). The role of the *rurales* during the Díaz regime is traced in PAUL J. VANDERWOOD, *Disorder and Progress: Bandits, Police, and Mexican Development* (1981). Biographies of prominent political figures of the period include RALPH ROEDER, *Juarez and His Mexico: A Biographical History,* 2 vol. (1947); OAKAH L. JONES, JR., *Santa Anna* (1968); STANLEY R. ROSS, *Francisco I. Madero: Apostle of Mexican Democracy* (1955, reissued 1970); MICHAEL C. MEYER, *Huerta: A Political Portrait* (1972); WILLIAM H. BEEZLEY, *Insurgent Governor: Abraham Gonzalez and the Mexican Revolution in Chihuahua* (1973); and JOHN WOMACK, *Zapata and the Mexican Revolution* (1969).

FRANK TANNENBAUM, *Mexico: The Struggle for Peace and Bread* (1950), is important for its observations on the political and social situation at the beginning of the 20th century. The labour movement is treated in RAMÓN EDUARDO RUIZ, *Labor and the Ambivalent Revolutionaries: Mexico, 1911–1923* (1976); and JOE C. ASHBY, *Organized Labor and the Mexican Revolution Under Lázaro Cárdenas* (1967). For other analytical works, see W. DIRK RAAT, *The Mexican Revolution: An Annotated Guide to Recent Scholarship* (1982). The relationship with Spain before World War II is discussed in T.G. POWELL, *Mexico and the Spanish Civil War* (1981). Specific features of the revolution are analyzed in JAMES W. WILKIE, *The Mexican Revolution: Federal Expenditure and Social Change Since 1910,* 2nd rev. ed. (1970). The aftermath is treated in HOWARD F. CLINE, *Mexico, Revolution to Evolution, 1940–1960* (1962, reprinted 1981); and DONALD HODGES and ROSS GANDY, *Mexico, 1910–1982: Reform or Revolution?,* 2nd ed. (1983), a Marxist interpretation. Later, comprehensive surveys include MICHAEL C. MEYER and WILLIAM L. SHERMAN, *The Course of Mexican History,* 3rd ed. (1987); and DANIEL COSÍO VILLEGAS *et al., A Compact History of Mexico,* 2nd ed. (1985; originally published in Spanish, 1973). DONALD C. BRIGGS and MARVIN ALISKY, *Historical Dictionary of Mexico* (1981), is a brief but useful reference source.

(E.C.G./An.Pa./H.B.P./J.J.Jo./H.F.C./M.C.M.)

Mexico City

Founded in the 14th century by the Aztecs, who named it Tenochtitlán, the future Mexico City soon became the centre of the largest empire in pre-Columbian Mesoamerica. Modern Mexico City (Spanish: Ciudad de México) is the capital of the United Mexican States and the centre of the country's political, economic, and cultural life. Although it was once called the "City of Palaces" and was said to have the world's "most transparent air," rapid population growth and industrial development have led to overcrowding, pollution, and social tensions. Still, the city retains considerable charm and has notable examples of colonial and modern architecture, as well as exceptional museums and parks.

Mexico City is located in the central Mexican plateau, in the Valley of Mexico—more properly a basin—just north of the Neo-Volcánica Range. Although in 1970 Mexico City was officially equated for the first time with the Federal District—the federally controlled area designated as the nation's capital—the term Mexico City continues to be used for the entire metropolitan area, which goes beyond the Federal District's boundaries to the north and falls well short of them to the south. The Federal District has an area of 571 square miles (1,477 square kilometres). By the 1980s the rapidly growing metropolitan area extended over about 425 square miles, of which only some 212 square miles were within the Federal District.

This article is divided into the following sections:

Physical and human geography

CHARACTER OF THE CITY

Mexico City is a metropolis of contrasts. Although it is one of the world's largest and most populous urban areas, the former small towns engulfed in its growth have preserved much of their traditional character. Distinctively Latin-American and proud of its origins—both Indian and Spanish—it has nonetheless acquired, by virtue of its proximity to the United States, a clear North American character in some areas. The city's colonial and 19th-century buildings stand side by side with steel-and-glass constructions. The wealth of the west side and of some of the southern suburbs contrasts with the poverty of the northeast and of the illegal settlements known as *ciudades perdidas* ("lost cities") in the metropolitan area.

Mexico City has long been a symbol of the centralization of power: first in the Aztec empire, then in the Viceroyalty of New Spain, and finally in independent Mexico. Thousands of government buildings in the urban area serve as reminders of the city's role in public administration. Resentment of the capital's perceived privileges has long been a source of friction with the rest of the country, but Mexico City and some of its monuments—such as Chapultepec Castle and the Independence Monument—are regarded nonetheless as symbols of the entire nation.

A centre of power

LANDSCAPE

The city site. Mexico lies in an endorheic (characterized by interior drainage) basin at an altitude of approximately 7,350 feet (2,240 metres). It is walled in by the sierras of Monte Alto and Monte Bajo to the west, the Sierra de las Cruces to the southwest, and the sierras of Ajusco and Chichinautzin to the south. Toward the east, the city ends in a plain that meets the Sierra Nevada, with its two extinct volcanoes, Ixtacihuatl (17,342 feet) and Popocatépetl (17,883 feet), which were once a familiar sight from Mexico City but are now usually obscured by pollution. To the north, Tepeyac Hill and the Sierra de Guadalupe were the traditional limit of the city, but new urban areas have developed around and beyond them.

The surrounding mountains

The island where the original Tenochtitlán was built—surrounded by lakes that would eventually be dried out—was also chosen as the site of the new colonial city. Construction expanded to the lake beds as these were desiccated, which accounts for the soft subsoil that has proved highly unstable during earthquakes. A gradual sinking of some downtown sections, a process that has threatened many historical landmarks, is also a consequence of the soft subsoil. Although the city's central area is flat, the land rises gently as it approaches the western and southwestern mountains.

Climate. Mexico City is located within the world's tropical zone, but high altitude accounts for its relative coolness. The annual median temperature is 64° F (18° C); seasonal changes are small. Night frosts occur in December and January, the coldest months, but even then temperatures rise to the mid-70s during the day. April and May are the warmest months. The rainy season, which usually lasts from late May until September, brings temperatures down and moderates the usual dryness of the air.

Air pollution—made up mostly of ozone, suspended particles, and sulfur dioxide—has affected the climate by partially blocking the Sun's rays. Poor air circulation out of the mountain-walled city aggravates pollution. The prevailing winds, especially strong during February and March, blow from the northeast and sweep dust particles into the city, although the partial regeneration of Lake Texcoco has begun to alleviate this problem. Thermal inversions often trap smog in the valley during winter.

Effects of air pollution

The weather is not homogeneous throughout the city. The higher and more wooded areas of the west and southwest are cooler and receive more rainfall than the rest. The north and northeast, largely depleted of vegetation, are the driest and hottest areas.

The city layout. The island where the Aztecs built their capital became the central area of Mexico City. The Zócalo (previously known as the Plaza Mayor and now officially called the Plaza de la Constitución) is the traditional hub of the city. On the Zócalo's northern side, close to the former site of the main Aztec temple, stands the Metropolitan Cathedral. The National Palace, formerly the viceroy's palace, which is the official seat of the republic's executive power, was built over the ruins of the Aztec emperor's palace. The colonial city extended just a few blocks around the Zócalo, and in that area, known as the historical centre, many buildings predating independence still stand.

The central plaza

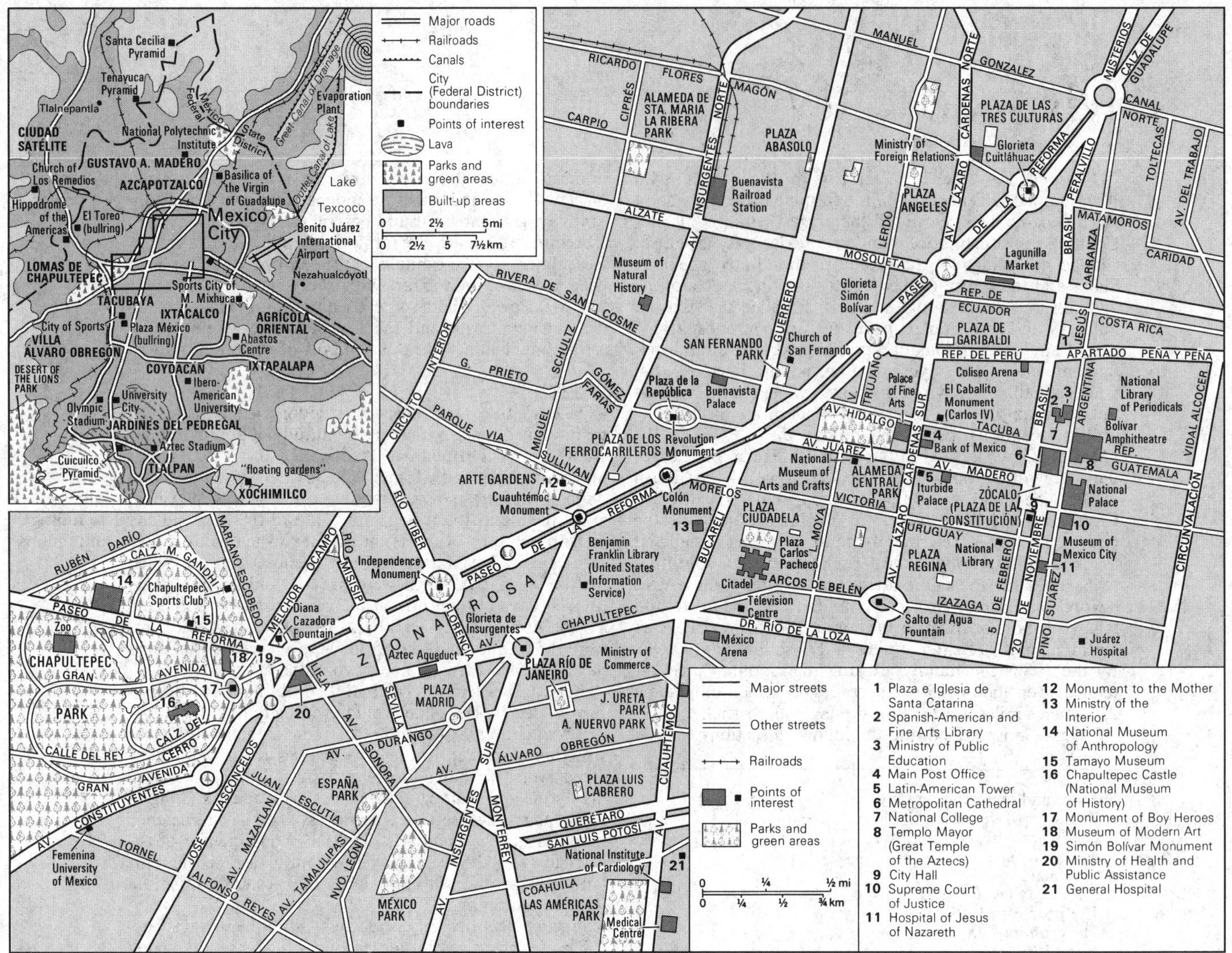

Central Mexico City and (inset) its metropolitan area.

The Alameda Central (Central Mall) roughly marks the western edge of the old colonial city. From its vicinity the Paseo de la Reforma—a wide, tree-lined boulevard—sweeps southwest toward Chapultepec. This wooded hill has been transformed into a public park, and its 18th-century castle is now a history museum. Upon reaching Chapultepec, Reforma turns west and advances into some of the city's wealthiest *colonias* (neighbourhoods), such as Polanco and Lomas de Chapultepec.

Chapultepec and environs

Avenida Insurgentes is Mexico City's main north–south axis. It crosses Paseo de la Reforma near the historical centre and continues both north and south to the end of the urban area. The Pink Zone ("Zona Rosa") is the main tourist and entertainment area. The city becomes increasingly residential and middle-class toward the south, although Avenida Insurgentes preserves its commercial and business nature. A number of former small towns in the south, such as Tacubaya, Mixcoac, San Ángel, and Coyoacán, have been incorporated into the city. Insurgentes traverses University City, the campus of the National Autonomous University of Mexico, before ending in Tlalpan, another formerly independent town and now the southern edge of the city. West of the southern portion of Insurgentes is the Pedregal de San Ángel, a wealthy residential *colonia* with notable examples of modern architecture.

At the southeastern tip of the city, Xochimilco, another small town subsumed by the city, is a popular tourist destination because of its *chinampas,* or "floating gardens," boats made out of reeds on which the Indians have grown plants since pre-Columbian times. The artificially preserved Xochimilco Lake is one of the few remnants of the old lake system in the basin. A number of middle-class *colonias* spread to the north of Xochimilco, but in the north the city becomes increasingly poor and more densely populated. East of the historical centre the Benito Juárez International Airport, once outside the city, is now surrounded by heavily populated working-class areas. North and northeast of the airport there are miles of poverty-ridden *colonias,* many lacking essential services. Outside the Federal District, but still part of the metropolitan area, lies Ciudad Nezahualcóyotl, one of the metropolis's poorest areas; it would be one of the largest cities in the country if measured on its own.

Xochimilco Lake

North of the historical centre stands Tlatelolco, a lower-middle-class residential development on the site of a former Indian city conquered by the Aztecs. Farther north is the Villa de Guadalupe Hidalgo, famed for its shrine of the Virgin of Guadalupe, a pilgrimage destination for Mexicans from throughout the country. Although "la Villa" was traditionally considered the northern edge of the city, urbanization has continued northward into the State of Mexico. To the northwest there are industrial zones, some within the Federal District (Azcapotzalco, for example) and some beyond it (Naucalpan). Farther northwest, around Ciudad Satélite, lies another cluster of middle-class residential suburbs, also in the State of Mexico.

Decentralization of commerce

Owing to the metropolitan area's enormous dimensions, each of its sections has developed its own commercial and service areas. The city centre, once the preferred middle-class shopping district, is now of marginal importance. Huge suburban shopping malls, such as Plaza Satélite in the northwest and Perisur in the south, have usurped the downtown area's commercial importance. The central Merced market, the city's main food-distribution centre

The Metropolitan Cathedral on the Zócalo in Mexico City.
Chip and Rosa Maria de la Cueva Peterson

since colonial times, was replaced in the 1980s by a modern supply centre (Abastos Centre) on the city's east end.

THE PEOPLE

Mexico City is one of the fastest-growing urban areas in the world. With a population of some 3,000,000 in 1950, it grew at rates of more than 3 percent annually in the following decades. By the 1980s it was the home of more than one-fifth of the country's population.

Racial composition

The city was traditionally inhabited by mestizos (people of mixed European and Indian descent) and criollos (Mexicans of European descent), but steady immigration from the countryside has given it a more Indian character. Although there is no formal racial discrimination, criollos constitute a disproportionate number of the upper and upper-middle classes.

Most Mexico City dwellers are Roman Catholic, although a number of Protestant churches have gained converts. There is also a small but influential Jewish community.

THE ECONOMY

Industry. Mexico City's metropolitan area accounts for more than 30 percent of the nation's industrial production. A trend to move heavy industry out of the city began in the 1950s, but a number of major plants remain within the urban area, especially in the northwest. The main industries are construction and the production of chemicals, plastics, cement, and yarns and textiles. Light industry is becoming predominant in the city's economy.

Commerce and finance. Because of the relative affluence of its residents and the fact that the city serves as the main supply centre for the country's central area, more than 40 percent of the nation's domestic sales occur in Mexico City. With the emigration of heavy industry, services constitute an increasingly important part of the local economy. Tourism is a major source of income.

Even more than other economic activities, Mexico's financial services are concentrated in the capital. The number of banking institutions, more than 50 in the late 1970s, dropped to less than 20 as a result of mergers following the government takeover of private banks in 1982. The country's only stock exchange operates in the city, where the Bank of Mexico, the central bank, is also located.

Transportation. Mexico City is the hub of the national transportation system. Five main highways link the capital with all regions of the country as well as with the United States and Guatemala. Railway lines run south, east, and north from the city. The Benito Juárez International Airport handles both national and international flights. In the late 1980s some flights began to land and depart from the Toluca airport in order to alleviate the former's perennial congestion.

The city's internal transportation system is chaotic and overextended. By the late 1980s close to 4,000,000 motor vehicles circulated in the urban area, and their number is growing rapidly. They creep at an average speed of about 12 miles an hour, and "rush hour" in many areas lasts virtually all day. In 1982 the Federal District's private bus system was expropriated by the government, while massive investments have been made to expand the efficient but overcrowded Metro (subway) system.

ADMINISTRATION AND SOCIAL CONDITIONS

Government. Most residents of Mexico City do not elect their own local government. The country's president appoints a regent, or mayor, who heads the administration of the Federal District. The regent appoints delegates who assume executive responsibility over the Federal District's 16 *delegaciones* (city districts), each of which functions with considerable autonomy. Many of these *delegaciones* have populations larger than those of most cities and some states within the country. The areas outside of the Federal District choose their own mayors (*presidentes municipales*) and participate in the election of the governor of the State of Mexico. Federal District residents vote for deputies (representatives) and senators to the federal Congress, as well as for the nation's president. In the late 1980s an elective advisory committee was established. Mexico City is the seat of the executive, legislative, and judicial powers of the country.

Administrative units

Services. Water supply has long been a problem for Mexico City. After its own reserves were virtually exhausted, expensive conveyance systems were built to bring drinking water from increasingly remote areas. The drainage system was partially renovated in the 1970s and '80s. Some electricity is produced within the city, but most is purchased from outside plants. The telephone system, always inadequate, suffered a major blow when the 1985 earthquake destroyed the city's main exchange; in the late 1980s a new decentralized system was installed. Propane gas, commonly used for cooking and for heating water, is distributed in portable tanks or by tanker trucks that fill home containers; home heating is virtually nonexistent.

Health. The oldest hospital in the Western Hemisphere—the Hospital of Jesus of Nazareth—was founded in Mexico City by Hernán Cortés in the early 16th century. The government operates numerous health facilities, including the gigantic General Hospital and the Medical Centre, a conglomerate of specialized units. There are also many private hospitals. Patients from throughout the country often travel to the capital for treatment.

Although sanitary standards are higher than in the rest of Mexico, gastrointestinal diseases remain common, particularly among lower-class children. Also prevalent are respiratory illnesses, a consequence of pollution, and psychological disorders stemming from overcrowding. With the improvement in general sanitary conditions, illnesses more characteristic of developed countries, such as cardiovascular problems and cancer, have become more common.

Education. Mexico City boasts a literacy rate of more than 90 percent, significantly higher than that of the rest of the country, and its educational facilities are unsurpassed in Mexico. The public school system is complemented by a large number of private schools. Dropout rates at the elementary and secondary school levels remain high.

The National Autonomous University of Mexico

The capital has the largest concentration of higher-education facilities in the nation. The National Autonomous University of Mexico, founded in 1551, is one of the largest in the world, with more than 350,000 students. Its buildings are beautifully decorated with murals by painter Diego Rivera and others. The National Polytechnic Institute and the Metropolitan Autonomous University are among the other important public institutions of higher education. Private universities include the Ibero-American

University, the Anáhuac University, and the United States International University. There are a number of specialized postgraduate and research institutions, including the prestigious College of Mexico.

CULTURAL LIFE

Mexico City has always been one of the prominent cultural centres of Latin America. There are several symphony orchestras and dozens of art galleries and museums, theatre groups, and dance companies in the city. The downtown Palace of Fine Arts is the traditional concert and opera hall. The University Cultural Centre, at the National University campus, houses the National Library, a major symphony hall, and a number of theatres. The National Museum of Anthropology is generally considered the world's finest in its specialty. Mexico City is also home for the country's most important art, music, and dance schools.

Mexico City is one of the most important book-publishing centres in the Spanish-speaking world, and more than 30 daily newspapers are published in the city. There are numerous news, literary, and other specialized magazines.

Each neighbourhood has its own parks and gardens. Chapultepec Park, the largest and most beautiful of these, encompasses about 1,600 acres (647 hectares) in the southwest. Its grounds contain museums, a zoo, botanical gardens, an amusement park, lakes, and fountains. Desert of the Lions ("El Desierto de los Leones"), another park 10 miles southwest of the city, occupies a wide expanse of mountains, pine forests, springs, and aqueducts. The Alameda Central, west of the Zócalo, was created in 1592.

The most popular spectator sports are association football (soccer) and bullfighting. Soccer is played in the Aztec Stadium and in the National University's Olympic Stadium. Plaza México is the largest bullring in the world. In addition, there are numerous sports complexes.

History

THE EARLY PERIOD

Origins. The Aztecs arrived in the Valley of Mexico in the 13th century. According to tradition, they founded Tenochtitlán ("Place of the High Priest Tenoch") after much wandering when they saw on an island in Lake Texcoco the sign that their god Huitzilopochtli had indicated—an eagle perched on a cactus, eating a serpent. Tenochtitlán quickly spread over the island, marshes, and swamps. As it developed into a city, it was divided into *calpulli,* or districts, each with communal lands and schools.

When the Spaniards led by Hernán Cortés arrived in 1519, Tenochtitlán had about 100,000 inhabitants. The island was connected to the mainland by three causeways—Tepeyac to the north, Ixtapalapa to the south, and Tacuba to the west—which converged on the ceremonial centre near the main temple and the emperor's palace.

The colonial city. Cortés razed Tenochtitlán in 1521 and constructed a Spanish city on its ruins. The conquerors divided the central area among themselves and relegated the defeated to the periphery. The city was chartered and its *cabildo,* or town council, recognized in 1522; it was given leadership over other *cabildos* of New Spain in 1535. It soon became the most important city of the Americas, with jurisdiction extending well into the present United States and as far south as Panama.

Rise to preeminence

Mexico City continued as a lakeside centre until constant floods necessitated the filling of the lakes of the valley floor. During the 17th century the capital comprised a well laid-out assemblage of homes, public buildings, churches, and convents. In their execution of European designs, the colonists and Indian artisans employed local *tezontle,* a light and porous volcanic rock, to create elaborate facades. This Baroque style reached its ultimate expression in the 18th century, the golden age of architecture in New Spain, after which Neoclassical ideas were introduced by the sculptor and architect Manuel Tolsá.

THE CITY AFTER INDEPENDENCE

Before the revolution. After the brief reign of Emperor Agustín de Iturbide of Mexico, the republican constitution of 1824 established the Federal District to centralize the country's government in Mexico City. The capital was captured by U.S. troops in the 1840s. During the anticlerical reform movement of the 1850s, all of the city's convents were either demolished or put to other uses. The city limits were expanded in 1865, when the Habsburg archduke Maximilian—then emperor of Mexico—built the Paseo del Emperador (now Paseo de la Reforma) to connect his palace with Chapultepec Castle. During the rule of Porfirio Díaz, from 1876 to 1911, Mexico City was modernized in the manner of Baron Haussmann's Paris. The Post Office and the Palace of Fine Arts exemplify the dominant French architectural influence. Also during this period the city undertook numerous public works and utilities projects, completing a drainage system in 1907 and introducing gas and electric lighting and streetcars.

Modernization under Díaz

The 20th century. During the Mexican Revolution (1910–17), the city became a battlefield. Disruption in rural areas resulted in an exodus from the countryside to the capital. In 1924 urban works were renewed with the construction of Avenida Insurgentes. French palaces were replaced with buildings designed in the modern style. The first skyscrapers were built in the 1930s, but the soft subsoil and the frequent seismic activity restricted them to modest proportions.

Mexico's prosperity and stability during the 1950s and '60s transformed the city. Public investment fueled growth during the 1970s, and especially during the oil-boom years of 1978–81. The collapse of petroleum prices, though, put a damper on public spending, beginning in 1982. The city continued to grow, but its services deteriorated. An earthquake shook the city in 1985, destroying many buildings and killing some 7,000 people. A new construction code enacted in 1987 took into account the soft subsoil of certain areas and the risks of high seismicity. Efforts to decentralize the federal public administration were made but with few apparent results.

BIBLIOGRAPHY

General works: Detailed maps of the city are provided in *Atlas de la ciudad de México* (1981), published by the DEPARTAMENTO DEL DISTRITO FEDERAL. BRANTZ MAYER, *Mexico as It Was and as It Is,* 3rd rev. ed. (1847), is a classic. Modern guidebooks include LORAINE CARLSON and NEIL CARLSON, *The TraveLeer Guide to Mexico City,* 2nd ed. (1981); and *Fodor's Mexico City and Acapulco, 1985* (1985). Brief summaries are found in such pictorial works as BOB SCHALKWIJK and J.M. COHEN, *Mexico City, México* (1965); and ALBERT MOLDVAY and ERIKA FABIAN, *Photographing Mexico City & Acapulco* (1980). Contemporary developments are discussed in SALVADOR NOVO, *New Mexican Grandeur* (1967, originally published in Spanish, 5th ed., 1967); HUMBERTO MUÑOZ, ORLANDINA DE OLIVEIRA, and CLAUDIO STERN, *Mexico City: Industrialization, Migration, and the Labour Force, 1930–1970* (1982); LOURDES BENERÍA and MARTHA ROLDÁN, *The Crossroads of Class & Gender: Industrial Homework, Subcontracting, and Household Dynamics in Mexico City* (1987); WAYNE A. CORNELIUS, *Politics and the Migrant Poor in Mexico City* (1975); and ALAN GILBERT and PETER M. WARD, *Housing, the State, and the Poor: Policy and Practice in Three Latin American Cities* (1985).

History: The artifacts of local history as preserved in Mexico City's museum collections are described in H.B. NICHOLSON and ELOISE QUIÑONES KEBER, *Art of Aztec Mexico: Treasures of Tenochtitlan* (1983); DORIS HEYDEN and LUIS FRANCISCO VILLASEÑOR, *The Great Temple and the Aztec Gods* (1984); and ELIZABETH HILL BOONE (ed.), *The Aztec Templo Mayor* (1987). A comprehensive history is provided in FERNANDO BENÍTEZ, *La ciudad de México, 1325–1982,* 3 vol. (1981–82). For early history, see HERNÁN CORTÉS, *Letters from Mexico,* trans. from Spanish by ANTHONY PAGDEN (1971, reissued 1986); and BERNAL DIAZ DEL CASTILLO, *Historia verdadera de la conquista de la Nueva España* (1632; new ed. by MIGUEL LEÓN-PORTILLA, 2 vol., 1984). On the colonial city, see FRANCISCO CERVANTES DE SALAZAR, *México en 1554,* 3rd ed. (1964); and JOHN E. KICZA, *Colonial Entrepreneurs, Families, and Business in Bourbon Mexico City* (1983). For the period from the 17th to the 19th century, see LUIS GONZÁLEZ OBREGÓN, *México viejo,* 10th ed. (1980); JOSÉ MARÍA MARROQUI, *La ciudad de México,* 3 vol. (1900–03, reissued 1969); JESÚS GALINDO Y VILLA, *Historia sumaria de la ciudad de México* (1925, reissued 1970); SILVIA MARINA ARROM, *The Women of Mexico City, 1790–1857* (1985); and WILLIAM H. BEEZLEY, *Judas at the Jockey Club and Other Episodes of Porfirian Mexico* (1987).

(S.S./F.Be.)

Michelangelo

Michelangelo was considered the greatest living artist in his lifetime, and ever since then he has been held to be one of the greatest artists of all times. A number of his works in painting, sculpture, and architecture rank among the most famous in existence. Although the frescoes on the ceiling of the Sistine Chapel (Vatican) are probably the best known of his works today, the artist thought of himself primarily as a sculptor. His practice of several arts, however, was not unusual in his time, when all of them were thought of as based on design, or drawing. Michelangelo worked in marble sculpture all his life and in the other arts only at certain periods. The high regard for the Sistine ceiling is partly a reflection of the greater attention paid to painting in the 20th century and partly, too, of the fact that it, unlike many of the artist's works in the other media, was completed.

Alinari/Art Resource, NY

Joseph of Arimathea (or, possibly, Nicodemus), detail of the "Pietà" by Michelangelo, *c.* 1550–55, which is thought to be a self-portrait. In the Duomo, Florence.

A side effect of Michelangelo's fame in his lifetime was that his career was more fully documented than that of any artist of the time or earlier. He was the first artist whose biography was published while he was alive, and there were two rival biographies. The first was the final chapter in the series of artists' lives (1550) by the painter and architect Giorgio Vasari. It was the only chapter on a living artist and explicitly presented Michelangelo's works as the culminating perfection of art, surpassing the efforts of all those before him. Despite such an encomium, Michelangelo was not entirely pleased and arranged for his assistant Ascanio Condivi to write a brief separate book (1553); probably based on the artist's own spoken comments, this account shows him as he wished to appear. After Michelangelo's death Vasari in a second edition (1568) offered a rebuttal. While scholars have often preferred the authority of Condivi, Vasari's lively writing, the importance of his book as a whole, and its frequent reprinting in many languages have made it the most usual basis of popular ideas. Michelangelo's fame also led to the preservation of countless mementos, including hundreds of letters, sketches, and poems, again more than of any contemporary. Yet despite the enormous benefit that has accrued from all this, in controversial matters often only Michelangelo's side of an argument is known.

Early life and works. Michelangelo Buonarroti was born March 6, 1475, to a family that had for several generations been small-scale bankers in Florence but had in the case of the artist's father failed to maintain its status. The father had only occasional government jobs, and at the time of Michelangelo's birth he was administrator of the small dependent town of Caprese. A few months later, however, the family returned to its permanent residence in Florence. It was something of a downward social step to become an artist, and Michelangelo became an apprentice relatively late, at 13, perhaps after overcoming his father's objections. He was apprenticed to the city's most prominent painter, Domenico Ghirlandajo, for a three-year term, but he left after one year, having (Condivi recounts) nothing more to learn. Several drawings, copies of figures by Ghirlandajo and older great painters of Florence, Giotto and Masaccio, survive from this stage; such copying was standard for apprentices, but few examples are known to survive. Obviously talented, he was taken under the wing of the ruler of the city, Lorenzo de' Medici, known as the Magnificent. Lorenzo surrounded himself at table with poets and intellectuals, and Michelangelo was included. More important, he had access to the Medici art collection, which was dominated by fragments of ancient Roman statuary. (Lorenzo was not such a patron of contemporary art as legend has made him; such modern art as he owned was to ornament his house or make political statements.) The bronze sculptor Bertoldo, a Medici friend and in charge of the collection, was the nearest to a teacher of sculpture he had, but Michelangelo did not follow his medium or in any major way his approach. Still, one of the two marble works that survive from the artist's first years is a variant on the composition of an ancient Roman sarcophagus, and Bertoldo had produced a similar one in bronze. This composition is the "Battle of the Centaurs" (*c.* 1492). The action and power of the figures foretell the artist's later interests much more than does the "Madonna of the Stairs" (*c.* 1491), a delicate low relief that reflects recent fashions among such Florentine sculptors as Desiderio da Settignano.

Apprenticeship with Ghirlandajo

Florence was at this time regarded as the leading centre of art, producing the best painters and sculptors in Europe, and the competition among artists was stimulating. The city was, however, less able than earlier to offer large commissions, and leading Florentine-born artists, such as Leonardo da Vinci and Leonardo's teacher, Verrocchio, had moved away for better opportunities in other cities. The Medici were overthrown in 1494, and even before the end of the political turmoil Michelangelo had left.

In Bologna he was hired to succeed a recently deceased sculptor and carve the last small figures required to complete a grand project, the tomb and shrine of St. Dominic (1494–95). The three marble figures are original and expressive. Departing from his predecessor's fanciful agility, he imposed seriousness on his images by a compactness of form that owes much to classical antiquity and to the Florentine tradition from Giotto onward. This emphasis on seriousness is also reflected in his choice of marble as his medium, while the accompanying simplification of masses is in contrast to the then more usual tendency to let representations match as completely as possible the texture and detail of human bodies. To be sure, although these are constant qualities in Michelangelo's art, they often are temporarily abandoned or modified because of other factors, such as the specific functions of works or the stimulating creations of other artists. This is the case with Michelangelo's first surviving large statue, the "Bacchus," produced in Rome (1496–97) following a brief return to Florence. (A wooden crucifix, recently discovered, attributed by some scholars to Michelangelo and now housed in the Casa Buonarroti, Florence, has also been proposed as the antecedent of the "Bacchus" in design by those who credit it as the artist's work.)

"Bacchus"

The "Bacchus" relies on ancient Roman nude figures as a point of departure, but it is much more mobile and more complex in outline. The conscious instability evokes the god of wine and Dionysiac revels with extraordinary virtuosity. Made for a garden, it is also unique among Michelangelo's works in calling for observation from all sides rather than primarily from the front.

The "Bacchus" led at once to the commission (1498) for the "Pietà," now in St. Peter's Basilica. The name refers not (as often presumed) to this specific work but to a common traditional type of devotional image, this work being today the most famous example. Extracted from narrative scenes of the lamentation after Christ's death, the concentrated group of two is designed to evoke the observer's repentant prayers for sins that required Christ's sacrificial death. The patron was a French cardinal, and the type was earlier more common in northern Europe than Italy. The complex problem for the designer was to extract two figures from one marble block, an unusual undertaking in all periods. Michelangelo treated the group as one dense and compact mass as before so that it has an imposing impact, yet he underlined the many contrasts present, of male and female, vertical and horizontal, clothed and naked, dead and alive, to clarify the two components. The artist's prominence, established by this work, was reinforced at once by the commission (1501) of the "David" for the cathedral of Florence. For this huge statue, an exceptionally large commission in that city, Michelangelo reused a block left unfinished about 40 years before. The modeling is especially close to the formulas of classical antiquity, with a simplified geometry suitable to the huge scale yet with a mild assertion of organic life in its asymmetry. It has continued to serve as the prime statement of the Renaissance ideal of perfect humanity.

"David"

On the side Michelangelo produced in the same years (1501–04) several Madonnas for private houses, the staple of artists' work at the time. These include one small statue, two circular reliefs that are similar to paintings in suggesting varied levels of spatial depth, and the artist's only easel painting. While the statue ("Madonna and Child") is blocky and immobile, the painting ("Holy Family") and one of the reliefs ("Madonna and Child with the Infant St. John") are full of motion; they show arms and legs of figures interweaving in actions that imply movement through time. The forms carry symbolic references to Christ's future death, common in images of the Christ Child at the time; they also betray the artist's fascination with the work of Leonardo. Michelangelo regularly denied that anyone influenced him, and his statements have usually been accepted without demur. But Leonardo's return to Florence in 1500 after nearly 20 years was exciting to younger artists there, and recent scholars have generally agreed that Michelangelo was among those affected. Leonardo's works were probably the most powerful and lasting outside influence to modify his work, and he was able to blend this artist's ability to show momentary processes with his own to show weight and strength, without losing any of the latter quality. The resulting images, of massive bodies in forceful action, are those special creations that constitute the larger part of his most admired major works.

The influence of Leonardo da Vinci

The middle years. After the success of the "David" in 1504 Michelangelo's work consisted almost entirely of vast projects. He was attracted to these ambitious tasks while at the same time rejecting the use of assistants, so that most of these projects were impractical and remained unfinished. In 1504 he agreed to paint a huge mural for the Florence city hall to form a pair with another just begun by Leonardo. Both murals recorded military victories by the city, but each also gave testimony to the special skills of the city's much vaunted artists; Leonardo's design shows galloping horses, Michelangelo's active nudes—soldiers stop swimming and climb out of a river to answer an alarm. Both works survive only in copies and partial preparatory sketches. In 1505 the artist began work on a planned set of 12 marble Apostles for the Florence cathedral, of which only one, the "St. Matthew," was even begun. Its writhing ecstatic motion for the first time shows the full blend of Leonardo's fluid organic movement with his own monumental power. This is also the first of Michelangelo's unfinished works that have fascinated later observers. His figures seem to suggest that they are fighting to emerge from the stone. This would imply that their incomplete state was intentional, yet he undoubtedly did want to complete all of the statues. He did, however, write a sonnet about how hard it is for the sculptor to bring the perfect figure out of the block in which it is potentially present. Thus, even if the works remained unfinished due only to lack of time and other external reasons, their condition, nonetheless, reflects the artist's intense feeling of the stresses inherent in the creative process.

Pope Julius II's call to Michelangelo to come to Rome spelled an end to both of these Florentine projects. The Pope sought a tomb for which Michelangelo was to carve 40 large statues. Recent tombs had been increasingly grand, including those of two popes by the Florentine sculptor Antonio Pollaiuolo, those of the doges of Venice, and the one then in work for Holy Roman Emperor Maximilian I. Pope Julius had an ambitious imagination, parallel to Michelangelo's, but because of other projects, such as the new building of St. Peter's and his military campaigns, he evidently became disturbed soon by the cost. Michelangelo believed that Bramante, the equally prestigious architect at St. Peter's, had influenced the Pope to cut off his funds. He left Rome, but the Pope brought pressure on the city authorities of Florence to send him back. He was put to work on a colossal bronze statue of the Pope in his newly conquered city of Bologna (which the citizens pulled down soon after when they drove the papal army out) and then on the less expensive project of painting the ceiling of the Sistine Chapel (1508–12).

The Sistine Chapel had great symbolic meaning for the papacy as the chief consecrated space in the Vatican, used for great ceremonies such as electing and inaugurating new popes. It already contained distinguished wall paintings, and Michelangelo was asked to add works for the relatively unimportant ceiling. Twelve Apostles were planned as the theme—ceilings normally showed only individual figures, not dramatic scenes. Traces of this project are seen in the 12 large figures that Michelangelo produced: seven prophets and five sibyls, or female prophets found in classical myths. The inclusion of female figures was very unusual though not totally unprecedented. Michelangelo placed these figures around the edges of the ceiling and filled the central spine of the long curved surface with nine scenes from Genesis: three of them depicting the creation of the world, three the stories of Adam and Eve, and three the stories of Noah. These are naturally followed, below the prophets and sibyls, by small figures of the 40 generations of Christ's ancestors, starting with Abraham. The vast project was completed in less than four years; there was an interruption perhaps of a year in 1510–11 when no payment was made.

Sistine ceiling

The work began at the end, with the Noah scenes placed over the entrance door, and moved toward the altar in the direction opposite to that of the sequence of the stories. The first figures and scenes naturally show the artist reusing devices from his earlier works, such as the Pietà, since he was starting on such an ambitious work in an unfamiliar medium. These first figures are relatively stable, and the scenes are on a relatively small scale. As he proceeded, he quickly grew in confidence. Indeed, recent investigations of the technical processes used show that he worked more and more rapidly, reducing and finally eliminating such preparatory helps as complete drawings and incisions on the plaster surface. The same growing boldness appears in the free, complex movements of the figures and in their complex expressiveness. While remaining always imposing and monumental, they are more and more imbued with suggestions of stress and grief. This may be perceived in a figure such as the prophet Ezekiel halfway along. This figure combines colossal strength and weight with movement and facial expression that suggest determination to reach a goal that is uncertain of success. Such an image of the inadequacy of even great power is a presentation of heroic and tragic humanity and is central to what Michelangelo means to posterity. Nearby the scene of the creation of Eve shows her with God and Adam, compressed within too small a space for their grandeur. This tension has been interpreted as a token of a movement away from the Renaissance concern with harmony, pointing the way for a younger generation of artists like Pontormo, often labeled Mannerists. Michelangelo's work on the ceiling was interrupted, perhaps just after these figures were completed. When he painted the second half, he seemed to repeat the same evolution from quiet stability to intricacy and stress. Thus he worked his way from the quietly monumental and harmonious scene of the creation of Adam to the acute, twisted pressures of the prophet Jonah. Yet in this second phase he shows greater inward expressiveness, giving a more meditative restraint to the earlier pure physical mass.

As soon as the ceiling was finished, Michelangelo reverted to his preferred task, the tomb of Pope Julius. In about 1513–15 he carved the "Moses," which may be regarded as the realization in sculpture of the approach to great figures used for the prophets on the Sistine ceiling. The control of cubic density in stone evokes great reserves of strength; there is richer surface detail and modeling than before, with bulging projections sharply cut. The surface textures also have more variety than the earlier sculptures, the artist by now having found how to enrich detail without sacrificing massiveness. Of about the same date are two sculptures of bound prisoners or slaves, also part of the tomb project but never used for it, since in a subsequent revised design they were of the wrong scale. Michelangelo kept them until old age, when he gave them to a family that had helped him during an illness; they are now in the Louvre. Here again he realized in stone types painted in many variants on the ceiling, such as the pairs of nudes that hold wreaths above the prophets' thrones. The complexity of their stances, expressive of strong feeling, was unprecedented in monumental marble sculpture of the Renaissance. The only earlier works of this nature were from the Hellenistic period of classical antiquity, well known to Michelangelo through the discovery of the Laocoön group in 1506. The old man and his two adolescent sons forming that group certainly stimulated the three statues by Michelangelo as well as the related figures on the ceiling. Yet the first of the ceiling figures in 1508 were not so affected; Michelangelo utilized the Hellenistic twists and complications only when he was ready for them, and he had been moving in this direction even before the Laocoön was found, as is evident in the case of the "St. Matthew" of 1505.

Julius II's death in 1513 cut off most of the funds for his tomb. Pope Leo X, his successor, a son of Lorenzo the Magnificent, had known Michelangelo since their boyhoods. He chiefly employed Michelangelo in Florence on projects linked to the glory of the Medici family rather than of the papacy. The city was under the rule of Leo's cousin Cardinal de' Medici, who was to be Pope Clement VII from 1523 to 1534, and Michelangelo worked with him closely in both reigns. The Cardinal took an active interest in Michelangelo's works. He made detailed suggestions, but he also gave the artist much room for decision. Michelangelo was moving into architectural design with a small remodeling project at the Medici mansion and a large one at their parish church, San Lorenzo. He approached such work with enthusiasm, caused no doubt by the large scale and the involvement with masses of stone to be manipulated expressively. The larger project never materialized, but Michelangelo and the Cardinal did better with a more modest related one, the new chapel attached to the same church for tombs of the Medici family.

The immediate occasion for the chapel was the deaths of the two young family heirs, named Giuliano and Lorenzo after their forebears, in 1516 and 1519. Michelangelo gave his chief attention up to 1527 to the marble interior of this chapel, to both the very original wall design and the carved figures on the tombs; the latter are an extension in organic form of the dynamic shapes of the wall details. The result is the fullest existing presentation of Michelangelo's intentions. Windows, cornices, and the like have strange proportions and thicknesses, suggesting an irrational, willful revision of traditional classical forms in buildings. Abutting these active surfaces, the two tombs on opposite walls of the room are also very original, starting with their curved tops. A male and a female figure sit on each of these curved bases; these are allegories symbolizing on one tomb day and night, according to the artist's own statement, and dawn and dusk on the other, according to early reports. Such personifications had never appeared on tombs before, and they refer, again according to Michelangelo, to the inevitable movement of time, which is circular and leads to death. The figures are among the artist's most famous and accomplished creations. The immensely massive figures of "Day" and "Dusk" are relatively tranquil in their mountainous grandeur, though "Day" perhaps implies inner fires. Both female figures have the tall, slim proportions and small feet considered beautiful at the time, but otherwise they form a contrast: "Dawn," a virginal figure, strains upward along her curve as if trying to emerge into life; "Night" is asleep, but in a posture suggesting stressful dreams.

The Medici Chapel

These four figures are naturally noticed more immediately than the effigies of the two Medici buried there, placed higher and farther back in wall niches. These effigies, more usual in execution, also form a contrast; they are traditionally described as active and thoughtful, respectively. Rendered as standard types of young soldiers, they were at once perceived not as portraits but as idealized superior beings, both because of their high rank and because they are souls beyond the grave. Both turn to the same side of the room. It has naturally been thought that they focus on the "Madonna," which Michelangelo carved and which is at the centre of this side wall, between two saints. The heads of the two effigies, however, are turned in differing degrees, and their common focus is at a corner of the chapel, at the entrance door from the church. On this third wall with the "Madonna" the architectural treatment was never executed.

The Laurentian Library

During the same years Michelangelo designed another annex to the same church, the Laurentian Library, required to receive the books bequeathed by Pope Leo; it was traditional in Florence and elsewhere that libraries were housed in convents. The design for this one was constrained by the existing buildings, and it was built on top of older structures. A small available area on the second floor was used as an entrance lobby and contains a staircase leading up to the larger library room on a new third floor. The stairhall, known as the *ricetto,* contains Michelangelo's most famous and original wall designs. The bold and free rearrangement of traditional building components goes still further, for instance, to place columns recessed behind a wall plane rather than in front of it as is usual. This has led to the work's being cited frequently as the first and a chief instance of Mannerism as an architectural style, when it is defined as a work that intentionally contradicts the classical and the harmonious, favouring expressiveness and originality, or as one that emphasizes the factors of style for their own sake. By contrast the long library room is far more restrained, with traditional rows of desks neatly related to the rhythm of the windows and small decorative detail in the floor and ceiling. It recalls that Michelangelo was not invariably heavy and bold but modified his approach in relation to the particular case, here to a gentler, quiet effect. For that very reason it has often been less noticed in the study of his work. At the opposite end of the long room, across from the stairway, another door led to a space intended to hold the library's rarest treasures. It was to be a triangular room, a climax of the long corridor-like approach, but this part was never executed on the artist's plan.

The sack of Rome in 1527 saw Pope Clement ignominiously in flight, and Florence revolted against the Medici, restoring the traditional republic. It was soon besieged and defeated, and Medici rule permanently reinstalled, in 1530. During the siege Michelangelo was the designer of fortifications. He showed understanding of modern defensive structures built quickly of simple materials in complex profiles that offered minimum vulnerability to attackers and maximum resistance to cannon and other artillery. This new weapon, which had come into use in the middle of the 14th century, had given greater power to the offense

Michelangelo as a designer of fortifications

in war. Thus, instead of the tall castles that had served well for defensive purposes in the Middle Ages, lower and thicker masses were more practical. The projecting points, which also assisted counterattack, were often of irregular sizes in adaptation to specific hilly sites. Michelangelo's drawings with rapid lively execution reflecting this flexible new pattern have been much admired, often in terms of pure form.

When the Medici returned in 1530, Michelangelo returned to work on their family tombs. His political commitment probably was more to his city as such than to any specific governmental form. Two separate projects of statues of this date are the "Apollo" or "David" (its identity is problematic), used as a gift to a newly powerful political figure, and the "Victory," a figure trampling on a defeated enemy, an old man. It was probably meant for the never forgotten tomb of Pope Julius because the motif had been present in the plans for the Julius tomb. Victor and loser both have intensely complicated poses; the loser seems packed in a block, the victor—like the "Apollo"—forms a lithe spiral. The "Victory" group became a favourite model for younger sculptors of the Mannerist group, who applied the formula to many allegorical subjects.

In 1534 Michelangelo left Florence for the last time, though he always hoped to return to finish the projects he had left incomplete. He passed the rest of his life in Rome, working on projects in some cases equally grand but in most cases of quite new kinds. From this time on a large number of his letters to his family in Florence were preserved; many of them concentrated on plans for his nephew's marriage, essential to preserve the family name. Michelangelo's father had died in 1531 and his favourite brother at about the same time; he himself showed increasing anxiety about his age and death. It was just at this time that the nearly 60-year-old artist wrote letters expressing strong feelings of attachment to young men, chiefly to the talented aristocrat Tommaso Cavalieri, later active in Roman civic affairs. These have naturally been interpreted as indications that Michelangelo was a homosexual, but such a reaction according to the artist's own statement would be that of the ignorant. The idea seems even less likely when one considers that no similar indications had emerged when the artist was younger. The correlation of these letters with other new events seems consistent instead with the view that he was seeking a surrogate son, choosing for the purpose a younger man who was admirable in every way and would welcome the role.

Michelangelo's poetry

Michelangelo's poetry is also preserved in quantity from this time. He apparently began writing short poems in a way common among nonprofessionals in the period, as an elegant kind of letter, but developed in a more original and expressive way. Among some 300 preserved poems, not including fragments of a line or two, there are about 75 finished sonnets and about 95 finished madrigals, poems of about the same length as sonnets but of a looser formal structure. In English-speaking countries people tend to speak of "Michelangelo's sonnets," as though all of his poems were written in that form, partly because the sonnets were widely circulated in English translations from the Victorian period, partly because the madrigal is unfamiliar in English poetry. (It is not the type of song well known in Elizabethan music, but a poem with irregular rhyme scheme, line length, and number of lines.) Yet the fact that Michelangelo left a large number of sonnets but only very few madrigals unfinished suggests that he preferred the latter form. Those written up to about 1545 have themes based on the tradition of Petrarch's love poems and a philosophy based on the Neoplatonism that Michelangelo had absorbed as a boy at Lorenzo the Magnificent's court. They give expression to the theme that love helps human beings in their difficult effort to ascend to the divine.

"The Last Judgment"

In 1534 Michelangelo returned after a quarter century to fresco painting, executing for the new pope, Paul III, the huge "Last Judgment" for the end wall of the Sistine Chapel. This theme had been a favoured one for large end walls of churches in Italy in the Middle Ages and up to about 1500, but thereafter it had gone out of fashion. It is often suggested that this renewal of a devout tradition came from the same impulses that were then leading to the Counter-Reformation under the aegis of Paul III. The work is in a painting style noticeably different from that of 25 years earlier. The pervasive colour harmony is a simple one of brown bodies against dark blue sky. The figures have less energy and their forms are less articulate, the torsos tending to be single fleshy masses without waistlines. At the top centre Christ as judge lifts an arm to save those on his right and drops the other arm to damn those on his left, suggesting in the idiom of the period a scale to weigh men in the balance. The saved souls rise slowly through the heavy air, as the damned ones sink. At the bottom of the wall skeletons rise from tombs, a motif taken directly from medieval precedents. To the right Charon ferries souls across the River Styx, a pagan motif which Dante had made acceptable to Christians in his *Divine Comedy* and which had been introduced into painting about 1500 by the Umbrian artist Signorelli. Michelangelo admired this artist for his skill in expressing dramatic feeling through anatomical exactitude.

The last decades. In his late years Michelangelo was less involved with sculpture and, along with painting and poetry, more with architecture, an area in which he did not have to do physical labour. He was sought after to design imposing monuments for the new and modern Rome that were to enunciate architecturally the city's position as a world centre. Two of these monuments, the Capitoline Square and the dome of St. Peter's, are still among the city's most notable visual images. He did not finish either, but after his death both were continued in ways that probably did not depart much from his plans.

Capitoline Square

The small Capitoline Hill had been the civic centre in ancient Roman times and was in the 16th century the centre of the lay municipal government, a minor factor in a city ruled by popes, yet one to which they wished to show respect. Michelangelo remodeled the old city hall on one side of the square and designed twin buildings for the two sides adjacent to it. He gave them rich and powerful fronts, using as his main device the juxtaposition of colossal columns, which rise through two stories to the top, with much smaller one-story columns crowded next to them. This invention creates a forcefully dynamic rhythm while also articulating in a rational way the structure behind the facades. He also produced a special floor design for the square between these two new buildings—an oval pattern that frames a statue at its centre (the ancient Roman monument of the emperor Marcus Aurelius) and gives the whole area the effect of a monumental room. Because of the hilly site, the square is not rectangular but wider on the city hall side and narrower on the opposite side, which was left open. This open side is the entrance for the public, reached by climbing a long flight of stairs. The visitor finds the two facades to his left and right inclined away from each other as they recede from the entrance; this counteracts the tendency of perspective to make walls seem to move nearer each other as they are farther off and so reinforces the effect of a grand expanse.

The dome of St. Peter's functions chiefly as a visual focus for the observer at a distance, representing a physical goal as well as expressing the dominant meaning of the city. It has been copied for this dual purpose many times, as, for instance, in the Capitol at Washington, D.C. It derives from the dome of the cathedral of Florence, which is 100 years older, perhaps the first great dome to be oriented chiefly outward in its effect rather than being meant chiefly to cover the interior. But it was Michelangelo's dome that gave this shift its universal acceptance. The dome, however, was not built until after Michelangelo's death, and the extent to which it follows his intentions has been much debated. As built by his successor, the dome is more pointed than the pure hemisphere seen in Michelangelo's best known project. But Michelangelo changed his ideas and may well have moved in that direction too.

During his life Michelangelo's major energy in working at St. Peter's was given to the lower part. He discarded the ideas of the architects who had been working on it just before him, approving only those of the original designer, Bramante. He reverted to the earlier plan for a church with four equal cross arms instead of the more conventional Latin cross plan of the more recent altered scheme. He also disliked the quantity of repeated smaller decorative elements added by the most recent architect, which diminished the effect of great size. He modified Bramante's interior in specifics, making it still more nearly a unified space. This is enclosed by huge semicircular sections of wall on the four sides, creating spaces comparable to the hemispherical space inside the dome. Most of his actual construction work was on the curving wall behind the altar, and there he carried still further the contrast between colossal and smaller supports next to each other, seen already on the Capitoline Hill. This time they are not load-carrying columns but thin pilasters that fit against the continuously curving walls on the exterior. They thus impart both a strong upward thrust and an equally strong horizontal rhythm as the direction of the wall continuously changes, producing an architecture of pulsing dynamism on a gigantic scale. One still can see the approach of the sculptor, who uses the projections and recessions of stone as his vehicle.

Around the base of the dome Michelangelo placed a columned walkway. The tops of the columns are tied to the dome by beams, but there is no roofing of the intervals between columns. Thus, the columns have the effect of flying buttresses on Gothic buildings, supporting the dome's heavy downward thrust. Yet the design is formally classical, and its horizontal aspect as a colonnade solves the problem of a visual transition between the dome and the horizontal lower structure of the building.

While remaining head architect of St. Peter's until his death, Michelangelo worked on many smaller building projects in Rome. He completed the main unit of the Palazzo Farnese, the residence of Pope Paul III's family. The top story wall of its courtyard is a rare example of an architectural unit fully finished under his eye. Some very imaginative and distinctive late designs, such as those for a city gate, the Porta Pia, and for the church of the Florentine community in Rome, were either much reworked later or never went beyond the plan stage in the form Michelangelo had proposed.

His last paintings were the frescoes of the Pauline Chapel in the Vatican, which still is little accessible to the public. Unlike his other frescoes, they are in the position normal for narrative painting, on a wall and not exceptionally high up. They consistently treat spatial depth and narrative drama in a way that brings them closer to other paintings of the age than to the artist's previous paintings. Among the artists Michelangelo came to know and admire was Titian, who visited Rome during the period of this project (1542–50), and the frescoes seem to betray his influence in colour. The poetry of his last years also took on new qualities. The poems, chiefly sonnets, are very direct religious statements suggesting prayers. They are no longer very intricate in syntax and ideas.

There are only two late sculptures, which Michelangelo did for himself, both presenting the dead Christ being mourned, neither one finished. The first and larger one was meant for his tomb, and the figure of the mourning Joseph of Arimathea (or, possibly, Nicodemus) is a self-portrait. (Michelangelo had introduced himself earlier in his works in the role of a sinner or penitent, notably in the "Last Judgment" in the face on the flayed skin of the martyred St. Bartholomew.) Becoming dissatisfied with this sculpture, Michelangelo broke one of the figures and abandoned the work. This constitutes still another variation on the theme of incompletion running through the artist's work. His last sculpture also went through several revisions on the same block of stone and in its current state is an almost dematerialized sketch of two figures leaning together. Michelangelo certainly had a powerful sense of his own imperfection, yet he was also aware of the quality of his work and angry at patrons for not meeting what he judged to be their obligations. He died on Feb. 18, 1564.

Assessment and influence. For posterity Michelangelo has always remained one of the small group of the most exalted artists, who have been felt to express, like Shakespeare or Beethoven, the tragic experience of humanity with the greatest depth and universal scope.

In contrast to the great fame of the artist's works, their visual influence on later art is relatively limited. This cannot be explained by hesitation to imitate an art simply because it appeared so great, for artists like Raphael were considered equally great but were used as sources to a much greater degree. It may be instead that the particular type of expression associated with Michelangelo, of an almost cosmic grandeur, was inhibiting. The limited influence of his work includes a few cases of almost total dependence, the most talented artist who worked in this way being Daniele da Volterra. Otherwise, Michelangelo was treated as a model for specific limited aspects of his work. In the 17th century he was regarded as supreme in anatomical drawing but less praised for broader elements of his art. While the Mannerists utilized the spatial compression seen in a few of his frescoes, and later the serpentine poses of his sculpture of "Victory," the 19th-century master Auguste Rodin exploited the effect of unfinished marble blocks. Certain 17th-century masters of the baroque perhaps show the fullest reference to him, but in ways that have been transformed to exclude any literal similarity. Besides Bernini, the painter Rubens may best show the usability of Michelangelo's creations for a later great artist.

MAJOR WORKS

SCULPTURE: "Madonna of the Stairs" (*c.* 1491; Casa Buonarroti, Florence); "Battle of the Centaurs" (*c.* 1492; Casa Buonarroti); "St. Petronius," "St. Proclus," and "An Angel" (1494–95; S. Domenico, Bologna, Italy); "Bacchus" (1496–97; Bargello, Florence); "Pietà" (1499; St. Peter's, Vatican City); "David" (1501–04; Accademia, Florence); "Madonna and Child" (1501–04; Notre-Dame, Brugge); "Madonna and Child with the Infant St. John" ("Taddei Madonna"; tondo, *c.* 1503; Royal Academy, London); "Madonna and Child" ("Pitti Madonna"; tondo, *c.* 1503; Bargello); "St. Matthew" (*c.* 1505; Accademia); "Moses" (*c.* 1513–15; for the tomb of Pope Julius II, 1505–45; S. Pietro in Vincoli, Rome); "Rebellious Slave" and "Dying Slave" (1513–16; Louvre, Paris); "Risen Christ" ("Christ Bearing the Cross"; 1519–20; Sta. Maria Sopra Minerva, Rome); four unfinished figures known as "Slaves" or "Prisoners" (*c.* 1520; Accademia); Medici tombs ("Dawn," "Dusk," "Day," "Night," "Giuliano de' Medici," "Lorenzo de' Medici," and "Madonna"; 1520–34; S. Lorenzo, Florence); "Apollo" ("David"; *c.* 1530; Bargello); "Victory" (*c.* 1532–34; Palazzo Vecchio, Florence); "Pietà" ("Deposition"; 1550–55; Duomo, Florence); "Rondanini Pietà" (1552–64; Castello Sforzesco, Milan).

DRAWINGS: Major collections: British Museum; Royal Library, Windsor; Ashmolean Museum, Oxford, Eng.; Casa Buonarroti, Florence; Teylers Museum, Haarlem, Neth.

ARCHITECTURE: Chapel of Leo X (dedicated to SS. Cosmas and Damian; facade, 1514; Castel Sant'Angelo, Rome); Laurentian Library (1523–59; S. Lorenzo, Florence); Palazzo Farnese (cornice of facade and top story wall of courtyard completed 1547; Rome); St. Peter's Basilica (dome designed 1557–61; Vatican City); Porta Pia (1561, Rome).

PAINTINGS: "Holy Family" ("Doni Tondo"; *c.* 1503–05; Uffizi, Florence); frescoes, Sistine Chapel ceiling (1508–12; Vatican City); "The Last Judgment" (1534–41; Sistine Chapel); "Conversion of St. Paul" (1542–45; Pauline Chapel, Vatican City); "Crucifixion of St. Peter" (1542–50; Pauline Chapel).

BIBLIOGRAPHY

Biographical works: For early sources of information, see GIORGIO VASARI, *Lives of the Most Eminent Painters, Sculptors & Architects,* 10 vol. (1912–15, reprinted 1976; originally published in Italian, 1550); and CHARLES HOLROYD, *Michael Angelo Buonarotti: With Translations of the Life of the Master by His Scholar, Ascanio Condivi, and Three Dialogues from the Portuguese by Francisco d'Ollanda,* 2nd ed. (1911). Other biographies include CHARLES H. MORGAN, *The Life of Michelangelo* (1960), an accurate interpretative record of the artist's life and accomplishments; HERBERT VON EINEM, *Michelangelo* (1973; originally published in German, 1959), a study of his character; HOWARD HIBBARD, *Michelangelo,* 2nd ed. (1985), a work for the general reader; ROBERT S. LIEBERT, *Michelangelo: A Psychoanalytic Study of His Life and Images* (1983), a historically balanced scholarly analysis; and DAVID SUMMERS, *Michelangelo and the Language of Art* (1981), which explores the historical background through the study of intellectual and philosophical terminology of the time.

Studies of creative output: The most detailed work of reference on all aspects of the artist and his work is CHARLES DE TOLNAY, *Michelangelo,* 5 vol. (1943–60, reissued 1969–70), which was strongly influenced by the author's theories of psychology as applied to the artist, as are most books on Michelangelo. ERWIN PANOFSKY, *Studies in Iconology: Humanistic Themes in the Art of the Renaissance* (1939, reissued 1972), contains a significant presentation of the relation of Michelangelo's work to Neoplatonism, but it is not accepted by all scholars. Other works include JOHANNES WILDE, *Michelangelo: Six Lectures* (1978), a knowledgeable and appreciative analysis, though the conclusions sometimes differ from those of other scholars; LINDA MURRAY, *Michelangelo: His Life, Work, and Times* (1984), a brief chronological overview; JAMES S. ACKERMAN, *The Architecture of Michelangelo,* 2nd ed. (1986), an analysis of the artist's buildings expressed in terms usually applied to sculpture; JOHN POPE-HENNESSY, *Italian High Renaissance and Baroque Sculpture,* 3rd ed. (1985), a lucid analysis of the work of other sculptors of the time side-by-side with Michelangelo's; and CARLO PIETRANGELI *et al., The Sistine Chapel: A New Light on Michelangelo: The Art, the History, and the Restoration* (1986), a collection of photographs documenting the restoration project, accompanied by critical essays of art historians and theologians.

Reproductions and sources: The following analytical collections can be recommended: MARIO SALMI (ed.), *The Complete Work of Michelangelo,* 2 vol. (1966); UMBERTO BALDINI, *The Sculpture of Michelangelo* (1982; originally published in Italian, 1981), containing an exhaustive collection of photographs; LUDWIG GOLDSCHEIDER (ed.), *The Sculptures of Michelangelo,* 2nd rev. ed. (1950), *The Paintings of Michelangelo,* 2nd ed. (1948), and *Michelangelo Drawings,* 2nd ed. (1966); FREDERICK HARTT, *Michelangelo Drawings* (1970, reprinted 1976); LUITPOLD DUSSLER, *Die Zeichnungen des Michelangelo: Kritischer Katalog* (1959); LEO STEINBERG, *Michelangelo's Last Paintings: The Conversion of St. Paul and the Crucifixion of St. Peter in the Cappella Paolina, Vatican Palace* (1975); *Complete Poems and Selected Letters of Michelangelo,* translated by CREIGHTON GILBERT, 3rd ed. (1980); and *Letters,* translated and edited by E.H. RAMSDEN (1963).

For further study of the artist's life and work, major bibliographies are a good starting point. See ERNST STEINMANN and RUDOLF WITTKOWER (eds.), *Michelangelo Bibliographie 1510–1926* (1927, reissued 1967); and LUITPOLD DUSSLER (ed.), *Michelangelo-Bibliographie, 1927–1970* (1974). For information on modern studies, see *RILA: International Repertory of the Literature of Art* (semiannual). Thematic lists of selected sources include CAROLE CABLE, *Michelangelo as an Architectural Draftsman* (1981); and LAURA S. KLINE, *Michelangelo's Architecture: A Selected Bibliography* (1983).

(C.E.G.)

Ancient Middle Eastern Religions

The religious beliefs, attitudes, and practices developed in the ancient Middle East (extending geographically from Iran to Egypt and from Anatolia and the Aegean Sea to the Arabian Peninsula, and temporally from *c.* 3000 to 330 BC, when Alexander the Great conquered much of the area) have had an enduring effect and influence on Western civilization. While this article treats only those religions of Middle Eastern antiquity that have not survived to modern times, special attention is given in the introduction to their role as antecedents of the major Western religions (*i.e.,* Judaism, Christianity, and Islām), all of which originated in the region. For full treatment of these "inheritors" of the Middle Eastern tradition, including also the surviving Zoroastrianism and Parsiism, see under the names of the individual religions.

For coverage of related topics in the *Macropædia* and *Micropædia,* see the *Propædia,* Part Eight, Division II, especially Section 822.

This article is divided into the following sections:

THE CULTURAL CONTEXT

General considerations

The ancient Middle East constituted an ecumene. The term ecumene comes from the Greek word *oikoumenē,* which means the inhabited world and designates a distinct cultural-historical community. The material effects of the commercial and cultural interconnections that permeated the component regions of the ancient Middle Eastern ecumene are richly supplied by archaeological excavations, which provide evidence of the spread of architectural, ceramic, metallurgical, and other products of ancient Middle Eastern man's industry. Manufacturing and services tended to be monopolized by professional guilds, including religious personnel specializing in sacrifices, oracles, divination, and other kinds of priestcraft. The mobility of such guilds throughout the entire area helps to explain the spread of specific religious ideas and techniques over great distances. Just as guild potters spread ceramic forms and methods, so also guild priests spread their religious concepts and practices, from the Indian Ocean to the Aegean Sea, and from the Nile River to Central Asia. The Greek poet Homer, in the *Odyssey,* noted the mobility of guildsmen, mentioning religious personnel as well as architects, physicians, and minstrels. Guild priests called *kohanim* were found at ancient Ugarit on the Mediterranean coast of northern Syria as well as in Israel; and Mycenaean Greek (Late Bronze Age) methods of sacrifice are similar to the Hebraic methods, which are preserved in many countries to this day in the traditional techniques of Jewish ritual slaughter.

The "archaeological revolution." The decipherment of Mesopotamian and Egyptian literatures in the 19th century opened new vistas of ancient Middle Eastern history. Hitherto, scholarly knowledge had been limited to the contents of classical Hebrew, Greek, and Latin literatures. Explorations and excavations in the Middle East yielded not only texts but an abundance of ancient objects of art, artifacts of daily life, and architecture, and thus have revolutionized scholarly knowledge of the ancient Middle East, including its religions. A ziggurat excavated at Babylon illustrates the form of the biblical Tower of Babel. The prototype of the biblical story of the Deluge has turned up in the Gilgamesh epic. A fragment (dating from about 1400 BC) of that Babylonian epic has been found at Megiddo in Israel, showing that the Mesopotamian version was current in Palestine before the Hebrews, under Joshua, conquered the land around 1200 BC. A previously little-known people, the Hittites, are, due to archaeological discoveries, now recognized as a major power of antiquity with a rich legacy of religious texts, especially rituals.

The earliest and certainly the most fundamental ancient Middle Eastern civilization—the Sumerian—had vanished without a reference in the literatures of the world. Now, Sumerology is an important field of investigation. Biblical studies have been greatly revolutionized by the tablets (1400–1200 BC) found from 1929 onward at Ugarit. It has become extremely difficult for anyone to keep abreast of the continually growing body of material, and very few scholars today feel secure enough to venture beyond limited areas.

By courtesy of the trustees of the British Museum

Kings and winged figures bearing offerings beside a sacred tree. Assyrian marble relief, reign of Ashurnasirpal II, *c.* 880 BC. In the British Museum.

Literary sources of knowledge of ancient Middle Eastern religion. Classical literature remains an important source for ancient Middle Eastern religion. The Roman historian Livy (59 or 64 BC–AD 17) wrote many descriptions of religious rites of the ancient Middle East. The Roman poet Virgil's (70–19 BC) *Aeneid* and *Eclogues* reflect Egyptian, Semitic, and Anatolian, as well as Greek, antecedents. The Greek biographer Plutarch's (AD 40/50–120/125) *De Iside et Osiride* ("Concerning Isis and Osiris") is still the best description of the Egyptian myth of Isis and Osiris and of the cult of the dead. The Greek satirist Lucian's (*c.* AD 120/125–190) *De Dea Syra* ("Concerning the Syrian Goddess") is of enduring value for an understanding of Canaanite religion. The writings of Herodotus, the 5th-century-BC Greek historian, remain an indispensable source for the cultural history and religion of the ancient Middle East. And due to the discovery of texts from Ugarit, the Homeric epic of the Greeks is now firmly linked to Middle Eastern literature.

The Old Testament as a source of knowledge

The Hebrew Bible is still the most important single source for knowledge of the ancient Middle East, reflecting life from Egypt to Iran, and from the Bronze Age beginnings to the Hellenistic Age. There is very little in the Old Testament that does not follow the types of religious literatures in the older Middle East: psalms, hymns, laws, rituals, prophecy, wisdom literature, and other types. Sometimes parts of the Bible are related in detail to specific outside sources. The Egyptian *Wisdom of Amenemope,* first published in modern times in 1923, for example, parallels Prov. 22:17–24:22 so closely that it effectively opened up the field of the comparative study of ancient Middle Eastern wisdom literature.

Middle Eastern worldviews and basic religious thought

THE CONCEPT OF THE SACRED

All of the ancient Middle Eastern people saw the agency of the gods in every aspect of life and nature. Everything on earth was regarded as a reflex of its prototype in the divine or sacred sphere, such as in the biblical description of the creation of man "in the image of God"; God was viewed as the primary reality of the universe, and man was seen as the reflection of that reality. In Egypt Thoth was the scribe in the pantheon. Mortal scribes were viewed as the human reflections of Thoth, and "the beak of the Ibis (*i.e.,* Thoth) is the finger of the Scribe" (*Wisdom of Amenemope,* ch. XV, 17:7).

Creation of the universe

The ancient Middle Eastern people believed that the universe resulted from the injecting of order (cosmos) into chaotic primordial beings or matter, followed by divine acts of creation. Gen. 1:1–3 says: "When God set about creating the heavens and the earth (*i.e.,* the universe), the earth was in a state of chaos and darkness was upon the face of the deep; and the Spirit of God was flying over the face of the waters. And God said, 'Let there be light!'; and there was light." Thus darkness (*i.e.,* evil) was preexistent. Moreover, the deep (*tehom* in Hebrew) is the same as the primordial dragon called Tiamat (cognate to the Hebrew *tehom*) in the Babylonian epic of creation. The first act of creation is God's evoking light (*i.e.,* the forces of good) by fiat. Accordingly, God is not responsible for the forces of evil, which were there before he embarked on the creative process. Proceeding by fiat he separated the water-containing earth from the water-containing heaven, confined the earth's waters to the bodies of water (leaving the rest as dry land), created the various species of vegetation, the heavenly bodies, the animal kingdom, and finally man who is to rule over the earth. All this takes six days, after which God rests on the seventh, so that the Sabbath crowns the epic of creation and imposes the obligation to observe the sabbath in keeping with the principle of *imitatio Dei* (the imitation of God).

The Babylonian creation epic (*Enuma elish,* "When on High") states that at first there existed only the male (Apsu) and female (Tiamat) gods of the deep. They raised a family of gods that were so unruly that Apsu resolved to destroy them. Rebellion and chaos ensued. Among the deities was Marduk, the god of Babylon. Since the main version of the epic of creation is the Babylonian, Marduk occupies the role of Creator. (In the Assyrian version, Ashur is important.) Tiamat, who had embarked on a course of destruction, was slain by Marduk, who cut her in two and used her carcass to create the universe. Out of half her body he fashioned the sky containing the heavenly bodies to mark the periods of time. The epic culminates in the glorification of Marduk and the establishment of his order. The *Enuma elish* was read on the Akitu, or New Year festival, at Babylon, to re-establish order, in accordance with sympathetic transference principles, by reciting Marduk's creation. The function of the Akitu is thus to rejuvenate society for the new year.

VIEWS OF MAN AND SOCIETY

The lack of hard and fast barriers between gods and men left room for hybridizing. The aristocracy, in particular, claimed some divine form of ancestry. Gilgamesh, a mortal king who ruled Uruk in Mesopotamia, was, according to the Gilgamesh epic, born of the goddess Ninsun, even as among the Greeks Achilles was accepted as the son of the goddess Thetis. Sometimes kings claimed to have two divine parents. King Keret, whose epic was found at Ugarit, claimed to be the son of El, the head of the pantheon, and of Asherah, El's wife. Every Egyptian pharaoh was hailed as "the son of Re" (the sun god). This does not, however, imply the absence of a human father. The concept was one of paternity at two levels; qualitative superiority emanated from the notion of divine paternity, but one's position in society came from the human husband of one's mother. Odysseus "the Zeus-begotten son of Laertes" (*Iliad* 10:144) was a hero because Zeus presumably impregnated his mother; but he was also king of Ithaca because his mother's husband was King Laertes of Ithaca. In this regard the birth and station of Christ differ only in that Mary was a virgin when she was divinely impregnated. Though the divine component of Christ is due to his divine paternity, his position as king of the Jews comes not from his heavenly Father but from Mary's husband, Joseph, who was descended from King David (Matt. 1).

In the ancient Middle Eastern world view, gods could become mortal, and men could become gods. Utnapishtim, the hero of the Babylonian Flood story, was deified together with his wife by the fiat of the great god Enlil: "Hitherto Utnapishtim has been but human; henceforth Utnapishtim and his wife shall be like us gods" (Gilgamesh epic 11:193–194). In the Hebrew Bible, God so loved Enoch (Gen. 5:24) and Elijah (II Kings 2:11) that he carried them aloft to heaven as immortals. But these were special cases, and in antiquity they set no precedent for common folk. Kings enjoyed deification regularly in Egypt, though in some other traditions only upon dying. The Hittite monarch Hattusilis III refers to his father's death as "when my father Mursilis became a god" (*Apology of Hattusilis,* line 22).

Purpose of man

From the ancient Middle Eastern point of view, man was created to serve the gods, and he does so in the hope that the gods appreciate it and will reward him for it. The gods need food and drink and depend on men to supply them. After the Flood the biblical Noah won God's goodwill, for "the Lord smelled the pleasing odor" (Gen. 8:21) of the tasty flesh and fowl offered up to him. Noah was following a long tradition, for Utnapishtim (Gilgamesh epic 11:155–161) had, after the Flood, offered sacrifices and libations to the gods who "crowded like flies" as they "smelled the sweet savor." Though gods depend on man, man also depends on the gods, and therefore service to the deities must be maintained for the welfare of the state, even as the family and the individual must do what the gods expect of them for domestic and personal welfare.

Everything on earth reflects a divine prototype, and all human affairs are divinely ordered and scrutinized. Gods may even build the cities destined to be their cultic centres and in which they are to reside, at least part of the time. The Greek god Poseidon built the walls of Troy, according to the *Iliad* (21:446–447). At Ugarit, Baal's temple was designed and built by Kothar-wa-Hasis, the god of arts and crafts. The Israelite King David gave his son Solomon plans for the Temple drawn up by Yahweh's (the Lord's) own hand (I Chron. 28:19).

National policy went hand in hand with theology. Ashur was the god of Assyria; the kings of Assyria were in theory his chief executive officers. Thus Sennacherib, king of Assyria, in undertaking a military campaign, recorded that it was not on his own initiative but in conformity with Ashur's will: "In my second campaign, Ashur my Lord impelled me." When the Hebrews and Transjordanians had a border dispute, Jephthah told the latter: "Will you not possess what Chemosh your god gives you to possess? And all that the Lord our God has dispossessed before us, we will possess" (Judg. 11:24). There was no such thing as secular policy in the ancient Middle East.

Since the king was the human agent of the god, he was exalted above other men. In Israel, the king was chosen by God to rule his people. God's representative was a priest or prophet who consecrated the king by anointing his head with oil. But the king of Israel was not divine, neither while on the throne nor after death.

The divinity of kings evoked certain fictions. By sucking the breasts of goddesses, crown princes imbibed a source of divinity. The baby pharaoh sucking the breasts of Isis (who was perhaps in real life represented by her high priestess) is a common motif in Egyptian art. In Mesopotamia, it was not the usual practice for kings to claim divinity, but now and then it cropped up. Naram-Sin (23rd century BC) prefixed the sign for divinity before his name and was officially a god. The same usage is attested among kings of the 3rd Dynasty of Ur (*c.* 2100 BC).

VIEWS OF BASIC VALUES AND ENDS OF HUMAN LIFE

Ethical emphases

The good life was one lived in accord with the regulations of one's god. In the realm of ethics and morals there was more international uniformity than there was in taboo and ritual. Honesty and kindness were universally recognized as good, theft and murder as bad. Wisdom literature tended to stress the same virtues and to condemn the same vices, regardless of the region and cult. It remained for the prophets of Israel to single out uncompromising virtue as the overriding consideration in the good life required by God. The most important factor in that system was "social justice," whereby the weak was always protected in conflicts of interest with the strong. This had an important place in what may be called "international religion"; *i.e.,* that governing relations between men from different areas belonging to different cults. That level of religion, called "fear of the gods," is tested when the strong man confronts the weak. The strong man who injures the weak lacks the fear of the gods; the strong man who helps the weak has the fear of the gods. This was religion transcending all the regional cults, and it came into play when strangers abroad were at the mercy of the local inhabitants. Odysseus in a foreign land wanted to know if the people there feared the gods or were lawless so that no stranger was safe (*Odyssey* 9:176). Abraham, too, was concerned in Philistia lest the inhabitants might kill him because there was no "Fear of God(s)" (Gen. 20:11). Men of all nations and all cults knew that only among god-fearing men was there decency or safety.

There was another common trend in international religion. No matter how polytheistic a cult may have been, it left a place for the god shared by all men. Theos, "God" (not merely "a god"), is in Homer; *pa netjer,* "the God," occurs in Egyptian exactly like Elohim, "(the) God," in Hebrew. Nebuchadrezzar, the 6th-century-BC Babylonian king, made Zedekiah, the Judaean king, swear by Elohim (II Chron. 36:13), the God of the universe for Babylonians and Hebrews alike. Similarly, when the Hebrews spoke of truth uttered by Pharaoh Necho, which fell on the deaf ears of the Judaean King Josiah, the text (II Chron. 35:21) states that Elohim, "God," had spoken through the mouth of the pharaoh.

In Egyptian religion (followed by Judaism, Christianity, and Islām), the concept of a happy afterlife depending on one's ethical and moral record in this world was developed. Vignettes in the various Egyptian books of the dead show the deceased's heart being weighed against the feather of truth in the balances before the scribe god Thoth, who records the text. When the Bible speaks of God as "who tests the heart and the kidneys" (Ps. 7:9; Jer. 11:20 and 20:12) it refers to the same concept.

MYTHS AS THE BASIC MODE OF RELIGIOUS THOUGHT

Purpose of myths

Myths were developed to account for the cosmos. How did the gods bring heavens, earth, plants, beasts, and human beings into existence? What is the divine origin of human institutions and of the ecumene? What divine process is responsible for prosperity or failure? To explain such basic questions etiological (origin or causal) myths were developed. For example, the attraction between man and woman (and the consequent institution of marriage) is explained by the myth that primeval man was one creature, subsequently divided into two parts, male and female, which are attracted to one another to regain their pristine unity. Aristophanes expresses this theory of sexual attraction in Plato's *Symposium.* Genesis relates the same theory in the familiar myth that a rib, taken out of Adam, was fashioned into Eve; and precisely because woman was taken out of man, man forsakes his father and mother to cleave unto his wife so that they become one flesh.

Myths are often invoked in magic (which, unlike religion, aims at compelling, instead of imploring, the gods). To banish evil from the life of a client, the magician may invoke the cosmic myth whereby the forces of good triumph over the forces of evil. Evil is depicted on a seal of the Akkad period (3rd millennium BC) in Mesopotamia as a seven-headed monster whose heads are being successively killed by good anthropomorphic (humanform) beings. At Ugarit, in mythological poems of the Late Bronze Age, the good gods Baal and Anath slay the wicked Leviathan of the Seven Heads, providing the precedent for the victory of good over evil. The Hebrews also nurtured this myth whereby God slays the many-headed Leviathan (Ps. 74:14) and will do so again at the end of days, to quell evil and establish good for all eternity (Isa. 27:1).

ASSOCIATION OF RELIGION WITH THE ARTS AND SCIENCES

Religion in the ancient Middle East was associated with both the arts and the sciences, though in the literature of the area it is very difficult to disentangle the secular from the sacred. Hymns, at one level, and omen or ritual texts, at another level, are clearly religious. But it would be difficult to categorize the Gilgamesh epic of Mesopotamia or the Homeric epics of Greece as definitely either secular or religious. They deal with human events or worldly problems, but the gods are constantly on hand. The same may be said for two Ugaritic epics, the epic of Keret and the epic of Daniel and Aqhat, which date from the Late Bronze Age. This also holds for the patriarchal narratives in the biblical book of Genesis about Abraham, Isaac, and Jacob, in which God and his messengers play the same kind of role in human affairs as do the gods in the Homeric or Ugaritic epics.

Religion had close ties with science as well as with literature and art. Astronomy, mathematics, and time reckoning are sciences in which the ancient Middle East made great strides at an early date, long before 3000 BC. Heavenly bodies were at the same time both deities and personified numbers. The planet Venus was the "star" that the Assyrians and Babylonians called Ishtar, which was at the same time both the goddess Ishtar and the deified number 15. The Moon was not only Earth's satellite but also the lunar deity Sin and the deified number 30. The most perfect number was one, for by advancing from zero to one men believed they proceeded from nonexistence to existence. Moreover, all other whole numbers were regarded as multiples of one, representative of the Creator, the Prime Mover, of the universe. The Egyptians called Re "the one One"; the Babylonians identified the divine "One" with Anu, the god of heaven. When the Hebrew prophet Zechariah (14:9) proclaimed "on that day the Lord will be one and his name one," he indicated that the Hebrews, like their neighbours, reckoned with sacred numbers and saw in the number one a symbol of the creator. Biblical monotheism, therefore, has more than one dimension, including not only the monotheistic principle that there is one God and none beside him, but also the mathematical principle of the primacy of "one" and its deification as the Prime Mover.

Significance of the number one

THE ROLE OF MAGIC

The loftier trends of ancient Middle Eastern religion did not as a rule threaten to eliminate magic. White, or protective, magic was never seriously discouraged. Black, or destructive, magic was frowned on by organized society, regardless of whether the official religion was monotheistic or polytheistic, because black magic makes its victims unfit for functioning productively in society. Section II of the Babylonian King Hammurabi's (Hammurapi's) code punishes witchcraft (as well as false accusations of witchcraft) with the death penalty. Moreover, all organized religion tended to oppose magic that circumvented the official clergy. King Saul of Israel had characteristically banned sorcery, driving it underground. Yet when he wanted guidance from the dead prophet Samuel, Saul consulted the Witch of Endor who was practicing her art illegally (I Sam. 28:6–25). She was able to call up the spirit of the prophet from the underworld, which, incidentally, illustrates one of the reasons why society opposes spiritualism. The witch, by claiming to bring the greatest authorities of the past onto the current scene, threatens the authority of the establishment.

Religious practices and institutions

NATURE: THE FRAMEWORK OF IDEAS AND PRACTICES

Fertility of agriculture, of edible animals, and of the human population was a paramount factor in the life and religion of the ancient Middle East. The forms that the fertility rites assumed varied from region to region, depending on climate and geography. Rain and dew were all-important in Canaan, but of little significance in Egypt. In both areas water was crucial, but the source of the life-giving water was entirely different. The agricultural year varied in the two regions. In Egypt the year was divided into three seasons: inundation, sowing, and harvest. In Canaan there were two seasons: the winter characterized by rainfall and the summer characterized by dew. The year was punctuated by different agricultural activities, as is indicated in the Gezer Calendar in which all 12 months

Seasonal patterns

Egyptian sepulchral stela by the craftsman Qaha, 19th dynasty. (Upper portion) The Syrian fertility goddess Qadesh stands atop a lion in the presence of the Egyptian fertility god Min (left) and the Syrian god of lightning and thunder Resheph (right). (Lower portion) The Syrian goddess Anath (seated right) and worshippers. In the British Museum.

are accounted for as times of profitable agricultural activity, with harvests in the rainless summer as well as in the green winter. Anxiety was caused by the uncertainty of rain in the rainy season and of dew in its season. All of the regions of the ancient Middle East schematized the blessing of good years and the threat of bad years in terms of seven-year cycles. A Mesopotamian text illustrating this is the Gilgamesh epic (8:101–113), in which the slaying of the hero Gilgamesh would initiate seven lean years. At Ugarit the slaying of the hero Aqhat evokes a curse depriving the land of rain and dew for seven (or, climactically, eight) years. The seven lean and seven fat years in the biblical story of Joseph in Egypt reflect the same system. In Egypt, of course, rain and dew are out of the picture; instead, generous Nile risings mean prosperity; inadequate risings in the season of inundation spells misery. A text of the Ptolemaic period (4th–1st century BC), purporting to record events of the Pyramid age, tells of seven lean years in the reign of Djoser (3rd dynasty; *i.e., c.* 2650–*c.* 2575 BC). The pharaoh appealed to the gods, who responded by restoring an abundant flow of the Nile.

The population desired the normal pattern of times and seasons, so that "seedtime and harvest, cold and heat, summer and winter, day and night, shall not cease" (Gen. 8:22). But since the seasonal pattern is not dependable, the need for order evoked a system of cycles: notably the sabbatical cycle. A Ugaritic liturgical text especially designed for this phenomenon aims at terminating a sabbatical cycle of privation and ushering in one of fertility by celebrating the birth and triumphal entrance of the Seven Good Gods, whose advent brings an abundance of food and wine.

Fertility rites

It was only natural that fertility rites should include sexual myths that were acted out dramatically. The Ugaritic text just alluded to describes El, the head of the pantheon, copulating with two human women. This has echoes in Hosea and Ezekiel where God, as in the Canaanite literary tradition, is referred to as having figuratively a love affair with two women, symbolizing Judah and Israel. The Hebrews, however, eventually eliminated sex from their official theology as well as their religious practices. Up to the time of King Josiah's reform (621 BC) there was a women's cult of Asherah (under *qedeshim* auspices [consecrated for fertility practices], according to II Kings 23:7) in the Jerusalem Temple, alongside the male cult of Yahweh. Asherah's devotees considered her the chief wife of Yahweh, even as she was the wife of El, head of the Canaanite pantheon, for in the Bible, El is identified with Yahweh. But Josiah eliminated the cult of Asherah, and official Judaism has since then left no place for other gods, which meant the elimination of every goddess. Popular religion, to be sure, persisted in the female fertility principle until the destruction of the Temple in 586 BC. In Judaean excavations Astarte figurines were found in private homes down to that time. Further purification of the Hebrew religion, which was intensified by the catastrophe of 586, put an end to the practice of pagan fertility rites, including the use of goddess figurines. Without goddesses there could be no sexual activity in the pantheon, and thus Judaism has developed without any divine mother figure.

The ancient Middle East made a place for homosexuality and bestiality in its myths and rites. In the Asherah cult the *qedeshim* priests had a reputation for homosexual practices, even as the *qedeshot* priestesses for prostitution. Israel eventually banned both the *qedeshim* and *qedeshot,* while in Ugarit the *qedeshim* and *kohanim* were priestly guilds in equally good standing. Baal is portrayed in Ugaritic mythology as impregnating a heifer to sire the young bull god. The biblical book of Leviticus (18:22–27) bans homosexuality and bestiality expressly because the Canaanite population had been practicing those rites, which the Hebrews rejected as abominations.

Ritual and myth

According to ancient views, the myth came first, and the rite imitated or reenacted it. This sequence, however, is not necessarily the order in which religion develops. Rites can be very tenacious; and when the origin of a rite has been forgotten, a myth has often been invented to explain it.

TYPES OF RELIGIOUS ORGANIZATION AND AUTHORITY

Religion occurs at different levels of society: personal, familial, local, national, and international. At the personal and international extremes there is need for but little organization. And yet in religion, as the ancient Middle Easterners saw it, there was a progression from one stage to the next. In the early myths of Genesis, God and Noah have direct personal relations. This leads to a covenant between God and all who went out of the ark: birds and beasts as well as mankind (Gen. 9:9–10). Through the sons of Noah and their descendants, who form the nations of the world (Gen. 10), there is a theoretical progress to international religion. This scheme of the relations between God and mankind, from the personal to the universal level, mirrors the historical record of religion. Judaism (followed later by Christianity and Islām) traces "the Religion" back to Abraham, who had personal and direct relations with God, as was customary in the ancient Middle Eastern milieu. Abraham's intimacy with God is similar to the intimacy between Odysseus and the Greek goddess Athena. The next step is a covenant between a particular deity and a particular person, binding the two together in a contractual relationship for all eternity from generation to generation. Such covenants were not rare; the Hittite King Hattusilis III made such a covenant with Ishtar. Abraham's covenant is unique simply because it was the only one destined to last in history.

The descendants of able men who established a dynasty or tradition would worship the God of their father, or fathers, and adhere to the original covenant. Gen. 31 portrays Jacob and Laban swearing by their respective ancestral gods: Jacob by the god(s) of Abraham and Laban by the god(s) of Nahor. Once a group expanded into a federation of clans or tribes, religious organization became necessary. A central shrine (such as the one at Shiloh in Israel) for amphictyonic (religious confederational) pilgrimage festivals required a professional priesthood and other religious personnel to take care of sacrifices, give oracular guidance, interpret dreams and omens, as well as to provide instruction. In an amphictyony of 12 tribes, each tribe could render federal service for religious and secular purposes, one month each year. A special tribe (such as the Levites in Israel, or the Magians in Iran) could be dedicated full time to cultic duties. A greater degree of centralization and organization of the cult would generally follow from the establishment of a powerful state. The cult of Marduk of Babylon spread in importance and influence because Babylon became the capital of a powerful kingdom in the time of Hammurabi (18th century BC) and of a mighty empire during the reign of Nebuchadrezzar (604–562 BC). The Egyptian cult of Amon-Re not only became powerful but took on the form of a universal religion as a result of the military and political triumphs of the rulers of Thebes, particularly during the reign of Thutmose III (1479–26 BC). Under Solomon, Jerusalem became the centre of a great commercial empire. The Temple of Solomon and its God, the God of Israel, were catapulted into an international prominence that was quite different from the national status that marked the extent of Hebraic religion previously. The new internationalism of Israel's involvements paved the way for the universality of the views of the prophets. The God of Israel was subsequently concerned with all mankind and not merely with one people in one small land. This ultimately meant the transformation of biblical religion from the cult of a single people to a more subtle, spiritual movement that required different organization and different personnel. The priesthood became defunct with the destruction of Herod's Temple and the cessation of sacrifices in AD 70. The new religious leaders (rabbis) were rather teachers and spiritual guides who were united by dedication to the same scripture. The spread of the devotees over the face of the Earth meant that they were now divided into regional groups, serving under different sovereigns, and the individual Jewish communities were organized independently, each with its own house of worship.

Professional priesthoods

There were various devices for holding an ethnic-religious group together even though it might be fragmentized into scattered communities. Laws of purity, especially those pertaining to diet, kept different groups apart. Each normally respected the other's rules, but the fact that each group had different taboos kept them from breaking bread together and mingling socially. They could do business with each other in the marketplace, but they could not fraternize in each other's homes. Above all, laws of purity were deterrents to intermarriage, the major factor that breaks up religious communities and encourages homogenization.

Laws of purity

(C.H.G.)

A SURVEY OF ANCIENT MIDDLE EASTERN RELIGIONS

Egyptian religion

The term Egyptian religion here refers to the indigenous religion of ancient Egypt from the Late Neolithic Period to the first centuries AD, and includes both folk traditions and the court religion of the pharaohs.

NATURE AND SIGNIFICANCE

Egyptian religion shared two characteristics with Egyptian culture in general: longevity and a development that, on the whole, was undisturbed by foreign influence. All manifestations of cultural and social life were so deeply permeated with religious ideas that an understanding of Egyptian culture is impossible without an understanding of Egyptian religion, and vice versa. Egyptian religion had a widespread influence on the neighbouring cultures of its time and on the cultures of later eras. One of the most striking aspects of Egyptian religion was the immense number of gods in human, animal, and material forms, who represented both the powers of nature and abstract ideas. They were never grouped systematically, though tendencies toward systematization were manifest in local groupings of gods and mythical associations. Another characteristic was their lack of distinct personality; *i.e.*, one god could easily be equated with another on the basis of one common feature or embodied power. In addition, they were all immanent, and there was no contrast between the divine and the world. The divinity of the world (cosmos, nature, mankind, society) implied a view of life that extended beyond physical life. The state of death was regarded as part of the well-ordered life cared for by the gods. Various material and ritual guarantees for life after death aided in the realization of this idea.

The divine world order

Thus the world appeared as a large, permanent unity in spite of the multitude of gods and their cults. It was regulated by the rule of pharaoh, whose main task was to establish *ma'at* instead of disorder. *Ma'at* stands for all order in life. The translations "order," "justice," and "truth" indicate its diverse aspects. In social life the demands of ethics help to realize *ma'at*.

By courtesy of the Egyptian Exploration Society; photograph, Oriental Institute, Chicago

King Seti I offering a figure of the goddess Ma'at to Osiris, Isis, and Horus. Relief from the temple of King Seti I, Abydos, early 13th century BC.

Characteristic of Egyptian religious thinking and national character was the toleration of ideas that, from the point of view of later cultures, contradict each other. This toleration was accompanied by the desire to retain ideas and forms once conceived, even when they had been replaced by new ones. As a consequence, the number of mythical, ritual, and theological creations increased in the course of time. It is difficult, therefore, to fix the time of origin and the primary life span of an idea that has become fixed in tradition.

The basic feature of religious feeling was optimism. Notions of an end of the world and skepticism rarely arose, as death was viewed as part of life and the realization of *ma'at* was always possible. Both magic and ritual acts were means to preserve the security of life, as they protected against danger and menace. Egyptian religion can therefore be classified among the typical ritual religions in which faith is less important than correct rites.

SOURCES OF MODERN KNOWLEDGE

Tombs

Nonliterary. Tombs provide sources for the knowledge of Egyptian religion in prehistoric as well as later times. Their offering places indicate belief in an afterlife: the dead need offerings of food and drink. A false door enables communication with the world of the living.

Funerary gifts and paintings. Real objects or models provided the deceased with household goods, articles of daily use, and servants, as in life. In the late Old Kingdom after *c.* 2250 BC, and in the First Intermediate Period (*c.* 2130–1939 BC), friezes of objects (*i.e.*, paintings of funerary gifts) were added. In this way, it was thought, the property of the dead could be preserved in case the tomb was plundered. From the early 4th dynasty (*c.* 2575–*c.* 2465 BC) on, tomb decorations (reliefs or paintings) occur. The main subjects are the so-called offering lists (lists of the food, drink, clothes, oils, and ointments that the dead needed) and representations of offering rituals and revivification ceremonies (*e.g.*, the "Opening of the Mouth," from the 18th dynasty—1539–1292 BC). In addition, there are the so-called scenes from life (agriculture, cattle breeding, crafts) and, occasionally, from the 6th dynasty (*c.* 2365–*c.* 2150 BC) on, representations of biographical events. Ritual scenes are not represented in tombs, and the king does not appear until the 18th dynasty. In the Old Kingdom (*c.* 2575–*c.* 2130 BC), the pyramid temples of the kings attest the existence of a royal funerary cult similar to that of private persons. From the 5th dynasty (*c.* 2465–*c.* 2325 BC) on the pyramid temples are decorated with scenes from the king's life.

Temples and images. The sun temples are limited to the 5th dynasty for the cult of the sun god, Re. Numerous temples for the gods date from the 18th dynasty to the time of the Roman emperors. The image of the god was kept in the holy of holies ("chamber of the cultic image"), where a daily offering ritual was performed. During festivals it was carried in procession before the public and taken to visit other temples. The ritual scenes decorating the temples of the New Kingdom (1539–1075 BC) enable scholars to determine to a large extent the function of the different rooms.

Sculptures of gods in human form are found from prehistoric times on (*e.g.*, Min of Coptos). The different gods are not distinguished by personal features but by attributes or shape—animal, hybrid, or human. Cult implements—portable wooden statues of gods, censers, libation vessels, altars, offering tables—provide clues to religious practices.

Literary sources. *Pyramid Texts and Coffin Texts.* The oldest text collections are the Pyramid Texts inscribed in the subterranean rooms of the pyramids of the kings and the queens from the end of the 5th (*c.* 2325 BC) to the end of the 6th dynasty (*c.* 2150 BC). They contain spells for the offering and funerary rituals, magical texts, and texts pertaining to the king's existence in the hereafter. The Coffin Texts (found on coffins of the First Intermediate Period and the Middle Kingdom—*c.* 2130–*c.* 1600? BC—and on several papyri) are a collection of spells for private individuals containing copious extracts from the Pyramid Texts, texts from the mortuary cult and the temple ritual, and purely mythological texts.

Book of the Dead. The latest collection is the Book of the Dead: spells written on papyrus and deposited with the dead in the tomb for their use in the hereafter (from the 18th dynasty to the Late Period). Although derived in part from the Coffin Texts, they retain little connection with rituals but are meant to provide the dead with power in the hereafter (which explains why there are so many spells for transformation of the dead into powerful beings). Best known is chapter 125, with the so-called negative

Psychostasia

Table 1: Major Gods and Goddesses

	alternative names	areas of responsibility	principal sanctuary	relations to other deities	symbols and emblems
Amon	Amen, Ammon, Amun	king of the gods; patron deity of the pharaohs; identified with the sun god Re as Amon-Re	originally Khnum, later Thebes	husband of Mut; member of the Theban triad	male figure with a ram's head, or a ram wearing the triple crown
Anubis	Anpu	god of the dead, particularly the aspects of the funeral cult and the care of the dead	Cynopolis	son of Re, or son of Osiris by Nephthys	black jackal, or a male figure with the head of a jackal or dog
Aton	Aten	represented the sun at its zenith; later, for a short time was made the chief and only god (with the exception of the pharaoh)	Akhetaton (Tell el-Amarna)	a form of the sun god Re	a red solar disk with rays terminating in hands
Atum	Tem, Tum	creator of gods, men, and the divine order; founder of the Heliopolitan Ennead; represented the setting sun	Heliopolis	merged with the cult of Re, becoming Atum-Re	old, bearded man wearing the double crown and carrying the *ankh;* sometimes, a male figure with the head of an ichneumon
Bast	Bastet, Ubasti	goddess of music, dance; originally symbolized the fertilizing warmth of the sun; during the New Kingdom thought to be a lioness war goddess	Bubastis	wife of Ptah; member of the Memphite triad; sometimes identified with Sekhmet	cat, or cat-headed woman, holding in her hand either a sistrum or an aegis
Bes	Bisu	originally, protector of the royal house; later, popular god of recreation; also associated with childbirth; the enemy of noxious beasts; protector and bringer of peace to the dead	originated in the Sudan; later adopted throughout Egypt	husband either of Beset, his female counterpart, or of Taurt	dwarf with large head, goggle eyes, protruding tongue, bowlegs, and a bushy tail
Buto	Edjo, Udjo, Wadjet, Wadjit	tutelary goddess of Lower Egypt; defender of the king; personification of the sun's burning heat	Buto	later thought to be the nurse of the infant god Horus	female figure wearing a *uraeus* or the red crown of Lower Egypt; or, a *uraeus* twined around a papyrus stem or as part of the king's diadem
Geb	Keb, Seb	god of the earth; the physical support of the world	Heliopolis	husband and brother of Nut; son of Shu and Tefnut; father of the Osirian gods	a goose or a male figure with his head surmounted by a goose
Hathor	Athyr	originally a personification of the sky; at Dandarah, goddess of festivity and love; protectress of women; at Thebes patroness of the region of the dead; later identified locally with tree, lion, or cow goddesses	originally, Dandarah; later, Ombos, Edfu, and western Thebes	daughter of Nut and Re	cow, cow-headed goddess, or goddess with a human head adorned with horns or cow's ears and heavy tresses framing her face
Horus	Hor	originally the god of Lower Egypt; later identified with the reigning king and thus the opponent of Seth	Nekhen, Edfu, later all of Egypt	son of Osiris	falcon or falcon-headed male figure
Isis	Aset, Eset	queen of the gods; great mother goddess figure; retriever and embalmer of the body of Osiris; protector of the child Horus	originally, Sebennytus; later spread throughout Egypt, the Near East, and the classical world	wife of Osiris; mother of Horus	female figure with both a vulture headdress and a throne or disk flanked by cow's or ram's horns on her head
Ma'at	Mayet	goddess of law, truth, and justice; served as the balance in the scale used to weigh the heart of the deceased	a deified abstract *par excellence;* thus, she had no single cult centre	daughter of Re; wife of Thoth	female figure standing or sitting on her heels, wearing an ostrich feather on her head
Min		personification of the generative force in nature; god of fertility and harvest; protector of desert travellers and god of the road	Coptos, Akhmīm	son of Re, or of Shu	ithyphallic bearded man, his crown surmounted by two tall plumes, and holding a flail or thunderbolt in his right hand
Mut		a vulture goddess of Thebes; a great and mighty divine mother	Thebes	wife of Amon-Re	female figure whose head or headdress was in the form of a vulture or who wears a heavy wig surmounted by the double crown
Nekhbet	Nekhebet	tutelary goddess of Upper Egypt; protectress of childbirth	Elkab (Nekheb)	daughter of Re; wife of Khenti-Amentiu or of Hapi	woman or vulture wearing the white crown of Upper Egypt; often shown spreading wings above king
Nut	Neuth, Nuit	goddess of the sky, arch of the heavens; protectress of the dead	Memphis and the Delta region; also, Dandarah	wife and sister of Geb; mother of the Osirian gods	elongated female figure arched over Shu; often wearing a water-pot or pear-shaped vessel on her head
Osiris	Usire	originally a fertility god and giver of civilization; later, with Re, the supreme god of Egypt and ruler of the dead	Busiris, Abydos	son of Nut and Geb; father of Horus	represented as a dead king in mummy wrappings, the hands holding the crook and flail and wearing the *atef* crown on his head
Ptah	Phthah	god of fertility, creator of the universe, maker of things; the patron of craftsmen and fine arts	originally Memphis, later, all of Egypt	husband of Sekhmet; father of Nefertum; member of the Memphite triad	mummified man with a shaven head his hands holding the *djed* symbol and a sceptre
Re	Phra, Ra	personification of the sun at its zenith; king of the gods and father of mankind; protector of kings; chief state god	Heliopolis	father of Shu and Tefnut, or, alternatively, son of Geb and Nut	falcon-headed man crowned with the sun disk encircled by the *uraeus;* held the *ankh* and a sceptre
Sebek	Sebeq, Sobk, Suchos	originally, perhaps associated with fertility, death, and burial; later, a protector of reptiles and patron of kings; occasionally, a personification of evil	Crocodilopolis; later, Ombos, Thebes, and Lake Moeris	son of Neith; sometimes identified with Seth or with Re (as Sebek-Re)	crocodile or crocodile-headed man wearing on his head either a solar disk and *uraeus* or a pair of horns surmounted by a disk and a pair of plumes
Sekhmet	Sekhet	warlike solar goddess	Memphis and the Delta region	wife of Ptah; mother of Nefertum; member of the Memphite triad	lioness or woman with a lion's head, on which she wore the solar disk and *uraeus*
Seth	Set, Setekh, Setesh	partner and rival of Horus in the Osirian myths	Ombos	brother or son of Osiris	the "typhonian animal": a composite creature with a grey hound's body, slanting eyes, square-tipped ears, and long forked tail
Shu		god of light and air and supporter of the sky; later, personification of the divine intelligence	Dandarah, Edfu, Apollinopolis Magna, Memphis	son of Re; husband and brother of Tefnut	male figure with an ostrich feather on his head
Thoth	Djhowtey	moon god; later the god of reckoning and of learning in general; inventor of writing, scribe of the gods; lord of magic	Hermopolis Magna	protector of Isis during her pregnancy; healer of her son Horus' injury; husband of Ma'at	male figure with an ibis' head on which were placed the moon crescent and disk

confession and the psychostasia (weighing of the soul) in the judgment of the dead.

Other texts. Further mortuary literature includes offering liturgies (already on a papyrus from the Old Kingdom), texts for the revivification ceremony ("Opening of the Mouth"), and guidebooks to the hereafter (from the 18th dynasty on: *Book of the Two Ways, Amduat,* and others). Ritual texts throwing light on the temple cult and hymns are preserved on temple walls and on papyri from the 18th dynasty on. Rare, however, are theological treatises like the "Memphite Theology," in which the creation of the world, its regulation by Ptah, and the supremacy of Memphis are confirmed theologically. Prayers are handed down in fixed formulas and, beginning in the 18th dynasty, in free form. Mythical subjects mainly are dealt with in ritual texts. Narrated myths form a part of the narrative literature, and the so-called tales are often built upon mythical material.

Later literary sources. The main source in the Old Testament is the story of Joseph in Genesis and Exodus. The Psalms and the apocryphal Wisdom of Solomon show Egyptian influence. Some things have been learned from the correspondence between the pharaohs and the rulers of Syria and Palestine preserved in Tell el-Amarna. The accounts of Greek and Roman historians and travellers are of particular value: Hecataeus of Miletus (6th century BC), Herodotus (5th century BC), Diodorus Siculus (1st century BC), Strabo, the geographer (1st century BC–1st century AD). Egyptian ideas in retouched form are to be found in Plutarch's *De Iside et Osiride* and Apuleius' *Metamorphoses* (*The Golden Ass*). Other important sources are the lexicographer Isidore of Seville (about AD 600) and the *Suda* Lexicon (late 10th century AD).

RELIGIOUS BELIEFS

The gods. Egyptian gods have different forms and personify different powers. There are numerous animal forms: bull gods like Apis at Memphis, Mnevis at Heliopolis, Buchis at Hermonthis; rams like Khnum at Elephantine and the ram of Mendes; falcons like Horus, the god of the king; doglike animals such as the god of the cemeteries, Anubis, and Wepwawet, the "Opener-of-the-Ways"; vulture goddesses like Mut in Karnak and Nekhbet in Elkab. They may also have a human form or a hybrid form with an animal head. Powers of nature like Re, the sun; Nut, the sky; Geb, the earth; and Thoth, the moon (and therefore "the reckoner of time"), are mainly rendered in human form but can also assume animal form (*e.g.,* Thoth as ibis or baboon). Ptah of Memphis, the creator-god; Min of Coptos, the god of fertility; Khons of Thebes as moon god; and Osiris as chthonian (underworld) fertility god are mostly human-shaped. Amon-Re of Karnak, usually in human form, can also have the form of a ram or a Nile goose and is looked upon as "breath of life," too. In theological theories each god is attributed as many powers as possible, hence the wide variety of divine manifestations.

Ma'at, the central conception of order, can be called a goddess insofar as she is represented as such, has a temple in Karnak, and is called "daughter of Re." But actually she is an abstract idea apart from the world of the gods.

Cosmogonies

Myths. Cosmogonies and other myths illustrate the order of the world and the cooperation of the gods. One cosmogony presents the image of a primeval hill emerging from the primeval flood (Nu) and bearing the first life. The Heliopolitan cosmogony says that the primeval god, Atum, spat out or coughed up the first couple of gods, Shu and Tefnut (air and moisture), or created them by self-generation. Shu separated heaven (Nut) from earth (Geb). These five gods are thought of as three generations. Osiris, the chthonian fertility god, is joined by Isis, his wife, and Seth, his murderer, who is married to Nephthys, the "Hostess of the House." Horus, the king's god and the son and heir of Osiris, rules here on earth. The myth of Osiris, the dead god, who begets a son out of the underworld, is connected with the cult of the first kings at Abydos. There, the so-called Osiris mysteries, annually reenacting the mysterious event, developed. To the Egyptian they mean the central point in his hope for life; to the Hellenists they symbolize the mysterious teachings of ancient Egypt. The connection of the gods of the Heliopolitan cosmogony with the gods of the Osiris family as "Children of Nut" makes up a family tree, reaching from the creator-god, Atum, to the ruling king, the "Living Horus."

Human nature and destiny. Man possesses spiritual power extending in part beyond his personal life.

Concepts of soul. First of all there is the *ka,* which, created with the person, can be defined as "vital force" and outlasts man. The bird-shaped *ba*-soul seems to be set free only after death. Gods too have *ba*- and *ka*-souls. The bird-shaped *akh*-soul is also preserved after death and can appear as a ghost or revenant. The heart is considered as the seat of the power of discrimination, and therefore the word "heart" also has the meaning "conscience." Image and name, which mainly play a part in magic, are to a certain extent regarded as independent.

Ethics. Ethics is part of social life. Its rules, preserved in biographies and teachings, do not refer to an absolute good or evil but are meant to guarantee a harmonious coexistence free from the use of force. They differ as to the social rank of the individual. They can be taught and aim to convince by common sense. It is only in the New Kingdom that ethics is directed at man's reflective nature and thus comes into intimate relationship with religion. The first conceptions of this kind can be found in the First Intermediate Period, but it is only later that they become popular belief. Right actions spring from a godfearing mind, and God inspires man's mind in the right way.

FORMS OF EGYPTIAN RELIGION

Funerary religion. Many rites deal with the provisions for life after death. The dead man's body is preserved by mummification; numerous amulets guarantee its invulnerability. Offerings at the burial and on funerary festivals in the tombs provide him with food and drink. The mortuary equipment, with all its useful and luxurious articles, is at his disposal. All serve the subsistence of the dead, who live in the tombs or return to them. Imagination created various conceptions of the hereafter. In one of them it is situated in heaven. The soul ascends or flies to heaven, lives among the stars or the entourage of the sun, and finds food and all its needs in the fields of the blessed. According to other conceptions, the hereafter is situated in the underworld. The soul finds its way there through passages and doors guarded by doorkeepers, trying to ward it off. It also has to cross watercourses. In books of the hereafter, the underworld is divided into 12 regions, visited by the sun on its nightly course, bringing life for a short period. The idea of a judgment of the dead developed from the hope that the dead person could find a tribunal in the hereafter, where he could sue for his claims. In the early period the dead king or Re or Osiris is the supreme judge. From the First Intermediate Period on, the conception changes; the dead person has to prove his right to enter the hereafter. It is not until the 18th dynasty that the classical picture of the judgment of the dead is formed, with Osiris

Conceptions of the afterlife

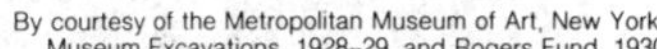
By courtesy of the Metropolitan Museum of Art, New York, Museum Excavations, 1928–29, and Rogers Fund, 1930

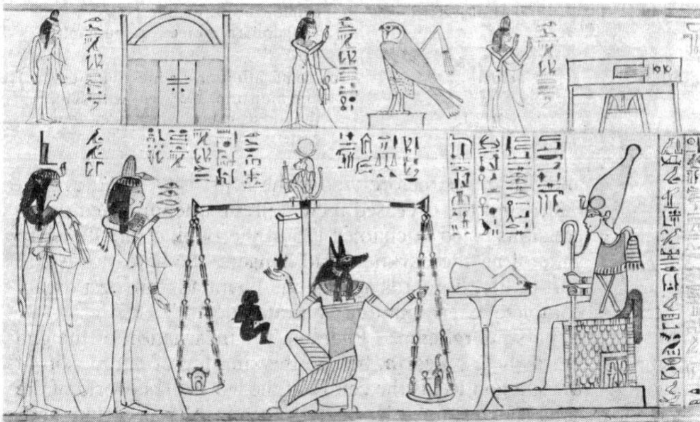
The judgment of the dead. While Osiris, the ruler of the dead, watches from his throne, the jackal-headed god Anubis weighs the heart of the deceased against the figure of Ma'at. Funerary papyrus from Thebes, *c.* 1025 BC.

Table 2: Minor Gods and Goddesses

	alternative names	areas of responsibility	principal sanctuary	relations to other deities	symbols and emblems
Anhur	Onouris	symbolized the creative power of the sun; frequently invoked against enemies and noxious animals	Sebennytus, This	probably a war-like personification of Re	warrior wearing a long embroidered robe and a headdress with four tall plumes; often carries a lance
Anuket	Anqet, Anquet	personification of the Nile as the nourisher of the fields	island of Sahal near Elephantine	second wife of Khnum; sister of Sati; member of the triad of Elephantine	woman wearing a crown of feathers and carrying a sceptre and the *ankh*
Apepi	Apep, Apophis, Rerek	personification of darkness and evil; attempted to obstruct the passage of the solar barque	as the embodiment of evil, Apepi had no worshippers	eternal enemy of the sun god Re	huge serpent
Hapi	Hap, Hep, Apis	god of the Nile, particularly of the inundation; bringer of fertility; nourisher of the gods and man	region of the First Cataract	husband of Nekhbet	bearded man coloured green or blue, with female breasts and a clump of water plants on his head
Khenty-Imentiu	Khenti-amentiu, Ophis (or Ophois)	warrior god; god of the dead until deposed by Osiris; at times piloted the sun's boat during its nocturnal voyage	Abydos, Asyûṭ	associated with Osiris during that god's conquest of the world, later identified with Upuaut (Wepwawet)	male figure with the head of a wolf or a jackal
Kheper	Khepera, Khepri	symbolized the daily cycle of the sun across the sky; sometimes thought to be a symbol of the rising sun	Heliopolis	one of the forms of the sun god Re	a scarab pushing the sun across the sky or a man with a scarab on his head
Khnum	Khnemu	god of the cataract region; earlier associated with the abyss of the netherworld; in some places thought to be the potter god who formed the world and its inhabitants	Elephantine	husband of Sati and Anuket; member of the triad of Elephantine	ram-headed male figure
Khons	Khensu, Khonsu, Chons	moon god; during the New Kingdom, an exoroist and healer	Thebes; later all of Egypt	adopted son of Amon and Mut	swathed figure with its head shaven except for the braid of royal progeny and the skull cap holding the lunar disk and crescent
Mont	Mentu, Month	war god of Upper Egypt; during the Middle Kingdom, lord of the sun and sky with Re	Hermonthis	a form of the sun god Re	male figure with the head of a hawk surmounted by the solar disk and two plumes; often carried a curved scimitar
Nefertum	Nefertem, Nefertemu	god of the lotus, thus having a life-giving aspect	Memphis	son of Ptah and Sekhmet (or Bast), third member of the Memphite triad	lion-headed man wearing a headdress composed of a lotus flower, two plumes and two menats
Neith	Neit	goddess of war and the loom	Sais	self-begotten virgin; according to some legends, the mother of Re	carried arrows crossed on an animal skin; on her head, wore the Red Crown of Lower Egypt or a weaver's shuttle
Nephthys	Nebhat	associate of Isis in the Osiris cycle	Heliopolis	mother of Anubis, wife of Seth; sister of Isis, Osiris, Seth, and Horus	female figure wearing horns and the solar disk on her head
Nu	Nun	personification of the primordial watery abyss from which the world was created; and, therefore, the oldest and wisest of all gods	Hermopolis	guarded Shu and Tefnut at birth	male or female figure, sometimes with the head of a frog; occasionally shown plunged up to his waist in water
Sati	Satet, Satis	goddess of the inundation and of fertility	Island of Sahal near Elephantine	principal wife of Khnum; sister of Anuket; member of the triad of Elephantine	female figure wearing the crown of the South and a pair of horns, and holding a sceptre and the *ankh* (or a bow and arrows)
Seker	Sokar, Sokaris	deity of darkness and decay in the earth	Memphis	identified with Ptah and Osiris as Ptah-Seker-Osiris	hawk or hawk-headed mummy
Seshat	Sesheta	goddess of writing and history; measurer of time; foundress of temples	Hermopolis Magna	principal wife of Thoth	female figure wearing a leopard skin and holding a writing reed and a scribe's palette; on her head, a crescent (or two turned-down horns) and two plumes
Taurt	Apet, Opet, Taweret, Thoueris	goddess of maternity, presided over childbirth; during the New Kingdom, a protective household deity	Thebes	often appeared with Bes	pregnant hippopotamus standing on hind legs and holding two plaits of rolled papyrus
Tefnut	Tefnet	personification of the life-giving dew and moisture; received, with Shu, the sun as it broke free from the eastern horizon	Heliopolis	sister and wife of Shu	lioness or a woman with the head of a lion wearing the solar disk and the *uraeus* (occasionally, represented as the *uraeus* itself)

and 42 judges, before whom the heart is weighed against *maʿat* and the deceased recites all the uncommitted transgressions listed in chapter 125 of the Book of the Dead. In spite of all the darkness and dangers, the hereafter is still part of life. It guards against the Egyptians' greatest dread: complete extermination, "repeated death."

Divine kingship: pharaoh as god

The state religion. Pharaoh, the incarnation of the god Horus here on earth, heir to the kingship of Atum, son of the sun god Re, is the centre of the world. The world of the gods is determined by his existence insofar as certain gods (Re, Atum, Ptah, etc.), following his example, acquire the rank of "King of the Gods," are arranged in dynasties, and are placed in traditional histories as godkings before the earthly kings. The existence of a legitimate pharaoh guarantees the order of the cosmos. This is expressed above all in the king's designation as "Lord of the Ritual." In theory he is the only priest who can perform the daily temple ritual and the festival rituals in accordance with *maʿat,* thus preserving the order of the cosmos, the fertility of the land, and the order and welfare of the empire.

The temple cult. The temple was "god's house," in which the god lived in the form of his cult statue. The daily ritual included the opening of the shrine, the decorating and dressing of the statue, and the offering of food and drink following the daily routine of the king.

Priesthood. The ritual was performed by official priests as representatives of the king. Knowledge of the ritual and maintenance of the rules of purity were the essential requisites for priestly service; a differentiation between priests and laymen seems to have occurred late. The priesthood itself consisted of numerous classes. Large temples had four main priests ("prophets"), numerous minor priests, singers, musicians, scribes, and temple employees. As each temple owned land, villages, workshops, and sometimes even quarries and foreign landholdings, it was virtually an independent economic unit, with personnel corresponding to its size. During the temple service, hymns and songs describing his nature and activity accompanied the appearance of the god. Formulas naming the objects (incense, food offerings, jewelry, clothes) and identifying both the ritual as a whole and the different objects with mythical elements were part of the ritual. Thus the ritual acts were elevated to a mythical level and drawn into manifold connections with mythical ideas.

Festivals. The numerous festivals were partly of local, partly of general importance. They were held on birthdays of gods, on special calendar days (New Year, first days of the months), at seasonal events (harvest festival), king's ceremonies (coronation, so-called jubilees), and victory celebrations. Important festivals lasted several days. Most of the temple festivals were connected with a procession of the god's image and often with a visit to other temples. On these occasions the god was visible to the public and gave oracles.

Religious, social, and economic roles. Since Egyptian religion was centred on temple ritual, individual faith (*i.e.,* personal piety) was never of primary importance and was therefore perceptible only in later periods. On the other hand, religion played a decisive part in social and economic life. A large part of the population was integrated into the official hierarchy of priests and temple personnel. As knowledge of the holy scriptures and the ability to interpret and reformulate them was required, the higher priesthood achieved a high standard of education. Since the temples were economic units, which at times owned large estates, they constituted a major factor in the national economy. The lands administered by them were in many cases more favourably taxed than private property.

Magic, divination, and popular religion. Magical power—through knowledge of the name, possession of the image, application of the "right" word, and the use of amulets—was a weapon in man's fight against supernatural powers. The boundaries between magic and ritual were fluid. The results desired from ritual actions (fertility, order in nature, etc.) can be ascribed to both magical power and divine activity. Oracles certainly date from early periods, but their importance increased from the New Kingdom on. Political decisions (*e.g.,* the election of the king) and personal affairs (*e.g.,* the beginning of a journey, the choice of a profession) as well as judicial investigations were brought before the god in the form of alternative questions and were apparently decided by movements of the image.

Oracles

Since the public was generally excluded from the temple cult (apart from festival processions), they turned to divine beings and objects outside the temples (*e.g.,* the "Western Peak" at Thebes) or to certain images of gods and kings in the outer districts of the temples (*e.g.,* "Ptah in the Door-Frame" at Madīnat Habu). Statues and tombs of famous deceased were also adored. Some of these "popular gods" were recognized by Egyptian theology and integrated into theological systems (*e.g.,* Imhotep, the architect of King Djoser, is first patron of scribes, later a god and the son of Ptah). The religious revival following the heresy of Amenhotep IV (Akhenaton) originated apart from the official theology and influenced religion for centuries.

RELIGIOUS SYMBOLISM AND ICONOGRAPHY

In accordance with the faculty for abstraction and the limited sense of individuality typical of Egyptian culture as a whole, the representation of religious conceptions was characterized by a series of religious symbols and emblems rather than by the creation of individual god figures. Of all the images of gods, that of Isis with the child Horus on her lap, perhaps the prototype of the Madonna with the Child, is the most noteworthy. The image of the youthful sun god on a lotus blossom also exerted an influence outside Egypt. Among the symbols that were used as ornaments were the *crux ansata* (the symbol of life), the divine eye as symbol of prosperity, the scarab beetle standing for eternal regeneration, the knot of Isis as protective symbol, the crook as sign of kingship, the winged sun as symbol of the sun god, the *djed*-pillar as symbol of endurance, and the *was*-sceptre (a shepherd's staff) and *nefer*-sign as symbols of both fortune and welfare. Significant among architectural forms are pyramids, obelisks, and cavetto cornices, the last, however, having no symbolic value.

HISTORICAL DEVELOPMENT

A large number of the gods go back to prehistoric times. The images of a cow and star goddess (Hathor), the falcon (Horus), and human-shaped figures of the fertility god (Min) can be traced back to that period. Some rites, such as the "running of the Apis-bull," the "hoeing of the ground," and other fertility and hunting rites (*e.g.,* the hippopotamus hunt), presumably date from early times. To explain the existence of a variety of gods at different places, the following theory is often referred to: Egypt consisted of numerous nomes, or provinces, each having its own gods. When they were united at the beginning of the 3rd millennium BC, they retained their local gods, thus creating the pantheon. This theory cannot be proved. Connections with the religions in southwest Asia cannot be traced with certainty. It is doubtful whether Osiris can be regarded as equal to Tammuz or Adonis or whether Hathor is related to the "Great Mother." There are closer relations with northeast African religions. The numerous animal cults (especially bovine cults and panther gods) and details of the ritual dresses (animal tails, masks, grass aprons, etc.) probably are of African origin. The kingship in particular shows some African elements, such as the king as the head ritualist (*i.e.,* medicine man), the limitation and renewal of the reign (jubilees, regicide), and the position of the king's mother (a matriarchal element). Some of them can be found among the Ethiopians in Napata and Meroe, others among Prenilotic tribes (Shilluk).

The pantheon as synthesis of earlier local gods

The religion of independent Egypt. The history of Egyptian religion is less one of change in cults and gods than one of change in ideas and beliefs within the existing mythological and ritual sphere. In the Old Kingdom the state religion in particular was developed: the king as Horus and son of Re at the head of an ordered and well-organized world. Evidence concerning personal beliefs is almost wholly lacking. The collapse of the Old Kingdom brought with it the dissolution of the old social and intellectual bonds. At this time questions concerning the origin of evil, the end of the world, the responsibility of man, and life in the hereafter were passionately discussed, with the traditional religious forms and figures receding into the background. The concept of the gods became personal and undogmatic.

Although the Middle Kingdom returned to the old forms, the following period showed that the ideas of the First Intermediate Period had not been lost. At the beginning of the New Kingdom, the Egyptian sphere expanded enormously. The boundaries of the empire reached from the Fourth Cataract of the Nile to the upper Euphrates, and the acquaintance with Syrian and Palestinian cultures and religions enriched Egyptian thinking. Foreign gods (Resheph, Astarte, Baal) were worshipped in Egypt. This expansion took place under the supremacy of the god Amon-Re at Karnak. Tensions with his priesthood led to the heresy of Amenhotep IV. Opposing the claim to authority of Amon-Re of Karnak and his priesthood and intending to give an all-uniting god to the empire, Amenhotep IV (Akhenaton) made the sun disk, Aton, the supreme god and proclaimed himself his only interpreter. The attempt to establish a new religion followed the old sun belief and was accompanied by the attempt to create a new style of life and art. His attempt failed because of the god's claim to exclusiveness, his struggle against the existing economic order, his political failure, and, last but not least, his underrating of the belief in Osiris. His death was followed by a restoration period, which tried to extinguish all traces of his innovations. The breakdown of the movement was followed by an apparent restoration

Amenhotep IV (Akhenaton): the Amarna heresy

of the traditional cults. But religious thought was strongly influenced by the rise of a feeling of guilt and sin that brought the individual into a new ethical relationship to the gods. Individual confessions and prayers and moral justifications of the teachings were symptomatic of the new religious climate.

In the Late Period various tendencies of religious development can be distinguished. The ethicizing and personalizing of religion continued. The importance of Amon-Re, who was closely linked to the policy of the New Kingdom, decreased, while that of Osiris and his so-called mysteries increased in response to the religious demands of the time. In addition, popular beliefs and their cults came increasingly to the fore: animal cults and oracles grew in number, local gods in importance. Cult prescriptions and purity laws apparently separated priests from laity to a greater extent than before. A discrepancy between cult forms and beliefs can be said to have begun.

Egyptian religion in the Greco-Roman world. When Egypt came under the rule of the Macedonian Ptolemies and later of the Roman emperors, the ancient cults continued to exist in their external forms. According to representations in the temples, the Ptolemaic kings and Roman emperors took the role of the pharaoh. Yet differences are still apparent. The layout of the temples (Dandarah, Edfu, Ombos, etc.) was standardized. All sorts of religious texts were written on temple walls, often in purposely mysterious spelling. A special cult for the Ptolemaic kings and queens was introduced in the temples, and some Hellenistic ideas seem to have been adopted and combined with native ideas by the Egyptian priests. The influence of the Egyptian on the Hellenistic mind was undoubtedly stronger than the reverse influence. In the Hellenic world Egyptian gods and cults were widely known through the histories of Hecataeus and Herodotus and the accounts of Greek merchants and mercenaries. Herodotus thought the Egyptian gods to be identical with the Greek ones (Zeus = Amon, Pan = Min, Athena = Neith, etc.).

For political reasons Ptolemy I Soter wanted to create a cult common to Egyptians and Macedonians. The deified Memphite Apis-bull, Osiris-Apis, became the prototype of the god Sarapis and acquired a Greek cultic image alleged to be from Sinope on the Black Sea. Its cultic centre was the new capital, Alexandria, whence the cult migrated to Europe more than to Egypt. The Hellenistic world, which favoured mystery religions with special zeal, adopted the cults of Osiris, Isis, and Horus (Harpocrates), transforming them in the manner of the mysteries of the late classical world. They were spread over the entire Roman Empire. The hymns to Osiris or Harpocrates preserved in Greek are translations of Egyptian texts. The conception of Isis as the goddess of navigation was formed in Alexandria. Not only Sarapis but also Osiris, Isis, and Horus adopted new forms in Hellenistic and Roman art; similarly Anubis was seen as a Roman warrior and Apis as an emperor. Particularly significant as the initiator of theosophy—a system of beliefs concerning God and the world based on mystical insights—is Hermes Trismegistos (in Egyptian, "Thoth the Very Great"), who is said to be the author of the Hermetic Scripts. As the so-called Thrice Great he was acknowledged by Christianity to some degree, because he was supposed to have expounded the Trinity. Egyptian theories often found their way, in many cases newly interpreted, into the philosophy of the late classical world (Plotinus, Neoplatonism) and Gnosticism—a Hellenistic religious movement that viewed spirit as good and matter as evil.

Mystery religions

Egyptian conversion to Christianity and the coming of Islām. Egypt was Christianized very early, probably in the time of the Apostles. St. Mark, the author of the First Gospel, is regarded as the founder of Egyptian Christianity. It is certainly no accident that the Egyptian Christian Church (the Coptic Church) adhered to the Monophysite theory that Christ had one nature (a view held heretical by the Council of Chalcedon in AD 451). This is surely connected with the Egyptian understanding of deity, which made a distinction between a divine and human person unnecessary. Besides that, however, hardly anything of ancient Egyptian religion can be found in Egyptian Christianity. Yet even after the Islāmic conquest (AD 641), many individual features have continued to survive in popular belief and may still be found in the veneration of saints, and in popular customs and superstitions. (E.O.)

Arabian religions

Under the name Arabian religions are grouped the cults that flourished in the Arabian Peninsula, or in adjoining areas among Arabic-speaking peoples, from earliest recorded times until the rise of Islām in the 7th century AD.

NATURE AND SIGNIFICANCE

In the modern world, Arabia has been so frequently and so thoroughly linked with the religious tradition of Islām that its pre-Islāmic religious history has received relatively little attention. Yet pre-Islāmic Arabia had a rich and diverse culture, in which the primitive and the cosmopolitan, the urban and the nomadic, often were found side by side.

Islām itself has done much to characterize its own background, for from its 7th-century beginnings Islām was presented as a new revelation, this time in Arabic, summing up the monotheistic tradition of the previous Jewish and Christian prophets. In so doing, it looked to revelations outside Arabia for its religious antecedents, explicitly rejecting as idols the local Arabian deities, and as superstition many of their religious practices. Classical Arab authors referred to what preceded the revelation of the Qur'ān as *jāhilīyah* ("ignorance," or, better, "barbarism"). Traditional Muslims, in short, have held Islām to be discontinuous with its Arabian past.

Some modern Western scholars, on the other hand, have attempted to see in pagan Arabian religion not only the antecedents of Islāmic religious practices but also a very early, if not original, strain of Semitic religion. The late-19th-century attempt to locate antecedent "causes" of biblical religion in the Middle East promised to be nearly as threatening to Christian and Jewish orthodoxy as the location of antecedents of Islām appeared to be for that faith. More recent scholarship, however, has sidestepped such theological issues, and in historical presentations, Arabian developments have also appeared more complex than earlier they had been thought to be.

SOURCES OF MODERN KNOWLEDGE

Documents from within ancient Arabia are fragmentary. Scholars must depend heavily, therefore, on other cultures' records of contact with Arabia. The earliest appear in the cuneiform annals of ancient Mesopotamia in certain scattered personal names, Arabic in form, in the 3rd millennium BC, and then in names of Arabian tribes, kingdoms, and even deities in the 1st millennium BC. A few Egyptian texts make similar mention of Arabic names.

Literary sources

Several biblical genealogies, reflecting Israelite tribal traditions before 1000 BC, record the Hebrews' sense of their close kinship and rivalry with the peoples of the desert fringe of Arabia. The account of a visit to King Solomon (died 922 BC) by an Arabian queen, reportedly Sabaean, suggests Israelite contact with the hinterland during the period of the Hebrew kingdoms.

The Greeks came to Arabia as traders, the Romans to its northern perimeter as both traders and rulers. Of the several classical authors (Arrian, Strabo, Origen, and others) who discuss Arabia, the 5th-century-BC Greek historian Herodotus is of chief interest because of his readiness to identify Arabian deities with the Greek gods of Olympus—both as to their function in the pantheon and as to their associations with the planets. In later Roman imperial times, southern Arabia was mentioned little, but northern Arabia continued to figure in literature, primarily in Syriac and Byzantine writings.

Poetry from central Arabia in the pre-Islāmic era was later recorded by Muslims, possibly with a certain degree of expurgation of pagan references; religion appears incidental in most of these pre-Islāmic odes, so that in some cases, for example, it is unclear to which community a poet belonged—pagan, Christian, or Jewish. Certain historians and geographers (Ibn Hishām, aṭ-Ṭabarī, Yāqūt, and especially al-Ḥamdānī in his *Iklīl*) wrote about pre-

Islāmic affairs. Also significant in the Arabic sources are the references to, and repudiation of, polytheism in the Qurʿān itself and the treatise of the Muslim author Ibn al-Kalbī (early 9th century AD) that is known as *Kitāb al-aṣnām* ("Book of Idols"). Finally, an uncertain but suggestive nonliterary source for Arabian culture is the survival of ancient customs and traditions among the Bedouin.

Inscriptions

The test of historical reconstructions based on any of the foregoing sources is the inscriptional and archaeological material of the pre-Islāmic Arabs themselves. Since the 1840s, thousands of inscriptions and graffiti have been recorded from the entire length of the Arabian Peninsula. These are in several dialects of Arabic, in addition to inscriptions by Arabs in the related Semitic languages known as Nabataean and Palmyrene. Most of the inscriptions consist only of the names and genealogies of their authors, with occasional prayers, drawings, or references to everyday activities—insignificant individually but instructive in the aggregate.

Only a few archaeologists have had the opportunity to excavate in Arabia in the 20th century; a few sanctuaries are known as a result of their work. Numismatic evidence for Arabian religion is slender, since Arabian coinage for a long time copied the well-known Athenian owl with little variety in symbols or legends.

THE HISTORICAL SETTING

South Arabia. The kingdoms of South Arabia, which are known to have flourished from the 1st millennium BC, included the kingdoms of Maʿīn, Sabaʾ, Qatabān, Awsān, Ḥaḍramawt, and Himyar. With a decline in economic fortunes after the 1st century BC because of changes in the Greco-Roman trade routes to India, the centre of population and cultural influence shifted northward from the Yemen to the Hejaz, which was ruled in the early Christian centuries by Ethiopia. Although the religion of South Arabia was polytheistic, the monotheistic communities of Jews and of Christians in the Hejaz gained in influence. The break of the Maʾrib Dam in the Yemen (*c.* AD 575), which brought about the total collapse of irrigation in the area, was an event that later Islāmic tradition considered as dramatizing the eclipse of ancient South Arabian culture.

Northern and central Arabia. The northern and central Arabian Peninsula contained both cities, at oases and on the desert perimeter, and nomadic populations. The name "Arabs" appears in historical sources during the 1st millennium BC; the Assyrian Shalmaneser III mentions "Gindibu the Arab" in an inscription commemorating the battle of Karkar in Syria (854 BC). In an inscription of the Assyrian king Tiglath-pileser III (died 727 BC) a kingdom of "Aribi" is mentioned. On the desert fringe of the Persian, Greek, and Roman empires, the caravan and oassis cities prospered. Most notable of these were Petra, the capital of the Nabateans, which flourished in the 1st centuries BC and AD; and the oasis of Palmyra, northeast of Damascus, which reached its zenith in the 3rd century AD. Arab kingdoms also arose on the frontiers of Persia: Characene in lower Mesopotamia and Mesene (Gerrha) on the Persian Gulf. From the 3rd to the 6th centuries the Lakhmid dynasty ruled al-Ḥīrah, a buffer state of the Sāsānian Persians and a centre of Arab Christianity, while the rival Byzantines sponsored the Ghassānid dynasty in 6th-century Syria.

PRE-ISLĀMIC DEITIES

Pre-Islāmic Arabian religion is commonly understood to be polytheistic. Of the many Arabian deities, only some of the more important will be mentioned here.

Astral deities

South Arabian deities. In the official cults of the South Arabian kingdoms, the devotees venerated most highly a triad of deities that were astral in character: the moon god, the sun goddess, and the god equated with the planet Venus. Each of these deities bore a variety of names, depending on the region, or on a particular attribute of the divinity. Chief among the triad was the moon god, who was the protector of the principal cities. The people of the various kingdoms and areas referred to themselves as his offspring, each under a different name: the Sabaeans were the children of Ilumquh ("God Is Power"), the Minaeans the children of Wadd ("Love"), the Qatabānians the children of ʿAmm ("Uncle"), and the people of Ḥadramawt the offspring of Sin (the name of the moon god in ancient Babylonia). In each region other names of the moon god appear, derived from aspects of the lunar cycle or other attributes. Next among the triad was Venus, the morning and evening star, named ʿAthtar, who also had a variety of attributes. Third was the sun goddess, whose principal name, Shams, was common to the various kingdoms, like ʿAthtar, but whose paired epithets, describing contrasting aspects, varied locally.

Despite the prominence of the name elsewhere among Semitic peoples, the god Il (El) appears to play a comparatively minor role in the South Arabian inscriptions. Some modern scholars have sought to explain this circumstance by equating Il with the moon god, but this opinion has not prevailed.

The remaining list of South Arabian deities is long, and many of them appear to have had a more particularized function than that of the major triad. Some were guardians of clans or of places, and two Qatabānian deities watched over boundaries and irrigation, respectively. Other deities' names, to cite only a few, were attributes, such as Yithaʿ ("Saviour"), Nasrum ("Eagle"), Raʿat ("He Who Instills Fear"), Dhū ʿAwdhān ("He Who Preserves"), and Mutībaqabt ("He Who Guarantees the Harvest").

El, or Ilāh, and Bel

North Arabian deities. Among the peoples around the northern perimeter of Arabia, "god," in the most generic sense, was El, or in a longer form of the same name, Ilāh. His veneration at a very early stage is attested by his appearance in theophoric names, that is, personal names of which one element is a divine name (the biblical name Gabriel is an example). Among nomadic tribes in particular, a residual sense of El as being the god par excellence remained until the time of Islām.

Astral or local deities, however, tended to displace El in the Nabataean and Palmyrene kingdoms. Although El was preserved in early Nabataean theophoric compounds, in Palmyra a more central place in the cult went to Bel (Baal, "Lord"), and in both Petra and Palmyra to Belshamin ("Lord of the Heavens"). With Bel, sometimes in a triad, the Palmyrenes associated Yarhibol, a solar deity, and Aglibol, a lunar deity; while Belshamin stood in a triadic relationship with the gods Malakbel, also a solar deity, and Aglibol.

Al-Lāt, Al-ʿUzzā, and Manāt. Among the Quúrʾān's references to its 7th-century pagan milieu are three goddesses, called daughters of Allāh: al-Lāt, al-ʿUzzā, and Manāt; these are also known from earlier inscriptions in northern Arabia. Al-Lāt ("the Goddess") may have had a role subordinate to that of El (Ilāh), as "daughter" rather than consort, but at aṭ-Ṭāʾif and a number of other sites in northern Arabia she is mentioned as al-Lāt-of-a-particular-place, as the local deity. At Palmyra she was equated with Athena. As for her two partners in the Qurʾānic triad, the goddess al-ʿUzzā ("Strong") was known among the Nabataeans, while Manāt ("Fate") was associated at Palmyra with the Greek Nemesis. Another principal goddess was Ruḍā, whose name is the feminine form of Arso, a deity whom Herodotus had mentioned in the 5th century BC along with al-Lāt as the sole recipients of worship among the Arabs.

Other indigenous deities. Other indigenous deities included the Nabataean Dhū-Sharā and Shaiʿ-ha-Qawm ("Protector of the People"), who also were invoked among neighbouring nomads. Local protectors were the deities named Gad ("Fortune"), often specified as the Gad of a particular place or, especially among the nomads, of a particular tribe.

The legacy of earlier Canaanite and Babylonian culture was noticeable on the northern perimeter of Arabia, particularly in Palmyra. There, the list of deities named or portrayed included the Babylonian gods Nergal (associated with Heracles) and Nabu or Nebo (associated with Apollo), the Syrian goddess Atargatis, and possibly the Babylonian goddesses Astarte (Ishtar) and Beltis (Beltu, feminine equivalent of Bel).

RELIGIOUS OBJECTS, PRACTICES, AND INSTITUTIONS

Sacred stones. A principal sacred object in Arabian religion was the stone, either a rock outcropping or a large boulder, often a rectangular or irregular black basaltic stone without representative sculptural detail. Such stones were thought to be the residences of a god—hence the term for them employed by Byzantine Christian writers in the 5th and 6th centuries: baetyl, from *bet ʾel,* "house of the god."

The baetyls

The best known baetyl is the Black Stone of the Kaʿbah at Mecca, which became the central shrine object of Islām. But there were others: Ibn al-Kalbī wrote of the square stone central to the cult of al-Lāt at aṭ-Ṭāʾif. Suidas, the compiler of a Greek lexicon and encyclopaedia of *c.* AD 1000, described the baetyl of Dhū-Sharā at Petra as a rectangular black stone on a gold base. There were baetyls at Ramm, southeast of Petra, of which the baetyl of al-Lāt-of-Bostra was in the form of a pedestal.

Just how sophisticated the Arabian peoples were in distinguishing the image from the deity is a matter of judgment. Perhaps the pedestal form indicated that the baetyl was the dwelling or throne of the god; a Nabataean term meaning "seat" apparently implies so, as does the etymology of baetyl itself, while the South Arabian term "the seat of the deities" may also imply the location of images in the temple. Some sources, however, associate the name of the deity with a word for stone or baetyl; some South Arabic texts refer to ʿAthtar as Hagar, "Stone." And a particular baetyl might have been venerated in and for itself; northern Syrians were reported to have venerated "Symbaetylos Leon"; *i.e.,* baetyl and lion in association. An inscription on an altar at Doura-Europus (Dura-Europos) on the Euphrates indicates that it was dedicated by a Syrian soldier to the ancestral god Zeus-Baetyl.

Sanctuaries. Characteristically, a Semitic sanctuary was a rectangular enclosure known as a *ḥaram,* "reserved space." Portions of it could be covered or roofed over with porticoes. An altar was central. There often was a well or cistern with water for ablutions, and a sacred tree on which might be hung offerings of visitors or trophies of war. The *ḥaram* served as a place of asylum for all living beings, including both men and animals. The trees growing in the area were likewise inviolate. The larger temples that have been excavated had many rooms, some denoted by words that imply kneeling, others implying burning. In small shrines, and particularly in household usage, one room might suffice for all such activity.

In North Arabian temples the image of the deity sometimes stood in the open air, or could be sheltered in a *qubbah,* a vaulted niche. Such a niche might be portable; a portable shelter is represented graphically on a Palmyrene relief. Not to be confused with the *qubbah* is the word *kaʿbah,* for a cube-shaped walled structure, which, though not portable, was constructed possibly after the shape of tents and served as a shelter for the sacred stones.

Considerable attention was given in Arabia to funerary practices and structures. Tombs were often as substantially built as temples, even more substantially in the case of the Nabataeans, who hollowed their tomb-facades out of the solid sandstone of the cliffs surrounding Petra. A standing stone, erected over the tomb, or at Palmyra often a mausoleum tower, was called a *nefesh* ("self" or "soul"), and symbolized the presence of the departed soul.

Pilgrimages

Ceremonies and customs. A principal public celebration of the Arabians was an annual pilgrimage, in which tribes who shared a common bond of worship of a deity at a specific sanctuary would reunite there. A pattern of ceremonial procession around the baetyl was common, and this pattern may be seen in the surviving Islāmic custom of the pilgrimage to Mecca. Processions played a great part in ritual, and divine images were sometimes brought out of the sanctuary and carried in them.

Another practice that left its influence on Islām was ceremonial abstinence. The South Arabian festival of Ḥalfān was a moratorium on the use of weapons. Certain times were specified for fasting and abstention from sexual relations.

Burnt offerings and sacrifices were common. Some inscriptions mention sacrifices of as many as 30 or 40 animals. Sacrifices sometimes took place in a pilgrimage context, following the ceremonial procession around the baetyl; the blood of the animal victim, or in some instances milk as a substitute, was placed on the altar or baetyl. Incense and libations also were used.

Ritual banquets

At public ceremonies in South Arabia the congregation stood, except for sacrificial banquets, when benches were used. Ritual banquets occurred in the northern areas, too. The Palmyrenes celebrated them reclining on couches, as depicted in their tomb reliefs; and "in the presence of the god," according to one text. Stone-carved benches suitable for banquets have been found at Petra and at other Nabataean sanctuaries.

Individual devotions included worship of household gods, and devotions to the astral deities were performed on the roof terraces of South Arabia. In many cases individuals made votive inscriptions, accompanied by drawings or symbols; some of these inscriptions are stylized in form, suggesting that the public ceremonial also followed a liturgy, though its text is not preserved. Among the many Bedouin graffiti in the northern regions are prayers that the deity will grant health and safety, booty and prosperity, and vengeance on enemies, or will blind anyone who effaces the inscription. South Arabian inscriptions likewise indicate concern for personal and public prosperity, including thanksgiving, but also seek expiation for transgressions, many of them ritual. People sought answers by means of divination through the use of dice, oracles, dreams, and visions. Amulets also were used, some of them not only bearing designs but naming the deity.

Religious personages and institutions. In northern Arabia, certain tribes looked after particular sanctuaries. In the role of custodian, a man would be known as a *kāhin,* "priest," but such personnel were not, as far as is known, set apart by ordination. In some circumstances, the head of a family or the chief of the tribe served as the chief officiant in religious functions; in cities such as Palmyra, it is more likely that the priestly function was carried out by specialized personnel.

The South Arabian temples had three ranks of priests and assistants. The interrelation of the priestly with the political organization in the ancient kingdoms can be noted in the title *mukarribs* (probably "procurators"), of Sabaʾ who were among the first to develop a centralized political power.

As an institution, the temple received gifts both in money and in kind, including harvest offerings and tithes. The gifts in kind might be buildings, lands (which would yield revenue), slaves, animals, images and furnishings, spices and incense, and other supplies. Among the temple's functions was included a legal one: because the gods were witness to judgments and contracts, the temple was the repository of legal and regulatory documents.

MONOTHEISM IN ARABIA

Despite all that has been said, present scholarly knowledge of ancient Arabia remains fragmentary and is based on arguments that fill in the unknown by an assumption of continuity with the known. These continuities often cut across long time spans and depend on assumed constant patterns of religious beliefs and practices among the Semitic peoples—an assumption that may ignore the tracing of developments, difficult when inscriptions are not easily datable.

Pre-Islāmic Arabian monotheism. Yet on one topic, namely monotheism, the views of many scholars show a marked interest in developmental change. This topic arises in two contexts: the possibility of an original monotheism anterior to Arabian polytheism, and the possibility of a monotheism as a late development out of Arabian polytheism.

Arguments for an original monotheism are based largely on the ubiquity of the word *īl, ilāh,* for "god" in Semitic languages. Each tribe started with its own single god, it has been argued, and a polytheistic pantheon was derived from a situation where tribes, failing to identify others' deities with their own, expanded the list. Whatever the speculative possibilities of such a theory, the Arabian situation was polytheistic at the time of the first surviving records of it.

External monotheistic influences

More fascinating and more tangible are the indications that in the last few pre-Islāmic centuries an Arabian monotheism developed. There were, of course, monotheistic influences from outside Arabia. Christian missionaries and traders from Syria, Mesopotamia, and Ethiopia brought a variety of teachings, and a Christian settlement flourished at Najrān near the Yemen. There were Jewish communities at Ṣanʿāʾ in South Arabia, and at Khaybar, Yathrib (Medina), and Taymāʾ farther north. In the 4th and 5th centuries AD, a few Sabaean inscriptions appear to have ascribed all supreme functions to Ilāh, calling him Merciful, and Lord of Heaven or Earth. One text calls him the Great One of Judah, and another speaks of his son Christ the Victorious. Other traditions were also in a position to have influence in Arabia, notably Zoroastrianism and Manichaeism in Mesopotamia. Despite the possibility of such influence, it has not so far been demonstrated in the inscriptions.

The ḥanīf. It may well have been the presence of Christians and Jews that set the stage in the Hejaz for the so-called *ḥanīf*s, men who found the old cult of the gods inadequate to their level of spirituality and monotheistic ideals, and who repudiated what they could not associate with Ilāh. A couple of Muḥammad's relatives, and early supporters, were reported to have been *ḥanīf*s. *Ḥanīf*s were not Christian; the word *ḥanīf* appears to be a Christian Syriac loanword meaning "heathen." But they were evidently monotheists, and, coming on the eve of Islām, they mark the passing of the old Arabian religion.

(W.G.O.)

Syrian and Palestinian religions

Syrian and Palestinian religions, originating in the Stone Age and continuing into Hellenistic times, absorbed religious beliefs and practices of other ancient Middle Eastern religions and transmitted them—as well as their own indigenous cultic phenomena—to biblical, Greek, and Roman religions. The Syrian and Palestinian religions influenced Judaism, Christianity, and Islām insofar as these religions reacted to Syrian and Palestinian religious beliefs and practices.

NATURE AND SIGNIFICANCE

At least as early as the 3rd millennium BC, the area comprising what was later known as Syria and Palestine was the home of a linguistically and ethnically mixed population and the meeting place of cultural influences from all sides: Egypt, Mesopotamia, and Asia Minor. This complexity increased in later centuries and had as its counterpart a very complex religious picture. The typical political unit in the area was a city-state of limited geographic extent. Each of these states had its own pantheon and cult, and within the larger states there might be different ethnic and social groups carrying on their distinct religious beliefs and practices.

Common features

Certain common features can be discerned, however. The religion of each of these peoples was characterized by the worship of numerous gods. These gods were mostly conceived in anthropomorphic terms and images and were identified with, or guardians of, important elements of the universe and vital aspects of nature and of human society. The competing powers in the divine world were thought to be organized, rather loosely, into a council of gods, in which the storm god played an especially dominant role. Images of the gods stood in their houses, the temples, where organized priesthoods saw to it that they were supplied with food and clothing. Important conceptions as to the nature of the world, and of human society, were embodied in myths, which often took the form of narrative poems of considerable length and complexity. The dominant concerns of official religion were for the economic bases of society—that is, for abundant crops and fertility of herds and flocks—and for the state, especially for the well-being of the ruling king and the continuance of his line. Scholars have reasonably full information only about the religion of the Canaanites—one of the ancient peoples of Palestine-Syria—as attested in the Ugaritic texts (see below *Sources*) from the Late Bronze Age (15th–13th century BC), supplemented by other materials; hence, for practical reasons, Canaanite religion must occupy a central place in a description of the area's religions. Fortunately, there is good reason to suppose that Canaanite religion was typical and representative and maintained its dominant characteristics through the centuries, so that knowledge of that religion probably indicates the general nature and features of most of the other religions of the area.

The religions of ancient Syria-Palestine are of great intrinsic interest because of the variety of phenomena they encompass and because of the great antiquity of the conceptions they preserve, some of which doubtless derive from the Stone Age (*c.* 4000 BC). But beyond this interest, these religions are of extraordinary importance to the student of ancient Israelite religion. On the one hand, Canaanite religion constituted the antithesis to Israelite religion; and, on the other hand, it supplied a rich heritage of religious language, ideas, and ritual practices on which the Old Testament writers drew to an extent that is only beginning to be realized. Furthermore, Syrian religion enjoyed a vogue not only in the Hellenistic world (3rd century BC–3rd century AD) but centuries earlier, in the Minoan-Mycenaean age (*c.* 3000–*c.* 1100 BC), it exercised an influence on early Greek religion.

SOURCES OF MODERN KNOWLEDGE

Evidence for reconstruction of the ancient Syrian and Palestinian religions has increased astonishingly within the last 50 years, due to materials recovered by excavation; even so, however, the record is full of gaps. Moreover, ancient religious texts tend to be more difficult to interpret than historical records, business documents, or other such recovered materials.

Old Testament, Greek, and Roman sources

The Old Testament was, until comparatively recent times, the most ancient of sources available to scholars for study of the religions of Syria-Palestine. It supplies the names of some major deities, such as Baal (male fertility god) and Asherah (female fertility goddess); some cultic terms; and evidence for the major concerns of the native religion. The story of the Israelite prophet Elijah's contest with the prophets of Baal on Mt. Carmel (I Kings 18) is especially rich in information. But biblical evidence is scattered, fragmentary, and limited in value by its polemical character. Greek and Latin sources have long been drawn on to fill in the gap in knowledge of this subject, especially for Punic religion—the Syrian-derived religion of Carthage in North Africa—and for Syrian religion in the Hellenistic world. Along with inscriptions and coins, scattered passages in classical writers shed light on Syrian religion. Thus, the Roman historian Dio Cassius (*c.* AD 150–235) describes the devotion of the Syrian-born Roman emperor Elagabalus (reigned AD 218–222) to the sun god of his native Emesa, and Apuleius (flourished 2nd century AD) paints a vivid picture of the obscene rites that attended the worship of the Syrian Goddess (*Metamorphoses* 8–9). *De Dea Syra* ("Concerning the Syrian Goddess"), attributed to the satirist Lucian (*c.* AD 120/125–*c.* 190), describes the temple and cult of the goddess at Bambyce (Hierapolis) in Syria. The 4th-century Christian historian Eusebius in his *Praeparatio evangelica* ("Preparation for the Gospel") gives extensive extracts from the "Phoenician History" of Philo of Byblos (2nd century AD), who in turn claims to have translated the work of one Sanchuniathon, a Phoenician priest. The work is a treatise on Phoenician religion, especially cosmogony (origin of the world) and theogony (origin of the gods). As long as no independent confirmation of its authenticity was available, it was possible to dismiss Philo's work as a farrago of elements current in Hellenistic religious syncretism, until the Ugaritic evidence referred to above confirmed its authenticity and antiquity. One can scarcely accept Philo's dating of Sanchuniathon to before the Trojan War (*c.* 12th century BC), but a leading biblical archaeologist, W.F. Albright (1891–1971), has dated him to about the 6th century BC.

Phoenician and Punic inscriptions were first effectively deciphered in 1837 by the German linguist H.F.W. Gesenius (1786–1842). Punic inscriptions are very numerous

Phoenician, Punic, and Ugaritic sources

but are mostly votive and provide little beyond the bare names of deities and a few epithets, plus theophoric names (those including the name of a god) of the offerers and some sacrificial terms. An inscription called the Sacrificial Tariff of Marseilles (2nd or 3rd century BC) lists various sorts of offerings and the payment due to the officiating priest in each case; a similar tariff from Carthage is also extant. Phoenician and Aramaic funerary, votive, and building inscriptions, the earliest of them dating to the 10th century BC, have been discovered in Syria-Palestine itself. Egyptian texts of the New Kingdom (18th–20th dynasties, *c.* 1567–*c.* 1085 BC) make fairly frequent mention of Syrian deities who had come to be venerated inside Egypt. A text in the Hittite language contains an originally Canaanite myth concerning Ilkunirsha (perhaps "El, Creator of the Earth") and his consort. Evidence for a very early stage of Semitic religion (early 2nd millennium BC) can be gleaned from Amorite theophoric personal names that have been preserved in cuneiform texts from Mari on the mid-Euphrates and from Alalakh in North Syria.

By far the most extensive and most important sources, however, are the Ugaritic texts. Since 1929, excavations at Ras Shamra on the Syrian coast opposite Cyprus have been yielding texts written in an alphabetic cuneiform script on clay tablets; the language—a Semitic tongue closely related to Phoenician and Hebrew—and the script are called Ugaritic from Ugarit, the ancient name of the city. Many of the tablets contain religious texts, myths, incantations, rituals, offering lists, and lists of gods. The tablets date from the Late Bronze Age, but the mythological texts may have been composed centuries earlier.

Written evidence is supplemented by a great quantity of strictly archaeological material from numerous excavations in Palestine and Syria: temples, cultic utensils, amulets, and images and symbols of the gods.

HISTORICAL AND SOCIAL BACKGROUND

Prehistory through the 3rd millennium BC. Behind the history of religion in Syria-Palestine stretches a long prehistory that is known only in fragments from the evidence of archaeology. By the 7th millennium BC, at Jericho, some characteristic elements of later religion can be discerned. British excavations of the prepottery Neolithic phase of the city discovered animal figurines that were probably votive offerings, and a figurine of a mother goddess proffering her breasts. A small shrine held a sacred standing stone, a type of cult object used very widely in later ages. Veneration of ancestors is attested for Stone Age Jericho in the groups of carefully preserved skulls, with plaster molded over the bones to reproduce the features of the living person.

Evidence of ancient religion at Jericho

By the 3rd millennium BC, when written evidence begins to be available in meagre quantity, Syria-Palestine was already inhabited by speakers of a Semitic language of a Canaanite type. Moreover, a large share of the ancient place-names are Semitic. Some, such as Beth Yerakh (House of the Moon god), shed a bit of light on the religion of this early time. Other place names suggest occupation of some areas by non-Semitic groups. Moreover, there is evidence that the Egyptians in the Old Kingdom (*c.* 2686–*c.* 2160 BC) already controlled Byblos on the Phoenician coast and exercised cultural and political influence over much of Syria-Palestine. Characteristic features of the religious history were thus already present—that is, a mixed population and an openness to foreign influence.

2nd millennium BC. In the early centuries of the 2nd millennium, the Amorites, a Semitic people, pushed into the centres of civilization all around the Fertile Crescent. At Mari on the Euphrates and also at many other sites in Syria and Mesopotamia, Amorites had gained the upper hand. The Egyptian Execration Texts (documents by means of which the Egyptians cursed their enemies) show that groups of Amorites also dominated throughout Palestine. Since many of the Amorite personal names—the only source for knowledge of the Amorite language—contain the name of a god and an assertion about the god, a reconstruction of some aspects of the religion is possible, though the limitations of the evidence are obvious.

Following the wave of Amorite settlement came a period of incursion by Hurrians and Indo-Europeans, beginning about the 18th century BC. By the 15th century BC, northern Syria was dominated by these elements, and many cities even in southern Palestine had kings with non-Semitic names. In the 15th century BC, kings with Indo-European names ruled a strong Hurrian state known as Mitanni, which controlled all of north Syria. The rise of the Hittite Empire spelled the end of Mitanni, and through the remainder of the Late Bronze Age, Syria-Palestine was the scene of a struggle for domination between Egypt and the Hittites. At the same time, the Akkadian language was in widespread use for communication between states throughout the Middle East, and scribes in Syria-Palestine were trained in the literary, religious, and scholarly works of Mesopotamia. Trade by sea with Cyprus, Crete, and the Aegean flourished. As might be expected, then, the Late Bronze Age presents a complex religious picture: a great many local cults were scattered throughout Syria-Palestine, and the possibilities for transmission and borrowing from one area to another were practically unlimited. A treaty (*c.* 1380 BC) of the Hittites with Mitanni illustrates the complexity in its list of the gods of Mitanni who are regarded as witnesses to the treaty, for the deities named include Hurrian figures such as Teshub, the storm god, and Shimegi, the sun god; the Indian gods Mitra, Varuṇa, Indra, and the Nāsatyas (later Aśvins); and originally Mesopotamian deities, such as Anu and Enlil.

Syncretistic developments

The political picture changed decisively at the transition from the Late Bronze to the Iron Age (*c.* 1200 BC). At about that time, certain peoples with ties to older nomadic groups established themselves as independent kingdoms in various parts of the region: the Aramaeans in various cities in Syria, down as far south as Damascus; the Ammonites, on the highlands east of the Jordan; Moab, east of the Dead Sea; and Edom, south of the Dead Sea. The Hittite Empire disintegrated, leaving behind a number of states in Syria that maintained Hittite cultural traditions. The "Sea Peoples," among them the Philistines, established themselves along the Mediterranean coast from the Egyptian border north to Dor on the coast of Palestine. Israel became master of most of Palestine west of the Jordan and held some lands east of the river. The direct descendants of the ancient Canaanites, the Phoenicians, were left in control of a small strip along the Syrian coast.

Only meagre evidence exists for the religion of the Aramaeans, Ammonites, Moabites, Edomites, and Philistines. Such evidence as survives suggests that they continued the traditions of Late Bronze Age polytheism in various ways, with no fundamental change in type. Even the non-Semitic Philistines worshipped gods under names familiar in the region for centuries before their arrival, such as the grain god Dagon and the fertility goddess Astarte. Israel introduced a new element, an exclusive monotheism that brought it into a life-and-death struggle with local religions.

1st millennium BC. The Phoenicians found an outlet for their energies in trade and colonization of lands bordering the Mediterranean, especially in Spain, Sardinia, and North Africa. Carthage, founded in the late 9th century BC according to tradition—a date that agrees well with modern research—became the principal Phoenician foundation. Carthage fell to Rome in 146 BC, but veneration of the old gods survived for centuries thereafter. In Syria-Palestine, although the old independent city-states were incorporated in successive empires—Assyrian, Neo-Babylonian, Persian, Hellenistic, and Roman—the local cults survived. At famous centres such as Baalbek, Emesa, and Hierapolis, a descendant of the ancient Canaanite religion flourished, and the Syrian goddess Atargatis was widely worshipped in the Eastern Roman Empire. After the triumph of Christianity, and later of Islām, vestiges of Syrian religion survived only at the level of folk religion.

MYTHOLOGY AND RELIGIOUS PHENOMENA

The gods. Ancient Ugaritic scholars prepared ordered lists of their gods, and one such order is followed here, omitting numerous minor figures. The first in the series of divine names is Il-a-bi, which admits various interpretations: "the god of the (or my) father(s)" or "the father god" or still others. The lack of certainty on this point

Storm god riding on a bull, brandishing a mace and thunderbolt. Relief from Arsian Tash; 8th century BC. In the Louvre, Paris.
Giraudon—Art Resource

leaves open the question as to whether this figure is in any way related to the "god of the fathers" or "the god of my father" frequently mentioned in the Old Testament stories of the patriarchs Abraham, Isaac, and Jacob.

El. The next deity is El, whose name is the same as the common noun "god," a word that appears in varying forms in most Semitic languages. El is the titular head of the pantheon and as such is called king. He is the father of the gods (except for Baal) and is also the creator of man. Phoenician and Aramaic texts give him the title Creator of the Earth, a title expanded in the Bible to "maker of heaven and earth" (Gen. 14:19). He is identified with the Hurrian Kumarbi and with Greek Cronos. El is thought of as an old man with a long gray beard and as such has the title "father of years" (other translations of the epithet have been preferred). As another epithet, "Bull," suggests, he was renowned for his sexual powers, both in myth and in artistic representations, where he is depicted with the attributes of the ithyphallic (having an erect penis) Egyptian god Min. As the "Kindly One, Merciful El," he is the bestower of good gifts on men in various mythic episodes. In one strange burlesque, he is almost a figure of fun, roaring drunk at his own party. In Ugaritic religion, El is relatively inactive compared to the storm god, Baal; but in Sanchuniathon, El is more active and rather sinister. Like the Greek Cronos (Saturn), he emasculates his father, Heaven, and he slays some of his children.

The Creator God

Dagon. Dagon (Dagan) comes next in the list, presumably because he, not El, was thought of as the father of Baal and because of his great importance in the city's cult, even though he plays no role in extant myth. The original meaning of the name is uncertain, but it became a common noun in Ugaritic and Hebrew for "grain," which sufficiently indicates that he was associated with fertility of crops. Worship of Dagon is attested at Mari almost a millennium earlier than at Ugarit, and Dagon later became the chief god of the Philistines.

Baal. Baal was the storm god and as such occupied a prominent place in both cult and myth. The ancient proper name of the deity is Hadad, but this title is much less common at Ugarit than Baal, which is also a common noun meaning "Lord, Master." As storm god, Baal is called "cloud rider," a title adopted in Israel for Yahweh (Ps. 68:4). He is also "the Prince" and "the Conquering One." His residence is on a mountain north of Ugarit on the Syrian coast whose Semitic name was Zaphon. The Hittite name was Khazzi, which becomes Kasios in later Greek references to the god and the mountain, the Canaanite Olympus. Under the title Baal-Zephon, the god was worshipped as a patron of sailors, a cult transferred to a site in the Egyptian delta near Pelusium. Though there is now no doubt that Baal/Hadad was a great god, comparable to Zeus in nature and importance, the situation is complicated by a number of factors. Since *baal* means "lord," it is often combined with place-names to form divine names of the pattern "Lord of such and such a place" (*e.g.,* Baal-peor, "Lord of Peor"). In some cases these names may designate a separate minor deity rather than the great storm god; on the other hand, the "baals" of various localities may in other cases be local manifestations of the one major figure. In a given case, it is often impossible to decide. In the Old Testament, a plural form, *ha-bealim* ("the Baals"), is of frequent occurrence. It may refer to a variety of local deities, but in many cases the plural is a "plural of majesty" referring to a single god; an honorific plural, *baaluma,* occurs at Ugarit.

Importance of the storm god

Yarikh and Kothar. Yarikh, "Moon," was a male deity widely and very anciently worshipped, but little mythological detail survives. In general, the sun—a goddess at Ugarit—and the moon and stars play relatively minor roles at Ugarit. Kothar was the Canaanite craftsman god, similar to the Greek Hephaestus. The name means "skillful," and his other title is Khasis, "clever."

Asherah, Anath, and Astarte. Three goddesses are especially prominent: Asherah, Anath, and Astarte. Asherah, the consort of El at Ugarit, has the fuller name "She who walks in the Sea" and is also called "Holiness." The Old Testament uses the name Asherah frequently, but usually for a wooden cult object associated with her worship rather than for the goddess herself. Astarte (Ashtoreth in the Old Testament) is a goddess of love and war, the approximate equivalent of Mesopotamian Ishtar. Overshadowed by Anath in Ugaritic mythology, she is much more prominent in cultic texts. In the Old Testament, she is the most frequently mentioned of the pagan goddesses; and her name is also a common noun, "sheep breeding."

Fertility goddesses

Anath is the chief Ugaritic goddess of love and war. The consort of Baal, she plays an important role in the myth of Baal's death and resurrection—that is, in the cycle of fertility and infertility in nature. Her outstanding trait is her ferocity in battle. In one scene, she wades in blood and wears heads and hands as ornaments. There is evidence that suggests a connection between Anath and the ferocious Indian goddess Kālī. In the Hellenistic period, Anath and Astarte are blended into a single figure, Atargatis. She is the "Syrian Goddess," whose cult was famous for its *galli,* devotees who voluntarily emasculated themselves for the goddess and thereafter dressed as women.

Mot, Melqart, Adonis, and other gods. Mot is what his name, "Death," implies, god of the dead and of all powers that oppose life and fertility. Resheph is a related figure, a god of the underworld and of pestilence. Some abstractions were deified and occur in the god lists, notably Mishor and Suduk, approximately "Justice" and "Righteousness." Many other deities are attested at Ugarit, and other sites swell the list of names.

The chief god of Tyre was Melqart, who was also head of the pantheon at Carthage. The name means "King of the city"—that is, "of the underworld city" in the most plausible interpretation. Greeks and Romans identified him with Hercules. Baal Hammon, perhaps "Lord of the Incense Altar," is mentioned only very rarely in inscriptions from Syria but becomes very important at Carthage, where the name occurs in hundreds of dedicatory inscriptions.

Carthaginian deities

Little is known of his nature. The principal Carthaginian goddess is Tanit (or Tinnit). No explanation of the name is generally accepted; usually it occurs in the form "Tanit face of Baal." Little of a positive nature can be asserted as to her nature, though, not surprisingly, she seems to have to do with the heavens and with fertility.

Adonis, whose name is a Semitic word, "Lord," is known only from relatively late non-Semitic sources. A youthful god of vegetation beloved of the goddess of love, he is according to one myth killed by a boar, his blood staining the river Adonis. Women took part in rites of mourning for him and set out ephemeral "Adonis gardens" in his honour. The cult reached Athens by the 5th century BC from Cyprus and was widespread in the eastern Mediterranean.

The chief god of Moab was Chemosh; his name occurs also in a list of gods at Ugarit, but little can be said about his nature; still less is known of Milkom, god of the Ammonites.

Myths and legends. *Theogony and cosmogony.* Philo of Byblos gives Sanchuniathon's account of the origins of the cosmos, the gods, and the arts of civilization. Many of the figures in the latter portion of the account can now be identified with ancient Canaanite deities, and in the sequence of divine generations, the account is strikingly like that of the Greek poet Hesiod's (flourished *c.* 800 BC) *Theogony* and the Hittite-Hurrian creation myth of Kumarbi, but sufficiently distinct to provide assurance that it is an ancient and independent variant of a common tradition. Thus, Sanchuniathon tells of four generations of gods: Eliun or Hypsistos ("the Most High"), Uranos, El (=Kronos), who castrates his father, and Demarus (=Zeus), all of this very like the *Theogony* and Kumarbi, but with numerous differences in details. This very archaic theogony is preceded by an atheistic cosmogony that is probably the product of later Phoenician speculative thought; it resembles the cosmogonies of the Pre-Socratic philosophers.

The Baal epic. From Ugarit comes the longest of known Canaanite myths, the Baal epic, probably composed in the early 2nd millennium BC. (The order of the separate tablets is not completely certain.) Baal is challenged to battle by the god Yamm (Sea). Equipped by Kothar with special clubs, Baal defeats Yamm. Baal, though supreme in power, has no house like those of the other gods; finally Kothar builds and equips a house for him, magnificent with gold and silver. After a gap in the text comes an episode in which Baal descends into the jaw of death, the god Mot. When the news reaches El, he mourns extravagantly, as does the goddess Anath, who then sees to the burial of Baal's body. She seeks out Mot and cuts him to pieces. Then Baal is resurrected and "the heavens rain oil, the watercourses flow with honey."

Other myths. Briefer myths recount the wedding of Nikkal, a moon goddess, to the moon god Yarikh, and El's seduction of two females, who bear the children Dawn and Dusk. Creatures of voracious appetite, they are driven into the wilderness; at this point the text breaks off. In one mythological fragment, Anath espies the beauty of her brother, then "she eats his flesh without a knife; she drinks his blood without a cup"—a striking parallel to the omophagy (eating of live victims, occasionally human) practiced by raving devotees of the Thracian and Phrygian god Bacchus. Elsewhere there is an allusion to Baal's defeat of Lotan, "the primeval serpent . . . the twisting serpent." Lotan is the same as the Hebrew Leviathan, and the same motif occurs in the Old Testament (*e.g.,* Isaiah 27), with Yahweh as the dragon slayer.

Legends. Other Ugaritic epics are less strictly mythological in that they involve human characters. The Keret epic concerns a king Keret whose sons have all died. In a vision, kindly El advises him to undertake a military campaign to get a new wife. After careful preparation, Keret besieges the city Udum and compels its king, Pabel, to grant him his daughter Hurriya in marriage. Hurriya bears Keret many children. In the last episode of the extant story, Keret falls ill and is saved only by El's healing intervention. The so-called *Aqhat Epic* concerns the sage, Danel (the ancient worthy Daniel mentioned in Ezekiel 14), who has no son. In response to Danel's prayer and offerings, El grants him a son, Aqhat. Later Danel gives Aqhat a marvellous composite bow made by Kothar. The goddess Anath covets it, but Aqhat spurns her and she arranges for him to be killed. Danel and his daughter Paghat discover the crime and take steps to avenge it; here the text breaks off.

PRACTICES AND INSTITUTIONS

The importance of sacrifice

Sacred customs and ceremonies. Animal sacrifice occupied a central place in the religion. Few details about the rites observed are known, but since much of the Ugaritic terminology is the same as later Israelite terminology (*e.g.,* "sacrifice," "burnt offering," "peace offerings," "wave offerings"), scholars contend that they are justified in conceiving Canaanite sacrificial practices to be similar in many respects to those of the Israelites. The animals commonly presented were sheep, goats, cattle, and birds; the Marseilles Tariff (see above) mentions also young deer and other game. The extent to which human sacrifice was carried on is uncertain, but there is no doubt that it was practiced to some extent, judging from biblical allusions and evidence for human sacrifice at Carthage. Sacred prostitutes, both male and female, were among the personnel of some shrines, but details as to the extent and significance of this institution are lacking.

Kings, priests, and prophets

Religious authorities. The king and queen were important religious figures, both because offerings and prayers were made for them and because they took a leading part in certain rituals, to judge from brief references in Ugaritic texts. The relatively elaborate official cult at Ugarit was led by a "chief priest" and by several lesser orders of priests. There were special temple singers and "drawers of water for the sanctuary" (compare the role of the biblical Gibeonites). The temples were economic as well as cultic centres. Estates were assigned to orders of priests, and a certain chief priest is said to have been also "chief of the shepherds"—that is, overseer of the temple flocks.

Prophets—that is, persons inspired by a god to deliver a message in his name—were a very ancient feature of the religion. In the Mari texts (dated *c.* 18th century BC), there are repeated references to ecstatics, some of them women, who appear unsolicited in the temples to deliver messages from the gods to the king. A similar phenomenon is attested for Byblos in the Wen-Amon report, an Egyptian text of about 1100 BC: a youth falls into an ecstatic state and delivers an oracle on behalf of the Egyptian envoy, which is respected by the ruler of Byblos. The prophets of the Tyrian Baal used dancing and self-laceration to achieve a state of frenzy (I Kings 18). A long charm against snakebite from Ugarit suggests that not only this variety of incantatory magic but others as well were cultivated in Syria—Palestine.

Shrines and festivals

Sacred places and sacred times. The temple, or house of god, was the place where the god, symbolized by his image, dwelt and thus the point at which heaven and earth met. Since, according to biblical tradition, Solomon's Temple was built by a Phoenician architect, the biblical descriptions apparently give us the fullest and most coherent idea of Syrian temple architecture. The basic tripartite plan, with porch, holy place, and most holy place, is illustrated in the small temple excavated at Tall Tainat in north Syria (9th–8th century BC). In addition to the elaborate temples in the cities, there were the more rustic shrines known as "high places" (Hebrew *bamot*), built on natural ridges or artificially built up and often associated with the cult of dead heroes. The principal cult objects were statues of the gods, but typical also is veneration of various deities in the form of unshaped stones, well exemplified in the black stone of Emesa that Elagabalus brought to Rome.

Very little is known about the sacred calendar of the region. At Ugarit, important sacrifices were offered on the day of the new moon and on the 14th of the month. Since the three great feasts of ancient Israel—that is, Unleavened Bread, Weeks (Pentecost), and Booths—were evidently native agricultural feasts originally, it is probable that from time immemorial the farmers of Syria-Palestine kept a spring festival at the beginning of barley harvest, a feast at the end of the grain harvest, and a fall vintage festival.

RELIGIOUS ART AND ICONOGRAPHY

Though excavations have yielded statues and reliefs depicting gods or symbols of the gods, it is frequently difficult to be certain about identification of a given representation with a particular deity known from written evidence. Baal and similar storm gods are frequently shown as riding on a bull and brandishing a mace or thunderbolts. The symbol of Tanit, very commonly found on Punic steles, is basically a triangle having a disk at its apex, with a horizontal bar in between; this basic form is often embellished. The source of the symbol and its significance are not known. In Syria-Palestine the most commonly found religious artifacts are small terra-cotta figurines depicting females, often naked and with exaggerated sexual characteristics. Some of these are probably intended to represent fertility goddesses, but none can be certainly identified with any one goddess. Winged human-headed lions (cherubim) and similar composite creatures are very frequent in Canaanite religious art, as in the cultic stand from Taanach (Palestine; 10th century BC). (D.R.H.)

Mesopotamian religions

The term Mesopotamian religions serves generally to designate the religious beliefs and practices of the Sumerians and Akkadians, who inhabited ancient Mesopotamia (modern Iraq) in the millennia before the Christian era. These beliefs and practices form a single stream of tradition. Sumerian in origin, it was added to and subtly modified by the Akkadians (Semites immigrating into the country from the West at the end of the 4th millenium BC), whose own beliefs were in large measure assimilated to, and integrated with, those of their new environment.

As the only available intellectual framework that could provide a comprehensive understanding of the forces governing existence and also guidance for right conduct in life, religion ineluctably conditioned all aspects of ancient Mesopotamian civilization. It yielded the forms in which that civilization's social, economic, legal, political, and military institutions were, and are, to be understood, as well as providing the significant symbols for poetry and art. In many ways it even influenced peoples and cultures outside Mesopotamia, such as the Elamites to the east, the Hurrians and Hittites to the north, and the Aramaeans and Israelites to the west.

HISTORICAL DEVELOPMENT

Cultural background. Human occupation of Mesopotamia—"the land between the rivers" (*i.e.*, the Tigris and Euphrates)—seems to reach back furthest in time in the north (Assyria) where the earliest settlers built their small villages some time around 6000 BC. The prehistoric cultural stages of Hassuna-Samarra and Halaf (named after the sites of archaeological excavations) succeeded each other here before there is evidence of settlement in the south—Sumer. There, the earliest settlements, such as Eridu, appear to have been founded around 5000 BC, in the late Halaf Period. From then on the cultures of the north and south move through a succession of major archaeological periods that in their southern forms are known as Ubaid, Warka, Protoliterate (during which writing was invented), and Early Dynastic, at the end of which—shortly after 3000 BC—recorded history begins. The historical periods of the 3rd millennium are, in order: Akkad, Gutium, 3rd dynasty of Ur; those of the 2nd millennium: Isin-Larsa, Old Babylonian, Kassite, and Middle Babylonian; and those of the 1st millennium: Assyrian, Neo-Babylonian, Achaemenian, Seleucid, and Parthian.

Periodization of Mesopotamian history

Politically, an early division of the country into small independent city-states, loosely organized in a league with the centre in Nippur, was followed by a unification by force under King Lugalzaggisi (*c.* 2375–2350 BC) of Uruk, just before the Akkadian period. The unification was maintained by his successors, the kings of Akkad, who built it into an empire, and—after a brief interruption by Gutian invaders—by Utukhegal (*c.* 2116–*c.* 2110) of Uruk and the rulers of the 3rd dynasty of Ur (*c.* 2112–*c.* 2004 BC). When Ur fell, around 2000 BC, the country again divided into smaller units, with the cities Isin and Larsa vying for hegemony. Eventually Babylon established a lasting national state in the south, while Ashur dominated a similar rival state, Assyria, in the north. From the middle of the 1st millennium onward, Assyria built an empire comprising, for a short time, all of the ancient Middle East. This political and administrative achievement remained essentially intact under the following Neo-Babylonian and Persian kings down to Alexander's conquest (331 BC).

Stages of religious development. The religious development—as indeed that of the Mesopotamian culture generally—was not significantly influenced by the movements of the various peoples into and within the area—the Sumerians, Akkadians, Gutians, Kassites, Hurrians, and Aramaeans (or Chaldeans). Rather it forms a uniform, consistent, and coherent Mesopotamian tradition changing in response to its own internal needs of insights and expression. It is possible to discern a basic substratum involving worship of the forces in nature—often visualized in nonhuman forms—especially those that were of immediate import to basic economic pursuits. Many of these figures belong to the type of the "dying god" (a fertility deity displaying death and regeneration characteristics) but show variant traits according to whether they are powers of fertility worshipped by marsh men, orchard growers, herders, or farmers. This stage may be dated tentatively back to the 4th millennium BC and even earlier. A second stage, characterized by a view of the gods as human in shape and organized in a polity of a primitive democratic cast in which each deity had his or her special offices and functions, overlaid and conditioned the religious forms and characteristics of the earlier stage during the 3rd millennium BC. Lastly, a third stage, characterized by a growing emphasis on personal religion involving concepts of sin and forgiveness, and by a change of the earlier democratic divine polity into an absolute monarchical structure dominated by the god of the national state—to the point of pious abstention from all human initiative, in absolute faith and reliance on divine intervention—characterizes the 2nd and 1st millennia BC. As a result of this development, since the ancient Mesopotamians were intensely conservative in religious matters and unwilling to discard anything of a hallowed past, the religious data of any period, and particularly those of the later periods, are a condensed version of earlier millennia that must be carefully analyzed and placed in proper perspective before it can be evaluated.

Characteristics of the stages of religious development

THE LITERARY LEGACY: MYTH AND EPIC

Present knowledge of ancient Mesopotamian religion rests almost exclusively on archaeological evidence recovered from the ruined city-mounds of Mesopotamia during the last century or so. Of greatest significance is the literary evidence, texts written in cuneiform (wedge-shaped) script on tablets made of clay or, for monumental purposes, on stone. Central, of course, are the specifically religious texts comprising god lists, myths, hymns, laments, prayers, rituals, omen texts, incantations, and other forms; but since religion permeated the culture, giving form and meaning to all aspects of it, any written text, any work of art, or any of its material remains, are directly or indirectly related to the religion and may further scholarly knowledge of it.

Among the archaeological finds that have particularly helped to throw light on religion are the important discoveries of inscribed tablets with Sumerian texts in copies of Old Babylonian date (*c.* 1800–*c.* 1600 BC) at Nippur and Ur, the Sumerian and Akkadian texts of the 2nd and 1st millennia from Ashur and Sultantepe, and particularly the all-important library of the Assyrian king Ashurbanipal (reigned 668–627 BC) from Nineveh. Of nonliterary remains, the great temples and temple towers (ziggurats) excavated at almost all major sites—*e.g.*, Eridu, Ur, Nippur, Babylon, Ashur, Calah, Nineveh—as well as numerous works of art from various periods, are important sources of information. The Uruk Vase, with its representation of the rite of the sacred marriage, the Naram-Sin stele (inscribed commemorative pillar), the Ur-Nammu stele, and the stele with the Code of Hammurabi (Babylonian king, 18th century BC), which shows at its top the royal lawgiver before the sun god Shamash, the divine guardian

Importance of archaeological discoveries

Detail of the stele inscribed with Hammurabi's code, showing the king before the god Shamash; bas-relief from Susa, 18th century BC. In the Louvre, Paris.

Giraudon—Art Resource

of justice, are important works of art that may be singled out. Also among important sources are the representations on cylinder seals and on boundary stones (*kudurrus*), both of which provide rich materials for religious iconography in certain periods.

Difficulties in interpretation of sources

In working with, and seeking to interpret, these varied sources two particular difficulties stand out: the incompleteness of the data, and the remoteness of the ancients from modern man, not only in time but also in experience and in ways of thought. Thus, for all periods before the 3rd millennium scholars must rely on scarce, nonliterary data only, and even though writing appears shortly before that millennium, it is only in its latter half that written data become numerous enough and readily understandable enough to be of significant help. It is generally necessary, therefore, to interpret the scarce data of the older periods in the light of survivals and of what is known from later periods, an undertaking that calls for critical acumen if anachronisms are to be avoided. Also, for the later periods, the evidence flows unevenly, with perhaps the middle of the 2nd millennium the least well documented and hence least known age.

As for the difficulties raised by differences in the ways of thinking between modern man and the ancients, they are of the kind that one always meets in trying to understand something unfamiliar and strange. A contemporary inquirer must keep his accustomed values and modes of thought in suspension and seek rather the inner coherence and structure of the data with which he deals, in order to enter sympathetically into the world out of which they came, just as, for example, in entering the sometimes intensely private world of a poem, or, on a slightly different level, in learning the new, unexpected meanings and overtones of the words and phrases of a foreign language.

Sumerian literature. Mesopotamian literature originated with the Sumerians, whose earliest known written records are from the middle of the 4th millennium BC. It constitutes the oldest known literature in the world; moreover, inner criteria indicate that a long oral-literary tradition preceded, and probably coexisted with, the setting down of its songs and stories in writing. It may be assumed, further, that this oral literature developed the genres of the core literature. The handbook genres, however, in spite of occasional inclusions of oral formula—*e.g.*, legal or medical—may generally be assumed to have been devised after writing had been invented, as a response to the remarkable possibilities that writing offered for amassing and organizing data.

Functions of Mesopotamian religious literature

The purpose underlying the core literature and its oral prototypes would seem to have been as much magical as aesthetic, or merely entertaining in origin. In magic, words create and call into being what they state—the more vivid and expressive they are the more they are believed to be efficacious—so by its expressiveness literature forms a natural vehicle of such creativity. In ancient Mesopotamia its main purpose appears to have been the enhancement of what was seen as beneficial. With the sole exception of wisdom literature, the core genres are panegyric in nature (*i.e.,* they praise something or other), and the magical power and use of praise is to instill, call up, or activate the virtues presented in the praise.

That praise is of the essence of hymns, for instance, is shown by the fact that over and over again the encomiast, the official praiser, whose task it was to sing these hymns, closed with the standing phrase: "O [the name of a deity or human hero], thy praise is sweet." The same phrase is common also at the end of myths and epics, two further praise genres that also belonged in the repertoire of the encomiast. They praise not only in description but also in narrative, by recounting acts of valour done by the hero, thus sustaining and enhancing his power to do such deeds, according to the magical view.

In time, possibly quite early, the magical aspect of literature must have tended to fade from men's consciousness, yielding to more nearly aesthetic attitudes that viewed the praise hymns as expressions of allegiance and loyalties, and accepted the narrative genres of myth and epic for the enjoyment of the story and the values expressed, poetic and otherwise.

Hymns, myths, and epics all were believed to sustain existing powers and virtues by means of praise, but laments were understood to praise blessings and powers lost, originally seeking to hold on to and recall them magically, through the power in the expression of intense longing for them and the vivid representation of them. The lamentation genre was the province of a separate professional, the elegist. It contained dirges for the dying gods of the fertility cults and laments for temples and cities that had been destroyed and desecrated. The laments for temples—which, as far as is known, go back no earlier than to the 3rd dynasty of Ur (*c.* 2112–*c.* 2004 BC)—were used to recall the beauties of the lost temple as a kind of inducement to persuade the god and the owner of the temple to restore it.

Penitential psalms lament private illnesses and misfortunes and seek to evoke the pity of the deity addressed and thus to gain divine aid. The genre apparently is late in date, most likely Old Babylonian (*c.* 19th century BC), and

By courtesy of the University Museum, University of Pennsylvania, Philadelphia

Tablet recounting the Sumerian story of the Flood, c. 2000–1500 BC, excavated from Nippur, Iraq. In the University Museum, University of Pennsylvania, Philadelphia.

in it the element of magic has, to all intents and purposes, disappeared.

The core genres of Mesopotamian literature were developed by the Sumerians apparently as oral compositions. Writing, which is first attested at the middle of the 4th millennium BC, was in its origins predominantly ideographical (picture or symbol writing) and long remained a highly imperfect means of rendering the spoken word. Even as late as the beginning of the Early Dynastic III Period in south Mesopotamia at the end of that millennium, the written literary texts preserved have the character of mnemonic (memory) aids only and seem to presuppose that the reader has prior oral knowledge of the text.

The significance of writing

As writing developed more and more precision during the 3rd millennium BC, more and more oral compositions seem to have been put into writing and with the 3rd dynasty of Ur (*c.* 2112–*c.* 2004 BC) a considerable body of literature had come into being and was being added to by a generation of highly gifted authors. Fortunately for its survival, this literature became part of the curriculum in the Sumerian scribal schools, studied and copied by student after student so that an abundance of such copies, reaching a peak in old Babylonian times, duplicated and supplemented each other as witnesses to the text of the major works. As many as 50 or more copies or fragments of copies of a single composition may support a modern edition, and many thousands more such copies probably still lie unread, buried in the earth.

Myths. The genre of myths in ancient Mesopotamian literature centres on praises that recount and celebrate great deeds. The doers of the deeds (creative or otherwise decisive acts), and thus the subjects of the praises, are the gods. In the oldest myths, the Sumerian, these acts tend to have particular rather than universal relevance, which is understandable since they deal with the power and acts of a particular god with a particular sphere of influence in the cosmos. An example of such myths is the myth of "Dumuzi's Death" that relates how Dumuzi (Producer of Sound Offspring), the power in the fertility of spring, dreamed of his own death at the hands of a group of deputies from the Nether World and how he tried to hide himself but was betrayed by his friend after his sister had resisted all attempts at making her reveal where he was.

Fertility myths

A similar, very complex myth, "Inanna's Descent," relates how the goddess Inanna (Lady of the Date Clusters) set her heart on ruling the Nether World and tried to depose her older sister, the queen of the Nether World, Ereshkigal (Lady of the Greater Earth). Her attempt failed, she was killed, and changed into a piece of rotting meat in the Nether World. It took all the ingenuity of Enki (Lord of Sweet Waters in the Earth) to bring Inanna back to life, and even then she was released only on condition that she furnish a substitute to take her place. On her return, finding her young husband Dumuzi feasting instead of mourning for her, Inanna was seized with jealousy and designated him as that substitute. Dumuzi tried to flee the posse of deputies who had accompanied Inanna, and with the help of the sun god Utu ("Sun"), who changed Dumuzi's shape, he managed to escape, was recaptured, escaped again, and so on, until he was finally taken to the Nether World, where the fly told his little sister Geshtinanna where he was, and she went in search of him. The myth ends with Inanna rewarding the fly and decreeing that Dumuzi and his little sister could alternate as her substitute, each of them spending half a year in the Nether World, the other half above with the living.

A third myth built over the motif of journeying to the Nether World is the myth of "The Engendering of the Moongod and his Brothers," which tells how Enlil (Lord Wind), when still a youngster, came upon young Ninlil (goddess of grain) as she—disobeying her mother—was bathing in a canal. He lay with her in spite of her protests and thus engendered the moon god Suen. For this offense Enlil was banished from Nippur and took the road to the Nether World. Ninlil, carrying his child, followed him. On the way Enlil took the shape first of the Nippur gatekeeper, then of the man of the river of the Nether World, and lastly of the ferryman of the river of the Nether World. In each such disguise Enlil persuaded Ninlil to let him lie with her to engender a son who might take Suen's place in the Nether World and leave him free for the world above. Thus three further deities, all underworld figures, were engendered: Meslamtaea (He Who Comes Out of the Meslam Temple), Ninazu (Water Sprinkler [?]), and Ennugi (the God Who Returns Not). The myth ends with a paean to Enlil as a source of abundance and to his divine word, which always comes true.

Most likely all of these myths have backgrounds in fertility cults and concern the disappearance of nature's fertility with the onset of the dry season or with the underground storage of food.

As Enlil is celebrated for engendering other gods that embody other powers in nature, so also was Enki in the myth of "Enki and Ninhursag," in which myth Enki lay down with Ninhursag (Lady of the Stony Ground) on the island of Dilmun (modern Bahrain), which had been allotted to them. At that time all was new and fresh, inchoate, not yet set in its present mold. There Enki provided water for the future city of Dilmun, lay with Ninhursag, and left her. She gave birth to a daughter, Ninshar (Lady Herb), on whom Enki in turn engendered the spider Uttu, goddess of spinning and weaving. Ninhursag warned Uttu, but Enki, proffering marriage gifts, persuaded her to open the door to him. After Enki had abandoned her, Ninhursag found her and removed Enki's semen from her body. From the semen seven plants sprouted forth. These plants Enki later saw and ate and so became pregnant from his own semen. Unable as a male to give birth, he fell fatally ill, until Ninhursag relented and—as birth goddess—placed him in her vulva and helped him to give birth to seven daughters, whom Enki then happily married off to various gods.

Not only the birth of gods but also the birth, or creation, of man is treated in the myths. The myth of "Enki and Ninmakh" relates how the gods originally had to toil for their food, dig irrigation canals, and perform other menial tasks until, in their distress, they complained to Enki's mother, Nammu, who took the complaints to Enki. Enki remembered the engendering clay of the Apsu (*i.e.,* the fresh underground waters that fathered him) and from this clay, with the help of the womb goddesses and eight midwife goddesses led by Ninmakh (another name for Ninhursag), he had his mother become pregnant with and give birth to man so that he could relieve the gods of their toil. At the celebration of the birth, however, Enki and Ninmakh both drank too much beer and began to quarrel. Ninmakh boasted that she could impair man's shape at will and Enki countered that he could temper even the worst that she might do. So she made seven freaks, for each of which Enki found a place in society and a living. He then challenged her to alleviate the mischief he could do, but the creature he fashioned (one suffering from all the ills and debilities of extreme old age) was far beyond her powers to cope with. Thus the many imperfections in man came into being.

The ordering, rather than the creation, of the world is the subject of another myth about Enki, called "Enki and World Order." Beginning with long praises and self-praises of Enki, it tells how he blessed Nippur (Sumer), Ur, Meluhha (Ethiopia), and Dilmun (Bahrain) and gave them their characteristics, after which he turned his attention to the Euphrates and Tigris rivers, to the marshes, the sea, and the rains, and then to instituting one facet after another of the economic life of Sumer: agriculture, housebuilding, herding, and so forth. The story ends with a complaint by Enki's granddaughter Inanna that she has not been given her due share of offices, at which he patiently pointed to various offices she had in fact been given and kindly added a few more.

The ordering of the world: cosmological myths

Another myth about the world order but dealing with it from a very different point of view concerns Enlil's son, the rain god Ninurta, called from its opening word "Lugal-e" ("O King"). This myth begins with a description of the young king, Ninurta, sitting at home in Nippur when, through his general, reports reach him of a new power that has arisen in the mountains to challenge him—*i.e.,* Azag, son of Anu (Sky) and Ea (Earth), chosen king by the plants and raiding the cities with his warriors, the stones. Ninurta sets out in his boat to give battle, and a

Shamash, the sun god, rising in the morning from the eastern mountains between (left) Ishtar (Sumerian Inanna), the goddess of the morning star, and (far left) Ninurta, the god of thunderstorms, with his bow and lion, and (right) Ea (Sumerian Enki), the god of fresh water, with (far right) his vizier, the two-faced Usmu.

By courtesy of the trustees of the British Museum

fierce engagement ensues in which Azag is killed. Afterward Ninurta reorganizes his newly won territory, builds a stone barrier, the *hursag,* the near mountain ranges, gathers the waters that used to go up into the mountains and directs them into the Tigris to flood it and provide plentiful irrigation water from Sumer. The *hursag* he presents as a gift to his mother, who had come to visit him, naming her Ninhursag, Lady of the Hursag; and lastly he sits in judgment on the stones who had formed the Azag's army. Some of them, who had shown special ill will toward him, he curses, and others he trusts and gives high office in his administration. These judgments give the stones their present characteristics so that, for example, the flint is condemned to break before the much softer horn, as it indeed does when the horn is pressed against it to flake it. Noteworthy also is the way in which order in the universe, the yearly flood and other seasonal events, is seen—consonantly with Ninurta's role as "king" and leader in war—under the pattern of a reorganization of conquered territories.

Other myths about Ninurta are "An-gim dím-ma" and a myth of his contest with Enki. The first of these tells how Ninurta, on returning from battle to Nippur, was met by Enlil's page Nusku, who ordered him to cease his boastful clamor and not scare Enlil and the other gods. After long speeches of self-praise, by Ninurta, further addresses to him calmed him and made him enter his temple gently. The second tale relates how he conquered the Thunderbird Ansud with Enki's help but missed the powers it had stolen from him, and how, resentful at this, he plotted against Enki but was outsmarted and trapped. Another Sumerian myth, the "Eridu Genesis," tells of the creation of man and animals, of the building of the first cities, and of the flood.

Epics. The genre of epics appears generally to be younger in origin than that of myths and apparently was linked—in subject matter and values—to the emergence of monarchy at the middle of the Early Dynastic Period. The works that have survived seem, however, all to be of later date. A single short Sumerian epic tale, "Gilgamesh and Agga of Kish," is told in the style of primary epic. It deals with Gilgamesh's successful rebellion against his overlord and former benefactor, Agga of Kish. More in the style of romantic epic are the stories of "Enmerkar and the Lord of Aratta," "Enmerkar and Ensuhkeshdanna," and the "Lugalbanda epic," all of which have as heroes rulers of the 1st dynasty of Uruk (*c.* 3500 BC) and deal with wars between that city and the fabulous city of Aratta in the eastern highlands. Gilgamesh, also of that dynasty, figures as the hero of a variety of short tales; some, such as "Gilgamesh and Huwawa" and "Gilgamesh and the Bull of Heaven" in romantic epic style, and others, such as "The Death of Gilgamesh" and "Gilgamesh, Enkidu and the Nether World," concern the inescapable fact of death and the character of afterlife.

Akkadian literature. The first centuries of the 2nd millennium BC witnessed the demise of Sumerian as a spoken language and its replacement by Akkadian. Because of its role as bearer of Sumerian culture, as the language of religion, literature, and many arts, however, Sumerian (much as Latin in the Middle Ages) continued to be taught and spoken in the scribal schools throughout the 2nd and 1st millennia BC. New compositions were even composed in it, grammatically more and more barbarous the greater the distance in time from when it was still alive.

Akkadian, when it supplanted Sumerian as the spoken language of Mesopotamia, was not without its own literary tradition. Writing, to judge from Akkadian orthographical peculiarities, was very early borrowed from the Sumerians. By old Babylonian times (*c.* 19th century BC), the literature in Akkadian, partly under the influence of Sumerian models and Sumerian literary themes, had developed myths and epics of its own, among them the superb Old-Babylonian Gilgamesh epic (dealing with the problem of death; see below *Epics*) as well as hymns, disputation texts (evaluations of elements of the cosmos and society), penitential psalms, and not a few independent new handbook genres—*e.g.,* omina, rituals, laws and legal phrasebooks (often translated from Sumerian), mathematical texts, and grammatical texts. A noticeable amount of translations from Sumerian is observable: incantation series like the *utukke limnuti* ("The Evil Spirits"), laments for destroyed temples, penitential psalms, and others. The prestige of Sumerian as a literary language, however, is indicated by the fact that translations were rarely, if ever, allowed to supersede the original Sumerian text. The Sumerian text was kept with an interlinear translation to form a bilingual work.

Canonization of Mesopotamian religious literature

The continued study and copying of literature in the schools, both Sumerian and Akkadian, by the middle of the 2nd millennium led to a remarkable effort of standardizing, or canonizing. Texts of the same genre were collected, often under royal auspices and with royal support, and were then sifted and finally edited in series that from then on were recognized as the canonical form. Authoritative texts were established for incantations, laments, omina, medical texts, lexical texts, and others. In myths and epics, such major and lengthy compositions as the Akkadian creation story *Enuma elish,* the Erra myth, Nergal and Ereshkigal, the Etana legend, the Gilgamesh epic, and the Tukulti-Ninurta epic were reworked or recreated.

Of special interest are philosophical compositions, in Akkadian called *Ludlul bel nemeqi,* "Let me praise the expert," and theodicies (justification of divine ways) that deal with the problem of the just sufferer, similar to the biblical Job. They constitute a high point in the genre of wisdom literature. From the 1st millennium BC the rise of factual historical chronicles and a spate of political and religious polemical writings reflecting the rivalry between Assyria and Babylonia deserve mention. Very late in the millennium, the first astronomical texts appeared.

Myths. The Akkadian myths are in many ways dependent on Sumerian materials, but they show an originality and a broader scope in their treatment of the earlier Sumerian concepts and forms; they address themselves more often to existence as a whole. Fairly close to Sumerian prototypes is an Akkadian version of the myth of "Inanna's Descent." An old Babylonian myth about the Thunderbird Ansud, who stole the tablets of fates and was conquered by Ninurta, who was guided by Enki's counsel, is probably closely related to the Sumerian story of Ninurta's contest with Enki.

Also important is an old Babylonian "Myth of Atrahasis," which, in motif, shows a relationship with the account of the creation of man to relieve the gods of toil in the "Enki and Ninmakh" myth, and with a Sumerian account of the flood in the "Eridu Genesis"; but the myth treats of these themes with noticeable originality and remarkable depth. It relates, first, how the gods originally had to toil for a living, how they rebelled and went on strike, how Enki suggested that one of their number—We, apparently the ringleader who "had the idea"—be killed and mankind created from clay mixed with his flesh and blood, so that the toil of the gods could be laid on man and the gods left to go free. But after Enki and the birth goddess Nintur (another name for Ninmakh) had created man, man multiplied at such a rate that the din he made kept Enlil sleepless. At first Enlil had Namtar, the god of death, cause a plague to diminish mankind's numbers, but the wise Atrahasis, at the advise of Enki, had man concentrate all worship and offerings on Namtar, and Namtar, embarrassed at hurting people who showed such love and affection for him, stayed his hand. Next Enlil had Adad, the god of rains, hold back the rains and thus cause a famine, but because of the same stratagem, Adad was embarrassed and released the rains. After this, Enlil, next planned a famine by divine group action that would not be vulnerable as the earlier actions by individual gods had been. Anu and Adad were to guard the heavens, he himself earth, and Enki the waters underground and the sea so that no gift of nature could come through to man. The ensuing famine was terrible. By the seventh year one house consumed the other and people began eating their own children. At that point Enki—accidentally he maintained—let through a wealth of fish from the sea and so saved man. With this, however, Enlil's patience was at an end and he thought of the flood as a means to get rid of humanity once and for all. Enki, however, warned Atrahasis and had him build a boat in which he saved himself, his family, and all animals. After the flood had abated and the ship was grounded, Atrahasis sacrificed, and the hungry gods, much chastened, gathered around the offering. Only Enlil was unrelenting until Enki upbraided him for killing innocent and guilty alike and—there is a gap in the text—suggested other means to keep man's numbers down. In consultation with the birth goddess Nintur, Enki then developed a scheme of birth control by inventing the barren woman, the demon Pashittu who kills children at birth, and the various classes of priestesses to whom birth giving was taboo.

The role of Atrahasis as the hero of the flood

The myth uses the motif of the protest of the gods against their hard toil and the creation of man to relieve it, which was depicted earlier in the Sumerian myth of "Enki and Ninmakh," and also the motif of the flood, which occurred in the "Eridu Genesis." The import of these motifs here is, however, new: they bring out the basic precariousness of man's existence; man's usefulness to the gods will not protect him unless he takes care not to annoy them, however innocently. He must stay within bounds; there are limits set for his self-expression.

The *Enuma elish*

A far more trustful and committed attitude to the powers that rule existence finds expression in the seemingly slightly later Babylonian creation story, *Enuma elish,* which may be dated to the later part of the 1st dynasty of Babylon (*c.* 1894–*c.* 1595 BC). Babylon's archenemy then was the Sealand, which controlled Nippur and the country south of it—the ancestral country of Sumerian civilization. This lends political point to the battle of Marduk (thunder and rain deity), the god of Babylon, with the Sea, Tiamat; it also accounts for the odd, almost complete silence about Enlil of Nippur in the tale.

The myth tells how in the beginning there was nothing but Apsu, the sweet waters underground, and Tiamat, the sea, mingling their waters together. In these waters the first gods came into being and generation followed generation. The gods represented energy and activity, and thus differed markedly from Apsu and Tiamat, who stood for rest and inertia. True to their nature the gods gathered to dance, and in so doing, surging back and forth, they disturbed the insides of Tiamat. Finally, Apsu's patience was at an end, and he thought of doing away with the gods, but Tiamat, as a true mother, demurred at destroying her own offspring. Apsu, however, did not swerve from his decision and he was encouraged in this by his page Mummu, "the original (watery) form." When the youngest of the gods, the clever Ea (Sumerian Enki), heard about the planned attack he forestalled it by means of a powerful spell with which he poured slumber on Apsu, killed him, and built his temple over him. He seized Mummu and held him captive by a nose rope.

In the temple thus built the hero of the myth, Marduk, was born. From the first he was the darling of his grandfather, the god of heaven, Anu, who engendered the four winds for him to play with. As they blew and churned up waves, the disturbing of Tiamat—and of a faction of the gods who shared her desire for rest—became more and more unbearable. At last these gods succeeded in rousing her to resistance and she created a mighty army with a spearhead of monsters to destroy the gods. She placed her consort Kingu ("Task[?]") at the head of it and gave him absolute powers.

When news of these developments reached the gods there was consternation. Ea was sent to make Tiamat desist, and then Anu, but to no avail. Finally Anshar, god of the horizon and king of the gods, thought of young Marduk. Marduk proved willing to fight Tiamat but demanded absolute authority. Accordingly, a messenger was sent to the oldest of the gods, Lahmu and Lahamu ("Silt[?]"), to call the gods to assembly, and in the assembly the gods conferred absolute authority on Marduk, tested it by seeing whether his word of command alone could destroy a constellation and then again make it whole, hailed him king, and set him on the road of "security and obedience," a formula of allegiance that based his power and authority on the pressing need for protection of the moment.

In the ensuing encounter with Tiamat's forces Kingu and his army lost heart when they saw Marduk. Only Tiamat stood her ground, seeking first to throw him off his guard by flattery about his quick rise to leadership, but Marduk angrily denounced her and the older generation: "The sons (had to) withdraw (for) the fathers were acting treacherously, and (now) you, who gave birth to them, bear malice to the offspring." At this Tiamat, furious, attacked, but Marduk loosed the winds against her, pierced her heart with an arrow, and killed her. Kingu and the gods who had sided with her he took captive.

Having thus won a lasting victory for his suzerain, King Anshar, he gave thought to what he might do further. Cleaving the carcass of Tiamat, he raised half of her to form heaven, ordered the constellations, the calendar, the movements of sun and moon, and, keeping control of atmospheric phenomena for himself, made the earth out of the other half of her, arranging its mountains and rivers. Having organized the various administrative tasks, he put their supervision in Ea's hands; to Anu he gave the tablets of fate he had taken from Kingu. His prisoners he paraded in triumphal procession before his fathers, and as a monument to his victory he set up images of Tiamat's monsters at the gate of his parental home. The gods were overjoyed to see him; Anshar rushed toward him and Marduk formally announced to him the state of security he had achieved. He then bathed, dressed, and seated himself on his throne, with the spear "Security and Obedience," named from his mandate, at his side. By now, however, the situation had subtly altered. The old fear and urgent need for protection was gone, but in its stead had come a promise held out by Marduk's organizational powers; so when the gods reaffirmed their allegiance to him as king they used a new formula: "benefits and obedience." From then on Marduk would take care of their sanctuaries and they, in turn, would obey him.

The building of Babylon

Marduk then announced his intention of building a city for himself, Babylon, with room for the gods when they come there for assembly; and his fathers suggested that they move there themselves to be with him and help in the administration of the world he had created. Next, he pardoned the gods who had sided with Tiamat and had been captured, charging them with the building tasks. Grateful for their lives, they prostrated themselves before him, hailed him as king, and promised to do the building.

Pleased with their willingness, Marduk magnanimously wanted to relieve them even from this chore and planned to create man to do the toil for them. At the advice of his father Ea, he then had them indict Kingu as instigator of the rebellion. Kingu was duly sentenced and executed, and from his blood Ea created man. Then Marduk divided the gods into a celestial and a terrestrial group, assigned them their tasks in the cosmos, and allotted them their stipends. Thus freed from all burdens, the gods wanted to show their gratitude to Marduk and as a token they took, of their own free will, for one last time, spade in hand to build Babylon and Marduk's temple Esagila. In the new temple the gods then assembled, distributed the celestial and terrestrial offices, the "great gods" went into session and permanently appointed the "seven gods of destinies," or better "of the decrees," who would formulate in final form the decrees enacted by the assembly. Marduk then presented his weapons and Anu adopted the bow as his daughter and gave it a seat among the gods. Lastly, Marduk was enthroned, and after the gods had prostrated themselves before him they bound themselves by oath—touching their throats with oil and water—and formally gave him kingship, appointing him permanently lord of the gods of heaven and earth. After this they solemnly named his 50 names expressive of his power and achievements. The myth ends with a plea that it be handed on from father to son and told to future rulers, that they may heed Marduk: it is the song of Marduk who bound Tiamat and assumed the kingship.

The motifs from which this myth is built up are in large measure known from elsewhere. The initial generation of the gods is a variant form of the genealogy of Anu in the great god list *An: Anum;* the threat to annihilate the disturbances of sleep are known from the Atrahasis and the Sumerian flood traditions; the battle of Marduk with Tiamat seems to stem from western myths of a battle between the thunder god and the sea; the organization of the universe after victory recalls the organization of conquered territory in "Lugal-e"; and the killing of a rebel god to create man to take over the gods' toil is found in the Atrahasis myth and—without the rebel aspect—in a bilingual creation myth found in Assur. New and original, however, is the way in which they have all been grouped and made dependent on the figure of the young king. The political form of the monarchy is seen as embracing the universe; it was the prowess of a young king that overcame the forces of inertia; it was his organizational genius that created and organized all; and it is he that—as his counterpart on earth, the human king—grants benefits in return for obedience. The high value set on the monarchy as a guarantor of security and order in the *Enuma elish* can hardly have seemed obvious in Babylonia in the first troubled years of Assyrian rule in the second quarter of the 1st millennium BC. From this period (*c.* 700 BC) comes a myth usually called the Erra epic, which reads almost like a polemic against *Enuma elish.* It tells how the god of affray and indiscriminate slaughter, Erra, persuaded Marduk to turn over the rule of the world to him while Marduk was having his royal insignia cleaned, and how Erra, true to his nature, used his powers to institute indiscriminate rioting and slaughter. Royal power here stands no longer for security and order, but for the opposite: license to kill and destroy.

The value of the monarchy

Two other Akkadian myths may be mentioned—both probably dating from the middle of the 2nd millennium—the myth of the "Dynasty of Dunnum" and the myth of "Nergal and Ereshkigal." The first of these tells of succeeding divine generations ruling in Dunnum, the son usually killing his father and marrying, sometimes his mother, sometimes his sister, until—according to a reconstruction of the broken text—more acceptable mores came into vogue with the last generation of gods, Enlil and Ninurta. This myth, as has been mentioned, underlies the Greek poet Hesiod's Theogony. The myth of Nergal and Ereshkigal relates the unorthodox way in which the god Nergal became the husband of Ereshkigal and king of the Nether World.

Epics. The quick rise of Sargon, the founder of the dynasty of Akkad (*c.* 2334–*c.* 2154 BC), from obscurity to fame and his victory over Lugalzaggisi of Uruk form the theme of several epic tales. The sudden eclipse of the Akkadian empire under Naramsin, attributed to that ruler's pride and the gods' retaliation, is the theme of "The Fall of Akkad." Akkadian epic tradition continues and gives focus to the Sumerian tales of Gilgamesh.

The Gilgamesh epic

The Akkadian *Epic of Gilgamesh* seems to have been composed in old Babylonian times but was reworked by a certain Sin-liqi-unninni later in the 1st millennium BC. It tells how Gilgamesh, the young ruler of Uruk, drives his subjects so hard that they appeal to the gods for relief. The gods create a wild man, Enkidu, who at first lives with the animals in the desert but is lured away from them and becomes Gilgamesh's friend. Together they vanquish the terrifying Huwawa, set by Enlil to guard the cedar forest in the West, and when on their return the goddess of Uruk, Ishtar, falls in love with Gilgamesh, is jilted by him, and sends the dread "bull of heaven" to kill him, he and Enkidu manage to kill the bull. At this point, however, their fortunes change. Enlil, angered at the killing of Huwawa, causes Enkidu to fall ill and die, and Gilgamesh, inconsolable at the death of his friend and terrified at the realization that he himself must someday die sets out to find eternal life.

After many adventures he reaches an ancestor of his, Utnapishtim, to whom the gods have granted eternal life, but his case proves to be a unique one and so of no help to Gilgamesh. Utnapishtim was rewarded for having saved human and animal life at the time of the great flood. Eventually, just as Gilgamesh is ready to return home he is told about a plant that rejuvenates and makes old men children again. Gilgamesh finds it and begins his return journey. But as the day is warm, when he passes an inviting pool, he leaves his clothes and the plant on the shore and goes in for a swim. A serpent smells the plant, comes out of its hole and eats it. Thus Gilgamesh's quest comes to naught. Eternal life is beyond man's grasp. The Gilgamesh epic is perhaps the most moving work in ancient Mesopotamian literature with its sharp contrast of values: the warrior's disdain of death and danger, which informs the early parts of the epic, and the haunting fear that drives Gilgamesh in the later parts.

Other Akkadian epics that deserve to be mentioned are the Etana epic, which tells how Etana, the first king, was carried up to heaven on the back of an eagle to obtain the plant of birth, so that his son could be born; and epic tales about Sargon of Akkad, one of which, the birth legend, tells of his abandonment in a casket on the river by his mother—much as the Hebrew Moses was abandoned—and his discovery by an orchardman, who raised him as his son. Another Sargon tale is "The King of Battle," which tells about conquests in Asia Minor to protect foreign trade. Naramsin is the central figure in another tale dealing with that king's pride and also relating the destructive invasions by barbarous foes. A late flowering of primary epic is the Assyrian Tukulti-Ninurta epic that deals with that king's wars with Babylonia. He reigned from 1245 to 1208 BC.

MESOPOTAMIAN WORLDVIEW AS EXPRESSED IN MYTH

The more completely a given culture is embraced, the more natural will its basic tenets seem to the people involved. The most fundamental of its presuppositions are not even likely to rise into awareness and be consciously held but are tacitly taken for granted. It takes a degree of cultural decline, of the loosening of the culture's grip on thought and action, before its most basic structural lines can be recognized and, if need be, challenged. Since culture, the total pattern within which man lives and acts, is thus not likely to be conceived of consciously and as a whole until it begins to lose its obvious and natural character, it is understandable that those myths of a culture that may be termed existential—in the sense that they articulate human existence as a whole in terms of the culture and show its basic structure—are rarely encountered until comparatively late in the history of a culture. Before that occurs, it is, rather, the particular aspects and facets of existence that are apt to claim attention.

In ancient Mesopotamia the oldest known materials, the Sumerian myths, have relatively little to say about creation; scholars must, for the most part, turn to the introductions of tales and disputations to infer how things were believed to be in the beginning. Thus, a story about the hero Gilgamesh refers in its introductory lines to the times: "after heaven had been moved away from earth, after earth had been separated from heaven." The same notion that heaven and earth were once close together occurs also in a bilingual Sumero-Akkadian text from Ashur about the creation of man. The actual act of separating them is credited to the storm god Enlil of Nippur in the introduction to a third tale that deals with the creation of the first hoe. From similar passing remarks scholars have inferred that the gods, before man came into being, had to labour hard at the heavy works of irrigation agriculture and dug out the beds of the Tigris and the Euphrates.

Cosmogony and cosmology. Though the "Eridu Genesis" may have come close to treating existence as a whole, a true cosmogonic and cosmological myth that deals centrally with the origins, structuring, and functional principles of the cosmos does not actually appear until Old Babylonian times, when Mesopotamian culture was entering a millennium and a half of doubts about the moral character of world government and even of divine power itself. Yet, the statement is a positive one, almost to the point of defiance. *Enuma elish* tells of a beginning when all was a watery chaos and only the sea, Tiamat, and the sweet waters under ground, Apsu, mingled their waters together and the original watery form that was personified served as Apsu's page. In their midst the gods were born. The first pair, Lahmu and Lahamu, represented the powers in silt; the next, Anshar and Kishar, those in the horizon. They engendered the god of heaven, Anu, and he in turn the god of the flowing sweet waters, Ea.

This tradition is known in a more complete form from an ancient list of gods called *An: Anum.* There, after a different beginning, Lahmu and Lahamu give rise to Duri and Dari, "the time-cycle"; and these in turn give rise to the powers for a circle to be Enshar and Ninshar, "Lord and Lady Circle." Enshar and Ninshar engender the concrete circle of the horizon, Anshar and Kishar, probably conceived as silt deposited along the edge of the universe. Next is the horizon of the greater heaven and earth, and then—omitting an intrusive line—heaven and earth, probably conceived as two juxtaposed flat disks formed from silt deposited inward from the horizons. *Enuma elish* truncates these materials and violates their inner logic considerably. Though they are clearly cosmogonic and assume that the cosmic elements and the powers informing them come into being together, *Enuma elish* seeks to utilize them for a pure theogony (account of the origin of the gods). The creation of the actual cosmos is dealt with much later. Also, the introduction of Mummu, the personified "original form," which in the circumstances can only be that of water, may have led to the omission of Ki, "Earth" who—as nonwatery—did not fit in.

The gods, who in *Enuma elish* come into being within Apsu and Tiamat, are viewed as dynamic creatures, who contrast strikingly with the older generation. Apsu and Tiamat stand for inertia and rest. This contrast leads to a series of conflicts in which first Apsu is killed by Ea; then Tiamat, who was roused later to attack the gods, by Ea's son Marduk. It is Marduk, the hero of the story, who creates the extant universe out of the body of Tiamat after he kills her. Marduk cuts her, as a dried fish, in two, making one-half of her into heaven—appointing there sun, moon, and stars to execute their prescribed motions—and her other half into the earth. He pierces her eyes to let the Tigris and Euphrates flow forth, and then, heaping mountains on her body in the east, he makes the various tributaries of the Tigris flow out from her breasts. The remainder of the story deals with Marduk's organization of the cosmos, his creation of man, and his assigning to the gods their various cosmic offices and tasks. The cosmos is viewed as structured as, and functioning as, a benevolent absolute monarchy.

Marduk as creator

The gods and demons. The gods were, as mentioned previously, organized in a polity of a primitive democratic cast. They constituted, as it were, a landed nobility, each god owning and working an estate—his temple and its lands—and controlling the city in which it was located. On the national level he attended the general assembly of the gods, which was the highest authority in the cosmos, to vote on matters of national import such as, for example, election or deposing of kings. The major gods also served on the national level as officers having charge of cosmic offices. Thus, for example, Utu, the sun god, was, in addition to taking care of the sun, the judge of the gods and in charge of justice and righteousness generally.

Highest in the pantheon—and presiding in the divine assembly—ranked An (Akkadian Anu), god of Heaven and responsible for the calendar and the seasons as they were indicated by their appropriate stars. Next came Enlil of Nippur, god of winds and of agriculture, creator of the hoe. Enlil executed the verdicts of the divine assembly. Equal in rank to An and Enlil was the goddess Ninhursag (also known as Nintur and Ninmakh), goddess of stony ground: the near moutain ranges in the east and the stony desert in the west with its wildlife—wild asses, gazelles, wild goats, etc. She was also the goddess of birth. With these was joined—seemingly secondarily—Enki (Ea), god of the sweet waters of rivers and marshes; he was the cleverest of the gods and a great troubleshooter often appealed to both by gods and by men. Of other gods may be mentioned Enlil's sons: the moon god Nanna or Sîn; the god of thunderstorms, floods, and the plough, Ninurta; and the underworld figures Meslamtaea, Ninazu, and Ennugi. Sîn's sons were the sun god and judge of the gods, Utu (the Akkadian Shamash), the rain god Ishkur (the Akkadian Adad), and his daughter, the goddess of war, love, and morning and evening star, Inanna (the Akkadian Ishtar). Inanna's ill-fated young husband was the herder god Dumuzi (the Akkadian Tammuz). The dread Nether World was ruled by the goddess Ereshkigal and her husband Nergal, a figure closely related to Meslamtaea and Ninurta. Earlier tradition mentions Ninazu as her husband.

Hierarchy of the gods

Demons played little or no role in the myths or lists of the Mesopotamian pantheon. Their domain was that of incantations. Mostly, they were depicted as outlaws; the demoness Lamashtu, for instance, was hurled from Heaven by her father An because of her wickedness. The demons attacked man by causing all kinds of diseases and were, as a rule, viewed as wind and storm beings. Consonant with the classical view of the universe as a cosmic state, it was possible for a person to go to the law courts against the demons; *i.e.,* to seek recourse before Utu and obtain judgments against them. Various rituals for such procedures are known.

Man: his origin, nature, and destiny. Two different notions about man's origin seem to have been current in ancient Mesopotamian religions. Brief mentions in Sumerian texts indicate that the first men grew forth from the earth in the manner of grass and herbs. One of these texts, the "Myth of the Creation of the Hoe," adds a few details: Enlil removed heaven from earth in order to make room for seeds to come up and, after he had created the hoe, he used it to break the hard crust of earth in Uzumua ("the flesh-grower"), a place in the Temple of Inanna in Nippur. Here, out of the hole made by Enlil's hoe, man grew forth.

The other notion presented the view that man was created from select "ingredients" by Enki, or by Enki and his mother Nammu, or by Enki and the birth goddess called variously Ninhursag, Nintur, and Ninmakh. In the myth of "Enki and Ninmakh" recounted above, Enki had man sired by the "engendering clay of the Apsu"—*i.e.,* of the waters underground—and borne by Nammu. The Akkadian tradition, as represented by the "Myth of Atrakhasis," had Enki advise that a god—presumably a rebel—be killed and that the birth goddess Nintur mix his flesh and blood with clay. This was done, after which 14 womb goddesses gestated the mixture and gave birth to seven human pairs. A similar—probably derived—form of this motif is found in *Enuma elish,* in which Enki (Ea) alone fashioned man out of the blood of the slain rebel leader Kingu. The creation of man from the blood shed by two slain gods is yet another version of the motif that appears in a bilingual myth from Ashur.

Man's nature, then, is part clay (earthly) and part god (divine). The divine aspect, however, is not that of a living god but rather that of a slain, powerless divinity. The Atrakhasis story relates that the *etemmu* (ghost) of the slain god was left in man's flesh and thus became part of man. It is this originally divine part of man, his *etemmu,* that was believed to survive at his death and to give him a shadowy afterlife in the Nether World. No other trace of a notion of divine essence in man is discernible; in fact, man by himself was viewed as being utterly powerless to act effectively or to succeed in anything. For anything he might wish to do or achieve, man needed the help of a personal god or goddess, some deity in the pantheon who for one reason or other had taken an interest in him and helped and protected him, for "Without his personal god a man eats not."

The divine and earthly nature of man

About man's destiny all sources agree. However man may have come into being, he was meant to toil in order to provide food, clothing, housing, and service for the gods, so that they, relieved of all manual labour, could live the life of a governing upper class, a landed nobility. In the scheme of existence man was thus never an end, always just a means.

INSTITUTIONS AND PRACTICES

City-state and national state. In early dynastic times, probably as far back as historians can trace its history, Mesopotamia was divided into small units, the so-called city-states, consisting of a major city with its surrounding lands. The ruler of the city—usually entitled *ensi*—was also in charge of the temple of the city god. The spouse of the *ensi* had charge of the temple of the city goddess, and the children of the *ensi* administered the temples of the deities who were regarded as children of the city god and the city goddesses. After the foundation of larger political units, such as leagues or empires, contributions were made to a central temple of the political unit, such as the temple of Enlil at Nippur in the Nippur league. On the other hand, however, the king or other central ruler might also contribute to the shrines of local cults. When, in the 2nd and 1st millennia, Babylonia and Assyria emerged as national states, their kings had responsibility for the national cult and each monarch supervised the administration of all temples in his domain.

The purpose of man in relation to the gods

Cult. In the cultic practices man fulfilled his destiny: to take care of the gods' material needs. Man therefore provided the gods with houses (the temples) that were richly supplied with lands, which man cultivated for them. In the temple the god was present in—but not bounded by—a statue made of precious wood overlaid with gold. For this statue the temple kitchen staff prepared daily meals from victuals grown or raised on the temple's fields, in its orchards, in its sheepfolds, cattle pens, and game preserves, brought in by its fishermen, or delivered by farmers owing it as a temple tax. Not only was the statue fed but it was also clad in costly raiments, bathed, and escorted to bed in the bedchamber of the god, often on top of the temple tower, or ziggurat. To see to all of this the god had a corps of house servants; *i.e.*, priests trained as cooks, bakers, waiters, and bathers, or as encomiasts (singers of praise) and musicians to make the god's meals festive, or as elegists to soothe him in times of stress and grief. Diversions from the daily routine were the great monthly festivals, and also a number of special occasions. Such special occasions might be a sudden need to go through the elaborate ritual for purifying the king when he was threatened by the evils implied in an eclipse of the moon, or in extreme cases there might be a call for the ritual installation of a substitute king to take upon himself the dangers threatening, and various other nonperiodic rituals.

Partly regular, partly impromptu, were the occasions for audiences with the god in which the king or other worshippers presented their petitions and prayers accompanied by appropriate offerings. These were mostly edibles, but not infrequently the costly containers in which they were presented, stone vases, golden boat-shaped vessels, etc., testified to the ardour of the givers. Appropriate gifts other than edibles were also acceptable—among them cylinder seals for the god's use, superhuman in size, and weapons for him, such as maceheads, also outsize.

To the cult, but as private rather than as part of the temple cult, may be counted also the burial ritual, concerning which, unfortunately, there is little known. In outgoing early dynastic times in Girsu two modes of burial were current. One was ordinary burial in a cemetery; the other, laying the body "in the reeds of Enki," is not clear, perhaps it denoted the floating of the body down the river into the canebrakes. Elegists and other funerary personnel were in attendance and conducted the laments seeking to give full expression to the grief of the bereaved and propitiate the spirit of the dead. In later times burial in a family vault under the dwelling house was frequent.

Sacred times. During most of the 2nd millennium each major city had its own calendar. The months were named from local religious festivals celebrated in the month in question. Only by the 2nd millennium did the Nippur calendar attain general acceptance. The nature of the festivals in these various sacred calendars sometimes reflected the cycle of agricultural activities, such as celebrating the ritual hitching up of the plows and, later in the year, their unhitching, or rites of sowing, harvesting, and other activities. The sacred calendar of Girsu at the end of the early dynastic period is rich in its accounting of festivals. During some of these festival periods the queen travelled through her domain to present funerary offerings of barley, malt, and other agricultural products to the gods and to the spirits of deceased charismatic human administrators.

The cycles of festivals celebrating the marriage and early death of Dumuzi and similar fertility figures in spring are structured according to the backgrounds of the various communities of farmers, herders, or date growers. The sacred wedding—sometimes a fertility rite, sometimes a harvest festival with overtones of thanksgiving—was performed as a drama: the ruler and a high priestess took on the identity of the two deities and so ensured that their highly desirable union actually took place. In many communities the lament for the dead god took the form of a procession out into the desert to find the slain god in his gutted fold, a pilgrimage to the accompaniment of harps and heart-rending laments for the god.

New Year Festival

Of major importance in later times was the New Year Festival, or Akitu, celebrated in a special temple out in the fields. Originally an agricultural festival connected with sowing and harvest, it became the proper occasion for the crowning and investiture of a new king. In Babylon it came to celebrate the sun god Marduk's victory over Tiamat, the goddess of the watery deep. Besides the yearly festivals there were also monthly festivals at New Moon, the 7th, the 15th, and the 28th of the month. The last—when the moon was invisible and thought to be dead—had a distinctly funereal character.

Administration. Supreme responsibility for the correct carrying out of the cult, on which the welfare of the country depended, was entrusted to the city ruler, or, when the country was united, the king. The city ruler and the king were, however, far more than administrators; they also were charismatic figures imparting their individual magic into their rule, thus creating welfare and fertility. In certain periods the king was deified; throughout the 3rd millenium, he became, in ritual action, the god Dumuzi in the rite of the sacred marriage and thus insured fertility for his land. The rulers of the entire 3rd dynasty of Ur (*c.* 2112–*c.* 2004 BC) and most of the dynasty of Isin (*c.* 2020–*c.* 1800 BC) were treated as embodiments of the dying god Damu and invoked in the ritual laments for him. As a vessel of sacred power the king was surrounded by strict ritual to protect that power, and he had to undergo elaborate rituals of purification if the power became threatened.

The role and functions of the priesthood

The individual temples were usually administered by officials called *sanga* ("bishops"), who headed staffs of accountants, overseers of agricultural and industrial works on the temple estate, and *gudu* (priests), who looked after the god as house servants. Among the priestesses the highest ranking were termed *en* (Akkadian *entu*). They were usually princesses of royal blood and were considered the human spouses of the gods they served, participating as brides in the rites of the sacred marriage. Other ranks of priestesses are known, most of them to be considered orders of nuns. The best known are the votaries of the sun god, who lived in a cloister (*gagûm*) in Sippar. Whether, besides nuns, there were also priestesses devoted to sacred prostitution is a moot question; what is clear is that prostitutes were under the special protection of the goddess Inanna (Ishtar).

Sacred places. Mesopotamian worshippers might worship in open-air sanctuaries, chapels in private houses, or small separate chapels located in the residential quarters of town; but the sacred place par excellence was the temple. Archaeology has traced the temple back to the earliest periods of settlement, and though the very early temple plans still pose many unsolved problems, it is clear that from the early dynastic period onward the temple was what the Sumerian (*e*) and Akkadian (*bîtum*) terms for it indicate; *i.e.*, the temple was the god's house or dwelling. In its more elaborate form such a temple would be built on a series of irregular artificial platforms, one on top of the other; by the 3rd dynasty of Ur, near the end of the 3rd millennium, these became squared off to form a ziggurat. On the lowest of these platforms a heavy wall—first oval, later rectangular—enclosed storerooms, the temple kitchen, workshops, and other such rooms. On the highest level, approached by a stairway, were the god's living quarters centred in the cella, a rectangular room with an entrance door in the long wall near one corner. The god's place was on a podium in a niche at the short wall farthest from the entrance; benches with statues of worshippers ran along both long walls, and a hearth in the middle of the floor served for heating. Low pillars in front of the god's seat seem to have served as stoppers for a hanging that shielded him from profane eyes. Here, or in a connecting room, would be the god's table, bed, and bathtub.

The structure and function of the temple

At a later time in Babylonia the dimensions of the cella with its adjoining rooms were greatly enlarged so that it became an open court surrounded by rooms. Only the section separated by the hanging remained roofed and became a new cella, entered from the middle of its long side and with the god in his niche in the wall directly opposite. The development in Assyria took a slightly different course. Here the original door in the long side moved around the corner to the short side opposite the god, creating a rectangular cella entered from the end wall.

The function of the temple, as of all of the other sacred places in ancient Mesopotamia, was primarily to ensure the god's presence and to provide a place where he could be approached. The providing of housing, food, and service for the god achieved the first of these purposes. His presence was also assured by a suitable embodiment—the cult statue, and, for certain rites, the body of the ruler. To achieve the second purpose, greeting gifts, praise hymns as introduction to petitions, and other actions were used to induce the god to receive the petitioner and to listen to, and accept, his prayers.

In view of the magnitude of such an establishment provided for the gods and the extent of lands belonging to them and cultivated for them—partly with temple personnel, partly by members of the community holding temple land in some form of tenure or another—it was unavoidable that temples should vie in economic importance with similar large private estates or with estates belonging to the crown. This importance, one may surmise, would lie largely in the element of stability that an efficiently run major estate provided for the community. With its facilities for producing large storable surpluses that could be used to offset bad years and with its facilities—such as its weaveries—the temple estates could absorb and utilize elements of the population, such as widows, waifs, captives, and others, who otherwise would have perished or become a menace to the community in one way or other. The economic importance of the temple primarily was local. The amount of foreign trade carried on by them apparently was small. The power behind foreign trade seems rather to have been the king.

The magical arts. In the ancient Mesopotamian view, gods and humans shared one world. The gods lived among men on their great estates (the temples), ruled, upheld law and order for men, and fought their wars. In general, knowing and carrying out the will of the gods was not a matter for doubt: they wanted the practice of their cult performed faultlessly, work on their estates done willingly and well, and they disapproved, in greater or lesser degree, of breaches of the moral and legal order. On occasion, however, man might well be uncertain: did a god want his temple rebuilt or did he not? In all such cases, and others like them, the Mesopotamians sought direct answers from the gods through divination, and conversely the gods might take the initiative and convey specific wishes through dreams, signs, or portents.

Belief in divination and astrology

There were many forms of divination. Of interest to students of biblical prophecy is recent evidence that prophets and prophetesses were active at the court of Mari on the Euphrates in Old Babylonian times (*c.* 1800–*c.* 1600 BC). In Mesopotamia as a whole, however, the forms of divination most frequently used seem to have been incubation—*i.e.,* sleeping in the temple in the hope that the god would send an enlightening dream—and hepatoscopy; *i.e.,* examining the entrails, particularly the liver, of a lamb or kid sacrificed for a divinatory purpose, to read what the god had "written" there by interpreting variations in form and shape. In the 2nd and 1st millennia large and detailed handbooks in hepatoscopy were composed for consultation by the diviners. Though divination in historical times was regularly presented in terms of ascertaining the divine will, there are internal indications in the materials suggesting that it was originally less theologically elaborated. Apparently it was a mere attempt to read the future from "symptoms" in the present, much as a physician recognizes the onset of a disease. This is particularly made clear in that branch of divination that deals with unusual happenings believed to be ominous. Thus, if a desert plant sprouted in a city—indicating that desert essence was about to take over—it was considered an indication that the city would be laid waste.

Related to the observation of unusual happenings in society or nature, but far more systematized, was astrology. The movements and appearance of the sun, the moon, and the planets were believed to yield information about future events affecting the nation or, in some cases, the fate of individuals. Horoscopes, predicting the character and fate of a person on the basis of the constellation of the stars at his birth, are known to have been constructed in the late 1st millennium, but the art may conceivably be older.

Witchcraft was apparently at all times considered a crime punishable by death. Frequently, however, it probably was difficult to identify the witch in individual cases, or even to be sure that a given evil was the result of witchcraft rather than of other causes. In such cases the expert in white magic, the *ashipu* or *mashmashshu,* was able to help both in diagnosing the cause of the evil and in performing the appropriate rituals and incantation to fight it off. In earlier times the activities of the magicians seem generally to have been directed against the lawless demons who attacked man and caused all kinds of diseases. In the later half of the 2nd, and all through the 1st millennium, however, the fear of man-made evils grew, and witchcraft vied with the demons as the chief source of all ills.

Belief in witchcraft

RELIGIOUS ART AND ICONOGRAPHY

The earliest periods in Mesopotamia have yielded figurines of clay or stone, some of which may conceivably represent gods or demons; certainty of interpretation in regard to these figurines is, however, difficult to attain. With the advent of the Protoliterate period toward the end of the 4th millennium BC, the so-called cylinder seal came into use. In the designs on these seals—often, it would seem, copies from monumental wall paintings now lost—ritual scenes and divine figures, recognizable from what is known about them in historical times, make their first appearance. To this period also belongs the magnificent Uruk Vase, with its representation of the sacred marriage rite. Until the early centuries of the 2nd millennium the cylinder seal remains one of the most prolific sources of religious motifs and representations of divine figures, but larger reliefs, wall paintings, and sculpture in the round greatly add to modern historians' understanding of who and what is rendered. In the 2nd and 1st millennia, the humble categories of clay plaques and clay figurines often contained representations of deities, and the numerous sculptured boundary stones (*kudurru*s) furnish representations of symbols and emblems of gods, at times identified by labels in cuneiform. To the 1st millennium belong also the magnificent colossal statues of protective genii (spirits) in the shape of lions or human-headed bulls that guarded the entrances to Assyrian palaces, and also, on the gates of Nebuchadrezzar's (died 562 BC) Babylon, the reliefs in glazed tile of lions and dragons that served the same purpose.

CONCLUSION

A religious development covering four millennia such as one finds in ancient Mesopotamian religions is obviously

Uruk Vase decorated with an offering scene to a goddess, rows of porters, and animals and plants; bas-relief, early 3rd millennium BC. In the Iraq Museum, Baghdad.

By courtesy of the Directorate General of Antiquities, Baghdad

of interest in and of itself. The tendencies that lead from a central concern with salvation from famine to salvation from attack, and finally to salvation from a sense of personal guilt, with the attendant deepening and enriching of the concept of the divine, invites close study. So also do the many moving and profound expressions of religious faith in the hymns, laments, and prayers of these religions. As one of the earliest religious systems in history to structure, and be itself structured by, the complexities of a high civilization, Mesopotamian religions are of significant interest to historians, historians of religion, and theologians. As a source from which religious insights, attitudes, and problems flowed into all of Western tradition, Mesopotamian religions are of lasting and great interest beyond themselves. (T.J./Ed.)

Iranian religions

The religions of the Iranian peoples, including the peoples of Iran proper, the Scythians, Sarmatians, and Alani, are characterized by a development of doctrines of salvation, a battle between good and evil, the afterlife, and a concept of a Saviour. Various forms of fire worship and burial rites that reflect certain eschatological views also are important in understanding the religions of the Iranian peoples that eventually exerted an influence on the religions of the Western world.

NATURE AND SIGNIFICANCE

The religious conditions of the ancient Iranian peoples who emerged out of a common Indo-Iranian origin sometime after 1700 BC to form the Iranian nation are largely unknown. The historical importance of the Iranian religions lies in the great role they played in Iranian developments and in the significant influence Iranian types of religion exercised in the West, especially on postexilic Jewish religion; on Hellenistic mystery religions, such as Mithraism; on Gnosticism; and on Islām, in which Iranian ideas are found both in Shīʿah, the most important medieval sect, and in popular eschatology (doctrines dealing with the last times).

In Iran itself the influence of the old religions lived on, not only in Zoroastrianism and in the various politico-religious movements that disturbed Iran during the first centuries of its Islāmic history but also in the cultural heritage of medieval and modern Iran, especially in art and literature.

The problems in the study of Iranian religions lie mainly in the sources and their character. To a great extent the sources are foreign to Iran and extant in many different languages. What purely Iranian sources there are date from many periods of the Iranian languages and are full of philological difficulties. In addition to the written sources, extremely valuable testimonies are offered by art and archaeology.

The most difficult problem of all is associated with the history of the Avesta, the holy book of the modern Parsis (Zoroastrians of India). Only the fourth part of the original Sāsānian (3rd–7th centuries AD) Avesta was saved after the Arab conquest of Iran in the 7th century. An enormous mass of religious traditions is preserved in Pahlavi (the language of the Sāsānian period) and new Persian literature. Hence the cardinal problem: how much of this textual matter may be traced back to lost Avestan tracts? The evaluation of the Iranian influence in older times depends on the answer to this question.

This influence is explained in terms of the characteristics of Iranian religions, which include: speculative vigour (*i.e.,* macrocosmic-microcosmic speculation); a theological conception of history; dualism; an optimistic monism; and eschatological and apocalyptic speculation (revelations on the character of the last times). The doctrines of the ages of the world and of the bodily resurrection of mankind are typical doctrines that had a great success outside Iran. Characteristics

All Iranian religions are religions of salvation. Everything is centred on individual and collective salvation. A central place is assumed by a Saviour, who is commissioned by God to bring revelation. Cyclical ideas about the history of the world are combined with the belief that the Saviour has been incarnated in human shape in order to bring a definite revelation. A special emphasis is given here to the concept of "mankind," for Primordial Man, who is the first Saviour, is called Mortal Life. Thus, divinity and humanity interpenetrate each other. The divine Saviour descends to the earth and is born in a human individual as his higher, spiritual element. Such is the background of the famous doctrine of "the saved Saviour." From this idea follows a belief in the ascension of the soul back to its original celestial home.

The idea of the king as a divine person results very largely from the expectation of a future Saviour. According to the royal legend, the birth and education of the king are characterized by miracles. When he is born his divine star appears in the sky. The king is thus conceived as a Saviour, and his enthronement introduces a new era, which is the return of a golden age. The ruler is possessed of the royal glory, called the *khvarnah,* which gives him good luck.

The Iranians' attitude to the world is coloured by either pessimism or optimism, according to the emphasis that is placed on the actual battle between Good and Evil in this present age and on the temporal triumph of Evil or on the definite victory of Good in the final period that is yet to come. From the pessimistic attitude the Iranian type of Gnosticism (which is a religious world view in which matter is viewed as evil and the spirit good) is born. Gnosticism derives from Iran its basic and much of its technical language.

HISTORICAL DEVELOPMENT

Early Indo-Iranian religion. Of the religion of the early Indo-Iranians there is little direct evidence, other than theophorous (god-bearing) personal names of the feudal nobility of the Mitanni kingdom, and the treaty of Suppiluliumas with Mattiwaza, king of Mitanni, dating from about 1380, in which are listed Mitra, Varuna, Indra, and the two Nāsatyas, the twin gods. To these is added a goddess with a Mesopotamian name, Allatum or Ellat. These deities represent the three cosmic and social functions: Mitra-Varuṇa are the rulers, of whom Mitra represents the juridical and Varuṇa the magic-priestly aspect; Indra is the god of the warrior function; Nāsatya and the goddess represent the nourishing function and the collective character of society.

Indo-Iranian deities

The theophorous personal names of Indo-Iranian type include also the names of the western high god Zurvān (time); Vayu, the god of the atmosphere, with affinities to the warrior function; and Arta, the cosmic order, representing such ethical concepts as right and truth.

Scythian religion. Of the north Iranian tribes the Scythians are best known from the religious point of view. Source material consists of Greek and Latin texts and inscriptions, theophorous personal names, monuments of art, tombs, and modern Ossetic (the language of the Ossetes, an Alan people of the Central Caucasus) folklore.

The pantheon, which is presented in accordance with the Indo-Iranian three-functional system (*i.e.,* the ruling, warrior, and supportive or collective functions), is introduced by Tabiti, the "flaming" goddess. Then follow a god of heaven, called Papeus, "Father," and a god corresponding to Mithra, whose name is either Oetosyrus or Goetosyrus, both representing the ruler function. The warrior function has as its representative a god corresponding to Verethraghna (the Iranian god of victory) in eastern Iran. His Scythian name is unknown. The goddesses Apia, "Water," and Artimpasa (Aphrodite Urania), "she who pays attention to Arti" (a notion signifying luck and fecundity), represent the third, the fertility and collective function. In the inscriptions there is mentioned a "Virgin," who probably is of the same type (or possibly identical with one of them). The enigmatic Thagimasadas (Poseidon), god of the running waters, which can be compared with the Ossetic Don Bettyr, probably also belongs to the third function.

Herodotus (5th-century-BC Greek historian) stated that the Scythians had no temples, altars, or statues. The war god, however, had as his sanctuary an enormous heap of bundles of firewood. Atop it was put an iron *akinakēs* (East Iranian word for a short sword) as the symbol of this god, to which the Scythians sacrificed every year sheep, horses, and captive enemies. They cut off the joined right arm and shoulder of every sacrificed enemy and threw it in the air. Ossetic folklore shows these huge bundles of wood to be destined for a gigantic pyre. From the animal sacrifices a priest offered a small part of the flesh and the bowels to the god, throwing it on the ground before him. No fire was used at sacrifices. Great sacrifices of horses were offered in connection with the funeral ceremonies.

Sacrifice and divination

Among ritual customs divination was prominent. Scythian diviners used rods of salix wood, of which the priest made a bundle. While pronouncing certain conjuration formulas, the priest placed the rods severally one on the other and then again put them together in a bundle. The diviners were called by Herodotus *enaries,* "manwomen" as he translates this term. He stated that the Great Goddess had given them the power of divination. They practiced another divination method, using linden bark. The name *enaries* itself is Iranian: *a-nar(a)-,* corresponding to *anandrieis,* as Hippocrates more accurately translated it. They outwardly changed their sex by dressing and speaking as women.

The cult of the hearth fire, especially that of the king, played a central role. Oaths of an especially solemn character were taken at the royal hearth.

A social-religious custom, which is confirmed by Ossetic folklore, was the yearly drinking party in every district, when only those who had killed an enemy during the past year were allowed to drink, while the other warriors, who were covered with shame, were relegated to a separate place. The giant bowl from which the heroes drank among the Ossetes is called *nārt-āmongā,* "indicator of the heroic man."

Funeral customs and eschatology are the best known parts of north Iranian religion. Excavations have in every point confirmed the descriptions given by Herodotus. Mourning rites were excessive; *i.e.,* they were expressions of sorrow given in a conventional ceremonial form. Herodotus mentioned these rites only in connection with royal funerals, but Ossetic customs show them to have been regularly practiced. Men beat themselves in their

Death rites and customs

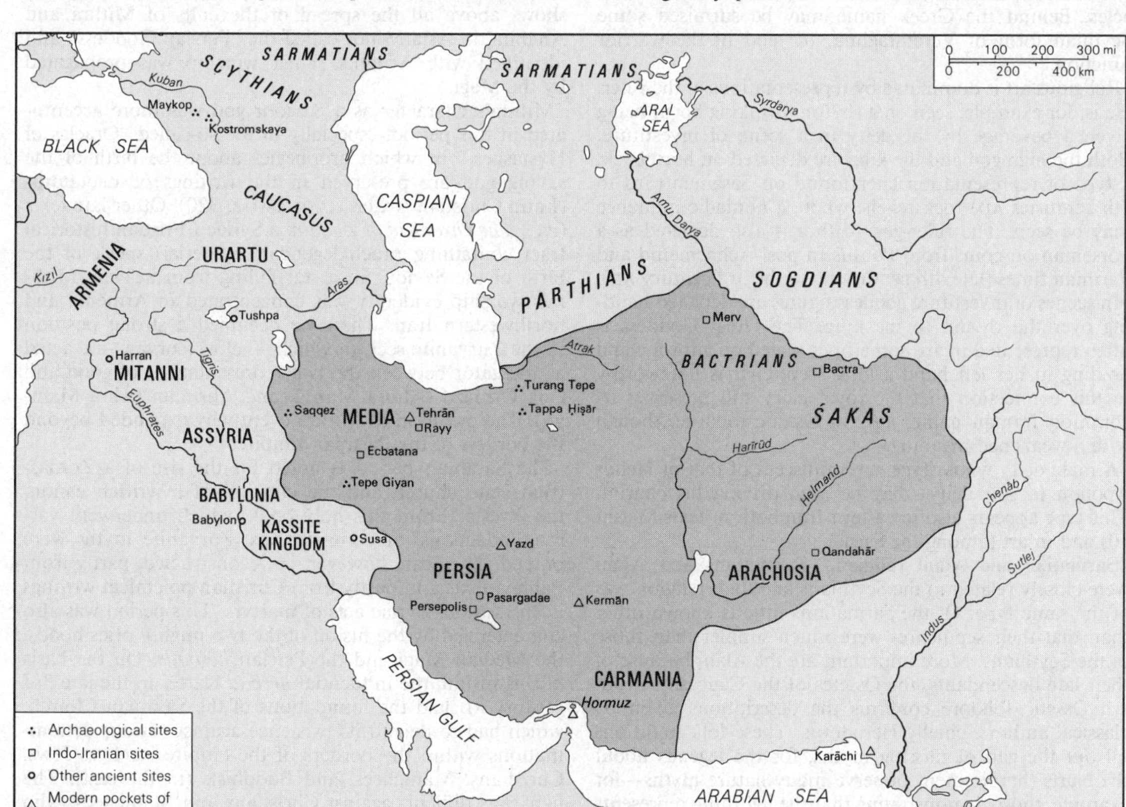

Significant religious sites and sites containing religious artifacts of ancient Indo-Iranian peoples, including those of peoples of adjacent areas and modern Zoroastrians.

faces, scratched their noses and cheeks, cut their hair, put arrows through their left hands, even cut away pieces of their ears. Women, besides scratching their faces, cut away their tresses or pulled out some of their hair and denuded their bosoms. A scene from a Buddhist painting in Central Asia shows Scythians indulging in such rites of mourning, which have been prevalent in all non-Zoroastrian forms of Iranian religion.

The disposal of the dead followed a certain pattern. There was, however, a difference between the burial of a king and a commoner. The royal tombs were covered with big mounds. A grave was dug that was supported by beams. The tomb itself was constructed with stones. Outside this grave chamber there were graves for the following of the king, people who were slaughtered in connection with the funeral. A corridor, covered by wood, led to the grave. Above the tomb a great tumulus (artificial mound) was heaped up.

The corpse was never burned, but the king was embalmed with wax. With the corpse were buried his arms and personal ornaments. In addition to his servants, horses also were slaughtered and buried.

Eschatological ideas among the Scythians can only be reconstructed from specimens of art, in which there is a scene representing the king before the seated Great Goddess in an act of communion, obviously after death. This scene must be compared with similar scenes described in the Zoroastrian text *Ḥadōkht Nask.*

North Iranian wall paintings from the graves of Panticapaeum depict banquet scenes. The motif of the funerary banquet has been depicted in a great many areas of the Iranian west.

Myth and art

Not much is known of the myths in general. Primordial Man, called Targitaos, had three sons: Lipoxais, Arpoxais, Kolaxais. Objects of gold fell from heaven: a golden bowl, a hatchet, and a plow and yoke. These objects symbolize the three social functions respectively. It is said that the youngest son, Kolaxais, got hold of these burning objects that had fallen from heaven, because before him the fire was extinguished. Kolaxais, the youngest son, accordingly served as the model for the two other sons.

Another mythical legend tells of the adventures of Heracles. Behind the Greek name may be surmised some Scythian form of Verethraghna, the god of the warrior function.

Religious art is dominated by representations of the ruler. He is, for example, seen on a rhyton (drinking horn) being given a beverage by the deity in a scene of investiture. Both the high god and the king are depicted on horseback, a type of representation later found on Sāsānian (3rd to 7th centuries AD) rock reliefs, where a nomadic influence may be seen. The ruler-god Mithra is also depicted as a horseman on coins from Pontus in post-Achaemenid and Parthian times (late 4th century BC to the 3rd century AD).

In scenes of investiture goddess figures are depicted handing over the rhyton to the king. The Great Goddess is often represented in art, sometimes seated on a throne and holding in her left hand a long sceptre. It is noteworthy in this connection that the royal glory still preserves its common Iranian name, *farr,* in Ossetic folklore, though with a weakened meaning.

A male deity whose type is reminiscent of that of Helios Apollon (a sun deity) may be seen driving his chariot. This type appears also in eastern Iran both in texts (Yasht 10) and in art (among the Śacas).

Sarmatian and Alani religion. Sarmatians and Alani were closely related to the Scythians and their religion was of the same type. Of the Sarmatians little is known other than that their sepulchres were much simpler than those of the Scythians. More important are the Alani because of their late descendants, the Ossetes of the Caucasus. Modern Ossetic folklore confirms the descriptions given by classical authors, chiefly Herodotus. These folk traditions fill out the gap of missing myths, for the legends about the Narts (heroic men) preserve many nature myths—for example, those demonstrating that the lightning represents the true nature of Batradz, and the sun that of Sozryko. A kind of trickster is Syrdon, of whom many adventures are told. Undoubtedly the three social groups among the Narts—the Boriats, the Alägats, and the Äxsärtägkats—represent the three social functions.

Eschatology

Important for the understanding of eschatology is the ceremony among the Ossetes called *bähfäldīsyn* ("horse blessing"). Here a speaker at the funeral gives a speech, called the "Horse-Speech," in which he describes the fate of the dead man and his way on horseback to the world of the Narts. In this description are mentioned the bridge over the river that he has to traverse and the interrogation of the soul at this bridge. If the dead man has been righteous the bridge is easy to pass; but if he has been unrighteous it is impossible to pass, because the bridge breaks down. The "Horse-Speech," for the popular eschatology of Iranian peoples, is highly instructive.

Median and Persian religion. The religions of the Medes and Persians in the pre-Zoroastrian periods were characterized by the presence of a powerful priesthood, the Median Magi. Their support of the Median Gaumāta's (pretender to the Achaemenid throne in 522 BC) seizure of power denied them their influence only for a short time, for already during the reign of Darius I (reigned 522–486), and still more under Xerxes I (reigned 486–465), they regained their position. The religion of the Magi has been styled syncretistic, and without doubt it was a blend of Zoroastrianism and the old religion of western Iranians.

Zurvān and Ahura Mazdā, and Mithra and Anāhitā

The high god of the Medes was Zurvān, god of time and destiny. Among the Persians, on the other hand, the major god was Ahura Mazdā. This fact constantly led to the assumption that the Achaemenid kings were Zoroastrians, but all we know about them speaks against their Zoroastrianism. The deities Mithra and Anāhitā, not accepted by Zoroaster, were worshipped in the west. The position of Mithra especially was very strong, as witnessed by his name being part of theophorous names of priests and nobles. The great festival Mithrakāna was dedicated to him.

While Ahura Mazdā and Mithra represented the first (ruling) function, Anāhitā was a goddess representative of the third (social) function. Her worship was characterized by cult images and also by small representations on gems. Equally revolutionary is the fact that temples appeared for the first time in Iranian religion in Achaemenid times.

The Parthian period (2nd century BC to 3rd century AD) shows above all the spread of the cults of Mithra and Anāhitā, in Asia Minor called the "Persian Goddess" and identified with Artemis. Their worship was propagated by the Magi.

Mithra's character as a Saviour god was more accentuated in this period, especially in the so-called "Oracles of Hystaspes," in which prophecies about the birth of the saving god are preserved in the writings of Lactantius (Latin Christian writer, *c.* AD 240–*c.* 320). Other late texts (*e.g., The chronicle of Zuqnin,* a Syriac Christian historical tract containing much legendary material) speak of the birth of the Saviour in a star falling from heaven. Mithra's worship evidently was concentrated in Armenia and northwestern Iran. There he occupied a strong position in the Zurvanite sect, in which—below Zurvān—he acted as mediator between the two representatives of good and evil, Ormazd (Ahura Mazdā) and Ahriman (Ahra Mainyu). The devotion to Mithra eventually expanded beyond the borders of the Parthian Empire.

The Sāsānian period is noted for the rise of a Zoroastrian state church and the creation of a written canon, the Avesta. From this holy book, which underwent various redactions, or compressions, Zurvanite myths were purged. They can, however, be reconstructed, partly from Pahlavi texts and partly from Christian polemical writings in the various Syriac acts of martyrs. This period was also characterized by the fusion of the two mighty priesthoods, the Median Magi and the Persian *hērbads.* On the basis of this fusion, the influential *hērbad* Kartēr in the late 3rd century AD laid the foundations of the Sāsānian Church, which had to defend its existence against various denominations within the borders of the empire, such as Jews, Christians, Manichees, and Buddhists (in the east). The fight was difficult against Christians and Manichees, who were severely persecuted. Nevertheless Christianity gained more and more ground and toward the end of the Sāsānian period seemed near a decisive victory, a development stopped by the Arab invasion, which ultimately led to the conversion of nearly the whole Iranian population and the emigration to India of many faithful Zoroastrians, the Parsis (see also ZOROASTRIANISM AND PARSIISM).

MYTHOLOGY

Creation. Creation myths have been preserved primarily in Zurvanite religion. Plutarch stated in *De Iside et Osiride* that Oromazes (the god of good) was born from the purest light but Areimanios (the spirit of evil) from the gloom, and that they strove in war with one another. The good god Oromazes created six gods: of good will, truth, good government, a maker of wisdom, maker of wealth, and maker of pleasures in beautiful things. These gods corresponded with the Zoroastrian *amesha spentas*. Areimanios created rival artificers, also six in number.

Struggle between good and evil

Oromazes withdrew himself from the Sun by as much as the Sun is withdrawn from the Earth and adorned the sky with stars. He then created 24 other gods and put them in an egg. But the gods born from Areimanios, being of the same number, bored through the egg, whence evil things have been mixed with the good.

A time fixed by Destiny will come, however, when Areimanios, bringing plague and famine, must be utterly destroyed by these and forced to vanish. The Earth having become flat and level, men shall have one life and one commonwealth, all being blessed and speaking one tongue.

According to the Magi, for 3,000 years in succession Oromazes or Areimanios rules and the other is ruled; for the next 3,000 years they fight and destroy one another's works, but finally Hades (*i.e.,* Areimanios) will fail. Men will become happy, neither needing food nor casting shadow, while Oromazes, the god who brought these things to pass, is quiet and at rest for a time.

The latter part of Plutarch's text goes back to the authority of the Greek historian Theopompus (*c.* 350 BC), whereas the origin of the former part is uncertain but also dates from Achaemenid times. The doctrines contained there are, however, old—and they are Zurvanite. Heaven, according to the Pahlavi religious text *Mēnōk i Khrat* ("Spirit of Wisdom"), is shaped as an egg. In the Zurvanite religious text of *Zātspram* I is described the attack launched by Ahriman (Areimanios) and his following against Ormazd (another name for Ahura Mazdā or Oromazes) in his heavenly light. It can be demonstrated on philological grounds that this text is based on lost Avestan passages, and these passages must have existed in oral tradition before the fall of the Achaemenid empire.

The two gods, the good one and the evil, are considered both as gods and as enemies, on an equal footing. The god of time and destiny, placed above them, is only hinted at, when it is said that there will come a time, fixed by destiny, when Areimanios will be utterly destroyed. The deity of destiny (Zurvān) accordingly decides the outcome of the war between good and evil, an outcome that will make an end of the "mingling" of evil with good (this "mingling," *gumēchishn,* is often alluded to in Pahlavi texts).

Supplementary details were offered by Eudemus of Rhodes (before 300 BC) in an observation preserved by the Greek philosopher Damascius (AD 453–*c.* 533). He stated:

> The Magi . . . call the intelligible and unified Whole, some (of them) Time, others (of them) Space. This results in a distinction either between a good god and an evil daemon, or between light and darkness. And the same people, after thus dividing the indivisible Nature, make a twofold classification of the more important elements, and set Oromazes over the one, and Areimanios over the other.

In Damascius' work the highest deity is time, also called space (in Pahlavi *swāsh,* or *spihr,* and *zamān*). Both Ormazd and Ahriman are represented, the one as the good and light, the other as the evil and dark. But Ahriman is here called not a god but only a daemon.

Cosmology. Cosmology (concerning the order of the universe), among the Magi in the west, is thus entirely dominated by Zurvanite conceptions, implying a double creation, one brought about by the good and the other by the evil principle.

Another aspect of cosmology is the macrocosmic-microcosmic speculation, now extant in the Pahlavi (late Zoroastrian) book *Bundahishn* XXVIII and other late writings. There is also correspondence between Man as a small World, and the World as a great Man. "Man's body, is a counterpart of the earthly World."

In the Iranian cosmology, God brought forth the whole creation by bearing it in his own body and producing everything from himself. First he created heaven from his head, earth from his feet, water from his tears, plants from his hair, and fire from his mind.

Creation out of God himself

The fact that God has created the universe out of his own body is alluded to in *Bundahishn* I, in which it is said that Ormazd by his act of creation has the position of "father and mother of creation." There the deity is conceived of as bisexual, a Zurvanite doctrine, for Ormazd obviously has taken the place originally occupied by Zurvān, who according to the myths clustering around him is both male and female. The birth of the cosmos as an embryo, proceeding from conception to birth, is a Zurvanite doctrine, for Zurvān is male-female, bearing in his womb the twins Ormazd and Ahriman. This is the myth propagated by the Magi. Originally the myth may have related only that the high god, being bisexual, produced from his womb the whole universe, composed of the elements. These elements, in non-Zoroastrian sources (*e.g.,* Manichaean texts), are called *mardaspanti* or *amahraspandān* (*amesha spenta*). The elements (*amahraspandān*) together form the universe, the body of the godhead; even in Zoroastrianism the *amesha spentas* are the various aspects of Ahura Mazdā. Zurvān out of himself produced Ormazd, who is composed of the elements; *i.e.,* the universe.

The gods. The deities in Iranian religions are to be classified according to the three-functional systems. Outside the north Iranian territory their names are: Mithra-Ahura Mazdā, representatives of the sovereign function; Verethraghna (in older times, Indra), representative of the warrior function; Vayu, a deity introducing the series of gods, associated with the same function; Anāhitā, the goddess of fertility, associated with the twin gods, Nāñhaithya, the social function. Already in remotest times the twin gods were probably called Haurvatāt (Health) and Ameretāt (Immortality). The functional series is concluded by the god of fire, here called Ātar, not the Indian Agni (but Agni once was a living deity in Iran, as well as India, as testified by the name Dāshtāgni). Some of these deities were accompanied by minor deities, such as Mithra, who had as his following, on the one hand, Sraosha ("Obedience," originally), Airyaman, and Rashnu ("the Righteous"), who, together with him, decided the fate of the deceased; and, on the other hand, the fertility goddess, Pārendi. The gods were divided in two classes: *ahura* and daeva, good ones and evil ones (the opposite of the Indian asura and deva). All the gods were interpreted spiritually by Zoroaster, but their functions were still preserved in his theological system.

Primordial Man was placed between gods and men. Various such primordial figures met in various parts of Iran: Yim, or Yima (child of the sun), Hōshang, and Gayōmart (first man). Yima was also the first ruler, the model of a sacral king. Gayōmart plays a major role in Zurvanite texts, extant in Pahlavi writings but based on lost Avestan passages.

Man. Man was composed of various spiritual forces, for which "soul conceptions," in referring to man's higher element, is a very inadequate term. Many of them belong to the common Indo-Iranian heritage. Most important of these spiritual forces are *ahu, vyāna, khratu, manah, urvan, tanu, kehrp,* and quite especially *daēnā.* The individual *manah* is part of the cosmic *manah,* in Manichaeism called the "Great Vohu Manah."

Still more significant is the *fravashi* (properly *fravarti*), meaning "protection," a kind of genius and at the same time the higher spiritual ego of man and his primoridal spiritual being. As ancestor-spirits the *fravashis* enjoyed worship in popular religion. The medieval Persian author al-Bīrūnī described the Fravardīgān festival, when food and drink were offered to the spirits of the dead, who during these days used to visit their families and occupy themselves with their affairs, although invisible to them. The *fravashis* are, however, also preexistent heavenly be-

The *fravashi* and the *daēnā*

ings and as such visualized as spear-carrying horsemen. In the great war between good and evil they are the allies of God. They are an Iranian equivalent of the Indian Maruts (followers of Indra, god of the warrior function) and of pre-Zoroastrian origin, chiefly associated with the second social function.

The notion of *daēnā* is also highly complex. In the text *Hadōkht Nask* II, in which the fate of the dead after death is related, the soul (*urvan*) of the righteous spends three nights near the corpse. Toward the end of the third night as dawn begins, a sweet-smelling wind is carried to the soul from the South. In this wind the soul sees its own *daēnā* in the shape of a beautiful 15-year-old virgin. Thanks to the good actions of the righteous soul, she has grown very beautiful. The soul then ascends through the three spheres of heaven, those of the stars, the moon, and the Sun, and finally arrives at "the Lights without beginning," the paradise, the place of the Godhead. This way upward is beset with perils, for demons are lying in ambush. Ahura Mazdā orders "spring butter" to be given to the soul, obviously some kind of food or drink of immortality.

The *daēnā* in this case should probably be compared with the paradise virgins of Indian eschatology who meet the ascending soul. The text, *Hadōkht Nask,* was probably written in the priestly Magian circles.

The bridge, *Chinvat peretu* (the "Bridge of the Requiter"), that is to be passed by the dead belongs to the Indo-Iranian heritage. The characteristic that it is sharp as a sword to the unrighteous and therefore impossible to pass appears also in Indian texts, and hence may be regarded as a common Aryan conception.

Eschatology. From individual eschatology the perspective widens to include the fate of the world and humanity. This general eschatology comprises what is called apocalyptic, in which God intervenes in history at the end of time. The world's process of development is conceived as a succession of four periods. A symbol of these ages of the world is the cosmic tree, on which there were four branches, one each of gold, silver, steel, and iron. These four branches were interpreted as corresponding to four periods of the world's history. The world, accordingly, had a brilliant beginning in a descending scale until its end. Zoroastrian tradition interpreted this symbol as a series of four successive reigns, starting with the period when Zoroaster received his revelation. Comparison with the corresponding Indian cyclical scheme, as well as with Zurvanite conceptions, however, demonstrates this fourfold scheme to comprise originally 12,000 years with 3,000 years in every period. It is probable that—as in India—each 3,000-year period was characterized by a certain colour as an alternative of a certain metal. The last period is, among other things, characterized by the fact that mankind is born smaller, with strength also being less than before. This characteristic must be a common Indo-Iranian notion, for it is paralleled by the Indian idea that in every age of the world men are born ever smaller and weaker. Pahlavi apocalyptic literature, in which these conceptions are also found, is based on lost Avestan texts, as can be proved by linguistic and literary analysis. Older attempts to assign Iranian apocalyptic speculations to a post-Christian or even post-Sāsānian age have thus been discredited.

The ages of the world

The last period is characterized by the final struggle between all good and evil powers. A symbol of evil is Azhdahāk (Avesta Azhi Dahāka), the Dragon, fought by the hero Thraētaona (or in other traditions Keresāspa). The Dragon here corresponds to the Indian dragon Ahi, or Vṛtra, killed by Indra. In the final battle a prominent place is taken by Mithra. Azhdahāk was not killed but only fettered on Mt. Damāvand. Now he is let loose and brings devastation everywhere, until Keresāspa kills him with his mace. This final battle is called the Great War and survives both in Zoroastrian and Manichaean traditions.

A central role is played by Mithra in the so-called Oracles of Hystaspes, spread in Greek language in the West more than 2,000 years ago. In it the birth of Mithra is alluded to, for it is said that God—to save the righteous among persecuted mankind—will send the "Great King" from heaven, who will annihilate the evil powers with fire and sword. This Great King is no one but the reincarnated Mithra.

Coming of the Saviour

Several Christian texts, based on Iranian traditions, describe the Saviour's miraculous birth. His star appears in the sky, bearing the image of a small boy, and descends in a column of light into a cave, where he is born out of the rock as a small child. The Magi, year after year, wait on the "Mount of Victories," hoping that the Saviour will be born. They present golden crowns as gifts to the newborn Saviour Mithra.

WORSHIP, PRACTICES, AND INSTITUTIONS

Temples and shrines. Indo-European peoples originally lacked temples, idols, and written religious traditions. The same holds true for the Iranian tribes who, however, in the west entered into contact with the Near Eastern culture and were influenced by it. For this reason in Achaemenid times temples existed (for example, in Susa and Persepolis) of modest size, protected by a roof, and housing the holy fire. Reliefs show the Great King officiating before the fire altar. Such altars are extant in Median territory from about 550 BC. The holy fire was also carried on portable altars.

Priesthood and soothsayers. Priests were of the same type as those in Vedic India and usually carried the same names. Thus there were *kavi, usig,* and *vifra,* all of whom possessed Indian correspondences. Both *kavi* and *vifra* denote the priest as an inspired person; *kavi* also is the appellation of members of a legendary dynasty. The term *usig* seems to signify a sacrificial priest. The *karapan,* mentioned together with *usig,* is to be connected with the Indian *kalpa* ("rite") and therefore may have been occupied with ritual practice in general. More specialized is the *zaotar,* the correspondence of the Indian *hotṛ.* His task probably was to praise the deity and carry out the libation. Zoroaster was a *zaotar.* At the sacrifice the *staotar* and the *zbātar* also fulfilled the function of praising the godhead. The *mathran* recited special formulas, as in India. The *āthravan* is likewise the same as the Indian *átharvan,* but it is impossible to define his special functions. All these categories are found in eastern Iran.

Western Iran was dominated by the Median Magi, as mentioned before. They were characterized by syncretistic, often deep speculations, coupled with a spirit of fanaticism. They were ancestors of the Sāsānian *mobed*s ("priests"), who had their centre in Shiz and propagated Zurvanite ideas and customs (*e.g.,* next-of-kin marriage). Their later subordinate colleagues, the *herbad*s of Fars, were fire priests like the Magi, and also carriers of oral tradition. Like the Magi, they accepted Zoroastrianism and had as their ancestors the *Haēthra paiti*s (possibly "fire priests").

Sacrifice. The priest, when sacrificing, recited with "a loud prayer" several sacrificial formulas. The *barsman*-bundle, his special attribute, was much used also among the northern tribes, even as an instrument of divination practice. It corresponds exactly with the Indian *barhis.* The twigs, kept together in a bundle, were spread out on the ground when a sacrifice was offered. The Magi killed the sacrificial animal with a mace, not a knife.

In addition to the *barsman,* the chief elements at a sacrifice were fire, the drinking of *haoma* (the juice of a mild narcotic plant), and libation. Fire was, however, not used to consume the sacrificial victim, which was not burned at all, but to call down the deities from heaven. The fire, Ātar, was the hearth fire. The fire ritual was organized in accordance with the three-functional system, the hearth fire being the starting point, from which the three fires were taken. Later they were associated with the three classes of society. Fire must always be burning and never quenched; it was a perpetual fire. The fire altar was the centre when the Iranian started constructing cult buildings. The *haoma* is the dialectal correspondence of Indian *soma* and was originally an alcoholic drink, conceived of as a drink of immortality, for it was called "averter of death," *haoma dūraosha.* Sacrifices of cattle, celebrated in honour of Mithra, the Slayer of the Bull, and excessive drinking of *haoma* were essential parts of a ritual looked upon by Zoroaster with great horror.

Rites and burial customs. Ritual acts besides sacrifice

Ordeals

were above all purification ceremonies and ordeal customs. The elements of purification were fire and water. Of these, fire was the more important. To prove a person's freedom from guilt, it was necessary for him to pass through a real pyre, nourished by fire taken from the sacred fire of a cult place. The deity was invoked to assist at the ordeal. In Zoroastrianism an ordeal with molten metal was used, and eschatological conceptions of how earth is purified through a huge stream of fire hinted at the importance of the ordeal fire.

Burial customs possessed a ritual character but were of different kinds in different parts of Iran. Four types were used: (1) exposure of the corpses so that the fleshy parts were consumed by dogs and birds of prey; (2) burning of the body, after which the ashes were collected in an urn; (3) burial in the ground, attested above all among northern tribes; and (4) embalming and burial in rock tombs, chiefly used in the burial of kings.

CONCLUSION

The evaluation of the influence exercised by Iranian religions depends upon a correct evaluation of the Pahlavi sources. The endeavour to analyze Avestan portions of this literature began only in the second half of the 20th century. When this task has been completed scholars will be in a position to form a more correct opinion of Iranian religion and to state with more certainty its importance as a type of religion independent of Zoroastrianism.

(G.Wn.)

Religions of Asia Minor

The religions of Asia Minor consist of the beliefs and practices of the ancient peoples and civilizations of the Anatolian Peninsula (modern Turkey), Soviet Armenia, Syria, and north Mesopotamia, including the Hattians, Hittites, Hurrians, Assyrian colonists, Urartians, Phrygians, and Luwians.

SOURCES OF MODERN KNOWLEDGE

Until comparatively recent times, the pre-Christian religions of Asia Minor were known only through the works of classical writers, supplemented by coins and the monuments reported by travellers. For the Greeks and Romans, Asia Minor was above all the home of the religion of Cybele, the Great Mother of the cult centred in Phrygian Pessinus. A monument such as the colossal, but much weathered, figure of a Hittite goddess carved high up on the slopes of Mt. Sipylus was of necessity ascribed by the 2nd-century-AD Greek traveller and geographer Pausanias to the Mother of the Gods (a title of Cybele), since no other ancient Anatolian goddess was known to him.

In the 19th century a series of inscriptions renewed interest in the ancient civilization of Asia Minor, and in the 20th century systematic excavations provided historians and archaeologists with vital new facts. The discovery of the royal archives of the Hittites at Boğazköy (ancient Hattusa) in 1907 made available for the first time a mass of indigenous literary evidence for an Anatolian civilization, a civilization belonging to the 2nd millennium BC, before the arrival of the Phrygians. Because of the discovery of these clay tablets, the religion of the Hittites necessarily predominates in any account of the religions of Asia Minor. Later Hittite history has been further clarified by the decipherment of the Hittite hieroglyphic inscriptions on monuments dating for the most part from the early centuries of the 1st millennium BC, after the downfall of Hattusa. For the same period, the cuneiform inscriptions of the kingdom of Urartu in the region of Lake Van contain some information on the religion of that area, though they are mostly concerned with other matters.

The clay tablets of Assyrian commercial colonists found at Kültepe, Alişar, and Boğazköy belong to the period immediately preceding the rise of the kingdom of Hattusa, but they contain little information bearing on the life of the indigenous population. For all earlier periods, scholars are dependent on the inarticulate data of archaeology—isolated finds, the interpretation of which leaves a large element of uncertainty.

PREHISTORIC PERIODS

The earliest evidence of religious beliefs has come to light at the mound of Çatal Hüyük, to the south of modern Konya. Here in four seasons of excavations (1961–65), James Mellaart discovered remains of a Neolithic village of mud-brick houses, many of which could be identified as shrines. They are dated by radiocarbon to *c.* 6500–5800 BC (calculated with a half-life of 5,730 years). Huge figures of goddesses in the posture of giving birth, leopards, and the heads of bulls and rams are modelled in high relief on the walls of some of these shrines. Others contain frescoes showing elaborate scenes such as the hunting of deer and aurochs, or vultures devouring headless human corpses. A series of stone and terracotta statuettes found in these shrines represent a female figure, sometimes accompanied by leopards and, from the earlier levels of excavation, a male either bearded and seated on a bull or youthful and riding a leopard. The main deity of these Neolithic people was evidently a goddess, a mistress of animals, with whom were associated both a son and a consort. Her character is vividly shown by a schist plaque carved to represent two scenes, a sacred marriage and a mother with child. The dead appear to have been excarnated in a mortuary outside the village by exposure to vultures, as shown in the painting, before being buried under the platforms in the houses.

Cults of goddesses

At Hacilar, near Lake Burdur, a somewhat later culture was unearthed by the same excavator, and here again were found statuettes of goddesses associated with felines; but, as in the later levels at Çatal Hüyük, the son or consort is absent.

Entirely different and far removed in time and place are the discoveries at Alaca Hüyük and Horoztepe in northern Anatolia. Here, dating from the latter half of the 3rd millennium BC (*c.* 2400–2200), were found royal tombs richly furnished with artifacts in bronze and precious metals. Beside the heads of skeletons lay female figurines; one such figure found in a grave at Horoztepe represents a mother nursing her child. Many of the objects found in these graves must have had ritual significance. At Horoztepe a bronze sistrum, or rattle, was found. But the outstanding feature of the graves at both sites is the occurrence of bronze standards, which may have been carried on poles. They are open-work objects of circular or occasionally rhomboid form and are adorned with figures of animals (bulls, stags, and, in one instance, felines), birds, flowers, and swastikas and other geometrical patterns. Other standards, consisting of simple statuettes of stags or bulls, also occur.

The archaeological finds of central Anatolia follow immediately after the period of these royal tombs from the Pontic region. Kültepe, near Kayseri, became in the 19th century BC the centre of the Assyrian trading outposts (*kārum*) already mentioned; but from the mound itself, from a level just prior to the foundation of the Assyrian colonies, have come a series of remarkable statuettes. The majority of these are abstract, disk-shaped idols without limbs; many of them have two, three, or even four heads, and others bear on their chests small male figures in relief, in one case accompanied by a lion. There can be little doubt that here again is a representation of a divine family—a mother goddess with consort and child or children. From a level at Boğazköy contemporary with Kültepe comes a limestone mold of a "mistress of animals," a nude goddess standing on a pair of felines and holding aloft an animal in either hand. Molds for a pair of figures, a bearded god and a goddess—the god carries various weapons or emblems, the goddess in most instances holds a baby—have been found at several sites at a somewhat later level.

Though the Old Assyrian tablets are concerned exclusively with commercial matters, the seal impressions that they bear contain a new and elaborate system of religious symbolism (iconography) that later reached its maturity under the Hittites. Here a whole pantheon of deities, some recognizably Mesopotamian, others native Anatolian, are distinguished by such features as dress, attendant animals, weapons, actions, and attitudes. Among them are several weather gods, all associated with a bull, but distinguished in various ways; the weather is depicted in the form of rain falling above the god. A bull alone, carrying an enigmatic pyramid upon its back, sometimes surmounted by a bird, is a particularly common motif and probably symbolizes a weather god. Other deities are a war god holding various weapons, a hunting god holding a bird or hare, a god in a horse-drawn chariot, another in a wagon drawn by boars, a goddess enthroned and surrounded by animals, a nude goddess, and several composite beings. On many seals the deity—and especially the bull with the pyramid—are shown receiving ritual offerings.

RELIGIONS OF THE HITTITES, HATTIANS, AND HURRIANS

An interval of only a few decades separates the end of the Assyrian colony period from the earliest records of the kingdom of Hatti, and for the next five centuries (*c.* 1700–1200 BC) the history of Asia Minor is well documented. The texts reveal a country inhabited by a number of distinct peoples. The Hittites in the centre, the Luwians in the south and west, and the Palaians in the north were speakers of related Indo-European languages. In the southeast were the Hurrians, comparatively late arrivals from the region of Lake Urmia. The Hattians, whose language appears to have become extinct, were most probably the earliest inhabitants of the kingdom of Hatti itself.

Each of these nations had its own pantheon, and individual cult centres had their own names for deities. The result is a bewildering number of divine names, and even when a deity is denoted not by a name but by a logogram (sign or signs standing for a word) to indicate weather god, sun god, moon god, etc., it seems that the deity of each city was regarded by the Hittite theologians as a distinct personality. There are even special weather gods, such as the weather god of the lightning, the weather god of the clouds, the weather god of the rain, the weather god of the palace, the weather god of the royal person, the weather god of the sceptre, and the weather god of the army, each again conceived as a separate personality. These were probably only manifestations or aspects of a single deity, and this is reflected to some extent in the iconography, the pattern of religious symbolism, in which, as in the preceding period, there is a well-defined and limited number of divine types. Shrines are distributed widely throughout the country.

Types of gods

The pantheon. The most widely worshipped deity of Hittite Anatolia was clearly the weather god, as befits a country dependent on rain for its fertility; and under the title "weather god of Hatti" he became the chief deity of the official pantheon, a great figure who bestowed kingship, brought victory in war, and probably represented the nation in its dealings with foreign powers. Thus the treaty with Egypt is said to be "for the purpose of making eternal the relations which the sun-god [of Egypt] and the weather-god [of Hatti] have established for the Land of Egypt and the Land of Hatti." His name in Luwian, and probably also in Hittite, was Tarhun (Tarhund); in Hattic he was called Taru, and in Hurrian, Teshub. He is associated with the sacred bull and appears on monuments either attended by a pair of divine bulls or driving over mountains in a chariot drawn by bulls. In the cult itself Tarhun may even have been represented by a bull. Often, deities were represented by a symbol on clubs and other weapons. An example is the rock carving of a sword deity in Yazılıkaya (Inscribed Rock) near Boğazköy. A human head tops the hilt, which is carved in the form of four crouching lions.

As Tarhun's spouse, the great goddess of the city of Arinna was exalted as patroness of the state. (Arinna has not been located, but it was situated somewhere in the heartland of the Hittite kingdom, within a day's journey of the capital.) Her name in Hattic was Wurusemu, but the Hittites worshipped her under the epithet Arinnitti. She is always called a sun goddess, and sun disks appear as emblems in her cult, but there are indications that she may originally have had chthonic, or underworld, characteristics. As "sun goddess of the earth" she might be identified with Lelwani, the ruler of the netherworld. The king and queen were her high priest and priestess.

The weather god of another city, who was named Nerik, was regarded as the son of this supreme pair, and they had daughters named Mezzulla and Hulla and a granddaughter, Zintuhi. Telipinu was another son of the weather god and had similar attributes. He was a central figure in the Hittite myths.

Solar and lunar deities

There was also a male sun god, distinct from the sun goddess of Arinna, a special form of whom was the "sun god in the water," probably the Sun as reflected in the waters of a lake. His name in Hittite was Istanu, borrowed from the Hattic Estan (Luwian Tiwat, Hurrian Shimegi). There was also a moon god (Hittite and Luwian Arma, Hurrian Kushukh, or Kushuh), but he plays little part in the texts. In the iconography, the sun god was represented in the robes of the king, whose title was "My Sun"; the moon god was shown as a winged figure with a crescent on his helmet, sometimes standing on a lion. According to official theology there also existed a sun god or goddess of the underworld. In this place resided the Sun on its journey from west to east during the night.

The god who is known from the Kültepe seals as the god of hunting appears frequently on Hittite monuments; he holds a bird and a hare, as at Kültepe, and he stands on a stag as his sacred animal. From descriptions of the statues it appears that this is the deity denoted in the texts by the logogram KAL, perhaps to be read Tuwata, later Ruwata, Runda. The war god also appears, though his Hittite name is concealed behind the logographic name ZABABA, the name of the Mesopotamian war god. His Hattic name was Wurunkatti, his Hurrian counterpart Astabi. His Hattic name meant "King of the land."

The Hittite goddess of love and war is similarly disguised under the logogram of the Babylonian ISHTAR; she was evidently much revered and was the special protectress of Hattusilis III. Her Hurrian name was Shaushka. As a warrior goddess she was represented as a winged figure standing on a lion with a peculiar robe gathered at the knees and accompanied by doves and two female attendants.

There was a mother goddess, Hannahanna "the grandmother," closely associated with birth, creation, and destiny, but the theologians appear to have regarded her as a minor deity.

It is impossible to enumerate the lesser deities, many of whom are mere names to scholars. Among them were deities of many mountains, rivers, and springs, and the spirits of past kings and queens who had "become gods" at death. Demons are conspicuous by their absence; sickness and misfortune were ascribed either to sorcery or to divine retribution.

During the later years of the Hittite kingdom, the state cult came under strong Hurrian influence. The sun goddess of Arinna and the weather god of Nerik were identified with the Hurrian queen of the gods, Hebat, and her son, Sharruma; and at a holy place near the capital (now named Yazılıkaya), where a rocky outcrop forming a natural open chamber was adorned with a series of 64 bas-reliefs that represented the national pantheon, every identifiable deity bears a Hurrian name, written in Hittite hieroglyphs. The central group is recognizable as the family of the sun goddess, but she is named Hepatu, her son Sharruma. They both stand on felines, she, perhaps, on a lion or lioness, and he on a panther. The Hittites had here already begun a process of assimilation.

Gods and men. The gods were imagined to have their own lives, though also needing the service of their worshippers, who in turn were dependent on the gods for their well-being. They lived in their temples, where they had to be fed, clothed, washed, and entertained. Part of their time, however, might be spent in heaven or in roaming the sea or the mountains. They might withdraw in anger and so cause life on Earth to wither and cease. One of the most characteristic rituals of the Hittites was the invocation by which a god who had absented himself was induced to return and attend to his duties by a combination of prayer and magic.

The relation between man and god resembled that between servant and master. "If a servant has committed an offence and confesses his guilt before his master, his master may do with him whatever he pleases; but because he has confessed his guilt . . . his master's spirit is appeased and he will not call that servant to account." Confession and expiation form the main theme of the extant royal prayers.

Divination. Divination, through which the cause of divine displeasure was ascertained, was of three kinds: augury (divination by flight of birds), haruspicy (divination by examining the entrails of sacred animals), and dice throwing, arts said to be practiced respectively by the "bird-watcher," the seer, and the "old woman." The omens, as interpreted by these experts, were either favourable or unfavourable, and would give a yes or no answer according to the sense of the question put to them. In this way, by a lengthy process of elimination, it was possible to determine the precise offence that required expiation. Divination was a science inherited by the Hittites from the Babylonian seers. Signs of the peoples' fate were thought to be sent by the gods, manifested in unusual occurrences. Haruspicy, as noted, was one of the most popular practices of divination. The liver and viscera of the sacrificial victim were examined, and according to their configuration it was decided whether the omen was favourable or unfavourable. Records of these practices have survived in large numbers, but they are also among the worst written of the Hittite tablets.

The cult. The Hittite records at Boğazköy give abundant evidence for a state religious cult. Religious ideals, for instance, are revealed in the prayers offered by various members of royalty and all important state matters, including royal decrees and treaties, were referred to certain deities. The clay tablets testify to a unification of religion and the state, for the state and monarchy were placed under the protection of national deities at the ancient capital of Hattusa.

Sacrifices and festivals

The proper conduct for temple personnel was laid down in a tablet of instructions that gives some insight into the organization of a temple. Divine vengeance is threatened against those who misappropriate food or drink brought for sacrifice, who admit unclean animals or unauthorized persons into the temples, who purloin vessels or implements belonging to the god, who fail to celebrate festivals at the proper time, and who desert their posts to spend the night with their wives.

Many extant texts consist of descriptions of festivals in which the king or queen is the chief officiant. These festivals were numerous, but their names are largely unintelligible. Many of them were seasonal. The preliminary details, such as the robing of the king and his entry into the temple, accompanied by various dignitaries and by musicians playing their instruments, differed little from one festival to another. Owing to the very large number of fragmentary texts, it has not yet been possible to discern special characteristics of the festivals. They invariably culminated in libations and frequently in a cultic meal. One such festival lasted 38 days and involved celebrations in a dozen different cities.

Burial customs. The tablets from Boğazköy have yielded much information about the burial practices of the Hittites. One tablet tells of a burial ritual for a king or queen that lasted 13 days and in which the body was cremated. In the usual Hittite fashion, the body was initially burned and the fire extinguished with potable liquids. The bones were then dipped in oil or fat and wrapped in cloth. A feast followed their placement on a stool in a stone chamber. Although cremations were practiced to a great extent, burial of the body in an earthen grave was not uncommon. In 1952 Kurt Bittel excavated a site near Yazılıkaya close to a natural rock outcrop. The site contained 72 burials, 50 of which were cremations. There was no indication to show that cremations were exclusively the right of the elite.

Mythology. In Anatolia itself myth seems to have remained on a rather primitive level and is mainly to be found embedded in magical or ritual texts. Writings of this type constituted a large portion of Hittite literature and indicate the prevalence of both black and white magic. Myths were consequently associated with magical rituals aimed at curing diseases, ensuring good fortune, dispersing evil spirits, and the like.

A particularly well-attested type of myth occurs in connection with the invocation of an absent god and tells how the god once disappeared and caused a blight on Earth, how he was sought and found, and eventually returned to restore life and vigour. In one such myth the weather god withdraws in anger and the search is conducted by the sun god (whose messenger is an eagle), the father of the weather god, his grandfather, and his grandmother Hannahanna. In another, it is Telipinu who is angry, and the gods who search are the sun god, the weather god, and Hannahanna, the grandfather being omitted. In both these versions, the missing god is found by a bee sent forth by Hannahanna. In another similar story, the sun god and Telipinu are both missing, not from anger, but because they have been seized by "Torpor," which has paralyzed nature. In yet another version, the weather god of Nerik is said to have gone down to the netherworld through a hole in the ground, apparently the hole from which the river Marassantiya (modern Kızıl Irmak) gushed forth, which suggests that this weather god may really have been a god of the underground waters.

Another myth, the "Slaying of the Dragon," connected with the Hattian city Nerik, was apparently recited at a great annual Spring festival called Purulli. It tells how the weather god fought the dragon and was at first defeated, but subsequently, by means of a ruse (of which there are two quite distinct versions), succeeded in getting the better of him and killing him. The ritual associated with this tale has not been identified but its primitive character establishes it as folklore.

Other mythological tales of Hittite and Hattian deities existed, but they are too fragmentarily preserved to give any connected story.

The elaborate epic of the struggle against Ullikummi, and the *Theogony,* though written in Hittite, are Hurrian in origin and refer to Hurrian and even Mesopotamian deities. The *Theogony* tells of the struggle for kingship among the gods. Alau, after holding the kingship for nine years, was defeated by Anu (the Babylonian sky god) and went down to the netherworld. Anu in his turn, after nine years, gave way to Kumarbi, a Hurrian god, and went up to heaven. Eventually the weather god Teshub was born, and though the god KAL apparently reigned for a period, and the end of the tale is lost, it is certain that Teshub was the final victor, for there are many allusions to the "former gods" who were banished to the netherworld by him. The conception itself derives from Babylonia.

The "Song of Ullikummi" tells of a plot by Kumarbi to depose Teshub from his supremacy by begetting a monstrous stone as champion. Ullikummi, the stone monster, grows in the sea, which reaches his waist, while his head touches the sky; he stands on the shoulder of Upelluri, an Atlas figure who carries heaven and earth. Teshub is warned of the danger and goes out to battle in his chariot drawn by bulls, but he fails and appeals for help to Ea (Babylonian god of wisdom). The latter orders the "former gods" to produce the ancient tool by which heaven and earth had once been cut apart (the only surviving hint of a Hittite creation myth), and with this he severs Ullikummi from the giant and so destroys his power. Again the end is lost, but it is certain that the final victory went to Teshub.

RELIGIONS OF SUCCESSOR STATES

When Hattusa fell, *c.* 1180 BC, the Luwians moved eastward and southward into Cappadocia, Cilicia, and North Syria. Here they formed a number of small successor kingdoms. Shortly afterward the Phrygians crossed the Bosporus from Thrace and occupied the centre of the Anatolian plateau, cutting off in the extreme southwest a remnant of the Luwian people, who became known as the Lycians and maintained their reverence for the Luwian gods Tarhun, Runda, Arma, and Santa into classical times.

The East Luwians, whose rulers used the Hittite hieroglyphic script to record their deeds, worshipped these same deities; but their chief goddess was Kubaba, who hardly appears in the archives of Hattusa except as the local goddess of Carchemish in Syria. Her prominence was due to political factors, for Carchemish was then the leading Hittite city.

The traditional Hittite iconography survived, but was gradually permeated by Aramaic and Assyrian influences. Orthostats (stone slabs set at the base of a wall) from Malatya on the Euphrates show Tarhun in his bull-drawn chariot receiving libations from a king dressed in his traditional robes, and there is a relief showing his battle with the dragon. At Carchemish was found a representation of the winged moon god with the sun god, both standing on a single lion. Kubaba on a stela appears enthroned, the throne resting on a lion. Runda (the Hittite Tuwata or KAL) is regularly symbolized by a stag's head or antler.

Urartu. In the far east of Anatolia, the Hurrian nation formed around Lake Van a new kingdom, which rose to considerable power, *c.* 900–600 BC. With few exceptions, the cuneiform inscriptions of this kingdom of Urartu are historical and reveal nothing of its religion, except the names of deities. The national god was Haldi, and he is associated with a weather god, Tesheba, a sun goddess, Shiwini (compare Hurrian Teshub and Shimegi), and a goddess, Bagbartu (or Bagmashtu). Haldi is represented standing on a lion, Tesheba on a bull, Shiwini as a goddess holding a winged sun disk above her head. The cult was practiced not only in temples (one of which is shown in detail on an Assyrian relief) but also in front of rock-hewn niches in the form of gates through which the deity was probably believed to manifest himself.

The Phrygians. Little would be known of the religion of the Phrygians but for the fact that in 204 BC the Roman Senate, on the instructions of the priests, who had consulted the Sibylline books, had the sacred black
Cybele stone of the Phrygian mother goddess, Cybele, or Cybebe, transported from Pessinus, together with her priests, and installed in a temple on the Palatine. As a result, there is much information about the cult and its mythology, though it must be remembered that during 200 years of Persian rule Anatolia had been exposed to many alien influences from the east, which may have affected this cult.

The high priest of Cybele was given the name of Attis, and—at least in later times—she was attended by a band of fanatical devotees called *galli,* whose orgiastic dancing, at the climax of which they castrated themselves in their ecstasy, was notorious.

The cult myth of these rites told how Cybele (known at Pessinus as Agdistis, from Mt. Agdistis in the vicinity) loved a beautiful youth named Attis. According to the earliest version, Attis was killed, as was the Syrian Adonis, by a boar. All later versions, however, refer to wild revelry and castration. Agdistis is a bisexual monster who is trapped by Bacchus and castrated; Attis is betrothed to a daughter of Midas (or Gallus, the king of Pessinus); the wedding guests are driven mad by Cybele, and first Midas, then Attis, castrates himself, the latter as he lies beneath a pine tree; in one version Attis is turned into a pine tree. A poem by Catullus describes how a young Greek wanderer named Attis was caught up in the revels and sacrificed his virility, only to be prostrated later with remorse. The "Phrygian rites" introduced into Rome by Claudius included the ceremonious felling of a pine tree to represent the dead youth and its transport in procession to the temple. Still later, the sacrifice of a bull and the belief in the resurrection of Attis were added to the cult.

How much of this myth belonged to the original cult of the Phrygian mother goddess is questionable. Herodotus, in describing the celebration of the rites by the legendary Scythian sage Anacharsis, mentions only that he did so in a grove, that he carried a timbrel (a small hand drum or tambourine), and that he fastened images about his person. There is no suggestion of orgiastic rites.

In Asia Minor itself, the cult of Cybele is marked by carved rock facades with niches or by rock-hewn thrones, on which the statue would be set; in front of these, the rites were celebrated in the open air. Cybele was a goddess of the mountains, out of which she was believed to manifest herself to her devotees. Representations of the goddess show her in her niche, sometimes flanked by lions, draped in a long garment and wearing a high polos (cylindrical crown or headdress) or with bared breasts and flanked by musicians. Her name and her association with the lion cannot be separated from the Hittite Kubaba, whose cult had spread from Carchemish to the borders of Phrygia; but the process by which this matronly figure was transformed into the Mountain Mother of the Phrygians can only be surmised.

The goddess Ma of Comana, despite her name (Mother), was regarded at least by the Romans as a deity distinct from Cybele and identified with the war goddess Bellona. Her relationship to the ancient Hittite-Hurrian goddess Hebat of Kummanni (= Comana) remains obscure, for there is no evidence that the latter was a goddess of war.

The god Men, who appears on numerous monuments of the Hellenistic period, was an equestrian moon god, later identified with Attis and with the Thracian Sabazius. He is basically the Persian moon god Mao, as (Artemis) Anaitis is the Persian Anahita.

CONCLUSION

Asia Minor shows a remarkable continuity in its worship. From the Neolithic Period, for 6,000 years, the population venerated a divine pair, mother goddess and weather god, the former in association with the lion, the latter with the bull; a divine son, associated with the panther; and a god of hunting whose symbolic animal was the stag. To the ancients, for whom the essence of a thing lay in its name, this continuity was less obvious than it is today. The many names under which the deities were known at different times and places appear to us of less significance, in a religious sense, than the constancy of the types. (O.R.G.)

BIBLIOGRAPHY

General: An excellent unified cultural history of the ancient Middle East is EDUARD MEYER, *Geschichte des Alterthums,* 2nd ed., 3 vol. (1907–37). More up-to-date, but very uneven, is the new edition of *Cambridge Ancient History,* now appearing in fascicles. A concise treatment is C.H. GORDON, *The Ancient Near East,* 3rd rev. ed. (1965). Biblical religion has an enormous bibliography. Among the many treatments is W.O.E. OESTERLEY and T.H. ROBINSON, *Hebrew Religion: Its Origin and Development* (1930). ROLAND DE VAUX, *Les Institutions de l'Ancien Testament,* 2 vol. (1958–60; Eng. trans., *Ancient Israel: Its Life and Institutions,* 1961), discusses Israelite religion and provides a copious bibliography. The best set of translations, with a bibliography for each text, is J.B. PRITCHARD (ed.), *Ancient Near Eastern Texts,* 2nd ed. (1955), updated by *The Ancient Near East: Supplementary Texts and Pictures Relating to the Old Testament* (1969). A handy, abridged version of Pritchard's works is available in a paperback edition, *The Ancient Near East: An Anthology of Texts and Pictures* (1958). Two excellent works providing a background for the whole subject are S. MOSCATI, *The Face of the Ancient Orient* (1962); and H. and H.A. FRANKFORT, *The Intellectual Adventure of Ancient Man* (1946).

Egyptian religion: H.B.C. BONNET, *Reallexikon der ägyptischen Religionsgeschichte* (1952), a dictionary of the names of gods, temples, and holy places, and religious terms of the pharaonic period and of the Ptolemaic and Roman times; J.H. BREASTED, *Development of Religion and Thought in Ancient Egypt* (1912) and *The Dawn of Conscience* (1934), two books that attempt to represent the historical development of the religious ideas and ritual customs; HENRI FRANKFORT, *Ancient Egyptian Religion: An Interpretation* (1961), a discussion of the special way of Egyptian understanding and thinking as a starting point of religious forms; HERMANN KEES, *Der Götterglaube im Alten Aegypten,* 2nd ed. (1956), a precise analysis of local gods, their forms and history, and the development of local cults; *Totenglauben und Jenseitsvorstellungen der alten Ägypter* (1956), a detailed study of the beliefs of the hereafter, the existence of the dead in the sky and in the netherworld, and the judgment of the dead; and *Das Priestertum im ägyptischen Staat* (1953), a discussion of the role and duties of the priesthood; K.H. SETHE, *Die altaegyptischen Pyramidentexte,* 4 vol. (1908–22), ritual texts written in the pyramids of the kings and queens of the 5th and 6th dynasties; a new translation and shorter commentary with supplements to these texts trans. by R.O. FAULKNER, *The Ancient Egyptian Pyramid Texts* (1969); ADRIAAN DE BUCK and A.H. GARDINER (eds.), *The Egyptian Coffin Texts,* 7 vol. (1935–61), texts written on wooden coffins (and a few papyri) in the time of the First Intermediate Period and the Middle Kingdom, especially important for the beliefs of this time; J.B. PRITCHARD (ed.), *Ancient Near Eastern Texts Relating to the Old Testament,* 2nd ed. (1955), translations of religious, literary, and historical texts from Egypt, Sumer, Mesopotamia, and Ugarit; THEODOR HOPFNER, *Fontes Historiae Religionis Aegyptiacae* (1922–25), excerpts from Greek and Latin authors relating to Egyptian religion from the time of Homer to the Middle Ages; R.T.R. CLARK, *Myth and Symbol in Ancient Egypt* (1960), an intelligible introduction to the mythological world with full interpretation of the great myths and explanations of the nature of the principal gods, their cult places, and major religious symbols; JOHN GARSTANG, *The Burial Customs of Ancient Egypt* (1907), an extensive description of the tombs of Beni Hassan and their equipment; ALEXANDRE MORET, *Du Caractère religieux de la royauté Pharaonique* (1902), a detailed description, though somewhat antiquated, of the dogma of the sacred kingship and its ceremonies at the birth, the coronation, at feasts, and at the death of the pharaohs; GEORGES POSENER, *De la Divinité du Pharaon* (1960), descriptions of the human character of the historical pharaohs and their image in literature; SERGE SAUNERON, *Les Prêtres de l'ancienne Égypte* (1957; Eng. trans., *Priests of Ancient Egypt,* 1960), the essential features of the Egyptian religion as shown by the description of the priesthood; FRANCOIS LEXA, *La Magie dans l'Égypte antique* (1925), a collection of magical texts and charms, amulets, sacred signs, and symbols of all periods; ERIK IVERSEN, *The Myth of Egypt and Its Hieroglyphs in European Tradition* (1961), on the survival of the Egyptian culture, especially the religion, in Mediterranean countries.

Arabian religions: GIORGIO LEVI DELLA VIDA, "Pre-Islamic Arabia," in N.A. FARIS (ed.), *The Arab Heritage,* pp. 25–57 (1944), is a readable treatment of ancient Arabian culture, with some references to religion. IRFAN SHAHID, "Pre-Islamic Arabia," in P.M. HOLT (ed.), *The Cambridge History of Islam,* vol. 1, pp. 3–29 (1970), stresses the displacement of the older cults by Christianity and Judaism. For further historical discussion, see ALBERT DIETRICH, "Geschichte Arabiens vor dem Islam," in B. SPULER (ed.), *Handbuch der Orientalistik,* vol. 2, sect. 4, pt. 2 (1966). Works on ancient Arabian religion, giving a review of the divinities and their functions, are based primarily on inscriptional material. Taking the simplest first: GONZAGUE RYCKMANS, "Les Religions arabes préislamiques," in M.M. GORCE and R. MORTIER (eds.), *Histoire générale des religions,* vol. 2, pp. 220–228, 593–605 (1960); JEAN STARCKY, "Palmyréniens, Nabatéens, et Arabes du nord avant l'Islam," and ALBERT JAMME, "La Religion sud-arabe pré-islamique," in M. BRILLANT and R. AIGRAIN (eds.), *Histoire des religions,* vol. 4, pp. 201–237, 239–307 (1956); and MARIA HOFNER, "Die vorislamischen Religionen Arabiens," in H. GESE, MARIA HOFNER, and K. RUDOLPH, *Die Religionen Altsyriens, Altarabiens und der Mandäer,* pp. 233–402 (1970). Extensive bibliographies may be found in these works and in YOUAKIM MOUBARAC, "Éléments de bibliographie sud-sémitique," *Revue des Études Islamiques,* 23:121–175 (1955) and 25:13–68 (1957). Readers limited to English may find the interpretations of JEAN STARCKY and ALBERT JAMME conveniently summarized in the article "Arabia," in the *New Catholic Encyclopedia,* vol. 1 (1967).

Syrian and Palestinian religions: For translations of Ugaritic texts and major Phoenician inscriptions, see J.B. PRITCHARD (ed.), *Ancient Near Eastern Texts Relating to the Old Testament,* 3rd ed. (1969). For the material remains of Canaanite religion, see Pritchard's *The Ancient Near East in Pictures,* 2nd ed. (1969). A one volume condensation of the earlier editions of both these works is available in paperback, *The Ancient Near East: An Anthology of Texts* (1958). G.R. DRIVER, *Canaanite Myths and Legends* (1956); and T.H. GASTER, *Thespis: Ritual, Myth and Drama in the Ancient Near East* (1950), contain some Ugaritic materials not in the Pritchard volume. E.H. GIFFORD, *Eusebius, Praeparatio Evangelica,* 4 vol. (1903), may be consulted for Philo of Byblos' Phoenician History in English. For the historical background, see W.F. ALBRIGHT, "The Role of the Canaanites in the History of Civilization," in G.E. WRIGHT (ed.), *The Bible and the Ancient Near East* (1961), and *Archaeology and the Religion of Israel* (1953), for an excellent summary sketch of Canaanite religion, rich in detail. M.H. POPE, *El in the Ugaritic Texts* (1955), is an important study of a major god. All the gods and myths are treated authoritatively by M. POPE and W. ROLLIG in H.W. HAUSSIG (ed.), *Wörterbuch der Mythologie,* vol. I (1965).

Mesopotamian religions: E.P. DHORME, *Les Religions de Babylonie et d'Assyrie* (1945), the standard survey of data on ancient Mesopotamian religions; H. FRANKFORT, *Kingship and the Gods* (1948), on the theme of the king as intermediator between men and gods, and *et al., Before Philosophy* (1951), an attempt at synthesis and religious interpretation; T. JACOBSEN, *Toward the Image of Tammuz,* ed. by W.L. MORAN (1970), a more detailed attempt at synthesizing, ordering, and interpreting data; J.B. PRITCHARD (ed.), *Ancient Near Eastern Texts Relating to the Old Testament,* 3rd ed. (1969), major sources in reliable translations; C.J. GADD, *Ideas of Divine Rule in the Ancient Near East* (1948), on the problems of divination and the communication between men and gods; S.A. PALLIS, *The Babylonian Akītu Festival* (1926), the first and only attempt to understand the meaning and function of the ritual drama; S.N. KRAMER, *The Sacred Marriage Rite: Aspects of Faith, Myth, and Ritual in Ancient Sumer* (1969), on the fertility cult.

Iranian religions: E. BENVENISTE, *The Persian Religion According to the Chief Greek Texts* (1929), the first effort to analyze the Greek texts; J. BIDEZ and FRANZ CUMONT, *Les Mages hellénisés,* 2 vol. (1938), fundamental for an understanding of the religion of the Magi outside Iran; A. CHRISTENSEN, *Les Types du premier Homme et du premier Roi,* 2 vol. (1918–34), a collection of texts in translation (slightly out of date, but the only existing work of this kind); G. DUMEZIL, *Légendes sur les Nartes* (1930), a collection of Ossetic texts with an analysis of their importance for the Scythian religion, and *Naissance d'archanges* (1945), fundamental for an understanding of the role of the *amesha spentas;* M. ROSTOVTZEFF, *Iranians and Greeks in South Russia* (1922), fundamental for Scythian culture and religion; G. WIDENGREN, *The Great Vohu Manah and the Apostle of God: Studies in Iranian and Manichaean Religion* (1945), an analysis of the concept of messenger and bringer of salvation in Iranian religion; *Iranisch-semitische Kulturbegegnung in partischer Zeit* (1960), the first effort to analyze cultural contacts between Parthian and Semite civilizations; and *Die Religionen Irans* (1965), a comprehensive textbook; O.S. WIKANDER, *Der arische Männerbund* (1938), fundamental for an understanding of the role of the social and cultic organizations in ancient Iran; R.C. ZAEHNER, *Zurvan: A Zoroastrian Dilemma* (1955), an important collection of Zurvanite texts.

Religions of Asia Minor: A. GOETZE, *Kleinasien,* in I. VON MULLER, *Handbuch der Altertumswissenschaft,* 2nd ed., vol. 3, pt. 1, sect. 3 (1957), a classic work covering all periods, and translations of Hittite texts in J.B. PRITCHARD (ed.), *Ancient Near Eastern Texts Relating to the Old Testament,* 3rd ed. (1969); E. AKURGAL and M. HIRMER, *The Art of the Hittites* (1962), an excellent presentation of Hittite and pre-Hittite art and iconography; M. VIEYRA, *Hittite Art, 2300–750 B.C.* (1955); SETON LLOYD, *Early Highland Peoples of Anatolia* (1967), a popular but excellent account of all periods, with many illustrations; O.R. GURNEY, *The Hittites,* rev. ed. (1961), a general description of Hittite civilization, and "Hittite Kingship," in S.H. HOOKE (ed.), *Myth, Ritual and Kingship* (1958); H.G. GUTERBOCK, "Hittite Religion," in V. FERM (ed.), *Forgotten Religions* (1950), and "Hittite Mythology," in S.N. KRAMER (ed.), *Mythologies of the Ancient World* (1961); J. MELLAART, *Catal Hüyük* (1967), an illustrated account of the evidence from Catal Hüyük and Hacilar; N. OZGUC, *The Anatolian Group of Cylinder Seal Impressions from Kültepe* (1965), an important publication of new discoveries; F. CUMONT, *The Oriental Religions in Roman Paganism* (1911), a classic; E.N. LANE, "A Re-Study of the God Men," in *Berytus,* vol. 17 (1968), a valuable summary of recent work on Men and Cybele; R.D. BARNETT, "Phrygia and the Peoples of Anatolia in the Iron Age," *Cambridge Ancient History,* rev. ed., vol. 2, ch. 30 (1967).

Milan

The destiny of Milan (Italian Milano), like that of many of the world's great cities, remains something of a historical paradox. There are powerful factors supporting the argument that Milan should have become the capital of a unified Italy, and this is the belief of many Milanese, in spite of the fact that the unity of Italy was actually born in Turin, rather than in Milan, in 1870. Milan, nevertheless, is the most industrious and vital city to have achieved prominence since the ancient land of Italy became aware of itself as a modern nation.

This article is divided into the following sections:

Physical and human geography

CHARACTER OF THE CITY

Contemporary Milan is the richest city of Italy and one of the richest of Europe, so far as money is concerned. When the Milanese assert that Milan is the moral capital of Italy they not only express the ancient regionalism typical of all Italy and known as *Campanilismo* (a reference to the church bell of each city) but they also refer to something intangible and yet authentic, for they are speaking of quality and values, historical as well as contemporary. And if the rest of Italy, Rome included, accepts this statement, or rather accepts the fact that the statement is made, it is because it is more than a simple claim. The claim is justified by contributions in every field—economic, cultural, and ideological—that the city of Milan, in modern times, and particularly since the unification of Italy, has made to the Italian nation. These contributions greatly exceed, even on a statistical basis, those made by all other Italian cities. When one remembers that in the 19th century a writer such as Stendhal, one of the giants of French culture, wished to proclaim himself "Milanese" in his epitaph, one must indeed believe in the fascination Milan exerted then, and still does, and of which the city is fully conscious. The fact that Milan is at a distance from much of the rest of Italy, that it is peripheral in a geographic sense, does not explain its position of second city, a position it has always pathetically and vainly fought. Some of the greatest European capitals are peripheral in this sense.

Competition with Rome

This role was the consequence of the immense historical importance and the enormous accumulation of myths and symbols that conferred on Milan's antagonist, Rome, an inevitable prestige; Rome became the heart of a future anticipated in the collective fantasies of the Italian people. This character is fundamental, because a capital is not simply the centre of a government or of administrative offices. In the 19th century Milan was the most European among Italian cities, but it was not strong enough to become the centre of Europe.

It was not by chance that Milan expressed its ideological greatness in the person of a poet, Carlo Porta (1776–1821). Porta wrote in the Milanese dialect and in so doing risked obscurity, both in his own country and abroad; but he was eager to give of his utmost self, aware that the use of Milanese coincided with the finest aspirations of his fellow citizens over the preceding century. Rome absorbed the values and language of a renascent Florence and integrated them throughout the centuries, as modern Rome demonstrates. In Rome, cinematography, which could never take root in Milan, in spite of numerous attempts, employs the mystery of the physiognomy and of the light of the city to recreate those classic elements, which, in Italy, may be called antique. This Milan cannot do. The majority of its intellectuals, writers, and artists, at least until the end of the post-World War II era, abandoned the city for Rome. Milan thus remained essentially an economic centre, succeeding, however—alone among Italian cities—in keeping alive an inquisitiveness and a spirit of polemic that involved not only these two cities but all the others in Italy as well. The increased importance of the mass media in Italy, particularly of the Milan-based television networks, has favoured the Milanese perspective; this has not, however, damaged the poetic image of Rome nor reduced the prosaic character of Milan.

THE LANDSCAPE

Site. Milan is set in the heart of the Po Basin of northern Italy, halfway across the immense plain spreading between the Ticino and Adda rivers. The site is 400 feet (122 metres) above sea level. To the north lies the great sweep of the southern flank of the Alps. Between this semicircle of mountains and the course traced by the Po River to the south, there lies a zone that is arid toward the north, but swampy near the Po, where it turns into an expanse of marshy groves and rice fields. It is at the line of demarcation between these two areas, which are strongly differentiated, that Milan has risen, although now only swamplands mark the site of the ancient city. The earliest inhabitants reinforced their defenses by means of the small watercourses of the Sèveso, the Nirone, the Lambro, and the Olona.

The physical setting of the city

Climate. Milan's climate is continental, with damp, chilly winters and hot, humid summers. Snow falls between December and February, and springtime is generally rainy. In winter temperatures range between 30° and 50° F (−1° and 10° C) and in summer between 68° and 86° F (20° and 30° C). Characteristic of the Po Basin, the city is often shrouded in fog; the removal of rice fields from the southern neighbourhoods has reduced the phenomenon, but this has been offset somewhat by the growth of an almost uninterrupted built-up area around the city that reduces local air circulation.

The city plan. Each period of historical crisis, advance, and consolidation has been reflected in the organic structure of Milan. For a thousand years the core of the city was located just southwest of the present cathedral, the Duomo, and was made up of the rectangular, four-gated city of Mediolanum, with roads thrusting out from each gate to the surrounding countryside, together with an irregular outer defense consolidated in Carolingian times. This core has influenced the city plan down to modern times. The period of dynastic struggle and the imposition of transalpine authority brought further changes. After the city was razed in 1162, an enlarged oval was constructed, the course of its outer walls still traceable in contemporary streets. Spanish domination brought the erection of still another outer ring resulting from the 16th-century reconstructions. This, too, can be traced in contemporary boulevards. Within the city centre, the main focus of activity centred on the Castello Sforzesco, a product of the 15th-century dynastic struggles, reinforced by the Spanish in the following century; the Piazza Mercanti, the centre of medieval economic activity; and the great Piazza del Duomo, laid out before the cathedral in 1489. Castle, cathedral, and a newer commercial area centred on the Piazza Cordusio, representatives of the motivating forces in Milanese life, dominate the modern city centre.

The basic plan

Several times since the late 19th century city planners have laid down the basis of a more organic plan, bypassing the traditional radial street plan, so that new districts might have wide streets and avenues intersecting at right angles. The centres of the newer suburban areas—Bollate, Novate Milanese, Cusano Milanino, Cinisello Balsamo, Sesto San Giovanni, and even Monza (nine miles [15 kilometres] away to the northeast)—are linked to the core of the ancient city by major arteries. Entire industrial districts have developed, particularly in the north and northeast and in the south and southwest. Unfortunately, while the periphery has been amply developed, the central nucleus has not benefited from a similar transformation, and the narrowness of the streets and squares creates problems for modern traffic. Since the end of World War II, practically all industrial growth has been concentrated in peripheral areas of the city. Industrial progress has reached such a level that a third of Milan's population is in some way connected with industrial construction. Heavy industries are concentrated outside the city boundaries, around Sesto San Giovanni. Since 1950 the city centre has fared badly under the influence of industrialization, with many old streets and buildings replaced haphazardly by massive blocks and skyscrapers containing apartments and offices. The Pirelli Building (1955–59), near the Stazione Centrale ("Central Station"), and the Olivetti Building in Via Clerici are among the few modern structures of architectural note.

THE PEOPLE

Immigration

Milan's population has shown a rapid increase since World War II. This increase has been due mainly to the flood of immigrants from the impoverished Italian south seeking improved conditions in the factories of the industrial north. Population pressure has resulted in the growth of slums and such shantytowns as Brianza, as well as in an expansion of the city itself. Milan has pressed outward into the surrounding countryside with renewed vigour, particularly to the northeast, toward Crescenzago, and to the south, toward Rogoredo and Vigentino. Milan's enormous urban expansion has contributed to its economic growth.

The Piazza d'Armi inside the walls of the Castello Sforzesco, Milan, and (right of centre) the Torre di Bona di Savoia. The castle is now an art museum.

THE ECONOMY

Industry. Milan, the most important economic centre of Italy, owes this fact to its geographical position. It is located at the centre of the traffic routes of the Val Padana and lies on the borderline between the advanced agriculture of the fertile irrigated plains to the south and the limited agriculture of the north. In addition, it is backed by an impressive industrial development. Milan's rich and extremely populous surroundings, differing from those of other large Italian manufacturing centres, increase the city's economic importance and potential for expansion. An extensive network of road and rail communications spreads toward the outlying areas and particularly toward the north, giving the city an economic advantage that other Italian cities do not possess.

Industrial products

The mechanical industries predominate; the production of automobiles, airplanes, motorcycles, major electric appliances, railroad materials, and other metalworking accounts for almost half of the work force. Textile manufactures (cotton, hemp, silk, and artificial fibres) are situated in the province of Milan, while in the city itself manufactures of ready-made clothing and designer fashions predominate. Milan's fashion industry has achieved great commercial importance, and the city contains the salons of some of the world's best known designers. Chemical production is also considerable. Besides large quantities of medicinal products, dyes, soaps, and acids are also manufactured. Also noteworthy to the city economy are graphic arts and publishing, as well as food, wood, paper, and rubber products. Milan's position as the electronic media centre of Italy has been augmented by the rapid growth of high-technology industries, including data processing and telecommunications.

Commerce. Commercial activity in the city has also been stimulated by industrial development. The largest wholesale markets of Italy are in Milan. Of greatest importance are the export trades, which include artificial fibres, cotton and wool goods, chemical products, and machinery. This enormous economic complex has benefited from the efficiency of the city's banks and of its stock market, which is the largest in Italy. Milan is the principal centre of exchange in Italy; every April the city hosts the International Sample Trade Fair (in Italy called Fiera Campionaria de Milano), which ranks as one of the major trade exhibitions in Europe.

Transportation. In addition to being a centre of production and exchange, Milan is also a national focus of transportation. The state-run railroads are integrated within the city landscape by means of a carefully designed and executed plan. The vast Piazza della Repubblica, for example, which contains the Pirelli Building and other tall buildings, is located on land formerly occupied by a railway station. Trade goods are sent and received at the Stazione Lambrate-Ortica. Two other stations serve for the transportation of passengers, five more for various kinds of merchandise. The largest railway loading site is the Stazione Centrale. Transalpine tunnels and other mainline connections link Milan with all parts of Europe, and there are many nonstop trains to and from major cities. The road network converging upon Milan is also important, carrying, as it does, an unceasing flow of foreign and domestic tourists. Besides being the focus of a number of major highways, Milan is also the starting point for the famous scenic route known as the Autostrada del Sole, which traverses the spine of the lengthy Italian peninsula. The metropolitan transportation service operates an extensive system of bus, tramway, and subway routes throughout the metropolitan area.

The Duomo, Milan.
Colour Library International

ADMINISTRATION AND SOCIAL CONDITIONS

Government. The city, technically the commune of Milan, capital of the province (*provincia*) of the same name and of the Lombardy Region (*regione*), is under the jurisdiction of the Republic of Italy. The government of the Italian state is composed of a central administration and of a peripheral or local administrative system, the latter having limited jurisdiction over a particular region. The most important division of the peripheral system is the prefecture (*prefettura*), at the head of which is the prefect, the highest authority of the executive power in the province of Milan. It supervises the activities of public administration. In its own area, the province performs the important functions of regulating health, sanitation, public works, welfare, education, agriculture, and commerce. The province of Milan, as all other Italian provinces, has a vice prefect, a counselor of prefecture, and an administrative and provincial assembly whose members, as well as its president, are selected by the prefect. The commune of Milan is administered by a council, chosen from a large assembly, and a mayor (*sindaco*). In the administrative elections of the communal council all electors registered in the province take part. The assembly and the mayor are elected by the communal council. The mayor is the head of the communal administration and represents the central government of the Republic of Italy. Mayoral responsibilities include performing marriage ceremonies, registering births and deaths, and maintaining safety and order on behalf of each citizen.

Regional innovations

The region and regional council, instituted in the early 1970s, are constituted as autonomous entities and have various prerogatives. Among these are the right to promulgate laws on matters related to the city so long as they do not infringe upon the national interest or the interest of other Italian regions. The regional authorities are the regional council, the assembly, and the president of the assembly. In the commune of Milan, the conciliation judge presides. The city is also divided into 20 zones, each of which has a council that can address matters of local concern.

Services. The central post office functions 24 hours per day. The city maintains a large, well-staffed streets and sanitation department, which endeavours to maintain both the cleanliness of the city and the health of its citizens. This task is made difficult, however, by overcrowding and poor housing conditions in some sectors. Health-care facilities are nonetheless generally good, and the city has a large network of publicly and privately run hospitals and clinics, as well as research facilities.

CULTURAL LIFE

The Duomo

The most striking of the monuments to be seen in contemporary Milan is the Duomo, a triumph of Gothic architecture; it is the third largest church of contemporary Europe, holding more than 20,000 people. Begun in 1386, it took five centuries to complete and rises over the area occupied at one time by the churches of Sta. Tecla and Sta. Maria Maggiore. The most imposing parts of the Duomo are its lateral aspects, its two top crosses, and the apse. In the latter, a powerful impression is made by the three immense Gothic windows of finely carved marble. The casing, of pink-tinged Italian marble, is to be found on all sides of the structure. At the lower level, it lends character to the small trilobate arches, capitals, and flowers; it also appears on the buttresses and, above them, runs along the crowning row of gigantic statues; above these, it covers the decorated water gutters and, finally, enhances the lacelike ornamental crest. The exterior of the cathedral is covered with a remarkable profusion of turrets, pinnacles, and more than 3,000 statues. Within are 52 pillars, each over 80 feet tall and more than 10 feet in diameter and bearing, instead of capitals, a crown of statues within their niches.

The most notable of the city's many palaces is the Palazzo di Brera, construction of which dates from 1651. Its architect, Francesco Maria Ricchino, infused the whole Milanese Baroque with his severe style. The Pinacoteca di Brera, one of the largest art galleries in Italy, contains a fine collection of north Italian painting. The building also contains the Biblioteca Nazionale Braidense, and its beautiful courtyard is dominated by Antonio Canova's statue of Napoleon. On the Corso Garibaldi stands S. Simpliciano, which according to tradition was founded in the 4th century by St. Ambrose. Its apse contains the 15th-century fresco "Coronation of the Virgin" by Ambrogio Bergognone. Other notable churches in the central area include S. Satiro, S. Eustorgio, S. Lorenzo Maggiore, and S. Babila. In Via Monte Napoleone, there are several handsome palaces, including the Bagatti-Valsecchi palaces. Leonardo da Vinci's fresco the "Last Supper," one of the most famous paintings of the Renaissance, is located in the former refectory of the Dominican monastery of Sta. Maria delle Grazie. Beyond the Piazza Cavour (which contains a monument to the great Italian statesman for whom it is named as well as the imposing and ultra-modern Centro Svizzero ["Swiss Centre"]) lie the public gardens, in which the Museo Civico di Storia Naturale (Museum of Natural History) stands. One of its most interesting exhibits is the Turati ornithological collection. The former Villa Reale, now the Galleria d'Arte Moderna e Padiglione d'Arte Contemporanea, is also nearby.

Libraries and universities

The Biblioteca Ambrosiana (founded 1609) and the Biblioteca Comunale are also of significance. Other excellent libraries are found in the universities, the philological clubs of the Instituto Lombardo Accademia di Scienze e Lettere, as well as in the Donati Foundation. The Archivio di Stato also contain an imposing collection. Milan is the seat of three universities: the Università Cattolica del Sacro Cuore (1920), one of the best Roman Catholic schools in Italy; the state-run Università degli Studi (1923); and the Università Commerciale Luigi Bocconi (1902). Other institutions of higher education include the Instituto di Ingegneria Nucleare, Centro di Studi Nucleari Enrico Fermi and the Conservatorio di Musica Giuseppi Verdi.

Milan's Teatro alla Scala (popularly called La Scala), constructed 1776–78 by the leading Neoclassical architect Giuseppe Piermarini, is one of the great theatres of the world. (Piermarini, incidentally, designed the Corso di Porta Romana, the first paved street of modern Europe.) The city also contains several other theatres, including the Lirica, the Odeon, and the Stabile, which is the home of one of Italy's major theatrical companies. There are also numerous motion-picture houses.

Sections of a network of communication and transportation canals, the Navigli, constructed in the 16th century, remain, especially in the southern part of the city. In the summer a tour boat makes trips on the canals between Porta Ticinese and the Po, passing by country estates that were built from the 16th to the 19th century for Milanese nobles.

Milan is the leading sports centre of Italy. Many of the facilities are located in San Siro, on the northwestern edge of the city. The Palazzo dello Sport is a splendid example of recreational architecture. The Ippodromo del Gallopo, a large horse-racing arena, is one of the best in Europe. The Mirabello course is also excellent. In addition, San Siro has a fine association football (soccer) stadium, a civic arena, and numerous other fields for various sports, among which the modern Vigorelli, for cycling races, is well known. The Lago Idroscalo, an artificial lake next to Linate airport, is also a popular recreation area. The Grand Prix automobile-racing circuit at nearby Monza has an international reputation.

History

THE EARLY PERIOD

Foundation and early growth. The earliest settlement on the site of Milan was founded by the Gauls about the year 600 BC, and in ensuing centuries it became the capital of a Celtic tribe known as the Insubres. At the time of the Roman conquest, 222 BC, Mediolanum, as it was then called, was already one of the most powerful cities of the region on the Roman side of the Alps known as Cisalpine Gaul. Under the emperor Augustus, it became a part of the 11th region of Italy, acquiring increasing prestige and economic power until it became the second city of the Western Roman Empire behind Rome itself. In the 3rd century AD, following the partition of the empire instituted by the emperor Diocletian, it was assigned as residence and main administrative centre for one of the two emperors. The emperor Constantine the Great declared it the seat of the Vicar of Italy. In the year 452, Attila the Hun devastated the city, and in 539 the Goths destroyed it. The city, however, did not entirely perish as a result of these barbarian incursions, and by the second half of the 10th century city life was surging with renewed vigour. Under the Carolingians (the region was incorporated into the dominions of Charlemagne in 774), life in Milan showed increased vitality, particularly through the efforts of Archbishop Ansperto da Biassono, who rebuilt and strengthened the fallen walls of the city in the late 9th century. Under Ariberto da Antimiano (1018–45), the political power of the archbishopric reached its apogee. This assumption of temporal power by the archbishops, dating from about 1000, can be considered as the origin of the subsequent greatness of Milan.

Early settlement

Establishment of the commune

In 1045, however, as a result of tensions engendered by the authority of the archbishops and because of the increasing growth and stability of the city as a whole, Milan constituted itself as a commune (*comune*), with permanent and autonomous governmental structures. In the resultant struggle for primacy among the cities of Lombardy, Milan became involved in a series of long battles against its less prosperous neighbours—Pavia, Cremona, Como, and Lodi. In 1111 the Milanese razed Lodi, and, after a bitter struggle lasting from 1118 to 1127, Como was destroyed. This was the pretext for the intervention of Frederick I Barbarossa, who decided to bring Milan under the direct authority of the central imperial power of his Holy Roman Empire. The city held out until 1162, when it yielded after a nine-month siege. Its fortifications were then razed, and the destruction of the city was such that the Milanese were forced to seek refuge in the surrounding countryside. The war blazed on until 1183, the year of the Peace of Constance, although Milan, rebuilt in 1167 under the auspices of the newly founded Lombard League, succeeded in playing a major role in the defeat of the German forces of Barbarossa at the Battle of Legnano in 1176. Its privileges rewon, the city attained a splendid economic florescence over the next 100 years.

Feudal conflicts. In the early years of the 12th century, however, the new industrial classes, in particular the guilds of the woolens and armaments workers, increased constantly in power and influence. The feudal nature of the relationship between the archbishop and his allies meant that the archbishop had to make enormous concessions to the emergent social and political forces among the citizenry in order to reinforce his own party, diminishing thereby the financial privileges of the church. Following the worsening of the relationship with Frederick II of Swabia, the Milanese proclaimed Pagano della Torre, a member of a family emerging as leaders of the less feudal of the city's power groupings, as their protector. The city forces were nevertheless defeated by the Emperor in the Battle of Cortenuova (1237). In the shadow of the subsequent struggle between the Torriani family and another powerful Milanese family, the Viscontis, the Signorial era was born. The Torrianis, leaders of the new popular forces, took the name of Guelfs; the Viscontis, followed by the aristocracy, headed the Ghibelline faction.

Dynastic struggles

In 1277 Ottone Visconti, archbishop of Milan, utterly defeated the enemy in the Battle of Desio. His nephew Matteo succeeded him, and, starting in 1311, Matteo and his heirs reigned as supreme lords of the city and of the surrounding state, replacing the political forms of the commune. Under this lordship, or *signoria,* the industrial and mercantile economy underwent rapid development, giving birth to further powerful coalitions of economic interests. But in 1450, Milan found itself besieged again. Francesco Sforza (1401–66), a ruthless and ambitious general, occupied the city and founded a new dynasty, basing his claim on his marriage to an illegitimate daughter of one of the Viscontis. A period of prosperity then began for Milan, based on the power of the Sforzas and the introduction of the silk industry. It was the golden period of the Italian Renaissance, typified by the splendour of the Sforza court.

The dynasty of the Sforzas, however, had but a short-lived enjoyment of power. In 1499 the Duchy of Milan fell into the hands of Louis XII, king of France, who was also a distant descendant of the Viscontis. In 1500 Ludovico Sforza (also called Il Moro) conquered the state but was defeated at Novara in the same year. The French continued to rule until 1513, at which point they were overthrown by Massimiliano Sforza, son of Il Moro, who had Swiss assistance. Francis I, successor to Louis XII, reconquered Milan in his renowned victory of Marignano (now Melegnano) in 1515. In accordance with the conditions of a peace treaty signed in 1529, Milan was once more returned to the Sforzas.

EVOLUTION OF THE MODERN CITY

In 1535 the incumbent duke died unexpectedly, and Milan and the entire Milanese state fell under the domination of the Habsburg emperor Charles V, who in 1540 invested his son—the future Philip II of Spain—with the duchy. Under Spanish rule—which was to last until 1706—the political and artistic elite of Milan rapidly succumbed. The dramatic period of dynastic struggle, which was also a period of economic growth, was to be replaced by a long period of economic stagnation and political decline associated with unimaginative foreign rule. In 1630 the city was struck by the great plague. This catastrophe was to be vividly portrayed by the local author Alessandro Manzoni (1785–1873) in his *I promessi sposi* (*The Betrothed*), a historical novel that is one of the finest artistic achievements of Italian and indeed European literature. The end of the desolation and squalor of the period of Spanish domination began with the outbreak, in 1701, of the War of the Spanish Succession, following the death of Charles II of Spain. In September 1706 Prince Eugene of Savoy entered Milan as its first Austrian governor, and the city passed thus from Spanish to Austrian rule. Although the first half of the 18th century was marked by neglect and oppression, after the Treaty of Aix-la-Chapelle (1748), the new rulers, in collaboration with the wealthy commercial classes of Milan, were able to foster a half-century of enlightened, if despotic, growth. This was particularly marked in the cultural domain. It is during this period that such figures as Cesare Beccaria, the outstanding criminologist and economist, and Pietro Verri, the gifted administrator and man of letters, were active. These and other members of a Milanese group known as the Società dei Pugni accepted the innovations of the theoreticians of the French Revolution, and this in spite of Austrian censorship. Neoclassical architecture also flourished. When, on May 15, 1796, the republican army of France, with Napoleon Bonaparte at its head, entered Milan, it was greeted enthusiastically, particularly by the middle classes. In 1797 the constitution of a Cisalpine Republic was promulgated. In 1805 Milan became the capital of the Kingdom of Italy, under Napoleon, who was crowned in the city. A true awakening then occurred in the consciousness of the Milanese people, as their city prospered from its domination of most of the Italian peninsula.

The city under Napoleon

These hopes were dashed, however, by the invasion and reestablishment of Austrian authority that followed the collapse of the Napoleonic Empire in 1814 and the Congress of Vienna the following year. This alien control of the new Lombardo-Veneto kingdom was to remain for nearly 50 years. Influenced by the new currents of Italian unity and nationalism known as the Risorgimento and smarting under the oppressive Austrian rule, the citizenry finally rose up in the "Cinque Giornate," the five days of March 18–22, 1848. In what has become one of the most celebrated episodes of the city's history, Milan was liberated from the Austrians for several months until the rebellion was finally brought under control. In spite of the fact that by Aug. 6, 1848, the brutal occupation forces of the aging Austrian commander Joseph Radetzky were once more in firm control of Milan, resistance forces of the city decided to continue their opposition to the invaders. Young men crossed the borders of Piedmont and Sardinia to enter the city's army. It remained for the second War of Italian Independence to finally liberate Milan from foreign control, and a few days after the Battle of Magenta (June 4, 1859), the people of Milan witnessed the triumphant entry of the two allies, Victor Emmanuel II and Napoleon III. The city—by now in the throes of an industrial revolution emphasizing metal products—was henceforth to be linked with the fate of the new Italian state, maintaining itself in a position of prime importance in the national economy. It also shared in the political development of the nation: on March 23, 1919, the formation of militant right-wing groups in the city marked the dawn of Fascism. Intense efforts at reconstruction healed the wounds of World War II, when the city suffered grave damage from intensive Allied bombing. The social and economic conflict that marked much of the city's development after the war found expression in the existence of a strong and aggressive Communist Party, whose influence continued unabated from the immediate postwar period through the ensuing decades of relative affluence.

Restoration and revolution

BIBLIOGRAPHY. For descriptions of the modern city, see FEDERICO ELMO (ed.), *Milan and Its Environs* (1955); EMIDIO BISSI, *Milan: An Artistic and Illustrated Guide-Book* (1958); and CARLO RIPA DI MEANA (ed.), *Tutta Milano: Tourist Guide* (1973). For architecture, see CARLO ROMUSSI, *Milano ne' suoi monumenti,* 3rd ed., 2 vol. (1912–13); NANCY A. HOUGHTON BROWN, *The Milanese Architecture of Galeazzo Alessi,* 2 vol. (1982), concentrating on Renaissance architecture; and GIACOMO C. BASCAPÈ, LUIGI MEDICI, and ULDERICO TEGANI, *Vecchia e nuova Milano* (1980); and YUKIO FUTAGAWA (ed.), *Carlo Aymonino, Aldo Rossi: Housing Complex at the Gallaratese Quarter, Milan, Italy 1969–1974* (1977), both of which provide views of modern architectural developments. City planning is addressed in MAURIZIO BORIANI *et al., La construzione della Milano moderna* (1982); and PATRIZIA GABELLINI, CORINNA MORANDI, and PAOLA VIDULLI (eds.), *Urbanistica a Milano, 1945–1980* (1980). GIORGIO LOTTI and RAUL RADICE, *La Scala* (1979; originally published in Italian, 1977), describes this cultural and historical landmark. Social and economic conditions of the contemporary city are studied in *Two Cultures, Two Cities* (1977), the proceedings of a symposium held in Toronto in 1976; and in JOHN R. LOW-BEER, *Protest and Participation: The New Working Class in Italy* (1978). The *Storia di Milano,* published by the Fondazione Treccani degli Alfieri, 16 vol. (1953–62), is the fullest historical account; but GIORGIO GIULINI, *Memorie spettanti alla storia di Milano,* new ed., 7 vol. (1854–57), is still useful for the Middle Ages. ELLA NOYES, *The Story of Milan* (1908, reprinted 1921), which provides an introductory account in English, focuses on the medieval town. Later historical sources include FRANCO FAVA, *Storia di Milano,* 3 vol. (1980–82); and RICHARD KRAUTHEIMER, *Three Christian Capitals: Topography and Politics* (1983).

(A.L.)

John Stuart Mill

John Stuart Mill was a British philosopher and economist, prominent as a publicist in the reforming age of the 19th century. He remains of lasting interest as a logician and an ethical theorist.

Early life and career. The eldest son of the British historian, economist, and philosopher James Mill, he was born on May 20, 1806, in his father's house in Pentonville, London. He was educated exclusively by his father, who was a strict disciplinarian. By his eighth year he had read in the original Greek Aesop's *Fables,* Xenophon's *Anabasis,* and the whole of the historian Herodotus. He was acquainted with the satirist Lucian, the historian of philosophy Diogenes Laërtius, the Athenian writer and educational theorist Isocrates, and six dialogues of Plato. He had also read a great deal of history in English. At the age of eight he started Latin, the geometry of Euclid, and algebra and began to teach the younger children of the family. His main reading was still history, but he went through all the Latin and Greek authors commonly read in the schools and universities and, by the age of 10 could read Plato and the Athenian statesman Demosthenes with ease. About the age of 12, he began a thorough study of Scholastic logic, at the same time reading Aristotle's logical treatises in the original. In the following year he was introduced to political economy and studied the work of the Scottish political economist and philosopher Adam Smith and that of the English economist David Ricardo.

While the training the younger Mill received has aroused

Mill.
By courtesy of the Gernsheim Collection, the University of Texas at Austin

amazement and criticism, its most important aspect was the close association it fostered with the strenuous character and vigorous intellect of his father. From his earliest days he spent much time in his father's study and habitually accompanied him on his walks. He thus inevitably acquired many of his father's speculative opinions and his father's way of defending them. But he did not receive the impress passively and mechanically. The duty of collecting and weighing evidence for himself was at every turn impressed upon the boy. His childhood was not unhappy, but there is no doubt that it was a strain on his constitution and that he suffered from the lack of natural, unforced development.

Effects of his education

From May 1820 until July 1821, Mill was in France with the family of Sir Samuel Bentham, brother of Jeremy Bentham, the English Utilitarian philosopher, economist, and theoretical jurist. Copious extracts from a diary kept at this time show how methodically he read and wrote, studied chemistry and botany, tackled advanced mathematical problems, and made notes on the scenery and the people and customs of the country. He also gained a thorough acquaintance with the French language. On his return in 1821 he added to his work the study of psychology and of Roman law, which he read with John Austin, his father having half decided on the bar as the best profession open to him. This intention, however, was abandoned, and in 1823, when he had just completed his 17th year, he entered the examiner's office of the India House. After a short probation he was promoted in 1828 to assistant examiner. For 20 years, from 1836 (when his father died) to 1856, Mill had charge of the British East India Company's relations with the Indian states, and in 1856 he became chief of the examiner's office.

In 1822 Mill had read P.-E.-L. Dumont's exposition of Bentham's doctrines in the *Traités de Législation,* which made a lasting impression upon him. The impression was confirmed by the study of the English psychologists and also of two 18th-century French philosophers—Étienne Bonnot de Condillac, who was also a psychologist, and Claude-Adrien Helvétius, who was noted for his emphasis on physical sensations. Soon after, in 1822–23, Mill established among a few friends the Utilitarian Society, taking the word, as he tells us, from *Annals of the Parish,* a novel of Scottish country life by John Galt.

Two newspapers welcomed his contributions—*The Traveller,* edited by a friend of Bentham's, and *The Morning Chronicle,* edited by his father's friend John Black. One of his first efforts was a solid argument for freedom of discussion in a series of letters to the *Chronicle* on the prosecution of Richard Carlile, a 19th-century English radical and freethinker. Mill seized every chance for exposing departures from sound principle in Parliament and courts of justice. Another outlet was opened up for him (April 1824) with the founding of the *Westminster Review,* which was the organ of the philosophical radicals. In 1825 he began work on an edition of Bentham's *Rationale of Judicial Evidence* (5 vol., 1827). He took part eagerly in discussions with the many men of distinction who came to his father's house and engaged in set discussions at a reading society formed at the home of English historian George Grote in 1825 and in debates at the London Debating Society, formed in the same year.

Public life and writing. The *Autobiography* tells how in 1826 Mill's enthusiasm was checked by a misgiving as to the value of the ends that he had set before him. At the London Debating Society, where he first measured his strength in public conflict, he found himself looked upon with curiosity as a precocious phenomenon, a "made man," an intellectual machine set to grind certain tunes. The elder Mill, like Plato, would have put poets under ban as enemies of truth; he subordinated private to public affections; and Landor's maxims of "few acquaintances, fewer friends, no familiarities" had his cordial approval. The younger Mill now felt himself forced to abandon these doctrines. Too much in awe of his father to make him a confidant, he wrestled with his doubts in gloomy solitude. He emerged from the struggle with a more catholic view of human happiness, a delight in poetry for its own sake, a more placable attitude in controversy, a hatred of sectarianism, and an ambition no less noble and disinterested but moderated to practical possibilities. Gradually, the debates in the Debating Society attracted men with whom contact was invigorating and inspiring. Mill ceased to attend the society in 1829, but he carried away from it the conviction that a true system of political philosophy was

Beginning of his mature thought

> something much more complex and many-sided than he had previously had any idea of, and that its office was to supply, not a set of model institutions but principles from which the institutions suitable to any given circumstances might be deduced.

Mill's letters in *The Examiner* in the autumn of 1830, after a visit to Paris, where he made the acquaintance of the younger liberals, may be taken as marking his return to hopeful activity; and a series of articles on "The Spirit of the Age" appeared in the same paper in 1831. During the years 1832 and 1833 he contributed many essays to *Tait's Magazine, The Jurist,* and *The Monthly Repository.* In 1835 Sir William Molesworth founded *The London Review,* with Mill as editor. It was amalgamated with *The Westminster* (as *The London and Westminster Review*) in 1836, and Mill continued as editor (latterly as proprietor, also) until 1840. In and after 1840 he published several important articles in *The Edinburgh Review.* Some of the essays written for these journals were reprinted in the first two volumes (1859) of Mill's *Dissertations and Discussions* and give evidence of the increasing width of his interests. Among the more important are "Thoughts on Poetry and Its Varieties" (1833), "Writings of Alfred de Vigny" (1838), "Bentham" (1838), "Coleridge" (1840), "M. De Tocqueville on Democracy in America" (1840), "Michelet's History of France" (1844), and "Guizot's Essays and Lectures on History" (1845). The twin essays on Bentham and Coleridge show Mill's powers at their splendid best and indicate very clearly the new spirit that he tried to breathe into English radicalism.

During these years Mill also wrote his great systematic works on logic and on political economy. His reawakened enthusiasm for humanity had taken shape as an aspiration to supply an unimpeachable method of proof for conclusions in moral and social science; the French positivist philosopher Auguste Comte had some influence here, but the main inspiration undoubtedly came from the English scientist and mathematician Sir Isaac Newton, whose physics had already been accepted as a model of scientific exposition by such earlier British philosophers as John Locke, David Hume, Jeremy Bentham, and James Mill. But he was determined that the new logic should not simply oppose the old logic. In his *Westminster* review (of 1828) of Richard Whately's *Elements of Logic,* he was already defending the syllogism against the Scottish philosophers who had talked of superseding it by a supposed system of inductive logic. He required his inductive logic

Works on logic and political economy

to "supplement and not supersede." For several years he searched in vain for the means of concatenation. Finally, in 1837, on reading William Whewell's *Philosophy of the Inductive Sciences* and rereading John F.W. Herschel's *Preliminary Discourse on the Study of Natural Philosophy,* Mill at last saw his way clear both to formulating the methods of scientific investigation and to joining the new logic onto the old as a supplement. *A System of Logic,* in two volumes, was published in 1843 (3rd–8th editions, introducing many changes, 1851–72). Book VI is his valiant attempt to formulate a logic of the human sciences—including history, psychology, and sociology—based on causal explanation conceived in Humean terms, a formulation that has lately come in for radical criticism.

Mill distinguished three stages in his development as a political economist. In 1844 he published the *Essays on Some Unsettled Questions of Political Economy,* which he had written several years earlier, and four out of five of these essays are solutions of perplexing technical problems—the distribution of the gains of international commerce, the influence of consumption on production, the definition of productive and unproductive labour, and the precise relations between profits and wages. Here for the most part Mill appears as the disciple of David Ricardo, striving after more precise statements and reaching forward to further consequences. In his second stage, originality and independence become more conspicuous as he struggles toward the standpoint from which he wrote his *Principles of Political Economy.* This was published in 1848 (2 vol.; 2nd and 3rd eds., with significant differences, 1849, 1852), and, at about the same time, Mill was advocating the creation of peasant proprietorships as a remedy for the distresses and disorder in Ireland. Thereafter, he made a more thorough study of Socialist writers. He was convinced that the social question was as important as the political question. He declined to accept property, devised originally to secure peace in a primitive society, as necessarily sacred in its existing developments in a quite different stage of society. He separated questions of production and distribution and could not rest satisfied with the distribution that condemned the labouring classes to a cramped and wretched existence, in many cases to starvation. He did not come to a Socialist solution, but he had the great merit of having considered afresh the foundations of society. This he called his third stage as a political economist, and he says that he was helped toward it by Mrs. Taylor (Harriet Hardy), who became his wife in 1851.

Activities during his married life

It is generally supposed that Mill writes with a lover's extravagance about Harriet's powers. He expressly says, indeed, that he owed none of his technical doctrine to her, that she influenced only his ideals of life for the individual and for society, and that the only work directly inspired by her is the essay on the "Enfranchisement of Women" (*Dissertations,* vol. 2). Nevertheless, Mill's relations with her have always been something of a puzzle.

During the seven years of his marriage Mill became increasingly absorbed in the work of the British East India Company and in consequence published less than at any other period of his life. In 1856 he became head of the examiner's office in the India House, and for two years, till the dissolution of the company in 1858, his official work kept him fully occupied. It fell to him as head of the office to write the defense of the company's government of India when the transfer of its powers was proposed. Mill opposed the transfer, and the documents in which he defended the company's administration are models of trenchant and dignified pleading. On the dissolution of the company, Mill was offered a seat in the new council but declined it and retired with a pension of £1,500. His retirement from official life was followed almost immediately by his wife's death at Avignon, France. He spent most of the rest of his life at a villa at Saint-Véran, near Avignon, returning to his house at Blackheath only for a short period in each year.

The later years. Mill sought relief by publishing a series of books on ethics and politics that he had meditated upon and partly written in collaboration with his wife. The essay *On Liberty* appeared in 1859 with a touching dedication to her and the *Thoughts on Parliamentary Reform* in the same year. In his *Considerations on Representative Government* (1861) he systematized opinions already put forward in many casual articles and essays. It has been remarked how Mill combined enthusiasm for democratic government with pessimism as to what democracy was likely to do; practically every discussion in these books exemplifies this. His *Utilitarianism* (in *Fraser's Magazine,* 1861; separate publication, 1863) was a closely reasoned attempt to answer objections to his ethical theory and to remove misconceptions about it. He was especially anxious to make it clear that he included in "utility" the pleasures of the imagination and the gratification of the higher emotions; and to make a place in his system for settled rules of conduct.

Mill also began to write again on the wider philosophical questions that had occupied him in the *Logic.* In 1865 he published both his *Examination of Sir William Hamilton's Philosophy* and his *Auguste Comte and Positivism,* but in both writings his motives were largely political. It was because he regarded the writings and sayings of Sir William Hamilton as the great fortress of intuitional philosophy in Great Britain that Mill undertook to counter his pretensions. In dealing with Comte, Mill distinguished sharply between Comte's earlier philosophical doctrine of Positivism and his later religion of humanity. The doctrine he commended (as he had frequently done previously) because he regarded it as a natural development of the outlook of George Berkeley and Hume; the religion he attacked because he saw in it merely another attempt to foist a priestly hierarchy upon suffering humanity. It is noticeable that Mill's language in these books is much closer to the language of Bentham and James Mill than it had been since his boyhood, and it was as an act of piety that in 1869 he republished his father's *Analysis of the Phenomena of the Human Mind* with additional illustrations and explanatory notes.

While engaged in these years mainly with theoretical studies, Mill did not remit his interest in current politics. He supported the North in the U.S. Civil War, using all his strength to explain that the real issue at stake in the struggle was the abolition of slavery. In 1865 he stood as parliamentary candidate for Westminster, on conditions strictly in accordance with his principles. He would not canvass or pay agents to canvass for him, nor would he engage to attend to the local business of the constituency. He was with difficulty persuaded even to address a meeting of the electors but was elected. He took an active part in the debates preceding the passage of the 1867 Reform Bill, and helped to extort from the government several useful modifications of the bill, for the prevention of corrupt practices. The reform of land tenure in Ireland (see his *England and Ireland,* 1868, and his *Chapters and Speeches on the Irish Land Question,* 1870), the representation of women (see below), the reduction of the national debt, the reform of London government, and the abrogation of the Declaration of Paris (1856)—concerning the carriage of property at sea during the Crimean War—were among the topics on which he spoke. He took occasion more than once to enforce what he had often advocated, England's duty to intervene in foreign politics in support of freedom. As a speaker Mill was somewhat hesitating, but he showed great readiness in extemporaneous debate. Elected rector of St. Andrews University, he published his "Inaugural Address" in 1867.

Mill in Parliament

Mill's subscription to the election expenses of the freethinker and radical politician Charles Bradlaugh and his attack on the conduct of Gov. E.J. Eyre in Jamaica were perhaps the main causes of his defeat in the general parliamentary election of 1868. But his studied advocacy of unfamiliar projects of reform had made him unpopular with "moderate Liberals." He retired with a sense of relief to Avignon. His villa was filled with books and newspapers; the country round it furnished him with a variety of walks; he read, wrote, discussed, walked, botanized. He was extremely fond of music and was himself a fair pianist. His stepdaughter, Helen Taylor (died January 1907), was his constant companion after his wife's death. Mill was an enthusiastic botanist all his life and a frequent contributor of notes and short papers to the *Phytologist.* During his last journey to Avignon he was looking forward to seeing the spring flowers and completing a flora of the locality.

Mill did not relax his laborious habits or his ardent outlook on human affairs. The essays in the fourth volume of his *Dissertations* (1875; vol. 3 had appeared in 1867)—on endowments, on land, on labour, and on metaphysical and psychological questions—were written for the *Fortnightly Review* at intervals after his short parliamentary career. In 1867 he had been one of the founders, with Mrs. P.A. Taylor, Emily Davies, and others, of the first women's suffrage society, which developed into the National Union of Women's Suffrage Societies, and in 1869 he published *The Subjection of Women* (written 1861), the classical theoretical statement of the case for woman suffrage. His last public activity was concerned with the starting of the Land Tenure Reform Association, for which he wrote in *The Examiner* and made a public speech a few months before his death; the interception by the state of the unearned increment on land and the promotion of cooperative agriculture were the most striking features in his program, which he regarded as a timely compromise in view of the impending struggle between capital and labour in Europe. His *Autobiography* and *Three Essays on Religion* (1874) were published posthumously.

Mill died at Avignon on May 8, 1873. A bronze statue of him stands on the Thames embankment in London, and G.F. Watts's copy of his original portrait of Mill hangs in the National Gallery there.

Influence and significance. Mill was a man of extreme simplicity in his mode of life. The influence that his works exercised upon contemporary English thought can scarcely be overestimated, nor can there be any doubt about the value of the liberal and inquiring spirit with which he handled the great questions of his time. Beyond that, however, there has been considerable difference of opinion about the enduring merits of his philosophy. At first sight he is the most lucid of philosophers. Many people have spoken of the marvelous intelligibility of his writing. Usually, however, it is not long before doubts begin to creep in. Although the lucidity remains, its span is seen to be somewhat limited, and one sometimes has the uneasy feeling that he is being equally lucid on both sides of a question.

Evaluation of Mill

Oddly enough, however, this judgment has not led to any neglect of Mill. Little attention is now paid to Hamilton or to Whewell, but Mill's name continually crops up in philosophical discussions. This is partly due to the fact that Mill offers a body of doctrine and a set of technical terms on many subjects (notably on induction) that have proved extremely useful in the classroom. But a more important reason is that he has come to be regarded as a sort of personification of certain tendencies in philosophy that it is regarded as continually necessary to expound or expose because they make such a powerful appeal to serious minds. Thus he is or says he is a Utilitarian; yet nothing, it is pointed out, could tell more strongly against Utilitarianism than certain passages in his writings. Then again, he is said to be an Empiricist (although he says himself that he is not), and his theories of the syllogism and of mathematics are constantly used to demonstrate the fatal consequences of this way of thinking.

It is misleading to speak without qualification of Mill's Utilitarianism. Nor is it sufficient to add that Mill modified the Utilitarianism that he inherited from Bentham and from his father in one way and another in order to meet the criticisms that it encountered in Victorian times. He does, it is true, sometimes give that impression (as in his essay *Utilitarianism*); but elsewhere (as in his essay *On Liberty*) he scarcely attempts to conceal the fact that his premises are completely independent of Bentham's. Thus, contrary to the common belief, it appears to be very hazardous to characterize offhand the precise position of Mill on any major philosophical topic. He sometimes behaved with a reckless disregard of consequences more suitable to a Romantic than to a Utilitarian. He is thoroughly romantic, again, and thoroughly representative of his age in the eagerness with which he seeks out and endeavours to assimilate every last exotic line of thought which shows any signs of vitality. He himself claimed to be superior to most of his contemporaries in "ability and willingness to learn from everybody," and indeed, for all his father's careful schooling, there was never anybody less buttoned up against alien influences than Mill. In his writings there can be discerned traces of every wind of doctrine of the early 19th century.

MAJOR WORKS

POLITICS AND ECONOMICS: *Essays on Some Unsettled Questions in Political Economy* (1844); *Principles of Political Economy,* 2 vol. (1848; 2nd and 3rd eds. with important differences, 1849, 1852); *On Liberty* (1859); *Considerations on Representative Government* (1861); *Utilitarianism* (1863); *On The Subjection of Women* (1869).

PHILOSOPHY AND RELIGION: *A System of Logic* (1843); *Examination of Sir William Hamilton's Philosophy* (1865); *Auguste Comte and Positivism* (1865); *Three Essays on Religion* (1874).

OTHER WORKS: Essays on "Bentham" (1838) and "Coleridge" (1840) in *Dissertations and Discussions,* 4 vol. (1859–75), also reprinted together with an introduction by F.R. LEAVIS (1950); *Autobiography,* ed. by Helen Taylor (1873).

BIBLIOGRAPHY. The definitive edition of the *Collected Works* is that edited by JOHN M. ROBSON *et al.,* in 17 vol. (begun in 1963); each volume has a full introduction, notes, and indexes.

Biography: The standard biography is M.ST.J. PACKE, *The Life of John Stuart Mill* (1954, reissued 1970), a fascinating book (including a bibliography), with interpretations sometimes too colourful. Mill's own *Autobiography* has been edited several times, for example by JACK STILLINGER (1969). Stillinger has also edited *The Early Draft of John Stuart Mill's Autobiography* (1961), written in 1853–54, which includes a much more vivid and intimate account of Mill's relations with his father and mother; it suggests a more gloomy picture of his childhood than does the final version. (This is not a work that Mill was himself prepared to publish.) ALEXANDER BAIN, *John Stuart Mill: A Criticism with Personal Recollections* (1882, reprinted 1969), will never be superseded; an excellent, rambling account by Mill's closest philosophical disciple, it refers to many conversations and quotes from letters now lost. F.A. HAYEK (ed.), *John Stuart Mill and Harriet Taylor* (1951, reprinted 1969), is full of details about the writing of Mill's works from the 1830s to 1858 (with gaps for times when they were meeting together); the painting of Harriet Taylor should not be missed. PEDRO SCHWARTZ, *The New Political Economy of J.S. Mill* (1972), is an intellectual biography; EUGENE R. AUGUST, *John Stuart Mill* (1975), is a biography for the general reader.

Comment and criticism: RICHARD P. ANSCHUTZ, *The Philosophy of J.S. Mill* (1953, reprinted 1969), a subtle and precise study presupposing a wide reading of the texts; KARL W. BRITTON, *John Stuart Mill: Life and Philosophy,* 2nd ed. (1969), an introductory book covering Mill's life and work—sympathetic but critical; ÉLIE HALÉVY, *The Growth of Philosophic Radicalism* (1928; new ed., 1949, reissued 1972; originally published in French, 1901–04), the standard comprehensive account of the school in which Mill was brought up, with issues fully analyzed and discussed (including a bibliography); JOHN P. PLAMENATZ, *The English Utilitarians,* 2nd ed. (1958, reissued 1966), a good account of the background and content of Mill's moral theory; JOHN M. ROBSON, *The Improvement of Mankind: The Social and Political Thought of John Stuart Mill* (1968), offering an account of Mill's life and of his mature views on morals, scientific method, politics, and sociology; MAURICE COWLING, *Mill and Liberalism* (1963), an eccentric account that imputes to Mill a strong strain of authoritarianism; DENNIS F. THOMPSON, *John Stuart Mill and Representative Government* (1976), an analysis of his *Considerations on Representative Government;* ALAN RYAN, *John Stuart Mill* (1970), an attempt to show that a single constant theory of inductivism underlies all Mill's writings; RICHARD HALLIDAY, *John Stuart Mill* (1976), arguing that behind Mill's eclecticism is a coherent pattern of thought; PETER WINCH, *The Idea of a Social Science,* ch. 3 (1958, reissued 1977), an attack on attempts to construct a causal science of human conduct; FRANCIS H. BRADLEY, *Ethical Studies,* 2nd ed. (1927, reissued 1962), in which the third essay is an attack on Mill's hedonism; G.E. MOORE, *Principia Ethica* (1903, reissued 1976), a very lively onslaught on Mill's Utilitarianism, often patently unfair; C.L. TEN, *Mill on Liberty* (1980), an interpretation of the conflict between his utilitarianism and his liberalism; J.O. URMSON, "The Interpretation of the Moral Philosophy of J.S. Mill," *Philosophical Quarterly,* 3:33–39 (1953), on moral rules; NEY MACMINN, J.R. HAINDS, and J. MCCRIMMON (eds.), *Bibliography of the Published Writings of John Stuart Mill* (1945, reprinted 1970).

(R.P.An./Ed.)

Milton

John Milton stands next to Shakespeare among English poets; his writings and his influence are a very important part of the history of English literature, culture, and libertarian thought. He is best known for his long epic poem *Paradise Lost,* in which his "grand style" is used with superb power; its characterization of Satan is one of the supreme achievements of world literature. Milton's prose works, however, are also important as a valuable interpretation of the Puritan revolution, and they have their place in modern histories of political and religious thought.

Milton, engraving by W. Faithorne, 1670. In the National Portrait Gallery, London.

By courtesy of the National Portrait Gallery, London

Milton was born in London on December 9, 1608. His grandfather, an Oxfordshire yeoman, had been a staunch Roman Catholic who had disinherited his son, the poet's father, for turning Protestant. John Milton, Sr., going to London, made his way to prominence and a comfortable fortune as a scrivener, or notary, and through the collateral business of private banking or moneylending. Milton was to pay repeated tributes to his father's generous concern with his education. One debt was in the way of music. The father was a composer of some repute, and the poet's lifelong devotion to music is attested by the warmth of his own allusions and by his early biographers. Of his mother (died 1637) Milton said only that she was well esteemed and known for her charities. He had an older sister, Anne, and a younger brother, Christopher, who became a lawyer.

Education and early poems. Milton was educated at St. Paul's School, London. The conventional date given for his admission is 1620, but it may have been as early as 1615. In addition to his regular schoolwork in Latin, Greek, and, later, Hebrew, the boy had instruction at home, perhaps partly in modern languages, from private tutors. Milton was a voracious student; he traced the initial cause of his later blindness to his having, from his 12th year, rarely quit his books before midnight. Along with a couple of Latin exercises that have survived, his earliest attempts at verse, made when he was 15, were rhymed paraphrases of Psalms 114 and 136. Milton's closest friend, at school and later, was Charles Diodati, the son of a prominent physician of Italian origin, who went from St. Paul's to Oxford; a less intimate friendship, which also lasted beyond school, was with Alexander Gill, the son of the headmaster.

Years at Cambridge

On April 9, 1625, Milton matriculated at Christ's College, Cambridge; he received his bachelor of arts degree in March 1629 and that of master in July 1632. His experience at Cambridge can be partly gathered from his abundant Latin verse and his seven Latin prolusions (public speeches that were expected to display the speaker's learning and rhetorical and argumentative powers). Apparently in March 1626 he clashed in some way with his tutor and was rusticated. He compared his "exile" at home in London to that of his beloved Ovid and rejoiced in the opportunity to read the books (here Classical plays) "that are my life" and to see beautiful girls while strolling. On his return he was assigned to another tutor and graduated at the normal time.

Milton's nickname at the university, "the Lady," was apparently bestowed because of his handsome and delicate features and a purity of mind and behaviour that disdained the diversions of his coarser fellows. During his seven years at Cambridge he seems to have moved from some unpopularity to general respect and, among dons and cultivated students, to high esteem. He did not love the Scholastic logic that dominated the curriculum; then, as well as later, he denounced it as barren. In his last prolusion (1631–32?) he proclaimed the fervent creed and dream of a young Renaissance Humanist who was at once a Christian, a Platonist, and—whether or not he had yet read Francis Bacon—a Baconian.

Meanwhile, Milton had been learning his craft and sometimes revealing his inner self in writing Latin verse. Neo-Latin poets, such as George Buchanan or the contemporary Hugo Grotius (whom Milton later met in Paris), enjoyed European fame; and students commonly celebrated academic and national events in what was then the normal language of the university world. The young poet's sensuous instincts were revealed in these Latin poems and were further displayed, along with his mastery of Italian, in six Italian pieces (1630?), with which may be linked his first English sonnet, "O Nightingale."

Earliest extant English poems

Early in 1628 Milton wrote the earliest of his extant English poems (apart from the two psalms), "On the Death of a fair Infant," an elegy, in the Elizabethan vein, on his baby niece, Anne Phillips. In part of an academic prolusion in English couplets ("At a Vacation Exercise," July 1628) he declared his devotion to his native language, a style free from eccentricity, and exalted themes concerning nature and man. And in the Latin "Elegy VI," addressed to Diodati in the Christmas season of 1629–30, he praised the light verse kindled by wine and love but turned from that to celebrate the ascetic purity of the heroic poet. The elegy ended with a reference to a poem he had just written, his first great poem in English, "On the Morning of Christ's Nativity." Such a poem, composed shortly after his 21st birthday, may be taken as a kind of announcement of his poetical coming of age and future direction, both in its religious theme and in its mastery of conception and form and image and rhythm. Probably in the long vacation of 1631 Milton wrote the companion poems "L'Allegro" and "Il Penseroso." Less ambitious in theme than the "Nativity," they have their own complexity, concealed beneath a unique grace and charm. They may be said to embody—and excel—the urbane decorum of the lyrical and reflective pieces of Ben Jonson—a quality already manifested in the tiny "Song: On May Morning" (1629–30?) and the "Epitaph on the Marchioness of Winchester" (1631). Milton had lately (1630) also written the lines "On Shakespear," which were printed in the Shakespearean Second Folio, 1632.

Milton's scholarly and literary gifts had from childhood marked him out in the minds of his family and teachers for the ministry; in his later prose he said he had refused to "subscribe slave" in a church governed by prelacy, but the date of his negative decision is not known. As his academic career approached its end, the problem of an occupation would come up, and the poem "Ad Patrem"—though some scholars link it with *Comus* (1634)—may well have been written in 1631–32. In this piece, with a mixture of filial gratitude, firmness, and confidence in poetry and himself, Milton assumes or urges that he should not be pushed into some basely lucrative profession by a father who has fostered his literary pursuits and is himself a devotee of the muses.

Horton period (1632–38). On taking his master of arts degree in July 1632, Milton retired to his father's house—until 1635 at Hammersmith, then at the country estate at Horton, near Windsor—and proceeded to give himself the liberal education Cambridge had not provided. It was in these years that he laid the foundation or set the direction of his liberal thinking. He sought to digest the mass of history, literature, and philosophy, to gain the "insight into all seemly and generous arts and affairs" needed by the citizen-poet who would be a leader and teacher. At times he suspended his labours to visit London in quest of books or something new in mathematics or music.

Self-education

An important landmark in Milton's early development is the sober sonnet "How soon hath Time," written on his 24th birthday. During recent years he had become a figure in the small university world; now he writes this sonnet while his contemporaries are forging ahead, and he has had six months of studious and outwardly unfruitful obscurity at home. But any uneasiness about his present and future is quieted in the earnest dedication of his life to his great Taskmaster's will. What might be called the first pledges toward the fulfillment of this self-consecration were two short religious poems, "On Time" and "At a Solemn Musick" (1632–33?). These are early renderings of the beatific vision that always kindled Milton's imagination. Both, in different sequence, contrast the grossness of temporal life, the jarring discord of sin, with the eternity and harmony of heaven and good.

The same contrast is sounded in the opening lines and carried through the whole of the masque known as *Comus.* During 1630–34, perhaps in 1632, Milton had, at the invitation probably of the musician Henry Lawes, written "Arcades," a miniature masque of Jonsonian courtliness. This presumably led to a request from Lawes for another masque. *Comus* was presented on September 29, 1634, before John Egerton, earl of Bridgewater, at Ludlow Castle, in Shropshire, in honour of his becoming lord president of Wales. *Comus* was Milton's first dramatizing of his great theme, the conflict of good and evil.

If *Comus* was, in a way, a song of innocence, "Lycidas" (written in November 1637) was a song of experience—Milton's first attempt to justify the ways of God to himself and to men. His former fellow collegian, Edward King, was drowned in a shipwreck in the Irish Sea in August 1637, and Milton was asked to contribute to a volume of elegies; "Lycidas," signed "J.M.," appeared at the end of an undistinguished collection of pieces in Latin, Greek, and English (1638). The pastoral convention had, from its Greek beginnings, proved its value as a dramatic vehicle—or mask—for almost anything that a poet wished to say. Milton, working as usual within a venerable tradition, as usual re-created it. He had no reason to feel deep personal sorrow, but the drowning of a virtuous and promising young man, on the threshold of service in God's church, brought home the whole enigma of life and death, of the rightness of things in a world where such events could happen. What if his own talents—which during his years of study he has been nurturing—should be cut off? It is impossible to summarize the complexities and depths of the poem, its reverberating solidity of reference, its rich variety of pace and tone, the artistic control that dominates turbulent emotions and ends with the high serenity of victory won. "Lycidas" may be the greatest short poem in the language.

Composition of "Lycidas"

Italian tour (1638–39). In May 1638, a year after his mother's death, Milton set off—with one servant—on a visit to Italy. He sojourned chiefly in Florence, Rome, and Naples. Milton and some of his early poems—not those in English—were cordially welcomed among men of letters and patrons and their academies. The experience, which he later described at length in *The Second Defence of the People of England* (1654) and alluded to elsewhere, warmed his heart and nourished his self-confidence. (It may be remembered that at home he had very little literary acquaintance and, outside a small circle, no poetic reputation.) To his host in Naples, Giambattista Manso, marquis of Villa, who had been the patron of Torquato Tasso and Giambattista Marino, Milton wrote a bread-and-butter epistle, "Mansus" (1638–39), which is one of his best Latin poems, a graceful apologia for English culture and a no less graceful statement of his own poetic standing and hopes. He wrote also an epistle to a Roman poet, Giovanni Salzilli, and several epigrams in praise of the singing of the famous Leonora Baroni. Though he mingled happily with Catholics and was a guest at a grand entertainment given by Cardinal Francesco Barberini, the staunch Protestant did not remain silent on matters of religion. He made a call—later recorded in "Areopagitica"—on the astronomer Galileo, who was in semicaptivity because his views on the universe conflicted with the doctrine of the Roman Church. Milton felt obliged to forgo a visit to Sicily and Greece because of news of mounting political tension in England, although, as he says, he lingered some time longer in Italy. In August 1638 Milton's friend Diodati died. Milton had been informed of his loss while in Italy; on his way home he stopped to see Diodati's uncle, Giovanni Diodati, who was professor of theology at Geneva.

Middle period (1641–60). Milton returned to England in July 1639, settled in a house in London, and prepared to take in pupils; the first ones were Edward and John Phillips, the sons of his sister Anne. His elaborate pastoral elegy on Diodati, "Epitaphium Damonis," was written apparently late in 1640 and privately printed. This has commonly been ranked at the head of Milton's Latin poetry, though dissenters may ask if the fact of its commemorating his dearly loved friend has not heightened its intrinsic merits.

Milton had returned to England with plans for an Arthurian epic (plans set forth briefly in "Mansus" and "Epitaphium Damonis"); like other ambitious poets of the Renaissance, he hoped to write the great modern heroic poem. But he was also deeply anxious about the Puritan cause. In his denunciation of hireling clergy in "Lycidas," Milton had virtually declared his Puritan allegiance, and the years 1641–60 he gave almost wholly to pamphleteering in the cause of religious and civil liberty. There is an important personal passage in his fourth tract, "The Reason of Church-government Urg'd against Prelaty" (1642), that shows it was a heavy sacrifice to put aside his craving for poetic immortality and leave off his cherished studies to "embark in a troubled sea of noises and hoarse disputes," but he could not be deaf to God's summons. And, as his work went on, he was sustained by the conviction that in his many and varied defenses of liberty he was, in another way, fulfilling his epic and patriotic aspirations. His first five pamphlets (1641–42) were contributions to the attack made on prelacy in the Anglican Church by a group of Presbyterian divines (called, from their initials, the "Smectymnuus" group). The attack was directed chiefly against its episcopal hierarchy, *The Book of Common Prayer,* and ritual, as being a compromise with Rome. The group urged a return to the democratic simplicity and purity of the apostolic church. Milton's first tract was "Of Reformation Touching Church Discipline in England" (1641). This begins by assailing the Anglican service and ends with a vision of the new and grand Reformation. In the personal passage in "The Reason of Church-government" Milton explains his religious conception of poetry and the deferment of his great epic because of what he feels to be his public duty.

Allegiance to Puritanism

Notoriety came in 1643, with Milton's "Doctrine and Discipline of Divorce" (enlarged edition 1644), followed by three more tracts in 1644 and 1645 on the same theme. His discussion was presumably hastened by his own marital disaster. In June (?) 1642, several months before the outbreak of the Civil War, Milton had married Mary Powell, the daughter of a Royalist squire of Oxfordshire who owed money to his father. Success could hardly be predicted for the marriage of a scholar and poet of 33 to an uneducated girl of half his age from a large, easygoing household. The young wife, visiting her family a little later, declined—doubtless with their backing—to

First marriage

return. The shock must have been especially severe for a man who—as one may infer from the anguished cries that recur in the "Doctrine"—had approached marriage not only with high hopes (and an unblemished past) but with earnest prayers; and there was no release from such a tragic mistake. In the tracts, Milton argued that the sole cause admitted for divorce, adultery, might be less valid than incompatibility, and that the forced yoke of a loveless marriage was a crime against human dignity. Both religious and philosophic tradition and the way of the world (including the usually meagre education given to girls) kept woman inferior to man; Milton, without denying that view, upheld a personal and Puritan ideal of marriage as an active bond of mutual love and mental companionship, an ideal that exalted women far above the level they occupied, say, in Cavalier poetry. He was, however, attacked as a libertine by Royalists and Presbyterians alike. In 1645 friends brought about a reunion between Milton and his wife; and in 1646, when the Powells had been ruined by the war, he took into his house, for nearly a year, the whole noisy family of 10. Three daughters, Anne, Mary, and Deborah, were born in 1646, 1648, and 1652. A son died in infancy. Mrs. Milton died a few days after Deborah's birth.

Milton's best known pamphlets (at any rate for modern readers) were published in 1644. "Of Education" is one of the last in a long line of European expositions of Renaissance Humanism. His aim was to mold boys into enlightened, cultivated, responsible citizens and leaders; its basis would be the study of the ancient classics, in due subordination to the Bible and Christian teaching. But he also gave notable emphasis to science. In "Areopagitica," on the freedom of the press, he writes as a scholar and poet and lover of books and reasserts above all his belief in the power of truth to win its way through free inquiry and discussion. The tract seems to have had very little effect in its own time.

On February 13, 1649, two weeks after the execution of Charles I, Milton's first political tract, "The Tenure of Kings and Magistrates," appeared. In it he expounds the doctrine that power resides always in the people, who delegate it to a sovereign but may, if it is abused, resume it and depose or even execute the tyrant. A month later he was invited to become secretary for foreign languages to Cromwell's Council of State. Hitherto a detached observer, Milton, in spite of his private studies, was doubtless eager to have a hand in the workings of government. He was not on the policy-making level, but he had the easy command of Latin needed for foreign correspondence. Also, as a publicist of demonstrated sympathy with the revolution, he was expected to continue his defense of the cause against the multiplying attacks on the regicides.

Secretary for foreign languages in the Council of State

Milton's first effort in this line was "Eikonoklastes" (October 1649), one of a number of answers to *Eikon Basilike*, a book edited from the King's papers by his chaplain, John Gauden; this ostensible self-portrait of the royal saint and martyr, catching the public in its first shock of horror over the execution, was one of the most potent pieces of propaganda in English history, and not even Milton could prevail against it.

During 1651 Milton was censor and supervisory editor of the chief Commonwealth newspaper, *Mercurius Politicus*, edited by Marchamont Needham. In this year appeared his Latin *Defence of the People of England.* Charles II, in exile, had engaged Claudius Salmasius (Claude Saumaise), the most eminent of classical scholars, to arraign the regicides (*Defensio Regia pro Carolo I*, 1649). Milton was less effective in legal argument than in discrediting Salmasius by personal abuse; like some other crusaders, he tended to see opponents as monstrous enemies of a sacred cause who must be destroyed by any means.

If he was, then and later, uplifted by the vanquishing of a renowned antagonist, he was inevitably and profoundly depressed by the loss of his eyesight; it had been failing for years, and blindness became complete in the winter of 1651–52. Milton was only 43, and the great poem was still unwritten. Blindness reduced his strictly secretarial duties, though he continued through 1659 as a translator of state letters.

Onset of blindness

The Second Defence of the People of England—also in Latin, since it was also addressed to Europe at large—was much more worthy of its subject and its author. In it he celebrated the achievements of the Commonwealth leaders (though he was bold enough to warn Cromwell against one-man rule). In 1659 two more tracts on church and state were published. In "A Treatise of Civil Power in Ecclesiastical Causes" Milton argued for religious freedom (except for Roman Catholics, since Catholicism had shown itself a danger to national security). In "Considerations Touching The likeliest means to remove Hirelings out of the church" he reasserted the ideal of a clergy of apostolic simplicity of life.

His last political pamphlet, "The Readie and Easie Way to Establish a Free Commonwealth," was published in March 1660 and again, enlarged, in April. It was an act no less courageous than futile, since machinery was patently moving to bring back Charles II (he made his triumphal entry on May 29). Milton's pamphlet is a cry of incredulity and despair from the last champion of "the good Old Cause." The glories of the Commonwealth, to which he himself had given 20 years and his eyesight, are being swept away by a nation of slaves "now choosing them a captain back for Egypt." The Restoration was the last and heaviest of Milton's many disillusionments.

Estimate of the prose works

The large bulk of Milton's prose—which fills four times as many volumes as his poetry—is read only by scholars, but much of it is important for several reasons. In an age of great prose, Milton's, at its best, has a very individual if often undisciplined greatness, and "Areopagitica" at least is a classic document and possession of the race. Moreover, as the record of Milton's growth (a leftward growth, in religion and politics) and of his dreams and disillusionments, his prose works are the essential introduction to *Paradise Lost, Paradise Regained,* and *Samson Agonistes,* providing a bridge between the radiant idealism of his youth and the much-tried faith and fortitude of his later years. In particular, his treatise *On Christian Doctrine* held a central place in his thoughts and labours. He seems to have finished it by *c.* 1658–60 (it was first printed and translated by Charles Sumner in 1825). Its importance is that it expounds, with differences, the theological frame of *Paradise Lost.* Viewed in perspective, most of Milton's essential beliefs are those of traditional Christianity, but—always on authority he finds in the Bible—he departs from orthodoxy on some points: God created the world not out of nothing but out of his own substance; God the Father, the Son, and the Holy Spirit are not a coequal Trinity but a descending order; man's soul dies with his body, until revived at the resurrection (this "mortalist" heresy, which is put into the mouth of the despairing Adam, had other adherents in England). Milton's conception of the Trinity, which is too complex for summary, is apparent to alert readers of *Paradise Lost,* though the poem did not disturb generations of the orthodox. More basic for the poem is Milton's denial of predestination (which, of course, is not a heresy). Brought up, like most Anglicans of his time, as a Calvinist, he regarded himself as one at least until 1644, but his final belief was in the Arminian doctrine—the salvation not of a predestined few but of all believers, who constitute the true elect. Milton above all insisted on man's rational freedom and responsible power of choice.

Sonnets and other poems (1642–58). Milton's early poems, in English, Latin, Greek, and Italian, were published at the beginning of 1646 (dated 1645). During the 20 years given to public affairs he was mostly cut off from poetry but did write 17 occasional sonnets, versified a number of Psalms, and began the composition of *Paradise Lost.* Some of the sonnets are deeply personal: two on his blindness (1651?–55) and one on the death in 1658, some months after childbirth, of his second wife, Katherine Woodcock, whom he had married in 1656.

The major sonnets have much poetical as well as autobiographical interest, and as a group they illustrate (with "Lycidas") both in texture and rhythm the beginnings of the grand style (which Milton may have learned partly from the 16th-century Italian poets Giovanni della Casa and Torquato Tasso) that was to have full scope in the epic. One is less conscious of sonnet structure and of rhymes than of a single massive unit that approaches a paragraph of Milton's blank verse.

Later life. The Restoration government executed the Commonwealth leader Sir Henry Vane the Younger and exhumed and hanged at Tyburn the bodies of Cromwell, Henry Ireton, and John Bradshaw. Milton himself, as a noted defender of the regicides, was in real danger. In the summer of 1660 a warrant was out for his arrest; he was kept in hiding by friends. In August the Act of Oblivion, granting pardon to most Commonwealth supporters, was passed. Milton was safe within its terms but was nevertheless taken into custody (and released on December 15). According to various early stories, his life was spared through the intercession either of the poet Andrew Marvell, who in 1657 had become a fellow secretary and was now a member of Parliament, or of the Royalist playwright Sir William Davenant, whose life Milton had earlier been the means of saving. It may have been decided that the blind writer was now harmless and that token proceedings against him would be enough.

Milton had given up the idea of composing a British epic. Instead he chose the most momentous event, next to the life and death of Christ, in the world's history—man's Fall from grace. It is not known when *Paradise Lost* was actually begun. Guesses have centred on 1655–58. Clearly, the lines on the poet's having fallen on evil days, in the prelude to book vii, were composed after the Restoration, and the whole may have been done pretty much in the order in which it stands. It was finished by 1665. The first edition of 1667 was in 10 books; this was reissued in 1668 and 1669, and in some of these issues Milton added the prefatory note on his use of blank verse and "The Argument." In the second edition (1674), along with some small revisions, books vii and x were each split into two; and the arguments, formerly grouped together, were placed at the head of the respective books. The main motives and events of *Paradise Lost* had precedent to a greater or lesser degree, though Milton handled them with powerful originality; like a Greek dramatist, he was reworking a story familiar in outline to his audience. His story, moreover, was one of unique truth, sacredness, and universal and eternal import, and it gave the poet the advantage of immemorial belief and association in the minds of his earlier readers. This advantage no longer operates in the same way—although, for modern readers, the fable still possesses at least the immemorial and universal import of archetypal myth.

Composition of *Paradise Lost*

As artist, Milton links himself, both proudly and humbly, with the ancients—especially Homer and the blind bards of Greek myth—but he regularly ranks his Christian theme above the themes of the pagan poets. As he had said long before, in explaining why he must postpone his epic, it was a work

> not to be obtained by the invocation of Dame Memory and her Siren daughters, but by devout prayer to that eternal Spirit who can enrich with all utterance and knowledge, and sends out his seraphim, with the hallowed fire of his altar, to touch and purify the lips of whom he pleases.

Milton's preface stressed the novelty and rightness of blank verse for a heroic poem. His manipulation of rhythm and sound is of course one of his supreme achievements. The continuous flow of his long sentences and paragraphs is naturally unlike the dramatic blank verse of Shakespearean dialogue, and it builds up a continuous onward pressure. As a modern master of rhythm, T.S. Eliot, has said, Milton's blank verse is never monotonous. The pattern of sound is so wedded to the pattern of sense that each is essential to the other.

In *Paradise Lost* (ix) Milton had spoken of "patience and heroic martyrdom" as themes unsung, though nobler than martial prowess, and this "better fortitude" was celebrated in *Paradise Regained* and *Samson Agonistes* (1671). *Paradise Regained* is a natural sequel to the long poem: Christ, the second Adam, wins back for man what the first Adam had lost. But Milton did not, as might have been expected, deal with the Crucifixion; instead, he showed Christ in the wilderness overcoming Satan the tempter, thereby proving his fitness for his ultimate trial and, in his human role, showing what man in general might achieve through strong integrity and humble obedience to the divine will. Although the poem has been found cold by the mass of readers and critics, it nevertheless has all the fire of Milton's religious and moral passion and his reverence for true heroism.

Paradise Regained and *Samson Agonistes*

For some readers, the drama of *Samson Agonistes* (published in the same volume with *Paradise Regained*) is the most powerful and completely satisfying of Milton's major works. It is by far the greatest English drama on the Greek model. The action, up to the reported catastrophe, is wholly psychological; it is the process by which Samson, "Eyeless in Gaza at the mill with slaves," moves from preoccupation with his misery and disgrace to selfless humility and renewed spiritual strength, so that he can once more feel himself God's chosen champion. The drama must owe a great deal of its power to Milton's sense of kinship with his hero; he has been eyeless in London among a nation of slaves. But the restraint of Milton's art shows itself very clearly: there is nothing in the drama that does not belong to the story of Samson.

Altogether, if *Samson* was his last work, it was a grand testament. Like Samson, Milton was able to conquer despair or to sublimate it in his last three great poems. These expressed, not his earlier revolutionary faith in men and movements, but a purified faith in God and the regenerative strength of the individual soul.

Last years

The poet's final 16 years of life, during which these three works were finished or composed, were—outwardly and in part inwardly—peaceful, although, along with sombre or uplifting thoughts of past and present, there were concrete troubles: a frugal domestic economy necessitated by greatly diminished resources; blindness and what was sometimes a more severe affliction, the pains of gout; and a degree of friction with his daughters, due probably to faults on both sides.

Apart from the publication of books, the chief events of these years were Milton's marriage (1663) to a third wife, the young and amiable Elizabeth Minshull, who survived him, and the removal, during the plague of 1665, to a house (now a Milton museum) at Chalfont St. Giles, Buckinghamshire.

Early biographers give pictures of a quiet daily routine. Milton got up at 4:00 AM and had the Hebrew Bible read to him. Meditation, reading, and dictation filled the time until midday dinner. His late and long poems were, of course, composed in his head, especially at night, as famous allusions in *Paradise Lost* indicate; when he was ready "to be milked," he would dictate, often with one leg flung over the arm of his chair. The taking of dictation, the correcting of copy, and reading aloud in various languages were services performed by paid assistants, his two nephews, his younger daughters, and friends and disciples. After dinner, says the 17th-century English antiquary John Aubrey, "he used to walk 3 or 4 hours at a time (he always had a garden where he lived)." In the evening there was reading of poetry, and he went to bed about 9:00, after a pipe and a glass of water. One refreshment was music, playing on the organ or viol and singing; "he would be cheerful even in his gout fits, and sing." And there were many, sometimes too many, callers—foreigners (who came to see the conqueror of Salmasius, not the poet) and English friends, old and young, such as men already mentioned, and the young Quaker Thomas Elwood, whom Milton helped with his Latin. In religion Milton had moved from the low-church Anglicanism of his parents to Presbyterianism to Independency to independence. In the latter part of his life, according to his early biographer John Toland, "he was not a professed member of any particular sect among Christians, he frequented none of their assemblies, nor made use of their peculiar rites in his family." But, as Dr. Johnson observed, suspending his Anglican hostility, "his studies and meditations were an habitual prayer." Milton died on November 8, 1674, "of the gout struck in," just before his 66th birthday. His burial in St. Giles', Cripplegate, was attended by "all his learned and great friends in London, not without a friendly concourse of the vulgar."

Reputation. Milton's reputation grew steadily after 1667 and was well established before Joseph Addison's papers on *Paradise Lost* appeared in *The Spectator* (1712); these were instrumental in extending the poet's fame to the Continent. His influence on 18th-century verse was immense. In the 19th century, two main streams of critical opinion are evident. On the one hand, the revolutionary Romantic poets Blake and Shelley launched the "Satanist" misinterpretation of *Paradise Lost* and made its author, like themselves, a rebel—their attitude is summed up in Blake's saying that Milton was of the devil's party without knowing it (in other words, that he had projected himself into Satan, who was the poem's real hero). On the other hand, other critics—also concentrating on the epic—threw overboard Milton's beliefs and ideas as long-dead fundamentalism and listened only to the organ voice.

The poet's influence waned during the Victorian age, and in the 20th century the new poetry and criticism launched by Ezra Pound and T.S. Eliot were strongly anti-Milton and pro-John Donne. But during the 1940s and 1950s a shift in critical attitudes took place, and dozens of books and hundreds of articles have been given to ideas and beliefs of the thinker, the publicist, and the poet, and have brought a new refinement of perception and analysis to the aesthetic study of Milton's poetry.

MAJOR WORKS

POEMS: *A Maske Presented at Ludlow Castle, 1634* [*Comus*], in an enlarged text, and "Lycidas" (1638) were both reprinted in *Poems* (1645), which included nearly all the other early pieces, "L'Allegro," "Il Penseroso," etc. The second edition (1673) reprinted the 1645 *Poems*, adding two early pieces and later sonnets; political reasons excluded four sonnets, addressed to Sir Thomas Fairfax, Cromwell, Sir Henry Vane, and the one to Skinner beginning "Cyriack, this three years' day." *Paradise Lost*, in 10 books, appeared in 1667 (revised in 12 books, 1674); *Paradise Regained* and *Samson Agonistes* were printed together in 1671.

PROSE: "Of Reformation Touching Church Discipline in England" (1641); "The Reason of Church-government Urg'd against Prelaty" (1642); "An Apology for Smectymnuus" (1642), three of Milton's five tracts against prelacy; "The Doctrine and Discipline of Divorce" (1643, enlarged 1644); "Of Education" (1644); "Areopagitica" (1644); "The Tenure of Kings and Magistrates" (1649); "Eikonoklastes" (1649), reply to John Gauden's *Eikon Basilike;* "A Treatise of Civil Power in Ecclesiastical Causes" (1659); "Considerations Touching The likeliest means to remove Hirelings out of the church" (1659); "The Readie and Easie Way to Establish a Free Commonwealth" (1660); *The History of Britain* (1670); "Of True Religion, Haeresie, Schism, Toleration, And . . . the growth of Popery" (1673); *A Brief History of Moscovia* (1682).

WORKS IN LATIN, GREEK, AND ITALIAN: (POEMS): *Poems* (1645) contained three Greek pieces and five Italian sonnets and a canzone. Most of the notable Latin poems are mentioned above; one other, "Elegy V" ("On the Coming of Spring"), was a fervently "pagan" celebration of awakening life and sexuality. (PROSE): The seven Latin speeches delivered at Cambridge and Latin letters to friends (published 1674); *Pro Populo Anglicano Defensio* (1651); *Pro Populo Anglicano Defensio Secunda* (1654); *Pro Se Defensio* (1655); *De Doctrina Christiana* (published 1825).

BIBLIOGRAPHY

Editions: The works of John Milton, 18 vol., with a useful 2-vol. index, was edited by Columbia University scholars (1931–40). HARRIS F. FLETCHER edited *Complete Poetical Works: Reproduced in Photographic Facsimile,* 4 vol. (1943–48). The complete prose, with translations of the Latin works and elaborate commentaries, was edited by D.M. WOLFE *et al.*, in 8 vol. (1953–82). *The Student's Milton,* ed. by FRANK A. PATTERSON, rev. ed. (1933, reissued 1961), has almost all the works in one volume, with some apparatus. A comprehensive one-volume annotated edition is *Complete Poems and Major Prose,* ed. by MERRITT Y. HUGHES (1957). Annotated editions of the complete poems are those of HELEN DARBISHIRE, 2 vol. (1952–55), with mainly textual notes; DOUGLAS BUSH (1965); JOHN CAREY and ALASTAIR FOWLER (1968, reissued 1980); and JOHN T. SHAWCROSS (1963; rev. ed., 1971). There are countless editions of selected poems. *The Prose of John Milton* was edited by J. MAX PATRICK *et al.* (1967).

Bibliographies: DAVID H. STEVENS, *Reference Guide to Milton: From 1800 to the Present Day* (1930, reprinted 1967); JAMES H. HANFORD and WILLIAM A. MCQUEEN, *Milton,* 2nd ed. (1979); C.A. PATRIDES (ed.), *Milton's Epic Poetry* (1967), including a full annotated reading list; and CALVIN HUCKABAY, *John Milton: An Annotated Bibliography, 1929–1968,* rev. ed. (1969). See also the descriptive survey in *English Poetry: Select Bibliographical Guides,* ed. by A.E. DYSON (1971). Current writings are recorded in the *Annual Bibliography of English Language and Literature,* published by the Modern Humanities Research Association; *MLA International Bibliography* (annual); and in *The Milton Quarterly.*

Biography and criticism: Milton's utterances on himself and his work are collected in JOHN S. DIEKHOFF, *Milton on Himself* (1939; 2nd ed., 1965). The six early biographies, by JOHN AUBREY and others, are in *Early Lives of Milton,* ed. by HELEN DARBISHIRE (1932, reprinted 1971); some of them are in PATTERSON, *The Student's Milton* (cited above). DAVID MASSON'S all-inclusive *Life of John Milton,* 6 vol., partly rev. (1881–96, reissued 1965), still has its uses. The standard modern biography is WILLIAM RILEY PARKER, *Milton,* 2 vol. (1968). Four small critical biographies are those of JAMES H. HANFORD, *Milton,* 2nd ed. (1979); KENNETH MUIR, *John Milton,* 2nd ed. (1960, reissued 1968); ÉMILE SAILLENS, *John Milton* (1964; originally published in French, 1959); and DOUGLAS BUSH, *John Milton* (1964). *The Life Records of John Milton,* 5 vol. (1949–58), is an exhaustive compilation by JOSEPH M. FRENCH of documents and references. A compendious account of the life and work is *A Milton Handbook,* 5th ed. (1970), by JAMES H. HANFORD and J.G. TAAFFE. See also CHRISTOPHER HILL, *Milton and the English Revolution* (1978); C.A. PATRIDES and RAYMOND B. WADDINGTON (eds.), *The Age of Milton: Backgrounds to Seventeenth-Century Literature* (1980), 11 essays; and JOAN WEBBER, *Milton and His Epic Tradition* (1979), a Jungian interpretation.

Early criticism is collected in JOHN T. SHAWCROSS (ed.), *Milton: The Critical Heritage* (1970), covering 1628–1731, and a sequel, *Milton, 1732–1801* (1972); and in *The Romantics on Milton,* ed. by JOSEPH A. WITTREICH (1970). Milton's Victorian repute is the subject of JAMES G. NELSON, *The Sublime Puritan* (1963, reprinted 1974). Twentieth-century criticism is surveyed in PATRICK MURRAY, *Milton: The Modern Phase* (1967); and K.L. SHARMA, *Milton Criticism in the Twentieth Century* (1971).

The huge proliferation of criticism and scholarship since about 1917 severely limits references. Some general surveys of the poetry and prose are: E.M.W. TILLYARD, *Milton* (1930; rev. ed., 1966); DAVID DAICHES, *Milton* (1957, reissued 1966); DOUGLAS BUSH, *English Literature in the Earlier Seventeenth Century* (1945; 2nd ed. rev., 1962, reissued 1976), ch. 12; and the modern biographies cited above. Collected studies by three eminent Miltonists are: MERRITT Y. HUGHES, *Ten Perspectives on Milton* (1965); JAMES H. HANFORD, *John Milton: Poet and Humanist* (1966); and ARTHUR S.P. WOODHOUSE, *The Heavenly Muse: A Preface to Milton,* ed. by HUGH MACCALLUM (1972). Miscellaneous papers appear in *Milton Studies,* ed. by J.D. SIMMONDS (vol. 1–12, 1969–78).

Studies of major poems, early and late, are DON C. ALLEN, *The Harmonious Vision* (1954, reissued 1979); MARJORIE H. NICOLSON, *John Milton* (1963, reissued 1971); JOSEPH H. SUMMERS (ed.), *The Lyric and Dramatic Milton* (1965); JOHN REESING, *Milton's Poetic Art* (1968); and BALACHANDRA RAJAN, *The Lofty Rhyme* (1970).

Early poems: The Latin, Greek, and Italian poems are treated by DOUGLAS BUSH and A.B. GIAMATTI in *A Variorum Commentary on the Poems of John Milton,* vol. 1 (1970). A.S.P. WOODHOUSE, DOUGLAS BUSH, and E.R. WEISMILLER deal with all the early English poems (and all the sonnets and psalms) in vol. 2 (3 pt.) of the same *Commentary* (1972). Three useful anthologies of essays are *John Milton: L'Allegro and Il Penseroso,* ed. by ELAINE B. SAFER and T.L. ERSKINE (1970); *A Maske at Ludlow: Essays on Milton's Comus,* ed. by JOHN S. DIEKHOFF (1968); and *Milton's Lycidas,* ed. by C.A. PATRIDES, rev. ed. (1983). CLEANTH BROOKS and J.E. HARDY, *Poems of Mr. John Milton* (1951), discusses the poems of the 1645 volume. Distinctive studies of major early poems are given in ROSEMOND TUVE, *Images and Themes in Five Poems by Milton* (1957). ALAN RUDRUM, *A Critical Commentary on Milton's "Comus" and Shorter Poems* (1967), is more popular. Another study of *Comus* is ANGUS FLETCHER, *The Transcendental Masque* (1971). The sonnets have been edited with commentaries by JOHN S. SMART (1921, reprinted 1966) and by E.A.J. HONIGMANN (1966); see also the *Variorum Commentary* above.

Paradise Lost: Modern criticism is analyzed by IRENE SAMUEL in *Critical Approaches to Six Major English Works,* ed. by R.M. LUMIANSKY and HERSCHEL BAKER (1968, reissued 1971). Among the scores of modern books, some are focussed on the theological and ethical "argument": JOHN S. DIEKHOFF, *Milton's Paradise Lost* (1946); DENNIS H. BURDEN, *The Logical Epic* (1967); STANLEY E. FISH, *Surprised by Sin* (1967, reissued 1971). Some more general studies are: C.S. LEWIS, *A Preface to Paradise Lost* (1942, reissued 1974); BALACHANDRA RAJAN, *Paradise Lost and the Seventeenth Century Reader* (1947, reissued 1967); A.J.A. WALDOCK, *Paradise Lost and Its Critics* (1947, reissued 1966), an attack that stimulated illuminating responses; ARNOLD STEIN, *Answerable Style* (1953); ISABEL G. MACCAFFREY, *Paradise Lost as "Myth"* (1959); JOSEPH H. SUMMERS, *The Muse's Method: An Introduction to Paradise Lost*

(1962, reissued 1981); ANNE FERRY, *Milton's Epic Voice* (1963, reissued 1983); LOUIS L. MARTZ, *The Paradise Within* (1964); NORTHROP FRYE, *The Return of Eden* (1965, reissued 1975); HELEN GARDNER, *A Reading of Paradise Lost* (1965, reissued 1971); ALAN RUDRUM, *A Critical Commentary on Milton's "Paradise Lost"* (1966); JOHN M. STEADMAN, *Milton and the Renaissance Hero* (1967), and *Milton's Epic Characters* (1968); GEORGE K. HUNTER, *Paradise Lost* (1980); and MURRAY ROSTON, *Milton and the Baroque* (1980). See also: WATSON KIRKCONNELL (ed.), *The Celestial Cycle: The Theme of Paradise Lost in World Literature* (1952, reissued 1967); JAMES H. SIMS, *The Bible in Milton's Epics* (1962); J. MARTIN EVANS, *Paradise Lost and the Genesis Tradition* (1968); and JOSEPH E. DUNCAN, *Milton's Earthly Paradise: A Historical Study of Eden* (1972).

Paradise Regained and Samson Agonistes: *Paradise Regained* and *Samson Agonistes* are treated in several books cited above. Others are ARNOLD STEIN, *Heroic Knowledge* (1957); BARBARA K. LEWALSKI, *Milton's Brief Epic* (1966); GALBRAITH M. CRUMP (ed.), *Twentieth Century Interpretations of Samson Agonistes* (1968); ALAN RUDRUM, *A Critical Commentary on Milton's "Samson Agonistes"* (1969); *Calm of Mind,* ed. by JOSEPH A. WITTREICH (1971); *The Prison and the Pinnacle,* ed. by BALACHANDRA RAJAN (1973); W. MACKELLAR, *Paradise Regained,* vol. 4 (1975), in the *Variorum Commentary* (see above, under *Early poems*); and MARY ANN RADZINOWICZ, *Toward "Samson Agonistes": The Growth of Milton's Mind* (1978).

Other studies: Studies of metrics and style include ROBERT BRIDGES, *Milton's Prosody* (1921, reprinted 1976); SAMUEL E. SPROTT, *Milton's Art of Prosody* (1953, reprinted 1978); FRANK T. PRINCE, *The Italian Element in Milton's Verse* (1954, reissued 1969); CHRISTOPHER RICKS, *Milton's Grand Style* (1963); and E.R. WEISMILLER, in vol. 2 of the *Variorum Commentary.* See also ROLAND M. FRYE, *Milton's Imagery and the Visual Arts: Iconographic Tradition in the Epic Poems* (1978).

Milton's political and religious thought is examined in some books already named (*e.g.,* ARTHUR S.P. WOODHOUSE, *The Heavenly Muse,* and *Prose Works,* ed. by D.M. WOLFE); in ARTHUR BARKER, *Milton and the Puritan Dilemma, 1641–1660* (1942, reprinted 1976); in WILLIAM HALLER, *The Rise of Puritanism* (1938), and *Liberty and Reformation in the Puritan Revolution* (1955); and in MICHAEL FIXLER, *Milton and the Kingdoms of God* (1964).

The nature and degrees of Milton's theological orthodoxy and "heresy" have caused controversy: see MAURICE KELLEY, *This Great Argument* (1941, reissued 1962), and vol. 6 of the *Prose Works* (cited above); C.A. PATRIDES, *Milton and the Christian Tradition* (1966, reprinted 1979); and WILLIAM B. HUNTER, C.A. PATRIDES, and J.H. ADAMSON, *Bright Essence* (1971).

Books on special subjects include IRENE SAMUEL, *Plato and Milton* (1947, reissued 1965), and *Dante and Milton* (1966); KESTER SVENDSEN, *Milton and Science* (1956); THOMAS KRANIDAS, *The Fierce Equation: A Study of Milton's Decorum* (1965); and MARCIA R. POINTON, *Milton and English Art* (1970). EDWARD S. LE COMTE compiled *A Milton Dictionary* (1961, reprinted 1969); and *A Milton Encyclopedia,* ed. by WILLIAM B. HUNTER, JR., 8 vol. (1978–80), includes a great many articles treating people, places, and institutions associated with Milton.

(D.B./Ed.)

Mimicry

Mimicry is a biologic phenomenon characterized by the superficial resemblance of two or more organisms that are not closely related taxonomically. This resemblance confers an advantage—such as protection from predation—upon one or both organisms through some form of "information flow" that passes between the organisms and the animate agent of selection. The agent of selection (which may be, for example, a predator, a symbiont, or the host of a parasite, depending on the type of mimicry encountered) interacts directly with the similar organisms and is deceived by their similarity. This type of natural selection distinguishes mimicry from other types of convergent resemblance that result from the action of other forces of natural selection (*e.g.,* temperature, food habits) on unrelated organisms.

In the most studied mimetic relationships the advantage is one-sided, one species (the mimic) gaining advantage from a resemblance to the other (the model). Since the discovery of mimicry in butterflies in the mid-19th century, a great many plants and animals have been found to be mimetic. In many cases the organisms involved belong to the same class, order, or even family, but numerous instances are known of plants mimicking animals and vice versa. Although the best-known examples of mimicry involve similarity of appearance, investigations have disclosed fascinating cases in which the resemblance involves sound, smell, behaviour, and even biochemistry.

A key element in virtually every mimetic situation is deception by the mimic, perpetrated upon a third party, which mistakes the mimic for the model. This third party may be the collective potential predators upon the mimic, potential prey of a predacious mimic, or even one sex of the mimic's own species. In some cases, such as host mimicry by parasites, the organism deceived is the model.

Because of the variety of situations in which mimicry occurs, a formal definition must rest upon the effect of certain key communicative signals upon the appropriate receiver and the resultant evolutionary effect upon the emitters of the signals. Mimicry may be defined as a situation in which virtually identical signals, emitted by two different organisms, have in common at least one receiver that reacts in the same manner to both signals because it is advantageous to react in that manner to one of them (that of the model), although it may be disadvantageous to react thus to the counterfeit signal.

The distinction between camouflage and mimicry is not always clear when only the model and the mimic are at hand. When the receiver is known and its reactions understood, however, the distinction is quite clear: in mimicry the signals have a special significance for the receiver and for the sender, which has evolved the signals in order to be perceived by the receiver; in camouflage the sender seeks to avoid detection by the receiver through imitation of what is neutral background to the receiver. For information on camouflage, see COLORATION, BIOLOGICAL.

For coverage of related topics in the *Macropædia* and *Micropædia,* see the *Propædia,* section 312.

This article is divided into the following sections:

BASIC TYPES OF MIMICRY

Batesian mimicry. In 1862 the English naturalist Henry W. Bates published an explanation for unexpected similarities in appearance between certain Brazilian forest butterflies of two distinct families. Members of one family, the Heliconiidae, are unpalatable to birds and are conspicuously coloured; members of the other family, the Pieridae, are edible to predators. Bates concluded that the conspicuous coloration of the inedible species must serve as a warning for predators that had learned of their inedibility through experience. The deceptively similar colour patterns of the edible species would provide protection from the same predators. This form of mimicry, in which a defenseless organism bears a close resemblance to a noxious and conspicuous one, is called Batesian, in honour of its discoverer.

Müllerian mimicry. Bates observed, but could not explain, a resemblance among several unrelated butterflies, all of which were known to be inedible. There seemed to be no reason for these species, each of which had an ample defense with which to back up the warning coloration, to be similar. In 1878 Fritz Müller, a German zoologist, suggested that an explanation for this so-called Bates's paradox might lie in the advantage to one inedible species in having a predator learn from another. Once the predator has learned to avoid the particular colour pattern with which it had its initial contact, it would then avoid all other similarly patterned species, edible and inedible. The initial learning experience of the predator often results in death or damage to the inedible individual that provided the lesson; there is thus some cost to the species that teaches the predator of its inedibility. Evidence indicates that there is little or no inherited recognition by certain predators; each individual learns of noxious or inedible species by sampling them. Other inedible species resembling the first, however, do not have to sacrifice individuals to teach this same predator, and the number of individuals sacrificed in educating the entire predator population is spread over all of the species sharing the same warning pattern. The tendency of inedible or noxious species to resemble each other is called Müllerian mimicry.

Edible and inedible butterflies

Aggressive mimicry. In some situations it is of advantage to a predator to resemble its prey, or a parasite its host. Aggressive mimicry, for which the phrase "a wolf in sheep's clothing" is an apt description, does not involve warning mechanisms. The mimic adopts certain of the recognition marks of its model in order to secure advantage over the model itself or over a third species that interacts with the model. The model may be mimicked during only a single stage of the life cycle, as in the case of parasitic cuckoos, the eggs of which resemble those of their hosts (see below *The occurrence of mimicry among plants and animals*), or the model may be a prey of the mimic's victim, as in the case of angler fishes, which possess rodlike spines tipped with a fleshy "bait" to lure other fishes within reach.

Automimicry. The phenomenon of automimicry involves the advantage gained by some members of a species from its resemblance to others of the same species. Males of many bees and wasps, although defenseless, are protected from predators by their resemblance to females that are equipped with stingers. Some butterflies are able to gain protection against predators through the ability to absorb, tolerate, and retain in the immature (larval) stage, poisons from the plants on which they feed. Individuals or even subpopulations of such butterflies may fail to acquire such protection, as a result of feeding on nonpoisonous plants, but they are avoided by predators that have sampled protected individuals of the same species.

Other forms. Many forms of mimicry do not fit neatly into any of the above categories. The roles of mimic, model, and receiver may be juxtaposed and multiplied to provide intricate and remarkable relationships, the unraveling of which may take years of study. One such case involves the South American coral snakes (*Micrurus*), long recognized as dangerously poisonous—which possess a brilliant red, black, and yellow ringed pattern—and several genera of nonpoisonous and mildly poisonous "false coral snakes" with nearly identical colour patterns.

Coral snake mimicry

WARNING SYSTEMS

The chemical basis for repulsion. Many plants are characterized by the production of large amounts of metabolic end products, often called secondary metabolites—complex chemicals that include alkaloids, terpenes, phenylpropanes, resins, lignins, saponins, flavonols, and anthocyanins—stored in the plant tissues. Many such substances are also found in animals that feed upon such plants. Some animals produce substances similar to the secondary metabolites of plants; they store these substances in glandular pockets (as in toads, salamanders, and some insects) or in musk glands (as in beavers and muskrats). Arthropods, particularly insects, are notable for the production of excretory substances that serve as means of defense. Millipedes of the family Glomeridae, for example, secrete a bitter substance (a quinazoline) that repels birds; similar substances, differing only slightly in molecular structure, are found in palms. The fact that a certain chemical substance is restricted to a specific function, such as sex attraction, does not necessarily mean that it was evolved solely for that purpose. It seems rather that natural selection follows the easiest course and makes use of substances already present, and sometimes widely distributed. If so, the appearance of such substances in other organisms is not too surprising.

Protective secretions

Among the chemical compounds that protect certain plants from insects or other animals that might feed on them are the cardenolides, or cardiac glycosides. These substances have a highly specific toxic effect on the vertebrate heart and also activate the nerve centre in the brain that causes vomiting. Because the amount necessary to cause vomiting is about half the amount necessary to cause death through heart failure, an animal that samples a plant containing cardenolides is not killed but survives with the knowledge that the plant is inedible. Certain milkweeds (*Asclepias*) that contain cardenolides are the primary food of the larvae of danaine butterflies, including the familiar monarch and queen butterflies (*Danaus plexippus* and *D. gilippus*). The larvae consume the poison without ill effects and retain it through the pupal stage to adulthood. As adult butterflies, they enjoy protection from vertebrate predators.

There is, of course, no such thing as complete protection. Just as danaine larvae are able to eat the protected milkweeds, some predators are able to prey upon the protected butterflies. Birds of the Old World bee eater family (Meropidae) and a few other birds are able to eat bees because the horny beak protects them from being stung while the insect is being killed and because they have evolved behavioral mechanisms for removing the stinger (usually by wiping the insect on a perch) before swallowing the prey. Rabbits are able to eat the extremely poisonous mushrooms of the genus *Amanita* without ill effects. The larvae of the Florida feather moth (*Trichoptilus parvulus*) consume the insect-trapping glands on the leaves of the sundew (*Drosera*).

The evolution of warning systems. *The selective advantage of warning.* When an organism possesses a mechanism that provides protection from predators, there is a further advantage in preventing the potential predator from even sampling the protected organism. By the act of learning of the danger, the predator may well kill or maim the individual if, for instance, the protected species must be tasted for its inedibility to become known. Many protected insects are provided with tougher skins than their unprotected relatives, but the sampling by a vertebrate predator is almost sure to do some damage. Many noxious organisms have evolved warning (aposematic) mechanisms that serve to identify them clearly to a predator who has had prior experience with the same or similar species.

Warning systems often rely primarily on bright colours, but these may be supplemented by olfactory, acoustic, or behavioral means. The New World skunks, for example, have a prominent black and white pattern that renders them clearly recognizable to potential nocturnal predators. When threatened, skunks perform a highly stylized display dance, thus ensuring that the predator will see and recognize the warning coloration.

Types of warning systems

Acoustic warning signals are often favoured over visual

ones because they allow the animal the option of remaining hidden. The rattlesnakes (*Crotalus* and relatives), which need protective coloration to avoid alerting their prey, are able to provide acoustic warning to large animals that threaten them. Many moths of the families Arctiidae and Ctenuchidae are foul-tasting but would be vulnerable to nocturnal predation by bats were it not for the emission of a series of high-pitched clicks, audible to bats, made when the moths hear the bats' own ultrasonic navigational pulses. That the moth clicks actually do serve as warnings is borne out by the fact that captive bats ignore thrown mealworms (which they normally eat) when the mealworms are accompanied by recorded moth clicks. Several species of edible moths also produce clicks and may be regarded as Batesian mimics of the unpalatable species.

The role of the receiver. In some cases, the animal who serves as the receiver of the warning signal reacts by means of an innate system that exists independently of experience. Generally, however, a predator must learn the significance of the warning signal through experience. If the predator is a slow learner, or if the warning signal is not sufficiently distinct to avoid confusion with beneficial sensory impressions that the predator receives, several experiences may be necessary. Natural selection, therefore, will favour warning systems that are devoid of ambiguity. Experimentation has shown that certain birds and mammals, at least, are capable of acquiring and retaining knowledge of some aposematic mechanisms from a single experience.

Combination of warning systems with concealing coloration. It is of obvious advantage for an aposematic organism to be able to control the display of the warning system, partly to minimize the amount of sampling, with its concomitant liability of injury, by naive receivers. Acoustic and chemical warning systems allow this. Many protected animals are coloured to match their backgrounds but provided with flash areas of warning coloration. Examples of these organisms are the tiger moths (certain of the Arctiidae), in which the hind wings are yellow or orange but are kept under the streaked brown forewings until the moth is molested.

THE OCCURRENCE OF MIMICRY AMONG PLANTS AND ANIMALS

Batesian mimicry. The stinging Hymenoptera (particularly the bees, wasps, and hornets), well protected from most predators and usually equipped with conspicuous warning coloration, are mimicked by insects of many other orders. Ladybird beetles (Coccinellidae) and leaf beetles (Chrysomelidae) are inedible and are provided with prominent colours and usually with contrasting spots. A whole group of Philippine roaches of the genus *Prosoplecta* mimics these beetles, having undergone profound modification to achieve the similarity. To simulate the short, rounded form of the ladybirds, the large hind wings of the roaches are rolled and folded in a manner unparalleled in other insects.

The order Lepidoptera abounds with Batesian mimics, the best known of which is a swallowtail butterfly, *Papilio dardanus,* a widespread African species. In many populations of this species the females are polymorphic; *i.e.,* a number of different types (morphs) of coloration are found, with each morph a mimic of a species of inedible butterfly of another genus (either *Danaus* or *Amauris*). In all populations, the males are nonmimetic, retaining the same yellow and black pattern throughout. The presence of polymorphism, coupled with the ability of the lepidopterist to breed and rear this species in the laboratory, makes this an apt species for the study of colour inheritance. Investigators have found that mimicry in *P. dardanus* depends upon the action of certain primary genes, the expression of which is switched on or off by modifier genes. The modifier genes reduce the number of possible morphs to the restricted number of mimetic forms. The effects of modifier genes are not carried to the offspring when members of different geographic races are crossed. This finding suggests that each set of modifier genes is adapted to the gene complex in which it normally occurs and in which it probably evolved.

Müllerian mimicry. Müllerian mimicry often occurs in groups of unrelated species, all noxious or inedible and all possessing the same conspicuous warning coloration. Such groups, called mimicry rings, often have associated Batesian mimics. It is not always easy to evaluate the palatability of members of such rings, and thus to distinguish Müllerian from Batesian mimics. Parallel Müllerian mimicry rings are known from South Africa, Borneo, and the tropical Americas; each contains such unrelated insects as malacodermoid and longicorn beetles, butterflies, true bugs, and spider wasps. In South America inedible butterflies of many distinct nymphalid subfamilies (Danainae, Ithomiinae, Acraeinae, and Heliconiinae) share the same warning coloration. Certain species show a highly perplexing divergence from the usual mimicry principles, however. It is axiomatic that maximum protection is gained by Müllerian mimics when all individuals employ the same signal, a principle known as signal standardization. Two species of *Heliconius* (*H. melpomene* and *H. erato*) are polymorphic, however, with each morph in one species duplicated by one in the other and with the morphs of each pair having virtually contiguous geographic ranges. Ecological and genetic evidence indicates that the racial divergence within these species was produced by differences in the abundance (or degree of protection) of different mimicry rings in different refuges, as have lasted for several thousand years, with the species coming to mimic whichever abundant, protected species was within reach by a single mutation.

Mimicry rings

Aggressive mimicry. Examples of aggressive mimicry are abundant and varied; each demonstrates its own particular variation of basic mimicry principles. The examples cited below illustrate a few of the remarkable extremes in the evolution of mimicry.

Parasitic worms. The flukes (Trematoda) are a class of parasitic worms belonging to the phylum Platyhelminthes. One species, *Leucochloridium macrostomum,* resides principally in the intestine of songbirds. The eggs of the parasite pass to the outside in the feces of the birds and are readily ingested by a terrestrial snail, *Succinea,* an inhabitant of waterlogged meadows and riverbanks. The parasite eggs hatch into the first larval form within the snail. The next stage, called the sporocyst, is strikingly green in colour and bears yellow-brown rings. The sporocyst develops in the snail tissues and carries several sacs of "spores," one of which is placed into each of the snail's tentacles, or eyestalks. The sac then begins to pulsate violently, at about 40 to 70 beats per minute. The tentacle of the snail becomes greatly enlarged and eventually is transformed into a transparent covering over the pulsating sporocyst. *Succinea* usually avoids light, but specimens with this parasite do not. When the snail appears with its conspicuous, pulsing eyestalks, birds mistake the eyestalks for insect larvae, bite them off, and eat them. Within the bird, the sporocyst then hatches into the final larval stage, which grows into an adult worm. In the meantime the snail's eyestalk regenerates, and the cycle is repeated when another sac passes into the new eyestalks. Because the sporocysts of other trematodes are neither brightly coloured nor mobile, it can be concluded that the colour and pulsation of *Leucochloridium* are adaptations for arousing the interest of the insectivorous birds. Under normal circumstances the host birds do not eat snails, so the sporocyst must imitate the bird's proper food in order to be eaten and to complete its life cycle in the bird host. The process represents an unusual case of aggressive mimicry, for the parasite manipulates its hosts and causes the bird to infect itself with the parasite.

Mimicry in the fluke

Another trematode, *Cercaria mirabilis,* is notable for its unusually large larvae form, called a cercaria. The size of this cercaria and its hopping mode of locomotion cause it to resemble a small, swimming crustacean or mosquito larva, with the result that fish mistake it for food and swallow it. Research on parasites of this kind is much easier when it is recognized that the larval stages often mimic the food of their respective hosts. Examination of the parasite often provides a suggestion as to the probable host.

Insect-luring plants. Newly hatched flesh flies (*Sarcophaga*), blowflies (*Calliphora*), and greenbottle flies (*Lu-*

cilia) are attracted to glistening droplets or imitations of droplets. The grass of parnassus (*Parnassia palustris*) has flowers with five nectar petals, which bear glistening buttons but no nectar. They attract flies, nevertheless, and reward them with nectar in two depressions on the upper surfaces of the petals. The insectivorous sundew (*Drosera*), on the other hand, presents a deceptive lure, consisting of glistening secretory droplets on the glandular leaves, which trap insects that are then dissolved with digestive juices.

Pitcher plants

The pitcher plants (*Nepenthes, Darlingtonia, Sarracenia, Cephalotus*) have juglike leaves, which may bear flowerlike markings near their openings. Some have a flap or hood that enhances the resemblance to a flower and prevents filling with rainwater. One form, *Nepenthes*, secretes nectar at the lip of the pitcher. A foraging insect landing on this apparent flower slips on the edge and falls in. A band of gland cells below the slippery region secretes an enzyme that digests protein. The lower part of the pitcher contains a watery mixture of digestive fluids.

The cleaner mimic. One of the few cases of mimicry reported among vertebrates is that of a so-called cleaner fish. This example involves a particularly close model imitation involving shape, coloration, and behaviour. The model, a wrasse (*Labroides dimidiatus*) of the Indo-Pacific Ocean, is known as a cleaner fish because it removes and eats externally attached parasites and, occasionally, damaged skin fragments from other marine fish. It occupies specific sites, or territories, on coral reefs, where, within a six-hour period, the individual cleaner may be visited by up to 300 other fish seeking its services. The other fish are attracted by the conspicuous black and white coloration of the cleaner and by its dancelike swimming pattern, in which the tail fin is spread and the posterior part of the fish oscillates up and down. The fish undergoing cleaning acts as though it were in a trance, while the cleaner fish cleans its body, including the inside of the mouth and gills. Even large predatory fish allow themselves to be cleaned, and the much smaller cleaner almost invariably emerges uninjured from their throats. It is quite apparent that the cleaners are protected from these predators although neither inedible nor capable of self-defense.

The wrasse model

At the cleaning stations of the cleaner fish, there is often found quite another fish, the sabre-toothed blenny (*Aspidontus taeniatus*). It is similar to the cleaner fish in size, coloration, and swimming behaviour, and it even exhibits the same dance as the cleaner. Fish that have had experience with the cleaner position themselves unsuspectingly in front of this mimic, which approaches carefully and bites off a semicircular piece of fin from the victim and eats it. After having been repeatedly bitten in this way, fish become distrustful even toward genuine cleaners. Observations in the wild indicate that younger fish are the principal victims of the mimic, whereas older fish avoid it whenever possible. It is unlikely that the ability to discriminate between the mimic and the model develops automatically with age and is independent of experience; this is borne out by the finding that adult fish kept in an aquarium and not previously exposed to the mimic confuse cleaner and mimic just as younger fish do. If such adult fish are kept with the mimics for a certain length of time, however, they eventually avoid these and the genuine cleaners. The obvious conclusion from these experiments is that other fish cannot distinguish between the model and the mimic without having had experience with both. Evidently victims of the mimic seek out and learn characteristics that enable them to distinguish between reliable and unreliable cleaners—that is, between the model and mimic, respectively. The most successful individuals among the mimics, therefore, are those that most confuse their victims. As a result, the further development of the mimic is steered in the direction determined by the characteristics of the cleaner; for example, the model occurs as a number of local races within its area of distribution, each of which shows its own peculiarities in coloration, such as a small or large black vertical stripe at the base of the pectoral fins or an orange-red spot on the flanks. In every case, the local population of the mimic shows the same special coloration as does the model in that particular area (see Figure 1).

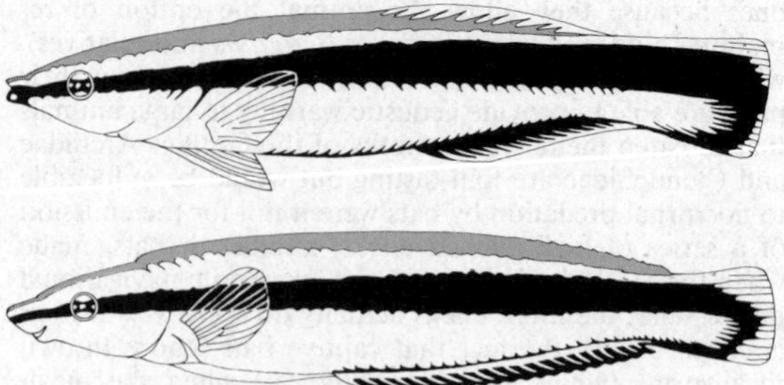

Figure 1: Differences and similarities between (top) the cleaner wrasse (*Labroides dimidiatus*) and (bottom) its mimic, the sabre-toothed blenny (*Aspidontus taeniatus*).

From W. Wickler, *Mimicry in Plants and Animals* (© 1968); used by permission of McGraw-Hill Book Co., Inc.

One of the interesting and highly unusual aspects of the cleaner–mimic relationship is that the individual characters of the mimicry pattern, especially the behavioral ones, have been traced to their origins. Certain characteristics, such as body size and shape and swimming pattern, amount to chance similarities. The mimic's drive to approach other fish, for example, is a specialization of a more general pattern, observable in non-mimicking relatives of the blenny, involving searching for food on suitable surfaces. The basic colour pattern of light and dark horizontal stripes is characteristic of fish that swim in open water, but the actual coloration of the mimicking blenny has been selected for closer resemblance to the cleaner wrasse. Interestingly enough, the blenny alters its coloration with its motivational state and adopts the appearance of the cleaner only under the specific conditions of self-confidence and intent to attack. As a group, blennies tend to wriggle while swimming, to counteract a strong tendency to sink at the tail. The sabre-toothed blenny, however, when confronted with danger holds the body stiffly without wriggling, allowing the hindquarters to sink somewhat, and advances solely by the use of the pectoral fins, in the manner common to wrasses. Superimposed on this motion is a nodding of the blenny's head, typical of approach-retreat conflict behaviour in blennies, but resulting in a simulation of the swaying dance of the cleaner. The combination of coloration and behavioral signals has a particular significance for the experienced visitor to the cleaner's station and causes it to adopt the posture that invites cleaning. In so doing, the visitor gives the mimic an opportunity to take a bite from a fin.

Behaviour mimicry

Fireflies. A form of aggressive mimicry that relies entirely on behaviour occurs in certain North American fireflies (Lampyridae). Males of these familiar nightflying beetles emit light bursts in flight according to highly specific patterns. The females, usually stationary, respond to the flash patterns of males of their own species with specific patterns of their own. The flying male responds to the appropriate female signal by approaching, landing, and courting. Most adult fireflies are short-lived and do not feed at all, but females of the genus *Photuris* have been found to feed on other beetles, including males of the genus *Photinus.* Upon perceiving a flashing male *Photinus,* the female *Photuris* responds with a flash that mimics the slower response time of the female *Photinus* (Figure 2). As the male *Photinus* approaches, the female *Photuris* even reduces the intensity of her flashes, to resemble more closely the weaker signals of the smaller female *Photinus.* The hapless male, after landing, is seized and eaten by the *Photuris.* In response to males of her own species, of course, the female *Photuris* gives a flash response quite different from that of *Photinus.*

Host mimicry by parasites. Another form of mimicry, sometimes considered an extension of aggressive mimicry, is mimicry of a host by its parasite. Most of the best-known examples occur among birds and represent some of the few known instances of mimicry in that class of animals.

Cuckoos. The European cuckoo (*Cuculus canorus*) is a brood parasite; *i.e.,* it lays its eggs in the nests of other birds, which act as foster parents for the young cuckoos. The most frequent foster parents are various species of small songbirds. Although the eggs of the various host

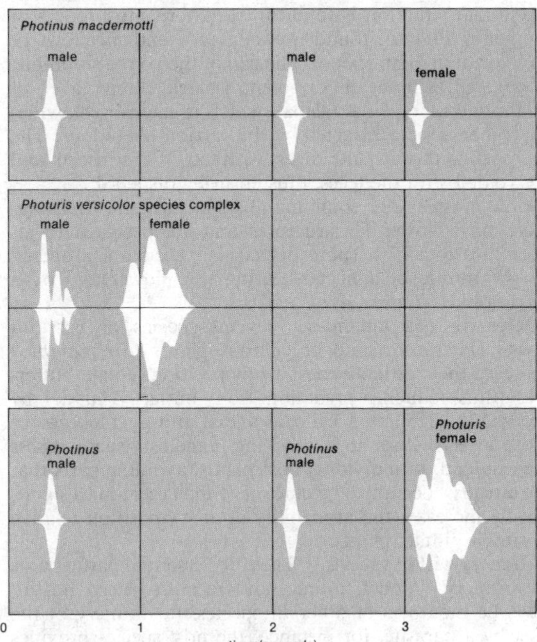

Figure 2: Comparative pulse rates of two genera of fireflies, *Photinus* and *Photuris*, showing (bottom) the deceptive response of *Photuris* female to *Photinus* male.

By courtesy of James E. Lloyd

species span a great range of colours and spotting, there is a striking correspondence in appearance between the eggs of the cuckoo and those of the host. Most small birds react unfavourably if they perceive a foreign egg in the nest and either abandon the nest, build another nest right over the first, or eject the strange egg. Each female cuckoo consistently lays eggs of one colour pattern and must therefore parasitize a particular host species. One survey has shown that of 1,642 cuckoo eggs laid in the nests of the correct (matching) hosts, only 8 percent were lost, whereas of 298 in the nests of the wrong hosts, 24 percent were lost. It is logical to conclude, therefore, that a cuckoo that lays its egg randomly, leaving the survival of the eggs to chance, would produce fewer offspring than one that selects hosts whose eggs match her own. Although the control of egg coloration is probably genetically determined, the choice of correct hosts is believed to be the result of a learning process that takes place when the female cuckoo is a nestling and learns to recognize her own foster parents.

Egg matching by cuckoos

Parasitic weaverbirds. Brood parasitism is also found in African whydahs, or widow birds, of the subfamily Viduinae of the weaverbird family, Ploceidae. Each species of whydah parasitizes a single species of estrildid finch (Estrildidae). In this case, egg colour does not seem to be a factor in acceptance of the parasite's egg, because both groups have pure white eggs. It has been argued that the whydah, many relatives of which have spotted eggs, have evolved white eggs in order to match those of their estrildid hosts.

Mimicry of mouth patterns

More significant than the mimicry of egg colour, however, is the highly specific pattern of spots and protuberances at the corners of the mouth (gape) and on the palate, tongue, and lower mandible of the nestling. This pattern, which varies from one species of finch to another, serves as a releaser for feeding behaviour on the part of the parents, which ignore any nestling that does not display the proper pattern for the particular species. In every species of parasitic weaverbird studied, the nestling has been found to match perfectly the mouth pattern of the estrildid host. In addition to mimicking the mouth patterns of their hosts, whydah nestlings also duplicate the specific begging calls and peculiar head movements of their hosts. The coloration of the juvenile plumage of the young whydah is identical to that of the host species, ensuring that the whydah will be fed after fledging. The digestive system of the young whydah is closely adapted to the particular type of food utilized by its host species, unlike that of the young cuckoo, which seems to be able to accept a variety of foods, from insects to mouse meat.

With each species of parasitic weaverbird closely committed to a single species of estrildid finch, it is obviously important that whydah species not hybridize, for the hybrid offspring would certainly not match either possible host in all of the important features. It is surprising to find seven forms of the paradise whydah (*Steganura*) so similar in appearance that they were once considered races of one species. Each of the seven, however, has its own estrildid host species, indicating that seven species of paradise whydah are represented.

As is frequently the case with closely similar bird species, hybridization is effectively prevented through the use of species-specific vocalizations by the males. An unusual feature of this situation is that each whydah species uses the same vocal pattern as its estrildine host. The young parasitic weaverbirds learn the songs of their host species during the critical learning period common to songbirds generally. As adults, the male whydahs use these estrildid vocalizations and gain response only from females that have been reared by the same foster species. This example is the only known one of a species-isolating mechanism consisting of vocalizations learned from another species. Vocal imitations by some bird species that have not been shown to give rise to mimicry systems are nevertheless frequently called mimicry.

Mimicry to effect pollination and dispersal. In some instances, plants have been found to rely on mimicry to attract insects as aids in pollination or in the dissemination of seeds or spores.

Orchids. Many flowering plants lure insects through the use of bright colours that indicate the presence of nectar. Some orchids mimic other flowering plants without offering any nectar, relying on those that do provide nectar to reward the nectar seekers.

Flowers that resemble female insects

A group of orchids, often known by such descriptive names as fly orchid, bee orchid, and spider orchid, carries the deception further, actually mimicking the insects themselves. The best-known orchids of this type are members of the genus *Ophrys*. The labellum (lip) of the *Ophrys* flower is a specialized median petal that acts as a dummy female of a species of bee or wasp (depending on the species of *Ophrys*), the resemblance being so close that males visit the flower in an attempt to copulate with the dummy female. In the course of precopulatory and copulatory movements, the visiting insect acquires the pollen sacs (pollinia) of the orchid and subsequently transmits them to other blossoms. A similar situation occurs in an Australian orchid, *Cryptostylis leptochila,* which bears a sufficient resemblance to the female of the ichneumon wasp *Lissopimpla semipunctata* to induce copulation by the male wasp.

An important feature in the mimicry of female insects by orchids is flower size. Flowers that are too small do not provide adequate stimulus for the copulatory attempts necessary to plant the pollinia on the insect. Conversely, if the flower is too large for the insect, the insect's head does not reach the stigma of the flower (the female receptor site for pollen), and the pollinia are not deposited on the insect.

The colour of the orchid's labellum is also important in attracting and properly orienting the male insect. The males are more attracted to dark than to light colours and to a contrasting dark spot on a light background. A velvety surface is a more effective attractant than a shiny one. The centre of the labellum of *Ophrys insectifera* bears a dark red spot, almost black, whereas the lateral lobes of the labellum are a somewhat lighter purple-red. Female wasps of the genus *Gorytes,* males of which are highly attentive to this orchid, are black dorsally with dark purple wings. Where the folded wings overlap over the female's body, there is a glistening area closely resembling the shiny central spot on the flower. The overall effect is further enhanced by movements of the flower in the wind.

Flowers that emit pheromones

Odour plays a particularly strong role in attracting male insects to the mimicking orchids. Some female Hymenoptera secrete odoriferous substances (pheromones) that initiate search behaviour in the males and guide them to the stationary females. Such attractant chemicals are usually limited in effectiveness to the producing species or a few close relatives. *Ophrys* flowers give off odours similar to, if not identical with, those produced by females of their associated insects. In a few cases the odour of the flower is a more potent attractant for the male than that of the appropriate female.

Carrion flowers, stinkhorn mushrooms, and mosses. A group of flowers are able to attract dung beetles (certain of the Scarabaeidae) and carrion flies (Calliphoridae) by mimicking the odours of dung or rotting flesh used by these insects as guides to sites for egg deposition. In some carrion flowers (*e.g., Stapelia*) the deception is so complete that blowflies actually lay their eggs in the flowers. The cuckoopint (*Arum maculatum*), which has a metabolic level unequaled among plants, spreads its odour over a wide area by an elevation of temperature that increases the vaporization rate of the volatile odour substance. An elaborate mechanism in the cuckoopint ensures that a pollen-laden visitor remains long enough to deposit the pollen. The sheath of the floral structure, upon which the insect lands, is made slippery by oil droplets with the result that the insect slides down into a cup equipped with a ring of spines to prevent escape. In trying to climb out, the insect deposits pollen on the tiny female flowers, from which the insect receives nectar. During the night, the male flowers mature and cover the resting insect with pollen. Then the spines shrink, and the insect is released (Figure 3). The production of the attractant odour occurs at midday, when many carrion-seeking insects are active, on the day before the male flowers mature; the timing of the cuckoopint's odour production is controlled by a substance produced by the male flowers six to 18 hours before maturity.

The trap of the cuckoopint

From W. Wickler, *Mimicry in Plants and Animals* (© 1968); used by permission of McGraw-Hill Book Co., Inc.

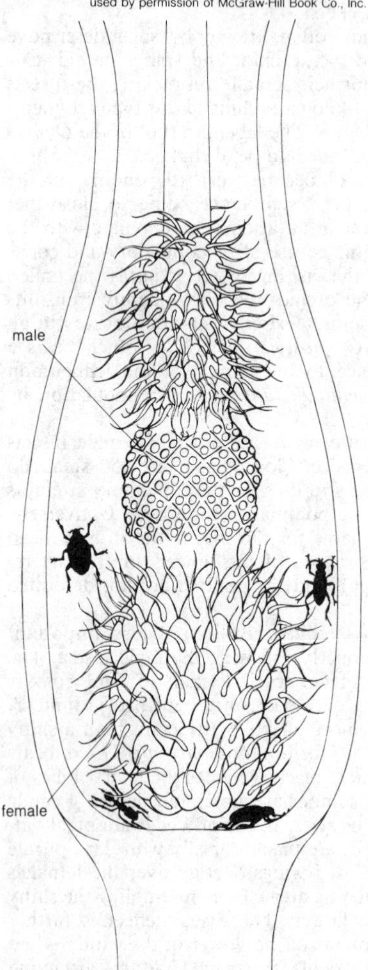

Figure 3: Flowers of the cuckoopint (*Arum maculatum*). The odour emitted by the flowers attracts insects that deposit pollen.

A similar situation is found in stinkhorn mushrooms of the genus *Phallus,* found in woodlands and meadows of the Northern Hemisphere. The cap of the young stinkhorn is covered with a thick, greenish-black, shiny layer of gelatinous spore slime (gleba), which is eaten by blowflies and other insects attracted by the carrion-like odour. The spores pass through the digestive tracts of the insects and are voided with the feces, thus ensuring dispersal.

Some mosses (*e.g.,* some members of the genus *Splanchnum*) have flowerlike structures that are designed to attract flies to aid in spore dispersal. Insects are attracted by the mimic of a nectar-bearing true flower and by a carrion-like odour.

Defensive egg dummies. Several species of passionflower (*Passiflora*) and cruciferous plants (*Streptanthus*) decrease their attractiveness to ovipositing female butterflies (thus reducing predation from butterfly larvae) by producing pigmented callosities that mimic the eggs of those insects. Prior to ovipositing, females visually assess the egg load on individual host plants, avoiding parts that are already "occupied." Removal of the egg mimics significantly increases the probability of an oviposition relative to similar, intact plants.

Mimicry within species. The three essential participants in mimicry—model, mimic, and receiver—need not always be members of different species. In mimicry of the host by a parasite, for instance, the host species provides both model and receiver. In another type of mimicry the mimic and receiver are members of the same species. An example of this type of mimicry is found in the small South American characoid fish *Corynopoma riisei,* in which the gill cover of the male is elongated into a thin, whitish stalk that terminates in a small, blackish plate. During courtship, the male raises the stalk and waves it jerkily in view of the female, who mistakes the tip of the stalk for an edible object, such as a tiny crustacean. As the female nears the male to grasp this supposed prey, mating takes place.

Egg mimicry in cichlid fishes

Another remarkable form of mimicry within the same species occurs in the African mouth-breeding cichlid fish of the genus *Haplochromis.* The female takes the eggs into her mouth immediately after they are laid, even before the male can fertilize them. The male, however, carries conspicuous yellow or orange spots near the base of the anal fin, which closely resemble the eggs of the particular species. Although the female is inhibited from eating while carrying eggs, she is strongly motivated to pick up loose eggs in her mouth. The male displays the fin spots to the female while releasing sperm; the female, as she attempts to pick up the false eggs, takes in sperm that fertilize the eggs in her mouth. In this case the model (real eggs), mimic (false eggs), and receiver (adult female) are all of the same species.

THE EVOLUTION OF MIMICRY

The effectiveness of warning systems. There is considerable experimental evidence to illustrate how effectively predators learn to avoid certain adverse stimuli. Chickens conditioned by electric shock to avoid drinking dark green water drank progressively more from paler solutions in proportion to the intensity of the colour. This experiment suggests that even an incomplete warning system provides a modicum of protection. The degree of protection provided is also affected by the strength of the punishment; after strong shocks the chickens drank only from very light coloured solutions. In the presence of severe punishment, an improved warning system made little additional effect once a threshold level was reached.

In other experiments, starlings (*Sturnus vulgaris*) were fed normal mealworms, two segments of which had been painted orange. To provide aposematic "models," the experimenter made other mealworms distasteful and painted the same segments green. "Mimics" were marked with green but not rendered unpalatable. There is no known instance in nature in which animals employ green for warning; there was therefore no possibility that the birds had already learned to avoid the experimental colour pattern. Before long the green-marked worms were completely avoided, regardless of palatability, even when the

Müllerian and other forms of mimicry

The odour of the pelican flower *Aristolochia grandiflora* attracts small flies that act as pollinating agents when they become trapped temporarily at the bottom of the flower.

The labellum (lip) of the flower of the orchid *Ophrys apifera* imitates a female bee; males attempting to copulate with the flower act as pollinators.

Mimicry in coral snakes and similar forms. (Left) venomous Eastern coral snake *Micrurus fulvius*; (centre) harmless king snake *Lampropeltis polyzona*; (right) moderately venomous rear-fanged false coral snake *Erythrolamprus aesculapii*.

Müllerian mimicry in unpalatable New World tropical butterflies.

Melinaea ethra (family Ithomiidae)

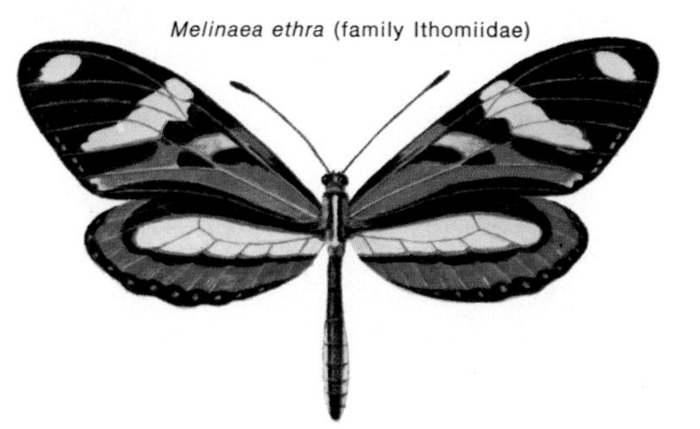

Mechanitis lysimnia (family Ithomiidae)

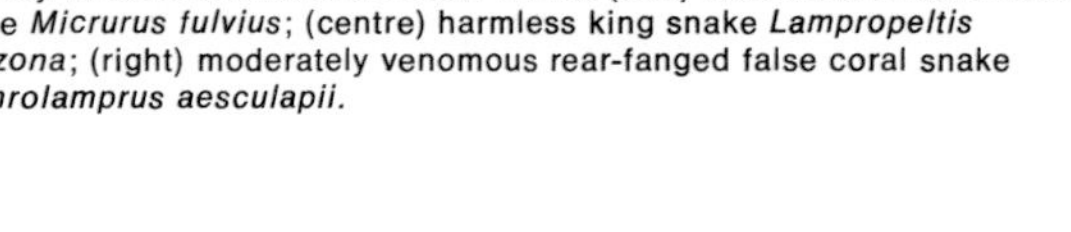

Lycorea halia (family Danaidae)

Heliconius narcaea (family Heliconiidae)

Painting by C. Olsen

The zone-tailed hawk is able to surprise its prey because of its resemblance in appearance and flight pattern to the carrion-feeding turkey vulture.

Aggressive mimicry in birds

Superficial resemblances of cuckoos to the sparrowhawk and shikra frighten other birds from their nests, allowing the cuckoos to deposit their eggs in them.

Eurasian sparrowhawk
Accipiter nisus

common cuckoo
Cuculus canorus

shikra
Accipiter badius

hawk cuckoo
Cuculus varius

The parasitic whydah deposits its eggs in the host finch's nest. The young whydah mimics the mouth pattern of the young estrildid finch, thereby triggering feeding behaviour by the estrildid host.

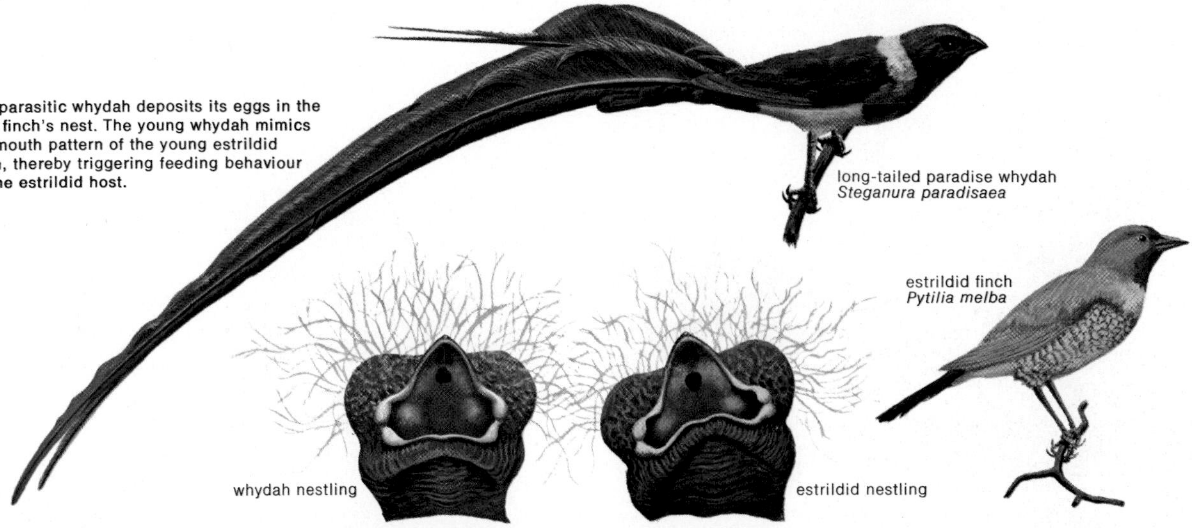

long-tailed paradise whydah
Steganura paradisaea

estrildid finch
Pytilia melba

whydah nestling

estrildid nestling

ratio of edible to distasteful was 60:40. This indicates that the number of mimics can exceed that of the model, when the resemblance is close, without loss of protection. When the ratio was increased to 90:10, 17 percent of the mimics were avoided, probably sufficient to a selective advantage in nature. Although a test bird would occasionally peck at a model, then reject it, the same action was sometimes shown to a mimic that it had picked up, suggesting that a premature response had been subsequently corrected.

The reconstruction of evolutionary pathways. Analysis and understanding of a given mimicry system require a rather comprehensive knowledge of morphology, behaviour, ecology, and mutual relationships of animals usually in different classes—for example, wasps (Hymenoptera), flies (Diptera), insect-eating amphibians, reptiles, birds, and small mammals. Tracing the evolution of such a complicated system requires a detailed acquaintance with a large group of forms related to each of the animals involved. Such data, in fact, are seldom available.

Mimicry and animal communication

Reconstructing the evolution of a case of mimicry within the same species, however, is relatively simple, requiring detailed knowledge of but one rather narrow taxonomic unit. Such a reconstruction is valuable, because mimicry is an indispensable tool in the study of the evolution of animal communication, and usually starts from conspicuously elaborated signals, which postulate a signal receiver interested in them. The receiver practically always has undergone a special molding toward optimal receiving of the signal. The mutual adaptations of the sender and the receiver must be examined separately.

This examination is easily made, so far as the evolution of a reaction or of a receiving mechanism is concerned, in all predators trying to find their prey and in all prey animals attempting to escape an approaching predator. The suppression of signals may be studied in predators trying to sneak up on a prey unnoticed. The elaboration of a signal, which must, of course, be important to the receiver, can only be studied after consideration of compensatory adaptations in the receiver and in situations where the sender has a one-sided interest in the signal. The deceiving signal can be derived only from one of two types: a signal developed by the receiver and another signal sender in their common interest or a signal emitted by another signal sender and made use of by the receiver only in its own interest. Both cases, by the definition given above, are called mimicry. An additional advantage is that the model is known to be the final stage toward which the mimic will evolve (so far as the signal characters are concerned), thus indicating a trend in evolution that is still operating and that probably over time will further elaborate the mimetic signals.

If the female *Haplochromis* fish were to discriminate between real eggs and the egg dummies of the male and were to stop reacting toward the latter, her eggs would remain unfertilized. In such cases of deceptive signals developed within the same species, natural selection operates against better signal discrimination on the part of the signal receiver.

The importance of the signal receiver. Fundamental characteristics of mimicry are determined mainly by behavioral properties of the signal receiver. A precise knowledge of the identity of the receiver and a thorough study of its behaviour are therefore indispensable for the understanding of mimicry. Moreover, mimicry gradually merges into other sender–receiver systems. Palatability is a matter of degree; whole ranges of distastefulness therefore exist, even in the mimics, model and mimic in the case of Müllerian mimicry being equally unpalatable and sharing the same warning coloration. Müllerian mimicry could be considered not to be true mimicry, after all, because no one is deceived, and it is impossible to designate one as model and the other as mimic.

Although all individuals of a given wasp species look alike and are all equally protected, this phenomenon is not usually called Müllerian mimicry, simply because the signals were not independently evolved, a property known as convergence. Because, however, the male wasps have no protective properties but retain their group-specific warning coloration, this is Batesian mimicry, although model and mimic are of the same species and their signals homologous (evolved from the same source). Convergence (or independent evolution) of the signal characters, therefore, is essential only for the so-called Müllerian mimicry, and thus Müllerian mimicry is distinguished from other cases of signal standardization. The typical (Batesian) mimicry merges into Müllerian mimicry if the difference between the consequences for the receiver of reacting similarly to model and mimic diminishes; and by homology of the signal characters it further merges into general signal standardization.

Mimicry and mimesis

An insect may be protectively coloured to resemble, for example, a wasp or a twig. In the first case the coloration is called mimicry, in the second, mimesis, or protective coloration. The difference lies within the signal receiver. If the mimetic signal does not release any reaction in the receiver, the mimic is said to exhibit mimesis. This distinction is illustrated by the experiments of the Dutch biologist L. de Ruiter with stick caterpillars, which, by virtue of their close resemblance to twigs, are protected against insect-eating birds. As soon as the number of "twigs" becomes too large, however, the bird develops an interest in them, attacks some real twigs, and also finds some caterpillars. If one positive experience with the caterpillar has the same weight as a negative one with the twig (the signal remaining unchanged), the relative abundance of caterpillars and twigs determines whether all twigs are mistakenly exterminated or whether the feeding reaction toward twiglike objects disappears, thus protecting the caterpillars.

This study again illustrates the importance of the bird's ability to decide correctly which is the model and further shows how easily an object (the twig) may quite involuntarily become a "mimic." Another example illustrating the importance of a correct model is found in the common farming relationship between ants and aphids. The protuberances, called the siphones and cauda, on the abdomens of aphids resemble respectively the bases of the antennae and labium of the ant's head. The aphid's abdomen is thus mistaken by the ant for the head of a fellow ant, thereby eliciting the food-begging response, which is identical with milking. Saturated ants in turn even try to feed the abdomens of the aphids. Aphid species with reduced abdominal siphones use their hind legs as antennae dummies, the movements elicited being originally defensive movements. This situation is exactly the way in which mimicry arises. Mimetic characters need not have evolved under the selection pressure of mimicking; in fact, their earliest evolutionary stages could not even have been brought about in this way. All cases studied thus far can be traced back to an incipient stage of deceptive resemblance, initiated as a preadaptive, nondirected by-product of preexisting species-specific features, thus providing a point of attack for new selective pressure.

The effects of selective pressure. The selective consequences for the signal receiver of responding to the model are always positive (the reaction would disappear if, on balance, it were unfavourable to the receiver). The mimic always has a selective advantage in releasing the reaction from the receiver. An unfavourable signal by the mimic would also disappear by natural selection.

The selective consequences of signaling by the model

The selective consequence for the model eliciting and obtaining the reaction from the receiver may be of several types. Consequences may be absent, if the model is an inanimate object on which natural selection does not act. They may be negative, if the model is non-aposematic (non-warning), such as the tiny crustacean, usually eaten by the signal receiver and mimicked by the male *Corynopoma* characin in order to attract the female. Or they may instead be positive, as in the wasp, which remains alive if it is avoided by the predator; in the cleaner, which feeds on parasites harmful to other fish; or in those hymenopteran females whose male-attracting signals are mimicked by certain orchids. Mutual interest is present between model and receiver in cases of aggressive mimicry where both parties belong to the same particular species and also in typical Batesian mimicry.

Constant learning by the signal receiver results in a strong selective pressure on the mimic against detectable differences from the model, but at the same time it also exerts a complementary strong pressure on the model to develop just such new differences from the mimic. Typically, it is the group of songbirds parasitized by cuckoos that has developed the most divergent egg-colour patterns; the group of estrildine finches parasitized by whydahs that has developed particular gape patterns; and among the cleaner wrasses the species *Labroides dimidiatus* mimicked by the blenny *Aspidontus* that develops into many different local races.

There is a boomerang effect, characteristic of the parasite–host relationship, that the more successfully a bird rears young cuckoos, the more certain it is that it will lose its own young, because they are killed off by the young cuckoo. Parasites that are too successful, therefore, harm themselves, for each female cuckoo needs several nests of the same host species for her eggs. In an area that contains particularly successful cuckoos, the number of reed warbler nests has been found to decrease from year to year, while the percentage of nests parasitized by cuckoos increases from year to year. This ratio means that a cuckoo that is too well adapted reduces the availability of its own hosts, while one insufficiently adapted kills off its own offspring. Presumably, selection in both directions produces a continual oscillation in the densities of hosts and cuckoos.

A similar dilemma is inflicted on human beings, who act as predators against weeds in crop fields and by winnowing select the wanted seeds from the usually smaller weed seeds. The flax dodder (*Cuscuta epilinum*), for example, which grows as a creeper around flax and linseed plants and damages them, originally had small seeds that could be easily separated from the larger flax seeds. By a mutation that produced twin seeds, the dodder has evolved the capability of being separated out and planted with the desirable flax seeds. This mutant of the flax dodder is now cultivated and spread by growers, despite being against their interests. In this case, the parasite mimics the protected plant, receiving the same protection.

The effects of geographic distribution and population density. It has been postulated that the model and the mimic should always occur in the same area—*i.e.,* be sympatric. They need not always be sympatric, however, but must always have a signal receiver in common: a model might be in Africa, for instance, and its mimic might be in Europe (or vice versa), functionally connected by a migratory bird.

Relative populations of model and mimic

Another postulate, that mimics must naturally be less numerous than their models, means, correctly stated, that the receiver has to meet the mimic less often than the model; this postulate is based on the assumption that one experience with the model has the same aftereffect, the same weight, as has one with the mimic. This assumption, however, has been proved not always to be so; in fact, the negative experience seems usually to be the stronger one. This negative experience may result from an encounter with the model (such as a wasp) or with the mimic (for example, the sabre-toothed blenny). There might very well be more wasp mimics than wasps, but in cases such as that of the cleaner wrasse mimic, it is probable that the mimic in fact has to be less numerous than the model. The protective power of the model, of course, is reduced with an increasing number of mimics, because the predator may eat larger numbers of them before his first encounter with the model.

The importance of mimicry to evolutionary theory. The mimicry hypothesis emerged in the middle of the Darwinian controversy and provided an ideal test case for the views of Charles Darwin and his contemporary Alfred Russel Wallace on the operation of natural selection in the evolutionary change of living organisms. It is now quite evident that the basic theory of natural selection is correct and that the theory is strengthened by many detailed studies of the process by which a mimetic resemblance is brought about and selected for. In addition, investigating suitable cases of mimicry provides important insight into the evolution of signals and the "semantization" process by which signals get their meaning.

BIBLIOGRAPHY. Significant aspects of mimicry are discussed in WOLFGANG WICKLER, *Mimicry in Plants and Animals* (1968; originally published in German, 1968); BASTIAAN J.D. MEEUSE, *The Story of Pollination* (1961), on insect–flower relationships; HUGH B. COTT, *Adaptive Coloration in Animals* (1940, reprinted 1966); BERTIL KULLENBERG, *Studies in Ophrys Pollination* (1961), on mimicry in orchids; and DENIS OWEN, *Camouflage and Mimicry* (1980). More research is described in THOMAS EISNER and EDWARD O. WILSON (comps.), *Animal Behavior: Readings from Scientific American* (1975), and *The Insects: Readings from Scientific American* (1977). Types of mimicry are discussed in G. PASTEUR, "A Classificatory Review of Mimicry Systems," *Annual Review of Ecology and Systematics,* 13:169–199 (1982). A series of articles in the *Philosophical Transactions of the Royal Society of London,* Series B, analyzes the mechanism of specific Batesian mimics: CYRIL A. CLARKE, PHILIP M. SHEPPARD, and I.W.B. THORNTON, "The Genetics of the Mimetic Butterfly *Papilio memnon L.,*" 254:37–89 (1968); CYRIL A. CLARKE and PHILIP M. SHEPPARD, "Further Studies on the Genetics of the Mimetic Butterfly *Papilio memnon L.,*" 263:35–70 (1971), and "The Genetics of the Mimetic Butterfly *Hypolimnas bolina L.,*" 272:229–265 (1975). Other journal articles on mimicry include J.R.G. TURNER, "Adaptation and Evolution in *Heliconius:* A Defense of Neo-Darwinism," *Annual Review of Ecology and Systematics,* 12:99–121 (1981); on plants, D. WIENS, "Mimicry in Plants," *Evolutionary Biology,* 11:365–403 (1978); SPENCER C.H. BARRETT, "Crop Mimicry in Weeds," *Economic Botany,* 37:255–282 (1983), and "Mimicry in Plants," *Scientific American,* 257(3):76–83 (September 1987); and on birds, P.K. MCGREGOR and J.R. KREBS, "Song Learning and Deceptive Mimicry," *Animal Behaviour,* 32:280–287 (1984).

(W.J.H.W.)

The Philosophy of Mind

One attribute that sharply distinguishes man from the rest of nature is his highly developed capacity for thought, feeling, and deliberate action. Here and there in other animals, rudiments, approximations, and limited elements of this capacity may occasionally be found; but the full-blown development that is called a mind is unmatched elsewhere in nature.

The task assumed by the discipline known as the philosophy of mind is to examine and analyze those concepts that involve the mind (including the very concept of the mind itself) in an attempt to discover the nature of each of these concepts, the relations between them, how they are to be classified, and how they are to be related to certain other concepts—especially to the concepts of matter and energy, the human body, and, in particular, the central nervous system.

It should be clear that the range of topics in the philosophy of mind goes far beyond what is intended in everyday discourse by "mind." When, for example, the layman speaks of someone as having "a good mind" or as pursuing "the pleasures of the mind," he is thinking of those particular activities that have to do with abstract reasoning, intellectual pursuits, and the exercise of intelligence. The "mind," as the term is used more technically in this article and in the philosophy of mind in general today, encompasses a variety of elements including sensation and sense perception, feeling and emotion, dreams, traits of character and personality, the unconscious, and the volitional aspects of human life, as well as the more narrowly intellectual phenomena, such as thought, memory, and belief.

The article is divided into the following sections:

PHILOSOPHY OF MIND AS A DISCIPLINE

In distinguishing the field of philosophy of mind from other sorts of investigation, one immediately obvious feature is its subject matter, the nature of mind and its various manifestations. This serves to distinguish it from empirical sciences such as astronomy and physics, which study matter in motion; from formal disciplines such as geometry and algebra, which study mathematical relationships; and from other fields of philosophy such as the philosophy of art and the philosophy of law. But subject matter alone does not serve to distinguish the philosophy of mind, since the mind is the subject of investigation of other disciplines as well—especially of psychology and of certain phases of biology, physiology, sociology, and anthropology. In comparison with these fields, it is by its method that the philosophy of mind is to be distinguished; for it proceeds not by the methods of empirical investigation—detailed sense observation, the formulation of predictions, the construction of experiments, inductive confirmation, the inventing and testing of contingent generalizations, theories, and laws—but by the method of philosophical reflection. That method consists of the examination of meanings, the analysis and clarification of concepts, the search for necessary truths, the use of deductive inference, reductio ad absurdum, and arguments with infinitely repeating terms and other forms of a priori reasoning, and the attempt to arrive at and evaluate the fundamental principles that underlie and justify the basic forms of human thought and endeavour.

Relation to other fields

Although the philosophy of mind is a distinct field of investigation, it has many important relations with other fields. First, its methods, being those of philosophy in general, are to be tested by the fruits that they have yielded in other areas: if a method has been successful in other areas, it is reasonable to try it here; if unsuccessful in other areas, it is suspect here. Second, the conclusions achieved in such fields as epistemology, metaphysics, logic, ethics, and the philosophy of religion are quite relevant to the philosophy of mind; and its conclusions, in turn, have important implications for those fields. Moreover, this reciprocity applies as well to its relations to such empirical disciplines as neurology, psychology, sociology, and history. Thus, the philosopher of mind must keep informed of developments in all related fields of investigation.

THE SEARCH FOR A CRITERION OF THE MENTAL

The bewildering variety of phenomena that fall under the heading of the mind or the mental was suggested earlier in a list. The question arises, however, whether there is some attribute that all of these mental phenomena have in common, something that characterizes them or that can serve as a criterion of the mental. More specifically, are there certain features that are either necessary or sufficient for mental phenomena?

Purposeful behaviour. Whenever a man watches a hungry animal using stealth and cunning in searching out, attacking, and killing its prey, he cannot but believe that the animal has a purpose and uses intelligence in achieving his goal. Whether it be a team of scientists designing a way of launching a man to the Moon, an ape figuring out how to screw two pieces of pipe together to get a banana that is out of reach, or—at a much lower level—a lobster trying to get out of a pot of boiling water, there seems to be a mind at work. Somewhere, as the phenomenon is traced farther down the ladder in the scheme of things toward inanimate matter, a line must eventually be drawn; but there is no agreement about where it should be drawn. It would be widely agreed that an ovum that has just been fertilized does not have a mind and that a normal adult does—but it is impossible to say exactly where in human development the change occurs. On the other hand, it would be just as erroneous to conclude that because there is no sharp dividing line there is no change as it would be to conclude that red and orange are the same colour because no sharp line divides them in the spectrum. In both instances there exists a transitional range within which the designation of a dividing line would be purely arbitrary; but at either end beyond that range a clear and definite difference is evident.

The question may then be raised as to how adequate purposeful activity is as a criterion of the mental. A major issue arises from the fact that a mechanical device can be built that exhibits the kind of activity ordinarily called purposeful—a surface-to-air missile, for example, so designed that it will hunt for a jet aircraft by searching for, and zeroing in on, the heat exhaust, thereby finding and destroying the aircraft. Such devices, known as "servomechanisms" (of which a thermostat is a simple example), achieve an end state by systematically diminishing any deviation from that predetermined end state. There are, in addition, the modern computers, capable of receiving, storing, and retrieving information, of making inferences, and of communicating information. Near the height of modern sophistication in machine technology are those machines, combining servomechanisms and computers, designed to roam the surfaces of other planets, gathering, processing, and sending back data and thus providing what would seem to be paradigms of purposeful behaviour and raising the question whether such systems are examples of minds at work. There are three possibilities worth considering: (1) one might continue to hold that purposeful behaviour is the criterion of the mental but argue that these devices do not really meet the criterion of exhibiting purposeful behaviour; (2) one might hold that the more complex of these devices do indeed have what can be called minds—simple and rudimentary, to be sure, but still minds—"artificial intelligences" that in a very literal sense have beliefs, think thoughts, solve problems, and achieve goals; or (3) one might give up the criterion of purposeful behaviour, or at least give it up as a *sufficient* condition of the mental.

Teleological mechanisms versus mental activity

Someone defending possibility (1) would attempt to find some feature of purposeful behaviour that could not be found in any mechanical device. He might hold, for instance, that the alleged purposes of mechanical devices are built in by their designers and that it is not up to the devices to choose their purposes. Against this line of argument, however, others might assert that for a large number of organisms the basic purposes are also built in through the genetic mechanisms of heredity: basic biological drives for food, reproduction, and safety govern most of their purposeful behaviour. People who accept this point of view argue that, in most cases, the organism is not really free to choose its purposes. On this argument, even human beings seem to display such built-in purposes; and it would be specious, at least in this instance, to deny them minds on this account.

Conceding that organisms have some built-in controls, the defender of the first possibility might then argue that the higher organisms have a flexibility that allows for the development of purposive methods that are novel. Machines, he would allege, solve problems only by the meth-

Machines, man, and inventiveness

ods designed into them, whereas creatures with minds can invent new methods. Against this line of argument others might argue that machines have been developed to use trial and error, analyze the outcomes of trends, and come up with new approaches that are more successful than earlier ones, and that, in an important sense, such machines might be called creative, since they "learn from experience" and use "ingenuity." Many observers assume that this trend in machine technology will continue and that machines will be developed with much, if not all, of the flexibility of many of the creatures that would unhesitatingly be acknowledged to have minds.

The basic issue, then, is whether a philosopher would want to say that a machine has a mind if it exhibits the flexibility in purposeful activity of, say, a normal seven-year-old child, who undoubtedly has a mind. In accepting possibility (2), the philosopher would maintain that such a machine does indeed have a mind and exhibits a wide range of the phenomena called mental. Many contemporary philosophers, however, would reject that thesis, considering it a needless flaunting of common sense and an affront to ordinary language to speak of a heat-seeking missile, for example, or even a lunar robot, as having a mind. Because something essential still appears to be omitted, further attempts are made below to determine the essence of the mind.

Intentionality. Another characteristic of the mental is sometimes thought to be found in certain ways in which an individual may be said to have something as his object. Thus, thinking, believing, desiring, and other such attitudes are thought to resemble one another in that they may be said to take an object, or to be directed upon an object, in a way quite unlike anything to be found in what is purely physical. "Intentionality" is the term for this way of being directed upon an object. The concept had been emphasized by some of the Scholastics and was introduced to modern philosophy in 1874 by a German philosopher and psychologist, Franz Brentano, and clarified and defended by a U.S. philosopher, Roderick M. Chisholm, in the 20th century.

The nature of intentionality. The idea of intentionality can be explicated in the following way: if one imagines three objects arranged as in Figure 1 and then supposes that the wind blows them so that they are arranged as in Figure 2, there results, from the physical point of view, simply a new arrangement. From a psychological point of view, however, something radically new also has been

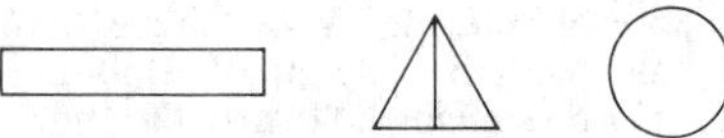

Figure 1: Three arbitrary physical objects in meaningless configuration (see text).

Added characteristic of aim or direction

introduced: one object now appears to be pointing to another—aimed at or directed toward it. It would seem that such pointing cannot be accounted for if the observer confines himself to the purely physical facts of the new configuration and that his mind has to be brought in to account for the feature of pointing to. Thus, intentionality is prima facie a reasonable candidate for the criterion of the mental.

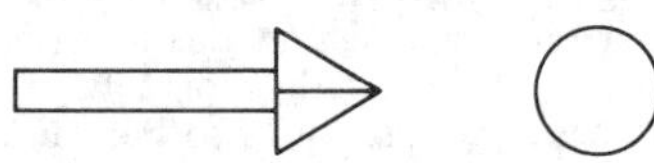

Figure 2: Physical objects with intentionality.

Intentionality is exhibited in a variety of phenomena. Thus, if a person experiences an emotion toward an object—*e.g.,* loves, fears, pities, envies, or reveres it—he has an intentional attitude toward it. Other examples of intentional attitudes toward an object are: looking for or expecting, believing in, doubting or conjecturing about, daydreaming, reminiscing, imagining, favouring, or disapproving—a list that seems to go on endlessly. Because it clearly comprises so many of the things that one thinks of as typically mental, intentionality, being of broader scope than purposefulness, would seem to be a more appropriate choice than purposeful behaviour for the criterion of the mental.

One of the characteristics of intentionality is what the Scholastics called "inexistence": a man may be intentionally related to an object that does not exist or to an event that does not occur. Thus, what a man looks for may not exist, and an event that he believes to occur may not occur at all. In contrast with such a nonintentional phenomenon as bumping into something, in which the object bumped into must be real, looking for something (an intentional act) does not necessarily imply that the object looked for exists. Similarly, in contrast with an explosion's resulting in the fact that many were hurt, a witness's believing that many were hurt (again an intentional act) does not imply the fact that many were hurt. Thus, existence and truth are irrelevant to intentionality.

Though this possible relationship to nonexistent objects as opposed to existent ones is a necessary feature of intentionality, it is not sufficient to define it, for there are phenomena that are equally concerned with nonexistent essences that are nonetheless nonintentional. "That lady resembles a mermaid," to use an example of Chisholm's, may be a true sentence even if mermaids, though having an essence, do not exist. Similarly, "That metal will ignite at temperatures above 1,000,000°" may be true whether or not such temperatures exist. Thus, intentionality requires further characterization if its scope is to be narrowed to exclude such examples as these.

Another characteristic of the intentional state is that not every description of its object will be appropriate. Assuming that his pen is the millionth pen produced this year, for example, a man may be in the intentional state of searching for it as his pen but not in a state of searching for the millionth pen produced this year; similarly, he may believe this is his pen and yet not believe that this is the millionth pen produced this year. This second feature of intentionality, often called "referential opacity," is such that a true sentence asserting an intentional state will become false when some alternative description of the object of that state is substituted for it (it is false that he is searching for the millionth pen).

There is no general agreement on the best way of conceiving of intentional phenomena. Brentano, at one point, thought of intentionality as being a relation between a subject and an entity, in which the entity is something that might or might not exist; but grave difficulties arise in the effort to characterize the ontological status of such an entity—*i.e.,* its kind of reality. More popular today are certain linguistic approaches: intentionality may be viewed, for example, as it was by Rudolf Carnap, a philosopher of science, and others, as a relation between a subject and a piece of language or, as it has been explained by others, as a relation between a subject and a linguistic practice or linguistic role. Under this view, the intentionality consists not in the relation of a subject to an *essence* (that of a millionth pen) but in its relation to a *sentence* ("This is the millionth pen . . . ") that has that alleged essence as its meaning. It remains to be seen whether such approaches will succeed in dealing with all intentional phenomena. It would seem to pose particular difficulty in those cases in which the intentional state is overtly directed toward some existent entity, with language playing a minor or null role, as in situations in which one feels anger, pity, or love toward someone; or when an animal is stalking its prey (which involves an intentional state). In such instances, an analysis in terms of linguistic attitudes would seem wide of the mark.

The scope of application of intentionality. The question of whether or not intentionality can apply to nonliving physical systems has become a controversial issue. If it can apply, then either intentionality would have to be given up as an exclusive criterion of the mental or else one would have to say that such systems exhibit some mental characteristics.

Application of intentionality to nonliving systems

It will be useful to consider a system designed for some purpose, taking the example again of the surface-to-air missile that searches for jet aircraft, and to ask whether it has intentionality. It does satisfy the first characteristic mentioned above: that it can be truly said to be a jet searcher regardless of whether there are or have been any jet aircraft (one could similarly design a unicorn searcher built to detect unicorns by their special horn). The question next arises whether some descriptions of the object are inappropriate. On the supposition that all and only jet aircraft have a component made of compound *X*, one can ask whether it would be true of the missile that it searches for things with a component made of compound *X*. It would seem that—unless this compound chances to be what the search system was sensitized to—the foregoing statement is a false, and thus an inappropriate, description of the device; and if so, it is plausible to regard the missile as a physical system with intentionality as that notion has been here characterized. An intentional physical system, however, would have to be of considerable complexity. One would not want to say that the left-hand complex in Figure 2 was pointed to the right-hand figure unless he had in mind that, if the right-hand figure were to shift its location, the left-hand complex would shift appropriately. If it did keep shifting appropriately, however, it would seem proper to say that it points to the right-hand figure. The question remains, however, whether *all* intentional phenomena are capable of appearing as instances in nonliving physical systems—whether such a physical system could have, for example, an emotion toward something, daydream about something, or be amused by something. Here it is very difficult to cite a plausible case; it would appear that one would have to strain such concepts considerably to apply them to nonliving systems.

The thesis that intentional phenomena are the essence of the mental thus seems problematic. Its suggestion that the jet-searching missile has a mind or partakes of the mental, as appeared in the discussion of the criterion of purposeful behaviour, would, to many scholars, appear to be quite implausible. Nor does it seem that the trouble lies in the limited number of intentional phenomena found in the missile. Even the lunar-exploration machines, with all of their flexibility and multiplicity of functions, would not be said by most analysts to have minds.

It might be possible to save intentionality as the criterion of the mental by insisting on the presence of such highly sophisticated intentional phenomena as emotions, daydreams, or amusement, but then one would have to deny minds to those human beings who lack a sense of humour, never daydream, or are cold-bloodedly unemotional, which does not seem correct either. Some progress can be made here if the question is asked whether intentionality is a necessary condition of all mental phenomena—whether there are any phenomena that are mental but nonintentional. Examples of a mental phenomenon that can most plausibly be said to be nonintentional are sensations, such as feeling pain, which lack both of the aforementioned characteristics of intentionality—inexistence and referential opacity. A man cannot feel a pain that, unbeknownst to him, does not exist; if he feels pain, there must be something he feels. Moreover, if a man feels pain, and the pain is identified with the effect of a tumour, then he does feel the effect of the tumour.

Sensations, which thus lack both of the characteristics of intentional phenomena, are not just an odd counterexample; not only do sensations comprise a large and central group of mental phenomena, but they also call attention to an important aspect of many other mental phenomena, viz., subjective experience. The arrow in Figure 2 may point to the circle, but it does not have the subjective experience of pointing, it does not feel itself pointing; and the jet-searching missile does not experience how it feels to be searching for jets. But when a person is in an intentional state, directed toward an object, he—at least sometimes—experiences, feels, or is aware of that directedness.

Clearly, this usage of "intentionality" differs somewhat from that found in medieval philosophy; and there are other features of the concept, not covered here, that are stressed by Phenomenologists and Existentialists.

Subjective experience. It is often maintained that the essence of the mental consists of states of consciousness taken as subjective experiences. When a person wakes up or regains consciousness after a general anesthetic, a host of experiences of colour and light, sounds, feelings, thoughts, and memories flood in on him. As far as his objective, observable behaviour is concerned, he may be lying unmoved and unmoving; but as far as his state of consciousness is concerned, he may be undergoing a series of subjective experiences.

Consciousness, "raw feels," discrimination

To take an example, when a person sees a scarlet patch, he experiences the homogeneous, spread-out, distinctive scarletness present before him. A blind or colour-blind person who has never experienced scarlet would not have the awareness of scarlet that the normally-sighted person has. He might have some vague idea, as did the hero of the story told by John Locke, a 17th-century British Empiricist:

> A studious blind man, who had mightily beat his head about visible objects, and made use of the explication of his books and friends, to understand those names of light and colours which often came in his way, bragged one day, that he now understood what scarlet signified. Upon which his friend demanding, what scarlet was? the blind man answered, It was like the sound of a trumpet.

This reply is not totally wide of the mark; but any sighted person will have a far more precise idea of scarlet than that. What he has and what the blind person lacks is something that philosophers have called the "raw feel" of scarlet, that peculiar and special way scarlet looks.

The subjective experience of scarlet is to be contrasted with the discrimination of scarlet things. One could imagine a blind person who was able to discriminate scarlet from other colours by the use of optical instruments (*e.g.*, spectroscopes with Braille printouts). But he would lack the subjective experience of the colour; he would not know the look of scarlet.

Defenders of this view would claim that there is a great variety of subjective experiences and that the experience of colours is only one of them. Sensations (*e.g.*, the experiences of pain, tickles, throbbings, pangs, nausea, and tiredness) provide another such example. Still other subjective experiences include: the experiencing of images (afterimages, memory images, and others); feelings of exultation, depression, pride, anger, fear, and love; and thoughts (imaginings, surmisings, doubtings, and recollectings). All of these are episodes, occurring at a particular time and place, in which the subject is in a state of awareness that has a particular content.

Adequacy as a criterion of the mental. The question now arises of how adequate subjective experience is as a criterion of the mental—whether, though it is obviously a sufficient condition for something to be mental, it is a sufficient condition for something to have a mind. The Scotsman David Hume, an 18th-century philosophical Skeptic and historian, once asked whether a creature that had but one state of consciousness could be said to have a mind and concluded that it could not. In his view, it takes, at the very least, a number of states of consciousness linked by memory before one would say that the creature has a mind; and it may be that there has to be a certain level of complexity in the nature and relation of the conscious states for there to be a mind.

The unconscious, dispositional, behavioral

It is doubtful, however, whether consciousness is a necessary condition for the mental. Before Sigmund Freud, it would have been widely agreed that the notion of unconscious mental phenomena was logically impossible—a contradiction in the very terms. That view had one important exception, however: Gottfried Wilhelm Leibniz, a 17th-century Rationalist and mathematician, held that there are *petites perceptions* of which the subject is unconscious. They are so slight, so similar to others, so familiar, or in such a crowd of other perceptions, that the subject is unaware of them at the time. One of the examples that Leibniz cited is the person who is unaware of the roar of the waterfall or the rumble of the mill if he has lived nearby for some time. Leibniz seemed to have had in mind what modern psychologists call "subliminal" perceptions, viz., those below the threshold of awareness but still capable of leaving some effects on the mind. But Leibniz confined unconscious states to perceptions; he would not have allowed unconscious beliefs, desires, emotions, or judgments.

It was Freud's great contribution to have discovered a range of phenomena of which the patient was unconscious but which were very much like typically mental phenomena, especially in their behavioral manifestations. In the light of such similarities, it was plausible to extend the concept of the mental to include these unconscious phenomena—especially since they were such that the patient could become conscious of them through hypnosis or psychotherapy. Freud postulated a mechanism that he called "repression" to explain why the patient is unconscious of them.

In addition to the subliminal and the unconscious, there are more familiar characteristically mental phenomena that do not consist of states of consciousness. When a man falls into a dreamless sleep, he does not lose all his beliefs or abandon all his goals, he does not cease wanting a better world or being artistic or imaginative or lazy, nor does he forget how to do arithmetic or speak French. A person is not jealous of someone only when thinking of him, nor does a businessman have confidence in the dollar only when concentrating on business. Obviously, these mentalistic characteristics can apply in a dispositional way to people who are not at that moment expressing or exhibiting the disposition.

Furthermore, as Gilbert Ryle has pointed out in great detail, a person may use his mind on many occasions without the feeling of subjective experiences. As he says,

> When we describe people as exercising qualities of mind, we are not referring to occult episodes of which their overt acts and utterances are effects; we are referring to those overt acts and utterances themselves. (This and the following quotations attributed to Ryle are from *The Concept of Mind* by Gilbert Ryle. Copyright © 1949 by Gilbert Ryle. Reprinted by permission of Barnes & Noble, Publishers, New York, Hutchinson Publishing Group Ltd., London.)

To be responsive to one's surroundings, to act intelligently, deliberately, with wit or good grace, to utilize arithmetic or logic, to be sympathetic or coldhearted, to drive alertly or absentmindedly—none of these requires the occurrence of subjective experiences or inner states of consciousness, the immediacy of feelings or sensations. In such activity, there may be nothing going on except performances of a particular kind, and there may be nothing more required except that under further circumstances other performances of a particular kind will be forthcoming. It is, thus, reasonable to conclude that subjective experience is not a necessary condition for the mental.

Ryle's charge of a category-mistake

Those who have put the private events of subjective experience at the centre of the mental have committed what Ryle calls a "category-mistake . . . represent[ing] the facts of mental life as if they belonged to one logical type or category, . . . when they actually belong to another." The mistake consists of taking talk about a person's mind as talk of events in a world parallel to the ordinary world but occult and mysterious. The truth, according to Ryle, is that

> to talk of a person's mind . . . is to talk of the person's abilities, liabilities and inclinations to do and undergo certain sorts of things, and of the doing and undergoing of these things in the ordinary world.

It would be rash, however, to draw the further conclusion that subjective experiences are in no way involved in whatever is mental. Returning to the case of Leibniz' *petites perceptions* that are not experienced, a person can be conscious of them in various ways, either before getting used to them or when they are alone or when their intensity or his own sensitivity is increased; and Freud's unconscious phenomena can become conscious phenomena under favourable conditions. The beliefs that an individual is not aware of in sleep are sometimes the objects of his consciousness, as are his moments of laziness and imaginativeness, his knowledge of arithmetic, and his goals. It is dubious that something that has no connection with states of consciousness could qualify as mental.

Core characteristics of subjectivity. Philosophers are still in deep disagreement on how to characterize what is peculiar to subjective experiences. Some hold that the existence of subjective experience indicates that there are peculiar events that do not occur in the public space–time world that everyone shares and has equal access to but occur only in a private world that each person has exclusively to himself, which he cannot share with others, and to which no one else has access.

The role of privacy

Ryle has called this view, with what he admits to be "deliberate abusiveness," "the dogma of the Ghost in the Machine." He characterizes the dogma as follows:

> Minds are not in space, nor are their operations subject to mechanical laws. The workings of one mind are not witnessable by other observers; its career is private. Only I can take direct cognisance of the states and processes of my own mind. A person therefore lives through two collateral histories, one consisting of what happens in and to his body, the other consisting of what happens in and to his mind. The first is public, the second private. The events in the first history are events in the physical world, those in the second are events in the mental world.

Are there private events? Even so adamant a critic of privacy as Ryle admits the existence of some private phenomena, chiefly dreams and daydreams, sensations, thoughts, and imaginings. He insists, however, that

> the sequence of your sensations and imaginings is not the sole field in which your wits and character are shown; perhaps only for lunatics is it more than a small corner of that field.

In Ryle's view, private events occupy a small and inessential place in the total range of mental phenomena; but they do occur.

The notion of privacy is really the conflation of two ideas: the metaphysical idea that mental events do not occur in space and the epistemological idea that mental events are objects of awareness solely to the person who is subject to them. Each of these may be considered in turn.

Nonspatiality of mental events

The Rationalist René Descartes, the earliest major philosopher of modern times, held that the essence of all that is nonmental consists in being extended in space. Turning this around and broadening it, one could say that the essence of the mental consists in the lack of spatiality; *i.e.,* the lack of shape, size, and, above all, location. If the philosopher confined himself to events, he would say that necessarily a physical event occurs in some place or other, but, necessarily, a mental event does not. It would be conceded that the person who experiences the mental event does typically have a location, and this leads to the question of why the event is not located where the person is located.

A defender of the nonspatiality criterion would argue that such ascriptions of location to mental events are very different from ascriptions of location for physical events. For a physical event, it is always possible to ask whether it occurred at some point, in some part, or throughout the location. Thus, if the temperature of a body of water rises, one can ask precisely where the rise occurred—at certain points, in certain parts, or throughout the volume. But if a thought occurs, it is senseless to ask whether it occurred throughout the area or only in some part of it. Furthermore, if the water undergoing the rise in temperature is in a box, it is reasonable to say that a rise in temperature occurred in the box; but if the person having a thought is in a box, it is senseless to say that a thought occurred in the box. So the sort of ascription of location is quite different for mental events, and the criterion can still be used to mark off the mental from the physical.

The question remains whether the sort of nonspatiality that is allegedly appropriate to the mental is peculiar to it. If such a physical event as recovering from an illness or changing shape is considered, it would appear also that it does not make sense to ask whether the event occurred throughout the whole volume, in some part, or at some point. Thus, it would seem that even this modified notion of spatiality does not uniquely distinguish the mental.

Privileged status of subjectivity. Other philosophers would interpret subjective experiences not as private events but as a special way of knowing certain events, specifically by introspection. This is called the "privileged access" view. John Locke, contrasting this way of knowing with sensation, called it "reflection," defining it as "that notice which the mind takes of its own operations and the manner of them." It is a way of being aware of one's own present states without the intervention or use of the senses. The emphasis here is on the way of knowing rather than on the events known. Someone who holds the privacy view will have to hold that there is some special way of knowing these special events, but someone who holds the privileged access view is not necessarily committed to holding that the events so known are in any way special. A person could hold that one and the same event can be known both by sense perception and in some other way. Being knowable by introspection would then be the characteristic that defines events as mental. Such an account, however, would not rule out that they may also be knowable by sense perception or by inference.

Objections and rejoinders

Some contemporary philosophers deny that there is any such special way of knowing. Ryle offers three objections: first, it would require that there be simultaneously multiple attentions—in the mental event itself and in the attending to that event; though it is not denied that such divisions of attention are possible, he suggests that they are more unusual and difficult to achieve than the proponent of introspection would have the reader believe; second, because there is obviously some upper limit to the number of simultaneous attendings that a person is capable of, there will have to be some mental acts of which a person is unaware, and if it is admitted that some mental events occur without being known in this special way, it is fair to ask whether one must assume that any of them are known that way; finally, for many states of mind—*e.g.,* extreme panic or fury—the person is so involved that he is incapable of taking note of them, yet such states are not, in consequence, suspect—the person involved is as sure that they occur as he is of any so-called mental events. There is thus no need to postulate this special way of knowing to account for man's knowledge of any such events.

It is not clear how compelling Ryle's objections are. It is admitted that attention can be divided, though it may be contended that it is unusual and difficult to achieve this division. Others would reply that it is a lot more common and easier than might be thought, that it occurs whenever a man takes note of his mental states. And from the fact that he cannot take note at the same time of very many of his mental states, it hardly follows that he never does; each could still be introspectable even if it was not actually introspected on that occasion. As for Ryle's third objection, it might be that some states of mind cannot be introspected, but it does not follow that none can be introspected; they might still be private for all that. Ryle, for instance, while denying introspection, admits retrospection, a capacity to recall one's states just after they occur. It would seem, however, that there is no important difference between a concurrent "introspection" and a prompt "retrospection." One advantage of retrospection is that it would explain an individual's self-knowledge of those events that are difficult to explain in terms of introspection; *e.g.,* extreme panic or fury.

Whether a person introspects or retrospects (the truth appears to be that sometimes he does the one, sometimes the other), he would still seem to have a kind of knowledge about his own present and recently past mental states that he does not have of the mental states of others and that others do not have of his. It is not possible either to introspect or to retrospect the mental states of others; the knowledge that a man has of the present and immediately past mental states of others must be based upon perceptions or inferences from perceptions, whereas the knowledge that he has of his own present and immediately past mental states need not be, and usually is not, so based.

Introspection as defining the mental

It is possible that the notion of introspection can thus be used to define the mental. Such a definition would be of the form: a mental event is an inner event that can be introspected. The difficulty remains, however, of how "introspected" is to be defined. If it is defined merely as "known without inference or sense perception," then it would seem to apply equally to the knowledge of certain bodily events that no one would want to call mental. An individual can know without sense perception, for example, that his heart is beating rapidly or that his fingers are crossed. To rule such cases out, one can include among the senses the kinesthetic sense that utilizes nerve endings within the body—those, for instance, that register the conditions of one's own muscles. But then it might appear that one must say that sensations are not mental phenomena, since the awareness of them typically involves such nerve endings. Such an admission, however, would be fatal for the privileged access view because sensations are precisely the sort of thing to which a person is supposed to have privileged access. If, on the other hand, the philosopher makes it a matter of definition that introspection applies only to the mental, then he cannot define the mental in terms of introspection. Thus, philosophers are at the present time faced with serious and unsolved difficulties in using the notion of introspection to define the mental.

Finally, it is significant here, as it was in the discussion of subjective experience, that to much of man's mental life and to many of the exercises of his mind—*e.g.,* employments of intelligence—he has no special privileged access; there are, in addition, the unconscious phenomena that are not introspectable. So introspection cannot be a necessary condition of the mental.

A clue to a more satisfactory criterion of the mental can be found in the attack on introspection cited above. There the difficulty was noted that there does not seem to be a way of distinguishing how an individual knows his mental state from how he knows such inner physical states as the rapid beating of his heart. But it may be argued that there does seem to be a difference between these two ways of knowing: specifically, it is clear how a person could be shown that he was mistaken in believing that his heart was beating rapidly; but it is by no means clear what would show a person that he was mistaken in believing himself to be feeling a particular throbbing, pounding sensation. For mental events, the subject's own beliefs are peculiarly authoritative. This authority only holds, of course, for present mental events; it is clear that many things could show that a person's belief about a past mental event of his was mistaken. It is sometimes claimed that what distinguishes mental events is their so-called indubitability—the fact that a belief by the subject that the event is occurring cannot be false or in error. However, the view that first-person, present-tense reports of mental events are indubitable has come under serious attack; to make such a report is to classify, and it is argued that it is always possible to err in classification.

Indubitability; incorrigibility; presumption

Instead of holding that such beliefs are indubitable, it is often more modestly maintained merely that such beliefs are "incorrigible," meaning that nothing will count as overthrowing (or correcting) such beliefs. A person who believes that he is experiencing a throbbing sensation may be mistaken; but there is nothing that will show an observer or him that he is mistaken, nothing that will entitle either of them to believe that he is mistaken. He may be experiencing a throbbing sensation even when no part of his body is actually throbbing, though the explanation for this curious fact might not be known.

It might be objected against the incorrigibility thesis that the same difficulty that arises for the alleged indubitability of first-person, present-tense beliefs about mental events also arises for their alleged incorrigibility. For if misclassification is possible, it would also seem possible to gather evidence that someone is misclassifying. If one could confuse a throbbing sensation with a different but somewhat similar sensation, it is reasonable to believe that this confusion could be known by others to have occurred. Perhaps the best that can be said for the incorrigibility thesis is that there is always a strong presumption that such beliefs are true, though this presumption can sometimes prove to be unwarranted. But then it is by no means clear that privileged authority is a unique criterion that distinguishes mental events, for such a presumption would also hold for many nonmental events as well (*e.g.,* the belief that one's heart is beating rapidly). Yet if the degree of presumptive force is taken into account, it is reasonable to say that it would be *comparatively* harder to overthrow beliefs about one's present mental events; and perhaps this is all that one needs to give the criterion force.

THE EXISTENCE AND STATUS OF THE MIND

The basic metaphysical issues in the philosophy of mind concern whether the mind exists and, if it does, what kind of existence it has and what its relation is to the rest of what exists. Materialists hold that only physical matter (and physical energy) exists. For those who hold, on the other hand, that the mind exists as an immaterial entity, there are dualistic theories for which both immaterial minds and material bodies exist, and immaterialistic theories for which only minds exist but not bodies. There are, finally, the so-called neutral monist theories for which the fundamental existents in nature are neither mental nor physical but some neutral stuff out of which both the mental and the material are formed.

History of Materialism

The mind as material. The basic contention of Materialism is that nothing exists but matter and its purely material properties, so that the concepts that are necessary and sufficient for describing and explaining matter will be necessary and sufficient for describing everything that exists. This view can be found in the early Greek philosophers. Thales of Miletus, who lived some 2,500 years ago (6th century BC) and who is generally regarded as the first philosopher in the Western tradition, is supposed to have held that all things are composed of water in some form or other; later thinkers added air, fire, and earth to the list of fundamental elements. The philosopher Anaxagoras of Clazomenae, born about 500 BC, introduced a new factor, *Nous* (Mind), which arranged all other things in their proper order, started them in motion, and continues to control them. There is still controversy as to how his concept of Mind is to be understood, but since he spoke of Mind as being "the finest and purest of all things" and as occupying space, it is likely that he did not think of it, as some later thinkers did, as nonmaterial stuff but rather as a very special kind of material stuff.

It was with the Atomists, Leucippus of Miletus and his disciple Democritus of Abdera, in the 5th and early 4th centuries BC, that Materialism was given its most developed statement. According to them, nature consists solely of an infinite number of indivisible particles, having shape, size, and impenetrability, and no further properties, and moving through an otherwise empty space. The shape, size, location, and movement of these particles make up literally all of the qualities, relations, and other features of the natural world. Such phenomena as sensations, images, sense perceptions, and thought—of particular interest to the philosophy of mind—are explicitly held to consist in the various qualities and relations of the particles.

Contemporary Materialists would, no doubt, wish to incorporate into their theory the latest findings of the physical sciences—the convertibility of matter and energy, the wave–particle duality, and the various subatomic particles and antiparticles with their peculiar properties, including the conservation of charge, direction of spin, and direction of time—but these would represent mere changes in detail. In broad outline, the theory would be the same.

Given the theory of Materialism in such broad outline, however, a serious question remains concerning the actual account to be given of such phenomena as sensations, images, perceptions, emotions, memories and expectations, desires, beliefs, thoughts, imaginings, and intentions. Among the possible views are those called eliminative Materialism, Behaviourism, and the central-state theory.

Eliminative Materialism. A philosopher might hold that there are no such things as sensations, images, perceptions, or emotions and that there never have been such. From this view, those who have believed in the existence of such things have simply been mistaken. A person might hold this view, called eliminative Materialism, on the grounds that all talk of such supposed phenomena is (1) meaningless verbiage, or (2) part of a set of theories that are outmoded, scientifically fruitless, and to be discarded, like theories about witches or the Homeric gods. On either account, it is implied that all such terms should be eliminated from the philosopher's vocabulary. There is a further doctrine, however, to the effect that all such talk is (3) meaningful but nondescriptive and without truth value. On this account, the proper function of such language is not to state facts but might be to prescribe or evaluate.

Two kinds of reductive Materialism

Among Materialistic views, the alternative to eliminative Materialism is some kind of reductive Materialism. According to this view, there are indeed such things as sensations, images, perceptions, and emotions, but they are only complicated forms of matter in motion. The philosopher may thus continue to use terms referring to such things (in contrast with eliminative Materialism), but he should keep in mind that no extra entities or features are being postulated over and above the physical entities with their physical features.

Behaviourism. If one asks reductive Materialists what sensations, images, and the like are, one will find that two alternatives have been proposed. The first is Behaviourism, the view that all such terms refer to the behaviour or movements of certain bodies, particularly of the higher animals. Thus, the Behaviourist would claim that to feel pain is to groan, writhe, blanch, moan, and so on, or at least to be disposed or tend toward such behaviour; to desire food is to engage in eating in the presence of food, in hunting in the absence of food, and so on, or at least to be disposed or tend toward such behaviour; and so also with all of the states and activities that one thinks of as mental.

Usually, Behaviourism is intended as a logical doctrine to the effect that the very meanings of the words referring to the mind, its mental states and activities, are to be analyzed in behavioral terms, that every mentalistic term is synonymous in meaning with some behavioral term. It is important to distinguish this view, logical Behaviourism, from the view of many psychologists that the most fruitful way to study psychological phenomena is to study human and animal behaviour. Such a view might be called methodological Behaviourism because it is actually the proposal that the science of psychology restrict itself to certain methods. It does not entail logical Behaviourism. Logical Behaviourism might also be distinguished from the view that psychological and behavioral terms, though not synonymous in meaning, have, as a matter of fact, the same denotation or reference, a view that might be called de facto Behaviourism.

Central-state theory. The second type of reductive Materialism is the central-state theory. In this view, mental states and activities are identical with states and activities within the body (hence this theory is sometimes called the identity thesis). In particular, they are identical with states and activities of the central nervous system or brain. Thus, to feel pain is for the brain to be in a particular state; to desire food is for the brain to be in another state.

Distinctions parallel to those for Behaviourism can be made for the central-state theory. A psychologist might hold that the only useful way of studying psychological phenomena is to study the central nervous system; this view might then be called methodological central-statism. A philosopher might hold that the very terms referring to the mind, its mental states and activities, are synonymous with neurological terms (or, more plausibly, that they *should* be taken to be synonymous—they obviously are not synonymous as language now stands). This position, which could be called logical central-statism, would differ from the eliminative Materialism mentioned above in that it would retain mentalistic terms rather than eliminate them but would redefine them neurologically. If this came to pass, such terms might eventually disappear, a result that eliminative Materialism would strive to achieve more directly.

Plato's *psychē;* Descartes's substances

The mind as immaterial. Plato was the first important figure in the Western tradition explicitly to defend the doctrine that the mind is an entirely nonmaterial entity—without such defining material properties as size, shape, or impenetrability—separate and distinct from the human body and able to exist apart from it. Plato used the Greek word *psychē* (traditionally translated as "soul").

Plato held that the mind (*psychē*) was in charge of the body and directed its movements. In his dialogue the *Phaedrus,* Plato spoke of the mind as having both appetitive desires and the higher desires and as having, in addition, a rational capacity to control, direct, and adjudicate between the two. This rational capacity of mind is the most valuable aspect of man, the part most worthy to be nurtured and developed, and the aspect of man most likely to be immortal (much of the dialogue concerning the last hours of Socrates, the *Phaedo,* is about these topics).

Dualism. Plato was a dualist; he believed in the existence of both material entities and immaterial ones. The most explicit statement of dualism, however, is found in the writing of René Descartes, who argued that mind and matter are two separate and distinct sorts of substances, absolutely opposed in their natures, each capable of existing entirely independently of the other.

The dualist is faced with the question of how, if at all, mind and matter are related to each other. Most dualists would agree that in rocks, tables, and other material things, matter exists alone and unrelated to mind; and that at what is called death (since for Descartes the soul is immortal), immaterial minds exist unrelated to matter. In the case of a living human being, however, there are two substances: a mind and a body. Thus, the question arises of how the relation between them is to be conceived. Any dualistic theory would have to account for certain obvious facts about human beings. When people's bodies are affected in certain ways—when subjected, for example, to bright lights, loud noises, rises in temperature—people often experience colours, sounds, or sensations of warmth or of pain. Again, when people experience certain things, their bodies undergo certain changes—they shut their eyes, they put their hands to their ears, they perspire, or their faces become pale.

Interactionism; epiphenomenalism; parallelism

There are various ways that dualists have proposed to account for these facts. The most straightforward position is interactionism, the view (held by Descartes) that mind and body are capable of affecting each other causally, so that what happens in the body can produce effects in the mind and vice versa. Descartes decided that somewhere within the nerve tissues of the brain was the place where the interactions occurred and chose the pineal gland as the precise point because of its central location. (It is now known that the pineal gland cannot perform the functions that Descartes attributed to it, though its precise functions are still unknown.)

It is an implication of interactionism that there cannot be a complete explanation of brain functioning exclusively in terms of the laws of neurology because of the intervention at crucial moments of the influences of the mind. This limitation has struck many scholars as an important difficulty. One way around it is epiphenomenalism, the view that the body can affect the mind but that the mind cannot affect the body. Mental events are mere by-products of brain activity, like the exhaust from an engine or the shadows cast by moving figures. When the mind would appear to be affecting the body, as when the experience of pain seems to cause one to grimace, the epiphenomenalist hypothesizes that the very brain state that produces the experience of pain also produces the grimace.

Dualists of either the interactionist or epiphenomenalist persuasion are committed to the existence of causal relations between body and mind. Some philosophers, struck by how entirely different mind and matter are supposed to be on the dualist hypothesis, have held it to be impossible that they could affect each other. Psychophysical parallelism avoids this difficulty by postulating that mind and body are like two perfect clocks, each with its own mechanism but in constant and uniform correlation with the other. Unfortunately, the analogy does not hold very well, for the mind does not seem to have the kind of internal mechanism that would account for any precise sequence of its successive states, and without such a mechanism it would be implausible to expect a constant but noncausal correlation between those states and states of the body.

Immaterialism. Some philosophers have held the doctrine of immaterialism, so named by Bishop George Berkeley, one of the classic British Empiricists, in whose view everything that exists is mental, "of the stuff that dreams are made of," and there is no such thing as the material. There are two major alternatives here: that reality consists of one vast, all-encompassing mind, or that it consists of a plurality of minds. The former position is sometimes called absolute Idealism; the latter, which Berkeley himself held, is sometimes called subjective Idealism.

Berkeley's mentalism

The philosophy of Berkeley represents a highly developed and energetically defended statement of the position that reality consists wholly of minds, the divine Mind and the multiplicity of finite minds that includes all men. Whatever exists does so either because it is a mind or because it is dependent upon a mind; nothing material exists. Berkeley argued that the notion of the material should play no role in one's thinking, for its existence is unverifiable, its postulation unnecessary, and, at bottom, the very notion is self-contradictory. How does Berkeley view the status of tables and chairs, rocks, the Moon, and all of the other apparently material things that everyone accepts as existing? Berkeley agreed that they do indeed exist but only as collections of ideas that exist in the mind of God and that are often caused by God to exist in the minds of men as well.

There are well-known difficulties in Berkeley's view. His account of the nature of tables and other objects cannot be accepted as an account of the meanings of these terms because it is implausible to think that the concept of a divine Mind is somehow part of their meaning. Nor does it seem a plausible scientific theory about such objects because of its ad hoc character and its lack of predictive value. If the notion of God is dropped, however, the philosopher is left with the phenomenalistic theory that such objects are collections of appearances. But phenomenalism also has serious difficulties; in particular, it cannot in the end account for the difference between real objects and illusions because it cannot provide an account of the difference between circumstances in which perceptions are veridical and those in which they are not.

The other variety of immaterialism, called absolute Idealism, derives from certain doctrines of Immanuel Kant and of the classical German Idealists who followed him—Johann Fichte, Friedrich Schelling, and G.W.F. Hegel—concerning the fundamental dependence of reality on mind or spirit in general. Among the several philosophers who have defended this view, there was, at the turn of the 20th century, F.H. Bradley, whose *Appearance and Reality* (1893; 2nd edition 1897) comprises its most systematic exposition and defense. Bradley denied that a plurality of minds exists and insisted that there is only one infinite Mind, Idea, or Experience that comprehends all of existence within it.

Neutral theories. Another important view has been that neither the mental nor the physical is really fundamental; each is an aspect of some underlying reality that is neither mental nor physical but neutral between them. There are many variants of such a view. Spinoza, a 17th-century Rationalist, held that the underlying substance, which encompassed all of reality and which he called God or Nature, had both thinking (the mental) and extension (the material) as attributes. A modern version of this position is that of Peter Strawson, a leading philosopher of the Oxford "ordinary language" school, who differs from Spinoza in holding that there is a multiplicity of substances, some of which are purely material and some of which are persons (thus he is not really a monist). Strawson conceives of persons as substances whose nature is to have both mental and physical attributes. Thus, one and the same substance can have both qualities, and the difference between the mental and the physical is conceived as a basic difference between the qualities.

Spinoza's substance and attributes

A different approach was suggested in some of Hume's writings and diversely stated by the Pragmatist William James and by various Positivists (Ernst Mach, Rudolf Carnap, and A.J. Ayer). They postulate a number of particular entities, experiences, that go to make up minds when they are related in certain ways, as by the laws of association and memory, and that go to make up bodies when the entities are related in other ways, as by the laws of perspective. Thus, a person's mind is conceived to be just the collection of his experiences, whereas a physical object is conceived to be just the collection of experiences that people can have of it. Here the difference between the mental and physical consists in the different kinds of relations obtaining between the neutral particulars, experiences.

Recently, it has been suggested by certain Linguistic philosophers that the difference between mind and body lies in two different kinds of language or conceptual systems: the physicalistic-conceptual language, on the one hand, with its spatiotemporal terms, and person-talk, on the other, with its reference to norms for assessing the rationality, moral responsibility, and ethical value of human actions.

Existentialist and Phenomenological views

Existentialist and Phenomenological philosophers have expressed similar conclusions, supported not so much by linguistic considerations as by general observations of man's condition as a being in the world, with a body, which he experiences and which, by its nature, affects his experience. Man can be viewed as a spatiotemporal aggregate, an object for observation, study, and manipulation, an instance of the laws of nature. But man can also be viewed as a self-moved mover, a being who alters himself and the world through the decisions he makes, who determines values and invests things with those values, who can make his life and his world according to the values that he determines, and who, in the end, can negate his values and even terminate his life by choice. Here the philosopher finds surprising similarities between some Analytic philosophers of the English-speaking world and the more speculative continental philosophers.

THE ANALYSIS OF MENTAL PHENOMENA

When the specific phenomena that go to make up the mental are considered, one finds that they all raise philosophical issues, only some of which can be sketched here. Mental phenomena are traditionally divided into three areas: the cognitive, which is concerned with knowledge; the affective, with feeling; and the volitional, with action. It is no longer believed that this division reflects the three so-called basic faculties that comprise the mind; nevertheless, as a very rough classification, it provides a convenient approach to the variety of mental phenomena.

The cognitive. Many philosophers since Plato have taken man's ability to know as the characteristic distinguishing him from all other animals. The very name of his species, *Homo sapiens,* means "man the knower."

Psychological aspect and phenomena

If one asks what knowledge is, he has raised the central problem of a major field of philosophy, epistemology (see EPISTEMOLOGY). But there is also a very important psychological aspect to knowledge, and that is where the philosophy of mind becomes relevant. It is often claimed, for example, that knowing that something is so entails believing that it is so; and the nature of belief lies clearly within the province of the philosophy of mind. Since a person does not lose a belief when he is not consciously attending to it, the approach to belief most in favour today is to treat it as a disposition, which, like all such, comes to open expression only sporadically. Other psychological phenomena falling within the area of the cognitive are attention, sense perception, understanding, memory, inference, and doubt. The view that each of these requires a subjective experience has been effectively refuted in the writings of Ludwig Wittgenstein, one of the seminal thinkers of modern Linguistic Analysis. Remembering that the oven is still turned on may consist in nothing but getting up in the middle of a conversation, going over to the oven, and turning it off, all the while animatedly continuing the conversation. But exactly why this is called "remembering that the oven is still on" is not clear. Perhaps the best that can be said is that there are analogies between such instances of remembering and other, more self-conscious instances. It is the task of the philosophy of mind to examine, classify, and analyze the relations among such phenomena.

The affective. Man has not only the capacity to know but also the capacity to respond emotionally to what he knows. A man may not only believe that some event will occur, but he may also dread it or welcome it. Concerning the things that a person knows, he may approve or disapprove, love or hate, pity or envy, enjoy or abhor. Here, although the subjective experience often plays an important role, it clearly is not the whole story. To enjoy doing something, as has been pointed out, is not to do the thing *and also* undergo a series of experiences of enjoyment; it may simply be to do the thing when circumstances permit and make efforts to avoid its cessation or interruption. But a disposition-to-behave approach will be less successful for other affective phenomena. For example, people have feelings about the past—regret, nostalgia, pride—feelings in which future behaviour plays a relatively minor role.

All of the affective phenomena so far considered have the property of intentionality, of being directed toward an object. It is clear, however, that this is not a sufficient condition for defining the affective, since it marks out too broad a scope—including, for example, believing, which, though intentional, falls not within the affective but within the cognitive. But neither does intentionality seem to be a necessary condition of the affective. Moods such as depression, anxiety, or joviality may not have any specific object, though it is sometimes replied that such emotions take as objects anything the person happens to think of. Sensations also do not seem to be intentional, even though they are usually classified as affects. One view is that sensations are really cognitions—the awareness of some bodily disturbance. The difficulty in trying to decide whether a sensation is an affect or a cognition further illustrates the inadequacy of the classification of mental phenomena into the cognitive, affective, and volitional.

The volitional. Intellect and emotion often come to expression in volition and action, important topics in the philosophy of mind—topics that comprise such concepts as motive, desire and purpose, deliberation, decision, intention, attempt, and action, both voluntary and involuntary.

Wittgenstein's question on action

There is a rough distinction to be made between the things that happen to a person and the things he does or makes to happen. If a person slips on the ice, it is something that happens to him; if he walks on the ice, it is something that he does. "Henry slid on the ice" is ambiguous: it may report something that happened to Henry or something that Henry did, depending upon the meaning. In this example, the observable event may be the same: from a photograph of Henry sliding on the ice one may not be able to tell which it is. The problem of action is primarily to understand this distinction and its ramifications. Wittgenstein once put the question this way: "And the problem arises: what is left over if I subtract the fact that my arm goes up from the fact that I raise my arm?"

There are a number of different answers: (1) Actions are events produced by causes of certain sorts—volitions or acts of will according to some theories; beliefs and desires under other theories; and simply persons or agents in yet another theory. (2) Actions are events that are "caused" in a special sense; they have a teleological rather than an efficient or mechanical cause, or an immanent (or originating) cause rather than one that is merely a reaction to, or modification of, an action coming from some other source. (3) Actions are events that are properly characterized and assessed in terms of rules of conduct, or principles of rational and ethical behaviour, and for which the agent is held responsible, liable, accountable, to be praised or blamed, rewarded or punished.

Any theory of action is expected to throw light on the issue of free will, a matter of great importance for ethical theory. If the philosopher holds that free will is compatible with determinism, any of the views above will allow for free will. Even if he holds that an action is not free if it has causes that eventually lie outside the agent, his view will be compatible with the various views of action unless he holds the version of (1)—that an action is an event produced by volitions or beliefs and desires—and also holds the additional thesis (2)—that volitions or beliefs and desires themselves have causes that lie outside the agent. Only then will there be no freedom of the will.

SOME METAPHYSICAL AND EPISTEMOLOGICAL ISSUES

Personal identity through time. A person, as he goes through life, changes in many ways; but he remains the person that he was. He is that person who was born on a certain day, that person who graduated 23rd in a particular high school class, who married on a certain date in a certain place; he has a particular identity through time. It is difficult to state what exactly it is that makes a person one and the same self through time.

Bodily versus psychological criteria

An obvious starting point is the fact that throughout a person's natural life he has the same body and that this is what makes him one and the same person throughout a particular period of time. But there are difficulties in this view. First, since the body cells are constantly being replaced and in some instances whole organs are transplanted, it is not clear what makes a particular body identical with a body that existed, say, 20 years earlier. A second difficulty arises through the hypothetical possibility of brain transplants; if two brains were interchanged, in all likelihood there would be a systematic interchange of memory, beliefs, personality and character traits, skills, and habits of thought and action. Such a transplant would incline one to say that not merely a small portion of each body had been interchanged but two people as well; for one also takes as a criterion of personal identity similarities through time of memory, personality, skills, and habits. After all, a man is often willing to say that this is the same person who did something in the past, not on the basis of knowing that it is the same body but on a quite different basis—that the person recounts the past situation with great accuracy, exhibits similar personal reactions, and displays the same skills.

Because two different kinds of criteria, bodily and psychological, are used for determining personal identity, it is possible to imagine instances of conflict in which the criterion of bodily identity would indicate that it is a different person but the psychological criteria would indicate that it is the same person and vice versa. The Austro-Czech novelist Franz Kafka, known for his nightmarish works, in his short story *Die Verwandlung* (1915; *The Metamorphosis*) tells of a person who awoke one morning to find, to his horror, that he had the body of a large insect. Although his family accepted his conclusion that he was the same person even though he had an entirely different body, others would have disagreed. There is still, in fact, considerable disagreement among scholars on this whole issue—on how to state precisely the bodily criterion; on whether there is a psychological criterion as well and, if so, how it is to be formulated; on what is the basic criterion of personal identity; and on what to say about instances in which criteria conflict.

Personal immortality. Many people believe that when the human body ceases to be a living system, there is not total annihilation of the person but that in some respect the person continues to exist. The philosopher of mind can put aside the various watered-down versions of immortality in which the person continues to exist in the remote sense that people still remember him or his works or that his influence continues through history. The philosopher does look with interest, however, on the claim that there is an immortality in which a person, in his survival, meets the psychological criteria of personal identity, of inheritance of memory, beliefs, habits, and personality characteristics.

Problems of meaning and fact

It is clear that a person's view of immortality will be affected by opinions that he holds about the relation of mind to matter. Given the versions of Materialism that urge the elimination of mental terms or their definition in bodily terms or that take bodily identity to be the basic criterion of personal identity, the very notion of survival after death is completely unintelligible. Many philosophers, however, reason that, since the notion of survival is intelligible, such versions of Materialism cannot be accepted. Central-state or identity theorists would admit survival to be an intelligible notion but would view it, like lightning without electricity, as something that never happens; they would thus be in agreement with many dualists, in particular epiphenomenalists and psychophysical parallelists. Even an interactionist would be free to accept or reject survival, as would a neutral monist.

If a philosopher holds that survival is an intelligible notion, he is still left with the further question of whether it ever happens. In the past there have been various a priori arguments for survival after death. Arguments based upon the nature of the self, such as its indivisibility, can be found in Plato's *Phaedo.* Kant argued that man's moral principles require survival as a postulate. But among those today who hold that survival is intelligible, it is widely agreed that a priori arguments will not do. If there is survival, they say, it is a contingent fact and not a necessity; one must thus look to empirical data for guidance. A survey of the evidence shows that the case against survival, though strong, is by no means conclusive. One thing is clear: if there is survival, the survivors can theoretically give firsthand testimony to it, whereas if there is no survival, there will be no one to give such testimony.

Knowledge of other minds. An important problem in the theory of knowledge has been the status of the belief in other minds, the belief that one's own consciousness is not the only consciousness in existence. Though few, if any, sane persons have seriously accepted solipsism (the view that one's own is the only consciousness), the grounds for rejecting it are not at all clear.

Again, as with the problems of personal identity and personal survival, one's view of the relation of mind to matter is relevant. On various Materialistic views, the problem reduces itself to that of justifying the belief in an external world that contains other bodies of the appropriate sort and with the appropriate behaviour. But for dualists and immaterialists, who hold that mental phenomena are something irreducibly different from the physical, there is the further question of whether that something is unique to oneself or whether there are other instances of it in the world.

Direct, transcendental, analogical approaches

Some scholars claim that individuals sometimes have direct awareness of the conscious states of others, either in telepathic experiences, moments of empathy, or even in everyday social intercourse. There is, moreover, a transcendental argument, found in Kant and defended by Strawson, holding that, unless a person could be confident of the existence of other minds, he could not be confident of the existence of his own mind. A different line of reasoning, the so-called argument from analogy, is based upon the similarities between one's own body and its behaviour, on the one hand, and other human bodies and their behaviour on the other. To pursue the argument, since a mind is known to be associated with one's own body, it is reasonable to conclude that another mind is associated with the body of another person. Finally, there is the view that the best way to explain the complex behaviour of other bodies, especially their ability to behave rationally, and in particular to speak and communicate information, is to postulate other minds at work.

None of these arguments compels strong conviction, certainly not the degree of conviction that all persons feel concerning the existence of other minds. Whether stronger arguments will be found, whether philosophers must admit that there is a considerable amount of faith required here, or whether they will reformulate their concepts of the mind in a more Materialistic way to bring them in closer accord with observable data remains to be seen.

Artificial intelligence. Remarkable progress in the development of high-speed electronic computers has led many philosophers to conclude that a suitably programmed computer with a sufficient memory capacity would have an actual mind capable of intelligent thought. The term artificial intelligence is used to denote the area of investigation that aims to develop computers with such capabilities.

Two questions are intensely debated in this field. First, what are the theoretical limits to what can be achieved in the way of artificial intelligence? Despite phenomenal progress in recent years, no computer yet devised even approximates in its capacity the multiplicitous powers of the human mind. However, it would be most unwise at present to make dogmatic predictions about future developments. Second, assuming that the optimistic hopes of artificial intelligence researchers are realized, would such devices literally have minds or would they be mere imitations of minds? It is already common linguistic practice to describe computers as having memories, making inferences, understanding one language or another, and the like, but are such descriptions literally true or simply metaphorical? One group holds that computers will never be more than tools employed by the human intelligence to aid its own thinking. Another group holds that human intelligence itself consists of the very computational processes that could be exemplified by advanced machines, so that it would be unreasonable to deny the attribution of intelligence to such machines. The issue may remain unresolved until researchers in artificial intelligence have had more time to determine the limits of computer capabilities.

BIBLIOGRAPHY. Various formulations of Materialism can be found in the writings of the pre-Socratic philosophers, especially LEUCIPPUS and DEMOCRITUS. PLATO'S dualism and his views on the nature of the soul appear in the *Phaedo, Timaeus, Phaedrus,* and books iv and x of the *Republic.* ARISTOTLE devoted a whole treatise, *De Anima* (*On the Soul*), to the subject, expressing a qualified Materialism. THOMAS HOBBES, *Leviathan* (1651), was radically Materialistic; whereas RENÉ DESCARTES, *Meditationes de prima philosophia,* 2nd ed. (1642), and other writings, presents a classic interactionist dualism. Dualism of the parallelist variety can be found in the writings of GOTTFRIED LEIBNIZ. BENEDICT DE SPINOZA, in his *Ethica* (1677), rejected both Materialism and dualism, expounding a double aspect theory. GEORGE BERKELEY, *Treatise Concerning the Principles of Human Knowledge* (1710), provides the classic statement and defense of Idealism (in his word, Immaterialism).

The contemporary interest in the philosophy of mind is largely a result of GILBERT RYLE'S brilliant and polemical *Concept of Mind* (1949, reprinted 1984). Also of great importance was the wholly new approach to all of philosophy taken by LUDWIG WITTGENSTEIN in his *Philosophical Investigations* (1953). There followed a spate of journal articles, some of the best of which are in the following anthologies: MYLES BRAND (ed.), *The Nature of Human Action* (1970); ANTONY FLEW (ed.), *Body, Mind, and Death* (1964); DONALD F. GUSTAFSON (ed.), *Essays in Philosophical Psychology* (1964); HAROLD MORICK (ed.), *Introduction to the Philosophy of Mind* (1970, reissued 1981); GEORGE PITCHER (ed.), *Wittgenstein: The Philosophical Investigations* (1966); ALAN R. WHITE (ed.), *The Philosophy of Action* (1968, reissued 1977); and OSCAR P. WOOD and GEORGE PITCHER (eds.), *Ryle* (1970). Selections written from Existentialist and Phenomenological perspectives are in STUART F. SPICKER (ed.), *The Philosophy of the Body* (1970). Introductory writings that include original contributions as well as balanced assessments are GERALD E. MYERS, *Self* (1969); ALAN R. WHITE, *The Philosophy of Mind* (1967, reprinted 1978); JEROME A. SHAFFER, *Philosophy of Mind* (1968); and COLIN MCGINN, *The Character of Mind* (1982). For analyses of particular mental phenomena, see G.E.M. ANSCOMBE, *Intention,* 2nd ed. (1963, reissued 1976); HARVEY RICHARD SCHIFFMAN, *Sensation and Perception,* 2nd ed. (1982), a good textbook; P.T. GEACH, *Mental Acts* (1957, reprinted 1971); STUART HAMPSHIRE, *Thought and Action,* new ed. (1982); ANTHONY KENNY, *Action, Emotion and Will* (1963, reissued 1976); ALASTAIR C. MACINTYRE, *The Unconscious* (1958, reissued 1976); NORMAN MALCOLM, *Dreaming* (1959, reissued 1976); R.S. PETERS, *The Concept of Motivation,* 2nd ed. (1969, reissued 1974); RICHARD TAYLOR, *Action and Purpose* (1966, reprinted 1973); and A.R. WHITE, *Attention* (1964). A.J. AYER, *The Concept of a Person* (1963); and CHRIS L. KLEINKE, *Self-Perception: The Psychology of Personal Awareness* (1978), deal with the problem of personal identity. The problem of one's knowledge of other minds is explored in HAROLD MORICK (ed.), *Wittgenstein and the Problem of Other Minds* (1967, reissued 1981); ALVIN PLANTINGA, *God and Other Minds* (1967); and JOHN WISDOM, *Other Minds,* 2nd ed. (1965). R.J. NELSON, *The Logic of Mind* (1982), offers a mechanistic approach to philosophy of mind; whereas JOHN ECCLES and DANIEL N. ROBINSON, *The Wonder of Being Human: Our Brain and Our Mind* (1984), poses strong opposition to the "human as machine" approach. The implications of artificial intelligence are examined in ALAN ROSS ANDERSON (ed.), *Minds and Machines* (1964); HUBERT L. DREYFUS, *What Computers Can't Do,* rev. ed. (1979); and DANIEL C. DENNETT, *Brainstorms* (1978, reissued 1981).

(J.A.Sh.)

Minerals and Rocks

A mineral is a solid element or inorganic compound that has a definite chemical composition and, in nearly all cases, a regular internal crystal structure. There are several thousand known mineral types, many of which constitute the basic building blocks of rocks, the masses of material that make up the Earth's crust and mantle. A few rocks consist of a single mineral or exclusively of natural volcanic glass, but most are aggregates of several minerals, and their properties are governed to a large degree by the properties of the individual minerals of which they are composed. The multitude of ways in which minerals combine accounts for the great variety of rocks that occur in nature. Rocks are commonly divided into three broad classes—igneous, sedimentary, and metamorphic—on the basis of origin. Each of these classes, in turn, is subdivided into numerous groups and types according to mineralogical composition and texture.

This article provides a summary of the chemical composition, morphology, occurrence, and origins of minerals and mineral associations. It treats the principal rock-forming minerals such as the silicates and clay minerals and the related rock varieties, indicating their physical properties, classification, and modes of formation. Additional information on the crystal structure of minerals can be found in the article MATTER: *Crystallography*. See also DRESS AND ADORNMENT: *Gems* for specific information about precious minerals. (Ed.)

This article is divided into the following sections:

THE NATURE OF MINERALS

Structure and composition

BASIC STRUCTURAL UNITS AND CHEMICAL BONDS

All minerals have regular arrangements (lattices) of atoms that have some geometrical symmetry. For each repeating unit cell, the smallest unit of a mineral that retains its basic structure and composition, there are sets of sites occupied by atoms at distances determined by the chemical bonding of the constituents involved. In quartz, for example, each silicon atom is surrounded by four oxygen atoms lying at the corners of a tetrahedron at a distance of 1.6 angstroms (one angstrom unit equals 10^{-8} centimetre). Each oxygen atom is close to two silicon atoms, and the whole atomic assemblage can be considered as an infinite framework of silicon–oxygen bonds. The crystal structure can be determined by X-ray-diffraction methods—*i.e.,* subjecting a crystal to radiation and employing Bragg's law, which relates the wavelength of radiation and the angle of diffraction of the radiation to the internal spacing of crystallographic planes. The cell dimensions, symmetry, and diffraction intensities provide unique identification.

Unit cell

From the geometrical distribution of atoms in the unit cell, and from the general principles of chemical bonding, the type of chemical bonding can be envisaged and used in the interpretation of mineralogic properties.

This topic is treated more fully in the article MOLECULES: *Chemical bonding,* and the four principal types that are of mineralogical concern will be but briefly described here. The first of these is ionic bonding, the permanent transfer of electrons from atoms to form ions, which undergo electrical attraction and repulsion. A second type is covalent bonding, in which clouds (groups) of electrons are shared between atoms. Metallic bonding involves the formation of an electron "gas" throughout an entire crystal. Van der Waals bonding, the fourth type, is a weak attractive force resulting from temporarily induced distortions of electron clouds. Most bonds are a mixture of more than one type.

Copper and gold typify metallic bonding and have atoms lying at the faces and corners of the cubic unit cell, so that each atom has 12 neighbours. Arsenic is only semimetallic; its structure is similar to that of copper or gold but is distorted so that it has three nearest neighbours to which it is partly bonded covalently.

Halite (common salt) typifies ionic bonding. The sodium and chlorine atoms lie in interpenetrating lattices, and the symmetry is such that each atom has six near neighbours.

Diamond is a prime example of covalent bonding. Carbon atoms lie in a tetrahedral arrangement with covalent bonds linking all atoms into a single edifice. In graphite, however, which also consists solely of carbon, the carbon atoms lie in layers or planes of hexagonal symmetry; they are bonded by covalent forces within the layer but by weak van der Waals forces between the layers.

Irrespective of the type of bonding, the crystal structure is

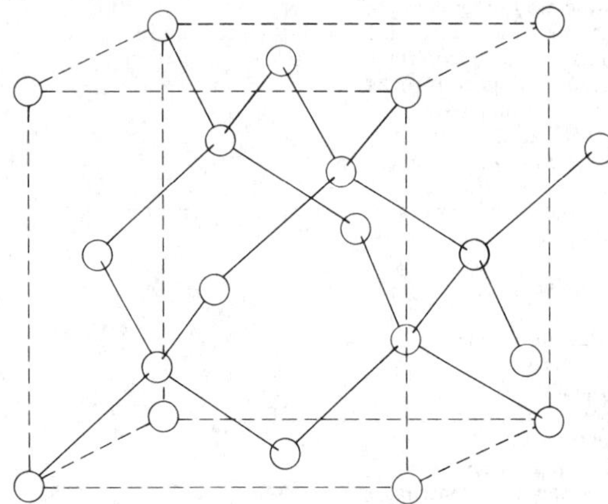
Figure 1: Structure of diamond. Positions of carbon atoms are shown by circles, direction of strong covalent bonds by the solid lines; dashed lines show the unit cell.

based on fascinating geometrical considerations. Even the most complex mineral structure has a simple underlying pattern that can be analyzed by using the principles of symmetry and topology (the study of geometric properties that are unchanged by continuous transformation). Complex structures are always distorted in response to subtle chemical forces not completely understood.

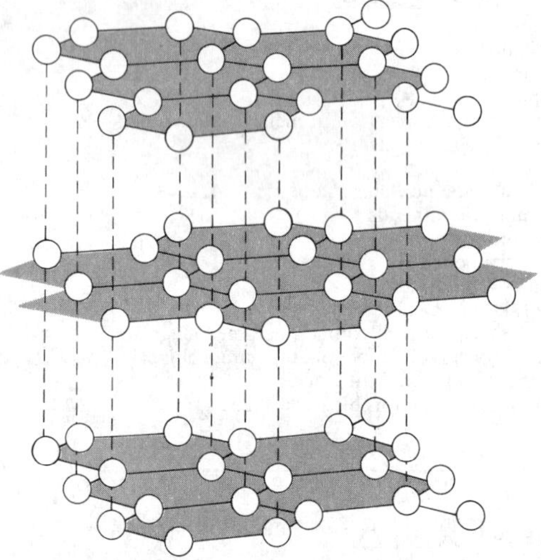
Figure 2: Structure of graphite. Each atom is bound triangularly to three neighbours, producing layers.

Close packing in mineral structures

The condensed nature of crystalline minerals results in close packing of near-spherical units in most ionic and metallic forms. Covalent forces require special bond angles that are inconsistent with simple concepts of close packing. On Earth, oxygen (O^{2-}) is the dominant anion (negatively charged ion), and it is larger than most of the cations (positively charged ions). The outer part of the Earth may be said roughly to consist of close-packed oxygen ions with the interstices occupied by cations.

The two simplest close-packed arrangements are cubic close packing and hexagonal close packing. The former is illustrated by the structure of copper and gold. There are two types of interstices, one type between six atoms (*i.e.*, six-coordinated) and one type between four. The halite structure, *e.g.*, consists of small sodium cations (Na^+) that occupy the six-coordinated holes between the large chlorine anions (Cl^-). Magnesium oxide (MgO) may exist deep in the Earth with the halite-type structure composed of large oxygen anions (O^{2-}) and small magnesium cations (Mg^{2+}). The second type of interstice can be envisaged from the diamond structure. If every alternate atom grows while the other half diminishes in size, the large ones ultimately will come into contact, and the small ones will just fill half the holes, leaving the other half empty.

Effect of ionic size

Ions have different inherent sizes, and the actual crystal structures result from minimizing the electrical potential. The complex structure of kaolinite, a clay mineral and aluminum silicate of composition $Al_2Si_2O_5(OH)_4$, serves as an example. Tiny silicon ions (Si^{4+}) lie between four large oxygen ions (O^{2-}) linked to form a hexagonal sheet. Large hydroxyl ions (OH^-) form another hexagonal sheet and also occur enmeshed with the oxygen sheet. Small aluminum ions (Al^{3+}) bond to four OH^- and two O^{2-}. The $Al_4Si_4O_{10}(OH)_8$ "sandwich" is electrically neutral and is bonded to adjacent sandwiches by weak and ionic van der Waals forces.

Many groups of minerals have the same topology in their crystal structure even though the actual cell dimensions are slightly different. This arises when the ratio of the ionic radii is within the tolerance for that particular structure type and when the ions have the appropriate charges. Examples of such isostructural minerals are calcite ($CaCO_3$), siderite ($FeCO_3$) and rhodochrosite ($MnCO_3$); halite (NaCl), sylvite (KCl) and periclase (MgO); diopside ($CaMgSi_2O_6$) and aegirine ($NaFeSi_2O_6$).

Polymorphic changes

Many chemical compositions yield more than one structural type, and these are known as polymorphs. Thus SiO_2 yields a host of polymorphs, including quartz, tridymite, cristobalite, coesite, and stishovite. The $CaCO_3$ composition occurs as calcite and aragonite. Under thermodynamic equilibrium, each polymorph would occur only for a specific range of temperature, pressure, and composition; however, a polymorph may grow metastably, or persist metastably—*i.e.*, resist change in response to small disturbances despite the fact that some other phase would be wholly stable under the same conditions—as a result of energy barriers to atomic movement. Other polymorphs are related merely by change of interatomic angles culminating in a symmetry change: the so-called high quartz changes to low quartz at 573° C (1,063° F), accompanied by a symmetry change from hexagonal to trigonal (see below *Quartz and other silica minerals*). Other polymorphic changes involve the atomic distribution between sites. Sanidine and microcline, two of the feldspars, are polymorphs of potash feldspar ($KAlSi_3O_8$) and differ in that microcline has the Al and Si atoms segregated each into its own sites, whereas sanidine has a random distribution.

Solid-solution series

An ideal crystal structure would yield a chemical formula with exact ratios: $CaMgSi_2O_6$, for example. Packing tolerance exists in most structures, however, and extensive atomic substitution (often called solid solution) is permitted. Solid solution is essentially the compositional variation of a single crystalline phase between finite limits without the appearance of a second phase. If the atomic substitution causes only minor structural distortions, which is the case for the common substitutions of silica (Si) and alumina (Al), then atomic substitution at temperatures above absolute zero is favoured on theoretical grounds. The extent of solid solution normally increases with temperature and may be complete. With falling temperature, dissolution or exsolution into two intergrown mineral phases may occur, or ordered structures may form.

Some minerals have unoccupied sites. Sulfides provide the best examples: pyrrhotite (iron sulfide) has a range of composition in which iron may be present in quantities equal to or down to eight tenths the amount of sulfur present. The formula is: $F_{1-x}S$, in which x varies up to 0.2; only in meteorites and in lunar samples is the end-member troilite (FeS) typical.

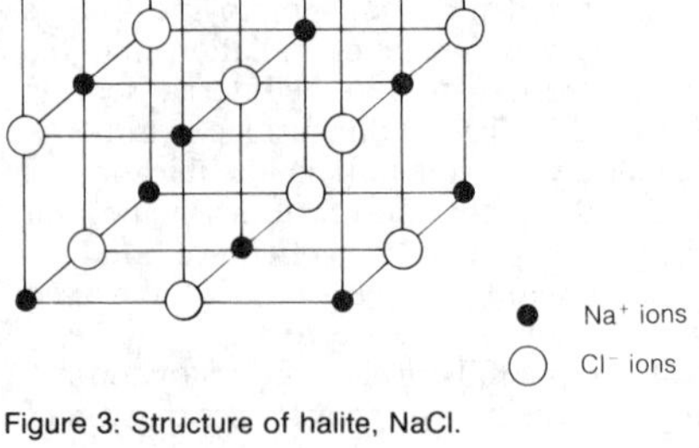

● Na^+ ions
○ Cl^- ions

Figure 3: Structure of halite, NaCl.

Figure 4: *Models of two types of crystal structures of minerals.* (Left) Crystal structure of fluorite, CaF_2, an example of strong ionic bonding. Red balls represent calcium and yellow balls fluorine ions. (Right) The structure of kaolinite, $Al_4Si_4O_{10}(OH)_8$; closely packed atoms in the composite slabs are held together by strong covalent and ionic forces. The slabs, however, are electrically neutral and only weakly held to one another by van der Waals bonding. Yellow balls represent oxygen atoms arranged in tetrahedra; silicon atoms occur within the tetrahedral pores and are not visible. Small brown balls are aluminum and blue are hydroxyl ions.

Ward's Natural Science Establishment, Inc.

In general, rock-forming minerals contain a bit of everything ranging from major constituents (over 1 percent), minor constituents (below 1 percent), and trace elements (parts per million or less). Only by combination of subtle analytical methods can the complete chemical analysis be obtained. The principles underlying the distribution of chemical elements in and between minerals are covered in CHEMICAL ELEMENTS: *Geochemical distribution of the elements.*

MORPHOLOGY

The shape of minerals obeys the rules of crystallography, which developed historically from the study of minerals. Museum collections naturally emphasize well-shaped crystals grown in cavities, but most minerals interfere with each other's growth in rocks. In analogous fashion, snowflakes contrast with block ice. Well-shaped crystals have characteristic angles between faces that are related to the dimensions and symmetry of the internal structure. Ideally, each group of faces related by the symmetry would be equally developed, thus providing the form; a set of six faces on a cube of galena or the prism faces on quartz are examples. Most minerals show several types of faces, and the relative development of each form yields the habit. Quartz from volcanic rocks usually grows as a hexagonal pyramid, whereas quartz from low-temperature veins is dominated by a hexagonal prism. Some minerals almost always show the same habit (*e.g.,* the icosahedral habit of garnet), but others (*e.g.,* feldspar) show major variations from one locality to another that are only partly correlative with obvious physical and chemical factors.

Certain crystals have pseudo-symmetry and during their growth incoming atoms may adopt a new configuration rather than adopting the old one. Such multiple crystals are called twins, even though many twins consist of more than two units. Easily recognized twinned minerals are staurolite, pyrite (the "iron cross"), sanidine (Carlsbad twin), aragonite, and spinel; in thin section, the twinning of microcline and plagioclase is often characteristic. Twinning also results from deformation and symmetry inversion as a consequence of changed pressure and temperature conditions.

Twins

By courtesy of (top left) Joseph and Helen Guetterman, Belleville, Illinois, (bottom left) the Field Museum of Natural History, Chicago, (bottom right) the Harvard Collection; photographs, (top left, bottom left) John H. Gerard—B Inc., (top right) Floyd R. Getsinger, (bottom right) Benjamin M. Shaub

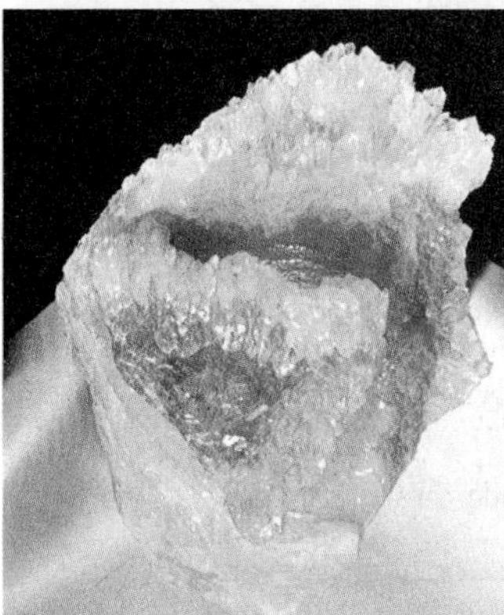

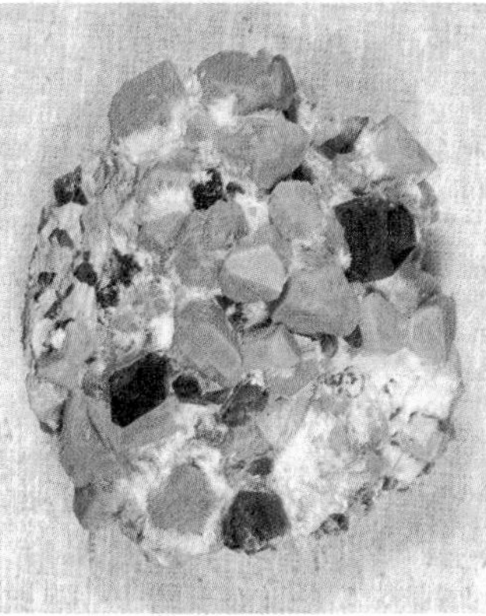

Figure 5: *Representative minerals that sometimes occur as euhedral crystals.*
Although in the minority, they receive the most attention because of their beauty and because they reflect the basic crystal form and structure of a particular mineral. (Top left) Wulfenite, $PbMoO_4$, from Mexico. (Top right) Calcite, $CaCO_3$, from Chihuahua, Mexico. (Bottom left) Rose quartz from Minas Gerais state, Brazil. (Bottom right) Microcline feldspar, $KAlSi_3O_8$, variety amazon stone, with smoky quartz, from Colorado.

Classification of minerals

Mineral nomenclature

Historically, mineral names were assigned haphazardly, with many errors and much redundancy. In spite of attempts to develop rational systems, the present conglomeration of proper names is useful, reasonably consistent, and fascinating from the etymological viewpoint. Since the 19th century, better understanding of crystal structure and chemical composition has led to slow refinement of mineral nomenclature. Since 1960, an international committee of nomenclature has reviewed new proposals for mineral names and attempted to remove redundancies. Generally speaking, a new mineral name is adopted only upon satisfactory evidence of (1) a significant change of chemical composition in a known structure type or (2) a completely new structure type of any composition. The discoverer has the right to propose a proper name (ending in "-ite") consistent with absence of confusion with an existing name. In complete solid solution (atomic substitution) series, a name is usually accepted for each of the constituents present. Gold and silver are such a pair, for example, and, if gold dominates, then gold is the name assigned for (Au,Ag); the name silver would be used for (Ag,Au). Minor constituents are represented by adjectival modifiers—*e.g.,* argentian tetrahedrite for minor Ag in $Cu_{12}Sb_4S_{13}$. Exceptions arise from such special features as changes of symmetry (*e.g.,* sanidine and anorthoclase in the feldspar group) and from historical precedent (*e.g.,* many subdivisions of olivine, plagioclase, and pyroxene). Names should be useful, reflecting the principal properties, and particularly complex mineral groups need many names even if they break some desired artificial system. Several thousand names are in common use, modified slightly from one language to another.

The first recorded classification was by the Greek philosopher Theophrastus. Subsequent schemes utilized mostly physical properties, but increasing chemical knowledge led to classifications based on chemical composition, such as that by a Swedish chemist, Axel Fredrik Cronstedt, in 1758. Major advances in both chemistry and mineralogy permitted James Dwight Dana, an American mineralogist, to develop his *System of Mineralogy* in 1837; the later editions of this work served as a primary reference source. Although ignorant of crystal structure, Dana proposed a system that correlates well with present knowledge. In this article, minerals are classified into 13 groups: (1) native elements; (2) sulfides, arsenides, and antimonides; (3) sulfosalts; (4) oxides and hydroxides; (5) halides; (6) carbonates; (7) nitrates and iodates; (8) borates; (9) sulfates; (10) chromates; (11) phosphates, vanadates, and arsenates; (12) tungstates and molybdates; and (13) silicates. In this

Dana's classification system

classification, the first group concerns single-element minerals with metallic or covalent bonding; the second two groups are principally metallic; the next two groups are principally minerals with ionic bonds, generally of equal strength; and the remaining groups have complex structures in which tightly bonded groups (*e.g.*, carbonate) are joined to ions by weaker bonds. The mineral groups are dominated by oxygen, which accords with its great geochemical abundance. In each group, isostructural minerals (*i.e.*, those with similar crystallographic structures) are placed together, and minerals are arranged on the basis of structural properties.

In the discussions that follow it is important to bear in mind that the Earth consists of three concentric shells—the crust, mantle, and core—which differ in chemical composition and in the conditions of pressure and temperature that prevail. Certain minerals that are known to form only under conditions of high temperature and pressure (*e.g.*, diamond) cannot form at the Earth's surface; others, which do form under surface conditions (*e.g.*, evaporites), cannot be expected to occur at depth in the mantle. For a detailed exposition of conditions in the Earth's crust, mantle, and core, see EARTH.

NATIVE ELEMENTS

The native elements consist of approximately 20 chemical elements that occur in nature in pure or nearly pure form. They are commonly divided into metals, semimetals, and nonmetals. Gold, silver, copper, and platinum are the most important metals. Rarer native metals include palladium, mercury, zinc, iron, tin, lead, and tantalum. The semimetals are comprised of arsenic, antimony, and bismuth. Sulfur, carbon in the form of diamond and graphite, and selenium and tellurium make up the nonmetals.

Native elements are rare at the Earth's surface because most chemical elements combine rapidly with oxygen, sulfur, and halogens. A few metallic elements such as platinum and gold are highly resistant, and various others, including copper, mercury, and iron, survive in special environments, although they are unstable in the presence of atmospheric gases or solutions. Sulfur and carbon (as diamond and graphite) are metastable with respect to oxygen but persist in special environments. Diamond is truly stable only at pressures that are equivalent to depths of several hundred kilometres in the Earth, and its persistence testifies to the difficulty of the transformation to graphite at the Earth's surface. Iron characteristically occurs in reducing environments (where oxygen is lacking), as typified in certain meteorites and in the Moon.

The crystal structures of the native elements are simple. In gold and silver, for example, atoms, held together by metallic bonds, are arranged in a configuration known as cubic closest packing, in which array each atom lies on a point of a face-centred cubic lattice (cubic arrangement with atoms in centres of faces) and is coordinated with 12 others. The unit of structure is a cubic unit cell containing four atoms. The metals crystallize in the isometric system, hexoctahedral class, space group Fm3m. Carbides, nitrides, and phosphides are normally classified with native elements, since the carbon (C), nitrogen (N), and phosphorus (P) atoms merely fill the interstices between the metal atoms. For more specific information about each of the elements mentioned above, see CHEMICAL ELEMENTS.

(J.V.S./Ed.)

SULFIDES, ARSENIDES, AND ANTIMONIDES

During melting of planetary material, sulfur combines with metals such as iron to form a liquid that is immiscible, or will not mix, with a silicate liquid. The sulfide-metal melt produces the native iron and troilite (FeS) that are seen in meteorites and in volcanic rocks from the Moon and are inferred to occur in the Earth's core. During the complex chemical processes of chemical differentiation near the Earth's surface, much of the sulfide is oxidized and hydrolyzed to form sulfates or gases, and some is converted to sulfur. Surviving sulfides, especially those in veins and hydrothermal deposits (those resulting from high-temperature solutions derived from magma), represent important ores of copper, zinc, silver, lead, mercury, and nickel. They also are the source of many less common metals such as cadmium, indium, rhenium, and selenium. These rarer metals occur in trace amounts in many common sulfides and are recovered in smelting and refining processes.

High symmetry of crystal form

Most of the sulfide minerals show high symmetry in their crystal forms. They have many of the properties of metals, such as metallic luster and electrical conductivity, characteristics that are attributed to metal–metal bonding in their structures. Arsenic and antimony tend to be associated with sulfur, though their semimetallic nature results in somewhat different properties. For convenience, the complex sulfosalt minerals (treated below) are separated from the sulfides, arsenides, and antimonides, most of which have simple binary (two-element) compositions.

Structural types. The sulfides, arsenides, and antimonides mostly have structures based on packing of small metal atoms between close-packed, large sulfur, arsenic, and antimony atoms. The six types of structural arrangements characteristic of nearly all sulfide minerals proper consist of this kind of close-packing combination of metal and sulfur.

The simplest and most symmetrical of the important structural types is the sodium chloride structure, in which each ion occupies a position within an octahedron composed of six oppositely charged neighbours. The most common sulfide mineral crystallizing in this manner is the ore mineral of lead, galena (PbS).

A type of packing that involves a disulfide ion in each of the octahedral positions in the sodium chloride structure is the pyrite structure. This is a high-symmetry structure and is that of the common iron sulfide, pyrite (FeS_2). A group of more complex sulfide minerals also exhibits this structure. Ullmannite, (Ni, Co, Fe) (Sb, As, Bi)S, in which the disulfide pairs in the pyrite structure are replaced by combinations of one of the B subgroup elements, Sb, As, or Bi, with a sulfide ion, is an example.

The second discrete structural type is that of sphalerite, ZnS, in which each metal ion and each sulfide ion is surrounded by four oppositely charged ions arranged tetrahedrally. In addition to sphalerite, metacinnabar, the less stable of two crystallographic forms of mercury (II) sulfide, and the selenide and telluride of mercury all crystallize with this structure.

A third structural type is that of the mineral fluorite (CaF_2). In this structure, the metal cation is surrounded by eight anions, and each anion in turn is surrounded by four metal cations. The reverse of this structure, that is, the metal cation surrounded by four anions and each anion surrounded by eight metal cations, is known as the antifluorite structure and is the arrangement of several of the more valuable precious metal tellurides and selenides, among which is hessite, Ag_2Te, silver telluride, the important ore mineral of silver.

Two structural arrangements that give rise to hexagonal symmetry are the wurtzite, ZnS, and molybdenite, MoS_2, structures. In the wurtzite structure, both metal and sulfide ions are surrounded by four of their opposite charge. The tetrahedral arrangement of ions gives rise to hexagonal symmetry and the second crystalline form of zinc sulfide. The other hexagonal structure is the molybdenite structure, in which the metal ion is coordinated with six sulfur ions and each sulfur ion is coordinated with three metal ions. This particular structure is markedly layered and gives rise to the characteristic platelike cleavage in molybdenite.

One series of five closely related sulfide minerals crystallizes in the spinel structure, common as an arrangement for oxide minerals, in which the oxygen or sulfur ions are close packed and the metal ions are in tetrahedral and octahedral coordination. In the series of cobalt and nickel sulfides (linnaeite series), nickel and cobalt occur in nearly continuously varying amounts in three named minerals between the two end members. The vacant sites and latitude for variation of composition in the spinel structure make this possible.

One mineral group—the argentite group—exists in the cesium chloride or body-centred cubic structure at elevated temperatures.

The structures described above are ideal ones; and when ionic charge and size are ideal, minerals that form in them give rise to crystal forms of high, usually isometric, symmetry. Certain combinations of metals and sulfur, however, can take the positions of monatomic ions in many of the structures and by distorting the ionic distances create crystal forms of lower symmetry. Examples of this are chalcopyrite, which through distortion of the sphalerite structure becomes tetragonal rather than isometric; and cinnabar, which through modifying the sodium chloride structure becomes hexagonal rather than isometric.

Occurrence. Sulfide minerals occur in all rock types. They may be syngenetic, that is formed at the same time and under the same conditions as those that formed the rock that encloses them. In other occurrences, they may be epigenetic, formed later than the rock that encloses them. Examples of syngenetic sulfides include pyrite in sedimentary rocks, such as shales or sandstones, chalcopyrite disseminated in felsic igneous rocks, and certain of the magmatic segregation deposits in which sulfide segregations occur conformably with rock structures.

Examples of epigenetic deposits of sulfide minerals are the common replacements of wallrock of veins by base- and precious-metal sulfides, the replacement of selected sedimentary beds by thick blankets of massive base-metal sulfides, and the deposition in open spaces of rocks of many sulfide mineral types. (J.V.S./S.R.Ty./Ed.)

SULFOSALTS

The general chemical formula of the sulfosalts is $X_aY_bS_c$, in which X is silver, copper, or lead; Y is arsenic, antimony, or bismuth; and S is sulfur. All of the 100 or so mineral species are rare and difficult to identify correctly without advanced techniques. The best known species are tetrahedrite-tennantite [$Cu_{12}(Sb,As)_4S_{13}$]; the ruby-silver group pyrargyrite-proustite [$Ag_3(Sb,As)S_3$]; enargite (Cu_3AsS_4); bournonite ($PbCuSbS_3$); and boulangerite ($Pb_5Sb_4S_{11}$).

Familiar species

Formerly it was believed that the sulfosalts were salts of complex hypothetical thioantimonic or thioarsenic acids (*e.g.*, $HSbS_2$, $H_{18}As_4S_{15}$, H_3AsS_3), but X-ray diffraction analyses indicate that the crystal structures of many sulfosalts are based on structural fragments of simpler compounds such as galena (lead sulfide; PbS) blocks and stibnite (antimony trisulfide; Sb_2S_3) sheets. No encompassing theory has been evolved to rationalize many of these curious compounds. The complexity of many of the structures evidently results from their having crystallized at low temperatures and the consequent high degree of ordering of the metal atoms. Syntheses of such compositions at higher laboratory temperature usually result in structures simpler than the complicated low-temperature forms.

Although sulfosalts are much rarer than the sulfide minerals with which they are often associated, some localities are truly remarkable for the variety of species encountered. At the Lengenbach Mine in Switzerland, for example, more than 30 distinct species have been recognized, 15 of which are not found elsewhere. Most sulfosalts have formed at low temperature in open cavities, usually in association with copper–zinc–arsenic sulfide ores. Very often they occur in cavities of calcite and dolomite, as at the Lengenbach Mine. Most are lead gray in colour with a metallic lustre, brittle (rarely malleable), crystalline, and difficult to tell apart without recourse to X-ray diffraction and electron microprobe analyses. The thallium-bearing sulfosalts often are deep red and transparent, as sometimes are the sulfosalts of silver. Nearly all sulfosalts occur as exploitable ores, often in association with other economic minerals, and solid solution is common. (J.V.S./Ed.)

OXIDES AND HYDROXIDES

The oxide minerals. Ice and quartz are the principal oxides on the Earth's surface. Cuprite (Cu_2O) occurs in oxidized copper deposits, and periclase (MgO) occurs rarely in marble but may be a major constituent of the deep mantle of the Earth.

The spinel group. The spinel group of minerals, with the general formula AB_2O_4 (representing two constituents, A and B, combined with oxygen, O) contains a wide range of natural minerals and artificial products. The structure consists of cubic close-packed oxygen atoms with A and B atoms in 4-fold and 6-fold interstices, respectively, giving a structural formula AB_2O_4. To balance the electrical charges (eight negative charges are given by O_4), one divalent cation (II) and two trivalent ones (III) are needed. Normal spinels have II in A and two III in B, whereas inverse spinels have III in A and II + III in B; disordered spinels also occur. The distribution of atoms depends on subtle chemical factors and on temperature. Natural spinels contain principally divalent magnesium, iron, manganese, and zinc; trivalent aluminum, iron, and chromium; and quadrivalent titanium, but spinels can be synthesized from many more elements. Spinel of any colour can be synthesized; natural gem spinel (typically ruby colour) mostly comes from gravels in southeastern Asia formed by weathering of metamorphosed aluminous limestone. Spinels occur as octahedral crystals, often exhibit twinning, and may be magnetic, depending upon the properties of the ions in the A and B sites.

Magnetite and chromite (the only ore of chromium) occur as accessories in basic and ultrabasic rocks (igneous rocks rich in iron and magnesium). Gravity settling produces rich ore bodies. Magnetite weathers and concentrates in beach sands; it also occurs in veins and metamorphosed rocks. The zinc spinels occur as ores in limestones and schists.

Oxides with the general formula R_2O_3 have cations coordinated 6-fold in hexagonally close-packed oxygens. Corundum (Al_2O_3) and hematite (Fe_2O_3) are isostructures. Ilmenite ($FeTiO_3$) has divalent iron and tetravalent titanium atoms alternating in the aluminum sites of corundum.

Corundum tends to occur naturally as hexagonal barrels or plates in high-temperature rocks rich in alumina and low in silica. Its hardness (9 on the Mohs scale, which ranges from 1 to 10; see below *Hardness*) results in corundum-rich rocks (*e.g.*, emery) being used as abrasives. Most commercial corundum is made synthetically in high-temperature furnaces by fusing bauxite, however. Clear, coloured crystals of natural corundum are prized gems, especially those showing asterism (a starlike effect visible in transmitted or reflected light). Gem-quality synthetic corundum is used in jewelry, clock and instrument bearings, and in crystal lasers. Coloured varieties result from substitution of metals for aluminum: chromium in red ruby and iron or titanium in blue or black sapphire. Asterism results from exsolution into oriented shapes obeying 6-fold symmetry.

Synthetic corundum

Hematite, the most important iron ore, occurs in beds resulting from precipitation of colloidal (very finely dispersed) iron weathered from iron-bearing rocks. Complex chemical and biological reactions occur involving other iron minerals. Massive or powdered hematite is reddish, but museum specimens often occur as metallic flakes or as kidney-shaped masses. Powdered hematite is used in red paint and for polishing (jeweller's rouge).

Ilmenite is an accessory mineral of iron- and magnesium-rich rocks on Earth and in lunar maria. Its high specific gravity (4.7) results in gravity concentrations in igneous rocks and in beach sands; these are exploited as titanium ores.

Rutile and uraninite. The rutile group comprises rutile (TiO_2), cassiterite (SnO_2), pyrolusite (MnO_2), and stishovite (SiO_2). The tetragonal structure—consisting of three mutually perpendicular crystallographic axes, two of which are of equal length and longer or shorter than the third—has six-coordinated cations and three-coordinated oxygens. Rutile and cassiterite occur as stout dark prisms with a Mohs hardness of about 6½. Rutile is an accessory in high-temperature rocks, and cassiterite occurs in hydrothermal veins. The high densities (4.2 and 7) and resistance to weathering result in concentration in beach sands and alluvium, forming principal ores of titanium and tin. Anatase and brookite are rare polymorphs of rutile. Synthetic rutile is used in jewelry.

Pyrolusite, braunite [$(Mn,Si)_2O_3$], manganite [$MnO(OH)$], and psilomelane (hydrated barium manganese oxide) are principal manganese minerals of variable composition and crystal structure composing fine-grained ores of manganese. Such ores form typically in bogs from colloidal solutions derived from weathered rocks or in veins.

Uraninite has an imperfect crystal structure (similar to that of fluorite), and the composition ranges from UO_2 to U_3O_8. It occurs in pegmatites (very coarse-grained igneous bodies) and in veins. Alteration to other uranium minerals (uranyl hydroxides and silicates) and redistribution by sedimentary and solution processes lead to complex chemical variations and geographic distribution of uranium ores. Minor occurrences of rich pitchblende ore are now supplemented by low-grade sources of uranium minerals. Thorium and rare earths are major constituents of uranium minerals.

The hydroxide minerals. All hydroxides are low-temperature minerals typically formed from products of aqueous alteration or from hydrothermal veins. The crystal structures consist of hexagonal layers of cations bonded to six hydroxyls or oxygens. Interlayer bonds are weak, and this results in soft crystals. Brucite [$Mg(OH)_2$] typically occurs in magnesium-rich rocks subjected to low-temperature hydrothermal action or metamorphism (*e.g.*, serpentinite and magnesian marbles). Hydrated iron and aluminum oxides occur everywhere on the Earth's surface and represent the stable forms, with respect to which other iron and aluminum minerals are metastable.

The aluminum ore, bauxite, consists of boehmite [AlO(OH)], diaspore [AlO(OH)], and gibbsite [$Al(OH)_3$] plus iron oxides. Clay and laterite soil consist principally of aluminum hydroxides. Alumina is resistant to leaching and may precipitate as hydroxides that render the soil incapable of sustaining agriculture.

Limonite is an iron ore containing goethite [FeO(OH)] and other hydrated iron oxides of complex structure. The hydrated iron oxides result from weathering of iron minerals in aqueous oxidizing environments. Most deposits are sedimentary, but some specimens occur in veins as crystals or stalactites (deposits suspended from the roofs of caverns).

HALIDES

Fluorine substitutes in silicates of high-temperature rocks and occurs as fluorite (CaF_2) in veins. Fluorite occurs in cubes, often beautifully coloured (but rarely red) from various trace substituents or lattice defects (the two most common defects in crystals are partial slippage along a crystallographic plane and a void or missing lattice element). The variety Blue John from Derbyshire, England, is used for ornamental vases, but the softness (hardness

Fluorite

of 4 on Mohs scale) precludes its use as a gem. Fluorite is the principal fluorine mineral, and increasing demand as an industrial flux and for fluorinated organic materials of high stability has led to reworking of many old galena deposits, with which fluorite is typically associated. Fluorite and fluorine glasses are valuable for their high optical refringence (refraction of light).

Chlorine, bromine, and iodine tend to end up in solutions, and form a major part of seawater. Evaporation of aqueous bodies leads to sequential precipitation of halide minerals as each successive solubility limit is reached (see below *Evaporites*). The resulting sedimentary deposits are structurally weak and are squeezed into salt domes. Halides also occur in volcanic sublimates.

Halite, or common table salt (NaCl), and sylvite (KCl) are isostructural minerals that occur as cubes or in massive deposits. Sylvite is more bitter than halite. Although transparent when pure, many specimens are coloured by impurities. Carnallite, a hydrous potassium magnesium chloride, is a deliquescent mineral that occurs at the top of many salt deposits.

Cerargyrite (AgCl) occurs in the oxidized zone of silver deposits as waxlike, ductile masses. Atacamite [$Cu_2(OH)_3Cl$] is a green secondary mineral in the oxidized zone of copper deposits in arid regions. Cryolite, a sodium fluoride (Na_3AlF_6), is a very rare mineral used as an electrolyte for industrial electrolysis of aluminum ores and now mostly synthesized from fluorite. (J.V.S.)

CARBONATES

Carbonate minerals are naturally occurring substances that contain the carbonate ion $CO2-_3$ as a major structural and compositional unit. As a group, the carbonates are rather soft minerals with hardnesses between 1 and 5 on the Mohs scale; and, with the exception of the uranyl and the alkali carbonates, they tend to be relatively insoluble in water. Because the carbonate ion reacts with the hydronium (hydrogen) ion to liberate carbon dioxide gas, the carbonates are characterized by their solubility, often with effervescence, in acids. The crystal structures of many carbonate minerals reflect the trigonal (threefold) symmetry of the carbonate ion, which consists of a carbon atom centrally located in an equilateral triangle of oxygen atoms. The planar structure of the carbonate ion also results frequently in highly anisotropic physical properties in the carbonates, such as the high birefringence (difference between the transmission of light in different crystal directions) characteristic of many carbonate minerals.

Calcite and dolomite

Two common carbonates, calcite ($CaCO_3$) and dolomite [$CaMg(CO_3)_2$], are among the most abundant and widely distributed minerals found on the surface of the Earth. As the principal constituents of limestones, dolostones, and marbles, these minerals have a wide variety of commercial uses. For example, these materials are extensively used for building and ornamental stone, for concrete and road stone, for the production of natural and portland cements, and as fluxes in steel-smelting processes. In addition, calcite crystals are vital components in the manufacture of optical polarizing prisms; certain limestones are used in lithography; and natural and precipitated calcite is used in the production of candy, chewing gum, food fillers, glass, pharmaceutical products (antacids, antibiotics, etc.), rubber, toothpaste, and many other commodities. Calcite also is used as an ore of metallic calcium and as a raw material in the manufacture of other chemical compounds of calcium. Dolomite and magnesite ($MgCO_3$), a carbonate closely related to calcite, are used as ores, as chemical sources of magnesium, and as major sources of refractory compounds (heat-resistant substances used as furnace linings).

The most important carbonate minerals, whether from

By courtesy of the (left) MacFall collection, (centre, right) Illinois State Museum; photographs, (left) Mary A. Root—EB Inc., (centre, right) John H. Gerard—EB Inc.

Figure 6: (Left) Azurite (blue) and reniform masses of malachite from Zacatecas, Mexico.
(Centre) Flat rhombohedral crystals of calcite from Anthony's Nose, Hudson River, New York.
(Right) Divergent needlelike aragonite crystals from Huttenberg, Austria.

the economic or the geologic point of view, belong to three major structural groups (calcite, dolomite, and aragonite) within the class of anhydrous normal carbonates, which are those minerals that contain only carbonate as an anion and no structural water. Alkali carbonates and bicarbonates such as nahcolite, trona, thermonatrite, and natron are relatively rare, and are of geologic interest because of their unusual mode of occurrence. Certain other carbonates, although geologically rare, may locally be concentrated in sufficient quantities to be economically important as minor ore minerals. Such minerals include malachite and azurite which because of their aesthetic appeal are highly prized by mineral collectors (see Figure 6), lanthanite, bastnaesite and related rare-earth carbonates, and hydrozincite, and various uranium and uranyl carbonates such as rutherfordine, andersonite, swartzite, bayleyite, and liebigite.

Calcite group. Calcite occurs in a wide variety of geological settings and frequently forms large, well-defined crystals. It displays the widest variety of crystal habits of any known substance; more than 600 different crystal forms have been reported. Despite this diversity of possible forms, only a few are commonly observed. Calcite exhibits essentially perfect rhombohedral cleavage. Because all calcite crystals will preferentially break along these planes, virtually all crystal fragments of calcite will possess this habit.

The crystal structure of calcite is hexagonal-rhombohedral. The structure can most easily be visualized as consisting of alternating planes of calcium ions and carbonate ions, arranged with hexagonal symmetry within each plane. This parallel planar arrangement of the carbonate ions accounts for the extreme anisotropy in many physical properties of calcite. The high birefringence (double refraction) of calcite arises from the fact that light vibrating parallel to the carbonate planes is propagated much more slowly than that vibrating perpendicular to the planes. This results in widely different indices and angles of refraction for light vibrating in the different directions. Consequently, unpolarized light will be resolved into two plane-polarized components, refracted at different angles by the calcite crystal. This separation of totally plane-polarized light rays is utilized in the construction of optical polarizing prisms. Other anisotropic properties related to the planar carbonate configuration include thermal expansion and linear compressibility. With increasing temperature, calcite expands in a direction perpendicular to the carbonate planes but contracts in the parallel directions. This leads to a decrease in the rhombohedral angle with increasing temperature. Conversely, increasing hydrostatic pressure causes a contraction perpendicular to the carbonate planes but expansion within the planes.

Chemical composition and variability

Chemically, most natural calcite is relatively pure. Divalent (doubly charged) cations may substitute for calcium but only to a very limited extent. Small amounts of Mg^{2+}, Fe^{2+}, or Mn^{2+} commonly may replace Ca^{2+}; less commonly, Zn^{2+}, Ni^{2+}, Cu^{2+}, Co^{2+}, Sr^{2+}, Ba^{2+}, or Pb^{2+} may be found. The presence of even such small amounts of the transition metal ions Mn^{2+}, Fe^{2+}, Co^{2+}, Cu^{2+}, or Ni^{2+} may be sufficient to impart pale colours to calcite; however, strong coloration of calcite is usually caused by the presence of other finely disseminated minerals that become included during growth of the calcite crystals.

The anhydrous normal carbonates of all divalent cations smaller than calcium also crystallize with the calcite structure, forming an isostructural series. Of these minerals, otavite, gaspeite, and cobaltocalcite have extremely limited occurrences. Smithsonite, although not widely distributed, occasionally occurs in sufficient quantity to be mined as an ore of zinc. Magnesite, siderite, and, to a lesser extent, rhodochrosite occur in sufficient abundance and distribution to be of interest both geologically and economically. These three minerals form complete solid solution series (complete atomic substitution is possible) with one another, and minerals of intermediate composition within these series have properties proportionately intermediate between those of the pure end members. Solid solution between these minerals and calcite is limited, perhaps by the differences in ionic size between Ca^{2+} and Mg^{2+}, Fe^{2+}, or Mn^{2+}. Instead, intermediate compounds are found, forming the isostructural group dolomite, ankerite, and kutnahorite.

Dolomite group. Of all carbonate minerals, dolomite is second only to calcite in abundance, distribution, and geologic and economic importance. Compositionally, dolomite may be described as calcite with exactly half the calcium ions replaced by magnesium. Structurally, this is accomplished by the replacement of alternate planes of calcium ions in the calcite structure with planes of magnesium ions. This lowers the symmetry and more reflections appear in the X-ray diffraction pattern. Dolomite commonly occurs as a massive mineral and is only rarely observed to form well-defined crystals.

As in the varieties of the calcite group, Fe^{2+} and Mn^{2+} can substitute freely for Mg^{2+} in the dolomite structure, resulting in solid solution series. Although intermediate members are uncommon, it is likely that a complete series exists between dolomite and kutnahorite. The pure cation-ordered compound $CaFe(CO_3)_2$ never has been observed in natural or in synthetic systems; though a wide range of compositions corresponding to ferroan dolomites and ankerites may be found in natural materials. Because this solid solution series is continuous, the distinction between ankerite and ferroan dolomite is arbitrary. The name ankerite is commonly applied to those species in which at least 20 percent of the magnesium positions of dolomite are occupied by iron.

Kutnahorite commonly contains some iron and is frequently deficient in calcium, indicating that the manganese ion is large enough to substitute in part for calcium in the dolomite structure. Dolomite and ankerite, however, are almost never deficient in calcium but frequently contain a small excess, indicating that magnesium and iron do not enter the calcium positions in dolomite, but that calcium may substitute in part for magnesium.

Aragonite group. The third major structural group of the anhydrous normal carbonates includes aragonite, the high-pressure polymorph of $CaCO_3$, and the carbonates of all divalent ions larger than calcium. Aragonite, although a reasonably common mineral in modern sedimentary environments, is thermodynamically unstable with respect to calcite and, given time, it should invert to the more stable calcite structure. Accordingly, aragonite is unknown in ancient geological deposits; however, aragonitic fossil shell material as old as 450,000,000 years (Ordovician Period) has been described.

Structure of aragonite

Although the structure of aragonite is orthorhombic, it is related to that of calcite. The aragonite structure may also be visualized as consisting of alternating layers of calcium and of carbonate ions; however, the calcium ions form a distorted hexagonal close-packed arrangement in aragonite rather than a cubic close-packed type of array as in calcite, and each layer of carbonate ions consists of two closely spaced parallel planes containing carbonate "triangles" of opposite directional configuration. The c-axis of the orthorhombic cell is perpendicular to the calcium and the carbonate layers. The hexagonal arrangement of calcium ions within each plane results in a pseudohexagonal symmetry for the structure, which is reflected in the morphology of many twinned crystals. (A.M.G./Ed.)

NITRATES AND IODATES

In the geochemical cycle, nitrogen becomes present in water as nitrate ions—as an end product of volcanic emissions and the breakdown of organic matter. In very arid climates, nitrate is deposited as soda-nitre ($NaNO_3$) and nitre (KNO_3). Because of the very high solubility, other evaporite minerals such as halite are precipitated first. Alkali nitrates are also produced by bacteria and by reaction of organic matter with salts. Only the Chile deposits are really significant commercially. Most nitrate for fertilizer results from synthesis using atmospheric nitrogen.

The nitrate and iodate minerals are structurally related to the carbonate minerals. The most important nitrates are soda-nitre, nitre, darapskite [$Na_3NO_3SO_4 \cdot H_2O$], and humberstonite [$Na_7K_3Mg_2(SO_4)_6(NO_3)_2 \cdot 6H_2O$]. Among the iodates are lautarite [$Ca(IO_3)_2$] and dietzeite [$Ca_2(IO_3)_2CrO_4$]. The iodates are much rarer than the nitrates and are distinguished from them by their yellow colour. The iodate minerals occur sporadically and are commonly intermixed with the nitrates.

BORATES

The boron ion is very small and exists in both triangular BO_3 and tetrahedral BO_4 groups. Furthermore, the groups condense into clusters, rings, and chains. In this respect, the crystal structure of the borates resembles that of the silicates.

Borate minerals occur principally in dried-up basins (playas) fed by waters rich in volcanic emanations; many complexities result from resolution, reprecipitation, and burial of deposits. The principal commercial borates are kernite [$Na_2B_4O_7 \cdot 4H_2O$], borax [$Na_2B_4O_7 \cdot 10H_2O$] of mule-train fame, and colemanite [$Ca_2B_6O_{11} \cdot 5H_2O$]. All are white and have complex crystal structures. Thermal stability is low. Molten borax dissolves many substances, the metallic elements of which can be identified from the colour of the resulting glass bead.

A group of rare borates containing beryllium, aluminum, or magnesium occurs in contact metamorphic deposits (where various rocks are heated at the contact with an igneous rock body intruded at high temperature) and hydrothermal veins. All but one are free of water, but many contain hydroxyl. The rare gem sinhalite ($MgAlBO_4$) has an olivine-like structure with B in fourfold coordination (see below *Olivines*). The ludwigite group occurs in contact-metamorphosed limestones.

Boracite ($Mg_3B_7O_{13}Cl$) occurs in evaporite beds with halides and sulfates, along with a complex group of hydrated magnesium and calcium borates.

SULFATES

Approximately 130 minerals contain sulfate ions. In the geochemical cycle, sulfides and volcanic emissions of sulfurous gases tend to become oxidized. Some sulfates result from local oxidation of ore sulfides, but large sulfate bodies result from evaporation of sulfatic solutions. Barite, celestite, and anglesite are isostructural minerals in which tetrahedral SO_4 groups provide 12 oxygen atoms around the large cations to yield the compositions $BaSO_4$, $SrSO_4$, and $PbSO_4$, respectively. Barite typically occurs in veins associated with lead ores as dirty, massive deposits. Its low solubility leads to sedimentary deposits from limestone weathering. Barite is readily identified from its heaviness (specific gravity of 4.5). Barite can participate in major solid solution with celestite, but the latter is usually pure. Celestite is a relatively rare mineral that may occur in a variety of sediments, probably as a precipitate from solutions; it also occurs in hydrothermal veins. Anglesite is a rare mineral formed in the oxidized zone of galena ores.

Anhydrite and gypsum

Anhydrite ($CaSO_4$) has a different structure because the smaller Ca cation is bonded to only eight oxygens of the SO_4 groups. The symmetry is orthorhombic (three mutually perpendicular crystal axes of unequal length), and three mutually perpendicular cleavages are characteristic. Anhydrite occurs in massive deposits interstratified with beds of gypsum, carbonates, and halides. Seawater precipitates anhydrite above 42° C (108° F), or at lower temperature upon evaporation. Gypsum is deposited at lower temperature or lower salinity. Some deposits of gypsum and anhydrite probably were derived by alteration of the other mineral; that is, by hydration or dehydration.

Gypsum ($CaSO_4 \cdot 2H_2O$) is an important economic mineral, being used extensively in wallboard and cements for the construction industry, as fillers in paper and paints, and as a soil dressing. Its softness (hardness of 2 on Mohs' scale) and the waxy surface of the massive variety alabaster permit use in statues and ornamental carvings. Most gypsum is massive and stained. Rare, transparent, well-developed crystals are called selenite. Fibrous forms are called satin spar. The weakly bonded structure contains water molecules and SO_4 groups in a monoclinic cell (three crystallographic axes of unequal length, two of which are perpendicular and the third inclined). Swallow-tailed twins are displayed commonly in mineral collections. Dehydration near 100° C (212° F) produces the hemihydrate used commercially as plaster of paris because it rehydrates to a solid aggregate of gypsum. Heating to 200° C (about 400° F) produces anhydrite. Gypsum occurs not only in evaporite deposits, as noted above, but also in low-temperature hydrothermal veins and as products of volcanic gases.

Epsomite ($MgSO_4 \cdot 7H_2O$) and kieserite ($MgSO_4 \cdot H_2O$) are just two of the six hydrates of magnesium sulfate deposited by appropriate solutions at characteristic temperatures and subject to hydration and dehydration reactions as conditions change.

Chalcanthite ($CuSO_4 \cdot 5H_2O$), antlerite [$Cu_3(SO_4)(OH)_4$], and brochantite [$Cu_4(SO_4)(OH)_6$] are the three common sulfates formed as alteration products of copper ores in arid regions. The copper ions cause rich blue (chalcanthite) and green colours (antlerite and brochantite).

In salt deposits, glauberite [$Na_2Ca(SO_4)_2$] and polyhalite [$K_2Ca_2Mg(SO_4)_4 \cdot 2H_2O$]are important minerals. Other notable sulfates include mirabilite ($Na_2SO_4 \cdot 10H_2O$), which occurs as an evaporation product of saline lakes and as a soil efflorescence, melanterite ($FeSO_4 \cdot 7H_2O$), a greenish-blue weathering product of iron sulfides. Alunite [$KAl_3(SO_4)_2(OH)_6$] and jarosite [$KFe_3(SO_4)_2(OH)_6$], are isostructural. Alunite results from alteration by sulfatic gases in volcanic regions, whereas jarosite is formed by alteration of iron ores.

(J.V.S./Ed.)

CHROMATES

The chromates are a rare and localized group of minerals that have formed from the oxidation of copper-iron-lead sulfide ores containing small amounts of chromium. Crocoite ($PbCrO_4$), an orange-red monoclinic mineral, is the best known of the chromates.

The structural unit of the chromate minerals is a tetrahedron formed from four oxygen atoms, each at one corner of a tetrahedron surrounding a central chromium atom. Each oxygen atom has a charge of −2, whereas the chromium atom has a charge of only +6; thus every CrO_4 tetrahedron has a net charge of −2, which is neutralized by metal ions outside the tetrahedron. Unlike the silicate or the borate minerals, which share oxygen atoms between tetrahedra, forming chains, sheets, rings, or frameworks, the chromate minerals share none and are thus anisodesmic.

(Ed.)

PHOSPHATES, VANADATES, AND ARSENATES

The phosphate minerals. The element phosphorus combines readily with oxygen. In the course of this oxidation, phosphorus becomes a positively charged atom (an ion) surrounded by and bonded to four oxygen ions that are arranged as a tetrahedron. This arrangement is called the orthophosphate ion, or more simply the phosphate ion; it is the basic building block of the more than 200 reported species of phosphate minerals. The phosphate tetrahedron has a net negative charge of three, and this can be supplemented by additional negative charges from hydroxyls (OH−) or halogens (*i.e.*, fluoride, chloride, bromide, and iodide). Cations (positively charged ions) then balance these charges. A simple classification of phosphate minerals consists of subdivision into the anhydrous group; the hydrous group with hydroxyls or halogens; and the hydrous group with hydroxyls or halogens and water.

Phosphate ion

Anhydrous phosphate minerals. Xenotime is an yttrium phosphate (YPO_4) that occurs as an accessory mineral in igneous rocks and pegmatites. The mineral generally is found as small, brown, tetragonal crystals—those referable to three mutually perpendicular crystallographic axes, two of which are of equal length and the third shorter or longer—which are similar in form, structure, and properties to zircon.

Berlinite is a rare aluminum phosphate ($AlPO_4$) mineral that has been found at a single locality in Sweden. The mineral resembles quartz in its form, structure, and properties.

Monazite [$(Ce,La)PO_4$] is an accessory mineral in igneous and metamorphic rocks and pegmatites. It is one of the most important of the phosphates because of its content of rare earth oxides. These comprise a group of elements of similar chemical properties that are used as additives in glass, alloys, and solid-state devices. Monazite is associated with zircon and titanium minerals in placer concentrates (alluvial deposits) derived from igneous (crystalline) rocks. The crystals of monazite are monoclinic (*i.e.,* referable to three unequal crystallographic axes, two intersecting obliquely and the third perpendicular to both of them), generally small, and euhedral (perfectly formed). They have a flattened tabular form with angular terminations. Although the cerium–lanthanum ratio of the mineral ordinarily is about 1:1, most monazite contains thorium that substitutes for the rare earths and causes metamictization (alterations caused by radioactive emanations) of the structure. Because of the range of composition and metamictization, the physical properties show considerable variation. Colour is tan to brown, and hardness on the Mohs scale ranges from 5 to 5.5. The cerium–lanthanum phosphate has a density of about 4.6, but thorium substitution results in increased density, to 5.4.

Whitlockite [$Ca_3(PO_4)_2$] is a rare phosphate mineral found in the Palermo pegmatite, New Hampshire, and also in some phosphorite rock and cave deposits. It is the simplest mineral in which the charge of the phosphate anion is satisfied by divalent cations (in this case by three calcium ions). The crystals are hexagonal (referable to three equal crystallographic axes that intersect at 120°, in a plane perpendicular to a fourth axis of different length) and clear or white.

Triphylite ($LiFePO_4$) is one end member of a solid solution series in which lithium and ferrous iron combine with the phosphate anion. Lithiophilite ($LiMnPO_4$) is the other end member, manganese replacing the iron. Hardness typically is 4.5, and density is about 3.3. Colour ranges from bluish-green for the ferrous member to yellow-brown for the manganese member. Triphylite and lithiophilite are both orthorhombic (referable to three mutually perpendicular crystallographic axes of unequal length) and have a structure similar to that of olivine, an iron–magnesium silicate. Thus, the phosphorus has tetrahedral (fourfold) coordination, and both the lithium and iron or manganese atoms are surrounded by six oxygens, which is octahedral coordination. Triphylite and lithiophilite occur in pegmatites and are commonly distinctive because of a dark altered surface or zone. Most material is massive, and rare crystals lack distinct faces.

Phosphate minerals containing hydroxyl or halogens. Apatite is the name for a mineral series that is subdivided with each name indicating the major halogen or hydroxyl; the general formula is $Ca_{10}(PO_4)_6(OH,F,Cl)_2$. Thus, there is fluorapatite (containing fluoride), chlorapatite (containing chloride), and hydroxylapatite (containing hydroxyl). The mineral exhibits toleration of extensive substitutions for phosphate and for calcium.

Most good crystals of apatite are fluorapatite, which occurs disseminated in igneous and metamorphic rocks and in ore deposits. Sedimentary rocks composed principally of fluorapatite are termed phosphorites or phosphate rock, which is a raw material for many industrial and agricultural products. Crystals of fluorapatite are euhedral hexagonal prisms that generally range from clear to various hues of yellow and green; crystals of all colours occur in nature, however. The mineral serves as the reference material for the hardness of 5 on Mohs scale. It has a density of 3.2 and is distinguished from beryl and quartz on this basis and by reason of its hexagonal form and inferior hardness.

Phosphorites

The apatite structure is basically a hexagonal column with six calcium ions, one at each corner of the hexagon in a plane. Each of these calcium ions is surrounded by eight oxygens. At the centre of the hexagonal column lies the fluoride ion that is surrounded by three calcium ions, in a plane parallel to that containing the six calcium, but at a different level in the structure. Two phosphorus ions lie off each join or connection of two of the calciums of the hexagonal ring. Each phosphorus ion shares oxygens with calcium of both the sixfold ring and the threefold group. Thus, the structure appears as a framework with hexagonal form and a central cavity; this cavity is blocked twice in a repeat (unit) distance by centrally located fluoride that is strongly bonded to three calcium ions, however. The great stability of this structure is shown by the lack of polymorphic transitions (changes to other forms) with heating and by a melting point in excess of 1,600° C (2,900° F).

Good crystals of hydroxylapatite are extremely rare. They occur in three known localities in talc schists (foliated metamorphic rocks) or serpentine rocks. Their rarity indicates that crystallizing apatite is a scavenger for minute quantities of fluoride in the system—which is why fluorapatite predominates in nature. Hydroxylapatite is similar to fluorapatite in properties and structure. Structural changes involve only the substitution of hydroxyl for fluoride.

Chlorapatite is rare. It is reported from some meteorites, and it occurs in gabbro (igneous rocks rich in iron and magnesium) and related rocks in southeastern Norway. The density of chlorapatite is about 3.2, and the structure is similar to that of other apatites but differs in the position of the halogen. Because the chloride ion is 1.8 Å (one angstrom unit [Å] equals 10^{-8} centimetre) in size, it lies between two of the triangular calcium planes and not within the plane, as does the fluoride ion. Thus, chloride is surrounded by six calciums compared to three for fluoride.

Phosphate minerals containing water. Brushite is very similar to gypsum ($CaSO_4 \cdot 2H_2O$) in form, structure, and physical properties, but in its composition HPO_4^{2-} replaces SO_4^{2-} of the gypsum, thus yielding the formula $CaHPO_4 \cdot 2H_2O$. Precipitated gypsum has a long prismatic or needlelike form, and usually the crystals are twinned. Brushite has a blocky prismatic form, and twinning, the intergrowth of two or more grains of the same

By courtesy of the (left) American Museum of Natural History, (centre) Ted and Elsie Boente collection, (top right) MacFall collection, (bottom right) American Museum of Natural History; photographs, EB Inc., (left) Emil Javorsky, (centre) John H. Gerard, (top right) Mary A. Root, (bottom right) Emil Javorsky

Figure 7: (Left) Monazite from Elk Mountain, New Mexico. (Centre) Wavellite from Buckville, Arkansas. (Top right) Fluorapatite on limestone from Renfrew, Ontario. (Bottom right) Vivianite from Wannon River, Victoria, Australia.

crystalline phase according to some crystallographic pattern, is much rarer than in gypsum.

At low temperature, brushite loses both water molecules and forms monetite ($CaHPO_4$). Both monetite and brushite are rare minerals, found in phosphorites formed from guano, and are the only phosphate minerals containing principally the HPO_4^{2-} ion, even though this ion is the most abundant phosphate ion in natural aqueous solutions.

Vivianite [$Fe_3(PO_4)_2 \cdot 8H_2O$] is monoclinic, with phosphate tetrahedrons linked with ferrous iron in octahedral coordination. This linking yields a sheet structure having a perfect cleavage in one direction; it is rare to find crystals or massive material lacking this cleavage. Vivianite, colourless when first mined, darkens rapidly to a very deep blue, or purple; it has a hardness of 1.5 to 2, a density of 2.7, and occurs as bladelike crystals. Vivianite occurs in gossans (hydrated iron oxide deposits that usually form above iron sulfide veins or ore bodies) or from the weathering of primary phosphate minerals of pegmatites. It is present in fossil teeth, bones, and in phosphatic shells or hard parts of organisms, to which it imparts a blue colour.

Phosphate minerals containing water and hydroxyl. Wavellite, with the formula $Al_3(PO_4)_2(OH)_3 \cdot 5H_2O$ is an aluminum phosphate containing water and hydroxyl. It is a secondary mineral found in near surface deposits of alumina-rich rocks. Wavellite has a hardness of 3.25 to 4, a density of 2.37, and crystallizes in the orthorhombic system. It tolerates limited substitution of ferric iron for aluminum, and this results in a colour range from yellowish-tan to light green.

Turquoise

Turquoise is a copper and aluminum phosphate containing water and hydroxyl with the formula $CuAl_6(PO_4)_4(OH)_8 \cdot 4H_2O$. It is a secondary mineral prized as a semiprecious material for polishing and carvings. Most turquoise occurs as cryptocrystalline-massive nodules or vein fillings; crystals are extremely rare. The mineral is triclinic (referable to three inclined crystallographic axes of unequal lengths) and is distinctive by reason of its green hue and waxy lustre. Bone turquoise is a name incorrectly applied to fossil teeth and bone coloured with vivianite.

Autunite is a secondary uranium phosphate mineral with the formula $Ca(UO_2)_2(PO_4)_2 \cdot 10\text{–}12H_2O$. It crystallizes in the tetragonal system, and specimens appear tabular, foliated, and even micaceous (in tablets, thin plates, and sheets). The mineral is distinctive by reason of its form, bright yellow to green-yellow colour, and strong fluorescence.

The vanadate minerals. The vanadates are compounds of vanadium and oxygen that have crystallized under extremely restricted conditions. The internal structures of various group members consist of vanadate tetrahedra (VO_4). Such vanadates are structurally and chemically similar to the phosphate minerals.

Carnotite [$K_2(UO_2)_2(VO_4)_2 \cdot nH_2O$] and tyuyamunite [$Ca_2(UO_2)_2(VO_4)_2 \cdot nH_2O$] are rare but widespread alternation products of vanadium and uranium ores. Their yellow colour is distinctive.

The arsenate minerals. The arsenates closely resemble both the phosphates and vanadates in their crystal structure and solubilities. In fact, many arsenate minerals form solid solutions with both mineral varieties.

Adamite [$Zn_2AsO_4(OH)$], erythrite [$Co_3(AsO_4)_2 \cdot 8H_2O$], and annabergite [$Ni_8(AsO_4)_2 \cdot 8H_2O$], which are oxidation and hydration products of zinc, cobalt, and nickel ores, are important arsenates. Mimetite [$Pb_5(AsO_4)_3Cl$] and vanadinite [$Pb_5(VO_4)_3Cl$] belong to the pyromorphite structural group. These minerals form by alteration of lead sulfides using components brought in from the breakdown of arsenides and vanadium-bearing minerals.

(D.R.S./J.V.S./Ed.)

TUNGSTATES AND MOLYBDATES

Wolframite and scheelite

Wolframite [$(Fe,Mn)WO_4$] and scheelite ($CaWO_4$) are the principal ores of tungsten. Wolframite occurs in high-temperature hydrothermal veins and altered rocks, and scheelite occurs by contact metasomatism of carbonate rocks.

Wulfenite ($PbMoO_4$) is a minor ore of molybdenum and occurs frequently in weathered lead ores. Spectacular orange-yellow square plates are familiar to mineral collectors. The crystal structure of wulfenite is similar to that of scheelite. The structural unit of these minerals is a tetrahedral group formed by four oxygen atoms at the corners of a tetrahedron surrounding a molybdenum or tungsten atom. Each MoO_4 or WO_4 tetrahedron has a net charge of −2, which is neutralized by metal ions outside the tetrahedron. Unlike the silicate or borate minerals, which form chains, rings, sheets, or framework structures by sharing oxygen atoms between adjacent tetrahedra, the molybdate and tungstate minerals share none; they are similar in this respect to the phosphate, vanadate, arsenate, and chromate minerals. Because the molybdenum ion and the tungsten ion have similar radii, they may substitute for one another within the structure of any naturally occurring example; thus, they tend to form solid solution series. (J.V.S./Ed.)

SILICATES

The high abundance of oxygen and silicon in the solar system, plus the separation of much of the iron metal and sulfide as an immiscible phase, leads to the dominance of silicates in the planets with physical properties similar to those of the Earth. On Earth, the crust and mantle essentially consist of silicates with only trivial amounts of other minerals. There are approximately 600 silicate minerals, but the major rock-forming minerals at the Earth's surface fall into the principal families of olivine, pyroxene, amphibole, mica, feldspar, quartz, aluminosilicates, feldspathoids, clay minerals, and zeolites. Each of these families is treated in a separate section, *The major rock-forming mineral groups.* A few general relationships, however, are described here to provide a framework within the overall subject of minerals.

The SiO_4 tetrahedra and SiO_6 octahedra. The fundamental unit of all silicates formed at low to moderate pressures is the silicate tetrahedron, an SiO_4 group in which one silicon atom (Si) is surrounded by and bonded to four oxygen atoms (O_4), each at the corner of a regular tetrahedron. Although this tetrahedron does show various distortions from regular shape in different minerals, it is not broken down until extremely high pressures, where silicon assumes a new coordination, forming SiO_6 groups, in which one silicon atom is surrounded by six oxygen atoms, each at the corner of an octahedron (a solid with eight triangular faces that looks like two pyramids joined at the bases). This increased coordination (four to six) results in the higher density minerals that would be expected at high pressure.

Silicate minerals can be thought of as three-dimensional arrays of oxygen atoms that contain void spaces where various cations can enter. Other than the tetrahedral and octahedral sites, the positions of the silicon atoms in 4-fold and 6-fold coordination, respectively, 8-fold and 12-fold sites, are also quite common. A correlation exists between the size of a cation and the type of a site it can occupy: the larger the cation, the greater the coordination, because large cations have more surface area for oxygen atoms to make contact with than small cations. The most common cations that occur in silicate minerals include, from smallest to largest, silicon (Si^{4+}), aluminum (Al^{3+}), ferric iron (Fe^{3+}), titanium (Ti^{4+}), magnesium (Mg^{++}), ferrous iron (Fe^{++}), lithium (Li^{+}), manganese (Mn^{++}), sodium (Na^{+}), calcium (Ca^{++}), and potassium (K^{+}). Tetrahedral (4-fold coordination) sites commonly are occupied by silicon and aluminum; octahedral (6-fold) sites by aluminum, iron, titanium, magnesium, lithium, manganese, and sodium; 8-fold sites by sodium, calcium, and potassium; and 12-fold sites by potassium.

Chemical substitution. Elements with similar ionic radii often can substitute for one another in a mineral. In such cases, a complete substitutional series may be found, as between magnesium silicate, Mg_2SiO_4, and iron silicate, $Fe_2^{2+}SiO_4$ (olivine minerals), for example. Between these pure magnesium and pure iron compounds, called end-members, substitution of one for the other can occur in any amount, and thus any magnesium-to-iron ratio may be observed in natural minerals. If the discrepancy in the size or charge, or both, of cations is large, only limited substitution, also called solid solution because one end-member can be thought of as being "dissolved" in the other, will be observed, and a miscibility gap may occur between compositional end-members.

Silicates as geothermometers and geobarometers

Silicate minerals act as tiny probes that record the detailed evolutionary history of the rocks that contain them. For example, the composition or crystal structure of a mineral may give clues to its temperature history (geothermometry) or pressure history (geobarometry). The amount of substitution (solid solution) between compositional end-members commonly increases with temperature, and thus the miscibility gaps usually decrease in size with increasing temperature. In addition, the way that cations are distributed between the different crystallographic sites in the oxygen three-dimensional network is commonly a function of temperature. For example, if a mineral contains two different cations and two different crystallographic sites, the distribution of the cations among the sites usually becomes more random with increasing temperature. Thus, when calibrated, the degree of substitution (solid solution) between compositional end-members and the degree of randomness (disordering) of cation distributions in a mineral structure is useful in deducing the thermal history of rocks.

The element aluminum plays an interesting role in silicate structures because it can enter both octahedral and tetrahedral sites. As pressure is increased, however, aluminum prefers octahedral coordination (6-fold) rather than tetrahedral (4-fold). This increased coordination of aluminum in silicates results in minerals with higher density, as would be expected from a high pressure of formation. Thus, in some silicates, it is possible to correlate the amount of aluminum in octahedral coordination with the pressure history of a rock.

Major silicate structural types. Because the basic building block of a silicate structure is the SiO_4 tetrahedron, most of the important rock-forming silicate minerals can be divided into groups based on the degree to which the SiO_4 tetrahedra are linked together (degree of polymerization).

A common structure is one that contains isolated SiO_4 groups (Figure 8A). If the charge on the silicon atom is considered as +4 and that on the oxygen as −2, a SiO_4 group has a total charge of $[1(+4) + 4(-2)]$, or −4. To achieve electrical neutrality in a silicate structure, therefore, cations must be present in addition to silicon; their charges must total +4 for each SiO_4 group.

Double tetrahedron groups

Another common silicate structure type has double tetrahedron groups (Figure 8B) in which one oxygen atom is shared by two tetrahedra. The formula for this structural group is Si_2O_7, and the charge on the group is $[2(+4) + 7(-2)]$, or −6. Thus, cations must be added with charges totalling +6 for each Si_2O_7 group for an electrically neutral structure.

Further polymerization may result in a third structure type—infinite single chains (Figure 8C) in which each tetrahedron shares two oxygen atoms. The formula for these chains is (SiO_3), with a charge of −2 on each SiO_3 group. Another type of chain, a double chain (Figure 8D), occurs when two single chains are linked by the sharing of one oxygen atom between every second tetrahedron on each chain. The formula can be derived by counting the silicon and oxygen atoms in a portion of the double chain and can be expressed as (Si_4O_{11}), in which each Si_4O_{11} group has a −6 charge. In both the single and double chain structures, the negative charges on the groups require additional cations in the structure.

A fourth basic structure type contains sheets of tetrahedra, in which each tetrahedron shares one oxygen atom with each of three other tetrahedra (Figure 8E); the basic unit in these sheets has the formula $(Si_4O_{10})^{4-}$. The tetrahedra link to form interconnected six-member rings.

The last structure type to be considered is an infinite three-dimensional network of tetrahedra, in which each tetrahedron shares all of its oxygen atoms. This framework structure has no residual negative charge; because it is electrically neutral, it does not contain appreciable amounts of any other cations.

Substitution of aluminum (charge +3) for silicon (charge +4) will change the negative residual charge on a silicate group; for example, if an aluminum atom is substituted for one silicon atom in the basic formula for a sheet structure, the formula $(Si_4O_{10})^{4-}$ becomes $(Si_3AlO_{10})^{5-}$. Thus, in the three-dimensional network structures (framework structures), substitution of aluminum for silicon leaves a residual charge on the framework, as in the feldspars.

Economic importance of silicate minerals. Silicate minerals have considerable economic importance. Tremolite and anthophyllite have been used for filtering fruit juices and chemicals. Montmorillonite (sometimes called bentonite) is used in drilling muds. Igneous and metamorphic silicate rocks are used for building and monumental materials. The very abundant feldspar minerals are used as additives in paint and as a mild abrasive as well as in the manufacture of glass and in ceramics. Some silicates are prized as gems; among these are emerald, aquamarine, and morganite, all varieties of beryl; peridot; moonstone, amazonstone, peristerite, and labradorite, all feldspars; garnet; jadeite and nephrite, the two forms of jade; opal, onyx, chalcedony; agate, bloodstone, and quartz, all forms of silica; staurolite; tourmaline; and zircon. Spodumene and lepidolite are ore minerals of lithium. Muscovite and

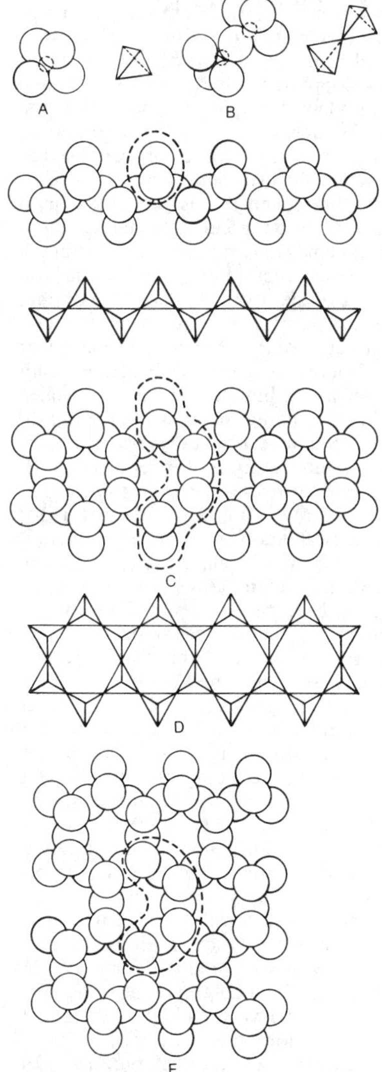

Figure 8: *Important silicate structure types.* (A) Isolated tetrahedra, with the formula $[SiO_4]^{-4}$. (B) Double tetrahedra, with the formula $[Si_2O_7]^{-6}$. (C) Single tetrahedral chain, in which the basic structural unit (in dashed ring) has the formula $[SiO_3]^{-2}$. (D) Double tetrahedral chain, in which the basic unit has the formula $[Si_4O_{11}]^{-6}$. (E) Sheet, in which the basic unit has the formula $[Si_4O_{10}]^{-4}$.

phlogopite are used in radio tubes, in capacitors, and in insulating of heating elements. Pyrophyllite is used in ceramics, paints, soap, textiles, cosmetics, and rubber. Quartz is sometimes used as an abrasive, and high-quality quartz crystals are used for precision electronic control components and for optical lenses. Andalusite, kyanite, and sillimanite are used in the preparation of mullite, a high-temperature refractory. Vermiculite is used for home insulation, concrete aggregate, agricultural chemicals, and fertilizers. Wollastonite is used in ceramics, especially for single-fired wall tile. Zircon is an ore mineral of zirconium and also of hafnium. (J.J.Pa./J.V.S./Ed.)

Properties of minerals

Simple visual and tactile estimations of mineral properties are increasingly augmented by complex techniques from the domain of solid-state physics.

MECHANICAL PROPERTIES AND SPECIFIC GRAVITY

Hardness. The simplest estimate of hardness involves scratching by reference minerals arbitrarily chosen for the Mohs scale in 1812 and placed in numerical order of increasing hardness: 1 talc, 2 gypsum, 3 calcite, 4 fluorite, 5 apatite, 6 orthoclase, 7 quartz, 8 topaz, 9 corundum, and 10 diamond. The scratch test must be made carefully because many minerals contain surface impurities. Quantitative estimates utilize the magnitude of indentation made by a known load applied to a known point (*e.g.*, the Vickers hardness test often applied to ore minerals). Each step on Mohs scale corresponds approximately to a doubling of the indentation. Hardness is a directional property, especially of kyanite, for which it varies on the cleavage face from 4 to 5 when scratched parallel to the long, or *c*, axis, and 6 to 7 in a direction that is perpendicular to it. The octahedral surface of diamond is the hardest of all minerals. The hardness tends to correlate with the strength of the bonds in the crystal structure, ranging from the van der Waals bonds of talc to the covalent bonds of diamond.

Mohs hardness scale

Cleavage, fracture, and parting. Strain beyond the elastic and plastic limit causes either irregular fracturing or cleavage along one or more planar surfaces. Fractures result from accidental irregularities, but cleavages are controlled by unequal (anisotropic) bonding strengths in different directions in the crystal structure; they always occur parallel to potential faces. The lubricating properties of graphite, talc, and molybdenite result from cleavage into tiny slippery flakes. Mica cleaves into thin, insulating plates that are useful in the electrical industry. In many minerals, chemical bonding is only weakly anisotropic, leading to imperfect cleavage. Parting resembles cleavage but is not an inherent property of the mineral; it results from various defects such as chemical changes and twinning.

Elasticity and strength. Under low stresses minerals are elastic, but under higher stresses some kind of permanent deformation occurs. In the Earth, velocity of seismic waves is related to these stresses (see EARTHQUAKES). The rigidity coefficients decrease with temperature and correlate with the type of chemical bonding and atomic packing. Metallic minerals are ductile (*e.g.*, will flow under high stress), and empirical relations for oxides and silicates are very useful.

Mineral deformation

The onset of permanent deformation occurs at lower stresses as the temperature rises. Controlled laboratory experiments, especially of carbonates and silicates, delineated the failure mechanism in terms of fracturing, twinning, and structural inversion. Particularly important are deformations induced by shock, produced naturally by meteorite impact and experimentally by explosions. The pressure and temperature rise very rapidly as the shock front passes, resulting in deformation, inversion to dense polymorphs, and finally melting as the peak pressure rises. Intensity of meteorite impact and nuclear explosions is calibrated by the deformation: for most natural silicates, melting occurs by about 0.5 megabar. Occurrence of coesite and stishovite, the high-pressure forms of SiO_2, is used as a criterion for meteoritic origin of circular features.

Specific gravity. The specific gravity of a mineral is the ratio of the mineral density to that of water at 4° C (39° F), and it varies from 0.92 for ordinary ice to 21 for platinum. Direct measurements of the ratio of weight to volume are affected by voids and impurities. Suspension in heavy liquids of mineral powder followed by determination of the heavy liquid provides higher accuracy. The density of a mineral can be calculated from its unit cell volume (determined by X-ray diffraction) and its chemical composition, assuming full atomic-site occupancy. Minerals are commonly separated in laboratories and industrial plants by suspension, or sinking, in liquids. Many monomineralic igneous rocks and economic-mineral deposits form by density separation.

MAGNETIC AND ELECTRICAL PROPERTIES

Minerals may be ferromagnetic, or attracted by a magnet (iron), ferrimagnetic (magnetite; used in primitive compasses), paramagnetic (all iron-bearing silicates), or diamagnetic—that is, repelled by a magnet (many iron-free silicates). The position of the magnetic field at the time of rock consolidation can often be determined from the magnetic direction of the constituent minerals (see below *Remanent magnetization*). Minerals are separated in the laboratory and commercially by passing them down an inclined chute between the jaws of an electromagnet. Certain ore bodies are located from their magnetic field, and subtle features of chemical forces and site distribution of atoms also are determined from techniques based upon magnetic properties.

Minerals range from electrical conductors (metals), to semiconductors, to nonconductors (mica and graphite). Minerals with good conductivity have metallic lustre, whereas most transparent ones have low conductivity. Natural and synthetic mica is widely used as an insulator. Nonconducting crystals with polar directions become electrically charged under compression (piezoelectricity) or upon heating (pyroelectricity). Quartz piezoelectric oscillators are used for generation of ultrasonic waves (militarily exploited for submarine detection) and provide highly stable frequency standards. Tourmaline pyroelectric crystals are used in pressure gauges.

Mineral conductivity

OPTICAL PROPERTIES

Light incident on the surface of a mineral is partly reflected, partly transmitted, and partly absorbed. Minerals

By courtesy of (top left, top right, bottom right) Ted Boente; photographs, John H. Gerard—EB Inc., (bottom left) Floyd R. Getsinger

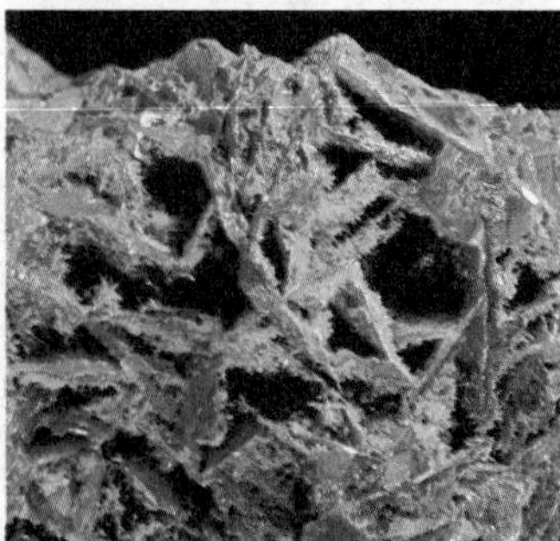

Figure 9: *Minerals in which colour is an intrinsic property of the species.*
(Top left) Brass-coloured chalcopyrite, $CuFeS_2$, from Ontario, Canada. (Top right) Red cinnabar, HgS, from Arkansas. (Bottom left) Yellow sulfur, from Racalmuto, Italy. (Bottom right) Green dioptase (a hydrous copper silicate) with orange-yellow wulfenite, $PbMoO_4$, from Arizona.

Figure 10: *Two types of crystalline aggregates at three levels of magnification.*
Most mineral crystals occur without faces (anhedral crystals) and as crystalline aggregates in the form of rocks. (Top left) Olivine crystals forming the monomineralic rock dunite, in which the individual crystals can scarcely be distinguished. (Centre left) Polished surface of the specimen (magnified 2 ×). Light green grains are olivine, dark spots are magnetite and serpentine. (Bottom left) Photomicrograph of the specimen in polarized light (magnified 12 ×). The different colours are due to the optical effect of the different orientations of the olivine crystals on the polarized light; most of the grains are olivine. (Centre right) Quartz, feldspar, biotite, and hornblende crystals forming the rock granite, a polymineralic aggregate. (Top right) Cut and polished surface of the rock (magnified 1½ ×). Large pink crystals are microcline feldspar, white ones are sodic plagioclase feldspar, small smoky ones are quartz, and black spots are biotite and hornblende. (Bottom right) Photomicrograph of the rock in polarized light (magnified 12 ×). White and gray crystals are quartz, light to dark bluish-gray ones are feldspar, those with irregular cross-hatching are microcline perthite, and those with finely ruled parallel lines are sodic plagioclase. Most of the green and brown crystals are biotite; the brown one in the centre is hornblende.
D.L. Weide

with a high reflectivity have metallic bonding, whereas those with a high transmissivity have ionic or covalent bonding. The optical properties vary with direction (except for isometric minerals—those in which properties are the same in all directions) and depend on the atomic nature of the crystal structure.

Colour of minerals

The colour of a mineral, as seen by the naked eye or at low magnification is a broad property that often depends on elusive factors. The colour of a metallic mineral is governed by the interaction of light with the surface. Some metallic minerals such as gold are chemically stable, yielding an intrinsic colour. Most are unstable, yielding a coating of a different colour (silver, copper, and many sulfide minerals). The intrinsic colour is yielded by rubbing the mineral on a porcelain plate to obtain a streak. The colour of a transparent mineral may be intrinsic (*e.g.,* green of the birthstone peridot), arising from interaction of the electromagnetic radiation with electrons, or it may be extrinsic, arising from inclusions (*e.g.,* reddish or whitish orthoclase). Intrinsic colours can arise from major constituents (divalent iron in peridot and copper in chalcanthite) or from minor constituents substituting into the crystal structure (chromium in ruby), or even from lattice defects. The colour may vary with the direction of light propagation (pleochroism), as in cordierite and alkali amphibole. Some minerals show a wide range of intrinsic colours (diamond, corundum, fluorite, beryl). The causes of some typical colours (blue and green of kyanite, green of the amazonite variety of microcline) are highly controversial despite extensive research. Sub-microscopic inclusions causing complex diffraction yield the remarkable light scattering of moonstone and labradorite. Flakes of iron oxide cause the light scattering of aventurine. Star gems (rubies, sapphires, garnets) contain sub-microscopic inclusions oriented in crystallographic planes. Although it can be helpful, colour is generally a poor guide to the identification of a mineral.

The reflected light from polished surfaces permits ready distinction between many opaque minerals on the basis of brightness, colour, and anisotropy (variation of properties with crystallographic direction) and is mandatory for study of ore minerals and host rocks.

Transparent minerals (especially in rocks) are commonly identified by transmitted light, using polarized light passing through thin sections or through fragments mounted in oil.

Most minerals have anisotropic optical properties, and incident light splits up into two polarized waves with different velocities. The plane of polarization and velocity vary with direction, and the principal indices of refraction, orientation of the optic axes, and variation of indices with wavelength (dispersion) and absorption of light serve to identify most transparent minerals, but the procedures are highly technical.

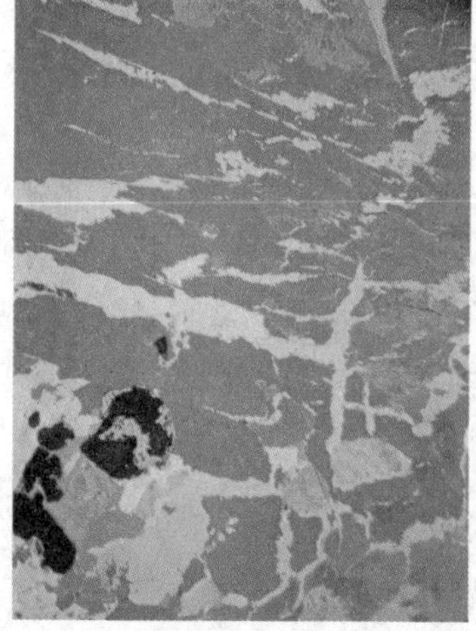

Figure 11: *Aggregation and intergrowth of ore minerals at megascopic and microscopic levels.* (Left) Aggregate of copper ore minerals (from Arizona) including bornite, Cu_5FeS_4 (reddish purple to iridescent blue where tarnished); covellite, CuS (dark blue); chalcopyrite, $CuFeS_2$ (yellow); and quartz and altered rock (white and light gray). (Centre) Photomicrograph of polished surface of what appears megascopically to be covellite (magnified 200 ×). The specimen is actually bornite that has been partly replaced by extremely fine-grained covellite (greenish-gray). (Right) Photomicrograph of central portion of polished surface to left, showing covellitized bornite (pink to red) more clearly (magnified 400 ×). Much more bornite is present than is apparent at lower magnifications. Also present are chalcocite, Cu_2S (gray), chalcopyrite (yellow), and tiny crystals of pyrite, FeS_2 (pale yellow), in the chalcocite veins.

By courtesy of (left) Ted Boente; photographs, John H. Gerard, (centre, right) Robert H. Carpenter

Advanced studies utilize a microscope fitted with a multi-axis stage for orienting the mineral; this permits the measurement of all optical properties. Routine studies of thin sections of rocks rely on the skill of the microscopist, who mentally correlates the properties seen in different grains. The degree of relief, polarization colour, position of optical extinction, shape, twinning, nature of inclusions, and other factors are all used to yield a probable identification.

THERMAL PROPERTIES

The thermodynamic properties are a function of pressure, temperature, chemical composition, and distribution of atoms in the crystal structure. Measurements are made of the specific heat, melting point, latent heats for change of state, thermal conductivity, and similar thermal properties. Differential thermal analysis involves detection of temperature discontinuities as heat is supplied at a constant rate: the discontinuities reveal structural changes that are diagnostic of some minerals (dehydration and structural readjustment in clays; bond-bending inversion in quartz; oxidation; structural breakdown).

RADIOACTIVITY

Minerals containing uranium and thorium provide commercial sources for nuclear energy and can be detected by radiation counters. The crystal structures of minerals containing thorium (zircon, allanite, thorite) commonly undergo a change of state by internal movement of recoiling atoms. Inclusions of these minerals in some other minerals are revealed in thin section by pleochroic halos; thus biotite is bleached.

Deliberate etching reveals the track of radioactive particles in minerals. The size of the track provides a measure of the energy of the particle. Study of minerals from the lunar surface is providing estimates of their exposure time to, and mass distribution of, cosmic rays.

Determining the ages of minerals

Several rock-forming minerals contain enough radioactive material to permit determination of the time since the radioactive material was incorporated in the mineral. The techniques involve accurate mass spectrometry and careful consideration of the thermal history of the mineral. The isotope potassium-40 decays to argon-40, but argon may be either lost or gained by diffusion, and thus misleading ages may be obtained. The uranium isotopes decay to lead isotopes, permitting a check on the concordance of the ages implied by the different decay series. The rubidium isotope, rubidium-87, decays to strontium-87, augmenting the abundance of the latter. Measurement of coexisting minerals with different amounts of rubidium and strontium permits estimation of the age at which the minerals formed together and the original isotopic ratio of the mineral system. Careful study permits selection of genuine ages from misleading ages, and the principal mineral-

Benjamin M. Shaub

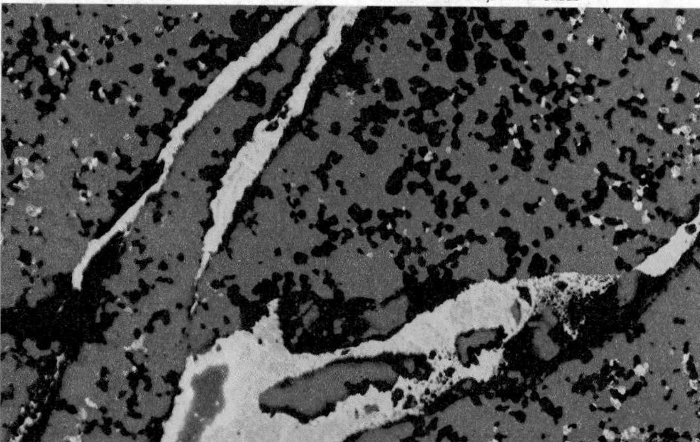

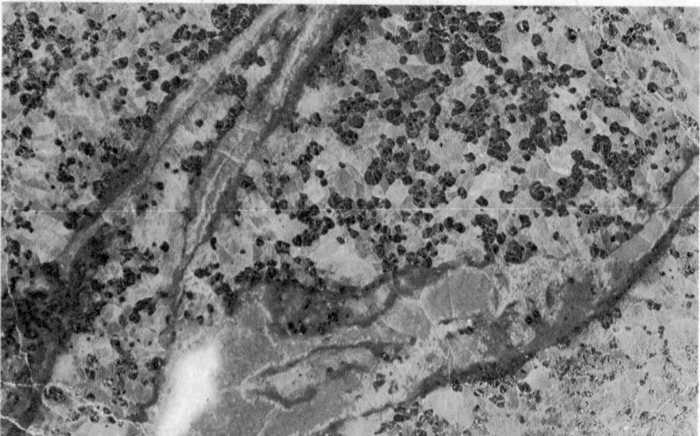

Figure 12: *Fluorescence in minerals.*
(Top) Specimen showing fluorescent colours resulting from ultraviolet irradiation of calcite (calcium carbonate; red fluorescence) with grains of franklinite (a zinc, manganese, and iron oxide; black because nonfluorescent) and veins and grains of willemite (a zinc silicate; green fluorescence), from Franklin, New Jersey. (Bottom) Same specimen in ordinary light, in which the willemite grains and veins are brownish gold and the franklinite grains are dark brown.

forming events on the Earth are dated (see GEOCHRONOLOGY). Isotope studies of meteorites and of terrestrial and lunar minerals yield crucial information on the chemical evolution of the solar system.

The distribution of stable isotopes between minerals, or between minerals and solution, depends on the temperature. The distribution of the isotopes oxygen-16 and oxygen-18 between silicates and oxides of rocks and the distribution of isotopes in biological carbonates yield estimates of their equilibrium temperatures.

LUMINESCENCE

The emission of light from a relatively cool mineral results from extremely complex electronic processes and from various energy sources. The luminescent colour bears no relation to the natural colour. Fluorescence excited by ultraviolet radiation permits rapid detection of certain minerals, including some uranium ores. Cathodoluminescence (excitation by accelerated electrons) is routinely used to identify some rock-forming minerals and to map variations of chemical composition as in carbonates and feldspars. Thermoluminescence is the emission of light released from stored energy levels by heating: it provides a crude estimate of the radiation and thermal history of certain minerals and rocks. Tri-boluminescence is the emission of light induced by mechanical deformation, as in sphalerite and fluorite. The electronic processes are known for very few luminescent minerals (*e.g.,* manganese substitution in red luminescing calcite). The phenomenon is erratically developed for most minerals, and for each mineral species there are several causes, including chemical substitutions and physical defects.

Fluorescence

Origin and distribution of minerals

Minerals result from a sequence of complex processes that began with chemical differentiation of the solar system to form planets and that ended, in many cases, with crystallization in rocks or ore bodies controlled by trivial local factors. The occurrence of minerals, therefore, involves a general understanding of geochemistry, geophysics, and petrology (the study of rocks), as well as special factors involved in the formation of ore deposits. Although spectacular advances have been made in these subjects during the 20th century, and particularly since 1950, the factors controlling mineral genesis are often controversial, and ideas can be expected to undergo revision.

The continuing changes on Earth and in the solar system result in mineralogic changes such that mineral genesis must be considered in terms of kinetic rather than static factors; most minerals become transformed to other minerals by reaction with air and water when they reach the Earth's surface, for example. The presence of water is essential because it permits concentration of elements to form ore bodies. The extreme dryness of the Moon inhibits formation of such types of ores, and, indeed, the number of mineral types found on the Moon is small. Under dry conditions, mineral concentrations arise principally from the processes of liquid immiscibility and from gravity settling of crystals from liquid. Under aqueous conditions, these processes are supplemented by incongruent solubility, by differential resistance to weathering, and by fluid transport and deposition. Biological processes also affect weathering and deposition on Earth.

Importance of water

In the magmatic domain, the classification of elements into lithophile, chalcophile, siderophile, and atmophile groups for those elements with an affinity for silicate, sulfur, iron, and oxygen, respectively, is extremely important in providing a guide to whether an element enters a mineral containing oxygen or sulfide or whether it occurs as a native element or enters the atmosphere. In the low-temperature aqueous domain, the relation between ionic charge and ionic radius controls whether an element is transported as a soluble complex anion (for example, the sulfate anion SO_4^{2-}) or a soluble cation (sodium, Na^+, for example) or whether it forms a hydrolysate, such as $Fe(OH)_3$, which is insoluble. The first two types may react to form a precipitate (*i.e.,* sodium sulfate [Na_2SO_4]). Finally, the availability of oxidizing material is important in determining the valence state of iron and manganese and in determining the extent and nature of alteration.

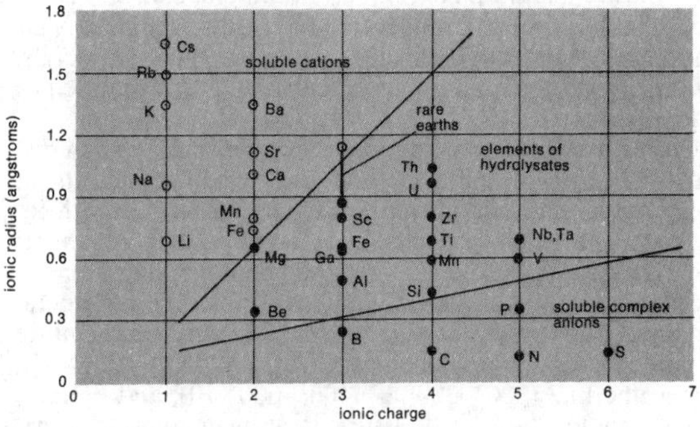

Figure 13: Consequences of ionic radius and ionic charge in geochemical processes (see text).

TERRESTRIAL MINERAL ASSOCIATIONS

Derivation from silicate magma. Volcanic rocks on Earth are extruded igneous rocks and are readily proved to have crystallized from a liquid silicate magma containing some water and volatile gases. Rocks of similar composition but of coarser grain size are recognized to have crystallized at some depth within the Earth. There is considerable controversy about the origin of such deep (plutonic) rocks, however, and about the origin of the magmas responsible for volcanic rocks. Almost certainly many processes, including melting, crystallization, annealing, remelting, and metasomatism (process of rock replacement), are involved. Particularly spectacular are kimberlite pipes (relatively narrow igneous bodies that extend downward into the Earth's crust) containing diamonds that probably were derived from depths of several hundreds of kilometres.

Igneous rocks are dominated by the silicate minerals (olivine, pyroxene, feldspar, quartz, feldspathoid, mica, amphibole); their differing proportions yield the various rock types. Accessory minerals (magnetite, ilmenite, sphene, zircon, apatite, allanite, fluorite, xenotime) occur in small quantities, but occasionally they are concentrated into ore bodies either by gravity separation or by later weathering.

During the crystallization of igneous rocks from silicate melts, the small amounts of water and volatile gases tend to concentrate, particularly in granites. This leads to the crystallization of especially large crystals. The concentrations may be small in volume (vugs) or may become large pegmatite bodies, commonly known as veins or dikes. Most pegmatites contain essentially the same minerals as the host rock, but a few pegmatites of great economic importance contain spectacular minerals of rare elements (*e.g.,* beryl, lepidolite, pollucite, cassiterite).

Metamorphic processes are commonly described as being either of contact or regional type. In the contact type, an intrusive magma heats an existing rock, producing a narrow zone of recrystallized minerals. Volatile gases from the magma may cause extensive alteration of the chemical composition, producing skarns. Such skarns may prove exploitable as ores.

Regional metamorphism involves burial (often of a sediment) followed by release to the surface after erosion. The pressure and temperature rise to a maximum and then fall. During the rise, the rock normally contains water, which acts as a catalyst for recrystallization. The water is essentially lost in the process, resulting in metastable persistence of minerals during cooling. Many sediments are rich in alumina and silica, resulting in the formation of aluminosilicates, cordierite, staurolite, and others, each of which forms at a specific range of temperature and pressure. Any type of rock may undergo metamorphism, however, resulting in extraordinary complexities that have been only partly resolved. Nevertheless, considerable progress has been made in estimation of pressure–temperature–time–composition relations for the great metamorphic cycles associated with sedimentation and mountain building (see also below *Metamorphic rocks*).

Typical metamorphic minerals in mineral collections are garnet, kyanite, staurolite, tremolite, idocrase, and wollastonite. Almost all silicates, and many other minerals, may occur in metamorphosed rocks; calcite in marble is a good example.

Veins, replacements, and secondary deposits. The crust of the Earth is unstable, and this condition results in extensive deformation and fracturing associated with igneous and other activity. The fractures form channels for aqueous solutions that deposit minerals; many are of economic value and are called ore deposits. The mineral deposits are loosely classified by the supposed temperature of deposition: hypothermal (300°–500° C [600°–900° F]); mesothermal (200°–300° C [400°–600° F]); and epithermal (up to 200° C). Pressure is also an important parameter. Typical minerals in this classification scheme are as follows: hypothermal—cassiterite, wolframite, scheelite; mesothermal—sulfides of copper, zinc, iron, and lead; epithermal—sulfides of antimony, mercury, silver, lead, zinc, and silver and gold as native metals. Gangue minerals (those associated minerals that are not of economic value) commonly include quartz and carbonates, among others; a few, such as fluorite and barite, may be of commercial value, however.

Gangue minerals

Solutions may percolate through porous rock, resulting in the precipitation of new minerals and alteration of old ones. Some of these replacement deposits, such as those of copper sulfides, have economic value.

Primary sulfides are unstable in the presence of air and water. A vein of primary sulfides becomes leached at the surface, producing a gossan (*e.g.*, decomposed rock) of quartz and iron oxides. Above the water table, oxidized and carbonate minerals such as malachite, azurite, and cuprite are formed. Below the water table, secondary sulfides such as chalcocite and covellite are precipitated.

In volcanic regions, escaping aqueous solutions mix with surface water to produce hot springs and fumaroles. Most of the deposited material is silica, but some deposits contain sulfur, sal ammoniac, sulfides, or oxides.

Sediments and precipitates. Upon exposure to water and air, most minerals break down to yield a residue and an aqueous solution. A few minerals such as quartz are highly resistant to alteration but are released by breakdown of other minerals to be concentrated into mechanical sediments. The products of breakdown proceed in several directions, depending on several chemical and mechanical factors. The hydrolysates form clays (mostly hydrated aluminosilicates), chert (silica), bauxite (alumina), and sedimentary iron silicates (glauconite, chamosite). Under oxidizing conditions, some iron and manganese become oxides. Under reducing (anaerobic) conditions, as in swamps, in the presence of sulfur-bearing material, iron sulfides and carbonates may be precipitated. Bacteria are increasingly recognized as important agents in both weathering and precipitation of such sediments.

Biological factors and the role of organisms

The soluble cations plus complex anions enter oceans and lakes, where they react with each other and with volcanic emanations plus the atmosphere. Biological organisms produce carbonates that yield limestone. Calcite and aragonite react with magnesium from seawater to form dolomite. Silica is incorporated by some organisms, such as the single-celled Radiolaria. Parts of the ocean floor and some lake beds are covered by nodules rich in manganese oxides containing other valuable elements. A host of complex organic and inorganic reactions occur in seawater, resulting in relatively small changes of composition. In lakes, the composition may change drastically as a result of variation of rainfall and of incoming and outgoing flows. Drying up of a basin leads to sequential precipitation of evaporite minerals as the successive solubility products are reached. The resulting layered beds of salt (*e.g.*, gypsum, halite, sylvite, carnallite) are of great value, especially as they are often associated with deposits of sulfur and petroleum.

Beach sands are commonly dominated by quartz grains sorted by prolonged mechanical processes. Heavy minerals may be concentrated into deposits of economic value (*e.g.*, gold, cassiterite, ilmenite, diamond).

Knowledge of marine and lake sediments is rapidly increasing as a result of deep drilling, dredging, and seismic studies. Marine sediments are composed of minerals derived from: rock fragments transported by rivers and ocean currents; windblown debris, such as desert sand and volcanic ash; chemical deposition, as in the case of carbonates, zeolites, and manganese nodules; death of biological organisms; and volcanic intrusions. The resulting minerals are slowly yielding evidence on the time of their deposition and the nature of the chemical environment. Ultimately the history of the ocean basins and continents will be derived from the mineral properties. For example, the recurrent beds of evaporite minerals in the Mediterranean Sea indicate cyclic sedimentation and dehydration associated with the differential movement of Africa and Europe. The concepts of sea-floor spreading and plate tectonics are being checked by the isotopic ratios of the minerals in these areas.

MINERAL ASSOCIATIONS OF THE MOON, PLANETS, AND METEORITES

Study of the lunar rock samples returned by the Apollo and Luna missions suggests that the most important factors controlling the formation of minerals on the Moon are: (1) crystal–liquid differentiation of material rich in basaltic components and low in volatile material, (2) an absence of biological processes, (3) absence of hydrothermal processes and water transport, (4) a high degree of reduction of transition metals and europium to low-valence states, and (5) liquid immiscibility.

Minerals of the lunar surface

The lunar maria (surface depressions) contain surface lava flows consisting of dominant pyroxene, plagioclase, olivine, and ilmenite plus about 30 other minerals. Troilite and native iron separated from a liquid immiscible with the silicate liquid. Spinel and armalcolite (an acronym from the American astronauts Armstrong, Aldrin, and Collins) are early minerals. The final products of crystallization contain an immiscible rhyolitic (equivalent to granite in composition) liquid associated with small amounts of apatite, whitlockite, pyroxferroite (a new mineral), zircon, and various other rare minerals.

The lunar surface is covered by fragmented minerals and rocks, some deformed by meteorite impact and others thermally sintered into breccia (rock consisting of coarse, angular fragments). Fragments rich in one mineral (either plagioclase or pyroxene or olivine) suggest mechanical processes for concentrating minerals by density fractionation in magma. Satellite photography and other remote studies of the surface indicate complex mineralogic variations over the surface that will be resolvable only by detailed exploration. Available data indicate that the highland regions are dominated by pyroxene and plagioclase, but most mineralogists and petrologists expect to discover many complex rocks in future lunar exploration. Occurrence of ice in shaded regions and of valuable mineral deposits cannot be ruled out, though the low content of hydrogen and of noble metals in Apollo rocks definitely indicates less favourable economic prospects than on Earth.

Martian and meteorite mineralogy

The mineralogy of Mars is speculative. Remote studies indicate polar caps composed principally of solid carbon dioxide (Dry Ice). The surface is heavily cratered in places but shows curious chaotic features elsewhere. The origin of the reddish colour is speculative; it may be due to iron oxide or to biological causes. Direct mineralogic studies were undertaken during the mid-1970s with unmanned landings. The high density of the planet Mercury suggests a mineralogy dominated by iron. The high surface temperature (near 500° C [900° F]) and high pressure (100 atmospheres, mostly CO_2) of Venus should cause an unusual mineralogy. Asteroids are prime targets for mineralogic study.

The origin of meteorites is controversial (see SOLAR SYSTEM: *Meteorites*). Their mineralogical and chemical properties are being pursued vigorously in an attempt to determine the development of the solar system. Important concepts governing the genesis of their minerals are: (1) condensation from a solar nebula falling in temperature, (2) mechanical accretion, (3) crystal–liquid fractionation plus metal–silicate immiscibility, (4) mechanical disruption, and (5) shock metamorphism upon collision of meteorites with the Earth. The high state of reduction results in minerals not occurring naturally on Earth.

The iron meteorites typically contain kamacite and taenite, iron and nickel alloys, troilite (FeS), cohenite (Fe_3C), schreibersite (Fe_3P), and similar mineral species. The stony meteorites are dominated by olivine, pyroxene, and plagioclase. Carbonaceous chondrites contain low-temperature minerals, including layer silicates and water-soluble salts (hydrated sulfates). Application of advanced techniques has resulted in discovery of many new minerals, including ringwoodite and majorite, high-pressure polymorphs of olivine and pyroxene. Some of the minerals not found on Earth are: osbornite (TiN); sinoite (SiON); oldhamite (CaS); lawrencite ($FeCl_2$); farringtonite [$Mg_3(PO_4)_2$]; and kosmochlor ($NaCrSi_2O_6$). Rare diamond apparently results from shock upon Earth impact.

The studies of meteorites and planets are changing the old parochial concept of mineralogy as a study of material from the Earth's surface. New concepts of solar mineralogy are developing rapidly as a result of exploration of the solar system, and studies of light from intergalactic regions suggest the presence of graphite and silicate grains.

Mineral synthesis and phase-equilibrium studies

Minerals are synthesized under controlled conditions to obtain information about how they form naturally and to produce commercially valuable products. Growth may occur under conditions of thermodynamic equilibrium, but commonly the first products of synthesis are metastable and only give way slowly to the stable materials. Even when the equilibrium conditions of mineral growth are known, care must be taken in the application to natural minerals. Kinetic factors are extremely important: indeed, if all mineralogic reactions achieved equilibrium, it would be impossible to obtain information about the mineralogic history of the solar system.

PROCESSES AND PRODUCTS OF MINERAL SYNTHESIS

Essentially all minerals have been synthesized, or can be expected to be synthesized, if the appropriate conditions are used. Some minerals that require complex atomic ordering have not been synthesized, however, presumably because of extreme sluggishness of atomic movement at low temperature. The most important examples are microcline and low-temperature varieties of plagioclase; their high-temperature equivalents with disordered atoms can be synthesized easily.

Several gem minerals are synthesized commercially, and the first synthesis of diamond in about 1950 resulted from technical advances of high-pressure research. Probably the most important synthetic minerals from an economic viewpoint are zeolite molecular sieves, which have revolutionized industrial catalytic processes. The synthetic relatives of the extremely rare mineral faujasite and other synthetic zeolites are used for a variety of processes utilizing petroleum. The industrial zeolites are metastable products produced by rapid reaction of alkaline material with aluminosilicate gels at temperatures around 100° C (212° F). Other important industrial minerals are crystals such as ruby used in lasers or in electronic equipment. Synthetic alumina minerals are used for industrial bearings and in clock movements. Synthetic quartz is used in optical equipment and piezoelectric oscillators. Synthetic diamond is a better abrasive than natural diamond.

Synthesis of individual minerals

Individual minerals are synthesized by choosing conditions of pressure, temperature, and bulk composition for which only one mineral phase crystallizes. Sulfide minerals can be synthesized easily by heating the appropriate source material in sealed silica tubes. Salts can be obtained by concentrating brine until the solubility product is exceeded. Refractory minerals such as corundum are synthesized by fusing alumina in a furnace using the Verneuil process, in which material melted by an oxyhydrogen torch crystallizes onto a seed forming a boule. Minerals stable only at elevated pressure, such as diamond, can be synthesized only in special high-pressure equipment.

Crystallization of some minerals proceeds rapidly only in the presence of a catalyst or flux. Fluxes may operate by producing a low-melting liquid from which the mineral crystallizes. The synthesis of diamond is promoted by catalyst or fluxes. Water is often an extremely effective flux; for silicates it increases crystallization velocities by many orders of magnitude.

Some minerals can crystallize only when the atmosphere is inert or controlled. Thus, ferrous minerals will grow only in the absence or near absence of oxygen gas: otherwise minerals like magnetite or hematite will form.

(J.V.S.)

PHASE EQUILIBRIA OF MINERAL SYSTEMS

The equilibrium assemblages of coexisting minerals are governed by various thermodynamic principles, discussed below according to the equilibrium temperatures and pressures involved. Mineral assemblages and pressure and temperature conditions believed to exist within the Earth at depths of about 100 kilometres can be reproduced in the laboratory. Such simulation enables researchers to deduce the kinds of mineralogical reactions that occur in the Earth's crust and upper mantle. The pressure–temperature (P–T) ranges of some of these reactions are shown in Figure 14.

From P.J. Wyllie, *The Dynamic Earth: Textbook in Geosciences* (1971); John Wiley & Sons

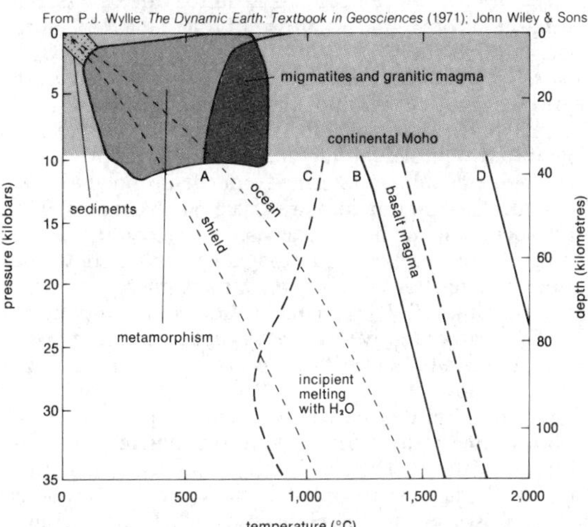

Figure 14: Ranges of pressure and temperature within which major geological processes occur. Dotted lines are estimated geotherms showing temperatures at specific depths beneath the oceans and beneath the continental shields (see text).

Metamorphism occurs up to pressures of about 10,000 atmospheres (one atmosphere is the pressure at sea level, 14.7 pounds per square inch), corresponding to the Moho depth—about 35 kilometres (22 miles) beneath the average continental crust. Line A marks the beginning of magma generation at higher temperatures. The upper mantle is believed to have a chemical composition between the plutonic rock types gabbro and peridotite. The subsolidus mineralogical changes occurring in gabbro and peridotite at pressures above 10,000 atmospheres are correlated with physical properties and boundaries within the Earth determined by geophysical methods. The zone above the line B shows conditions for the generation of basaltic magmas by partial fusion of mantle peridotite. Incipient melting can occur between the lines B and C in the mantle if traces of water are present. Geochemical reactions, like other chemical reactions, may be reversible; that is, the products of the reaction may themselves react to reform the original substances. If the rate of formation of the products and the rate of reformation of the original reactants are equal, the reaction is in equilibrium. The rate of a chemical reaction is expressed in terms of concentration, and the ratio of the two rates is embodied in what is known as the law of mass action, which is used to interpret the phenomena of geochemical equilibrium. (J.V.S./P.J.W./Ed.)

Basic concepts and laws. *Systems, phases, and components.* In the thermodynamic sense, any given system is an assemblage of material bodies interacting among themselves and distinguished from the surrounding medium by certain characteristics. Conditions in the Earth do not correspond precisely to those of ideal thermodynamic systems, but the latter provide concepts for the study of natural systems.

Closed and open systems

A closed system is one with walls that permit exchange of heat with the surroundings but no exchange of matter and is characterized by a fixed chemical composition. An open system can exchange heat and matter with the surrounding medium under controlled conditions. In geochemistry, the word system is usually used to describe the whole range of compositions that can be produced by mixing specified end-members (components).

The material within a system can exist in solid, liquid, or vapour state, given appropriate conditions of P and T. Each homogeneous portion of a system differing in composition or state and bounded by a surface is called a phase. Phases can theoretically be separated from each other by mechanical methods.

Components are defined as the smallest number of independently variable composition terms that are necessary and sufficient to express algebraically the compositions of all phases present in a system at equilibrium. Systems may be classified as one-component (unary), two-component (binary), etc., or multi-component, according to the number of components required to express the compositions of the phases present through the P–T range under consideration.

Phase diagrams and the phase rule. When minerals are heated they may change into other polymorphic forms (*i.e.*, they may change in crystalline structure), they may dissociate into two phases, or they may melt; at high pressures, many minerals are transformed into dense polymorphs. All of these transformations are called phase changes. The most successful method yet devised for recording phase changes is the use of phase diagrams, which show the equilibrium relationships among various phases in terms of the variables T, P, and concentrations of components (X). These are intensive parameters (*i.e.*, specific properties), the magnitudes of which do not depend on the size of the system.

For material of a given composition, such as granite or gabbro in the crust or peridotite in the mantle, the composition is defined. The phase changes can then be plotted on a P–T diagram. In order to show the compositions of the phases at various points, supplemental diagrams are required. There are $(n-1)$ independent concentration variables in an n-component system, n representing any given number. Graphical representation of phase compositions in a four-component system thus requires three dimensions, or a tetrahedron; for more complex systems, graphical representation is difficult.

The number of the variables P, T, and X, which must be arbitrarily fixed in order to define completely the state of a system at equilibrium, is called the number of degrees of freedom (f), or the variance of the system. The variance is the largest number of intensive parameters that can change independently of each other without decreasing the number of coexisting phases. A divariant ($f=2$; that is, there are two degrees of freedom) phase assemblage occupies an area on a P–T phase diagram; P and T can be changed independently of each other, and the number of phases does not change. At a given P and T, however, the compositions of the phases are fixed because there are no more degrees of freedom. A univariant ($f=1$) phase assemblage traces a line, and an invariant ($f=0$) phase assemblage can occur only at a single point on a P–T diagram.

The variance of a system is defined for p coexistent phases, each of which contains the same c independently variable components, by the Gibbs phase rule: $f=c-p+2$. The number 2 arises from two assumptions: (1) that the state of the system is defined by the concentration variables and only two others, namely, P and T—if other variables have to be taken into account, such as the force of gravity, electrical fields, or surface effects, then the number 2 has to be modified; (2) that the pressure is constant throughout the system, in particular across each interface. The second assumption is not true in the case of osmotic equilibrium between two liquids, and it is possible to have a system in which the pressure on the fluid phase is less than the pressure on solid phases; these conditions occur within the Earth. If there are two independent pressure variables in a system, then the "operating" phase rule becomes $f=c-p+3$.

Systems in the Earth's crust

The mineralogical phase rule. The mineralogy of rocks suggests that a close approach to chemical equilibrium is attained during many deep-seated processes. Consider a block of the crust of uniform composition with the same assemblage of minerals throughout; this assemblage may be treated as a system. During its formation the pressure varied from the top to the bottom of the block. The geotherms (lines showing the temperatures at specific depths) in Figure 14 indicate that the temperature also would have varied, as a function of pressure. The mineral assemblage present is therefore at least divariant. For a divariant closed rock system with P and T the only intensive variables, the Gibbs phase rule becomes: $2=c-p+2$, or $p=c$. The variance may be greater than 2, and, for equilibrium mineral assemblages formed in finite rock masses within the Earth, the Norwegian mineralogist Victor Moritz Goldschmidt stated the mineralogical phase rule: $p \leq c$ (p is less than or equal to c), or the maximum number of minerals that can coexist in rocks in stable equilibrium is equal to the number of components.

The phase rule for open systems. When solutions and magmas migrate within the Earth, geochemical reactions and equilibria can be represented in terms of open rather than closed systems. In a thermodynamic model for an open system there are two kinds of components: inert and mobile. Inert components, c_i, remain with the system; their concentrations are defined by the initial conditions. Perfectly mobile components, c_m, can migrate in or out of the system during reactions; the chemical potentials of the mobile components are defined by conditions external to the system, regardless of what happens in the system. The state of an open system is defined in terms of P, T, x_i for the inert components and the chemical potentials of the mobile components. The phase rule for such a system is $f=c_i-p+(2+c_m)$. A finite rock mass at equilibrium under these conditions has at least $2+c_m$ degrees of freedom, and the mineralogical phase rule for an open system therefore becomes $p \leq c_i$, or the maximum number of minerals that can coexist in rocks is equal to the number of inert components. The number of mobile components in a rock system, according to this rule, equals the difference between the total number of components (c_m+c_i) and the maximum number of minerals observed in the rock.

Many rock systems have been open to components such as water (H_2O) and carbon dioxide (CO_2), but it is probably rare for conditions to approach those of the model thermodynamic open system. Rocks are usually permeated by a limited amount of pore fluid (*i.e.*, a film, varying in thickness and nature, between the grains of a rock), and reaction of the fluid with the minerals changes its composition and the chemical potentials of the mobile components in the fluid. Only if large quantities of fluid flow through a rock, as in metasomatic processes (*i.e.*, replacement processes, in which new minerals of different chemical composition are produced by the introduction of material from external sources), are conditions in the thermodynamic open systems likely to be approximated. Components may be mobile but only rarely perfectly mobile.

Phase equilibria of mineral assemblages. *One-component, two-component, and multi-component systems.* There are several approaches to the use of phase equilibria concepts that apply to petrological (*i.e.*, ore, mineral, and rock) and geochemical investigations. One approach is to study the phase relationships of a single mineral. For example, Figure 15 shows univariant phase transition boundaries for the one-component systems silicon dioxide (SiO_2), calcium carbonate ($CaCO_3$), and aluminum silicate (Al_2SiO_5). These boundaries provide limits for the conditions of formation of rocks containing the polymorphs involved. Another approach is to study a synthetic mineral assemblage or system, as a model for the more complex rock system under consideration. A third approach is to work with whole-rock multi-component systems and to determine the conditions for the occurrence of specific

Study of synthetic mineral assemblage

reactions; the conditions can be plotted on P–T diagrams, but the compositions of phases involved have to be represented separately.

Solid–solid reactions. Several types of solid–solid mineral reactions are shown in Figure 15. There are polymorphic transitions in unary systems as mentioned above. Minerals that are stable in the Earth's crust may become unstable at high pressures, as shown by the breakdown of plagioclase feldspar (albite–anorthite solid solutions) to

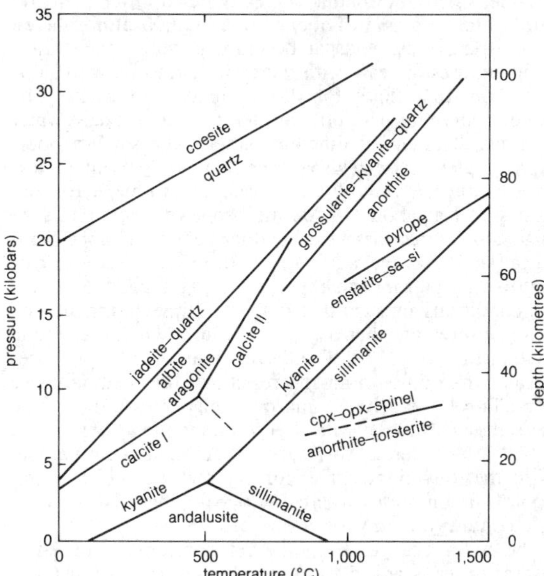

Figure 15: Solid–solid phase transitions in simple mineral systems. Abbreviations: cpx—clinopyroxene; opx—orthopyroxene; sa—sapphirine; si—sillimanite.

yield quartz and the dense minerals jadeite, kyanite, and zoisite. The stability range may be affected considerably if other minerals are involved. The reaction of anorthite with forsterite is shown at pressures much lower than the breakdown of anorthite alone. Many minerals can form stably only at high pressures, as illustrated by the formation of pyrope garnet from three other minerals. Changes of temperature or pressure may affect the compositions of coexisting minerals, and this is another important type of solid–solid reaction, one that cannot be illustrated conveniently on a P–T diagram.

The reactions in Figure 15 are univariant. In multicomponent rock systems, many similar reactions are divariant or multi-variant, and they occur through a transition interval. One of the most significant is the transformation of gabbro, a rock that generally consists of calcic plagioclase and augite (a clinopyroxene), to eclogite, a rock with the same composition but different mineralogy. This involves transitions similar to the reactions plotted in Figure 15; plagioclase and augite become unstable, and jadeitic pyroxene and pyrope are produced at their expense. Experimental determination of this transformation is difficult because reaction rates are extremely slow at temperatures below 900° C (1,650° F).

Dissociation reactions. Carbonates and hydrous minerals are stable only to their dissociation temperatures. The general shape of univariant dehydration reactions is shown in Figure 16 by the curves for serpentine, muscovite, amphibole, and phlogopite; and the curve for magnesite is the sole example given of a decarbonation reaction. The dissociation temperatures of individual minerals are lowered if other minerals become involved, as shown by the curves for serpentine + brucite and muscovite + quartz.

The curves for hydrous or carbonated minerals and assemblages show the maximum temperatures for their stability under subsolidus conditions (*i.e.*, below the melting temperatures of the chemical system). Dissociation temperatures are lowered if the partial pressure of the volatile component involved, water (H_2O) or carbon dioxide (CO_2), respectively, is decreased compared to the total pressure on the solid minerals. This condition can arise in natural rock systems if the pore fluid contains additional components or if the pore fluid pressure is less than the load pressure, a condition that could occur if the vapour released migrates away from the rock. The dashed line for total pressures greater than 2,000 atmospheres shows the dissociation of muscovite + quartz if $P\,H_2O$ is maintained constant at 2,000 atmospheres. This line is a contour for constant $P\,H_2O$ on a divariant surface for the reaction in a system in which there are three independent variables, P_{total}, $P\,H_2O$, and T (see discussion of open systems).

Behaviour of rock-forming minerals

The temperature of dissociation increases with pressure, and for many minerals melting temperatures may be reached. Invariant points in Figure 16 show the pressures above which phlogopite, muscovite, and muscovite + quartz dissociate to yield a liquid rather than a vapour phase. Some amphibole minerals behave the same. In the presence of a liquid phase, in contrast with the subsolidus dissociation reactions, the stability temperatures for hydrous minerals are increased if the partial pressure of water (H_2O) is decreased compared with the total pressure, shown by the curves for phlogopite in Figure 16.

With increasing pressure, the slope of the curve (dP/dT) of dissociation reactions, representing the rate of change of Pressure with Temperature, also increases toward the vertical. The slope for the dissociation curve of amphibole changes from positive to negative at pressures above about 18,000 atmospheres, in which region magnesian garnet and jadeitic pyroxene are produced; the change in slope from positive to negative is thus related to the gabbro–eclogite phase transition and the formation of dense minerals.

Geological processes include not only dissociation reactions but also hydration and carbonation reactions. The univariant curves and associated divariant surfaces for open systems provide P, T, and composition limits. The proportions of water and carbon dioxide in migrating solutions determine whether an assemblage including hydrous minerals becomes carbonated or whether one including carbonates becomes hydrated. Experimental determination in the laboratory establishes values for equivalent reactions occurring in open systems in the Earth.

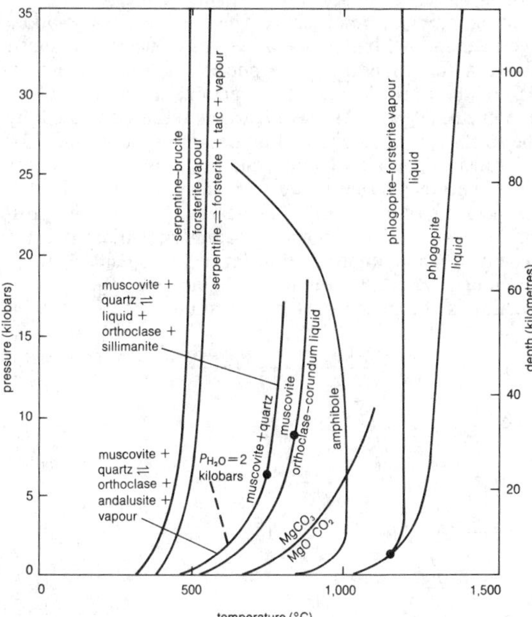

Figure 16: Dehydration and decarbonation relations in mineral systems.

Melting reactions. In Figure 17B the univariant melting curve for a one-component system, albite, is shown. At fixed pressure albite melts completely at constant temperature. The effect of pressure is to increase the melting temperature; the slope of the melting curve (dP/dT) is steep and positive. The subsolidus curve for the breakdown of albite to form jadeite + quartz meets the albite melting curve at an invariant point; at higher pressures the system becomes binary, and the melting reaction becomes jadeite + quartz ⇌ liquid. This reaction is univariant, but for mixtures of jadeite and quartz that do not have the composition of the liquid produced (this is fixed at a given P and T, as shown by application of the phase rule), the mineral assemblage melts through a temperature interval, beginning at the univariant curve. (The reverse curvature for the albite melting curve below the invariant point is part of a complex series of changes.)

From A. Boettcher and P. Wyllie, "Phase Relationships in the System $NaAlSiO_4$–SiO_2–H_2O to 35 Kilobars Pressure," *American Journal of Science*, Vol. 267 (1969)

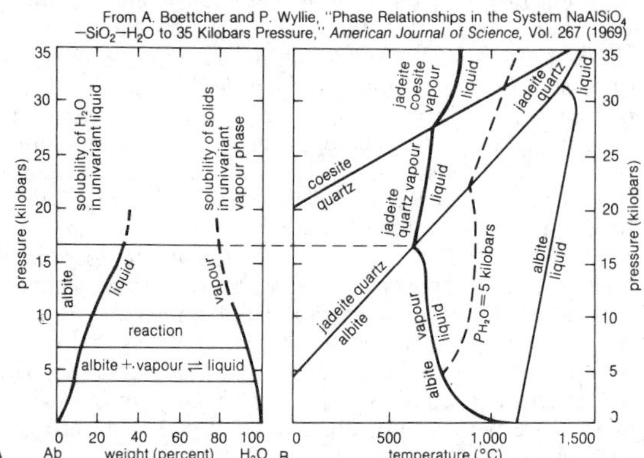

Figure 17: *Phase relationships for composition on the join albite–water.*
(A) Variations in composition of phases for the reaction albite + vapour = liquid. (B) Univariant melting curves and solid–solid transitions (see text).

Multi-component rock systems also have melting intervals. The curve for the beginning of melting of peridotite is shown in Figure 18, with a steep positive slope. The melting interval for peridotite is indicated in Figure 14 between the lines B and D. The composition of the liquid produced by partial melting of the peridotite, within a temperature interval above the solidus, corresponds in composition to basaltic magmas; the composition varies with temperature above the solidus, and with pressure.

Melting in the presence of water. Also shown in Figure 17B is the effect of water vapour under pressure on the melting temperature of albite. There is initially a marked decrease in melting temperature; this effect is reduced above a few thousand atmospheres, but the slope (dP/dT) of the univariant reaction remains negative until albite breaks down. At the invariant point generated by the formation of jadeite and quartz, the solidus curve for mixtures in the albite–water composition range changes slope, becomes ternary, and with increasing pressure the temperature of melting for jadeite and quartz in the presence of water vapour increases. Another invariant point is generated where quartz is transformed to coesite. If there is enough water to saturate the liquid (see Figure 17A), melting is completed on the univariant curve for the binary mineral-water system, but for the ternary system, the univariant solidus curve is the beginning of melting; only mixtures corresponding to the first liquid produced melt at one temperature.

Effect of excess water

This melting pattern is general for minerals in the presence of excess water. The effect of water vapour under pressure on the temperatures of beginning of melting of the major crustal rock types is shown in Figure 18. These reactions follow the same pattern; there is a low-pressure regime, where the solidus curves trend to lower temperatures, and at pressures above about 15,000 atmospheres, where plagioclase feldspar becomes unstable, the solidus temperatures increase with increasing pressure, with slope approximating those for dry minerals and rocks. The solidus curve for peridotite in the presence of excess water exhibits a somewhat different pattern; the small proportion of plagioclase feldspar that may be present at low pressures reacts with olivine to yield aluminous pyroxenes and spinel at about 10,000 atmospheres (Figure 15). At higher pressures there is a gradual change in slope from negative to positive, associated with the formation of garnet peridotite from spinel peridotite (see Figure 15).

Effect of water deficiency

If conditions are such that $P_{H_2O} < P_{total}$, then the melting temperatures are increased, as is illustrated for a simple system in Figure 17B. The dashed line for total pressures greater than 5,000 atmospheres shows the melting curve for albite (or jadeite + quartz at high pressures) in the presence of vapour with P_{H_2O} maintained constant at 5,000 atmospheres. This curve is approximately parallel with the univariant curves for dry melting, which correspond to conditions where $P_{H_2O} = 0$. This dashed curve is a contour on a divariant surface.

The main changes in phase relationships produced if excess water is added to a dry rock are that solidus and liquidus temperatures are lowered, the melting interval between solidus and liquidus is increased, and hydrous minerals such as mica and amphibole are stabilized; these relationships become involved in reactions including a liquid (see Figure 16). For a granodiorite (a plutonic rock) with excess water at a fixed pressure of 2,000 atmospheres, Figure 19 shows the successive equilibrium assemblages, bounded by isothermal reaction lines, within the melting interval (see composition IV); the temperature interval is 270° C (490° F). For the dehydrated granodiorite composition (I), the melting interval is only 130° C (230° F), between n' and n.

Most natural conditions are water deficient, and the reactions through the melting interval of a rock are more like those for compositions II or III in Figure 19. The shaded area left of line a–b–c–d is vapour absent; there is insufficient water to saturate the liquid and hydrous minerals in the assemblages. The main changes caused by passing from the vapour-present phase fields into the vapour-absent phase fields, with progressive decrease in water content (and in P_{H_2O}), are that the liquidus temperature increases, the temperature interval between solidus and liquidus increases, the temperature stabilities of the hydrous minerals (biotite and hornblende) increase, and the amount of liquid in a given temperature interval above the solidus decreases. In composition II, containing no vapour-phase subsolidus, the temperature of beginning of melting is about 160° C (290° F) higher than for subsolidus assemblages with vapour; melting does not begin until biotite begins to dissociate, releasing water to dissolve in the liquid.

In the P–X diagram of Figure 17A are shown the compositions of the three phases, albite (Ab), liquid (L), and vapour (V), involved in the univariant melting reaction Ab + V ⇌ L, at pressures up to the invariant point at which albite breaks down. The line for the liquid composition gives the solubility of water (H_2O) in the silicate liquid as a function of pressure, and similarly the line for the vapour composition gives the solubility of the solid components in the vapour phase; the temperature varies along these curves, as shown by the corresponding reaction curve in Figure 17B. Experimental data are sparse, but the general pattern for other silicate minerals and rocks at pressures up to 10,000 atmospheres appears to be similar to that illustrated, although specific solubility values vary with the composition of the minerals and rocks involved.

From *Journal of Geology*,

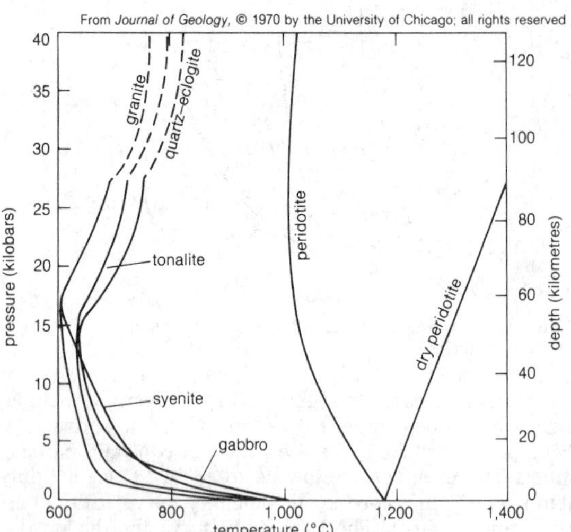

Figure 18: Melting points of major rock types in the presence of water with $H_2O = P_{total}$, compared with the solidus for dry peridotite.

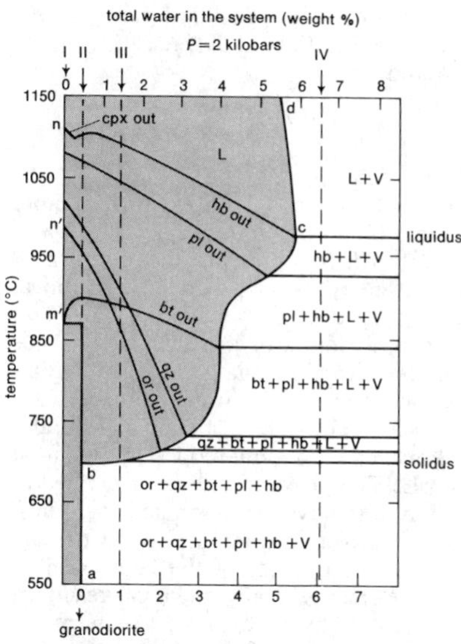

Figure 19: The system anhydrous granodiorite-water, showing the melting interval for system with excess water (IV), for water-deficient conditions (III and II), and for the dehydrated rock (I). Abbreviations: or—alkali feldspar; qz—quartz; bt—biotite; pl—plagioclase; hb—hornblende; cpx—clinopyroxene; L—liquid; V—vapour.

From *Journal of Geology*, © 1971 by the University of Chicago; all rights reserved

The solid components usually dissolve in the vapour phase in proportions different from their proportions in the mineral or rock, an effect that becomes more marked as the total solubility increases. At a given pressure, the solubility of water in silicate liquids decreases as the temperature increases, and the solubility of solid components in the vapour phase increases.

Reactions involving other volatile constituents. The dashed line in Figure 17B shows the effect of insoluble volatile components on the melting temperatures. If other volatile components more soluble in the silicate liquid than water are added, then melting temperatures are lowered. Experiments have been conducted using dilute acids or salt solutions. Experimental techniques have been developed for controlling oxygen fugacities (the pressure of a perfect gas is called the fugacity; it may be derived mathematically from measured pressure) at low levels of the order of 10^{-30} atmospheres while $P\,H_2O$ is controlled independently at pressures up to several thousand atmospheres. These techniques make possible evaluation of the effect of oxygen fugacity and the oxidation state of iron on the stability ranges and melting reactions of iron-bearing minerals and rocks. The study of systems containing sulfur as a component has bearing on the origin of ore deposits, and attention has been directed toward experimental determination of the solubilities of sulfides in solutions. Another type of experimental study deals with the distribution of oxygen isotopes among minerals and fluids as a function of temperature.

Geological thermometry and barometry. A P–T phase diagram based on mineral reactions measured in the laboratory is an effective means of estimating temperatures and pressures of formation of rocks on the basis of their mineralogy. Some reactions are suitable for estimating temperatures, and others for estimating pressures.

Other aspects of geochemical reactions or equilibria provide similar information. The compositions of coexisting minerals, for example, are usually sensitive to changes in temperature and only slightly changed by pressure. Calibration by experimental studies provides temperature estimates within specific mineral facies. Other combinations are sensitive to pressure changes. The distribution of oxygen isotopes among coexisting minerals is a function of temperature, and this fact provides another geological thermometer that has been calibrated by high pressure geochemical experimentation. (P.J.W./Ed.)

Low-temperature, low-pressure studies of geochemical equilibria. Studies of this kind are concerned with the processes that take place between the lowest temperature on Earth and approximately 400° C (750° F), and between near vacuum and several kilobars of pressure (one bar = 0.987 atmosphere = 14.7 pounds per square inch). Such mineral reactions at the Earth's surface generally occur in the presence of aqueous solutions (*e.g.,* those characteristic of the ocean environment or the hydrosphere) and are governed by the oxidation–reduction conditions as well as the concentrations of cations and anions in the solutions. Difficulty of obtaining equilibrium at low temperatures has led to a major attempt to calculate the stability of mineral assemblages from the measurable thermodynamic properties of the individual minerals. Combination of these calculations and observations of both synthetic and natural mineral assemblages has produced a good understanding of mineralogic processes at the Earth's surface, but the details are complex. Some principles of special relevance to understanding geochemical equilibria at low temperatures and pressures are considered below, as are geochemical diagrams that are employed to delimit environmental conditions. (J.V.S./Ed.)

Standard state, activity, and activity coefficient. A standard state for a given substance is the sum of its physical and chemical properties at an arbitrary set of reference conditions; a standard state may be varied for convenience, depending on the problem. In its standard state, the activity of a pure phase is defined as unity. The standard state of a pure solid phase (whether an element or compound), for example, is generally chosen at a specified temperature and, usually, at one atmosphere total pressure. Thus, the standard state of the mineral corundum, Al_2O_3, at 35° C or 95° F (308.16 K) would be written $Al_2O_{3\,\text{corundum}}$, 308.16° and would have unit activity.

Free energy and equilibrium. If a system is not at equilibrium, it will tend to react spontaneously with a release of energy. The so-called Gibbs free-energy function, ΔG, provides a true measure of the driving force of a chemical reaction because free energy connotes the available work that can be done by a system. The Gibbs free energy of reaction is the sum of the free energies of formation of products less the sum of the free energies of formation of reactants; that is: Gibbs free energy

$$\Delta G_R{}^0 = \Sigma \Delta G_{f\,\text{products}} - \Sigma \Delta G^0{}_{f\,\text{reactants}},$$

in which $G_R{}^0$ is the free energy of the reaction and the Greek letter sigma, Σ, represents a summation. When $\Delta G_R{}^0$ is zero, there is no net chemical work obtainable; the system is at equilibrium. If $\Delta G_R{}^0$ is negative, the process may proceed spontaneously; a positive value means that work (energy) must be put into the system for the reaction to proceed. The equilibrium constant can be calculated from $\Delta G_R{}^0$ according to the relation

$$\Delta G_R{}^0 = -RT\ln K_{eq},$$

in which R is a constant, T is temperature, and $\ln K_{eq}$ is the natural logarithm of the equilibrium constant.

The standard state for the calculation of free-energy values is commonly taken as that of the pure substance at 25° C or 77° F (298.16 K) and one atmosphere total pressure. Because natural systems of interest are commonly at some temperature other than 25° C, it is necessary to extrapolate free-energy data from 25° C to the temperature of the natural system. This may be done by using an equation (Gibbs–Helmholtz), which states that at constant pressure the free energy equals the heat of reaction plus the product of temperature and the rate of change of free energy with temperature, namely:

$$\Delta G = \Delta H + T\left(\frac{\partial \Delta G}{\partial T}\right)_P,$$

in which ΔH is enthalpy or heat of reaction (enthalpy is the heat change during a chemical process at constant pressure) and

$$\left(\frac{\partial \Delta G}{\partial T}\right)_P$$

is the rate of change of free energy with temperature at constant pressure. By mathematical operations on the last two equations, the so-called van't Hoff equation relating the change in equilibrium constant with change in temperature to the enthalpy and absolute temperature is obtained:

$$\left(\frac{\partial \ln K_{eq}}{\partial T}\right)_P = \frac{\Delta H}{RT^2},$$

in which the symbols are as previously defined. This equation may be used to calculate equilibrium constants at temperatures other than 25° C. It generally provides a fair approximation only if the actual temperature is not far from 25° C. For larger variations, the assumption that ΔH is independent of temperature (which is explicit in the van't Hoff equation) is invalid.

Pressure changes also affect the rate of change of the Gibbs free-energy function. The rate of change of free energy with change of pressure at constant temperature is equal to the change in volume, namely:

$$\left(\frac{\partial \Delta G}{\partial P}\right)_T = \Delta V_R,$$

in which ΔV_R is the molal volume change of the reaction. It is calculated in a manner similar to the Gibbs free energy of reaction.

In most natural systems both temperature and pressure are subject to change. If the compositions of the phases do not change during a reaction (*e.g.*, during congruent dissolution) and if the system remains at equilibrium, then the Clausius–Clapeyron equation, which defines the rate of change of pressure with respect to temperature is useful. This can be expressed

Clausius–Clapeyron equation

$$\frac{dP}{dT} = \frac{\Delta H_R}{T\Delta V_R},$$

in which ΔH_R is the total enthalpy change of the reaction, T is absolute temperature, and ΔV_R is again the molal volume change.

Nernst equation and Eh-pH relation. In order to understand chemical reactions that involve an exchange of electrons, it is necessary to measure the electromotive force (emf) of the reaction. If the reaction is reversible, then the reversible emf, E^0, is related to the Gibbs free energy of reaction $\Delta G_R{}^0$ by the expression

$$\Delta G_R{}^0 = nE^0F,$$

in which n is the number of electrons involved in the reaction, E^0 is the calculated potential of the cell when all species are at unit activity, and F is the faraday (*i.e.*, the quantity of electricity transferred per equivalent weight of an element or ion). The cell potential can be shown to be related to the natural logarithm of the equilibrium constant by:

$$E^0 = -(RT/nF)\ln K,$$

in which K is the equilibrium constant, T is absolute temperature, R is a constant, and n and F are as defined above. In most chemical reactions the activity of all species is generally not unity, in which case the free-energy function equals the free energy of the reaction plus the product of temperature and the logarithm of the equilibrium constant:

$$\Delta G = \Delta G_R{}^0 + RT\ln K,$$

in which ΔG is the free energy function, $\Delta G_R{}^0$ is the free energy of the reaction, T is temperature, R is a constant, and K is the equilibrium constant.

The cell potential can be related to the equilibrium constant by:

$$\text{Eh} = E^0 + (RT/nF)\ln K,$$

in which Eh is the potential measured against the standard hydrogen-electrode reaction involving the decomposition of hydrogen to hydrogen ions plus electrons (which, by convention, has an emf equal to zero) and E^0 is again the potential when all ionic species are at unity activity. This is a form of the Nernst equation; at standard pressure (one atmosphere) and temperature (298.16 K), the factor (RT/nF) can be reduced and

$$\text{Eh} = E^0 + \frac{0.05916}{n}\log K.$$

Many chemical elements are capable of existing in more than one valence state (*i.e.*, combining capacity, the numerical expression of which represents the number of electrons an atom can gain, lose, or share in a chemical reaction). Thus, iron may exist as metallic iron with no net charge, as the ferrous ion with a net charge of plus two, or as the ferric ion with a net charge of plus three. In addition, complex ions, such as the iron hydroxide ions $Fe(OH)^{2+}$, $Fe(OH)^+{}_2$, and $FeO(OH)^-$, are possible under appropriate conditions of oxidation–reduction potential (redox, or Eh) and pH. The pH of a solution is defined as the negative logarithm of the hydrogen-ion activity. Thus, if the activity of the hydrogen ion is $10^{-7.3}$, then the pH of the solution is plus 7.3. Because of the large number of similarly behaving elements, many chemical reactions in geologic environments may be expressed in terms of Eh, or pH, or by a combination of Eh and pH. For this reason, Eh-pH diagrams (the plotted relations of Eh and pH) provide an excellent pictorial method for portraying such reactions. By drawing lines on these diagrams to denote the activity of each possible dissolved species, the oxidation–reduction potential of the environment can be estimated from study of the solid phases present and from determination of the activity of dissolved species in equilibrium with the solid phases.

Use of Eh-pH diagrams to depict elements in more than one valence state

Reaction types. One of the primary tasks of low-temperature studies is to determine which minerals are in equilibrium with their physical and chemical environment. This can be done by means of calculations that utilize the equations cited thus far. Examples of solid-solid reactions and those involving solids and pure water are considered below.

There are many reactions involving only solids that are geologically important. Any reaction for which free-energy data exist can be tested by means of the Gibbs free-energy equation. The reaction of calcite, $CaCO_3$, with magnesite, $MgCO_3$, to produce dolomite, $CaMg(CO_3)_2$, provides a common example. If the reaction occurs at 25° C and one atmosphere pressure and if the solids are pure, then they are in their standard states and have unit activity. Under these conditions, the reaction can be written

Solid–solid reactions

$$CaCO_3 + MgCO_3 = CaMg\,(CO_3)_2.$$

Applying the relation that the free energy of reaction is equal to the free energy of the products (dolomite) minus the free energy of the reactants (calcite and magnesite) yields:

$$\Delta G_R{}^0 = \Delta G^0{}_{\text{dolomite}} - (\Delta G^0{}_{\text{calcite}} + \Delta\, G^0{}_{\text{magnesite}});$$

and substituting the appropriate free energy values at 25° C and one atmosphere of pressure:

$$\Delta G_R{}^0 = (-516.56) - (-269.98 - 246.11) = -0.47 \text{ kilocalorie per mole.}$$

Because the free energy of reaction is negative, this means that dolomite is the stable mineral at the given conditions of temperature and pressure. That is, it would require an input of +0.47 kilocalorie to drive the reaction in the opposite direction, converting dolomite to calcite and magnesite.

Reactions that involve only solids and pure water can be treated similarly to solid–solid reactions, because the activity of pure water is unity. An example of importance in nature is the reaction: anhydrite, $CaSO_4$, plus water, H_2O, to yield gypsum, $CaSO_4 \cdot 2H_2O$. This is written

Solids and pure water

$$CaSO_4 + 2H_2O = CaSO_4 \cdot 2H_2O.$$

Applying again the relation that the free energy of the reaction is equal to the free energy of the products minus the free energy of the reactants:

$$\Delta G_R{}^0 = \Delta G^0{}_{\text{gypsum}} - (\Delta G^0{}_{\text{anhydrite}} + 2\Delta G^0{}_{\text{water}})$$

$$\Delta G_R{}^0 = 429.19 - (-315.56 + 2(-56.9)).$$

In this instance, the free energy of the reaction is

$$\Delta G_R{}^0 = -0.25 \text{ kilocalorie per mole.}$$

Thus, this reaction also tends to go in the direction of the product (gypsum) at 25° C and one atmosphere pressure. One of the reasons that the hydration (addition of water) of anhydrite is important is that a mole of gypsum is much less dense than a mole of anhydrite. If, therefore, hydration occurs in confined space, as in the subsurface environment, the pressure may be significantly increased. Also, the reaction gives off heat and consequently changes both the pressure and the temperature of the system.

Partial-pressure diagrams

Geochemical diagrams. It is often convenient to portray diagrammatically the relations between mineral species in order to better understand their origin and mode of occurrence. One such diagram of broad practical value is the partial-pressure diagram. Any reaction that can be written so as to include a gas phase can be illustrated on such a diagram. As shown in Figure 20, which portrays the copper–sulfur–oxygen system, the lines on the diagram that

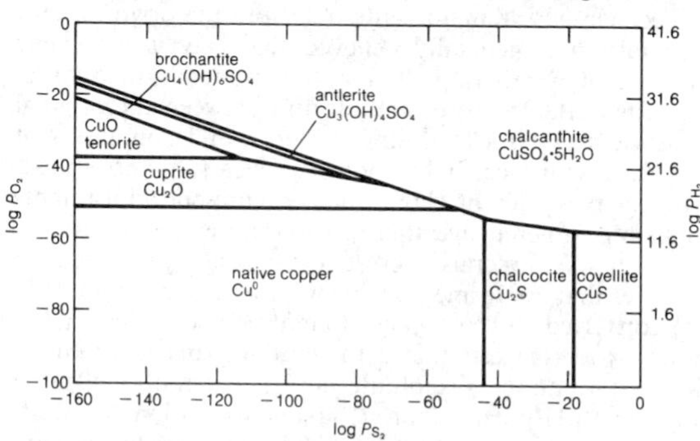

Figure 20: Partial-pressure diagram of the Cu-S-O system with water as a mobile excess compound, at 25° C and one atmosphere total pressure (see text).

separate solid phases represent the equilibrium condition between the two minerals. The reaction whereby native copper, Cu, reacts with sulfur, S, to produce chalcocite, Cu_2S, for instance is expressed by:

$$2Cu + {}^1\!/\!{}_2S_2 = Cu_2S,$$

and the equilibrium constant (K) is

$$K = \frac{1}{\sqrt{P\,s_2}},$$

in which Ps_2 is the partial pressure of sulfur gas in the system. The free energy of this reaction is −30.2 kilocalories, and the equilibrium constant, K, is $10^{22.14}$; for this value of K, the partial pressure of sulfur at which the two minerals, Cu and Cu_2S, are in equilibrium is therefore $10^{-44.28}$. This is the position of the phase boundary on Figure 20. In like manner, boundaries involving oxides can also be calculated. Those reactions that involve only oxygen or sulfur in the gas phase plot as either horizontal or vertical lines on the figure. Those reactions that involve both gases plot as slanted lines. The slope depends on the relative amounts of the two gases involved. The diagram indicates that one could find Cu and Cu_2O in the same geological environment but that the pair Cu plus CuO is not geochemically stable; the two phases should always be separated by Cu_2O. The diagram also indicates that Cu_2O, CuO, and $Cu_4(OH)_6SO_4$ can coexist at a unique combination of gas pressures. The point where all three phases occur is commonly called a triple point.

Eh–pH diagrams

Another common geochemical diagram is the Eh–pH plot in Figure 21. By means of the Nernst equation, which relates the potential electromotive force of a reaction to the equilibrium constant, a picture can be constructed of mineral relations for elements that commonly exist in several valence states. Copper provides a useful example because it can exist in nature as the element Cu^0 and in both the cuprous (Cu^+) and cupric (Cu^{2+}) states.

The upper slanted boundary on Figure 21 represents the conditions under which water decomposes to oxygen. The reaction, at one atmosphere pressure and 298.16 K (25° C, or 77° F) is

$$2H_2O = O_2 + 4H^+ + 4e^-,$$

in which the products of decomposition are four hydrogen ions (H^+) and four electrons (e^-), in addition to oxygen (O_2). The equilibrium constant in this case is simply the logarithm of the activity of the hydrogen ions (α_{H+}) raised to the fourth power because four ions are present. Thus, the Nernst equation relating cell potential and the equilibrium constant is:

$$\text{Eh} = E^0 + \frac{0.059}{4}\log(a_{H+})^4,$$

in which Eh is the potential of the reaction measured against the hydrogen electrode half cell (emf = 0), and E^0 is the potential when all ionic species are at unit activity. Because pH is defined as the negative logarithm of the activity of the hydrogen ion ($-\log \alpha_{H+}$):

$$\text{Eh} = E^0 - 0.059\ \text{pH}.$$

This basic relationship defines the slope; by using the free energy relationship to cell potential previously given ($\Delta G_R{}^0 = nE^0F$) it is possible to solve E^0 and obtain:

$$\text{Eh} = 1.23 - 0.059\ \text{pH}.$$

In like manner, it is possible to solve for the intercept and slope of the bottom boundary on Figure 21, which represents the conditions under which water breaks down to hydrogen gas at one atmosphere pressure.

Lines between various pairs of copper-bearing minerals on Figure 21 represent equilibrium conditions between those pairs. Considering the conditions under which native copper is oxidized to cuprite, Cu_2O, for example:

$$2Cu^0 + H_2O = Cu_2O + 2H^+ + 2e^-,$$

in which Cu^0 is native copper, reacting with water to produce cuprite, hydrogen ions, and two electrons (e^-). The slope and intercept on the diagram can be determined in the manner given above for the $H_2O : O_2$ relation.

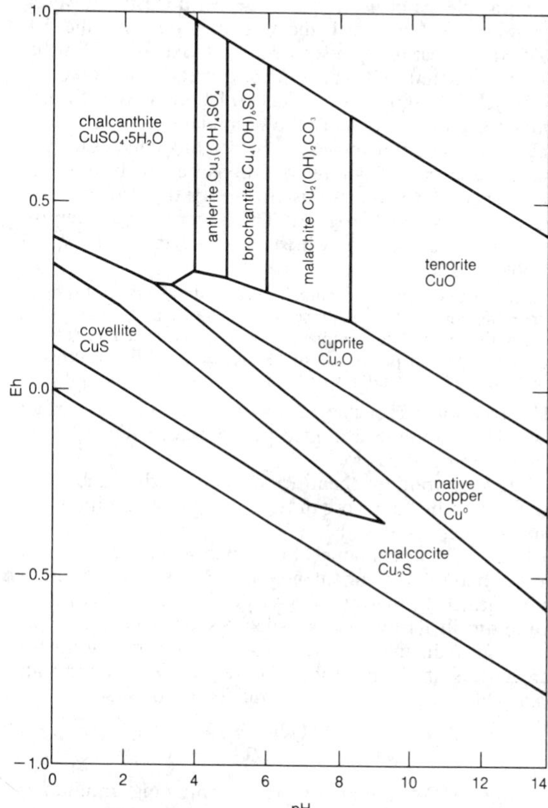

Figure 21: Eh–pH diagram of stability relations in the system Cu-S-C-H_2O at 25° C and one atmosphere pressure (see text).

Those reactions that do not involve a change in valence state (*i.e.*, only involve dissolved species but no electrons) have phase boundaries that plot as vertical lines on the diagram. This means the reaction is independent of Eh and occurs only at a given concentration of dissolved species and fixed pH. The equilibrium boundary between the copper minerals tenorite, CuO, and malachite, $Cu_2(OH)_2CO_3$, can be obtained from the reaction

$$Cu_2(OH)_2CO_3 = 2CuO + HCO_3^- + H^+,$$

in which malachite dissociates to produce cuprite, bicarbonate ion (HCO_3^-), and hydrogen ion (H^+). The free energy of the reaction and the equilibrium constant can be obtained as before, and because the activity of total carbon species is fixed for the entire diagram, the pH can readily be computed.

Use of geochemical diagrams with ore deposits

Such diagrams are useful in understanding ore deposits. Under increasingly oxidizing conditions, for instance, but without much change in pH, a buried deposit consisting of copper, Cu, and copper sulfide, Cu_2S, will change to malachite ($Cu_2(OH)_2CO_3$) and possibly also brochantite ($Cu_4(OH)_6SO_4$) toward the surface of the Earth. This is because the geochemical conditions become increasingly oxidizing (the Eh increases) from deep within the Earth's crust toward its surface. Thus, the occurrence at or near land surface of the secondary enrichment minerals, such as brochantite, antlerite, malachite, azurite, or tenorite, may indicate a large copper deposit lying below.

Significant geochemical equilibria in nature. *Uranium–vanadium equilibrium.* The search for radioactive materials after World War II provided a great impetus for scientists to study chemical equilibrium because of complex problems associated with the origin and occurrence of uranium ores. Principles of modern low-temperature geochemistry were largely developed during this period of exploration for radioactive ores. Before about 1950, the chief uranium ore in the United States was carnotite, a hydrated, potassium-bearing uranium, and vanadium oxide compound ($K_2(UO_2)_2V_2O_8 \cdot 0$ to $3H_2O$), and it was believed to be a primary mineral precipitated during deposition of the surrounding sediments. The mineral is fully oxidized; uranium has a valence of six (U^{6+}) and vanadium a valence of five (V^{5+}). In deeper deposits, however, ore was found in which the valence states U^{4+} and V^{3+} existed, indicating a lesser degree of oxidation. Further search and study ultimately proved that uraninite (UO_2), in which uranium has a valence of four, is the primary mineral, and carnotite is the secondary mineral resulting from oxidation processes. Before this conclusion was reached, several important questions had to be resolved in order to develop a consistent theory that led to a successful exploration program. The American geochemists R.M. Garrels and C.L. Christ have succinctly stated the problem as follows,

> . . . if an unoxidized uranium ore consists of uraninite, montroseite, and pyrite, with some sphalerite and galena, will oxidation yield the complex mineral assemblages observed? What oxidation products can coexist stably? Which minerals will oxidize first under near equilibrium conditions?

The solution was achieved by superposition of various Eh–pH diagrams constructed in the manner described in the foregoing discussion.

Details of uranium chemistry explain much of the origin and occurrence of its ore minerals. Although uranium has many valence states (+2, +3, +4, +5, and +6), only the +4 and +6 states are of geologic interest. Vanadium exists in the natural state in valences of +3, +4, and +5 and is complicated further by the great variety of complex ions. Uranium in its two lowest valence states is a sufficiently powerful reducing agent to decompose water to form hydrogen gas; in the presence of water, the +5 valence state is unstable with respect to +4 and +6 as follows:

$$\underset{(U=+5)}{2UO_2^+} + 4H^+ = \underset{(U=+6)}{UO_2^{+2}} + U^{+4} + 2H_2O.$$

in which UO_2^+ is uranium oxide containing uranium in the +5 state and UO_2^{+2} is uranium oxide containing uranium in the +6 state. The transition from valence state +4 to +6 occurs in the following reaction:

$$U^{4+} + 2H_2O = UO_2^{2+} + 4H^+ + 2e^-,$$

in which uranium in the +4 state combines with water to produce U^{+6}-bearing uranium oxide, from hydrogen ions (H^+) and two electrons (e^-). The reaction has a potential ($E^0 = +0.33$ volt) that is within the normal range for redox potentials in nature. By obtaining equilibrium constants from free-energy data for various reactions, as discussed in the section on principles and techniques, it is quite easy to explain why the particular minerals are stable in the selected environments in which the ores exist.

Kaolinite–gibbsite equilibria. The distribution, origin, and formation of clay minerals demonstrate another group of chemical reactions that occur in nature. Clay minerals are hydrous aluminum silicates, and many contain other metals, primarily magnesium, iron, calcium, sodium, and potassium. The chemical composition of clay does not determine its properties, such as degree of plasticity and capacity for ion exchange. The primary control on clay properties is structure of the clay minerals, which may be examined by X-ray-diffraction cameras and electron microscopes. Many intriguing and unanswered questions of geochemistry remain centred around the origin of clay minerals. It is generally believed that clay is the stable product of weathering; that is, the minerals that represent final attainment of equilibrium between the original constituents of rock-forming minerals and conditions at the Earth's surface. It has not been clearly demonstrated whether the different clay minerals represent adjustments to slightly different weathering environments, or whether some of the minerals represent metastable intermediate varieties that are formed during weathering and ultimately are converted to other clay minerals. Experimental laboratory work suggests that acid solutions (pH less than 7) favour formation of kaolinite, and that basic or alkaline solutions (pH greater than 7) favour formation of montmorillonite. This conclusion is partly corroborated by data on the geologic occurrence of the two minerals.

Kaolinite is commonly the chief clay mineral in soils on well-drained slopes in humid climates, where abundant vegetation makes soil solutions acid and where cations are effectively leached away (the percolating action of groundwater). Montmorillonite is characteristic of soils in less humid climates, where soil solutions are mainly alkaline and where cations are moved less rapidly. Illite is formed in environments with a high concentration of potassium ion and can be formed from montmorillonite. Illite is the common clay mineral in alkaline soils of desert areas.

The formation of bauxite

Another question of long standing has been the formation of bauxite, the important aluminum ore. The essence of the problem of origin of bauxite lies in the relation be-

From Robert M. Garrels and Charles L. Christ, *Solutions, Minerals, and Equilibria*, p. 358 (1965); Harper and Row

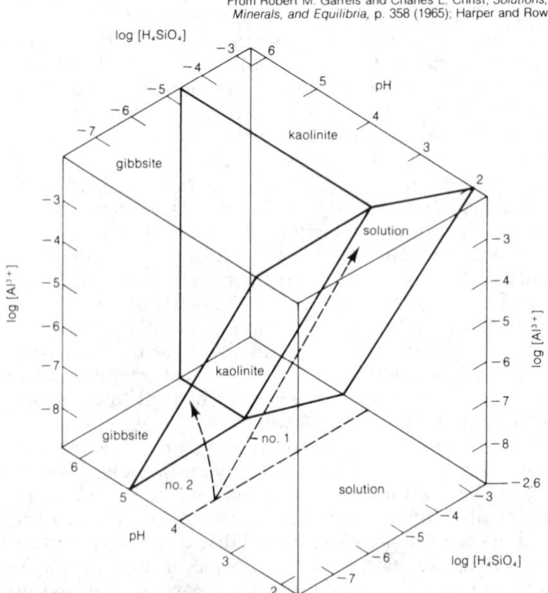

Figure 22: Gibbsite-kaolinite solution relations at 25° C and one atmosphere pressure, for acid conditions (see text).

tween kaolinite, $H_4Al_2Si_2O_9$, and gibbsite, $Al_2O_3 \cdot 3H_2O$. In many geological areas, kaolinite is the mineral that precedes the final dissolution of solids by agents of weathering. In other areas, the persistent mineral is gibbsite.

If equilibrium between kaolinite, gibbsite, dissolved silica, and water is assumed, then the following reaction can be written:

$$\underset{\text{kaolinite}}{H_4Al_2Si_2O_9} + \underset{\text{water}}{5H_2O} = \underset{\text{gibbsite}}{Al_2O_3 \cdot 3H_2O} + \underset{\text{dissolved silica}}{2H_4SiO_4}.$$

Severe leaching conditions generally are accepted as required for the formation of gibbsite, and the pore water must be reasonably pure; its activity therefore is fixed at unity. The equilibrium constant for the reaction is $K_{eq} = [H_4SiO_4]^2$, and the free energy of the reaction is +12.7 kilocalories. Equilibrium is attained between gibbsite and kaolinite at a fixed value of the activity (= concentration) of dissolved silica of about two parts per million of dissolved silica. At any lower value of dissolved silica, kaolinite should tend to dissolve, leaving a residuum of gibbsite.

The stability of gibbsite (Al_2O_3) can be shown (Figure 22) as a volume on a diagram using pH, Al^{3+}, and dissolved silica (H_4SiO_4) as variables, even though its stability alone is independent of H_4SiO_4. The boundary between gibbsite and kaolinite is a plane representing a fixed activity of H_4SiO_4. At H_4SiO_4 activities greater than this value, kaolinite can be expected to dissolve congruently and thus leave no gibbsite residue. The prevalence of kaolinite in the upper levels of most soils formed under strong leaching conditions leads to the prediction that most soil-solution compositions are toward the rear of Figure 22.

The dashed arrows show the change in solution composition that results if kaolinite dissolves at a fixed pH. Under such conditions, the ratio of H_4SiO_4 to Al^{3+} in solution is maintained at unity. If a kaolinite soil is subjected to leaching by rainwater, with pH fixed at 4, perhaps by living plants or decomposing organic materials that release carbon dioxide, CO_2, to the soil water, the solution composition will change as indicated by arrow 1, and the soil field intersected is that of kaolinite. In other words, kaolinite dissolves congruently to leave a kaolinite residue. If there is no pH buffering (*i.e.*, stabilizing action by dissolved substances that release hydrogen ion) hydrogen ion (H^+) will be used up when kaolinite dissolves, and the solution composition will change along a path similar to that shown by arrow 2, indicating incongruent solution of kaolinite to produce a gibbsite residue.

The diagram thus leads to a hypothesis concerning some major controls on the formation of bauxite and serves to show the utility of such methods of representation as stimuli to the collection of data about relations that might not otherwise be deduced. Most soils in areas of high rainfall and concomitant high leaching rates are kaolinitic; they also tend to have low pH values. The low pH apparently results in part from a high carbon dioxide content in the soil atmosphere, an effect induced by decomposition of organic materials in the soil and in part from pH lowering at the surfaces of roots. Perhaps under exceptional conditions of high rainfall and high temperature, bacterial decomposition is so rapid that carbon dioxide resulting from organic decomposition passes directly into the atmosphere, and the soils are so heavily leached that plant ground cover is relatively sparse. If these conditions occur, rainwater descending through the soil will be relatively unbuffered, and gibbsite residue could result. Whatever the details of the explanation, it does appear that the requirement of abundant unbuffered soil water for bauxite formation is in accordance with the occurrence of low silica–high alumina soil residues. (B.B.H./Wi.B./Ed.)

THE MAJOR ROCK-FORMING MINERALS

Importance of silicates

As previously noted, silicates constitute the principal rock-forming minerals. The igneous rocks that make up more than 90 percent of the Earth's crust all consist of silicates, namely feldspars (nearly 60 percent), amphiboles and pyroxenes (about 17 percent), quartz and other silica minerals (12 percent), and micas (about 4 percent), with olivines, feldspathoids, and zeolites in smaller amounts. Technically speaking, the zeolites are not primary rock formers, but they are widely distributed. Sedimentary and metamorphic rocks, which comprise the balance of the crust, also contain large quantities of silicates. The weathering of rocks exposed at the Earth's surface, along with hydrothermal processes, produces various groups of minerals known as the clay minerals. These, in turn, form the metamorphic rock slate and such sedimentary rocks as shale, limestone, and dolomite. Each of the above-mentioned mineral groups is described in the following section. (Ed.)

Feldspars

The feldspars are aluminum silicate minerals that not only make up a large percentage of the rocks exposed at the Earth's surface but comprise an appreciable fraction of all soils, marine clays, and other unconsolidated sediments. They are principal elements in rock classification, are widely used in the glass and ceramics industry, and some provide ornamental stone and semiprecious gems.

GENERAL IDENTIFICATION OF THE FELDSPAR MINERALS

Characteristic of the feldspar group of minerals are solid solution series—*i.e.*, a single crystalline phase whose chemical composition can vary between finite limits that are called end-members. There are three such end-members in the feldspar group, namely, orthoclase, a potassium aluminum silicate ($KAlSi_3O_8$); albite, a sodium aluminum silicate ($NaAlSi_3O_8$); and anorthite, a calcium aluminum silicate ($CaAl_2Si_2O_8$). At temperatures above 700° C (1,300° F) there is complete solid solution between orthoclase and albite. The minerals involved have compositions that vary between pure potassium feldspar and pure sodium feldspar; these constitute the alkali feldspar series. There is also complete solid solution at high temperature between the end-members albite and anorthite. These minerals theoretically vary between pure sodium feldspar and pure calcium feldspar and are called the plagioclase feldspar series. There is commonly a certain amount of potassium in the plagioclase feldspars and some calcium in the alkali feldspars. This is, however, generally not greater than 10 percent of the feldspar molecule. Other elements that enter the feldspars in appreciable amounts are barium, rubidium, and strontium. The barium feldspar ($BaAl_2Si_2O_8$), known as celsian, is very rare, and minerals with compositions intermediate to celsian and potassium feldspar are known collectively as hyalophane.

The importance of the feldspars in the classification of igneous rocks is such that the alkali and plagioclase series of minerals are further subdivided. The plagioclase series is designated in terms of the fraction of the albite (Ab) component and anorthite (An) component in each intermediate mineral. Because Ab plus An must total 100 percent in each mineral, the content of only one of the end-members need be specified. That is: albite (Ab = 100–90), oligoclase (Ab = 90–70), andesine (Ab = 70–50), labradorite (Ab = 50–30), bytownite (Ab = 30–10), and anorthite (Ab = 10–0).

In the alkali series the feldspar names are related to the structural state as well as to chemical composition. At temperatures above 700° C there is complete solid solution from albite through anorthoclase to high sanidine. At lower temperatures intermediate members of the series consist of intimate intergrowths of a sodium-rich and a potassium-rich feldspar; these intergrowths have the general name perthite. Perthites are subdivided according to their size: those called perthites are visible to the naked eye; microperthites are visible only under the microscope; and cryptoperthites are invisible under the microscope. It may seem that the name cryptoperthite would be of little use; an optical effect observed in moonstone, however, indicates that the mineral is a cryptoperthite. In addition, X-ray-diffraction analysis will indicate the occurrence of a sodium–potassium feldspar consisting of two phases intergrown on a submicroscopic scale.

Besides its use in the glass and ceramics industry, feldspar has replaced silica in scouring powders because of the health hazard caused by some silicas in the manufacturing process. China clay, used for making good quality china, is mainly composed of the clay mineral kaolin [$Al_2Si_2O_5(OH)_4$]—a decomposition product of feldspar.

Feldspar-bearing rocks have been used as decorative stones, the most spectacular being the larvikite (from Norway) and anorthosites containing labradorite, which show pronounced iridescence. Many building stones depend on pink feldspars for their beauty, and some feldspars are used as semiprecious gemstones. The chief varieties are moonstone, a cryptoperthite showing pronounced pale-blue iridescence; and aventurine feldspar, or sunstone, plagioclase or orthoclase containing oriented flakes of hematite that produce a copper-coloured lustre called schiller. Orthoclase and labradorite that exhibit a pale-yellow colour because of the presence of small amounts of iron are also used in jewelry.

CRYSTAL STRUCTURE

Feldspars crystallize in the monoclinic or triclinic system. Crystals in the monoclinic system are referable to three unequal crystallographic axes; one axis is perpendicular to the other two, which are not at right angles to each other. In the triclinic system there are three unequal axes, each of which is inclined with respect to the other two. Crystals in this system show the lowest order of symmetry of all minerals, but the feldspars show strong pseudo-symmetry.

Silicon–aluminum ratios

All the feldspars are made up of SiO_4 and AlO_4 tetrahedra (*i.e.,* there are four oxygen atoms at the vertexes surrounding and bonded to a central silicon or aluminum atom) that are linked together in a three-dimensional framework by the sharing of oxygen atoms between adjacent tetrahedra. Potassium, sodium, calcium, or barium occupy the cavities in the framework. When two tetrahedra are linked by an oxygen atom, the centres of both cannot be occupied by aluminum atoms, and therefore substitution of silicon by aluminum in tetrahedral (4-fold) coordination cannot exceed 50 percent. In $KAlSi_3O_8$ and $NaAlSi_3O_8$ the replacement is 25 percent, whereas in $CaAl_2Si_2O_8$ it is 50 percent, and thus, in the plagioclase series, the replacement of silicon by aluminum is between 25 and 50 percent.

In the structure of $CaAl_2Si_2O_8$, the silicon and aluminum tetrahedra must be very systematically arranged; every silicon tetrahedron is surrounded by four aluminum tetrahedra and vice versa; this means that the structure is ordered with respect to silicon and aluminum. In all other feldspars, the aluminum content is lower than the 1:1 ratio of aluminum to silicon in anorthite, and this permits the existence of aluminum and silicon disorder. It is this factor that is chiefly responsible for the differences between feldspars that crystallize after being quickly cooled from a high temperature, such as those in lavas, and those that may have formed at high temperatures but only after cooling slowly over a long period of time, so that they can equilibrate at a low temperature.

Although the feldspars have framework structures, these structures can be considered as being made up of linked chains that are parallel to the *a* axis, formed of linked rings of four tetrahedra that, when viewed along the *b* axis, present a zigzag appearance (see Figure 23).

The two prominent cleavages (*i.e.,* the tendency to split along preferred crystallographic directions) of the feldspars are (010) and (001) and these break only the bonds linking the chains. The only monoclinic feldspars are the potassium-rich alkali feldspars sanidine and orthoclase. Sanidine microperthites and sanidine cryptoperthites frequently appear to be monoclinic; because they consist of an intimate intergrowth of a monoclinic potassium phase and a triclinic sodium phase, however, they cannot be described as monoclinic in the strict sense. High albite and solid solutions with a small amount of potassium acquire monoclinic symmetry at elevated temperature but automatically revert to triclinic symmetry on cooling.

Sanidine and orthoclase

The sanidine structure. The structure of sanidine (Figure 24) can be used to illustrate the crystal structure of all the feldspars. Because sanidine has monoclinic symmetry, only one-half of the cell need be shown; the other half is its mirror image. The chains parallel to the *a* axis can be seen in this projection, and the positions of the potassium atoms are also indicated at heights 0 and 50. The oxygens at the corners at height 15 and halfway along the "a" cell edge at height 35 are those that link this chain to adjacent chains.

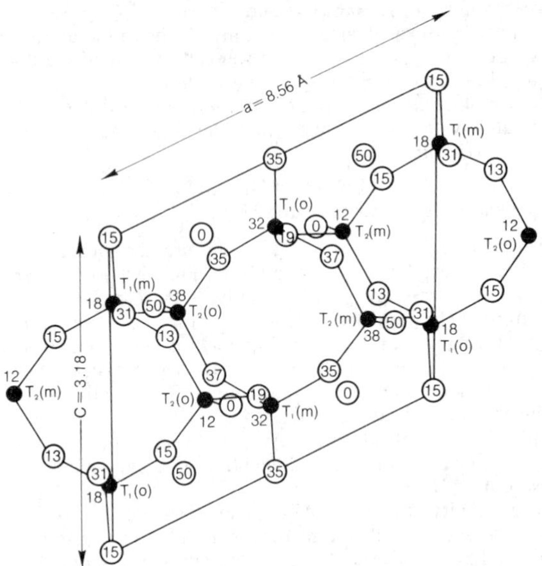

Figure 24: The structure of sanidine, showing one half of the unit cell. The projection is parallel to (010).

Reprinted from W.L. Bragg: *Atomic Structure of Minerals.* Copyright 1937 by Cornell University. Used by permission of Cornell University Press

From W. Taylor, "The Structure of Sanidine and other Feldspars," *Zeitschrift fur Kristallographie,* vol. 85 (1933)

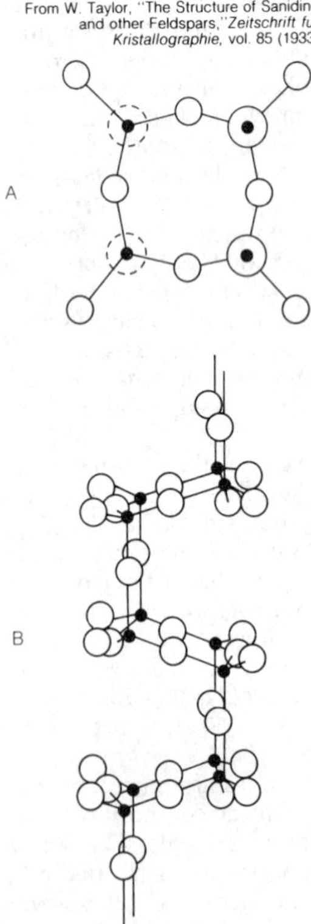

Figure 23: (A) Idealized rings formed from SI-O or Al-O tetrahedrons in feldspar structures. (B) Chains formed by linking the tetrahedral rings. These chains lie parallel to the "a" crystallographic axis.

Silicon and aluminum sites

There are a total of 16 (aluminum + silicon) atoms in the cell; these occupy two 8-fold sites, which are usually designated T_1 and T_2. In the triclinic potassium feldspar microcline, however, the eight T_1 sites are replaced by four T_1(o) sites and four T_1(m) sites, and, likewise, the eight T_2 sites are replaced by four T_2(o) sites and four T_2(m) sites. This nomenclature has been incorporated in Figure 24 to indicate the different tetrahedral sites in triclinic potassium feldspar, but it should be understood that, in sanidine, T_1(o) is equivalent to T_1(m) because these are related by a diad axis—*i.e.*, one of twofold symmetry in which the same crystal relations obtain after rotation of 180°.

As noted above, the different distribution of the aluminum and silicon atoms in these tetrahedral sites is the cause of the difference between high sanidine (the highest temperature potassium feldspar) and maximum microcline (the lowest temperature potassium feldspar). In high sanidine, the silicon and aluminum atoms are completely randomly distributed between T_1 and T_2 types of sites, whereas, in microcline, the aluminum atoms are almost all concentrated in the T_1(o) sites, and the silicon atoms occupy the T_1(m), T_2(o), and T_2(m) sites. All degrees of ordering exist, from high sanidine through low sanidine, orthoclase, and intermediate microcline to maximum microcline. The transition from monoclinic to triclinic symmetry occurs when the T_1(o) and T_1(m) sites have different statistical aluminum contents.

A similar relationship holds between high albite and low albite except that, because both are triclinic, the nomenclature for the tetrahedral sites of the highest temperature and lowest temperature forms are the same. Because of the smaller size of the sodium atom compared with the potassium atom, there is a tendency for the framework partially to collapse. The elongation of the sodium atom may be due to random occupation of two sites and is greater in the high-temperature form.

Although the alkali feldspars form a complete solid solution at high temperatures, natural feldspars of composition near $Ab_{50}Or_{50}$ (one-half albite and one-half orthoclase) are invariably unmixed (*i.e.*, have separated upon cooling) to some extent; the degree of unmixing depends on the rate of cooling. There is some evidence that feldspars that have cooled rapidly are initially homogeneous but will unmix gradually even at temperatures as low as 150° C (300° F). Feldspars that have cooled slowly to low temperatures consist of almost pure low albite and pure potassium feldspar in an intimate intergrowth. Between these two extremes there are all intermediate stages in degrees of unmixing. It should be noted that, whereas the sodium-rich phase is highly disordered in the case of high-temperature perthites and highly ordered in the case of low-temperature perthites, the same is not true of the potassium-rich phase, wherein there are all possible gradations in the degree of order.

Plagioclase structures. Structural variation with composition of the plagioclase feldspars is shown in Figure 25. Although the phase diagram of the plagioclase feldspars usually shows complete solid solution between albite and anorthite at high temperature, pure anorthite has a 14 Å *c* axis even at the highest temperature, whereas albite has a 7 Å *c* axis. In the case of pure anorthite, the aluminum and silicon distribution is completely ordered; this is primitive anorthite. With the substitution of sodium for calcium and the accompanying replacement of some of the aluminum by silicon, the primitive anorthite structure gives way to body-centred anorthite (a structure with atoms at each corner and one in the centre) that also has a 14 Å *c* axis. The intermediate plagioclases are briefly described under *Iridescence*.

Peristerite structure

The peristerite structure occurs in low-temperature feldspars in the composition range An_2 to An_{16} (see Figure 25). This structure results from an intimate intergrowth of two phases, one being pure albite with the low albite structure, the other of oligoclase composition but with a lower concentration of aluminum in the T_1(o) site than in low albite. It seems fairly certain that this structure results from exsolution of an originally homogeneous phase, but the precise nature of the reaction has not yet been determined. The iridescence shown by peristerites is caused by the intergrowth of the two phases, but all specimens having this structure do not show iridescence.

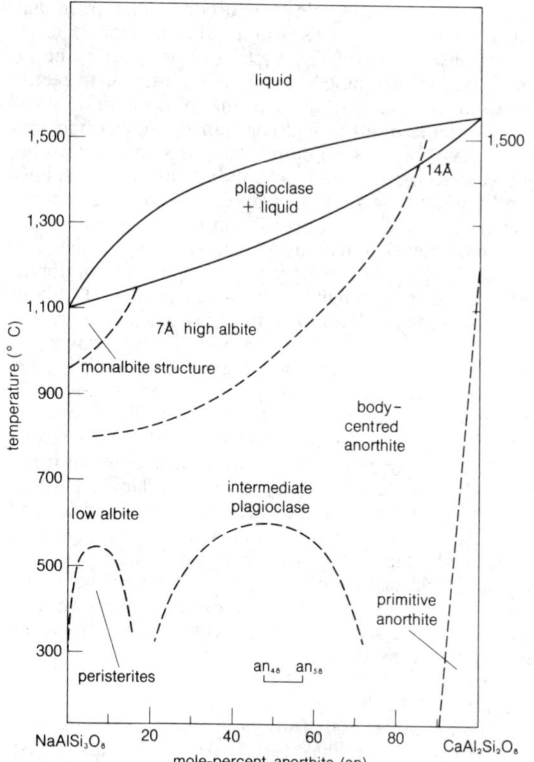

Figure 25: Plagioclase system, showing structural variations with compositional change within the system.

From J.V. Smith and P.H. Ribbe, "Atomic Movements in Plagioclase Feldspars: Kinetic Interpretation," in *Contr. Mineral. and Petrol.*, Bd. 21, S. 157–202 (1969); Berlin-Heidelberg-New York: Springer

TWINNING IN FELDSPARS

Twinning is the intergrowth of two or more grains of a given crystalline material according to some definite pattern or arrangement called a twin law. The twin laws common in feldspars can be divided into those that apply only to the triclinic crystals (in which the axis or plane of twinning corresponds to the symmetry axis or symmetry plane in monoclinic crystals) and those that apply either to the monoclinic or triclinic crystals.

Carlsbad, Manebach, and Baveno twins

Twinning in monoclinic and triclinic crystals. The twin laws that commonly are found in both monoclinic and triclinic crystals are called Carlsbad, Manebach, and Baveno (see Figure 26). The twins result from the zigzag chains of one part being joined to those of the other part by the oxygen atoms, which provide the linkages between the chains of a single untwinned crystal. In the case of Carlsbad twinning, the twin-axis lies in the plane perpendicular to the *b* axis and is described as a parallel twin. The Manebach and Baveno twins, in which the twin-axis is perpendicular to the twin plane are normal twins.

Albite and pericline twins

Twinning restricted to triclinic crystals. Twin laws that occur only in triclinic crystals are very numerous, but many of the laws are of rare occurrence. The two most common types are according to the so-called albite and pericline laws, and these are frequently found in the same crystal. The albite twin is a normal twin, whereas the

From A. Deer, R. Howie, and J. Zussman, *Rock-Forming Minerals*, vol. 4 (1963); Longman Group Ltd.

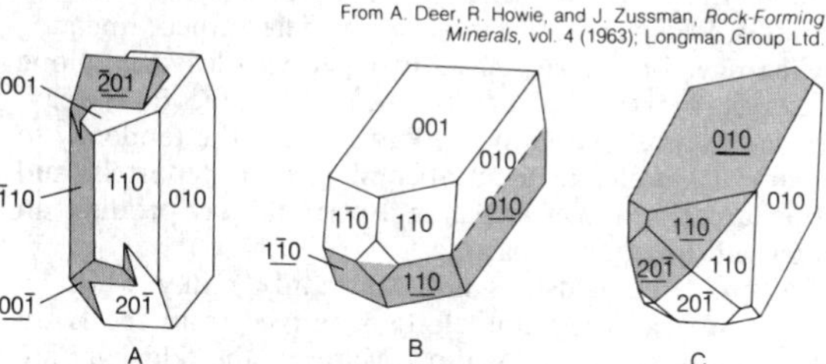

Figure 26: Common feldspar twins. (A) Interpenetrant Carlsbad twin. (B) Manebach twin. (C) Baveno twin.

pericline is a parallel twin that occurs in an irrational plane containing the *b* axis. Albite twinning represents an attempt on the part of the crystal to retain the plane of symmetry, and pericline twinning is an attempt to retain the axis of twofold symmetry of the monoclinic crystals. In two varieties of alkali feldspar, namely, microcline and anorthoclase, there is no doubt that the symmetry of the crystals was originally monoclinic; but the crystals subsequently inverted to triclinic symmetry, and, in doing so, twinning occurred according to both twin laws. This condition has been described as M-type twinning to indicate the origin in a monoclinic crystal; this type of twinning is readily detected by single crystal X-ray studies. It also is recognized optically because of the crosshatched, or tartan, appearance of the crystals when viewed in thin section.

In plagioclase feldspars the original symmetry of the crystals was triclinic, and the twinning may be primary (formed during crystallization), or it may be secondary (formed subsequent to crystallization, perhaps by deformation). The appearance of the twinning is different from that shown by M-type twinning in that lamellae (thin layers, seen as lines in thin sections) of one twin are frequently cut off by twin lamellae approximately at right angles, and so the tartan effect is not produced.

In the plagioclases the position of the pericline twin lamellae depends both on the chemical composition and on the structural state. It may indicate a relict structural state in certain instances.

PHYSICAL PROPERTIES

Hardness. In general, feldspars are quoted as having hardness 6 to 6.5 on the Mohs scale of hardness. Thus, feldspars are just softer than most minerals that are used as gemstones. Albite is just slightly harder than orthoclase, and, in the plagioclase series, there is a very slight decrease in hardness from albite to anorthite. Detailed study of indentation hardness of the plagioclase feldspars reveals two inflections in the curve of hardness plotted against composition; these inflections occur at An_{25-30} and An_{45-55}. It has been tentatively suggested that these may be correlated with structural breaks in the plagioclase series. Hardness is a property that is not easy to measure accurately and consequently has very limited value as a means of identification of individual feldspars.

Table 1: Densities of Feldspar Group End Members

	high form	low form
$KAlSi_3O_8$	high sanidine 2.558–2.560	microcline 2.560–2.564
$NaAlSi_3O_8$	high albite 2.606	low albite 2.624
$CaAl_2Si_2O_8$		anorthite 2.760

Specific gravity. The densities of the feldspars are dependent on both chemical composition and structural state, but, toward the anorthite end of the plagioclase series, the differences in structural state gradually disappear, and so also do density differences.

Accurate measurements of density are difficult to make because inclusions and flaws in crystals are common. Consequently, densities usually are calculated from the unit cell volume and molecular weight. Unfortunately, small errors in the cell volume may result in noticeable errors in density. The densities of the two forms of potassium feldspar are roughly the same because the cell volumes appear to be nearly identical, whereas, in the case of sodium feldspar, there is a significant difference in cell volume. The relation between density and composition for the two series of feldspars is, as far as can be determined, linear.

Cleavage. Feldspars have two perfect cleavages along the crystallographic planes (001) and (010); the (001) cleavage is the most pronounced. Parting (*i.e.*, the tendency to separate) parallel to a number of faces is reported, and lamellae of sodium feldspar in a perthite may produce an apparent direction of parting.

Colour. The feldspars are commonly milky white in colour; indeed, the name albite is derived from the Latin word *albus*, meaning "white." Many of the feldspars are transparent with a yellowish or green colour, and sometimes they are translucent. Feldspars frequently are reddish brown in colour due to staining by iron, more commonly in potassium-rich feldspars. Some have a small amount of iron in their structure and occur as transparent yellowish crystals. The latter are either iron-bearing orthoclases or iron-bearing labradorites, both of which are used as semiprecious gemstones. Their perfect cleavage is a disadvantage in this connection. Feldspars that are green in colour are called amazonite. When transparent they are used as gemstones and when cloudy as decorative stones.

Figure 27: (Left) Microcline, Pikes Peak, Colorado. (Right) Albite, Amelia Court House, Virginia.

By courtesy of The American Museum of Natural History, New York; photographs, E. Javorsky—EB Inc.

Play of colours

Iridescence. The property of iridescence is shown by different types of feldspars. Moonstones, which are alkali feldspars that are made up of a submicroscopic intergrowth of potassium-rich and sodium-rich feldspar, usually have a very attractive pale-blue iridescence and are used as semiprecious gemstones. Plagioclases in the albite–oligoclase composition range (peristerites) that consist of submicroscopic lamellae of two phases, one of which is almost pure albite, also show iridescence. The name is derived from the Greek word *peristera* in allusion to the resemblance of the iridescence colour to that of a pigeon or dove.

Some feldspars in the labradorite composition range show a play of colours that varies through red, gold, brown, yellow, blue, and green. Although there is some overlap, the colours are related to the bulk composition of the sample: blue may be shown by samples of composition $An_{48.5}$–An_{52}; green to yellow, by An_{52}–$An_{55.5}$; and orange to red, by An_{55}–$An_{58.5}$ (Figure 25). The potassium content apparently is critical as to whether iridescence is produced or not, because all specimens that lack iridescence have less than 2.1 mole (gram-molecular weight) percent of orthoclase. Although many workers have tried to explain this effect, there is no consensus of opinion as to its cause. If it is caused by an intergrowth of two phases, then these are extremely similar in structure. Recent work on this

By courtesy of the Department of Geology, The University of Manchester, England; photographs, Susan Maher

Figure 28: (Left) Moonstone showing pale-blue iridescence, origin unknown. (Top right) Polished slab of labradorite showing iridescence colours and polysynthetic twinning, from Labrador. (Bottom right) Aventurine feldspar showing schiller produced by flakes of hematite, from Bjordammen, Norway.

topic suggests that unmixing into two phases appears to be the most likely explanation of this phenomenon.

The property of schiller is shown by a type of feldspar known as aventurine, sometimes known as sunstone. The feldspar is usually of oligoclase composition but is sometimes potassium feldspar. The appearance is that of a copper-coloured schiller due to oriented hematite lamellae. When the specimen is heated above 1,200° C (2,200° F), these lamellae disappear, presumably due to solid solution in the feldspar, and they may reappear on annealing at 1,000° C (1,800° F).

Strong pseudo-symmetry

Crystal form and habit. The feldspars have fairly strong pseudosymmetry, and in the triclinic feldspars this is the cause of polysynthetic (multiple) twinning. This is in some instances hexagonal pseudosymmetry, with the *c* axis serving as the sixfold axis (*i.e.*, one that reveals the same crystal relations with each 60° rotation.

Orthoclase and microcline commonly have prismatic habit, whereas sanidine is frequently tabular (see Figure 29). Albite in pegmatites forms very thin tabular crystals parallel to (010)—a plane parallel to *a* and *c;* this is called

From A. Deer, R. Howie, and J. Zussman, *Rock-Forming Minerals*, vol. 4 (1963); Longman Group Ltd.

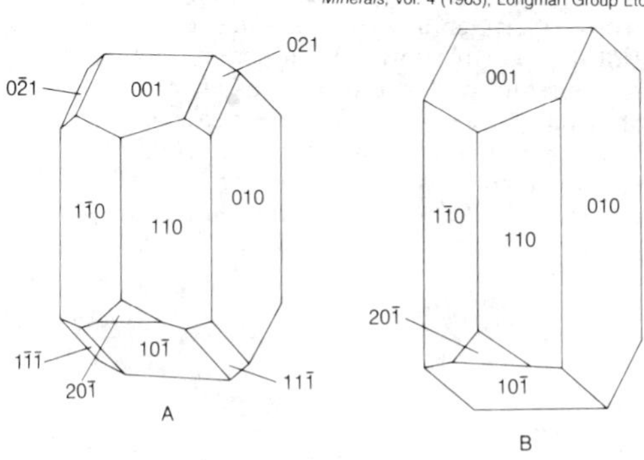

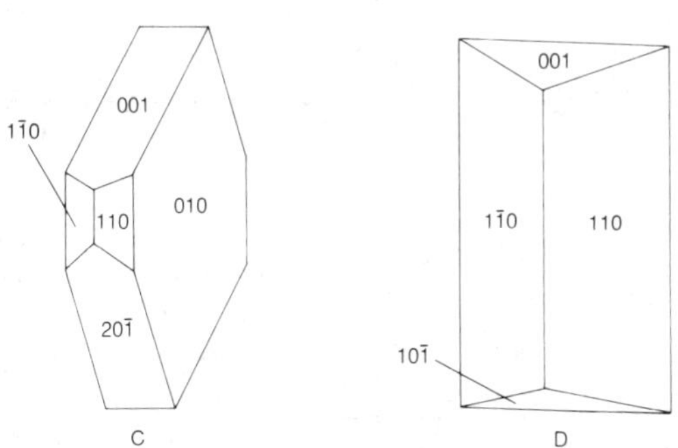

Figure 29: *Common feldspar habits.*
(A) and (B) prismatic habit of orthoclase, microcline, and plagioclase; (C) tabular habit of sanidine; (D) adularia habit.

cleavelandite. Pericline is a variety of albite found in low-temperature veins. Pericline is characteristically elongated along the *b* axis and has simple pericline twinning. The pericline twin law is named from this variety of feldspar.

The feldspars of some volcanic rocks in Norway are rather unusual in that, like adularia, they have a rhomb-shaped outline.

Optical properties. Optical properties of minerals require specialized knowledge both for determination and understanding. Although there are other optical properties of significance with regard to the feldspars, only refractive index—the ratio of the velocity of light in a vacuum (in air, as commonly measured) to that in the mineral—will be discussed here.

Refractive indices

Refractive indices of feldspars depend on chemical composition and, to a lesser extent, on the structural state. A graph of refractive indices and composition of alkali feldspars clearly indicates that the substitution of potassium for sodium has a small effect on the refractive index.

Table 2: Optical Properties of Feldspar Group End Members

	refractive indexes			optic axial angles	extinction angles	
	α	β	γ		(001) section	(010) section
High sanidine	1.518	1.522	1.522	(−) 64°	0	(+) 2°
Orthoclase	1.519	1.524	1.526	(−) 32°	0	(+) 5°
Microcline	1.522	1.526	1.529	(−) 70°–80°	(+) 5–15°	(+) 5°
High albite	1.527	1.532	1.534	(−) 45°–55°	(+) 0°–2°	+ 9°
Low albite	1.529	1.533	1.539	(+) 78°	(+) 3°	+ 20
Anorthite	1.575	1.584	1.589	(−) 77°	(−) 43°	(−) 39°

Measurements must be very accurate to have any value for determining chemical composition. Minor elements such as calcium, strontium, and barium also affect the plot, so that little useful information on alkali feldspars can be obtained by measuring approximate refractive indices except to indicate whether they are potassium- or sodium-rich compositions. In the plagioclase series, on the other hand, measurements of refractive indices have long been recognized as having useful determinative value, but, unless the structural state is known, the accuracy is not as great as might be desired, particularly for sodium-rich compositions.

An alternative method, very useful for relatively unzoned crystals, consists of fusing the crystals to a glass and then measuring the refractive index of the glass. A curve relating chemical composition to the refractive index of the glass for synthetic feldspar glasses may then be used for analysis. Because feldspars are frequently chemically zoned, sometimes in a very complex manner, it may be desirable to determine the composition of the separate zones, a distinction usually made by optical determinations; but, because this measurement depends on both structural state and chemical composition, an accurate knowledge of one of these must be obtained by some other method. A large number of optical techniques for determining the compositions of feldspars are available. These methods have become largely outdated, however, with the increasing availability of the electron microprobe.

PHASE EQUILIBRIA OF FELDSPAR SYSTEMS

Alkali feldspars. At atmospheric pressure pure potassium feldspars and compositions from pure orthoclase (Or) to about $Or_{50}Ab_{50}$ melt incongruently (*i.e.*, they react with the liquid to produce a new solid phase) and yield leucite plus liquid (see Figure 30). The

$$NaAlSi_3O_8{-}KAlSi_3O_8$$

system is not binary for those compositions above the beginning of melting. For all temperatures below the beginning of melting, however, the relations can be represented in a temperature–composition diagram. There is a minimum melting relationship, and the minimum is near $Or_{35}Ab_{65}$, as shown in Figure 30.

Importance of the solvus

The most important feature of the diagram is that it is dominated by a solvus (a boundary between a homogeneous field of solid solution and a field of two or more solid phases derived from the homogeneous one), whose crest lies at some temperature above 700° C. The experimentally determined solvus has a crest at about 690° C (1,274° F) at a water pressure of two kilobars, but this was determined using completely disordered feldspars: it is likely that some aluminum–silicon order is present in the crystals stable at this temperature, and the effect is to raise the crest of the solvus. The exact location of the solvus cannot be determined precisely because there will be an infinite number of metastable solvi, depending on the degree of aluminum–silicon order in the specimens used to define the solvus. Thus, the solvus shown is drawn only approximately, on the assumption that its crest is above 700° C and near $Or_{50}Ab_{50}$, and in the knowledge that low albite and maximum microcline show a limited solid solution of potassium and sodium, respectively.

The dashed line sloping from 930° C (1,706° F) at albite composition and intersecting the solvus represents the nonquenchable monoclinic–triclinic inversion in sodium-rich alkali feldspars; below the solvus this is denoted by a

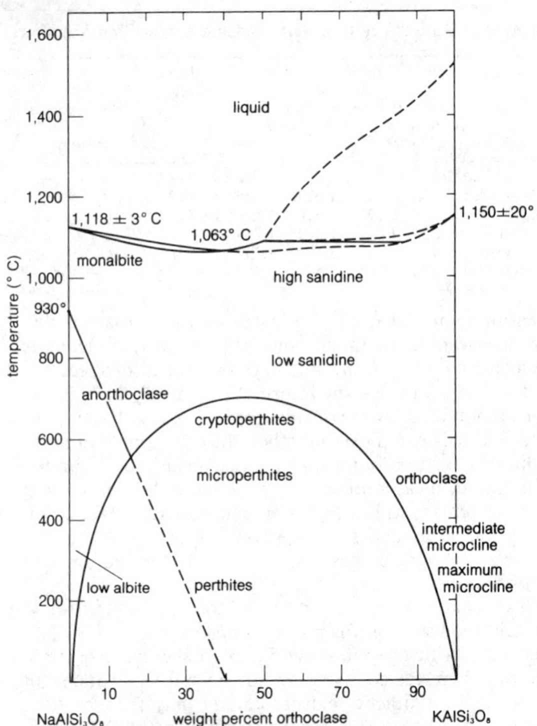

Figure 30: The alkali feldspar system, showing the liquidus, solidus, and subsolidus relations (see text).

From N. Bowen and O. Tuttle, "The System $NaAlSi_3O_8$-$KAlSi_3O_8$-H_2O," *Journal of Geology*, vol. 58 © 1950; the University of Chicago Press

dotted line to indicate that it is metastable in this region.

Temperature ranges for the stabilities of the various forms of sodium and potassium feldspars cannot be shown because they are not accurately defined, there being a gradual transition from the highest to the lowest temperature form (see Figure 30). The boundary between anorthoclase and sanidine is at $Or_{40}Ab_{60}$ because single-phase crystals of a composition more sodium rich than this are triclinic at room temperature, and compositions more potassium rich are monoclinic at room temperature.

At a water pressure of five kilobars, the melting curves on this system are lowered considerably because of the incorporation of water in the silicate melt, and the minimum is replaced by what appears in projection to be a eutectic (*i.e.*, the lowest melting point possible in mixtures of components that do not form solid solutions). The degree of aluminum–silicon disorder in the two feldspars in equilibrium with the liquid at the temperature of this pseudo-eutectic is likely to be very high; hence the stable solvus close to the melting curves might be expected to be that determined experimentally. The effect of pressure on the solvus is to raise it slightly. (See Figure 32.)

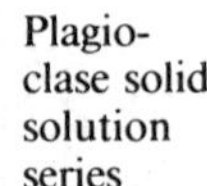

Plagioclase feldspars. At high temperature the plagioclase feldspars form a solid solution series with no maximum or minimum. At lower temperatures the phase diagram is extremely complex (Figure 25). The form of sodium feldspar stable at the melting point is monoclinic albite, but, with increasing calcium this quickly gives way to a triclinic form with a 7 Å *c* axis, which extends across the diagram to near anorthite, where the body-centred form with a 14 Å *c* axis is the stable form. The relations at the anorthite end of the series are extremely complex, and recent studies suggest a possible solvus for bytownite compositions. At the albite end of the series, where the peristerites are found in the composition range An_2–An_{16}, it is likely that these represent a solvus, although it has not been proved experimentally, nor has the temperature of the crest of this possible solvus been determined. At high water pressures the solidus and liquidus are lowered, but the shape of the plagioclase loop is not greatly changed.

The melting relations also have been determined in the absence of water at pressures of one bar and 10 and 20 kilobars (Figure 31). At 10 kilobars anorthite melts incon-

By courtesy of Carnegie Institution of Washington

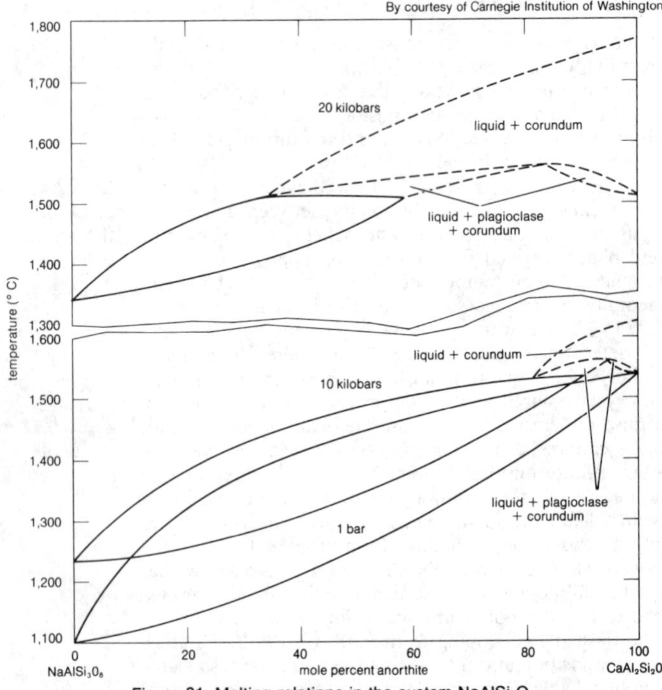

Figure 31: Melting relations in the system $NaAlSi_3O_8$–$CaAl_2Si_2O_8$ at one bar, 10 kilobars, and 20 kilobars (see text).

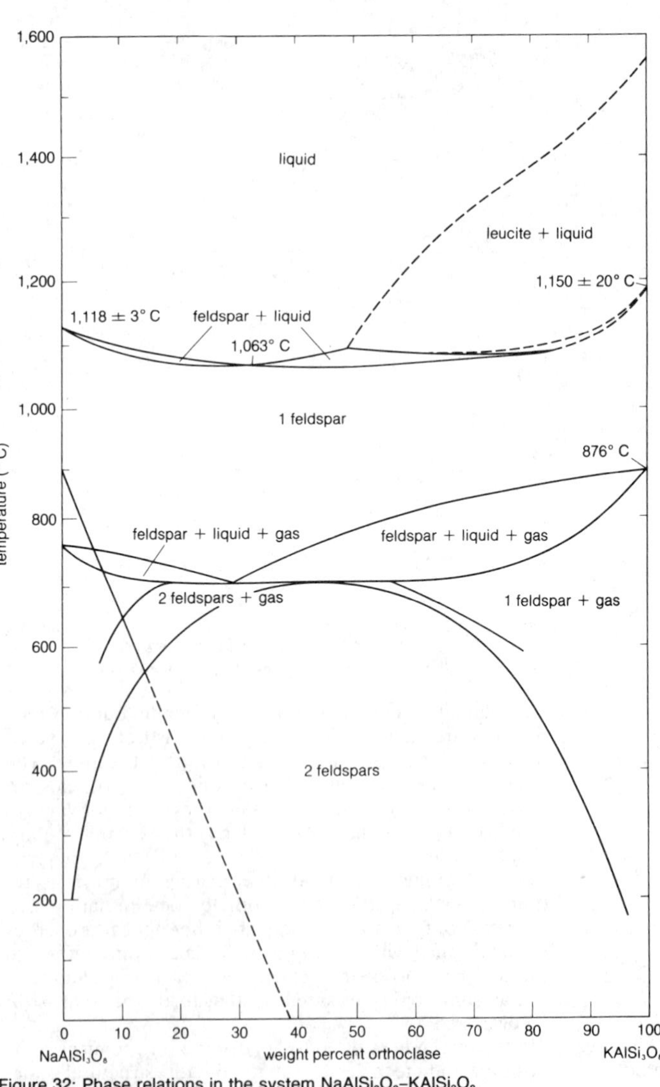

Figure 32: Phase relations in the system $NaAlSi_3O_8$–$KAlSi_3O_8$ at atmospheric pressure and at $P_{H_2O} = 5$ kb, showing the effect of P_{H_2O} on the melting point (see Figure 30) and the solvus.

gruently to corundum + liquid, and at higher pressures the corundum + liquid field extends to more sodium-rich compositions. At 26 kilobars congruent melting occurs only between pure albite and $Ab_{85}An_{15}$. At pressures above 32 kilobars albite melts to jadeite + liquid, so that above this pressure no plagioclase of any kind can crystallize from a melt.

Ternary system. Phase relations in the ternary feldspar system (*i.e.,* the sodium–potassium–calcium feldspar system) have not been completely determined experimentally, mainly because of the viscosity of the melts and the difficulty of attaining equilibrium. At atmospheric pressure only the liquidus surface has been determined, and, because of the incongruent melting of potassium-rich compositions, the system is quaternary.

Crystallization in this system is exceedingly complex because the two solid phases are ternary solid solutions, and with falling temperature these solid solutions approach each other in composition. For certain bulk compositions it can be shown that, at some stage during equilibrium crystallization, one of the feldspars present may be dissolving while the other is precipitating. Different bulk compositions behave differently, and a detailed discussion of the variations in crystallization paths is beyond the scope of this discussion. (W.S.MacK./Ed.)

Amphiboles

The amphiboles occur in a wide variety of igneous rocks and metamorphic rocks, less commonly in sedimentary rocks, and rarely in meteorites. Common forms include long prismatic crystals, radiating columnar aggregates, silky fibres, or irregularly shaped grains that typically exhibit well-developed planes of prismatic cleavage (tendency to split parallel to certain crystallographic directions). These planes meet at angles of about 55° and 125° and yield cleavage fragments that are diamond-shaped in cross section.

Amphiboles may be white, gray, green, brown, black, blue, or violet; iron-poor varieties, however, can be colourless or nearly so. They exhibit a hardness on the Mohs scale between 5 and 6.5, yield water when heated in a closed tube, fuse in a flame with difficulty, and dissolve slowly in hydrofluoric acid but are virtually unaffected by other acids. The optical property of pleochroism (colour absorption varying with direction), which sometimes aids in mineral identification, usually is distinct, increasing in intensity with increasing transition metal ion content; it may be weak or absent, however, in amphiboles lacking these ions.

Economic importance

Few amphibole minerals are of economic importance. Fibrous anthophyllite, actinolite, and crocidolite (a variety of magnesioriebeckite–riebeckite) are used as substitutes for chrysotile asbestos. Their heat-resistant properties and tensile strength, however, are less than that of chrysotile, and they are not as suitable for spinning. The aggregate called jade, used extensively by Oriental and Mayan peoples for ornamental purposes, is of two types. The more highly prized type consists of the pyroxene mineral jadeite. The other, usually called nephrite jade, is an amphibole and consists of a yellowish or spinach green, translucent-to-opaque, compact, dense aggregate of finely interfelted tufts of actinolite fibres.

CHEMICAL COMPOSITION

The chemistry of the amphibole group is complex and variable because of the possible ionic substitution between certain end-members. A typical amphibole often contains 10 or more of the most abundant elements in the Earth's crust. A generalized structural formula is:

$$W_{0-1}X_2Y_5(Z_4O_{11})_2(OH,F,O,Cl)_2,$$

in which W refers to ions of radius one Å (one angstrom unit [Å] equals 10^{-8} centimetre) and larger, chiefly potassium (K^+) and sodium (Na^+), which may or may not be present; X refers to ions of radius 0.7 to 1.1 angstroms, chiefly calcium (Ca^{2+}), sodium (Na^+), ferrous iron (Fe^{2+}), magnesium (Mg^{2+}), manganese (Mn^{2+}), and lithium (Li^+); Y refers to ions of radius 0.5 to 0.9 angstrom, chiefly magnesium (Mg^{2+}), ferrous iron (Fe^{2+}), ferric iron (Fe^{3+}), aluminum (Al^{3+}), manganese (Mn^{2+}), and titanium (Ti^{4+}); and Z refers to small, highly charged cations, chiefly silicon (Si^{4+}) but to a lesser extent aluminum (Al^{3+}) and ferric iron (Fe^{3+}), and rarely beryllium (Be^{2+}). The ionic substitution is determined, in general, by the radius of the ion, by the requirement for electrostatic neutrality (*i.e.,* that the positive and negative charges balance) in the final formula unit, and by the chemical environment and pressure-temperature conditions that existed during formation. Amphibole minerals can be classified chemically into one of three groups: magnesium–iron-, sodic-, or

By courtesy of Howard W. Jaffe and Peter Robinson

Figure 33: Photomicrograph of a three-amphibole assemblage from the Partridge formation of Middle Ordovician age near Quabbin Reservoir, Massachusetts. The light brown grain filling the centre of the micrograph is anthophyllite exhibiting incipient prismatic cleavage characteristic of amphiboles. The darker brown grain, which is an oriented intergrowth enclosed by anthophyllite, is hornblende showing cleavage and exsolution lamellae of $P2_1/m$ cummingtonite. Subjacent to the hornblende is a smaller brownish grain of $P2_1/m$ cummingtonite with fine exsolution lamellae of hornblende.

calcic-amphibole, depending on whether Mg-Fe, Na, or Ca is the predominating X cation. Selected end-member representatives are enumerated in Table 3 together with some characteristic physical properties.

CRYSTAL STRUCTURE

Amphibole chains and layers

The fundamental structural unit in almost all silicate minerals is the SiO_4 tetrahedron. The structure types of the different silicates can be related to the various ways the

By courtesy of the (left, right) Field Museum of Natural History, Chicago, (centre) Joseph and Helen Guetterman Collection; photographs, John H. Gerard—EB Inc.

Figure 34: *Three important members of the amphibole group.*
(Left) Hornblende from Chester, Massachusetts. (Centre) Actinolite crystals with talc from Washington. (Right) Crocidolite (tigereye) from Orange River, South Africa.

Table 3: Selected (Mg, Fe)-, and Ca-Amphibole End-Members with Characterizing Chemical and Physical Properties

amphibole	W_{0-1}	X_2	Y_5	Z_8O_{22}	$(OH,F,O)_2$	specific gravity	refractive indices α	β	γ	crystal system	space group symmetry	unit cell parameters a	b	c	β
(Mg, Fe)-															
Anthophyllite	0	Mg_2	Mg_5	Si_8	$(OH)_2$	2.95	1.587	1.602	1.613	orthorhombic	Pnma	18.61	18.01	5.24	90°
Gedrite	0	Mg_2	Mg_3Al_2	Si_6Al_2	$(OH)_2$	3.18	1.642	1.655	1.661	orthorhombic	Pnma	18.53	17.74	5.25	90°
Protoamphibole	0	$(Mg, Li)_2$	Mg_5	Si_8	F_2	2.92	1.575	1.587	1.593	orthorhombic	Pmnm	9.33	17.88	5.29	90°
Cummingtonite	0	Fe_2	Mg_5	Si_8	$(OH)_2$	3.10	1.643	1.650	1.663	monoclinic	C2/m	9.30	18.14	5.19	102.1°
Grunerite	0	Fe_2	Fe_5	Si_8	$(OH)_2$	3.54	1.688	1.711	1.731	monoclinic	C2/m	9.59	18.43	5.34	101.9°
$P2_1/m$ clino-amphibole	0	$(Fe, Mn)_2$	$(Mg, Fe)_5$	Si_8	$(OH)_2$		1.621	1.632	1.643	monoclinic	$P2_1/m$	9.55	18.01	5.30	102.6°
Na-															
Glaucophane II	0	Na_2	Mg_3Al_2	Si_8	$(OH)_2$	3.03	1.594	1.612	1.618	monoclinic	C2/m	9.64	17.73	5.28	103.6°
Magnesioriebeckite	0	Na_2	$Mg_3Fe_2^{3+}$	Si_8	$(OH)_2$	3.15	1.656	1.671	1.672	monoclinic	C2/m	9.73	17.95	5.30	103.3°
Riebeckite	0	Na_2	$Fe_3^{2+}Fe_2^{3+}$	Si_8	$(OH)_2$	3.40	1.702	1.712	1.719	monoclinic	C2/m	9.73	18.06	5.33	103.3°
Ca-															
Richterite	Na	NaCa	Mg_5	Si_8	$(OH)_2$	3.0				monoclinic	C2/m	9.89	17.96	5.26	104.3°
Tremolite	0	Ca_2	Mg_5	Si_8	$(OH)_2$	2.97	1.600	1.614	1.627	monoclinic	C2/m	9.83	18.05	5.27	104.5°
Ferrotremolite	0	Ca_2	Fe_5	Si_8	$(OH)_2$	3.40	1.672	1.686	1.693	monoclinic	C2/m	9.97	18.34	5.30	104.5°
Pargasite*	Na	Ca_2	Mg_4Al	Si_6Al_2	$(OH)_2$	3.0	1.624		1.645	monoclinic	C2/m	9.91	17.99	5.26	105.3°
Ferropargasite*	Na	Ca_2	$Fe_4^{2+}Fe^{3+}$	Si_6Al_2	$(OH)_2$	3.4	1.700		1.718	monoclinic	C2/m	9.95	18.14	5.33	105.3°
Hastingsite*	Na	Ca_2	$Fe_4^{2+}Fe^{3+}$	Si_6Al_2	$(OH)_2$	3.5	1.702		1.728	monoclinic	C2/m	9.98	18.15	5.32	105.2°
Joesmithite	(Ca, Pb)	Ca_2	$(Mg, Fe^{2+}, Fe^{3+})_5$	Si_6Be_2	$(OH)^2$	3.83	1.747	1.765	1.78	monoclinic	P2/a	9.88	17.88	5.24	105.7°

*Hornblende.

tetrahedra are linked together into larger units. In pyroxene, SiO_4 tetrahedra are linked in infinite single chains of SiO_3 composition, whereas the amphiboles are made up of double chains in which the tetrahedra alternately share two and three oxygen atoms; this arrangement leads to an oxygen/silicon ratio of 11 to 4 (see Figure 35). The crystal structure of amphibole is characterized by layers of interlocking (Z_4O_{11}) infinite double chains (Figure 36) consisting of tetrahedra linked together into arrays of O(3)-centred six-membered rings, O(3) representing hydroxyl, fluorine, oxygen, or (rarely) chlorine.

In Figure 36, A and B represent idealized drawings of the structure of a clinoamphibole viewed down *c* (commonly the vertical or upright crystallographic axis) and a^* [a^* is perpendicular to (100)—a plane that intersects the *a*-axis at unit distance and is parallel to the other two crystallographic axes], respectively, together with the nomenclature of the atoms in the asymmetric unit. The chains in these drawings parallel (100) with their endless dimensions lying along *c*. Along the *b*-axis the chains are juxtaposed and alternate in orientation, with the apices of the ZO_4-tetrahedra pointing successively up and down along a^*. The O(4) oxygen anions of each chain dovetail with the O(1) and O(2) oxygen anions of adjacent chains, locking them together into layers. The layers, stacked parallel to (100), are bonded together by *X* and *Y* cations that are coordinated between narrow hexagonal strips consisting of O(1), O(2), O(3), and O(4), the coordination being affected by a stagger of about *c*/3 between adjacent layers. The *Y* cations occur in more or less perfect octahedra designated M(1), M(2), and M(3), whereas the *X* cations are in irregular sixfold to eightfold coordination polyhedra designated M(4). When present, the *W* cations are distributed about the *A*-site, which is located in the relatively large cavity formed by eight oxygen anions at the backs of adjacent chains. The good to perfect prismatic cleavage, diagnostic of the mineral, passes through the structure parallel to these chains by stepping successively along their backs through the *A*-site and thence to periphery of the next layer. The crystal structures and physical properties of many of the amphiboles are remarkably similar to those of the clinoamphibole shown. All consist of layers of interlocking double chains of ZO_4-tetrahedra bonded together by *X* and *Y* cations. Different structural types arise, however, because of different layered stacking sequences, the occurrence of chains of two slightly different geometries, or variations of cation ordering and composition.

From Deer, Howie, and Zussman, *Rock-Forming Minerals*, vol. 2, p. 204, fig. 53a (1962), Longman Group Ltd.

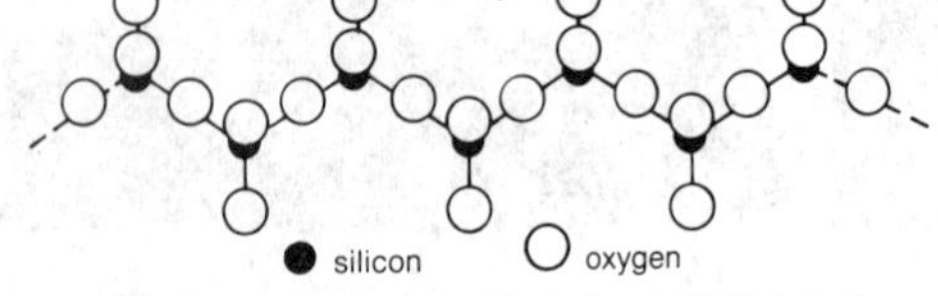

Figure 35: Comparison of amphibole band $(Si_4O_{11})_n$ and pyroxene chain $(SiO_3)_n$ (see text).

OCCURRENCE AND DISTRIBUTION

Magnesium–iron amphiboles

The magnesium–iron amphiboles are for the most part confined to metamorphic rocks and crystallize in both the orthorhombic and monoclinic systems. The orthorhombic varieties are represented in nature by the anthophyllites, in which the Mg/Mg + Fe ratio may reach 0.4, and by the gedrites (essentially aluminous anthophyllites), in which aluminum may substitute for magnesium or iron in *Y* and for silicon in *Z*. The gedrites, however, can be quite iron-rich. Magnesium-rich anthophyllites are commonly found in contact zones where granitic dikes have intruded ultramafic (iron- and magnesium-rich) rocks and in metamorphosed siliceous dolomites (calcium magnesium carbonate rocks). Iron-rich anthophyllites occur in ultramafic bodies such as peridotites, which have been partially hydrated at moderate temperatures. In the presence of alumina, as in rocks that contain such minerals as cordierite or plagioclase, the amphibole composition approaches that of a gedrite. Environments that are relatively low in sodium, potassium, calcium, and manganese, however, are essential for crystallization of anthophyllite or gedrite alone.

The monoclinic varieties, called cummingtonites, commonly seem to require an Fe/Fe + Mg ratio of 0.4 or more. If this ratio is close to 1.0, the amphibole is called grunerite, a form that is stable only at the lower oxidation states. Manganese is normally the third most abundant cation in *X* and *Y*, whereas aluminum, sodium, and calcium are characteristically low. Cummingtonites are commonly found in iron formations, such as those in Labrador and Minnesota, where they are associated with quartz, iron oxides, carbonates, and iron-rich sheet silicates. The existence of a monoclinic form not commonly reported ($P2_1/m$) that can be changed by heating at 40° C (104° F) and one atmosphere pressure into the more commonly reported monoclinic form (C2/m) has been demonstrated. Assemblages that include orthorhombic and monoclinic amphiboles have been reported in zones between metamorphosed iron-rich volcanic rocks and clay-rich sediments. Nevertheless, because many nat-

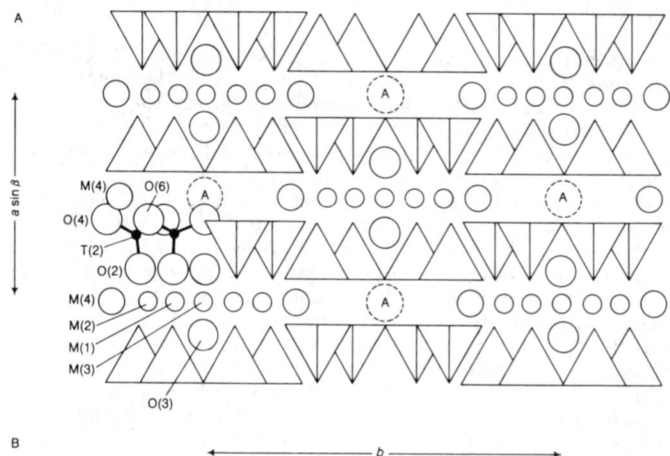

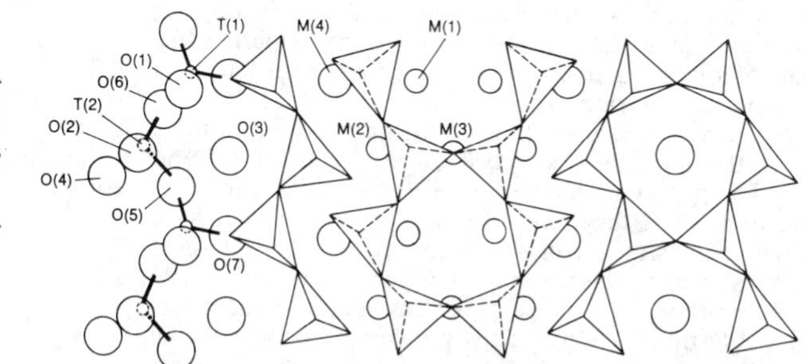

Figure 36: The crystal structure of C2/m clinoamphibole viewed (A) along the c-axis and (B) down the a-axis; T(1) and T(2) represent substitution sites (see text).

ural environments contain significant amounts of sodium, potassium, and calcium, the magnesium–iron amphiboles are the least abundant of the three amphibole groups.

Sodic amphiboles

Sodic amphiboles are typified by the minerals glaucophane, magnesioriebeckite, and riebeckite (see Table 3). Figure 37 illustrates their chemical variation in nature and the control of rock bulk composition on their chemistry. The ferroglaucophane corner in Figure 37 represents a composition that does not appear to be common.

Glaucophane and magnesioriebeckite occur principally in low-grade (altered at relatively low temperatures) metamorphic rocks. The association of glaucophane with lawsonite, $CaAl_2Si_2O_8 \cdot 2H_2O$, and/or one of the carbonate minerals (*e.g.*, calcite or aragonite, polymorphs of $CaCO_3$), constitutes one of the characteristic assemblages of the so-called blueschist metamorphic facies (rock types). Such rocks represent relatively high pressures (five to eight kilobars) and low temperatures of recrystallization (100° to 300° C [210° to 570° F]). Glaucophane is most abundant in rocks of basaltic bulk composition in this facies. In environments high in aluminum, magnesium, iron, and alkalis, solid solutions toward magnesioriebeckite result. These solid solutions, intermediate members of which are called crossite, may also occur at the low temperatures but less elevated pressures of the greenschist metamorphic facies. In most greenschists, however, the amphiboles are calcic varieties, so that the presence of sodic forms represents departures from basaltic composition toward high soda and low lime.

Riebeckites have low thermal stability and are most common in the lowest temperature, last-to-crystallize, silica-rich igneous rocks, such as pegmatites. They also form in the greenschist and blueschist facies in recrystallized iron-rich cherts. The dark green to black amphibole that occurs in some granites and syenites, though often called riebeckite, is probably more nearly an arfvedsonite; it exhibits a higher soda content and higher Fe^{2+}/Fe^{3+} ratio than riebeckite. Authigenic (formed *in situ*) riebeckite–magnesioriebeckite has been reported from the Green River Shales and evaporites in Utah. The temperature of growth must have been in the range of 25° to 50° C (75° to 120° F), and, accordingly, these sodic forms may be stable at lower temperatures than any other members of the amphibole group. In contrast, there are no documented reports of magnesium–iron or calcium varieties forming naturally at temperatures as low as even 100° C. These latter species weather and decompose to clays and oxides, indicating that their lower temperature of stability lies above that of the sedimentary environment.

Calcic amphiboles

Calcic varieties are the most widespread and volumetrically abundant members of the amphibole group. For purposes of discussion, two subgroups may be distinguished: (1) the tremolite–ferrotremolite series (intermediate members being called actinolites), which contain little or no aluminum and lack *W* cations (vacant *A*-site), and (2) the hornblendes, which include the majority of other calcium amphiboles.

Tremolite is a common mineral in metamorphosed siliceous dolomites and limestones and in ultramafic rocks metamorphosed at low grade. It can be found in high-temperature carbonate-free rocks (sillimanite zone) but forms at much lower temperature in the presence of carbon dioxide, which is the common case. Thus, its occurrence normally implies only a low-grade metamorphic environment. Actinolites form in rocks of basaltic composition because such rocks contain more iron than carbonates. Actinolites are a common and diagnostic feature of greenschist facies conditions. The change from low-grade to high-grade metamorphic conditions is accompanied by a concomitant change in calcium-amphibole composition from actinolite to hornblende.

Hornblendes

Hornblendes have a wide compositional range and are chemically the most complex of the natural amphiboles. Entire metamorphic terranes are composed chiefly of hornblende plus plagioclase feldspar (a rock called amphibolite). Higher temperature conditions of origin are commonly reflected by increased aluminum, titanium, sodium, and potassium content. The maximum amount of substitution of aluminum for silicon in *Z* is about 25 percent (two of the eight *Z* cations in the formula unit) with the aluminum ordering into the T(1) tetrahedra of the chain (Figure 36). The pargasite–hastingsites are hornblende end-members illustrative of the maximum substitution of aluminum for silicon.

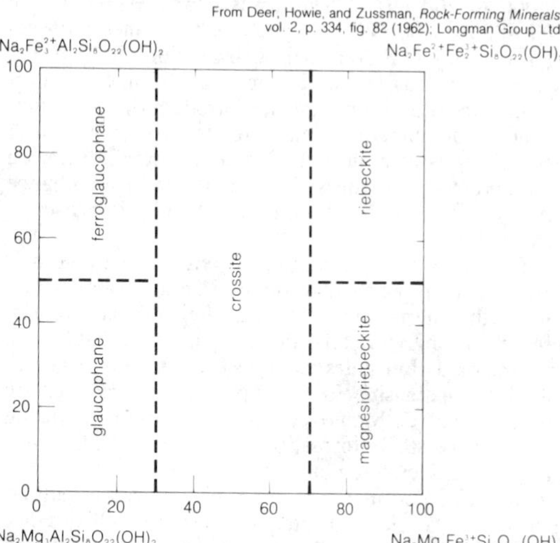

Figure 37: Variation in the chemical composition and nomenclature of the glaucophane–riebeckite amphiboles.

Hornblendes have sufficient thermal stabilities to be stable in magmas; thus they are common and very abundant in such plutonic igneous rocks as diorites, quartz diorites, and granodiorites. Hornblendes also occur as phenocrysts (large single crystals) in andesitic lavas but normally are much less abundant in volcanic rocks because the volcanic conditions of relatively low water pressure and high temperature are outside amphibole stability. The iron-rich hornblende hastingsite is found in many granites, syenites, and certain other alkali-rich rocks.

Calcium amphiboles are found as detrital grains (those

derived from pre-existing rocks and then transported) in heavy mineral (*i.e.,* of specific gravity greater than that of quartz [2.65] and other relatively light minerals) suites (sets) of sedimentary rocks. Actinolite seems to be less abundant than hornblende. In general, amphiboles represent a decreasing percentage of the suite with increasing age because of a relatively low resistance to weathering and post-depositional changes.

EXPERIMENTAL STUDIES OF AMPHIBOLE STABILITYAND PHASE RELATIONS

Synthesis of amphiboles

Experimental studies of the stability and phase relations of amphiboles date back only to the 1950s. Since that time a number of the end-member compositions have been synthesized successfully. The decomposition of amphiboles at a given pressure with increasing temperature gives rise to assemblages that may include the phases pyroxene, quartz, olivine, plagioclase, garnet, oxides, liquid, and/or vapour. The chemically simpler amphiboles, such as anthophyllite or tremolite, may be represented by an assemblage of equivalent bulk composition consisting of only two or three minerals. The chemically more complex amphiboles, however, represented by hornblende, may either decompose or melt incongruently (react with the liquid phase) to as many as five other minerals. Thus, many rock compositions, if they could be recrystallized in the presence of water at 300° to 800° C (570° to 1,470° F) and pressures of 500 to 5,000 bars, would consist predominantly of amphibole.

Adequate experimental work has been completed to allow generalizations on the effect of compositional changes on amphibole thermal stability. One of the most dramatic increases in high temperature stability of amphibole comes about if magnesium is substituted for ferrous iron (200°–400° C [390°–750° F]). Equally important is the substitution of fluorine for the hydroxyl (OH) ion. Some synthetic fluoramphiboles appear to be stable up to 1,100°–1,200° C (2,000°–2,200° F) at one atmosphere pressure, which is 600°–800° C (1,100°–1,470° F) higher than for species containing only OH. Whether such relations hold at elevated pressures has yet to be determined. Substitution of ferric iron for aluminum and the introduction of sodium into the *A*-site lead to increases in stability of the order of tens of degrees Celsius only. If aluminum is introduced into *Y* and *Z* along with sodium in *W,* as in the change from tremolite to pargasite, thermal stability increases as much as 200° C.

For any amphibole containing elements of variable oxidation state (*e.g.,* iron, manganese, titanium), the oxygen fugacity (the thermodynamic equivalent of partial pressure) will strongly modify the stability relations. With increasing oxidation states, the upper temperature stability limit of ferropargasite, for example, can be reduced by more than 300° C. Moreover, under conditions oxidizing enough for the stable formation of hematite (Fe_2O_3), ferropargasite and ferrotremolite are unstable.

The pure iron end-members are rarely realized in nature. Experimental studies indicate, however, that this is not caused by the instability of such structures. The principal causes are: (1) the iron members have much more limited thermal ranges compared to their magnesium counterparts, (2) the oxygen fugacity–temperature conditions necessary for the formation of the iron members occur rarely in nature, and (3) rock bulk compositions normally are not sufficiently iron-rich to permit the formation of such amphiboles.

Geological evidence suggests that the oceans and atmosphere of the Earth developed with time through emission or release of gases from the mantle (the zone beneath the crust) during volcanism. Accordingly, interest has centred on amphiboles as possible compounds containing water in the mantle. Work shows that these phases have lowered thermal stabilities at fluid pressures of 15 to 30 kilobars compared to pressures up to 15 kilobars. Nevertheless, the stable existence of amphiboles to depths of 50 to 70 kilometres (30 to 45 miles) in the Earth is not precluded. The storage of water in amphiboles under upper mantle conditions is thus a very real possibility.

Amphiboles in the Earth's mantle

(G.V.G./M.C.G.)

Pyroxenes

Occurrence and use

The name pyroxene is derived from the Greek *pyro,* "fire," and *xenos,* "stranger," in allusion to the occurrence of the mineral in volcanic rocks, which was initially thought to be accidental rather than indigenous. Pyroxenes are the principal minerals in many kinds of igneous and metamorphic rocks, however, and they occur in meteorites and lunar samples as well. Omphacite, a variety rich in sodium and aluminum, and aluminous enstatite are thought to be abundant in the Earth's mantle, and analysis of the radiation emitted by certain cool stars reveals the probable presence of pyroxenes throughout the known universe.

Certain pyroxenes are useful as economic mineral guides, or indicators: johannsenite is generally associated with copper, zinc, and lead ores; omphacite occurs with diamond in kimberlites (relatively rare igneous rocks that are rich in iron and magnesium); and spodumene and aegirine (lithium aluminosilicate and sodium ferrisilicate minerals, respectively) are often indicators of pegmatites—very coarse-grained crystalline rocks that commonly contain a rare-mineral assemblage. Aside from this usage as indicators or guide minerals, only jadeite, nephrite—ornamental jade—and spodumene, a commercial source of lithium, are of economic importance.

Form, habit, and colour

All pyroxene species exhibit a prismatic crystal form in which the angles between crystal faces are about 87° and 93°. The pyroxenes have good cleavages parallel to these directions—*i.e.,* they tend to split along planes that have these trends. As a consequence, the pyroxenes possess nearly square cross sections when viewed perpendicularly to their principal cleavage directions, and this characteristic is diagnostic. Most of the pyroxenes in rocks in the Earth's crust, however, occur as irregularly shaped grains; short, stubby, prismatic crystals are less common.

Aegirine commonly occurs as long, needle-like crystals, and spodumene as prismatic crystals as long as 12 metres (40 feet) and two to six feet wide. These two minerals are associated with very coarse-grained pegmatites.

The colour of pyroxenes varies with slight changes of chemical composition: augite is brown or green; diopside is either colourless or white to green; and aegirine is green to greenish black. Some varieties of jadeite and spodumene may be violet or pink.

CLASSIFICATION AND PROPERTIES

Variation of composition and physical properties

Mineral names and groups. The naming of a pyroxene depends upon its major element composition and crystal system, and the more refined aspects of minor element content and crystal structure often require prefixes. Diopside, for example, is primarily a calcium (Ca) magnesium (Mg) silicate ($CaMgSi_2O_6$) and crystallizes in the monoclinic system, which refers to three unequal crystallographic axes, two intersecting obliquely and the third perpendicular to these two. Diopside has the basic pyroxene crystal structure but differs in detail from another monoclinic pyroxene such as spodumene. A trace content of chromium also is sufficient in some cases to warrant the name chrome diopside. Enstatite is primarily magnesium silicate ($Mg_2Si_2O_6$) and usually crystallizes in the orthorhombic system, which refers to three unequal crystallographic axes that are mutually perpendicular, but polymorphism (the ability of a mineral species to occur in different forms) gives rise to other crystal structures with the same composition. These may be orthorhombic such as protoenstatite or monoclinic such as clinoenstatite. A trace content of aluminum may warrant the name aluminous enstatite. For diopside, a marked increase of iron in place of magnesium leads to hedenbergite; magnesium in place of calcium leads to clinoenstatite; and magnesium and iron in place of calcium yield augite and ultimately pigeonite. This subgroup of pyroxenes, can first be expressed chemically in terms of three end-members (pure compounds): calcium silicate ($Ca_2Si_2O_6$), magnesium silicate ($Mg_2Si_2O_6$), and iron (Fe) silicate ($Fe_2Si_2O_6$).

The pyroxene formulas listed in Table 4 are relevant only to these end-member compositions, and the sections of this article on crystal structure and chemical composition explain the relationships between these and the more

Table 4: The Pyroxene Minerals

mineral	chemical formula	unit-cell dimensions* a	b	c	density (g/cm³)
Diopside	$CaMgSi_2O_6$	9.73	8.91	5.25	3.25
Hedenbergite	$CaFe^{2+}Si_2O_6$	9.85	9.02	5.26	3.54
Enstatite	$Mg_2Si_2O_6$	18.23	8.81	5.19	3.21
Ferrosilite (Ortho)	$Fe_2^{2+}Si_2O_6$	18.43	9.06	5.26	3.96
Aegirine (or Acmite)	$NaFe^{3+}Si_2O_6$	9.65	8.79	5.29	3.56
Jadeite	$NaAlSi_2O_6$	9.50	8.61	5.24	3.25
Spodumene	$LiAlSi_2O_6$	9.50	8.30	5.24	3.16
Johannsenite	$CaMnSi_2O_6$	9.83	9.04	5.27	3.45

*The unit cell is the smallest volume that will provide a representative sample of the atomic and molecular groups that comprise a mineral. Dimensions are given along the three crystallographic axes (designated *a*, *b*, and *c*) in angstrom units (one angstrom unit equals 10^{-8} centimetre).

common intermediate variants. The general composition of the pyroxenes, in fact, must be expressed as: XYZ_2O_6, in which X is zero or one, Y is one or two, and $X + Y = 2$. The compositional range can be indicated by the array of possible substituting elements—*i.e.*, X = calcium, sodium, or, less commonly, lithium; Y = magnesium, iron, aluminum, or, less commonly, manganese, nickel, chromium, and titanium; and Z = silicon, but aluminum or ferric iron also may occur.

Certain optical properties serve to differentiate the pyroxenes, but other physical properties tend to be rather uniform. The hardness of these minerals is 6 to 6½ on Mohs scale, the lustre is vitreous or glassy, and the form and habit also tend to be rather similar because of the

After Bragg, 1937, Jong, 1959, in Deer, Howie, and Zussman, *Rock-Forming Minerals*, vol. 2 (1968); Longman Group Ltd.

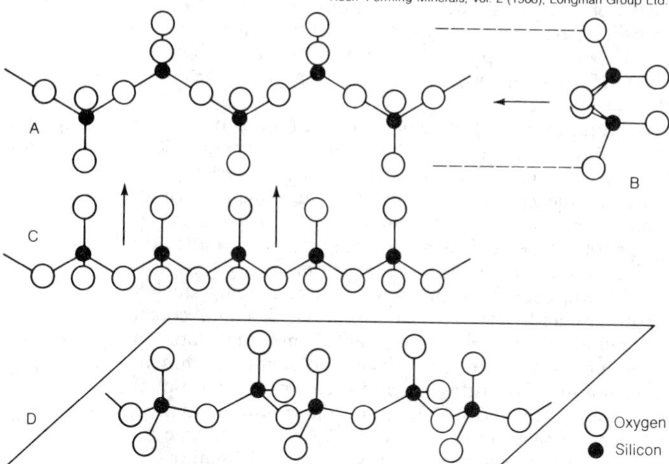

Figure 38: Single pyroxene chain, $(SiO_3)\,n$, in three projections (A) on (100), (B) along the *z* direction, (C) along the *y* direction, as well as (D) in perspective.

good cleavage at 87° and 93° as previously noted. Density variations (see Table 4) are diagnostic of iron enrichment.

Basic pyroxene chain structure

Crystal structure. The crystalline structure of all pyroxene minerals, like that of other silicates, consists basically of four oxygen atoms arranged as a tetrahedron with a silicon atom at its centre. These tetrahedra are linked in the form of chains, a structure similar to that of the amphiboles. The linkage is effected by the sharing of two oxygens between neighbouring tetrahedra in the chain, so that the basic formula becomes one silicon (Si) to three oxygens (O), or SiO_3. Identical units of the chain are repeated at approximately 5.3-Å (one angstrom unit [Å] equals 10^{-8} centimetre) intervals; this direction defines the *c*-axis of the crystal, and the distance is the dimension of the unit cell in the *c*-direction. The linkage of a pyroxene chain viewed from various directions is shown in Figure 38.

The diopside structure consists of only one type of chain, which is also characteristic of jadeite, augite, and protoenstatite. In contrast, the clinoenstatite and pigeonite structures consist of two structurally distinct SiO_3 chains. The orthorhombic pyroxenes have a unit cell that is derived by twinning of the latter structure along the *a*-axis. In spodumene there is a slight deviation whereby two different kinds of SiO_4 tetrahedra alternate along one kind of chain, and in omphacite this alternation occurs along each of two kinds of chain to produce a low-symmetry structure capable of accommodating a wide variety of cation (positively charged atom) sizes.

The diopside structure

The tetrahedra may show some substitution of silicon by aluminum and, less commonly, by traces of ferric iron or titanium. Most of the important cations other than silicon, however, occur as layer cations that are linked to the chain oxygens to form cation–oxygen polyhedra. Thus, the chains themselves are linked together by these cations to form a structure that is weakest parallel to the dominant cleavage direction of all pyroxenes.

The diopside structure may be taken as an example. Calcium and magnesium are divalent (doubly charged) cations that fulfill charge balance requirements to give the formula $CaMg(SiO_3)_2$. These cations lie in octahedral layers parallel to (100)—*i.e.*, a plane that intersects the *a*-axis and is parallel to *b* and *c*—but occur in two crystallographically distinct cation sites. The small magnesium ion (ionic radius = 0.78 Å) lies in the M_1 site and is linked with six oxygen atoms to form a fairly regular octahedron. The larger calcium ion (ionic radius = 1.06 Å) in the M_2 site, however, is linked with eight oxygens. Chemical substitution within the pyroxene group allows the M_1 site to be occupied by many small cations such as magnesium, ferrous and ferric iron, aluminum, or manganese. The M_2 site is usually occupied by the larger cations such as calcium or sodium, but in calcium-poor pyroxenes the site is occupied by smaller cations such as magnesium or ferrous iron in hypersthene or sodium in jadeite; the M_2 polyhedra are then distorted octahedra. In the pigeonite structure, which is somewhat problematical, disordered calcium and ferrous iron probably occupy the M_2 site in irregular 7-fold coordination (*i.e.*, surrounded by and bonded to seven oxygens), whereas M_1 is occupied by disordered magnesium and ferrous iron in regular 6-fold coordination. This condition may, in fact, be an average of randomly arranged domains of diopside-type and clinoenstatite-type structures.

The simpler structure of diopside is illustrated in Figure 39, in which the M_2 site is occupied by calcium in 8-fold coordination and the M_1 site by magnesium in 6-fold coordination. Hedenbergite differs by the presence of ferrous iron rather than magnesium in the M_1 site, and in the common augite both sites must be disordered between calcium, magnesium, and ferrous iron.

In the calcium-poor pyroxenes, the structural relations are more complex and lead to polymorphism. Magnesium silicate ($Mg_2Si_2O_6$) is an example. Three structural forms exist: clinoenstatite, rhombic enstatite, and protoenstatite. In these, successive tetrahedral slabs are related by glide-planes of symmetry parallel to (100), the glide component acting along either direction of the *c*-axis.

Chemical composition. The term common pyroxenes is applied to the great majority of minerals with compositions

After Warren and Bragg, 1928, in Deer, Howie, and Zussman, *Rock Forming Minerals*, vol. 2, fig. 14 (1963); Longman Group Ltd.

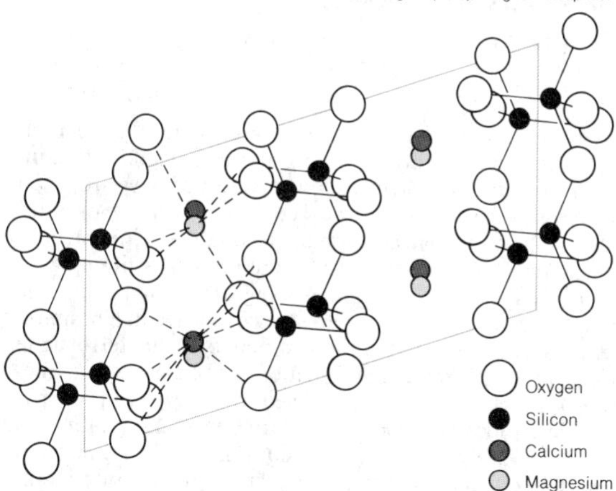

Figure 39: Idealized structure of diopside as viewed along the *y* direction.

Figure 40: Photomicrographs of various pyroxene minerals in thin sections (illuminated with polarized light). (Left) Augite phenocryst (large, individual, gray crystal) in basalt lava, showing characteristic basal octagonal form and square-segmentation cleavage (magnified about 16.5 ×). (Centre) Titanaugite crystal (yellow) showing typical hourglass zoning (magnified about 13.2 ×). (Right) Gabbro with two pyroxenes, a calcium-rich augite (blue-red and green) enclosed by a calcium-poor pigeonite crystal; clinohypersthene in thin lamellae has separated from the calcium-rich augite, and augite has separated from the pigeonite before it inverted to hypersthene (gray; magnified about 21.1 ×).

By courtesy of G. Malcolm Brown

The pyroxene quadrilateral

that can be expressed in terms of their calcium silicate ($Ca_2Si_2O_6$), magnesium silicate ($Mg_2Si_2O_6$), and iron silicate ($Fe_2Si_2O_6$) molecular contents. Compositions plotted on a triangular diagram show distinct pyroxene groupings that are of the greatest significance. No pyroxenes plot in that part of the diagram more calcic than the join (boundary line between phases) at $CaMgSi_2O_6$ and $CaFeSi_2O_6$ because of the structural prohibition of calcium from entering the M_1 sites. The common pyroxene quadrilateral is shown in Figure 41.

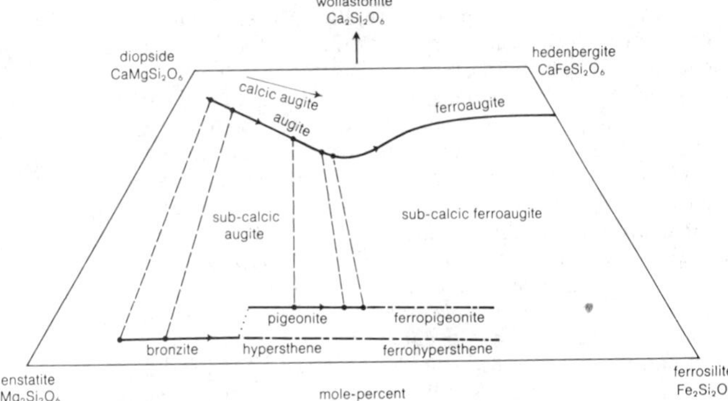

Figure 41: Common pyroxene quadrilateral showing the compositional ranges for various pyroxenes.

The nomenclature of the common clinopyroxenes was once based on subdivision of the quadrilateral, but the rigidity of the nomenclature and the orientation of the boundary lines between each named type proved unsatisfactory. It is now known that relationships within and between the common pyroxenes simplify the diagrammatic representation of their compositional fields within the quadrilateral.

Pyroxenes plotting close to or on the diopside–hedenbergite join are found only in metamorphosed calcium silicate rocks, for example by the reaction

$$\underset{\text{dolomite}}{CaMg(CO_3)_2} + \underset{\text{quartz}}{2SiO_2} \rightleftharpoons \underset{\text{diopside}}{CaMgSi_2O_6} + \underset{\text{carbon dioxide.}}{2CO_2}$$

The calcic augites occur in alkali basalts and their derivatives and are usually richer in aluminum and titanium than the augites. The calcic augites do not have iron-rich variants because their parent magmas generally produce liquids from which aegirine-augite and aegirine precipitate. The titanium-rich varieties are known as titanaugites and often exhibit hourglass zoning. The augites are the most common pyroxenes and show extensive magnesium–iron substitution to give the distinctive augite–ferroaugite trend line. Extreme fractionation of tholeiitic (olivine-poor) basalt magma is depicted by this trend of pyroxenes: diopsidic augite in ultramafic rocks (composed almost entirely of iron magnesium silicate), to augite in less mafic gabbroic rocks, to ferroaugite in intermediate, dioritic rocks (containing some quartz and sodium feldspar), and to ferrohedenbergite in acid, granitic rocks (rich in silica). The subcalcic augites and subcalcic ferroaugites occur as metastable phases in the quickly cooled groundmass (fine-grained crystalline bulk) of lavas. The tholeiitic suite of differentiated rocks generally contain, in addition to a member of the augite series, a calcium-poor pyroxene with, approximately, either 5 percent (bronzite) or 10 percent (pigeonite) of calcium silicate. The ultramafic rocks usually contain a bronzite, the gabbroic rocks a pigeonite, the intermediate rocks a ferropigeonite, and the acid rocks have no calcium-poor pyroxene. Certain intermediate rocks, notably the andesite and dacite lavas, contain hypersthene or ferrohypersthene instead of a pigeonitic phase.

The enstatite–ferrosilite pyroxene series is not fully represented on the quadrilateral. The nomenclature, based on ferrosilite percentage, is: enstatite (0–10 percent), bronzite (10–30 percent), hypersthene (30–50 percent), ferrohypersthene (50–70 percent), eulite (70–90 percent), ferrosilite (90–100 percent).

Aluminum and other elements

The aluminum (Al) content of the common pyroxenes varies with temperature and pressure of crystallization, and, in cases in which two pyroxenes are present, it is higher in the calcium-rich phase. In ultramafic nodules from basalt, enstatites contain up to 5.5 percent (average about 1.5 percent in lava orthopyroxenes), and calcic augites contain about 6.5 percent alumina (Al_2O_3). Compared with coexisting olivines, pyroxenes show higher chromium and vanadium and lower nickel and cobalt contents. With fractionation, augites show depletion in chromium, vanadium, and nickel and slight enrichment in scandium. Coexisting calcium-rich and calcium-poor pyroxenes have a distribution of magnesium and iron between the phases that may ultimately be a valuable indicator of the pressure and temperature of formation. At present the distribution is too much influenced by other factors, including the oxidation state of the iron and aluminum content, to be dependable.

The less common pyroxenes have a more simple chemistry, which is expressed chiefly by the formulas in Table 4. In aegirines the main replacement is sodium and ferric iron by calcium, magnesium, and ferrous iron to give aegirine augites, although varieties with up to 4 percent vanadium oxide and 5 percent manganese oxide have been reported. Ferroan johannsenite with about 13 percent iron oxide is transitional to hedenbergite. Omphacite (rich in sodium and aluminum) and fassaite (rich in aluminum and ferric iron) are otherwise of diopside composition.

PHASE RELATIONS AND STABILITY

Pyroxenes can be formed over a very wide range of temperatures, representing their stability in low-grade metamorphic rocks (subject to low temperatures and pressures), at the one extreme, and ultramafic nodules from upper-mantle sources, at the other. Diopside is formed under low carbon dioxide pressures at 300° C (570° F) from dolomite and silica and from a diopside melt at 1,391° C (2,536° F). The stability fields of pyroxenes are relatively larger at higher temperatures, however, and the more common phases are found in igneous and high-temperature metamorphic environments. Hydrothermal (referring to hot,

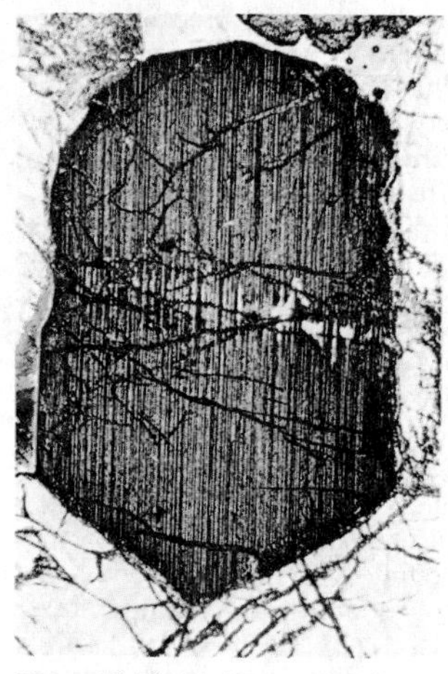

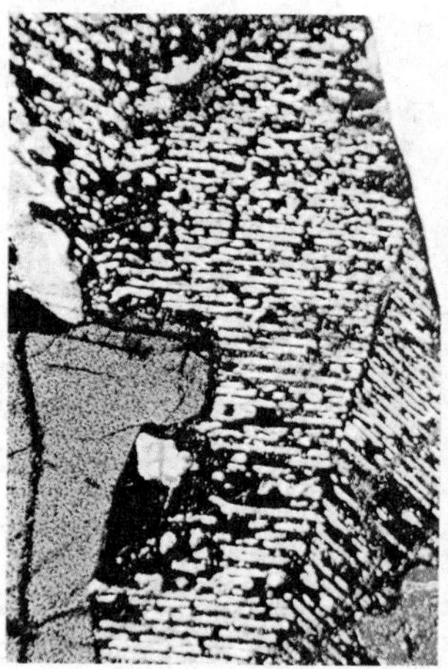

Figure 42: Photomicrographs of various thin sections containing pyroxene minerals; all show separation within a mineral grain of distinct phases due to further cooling after the grain had solidified (illuminated by polarized light). (Far left) Bronzite crystal from an ultramafic rock; thin lamellae of a calcium-rich species, probably pigeonite, have separated from the bronzite, and the host (grayish) thus has a very low calcium content (magnified about 40 ×). (Left) Twinned crystal of inverted pigeonite from a gabbro. Augite, seen as brightly coloured thin lamellae with herringbone texture because of the twinned relationship, has separated from the pigeonite; further cooling has caused the host, gray-coloured hypersthene, to change symmetry (invert; magnified about 22 ×). (Right) Inverted pigeonite from a more slowly cooled gabbro than that at left; as a result, the augite lamellae are wider, and after inversion more augite has separated from the hypersthene host (magnified about 70.4 ×). (Far right) Complex separation of augite from an inverted pigeonite (magnified about 70.4 ×).

By courtesy of G. Malcolm Brown

water-rich fluids derived from magma) alteration usually produces amphibole or chlorite, but pyroxenes are generally resistant accessories in detrital sediments.

Pressure–temperature conditions

The pyroxene quadrilateral (Figure 41) has been studied extensively. Diopside (di) has no known polymorphs, and its pressure–temperature phase diagram is a simple melting curve: at low pressures the rate of change of temperature with pressure is 15° C (59° F) per kilobar. Enstatite (en) melts incongruently (accompanied by reaction with the liquid) at low pressures but congruently at about 2.3 kilobars. With respect to the di-en join at atmospheric pressure (Figure 43), reaction and crystallization result in two coexisting pyroxenes at temperatures below 1,400° C (2,550° F), calcium-rich and calcium-poor. The calcium-poor phase at solidus temperatures (see above *Phase equilibria of mineral systems*) is a protoenstatite solid solution

From F.R. Boyd and J.F. Schairer, "The System $MgSiO_3$-$CaMgSi_2O_6$," *Journal of Petrology*, Vol. 5, no. 2 (1964); Oxford University Press

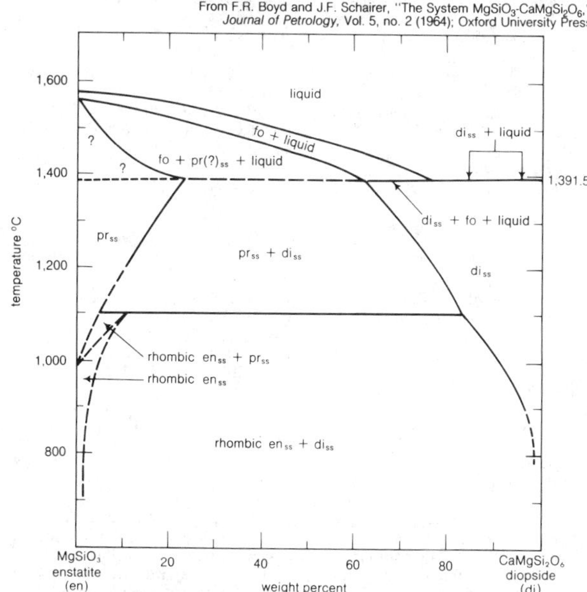

Figure 43: Equilibrium relations along the enstatite–diopside join. The phases of various mixtures of pure enstatite (en) and pure diopside (di) are shown as a function of temperature at atmospheric pressure. Other phases shown are protoenstatite (pr) and forsterite (fo), an olivine with the composition Mg_2SiO_4.

(single crystalline phase that varies in composition within finite limits), and the calcium-rich phase is an augite solid solution. At subsolidus temperatures each phase exsolves the other phase and changes composition along the domed limbs of the curve. At about 1,100° C (2,000° F), the protophase inverts to a slightly more calcic, orthorhombic phase that then continues to exsolve diopside to 800° C (1,470° F) or lower. This bears general comparison with natural pyroxenes, except that the protoenstatite phase is rare. It inverts to clinoenstatite on quenching and ceases to be stable above about eight kilobars.

Pyroxenes in the hedenbergite (Hd)–ferrosilite (Fs) system are not stable at liquidus temperatures (above the liquidus temperature a system is completely liquid), the higher temperature equivalents being ferriferous wollastonite, fayalitic olivine, and a silica phase (see Figure 44). Ferrohedenbergite is stable below about 950° C (1,750° F), but ferrosilite is totally unstable at these low pressures. Pressure increases the stability field of hedenbergite, and at about 13 kilobars the iron wollastonite field is eliminated. At about 17 kilobars, ferrosilite is stable and melts congruently, although the high-temperature liquidus phase has a problematical pyroxene structure.

The diopside–enstatite and enstatite–ferrosilite phase relations would be simple solid solutions between each end-member if it were not for the complexities shown on Figures 43 and 44. Natural pyroxene occurrences indicate the need for a restudy of the enstatite–ferrosilite system, of the effect of diopside on hedenbergite phase relations, and of compositional joins within the quadrilateral.

Confirmation by mineral synthesis

The broad natural relations shown in Figure 41 are confirmed by synthetic studies. Augite and bronzite coexistence, for example, results from the demonstrated instability of protopyroxene at moderate pressures and iron content. Inversion to clinoenstatite from protoenstatite occurs in a Papuan lava and in enstatite–chondrite meteorites. Pigeonite is stable at high pressures on the diopside–enstatite join but in nature is only found in the composition range shown on Figure 41, coexisting with augite. Inversion of pigeonite occurs in slowly cooled gabbros and dolerites unless they are iron-rich. The inversion product is orthorhombic hypersthene, with augite exsolution lamellae (thin layers) that indicate the previous monoclinic structure. Exsolution at 1,000° C and inversion at 980° C have been shown by experimental studies at zero pressure. The cessation of the calcium-poor pyroxene trend (Figure 41) is explained by ferrosilite instability, the end point

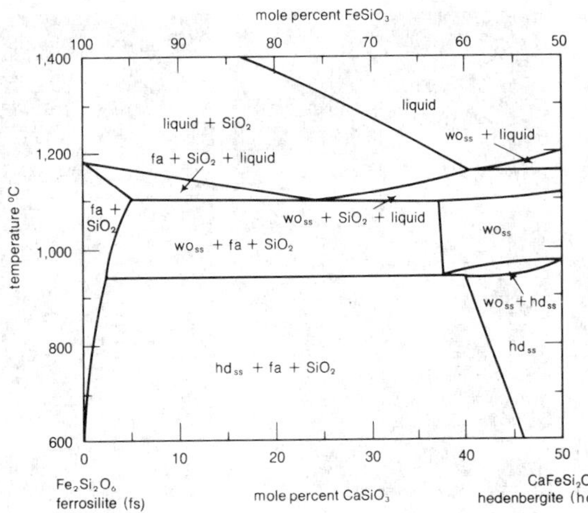

Figure 44: Equilibrium relations for the iron-rich pyroxenes along the ferrosilite–hedenbergite join. The phases of various mixtures of pure ferrosilite (fs) and pure hedenbergite (hd) are shown as a function of temperature at atmospheric pressure. Other phases, the result of the instability of pyroxenes at elevated temperatures, are iron-rich wollastonite (wo), the olivine fayalite (fa) with a composition of Fe_2SiO_4, and silica (SiO_2).

From D.H. Lindsley, G.M. Brown, and I.D. Muir, *Mineralogical Society of America Special Paper 2* (1969)

of the calcium-rich trend coincides with the minimum for $Wo_{ss} + Hd_{ss}$ shown on Figure 44, and the absence of iron wollastonites in all but low-pressure environments is also confirmed.

The occurrence of Tschermak's molecule

Aluminous pyroxenes contain the so-called Tschermak's molecule ($CaAl_2SiO_6$), which alone is stable above 1,150° C (2,100° F) and 11 kilobars. This molecule and the magnesium aluminum silicate molecule ($MgAl_2SiO_6$) are molecular expressions of the aluminum that can enter pyroxene structures at high pressure. In magnesium silicate ($MgSiO_3$), the alumina (Al_2O_3) solubility increases from 2.5 percent at atmospheric pressure to 14–19 percent at 20 kilobars, but it decreases at higher pressures. Diopside, however, can contain 12–15 percent Al_2O_3 at atmospheric pressure. Ferric diopsides contain ferri-Tschermak's molecule ($CaFe_2SiO_6$) produced, with andradite garnet and quartz, by oxidation of augites. More sodium in the magma would lead to formation of aegirine (acmite), which melts incongruently to hematite + magnetite + liquid up to 45 kilobars and from low to high oxygen pressures. Experiments at 40 kilobars suggest complete solid solubility between acmite and jadeite. Jadeite (from albite + nepheline) is only stable above about 17 kilobars (900° C [1,650° F]), and jadeite + quartz (from albite) is stable above about 25 kilobars at similar temperatures. Omphacite is a jadeite–diopside solid solution with a fairly wide pressure-stability range if viewed in isolation from other phases. At 30 kilobars, it splits into jadeitic and diopsidic phases at about 1,450° C (2,640° F). Spodumene is the high-pressure member of three polymorphs with lithium aluminum silicate compositions ($LiAlSi_2O_6$). At 10 kilobars and 900° C, it converts to a form called β-eucryptite, so that its low-pressure pegmatite environment must imply crystallization well below 900° C.

(G.M.B.)

Quartz and other silica minerals

Silica minerals make up approximately 12 percent of the Earth's crust and are second only to the feldspars in mineral abundance. Free silica occurs in many crystalline forms with a composition very close to that of silicon dioxide (SiO_2), 46.75 percent by weight of silicon and 53.25 percent oxygen. Quartz is by far the most commonly occurring form. Tridymite, cristobalite, and the hydrous silica mineral opal are uncommon, and vitreous (glassy) silica, melanophlogite, coesite, and stishovite have been reported from only a few localities. Several other forms have been produced in the laboratory but have not been found in nature.

Uses of quartz

Quartz is the only natural silica mineral used in significant quantities; millions of tons are consumed annually by many industries. The sand that is an essential ingredient of concrete and mortar is largely quartz, as are the sandstone and quartzite used as building stones. Crushed sandstone and quartzite are used for road and railway construction, roofing granules, and for riprap—erosion-control linings of river channels. Quartz is hard (7 on Mohs scale of mineral hardness) and resists fracture because it lacks easy cleavage. These properties, combined with its ready availability, lead to its use as a sandpaper abrasive and in sandblasting; for polishing and cutting glass, stone, and metal; and for providing traction on stairs, streets, and rails. Large amounts of relatively pure quartz are used in refractory products, such as insulating and firebricks, foundry molds, and electrical insulators, because of the combination of its high melting temperatures, low coefficients of expansion, inertness of the high-temperature forms of silica, and low costs.

Relatively pure quartz is required in large tonnages as an ingredient for glass and porcelain manufacture. High purity quartz is fused to make premium grades of chemical and optical glass for which one or more of its desirable properties of low thermal expansion, high-shape stability, elasticity, low solubility, and transparency to various kinds of light can justify the greatly increased costs involved. Fibres of vitreous silica are essential for precision instruments, such as balances, galvanometers, and gravimeters. Large tonnages of quartz of various qualities are used as raw materials for processes in which silica is not the final product. These include the production of water glass, or sodium silicate, various sols—very fine dispersions of solids in liquids—that are used as hydrophobic coatings, organic silicates and silicones, silicon carbide, silicon metal, smelting flux, and alloying in metallurgy.

Quartz and its varieties have been used since antiquity as semiprecious gems, ornamental stones, and collector's items. Precious opal, a hydrous form of silica, has been a gemstone since Roman times.

Table 5: Some Physical Properties of Silica Minerals

phase	symmetry	cell* parameters	specific gravity	hardness
Quartz (α-quartz)	hexagonal; trigonal trapezohedral	a = 4.913Å c = 5.405Å	2.651	7
High quartz (β-quartz)	hexagonal; hexagonal trapezohedral	a = 4.999Å c = 5.457Å at 575° C	2.53 at 600° C	7
Low tridymite	monoclinic (?)	a = 18.54Å b = 4.99Å c = 23.83Å β = 105.6°	2.26	7
High tridymite	orthorhombic	a = 8.74Å b = 5.05Å c = 8.24Å at 200° C	2.20 at 200° C	7(?)
Low cristobalite	tetragonal	a = 4.97Å c = 6.93Å	2.32	6–7
High cristobalite	isometric	a = 7.15Å at 1,300° C	2.20 at 500° C	6–7
Keatite	tetragonal	a = 7.456Å c = 8.604Å	2.50	?
Melanophlogite	isometric	a = 13.402Å	1.99	6–7
Coesite	monoclinic	a = 7.16Å b = 12.39Å c = 7.16Å β = 120°	2.93	7.5
Stishovite	tetragonal	a = 4.179Å c = 2.665Å	4.28	?
Vitreous silica	amorphous	—	2.203	6
Opal	poorly crystalline or amorphous	—	1.99–2.05	5.5–6.5

*The unit cell of a mineral is the smallest volume that contains a complete sample of the atomic composition and symmetry. It is described in terms of crystallographic axes and the angles at which they intersect. These axes are designated *a*, *b*, and *c* when of unequal length (monoclinic and orthorhombic symmetry); if *a* equals *b*, then only *a* and *c* cell lengths are given, and if *a*, *b*, and *c* are all equal (isometric symmetry) then only *a* is given. Hexagonal symmetry is related to three *a* axes of equal length that are 120° apart; the *c* axis is perpendicular to the plane containing these *a* axes. In monoclinic symmetry, two axes intersect obliquely, and the angle formed is designated β.

PHYSICAL AND CHEMICAL PROPERTIES

The crystallographic structures of the silica minerals, except stishovite, are three-dimensional arrays of linked tetrahedra, each consisting of a silicon atom coordinated by four oxygen atoms. The tetrahedra are usually quite regular, and the silicon–oxygen bond distances are 1.61 ± 0.02 angstrom (Å). Principal differences are related to the geometry of the tetrahedral linkages, which may cause small distortions within the silica tetrahedra. High pressure forces silicon atoms to coordinate with six oxygen atoms, producing nearly regular octahedra in the stishovite structure.

The silica minerals when pure are colourless and transparent and have a vitreous lustre. They are nonconductors of electricity and are diamagnetic (inert in a magnetic field). All are hard, strong, and fail by brittle fracture under an imposed stress.

Relatively high symmetry of silica minerals

Some of the more important physical properties of the silica minerals are compared in Table 5. All except low tridymite and coesite (among the crystalline varieties) have relatively high symmetry. There is a linear relationship between the specific gravity values listed in Table 5 and the arithmetic mean of the indices of refraction (measures of the velocity of light that is transmitted in different crystallographic directions) for silica minerals composed of linked tetrahedra. This relationship (Figure 45) does not

From B.J. Skinner and D.E. Appleman, *American Mineralogist* (1963); Mineralogical Society of America

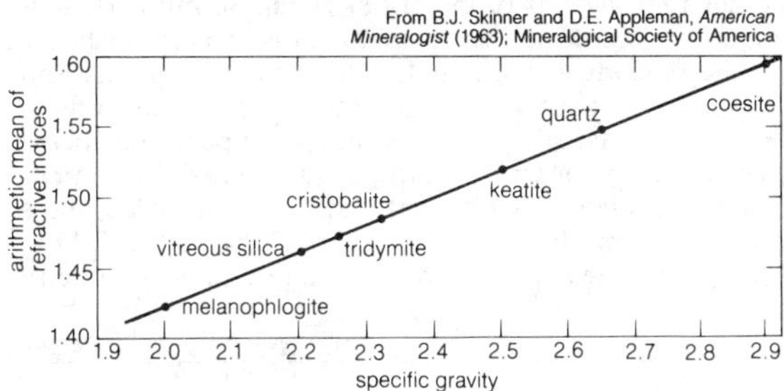

Figure 45: The linear plot obtained for silica minerals made up of linked tetrahedra (see text).

extend to stishovite because it is not made up of silica tetrahedra. Melanophlogite is notable because it plots below vitreous silica on the graph; one other poorly defined silica polymorph, called silica W, may also plot below vitreous silica. The specific gravities of silica minerals are less than those of most of the dark-coloured silicate minerals associated with them in nature; in general, the lighter coloured rocks have lower specific gravity for this reason.

Silica minerals are insoluble to sparingly soluble in strong acids except hydrofluoric acid. There is a fair correlation between specific gravity and the solubility in hydrofluoric acid. The less dense phases dissolve rapidly in cold acid; quartz dissolves slowly in cold acid and rapidly in hot; coesite is nearly insoluble in cold and slowly soluble in hot acid; and stishovite is nearly insoluble even in hot hydrofluoric acid. All silica minerals are dissolved by strong alkali, particularly in hot and concentrated solutions, and by some fused salts, such as ammonium bifluoride.

INDIVIDUAL SILICA MINERALS

Quartz. Quartz occurs in many varieties in almost all types of igneous, sedimentary, and metamorphic rocks. It has also been found in meteorites and in some lunar rocks.

Left-handed and right-handed quartz crystals

Quartz crystals lack a centre of symmetry or planes of symmetry and have one crystallographic axis (c) perpendicular to three polar axes (a) that are 120° apart. One end of a polar axis is different from its other end; when mechanical stress is applied on such an axis, opposite electrical charges develop on each end. This leads to important applications in electronics as a frequency control and in pressure gauges and other devices. The lack of symmetry planes parallel to the vertical axis allows quartz crystals to occur as two types: left-handed or right-handed (enantiomorphism). Left-handed quartz is less than 1 percent more abundant than right-handed quartz. The structural tetrahedra spiral upward through the crystal in the sense of the handedness parallel to the c axis. Similarly, if polarized light—which is light vibrating in a single plane—is transmitted by a quartz crystal along the c axis direction, the plane is rotated in the direction of the handedness by tens of degrees per millimetre, the amount depending on the wavelength of the light. This property is used in the manufacture of optical instruments such as monochrometers.

Twinning is ubiquitous in quartz, even if not conspicuous to the eye. One general class of twins occurs with the two sets of a axes parallel to each other, and the twinned portions may be complexly intergrown so that they penetrate each other. When the two crystals are of the same handedness and the a axes are of opposite electrical polarity, such twinning constitutes the Dauphiné law, which is also known as electrical twinning. When one of the crystals is left-handed and the other right-handed, this also causes the parallel a axes to be of opposite electrical polarity; this type is called Brazil, or optical, twinning. In another general class of quartz twins, the sets of a axes of the twinned crystals are inclined to each other, and

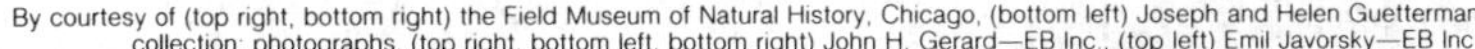
By courtesy of (top right, bottom right) the Field Museum of Natural History, Chicago, (bottom left) Joseph and Helen Guetterman collection; photographs, (top right, bottom left, bottom right) John H. Gerard—EB Inc.; (top left) Emil Javorsky—EB Inc.

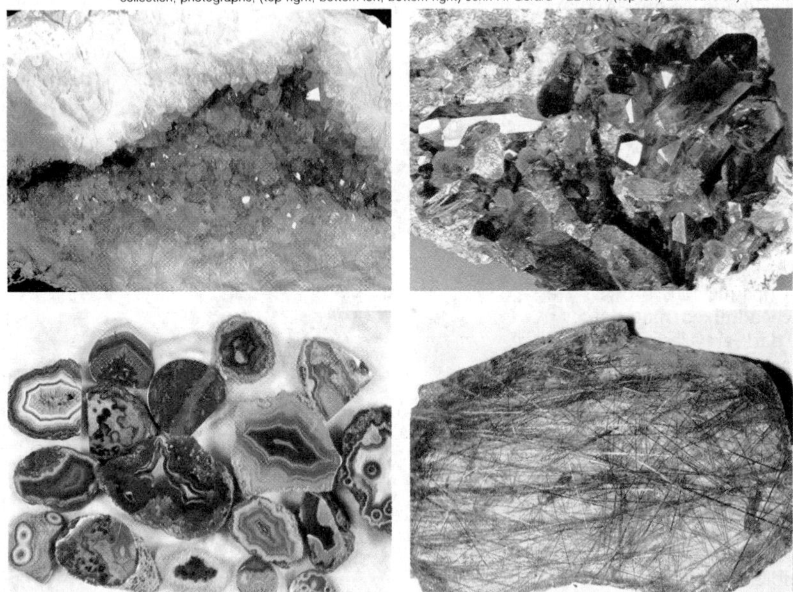

Figure 46: *Quartz varieties.*
(Top left) Amethyst geode from Nova Scotia. (Top right) Smoky quartz from St. Gotthard, Switzerland. (Bottom left) Quartz agate from Mexico. (Bottom right) Rutilated quartz from Madagascar.

the crystals ordinarily do not penetrate one another. This twinning is the Japan law.

The requirements for high purity crystals free from twinning for electronic frequency applications have led to the development of industrial synthesis methods based on the differences in silica solubility with temperature. Nutrient crystals are placed in the hot portion of a solution-filled autoclave, and an oriented seed crystal free from twinning is placed in the cooler portion. Crystals weighing thousands of grams can be grown in a few weeks.

Quartz shows less range in chemical composition than do most other minerals, but it commonly contains tens to hundreds of parts per million of aluminum atoms substituting for silicon atoms, with charge balance maintained by the incorporation of small atoms, such as hydrogen, lithium, or sodium. Titanium, magnesium, or iron atoms substituting for silicon atoms also have been reported, but anionic substitution (*i.e.*, substitution for the negative ion, oxygen) is limited because the linkage of the tetrahedra is disrupted.

Colours of quartz varieties

Coloured varieties of quartz are numerous and have many causes. Most colours result from mechanically incorporated admixtures within fine-crystallized or granular quartz, but some coarse-crystallized varieties, such as amethyst (violet), citrine (yellow), milky quartz, smoky quartz or morion (black), or rose quartz, may be coloured by ions other than silicon and oxygen that occur within the crystal structure (see Figure 46). Small fractions of 1 percent by weight of iron, aluminum, manganese, titanium, hydrogen, and small alkali atoms, such as lithium and sodium, have been shown to be the cause of different colours. Heat treatment or various irradiation treatments under oxidizing or reducing atmospheres are used to change one coloured variety to another. Citrine is commonly produced by heat treating amethyst at 250°–400° C (500°–750° F), for example.

Quartz may contain inclusions of other minerals, such as rutile (rutilated quartz), asbestiform amphiboles (tigereye is the yellow-brown variety from South Africa; hawk's-eye, the blue variety), or platy minerals, such as mica, iron oxides, or chlorite (aventurine).

Chalcedony. Chalcedony is white, buff, or light tan, finely crystallized or fibrous quartz that forms rounded crusts, rinds, or stalactites (mineral deposits suspended from the roofs of caverns) in volcanic and sedimentary rocks as a precipitate from moving solutions. If chalcedony is conspicuously colour banded, it may be called agate; onyx is agate with alternate bands of white and black or dark brown. Some concentrically banded "eye" agate nodules contain cores of coarsely crystalline quartz, and other agates are mottled or variegated in colour. Arborescent or dendritic (branching) dark-coloured patterns set in a lighter field are called moss agate or Mocha stone. Translucent red chalcedony is called carnelian, and translucent brown shades are called sard; both are pigmented by admixed iron oxides.

Chrysoprase, plasma, and prase are names for green varieties of chalcedony coloured by admixed green minerals, such as chlorite, fibrous amphiboles, or hydrous nickel silicates. Bloodstone and heliotrope are green chalcedony with red spots. Much chalcedony is coloured by artificial methods.

Jasper, chert, and flint. Jasper is opaque red, brown, or yellow quartz that contains much admixed material. Touchstone, or basanite, is black or dark gray jasper that has been used to estimate the composition of precious alloys by the colour of their streak (powder). Chert and flint are finely crystallized varieties of gray to black quartz that occur as nodules or bands in sedimentary rocks.

High quartz (β-quartz). High quartz, or β-quartz, is the more symmetrical form quartz takes at sufficiently high temperatures (about 573° C [1,063° F] at one atmosphere of pressure), but the relationship is pressure-sensitive (see Figure 47). High quartz may be either left- or right-handed, and its *c* axis is one of sixfold symmetry rather than threefold; thus, many twin laws of ordinary quartz cannot occur. High quartz twins typically involve inclined sets of axes. High quartz can form directly from silicate magma or from high-temperature gases or solutions. It invariably undergoes the transition to ordinary quartz (low quartz) on cooling, and all ordinary quartz, when heated above the transition temperature, is transformed into high quartz. The transformation involves only displacement of the linkage between the tetrahedra, and no bonds are broken. Much quartz that formed originally as high quartz in volcanic rocks has lost all morphological or twinning evidence of its origin and is virtually indistinguishable from ordinary quartz on any other basis.

Transition from high quartz to low quartz

Tridymite. Tridymite may occur as a primary magmatic phase (*i.e.*, as a direct result of crystallization from a silicate melt) in siliceous rocks but is most abundant in voids in volcanic rocks where it probably was deposited metastably from hydrous gases. Tridymite also forms in contact-metamorphosed rocks. It has been found in meteorites and is common in lunar basalts. It occurs in quantity in firebricks and other siliceous refractories. Natural tridymite has no specific commercial use.

The tridymite structure

Tridymite characteristically forms thin plates made up of three crystals in twin relationships; hence the name, which means triplet. The tridymite structure can be considered as cross-linked hexagonal sheets of tetrahedra perpendicular to the *c*-axis that approximate hexagonal closest packing of the oxygen atoms. These sheets may be stacked in regular, random, or irregular sequences, and the stacking can be different in parts of the same crystal. So much crystallographic complexity results that confusion exists as to the precise stacking arrangements. The stacking sequence and tetrahedral linkage within a sheet can change easily with temperature change, the transition temperatures being sensitive to the original stacking sequence and the composition. The high tridymite that is stable at one atmosphere pressure, from about 867°to 1,470° C (1,593° to 2,678° F), contains two sheets and has orthorhombic symmetry

From F.R. Boyd and J.L. England, *Journal of Geophysical Research*, vol. 65, p. 752 (1960)

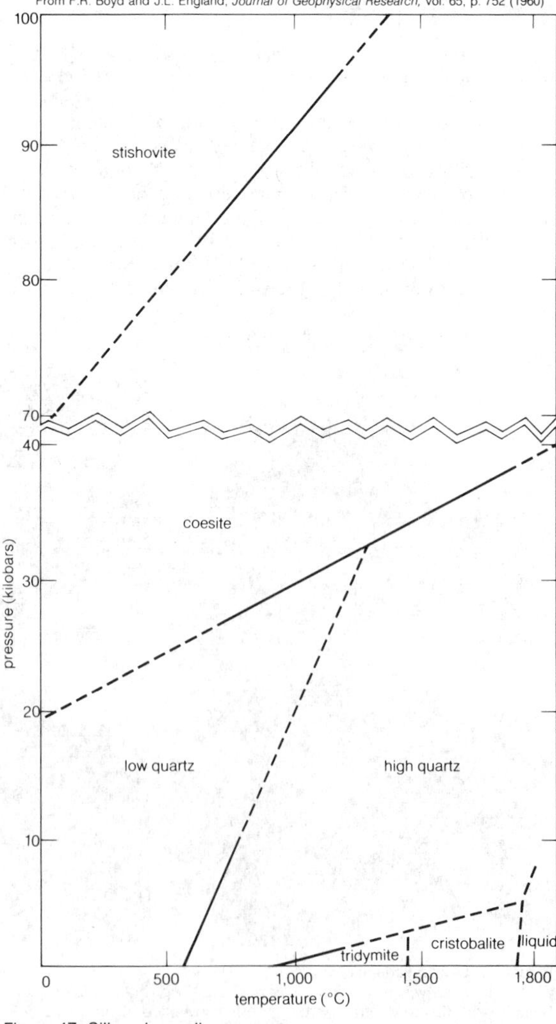

Figure 47: Silica phase diagram.

(related to three mutually perpendicular crystallographic axes of unequal length), though it is dimensionally hexagonal. Tridymite retains an orthorhombic cell as a subcell at lower temperatures but may contain as many as 20 sheets. Such tridymite also has pseudohexagonal symmetry (*i.e.*, appears to have sixfold symmetry but does not), but most carefully studied samples are actually monoclinic at room temperature. Terrestrial low tridymite does not show the characteristic monoclinic supercell of extraterrestial samples. This probably is related to the influence of conditions of formation on stacking sequences. Tridymite transforms sluggishly to quartz because the transformation requires tetrahedra to be disrupted and relinked.

Tridymite can be synthesized with high purity, but natural material commonly contains as much as 2 percent by weight of sodium and aluminum oxides substituting for silica, as well as fractions of 1 percent of titania, ferric iron, magnesia, calcium oxide, or potassium oxide.

Cristobalite. Cristobalite is probably more abundant in nature than tridymite, although it seldom forms as distinctive crystals. The devitrification (transformation from the glassy to the crystalline state) of siliceous volcanic glasses yields abundant tiny crystallites of cristobalite, and the mineral is also deposited metastably from hot hydrous gases in cavities and cracks of many volcanic rocks. It has been found in lunar basalts and in meteorites and is common in silica refractories exposed to very high temperatures.

Cristobalite is made up of sheets of silica tetrahedra that can be considered to be stacked in sequences of three sheets normal to a threefold axis; this approximates cubic closest packing of the oxygen atoms. Isometric high cristobalite is the stable phase at one atmosphere of pressure from about 1,470° C (2,678° F) to melting, and this form can be supercooled to the range 270°–175° C (520°–350° F) before it transforms reversibly to a metastable tetragonal form. The latter is called low cristobalite and shows complex polysynthetic twinning (twins of three or more individual crystals conforming to the same twin law). As might be expected from its open structure and high temperature of origin, substitution of small alkali and aluminum atoms for silicon atoms may amount to several percent in cristobalite, and minor amounts of other coupled substitutions are known.

Opal. Opal is poorly crystalline or amorphous hydrous silica that is compact and vitreous and most commonly translucent white to colourless. Precious opal reflects light with a play of brilliant colours across the visible spectrum, red being the most valued. Opal forms by precipitation from silica-bearing solutions near the Earth's surface. Electron microscopy has shown that many opals are composed of spheres of tens to a few thousand angstrom units in size that are arranged in either hexagonal or cubic close packing. The spheres are composed of hydrous silica that may be either almost cristobalite-like, tridymite-like, mixtures of both, or random and nondiffracting. The specific gravity and refractive index are lower than those of pure silica minerals and tend to fall along lines extending from cristobalite, tridymite, and vitreous silica (see Figure 45) toward the point for water (the index of refraction of water is 1.33, and the specific gravity is 1). The play of colours in precious opal arises from domains of regularly oriented spheres that satisfy Bragg's law (relating the angle of reflection of X-rays from a crystal to the spacing of crystallographic planes and the wavelength of the incident radiation) for the wavelength of visible light observed. When heated, opal may lose as much as 20 percent of its weight of water, fracture, and then crystallize to one of the silica minerals described above.

Arrangement of spheres in opal

Opal usually contains 4 to 9 percent water, but lower and much higher values have been observed. The contents of alumina, ferric oxide, and alkalis are variable but may amount to several percent in light coloured opals and more if pigmenting minerals are also present. Precious opal has been synthesized. Opaline silica is a friable hydrous silica found near hot springs and geysers.

Supercooled liquid silica

Vitreous silica. Vitreous silica is supercooled liquid silica. It has been observed in nature as the result of fusion of quartz by lightning strikes or by shock associated with large meteorite impacts and may approach artificial, very pure silica glass in composition and physical properties.

Melanophlogite. Melanophlogite is a cubic silica mineral with a gas-hydrate structure containing many large voids. In nature these are filled with 6 to 12 percent by weight of compounds of hydrogen, carbon, and sulfur, which may be necessary for mineral growth. If these compounds are destroyed by heating, they do not cause the crystal to collapse, but the free carbon formed does darken it. Melanophlogite occurs with bitumen and forms at temperatures below 112° C (234° F) on native sulfur crystals in Sicily.

Keatite. Keatite is a tetragonal form of silica known only from the laboratory, where it can be synthesized metastably over the range of temperatures from about 300° to 600° C (600°–1,200° F) and 400 to 4,000 bars (standard atmospheric pressure at sea level is 1,013.3 millibars, or slightly more than one bar, which equals 760 millimetres of mercury) in the presence of steam. It has negative thermal expansion along the *a* axes and positive thermal expansion along the *c* axis, so that the overall expansion is very low or negative.

Coesite and stishovite. Coesite and stishovite are rare dense forms of silica observed in nature only where quartz-bearing rocks have been severely shocked by a large meteorite impact, such as Meteor Crater, Arizona. Coesite is made up of tetrahedra arranged like those in feldspars. Stishovite is the most dense form of silica and consists of silicon that is octahedrally coordinated with oxygen. Both coesite and stishovite have been synthesized and found to be stable only at high pressures (Figure 47).

OCCURRENCE IN MAGMAS AND SOLUTIONS

Silicon and oxygen are the two most abundant elements in the Earth's crust, in which they largely occur in combination with other elements as silicate minerals. Free silica, SiO_2, appears as a mineral in crystallizing magma only when the relative abundance of SiO_2 exceeds that of all other cations available to form silicates. Silica minerals thus occur only in magmas containing more than about 47 percent by weight of SiO_2 and are incompatible with minerals with low cation/silica ratios—such as olivine, nepheline, or leucite. Basaltic and alkalic igneous magmas therefore can crystallize only minor amounts of silica minerals, and sometimes none are produced. The gas released from such rocks can dissolve the silica components, however, and later precipitate it as silica minerals upon cooling. The amount of silica minerals crystallized from magma increases with increasing silica content of magma, reaching 40 percent in some granites and rhyolites. In granitic pegmatite, where a hydrous gas was present in addition to magma, igneous-appearing rocks composed largely or almost completely of quartz can occur because of transport of silica through the hydrous gas.

Occurrence of free silica

Solubility of silica minerals. The solubility of silica minerals in natural solutions and gases is of great importance. The solubility of all silica minerals increases regularly with increasing temperature and pressure (Figure 48) except in the region of 340°–550° C (640°–1,020° F) and 0–600 bars, where retrograde solubility occurs because of changes in the physical state of water. The solubility of quartz in steam reaches at least 22 percent by weight at 10,000 bars and 1,055° C (1,931° F). The solubility of silica increases in the presence of anions such as OH^- and CO_3^-, which form chemical complexes with it.

Quartz is the least soluble of the forms of silica at room temperature. In pure water its solubility at 25° C (77° F) is about 6 parts per million, that of vitreous silica being at least 10 times greater. The amount of dissolved silica in hot springs has been utilized to measure the temperature at the depth from which the water emanates, because the major control of silica solubility appears to be with quartz. Typical temperate climate river water contains 14 parts per million of silica, and enormous tonnages of silica are carried away in solution annually from weathering rocks and soils. The amount so removed may be equivalent to that transported mechanically in many climates. In tropical climates, waters enriched in organic acids may leach silica completely to form lateritic residual soils enriched

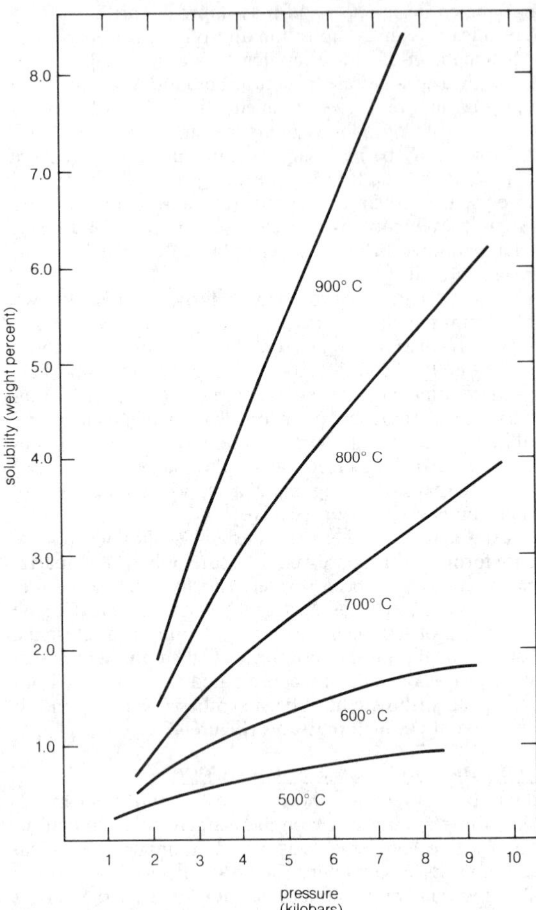

Figure 48: Solubility of quartz in pure water.
From G.M. Anderson and C.W. Burnham, *American Journal of Science*, vol. 263 (1965)

in hydrous iron and aluminum oxides. Silica dissolved in moving groundwater may form hollow spheroids lined with crystals called geodes, or it may cement loose sand grains together to form concretions and nodules or even entire sedimentary beds into sandstone, which, when all pore space is eliminated by selective solution and nearby deposition during metamorphism, form tough, pore-free quartzite.

The silica content of seawater is highly variable because it is removed by plankton (floating organisms). An estimate for average upper ocean waters is 4.3 parts per million, but values of 0.1 part per million can occur at the surface. Deep sea sediments are highly siliceous from the accumulation of the siliceous skeletons of single-celled plants and animals (diatoms and radiolaria), sponges, and other organisms.

Rock crystal, spring deposits, and glass sands

Gases or solutions escaping from cooling rocks, especially volcanic or intrusive igneous rocks, commonly are saturated with silica and other compounds that, as they cool, precipitate quartz along their channelways to form veins. It may be fine-grained (as chalcedony), massive granular, or in coarse crystals as large as tens of tons. Most natural colourless quartz crystals—the "rock crystal" in collections or in jewelry and electronic and optical apparatus—were formed in this way. Areas for rock crystal include the Swiss Alps; Herkimer County, New York; Minas Gerais, Brazil; Hot Springs, Arkansas; and Madagascar.

The emergence of heated silica-bearing solutions onto the surface results in rapid cooling and the loss of complexing anions. Rapid precipitation of fine-grained silica results in formation of siliceous sinter or geyserite, as at Mammoth Hot Springs in Yellowstone National Park.

Quartz is mechanically resistant and relatively inert chemically during rock weathering in temperate and cold climates. Thus, it becomes enriched in river, lake, and beach sediments, which commonly contain more than one-half quartz by weight. Some strata consist almost entirely of quartz over large lateral distances and tens or hundreds of metres in thickness. Known as glass sands, these strata are important economic sources of silica for glass and chemical industries. Quartz-bearing strata are abundant in metamorphic terrains. The reincorporation of free silica into complex silicates and the solution and redeposition of silica into veins is characteristic of such terrains.

The silica phase diagram. The pressure-temperature fields of stability of silica minerals as presently understood are shown in Figure 47. The experimentally determined boundaries are drawn with heavy lines. No data have been obtained for certain boundaries because of slow reaction rates or difficulties in obtaining the required conditions. Traces of water, for example, are necessary for reactions to take place over much of the diagram. Stability fields are not shown for keatite, melanophlogite, opal, or the low forms of tridymite and cristobalite because they have not been demonstrated. Quartz is the stable phase of silica under the physical conditions that prevail over most of the Earth's crust. Coesite is possible at depths of about 100 kilometres (60 miles) in the Earth's mantle, but free silica is not thought to be abundant there. Stishovite would require even greater depths of burial, and no rocks that occur on the Earth's surface have been buried so deeply. (D.B.S.)

Micas

The micas are characterized by their highly perfect cleavage, yielding thin laminae. The name is from the Latin *mica* ("grain"). The principal members of the group are muscovite, biotite, and lepidolite. These are aluminosilicates with potassium, magnesium, iron, or lithium, and hydroxyl and fluorine. The micas as a group are highly variable in chemical composition, physical and optical properties, and mode of occurrence, but all are based on a relatively simple crystal-structure unit.

Importance and uses

Because some micas are poor electrical conductors, they are used in the construction of electrical equipment. Some micas are also poor heat conductors, transparent, and relatively resistant to water corrosion; these have been useful as stove windows and boiler-gauge packings. Ground mica is commonly employed as a filler, lubricant, absorbant, dusting powder, and packing material. It is used in the manufacture of wallpaper, roofing paper, and paints. It is employed for special effects by decorators and toy manufacturers—for example, as "frosting" or Christmas tree "snow." Sheets of mica are used to make plates of precise thickness for use in the analysis of polarized light. Lepidolite is an important source of lithium and rubidium salts. Some of the synthetic micas are used as electrical insulators and in special delicate electronic instruments.

The common micas are rich in potassium and also contain some strontium and rubidium, which are essential elements involved in the age determination of minerals and rocks. The abundance of the elements involved in the decay of the isotope (isotopes are elements with the same atomic number but different atomic weights) potassium-40 to argon-40, and of rubidium-87 to strontium-87, in a mica can be measured with precision and the absolute age of the mineral calculated in millions of years. Metamorphism of the micas often affects the relative abundance of these elements, so that the micas usually record the last geological event or episode of metamorphism and not the date of their initial growth in the Earth.

Occurrence of micas and their mining

The micas occur in all terrestrial rock types—igneous, metamorphic, and sedimentary. They are absent in rocks so far recovered from the lunar surface, however. Members of the group are found under the entire range of pressures and temperatures that reflect geological conditions: thus, micas occur in lavas, schists, granites, marbles, soils and deep-sea sediments, mineralized veins, pegmatites, alteration zones, and in products of weathering of other minerals. Each particular mica type is limited in occurrence to a certain range of variables (such as composition, temperature, and pressure) of the geological environment, and some micas are found only in specific rock types. A characteristic occurrence is in granite (see Figure 49), in which biotite and muscovite usually form. Phlogopite is common

Figure 49: (Left) Single crystals of muscovite on feldspar. (Centre) Packing model of muscovite. (Right) Thin section of two-mica granite.
(Left) Joe J. Holdaway, (centre) B.M. Sharib, (right) Hatten S. Yoder, Jr.

both in ultrabasic rocks such as dunites and peridotites and in dolomitic marbles. Fine-grained white micas, or sericite, particularly muscovite, form in the early stages of metamorphism of sediments and are closely associated with biotite. During retrograde metamorphism (the occurrence of one episode of intense metamorphism followed by subsequent, less intense episodes) the aluminous silicates are altered to sericite; these silicate minerals include andalusite, kyanite, sillimanite, cordierite, and staurolite, as well as the feldspars. The illites, a group of clay minerals, are partly of mica and are a common constituent of soils and deepsea sediments. Glauconite, another type of clay mineral, also occurs in marine deposits. Celadonite is an alteration product of some igneous rocks. Lepidolite is mainly found in veins and pegmatites, often in parallel growths with muscovite.

The mining of mica is difficult because the mica books (crystalline blocks that cleave or split readily into thin mica sheets) are readily damaged by rough handling. Methods of extraction are therefore primitive and necessarily wasteful; the veins and pegmatites are usually worked by quarrying, but underground excavation may be economical. The books are split and trimmed by hand; sorted according to size, transparency, colour, and freedom from spots or strains; and the scrap is ground. The production of mica sheets seldom exceeds 10 percent of the total mine output. Mining is conducted primarily in the United States (North Carolina, Idaho, South Dakota), India, the Republic of South Africa, the Soviet Union, Brazil, Argentina, Canada, and Madagascar.

PHYSICAL PROPERTIES

Wide colour variation

The different kinds of mica (see Table 6 for principal members) vary greatly in colour and are frequently zoned (*i.e.*, there are concentric colour bands). Muscovite is commonly colourless and may be gray, brown, light green, lavender, or ruby red. The biotites are commonly black, brown, green, yellow, and occasionally are colourless. High ferric iron content tends to make the crystals green, whereas high titanium oxide content gives a reddish brown colour. Intermediate proportions of titanium and ferric iron tend to produce colours of yellowish or greenish brown. Pink, violet, yellow, gray, red, brown, and green are the colours displayed by the lepidolites. Paragonite is colourless. The luster varies from pearly, as in muscovite, to submetallic, as in lepidomelane.

Table 6: Principal End-Members of the Mica Group*

	X	Y	Z	O_{10}	$(OH, F)_2$
Dioctahedral					
Muscovite	K	Al_2	$AlSi_3$	O_{10}	$(OH)_2$
Ferrimuscovite	K	Fe_2^{+3}	$AlSi_3$	O_{10}	$(OH)_2$
Paragonite	Na	Al_2	$AlSi_3$	O_{10}	$(OH)_2$
Margarite	Ca	Al_2	Al_2Si_2	O_{10}	$(OH)_2$
Celadonite	K	$MgFe^{+3}$	Si_4	O_{10}	$(OH)_2$
Al-celadonite (leucophyllite)	K	MgAl	Si_4	O_{10}	$(OH)_2$
Trioctahedral					
Phlogopite	K	Mg_3	$AlSi_3$	O_{10}	$(OH)_2$
Na-phlogopite	Na	Mg_3	$AlSi_3$	O_{10}	$(OH)_2$
Annite	K	Fe^{+2}	$AlSi_3$	O_{10}	$(OH)_2$
Clintonite	Ca	Mg_3	Al_2Si_2	O_{10}	$(OH)_2$
Eastonite	K_2	Mg_5Al	Al_3Si_5	O_{20}	$(OH)_4$
Iron-eastonite	K_2	$Fe_5^{+2}Al$	Al_3Si_5	O_{20}	$(OH)_4$
Polylithionite	K	Li_2Al	Si_4	O_{10}	F_2
Trilithionite	K	$Li_{1.5}Al_{1.5}$	$AlSi_3$	O_{10}	F_2
Intermediate					
Unnamed synthetic	K	$Mg_{2.5}$	Si_4	O_{10}	$(OH)_2$
Siderophyllite	K	$Fe_{1.66}^{+2}Al$	$Al_{1.33}Si_{2.67}$	O_{10}	$(OH)_2$
Lepidomelane	K	$Fe_{1.66}Fe^{+3}$	$Al_{1.33}Si_{2.67}$	O_{10}	$(OH)_2$

*General formula is: $XY_{2-3}Z_4O_{10}(OH, F)_2$.

Most occurrences of the micas yield fine-grained crystals; the largest crystals are found in veins and pegmatites. The largest book of mica discovered was 4.3 metres (14 feet) in diameter and 10 metres (33 feet) long. Paragonite is especially fine-grained, occurring in massive scaly aggregates. Where colourless micas occur in two size ranges, the smaller size range can usually, but not always, be attributed to paragonite and the larger to muscovite.

Form and cleavage

When well formed, the crystals are usually tabular with hexagonal or pseudo-hexagonal outline; hence, six-sided prisms are common. The perfect basal cleavage yields thin laminae that are usually elastic. Some varieties, margarite for example, have brittle laminae. The perfect basal cleavage (perpendicular to the sides of the prism form) reflects the layered character of the internal crystal structure. The cleavage laminae are not equal in thickness throughout but may exhibit a series of steps. Each step is exactly equal to, or a multiple of, a crystal structure unit. These steps are also observed in the spiral growth of mica crystals.

When a cleavage flake is struck a sharp blow with a blunt needle point, a six-rayed star of cracks, or percussion figure, develops. A similar set of cracks develops 30 degrees from the percussion set when a blunt punch is pressed against crystal; these cracks, the pressure figure, coincide with secondary parting planes in the crystal. Such parting planes are inclined to the basal cleavage and often are mistaken for true crystal faces. The percussion figure is a useful aid in determining the orientation of the crystal symmetry in the absence of faces. Micas in the vicinity of a shear zone (zone of deformation in the Earth's crust) show kink banding. Kink bands are narrow, sharply bounded by plane surfaces inclined to the cleavage, and are parallel or subparallel. They indicate strong local deformation by translation gliding (slippage of crystal structure) whose precise nature is as yet undefined. Kink bands are displayed particularly well in micas in the sheared schists and cataclastic rocks (greatly deformed metamorphic rocks) of Scotland and Austria, and have been noted in mica-bearing rocks shocked by meteorite impact. Kink bands have been produced in laboratory studies of natural mica.

The hardness of the micas is anisotropic (that is, it varies with direction in the crystal) and ranges from 2.5 to 4.5 on the Mohs scale of mineralogical hardness. The specific gravity ranges from 2.8 to 3.4, and the indexes of refraction (measure of light transmission) from 1.535 to 1.705. Bi-refringence (double refraction) is strong in the micas, meaning that the speed of light transmission varies greatly with crystal direction. The dark-coloured micas exhibit strong pleochroism; that is, different colours are exhibited in different directions. Inclusions are common in the micas and sometimes produce pleochroic halos (concentric colour bands). Dark spots in micas are often a result of radiation damage from included zircons, which contain radioactive chemical elements. The micas often enclose flattened crystals of garnet, tourmaline, quartz, and magnetite in thin plates between the sheets. Minute acicular (needlelike) inclusions arranged parallel to the rays of the percussion figure, particularly in phlogopite, give rise to asterism similar to that observed in rubies and sapphires.

Alteration and weathering

Muscovite and clintonite are relatively insoluble in acids, whereas biotite, lepidolite, and margarite are attacked by acids, leaving a residue of silica. Most micas yield water on ignition. The structure of muscovite can be completely destroyed by prolonged grinding in the laboratory and appears to be similarly affected when the mineral is transported in streams and rivers. Alteration of muscovite usually results in a loss of alkalies and hydration, producing a mixed-layer mineral with montmorillonite (a clay mineral). Strong alteration may produce the clay minerals kaolinite or gibbsite with quartz. The farmer tends to restore most of the lost alkalies in the soil micas by using potash fertilizer; that potash is unavailable to the crop because it is taken up by the micas. The exchange of alkalies in micas is reversible, but slight irreversible structural changes appear to occur. Muscovite, for example, can be converted to paragonite in solutions rich in sodium chloride, and paragonite can be converted to muscovite in solutions containing potassium chloride. The biotites on alteration are converted to chlorites. Potash feldspar, rutile, hematite, magnetite, or serpentine may also be produced. Weathering of biotite usually changes it to a soft brown or yellow mineral with a bronze luster, vermiculite.

CRYSTAL STRUCTURE

The fundamental unit of structure of the micas (see Figure 50) has been deduced by X-ray analysis of single crystals. It consists of two sheets of oxygen tetrahedra containing silicon and, usually, some aluminum. Each sheet consists of tetrahedra linked at each of three corners to form a hexagonal or pseudo-hexagonal array with all the bases parallel and all the vertexes pointing the same way. The two sheets are parallel and have opposing vertexes. These sheets are held together by magnesium or other ions, which are coordinated with two apical oxygens and one hydroxyl from one sheet and two apical oxygens and one hydroxyl from the opposite sheet, forming an octahedron. The hydroxyls occupy the centres of the hexagonal or pseudo-hexagonal arrays of apical oxygens. The structure is a succession of such double sheets with alkali atoms (*e.g.*, potassium) between them, the alkali atoms located between the hexagonal or pseudo-hexagonal arrays formed by the basal oxygens of the adjoining double sheets. The alkali atoms are thereby in twelvefold coordination, occupying the centre of a hexagonal prism formed by six basal oxygens from each of the adjoining sheets.

From R.E. Grim, *Clay Mineralogy* (1953); McGraw-Hill Book Co., Inc.

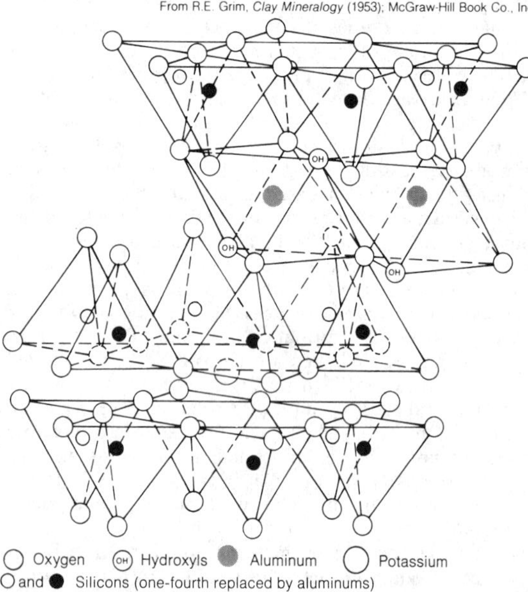

Figure 50: Structure of 1M muscovite (see text).

The general structure may be represented by the formula $XY_{2-3}\ Z_4O_{10}\ (OH,F)_2$, in which X in 12-fold coordination may be potassium, sodium, calcium, or barium; Y in sixfold coordination may be magnesium, ferric or ferrous iron, aluminum, lithium, manganese, and, rarely, chromium, vanadium, and titanium; and Z in fourfold coordination may be silicon and aluminum (see Table 6).

Polymorphism in micas

Minerals having the same chemical composition and different structures are called polymorphs. The simple structural unit described above has monoclinic symmetry; that is, it is related to three unequal crystal axes, two of which intersect obliquely and the third perpendicularly to the others. If successive units are stacked on top of each other with precisely the same orientation, the repeating unit of the mica is described as having a one-layer monoclinic structure (1M). If successive units are stacked with different orientations in a regular way, different structures (polymorphs) result. The symmetry of the surface of the unit restricts the number of ways in which successive units may be stacked. The structures resulting from the various types of stacking may be described by the number of layers involved and the symmetry produced. The following structures have been observed in addition to the 1M: two-layer monoclinic, type one ($2M_1$); two-layer monoclinic, type two ($2M_2$); and two-layer orthorhombic (2O). Crystal symmetry in the orthorhombic system is related to three unequal and mutually perpendicular crystal axes: three-layer trigonal (3T)—a division of the hexagonal system in which crystal symmetry is related to three equal crystal axes that intersect at angles of 120 degrees and a fourth unequal axis that is perpendicular to these three; eight-layer triclinic (8TC)—crystal symmetry in the triclinic system is related to three unequal and mutually oblique crystal axes; twelve-layer monoclinic (12M); and eighteen-layer monoclinic (18M). Other more complex structures exist. A structure in which the units are randomly stacked also has been found. In addition, a six-layer hexagonal (6H) structure has been predicted but not found in nature. It should be emphasized that the structure of a ($2M_1$) mica, for example, is not exactly equivalent to two (1M) layers properly stacked. The internal strains and resulting distortions of the polyhedra produced by the various types of stacking yield new structures that, although very closely related, are not merely multiples of the simple structural unit as in polytypism. A single hand specimen may contain several polymorphs, but the biotites usually are (1M), the muscovites ($2M_1$), and the lepidolites ($2M_2$). Randomly stacked micas and mixed-layers with other layered minerals, such as montmorillonite, are common in sediments.

CHEMICAL COMPOSITION

Rare micas and hydromica

The various species of the mica group may be described for the most part as consisting of variable proportions of ideal end-members. Actual compositions are complex because of chemical substitutions. The group may be divided into those micas having two atoms in octahedral coordination (Y position), called the di-octahedral micas; those with three atoms in octahedral coordination, the tri-octahedral micas; and those containing between two and three atoms in octahedral coordination, the intermediate micas. The ideal end-members are listed in Table 6: the various atoms are arranged according to their structural position. Broadly speaking, the white micas, commonly referred to as sericite when fine grained, consist of muscovite, paragonite, or both. These form a limited series of solid solutions. Common glauconite consists of about two-thirds celadonite and one-third muscovite. It is not known whether glauconite is a true compound or a random mixed-layer structure, a structure consisting of discrete structural units of both muscovite and celadonite. Illite, a field designation for some sedimentary micas, is a mixed-layer mineral usually consisting of muscovite and montmorillonite. Common biotite is widely variable in composition and incorporates in solid solution various proportions of phlogopite, annite, eastonite, iron–eastonite, siderophyllite, and lepidomelane. The biotites do not form solid solutions with muscovite. Lepidolite consists mainly of polylithionite and trilithionite and forms limited solid solutions with muscovite and paragonite. There is no known complete series of solid

Table 7: Maximum Thermal Stability of Synthetic End-Member Micas
(temperature in °C)

reaction	pressure in kilobars					
	0.5	1.0	2.0	5.0	10.0	20.0
Celadonite ⇄ ferriphlogopite + ferrisanidine + quartz + H_2O		405	420			
Paragonite ⇄ albite + corundum + H_2O	520	535	565	630	675	
Muscovite ⇄ sanidine + corundum + H_2O	635	655	690	710	740	
Annite + oxygen ⇄ kalsilite + leucite + fayalite + magnetite + H_2O	745	785	825			
Ferriannite ⇄ fayalite + magnetite + wüstite + liquid + H_2O		835	825			
Phlogopite ⇄ forsterite + liquid			1,220	1,265	1,305	1,340
Muscovite + quartz ⇄ sanidine + andalusite (or sillimanite) + H_2O		525	600	690		
Phlogopite + quartz ⇄ sanidine + enstatite + liquid + H_2O	820	820	820			

solutions between a di-octahedral and a tri-octahedral mica.The rare micas include: a vanadium-rich mica (roscoelite), a chromium-rich mica (fuchsite), a manganese-bearing mica (manganophyllite), an aluminum-free mica (taeniolite), and a lithium–iron mica (zinnwaldite). Some mica samples yield more water on chemical analysis than that indicated by their formula. These are erroneously referred to as hydromica; in fact, they are mixtures or mixed-layered minerals of mica and a more hydrous mineral such as montmorillonite. A true hydromica, in which the hydronium ion, H_3O^+, replaces potassium, has not as yet been demonstrated in natural micas. The micas in some localities contain other volatile constituents such as ammonia and chloride in addition to hydroxl and fluoride.

EXPERIMENTAL STUDY OF MICAS

Synthesis. Micas very closely approaching the properties of those found in nature have been synthesized in the laboratory; these include phlogopite, muscovite, paragonite, margarite, clintonite, annite, ferriannite, eastonite, siderophyllite, and celadonite. In addition, some end-member micas, possibly occurring as very minor solid solutions in other natural micas, have been made. Some of the fluorine end-members, such as fluorophlogopite, fluoromuscovite, fluoroparagonite, as well as polylithionite and trilithionite, have been synthesized. Na-phlogopite is another synthetic end-member. Other compounds having the mica structure, but not found in nature, have been prepared for special commercial applications. Examples of successful synthesis include fluorine (F) aluminosilicates that contain barium (Ba), magnesium (Mg), potassium (K), and nickel (Ni). The formulae of such compounds are: $BaMg_3Al_2Si_2O_{10}F_2$; $KNi_3AlSi_3O_{10}F_2$; and $KMg_2MnAlSi_3O_{10}F_2$. The hydrous micas are grown in steel pressure vessels capable of withstanding high water pressures, and the fluoromicas are grown from melts in platinum, graphite, or bonded silicon carbide crucibles at approximately atmospheric pressure. A few crystals in excess of 26 square centimetres (four square inches) and 0.3 centimetre (1/8 inch) in thickness have been produced from fluoride melts. Smaller synthetic fluoromica crystals have been bonded into large sheets and other forms.

Environmental temperatures and pressures required for mica formation

Stability limits. The geological conditions under which a specific composition or polymorph of mica may be found are limited. Phlogopite ranges in occurrence from the relatively low temperature and pressure environment in which marbles are believed to have formed to the high temperature and pressure environment of some ultrabasic rocks. In fact, phlogopite will grow in hot silicate liquids (magma) and persist in the lava flows that appear at the surface of the Earth. Other micas such as lepidolite, however, are confined to the moderate temperatures and pressures of environment in which pegmatites are formed. The glauconites are confined almost exclusively to marine sediments and to low-temperature and low-pressure environments. These qualitative restrictions deduced from field observations do not fully describe the limits of stability of a mica because of the constraints imposed by the available compositions, temperatures, and pressures in the Earth. Quantitative measure of the limits of stability have been carried out in the laboratory, where composition, temperature, and pressure can be varied at will. Data are available on many of the pure end-member compositions listed in Table 6, as well as on compositions generated by mixtures of two or three end-members. The measured maximum stability limits in the pressure–temperature region studied for some micas are listed with their decomposition or breakdown products in Table 7. For reference, the pressure in the crust of the Earth increases with depth at an average rate of about one kilobar per 3.66 kilometres (273 bars per kilometre [434 atmospheres per mile]). In general, the thermal stability of mica increases rapidly with pressure initially and then increases at a slow rate at pressures above about two kilobars. The stability of phlogopite at very high pressures is noteworthy; it is a mineral that is likely to be present in the Earth's mantle and is of particular interest because of its water and potassium content. The potassium content has great bearing on heat production in the mantle because it is a radioactive element, and water tends to lower the melting temperatures in the mantle and thus affect magma production.

The stability of a mica is also dependent on the presence of other minerals and the composition of the ambient fluid (mainly water). In Table 7 the results of studies on micas themselves, and when in the presence of quartz (SiO_2), are given. The muscovite + quartz reaction is important because it is prominent in the metamorphism of shales or clay-rich sediments. In addition, the stability of muscovite appears to be influenced by the potassium ion–hydrogen ion ratio in the fluid; and the magnesium–iron ratios, especially in biotite, are sensitive to the presence of sulfur. The presence of fluorine enlarges the thermal range of stability of the hydrous tri-octahedral micas. (H.S.Y.)

Olivines

The olivines are closely related on chemical and structural grounds. The name olivine alludes to the quasi-olive green colour of the most abundant varieties, forsterite and fayalite, which are silicates of magnesium and ferrous iron, respectively. Other members of the group may contain manganese or calcium in addition to, or substituting for, iron or magnesium; among these, the more important named varieties are tephroite (containing manganese), monticellite (calcium and magnesium), kirschsteinite (calcium and iron), and glaucochroite (calcium and manganese). These varieties and some of their physical properties are listed in Table 8. The olivine minerals that contain magnesium and iron are generally believed to be among the most important minerals in the Earth's upper mantle. They are particularly characteristic of basic and ultrabasic igneous rocks; that is, rocks that are relatively poor in silica and rich in iron and magnesium that

Table 8: Some Physical Properties of the Olivines

end members	composition	specific gravity	hardness on Mohs scale	unit cell dimensions*		
				a	b	c
Forsterite	Mg_2SiO_4	3.22	7	4.756	10.195	5.918
Fayalite	Fe_2SiO_4	4.39	6½	4.817	10.477	6.105
Tephroite	Mn_2SiO_4	3.78	6	4.90	10.60	6.25
Monticellite	$CaMgSiO_4$	3.08	5½	4.815	11.08	6.37
Kirschsteinite	$CaFeSiO_4$	—	—	—	—	—
Glaucochroite	$CaMnSiO_4$	3.41	—	4.92	11.19	6.51

*The unit cell is the smallest volume of a mineral containing a complete sample of the atomic or molecular groups that comprise it. Unit cell dimensions along the three crystallographic axes (*a*, *b*, *c*) are given in angstrom units (one angstrom equals 10^{-8} centimetres).

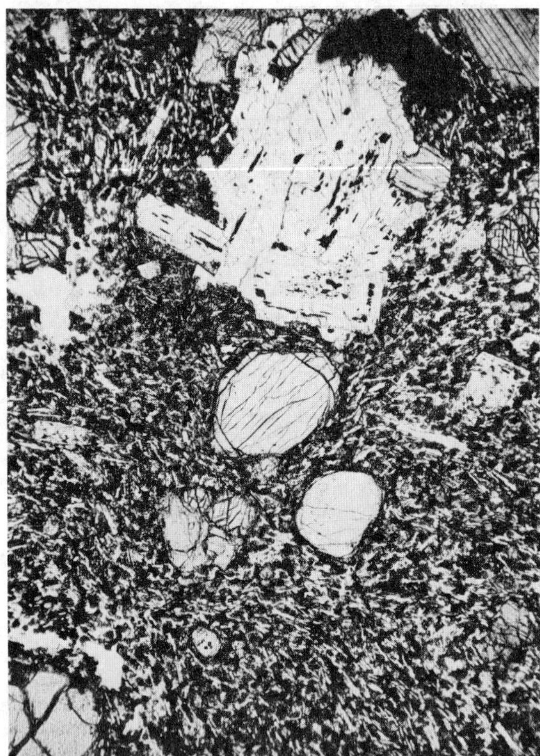

Figure 51: Phenocryst of olivine (centre) in a fine-grained groundmass; olivine basalt from Ookala, Mauna Kea, Hawaii (magnified 28 ×).

By courtesy of C.E. Tilley

crystallize from molten material within the Earth (Figure 51). They also occur in metamorphic rocks, lunar basalts, and in some meteorites. When clear and of good colour, magnesium-rich olivine is used as a gemstone and has the names peridot (for dark-coloured varieties) and chrysolite (light-coloured). Because of its high melting point and resistance to chemical reagents, magnesium olivine is an important refractory material—*i.e.,* it can be used in furnace linings and in kilns when other materials are subjected to heat and chemical processes.

COMPOSITION AND STRUCTURE

Solid-solution series

Chemical composition. The most abundant olivines are intimate mixtures of forsterite, pure magnesium silicate (Mg_2SiO_4), and fayalite, pure ferrous silicate (Fe_2SiO_4); most of the naturally occurring specimens are intermediate in composition to these two pure compounds, called end-members, and have the general chemical formula $(Mg,Fe)_2SiO_4$ (Figure 52). The members of this mixture, the forsterite–fayalite solid-solution series (a single crystalline phase that varies in composition between finite limits—*i.e.,* the end-members), are given the general mineral name olivine. The name forsterite is restricted to those species with no more than 10 percent iron substituting for magnesium; fayalite (from Fayal Island in the Azores, where it was believed to occur in a local volcanic rock but probably was obtained from slag brought to the island as ship's ballast) is restricted to species with no more than 10 percent magnesium substituting for iron. Species intermediate in composition to forsterite and fayalite are also named; from most magnesium-rich to most iron-rich they are: chrysolite (90–70 percent Mg), hyalosiderite (70–50 percent Mg), hortonolite (50–70 percent Fe), and ferrohortonite (70–90 percent Fe).

From *American Journal of Science*, vol. 29 (1935)

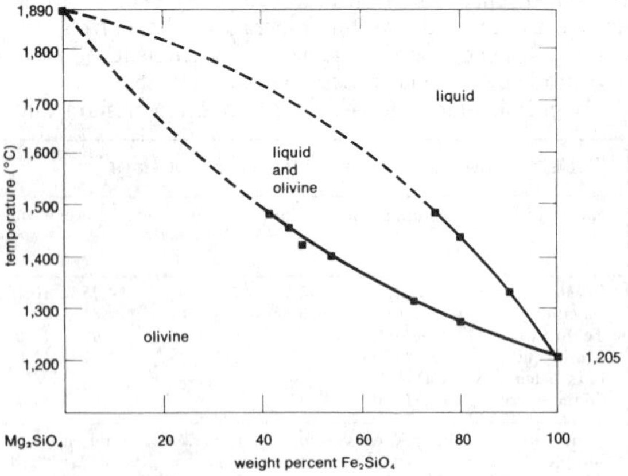

Figure 52: Equilibrium diagram of the system Mg_2SiO_4–Fe_2SiO_4.

The continuity in the forsterite–fayalite series has been verified experimentally. At the magnesium-rich end of the solid solution series, natural crystals may contain very small amounts of calcium, nickel, and chromium; the iron-rich members near the other end of the series may incorporate small amounts of manganese and calcium. Apart from ferrous iron, the crystalline structure of the olivines is also capable of accommodating relatively small amounts of ferric iron; dendrites (small branching crystals) of magnetite or chromite found oriented with respect to some crystallographic direction within such olivines may be attributed to exsolution (that is, to precipitation while cooling in the crystalline state). But the presence of relatively large amounts of ferric oxide in the analyses of olivines clearly indicates either an advanced state of oxidation or the mechanical inclusion of co-precipitating magnetite upon crystallization from the magma.

X-ray diffraction data for powders of synthetic forsterite and fayalite permit estimation of the composition of any solid solution between these two end-members to an accuracy of better than 4 percent.

In addition to the forsterite–fayalite series, other complete solid-solution series exist among the various olivine minerals. Fayalite is soluble in all proportions with ash-gray tephroite (from Greek *tephros,* "ashen"), pure manganese silicate (Mn_2SiO_4); the intermediate in the series is knebelite ($FeMnSiO_4$). Tephroite and knebelite come from manganese and iron-ore deposits, from metamorphosed manganese-rich sedimentary rocks, and from slags.

By courtesy of the Crystallography Laboratory, University of Amsterdam

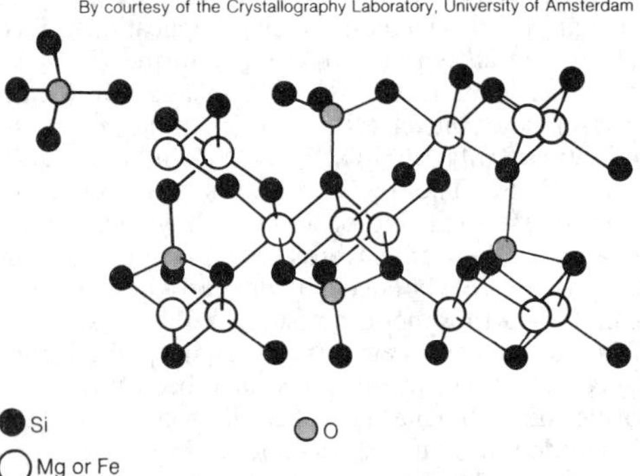

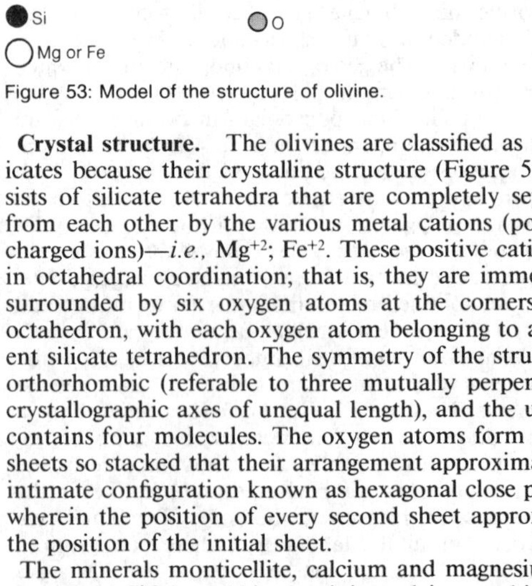

Figure 53: Model of the structure of olivine.

Crystal structure. The olivines are classified as nesosilicates because their crystalline structure (Figure 53) consists of silicate tetrahedra that are completely separated from each other by the various metal cations (positively charged ions)—*i.e.,* Mg^{+2}; Fe^{+2}. These positive cations are in octahedral coordination; that is, they are immediately surrounded by six oxygen atoms at the corners of an octahedron, with each oxygen atom belonging to a different silicate tetrahedron. The symmetry of the structure is orthorhombic (referable to three mutually perpendicular crystallographic axes of unequal length), and the unit cell contains four molecules. The oxygen atoms form parallel sheets so stacked that their arrangement approximates the intimate configuration known as hexagonal close packing, wherein the position of every second sheet approximates the position of the initial sheet.

The minerals monticellite, calcium and magnesium silicate ($CaMgSiO_4$), and kirschsteinite, calcium and iron silicate ($CaFeSiO_4$), have essentially the same structure as the forsterite–fayalite minerals, but the calcium atoms are so placed that the magnesium and iron atoms are restricted to certain positions.

MINERALOGICAL CHARACTERISTICS

Banded structures

Physical properties. The specific gravity and hardness of the olivines are listed in Table 8. There are at least two cleavages—*i.e.,* the tendency to split along preferred crystallographic directions (perpendicular to the *a* and *b* axes in this case)—both of which are better developed in the iron-rich varieties. Forsterite contained in certain ultrabasic rocks may show a banded structure when observed in thin sections with a polarizing microscope; in some dunites (a rock consisting nearly entirely of olivine), for example, olivine is preferentially oriented so that the cleavage plane perpendicular to the *b* axis is parallel to the microscopic laminated structure of the rock. Individual grains of olivine within such rocks typically appear as oriented bands with angles of up to 10 degrees between them. Such banding, which is undoubtedly the product of incipient mechanical deformation, also can be observed within the olivine nodules of some basalts.

To the unaided eye pure forsterite appears colourless, but as the content of ferrous oxide increases, specimens show yellow-green, dark-green, and, eventually, brown to black tints. In thin sections under the microscope, however, even pure fayalite appears pale yellow. Pure tephroite is gray, and monticellite also appears gray or colourless.

Some variations of optical properties observed in natural olivine crystals probably result from small but varying replacements of magnesium and iron by calcium and manganese and of silicon by titanium, chromium, and ferric iron.

Crystal habit and form. The magnesium-iron olivines occur most commonly as compact or granular masses. Except for the well-shaped phenocrysts (single crystals) of such olivines found embedded in the fine-grained matrices (groundmass) of basalts (see Figure 51), distinctly developed crystals are relatively rare. The phenocrysts in basalts are characterized by prominent pinacoid (*i.e.,* having a pair of parallel faces) and prism faces, so that their cross sections often appear six- or eight-sided. With fayalite the morphology is often simple. Monticellite and tephroite commonly show prominent pyramidal faces. Twinning is not very frequently observed. When twinning does occur, trillings (the intergrowth of three grains) may be produced and, in monticellite, six-pointed star shapes, as reported from the Highwood Mountains in Montana.

OCCURRENCE IN NATURE

In igneous and metamorphic rocks. The magnesium-iron olivines are essential minerals in basic and ultrabasic rocks. Their composition in these rocks ranges from Fo_{92} (92 percent forsterite by molecular weight) in dunites and

From J.F. Schairer and H.S. Yoder, Jr., "Crystal and Liquid Trends in Simplified Alkali Basalts," *Carnegie Institution of Washington Year Book 63*, p. 65, 1964

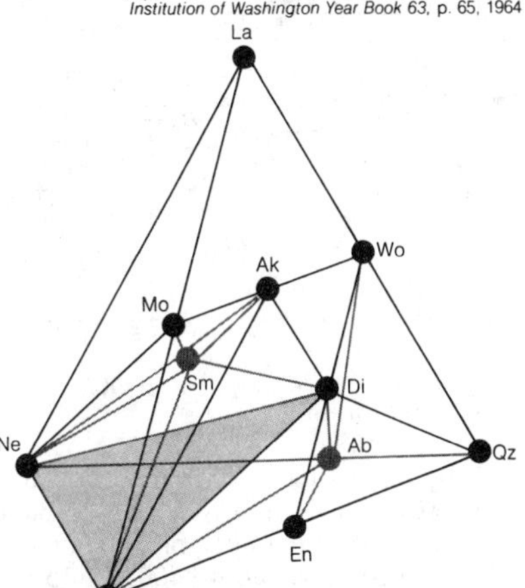

Figure 54: Expanded basalt tetrahedron showing mineral associates of magnesium-iron olivine (see text for explanation of symbols).

The basalt tetrahedron

about Fo_{88} in peridotites through the interval Fo_{88}–Fo_{50} in basalts, gabbros, and dolerites. The minerals associated with olivine in basalts and in gabbros are indicated in the expanded basalt tetrahedron (see Figure 54). This tetrahedron represents the chemical relationships between the minerals larnite (La), nepheline (Ne), forsterite (Fo), and the various phases of silica (Qz). These minerals are shown at the corners of the tetrahedron, which represent the pure compounds. Moving along the edges and faces of the tetrahedron from one corner increases the content of the other mineral phases. Thus, along the edges and faces of this tetrahedron are located the intermediate phases enstatite (En), albite (Ab), wollastonite (Wo), monticellite (Mo), diopside (Di), akermanite (Ak), and sodamelilite (Sm). On the tetrahedron, the four points representing the minerals nepheline, forsterite, quartz, and diopside form the corners of another tetrahedron, the simple basalt tetrahedron: Ne - Fo - Qz - Di. The three points Di, Ne, and Fo define a critical plane (shaded) of undersaturation with respect to silica. This plane separates the basic mineral assemblages of the simple basalt tetrahedron, which contain plagioclase (Ab) and olivine (represented below the plane) from the olivine-bearing ultrabasic mineral assemblages that are devoid of plagioclase but contain monticellite (Mo) and melilite (Ak) (represented above the plane).

Olivines richer in iron than Fa_{50} are less common; they do occur in the iron-enriched layers of some intrusive rocks, however. Fayalite itself occurs in small amounts in some silicic volcanic rocks, both as a primary mineral and in the lithophysae and vugs (bubble-like hollows) of rhyolites and obsidians (volcanic glass). It also occurs in acidic plutonic rocks such as granites, in association with iron-enriched amphiboles and pyroxenes.

Olivines also occur in metamorphic environments. Both forsterite and monticellite typically develop in the zones in which igneous intrusions make contact with dolomites. Forsterite tends to develop at lower temperatures than monticellite as the process of decarbonation in the contact zone progresses. Fayalitic olivines develop within metamorphosed iron-rich sediments. In the quaternary (*i.e.,* four-component) system Fe_2O_3 - FeO - SiO_2 - H_2O, fayalite is associated with the minerals greenalite (iron-serpentine), minnesotaite (iron-talc), and grunerite (iron-amphibole) in various metamorphic stages. In chemically more complex environments, which, in addition to the above components, also involve lime (CaO) and alumina (Al_2O_3), fayalite may be associated with hedenbergite, eulite (iron-rich orthopyroxene), grunerite, and almandine (iron-garnet).

In meteorites and in the Earth's mantle. In meteorites, the olivine is usually a forsteritic variety containing only Fa_{15} to Fa_{30}. In the Nakhla (Egypt) meteorite, an achondrite, the olivine is more ferrous, however, containing as much as Fa_{65}. In the chondrites (stony meteorites), the olivine commonly is incorporated in the distinctive spheroidal bodies referred to as chondrules, which range up to one millimetre in diameter.

Relation to the spinel structure

Because the rocks of the upper mantle directly below the Mohorovičić discontinuity (see above) are believed to consist of peridotite and garnetiferous peridotite that contain olivines as their most abundant minerals, it is important to establish their behaviour when subjected to high pressures. Study of the olivine-like compound magnesium germanate, Mg_2GeO_4, showed that it has polymorphs that have both olivine and spinel structure. In the spinel structure, the oxygen atoms are arranged in cubic close packing (in which the position of every third layer repeats that of the initial layer) instead of hexagonal close packing (in which the position of every second layer repeats that of the initial layer) of the olivine structure. The spinel form of Mg_2GeO_4 was found to have a density exceeding that of the olivine form by 9 percent. In 1936 it was suggested that at high pressures Mg_2SiO_4 might also transform to a spinel structure; this suggestion was adopted in 1937 as a basis for explaining the so-called 20°-discontinuity, an observed seismic discontinuity in the mantle at a depth of about 400 kilometres (250 miles).

In 1966 it was shown that each of the three synthetic olivines, Fe_2SiO_4, Ni_2SiO_4, and Co_2SiO_4, could be transformed directly to a spinel structure at a temperature of

700° C (1,300° F) and at pressures below 70 kilobars (the bar is a unit of pressure equal to atmospheric pressure about 100 metres above sea level). These spinel structures were denser by approximately 10 percent than the corresponding olivine structures. In 1968 a series of synthetic magnesium and iron olivines was subjected to a range of pressures between 50 and 200 kilobars (700,000 and 3,000,000 pounds per square inch) at a temperature of 1,000° C (1,830° F). In the composition range Fe_2SiO_4 to $(Mg_{0.8}Fe_{0.2})_2SiO_4$, these olivines were transformed completely to their spinel polymorphs, which are isometric crystals (referable to three mutually perpendicular crystallographic axes of equal length), with an accompanying increase in density of 10 percent. In the composition range $(Mg_{0.8}Fe_{0.2})_2SiO_4$ to Mg_2SiO_4, however, the olivines were transformed to another orthorhombic structure (called β-orthosilicate) at a pressure of about 130 kilobars (1,900,000 pounds per square inch) and a temperature of 1,000° C. This β-phase polymorph, with a density only 8 percent greater than that of the corresponding olivine structure, is believed to be the stable phase in the field of its synthesis. The change in the crystalline structure of olivine to its spinel polymorph, accompanied by a change in the structure of magnesium-iron pyroxenes to a new garnet-like structure at depths of 350 to 450 kilometres (220 to 280 miles) in the mantle, is believed to be responsible for the observed abrupt change in the velocity of seismic waves at these depths (see also EARTHQUAKES).

The spinel polymorph of olivine has been recorded in the Tenham (Queensland) chondrite as pseudomorphs after olivine. Portions of some large grains of olivine immediately adjacent to black, shock-generated veins are recognized as transforms to the spinel phase; the associated plagioclase feldspar was converted to maskelynite. The composition of the spinel phase in the meteorite has been analyzed by means of an electron probe and found to be $(Mg_{0.75}Fe_{0.25})_2SiO_4$; in thin sections it appears blue-gray to violet-blue. It has been named ringwoodite after A.E. Ringwood, an Australian earth scientist who synthesized spinel phases with compositions and properties close to those of the mineral found in the meteorite. More recently, ringwoodite also has been found in the Coorara (Western Australia) meteorite in association with a garnet phase. The β-phase polymorph has not yet been observed in shocked meteorites—*i.e.,* those that have undergone impact shock—but it is highly probable that it, too, exists in relative abundance within the Earth's mantle.

Other occurrences. Knebelite olivines are restricted to iron-manganese ore deposits, to their associated skarn (lime-bearing silicate rocks) zones, and to metamorphosed manganiferous sediments. At Franklin, New Jersey, tephroite and glaucochroite occur in the same deposit as roepperite, a knebelite containing 10.7 weight percent zinc oxide (ZnO).

Sources of monticellite

Monticellite occurs in some alkali peridotites and within limestones near their contact with peridotites. Pure kirschsteinite is known only from slags and has not yet been observed as part of a natural mineral assemblage. The most plausible natural environments for kirschsteinite should be altered limestones, and it is possible that the mineral has remained unrecognized in such rocks because its optical properties (the chief means of identification) are similar to those of the much more common magnesium-iron olivines. A kirschsteinite containing 31 percent by weight of other olivines, particularly monticellite, has been reported from a nepheline-melilite in north Kivu Region, Zaire.

Glaucochroite, pure calcium and manganese silicate ($CaMnSiO_4$), is rare, reported only from a deposit in Franklin, New Jersey, where it occurs with tephroite. The limited availability of manganese in parent magmas is thought to account for the rarity of minerals intermediate in the solid solution series between the calcium-rich olivines monticellite, glaucochroite, and kirschsteinite.

Alteration products and weathering. Olivines gelatinize in even weak acids and offer little resistance to attack by weathering agents and hot mineralizing (hydrothermal) solutions. The forsteritic olivines are altered principally through leaching, which results in the removal of magnesium and the addition of water and some iron. The chemical reactions are usually complex and involve hydration, oxidation, and carbonation. The fayalitic olivines are altered principally through oxidation and the removal of silica. The usual products of alteration are the minerals serpentine, iddingsite, and bowlingite, all of which may occur as pseudomorphs (forms with the outward appearance of the original mineral but which have been completely replaced by another mineral). Serpentine, which is the most common alteration product of olivine in ultrabasic rocks, often is accompanied by magnesite. Iddingsite and bowlingite are variable in composition and, even though they appear optically homogeneous, each actually consists of an intimate mixture of several distinct minerals. X-ray diffraction analyses of iddingsite show that the mineral goethite (FeO · OH) is a frequent component. Also included with the mixture may be hematite (Fe_2O_3), as well as a silicate phase whose structure, even though very irregular and disordered, appears to be related to that of the clay minerals vermiculite or montmorillonite. Iddingsite develops almost exclusively from the olivines of extrusive and hypabyssal (minor intrusive, such as sill and dike) rocks and practically never from the olivines of plutonic and metamorphic rocks. The process of "iddingsitation" of olivine may set in even before the complete consolidation of the lava or the hypabyssal magma. This is evident from the observation of rock textures in which shells of iddingsite surrounding a core of olivine are, in turn, surrounded by more unaltered olivine.

Olivine in beach sands

The mechanical weathering of olivine-rich rocks leads to the release of olivine particles that, in the absence of much chemical weathering, may accumulate to produce green or greenish-black sands. Conspicuous examples of such sands occur on the beaches of the islands of Oahu and Hawaii, particularly at Diamond Head (Oahu) and South Point (Hawaii). Alluvial sands rich in olivine are also known from the Navajo County of Arizona and from New Mexico; these sands provide clear olivine used in jewelry.

EXPERIMENTAL STUDIES

The general stability fields of the olivines are shown in Figure 55, on which the olivines, pyroxenes, and silica phases present are plotted. With regard to olivine end-members, forsterite is readily prepared by heating its component oxides (2MgO and SiO_2) to temperatures of at least 500° C (900° F) at water-vapour pressures of from 140 to 2,800 atmospheres (2,000 to 4,000 pounds per square inch). Although forsterite remains stable in contact with water vapour at all temperatures above 400° C (750° F), below this temperature it is attacked by water, yielding serpentine and brucite:

From American Journal of Science, vol. 29 (1935)

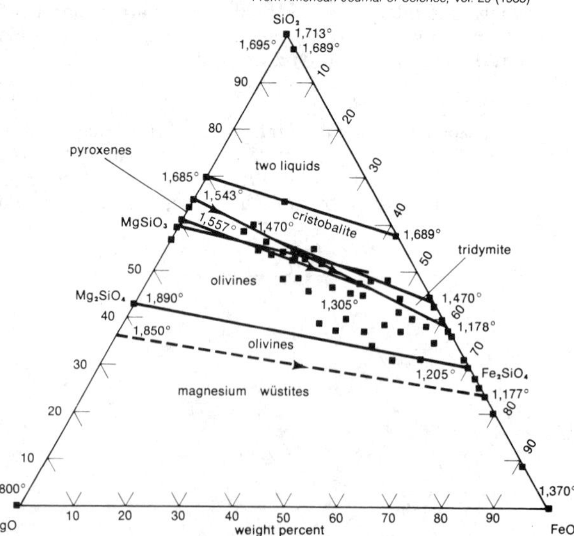

Figure 55: Equilibrium diagram of the system $MgO-FeO-SiO_2$. Temperatures are given in degrees Celsius.

$$\underset{\text{forsterite}}{2Mg_2SiO_4} + \underset{\text{water}}{3H_2O} \rightleftharpoons \underset{\text{serpentine}}{H_4Mg_3Si_2O_9} + \underset{\text{brucite}}{Mg(OH)_2}.$$

Fayalite also can be prepared hydrothermally from iron oxide and silica ($2FeO + SiO_2 \rightleftharpoons Fe_2SiO_4$) at low partial pressures of oxygen and at temperatures above 250° C (480° F). Below this temperature, fayalite is unstable in contact with water, and hydrous phases such as greenalite, accompanied by magnetite, appear instead.

Experimental studies are important for the interpretation of the role of olivine in rocks. In synthetic systems fayalite is quite stable even in the presence of free silica, but forsterite is unstable unless the system is undersaturated with respect to silica. In the binary system $MgO - SiO_2$ the stability field of the pyroxene-like metasilicate called protoenstatite separates the stability field of forsterite from that of cristobalite. Upon heating to nearly 1,560° C (2,840° F), the pyroxene melts according to the reaction: $2MgSiO_3 \rightleftharpoons MgSiO_4 + SiO_2$. This relationship, called incongruent melting because the solid and the melt are not identical, is carried over into the ternary system $CaO - MgO - SiO_2$, involving diopside, forsterite, and silica, and into the quaternary system $Al_2O_3 - CaO - MgO - SiO_2$, involving anorthite, diopside, forsterite, and silica. The reverse reaction occurs when forsterite, in contact with the liquid, cools to the incongruent melting temperature. It is recorded in basic and ultrabasic rocks in which partially resorbed crystals of olivine are encased in a shell of pyroxene, the product of the incongruent melting reaction.

Unlike the $MgO - SiO_2$ system, the binary system $FeO - SiO_2$ (Figure 56) has no metasilicate phase ($FeSiO_3$) intervening at liquidus temperatures, and there is no obstacle to the coexistence of fayalite (Fe_2SiO_4) with tridymite (SiO_2). But at 1,205° C (2,201° F), fayalite undergoes incongruent melting, with the separation of metallic iron and the simultaneous enrichment of the liquid in Fe_2O_3. This incongruent melting is characteristic of all phase assemblages in the system $FeO - SiO_2$. (C.E.T.)

From *American Journal of Science*, vol.29 (1935)

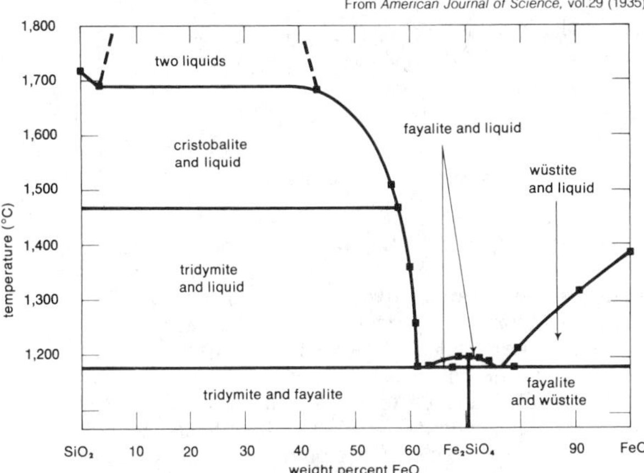

Figure 56: Equilibrium diagram of the system $FeO-SiO_2$.

Feldspathoids

The feldspathoids are a group of aluminosilicate minerals that contain the alkali metal sodium and, in some varieties, potassium and calcium. Because extensive chemical substitution occurs in natural feldspathoids, their compositions and crystal structure vary widely and, hence, their physical properties show great variation. Nevertheless, they are often identifiable in the field on the basis of colour, crystal form, and geological environment. Chemically, the feldspathoids lie between the feldspars, the structure of which contains no extraneous molecules (*i.e.*, water, sulfate, or carbonate) and permits slow chemical substitution for the metal ion present, and the zeolites, the structure of which has relatively large spaces that may contain a large number of extraneous molecules and readily permits the exchange of its metal ions—a characteristic that lends water-softening ability to the zeolites. The distinction between feldspathoids and zeolites is somewhat arbitrary, however, and is based more on historical custom than on strict scientific rules (see below *Zeolites*).

Figure 57: Typical scapolite (wernerite) crystal, with a tetragonal prism capped by a pyramid, Pierrepont, New York.

By courtesy of the American Museum of Natural History, New York; photograph, Lee Boltin

Economic importance

The most important feldspathoids are nepheline (nephelite), which is the most abundant mineral of the alkaline rocks, and leucite. Others, including analcime, sodalite, lazurite, noselite (nosean), haüynite (haüyne), and cancrinite, are relatively rare. The feldspathoid group is of minor economic importance; nepheline, however, is mined in large quantities in Ontario and the Kola Peninsula as a source of soda, silica, and alumina for glass and ceramic products. It also is used in the Soviet Union in the production of alumina and cement. Leucite has been used in Italy as a fertilizer and as a source of alum.

Lazurite-rich rock formerly was crushed to provide ultramarine, an intense blue pigment long used in painting, printing, and colouring of ceramics, but since the synthesis of ultramarine in 1828, synthetic ultramarine of various shades of blue has replaced the rare and expensive natural product. Blue sodalite and massive lazurite are used as

By courtesy of (right) Northwestern University Geology Department, Evanston, Illinois; photographs, (left, centre) Katherine H. Jensen—EB Inc., (right) Mary Root—EB Inc.

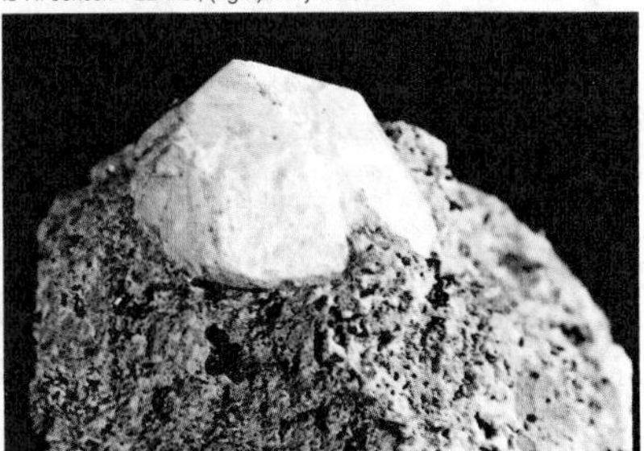

Figure 58: (Left) Typical trapezohedral analcime crystals, the Alps, northern Italy. (Centre) Sodalite (blue), cancrinite (yellow), nepheline (greasy luster), feldspar (white), and ferromagnesine minerals (black) in a syenite, Litchfield, Maine. (Right) Leucite crystals, with typical trapezohedral shape, weathered out of volcanic rock, Vesuvius, Italy.

ornamental stones and inlays; the latter rock is called lapis lazuli when it is of gem quality.

The feldspathoids have a crystal structure that is a continuous framework of linked silicate tetrahedra (SiO_4^{2-}), in which a silicon atom is surrounded by and bonded to four oxygen atoms arranged at the corners of a tetrahedron; aluminum replaces silicon in some of the tetrahedrons. Each oxygen atom is part of two tetrahedrons and provides the linking necessary for a continuous structure. Alkali metals and other large atoms and molecules occupy the holes (spaces) between the oxygen atoms. It is the open framework that permits extensive chemical substitutions in the feldspathoids.

The feldspathoids are characteristic of rocks that are relatively poor in silica and rich in alkalies and aluminum. In these rocks they form as a substitute for the more common feldspars (hence, the German name for the group, *Feldspat Vertreter,* "feldspar substitute,"), which require a higher silicate to alkali ratio. The feldspathoids can never occur in rocks that contain free silica (quartz; SiO_2) as an original constituent. They occur in a variety of alkali-rich rocks, including volcanic, plutonic, metamorphic, replacement, skarn, and precipitated varieties. Analcime, nepheline, and leucite, for example, occur as phenocrysts (single crystals in a finer matrix), and analcime is also precipitated in saline lakes and occurs on the sea floor.

CHEMICAL COMPOSITION AND CRYSTAL STRUCTURE

Classification of the feldspathoids

Because extensive chemical substitution occurs in natural feldspathoids, a wide range of compositions and associated crystal structures is represented by members of this mineral group. Classification of the feldspathoids, therefore, is best accomplished by grouping members on the basis of chemical composition and structure. Such a classification is presented in Table 9, which lists mineral composition, crystal system, and unit cell dimensions. It should be noted that the compositions of most feldspathoids range widely about the ideal formulae that are listed.

The reasons for this classification of feldspathoids will be apparent from consideration of the several feldspathoid groups, the first of which is the nepheline group.

The nepheline group. Nepheline, kalsilite, and kaliophilite have structures similar to that of the high-temperature form of silica called tridymite, and the structure of carnegieite is similar to another form of silica called cristobalite.

The idealized structure of kalsilite has potassium atoms occupying the centres of the large voids in a framework that contains sheets of tetrahedra. The vertices of these tetrahedra are oxygen atoms, and at their centres are silicon and aluminum atoms. Alternate tetrahedra point up (U) like an Egyptian pyramid and share one oxygen (at the tetrahedron's base) with each of three tetrahedra pointing down (D), as shown in Figure 59. The next higher sheet

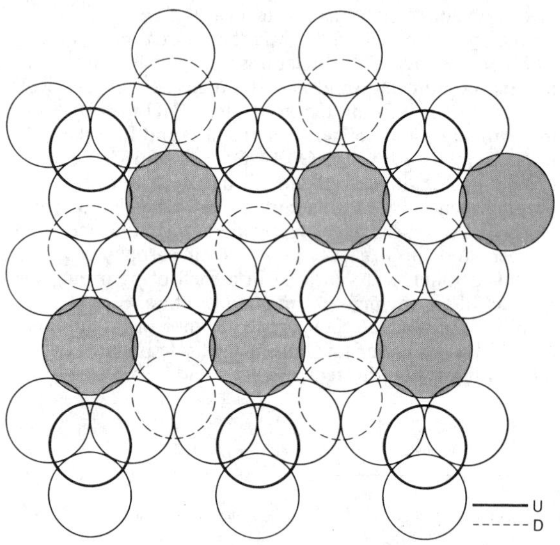

Figure 59: Crystal structure of kalsilite (see text).

is joined to the first sheet by sharing of oxygen atoms at the top of U tetrahedra so that, in projection, U of the first sheet is under D of the next higher sheet. D of the first sheet comes over U of the next lower sheet. In this structure the oxygen atoms are arranged in the stacking pattern called hexagonal close packing. When smaller sodium atoms substitute for the potassium atoms, the framework buckles to reduce the size of the cavities. For ideal nepheline, there are three small holes for sodium and one large hole for potassium. The expanded kalsilite is able to accommodate only a few sodium atoms before it buckles to the nepheline structure, which can accommodate an extremely large range of compositions. The cell dimensions (see Table 9) change with the chemical substitution, and the chemical composition can be estimated from X-ray diffraction data (see MATTER: *Crystallography*). Not only does nepheline permit sodium–potassium substitution, but it also permits substitution of silicon for aluminum with corresponding absence of alkali atoms to adjust the charges. Kaliophilite and other rare minerals have different degrees of distortion. The relation between tridymite and cristobalite frameworks is analogous to hexagonal and cubic close packing of equal spheres; in hexagonal close packing, every second layer is oriented the same as the original layer, whereas in cubic close packing every third layer has that orientation. At high temperatures, nepheline of composition $NaAlSiO_4$ changes to carnegieite, the cristobalite-like framework of which consists of identical sheets of U and D tetrahedra, but every third sheet is rotated by 60° with respect to the ideal tridymite structure. Upon cooling, the high-order, isometric (cubic) symmetry of carnegieite changes discontinuously at 690° C (1,275° F) to low-order symmetry as a result of framework collapse. The crystal system of this carnegieite may be triclinic, as indicated in Table 9.

Nepheline that has been annealed in metamorphic rocks shows complex X-ray patterns that indicate a special arrangement of atoms. Nepheline from volcanic rocks typically deviates considerably from the composition $Na_3KAl_4Si_4O_{16}$, whereas nepheline from low-temperature environments is much closer to this ideal formula. Calcium commonly substitutes for sodium and iron for aluminum.

Table 9: Classification of Feldspathoids According to Composition and Structure

	idealized composition	crystal system*	unit cell dimensions†
Nepheline	$Na_3KAl_4Si_4O_{16}$	hexagonal	a 10.0, c 8.4
Kalsilite	$KAlSiO_4$	hexagonal	a 5.1, c 8.7
Kaliophilite	$KAlSiO_4$	hexagonal	a 26.9, c 8.5
Carnegieite (high)	$NaAlSiO_4$	isometric	a 7.3
Carnegieite (low)	$NaAlSiO_4$	triclinic?	?
Leucite (high)	$KAlSi_2O_6$	isometric	a 13.4
Leucite (low)	$KAlSi_2O_6$	tetragonal	a 13.7
Analcime	$NaAlSi_2O_6 \cdot H_2O$	isometric	a 13.7
Sodalite	$Na_4Al_3Si_3O_{12}Cl$	isometric	a 8.9
Hydroxysodalite	$Na_4Al_3Si_3O_{12}OH$	isometric	a 8.9
Noselite (nosean)	$Na_8Al_6Si_6O_{24}(SO_4)H_2O$	isometric	a 9.1
Haüynite (haüyne)	$Na_6Ca_2Al_6Si_6O_{24}(SO_4)_2$	isometric	a 9.1
Cancrinite	$Na_6Ca_2Al_6Si_6O_{24}(CO_3)_2 3H_2O$	hexagonal	a 12.7, c 5.1
Natrodavyne	$Na_{10}Al_6Si_6O_{24}(CO_3)_2 \cdot xH_2O$	hexagonal	a 12.7, c 5.1
Vishnevite	$Na_8Al_6Si_6O_{24}(SO_4)3H_2O$	hexagonal	a 12.7, c 5.1
Scapolite	(family name)		
Marialite	$Na_4Al_3Si_9O_{24}Cl$	tetragonal	a 12.1, c 7.6
Meionite	$Ca_4Al_6Si_6O_{24}CO_3$	tetragonal	a 12.2, c 7.6

*In the isometric system crystals are referable to three mutually perpendicular crystallographic axes of equal length. Tetragonal crystals also are referable to three mutually perpendicular axes, two of which are of equal length and the third longer or shorter. In the hexagonal system three axes of equal length intersect at angles of 120° and are perpendicular to a fourth axis that may be longer or shorter. The three axes of triclinic crystals are inclined relative to each other and are of differing lengths. †The unit cell is the smallest volume that contains a complete sample of the atomic or molecular groups that comprise a particular mineral. Dimensions are given in angstrom units (one angstrom equals 10^{-8} centimetres), and the letters *a* and *c* refer to directions along the crystallographic axes. In the isometric system all axes are of equal length and only one value (*a*) is given. Similarly, in the tetragonal system *a* refers to the two axes that are of equal length and *c* to the third, and in the hexagonal system *a* represents the cell dimensions along each of the three axes of equal length and *c* represents the fourth.

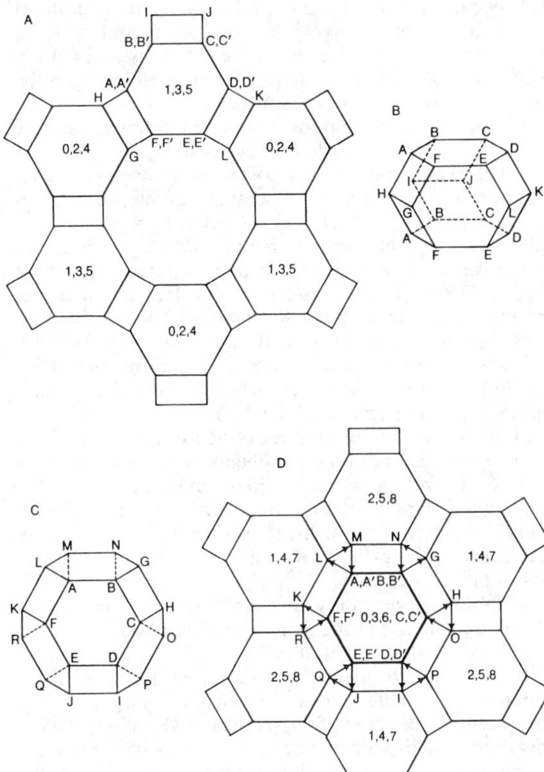

Figure 60: Two-dimensional projections of three-dimensional aluminosilicate frameworks of cancrinite and sodalite.
The Si and Al atoms occur at the line intersections and oxygen atoms at the middle of the line segments. In cancrinite (A), there are hexagonal rings superimposed so that they lie either at heights 0,2,4, etc., or at 1,3,5, etc. The edges of the rings form tilted squares. In (B) a perspective diagram shows the unit formed from the labelled intersections of (A). In sodalite (C), the hexagonal rings superimposed at 0,3,6, etc., 1,4,7, etc., and 2,5,8, etc., forming truncated octahedra as shown by the perspective drawings of (D). Corresponding intersections are labelled. The upper hexagonal face of a truncated octahedron is emphasized in (C), and descending lines are shown by the arrows.

Leucite and analcime. Leucite has an aluminosilicate framework that is too complex to describe here: four-, six-, and 12-membered rings of tetrahedra occur in the framework. Above 625° C (1,150° F) leucite has isometric symmetry, with potassium atoms vibrating at the centre of the large cavities; below 625° C the framework buckles sharply, producing a one-sided distortion and reduction of size of the cavities occupied by the potassium atoms. The mineral pollucite, a cesium-bearing hydrated aluminosilicate ($CsAlSi_2O_6 \cdot H_2O$), remains isometric at all temperatures because the cesium atoms are large enough even without thermal vibration to hold the framework in a regular configuration.

Modifications of analcime

Analcime has the same structural framework as leucite, but the smaller sodium atoms are each accompanied by a water molecule, thereby precluding structural distortion. Analcime occurs in three modifications, which probably result from different arrangements of aluminum and silicon atoms among the tetrahedra. Synthetic analcime has a random (disordered) distribution of aluminum and silicon atoms, but the atoms in some natural analcimes that were slowly annealed have a regular arrangement.

Analcime and leucite have incomplete sodium–potassium substitution. Analcime commonly contains some calcium, but there is a major gap between its composition and that of the zeolite mineral wairakite ($Ca_{0.5}AlSi_2O_6 \cdot H_2O$). The synthetic analcimes range in composition from $Na_{1.2}Al_{1.2}Si_{1.8}O_6 \cdot 0.9H_2O$ to $Na_{0.75}Al_{0.75}Si_{2.25}O_6 \cdot 1.1H_2O$; natural analcimes cover about half of this composition range. Analcimes formed at higher temperatures approach more closely the ideal formula; silica-rich analcimes form by reaction of volcanic ash with salt water. Analcime technically may be classed as a zeolite mineral because the water is removed reversibly by heating up to 150° C (300° F) and the alkali atoms can be ion exchanged reversibly.

The sodalite and cancrinite groups. The sodalite and cancrinite groups have aluminosilicate groups related in an elegant way (see Figure 60). In sodalite the aluminum and silicon atoms lie at the corners of imaginary truncated octahedra (the Archimedean semiregular polyhedron, which has eight hexagonal faces formed by truncating the six corners) close packed on the hexagonal faces to fill the space completely. Although the symmetry is isometric, it appears to be hexagonal when viewed perpendicular to one set of imaginary faces; there are three sets of parallel hexagonal faces that are so stacked one behind the other that in projection they appear to have a hexagonal orientation around a central hexagonal face. The centres of the hexagonal faces in sodalite have positions that are analogous to the cubic close packing of spheres.

In cancrinite, two sets of hexagonal faces are stacked one behind the other so that in projection they form a hexagonal pattern around a rather large 12-sided void. The centres of the hexagons in this case have positions analogous to hexagonal close packing of spheres.

In sodalite all of the cavities between the oxygen atoms (which lie nearly at the centres of the edges of the truncated octahedron) are near spherical and are connected by apertures in the six-membered rings. In cancrinite there are much larger cavities connected by 12-membered rings, and, in addition, there are smaller cavities. The large cavities and channels permit easy movement of atoms. In the sodalite group, the large chlorine, sulfate, or sulfide units fit nicely in the truncated octahedra, while the sodium atoms lie close to the six-membered rings of oxygen atoms. In cancrinite the carbonate group lies at the centre of the large cavities, while the sodium atoms and water molecules occupy other convenient positions.

Structures of the scapolite group

The scapolite group. The aluminosilicate framework of scapolite, sometimes also called wernerite, is composed of two types of four-membered rings of tetrahedra. One type has alternate tetrahedra pointing upward (U) and downward (D), and the other type has tilted tetrahedra (T_1, T_2), each of which has an innermost edge that is horizontal and an outermost edge that is vertical; the rings of T_1 and of T_2 tetrahedra are at different levels (see Figure 61). These four-membered rings are so linked that each U tetrahedron has a D tetrahedron above it and a T_2 tetrahedron below it and to the side, whereas each D tetrahedron has a U tetrahedron below it and a T_1 tetrahedron above it and to the side. This arrangement forms vertical five-membered rings composed of two U, two D, and one T tetrahedra.

Chlorine atoms or carbonate groups lie in the large cavities between the T rings. Calcium atoms occur in the

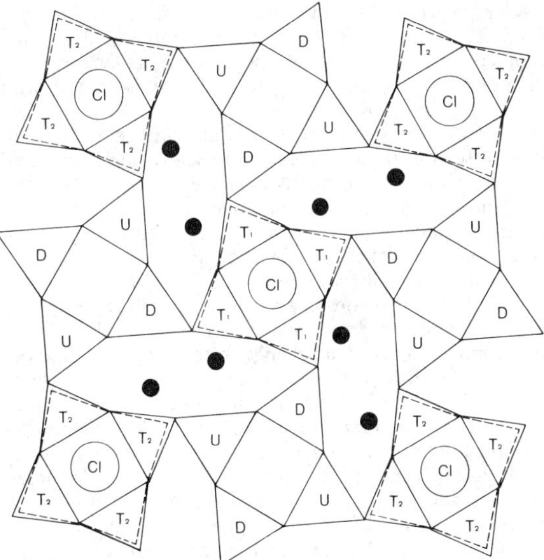

Figure 61: Scapolite structure shown as two-dimensional projection. (See text for explanation of U, D, and T.) Chlorine atoms lie in cavities marked Cl, while Ca atoms occupy in projection the places marked by heavy dots.

elongated cavities bonded to oxygen atoms and to chlorine atoms or carbonate groups.

The distribution of aluminum and silicon atoms in scapolite is complex. In all framework structures, the best electrostatic stability results when not more than one aluminum atom is attached to each oxygen. In marialite, each aluminum atom alternates with three silicon atoms in conformity with this rule. In pure meionite with one aluminum atom for each silicon atom, this rule would be violated because no more than two aluminum atoms would be placed in the five-membered rings. Indeed, few if any scapolites closely approach the meionite composition. The relatively low-order symmetry of at least some scapolites is probably caused by special ordering patterns of the aluminum and silicon atoms and perhaps by special orientations of carbonate molecules.

PHYSICAL PROPERTIES OF FELDSPATHOIDS

Identification of feldspathoids

The physical properties of feldspathoids are rather variable because of the extensive chemical substitutions. Visual examination of hand-sized specimens or microscopic study of thin sections often permits qualitative identification of feldspathoids, but X-ray diffraction and chemical analysis, especially with the electron microprobe, are desirable for quantitative identification. Simple chemical tests also are useful. Feldspathoids decompose in weak mineral acid because of the high aluminum content, and this serves to distinguish them from feldspar. The hardness of all feldspathoids is 5–6 on the Mohs scale.

Nepheline has a specific gravity of 2.56–2.66, is usually white or gray, has a greasy lustre, and is shapeless in plutonic rocks; simple hexagonal prisms are the predominant form in volcanic rocks. Basal and prismatic cleavages (mineral surfaces that parallel crystallographic planes, along which the mineral tends to split) are poor, and the mineral rarely exhibits twinning—*i.e.*, intergrowths of two or more grains in accord with some preferred crystallographic surface or orientation.

Kalsilite is similar to nepheline, but the specific gravity is 2.59–2.62 and its optical properties differ. The most distinctive property for diagnostic purposes is the potassium/sodium ratio, which can be determined by X-ray diffraction.

Leucite and analcime are white, gray, or pink and usually have trapezohedral forms. Leucite shows intimately twinned crystals on the dodecahedron faces when viewed in thin section, and analcime exhibits very poor cleavage. Specific gravity ranges from 2.45–2.50 for leucite and from 2.24–2.29 for analcime. The minerals are best distinguished optically.

Sodalite, noselite, and haüynite can occur in almost any colour when in hand-specimen size, but they are colourless or pale blue in thin section. Specific gravities range from 2.3–2.5, and dodecahedral or shapeless forms are characteristic. Members of the sodalite group are best differentiated chemically because all are isometric with similar optical properties.

Cancrinite and vishnevite also exhibit almost any colour. In thin section these minerals are usually colourless, and perfect prismatic cleavage is characteristic. Specific gravities range from 2.3–2.5, and their perfect cleavage and different optical properties serve to distinguish these minerals from those of the scapolite group.

Scapolite is usually white but, again, colour can be variable. Tetragonal prisms capped with pyramids are typical forms. Major property changes are associated with the structural–compositional change from marialite to meionite. Specific gravity varies from 2.5–2.6 in marialite to 2.6–2.8 in meionite. The optical properties of scapolite, marialite, and meionite vary with the sodium/calcium ratio and thus provide a good estimate of composition. In addition to their optical properties, the scapolite minerals are distinguished from feldspar minerals by their cleavage angle and absence of twinned crystals and from cancrinite by their lesser solubility in hydrochloric acid.

SYNTHESIS AND NATURAL OCCURRENCE

The natural occurrence of minerals can be treated from a geographic viewpoint, but knowledge of the reasons for such occurrences or the interpretation of the conditions of formation stems largely from experimental data on mineral synthesis. In this sense, the synthesis and natural occurrence of the feldspathoids are best considered jointly, particularly because they commonly grow and develop under metastable conditions; that is, conditions that may permit further change before final stability.

Mineral stability fields

Nepheline and kalsilite. At low temperatures, the stability fields (as a function of temperature for varying compositions between $NaAlSiO_4$ and $KAlSiO_4$) of nepheline and kalsilite are separated by an area in which the two phases do not mix and thus coexist. At temperatures of less than 400° C (750° F) the boundary (solvus) of this area approaches the compositions $KAlSiO_4$ and $KNa_3Al_4Si_4O_{16}$. Nepheline inverts to carnegieite at 1,250° C (2,280° F), and kalsilite inverts to an orthorhombic form (one referable to three mutually perpendicular but unequal crystallographic axes) at 900° C (1,650° F).

Kalsilite occurs in volcanic rocks rich in potassium from Uganda, Zaire, and Italy as phenocrysts (isolated crystals) and in the groundmass (fine-grained matrix). Some phenocrysts consist of an intergrowth of kalsilite with nepheline resulting from breakup of a high-temperature, potassium-rich nepheline. Kalsilite also occurs in the linings of blast furnaces.

Kaliophilite occurs only in ejected blocks from Italian volcanoes, where it probably grew metastably at a temperature of about 1,000° C (1,830° F).

Nepheline–leucite–analcime. The occurrence of these minerals is intimately related to that of feldspar in the three-component system SiO_2–$NaAlSiO_4$–$KAlSiO_4$. To delineate the stability fields of these minerals it is necessary to consider temperature, hydrostatic pressure, and the pressure of water vapour. In laboratory synthesis, pressure commonly is applied in the form of water vapour. When the crystal products are anhydrous (*i.e.*, waterless), the addition of water acts merely as a catalyst promoting the growth rate. When analcime or melt is involved, however, the water actually enters the silicate material.

Figure 62 shows the composition ranges for the crystallization of the first mineral from a silicate melt containing

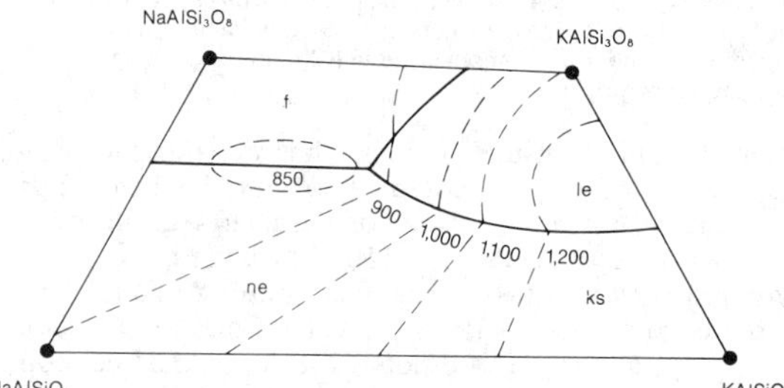

Figure 62: Composition regions at which nepheline (ne), kalsilite (ks), leucite (le), and sanidine feldspar (f) are the first to crystallize from the melt at 1,000 atmospheres H_2O pressure. Temperatures in °C (some estimated) are shown by contours. The boundary between the nepheline kalsilite fields is probably near the 1,200° C contour.

excess water at a pressure of 1,000 atmospheres. The contours show the temperatures for the beginning of crystallization: generally 200°–400° C (390°–750° F) lower than for the dry system. In agreement, kalsilite, leucite, nepheline, and alkali feldspar occur as phenocrysts in volcanic rocks of appropriate chemical composition.

When the liquid has been consumed by crystallizing minerals, the minerals that coexist over temperatures ranging down to 700° C (1,300° F) are as shown in Figure 63. Nepheline coexists with either sanidine feldspar, feldspar + leucite, or leucite + kalsilite. At temperatures below 500° C (930° F), leucite is no longer stable, and sanidine feldspar is replaced by microcline and albite.

The natural occurrence of leucite is compatible with the laboratory syntheses because leucite occurs only in potassium-rich volcanic rocks. Important localities are Leucite Hills, Wyoming; central Montana; Rome; Uganda; and Zaire. Pseudo-leucite is the name for trapezohedral crystals of a mixture of nepheline and feldspar plus al-

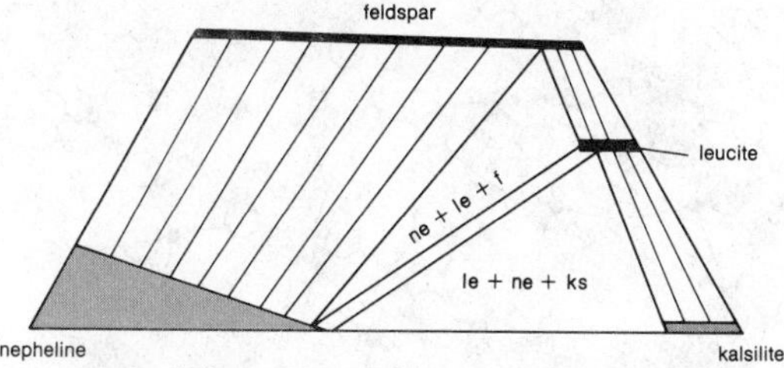

Figure 63: Composition regions in which feldspathoids coexist at temperatures from 700° C to the beginning of melting. In the triangles, three minerals coexist. In the shaded areas one mineral exists. In the striped area two minerals coexist with compositions represented by the ends of the line.

teration products. Their origin is controversial, a probable explanation is that phenocrysts of leucite, containing sodium, are reconstituted as nepheline and feldspar.

Origin and distribution of nepheline and analcime

Nepheline is the most abundant mineral of the alkaline rocks, such as nepheline-syenites and gneisses, in which it is typically associated with feldspars. Whether these rocks form by igneous processes or by the chemical alteration of sediments by sodium-rich fluids is controversial. Famous localities are the Haliburton-Bancroft area of Ontario; Oslo, Norway; and Alnö, Sweden; Norra Kärr, Finland; and Kola Peninsula, Russian Soviet Federated Socialist Republic. Local reaction of silica-poor magma with carbonate-rich sediments produces other nepheline-bearing rocks in the British Isles at Camas Mor, Muck, and Scawt Hill. Nepheline commonly is accompanied by sodalite, cancrinite, or scapolite. Nepheline in volcanic rocks is glassy, but in deep-seated rocks it has a greasy lustre that is caused by alteration to cancrinite and other minerals. Nepheline occurs in walls of furnaces. In the chemical industry, the $NaAlSiO_4$ composition at temperatures near 100° C (212° F) in aqueous solution yields an important zeolite known as Type A.

Analcime has a tremendous range of environmental occurrences. Under high water pressure, analcime replaces nepheline and feldspar as the mineral first crystallizing from a melt of potassium-poor material. This explains its occurrence as phenocrysts in extrusive rocks, such as phonolites and trachybasalts. At lower pressures, analcime is not stable with a liquid, but it occurs at lower temperatures for a composition range overlapping that of $NaAlSi_3O_8$. The occurrence of analcime in vesicles of basalts and in wide areas of very low-grade (slightly altered) metamorphosed sediments, such as volcanic ash in New Zealand, is consistent with laboratory syntheses up to 200° C. Volcanic ash commonly alters in the presence of solutions (or in lake beds or on the ocean floor) to a variety of zeolites or clay minerals. Analcime is increasingly common in the older rocks, thus indicating that it is more stable than erionite, mordenite, and other zeolites. Silica-rich analcime transforms slowly to albite.

Analcime also precipitates from lakes that are fed by alkaline waters. Huge beds of analcime-rich rocks, tens of feet thick and covering thousands of square miles in Wyoming, Utah, the Sahara, and Zaire, show no evidence of residual volcanic ash and are believed to have originated by direct precipitation.

Sodalite and cancrinite groups. The stability conditions of the sodalite and cancrinite groups are poorly known, partly because of the metastable growth of these minerals and partly because of extensive chemical substitutions that may occur. Because of the special relation between their framework geometry, sodalite and cancrinite minerals can be polymorphous. Cancrinite contains more water and therefore is the low-temperature phase.

Cancrinite grows from 200° to 1,250° C (390° to 2,300° F), at which temperature it melts to nepheline plus liquid. Hydroxycancrinite grows up to 800° C (1,470° F). Natrodavyne breaks down above 600° C (1,100° F) to a sodium carbonate form of noselite. Continuous chemical substitution exists between noselite and haüynite but not with sodalite. Hydroxysodalite has been synthesized extensively during growth of zeolite molecular sieves. Noselite and haüynite typically occur in volcanic rocks, which is consistent with the data for breakdown of natrodavyne. Noselite occurs in phonolites of the Cape Verde Islands and Wolf Rock, Cornwall, and in ejected blocks of Laacher See, Rhine district. Haüynite occurs in Italian and Laacher See volcanoes and in alnöite rocks at Oka, Quebec, and Winnett, Montana.

Famous feldspathoid localities

Chlorine-rich sodalites occur in both volcanic and plutonic rocks and in metasomatic rocks, indicating a very wide temperature range of formation. Famous localities include the nepheline–syenites of Litchfield, Maine; Rhodesia; Korea; nepheline–syenite pegmatites of Burma, the Republic of Guinea, and Bearpaw Mountains, Montana; phonolites of Scotland and the Sahara; trachytes of Naples and Laacher See. In Angola, sky-blue crystals as long as 20 centimetres (eight inches) occur. The hackmannite variety, characterized by a pink colour that fades on exposure to light, occurs in Bancroft, Ontario; Magnet Cove, Arkansas; Kola Peninsula; and Korea.

Cancrinite minerals typically occur as alteration products of nepheline and feldspar or by contact metamorphism of a limestone by an igneous intrusion. Famous localities are at Alnö, Sweden; Fen district, Norway; Iivaara, Finland; and Iron Hill, Colorado.

The scapolite group. Very little is known about the stability of scapolite minerals: indeed, the first proven syntheses were accomplished only in 1962. Scapolite does not occur as phenocrysts in volcanic rocks and, typically, is a metamorphic and metasomatic (completely replaced by chemical substitution) mineral requiring the availability of carbonate and sulfate. The principal occurrences are in regionally metamorphosed rocks of all metamorphic grades in Quebec and Ontario; hydrothermally altered igneous rocks associated with iron ores at Kiruna, Sweden, and Bucks County, Pennsylvania; contact skarns between limestone and igneous rocks in Queensland, Australia; and metamorphosed volcanic blocks of Laacher See. (J.V.S.)

Zeolites

The zeolites comprise another significant group of aluminosilicate minerals. They contain alkali and alkaline-earth metals, such as sodium, potassium, and calcium, as well as water molecules within their structural framework. The latter is relatively porous, enclosing interconnected cavities in which the metal cations (positively charged atoms) and water molecules reside. Because of the presence of water, the zeolites swell and boil upon heating, and they were named by the Swedish mineralogist A.F. Cronstedt, in 1756, in allusion to this property (*i.e.,* from the Greek *zein,* "to boil" and *lithos,* "stone").

Economic importance

The cations and the water molecules have considerable freedom of movement within the framework of aluminum, oxygen, and silicon atoms; this gives the zeolites the cation exchange and reversible dehydration properties for which they are noted. The porous framework of the zeolites enables them to act as molecular sieves—*i.e.,* they are used to separate molecular mixtures on the basis of the size and shape of molecular compounds or for the selective adsorption of gases. These unique properties are utilized in diverse industrial processes such as the purification of water as well as other liquids and gases, chemical separations, catalysis, and the decontamination of radioactive wastes.

More than 30 distinct species of zeolites occur in nature. Numerous zeolites have been synthesized, but many of these have no natural counterparts. Although the crystal habit is an adequate basis for the identification of some zeolites and optical properties for others, most zeolites can be positively identified only through X-ray diffraction methods, which involve the analysis of radiation scattering by powdered samples. This method is particularly well suited for the identification of zeolites in fine-grained rocks from which the individual minerals cannot be isolated.

STRUCTURE AND COMPOSITION

Crystal structure. The fundamental building block of the zeolites is a tetrahedron of four oxygen atoms surrounding a small silicon or aluminum atom. The structural framework of zeolites consists of SiO_4 and AlO_4 tetrahedra so arranged that each oxygen is shared between two tetrahedra. Thus, the atomic ratio O/(Al + Si) is equal to two. Because aluminum has one less positive charge than silicon, the framework has a net negative charge of one and is neutralized by the exchangeable cations. Each sodium or potassium ion, with one positive charge, can balance one aluminum; but each calcium ion, with two positive charges, can balance two aluminums. Feldspars and feldspathoids also have framework structures, but their structures are more compact than those of the zeolites.

Classification of zeolite structures

Zeolite structures can be classed into three groups based on the kinds of linkages of the tetrahedra: (1) linkages more numerous in one crystallographic direction than in a plane at right angles to it, (2) linkages more numerous in one plane than in the direction at right angles to it, and (3) linkages similar in all directions. The fibrous zeolites, such as natrolite, mesolite, scolecite, and thomsonite, are characteristic of the first group. Platy zeolites, including heulandite, stilbite, and brewsterite, are typical of the second group. Representative zeolites of the third group include faujasite, gmelinite, and chabazite. The structures of natrolite, brewsterite, and chabazite were chosen to illustrate the three groups and are diagrammatically represented in Figures 64, 65, and 66.

Adapted from W.M. Meier, *Zeitschrift fur Kristallographie* (1960)

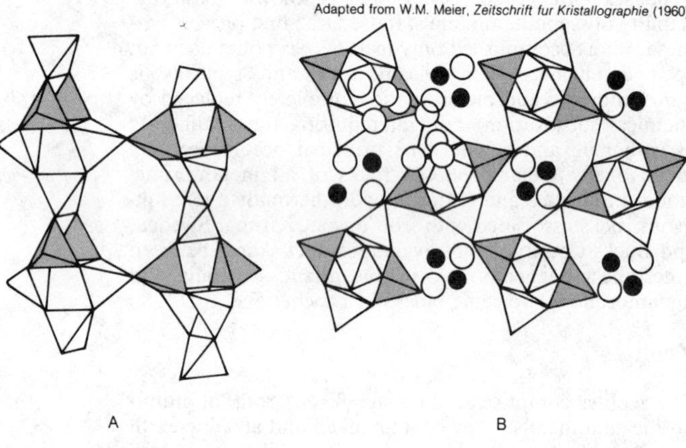

Figure 64: (A) Chains in natrolite. The lower SiO_4 tetrahedra of a chain are linked to the upper AlO_4 of neighbouring chains. (B) Projection of the natrolite structure showing placement of sodium ions and water molecules.

The structure of natrolite (Figure 64) consists of silicon and aluminum tetrahedra linked to form chains in the *c* direction (the vertical crystallographic axis). The repeating unit of each chain is five tetrahedra that have a dimension of about 6.6 angstroms (Å) in the *c* direction. Chains are linked laterally by shared apical oxygen atoms: the lower SiO_4 tetrahedra of one chain are linked to the upper AlO_4 tetrahedra of neighbouring chains. The fibrous nature of natrolite is explained by the relatively few bonds linking chains laterally as compared with the bonds within the chains. Natrolite has channels (with a minimum free diameter of 2.08 Å) parallel to the *c* axis and a system of intersecting channels (with a minimum free diameter of 2.60 Å) between neighbouring chains. Sodium atoms and water molecules lie within the channels. Each sodium is surrounded by six oxygens, and each water molecule is close to two sodium atoms.

The structure of brewsterite consists of layers of tetrahedra that are formed from linked four-, six-, and eight-membered rings (Figure 65). The layers are cross-linked by additional tetrahedra, forming a framework that also contains many tilted five-membered rings. Figure 65 is a projection of the structure down the *a* axis (crystallographic direction) and shows the paucity of bonds across the *b* axis that accounts for the typical platy cleavage (tendency to split) of brewsterite. There are two sets of intersecting channels that lie parallel to the *a* and *c* axes, and each set is controlled by apertures formed from eight-membered rings. The strontium atoms lie near the intersections of the channels and are in contact with five water molecules.

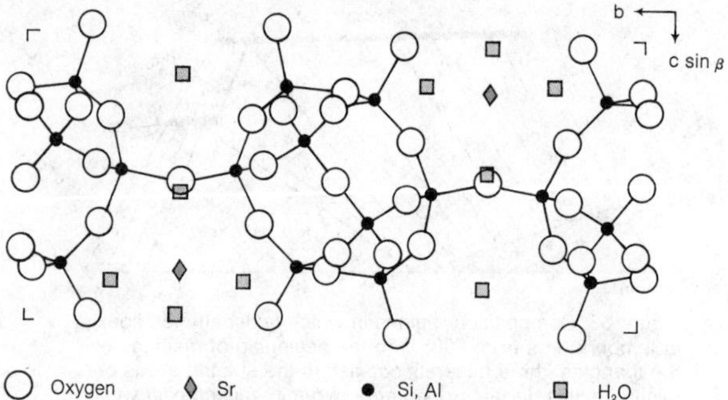

Figure 65: *Structure of brewsterite.*
Projection down the *a* axis shows the locations of cations and water molecules as well as the paucity of tetrahedral bonds across the mirror planes at b = 1/4 and 3/4, in conformity with the observed {010} cleavage. The lower and upper halves of the eight-membered rings may be seen in the top and bottom, respectively, of the diagram; these rings, which may be visualized by extension into neighbouring cells, provide the narrowest parts of the channel.

Adapted from A.J. Perrotta and J.V. Smith, *Acta Crystallographica* (1964)

The six-membered rings of chabazite

The structure of chabazite is built of double six-membered rings of tetrahedra that form hexagonal prisms. The centres of the prisms occupy the corners of the rhombohedral cell, and the prisms are linked to form one large cage per unit cell (Figure 66). Each cage has six octagonal, two hexagonal, and 12 quadrilateral faces and is connected to six neighbouring cages by apertures of eight-membered rings. The eight-membered rings permit adsorption in all directions but limit it by the minimum free diameter of 3.9 Å. Thus, argon and methane, with relatively small diameters, are adsorbed, but isobutane (diameter 5.6 Å) is excluded. Dehydration of chabazite causes distortion of the eight-membered rings so that the free area is elliptical, with dimensions of 4.4 Å by 3.1 Å. Water molecules and the calcium atoms lie within the cavities of the framework.

Chemical composition. Most natural zeolites show considerable variation in chemical composition, including variation in the water content, the cation content, and the Si/Al ratio. The most common cations in natural zeolites are sodium, potassium, and calcium; barium, strontium, and magnesium are also found in some, however. Barium is the predominant cation in the zeolite harmotome. Although potassium occurs in many zeolites, it generally is not the predominant cation, probably because of its relatively large size.

Adapted from J.V. Smith, F. Rinaldi, and L.S.D. Glasser, *Acta Crystallographica* (1963)

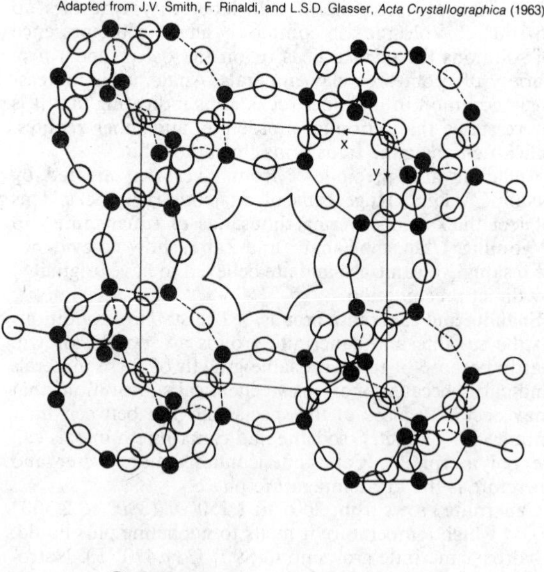

Figure 66: *Structure of chabazite.*
Rhombohedral *c*-axis projection showing the framework of constituents. The relative actual size of the oxygen atoms is about 2½ times greater than shown, and the free area of the eight-membered ring is outlined in the centre.

Si/Al ratios

The actual number of sodium, potassium, and calcium atoms in the formula of a zeolite must be related to the Si/Al ratio by the charge relation Na + K + 2Ca = Al. Substitution of Al^{3+} for Si^{4+} in the framework of a zeolite requires the presence of a cation to maintain the charge balance. The maximum substitution of Al^{3+} for Si^{4+} results in a Si/Al ratio of one. Thomsonite, gismondine, and gonnardite are the only natural zeolites that have Si/Al ratios close to one. A commercially important zeolite called type A has been synthesized with a Si/Al ratio of one. The minimum substitution of Al^{3+} for Si^{4+} is in mordenite, which has a Si/Al ratio of about five. Like the feldspars, zeolites show replacement of the type calcium and aluminum for sodium, potassium, and silicon [CaAl $\rightleftharpoons$ (Na,K)Si]. Replacement of calcium for sodium and potassium [Ca $\rightleftharpoons$ 2(Na,K)] also occurs and does not involve the framework constituents. Replacement of the latter type can occur in zeolites at any time after their crystallization. The Si/Al ratio of a zeolite is probably determined at the time of crystallization, and it is not subsequently modified because of the difficulty of moving silicon and aluminum atoms in the framework.

Some investigators have found a relationship between the water content of zeolites and the kind of exchangeable cation in the structure. In a general way the water content of a zeolite increases with decreasing radius of the cation. The water content is also greater for a bivalent cation than for a univalent cation of the same radius.

PROPERTIES OF ZEOLITES

Physical properties. When they are pure, zeolites are colourless or white, but many specimens are coloured gray, pink, yellow, or green by minute inclusions of iron oxides, clay minerals, or other impurities. The specific gravity of zeolites is notably low as a consequence of their porous structures. Except for barium-rich zeolites, the specific gravity is 1.9 to 2.4 (the specific gravity of common quartz is 2.65 and that of most iron-bearing minerals is greater than 3.0); most zeolites are in the range of 2.0 to 2.3, however. Barium-rich zeolites such as harmotome and edingtonite have a specific gravity of 2.4 to 2.8. The hardness of zeolites is about 3.5 to 5.5 on the Mohs scale.

Crystal habits

The crystal habits of zeolites vary, but most can be classed into three groups: (1) fibrous or prismatic, (2) platy or bladed, and (3) equant, or of approximately equal dimensions in all directions. Natrolite, mesolite, and scolecite typically occur as slender prisms or tufts of hairlike crystals. Parallel intergrowths of natrolite with mesolite are especially common. Heulandite and stilbite are representative of the platy or bladed group. Stilbite belongs to the platy group but also occurs in sheaflike aggregates (Figure 67). Chabazite belongs to the equant group and typically occurs as rhombohedral crystals. Some mineralogists have correlated the composition of certain zeolites with their habit. For example, thomsonite is typically acicular (needlelike) or prismatic, but silica-poor varieties tend to form short prisms or plates.

Optical properties. The indices of refraction (a measure of the velocity of transmission of light in certain crystallographic directions) of zeolites are relatively low for silicate minerals. They are in the range of 1.48 to 1.52 (the index of refraction of water is about 1.33 and that of diamond is 2.42) and are sensitive to changes in the water and cation contents as well as changes in the Si/Al ratio. Some zeolites, particularly the fibrous ones such as natrolite and mesolite, show first a decrease in indices on dehydration but then an increase in indices as dehydration proceeds. They decrease markedly with an increase in the Si/Al ratio. Such behaviour has been well documented for chabazite, phillipsite, and thomsonite.

Cation exchange. The ability of cations in zeolites to exchange with other cations in aqueous solutions was first reported in 1858; since then, a wide range of exchange behaviour has been observed. The cation-exchange properties depend on the size and charge of the cations and the structure of the particular zeolite mineral involved. At relatively low concentrations and ordinary temperatures, the extent of cation exchange generally increases with increased charge and atomic number (the number of protons or positive charges in the atom's nucleus) of the exchangeable cation. The extent of exchange is less predictable at high concentrations and high temperatures. The number of different cations that can undergo exchange increases as the zeolite structure becomes more open. Faujasite, one of the most open natural zeolites, shows extensive exchange with all the above cations as well as with bivalent cations and large organic cations. Many zeolites show only little or no structural modification of the framework during cation exchange. A drastic structural modification or even destruction of the structure accompanies the exchange of certain cations in some zeolites. The structure of the synthetic type A zeolite is completely destroyed when exchanged with barium (Ba^{2+}), copper (Cu^{2+}), or iron (Fe^{3+}). The thermal stability of some zeolites is improved by exchange with large cations, such as rubidium (Rb^{+}) and cesium (Cs^{+}). Chabazite remains stable above 1,000° C (1,830° F) when exchanged with these cations.

Factors influencing exchange

Water softening by zeolites

The cation-exchange behaviour of zeolites has been utilized to soften water. Hard water is caused by the presence of calcium ions and can be softened by passing it through a bed or tank of sodium zeolite. Calcium enters the zeolite and displaces the sodium to make the water "soft" (hard water is commonly defined as water containing calcium and magnesium salts because these constituents are highly insoluble and prevent lathering with soap). The zeolite eventually becomes saturated with calcium and loses its effectiveness. It can be easily regenerated, however, by flushing it with a saturated brine of sodium chloride; this reverses the exchange. Ion-exchange resins have replaced zeolites in water softening and most other cation-exchange applications. Considerable interest in zeolites has been recently generated by the nuclear energy industry, however. Clinoptilolite was found to be effective in the extraction of cesium and strontium from radioactive wastes.

Dehydration. The reversible dehydration property of zeolites was discovered in 1857. When most zeolites are heated, the water is given off continuously rather than in separate stages at certain temperatures. The dehydrated zeolite can then readsorb the original amount of water when exposed to water vapour. Recent investigations show that some zeolites such as phillipsite and gismondine lose and gain water in a stepwise manner. These zeolites and others undergo drastic structural modifications during dehydration at temperatures below 200° C (390° F). Chabazite, on the other hand, dehydrates continuously and shows only a slight shrinkage of the unit cell parameters. Detailed

By courtesy of (left, far right) the Field Museum of Natural History, Chicago; photographs, EB Inc., (left, far right) John H. Gerard, (far left, right) Katherine H. Jensen

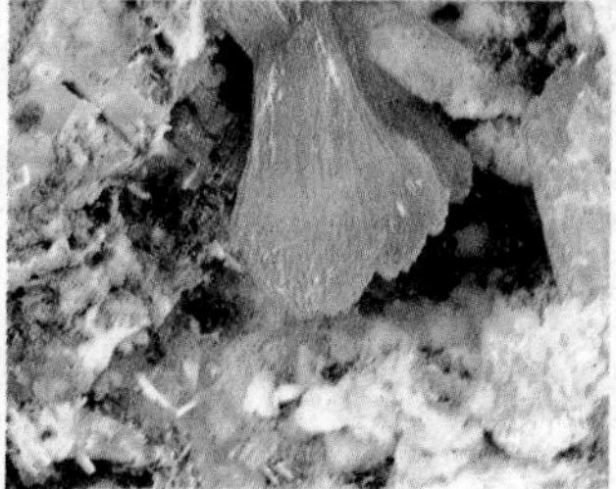

Figure 67: *Crystal habits of zeolites.*
(Far left) Tufts of hairlike natrolite crystals from Moore's Station, New Jersey. (Left) Platy heulandite from Cape Split, Nova Scotia. (Right) Sheaflike aggregate of stilbite from Paterson, New Jersey. (Far right) Equant rhombohedrons of chabazite from Nova Scotia.

structural studies of dehydrated chabazite reveal minor framework changes and major shifts of the calcium atoms. Apertures to cavities in the framework of chabazite also change in size and shape. Fully hydrated laumontite is rarely found in nature. On exposure to the atmosphere, laumontite loses about one-eighth of its water and changes to a partially dehydrated form known as leonhardite with distinctive optical properties.

Molecular-sieve properties. When zeolites are dehydrated, the remaining crystalline solid is characterized by molecular-sized voids that have a large internal surface area. As early as 1909 it was learned that dehydrated zeolites could reversibly adsorb gaseous iodine, mercury, and ammonia, as well as water. It was noted that dehydrated chabazite adsorbed methyl and ethyl alcohol but virtually excluded the relatively large molecules of acetone, ether, and benzene. When the significance of this selective behaviour was recognized, the term molecular sieve was proposed for the zeolites.

The molecular-sieve properties of zeolites depend not so much on the size or volume of the voids in the framework but rather on the size of the apertures that connect the voids. The zeolites differ in the sizes of their apertures; that of phillipsite, for example, is 4 Å and that of faujasite is 8 Å. The size of the apertures can be modified by controlling the temperature and the exchangeable cations. The framework of zeolites is not totally rigid, and the size of the apertures can be reduced by lowering the temperature. Cations are located in and near the apertures and therefore partially block them. Aperture size can be increased by reducing the number or size of the cations through cation exchange.

Applications of sieve properties

Diverse industrial applications are possible with dehydrated zeolites by careful choice of the zeolite and by control of the exchangeable cations and the temperature. In addition to uses as drying agents for liquids and gases, the zeolites are effective in such processes as separation of straight-chain paraffins from branched-chain or cyclic hydrocarbons, upgrading the octane number of gasoline by removal of straight-chain constituents, and separation of saturated hydrocarbons from undersaturated hydrocarbons. Zeolites have also found wide application as carriers for certain catalysts that were previously unusable because of their high volatility. Synthetic zeolites are preferred over natural zeolites for most industrial applications because of their uniform chemical composition and crystallinity.

OCCURRENCE AND ORIGIN

In igneous and metamorphic rocks. Zeolites occur in rocks that are diverse in lithology (type) and age and in many different geological environments. The most common occurrences are in the cavities and fractures of igneous rocks, particularly volcanic rocks. Most of the large, attractive zeolite specimens in museum collections have been obtained from igneous rocks. Zeolites are also found in metallic-ore deposits and hot-spring deposits, such as those at Wairakei, New Zealand, and Yellowstone National Park, U.S. In recent years, zeolites have been recognized as important rock-forming constituents in low-grade metamorphic rocks and in a variety of sedimentary rocks. The zeolites in sedimentary rocks are very finely crystalline and do not appeal to mineral collectors; deposits of this type are voluminous and have economic potential for many industrial processes, however.

Cavities and fractures in basalt

Nearly all of the zeolites can be found as cavity and fracture fillings in basaltic rocks. Innumerable occurrences have been reported from volcanic terranes. In the United States, zeolites are especially abundant in the Cenozoic (the last 65,000,000 years of Earth history) basaltic plateaus of Washington, Oregon, and Idaho; at Table Mountain, near Golden, Colorado; and in the Mesozoic (65,000,000 to 225,000,000 years ago) basalt and diabase of northeastern New Jersey. The Table Mountain locality has yielded fine specimens of chabazite and the fibrous zeolites—thomsonite, mesolite, and scolecite. Zeolites are also of common occurrence in the basalts along the Bay of Fundy, between Nova Scotia and New Brunswick; eastern Iceland, especially at Berufjördhur; and at Garron Point in County Antrim, Northern Ireland. Successive growths of several zeolites in a single cavity or fracture are typical of these occurrences in basaltic rocks. More than one generation of a zeolite species is common at some localities. Other contemporaneous minerals are generally associated with zeolites in basaltic rocks. These include quartz, calcite, apophyllite, and epidote.

In sedimentary rocks. Zeolites are among the most common secondary silicate minerals that occur in sedimentary rocks. Since the discovery in 1891 of phillipsite in deep-sea sediments, zeolites have been reported from many different sedimentary rocks and depositional environments. These zeolites are finely crystalline, commonly only five to 100 micrometres (one micrometre = 0.001 millimetre) in size, and their recognition and identification was virtually impossible until the widespread use of X-ray techniques. Unlike the varied suite of zeolites in the cavities of basaltic rocks, the zeolites in sedimentary rocks are limited to six species: chabazite, clinoptilolite, erionite, heulandite, mordenite, and phillipsite. Clinoptilolite is by far the most common. Zeolites are particularly abundant in deposits of alkaline, saline lakes. These bedded deposits generally consist of two or more zeolites that are associated with clay minerals, silica minerals, or feldspar. Beds consisting almost entirely of one zeolite, however, have been found in the Cenozoic continental deposits in the desert areas of the western United States. Other significant occurrences of zeolites in sedimentary rocks have been reported from the rift valleys of eastern Africa; Honshu, Japan; South Island, New Zealand; and the Soviet Union.

Factors that govern zeolite formation. The zeolites are secondary or authigenic minerals—*i.e.,* they are formed in place, in contrast to detrital or transported minerals. Although zeolites in hot-spring deposits may have formed at temperatures as high as 250° C (480° F), most zeolites crystallized at temperatures considerably below 100° C (212° F). Conditions favourable for the formation of zeolites include alkaline water enriched in alkalies and a readily available source of silicon and aluminum. Zeolites form as a result of the reaction of interstitial fluid with glassy or aluminosilicate mineral constituents of the host rock. The interstitial fluid originated as either percolating meteoric water (derived from rainfall) or connate water (that within the Earth). Rhyolitic volcanic glass in sedimentary deposits is particularly susceptible to alteration in the post-depositional environment. Rocks originally rich in shards of volcanic glass now commonly consist of zeolites that have preserved the original form of the glass particles (Figure 68). Those factors that determine which

Conditions favourable for zeolite formation

By courtesy of the U.S. Geological Survey

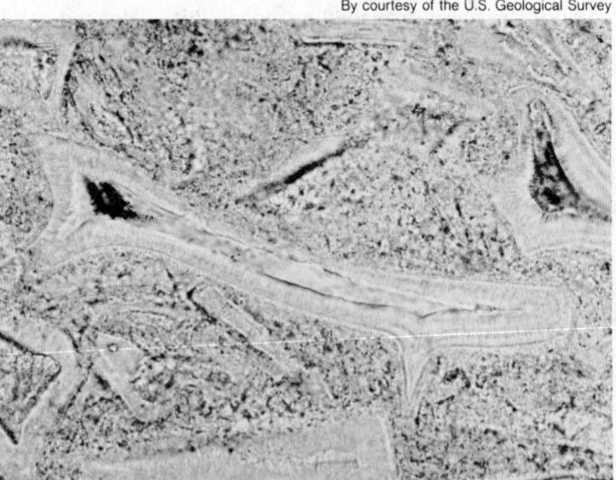

Figure 68: Photomicrograph of a zeolite tuff showing the preservation of the form of glass shards by fibrous clinoptilolite (magnified about 186 ×).

one of the many zeolites will crystallize in a rock are mostly unknown. The following are important, however: the porosity, permeability, and composition of the host rock; the depth of burial, inasmuch as this affects the temperature and pressure; and the chemistry of the interstitial fluid, including the pH (a measure of the acidity or alkalinity), salinity, and the proportion of cations present.

Zeolites have been synthesized in the laboratory from

Synthesis of zeolites

a wide range of materials, including glasses, gels, metal oxides, and crystalline aluminosilicate minerals. Some of these zeolites have natural counterparts, but many are not found in nature. A commercial synthesis utilizes highly reactive aluminosilicate gels (jellylike material consisting of very fine grained suspended particles) prepared from aqueous solutions of sodium aluminate, sodium silicate, and sodium hydroxide. Zeolites are then crystallized from the gels at temperatures ranging from room temperature to about 150° C (300° F) and at atmospheric pressure. The resulting zeolite species depends on the initial composition of the gel, the crystallization temperature, and the type of reactant employed.

Data on the stability fields of the zeolites are especially meagre because they crystallize metastably in most laboratory experiments (*i.e.,* they are subject to further change or modification under existing conditions of pressure and temperature). The physical state of the initial materials is commonly more important than bulk composition in determining which zeolite will form. (R.A.S./Ed.)

Clay minerals

Clays are composed essentially of silica, alumina, and water, and appreciable quantities of iron, alkalies, and alkaline earths are frequently present. Until recently there were no analytical techniques by which to determine the precise nature of the components of these elements in clays. X-ray diffraction techniques developed in the 1920s, followed a few years later by improved microscopic and thermal procedures, established that clays are composed of a few groups of crystalline minerals. Small amounts of amorphous material occur in some clays and varying amounts of such minerals as quartz, feldspar, mica, and iron oxides may also be present. The clay mineral components provide the essential characteristics and properties of clay, however.

Clay minerals occur in flake-shaped, lath-shaped, and needle-shaped units. The individual units are measured in angstroms (Å = 10^{-4} micrometres) but they occur in clays in booklike particles, aggregates of flakes, or bundles of laths and needles that are of the order of microns in diameter. Kaolin-type clay, for example, is essentially an aggregation of book-shaped units of sheets of the clay mineral kaolinite.

STRUCTURE AND COMPOSITION

Numerous classifications that vary in detail have been suggested for the clay minerals. It is generally agreed, however, that they can be classified on the basis of variations of atomic structure and chemical composition into the following groups: (1) allophane; (2) kaolinite; (3) halloysite; (4) smectite; (5) illite; (6) chlorite; (7) vermiculite; (8) sepiolite, attapulgite, and palygorskite; (9) mixed-layer clay minerals. Information on and structural diagrams for these groups are given below.

The composition and structure of the clay minerals has been determined largely by X-ray diffraction methods. Diffraction data for the clay minerals, as well as data on their infrared spectra, which can be related to chemical composition, are available in the clay-mineral literature.

From R. Grim, *Clay Mineralogy* (Copyright 1968); used with permission of McGraw-Hill Book Company

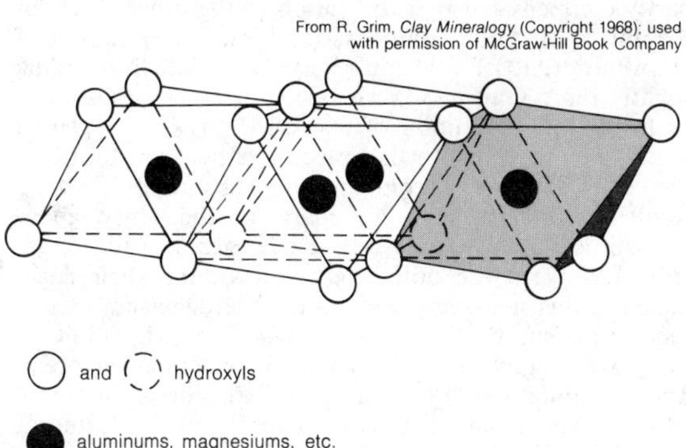

Figure 69: Single octahedral unit (shaded) and the sheet structure of octahedral units.

The atomic lattices of most of the clay minerals consist of two structural units. In the first, two sheets of closely packed oxygen atoms or hydroxyls have aluminum, iron, or magnesium atoms sandwiched between them. Each metal atom is in the centre of, and equidistant from, six oxygens arranged in an octahedron (Figure 69). This is called the gibbsite structure when aluminum predominates; only two-thirds of the possible central positions are filled, and the structure has the formula $Al_2(OH)_6$. It is called the brucite structure when magnesium predominates; in this case all of the central positions are filled, and the structure has the formula $Mg_3(OH)_6$.

In the second unit, a silicon atom is at the centre of and equidistant from four oxygens or hydroxyls arranged to form a tetrahedron (Figure 70). These are joined at their bases into a hexagonal network that is repeated indefinitely. The tips of all of the tetrahedrons point in the same direction, and the bases of all tetrahedrons are in the same plane; the sheet formed has the formula $Si_4O_6(OH)_4$.

From R. Grim, *Clay Mineralogy* (Copyright 1968); used with permission of McGraw-Hill Book Company

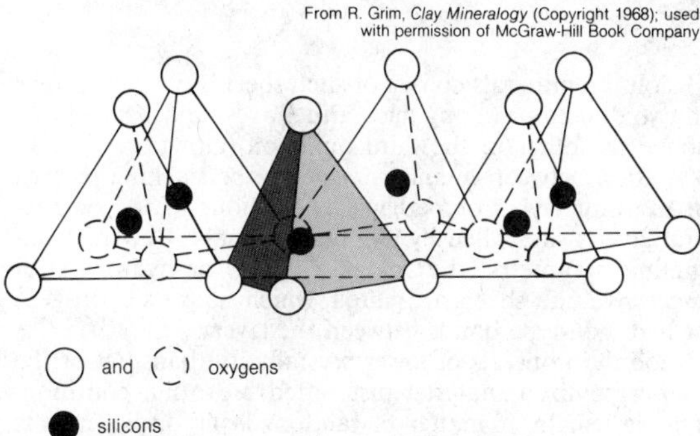

Figure 70: Single silica tetrahedron (shaded) and the sheet structure of silica tetrahedra arranged in hexagonal network.

Distortion of structural units

Recent detailed structural investigations have shown that consideration must be given to the substantial distortion of the clay mineral structural units to allow them to fit into determined unit cell dimensions of the minerals. Thus opposing rotation (from a few degrees to a theoretical maximum of 30°) of alternate tetrahedrons distorts the ideally hexagonal network of silica tetrahedrons and produces a ditrigonal (literally, doubly triangular) surface symmetry. Departure from geometrical regularity frequently occurs in the octahedral layer when the upper and lower equilateral triads of anions rotate around one central metal atom. In experiments with kaolinite it has been observed that rotation around aluminum sites in the upper triads is +6.5° and in the lower triads is −4°.

Sepiolite, attapulgite, and palygorskite are fibrous clay minerals and are composed of different structural units. Their configurations will be discussed later.

Allophane. Allophane is the name given to an amorphous inorganic compound found in some clays. Such material may be considered as composed of tetrahedral and octahedral units that are arranged in too irregular a fashion or on too small a scale to provide X-ray diffraction effects. In some cases such material has sufficient order to diffract electrons, although not X-rays.

The chemical composition of allophane is variable. It has been observed that some specimens resemble halloysites, whereas others have a composition more like smectites. Also, some allophane samples contain notable amounts of sulfate and phosphate compounds.

Kaolinite. The kaolinite structural unit (Figure 71) consists of a tetrahedral and octahedral sheet, so arranged that a common layer is formed by one of the anionic layers of the octahedral sheet and the tips of the silica tetrahedra. In this common layer silicon and aluminum atoms share two-thirds of the anions, which then become O instead of OH. Out of all the possible positions for aluminum in the octahedral sheet only two-thirds are filled and charges are balanced within the structural unit. The structure has the formula $(OH)_8Si_4Al_4O_{10}$, and its theoretical composition, as oxides, is SiO_2, 46.54 percent; Al_2O_2, 39.50 percent; H_2O, 13.96 percent. Analysis shows very little substitution occurring within the lattice.

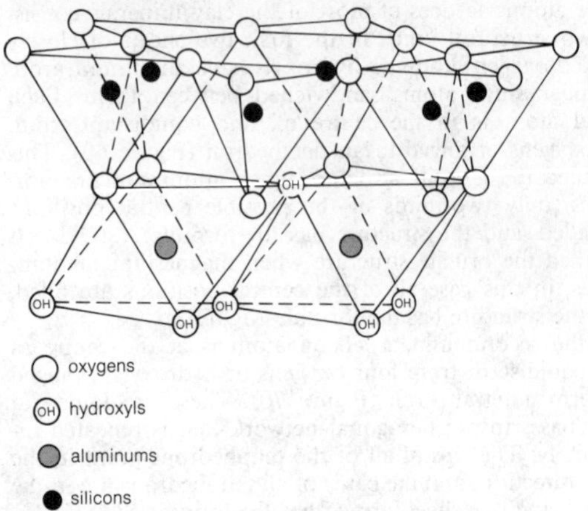

Figure 71: Structure of the kaolinite layer (see text).

From R. Grim, *Clay Mineralogy* (Copyright 1968); used with permission of McGraw-Hill Book Company

Kaolinite minerals consist of such sheet units continuous in two directions (along the *a* and *b* axes) and stacked one above the other in the third direction (along the *c* axis). Variation between members exists in the stacking pattern of the unit layers or perhaps in positions of the octahedral layer's sites filled by aluminum atoms. Kaolinite has triclinic symmetry; the anions (oxygens or hydroxyls) of successive unit sheets are paired, which suggests hydrogen- or hydroxyl-type bonds between the layers.

Triclinic symmetry of kaolinite

Kaolinite minerals of lower crystallinity than that of the well-crystallized material just noted are quite common. This is usually a matter of random layer displacements parallel to the *b* axis. Also, in poorly crystallized kaolinite, it is quite conceivable that the vacancy in octahedral positions may occur in different sites of each layer.

Halloysite. One of the two forms of halloysite has the composition $(OH)_8Si_4Al_4O_{10}$ and the other has the composition $(OH)_8Si_4Al_4O_{10} \cdot 4H_2O$; the latter form irreversibly dehydrates (loses the four water molecules) to the former at relatively low temperatures (60° C). The dehydrated form has a basal spacing about the thickness of a kaolinite layer or about 7.2 Å, and the hydrated form has a basal spacing of about 10.1 Å; the difference between them, 2.9 Å, is about the thickness of a sheet of water one molecule thick. Consequently, the layers of kaolinite in the hydrated form are separated by monomolecular water layers. These are lost during the transition from the hydrated to the dehydrated form. X-ray diffraction shows the absence of sharp *hkl* (faces perpendicular to the *a, b,* and *c* axes, respectively) reflections in the dehydrated form, which is explained by displacement parallel to both the *a* and *b* directions in a highly random manner.

Electron micrographs have shown the tubular nature of much halloysite. Recent studies have indicated that the tubes are commonly prismatic rather than round in cross section.

Smectite. The structural units (Figure 72) of smectite consist of two silica tetrahedral sheets with a central alumina octahedral sheet. The tips of each tetrahedral sheet all point in toward the centre of the unit, and combine with one octahedral sheet to form a common layer; atoms common to both layers become O instead of OH. The units are continuous in two directions and are stacked one above the other.

In the stacking of the silica-alumina-silica units, a weak bond is formed and an excellent cleavage results between the outside (oxygen) layers of each unit because they are adjacent to similar layers of neighbouring units. The particular distinction of the smectite structure from the other types is that water and other polar molecules (as certain organic substances) can, by entering between the unit layers, cause the lattice to expand in the direction of stacking (along the *c* axis). Thus this dimension may vary from about 9.6 Å, when there are no polar molecules between the unit layers, to nearly complete separation of the individual layers.

Without considering lattice substitutions, the theoretical formula of the smectite structural unit is $(OH)_4\ Si_8Al_4O_{20} \cdot nH_2O$ (interlayer); without considering the interlayer material the theoretical composition, as oxides, is SiO_2, 66.7 percent; Al_2O_3, 28.3 percent; and H_2O, 5 percent.

In actuality, smectite always differs from this theoretical formula because substitution occurs within the lattice. Aluminum or phosphorus may substitute for silicon in the tetrahedral sheets, and magnesium, iron, zinc, nickel, lithium, and others may substitute for aluminum in the octahedral sheet. Substitution of aluminum (Al^{3+}) for silicon (Si^{4+}) in the tetrahedral sheets seems to be limited to less than 15 percent. In the above formula, only two thirds of the possible positions in the octahedral sheet are filled; one magnesium (Mg^{++}) ion may substitute for one aluminum (Al^{3+}) ion, which continues to leave the structure with only two-thirds of the octahedral sites filled; or three magnesium (Mg^{++}) ions may substitute for two aluminum (Al^{3+}) ions, in which case all possible octahedral positions are filled. These substitutions vary from few to complete within the octahedral sheet. Total replacement of aluminum by magnesium yields saponite; replacement by iron yields nontronite; by chromium, volkhonskoite; and by zinc, sauconite.

Substitutions for silicon

From R. Grim, *Clay Mineralogy* (Copyright 1968); used with permission of McGraw-Hill Book Company

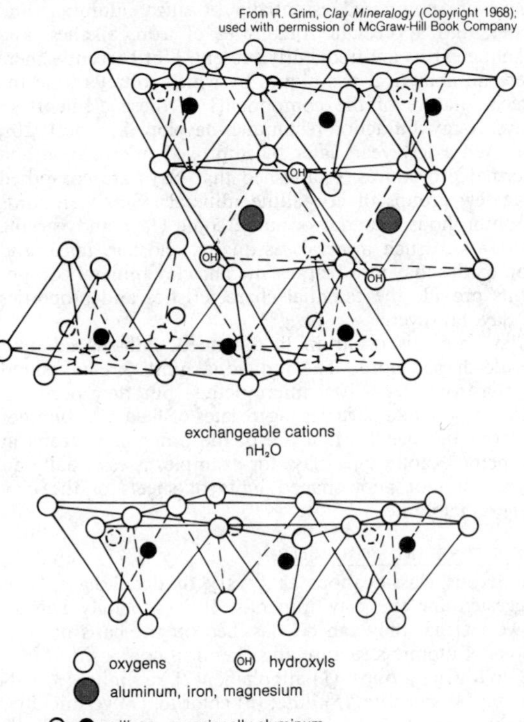

Figure 72: The structure of smectite.

Smectite also differs from the theoretical formula because the lattice charge is always unbalanced by the substitution of ions of different valence (as Mg^{++} for Al^{3+}; or Al^{3+} for Si^{4+}); the imbalance may occur in the tetrahedral or octahedral sheet or in both, and that in one sheet may be partly compensated by substitution in the other sheets of the unit layer. Thus, compensation for the substitutions of aluminum (Al^{3+}) for silicon (Si^{4+}) may result from filling slightly more than two-thirds of the octahedral positions, or from the substitution of hydroxyl ions for oxygen in the octahedral layer. In the smectite lattice, substitutions, including the internal compensating substitutions, always result in about the same net charge on the lattice, about two-thirds unit per unit cell. Exchangeable cations adsorbed between the unit layers and around their edges balances this net-charge deficiency; the deficiency would require the substitution of one magnesium (Mg^{2+}) ion for every sixth aluminum (Al^{3+}) ion, for example, or about one aluminum (Al^{3+}) ion for every sixth silicon (Si^{4+}) ion.

Illite. Micas have a basic structural unit the same as that of smectite (two silica tetrahedral sheets sandwiching an octahedral sheet), but some of the silicons are always replaced by aluminums. This results in a charge deficiency that is balanced by potassium ions between the unit layers. The sheet thickness (c-axis dimension) is fixed at about 10 Å. Some of the micas, such as muscovite, are dioctahedral and only two-thirds of the possible octahedral positions are filled with aluminum atoms. Other micas are trioctahedral and all of the octahedral positions are filled with magnesium (Mg^{2+}) or iron (Fe^{2+}, Fe^{3+}) ions. Various polymorphic forms of the micas occur, depending on the stacking arrangement of the unit layers.

Hydrous micas

The several ways in which the illite clay minerals, sometimes called the hydrous micas, differ from the well-crystallized micas may be exhibited by any single sample. In the micas one-fourth of the silicon (Si^{4+}) ions are replaced by aluminum (Al^{3+}) ions, whereas in the illites only about one-sixth are replaced; thus there is less substitution of aluminum (Al^{3+}) for silicon (Si^{4+}) in the illites. As a result, the illites have a higher silica-to-alumina molecular ratio than the well-crystallized micas, with a net-unbalanced-charge deficiency reduced from two per unit cell to about 1.3 per unit cell. Other cations such as calcium, magnesium, or hydrogen (Ca^{++}, Mg^{++}, H^{+}) may partially replace the potassium ions between the unit layers. Some randomness occurs in the stacking of the layers, and illite particles occurring naturally are of small size, one to two microns or less.

The characteristics of the illite clay minerals thus differ from those of the well-crystallized micas. The 10 Å diffraction line shown by the micas as a characteristic diffraction effect is shown by illite; due to small particle size, variation in the interlayer cation, and occasional slight interlayer hydration, however, it is often modified into a band that tends to tail off slightly toward the low angle region. The potassium ions may be replaced by hydronium ion, $(H_3O)^+$, to account somewhat for the reduced potassium content and the interlayer hydration. Because of the poor crystallinity of illite, its small particle size, and its intimate mixing with other clay minerals, it is usually impossible to determine its polymorphic form.

Chlorite. The structure of the chlorite minerals consists of alternate micalike and brucitelike layers (Figure 73) about 14 Å thick. General composition of the micalike layers is $(OH)_4(Si,Al)_8(Mg,Fe)_6O_{20}$, and that of the brucitelike layers is $(Mg,Al)_6(OH)_{12}$. The micalike layer is unbalanced by substitution of aluminum (Al^{3+}) ions for silicon (Si^{4+}) ions; the ensuing charge deficiency is balanced by an excess charge in the brucite sheet caused by the substitution of trivalent aluminum (Al^{3+}) for divalent magnesium (Mg^{2+}).

From R. Grim, *Clay Mineralogy* (Copyright 1968); used with permission of McGraw-Hill Book Company

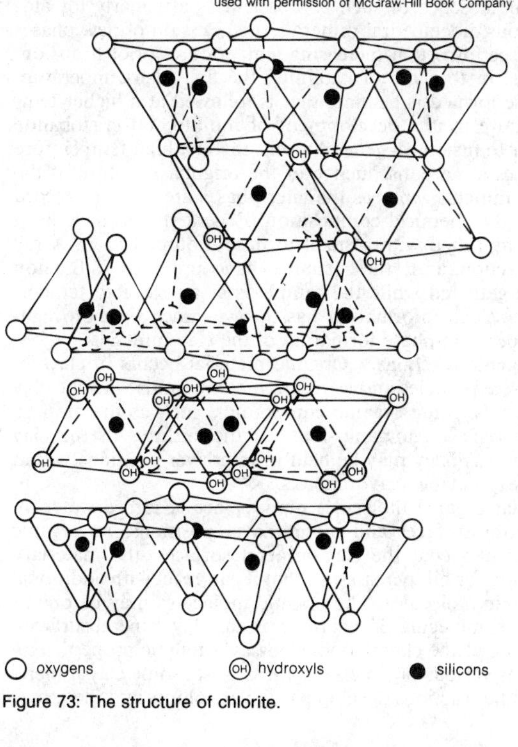

oxygens   hydroxyls   silicons

Figure 73: The structure of chlorite.

Various members of the chlorite group differ in the kind and amount of substitutions within the brucite layer and within the tetrahedral and octahedral positions of the mica layer, in the detailed orientation of successive octahedral and tetrahedral layers, in the relation of the mica to brucite layers, and in the stacking of successive chlorite units. The symmetry of specimens also is variable. The range of polymorphic forms of chlorite in clay minerals has not been established. Available evidence suggests that clay-mineral chlorites differ from well-crystallized material in the random stacking of layers and in hydration. Because chlorite in clay generally occurs mixed with other clay minerals, diffraction data permit only the identification of a mineral with a fixed thickness of 14 Å and not the polymorphic form.

Vermiculite. The vermiculite unit structure consists of sheets of trioctahedral mica or talc separated by layers of water molecules; these layers occupy a space about two water molecules thick (4.98 Å). Substitutions of aluminum (Al^{3+}) for silicon (Si^{4+}) constitute the chief imbalance but the net-charge deficiency may be partially balanced by other substitutions within the mica lattice; there is always a residual net-charge deficiency of 1 to 1.4 per unit cell, however. Exchangeable cations occur chiefly between the mica layers to satisfy the charge deficiency: in the natural mineral, the balancing cation is magnesium (Mg^{++}), sometimes with a small amount of calcium (Ca^{++}) also present; the cation-exchange capacity is the same as smectite, or somewhat higher.

Heating vermiculite to temperatures as high as 500° C (900° F) drives the water out from between the mica layers, but the mineral quickly rehydrates at room temperature. The vermiculite lattice, therefore, can expand, but the expansion is restricted to about 4.98 Å, or the thickness of two water layers.

Sepiolite, attapulgite, and palygorskite. The important structural element in the fibrous clay minerals is the amphibole double silica chain, which is oriented parallel to the c axis. There are two distinct fibrous clay minerals, one type called attapulgite or palygorskite, and the second type similar to sepiolite. The attapulgite structure consists of double silica chains with oxygen linking the chains together at their longitudinal edges. The apexes of the tetrahedrons in successive chains point in opposite directions, and the linked chains, thus, form a kind of double-ribbed sheet of two rows of tetrahedral apexes that alternate between the top and bottom of the sheets. The apexes of successive sheets point together and aluminum or magnesium or both in octahedral coordination link the apex oxygens. Similarity exists between this octahedral layer and that in the layer clay minerals, but it is continuous in only one direction. It is completed by hydroxyl groups in the centres and at the open sides. A weak link through the oxygen of the silica chains in the ribbed layer causes the mineral to have a good cleavage parallel to the c axis. The interstices between the amphibole chains are filled by chains of water molecules running parallel to the chains. The cavities accommodate four molecules of water per unit cell, which would account for the dehydration loss at low temperatures. The names attapulgite and palygorskite are used interchangeably for a clay mineral with this structure.

The structure of sepiolite is similar to that of attapulgite, except that three pyroxene chains are linked to form two continuous amphibole-type chains. The b dimension of sepiolite therefore is about one-third greater than that of attapulgite. Substantially all of the octahedral positions in the sepiolite structure are populated with magnesium ions, but there is some replacement by aluminum and iron in attapulgite.

Mixed-layer minerals. Many clay materials are mixtures of more than one clay mineral. One kind of mixture consists of discrete clay-mineral particles in which there is no preferred geometric orientation of one particle with respect to the surrounding clay-mineral particles. Another kind is the interstratification of the layer clay minerals where the individual layers are composed of only a single or a few alumino-silicate sheets. These mixed layer structures result from the strong similarity that exists between the layers of the different clay minerals, all of which are composed of silica tetrahedral-hexagonal layers and closely packed octahedral layers of oxygens and hydroxyl groups. Therefore, mixed-layer structures occur as stable as those composed of a single kind of layer.

Regular interstratification

These structures of mixed-layer clay minerals are of two different types. The interstratification may be regular, with the different layers regularly repeated in the stacking sequence. In such cases distinctive characteristics result; the unit cell is equivalent to the sum of the component layers and regular reflections are obtained. Chlorite, composed of regularly alternating mica and brucite layers, is an example of a regular mixed-layer mineral.

Random, irregular interstratifications of layers also exists, with no uniform repetition of layers. The mineral glauconite frequently exhibits this structure, with a random interstratification of smectite and illite. Mixed-layer structures are very common in clays and soils. The precise identification of the components of such structures requires detailed X-ray diffraction analyses.

CHEMICAL AND PHYSICAL PROPERTIES

Ion exchange. Clay minerals are able to adsorb certain positively and negatively charged particles (cations and anions) and retain them around the outside of the structural unit in an exchangeable state. The exchange reaction differs from simple sorption because it is stoichiometric (involving equal amounts), and it generally does not affect the silica-alumina structure. The range of the cation and anion exchange capacities of the clay minerals is given in Table 10.

Table 10: Exchange Capacities of Clay Minerals
(milliequivalents per 100 g)

cation-exchange capacity		anion-exchange capacity (approximate)	
Kaolinite	3–15	Smectite	23
Halloysite ($2H_2O$)	5–10	Nontronite	20
Halloysite ($4H_2O$)	40–50	Saponite	21
Smectite	80–150	Vermiculite	4
Illite	10–40	Kaolinite	13, 3
Vermiculite	100–150		
Chlorite	10–40		
Sepiolite-attapulgite-palygorskite	3–15		

Causes of anion exchange

Exchange capacities vary with particle size, perfection of crystallinity, and nature of the adsorbed ion; hence, a range of values exists for a given mineral rather than a single specific capacity. Cation-exchange capacity results from broken bonds around the edges of the structural units, which give rise to unsatisfied charges. Substitutions within the lattice structure (for example, trivalent aluminum for quadrivalent silicon) and possibly the hydrogen of exposed hydroxyls, also provide cation exchange capacity. Anion-exchange capacity may be due to (1) the replacement of hydroxyl ions at the edges of the lattice structures, (2) adsorption because of the geometry of the anion in relation to the geometry of the clay-mineral structural units (the adsorption of phosphate at the edges of silica tetrahedrons), for example, and, possibly, (3) unbalanced electrical charges within the lattice, such as that which would result from an excess of aluminum in octahedral positions.

The rate of ion exchange varies with clay mineral type and the nature and concentration of the ions. In general, the reaction for kaolinite is most rapid, being almost instantaneous. It is slower for smectite and for attapulgite, and requires even longer time, perhaps hours or days, to reach completion for illites. Under a given set of conditions the various cations are not equally replaceable and do not have the same replacing power. Calcium, for example, will replace sodium more easily than sodium will replace calcium.

The ion exchange properties of the clay minerals are extremely important because these properties determine their physical characteristics and economic use. The availability and retention of fertilizers in soils, plasticity, and other clay properties, depend to a great extent on ion exchange in general and on the identity of the exchange cation.

Clay-water relations. Clay materials contain water in several forms. The water may be held in pores and may be removed by drying under ambient conditions. Water also may be adsorbed on the surface of the clay mineral structures and in smectites, vermiculites, and attapulgites; this water may occur in interlayer positions or within structural channels. Finally, the clay mineral structures contain hydroxyls that are lost as water at elevated temperatures.

Adsorbed water may be removed by heating to temperatures of the order of 100°–200° C (212°–390° F) and in most cases is regained readily at ordinary temperatures. It is generally agreed that this adsorbed water, directly adjacent to the clay mineral surfaces, has a structure other than that of liquid water. As the thickness of the adsorbed water increases outward from the surface, the nature of the water changes abruptly or gradually to that of liquid water. Ions and molecules adsorbed on the clay mineral surface exert a major influence on the thickness of the adsorbed water layers and on the nature of this water. The nonliquid water may extend out from the clay mineral surfaces as much as 60–100 Å.

Hydroxyl ions are driven off by heating clay minerals to temperatures of 400°–700° C (750°–1300° F). The rate of loss of the hydroxyls and the energy required for their removal are specific properties characteristic of the various clay minerals. The reaction for dioctahedral minerals (in which only two-thirds of the possible octahedral positions of aluminum are occupied by other cations) such as kaolinite is abrupt, whereas the loss takes place rather gradually in trioctahedral minerals (in which all possible octahedral positions of aluminum are occupied by other cations) such as the micas.

Differential thermal analysis procedures

Differential thermal analysis is a procedure for measuring the temperatures at which thermal reactions take place, and the intensities of these reactions, when materials are heated to elevated temperatures. The reactions for the loss of hydroxyls are endothermic (involve heat absorption), and reactions for the development of new crystalline phases at elevated temperatures are endothermic or exothermic (generate heat). Characteristic differential thermal curves can be used as diagnostic criteria for identifying the various clay minerals.

High-temperature reactions. When hydroxyls are lost by heating, the lattice structure may be destroyed or simply modified, depending on the composition and structure of the clay minerals. In the presence of fluxes, such as iron or potassium, fusion may follow dehydration very quickly. In the absence of such components, particularly for aluminous dioctahedral minerals, a succession of new phases may be formed at increasing temperatures prior to fusion. Thus, in the case of kaolinite, the first high-temperature phase formed is a spinel that is followed at a higher temperature by the development of mullite and cristoballite prior to fusion. In general terms, the first high-temperature phases are a consequence of the original structure of the clay mineral, whereas the later phases are more in accord with the chemical composition. Recent studies have been accomplished with a small furnace mounted in an X-ray diffraction unit; these studies have provided diffraction data gathered while the sample is at an elevated temperature. Such information has thrown much light on high-temperature-phase formation of the clay minerals.

Organic reactions. Organic material occurs in clays in discrete particles and as reaction compounds with the clay minerals. Ionic organic compounds, such as the amines, may replace inorganic ions on the surfaces of the clay minerals. They may be held in interlayer positions within the expandable clay minerals.

Polar organic molecules may replace adsorbed water on exterior surfaces and in interlayer positions. As organic molecules coat the clay mineral surfaces, the material's affinity for oil increases, so that it can react with additional organic molecules. The organic molecules may be one or several molecular layers thick on the clay mineral surfaces.

Catalytic properties

Some of the clay minerals possess catalytic properties towards various organic substances. Also, some clay mineral organic reactions develop particular colours and these may

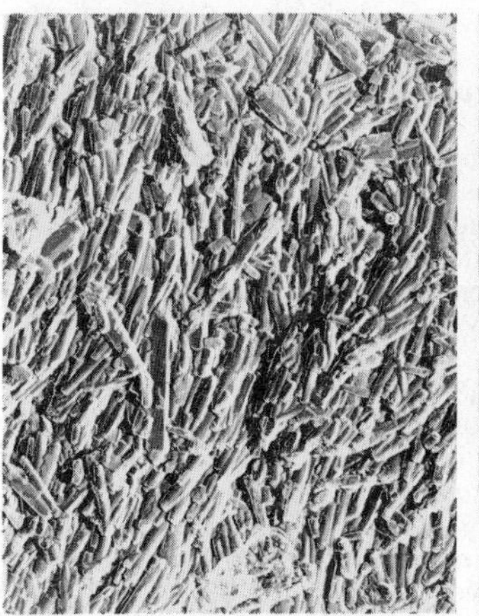

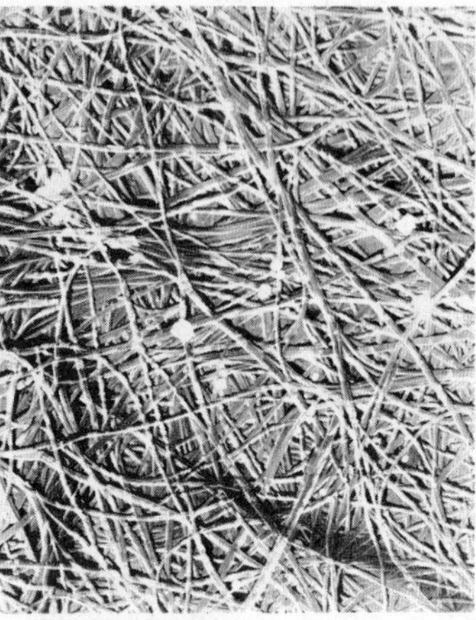
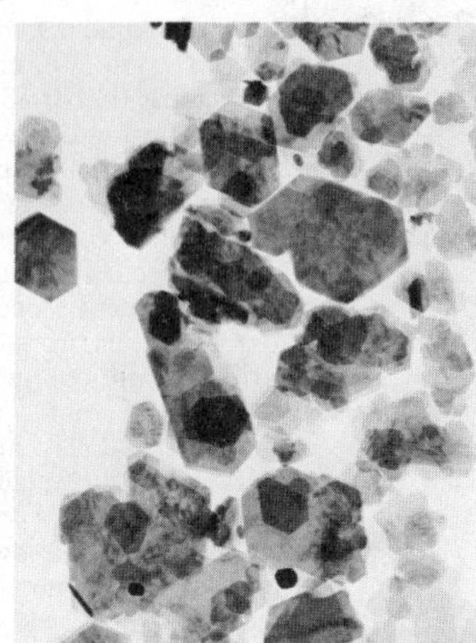

Figure 74: *Electron micrographs of clay minerals.*
(Left) Tubular units of halloysite (magnified about 8,400 ×). (Centre left) Broad, undulating mosaic sheets of smectite (magnified about 3,750 ×). (Centre right) Elongated, lath-shaped units of attapulgite (magnified about 9,475 ×). (Right) Six-sided kaolinite flakes (magnified about 22,000 ×).
By courtesy of the Smithsonian Institution, Washington, D.C.; photographs, Kenneth M. Towe

be of diagnostic value in identifying specific clay minerals. Organically clad clay minerals are used extensively in paint, ink, and plastics.

Optical properties. Clay mineral particles are commonly too small for the measurement of optical properties. Oriented aggregates that are large enough for optical measurements can, however, be prepared by allowing the flake-shaped clay mineral particles to settle from a clay water suspension on a horizontal surface. The particles settle with one flake on top of another so that their basal plane surfaces are essentially parallel. Though optical properties can be measured in oils, optical characteristics will change because some of the clay minerals will adsorb such oils. Moreover, optical data from interlayered structures can easily be mistaken for that of a single mineral.

Size and shape. The size and shape of clay minerals have been determined by electron micrographs (Figure 74). Allophane, the amorphous clay mineral, shows no definite morphology. Kaolinite occurs as well-formed six-sided flakes, frequently with a prominent elongation in one direction. Particles with maximum surface dimensions of 0.3 to about 4 micrometres, and thicknesses of 0.05 to about 2 micrometres are common. The flakes of disordered kaolinite have poorly developed hexagonal outlines. Halloysite commonly occurs as tubular units with an outside diameter ranging from 0.04 to 0.19 micrometre.

Electron micrographs of smectite frequently show broad undulating mosaic sheets. In some cases, the flake-shaped units are discernible but frequently they are too small to be seen individually.

Illite occurs in poorly defined flakes commonly grouped together in irregular aggregates. Many of the flakes have a diameter of 0.1 to 0.3 micrometre, and the thinnest flakes are approximately 30 Å thick. Little information is available regarding the vermiculite and chlorite minerals, but based on structural considerations they probably are similar in character to the illites.

Electron micrographs show that attapulgite occurs as elongated laths, singly or in bundles. Frequently the individual laths are many microns in length and 50 to 100 Å in width. Sepiolite occurs in similar lath-shaped units but the laths are somewhat thicker and shorter than in attapulgite.

Surface-area measurements indicate that the value for kaolinite is about 15–20 square metres per gram, whereas illite is 80–90 square metres per gram and halloysite is about 40 square metres per gram. The theoretical surface area of smectites, when dispersed to nearly unit cell dimensions, is 8×10^6 square centimetres per gram. However, values similar to those of illite are frequently obtained because the nitrogen does not penetrate between the layers.

Solubility of the clay minerals. Solubility of the clay minerals in acids varies with the nature of the acid, the acid concentration, the acid to clay ratio, the temperature, and the duration of treatment. It also varies as a function of heating of the clay minerals and the firing temperatures prior to the acid attack. In general the acid first attacks the adsorbed cations and then the components of the octahedral part of the clay mineral structure. Frequently the silica sheets are not attacked and the morphology of the clay minerals may be retained after solution of all components except silica.

In alkaline solutions a cation exchange reaction first takes place and then the silica part of the structure is attacked. The reaction depends upon the same variables as those stated for acid reactions.

OCCURRENCE OF THE CLAY MINERALS

Soils and recent sediments. All types of clay minerals have been reported in soils. Kaolinite is the dominant component and in some instances the only component in podsols (soils rich in ash and organic matter). Varying amounts of illite and smectite are also usually present.

Illite and smectite, with occasional small amounts of kaolinite, occur in prairie soils and smectite and illite predominate in soils of arid regions and in chernozems (black, fertile soils). Attapulgite has been reported in a few desert soils and kaolinite is the dominant component in laterites (residual soils).

Soil composed of illite and chlorite is better suited for agriculture than kaolinitic soils because of their relatively high ion-exchange properties and, hence, their capacity to hold plant nutrients. Moderate amounts of smectite in soils are advantageous for the same reason but when present in large amounts (50 percent ±), smectite is detrimental because it is impervious and has too great a water-holding capacity.

Illite and chlorite in marine sediments

Illite and chlorite are the dominant clay minerals in marine sediments that are accumulating in the seas today. Smectite also may be present and in some areas, such as the Gulf of Mexico, it is relatively abundant. Kaolinite also is common but is usually in small amounts.

Sediment accumulating under nonmarine conditions may have any clay mineral composition. Under highly saline conditions in desert areas, however, illite, chlorite, or attapulgite or both are likely to develop, depending on the nature of the cation that is present.

Ancient sediments. Analyses of many ancient sediments in many parts of the world indicate that smectite is much less abundant in sediments older than the Mesozoic Era than in younger sediments. The available data also suggest that kaolinite is less abundant in very ancient sediments than in those deposited after the Devonian Period. Stated another way, the very old argillaceous (clay-rich) sediments are largely composed of illite and chlorite. Attapulgite and sepiolite have not been reported in sediments older than the Tertiary Period.

Material classed as clay may have any clay mineral composition. In some instances, the component is a single clay mineral, but more often there is a mixture of clay minerals. Materials that are described as shales because they are relatively hard and have a laminated character frequently are composed of illite and chlorite. Smectite is a common component of many shales of Mesozoic and younger ages. Kaolinite is a common component of some shales but it usually occurs in minor amounts. Sepiolite-attapulgite minerals frequently occur in argillaceous sediments associated with ancient saline deposits. Smectite, illite, and chlorite also are common components of such sediments.

Kaolinite in shales

Slates appear to be composed primarily of illites and chlorites. These clay minerals generally have a relatively higher degree of crystallinity in slates than when found in clays. Kaolinite has been reported in some slates, particularly those that have relatively low schistosity (subparallel arrangement of mineral components due to metamorphic pressures).

The clay minerals found in carbonate rocks are chiefly illite and chlorite. Kaolinite and smectite are sometimes present in small amounts; however, smectite and attapulgite may be an important constituent in the younger carbonate rocks.

Kaolinite and illite have been reported in various coals. The data are insufficient, however, to indicate whether there is any general relationship between the nature of the clay mineral component and the character and age of the coals.

Bentonite generally is defined as a clay composed largely of smectite, which has high colloidal, plastic, and adsorption properties. Much bentonite has formed by the devitrification of volcanic ash *in situ.* Other clays that have been called bentonite have formed by hydrothermal processes and, possibly, by weathering.

Hydrothermal deposits. All of the clay minerals, except attapulgite, have been found as alteration products associated with hot springs and geysers and as aureoles around metalliferous deposits. Frequently there is a zonal arrangement of the clay minerals around the source of the alteration; mica and kaolinite are close to the source whereas chlorite and smectite are more distant.

ORIGIN OF THE CLAY MINERALS

All of the clay minerals, with the possible exception of halloysite, have been synthesized from mixtures of oxides or hydroxides at moderately low temperatures and pressures. Kaolinite tends to form in alumina-silica systems without alkalies or alkaline earths. Illite is formed when potassium is added to such systems, and smectite or chlorite is formed when magnesium is added depending on the concentration of the magnesium. The clay minerals can be synthesized at ordinary temperatures and pressures if the oxides are mixed together very slowly and in great dilution.

Weathering processes. The formation of the clay minerals by weathering processes is determined by the nature of the parent rock, climate, topography, vegetation, and the time period during which these factors have operated. Climate, topography, and vegetation influence weathering processes by their control of the character and direction of movement of water through the weathering zone (see also GEOMORPHIC PROCESSES: *Weathering*).

When the dominant movement of water is downward through the alteration zone, any alkalies or alkaline earths tend to be leached and primary minerals containing these components are first degraded and then broken down. If the leaching is intense, then after the removal of the alkalies and alkaline earths the aluminum or silica may be removed from the alteration zone. This will depend on the pH (index of acidity–alkalinity) of the downward-seeping waters. The pH of such water is determined, in turn, by the climate and cover of vegetation. Under warm and humid conditions, with long wet and dry periods, the surface organic material tends to be completely oxidized. The downward-seeping waters therefore are neutral or perhaps slightly alkaline and silica will be removed, whereas alumina and iron will be left behind and concentrated. The result is a lateritic type of soil. Under more temperate conditions, the surface organic material is not completely oxidized and the downward-seeping water contains organic acids. In this case, alumina and iron oxides are leached and the silica is left behind; podsolic types of soils will develop.

In dry areas the dominant movement of water is not downward and leaching does not take place. The alkalies and alkaline earths remain close to the surface and chernozem soils containing illite, chlorite, and smectite, will develop. In extremely dry desert areas where the concentration of magnesium is particularly high, the formation of attapulgite has been reported.

Other changes. As the clay minerals are transported from freshwater to a marine environment a definite regrading of the micas takes place. Illite and chlorite tend to develop from smectites by the respective adsorption of potassium and magnesium from sea water. Diagenetic changes tend to occur during sedimentation and compaction and similar changes take place when metamorphic processes are involved.

In the development of clay minerals by natural hydrothermal processes, the presence of alkalies and alkaline earths influence the resulting products in the same manner as shown by synthesis experiments.

INDUSTRIAL USES OF THE CLAY MINERALS

Clays composed of kaolinite are required for the manufacture of porcelain, whiteware, and refractories. The absence of iron in this clay mineral gives it a white burning colour, and the absence of alkalies and alkaline earths gives it a very high fusion temperature that makes it refractory. Whiteware bodies frequently contain talc, feldspar, and quartz, in addition to the kaolinite clay, in order to develop desirable shrinkage and burning properties. If the kaolinite is poorly crystalline the clay will have higher plastic and bonding properties. Clays composed of a mixture of clay minerals, in which illite is most abundant, are used in the manufacture of brick, tile, stoneware, and glazed products. Small proportions of smectite in such clays provide good plastic properties, but in large amounts smectite is undesirable because it causes too great a degree of shrinkage.

Bentonite clays composed of smectite are used primarily in the preparation of muds for drilling oil wells. This type of clay, which swells to several times its original volume in water, provides desirable colloidal and wall-building properties. Attapulgite clays also are used because of their resistance to flocculation (grouping or clustering of individual grains or flakes) under high salinity conditions. Certain clay minerals, notably attapulgite and some smectites, possess substantial ability to remove colour bodies from oil. These so-called Fuller's earths are used in processing many mineral and vegetable oils. Acid treatment of some smectite clays increases their decolourizing ability. Much gasoline is manufactured by using catalysts prepared from either smectite, kaolinite, or halloysite types of clay minerals. The preparation may be by acid treatment to modify the structure, or by the use of kaolinite and halloysite as a source of alumina and silica for the synthesis of new zeolite-type structures.

Fuller's earth

Large tonnages of kaolinite clays are used to fill and coat paper. The coating clays are washed to free them from grit and then are processed by physical and chemical techniques to improve their whiteness and viscosity. In general, well crystallized kaolinite that cleaves easily into thin flakes is desired. Attapulgite clays are used in the preparation of no-carbon-required paper because of the colour they develop during reactions with certain colourless organic compounds.

Large tonnages of bentonite are used as bonding agents in foundry sands for casting metals. Some poorly crystallized illites and kaolinites are also used for this purpose. Bentonite is combined with lime and coke to pelletize finely ground iron ore; this renders it suitable for use in blast furnaces. Because many clay minerals have aluminum oxide contents of the order of 30 to 40 percent, they are potential ores of aluminum. A variety of processes have been developed to extract this metal from clays but clays are not yet competitive with bauxite as a source of aluminum. Extremely large tonnages of reasonably pure clay, preferably of the kaolinite type, would be required for this purpose.

Clays have a tremendous number of miscellaneous uses and for each use a particular type of clay with particular properties is important. For example, attapulgite and smectite clays are used as carriers for insecticides and pesticides. Smectite clays are used as plasticizing agents, and kaolinite clays are used as extenders and fillers in a large number of organic and inorganic bodies. Kaolinite and smectite clays also are used in a variety of pharmaceutical and medicinal preparations.

Smectite and kaolinite clay minerals can be coated with organic molecules for use in many organic systems. Often such organic-clad clays are tailor-made to fit a particular organic system, and thus become an integral part of the system rather than a simple diluent. (R.E.G.)

PHYSICAL PROPERTIES OF ROCKS

Rocks are, as previously noted, aggregates of mineral grains or crystals, and their physical properties are to a large extent governed by the properties of the individual minerals that compose them. In a rock, the individual mineral properties are averaged in accordance with the relative proportions and orientations of the various mineral crystals present. Because of this averaging, the properties of rocks can usually be considered as isotropic (uniform in all directions), although most minerals individually are in fact anisotropic. Rocks in which the crystals are not oriented at random, such as schist and slate, show a definite anisotropy reflecting that of the individual minerals.

The averaging of mineral properties provides a valid basis for most of the bulk properties of crystalline rocks—that is, rocks composed of a dense, interlocking aggregate of mineral crystals. Most igneous and metamorphic rocks, such as granite, basalt, marble, and gneiss, are of this type. Glassy rocks, such as volcanic glass, are noncrystalline and have properties similar to those of artificial glasses. For clastic rocks, composed of an aggregate of originally loose mineral or rock fragments subsequently cemented together, important additional factors governing the physical properties are the grain packing and contact geometry, the amount and distribution of void space (porosity), and the nature of the cementation.

Physical properties of rocks are influenced by pressure and temperature. In addition to effects characteristic of the individual mineral components, there are distinctive phenomena related to the granular and void structure of rocks. In particular, the presence of water or other pore fluids has an important influence on some properties.

Although most of the physical properties described here can be measured with reasonable precision for an individual rock specimen, the measured values vary substantially, often by as much as 50 percent, from specimen to specimen of a given rock type and even from specimen to specimen of rock from a single, apparently homogeneous parent mass or formation. This statistical variability is an inherent attribute of rocks, resulting from their complex constitution and the consequently large number of variable details of chemical composition and granular structure that can influence the physical properties. It contrasts with the better defined properties of individual minerals, although these, too, are subject to some variability resulting from variations in chemical composition and internal structure. Because of variability, precise figures for the physical properties of a particular rock type cannot be stated: instead only representative values that convey the general magnitude to be expected. Whenever precise figures are needed, a thorough statistical study of the rock mass of interest is called for. Some of the aggregate physical properties of large rock masses *in situ* (in their natural locations) in the Earth are significantly affected by gross inhomogeneities, such as fractures that occur on a scale so coarse that they cannot readily be sampled in specimens appropriate for laboratory tests. Also, the act of sampling itself may disturb the rock so as to alter some of its physical properties. In such cases, the physical properties of interest must be measured *in situ* by field methods.

Statistical variability

Volumetric properties

DENSITY

Table 11 gives ranges of observed density for several important rock types. For a pore-free rock, the density ρ is a volume-weighted average of the densities of the individual mineral components—that is, the sum of the volume fraction of each mineral times its density. Among the plutonic rocks—*i.e.,* crystalline rocks of deep-seated igneous origin—the density increases systematically from granite, composed mostly of the minerals feldspar (density 2.56 grams per cubic centimetre, abbreviated g/cm^3) and quartz (2.65 g/cm^3), to peridotite and eclogite, composed mostly of the minerals pyroxene (3.4 g/cm^3), olivine (3.5 g/cm^3), and garnet (3.8 g/cm^3). This density increase plays an important role in the structure of the Earth: plutonic rocks ranging in composition from granite to diorite form the continental masses and essentially float in a dense substratum of peridotite and eclogite, which lies below depths of 10 to 50 kilometres (six to 30 miles).

The range in densities indicated for the individual crystalline rocks in Table 11 mainly reflects variations in mineral and chemical composition among rocks to which the specific names are applied. The average density of fresh rock samples of the types listed is near the middle of the ranges given. Glasses are generally less dense than crystalline solids of the same composition, as illustrated by obsidian, which is volcanic glass of granitic composition.

POROSITY

The bulk densities of clastic rocks and of vesicular lavas (the name given to lavas with frozen-in gas bubbles) are reduced significantly by the void space present. The resulting porosity is important in providing storage space for water or petroleum in the rocks. Porosity η is defined as the ratio of void volume to bulk volume (solid plus voids). Typical values are given in Table 11. If the void-free solid material is of density ρ_s, then the porous solid has bulk density (ρ_b) equal to the void-free density times the quantity one minus porosity—*i.e.,* $\rho_b = \rho_s\,(1 - \eta)$, or $\rho_b = \rho_s\,(1 - \eta/100)$, if η is expressed in percent, as in Table 11.

The large range of densities for basalt in Table 11 reflects variations in porosity attributable to gas vesicles. The porosity of vesicular lavas increases with the amount of volatile material (such as water) dissolved in the original rock melt. Separation of gas bubbles is inhibited by solidification at depth, under pressure. Thus, Hawaiian

Density range in basalt

Table 11: Densities and Porosities of Important Rock Types

	characteristics	density ρ g/cm^3	porosity η (percentage)
Granite	crystalline, plutonic, sialic	2.5–2.8	0.3–1.5
Diorite	crystalline, plutonic, intermediate	2.7–3.0	0.5±
Gabbro	crystalline, plutonic, mafic	2.9–3.1	0.5±
Peridotite	crystalline, plutonic, ultramafic	3.1–3.3	0.5±
Eclogite	crystalline, plutonic, ultramafic	3.3–3.6	0.5±
Gneiss	crystalline, metamorphic	2.6–3.1	0.5±
Schist	crystalline, metamorphic	2.7–3.0	0.5±
Slate	crystalline, metamorphic	2.7–2.85	4±
Quartzite	crystalline, metamorphic	2.64±	0.5±
Marble	crystalline, metamorphic	2.6–2.8	0.4–2
Obsidian	glassy, volcanic	2.3–2.4	low
Basalt glass	glassy, volcanic	2.7–2.85	low
Basalt	crystalline–glassy, volcanic	2.2–3.0	1–30
Scoria	crystalline–glassy, volcanic, vesicular	1.4–2.4	10–50
Pumice	glassy, volcanic, vesicular	0.5–1.1	60–90
Sandstone	clastic, young (Tertiary)	1.9–2.2	10–35
Sandstone	clastic, old (Paleozoic)	2.3–2.5	5–25
Shale	clastic, young, shallow (<0.5 km)	1.8–2.2	15–35
Shale	clastic, young, deep (>2 km)	2.4–2.5	9–11
Shale	clastic, old, deep	2.6–2.7	4–7
Chalk; coquina	clastic, shell aggregates	1.2–2.2	15–55
Limestone	crystalline–clastic, shell fragments	2.5–2.7	0.1–15
Tuff	clastic, volcanic shards	1.4–1.5	35–40

basalts solidified on the ocean floor at depths less than 800 metres (2,600 feet) are vesicular and have densities less than 2.8 g/cm^3, whereas those formed deeper than 4,000 metres (13,000 feet) are almost vesicle free and have densities close to 3.0 g/cm^3. The most highly vesicular volcanic rocks, called pumice, have densities so low that they float on water.

Porosity of elastic rocks

The porosity of clastic rocks is highly variable and depends on the original shape and packing arrangement of the fragments, the amount of subsequent compaction, and the amount of void space filled by cementation. Rounded mineral or rock fragments, such as sand or gravel, pack initially to a porosity of 30–50 percent, which is reduced to 25–35 percent by compaction. Lower porosities are achieved when a wide range of particle sizes is present, so that the finer particles can fill the interstices among the coarser ones. Unconsolidated (*i.e.,* loose) sand and gravel are converted into sandstone and conglomerate by cementation, and the porosity is thereby reduced to 5–30 percent. As the rocks become older, additional cementation accumulates and the porosity decreases further (Table 11).

The packing properties of animal shells and shell fragments give high initial porosities for coquina (limestone composed of coarse shell debris) and chalk (limestone composed of shells of micro-organisms). In ordinary limestones, void spaces among shell fragments tend to be filled with fine calcite or aragonite detritus. Compaction can occur through solution and reprecipitation of these readily soluble minerals, leading in some cases to a rock of very low porosity.

Porous clastic rocks *in situ* in the Earth are generally saturated with water, the upper limit of saturation being called the water table. If the pores are completely filled with water, the bulk density ρ_b is increased by an amount equal to η, the porosity, over the density of the dry rock, which is the density given in Table 11. The volume fraction of water that is absorbed by an initially dry rock specimen is called the sorption or apparent porosity. In the laboratory, sorption is usually about half the total porosity. Under the pressures at depth in the Earth, however, the water content probably approaches the total porosity.

Mechanical properties

When an external force acts on a body, such as a rock, and there is a change of volume or shape, called a strain, internal forces will be transmitted throughout its interior. An internal force and its force of reaction acting across an imaginary plane that separates two parts of the body is known as stress, and the magnitude of the stress is measured in force per unit area of the imaginary plane. The unit of stress is the bar, defined as 10^6 dynes per square centimetre; to a good approximation it equals one atmosphere (14.7 pounds force per square inch) or one kilogram weight per square centimetre.

Among types of response to externally applied stress, distinction is made between elastic properties, in which the strain is reversible (recoverable on unloading), and nonelastic properties, in which it is not. In elasticity, strain is usually proportional to stress, and the constant of proportionality is called an elastic constant: specific examples discussed below are the elastic compressibility, bulk modulus, Young's modulus, and shear modulus. The response under the simplest type of stress, hydrostatic pressure, is usually considered separately from the response to directed, nonhydrostatic stress; hydrostatic behaviour is in principle only a special case of nonhydrostatic, but phenomena of different types are important under the two different types of stress.

ELASTIC PROPERTIES

Compressibility. The density of rocks under the high pressures at depth in the Earth is increased as a result of compressibility (reduction in volume). Bulk compressibility β is defined in terms of the increase of bulk density ($\Delta\rho_b$) that occurs on raising the pressure by a small amount (ΔP), at constant temperature, and is equal to the fractional bulk density increase divided by the pressure increase. The density increase considered in this definition is that which results from elastic compression; any loss of volume that is not recovered on releasing the pressure represents compaction (see below).

Compressibility of jacketed rock

When pressure is applied to a rock specimen by means of a fluid that permeates the pores, there is no compaction, and the compressibility observed is an average of the elastic compressibilities of the individual mineral components. On the other hand, when the rock is kept dry by a fluid-impermeable jacket enclosing the specimen, compaction may occur, and, in addition, the elastic compressibility is usually much greater than an average taken of the mineral components. The same behaviour is observed also for jacketed wet specimens vented so that the pore fluid can escape at low pressure. This arrangement simulates the conditions of compression experienced by rocks at depth in the Earth's crust, because rock permeability (discussed later) allows the pore fluids to escape, and the pore fluid pressure is usually only about a third the total overburden pressure.

The high compressibility of jacketed rock specimens is caused by closure of pore space under pressure. This effect is marked even for crystalline rocks of low porosity. As the pressure on a specimen is raised and the pores close, the compressibility decreases markedly. Low- and high-pressure compressibilities measured for rocks of several types are given in Table 12. Above a pressure of about 2,000 atmospheres, the compressibility becomes nearly constant, because substantially all of the pores that can close are already closed. Pores capable of closing over the pressure range zero to 2,000 atmospheres must be narrow cracks; hence the great increase in compressibility at low pressure is said to be due to crack porosity. The cracks probably lie mainly along the boundaries between mineral grains. Pores of roughly equidimensional shape (such as vesicles and interstitial spaces between clastic grains) do not close up rapidly with pressure and contribute only moderately to the compressibility, but the contribution must continue to much higher pressures than that caused by the crack porosity. The drop in compressibility with pressure is much larger in the case of crystalline rocks that formed at depth than it is in those that formed near the surface, suggesting that the cracks opened as a result of the pressure release that followed formation of the deep-seated rocks.

Table 12: Elastic Properties of Rocks at Low and High Confining Pressure*

	compressibility β (10^{-6} bar^{-1})		moduli at low P (10^6 bar)			moduli at high P (10^6 bar)			Poisson's ratio ν	
	low P	high P	K	E	G	K	E	G	low P	high P
Granite	8	2.0	0.1	0.3	0.2	0.5	0.6	0.4	0.05	0.25
Gabbro	4	1.1	0.3	0.9	0.6	0.9	0.8	0.5	0.1	0.2
Dunite	—	0.8	1.1	1.5	0.5	1.2	1.7	0.7	0.3	0.27
Obsidian	2.8	2.8	0.4	0.7	0.3	—	—	—	0.08	—
Basalt	2.2	1.3	0.5	0.8	0.3	0.8	1.2	0.4	0.23	0.25
Gneiss (granitic)	11	1.9	0.1	0.2	0.1	0.5	0.7	0.3	0.05	—
Marble	9	1.3	0.1	0.4	0.2	0.8	0.7	0.3	0.1	0.3
Quartzite	7.6	2.4	—	—	—	0.5	1.0	0.4	—	0.07
Sandstone (2.3 g cm^{-3})	14	—	0.07	0.2	0.08	—	—	—	0.1	—
Shale	~25	~5	0.04	0.1	0.05	—	—	—	0.04	—
Limestone	1.3	1.3	0.8	0.6	0.2	—	—	—	0.30	—

*Low pressure—approximately one atmosphere; high pressure—approximately 3,000 atmospheres.

Once any initial crack porosity has been removed by application of pressure, the compressibility of a rock is an average of the compressibilities of the mineral components. The averaging process is complex, however, because an aggregate of grains having different and generally anisotropic compressibilities cannot compress uniformly but instead develops a complex pattern of stresses and strains varying from grain to grain. An exact method of calculating the compressibility of a rock from the compressibilities of its mineral components is not known, but limits on the compressibility can be set by two types of average: (1) the so-called Reuss average (after the German physicist A. Reuss), which is the volumetrically weighted average of the compressibilities of the mineral components; and (2) the Voigt average (after Woldemar Voigt), in which the reciprocal compressibility (called the bulk modulus) is calculated as the volumetrically weighted average of the bulk moduli of the components. The true compressibility must lie between these two averages. The Voigt average can be applied to estimate the compressibility of a rock with quasi-spherical pores by treating the pores as components of zero bulk modulus.

Reuss average and Voigt average

Nonlinear compressibility. Over a pressure range from about 2,000 to 10,000 atmospheres (or zero to 10,000 atmospheres for a rock with no initial crack porosity), the compressibility can be considered to be linear in the sense that the compression increases in direct proportion to the pressure, and the compressibility coefficient β is practically constant. Over a wider pressure range, however, such as the range zero to 2,000,000 atmospheres that occurs within the Earth, deviations from linearity become significant. Theories of finite elastic strain have been developed to deal with compressibility as a function of pressure over this wide pressure range. It is found empirically that for many rocks the bulk modulus K (reciprocal compressibility $1/\beta$) is to a good approximation a linearly increasing function of pressure: K is equal to the bulk modulus at zero pressure (K_0) plus a constant (K') times the pressure P, or $K = K_0 + K'P$. The corresponding rock density (ρ) as a function of pressure is given by the density (ρ_0) at zero pressure times the quantity 1 plus the ratio of pressure to zero-pressure bulk modulus raised to the power $1/K'$, or

$$\rho = \rho_0(1 + P/K_0)^{1/K'}.$$

The dimensionless quantity K' (an arithmetic value without units) has a value in the range four to six for most rocks. It plays an important role in reasoning about the internal density and composition of the Earth.

Nonhydrostatic stress. When a cylindrical specimen is compressed along its length, while laterally unconfined, the compressive stress σ is related to longitudinal elastic strain e_{long} by Young's modulus (after Thomas Young, an English physicist). Young's modulus (E) is equal to the ratio of stress to strain, or $E = \sigma/e_{long}$. The ratio of lateral expansion e_{lat} to longitudinal compression $-e_{long}$ is Poisson's ratio (after a French mathematician, Siméon-Denis Poisson). Poisson's ratio (ν) is thus $\nu = -e_{lat}/e_{long}$. (The longitudinal or lateral strain e is the ratio of change in specimen length, Δl, or width, Δw, to the corresponding initial dimension l or w: $e_{long} = \Delta l/l$, $e_{lat} = \Delta w/w$.) When a specimen is loaded in shear—that is, with stress parallel to a particular plane—the ratio of shear stress (τ) to shear strain (γ) is the shear modulus, $G = \tau/\gamma$ (see MECHANICS). Values of the moduli and Poisson's ratio for several rock types are listed in Table 12. Because of the large typical variation of measured moduli from specimen to specimen, the figures in Table 12 are given only to one decimal and convey only the general magnitudes to be expected for the given rock types. The greatest source of variation is crack porosity. As the stress is increased, some of the cracks become closed; hence, Young's modulus increases with compressive stress σ. The cracks that tend to close are aligned transverse to the direction of compression; hence, Poisson's ratio is low (about 0.1) initially, at low σ, and increases with σ, approaching generally a value near 0.25 when the cracks become closed. Similar effects are produced by hydrostatic confining pressure. The high pressure values given in Table 12 represent rocks from which crack porosity has been eliminated.

For isotropic materials, Young's modulus, the shear modulus, and Poisson's ratio are, in principle, related by the condition that Poisson's ratio (ν) is equal to the ratio of Young's modulus (E) to twice the shear modulus (G), less 1, or $\nu = E/2G - 1$. Similarly, the moduli E and G are related to the bulk modulus K and Poisson's ratio ν by: $E = 3K(1 - 2\nu)$ and $G = 1.5K(1 - 2\nu)/(1 + \nu)$. Tabulated values do not always satisfy these relations because the values may have been measured on different specimens, under different conditions, or by different techniques or because the specimens may not have been fully isotropic. For $\nu = 0.25$, it is expected that $E = 1.5K$ and $G = 0.6K$; these expectations are realized to a rough approximation by the modulus values in Table 12. Limits on the moduli E and G can be estimated from the elastic properties of the mineral components by methods similar to those already discussed for the compressibility.

Cause of elastic anisotropy

Elastic anisotropy occurs when the mineral components have a preferential alignment, as in gneiss (a type of metamorphic or altered rock), schist, and slate. In a schist with highly aligned flakes of mica, Young's modulus measured parallel to the plane of alignment can be as much as three times as large as when it is measured perpendicular to this plane, and an even larger anisotropy in the shear modulus can occur. Actually observed elastic anisotropies of rocks are, however, generally much smaller. Preferential alignment of unclosed microscopic cracks can also cause elastic anisotropy.

Elastic waves. When a rock is subjected to oscillatory loading, waves of oscillating displacement and stress, much like sound waves, are propagated through it. These waves are of two types: longitudinal or compressional waves (P waves), in which the displacements occur along a direction parallel to the direction of propagation; and the transverse or shear waves (S waves), in which the displacements occur at right angles to the direction of propagation. P waves propagate with a velocity (υ_P) that is equal to the square root of the density (ρ) divided into the sum of the bulk modulus and 4/3 times the shear modulus $\upsilon_P = \sqrt{(K + \frac{4}{3}G)/\rho}$ whereas S waves propagate with a velocity (υ_s) that is equal to simply the square root of the ratio of the modulus G to the density: $\upsilon_s = \sqrt{G/\rho}$. The velocities can be calculated from static test data such as those in Table 12, but they are often measured directly for comparison with velocities at depth in the Earth as inferred by seismology. At low pressures, crack porosity causes the moduli, and hence the velocities, to be low and erratic, but above a confining pressure of about 2,000 atmospheres the intrinsic velocity, representing an average over the mineral components, is realized. Values for several rock types are listed in Table 13. Higher values are shown by the denser

Table 13: Elastic Wave Velocities for Rocks at Low and High Confining Pressure (km/sec)

	low P*		high P†	
	V_P	V_S	V_P	V_S
Granite	5.3	2.3	6.3	3.6
Diorite	5.4	3.1	6.6	3.7
Gabbro	6.5	3.5	7.1	3.8
Dunite	7.4	4.2	8.0	4.5
Eclogite	7.0	4.0	7.8	4.5
Diabase	6.3	3.2	6.8	3.8
Basalt	5.6	3.0	—	—
Marble	5.8	3.2	6.7	3.5
Quartzite	5.6	—	6.2	4.0
Slate	4.3	2.9	—	—
Sandstone‡	2.2	—	4.5	—
Shale‡	2.1	—	4.4	—
Limestone‡	2.8	1.1	6.4	3.0
Clay	1.6	0.7	—	—

*Approximately one atmosphere. †Approximately 4,000 atmospheres. ‡Velocity for young, porous sediments at shallow depth is given in low-P column; those for old, dense sediments at substantial depth (~4 km) are given in the high-P column.

rock types, reflecting the fact that denser minerals generally have elastic moduli that are increased much more than in proportion to their increased density. When, however, the density increase is due primarily to a substitution of iron for magnesium or aluminum in the mineral composition, relatively little increase in elastic moduli occurs, and the elastic wave velocities drop. Empirical observations are summarized by the following approximate formula relating *P*-wave velocity (in kilometres per second) to rock density ρ (grams per cubic centimetre) and the average value of the atomic weights of the constituent atoms (symbolized $\bar{A}$): $\upsilon_P \approx 7.3 + 3.1(\rho - 3.0) - 0.5(\bar{A} - 21)$. For most igneous rocks $\bar{A}$ is near 21, except for rocks notably enriched in iron, for which it can approach 30. For mica-rich rocks in which the mica flakes are strongly aligned, such as mica schist, an appreciable velocity anisotropy is expected; for example, the *P*-wave velocity parallel to the foliation (plane of mica alignment) can be as much as 1.8 times higher than that perpendicular to the foliation of the schist.

Elastic waves are subject to attenuation, a decrease in wave amplitude, which results from imperfections in elasticity, called internal friction, delayed elasticity, or viscoelasticity. The attenuation is measured in terms of the specific damping capacity *b*, which is the fraction of the elastic energy lost from the wave per cycle of oscillation. (It is often reported in terms of the quality factor [*Q*], defined as equal to the numerical factor 2π divided by the specific damping capacity, *i.e.*, $Q = 2\pi/b$.) For crystalline rocks, specific damping capacities are typically in the range from 0.5 to 10 percent per cycle under ordinary conditions. Porous clastic rocks such as sandstone and shale often show high attenuation (with a specific damping capacity [*b*] of about 10 to 50 percent per cycle). The attenuation under ordinary conditions is dominated by frictional losses that arise from sliding across microscopic cracks; variability in characteristics of crack porosity is responsible for the wide scatter in observed attenuations. About 5,000 atmospheres of confining pressure inhibits attenuation due to crack sliding and reduces *b* to less than 2 percent per cycle. The remaining attenuation is due to a variety of mechanisms, which have not yet been thoroughly elucidated, because of the complex composition and structure of rocks. The known individual loss mechanisms have a marked dependence on frequency of the elastic wave, but the aggregate effect caused by superposition of many mechanisms is an observed specific damping capacity that shows no definite dependence on frequency over a wide range of frequencies, from those used in typical laboratory experiments, 10^2 to 10^6 hertz (cycles per second), to those encountered in observed seismic waves, 10^{-1} to 10^{-3} hertz. Increase of temperature generally causes an increase in attenuation, but at depth in the Earth's mantle the inhibiting effect of pressure dominates, and *b* is low (approximately 0.5 percent per cycle). A conspicuous increase in attenuation, by as much as a factor of 2, occurs when a rock begins to melt. Partial melting is probably responsible for the relatively high attenuation (about 5 percent per cycle) for seismic *P* waves traversing the low-velocity zone in the Earth at a depth of about 200 kilometres (125 miles). In general, attenuation for *S* waves appears to be larger than for *P* waves by about 50 percent.

Temperature and pressure effects

NONELASTIC PROPERTIES

Permanent deformations, nonrecoverable on unloading, become detectable normally at stresses of 10 to 100 bars in mechanical tests on rocks. At the much lower stresses in typical elastic waves, there is some deviation from reversible elastic behaviour, as indicated by attenuation, but permanent deformations are small and generally remain undetected. Except for compaction, the nonelastic properties of rocks appear only under directed stress. A representative curve of stress σ as a function of strain *e* in a mechanical test is shown in Figure 75. In the elastic range of the curve, from *O* to *Y*, some deviation of the curve from an ideal straight line usually occurs, as shown, because of crack closure. The knee in the curve at *Y* represents the onset of permanent, nonrecoverable strain and is called the yield point. The permanent strain is evident on unloading, which follows the path from *W* to *S*. At point *R*, rupture occurs, and the load that the rock can support (stress) drops abruptly to zero. The amount of permanent strain accumulated between *Y* and *R* is a measure of the ductility of the specimen. Under ordinary conditions, most rocks are brittle—*i.e.*, rupture with little or no ductile deformation—and the rupture point *R* essentially coincides with the yield point *Y*.

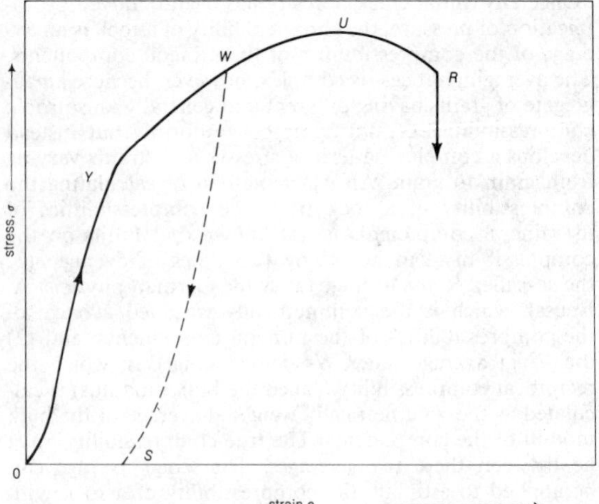

Figure 75: A typical stress–strain curve for rock. *Y* is the yield point (beginning of plastic failure), *U* the point of ultimate strength, and *R* the point of rupture. *WS* represents unloading before rupture (see text).

Compaction. Porous rocks composed of or cemented by relatively weak minerals, such as clay, undergo significant compaction under pressure, the weak grains deforming inelastically into the pore spaces. Thus the porosity of shale decreases substantially with depth of burial (Table 11). For porous sandstones, compaction is normally minor because the tight packing of strong grains (quartz or feldspar) provides mechanical support for the cementing material, which is itself often a strong mineral (calcite or quartz). Under high pressures (approximately 10,000 atmospheres), however, the strong grains themselves fail and porosity is eliminated. No standard measure of compaction as a physical property is available.

Brittle rupture. In most practical situations in which rocks are used as building or foundation materials, their strength is limited by brittle failure. The sudden release of stored elastic energy that occurs in brittle failure of rocks below the surface of the Earth is the source of the seismic disturbances in earthquakes, and in deep mines

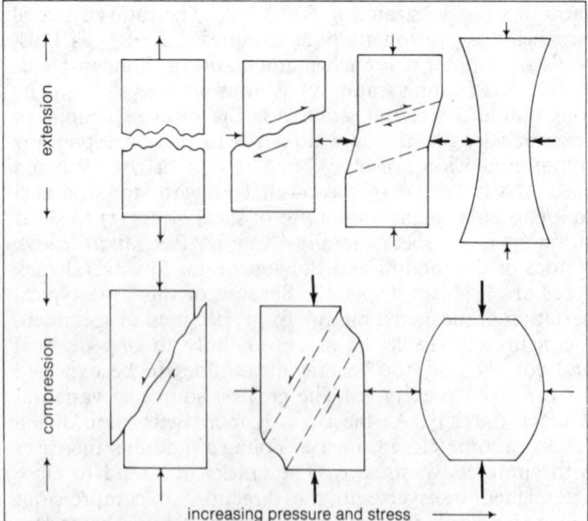

Figure 76: Stages of transition from brittle to ductile failure, as seen in laboratory tests on cylindrical specimens. (Top) The vertical axis is of relative extension, (bottom) of compression. (Left) Extension and shear fracture are illustrated, and (left to right) a progressive increase in confining pressure is shown. Bold arrows indicate directions of greater relative stress.

it takes place in "rock bursts," causing violent damage. In brittle failure, the rock loses cohesion and splits into two or more pieces along fracture surfaces. Two types of fracture are distinguished (see Figure 76): (1) extension fracture, in which perpendicular separation occurs across a surface oriented at right angles to the direction of greatest tensional (pulling apart) stress; and (2) shear fracture, or faulting, in which there is lateral (shear) displacement across a fracture surface inclined at about 25° to the direction of greatest compressive stress. In extension fracture, the stress supported by the rock always drops abruptly to zero. In shear fracture, an abrupt stress drop usually occurs, but the stress does not drop entirely to zero because of sliding friction across the fracture surface; under some conditions the friction is large enough to prevent any stress drop when the fracture or fault develops. Cylindrical rock specimens fail by extension fracture when loaded in unconfined tension and by shear fracture in unconfined compression, or in compression with superimposed confining pressure. Under intermediate states of stress there is a transition from shear to extension fracture, in which the orientation and nature of the fracture surfaces change progressively.

Shear fracture

The stress required to cause brittle failure in an unconfined compression test is called the compressive strength or crushing strength and, in a tensile test, the tensile strength. Representative values are given in Table 14. The tensile strength of a rock is typically only one-tenth to one-twentieth the compressive strength. Because of effects of internal friction, the strength increases substantially with pressure. In compression tests with superimposed pressure, the strength, measured as the difference between axial compressive stress σ and lateral confining pressure P at failure, increases linearly with the pressure: the strength $(\sigma - P)$ is equal to the unconfined crushing strength (C_0), plus the product of a coefficient (s) times the bulk confining pressure (P); *i.e.*, $(\sigma - P) = C_0 + sP$. The coefficient (s) determines the frictional contribution to the strength and commonly has a value in the range three to 10 (Table 14). At a depth of five kilometres (three miles) in the Earth, where pressure is of the order of 1,500 atmospheres, the frictional contribution (sP approximately 9,000 bars) greatly exceeds the contribution from internal cohesion (C_0 is approximately 2,000 bars).

Crushing strength

If a rock contains pore fluid under a pressure p, the strength is reduced accordingly: the pressure quantity that is effective in governing the strength according to the formula above is the confining pressure (P) less the pore pressure (p), thus $(\sigma - P) = C_0 + s(P - p)$. The quantity $(P - p)$ is called the effective confining pressure and plays and important role in the mechanical properties of rocks. It is thought that the pumping of water into the ground under high pressure has, by decreasing the effective confining pressure, been responsible in some instances for reducing the strength of rocks to the point where faulting and earthquakes have occurred. There is evidence that, even in the absence of significant pore pressure, the presence of pore water reduces the strength of sandstones about 50 percent below that of the dry rocks.

Brittle failure of solid rock is controlled by the presence of microscopic flaws that reduce the strength greatly from what is theoretically possible for perfect mineral crystals. These flaws are doubtless closely related to the cracks responsible for anomalies in compressibility and elastic moduli, discussed above. The Griffith theory of failure proposed by the English engineer A.A. Griffith supposes that at the microscopic level the cracks grow by tensile fracture. The theory is applicable to rocks if the additional assumption is made that slippage across the cracks is restrained by friction. If the coefficient of friction is μ, the theory predicts a linear dependence of strength on effective confining pressure, with coefficient $s = 2\mu/(\sqrt{1+\mu^2} - \mu)$. In the Coulomb-Navier-Mohr theory of failure resulting from the work of a French physicist, Charles-Augustin Coulomb, a French engineer, Claude-Louis-Marie Navier, and a German engineer, Otto Mohr, which predicts the same relationship but is conceptually less satisfactory, the quantity μ is called the coefficient of internal friction. (It should not be simply equated with the internal friction that causes elastic wave attenuation.) The theory predicts that the fracture surface should be oriented relative to the compression axis at an angle (θ) that is 45° minus half the angle whose tangent is μ, thus $\theta = 45° - \frac{1}{2}\tan^{-1}\mu$. It also assigns to each rock a quantity called the cohesive strength, which is the shear stress necessary to cause failure across a potential fracture surface in the absence of any frictional constraint; the cohesive strength (τ_0) is related to the crushing strength (C_0) as follows: $\tau_0 = \frac{1}{2}C_0(\sqrt{1+\mu^2} - \mu)$. The cohesion τ_0 is of the order 100 bars for clastic rocks and 500 bars for crystalline rocks. The values of μ needed to account for s in the observed pressure dependence of rock strength are reasonable as coefficients of friction, being near unity (Table 14). The predicted fracture orientation angles (Table 14) are in rough agreement with observation, except in the transition from shear to extension fracture. The strength quantities C_0 and τ_0 vary approximately as the inverse square root of the size of mineral grains (the individual crystals or particles of which the rock is made) as is predicted by the Griffith theory: in finer grained rocks microscopic cracks tend to be shorter than in coarser grained rocks; hence the finer grained rocks are stronger.

In rocks with planar anisotropy, such as slate, fractures tend to develop preferentially parallel to the plane of weakness, even when it is misoriented by as much as 30° from the fracture orientation predicted from the theory for isotropic materials. Such fracture, along planes of a definite orientation, is called cleavage. Even apparently isotropic rocks such as granite show a significant tendency in quarrying to split preferentially along certain planes, called the "rift" and "grain" of the rock.

Individual measurements of the crushing and tensile strengths of rocks often show wide fluctuations, typically by as much as 50 percent from the average values for rock from a given source. This wide scatter is probably a result of uncontrollable variations in characteristics of crack porosity from sample to sample. Variations in average values among rocks of the same type from different sources are also large; hence the figures given in Table 14 should be viewed as representative examples only.

Repeated brittle failure. In the Earth, brittle failure commonly occurs in fault zones, in which the rocks have a previous history of failure and are pervaded by pre-existing fractures; this is a situation distinctly different from the failure of virgin rock, described above. If the fractures are not healed by cementation, the rock in bulk has already lost cohesion and has no tensile strength. In

Table 14: Brittle Strength Parameters for Rocks

	tensile strength T_0 (kbar)	crushing strength C_0 (kbar)	pressure dependence s	cohesion τ_0 (kbar)	internal friction μ	fracture angle θ (in degrees)	
						predicted	observed
Granite	0.2	2.3	7.3	0.39	1.3	19	26
Granodiorite	—	1.1	9.7	0.17	1.5	17	—
Diabase	0.4	4.9	3.8	0.87	0.9	24	26
Basalt	—	2.2	5.6	0.44	1.1	21	—
Gneiss (dioritic)	—	1.1	9.0	0.18	1.4	18	—
Dolomite marble	0.1	1.5	2.1	0.38	0.8	26	17
Quartzite	0.3	4.6	8.4	0.76	1.4	18	25
Limestone	—	1.1	11.6	0.15	1.6	16	—
Sandstone	—	0.5	4.9	0.11	1.0	23	—
Siltstone	—	0.03	8.3	0.005	1.4	18	—

Types of friction

compression, in which the rock fails largely by slipping on the pre-existing fractures, however, the friction across these surfaces determines the strength; at depths of several kilometres it is substantial (thousands of bars), unless the effective pressure is reduced by an abnormally high pore pressure. The pre-existing fractures contain comminuted (pulverized) rock debris produced by previous slippage; hence the failure properties are related to those of incoherent granular materials such as sand or soil. Of great importance is the distinction between two contrasting types of frictional behaviour: (1) stable sliding, in which the coefficient of friction (a measure of the resistance to sliding) remains essentially constant as slip progresses across the fracture surface; and (2) stick-slip friction, in which the initiation of sliding is accompanied by a large and abrupt drop in the coefficient of friction. Stick-slip friction results in sudden stress release, the cause of earthquakes, whereas stable sliding allows a slow creeping motion across the faults, without earthquakes. Increased temperature and decreased pressure promote stable sliding instead of stick-slip friction. The physical conditions controlling the two types of frictional behaviour have important influence on the causes, locations, and hazards caused by earthquakes.

Brittle-ductile transition. By raising fracture strength, confining pressure inhibits brittle failure and allows other mechanisms of yielding to occur, which produce a more or less homogeneous permanent deformation and constitute ductile failure (Figure 76). The pressure required to effect the transition from brittle to ductile failure is relatively small (1,000 atmospheres or less) for rock materials of low plastic yield strength, such as limestone, shale, and rock salt. At ordinary temperatures, most igneous and metamorphic rocks and also clastic rocks well cemented by silica begin to show ductile behaviour only at pressures of 10,000 to 30,000 atmospheres, because the directed stress needed to cause plastic deformation in the silicate minerals of these rocks is high. The pressure variable pertinent to the brittle-ductile transition is the effective pressure, as defined above, rather than the total pressure. Intermediate between brittle failure at low pressure and true plasticity at high pressure is a type of deformation behaviour called cataclastic, in which the rock fails in a ductile manner as viewed macroscopically but in which on the microscopic scale there is progressive comminution of the mineral grains by local fracturing distributed microscopically throughout the specimen. Cataclastic deformation occurs under conditions where the internal friction of virgin rock is enough lower than the sliding friction on already formed fracture surfaces that slippage is inhibited on fractures once formed, and brittle failure therefore spreads pervasively through the rock. Increase of temperature promotes true rock plasticity at the expense of cataclastic flow and lowers the brittle-ductile transition pressure. The explanation for this is that temperature has a much greater effect in lowering the plastic yield stresses of minerals than in lowering the cohesions or internal frictions.

PLASTICITY

Types of crystal deformation

In true plastic yielding of rock, intra-crystalline plastic deformation of the individual mineral grains takes place. Crystals, composed of uniform layers, or planes, of atoms, deform plastically by two distinct mechanisms: (1) translation gliding, in which individual atomic planes appear to slip past one another, leaving the basic crystal structure unchanged; and (2) mechanical twinning, in which the atomic planes slip through a definite fraction of the crystallographic repeat distance, in such a way as to produce a new crystal in twinned orientation relative to the original. The displacements of the atomic planes are made possible by the motion of crystal dislocations and are crystallographically controlled: each mineral has definite crystallographic planes (called slip planes) across which translation gliding or mechanical twinning can take place by slip in a definite crystallographic direction. Mechanical twinning produces visible twin lamellae (layers) in the individual crystals, which are a feature of deformed marbles. Translation gliding leaves less obvious traces but can result in a bending of the individual crystals, which is often found in the quartz grains of deformed rocks.

Critical resolved shear stress

For each set of potential slip planes in a given mineral under given conditions, a certain definite shear stress acting across the planes in the direction of slip is necessary to initiate slip; it is called the critical resolved shear stress. For the appropriate planes in calcite this stress is about 80 bars for mechanical twinning and about 1,200 bars for translation gliding at 24° C (75° F) and 3,000 atmospheres confining pressure. With the exception of sheet silicates (clays and micas), silicate minerals generally have high critical shear stresses, in the range 2,000 to 30,000 bars.

Cause of hardening

Once the critical shear stress for a set of slip planes is reached, substantial plastic shear strain can occur by slip across these planes; ideally there is only a modest further increase in stress (called work hardening), so that the stress-strain curve has a sharp knee at the yield point *Y* (Figure 75), with a low slope above that point. In a rock, the individual crystals cannot yield simultaneously because, with their various orientations, the potential slip planes in different grains have widely different resolved shear stresses for a given stress applied to the rock as a whole. Moreover, the slip systems of adjacent grains in a rock are not generally compatible, and the crystals therefore tend to interfere with one another during plastic flow, distrupting one another and causing increased work hardening. The result of these effects is that the plastic yielding of a rock occurs less sharply and at substantially higher stresses than that of individual crystals of its component minerals. The stress-strain curve has a broad, rounded knee at *Y* (Figure 75) and a substantial slope above *Y*. Because of this, a meaningful statement of the plastic yield strength of a rock requires specification of the strain to which the quoted strength refers. Strengths observed for several rock types at 2 percent strain are listed in Table 15. Because of substantial variation in results from one experiment to another, only rough, generalized figures are given. The ultimate strength, which is the maximum stress reached in a loading test (*U* in Figure 75), is often substantially higher than the yield strength because of work hardening. The strain range of ductile behaviour is usually terminated by brittle failure (*R* in Figure 75), which occurs when the deforming stress has risen to the point at which the confining pressure is no longer able to inhibit fracture. Contributing to it is a progressive deterioration of the rock texture caused by structural flaws generated in plastic flow; these flaws reduce the cohesion.

Table 15: Plastic Yield Strength of Rocks

	temperature (°C)	pressure (kbar)	plastic yield strength at 2% strain (kbar)	ultimate strength (kbar)
Granite	500	5	10	11.5
	800	5	5	6
Gabbro	500	5	4	8
Peridotite	500	5	8	9
	800	5	5.5	8
Basalt	500	5	8	10
	800	5	2	2.5
Marble	24	2	2.5	5.5
	500	3	1	2
Quartzite	500	8	21	22
	1,000	8	7*	10
	1,000	8	4†	5
Limestone	24	2	4.5	5.5
	500	3	2.5	3
Dolomite	24	2	6	7
	500	5	4	6.5
Shale	24	2	1.5	2.5
Rock salt	24	1	0.5	1

*At strain rate of 2.4 percent per minute. †At strain rate of 0.2 percent per minute.

In conformity with the fact that sliding friction is not involved in the plastic yield process, pressure has only a slight effect on the plastic yield strengths of minerals and rocks. The effect is a modest increase in strength, comparable to the increase in elastic bulk modulus with pressure, discussed earlier. Increase of temperature, on the other hand, lowers the yield strength substantially (Table 15). Truly plastic behaviour of igneous and metamorphic rocks containing strong silicate minerals is generally observed only above temperatures of about 600° C (1,100° F). The effect of temperature is even more dramatic when water is present: the yield strength of quartz at 600° C drops from 20,000 to 1,500 bars when water is made available. It is thought that water causes this effect by breaking some of the strong silicon-oxygen bonds in the silicate minerals. The phenomenon of water weakening explains the seeming contradiction between the great rigidity of quartz as observed in most laboratory tests and the abundant evidence of plasticity in the quartz of natural rocks, even in rocks that must have been deformed at only relatively low temperatures.

TIME-DEPENDENT DEFORMATION: CREEP

When a rock placed under load experiences a strain that does not appear immediately but instead appears gradually as time progresses, the phenomenon is called creep. The slow, drifting motion of the Earth's continents and oceanic plates (rigid, slablike regions of the ocean floor) is a surface indication of creep taking place in the rocks at depth. At ordinary temperatures, the creep rate immediately after the initial loading of a specimen may be relatively large, but it decreases with time. Transient creep, as this is called, yields only a limited total strain; it may, however, affect the use of rock as a building material under high loads. Transient creep of this kind is due primarily to a gradual loosening of the granular texture of the rock. At high temperatures (within a few hundred degrees Celsius of the onset of melting) steady-state creep makes its appearance; this is a type of creep in which, after possible initial transients, the creep settles down to a steady rate under fixed stresses. Although the rate may be low, it can lead cumulatively to large deformations when continued over the millions of years of geologic time. The required stress need not exceed the plastic yield stress, and the strain rate may be so low as to be undetectable in laboratory tests on rocks.

For creep, the physically significant relationship is not between stress and strain but between stress and strain rate. If the relationship is linear, so that strain rate is directly proportional to stress, the creep behaviour is similar to the flow of a viscous fluid except that the deforming material is a crystalline solid rather than an amorphous liquid. The ratio of shear stress to shear strain rate is called the effective viscosity. Certain creep phenomena in the Earth, such as the slow rise of Scandinavia due to removal of the continental ice-sheet load at the end of the Ice Age (called postglacial rebound), have been interpreted in terms of linear creep and imply an effective viscosity of about 10^{22} poise (dyne sec cm^{-2} unit) for rocks in the outer part of the Earth's mantle. The flow of glacier ice corresponds to an effective viscosity of roughly 10^{14} poise. For comparison, the viscosity of water is 0.01 poise, and the viscosity of molten lava is in the range 10^4 to 10^5 poise at temperatures of 1,000°–1,100° C (1,800°–2,000° F). With an effective creep viscosity of 10^{22} poise, a rock specimen loaded in compression at 1,000 bar would undergo a total strain of 10^{-6} (one millionth) in a year's time.

Effective viscosity

Laboratory experiments on limestone, marble, dunite (an olivine-rich rock), rock salt, and ice have shown that over the range of measurable strain rates, the creep behaviour is markedly nonlinear. The same is observed in the high-temperature creep of metals. The type of nonlinearity commonly found in the relation between stress σ and strain rate (*i.e.*, change of strain with time, symbolized $\dot{e}$) has the form, strain rate equals a constant (k) times stress raised to a power n, or $\dot{e} = k\sigma^n$. Values commonly found for the exponent n range from 3 to 7, rather different from a value of 1, which represents linear creep. Linear and nonlinear creep behaviour are compared in Figure 77. Because of the observed creep nonlinearity, strain rates increase much more rapidly than in simple proportionality to stress. The effective creep viscosity decreases as the stress increases. At low stresses, there is hardly any creep, and as the stress rises above a level of order σ_0 in Figure 77, the strain rate increases rapidly, so that the behaviour is somewhat like that of a plastic material with yield stress σ_0. Creep rates in the Earth are probably less, in general, than the experimentally studied range, and it is possible that at the lower stresses the creep behaviour tends toward linearity.

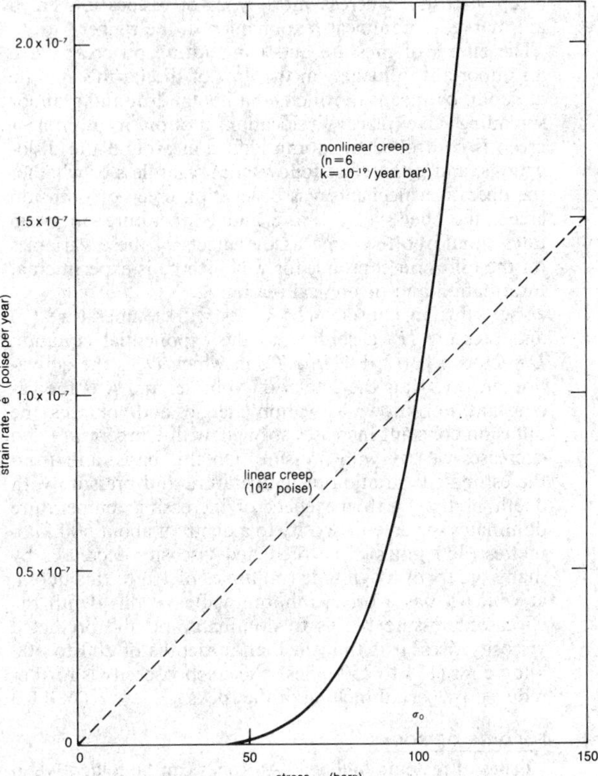

Figure 77: Comparison of stress versus strain–rate curves for linear and nonlinear creep. Linear creep is shown for a rock that deforms to a substantial strain ($e \sim 1$) under a stress of 100 bars applied for 10,000,000 years, a geologically typical period of rock deformation. Nonlinear creep is plotted for a material that behaves approximately as a plastic material with yield stress $\sigma_0 \sim 100$ bars.

Rock creep can take place by intra-crystalline deformation of the individual mineral grains, made possible by a motion of crystal dislocations that is similar to what occurs in crystal plasticity, except that the dislocation motion is time dependent, and the dislocations can move out of the plastic slip planes, with the help of atomic diffusion. This type of creep may be called dislocation creep. (In technical practice, distinctions between different types of dislocation creep are made.)

Dislocation creep is usually accompanied by recrystallization, an important process that modifies the crystalline texture through lateral migration of the grain boundaries and through nucleation and growth of new crystal grains in the rock. By allowing new fresh crystals to grow at the expense of old deformed ones, recrystallization serves to anneal the disturbances in the crystalline texture generated by intra-crystalline creep or plasticity. As a result of recrystallization, deformed rocks commonly have a texture much different from the parent rock.

A second creep mechanism, found to be important in the creep of ceramic materials at high temperature, is the diffusion of atoms along the grain boundaries, or from one grain boundary to another through the intervening crystal grain. This has an effect much like dissolution of the grains on some sides and growth of the grains by precipitation of dissolved material on other sides. It allows the grains to change their external shape and thus the polycrystalline aggregate as a whole to deform, without any intra-crystalline deformation of the grains themselves. The resulting progressive deformation under stress is called diffusion creep. Because the rate is limited by the distance that the atoms must diffuse, it is inversely proportional to the grain size; fine-grained materials, with grain sizes in the micron range, are most prone to show diffusion creep.

It is not yet known whether the creep of rocks at depth in the Earth is primarily due to dislocation creep or to diffusion creep. The distinction is important, because diffusion creep is a strictly linear process giving a stress-independent creep viscosity, whereas most types of dislocation creep are markedly nonlinear (exponent n in the range 3 to 7).

Creep of Earth's mantle

The effects of pressure and temperature on creep have an important influence on the flow of the Earth's mantle at depth, by means of which continental drift and seafloor spreading take place. Dislocation motion in nonlinear creep is controlled by atomic diffusion around the dislocations, and it therefore follows that regardless of whether the operative mechanism is dislocation creep or diffusion creep, the effects of pressure and temperature on creep rates should be the same as the effects of these variables on the diffusion constant, for which there is experimental information and theoretical reasoning.

The diffusion constant (D) varies with temperature (T) and pressure (P) according to the exponential equation $D = D_0 \exp[-(Q_a + V_a P)/RT]$, in which Q_a is the activation energy, V_a is the activation volume, and R is the gas constant. For known activation energies and volumes, the diffusion constant increases strongly with temperature and decreases weakly with pressure. On this basis, and from the estimated variation of temperature and pressure with depth in the Earth the effect of increasing temperature dominates the creep viscosity to a depth of about 500 kilometres (300 miles). The predicted viscosity decreases by many orders of magnitude (multiples of 10) to this depth, at which it has a broad minimum. Below this depth the effect of pressure begins to dominate and the predicted viscosity rises. It is thought that, at depths of 200 to 400 kilometres (125 to 250 miles), the creep viscosity is further reduced by partial melting of the rocks. (W.B.K.)

FOLDING OF ROCKS

Types of tectonic folding. All rocks can be folded when the stress is sufficient to produce permanent strain, but folds are more obvious where original planar structures (such as bedding or schistosity) were deformed during the total strain. In the mobile belts, fold wavelengths (distance from crest to crest) vary from a few millimetres to several kilometres. Traditionally, most geologists have recognized three types of folding, but gradations between these are readily found in nature.

Flexure folding. The rock is structurally homogeneous (containing no planes of mechanical discontinuity) and no planes of discontinuity develop during flexure folding. A sheet of India rubber or modelling clay is an appropriate analogue—when folded, the concave side is compressed and the convex side is stretched without fracture development. Such strain is relatively rare in rocks.

Slip folding. The rock is structurally homogeneous but the stress induces a single set of parallel slip planes (S') during slip folding. Folds of this type are common in slates where colour banding or very minor compositional differences define original bedding (S_0) that is folded by differential slip along innumerable new S' planes. The geometry can be illustrated with a deck of cards (Figure 78A). A heavy line can be drawn around the cards to represent bedding (S_0), and it can be assumed that the cards are a solid homogeneous mass before deformation and that the planes (S') between the cards result from the stress; differential slip on these induced planes produces folds in S_0 that are variously called slip, similar, or bending folds. The genetic term bending fold implies folding caused by motion transverse to bedding that was not generated by compression along the rock layers (S_0).

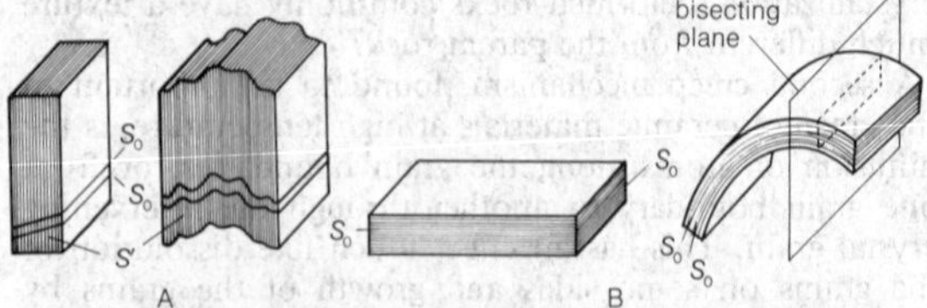

Figure 78: Simple fold models illustrated by decks of cards. (A) Slip folding of bedding S_0 along slip planes S'. (B) Flexural-slip folding of bedding S_0 (see text).

Flexural-slip folding. The initial rock has planes of mechanical discontinuity (*e.g.,* well-marked bedding planes) along which slip can occur during stress. A deck of cards can also illustrate such folding if the separation between the cards is assumed to correspond to original bedding (S_0). Compression or shortening parallel to the layering (or bending of the layers) causes folding with slip (S') between the cards parallel to bedding (S_0); the result is variously called flexural-slip, parallel, or buckling folds (Figure 78B).

Successive rock layers tend to be mechanically dissimilar during folding. Well-bedded sandstones, for example, may respond by flexural slip while interstratified silts and clays may develop slip-fold characteristics. Such complex relationships are common. Rock between the successive slip planes of flexural-slip folds is also strained during folding, but whether by flexure or by one of the other types of folding is not entirely clear.

Theoretically, the geometries are simple and distinct. In ideal flexural-slip or parallel folds (Figure 79A), the orthogonal thickness (t) of each bed remains constant whereas "thickness" (T) measured parallel to the bisecting plane of the fold changes from point to point. By contrast, in slip folds the orthogonal thickness (t) varies while T remains constant (Figure 79B). It has generally been assumed that flexural-slip and slip folds are the dominant types in nature, with the former more common. These models have been recognized since 1896, but recently it has been noticed that few folds really have these geometries. In fact, most folds appear to depart markedly from the ideal t and T relationships, which calls into question the basic hypotheses about fold formation. In an attempt to explain this anomaly, it has been suggested that, after the initial fold formation, continued compression causes the structure to be flattened in the plane normal to the original maximum stress (*i.e.,* flattening approximately in the bisecting plane). Limited published t and T data for natural and experimentally produced folds make it difficult to evaluate the flattening hypothesis. If "flattening" is as common in numerous environments as has been suggested, most ideal fold shapes must be distorted.

Departure from ideal fold geometries

From J. Ramsay, *Journal of Geology*, vol. 70 (1962); University of Chicago Press

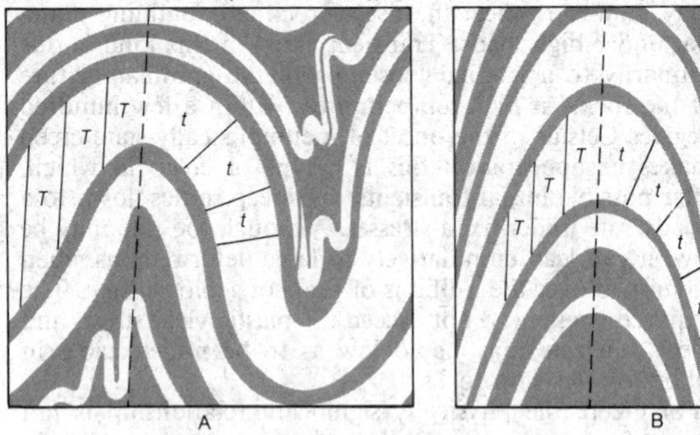

Figure 79: Geometrical features of (A) ideal flexural-slip folds and (B) ideal slip or similar folds (see text).

The terms flexural-slip, slip, and flexure fold clearly have genetic implications suggesting that the kinematic mode of formation is known unequivocally and that the folds conform to the t and T specifications. For this reason, many geologists use the older terms, similar and parallel folds, instead of slip and flexural-slip folds, respectively. The older terms refer to what now appears to be rare, idealized geometry; supposedly, in slip folds, successive folded layers have similar shape, whereas, in flexural-slip folds, boundaries between successive layers are parallel (Figure 79). Following the genetic terminology developed in strength-of-materials studies, some geologists prefer the terms bending and buckling folds.

Nontectonic folding. The development of small, nontectonic folds in relatively unconsolidated surficial rocks and recently deposited sediments is also important. Submarine sliding and slumping is widespread and more important; the process produces small folds contemporaneously (or nearly so) with sedimentation. Gravitational slip along bedding planes prior to additional sedimentation means that the folds affect only a metre or two of sediment; the underlying strata and the overlying (as yet undeposited) strata are unaffected. Lithified examples seen in outcrop can look deceptively like tectonic folds. Following tectonic deformation, the superposed tectonic folds make it difficult to recognize the earlier soft-sediment structures; a good example of this situation was described in graywackes from the Appalachian mobile belt of Newfoundland. Gravitational creep and flow in sedimentary rocks that are exposed in deeply dissected terrain on land causes crumpling and folding in disturbed zones up to a few metres thick, several good examples from the Italian Apennines have recently been described.

Under special conditions, numerous other soft-sediment folds can develop in largely unconsolidated sediments. For example, differential compaction, extrusion of water during compaction and dewatering, and decay of ice bodies within periglacial areas are examples of conditions that can induce minor fold structures.

Relation of joints and faults to folding. It is widely believed that joints (fractures along which little or no displacement has occurred) and faults have as a common origin the deformative stress that occurs during a phase of folding. Many cylindrical and conical folds are associated with well-developed cross joints (normal to fold axis) and longitudinal joints (parallel to axial surface). Less pronounced diagonal joints occur as paired (conjugate) sets symmetrical to the cross and longitudinal joints but more closely inclined to the former. Joints tend to be of two types: (1) tension fractures characterized by clean granular breaks (sometimes with plumose, or radiating, patterns reflecting the spreading fracture through the rock) oriented parallel to the maximum-stress axis and perpendicular to the minimum-stress axis; (2) shear fractures occurring as conjugate sets with slight offsets and slickensided surfaces; these joints or faults develop in planes parallel to the median stress direction, and they have an acute angle between them that is bisected by the maximum-stress direction. Slickensides are grooves or striations on joint or fault surfaces produced parallel to the last direction of forceful movement of one face across the other. Close relationships between joint sets and fold geometry are widespread and, when actually established, fracture-pattern analysis can have far-reaching significance in determining the orientation of tectonic forces responsible for regional structures (*e.g.*, anticlines and mountain uplifts).

Where there appears to be a clear genetic interrelationship between joints and folds, the fracture density tends to be greater in thinner rock units and in the more brittle rocks. Fracture frequency is commonly correlative with the degree of bed curvature, so that fold flanks have fewer fractures than the closures; such fractures, seen on fold profiles, have sometimes been called fracture cleavage, but they are true joints and should be differentiated from cleavage or foliation. Foliation, unlike joints, is characterized by a splitting parallel to a preferred mineral orientation (*e.g.*, schistosity or slaty cleavage). Occasionally, this type of fracture and slaty cleavage grade into each other; this is additional evidence for foliation and folding being concomitant and genetically related. In metamorphic rocks, tensional-joint formation is commonly aided by the foliation, which customarily parallels the fold axial surfaces.

Propagation of basement joints

In many other situations, joints appear to be independent of the stress field that previously effected strain of the rocks. Sedimentary rocks on stable cratonic areas, for example, are commonly almost unfolded or folded only very mildly. Such rocks are invariably jointed, however, and the joint patterns remain remarkably constant in orientation over vast areas, although varying in frequency from one rock type to another. Similarly, the highly folded and metamorphosed shield areas are characteristically transected by regional joint sets bearing no easily discerned relationship to the local structural geometry. Such joints apparently reflect major regional stress phenomena. Sometimes consistent offsets suggest shear components. More commonly, three mutually perpendicular (orthogonal) joint sets are dominant—two nearly vertical and one approximately horizontal. This suggests that basement joints—those in the oldest crystalline rocks at the bottom of the sequence—were propagated into the overlying cratonic rocks (and even into Pleistocene sedimentary rocks) by either (1) continuation of the processes that produced the original basement joints or (2) relatively small vertical movements on the old joints causing extension of those joints up into the overlying rocks. (E.H.T.W.)

RESPONSE TO SHOCK WAVES

Impacts of meteoroids on the Earth, Moon, and other planets subject rock to severe stresses on short time scales (fractions of a second). Similar effects are produced by artificially generated shock waves, for which the duration is measured in thousandths of a second; shock pressures as high as 1,000,000 atmospheres have been generated. The point of mechanical failure for a rock is reached early in the shock event. Failure by brittle fracture is abundant both in shock-wave experiments and in cratering impact events: the rock is shattered into many fragments. There is often evidence, however, of plastic deformation (translation gliding, bending, twinning) of the mineral components. A novel and diagnostic type of shock failure is by partial or complete phase change: either by melting or by conversion to glass in the solid state or by transformation to high-pressure mineral phases. As a result of failure, rocks approach a hydrostatic condition at the peak pressure of the shock wave. Hence shock experiments can be used to obtain compressibilities up to very high pressures.

HARDNESS AND FRIABILITY

The characteristics of hardness and friability (the resistance of a rock to crumbling into grains) are important in the practical usage of rock materials. Although the hardness of the individual minerals in a rock is a well-defined property, the aggregate, made up of grains of differing hardness, has no single, definite hardness. A rock such as granite, composed mostly of minerals of hardness 6 to 7 on the Mohs scale, has a relatively definite, high hardness, whereas a sandy shale has attributes of hardness varying from 1 to 7. The ability of a rock to scratch or abrade other materials is a reflection, by and large, of the hardest abundant mineral component, whereas the extent to which the rock is scratched or abraded by other objects reflects the softest abundant component. Friability, the readiness with which mineral grains are separated from the rock, is also related to the weakest abundant component, usually the cementing mineral in a clastic rock.

Thermal properties

SPECIFIC HEAT

Heat capacity

The heat capacity of a rock is a mass-weighted average of the heat capacities of its mineral constituents (*i.e.*, sum of the heat capacity of each mineral times its mass fraction). Figure 80 shows heat capacity as a function of tempera-

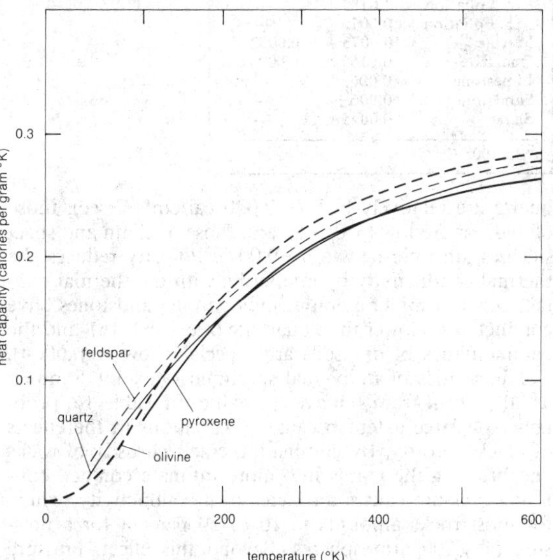

Figure 80: Specific heats (at constant pressure) of rock-forming minerals, as a function of temperature. Weighted averages of these curves give the specific heats of common rocks.

ture for important rock-forming silicate minerals and thus outlines the range of possible variation of the heat capacities of common silicate rocks. Because the mean atomic weight $\bar{A}$ of most rock-forming minerals is near 21, the high-temperature specific heat (Dulong-Petit value) is near 0.3 calorie per gram degree Celsius. This value is reached only above temperatures of about 1,000° C (1,830° F), because the strong interatomic bonds, especially silicon–oxygen, inhibit excitation of some of the thermal vibrations at lower temperatures. The heat capacity is roughly half the limiting Dulong-Petit value at room temperature. The presence of water, either mechanically included (in pores) or in chemical combination (hydrous minerals), adds appreciably to the heat capacity; anomalously high apparent heat capacities are shown over ranges of temperature in which water is driven off on heating, either by volatilization or by thermal breakdown of hydrous minerals.

THERMAL CONDUCTIVITY

The rate at which heat escapes from the Earth's interior to the surface is controlled by thermal conductivity, and this property affects the suitability of rock as a building material, for which its insulating capability is important. The conductivity of a rock is a somewhat complex average over the conductivities (generally anisotropic) of its component minerals modified by effects of porosity. As shown in Table 16, crystalline silicate rocks have conductivities generally in the range from about 0.004 to about 0.008 calorie per centimetre degree Celsius second (abbreviated cal/cm° C sec), the lower values being typical of silicate rocks relatively rich in magnesium and iron, such as basalt and gabbro, whereas the higher values are typical of rocks rich in silica and alumina, such as granite and granodiorite. The variations reflect the fact that the conductivities of quartz are relatively high (~ 0.020 cal/cm° C sec), those of feldspar are low (~ 0.005), and those of chain and sheet silicates are intermediate (~ 0.007). Porosity reduces the thermal conductivity by interfering with the thermal contact between mineral grains; thus porous sandstones have conductivities lower than quartzite (see Table 16), and the conductivities of dry soils are especially low (~ 0.0004). Conductivities of individual specimens vary by as much as 20 percent from the average values in Table 16, probably to a large extent because of variations in the effects of crack porosity. By eliminating crack porosity of rocks and bringing the grains into more intimate contact, confining pressure causes an increase in conductivity, which for most rocks amounts to 10 to 20 percent for a pressure of 1,000 atmospheres. Beyond this effect, pressure has little effect on conductivity. Saturation of the pores with water causes an increase in conductivity similar to that obtained by closing the pores under pressure. The conductivity of mica is about six times greater parallel to the micaceous sheets (mica layers) than perpendicular to them; hence, rocks with abundant, well-aligned mica flakes have anisotropic conductivity; this is illustrated by gneiss and phyllite in Table 16.

Porosity and thermal conductivity

Table 16: Thermal Conductivities of Rocks
(mean values)

	thermal conductivity k(cal cm^{-1} °C^{-1} sec^{-1})	
	at 20° C	at 200° C
Granite	0.0078	0.0066
Granodiorite	0.0071	0.0057
Diabase	0.0053	0.0051
Gabbro	0.0051	0.0050
Anorthosite	0.0042	0.0044
Dunite	0.012	0.0081
Basalt	0.004	0.004
Gneiss		
‖ Foliation	0.0082	0.0074*
⊥ Foliation	0.0059	0.0055*
Phyllite		
‖ Foliation	0.0183	—
⊥ Foliation	0.0079	—
Marble	0.0073	0.0052
Quartzite	0.015	0.009
Limestone	0.006	—
Sandstone	0.006±	—
Shale	0.0045±	—

*At 100° C.

Glassy rocks, like glasses generally, have a low thermal conductivity (~ 0.002 cal/cm° C sec), which increases with temperature. In contrast, increasing temperature reduces the conductivities of most crystalline materials, as shown by the data for rocks in Table 16. The decrease in conductivity is large for quartz, but for feldspars it is small, and, in fact, calcium-rich feldspar shows a small increase, indicated by the data for anorthosite in Table 16. These differences in behaviour account for the fact that sialic rocks show a larger drop in conductivity with temperature than do mafic rocks. The drop in conductivity tends to cause the geothermal gradient to increase with depth in the Earth, for a constant flux of heat escaping outward. Above temperatures of about 1,600° C (2,900° F), however, conductivities begin to increase with temperature, because transport of heat by thermal radiation through the solid becomes significant; radiative transfer probably makes an important contribution to heat conduction in the Earth's mantle.

THERMAL EXPANSION

The increase in volume of a rock specimen with temperature is expressed in terms of the coefficient of volumetric thermal expansion. The coefficient α is equal to the reciprocal of the specimen volume (V) times the ratio of the increase in specimen volume (ΔV) that occurs for a small temperature increase (ΔT) to that temperature increase, or $\alpha = (1/V)(\Delta V/\Delta T)$. Similarly the increase ΔL in linear dimension (L) of the specimen is expressed in terms of the coefficient of linear thermal expansion $\Delta L/L\Delta T$. It is equal to $\alpha/3$, for isotropic specimens. The volumetric expansion is of particular importance in estimating the density of rocks at the high temperatures within the Earth and in assessing the possibility that temperature gradients in the Earth will cause convective motion analogous to the convection of a viscous liquid. The linear expansion is important where rock must remain fitted to other structural materials over wide variations in ambient temperature. Most rocks have a volumetric expansion coefficient in the range $1.5–3.3 \times 10^{-5}$ per degree Celsius under ordinary conditions. Quartz-rich rocks, especially sandstone and quartzite, have the highest values, indicating a relatively high thermal expansion of quartz itself. Thermal expansion coefficients increase substantially with temperature. At the microscopic level, the thermal expansion of a rock is a complex affair, because of the generally anisotropic character of the expansion of the individual minerals and the differences in expansion from grain to grain. A complex pattern of stresses is set up in the grains, controlled by the thermal expansions and the various elastic properties. To some extent the stresses are relieved by opening up of microscopic cracks, and a part of the measured expansion, probably about 10–20 percent, thus represents increase in crack porosity. Crack opening is not entirely reversible, so that the contraction on cooling generally is less than the expansion during the previous heating, and the expansions on successive heatings may differ. Because of the cracking, prolonged thermal cycling causes mechanical disintegration of rocks into their granular components. These effects are inhibited by confining pressures sufficient to keep the cracks closed.

Thermal cycling

RADIOACTIVE HEAT PRODUCTIVITY

Of importance in determining the temperature and thermal evolution of the Earth's interior is the heat produced by absorption of radiation that is emitted from radioactive elements in the rocks. Significant contributions come from the nuclear decay of potassium-40, thorium-232, uranium-235, and uranium-238. In Table 17, average rates of heat production are given for several major rock types, including chondritic meteorites (meteorites imbedded with nodules of certain materials), which are considered to represent a possible composition for the Earth's mantle. The great enrichment of the radioactive heat producing elements in the more sialic rock types of the Earth's crust is

Table 17: Radioactive Heat Generation by Rocks

	heat production (10^{-6} cal g^{-1} $year^{-1}$)			
	from U	from Th	from K	total
Granite	3.4	4.0	1.1	8.5
Granodiorite	1.9	1.8	0.7	4.4
Diorite	1.5	1.7	0.3	3.5
Gabbro, basalt	0.7	0.5	0.1	1.3
Dunite, eclogite*	0.001–0.04	0.0002–0.04	0.0002–0.01	0.001–0.09
Chondrite	0.009	0.009	0.023	0.04
Sandstone*	2.2	1.2	0.4	3.8
Shale	2.7	2.4	0.7	5.8
Limestone	1.6	0.3	0.1	2.0

*Shows very wide variation.

evident in Table 17 and has important consequences in the thermal history of the Earth, the generation of magmas, and volcanism. The average geothermal heat flow at the Earth's surface (1.2×10^{-6} calorie per square centimetre per second) could be generated by a layer of granite only 16 kilometres (10 miles) thick, somewhat thinner than the typical thickness of the continental crust, whereas some 300 kilometres (185 miles) of chondritic material would be required.

MELTING

Rocks begin to melt at temperatures somewhat lower than the melting points of any of their constituent minerals, and melting occurs over a range of temperatures, from the first appearance of liquid to the final disappearance of the last crystals. Melting points of the common anhydrous (non-water-bearing) rock-forming silicates lie between 1,100° and 1,800° C (2,000° and 3,300° F). The lowest melting mixture of these has the composition of granite (mainly quartz and potassium-sodium feldspar) and begins to melt at 950° C (1,750° F). The temperature of first melting does not depend on the relative proportions of the different minerals present and hence is the same for granitic rocks of diverse compositions, representing different proportions of quartz, potassium feldspar, and sodium feldspar. The temperature of first melting does depend, however, on which minerals are present and on their individual compositions. Thus the more mafic igneous rocks such as diorite and basalt, which lack quartz and potassium feldspar and which contain a calcium-rich sodium feldspar, begin to melt at higher temperatures, approaching 1,100° C. Ultramafic rocks such as peridotite, containing only pyroxene and olivine, begin to melt at 1,350°–1,550° C (2,450°–2,800° F). The completion of melting is sensitive to the mineral proportions in the rock. Most granites have a narrow melting range, because their bulk compositions are close to that of the first-formed melt. Increasing the proportion of a mineral constituent of high melting point widens the melting range by raising the completion of melting. Thus mafic rocks, containing substantial amounts of high-melting iron-magnesium silicates, have melting ranges 200°–300° C (390°–570° F) wide.

Melting points of rock-forming silicates

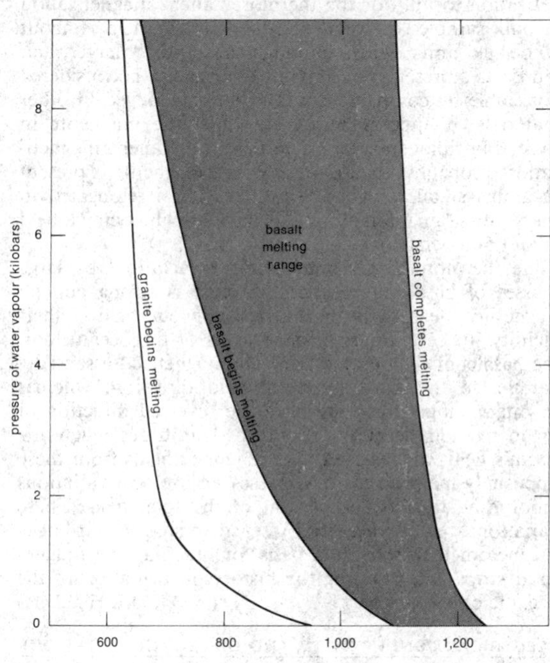

Figure 81: Melting range for basalt (shaded) and temperature of beginning of melting for granite, as a function of water-vapour pressure.

Melting of rocks is greatly affected by the presence of water vapour under pressure, because water can dissolve in silicate melts. Increasing the water-vapour pressure to a few thousand bars lowers the first melting of granite from 950° to 650° C (1,740° to 1,200° F) and causes water to dissolve in the melt to the extent of several percent. The effect of water-vapour pressure in lowering the melting range of basalt and the first melting temperature of granite is shown in Figure 81. Similar considerations apply to the melting of metamorphic and sedimentary rocks of similar compositions.

Importance of water vapour under pressure

Another important effect of water vapour under pressure is to increase the stability of hydrous minerals, such as mica and amphibole. When heated at atmospheric pressure, these minerals break down to anhydrous minerals (with release of water) at temperatures of only 500°–700° C (930°–1,300° F), well below the start of melting. Raising the water-vapour pressure both lowers the onset of melting and raises the stability of the hydrous minerals against breakdown, so that it becomes possible for them to melt or, on cooling, to crystallize from a rock melt. The fact that these minerals actually formed in many igneous rocks at the time of initial crystallization shows that substantial pressures of water vapour must have operated on the parent magmas.

Electric and magnetic properties

In deciphering the history of the Earth's magnetic field and the wandering motions of the continents and in estimating temperatures in the Earth's interior, electric and magnetic properties of rocks play an important role. They are also utilized in methods of geophysical exploration.

MAGNETIC SUSCEPTIBILITY

Application of a magnetic field (H) to a rock specimen induces a magnetization (M) that is generally proportional to the field; the proportionality constant (symbolized by χ, the Greek letter chi) in the equation $M = \chi H$ is the magnetic susceptibility (see ELECTRICITY AND MAGNETISM). Substances are classified as paramagnetic or diamagnetic accordingly as χ is positive or negative. In a paramagnetic material, the directions of the inducing magnetic field and the induced magnetization are the same, whereas in a diamagnetic material they are opposite. Most minerals are weakly diamagnetic, with magnetic susceptibilities of about -10^{-6}. Minerals containing iron, manganese, and related elements (transition elements in the periodic table), whose atoms act as individual little magnets, are paramagnetic and typically have magnetic susceptibilities of about $+10^{-4}$. Certain paramagnetic materials typified by iron and the common magnetic mineral magnetite have abnormally large susceptibilities (χ is approximately 1 to 10^{+3}) and are called ferromagnetic. In these materials, the individual atomic magnets (*e.g.,* iron atoms) align themselves spontaneously to produce a magnetization even in the absence of an inducing field. A ferromagnetic mineral normally shows little or no net magnetization in bulk because the spontaneous magnetization occurs in microscopic regions, called domains, the magnetic orientations of which point in diverse directions, and which therefore cancel out on the average. Application of a magnetic field causes progressive reorientation of the domains, inducing a net bulk magnetization. The corresponding susceptibility varies with field strength and magnetic history, but it is always large—so large that the bulk magnetic susceptibility of rocks is dominated by their content of ferromagnetic minerals (mainly magnetite), even though these are present only as minor constituents. The magnetic susceptibility χ of most rocks is approximately 0.3 times the magnetite content expressed as volume fraction. Because of regularities in the chemical processes of rock formation, magnetite tends generally to be more abundant in more mafic rock types; hence the susceptibilities of basalts and gabbros (commonly $\chi \sim 10^{-3}$) are as a rule larger than those of most granites, granitic gneisses, and sandstones ($\chi < 10^{-4}$).

Rocks of higher than normal magnetic susceptibility at depth beneath the Earth's surface tend to enhance the Earth's magnetic field locally in the same way that an iron core enhances the field of an electromagnet. The resulting local variations in the Earth's field provide a geophysical tool for assessing the distribution of rock types at depth, especially ore bodies containing magnetic minerals. (W.B.K.)

REMANENT MAGNETIZATION

The variety of magnetite called lodestone is the oldest known example of a ferromagnetic material in which remanent magnetization is retained in the absence of an inducing magnetic field, forming a permanent magnet. Remanent magnetization results from some non-randomness in the orientations of magnetic domains. Rocks containing ferromagnetic minerals can acquire a remanent magnetization that results from the magnetizations of the individual grains.

Temperature and magnetization. The rocks most strongly magnetized are those of igneous origin, namely those rocks thrust up to the Earth's surface in a molten state. Volcanic extrusions of lava and intrusive dikes (tabular bodies that penetrate pre-existing rocks and structures) are examples. These materials contain relatively large amounts of iron oxide minerals and are commonly formed at temperatures greater than about 1,000° C (1,830° F). This temperature is much above the Curie temperature of the magnetite minerals (575° C [1,067° F]), above which ferrimagnetic minerals lose their remanent magnetic characteristics. Hematite loses its remanence above 675° C (1,247° F). This is called the Neel temperature in antiferromagnetic minerals. Upon cooling at the Earth's surface these minerals become strongly magnetized in the direction of the ambient Earth's magnetic field. The temperature at which the rock acquires its magnetization upon cooling in a magnetic field is the blocking temperature. The blocking temperature depends largely on the size and shape of the magnetic domains. Such rocks are said to have acquired thermoremanent magnetization (TRM) because the magnetization is retained after the temperature falls to that of the surface environment and the field is removed. This magnetization is very stable and subsequent exposure of rocks with TRM to magnetic fields several orders of magnitude stronger than the magnetizing field cannot appreciably change the original magnetization.

Thermoremanent magnetization

Acquisition of magnetization. There are several ways in which a specimen may acquire magnetization in an ambient magnetic field; these include:

1. Thermoremanent magnetization (TRM) is as described above.
2. Isothermal remanent magnetization (IRM) is a weak magnetization acquired in a strong magnetic field at constant low temperature, much below the Curie temperature, and in only a matter of minutes. This magnetization is considered soft (less stable) as compared to TRM.
3. Chemical remanent magnetization (CRM) is acquired in a weak magnetic field when new magnetic mineral grains are formed during such chemical reactions as oxidation and dehydration. These reactions occur at low temperatures much below the Curie temperature. The CRM is much like TRM in its strength and stability characteristics.
4. Viscous remanent magnetization (VRM) is acquired at constant low temperature in a weak magnetic field over a time period on the order of millions of years. It is a relatively strong and hard magnetization compared to IRM. The regular thermal agitation of the magnetic domains eventually orders the mineral grains to produce a coherent magnetization.
5. Detrital remanent magnetization (DRM) arises when small magnetic grains that already possess remanent magnetization fall through the Earth's atmosphere or through water and are subjected to the Earth's ambient magnetic field. The grains align themselves to produce an appreciable magnetic effect that is quite stable.

Less frequently encountered types of magnetization include piezoremanent magnetization (PRM), which arises when stress is applied to a specimen in a magnetic field; inverse-type thermoremanent magnetization (ITRM), due to anomalous changes in crystal structure with temperature in the presence of a magnetic field; and anhysteretic remanent magnetization (ARM), which sometimes arises in rock specimens when an external alternating magnetic field is decreased from a maximum value to zero in the presence of a constant magnetic field. In addition many materials acquire a strong magnetization when they are struck by lightning. It is important to note than an existing magnetic field must always be present when a rock is magnetized, regardless of the method.

The total magnetization of a rock may be due to the sum of any or all of these types of remanent magnetization and to a nonremanent (induced) magnetization as well. The ratio of the strength of remanent to induced magnetization is called the (Koningsberger ratio) Q. This ratio has been found to be nearly zero for some sedimentary rocks and characteristically high, approaching 100, for certain marine lava rocks.

Primary magnetization of igneous rocks

The primary or original magnetization of most igneous rocks is generally considered to be TRM. The magnetization of sedimentary rocks is more complex. Certain sediments are believed to contain both CRM and DRM components of primary magnetizations. The former probably results from chemical changes shortly after the sediments are deposited on the sea floor, whereas the latter is acquired as the sediment particles slowly accumulate. The primary magnetization is believed to be acquired in most rocks soon after the rock is formed.

On the basis of that assumption, rock magnetization provides a record of the Earth's magnetic field as it existed at the time of rock formation. This record tends to be obscured by magnetization components impressed later, under changed magnetic fields. Fortunately, however, these later components can often be removed by suitable heat and alternating-field demagnetization treatments without destroying the original magnetization. The permanence of a given magnetization is measured in terms of the corresponding coercive field, which is the strength of the reversed magnetic field required to reduce the bulk magnetization to nil. For the thermoremanent magnetization in bulk samples of magnetite, the coercive field is about 20 oersted units, which, although substantially larger than the Earth's present field (about 0.5 oersted), is considered not stable by comparison with what is achieved in other materials. It appears nevertheless that the magnetite in rocks contributes to the stable thermoremanent magnetization, probably because much of the magnetite is present as grains smaller than the domain size; if elongated in shape, these one-domain grains have a high coercive field (about 500 oersted).

The thermoremanent magnetization acquired by large masses of basalt in the oceanic crust is strong enough to modify measurably the Earth's magnetic field in their vicinity. In certain strip-shaped areas of the ocean floor, the basalts of the oceanic crust are magnetized essentially parallel to the Earth's present field direction, whereas in intervening strips they have the reversed direction of magnetization because they formed at times when the Earth's field was reversed. The magnetic fields from these oppositely magnetized rock masses set up local variations amounting to about 1 percent of the total field. These variations, readily detected by sensitive ship- or air-borne magnetometers, provide a basis for mapping the magnetized strips and inferring the history of formation of the oceanic crust. (W.B.K./J.R.H./J.D.P.)

ELECTRICAL CONDUCTIVITY AND DIELECTRIC BEHAVIOUR

The common rock-forming minerals (silicates, oxides, carbonates, sulfates) are electrical insulators, having resistivities higher than about 10^8 ohm metres (units of ohm times metre) at ordinary temperatures. Many ore minerals (sulfides and sulfosalts) and some oxides (notably magnetite and ilmenite, which are common accessory minerals in rocks) are electronic semiconductors, with resistivities in the range of 10^{-4} to 10^{4} ohm metres. Metallic conductors are rare in nature, with the exception of graphite. The electrical conductivity of rocks depends on mineral content, texture, and porosity in a way similar in most respects to the thermal conductivity. Crack porosity increases the resistivity of dry rocks. A conductive minor mineral component such as graphite, magnetite, or pyrite gives only a modest increase in bulk conductivity if present as isolated grains but gives a large increase if distributed in interconnected networks, such as interstitial cementation in a clastic texture, intersecting fracture fillings, or dendritic (branching) growth structures. Resistivities of slates, for example, are normally several thousand ohm metres but can be reduced to less than one ohm metre by a content of graphite and pyrite amounting to only a few percent.

Resistivities of dry igneous rocks approximate 10^{10} ohm metres at room temperature. Above about 500° C (930° F), the resistivity begins to drop rapidly with temperature. Atoms displaced by thermal agitation out of their stable sites in mineral structures can diffuse through the structures under the force of the electric field, and at high temperatures this type of ionic or electrolytic conduction dominates the electrical behaviour of insulating minerals. Its temperature dependence follows the exponential form for thermally activated processes: $1/\rho = A \exp(-Q/RT)$, in which $1/\rho$ is conductivity [reciprocal resistivity, expressed as $\text{ohm}^{-1}\ \text{m}^{-1}$—that is, 1/(ohm metre)], A is a constant, Q is the activation energy for the conduction process, and R is the gas constant (2 calories per mole per kelvin). For olivine, which is thought to be a major constituent of the outer part of the Earth's mantle (in the rock peridotite), the constant A is 5 $\text{ohm}^{-1}\text{m}^{-1}$ and the activation energy is 16 kilocalories per mole; the resistivity falls from about 10^{6} ohm metres at 200° C (390° F) to about 10^{2} ohm metres at 1,000° C (1,830° F). The resistivities of rocks in the Earth's interior can be calculated from the magnetic effects of currents induced in the interior by current flow in the ionosphere. Resistivities so determined decrease from about 10^{3} ohm metres in the lower part of the crust to one ohm metre in the upper mantle, at a depth of about 600 kilometres (370 miles), and to the order of 10^{-2} ohm metres in the lower mantle. This is doubtless the effect of temperature increase inward. Because ionic conductivity, like diffusion, has a substantial activation volume, it is inhibited by the high pressures in the mantle, and it therefore seems likely that the high conductivities of rocks in the deep mantle are due to appreciable electronic semiconduction at the high temperatures prevailing there.

Resistivity in the Earth's interior

In the shallower parts of the crust, at depths less than about six kilometres, where because of the relatively low confining pressure (less than 2,000 atmospheres) the rocks retain some crack porosity, their electrical properties are dominated by the presence of water. Pure water is a reasonably good insulator (its resistivity is 2×10^{5} ohm metres), but the water present in rocks (groundwater, connate water [water trapped during rock formation]), is moderately conductive due to the presence of dissolved salts; resistivities are commonly in the range one to 10 ohm metres and less commonly as low as that of seawater (0.2 ohm metre) or even lower. Except for rare rock types containing substantial amounts of conductive minerals, the resistivities of water-saturated rocks do not depend on the mineral resistivities but are instead proportional to the resistivities of the contained water and depend sensitively on the amount and nature of the pore space. It is found empirically that for a given type of porosity, the resistivity ρ varies approximately as the inverse square of the porosity η: $\rho = a\,\rho_w \eta^{-2}$. Here a is a constant and ρ_w is the resistivity of the contained water. The empirical constant a depends on the type of porosity: for clastic rocks (interstitial porosity) it is about 0.7, whereas for volcanic rocks it is larger (~1.5), indicating the relatively poor connectivity of the vesicular pore space. Crack porosity is the most effective source of rock conductivity, the value of the constant a for crystalline rocks being about 0.3. It has been found that the increase in crack porosity that occurs in stressed rocks just before brittle failure can be detected by a corresponding decrease in resistivity, thus providing a possible method for anticipating the occurrence of fracture in the Earth, and hence the resultant earthquakes and earth tremors.

Earthquakes predicted by resistivity

For rocks only partially saturated with water, which occur above the water table, the resistivity increases as expected for a reduced porosity corresponding to that portion of the pore space actually occupied by water. Beyond a certain reduction in water content, corresponding to about half of the total porosity, the resistivity increases more rapidly, probably because the connectivity of thin films of water between the mineral grains becomes severed as the water content becomes increasingly lower.

Information about the average resistivities of rocks down to depths of about 100 metres (330 feet) in the Earth is obtained by electromagnetic measurements at radio frequencies. It is found that younger sedimentary rocks generally show resistivities less than 40 ohm metres, older sedimentary rocks and volcanic rocks are intermediate (40–100 ohm metres), and crystalline rocks of low porosity show resistivities greater than 100 ohm metres.

In addition to setting up current flow, an electric field (E) causes the displacement of bound charges in a material medium, creating a state of electric charge displacement called the polarization (P). It is analogous to the magnetization produced by a magnetic field and obeys a similar linear relation between polarization and the electric field producing it: $P = \alpha E$, in which α is the polarizability of the medium, analogous to the magnetic susceptibility χ. The constant α may be calculated directly from a measured quantity, the dielectric constant, $\varepsilon = 1 + 4\pi\alpha$. The dielectric constant is highest in a static (steady state) electric field and generally decreases in alternating fields of progressively higher frequency. At the frequencies of visible light, the dielectric constant equals the square of the refractive index and ranges from 2.3 to 3 for the common rock-forming minerals; at radio frequencies, ε is generally two to three times larger. The corresponding bulk dielectric constants for rocks are given to a reasonable approximation by a volume-weighted average over the mineral components. The effect of porosity can be included by treating the pore space as a component with dielectric constant 1. Water-saturated pore space can also be included, provided account is taken of the great dielectric dispersion (change of ε with frequency) of water near 10^{11} hertz, the dielectric constant dropping from a value of about 85 at lower frequencies to about 5 at higher frequencies.

Rocks containing appreciable amounts of moisture, even absorbed moisture, begin to show departures from the above type of behaviour at frequencies less than about 10^{6} hertz. Below about 10^{4} hertz, the apparent dielectric constant measured by standard techniques begins to increase rapidly with decreasing frequency; the values reported at low frequencies, below one hertz, are prodigious (10^{5} to 10^{8}), higher by many orders of magnitude than the static (zero hertz) dielectric constants of any of the mineral components or water. The high apparent values are probably caused by the flow of electric currents that are unable to pass freely through the rock, owing to internal obstructions along the conductive water films in the rock and to electrochemical blocking either internally or at the measuring electrodes. When the currents are blocked in this way, they result in what appear to be displacements of bound charge and give a large apparent contribution to the dielectric constant ε. The product $\varepsilon\rho\omega$ (in which ρ is the bulk resistivity and ω is the frequency), is found to be nearly frequency-independent over a wide frequency range, from 10^{3} hertz to as low as 10^{-3} hertz. Because the resistivity appears frequency-independent, the apparent dielectric constant at low frequencies thus varies inversely as the frequency. The reciprocal product $1/\varepsilon\rho\omega$ is known as the loss tangent and is the fractional power dissipated per cycle of oscillation of the electric field; it is thus analogous to the specific damping capacity b for elastic waves, which for rocks shows a similar frequency independence. Loss tangents are more useful than dielectric constants for characterizing rocks electrically at frequencies below 1,000 hertz.

Other significant physical properties

HYDRAULIC CONDUCTIVITY

Although porosity indicates the capacity of a rock to store fluids such as water or petroleum, the usefulness of this storage capacity depends on the readiness of extraction or recharge, which is controlled by the permeability (hydraulic conductivity). This is defined in terms of the volume of fluid that will flow per unit time through a rock cross-sectional area under a specified pressure gradient driving the fluid forward. The driving pressure is the excess over the simple hydrostatic pressure that would be present in the fluid at rest and is expressed in terms of the excess fluid head (h). Darcy's law (after Henri Darcy, the French engineer) states a linear relationship between the volume of fluid and the pressure gradient (the decrease in pressure with distance x in the direction of flow, $-dh/dx$) along the fluid flow path: the volume (Q) of fluid flowing through a rock per unit time is equal to the cross-sectional area (A) times the permeability (K) times the driving pressure gradient—*i.e.*, $Q = -AK\,dh/dx$. In engineering practice, Q is expressed in gallons per day and A in square feet; so that, if h and x are taken in the same units, the permeability K has dimensions gallons per day per square foot, a unit also called the Meinzer (after Oscar Meinzer, an American hydrologist). The values of K in these units vary from less than 10^{-5} for crystalline rocks to 10^{6} for gravel; some intermediate values for the permeability of various rock materials to water at 25° C (77° F) are sandstone 10^{-2}–10^{2}, shale 10^{-6}–10^{-4}, limestone 10^{-4}–10, and sand 10^{-2}–10^{4}. Permeabilities for other fluids, or for water at other temperatures, can be obtained from the fact that the permeability is inversely proportional to the fluid viscosity.

Darcy's law

Although the more porous rocks generally have higher permeability, the relationship is greatly affected by the type of porosity: interstitial porosity in a clastic texture, where the pore spaces interconnect, gives a much greater permeability than does vesicular porosity. For porosities of a given geometrical type, the permeability varies directly as the square of the pore dimensions, hence coarse detritus and coarse-grained clastic rocks have much higher permeabilities than their finer-grained counterparts. The strong dependence on pore size distinguishes hydraulic conductivity sharply from electrical conductivity. The wide range of observed permeability values for rock materials of a given type (*e.g.*, 10^{-2}–10^{4} for sand) indicates the influence on pore sizes of various factors in addition to clast size: size sorting, compaction, clast shapes, cementation, etc. Thus clean sands have much higher permeabilities than clay-rich sands, whose interstices tend to be blocked by clay. Crystalline rocks have not only small total porosity, but also thin pores (cracks), and the permeability of sound specimens is for practical purposes nil. Masses of crystalline rock undergound, however, usually show some bulk permeability because of the presence of macroscopic fractures (joints, faults) on a coarse scale; this type of fracture permeability cannot be assessed primarily from laboratory tests on small rock samples.

OPTICAL PROPERTIES

The effects of rocks on visible light are best considered in terms of the optical properties of the individual component minerals, and are best observed in slices of rock about 30 micrometres thick. To the naked eye, the striking optical feature of many rocks is their colour, which derives from the colour of one or more mineral constituents. Striking colours are often caused by minor and petrologically insignificant mineral components, as, for example, in the pink colour of some granites. In most common rocks the colour effects are dominated by iron-containing minerals. Reds, browns, and ochre yellows are caused by oxides or hydrous oxides of ferric iron, and greens by silicates of ferrous iron or by finely divided silicates or hydrous silicates of both ferrous and ferric iron. Less commonly, other metal ions with distinctive absorption spectra in the visible range are responsible for striking rock colourations, when there is local enrichment of the comparatively rare minerals containing these ions: thus blue from copper, pink from manganese or cobalt, green from chromium or nickel, yellow from cadmium, orange from chromium or molybdenum, red from mercury, etc.

Colour effects

The lustre of rock surfaces depends on the component minerals, modified by the effects of grain size: coarse-grained minerals display their inherent lustre, whereas fine-grained aggregates generally are dull. Rock weathering produces a dull lustre because it involves chemical alteration of the original coarse-grained minerals to aggregates of clay and other fine particles. (W.B.K.)

IGNEOUS ROCKS

Igneous rocks are, as discussed earlier, the predominant solid constituents of the Earth, formed through the cooling of molten or partly molten material at or beneath the Earth's surface. As the products of natural melts or magmas, igneous rocks are distinguished from sedimentary rocks, which in general represent either surface accumulations of fragmental materials or mineral precipitates from surface waters. They are also distinguished from metamorphic rocks, which result from the transformation of preexisting solid rocks at depth beneath the surface of the Earth.

Insight to the mineralogical and textural properties of igneous rocks can be gained from their microscopic examination in polarized light, whereas certain aspects of rock structure and origin can be deduced from field study. Experimental work also is of great importance, however. Serious efforts to apply the results of experimental investigation toward an understanding of igneous processes date from nearly two centuries ago, when a Swiss physician, Horace de Saussure, fused several kinds of granitic rocks in his laboratory. In 1798 the English scientist Sir James Hall demonstrated that basaltic rock could be melted and then resolidified to yield either dark-coloured glasses or crystalline mineral aggregates like those in the parent rocks, depending upon the rate of cooling. Half a century later, two French investigators, Élie de Beaumont and Gabriel-Auguste Daubrée, successfully synthesized numerous minerals and rocks. Then, beginning in 1878, more systematic work by two other French scientists, Ferdinand Fouqué and Auguste Michel-Lévy, yielded valuable data on the melting and crystallization of rocks and rock-forming minerals. In several of their syntheses, Fouqué and Michel-Lévy demonstrated the important effects of steam and other fluxing agents (substances used as an aid in fusing and in melting other substances) in promoting crystallization. That the laws of solutions can be applied to magmatic liquids, as first suggested in 1861 by the German chemist Robert Bunsen, was confirmed during the period from 1884 to 1906 by Johan Vogt, a Norwegian geologist and petrologist, who studied the behaviour of silicate slags and drew many parallels with crystallization processes in magmas.

Early experimental work

More rigorous application of the laws of physical chemistry to igneous petrology began at about the turn of the present century, most notably with establishment in 1904 of the Geophysical Laboratory of the Carnegie Institution in Washington, D.C. As techniques were improved and refined in this and in a growing number of other specially equipped laboratories, the experimental approach became increasingly valuable as a controlled simulation of magmatic and allied processes. Perhaps most important, it was combined with theoretical principles to provide a sound basis for determining what can happen and what should not happen in the formation of igneous rocks.

Petrology in the present century has been progressively extended beyond description and classification to include detailed studies of igneous rock masses, their internal structure and compositional variations, and their relationships with other rocks. The generation, emplacement, and consolidation of magmas as chemical systems have been considered in terms of the Earth's thermal budget, compositional inhomogeneities, and structural history; and the timing of many significant crustal events has been established in more recent years through the age dating of igneous rocks by radiometric methods.

Properties of igneous rocks

Igneous rocks form the bulk of the Earth's crust; thus, the crust is mainly a complex product of volcanic and plutonic processes. The geologic record indicates that igneous activity has been widely distributed in space and time and that it has varied considerably in both environment and scale. Its expressions at the Earth's surface have ranged from isolated small eruptions of volcanic ash to vast outpourings of basaltic lava; and at depth, from injection of thin stringers of magma to the emplacement of enormous igneous cores in developing mountain ranges. Magmatic activity has played a vital part in the spreading of ocean basins and has made the principal contributions to the oceanic crust; it also has been closely related to repeated thrusting of oceanic crust beneath the continents. Igneous rocks define much of the present landscape and have directly yielded a variety of materials for the use of mankind. Further, many kinds of valuable mineral deposits are genetically related to them.

Nearly 1,500 different names have been suggested for various igneous rocks, of which about 900 are valid expressions of distinctive rock types. The number is so large because these rocks represent a wide variety of chemical systems and conditions of formation, and because there are so many different physical and chemical bases for description and characterization. The more important of these variations and bases are described below.

CHEMICAL COMPOSITION

The nine principal elements of igneous rocks

Analyses of thousands of igneous rocks indicate that only nine elements—oxygen, silicon, aluminum, iron, calcium, sodium, potassium, magnesium, and titanium—account for more than 99 percent of their total composition. Oxygen and silicon together constitute nearly 75 percent by weight and 93 percent by volume of this total, and aluminum and iron are dominant among the remaining elements. It is interesting to note that many elements of considerable economic value, such as carbon, nickel, copper, lead, zinc, and uranium, are present in igneous rocks at very low levels of average concentration.

Because oxygen is the overwhelmingly preponderant constituent, it is common practice to indicate the chemical composition of igneous rocks in terms of oxides. Table 18 shows the ordinary ranges in levels for the major oxides, and Table 19 shows the percentage of contained silica (SiO_2) in igneous rocks, a useful basis for making the broad distinctions listed. Rocks that are relatively rich in silica and alumina also are referred to as sialic (from the chemical symbols for silicon and aluminum); those relatively rich in iron, magnesium, or certain other constituents are referred to as femic (from the symbols for iron and magnesium). All acid and a few intermediate rocks are called oversaturated because they contain SiO_2 in sufficient abundance to form quartz or other silica minerals in addition to the amounts of silica required to form all other mineral constituents that are present. Correspondingly in this context, undersaturated rocks, which include all ultrabasic as well as some basic and intermediate types, are characterized by a deficiency of SiO_2. Such rocks commonly contain minerals that cannot exist in equilibrium with free silica. Other igneous rocks generally are regarded as essentially saturated in terms of silica.

Table 18: Major Oxide Constituents of Igneous Rocks

constituent	common range (weight percent)	approximate average value (weight percent)
Silica (SiO_2)	35–78	59.1
Alumina (Al_2O_3)	10–21	15.4
Ferric oxide (Fe_2O_3)	0–7	3.1
Ferrous oxide (FeO)	0–10	3.8
Calcium oxide (CaO)	0–12	5.1
Magnesium oxide (MgO)	0–20	3.5
Sodium oxide (Na_2O)	1–7	3.8
Potassium oxide (K_2O)	0–7	3.1
Water (H_2O)	0–2	1.2

Source: Based on approximately 6,000 analyses of fresh rocks and in part adapted from W.A. Richardson and G. Sneesby, "The Frequency Distribution of Igneous Rocks: I. Frequency Distribution of the Major Oxides in Analyses of Igneous Rocks," *Mineralog. Mag.*, (1922).

Table 19: Silica Content in Igneous Rocks

general designation of rock	percentage of silica (SiO_2)*
Acid or silicic	>66
Intermediate	55–66
Subsilicic	
Basic	45–55
Ultrabasic	<45

* >—greater than; <—less than.

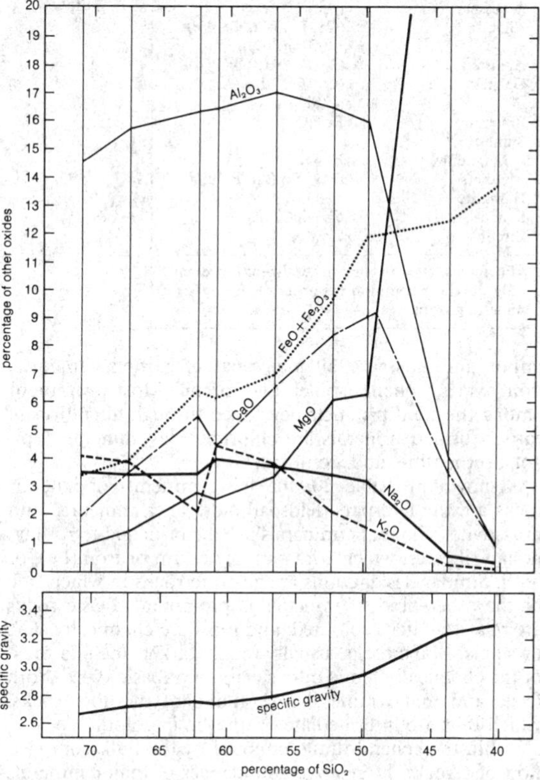

Figure 82: Silica variation diagram, showing trends in chemical composition and specific gravity among the most important groups of igneous rocks.

Alumina tends to be most abundant in the intermediate rocks; CaO in intermediate to basic rocks; and Fe_2O_3, FeO, and MgO in basic and ultrabasic rocks. The alkalies Na_2O and K_2O are much less abundant in such rocks; instead, they are generally concentrated in intermediate to silicic types. Rocks that are relatively rich in the alkalies are known as alkalic or alkaline, the latter term sometimes being restricted to an important group of alkali-rich rocks that contain relatively low percentages of silica and, hence, are undersaturated. Abundance relationships between SiO_2 and the other major oxides of igneous rocks are shown graphically in Figure 82.

MINERAL COMPOSITION

Only a small number of mineral groups are abundantly represented among the common igneous rocks (see above *The major rock-forming minerals*). All are silicates or aluminosilicates, and together they include all of the essential (definitive) minerals and most of the varietal minerals in the major rock types that have been named. The most widespread accessory constituents, ordinarily present in

Table 20: The Common Minerals of Igneous Rocks

mineral groupings	generalized composition*
Essential and varietal	
Felsic	
Quartz, tridymite, cristobalite	SiO_2
Feldspars	
Plagioclases	$(Ca, Na)(Al, Si)_4O_8$
Alkali feldspars	$(K, Na)AlSi_3O_8$
Feldspathoids	
Nepheline	$(Na, K)AlSiO_4$
Leucite	$(K, Na)AlSi_2O_6$
Muscovites	$(K, Na)Al_2(OH)_2 AlSi_3O_{10}$
Mafic	
Olivines	$(Mg, Fe)_2SiO_4$
Pyroxenes	$(Ca, Na)(Mg, Fe, Al)(Si, Al)_2O_6$
Amphiboles	$(Ca, Na)_2(Mg, Fe, Al)_5(OH)_2(Al, Si)_2Si_6O_{22}$
Biotites	$K(Fe, Mg)_3(OH)_2 AlSi_3O_{10}$
Accessory	
Allanite	$(Ca, Fe)_2(Al, Ce, Fe)_3(OH)(SiO_4)_3$
Apatite	$Ca_5(F, OH, Cl)(PO_4)_3$
Garnets	$(Ca, Fe, Mg)_3(Al, Fe)_2(SiO_4)_3$
Ilmenite	$FeTiO_3$
Spinels	
Magnetite	Fe_3O_4
Others	$(Mg, Fe)(Al, Fe)_2O_4$
Hematite	Fe_2O_3
Sphene	$CaTiSiO_5$
Zircon	$ZrSiO_4$

*Formulas, even though generalized, represent only the most common members of the mineral groups.

minor amounts, are allanite, apatite, garnets, ilmenite, iron oxides, sphene, spinel, and zircon. Most prominent among the solid products developed through alteration of earlier formed minerals are chlorites, clay minerals, epidote, serpentine, and iron oxides.

As shown in Table 20, the felsic minerals of igneous rocks are the feldspars, feldspathoids, silica minerals, and muscovite. The mafic minerals are the principal ferromagnesian silicates, which contain magnesium or iron (Fe), or both. Similar designations are given to rocks in which one or the other kind of minerals is prominent. Felsic rocks are relatively light coloured, and most are chemically salic or silicic. Mafic rocks, usually much darker, include most of the chemically femic or basic and ultrabasic types. Both felsic and mafic minerals are abundant in other rocks, which thus are intermediate or uneven in colour.

Within the general limits imposed by the bulk composition of a rock, the relative abundances of major minerals are further limited by their own compositional requirements (Table 20). The high atomic ratio (3:1) of Si to Al and Si to K + Na in alkali feldspars, for example, demands so much silica that the relatively sialic and alkali-rich rocks in which these feldspars are abundant must also be very rich in total SiO_2 if significant amounts of quartz are present. But in the plagioclase feldspars the Si to Al ratio ranges downward to 1:1, and the Si to Na + Ca ratio ranges downward to 2:1. Therefore, these rocks require smaller percentages of silica. This explains why many relatively sialic rocks with high ratios of plagioclase to alkali feldspar contain quartz even though they are not extremely rich in total SiO_2. The effects of these differences in silica requirements can be large because the feldspars are so abundant. This abundance is the main reason why the oversaturated rocks span a fairly broad range in SiO_2 content.

Because the ratio of Ca + Na + K to Al is slightly greater than unity in the average igneous rock, all aluminum in such a rock could be fixed in the form of felsic minerals unless there were substantial amounts of calcium in one or more of the mafic minerals (Table 20). This is in reasonable accord with the 1:1 ratio of Na + K to Al in the alkali feldspars and the feldspathoids and with the somewhat smaller average ratio of Ca + Na to Al in the plagioclases. Where aluminum is present in greater than average abundance, the excess over that required to form feldspars or feldspathoids ordinarily appears in the form of muscovite, biotite, aluminous pyroxenes or amphiboles, accessory minerals, or some combination of these. On the other hand, an excess of alkalies over aluminum commonly results in the development of alkali-bearing pyroxenes, amphiboles, or accessory minerals.

These and other examples can be useful, up to a point, in relating mineral composition to rock chemistry. The compositional constraints that must be involved in the distribution of constituents within igneous rocks explain why certain mineral pairs such as quartz–leucite, quartz–nepheline, quartz–magnesian olivine, and muscovite–pyroxene are not found as products of magmatic crystallization. Such knowledge of compositional constraints permits remarkably accurate predictions concerning the mineralogy of some rocks with known bulk composition, but it is possible for widely different mineral assemblages to exist among rocks of almost identical composition.

TEXTURAL FEATURES

The texture of an igneous rock normally is defined by the size and form of its constituent mineral grains and by the spatial relationships of individual grains with one another and with any glass that may be present. Texture can be described independently of the entire rock mass, and its geometric characteristics provide valuable insights into the conditions under which the rock was formed.

Degree of crystallinity

Among the most fundamental properties of igneous rocks are crystallinity and granularity, two terms that closely reflect differences in magma composition and the differences between volcanic and various plutonic environments of formation. Crystallinity generally is described in terms of the four categories shown in Table 21.

Table 21: Crystallinity Categories of Igneous Rocks

crystallinity	rock term
Entirely crystalline	holocrystalline
Crystalline material and subordinate glass	hemicrystalline or hypocrystalline
Glass and subordinate crystalline material	hemihyaline or hypohyaline
Entirely glassy	holohyaline or hyaline

Those holocrystalline rocks in which mineral grains can be recognized with the unaided eye are called phanerites, and their texture is called phaneritic; some examples are shown in Figure 83. Those with mineral grains so small that their outlines cannot be resolved without the aid of a hand lens or microscope are termed aphanites, and their texture is termed aphanitic; some examples are shown in Figure 83. Aphanitic rocks are further described as either microcrystalline or cryptocrystalline, according to whether or not their individual constituents can be resolved under the microscope. The sub-aphanitic, or hyaline, rocks are referred to as glassy in terms of granularity.

Aphanitic and glassy textures represent relatively rapid cooling of magma and, hence, are found mainly among the volcanic rocks. Slower cooling, either beneath the Earth's surface or within very thick masses of lava, promotes the formation of crystals and, under favourable circumstances of magma composition and other factors, their growth to relatively large sizes. The resulting phaneritic rocks are so widespread and so varied that it is convenient to specify their grain size as shown in Table 22.

Table 22: Categories of Rock Grain Size

terms in common use	general grain size	
	igneous rocks in general	pegmatites
Fine grained	<1 mm	<1 in.
Medium grained	1–5 mm	1 in.–4 in.
Coarse grained	5 mm–2 cm	4 in.–12 in.
Very coarse grained	>2 cm	>12 in.

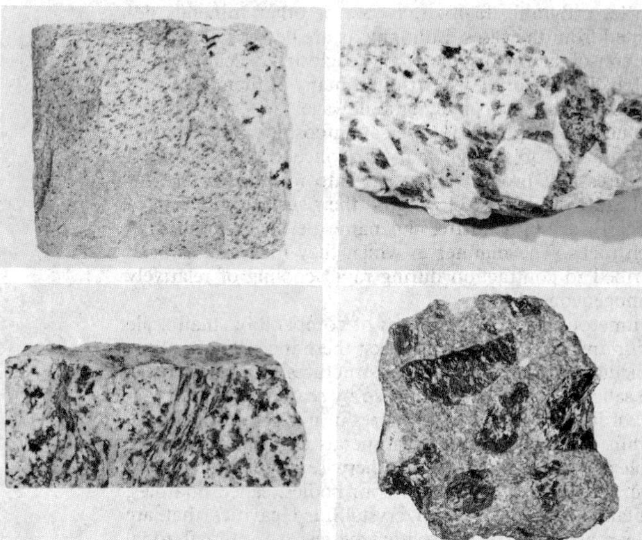

Figure 83: *Textural and structural features of typical phaneritic intrusive rocks.*
(Top left) Fine-grained quartz monzonite in contact with coarse-grained leucocratic granite, Milford, Massachusetts. (Top right) Coarse-grained quartz monzonite grading downward into coarser grained pegmatite, Milford, New Hampshire. (Bottom left) Coarse-grained granite showing flow structure formed by movements in the magma during late-stage crystallization, Conway, New Hampshire. (Bottom right) Very coarsely porphyritic lamprophyre (camptonite) with anhedral phenocrysts of hornblende, near Hoover Dam, Arizona–Nevada border. The specimens range from four to six inches in maximum dimension.
Richard H. Jahns

The general grain size ordinarily is taken as the average diameter of dominant grains in the rock; for the pegmatites, which are special rocks with extremely large crystals, it can refer to the maximum exposed dimensions of dominant grains. Most aphanitic rocks are characterized by mineral grains less than 0.3 millimetre (0.01 inch) in diameter, and those in which the average grain size is less than 0.1 millimetre (0.004 inch) commonly are described as dense.

A major part of rock texture is fabric or pattern, which is a function of the form and outline of its constituent grains, their relative sizes, and their mutual relationships in space. Many specific terms have been employed to shorten the description of rock fabrics, and even the sampling offered here may seem alarmingly extensive. It should be noted, however, that fabric provides some of the most useful clues to the nature and sequence of magmatic crystallization.

The degree to which mineral grains show external crystal faces can be described as euhedral or automorphic (fully crystal faced), subhedral or hypautomorphic (partly faced), or anhedral or xenomorphic (no external crystal faces). Quite apart from the presence or absence of crystal faces, the shape, or habit, of individual mineral grains is described by such terms as equant, tabular, platy, elongate, fibrous, rodlike, lathlike, needlelike, and irregular. A more general contrast can be drawn between grains of equal (equant) and inequal dimensions. Even-grained, or equigranular, rocks are characterized by essential minerals that all exhibit the same order of grain size, but this implied equality need not be taken too literally. For such rocks the combination terms automorphic-granular, hypautomorphic-granular, and xenomorphic-granular are applied according to the occurrence of euhedral, subhedral, and anhedral mineral grains within them. Many fine-grained xenomorphic-granular rocks are more simply termed sugary, saccharoidal, or aplitic.

Porphyritic texture

Rocks that are uneven grained, or inequigranular, are generally characterized either by a seriate fabric, in which the variation in grain size is gradual and essentially continuous, or by a porphyritic fabric, involving more than one distinct range of grain sizes. Both of these kinds of texture are common. The relatively large crystals in a porphyritic rock ordinarily occur as separate entities, known as phenocrysts, set in a groundmass or matrix of much finer grained crystalline material or glass (see Figure 84). The size of phenocrysts is essentially independent of their abundance relative to the groundmass, and they range in external form from euhedral to anhedral. Most of them are best described as subhedral. Because the groundmass constituents span almost the full ranges of crystallinity and granularity, porphyritic fabric is abundantly represented among the phaneritic, aphanitic, and glassy rocks.

The sharp break in grain size between phenocrysts and groundmass reflects a corresponding change in the conditions that affected the crystallizing magma. Thus, the phenocrysts of many rocks probably grew slowly at depth, following which the nourishing magma rose to the Earth's surface as lava, cooled much more rapidly, and congealed to form a finer grained or glassy groundmass. Other porphyritic rocks may well reflect less drastic shifts in position and perhaps more subtle and complex changes in conditions of temperature, pressure, or crystallization rates. Many phenocrysts could have developed at the points where they now occur, and some may represent systems with two fluid phases, magma and coexisting gas. Appraisals of the composition of phenocrysts, their distribution, and their periods of growth relative to the accompanying groundmass constituents are important to an understanding of many igneous processes.

The articulation of mineral grains is described in terms of planar, smoothly curved, sinuous, sutured, interlocked, or irregular surfaces of mutual boundary. The distribution and orientation of mineral grains and of mineral grains and glass are other elements of fabric that can be useful in estimating the conditions and sequence of mineral formation in igneous rocks. The following are only a few of the most important examples:

Directive textures are produced by the preferred orientation of platy, tabular, or elongate mineral grains to yield grossly planar or linear arrangements; generally a result of magmatic flowage.

Graphic texture refers to the regular intergrowth of two minerals, one of them generally serving as a host and the other appearing on surfaces of the host as striplike or cuneiform units with grossly consistent orientation; the graphic intergrowth of quartz in alkali feldspar is a good example.

Ophitic texture is the association of lath-shaped euhedral crystals of plagioclase, grouped radially or in an irregular mesh, with surrounding or interstitial large anhedral crystals of pyroxene; it is characteristic of the common rock type known as diabase.

Richard H. Jahns

Figure 84: *Textural and structural features of typical aphanitic and glassy volcanic rocks.*
(Top left) Vesicular basalt with large crystals of plagioclase (labradorite), Sonora, Mexico. (Top right) Porphyritic andesite with bladelike phenocrysts of hornblende in aphanitic matrix, Mount Shasta, California. (Bottom left) Aphanitic basalt with scattered white crystals of plagioclase, Lassen Peak, California. (Bottom right) Felsite with taffy-like flow layering, Iron Mountain, New Mexico. The specimens are from four to five inches in maximum dimension.

Poikilitic texture describes the occurrence of one mineral that is irregularly scattered as diversely oriented crystals within much larger host crystals of another mineral.

Reaction textures occur at the corroded margins of crystals, from the corrosive rimming of crystals of one mineral by finer grained aggregates of another, or as a result of other features that indicate partial removal of crystalline material by reaction with magma or other fluid.

Replacement textures occur where a mineral or mineral aggregate has the external crystal form of a pre-existing different mineral (pseudomorphism) or where the juxtaposition of two minerals indicates that one was formed at the expense of the other.

Finally, crystal zoning describes faintly to very well defined geometric arrangements of portions within individual crystals that differ significantly in composition (or some other property) from adjacent portions; most common are successive shells grouped concentrically about the centres of crystals, presumably reflecting shifts in conditions during crystal growth.

STRUCTURAL FEATURES

The structure of an igneous rock is normally taken to comprise the mutual relationships of mineral or mineral–glass aggregates that have contrasting textures, along with layering, fractures, and other larger scale features that transect or bound such aggregates. Structure often can be described only in relation to masses of rock larger than a hand specimen, and most of its individual expressions can be closely correlated with physical conditions that existed when the rock was formed.

Vesicles and amygdules

Small-scale features. Among the most widespread structural features of volcanic rocks are the porelike openings left by the escape of gas from the congealing lava. Such openings are called vesicles, and the rocks in which they occur are said to be vesicular. Where the openings lie close together and form a large part of the containing rock, they impart to it a slaglike, or scoriaceous, structure. Their relative abundance is even greater in the type of sialic glassy rock known as pumice, which is essentially a congealed volcanic froth. Most vesicles can be likened to peas or nuts in their ranges of size and shape; those that were formed when the lava was still moving tend to be flattened and drawn out in the direction of flow. Others are cylindrical, pearlike, or more irregular in shape, depending in part on the manner of escape of the gas from the cooling lava; most of the elongate ones occur in subparallel arrangements.

Many vesicles have been partly or completely filled with quartz, chalcedony, opal, calcite, epidote, zeolites, or other minerals. These fillings are known as amygdules, and the rock in which they are present is amygdaloidal. Some are concentrically layered, others also include centrally disposed series of horizontal layers, and still others are featured by central cavities into which well-formed crystals project.

Features of glassy rocks

Spherulites are light-coloured subspherical masses that commonly consist of tiny fibres and plates of alkali feldspar radiating outward from a centre. Most range from pinpoint to nut size, but some are as much as several feet in diameter. The relatively large ones tend to be internally complex and to contain concentric shells of feldspar fibres with or without accompanying quartz, tridymite, or glass. Spherulites occur mainly in glassy volcanic rocks; they also are present in some partly or wholly crystalline rocks that include shallow-seated intrusive types. Many evidently are products of rapid crystallization, perhaps at points of gas concentration in the freezing magmas. Others, in contrast, were formed more slowly, by devitrification (formation of minute crystals) of volcanic glasses, presumably not long after they congealed and while they were still relatively hot.

Lithophysae, also known as stone bubbles, consist of concentric shells of finely crystalline alkali feldspar separated by empty spaces; thus, they resemble an onion or a newly blooming rose. Commonly associated with spherulites in glassy and partly crystalline volcanic rocks of salic composition, many lithophysae are about the size of walnuts. They have been ascribed to short episodes of rapid crystallization, alternating with periods of gas escape when the open spaces were developed by thrusting the feldspathic shells apart or by contraction associated with cooling. The curving cavities commonly are lined with tiny crystals of quartz, tridymite, feldspar, topaz, or other minerals deposited from the gases. Lithophysae are developed early in the consolidation history of the enclosing volcanic rocks and, like early-formed spherulites, many of them show the effects of subsequent magmatic flowage.

Some glassy rocks of silicic composition are marked by domains of strongly curved, concentrically disposed fractures that promote breakage into rounded masses of pinhead to walnut size. Because their surfaces often have a pearly or shiny lustre, the name perlite is applied to such rocks. The manner in which they fracture has been ascribed to contraction during rapid cooling of relatively homogeneous glass.

Numerous structural features of comparably small scale occur among the intrusive rocks; these include miarolitic, orbicular, plumose, and radial structures. Miarolitic rocks are salic phanerites distinguished by scattered pods or layers, ordinarily several centimetres in maximum thickness, within which their essential minerals are coarser grained, subhedral to euhedral, and otherwise pegmatitic in texture. Many of these small interior bodies, called miaroles, contain centrally disposed crystal-lined cavities that are known as druses or miarolitic cavities. An internal zonal disposition of minerals also is common, and the most characteristic sequence is alkali feldspar with graphically intergrown quartz, alkali feldspar, and a central filling of quartz. Miarolitic structure probably represents local concentration of gases during very late stages in consolidation of the host rocks.

The term orbicular is applied to rounded, onion-like masses with distinct concentric layering that are distributed in various ways through otherwise normal-appearing phaneritic rocks of silicic to basic composition. The layers within individual masses are typically thin, irregular, and sharply defined, and each differs from its immediate neighbours in composition or texture. Some layers contain tabular or prismatic mineral grains that are oriented radially with respect to the containing orbicule and, hence, are analogous to spherulitic layers in volcanic rocks. The minerals of most orbicules are the same as those of the enclosing rock, but they are not necessarily present in the same proportions. The concentric structure appears to reflect rhythmic crystallization about specific centres, commonly at early stages in consolidation of the general rock mass.

The normal fabric of some relatively coarse-grained plutonic rocks is interrupted by clusters of crystals with radial grouping but without concentric layering. A characteristic plumelike, spraylike, or rosette-like structure is imparted by the markedly elongate form of the participating crystals or crystal aggregates, which seem to have developed outward from common centres by direct crystallization from magma or by replacement of pre-existing solid material.

Large-scale structural features. Many kinds of larger scale features occur among both the intrusive and the extrusive rocks (see Figure 85). Most of these are mentioned

Richard H. Jahns

Figure 85: Irregular branching dikes and tongues of medium-grained quartz diorite in darker coloured gabbro and metamorphic rocks, near Escondido, California. The boundaries are sharply defined, and very thin, straight stringers of light-coloured aplite transect all the other rocks.

later in connection with rock occurrence or are discussed in other articles, but several are properly introduced here:

Clastic structures. Various features that express the accumulation of fragments or the rupturing and dislocation of solid material. In volcanic environments they generally result from explosive activity or the incorporation of solid fragments by moving lava; as such, they characterize the pyroclastic rocks. Among the plutonic rocks, they appear chiefly as local to very extensive zones of pervasive shearing, dislocation, and granulation, commonly best recognized under the microscope. Those developed prior to final consolidation of the rock are termed protoclastic; those developed after final consolidation, cataclastic.

Flow structures. Planar or linear features that result from flowage of magma with or without contained crystals. Various forms of faintly to sharply defined layering and lining typically reflect compositional or textural inhomogeneities, and they commonly are accentuated by concentrations or preferred orientation of crystals, inclusions, vesicles, spherulites, and other features.

Fractures. Straight or curving surfaces of rupture directly associated with the formation of a rock or later superimposed upon it. Primary fractures, distributed on various scales and in various patterns, generally can be related to emplacement or to subsequent cooling of the host rock mass. The columnar jointing found in many basic volcanic rocks is a typical result of contraction upon cooling.

Inclusions. Rounded to angular masses of solid material enclosed within a rock of recognizably different composition or texture. Those consisting of older material not directly related to that of their host are known as xenoliths, and those representing broken-up and detached older parts of the same igneous body that encloses them are termed cognate xenoliths or autoliths.

Xenoliths and autoliths

Pillow structures. Aggregates of ovoid masses, resembling pillows or grain-filled sacks in size and shape, that occur in many basic volcanic rocks. The masses are separated or interconnected, and each has a thick vesicular crust or a thinner and more dense glassy rind. The interiors ordinarily are coarser grained and less vesicular. Pillow structure is formed by rapid chilling of highly fluid lava in contact with water or water-saturated sediments, accompanied by the development of budlike projections with tough, elastic crusts. As additional lava is fed into each bud, it grows into a pillow and continues to enlarge until rupture of the skin permits escape of fresh lava to form a new bud and a new pillow.

Segregations. Special types of inclusions that are intimately related to their host rocks and in general are relatively rich in one or more of the host-rock minerals. They range from small pods to extensive layers and from early-stage crystal accumulations formed by gravitational settling in magma to very late-stage concentrations of coarse-grained material developed in place.

Zonal structures. Arrangement of rock units with contrasting composition, or texture, in an igneous body, commonly in a broadly concentric pattern. Chilled margins, the fine-grained or glassy edges along the borders of many extrusive and shallow-seated intrusive bodies, represent quick freezing, or quenching, of magma along contacts with cooler country rock. Other kinds of zones generally reflect fractional crystallization of magma and are very useful in tracing courses of magmatic differentiation, as will be noted later.

COLOUR AND SPECIFIC GRAVITY

Differences between the inherently light colours of the felsic minerals and the darker colours of most mafic minerals can be useful indications of general rock composition. Colour index, which is either employed directly or is implied in nearly all classifications of igneous rocks, is simply the sum of the mafic minerals expressed as a volume percentage of the entire rock. It is correlated with the common descriptive terms shown in Table 23.

Colour index

Table 23: Terminology Based on Colour Index

rock term	colour index
Leucocratic	<30
Mesocratic	30–60
Melanocratic	60–90
Hypermelanic	>90

The colour index may or may not correspond to the gross colour of a rock in terms of lightness or darkness. Many of the iron-poor mafic minerals, for example, are pale green, gray, or otherwise not dark coloured. Thus, a rock rich in a magnesian olivine may be lighter coloured than one rich in a dark-gray plagioclase, despite its much higher colour index. Colour also can be misleading if taken as a guide to the composition of individual minerals or of very fine-grained or glassy rocks. Thus, crystals of alkali feldspar in many coarse-grained leucocratic rocks are dark reddish brown, and many highly silicic volcanic glasses appear dark gray or black. The more meaningful colour index, dependent on recognition of component minerals, is readily determinable only among the phanerites.

Most light-coloured rocks also are light in weight, and hence there is a fairly consistent relationship between colour index and specific gravity (the ratio of the weight of a substance to the weight of an equal volume of water, the specific gravity of which is expressed as 1). Specific gravity ranges between extremes of 2.6 and 3.4 among the more common igneous rocks (Figure 82) and between 2.7 and 2.9 for most leucocratic and mesocratic rocks without vesicles or other large voids. Both specific gravity and colour index tend to increase with increasing percentages of iron and magnesium and with increasing ratios of iron to magnesium and calcium to alkalies.

Classification of igneous rocks

CLASSIFICATIONS BASED ON MINERALOGY AND TEXTURE

An ideal classification would clearly relate origin and mode of occurrence, mineral and chemical composition, and all major physical properties for the many known kinds of igneous rocks. These features are interrelated in such complex ways, however, that the ideal cannot even be approached without introducing cumbersome qualifications and details. Thus, most practical classifications are based primarily upon elements of composition and texture, and they represent various compromises among such factors as adequate coverage of the most common rock types, simplicity and consistency, adaptability for work without a microscope, and retention of long-established concepts and terms.

One kind of useful compromise is illustrated in Table 24. The lines in this chart are drawn solely for convenience in recognizing general positions of the indicated properties and names; they are not intended to suggest that clear-cut breaks exist between adjoining categories, as the actual situation in nature ordinarily is one of transition. The igneous rocks are divided into clans on the basis of mineral composition and implied chemical composition, and the arrangement of the clans reflects progressive increases in colour index and specific gravity from left to right. A general shift from acid rocks to basic and ultrabasic rocks occurs in the same direction, although between the granite and diorite clans there are alternations among clans of oversaturated rocks and ones of saturated or undersaturated rocks. Salic alkaline rocks, such as nepheline syenite and phonolite—here included with the syenite clan—are sometimes treated as members of a separate clan. Another alkaline clan of basic rocks, such as leucite basalt and the alkali gabbros, could be similarly distinguished from the normal gabbro clan.

Rock clans

Quartz, alkali feldspar, and plagioclase are the essential minerals used to define nearly all of the clans in Table 24. Those clans in the left-hand and central parts of the chart are characterized by high percentages of total feldspars; those in the right-hand part, by percentages of feldspars decreasing to a minimum in the ultrabasic clan. Comparison with Figure 86 will indicate how the ratio of alkali feldspar to plagioclase, an important element of this classification, decreases progressively from left to right in the chart and how plagioclase composition shifts from sodic to calcic in

Table 24: General Megascopic Classification of Igneous Rocks

rock clan		granite	syenite	quartz monzonite (adamellite)	monzonite	grano-diorite	quartz diorite (tonalite)	diorite	gabbro	ultrabasic rocks
general trends	colour	light					intermediate			dark
	colour designation	leucocratic				mesocratic		melanocratic		hypermelanic
	specific gravity	low					intermediate		high	
	major constituents	felsic minerals							mafic minerals	
principal felsic essential minerals	ratio of alkali feldspar to plagioclase	2:1 or greater		2:1 to 1:2		1:2 to 1:7	1:7 or less	1:2 or less	alkali feldspar rare or absent	feldspars rare or absent
	quartz	with quartz	without quartz	with quartz	without quartz	with quartz		without quartz		
textural categories (volcanic—plutonic; extrusive—occurrence—intrusive)	*phanerites* even- or uneven-grained, porphyritic or nonporphyritic	granite	syenite nepheline syenite*	quartz monzonite (adamellite)	monzonite (syeno-diorite)	grano-diorite	quartz diorite (tonalite)	diorite	gabbro alkali gabbro* anorthosite† diabase	peridotite pyroxenite hornblendite dunite magmatic ores
		aplites								
		pegmatites								
	aphanites porphyritic or nonporphyritic	rhyolite	trachyte phonolite*	quartz latite (rhyodacite)	latite (trachy-andesite)	quartz latite	dacite (rhyodacite)	andesite	lamprophyres basalt scoria	‡
		felsites								
	glasses porphyritic	vitrophyres			‡	‡	‡		tachylyte (sideromelane)	‡
	glasses non-porphyritic	obsidian pitchstone pumice perlite			‡	‡	‡		palagonite	‡
					‡	‡	‡	‡	‡	‡
	fragmental rocks clastic	tuffs, volcanic breccias, and agglomerates								§

*Sometimes considered to represent a separate alkali-rich clan characterized by essential alkali feldspars or feldspathoids or both. †Unusually felsic member of gabbro clan with predominant plagioclase. ‡Representatives of clan unknown or extremely rare. §Represented mainly by special kinds of intrusive breccias.

the same direction. The crystalline rocks in four of the clans contain quartz to the extent of 10 percent or more in the granite clan and five percent or more in the others. Rocks of the remaining clans contain lesser amounts or are quartz free, as jointly indicated by "without quartz" in Table 24 (see also Figure 86). The megascopic distinction between the diorite and gabbro clans can be drawn from the relative abundances of felsic and mafic minerals or, alternatively, on the basis of the principal mafic minerals, amphibole in the dioritic rocks and pyroxene or olivine in the gabbroic ones.

The chemical trends among common representatives of the major clans are shown in the silica variation diagram of Figure 82. Here the rocks are arranged from left to right in order of decreasing SiO_2 content, from acid to ultrabasic types. Minor differences between this order and

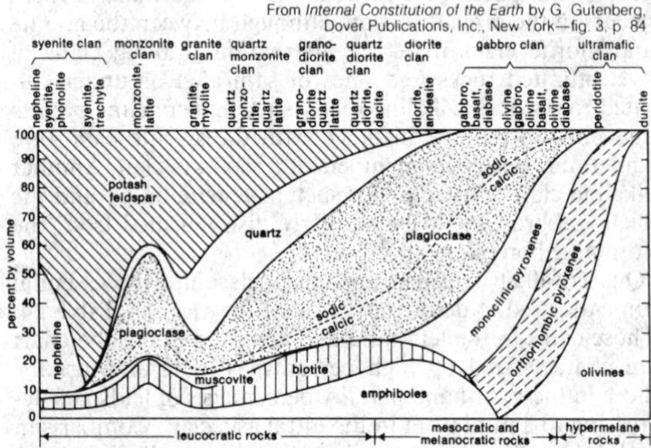

Figure 86: Semi-quantitative representation of mineral composition among the major igneous rock clans and families. The alkali feldspars are represented by the potash feldspar field plus the upper part of the sodic plagioclase field.

that of clans in the classification chart, which is based mainly upon feldspar ratios and colour index, correspond to reversed trends in the plots for Na_2O and K_2O in the variation diagram. The reversals are attributable chiefly to differences in the ratio of alkali feldspar to plagioclase, as already noted in connection with rock composition. On this score, the abundance of quartz in rocks of the quartz diorite to granite range, with SiO_2 contents of 62 percent to more than 70 percent, correlates with the range in which the general trend in CaO content is opposite from those of Na_2O and K_2O.

Major elements of texture provide a means for dividing the various clans into rock families that are represented among the phanerite, aphanite, glass, and fragmental categories. Three of these four textural groups include porphyritic rock types, but an additional category of porphyries is commonly employed to distinguish rocks with more than 20 percent of phenocrysts in groundmasses that are fine-grained, aphanitic, or glassy. The individual rock names noted in the chart are those in most general use, and several other common names that are synonymous or nearly so are shown in parentheses. Typical rock types can be designated texturally and related to geological occurrence, as indicated by the examples from the granite and gabbro clans shown in Table 25.

Exceptions to the classification scheme

Some common rock types are exceptional relative to some aspect of the scheme of classification, others do not fit readily into a single category, and many others are so fine-grained (or glassy) that they must be grouped on the basis of chemical composition rather than essential mineralogy. Thus, anorthosite, though a felsic rock, is a legitimate member of the gabbro clan because of its close genetic associations with more typically basic rocks; and diabase, a more mafic rock distinguished by ophitic texture, is found in both plutonic and volcanic environments. Wide ranges in composition characterize the aplites, which

Table 25: Geologic Occurrence and Textural Designation of Typical Rock Types

typical geologic occurrence	general textural designation	rock family*
Plutonic, intrusive		
Abyssal	phanerite	granite (hornblende-biotite granite); gabbro (olivine gabbro)
Hypabyssal	porphyry	rhyolite porphyry (biotite rhyolite porphyry); basalt porphyry (augite basalt porphyry)
Volcanic, extrusive		
	aphanite	rhyolite (spherulitic rhyolite); basalt (scoriaceous basalt)
	glass	rhyolite (obsidian); basalt (tachylite)
	pyroclastic rock	rhyolite (crystal tuff); basalt (basalt agglomerate)

*Example of specific rock type is given in parentheses.

are felsic rocks with fine-grained, sugary texture, and the pegmatites, generally felsic rocks that are in part extremely coarse-grained. Individual occurrences are identified by such combination terms as granodiorite aplite and granite pegmatite, and most can be variously assigned to the granite, syenite, and quartz monzonite clans. The lamprophyres—in effect extending across the diorite, gabbro, and ultrabasic clans—are special mesocratic to hypermelanic porphyritic rocks with alkaline groundmasses. They ordinarily are classified according to their dominant mafic minerals; like other and more abundant types of alkaline rocks, they have been subdivided into a host of specifically named varieties.

Light-coloured aphanites with relatively few phenocrysts or none at all are simply termed felsites, and those light-coloured porphyries in which the phenocrysts cannot be readily identified are referred to as felsite porphyries. Obsidian is relatively massive volcanic glass with vitreous lustre. Pitchstone also is massive but generally contains more water, has a resinous or pitchy lustre, and is more extensively cracked. Both these natural glasses tend to be dark coloured, mainly because of finely divided mafic accessory constituents, but they are compositional correlatives of only the most leucocratic types among the holocrystalline rocks. A similarly restricted range characterizes their porphyritic equivalents, the vitrophyres. Pumice and perlite, distinguished, respectively, by froth and fracture structures, have a compositional range that extends little beyond that of the granite clan. The basic part of the rock spectrum is represented among the glasses by tachylite, which generally is dark coloured and crowded with tiny crystals, and by palagonite, which contains substantial amounts of water and has a duller lustre. The name palagonite also is applied to yellowish and brownish rocks consisting of altered basaltic glass with or without grains or fragments of plagioclase and mafic minerals.

Pyroclastic rocks

The pyroclastic rocks are those formed partly or wholly of solid fragments accumulated during volcanic eruptions. Agglomerates are coarse accumulations of lava clots and bombs that were erupted in a liquid or plastic state, and breccias consist mainly of angular blocks that were solid when accumulated from volcanic vents or incorporated within moving lava. Both blocks and bombs are greater than 32 millimetres (1.3 inches) in diameter. Fragments with diameters in the range 4–32 millimetres (0.16–1.3 inches) comprise lapilli (rounded) and cinders (rough, angular); smaller fragments include volcanic ash, sand, and dust. Combinations of the finer grained materials constitute volcanic tuffs and the matrices of tuff breccias. Tuffs can be subdivided into lithic, crystal, and vitric types according to whether they consist principally of crystalline rock fragments, separate crystals and crystal fragments, or bits of glass, respectively. Welded tuffs, often mistaken for congealed lava, are composed primarily of particles that were sufficiently hot and plastic to be fused together at the time of deposition or emplacement.

CLASSIFICATION ACCORDING TO CHEMICAL COMPOSITION

Classifications based upon chemical composition have fundamental advantages over all other schemes. They directly and quantitatively relate rocks to one another as products of natural chemical systems; they also permit useful comparisons of rock types with the results of experimental investigations on synthetic systems of known composition. Such schemes, which begin with compositional information that can be no more than inferred in classifications like that shown in Table 24, are of special value in dealing with very fine grained or glassy rocks. The required data, however, can be obtained only from chemical analyses or, less satisfactorily, from calculations based upon mineral composition. And, when such data are available, they apply more to magmas than to rocks unless the data are combined with knowledge of texture, mineral content and sequence, and geologic occurrence of the rocks involved.

Most chemically based classifications express certain definite combinations of constituents that are well known among the principal rock-forming minerals. In the widely used CIPW system (the letters refer to the last names of the four men who devised the system), for example, a given rock analysis is recast in the form of "standard mineral molecules" to yield the norm, an assemblage of specifically selected minerals that theoretically could have developed from a magma of the indicated bulk composition. The rock is then classified according to the proportions of calculated normative minerals. All minerals of the norm actually are present in many rocks, but in most rocks some are not. Also, the assemblage of minerals actually present, known as the mode, commonly includes some that are not considered in the "standard" normative suite. Nonetheless, major constituents such as quartz and the feldspars generally appear in both the norm and mode of a given rock.

Formation of igneous rocks

NATURE OF MAGMAS

Ionic constituents

Magmas are chemically complex fluid systems that differ in many ways from ordinary solutions, in which water is the solvent and the dominant constituent. They can be thought of as mutual solutions, or melts, of rock-forming components that are variously present as simple ions (atoms that carry positive or negative electric charges), as complex ions and ionic groups, and as molecules. The most abundant of the simple ions in common magmas are such singly and doubly charged cations (positive ions) as Na^+, K^+, Ca^{2+}, Mg^{2+}, and Fe^{2+}. Because these ions can move about rather freely in the system, they occupy no fixed positions with respect to other ions that are present. In contrast, the smaller and more highly charged cations, notably Si^{4+}, Al^{3+}, and (to a lesser degree) Fe^{3+}, are surrounded or screened by O^{2-} ions and other anions (negative ions) to form parts of relatively stable complex ions such as $(SiO_4)^{4-}$, $(AlO_4)^{5-}$, and $(FeO_6)^{9-}$. Simple anions, including F^-, Cl^-, O^{2-}, and $(OH)^-$, ordinarily are present in much smaller amounts. Water, hydrochloric acid (HCl), hydrogen fluoride (HF), carbon dioxide (CO_2), and other volatile molecular substances occur as well, generally in equilibrium with ionic forms such as $(OH)^-$, Cl^-, F^-, and $(CO_3)^{2-}$.

Because the bond that unites silicon and oxygen is a remarkably strong one, $(SiO_4)^{4-}$ ions are stable in magmas even at very high temperatures. They also tend to join with one another, or polymerize, to form more complex anionic groups, a tendency that is especially great in the more silicic magmas. The joining is accomplished by a sharing of oxygen ions between adjacent silicon ions to form Si-O-Si bridges like those in many silicate and aluminosilicate minerals; in the simplest such case, $(Si_2O_7)^{6-}$ ions are the result. Because the $(AlO_4)^{5-}$ ions also have a strong tendency to polymerize, most of the large ionic groups in magmas probably contain both silicon and aluminum ions. These groups, which resemble the frameworks of many rock-forming minerals but are geometrically less regular, significantly affect the viscosity and crystallization of magmas.

Viscosity of magmas

The viscosity of magmas, which spans an enormous range of values, affects their flow behaviour, the movements of crystals and inclusions of foreign matter within them, the diffusion of materials through them, and the growth of crystals from them. It increases greatly with decreasing temperature and less markedly with increasing pressure. Viscosity also can be governed in part by the amount and distribution of any solid materials or bubbles of gas present. Finally, it varies considerably among magmas of differing gross composition, mainly because of the differences in the degree of Si-O and Al-O polymerization. Thus, highly silicic magmas generally are more viscous than basic ones by several orders of magnitude, a difference reflected by contrasts in the eruptive behaviour of rhyolitic and basaltic lavas. The presence of volatile constituents can markedly increase the fluidity of magmas, even those that are rich in SiO_2. This effect has been attributed to the breaking of Si-O-Si bridges (depolymerization) through substitution of ions such as F^- and $(OH)^-$ for shared O^{2-} ions in elements of the polymerized groups.

A typical magma can be broadly viewed as an assemblage of relatively large and rather closely packed oxygen ions, among which some cations have considerable mobility; others, such as Si^{4+} and Al^{3+}, tend to occupy positions that are more fixed. The entire system is a dynamic one, however, and even the largest of the Si-O and Al-O ion groups are constantly changing form and position as bonds are broken and new ones are established. If the magma quickly loses thermal energy and cools to a glass, these internal movements are sharply restricted, and the various constituents become essentially frozen in position. If cooling is slower, the contained complex ions and polymerized ion groups have time to assume more regular arrangements and to be stabilized by cations of appropriate size, charge, and other properties. Crystalline solids are thereby formed. Their regular internal structure is relatively conserving of space, and hence they have somewhat higher specific gravities than the magma from which they were nourished.

CRYSTALLIZATION FROM MAGMAS

Regardless of their cooling rates, magmas consolidate over ranges of temperature that vary with composition and generally amount to hundreds of degrees. Completely fluid basaltic lavas generally have temperatures in the range of 1,000° to 1,150° C (1,830° to 2,100° F), and during the course of their solidification they may retain some capacity for flowage at temperatures as low as 700° C (1,300° F). Rhyolitic lavas have lower initial temperatures, generally in the range of 850° to 950° C (1,560° to 1,740° F), and most lavas of intermediate composition seem to have correspondingly intermediate temperatures between this and the basaltic range. Plutonic magmas of basic composition probably are emplaced chiefly in a temperature range similar to that of basic lavas, and those of more silicic composition in the range of 800° to 950° C (1,470° to 1,740° F). There is little reason to believe that magmatic temperatures on or within the Earth's crust are significantly higher than about 1,150° C, except for some plutonic magmas of ultrabasic composition and possibly some basic lavas under special conditions of gas discharge.

Magmatic temperatures

Crystallization of most intrusive magmas probably begins at temperatures between 800° and 1,100° C (1,470° and 2,000° F) and continues through ranges of a few tens of degrees to as much as 300°. The levels and lengths of these ranges depend mainly upon compositional factors, including any volatile fluxing agents that may be present. Thus, many granitic magmas containing dissolved water, for example, may not be completely solidified until they cool to points within the 600°–700° C (1,100°–1,300° F) range. Special types of volatile-rich magmas, such as those that form pegmatites and lamprophyres, can remain partly fluid at temperatures below 600° C.

The melting points of all important rock-forming substances except ice are raised by increasing pressure, a significant factor in the generation and emplacement of magmas. Because pressure also affects, in contrasting degrees, the respective solubilities of different minerals in magmas, it exercises some control on the sequence of crystallization. More importantly, it strongly controls the amounts of water and other substances that a magma can hold in solution. And, where such substances are present as a separate dense gas phase at high pressures, they can exercise a significant solvent action on silicate minerals.

Prevailing pressures

The confining pressure exerted upon a lava flow at the Earth's surface is essentially one atmosphere (about one kilogram per square centimetre); that upon a body of intrusive magma is related mainly to the weight of the overlying column of rocks. Where pressure is equivalent to this weight, it is termed lithostatic pressure. This pressure increases at a rate of about 100 atmospheres for every 375 metres (1,300 feet) of depth beneath a cover of silicic igneous rocks or the lighter coloured sedimentary rocks and their metamorphic counterparts. It increases at higher rates in the more basic, denser parts of the Earth's crust. The rates of increase are by no means uniform in detail, however, because the crust is far from homogeneous.

Most large bodies of intrusive magma probably crystallize under confining pressures ranging from about 1,000 to 10,000 atmospheres. A notable range in pressure also must be expected for any single body with a large vertical extent, the result of progressive changes, with increasing depth, in the lithostatic load, the mass of overlying magma, and the Earth's gravitational field. A directed pressure also is present where the magma is under stress other than that due to load, as in regions of crustal compression. Magmas that reach points high in the Earth's crust also can be under confining pressures that are less than the prevailing lithostatic pressures if water-filled fissures or other interconnected openings traverse the column of overlying rocks. The term hydrostatic pressure is applied in such situations, as its effective value relates to the water rather than to the denser rocks.

PHASE EQUILIBRIA IN SILICATE MELTS

The apportioning of constituents among the mineral phases in a crystallizing magma is a complicated process that is governed primarily by temperature, pressure, and composition of the system. Many textural and structural features in igneous rocks indicate that the contained minerals were formed in part simultaneously and in part sequentially, and this is confirmed by phase-equilibrium studies in the laboratory.

Diopside-anorthite equilibria

Under a pressure of one atmosphere, the pyroxene diopside ($CaMgSi_2O_6$) melts at a temperature of 1,391° C (2,536° F), and the plagioclase anorthite ($CaAl_2Si_2O_8$) melts at 1,553° C (2,874° F). When a mixture of these two substances is heated, however, melting begins at only 1,274° C (2,293° F) and yields a liquid with a composition corresponding to 57 percent diopside and 43 percent anorthite (see Figure 87). Continued melting under equilibrium conditions generates increasing amounts of this same liquid at a constant temperature of 1,274° C until all of one substance melts. The remainder of the other substance then melts as the temperature rises. Viewing the process in reverse (and referring to Figure 87), the cooling

From American Journal of Science, vol. 240 (1942)

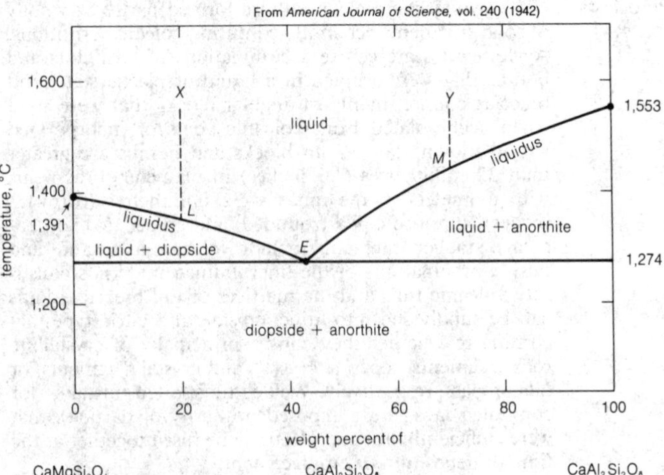

Figure 87: Equilibrium diagram showing melting and crystallization relationships of diopside and anorthite in the system $CaMgSi_2O_6$–$CaAl_2Si_2O_8$ at a pressure of one atmosphere.

of a melt with composition *X* begins to yield crystals of diopside at a temperature near 1,350° C (2,460° F; point *L*). With further cooling, additional diopside forms at steadily decreasing temperature, and the liquid becomes progressively enriched in $CaAl_2Si_2O_8$ until, at 1,274° C, anorthite begins to crystallize at what is termed the eutectic point (*E* in the diagram). The path of diopside crystallization thus far completed is represented by the line *LE*, a part of the liquidus for the system. The liquidus is the line along which liquid and solid phases are in equilibrium and above which no solid phase can exist in equilibrium.

Once the eutectic point is reached, the remaining liquid is used up in simultaneous crystallization of diopside and anorthite in a constant ratio and at a constant temperature to form a eutectic mixture of composition *E*. Because of the presence of earlier formed diopside, the overall ratio of the two minerals in the final solid product corresponds to the initial composition *X*. Similar relationships obtain if the composition of the initial melt is richer in the $CaAl_2Si_2O_8$ component, as represented by *Y* in the diagram, except that anorthite now begins to crystallize at the liquidus (point *M*). It continues to form until the eutectic point *E* is reached, when diopside also begins to appear. In the special case of an initial liquid with eutectic composition, crystallization begins and ends with a eutectic mixture at a constant temperature of 1,274° C.

Eutectic melting relationships characterize many pairs of minerals, among them diopside–albite, diopside–leucite, enstatite–quartz, quartz–albite, albite–olivine, and albite–nepheline. Other pairs, in marked contrast, form solid solutions; these include such important rock-forming constituents as the olivines, plagioclases, and alkali feldspars (see also above).

BOWEN'S REACTION SERIES

By correlating observations of mineral relationships in igneous rocks with data from experimental studies, the American petrologist Norman L. Bowen identified the principal reactions that can take place during crystallization of ordinary magmas. He ordered the most common mineral products into two reaction series, one continuous and the other discontinuous. The former comprises the plagioclase feldspars and represents a general solid–solution relationship; *i.e.*, one in which there is continuous variation in feldspar. The discontinuous series, comprising reaction pairs of mafic mineral groups, indicates that under many circumstances olivines react with residual liquid to form pyroxenes, that pyroxenes react with residual liquid to form amphiboles, and that amphiboles similarly react to form biotites. Within each of these groups are solid solutions that bespeak continuous reaction; the discontinuous reactions occur only between groups and series of compounds in a crystallizing melt.

The continuous and discontinuous series

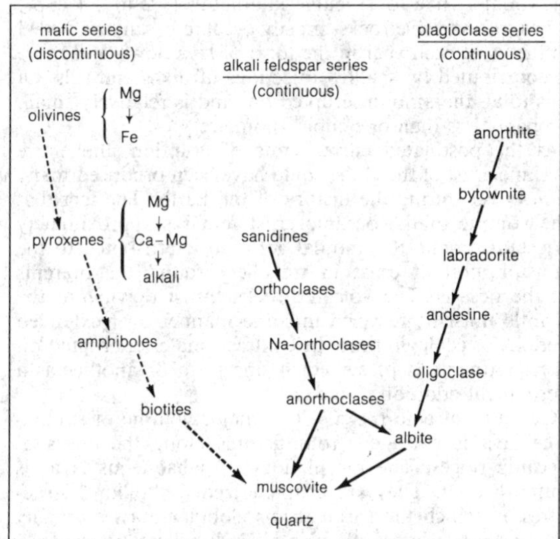

Figure 88: Trends in the major reaction series that occur among the crystalline igneous rocks.

The two series generally are shown in a Y-shaped arrangement (Figure 88) in order to suggest their gradual convergence toward a single series, and a third series can be added to represent continuous reaction among the alkali feldspars and their merging with sodic members of the plagioclase series. The diagram indicates the progression of events to be expected as magmas cool, and relative temperatures are implied in the vertical distribution of its various parts. Minerals in the relatively low-temperature region of convergence, chiefly the stem of the Y, are not included on the general basis of reaction relationships. Instead, these minerals with adjacent members of the feldspar series reflect various approaches to eutectic crystallization.

The mineral groups of the mafic series differ markedly from one another in terms of crystal structure. As shown in Figure 89, the discontinuous reactions involve changes in structural arrangements from isolated SiO_4 groups (olivines) to single chains (pyroxenes) to double chains (amphiboles) to sheets (micas). This is in contrast to the consistent presence of three-dimensional framework struc-

Adapted from H. Von Eckermann, *Sime Notes on the Reaction Series*

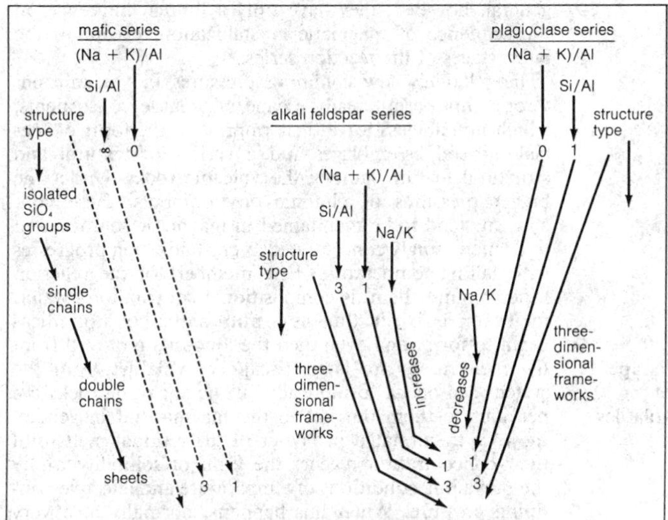

Figure 89: Principal trends in composition and structure type among minerals of the reaction series shown in Figure 88.

tures in the other series. A noteworthy chemical convergence of all three series results from the compositional shifts within each of them. Thus, initially different atomic ratios of Si to Al converge to a common value of three, and the ratios of Na + K to Al to a common value of one. Muscovite and quartz do not reflect these trends, which is compatible with their positions farther down on the diagram and outside the region of reaction relationships.

The reaction series not only express broad compositional trends between liquid and crystals during the cooling of a magma, but they also suggest what can happen when it is in contact with foreign solid materials. If a foreign mineral belongs to one of the reaction series but represents an earlier stage of that series than the minerals being crystallized from the magma, it can be converted by reaction to later stage minerals, just as if it had been formed earlier from the magma. If it represents a later stage, it can be dissolved by the magma. A foreign mineral that does not belong to one of the series also will tend to react with the magma, thereby causing shifts in composition of both the liquid and the crystalline phases being formed from it. In addition, a magma might also react to some extent with the surrounding wall rock, affecting its composition. Consequently, new mineral assemblages could form.

The presence of a certain mineral in an igneous rock does not necessarily indicate that it was developed by reaction from another mineral higher in its series, because the overall composition of the system dictates whether or not certain minerals can form. A calcium-free magma, for example, can yield no diopside or intermediate plagioclase, and a potassium-free magma can yield no orthoclase or leucite. Some magmas, in effect, encompass the entire span of the reaction series; whereas others complete their crystallization in the upper parts, and still others begin theirs in the lower parts. Finally, the specific courses of crystallization can vary considerably with respect to the timing of events within and between the reaction series, in part because of the fractionation of different elements among the many solid phases forming in a typical system. Despite these and other complexities of detailed application, the reaction principle is an extremely valuable indicator of general sequence and compositional trends in magmatic processes.

VOLATILE CONSTITUENTS AND LATE MAGMATIC PROCESSES

Influences on the properties and behaviour of magmas

Effects of water and other volatiles. Water and most other volatile substances profoundly influence the properties and behaviour of magmas in which they are dissolved. They reduce viscosity, lower temperatures of crystallization by tens to hundreds of degrees, and participate directly in the formation of minerals that contain essential hydroxyl (OH) or elements such as the halogens. They also increase rates of crystallization and reaction, especially when they are present as a fluid phase distinct from the magma. In general, however, they have only a limited influence on the sequence of magmatic crystallization, except in the latest stages of the reaction series.

The relatively low confining pressures in volcanic environments permit ready escape of volatile constituents, which nonetheless leave their imprint in the form of special mineral assemblages and a variety of textural and structural features among the volcanic rocks. Under the higher pressures of plutonic environments, these constituents tend to be maintained in magmatic solution and to be increasingly concentrated as crystallization progresses with falling temperature. Few members of the reaction series require them as compositional contributors; water, for example, is not thus used until amphiboles or micas begin to form, and even then the amounts removed from the melt rarely are large. Escape of volatiles from the system can occur "osmotically" if the enclosing rocks are pervious to them but not to the magma, but in general they are fractionated in favour of the residual melt until their concentration reaches the limit of solubility under the prevailing conditions of temperature and effective confining pressure. When this happens, normally at a very late stage of magmatic crystallization, they are exsolved from the melt as a separate fluid phase that under most circumstances is a supercritical gas. This process has been referred to as resurgent boiling, a somewhat misleading term because the exsolved fluid is not necessarily expelled from the system.

Escape of volatiles

Pegmatites and late-stage mineralization. Coexistence of residual magma and a volatile-rich fluid (generally aqueous) promotes the partitioning and segregation of constituents, as well as the growth of very large crystals.

Richard H. Jahns

Figure 90: Giant lathlike crystals of spodumene in very coarse-grained pegmatite, Harding mine, Dixon, New Mexico. These crystals, 1.2 to 3 metres (four to 10 feet) long, have been warped, cross fractured, and "healed" with quartz (dark). Spodumene, a lithium pyroxene, forms the largest crystals known among the igneous rocks.

The exsolved fluid, with its very low viscosity, not only can move readily through open spaces in the nearly solid igneous rock and in adjacent rocks but also serves as a medium through which various substances can diffuse rapidly in response to concentration gradients. Thus, it plays an important role in the formation of such special rock types as the pegmatites (Figure 90) and lamprophyres, special features such as miaroles and plumose mineral aggregates, and many kinds of ore deposits whose constituents are derived from the original magma.

Most plutonic systems remain at elevated temperatures for long periods of time after all magma has been used up, and during these periods hydrothermal conditions normally obtain. These depend upon the continued presence of a typically aqueous fluid that further facilitates crystallization and exchanges of materials. It speeds up exsolution within homogeneous solid phases and devitrification of any glass that may be present, and it is a potent agent in the alteration, leaching, and replacement of minerals. Rock textures thereby are modified, especially along boundaries between original mineral grains, and details of composition also can be much changed. In some instances the bulk chemistry of the rock is markedly affected.

Among the constituents commonly added during hydrothermal alteration are water, hydroxyl, carbon dioxide, boron, fluorine, chlorine, and sulfur. Calcium and magnesium ordinarily are subtracted, silicon is either added or subtracted, and aluminum and the major alkalies are shifted about in complex ways. The alterations favour development of phases such as albite, carbonates, chlorites, clay minerals, epidotes, iron oxides, micas, silica minerals, talc, and zeolites, and many of them are accompanied by gross changes in volume. (R.H.J.)

Occurrence of igneous rocks

EXTRUSIVE IGNEOUS ROCKS

The behaviour of magma at the Earth's surface is governed by an interplay of factors that include scale and rate of extrusion, timing of extrusive episodes, shape and distribution of vents, nature of the surrounding rocks, configuration of the surface that is occupied, and the temperature, composition, and gas content of the magma itself. The natural result is a great variety of volcanic bodies with considerable ranges in form and size. Some of them express relatively quiet effusions of lava, and others express explosive production of pyroclastic debris.

Rates and volumes of eruption. The average rate of production of extrusive igneous rocks is not much different today from what it has been during most of geologic time. Although there have been episodes when volcanism was especially intense in certain regions, there is no evidence that the average volcanicity over long periods of time has either declined or increased by any substantial factor. Approximately five to 10 cubic kilometres (1.2 to 2.4 cubic miles) of extrusive rocks, mostly oceanic basalt, are added to the crust each year in the form of lava flows, and more is contributed by shallow injections of dikes and sills. Of this total, the amount erupted on land is relatively small, probably less than one cubic kilometre.

At the postulated current rate of eruption, the entire oceanic crust of the globe could have been produced many times over during the history of the Earth. The fact that the volume of the oceanic crust remains approximately constant despite this annual addition is attributed to the consumption of crust in trenches around the margins of the oceans. The volcanic rocks thrust down into the mantle must be recycled in some manner over extended periods of geologic time. In contrast, material erupted on the continents is preserved in one form or another as a permanent addition to the crust.

Oceanic volcanic rocks. The major volume of submarine lava is extruded from fissures along the crests of oceanic ridges. The morphology of subaqueous lavas is quite distinct. They are characterized by "pillow" structures, in which the basalt forms globular masses roughly the size and shape of pillows. Each pillow has a dark, glassy shell of quickly chilled lava encasing a crystalline interior that cooled more slowly. Under the pressure of

Interaction of submarine lavas and seawater

several thousand metres of water, there is little exsolution of the water vapour and other gases that are dissolved in fluid basalt, so that gas bubbles (vesicles) are small or totally absent. At shallower levels and lower water pressures, the size and number of vesicles increase. On the submarine slopes of Hawaii, for example, there is a progressive increase in the proportion of gas cavities in the lavas from the base of the volcano up to sea level. At shallow depths, where bubbles expand to a large volume and expose a wider surface area to the quenching action of water, the glass may shatter into myriads of small, angular fragments. Masses of this material, sometimes referred to as hyaloclastites, may accumulate in deposits several hundreds of metres thick in which the lavas have disintegrated to the point where they are unrecognizable as distinct flow units. Alteration and hydration of this fragmental glass advance rapidly and convert it to palagonite, a yellowish-brown mixture of clay and other secondary minerals. Chemical alteration of basalt in seawater results in a steady loss of sodium, calcium, manganese, and magnesium and a gain of potassium, titanium, iron, and water.

Prolonged activity at a centralized submarine vent produces broad symmetrical cones, or "shield volcanoes," that may reach enormous size. According to recent estimates, there are more than 20,000 submarine volcanoes with a relief of more than 1,000 metres (3,300 feet). Although only a small number of these volcanoes grow large enough to reach the surface and emerge as islands, there are hundreds, if not thousands, of submarine volcanoes that exceed the height and volume of Mt. Etna, in Sicily, the largest volcano on land.

Oceanic basalts, such as those of Hawaii or the Galápagos Islands, are erupted at temperatures between 1,050° and 1,200° C (1,920° and 2,200° F). Their viscosity is unusually low (about 2,000 to 4,000 poises), so that the flows move rapidly down gentle slopes toward the sea. Lava with a smooth or ropelike surface texture, called pahoehoe by the Hawaiians, is common, especially near the source, but a clinkery scoriaceous type of lava, called aa, is also abundant. Many of the lava eruptions come from radial or concentric fissure vents around the summit. Eruptions from fissures on the flanks of Hawaiian volcanoes produce especially voluminous flows, commonly at rates as high as 10,000 to 20,000 cubic metres (353,000 to 706,000 cubic feet) per day. The average rate of outpouring during historic time for the island of Hawaii is approximately 0.025 cubic kilometres (0.006 cubic miles) per year.

Tholeiitic and alkali basalts

Basalts are by far the dominant rocks of the oceanic environment. They account for all but a minute fraction of submarine lavas and at least 90 percent of the volume of most oceanic islands. The basalts, though superficially uniform, vary significantly within certain broad compositional limits. Most common are the tholeiitic basalts, which normally contain about 50 percent silica (Table 26) and crystallized labradorite, augite, titaniferous magnetite, and in some cases a calcium-poor pyroxene. Olivine may be abundant as large crystals (phenocrysts), but it is not found as a stable mineral in the fine-grained matrix. The dark iron-magnesium minerals account for more than 40 percent of the volume. Basalts of this type are by far the most abundant submarine lavas, and they make up a major portion of many volcanic islands, such as Hawaii and Iceland.

With decreasing silica content and a corresponding increase in sodium, potassium, magnesium, and titanium, tholeiitic basalts grade into the somewhat less common group of alkali basalts (Table 26). Olivine is an important constituent of the fine-grained matrix of these rocks; the augite is richer in titanium; and calcium-poor pyroxenes are absent. Basalts of this type appear in the late stages of activity in Hawaii; but elsewhere in the oceans, especially on islands far removed from the oceanic ridges, they may be the only type of basalt in the emergent part of the volcano. Extreme varieties of alkali basalt grade into basanites, which, in addition to the other minerals just named, contain a silica-deficient aluminous mineral, such as nepheline.

Table 26: Chemical Composition of Typical Oceanic Volcanic Rocks
(percentages by weight)

	tholeiitic basalt	alkali basalt	nepheline basanite	icelandite	mugearite	trachyte	phonolite
SiO_2	49.5	46.5	44.3	59.3	51.9	65.3	55.8
TiO_2	2.0	3.0	2.6	1.1	2.6	0.7	0.3
Al_2O_3	14.5	14.6	12.8	14.5	16.0	14.8	19.2
Fe_2O_3	3.0	3.3	3.4	3.4	4.2	3.2	2.3
FeO	8.5	9.1	9.2	4.6	6.3	1.5	0.9
MnO	0.2	0.1	0.2	0.1	0.2	0.1	0.1
MgO	6.6	8.2	11.0	2.0	3.7	0.6	0.2
CaO	10.6	10.3	10.5	4.8	6.3	1.2	0.9
Na_2O	2.1	2.9	3.6	4.4	5.2	6.1	9.8
K_2O	0.4	0.8	1.0	2.1	2.0	3.0	5.7
P_2O_5	0.3	0.4	0.4	0.5	0.8	0.2	0.1

Rocks of the orogenic system. The igneous rocks that are erupted in the course of development of mountain-building systems have a character and a geologic association that are distinct from those of the igneous rocks of the oceans. Modern examples are closely related to the linear volcanic belts, trenches, and zones of earthquake activity that follow the boundaries between some of the oceanic and continental regions, and it seems likely that similar relations prevailed in the past.

Spilites and keratophyres

In the early geosynclinal stages—when large volumes of clastic sediments such as sandstones are accumulating in a subsiding trough—volcanic rocks are normally erupted from vents near the landward margin of the deepest part of the geosyncline. These vents may not necessarily be large composite cones; many are probably fissures. Basaltic and andesitic pyroclastic material and detritus from subaerial erosion contribute a large volume to the sedimentary material poured into the trough. At the same time, submarine lavas or shallow intrusions of dikes and sills are interlayered with the sediments. Many submarine lavas from this environment have unusually high sodium contents and distinctive mineral assemblages. Basalts of this type are called spilites, and the more siliceous rocks, keratophyres. Both contain a sodic plagioclase—albite or oligoclase—and abundant chlorite, greenish pyroxene, epidote, and calcite. To a large degree, these rocks owe their present compositional features to low-grade metamorphism under submarine conditions. Not all submarine lavas of this environment are spilites; nor are all spilites confined to the orogenic association—they have also been reported from modern oceanic ridges. It is believed, therefore, that many of the basaltic lavas found in geosynclinal sediments were erupted much earlier on the floor of the deep ocean basin far from their present site, were subjected to various degrees of alteration, and were then carried into the trench as part of the oceanic crust. In this sense, they belong to the true oceanic series considered in the preceding section.

The great majority of orogenic volcanic rocks are erupted from large andesitic cones, much like those that are seen today in the island arcs and continental margins of the circum-Pacific. They normally form a belt parallel to an oceanic trench, about 100 to 150 kilometres (60 to 90 miles) away from the trench on the continental side. Strong negative-gravity anomalies are found near the axis of the trench, and positive ones are common, though less distinct, along the volcanic axis.

Andesitic volcanoes

The lavas of even the largest andesitic cones are much less voluminous than those of oceanic volcanoes. Individual eruptions seldom produce more than a few thousand cubic metres of lava, and there are usually long intervals between events, especially in older volcanoes. The proportion of explosive pyroclastic ejecta is higher than that of oceanic volcanoes and in some regions may account for a larger volume than lava.

The calc-alkaline suite

In contrast with the great diversity of oceanic rocks, the extrusive rocks of tectonically active zones are relatively similar wherever they occur. They belong to what is commonly called the calc-alkaline series because of their relatively high proportion of plagioclase components. Andesite is by far the most voluminous and characteristic rock of this suite. Although there are minor variations that distinguish the andesites of island arcs, continental margins, or interior regions of continents, almost all of them share several principal features in common. They contain between 53 and 60 percent silica and have very abundant plagioclase; dark minerals, such as pyroxene, hornblende, and magnetite, make up less than 40 percent of their volume. Although the rocks are rich in silica and rarely have olivine, few contain quartz. Almost all of the calc-alkaline rocks are markedly porphyritic; that is, they have an important fraction of crystals, mainly plagioclase, that are much larger than the minerals of the matrix in which they are set.

Basalt, normally rich in alumina, commonly appears early in an episode of orogenic volcanism and may form the broad base upon which the large andesite cones are subsequently built. Basalt may also be erupted at late stages as small flows from scattered subsidiary vents around the flanks of the main cones, but in some regions, such as parts of the Cascade Range of the Pacific Northwest, it is absent or trivial in volume.

Differentiated rocks, such as dacite and rhyolite, differ from andesite in that they have fewer iron-magnesium minerals and more alkali feldspar and quartz. Typical chemical compositions of members of the calc-alkaline suite are given in Table 27. Dacite and rhyolite are often

Table 27: Chemical Composition of Typical Continental Volcanic Rocks
(percentages by weight)

	high-alumina basalt	andesite	dacite	rhyolite	lamprophyre
SiO_2	52.8	58.6	63.6	74.6	40.7
TiO_2	1.1	0.8	0.6	0.2	3.9
Al_2O_3	18.0	17.5	16.7	12.6	16.0
Fe_2O_3	3.4	3.2	2.2	1.3	5.4
FeO	5.7	3.5	3.0	1.0	7.8
Mn	0.1	0.1	0.1	0.0	0.1
MgO	4.7	3.2	2.1	0.1	5.8
CaO	9.3	6.3	5.3	0.6	9.2
Na_2O	3.1	3.8	4.0	4.2	3.5
K_2O	1.3	1.7	1.8	4.7	2.0
P_2O_5	0.5	0.2	0.2	0.2	0.6

erupted from mature andesitic volcanoes as viscous flows or, more often, as pumiceous pyroclastic ejecta. They rarely constitute a large part of andesitic cones in orogenic belts, but they have been erupted in great volumes from linear or arcuate fissures that may be unrelated to older andesitic volcanoes. This latter type of occurrence is discussed more fully below.

Evidence from experimental studies

Andesites have been ascribed to at least three major genetic processes—differentiation of basaltic magma by crystal fractionation, contamination of basaltic magma with granitic material of the continental crust, and generation of a primary magma by partial melting of the mantle. Experimental studies have shown that basaltic liquids can differentiate to andesitic compositions under conditions where olivine, pyroxene, and abundant magnetite crystallize and settle out of the magma. A condition essential to this process is a high oxidation state of the liquid; this may be induced by the water-bearing sedimentary and metamorphic rocks through which andesites must rise to reach the surface.

Continental flood lavas. The most voluminous extrusions of lava in the geological record are the vast sheets of basalt that have poured out in several regions at widely spaced intervals of time. The lava flows of Iceland are the only modern example, and these are relatively small compared with prehistoric flows in other regions. The 1783 eruption of the Icelandic volcano Laki spread 12.3 cubic kilometres (three cubic miles) of basalt over an area of 565 square kilometres (220 square miles). This is a relatively small flow compared with some of the lavas that were erupted on the Columbia River plateau some 10,000,000 to 15,000,000 years ago and covered an area of about 500,000 square kilometres (193,000 square miles). Some of the Columbia River lavas have been traced as far as 150 kilometres (90 miles) and have volumes as great as 300 cubic kilometres (72 cubic miles). Other examples of flood lavas are the Late Cretaceous and Early Tertiary (about 65,000,000 years ago) Deccan basalts of India, which still cover an area of 650,000 square kilometres (251,000 square miles), and the Jurassic (136,000,000 to 190,000,000 years ago) Paraná basalts of Paraguay and Brazil, which cover more than 750,000 square kilometres (290,000 square miles).

In all of these regions, the source vents were long fissures rather than cones with central vents. The high fluidity of the lavas produced wide areas of low relief that never rose much above sea level, despite the great thickness of accumulated lavas. Subsidence of the base of the volcanic pile seems to have kept pace with the outpouring of lavas on the surface.

Siliceous ignimbrite sheets

The only other igneous extrusive rocks that approach the extent of flood basalts are the silica-rich ignimbrite sheets that have been erupted from fissure vents to spread over wide areas of the continents. These rocks differ from basalt both in composition and in their mode of eruption. They must have contained large amounts of gas, which exsolved and disrupted the liquid as it emerged from the vent, but, instead of being ejected vertically as in normal pyroclastic eruptions, the hot fluidized mixture of gas, magma, and crystals flowed with great mobility as a turbulent cloud across the surface. Few eruptions of this type have been observed during historic times, and those few examples that have been described by eyewitnesses were all small, but there is plentiful evidence that very large eruptions of this type covered wide areas in the past. Much of Nevada, Utah, and adjacent parts of the Great Basin of the western United States were once covered by ignimbrites to depths of several hundred metres. Similar deposits are found in western Mexico, central Honduras, and along the western slope of the Chilean Andes. Most of these examples were erupted during Tertiary time (from 2,500,000 to 65,000,000 years ago), but some of the ignimbrites of North Island, New Zealand, have been erupted within the last few thousand years. (A.R.McB./Ed.)

INTRUSIVE IGNEOUS ROCKS

Intrusive igneous rocks result when magma cools and solidifies below the surface of the Earth. During intrusion, the magma must either displace or dissolve the surrounding rock (called country rock) to make room for itself. The intrusive contact (the surface along which intrusive rock touches the country rock) commonly cuts across the structures of the preexisting rock, suggesting a vertical rise of magma under pressure (see below *Emplacement of magma*).

Occurrence

Intrusive igneous rocks make up the deeply eroded portions of some mountain ranges (*e.g.*, the Sierra Nevada of California and large parts of the Andes), but in others (including the Appalachians, Pyrenees, Himalayas, and the Atlas Mountains) these rocks are subordinate to metamorphic (altered) rocks and deformed sedimentary rocks. On a smaller scale, individual volcanic mountains, when deeply dissected by erosion, reveal intrusive cores formed by magma that froze in the throats of the volcanoes. Mt. Kenya, Tahiti Nui, and Mt. Pelée are examples of volcanic cones reinforced against erosion by resistant intrusive spines and ribs (see Figure 91). The "swelling" of volcanoes shortly before eruption and studies of old, deeply eroded volcanoes indicate that a large portion of a volcanic cone may be intrusive rock, rather than extrusive or pyroclastic material.

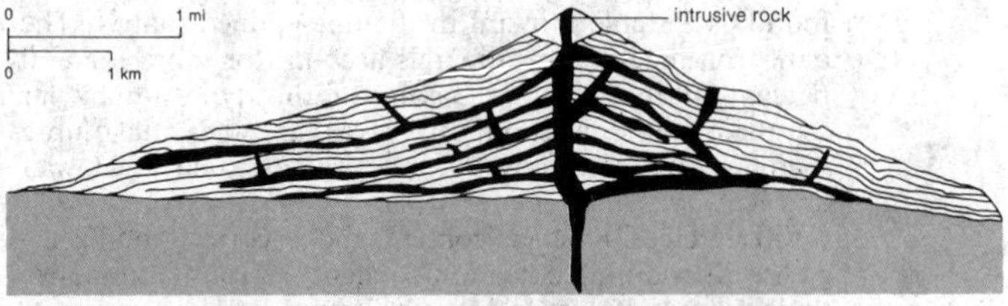

Figure 91: Cross section of a volcano showing intrusive rock in the form of a central neck or spine giving rise to ribs.

In all of the continents, intrusive igneous rocks make up approximately half of the ancient shield areas, or so-called basements, forming a rigid, stable foundation beneath veneers of younger extrusive, pyroclastic, and sedimentary rocks.

The most practical mineralogical classification of intrusive igneous rocks utilizes the following data: presence or absence of quartz or feldspathoids; proportions of quartz, feldspathoids, alkali feldspar, plagioclase feldspar, and mafic minerals.

The presence or absence of quartz (SiO_2) or of the feldspathoids, the commonest of which is nepheline, is significant because quartz and feldspathoids cannot coexist in the same igneous rock. Such chemical reactions as the combination of nepheline and quartz to yield albite, namely,

$$\underset{\text{(nepheline)}}{NaAlSiO_4} + \underset{\text{(quartz)}}{2SiO_2} = \underset{\text{(albite, sodium feldspar)}}{NaAlSi_3O_8},$$

produce feldspar until all the quartz or all the feldspathoid is consumed. The presence or absence of quartz or feldspathoids therefore provides an absolute criterion based upon the degree of silica saturation. If a rock contains sufficient silica to make quartz, the rock is silica oversaturated, and, if the rock contains so little silica that feldspathoids are stable, it is silica undersaturated. Magnesium-rich olivine is another mineral that is stable only in silica-undersaturated rocks. Some rocks have ratios of silica to sodium, potassium, and aluminum such that alkali feldspar but neither quartz nor feldspathoids is stable; such rocks are called silica saturated.

Aside from quartz and feldspathoids, which make up less than 50 percent of most rocks and may be entirely absent in some, the other important mineral groups are feldspars and mafic minerals.

Major intrusive rock types. *Ultramafic rocks.* These rocks, characterized by a content of at least 90 percent mafic minerals, are further classified on the basis of the percentage of olivine, pyroxene, or carbonate minerals present (see Table 28).

Laboratory experiments show that ultramafic rocks become molten at very high temperatures. On the other hand, field relations indicate that many such rocks were intruded as solid masses (no molten material was present) and therefore are not strictly igneous. Country rock near the intrusive contacts with ultramafic rocks rarely shows any effect of strong heating, which is in conflict with the laboratory investigations. Regardless of the degree of care with which such experiments are performed, however, it must be asked whether they imitate the actual processes taking place in nature. As a solution to the conflict between field and laboratory evidence, some recent experiments suggest that addition of small amounts of potassium will lower the melting temperatures of ultramafic rocks by several hundred degrees. These results indicate that ultramafic rocks could be intruded as relatively cool magma and thus be incapable of intensely baking the adjacent rocks. Upon solidification of the magma, the potassium would likely be released and carried away in solution. The existence of ultramafic magmas is demonstrated by the recent recognition of ultramafic lava flows in South Africa, Western Australia, Cyprus, and Siberia.

The Earth's mantle (the zone beneath the crust) is thought to be made up of ultramafic rock, specifically peridotite. One line of evidence leading to this conclusion is the presence of ultramafic fragments within some intrusive and extrusive rocks that have been carried upward by magma and frozen within the igneous rock. Some such fragments contain assemblages of minerals that should have formed, according to experiments, at depths exceeding 100 kilometres (60 miles).

Serpentinites

Ultramafic rocks are highly susceptible to mineralogical changes produced by reaction with water at low temperatures. The olivine and pyroxene originally present may be completely replaced by the mineral serpentine, a hydrous magnesium silicate. Serpentinites, altered ultramafic rocks, occur in belts outlining the trends of ancient eroded mountain ranges and, according to one current hypothesis, represent slices of mantle pushed into the crust during collision of migrating oceanic and continental crustal plates. Serpentinites are commercially important as sources of talc and asbestos. Unaltered and serpentinized ultramafic rocks are the major sources of chromium and platinum.

Kimberlite is a mica-bearing peridotite that contains large crystal fragments of olivine, pyroxene, garnet, chromite, and phlogopite in a fine-grained groundmass of serpentine and carbonates. Most kimberlites were intruded explosively at shallow depths, but apparently the rock was derived from great depth. Ultramafic fragments, presumed to be from the Earth's mantle, make up nearly half the volume of most kimberlites.

Carbonatites are ultramafic rocks composed largely of carbonate minerals. They are widely distributed on the continents in the form of small intrusive bodies and in nearly all known instances are associated with feldspathoidal rocks.

Gabbroic rocks. The major minerals of gabbro are plagioclase and pyroxene; other common constituents are olivine, amphibole, and biotite. Quartz, or feldspathoids, and alkali feldspar may be present in minor amounts. Gabbro is medium- to coarse-grained and consists of plagioclase crystals partly surrounded by pyroxene (see Figure 92). Other minerals may be enclosed by individual pyroxene grains or may fill spaces between plagioclase and pyroxene. If gabbro contains olivine and sulfides, these minerals may break down, staining the polished surface with rust. Small to very large intrusive bodies of gabbro (up to hundreds of cubic kilometres) are widespread in

Table 28: Classification of Intrusive Igneous Rocks* (in percentage)

	olivine	pyroxenes	carbonates	
Ultramafic rocks (mafic minerals 90–100% of total rock)				
Dunite	90–100	—	—	
Peridotite	30–90	—	—	
Pyroxenite	—	70–100	—	
Carbonatite	—	—	70–100	
	mafic minerals	quartz	plagioclase / total feldspar	anorthite in plagioclase
Gabbroic rocks				
Gabbro (diabase, basalt)	10–90	0–10	90–100	50–100
Diorite (andesite)	10–90	0–10	90–100	0–50
Anorthosite	0–10	0–10	90–100	—
Quartz diorite (quartz andesite)	0–90	10–50	90–100	—
Granitic rocks				
Granite (rhyolite)	0–90	10–50	0–65	—
Granodiorite (dacite)	0–90	10–50	65–90	—
Monzonite (latite)	0–90	0–10	35–90	—
Syenite (trachyte)	0–90	0–10	0–35	—
Feldspathoidal rocks (phonolite)	0–90	†	0–100	—

*Names of fine-grained equivalents, either intrusive or extrusive, are given in parentheses. †Feldspathoids present.

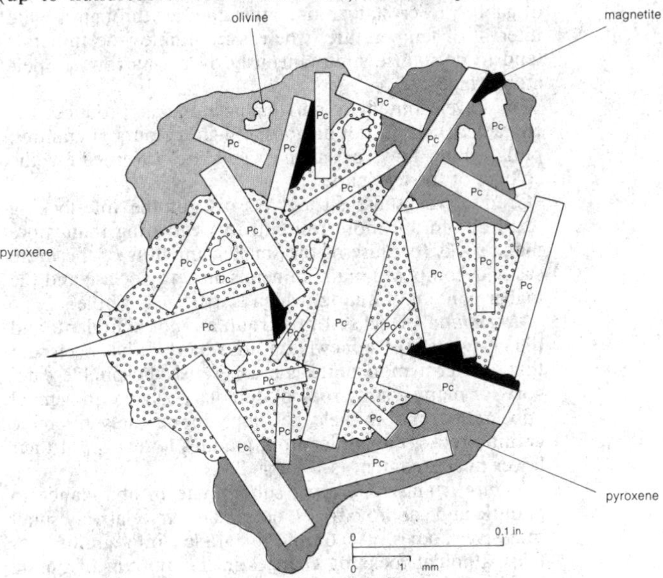

Figure 92: Typical texture of gabbro. Pc = plagioclase; irregular grains of olivine and magnetite, and pyroxenes of differing texture, are distributed as shown.

the continents and probably in the oceanic crust as well.

Diorite

The rock name diorite, from the Greek word meaning "to distinguish," refers to the necessity and difficulty of setting this type apart from gabbro. Arbitrarily but on sound chemical grounds, this distinction is made according to the composition of the plagioclase. In many examples of diorite, amphibole takes the place of pyroxene, and the texture, even if the major minerals are plagioclase and pyroxene, is not the same as the typical texture of gabbro. In diorite, the feldspar and the mafic minerals tend to form irregular, interlocking grains, and there is no strong tendency for one mineral consistently to be surrounded by another.

Diorite occurs in many small intrusive bodies that commonly are unrelated to and older than other intrusive rocks in the same area. The equivalent extrusive rock, andesite, is much more abundant than diorite. The reason for this disparity may be a tendency for geologists to apply the term andesite to rocks that are really finegrained equivalents of rocks other than diorite.

Anorthosite is relatively rare and has two distinct modes of occurrence; one is in small and usually layered bodies within gabbroic and ultramafic rocks, and the other is in large masses that cover several hundred square kilometres, associated with granite and syenite. The large masses, all ranging from 1,100,000,000 to 1,700,000,000 years old, are found in southern Africa, India, North America, and Scandinavia. The restriction of these massive anorthosite bodies in space and time remains a puzzle. Extrusive equivalents of anorthosites are unknown.

Quartz diorite. As implied by the name, this rock contains more quartz (is more strongly silica oversaturated) than diorite, but it differs from diorite in its field relations. Quartz diorite occurs as large intrusive bodies that formed approximately at the same time as neighbouring granitic rocks. It grades into the granites through a decrease in the ratio of plagioclase to total feldspar.

Granitic rocks. Intrusive rocks of this group are abundant, forming large portions of some mountain ranges as well as smaller isolated intrusions. Petrologists distinguish several rock types within this group, according to the ratio of plagioclase to total feldspar. Mafic minerals, usually far less abundant than in gabbro and diorite, are amphiboles and micas, rarely pyroxene and iron-rich olivine.

Granitic texture and colour

The texture of granitic rocks differs markedly from that of gabbro. Plagioclase feldspar, as in gabbros, may be bounded by crystal faces. The mafic minerals are more likely to show well-developed crystal forms in granitic than in gabbroic rocks. Quartz and alkali feldspar usually form irregular grains interlocking in a jigsaw-puzzle fashion (see Figure 93). The textural differences between gabbro and granite are partly due to the tendency of minerals of gabbro to crystallize one after another through a wide interval of temperature, whereas in granites the minerals tend to crystallize simultaneously over a narrow temperature range.

The lower content of dark mafic minerals produces the characteristic (but not diagnostic) light colours of granites: pink, white, gray, or green shades are governed by the colours of the feldspars.

Granitic rocks are strong (because of the interlocking texture) and are more resistant to weathering than more mafic rocks (because of the smaller amounts of the more easily decomposed mafic minerals and plagioclase and the higher content of quartz, which is extremely stable).

Monzonite. Rocks of this group are not abundant, and the group itself is somewhat a miscellany. It has been said that the term monzonite is a generously hospitable category for many a stray rock of dubious pedigree. In general appearance and in field relations monzonites resemble granitic rocks; they differ from granites by reason of their lower quartz content (see Table 28).

Syenite. This rock type, subordinate in abundance to granitic and gabbroic rocks, occurs only in relatively small intrusive bodies. It commonly grades into granitic or feldspathoidal rocks by changes in the amount of quartz or feldspathoid. Syenites, by definition, are silica saturated, containing neither a great excess nor deficiency of silica.

Feldspathoidal rocks. These silica-undersaturated rocks form small but widespread intrusive bodies. Although these rocks make up no more than 1 or 2 percent of the mass of all intrusive igneous rocks, nearly half the names applied to igneous rocks have been coined for members of this group.

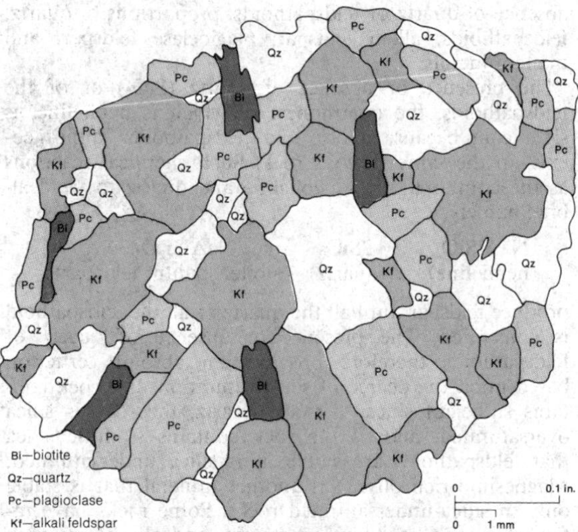

Figure 93: Typical texture of granite.

Distribution of intrusive igneous rocks. The locations of magmatic intrusion are varied. Gabbroic magma approaches the Earth's surface under the ocean floor and along the crests of mid-oceanic ridges, as well as on the continents. Granitic magma, in contrast, seems confined to continental crust. Continental margins, where the major plates that comprise the continents and ocean basins are colliding, are sites of ultramafic and intermediate (quartz-diorite and granodiorite) magma injection, whereas stable continental interiors seem more susceptible to intrusion by granite, kimberlite, carbonatite, and feldspathoidal magmas. Much more field and laboratory work is needed before a unifying theory can be erected to explain the segregation of different magma types in different crustal environments. At present, petrologists are not certain of the degree to which such segregation has occurred.

Emplacement of magma. Magma can make room for itself in several ways as it invades the crust. By means of the process called stoping, magma can detach fragments of country rock, which may sink or become assimilated. Piecemeal stoping is an inefficient mechanism of intrusion and usually occurs on a minor scale, serving only to modify contacts of intrusions that were emplaced in other ways.

On a much larger scale, magma can break loose portions of the overlying crust, extending all the way to the Earth's surface. Such blocks may founder in a pool of magma (Figure 94), resulting in large-scale subsidence called caldron subsidence) at the surface and catastrophic eruption of volcanic rocks. Shallow intrusive bodies thus formed have the outlines of crude rings. Successive intrusions,

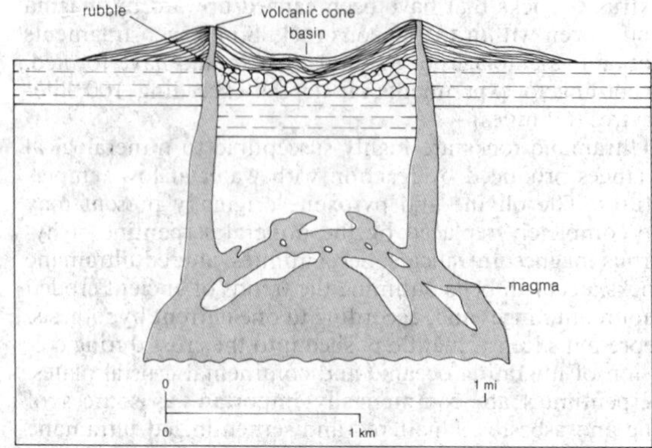

Figure 94: Caldron subsidence in cross-section. A central block of crust has sunk into magma. The surface expression is a basin (caldera) floored by rubble (breccia) and ringed by volcanic cones. The subsidence may be repeated.

generally younger toward the centre, build up forms that are termed ring complexes.

Instead of breaking and swallowing its wall rock, magma can shoulder it aside by forcible intrusion. Diapirism, the rise of a vertical columnar plug (diapir) of less dense rock or magma piercing through more dense rock, forms igneous as well as non-igneous intrusions; among the latter, salt domes are the most common. Rather than forcing its way upward in a vertical pipe, magma may find it less effort to follow fractures or other surfaces of weakness in the country rocks, prying them apart.

Forms of intrusive bodies

The forms of intrusive igneous bodies (Figure 95) are controlled by several factors: the stress field in that particular volume of crust (in turn related to depth and to tectonic setting); the behaviour of the country rock (whether it is homogeneous or layered, brittle or plastic); the viscosity and density of the magma; and the rate of intrusion.

Volcanic necks, such as Devil's Tower, Wyoming, and Ship Rock, New Mexico, are the intrusive fillings of the central conduits of volcanoes (Figure 91).

Dikes are magma-filled fractures that cut across the structure of the country rock. Sills form when magma congeals in fractures that are parallel to layering of the country rock. Horizontal or gently dipping sills, such as the Palisades Sill along the west bank of the Hudson River, must have formed at shallow depths in order to have permitted the magma to lift its roof of overlying rocks.

Laccoliths are sills with updomed roofs; lopoliths sag in the centre. Lopoliths are considerably larger than laccoliths and, as a general rule, are composed of more mafic rocks. Lopoliths are apparently fed by dikes that form narrow keels at the bases of the intrusions.

Larger intrusive bodies are usually irregular in form and are classified arbitrarily according to the size of their area presently exposed. Plugs, stocks, and batholiths, in increasing order of size, complete the roster of intrusive forms. Batholiths are defined as intrusive bodies that crop out over areas greater than 100 square kilometres (40 square miles), were not intruded as one pulse of magma but grew by successive intrusions, and consist of more than one rock type (usually ranging from quartz diorite to granite). Intrusive bodies of unknown or unspecified shape are called plutons, a general term for all such bodies except dikes, sills, and volcanic necks. (D.S.B./Ed.)

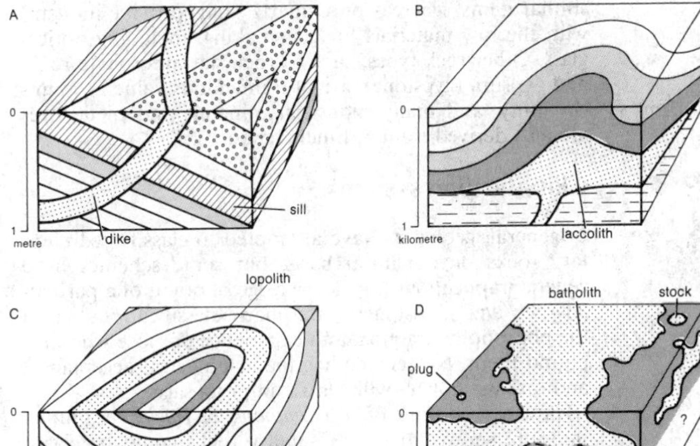

Figure 95: Forms of intrusive igneous rock bodies in hypothetical sections of Earth strata. Note the change of scale from A through D.

SEDIMENTARY ROCKS

Definition, formation, and significance

Sediments are deposits of solid material that accumulate upon the Earth's surface under the influence of various mediums (water, ice, wind, gravity) and under the normal conditions of temperature and pressure that exist at the surface. Sedimentary rocks are the lithified equivalents of sediments, whether derived from previously formed rocks and minerals or from chemical and biochemical deposition. The processes of physical and chemical weathering prepare loose detrital sediment such as clay, silt, sand, and gravel for the processes of transportation, by gravity, mudflows, running water, glaciers, and wind action. These particles are transported to depositional sites—deserts, alluvial fans, submarine shelves and slopes, and deltas in lakes and oceans, among others. Upon reaching a site of deposition, the sediment is converted to sedimentary rocks by cementation, compaction, and induration. Hence, there is both a detrital fraction (the transported sediment) and a chemical fraction (various chemical precipitates) that make up the final sedimentary rock.

Agents of transportation may sort out discrete particles, such as gravel to form conglomerate, sand to form sandstone, or silt and clay to form siltstone and claystone, which are called shale. Chemicals in solution in water bodies are precipitated or flocculated out to form certain types of limestone, dolostone, gypstone, rock salt, and other chemical sediments. Detrital particles of limestone may accumulate mechanically like any other sand, eventually forming limesand. Sedimentary rocks form only about 5 percent by volume of all rocks of the Earth's crust. The area of outcrop and exposure of sedimentary rocks, however, is about 75 percent of the total land area. The percentage probably is greater for ocean basins, though volcanic material is also being added to the daily increment of accumulation upon ocean floors. Sediments and sedimentary rocks therefore form only a thin, surficial veneer upon the Earth. Geologists have measured the thicknesses of outcropping sedimentary rocks and have calculated that the average thickness is about 2.4 kilometres (1.5 miles); thicknesses range from eight to 16 kilometres (five to 10 miles) when a composite rock section is considered.

During all of geologic time, sediment has formed at various places on Earth and in the oceans, ultimately to become compacted and cemented into sedimentary rocks. The process continues today, and during an average 24-hour period, for example, approximately 2,000,000 tons of sediment are transported by the Mississippi River past New Orleans, to accumulate in the Mississippi River Delta or in the Gulf of Mexico. The entire area is very slowly subsiding—*i.e.,* the crust of the Earth beneath the northern Gulf of Mexico is sagging—and the rate of sediment income just about balances the rate of subsidence. This is, therefore, a modern depositional site, and the sediment that accumulates today will eventually be transformed into sedimentary rocks in the future.

Fossil record

When properly understood and interpreted, sedimentary rocks reveal the story of past life groups (fossils) and of the evolutionary advancement from simple to complex organisms in the plant and animal kingdoms. They also provide information on ancient geography, termed paleogeography, because a map of the distribution of sediments that formed in shallow oceans will indicate relationships of seas to landmasses in the past. It is also possible to study rock deformation—the various folds or bends in the strata and the faults that displace stratified rocks—and to determine the history of the formation of ancient mountain chains.

It is almost impossible to assess the importance of sedimentary rocks in terms of economics, because these rocks contain essentially the world's entire store of oil and gas, coal, phosphates, salt deposits, groundwater, and other natural resources. Sedimentary rocks are valuable as building stones, trim stone, patio slabs, and the like, and limestones also are sedimentary in origin. Limestones are used in cement making, in toothpastes and tooth powders, and in paints and chemicals. They serve as flux in steel plants, as crushed rock for highway construction, and for making burnt lime for mortar. Shales of certain types are used in the brick industry and to make clay pipes and similar items, whereas pure quartz sands provide industry with the raw materials for glassmaking, including optical glass. Other rock types, such as rock salt, phosphate rock, and gypsum (gypstone), are of tremendous value in man's economy, and many industrial minerals and metal ores are also derived from sedimentary rocks.

Classification systems

In general, geologists have attempted to classify sedimentary rocks on a natural basis, but some schemes have genetic implications (*i.e.,* knowledge of origin of a particular rock type is assumed), and many classifications reflect the philosophy, training, and experience of those who propound them. No scheme has found universal acceptance, and discussion here will centre on proposals.

The early editions of *A Handbook of Rocks,* beginning in 1896, showed that sedimentary rocks could be classified into clastic, chemical, and organic groups. A major contribution was made by the American geologist A.W. Grabau in 1904 in his *On the Classification of Sedimentary Rocks* and his revisions in 1913 of the monumental work *Principles of Stratigraphy.* Grabau combined textural and compositional terms in classifying and describing sedimentary rocks, and he distinguished between exogenetic and endogenetic types; the former are chiefly mechanical or clastic, having been derived from fragments of older rocks, whereas the latter are the nonclastic rocks and are chemical, organic, or biochemical in origin. His scheme of classifying sedimentary rocks involved the use of such prefixes as hydro- (for water-laid rocks), anemo- (for wind-deposited rocks), auto- (crushed or shattered rocks), and atmo- (rocks formed *in situ*). They were compounded with other terms designating composition and size, including rudaceous (gravelly texture), arenaceous (sandy texture), and lutaceous (silty and clayey texture). Many of Grabau's rock names have gained wide acceptance today, although the spelling has been changed slightly. The names calcirudite, calcarenite, and calcilutite—referring to calcareous conglomerate, sandstone, and shale—are popular, for example, among sedimentary petrologists.

Grabau's contribution

The book *Rocks and Rock Minerals* was first published in 1908, and it has enjoyed various revisions. Sedimentary rocks are classified there according to their physical characteristics and composition into detrital and nondetrital rocks (see Table 29).

Table 29: Terms Designating Composition and Physical Characteristics

detrital rocks	nondetrital rocks
Rudites (coarse)	**Precipitates**
Conglomerates (rounded clasts)	Chemical precipitates
Breccias (angular clasts)	(rocks formed by precipitation from seawater or freshwater)
Basal, or transgression	Evaporites (products of evaporation from saline brines)
Fanglomerates (in alluvial fans)	Duricrust rocks (hardened surface or mean-surface layer of any composition)
Tillites (glacially transported)	**Organic**
Arenites (medium-grained)	Zoogenic (made up of hard parts of animals; *e.g.,* crinoidal limestone)
Sandstone	Phytogenic (made up of plant remains; *e.g.,* algal limestone)
Arkose (feldspar-rich)	
Graywacke (sandstone with mud matrix)	
Quartzite (orthoquartzite)	
Lutites (fine-grained)	
Siltstone	
Shale	
Mudstone or claystone	
Argillite	
Loess (transported and deposited by wind)	

Other attempts were made to classify sedimentary rocks, and in 1948 a significant advance occurred. In that year three definitive articles were published in the *Journal of Geology* by the American geologists F.J. Pettijohn, R.R. Shrock, and P.D. Krynine. These classifications may be said to have provided the basis for all modern discussion of the subject. The nomenclature associated with several schemes of classifying clastic and nonclastic rocks will be discussed in the sections immediately following, but a rough division of sedimentary rocks based on chemical composition is shown in Figure 96.

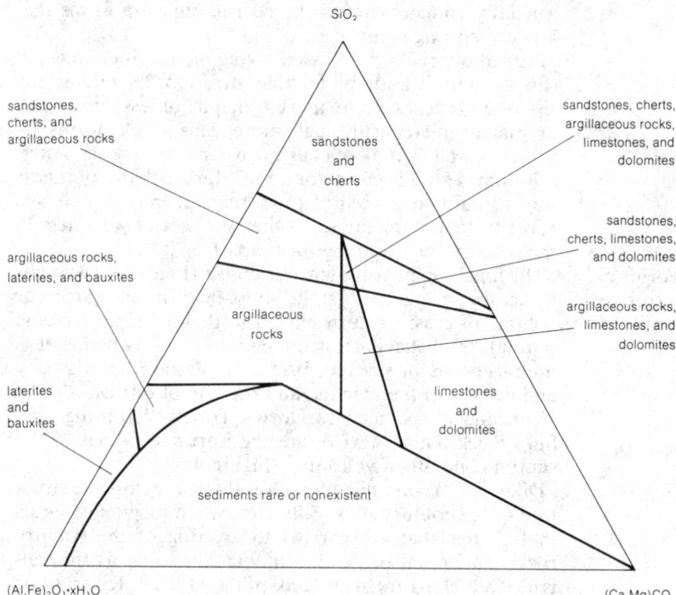

Figure 96: Chemical composition of sedimentary rocks.
From B. Mason, *Principles of Geochemistry* (1966); John Wiley and Sons

CLASTIC ROCKS

An obvious physical feature of many rocks is texture; that is, the size, shape, and arrangement of the constituent grains. Texture may be coarse, medium, fine, or amorphous. When it is fragmental, and discrete grains can be recognized, the rock is a clastic sedimentary rock. Clastic material, for the most part, has been transported to the site of deposition and includes the gravelly sediment that forms conglomerate (if the particles are abraded and somewhat rounded) and breccia (if composed of angular particles). The following size grades can be recognized among coarse clastic sediments: granules; pebbles; cobbles; and boulders, or blocks (see Table 30). Medium clastics include the various sandstone (arenite) types; and fine clastics are the siltstones, mudstones, and shales. Some petrographers further subdivide sandstones as coarse, medium, and fine and may similarly classify fine clastic rocks.

Texture as a basis

There are many ways of classifying coarse, clastic sedimentary rocks. One such scheme is that of Grabau, previously mentioned, but the simplest method consists of giving a name together with a brief meaningful description of the characteristics of a particular conglomerate. Such a statement is, of course, applicable to all types of sedimentary rocks and need not be confined to the conglomerates. Thus, a pebble conglomerate means what the name implies—a coarse, clastic sedimentary rock whose discrete particles range from four to 64 millimetres (0.2 to 2.5 inches) in diameter. A description is necessary, however, to indicate the rock types that compose this variety of conglomerate. If the clasts, for example, consist of nearly equal amounts of granite and gneiss (crystalline and metamorphic rock types, respectively), such a rock could be called a granite–gneiss pebble conglomerate.

According to Pettijohn, gravels collected by ordinary water currents have an intact framework (*i.e.,* the clasts are in close proximity) and may be termed orthoconglomerates. Those deposited by mudflows, subaqueous turbidity flows and slides, and glacial ice tend to have a disrupted framework and may be termed paraconglomerates. As a further distinction, those conglomerates composed of a single rock type are termed oligomictic, whereas those containing many rock types are termed polymictic. This is but a sampling of the possible nomenclature for coarse clastic rocks.

Sandstones have long intrigued geologists, largely because of their relative abundance in the geologic column; they are present in rocks of every age and are also forming today. Certain groups of geologists have devoted great effort to the classification of these medium-textured, clastic sedimentary rocks, but no attempt will be made here to review all of the many schemes. There has been an

Three-component and other schemes

Table 30: Size Limits of Common Grades and Rock Terms

size	sedimentary particles: rounded, subrounded, subangular — fragment		sedimentary particles: rounded, subrounded, subangular — aggregate	sedimentary particles: angular — fragment	sedimentary particles: angular — aggregate	volcanic particles — fragment	volcanic particles — aggregate
	boulder	"roundstone"	boulder gravel boulder conglomerate	block		block*	volcanic breccia
256 mm							
	cobble		cobble gravel cobble conglomerate	...	breccia	bomb†	agglomerate
64 mm							
	pebble		pebble gravel pebble conglomerate	...		— 32 mm — lapilli — 4 mm —	lapilli tuff
4 mm							
	granule		granule gravel	...			
2 mm							
	sand		sand sandstone	...	— 1 mm — grit — ½ mm —	coarse ash	coarse tuff
1/16 mm						— ¼ mm —	
	silt		silt siltstone	...			
1/256 mm						fine ash	fine tuff
	clay		clay shale	...			

*Broken from previously consolidated igneous rock. †Solidified from plastic material while in flight.
Source: from F.J. Pettijohn, *Sedimentary Rocks*.

effort on the part of one group of researchers to maintain the name sandstone, whereas others prefer to perpetuate the name arenite. Moreover, some authorities favour a classification based on the quartz–feldspar–clay content of a rock, whereas others consider the presence of rock fragments to be of principal significance (see below *Sandstones*). Classification schemes have been presented in the form of triangles, in which the three components used for classification occupy the corners, and in the form of tetrahedrons, which are more complicated but permit the use of four end members, or rock components.

Siltstone

Shale is a fine-textured clastic sedimentary rock with a preponderance of detrital components, having been indurated from silt and clay. Some term shale a siltstone if it has an average grain size between 1/16 and 1/256 millimetre (0.0025 and 0.0002 inch) and claystone if discrete particles are mostly smaller than 1/256 millimetre, which is clay-size detrital material. Shales can contain carbonates but not in excess of 50 percent of the bulk of the rock; otherwise, they fall into the limestone or dolostone scheme of classification (see below *Shales*).

NONCLASTIC ROCKS

Nonclastic sedimentary rocks differ in many respects from their clastic counterparts, and there is no single classification that has been universally accepted. This is a reflection of the great variation in mineral composition, textures, and other properties of these rock types.

Limestones and dolostones, commonly called dolomites, make up the bulk among the nonclastic sedimentary rocks. Such rocks as ironstones (limonite, goethite, hematite, siderite, and chamosite), phosphorites (phosphate rock), coal- and oil-bearing rocks, carbonaceous and bituminous shales and limestones, evaporites (rock salt, gypsum, and other salts), chert, opal, and chalcedony occur in much lesser abundance, although locally these noncarbonate (or low-carbonate), nonclastic sedimentary rocks may form thick and widespread deposits. Classification schemes that would incorporate all types of noncarbonate, nonclastic sedimentary rocks have not been set forth, because no triangular or tetrahedral scheme could accommodate them all. Several of the major types of nonclastic rocks are shown in the tetrahedron in Figure 97. The organic corner of the tetrahedron identifies such nonclastic rocks as coal, lignite, and some richly bituminous rocks. Some carbonates and clastic material may be present, but these commonly compose much less than 50 percent of the bulk of such rocks. Coal consists principally of plant material that has been converted to a type of hydrocarbon, but it can pass into a carbonaceous shale, which is a clastic sedimentary rock. Similarly, an oil-rich nonclastic rock can grade into bituminous (petroliferous) shale, sandstone, or limestone. The same kinds of gradational possibilities occur in phosphatic, siliceous, and ferruginous rocks, and the tetrahedron in Figure 97 is designed to aid in locating and identifying the more common nonclastic sedimentary rocks.

Limestones are, for the most part, originally deposited carbonate rocks and consist of 50 percent or more of calcite or aragonite (both $CaCO_3$). Dolostones are mostly secondary deposits or replacements of limestones; that is, the mineral dolomite $[CaMg(CO_3)_2]$ replaces the calcite of limestones during diagenesis (postdepositional processes). Some very fine textured dolostones do form directly by precipitation from marine and lake brines in restricted environments, however, and these are primary deposits (see below *Limestone and dolomites*).

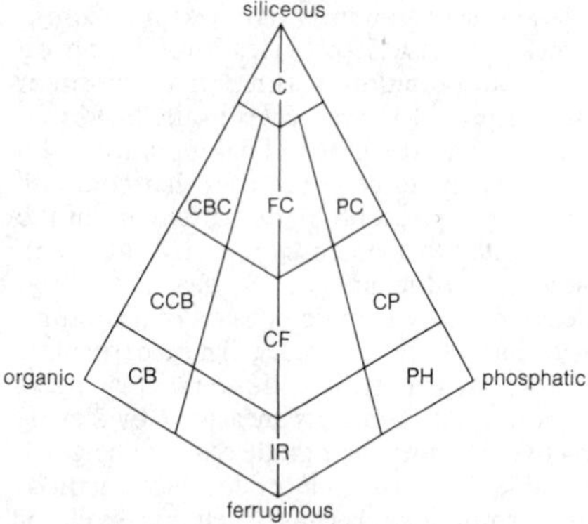

Figure 97: Common noncarbonate, nonclastic sedimentary rocks. C—cherts; CBC—carbonaceous chert; FC—ferruginous chert; PC—phosphatic chert; CCB—cherty carbonaceous rock; CF—cherty ironstone; CP—cherty phosphorite; CB—carbonaceous rock; PH—phosphorite; and IR—ironstone.

Crusts, soils, and weathering products

Not really amenable to classification but of sufficient significance to warrant mention are some sedimentary crusts, soils, and weathering products. Duricrusts are peculiar deposits formed on gently sloping erosion surfaces in many parts of the world, consisting of armour-like precipitates that result from upward capillary migration of groundwaters during periods of aridity. Various carbonates are precipitated from these rising groundwaters, and aluminous, ferruginous, and siliceous materials also may form.

Residual soils are the products of weathering formed *in situ*. The character of these deposits results from the interaction of climate, drainage, and type of the parent rock. Regolith is a mantle of loose, incoherent rock material, of any origin or nature, which blankets the parent rock; saprolith is essentially the same; and saprolite is thoroughly decomposed, earthy, but not transported rock. It is a residual clay, silt, or other substance. In the piedmont area of North and South Carolina it commonly is reddish in colour and results from rather thorough decomposition *in situ* of old Paleozoic (225,000,000 to 570,000,000 years old) crystalline rocks. In humid regions the residual materials are enriched in hydroxides of aluminum and ferric iron during processes of weathering, and the end product is called laterite. It also is reddish in colour, and its formation requires high rainfall and high temperatures. Bauxite is a residual clay-size weathering product that is formed *in situ*, consisting largely of hydrated alumina (essentially $Al_2O_3 \cdot 2H_2O$). The principal ores of aluminum are obtained from bauxite; it is commonly gray to light gray in colour. Scree and talus are angular fragments of rock that occur at the bases of cliffs from which they were derived by weathering and erosion. Paleosols are buried soils, especially those developed during an interglacial episode and buried by later advances of ice. They are "fossil" soils and can occur interlayered in other types of sedimentary rocks. A final sedimentary material in this general category is sapropel, an aquatic ooze and sludge rich in organic matter.

Properties of sedimentary rocks

TEXTURE

Texture concerns the physical makeup of rock, namely, the size, shape, and arrangement (packing and fabric) of the discrete grains or elements of a sedimentary rock. Whereas mineral or chemical composition of sedimentary rock must be determined in order to classify these rocks and interpret their depositional history correctly, texture relates to the physical parameters of size grades: sorting, skewness of the size distribution, and the degree of particle abrasion, among others. Two main natural textural groupings exist for sedimentary rocks, namely, clastic (or fragmental) and nonclastic (commonly crystalline). A few rare types of sedimentary rocks are said to have an amorphous texture, but with the advent of the electron microscope many of these so-called featureless rocks were found to have a detrital or crystalline texture or both.

Grain size. Particle size is an important textural parameter of clastic rocks, because it provides information on the conditions of transportation, sorting, and deposition of the sediment and provides some clues to the history of events at the depositional site prior to final induration. To determine the sizes of the discrete particles that compose a sedimentary rock can pose a problem, particularly if the rock is firmly indurated (cemented, compacted, lithified). Various methods of setting up grade scales have been devised; a grade scale is a systematic division of a continuous range of sizes into classes or grades. Thus, particulate materials that make up sediments and sedimentary rocks can be weighed and their diameters measured by sieving through screens to determine their grade scales. The grade scale given in Table 31 is still one of the best methods of standardizing terminology, because each size grade or class differs from its predecessor by the constant ratio of 1:2, and each has a specific name to identify the particles included within it. The scale is a geometric grade scale, with a constant ratio between classes, and is well adapted to the description of sediments, because it gives equal significance to size ratios, whether the ratios relate to gravel, sand, silt, or clay. The gravels and sands can be separated into discrete grade scales or size grades by using screens or sieves whose openings correspond to metric sizes. Silts and clays are relegated to their respective size grades by utilizing their settling velocities in water or in air to separate one size from another.

Size grades and grade scales

Table 31: Particle-Size Classification

grade limits (diameters in mm)	name	grade limits (diameters in mm)	name
Above 256	boulder	1/2–1/4	medium sand
256–128	large cobble	1/4–1/8	fine sand
128–64	small cobble	1/8–1/16	very fine sand
64–32	very large pebble	1/16–1/32	coarse silt
32–16	large pebble	1/32–1/64	medium silt
16–8	medium pebble	1/64–1/128	fine silt
8–4	small pebble	1/128–1/256	very fine silt
4–2	granule	1/256–1/512	coarse clay
2–1	very coarse sand	1/512–1/1,024	medium clay
1–1/2	coarse sand	1/1,024–1/2,048	fine clay

Source: C.K. Wentworth (1922).

Sorting of grains. The sorting of clastic sedimentary rocks measures the thoroughness with which a sediment has been winnowed by wind, washed by water, or worked by other transporting agents. The degree of sorting is a valuable indicator of the rate of sedimentation and the probable environment of deposition.

Determination of the degree of sorting in the laboratory with unconsolidated (or disaggregated) gravels and sands is readily accomplished, using a nest of sieves (screens) whose openings correspond to the grade sizes of the Wentworth or other scale. Sizes of silts and clays are determined in the laboratory using air elutriation or in settling tubes filled with water. Discrete size grades are separated according to their settling rates, and the percentage of material occurring in each size grade is obtained directly.

In order to determine the degree of sorting of indurated sedimentary rocks, a slabbed surface is prepared by cutting the rock, and the surface is then etched with acid or otherwise treated to cause the grains to stand out in relief. The grains can then be studied and counted.

All methods of ascertaining the grade sizes of clastic sediments and of sedimentary rocks result in compilation of data relating to the size frequency distribution. These data can be plotted in tabular form, as histograms (bar graphs), as size frequency curves, or as cumulative curves. Numerous techniques have been devised to illustrate these data; Figure 98 shows a few possibilities.

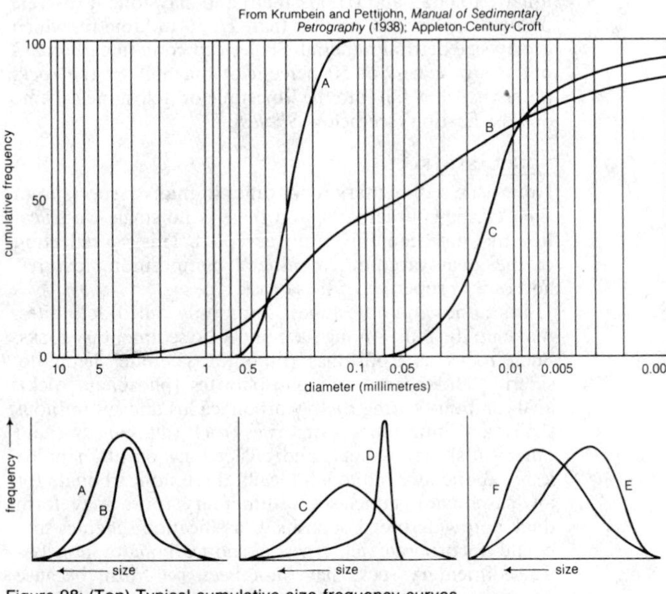

Figure 98: (Top) Typical cumulative size frequency curves for (A) beach sand; (B) glacial till; (C) loess. (Bottom) size frequency distribution curves for sediments that are (A) normal; (B) normal and peaked; (C) normal and scattered; (D) skewed to right and peaked; (E) asymmetrical, skewed to right; (F) asymmetrical, skewed to left.

Size frequency distribution

Some characteristics of size frequency distributions include skewness (measurement of the symmetry of a histogram or of a size frequency curve), kurtosis (degree of peakedness of the histogram or curve), and the mean, or average (measurement of the central tendency), as well as the quartiles. Some of these characteristics are shown in Figure 98. The advantages of these parameters is that they systematize determination of the degree of sorting of clastics and of the precise percentages of discrete grade sizes and designation of the clastic mixture as unimodal, bimodal, or even polymodal. These facts permit interpretation of the environment of sedimentation for the particular suite of sediments or sedimentary rocks involved.

Grain roundness. Clastic rocks become abraded during their transit, and some degree of rounding usually occurs. Conglomerates, for example, are roundstones in that they have been abraded, and most (if not all) sharp corners have been worn off. Breccias, by contrast, are sharpstones and display varying degrees of angularity. The same is true of the arenities, or sandstones; thus, it is important to obtain some measurement of the degree of abrasion or perfection of roundness. Some geologists prefer to arrange sand grains in order of increasing abrasion, from those that are almost entirely unabraded and are thus angular to those that are well rounded. Figure 99 illustrates this arrangement, which is commonly used.

From F. Pettijohn, *Sedimentary Rocks*, 2nd Edition (1957); Harper and Row

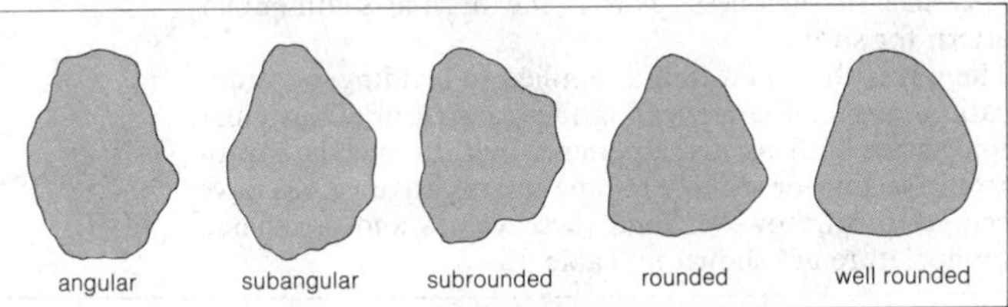

Figure 99: Roundness classes of sedimentary particles.

Grains that are angular have maximum sharpness around their edges and show minimum abrasion on corners. Subangular grains indicate that the edges and corners have been abraded but retain their original form, and their original surfaces are relatively little worn. Subrounded grains denote considerable attrition and abrasion, so that the entire surface has been worn from faces, angular grains, and crystal boundaries to a relatively smooth texture. Rounded grains approximate roundness and sphericity; edges, corners, and original surfaces have been so abraded that the entire remaining surface of the grain forms a smooth, broad curve. If some grains display perfect roundness and sphericity they may be termed well rounded.

Carbonate texture. Carbonate clastic rocks are similar in texture and may be lithoclastic or bioclastic. Lithoclastic means that the allogenic (detrital) materials are mainly inorganic and consist of grains of different kinds of minerals and rocks or rock fragments that are transported and redeposited as detrital grains and matrix. Thus, an arenite that consists of 50 percent or more (by bulk or by exposed area) of clasts of limestone derived from an earlier formed rock or partly indurated lime mud should be termed lithocalcarenite. Bioclastic indicates that the texture and composition is derived from allogenic materials that are high in organic material, commonly containing a variety of abraded skeletal fragments that have been transported and deposited as detrital material. The source of the clastic material is skeletal fragments, ranging in size from lutites (clays) and comminuted fossil detritus to calcarenite and even to rudaceous (gravelly) textured sediment, the calcirudites. Thus, a biocalcarenite is a clastic carbonate sedimentary rock consisting primarily of sand-size abraded skeletal grains; 50 percent or more of such a rock consists of sand-size fossil fragments.

Crystalline carbonate sedimentary rocks

Many carbonate sedimentary rocks are crystalline, however, rather than granular. In terms of crystal size, they can range from the macrocrystalline or megacrystalline—visible to the unaided eye—through those that are microcrystalline and cryptocrystalline (not visible). The term aphanic is useful to describe the texture of most micrites (and micritic limestones) and dolomicrites; individual crystals and grains (if present) are less than 0.01 millimetre (0.0004 inch) in size. A second designation, phaneric, refers to discrete particles, crystals, and grains that are larger than 0.01 millimetre in size, commonly visible to the unaided eye.

In addition, some degree of perfection of crystallinity can be noted in crystalline sedimentary rocks. Euhedral is a term applied to those crystals that are bounded by their own crystal faces, resulting in a relatively high degree of crystalline geometry. Those crystals whose faces are of a lower degree of perfection than euhedral forms are termed subhedral. Those crystals that are not bounded by their own crystal faces and have their outlines impressed on them by adjacent crystals are termed anhedral. They have a degree of geometry lower than subhedral forms. For further discussion of carbonate textures see below *Limestone and dolomites.*

MASS PROPERTIES

Discussion of sedimentary rocks thus far has related to the problems of their classification and to some of the textural characteristics of sediments and sedimentary rocks. The association of the discrete particles in their aggregate, or bulk, state and the whole rock and its mass properties also warrant consideration. Some of the more significant of these properties are discussed here, in alphabetical order.

Cementation. The precipitation of mineral matter in the interstices of a clastic sediment provides cementation, particularly during and shortly following sedimentation. The final product is an indurated rock.

Cohesiveness. Cohering, or sticking together by surface forces, normally is displayed by unconsolidated (to weakly indurated), fine-textured clastic and carbonate sediments of particle size less than 0.01 millimetre.

Colour. The overall hue of sediment results from a combination of various grain colours, mineral inclusions, surface coating, weathered surfaces, matrix colour, and nature and hue of the cementing materials.

Compactibility. Rock becomes compacted when porosity is reduced in response to a decrease in volume under load. Finely textured sediments, such as silt and clay, normally are compacted more than sands and gravels.

Density. The mass per unit bulk volume of the sediment or rock, or its density, is a measure of the degree of packing of the components.

Elasticity. The ability of a strained body to recover its size and shape after deformation is its elasticity. If a rock such as shale, for example, is slowly bent, the degree to which it is able to regain its original size and shape without fracturing is a measure of its elasticity.

Electrical resistivity. Resistance to the passage of an electric current depends, of course, upon the nature of the sediment and the fluid content in its open spaces. Knowledge of the electrical resistivity of the various types of sedimentary rocks helps geologists to locate oil, gas, and water deposits below ground.

Magnetic susceptibility. Magnetization is acquired by rocks when in a magnetic field. In sediments, the susceptibility is largely related to the amount of magnetic minerals (magnetite, for example) that is present.

Packing. The mutual spatial relationships among the grains of a rock, or packing, reflect the degree to which grains are in contact with or interlocked among their neighbours.

Permeability. The ease of fluid flow through rocks, or permeability, is strongly influenced by particle size; coarse gravel, for example, has large openings among the cobbles and boulders, affording easy passage for fluids. Sands also have high permeability values, whereas clays (which have high cohesiveness) have low ones.

Porosity. Porosity, or the actual pore space in a rock, is expressed in percentages. Porosity is a function of the uniformity of particle size and shape and of the state of packing of the particles.

Radioactivity. In sediments radioactivity is expressed in units equivalent to 10^{-12} gram of radium per gram of rock. Measured values average about 4.1 for pure quartz sandstones, 4.0 for limestone, 11.3 for gray shale, and 22.4 for dark-gray to black shale.

GEOCHEMICAL PROPERTIES

Allogenic and authigenic minerals

Minerals that make up sedimentary rocks are of two principal types, namely, allogenic (detrital) and authigenic. The former are obtained during the processes of weathering and are transported to or within the depositional site, whereas authigenic minerals form *in situ* within the depositional site in response to geochemical processes. The geochemical properties of sedimentary rocks, whether clastic or nonclastic, therefore result from certain chemical properties they inherited from earlier formed rocks and from the properties induced upon them during postdepositional epochs. Many igneous rocks contain minerals that are radioactive (some feldspars and zircon, for example). When such minerals occur as detrital grains in clastic sedimentary rocks, their absolute age and the source can generally be determined. Because only a few such minerals are commonly incorporated, however, the use of isotope techniques to determine the time of deposition of sedimentary rocks is limited.

Various clay minerals are present in sedimentary rocks and are of particular importance in most shales and in some limestones. Some of these clays are no more than fine to very fine textured detrital particles, whereas some may form authigenically in the site of deposition. Some of the important clays include kaolinite, halloysite, montmorillonite, illite, vermiculite, and chlorite (see above *Clay Minerals*).

Some zeolites are authigenic in origin, and their presence may shed light on the environmental conditions under which they formed. The zeolite analcite ($NaAlSi_2O_6 \cdot H_2O$), for example, commonly indicates formation that has taken place in lakes (such as the Green River Formation of Utah, Colorado, and Wyoming). Heulandite, $(Ca, Na_2)(Al_2Si_7O_{18} \cdot 6H_2O)$, results from the interaction of volcanic glass and saline waters that are commonly marine. In addition to zeolites, trace elements that are present in sedimentary rocks provide indications of either freshwater or marine environments. Marine clays may contain about 100 to 200 parts per million of boron, whereas freshwater clays have only about 10 to 50 parts per million.

Diagenesis of sediments

The term diagenesis is a designation for all processes that act on sediments after their deposition. Such postdepositional processes may take place hundreds or even millions of years after sediment finally comes to rest; they include (1) formation of new minerals, (2) redistribution and recrystallization of substances in sediments, and (3) lithification. Diagenesis, therefore, includes all physicochemical, biochemical, and physical processes modifying sediments in the time between their deposition and their lithification at the low temperatures and pressures characteristic of surface and near-surface environments. Dolomitization is one process of diagenesis, whereby limestone is changed to dolostone.

FABRIC

Fabric is the orientation or the lack of it of the elements of a rock. The texture of a rock therefore defines the fabric, because it is the arrangement or orientation of clasts and crystals in these rocks that controls its fabric—it is the way the rock is put together. Packing is a factor in the fabric because it concerns the spacing of the elemental constituents of sediments and sedimentary rocks, and this in turn determines the density. Genetically, there are two principal varieties of fabric, namely, primary (depositional or appositional) and secondary (or deformational). Primary fabric is syngenetic (it is determined while sediment is accumulating), whereas a deformation fabric is produced as a postdepositional process by external stress on the rock. It results from a rotation or from movements of the constituent elements under stress or from the growth of new elements. Fabric in clastics such as conglomerates and sandstones can be determined by plotting dimensional directions, such as the long axes of pebbles or quartz-sand grains. Fabric in shales can be ascertained by plotting the platelike arrangement of mica and other clays and in carbonate rocks by plotting directional properties of clasts (pellets, skeletons, oolites) or of crystals and crystal patterns.

Sedimentary structures

EXTERNAL STRATIFICATION

Stratification (or bedding) is expressed by rock layers (units) of a general tabular or lenticular form that differ in rock type or other characteristics from the material with which they are interstratified (sometimes stated as interbedded, or interlayered). These beds, or strata, are of varying thickness and areal extent. The term stratum identifies a single bed, or unit, normally greater than one centimetre in thickness and visibly separable from superjacent (overlying) and subjacent (underlying) beds, or units. "Strata" refers to two or more beds, and the term lamina is sometimes applied to a unit less than one centimetre in thickness. Thus, lamination consists of thin units in bedded, or stratified, or layered, sequence in a natural rock succession, whereas stratification consists of bedded layers, or strata, in a geologic sequence of interleaved sedimentary rocks.

The individual beds, or layers, in an interbedded succession of rock strata will rarely be of approximately equal thickness. Examples do exist, however, notably in varved deposits, which are laminated to thinly stratified layers of sediment that reflect seasonal or annual rhythms. For the preponderance of stratified sedimentary rocks the arrangement is one of unequal thickness, ranging from very thin laminae to discrete beds that measure a few to many feet in thickness. This is the normal sedimentary pattern for strata.

The terms thick and thin as applied to bedding, or stratification, are relative, reflecting the training of a particular geologist as well as his experience with a specific stratigraphic section or sections. Some quantitative values have been set forth, however, and these values and associated nomenclature are shown in Table 32.

Table 32: Quantitative Terms to Describe Layered Sedimentary Rocks

descriptive terms for stratification	descriptive terms for cross-stratification	thickness	descriptive terms for splitting
Very thick-bedded	very thickly cross-bedded	greater than 6 ft	massive
Thick-bedded	thickly cross-bedded	3 ft to 6 ft	blocky
Medium-bedded	medium cross-bedded	1 ft to 3 ft	slabby
Thin-bedded	thinly cross-bedded	1 in. to 1 ft	flaggy
Laminated	cross-laminated	2 mm to 1 in.	platy (or shaly)
Thinly laminated	thinly cross-laminated	less than 2 mm	papery

BEDDING TYPES AND BEDDING-PLANE FEATURES

Types. It is common to discover a rhythmic pattern in a pile of stratified sedimentary rocks represented by a repetitive sequence of rock types. In most instances of such cyclic sedimentation, the bedding, or stratification, is horizontal or essentially so; that is, the transporting, sorting, and depositing agents of wind, running water, and lake and ocean currents and waves accumulated the laminae and strata in flat-lying or horizontal arrangement. They are termed well-bedded, a type of primary stratification.

Primary stratification in sediments and sedimentary rocks can be cross-bedded (cross-stratified), graded, and imbricate and can also display climbing laminae, ripples, and beds. A simplified classification of cross-stratification into three principal types (simple, planar, and trough) is shown in Figure 100.

Graded and imbricate bedding

Graded bedding simply identifies beds, or strata, that grade upward from coarse-textured clastic sediment at their base to finer textured materials at the top (Figure 101). The stratification may be sharply marked so that one layer is set off visibly from those above and beneath it. More commonly, however, the layers are blended. This variety of bedding results from a check in the velocity of the transporting agent, and thus coarse-textured sediment (gravel, for example) is deposited first, followed upward by pebbles, granules, sand, silt, and clay. It is commonly associated with submarine density currents.

Imbricate bedding is of a shingle structure in a deposit of flattened or disk-shaped pebbles or cobbles (Figure 101). That is, elongated and commonly flattened pebbles and cobbles in gravelly sediment are deposited so that they overlap one another like roofing shingles. Imbricate

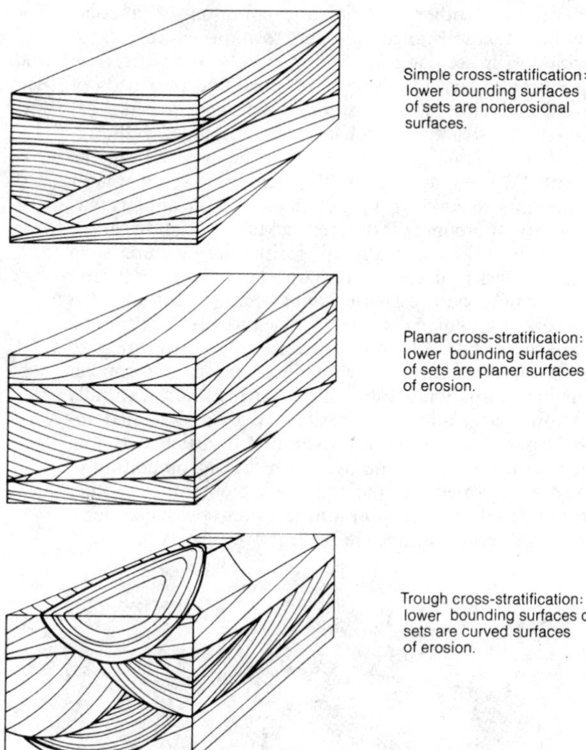
Simple cross-stratification: lower bounding surfaces of sets are nonerosional surfaces.
Planar cross-stratification: lower bounding surfaces of sets are planer surfaces of erosion.
Trough cross-stratification: lower bounding surfaces of sets are curved surfaces of erosion.

Figure 100: Basic elements of cross-stratification classification.

By courtesy of E.D. McKee and G.W. Weir, *Geological Society of America Bulletin*, vol. 64 (1953); Geological Society of America

bedding forms where high-velocity currents move over a stream bed or where strong currents and waves break over a gradually sloping beach, thereby forming beach shingle.

Growth structures

Growth structures in sedimentary rocks are *in situ* features that accumulate largely as the result of organic buildups within otherwise horizontal or nearly flat-lying strata. Reefs and stromatolites are two common varieties of such growth structures. Reefs can consist of corals or any other organisms capable of constructing a rigid topographic deposit of carbonate in strongly agitated but shallow lake or ocean realms. Stromatolites are largely wavy-crinkly laminae or thin layers of carbonate that form when algae precipitate the lime from solution into a buildup superficially resembling heads of cabbage or lettuce. A rather exotic growth structure is travertine; this calcium carbonate deposit is more common to caves in the form of stalactites, stalagmites, columns, and other dripstone, but it can also form in other openings in limestones, such as faults and joints.

Bedding-plane features. Upper surfaces of beds commonly display primary sedimentary features that are classified as bedding-plane structures. A three-dimensional view may be obtained if some of these can be seen from the side as well as from the top of a pile of strata. They include such features as ripples (ripple marks), climbing ripples, rills, pits, mud cracks, trails and tracks, salt and ice casts and molds, and others. Bedding-plane markings and irregularities can be allocated to one of three classes: (1) those on the base of a bed (load and current structures and organic markings); (2) those within a bed (parting lineation); and (3) those on top of a bed (ripple marks, pits, impressions, mud cracks, tracks and trails of organisms, and others).

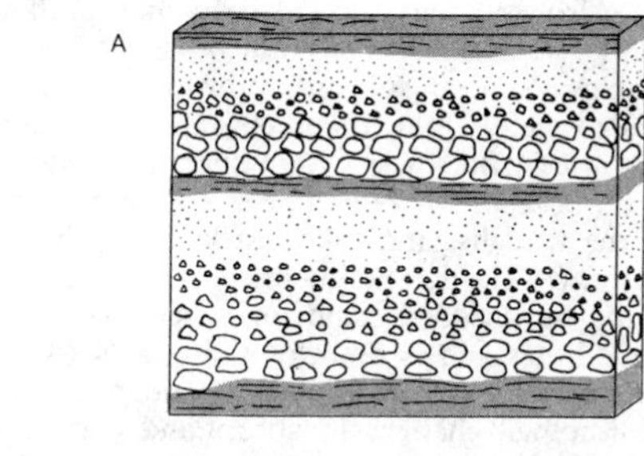
A

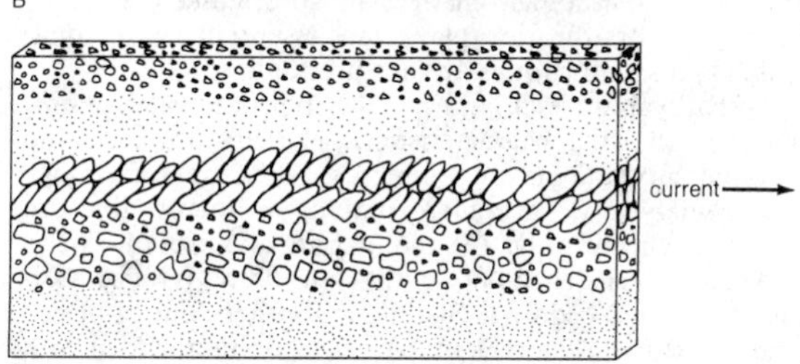
B
current

Figure 101: (A) Graded bedding. (B) Imbricate bedding.

DEFORMATION STRUCTURES

In addition to sedimentary structures that are normally associated with bedding planes, there are other sedimentary structures that result from deformation during or shortly after sedimentation but before induration of the sediment into rock. These are nontectonic features; that is, they are not bends and folds brought about by metamorphism or other causes. Deformation structures can be grouped into several classes, as follows: (1) founder and load structures, (2) convoluted structures, (3) slump structures, (4) injection structures, such as sandstone dikes or sills, and (5) organic structures. Pillow and convoluted structures are shown in Figures 102 and 103, and a plunge-trough structure in Figure 104.

Structures found on the bottom of a bed are called sole markings, because they formed on the "sole" of the bed. Sole marks are commonly formed on sandstone and limestone beds that rest upon shale beds. They are termed casts, because they are fillings of depressions that formed

Casts

From F.J. Pettijohn and P.E. Potter, *Atlas and Glossary of Primary Sedimentary Structures*; Springer-Verlag New York Inc.

Figure 102: Cross section of a large pillow structure in Thorold Sandstone (Silurian). New Jolly road cut, Hamilton, Ontario, Canada.

on the surface of the underlying mud. They originate (1) by unequal loading upon the soft and plastic wet mud, (2) by the action of currents across the upper mud surface, or (3) by the activities of organisms on this surface. Load casts form as the result of downsinking of sandstone or limestone into the mud beneath. Current marks can form by the action of water currents on upper surfaces of the beds or by "tools" (such as wood and fossils) that are transported by currents over soft sediment.

A special variety of deformation structure that is common (but not necessarily limited) to limestones is the stylolite, a unique zigzag line that crosses rock surfaces. Stylolites may result from pressure-solution phenomena, which form a sutured pattern during compaction of wet sediment. Being common to limestones, they ordinarily form parallel to the horizontal bedding, or they parallel foreset bedding and cross-bedding. They may form at other angles in newly deposited sediment. The amplitude of the zigzag or up-and-down suture pattern is a measure of the amount of material that was dissolved and removed during compaction of the sediment.

Figure 103: Convolute lamination, Krosno Beds (Oligocene), from Mymon, central Carpathians, Poland.

From F.J. Pettijohn and P.E. Potter, *Atlas and Glossary of Primary Sedimentary Structures*; Springer-Verlag New York Inc.

Sedimentary environments

"Sedimentary environment" refers to the complex of physical, chemical, and biological conditions under which a sediment accumulates. These conditions largely determine the properties of sediments deposited within the environment. A sedimentary rock, however, is a product not only of the environment but also of the transporting agent(s) involved. Moreover, its composition, texture, and other characters are determined to a large degree by the makeup of the source area (the provenance).

Any attempt to classify environments of sedimentation must take into account that there are not only marine and nonmarine realms of sedimentation but also mixed or transitional environments in nature.

Marine environments include the nearshore, rather shallow littoral zone, the offshore, moderately shallow zone, and deepwater realms. For mixed marine and nonmarine environments, such names as supralittoral, supratidal, and foreshore may be applied to that realm between the beach (or berm) and the water's edge at normal high tide. Other environments include the beach, estuary, and delta. Each environment, regardless of the name assigned, is associated with a set of criteria that constitutes its hallmark. The most commonly cited criteria for the recognition of sedimentary environments and source areas follow.

MARINE ENVIRONMENT

The marine environment consists of the shallow and deep littoral zones and the deepwater realm, as previously stated. The shallow littoral zone (high-energy or agitated realm) has the following characteristics: (1) gravelly, coarse

Harold J. Bissell

Figure 104: Plunge-trough filling in Queantoweap Sandstone (Permian) southwest of Las Vegas, Nevada.

The shallow and deeper littoral

bioclastic, and other materials are common; (2) moderately high textural range (boulders to mud) is present; (3) marine fossils are common and may be mixed with some nonmarine forms; (4) there is interbedding into beds of gravel, sand, silt, and clay, some of which are lenslike; (5) sedimentary structures such as ball-and-pillow, roll-and-plunge, and high-angle cross-bedding (Figure 105) may be present; (6) the map pattern of outcropping sediments or sedimentary rocks consists of elongate and linear belts parallel to the shoreline; (7) different textural variations grade laterally as well as vertically; (8) sedimentary features such as ripple marks, rill marks, rain and bubble pits, and mud cracks should be present in some beds; (9) within short distances (particularly at right angles to the depositional strike) there should be an apparent range in thickness of the various strata; (10) individual beds, lenses, and smaller units may display fair to excellent sorting, both texturally and mineralogically; (11) fossil bivalves and related invertebrates commonly are broken and disarticulated and, when cemented and indurated, form a conglomeration of shell debris termed coquina; (12) reefs, bioherms, and other organic buildups are common in limestone successions; and (13) disconformities are present or rather common.

From F.J. Pettijohn and P.E. Potter, *Atlas and Glossary of Primary Sedimentary Structures*; Springer-Verlag New York Inc.

Figure 105: Cross-bedding in calcareous sandstone of Loyalhanna Limestone (Mississippian), current from right to left. From abandoned quarry, Westmoreland County, Pennsylvania.

The deeper littoral zone (low-energy, minor agitated realm) has the following characteristics: (1) the average sediment is fine-sandy, silty, clayey, and limestone-dolostone; (2) moderately low textural range (local lenses only of gravelly material) is present; (3) lamination and stratification are fair to excellent; sorting is excellent; (4) marine fossils range from bedded shells with articulated valves to sparse isolated remains; (5) individual units as well as bedded geologic successions will be areally extensive, recognizable over a range from scores to hundreds of kilometres; (6) discrete strata, members, and formations do not vary greatly in thickness within short to moderate distances; (7) ripple marks may be present but commonly lack shells in the troughs, and mud cracks and raindrop prints are absent; (8) clastic and chemical sediments may interleave, or be interbedded; sandstones, siltstones, and shales may have limestone or dolostone interbeds; (9) lateral lithologic changes are subtle and extend over large areas; vertical lithologic changes are abrupt and sharp; (10) bedding or stratification planes are essentially horizontal; and (11) disconformities are not pronounced.

The bathyal, abyssal, and hadal zone (deepwater realm) has the following characteristics: (1) there are very fine textured silty and clayey sediments; (2) the textural range is extremely low, particularly among sediments that are silty and clayey only; (3) radiolarian and ribbon cherts and siliceous shales are present; (4) turbidites (graded sediments), graded bedding, chaotic, and other "out-of-place" coarse-textured materials may be sharply interbedded with finer sediments; (5) fossils of deepwater realms are present but scanty; turbidities may contain fossils obtained from the littoral zone or even from land areas; (6) burrowing structures may be present; (7) red and blue muds, possibly of volcanic-ash source, may be present; and (8) beds commonly range from thin to laminated and finely laminated and are not areally extensive.

MIXED MARINE AND NONMARINE ENVIRONMENT

The mixed environment consists of the supralittoral zone, the beach, and the deltaic zones. The supralittoral zone has the following characteristics: (1) restricted environments have aphanic dolostone with algal crusts; (2) deposits are thin and not areally extensive, in bands parallel to coastline; (3) high-energy, high-storm deposits may have littoral fossils crudely mixed with supralittoral dolostones; (4) mud cracks and raindrop prints may be present; and (5) tree stumps may be in place or logs may be present in chaotic jumble.

Beach, deltaic, and lacustrine environments

The beach zone has the following characteristics: (1) sandstones are cross-bedded with moderate- to high-inclination on foreset beds; (2) low textural range is present within cross-bedded sands; (3) stranded shells interlayered in beach sands display wave abrasion; some may represent life-forms common to the littoral zone, now stranded on the beach; (4) where beach shingle of flattened, disk-shaped pebbles is present, an imbricate structure is evident; (5) beach gravel (conglomerate) contains shells derived from the littoral zone crudely intermixed with gravel; (6) deposits are arranged in linear bands parallel to the coastline; (7) beach conglomerates are well cemented, in modern and ancient deposits; (8) land-derived logs and stumps and land-derived sediments are present; and (9) wind ripple marks and excellent sorting is present locally.

The deltaic zone has the following characteristics: (1) sandstones are arranged in linear bodies and are well sorted, with low textural range; (2) foreset dips (even in excess of 35°) are prevalent in the direction of streamflow; (3) lenses, pockets, and thin layers of carbonaceous shales are present; (4) much vegetation is derived from land; (5) there are rapid lateral and vertical lithologic changes; (6) tree stumps may occur in growth position; (7) mixtures of marine and nonmarine fossils are present; (8) there is a high textural range, except for localized thin units; (9) there are various sedimentary structures: scour, ball-and-pillow, burrowed units, roll-and-plunge, and slump overturning; (10) channel cut-and-fill features are present; (11) coarse-textured sediments grade into finer textured sediments; and (12) localized lacustrine deposits are present.

NONMARINE ENVIRONMENT

The nonmarine environment consists of the lacustrine, eolian, fluvial, and glacial realms. The lacustrine realm (nearshore) has the following characteristics: (1) sediments are medium to coarse textured (sandstones to conglomerates); (2) there is a high textural range (boulders to clay—conglomerates to shales); (3) there is a strong contrast in bed thickness and areal extent; (4) some well-sorted pockets, lenses, and thin beds are present; (5) cross-bedding is characteristic; (6) fossils from surf or high-energy realm and some from land are present; (7) shingle gravels may be present; (8) there are contrasting vertical and lateral lithologic changes; (9) stratification planes may dip in all directions; (10) marsh mucks, delta lobes, channel cut-and-fill structures are present; (11) units are not uniformly thick or of areal extent; and (12) washed-in land plants (stumps, logs, and leaves) are present.

In areas of still water the lacustrine realm will exhibit different characteristics, which may be summarized as follows: (1) material is fine textured, and siltstones, shales, and mudstones are common; (2) there is a low textural range (silt to clay), except where turbidity currents have introduced coarse materials from land or nearshore; (3) definite, well-sorted layers and varves are common; (4) laminae and beds are rather uniform in thickness; (5) fossil fish, bivalves, and other organisms of lake origin are present; (6) sediment is distributed continuously over large or small areas, according to the size of the lake; (7) evaporites and saline sediments may be present; (8) aphanic dolostones may be common; (9) oolites, pisolites, oncolites, and other accretionary limestone accumulations may be present; (10) tufa, travertine, and similar limestone buildups may be present; (11) bioherms are common and extensive; (12) montmorillonite clays are common; and (13) if present, illite clays contain little (10 to 50 parts per million) boron.

The eolian, fluvial, and glacial environments

The eolian realm has the following characteristics: (1) the textural range is low (fine-textured sandstones, extremely well sorted; if silty, well-sorted "adobes" or loess); (2) sediments are prominently cross-bedded into large-scale, sweeping, and festoon types; (3) they are sorted into irregular beds and lenses; (4) sediment is porous if original depositional fabric is preserved; (5) stratification planes are rarely horizontal and commonly dip up to 33°; (6) stratification planes may be crisscrossed and dip in all directions; (7) sand grains may display tiny pits resulting from sand blasting; (8) sand grains commonly are rounded to well rounded and spherical; (9) there is a strong contrast in thickness laterally and vertically; (10) fossils, if any, are of terrestrial forms; footprints may be present; and (11) ripple marks and raindrop imprints may show on cross-beds.

The fluvial realm has the following characteristics: (1) the textural range is high (blocks and boulders to mud or shale); (2) the sediment is nonsorted to poorly sorted; (3) it is lenticular in form—units thicken and thin rapidly and change in lithology; (4) channel sands and cut-and-fill structures are common; (5) log jams and logs in ancient stream channels may be common; (6) lenses and pockets of gravel may occur in fine sediment; (7) the sediment is distributed in belts (river flats and piedmont alluvial plains); some beds are linear "shoestring" sands with definite trends as distributaries or master-channel deposit; (8) when discrete sands of shoestring nature are mappable, a prevailing one-direction dip is characteristic; only locally are small opposing dips present; (9) the deposit diminishes in thickness uniformly in the direction of the divergence of dips; (10) lithologically, the sediment is likely to be heterogeneous; and (11) fossils, if present, are disarticulated, broken, and highly mixed.

The glacial realm has the following characteristics: (1) sediment is heterogeneous and largely nonsorted and may rest on glacially striated bedrock; (2) there is a high textural range, ranging from rock flour to unusually large blocks and boulders; (3) there is no stratification, except by glaciofluvial streams or as varves in glacial lakes; (4) most sediment is angular to subangular, unless derived from an already rounded conglomerate or gravel; (5) variation in thickness within short distances is unusually high; (6) sediment commonly is foreign to the area of outcrop (*e.g.,* granitic and metamorphic rocks may occur far from their source area); (7) large angular and subangular blocks enclosed in tillites may display striations; (8) bases of glacial deposits contrast sharply with the substrate on which they rest; (9) deposits may contain paleosols (*i.e.,* buried soil horizons); and (10) fossils, if any, are of terrestrial origin, save for fossils ripped from sediments over which the glacial material was transported. (H.J.Bi./Ed.)

Important sedimentary rock types

CONGLOMERATES, BRECCIAS, AND TILLITES

Distinguishing characteristics

As noted above, conglomerates and breccias are rocks composed of coarse fragments of pre-existing rocks that are held within a matrix of finer particles. The name conglomerate is from the Latin *conglomeratus* ("lumped together"). The rock essentially is consolidated gravel, and the coarse components, or clasts, have been individually transported and worn down by abrasion and solution before deposition. Any clastic deposit coarser than sand size (two millimetres [0.078 inch] in diameter) may be called a conglomerate, but the term usually is restricted to water-laid sediments. Thus, conglomerates are distinct from tillites, which are presumed to be ice-transported and, hence, of glacial origin. A breccia consists of unworn, generally angular, fragments. Sometimes the term rudite is used to embrace both conglomerates and breccias. Coarse clastic rocks are generally considered to bear witness to upheavals in Earth history; faulting, mountain building, marine transgressions, glaciations, and volcanism are the processes principally responsible for production of the requisite fragments. This view must be slightly qualified—at least with respect to faulting and mountain building—because in addition to the undeniable requirements of suitable source rocks and some relief, the agency of transport involved must be competent to transport coarse gravels to a site of deposition. Although it is generally true that coarse debris is derived from fault-block mountains and similar terrain, climate—and water discharge, its derivative—is at least of equal importance in the creation of conglomerates through fluvial processes. The occurrence of conglomerates and breccias in the geological record is therefore significant as long as transport requirements can be assumed to have been met; their presence often has helped to define stratigraphic boundaries. Because of their permeability, conglomerates provide good drainage and act as aquifers (water-bearing layers) underground. This property is of increasing importance in an age of urban and industrial expansion. The importance of these coarse sedimentary rocks to man is perhaps greatest with regard to their mineral content. Valuable heavy minerals such as gold, gemstones, tin, and tungsten settle together with stream gravel once they are freed by weathering, and this creates easily worked placer deposits. At depth within the Earth, on the other hand, brecciated zones are favourable locations for the occurrence of ore veins and other mineral deposits.

Composition, texture, and structure. Rocks that disintegrate easily on weathering, such as granite, mica schist, and shale, can only contribute coarse particles if mechanical erosion is fairly rapid; fragments that are fissile (split easily, like slate) or easily abraded and reduced in size cannot survive much transport. Thus, many common rock types are rare as conglomerate components. On the other hand, tightly knit siliceous rocks such as chert, metamorphic quartzite, vein quartz, and rhyolite are almost indestructible, and, for this reason, they are disproportionately represented. The matrix consists of primary components deposited together with the clasts and secondary material that is introduced or formed later. The primary matrix of a conglomerate, trapped between the accumulating pebbles, is commonly sandy. Most sand grains are quartz, so the matrix also contributes to the silica-rich composition of conglomerates.

Primary matrix of conglomerates

Tillites and breccias are formed by less selective processes, and their composition closely reflects the rocks from which they were derived. Mechanically weak components are crushed to produce a primary matrix that is, therefore, often clay rich. The various kinds of brittle rocks present will contribute clasts.

Because no two clasts are alike, only general descriptions can be given unless some property has been measured on a sufficient number of clasts and treated statistically. And because clasts are not regular solids, simple yet significant parameters of such properties as shape and roundness are hard to devise. Clasts are shaped by breaking until reentrants (inward projecting hollows) are eliminated and no dimension greatly exceeds the others. Transport also blunts sharp edges, producing increasing roundness by grinding and bumping, until tough, water-worn pebbles may approximate the perfect roundness of an ellipsoid.

In conglomerates, shape depends largely on the internal structure of the clasts; fissile rocks, for example, occur as disk- or blade-shaped pebbles. Roundness, however, depends on the distance of transport. Tillite components tend toward irregular, faceted shapes and slightly rounded edges, both due to grinding. In most breccias, the fragments are naturally angular; in fact, the degree of roundness is commonly used to distinguish, or even to define, conglomerates and breccias. There are a few rocks in which the components have not been worn by transport but were rounded to begin with; application of the roundness criterion will lead to classification of such rocks as conglomerates, although genetically they belong with the breccias.

In terms of size a conglomerate can consist of pebbles, boulders, or cobbles; the overall rock may be well or poorly sorted, however. Maximum size depends on the power or competence of the transport medium, whereas sorting depends on the mode of transportation. Most water-laid conglomerates are pebbly and fairly well sorted to well sorted, whereas boulders that exhibit no sorting by size are typical of tillites. A cross section through a conglomerate does not cut through most clasts at their greatest circumference; for this reason, both size and sorting of a conglomerate appear to be less than they actually are (Figure 106).

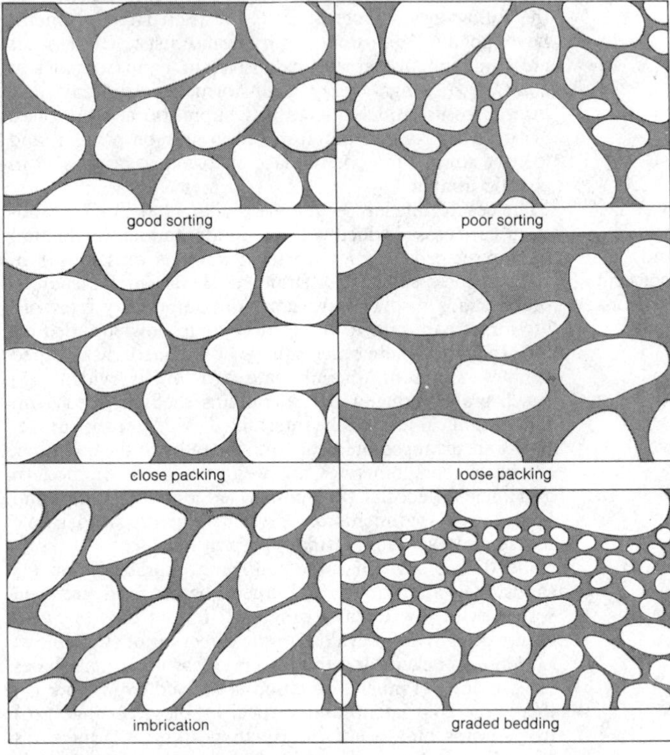

Figure 106: Textures and structures of conglomerates.

Packing is called close if neighbouring clasts are touching and if the near-maximum number is crammed into a given space, occupying about 75 percent of the space available. The interstices only are filled by matrix in this case. In a loose packing, the matrix largely envelops the clasts. If matrix preponderates, the rock is called a pebbly sandstone or pebbly mudstone; "boulder clay" is not a descriptive term but applies exclusively to coarse glacial tills.

Bedding (layering or stratification) in conglomerates, if apparent at all, is typically thick and lenticular. Graded bedding, in which size decreases from bottom to top, is common: as agitated waters rarely subside at once, declining transport power causes a gradual upward decrease in maximum clast size. Relative to the bedding, the pebbles in sandy conglomerates tend to lie flat, with their smallest dimension vertical and the greatest aligned roughly parallel to the current. But in closely packed conglomerates, there often is a distinct imbrication; that is, flat pebbles overlap in the same direction, like roof shingles. Imbrication is upstream on riverbeds and seaward on beaches. Tillites are massive and do not exhibit bedding. Breccias, however, may be massive, bedded, or flow layered.

Porosity is the volume percentage of "void" (actually, fluid- or air-filled) space in a rock, whereas permeability is defined by the rate of flow of water, at a given pressure gradient, through a unit volume. Conglomerates are among the most porous of rocks, and, because the chief resistance to flow is due to friction and capillary effects, coarseness makes a conglomerate more permeable—by a factor of tens or hundreds—than an equally porous but fine-grained sandstone. Conglomerates therefore provide excellent surface drainage and are to be avoided as dam and reservoir sites. Underground, they hold water reserves that are easily released through wells.

On the other hand, the occurrence of a clayey matrix will make the rock practically impermeable. Tillites and boulder clays make excellent dams, both natural and artificial. Fault breccias are either more or less permeable than the unfragmented rock they traverse. For these reasons, conglomerates and breccias are a major concern of hydrology.

Postdepositional changes

The permeability of conglomerates favours cementation by precipitated mineral substances. Very little of this "secondary matrix"—commonly silica or calcium carbonate—is needed to bond a conglomerate into a firm and coherent rock. Much of it is furnished by preferential solution within the deposit itself, either of fine matter in the primary matrix, or at points where clasts touch each other and pressure is concentrated. Interpenetrating pitted, or even sutured, pebbles bear witness to this phenomenon.

Where packing is loose and clay is a major constituent of the matrix—as in tillites and mudflow breccias—consolidation can be attained by simple compaction: volume and porosity are reduced and interstitial water expelled by increasing overburden or tectonic compression (caused by Earth movements such as mountain building). In calcareous breccias, recrystallization of the primary matrix is often a major factor. Many of the ornamental marble breccias of commerce really belong in this category, though some—such as serpentine breccia—are true marbles in the sense that they have been metamorphosed.

Conglomerates often are metamorphosed to quartzites in which the clasts remain discernible. Simultaneous tectonic deformation (folding and squeezing) produces conglomerate quartzites in which the original pebbles are all flattened to parallel blades or stretched parallel to the fold axes to form long rods.

Origin of conglomerates. The formation of a conglomerate is governed by three conditions, namely, (1) a source area that produces rock fragments, (2) moving water capable of transporting the clasts, and (3) a depositional site or trap where the transport energy fails. Suitably hard rocks must crop out in the source area, and their denudation must be rapid enough to outpace solution and disintegration by chemical weathering, which would, of course, preclude the production of clasts. Steep or arid mountain ranges, active fault scarps, and retreating rocky coasts are thus the major sources of conglomerates.

Transport and deposition

A water current moves stones by traction—rolling them along the bottom and sorting, shaping, and rounding them in the process. But water cannot transport even small pebbles unless it flows faster than one to 1.5 metres (five feet) per second. Such bottom velocities are exceeded by many rivers and by tidal currents and wave eddies in shallow water, but not by offshore marine currents; thus the formation of conglomerates is restricted to continents and their coastal waters. Streams move their coarsest load only during intermittent flood stages, which is another reason why an arid climate favours the formation of conglomerates.

Deposition will occur where the moving water no longer meets energy requirements of its load. This commonly takes place when a stream debouches into a wide valley or plain. Obstructed by its own deposited loads, the course will be deflected frequently and conglomerates or pebbly sandstones will spread out to form a conical alluvial fan. The rocks formed by ancient fans are sometimes called fanglomerates. Along a mountain front or scarp, fans coalesce to form a wedge of sediment that also is called a piedmont deposit. Amid sandy flood deposits in such regions, conglomeratic strings, lenses, and other traces mark abandoned stream channels.

Surf that undermines a steep rocky coast will produce fragments that are very well rounded. If the sea continues to encroach upon a subsiding land area, a transgression conglomerate, extended but thin, is gradually spread like a blanket over the abraded surface. As the coast recedes, this becomes covered by offshore sands and clays, and the initial coarse deposit is designated a basal conglomerate.

Origin of tillites. A tillite is, by definition, an ancient, consolidated till and must therefore be of glacial origin. In the case of Recent tills (those formed during the last 10,000 years), the connection wth glaciers or ice sheets is still in evidence. For the much more extensive Pleistocene tills (formed during the interval from 10,000 to 2,500,000 years ago), the relationship to ice also can be demonstrated convincingly. This is not true, however, for many formations that predate Pleistocene time, and the designation tilloid—meaning merely till-like—is often preferable. Tills are of two kinds: the local moraines (ridges of debris marginal to glaciers) of mountain glaciers and the great till blankets that were spread over lowlands by ice sheets. Only the latter have a good chance of becoming preserved in the geological record. But ice sheets imply a glacial age, and glaciations are exceptional episodes in the Earth's history. True ancient tillites, therefore, are rare and very interesting formations.

Origin of breccias. Breccias can be loosely classified with respect to origin as residual, intraformational, mudflow, impact, collapse, tectonic, and volcanic.

Residual breccias consist of rubble produced by mechanical weathering, not far removed from its place of origin. As opposed to conglomerates, the clasts should show no evidence of transport and be angular in shape and poorly sorted; all kinds of transitions occur, however. Slope breccias (Figure 107) accumulate as scree (hillslope talus or rubble) along the lower parts of mountain slopes. In deserts, rubble is periodically removed from the hillsides by sheetfloods and spread into the intervening basins to form a deposit often called, as in ancient fan deposits in general, fanglomerate. If the finer fractions are carried away, leaving only coarse rubble, a lag breccia results.

By courtesy of Ernst ten Haaf

Figure 107: Quartzite slope breccia of Cambrian age from Ardennes, Belgium.

Intraformational and mudflow breccias

Intraformational breccias are derived from, and intercalated between, contemporary sediments; they are typical of shallow marine environments where the seabed is likely to be torn up from time to time by storms or shifting tides. If the sediment involved was still loose, it will settle again as an ordinary bed; but, if there had been some prior consolidation, a blanket or channel of breccia is produced. The designation sedimentary breccia is commonly, and rather confusingly, restricted to this kind of origin. If consolidation was slight, the clasts will appear as rounded or convoluted lumps; but limestones, which tend to indurate rapidly, often form angular breccias that are sometimes called sharpstone conglomerates. An apron of reef breccia (reef talus) surrounds the base of coral and algal reefs attacked by surf.

Mudflow breccias are formed when a mass of partly consolidated sediment slides downslope with enough clay present to permit plastic flow to occur. Brittle beds are then broken up to contribute angular, unsorted clasts scattered through the clay matrix. On land, mudflows are common on steep hillsides, creeping down slowly (landslip) or descending catastrophically (lahar); but the resulting breccias stand little chance of ultimately escaping erosion. On the other hand, the geological record reveals many mudflow breccias that are intercalated with offshore marine formations. Some are mere intraformational slump breccias of local, contemporaneous sediment; but others have evidently travelled far on a gentle slope, because they involve exotic clasts, often of various ages. The designation olistostrome has come into use for the latter type.

Figure 108: Tilted conglomerates of the Pyrenean Molasse at Peña de Oroel near Jaca, Spain.

By courtesy of the Geological Institute, Utrecht

Angular clasts, provided by the breaking up of coherent rocks in the flow, remain unsorted and may range up to mountain size. If loose gravel or boulders have slid down from coastal deposits, the result is a pebbly mudstone or a boulder bed. Formerly, many boulder beds have been mistaken for tillites. The term *mélange* is used to designate some coarse, variegated breccias of disputed origin.

Impact breccias, thought to have been produced by the fall of large meteorites, are rare on Earth but may prove to be common on the Moon. Minute breccias with a glassy matrix that may have originated in this manner were among the samples of moon rocks collected on the first U.S. Apollo mission to the Moon.

Collapse breccias are caused by postdepositional dissolution or shrinking of certain beds in a series. The transition of gypsum to anhydrite and, to a lesser extent, the secondary dolomitization of limestone, entail a loss of volume that favours brecciation of these rocks and of overlying beds. False breccias can be produced by partial dolomitization along cracks and joints in a limestone that has never been broken up.

Tectonic breccias are formed from rocks strained beyond the plastic limit and are associated with faulting. Little is known about the conditions that make some faults appear as clean-cut planes and others as zones of fault breccia many metres thick. The matrix of a tectonic breccia may be largely primary, consisting of finely ground rock flour, or secondary, precipitated from percolating solutions. On deep-reaching fault zones, these solutions have often been ascending and metalliferous, making tectonic breccias of importance to mining. (E.t.H./Ed.)

SANDSTONES

The weathering of rocks into their constituent mineral grains yields great quantities of sand-sized particles. This material is carried down rivers to the coast where it accumulates as dunes on beaches and as submarine bars, deltas, and other offshore deposits. Gradual consolidation converts such sand deposits into sandstone.

Grain size

Sandstones generally are defined as consisting mainly of grains between 0.06 and two millimetres (0.002 and 0.078 inch) in diameter; they grade on the one hand into conglomerates and breccias and on the other into siltstones and shales. When the proportion of shell fragments, oolites, and other biogenic material increases, they also grade into limestones.

Most sandstones are resistant to erosion, and they form about one-fourth of the sedimentary rocks of the earth's crust and thus create the backbone of many mountain ranges, such as the Appalachians, Carpathians, Pennines, and Appenines. Sandstone beds that are gently folded or nearly horizontal tend to form plains and uplands on which poor soils develop.

Sandstone components and colour. There are three basic components of sandstones. These are (1) detrital grains, mainly transported, sand-sized minerals such as quartz and feldspar; (2) a detrital matrix of clay or mud, which is absent in "clean" sandstones; and (3) a cement that is chemically precipitated in crystalline form from solution and that serves to fill up original pore spaces. The conversion of any sediment to rock is called diagenesis. Most diagenesis is caused by cementation, but some occurs by the recrystallization of clay minerals. Some sandstones that have no cement and little or no clay matrix are loose enough to be crushed with the fingers. Sandstones bonded with calcite or iron oxide cements are moderately hard. The hardest of all sandstones are those in which the pore spaces have been completely filled with chemically precipitated quartz cement, particularly if this quartz is in crystallographic continuity with detrital quartz grains. In this event, the quartz has the strength that would be attributable to a single mass. The original, detrital quartz grain is separated from the overgrowth by a thin line of water bubbles, clay, or hematite (iron oxide). These thoroughly cemented, quartz-rich rocks, or quartzites, form some of the hardest, most resistant rocks in the Earth's crust. The Tuscarora Quartzite of Silurian (395,000,000 to 420,000,000 years ago) age, for example, makes the high ridges in most of the Appalachian Mountains.

Other minerals that may occur as cement in sandstones include feldspar, gypsum, barite, dolomite, opal, pyrite, and chert, among others. Deep burial of sandstones may produce more unusual cements, such as zeolites or chlorite, and the original clay matrix may be recrystallized to micas. Electron luminescence examination of thin sections of such formations can reveal special features of cementation that are not visible by any other means. For the identification of very fine-grained or complex minerals such as clays or zeolites, X-ray diffraction may be necessary.

The colour of a sandstone depends upon its detrital grains and bonding material. An abundance of potassium feldspar often gives a pink colour; this is true of many arkoses, which are feldspar-rich sandstones. Fine-grained, dark-coloured rock fragments, such as pieces of slate, chert, or andesite, however, give a salt-and-pepper appearance to a sandstone. Iron oxide cement imparts tones of yellow, orange, brown, or red, whereas calcite cement imparts a gray colour. A sandstone consisting almost wholly of quartz grains cemented by quartz may be glassy and white. A chloritic clay matrix gives a greenish-black colour and extreme hardness; such rocks are graywackes.

Formation of sandstones today. Sandstones occur in strata of all geologic ages. Much of man's understanding of the depositional environment of ancient sandstones comes from detailed study of sand bodies forming today. One of the clues to the origin is the overall shape of the entire sand deposit. Inland desert sands today cover vast areas as a uniform blanket; some ancient sandstones in beds a few hundred metres thick but 1,600 kilometres or more in lateral extent, such as the Mesozoic Nubian Sandstone of North Africa, also may have formed as blankets of desert sand. Deposits from alluvial fans form thick, fault-bounded prisms. River sands today form "shoestring-shaped" bodies, tens of metres thick, a few hundred metres wide, up to 60 kilometres or more long, and usually oriented perpendicularly to the shoreline. In meandering back and forth, a river may construct a wide swath of sand deposits, mostly accumulating on meander-point bars. Beaches, coastal dunes, and barrier bars also form "shoestring" sands, but these are parallel to the shore. Deltaic sands show a fanlike pattern of radial, thick, finger-shaped sand bodies interbedded with muddy sediments. Submarine sand bodies are diverse, reflecting the complexities of underwater topography and currents. They may form great ribbons parallel with the current; huge submarine "dunes" or "sand waves" aligned perpendicularly to the current; or irregular shoals, bars, and sheets. Some sands are deposited in deep water by the action of density currents, which flow down submarine slopes by reason of their high sediment concentrations and, hence, are called turbidity currents. These characteristically form thin beds interbedded with shales; sandstone beds often are graded from coarse grains at the base to fine grains at the top of the bed and commonly have a clay matrix.

Bedding structure. One of the most fruitful methods of deciphering the environment of deposition and direction of transport of ancient sandstones is detailed field study of the sedimentary structures.

Bedding-plane markings and cross-bedding

Bedding in sandstones may be tens of feet thick, but it can range downward to paper-thin laminations, expressed by layers of clays, micas, heavy minerals, pebbles, or fossils. Flagstone breaks in very smooth, even layers a few inches thick and is used in paving. Thin, nearly horizontal lamination is characteristic of many ancient beach sandstones. Bedding surfaces of sandstones may be marked by ripples (almost always of subaqueous origin), by tracks and trails of organisms, and by elongated grains that are oriented by current flow (fossils, plant fragments, or even elongated sand grains). Sand grain orientation tends to parallel direction of the current; river-channel trends in fluvial sediments, wave-backwash direction in beach sands, and wind direction in aeolian sediments are examples of such orientation.

A great variety of markings, such as flutes and scour and fill grooves, can be found on the undersides of some sandstone beds. These markings are caused by swift currents during deposition; they are particularly abundant in sandstones deposited by turbidity currents.

Within the major beds, cross-bedding is common. This structure is developed by the migration of small ripples, sand waves, tidal-channel large-scale ripples, or dunes and consists of sets of beds that are inclined to the main horizontal bedding planes. Almost all sedimentary environments produce characteristic types of cross-beds; as one example, the lee faces of sand dunes (side not facing the wind) may bear cross-beds as much as 33 metres (100 feet) high and dipping 35°.

Graded beds, slump structures, and fossils

Some sandstones contain series of graded beds. The grains at the base of a graded bed are coarse and gradually become finer upward, at which point there is a sharp change to the coarse basal layer of the overlying bed. Among the many mechanisms that can cause these changes in grain size are turbidity currents, but in general they can be caused by any cyclically repeated waning current.

After the sand is deposited, it may slide downslope or subside into soft underlying clays. This shifting gives rise to contorted or slumped bedding on a scale of centimetres to tens of metres. Generally these are characteristic of unstable areas of rapid deposition.

Local cementation may result in concretions of calcite, pyrite, barite, and other minerals. These can range from sand crystals or barite roses to spheroidal or discoidal concretions tens of metres across.

The fossil content also is a useful guide to the depositional environment of sandstones. Desert sandstones usually lack fossils. River-channel and deltaic sandstones may contain fossil wood, plant fragments, fossil footprints, or vertebrate remains. Beach and shallow marine sands contain mollusks, arthropods, crinoids, and other marine creatures, though marine sandstones are much less fossiliferous than marine limestones. Deepwater sands are frequently devoid of skeletal fossils, although tracks and trails may be common. The fossils are not actually structures, of course, but the living organisms are able to produce these.

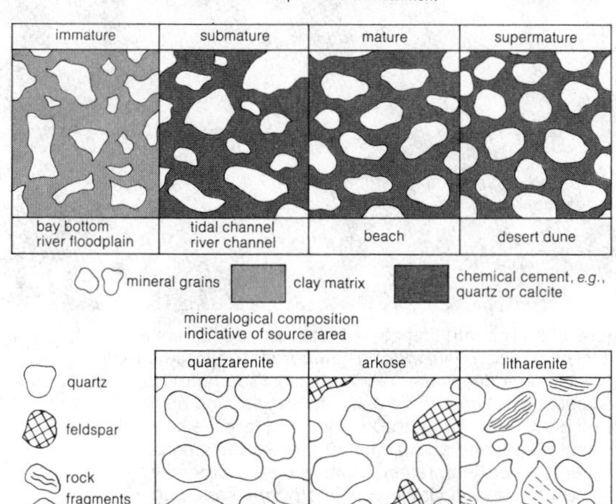

Figure 109: Textural maturity and mineralogical composition of sandstones from various environments.

Burrowing by organisms, for example, may cause small-scale structures, such as eyes and pods or tubules of sand.

Textures. The texture of a sandstone is the sum of such attributes as the clay matrix, the size and sorting of the detrital grains, and the roundness of these particles. To evaluate this property, a scale of textural maturity that involved four textural stages was devised in 1951. These stages are described as follows.

Degree of textural maturity

Immature sandstones contain a clay matrix, and the sand-sized grains are usually angular and poorly sorted. This means that a wide range of sand sizes is present. Such sandstones are characteristic of environments in which sediment is dumped and is not thereafter worked upon by waves or currents. These environments include stagnant areas of sluggish currents such as lagoons or bay bottoms or undisturbed sea floor below the zone of wave or current action. Immature sands also form where sediments are rapidly deposited in subaerial environments, such as river floodplains, swamps, alluvial fans, or glacial margins. Submature sandstones are created by the removal of the clay matrix by current action. The sand grains are, however, still poorly sorted in these rocks. Submarine sandstones are common as river-channel sands, tidal-channel sands, and shallow submarine sands swept by unidirectional currents. Mature sandstones are clay free, and the sand grains are subangular; but they are well sorted, that is, of nearly uniform particle size. Typically, these sandstones form in environments of current reversal and continual washing, such as on beaches. Supermature sandstones are those that are clay free; well sorted; and, in addition, those in which the grains are well rounded. These sandstones probably formed mostly as desert dunes, where intense aeolian abrasion over a very long period of time may abrade sand grains to nearly spherical shapes.

More detailed study of texture, first accomplished in 1898, involved grain-size analysis, and the establishment of the following grain-size terms: 1–2 millimetres (0.039–0.078 inch), very coarse sand; 0.5–1.0 mm (0.019–0.039 in.), coarse sand; 0.25–0.5 mm (0.009–0.019 in.), medium sand; 0.125–0.25 mm (0.0045–0.009 in.), fine sand; and 0.062–0.125 mm (0.0022–0.0045 in.), very fine sand. For purposes of analysis, the cement is removed chemically, and the sandstone is carefully broken down into its constituent detrital grains. These grains are then filtered through a stack of sieves with fixed, decreasing mesh size. Size can also be measured by allowing the grains to settle in a water column (the larger grains settle more rapidly). From these analyses a size frequency distribution showing the weight of grains in each size class can be constructed. Often an analysis of a beach or river sand will show a typical Gaussian curve or bell-shaped size distribution. A logarithmic transformation (the φ scale) invented in 1934 greatly facilitates statistical analysis. The main parameters it measures are mean size, standard deviation (a measure of sorting), skewness (symmetry of the frequency distribution), and kurtosis (peakedness).

Such information is useful in identifying depositional environments. For example, dune sands in all parts of the world tend to be in the 0.12–0.25 mm (0.0022–0.0045 in.) mean size range, because sand of that size is easiest to move by winds. Desert floor sediments tend to be bimodal or polymodal, with two (or more) abundant sizes of grains with a gap in between. Dune and beach sands exhibit the best sorting, and river and shallow marine sands are less well sorted. Such sediments as glacial tills, river-floodplain deposits, and submarine sands in areas of sluggish currents have much poorer sorting. Skewness serves to separate beach sands, which are often negatively skewed (with a tail of coarse grains), from dune and river sands, which tend to be positively skewed (with a tail of fine grains). Kurtosis is valuable in identifying sediments that have come from a mixture of two materials, such as beach sands blown into a muddy lagoon.

Shape and roundness

Careful analysis of grain roundness and grain shape also can aid in distinguishing the high-abrasion environments of beach and especially dune sands from those of fluvial or marine sands. Rounding takes place much more rapidly in sands subjected to wind action than in water-laid sands. In general, coarser sand grains are better rounded than

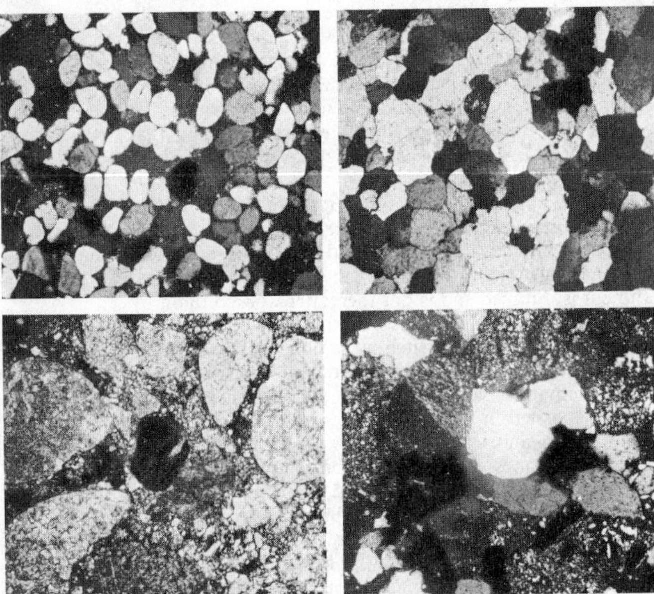

Figure 110: (Top left) Cambrian quartzarenite, cemented with calcite and typical of those formed originally as dune sands. (Top right) Silurian Tuscarora quartzite, a former beach sand. Quartz sand grains are well rounded and are completely cemented by quartz overgrowths visible as clear rims around the "dusty" detrital nuclei. (Bottom left) Submature calclithite of the Ordovician Marathon Formation. (Bottom right) Chert-arenite consisting of about 50 percent quartz and 50 percent chert (finely speckled). It probably is a channel sandstone derived from older sedimentary rocks. (All photographs magnified about 50 ×.)

By courtesy of R.L. Folk

finer grains because the coarser ones hit bottom more frequently and also hit with greater impact during transport. Sand grains may also have polished, frosted, pitted, or otherwise characteristic surfaces. These depend on the grain size, the agent of transport, and the amount of chemical attack. For example, polish can occur on medium-grained beach sands and fine-grained desert sands and can also be produced chemically by weathering processes.

Mineral composition. Mineralogical study of sandstones has proceeded along two distinct lines. One method involves cutting a thin section (0.03 mm [0.0012 in.] thick) from the rock for examination of the mineralogy, cementation, texture, and structures with a petrographic microscope. This thin section approach was first used in the 1870s. Another method is to disaggregate the sand and place the grains in a heavy liquid such as bromoform (density about 2.8). This concentrates the heavy minerals that are present in minute amounts (0.01 to 1 or 2 percent of the rock) for detailed microscopic study. These methods offer valuable clues to source area composition.

Although sandstones may be composed of any mineral, the most common mineral is quartz (SiO_2), which comprises about 80 percent of the average sandstone; a few sandstones, however, lack quartz entirely, whereas others contain more than 99 percent quartz. Microscopic study reveals a great many types of quartz, recognizable by their appearance in polarized light and by inclusions of gas or liquid bubbles or other substances. Volcanic quartz, various types of metamorphic quartz, hydrothermal quartz, and other varieties are known. Other detrital minerals of common occurrence are the feldspars and micas. The abundance of these chemically less resistant silicates has been used as a climatic indicator. Sand-sized fragments of older fine-grained rocks (*e.g.*, chert, slate, basalt) are common in many sandstones. Clay matrix, if present, may consist of the minerals illite, kaolinite, montmorillonite, or clay-sized micas. Some marine sandstones contain an abundance of pellets of glauconite (greensands) or phosphates in the form of bones, teeth, scales, or chemical precipitates. These sands are useful as fertilizers.

Classification of sandstones. There are many different systems of mineralogic classification of sandstones. The system presented here is that of R.L. Folk (1966), based upon the concepts of P.D. Krynine, an American sedimentologist, and others. In it sandstones are divided into three main groups based on percentages of quartz, feldspar, and rock fragments. Clays are considered only in the textural part of the name (*e.g.*, clayey fine sandstone), and cements and accessory minerals are handled by descriptive adjectives. Rocks whose sand grains consist of more than 95 percent quartz are termed quartzarenites. If the sand grains consist of more than 25 percent feldspar, the rock is termed arkose; if the feldspar content is between 5 and 25 percent it is "subarkose." Sandstones with more than 25 percent rock fragments are called litharenites and are further subdivided according to the nature of the rock fragments (see below). "Sublitharenite" contains 5 to 25 percent rock fragments.

Quartzarenites. Quartzarenites are usually white but may be any other colour; cementation by hematite, for example, makes them red. They are usually well sorted and well rounded (supermature) and often represent ancient dune, beach, or shallow marine deposits. Characteristically, they are ripple marked or cross-bedded and occur as widespread thin blanket sands. On chemical analysis, some are found to contain more than 99 percent SiO_2 (silicon dioxide, or silica). Most commonly they are cemented with quartz, but calcite and iron oxide are common cements.

This type of sandstone is widespread in stable areas of continents surrounding the craton (a stable area), such as central North America (St. Peter Sandstone, Ordovician), central Australia, or the Russian Platform, and are particularly common in Paleozoic strata. Quartzarenites have formed in the past when large areas of subcontinental dimensions were tectonically stable (not subject to uplift or deformation) and of low relief, so that extensive weathering could take place, accompanied by prolonged abrasion and sorting. This process eliminated all the unstable or readily decomposed minerals such as feldspar or rock fragments and concentrated pure quartz together with trace amounts of such resistant heavy minerals as zircon and tourmaline. Occasionally, deeply subsiding basins adjoining stable cratons were filled with many thousands of feet of quartzarenite. Quartzarenites also form in geosynclines (large depositional troughs that are loci of mountain

By courtesy of R.L. Folk

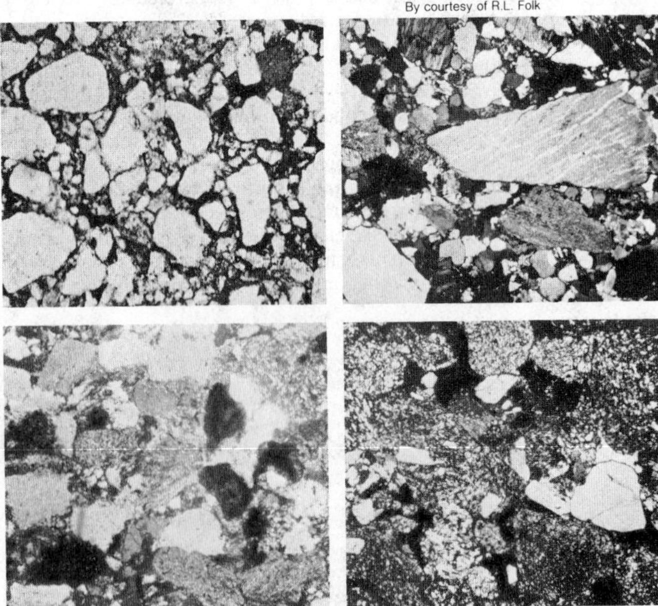

Figure 111: (Top left) Immature Devonian quartzarenite with clay matrix. This rock originated from turbidity-current deposition in a deepwater marine basin. (Top right) Precambrian submature arkose with angular and poorly sorted grains. (Bottom left) Devonian phyllarenite consisting of about 50 percent quartz and 50 percent metamorphic rock fragments (speckled grains). (Bottom right) Carboniferous volcanic arenite with clay matrix and poorly sorted grains of volcanic rock fragments containing tiny feldspar laths. This sandstone was deposited in an island arc area. (All photographs magnified about 50 ×.)

building) if the source area is sufficiently stable to permit beach abrasion and chemical weathering to remove rock fragments and feldspars. Apparently this was the origin of the Tuscarora Quartzite (Silurian) of the Appalachians.

Arkosic sandstones. Arkosic sandstones are of two types. The most common of these is a mixture of quartz, potash feldspar, and granitic rock fragments. Chemically, these rocks are 60–70 percent SiO_2 and 10–15 percent aluminum oxide (Al_2O_3), with significant amounts of potassium (K), sodium (Na), and other elements. This type of arkosic sandstone, or arkose, can form wherever block faulting of granitic rocks occurs, given rates of uplift, erosion, and deposition that are so great that chemical weathering is outweighed and feldspar can survive in a relatively unaltered state. These rocks are usually reddish, generally immature, very poorly sorted, and frequently interbedded with arkose conglomerate; alluvial fans or fluvial aprons are the main depositional environments. The Triassic Newark Group of Connecticut is a classic example of this type of arkosic sandstone.

Arkose

Arkoses also form under desert (or rarely Arctic) conditions in which the rate of chemical decomposition of the parent granite or gneiss is very slow. These arkoses generally are well sorted and rounded (supermature) and show other desert features, such as aeolian cross-beds (of wind origin), associated gypsum, and other evaporitic minerals. The Precambrian Torridonian Arkose of Britain is thought to be of desert origin. Basal Sands deposited on a granitic-gneissic craton (stable continental interior) are also usually arkosic. Subarkose sandstones (*e.g.,* Millstone Grit, Carboniferous of England) have a feldspar content that is diminished by more extensive weathering or abrasion or by dilution from nonigneous source rocks.

Less commonly, arkoses may contain plagioclase feldspar (sodic to calcic types) as the dominant variety. These generally result from volcanic activity and are frequently associated with volcanic rock fragments and a chlorite matrix.

Litharenites. Litharenites occur in several subvarieties, but they are normally gray or of salt-and-pepper appearance because of the inclusion of dark-coloured rock fragments. Most commonly, fragments of metamorphic rocks such as slate, phyllite, or schist predominate; this dominance produces the phyllarenite variety of sandstone. If volcanic rock fragments such as andesite and basalt are most abundant, the rock is a volcanic arenite. It is termed a vitric arenite if glass predominates. These sandstones are transitional to tuffs (derived from volcanic dust and ash). Finally, if chert or carbonate rock fragments prevail, the rock is a chert arenite or calclithite.

Litharenites are a diverse family of rocks that in general were formed by rapid deposition under unstable tectonic conditions. Among the subvarieties, the phyllarenite is most common. It is a typical sandstone of geosynclines in which a low-rank (low temperatures and pressures of origin) metamorphic source of fold mountains with slates and phyllites has been exposed. These sandstones are usually rich in mica and texturally immature; the SiO_2 content is 60–70 percent; Al_2O_3 is 15 percent; and potassium, sodium, iron, calcium, and magnesium are present in lesser amounts. Most examples are deposited as fluvial apron, deltaic, coastal-plain, and shallow marine sandstones, interbedded with great thicknesses of shale and frequently with beds of coal or limestone. If laid down in an oxidizing environment, such as a well-drained river system, they are reddish (*e.g.,* Devonian Catskill Formation of New York or the Devonian Old Red Sandstone of England). Many sandstones of the Appalachians are phyllarenites, and they are common in the Carpathians and many other mountain chains. Heightened abrasion in the beach environment eliminates the soft rock fragments, and the rock may pass into a subphyllarenite; these are often good oil reservoirs, such as the Devonian Bradford Sand of Pennsylvania.

Volcanic arenites occur mainly in unstable, island-arc volcanic regions, such as the Paleozoic Tasman Geosyncline of Australia, and they also are deposited as continental beds derived from the erosion of volcanic terranes. Chert arenites and calclithites result from rapid erosion of uplifted chert and carbonate mountain tracts, respectively. Many of these are alluvial fan deposits that front areas of intense faulting. Calclithites are common among the younger sandstones of the Alps and Slovak Carpathians.

The study of heavy minerals reveals many details about changes in source area and climate and aids in the correlation of sandstones. Quartzarenites contain only the most durable and chemically stable heavy minerals, such as tourmaline, zircon, and magnetite; yet these minerals may be present in a great number of varieties based upon colour, shape, and inclusions. Arkose and litharenite specimens often have upward of 20 species of heavy minerals, such as rutile, pyroxene, epidote, amphibole, kyanite, staurolite, and monazite. More than 100 heavy minerals are known to occur in sandstones, and in some places (Florida, Brazil, Queensland) they form black sand beaches from which the minerals can be commercially mined. In sea-bottom sediment, heavy minerals occur in distinct geographic provinces, indicating derivation from diverse source areas and revealing the direction of marine currents. (R.L.F.)

Graywackes. Graywacke is the name applied to generally dark-coloured, very strongly bonded sandstones that consist of a heterogeneous mixture of rock fragments, feldspar, and quartz of sand size, together with appreciable amounts of mud matrix. Almost all graywackes originated in the sea, and many were deposited in deep water by density (turbidity) currents.

Graywackes typically are poorly sorted, and the grain sizes present range over three orders of magnitude—*e.g.,* from 2 to 2,000 micrometres. Commonly, the coarsest part of a graywacke bed is its base, where pebbles may be abundant. Shale fragments, which represents lumps of mud eroded from bottom sediments by the depositing current, may be concentrated elsewhere in the bed.

Characteristics of graywackes

Many graywackes contain much mud, typically 15–40 percent, and this increases as the mean grain size of the rock decreases. The particles forming the rock are typically angular. This, and the presence of the interstitial mud matrix, has led to these rocks being called "microbreccias." The fabric and texture indicate that the sediments were

By courtesy of K.A.W. Crook, the Australian National University, Canberra

Figure 112: *Sedimentary structures in graywackes.*
(Left) Interbedded shales and graywackes, Lower Silurian Aberystwyth Grits, Wales. (Centre) Bed of very coarse Upper Cambrian graywacke, showing graded bedding and load casting, Denison Range, Tasmania. (Right) Groove molds on underside of graywacke bed, Middle Silurian Denbigh Grits, Wales.

carried only a short distance and were subject to very little reworking by currents after deposition.

The most widespread internal structure of graywackes is graded bedding (Figure 112), although some sequences display it poorly. Sets of cross strata more than three centimetres (1.28 inches) thick are very rare, but thinner sets are very common. Parallel lamination is very common, and convolute bedding is usually present. These internal structures are arranged within graywacke beds in a regular sequence. They appear to result from the action of a single current flow and are related to changes in the hydraulics of the depositing current. In some beds, the upper part of the sequence of structures is missing, presumably because of erosion or nondeposition. In others, the lower part is missing. This has been attributed to change in the hydraulic properties of the depositing current as it moves away from its source and its velocity decreases to the point at which the first sediment deposited is laminated, rather than massive and graded as is the case closer to the source.

The most typical external structures of graywacke beds are sole markings, which occur on their undersurfaces. Flute and groove molds (Figure 112) are the most characteristic, but many other structures have been recorded.

The upper surfaces of graywacke beds are less well characterized by sedimentary structures. The most typical are current lineation and various worm tracks, particularly the highly sinuous form *Nereites.* Apart from these trace fossils, graywackes are usually sparsely fossiliferous. Where fossils occur they are generally free-floating organisms (graptolites, forams) that have settled to the bottom, or bottom-living (benthic), shallow-water organisms displaced into deeper water as part of the sediment mass.

Role of quartz in composition of graywackes

The mineralogical composition of graywackes varies widely. Three groups can be recognized in terms of the content of free quartz grains of sand size. The first contains less than 15 percent free quartz and is derived from igneous rocks. It comprises two types of volcanic derivation, plagioclase graywacke, volcanic lithic graywacke, and serpentine graywacke, which is derived from serpentinite, a subcrustal rock. Of these, volcanic lithic graywacke is by far the most abundant. Sequences in which it occurs usually contain some beds of plagioclase graywacke. Serpentine graywacke is rare but is important because it reflects a deep rupture of the Earth's crust.

Quartz-poor graywackes are widespread in eastern Australia and around the margins of the Pacific and Caribbean but also occur within continents—for example, in the Urals. Serpentine graywacke is recorded from Colombia and the Solomon Islands.

Graywackes with from 15 to 65 percent free quartz form the second group. They are of varied composition and origin. Some are almost devoid of feldspar and are derived from sedimentary and low-grade metamorphic rocks. Others, richer in feldspar, are from heterogenous source areas containing volcanic, plutonic, metamorphic, and sedimentary rocks. Still others come from sources in which granite is widespread. The typical graywackes of North America and Europe are representatives of this group. Representatives also occur in New Zealand and eastern Australia.

The third group of graywackes (the subgraywackes of some authors) contains from 65 to 95 percent free quartz. These quartz-rich varieties exhibit the same dark colour and sedimentary structures as those poorer in quartz. They occur in thick geosynclinal sequences (deposits in great subsiding troughs), either as the dominant rock type or as a minor component with more common graywackes of the second group. Their high quartz content reflects source areas dominated by quartz-rich igneous, sedimentary, and metamorphic rocks or more heterogenous source areas in which intense chemical weathering eliminates the less stable minerals before the sediment is finally deposited.

Depositional sites, geosynclines, and Earth history

Three major depositional sites for contemporary graywackes have been recognized. The first sites, recognized early in the history of geology, are the deepsea troughs adjoining fold mountain ranges, as, for example, those off the west coast of North and South America. These troughs have been the traditional site for ancient graywackes, especially those containing intermediate amounts of quartz. The second depositional sites, recognized rather more recently, are the troughs adjoining volcanic island arcs—for example, in Indonesia and Melanesia. These are the traditional sites of accumulation of volcanic graywackes. The third sites, recently recognized, are the continental rises along the margins of continents that lack adjacent high relief, as, for example, the east coast of North America. This latter has not been cited so far to explain any particular type of graywacke, but analyses of modern North Atlantic sediments and considerations of the composition of ancient graywackes suggest that it is the typical site of accumulation of quartz-rich graywackes.

There is an intimate relationship between these depositional sites and geosynclines. The first and second sites have long been recognized as the modern analogues of ancient geosynclines. More recently the continental rise has been suggested by R.S. Dietz, an American marine geologist, as the precursor of many fold mountain belts that have been regarded as sited on old geosynclines.

Because of their association with geosynclines and their occurrence in thick sequences that have subsequently been folded, graywackes are taken to indicate zones of tectonic activity (folding and faulting) in the Earth's crust. They are generally regarded as pre-tectonic deposits, with respect to the basin in which they occur. They can also be contemporaneous with deformation of an adjoining earlier-filled basin that becomes the source of the graywacke sequence. Insofar as the Atlantic continental rise of North America is a modern graywacke accumulation, graywackes may also reflect tectonic quiescence with respect to both source and the basin of deposition.

The feature common to all modern depositional sites is that they adjoin land masses in areas of high submarine relief. The land mass may be the seismic or aseismic margins of a continent, or the margins and interstices of juvenile continental crust, the island arcs. Thus, all occurrences are related to major discontinuities in the Earth's crust. The quartz-poor graywackes include such types as serpentine graywacke; these reflect the emergence of subcrustal material at the Earth's surface, an intimate part of mountain building processes. (K.A.W.C./Ed.)

Special types of sandstones. Certain types of sandstones are defined by special features; they may have any mineral composition and form in a wide range of environments. Flysch was originally a European term for thick sequences of rhythmically interbedded sandstone and shale in beds a fraction of a centimetre to a few metres thick. Most workers in geology believe that the sands have been deposited by turbidity currents; the beds are thought to fill deepwater marine geosynclines with rapid sediment influx fed by rising mountain chains.

Molasse is also a European term. It refers to sandstones that are deposited on top of flysch. They are coarser grained than flysch; tend to be shallow marine, fluvial, or alluvial fan deposits; and are thought by workers to represent the peak of the mountain-building, when mountains are at their maximum height. In theory, as a mountain chain rises, the resulting deposits should grade from deepwater dark shales into flysch sands and shales, and finally into continental, molasse sands and conglomerates. Redbed is a general term referring to red shales, sandstones, and conglomerates. The problem of the significance and origin of the red colour has intrigued geologists for more than 100 years. Doubtless this type of sediment can originate in many ways, the only requisite being survival of the red hematite (iron oxide) pigment in an oxidizing environment. Redbeds form in many environments, from alluvial fans to fluvial, deltaic, and shallow marine areas. Some geologists think that redbeds are the result of hot desert climates, whereas other scientists believe that hot humid climates with seasonal rainfall are responsible for them; still other investigators think that they are caused by post-depositional alteration not necessarily related to climate.

Uses of sandstones. The most valuable aspect of sandstone depends on its natural storage capacity for underground fluids: water, oil, and natural gas. Many sandstones contain an interconnected spongelike network of tiny pores. Porosity is a measure of the total volume of holes in the rock and may range up to 35 percent for some sandstones, although an average oil sand has 10–20

Sandstone reservoirs

percent porosity. Permeability is a measure of the rate at which a fluid may pass through a rock and is greater if the pores are large and well interconnected. Both permeability and porosity are at a maximum in coarser sands that are well sorted and lack both clay matrix and chemical cement. Many sandstones are so tightly bonded with clay or cement that they are for practical purposes devoid of useful porosity and are useless as fluid reservoirs.

Approximately half the world's oil comes from sandstone strata. A typical porous sandstone is folded and faulted by tectonic movements. One common site of occurrence of oil is in anticlines (arch-shaped folds), wherein the three fluids arrange themselves in order of density, with water filling the pores at greatest depths, then oil, and finally gas on top. Early oil prospectors concentrated on searching for oil in anticlines. Another type of oil trap is one in which a sandstone gradually decreases in porosity in a lateral direction, and the migration of oil is stopped at the porosity–permeability barrier where an oil pool may accumulate. Most good oil sands are of deltaic, beach, or shallow marine origin.

Sandstones provide a very valuable reservoir of water. The Dakota Sandstone in the western United States, for example, provides artesian-well water for a widespread area of the Great Plains. Sandstone aquifers are of great importance in most developed countries.

Building stone and glass sands

An important use of sandstones is in the construction industry. Relatively clay-free, little-cemented sands or sandstones are crushed and sieved for use in concrete, plaster, or as fill in the manufacture of bricks, asphalt paving, etc.

Glass sand requires easily crushable, medium-grained quartzarenite sandstones of the highest purity, often over 99 percent SiO_2 and particularly low in iron oxides and aluminum (under 0.1 percent and 0.2 percent, respectively). The Devonian Oriskany Sandstone of West Virginia and Pennsylvania supports an important glass industry. Ganister is a tough, quartz-cemented sandstone used as firebrick in industrial furnaces.

Certain sandstones are used as a source of commercially valuable heavy minerals (titanium, zirconium, rare earths), and some sandstones in the American Southwest are cemented with uranium minerals and form a valuable ore of this element. (R.L.F./Ed.)

SHALES

The finest-grained clastic rocks, consisting of particles finer than sand size (0.06 to two millimetres [0.002 to 0.078 inch]) derived principally from the weathering of continental (*i.e.,* nonmarine) rocks, are designated as shales or lutites. Those lutites that are laminated (bedding thicknesses are less than one centimetre) and fissile (tend to split into thin layers, generally parallel to bedding) or both are called shales. A bipartite name is often used, with a prefix such as clay, silt, or mud indicating the dominant grain size and the suffix shale or stone indicating the presence or absence of lamination and fissility. Commonly the term shale is used interchangeably with lutite, perhaps because such shales make up 50 percent of all sedimentary rocks, and a lutite fraction is a significant component in many more.

In addition to weathered continental debris, many shales contain appreciable chemical precipitates and volcanically derived components. Fragments of hard parts of calcareous and siliceous microorganisms and fine particles of calcium carbonate that are precipitated by chemical or biochemical means are often present. Organic matter also is commonly an important component. Some fine-grained material is formed by chemical alteration *in situ,* partly as the reaction product of original fine clastic detritus (transported particles) but mostly by reaction of volcanic flows and ejecta with sea (or lake) water to form clay minerals and zeolites by reaction of volcanic flows and ejecta with sea (or lake) water, forming extensive marine volcanic muds or continental bentonite (a type of clay) beds.

General properties. The properties of shales are largely determined by the fine grain size of the constituent minerals. The accumulation of fine clastic detritus generally requires a sedimentary environment of low mechanical energy (one in which wave and current actions are minimal), although some fine material may be trapped by plants or deposited as weakly coherent pellets in more agitated environments. The properties of the clay mineral constituents of lutites are particularly important, even when they do not make up the bulk of a rock. The clay minerals have a platy (rarely fibrous) form and are electrically charged with charge balance achieved by associated ions. The plates may bond together face-to-face, and the interlayer and edge ions may be exchangeable with ions from surrounding waters. The clays also may absorb water; hydration of interlayer cations (positively charged atoms) leads to clay swelling that ranges from a few angstrom units to a widely dispersed state. The charge interactions between clay particles allows their association in a very open fabric of high porosity but low permeability. The potential in such materials for variation of fabric leads to plasticity at moderate water content: at higher water content the sediment may undergo sudden liquefaction (a process known as thixotropic behaviour).

The average abundance of organic matter in shales is about 1 percent, compared with 0.3 percent in limestones and 0.05 percent in sandstones; lesser amounts exist in the open ocean muds, and more than 30 percent is contained in muds entrapped in marsh environments. More than 75 percent of all buried organic matter is found in shales. With abundant deposition of suitable types of organic matter and its preservation in the sediment, the complex sequence of events leading to petroleum accumulation may begin. Low-temperature thermal degradation produces disseminated hydrocarbons, and, if the hydrodynamic situation is suitable, these may migrate to porous reservoir rocks. Further maturation and gravitational segregation may then lead to economic accumulations of natural gas and crude oil.

Kerogen as a component of oil shales

Some organic-rich shales, called oil shales or kerogen shales, contain kerogen (a chemically complex mixture of solid hydrocarbons from macerated plant matter) in sufficient amounts to make feasible petroleum production by distillation.

Mineralogy and chemistry. The mineralogy of shales is highly variable. In addition to clay minerals (60 percent), the average shale contains quartz and other forms of SiO_2, notably amorphous silica and cristobalite (30 percent), feldspars (5 percent), and the carbonate minerals calcite and dolomite (5 percent). Iron oxides and organic matter (around 0.5 and 1 percent, respectively) are also important. Older estimates greatly underestimated clay minerals because of incorrect assignment of potassium to feldspar minerals. The most abundant clay mineral is illite; montmorillonite and mixed-layer illite-montmorillonite are next in abundance, followed by kaolinite, chlorite, chlorite-montmorillonite, and vermiculite. The quartz-to-feldspar ratio generally mirrors that of associated sands. In pelagic (deep-sea) sediments, however, feldspar may be derived from local volcanic sources, whereas quartz may be introduced from the continents by wind, upsetting simple patterns. A large number of accessory minerals occur in shales. Some of these are detrital (*i.e.,* are transported grain fragments), but diagenetic or *in situ* varieties (*e.g.,* pyrite, siderite, and various phosphates) and volcanically derived varieties (*e.g.,* zeolites, zircon, biotite) have been noted.

Relation to igneous rocks

The bulk of the weathering products of igneous rocks are incorporated in shales, and it is not surprising that the average shale is chemically little different from the average igneous rock. The differences reflect mainly the differentiation or selective distribution of sodium and magnesium to seawater, calcium and magnesium to limestones, and silicon to sandstones. One estimate of average shale composition in percent by weight is SiO_2, 58.1; Al_2O_3, 15.4; Fe_2O_3, 4.02; FeO, 2.45; MgO, 2.44; CaO, 3.11; Na_2O, 1.3; K_2O, 3.24; CO_2, 2.63; H_2O (110° C), 5; and other components, 2.31. Many trace metals are enriched in shales, particularly in organic-rich varieties. Variations in shale composition, generally quite minor, may reflect the silt-to-clay ratio, differential leaching of the source rock, the relative importance of biogenic components, and depositional variations in mineralogy throughout a basin. Pelagic muds of the South Pacific volcanic province differ from average shale, particularly in their greater abundance of soda

(Na_2O), and geochemical calculations suggest that some shales (and some limestones also) may have an important volcanic component. The influence on shale composition will depend on the extent to which the calcium, magnesium, and iron leached from the (basaltic) volcanic material either form carbonates and iron oxides (admixed with the plagioclase feldspar, clay minerals, and zeolites of the residual mud) or are removed and deposited elsewhere.

Older shales tend to differ chemically from modern ones. It is sometimes difficult to determine whether this reflects variations in weathering and depositional conditions through time or whether the older shales sampled simply reflect selective preservation of certain environments and increased frequency of samples subjected to higher grades of diagenesis (*i.e.*, of alteration during the processes of rock formation)—metamorphism and metasomatism. Lower values of carbon dioxide and water in older shales represent loss during incipient metamorphism. Studies of younger shales show increased reduction of iron (accompanying oxidation of organic matter) with increasing depth of burial. The higher Fe^{2+}:Fe^{3+} ratio found in older shales probably reflects this, although iron compounds may have been exposed to less efficient oxidation processes on weathering or to more reducing depositional environments on a younger Earth. Other major elements decrease, relative to chemically inert alumina, potassium, and, possibly, total iron increase in older shales.

Colour. The colours of the common abundant minerals in shales are nearly white. The wide variety of rock colour observed is caused by small amounts of finely disseminated pigmenting material. The common pigments are organic matter and various iron-bearing minerals. A high organic content, often supplemented by very fine pyrite, gives a black colour. In general, the higher the organic content, the darker the shale, but in oil shales this may lead to a brown colur. The colour of iron-bearing minerals is controlled by oxidation state rather than by abundance of iron, and local variations in oxidation potential (*e.g.*, local concentrations of decomposing organic tissue, worm burrowing, or periodic exposure and aeration of tidal flats) may lead to colour mottling or banding. Hematite and limonite (ferric iron) impart reddish and purple colours. Blue, green, gray, and black colours generally indicate reducing conditions and ferrous iron, although the green clay mineral glauconite is rich in ferric iron. Many calcareous and siliceous shales are devoid of pigment and exhibit light gray or buff colour. In general, marine muds of the continental slope and continental rise are blue or green, whereas deep-sea muds are red.

Structure. Some shales, particularly those formed in lagoons, small lakes, or on floodplains, occur in relatively elongate or lenticular formations. The geographic requirements for a low-energy depositional environment of muds, however, coupled with their generally low depositional rates, lead to the common occurrence of shales in extensive thin sheets. The wide extent of the environment may allow persistence over long time periods, and shale sequences thousands of metres thick are found in geosynclinal regions where great depositional troughs existed in the Earth's crust. By contrast, the high-energy environment of sand deposition is usually restricted to relatively narrow zones such as river channels and along shorelines, and sheet formation requires lateral migration of such environments through time. The wide extent of some shale formations, a few metres thick and of different age in different localities, also requires environment migration. The source of the sediments may affect formation geometry. The silty muds of river deltas occur as lobate masses. In these, as in other subaerial environments, formations are often quite irregular.

Bedding thickness and extent

Shales are generally characterized by very thin bedding or lamination because of grain-size variations or changes in mineralogy (*e.g.*, different proportions of calcite or organic matter). Some, but by no means all, of these may reflect seasonal variations in mineral detritus or biologic productivity. Silt rarely forms thick deposits, except in windblown loess deposits. When not intimately associated with clays or sands, it occurs as thin lenses within the shales. Thick, homogeneous clay sequences are more common. The silts show the current scour and cross-bedding (micro-cross-bedding) features associated with sands. Water-saturated silts are particularly susceptible to differential compaction and soft sediment flowage. Dewatering of muds may lead to mud cracks. These are susceptible to re-erosion and transport as soft shale pellets, some being hydraulically equivalent to sand grains. On close examination, massive clay shales are often found to consist of aggregates of pellets. These may be transported clay floccules, re-eroded shale pellets, or fecal pellets. Burrowing by mud-dwelling organisms may homogenize sediments by wholly or partially destroying depositional laminae. Many shales are characterized by nodules and concretions because of element migration and accumulation under chemical gradients set up largely by localized accumulation of decaying biologic tissue.

Role of water content

Fabric. The water content of detrital sediments is, in general, inversely related to particle size, and some freshly deposited muds may contain up to 90 percent water by volume. The fabric of muds and shales is strongly influenced by the properties of the clay minerals, in particular their small size, high specific surface, platy morphology, and properties of water absorption and cation exchange. Depending on the type of clay minerals and the nature of the geochemical environment, the particles may be deposited individually from a dispersed state or as floccules (face-to-face, edge-to-edge, or face-to-edge associations of clay plates). The freshly deposited mud undergoes particle rearrangement and dewatering, either by subaerial dehydration (leading to mud cracks), by spontaneous expulsion of water from an unstable gel (syneresis), or as a result of the pressure of newly deposited sediments. At moderate water contents the sediments exhibit plastic behaviour, and structures caused by foundering and flow are common. Large-scale flowage may lead to diapiric (piercement type) mud intrusion. Muds with higher water content are metastable, and, when subjected to stress by earthquakes, sediment load, etc., the interparticle bonds may be broken, the particles will pack more closely, and oversaturation with water may lead to sudden initiation of flow as a viscous liquid.

The best fissility in shales is associated with a high degree of orientation of clay plates parallel to bedding. This may be the result of compactional rearrangement of flocculated particles or, perhaps, of diagenetic growth of clay minerals with orientation influenced by overburden pressure, but in most cases it is developed early, at deposition or during the first few metres of burial. This preferred orientation may result from the settling of clay plates particle by particle from a dispersed state or by particle rearrangement, a process for which a high initial water content appears necessary. Biogenic siliceous and calcareous matter decrease fissility. A high organic content and perhaps also deposition from low-salinity waters are associated with high fissility, apparently through their effect on promoting clay dispersion or weak flocculation.

Origin of shales. *Transportation and deposition of sediments.* The formation of fine-grained sediments generally requires weak transporting currents and a quiet depositional basin. Water is the common transporting medium, but ice-rafted glacial flour (silt produced by glacial grinding) is a major component in high-latitude oceanic muds, and windblown dust is prominent, particularly in the open ocean at low and intermediate latitudes. Shale environments thus include the deep ocean; the continental slope and rise; the deeper and more protected parts of shelves, shallow seas, and bays; coastal lagoons; interdistributory regions of deltas, swamps, and lakes (including arid basin playas); and river floodplains. The deep-sea muds are very fine, but an orderly sequence from coarse sediments in high-energy nearshore environments to fine sediments at greater depths is rarely found. Sediments at the outer edges of present-day continental shelves are commonly sands, relict deposits of shallower Pleistocene (from about 10,000 to 2,500,000 years ago) glacial conditions, whereas muds are currently being deposited in many parts of the inner shelf. The nearshore deposition of clay minerals is enhanced by the tendency of riverborne dispersed platelets to flocculate in saline waters (salinity greater than about four parts per 1,000) and to be deposited just beyond the agitated estuarine environment as aggregates hydraulically equivalent to coarser particles. Differential flocculation leads to clay-mineral segregation, with illite and kaolinite near shore and montmorillonite farther out to sea. Advance of silty and sandy delta-slope deposits over clays also leads to complex grain-size patterns.

Shales may be deposited in environments of periodic agitation. Sediments deposited on submarine slopes are frequently mechanically unstable and may be redistributed by slumping and turbidity currents (density currents that result from an increase in sediment concentration) to form thick accumulations (possible present-day eugeosynclinal equivalents) on the lower continental slope and rise. Part of the shale in many graywacke-shale alternations may be of turbidite origin. Fine sediment can be deposited in marshes and on tidal flats. Trapping by marsh plants and binding of muds in fecal pellets are important. Because of electrochemical interactions among fine particles, muds plastered on a tidal flat by an advancing tide are difficult to re-erode on the ebb. This may lead, as in the present-day Waddenzee, in The Netherlands, to a size increase from nearshore tidal flat muds to lag sands seaward. Fine floodplain sediments may dry out to coherent shale pellets, and these, on re-erosion, can be redistributed as sands and gravels.

Reaction with seawater

Diagenetic changes. The minerals deposited in a sedimentary basin may not be in physicochemical equilibrium among themselves and with the water. At any point on the sea floor, for example, there are too many aluminosilicate minerals to constitute an equilibrium assemblage, and common biogenic constituents (amorphous silica, magnesium-calcite, and aragonite) are metastable. Diagenetic reconstitution (alterations following deposition but prior to final lithification) is expected because of observed changes in water composition in laboratory experiments; there is some evidence for such reaction in nature. Clays entering the sea undergo a rapid re-equilibration of their exchange cations, and potassium and chloritic (iron- and magnesium-rich) interlayers may become strongly incorporated in some clays. Diagenetic palygorskites are associated with midoceanic ridge hydrothermal activity. Most unequivocal examples of marine diagenesis involve iron-rich clays. For example, glauconite and chamosite are shown to be diagenetic by their virtual restriction to marine sediments and to specific depth zones in present seas, by their occurrence in special micro-environments (concentrations of organic tissue), and by the smaller number of clay mineral types in glauconite pellets than in the surrounding muds. The montmorillonites formed with zeolites from volcanic material in the oceans are also iron rich.

The distribution of clay minerals in the present deep ocean can be related to source-area mineralogy and wind- and water-current patterns. Chlorite is concentrated at high latitudes where mechanical (glacial) weathering is dominant, whereas low-latitude concentration of kaolinite reflects intense chemical weathering on the adjacent continents. Illite (and quartz) concentrations in the central North Pacific are related to the path of midlatitude jet streams. Only the montmorillonite (and zeolite) concentration of the South Pacific, Indian Ocean, and Red Sea indicates extensive diagenesis, utilizing chemically reactive volcanic material. Nearshore gradients of proportion of different clay minerals are better explained by transport phenomena such as differential flocculation than by extensive diagenesis. Reaction is limited by the relatively short exposure time of clay minerals before burial (about one year) and the armouring of grains by reaction products.

The euxinic environment

Little further reaction occurs among the silicates on shallow burial, but dissolved silica levels are raised by the solution of siliceous diatoms, one-celled marine organisms, and bacterial attack of organic matter releases nutrient elements and alters the physicochemical properties of the sediment. In some cases, this leads to the formation of diagenetic sulfides and phosphates. This is particularly important in euxinic environments, in which stagnant conditions prevent introduction of oxygen to bottom waters from the atmosphere. Considerable amounts of organic matter (black shales) with their nutrient elements and adsorbed trace metals are thus incorporated into the sediment rather than being oxidized in the sea floor. With increased temperature of deeper burial (several thousand metres), extensive reconstitution of the silicates and carbonates occurs. The most obvious change is the evolution of montmorillonite, through mixed-layer minerals, toward illite and chlorite. Kaolinite and some feldspars and micas become unstable, and their breakdown provides elements for new mineral growth. There may be some additions from greater depth and some element exchange with associated sands, however.

Shales of economic value. Black shales are often of economic importance as sources of petroleum products and metals, and this importance will probably increase in the future. The lacustrine Eocene Green River Shales of Colorado–Wyoming–Utah are potentially rich petroleum sources and are undergoing exploratory extraction. Bituminous layers of the Early Permian Irati Shales of Brazil are similarly important. These shales contain the remains of the marine reptile *Mesosaurus,* also found in South Africa, and have played a prominent part in the development of the concepts of continental drift. The very widespread thin Chattanooga Shale (Devonian-Mississippian) of the eastern United States has been exploited for its high (up to 250 parts per 1,000,000) uranium content. The Permian Kupferschiefer is a bituminous shale rich in metallic sulfides of primary sedimentary or early diagenetic origin; it covers a large area of central Europe as a band generally less than one metre thick, and in East Germany and in Poland there is sufficient enrichment in copper, lead, and zinc for its exploitation as an ore. (K.C.B./Ed.)

LIMESTONES AND DOLOMITES

Limestones and dolomites consist of more than 50 percent carbonate minerals, mainly calcite (calcium carbonate, $CaCO_3$) and dolomite (calcium magnesium carbonate, $CaMg(CO_3)_2$). For this reason, they are commonly referred to as carbonate rocks.

Calcite and dolomite as chief constituents

Although their distinction is based on their rather uniform mineralogical composition, limestones and dolomites are formed by a wide variety of processes. A limestone may be produced by the cementation of carbonate sand grains derived by erosion of a former carbonate landform (*e.g.,* island, hill, plateau); in this case it is a clastic rock, a sandstone, whose grains have been transported and deposited in accord with the laws of hydraulics. On the other hand, a limestone might result from direct precipitation in seawater, in which case it is a chemical rock, like salt, whose formation has been governed by such factors as water temperature and pressure, and the concentration of the solution. In still another category are carbonate bodies, such as reefs, that have been constructed principally by sedentary organisms; in this case the rock-forming process is skeletal secretion by physiological means. Since the three types of carbonate sediments may be mixed while they are still in the depositional environment or may be modified by various postdepositional changes, the final product may be a rock with a very complicated history.

Limestones and dolomites have long fascinated geologists and paleontologists because of their rich fossil content. Much existing knowledge of the Earth's chronology and evolution has been derived from study of fossils included in carbonate rocks. They represent about 20 percent of all sedimentary rocks and occur in all continents, in strata of every age—from Precambrian to Quaternary.

Physical and chemical characteristics. *Mineral and chemical composition.* As mentioned earlier, the most important rock-forming carbonate minerals are calcite, aragonite, and dolomite. Other carbonate minerals of the calcite family are magnesite ($MgCO_3$), rhodochrosite ($MnCO_3$), and siderite ($FeCO_3$); these occur in restricted environments and are quantitatively of limited importance.

Calcareous sediments forming today in tropical and subtropical shallow seas consist predominantly of aragonite and magnesium-rich calcite. Both minerals are metastable, however, and change quickly with geological time. All limestones of Precambrian to Tertiary age (*i.e.,* older than 2,500,000 years) consist of normal calcite; that is, cal-

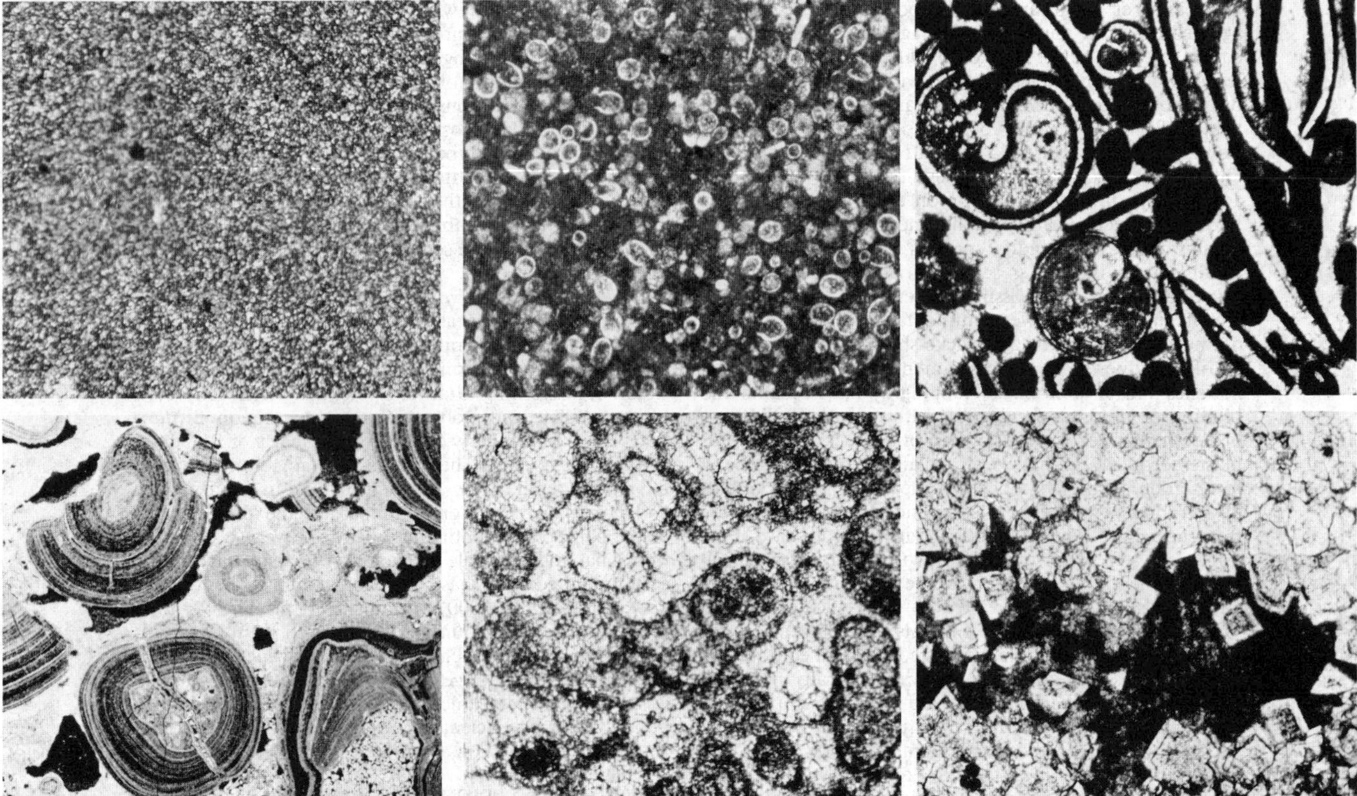

Figure 113: *Photomicrographs of carbonate rocks.*
(Top left) Micritic limestone, Triassic (magnified 18 ×). (Top centre) Micritic skeletal limestone, Upper Jurassic (magnified 25 ×). (Top right) Skeletal oolitic limestone, with clean calcite cement, Lower Triassic (magnified 18 ×). (Bottom left) Pisolitic dolomite, Upper Triassic (magnified 5 ×). (Bottom centre) Lump limestone, recrystallized, Permian (magnified 18 ×). (Bottom right) Diagenetic dolomite growing at the expense of existing micritic material, Middle Triassic (magnified 15 ×).
By courtesy of A. Bosellini

cite with a low magnesium content. This is because the rocks have undergone diagenetic processes that changed their original mineralogical character. Only limestones formed in deep or cold marine environments have undergone no transformation; they were made of normal, low-magnesium calcite from the outset.

Minor constituents

Minor constituents also are commonly present in limestones and dolomites. These may be finely disseminated throughout the rock (*e.g.,* clay minerals, iron oxides, bituminous matter), present as individual grains (*e.g.,* glauconite, pyrite, quartz, and feldspar), or segregated into large nodules (*e.g.,* chert or flint). Compositional gradations are common, and many classification schemes have been used. In the chemical sense, however, carbonate rocks are rather simple because they reflect their mineralogical composition. Calcium and magnesium oxides and carbon dioxide are the most important constituents, forming more than 95 percent of the rock in many cases. When impure carbonates are involved, other constituents, such as silica, alumina, iron oxides, phosphorus, and sulfides, may contribute notably to the bulk composition.

Depositional textures. The two main classes of carbonate rocks are mechanically deposited carbonates, those with particulate texture, and carbonates grown in place, either by biological activity (reefs) or chemically accreted (tufa, travertine, caliche, and speleothems, or cave deposits). The mechanically deposited carbonates constitute the most important group; the other types are of more limited extent.

The particulate material consists of a mixture of various particles (grains) immersed in a finer matrix (lime mud). The rigid grain framework creates a pore system that permits the transmission and storage of fluids. Subsequently, this pore system may become partially or completely filled by a chemical precipitate (cement). The particles and their matrix produce varying rock textures, depending upon their arrangement, and the textures of limestones and dolomites exert a controlling influence on porosity and permeability and, in turn, on rock suitability as a reservoir for oil or water. Five major types of grains are recognized in carbonates; namely, skeletal, detrital, pellets, lumps, and coated grains.

Grains consisting of whole and fragmented skeletons of marine plants and animals are called skeletal grains. Unlike other kinds of grains, they usually have a precise internal structure resulting from a regular crystal arrangement. A wide variety of marine organisms (mollusks, algae, corals, echinoderms, sponges, and foraminifera) of quite different character contribute their skeletal remains. Accordingly, different kinds of skeletal sediments may form.

Grains made of debris derived from pre-existing rocks are called detrital grains. They may originate during deposition as pieces broken from poorly consolidated sediments (intraclasts) or as pieces broken from rigid rocks (lithoclasts). Detrital grains usually have sharp angular corners, may show an internal texture derived from the source rock, and a single specimen may be essentially of one or of varied rock types.

Intraclasts form after the sediment becomes sufficiently coherent if there is an agent able to break it; they are abundant where erosion, dynamic energy—generally in the form of waves and currents—and burrowers occur. Intraclasts can be formed from carbonate mud when it is compacted or when it dries out, but in carbonate sands, rapid cementation (filling of the pores by a chemical precipitate) must occur. It is easier for sediments to become compacted or desiccated than cemented; thus, intraclasts usually have a fine-grained (mud) texture.

Lithoclasts form when carbonate rocks are exposed and eroded. They usually are related to land areas, such as a carbonate tropical island. They may represent minor unconformities, or interruptions in the depositional sequence.

Grains of mud lacking significant internal structure are called pellets; they usually have an ovoidal or subspherical shape. They are a polygenetic group of grains, because some of them are of fecal origin (fecal pellets); whereas others (grains of matrix) may represent processes of physical accretion, diagenetic (postdepositional) alterations of skeletal grains, and recrystallization; and still others may represent bits of lime mud torn from the sea floor and rolled around before coming to rest. Genetically, the latter should belong to the intraclast category, but because of their small size it is impossible to recognize their detrital origin.

Lumps are composite grains (*i.e.,* aggregates of particles, generally pellets), in which the single element protrudes from the principal body and gives it a characteristic lobate outline. In Recent sediments (those formed during the last 10,000 years) various forms can be distinguished (grapestones—forms resembling bunches of grapes—botryoidal lumps, friable aggregates); in ancient carbonates they are regarded as a single group. Lumps form in environments in which grains lying on the sea bottom tend to cement together; they occur in carbonate sand tongues controlled by tidal currents that flow through inter-key channels and are frequently associated with oolitic sands described below.

Grains having concentric or enclosing layers of calcium carbonate around a central nucleus are called coated; the most common types are oolites, pisolites, and algae-encrusted grains. Oolites (from the Greek *ōon,* "egg," and *lithos,* "stone") are subspherical grains less than two millimetres in size; if bigger, they are called pisolites. The nucleus is generally a skeletal grain, a pellet, or, more rarely, a quartz grain; some oolites may display a radial structure.

Origin of oolites

There are various theories of the origin of oolites. The first, introduced a century ago, is called the "snowball" theory. According to this theory, seawater is presumed to be crowded with suspended aragonite crystallites in a particular place; as they roll on the bottom or float in the water, particles of whatever origin, possibly coated with adhesive mucilaginous organic material, capture the crystallites, which adhere to their surfaces. As a result of the continuous movement caused by waves and tidal currents, the small grains grow just like a snowball rolling downhill. A second theory explains oolite growth by chemical precipitation producing crystals perpendicular to the grain surface; as the grain rolls, these crystals break and lie on the surface, trapped by the organic mucilage. A third theory attributes oolite origin to the presence of protenic matter that supposedly controls precipitation and orientation of crystals.

Matrix material. This is generally a very fine lime mud, now almost universally called micrite (originally from the contraction of the words microcrystalline calcite). Micrite, which applies to both consolidated and unconsolidated carbonate mud, is the carbonate analogue to the mud that occurs between the framework grains of many land-derived sands. There is considerable controversy over the size limit that is to distinguish matrix (micrite) from grains; four, 20, 30, 60, and 125 micrometres have been proposed.

Structures in carbonate rocks. Mechanically deposited carbonate rocks show the same structures that are present in terrigenous (land-derived) rocks: cross-bedding, graded bedding, ripple marks, mud cracks, laminations, and cut-and-fill structures (pockets formed by erosion and subsequently filled with sediment) may be well displayed in many limestones. There are some structures that are peculiar to carbonate rocks, however; stromatolites (fossil algae), stylolites (columns or veins that are inclined to the beds), nodular bedding, and various solution features are a few examples.

Stromatolites, bioherms, and reefs

Stromatolites are organic-sedimentary structures composed of flat, undulated, or cabbage-like laminations; these are built by dense mats consisting primarily of blue-green algae, which selectively trap and bind sediment particles among their mucilaginous filaments. Stromatolites range in age from the early Precambrian (perhaps 2,500,000,000 years old) to the Recent, although they are most abundant in the Precambrian and Lower Paleozoic (about 400,000,000 to 570,000,000 years ago). Recent stromatolites are forming in littoral (near shore) environments in south Florida and in the Bahamas; spectacular examples are those of Shark Bay (Western Australia), where stromatolitic columns more than one metre tall occur. These have an elliptical cross section, the long axis being oriented with the prevailing current. Similar current-oriented stromatolites have been discovered in the Precambrian of the Northwest Territories, in Canada.

Biohermal and reef structures are other typical structures of carbonate rocks. Bioherms are domelike, moundlike, or otherwise circumscribed masses built exclusively or mainly by sedentary organisms and enclosed in a normal rock of a different lithologic character. They vary in size and shape and may be as small as a few centimetres or impressive structures several kilometres across and hundreds of metres thick. Algae, stromatoporoids, coral, crinoids, and mollusks are among the most common constituents.

Origin of limestones and dolomites. *Source material and its transportation.* Limestones originate mainly through lithification (transformation to rock) of loose carbonate

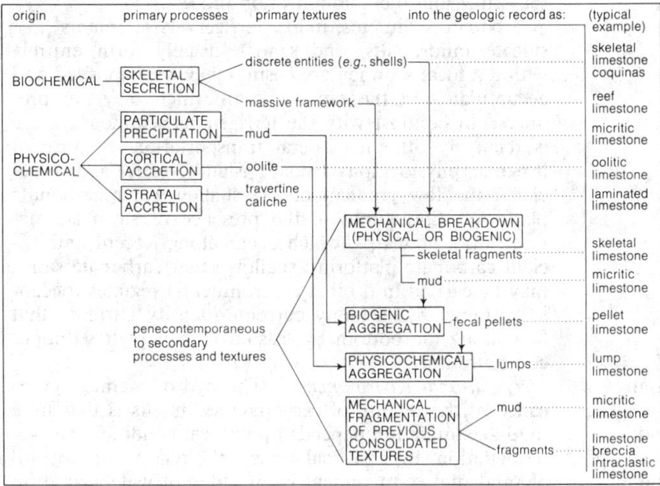

Figure 114: The origins of limestones.

sediments. Exceptions are deposits like travertine or reefs, which are lithified in their original state. The primary origin of most limestones is attributable to biochemical or physicochemical processes.

Skeletons of marine plants and animals are produced biochemically, through skeletal secretions. If cemented, these skeletal sediments may be transferred directly into the geologic record as skeletal limestones, reefs, or bioherms. Otherwise, they may undergo early diagenetic processes like biogenic breakdown or biogenic and physicochemical aggregaton. In this way, muds, fecal pellets, and lumps can be produced from carbonate matter of biochemical origin, and such rocks as micritic limestones, pellet limestones, and lump limestones will be formed.

Lime muds, oolites, and travertine are produced physicochemically, through particulate precipitation and layered accretion, although travertine may also be controlled by algal activity. These carbonate deposits may become micritic limestones, oolitic limestones, and laminated limestones, respectively.

Both biochemically derived and physicochemically derived carbonate sediments may be mechanically fragmented after early consolidation, and clastic sediments and rocks such as limestone breccias, intraclastic limestones, and carbonate mudstones may be produced.

The dolomite problem

Poor knowledge of the origin of ancient dolomites, which are widespread, together with the apparent lack of dolomite in Recent sediments, created the "dolomite problem," which was debated for many years. All this was abruptly changed with the development of X-ray diffraction techniques. In the last few years dolomite has been discovered in Recent sediments, and an understanding of its origin and occurrence in the geologic record has been gained.

All the Recent dolomite occurs in a particular environment; namely, hypersaline lakes or lagoons, and supratidal areas (Persian Gulf, Bahamas, Florida, The Netherlands Antilles). Hypersalinity is the hallmark.

Hypersalinity in marginal marine environments and in intermontane basins may result because of excess of evaporation over rainfall; interstitial waters in the sediments transpire upward and evaporate at the sediment–air interface. This process is common in intertidal and supratidal flats in the tropics. Hypersalinity may also result when evaporation exceeds precipitation plus runoff, thus increasing the concentration and density of the waters in lagoons and shallow coastal seas. The heavy brine that is formed sinks and flows seaward down the sloping shelf. If, however, this reflux to the sea is prevented by natural barriers such as reefs or sills, the brine migrates to the lowest possible topographic depressions and seeps slowly through the underlying sediments, which are progressively dolomitized.

Hypersaline brines are also responsible for a subsurface process by which older calcareous rocks can be transformed into dolomites. Volcanic activity, faults, and special subsurface traps or other conditions control the migration of the brines and the dolomitization process.

Carbonate sediments, unlike terrigenous sediments (*i.e.,* silicate muds, silts, and sands), usually form entirely within a local sedimentary basin—they are deposited and accumulated in the same area in which they are produced. In contrast with the terrigenous sediments, there is relatively little net lateral transportation, because of irregular physiography (shoals, islands, reefs) and, especially, the low gradient of the shallow-water carbonate platforms. Sometimes in the presence of steep submarine slopes or scarps, which occur along Recent and ancient carbonate platforms, shallow-water carbonate sands may be carried into other environmental regimes (oceanic bottoms) by turbidity currents (density currents that flow along the bottom by reason of their high sediment concentration).

High-energy and low-energy environments

Depositional environments. The hydrodynamic significance of the texture of carbonate sediments is that lime mud accumulation depends upon local conditions of water agitation. In a particular rock, the relative proportion of mud matrix to cement is an index of water agitation or mechanical energy. Depositional areas of "high energy" are inferred to produce clean, well-sorted, coarse-grained carbonate sediments, whereas areas of "low energy" are held to be responsible for muddy deposits. High-energy sites are beaches, surf zones, dunes, and tidal channels. Carbonate muds generally accumulate in protected areas such as lakes, lagoons, deep-sea basins, and areas on the lee side of major islands situated on oceanic banks.

Carbonate rocks form in various environments; namely, continental, marine, or transitional. Most of them are formed in shallow marine and transitional zones of the tropical seas. Criteria that help to distinguish different environments of deposition may be found in grain types, sedimentary structures, geometry of sedimentary bodies, fossil content, and stratigraphic relationships with the rocks that are adjacent, both laterally and vertically. Diagnosis usually is achieved by the association of various distinctive elements.

Diagenetic changes. The carbonate rocks observed in the geologic record have undergone diagenetic processes over long periods of time, altering them partially or even completely. The late diagenetic changes occurring in a sediment are a response to pressure, temperature, the nature of the fluids moving through the pores, and the physical and chemical properties of the original sediment.

The first change occurs in grain mineralogy when magnesium-rich sediments pass to magnesium-poor calcareous rocks. The result is a complete change of mineralogy of the grains, but with retention of their original depositional texture. The exact mechanism by which removal of magnesium takes place is not yet fully understood.

Cement is the most important textural diagenetic element and the most important single element in the lithification (rock-forming) process. It consists of a chemical precipitate that fills voids within the sediment. The pore space may have existed originally between the grains or may have been created by desiccation or selective dissolution of the lime mud matrix. The most common mineral cement is calcite, but dolomite, anhydrite, and siliceous cements also occur. Cement appears as a clear, coarse mosaic and commonly begins as euhedral (well-formed) crystals that grow radially outward from the grains or from the cavity walls. Sometimes cementation is incomplete, and the available space may be filled with finer diagenetic sediment, called "crystal silt."

Recrystallization

Recrystallization is another important diagenetic process that is responsible for the obliteration of the original depositional textures; a mass of large interlocking crystals, which may strongly resemble cement, is the final product. The process, which consists of grain or crystal enlargement, may operate in either fine-grained or coarse-grained sediments, and it may be selective, involving only parts of the material, or complete. Apparently, lime mud matrix is the textural element most sensitive to recrystallization.

Economic significance of carbonate rocks. In the last few decades enormous petroleum reservoirs have been discovered in carbonate rocks in the Middle East, the Canadian Rockies, west Texas, and many other parts of the world. Some of these oil fields are localized in fossil reefs, such as Norman Wells (northern Canada), Leduc (Alberta), the Permian Basin of Texas, New Mexico, and the Tampico area (Mexico).

Carbonates have a large variety of economic uses. As building stone, limestones and dolomites are used for monuments, exterior and interior facings, and flooring of several kinds. Crushed rock is used for railroad ballast, riprap fill (broken rock used to protect structures from natural processes of erosion) around the bases of dams and piers, filter beds in sewage treatment, and surfacing for airports. The heating of limestones and megnesian limestones to temperatures of 900°–1,000° C (1,650°–1,830° F) will dissociate calcium carbonate and yield carbon dioxide and lime for commercial use. Lime has major applications in the construction industries, for the manufacture of glass, and for agricultural purposes. Carbonate rocks are also common host rocks for many ore deposits, because they are easily attacked by high-temperature solutions that precipitate ore minerals. (A.Bo./Ed.)

SILICEOUS ROCKS

The siliceous rocks are those sedimentary rocks that consist largely or almost entirely of free silica (SiO_2), in the form either of quartz or varieties of amorphous silica and cristobalite. By custom the term includes rocks that have formed as chemical precipitates of one type or another but exclude rocks high in free silica content that are of detrital or fragmental origin, such as the quartz arenites, those sandstones composed almost entirely of quartz grains. Though many of the siliceous sediments are relatively pure silica, the same rock types may be mixed with clays, carbonates, or detrital grains of sand and silt so that they are impure. By far the most abundant type of siliceous rock is chert, a common constituent of strata of every age and character.

Chert and flint

Types of siliceous rocks. Chert is a dense, more or less microcrystalline rock, composed of chalcedony and quartz, that occurs in beds and nodules. Flint, a term that is used synonymously with chert, tends to be used more for references to artifacts such as arrowheads. Various other names have been used for chert, including silexite, hornstone, and phthanite. Porcellanite is a variety of chert, equally dense and hard, that breaks in the manner of unglazed porcelain. Jasper is a coloured chert; the most abundant variety is mixed with iron oxide that makes it red and brown in colour. Such rocks contain much nonsiliceous material, chiefly clay and calcium or magnesium carbonate (calcite or dolomite). Novaculite is a bedded chert (deposits exhibit stratification); the name has been applied mainly to formations of Paleozoic age in the Ouachita Mountains of Arkansas and Oklahoma and, to some extent, to rocks of the same age in the Marathon Mountains of Texas.

Occurrence. Many siliceous rocks called chert are composed almost entirely of siliceous fossils. Thus, diatoms (one-celled marine plants) sink to form diatomaceous oozes on the sea floor, which ultimately may become diatomaceous earths or, if well indurated, diatomite, a hard rock. In the same way, radiolaria (one-celled marine animals) form oozes, earths, and radiolarites. The radiolarians or radiolarian cherts of the Alpine chain are the most famous representatives in the geologic column (the strata that represent all of geological time). Other names used for siliceous fossil earths are infusorial earth, or kieselguhr, and tripoli.

Yet another mode of occurrence of siliceous deposits is as sinters and encrustations formed by evaporation in and around hot springs. There are many names applied to these kinds of deposits; most frequent are siliceous sinter, geyserite (if associated with geysers), and fiorite. The areal extent and total volume of the deposits associated with hot springs and geysers are relatively small, but it is not known how much silica is deposited under the sea or in the interstices of rocks by rising hydrothermal solutions. In contrast, the areal extent and volume of cherts, both bedded and nodular, is large. Some formations containing abundant chert are known to have covered many tens of thousands of square miles in their former extent. Cherts also may be a prominent constituent of many stratigraphic sections (the sequence of strata in a given locale); and though quantitatively small compared to the total amount of clastic rocks and limestone, they are probably the most abundant chemically precipitated rock type after limestone. Much of their total volume is distributed in small beds and nodules, mainly in carbonate rock sections, and tends to be underestimated.

Various forms of siliceous rocks have found a wide variety of uses since prehistoric times. The earliest important use was that of chert or flint for the making of weapons in early prehistoric cultures. Another former use for flint was its use in firearms. In modern times chert pebbles have been found useful as grinding agents in ball mills. Diatomaceous earths are used for fine abrasives (as are crushed cherts of various kinds), for molded refractories, and for some fluid filtering purposes. As a major source of silica, the siliceous rocks can be used as the raw material for the making of portland cement, as crushed rock for secondary roads, and as raw material for the making of chemical compounds of silicon. In some localities they are used for building stone.

Physical properties. *Colour.* The diverse origins of siliceous rocks are reflected in the variety of their physical characteristics. Cherts range from almost pure white through tones of cream and buff to dark grays and blues and black. The colours come from impurities, the most common of which are iron impurities, usually finely disseminated ferric oxide (hematite), that colour the rock yellow, brown, and red. The jaspers may represent various mixtures of hematite and silica. Included clay gives a gray or gray-blue colour, whereas finely dispersed organic matter produces a dark blue or black colour. Diatomaceous and radiolarian oozes and earths are white to cream coloured unless they are mixed with large amounts of clay. The sinters and geyserites are white to varying shades of gray.

Porosity, hardness, texture, and composition. The porosity of cherts is very low, usually less than a few percent; and electron micrographs have shown that this porosity is distributed as very tiny cavities and holes. Thus, the permeability is immeasurably small. In contrast, the diatomaceous earths may be very porous and permeable; the pore space between the fossil skeletons may be as high as 50 percent if the rock is not cemented at all. The bulk specific gravity (density of a bulk specimen) of the rock, therefore, may range from a value near that of quartz (2.65) to very low values, depending on its porosity. The cherts tend to have relatively high specific gravities and will be particularly high if much iron is included. Almost all cherts are hard, and some particularly dense varieties may approach seven (the value of quartz) on the Mohs scale of hardness. The siliceous earths are softer because of the friability of the skeletal remains of diatoms and radiolaria, although the silica substance itself is hard. Chert is brittle and breaks with a conchoidal fracture, two properties that made it so suitable for prehistoric arrows, spears, and axes.

The composition of cherts, in terms of free silica present, ranges from opaline silica, a type of amorphous silica, through a form of disordered cristobalite similar in some respects to amorphous silica, to a chalcedonic silica that consists largely of microcrystalline quartz, perhaps with an admixture of cristobalite or amorphous silica. Composition varies with age; the oldest cherts are entirely microcrystalline quartz, whereas younger rocks have more amorphous silica or cristobalite. The siliceous oozes and earths are composed entirely of the untransmuted skeletons of diatoms and radiolaria, which are amorphous silica. The common nonsilica components of siliceous rocks—carbonate (calcite and dolomite), clay minerals, and iron oxides—contribute calcium, magnesium, sodium, potassium, aluminum, and iron, the presence of which is shown by chemical analyses. There is usually a finegrained fraction of detrital quartz in cherts. The texture of cherts under the microscope is that of a fine-grained microgranular rock composed of interlocking and intergrown tiny crystals of quartz. Chalcedonic quartz, commonly present in many cherts, is composed of radiating sheaves and fibres of material whose index of refraction (ratio of velocity of light in air to the velocity in the substance) is slightly lower than that of quartz (1.54; 1.55), a property that may be the result of occluded water in tiny holes in the structure. Opaline silica is isotropic (its properties of light transmission are the same in all directions) with an index of refraction from 1.41 to 1.46. Electron microscopy of cherts has revealed a great range of textures, ranging from equigranular to those exhibiting complex intergrowths of different size crystals with varying morphology. The oldest fossils known, those of cells of primitive algae, have been noted by microscopic and electron microscopic studies of Precambrian cherts.

Bedding and sedimentary structures. The bed-thickness characteristics of siliceous rocks are linked to their composition and origin. The bedded cherts are those that show continuous beds of wide areal extent, with more or less uniform thickness. Such beds usually range in thickness from less than an inch to a foot and are most commonly several inches thick. A succession of these layers makes up a thicker unit of chert, varying from one foot to hundreds of feet in thickness. The beds may alternate with beds of siliceous clay or shale or with limestones and dolomites.

Chert nodules and horizons

In contrast, the nodular cherts have a much more uneven bedding development. The chert beds may be stratigraphic horizons (zones that represent a given time interval) along which many chert nodules occur, or they may be continuous beds that pinch and swell, composed of coalesced nodules. Some formations have been traced laterally from a zone in which a few nodules are present, through one in which nodules are abundant, to one in which the nodules are completely coalesced to make a continuous bed. The siliceous earths tend to be more or less evenly bedded.

The common sedimentary structures of cherts are the nodules. A nodular character, however, is entirely missing from the bedded cherts. In some bedded cherts one can sometimes see faint traces of current bedding and ripples.

From R. Siever, *American Mineralogist*, vol. 42 (1957)

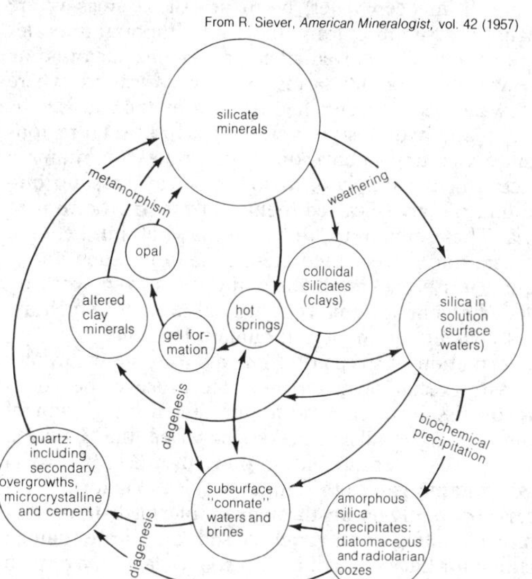

Figure 115: Silica cycle.

Bands of reddish or brownish colour are common in many cherts; they may cut across the bedding and thus indicate their postdepositional origin. Cherts are in some places deformed by contemporaneous or postdepositional movements that give rise to contorted bedding, intrusions of a chert layer into overlying or underlying beds, and brecciation, the breakage and reconsolidation of angular chert fragments. One variety of siliceous rock is actually a silicified limestone; some of these limestones were originally oolitic, that is, they were composed of rounded carbonate grains that had formed by precipitation about various nuclei. Thus, in a few instances, a siliceous oolite rock results. None of the primary siliceous rocks, the bedded cherts, contains such oolites, and the nodular cherts are oolitic only when the nodules have replaced sections of oolitic limestone.

Origin of the siliceous rocks. The origin of chert and the siliceous rocks has been the subject of controversy for as long as the rocks have been studied (Figure 115). There is little doubt as to the origin of the diatomaceous and radiolarian oozes and earths. Sediments in all stages of development have been found. It is clear that they form by the sedimentation of the shells and other hard parts of siliceous organisms that live in surface waters, such as diatoms, radiolaria, and silicoflagellates, together with the spicules of siliceous sponges. It is probable that portions of such shells, or the entire shells of the most fragile species, dissolve as they fall through the lower part of a seawater column that is undersaturated with respect to silica. Freshwater diatomaceous earths form in lakes as they do in the oceans. The transformation of such unindurated (relatively soft) siliceous sediments into hard cherts has been partly traced by studies of Tertiary cherts that show all intermediate stages. The hardness and denseness of the cherts comes from the precipitation of silica in the void spaces between skeletal fragments, the source of the silica being the more soluble parts of the skeletons themselves. The net result of the dissolution and reprecipitation process is the making of a hard rock out of soft sediment, with an accompanying loss of many identifiable fossils and an increase in bulk density of the rock. Although the fossils in older cherts, those of the Paleozoic, are harder to see, they contain siliceous sponge spicules and radiolarians. The Precambrian cherts, however, contain no recognizable fossil remains other than the organic remains of algae; and it is doubtful that such algae secreted silica at that early evolutionary stage.

Role of organisms and their remains

The interrelation of siliceous organisms, sedimentary deposits, and the geochemistry of oceans or lakes is fairly well understood. Most of the silica-secreting organisms require silica as an essential nutrient, usually coupled with phosphate. As a result, abundant populations of these organisms are found in those surface waters of the oceans overlying upwellings that supply sufficient quantities of nutrients from deep water, or in nearshore areas where nutrients are supplied from the land. Important locales for the supply of dissolved silica are regions surrounding active volcanoes or submarine extrusive volcanics, where the seawater becomes enriched in silica by the continuous alteration and hydrolysis of volcanic glass. In such regions the silica-secreting population more or less maintains a balance with the supply of dissolved silica; the solid biogenic amorphous silica sediments sink to the bottom of the sea. These organisms, then, are the vital link between volcanism and siliceous sediment formation. Such an association has been known for many years from work on bedded cherts in volcanic geosynclinal terrains, which are sites of ancient and modern mountain building.

Volcanism and the supply of silica in oceans and lakes

The formation of siliceous sediments in some freshwater lakes is the result of much the same process, the abundance of dissolved silica promoting extensive growth of diatoms. In some alkaline lakes, however, the dissolved solids in the water inhibit or prevent much biological growth, and inorganic precipitates of silica may form. This process apparently occurs through an intermediate mechanism precipitating first a variety of sodium silicate (named magadiite for Lake Magadi in Africa) that later converts to free silica by the leaching of sodium. Such alkaline lakes are almost all restricted to volcanic-rich terrains, where the source of dissolved silica and alkalies comes from alteration of volcanic material, demonstrating again a clear relationship between volcanism and chert formation.

Origin of nodular chert. The origin of the nodular cherts is tied to a much different kind of environment. Where the bedded cherts show little or no evidence of postdepositional origin other than cementation and have every appearance of a primary sedimentary deposit, the nodular cherts in limestones appear to be almost entirely the product of diagenesis, whereby the rock is extensively altered after deposition. The evidence for this is the commonly seen replacement texture, in which primary sedimentary features, such as fossils, bedding, and oolites, are partially or completely replaced by secondarily precipitated silica. A key observation in such rocks is the presence of the remains of siliceous organisms in the chert nodule—usually sponge spicules and radiolaria in Paleozoic formations—and the absence of such fossils in the limestone bed between nodules. Because it is most unlikely that the original fossil distribution bore any relation to the nodules, which follow somewhat braided paths and cut across bedding, it must be concluded that the fossils were originally distributed more or less evenly through the largely limy sediment and that subsequently silica through much of the rock dissolved and reprecipitated as inorganic silica in the form of nodules. Such redistribution of silica in an early stage of diagenesis may have been caused by localized clumpings of decaying organic matter in the sediment. These could give rise to a lateral variation in pH (acidity-alkalinity index) and dissolved organic matter, both of which are known to affect the solubility of silica.

The nodules are typically distributed along some bedding planes but are absent in others, even though there seem to have been no obvious differences in permeability between the beds. This suggests that the beds that contain nodules were laid down during times in which the silicasecreting organisms were particularly abundant. The lateral variation between the occurrence of occasional nodules and their coalescence to form lumpy beds of continuous nodular chert suggests that the population of organisms increased toward the source of dissolved silica. Because there seems to be no association with volcanic activity for most of these formations, the source was probably solid and dissolved land-derived material from a nearby shoreline.

Mixed siliceous sediments. The mixed siliceous sediments, those intermediate between chert and shale or chert and limestone, are the products of varying amounts of dilution of the chemically precipitated silica by solid terrigenous detritus or by biogenically formed carbonate. Some highly siliceous shales have been shown to have formed by diagenetic redistribution of siliceous organisms; others show no identifiable fossil remains and may be the result of redistribution and cementation by nonbiogenic silica. The source of the nonbiogenic silica may have been groundwaters that were enriched with silica by passing through volcanic rocks in some stage of weathering and alteration. By convention, siliceous shales do not include very silty shales, which contain large amounts of fine-grained detrital quartz and thus show high proportions of SiO_2 in a chemical analysis.

Many types of both clastic and chemical sediments may become impregnated with secondarily precipitated silica; sandstones that have become completely cemented by silica are the most common. If the original sandstone were composed chiefly of quartz grains, the cemented rock, which may have the appearance of a true quartzite in which the rock splits across the grains of sand, is practically a monomineralic rock. It is less common to find sandstones with smaller quantities of quartz completely cemented by silica. The silica may be the result of pressure solution, a process by which quartz grains dissolve at points of grain-to-grain contact and the whole rock loses pore space and becomes more compact. Other sources of silica are clay minerals, which under appropriate chemical conditions may transform to a less siliceous clay, releasing silica into solution in the process.

Modern siliceous analogues. Though contemporaneous siliceous oozes and freshwater silica deposits are clearly the modern analogues of the process that formed many of the ancient siliceous rocks, until recently there have been few observations in modern sediments of opaline silica forming as an early diagenetic product. Small amounts of opaline silica have been found in the Coorong Swamp, an intermittently hypersaline and desiccated inlet of the sea in South Australia. A program of deep drilling in the bottom sediments of the oceans of the world, initiated in 1968 by the U.S. National Science Foundation, has resulted in knowledge of the commonplace and relatively abundant occurrence of chert and other siliceous sediments in the stratigraphic columns beneath the deep sea. Such cherts appear to be similar to their ancient continental analogues and to have formed in the same way, that is, by diagenetic reorganization of a biogenic silica deposit. The occurrence of these deep-sea cherts is proof that siliceous deposits need not be uplifted or subject to any special conditions to become cemented; the norm is an isochemical redistribution of silica, in which there is no addition or subtraction of material from outside the bed. (R.Si.)

PHOSPHORITES

Most of the phosphorus in the Earth's crust and in phosphorites, or phosphate rocks, occurs in minerals of the apatite family of calcium phosphates. Nearly all of the phosphate fertilizers and phosphorus for industrial uses are obtained from phosphorites. Thus the availability of large quantities of this variety of sedimentary rock is of primary importance to agricultural and industrial nations.

Commercial importance

Occurrence and characteristics. Marine phosphorites are blanket-like deposits that form on the sea floor as the result of organic or inorganic precipitation of carbonate-fluorapatite from seawater, generally in low latitudes in areas where cold, phosphate-rich water upwells onto the continental shelves. They are commonly associated with beds of black carbonaceous shale, chert or diatomite, sandstone, and minor amounts of limestone. The phosphatic layers consist mainly of pellets and nodules ranging from less than 0.1 to 20 millimetres (0.004 to 0.8 inch) or more in diameter. Fish teeth, scales, and bones, phosphatic brachiopod shells, and casts of small pelecypods and other fossils are common in many deposits. Individual layers are as much as 4.7 metre (15 feet) or more in thickness, may extend over hundreds of square kilometres, and contain millions or even billions of tons. Unweathered deposits, including those found on the present sea bottom, commonly do not contain more than about 30 percent phosphorus pentoxide (P_2O_5), but deposits that have been enriched by the leaching and oxidation of impurities may contain as much as 38 percent. Less phosphatic sandstones and shales are upgraded by separating the phosphatic particles from the matrix by screening, washing, or flotation. The marine phosphorites and some of the associated black shales contain many minor metals, some of which may be recoverable as by-products. Examples are vanadium, uranium, zinc, rare earths, and selenium.

Igneous apatite deposits are found as inclined sheets or irregular masses of intrusive igneous rock, veins, or replacement bodies, which are derived from the cooling and crystallization of silicate melts within the Earth's crust. They are associated with other rocks of igneous origin, such as nephelite-syenite and carbonatite, and, in many places, with magnetite or ilmenite ores. The apatite masses range in size from thousands to millions of tons and may contain as much as 35 percent P_2O_5 (in the fertilizer industry the phosphate content is sometimes also reported as bone phosphate of lime [BPL] or tricalcium phosphate [TPL], both of which are equal to 2.18 times the P_2O_5 content). The richest deposits are used without beneficiation. The phosphate in some of the apatite-bearing ilmenite and magnetite ores is recovered as a by-product of the milling or smelting of the titanium or iron ore.

Residual phosphate deposits develop by decomposition of phosphatic limestones, located within humid and tropical climatic regions. These deposits, consisting of phosphate pellets and nodules left behind when the calcium carbonate of the limestone is removed by solution, lie on an irregularly weathered bedrock surface. In hilly country, residual phosphate deposits are narrow and conform to the outcrop pattern of the strata; but in valleys or flat country, the deposits are blanket-like. These deposits may be several feet or more in thickness and contain 30 to 38 percent P_2O_5. Phosphate reserves in residual deposits amount to many millions of tons.

Phosphatized rocks develop in regions of tropical and subtropical climate when phosphate dissolved from phosphatic rocks or guano by percolating water is again deposited, by reprecipitation, in openings or replaces the minerals of limestone, igneous rocks, or clay that lie at a lower horizon. Where the phosphatized rocks are limestone, the deposits consist of apatite; but where the phosphatized rocks are igneous rocks or clay, the deposits are iron or aluminum phosphates such as strengite, crandallite, and wavellite. Some phosphatized rocks contain as much as 38 percent P_2O_5, and reserves in individual deposits may be scores of millions of tons.

River-pebble deposits consist of phosphate pellets and nodules weathered out of marine phosphatic limestone, located in humid climatic regions of low relief. The pellets and nodules are reconcentrated by stream action. Most river-pebble deposits do not contain sufficient phosphate to be mined profitably. (V.E.McK./Ed.)

EVAPORITES

Evaporites constitute a group of sedimentary rocks that form by the precipitation of salts in restricted water bodies such as inland seas, semi-isolated coastal waters, lagoons, and terrestrial playa lakes. When such water bodies are subject to evaporation losses that equal or exceed the water supplied by rainfall, runoff, groundwater flow, or the open sea, the salts in solution become concentrated and, by definition, the salinity increases. Ultimately a saline brine will form and salts will begin to precipitate from the brine. Because evaporation is the principal cause of the salt concentration and precipitation, the individual minerals and the deposits as a whole—whether marine or nonmarine in origin—are termed evaporites, after the process.

Occurrence

More than 80 minerals have been identified in evaporites of marine origin. These are principally carbonates, sulfates, and chlorides, with some borates, silicates, and other mineral groups. Evaporites formed in nonmarine environments may contain many of the same mineral species, but, as a generalization, they exhibit still greater diversity. This is because the composition of seawater is everywhere more nearly constant than the waters that feed playa lakes, which reflect the vagaries of neighbouring source areas. Borates, nitrates, and sulfocarbonates occur more often in nonmarine evaporites.

Evaporites occur in strata of every geological system, beginning with the Cambrian Period, 570,000,000 years ago. They are widespread, occurring on every continent, but a gradual restriction toward the Equator is evident from consideration of their distribution through time. This fact, combined with the need for high evaporation rates, has led many authorities to believe that evaporites are good paleoclimatic indicators—*i.e.,* that their occurrence signifies the existence of a generally arid climate at the time of their formation.

Sites of modern deposition

Areas of modern evaporite formation tend to sustain this view; noteworthy occurrences include: Great Salt Lake, the Death Valley salt pan, and many other playa lakes in the western United States, Chile, Australia, and other arid areas; Kara-Bogaz-Gol Gulf in the eastern part of the Caspian Sea; coastal lagoons along the margins of the Persian Gulf; the Rann of Kutch in India, Lake Larnaca, Cyprus; Lake Assal, Djibouti, the Dead Sea, between Israel and Jordan; and parts of the Red Sea. In each of these cases, the climate is generally arid, evaporation rates are high, and water salinities are about seven to 10 times that of normal seawater, except in the rainy season.

In addition to their possible paleoclimatic significance, evaporites are of much interest for paleogeographic reasons; this stems from the occurrence of thick deposits in nature. It has long been known, for example, that evaporation of a column of seawater 100 metres (330 feet) in height would lead to deposition of a salt bed only 150 centimetres (60 inches) thick. Moreover, only four centimetres (1.5 inches) of this salt would be gypsum (or anhydrite), a mineral that is present in beds whose aggregate thickness is as great as 500 metres (1,640 feet) or more in some sequences. The quantities and depths of water required to produce 500 metres of anhydrite are so vast that it has long been obvious that some resupply mechanism must be involved.

The paleogeographic or environmental setting is still subject to debate, however. Aside from clearly continental playa deposits, the association of some evaporites with coral-reef deposits, red beds, or fluvial structures suggests shallow-water or terrestrial environments. Indeed, there are many authorities who would interpret most deposits as originating in this way. Others, however, argue for deep-water basins, and still a third idea involves a two-layer aqueous system in which a lower brine layer is exposed intermittently to evaporation.

Importance to man

Evaporites are of considerable importance to man. They are the source for the world's supply of common salt (halite), gypsum, and much potash and magnesium. Borates and nitrates of economic importance also are derived from evaporite deposits. In addition, salt beds that are confined by the weight of overlying sedimentary rocks eventually tend to rise upward through this overburden, forming salt domes. These salt structures are intimately related to petroleum and natural gas occurrences in many parts of the world because they trap or block the subsurface migration of oil and gas and cause its accumulation.

Evaporite mineralogy. Evaporite mineralogy appears formidable to the uninitiated because of the large number of mineral species involved and the unfamiliar ring of their names and chemical formulas. Examination of some relatively common evaporite minerals, however, reveals that a somewhat restricted set of constituents is present (see Table 33). The minerals are categorized in four principal groups: carbonates, sulfates, chlorides, and borates and nitrates. The four principal cations (positively charged ions) associated with these groups are sodium, calcium, potassium, and magnesium, which are, of course, the principal salts in seawater. Table 33 also reveals that several pairs of mineral species are distinguished solely by reason of different numbers of water molecules contained in their crystal structure. Gypsum and anhydrite; vanthoffite and bloedite; and colemanite and inyoite are paired examples of this fact.

Classification of evaporite minerals

Table 33: Some Relatively Common Evaporite Minerals*

	formula
Carbonates	
Calcite	$CaCO_3$
Aragonite	$CaCO_3$
Magnesite	$MgCO_3$
Dolomite	$CaCO_3 \cdot MgCO_3$
Natron	$Na_2CO_3 \cdot 10H_2O$
Trona	$Na_2CO_3 \cdot NaHCO_3 \cdot 2H_2O$
Nahcolite	$NaHCO_3$
Pirssonite	$Na_2CO_3 \cdot CaCO_3 \cdot 2H_2O$
Gaylussite	$Na_2CO_3 \cdot CaCO_3 \cdot 5H_2O$
Sulfates	
Anhydrite	$CaSO_4$
Gypsum	$CaSO_4 \cdot 2H_2O$
Glauberite	$CaSO_4 \cdot Na_2SO_4$
Thenardite	Na_2SO_4
Mirabilite	$Na_2SO_4 \cdot 10H_2O$
Aphthitalite	$(K,Na)_3Na(SO_4)_2$
Vanthoffite	$3Na_2SO_4 \cdot MgSO_4$
Bloedite	$Na_2SO_4 \cdot MgSO_4 \cdot 4H_2O$
Loeweite	$6Na_2SO_4 \cdot 7MgSO_4 \cdot 15H_2O$
Kieserite	$MgSO_4 \cdot H_2O$
Hexahydrite	$MgSO_4 \cdot 6H_2O$
Epsomite	$MgSO_4 \cdot 7H_2O$
Langbeinite	$K_2SO_4 \cdot 2MgSO_4$
Leonite	$K_2SO_4 \cdot MgSO_4 \cdot 4H_2O$
Picromerite	$K_2SO_4 \cdot MgSO_4 \cdot 6H_2O$
Polyhalite	$K_2SO_4 \cdot MgSO_4 \cdot 2CaSO_4 \cdot 2H_2O$
Celestite	$SrSO_4$
Barite	$BaSO_4$
Chlorides	
Halite	$NaCl$
Sylvite	KCl
Bischofite	$MgCl_2 \cdot 6H_2O$
Carnallite	$KCl \cdot MgCl_2 \cdot 6H_2O$
Kainite	$4KCl \cdot 4MgSO_4 \cdot 11H_2O$
Borates and nitrates	
Colemanite	$Ca_2B_6O_{11} \cdot 5H_2O$
Inyoite	$Ca_2B_6O_{11} \cdot 13H_2O$
Priceite	$Ca_4B_{10}O_{19} \cdot 7H_2O$
Kernite	$Na_2B_4O_7 \cdot 4H_2O$
Borax	$Na_2B_4O_7 \cdot 10H_2O$
Ulexite	$NaCaB_5O_9 \cdot 8H_2O$
Searlesite	$Na_2O \cdot B_2O_3 \cdot 4SiO_2 \cdot 2H_2O$
Boracite	$Mg_3B_7O_{13}Cl$
Niter	KNO_3
Soda niter	$NaNO_3$

*The formulas are written as shown for reasons of convenience and ease of distinguishing the cationic and anionic elements and groups involved. Dolomite, for example, is commonly expressed chemically as $CaMg(CO_3)_2$, rather than the form listed above.

Having said this, it must be admitted that variety is one of the hallmarks of evaporite mineralogy. In addition to the minerals listed in Table 33 there are perhaps another 70 species that have been identified in marine and nonmarine deposits. They include some fluorides (fluorite and sellaite), iron oxides (magnetite, hematite, and limonite), silicate minerals (quartz, opal, and talc), clay minerals (kaolinite, illite, and sepiolite), phosphates (goyazite), sulfides (pyrite), and even native elements (sulfur).

Origin of evaporites. The origin of evaporites is rather simple in the sense that all deposits are derived by evaporation of water bodies. Beyond this, complexities arise because the variability of conditions in nature can give rise to the great mineral diversity already noted, and because a number of possible environments of deposition are involved.

Nonmarine environment. Evaporite deposition in the nonmarine environment occurs in closed lakes—those without outlet—in arid or semi-arid regions. Such lakes form in closed interior basins or shallow depressions on land where drainage is internal and runoff does not reach the sea. If water depths are shallow or, more typically, somewhat ephemeral, the term playa or playa lake is commonly used.

Hydrology of closed lakes

Hydrologic inflow to closed lakes consists principally of precipitation and surface runoff, both of which are small in amount and variable in occurrence in arid regions. Groundwater flow and discharge from springs may also provide water input in some cases, but evaporation rates are high and are always considerably in excess of precipitation and surface runoff. When sporadic or seasonal storms occur, they give rise to a sudden surge in water inflow. Because the closed lake lacks an outlet, it can respond to such circumstances only by increasing its surface area and water depth. Subsequent evaporation will reduce the volume of water present to the prestorm or normal amount; fluctuation of the lake level, therefore, is characteristic of the environment.

Changing lake levels and water volumes give rise, in turn, to fluctuating salinity values. Salinity is a measure of the total salt content. Salinity variations affect equilibrium relations between brine and minerals and lead to much solution and reprecipitation of evaporites in the nonmarine environment.

Shallow marine environment. Evaporite deposition in the shallow marine environment (sometimes termed the salina) occurs in desert coastal areas, particularly along the margins of such semi-restricted water bodies as the Red Sea, Persian Gulf, and Gulf of California. Restriction is, in general, one of the critical requirements for evaporite deposition because free and unlimited mixing with the open sea would easily overcome the high evaporation rates of arid areas and dilute these waters to near-normal salinity. The semi-restriction referred to cannot, in fact, prevent a great deal of dilution by mixing; coastal physiography is the principal factor involved in brine production.

Deep-basin environment. As in all instances of evaporite formation—including nonmarine formation—evaporation must generally exceed precipitation and surface runoff in the deep-basin environment. The principal physiographic requirement is the presence of a barrier sill to prevent unlimited mixing of water within the basin with that of the open sea. This physical configuration is quite similar to that of the Mediterranean Sea, most of the Norwegian fjords, and the Red Sea proper.

Figure 116 illustrates the probable sequence of events. In the formative stage (Figure 116A), incoming seawater

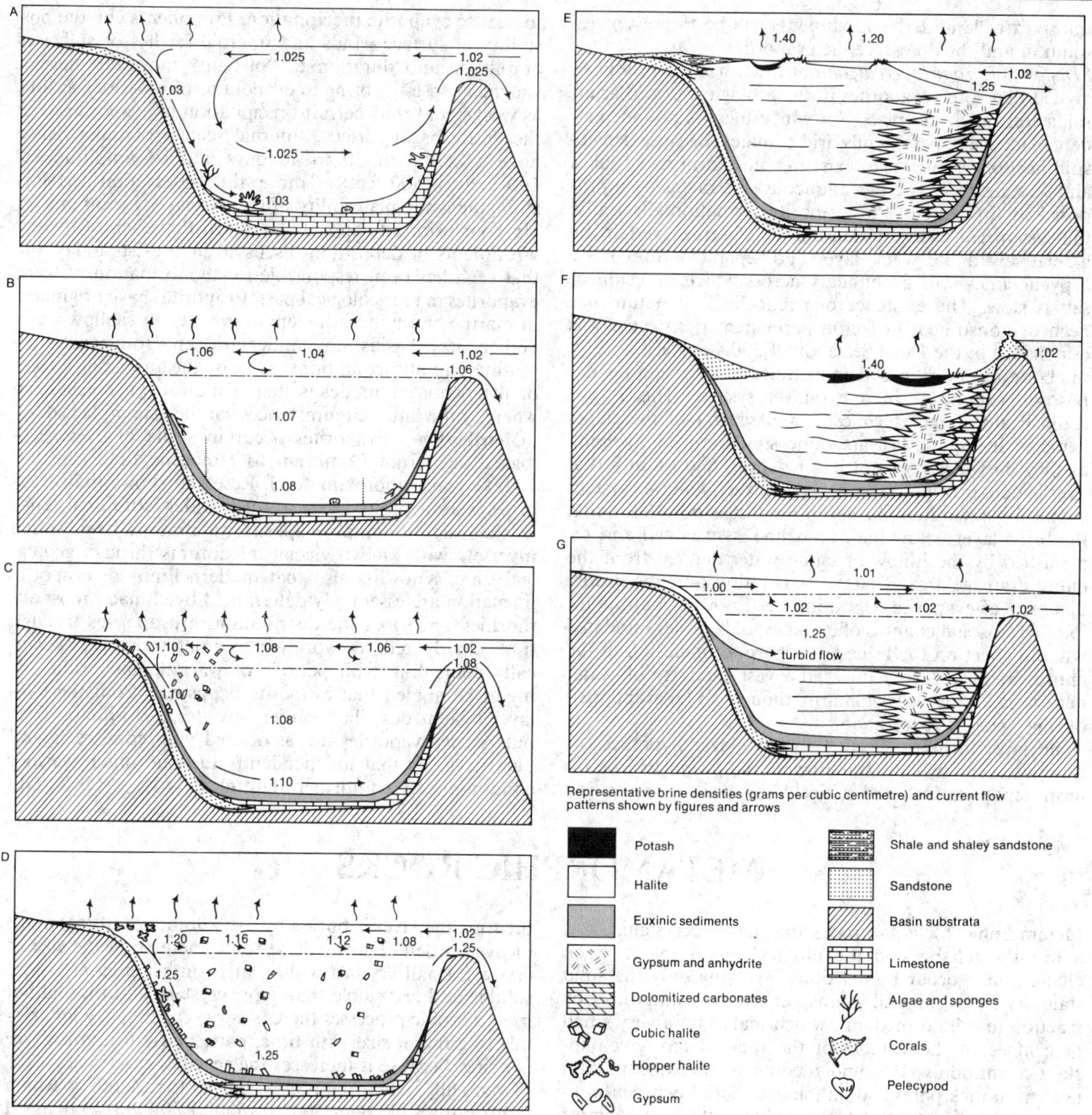

Figure 4: *Model of deepwater evaporite deposition.*
(A) Formative stage. (B) Euxinic stage. (C) Ephemeral stage. (D) Permanent evaporite stage.
(E–G) Alternative terminal stages (see text).

From R. Schmalz, "Deep Water Evaporite Deposition: A Genetic Model" (1969); American Association of Petroleum Geologists

of density 1.02 grams per cubic centimetre (subsequently abbreviated here as g/cm^3) gives rise to water of density 1.025 g/cm^3 within the basin because of surface evaporation. Toward the landward margin of the basin, the density further increases, and the circulation caused by the sinking of denser water is as shown. Conditions in the Mediterranean Sea today closely resemble those depicted here for the formative stage.

The continual sinking of dense brines formed at the surface ultimately displaces all of the waters of normal or near-normal density within the basin, and stagnant bottom water, lacking oxygen, is formed. This is the euxinic stage (Figure 116B), in which normal carbonate deposition ceases and is replaced by the accumulation of dark, sulfide-rich, organic muds. Bottom-water densities attain values of about 1.08 g/cm^3 and marine life generally perishes.

Continued surface evaporation will lead to precipitation of the first evaporite mineral, gypsum, when densities of about 1.10 g/cm^3 are attained in the distal parts of the basin. This is termed the ephemeral stage (Figure 116C) because the gypsum crystals will redissolve as they sink to ward the bottom through water of lesser density (1.08 g/cm^3) that is not yet fully saturated with respect to calcium sulfate.

The permanent evaporite stage is finally reached when very dense water fills the entire basin to the depth of the sill (Figure 116D). At the density shown (1.25 g/cm^3), gypsum, anhydrite, and halite could accumulate on the basin bottom without the occurrence of re-solution. Depending upon the salinity (density) variations that occur through time, a variety of evaporite minerals and mineral sequences could be deposited under the conditions here associated with the permanent stage of development.

Preservation of deposits

Evaporite deposition in the deep-basin environment is therefore limited chiefly by basin depth; the great thicknesses of many known deposits can be accounted for by this model. With regard to the ultimate fate and degree of preservation of deep-basin evaporites after basin filling, several alternatives are possible. Figure 116E shows one such alternative. The deep basin has been completely filled and salt flat or salina-like conditions prevail at the surface. Normal sedimentation, associated with shoreline shifts of the shallow marine environment, will preserve the thick evaporite deposit.

If sea level should fall or if the basin and its sill should rise because of uplift of the Earth's crust, the influx of seawater will be effectively cut off and the deep-basin evaporites easily preserved (Figure 116F). The thick salt deposits of the Ethiopian Danakil Depression may reflect this postulated condition.

Finally, climatic change may interrupt basin filling during the permanent stage. Even in the instance of much freshwater inflow (Figure 116G), the combined effect of the immediately overlying saline brine and the basinward transport of land-derived sediments will be to prevent resolution and thus preserve the evaporites.

Deposition from layered solutions. It has recently been argued that some evaporites in the geological record accumulate at times and places for which there is no independent evidence of persistently arid climates. Because density stratification is known to exist in some form in all lakes and seas, a simple two-layer aqueous system has been proposed as fundamental to evaporite formation. Basically, the system consists of a dense layer of brine overlain by a relatively dilute water layer and separated from it by a pycnocline—*i.e.*, a boundary across which diffusion of salt is slow. The existence of pycnoclines in nature has been demonstrated; in fact, a permanent pycnocline was established in the Dead Sea about 1,500 years ago.

Laboratory work has demonstrated that evaporite deposition can occur in a two-layer system. This is not a drastically different concept, and several of the stages depicted in Figure 116 are quite similar to it, involving as they do water layers of lesser density and salinity that overlie denser brines. Two aspects of the two-layer system should be noted here, however. First, it is postulated that the brine layer below the pycnocline is sustained and replenished by the inflow of saline water derived from the entire drainage area. That is, evaporation over the immediate site of evaporite deposition need not be continuous; local or seasonal changes of climate can be accommodated without effect on the brine layer. Second, inclusion of the entire drainage area reduces the vast quantity of water per unit area that is customarily thought to be evaporated during evaporite deposition.

Brine exposure by seiches

The most tortuous facet of the two-layer hypothesis is a requirement that the brine below the pycnocline be intermittently exposed and subjected to surface evaporation to induce evaporite precipitation. Proponents cite the possibility of surface winds and internal seiches of sufficient amplitude and duration to "pile up" the dilute surface waters, expose the brine to evaporation for periods as long as weeks, and thus permit precipitation of evaporites over the entire basin surface. Internal seiches of Lake Baikal have a period of 30 to 40 days and an amplitude of 150 metres (500 feet) or more; this observation certainly strengthens the plausibility of the two-layer hypothesis.

In conclusion, it can only be added that each of the environments of deposition discussed here exists today and that each has been responsible for the formation of some evaporites in the geological past. Evaporites have originated in marine and nonmarine environments, in shallow water and in deep basins, and under arid and somewhat fluctuating climatic conditions. One of the principal virtues of the two-layer model is that it indicates a mechanism whereby the latter circumstances can be accomplished.

Distribution. Evaporites occur in strata of every geological age, from Cambrian to Holocene time (the last 10,000 years, approximately). Research shows that evaporites were deposited over a much wider latitudinal range in the past, and that evaporite maximums have varied inversely with known glacial maximums through geological time. Knowing also that modern limits of evaporite formation are essentially determined by climate, most authorities agree that the distribution of evaporites through time closely reflects worldwide climatic change, specifically coinciding with periods of warmth and aridity. It might be argued that evaporite deposition from the two-layer system described earlier obviates the climatic link; but Arctic evaporites are associated with coral reefs and plant remains that independently indicate much warmer conditions at high northern latitudes. (L.K.L./Ed.)

METAMORPHIC ROCKS

Metamorphic rocks are rocks that have recrystallized as a result of changes in the physical environment. Such changes may occur by reactions involving only the solid state (*i.e.*, the mineral grains) or, more commonly, by reaction in a fluid medium, which makes up a very small percentage of the volume of the rock at any given instant. Commonly, the fluid medium is an aqueous film present in rock pores and on the boundaries between mineral grains. In a sense, metamorphic rocks are the most common rock types of the solid Earth, primarily because the Earth is a dynamic system whose temperatures and pressures tend to fluctuate in space and time. Because the pressure-temperature (*P–T*) conditions to which rocks of all igneous and sedimentary types may be subjected are almost infinite, the variety of metamorphic rock types is very large indeed.

Metamorphic alterations. A very simple mineralogical system and its response to changing pressure and temperature provide a good illustration of what occurs in metamorphism. An uncomplicated sediment at the Earth's surface, a mixture of the clay mineral kaolinite [$Al_4Si_4O_{10}(OH)_8$] and the mineral quartz (SiO_2), provides a good example. Most sediments have small crystals or grain sizes but great porosity and permeability, and the pores are filled with water. As time passes, more sediments are piled on top of the surface layer, and it becomes slowly buried. Accordingly, the pressure to which the layer is subjected increases because of the load on top, or overburden. For rocks with a density of two to three grams per cubic centimetre, the pressure will increase by 200 to 300 bars above for each kilometre of overburden. At the same time, the temperature will increase because of radioactive heating within the sediment and heat flow from deeper levels within the Earth. On the average, the temperature increases by about 30° C for each kilometre (87° F per mile) of burial.

In the first stages of incremental burial and heating, few chemical reactions will occur in the sediment layer, but the porosity decreases, and the low-density pore water is squeezed out. This process will be virtually complete by the time the layer is buried by five kilometres (three miles) of overburden. There will be some increase in the size of crystals; small crystals with a large surface area are more soluble and less stable than large crystals, and throughout metamorphic processes there is always a tendency for crystals to grow in size with time, particularly if temperature is rising, because it increases the speed of reaction.

Eventually, when the rock is buried to a depth at which temperatures of about 300° C (600° F) obtain, a chemical reaction sets in, and the kaolinite and quartz are transformed to pyrophyllite and water:

$$\text{kaolinite + quartz} \rightarrow \text{pyrophyllite + water}$$
$$Al_4Si_4O_{10}(OH)_8 + 4SiO_2 \rightarrow 2Al_2Si_4O_{10}(OH)_2 + 2H_2O.$$

The exact temperature at which this occurs depends on the fluid pressure in the system, but in general the fluid and rock-load pressures tend to be rather similar during such reactions. The water virtually fights its way out by lifting the rocks. Thus, the first chemical reaction is a dehydration reaction leading to the formation of a new hydrate. The water released is itself a solvent for silicates and promotes the crystallization of the product phases.

If heating and burial are continued, another dehydration sets in at about 400° C (750° F), in which the pyrophyllite is transformed to andalusite and quartz and water:

A second dehydration reaction

$$\text{pyrophyllite} \rightarrow \text{andalusite + quartz + water}$$
$$Al_2Si_4O_{10}(OH)_2 \rightarrow Al_2SiO_5 + 3SiO_2 + H_2O.$$

After the water has escaped, the rock becomes virtually anhydrous, containing only traces of fluid in minute and small inclusions in the product crystals. Both of these dehydration reactions tend to be fast, because water, a good silicate solvent, is present.

Although the mineral andalusite is indicated as the first product of dehydration of pyrophyllite, there are three minerals with the chemical composition Al_2SiO_5. Each has unique crystal structures, and each is stable under definite *P–T* conditions (Figure 117). Such differing forms with identical composition are called polymorphs. If py-

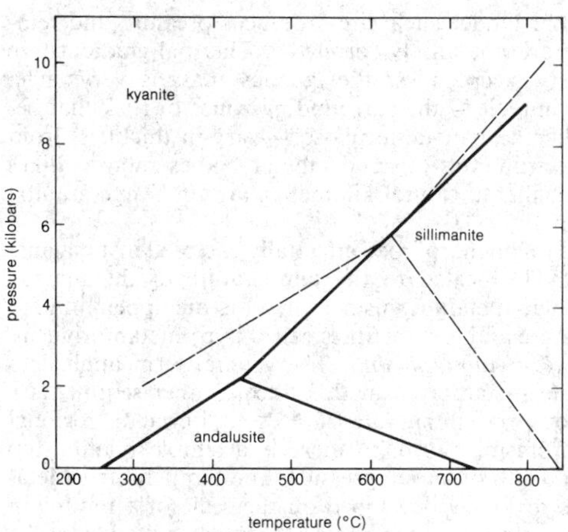

Figure 117: Pressure–temperature regions where the three polymorphic modifications of Al_2SiO_5 are stable. The dashed and solid lines are boundaries provided by different laboratories (see text).

rophyllite is dehydrated under high-pressure conditions, the polymorph of Al_2SiO_5 formed would be the mineral kyanite (the most dense polymorph). On the other hand, if the original temperature gradient persists, then at a depth of burial corresponding to about 700° C (1,300° F) the polymorphic transformation from andalusite to sillimanite will occur:

$$\begin{array}{c}\text{andalusite} \rightarrow \text{sillimanite}\\ Al_2SiO_5 \rightarrow Al_2SiO_5\end{array}$$

Sillimanite is more stable than andalusite at high temperatures, but, unless a small amount of water is present in the rock, this reaction may not go to completion even in geological time. If sillimanite does form, however, then the temperature range within the Earth's crust will preserve the sillimanite–quartz assemblage unchanged.

If the forces leading to burial and sinking are reversed when the base of the sedimentary column has reached the sillimanite stage, then the thick column may be pushed up into a mountain range, permitting its observation. The reactions that proceeded during burial tend not to be reversed: with the water of the original sediments gone, the hydrates cannot reform, and chemical reaction rates are always faster in response to rising than to lowering temperatures. The re-exposed column would reveal the metamorphic history of the pile of sediments.

The types of reaction cited here are typical of all metamorphic changes. Gases are lost (hydrates lose water, carbonates lose carbon dioxide), and mineralogical phases undergo polymorphic or other structural changes; low-volume, dense mineral species are formed by high pressures, and less dense phases are favoured by high temperatures. Considering the immense chemical and mineralogical complexity of the Earth's crust, it is clear that the number of possible reactions is vast. In any given complex column of crustal materials some chemical reaction is likely for almost any incremental change in pressure and temperature. This is a fact of immense importance in unravelling the history and mechanics of the Earth, for such changes constitute a vital record and are perhaps the primary reason for the study of metamorphic rocks.

Observations show that pressure is only rarely hydrostatic (equal in all directions) at any point within the Earth's crust. In real cases, consequently, stresses operate that may lead to flow or fracture of materials. Such occurrences produce certain characteristic fabrics or structures in metamorphic rocks that may be observed at the level of the orientation of small crystals in a rock or as a pattern of folds in a mountain range. One of the principal characteristics of most metamorphic rocks is that the arrangement of crystals is not isotropic, or random, but that there is a strong preferred orientation related to the direction of stress components of pressure.

Economic aspects of metamorphic rocks. Many metamorphic reactions result in the gain or loss of water and other volatile compounds, such as the gaseous forms of hydrogen sulfide, carbon dioxide, and hydrochloric acid. At moderate temperatures and pressures, a good solvent for silicates is water; for carbonates, carbon dioxide in water; and for sulfides and elements such as gold, sodium chloride in water. Because large quantities of fluids may take part (perhaps 5 percent by weight of the rocks) in metamorphism, these fluids may transport economically important quantities of other minerals, which either may form deposits in veins or be disseminated in more permeable rocks. Various types of veins often have a very simple mineralogy and are characteristic of metamorphic rocks.

Formation of ore deposits

A large number of ore deposits are formed in metamorphic rocks. Practically all gold concentration occurs during metamorphism, even though sedimentary processes may lead to reworking and further concentration. Most important among the many other elements characteristically associated with metamorphic processes are copper, tungsten, zinc, lead, and mercury.

Other metamorphic rocks have useful application as building materials, often because of their peculiar grain sizes and fabrics. Thus, slates characterized by their ability to split or show slaty cleavage have applications wherever erosion- and corrosion-resistant thin materials are wanted. The uses of marble are associated with the increased grain size resulting from the metamorphism of limestones. Serpentines find application because of their beauty when polished; they form during metamorphism by the hydration of certain classes of basic igneous rocks (peridotites and dunites). At times, nickel deposits form during this process. Some metamorphic minerals are of value because of their physical properties or purity. Thus, garnet is often used in abrasives and kyanite as a source of pure aluminum silicate in certain refractory materials.

Formation and classification of metamorphic rocks

The common metamorphic rocks observed on the Earth's surface, in mountain ranges and areas of deep erosion, are formed from materials within the crust. The average thickness of the crust is around 30 kilometres (20 miles) under the continents and six to eight kilometres (four to five miles) under the oceans. These thicknesses correspond to load pressures on the order of 10 kilobars and two to three kilobars, respectively (one kilobar is very nearly 1,000 atmospheres pressure). Occasionally, crustal thickness may approach 60 kilometres (40 miles), and, hence, pressures may approach 20 kilobars. From place to place on the Earth's surface, thermal gradients are quite variable. The average figure quoted is about 30° C per kilometre of depth, but in some regions the thermal gradient is much less (about 10° C per kilometre), and in some active hydrothermal regions it may exceed 100° C per kilometre (300° F per mile) (see EARTH). If the temperature at any point in the crust becomes very high, melting will commence, and metamorphic processes will give way to igneous processes. Thus, the melting temperatures of common rocks (800° C [1,500° F] for granites; 1,200° C [2,200° F] for basalts) represent the upper limits of metamorphic temperatures, and in a general way the limits of formation of common metamorphic rocks can be considered to be 100°–1,200° C (200°–2,200° F) and 1–20,000 bars.

Because most of the Earth's mantle (the region beneath the crust) is solid, metamorphic processes may also occur there. Mantle rocks are seldom observed at the surface, because they are too dense to rise, but occasionally a glimpse is presented by their inclusions in solid volcanic materials and in rapid gaseous volcanic extrusions. Such rocks may represent samples from a depth of a few hundred kilometres, where pressures of about 100 kilobars may be operative. The class of rocks known as kimberlites, which contains diamond, the high-pressure form of carbon, is an example. Experiments at high pressure have shown that few of the common minerals that occur at the surface will survive at depth within the mantle without changing to new high-density phases in which atoms are packed more closely together. Thus, the common form of SiO_2, quartz, with a density of 2.65 transforms to a new phase, stishovite, with a density of 4.29. Such changes are of critical significance in the geophysical interpretation of the Earth's interior.

The Earth's oldest rocks

Geologists believe the Earth is about 4,600,000,000 years old. This is also the age of meteoric materials and probably the age of the Moon. The oldest rocks on Earth are found on the continents; ages of about 3,500,000,000 years from Africa and the Soviet Union have been substantiated. These ages were obtained from analyses of igneous rocks, but the rocks themselves intrude metamorphosed sedimentary rocks. The oldest rocks found on Earth at this time are metamorphic rocks from Greenland with an age of 3,800,000,000 years. It may be argued, therefore, that the oldest rocks on Earth are metamorphic and that metamorphic processes of the same type as those existing today have been operating since the earliest times, when the Earth was cool enough to allow fragments of the crust to survive. Thus, metamorphic processes affect almost all rocks except those that are being formed at the surface today.

Because metamorphism represents a response to changing physical conditions, those regions of the Earth's surface where dynamic processes are most active will also be regions where metamorphic processes are most intense and easily observed. The vast region of the Pacific margin, for example, with its seismic and volcanic activity, is also a region in which materials are being buried and metamorphosed intensely. In fact, the margins of continents and regions of mountain building are also regions where metamorphic processes proceed with intensity. But in quiet places, where sediments may accumulate at slow rates, less spectacular changes occur; these record changing, conditions of pressures and temperatures that act upon each mineral grain. Metamorphic rocks are therefore distributed throughout the geologic column.

TYPES OF METAMORPHISM

It is convenient to distinguish several general types of metamorphism in order to simplify the description of the various metamorphic phenomena. Recognized here are contact, regional, hydrothermal, dynamic, and retrograde metamorphism, each of which will be described in turn.

Contact metamorphism. Whenever the crust is invaded at any level by silicate melts (magmas, from which igneous rocks crystallize within the Earth), they perturb the normal thermal regime and cause a heat increase in the vicinity. If a mass of basaltic liquid coming from the upper mantle is trapped in the crust and crystallizes there, it will heat up the surroundings; and the amount of heating and its duration will be a direct function of the mass of igneous material and its shape. Contact-metamorphic phenomena thus occur in the vicinity of hot igneous materials and at any depth. Under such circumstances pressure and temperature are not simply correlated. Thermal gradients are often very steep unless the igneous mass is very large. Contact aureoles—the surrounding zones of rock that become altered or metamorphosed—vary in thickness from several centimetres (around tabular bodies such as dikes and thin sills) to several kilometres (around large granitic intrusions).

Contact-aureole thickness

If small fragments of rock are totally enclosed in a magma, they may be heated to the temperature of the magma itself. Their metamorphism represents an upper limit to temperature and is sometimes called pyro-metamorphism.

Regional metamorphism. The general term applied to large-scale metamorphism that affects either sedimentary or igneous rocks that are subject to burial is regional metamorphism. Normally there is a simple relationship between depth of burial, pressure, and temperature. Metamorphic rocks are developed on the scale of a mountain range, but among systems (*e.g.,* the Alps or the Urals) the pattern of thermal gradients may differ. Stress is normally operative, and the rocks produced by regional metamorphism have a well-developed fabric.

When low pressures are associated with regional metamorphism, the term burial metamorphism is applied. It occurs on a large scale, and the general distinguishing feature is the presence of a rather low-temperature mineral assemblage and often a lack of any pronounced mineral fabric.

Hydrothermal metamorphism. Changes that occur in rocks near the surface, where there is intense activity of hot water, are categorized as hydrothermal metamorphism. Such areas include Yellowstone National Park, United States; Wairakei, New Zealand; and the Salton Sea, California. It is now generally recognized that the circulating groundwaters that often become heated by proximity to igneous materials produce the metamorphism. Migration of chemical elements, vein formation, and other kinds of mineral concentration may be extreme on account of the large volumes of water circulated.

Dynamic metamorphism. When directed pressure or stress is the dominant agent of metamorphism, it is termed dynamic; other terms are dislocation, kinematic, and mechanical metamorphism. Mineralogical changes occurring on a fault plane provide an obvious example. In some such cases, the action may simply be a grinding up of existing grains or realignment of minerals that have nonequidimensional crystals. If the action is intense, friction may even lead to melting.

The general irreversibility of metamorphic reactions

Retrograde metamorphism. Two reasons explain why metamorphic reactions that occur in response to rising pressure and temperature are not reversed when the rocks ultimately are returned to the Earth's surface, when pressures and temperatures are lower. First, if prograde (initial) reactions involve loss of volatile constituents such as water and carbon dioxide, then, unless these can be supplied again during unloading (erosional stripping away of the overlying rocks), the changes cannot be reversed. This is the most general case. Second, reaction rates generally increase with temperature; thus, prograde reactions are faster than retrograde reactions. Nevertheless, there are few metamorphic rocks that do not show at least some traces of retrograde processes, and these traces may record details of the unloading history.

Metamorphic grade refers to the pressure–temperature relations that are associated with particular metamorphic minerals or mineral assemblages. High-grade metamorphism involves minerals produced under high temperatures and pressures; low-grade metamorphism, the reverse. When rocks are subjected to more than one metamorphic event, the first event may be of a higher or lower grade than subsequent events. If the first metamorphic event affected a given rock at a higher grade than conditions of a later event, the rock may be quite unresponsive chemically, even though new deformation structures may appear. But, if the later metamorphic phase carries the rock into higher grades, the first event may be obliterated, totally or partly. Careful studies of rock textures may reveal the primary metamorphism. Rocks that are products of dry metamorphism, such as eclogites and granulites, are

By courtesy of W.S. Fyfe

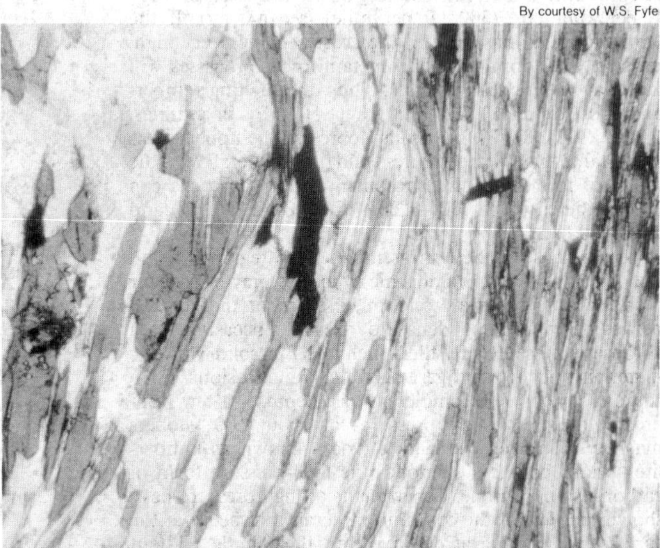

Figure 118: Photomicrograph of a staurolite–biotite schist from Scotland showing strong orientation of biotite crystals (dark) in a matrix of quartz and feldspars (magnification 50 ×).

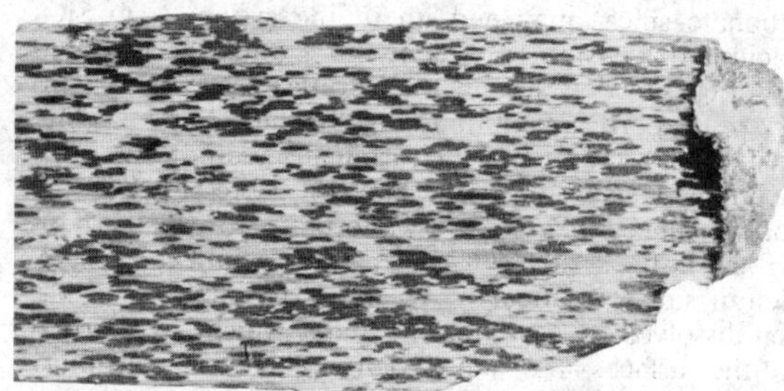

Figure 119: Cross-sectional view of a spotted phyllite from Cornwall, showing the intense stretching of spots (chlorite) in the quartz-rich (white) matrix.

By courtesy of W.S. Fyfe

highly susceptible to later events. Low-grade facies such as glaucophane-lawsonite schists are also likely to be altered by later, higher grade changes.

TYPES OF METAMORPHIC ROCKS

Because of the diverse chemistry, mineralogy, and primary origin of metamorphic rocks and because of the diverse fabrics or textures that may develop depending on the stresses that may operate during their formation, there is no simple, universally used classification of these rocks. In addition, different countries may have their own special terms. In general, any classification of metamorphic rocks tends to stress either their fabric, mineralogy, or primary origin. Some of the most common metamorphic rock types will be described here.

Schist. Rocks in which metamorphic minerals are easily seen by eye or hand lens and in which the mineral grains have a highly orientated fabric are called schists (Figure 118). Grains of acicular (needlelike) or platy minerals (amphiboles and micas) tend to lie with their long directions parallel or their planar directions parallel. Often the rocks show a pronounced mineralogical layering; quartz layers a few millimetres or centimetres in thickness may lie between mica layers, for example. Other words often qualify schist: greenschist is a schist rich in the green mineral chlorite; blueschist is rich in the blue amphibole, glaucophane; mica-schist is rich in mica; and a graphite-schist is rich in graphite. Schists that are rich in the amphibole hornblende and are often derived by metamorphism of common igneous rocks of the basalt–gabbro type are called amphibolites.

Pronounced mineralogical layering in schists

Slate. A very fine grained metamorphic rock (usually developed from clay-rich sediments) exhibiting perfect planar layering and perfection of splitting into layers (slaty cleavage) is slate. Such rocks are normally rich in micas and chlorites. As the intensity of metamorphism increases, a few large crystals may grow (porphyroblasts); such slates are sometimes termed spotted slates. As metamorphism proceeds, the average crystal size increases, and mineral segregation develops; the rock then may be termed a phyllite (Figure 119).

By courtesy of W.S. Fyfe

Figure 120: Typical granitic gneiss from Africa with large crystals of feldspar and a matrix containing dark biotite flowing around them.

Gneiss. A gneiss is produced by intense metamorphism, at high temperature and pressure. The grain size is coarser than that in schists, and layering is often well developed; mineral orientation is less perfect than in schists, however. Very common granitic gneisses (Figure 120) of Precambrian (more than 570,000,000 years in age) areas have been derived from metamorphism of granitic igneous rocks.

Hornfels and granulite. The hornfelses are formed by contact metamorphism, often show little sign of the action of directed pressure. They are fine-grained rocks in which crystals show little orientation. Granulites are products of ultrametamorphism (perhaps often the residue from partial fusion and melting). They tend to be coarse-grained and lack minerals such as amphiboles and micas capable of exhibiting strong orientation. Often they may resemble igneous rocks in appearance.

Hornfels as a product of contact metamorphism

Marble. Rocks derived from the metamorphism of carbonate sediments containing calcite or dolomite are marbles. The main result of metamorphism is an increase in grain size. Because of the rather equidimensional habit of calcite and dolomite crystals, they rarely appear schistose unless they contain other minerals such as mica.

Mylonites and cataclastites are rocks in which the texture is the result of mechanical shattering of grains. Often they show only slight if any development of new minerals. They form on fault planes or in zones of intense shearing. If the crustal rocks have an appropriate composition, phyllonites may develop where new mica crystals grow parallel to the shearing direction. If shearing is extreme, melting may occur, locally producing a pseudo-tachylite. Tachylite is a term applied to certain types of glasses formed by rapid cooling of molten rocks.

Other classes. Most of the above terms indicate structural or fabric classification of metamorphic rocks. Sometimes terms are used to indicate chemical features. Several types of schists, for example, include the following: pelitic schists contain much Al_2O_3 and often are derivatives of clayrich sediments; quartzofeldspathic schists are high in SiO_2 and feldspars and often are derivatives of sandstones or quartz-rich igneous rocks; calcareous schists have a high content of lime (CaO) and often are derivatives of impure limestones, dolomites, or calcareous muds; and basic schists contain the elements of basic igneous rocks, namely, calcium, magnesium, and iron.

In addition to the fabric and chemical features of rocks, the primary origin of the material that has been metamorphosed serves as the basis of such names as metagraywacke, the metamorphic product of the voluminous sediment type called graywacke; meta-basalt, which is derived from basalt; and meta-sediment, a general term stressing the sedimentary origin of the metamorphic rocks.

Meta-sediment

Physical and chemical characteristics

METAMORPHIC MINERALS

It is clear that many more metamorphic minerals than igneous or sedimentary minerals might be expected to exist, simply because the conditions of formation of metamorphic minerals cover a much wider range of temperatures and pressures than those of igneous or sedimentary environments. The most common characteristic minerals of metamorphic rocks are listed in Table 34. Generally, if such minerals are found well developed in a rock, then the rock will be metamorphic. Under some conditions, however, a sediment may contain such mineralogical debris, as from metamorphic rocks that are being weathered and eroded. In such a case, fabric and microscopic study may be needed to identify the rock as metamorphic. To stress changes that occur in response to increasing temperature and pressure, the common metamorphic minerals are listed in that order—*e.g.,* quartz is associated with the lowest temperatures and pressures. Minerals marked with an asterisk may have a wide range of stability; quartz, for example, may be stable in sediments, igneous melts, or almost any type of metamorphic rock. Phases marked with a dagger (†) are minerals of a composition for which more than one form (polymorph) may be found. In some cases

Table 34: Common Minerals of Metamorphic Rocks

mineral	composition
Quartz*†	SiO_2
Kaolinite	$Al_4Si_4O_{10}(OH)_8$
Montmorillonite	$(\frac{1}{2}Ca, Na)_{0.7}(Al, Mg, Fe)_4[(Si, Al)_8O_{20}](OH)_4 \cdot nH_2O$
Albite*	$NaAlSi_3O_8$
Calcite*†	$CaCO_3$
Dolomite*	$CaMg(CO_3)_2$
Analcite	$NaAlSi_2O_6 \cdot H_2O$
Laumontite*	$CaAl_2Si_4O_{12} \cdot 4H_2O$
Adularia†	$KAlSi_3O_8$
Chlorite*	$(Mg, Al, Fe)_{12}[(Si, Al)_8O_{20}](OH)_{16}$
Prehnite	$Ca_2Al(AlSi_3O_{10})(OH)_2$
Pumpellyite	$Ca_4(Mg, Fe^2)(Al, Fe^3)_5O(OH)_3(Si_2O_7)_2(SiO_4)_2 \cdot 2H_2O$
Stilpnomelane	$(K, Na, Ca)_{0-1.4}(Fe^3, Fe^2, Mg, Al, Mn)_{5.9-8.2}(Si_8O_{20})$ $(OH)_4(O, OH, H_2O)_{3.6-8.5}$
Epidote*	$Ca_2Fe^3Al_2O(OH)(Si_2O_7)(SiO_4)$
Muscovite*	$KAl_2(AlSi_3O_{10})(OH)_2$
Magnetite*	Fe_3O_4
Hematite*	Fe_2O_3
Pyrite	FeS_2
Glaucophane	$Na_2Mg_3Al_2(Si_8O_{22})(OH, F)_2$
Jadeite	$NaAlSi_2O_6$
Omphacite	a complex solid solution mainly of $NaAlSi_2O_6 - CaMgSi_2O_6 - NaFeSi_2O_6$
Lawsonite	$CaAl_2(Si_2O_7)(OH)_2 \cdot H_2O$
Aragonite†	$CaCO_3$
Magnesite	$MgCO_3$
Tremolite	$Ca_2Mg_5(Si_8O_{22})(OH)_2$
Actinolite	$Ca_2(Mg, Fe)_5(Si_8O_{22})(OH)_2$
Talc	$Mg_3(Si_4O_{10})(OH)_2$
Serpentine†	$Mg_3(Si_2O_5)(OH)_4$
Hornblende*	$(Na, K)_{0-1}Ca_2(Mg, Fe^2, Fe^3, Al)_5(Si_{6-7}Al_{2-7}O_{22})(OH, F)_2$
Plagioclase*	$(NaAlSi_3O_8, CaAl_2Si_2O_8)$
Kyanite†	Al_2SiO_5
Sillimanite†	Al_2SiO_5
Andalusite†	Al_2SiO_5
Microcline†	$KAlSi_3O_8$
Garnet*	a complex solid solution of
	pyrope $Mg_3Al_2Si_3O_{12}$
	almandine $Fe^2_3Al_2Si_3O_{12}$
	spessartite $Mn_3Al_2Si_3O_{12}$
	grossularite $Ca_3Al_2Si_3O_{12}$
	andradite $Ca_3Fe^3_2Si_3O_{12}$
Staurolite	$(Fe^2, Mg)_2(Al, Fe^3)_9O_6(SiO_4)_4(O, OH)_2$
Chloritoid	$(Fe^2, Mg, Mn)_2(Al, Fe^3)Al_3O_2(SiO_4)_2(OH)_4$
Anthophyllite	$Mg_7Si_8O_{22}(OH)_2$
Orthoclase†	$KAlSi_3O_8$
Anorthite	$CaAl_2Si_2O_8$
Diopside	$CaMgSi_2O_6$
Phlogopite*	$KMg_3(AlSi_3O_{10})(OH)_2$
Scapolite	$(Na, Ca, K)_4[Al_3(Al, Si)_3Si_6O_{24}](Cl, SO_4, CO_3OH)$
Biotite*	$K_2(Mg, Fe^2)_{6-4}(Fe^3, Al, Ti)_{0-2}(Si_{6-5}Al_{2-3}O_{20})(OH, F)_4$
Cordierite	$Al_3(Mg, Fe^2)_2(Si_5AlO_{18})$
Wollastonite	$CaSiO_3$
Forsterite	Mg_2SiO_4
Hypersthene	$(Mg, Fe)SiO_3$
Enstatite	$MgSiO_3$
Tridymite†	SiO_2
Corundum	Al_2O_3
Periclase	MgO
Mullite	$3\,Al_2O_3 \cdot 2\,SiO_2$
Sanidine†	$KAlSi_3O_8$
Larnite	Ca_2SiO_4

*Indicates wide range of stability. †Indicates more than one form (polymorph) exists.

a single mineral may be characteristic of a metamorphic facies, but more commonly an assemblage is needed to indicate conditions of metamorphism.

Metamorphic minerals display the complete range of silicate structural types from low-density, open-type structures (*e.g.*, zeolites) to high-density phases, such as garnets and jadeite. Changes in the atomic structural arrangement reflect the geothermal regime quite clearly.

ROCK COMPOSITION

Relation of metamorphic and original rock composition

Common metamorphic rock types have essentially the same chemical composition as what must be their equally common igneous or sedimentary precursors. Common greenschists have essentially the same compositions as basalts; marbles are like limestones; slates are similar to mudstones or shales; and many gneisses are like granodiorites. In general, then, the chemical composition of a metamorphic rock will closely reflect the primary nature of the material that has been metamorphosed. If there are significant differences, such differences tend to affect only the most mobile (soluble) or volatile elements; water and carbon dioxide contents change significantly, for example. An impure limestone in the system $CaCO_3$–SiO_2 (calcium carbonate–silica) may end up in the system CaO–SiO_2 (calcium oxide–silica). An extreme example is provided by buried salt deposits. In their primary state the chemistry of evaporites commonly falls in the system $CaCO_3$–$NaCl$–$CaSO_4$–H_2O (calcium carbonate–sodium chloride–calcium sulfate–water). They are not represented in the more advanced stages of metamorphism except perhaps by rocks in the system $CaCO_3$–$CaSO_4$ (calcium carbonate–calcium sulfate). Often the greatest part of the rock has been dissolved by metamorphic fluids, which have carried it to the surface. These fluids, rich in halides, or salts, may play a key role in the transport of ore minerals.

Metamorphic rocks only rarely exhibit a chemical composition that is characteristically "metamorphic." This statement is equivalent to saying that diffusion of materials in metamorphism is a slow process, and various chemical units do not mix on any large scale. But occasionally, particularly during contact metamorphism, diffusion may occur across a boundary of chemical dissimilarity leading to rocks of unique composition. If a granite is emplaced into a limestone, the contact region may be flooded with silica and other components leading to the formation of a metasomatic rock. Often such contacts are chemically zoned. A simple example is provided by the metamorphism of magnesium-rich igneous rocks in contact with quartz-rich sediments. A zonation of the type serpentine–talc–quartz may be found such as:

$$Mg_6(Si_4O_{10})(OH)_8/Mg_3(Si_4O_{10})(OH)_2/SiO_2.$$

In this case the talc zone has grown by silica diffusion into the more silica-poor environment of the serpentine. Economic deposits are not uncommon in such situations; *e.g.*, the formation of the $CaWO_4$ (calcium tungstate) scheelite when tungstate in the form of WO_3 moves from a granite into a limestone contact. The reaction can be expressed as:

$$\underset{\text{calcite}}{CaCO_3} + WO_3\ (\text{solution}) \rightarrow \underset{\text{scheelite}}{CaWO_4} + CO_2\ (\text{gas}).$$

METAMORPHIC FACIES

Metamorphic petrologists working on contact metamorphism early in the 20th century introduced the idea of metamorphic facies to correlate metamorphic events. The concept was first defined in 1914 by a Finn, Pentti Eelis Eskola, as any rock of a metamorphic formation that has attained chemical equilibrium through metamorphism at constant temperature and pressure conditions, with its mineral composition controlled only by the chemical composition. In current usage, a metamorphic facies (Figure 121) is a set of metamorphic mineral assemblages, repeatedly associated in space and time, such that there is a constant and therefore predictable relation between mineral composition and chemical composition.

The facies concept is basically observational. In a layered sequence of sediments, for example, if each layer exhibits a different chemical composition, then it is reasonable to suppose that the different minerals within any single layer represent a response to similar conditions. In other words, the rocks belong to the same facies. In another region, in which the composition is equivalent to that in only one of

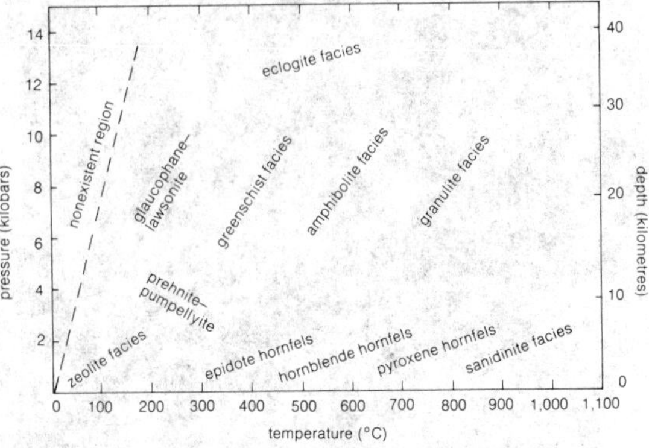

Figure 121: Approximate pressure–temperature regions of the major metamorphic facies (see text).

the sediment layers in the first sequence, the facies concept permits correlation with the more complex assemblages. A facies is defined by a set of rock types, but the naming of facies tends to follow some single common type. The greenschist facies is named after schists formed from basaltic compositions; other facies, such as the zeolite facies, are named after some characteristic mineral type in the rock; still others are named after a textural feature. The definitions of facies suggest that during most metamorphic processes there is a close approach to some equilibrium state, and experimental studies of metamorphic processes substantiate this deduction.

Grades, zones, and facies series

The intensity of metamorphism is called metamorphic grade. A line on a map where the grade of metamorphism is similar would be called an isograd. During regional mapping of metamorphic rocks it is common to record where a particular mineral appears in progressive metamorphism. If the mineral was biotite or garnet in rocks of the greenschist facies, this would be recorded as the biotite or garnet zone. Zones of development of various minerals in contact metamorphism are often mapped and indicate the type of thermal gradient around an igneous intrusion.

If the thermal gradient is very low (high pressure at low temperature), transitions will occur from zeolite facies to glaucophane-schist facies with increasing burial. If the gradient is moderate, the transitions involve zeolite facies that lead to greenschist facies that lead to amphibolite facies that lead to facies of still higher grades. The concept of facies series arises from the attempt to describe and emphasize such major geothermal trends, which have great significance in the major features of Earth dynamics. Thus, the zeolite-glaucophane-schist trend is found only when the rate of downbuckling of the crust is very fast. This type of motion occurs on continental margins and is associated with continental drift.

TEXTURES AND FABRICS

The study of the fabric of metamorphic rocks has become a highly specialized subject. Modern work has been based on the classic investigation in 1930 of Bruno Sander of Innsbruck, Austria. The study of fabric or structure may reveal the nature and direction of forces acting during dynamic processes within the Earth. If hydrostatic forces prevailed, there would be no reason for the crystals in a rock to show pronounced preferred orientation of their axes, but such preferred orientation of crystals and mineral grains is perhaps the most striking difference between a metamorphic rock and other rock types.

The most obvious features of a metamorphic rock are certain planar features that are often termed s-surfaces. The simplest planar features may be primary bedding (akin to the layering in sedimentary rocks). As the rock crystallizes or recrystallizes under directed pressure, new crystals may grow in some preferred direction, sometimes subparallel to the primary bedding but often at new angles defining new planar structures. At the same time, folding of layers may occur, leading to folds on scales with amplitude of kilometres or millimetres. Fabric symmetry may be represented by nature of deformed fossils, pebbles in a conglomerate, or any objects with a known shape prior to deformation (Figure 122).

By courtesy of J. Ramsay, Imperial College, London

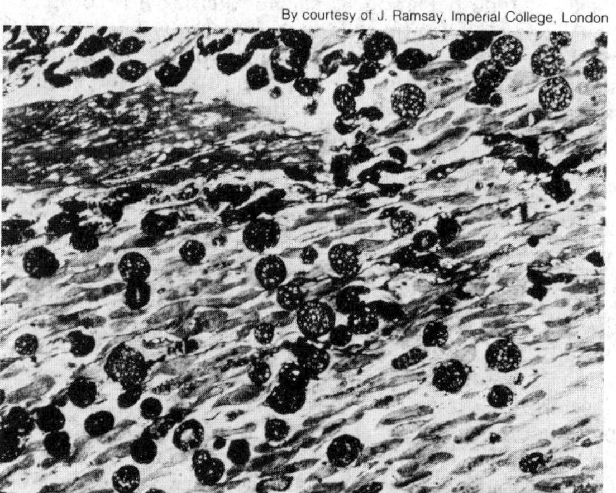

Figure 122: A deformed dolomite–calcite marble from Sardinia containing spherical fossil objects (oolites) about three millimetres (0.12 inch) in size. Oolites made of dolomite (black circles) are not deformed. Oolites made of calcite (gray), a weaker solid, are smeared out in S forms.

Figure 123: A large garnet crystal (enlarged; one centimetre [0.4 inch]) growing in a quartz–mica matrix. The garnet contains trails of inclusions and has rotated during growth in the flowing rock medium.

By courtesy of J. Ramsay, Imperial College, London

A few terms that commonly are used to describe several types of preferred orientation in metamorphic rocks include foliation, a general term describing any type of s-surface, bedding, or crystal orientation; slaty cleavage, a planar structure leading to facile cleavage that is normally caused by the preferred orientation of mica crystals; schistosity, a term used to describe repetitive and pronounced foliation of the type that is present in schists; and lineation, which is any linear structure, such as the axis of the fold, grooves on a fault plane, or the direction of stretching of pebbles.

Crystalloblastic fabric and laminations

The various mineral phases of a metamorphic rock have different physical properties and symmetries. When a rock is subjected to recrystallization in a stress field, different substances will behave differently according to such physical properties and symmetries. Some crystals always tend to grow in better formed crystals than others; rates of nucleation may differ, and this can lead to different patterns of growth of crystals—there may be a few large crystals or a mass of small crystals. Minerals can be arranged in order of their tendency to form crystals showing planar surfaces, namely, magnetite, garnet, epidote, mica, calcite, quartz, and feldspar. Crystals that tend to form large single crystals (*e.g.,* garnet) are termed porphyroblasts. Porphyroblastic crystals and their contained inclusions often record details of the mechanism of deformation and flow. A spectacular example is provided by the so-called snowball garnets, which have spiral trails of inclusions that indicate rotation during growth (Figure 123).

There is a tendency for many types of metamorphic rocks to become laminated, and the separate laminae may have distinct chemical compositions. A rather homogeneous sediment may become inhomogeneous on a minute scale. When graywackes are metamorphosed within the greenschist facies, for example, laminae rich in quartz and feldspar alternate with others rich in epidote, chlorite, and muscovite. The precise causes of this process are not well known, but it must result from a combination of extensive deformation accompanied by recrystallization. In a sense, it is a type of flow unmixing. It is often important to recognize that this structure need have no relation to original bedding in the unmetamorphosed sediments.

Rocks of the principal facies

FACIES ASSOCIATED WITH CONTACT METAMORPHISM

Possibly the simplest of all types of metamorphic processes to envisage are those in which hot silicate liquids are intruded into rocks at rather shallow depths. The hot liquids heat up the originally cool rocks, and the extent of the aureole that is formed depends on the size of the intruding igneous body and its temperature. The contact metamorphic rocks of the aureole zone often lack any obvious schistosity or foliation. The facies associated with contact metamorphism include the sanidinite, pyroxenite-hornfels, hornblende-hornfels, and albite-epidote-hornfels facies.

Sanidinite facies. Rocks of the sanidinite facies are represented by small fragments of aureole materials that have often been totally immersed in silicate liquids or by the aureole rocks surrounding volcanic pipes. Very high temperatures are attained, often at very low pressures. The dominant feature of the mineralogy of this facies is an almost complete lack of minerals containing water or carbon dioxide. Many of the minerals show similarity to those of igneous rocks themselves. If the duration of heating is short, adjustment to the imposed temperature is often imperfect.

Typical pelitic rocks

Pelitic rocks (high in Al_2O_3) contain minerals such as mullite, sillimanite, sanidine, cordierite, spinel, hypersthene, anorthite, tridymite, and even glass. One of the classic localities of such rocks is the island of Mull, off the west coast of Scotland, but in most regions of volcanism such rocks can be found.

Calcareous rocks (originally impure limestones or dolomites) tend to lose almost all their carbon dixoide, but pure calcite may survive. Typical metamorphic minerals are: quartz, wollastonite, anorthite, diopside, periclase, and in some places (the classic is Scawt Hill in Northern Ireland) an array of complex calcium silicates such as spurrite, larnite, rankinite, melilite, merwinite, and monticellite. These minerals result from the addition of varying amounts of silica to impure mixtures of calcite and dolomite. In a general way the minerals of this facies are reminiscent of those of industrial slags.

Pyroxene–hornfels facies. Rocks of the pyroxene–hornfels facies are characteristically formed near larger granitic or gabbroic bodies at depths of a few kilometres or at pressures of a few hundred bars. The mineral assemblages are again largely anhydrous, but, unlike the sanidinite facies, the minerals reflect distinctly lower temperatures. One of the classic descriptions of such rocks is from the Oslo district of Norway.

In pelitic rocks, minerals such as quartz, orthoclase, andalusite, sillimanite, cordierite, hypersthene, and plagioclase occur. Sometimes the hydrate biotite is developed. In calcareous rocks the minerals found include plagioclase, diopside, grossularite, vesuvianite (a hydrate), wollastonite, and sometimes the more complex calcium silicates monticellite, melilite, spurrite, tilleyite, and clinohumite.

Hornblende–hornfels facies. A generally deeper level of contact metamorphism where pressures of a few kilobars may be active is represented by the hornblende–hornfels facies. Hydrated phases become stable, and the transition to regional metamorphism becomes apparent. Because of the generally greater depth, this type of aureole is often superposed on a more normal metamorphism, and the rocks may appear schistose and show the development of new thermally generated minerals on a pre-existing assemblage. This type of metamorphism develops the classic "spotted" texture in which new porphyroblasts grow in slates and phyllites of a previous episode of metamorphism. Typically, these rocks are developed near most of the world's large granite batholiths, where these have moved to higher levels in the Earth's crust.

Typical minerals of pelitic assemblages include quartz, muscovite, biotite, andalusite, sillimanite, cordierite, plagioclase, microcline, and staurolite. Calcareous assemblages include calcite, quartz, diopside, grossularite, plagioclase, wollastonite, brucite, talc, forsterite, tremolite, and clinozoisite. Basaltic compositions include plagioclase, hornblende, diopside, quartz, biotite, and almandine garnet.

When rather pure limestone and dolomite come into direct contact with granitic rocks, elements such as silicon, iron, magnesium, and aluminum diffuse into the limestone, forming spectacular rocks termed skarns. These rocks often consist of large garnet crystals (grossularite) with green diopside and vesuvianite or epidote.

Formation of spectacular skarns

Albite–epidote–hornfels facies. Rocks of the albite–epidote–hornfels facies are characteristically found as the outer zones of contact aureoles where the thermal episode fades out and the rocks pass into their regional grade of metamorphism. The mineral assemblages are quite similar to those found in regional greenschist-facies metamorphism, except for the presence of low-pressure phases such as andalusite. Characteristic minerals include quartz, muscovite, biotite, chlorite, andalusite, actinolite, calcite, dolomite, albite, and epidote.

Conditions of formation of the contact facies. The mineralogical reactions included in the rocks described above are varied, and laboratory studies have provided a rather exact picture of the conditions of formation of these facies. It should be stressed that all correspond to conditions of pressure and temperature such that a thermal accident or abnormal thermal gradient is necessary to produce the observed mineral phases. This accident is the rise of silicate melt from depth.

FACIES ASSOCIATED WITH REGIONAL METAMORPHISM

Regional metamorphism is associated with the major events of Earth dynamics, and the vast majority of metamorphic rocks are so produced. They are the rocks involved in the cyclic processes of erosion, sedimentation, burial, metamorphism, and mountain building, events that are all related to major convective processes in the Earth's mantle. Two particular trends of facies can be noted: a cold trend, in which the geothermal gradient is low (about 10°–15° C per kilometre [30°–45° F per mile]), leading from zeolite facies to glaucophane schist facies; and the more general trend for normal gradients (20°–30° C per kilometre [57°–87° F per mile]), from zeolite facies to greenschist facies to amphibolite facies to a zone of crustal fusion. In almost all such crustal events at different times and places, however, there is uniqueness as well as conformity to a general pattern. Metamorphic events in the European Alps, the Urals, and the Himalayas all show specific differences: to unravel such differences and their significance is a great task of metamorphic petrology.

Zeolite facies. In the zeolite facies, sediments and volcanic debris show the first major response to burial. Reactions are often not complete, and typical metamorphic fabrics may be poorly developed or not developed at all. This is the facies of burial metamorphism.

The facies of burial metamorphism

The zeolite facies was first described from southern New Zealand, but similar rocks have now been described from the rocks of many younger mountain regions of the Earth, particularly around the Pacific margin and the European Alps. Typically, the rocks are best developed where reactive volcanic materials (often partly glassy) are common and the characteristic minerals include zeolites, which are low-density, hydrated silicates, stable at temperatures rarely exceeding 300° C (570° F). Typical mineral assemblages include heulandite, analcite, quartz with complex clay minerals (montmorillonite), micaceous phases such as chlorite and celadonite, and the potassium feldspar, adularia. At higher grades of metamorphism, the zeolite laumonite and the feldspar albite dominate the mineral assemblage. In New Zealand these are developed in a rock column that is about 15 kilometres (nine miles) thick. Calcareous rocks (impure limestones) show very little response to this grade of metamorphism.

Prehnite–pumpellyite facies. Along with the zeolite facies, the prehnite–pumpellyite facies received little attention until about 1950. The first rocks of the facies were described in New Zealand and the Celebes. The facies is transitional, bridging the path to the glaucophane–lawsonite facies or the greenschist facies. It is particularly well developed in graywacke-type sediments. The two minerals prehnite and pumpellyite replace the zeolite minerals of the zeolite facies and are themselves replaced by epidote minerals in the greenschist facies and by lawsonite and pyroxenes in the glaucophane–lawsonite facies. Typical minerals in this facies are quartz, albite, prehnite, pumpellyite, chlorite, stilpnomelane, muscovite, and actinolite. Almost all the minerals are hydrated, and, except for chlorite, they bear little resemblance to the minerals of sediments.

Again, the facies has been most described from younger mountain ranges of the Pacific margin.

Glaucophane–lawsonite schist facies. Rocks of the glaucophane–lawsonite schist facies represent deep metamorphism under conditions of a low thermal gradient. The characteristic locale for this type of metamorphism appears to be along a continental margin being underthrust by an oceanic plate. Regions in which glaucophane schists are found are also regions of great seismic and volcanic activity, such as the Pacific margin. The best described examples of this class of metamorphism come from California, Japan, New Caledonia, Celebes, the Alps, and the Mediterranean region. At present there are no known examples of glaucophane schists predating the Paleozoic Era (570,000,000 to 225,000,000 years ago). Because of the presence of the blue amphibole glaucophane (this facies is also sometimes termed the blueschist facies) and minerals such as garnet and jadeite, these schists are among the most attractive of metamorphic rocks.

Characteristic minerals of the facies include quartz, glaucophane, lawsonite, jadeite, omphacite, garnet, albite, chlorite, muscovite, paragonite, epidote, and kyanite. In calcareous rocks, calcite may be replaced by the high-pressure polymorph aragonite. Lawsonite, aragonite, and jadeite are found in no other metamorphic facies. In general, the facies is characterized by many high-density minerals reflecting a high pressure of formation.

Greenschist facies. The greenschist facies was once considered the first major facies of metamorphism proper. The name comes from the abundance of the green mineral chlorite in such rocks (Figure 124). Because chlorite and muscovite are ubiquitous and because both exhibit a platy crystal habit, these rocks normally show a highly developed foliation and often exhibit strong metamorphic differentiation. They have been described from practically every metamorphic terrain on Earth from earliest Precambrian to the young mountain regions. In fact, many of the Earth's oldest rocks (about 3,000,000,000 years old) of the continental-shield areas are in this facies, classic examples of which are in the Appalachians, Scottish Highlands, New Zealand, the European Alps, Japan, and Norway.

By courtesy of W.S. Fyfe

Figure 124: A typical greenschist from Scotland; the gray minerals are biotite and chlorite showing strong preferred orientation. The black crystals are magnetite, and the white areas are albite–quartz. Epidote and calcite are also present (magnification 50 ×).

The dominant minerals of greenschists formed from silicate-rich sediments include quartz, albite, muscovite, chlorite, epidote, calcite, actinolite, magnetite, biotite, and paragonite. Minerals less common include the manganese-rich garnet spessartite, stilpnomelane, kyanite, rutile, sphene, pyrophyllite, and chloritoid. Calcareous rocks are dominated by calcite, dolomite, and quartz; the major carbonate minerals are thermally stable. It is only when large quantities of water flush away carbon dioxide or keep its partial pressure low that carbonate-silicate reactions take place liberating carbon dioxide. The typical minerals of this facies have low water contents as compared to the zeolite facies minerals.

Amphibolite facies. The amphibolite facies is the common high-grade facies of regional metamorphism, and, like the greenschist facies, such rocks are present in all ages from all over the world. Their characteristic feature is the development of the most common amphibole, hornblende, in the presence of a plagioclase feldspar and garnet. The rocks are normally highly foliated or schistose. Many zones or isograds subdividing the facies have been recognized, and classic studies have been made in the Scottish Highlands, New Hampshire, Vermont, Switzerland, and the Himalayas.

Hornblende, the most common amphibole

Characteristic minerals derived from pelitic rocks are quartz, muscovite, biotite, garnet, plagioclase, kyanite (sillimanite), staurolite, and orthoclase. Minerals derived from basaltic rocks include hornblende, plagioclase, garnet, epidote, and biotite. Those derived from calcareous rocks are calcite, diopside, grossularite (garnet), zoisite, actinolite (hornblende), scapolite, and phlogopite. Minerals from magnesium-rich ultrabasic rocks are chlorite, anthophyllite, and talc. In most common types, water is present only in minerals of the mica and amphibole families, and, with their water contents of only about 1 to 3 percent, dehydration is nearing its metamorphic climax.

Conditions of formation of the regional metamorphic facies. Most workers on the metamorphic facies of regional metamorphism considered above agree that progressive metamorphic reactions occur in a regime in which fluid pressure is about the same as the lithostatic (rock) pressure. Furthermore, because water is the common fluid phase and will be diluted by CO_2 (carbon dioxide) only in exceptional circumstances, the fluid pressure will approximately equal the pressure of water. Current thought on the regions of formation of metamorphic facies is shown in Figure 121, where the coordinates are the pressure of water and temperature. No matter how imperfect these estimates are in absolute terms, there is little doubt about their relative significance: they emphasize the uniqueness of metamorphic events.

THE ECLOGITE AND GRANULITE FACIES

The fact that the eclogite and granulite facies have no hydrated phases has led to considerable debate as to the place of such rocks among other metamorphic facies. They could represent dry equivalents of other metamorphic rocks, or their conditions of formation may be unique. Experimental studies have shown the extreme thermal stability of hornblende in rocks of basaltic composition. If a crustal rock contains this mineral, then at moderate pressures its dehydration reactions may lead to partial melting of the crust and the onset of igneous phenomena.

Eclogite facies. Eclogite facies are recognized only in rocks whose composition is near that of basalt. Two minerals dominate the mineralogy—omphacite pyroxene and garnet. The garnet is rich in the high-pressure species pyrope, and the omphacite is rich in the high-pressure pyroxene jadeite. Small amounts of minerals such as kyanite, the hydrate zoisite, and hornblende may be present. The rocks are of high density and frequently show little or no schistosity.

Because of the high density and composition, it was proposed long ago that part of the upper mantle might be made of eclogite. Such a view is supported by eclogitic intrusions in volcanic rocks and by eclogitic inclusions in diamond-bearing kimberlite, which must come from the upper mantle. Some workers also think that eclogites found in metamorphic terrains in Norway, California, and the European Alps could also come from the mantle by tectonic processes (crustal movements). Some eclogites are known to have been produced within the crust from former surface materials (*e.g.,* basalt lava flows). It also is known that eclogites form over a wide range of temperatures, perhaps from 400° to 1,000° C (750° to 1,830°

Upper mantle as source of eclogite

F). These conditions overlap greenschist, amphibolite, and granulite facies temperatures.

Experimental studies have demonstrated that eclogites can be stable (except under certain upper-mantle conditions) only if water pressure is much lower than load pressure. The facies represents dry, high-pressure metamorphism of basaltic materials. The exact mechanism by which these metamorphic reactions take place is still a matter of considerable argument.

Granulite facies. The granulite facies is an anhydrous facies that develops gradationally from amphibolites but without any suggestion of a desiccated environment. Granulite-facies rocks are often found best developed in ancient Precambrian-shield areas of the continents. No large-scale development of such rocks has been observed in post-Cambrian metamorphism.

Rocks of this facies frequently have a granular texture quite similar to plutonic igneous rocks. Schistosity is only weakly developed. Typical minerals of the facies are quartz, alkali feldspar, garnet, plagioclase, cordierite, kyanite, sillimanite, and hypersthene. In calcareous members, dolomite, calcite, diopside, and forsterite occur; and it is in this facies that minerals of the scapolite family are best developed. Small amounts of hornblende are often present. A rare mineral occurring in this facies is sapphirine. The rock type charnockite (from Tamil Nadu, India), essentially a hypersthene granite, is normally included in this facies.

It appears from experimental studies that during ultrametamorphism, when melting starts, the basic reactions to take place are of the type:

$$\text{biotite} + \text{other minerals} \rightarrow \text{melt} + \text{residue}$$

$$\text{hornblende} + \text{other minerals} \rightarrow \text{melt} + \text{residue.}$$

The probable process of granulite formation

The first melts to form are partly wet granitic or granodioritic melts, and phases such as biotite and hornblende break down by producing a partly wet melt from the least refractory phases in the rocks. They would persist to much higher temperatures in systems of their own composition. The residue in the above equations is a granulite-facies metamorphic rock containing phases such as pyroxene and sillimanite or kyanite. Thus it is probable but certainly not universally proved that most granulites are formed only in the presence of a silicate liquid. This liquid may, of course, move to higher crustal levels. As with eclogites, this facies represents metamorphism in which the partial pressure of water is lower than total pressure. Granulites may be very common rocks in the base of the crust. The lowering of pressure is caused by solution and dilution of water in a silicate melt. Rocks whose appearance suggests that they were once a mixture of liquid and solid parts are often called migmatites.

Distribution of metamorphic rocks

A high-grade metamorphic rock is one that formed at a depth of tens of kilometres and subsequently returned to the surface. Hence, metamorphic regions are also regions of former or recent intense orogeny (mountain building). More stable regions of the Earth's crust tend to be covered with sediments, and only deep drilling will reveal the metamorphic rocks below.

The Earth's crust is made up of two basic units, the continents and ocean basins. Exploration of ocean floors has revealed that old, thick sedimentary piles are missing. Doubtless this is related to the processes of continental drift or sea-floor spreading; sediments are continuously swept up by continental motion and are added to the continents or returned to the upper mantle. (See also PLATE TECTONICS.) Nearly all studies of metamorphic rocks have concentrated on the continents for this reason.

There are few large areas of the Earth's crust that are not affected by some type of igneous event from time to time. Although the intensity of volcanism may be focussed in certain geographic regions (*e.g.*, the Pacific margin), volcanism appears to be a rather random phenomenon, at times even occurring in the stable shield areas of the continents. In this sense, contact-metamorphic events may be found almost everywhere at almost any time on Earth. But these metamorphic events are of trivial volumetric significance compared to those of regional or burial metamorphism.

Belts of mountain building and shield areas

During the past 500,000,000 years or so of Earth history, major tectonic, seismic, igneous, and metamorphic events have been concentrated on continental margins (Figure 125). This has been a period of depression and uplift of the Earth's crust associated with the formation of the present continental distribution. The processes are still going on at dramatic rates in ocean trench environments. These modern regions of activity form immense linear belts. One such belt runs virtually around the entire Pacific margin and another through the Mediterranean and southern Asia to fuse with the circum-Pacific belt. It is in these belts that the spectacular development of zeolite facies, prehnite–pumpellyite facies, glaucophane-schist facies, and, occasionally, eclogite facies, as well as the more universal facies of regional metamorphism, have occurred. The granulite facies is almost missing.

The central and often dominant feature of most continents is their vast Precambrian-shield area; examples include the Canadian Shield, Brazilian Shield, African Shield, and Australian Shield. In these rocks, dating reveals ages of 1,000,000,000 to 3,500,000,000 years, and they have been little affected by tectonic events postdating the Cambrian. But these shield areas are themselves complex. They consist of vast areas of granitic or granodioritic gneisses. Inside them, between them, and overlapping onto them are belts of sedimentary rocks quite like those in modern sedimentary belts of the Pacific margin or European Alps. These rocks are frequently metamorphosed in the greenschist, amphibolite, and granulite facies. Low-temperature facies and, in particular, low-temperature–high-pressure facies are missing—or have not yet been found. From marginal areas of these stable shield areas, a complex array of processes has been documented covering the past few hundred million years. The Caledonian orogeny (at the close of the Silurian Period) produced tectonic–metamorphic events along the east coast of North America, Greenland, the British Isles, Fennoscandia, Central Asia, and Australia. The Hercynian, or Variscan, orogeny followed about 300,000,000 years ago, affecting subparallel regions and the Urals and European Alps. In fact, the shield margins appear to have been subjected to a more or less constant battering by forces both destroying and rebuilding the margins of these protocontinents. As geologists study Precambrian areas in greater detail, the number of metamorphic and orogenic events recognized on a global scale increases.

Tectonic-metamorphic events associated with the Caledonian orogeny

It is the great task and problem of those who study metamorphic rocks to deduce the record of Earth dynamics and thermal history from metamorphic rocks. Among the questions to be answered are (1) whether the pattern of facies development through time—*e.g.*, the granulite facies in the Archean to glaucophane–lawsonite facies in the Tertiary—is a reflection of a cooling Earth and the decline of radioactivity in the crust and (2) whether the increase in size of global tectonic–metamorphic belts through time reflects changes in convective patterns in the mantle.

As understanding of the pressure–temperature regimes of metamorphism increases, and as knowledge of rock mechanics and fluid motion during metamorphism also increases through field and laboratory studies, it may become possible to understand the details of the motion of the chemical elements during such processes and hence much of the subject of economic geology or the search for man's essential raw materials. (W.S.F.)

BIBLIOGRAPHY

The nature of minerals: Standard references and basic textbooks include I. VANDERS and P.F. KERR, *Mineral Recognition* (1967); P.E. DESAUTELS, *The Mineral Kingdom* (1968); F.H. POUGH, *Field Guide to Rocks and Minerals* (1953). I. KOSTOV, *Mineralogy* (Eng. trans. 1968); L.G. BERRY and B.H. MASON, *Mineralogy* (1959); C.S. HURLBUT, *Dana's Manual of Mineralogy*, 17th ed. (1959); E.N. CAMERON, *Ore Microscopy* (1961); E.W. HEINRICH, *Microscopic Identification of Minerals* (1965); P.F. KERR, *Optical Mineralogy*, 3rd ed. (1959); J. SINKANKAS, *Mineralogy: A First Course* (1966). C. PALACHE, H. BERMAN, and C. FRONDEL, *Dana's System of Mineralogy*, 7th ed., 3 vol. (1944–62), see also earlier edi-

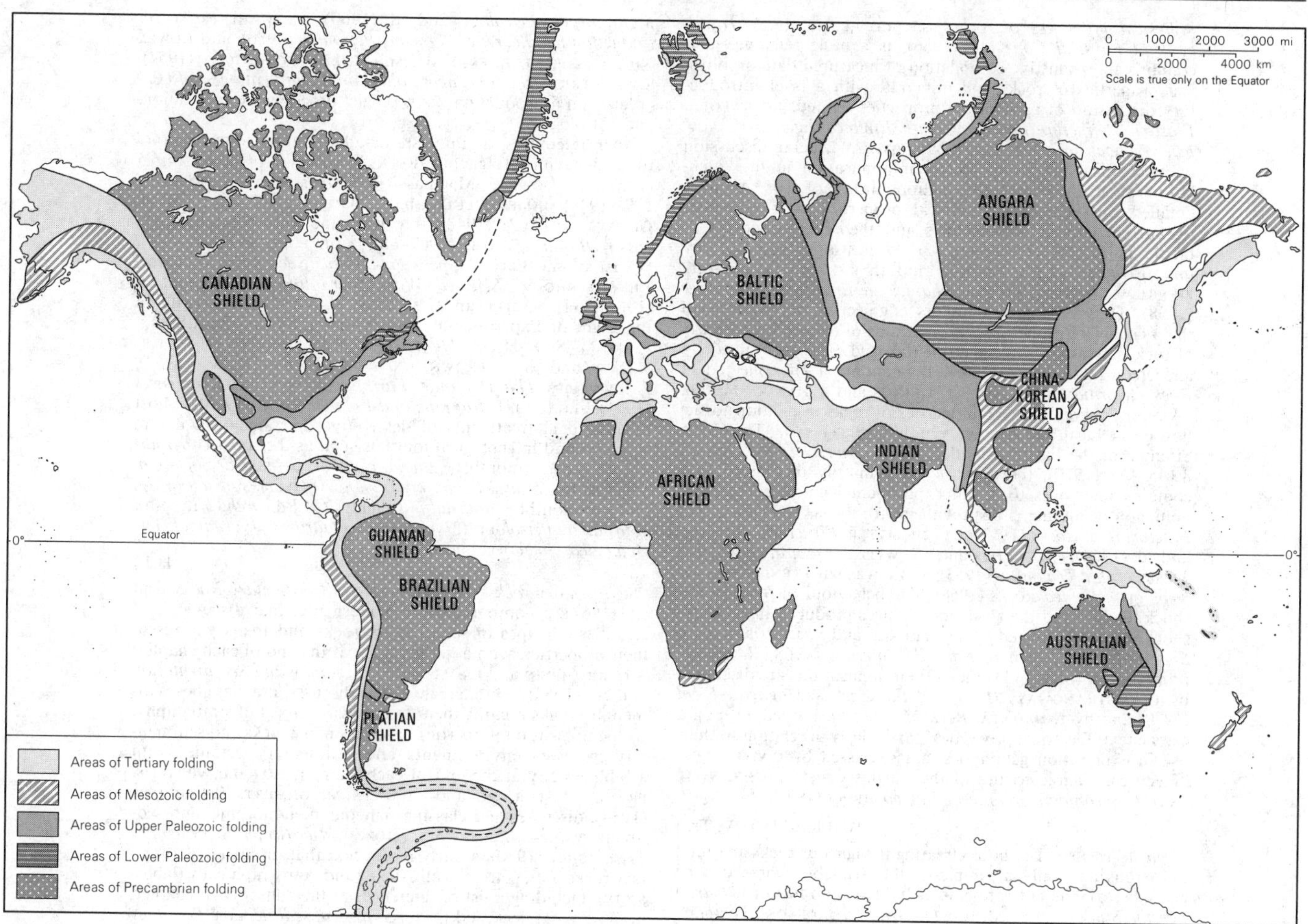

Figure 125: Tectonic units of the continents: shields and orogenic (fold) belts.

From J. Umbgrove, *The Pulse of the Earth*

tions for silicates and early data; W.A. DEER, R.A. HOWIE, and J. ZUSSMAN, *Rock-Forming Minerals,* 5 vol. (1962); W.L. BRAGG, G.F. CLARINGBULL, and W.H. TAYLOR, *Crystal Structures of Minerals* (1965). J.F. NYE, *Physical Properties of Crystals* (1957); L.V. AZAROFF, *Elements of X-Ray Crystallography* (1968); F.C. PHILLIPS, *An Introduction to Crystallography,* 2nd ed. (1956). B.H. MASON, *Principles of Geochemistry,* 3rd ed. (1966); R.M. GARRELS and C.L. CHRIST, *Solutions, Minerals, and Equilibria* (1965); KEITH LYE, *Minerals and Rocks* (1980).

(J.V.S./Ed.)

Major rock-forming minerals: W.A. DEER, R.A. HOWIE, and J. ZUSSMAN, *Rock-Forming Minerals,* vol. 4, *Framework Silicates* (1963), includes an extensive, well-illustrated section on the feldspars; T.F.W. BARTH, *Feldspars* (1969), a good modern text on the mineral group; A.S. MARFUNIN, *The Feldspars: Phase Relations, Optical Properties and Geological Distribution* (1966; orig. pub. in Russian, 1962). W.G. ERNST, *Amphiboles* (1968), a good review of the crystal chemistry, experimentally determined phase relations, and occurrence of amphiboles—cell parameters and indexes of refraction of a number of synthetic end-member amphiboles are included; J.J. PAPIKE *et al., Pyroxenes and Amphiboles: Crystal Chemistry and Phase Petrology* (1969), contains studies by X-ray diffraction, optical, electron paramagnetic resonance, Mössbauer, electron microprobe, and synthesis techniques of the amphiboles and pyroxenes; AMERICAN GEOLOGICAL SOCIETY, *Short Course on Chain Silicates* (1966), a summary of modern research on pyroxene and amphibole mineralogy, much of which is otherwise unpublished; G.M. BROWN, "Mineralogy of Basaltic Rocks," in H.H. HESS and A. POLDERVAART (eds.), *Basalts* (1967), a modern review of the structures, chemistry, and phase relations of the more common pyroxenes, with references to papers on subsolidus exsolution and inversion (extensive bibliography). H.C. DAKE, F.L. FLEENER, and B.H. WILSON, *Quartz Family Minerals* (1938), a popular illustrated account of quartz varieties and localities for the mineral collector; CLIFFORD FRONDEL, *Dana's System of Mineralogy,* 7th ed., vol. 3, *Silica Minerals* (1962), an encyclopaedic treatise of all aspects of the mineralogy of silica minerals through early 1962, with historical perspective and attention to localities; R.B. SOSMAN, *The Phases of Silica* (1965), a treatment from the physical chemist's point of view with the strengths and weaknesses of each observation or experiment critically examined—helpful discussions of solutions, gels, and phase equilibria with water; R.W.G. WYCKOFF, *Crystal Structures,* 2nd ed., vol. 1 (1963), a detailed and critical evaluation of the crystal structures of silica minerals. DEER, HOWIE, and ZUSSMAN, *Rock-Forming Minerals,* vol. 3, *Sheet Silicates,* pp. 1–102 (1962), contains discussion and detailed references on mineralogical properties, structure, polymorphism, chemical composition, occurrence, synthesis, and stability of micas. Mineral associates of olivine in basaltic rocks are covered in J.F. SCHAIRER and H.S. YODER, JR., "Crystal and Liquid Trends in Simplified Alkali Basalts," *Yb. Carnegie Instn. Wash., 63,* pp. 65–74 (1964). A further summary is by H.S. YODER, JR. and C.E. TILLEY, "Origin of Basalt Magmas: An Experimental Study of Natural and Synthetic Rock Systems," *J. Petrology,* 3:342–532 (1962). For phase transformations of olivine in meteorites and in the Earth's mantle, see R.A. BINNS, "$(Mg,Fe)_2SiO_4$ Spinel in a Meteorite," in *Physics of the Earth and Planetary Interiors,* vol. 3, pp. 156–160 (1970). C.B. AMPHLETT, *Inorganic Ion Exchangers,* ch. 3 (1964), treats the exchange and sieve properties of natural and synthetic zeolities; R.L. HAY, "Zeolites and Zeolitic Reactions in Sedimentary Rocks," *Spec. Pap. Geol. Soc. Am. 85* (1966), a comprehensive review of the occurrence and genesis of zeolites in sedimentary and low-grade metamorphic rocks; J.V. SMITH, "Structural Classification of Zeolites," *Spec. Pap. Mineralog. Soc. Am. 1* (1963), a review and classification of the crystal structures of zeolites. G. BROWN (ed.), *X-Ray Identification and Crystal Structures of Clay Minerals,* 2nd ed. (1961), a comprehensive consideration of the atomic structure and X-ray diffraction characteristics of the mineral components of clays; R.E. GRIM, *Clay Mineralogy,* 2nd ed. (1968), a discussion of the structure, properties, origin, and mode of occurrence of the clay minerals. See also RICHARD S. MITCHELL, *Mineral Names* (1979), an explanation of name derivations.

(W.S.MacK./G.V.G./M.C.G./G.M.B./D.B.S./H.S.Y./C.E.T./R.A.S./R.E.G./Ed.)

Physical properties of rocks: S.P. CLARK, JR. (ed.), *Handbook of Physical Constants* (1966), is a basic reference that contains an exhaustive compilation of measured data on physical properties of rocks and minerals, with a brief introductory discussion of each of the properties treated. J.C. JAEGER, *Elasticity, Fracture and Flow, with Engineering and Geological Applications,* 3rd ed. (1969), gives a general discussion of mechanical properties and their application to the calculation of stresses and deformations in the Earth. A more detailed treatment of mechanical properties, with emphasis on current experimental studies and theoretical concepts of brittle failure, is contained in C. FAIRHURST (ed.), *Failure and Breakage of Rock* (1967); and in K.G. STAGG and O.C. ZIENKIEWICZ (eds.), *Rock Mechanics in Engineering Practice* (1968). These works also discuss engineering applications of the mechanical properties, and methods of testing, particularly of rock masses *in situ.* Experimental studies of rock plasticity and creep pertinent to geological phenomena are collected in *Rock Deformation,* ed. by D.T. GRIGGS and J. HANDIN (1960).

A recent survey of creep properties of rocks in relation to the flow of the Earth's mantle is given by J. WEERTMAN, "The Creep Strength of the Earth's Mantle," *Rev. Geophys. Space Physics,* 8:145–168 (1970); the approach is primarily theoretical, but contains references to recent experimental studies. The phenomenon of folding is dealt with in J.G. RAMSAY, *Folding and Fracturing of Rocks* (1967); L.U. DE SITTER, *Structural Geology,* 2nd ed. (1964); F.J. TURNER and L.E. WEISS *Structural Geology of Metamorphic Tectonites* (1963); and E.H.T. WHITTEN, *Structural Geology of Folded Rocks* (1966). The behaviour of rocks under shock loading and the structural changes produced in rocks by shock waves are treated by B.M. FRENCH and N.M. SHORT (eds.), *Shock Metamorphism of Natural Materials* (1968). Magnetic properties of rocks and some of their applications are discussed by D.W. STRANGWAY, *History of the Earth's Magnetic Field* (1970) and by T. NAGATA, *Rock Magnetism,* rev. ed. (1961), a classic text. Electrical properties, particularly in relation to their use in exploration geophysics, are discussed by G.V. KELLER, "Electrical Characteristics of the Earth's Crust," in J.R. WAIT (ed.), *Electromagnetic Probing in Geophysics* (1971).

(W.B.K./E.H.T.W./Ed.)

Igneous rocks: Textbooks treating the igneous rocks are quite numerous and only a sample of the available works can be given here. General treatments include ALFRED HARKER, *Petrology for Students,* 8th ed. rev. (1954); K.C. JACKSON, *Textbook of Lithology* (1970); J.F. KEMP, *A Handbook of Rocks,* 6th ed. rev. and ed. by F.F. GROUT (1940); L.V. PIRSSON, *Rocks and Rock Minerals,* 3rd ed. rev. by ADOLPH KNOPF, (1947); S.J. SHAND, *The Study of Rocks,* 3rd ed. rev. (1951); and G.W. TYRRELL, *The Principles of Petrology: An Introduction to the Science of Rocks,* 2nd ed. (1929, reprinted 1963). Among the more advanced textbooks available that treat nomenclature, classification, and theoretical igneous petrology, the following works are recommended to the interested reader: T.F.W. BARTH, *Theoretical Petrology,* 2nd ed. (1962); BRIAN BAYLY, *Introduction to Petrology* (1968); N.L. BOWEN, *The Evolution of the Igneous Rocks* (1928; republished with new introduction by J.F. SCHAIRER, 1956); C.W. CROSS *et al., Quantitative Classification of Igneous Rocks, Based on Chemical and Mineral Characters, with a Systematic Nomenclature* (1903); R.A. DALY, *Igneous Rocks and the Depths of the Earth* (1933, reprinted 1968); ARTHUR HOLMES, *The Nomenclature of Petrology* (1920, reprinted 1971); ALBERT JOHANNSEN, *A Descriptive Petrography of the Igneous Rocks:* vol. 1, *Introduction, Textures, Classifications and Glossary,* 2nd ed. (1939); vol. 2, *The Quartz-Bearing Rocks* (1932); vol. 3, *The Intermediate Rocks* (1937); and vol. 4, pt. 1, *The Feldspathoidal Rocks,* pt. 2, *The Peridotites and Perknites* (1938); S. J. SHAND, *Eruptive Rocks,* 3rd. ed. (1949); F.J. TURNER and JOHN VERHOOGEN, *Igneous and Metamorphic Petrology,* 2nd ed. (1960); E.E. WAHLSTROM, *Introduction to Theoretical Igneous Petrology* (1950); and HOWEL WILLIAMS, F.J. TURNER, and C.M. GILBERT, *Petrography* (1954). R.V. DIETRICH, *Stones, Their Collection, Identification, and Uses* (1980), an introduction to geologic processes, classification, and petrology.

Other references of interest include ROBERT BALK, "Structural Behavior of Igneous Rocks," *Mem. Geol. Soc. Am. 5* (1937); N.L. BOWEN, "Magmas," *Bull. Geol. Soc. Am.,* 58: 263–279 (1947); JAMES GILULLY (ed.), "Origin of Granite," *Mem. Geol. Soc. Am. 28* (1948); H.H. HESS and ARIE POLDERVAART, (eds.), *Basalts,* 2 vol. (1967–68); ARIE POLDERVAART, (ed.), "Crust of the Earth," *Spec. Pap. Geol. Soc. Am. 62* (1955); J.J. SEDERHOLM, *Selected Works: Granites and Migmatites* (1967); O.F. TUTTLE and N.L. BOWEN, "Origin of Granite in the Light of Experimental Studies in the System $NaAlSi_3O_8$–$KAlSi_3O_8$–SiO_2–H_2O," *Mem. Geol. Soc. Am. 74* (1958); L.R. WAGER and G.M. BROWN, *Layered Igneous Rocks* (1967); P.J. WYLLIE, *The Dynamic Earth: Textbook in Geosciences* (1971); and (ed.), *Ultramafic and Related Rocks* (1967). A host of additional treatments of descriptive and analytical nature can be found in geological journals such as the *American Journal of Science* (monthly), *Bulletin of The Geological Society of America* (monthly), *Economic Geology* (8/year), *Journal of Geology* (bimonthly), *Journal of Geophysical Research* (3/month), *Journal of Petrology* (3/year), and *Quarterly Journal of The Geological Society* (London).

(R.H.J.)

Sedimentary rocks: F.J. PETTIJOHN, *Sedimentary Rocks,* 2nd ed. (1957), a comprehensive, modern text that discusses and classifies all types of sedimentary rocks and treats various of their properties, with a bibliography at the end of each chapter; W.C. KRUMBEIN and L.L. SLOSS, *Stratigraphy and Sedimentation* 2nd ed. (1963), a modern text that discusss and classifies sedimentary rocks relating them to the twin subject of stratigraphy, with emphasis on properties of sedimentary rocks and sedimentary processes, environments, and sedimentary tectonics, with a bibliography at the end of each chapter; HOWELL WILLIAMS, FRANCIS J. TURNER, and CHARLES M. GILBERT, *Petrography* (1954), discusses and classifies igneous metamorphic, and sedimentary rocks; ALBERT V. CAROZZI, *Microscopic Sedimentary Petrography* (1960), a fairly recent text that discusses sedimentary rocks both petrologically (field) and petrographically (laboratory), including a list of references at the end of each chapter; ROBERT E. CARVER, (ed.), *Procedures in Sedimentary Petrology* (1971), a modern text that treats in an excellent manner the procedures that should be followed in any investigation of sedimentary rocks, with 29 outstanding scholars each contributing a section of his specialty, including lists of references at the end of each section.

(H.J.Bi.)

Metamorphic rocks: Fundamental texts treating all aspects of the mineralogy and petrology of metamorphic rocks include: T.F.W. BARTH, C.W. CORRENS, and P. ESKOLA, *Die Entstehung der Gesteine* (1939); W.S. FYFE, F.J. TURNER, and J. VERHOOGEN, *Metamorphic Reactions and Metamorphic Facies* (1958); A. HARKER, *Metamorphism,* 2nd ed. (1939); B. MASON, *Principles of Geochemistry,* 3rd ed. (1966); F.J. TURNER, *Metamorphic Petrology* (1968); J. VERHOOGEN *et al., The Earth* (1970); H. WILLIAMS, F.J. TURNER, and C.M. GILBERT, *Petrography: An Introduction to the Study of Rocks in Thin Sections* (1954); and H.G.F. WINKLER, *Die Genese der metamorphen Gesteine* (1965; Eng. trans., *Petrogenesis of Metamorphic Rocks,* 1965). The structure and fabric of the metamorphic rocks are covered in books such as: B. SANDER, *Gefügekunde der Gesteine* (1930); A. SPRY, *Metamorphic Textures* (1969); and F.J. TURNER and L.E. WEISS, *Structural Analysis of Metamorphic Tectonites* (1963).

(W.S.F.)

Modernization and Industrialization

Modern society is industrial society. To modernize a society is, first of all, to industrialize it. Historically, the rise of modern society has been inextricably linked with the emergence of industrial society. All the features that are associated with modernity can be shown to be related to the set of changes that, no more than two centuries ago, brought into being the industrial type of society. This suggests that the terms industrialism and industrial society imply far more than the economic and technological components that make up their core. Industrialism is a way of life that encompasses profound economic, social, political, and cultural changes. It is by undergoing the comprehensive transformation of industrialization that societies become modern.

Modernization is a continuous and open-ended process. Historically, the span of time over which it has occurred must be measured in centuries, although there are examples of accelerated modernization. In either case, modernization is not a once-and-for-all-time achievement. There seems to be a dynamic principle built into the very fabric of modern societies that does not allow them to settle, or to achieve equilibrium. Their development is always irregular and uneven. Whatever the level of development, there are always "backward" regions and "peripheral" groups. This is a persistent source of strain and conflict in modern societies. Such a condition is not confined to the internal development of individual states. It can be seen on a global scale, as modernization extends outward from its original Western base to take in the whole world. The existence of unevenly and unequally developed nations introduces a fundamental element of instability into the world system of states.

Modernization seems to have two main phases. Up to a certain point in its course, it carries the institutions and values of society along with it, in what is generally regarded as a progressive, upward movement. Initial resistance to modernization may be sharp and prolonged, but it is generally doomed to failure. Beyond some point, however, modernization begins to breed discontent on an increasing scale. This is due in part to rising expectations provoked by the early successes and dynamism of modern society. Groups tend to make escalating demands on the community, and these demands become increasingly difficult to meet. More seriously, modernization on an intensified level and on a world scale brings new social and material strains that may threaten the very growth and expansion on which modern society is founded. In this second phase, modern societies find themselves faced with an array of new problems whose solutions often seem beyond the competence of the traditional nation-state. At the same time, the world remains dominated by a system of just such sovereign nation-states of unequal strengths and conflicting interests.

Yet challenge and response are the essence of modern society. In considering its nature and development, what stands out initially at least is not so much the difficulties and dangers as the extraordinary success with which modern society has mastered the most profound and far-reaching revolution in human history.

This article discusses the processes of modernization and industrialization from a very general and primarily sociological point of view. It does so also, it should be remembered, from a position within the very processes it describes. The phenomena of industrialization and modernization that are taken to have begun some two centuries ago and that were not until much later identified as distinct and novel concepts have not yet arrived at any recognizable closure. The end of the story, if there is one, is thus not in sight, and the question of an ultimate judgment on the nature and value of this vast historical movement is unanswerable.

For coverage of related topics in the *Macropædia* and *Micropædia,* see the *Propædia,* sections 521, 524, and 712.

The article is divided into the following sections:

Becoming modern

THE REVOLUTION OF MODERNITY

If one imagines all of human social evolution charted on a 12-hour clock, then the modern industrial epoch represents the last five minutes, no more. For more than half a million years, small bands of what we may agree were human beings roamed the earth as hunters and gatherers. With simple stone tools and a social order based on kinship ties they successfully preserved the human species against predators and natural calamities. In observing contemporary Australian Aborigines, the San (Bushmen) of southern Africa, the Eskimo, the Negritos in Malaysia and the Philippines, and Pygmy groups in Africa, a glimpse may be had of the social life of the Paleolithic period (Old Stone Age)—the oldest and most enduring type of human society.

About 10,000 BC some of these hunters and gatherers took to cultivating the earth and domesticating animals. It is this process that is somewhat misleadingly called the Neolithic revolution, implying that new stone tools were at the root of this vast change. It is now generally accepted that the new technology was not the principal factor. Nevertheless what took place was undoubtedly a revolution. Mobile bands became settled village communities. The development of the plow raised the productivity of the land a thousandfold, and in response the human population of the planet increased dramatically. More significantly, herding and agriculture for the first time created a surplus of food. This allowed some members of the population to abandon subsistence activities and become artisans, merchants, priests, and bureaucrats. This division of labour took place in a newly concentrated physical environment. In the 4th millennium BC cities arose, and with them trade, markets, government, laws, and armies.

The agricultural revolution

The technology and social organization of the Neolithic revolution remained the basis of all civilization until the coming of industrialism. With remarkably few additions—the invention of the stirrup was an important one—what served ancient Mesopotamia and ancient Egypt of the third and second millennia BC served as the foundation of all the states and empires of the ancient world, from China and India to Greece and Rome. And it served equally the European Middle Ages, which in some respects, notably in technology, actually fell back from the achievements of the ancient world. Not until the 17th and 18th centuries in Europe did humankind make another leap comparable to that of the Neolithic revolution.

It is against this very slowly evolutionary background that the revolution that underlay modernity must be seen. It is one of just two quantum jumps that human social evolution has made since the primal hunting and gathering stage of early *Homo sapiens*. The Neolithic or agricultural revolution produced, paradoxically, urban civilization; the Industrial Revolution lifted humankind onto a new plane of technological development that vastly increased the scope for transforming the material environment. In its speed and scale the change brought about by the Industrial Revolution has had, indeed, a greater impact on human life than the Neolithic revolution. Neolithic civilization remained throughout confined by a sharply limited technical and economic base; industrial civilization knows no such limits. Nevertheless, an understanding of agrarian society is essential to the analysis of industrial society, for it is largely through the contrast with its agrarian past that modern society stands out. The meaning of the modern is to be found as much in what it renounces as in what it aspires to.

THE WEST AND THE WORLD

It is not fully understood what produced the leap into modernity and why, just as some groups of hunters and gatherers gave rise to agrarian society, some agrarian societies gave rise to industrial society. What is clear is that it took place between the 16th and 18th centuries and that it began in the countries of northwestern Europe—especially England, the Netherlands, northern France, and northern Germany.

This could not have been expected. Compared to the Mediterranean, not to mention Arabic and Chinese civilizations, northwestern Europe early in the 16th century was backward, technically and culturally. In the 16th and 17th centuries it was still absorbing the commercial and artistic innovations of the Italian city-states of the Renaissance and making piratical raids, where it could, on the wealthy Spanish empire. It seemed an unlikely candidate for future economic leadership of Europe. Yet it was there that the changes took place that propelled those particular societies into the forefront of world development.

One reason advanced for this is that northwestern Europe was the origin and heartland of the Protestant Reformation of the 16th century. In his great work *The Protestant Ethic and the Spirit of Capitalism* (1904), the German sociologist Max Weber suggested that Roman Catholicism and to an even greater extent such Eastern religions as Hinduism and Buddhism were essentially otherworldly religions. They placed doctrinal emphasis on religious contemplation and the life hereafter. Protestantism, on the other hand, was predominantly a "this-worldly" religion. It broke down the distinction between the church and the world, between the monastery and the marketplace. Every man was a priest; everything he did, at work or at play, he did in the sight of God. Weber sought to show that Protestantism, and especially its Puritan variety, developed a particular type of character that valued frugality and hard work. Protestantism particularly promoted a work ethic. For the Protestant, all work, all occupations, were in a sense a religious vocation. Work was to be pursued with a fitting seriousness and order, in a spirit of rational enterprise that eschewed waste and frivolous adventurism. Such an attitude was admirably suited—though not intentionally—to the development of industrial capitalism. The Protestant nations, therefore, according to Weber, invented modern capitalism and so launched the world on a course that it still follows. Some later historians have disputed Weber's thesis and have adduced evidence that the early development of capitalism and of industrial organization preceded the rise of Protestantism. In either case, their mutual accommodation remains striking.

Weber's thesis

In a similarly persuasive way, the rationality of the Protestant work ethic has seemed linked to the development of modern science. This, too, took place largely in northwestern Europe in the course of the 17th century. In no other place, at no other time, was there anything like the scientific revolution of these years in England, France, and the Netherlands. It is true that the Industrial Revolution, in its early phases at least, did not depend on the theoretical science of Isaac Newton, Robert Boyle, or others of the period. What was crucial was the rationalist culture and the scientific habits of mind that this culture nurtured. Moreover, the scientific method of observation, hypothesis, experimentation, and verification could be applied not only to nature but also to society. Eventually, toward the end of the 18th century, what would later be called social science—economics and sociology especially—began to find a place alongside natural science. The scientific outlook—skeptical, autonomous, applying fixed standards of observation to continually changing phenomena, to reach conclusions that were never to be considered more than provisional—became the hallmark of modern society.

The scientific temper

Already, by the 17th century, western Europe had embarked on the course of transoceanic expansion that was to become one of its most notable features in the succeeding centuries. The colonization of America, although uneven, added a vast new domain to the West. In wealth, resources, and physical power, the West took a commanding lead over the rest of the world. From the enormous potentialities of science and industry, it acquired a momentum and a dynamism that pointed to a future immeasurably grander than anything previously achieved. For the first time, moralists and philosophers began to conceive of the possibility that the modern world might come to be the equal and even the superior of the ancient world of Greece and Rome. The idea of progress, and with it that of modernism, was born. The world was growing in power and enlightenment and, so far as anyone could see, would continue indefinitely to do so. Western society was not merely plunging ahead on its own; it was paving the way for the rest of the world. As Karl Marx said, albeit two centuries later, "The country that is more developed industrially only shows, to the less developed, the image of its own future."

THE DUAL REVOLUTION

Modern society owes its origin to two great upheavals in the 18th century, one political, the other economic. Both were part of a broader pattern of change that, since the Renaissance and Reformation, had set the West on a different path of development from that of the rest of the world. This pattern included the individualism and, in the end, the secularism, that was the Protestant legacy. It also included the rise of science, as a method and as a practice. Both of these culminated in explosive events toward the end of the 18th century. The first helped provoke political revolutions in America and France. The second, in creating an atmosphere conducive to technological innovation, was one of the chief elements in the emergence of the Industrial Revolution in Great Britain.

The American and French revolutions established the political character of modern society as constitutional and democratic, meaning not necessarily that every government thenceforward was of such character but that even those most conspicuously not so frequently claimed to be. From the time of those revolutions it became clear to practically all thinkers that no political system could now claim legitimacy that was not in some sense based on "the will of the people," constitutionally expressed. It was this message that was so brilliantly spelled out by the clear-sighted French aristocrat Alexis de Tocqueville in his works, *The Ancien Régime and the Revolution* (1856) and *Democracy in America* (1835–40).

Political origins of modern society

That the new democratic legitimation could be, and would be, claimed by popular or constitutional dictatorships such as those of Napoleon III in France or Adolf Hitler in Germany only showed how central the double ideal of democracy and constitutional justification had become. But they were not infinitely malleable. The idea of tacit or implicit popular consent, resorted to by several old-fashioned monarchies and empires, fell before the march of modern democratic theory as developed from the American and French revolutions. In the United Kingdom this was done through a gradual extension of the franchise in the 19th century. In Russia and in eastern and central Europe, violent revolution, defeat in war, and centrifugal nationalist tendencies turned out to be the means by which autocratic intransigence was overcome.

The democratic constitutional state

But however accomplished—whether grudgingly conceded, seized in popular revolution, or imposed by modernizing elites—the democratic constitutional state has come to be accepted as in principle the only fully legitimate polity of modern society. States that deviate from the norm, as, for instance, the communist states of eastern Europe or the military dictatorships of Africa and Latin America, feel compelled to offer elaborate justifications of their conduct. These are sometimes outright denials that the regime in question is the antithesis of a constitutional democracy; generally, however, they take the form of pleading special or emergency conditions. Full democracy, at some time in the future, remains the professed goal. The doggedness with which most of this casuistry is advanced, often in the teeth of observable evidence to the contrary, is the clearest testimony to the normative strength of the democratic ideal in modern society.

Self-determination

The American Revolution added a further ingredient to the political form of modern society. It asserted the principle of self-determination. Only those states were legitimate in which a people of common culture ruled for themselves a common territory. Foreign rule, or rule by an alien elite, as in the Ottoman and Habsburg empires, was unnatural. Only nation-states were natural political entities; only they were legitimate. "National self-determination" became one of the most powerful catchphrases of the liberal and radical ideologies that largely shaped the modern states of the 19th and 20th centuries.

That self-determination could be a highly ambiguous demand, as with democracy, was shown especially in the experience of central and eastern Europe, where the question of whose presumed nationality should be the basis of the state divided ethnic groups bitterly and murderously. Who, in the extremely mixed domains of what was Austria-Hungary before 1918, was to constitute an autonomous national group—Magyars, Slovaks, Croats, Serbs, Romanians? Only force would resolve the issue, so that modern Romania ended up with substantial Magyar and Saxon minorities inside its national boundaries while Yugoslavia contained a number of ethnic groups not much less various than those of the Austro-Hungarian monarchy which in part it was created to replace. But, once again, it was not the practical difficulties that mattered. As with democracy, it was the pure ideal of nationalism that became the irresistible force. And, once invented by the West, it could not be contained there. Along with democracy, it was one of the ideals absorbed by the colonies of the Western powers, and it became a powerful factor in the dissolution of Europe's overseas empires.

Industrial revolution in Britain

If the American and French revolutions laid down the political pattern of the modern world, the Industrial Revolution in Great Britain laid down the economic pattern. The changes that took place in Britain during the 19th century became almost a prototype of industrialization. To choose to industrialize—and not so to choose meant risking backwardness and dependence—was to imitate consciously the British Industrial Revolution. Great Britain was the pioneer industrial nation of the world; there simply was no other model to fix on. Even later, when it was clear that the British method of industrialization might not be exclusively valid or universally applicable, the general form of society that emerged in the course of the Industrial Revolution was widely regarded as typical.

Certain episodes and tendencies in the British case were pointed to as characterizing industrial development as such. These included the movement from the land to the cities, the massing of workers in the new industrial towns and factories, and the rise of new distinctions between family life and work life, and between work and leisure as notions meaningful to large classes of persons. Such features, with various others, were compounded into a powerful image of industrialism as a whole and wholly new social system and way of life.

The British themselves, it should be noted, did not contribute much to the promulgation of this image of industrialism, at least insofar as it was turned into a systematic account of society. Certain powerful symbols and images of urban and industrial life were indeed picked up from such English novelists as Charles Dickens and Elizabeth Gaskell. But it was left to others, from societies only just beginning to industrialize, to blend these artistic impressions (many of them not at all celebratory) into a systematic analysis of the new society. Foreigners such as Alexis de Tocqueville, Friedrich Engels, and Karl Marx observed and reflected on the changes they saw in England. They were convinced that what was happening in Britain would be repeated, more or less exactly, in other societies as they underwent industrialization. Industrial Britain could be seen, therefore, as a social laboratory of inestimable value to those other societies. In works such as Engels' *The Condition of the Working Class in England in 1844* (1845), and Marx's *Das Kapital* (1867–1894), British experience was examined for the light it shed on the general process of industrialization and for what it suggested of future developments, there and elsewhere. Through such works, the British Industrial Revolution became the property not just of the British nation but of the whole world. All societies, it was felt, would have their "Coketowns," the generic industrial town of Dickens' *Hard Times* (1854); all would have industrializing ideologies and institutions of the kind—referred to by Germans as *Manchestertum*—that 19th-century observers came to associate with the world's leading industrial city. Manchester was indeed the symbol of the new industrial society, and hence the image of the world's future. "The age of ruins is past," declared the British politician and novelist Benjamin Disraeli in his novel *Coningsby* (1844). "Have you seen Manchester?"

Industrialization as symbol

One consequence of this tendency to generalize the British experience was that the idea of industrialism itself grew in scope and significance. It came to symbolize and to embody not just the economic and technological changes that lay at its heart, but other political, social, and cultural changes that appeared to be organically connected with it, whether as causes, concomitants, or consequences. Thus, the democratic movement triggered by the American and French revolutions was seen as the necessary political transformation that, sooner or later, must accompany all movement toward an industrial society. Similarly, changes in urban life, in family form, in individual and social values, and in intellectual outlook, were all seen as linked to industrialism. Industrial society came to stand as the epitome of modern society. And through the lens provided by industrialism, earlier developments, such as Protestant individualism and the scientific revolution, came to be seen as preconditions or presentiments of industrialism, elements incorporated into a systematic and more comprehensive movement that had its own compelling logic and momentum. Industrialism, it came to be agreed, was a package and had to be purchased as such.

The nature of modern society

GENERAL FEATURES

Modernity must be understood, in part at least, against the background of what went before. Industrial society emerged only patchily and unevenly out of agrarian society, a system that had endured 5,000 years. Industrial structures thus took much of their characteristic form and colour from the rejection, conscious or unconscious, of preindustrial ways. Industrialism certainly contained much that was new, but it remained always at least partly an idea that in both its theory and its practice was to be understood as much by what it denied as by what it affirmed. The force of the modern has always been partly a reactive force, a force that derived meaning and momentum by a comparison or contrast with, and by rejection or negation of, what went before.

Considered at the most general level, this point suggests a view of modernization as a process of individualization, differentiation or specialization, and abstraction. Put more concretely: first, the structures of modern society take as their basic unit the individual rather than, as with agrarian or peasant society, the group or community. Second, modern institutions are assigned the performance of specific, specialized tasks in a social system with a highly developed and complex division of labour; in this they stand in the sharpest possible contrast with, for instance, the family in peasant society, which is at once the unit of production, consumption, socialization, and authoritative decision-making. Third, rather than attaching rights and prerogatives to particular groups and persons, or being guided by custom or tradition, modern institutions tend to be governed and guided by general rules and regulations that derive their legitimacy from the methods and findings of science. In principle at least, they are not the agents of particular individuals, such as a king or priest, endowed with divine or prescriptive authority, but act according to the rational and impersonal precepts formulated by "experts."

Contrasts with traditional society

These contrasts by no means complete the characterization of modern society, nor are they the only ones that might be drawn. Nevertheless, they do illustrate the dependence of the concept of modernity on past structures that form the basis of comparison and exclusion. Indeed, it is such a set of contrasts, not necessarily carefully distinguished, that most people have in mind when they speak of modern as opposed to traditional society.

With regard to the more positive features of industrialism, industrial society can best be thought of as consisting of an economic core around which other, noneconomic structures crystallize. In Marxist terminology, this is rendered in the more deterministic form of an economic base conditioning a noneconomic "superstructure." This seems unnecessarily rigid and misleading. The relation of the economic to the noneconomic realm is mutual and interactive, as can be seen by considering the impact of scientific ideas on economic and technological development. Still, it is true to say that, fundamentally, it is the economic changes that most dramatically affect industrial society.

ECONOMIC CHANGE

Economic historians and theorists have been inclined to stress economic growth as the central defining feature of an industrial as opposed to a nonindustrial economy. Thus, the British historian Edward Anthony Wrigley (b. 1931) declared that "industrialization is said to occur in a given country when real incomes per head begin to rise steadily and without apparent limit." The American economic historian W.W. Rostow (b. 1916) popularized a similar conception in suggesting that with industrialization, the economy at a certain point "takes off" into "self-sustained growth"; all the relevant statistical indexes of the economy—investment, output, growth rate, and so on—take sudden, sharp, almost vertical upward turns.

Underlying this phenomenon of growth are certain core components of the industrial system. These include technological change, whereby work is increasingly done by machines rather than by hand; the supplementing or replacement of human and animal power by inanimate sources of energy, such as coal and oil; the freeing of the labourer from feudal and customary ties and obligations, and the consequent creation of a free market in labour; the concentration of workers in single, comprehensive enterprises (the factory system); and a pivotal role for a specific social type, the entrepreneur.

Core components of the industrial system

It would be easy to vary and extend this list. Not all components are of equal importance, nor are all equally indispensable to the industrial economy. They are drawn largely from the experience of the first industrializing nations, in western Europe and North America. Later industrializers were able to dispense with some of them, or at least to try to do so. The Soviet Union, for instance, industrialized on the basis largely of forced rather than free labour and made a point of doing away with entrepreneurs, while in Japan the entrepreneur was throughout stimulated and sustained by strong state involvement in industrialization. Moreover, it should be remembered that states—as, for instance, Denmark and New Zealand—can industrialize largely through the commercialization and mechanization of agriculture. Agriculture simply becomes another industry; farms are simply rural factories.

Even in this latter case, there is no place for a distinctively rural way of life in industrial society. Mechanization brings an increase in productivity that renders a large portion of the rural labour force superfluous. Even where agriculture remains an important part of the industrial economy, the proportion of the labour force employed in agriculture drops steadily with industrialization. This is the "sectoral transformation" that is one of industrialization's clearest and most obvious effects. A majority of the work force comes to be employed in the production of manufactured goods and in services rather than in the primary sector of agriculture. In both the United Kingdom and the United States, for instance, by the mid-1970s more than 95 percent of the employed population were in manufacturing and services and less than 5 percent in agriculture. Japan, as an example of a late developer, shows the same pattern: in 1970, more than 80 percent of the employed population were in manufacturing and services, and less than 20 percent in agriculture. These figures should be compared with the normal condition of preindustrial agrarian societies, where typically 90 percent of the adult population are peasant farmers or farm workers.

Agricultural productivity and labour

The vast increase in agricultural productivity which this sectoral change in employment signals is characteristic of industrialism. Industrial society breaks through the historic limits of scarcity. In the past, the potential for economic growth was always cut short by Malthusian checks on population, by limitations of food supply, or by the shortage of easily available raw materials such as wood. Industrialization permits the creation of large food surpluses that can feed a largely urban population. The entire world, both on land and in the sea, is scoured for raw materials and further energy sources to supply industry. Science has so far proved remarkably effective at finding substitutes for those sources that have dried up and those materials that have become dangerously scarce. The British economist John Maynard Keynes suggested that, for the first time in human history, "the economic problem may be solved," and that "the economic problem is not the permanent problem of the human race." In the mid-1980s it still seemed reasonable to believe that industrialism promised growth for the foreseeable future, even that it might bring abundance to all.

POPULATION CHANGE

There have been two major population explosions in the course of human social evolution. By the end of the Paleolithic period the world's human population is estimated to have been between five and six million (an average of 0.1 person per square mile [0.04 person per square kilometre] of the Earth's land area). Following the Neolithic or agricultural revolution, the population made its first major leap, reaching over the short span of 8,000 years around 150 million by the year 1000 BC (2.6 persons per square mile). For the next two and a half thousand years there was relatively little change. World population had reached about 500 million by the middle of the 17th century. During this time any tendency for population to grow was punished by the Malthusian checks of starvation and pestilence. Only with the Industrial Revolution of the 18th century did population break out again from its Malthusian fetters.

From about 1700 there was a second and far more rapid population explosion. Since the late 1600s the world's population has increased more than eightfold, reaching 4.8 billion by the mid-1980s. On current projections it is expected to reach more than six billion by the year 2000 (which will mean an average of 42 persons per square kilometre of the Earth's land area). This gives some measure of the difference between the two population revolutions of human history: there has been a dramatic acceleration not simply in population but in the rate of increase of population since industrialization took hold. Between 1650 and 1850 the average annual rate of increase of the world's population doubled; it doubled again by the

Industrial revolution and population

1920s, and more than doubled, once more, by the 1970s.

If the time taken to double the world's population over the past 350 years is taken as a measure, then the doubling time is seen to have been shrinking fast. It took 200 years, to 1825, to double the world's population from 500 million to one billion. It took only 100 years to achieve the next doubling, bringing the total to two billion by 1930; and only 45 years to achieve yet another doubling, to four billion by 1975. There were signs of slowing in the last part of the 20th century, and clearly this accelerating pace could not last indefinitely. Even so, many experts predicted eight billion by early in the 21st century, a reduction in the doubling time to about 40 years.

It was in western Europe, with the Industrial Revolution, that the second population revolution began. Europe's population doubled during the 18th century, from roughly 100 million to almost 200 million, and doubled again during the 19th century, to about 400 million. It was in Europe, too, that the pattern first emerged that has come to be known as the "demographic transition" (see POPULATION). The populations of nonindustrial countries are normally stable (and low) because high birth rates are matched by high death rates. With industrialization, improvements in medical knowledge and public health, together with a more regular food supply, bring about a drastic reduction in the death rate but no corresponding decline in the birth rate. The result is a population explosion, as experienced in 19th-century Europe. In time, however, as European societies showed in the early 20th century, the urbanized populations of industrial societies voluntarily lower their birth rates and population growth flattens out. A new population plateau is reached. Japan, industrializing some 50 years later than the West, provided an almost textbook demonstration of the pattern of the demographic transition. Its population grew rapidly after 1870, during its industrializing phase, and leveled off equally rapidly after World War II. In an even more speeded-up form, the Soviet Union in its century of industrialization that began in the 1880s illustrated the link between industrialization and population.

Demographic transition

Does the demographic transition hold good for the developing societies known as the Third World? Nearly all of these countries experienced rapid population growth after World War II, at rates greater than had ever occurred anywhere in the West. Western aid and medical science spectacularly reduced the high death rates, often by more than 50 percent. But, unlike those in the West, the high birth rates showed little tendency to fall. Determined efforts in a few countries, such as Singapore, Sri Lanka, and China, were beginning to yield some results by the 1980s. But on the whole the attempts by national governments and international agencies to persuade non-Westerners to have smaller families had failed. One result was the persistence of predominantly youthful populations in societies that could least afford the burden of feeding and educating their nonproductive young. People under 15 made up more than 40 percent of the populations of the Third World, as compared with between 20 and 30 percent in the industrialized world.

Third World demographics

It was argued that the birth rate remained stubbornly high in these societies partly because industrialization was so slow and fragmentary in the Third World. In addition, where any significant development had taken place, as in Brazil or Malaysia, it had only really affected a small elite; the mass of the people were untouched. Thus, the reasons people in the industrialized West chose to have fewer children lacked cogency in underdeveloped countries. It remained rational for the bulk of the population to continue to have large families both to share in manual labour and to provide security for parents in their old age. Lower fertility would come, it was argued, when wealth was more evenly distributed and social security systems well established.

URBANISM AS A WAY OF LIFE

Industrialism does not simply increase numbers; it distributes them in particular ways, concentrating mass populations in cities. Modern life is unquestionably urban life.

It may be argued that it was in the cities of ancient Mesopotamia, Egypt, Greece, and Rome that a distinctively urban existence was first brought to that pitch of refinement that signifies an advanced civilization. Certainly for those fortunates who were free citizens the Athens of Pericles provided an agreeable existence. The Italian cities of the Renaissance, too, provided a distinctly urban culture.

Industrial urbanism differs from preindustrial urbanism in two ways. The first is in its quantitative reach and intensity; the second is in the new qualitative relationship it sets up between the city and society.

For all the culture and sophistication of the preindustrial city, it remained a minority experience. Full participation in urban life was available to no more than the 3 or 4 percent of the population who were city dwellers in 3rd-millennium-BC Egypt and Mesopotamia and to the 10 to 15 percent of Romans who lived in cities at the zenith of imperial Rome (but who were heavily dependent on food supplies from North Africa). These latter represent a high point of preindustrial urbanism.

Industrialization brings a growth in trade and manufactures. To serve these activities it requires centralized sites of production, distribution, exchange, and credit. It demands a regular system of communications and transport. It multiplies the demand that political authorities establish a dependable coinage, a standard system of weights and measures, a reasonable degree of protection and safety on the roads, and regular enforcement of the laws. All these developments conduce to a vast increase in urbanization. Whereas in typical agrarian societies 90 percent or more of the population are rural, in industrial societies it is not uncommon for 90 percent or more to be urban.

Demands of industrialization

The growth of cities with industrialization can be illustrated by the example of the United Kingdom. In 1801 about a fifth of its population lived in towns and cities of 10,000 or more inhabitants. By 1851 two fifths were so urbanized; and if smaller towns of 5,000 or more are included, as they were in the census of that year, more than half the population could be counted as urbanized. The world's first industrial society had become its first truly urban society as well. By 1901, the year of Queen Victoria's death, the census recorded three-quarters of the population as urban (two-thirds in cities of 10,000 or more and half in cities of 20,000 or more). In the span of a century a largely rural society had become a largely urban one.

The pattern was repeated on a European and then a world scale as industrialization proceeded. At the beginning of the 19th century, continental Europe (excluding Russia) was less than 10 percent urbanized, with respect to cities of 10,000 or more; by the end of the century it was about 30 percent urbanized (10 percent in cities with 100,000 or more), and by the mid-1980s, the urban population was more than 70 percent. In the United States in 1800, only 6 percent of the population lived in towns of 2,500 or more; in 1920 the census reported that for the first time more than half of the American people lived in cities. By the mid-1980s this had risen to nearly 75 percent—about the same as Japan's urban population—and more than two-fifths of the population lived in metropolitan areas of one million or more. Taking the world as a whole, in 1800 no more than 2.5 percent of the population lived in cities of 20,000 or more; by 1965 this had increased to 25 percent, and by 1980 to 40 percent. It is estimated that by the year 2000 about half the world's population will be urban, by this measure. At the same time there has been a great growth of very large cities, of a type virtually unknown in the preindustrial world. Cities of more than one million inhabitants numbered 16 in 1900, 67 in 1950, and 250 in 1985.

Western urbanization

As with population growth, it was in the underdeveloped nations that the fastest rates of urban growth were to be found. The rapidly expanding population of a countryside unable to support it sought the city for both escape and opportunity, though in many cases it was a perilous choice. Between 1900 and 1950, while the world's population as a whole grew by 50 percent, the urban population grew by 254 percent; but in Asia urban growth was 444 percent and in Africa 629 percent. By the mid-1980s, Africa and Asia were about 30 percent urbanized, and Latin America

Third World urbanization

nearly 70 percent so. Cities such as São Paulo (15 million), Mexico City (17 million), and Calcutta (10 million), had mushroomed to rival and even overtake in size the large cities of the developed West and Japan.

But while urbanization in the underdeveloped nations repeats some of the more distressing features of its Western counterpart—overcrowding, unsanitary conditions, and unemployment—the compensation and eventual remedy of economic growth has been largely lacking. With some partial exceptions, such as Brazil, Mexico, Singapore, and Hong Kong, the underdeveloped world has known urbanization without industrialization. The result has been the rapid growth of shantytowns on the edges of the big cities. It has been estimated that about four or five million families in Latin America live in shantytowns.

Urbanism cannot be understood simply by statistics of urban growth. It is a matter, too, of a distinctive culture and consciousness. Urbanism is a way of life, as classically analyzed by the German sociologist Georg Simmel and the American sociologist Louis Wirth. City life, with its tendency to nervous overstimulation, may lead to a bored and blasé attitude to life. It may encourage frivolous and fleeting cults and fashions. It can detach people from their traditional communal moorings, leaving them morally stranded and so inclined to harbour unreal expectations and feverish dreams. In the very number of social contacts it necessarily generates, it may compel individuals to erect barriers to protect their privacy. Individuals may be forced into an attitude of reserve and isolation. Hence, as Simmel noted, the superficial paradox that "one nowhere feels as lonely and lost as in the metropolitan crowd."

Urban culture

At the same time, cities promote diversity and creativity. They attract the best and the brightest. If anything is to be accomplished in modern society, it almost certainly will be in the city. Karl Marx spoke of "the idiocy of rural life." Only in cities, many sociologists have felt, are human beings able to realize to the full all their potentialities. Cities are the forcing house of change and growth. "Great cities," declared the French sociologist Émile Durkheim, "are the uncontested homes of progress; it is in them that ideas, fashions, customs, new needs are elaborated and then spread over the rest of the country. . . . Minds naturally are there oriented to the future."

But whether they deplored or praised urban life, most commentators have agreed that, with industrialism, the city moved into a pivotal new relation with society as a whole. Preindustrial cities were islands in an agrarian sea. They hailed each other across vast alien tracts of nonurban life, which remained largely indifferent to and unaffected by their practices. Essentially they were parasitic on the countryside and on the peasant masses whose agricultural labour sustained them. Their disappearance not only would not have mattered to the peasants but would in most cases have been welcomed.

With industrial urbanism, this relationship was reversed. The countryside now became dependent on the city. It became an integral but peripheral part of a single economic system that was centred on the cities. Largely emptied of people, the countryside was now in effect simply another theatre of industrial operations for city merchants and bankers. Political and economic power resided in the city; industrial and financial corporations became the dominant landowners, replacing individual proprietors. Except in pockets largely maintained as quaint retreats for tourists, rustic life virtually disappeared; certainly it no longer significantly affected the values and practices of the larger society. What remained of "country life" was often little more than a persuasive and nostalgic motif in the hands of advertising copywriters, preying on the fantasies of city dwellers.

The city became both the symbol and the reality of industrial society as a whole. No longer, as in the past, standing in a merely mechanical relation to other parts of society, the city took its place at the centre of an increasingly organic whole. Industrialism created a centralized web of social relationships, and the city was the node. It dictated the style and set the standard for the whole society, imposing on all its own economic, political, and cultural framework.

WORK AND THE FAMILY

In preindustrial or nonindustrial society the family is the basic unit of production. All its members engage in a cooperative set of subsistence activities. In a typical example from early 18th-century England, the man might be a weaver and his wife a spinner, with the younger children acting as assistants in the joint domestic enterprise. Mixed in with this wage or piece labour would probably be the cultivation of a small plot of land, together with access to common land to forage for fuel and to hunt small game. The family need not necessarily be very large—in northwestern Europe and North America it seems to have been relatively small—but on the whole additional members are an economic asset as the value of extra hands to work outweighs the cost of extra mouths to feed. The family is a collective enterprise; all its members regard themselves as part of that collectivity and their contributions as adding to a common store; servants or other nonfamily members, such as apprentices, are "adopted" or treated as family members, for no other binding personal relationships but family ones are recognized. The family and its members are society in miniature.

The family as the unit of production

Industrialization radically disrupts this more or less autonomous family economy. It takes away the economic function of the family, and reduces it to a unit of consumption and socialization. Production moves away from the household to the factory. The commons are enclosed, and the land commercially exploited for national and international markets. Some individuals become the owners and the managers of the new system. But the bulk of family members must become either landless agricultural labourers or, increasingly, workers in the factories of the new industrial towns. In either case, the family becomes immediately dependent for its livelihood on structures and processes external to itself. It lives by the jobs and wages of its members, and these are affected by forces which it barely comprehends, still less controls.

In the early stages of industrialization, the family will likely struggle to maintain its traditional collective unity. Its members, whether employed as farm workers in the country, industrial workers in the towns, or domestic servants in well-to-do urban homes, continue to pool their resources. They make regular visits home and continue to think of themselves as a collectivity. Their wages still contribute to a common family fund, which is used to support the nonworking young as well as temporarily unemployed members and to provide for members in sickness and old age. In the absence of a comprehensive system of social security, the family itself continues to fulfill the role. In these circumstances, as in the past, a large family can be as much an asset as a burden. For a considerable time, therefore, large families, especially among the working classes, continue to be the norm in industrializing society.

Eventually the forces of individualization, whose gross effects on the industrial economy and the society at large are so striking, also affect the family. Its members, male and female, increasingly come to think of their wages as their own, to be disposed of as they individually see fit. This attitude is encouraged by the increasing availability of attractive consumer goods. At some point it becomes economically and politically necessary for the state to step in to provide for those members unable to earn their own living, either because they are chronically unemployed, or because they are too young, too sick, or too old. The family role thus shrinks further to little more than childrearing, and even here it has to compete with the school, peer groups, and child-care agencies. For its older members, the family becomes merely the domicile and the locus of recreation and a certain amount of sociability. Its members may spend a good deal of time at home, but their minds are formed more by influences operating outside it. Their lives are led largely outside the family, in their work and in association with nonfamily friends and colleagues. They no longer find their identity within a collective family identity. Hence the tendency of young adults to marry young, to break away from their families of origin, and to set up their own independent families.

Fragmentation of the family

Shorn of so many traditional functions, the family becomes almost exclusively the sphere of private life. It attends to the needs of children and the emotional and sexual satisfaction of the spouses. A small unit is best suited to these tasks. The extended families of the preindustrial and early industrial periods, which sometimes included grandparents and married offspring to three or more generations, give way to the small, two-generation nuclear family of parents and dependent children only. Whether or not the nuclear family precedes industrialization—as, for instance, it seems to have done in England—in industrial society it certainly becomes the norm.

With the shrinking and privatization of the family, the importance of work grows correspondingly. It becomes the principal source of individual identity. In preindustrial society, the question of who one is is likely to be answered in terms of place of origin or family membership: I am John of Winchester, or John, Robert's son. In industrial society the question is typically answered in terms of one's occupation in the formal economy. The occupational role, as miner or machinist, clerk or cleaner, becomes the determining and defining role. It is the source of one's identity, status, and income. Work, throwing off its religious justifications, itself becomes a religion. Not to work, to be unemployed, is to be stigmatized as much in one's own eyes as in the eyes of society.

Work as identity

Work is redefined as applying almost exclusively to formal employment in the industrial economy. All other kinds of work—unpaid domestic work, voluntary work, work done for friends or family, child-rearing—are devalued and treated as marginal or "unproductive." The paradox is that the elevation of employed work is accompanied by a decisive fragmentation of work as an activity. Industrialization brings about a massive increase in the division of labour. But this involves not just, as in preindustrial urban life, a specialization of crafts and the rise of new occupations. More significant is a new kind of division of labour, what Adam Smith and Karl Marx called the "detailed" division of labour, in the work task itself. The set of tasks involved in the making of a whole product, which was previously performed by a single artisan or worker, is now broken apart and allocated to a number of different individuals. In his famous example of a pin manufactory, Adam Smith showed how, by dividing the task of pin-making into some 18 distinct operations, each performed by "distinct hands," productivity could be increased more than a thousandfold. It was this form of the division of labour that became the source of the fantastic productivity of the industrial system, especially once Henry Ford had organized it around the continuously moving assembly line and the American pioneer in scientific management Frederick W. Taylor had supplied an engineering method for the splitting of any task into its simplest operations.

Division of labour

The English social critic John Ruskin pointed to one consequence of this new division of labour when he said that "it is not, truly speaking, the labour that is divided, but the men." The problem of motivating the work force, of providing sufficient inducement to work discipline and performance when the tasks themselves were so intrinsically uninteresting, haunted all industrial societies. But the new division of labour itself pointed, rather ominously, to the likely resolution of this problem. Once tasks had been so minutely subdivided that the least skilled worker could do them, the next step was to mechanize the tasks and dispense with the human worker altogether. Full automation was in some sense implicit in the principle of the division of labour from the very start. It is ironic that a social process that had in its early stages put work at its very centre should also, in its further evolution, threaten to take it away altogether from its citizens.

SOCIAL STRUCTURE

Given the importance of economic institutions in general, and of employment in particular, it is not surprising to find that industrial society tends to produce a new principle in the ordering and ranking of individuals. Economic position and relationships become the key to social position and class membership. This is new, at least in its extent. While wealth or the lack of it were always important in determining social position, they were not usually the sole or even the central determinant. In all nonindustrial societies, attributes of tribal membership, race, religion, age, and gender are of equal and often greater importance in assigning individuals to a position in the social hierarchy. In the traditional Indian caste system, for instance, the religious eminence of even the poorest Brahman marks him out as a member of the highest and most esteemed caste.

Industrial society tends to subordinate all these preindustrial principles of ranking to the economic one. One's position in the system of production or, more generally, in the marketplace assigns one to a particular class or group. Ownership of property, level of education, and type and degree of training all affect one's market position. Karl Marx was convinced that in the course of its development capitalism—the only form of industrialism he considered—would eventually throw up only two main economic classes, the propertyless workers, or proletariat, and the capitalist owners, or bourgeoisie.

Primacy of economic status

One reason why Marx's prediction has not come to pass in any developed society is that, though perhaps dominant in the long run, economic relationships have not so sweepingly eliminated other noneconomic considerations. Older sources of identity have continued to exert considerable power. Groups based on ethnic, religious, and regional ties have overlapped with and occasionally submerged those based solely on the tie of economic interest. Thus, the working class of Northern Ireland has preferred to stress its Protestant identification over its proletarian one. Workers and capitalists in the Basque and Catalan regions of Spain have united in a long, drawn-out opposition to the central government in Madrid. In the United States, racial identity has continued to override any other based on income or occupation.

This is one way in which it is brought home that even radical changes do not necessarily disrupt all continuities. There are gainers and losers in the process of change, and the losers are apt to hark back to past ways and values. Industrialization, while making a fundamental break with earlier forms of society, does not abolish all the elements of traditional society.

SECULARIZATION AND RATIONALIZATION

At the most abstract level of analysis, modernization leads to what Max Weber called "the disenchantment of the world." It eliminates all the superhuman and supernatural forces, the gods and spirits, with which nonindustrial cultures populate the universe and to which they attribute responsibility for the phenomena of the natural and social worlds. In their place it substitutes as the sole cosmology the modern scientific interpretation of nature. Only the laws and regularities discovered by the scientific method are admitted as valid explanations of phenomena. If it rains, or does not rain, it is not because the gods are angry but because of atmospheric conditions, as measured by the barometer and photographed by satellites.

Specifically, modernization involves a process of secularization; that is, it systematically displaces religious institutions, beliefs, and practices, substituting for them those of reason and science. This process was first observable in Christian Europe toward the end of the 17th century. (It is possible that there is something inherently secularizing about Christianity, for no other religion seems to give rise spontaneously to secular beliefs.) At any rate, once invented in Europe, especially Protestant Europe, secularization was carried as part of the "package" of industrialism that was exported to the non-European world. Wherever modern European cultures have impinged, they have diffused secularizing currents into traditional religions and nonrational ideologies.

Although secularization is a general tendency or principle of development in modern societies, this does not imply that religion is driven out altogether from society. Against a deep background of tradition, it inevitably leaves many religious practices in place and may even stimulate new ones. Religious rituals, such as Christian baptism and church weddings, persist in all industrial societies; the church may, as in England and Italy, continue to play an important moral and social role. The majority of the population may hold, however insecurely, traditional religious beliefs alongside more scientific ones. There may even

Persistence of religious practice

be, as in the United States, waves of religious revivalism, involving large sections of the population.

It is nonetheless true that all such religious phenomena, real as they may be in the lives of believers, lose their centrality in the life of the society as a whole. As compared with their place in traditional society, they increasingly take on the character of marginal, even leisure-time, activities. They no longer embody that crucial legitimating power that religious activities have in all nonindustrial societies. The religious establishment is aware that to confront the modern state too openly is to risk disestablishment, as in France, or even, as in communist societies, dissolution. Baptisms and church weddings persist as much for social reasons as from belief in their religious significance.

Secularization is but one manifestation of a larger cultural process that affects all modern societies: the process of rationalization. While this process is epitomized by the rise of the scientific worldview, it encompasses many more areas than are usually associated with science. It applies, for instance, to the capitalist economy, with its rational organization of labour and its rational calculation of profit and loss. It applies also to artistic developments, such as the rational application of the geometry of perspective in painting and the development of a rational system of notation and rational harmonic principles in music. For Max Weber, the most careful student of the process, it referred above all to the establishment of a rational system of laws and administration in modern society. It was in the system of bureaucracy, seen as the impersonal and impartial rule of rationally constituted laws and formal procedures, that Weber saw the highest development of the rational principle. Bureaucracy meant a principled hostility to all traditional and "irrational" considerations of person or place, kinship or culture. It expressed the triumph of the scientific method and scientific expertise in social life. The trained official, said Weber, is "the pillar both of the modern state and of the economic life of the West."

The role of bureaucracy

Weber was aware that bureaucracy has two faces. It can also be despotic and irrational in actual operation. The triumph of the principle does not guarantee its strict performance in practice. Rationalization is a process that operates at the highest, most general level of social development. It would be surprising if its effects were to be found in every nook and cranny of modern society. Everywhere one should expect to find the persistence of nonrational and even antirational attitudes and behaviour. Superstition is one example; the occasional rise of personal, charismatic leadership breaking through the rationalized routines of bureaucracy is another. These should not be thought of simply as vestiges of traditional society. They are also the expressions of essential needs, emotional and cultural, that are in danger of being stifled in a scientific and unillusioned environment.

Weber stressed another significant point. Rationalization does not connote that the populations of modern societies are, as individuals, any more reasonable or knowledgeable than those of nonindustrial societies. What it means is that there is, in principle, scientifically validated knowledge available to modern populations, by which they may, if they choose, enlighten themselves about their world and govern their behaviour. In practice, as Weber knew, such knowledge tends to be restricted to scientifically trained elites. The mass of the population of a modern society might in their daily lives be relatively more ignorant than the most primitive savage, for the savage usually has a comprehensive and working knowledge of the tools he uses and the food he consumes, whereas modern man may well use an elevator without the slightest idea of its working principle or eat food manufactured in ways and with materials of which he is totally unaware.

SOCIAL PROBLEMS

Two faces of modernity

As with bureaucracy, so with most other features: they show the two faces of modernity. One is dynamic, forward-looking, progressive, promising unprecedented abundance, freedom, and fulfillment. The other shows the dark side of modernity, the new problems that modernity brings in its wake by virtue of the very scale and novelty of its achievements. Social progress is matched by social pathology.

Thus, the historic achievement of becoming able to feed a large population brings with it crowding, pollution, and environmental destruction. Quiet, privacy, and space become scarce and increasingly treasured commodities. Massed together in cities, seeking rest and recreation, the populations of industrial societies force open the whole world to tourism. Soon every rural haven, every sunswept coast, is turned into an administered holiday camp, each a uniform replica of the rest. The industrial principle of mass production and distribution can readily be turned from the production of goods to that of services, including those of leisure and entertainment.

Urban-industrial life offers unprecedented opportunities for individual mobility and personal freedom. It also promises the attainment of dazzling prizes, in wealth and honours, for those with the enterprise and talent to reach for them. The other side of the coin is the loneliness of the city dweller and the desolation of failure for those many who cannot win any of the prizes. As Durkheim analyzed it, the individual is placed in the pathological condition of anomie. He experiences "the malady of infinite aspirations." The decline of religion and community removes the traditional restraints on appetite, allowing it to grow morbidly and without limit. At the same time the competitive modern order that stimulates these unreal expectations provides insufficient and unequal means for their realization. The result is an increase in suicide, crime, and mental disorder.

Anomie and alienation

Industrial work, too, exacts a high price for the enormous increase in productivity brought about by the intensified division of labour. Karl Marx offered the most systematic analysis of this price under the heading of "alienation." The industrial worker feels estranged from the activity of work because his task is so fragmented, undemanding, and meaningless. He does not realize himself, his human potential, in his work. Unlike traditional craft work, for instance, it does not call on his constructive and creative faculties. The industrial worker also feels alienated from the product of his work, for he has no control over its manufacture, nor over the terms and conditions of its disposal. As the dynamic sum of its parts, the industrial system of production is phenomenally powerful; but this power is achieved at the cost of reducing one class of those parts, the human workers, to mere "hands," mere semblances of humanity. Eventually, Marx hoped, the surplus wealth produced by the industrial system would free workers altogether from the necessity of work; but until that time the degraded condition of the worker would be the most eloquent testimony to the dehumanization wrought by the system.

Marx's optimism about the future was perhaps as excessive as his pessimism about his present. But he was by no means the only one who felt that industrial society demanded too high a price of many of its members. Repeatedly, industrialism was found to have created new and apparently ineradicable pockets of poverty. Despite steady economic growth, it was the persistent finding throughout the industrial world that between 15 and 20 percent of the population remained permanently below officially defined levels of poverty. It appeared that industrialism by its very mechanism of growth created a "new poor," who for whatever reason—deprived backgrounds, low enterprise, low intelligence—were unable to compete according to the rules of the industrial order. The communal and kinship supports of the past having withered away, there was no alternative for the failed and the rejected but to become claimants and pensioners of the state.

There were other victims, too. The small nuclear family offered, to a greater extent than ever before, the opportunity for intense privacy and emotional fulfillment. But the very intensity of these relationships seemed to put an intolerable burden on it. Added to that, the family survived as the only remaining primary group in society, the only social unit where relationships remained primarily personal and face-to-face. Elsewhere bureaucratic or commercial relationships prevailed. The nuclear family was called upon to do all the work of restoration and repair of its members on their return from the impersonal, large-scale, bureaucratic world of work and, increasingly, play.

Stress of the nuclear family

Under this unprecedented pressure it began to show all the classic symptoms of distress. Adolescent alienation and teenage rebellion became accepted features of modern family life. Divorce rates soared; and when people sought to remarry—"the triumph of hope over experience"—their second marriages proved even less stable than their first. There was a steady increase in the incidence of one-parent families, usually headed by a woman.

Modernization, finally, put a number of new political and cultural problems on the agenda. The decline of local communities, and the great growth in the scale of all social institutions and especially the acceleration of political centralization, put a strain on civic loyalties and the willingness of people to participate in political life. As mass political parties came to monopolize civic life, individual citizens retreated increasingly into private life. Political apathy and low turnouts at elections became matters of serious concern, calling into question the democratic claims of modern liberal societies. A similar concern centred on the spread of mass communications, which in the 20th century came to dominate the cultural life of modern societies. The uniformity and conformity bred by the press, radio, and television threatened, albeit passively rather than directly, the pluralism and diversity on which liberal society prided itself and which it regarded as its chief security against totalitarian challenge.

Together, political and cultural centralization and uniformity were interpreted as evidence of the creation of a "mass society." Tocqueville had warned that individuals lacking strong intermediate institutions with which to identify would become atomized, and in their anonymity and powerlessness might look to the protection of strong men and strong governments. Once more, this outcome had to be seen as a possibility, not an inevitability. Pluralism remained strong in many societies. But the rise and success of totalitarian movements in some industrial societies showed that the tendencies were real and suggested that they were present in some degree in all modern societies.

Modern society and world society

WESTERN AND NON-WESTERN ROUTES TO MODERNITY

The Western experience of industrialization, as has been noted, served as the model for world industrialization. To become modern was to become something like Western industrial society. Non-Western societies were not always given much choice in the matter. As formal colonies or informal clients of Western powers they often found themselves being "developed" in a Western direction before they were permitted to take political control of their own destinies. Once on the way, there was no turning back. But even where an element of choice existed, it remained the consensus that the only viable form of society in the modern world was industrial society. Only industrial societies could be active agents in the world system. All others must remain clients or dependents. Japan demonstrated this better than any other nation. From a poor nation humiliated at the hands of the West in the mid-19th century, Japan rose through industrialization to become one of the most powerful societies in the world. More pointedly, Japan showed that, by meeting the challenge of industrialization, a non-Western society could become not merely the equal but the superior of some of the strongest Western powers.

Japan confirmed what Western experience had already made clear: There are several routes to modernity. In the 19th century Britain, Belgium, France, and the United States industrialized largely on the basis of the individual entrepreneur and the free market economy. In Germany, and even more in Japan, the state and political elites played a major role, organizing credit, coordinating and planning development, and restricting foreign access to home markets in the interests of native industry. Later still came the even more centralized authoritarian model of modernization under the aegis of the one-party state. Taking their lead from the Soviet Union, following the Russian Revolution of 1917, many developing countries in Asia, Africa, and Latin America sought to industrialize according to economic plans drawn up by political elites and stringently imposed on their populations. Even where, as in India, formal liberal democracy was instituted, industrialization was largely guided by a single national party—usually the one identified with the struggle for independence from colonial rule, as was the Indian National Congress party. In any case, there were plenty of socialisms to choose from. There were the African socialisms of Kwame Nkrumah's Ghana and Julius Nyerere's Tanzania, the Chinese socialism of Mao Zedong, the Cuban socialism of Fidel Castro, or the Yugoslav socialism of Josip Broz Tito. All could aspire to be models of development to Third World societies.

Socialist paths to development

Japan and the Soviet Union suggested, in their different ways, that there was a general pattern of late development, appropriate to all those nations that attempted to industrialize in the shadow of already formidable industrial powers. This pattern variously involved strong protectionism, directed labour, control of unions, and central supervision of banking and credit. It also meant circumventing the sharp division between management and workers that hampered most early Western industrializers and that continued to worry them in their later industrial history. Above all, late developers put the power of the state at the centre of the modernizing effort. The state was the prime mover and guardian of the whole enterprise. Unlike Britain or the United States, where the state—at any rate in the early stage—encouraged development more or less passively, keeping the peace and enforcing the laws and perhaps arranging for some free land (as for the railroads in the United States), in countries such as Japan, the Soviet Union, and China the state directed the industrializing process from the start and supervised it closely throughout. The state made the major decisions about investment, transport and communications, and education. It developed the media of mass communications as agencies of mass socialization. Whether or not, therefore, the economy was formally nationalized, in practice economic development was placed firmly under national auspices and directed to nationalist ends.

ONE WORLD OR MANY?

Japan has been, so far, the only non-Western country in the world to become fully industrialized. It may be significant that it began its industrialization in the 19th century, while the West was still itself industrializing and before it had built up a truly commanding lead. The same is true of Russia, the only other major case of industrialization outside western Europe and North America (taking South Africa and Australia as "European"). In the 20th century it has become increasingly clear that industrialization is not something that nations can decide to do or how to do entirely by themselves. They operate within a context of world industrialization, in a world system of states of decidedly unequal wealth and power.

The nations of this world system can be categorized according to political or economic criteria. Applying the former results in the familiar "West–East" divide. This is primarily an ideological division between the developed capitalist nations, such as the United States, West Germany, and Japan (counted ideologically as Western), and the developed communist or state-socialist nations, such as the Soviet Union, East Germany, and Hungary. Attached to these are, respectively, underdeveloped capitalist nations, such as Bolivia and Bangladesh, and underdeveloped communist nations, such as China and Cuba.

West–East and North–South

A more significant and in many ways more interesting division arises from placing primary emphasis on the level of economic development, with political or ideological differences as subsidiary matters. This approach yields the "North–South" divide. With some anomalies—South Africa, Australia—the world is seen as divided essentially between the wealthy and powerful countries of the Northern Hemisphere, and the poor, less developed countries of the Southern Hemisphere. But the North–South dichotomy, though useful in debate, is inaccurate and misleading. A more precise economic model of the world system distinguishes among the superpowers, the United States and the Soviet Union; other developed countries, such as Japan, Great Britain, and Hungary; and the underdeveloped countries, such as China and Bolivia. We then have First, Second and Third Worlds. (In many other uses of these terms, First and Second refer separately to the superpowers and their developed allies; but a less political categorization is preferred here.)

The attraction of this model is that it points up the interconnections and flow of power in the world system. It shows especially the global dominance of the superpowers, which, despite their usually conflicting ideological and strategic interests, share a common interest in maintaining their world political and economic leadership. In competing with each other the superpowers draw into their respective spheres of influence the less powerful countries of the Second and Third Worlds; but, in order to maintain the balance of power, they may also in effect collude, choosing on occasion to ignore opportunities to gain at each other's expense in order to stifle political movements which seek too independent a third way.

A further refinement of the economic model looks past the level of three worlds of development to a single underlying and developing world system. Based on a historical perspective, this view, advanced especially by the American theorist Immanuel Wallerstein (b. 1930), argues that there is but a single world economy, the capitalist world economy, which has been expanding since the 17th century. This economy has, over the centuries, been expanding outward from its northwestern European base to take in an increasingly large portion of the globe. Eastern European societies are seen as full participants in this system and are accordingly regarded not as aberrant socialist economies but as "collective capitalist firms." Countries can be classified according to their nearness to the centre of the system. There are "core countries," such as the United States and Japan; "semi-peripheral countries," such as Brazil, most eastern European states, and China; and "peripheral countries," such as Cuba and most of the poor countries of Africa and Asia. Depending on economic fortunes and fluctuations, as well as the logic of the developing system itself, countries can move in and out of these categories—Russia, for instance, moved from semi-periphery to core, and India from periphery to semi-periphery.

The world economy

The plausibility and appeal of this model lie in its recognition of the growing internationalization of the industrial economy. Nation-states, whether capitalist or communist, are becoming increasingly subordinate to world economic developments. The politics of energy—oil, gas, nuclear power—are world politics (just as, for some considerable time, military strategy has been world strategy). Decisions about capital investment and growth are made in a world context and on a world scale. The giant multinational corporations are the most significant new actors on the world stage. They have been establishing a new international division of labour. From their point of view, it makes more sense to manufacture goods in South Korea or Taiwan, where labour is still cheap and governments compliant, than in the United States or Britain, where labour is expensive and regulation stringent. Such high-level functions as central planning and research and development can be retained in their Western homelands, where there are the necessary reserves of highly trained professional and scientific personnel. Profits can be declared in those countries where taxes are lowest. In such a way do the multinationals illustrate, even embody, the interdependence of core and periphery nations.

The role of multinationals

Postmodern and postindustrial society

NEW DEVELOPMENTS IN ECONOMIC AND SOCIAL STRUCTURE

Industrialism, at least within our experience of it for more than 200 years, never reaches a point of equilibrium or a level plateau. By its very principle of operation, it ceaselessly innovates and changes. Having largely eliminated the agricultural work force, it moves on manufacturing employment by creating new automated technology that increases manufacturing productivity while displacing workers. Manufacturing, from accounting for a half or more of the employed population of industrial societies, shrinks to between a quarter and a third. Its place is filled by the service sector, which in fully industrial societies comes to employ between a half and two-thirds of the work force and to account for more than half of the gross national product. Most service occupations—in government, health and education, finance, leisure and entertainment—are white-collar. The typical industrial worker is now not the blue-collar worker but the white-collar worker, or indeed the "pink-collar" worker, as someone called her, since the majority of service workers are women.

The service economy

The move to a service society is marked by a great expansion in education, health, and other private and public welfare services. The population typically becomes not just healthier, better housed, and better fed, but also better educated. Most young people complete secondary- or high-school education; between a quarter and a half of them go on to full-time higher education. Professional and scientific knowledge becomes the most marketable commodity. The "knowledge class" of professional, scientific, and technical workers becomes the fastest-growing occupational group. The link between pure science and technology, loose and uncertain in the early stages of industrialization, becomes pivotal. New industries, starting with chemicals and pharmaceuticals and later including the aeronautical, space, and nuclear industries, are created by developments in pure science and depend largely on theoretical research. Theoretical knowledge in the social sciences also comes to be widely applied, as in Keynesian management of the national economy and in complex models of technological and economic forecasting.

Struck by these changes, as compared with the classic forms of industrial society of the 19th and early 20th centuries, some theorists, notably the American sociologist Daniel Bell, have discerned a movement to a new postmodern or postindustrial society. Such conclusions may be premature. Most of the changes characterizing late industrialization can be seen as the results of long-term developments implicit in the process of industrialism from the start. The rise of service industries has emerged in part from the increase in leisure and in disposable wealth and in part from the continuing process of mechanization and technical innovation, which constantly raises manufacturing productivity by replacing human labour with machines. It can also be seen as the consequence of the growth of multinational corporations, and specifically of their strategy of removing their manufacturing operations to Third World countries, while retaining their service operations in the developed world. This, too, is the result of the increase in scale and complexity of industrial organization, a clear tendency from the very start. The growth of knowledge-based industries, finally, represents no break with the past. Science has always been at the base of industrialism, and its closer union with industry and society in the 20th century is simply the fulfillment of modernization's rationalizing drive.

But, while there may be no new society, these changes do add a new dimension to modern societies. Beyond a certain point in economic development, new values and problems emerge. The activities of the multinationals seem to encourage a process of "de-industrialization" in many modern societies, a drastic decline in manufacturing output and employment as these functions shift to the Third World. While services have for the time being filled the breach, it cannot be assumed that such a balancing will continue, at least as far as employment is concerned. The new microelectronic technology, itself simply the latest wave of industrial tools, has made inroads into service employment faster than more traditional industrial machines displaced manufacturing workers. The application of computers to information processing in a wide range of service work may threaten in turn to displace the vast mass of routine white-collar workers. Nor are the jobs of the more skilled workers necessarily much safer: Computer-aided design may take over much of the draftsman's and architect's work as computer-aided manufacturing equipment displaces skilled machinists; electronic audio-visual equipment may to a large extent take the place of the classroom teacher; and self-service diagnostic software may eliminate many tasks of the nurse and doctor.

Effects of the computer

NEW PATTERNS OF URBAN LIFE

Many features of modernity, intensified beyond a certain level, produce a reactive response. Urbanization, having reached some practical saturation point, leads to suburbanization, the desire to live in neighbourhoods with green spaces and at least a breath of country air. As the suburbs fill up, the more prosperous citizens become exurban: they colonize the villages and small towns of the countryside within commuting distance of their work in the city. Aiding this trend is the industrial decentralization and depopulation of many cities, as old manufacturing industries decline and new service industries move out to the suburbs and small towns. For the first time since the onset of industrialization, the countryside begins to gain population and the cities to lose it. According to the 1980 U.S. census, cities such as St. Louis, Buffalo, and Detroit lost between 35 and 47 percent of their populations over a 30-year period. London lost almost 15 percent of the population of its inner boroughs between 1961 and 1971, and Liverpool almost 25 percent of its population in the 20-year period to 1971.

But there is a deceptive aspect to this movement. The familiar forces of industrialism, here as elsewhere, continue to dominate the process. Suburbanization and exurbanization do not mean deurbanization. On the contrary, they amount to a spreading of urban life over greater and greater areas. They are simply the filling up, at lesser but still urban densities, of larger areas and regions. From the old city develops the metropolitan area, comprising a large city of around 10 million people together with a surrounding community socially and economically dependent on it. The metropolitan areas themselves tend to merge into even larger urban agglomerations, the megalopolises, which serve populations of 40 million or more.

The megalopolis

The biggest of these is "Boswash," the chain of contiguous cities and surrounding regions that stretches from Boston to Washington, D.C., along the northeastern seaboard of the United States. Others in the United States include the Chicago–Pittsburgh area around the Great Lakes and the San Francisco–San Diego region along the California coast. There are emerging megalopolises in Britain in the region between London and the Midland cities, in West Germany in the industrial basin of the Ruhr, and in Japan in the Tokyo–Osaka–Kyoto complex.

The Greek architect and city planner Constantinos Apostolos Doxiadis argued that this process is part of a long-term evolution that must eventually culminate in the world-city, or "Ecumenopolis." This remarkable object will incorporate areas reserved for recreation and agriculture as well as desert and wilderness conservation areas, but essentially it will be a web of interconnected cities throughout the world, all closely linked by rapid transport and electronic communication, and all contributing to a single functional unity. In Ecumenopolis, the entire land surface of the globe will have become recognizably the dwelling place of urbanized humanity.

Embedded in this process is a contradictory pattern typical of late industrial life. Subjectively, individuals wish to escape from the city. They leave the congested and declining older urban centres only to find themselves cocooned by larger urban structures in the region at large. The objective structural forces of industrialism have in no way abated. But increasingly they give rise to reactions and behaviour that have a de-modernizing character.

Thus there is reaction against large-scale bureaucratic organization. "Small is beautiful," declare the protesters as they seek to reestablish communal and craft environments characteristic of the preindustrial period. Parallel with this is a movement to promote "alternative" and "intermediate" technology, which aims to design tools that restore to the human worker the potential to use and express skill and creativity.

At the political level, too, there is reaction against large scale and centralization. In many industrial societies, such as those of Britain, France, and Canada, there have been strong regional movements demanding autonomy or outright independence. Often these are areas, such as Scotland in Britain, where at least substantial minorities wish to restore historic nations that have been incorporated into larger, more centralized states. Such movements derive momentum from the internationalization of the world economy and polity, which, over the world generally, gives rise to wholly new nationalisms as well. Lacking economic and often genuine political self-government, small societies assert their cultural identity and clamour—and sometimes fight—for autonomy. New nations emerge, although their main symbols of independence may be no more than a national anthem and an international airport.

The rise of new nationalisms

The assertion of cultural values opposed to modernity is a general characteristic of late industrialism. This may take the form of a revival of ethnicity, a claim for a culture and way of life that often harks back to older communal traditions and which denies the legitimacy of any uniform culture propagated by the large nation-state. Thus in the United States blacks, Hispanics, American Indians, and many other groups have made strong claims on behalf of a distinctive ethnic way of life which they variously seek to defend against the encroachments of the national culture. Protests against rationality and uniformity are seen, as well, in the successive waves of youth cultures and religious revivals that have marked late industrial society. Objectively, it is clear that the large-scale bureaucratic institutions of society continue to give the main direction to national life. All revolts break against their indispensability to modern society. But subjectively these institutions are incapable of satisfying the emotional and social needs of individuals. The consequence is the repeated rise of subcultures, often of bizarre mystical or hedonistic kinds, which aim in their practice to reverse the main features of modernity and which give their members a sense of participation and belonging of an almost tribal nature. Central to most of these antinomian movements and ideologies is a wholesale rejection of the scientific worldview, which is depicted as alienating and dehumanizing.

The role of subcultures

To embark on modernization is to be caught up in a whirligig. Once started, the ceaselessly spinning motion seemingly cannot be stopped or even slowed for long. A nation that modernizes is set upon a path of development that carries its own logic and an inseparable mixture of good and bad. Without question, modern society brings progress in the form of material abundance. Less certainly, it brings increasing control of the natural and social environment. But its scientific and technological achievements are bought at some cost to spiritual and emotional life. Moreover, in unifying the world, modernization establishes uniform standards, albeit higher ones in many cases than previously prevailed. But at the same time it ensures that failures and disasters will also be magnified on a world scale. There are no retreats and escape routes, except those which modern society itself invents as pastimes. The world becomes one and its fate that of all its inhabitants.

To measure the balance of gains and losses in modernity, and to increase the former against the latter, require forms of social accounting and social engineering that have so far largely defied the efforts of social science and government. But in practice this does not matter. No one can wait for that problem to be solved, if it ever can be. To modernize is to take everything, the bad with the good, and not to modernize is to play no part in the life of contemporary humanity. One of the unusual, and historically unprecedented, aspects of modernization is that it leaves no choice in the matter.

BIBLIOGRAPHY

General surveys of modernization: ALEXIS DE TOCQUEVILLE, *Democracy in America*, 4 vol. (1835–40; originally published in French, 1835–40), available also in many later revised editions, both of the original French edition and of Henry Reeve's translation, provides the classic statement of the "democratic revolution" in modern society, with a finely blended mixture of the author's hopes and fears. For an introduction to Marx's passionate, often indignant appraisal of modern industrial capitalist society, with suggestions of how capitalism might be superseded, see KARL MARX, *Selected Writings*, ed. by DAVID MCLELLAN (1977). ÉMILE DURKHEIM, *The Division of Labor in Society* (1984; originally published in French, 1893), is a guardedly optimistic exploration of the growth of modern society and of hopes for the future, in a new translation by W.D. HALLS. MAX WEBER, *The Protestant Ethic and the Spirit of Capitalism*

(1930, reissued 1985; originally published in German, 1904), is a classic discussion of values that underlie industrial society.

The explorations begun in these classic works continues in the writings of the second half of the 20th century: IRVING L. HOROWITZ, *Three Worlds of Development: The Theory and Practice of International Stratification*, 2nd ed. (1972), studies the impact of the West on modernization in the non-Western world; PETER L. BERGER, BRIGITTE BERGER, and HANSFRIED KELLNER, *The Homeless Mind: Modernization and Consciousness* (1973), analyzes the social tensions, pains, and conflicts that accompany modernization; SZYMON CHODAK, *Societal Development* (1973), surveys in critical detail the theories of modernization and development; PETER WORSLEY, *The Three Worlds: Culture and World Development* (1984), compares earlier Western modernization with that taking place in the rest of the world today; RICHARD L. RUBENSTEIN (ed.), *Modernization: The Humanist Response to Its Promise and Problems*, new ed. (1985), offers scholarly essays examining religious and philosophical aspects of modernization; and THEODORE H. VON LAUE, *The World Revolution of Westernization: The Twentieth Century in Global Perspective* (1987), explores modernization and development as adaptation to Western influences.

Industrialization as economic change and development: CARLO M. CIPOLLA, *Before the Industrial Revolution: European Society and Economy, 1000–1700*, 2nd ed. (1980; originally published in Italian, 1974), offers a historical survey focusing on the economic conditions of preindustrial Europe; W.W. ROSTOW, *How It All Began: Origins of the Modern Economy* (1975), surveys economic history from the beginning of the 17th to the end of the 19th century; DAVID S. LANDES, *The Unbound Prometheus: Technological Change and Industrial Development in Western Europe from 1750 to the Present* (1969), discusses the first Industrial Revolution and its spread throughout Europe and the wider world; SIDNEY POLLARD, *Peaceful Conquest: The Industrialization of Europe, 1760–1970* (1981), examines the original act of European industrialization and its further progress since. Patterns of industrialization in their historical development throughout the world are compared in TOM KEMP, *Industrialization in Nineteenth-Century Europe*, 2nd ed. (1985), *Historical Patterns of Industrialization* (1978), and *Industrialization in the Non-Western World* (1983). Philosophical and political aspects of industrialization as reflected in traditional understanding of market behaviour and economic laws are analyzed in GREGORY CLAEYS, *Machinery, Money, and the Millennium: From Moral Economy to Socialism, 1815–1860* (1987). KARL POLANYI, *The Great Transformation* (1944, reprinted 1985), explores the novelty of the modern market economy and the social and political problems arising from it; IMMANUEL WALLERSTEIN, *The Capitalist World-Economy* (1979), presents modernization as the growth of a capitalist world economy, dominated by the powerful capitalist nations; HENRY BERNSTEIN (comp.), *Underdevelopment and Development: The Third World Today* (1973), offers a collection of theoretical and empirical essays with a Marxist and neo-Marxist slant; and DAVID GOODMAN, BERNARDO SORJ, and JOHN WILKINSON, *From Farming to Biotechnology: A Theory of Agro-Industrial Development* (1987), studies the impact of modernization and industrialization on agriculture.

Demographic change: ROBERT I. ROTBERG and THEODORE K. RABB (eds.), *Population and Economy: Population and History from the Traditional to the Modern World* (1986), is a collection of excellent scholarship, exploring demographic dynamics of preindustrial society; H.J. HABAKKUK, *Population Growth and Economic Development Since 1750* (1971), is a monographic history covering both Europe and developing countries; JAMES C. RILEY, *Population Thought in the Age of the Demographic Revolution* (1985), discusses, in a somewhat technical style, the influence of demographic ideas on social policies and choices; R.K. KELSALL, *Population*, 4th ed. (1979), presents a sociological survey; PAULA ENGLAND and GEORGE FARKAS, *Households, Employment, and Gender: A Social, Economic, and Demographic View* (1986), provides an interdisciplinary explanation of the influence of main demographic trends on modern and postmodern society; MICHAEL S. TEITELBAUM and JAY M. WINTER, *The Fear of Population Decline* (1985), is a readable examination of demographic and political aspects of negative growth of population in developed economies at the end of the 19th and beginning of the 20th centuries; and WILLIAM ALONSO (ed.), *Population in an Interacting World* (1987), is a collection of contemporary studies on the connection between population development and social change.

Urbanization as a way of life: PAUL M. HOHENBERG and LYNN HOLLEN LEES, *The Making of Urban Europe, 1000–1950* (1985); offers a well-illustrated socioeconomic history of urbanization, modernization, and industrialization. Collections of shorter writings on urban history, sociology, culture, and economics, sampling both classic works and contemporary studies, include RICHARD SENNETT (comp.), *Classic Essays on the Culture of Cities* (1969); PHILIP ABRAMS and E.A. WRIGLEY (eds.), *Towns in Societies: Essays in Economic History and Historical Sociology* (1978); FUAD BAALI and JOSEPH S. VANDIVER (eds.), *Urban Sociology* (1970); and GINO GERMANI (ed.), *Modernization, Urbanization, and the Urban Crisis* (1973). JANE JACOBS, *Cities and the Wealth of Nations: Principles of Economic Life* (1984), explores the role of cities in economic development. Theories explaining the relationship between urbanization and modernization are surveyed in R.J. HOLTON, *Cities, Capitalism, and Civilization* (1986). E.A. WRIGLEY, *People, Cities, and Wealth: The Transformation of Traditional Society* (1987), examines major issues of change from rural into urban society. Sociological studies of urbanization include BRIAN J.L. BERRY, *The Human Consequences of Urbanization: Divergent Paths in the Urban Experience of the Twentieth Century* (1973); R.E. PAHL, R. FLYNN, and N.H. BUCK, *Structures and Processes of Urban Life*, 2nd ed. (1983); and EDWARD KRUPAT, *People in Cities: The Urban Environment and Its Effects* (1985).

The nature of work: CLARK KERR *et al.*, *Industrialism and Industrial Man: The Problems of Labour and Management in Economic Growth*, 2nd ed. (1973), sees the apparatus of production as an all-conquering world system, with its own inner logic and dynamism. Development of society where work for industrial production or related service is an issue of survival is studied in KRISHAN KUMAR, *Prophecy and Progress: The Sociology of Industrial and Post-Industrial Society* (1978); KENNETH THOMPSON (ed.), *Work, Employment, and Unemployment: Perspectives on Work and Society* (1984); REINHARD BENDIX, *Work and Authority in Industry: Ideologies of Management in the Course of Industrialization* (1956, reprinted with a new introduction, 1974); HERBERT G. GUTMAN, *Work, Culture, and Society in Industrializing America: Essays in American Working-Class and Social History* (1977); and HARRY BRAVERMAN, *Labor and Monopoly Capital: The Degradation of Work in the Twentieth Century* (1975). ARNE L. KALLEBERG and IVAR BERG, *Work and Industry: Structures, Markets, and Processes* (1987), is an interdisciplinary examination of the role of work in economic development; and PATRICK JOYCE (ed.), *The Historical Meaning of Work* (1987), offers observations on historical and social changes in cultural and ideological dimensions of work in the West during the last two centuries.

Family in industrial society: FRANCES GIES and JOSEPH GIES, *Marriage and the Family in the Middle Ages* (1987), looks at one thousand years of family history to the end of the preindustrial period; PETER LASLETT, *The World We Have Lost: Further Explored*, 3rd ed. (1984), examines the English household of the preindustrial period; and LLOYD BONFIELD, RICHARD M. SMITH, and KEITH WRIGHTSON (eds.), *The World We Have Gained: Histories of Population and Social Structure* (1986), is a collection of essays on family history from the 14th to the 20th century. The modern family is treated in EDWARD SHORTER, *The Making of the Modern Family* (1975); and MICHAEL YOUNG and PETER WILLMOTT, *The Symmetrical Family* (1974, reissued 1984). SYLVIA ANN HEWLETT, ALICE S. ILCHMAN, and JOHN J. SWEENEY (eds.), *Family and Work: Bridging the Gap* (1986), analyzes the complex evolutionary relationship between these two social institutions. Specific features of family in industrialized states are surveyed in JAMES DICKINSON and BOB RUSSELL (eds.), *Family, Economy & State: The Social Reproduction Process Under Capitalism* (1986).

Changes in social structure and understanding of social problems: S.N. EISENSTADT (ed.), *Readings in Social Evolution and Development* (1970), gathers together classic essays of 19th- and 20th-century authors; BERT F. HOSELITZ and WILBERT E. MOORE (eds.), *Industrialization and Society* (1963), analyzes the general impact of modernization on social structure and social institutions; JASON L. FINKLE and RICHARD W. GABLE (eds.), *Political Development and Social Change*, 2nd ed. (1971), studies the political consequences of development, particularly in Third World societies; and EMANUEL DE KADT and GAVIN WILLIAMS (eds.), *Sociology and Development* (1974), emphasizes the interrelationship of the developed and developing societies. Contemporary social structures are discussed in SALVADOR GINER and MARGARET SCOTFORD ARCHER (eds.), *Contemporary Europe: Social Structures and Cultural Patterns* (1978); ANTHONY GIDDENS, *The Class Structure of the Advanced Societies*, 2nd ed. (1981); and JACQUES ELLUL, *The Technological Society* (1964; originally published in French, 1954). Dilemmas and problems posed for societies by modernization are outlined in REINHARD BENDIX, *Embattled Reason: Essays on Social Knowledge*, 2 vol.: vol. 1, 2nd rev. ed. (1988), vol. 2 (1989); FRED HIRSCH, *Social Limits to Growth* (1976); ADRIAN ELLIS and KRISHAN KUMAR (eds.), *Dilemmas of Liberal Democracies: Studies in Fred Hirsch's 'Social Limits to Growth'* (1983); and WILLIAM LEISS, *The Limits to Satisfaction: On Needs and Commodities*, rev. ed. (1978). (Kr.K.)

Molecules: Their Structure, Properties, and Forms

A molecule is a group of atoms bonded together strongly enough to establish a separate identity and act together as a unit and, consequently, to have a constant mass and atomic composition. Atoms and molecules are the chief intellectual abstractions of chemistry. Atoms are the fundamental building blocks from which molecules are constructed, and molecules the smallest particles of a pure compound that retain its characteristic properties. Although there are only about 100 different kinds of atoms (see ATOMS: *Components of an atom;* CHEMICAL ELEMENTS: *Periodic law and table*), they combine in tens of millions of different molecules (see CHEMICAL COMPOUNDS), and chemists add new kinds of molecules at a rate of more than 100,000 per year. Atoms and molecules undergo physical change without change in number or kind; atoms participate in chemical reaction without change in number or kind, but they can be transformed in nuclear reactions; molecules can be transformed in chemical reactions. It is a fundamental problem of chemistry to determine the arrangement of atoms in molecules and to elucidate their bonding forces.

This article is divided into the following sections:

Molecular weight

Historic development of atomic-molecular theory

Although the idea of molecular weight is accepted today, it evolved only slowly. As modern atomic-molecular theory was developed and the existence of discrete molecules asserted, the Italian physicist Amedeo Avogadro postulated (1811) that equal volumes of different gases would contain the same number of molecules if the temperature and pressure were the same. Therefore, if equal volumes of two gases were weighed under identical conditions of temperature and pressure, the weights would compare exactly as the masses of single molecules. Stanislao Cannizzaro, an Italian chemist, revived Avogadro's concept in 1858 and showed its significance by analyzing existing measurements of gas densities. He was able to rationalize the molecular weights and chemical formulas of the well-known gases, and molecular weight came to be accepted as one of the fundamental properties of any chemical compound.

The number of molecules in one millilitre (ml) of gas is about 10^{19} at room temperature and atmospheric pressure. Although gas densities vary, a value of 0.001 gram per millilitre is common. The mass of a single gas molecule would then be about 10^{-22} gram. Because this mass is not directly measurable, other ways of determining molecular weight are required, and a scale of relative values has been built around the concept of a mole (*i.e.,* the amount of a substance in grams that corresponds to the sum of the atomic weights of all the atoms that make up the molecule; the atomic weight of the atom of an element is defined as its mass as compared with the mass of the atom of carbon-12). A mole of a substance is considered to contain exactly the same number of molecules as there are atoms in 12 grams of the pure carbon isotope carbon-12: 6.022×10^{23} atoms of carbon. This number is called Avogadro's number or, in some literature, Loschmidt's number.

The molecular weight of a substance is defined as the weight in grams of one mole of the substance; that is, the actual weight in grams of 6.022×10^{23} molecules. Molecular weights are expressed in grams per mole (or daltons, a term common in the field of biological chemistry, although it has not been approved by the International Union of Pure and Applied Chemistry). Molecular weights range into the millions, as shown by Table 1.

All molecules over this range of molecular weights can be at least conceptually separated from one another for some measurement of molecular weight. For many solids with molecules that cannot be separated into a gaseous state, it is possible to find a solvent that will dissolve the substance and thus separate the molecules so that their weights can be determined.

Table 1: Approximate Molecular Weights

molecule	structure	molecular weight (in grams/mole)
Hydrogen	H_2	2
Sucrose (sugar)	$C_{12}H_{22}O_{11}$	342
Insulin	51 amino-acid residues	5,700
Polyesters	$(O(CH_2)_5CO)_n$	10,000–20,000
Hemoglobin	587 amino-acid residues	65,000
Synthetic rubbers	$(CH_2{-}CH{=}CH{-}CH_2)_n$	100,000
Myosin		600,000
Polystyrene	$(C_6H_5CHCH_2)_n$	50,000,000
Nucleic acids	phage DNA	130,000,000 and greater
Dextrans	polysaccharides	up to 500,000,000

This simple procedure is subject to two frequent chemical complications: (1) The solution of the dissolved molecules often results in chemical reactions that produce associated or dissociated species rather than a simple, unchanging molecular species. (2) Solids such as sodium chloride (NaCl) have a neat geometrical arrangement of sodium ions and chloride ions in the solid state, but they have a disordered arrangement of ions and no clearly defined molecular species of NaCl in the solution state (in which the ions dissociate and move about in accordance with electrochemical factors). In both these cases the simplest chemical formula that represents the proper chemical composition is assumed, and the molecular weight is assigned to that formula. If alcohol, for example, has a structure for which the simplest formula is C_2H_5OH, its molecular weight is found by multiplying the number of atoms in this formula by their atomic weights as found in the atomic-weight tables: that is, 2 atoms of carbon $\times (12.011) + 1$ atom of oxygen $\times (15.999) + 6$ hydrogen atoms $\times (1.008) = 46.069$. This weight of alcohol—*i.e.,* 46.069 grams—then constitutes one gram mole. Often when dealing with known simple materials such a calculation is sufficient. For unknown substances or known substances in a totally new environment, one of the methods discussed below is used.

PRINCIPLES OF MOLECULAR-WEIGHT DETERMINATION

The three methods of determining the molecular weight of uncharged molecules are based respectively on thermodynamic theory, on kinetic theory of transport phenomena, and on known spatial arrangements of atoms in the solid state. A fourth method, mass spectrometry, can be used on species that can be ionized; *i.e.,* given an electrical charge either by adding or by removing one or more electrons from the structure.

Thermodynamic methods

The thermodynamic methods of molecular-weight determination rely on the equation of state for gases or the equation of state for solutions. The laws concerning the physical behaviour of gases are among the most useful in science, but they are based upon the concept of an ideal gas in which each molecule is, in effect, a point without volume, without any attraction or repulsion toward other points, and with perfect resilience in collisions. The molecules of a real gas have volume and are attracted to or repelled by one another; they often have electrical charges and magnetic properties, and they have a true mass that makes them react to the gravitational field. They may react chemically under certain conditions, and they spin and tumble about. Their internal structure is such that they can absorb energy or lose it in ways that may or may not affect their motion. In an ideal gas the volume (V), pressure (P), temperature (T), and a constant of proportionality (R) are related in such a way that the volume is directly proportional to the temperature and to the constant and is inversely proportional to the pressure, which can thus be expressed by the equation: $V = RT/P$. This relationship is true with R only if one mole of gas is considered. If the gas has a mass m and its molecular weight is M, then the number of moles is m/M, and the equation may be rewritten pressure times volume is equal to constant times temperature times mass divided by molecular weight, or: $PV = RT(m/M)$. Molecules in a solution may be considered to behave somewhat like gases, and an equation of state can be derived for solutions following the same sort of reasoning as with gases, with the additional factors that dominate the liquid state. If π represents osmotic pressure (defined below) as analogous to gas pressure, and C_2 is the concentration of dissolved molecules, analogous to the weight of gas molecules, then the van't Hoff relation for the equation of state for solutions is written $\pi = RT(C_2/M)$. Although ideal gases and ideal solutions are never encountered, the ideal is approached with increasing dilution. Furthermore, if measured quantities are extrapolated to infinite dilution, the use of ideal-gas or ideal-solution laws is usually justified.

Transport and other methods

Transport phenomena include the movement of a variety of properties through a system; *e.g.,* heat. The transport methods of molecular-weight determination depend on the relationship of the size of the molecule to the diffusion, or spreading of concentration, the viscosity (*i.e.,* a liquid's internal resistance to flow), or sedimentation (*i.e.,* the settling of finely divided particles from a liquid) of the molecules, whether in the gaseous or dissolved states. Other transport methods rely on the heat conduction or electrical mobility. If a simple shape can be assumed for the molecule, there is a direct relationship of size, mass, and density. Historically these methods were used for determining Avogadro's number, but today they are seldom used for molecular-weight determinations of small molecules except under special experimental conditions.

The geometrical arrangements of the molecules and their constituent atoms can sometimes be clearly determined in the crystalline state (*e.g.,* when X-rays are passed through a thin slice of a crystal to fall on a photographic plate, the two-dimensional pattern on the plate can be interpreted in terms of the three-dimensional structure of atomic nuclei that deflected the X-rays); in such instances, it is easy to calculate the average volume occupied by the molecule. By multiplying the average molecular volume by the macroscopic crystal density, the average mass of a molecule can be determined. The molecular weight can then be determined quite accurately using Avogadro's number. This method is obviously limited to a few well-studied compounds and is not used for routine molecular-weight determinations.

If the molecule can be ionized (*i.e.,* given an electrical charge by either adding or removing electrons), the ionized sample can be fed into a mass spectrometer, in which the heavier molecules are separated from the lighter. The ratio of mass to charge can be accurately determined (see below *Methods of molecular-weight determination*). Since the ions are frequently of low charge, it is possible to determine ion mass. Using Avogadro's number, the molecular weight can be determined. This method is extremely accurate but is restricted to low molecular weights. Because of its speed, it is used extensively in the petroleum industry.

Application of methods

For an unknown compound the thermodynamic and transport methods discussed above are usually used, unless the molecule is of low molecular weight or the substance is gaseous. In the latter cases the mass spectrograph may be preferred. The thermodynamic and transport types of measurement can be simply and inexpensively performed. From an operational point of view, molecular-weight measurements by the thermodynamic and transport methods generally require that: (1) the substance be used in a solution, (2) the solution be sufficiently dilute that van't Hoff's law is obeyed, and (3) the substance be a pure chemical compound, not a mixture of different molecules.

Frequently, the substance is not a pure chemical compound; petroleum samples, for example, are often mixtures of several hydrocarbons, the boiling points of which are close together. Furthermore, polymer samples, such as plastics, rubbers, or wood, are always mixtures of differing molecular weights (see below *Molecular-weight distributions*). Even pure proteins often occur with small traces of other similar components. The best representation of any mixture is a frequency count of all components, as is routinely done with petroleum samples, using the mass spectrometer. With samples of higher molecular weight, however, such as polymers and proteins, the same techniques are not applicable; average molecular weights must be given. In averaging, the different molecules are counted either by number or by weight. In the first case, the molecular weight is called a number-average molecular weight and, in the second, a weight-average molecular weight.

METHODS OF MOLECULAR-WEIGHT DETERMINATION

Gaseous-state methods. *Density.* The measurement of gas densities to determine the molecular weight of a gas is an application of the ideal-gas law, which can be used with any volatile liquid or solid. Sensitivity of the method is low because large vessels must be weighed to determine the mass and volume of the gas. Real molecules are not simple points in space as the ideal-gas law assumes, and, accordingly, a pressure-dependent term must often be added to the ideal-gas law. At one atmosphere pressure, the correction is less than 1 percent for very simple gases.

Effusion. The general theory of diffusion (the expansion of a gas as a result of its internal pressure, brought about by the incessant motion and collisions of its molecules) indicates that the rate of diffusion will be inversely proportional to the mass of the diffusing particle; *i.e.,* the more massive particle diffuses more slowly. Effusion of a gas through a small hole can be used to measure the ratios of molecular weight of any two gases. The rates of effusion R_1 and R_2, of two species, for example, are related to the square roots of their molecular weights (M_1 and M_2) inversely and therefore can be expressed numerically as $\frac{R_1}{R_2} = \sqrt{\frac{M_2}{M_1}}$, all other variables being constant.

Formula for effusion methods

In the mass spectrometer, the rate at which molecules enter or leave the ion chamber (a process of effusion) is measured, a technique that allows analysis of mixtures by molecular weights.

Mass spectrometry. The mass spectrometer is so sensitive that it can distinguish between isotopes (atoms of the same element that differ in atomic mass) in molecules of low molecular weight. Thus, in many reactions the changes in molecular weight of the molecules involved can be followed through isotope or heavy atom exchange. The amount of material required for analysis is small (less than 0.1 millilitre of gas). Mass spectrometers are used in refinery operations to make automatic molecular-weight determinations of petroleum fractions. The limited range of the mass spectrometer is its only major disadvantage in this application. It is suitable only for a range of molecular weight (for a unit electrical charge) of up to several thousand grams per mole and is generally used for molecular weights no greater than 500 grams per mole. Another disadvantage is that, after the sample is volatilized inside the instrument, only fragments of the original molecule remain to be measured.

Solution methods using colligative-property measurements. Solution methods are in general use because they can be inexpensive, and they cover a very large molecular-weight range, about 100 grams per mole to greater than 100,000,000 grams per mole. They also can vary from simple thermodynamic methods to transport methods that are based on thermal conduction and mass transport. Solution methods usually are separated into those that count numbers of molecules (colligative properties) and those that count weights of molecules.

Osmotic pressure. When molecules of the substance to be measured are placed in a solvent, they affect the energy of the solvent molecules so that the latter no longer have the same chemical potential (or internal pressure) as the pure solvent. If the pure solvent is separated from the solution by a membrane that is impermeable to all but solvent molecules, these will migrate through the membrane from a higher to a lower concentration of solvent; *i.e.,* from the pure solvent side to the solution side. Pressure applied to the solution will inhibit the migration, and the exact pressure that must be applied to bring about equilibrium between solution and solvent is called the osmotic pressure. This is a direct measure of the effect of the substance whose molecular weight is sought upon the chemical potential of the solvent, and experiments show that osmotic pressure (π), as was stated earlier, equals the product of the concentration of dissolved molecules (C_2), the temperature (T), and the gas constant (R) from the ideal-gas law, divided by the molecular weight (M) of the dissolved molecules. Rearranging this, the equation may be written: $M = RTC_2/\pi$. As with the gas equation of state, all of the solution measurements are conducted at low concentrations or are extrapolated to zero concentration, in order to minimize the discrepancy between an ideal state and the actuality, in which molecules affect one another in various other ways as well.

Automatic osmometers

In recent years automatic osmometers have become commercially available. They are not more accurate than simple osmometers using capillary tubes, but they are faster. With corrections for diffusion through the membrane, osmotic-pressure measurements have accurately measured the molecular weight of sucrose ($M = 342$ grams per mole). Osmometers have been used to measure M as high as 1,000,000 grams per mole.

Vapour pressure. The vapour pressure of a pure solvent is always lowered when the substance to be measured is added to it, because the concentration of solvent molecules at the surface is reduced. The solvent molecules have fewer chances at the surface to exert a pressure. Such small pressure differences, however, are generally so difficult to measure that the technique is not used routinely for molecular-weight determinations.

Vapour-pressure osmometer. Differences in vapour pressure can be measured by thermistors, devices that employ semiconductors to measure minute changes in temperature. If a thermistor has a drop of solution and a drop of solvent, with only a small air gap separating the drops, the different rates at which vapour is transported between the drops cause a temperature difference that the thermistor can sense. This temperature difference can be related to the molecular weight of the solute. The technique needs to be calibrated with known compounds, but the measurement has become common in organic- and polymer-chemistry laboratories. The range is limited to a few thousand grams per mole in molecular weight.

Boiling point and freezing point. When a compound is dissolved in a solvent, the chemical potential of the solvent is reduced, and the freezing point of the resulting solution becomes lower than that of the pure solvent. The difference in temperature is inversely proportional to the molecular weight of the solute. Again, the phenomenon may be explained in terms of the concentration of solvent molecules. A solution also has a higher boiling point than the pure solvent, and the difference in temperature is, as with the freezing point, inversely proportional to the molecular weight (the greater the difference the smaller the molecular weight). The elevation of the boiling point, however, is less sensitive than the lowering of the freezing point because of the higher heat of vaporization. The method is used in teaching because it is inexpensive, using only a thermometer and a water bath. Its range is generally less than 5,000 grams per mole.

Other solution methods. *Equilibrium sedimentation.* If a sample solution is centrifuged (spun in a container shaped like a test tube) at extremely high speed, the dissolved molecules may collect in the region at the bottom of the tube. The process of concentrating the solution near the bottom of the tube, however, sets off an osmotic driving force that tends to make the dissolved molecules diffuse back into now less-concentrated solvent. If the experiment is carried out carefully, the two forces are balanced and a very simple determination of molecular weight is possible through the osmotic equation of state (as explained above). The range of molecular weights that can be determined is enormous because the buoyancy of the medium and the speed of the centrifuge rotation can both be altered. In many ways measurement of solutions with the centrifuge, using the product of mass and buoyancy, are analogous to measurement with the mass spectrometer of gas, using a ratio of mass and charge. The method is capable of great accuracy and is fast. Its primary application has been in biological chemistry.

Light scattering. Fluctuations of concentration in a solution were analyzed by Einstein and found to be proportional to the change of osmotic pressure with concentration. To make a concentration fluctuation requires working against the osmotic forces in the solution, *i.e.*, the tendency for the ratio of solute to solvent molecules to become uniform throughout the solution. If a light beam strikes a solution in which there are fluctuations of concentration, it will be scattered. The Dutch chemist Peter Debye during World War II showed how the intensity of scattered light could be measured and applied to the analysis of the molecular weights of synthetic rubber through the osmotic equation of state. There is no limit in range for this method and it can be very precise, but extreme care is necessary to get meaningful results. Most polymer and biological laboratories use this method.

X-ray crystallography

Solid-state measurements. In the technique of X-ray crystallography, extremely thin sections of solid sample are bombarded with X-rays, which are deflected by the pattern of nuclei in the sample to emerge in a pattern that can be photographed. This technique is so complex that it is used only for exceedingly important materials that cannot be dissolved in any useful solvent. In principle, a large molecule that is completely homogeneous could be analyzed by viewing its entire length by high-resolution electron microscopy. In practice, estimates of molecular weight can be made for any dispersed particle thought to be a single molecule if the densities can be guessed from other experiments.

Relative methods based on molecular size. *Sedimentation rate and diffusion constant.* The sedimentation velocity and free diffusion methods assume that certain laws are obeyed, and, from this assumption, the molecular weight can be determined. If both diffusion and sedimentation measurements are made, the need for the assumption is eliminated. These methods are seldom used for measuring molecular weight.

Intrinsic viscosity. A molecule turning over as it is moved in the flow of a solution has friction properties; a viscometer is used to make intrinsic viscosity measurements from which the molecular weight can be calculated. Einstein solved the problem very generally for spherical particles. The method is also used extensively for determining the molecular weight of polymers.

Gel permeation chromatography (GPC). The most recent development in routine methods of molecular-weight determination is gel permeation chromatography. Gels are semisolids consisting of two components—a liquid dispersed through a network of solid material. In chromatography, a solution is passed through a medium that has a stronger affinity for one of the dissolved compounds, which settles out first and thus is separated. Gels that have very well defined holes have been made of polystyrene and dextrans; when a solution passes through a column of the gel, the smaller molecules can diffuse into the holes and therefore are retained longer in the gel column. The larger molecules, not able to get into the holes, move through the column faster. Using calibration with known materials, the technique has worked effectively throughout a molecular-weight range of from a few hundred to many million grams per mole.

MOLECULAR-WEIGHT DETERMINATIONS OF MACROMOLECULES

Very large molecules—that is, molecules with molecular weights greater than 20,000 grams per mole and perhaps up to 1,000,000,000 grams per mole—have become extremely important in industry and biochemistry. Plastics, rubbers, thickeners, paints, wood, paper, proteins, nucleic acids, polypeptides, and polysaccharides are of this type. As recently as the 1920s, these molecules were considered to be aggregates of smaller molecules rather than single large molecules, and their molecular-weight determination has been an extremely important development.

Effect of bonding in gels

Gels. Gels exist as macromolecules, but their molecular weight is immeasurably large. A gel is not really a dissolved molecule but rather a separate continuous phase (a phase is a state of matter such as solid, liquid, or gas). From a molecular point of view, a gel is analogous in three dimensions to the coupling of many short segments of threads in a two-dimensional mesh fabric. Such gels can be held together as a mesh by covalent bonds or hydrogen bonds. If the bonding forces are covalent, the gel cannot be handled by any of the above methods, and the molecular weight tends toward infinity, but the gel will have a particle size almost large enough to be observed by the unaided eye. Vulcanized rubber is typical of this type of gel. Gelatin is typical of a protein gel that can be dissolved in special solvents or at higher temperatures and become individual chains that are no longer in a gel structure. These single chains can then be analyzed for their molecular weight.

Molecular-weight distributions. Although biological processes tend to produce relatively uniform macromolecules, industrial synthetic polymerization processes produce a rather broad range of groups of molecules. In terms of molecular weights, the proteins are said to be monodisperse in molecular weight, while the polymers are polydisperse.

Petroleum, a natural product, can be treated in a refinery to separate fractions that are more or less uniform, and thus the molecular weights of the components can be determined. A detailed accounting of all of the molecular weights in a truly polydisperse system, however, cannot be obtained. Instead, a statistical description, called the molecular-weight distribution (MWD), may be obtained.

Industrial techniques

In polymers, the existence of small amounts of other components of lower or higher molecular weight is important. Industrially, optimum processability and strength are related to the type of molecular-weight distribution. The presence of dimers or trimers (molecules consisting of two or three identical subunits), or degraded material from a biological macromolecule, gives insight into many kinds of biochemical processes; consequently, the fast elucidation of the MWD has been a goal of macromolecular chemistry. This goal has been achieved by gel permeation chromatography and by a process called boundary spreading in the ultracentrifuge (extremely high speed of rotation and, consequently, better separation of particles). Previously, time-consuming separation by fractionation schemes was required. In both these faster techniques, however, the molecular-weight distribution may be reported incorrectly, because the analysis assumes that only linear molecules are present in the sample whereas the sample may also contain branched and complicated ring and other types of molecular structures.

Branched molecules. Both natural and synthetic polymers have nonlinear, branched molecules. For the problem of samples that are mixtures of linear and branched polymers, as well as for many other problems, the equilibrium-sedimentation method is useful because it offers the greatest versatility in determining a true molecular-weight distribution.

Insoluble polymers. Commercial polymers may have such high melting points that the operations of solution chemistry are difficult to carry out. One popular product has never had an accurate molecular-weight description because the solutions must be handled at 300° C (about 600° F). New special-purpose polymers are often high melting. To determine their molecular weights, experimenters have used correlations of molecular weight with viscoelastic properties and mechanical strength found in other, lower melting polymer systems. For example, cellulose is difficult to characterize because it must be dissolved in chemically active solvents, and such solvents may alter the cellulose. This is the case with many polymers.

End-group analyses. If the polymer has identical subunits, the ends of the molecule can often be analyzed chemically because they are different from all the other chemical units in the chain and will react with reagents. The molecular weights of food additives, foaming agents, and other intermediate-molecular-weight polymers are determined by chemical analysis of the number of ends. If the ends can be counted, the number of chains is known, and the average mass per chain, or molecular weight, can easily be determined.

Nonideal solutions. All macromolecules, as a result of their size, are affected in many ways and therefore have large additive terms, in addition to the van't Hoff relation, for molecular weight. To avoid such factors as much as possible, macromolecules must be measured in very dilute solutions and the resultant molecular weight extrapolated to infinite dilution. All early work in this field is now of limited value because this effect was not fully understood. Sometimes a poor solvent, which then ensures a more ideal solution, is used to minimize the extrapolation. Biological macromolecular systems and synthetic polyelectrolytes are always nonideal because of the charges on the molecules, and they must be analyzed for their molecular weight with special experimental care.

Biological macro-molecular systems

Association of macromolecules occurs in biological macromolecules, such as insulin, and in synthetic polymers such as polyvinyl chloride. Like any other association equilibrium with similar small-molecular-weight systems, the problem can often be avoided by using a more active solvent or by studying the change of molecular weight with dilution or temperature or both.

(D.McI.)

Molecular structure

GENERAL CONSIDERATIONS

The simplest molecule is that of hydrogen, H_2, in which two hydrogen atoms are joined together. The minute mass of these particles is suggested by the fact that one gram of hydrogen contains more than 10^{23} hydrogen molecules. Molecules range in size and complexity from hydrogen to molecules within living organisms that may contain many millions of atoms. In the case of two-atom, diatomic, molecules, such as those of hydrogen, nitrogen (N_2), oxygen (O_2), or hydrogen chloride (HCl), the only question about the molecular structure would be the distance between the two joined atoms. Adding an oxygen atom to the hydrogen molecule to make water (H_2O) raises several other questions. Water molecules could consist of chains with a terminal or a central oxygen atom, H—H—O or H—O—H; the chain could be straight or bent. If it is not straight, the angle of bend as well as the distances between the centres of the atoms must be known in order to specify the molecular structure. For molecules with larger numbers of atoms, three-dimensional shapes must be considered. While water, for example, has two hydrogen atoms attached at an angle of 104.5° to a central oxygen atom, hydrogen peroxide (H_2O_2) has two hydrogen and two oxygen atoms joined in a structure known to have the shape:

Structural possibilities with water

```
        H
       /
    O—O
   /
  H
```

Historical background of structural concepts. Early in the 19th century an English chemist, John Dalton, proposed his atomic theory, and the precise distinction between atoms and molecules was first drawn in 1811 by Amedeo Avogadro. It was not until 1858, however, that his countryman Stanislao Cannizzaro showed that all physical and chemical facts confirmed the validity of Avogadro's conclusions and that the distinction reconciled many contradictory experimental results accumulated since the beginning of chemistry as a science. It was then recognized that molecules can possess three-dimensional shapes formed by connected (bonded) atoms. The contributions of another generation of chemists and a great deal of controversy were required, however, to ready the problem of molecular structure for solution, but the final steps in discarding the earlier, flat-molecule theory were taken by chemists Jacobus Henricus van't Hoff of The Netherlands and Joseph-Achille Le Bel of France. Van't Hoff's ideas, summarized in his book *Chemistry in Space,* were ferociously attacked by one of the leading chemists of the day. Thanks to this controversy the idea of geometrical relations within molecules became widely known and accepted.

During the same period, the concept that matter is in continual motion (kinetic-molecular theory) prevailed over the concept that matter is in a state of static equilibrium. Thus, the geometrical relationships of atoms within molecules cannot be considered as fixed. In addition to the movements of the molecules themselves through the gases and liquids that they constitute (translation), the various parts of the molecular structure itself are in continuous motion. This internal motion may take the form of vibrations in which atoms and groups of atoms move back and forth, increasing and decreasing the distances between them (stretching) and opening and closing the angles made by their bonds (bending). In complex molecules, groups may rotate about portions of the structure. These motions are fast and frequent, typical vibrations taking place on a time scale of 10,000,000,000,000 (10^{13}) per second; rotations are somewhat slower (typically 100,000,000,000 [10^{11}] per second). Because of this flexibility, molecular dimensions are taken as time-averaged values of the positions of the atoms. At higher temperatures, the atoms take longer and more violent excursions from their equilibrium positions, and new patterns of motion sometimes become possible. Molecular structure thus depends upon temperature.

Internal motions of atoms

In addition, the exact dimensions of molecules vary according to the situation in which they are studied. Thus, somewhat different measurements are obtained for molecules in the three phases, solid, liquid, and gas, or dissolved in solution or adsorbed on a surface. Drastic changes from the normal form have been found in determining structures of molecules carrying excess charges (called ions or radicals) and those possessing excess energy (excited-state species).

Structural theories. *Quantum mechanical approach.* No truly adequate theory of molecular structure is yet available. The detailed structure of complex molecules cannot be predicted but must be obtained from experiment. Recent studies, however, have been specifically directed toward the development of theories that could yield structural information.

One approach is through quantum mechanics (see MECHANICS: *Quantum mechanics*), in which an orbiting electron is considered to have the characteristics of a wave; treating the electron standing waves (atomic orbitals) mathematically allows determination of how pairs and groups of atoms come together to form joint orbitals (bonds). Such an approach relies on data from experiment in conjunction with approximate mathematical methods utilizing high-speed computers, but only the simplest systems can be calculated exactly. To achieve a strong bond, the electron orbitals of the atoms involved must overlap in space as much as possible (see below *Chemical bonding*); and since atomic orbitals are themselves directed in space, the resulting bonds must conform to their arrangements. The quantum-mechanical approach leads to correct predictions concerning the shape of only simple molecules; for example, the bent shape of the water molecule.

Electrostatic approach. An alternative approach is to consider the molecule as a system in electrostatic balance—the attraction between electrons and their nuclei (because they have opposite charges) tending to be maximum and the repulsion between electrons (because they carry the same charge) tending to be minimum. The attraction between each nucleus and the electrons of an adjacent nucleus is also of primary importance in bonding atoms. In this view, the most likely shape of the molecule will be the one that best meets these electrostatic requirements. Those pairs of electrons farthest from the nucleus of a central atom of a group are considered to be important in determining the molecular structure of the group. To minimize the repulsion between centres of negative charges, the system adopts the most balanced arrangement possible; when there is more than one pair, each takes up a position as far as possible from the others, while remaining as close as possible to the nucleus. Two electron pairs thus place themselves on opposite sides of the nucleus to give a linear (180°) relationship; three pairs lead to a trigonal planar arrangement, with bond angles of 120°; four to a tetrahedral arrangement, with angles of 109°28′; six to an octahedron, with 90° angles; etc. The electron pairs can be either shared with a second atom (bonding) or lone pairs (nonbonded). Shared pairs are drawn out between two positive centres and lie farther from other pairs of electrons on the same atom, and their repulsive effect is thus somewhat reduced. Unshared pairs,

Shared and unshared pairs

on the other hand, are under the influence of only one positive centre and, because of their proximity, create the severest repulsions. The relative repulsive power is thus, in descending order, lone pair–lone pair, lone pair–bonding pair, bonding pair–bonding pair; this is also the order in which distortion (opening) of bonding angles has been found experimentally for molecules taking the regular geometric shapes listed above.

No perfectly regular solid figures exist with five or seven points (or vertices); the electron pairs are, however, well separated in the semiregular trigonal and pentagonal bipyramidal shapes, and there are many molecules of those kinds.

The structure adopted by a molecule must also meet the spatial requirements of its constituent atoms and groups of atoms. The exact dimensions of atoms are not known, but the volumes occupied by given numbers of atoms are largely incompressible. No amount of force generated in one part of a structure can bring about interpenetration of atomic volumes in another. These spatial requirements are a controlling factor in molecular geometry.

CHEMICAL BONDS AND MOLECULAR SHAPES

The basic laws of chemistry give the number of attachments, usually variable, that each atom is capable of making with other atoms. The restriction against atoms occupying the same volume guides their packing together to fill space. Distances and angles between atoms are adjusted to maximize attractive (bonding) interactions and to minimize electrostatic repulsions. On these principles a bewildering variety of molecular shapes and sizes are constructed. The range of structural possibilities is difficult to comprehend and impossible to represent adequately on the printed page, first because most molecules have three-dimensional shapes and, second, because all are in rapid, dynamic motion. Static, two-dimensional figures in which atomic symbols are placed at equilibrium positions in the structure are nevertheless the most useful way of representing molecular structures.

Organic compounds

Chains. The chemistry of carbon, the archetypal participant in shared-electron-pair (covalent) bonds, is the basis of organic chemistry. Carbon and hydrogen together form a fantastic number of compounds; those containing only the two elements are called hydrocarbons. These have derivatives that contain other elements as well. All are called organic compounds, because it was thought at one time they could be made only by living organisms. The simplest hydrocarbon is methane, with the formula CH_4, in which carbon directs four equivalent bonds toward the vertices of a tetrahedron, so that methane can be represented structurally as:

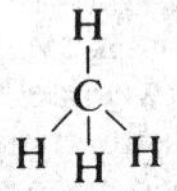

```
    H
    |
    C
   /|\
  H H H
```

Ethane, with an empirical formula of C_2H_6, can be considered to be constructed by replacing one of the hydrogen atoms of methane by a CH_3 group, thus

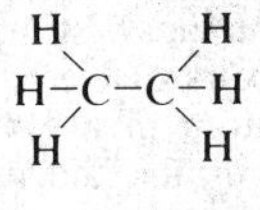

```
 H     H
  \   /
H-C-C-H
  /   \
 H     H
```

This arrangement can also be written without showing the hydrogens:

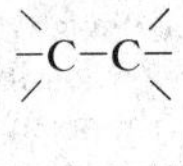

```
 \   /
 -C-C-
 /   \
```

Repeating the same operation and replacing a hydrogen atom of ethane by another CH_3 group leads to propane, C_3H_8:

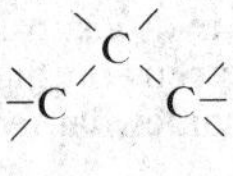

```
    \ /
     C
   /   \
 -C     C-
 /       \
```

A hydrogen atom on a terminal, or end, carbon can again be replaced with a CH_3 group, to produce butane, C_4H_{10}:

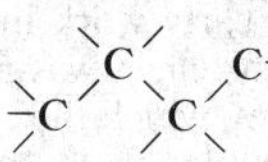

```
   \ /   \ /
    C     C-
   / \   /
 -C    C
 /    / \
```

from which the same process produces pentane, C_5H_{12}:

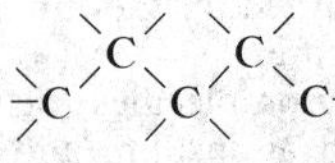

```
   \ /   \ /
    C     C
   / \   / \
 -C    C     C-
 /    / \     \
```

etc. This series of hydrocarbon compounds in which the carbon atoms always form a straight chain can be extended indefinitely. In actuality, the light, shorter chain hydrocarbons are derived from natural gas, which is a mixture of straight-chain hydrocarbons having one to four carbon atoms (in abbreviated form, C_1 to C_4); bottled fuel gas is usually C_3 or C_4; gasoline is C_6–C_{10}, kerosene is C_{10}–C_{18}, and paraffin waxes are greater than C_{20}; and polyethylene consists of chains of as many as 5,000 or more of the same CH_2 units that first occur in propane (see CHEMICAL COMPOUNDS: *Hydrocarbons*).

Rings. Compounds that consist of ring structures of various sizes can be formed by connecting the ends of chains, as in C_3 to C_6 hydrocarbons represented diagrammatically below:

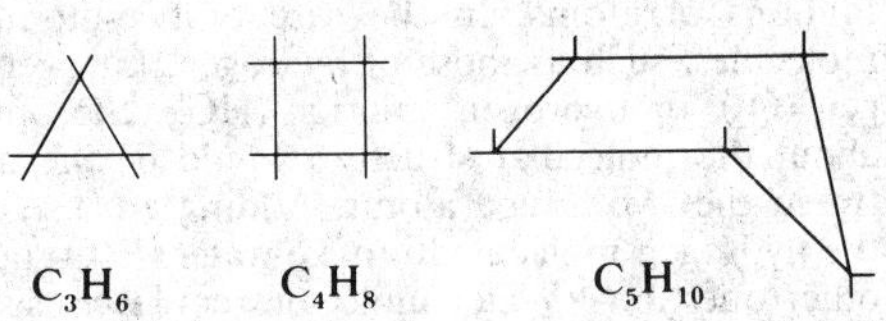

C_3H_6 C_4H_8 C_5H_{10}

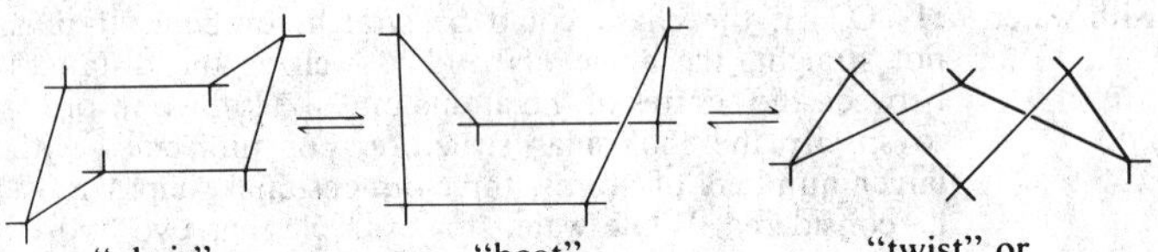

"chair" "boat" "twist" or "skew-boat"

C_6H_{12}

The names of ring compounds are made up of their straight-chain names combined with the prefix cyclo-. Cyclopropane, C_3H_6, is highly reactive, because the interior 60° angles of the three corners bring electrons that are mutually repulsive into close proximity. The cyclobutane (C_4H_8) molecule, with interior angles of 90°, is also easily decomposed. A pentagon has interior angles of 108°, close to the tetrahedral angles of 109°28′, which are the normal bonding angles of carbon, and, therefore, cyclopentane (C_5H_{10}) is quite stable. The puckered form that it adopts minimizes hydrogen contact. It might be thought that, as larger numbers of carbon atoms join rings, the molecules would become less stable again, since the interior angles of the planar figures become larger than 109°28′; for example, 120° in the hexagon. The problem does not arise, however, because of the possibility of reducing the angles by puckering the structure and eliminating a flat configuration. The C_6 cyclohexane molecule (C_6H_{12}) can exist in a "chair," a "boat," or a "twist," or "skew-boat," form, all involving tetrahedral angles at the carbon atoms while minimizing hydrogen-atom repulsions. The molecules flip rapidly from one form to another at room temperature. Stable hydrocarbon rings with more than 30 carbon atoms are known.

Puckered rings

More complex ring types are represented by bicyclobutane and bicyclooctane and the fused-ring systems such as those found in steroids.

Since the mid-20th century, chemists have been synthesizing a spectacular number of hydrocarbons with unusual polyhedral structures. Some examples of these compounds, along with their highly descriptive, non-technical names, are given below:

Silicon and oxygen in minerals

cubane asterane prismane

basketane twistane birdcage

propellanes iceane paddlewheelane

Efforts are under way to add the following:

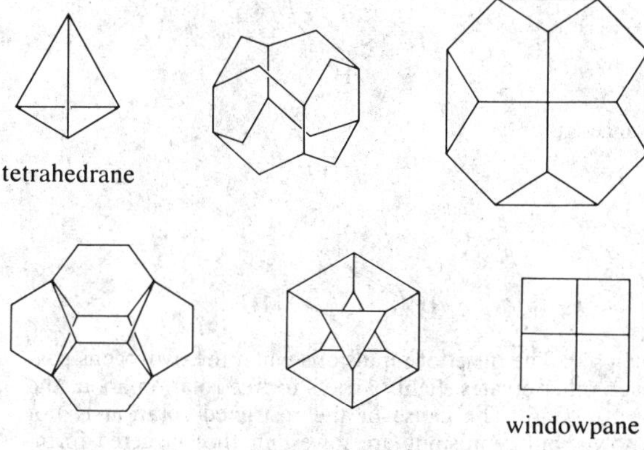

tetrahedrane

windowpane

The idea of what constitutes a molecule has itself been modified by the synthesis of linked rings:

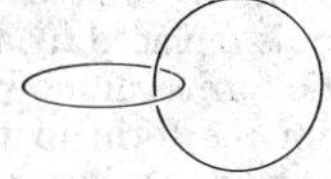

As carbon and hydrogen form the basis of the organic world, so are silicon (Si) and oxygen (O) the basic elements of the mineral world, and the linkages represented by $-\overset{|}{\underset{|}{\mathrm{Si}}}-\mathrm{O}-$ form the backbone of molecular structures.

Small numbers of these individual oxygen–silicon units are found in the soft rocks, such as talc; long chains of them give rise to fibrous minerals such as asbestos; planar sheets form the two-dimensional structure of mica, while quartz contains the same $-\overset{|}{\underset{|}{\mathrm{Si}}}-\mathrm{O}-$ units cross-linked into three-dimensional arrays. Lately, materials have been made that can be viewed as the organic derivatives of these rock forms. For example, CH_3 groups are bonded to silicon atoms, which are linked through oxygen into long chains. These materials, called silicones, combine advantages of the strong oxygen–silicon backbone with the tractable nature of organic compounds.

Chelates. Hydrocarbons can be modified by the substitution of other atoms for carbon. When a carbon atom in a ring is replaced by another kind of atom, the compound is called heterocyclic, and it adopts conformations that accommodate the particular spatial, or steric, requirements of the heteroatom, the noncarbon atom in the ring. Incorporation of heteroatoms and groups into hydrocarbon molecules often confers special properties, including the ability to form additional bonds, typically to a charged metal atom (ion), in what are called coordination compounds. Examples are provided by molecules with two or more heteroatom sites juxtaposed spatially to enable them to attach simultaneously to a single metal ion. Such compounds, called chelates, after the Greek for "crab's claw," can be synthesized in bidentate (two active sites), tridentate, etc., varieties. If the spacing between the heteroatoms is just appropriate to hold a metal ion of a certain size, the chelating action will be selective. The hexadentate compound ethylenediaminetetraacetic acid (EDTA), for example, has its six points of attachment so arranged that it can wrap itself around a lead atom and remove that element from the body in cases of lead poisoning. Other complexing agents of biological importance include heterocycles fused into large, flat rings, leaving a central hole into which the heteroatoms protrude. The porphyrins are such a class, with four nitrogen atoms in a central opening just large enough to fit a metal ion. Hemoglobin and chlorophyll consist of porphyrin rings in which iron and magnesium are held, respectively. Chelating agents have been synthesized that mimic the natural materials but differ from them in potentially important ways.

Heteroatoms

Novel shapes. Other novel molecular shapes are found in compounds in which metal atoms are sandwiched between the planar faces of hydrocarbon rings; for example, ferrocene, $(C_5H_5)_2Fe$, and dibenzenechromium, $(C_6H_6)_2Cr$, in which the ring planes are parallel, and stannocene, $(C_5H_5)_2Sn$, with an angular sandwich structure. These and other synthetic organometallic compounds are the fruits of attempts to break elements out of intractable, inorganic compounds such as salts and oxides or tough metallic forms and to incorporate them into molecules with useful and interesting properties. The operation involves the replacement of the inorganic or metallic lattice bonds with bonds to hydrogen or organic groups. The element boron, for example, forms an icosahedral structure (having 20 faces), and a hydrogen derivative of this structure has been prepared, with the formula $B_{12}H_{12}^{2-}$, along with several smaller borane molecules, which can be viewed as derivatives of icosahedral boron fragments. Carboranes, with formulas such as $B_{10}H_{10}C_2H_2$, have two icosahedral vertices substituted by carbon. In a similar way, there have been syntheses of organic derivatives of a large number of the familiar metals that preserve the clusters of atoms found in the metals themselves.

Polymers. When a simple molecule is bonded to itself or to a few other simple molecules to form long chains, the result is a polymer, or macromolecule. Polymers constitute a special class of molecular structure because of their giant size and because any given sample is always a mixture of molecules of various sizes. It is possible to distinguish one-dimensional, chain, or linear, structures, such as the natural polymers in unvulcanized rubber, silk, and asbestos and the artificial polyethylene and silicone fluids; two-dimensional macrostructures such as those formed by mica and graphite; and three-dimensional structures such as quartz or diamond. In fact, a perfect crystal of diamond (one of the forms of carbon) could be considered to be a single, giant molecule, owing its extraordinary hardness to the four strong electron-pair bonds radiating from each carbon atom to four other carbon atoms. Some of the polyhedral hydrocarbon compounds mentioned above can be considered to be fragments of the diamond structure. The constituent units of a linear polymer may be arranged at random, as was the case of all artificially produced polymers made before 1954, or in some highly ordered manner, as is the case of materials such as natural rubber and the artificial materials produced after the discovery (1954) of a special type of polymerization, called stereospecific.

Spatial structures

Special problems in molecular structure arise with proteins. The basic constituents of proteins are molecules with two different group properties (bifunctional molecules). These properties are provided by two functional groups attached to the molecule, in this case an acid group and a base group, in compounds called α- (alpha-) amino acids. The acid (carboxyl) end of one such molecule can act on the base (amino) end of another to form a molecule of water, which is released, and a bond called the peptide link between the remaining parts of each molecule. Using R— to represent the body of an α-amino acid, the formula is $H_2N{-}CHR{-}COOH$, H_2N being the amino group and COOH the acid group. The reaction between any two amino acids (R_1 and R_2) is:

Protein structures

$$H_2N{-}CHR_1{-}COOH + H_2N{-}CHR_2{-}COOH$$

$$\longrightarrow H_2N{-}CHR_1{-}CONH{-}CHR_2{-}COOH + H_2O.$$

Repeating this process over and over, each time eliminating a molecule of water, produces a polypeptide chain. The various amino acids are distinguished by the nature of the R groups; because 23 amino acids have been recognized as constituents of proteins, the number of different sequences in which they can polymerize is practically unlimited.

The order of the amino acids in the polypeptide chains is called the primary structure, and the first such sequence was determined in 1952 by an English chemist, Frederick Sanger, for the protein insulin. The regular way in which the polypeptide chains are arranged in space to form a protein molecule is called the secondary structure. The principal type is called the alpha helix. The polypeptide chain can be folded into the spiral form with about four amino acid units per turn. Many fibrous proteins, including hair and muscle, consist of these polypeptide helices twisted about one another to form cables. In 1960 investigation of the protein myoglobin revealed that its single polypeptide chain coils into eight short, helical segments separated by nonhelical sections. This arrangement of the three-dimensional structures is the tertiary structure, while the combination of two or more polypeptide chains constitutes the quaternary structure.

Possibilities for variety in molecular structure are expanded by the freedom to arrange the same group of atoms in more than one way to form different structures, a phenomenon called isomerism. The properties of a compound are determined not only by its chemical composition but also by the arrangement of its constituent atoms in space. Two substances are isomers if they have identical chemical composition and molecular weight but differ in molecular structure (see below *Isomerism*).

TIME-DEPENDENT PROPERTIES

Motions preserving molecular integrity. The rather static world of experience is, at the molecular level, only the blur of ceaseless, dynamic motion. Gas molecules in a room atmosphere have speeds of 10^4–10^5 centimetres per second (200–2,000 miles per hour) and collide with each other about 10^{10} times per second. Since a typical frequency of rotation is 10^{11} times per second, such a molecule completes 10 rotations between collisions. Molecular bonds typically vibrate with a frequency of about 10^{13} per second, and, therefore, bonds vibrate about 100 times during each molecular rotation and about 1,000 times between collisions in the gases in a room atmosphere.

Molecular motion in liquids

Molecular motion in the liquid phase is more difficult. Translation is impeded because the molecules are tightly packed. Even rotations will be relatively rare unless the molecules are almost spherical or are nearly cylindrical about one axis. Rotations tend to be transformed into oscillations or twisting motions and the translations into a rapid back and forth bouncing off nearest neighbours. The frequency of collision is great, about 10^{12} per second, because the molecules are so close; the bond vibration frequencies, however, will still be higher by almost tenfold.

Translation ceases on solidification; molecules oscillate and, where space permits, rotate about fixed equilibrium positions.

Flexibility is, then, a chief characteristic of molecules, and it is restrained only by powerful forces. The various types of molecular motions that contribute to this flexibility are summarized below.

Vibration. A diatomic (of two atoms) molecule can vibrate in only one way. This vibration consists of an in-phase motion of the two atoms toward and away from their centre of mass along the internuclear axis (comparable to the motions of a pair of weights connected by a spring). By in-phase is meant that the atoms pass through their mean positions and reach their turning points simultaneously. Such vibrations along bond axes are called stretching motions. The amplitude of such motion is typically about 10 percent of the bond length.

A bent, triatomic (of three atoms) molecule, such as water, HOH, can execute three fundamental modes of motion: a concerted compression and stretching of the two O—H bonds: an asymmetrical motion by which one O—H stretches while the other compresses; and a bending motion in which the H/O\H angle opens and closes. If such a triatomic unit is held by its centre atom in a more complex system, this last scissoring motion will be accompanied by twisting, wagging, and rocking torsions. Planar (in one plane) molecules undergo out-of-plane deformations of terminal atoms; cyclic molecules undergo simultaneous stretching apart of the ring atoms (called breathing). Bending requires less energy than stretching.

Rotation. Detailed consideration of the rotational motions of groups within molecules led in 1937 to the recognition of several new possibilities. Viewing the ethane molecule, C_2H_6, for example, down its central C—C axis, reveals two extreme positions for the hydrogen atoms:

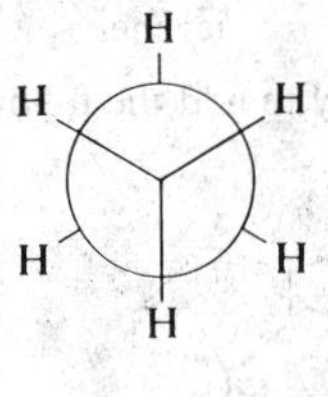

staggered, and

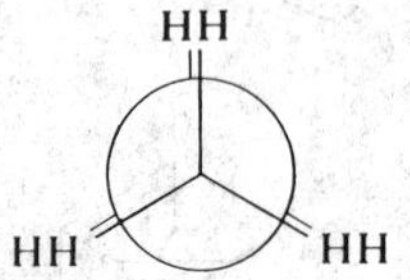

eclipsed. The onset of repulsions when the hydrogens pass each other creates slight barriers to free rotation about the C—C bond. The cause of the restricted rotation is not known, but repulsions are lowest in the staggered form. Rotation from one staggered form (called rotamer) to another is very rapid at room temperature.

Rotamers

The barrier to free rotation is raised when one hydrogen on each ethane carbon is replaced by a CH_3 group to give *n*-butane. Six rotameric forms can now be drawn, with the barrier decreasing from the form in which the two CH_3 groups are eclipsed to the most favourable staggered form with the two groups farthest apart. In the structural forms below, rotamers (ii) and (iii) and (iv) and (v) constitute enantiomorphic pairs:

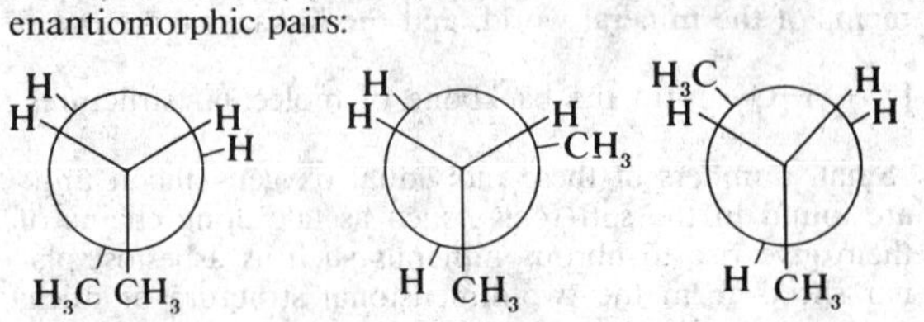

(i) (ii) (iii)
eclipsed

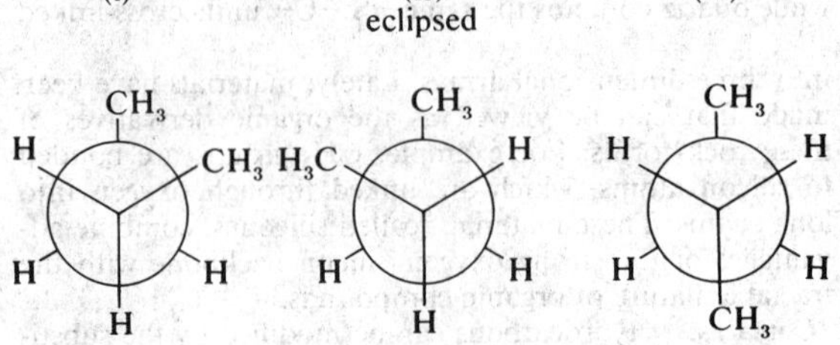

(iv) (v) (vi)
staggered

Rotation at room temperature is too rapid to permit isolation of the individual rotamers.

Another form of motion, called pseudorotation, was postulated in 1960 to explain the rapid interchange of the positions of atoms in trigonal bipyramidal molecules. A similar twisting of CH_2 units is now thought to be responsible for the easy interconversion of conformation in cyclic hydrocarbons; *e.g.,* in cyclohexane (see above). Such pseudorotations have very low energy requirements and take place easily and rapidly at room temperature. The individual conformers of cyclohexane (boat, chair, and twist, or skew-boat) cannot be isolated.

Inversion. Ammonia, NH_3, and its substituted derivatives, called amines, are pyramidal molecules. If the three groups attached to nitrogen are different, two forms with nonsuperimposable mirror images should exist. No such optical isomer has ever been isolated, however, because pyramidal molecules of this type undergo a rapid motion by which the pyramid becomes inverted. In this vibration the nitrogen atom oscillates through the plane of the three attached groups, much as an umbrella can turn inside out. The inversion frequency of ammonia is over 10^{10} times per second. Substitution of bulky groups for hydrogen slows the inversion rate somewhat.

Fluxional molecules. Several organometallic molecules are now known in which a metal atom rapidly changes its point of attachment from one to another of the carbon atoms of a hydrocarbon ring or chain. In the first recognized example, mercury (Hg) in $(C_5H_5)_2Hg$ was shown in 1954 to exchange its bonding position about the five carbons of the C_5H_5 ring. The bromine–magnesium (BrMg) unit in $CH_2{=}CHCH_2MgBr$ appears bonded to one, then another of the terminal carbon atoms. Such nonrigid structures have been described as "ring whizzers" or "chain swingers" or, more simply, as fluxional.

Nonrigid structures

Despite the possibility of more complex flexible torsions, some types of which can occur simultaneously, molecular vibrations involving each bond and group of bonds are always in progress. Each of the motions described above occurs with a characteristic frequency, energy, and rate.

Motion in which molecular integrity is disrupted. *Dissociation.* Stretching movements of sufficient energy will disrupt the bond between two vibrating atoms, with several possible results, depending upon the final disposition of the electrons in the broken bond.

In heterolytic fission (breaking into differing parts) of a bond, both electrons remain with one fragment, making it an ion with one excess negative charge, while the other fragment, lacking an electron, becomes an ion with one positive charge. In water, hydrogen is a typical positive ion (H+); molecules releasing H+ are called acids. Hydroxide ion (OH−) is a typical negative ion in water; molecules releasing OH− are called bases. In water these ion products of heterolytic fission are separated and stabilized by oppositely charged centres in the medium, the ionic molecules, like other charged particles, obeying the physical law of being attracted by opposite and repelled by similar charge.

Homolytic fission (separation into two neutral atoms or groups) of bonds leaves each fragment with a balance of charges, but each possesses an odd number of electrons. Such fragments, called radicals, are usually reactive since they can readily form new electron pair bonds with other odd-electron species. Homolytic fission of bonds occurs when molecules are subjected to heat or radiation.

Addition or coordination compounds are made up of constituent molecules that can exist independently and that return to their independent state upon dissociation of the complex. One example is the complex formed reversibly with oxygen by hemoglobin, which transports oxygen through the bloodstream. Dissociation of the complex in the tissues releases oxygen molecules for oxidation of foodstuffs and frees hemoglobin for return to the lungs and repetition of the cycle.

Exchange reactions. Change in position among easily displaced atoms or groups in gases and liquids is common and can be assumed to take place at some rate among most linkages. Readily changed hydrogen linkages represent an extreme case; the exchange of hydrogen between H_2O molecules in liquid water is particularly fast.

Interconversion of isomers. The pure substance acetaldehyde (C_2H_4O) furnishes an example of tautomerism, a condition in which isomers change into each other easily and ordinarily exist together in equilibrium. It has the chemical and physical properties expected for a mixture of two different structures, one with a carbon–carbon double bond ($>C=C<$) and an oxygen–hydrogen (OH) group and the other with a carbon–carbon single bond (—C—C—) and a carbon–oxygen ($>C=O$) double bond. The two isomers undergo rapid interconversion within the molecule through exchange of hydrogen between carbon and oxygen in the structure to give the keto ($CH_3{-}CH{=}O$) and enol ($CH_2{=}CH{-}OH$) forms. These changes take place too rapidly to permit separation from the mixture under ordinary conditions.

Isomerization. In many cases the interconversion of isomers is so easy that the individual isomers cannot be isolated. Optical isomers capable of fast, reversible transformation into a symmetric arrangement, for example, will always exist as an equal mixture of dextrorotatory and levorotatory forms; *e.g.,* the enantiomorphic rotamers of *n*-butane. Tautomeric exchange of hydrogen is within the molecule and fast. Just as fast is the migration of metal atoms in the constantly changing fluxional molecules. At the other extreme lie hydrocarbon and oxygen-silicon isomers, which are stable because the rupture of several strong, inert bonds is necessary to rearrange the structure; for example, mirror image (enantiomorphic) crystals of quartz have retained their identity for eons. Between the two extremes are many molecular rearrangements of stable substances that can be brought about under mild conditions by heat or chemicals.

MOLECULAR STRUCTURE AND GENERAL PROPERTIES OF MATTER

The bulk materials of experience are made up of tremendous numbers of atoms or molecules, and the macroscopic properties of materials can usually be generalized from the properties of the constituent units. Behaviour of molecular materials can be understood through knowledge of molecular structure and intermolecular forces. In this way, the nature of known materials is learned and possibilities for new materials are realized.

Physical properties. Those characteristics of molecules generally classified as physical are due to molecular size and shape, forces between molecules, and their interaction with electromagnetic radiation and fields.

Size and shape effects. A collection of molecules fits into a regular crystalline arrangement according to the same rules of geometry as the packing of large objects. Molecular crystalline arrangements conform to various shapes known in solid geometry. Bulk crystalline form can also reflect the shape of the molecules making up the crystal, as demonstrated by Pasteur's identification of right- and left-handed crystal shapes composed of enantiomorphic molecules, solutions of which rotate the plane of polarized light in opposite directions. Long-chain molecules often form fibrous crystals, and sheetlike molecules form layer lattices. Other bulk properties are similarly related to molecular characteristics. Rubber, for example, is an aggregate of very long molecules intertwined in a random way. Unvulcanized rubber is sticky because the molecules tend to pull away from each other. Vulcanized rubber has been heated with sulfur, which forms bridges of sulfur-atom chains linking the rubber molecules together; small amounts of sulfur (few cross-links) lead to soft rubber, larger amounts of sulfur to much harder materials. Rubber's elasticity arises from the reversible stretching of the randomly twisted and coiled molecules, under stress, into a more ordered, chainlike arrangement.

Structure of rubber

Size and shape are important in other respects; for example, in diffusion of molecules through channels in rigid mineral forms or in nonrigid, biological membranes. Only a single dimension may be critical, as in the case of a rodlike molecule passing through an orifice or of a long-chain structure passing through a membrane channel that its branched isomer cannot penetrate.

Intermolecular forces determine whether a substance will be found in gas, liquid, or solid phase. Strong attractive forces result in solidification, even for the lightweight lithium hydride, while weak attractive forces between the much heavier radon atoms are easily disrupted, and radon exists as a gas at room temperature. When intermolecular forces are relatively constant through a series of molecules, their size and shape can determine the phase. The saturated hydrocarbons are an example: methane, CH_4, is a gas; isooctane, C_8H_{18}, is a liquid; and triacontane, $C_{30}H_{62}$, is a waxy solid. Shape is also important. The chain molecule decane, $C_{10}H_{22}$, is a liquid at room temperature, but the flat, fused-ring naphthalene, $C_{10}H_8$, of similar mass, packs efficiently into a crystal and is solid under the same conditions. Attaching one carbon–hydrogen group (CH_3) to naphthalene can disrupt the layer packing and make the methyl derivative a liquid at room temperature.

Intermolecular forces. At very short distances, all atoms and molecules attract each other. In the absence of other more powerful forces, weak attractions account for liquefaction and, as temperature is lowered, eventual solidification. At the other extreme are the powerful forces of electrical attraction between oppositely charged ions. Crystalline lattices are typical of ionic aggregates. Between the two extremes are electrically neutral molecules with, nevertheless, concentrations of negative charge in one part of the molecule and of positive charge in another; such molecules are electric dipoles (just as bar magnets are magnetic dipoles) and are called polar, as compared with nonpolar molecules, in which the charges are evenly distributed. The oppositely polarized ends of two molecules will attract one another. Molecules consisting of two atoms of the same element, $A-A$, are nonpolar. On the other hand, all heteronuclear (containing different kinds of atoms) diatomic molecules, $A-B$, are polar, since the electrons joining A and B will inevitably lie closer to one atom or the other, thereby distorting the electrical balance of the system. The presence of the electric dipole can be experimentally verified, since in an electric field the molecules, like the magnets, will align themselves with the electron-rich end toward the positive pole. The extent of the imbalance, called the dipole moment, is a vector quantity (*i.e.*, it has both magnitude and direction), and vector addition can be used to relate the measured dipole moment of a complex molecule to the individual contributions of the bonds that make it up. Linear $A-B-A$ molecules made up of polar bonds between oxygen and carbon, $O{=}C{=}O$, for example, have no net polarity because the two equal and oppositely directed dipolar $C=O$ vectors cancel each other. The polarity of the water molecule, on the other hand, was used by a Dutch scientist, Peter Debye, to show that the $H-O-H$ system is bent, since only in that shape could the two dipolar $O-H$ vectors add to give a net dipole moment for the molecule.

Polar molecules

The electron-rich ends of polar molecules attract the electron-poor ends of their neighbours. This attraction, while much weaker than the force between charged ions, imparts important properties to polar water molecules. The dipole vectors in the water (H_2O) molecule produce an attraction called hydrogen bonding in liquid water and ice. These intermolecular hydrogen bonds are only 5 to 10 percent of the strength of the covalent $O-H$ bonds in the water molecules themselves but account for most of water's unique properties, including its liquid state under mild terrestrial conditions, while the combination of hydrogen with the 20 elements most resembling oxygen are all gases under the same conditions, despite the much greater mass of most of them. In freezing, water expands into a structure that permits the most effective hydrogen bonding of its molecules, and as a consequence ice is less dense than liquid water and floats on its surface. Water is one of the very few materials known in which the solid form does not sink in the liquid. The electron-rich end of the water molecule is drawn even more strongly to positively charged ions than is the opposite end to negative ions. Water is thus an excellent solvent for compounds, such as salts, which give ions, as well as for other polar molecules such as alcohol or sugar. Nonpolar molecules, such as those found in oils, do not mix with water. In general, "like dissolves like" as far as molecular polarity is concerned, but oil and water can be made to mix in the presence of soaps or detergents, the molecules of which are constructed with highly polar, water-soluble groups to which are attached long oil-soluble hydrocarbon chains. Washing action combines the two unlike types of materials into an emulsified mixture with the soap molecules.

Soap structure

Resonance with radiation. Each of the different types of molecular flexibility considered under time-dependent phenomena has a characteristic rhythm of oscillation or frequency. That molecules can oscillate only with certain allowed frequencies is the result of quantum-mechanical laws that govern the behaviour of minute particles. Similarly, molecules can absorb energy only in certain characteristic amounts. The absorption can stimulate more rapid rotations or vibrations or excite bonding electrons to higher energies. Radiation is described by frequencies or energies characteristic of its position in the electromagnetic spectrum (listing of the wavelengths and frequencies of electromagnetic radiation).

Molecular spectroscopy is based upon the absorption of electromagnetic radiation by molecules. Just as dishes in a cupboard can be made to rattle when certain notes are sung, particular types of motions in certain regions of a molecule will resonate with radiation of selected frequencies or energies. In order of decreasing energy, electronic excitation is generated by ultraviolet or visible light, molecular vibrations by infrared radiation, and rotations by far-infrared and microwave radiation.

Chemical properties. In general, the overall chemical behaviour of molecules is determined by the nature of the chemical bonds and the atoms they join. Subtle changes can arise in more complex systems, however, from the way certain portions of the structure are positioned. Reaction rates and whether a given reaction will take place at all are often governed by these spatial, or steric, factors. Chemical reactions in living organisms are almost always controlled by detailed molecular structure. This is evident in the requirement for particular isomers, such as for left-handed amino acids in food, versus the right-handed structure, which cannot be digested. Chemical processes in biology are apparently governed by the ability of sometimes highly complex molecular aggregates to fit together in space. The double helix structure of deoxyribonucleic acid, DNA, is an example: the cylindrical form brings complementary portions of the two strands together in a hydrogen-bonding interaction between matched base groups. For the interwound strands to be held together by hydrogen bonding, the sequence of the bases on the two strands must be complementary; this sequence is the information used in constructing new strands. The order on one of the strands is used alone in the production of a slightly different polymer, similar to DNA, called ribonucleic acid, RNA, which serves as the pattern upon which amino acids are brought together and incorporated into new linear protein polymers. Viruses carry RNA units, which invade cells and cause destructive changes in their functioning. Changes in the order of the units in DNA, which can be brought about by radiation with enough energy to disrupt chemical bonds or by other molecular agents (mutagens), produce mutations. Biochemists have synthesized a number of biologically active materials in the laboratory, including an exact copy of the DNA in a virus and a yeast gene (an element that transmits hereditary characters).

Structure of DNA

Through investigations into the genetic materials of creatures lower on the evolutionary ladder, the molecular background of human life is revealed. Work continues on correcting hereditary defects, by supplying missing genes, and even of designing DNA and RNA molecules that could lead to forms of life that are not now known.

STRUCTURE DETERMINATION

Information about molecular structure, once limited to inferences derived from gross physical properties and chemical reactions of compounds, has been greatly expanded through the techniques of spectroscopy and diffraction. Some of these techniques are now used routinely by the

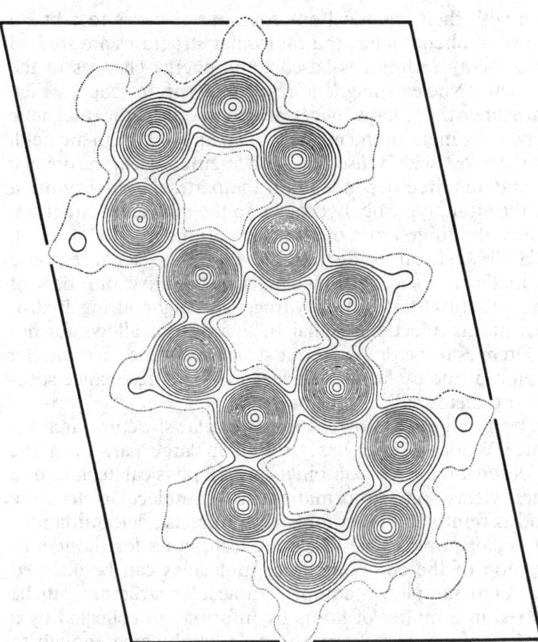

Figure 1: Electron-density map of anthracene, $C_{14}H_{10}$, drawn from X-ray-diffraction data. Contour lines are drawn at density intervals of one-half of an electron per angstrom (see text).

From E. Braude and F. Nachod (eds.), *Determination of Organic Structures by Physical Methods* (1955); Academic Press

practicing chemist and can give, within minutes, data from which the nature of molecular structure can be inferred. Other techniques, especially diffraction, are capable of determining the dimensions of molecules, but long periods of time are required to collect the data and laborious computations to interpret it. Such methods are used by a relatively few expert chemists.

Precise methods. *Microwave spectroscopy.* Rotational characteristics can, in principle, provide information about molecular dimensions, since the frequency of a body's rotation is governed by its moment of inertia (its tendency to continue in motion), which in turn depends upon the masses and the distances between them. With knowledge of the precise masses of atoms, precise distances can be calculated from rotational data. In practice, the microwave technique (a microwave is electromagnetic radiation of between one and 100 centimetres in wavelength) has been limited to relatively simple polar molecules in the gas phase. It has shown, for example, that the two hydrogen atoms in the water molecule are about one angstrom (10^{-10} metre) from the oxygen atom and that the angle formed by the three atoms is 104.5°.

Electron diffraction. Electron beams passing through a sample of molecules are diffracted (scattered). Such radiation cannot penetrate deeply into matter, but the pattern of diffraction of electrons by gaseous samples can be used to obtain molecular dimensions. Molecules of a gas are relatively far apart and so no intermolecular diffraction effects occur; instead, it is the relative dispositions of the atoms in space within each molecule that determine the diffraction pattern. In using this method a molecular structure is assumed, the intensities of the diffracted beams that it would cause are calculated, and the observed values are compared with those predicted to determine the validity of the assumed model. In practice, the technique is used for fairly simple, somewhat symmetrical, gaseous molecules, but different structural arrangements cannot always be distinguished. Electron-diffraction patterns of small molecular fragments boiled off the surfaces of refractory salt crystals, such as sodium chloride (NaCl), have been studied at high temperatures.

X-ray and neutron-beam diffraction. X-rays are scattered far less than electrons and can penetrate deep into crystalline solids. Each atom of the regular arrangement within a crystal can diffract X-rays, and the manner of diffraction within molecular crystals depends upon the shape and size of the molecules and on their positions and orientation in the crystal. The X-ray diffraction patterns are compared with prior calculations based on plausible assumptions, in a trial and error process ideally suited to a computer. This technique has been developed into the most effective method available for the determination of detailed molecular structure. Because hydrogen atoms have far less scattering power than heavier atoms, the positions of hydrogen atoms in complex molecules usually cannot be obtained from X-ray data. Neutrons, on the other hand, are scattered by all atoms to a similar extent, and therefore the positions of hydrogen atoms can be readily established, even when very much larger atoms are present. To obtain neutron beams of the necessary intensity, however, requires a nuclear reactor, and neutron-diffraction studies can be carried out only in few laboratories. X-ray diffraction requires only that the molecules be in a crystalline, not glassy, solid. Liquids and gases can be studied as crystals at low temperatures.

Limitations of X-ray diffraction

Many techniques have been devised to reduce the labour of calculating structures from diffraction data. Structures of simple molecules, once requiring months of computation, can be solved with great accuracy in a matter of days, using computers. An example is the electron-density-distribution map of the molecule anthracene, $C_{14}H_{10}$, from X-ray data, which verified the chemist's intuitive concept represented in its structural formula

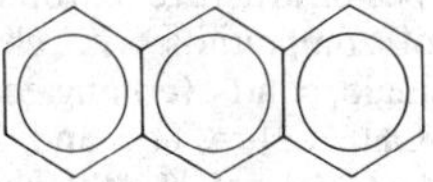

(see Figure 1). The structure of DNA, proposed in 1953 from X-ray data, was a breakthrough toward understanding the fundamental chemistry of life (see Figure 2).

From J. Robertson, *X-ray Diffraction*, vol.1, (1955); Academic Press

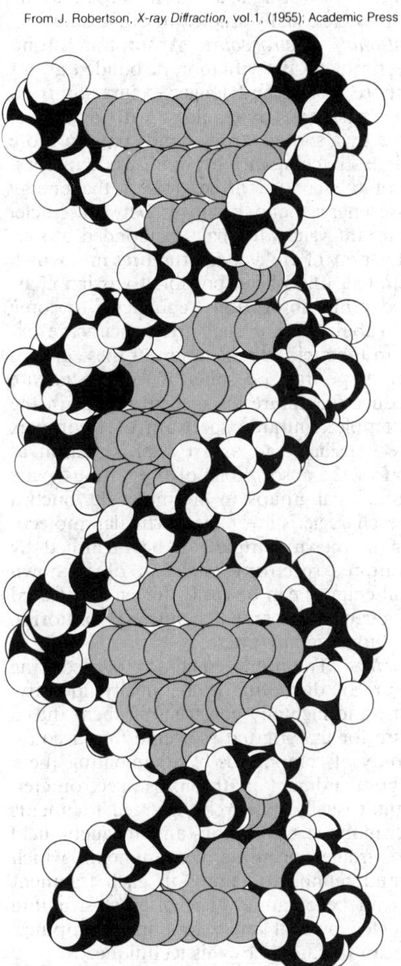

Figure 2: Schematic drawing of DNA double helix molecule.

Inferential methods. In recent years there has been rapid growth in experimental methods based on some physically measurable property that varies according to molecular structure. This category includes spectroscopic techniques, in which a beam of radiant energy is dispersed by a sample and its component waves are then arranged in order of their wavelengths; these techniques are commonly used to give information that can be related to molecular structure. In most cases it is not possible to make theoretical predictions about the relationship between molecular structures and the measured property from established principles. The practicing chemist, therefore, relies upon assumed similarities to measurements on compounds of known structure. The information thus obtained for the solution of new problems is inevitably circumstantial; a choice must often be made between a number of apparently reasonable interpretations. In this respect, especially, additional data from other physical methods can be of great value.

Ultraviolet and visible (electronic) spectroscopy. Stable compounds of low molecular weight are electronically excited only by radiation in the higher energy ultraviolet region of the spectrum; and water, carbon dioxide, ethyl alcohol, and other compounds of low weight are thus colourless. Colour in a compound indicates the presence of easily excited electrons, and certain functional groups or types of structure (chromophores) provide colour. In series of compounds with chains of alternating double and single bonds (conjugated), such as 1,3-butadiene, $H_2C{=}CH{-}CH{=}CH_2$, and 1,3,5-hexatriene, $CH_2{=}CH{-}CH{=}CH{-}CH{=}CH_2$, the absorption of radiation, corresponding to electronic excitation, progressively falls in required radiant energy through the ultraviolet into the visible region, with the compound with eight double bonds showing colour. Double bonds isolated in a molecular structure can thus be distinguished from those that are conjugated. Samples are usually studied in dilute solution.

Significance of colour in compounds

Infrared (vibrational) spectroscopy. Absorption of infrared radiation stimulates the vibration of bonded atoms and groups to more violent and longer excursions from their equilibrium positions. By analogy with a pair of weights connected by a spring, strong bonds require more energy to stimulate stretching and bending, while increasing the masses of the bonded atoms lowers the energy required. Because energies and distances between nuclei are relatively constant values for pairs of bonded atoms, despite the great variety of molecular structures into which they are incorporated, it has been possible to assign characteristic infrared group-absorption frequencies to some pairs of atoms. Tabulations of such frequencies are exceedingly useful in the rapid identification of these groups from their infrared spectra, and shifts of frequencies are often used to deduce the nature of adjacent groups in the molecule. The complete infrared spectrum of a complex molecule can be considered to a first approximation as the superposition of the absorptions of the various pairs of atoms and functional groups in the molecule. Such a spectrum will be characteristic of the particular molecular structure; an unknown sample can be identified by comparing its infrared spectrum with that of a known compound. Small changes can be easily detected. Infrared spectroscopy is in general use in all chemical laboratories. Samples can be studied in any phase.

Mass spectrometry. Traditional methods of deducing molecular structure by disrupting it chemically, identifying the fragments, and mentally constructing them into a plausible structure for the original molecule find a counterpart in the study of compounds by fragmenting them under electron bombardment in the mass spectrometer. The masses of the (usually positively) charged fragments so produced are analyzed by electric- and magnetic-field separation, and extremely accurate measurements, which allow the type and number of atoms in each fragment to be specified, can be obtained. The original structure can be reconstructed by trial and error, on a computer. Minute samples can be studied by this technique.

Nuclear magnetic resonance. Except for mass and electric charge, nuclear properties were once of little interest to the chemist. Today it is known that interactions of nuclei with their chemical environment give rise to a broad range of phenomena, and molecular structures are studied with many techniques based upon energy changes in the nucleus. Nuclear-magnetic-resonance spectroscopy, which measures the energy necessary to reorient the magnetic dipole moment of the nucleus in an applied magnetic field, is the most widely used of such methods. The resonance energy required depends upon the particular environment of the atom, typically hydrogen, in the molecular structure. Thus, the three types of hydrogen atoms in ethyl alcohol, CH_3CH_2OH, can be distinguished, and the signal response is in the ratio 3:2:1, which tells the relative numbers of the structurally distinct hydrogens. Neighbouring hydrogen atoms affect the signal in a way that allows further inferences to be drawn about structure in the surrounding region of the molecule. Nuclear magnetic resonance spectra are measured in solution.

The prodigious progress in molecular-structure analysis since World War II has resulted in large part from the widespread use of combinations of physical techniques; each yields some information about molecular structure and is reinforced by complete and precise determinations of key examples. The foregoing techniques for the identification of the components of molecules can be adapted to micro samples; a complex molecular structure can be solved in a matter of hours by information collected by a battery of methods from a sample barely large enough to see.

In the middle of the 19th century, the gifted British physicist James Clerk Maxwell wrote:

> A molecule is the smallest possible portion of a particular substance. No one has ever seen or handled a single molecule. Molecular science, therefore, is one of those branches of study which deal with things invisible and imperceptible by our senses, and which cannot be subjected to direct experiment.

The basic concepts have not changed. What has changed is that increasingly indirect physical effects have been found to be understandable in terms of molecular structure. The insights obtained from the application of these experimental techniques to problems of molecular structure have provided the major stimulus to mid-20th-century chemistry as a science and are beginning to have similar effect in the world of biology.

(F.C.N./J.J.Z.)

Isomerism

The laws of chemical bonding sometimes permit a given set of atoms to be combined in more than one way, so that two or more substances may exist that have identical chemical composition but different atomic arrangements. Such substances are called isomers, and the phenomenon is known as isomerism. The term was derived in 1830 by a Swedish chemist Jöns Jacob Berzelius, probably from the Greek words *isos* ("same") and *meros* ("part").

Isomerism is important because the properties of chemical substances depend not only on the number and kinds of atoms present but also on their arrangement. Two isomeric substances may have different physical, chemical, and biological properties; to comprehend these differences it is necessary to understand how the substances differ structurally. Sometimes rather subtle structural differences or configurations in otherwise identical molecules determine whether a substance is rendered toxic or harmless, explosive or inert, or effective or inactive as a drug.

GENERAL CONSIDERATIONS

Atomic structure. The composition of matter, knowledge of which is necessary for an understanding of isomerism, is best understood in terms of the existence of atoms. As previously noted, atoms can combine with each other in different ways. There are millions of distinguishable forms of matter, all built up from only about 100 different kinds of atoms, each kind comprising one of the chemical elements. Atoms, in turn, are composed of a few kinds of even simpler particles combined in an orderly way that underlies the occurrence of groups of elements having related properties.

Practically all the mass of an atom is concentrated in

its nucleus, which contains protons, each possessing a positive electrical charge, and neutrons, which are electrically uncharged. Surrounding the nucleus is a cloud of electrons, particles with very little mass but each with a negative electrical charge. The electrons occupy regions of space called orbitals, which differ in shape, orientation, and average distance from the nucleus. The orbitals, each of which can accommodate two electrons, are arranged in shells of increasing distance from the nucleus, each successive shell being composed of a larger number of orbitals.

The electrons in a given atom are distributed among the orbitals so as to strike a balance between the attraction of the nucleus for all the electrons and the repulsion between each electron and all the others. In any atom, the electrons occupying the outermost shell are the least tightly bound to the nucleus and, thus, are the ones affected by the approach of other atoms; that is, these outermost, or valence, electrons, are those involved in chemical reactions and bond formation. Fundamentally, isomerism involves alternate patterns of bond formation between specific atoms in a molecule.

Ionic compounds

Electronic structure and bonding. Certain arangements of electrons are more stable than others; *e.g.,* the presence of eight electrons (the maximum possible) in the outermost shell represents an especially stable condition. Atoms having only a few valence electrons and eight electrons in the next underlying shell tend to lose their valence electrons: the resulting particle (no longer an atom, but an ion) has fewer electrons than protons and is positively charged. Similarly, an atom needing only a few electrons to complete an outermost shell of eight tends to gain the needed electrons, also becoming an ion (in this case, negatively charged). Oppositely charged ions attract each other and form crystalline compounds in which each ion occupies a position in a definite latticelike pattern. The ionic bonds existing in these structures do not connect any particular pair of ions but act equally in all directions. The compositions of these compounds are expressed by formulas indicating the proportions of the various ions: the compound sodium chloride (common salt) contains equal numbers of sodium ions (denoted by the symbol of the element and a superscript signifying the electrical charge, Na^+) and chloride ions (Cl^-), and its formula is NaCl. Isomerism is concerned less with this kind of bonding than with another type, called covalent.

Atoms that could be converted into ions only by the gain or loss of several electrons often form compounds by a different process. Rather than gaining or losing electrons outright, two atoms will take up positions close together so that each can provide one, two, or three electrons in the formation of a single, double, or triple covalent bond. In these compounds, specific groups of atoms remain linked together by the interaction of the shared electrons in stable associations—namely, molecules. Formulas of covalent compounds express the exact numbers of atoms of the various elements present in a molecule, rather than simply the ratio in which they occur (as in formulas of ionic compounds). For example, the formula C_2H_4 represents a molecule of the compound ethylene, containing two atoms of carbon (C) and four of hydrogen (H). The molecules of numerous other substances are made up solely of carbon and hydrogen atoms that are combined in the same 1:2 ratio as in ethylene (a fact expressed by saying that they all have the empirical formula CH_2). However, they are all different from ethylene, having definite compositions such as C_3H_6, C_4H_8, C_5H_{10}, etc.

Molecular and structural formulas

By analyzing a pure chemical compound one can determine the percentage by weight of each element present. This information, together with knowledge of the atomic weights and the molecular weight, permits one to calculate a formula, called a molecular formula, that tells how many atoms of each element are present in a molecule of the substance. An example is H_2O, for water. Such formulas do not show the order of attachment of the atoms. The laws of chemical bonding require, for example, that the two hydrogen atoms in a water molecule be bound to the oxygen atom and not to one another, as expressed by the formula H—O—H (not H—H—O). Such formulas, called structural formulas, give more information than molecular formulas because in addition to composition, they show the order of attachment of the atoms.

(H.Ha.)

Development of the concept of isomerism. The first such sets of compounds identified were the explosive fulminates (salts of fulminic acid) prepared in 1824 by the German chemist Justus von Liebig and the inactive cyanates (salts of cyanic acid) prepared in the following year by another German chemist, Friedrich Wöhler. At first, each man thought the other wrong, since the formulas for the two salts proved to be the same, but they soon met and in a common series of experiments showed that both parent acid compounds possessed the same atoms, of carbon, hydrogen, oxygen, and nitrogen. The French scientist Joseph-Louis Gay-Lussac correctly concluded that the spatial arrangement of atoms in the two compounds must be different. Cyanic acid has the formula HOCN, while fulminic is HONC. It remained for Berzelius to formulate a precise definition of the concept of isomerism.

(F.C.N./J.J.Z.)

The possibilities for isomerism increase with increasing molecular complexity. Though only one structure is possible for a diatomic (two-atom) molecule (say, $A-B$), there are three theoretically possible linear triatomic (three-atomic) molecules in which the three atoms are different: $A-B-C$, $A-C-B$, and $B-A-C$, but $A-B-C$ and $C-B-A$ are identical. Redundancy tends to reduce the number of possible isomers; for example, if C is replaced by another A, the number of possibilities for the resulting linear A_2B is reduced to two: $A-A-B$ and $A-B-A$. Many possibilities may also be eliminated by restrictions imposed by the laws of chemical bonding.

Subdivisions of isomerism

For convenience, the subject of isomerism is usually treated under two main subdivisions, structural isomerism and stereoisomerism. In structural isomers the order of attachment of the atoms, one to another, differs. In stereoisomers the attachment sequence is the same, but the atoms are located differently in space. To illustrate this distinction, consider triatomic molecules composed of atoms A, B, and C. Molecules $A-B-C$ and $A-C-B$ would be considered structural isomers because they differ in the order of attachment of the atoms. Either of these

$A-B-C$ $\overset{B}{A \diagup \; \diagdown C}$

molecules, however, could conceivably exist in more than one geometric form, say, linear and "bent":

Stereoisomers

Two chemical substances with molecules differing in this manner would be called stereoisomers; the phenomenon of stereoisomerism is particularly important among compounds that occur in nature (carbohydrates, proteins, and enzymes).

Isomerism is not rare; it pervades the study of chemistry and is encountered with compounds of virtually every known element. The significance and generality of the phenomenon were recognized earliest, however, in connection with the study of organic compounds, particularly those that occur in nature. Most of the examples that are used in this discussion to illustrate the principles of isomerism will be taken from organic chemistry. The principles are general, however, and one major portion of this section deals with the stereoisomeric compounds of elements other than carbon.

Early in the 19th century, reliable analytical methods were developed to permit the accurate determination of the percentage composition of various substances. It was soon noted that occasionally two obviously different chemical substances had identical compositions. To explain these observations, a French chemist, Michel-Eugène Chevreul, in 1818 defined a "chemical species" as being formed from the same elements in the same proportions and in the same arrangement. At that time, however, the distinction between substances with molecules of a given composition and with multiples of that composition (*i.e.,* C_2H_4 and C_4H_8) was not clear. In 1830 Berzelius noted the cyanate–fulminate results mentioned above and also referred to two other well-known organic compounds that have identical composition (tartaric and racemic acids, both isolated from grapes) as isomeric bodies. A year later he called attention to the generality of the phenomenon with five examples (only three of which were actually correct) and clearly distinguished between isomerism and what he called polymerism (*i.e.*, C_2H_4, C_4H_8, etc.). The term polymerism has since gone out of use, and the word polymer has quite a different chemical meaning.

STRUCTURAL ISOMERISM

Functional group isomers. The arrangement, or order of attachment, of atoms in a molecule is not arbitrary but is governed by the rules of chemical bonding. Only certain arrangements or structures are permissible. In neutral molecules, for example, carbon atoms may not be attached to more than four other atoms (for nitrogen, oxygen, and hydrogen, other elements commonly present in organic compounds, the numbers are three, two, and one, respectively). Thus, only two structural formulas consistent with these bonding rules are possible for the molecular formula C_2H_6O:

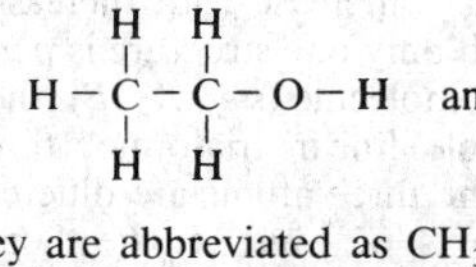

$$\begin{matrix} & H & & H & & & \\ & | & & | & & & \\ H- & C & - & C & -O-H \\ & | & & | & & & \\ & H & & H & & & \end{matrix} \quad \text{and} \quad \begin{matrix} & H & & & & H & \\ & | & & & & | & \\ H- & C & - & O & - & C & -H \\ & | & & & & | & \\ & H & & & & H & \end{matrix}$$

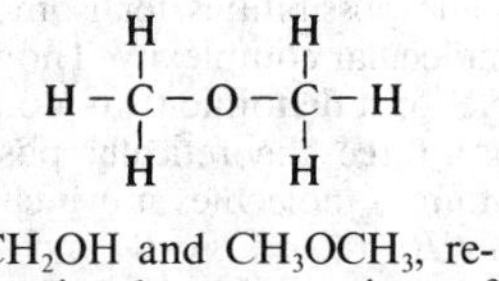

They are abbreviated as CH_3CH_2OH and CH_3OCH_3, respectively. (These are two-dimensional representations of three-dimensional structures. The formula

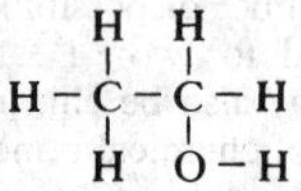

$$\begin{matrix} & H & & H & \\ & | & & | & \\ H- & C & - & C & -H \\ & | & & | & \\ & H & & O & -H \end{matrix}$$

is considered identical with the first formula above because it preserves the same order of attachment of the atoms one to another. The consequences of the three dimensionality of molecules are considered later in this discussion.) In each structural formula, each carbon atom is attached to four other atoms, the oxygen atom to two other atoms, and each hydrogen atom to only one other atom. All other conceivable structural formulas (for example, C—C—H—H—H—H—H—H—O) violate the laws of chemical bonding.

Alcohols and ethers

In agreement with bonding theory, there are two and only two known chemical substances with the molecular formula C_2H_6O. One isomer, called ethyl alcohol (or ethanol), is a liquid that boils at 78.5° C (173.3° F). The other isomer, called dimethyl ether, is a gas at room temperature and boils at −23° C (−9° F). The great difference in boiling points of these two isomers emphasizes the importance of molecular structure (not just composition) in determining the properties of chemical substances.

The choice as to which substance has which structure can be made by studying the chemical reactions of each. For example, ethanol reacts with the metal sodium (Na) at room temperature to liberate one-sixth of its hydrogen content as hydrogen gas; the other reaction product is a substance with the molecular formula $NaOC_2H_5$. In contrast, dimethyl ether is inert toward sodium under the same reaction conditions. Because one of the six hydrogens in the formula CH_3CH_2OH is unique (attached to oxygen, rather than carbon), but all six hydrogens in the formula CH_3OCH_3 are equivalent, it is reasonable to assign the structure with the hydroxyl (—OH) group to ethanol. Other chemical and physical methods for determining organic structures confirm this conclusion.

Ethanol and dimethyl ether are members of two important classes of organic compounds, alcohols and ethers respectively, which have the general formulas *R*—OH and *R*—O—*R′* (*R* and *R′* stand for certain organic groups). Members of such classes of compounds have a common functional group (—OH for alcohols, —C—O—C— for ethers) and, for this reason, show similar chemical behaviour (for example, most alcohols react with sodium to give hydrogen). Ethers and alcohols are considered to be functional group isomers. For every alcohol with two or more carbon atoms, there is at least one isomeric ether (for another example, 1-propanol [$CH_3CH_2CH_2OH$] and ethyl methyl ether [$CH_3OCH_2CH_3$], both C_3H_8O).

Some other common classes of organic compounds are acids ($R-\overset{O}{\overset{\|}{C}}-OH$), aldehydes ($R-\overset{O}{\overset{\|}{C}}-H$), ketones ($R-\overset{O}{\overset{\|}{C}}-R'$), and esters ($R-\overset{O}{\overset{\|}{C}}-O-R'$). Table 2 shows some of the functional group isomers of molecules, all of which have the molecular formula $C_3H_6O_2$, together with their known melting points and boiling points.

Table 2: Comparison of Isomers of $C_3H_6O_2$

structural formula	class	name	boiling point (°C)	melting point (°C)
$CH_3CH_2-\overset{O}{\overset{\|}{C}}-OH$	acid	propionic acid	141	−20.8
$CH_3-\overset{O}{\overset{\|}{C}}-CH_2OH$	keto-alcohol	acetol	145–146	−17
$CH_3-\overset{O}{\overset{\|}{C}}-OCH_3$	ester	methyl acetate	57–59	−98
$H_2C-CH-CH_2OH$ (ring through O)	ether-alcohol	glycidol	166–167	—
$CH_3OCH_2-\overset{O}{\overset{\|}{C}}-H$	ether-aldehyde	methoxyacetaldehyde	92.3	—
H_2C-CH_2, O, O, CH_2 (ring)	cyclic diether (or acetal)	1,3-dioxolane	78	−95

The list is far from exhaustive for all $C_3H_6O_2$ isomers but illustrates some of the unique properties of these substances, which differ from one another in the arrangement of atoms within each molecule.

Positional isomers. It is common to have isomers within the same class of compounds. In the alcohols with the molecular formula C_3H_8O, for example, the hydroxyl group may appear on an end carbon of the three-carbon chain, or it may be attached to the central carbon atom in the chain.

$$\overset{3}{C}H_3\overset{2}{C}H_2\overset{1}{C}H_2OH \qquad \overset{1}{C}H_3\overset{2}{C}H\overset{3}{C}H_3 \ (\text{OH on C-2})$$

1-propanol bp 97° C — 2-propanol bp 82° C

Such isomers, called positional isomers, frequently have similar, though not identical, chemical properties. Both propanols, for example, are completely miscible with water, and both of them react with sodium to give hydrogen, etc.

There are, however, examples of positional isomers that have grossly different properties. This condition is especially true of substances with two (or more) functional groups that may or may not be able to interact with one another, depending upon the carbon-atom framework to which they are attached. Examples are particularly common among aromatic compounds. Phthalic acid ($C_8H_6O_4$), with two acid groups attached to adjacent carbon atoms of a benzene ring, loses water to form a cyclic anhydride when heated above 180° C (360° F).

Aromatic compounds

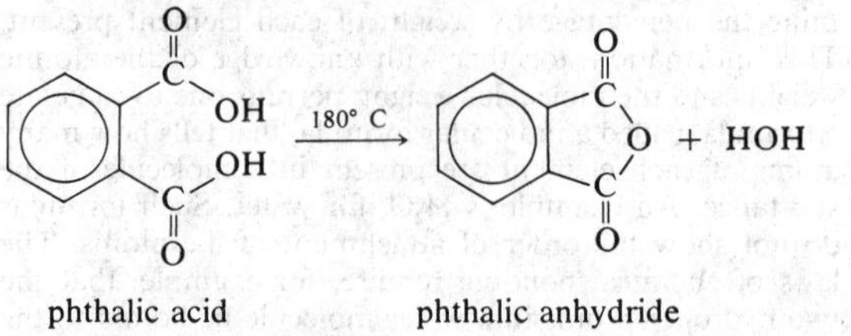

$$\text{phthalic acid} \xrightarrow{180^\circ C} \text{phthalic anhydride} + HOH$$

phthalic acid — phthalic anhydride

Isophthalic and terephthalic acids (also $C_8H_6O_4$), in which the acidic groups are farther apart, cannot react analogously.

isophthalic acid terephthalic acid

Physiological properties of isomeric substances may also depend on the relative location of the functional groups present. The two possible positional isomers of aspirin are almost totally devoid of biological activity.

aspirin positional isomers of aspirin

Tautomerism. Certain isomers may spontaneously interconvert more rapidly than they react with another compound. They are incapable of isolation. The phenomenon is called tautomerism (probably from Greek *tauto,* "the same"). A substance capable of existing in two (or more) tautomeric forms may exhibit chemical properties that correspond to each isomeric structure. The classic example is the compound ethyl acetoacetate ($C_6H_{10}O_3$) studied in the 1860s; it was considered by some chemists to have structure A (with alcohol and carbon–carbon double-bond functions) but by others to have the ketone structure B.

Ethyl acetoacetate

$$CH_3\overset{OH}{\overset{|}{C}}=CH\overset{O}{\overset{\|}{C}}OCH_2CH_3 \qquad CH_3\overset{O}{\overset{\|}{C}}CH_2\overset{O}{\overset{\|}{C}}OCH_2CH_3$$

A (enol) B (keto)

two tautomeric structures of ethyl acetoacetate

Each group of workers observed chemical reactions of the substance that were consistent with their formulation of the structure. The two structures differ in the location of a hydrogen atom: in A it is attached to oxygen and in B to carbon. It is now known that such structures rapidly interconvert at room temperature. Both groups of investigators were correct; ethyl acetoacetate is a mixture of the enol (A, 7.5 percent) and keto (B, 92.5 percent) forms.

enol keto

In 1911 a German chemist, Ludwig Knorr, succeeded in separating the two isomers at low temperatures (−78° C [−108° F]), but each, when permitted to attain room temperature, gave the equilibrium mixture—the mixture of constant composition that results from continuous conversion of each tautomer into the other.

Many other functional groups, besides ketones and enols, may exist in tautomeric equilibrium; in all cases, a hydrogen atom (proton) may occupy one of two possible sites. Examples include

amide imine-ol nitro aci form

imine ene-amine thione ene-thiol

Glucose (commonly known as blood sugar) exists as an equilibrium mixture of the three tautomeric structures shown (all $C_6H_{12}O_6$).

β-form open-chain form

α-form

tautomeric forms of glucose

In aqueous solution at room temperature the composition is 65 percent β (beta) and 35 percent α (alpha), with less than 0.1 percent of the intervening open-chain structure. The interconversion of cyclic and acyclic structures is sometimes called ring-chain tautomerization.

In all of the examples of tautomerism discussed so far, a hydrogen atom (and in other cases, some other atom) changes its location. An entirely different type of tautomerism has been recognized, which involves only a redistribution of bonds and small changes in interatomic distances and angles. For example, at 100° C (212° F) the eight-membered ring hydrocarbon shown (C_8H_{10}) is in equilibrium with the structure with a six- and a four-membered ring (also C_8H_{10}).

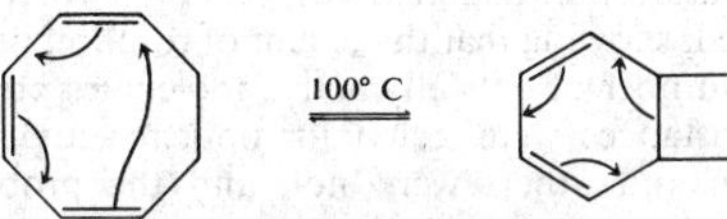

The interconversion can be accomplished by moving the bonds as shown by the arrows. The two isomers, which are readily separable at room temperature, are called valence tautomers.

Valence tautomers

STEREOISOMERISM

Stereoisomers (Greek *stereos,* "solid") have identical structural formulas, but the atoms are located differently in space. Stereoisomerism is often subdivided into geometric (or *cis–trans*) and optical isomerism, though this separation arises more out of the historical development of the subject than out of logic, because geometric isomers may or may not also be optical isomers. The latter type of isomerism, being more general, will be discussed first.

Optical isomerism. *Polarized light.* The history of stereoisomerism is intimately connected with the concept of optical activity, a consequence of the interaction of molecules with polarized light. In an ordinary light beam, the electromagnetic waves vibrate in all planes perpendicular to the direction of propagation of the beam. Ordinary light divides into two rays when passed through a properly oriented crystal of Iceland spar (crystalline calcium carbonate), and each ray consists of waves vibrating in a single plane. Such a light beam is said to be plane-polarized.

A Nicol prism, invented in 1828 by the Scottish physicist William Nicol, is a device made up of two pieces of Iceland spar in such a way that one of the two polarized rays passes through and the other is deflected. In a polarimeter there are two Nicol prisms or other polarizing devices through which a light beam passes in turn; the beam will pass through and be visible to an observer or detector only if the two prisms are parallel. The light will be totally cut off if the second prism (called the analyzer) is at right angles (90°) to the first prism (called the polarizer).

A quartz plate obtained by cutting a quartz crystal perpendicular to the crystal axis causes rotation of the plane of plane-polarized light. The phenomenon can best be observed by placing the quartz plate between the polarizer and analyzer of a polarimeter that has first been set with the two prisms at right angles. Before the quartz plate is placed in the instrument, no light passes through the second prism. With the plate between the prisms, some light passes through the second prism, which must now be rotated through a definite angle to cut off the light beam again. A substance, such as the quartz plate, is said to be optically active if it possesses the ability to rotate the plane of plane-polarized light. The angle through which the second crystal must be rotated to restore the original condition is called the optical rotation of the optically active substance and is given the symbol α.

Enantiomorphs

Two kinds of quartz crystals exist that differ only in the location of two facets that cause the crystals to be nonidentical mirror images (comparable to a right and left glove). Because of the mirror-image relationship, they were called enantiomorphs (Greek *enantios,* "opposite," and *morph,* "form"). Plates of the same thickness from the two kinds of quartz rotate plane-polarized light equally but in opposite directions. The form that rotates the plane to the right when the viewer faces the light source is called dextrorotatory (*d;* sometimes designated +), and that to the left levorotatory (*l;* sometimes designated −).

Molecular dissymmetry. A French physicist, Jean-Baptiste Biot, laid the foundation for modern stereochemistry when he found, in 1815, that substances other than quartz are optically active. These included an alcoholic solution of camphor, laurel oil, lemon oil, and turpentine, the latter even in the vapour phase. Because these substances are not crystalline, such rotation must clearly be associated with the structures of the individual molecules and not necessarily with their dissymmetric arrangement in a solid. (An object is dissymmetric if it is non-superimposable on its mirror image.) This notion was supported by the finding that if the concentration (say of sugar in water) was doubled, the observed rotation was also doubled, showing that the extent of rotation depended upon the number of optically active molecules present.

Many substances were tested for optical activity; some were active and others were not, and the problem remained to discern what molecular property caused the difference. Among the active compounds was tartaric acid, first isolated from grape tartar and found to be dextrorotatory. Another acid from the same source, called racemic acid (Latin *racemus,* "bunch of grapes"), was found to be optically inactive. Yet both acids had identical compositions and otherwise very similar properties, now known to be accounted for by the same structural formula ($C_4H_6O_6$).

$$HO-\overset{O}{\overset{\|}{C}}-\underset{OH}{\overset{H}{C}}-\underset{OH}{\overset{H}{C}}-\overset{O}{\overset{\|}{C}}-OH$$

Tartaric and racemic acids

Louis Pasteur, in 1848, noticed that crystals of the tartrate salt were of a single type with facets that caused the crystals to be dissymmetric. Crystals of the racemate salt, however, were of two types: one identical with those of the tartrate salt, and the other having a mirror-image relationship (enantiomorphic) with the tartrate crystals. Pasteur carefully separated the two types of racemate crystals. One set, when dissolved in water, was dextrorotatory, with an optical rotation identical to that of the tartrate salt. The other set gave solutions that rotated the plane-polarized light to the same extent but in the opposite direction. When equal weights of the two types were dissolved and mixed, the resulting solution was optically inactive. Clearly, racemic acid was optically inactive because it consisted of a 50 : 50 mixture of two types of molecules, one of which was identical with tartaric acid and the other of which was related to it as an object and its mirror image. Pasteur realized that optical activity is caused by a dissymmetric grouping of the atoms in a molecule, but he failed to discern the structural feature that accounts for the dissymmetry.

A German chemist, Friedrich August Kekule von Stradonitz, recognized that carbon usually has a valence of four and that complex organic structures can be produced by linking carbon atoms in chains or rings (see below *Chemical bonding*). In 1874 Jacobus Henricus van't Hoff in The Netherlands and Joseph-Achille Le Bel in France independently made the connection between the quadrivalence of carbon and Pasteur's suggestion that optical activity is caused by molecular dissymmetry. They noted that a structural feature that causes a molecule and its mirror image to be non-superimposable is necessary for the existence of optical activity and that every optically active compound of which the structure was known at that time had at least one carbon atom that was combined with four different groups. Examples (the pertinent carbon atoms are marked with an asterisk):

$$CH_3-\underset{OH}{\overset{H}{C^*}}-CO_2H \qquad HO_2C-CH_2-\underset{OH}{\overset{H}{C^*}}-CO_2H$$

lactic acid — malic acid

$$HO_2C-CH_2-\underset{NH_2}{\overset{H}{C^*}}-CO_2H \qquad CH_3-CH_2-\underset{CH_3}{\overset{H}{C^*}}-CH_2OH.$$

aspartic acid — active amyl alcohol

Whenever both members of a pair of optical isomers were known, all chemical and physical properties (melting point or boiling point, etc.) were identical, the only difference being the sign (not the magnitude) of the optical rotation. Accordingly, the isomers seemed to differ from one another only in a right- and left-handed manner. Both chemists pointed out that if the four different groups about a carbon atom were located at the corners of a tetrahedron, two arrangements were possible, which are related to one another as an object and its non-superimposable mirror image. This is shown in the formulas below, in which the dashed lines and wedges represent bonds extending, respectively, away from and toward the reader, and full lines represent bonds lying in the plane of the paper.

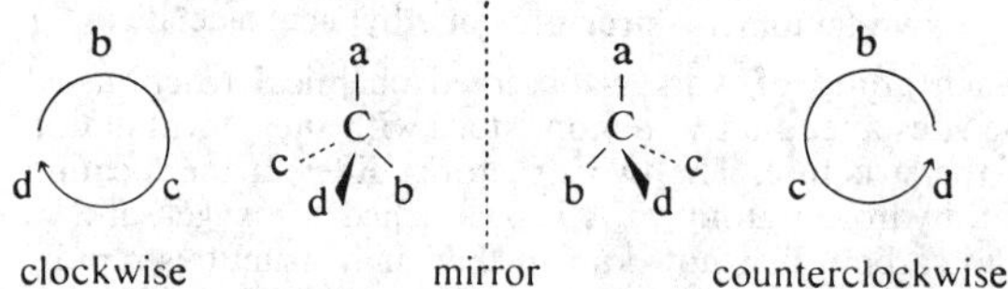

If each molecule is viewed down the C–a bond axis, the remaining groups b–c–d occur in either a clockwise or a counterclockwise sequence, thus emphasizing that the feature that distinguishes the two structures is one of handedness. The correctness of the proposals of van't Hoff and Le Bel has now been established unequivocally through the application of many physical and chemical techniques.

Chirality

Symmetry elements of molecules. The property of handedness is called chirality (Greek *cheir,* "hand"). Just as it is easy for two right-handed (or left-handed) persons to shake hands but impossible to shake a right hand with a left hand in the usual way, so molecules may interact differently with one another depending on their chirality. Because many molecules that occur in nature are optically active and chiral, their chemical behaviour cannot be understood without some understanding of stereoisomerism.

Whether a molecule is chiral or achiral depends on the presence or absence of certain symmetry elements. The most important are axes, centres, and planes. An axis of symmetry is one that passes through a molecule (or object) in such a way that rotation about the axis brings the molecule repeatedly into a position indistinguishable from its original one. If in one complete rotation through 360°, four indistinguishable positions are obtained, the axis is said to be one of fourfold symmetry; in general, if n such positions are obtained, an n-fold axis of symmetry is present. (The performance of such a rotation or any other test for a symmetry element is called a symmetry operation.) The line perpendicular to the plane of a square and passing through its centre is a fourfold symmetry axis. A centre of symmetry is a point within a molecule (or object) such that a straight line drawn from any part of the molecule to the centre and extended an equal distance on the other side encounters an equivalent part of the molecule. Squares and spheres have centres of symmetry. A plane of symmetry is one that passes through a molecule (or object) so that one side of the plane is the exact reflection of the other side, the plane acting as a mirror.

Molecules with a centre, plane, or axis of symmetry are superimposable upon (or identical with) their mirror images. Such molecules are achiral, or symmetric. Examples are a sphere, a cube, and a baseball and bat. Molecules that lack these symmetry elements are chiral, or dissymmetric; they are not superimposable on their mirror images. Common chiral objects are gloves, screws, and spiral staircases. A chiral molecule or object is said to be asymmetric if it lacks all of the symmetry elements, even including a simple axis.

Symmetry and optical activity. The chirality of an object cannot be determined by its interaction with an achiral (symmetric) object but only with another chiral object. For example, a left-handed baseball player can use the same bat (which is achiral, having an infinite number of symmetry planes through its long axis) or ball (also achiral, with a centre of symmetry) as a right-handed player, but he cannot use the same glove (which is chiral, or asymmetric, being like the players, left- or right-handed).

The same situation prevails with mirror-image chiral molecules. They react identically with achiral molecules, and their properties that do not depend on chirality (such as melting and boiling points) are identical. They behave differently, however, toward other chiral molecules (these differences are the basis for much of the specificity of many biochemical reactions, such as those of enzymes) and have different chiral physical properties, such as the direction in which they rotate plane-polarized light or their solubility in solvents of which the molecules are chiral.

Molecules with an asymmetric carbon atom. A carbon atom to which four different atoms or groups of atoms are attached is called an asymmetric carbon atom. Such an atom can serve as a focus of dissymmetry, or handedness, and in modern terminology is called a chiral centre. Typical of such compounds is lactic acid, a naturally occurring, optically active compound important in several biological processes. In the formula at the left, the asymmetric carbon atom is marked with an asterisk.

Lactic acid

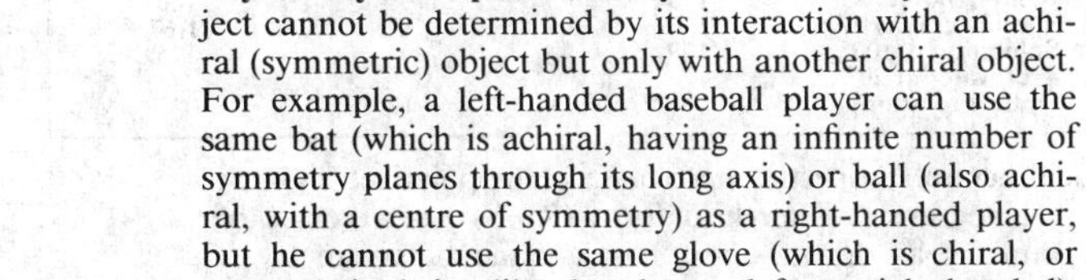

$H_3C-C^*(H)(OH)-CO_2H$ — lactic acid

mirror

l-lactic acid: C with CO_2H, H_3C, OH, H | d-lactic acid: C with HO_2C, HO, H, CH_3 —rotate 180°→ C with CO_2H, H_3C, H, OH

lactic acid | *l*-lactic acid | *d*-lactic acid

The two non-superimposable mirror-image structures, or enantiomers, are also shown. They represent two chemical substances that have the same molecular and structural formulas but differ in the location of the atoms in three-dimensional space (*i.e.,* they are stereoisomers). One form of lactic acid, the levorotatory (or *l*) isomer, is found in sour milk, whereas the other enantiomer, dextrorotatory (or *d*), is produced when muscle tissue performs work. The two lactic acids not only rotate plane-polarized light in opposite directions but also differ in biochemical reactivity. For example, the enzyme lactic acid dehydrogenase (which is chiral) can readily distinguish between the two stereoisomers; it converts *d*-lactic acid (but not the *l*-isomer) to pyruvic acid. In contrast, achiral chemical reagents readily convert both forms of lactic acid to pyruvic acid.

A given amount of one form of lactic acid will rotate plane-polarized light through the same angle but in the opposite direction from an equal amount of the mirror image form. This characteristic applies to all pairs of enantiomers. Consequently, a mixture containing equal amounts of two enantiomers will be optically inactive, the two rotations exactly cancelling one another. Such a mixture is called a racemic mixture (named after the first such mixture, *d*- and *l*-tartaric acids, studied by Pasteur).

In the structure of lactic acid the molecule lacks a plane or centre of symmetry; it also lacks a symmetry axis and is therefore asymmetric. It is instructive to make two of the groups attached to the (formerly) asymmetric carbon atom identical. If, for example, the hydroxyl (—OH) group in lactic acid is replaced by a hydrogen atom, giving propionic (propanoic) acid, then the molecule will possess a plane of symmetry; the plane of the paper bisects the H—C—H angle and contains the other groups.

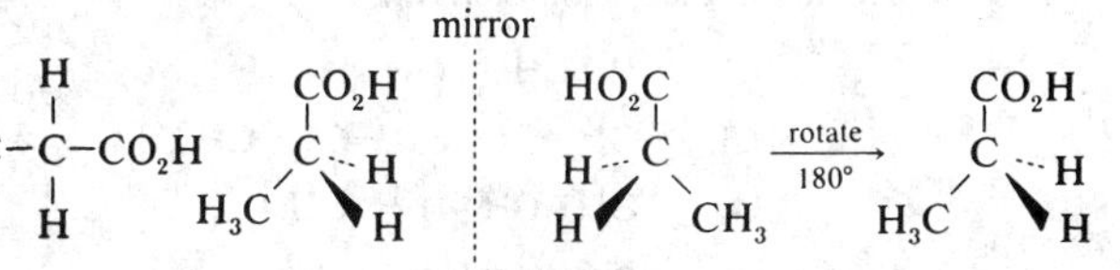

mirror

$H_3C-C(H)(H)-CO_2H$ | C with CO_2H, H_3C, H, H | C with HO_2C, H, H, CH_3 —rotate 180°→ C with CO_2H, H_3C, H, H

propionic acid

The substance is therefore achiral and, as the above drawing shows, has a mirror image that is, in fact, identical with or superimposable on itself. Consequently, propionic acid is known in only one form, which is optically inactive. The asymmetric carbon atom is, therefore, the structural feature that imparts chirality to lactic acid.

Configuration refers to the arrangement of atoms in space that characterizes a particular stereoisomer. Enantiomers are said to have opposite configurations. Before 1950 no method to determine the absolute configuration of any dissymmetric molecule was known. For example, it was not known whether *l*-lactic acid had the configuration shown above or its mirror-image configuration (*i.e.,* which structure fit with which sign of rotation), although through chemical interconversions many relative configurations had been established. For example, *l*-lactic acid, isolated from sour milk, is converted by treatment with methyl alcohol to an ester, methyl lactate, also levorotatory.

Absolute configurations

$$CH_3CH(OH)CO_2H + CH_3OH \longrightarrow CH_3CH(OH)CO_2CH_3 + H_2O$$

l-lactic acid | methyl alcohol | methyl lactate (levorotatory) | water

Because no bonds to the asymmetric carbon were broken during this reaction, it is safe to conclude that *l*-lactic acid and *l*-methyl lactate have the same relative configurations, even though the absolute configuration of each was not known.

In 1951 Dutch scientists established the absolute configuration of *d*-tartaric acid. Because it had already been related configurationally to many other optically active compounds, their absolute configurations (including those shown here for the lactic acids) became known. Since 1951 the absolute configurations of many optically active substances and various conventions for describing them have been established.

Molecules with more than one asymmetric carbon atom. The molecules of many substances in nature, such as the common sugars and other carbohydrates, contain more than one asymmetric carbon atom. Recognizing this possibility, van't Hoff formulated rules predicting the numbers of stereoisomers that may exist in such instances. If the two possible configurations at a single chiral centre are designated R (Latin *rectus,* "right") and S (Latin *sinister,* "left"), respectively, then a substance which has two different chiral centres may exist in four stereoisomeric forms, as shown by the chart below (the numbers in the parentheses represent the two chiral centres).

molecules with two different chiral centres

R(1)–R(2)
S(1)–S(2) } enantiomers

R(1)–S(2)
S(1)–R(2) } enantiomers

Since R(1) is considered to be the mirror image of S(1), etc., molecules R(1)—R(2) and S(1)—S(2) constitute one pair of enantiomers; similarly, R(1)—S(2) and S(1)—R(2) are another enantiomeric pair. It is easy to show that if a molecule has three chiral centres, there are eight possible stereoisomers; four chiral centres permit 16 stereoisomeric structures (eight pairs of enantiomers). This possibility is not at all uncommon. For example, *d*-glucose, the sugar present in blood, is one of 16 isomeric sugars, each of which has the same molecular and structural formula but differs from the others in the configurations at one or more of the four asymmetric carbon atoms present in the molecule (marked with asterisks).

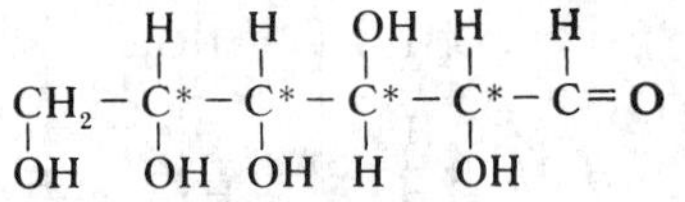

$$\begin{array}{cccccccccc} & & H & & H & & OH & & H & & H \\ CH_2 & - & C^* & - & C^* & - & C^* & - & C^* & - & C{=}O \\ OH & & OH & & OH & & H & & OH & & \end{array}$$

structural formula for *d*-glucose and its 15 stereoisomers

The van't Hoff rule summarizes the situation: if a molecule has *n* different chiral centres, it is capable of existing in 2^n stereoisomeric structures.

An extremely far-reaching concept in stereoisomerism develops if one considers, in the chart of molecules with two different chiral centres, the relationship between any two molecules that are not enantiomers—for example, R(1)—R(2) and R(1)—S(2). These substances have the same configuration (*i.e.,* R) at centre (1) but opposite configurations at centre (2). These substances are therefore stereoisomers but not mirror images (enantiomers). Compounds related in this way are called diastereomers (or diastereoisomers). Because they are not mirror images, two compounds that are diastereomers may differ in all properties, not only those that are chiral. They may have different melting points, boiling points, densities, and solubilities in various solvents; and they react differently with all chemical reagents, whether chiral or achiral. If dissymmetric, they interact with plane-polarized light but need not rotate the light in opposite directions nor to the same extent. In short, diastereomers may behave as differently from one another as any two chemical substances. For example, *d*-mannose is a sugar that is known as a diastereomer of *d*-glucose; they have identical configurations at three chiral centres and opposite configurations at only one of the four asymmetric carbon atoms. Yet *d*-mannose melts 14° C (25° F) lower than *d*-glucose and is also three times as soluble in water.

Diastereomers

A special case of stereoisomerism arises when a molecule possesses two identical asymmetric carbon atoms; that is, the two carbon atoms have the identical four different groups attached. In this case, the total number of possible stereoisomers decreases from four to three, as shown in the chart below. Because the two chiral centres are identical, they are designated by the same number; *i.e.,* (1).

molecules with two identical chiral centers

R(1)–R(1), S(1)–S(1) } enantiomers (optically active)

R(1)–S(1) meso form (optically inactive)

The form R(1)—S(1), though it possesses chiral centres, is achiral and optically inactive because the two chiral centres are equal and opposite. In other terms, because S(1) is the mirror image of R(1), the molecule has a plane of symmetry (and is therefore achiral). Such substances are called meso forms.

R(1) ┼ S(1)

plane of symmetry

The structure of tartaric acid, which has two identical asymmetric carbon atoms, indicated by asterisk, is shown in the following diagram.

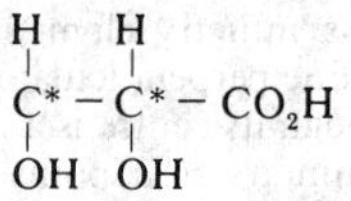

$$\begin{array}{ccccccc} & & H & & H & & \\ HO_2C & - & C^* & - & C^* & - & CO_2H \\ & & OH & & OH & & \end{array}$$

tartaric acid

Each asymmetric carbon atom has the same four groups attached, $-H$, $-OH$, $-CO_2H$, and $-CH(OH)CO_2H$. Tartaric acid exists in three stereoisomeric forms having the structures shown in the three-dimensional drawings of Table 3. Two structures (R—R and S—S) form an enantiomeric pair and are optically active; they have identical achiral properties but rotate plane-polarized light in opposite senses. The third form (R—S) has a centre of symmetry as drawn, or it has a plane of symmetry if one asymmetric carbon is rotated 180° about the bond that joins the two asymmetric carbons. This structure is therefore achiral, optically inactive, and a meso form. The meso form is a diastereomer of the optically active forms and therefore differs from them in its properties.

Table 3: Properties of the Three Isomers of Tartaric Acid

	R–R	S–S	R–S
Structure	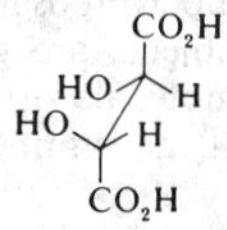 CO_2H / HO–C–H / HO–C–H / CO_2H	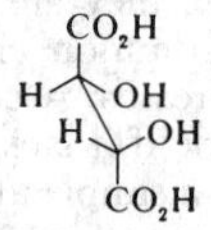 CO_2H / H–C–OH / H–C–OH / CO_2H	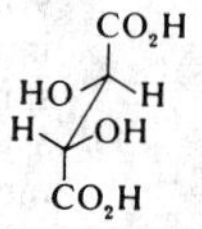 CO_2H / HO–C–H / H–C–OH / CO_2H
Melting point, °C	170	170	140
Specific gravity	1.76	1.76	1.67
Solubility, g/100 g of water at 20° C	139	139	125
Optical rotation	+12°	−12°	0°

Conformational isomers. Several classes of molecules have been devised in which the interconversion of enantiomeric dissymmetric conformers is prevented by placing, in strategic positions, large groups that restrict what would otherwise be fairly free rotational motions. Certain substituted biphenyls constitute a well-studied example. Biphenyl (I) itself is a hydrocarbon in which two benzene rings are joined by a single bond. The two rings may be coplanar or mutually perpendicular, or they may assume any twisted conformation between these extremes.

Biphenyls

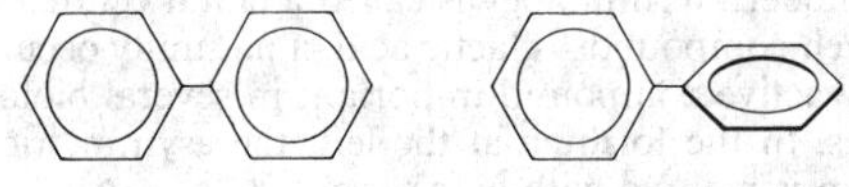

coplanar I perpendicular

two conformations of biphenyl

The coplanar conformation has three planes of symmetry, and the perpendicular conformations and the twisted conformations are readily interconverted by a simple rotational motion about the bond that joins the two benzene rings, biphenyl itself is achiral and optically inactive.

If two large and different groups (say, A and B) are placed on the ring positions (called the ortho positions) adjacent to the bond that joins the two rings, the planar arrangement, which brings these groups very close to one another in space, becomes less stable than any of the twisted conformations.

A A / B B A B / B A

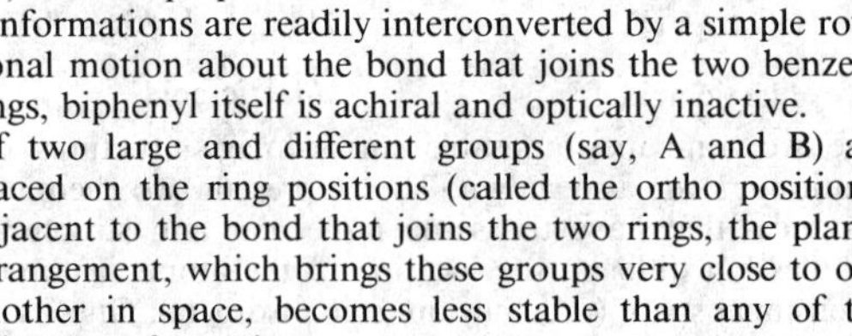

two planar conformations that are unstable when A and B are large groups

Consequently, the symmetric, or achiral, coplanar conformation becomes very difficult to achieve. Any twisted conformation, including the one in which the rings are mutually perpendicular, is dissymmetric because of the difference in the two substituents, A and B. An end-on view of the two enantiomers shows their chirality.

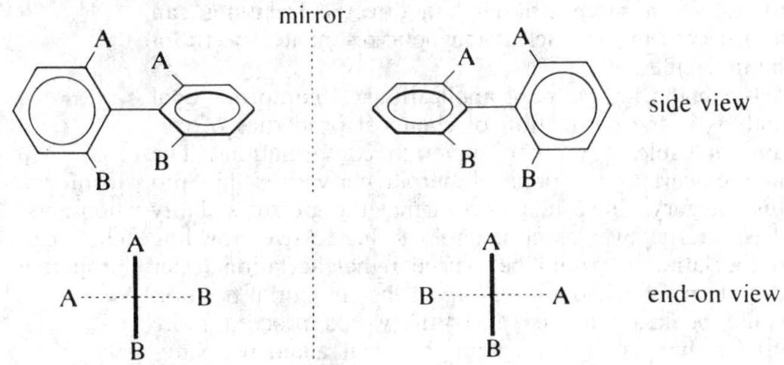

mirror

A A A A

side view

B B B B

A A

A B B A end-on view

B B

chiral, optically active biphenyls

The substances represented by the two structures are distinct from one another, constituting a pair of enantiomers that differ from one another in all chiral properties. Commonly, A and B are large groups such as methyl ($-CH_3$), nitro ($-NO_2$), or carboxyl ($-CO_2H$); the larger the groups, the more difficult for the molecule to pass through the planar conformation, a process that interconverts the two enantiomers. If two of the groups on either of the rings are identical, the substance is achiral and optically inactive, even though the rings cannot easily become coplanar, because the easily achieved conformation with the two rings mutually perpendicular has a plane of symmetry. It is essential that A and B be different; of course, all four groups may be different without affecting the possibilities for having two separable optical isomers. (H.Ha.)

In organic molecules, the valence bonds limit considerably the positions in space that the atoms can take. Nonetheless, because the various parts of the molecule are free to rotate about many of these valence bonds, the molecule can still assume any of a large number of three-dimensional shapes, or conformations. For several reasons, however, some conformations are more stable than others (see below) and represent the true state of the molecule under normal circumstances. In general, there is a correlation between the preferred conformations of the molecules of a substance and the chemical and physical properties of that substance. The study of the factors that determine which conformations are preferred and of the correlations between these conformations and the properties of the substance in question is called conformational analysis.

Conformational analysis

In the 1940s and 1950s Odd Hassel of the University in Oslo and Derek H.R. Barton of Imperial College of Science and Technology (London) were active in developing the principles of conformational analysis; in 1969 they were jointly awarded the Nobel Prize for Chemistry.

Rotational conformations. Initially it was assumed that completely free rotation was possible about any single bond between carbon atoms in a molecule. In 1936 chemical physics showed that restriction of rotation about single bonds was common to all organic compounds and that certain arrangements of bonded atoms in space were preferred. Sir Walter Norman Haworth (1929) defined the word conformation as an arrangement in space of the atoms of a molecule of defined configuration that is not superposable upon any other arrangement. From this it follows that an infinite number of conformations are possible even for as simple a molecule as ethane, CH_3CH_3.

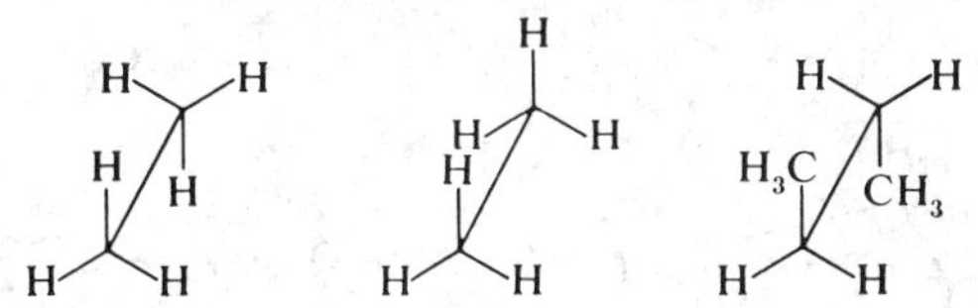

II III IV

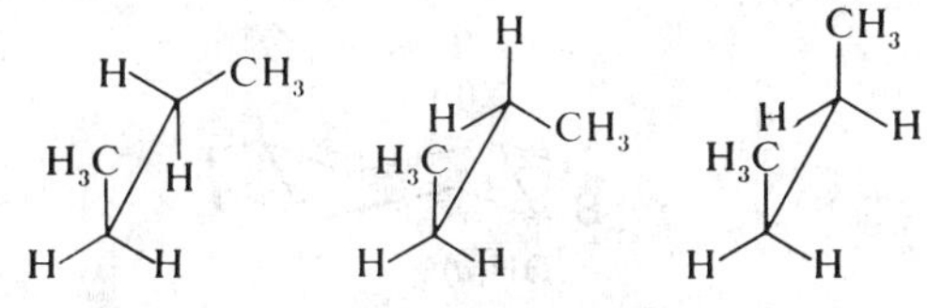

V VI VII

Staggered conformation

Only two extreme conformations, shown in II and III, however, need be considered. In II, the staggered conformation, the hydrogen atoms are as far away from each other as is possible and the energy of the system is at a minimum, whereas in III the hydrogen atoms are as close as is possible and the energy is at a maximum. The energies of the infinite number of conformations that lie between these two extremes are also intermediate. Thus ethane at normal temperatures will exist mainly in II, but as the temperature of the gas is raised—*i.e.,* as energy is introduced into the system—an increasing proportion of it will adopt conformations of higher energy.

In *n*-butane ($CH_3CH_2CH_2CH_3$), there are four limiting conformations shown in IV, V, VI, and VII. That with lowest energy is IV, in which the methyl groups are as far apart as is possible; next comes the staggered arrangement V, in which the methyls are fairly close together. Of the high-energy arrangements, VII, in which the methyls are opposed, is less stable than VI, in which methyl is opposed to a hydrogen. Thus it can be seen that, in general, the preferred conformation is that in which the largest groups are farthest apart; this is due to the interaction of the nonbonded atoms whose electron atmospheres repel each other.

The barriers to free rotation in ethane, *n*-butane, and related molecules are only of the order of a few kilogram calories per mole. Although this is sufficient to ensure that the molecules exist in the preferred staggered conformations, it is far too small to allow the separation of stable isomers.

Conformations of cyclohexane derivatives. In 1890 H. Sachse pointed out that, if the valency angles of carbon were retained at the natural tetrahedral angle of 109°28′, then cyclohexane (C_6H_{12}) could exist in two conformations free of angle strain. These are usually designated the chair (VIII) and boat (IX) conformations. In VIII all the bonds are staggered with respect to their neighbours (see also X), whereas in IX there are four pairs of opposed interactions. Thus it would be expected that the chair conformation (VIII) would be the more stable. This condition has, in fact, been established experimentally beyond any question, a direct physical proof being provided by the electron diffraction work of Odd Hassel (1948) and supported by the statistical mechanical studies of Kenneth S. Pitzer (1948).

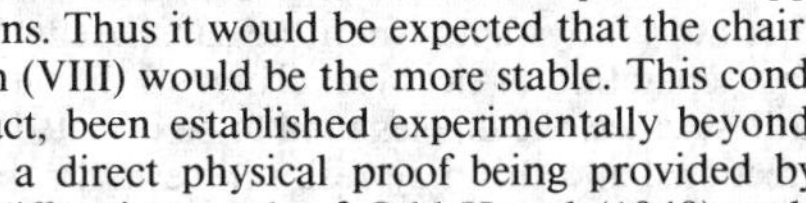

VIII IX

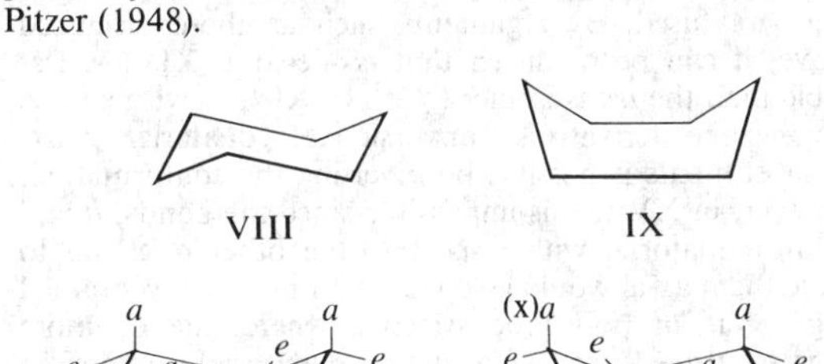

X XI

In the chair conformation, two geometrically distinct types of carbon-hydrogen bond are present (see X). Six of the bonds are parallel to the threefold axis of symmetry of the ring and are called axial bonds (D.H.R. Barton, Hassel, Pitzer, and Vladimir Prelog, 1954).

The other six carbon-hydrogen bonds, placed in a belt around the molecule, are called equatorial (*e*). The conformation X can be converted to the boat conformation (IX) or it can be inverted to the alternative, but in every way equivalent, chair (XI) simply by movement of the carbon atoms through a plane. In this process an equatorial hydrogen—say (x) in X—becomes axial ([x] in XI) and vice versa. The energy needed to effect this process is only a few kilogram calories, and therefore it is not possible to isolate boat and chair conformational isomers in cyclohexane or its derivatives at ordinary temperatures.

Monosubstituted cyclohexanes can, in principle, have the substituent in the axial or equatorial arrangement, the two alternatives being different conformations of the

Equatorial conformation favoured

molecule. In fact, it is the equatorial orientation that is favoured, except in unusual circumstances. In the equatorial conformation (XII), the substituent X is close enough in space to interact only with the two equatorial and two axial hydrogens on the carbon atoms proximate to the C—X bond; *i.e.*, four 1 : 2 H:X interactions. Similarly in the axial conformation (XIII), the substituent interacts with the two equatorial hydrogens on the adjacent carbon atoms and with the two axial hydrogens on the next but one carbon atoms; *i.e.*, two 1 : 2 H:X and two 1 : 3 H : X interactions. When the substituent is hydrogen, it is found by examining models that the 1 : 2 hydrogens are the same distance apart as the 1 : 3 axial hydrogens and thus have the same repulsive energy, but if any substituent larger than hydrogen is introduced, then the 1 : 3 axial distance is smaller than the 1 : 2 distance and the latter will therefore have a smaller energy of interaction.

So it may be concluded that, in general, substituted cyclohexanes tend to exist mainly in the conformation in which the largest group is in the equatorial position or, if more than two substituents are present, with the largest

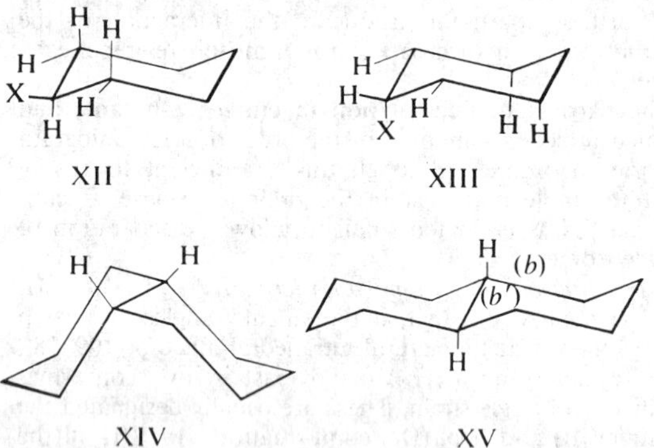

number of groups in the equatorial positions. This general rule does not always hold when the substituents have appreciable separation of electrical charge or dipole moment for, in these cases, the dipoles tend to be oriented in opposite directions, and this may result in several substituents with axial orientations.

In compounds of the decalin series, two cyclohexane rings are fused. By arguments such as those discussed above, it can be predicted that *cis*-decalin (XIV) is less stable than the *trans* isomer (XV). In XIV, as with simple cyclohexane derivatives, conversion of equatorial to axial substituents is possible by inverting the conformation; however, in XV this is impossible since the bonds, *b* and *b′*, are equatorial with respect to the other ring and to make them axial would give rise to an impossibly strained ring. Thus in polycyclic systems, where one or more rings are *trans*-fused, the axial and equatorial isomers are not interconvertible. It is in these cases, where the rigidity of the molecule prevents there being any ambiguity about the orientation of substituents, that conformational analysis has made its most important contributions. The fundamental tenet of conformational analysis is that the preferred conformation of a molecule can be related to its physical and chemical properties. This tenet was first shown in polycyclic systems in 1950 by Barton, mainly with examples from the steroid field.

Applications of conformational analysis. Conformational analysis is used chiefly in two ways: (1) to correlate directly the properties of molecules with their preferred conformations and (2) to analyze the interplay of conformational preference with the geometrical requirements of the transition state in organic reactions.

In the first class may be grouped such properties as specific bands in the infrared or ultraviolet spectrum of a compound. For example, in α-halocyclohexanones if the halogen is equatorial, the infrared maximum of the carbonyl group is displaced, but if the halogen is axial the frequency remains unchanged. In the ultraviolet spectrum the opposite holds true; thus in an axially substituted α-haloketone there is a displacement of the ultraviolet maximum but not in the corresponding equatorial compound. Even more striking and direct correlations can be observed in the nuclear magnetic resonance spectra of the molecules.

Conformation and chemical properties

Also in the first class of applications of conformational analysis is the correlation of chemical properties of certain molecules with their preferred conformations. The rates of certain reactions of steroid derivatives fall into this category. Since it is known that the greater stability of equatorial over axial alcohols is due to overcrowding in the latter, it would be expected that acylation (ester formation) of a hydroxyl group in the equatorial position would be less hindered and thus would proceed more rapidly than is the case with the axial analogue. Similarly, it would be predicted that hydrolysis, or cleavage, of equatorial esters would occur more rapidly than it would in the case of the corresponding axial compounds. This has been amply proved in the case of various steroidal alcohols where the axial and equatorial pairs were examined with hydroxyl groups at the positions numbered in XVI. That the equatorial alcohol is more stable than the axial has also been demonstrated in these steroidal alcohols, mainly by reduction of the corresponding ketone with sodium and an alcohol to an equilibrium mixture of the axial and equatorial isomers. In all cases, the equatorial alcohol preponderates and hence must be the more stable. The greater stability of the equatorial over the corresponding axial substituent has been demonstrated for numerous other groups in various environments, especially in rigid fused-ring systems such as steroids and triterpenes, where the configuration of a substituent defines its conformation.

Conformation and reaction mechanisms

This ability to define unambiguously the conformation of a compound is particularly important in the second way in which conformational analysis is applied; *i.e.*, the analysis of reaction mechanisms. Although flexible compounds such as substituted cyclohexanes usually exist in one preferred conformation, this does not mean that they must react in this form. For example, bromocyclohexane exists mainly in the equatorial conformation, but it is

XVI

XVII XVIII

XIX XX

XXIII XXI

XXII

almost certain that when it is dehydrobrominated to cyclohexene, the form that reacts is the axial form. Thus it is in rigid systems with well-defined conformation (where such transformation cannot occur) that conformational analysis can be applied most fruitfully to the study of reaction mechanisms.

The transition state of lowest energy for an ionic bimolecular elimination reaction requires that the four centres involved be in one plane. This is fulfilled in conformationally rigid cyclohexane systems by *trans*-1,2-diaxial substituents, but not by *trans*-1,2-diequatorial substituents or by either of the *cis*-(equatorial-axial) isomers.

For example, 5α,6β-dibromocholestane (represented in partial formulation by XVII) has two axial bromine atoms. It is debrominated by iodide ion much faster than its 5β,6α-isomer (XVIII), where both bromines are equatorial. As a corollary to this rule, it has also been established that addition of electrophilic, or positive charged, reagents to double bonds gives the *trans*-diaxial product; in most cases this is the thermodynamically less stable one. Thus cholest-2-ene (XIX) gives mainly the diaxial 2β,3α-dibromocholestane (XX). Similarly, it has been shown that epoxides, such as cholest-2-ene α-epoxide (XXI), give the diaxial product (*e.g.*, XXII) on ring opening, although they could conceivably give the stabler diequatorial products; *e.g.*, XXIII. Conversely it has been shown that the diaxial halohydrins on treatment with alkali reform the epoxide ring much more rapidly than do the corresponding diequatorial compounds.

The initial application of conformational analysis to rigid cyclohexane systems, particularly to steroids, by Barton in the 1950s at once rationalized a large body of existing steroid chemistry, which had not been readily comprehensible under standard stereochemical considerations. With conformational analysis, otherwise inexplicable variations in the physical and chemical properties of steroid derivatives were made understandable. Further, the application of the principles of conformational analysis to the steroid field facilitated the rapid development of new partial and total syntheses of steroid derivatives in subsequent years.

Extensions of conformational analysis. Although conformational analysis can be more favourably applied to rigid cyclohexane systems, it has also been widely and fruitfully used in aliphatic and heterocyclic systems, and also in large- and small-ring compounds, though the latter do not have the symmetrical perfection of the cyclohexane ring. The substitution of heteroatoms such as nitrogen and oxygen for one or more of the carbon atoms of a cyclohexane ring causes only a slight distortion of the chair conformation. In consequence, the generalizations that have been found pertinent in cyclohexane chemistry can be carried over in main part to heterocyclic analogues. Thus tetrahydropyran ($C_5H_{10}O$) may be represented by the

Conformations of heterocyclic systems

O

XXIV

conformation XXIV. Many of the compounds of carbohydrate chemistry contain the tetrahydropyran ring, and it has been shown that the chair conformation (XXIV) is adopted wherever possible. In macromolecular chemistry, as well, conformational principles are extremely important. The conformations of natural macromolecules are of considerable importance in determining their biological activity. (D.H.R.B./J.K.S.)

Helical molecules. The helix is a common chiral structure; it may be left- or right-handed, and the two types of helices are related to one another as an object and its nonsuperimposable mirror image (*i.e.*, they are enantiomers). Helical structures are fairly common in molecules that occur in nature, the best known examples being the double helix of DNA (deoxyribonucleic acid) and the α-helix of many proteins. These substances are optically active, but their structures also contain many units with asymmetric carbon atoms, and one cannot easily dissociate the optical activity caused by these chiral centres from the optical activity caused by the helicity of the molecule.

Geometric isomers. *Cis-trans isomers.* Rotation about carbon–carbon double bonds usually requires considerably more energy than rotations about single bonds. As a consequence, compounds of the type Cab=Cab, in which a differs from b, exist as stereoisomers. Because all of the atoms ordinarily lie in a plane, this plane constitutes a

cis — trans

a pair of geometric isomers

plane of symmetry, and molecules of this type usually are not optically active (unless a or b itself is chiral). This type of isomerism is called geometric, or *cis-trans*, isomerism. *Cis-trans* isomers of this type can also be considered as diastereomers because they are stereoisomers that are not mirror images. They differ from one another, therefore, in their chemical and physical properties.

The existence of geometric isomers was predicted by van't Hoff in 1874, and specific examples were recognized within the next two decades. Maleic and fumaric acids constitute the classic examples. Both have the structural formula $HO_2C-CH=CH-CO_2H$, but they differ in all

Maleic and fumaric acids

Table 4: Comparison of the Properties of Maleic and Fumaric Acids

	maleic acid (*cis*)	fumaric acid (*trans*)
Melting point	130°–131° C	287° C
Solubility in water, g/100 ml at 25°	78.8	0.7
Density, g/ml	1.590	1.635
Acidity constants (p*Ka*'s)	1.9; 6.5	3.0; 4.5
Toxicity	toxic	nontoxic; an intermediate in metabolic processes

physical properties (see Table 4). They are readily distinguished by their thermal behaviour. Maleic acid, on being heated above 140° C (284° F), loses water and forms a cyclic anhydride. Under the same conditions, fumaric acid is unaffected.

maleic acid $\xrightarrow{140°}$ maleic anhydride + H_2O

fumaric acid $\xrightarrow{140°}$ no change

This result suggests that maleic acid must have the two acidic groups in the *cis* arrangement, in which they are close enough to interact (compare with the distinction of phthalic acid from its positional isomers, above).

If more than one carbon–carbon double bond is present in a molecule, the number of possible isomers may be increased. Four geometric isomers of the hydrocarbon $CH_3CH=CHCH_2CH=CHCH_2CH_3$ are possible:

cis–cis — *cis–trans*

trans–cis — *trans–trans*

Many biological materials, such as the carotenes, retinenes, and unsaturated fats, contain several carbon–carbon double bonds, the geometry of which is significant in governing their biochemical function.

Allenes. A special case of isomerism arises in molecules that are known as allenes, Cab═C═Cab, in which two double bonds are immediately adjacent to one another. The substituents at one end of the allene system are in a plane at right angles to the plane of the substituents at the other end. As with the biphenyls, the chirality is best seen from an end-on view. If a is different from b, two optically active enantiomers exist. This possibility was recognized by van't Hoff in 1874, but the first actual

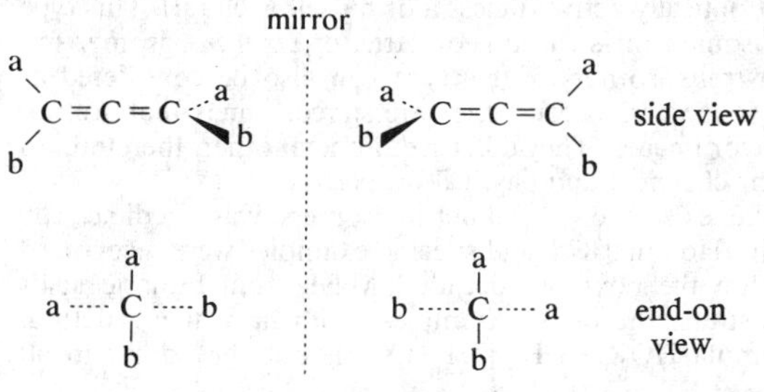

mirror

side view

end-on view

isomerism of allenes

example was not observed until 1935. Allenes have no chiral centre but a chiral axis, which is analogous to that in the biphenyls. They are conformational isomers that are prevented from interconversion because rotation about carbon–carbon double bonds does not ordinarily occur at room temperature. In this sense they are analogous to *cis-trans* isomers.

Cyclopropanedicarboxylic acids

Cyclic molecules. Molecules that have cyclic structures may also exhibit geometric isomerism. The 1,2-cyclopropanedicarboxylic acids provide a good example and also illustrate the occasional interrelation that exists between geometric and optical isomers. The three carbon atoms of a cyclopropane ring form a plane; because two bonds of each ring carbon atom extend above and below that plane, the acid groups may lie on the same (*cis*) or opposite (*trans*) side of the ring, as shown in Table 5. The two types of geometric isomers differ in all properties and can be readily distinguished because the *cis* isomer forms a cyclic anhydride on being subjected to heat, but the *trans* isomer does not (compare with maleic and fumaric acid). Each form has two identical asymmetric carbon atoms, marked in the drawings with asterisks (analogous to those in the tartaric acids). Consequently, the *cis* isomer can also be regarded as a meso form (it has a plane of symmetry—the perpendicular bisector of the bond that joins the two asterisked carbon atoms—and is therefore achiral and optically inactive). The *trans* isomer has no plane or centre of symmetry and is consequently chiral and exists in two non-superimposable mirror-image forms as shown.

Geometric isomerism occurs in rings of all sizes, even if they are not planar, because the ring can always be regarded as having two sides. Menthol, which is the major constituent of peppermint oil, provides an instructive example. The hydroxyl (−OH) group is *cis* to the methyl ($-CH_3$) group because each group is attached to the upper one of the two bonds of the carbon atom in the six-membered ring. The hydroxyl group is *trans* to the isopropyl [$CH(CH_3)_2$] group because the latter is attached to the lower of the two bonds of the ring carbon atom.

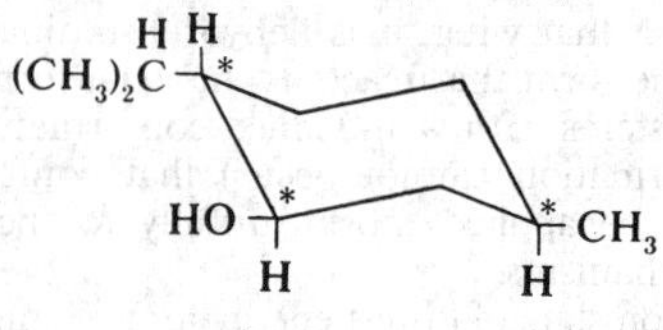

l-menthol

The methyl and isopropyl groups are also *trans* to one another. Menthol, however, has no plane or centre of symmetry and is therefore chiral and optically active. Indeed, because there are three different asymmetric carbon atoms (marked in the drawing with asterisks), there are $2^3 = 8$ possible and known stereoisomers of the substance (four pairs of enantiomers, in accord with the van't Hoff rule).

Molecules with planar chirality. Examples of enantiomerism that arise from chiral centres (asymmetric carbon atom) and chiral axes or helicity (biphenyls, allenes) have been described. There is a third case in which neither a centre nor an axis can be defined as the focus of chirality, but a chiral plane can be identified, the dissymmetry being caused by the location of atoms or groups on one or the other side of that plane. Cyclic molecules that contain a *trans* carbon–carbon double bond in the ring, such as *trans*-cyclooctene, constitute typical examples of planar chirality.

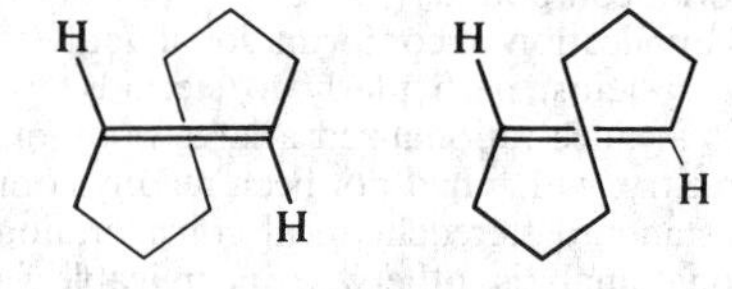

enantiomers of *trans*-cyclooctene

Trans-cyclooctene

The plane containing the carbon-carbon double bond is a chirality plane, the carbon chain lying behind or in front of that plane. The mirror-image structures are not superimposable and were successfully separated and shown to be optically active in 1963.

The separation and interconversion of chiral molecules. Synthesis of a chiral substance in the laboratory from achiral precursors always results in a mixture that contains equal amounts of the two enantiomers; *i.e.*, a racemic modification. The point is illustrated with the synthesis of the two enantiomers of bromopropionic acid from the achiral (symmetric) precursors propionic (propanoic) acid and bromine. Either of two hydrogen atoms of propionic acid is equally easily replaced by bromine, thus giving the two enantiomers of bromopropionic (bromopropanoic) acid in equal amounts. It therefore becomes important, if pure enantiomers are to be obtained in the laboratory, to have ways of separating (or resolving) enantiomers. The process is called resolution. Because their achiral physical properties are identical, enantiomers cannot be resolved by the physical methods (distillation, crystallization, or chromatography) normally used to isolate pure substances.

One method of resolution, the mechanical separation of dissymmetric crystals used with the tartaric acids by Pasteur, is possible only in fortuitous situations in which the racemic mixture forms such crystals, however; it is primarily of historic interest. Several other methods of res-

Table 5: Comparison of the Geometric Isomers of 1, 2-Cyclopropanedicarboxylic Acids

	cis (meso form)	*trans* (pair of enantiomers)
Structure	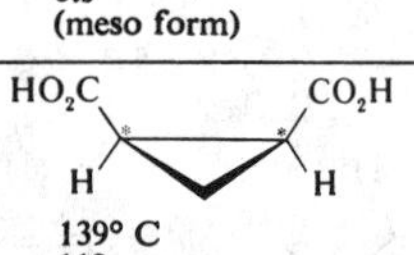 HO_2C, CO_2H / H, H	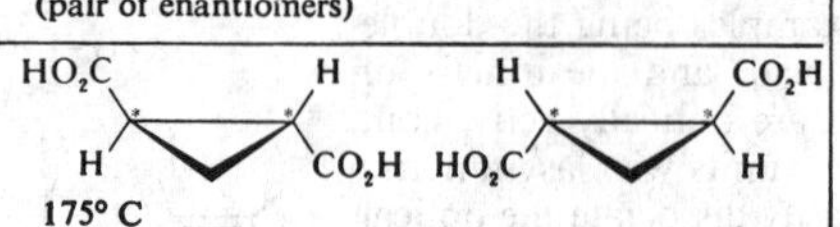 HO_2C, H / H, CO_2H ; H, CO_2H / HO_2C, H
Melting point	139° C	175° C
Solubility in water, g/100 g at 20° C	112	19
Optical rotation	0°	±84°

$$2\left[\begin{matrix}H & & H\\ & C & \\ H_3C & & CO_2H\end{matrix}\right] + 2Br_2$$

propionic acid

$$\longrightarrow \begin{matrix}Br & & H\\ & C & \\ H_3C & & CO_2H\end{matrix} + \begin{matrix}H & & Br\\ & C & \\ H_3C & & CO_2H\end{matrix} + 2HBr$$

50:50 mixture of bromopropionic acid enantiomers

olution are generally employed, the two most important involving diastereomeric salts or enzymatic processes.

The most generally practical procedure for resolving a racemic modification involves converting the enantiomers, by reaction with an optically active substance, into compounds that are diastereomers. Because diastereomers are not mirror images, they do not have identical physical properties and may be separated by ordinary means, such as fractional crystallization. After the diastereomers are separated, they are converted back into the original reactants. This method, first developed by Pasteur, has many modifications. The selective adsorption of enantiomers on optically active adsorbents and selective extraction with optically active solvents are based on the same principle.

Use of enzymes

Enzymes often react with only one of two enantiomers. Pasteur found that the mold *Penicillium glaucum,* for example, when grown in the presence of racemic ammonium tartrate, consumed only the *d*-isomer, leaving the *l*-tartrate unchanged. The reason for the discrimination by the enzyme is that it is chiral and interacts differently with the two (chiral) enantiomers. The situation is analogous to the interaction of a right hand with a pair of gloves: only the right-handed glove will fit, and the left-handed glove will remain unused.

The resolution methods just described all depend on the presence of another dissymmetric compound; *i.e.,* dissymmetry is propagated rather than created. There remains the interesting question of the ultimate origin of molecular dissymmetry or how the first optically active compound was formed. Essentially, two possibilities have been discussed. Some substances, such as urea, are symmetric on the molecular scale but form dissymmetric crystals. It is possible that the first organic compounds were resolved by occlusion in the dissymmetric cavities of such crystals. Alternatively, a synthesis carried out in the presence of some dissymmetric physical agent may lead to a preponderance of an enantiomer. Le Bel pointed out that in the presence of light polarized in a peculiar way, the formation of a substance with an asymmetric carbon atom need not give equal amounts of the two enantiomers; much later his proposal was verified experimentally. Because light reflected from the surface of the ocean is polarized in the necessary way by the Earth's magnetic field, this proposal offers one reasonable explanation for the origin of optically active substances.

Racemization is the conversion of an optically active substance into its enantiomer by a process that ultimately results in a 50 : 50 mixture. The process may be brought about by a number of agents—such as by treatment with heat, acids, bases, light, or catalysts—that cannot be dealt with in a general way because the methods depend on the structure and chemical behaviour of the particular dissymmetric substance. Usually in laboratory syntheses of chiral natural products—as, for example, proteins from the individual, optically active amino acids—racemization is an undesirable process, and measures customarily are taken to minimize it.

STEREOISOMERISM OF ELEMENTS OTHER THAN CARBON

The possibilities for stereoisomerism about a central atom depend on the geometric orientation of its bonds. These may be directed toward the vertices of a tetrahedron (as with carbon bound to four other groups), or of many other figures, including simple pyramids, trigonal bipyramids, squares, octahedra, etc.

Tetrahedral structures. Several other elements form tetrahedral compounds analogous to those of carbon. If an atom of one of these elements is joined to four different groups, the racemic forms may be resolvable into the two enantiomers. The first successfully resolved examples of such compounds were ammonium salts, the positive ion of which had a tetrahedral nitrogen (N) atom with four different organic groups attached.

$$\left[\begin{matrix} & a & \\ & N & c\\ b & & d\end{matrix}\right]^{+} X^{-}$$

a tetrahedral ammonium ion

Analogous ions with phosphorus or arsenic in place of the nitrogen have been resolved, as have similar neutral molecules with silicon, germanium, or tin as the central atom.

Though certain other metals also form tetrahedral compounds or complexes (see CHEMICAL COMPOUNDS: *Coordination compounds*), the groups, or ligands (Latin *ligare,* "to tie"), that are bound to the metal often are readily replaced by solvent molecules or by other ligands. This situation permits rapid interconversion of the enantiomers, and usually only the racemic modification can be isolated; but, if two of the ligands are joined to one another so as to form a ring with the metal atom, the complexes are more stable, and the separate isomers can be prepared. Examples of the type shown below, with beryllium, boron, zinc, or copper as the metal M, are known:

Replacement of ligands

[two cyclic complexes: a–M–a with b, b ring-linked; mirror images]

Because of the cyclic structures, the four groups need not necessarily be different from one another. These complexes have a chirality axis (through the metal and bisecting both a–M–b angles) and are analogous to the allenes, or optically active biphenyls.

Neutral nitrogen compounds are usually trivalent and, in addition to the three attached groups, have one unshared pair of electrons on the nitrogen atom.

A ⇌ B ⇌ A (pyramidal N with groups a, b, c)

The geometry is pyramidal, with the nitrogen at the apex, and in principle two enantiomers (A and B) are possible. The absence of a fourth group, however, permits the molecule to undergo an inversion, like an umbrella in a strong wind, that interconverts the two enantiomers, as shown. It has been found that certain groups (such as chlorine or fluorine atoms for a, b, or c) slow down this motion, and separate isomers have been isolated. If the nitrogen in the above formulas is replaced by sulfur or selenium as the central atom, the resulting compounds do not undergo the umbrella-like inversion process and are readily resolvable into stable, optically active enantiomers.

When nitrogen is bound to carbon by a double bond, two isomers are possible. These are analogous to the *cis–trans*

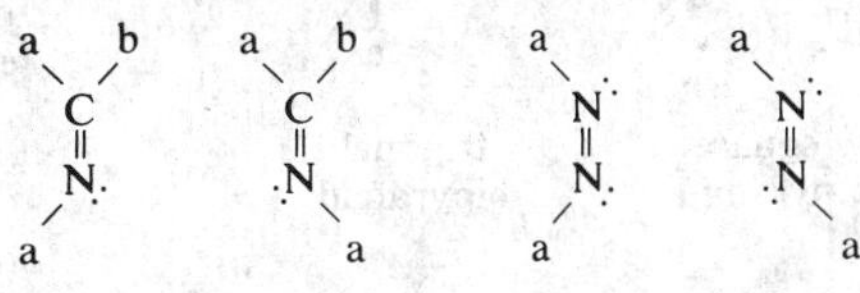

syn and *anti* isomers of C = N compounds

syn and *anti* isomers of N = N compounds

Syn and *anti* isomers

isomers of compounds having a carbon–carbon double bond. The terms *syn* and *anti* used with nitrogen compounds have the same meaning as *cis* and *trans,* and an electron pair (on the nitrogen) takes the place of an atom or group of atoms in the carbon analogue. The structures have a plane of symmetry (the plane of the paper, as drawn) and are therefore achiral. The geometric isomers (or diastereomers) are usually separable, and they differ in all achiral properties. Classes of compounds that exhibit this type of isomerism are oximes, hydrazones, semicarbazones, imines, and others. The analogous compounds with a nitrogen–nitrogen double bond (azo compounds) exhibit entirely analogous behaviour.

Square planar structures. The other common geometry (besides tetrahedral) in molecules with four groups attached to a central atom is square planar. If the four groups are all different (Mabcd), three geometric (or diastereomeric) isomers are possible:

b, a – M – c, d   c, a – M – d, b   d, a – M – b, c

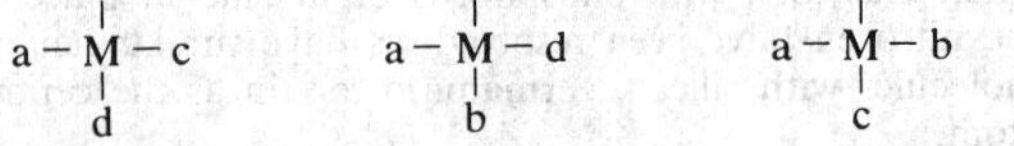

All three are achiral, the plane that includes all five atoms constituting a plane of symmetry. The three structures are distinct, however, as can readily be seen by noting that the group opposite (or *trans*) to a is different in each isomer. Much more common are complexes of the type Ma_2b_2, which can exist in two forms: *cis* and *trans.* A typical example is dichlorodiammineplatinum (II), $Pt[Cl_2(NH_3)_2]$, which has been isolated in each of the two isomeric structures.

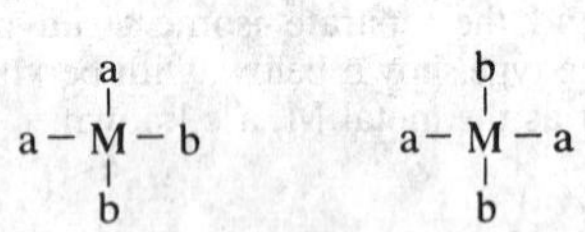

a, a – M – b, b   b, a – M – a, b

cis   *trans*

Similar compounds containing palladium, nickel, gold, rhodium, or iridium as the central metal atom are known.

In some relatively rare instances, both the square and the tetrahedral geometry are possible for a given central atom.

b, a – M – a, b   a, M, a, b, b

Examples have been found for M = cobalt or nickel, a specific case being dibromobis(benzyldiphenylphosphine) nickel(II), in which a = Br and $b = P(C_6H_5)_2(CH_2C_6H_5)$. This compound constitutes a specific example of the possibility mentioned in the first part of this discussion: that two substances may subsequently differ only in the bond angles, with a consequent different location of the atoms in space.

Trigonal bipyramidal structures. Phosphorus (P) forms some compounds (for example, the pentafluoride PF_5) in which five groups are attached to the phosphorus atom. In these and other compounds in which five groups are attached to a single central atom, the most common geometry is the trigonal bipyramid. The central atom lies in a plane defined by three of the attached groups; the remaining two groups lie along an axis perpendicular to that plane.

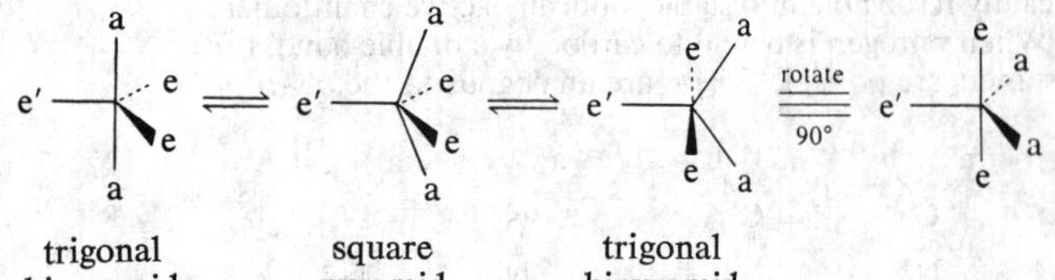

trigonal bipyramid ⇌ square pyramid ⇌ trigonal bipyramid (rotate 90°)

Thus, two different types of groups can be distinguished, called equatorial (e) and apical (a), respectively; and, in special cases in which the groups are not structurally identical, isomerism becomes possible. Separation of such isomers is usually not possible, however, because there exists a relatively easy mechanism for their interconversion. If one group, say e′, is held in a fixed position, then a small motion of the apical groups toward the remaining two equatorial groups, thus decreasing the angle between them, changes the geometry to that of a square pyramid. (Some compounds of zinc and nickel are known to have this geometry.) A counter motion of the two e groups, widening the angle between them, converts the structure back to a trigonal bipyramid, but the groups that were formerly apical are now equatorial, having exchanged places with two of the original equatorial groups. Because the equatorial plane is rotated 90° by these motions, the entire process is called pseudorotation. Trigonal bipyramidal structures are important as intermediates in the reactions of many phosphorus compounds; and, because of their widespread presence in many biological systems, much attention has been focussed on such compounds.

Pseudorotation

Octahedral structures. The most common geometry for substances with six ligands around a central atom is the octahedron. The metal atom lies in a plane that contains four of the ligands; the remaining two ligands lie on an axis that is perpendicular to this plane and passes through the metal atom. This structure permits the existence of a large number of stereoisomers, and many of these have been obtained, with such metals as cobalt, chromium, rhodium, iridium, ruthenium, or platinum as the central atoms. If all six groups attached to the metal are different (*i.e.,* Mabcdef), 15 pairs of enantiomers are possible, though no one has yet succeeded in obtaining all the theoretically possible isomers of such a molecule. Much more common are compounds in which several of the attached groups are identical, such as Ma_3b_3 or Ma_4b_2. Each of these may exist as geometric (*cis–trans*) isomers.

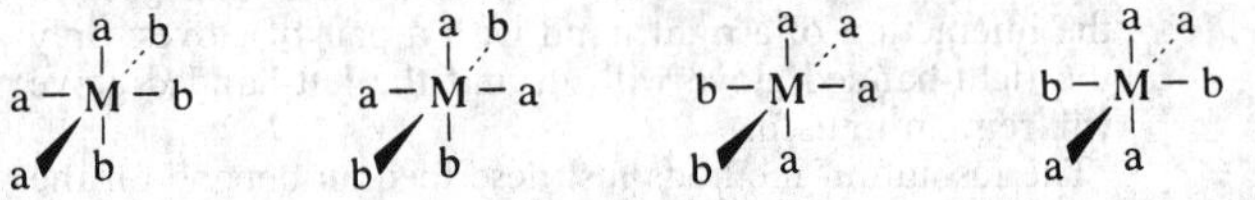

cis Ma_3b_3 *trans* Ma_3b_3 *cis* Ma_4b_2 *trans* Ma_4b_2

Cis isomers have all like groups adjacent (90° angles), but *trans* isomers have at least one pair of like groups in opposite positions (180° angles). Each of these structures has at least one symmetry plane; therefore, species of this type are achiral, but because they are pairs of diastereomers, they differ in all achiral properties. Specific examples are the platinum (Pt) and cobalt (Co) complexes with ammonia (NH_3) and chloride ion (Cl^-), trichlorotriammineplatinum (IV), $[Pt(NH_3)_3Cl_3]^+$, and dichlorotetramminecobalt (III), $[Co(NH_3)_4Cl_2]^+$.

When two or more of the ligands are chemically linked, a great variety of isomeric structures become possible, even when the ligands are identical. Compounds of the $[M(\widehat{aa})_3]$ type for example, may exist in two enantiomeric structures, as shown below.

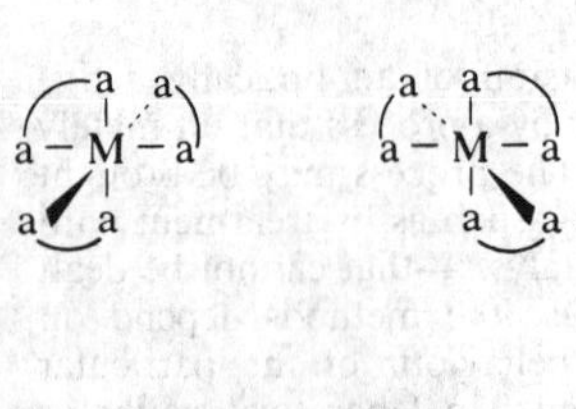

a pair of enantiomers 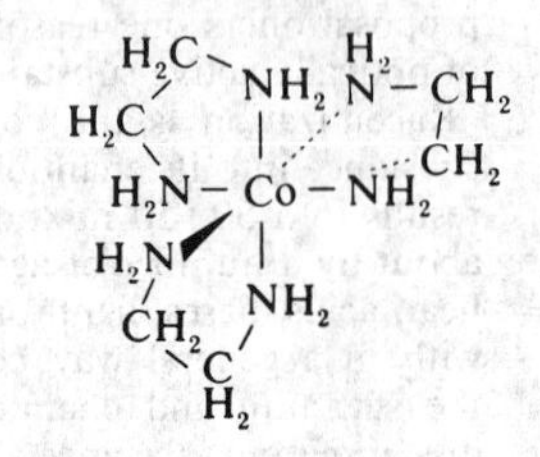   (+)-isomer

The dextrorotatory isomer of the complex cobalt ion tris (ethylenediamine)cobalt(III), $[Co(NH_2CH_2CH_2NH_2)_3]^{3+}$, for example, has the absolute configuration corresponding to the general structure at the left.

Complexes of the type $[M(\widehat{aa})_2b_2]$ are also common; *cis* and *trans* geometric isomers are possible. The *cis* form may exist as either of two optically active enantiomers, but the *trans* form has several planes of symmetry and is optically inactive. The stereoisomers of a cobalt complex ion provide a specific example.

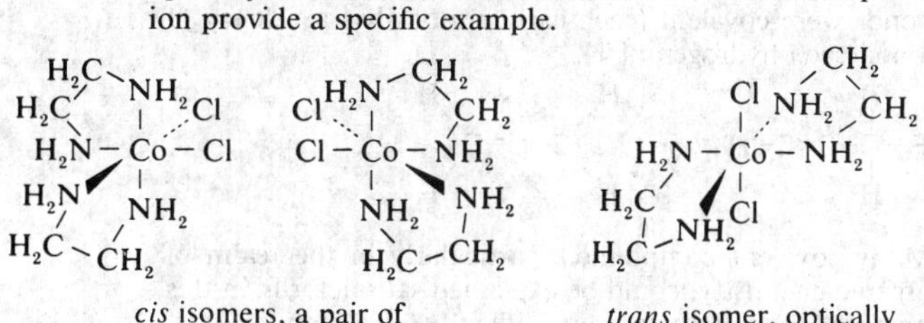

cis isomers, a pair of enantiomers

trans isomer, optically inactive

The *cis*-cobalt ions are violet, although the *trans* isomer is green. Many other possibilities for isomerism can be realized with octahedral structures through variations in the types of ligand attachment; those presented here are merely illustrative. Many structures are also known with more than six (seven to 12) groups around a central atom. The possibilities for isomerism increase with the molecular complexity, but such systems have not been studied as extensively as those with six or fewer groups around the central atom.

Other types of isomerism. Several rather common types of isomerism in coordination compounds are analogous to the structural isomerism of organic compounds. For example, in the linkage isomers $[Co(NH_3)_5NO_2]^{2+}$ and $[Co(NH_3)_5ONO]^{2+}$, the nitro ($-NO_2$) and nitrito ($-ONO$) groups are linked to the central cobalt atom by a nitrogen or oxygen atom, respectively. This situation is analogous to the functional group isomerism of organic compounds. Ionization isomerism, as, for example, with $[Co(NH_3)_4Cl_2]^+NO_2^-$ and $[Co(NH_3)_4ClNO_2]^+Cl^-$ in which the nitro group and a chloride ion interchange places, is a counterpart of positional isomerism in organic compounds. The three isomeric chromic chloride hydrates, $CrCl_3 \cdot 6H_2O$, constitute a particularly striking example; $[Cr(H_2O)_6]Cl_3$ is violet, but $[Cr(H_2O)_5Cl]Cl_2 \cdot H_2O$ and $[Cr(H_2O)_4Cl_2]Cl \cdot 2H_2O$, in which one or two chloride ions replace water molecules in the octahedral arrangement around the chromium atom, are green. Yet another type of positional isomerism is found in compounds in which the negative and positive ions are complex. The distribution of different ligands between the two ions gives rise to coordination isomers, as with the cobalt–chromium complexes:

$$[Co(NH_3)_6]^{3+}[Cr(CN)_6]^{3-} \text{ and } [Cr(NH_3)_6]^{3+}[Co(CN)_6]^{3-}.$$

DYNAMIC APPLICATIONS OF STEREOCHEMISTRY

This section has dealt almost exclusively with the recognition, delineation, and classification of stable isomers, but there are also dynamic aspects of the subject of isomerism. Intermediate between the reactants and the products in any chemical reaction lies a transition state. or transition complex, in which some chemical bonds in the reactants have been partially broken, and new chemical bonds, which will appear in the products, have partially formed. As with stable compounds, possible transition states for a chemical reaction may be isomeric; some may be enantiomeric, others diastereomeric, with different consequences for the outcome of the reaction (*i.e.,* products with different structures may be obtained, depending on the relationship between the various transition states). As an illustration, the following reaction may be considered.

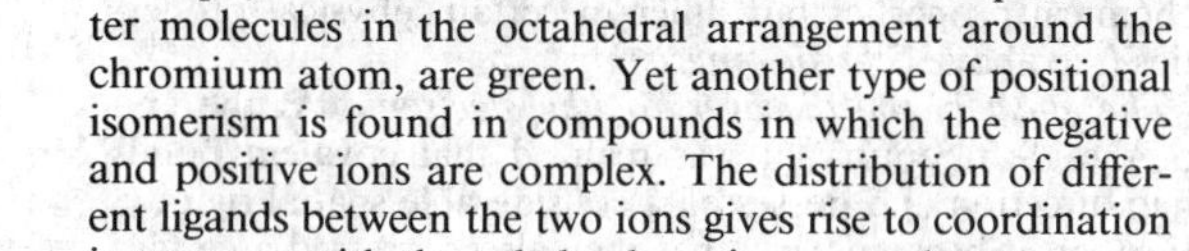

$$CH_3-\overset{H}{\underset{Br}{C^*}}-CH_2CH_3+Br_2 \longrightarrow CH_3-\overset{H}{\underset{Br}{C^*}}-\overset{H}{\underset{Br}{C^*}}-CH_3+HBr.$$

One reactant is asymmetric (has an asymmetric carbon atom, marked with an asterisk); the other (bromine) is symmetric. Although it might at first be thought that there would be a 50–50 chance of replacing either hydrogen of the $-CH_2-$ group by a bromine atom, this is not true. The presence of a nearby asymmetric centre makes the two hydrogens stereochemically distinct, as the following structures show.

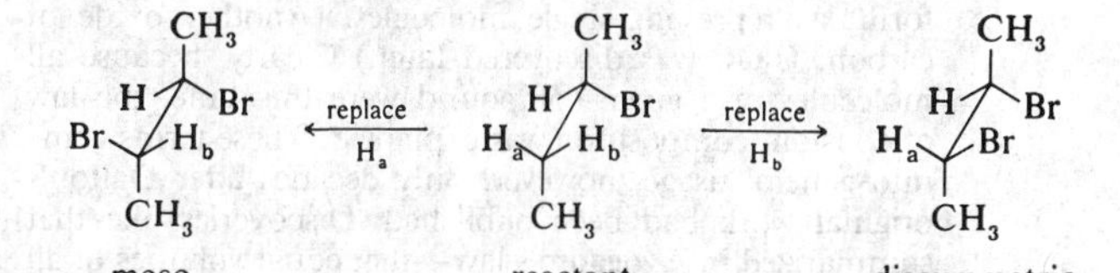

meso (optically inactive) ← replace H_a ← reactant → replace H_b → dissymmetric (optically active)

No matter what conformer of the reactant is drawn, H_a will always be in a different chemical environment (say, between H and CH_3) with respect to its neighbours than H_b (say, between CH_3 and Br). Replacement of H_a gives a meso product; but, if H_b is replaced, one of two enantiomers is produced. The products are diastereomers, as are the transition states leading to them. Because the transition states are not enantiomers, they need not be formed in equal amounts; consequently, the products are also not formed in equal amounts, and the reaction is said to be stereoselective (in this case, the product is 70 percent meso, 30 percent racemic). If one diastereomeric transition state is very much stabler than another, the reaction may proceed exclusively along the path that includes the stable form, in which case the product consists of only one stereoisomer, and the reaction is said to be stereospecific. Most biochemical processes are of this type. For example, only *d*-glucose (not the *l*-isomer) is fermentable by yeast or usable in cell metabolism; only one configuration of amino acid enantiomers is usable in protein synthesis, etc. The reason for the very high degree of stereospecificity of most biochemical reactions is that it is virtually impossible for the wrong enantiomer to fit into or react at the active site of an enzyme; that is, only one of the two diastereomeric transition states is accessible. Similar results are sometimes obtained with nonenzymatic catalysts, as in the formation of stereoregular polymers (see CHEMICAL COMPOUNDS: *Polymers*). (H.Ha.)

Stereoselective and stereospecific reactions

Chemical bonding

Chemical bonds hold atoms together in various kinds of associations, such as those in molecules, crystals, and metals. In every neutral atom the number of positive charges on the nucleus (the atomic number) holds an equal number of negatively charged electrons clustered about the nucleus in a pattern characteristic for each element. Chemical bonds result when a few electrons (ordinarily an even number) are attracted simultaneously by more than one atomic nucleus (ordinarily two) and thereby serve to hold those nuclei close together. All chemical reactions are explained according to changes in the electron structures of the atoms, whether bonds are made or broken.

NONQUANTUM TREATMENT OF CHEMICAL BONDING

Early theories of chemical bonds. The idea that matter is made up of a large number of discrete particles somehow linked together dates back to Roman times, but it did not attain significance as a scientific hypothesis until the early part of the 18th century, when physical scientists interpreted the behaviour of gases in terms of simple kinetic (pertaining to motion) theory. Later in the same century, chemists began to weigh carefully all reactants and all products (gravimetric measurement) of chemical changes and were able to formulate laws governing such changes. Among these was the law of constant composition, which stated that a pure compound always has the same composition. As noted previously, John Dalton of England hypothesized, early in the 19th century, that these chemical observations were most readily explained by what he called an atomic theory, according to which all atoms of the same element were identical to each other and different from the atoms of all other elements and, in the formation of compounds, atoms of the elements, being indivisible, were joined together in simple whole numbers. Thus, the elements carbon and oxygen formed a compound, carbon monoxide, and also a compound, carbon dioxide. If C represents a single carbon atom and O an oxygen atom, the two compounds have the chemical formulas CO and CO_2, respectively, and such formulas represent single molecules. (Another oxide of carbon, C_3O_2, was discovered later.) Clearly, because all molecules of a given compound were the same, the law of constant composition was explained. These terms came into general usage, however, only decades after Dalton's original work had been published. Discoveries like that summarized in Avogadro's law—that equal volumes of all gases at the same temperature and pressure have equal numbers of molecules—enabled molecular weights to be determined on an arbitrary scale of comparisons in which the hydrogen atom was given a mass of one; later, the standard became oxygen, with a mass of 16 and, recently, by international agreement, carbon was selected for the standard (the isotope carbon-12). This basic knowledge of molecular masses was a necessary preliminary to theories concerning the nature of the chemical bonds holding atoms together in molecules.

Valence. About the middle of the 19th century, the first modern theory introduced the concept of valency to represent the combining capacity of an atom with a number: the valence of an element was the number of hydrogen atoms each atom of the element could combine with. Hydrogen was selected as the unit element because a single atom of hydrogen could never be found to combine with more than one atom of any other element. Thus, atoms of elements that combined with only one hydrogen atom were said to have a valency of 1, for example, chlorine (symbol Cl), while, for example, oxygen, nitrogen, and carbon (symbols O, N, C) had valencies of 2, 3, and 4, respectively. The compounds formed with hydrogen could then be represented quite simply by the numbers of symbols for the elements involved: hydrogen chloride, HCl; water, H_2O; ammonia, NH_3; methane, CH_4. Other molecules were also capable of such simple representation: an oxygen molecule was O_2; carbon dioxide, CO_2, etc.

Electrovalent bond. Early in the 19th century it was realized that there were two types of compounds, later termed electrovalent and covalent. The former, when dissolved in water, were capable of conducting an electric current, while the latter were not. As it became clear that electrically neutral atoms could acquire electrical charges, the concept developed that a charged atom was an independent particle; it was given the name ion and symbolized with a plus or minus superscript, indicating the charge, following the symbol for the element. Thus, the sodium atom could produce a positively charged sodium ion, symbolized as Na^+. Likewise, chlorine could produce negative ions, symbolized Cl^-. If this ionization occurred in a water solution, the ions were stable, so that the compound sodium chloride (common salt) could be regarded as composed of sodium and chlorine ions: Na^+Cl^-. Early in the 20th century it was shown that even solid crystals of sodium chloride consisted of independent sodium and chloride ions arranged in an orderly fashion, so that the positive ions were always balanced by negative ions. All electrovalent compounds have this general structure.

Discovery of ions

Covalent bond. As discussed earlier, covalent compounds do not involve ions. It was observed that two molecules, each made up of the same number of similar atoms (*e.g.,* methylacetylene and allene, both having the formula C_3H_4) could be chemically and physically different. Compounds having the same composition but different properties were named isomers. The only possible explanation for isomerism is that the molecules had different arrangements of the atoms and that these different arrangements were capable of a considerable persistence. An empirical hypothesis was needed to describe how the atoms were joined together, and so the chemical bond, or the covalent bond, was proposed. For many years nothing at all was known about the structure of the covalent bond, but a great deal of information was assembled about its properties. In one representation of the bond it was a line, and the symbol for each atom had as many lines attached to it as the atom had valences. Thus sodium was symbolized Na—, chlorine was Cl—, oxygen —O—, carbon, =C=. In a molecule, a single bond between two atoms consisted of one line from each symbol, but the two lines between bonded atoms were shown simply as a single shared line. Thus, the molecule C_3H_4 could be represented as having either of two possible structures in which all bonds were covalent (each carbon atom has a valency of 4 and each hydrogen of 1):

```
    H                  H         H
    |                   \       /
H—C—C≡C—H     or         C=C=C
    |                   /       \
    H                  H         H
```

Many covalent compounds, particularly in the realm of organic chemistry, could be explained satisfactorily in this manner, though there were difficulties. Carbon dioxide, CO_2, was clearly O=C=O, for instance; but how was carbon monoxide, CO, to be explained if carbon had a valency of 4 and oxygen a valency of 2? There were similar difficulties, but the overall success was so great that the difficulties were not allowed to invalidate the theory.

Difficulties of early theories

Stereoisomers. Toward the end of the 19th century, it became necessary to consider the arrangements of atoms in three dimensions. It was necessary to suppose that the four bonds from a carbon atom were directed from the central nucleus to the four corners of a regular tetrahedron, in order to explain why molecules having four different groups attached to the same carbon atom had isomers. It was realized that, if four different groups were attached tetrahedrally to the same carbon atom, two different molecules, which were mirror images of one another, were possible; for example, the carbon atom joined to four atoms signified by P, R, S, and Q can have the following different structures:

```
   P            P
   |            |
   C            C
  / | \       / | \
 R  |  Q     Q  |  R
    S           S
```

The C and P atoms lie in the plane of the page, S projects upward from the page and R and Q lie behind. Substances of this type of mirror-image organization have the same chemical properties but differ in certain physical properties (see above *Stereoisomerism).*

The effect of the discovery of the electron. At the end of the 19th century, it was realized that covalent bonds had direction and possessed a considerable spatial rigidity. Further, it became clear that they also possessed a certain degree of independence of one another; *e.g.,* the carbon–hydrogen bonds in compounds as different as methane and chloroform, (formulas CH_4 and $CHCl_3$, respectively) behaving in a similar manner. It was at this stage in history that the English physicist J.J. Thomson discovered the electron. It was soon realized that the covalent bond consisted of electrons being shared and that electrovalent bonds resulting from the formation of ions took place by electron transfer from one atom to another. The subsequent development of the theory of chemical bonding is therefore almost entirely a development of its electronic interpretation.

Early electronic theory of valency. Experiments early in the 20th century showed that atoms were mostly empty space, being made up of a small, heavy nucleus with positive charge around which at a distance were clustered the much lighter negatively charged electrons, the number of which was equal to the positive charge on the nucleus—*i.e.,* to the atomic number of the element, which is the basis of the periodic table of the elements.

Periodic properties of the elements. The modern periodic table of the elements, proposed in the 1860s, was based on the relative atomic weights of the elements, and it contributed to the theories of chemical reaction. Early in the 20th century, the basis for the periodic table became the nuclear and electronic structure, and chemical bonding, since then, has been understood with reference to this arrangement of the elements, which emphasizes valence properties as a function of the electronic structure. If the known elements are arranged in sequence according to their atomic numbers (the number of protons in the nucleus) their chemical and physical properties will be periodic; that is, similarities in properties will recur at regular intervals in the sequence of elements. Thus, elements that form a certain type of strong acid with hydrogen

The periodic table of the elements

(fluorine, chlorine, bromine, iodine) do not directly follow one another in the sequence but are separated by a recurring number of other elements. The sequence may be broken up, therefore, into periods, and, when these are placed horizontally under one another, vertical groups of elements will have similar properties. This is so because the internal structure of atoms, as they become larger and more massive, have recurring similarities. The electrons are grouped into arrangements called shells and subshells, each shell having a maximum number it can hold. Their arrangement is largely the result of quantum mechanical effects summarized in the so-called Pauli principle. The energy required to remove an electron is an important property. Some elements tend to lose electrons easily and thereby be left with a net positive charge; these are the metals. Nonmetallic elements have a great affinity for electrons and will accept them into their structure, thereby acquiring a net negative charge. Such charged atoms are called ions. This tendency to gain or lose electrons, with resulting changes in the total energy, forms the basis of one type of chemical bonding.

Structure of the noble gases

The noble gases, members of Group 0 in the periodic table (helium, neon, argon, etc.), have key positions in the sequence of elements because their electron structures are the stablest. All other elements tend toward this arrangement, gaining, losing, or sharing electrons to achieve it and forming compounds or ions to do so. (The empirical formulas for compounds are simply a numerical count of the atoms that are bonded together through electron structures, the atoms being represented by their symbols, followed by the number present in the molecule; for example, sulfuric acid is written H_2SO_4, which means two atoms of hydrogen, one atom of sulfur, and four atoms of oxygen.)

Shell theory and ionic bonds. The behaviour of the lighter elements suggests that the orbiting electrons occur in shells at various distances from the nucleus. The helium atom, for instance, atomic number 2 (see periodic table), contains two electrons. Apparently this arrangement must have a high stability, because the helium atom forms no chemical compounds; *i.e.,* it is not disrupted by collisions with other atoms. The lithium atom, atomic number 3, however, with three electrons, readily loses one electron to form an ion that still contains two electrons and is also very stable. The next element showing behaviour similar to that of helium is neon, the atom of which contains 10 electrons arranged in a stable inner shell of two (like those of helium) and an outer shell of eight electrons that is also very stable. Moreover, this number of electrons is attained also in the stable ions of oxygen (O^{2-}), fluorine (F^-), sodium (Na^+), and magnesium (Mg^{2+}), showing again the high stability of this outer shell of eight electrons, sometimes called the octet. Oxygen has six outer electrons but its ion has gained two, making a total of eight; fluorine has seven outer electrons, but it gains one in forming the ion; sodium, with 11 electrons, one outermost, loses that one to form a positive ion with only eight electrons outermost; magnesium loses two electrons to form its ion with eight. The argon atom, atomic number 18, contains 18 electrons, and the stability of this number is demonstrated by the formation of the ions of sulfur (S^{2-}), chlorine (Cl^-), potassium (K^+), and calcium (Ca^{2+}). The electron configuration of these ions may be assumed to consist of three shells containing two innermost, eight central, and eight outermost electrons, respectively. With this structure, the formation of the simple electrovalent compounds is understandable as being a consequence of electron transfer. The process is illustrated in the following equation of the reaction between sodium, Na, and fluorine, F; the dots represent electrons in the outermost shell only:

$$Na\cdot + \cdot\ddot{\underset{..}{F}}: \longrightarrow [Na]^+ + [:\ddot{\underset{..}{F}}:]^-$$

Such an electron transfer usually requires heat energy (*i.e.,* the reaction is usually endothermic), but the ultimate stability of electrovalent compounds, in the solid state, resides in the lowering of energy (called the ionic lattice energy of the crystal) resulting from the interionic electrostatic forces so that, overall, the total energy of the products is less than that of the reactants, and the energy falls. In solution, the overall lowering of the energy results from the separation by water molecules of the ions, a process called solvation. If a sodium atom were to form the ion Na^{2+}, the energy required to remove the second electron would be considerably larger than that required to remove the first, because the second electron would have to come from the inner, closed shell of eight in the ion Na^+, and the nucleus, still with its total of 11 positive charges, would hold each of those eight with greater affinity than the outermost electron is held when there are 11 electrons. Consequently, even though the electrovalent compound $Na^{2+}(F^-)_2$ would have a higher lattice energy than the compound Na^+F^-, this would not be large enough to compensate the energy required to form the ion Na^{2+}. In fact, the compound NaF_2 is unknown, being impossible in terms of energy content. The stability of the shell of eight provides a most satisfactory guide for the formation of ions for elements with atomic numbers less than 21 (the atomic number of the element scandium, Sc).

The Lewis structures

Octet and covalent bond. The above consideration led G.N. Lewis, a U.S. chemist, to emphasize the importance of the group of two and the group of eight electrons, called the pair and the octet. He used their stability, together with the concept of "electron sharing," in explaining covalent compounds. It was supposed that a covalent bond consisted of two electrons, one provided by each atom. Each of the shared electrons contributed to the outermost shells of both atoms and thus stability was achieved, just as in electrovalent compounds, with a shell of two for hydrogen and of eight for carbon, nitrogen, oxygen, fluorine, and the corresponding elements of the second short period in the periodic table, silicon, phosphorus, sulfur, and chlorine. Below are examples of electronic covalent structures, using dots to represent outershell electrons, for the compounds with the empirical formulas CH_3NH_2, CH_2O, HF, and HOCl:

```
  H          H                        
H:C:N:H       .C: :O.      H:F:      H:O:
  H H        H                       :Cl:
```

It was supposed that the octet was made up of four pairs which were either shared or unshared (lone pairs), each of the four pairs being disposed tetrahedrally (at the four corners of a tetrahedron) around the atom. A tetrahedral distribution of covalent bonds of carbon and silicon atoms was postulated, as well as the pyramidal arrangement for nitrogen and phosphorus atoms and a nonlinear arrangement for oxygen and sulfur atoms.

Coordinate bond. In some cases, electron-pair bonds could be formed with both electrons being donated by one atom only. Such a bond was called a coordinate bond and may be illustrated by a group of compounds called the oxo acids of chlorine. Using dots for the outershell electrons, the structures are:

```
                          H            H
 H         H             :O:          :O:
:O:       :O:            :Cl:O:     :O:Cl:O:
:Cl:      :Cl:O:         :O:          :O:
```

To indicate covalent bonds, a line was used, and the symbol usually employed for the coordinate bond was an arrow indicating the donation of the electrons, so that the oxo acids of chlorine could also be written as:

```
H       H        H          H
|       |        |          |
O       O        O          O
|       |        |          |
Cl      Cl→O     Cl→O     O←Cl→O
                 ↓          ↓
                 O          O
```

The assumed stability of the octet provided a most successful hypothesis for elements of low atomic number, and certain earlier difficulties were removed. Carbon monoxide, for instance, could have the structure

:C:::O: or C≦O

Some difficulties remained, however; nitrogen oxide (NO), nitrogen dioxide (NO_2), and chlorine dioxide (ClO_2), each of which contains an odd number of electrons, are violations of the electron-pair concept.

In addition, the fluorides of phosphorus, PF_5, and sulfur, SF_6, were known. Since the bonds in these compounds behaved as single bonds, the most likely electronic structures were:

```
  F            F
F:  .        F.:.F
  P :F  and   :S:
F :.         F.:.F
  F            F
```

Expansion of the octet

Such a configuration required the assumption that the second shell could be expanded beyond the octet. (This discussion is still concerned with elements lighter than argon.) Empirically it appeared that the limit of this expansion was six pairs, the groupings SF_6, PF_6^-, and SiF_6^{2-} being known, but no molecules or ions that required an outermost bonding shell with more than 12. The sulfate ion, SO_4^{2-}, could then be represented by:

```
:O: :O:          :O: :O:
    S      or        S
:O: :O:          :O: :O:
```

Nevertheless, the employment of the Lewis electron-pair bond was still based largely on empiricism and, in fact, it was only slightly less empirical than the 19th-century chemical bond, but its electrical character did serve to guide, in most important ways, the assembly of empirical knowledge. A particularly important example lay in the field of organic chemistry, where physical organic chemists were able to interpret subtle differences in behaviour by considering the polarization and polarizability (*i.e.,* the unequal distribution of charges to produce concentrations, or poles, of positive and negative charge) of the electronic bond; it led to concepts (such as the inductive effect) that have been vitally important in modern research.

This phase in the history of chemical-bond theory ended with quantum mechanics and the provision of the basic equation governing electronic behavior. The application of the equation proved so difficult that empirical development continued to be a most important aspect of research.

Before studying the effect of quantum mechanics it is necessary to consider the earlier quantum theory and its importance to the understanding of atomic structure, a necessary precursor to the understanding of molecular structure and chemical bonding.

Atomic structure and bonding. In the first decades of the 20th century, development within the physical sciences was dominated by the quantum theory proposed in 1900 by Max Planck, a German physicist. Niels Bohr, a Danish physicist, and, later, others applied the quantum theory to atomic structure.

Electron arrangement. It was concluded that because energy was absorbed in finite quanta, or measurable units, by electrons, only certain electron orbits could occur; *i.e.,* an electron could not have energy in any amount but only in multiples of a finite quantity. These quantized orbits were designated and distinguished from one another by three quantum numbers that finally assumed the following pattern. The principal quantum number, n, was related primarily to the size of the orbit and could have any integral value. These are the "shells," designated from innermost outward as K, L, M, N, O, P, etc. The subsidiary quantum number, designated as l, was related to the shape of the orbit. It could have the integral values for a given value of n from 0 to $(n-1)$, and it measured the angular momentum (resulting from orbital motion) of the electron. The third quantum number, designated m, was related to the orientation of the orbit and represented a magnetic property. It could have the integral values for any given value of l from $-l$ to $+l$. The letters s, p, d, f (sometimes called subshells) are used to represent the value of the l quantum number, being equivalent to $l = 0$, 1, 2, 3, respectively. Hence, an orbit having $n = 3$ and $l = 1$ is described by the symbol $3p$. There are three such orbits, $3p_{-1}$, $3p_0$, and $3p_1$, in which the magnetic quantum number is given as a subscript. In atoms containing a number of electrons, the order of binding of the orbits is $1s$, $2s$, $2p$, $3s$, $3p$, $4s$, $3d$, $4p$, $5s$, $4d$, $5p$, $6s$, $4f$, $5d$, $6p$, $7s$. Later it became necessary to assume that the electron had an intrinsic angular momentum (*i.e.,* it had a spin). A fourth quantum number was added, called the spin quantum number, which measured the orientation of this spin angular momentum about a given axis, prescribed, say, by a magnetic field; the spin angular momentum could have only two values, and two values of the spin quantum are, therefore, possible, designated as plus or minus one-half

The quantum numbers

Table 6: Whole Orbital Occupation for the Least Energy States of a Number of Elements

element	1s	2s	2p	3s	3p	3d	4s	4p	4d	4f	5s	5p	5d	6s	6p	7s
Hydrogen	1															
Helium	2															
Lithium	2	1														
Elements between lithium and neon omitted																
Neon	2	2	6													
Sodium	2	2	6	1												
Elements between sodium and potassium omitted																
Potassium	2	2	6	2	6		1									
Elements between potassium and scandium omitted																
Scandium	2	2	6	2	6	1	2									
Elements between scandium and zinc omitted																
Zinc	2	2	6	2	6	10	2									
Gallium	2	2	6	2	6	10	2	1								
Elements between gallium and rubidium omitted																
Rubidium	2	2	6	2	6	10	2	6			1					
Elements between rubidium and yttrium omitted																
Yttrium	2	2	6	2	6	10	2	6	1		2					
Elements between yttrium and palladium omitted																
Palladium	2	2	6	2	6	10	2	6	10							
Elements between palladium and indium omitted																
Indium	2	2	6	2	6	10	2	6	10		2	1				
Elements between indium and cesium omitted																
Cesium	2	2	6	2	6	10	2	6	10		2	6		1		
Elements between cesium and lanthanum omitted																
Lanthanum	2	2	6	2	6	10	2	6	10		2	6	1	2		
Cerium	2	2	6	2	6	10	2	6	10	2	2	6		2		
Elements between cerium and ytterbium omitted																
Ytterbium	2	2	6	2	6	10	2	6	10	14	2	6		2		
Lutetium	2	2	6	2	6	10	2	6	10	14	2	6	1	2		
Elements between lutetium and mercury omitted																
Mercury	2	2	6	2	6	10	2	6	10	14	2	6	10	2		
Thallium	2	2	6	2	6	10	2	6	10	14	2	6	10	2	1	
Elements between thallium and francium omitted																
Francium	2	2	6	2	6	10	2	6	10	14	2	6	10	2	6	1
Elements following francium omitted																

($\pm\frac{1}{2}$). From spectroscopic and other evidence, Wolfgang Pauli concluded that it was impossible for two electrons in an atom to have the same four quantum numbers. As a consequence, each orbit had a capacity of two electrons spinning in different directions. Accordingly, every electron in any atom can be defined according to the position it occupies in terms of the four quantum numbers. When an electron's energy was increased, it acquired different quantum numbers. The *s* orbitals could each hold two electrons; a set of *np* orbitals, with a given value of *n*, could hold six; a set of *nd*, 10, and a set of *nf*, 14. Atomic structures, defined by occupancy of orbitals, were then formed according to the principle whereby a number of electrons appropriate to the given atom or ion were "fed" into the sets of orbitals in order of their energy, each receiving electrons up to its capacity. The number of electrons in any subshell is indicated by a superscript, thus: $2s^2$ means two electrons in the *s* subshell of the second (*L*) shell; $3d^6$ means six electrons in the *d* subshell of the third (*M*) shell. The electronic structures of atoms occupying key positions in the periodic table are given in their ground, or least energy, states in Table 6.

The stable configuration

The stability of the electron pair in helium and in bonded hydrogen is accounted for by the completion of the $n = 1$ shell. The stability of the octet for elements in the next period (ending with neon) is caused by the completion of the $n = 2$ shell (one $2s$ and three $2p$ orbits). In the next period (ending with argon), the stability of the octet is caused by the filling of the $3s$ and $3p$ orbits. In these elements, however, the $3d$ orbits are also available, and it has been proposed that this is why the shell can be expanded beyond four pairs. This is not possible with the $n = 2$ shell, because the *l* quantum number is limited to 0 and 1 when $n = 2$. Consequently, nitrogen does not form pentavalent compounds whereas phosphorus does.

Ion formation by transition elements. The formation of ions by the transition elements will now be examined. These are the elements in the centre of the table and they are classified as metals; *i.e.,* they tend to lose electrons in chemical reactions. Iron forms two simple ions: Fe^{2+} and Fe^{3+}. The electronic structure of the neutral iron atom, Fe, is $1s^22s^22p^63s^23p^63d^64s^2$; that of iron (II) ion (the iron atom having lost two electrons), Fe^{2+}, is $1s^22s^22p^63s^23p^63d^6$, and that of iron (III) ion (the atom having lost three electrons), Fe^{3+}, is $1s^22s^22p^63s^23p^63d^5$. There is no question here of losing electrons to achieve an octet structure as former theory assumed. The removal of one electron from an iron atom requires considerable energy, the removal of a second more, of a third still more, and so on. There is no sudden rise, however, in the energy to remove a further electron as there was with sodium's second electron (discussed above). With the iron atom, electrons are being removed from $4s$ and $3d$ levels, the binding energies of which are not very different. The rise occurs because successive electrons are being withdrawn from an ion that has successively increasing, unbalanced positive charges. In forming a series of compounds with chlorine (the iron chlorides), the electrons removed from iron are transferred to chlorine to give chloride ions. One can envisage the formation of the following iron chloride compounds, with their formulas: iron monochloride, Fe^+Cl^-; iron dichloride, $Fe^{2+}(Cl^-)_2$; iron trichloride, $Fe^{3+}(Cl^-)_3$; iron tetrachloride, $Fe^{4+}(Cl^-)_4$; etc. The lattice energy (that required to separate an ion from the lattice of ions forming the solid crystal) of these compounds (all are salts) would increase steadily.

Role of lattice energy

The question is, therefore: to what extent can the lattice energy outweigh the energy required to transfer an electron from the iron atom to the chlorine atom? The monochloride, FeCl, is unknown because the gain in lattice energy in forming the dichloride, $FeCl_2$, from FeCl is much more than sufficient to outbalance the energy to remove the second electron from the iron atom. At the next stage (going from $FeCl_2$ to the trichloride, $FeCl_3$), the energies are fairly evenly balanced, so both can be prepared. But the energy required to remove the fourth electron is so great that the increase in lattice energy between $FeCl_3$ and the tetrachloride, $FeCl_4$, would be inadequate to provide it. Hence, $FeCl_4$ is an impossible compound, energetically. Consequently, only the $FeCl_2$ and $FeCl_3$ forms are known.

Such variable valency in the other transition elements can be explained similarly. The valency differences are single when simple ions are formed. The energy required to produce highly charged ions is usually prohibitive for simple electrostatic reasons so that vanadium (V), for example, forms the ions V^{2+} and V^{3+}, but it is tetravalent only in the oxide VO_2, and shows a valency of 5 in such compounds as $VOCl_3$. The relative stability of the different valency states depends on the energy required to remove the electrons. In the series of transition elements iron, cobalt, nickel (Fe, Co, Ni), of increasing atomic number, electrons become increasingly difficult to remove, so that, while the ions Fe^{2+} and Fe^{3+} have comparable stability, the cobalt ion Co^{3+} is more difficult to form, and the nickel ion Ni^{3+} extremely so. With the next element, the copper ion Cu^{3+} is unknown, and, in fact, it becomes possible to form the ion Cu^+ in addition to the ion Cu^{2+}.

Complex ions. Another feature of transition-metal ions is the ease with which they form complex ions. Thus, the iron(II) ion Fe^{2+} combines with cyanide ions, CN^-, to give the hexacyanoferrate(II) ion, $Fe(CN)_6^{4-}$. The Fe^{2+} ion has 12 fewer electrons than the next inert gas, krypton. Six electron-pair coordinate links from the cyanide ions to the iron, therefore, provide for the metal atom the same electron shell as that for krypton. The role of the cyanide ion in donating electrons to the iron ion makes the cyanide a ligand, which is defined in any compound as the atom or ion that provides some or all of the bonding pair of electrons to a central atom. Also, from Fe^{3+} the hexacyanoferrate(III) ion, $Fe(CN)_6^{3-}$, is formed, in which the iron atom is associated with a number of electrons that is one short of that for krypton. Many other complex ions are known in which the ligands can all be regarded as being bound to the central positive ion by lone pairs on the ligand, though the extent to which these are incorporated into the electron shells of the central atom varies.

Ligands

The shape of these complexes has aroused great interest. Ions such as $Fe(CN)_6^{4-}$ are octahedral; that is, the attached groups are located at the corners of an octahedron. Ions such as tetrachloromercurate(II), $HgCl_4^{2-}$, are tetrahedral, but tetracyanonickelate(II), $Ni(CN)_4^{2-}$, is square planar. The explanation of these shapes will be considered later. More recently, interest has shifted from the shape to the study of the spectra (*i.e.,* the spectroscopic analysis of radiation absorbed and emitted by molecules gives evidence concerning their structure) of these complexes.

QUANTUM-MECHANICAL TREATMENT OF CHEMICAL BONDING

The early electronic theory of valency was, as has been said, largely empirical, and the older quantum theory was, in many respects, arbitrary. It dealt quantitatively with a few atomic properties, but it was completely unsuccessful in selecting quantized molecular orbits or making calculations of the energies of electrons in molecules. In 1924, Louis de Broglie examined the possibility that particles such as electrons might show, in addition to properties of matter, other properties explicable only in terms of wave propagation. That electrons had wave properties was demonstrated by diffraction experiments. This observation was followed, in 1926, by a wave equation proposed by Erwin Schrödinger, that provided, for the first time, an equation capable, in principle, of calculating the energy of any electronic system in any potential field. (Werner Heisenberg simultaneously devised an equivalent scheme.) Hence, the energies of atoms and molecules could be calculated, in principle, exactly. Moreover, the equation allowed immediate approximate calculation. Researchers using this new wave mechanics obtained a value for the dissociation energy of the hydrogen molecule that was about three-quarters of the true one. No comparable success had ever been achieved before, yet, in less than 10 years, others calculated this dissociation energy almost exactly. The discovery of the electron in 1897 had revealed the material of the chemical bond, but the introduction of quantum mechanics was perhaps even more important because, with it, the mechanics, dynamics, and energetics of these electrons could be, in principle, calculated ex-

Wave equation

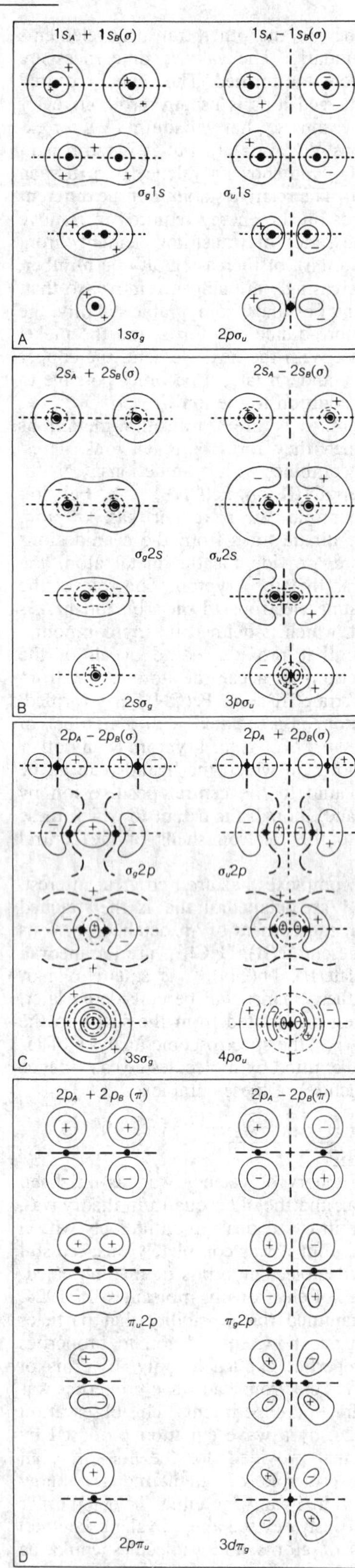

Figure 3: *Transition from separated-atom orbitals to united-atom orbitals for symmetric diatomic molecules.*
(A) Separated 1*s* orbitals to 1*s* (bonding) and 2*p* (antibonding) in the united atom. (B) Separated 2*s* orbitals to 2*s* (bonding) and 3*p* (antibonding). (C) Separated σ2*p* orbitals to 3*s* (bonding) and 4*p* (antibonding). (D) Separated 2*p*π orbitals to 2*p* (bonding) and 3*d* (antibonding). These diagrams show general form of changes and are not accurate in detail.

actly. The difficulty lay in the labour and length of such calculations, even for systems containing only two nuclei and only five or six electrons. Progress with exact calculations has been slow, and even with computers it remains slow. Consequently, less than exact quantum-mechanical calculations involving various approximations and varying degrees of empiricism have assumed prominence, and new procedures and fresh variants are proposed and tested all the time. Moreover, the new mechanics has naturally modified the scientific attitude to certain physical models and has introduced new ones. Though qualitative instead of quantitative, these attitudes are of great importance. Unfortunately, the natural desire to describe the quantum-mechanical phenomena in essentially classical and pictorial terms has produced a jargon such that those with little knowledge of quantum mechanics often have difficulty in separating the concepts that arise as a consequence of the approximations from those that are fundamental.

Atomic and molecular states and orbitals. Max Planck's quantum theory, in the hands of Niels Bohr, showed that stationary energy states could exist for atoms. Associated with each stationary state of the hydrogen atom (containing one electron) was an orbit, designated by three quantum numbers, *n, l,* and *m; i.e.,* each orbit was defined by three numbers representing different kinds of energy states. In atoms with more than one electron, the electrons moved in several of these orbits, which were, by definition, associated with fixed energy levels; that is, quantized orbits. Quantum mechanics does not permit the degree of spatial precision implied by an orbit and, therefore, the orbits are replaced by the concept of orbitals.

Stationary state

In the 1930s Robert Sanderson Mulliken and others studied molecular energy states and the form of electron orbitals in molecules rather than in atoms. They first investigated symmetrical diatomic molecules (*e.g.,* those consisting of two atoms, of the same or different elements with comparable electronegativities), relating molecular orbitals to those of the component atoms of the molecule and tracing the changes that occur during the transition of configurations from those of widely separated atoms through the molecule to the united atom produced when the two nuclei became coincident—*i.e.,* fused into one nucleus. Schematic representations of the formation of united-atom orbitals from separated-atom orbitals and the energy relations are given in Figures 3 and 4.

To understand schematic representation of chemical bonding, a wider background is required than can be given here. (For such information see the articles ATOMS; CHEMICAL ELEMENTS; MECHANICS: *Quantum mechanics.*) When two atoms initially separated are brought together to form a molecule, the electrons in their outermost electron shell, also called the valence electrons, and, in some cases, electrons from an inner shell combine, usually in pairs, and constitute the chemical bond (a covalent bond) that holds the atoms together. The valence electrons in the separated atoms occupy orbitals within the electron shell, designated as *s, p, d,* and *f,* orbitals corresponding to some orientation with respect to the nucleus (*e.g.,* an *s* orbital is spherically symmetrical; each of the three *p* orbitals is symmetrical about an axis running through the nucleus). An electron shell represents an energy level; integers called the principal quantum number (n) represent an ordering of the electron shells according to increasing energy levels. The letters *K, L, M, N,* etc., are also used to represent the ordering of the electron shells; *i.e., K* represents $n = 1$; *L* represents $n = 2$. In atoms with fewer electrons, the orbitals within a shell have energies that are only slightly different from one another. For atoms with more electrons (hence more electron shells), the energy values of some orbitals, usually the *d* and *f* orbitals in a certain shell, overlap with the next higher energy shell. A complete description of an atomic orbital consists of a designation of the electron shell followed by the type of orbital—*i.e.,* 1*s* for the *s* orbital in the *K* ($n = 1$) shell.

Covalent bond in terms of orbitals

When two atoms unite to form a molecule, certain orbitals combine, forming a new orbital that encompasses the two atomic nuclei (a molecular orbital). One way in which a molecular orbital is formed is by the combination

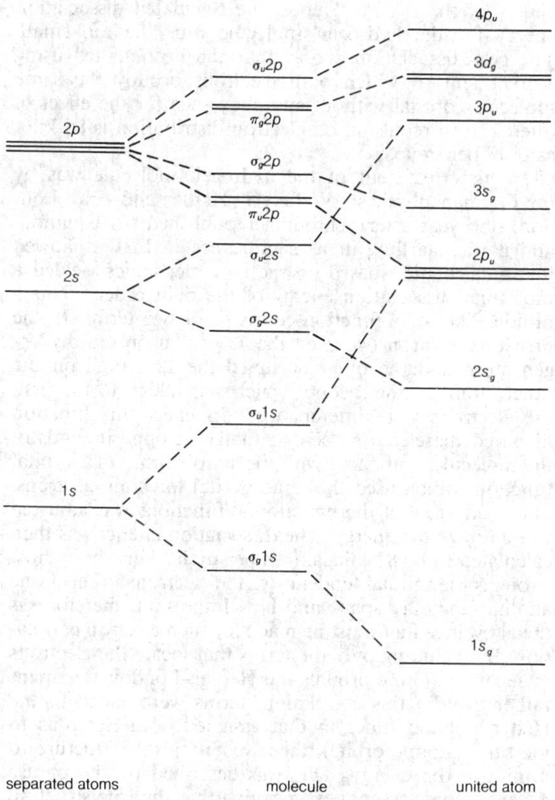

separated atoms molecule united atom

Figure 4: Energy level relationships, not drawn to scale. (See text.)

of similar atomic orbitals. Each pair of similar orbitals (*e.g.*, 1*s* on each atom) leads to two molecular orbitals; one is the sum of the two atomic orbitals creating a new orbital that encompasses the two nuclei, but the other is the difference of the two orbitals creating a new orbital consisting of two parts, each one on either side of the two nuclei (in physical terms, this type of orbital is nodal). The molecule whose bonding electrons occupy orbitals with a node tends to be unstable, and this type is called an antibonding orbital. Molecular orbitals are represented by the same symbols used for atomic orbitals (*e.g., s, p, d,* etc.) together with the Greek symbols sigma (σ) or pi (π) corresponding to symmetrical or antisymmetrical orbitals, a symmetrical orbital being one that does not change its sign when rotated about an axis lying in the molecular plane. Occasionally, the Greek symbols are also included in the description of atomic orbitals. The subscripts *g* and *u* distinguish between bonding and antibonding orbitals.

Anti-bonding orbitals

Figure 5 shows the pattern of orbitals and the energy levels in a given state of a given molecule. In assigning electrons to the orbitals, each electron will be represented

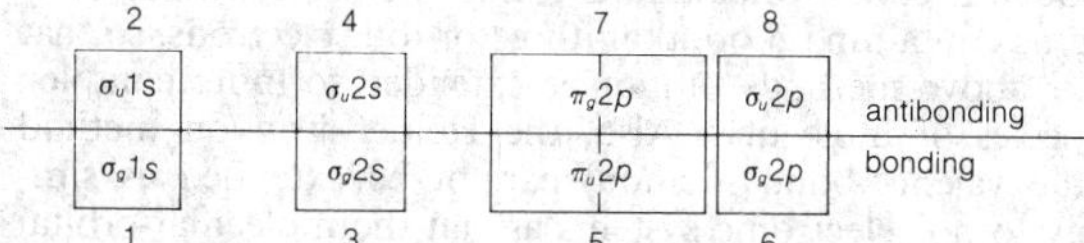

Figure 5: Orbital patterns. Numbers represent order on an energy scale. Compare Figures 3 and 4.

by an arrow, the orientation of spin (+½ or −½) being indicated by the direction of the arrow (up or down). Figure 6 shows the orbital occupation for the ground states of H_2^+, H_2, He_2^+, He_2, Li_2^+, Li_2, 2Be, B_2, C_2, N_2^+, N_2, O_2^+, O_2, O_2^-, F_2, and 2Ne. Two helium atoms do not form a bond because the effect of the antibonding electrons cancels that of the bonding ones. The pattern of dissociation energies, force constants, and equilibrium lengths confirms these bond orders. The electrons enter the orbitals in their energetic order. When two orbitals of equal energy accommodate two electrons they occupy the separate orbitals with spins parallel. The number of chemical bonds is obtained by subtracting the number

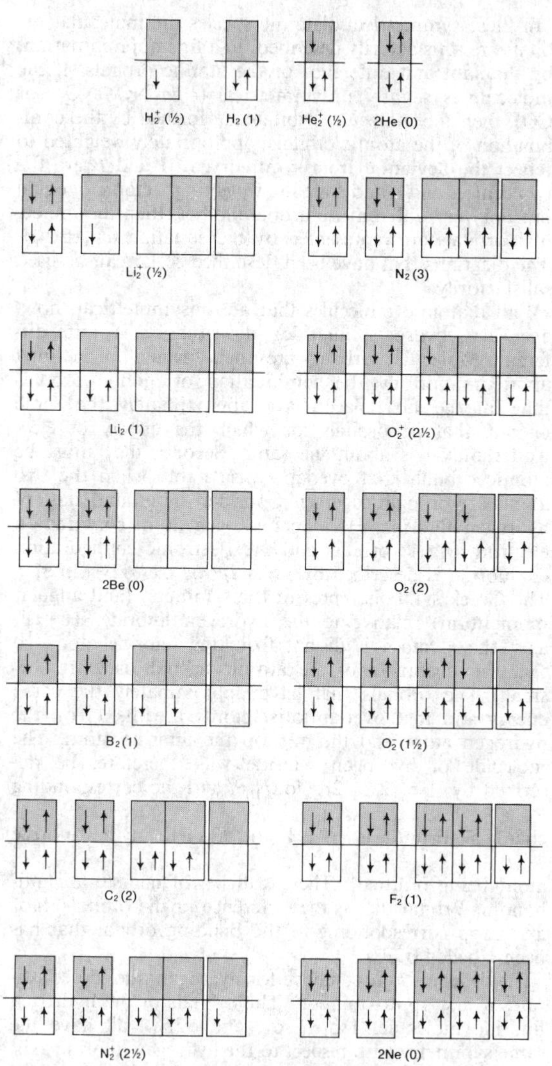

Figure 6: Orbital occupation of lowest states of several symmetrical diatomic systems containing from one to 20 electrons. Number of chemical bonds shown in parentheses. The shaded boxes represent antibonding orbitals; the unshaded boxes, bonding orbitals.

of electrons in antibonding orbitals from the number in bonding orbitals and then dividing by two.

The presence of two electrons with the same spin in the corresponding bonding and antibonding orbitals is equivalent to one electron on one atom and one on the other, as was pointed out by the British physicist Sir John Lennard-Jones. Using this principle and employing crosses and circles for electrons with opposite spin together with a line for a pair of crosses and circles, one arrives at the chemical formulas in the diagram below for the diatomic molecules in Figure 4 above.

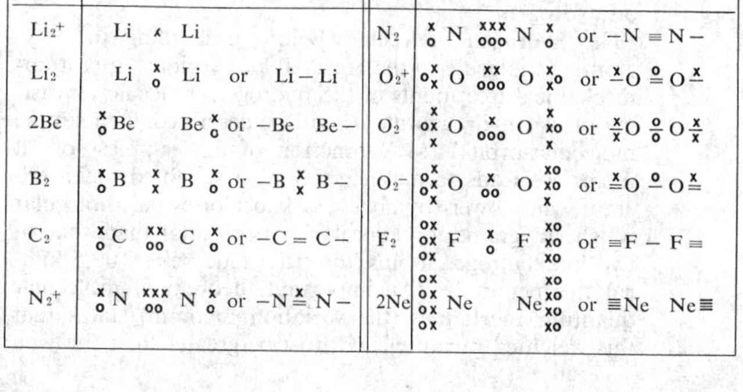

H_2^+	H x H	H_2	H $\substack{x\\o}$ H or H − H
He_2^+	x He o He x	2He	$\substack{x\\o}$ He He $\substack{x\\o}$ or −He He−
Li_2^+	Li x Li	N_2	$\substack{x\\o}$ N $\substack{xxx\\ooo}$ N $\substack{x\\o}$ or −N ≡ N−
Li_2	Li $\substack{x\\o}$ Li or Li − Li	O_2^+	$\substack{o\,x\\x}$ O $\substack{xx\\ooo}$ O $\substack{x\\x\,o}$ or $\overset{x}{-}$O $\overset{o}{\equiv}$ O $\overset{x}{-}$
2Be	$\substack{x\\o}$ Be Be $\substack{x\\o}$ or −Be Be−	O_2	$\substack{x\\ox\\x}$ O $\substack{x\\ooo}$ O $\substack{x\\xo\\x}$ or $\frac{x}{x}$O $\frac{o}{o}$ O $\frac{x}{x}$
B_2	$\substack{x\\o}$ B $\substack{x\\x}$ B $\substack{x\\o}$ or −B $\substack{x\\x}$ B−	O_2^-	$\substack{o\,x\\o\,x\\x}$ O $\substack{x\\oo}$ O $\substack{xo\\xo\\x}$ or $\overset{x}{=}$O $\overset{o}{-}$ O $\overset{x}{=}$
C_2	$\substack{x\\o}$ C $\substack{xx\\oo}$ C $\substack{x\\o}$ or −C = C−	F_2	$\substack{ox\\ox\\ox}$ F $\substack{x\\o}$ F $\substack{xo\\xo\\xo}$ or ≡F − F≡
N_2^+	$\substack{x\\o}$ N $\substack{xxx\\oo}$ N $\substack{x\\o}$ or −N $\overset{x}{=}$ N−	2Ne	$\substack{ox\\ox\\ox\\ox}$ Ne Ne $\substack{xo\\xo\\xo\\xo}$ or ≣Ne Ne≣

Symmetrical diatomic molecules

In these symmetrical diatomic species the molecular orbitals are satisfactorily described, to a first approximation, by the sum and difference of the atomic orbitals. If the molecule is slightly unsymmetrical (*e.g.*, NO, NO^+, or CO), then the molecular orbitals are formed by the combination of the atomic orbitals, appropriately weighted to reflect the deviation from symmetry; if A and B are the two centres and a and b are the weighting factors not equal but not very different from one another, then the molecular orbitals are represented by the equation $a\psi_A \pm b\psi_B$. The diagrams that have been described so far can be used satisfactorily.

With diatomic molecules that are unsymmetrical, however (*e.g.*, hydrogen fluoride), the situation is quite different. Molecular orbitals are then formed in the first approximation by the combination of atomic orbitals that, in the first place, have approximately the same energy; that is, orbitals for which the energy of electron removal is about the same. Second, they must be atomic orbitals that overlap considerably when the two atoms are brought together. Consider the ground state of hydrogen fluoride, HF; the hydrogen atom contains an electron in a $1s$ orbital, and the electronic configuration in fluorine is described by $1s^2 2s^2 2p^5$ or $\sigma 1s^2 \sigma 2s^2 \pi 2p^4 \sigma 2p$. The Greek symbols represent the symmetry (and angular momentum) relative to the hydrogen fluoride, H − F, axis; the H atom is distant from the fluorine atom, so that the distortion of the atomic orbitals is extremely small. The orbitals that have approximately the same energy and that overlap satisfactorily are the $1s$ on the hydrogen atom and the $\sigma 2p$ on the fluorine atom. The molecule of hydrogen fluoride will, therefore, be described by: $1s\sigma_F{}^2 2s\sigma_F{}^2 2p\pi_F{}^4 \sigma 2p_{HF}{}^2$, and the corresponding chemical formula is $-\overset{|}{\underset{|}{F}}-H$ (the K shell on the fluorine atom being omitted). There will be, of course, an antibonding orbital that is the difference of the orbitals $2p\sigma_F$ and $1s\sigma_H$ corresponding to the bonding orbital that has been labelled $\sigma 2p_{HF}$.

The description used above for hydrogen fluoride constitutes a first approximation. The orbitals of the hydrogen fluoride molecule, $1s\sigma_F$, $2s\sigma_F$, and $\sigma 2p_{HF}$, all have the same symmetry with respect to the hydrogen fluoride axis. They are axially symmetric. A better description will be obtained by allowing mixing of some orbitals. The $1s\sigma_F$ orbital (K shell) is, however, so much lower in energy than the others that it will not mix in very much. If $2s\sigma_F$ and $2p\sigma_F$ are combined with the same sign, the resulting orbital projects more toward the proton, while if they are combined with opposite sign, the resulting orbital projects away from the proton. The improved orbitals are formed by the addition of all the atomic orbitals, as shown in the equation, in which a, b, and c represent the weighting factors: $a2s\sigma_F + b2p\sigma_F + c1s\sigma_H$, where a is smaller than b and c, and by the difference of the two orbitals of the fluorine atom, $d2s\sigma_F - e2p\sigma_F$, d being much greater than e (a to e are all positive). The first orbital accommodates the bonding pair (*i.e.*, the electron pair that constitutes the chemical bond between hydrogen and fluorine), the latter the lone pair on the fluorine atom. The bond diagram, therefore, is not altered. The combinations of $2s\sigma_F$ and $2p\sigma_F$ are called hybrid orbitals, and the procedure of mixing atomic orbitals in this way is termed hybridization. In this case the bonding orbital is formed by combining a $2s2p$ hybrid orbital on fluorine with a $1s$ orbital on hydrogen.

Hybridization

The hydrogen molecule. Before proceeding to polyatomic molecules, the results of various quantum-mechanical treatments of the hydrogen molecule consisting of two hydrogen atoms will be described. The simple molecular-orbital (MO) function of this simplest of all molecules leads to an energy (*e.g.*, a weighted mean energy) value lower (by about 70 kilocalories per molecular weight in grams, or kilocalories per mole) than that of two free hydrogen atoms (the true value being 109.5 kilocalories per mole). An important theorem of molecular quantum mechanics (the variation theorem) states that this weighted mean energy must be greater than the true energy of the system. Hence, the calculated dissociation energy for the hydrogen molecule must be too small. The best dissociation energy that can be obtained using a treatment in which both electrons occupy the same molecular orbital without any allowance for the effect of interelectron repulsion on electron distribution is 85 kilocalories per mole.

The first treatment of the hydrogen molecule was by the German physicists Walter H. Heitler and Fritz London, one year after Schrödinger published his equation, and it was startling in its significance in that it showed that a calculation based on the new mechanics yielded a molecular dissociation energy of the right order of magnitude. The wave function consisted of two terms. In the first, one electron occupied the $1s$ orbital on one hydrogen atom and the other occupied the $1s$ orbital on the other atom. In the second, which was added to the first, the electrons were interchanged. In effect this function favoured the electrons being situated at opposite ends of the molecule, compared with the simple molecular-orbital function, which used the same orbital for both electrons. Later, the scale of the two atomic functions was adjusted to minimize the energy. The dissociation energy was then calculated to be 87 kilocalories per mole. This shows how strong is the mutual tendency of the electrons to repel one another and stay apart, and how important, therefore, is the allowance that must be made for such electron correlation. By including only the terms that locate the electrons in separate atomic orbitals the Heitler–London treatment rather overdid this correlation; terms were added to the Heiter–London function that assigned both electrons to the same atomic orbital, then weighting this structure to minimize the energy. This was described by the phrase covalent–ionic resonance, meaning that the true structure lay between the two extremes or that the structure could be best described by assuming that its details were considered a combination of two possible structures, one ionic and the other involving an idealized nonpolar covalent bond. The terms in the Heitler–London equations were taken to represent the truly covalent form, using a line to represent the pair of bonding electrons: H—H. Assigning both electrons to the same atom is symbolized as an association of negative and positive ions: H^-H^+ and H^+H^-. Linus Pauling, a U.S. chemist, proposed the name resonance for this mixing of wave functions, the mixing being used to achieve a better total wave function.

Covalent–ionic resonance

Consequently, though it appeared first in time, the Heitler–London function is perhaps best regarded as one that includes (in fact, overincludes) some allowance for electron correlation in the simple molecular-orbital function. Later, electron correlation was added specifically in the function, values involving the interelectron separation being included. This was first done in the mid-1930s to achieve a dissociation energy only slightly less than the true value. This magnificent achievement was improved 25 years later by researchers who obtained a dissociation energy more precise than the existing experimental value.

Such accurate calculations cannot be performed for systems containing more than three or four electrons, so that the above methods cannot be extended to more complex species of molecules. Also, the Heitler–London method (the valence-bond method) cannot be extended as simply to polyelectronic systems as can the molecular-orbital method. Consequently, molecular quantum mechanics in the post-World War II period has been almost entirely based on the molecular-orbital method. An additional reason for this is that orbitals that are unoccupied are given by conventional molecular-orbital calculations. This means that electronic excitation can be described, and, hence, the spectra of molecules can be discussed and even predicted (the absorption and emission of electromagnetic radiation, such as light, is related to changes in occupation of the electron orbitals; the pattern of emitted or absorbed radiation is called the spectrum, and it is studied by spectroscopic methods). In fact, one development that has been associated with the growth of the molecular-orbital method has been an increased interest in visible and ultraviolet spectra, though it is not easy to say which is cause and which is effect.

The molecular spectrum

The simple molecular-orbital function for the hydrogen molecule is that in which both electrons are assigned to the same orbital. If the two atoms are labelled *A* and *B*, then their electrons occupy the $1s_A$ and $1s_B$ orbitals; in the molecule they occupy the orbital that can be most simply designated by $(1s_A + 1s_B)$. In the same way that the Heitler–London function was improved by adding ionic terms to covalent terms (resonance), the simple molecular-orbital function can also be improved by adding other functions that involve assigning electrons to other molecular orbitals. This procedure is called configuration interaction, but in principle it is the same as resonance. For instance, a second function in which both electrons are assigned to the antibonding orbital $(1s_A - 1s_B)$ can be added with a weight or value that minimizes the energy. Additional configuration, to an extent that is limited only by the availability of computer time and capacity, can be used by assigning both electrons to the 2*s* bonding orbitals or both to the 2*s* antibonding orbital. In addition, the configuration that includes *p* orbitals can be used. The use of configuration interaction serves to adjust the precise spatial form (the three-dimensional geometric shape) of the wave function and also to allow for electron correlation. It is a procedure that has come to be widely used in calculations for polyatomic molecules.

Simple polyatomic molecules. It is best to begin a study of polyatomic molecules with those symmetric molecules consisting of two hydrogen atoms bonded to a single atom of any element with an atomic number between those of beryllium (Be) and oxygen (O) in the periodic table. If H represents the hydrogen atoms and A the other atom, then HAH is the formula. As with diatomic molecules, the molecular orbitals are constructed by taking linear combinations of atomic orbitals (LCAO). The *K*-shell orbital (the innermost shell, for which $n = 1$, and containing only two electrons, both in the *s* orbital) on the atom A is little changed in molecule formation, so that the valence-, or outermost, shell atomic orbitals (in the case of these elements the *L* shell, for which $n = 2$) to be combined with one another are the two atomic orbitals of the hydrogen atom, designated as $1s_H{}'$ and $1s_H{}''$, and the 2*s* and 2*p* orbitals on the atom of element A.

Symmetry of a polyatomic molecule

If the HAH molecule is bent, there are two planes of symmetry; one of the whole molecule cutting through HAH, and another one perpendicular to the first plane and passing through the A atom only, thus dividing the two AH bonds on either side onto opposite sides of the plane. Molecular orbitals must be symmetric or antisymmetric to this plane. The contributing atomic orbitals remain the same. These orbitals can be diagrammed, and a study of the diagrams enables certain predictions to be made.

In beryllium hydride, BeH_2, there are four electrons outside the *K* shell ($n = 1$), and the molecule is linear. Lithium hydride ion, LiH_2^+, has two electrons outside the *K* shell and is probably bent, and it is better to write it as a combination of the lithium ion and a hydrogen molecule: Li^+H_2. The fifth electron in boron hydride, BH_2, makes the molecule bent, the third orbital (for the fifth electron) strongly favouring a nonlinear form. The molecule of the hydride of carbon, CH_2, with no unpaired electrons (singlet) is also bent. On the other hand, the lowest (triplet) state of CH_2 (with two unpaired electrons) is linear, which could not be anticipated directly from the diagram. The hydride of nitrogen, actually the amine radical NH_2, with seven electrons, and the hydride of oxygen, actually water, OH_2, with eight electrons outside the *K* shell, are both bent, as would be expected from the diagram. It is interesting that the angles formed by the two hydrogens in CH_2, NH_2, and OH_2 are almost the same (104°, 103¼°, 104½°), confirming that the effect of filling the fourth (2*p*) orbital in the *L* shell has no effect on shape; it remains a 2*p* atomic orbital whether the molecule is linear or bent.

Diagrams of a similar kind that have been drawn for other systems have proved to be extremely useful and have maintained their basic correctness extraordinarily well with the passage of time.

In the case of diatomic molecules, the situation outlined was that two electrons with parallel spins (*i.e.*, unpaired electrons) occupying corresponding bonding and antibonding orbitals could be regarded equally as occupying the component atomic orbitals, which are, in fact, the sum and difference of the bonding and antibonding orbitals. Analogously, in the present case with three atoms, electrons with the same spin occupying the two bonding orbitals can equally be regarded as occupying sum and difference orbitals. Likewise, the nonbonding orbitals in the bent molecule can be transformed into two equivalent orbitals capable of accommodating lone pairs. In this way it is possible to arrive at an equal formulation that does, however, correspond to the more classical concepts of chemical bonds. The correspondence between this and the conventional molecular-orbital formulation can be shown. These two formulations are equal to one another. The first, the simple molecular-orbital formulation, is the more suitable one for discussing and describing electron excitation and electron removal and addition. The latter is more suitable for considering more conventional chemical behaviour, which historically has been more usually examined on the basis of localized chemical bonds. If the description of two electrons occupying the same bond orbital is modified to resemble that used by Heitler and London for the bond in the hydrogen molecule, then the conventional valence-bond molecular wave function is obtained.

The compound acetylene, C_2H_2, containing four atoms, can be treated in the same way. The 1*s* orbitals on the two hydrogen atoms and the 2*s* and 2*p* orbitals on the two carbon atoms combine together to give three molecular orbitals that are symmetric to the central plane and three that are antisymmetric to the central plane. Of the first group, two are bonding (one mainly C—H bonding and the other mainly C—C bonding), while one is antibonding. Of the second group, one is mainly C—H bonding, while two are antibonding. The three bonding orbitals contain electron pairs and can be transformed to give an alternative description based on localized C—H and C—C bond orbitals. The degenerate pair of 2*p* orbitals on the two carbons combine to give a degenerate pair of C—C-bonding orbitals and a degenerate pair of antibonding orbitals. The bonding pairs are filled. Consequently, the C—C bond is a triple bond.

Structure of ozone

The next example is ozone, a molecule consisting of three oxygen atoms, O_3. Two end atoms of oxygen are bonded to a central one. The arrangement is nonlinear, and all the bonding and nonbonding orbitals are fully occupied, while the antibonding orbitals are empty. Combinations that give localized orbitals can be made. If each localized orbital is represented by a line, the disposition of these orbitals will show that two orbitals are bonding and five are nonbonding. Again, the bonding and nonbonding orbitals contain electron pairs. These orbitals are referred to, rather loosely, as the pi or π-orbitals; however, it is not possible to transform the description based on the filled π-bonding and π-nonbonding orbitals into one single localized description, though it is possible to transform the molecular-orbital description into a combination of localized descriptions.

Quantum-mechanical calculations. The first molecular quantum-mechanical calculation was that of Heitler and London for the hydrogen molecule. As stated earlier, this has been improved with the help of the variation theorem, so that now an effectively exact treatment of the hydrogen molecule exists. Extension of such exact methods to other molecules has been slow, even though the speed and capacity of computers has greatly increased.

Approximate treatments are basically of two kinds: (1) nonempirical, in which calculations are based on an approximate wave function but an exact expression for the potential and kinetic energies, the success depending on the completeness and flexibility of the function and the art and skill with which it is chosen; (2) empirical, in which a full or approximate energy expression may be used together with an approximate wave function, the values of integrals being chosen to reproduce certain experimental results (some integrals are often set equal to zero) and these used to derive others.

The best known empirical calculations are those that treat the π-orbitals of certain types of molecules called conjugated (butadiene, benzene, naphthalene, pyridine, etc.) using a method called linear combinations of atomic

Improvements in calculations

orbitals. This treatment simplifies the calculation to the point that only integrals involving orbitals on the same and adjacent atoms are used, others being assumed to be zero. Moreover, the treatment considers each electron separately, giving the energy as a sum of one-electron energies. This treatment is an extremely simple one, and it yields bond energies, ionization potentials, charge distribution, and other quantities. Improved by many workers, it has been extremely valuable in the development of the quantitative and semiquantitative application of quantum mechanics. The changes introduced usually involved increased complexity and the inclusion of integrals that earlier treatments had omitted. Allowance was also made increasingly for the effect of neighbouring atoms.

Self-consistent field method. In the first decade of quantum mechanics, what is called the self-consistent field method for treating atoms was developed. Using a system of successive approximation, each occupied orbital was determined to satisfy the Schrödinger equation for the nuclear field plus that arising from the averaged distribution of the other electrons. Originally, electron exchange was not included in the function, but this was added later in a special form and has been extended to molecules. The molecular orbitals are constructed from a set of atomic orbitals. The more of these that are included in the basis set, the better is the accuracy achieved. A minimum basis set contains the smallest possible number of atomic orbitals. Calculations have been carried out, using minimum basis sets, for a number of molecules containing atoms of the first and second short periods in the periodic table, and questions of bonding have been investigated; calculations with larger basis sets have been made for simple molecules. Bond lengths and other properties are obtained in satisfying agreement with experiment. Such self-consistent field calculations approach the best that can be achieved by functions that assign electrons to molecular orbitals in pairs, and they approach this limit more closely the larger the basis set. The effect of electron repulsion between orbitals is included, but the mutual effect within the pairs is not. The method must always, therefore, be limited, and, in fact, because of this, occasionally it fails completely. The diatomic fluorine molecule, F_2, for example, is calculated to be unstable relative to two fluorine atoms. The difference between the best value for the calculated energy and the true energy is called the correlation energy; it is a measure of the energy reduction arising from the tendency of the electrons within the pairs to keep apart.

Trends in calculating molecular bond structures

Extension of method. In order to make it possible to extend the self-consistent field method to larger molecules of greater chemical interest, various empirical developments have been made. To begin with, all integrals involving overlap distributions arising from different atomic orbitals were set equal to zero; however, this was found to be an excessive simplification, and, at the present time, various empirical methods that involve an intermediate neglect of differential overlap are being developed and employed. They have achieved considerable success, sometimes as an aid to interpretation and sometimes in providing useful numerical results. It should be stressed that their strength lies in their empirical approach, which derives the values of the integrals used from appropriate experimental data. The reason they have great merit is that all electrons are included.

Many special methods have been introduced, but all too frequently the greater complexity limits their range of application. Special mention ought to be given to empirical and nonempirical methods of attempting to determine electron correlation energy so that the power of the self-consistent field method can be made more useful.

The ultimate aim, of course, must be to increase the range of accurate calculations, and some of the work done suggests that progress is possible. It is quite clear, however, that at present only approximate methods, both of an empirical and of a nonempirical kind, are available for many species of great chemical interest.

Hydrogen bonding

Other bonding effects. The most important types of chemical bonding to the chemist are electrovalent and covalent. There is an important special kind, however, in some molecules, called hydrogen bonding. It occurs, for example, in the association of two water molecules in which one hydrogen of one molecule is oriented toward the oxygen of the other molecule. It is also present in a particularly strong form in the hydrogen difluoride ion, HF_2^-, in which the hydrogen nucleus, or proton, lies between the two fluorine atoms. The dissociation energy of most hydrogen bonds is about five kilocalories per mole, which is approximately one-tenth that of most covalent bonds. The hydrogen bond results when the hydrogen atom in a molecule carries a residual positive charge and the receptor atom in the other molecule is negative and contains lone electron pairs. Hydrogen bonding may be intermolecular, as shown in the above example, or intramolecular, as in *o*-chlorophenol, the hydrogen of the hydroxyl being attracted by a lone pair on the neighbouring chlorine atom. Association resulting from hydrogen bonding can produce increased viscosity and increased boiling point in liquids, and it can be of great importance in crystalline structures (*e.g.,* ice and oxalic acid), as well as in such organic molecules as proteins.

Metallic bonds. The bonding in metals and alloys is another form of internuclear binding with distinctive properties. In this case, the valence-shell electrons are strongly delocalized and, therefore, treatments concentrating on this feature are important. The overlap of orbitals of the array of atoms in a solid metal produces bands of energy levels, the constituent orbitals of which are often only partly filled. Electronic properties (*e.g.,* conductivity) have been treated successfully using this approach.

Bonds in crystals. In solids and liquids instantaneous polarization forces between atoms and molecules, called van der Waals forces, are important. They provide the cohesive forces in the crystals of covalent compounds, and they are also important in the interaction of nonbonded atoms in molecules. They do not produce what is normally understood to be a chemical bond, however.

Stereospecific reactions

There has been great interest recently in stereospecific reactions, in which there is a close relationship between the three-dimensional geometry of reactants and products. The relation observed can be explained by considering the symmetry of the molecular orbitals and the requirement that the new bond must be formed by the overlap of those lobes of the contributing orbitals that have the same sign. The interpretation of these results has provided one of the great recent triumphs of molecular-orbital theory.

EXPERIMENTAL OBSERVATIONS OF BONDING

From measured heats of combination and other laboratory data, it is possible to derive the heats of formation of molecules from atoms. This can lead to a set of bond energies. It is found that the energy of a particular bond (*e.g.,* the carbon–hydrogen bond) remains fairly constant through a range of molecules. Discrepancies between heats of formation calculated by transferring the value of bond energies in one molecule to another and observed values led to concepts such as resonance.

Molecular dipole moments (the electrical moment of a molecule that has one end positive, the other equally negative) obtained by measuring dielectric constants reflect the overall electron distribution and have been used to assess quantum-mechanical calculations of molecular structures. Changes of dipole moments during molecular vibrations are also useful in the discussion of charge distribution. Molecular polarizabilities and their changes upon distortion as derived from spectroscopic studies (specifically, Raman spectra) also provide information about electronic structures.

Molecular shape, bond length, and bond angles are particularly important in the consideration of electronic structures. There is, in carbon–carbon bonds, for example, a relation between observed bond length and calculated bond order. The interpretation of these quantities has been most important in the development of the application of quantum mechanics to molecular structure. Experimental methods used, include spectroscopy, and electron, neutron, and X-ray diffraction.

The nuclei can be used to probe the electronic structures of molecules; for instance, in nuclear magnetic resonance spectroscopy (the study of radiation absorbed by the nucleus when it is placed in a magnetic field), the nuclear magnetic moment (the nucleus acting as a magnet) interacts with the surrounding electrons, called the electron cloud, and the position of absorption (*i.e.*, the chemical shift) can be used to obtain information about this electron cloud and the way in which it is affected by bonding. Other interactions of the nucleus and the electric field at the nucleus can also be used to obtain information about the surrounding electrons. Experimental data are obtained from microwave spectra. The radiation absorbed on reorienting electron spin can be used to study the spin distribution within a molecule. This is valuable for checking the wave functions of radicals. Also, particularly for inorganic complex ions, measurements of magnetic susceptibility are valuable for determining such quantities as the number of electrons possessing unpaired spins. These data are invaluable in the determination of electronic structures.

Photoelectron spectroscopy

Since the 1960s the distribution of the energy of electrons ejected from molecules by quanta of electromagnetic radiation has been widely studied. Called photoelectron spectroscopy, it provides the best means of determining molecular-orbital energies and has proved invaluable because the results obtained experimentally are related directly to those obtained from molecular-orbital calculations. Ultraviolet and visible spectra give differences of energies between molecular-orbital energies and are therefore also valuable for obtaining information of a similar kind. In fact, the growth of molecular-orbital calculations has been encouraged by their ability to interpret the energies of electronic excitation and removal.

There are, therefore, many methods for making observations on the spatial distribution of the electrons and their energies. Because the electrons provide chemical bonding, such observations are of direct importance to understanding the phenomenon. The development of further understanding of electronic structure and chemical bonding depends, therefore, on bringing together the quantum-mechanical theory of electronic behaviour and those molecular properties that are most directly related in one way or another to the electronic distribution.

(Ed.)

BIBLIOGRAPHY

Molecular weight: J.R. PARTINGTON, *An Advanced Treatise on Physical Chemistry,* vol. 1 (1949), presents original references to early work in molecular weights and basic equations. See also the same author's *A History of Chemistry,* vol. 4 (1964), for a detailed account of the historical development. The development of molecular weight as a concept is carefully woven into the fabric of the whole kinetic-molecular hypothesis in JAMES B. CONANT and LEONARD K. NASH (eds.), *Harvard Case Histories in Experimental Science,* vol. 1 (1957). Other recommended works include: E.A. MOELWYN-HUGHES, *Physical Chemistry,* 2nd rev. ed. (1961), an excellent general reference book in physical chemistry; F.W. BILLMEYER, *Textbook of Polymer Science* (1971), a readable account of all aspects of polymer science; and C. TANFORD, *Physical Chemistry of Macromolecules* (1961), an excellent physical-chemical introduction to biomacromolecules.

(D.McI.)

Molecular structure: Introductory works include O.T. BENFEY, *From Vital Force to Structural Formulas* (1964); F.C. NACHOD and R.F. BRILL, "Molecular Structure," in the *Kirk-Othmer Encyclopedia of Chemical Technology,* vol. 9 (1952), the status of knowledge on this subject in the early 1950s; J.D. WATSON, *The Double Helix: A Personal Account of the Discovery of the Structure of DNA* (1968), an informative and readable account describing the work of the Nobel prize winners, Watson and Crick.

For more advanced treatment, see W.S. BREY, JR., *Physical Methods for Determining Molecular Geometry* (1965); E. CARTMELL and G.W.A. FOWLES, *Valency and Molecular Structure,* 3rd ed. (1966); C.A. COULSON, *Valence,* 2nd ed. (1961); G. KARAGOUNIS, *Einführung in die Elektronentheorie organischer Verbindungen* (1959; Eng. trans., *Introductory Organic Quantum Chemistry,* 1962); F.C. NACHOD *et al.* (eds.), *Determination of Organic Structures by Physical Methods,* 4 vol. (1955–71; vol. 5 in prep.); LINUS PAULING, *The Nature of the Chemical Bond and the Structure of Molecules and Crystals,* 3rd ed. (1960); and with ROGER HAYWARD, *The Architecture of Molecules* (1964); R.M. SILVERSTEIN and G.C. BASSLER, *Spectrometric Identification of Organic Compounds,* 2nd ed. (1967).

(F.C.N./J.J.Z.)

Isomerism: For the historical development of the concept of isomerism, see J.R. PARTINGTON, *A History of Chemistry,* vol. 4 (1964). General discussions of organic stereochemistry are found in KURT MISLOW, *Introduction to Stereochemistry* (1965); E.L. ELIEL, *Stereochemistry of Carbon Compounds* (1962) and *Elements of Stereochemistry* (1969); the latter volume contains a short section on inorganic stereochemistry. Less detailed accounts of organic stereochemistry and isomerism are found in standard organic chemistry texts, such as C.R. NOLLER, *Chemistry of Organic Compounds,* 3rd ed. (1965); and LOUIS F. and MARY FIESER, *Advanced Organic Chemistry* (1961). Two inorganic chemistry texts that survey inorganic isomerism and contain references to more specialized sources are F.A. COTTON and GEOFFREY WILKINSON, *Advanced Inorganic Chemistry,* 2nd ed. (1966); and A.F. WELLS, *Structural Inorganic Chemistry,* 3rd ed. (1962). Specialized books on isomerism and stereochemistry include H.H. JAFFE and MILTON ORCHIN, *Symmetry in Chemistry* (1965); J.W. BAKER, *Tautomerism* (1934); E.L. ELIEL *et al., Conformational Analysis* (1965); and J.D. MORRISON and H.S. MOSHER, *Asymmetric Organic Reactions* (1971). Continuing series that have short chapters on recent developments include W. KLYNE (ed.), *Progress in Stereochemistry;* and N.L. ALLINGER and E.L. ELIEL (eds.), *Topics in Stereochemistry.*

(H.Ha.)

Conformational analysis: D.H.R. BARTON, "The Conformation of the Steroid Nucleus," *Experientia,* 6:316–329 (1950), the first paper in which the significance of conformational analysis for organic chemistry was explicitly suggested; and with R.C. COOKSON, "The Principles of Conformational Analysis," *Q. Rev. Chem. Soc.* 10:44–82 (1956), a summary of the field as it had developed in its qualitative aspects between 1950 and 1956; M.S. NEWMAN (ed.), *Steric Effects in Organic Chemistry* (1956), a good collection of review articles on stereochemistry that includes authoritative chapters on conformational analysis; E.L. ELIEL *et al., Conformational Analysis* (1965), an authoritative summary.

(D.H.R.B./J.K.S.)

Chemical bonding: Historical works include G.N. LEWIS, "The Atom and the Molecule," *J. Am. Chem. Soc.,* 38:762–785 (1916), the electron-pair bond concept introduced by its originator; N.V. SIDGWICK, *The Electronic Theory of Valency* (1927), a clear statement of the pre-quantum mechanics position; LINUS PAULING, *The Nature of the Chemical Bond and the Structure of Molecules and Crystals,* 3rd ed. (1960), the pre-war position.

For textbooks on chemical bonding, see H. EYRING, J.E. WALTER, and G.E. KIMBALL, *Quantum Chemistry* (1944), an explanation of the techniques of quantum chemistry; F.O. RICE and E. TELLER, *The Structure of Matter* (1949), for the general reader; Y.K. SYRKIN and M.E. DYATKINA, *Structure of Molecules and the Chemical Bond* (1950; orig. pub. in Russian, 1946), based on Pauling's approach; C.A. COULSON, *Valence,* 2nd ed. (1961), an introduction to the semiquantization application of quantum mechanics; K.S. PITZER, *Quantum Chemistry* (1953), an account of the qualitative importance of quantum mechanics; J.W. LINNETT, *Wave Mechanics and Valency* (1960), a simple introduction; *The Electronic Structure of Molecules* (1964), description of a particular approach; J.C. SLATER, *Electronic Structure of Molecules* (1963), a lengthy analysis; J.C. SPEAKMAN, *A Valency Primer* (1968), a qualitative introduction for the beginner; M.W. HANNA, *Quantum Mechanics in Chemistry,* 2nd ed. (1969), an introductory book.

(Ed.)

Molière

Although the sacred and secular authorities of 17th-century France often combined against him, the comic genius of Jean-Baptiste Poquelin, known as Molière, emerged finally to win him eventual acclaim as the greatest of all French writers. Comedy had a long history before Molière, who employed most of its traditional forms, but he succeeded in inventing a new style that was based on a double vision of normal and abnormal seen in relation to each other—the comedy of the true opposed to the specious, the intelligent seen alongside the pedantic. An actor himself, Molière seems to have been incapable of visualizing any situation without animating and dramatizing it, often beyond the limits of probability; though living in an age of reason, his own good sense led him not to proselytize but rather to animate the absurd, as in such masterpieces as *Tartuffe, L'École des femmes, Le Misanthrope,* and many others. It is testimony to the freshness of his vision that the greatest comic artists working centuries later in other media, such as Charlie Chaplin, are still compared to Molière.

Beginnings in theatre. Molière was born (and died) in the heart of Paris. The registers showed that he was baptized on January 15, 1622, as Jean-Baptiste Poquelin. His mother died when he was 10 years old; his father, one of the appointed furnishers of the royal household, gave him a good education at the Collège de Clermont (the school that, as the Lycée Louis-le-Grand, was to train so many brilliant Frenchmen, including Voltaire). Although his father clearly intended him to take over his royal appointment, the young man renounced it in 1643, apparently determined to break with tradition and seek a living on the stage. That year he joined with nine others to produce and play comedy as a company under the name of the Illustre-Théâtre. His stage name, Molière, is first found in a document dated June 28, 1644. He was to give himself entirely to the theatre for 30 years and to die exhausted at the age of 51.

A talented actress, Madeleine Béjart, persuaded Molière to establish a theatre, but she could not keep the young company alive and solvent. In 1645 Molière was twice sent to prison for debts on the building and properties. The number of theatregoers in 17th-century Paris was small, and the city already had two established theatres, so that a continued existence must have seemed impossible to a young company. From the end of 1645, for no fewer than 13 years, the troupe sought a living touring the provinces. No history of these years is possible, though municipal registers and church records show the company emerging here and there: in Nantes in 1648, in Toulouse in 1649, and so on. They were in Lyon intermittently from the end of 1652 to the summer of 1655 and again in 1657, at Montpellier in 1654 and 1655, and at Béziers in 1656. Clearly they had their ups as well as downs. These unchronicled years must have been of crucial importance to Molière's career, forming as they did a rigorous apprenticeship to his later work as actor-manager and teaching him how to deal with authors, colleagues, audiences, and authorities. His rapid success and persistence against opposition when he finally got back to Paris is inexplicable without these years of training. His first two known plays date from this time: *L'Étourdi ou les contretemps* (*The Blunderer,* 1762), performed at Lyon in 1655, and *Le Dépit amoureux* (*The Amorous Quarrel,* 1762), performed at Béziers in 1656.

First success

The path to fame opened for him on the afternoon of October 24, 1658, when, in the guardroom of the Louvre and on an improvised stage, the company presented Corneille's *Nicomède* before the king, Louis XIV, and followed it with what Molière described as one of those little entertainments which had won him some reputation with provincial audiences. This was *Le Docteur amoureux* ("The Amorous Doctor"); whether it was in the form still extant is doubtful. It apparently was a success and secured the favour of the King's brother Philippe, duc d'Orléans. It is difficult to know the extent of the Duc's patronage, which lasted seven years, until the King himself took over the company known as "Troupe du roi." No doubt the company gained a certain celebrity and prestige, invitations to great houses, and subsidies (usually unpaid) to actors, but not much more.

From the time of his return to Paris in 1658, all the reliable facts about Molière's life have to do with his activity as author, actor, and manager. Some French biographers have done their best to read his personal life into his works, but at the cost of misconstruing what might have happened as what did happen. The truth is that there is little information except legend and satire. The fact that authors like Montaigne, Plutarch, Julius Caesar, and Seneca may have been in his library (according to a legal inventory of 1708), for example, does not mean that his plays should be read with the doctrines of such authors in mind.

Although unquestionably a great writer, Molière was not an author in the usual sense: he wrote little that could be called literature or even that was meant to be published—some poems and a translation of the ancient Latin writings of Lucretius, incomplete. His plays were made for the stage, and his early prefaces complain that he had to publish to avoid exploitation. (Two of them were in fact pirated.) He left seven of his plays unpublished, never issued any collected edition, and never (so far as is known) read proofs or took care with his text. Comedies, in his view, were made to be acted. This fact was forgotten in the 19th century. It took such 20th-century actors as Louis Jouvet, Charles Dullin, Jean-Louis Barrault, and Jean Vilar to present a new and exact sense of his dramatic genius.

"Molière," oil painting by Pierre Mignard. In the Musée Condé, Chantilly, France.

By courtesy of the Musee Conde, Chantilly, France; photograph, Girandon—Art Resource

Nor was he at all a classical author, with leisure to plan and write as he would. Competition, the fight for existence, was the keynote of Molière's whole career. To keep his actors and his audiences was an unremitting struggle against other theatres. He won this contest almost single-handed. He held his company together by his technical competence and force of personality.

Molière's first Paris play, *Les Précieuses ridicules* (*The Affected Young Ladies*), prefigured what was to come. It centres on two provincial girls who are exposed by valets masquerading as masters in scenes that contrast, on the one hand, the girls' desire for elegance coupled with a lack of common sense and, on the other, the valets' plain speech seasoned with cultural clichés. The girls' fatuities, which they consider the height of wit, suggest their warped view of culture in which material things are of no account. The fun at the expense of these affected people is still refreshing and must have been even more so for the first spectators.

Molière's Paris theatres

Les Précieuses, as well as *Sganarelle* (first performed in October, 1660), probably had its premiere at the Théâtre du Petit-Bourbon, a great house adjacent to the Louvre. The Petit-Bourbon was demolished (apparently without notice), and the company moved early in 1661 to a hall in the Palais-Royal, built as a theatre by Richelieu. Here it was that all Molière's "Paris" plays were staged, starting with *Dom Garcie de Navarre, ou le prince jaloux* in February 1661, a heroic comedy of which much was hoped; it failed on the stage and succeeded only in inspiring Molière to work on *Le Misanthrope.* Such failures were rare and eclipsed by successes greater than the Paris theatre had known.

Scandals and successes. The first night of *L'École des femmes* (*The School for Wives*), December 26, 1662, caused a scandal as if people suspected that here was an emergence of a comic genius that regarded nothing as sacrosanct. Some good judges have thought this to be Molière's masterpiece, as pure comedy as he ever attained. Based on Paul Scarron's version (*La Précaution inutile,* 1655) of a Spanish story, it presents a pedant, Arnolphe, who is so frightened of femininity that he decides to marry a girl entirely unacquainted with the ways of the world. The delicate portrayal in this girl of an awakening temperament, all the stronger for its absence of convention, is a marvel of comedy. Molière crowns his fantasy by showing his pedant falling in love with her, and his elephantine gropings toward lovers' talk are both his punishment and the audience's delight.

From 1662 onward the Palais-Royal theatre was shared by Italian actors, each company taking three playing days in each week. Molière also wrote plays that were privately commissioned and thus first performed elsewhere: *Les Fâcheux* (*The Impertinents,* 1732) at Vaux in August 1661; the first version of *Tartuffe* at Versailles in 1664; *Le Bourgeois Gentilhomme* at Chambord in 1670; and *Psyché* in the Tuileries Palace in 1671.

Marriage to Armande Béjart

On February 20, 1662, Molière married Armande Béjart. It is not certain whether she was Madeleine's sister, as the documents state, or her daughter, as some contemporaries suggest. There were three children of the marriage; only a daughter survived to maturity. It was not a happy marriage; flirtations of Armande are indicated in hostile pamphlets, but there is almost no reliable information.

Molière cleverly turned the outcry produced by *L'École des femmes* to the credit of the company by replying to his critics on the stage. *La Critique de L'École des femmes* in June 1663 and *L'Impromptu de Versailles* in October were both single-act discussion plays. In *La Critique* Molière allowed himself to express some principles of his new style of comedy, and in the other play he made theatre history by reproducing with astonishing realism the actual greenroom, or actors' lounge, of the company and the backchat involved in rehearsal.

The quarrel of *L'École des femmes* was itself outrun in violence and scandal by the presentation of the first version of *Tartuffe* in May 1664. The history of this great play sheds much light on the conditions in which Molière had to work and bears a quite remarkable testimony to his persistence and capacity to show fight. He had to wait five years and risk the livelihood of his actors before his reward, which proved to be the greatest success of his career. Most men would surely have given up the struggle: from the time of the first performance of what was probably the first three acts of the play as it is now known, many must have feared that the Roman Catholic Church would never allow its public performance.

Undeterred, Molière made matters worse by staging a version of *Dom Juan, ou le festin de Pierre* with a spectacular ending in which an atheist is committed to hell—but only after he had amused and scandalized the audience. *Dom Juan* was meant to be a quick money raiser, but it was a costly failure, mysteriously removed after 15 performances and never performed again or published by Molière. It is a priceless example of his art. The central character, Dom Juan, carries the aristocratic principle to its extreme by disclaiming all types of obligation, either to parents or doctors or tradesmen or God. Yet he assumes that others will fulfill their obligations to him. His servant, Sganarelle, is imagined as his opposite in every point, earthy, timorous, superstitious. These two form the perfect French counterpart to Don Quixote and Sancho.

Setbacks and harassment by the authorities

While engaged in his battles against the authorities, Molière continued to hold his company together single-handedly. He made up for lack of authors by writing more plays himself. He could never be sure either of actors or authors. In 1664 he put on the first play of Jean Racine, *La Thébaïde,* but the next year Racine transferred his second play, *Alexandre le Grand,* to a longer established theatre while Molière's actors were actually performing it. He was constantly harassed by the authorities. These setbacks may have been offset in part by the royal favour conferred upon Molière, but royal favour was capricious. Pensions were often promised and not paid. The court wanted more light plays than great works. The receipts of his theatre were uncertain and fluctuating. In his 14 years in Paris, Molière wrote 31 of the 95 plays that were presented on his stage. To meet the cumulative misfortunes of his own illness, the closing of the theatre for seven weeks upon the death of the Queen Mother, and the proscription of *Tartuffe* and *Dom Juan,* he wrote five plays in one season (1666–67). Of the five, only one, *Le Médecin malgré lui* (*The Doctor in Spite of Himself,* 1914), was a success.

In the preceding season, however, *Le Misanthrope,* almost from the start, was treated as a masterpiece by discerning playgoers, if not by the entire public. It is a drawing-room comedy, without known sources, constructed from the elements of Molière's own company. Molière himself played the role of Alceste, a fool of a new kind, with high principles and rigid standards, yet by nature a blind critic of everybody else. Alceste is in love with Célimène (played by Molière's wife, Armande), a superb comic creation, equal to any and every occasion, the incarnate spirit of society. The structure of the play is as simple as it is poetic. Alceste storms moodily through the play, finding no "honest" men to agree with him, always ready to see the mote in another's eye, blind to the beam in his own, as ignorant of his real nature as a Tartuffe.

The church nearly won its battle against Molière: it prevented public performance, both of *Tartuffe* for five years and of *Dom Juan* for the whole of Molière's life. A five-act version of *Tartuffe* was played in 1667, but once only: it was banned by the President of Police and by the Archbishop on pain of excommunication. Molière's reply was to lobby the King repeatedly, even in a military camp, and to publish a defense of his play called *Lettre sur la comédie de l'Imposteur.* He kept his company together through 1668 with *Amphitryon* (January 13), *George Dandin* (Versailles, July 18), and *L'Avare* (September 9). Sooner or later so original an author of comedy as Molière was bound to attempt a modern sketch of the ancient comic figure of the miser. The last of his three 1668 plays, *L'Avare,* is composed in prose that reads like verse; the stock situations are all recast, but the spirit is different from Molière's other works and not to everyone's taste. His miser is a living paradox, inhuman in his worship of money, all too human in his need of respect and affection. In breathtaking scenes his mania is made to suggest cruelty, pathological loneliness, even insanity. The play is too stark for those who expect laughter from comedy; Goethe started the dubious fashion of calling it tragic. Yet, as before, forces of mind and will are made to serve inhuman ends and are opposed by instinct and a very "human" nature. The basic comic suggestion is one of absurdity and incongruity rather than of gaiety.

His second play of 1668, *George Dandin,* often dismissed as a farce, may be one of Molière's greatest creations. It centres on a fool, who admits his folly while suggesting that wisdom would not help him because, if things in fact go against us, it is pointless to be wise. As it happens he is in the right, but he can never prove it. The subject of the play is trivial, the suggestion is limitless; it sketches a new range of comedy altogether. In 1669, permission was somehow obtained, and the long run of *Tartuffe* at last began. More than 60 performances were given that year alone. The theme for this play, which brought Molière more trouble than any other, may have come to him when a local hypocrite seduced his landlady. Of the three versions of the play, only the last has survived; the first (presented in three acts played before the King in 1664) probably portrayed a pious crook so firmly established in a bourgeois household that the master promises him his daughter and disinherits his son. At the time it was common for lay directors of conscience to be placed in families to reprove and reform conduct. When this "holy" man is caught making love to his employer's wife, he recovers by masterly self-reproach and persuades the master not only to pardon him but also to urge him to see as much of his wife as possible. Molière must have seen even greater comic possibilities in this theme, for he made five acts out of it. The final version contains two seduction scenes and a shift of interest to the comic paradox in Tartuffe himself, posing as an inhuman ascetic while by nature he is an all-too-human lecher. It is difficult to think of a theme more likely to offend pious minds. Like Arnolphe in *L'École des femmes,* Tartuffe seems to have come to grief because he trusted in wit and forgot instinct.

The long run of *Tartuffe*

Last plays. The struggle over *Tartuffe* probably exhausted Molière to the point that he was unable to stave off repeated illness and supply new plays; he had, in fact, just four years more to live. Yet he produced in 1669 *Monsieur de Pourceaugnac* for the King at Chambord and in 1670 *Le Bourgeois Gentilhomme.*

Le Bourgeois Gentilhomme treated a contemporary theme—social climbing among the bourgeois, or upper middle class—but it is perhaps the least dated of all his comedies. The protagonist Jourdain, rather than being an unpleasant sycophant, is as delightful as he is fatuous, as genuine as he is naïve; his folly is embedded in a bountiful disposition, which he of course despises. This is comedy in Molière's happiest vein: the fatuity of the masculine master is offset by the common sense of wife and servant.

Continuing to write despite his illness, he produced *Psyché* and *Les Fourberies de Scapin* (*The Cheats of Scapin,* 1677) in 1671. *Les Femmes savantes* (*The Blue-Stockings,* 1927) followed in 1672; in rougher hands this subject would have been (as some have thought it) a satire on bluestockings, but Molière has imagined a sensible bourgeois who goes in fear of his masterful and learned wife. *Le Malade imaginaire* (first performed 1673; Eng. trans., *The Imaginary Invalid*), about a hypochondriac who fears death and doctors, was Molière's last play. It is a powerful play in its delineation of medical jargon and professionalism, in the fatuity of a would-be doctor with learning and no sense, in the normality of the young and sensible lovers, as opposed to the superstition, greed, and charlatanry of other characters. During the fourth performance of the play, on February 17, 1673, Molière collapsed on stage and was carried back to his house in the rue de Richelieu to die. As he had not been given the sacraments or the opportunity of formally renouncing the actor's profession, he was buried without ceremony and after sunset on February 21.

Molière's collapse on stage and death

Molière as actor and as playwright. Molière's acting had been both his disappointment and his glory. He aspired to be a tragic actor, but contemporary taste was against him. His public seemed to favour a tragic style that was pompous, with ranting and roaring, strutting and chanting. Molière had the build, the elasticity, the india-rubber face, as it has been called, of the born comedian. Offstage he was neither a great talker nor particularly merry, but he would mime and copy speech to the life. He had the tireless energy of the actor. He was always ready to make a scene out of an incident, to put himself on a stage. He gave one of his characters his own cough and another his own moods, and he made a play out of actual rehearsals. The characters of his greatest plays are like the members of his company. It was quite appropriate that he should die while playing the part of the sick man that he really was.

The actor in him influenced his writing, since he wrote (at speed) what he could most naturally act. He gave himself choleric parts, servants' parts, a henpecked husband, a foolish bourgeois, and a superstitious old man who cursed "that fellow Molière." (The comparison with Charlie Chaplin recurs constantly.) Something more than animal energy and a talent for mime was at work in him, a quality that can only be called intensity of dramatic vision. Here again actors have helped to recover an aspect of his genius that the scholars had missed, his stage violence. To take his plays as arguments in favour of reason is to miss their vitality. His sense of reason leads him to animate the absurd. His characters are imagined as excitable and excited to the point of incoherence. He sacrifices plot to drama, vivacity, a sense of life. He is a classical writer, yet he is ready to defy all rules of writing.

To think of Molière as a cool apostle of reason, sharing the views of the more rational men of his plays, is a heresy that dies hard; but careful scrutiny of the milieu in which Molière had to work makes it impossible to believe. The comedies are not sermons; such doctrine as may be extracted from them is incidental and at the opposite pole from didacticism. Ideas are expressed to please a public, not to propagate the author's view. If asked what he thought of hypocrisy or atheism, he would have marvelled at the question and evaded it with the observation that the theatre is not the place for "views." There is no documentary evidence that Molière ever tried to convey his own opinions on marriage, on the church, on hell, or on class distinctions. Strictly speaking, his views of these things are unknown. All that is known is that he worked for and in the theatre and used his amazing power of dramatic suggestion to vivify any imagined scene. If he has left a sympathetic picture of an atheist, it was not to recommend free thought: his picture of the earthy serving man is no less vivid, no less sympathetic. Scholars who have tried to make his plays prove things or to convey lessons have made little sense of his work and have been blind to its inherent fantasy and imaginative power.

The heresy of Molière as a propagandist

Since the power of Molière's writing seems to lie in its creative vigour of language, the traditional divisions of his works into comedies of manners, comedies of character, and farce are not helpful: he does not appear to have set out in any instance to write a certain kind of play. He starts from an occasion in *Le Mariage forcé* (1664; *The Forced Marriage,* 1762) from doubts about marriage expressed by Rabelais's character Panurge, and in *Le Médecin malgré lui* he starts from a medieval fable, or *fabliau,* of a woodcutter who, to avoid a beating, pretends he is a doctor. On such skeleton themes Molière animates figures or arranges discussion in which one character exposes another or the roles are first expressed and then reversed. It is intellectual rhythm rather than what happens, the discussion more than the story, that conveys the charm, so that to recount the plot may be to omit the essential.

His unique sense of the comic. The attacks on Molière gave him the chance in his responses to state some aesthetic home truths. Thus, in *La Critique de L'École des femmes,* he states that tragedy might be heroic, but comedy must hold the mirror up to nature: "You haven't achieved anything in comedy unless your portraits can be seen to be living types . . . making decent people laugh is a strange business." And as for the rules that some were anxious to impose on writers: "I wonder if the golden rule is not to give pleasure and if a successful play is not on the right track."

The attacks on *L'École des femmes* were child's play in comparison with the storm raised by *Tartuffe* and *Dom Juan.* The attacks on them also drew from the poet a valuable statement of artistic principle. On *Dom Juan* he made no public reply since it was never officially condemned. The documents in defense of *Tartuffe* are two placets, or petitions, to the King, the preface to the first edition of 1669 (all these published over Molière's own name), and the *Lettre sur la comédie de l'Imposteur* of 1667. The placets and preface are aesthetically disappointing, since Molière was forced to fight on ground chosen by

Concept of comedy

his opponents and to admit that comedy must be didactic. (There is no other evidence that Molière thought this, so it is not unfair to assume that he used the argument only when forced.) The *Lettre* is much more important. It expresses in a few pregnant lines the aesthetic basis not only of *Tartuffe* but of Molière's new concept of comedy:

> The comic is the outward and visible form that nature's bounty has attached to everything unreasonable, so that we should see, and avoid, it. To know the comic we must know the rational, of which it denotes the absence and we must see wherein the rational consists . . . incongruity is the heart of the comic . . . it follows that all lying, disguise, cheating, dissimulation, all outward show different from the reality, all contradiction in fact between actions that proceed from a single source, all this is in essence comic.

Molière seems here to put his finger on what was new in his notion of what is comic: a comedy, only incidentally funny, that is based on a constant double vision of wise and foolish, right and wrong seen together, side by side. This is his invention and his glory.

A main feature of Molière's technique is a mixing of registers, or of contexts. Characters are made to play a part, then forget it, speak out of turn, overplay their role, so that those who watch this byplay constantly have the suggestion of mixed registers. The starting point of *Le Médecin malgré lui,* the idea of beating a man to make him pretend he is a doctor, is certainly not subtle, but Molière plays with the idea, makes his woodcutter enjoy his new experience, master the jargon, and then not know what to do with it. He utters inanities about Hippocrates, is overjoyed to find a patient ignorant of Latin, so that he need not bother about meaning. He looks for the heart on the wrong side and, undeterred by having his error recognized, sweeps aside the protest with the immortal: "We have changed all that." The miser robbed of his money is pathetic, but he does not arouse emotions because his language leads him to the absurd " . . . it's all over . . . I'm dying, I'm dead, I'm buried." He demands justice with such intemperance that his language exceeds all reason and he threatens to put the courts in the court. Molière's *Misanthrope* is even more suggestive in his confusion of justice as an ideal and as a social institution: "I have justice on my side and I lose my case!" What to him is a scandal of world order is to others just proof that he is wrongheaded. Such concision does Molière's dramatic speech achieve.

A French genius. When Voltaire described Molière as "the painter of France," he suggested the range of French attitudes found in the plays, and this may explain why the French have developed a proprietary interest in a writer whom they seem to regard in a special sense as their own. They stress aspects of his work that others tend to overlook. Three of these are noteworthy.

First, formality permeates all his works. He never gives realism—life as it is—alone, but always within a pattern and a form that fuse light and movement, music and dance and speech. Modern productions that omit the interludes in his plays stray far from the original effect. Characters are grouped, scenes and even speeches are arranged, comic repartee is rounded off in defiance of realism.

Second, the French stress the poetry where foreigners see psychology. They take the plays not as studies of social mania but as patterns of fantasy that take up ideas, only to drop them when a point has been made. *Le Misanthrope* is not considered as a case study or a French *Hamlet* but as a subtly arranged chorus of voices and attitudes that convey a critique of individualism. The play charms by its successive evocations of its central theme. The tendency to speak one's mind is seen to be many things: idealistic or backbiting or rude or spiteful or just fatuous. It is in this fantasy playing on the mystery of self-centredness in society that Molière is in the eyes of his own people unsurpassed.

A third quality admired in France is his intellectual penetration in distinguishing the parts of a man from the whole man. Montaigne, the 16th-century essayist who deeply influenced Molière, divided qualities that are acquired, such as learning or politeness or skills, from those that are natural, such as humanity or animality, what might be called "human nature" without other attributes. Molière delighted in opposing his characters in this way; often in his plays a social veneer peels off, revealing a real man. Many of his dialogues start with politeness and end in open insults.

Molière opposed wit to nature in many forms. His comedy embraces things within the mind and beyond it; reason and fact seldom meet. As the beaten servant in *Amphitryon* observes: "That conflicts with common sense. But it is so, for all that." (W.G.Mo./Ed.)

MAJOR WORKS

Les Précieuses ridicules (first performed 1659, published 1660; trans. by B.H. Clark, *The Affected Young Ladies,* 1915); *L'École des femmes* (1663; trans. by the Earl of Longford, *The School for Wives,* 1948; and by M. Malleson, 1954); *Le Tartuffe, ou l'imposteur* (first version 1664, present version 1669; trans. by M. Malleson, *The Imposter,* 1950); *Dom Juan, ou le festin de Pierre* (1665; trans. by J. Ozell as *Don John; or, The Libertine,* 1665 and rev. and augmented by O. Mandell, 1963); *Le Misanthrope* (first performed 1666, 1667; adapted by W. Wycherly, *The Plain-Dealer,* 1677; trans. by M. Malleson, 1955); *L'Avare* (1669; trans. by H. Fielding as *The Miser,* 1733; by M. Malleson, 1950; and by K. Cartledge, 1962, with the same title); *Le Bourgeois gentilhomme* (1670; trans. by M. Malleson, *The Prodigious Snob,* 1952); *Les Femmes savantes* (1672; trans. by V. Beringer and M. Down, *The Blue-Stockings,* 1927); *Le Malade imaginaire* (1674; trans. as *The Imaginary Invalid* by B.H. Clark, 1925; by M. Malleson, 1959; and B. Briscoe, 1967; and as *The Hypochondriac* by H. Baker and J. Miller, 1961).

BIBLIOGRAPHY

Editions: Collected editions of Molière's works include those by C. VARLET DE LA GRANGE, 8 vol. (1682); by M.A. JOLLY, 6 vol. (1734); by EUGÈNE DESPOIS and PAUL MESNARD in the "Grands Écrivains de la France Series," 13 vol. (1873–1900); by RENÉ BRAY in the "Belles Lettres Series," 8 vol. (1935–52); by GUSTAVE MICHAUT, 11 vol. (1949); by ROBERT JOUANNY in the "Garnier Series," 2 vol. (1962); and by GEORGES COUTON in the "Pléiade Series," 2 vol. (1971). Among editions of particular plays those of *L'Avare* by CHARLES DULLIN (1946), of *Le Malade imaginaire* by PIERRE VALDE (1946), of *Tartuffe* by FERNAND LEDOUX (1953), and of *Le Misanthrope* by GUSTAVE RUDLER (1947) deserve special mention.

Biography: Earlier literature is superseded by GUSTAVE MICHAUT, *La Jeunesse de Molière* (1922, reprinted 1968), *Les Débuts de Molière à Paris* (1923, reissued 1968), and *Les Luttes de Molière* (1925, reissued 1968). See also JOHN L. PALMER, *Molière: His Life and Works* (1930, reprinted 1970); GUSTAVE MICHAUT (ed.), *Molière: raconté par ceux qui l'ont vu* (1932); GEORGES MONGRÉDIEN, *La Vie privée de Molière* (1950); GERTRUD MANDER, *Moliere* (1973; originally published in German, 1967); and RENÉ BRAY, *Molière, homme de théâtre,* new ed. (1963, reissued 1972). Official documents have been collected in MADELEINE JURGENS and ELIZABETH MAXFIELD-MILLER, *Cent Ans de recherches sur Molière, sur sa famille et sur les comédiens de sa troupe* (1963).

Theatrical history: HENRY C. LANCASTER, *A History of French Dramatic Literature in the Seventeenth Century,* pt. 3 (1936, reprinted 1966); ANTOINE ADAM, *Historie de la littérature française au XVIIe siècle,* vol. 3 (1956); PIERRE MÉLÈSE, *Le Théâtre et le public à Paris sous Louis XIV* (1934, reprinted 1976); THEODORE VAN VREE, *Les Pamphlets et libelles littéraires contre Molière* (1933); and BURT E. and GRACE P. YOUNG (eds.), *Le Registre de La Grange,* 2 vol. (1947, reprinted 1977). On particular plays, see ANTOINE ADAM, "La Genèse des 'Précieuses ridicules,' " *Revue d'histoire de la philosophie et d'histoire générale da le civilisation,* 14–16 (January–March 1939); JACQUES ARNAVON, *Le Misanthrope de Molière* (1930, reprinted 1970), and *L'École des femmes de Molière* (1936); and RENÉ JASINKI, *Molière et le Misanthrope* (1951, reissued 1970).

General criticism: PAUL F. SAINTONGE and R.W. CHRIST, *Fifty Years of Molière Studies: A Bibliography, 1892–1941* (1942, reissued 1977); ROGER JOHNSON, EDITHA S. NEUMANN, and GUY T. TRAIL (eds.), *Molière and the Commonwealth of Letters* (1975), a study that includes Paul Saintonge's "Thirty Years of Molière Studies: A Bibliography, 1942–1971"; LAURENCE ROMERO, *Molière: Traditions in Criticism, 1900–1970* (1974); WILL G. MOORE, *Molière: A New Criticism* (1949, reprinted 1973); JACQUES GUICHARNAUD, *Molière, une aventure théâtrale. Tartuffe, Dom Juan, Le Misanthrope* (1963); HAROLD C. KNUTSON, *Molière: An Archetypal Approach* (1976); and NICHOLAS GRENE, *Shakespeare, Jonson, Molière: The Comic Contract* (1980), a comparative study.

Mollusks

The phylum Mollusca (mollusks) is one of the most numerous groups in the animal kingdom after the insects and vertebrates. Each class includes an ecologically and structurally immense variety of forms (Figure 1): the shell-less Caudofoveata; the narrow-footed gliders (Solenogastres); the serially valved chitons (Placophora or Polyplacophora); the cap-shaped neopilinids (Tryblidia); the limpets, snails, and slugs (Gastropoda); the clams, mussels, scallops, oysters, and cockles (Bivalvia); the tubiform to barrel-shaped tusk shells (Scaphopoda); and the nautiluses, cuttlefishes, squids, and octopuses (Cephalopoda).

In this article the biology and classification of mollusks are first considered in general terms; more detailed information on the three major classes (Gastropoda, Bivalvia, and Cephalopoda) follows.

For coverage of related topics in the *Macropædia* and *Micropædia,* see the *Propædia,* section 313, and the *Index.*

The article is divided into the following sections:

MOLLUSKS: THE PHYLUM MOLLUSCA

GENERAL FEATURES

Size range and diversity of structure. The range in size and structure is an adaptation to the environment. Typical molluscan features may be altered, or even lost, depending on the subgroup. Among the cephalopods the giant squids (*Architeuthis*), the largest living invertebrates, attain a body length of eight metres (more than 26 feet); with the tentacle arms extended, the total length reaches to 22 metres. Other cephalopods exceed a length of one metre. Many of the remaining molluscan classes show a large variation in size: among bivalves the giant clam (*Tridacna*) ranges up to 135 centimetres (four feet) and the pen shell (*Pinna*) from 40 to 80 centimetres; among gastropods the sea hares (*Aplysia*) grow from 40 to 100 centimetres and the Australian trumpet, or baler (*Syrinx*), up to 60 centimetres; among placophores the gumshoe, or gumboot chiton (*Cryptochiton*), achieves a length up to 30 to 43 centimetres; and, among solenogasters, *Epimenia* reaches a length of 15 to 30 centimetres. Finally, gastropods of the family Entoconchidae, which are parasitic in echinoderm sea cucumbers, may reach a size of almost 1.3 metres. In contrast, there are minute members, less than one millimetre (0.04 inch) in size, among the solenogasters and gastropods.

Adaptations

Distribution and abundance. The mollusks have adapted to all habitats except air. Although basically marine, bivalves and gastropods include freshwater species. Gastropods have also adapted to land, where the almost 17,500 species occupy most existing niches. Found on rocky, sandy, and muddy bottoms or substrates, mollusks burrow, become cemented to the surface, or are free-swimming.

Mollusks are of worldwide distribution, but there is a preponderance of some groups in certain areas of the world. The close association of many molluscan groups with their food source—whether by direct dependence on a specific food supply (*e.g.,* plant-eating, or herbivores) or by involvement in food chains—limits their geographic distribution; for example, bivalves of the family Teredinidae (shipworms) are associated with driftwood. In general, cold-water regions support fewer species.

Importance to humans. Mollusks are of general importance within food chains and as members of ecosystems. Certain species are of direct or indirect commercial and even medical importance to humans. Most bivalves contribute to the organic turnover in the intertidal (littoral) zones of marine and fresh water because, as filter feeders, they filter up to 40 litres (10 gallons) of water per hour. This filtering activity, however, may also seriously interfere with the various populations of invertebrate larvae (plankton) found suspended and free-swimming in the water.

Conchifera (a subphylum including the tryblids, gastropods, scaphopods, bivalves, and cephalopods) are a source of food for many cultures and therefore play an important role in the fishing industries of many countries. Conchifera also are used in the fabrication of ornaments and in pearl and mother-of-pearl industries.

NATURAL HISTORY

Reproduction and life cycles. Mollusks are primarily of separate sexes, and the reproductive organs (gonads) are simple. Reproduction via an unfertilized gamete (parthenogenesis) is also found among gastropods of the subclass Prosobranchia. Most reproduction is by sexual means: eggs and sperm are released into the water, where fertilization takes place; in prosobranch gastropods, water currents may cause a simple internal fertilization within the mantle cavity. Both male and female reproductive organs may be present in one individual (hermaphroditism) in some classes, and various groups exhibit different adaptations to this body form. For example, in bivalves and prosobranch gastropods, male and female gonads are functional at separate times and in rhythmic and consecutive patterns (successive hermaphroditism). Conversely, male and female gonads are functional at the same time

Methods of reproduction

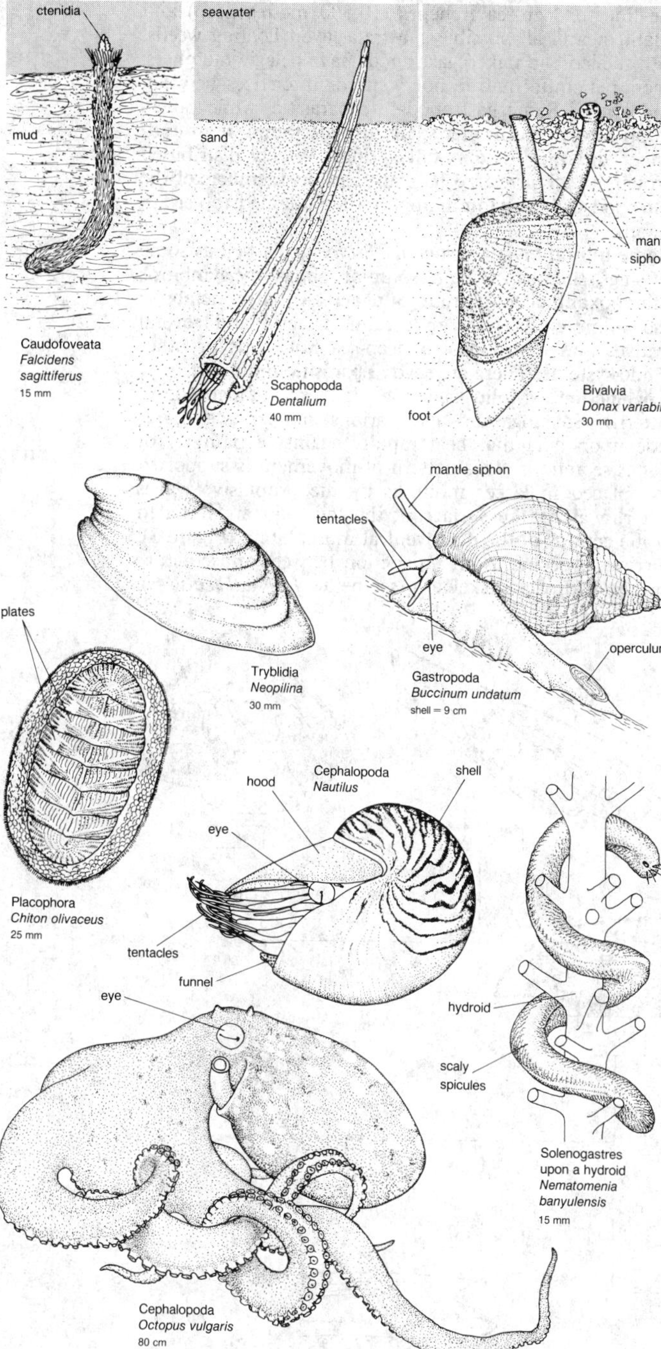

Figure 1: Body plans of mollusks.

From (*Falcidens, Nematomenia*) L.v. Salvini-Plawen in *Die Neue Brehm' Bucherei* (1971), A. Ziemsen-Verlag, Wittenberg; (*Dentalium, Nautilus*) T.I. Storer and R.L. Usinger, *General Zoology* (1965), McGraw-Hill, New York; (*Donax*) R. Barnes, *Invertebrate Zoology* (1974), W.B. Saunders, Philadelphia; (*Chiton*) L.v. Salvini-Plawen in K.M. Wilbur (ed.), *The Mollusca*, vol. 10 (1985), Academic Press, London; (*Buccinum*) adapted from K.-J. Gotting, *Malakozoologie* (1974), G. Fischer Verlag, Stuttgart; (*Octopus*) L.v. Salvini-Plawen in R. Reidl (ed.), *Fauna und Flora des Mittelmeeres* (1983), Paul Parey Scientific Publishers, Hamburg and Berlin

(simultaneous hermaphroditism) in solenogasters and the gastropod subclass Euthyneura.

Fertilization by transfer of capsules containing sperm (spermatophores) typically occurs in cephalopods and some gastropods. In cephalopods, transfer of spermatophores is usually combined with copulation by a modified arm, or hectocotylus. Copulation in solenogasters, often by means of a special genital cone, may be supported by copulatory stylets. Various penis formations, in part with copulatory stylets, or darts, are widely found in gastropods.

Eggs are laid singly, in heaps, or as spawn, generally on some hard surface and often within capsules. Squids of the suborder Oegopsida and some gastropods have eggs that are suspended in the water. Fertilized eggs commonly undergo spiral cleavage. The eggs of cephalopods, on the other hand, possess a large amount of yolk, which displaces the dividing cells and causes a characteristic type of development.

Larvae (Figure 2) are originally free-swimming and lecithotrophic. The resulting larva in primitive forms is a pericalymma (test cell) larva in which the embryo is protected below a covering (test) of cells provided with one to four girdles of cilia, at the apex of which is a sensory plate of ciliated cells. After the developing juvenile has grown out apically of the test (which then is lost), the animal settles and develops into an adult. The test in other lecithotrophic larvae is restricted to a preoral girdle of ciliated cells (the prototrochus) and is called the pseudotrochophore larva. In more advanced mollusks the pseudotrochophore larva develops into a veliger larva (in marine gastropods) or into a rotiger larva (in bivalves). In these planktotrophic larvae, the girdle of ciliated cells widens to form a velum that entraps food. As the larva continues to develop, the shell, mantle cavity, and foot begin to appear; in case of planktotrophy, a characteristic larval shell interconnects the embryonic and adult shells. After a specific amount of time, the larva metamorphoses into an adult.

Development

Secondary (newly evolved) larvae are developed among freshwater bivalves and in some cephalopods. Maternal protection of the developing eggs (brood) is not unexceptional behaviour in solenogasters, bivalves, and certain gastropod adults. Direct development without a larval stage or the bearing of live young from a yolky egg, or both, are typical in cephalopods and most nonmarine gastropods. Many species go through two breeding seasons per year, whereas in cephalopods mating or egg laying appears to be rapidly followed by death effected by hormones.

Habitats, feeding habits, and associations. Caudofoveates burrow in muddy sediments at depths of 10 to more than 7,000 metres (33 to 23,000 feet) and consume microorganisms and loose organic material (detritus). In contrast, solenogasters prey on some members of the class Cnidaria (*e.g.,* hydroids and corals) in five to 6,850 metres of water, on clay or muddy sand, or directly upon hydroid or coral colonies. Placophores cling to hard bottoms of the intertidal zone, scraping algae from the rock surfaces by using their strong rasping teeth (radula); several members of the placophore family Lepidopleuridae

From L.v. Salvini-Plawen in R. Reidl (ed.), *Fauna und Flora des Mittelmeeres* (1983), Paul Parey Scientific Publishers, Hamburg and Berlin

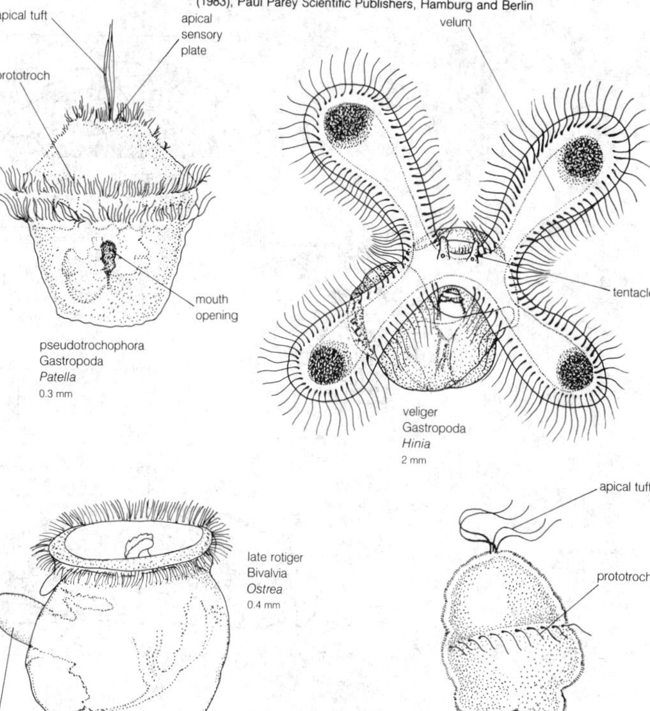

Figure 2: Types of larvae.

consume detritus found at depths down to 7,000 metres, and Hanleyidae as well as Hopaliidae even depend on animal food. The few extant members of the class Tryblidia inhabit secondary hard bottoms at depths of 175 to 6,500 metres and capture detritus by means of head appendages (velum) around the mouth. The scaphopods dwell in sand or sandy mud down to 7,000 metres and nourish themselves on protozoa, crustaceans, or small mollusks captured by the filamentous head tentacles (captacula). Except for the carnivorous septibranch anomalodermata, all bivalves are ciliary suspension feeders, using food-sorting organs near the mouth (labial palps) and respiratory gills modified to assist in feeding (ctenidia). Found in marine and fresh water, bivalves burrow into sediments to depths of 10,700 metres or attach themselves to hard surfaces by means of tough threads secreted by the byssus gland in the foot. Cephalopods are generally carnivores, feeding on crustaceans and fishes, but some have adapted a microvorous diet of detritus and microscopic organisms and plants. Some cephalopods are offshore (pelagic) jet swimmers, moving from the surface to depths of 5,400 metres, while others dwell near the bottom (benthic) at depths of 8,100 metres.

Gastropod diversity

The greatest ecological diversity is shown by the gastropods. The marine members are found from the spring-tide line to deep-sea trenches (10,500 metres deep) and inhabit nearly all possible substrata, even floating weeds. Both shelled and naked gastropods have pelagic members; others penetrate marine hot vents or interstices between sand grains. Some gastropods are parasitic, while others are predatory. Freshwater snails also are found in groundwaters and may inhabit hot springs. Widely distributed throughout all terrestrial habitats, various members of the gastropod order Stylommatophora are adapted to certain regions.

Some littoral bivalves, such as *Tridacna,* as well as some sea slugs, such as *Aeolidia,* share an obligatory symbiosis with zooxanthellae (a group of algae). Another metabolic association exists between certain bacteria and several bivalves and gastropods of deep-sea hot vents or other sulfide systems. There are several parasitic mollusks.

Locomotion. Mollusks have a wide range of locomotory patterns. Solenogasters and various smaller gastropods glide upon cilia that beat rapidly against a pathway of mucus secretions. This pattern of movement is supported or replaced in larger mollusks by the propulsive waves that run along the surface of the foot and are initiated by the actions of the dorsoventral musculature (Figure 3). Burrowing occurs as an interaction between musculature and the hydrostatic skeleton (see below *Internal features*);

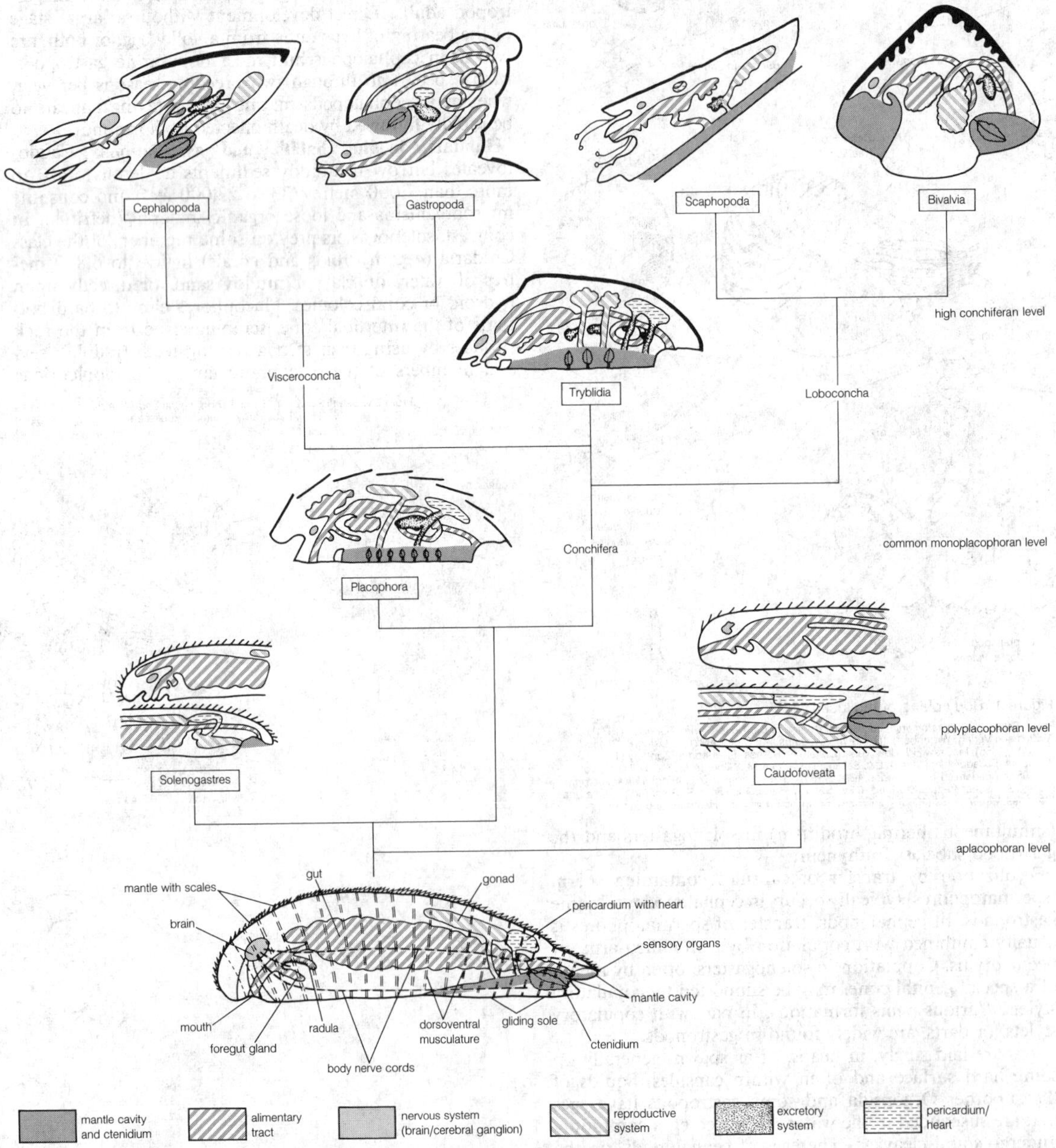

Figure 3: Organizational levels and body diagrams of the eight classes of mollusks evolved from a hypothetical generalized ancestor (archi-mollusk).

it is performed in caudofoveates and several sea slugs by the whole anterior body but is restricted to the foot in scaphopods, bivalves, and some specialized gastropods.

Various bivalves (*e.g.,* cockles) and snails may perform rapid twists or jumps through violent flexion of the foot. Buoyancy floating and jet propulsion are found in cephalopods; floating is also known in gastropods, and swimming of a different kind is practiced in gastropods of the subclass Opisthobranchia as well as in scallops and related bivalves. Octopods use their arms to crawl or even to swim or float with the help of the body skin interconnecting the arms (interbrachiate web). Some bivalve groups bore into hard surfaces by secreting strong chemicals that dissolve the substrate or by drilling, using the shell and radula. A sedentary (sessile) way of life has been adopted by many bivalves and some wormlike internal parasites of gastropods.

Features of defense. The external cover that extends over the mantle may consist of a hardened epithelial layer called a cuticle, separate calcareous plates, or a shell. The mantle cover is one of the most important protective devices, the key characteristics of which were already present at the beginning of molluscan evolution. Another defense includes the ability of most solenogasters and chitons to roll the body up. Chitons, neopilinids, and limpets can adhere firmly to the substrate by a powerful suction pad foot. Protection is also afforded if the animal is able to withdraw into its shell; a snail has the added advantage of having a hardened plate (operculum) on the foot that covers the shell opening (auricle) once the animal has withdrawn. Burrowing by caudofoveates, scaphopods, many bivalves, and some gastropods is a protective behaviour when used to escape predators.

Chemicals, poisons, and camouflage

In many gastropods, slippery mucus is secreted from mantle extensions, or parapodia, as a defense against larger predators, such as the echinoderm starfish. In scaphopods, mucus is secreted against an aggressor from the anterior mantle. Certain molluscan subgroups secrete noxious chemicals either as a poisonous secretion of the salivary glands or as distasteful acids in mantle cells. Glandular secretions by solenogasters or the gastropod superfamily Eolidacea prevent the stinging nettle capsules (nematocysts) of cnidarians, when consumed, from expulsing the stingers; moreover, the gastropods are able to store and then use the capsules when attacked by a predator. Some mollusks secrete fluids to divert or frighten a predator, to provide camouflage, or to inhibit the predator's sense of smell. For example, the ink in cephalopods, the luminous cloud secreted by some deep-sea squids, and the purple fluid from the sea hare (*Aplysia;* a gastropod of the subclass Opisthobranchia) distract and confuse the predator and conceal the prey. Camouflage or frightening coloration are effective in protecting cuttlefishes, octopuses, and sea slugs, as well as other gastropods.

FORM AND FUNCTION

The highly varied evolutionary development of basic molluscan features has left only a few characters that may be taken as typical. As a result, molluscan form varies much among levels and subgroups (Figure 3).

External features. The most obvious external molluscan features are the dorsal epidermis called the mantle (or pallium), the foot, the head (except in bivalves), and the mantle cavity. The mantle in caudofoveates and solenogasters is covered by cuticle that contains scales or minute, spinelike, hard bodies (spicules), or both (aplacophoran level). The placophores develop a series of eight plates or valves still surrounded by a girdle of cuticle with spicules; in all other mollusks (the Conchifera), the mantle secretes an initially homogeneous shell (monoplacophoran level). The mantle and shell are laterally compressed in scaphopods and bivalves; in gastropods and cephalopods the head is free of the mantle and shell. In bivalves a dorsal hinge ligament joins two valves, which are further held together by two adductor muscles with attachment points on the inner aspect of each valve.

The body

The body of the mollusk, containing all the visceral elements, such as the alimentary tract, gonads, and heart, is connected to the mantle by dorsoventral musculature. The head, when present, has tentacles called captacula in scaphopods, labial palps in bivalves, head tentacles in gastropods, and arms in cephalopods. The primitive ciliary gliding surface with forward pedal and sole glands is reduced in caudofoveats and some gastropods, as well as in some bivalves, and it is narrowed to a ridged tract in solenogasters as well as some members of the placophore genus *Cryptoplax.* The foot forms an anteriorly elongated and slendered burrowing organ in scaphopods, is ax-shaped to vermiform in bivalves, and is modified to a siphon or funnel in cephalopods. Among gastropods of the subclass opisthobranchia the foot may be extended laterally to form swimming lobes (parapodia).

The mantle, or pallial, cavity is found between the mantle rim and the body. The pallial complex is a collection of structures at the roof of the mantle cavity and typically contains at least one pair of lamellate gills (ctenidia), a thick layer of glandular epithelium called mucus tracts or hypobranchial glands, and the outlets for the digestive, excretory, and reproductive systems. A loss of the ctenidia (along with the mucus tracts) is seen in scaphopods, advanced gastropods, septibranch bivalves, and solenogasters. Placophores, tryblids, nautilid cephalopods, and some gastropods have a multiple number of ctenidia.

Internal features. *Muscles and tissues.* The internal molluscan organization is almost entirely soft-bodied. The body cavity is filled with fibrous tissue or fluid-filled spaces (hemocoel), or both. The tissues, hemocoel, and body wall act as a hydrostatic skeleton for shape and support; when filled with fluid, the hemocoel expands against the body wall and fibrous tissues, providing a rigid framework. This same framework provides a structure against which the animal can exert internal pressure when protruding the foot from the shell during burrowing. Conversely, extrusion of the head and foot from the shell in the supraclass Visceroconcha (gastropods and cephalopods), shell elevation in gastropods, and the rapid expansion and contraction of the mantle required for jet propulsion in cephalopods of the subclass Coleoidea are the result of a more complicated system carried out by the antagonistic actions of muscles working in opposition to other muscles.

Hydrostatic skeleton

The basic sets of muscle systems, fully retained only in solenogasters, include the subintegumental musculature below the mantle; a pair of longitudinal muscle bundles below the mantle margins, which roll the body up and which are almost disintegrated in conchiferans; and the dorsoventral musculature, which is reduced in caudofoveates and shell-less gastropods and which in shelled gastropods forms the columellar muscles.

The nervous system and organs of sensation. In the nervous system typical of mollusks, a pair of cerebral ganglia (masses of nerve cell bodies) innervate the head, mouth, and associated sense organs. From the dorsal cerebral ganglia, two pairs of longitudinal nerve cords arise: a pair of lateral (pleural) nerve cords, often forming pleural ganglia (which innervate the mantle), and a ventral pair of pedal nerve cords, often forming pedal ganglia (which innervate the foot). In primitive forms both cords are interconnected by lateral branches of nerve fibres. A buccal nerve loop with paired ganglia generally supplies the radular apparatus in the head. Posterior paired visceral ganglia, when present, innervate the viscera. Other mollusks have various grades of ganglia formations, all of which may be concentrated anteriorly. Because of torsion, special nerve configurations are found in gastropods; in cephalopods a cartilaginous capsule encloses the concentrated mass of ganglia.

Sense organs

Supplied by the most posterior aspect of the lateral nerve cords, a paired chemoreceptive sense organ (the osphradium) monitors the water currents of the mantle cavity. This organ has regressed in scaphopods, some cephalopods, and higher gastropods. Pluricellular mantle papillae, which penetrate the cuticle, the valves, and the shell in some conchifers, are differentiated in placophores as photoreceptors. Aside from the cerebral eyes in Visceroconcha, there are photoreceptors on the mantle margins of autobranch bivalves. Orientation in different gastropods is evidenced by reaction to polarized light, which in part serves for homing. Homing in other gastropods and in the placophores that flee from light appears to be performed by chemoreception along their mucus trails.

The digestive system. The primitive alimentary tract is straight, and the foregut contains glands and chitinized teeth, called the radula, upon a tough membrane or ribbon underlain by a mass of compact tissue as a support and operated by musculature. In bivalves and some other mollusks the whole radular apparatus is reduced. The radula is used to bite, tear, and scrape various food materials. The different structural aspects of the radula in caudofoveates, solenogasters, and gastropods serve in classification. The differentiation of a more flexible radular structure, called the flexoglossate type, among the primitive subclass Archaeogastropoda subsequently enabled successful radiation into diverse habitats. Jaw formation is characteristic for conchifers.

The midgut and digestion

The midgut in caudofoveates divides into a hindgut and a large ventral sac for enzyme production. In contrast, the midgut in placophores and conchifers is subdivided into a slender esophagus with a pair of glandular pouches, a distinct stomach with a pair of digestive glands, and a slender, often looped intestine. In primitive conchifers the stomach is of the so-called style sac type. The esophagus opens into an anterior elaboration of the stomach into which the enzymes from the style sac, an area separated by ridges, also are released; the tapered end of the stomach leads to the intestine. Cilia that line the style sac churn the stomach contents and form a long food-laden mucous mass called a protostyle, which abuts a chitinous area of epithelium in the stomach. Usually found within the style sac is a rod, called the crystalline style. The protostyle or the crystalline style are fully retained in the bivalves and gastropods that subsist on small microorganisms and detritus. The protostyle or crystalline style may vary in form among the bivalves. Digestion in primitive forms appears to have been both intracellular and extracellular, such as is still the case in solenogasters, many bivalves, and most gastropods. In advanced levels either intracellular or extracellular digestion appears to be exclusively elaborated—*e.g.,* advanced crystalline style and intracellular.

Open circulatory system

The circulatory system. Mollusks possess an open circulatory system in which body fluid (hemolymph) is transported largely within sinuses devoid of distinct epithelial walls. The posteriodorsal heart enclosed in a pericardium typically consists of a ventricle and two posterior auricles. Hemolymph is drained from ctenidia, gills, or other specialized respiratory epithelia into the respective auricles. The ventricle pumps the hemolymph through a middorsal sinus (in solenogasters and scaphopods) or vessel (aorta) into the body tissues. Hemolymph drains from the tissues into the gills, whence it returns to the auricles.

The respiratory pigment is commonly dissolved in the fluid, either as hemoglobin (as is especially the case in bivalves) or more generally as hemocyanin; in more-advanced forms, hemoglobin is bound to blood cells. In placophores and conchifers (but not in the caudofoveates and the solenogasters) the heart is also the site of the purifying ultrafiltration, and the waste products are then discharged into the pericardium and via a pair of pericardial outlets modified to excretory organs (emunctoria, such as false kidneys or nephridia).

The reproductive system. In adult cephalopods and some other representatives the paired dorsal gonad retains the developmental connection with the pericardium. In caudofoveates and solenogasters, eggs or sperm are discharged into the pericardial cavity, and from there the pericardial outlets transport them to the environment, where fertilization takes place. In more-advanced mollusks there are usually separate ducts to transport the gametes (gonoducts): a pair of gonoducts, called oviducts for the female gametes and spermiducts, or vasa deferentia, for the male gametes, leads the egg and sperm, respectively, to the mantle cavity. Glands to secrete protective coatings around the egg may be present. In gastropods the left gonad is reduced, and after torsion only the right gonad is operational, leaving the internal body asymmetrical; similar asymmetries also may be found in other molluscan subgroups.

Hormones

The endocrine system. Hormone production is not well documented in mollusks other than gastropods and cephalopods. Antagonistic neurohormonal control of reproductive activity and metabolic processes is performed in the gastropods through cerebral dorsal bodies and lateral lobes or juxtaposed organs and in the cephalopods through optic glands. In cephalopods, the hormones also effect death by starvation after the mollusk has deposited its eggs or has mated. Neurosecretions by cells outside the nerve cell bodies (ganglia) have been described in gastropods and cephalopods, the released hormones diffusing through the tissues rather than being concentrated in special organs.

Heart rate in mollusks plays a crucial role in many metabolic processes, including excretion; hormones that affect the heart are released from the wall of veins in cephalopods or, in gastropods, from the subesophageal ganglia, the junction between the auricles and the ventricle. Insulin-like hormones shed from gastropods and bivalves by certain midgut cells control the amount of glucogen (a storage form of sugar) kept as a reserve nutrient.

EVOLUTION AND PALEONTOLOGY

There are no known fossil records of caudofoveates and solenogasters. Both placophores and conchifers date from the earliest Cambrian time (some 570 to 550 million years ago). These records exclude the scaphopods and cephalopods but include the extinct Merismoconchia, Helcionellida, and Rostroconchia. Most of these fossils represent fairly small organisms of about one to five millimetres (0.04 to 0.2 inch), which metabolically parallel the primitive lecithotrophic, rather than planktotrophic, larval development. The oldest known cephalopods are of the Late Cambrian epoch (which ended some 505 million years ago) and subsequently had a remarkable radiation, including the dominant Ammonites (predominantly spirally coiled cephalopods with complicated sutures between chambers and shell—some 10,000 fossil forms—until the Cretaceous (about 100 million years ago). Extinct bivalves (about 15,000 forms) exceed in number the recent fauna. Scaphopods have not been recorded before the Middle Ordovician (some 450 million years ago).

The fossil record gives little clue as to how the mollusks originated and how the eight classes differentiated in Precambrian times. The evolutionary pathway must thus be largely inferred from comparative anatomy and development. The common archimolluscan base, in spite of the large number of fossils of the ancestors of gastropods and bivalves, was probably of shell-less (aplacophoran) organization; that in turn appears to have been differentiated from some flatwormlike organization that adapted the mantle cover rather than from a coelomate segmented construction. Most obvious is the subsequent elaboration of the mantle cover defining the aplacophoran, the placophoran, and (by fusion) the conchiferan (monoplacophoran) level of organization. The realization that the organization of the mantle and mantle cavity in caudofoveates and solenogasters reflects two separate evolutionary lines also discloses conservative molluscan characters. The solenogasters appear to be linked by developmental characters with the placophores; they have retained, however, the most primitive alimentary tract (in that the radular membrane is poorly elaborated, and no midgut gland is separated). The latter was reorganized at the placophore level and overtaken in the conchifers. The subradular organ, the arrangement of the dorsoventral musculature, the three-layered shell structure with enclosed mantle papillae, and the excretory system also demonstrate the placophore heritage in the tryblids, which are the more primitive of the conchifera. Subsequently this radiated into two branches called subclades: the supraclass Loboconcha (or Diasoma), including the suspension-feeding bivalves, and the infaunal scaphopods, sharing a common ancestor in the fossil class Rostroconchia. These groups have a mantle with the shell enlarged in width to envelop the soft body as well as an anterior elongated foot to live on the bottoms of mobile particles (sand, mud). In contrast, a free head with cerebral eyes is set off from the mantle and shell in the supraclass Visceroconcha, including the gastropods and the cephalopods; both share a posterior mantle cavity, lateral (or pleural) nerve cords medial to the dorsoventral musculature, and an antagonistic muscle system (see above *Internal features: Muscles and tissues*). The relation of the fossil order Bellerophontacea is controversial.

CLASSIFICATION

This classification is a consensus of recent views mainly of Luitfried v. Salvini-Plawen and Gerhard Haszprunar, generally based on those of Kenneth J. Boss.

Annotated classification.

PHYLUM MOLLUSCA

Unsegmented, soft-bodied metazoans with mantle (or pallium) covered by cuticular or calcareous secretions, or both; ventral body with head region; and ciliar to muscular locomotion organ; lamellate gills (ctenidia); paired chemoreceptive sense organ (osphridia); nervous system tetraneurous with cerebral ganglia, buccal loop, and 2 pairs of longitudinal body cords, though often concentrated; pronounced dorsoventral musculature; pharyngeal teeth (radula); hemocoelic body cavity with coelomatic pericardium and gonosacs; originally the sexes are separate; development includes spiral cleavage and a primitively lecithotrophic trochus larva; about 50,000 marine, limnic, and terrestrial species.

Class Caudofoveata (Aplacophora partim, or **Chaetodermatida;** mudmoles)

Worm-shaped; covered by cuticle and aragonitic scales; ventral gliding area reduced; mantle cavity terminal with 1 pair of ctenidia; midgut with ventrally separated sac; adapted to burrowing habits in mud; marine in 10–7,000 m; 2 mm to 14 cm; about 100 species in 3 families.

Class Solenogastres (Aplacophora partim, **Ventroplicida,** or **Neomeniidea;** narrow-footed gliders)

Narrowed body and gliding sole (foot); mantle with cuticle and aragonitic scales or spicules, or both; mantle cavity modified; no true ctenidia; radular membrane rudimentary; midgut straight without separate glands; hermaphroditic; epibenthic predators of or epizoic on Cnidaria; marine in 5–6,850 m; 0.8 mm to 30 cm; about 200 species in 4 orders.

Class Placophora (Polyplacophora or **Loricata;** chitons)

Generally flattened body and broad foot; mantle covered with cuticle and spicules; 8 middorsal serial shell plates (valves) enclosing photoreceptive papillae (aesthetes); mantle cavity peripedal with multiple pairs of ctenidia; marine; mainly algae-scraping on hard bottoms in 0–7,000 m; 3 mm to 43 cm; about 600 species in 3 orders.

Class Tryblidia (Monoplacophora or **Galeroconcha** partim; neopilinids)

Cap-shaped shell; head with 2 pairs of appendages; mantle cavity peripedal with 5–6 pairs of modified ctenidia; 5–6 pairs of excretory organs; 2 pairs of heart auricles and gonads; marine detritus feeders in 175–6,500 m; 1.5 to 37 mm; 12–15 species in 1 family.

Class Bivalvia (Pelecypoda, Acephala, or **Lamellibranchiata;** clams, mussels, oysters, scallops, and cockles)

Laterally compressed body; 2 middorsally hinged valves; posterior mantle often extended to form siphons; head with labial palps, foot ax-shaped to vermiform; peripedal mantle cavity with 1 pair of ctenidia mostly modified to large plates of lamellae; buccal mass (jaws and radula) reduced; predominantly ciliary suspension feeders burrowing in soft sediments or attached by byssus gland of foot on hard substrata in 0–10,700 m; 1 mm to 1.35 m; 3 subclasses: Ctenidiobranchia (Nuculida), Palaeobranchia (Solemyida), Autobranchia (lamellibranch and septibranch bivalves); about 6,000 marine and 2,000 limnic species.

Class Scaphopoda (Solenoconcha; tusk shells)

Midventrally fused mantle and tubiform to barrel-shaped shell; head with tubular snout and 2 bunches of slender tentacles (captacula); foot pointed and cylindrical; no ctenidia and distinct blood vessels; no heart auricles; radula strong; microcarnivores; marine burrowers in soft sediments, in 0–7,000 m; 2 to 150 mm; about 350 species in 2 orders.

Class Gastropoda (limpets, snails, and slugs)

Mantle cavity undergoes torsion and often secondarily "detorsion"; shell mostly coiled with operculum; head free with paired eyes; left reproductive organs reduced; immense ecological and structural variability; 0.3 mm to more than 1 m; about 40,000 marine, limnic, and terrestrial species.

Subclass Streptoneura

Mostly marine limpets or operculate snails; 3 ganglia at visceral loop; orders include Archaeogastropoda (long cerebropleural connectives) and Apogastropoda (bifurcate tentacle nerves, 2 pedal commissures).

Subclass Euthyneura

Marine, limnic, or terrestrial snails and slugs without operculum; visceral loop with additional parietal ganglia; hermaphroditic; supraorders include Opisthobranchia (marine with Hancock's organs or derivates) and Aeropneusta (mostly limnic and terrestrial with procerebrum/cerebral glands) with orders Gymnomorpha and Pulmonata.

Class Cephalopoda (Siphonopoda; nautiluses, cuttlefishes, squids, and octopuses)

Dorsoventrally elongated body; shell straight, coiled, or almost highly regressive, originally chambered and pierced by a siphuncular tube; head free with paired eyes and 1 or 2 circles of 8–10, or about 90, tentacles (perioral arms); foot modified as a funnel for jet locomotion; mantle cavity restricted to posterior body with 2 ctenidia; alimentary tract with strong jaws and predominantly with a rectal ink sac; nervous system extremely concentrated; about 600 recent species (some 10,000 fossil forms) of 1 cm to 8 m (+14 m arms) in size; basically pelagic marine carnivores from the surface to 5,400 m depth or benthic to 8,100 m; 4 subclasses are Palcephalopoda (Orthoceroida; fossils); Nautiloida (fossil groups and 3–5 recent species); Ammonoida (fossils); and Coleoida (fossils and 4 recent orders).

Critical appraisal. The long-standing classification of Caudofoveata and Solenogastres within one class (Aplacophora) is not tenable. The configuration of the mantle cavity in each group clearly contradicts the derivation of one from the other, and neither possesses a single commonly derived character that would demonstrate closer relationship other than in an archimolluscan ancestry. A similar condition refers to the bivalve subclasses Ctenidiobranchia and Archaeobranchia, often united below one single taxon (Protobranchia).

The term Amphineura, formerly comprising the Polyplacophora (placophores) and Aplacophora (caudofoveates and solenogasters) within one subphylum (side by side with the subphylum Conchifera), is misleading and out-of-date; it may be replaced by the more appropriate term Aculifera.

The term Monoplacophora is not used here because evolutionarily it equalizes the conchiferan level (in contrast to the polyplacophore and aplacophore levels), and classificatorily it is a junior synonym of Tryblidiacea. Moreover, as is the taxon Galeroconcha, it is in part also taken to include several fossil groups (*e.g.,* Bellerophontacea) of still uncertain relationships.

The familiar three divisions of the Gastropoda into Prosobranchia, Opisthobranchia, and Pulmonata is no more satisfying and, according to the nervous system, is generally replaced by Streptonra and Euthyneura.

The popular term Cephalopoda ("head-footed" mollusks) is a misnomer scientifically since the innervation evidences the siphon, or funnel, with its pedal-funnel gland (rather than the perioral arms) as the equivalent of the foot. Siphonopoda is often preferred. (L.v.S.-P.)

MAJOR MOLLUSK GROUPS

Gastropods (snails and slugs)

Gastropod, which means "belly-footed," refers to the broad tapered foot on which these animals glide. The class comprises the snails, which have a shell into which the animal can withdraw, and the slugs—snails whose shells have been reduced to an internal fragment or completely lost in the course of evolution. Gastropods are among the few groups of animals to have successfully radiated in the ocean, fresh waters, and on land. Because of the challenges presented by these diverse habitats, gastropods are very difficult to characterize. A few are used as food, a very few transmit animal diseases (only a fraction of these have been found to carry the agents of human and animal disease), and the shells of some are used as ornaments or in making jewelry. The main role of gastropods is as scavengers, feeding on dead plant or animal matter, or as predators.

GENERAL FEATURES

Size range and diversity of structure. Some adult marine snails (*Homalogyra*) and forest-litter snails (*Stenopylis, Punctum*) are less than one millimetre (0.04 inch) in diameter. At the other extreme, the largest land snail, the African *Achatina achatina,* is almost 20 centimetres (eight inches) long. The largest freshwater snails, *Pomacea* from South America, reach nearly 10 centimetres in diameter, and the largest marine snail, the Australian *Syrinx aruanus,* occasionally grows to more than 0.6 metre (two feet). The longest snail probably is *Parenteroxenos doglieli,* which lives as a parasite in the body cavity of a sea cucumber: it grows to be almost 130 centimetres (50 inches) in length, although it is only 0.5 centimetre (0.2 inch) in diameter. Most snails are much smaller, and probably 90 percent of all adult snails are less than one inch in maximum dimension.

Variations in shape

Snails show a tremendous variety of shapes, based primarily upon the logarithmic spiral (Figure 4). They can be coiled flatly in one plane, as in *Planorbis;* become globose with the whorls increasing rapidly in size, as in *Pomacea;* have the whorls become elongate and rapidly larger, as in *Conus* and *Scaphella;* have a few flatly coiled whorls that massively increase in width, as in *Haliotis;* become elongated spike-shaped, as in *Turritella;* or adopt a limpet shape, as in *Fissurella.* Often a number of such shapes can be found within a single family, but such marine families as the Terebridae, Conidae, and Cypraeidae are conservative in shape.

Traditionally, the three main gastropod groups are the prosobranchs, the opisthobranchs, and the pulmonates. The prosobranchs generally secrete a massive shell into which the animal can withdraw. The operculum, an often calcified disk situated on the rear part of the foot, fills the shell aperture when the snail is inside the shell, protecting the animal against predation and dessication. The body structure shows relatively minor variations. The opisthobranchs are marine species that often have a reduced or absent shell and very colourful bodies. The pulmonates are snails and slugs that lack an operculum but show complex and highly varied body structures. They have a "lung" or pulmonary cavity that serves also as a water reservoir. It long has been recognized that these groups probably represent similar morphology derived independently several times in the more than 400 million years since the origin of the gastropods.

Distribution and abundance. Of the probable 65,000 species, 30,000 are marine, 5,000 live in fresh water, and 30,000 live on land. In general, oceanic gastropods are most diverse in number of species and in structure in tropical areas; several hundred species (most of which are comparatively rare) can be found in a complex coral reef habitat. This is in contrast with Arctic or subarctic coasts, where the few species that are present are common. A

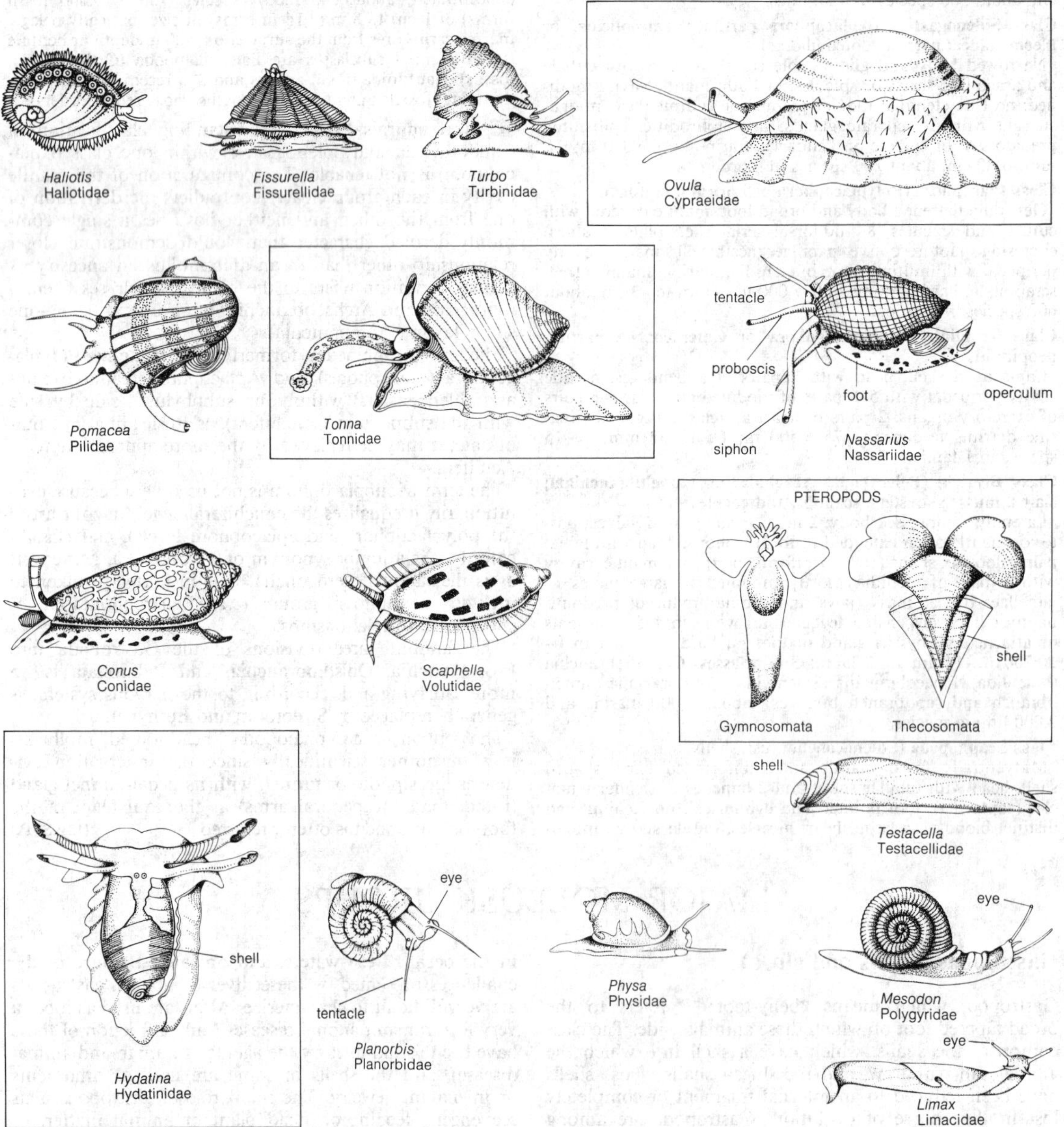

Figure 4: Diversity among gastropods.

number of deep-sea species are known, and a significant snail fauna is associated with hydrothermal vents. Most marine species have relatively large ranges.

Freshwater snails are common in ponds, streams, marshes, and lakes. Usually only a few species are found at one place, but each species will have a rather wide range. Most species are common and feed on algae or dead plant matter. In a few relatively old river systems and lakes—in particular, Baikal in Siberia, Titicaca in South America, Ohrid in Yugoslavia, the Mekong basin in Southeast Asia, and the African Rift lakes—extensive and complex radiations of snails have occurred in comparatively recent geologic time, producing a large number of species.

Adaptations to terrestrial life

Land snails are marginally, but very successfully, terrestrial. When actively moving, they continuously lose water. During periods when water is unavailable, they retreat into their shells and remain inactive until conditions improve. They hibernate during winter periods, when water is locked into snow or ice, and estivate during periods of summer drought. Land snails have been found above the snow line; species of *Vitrina* crawl on snowbanks in Alpine meadows. Other species inhabit barren deserts where they must remain inactive for years between rains.

Only in such favourable areas as New Zealand, Jamaica, northeastern India, and the wet forests of Queensland (Australia) 30 to 40 different species can be found together; in some parts of western Europe 20 species can be found together, while in most of North America less than 10 species live together. In many desert regions, only one or two species are found, and they have significant feeding specializations.

The actual local abundance of snails and slugs can be spectacular. Millions of some brackish water and freshwater species can live on small mud flats. An acre of British farmland may hold 250,000 slugs, and a Panamanian montane forest was estimated to have 7.5 million land snails per acre. Despite this abundance, snails and slugs often pass unobserved. Land and freshwater species often stay hidden during the day and are active at night. Most marine species, as well, are nocturnal, and the shells of many of these species are so heavily covered with algae and other encrusting organisms that they may be mistaken for bits of rock.

Importance to humans. From earliest times, humans have used many species of snails as food. Periwinkles (*Littorina*) in Europe and South Africa, queen conchs (*Strombus gigas*) in the West Indies, abalones (*Haliotis*) in California and Japan, and turban shells (*Turbo*) in the Pacific are the most frequently eaten marine snails. Occasionally limpets and whelks are used for food, but they are more commonly used as fish bait. Freshwater snails rarely are eaten. Land snails of the family Helicidae have been eaten in the Middle East and Europe since prehistoric times. Today, many tons of the European edible snails *Helix aspersa* and *H. pomatia* are raised on snail farms or collected wild. Several species of *Otala* and *Eobania* from Morocco and Algeria are exported for food.

In some places, introductions of *Achatina* and *Helix* have resulted in damage to crops and gardens by these rapidly multiplying snails. California orange groves are plagued by *H. aspersa.* Many slugs accidentally introduced from Europe to both the West Coastal and the Eastern to Midwestern United States are a continual nuisance in home gardens. Freshwater snails of the family Bythinidae sometimes become so numerous that they clog the filter systems of pumping stations.

Shells of certain snails are highly prized by collectors. The operculum of some *Turbo* species is used in making earrings; cameos are cut from the shell of the Red Sea snail *Cassis rufa.* Abalone shells are used in many cultures for decorative purposes; the shell of the golden cowrie (*Cypraea aurantium*) served at one time as a badge of a chief in Fiji. Strings of shells have been used as money.

Intermediate hosts of disease organisms

More serious effects are caused by the few freshwater snails (*Pomatiopsis, Bulinus, Biomphalaria*) that serve as intermediate hosts for worms parasitic of humans. Schistosomiasis is a disease caused by minute blood flukes (schistosomes). Both snails and flukes are most common in areas where fields are irrigated. Schistosomes also parasitize birds and mammals. A skin rash called swimmer's itch results from bird schistosomes trying, only partly successfully, to penetrate human skin. They die in the upper skin layers, and their decomposition causes local infection. Other health problems are caused by several snails and slugs (*e.g., Bradybaena, Angustipes, Veronicella*) that serve as intermediate hosts for the rat lungworm. If an infected land snail or slug is accidentally chopped up in a salad and eaten, the worm can migrate to the brain and encyst, causing moderate to severe damage.

Most gastropods, however, are useful to humans in that they help decompose dead plants and animals into substances that can be used by plants to manufacture new organic compounds. In both field and forest, as in ponds, rivers, and oceans, gastropods are an important part of the decomposer community, and some are significant predators.

NATURAL HISTORY

The colonization of freshwater and terrestrial habitats by gastropods is due to the plasticity of their body and considerable alteration in both structure and function of specific organ systems. Most major groups of organisms primarily inhabit one of the three great biospheres (ocean, fresh water, or land)—the gastropods are successful in all three.

Reproduction and life cycles. Gastropods originated in the oceans, and relics of this fact are preserved in the early life history of freshwater and land species. Only in the most primitive prosobranchs are the gametes released into the water for fertilization to take place outside the female. The fertilized egg hatches into a free-swimming form (trochophore larva). Upon the expansion of the ciliary girdle of the trochophore larva into large, heavily ciliated swimming lobes (vela), the larva, called a veliger, undergoes torsion, a 180° rotation of the fleshy organs from a posterior to an anterior position behind the head. Torsion is an embryological distinction of the gastropods (see Figure 5). Torsion

From J.E. Morton, *Molluscs*, 4th ed. (1967); Hutchinson Publishing Group Ltd.

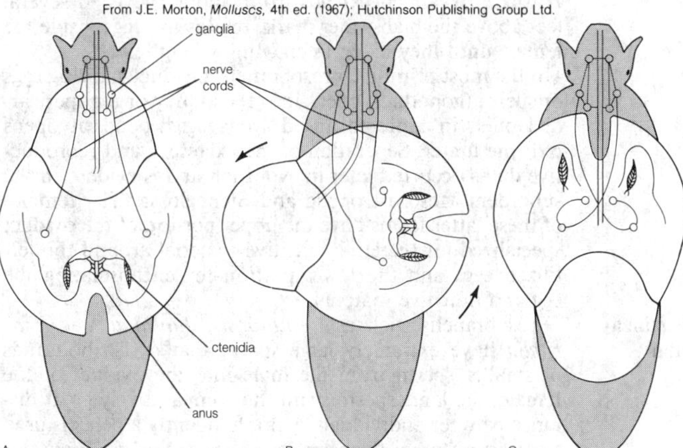

Figure 5: *Torsion.*
(A) Before torsion. (B) 90° rotation. (C) Torsion completed (180° rotation).

In some species the veliger stage may persist for a long period of larval life. The veliger has a small shell into which the velar lobes and head can be withdrawn and a larval heart that seems to exist solely to provide circulation in the velar lobes. Food consists of diatoms (an algae group) and small plankton collected by ciliary currents of the velum and channeled by the currents into the mouth. Special excretory cells located on either side of the mouth and the larval heart disappear when the veliger settles to the bottom and changes into a crawling snail. Upon settling, the snail starts a typical pattern of rapid growth until sexual maturity, at which point growth either ceases or is greatly slowed because energy is being diverted to the production of the next generation. In opisthobranchs and many pulmonates, the life span is about one year, although there are notable exceptions. Prosobranchs in general seem to have a much longer life span, with some species of the freshwater *Vivipara* having lived 20 years Life span in captivity. Some Sonoran Desert snails from California have been revived after eight years in estivation. Such desert species may have a life span of 20 to 50 years.

Several trends are evident in gastropod evolution from this basic pattern. First, there is a tendency toward the development of structures to permit internal fertilization. Pallial reproductive tubes of male and female become closed tubes, and a male copulatory organ develops on the right side of the head for transmission of sperm to the female. Second, the trochophore and veliger stages tend to be passed within an egg capsule provided with a food supply, rather than as free-swimming immature organisms that must find their own food. At first, provision of nutriment for the young probably involved laying eggs in a mucous mass. As evolution progressed, capsules containing yolk and with a protective cover might have been laid singly or in masses. Still later forms may have provided parental care of the eggs or egg mass. Finally the eggs are retained inside a brood pouch or the uterus until the young are ready to hatch (ovoviviparity). Third, there are tendencies toward sex reversal and the development of hermaphroditism—the presence of both male and female sex organs in one animal; nearly all opisthobranchs and pulmonates are hermaphrodites.

Such changes occurred more than once during gastropod evolution, and there is no clear pattern of changes that would suggest relationships. The differences correlate with habitat and frequently are seen within species of one genus. *Littorina,* on the English coasts, is a classic example: *L. neritoides* lives in crevices of exposed rocks above normal high water but releases floating (pelagic) egg capsules during fortnightly high tides or storms; *L. littorea,* on the lower half of the shore, also has pelagic egg capsules, which hatch six days later into veligers; *L. littoralis,* which lives on seaweeds that are rarely exposed by the tides, deposits gelatinous egg masses on the seaweeds, and the larvae pass through the veliger stage in the egg mass, emerging in two to three weeks as crawling young; and *L. saxatilis,* which extends from midtide level to several feet above the high-water mark, retains the eggs inside the female until they hatch as crawling young.

In the most primitive prosobranchs the duct carrying eggs or sperm (gonoduct) opens into the kidney or renopericardial duct; in more-advanced archaeogastropods it opens into the ureter. Separation of the excretory and reproductive ducts occurred later in evolution and is evident in the suborders Mesogastropoda and Stenoglossa. The females of these latter forms have the upper portion of the oviduct specialized for secreting nutritive material around the fertilized eggs and the lower portion for encapsulating the egg and nutritive material.

Fertilization

Prosobranchs such as *Cerithiopsis, Janthina,* and *Turritella* have extremely large sperm that carry thousands of smaller sperm from the male into the oviduct of the female; the large sperm swim the comparatively great distance between individuals. More frequently a penis is used to insert a stream of sperm into a special storage organ or the oviduct. In the opisthobranch *Limapontia* the penis stylet injects sperm through the body wall into a storage organ (bursa) of the mate.

Internal fertilization is necessary for land gastropods. The more primitive species directly transfer a stream or gelatinous mass of sperm by insertion of the penis. One individual can act as a male and the other as a female, or copulation can be reciprocal. During evolution, loosely adherent masses of sperm gave rise to enclosed packets of sperm and then to horny or calcareous sperm bundles (spermatophores) with elaborately ornamented exteriors. It is not uncommon for there to be as many as 12 such spermatophores inside the bursa of a female. Closely related species show clear differences in the number and spacing of exterior spikes. Undoubtedly, this difference provides a method of species recognition among these snails. Other pulmonates depend on explicit courtship patterns (such as the slugs from the family Limacidae) or structural differences in the penis (as in the land snails of the family Endodontidae) to distinguish close relatives.

Sex reversal

Most members of the prosobranch family Calyptraeidae begin life as fully functional males but, after a transitional phase, spend their remaining life span as females. *Crepidula* species normally attach to one spot when young and rarely move again. Other members of the species frequently attach to the shell surface of a settled individual, forming piles of as many as 19 specimens. The younger ones on top are male, the old ones on the bottom female, and those in the middle are intermediate in sex. Isolated young individuals function as males for only a week or two, but young males in a pile remain male for a longer period, through some unidentified influence of the larger females underneath. Some limpets also undergo sex reversal.

Egg production is correlated with the degree of care given the eggs or young. The extremes are the production of enormous numbers of eggs, which receive no care and hence suffer mass mortality (a fraction of 1 percent surviving), and the production of only one or two eggs, which receive intensive care. There are many gradations between the extremes. Many members of the suborders Mesogastropoda and Stenoglossa produce egg capsules that may contain from one to more than 1,000 eggs. In *Busycon,* for example, each capsule may contain up to 1,000 eggs, but extensive cannibalization occurs among the early hatched young and upon unhatched eggs in the capsule. *Strombus* can lay a tubular string of eggs 23 metres (75 feet) long, with up to 460,000 eggs. Many *Conus* cement up to 1.5 million eggs in capsules on the undersides of rocks. Opisthobranchs weave delicate ribbons of eggs in colourful sheets—sometimes up to 50 millimetres (two inches) of ribbon per hour—that contain many millions of eggs. In these cases, the eggs hatch into swimming veligers. Freshwater snails frequently deposit eggs in capsules on plant leaves or rocks, but the number of eggs is much less than in the marine gastropods.

Parental care of eggs

Direct care of the eggs is given in different ways. A small trochid, *Clanculus bertheloti,* deposits its eggs in grooves on the shell surface and covers them with a sheet of mucus to hold them in place; many *Neptunea* simply cement the egg capsules to their shell surface. Many *Crepidula* deposit a mass of 5,000 to 20,000 eggs under the shell edge just in front of the female's foot, brooding them until they hatch as veligers. Freshwater viviparids and thiarids have either uterine or neck brood pouches, in which the fertilized eggs develop to a crawling stage. The vermetid *Stephopoma* and the acmaeid *Acmaea rubella* brood their young in the mantle cavity between the fleshy body and the shell. A number of endodontid land snails on Pacific islands deposit their eggs in the umbilicus, an opening in the shell base. In one species, *Libera fratercula,* the young gnaw their way out through the apex of the maternal shell. One pteropod, *Hydromeles,* has an internal brood chamber that apparently ruptures, freeing the young into the body cavity of the parent; it is suspected that the escape of the young results in the parent's death.

Even without direct care of the eggs, land snails generally lay fewer than 200 eggs at a time. This reflects the different problems encountered on land and the lower mortality of larvae that are protected within the egg coverings. Many slugs and some snails bury egg masses in soil or under moist pieces of bark. Others, such as *Discus,* scatter their eggs singly over bark and decaying wood. One tropical genus (*Amphidromus*) rolls a leaf into a tube, seals one end with mucus, and lays its eggs in the cylinder thus formed. The South American *Strophocheilus* lays one large egg about four centimetres (1.5 inches) long. Among the many ways in which land snails minimize losses from drying is the adoption of ovoviviparity, or the hatching of eggs within the parent's body.

The evolutionary trend from the simple release of eggs and sperm toward the provision of a large quantity of nutritive materials and protective encapsulation of each fertilized egg has resulted in an increase in the size of the organs that provide these abilities as well as a reduction in the sizes of the ovary and testis. The shift to direct transfer of sperm masses has led to evolution of both complex structures for species recognition and complicated behaviour to assure species identity.

Ecology and habitats. Although all levels of the ocean are inhabited by snails, they are in greatest abundance in and just below the tidal zones, where the most abundant quantities of food may be found. The extent of their effect on a coastline is indicated by the estimate that an average population of 860 million *Littorina* on one square mile of rocky shore ingests 2,200 tons of material each year, only about 55 tons of which is organic matter. Limpets of all types are even more influential in such habitats, browsing and grazing on the algae and sessile animals. One interesting characteristic of limpets is that of homing. Numerous species have the tendency to settle on one spot and to feed on regular pathways radiating from this home base, to which they return for rest or under stressful conditions.

Snail damage to rocky coasts

Some larger prosobranchs are selective herbivores, cutting off one- to two-centimetre (0.4- to 0.8-inch) strips of seaweed for swallowing. More characteristic of the sand and mud flats are scavengers that indiscriminately take in surface debris; scavengers are found in various groups, including limpets, strombids, and nassariids. Carnivores include both surface hunters and burrowing forms such as the naticids. As an adaptation to sedentary life, several families have adopted mucociliary feeding by collecting food particles from water currents. Sensory reception to detect prey is highly developed in many carnivores.

Janthina builds a float of air bubbles in mucus; the float is attached to the middle part of the foot. Heteropods swim either by undulations of the foot or by the action of fleshy fins. Pelagic opisthobranchs show almost every conceivable type of swimming mechanism and are at times extremely abundant on the ocean surface. Many opisthobranchs and most small freshwater pulmonates can glide on the underside of the surface film of the water but are not able to swim.

Diversity of mollusks in the ocean has resulted from specialization in food resources. Temperature and salinity are the prime physical factors limiting range extensions, usually by preventing successful breeding rather than by preventing settlement and growth of young.

Adaptations to fresh water and land

Migration of the snails into fresh water and onto land required a number of new adaptations. Snails had extra problems to solve, relating to their basic feeding and reproductive patterns. In the ocean, dispersal can take place by way of a veliger stage transported passively by currents and waves. In streams and rivers such a means of dispersal would result in downstream spread only. Because of this, the veliger stage was suppressed; instead, many freshwater prosobranchs brood the young inside the female, and pulmonates attach egg capsules to rocks, to vegetation, or to other snail shells. This essentially restricts snail dispersal to individual movement. In prosobranchs with separate sexes, the freshwater distributions closely follow drainage systems, because, in order to colonize a new body of water, either a pregnant female must be transported or both a male and a female must arrive at about the same time. The majority of pulmonates in fresh water are hermaphrodites and are capable of self-fertilization as well as cross-fertilization with other individuals. As a result, any pulmonate entering a new body of water can establish a considerable population of that species in a short time. For this reason, isolated ponds often have several species of pulmonates but only rarely prosobranch gastropods. In crawling over waterweeds, the pulmonates frequently come in contact with the feet or feathers of wading birds, to which they adhere accidentally by mucus secretion and are carried to a new pond.

Land snails avoid dessication in several ways. Prosobranchs retreat into their shells, and the operculum effectively seals the opening against the exterior. In the tropics, land operculates have developed elaborate breathing tubes to allow gas exchange during dry periods and yet minimize water loss. Pulmonates lack an operculum, but a great number of the forms secrete either simple mucous coverings (epiphragms) across the shell aperture or, in some of the more arid areas, a calcium-impregnated seal that can be almost as thick as the shell itself. Most land snails, however, have adjusted to life on land primarily through behaviour patterns. They stay in areas of high moisture or retreat into damp niches during short dry spells. A few burrow into soil. *Sonorella* species survive by remaining dormant during the years between rains; the genital structures of many individuals are reduced or lost to minimize use of energy in reproductive activities.

Tree snails

Only in the wet and warm tropics have tree snails been able to develop. These species have brightly coloured shells that usually are much thinner than those of their terrestrial counterparts. In the humid mountain regions of the world, where a constant supply of moisture is available throughout the year, there has been a marked tendency toward reduction of the shell and the evolution of slugs. This tendency probably results from two different selective pressures that reinforce each other. The shell, which is useful primarily in providing protection against dessication, is no longer needed when moisture is plentiful. Secondly, construction of the shell requires that a large quantity of calcium be readily available; calcium is generally in short supply on the slopes of volcanic mountains. With the need for the shell lessened and the primary constituent in short supply, any mutation favouring shell reduction is advantageous. Although most species of slugs seem to have evolved in mountain areas, their spread into lowlands has been greatly aided by crop irrigation and garden watering.

By far the majority of land snails occupy the surface litter and upper soil zone. This microhabitat is generally moist, and food is plentiful in the form of decaying animals and plants as well as fungi. Most land snails have shells that are drab in colour and inconspicuous. Frequently, the shell surface is highly sculpted. The minute species (less than three millimetres [0.1 inch] in diameter) face a problem of predation by small arthropods. The normal instinct of a snail to withdraw into its shell is of no help, since the predator simply follows the snail into its shell. Elaborate barriers that narrow the shell opening and tiny spines along the opening must provide some protection, since this construction occurs in more than 12 pulmonate families.

Most land snails feed directly on decaying plant matter, which is a simple shift in feeding behaviour from the primitive browsing of their marine ancestors. The carnivorous habit probably evolved through a transition period of carrion eaters. Many slugs feed on dead animal matter as well as plants. Pursuit and capture of other snails or earthworms demand increased sensory equipment and more rapid motion. Most carnivores, such as *Euglandina,* have greatly elongated bodies for reaching further into the shells of their victims.

Locomotion. The foot is the organ of locomotion in land gastropods. In swimming and sessile forms, however, the foot is greatly reduced and in many groups greatly modified. The normal progression of a snail is by muscular action, with a series of contraction waves proceeding from the posterior to the anterior end of the gliding portion of the foot. This type of progression is called monotaxic locomotion. A few groups have the foot divided into right and left halves, with separate waves moving on each side, a condition termed ditaxic locomotion. Certain species move by the beating action of cilia of the foot on the mucous sheet secreted by the anterior part of the foot. When the foot is narrow, as in *Strombus* and *Aporrhais,* the animal moves in fits and starts, tumbling along by a digging action of the foot and the pointed operculum. Most prosobranchs are relatively slow-moving, with a speed of less than eight centimetres (about three inches) per minute, although *Haliotis* has been reported to move at almost 10 times that rate.

Movement by contraction of the foot

Many opisthobranchs employ monotaxic locomotion; some can glide on the underside of water-surface films through ciliary action. Swimming has been achieved in a number of ways. Body undulations propel such large snails as *Dendronotus* and *Melibe.* Pteropods, *Gastropteron, Akera,* and others move foot flaps (parapodia) to provide motion. The sea hare, *Aplysia,* uses an inchwormlike progression, and some nudibranchs swim by beating accessory breathing organs (cerata).

Freshwater pulmonates use ciliary action on a bed of mucus secreted by the snail. Many snails, especially *Physa,* can form a cord of mucus from the water surface to the bottom.

Land pulmonates depend upon a combination of muscular action and cilia for locomotion. In many of these species the foot is divided longitudinally into three parts, with locomotor activity being confined to the central section, which glides on a mucous track. An additional use of slime by slugs is in the act of mating. A slime rope is secreted from which the mating pair of slugs are able to suspend themselves. If irritated, slugs can secrete copious quantities of slime. This reaction is the basis for one of the most effective methods of controlling slugs: spreading enough ashes in slug-infested areas causes exhaustion and death of the animals through the overproduction of slime.

Some of the small, tropical, brightly coloured sluglike species will, when disturbed, travel at a very high rate of speed with the anterior half of the foot lifted off the ground. They can continue moving at this pace for a distance of almost a metre at a rate faster than one metre per minute in snails less than two to three centimetres (or about one inch) in body length. Large species, such as *Achatina* or *Strophocheilus,* are much slower, although carnivores are usually relatively fast-moving.

Food and feeding. As in all molluscan groups except the bivalves, gastropods have an odontophore at the anterior end of the digestive tract. Generally, this organ forms a broad ribbon (radula) covered with a few to many thousand "teeth" (denticles). The radula is used in feeding: muscles extrude the radula from the mouth, spread it out, and then pull it back into the mouth, carrying particles or pieces of food and debris into the esophagus. Although attached at both ends, the radula grows continuously during the gastropod's life, with new rows of denticles being formed posteriorly to replace the worn denticles cast off at the anterior end. Both form and number of denticles vary greatly among species—the differences correlating with food and habitat changes. Radular denticles are shown in Figure 6.

The odontophore: a rasping organ

Evidently, the most primitive type of gastropod feeding involved browsing and grazing of algae from rocks. Some species of the order Archaeogastropoda still retain the basic rhipidoglossan radula, in which many slender marginal teeth are arranged in transverse rows. During use, the outer, or marginal, denticles swing outward, and the radula is curled under the anterior end of the odontophore. The latter is pressed against the feeding surface, and, one row at a time, the denticles are erected and scrape across the surface, removing fine particles as the odontophore is withdrawn into the mouth. As the marginals swing inward, food particles are carried toward the midline of the radula and collected into a mucous mass. By folding the teeth inward, damage to the mouth lining is avoided and food particles are concentrated. Mucus-bound food particles are then passed through the esophagus and into the gut for sorting and digestion.

From this basic pattern, numerous specializations have developed, including docoglossate, taenioglossate, rachiglossate, and toxoglossate radulae. Many limpets, which scrape algae directly from rock surfaces, have a docoglossate radula, with the marginals greatly reduced in number. When the radula is extruded, in *Patella,* for example, several rows of denticles on the lower odontophoral margin are pressed against the surface. There is no elevation of single rows and no lateral movement of the few marginals. Consequently, wear against the rock surface is great, and, although the denticles are heavily impregnated with mineral salts, tooth damage and loss is extensive. In rock-grazing species, replacement and growth are relatively rapid, and the radula is very long in relation to shell size.

Wear and replacement of teeth

Mesogastropods have a taenioglossate radula, in which a central tooth is flanked on either side by three laterals, for a total of seven denticles. This highly flexible pattern has allowed great diversity in feeding by alteration of cusp and tooth size. Often members of a genus may show striking differences. The limpetlike *Hipponyx antiquatus* attaches permanently in rock crevices or on clamshells and feeds on the organic debris that can accumulate. Other limpetlike, or burrowing, mesogastropods collect food particles off the gill and pass them into the mouth by cilia. *Hipponyx* and *Aporrhais* grasp the trapped particles with the radular teeth, whereas in *Crepidula* a food-laden mucous cord is formed, bits of which are torn off by the radula.

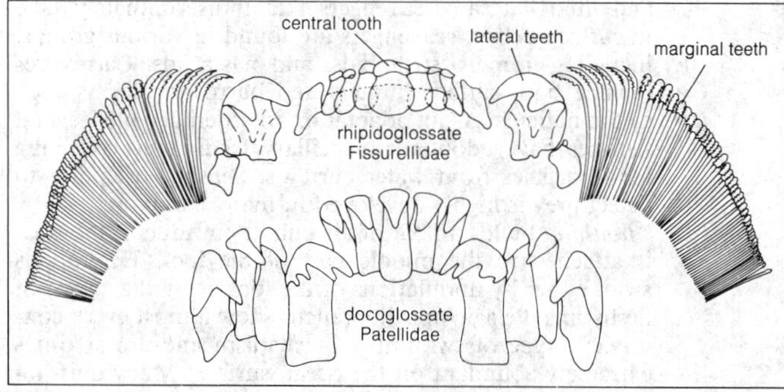

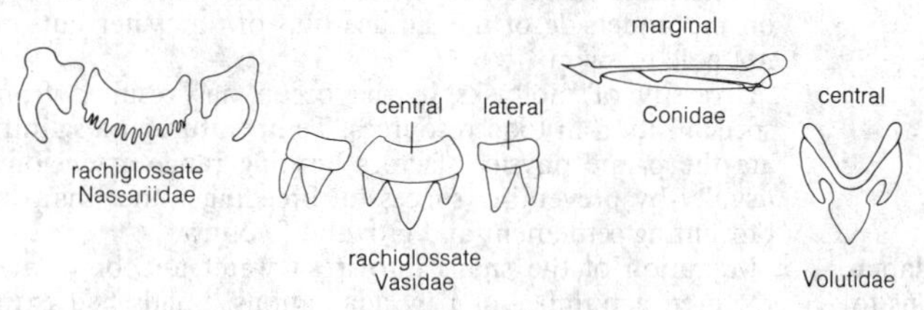

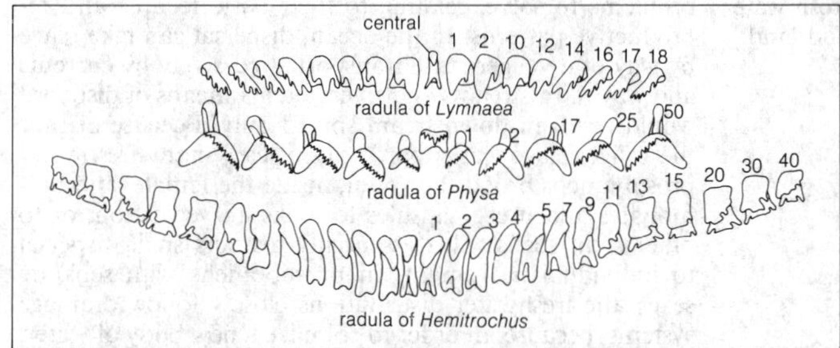

Figure 6: Gastropod radulae and types of teeth.

Gastropods that feed on sessile animals have evolved an extensible proboscis capable of reaching into narrow openings. Such minute sponge feeders as *Triphora* extend the slender proboscis into the openings of a sponge to reach delicate fleshy cells. Similarly, many cowries feed on sea squirts (ascidians). Numerous mesogastropods and prosobranch-opisthobranch transition groups are external parasites (ectoparasites) on larger animals. A few are internal parasites (endoparasites) of echinoderms.

Floating snails

Floating snails such as *Janthina* drift along until they contact prey. Certain mesogastropods are active swimmers; one, *Pterotrachea,* has the foot modified into a small sucker for holding prey. Mesogastropods of the families Naticidae and Doliidae feed upon bivalves and echinoderms. The naticids use their large foot to hold the prey while they drill through the bivalve shell. A combination of mechanical rasping by the radula and chemical loosening of the calcium by secretions produces a hole in the bivalve shell through which the proboscis is inserted to enable the naticid to feed upon the soft tissues.

In stenoglossans the basic radular type is rachiglossate, with only three denticles—a central and two laterals. Families such as the Buccinidae and Nassariidae include carnivores and scavengers. Members of the family Muricidae are predators that may use either a secretion to bore holes into shells or the physical force of their proboscis to pry into shelled prey. Many genera (*e.g., Busycon, Fasciolaria,* some *Murex*) use part of their shell to wedge open a clam for feeding.

Finally, the toxoglossate radula has only two teeth, which are formed and used alternately. Most toxoglossate gastropods inject a poison via the functional tooth. Prey selection usually is highly specific. Although many cones hunt polychaete worms, others prey on gastropods or fishes, using the radular tooth as a harpoon, with poison being injected into the prey through the hollow shaft of the tooth. Several of the large fish-eating cones, which produce a potent nerve poison, have been known to kill humans.

Opisthobranch gastropods show less clearly defined types of radular structure. Anaspideans such as *Dolabella* may have as many as 460 teeth per row with a total of 25,000 denticles; sacoglossans have only one longitudinal row of teeth. In terms of feeding, opisthobranchs are extremely varied. Besides the algae-sucking sacoglossans, *Aplysia* cuts up strips of seaweed for swallowing, and a number of the more primitive species feed on algae encrusted on rocks. Perhaps the majority of opisthobranchs, including the sea slugs, are predators on sessile animals, ascidians and coelenterates being especially favoured. Pyramidellids are ectoparasites on a variety of organisms. Some of the pteropods are ciliary feeders on microorganisms.

Pulmonate modifications for feeding

Pulmonate gastropods are predominantly herbivores, with only a few scavenging and predatory species. Basically, on the radula there is a central tooth flanked by a few to many denticles, which may be differentiated into laterals and marginals. The central tooth may be reduced in size or lost, whereas the other teeth show modifications correlated with diet. Primitively, the pulmonate radular tooth has three raised points, or cusps (*i.e.,* is tricuspid), but modifications involving splitting of cusps or reductions to one cusp are numerous. With each successive appearance of a carnivorous type during evolution, however, the teeth have been reduced in number, each tooth usually having one long, sickle-shaped cusp.

Much of the diversity achieved by the gastropods relates to the evolutionary shifts in radular structure, which have led to exploitation of a variety of food sources. Predators capable of swimming, surface crawling, and burrowing to capture prey have evolved among the prosobranchs and opisthobranchs; predators that produce chemical substances for entering the shells of their prey have evolved among the mesogastropods (family Naticidae and superfamily Tonnacea), stenoglossans (family Muricidae), and a nudibranch opisthobranch (*Okadaia*); and, in the pulmonates, predation and thus a carnivorous diet have evolved at least 12 times.

FORM AND FUNCTION

Gastropods present such a variety of structures and adaptations that few all-encompassing characteristics can be presented. A detailed presentation on the radula and reproductive changes, which are keys to understanding gastropod diversification, has been given above. The following survey focuses on the external shell and the body.

The shell. The typical snail has a calcareous shell coiled in a spiral pattern around a central axis called the columella. Generally, the coils, or whorls, added later in life are larger than those added when the snail is young. At the end of the last whorl is the aperture, or opening. The shell is secreted along the outer lip of the aperture by the fleshy part of the animal called the mantle, first by outward additions to the shell lip and then by secretion of inner thickening layers. The outer layer, or periostracum, is a mixture of proteins known as conchin. Inner layers of calcium carbonate interlace with a network of conchin and are impregnated with a variety of mineral salts. The calcium usually is in the form of calcite crystals in marine species and aragonite crystals in terrestrial species, but mixtures of crystal types do occur.

Shell ornamentation

Modifications and ornamentations of the basic shell are widely variable. Frequently, the shell is altered into a nonspiral cap or a cup-shaped limpet form as an adaptation to life in swift currents (the freshwater family Ancylidae) or amid pounding waves on rocks (the marine families Acmaeidae, Patellidae, Fissurellidae, and Calyptraeidae). In many groups, such as the abalones (the family Haliotidae), only traces of spiral coiling are evident, because the rate of successive whorl widths is so large that the last, or body, whorl occupies more than 90 percent of the shell volume. Elaborate surface sculpture, including knobs and spines, develop as protection against predation. In a few species of the genera *Leucozonia* and *Acanthina,* a spine on the lip edge is used to wedge open clam valves so that the snail can feed. As implied earlier, land gastropods in dry regions tend to have very thick shells; on the other hand, those in very humid mountain situations have thin shells or none at all. Many carnivorous snails have the calcareous part of the shell greatly reduced.

The body. The gastropod body consists of four main parts: visceral hump, mantle, head, and foot. The body is attached to the shell either by one columellar muscle or by a series of muscles. Typical snails can withdraw the head and foot into the shell, but numerous species have shells so reduced in size as to be unable to contain the body; slugs, of course, have either an internal shell vestige or no shell at all.

The mantle cavity

The visceral hump. The visceral hump of gastropods is always contained within the shell; it generally holds the bulk of the digestive, reproductive, excretory, and respiratory systems (Figure 7). A significant part of the visceral hump consists of the mantle, or pallial, cavity. In both prosobranchs and shelled opisthobranchs this is a cavity completely open anteriorly; in pulmonates it is closed except for a narrow pore. The upper surface of the mantle cavity serves a respiratory function. In marine species the ciliated lining of the mantle cavity produces a water current that passes posteriorly across the gill, or

From (B) *Treatise on Invertebrate Paleontology;* courtesy of the Geological Society of America and the University of Kansas Press

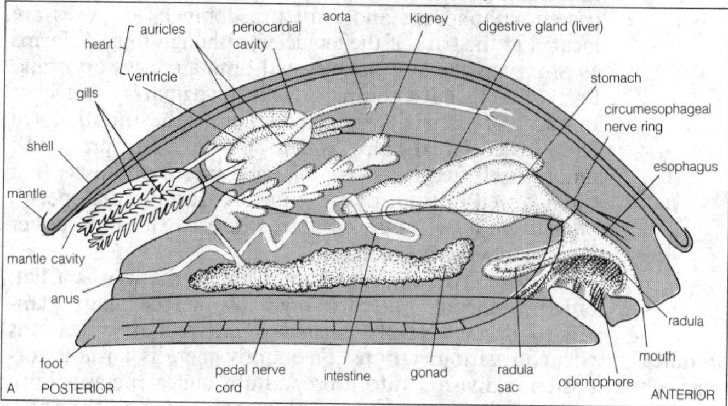

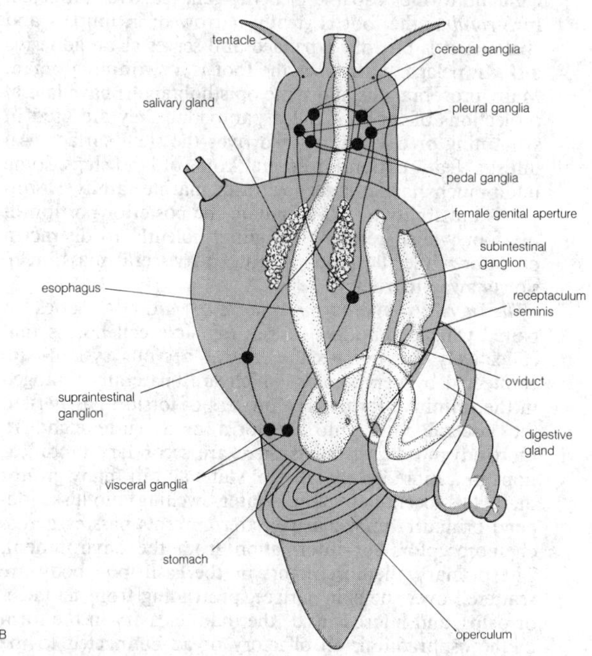

Figure 7: *Adult gastropod structure.* (A) Primitive. (B) Advanced.

ctenidium, and the osphradium, which is thought to be a sensory receptor that can detect chemical changes in the environment. Both organs lie on the left anterior side of the cavity. The water current sweeps across the posterior part of the mantle cavity, where the nephridiopore, or kidney opening, lies; the water current then passes anteriorly along the right margin past the anus, through which undigested particles of food are eliminated, and usually moves past the gonopore, through which sexual products are released.

The mantle cavity serves as a space for the head and foot when these organs are retracted. Many land pulmonates apparently also use the mantle cavity to retain water. Prosobranchs use the operculum, the horny or calcareous disk located on the back of the foot at the posterior end, to seal the shell opening after the head and body have been retracted.

Operculum

The mantle. The mantle is the fleshy lining of the outer wall of the shell; it roofs the mantle cavity. At its anterior end lie glandular tissues that deposit the various shell layers. In terrestrial forms with reduced shells, various lobes and laps extend anteriorly over the neck and head or are reflected back over the shell surface. These are highly vascularized and probably serve both in respiration and in water balance of the body. Many marine forms have the mantle collar extended forward and rolled into a siphon, which functions in both food location and chemoreception.

The head. Generally, the head is bilaterally symmetrical, bearing one or two pairs of tentacles, often with accessory palps, and the mouth in the middle of the ventral margin. In stylommatophoran land snails the upper tentacles, or ommatophores, are invaginable (capable of being rolled in), and the eyes are borne at the tips. In freshwater basommatophorans and most prosobranchs the eyes are located at the base of the tentacles, although in such forms as *Strombus* the eyes are elevated onto an accessory stalk. Prosobranchs have contractile (not invaginable) tentacles. In carnivorous snails the lateral lips of the mouth form lobes called labial palps, which help to locate prey. The mouth itself frequently is prolonged into a proboscis that extends well in front of the tentacles. Carnivorous species often have a proboscis capable of great extension, either invaginable or contractile.

The foot. Although the basic form of the foot is a flat, broadly tapered, muscular organ, which is highly glandularized and usually ciliated, numerous modifications occur in various groups. Frequently there is an anterior-posterior division into a propodium and a metapodium, with the former capable of being reflexed over the shell. In *Strombus* the foot is greatly narrowed; in limpets and abalones it is broadly expanded and serves as an adhesive disk. In pelagic gastropods the foot is a swimming organ. Many prosobranchs and some opisthobranchs have lateral projections of the foot called parapodia; they are used in swimming or else are reflexed over the shell surface. An unusual feature found in several kinds of land slugs, some nudibranchs, and the stenoglossan marine family Harpidae is the ability to self-amputate the posterior portion of the foot, which remains wriggling violently to distract a predator while the anterior foot and visceral mass creep slowly away to safety.

Modifications of the foot

The nervous system and sense organs. A series of paired ganglia (knotlike masses of nerve cell bodies that collectively function as the central nervous system) are connected by nerve cords, which are bilaterally arranged in the primitive forms. The process of torsion has twisted the visceral cords into the form of a figure eight. In more-advanced gastropods there are secondary modifications to a more nearly bilateral state, and in many groups there has been detorsion. Water-dwelling mollusks depend primarily upon ciliary water currents passing across chemoreceptors for information from the environment. The primary chemoreceptors in the gastropod body are scattered over the skin surface, protruding from tentacles or palps, and housed inside the mantle cavity in the form of the osphradium, an olfactory organ connected to the respiratory system. Sense organs are more highly developed in carnivores than in herbivores. Eyespots, located at the base (most gastropods) or tip (land pulmonates) of the eye tentacles, are primarily light-sensitive rather than image-forming. A pair of statocysts, thought to be balancing organs, is present in nonsessile taxa.

Digestive system. The radular motion conveys food particles into the mouth, and ciliary currents move the food through the tract, except in carnivores, where muscular action plays an important role. Various salivary and digestive glands secrete enzymes into either or both the buccal cavity and the stomach, where digestion takes place. The apical digestive gland, or "liver," can store digested food for use during periods of inactivity.

The excretory system. There are two kidneys, or nephridia, in only the primitive gastropods, such as the archaeogastropods, while, in the advanced forms, one kidney is small or lost. The kidney plays different roles, depending upon the environment in which the snail lives. Most marine gastropods have the same total concentrations of solutes as in the surrounding seawater, and thus a small osmotic differential (*i.e.,* an equilibrium) exists between the water leaving and that entering the cell. Little energy is needed therefore to prevent the cells from losing or gaining too much water. Freshwater gastropods, however, have a higher total solute concentration than that of the surrounding water. The kidney must expend energy to control water balance (osmoregulation). The flow of water through the mantle cavity is restricted in freshwater species by the closure of the mantle cavity by the mantle collar. Land prosobranchs have an open mantle cavity and, in order to conserve water, secrete nearly crystalline urine. Land pulmonates have a ureteric groove or closed ureter that resorbs water from the urine. In both marine and freshwater species, ciliary water currents sweep the excreted matter out of the mantle cavity.

Respiration. In marine and freshwater gastropods, respiration takes place as water currents pass across the gill surfaces within the mantle cavity in most species with spiral shells, across gill elements along the sides of the bodies in most limpets, or through projections from the body surface in sea slugs or taxa with reduced shells. The upper surface of the mantle cavity is heavily vascularized in land snails, which use muscular contractions to pump air in and out of the small respiratory pore at the anterior edge of the mantle cavity. In some land slugs or tropical snails with reduced shells, respiratory functions have shifted either to external projections from the mantle collar or to the skin as the area of mantle roof available for respiration has decreased in size.

The reproductive system. The primitive archaeogastropods retain two nephridia; the right nephridium provides the passage for eggs or sperm from the ovary or testis to the mantle cavity. The sexes are separate in nearly all prosobranchs, although in a few taxa, such as *Crepidula,* an animal begins life as a male and then changes to a female later. Both the opisthobranchs and pulmonates are hermaphroditic, often protandrous (male gonads maturing first), but many taxa when fully adult become simultaneous hermaphrodites (male and female gonads are functional at the same time). Internal fertilization is common in the more advanced marine taxa but mandatory in the freshwater and terrestrial groups. A very few gastropods are parthenogenetic (gametes developing without fertilization).

Features of defense. Warning coloration is found in some of the brilliantly coloured shells and bodies of carnivorous marine snails that possess highly toxic poisons. Similar bright colours characterize some land snails and slugs that secrete noxious chemicals and thus will be sampled only once by a predator. Camouflage coloration provides partial protection against predation by some European land snails.

EVOLUTION AND PALEONTOLOGY

The basic trends in snail evolution involve changing from a herbivorous to a carnivorous diet, shifting from the ocean to freshwater and terrestrial life, and adopting a sluglike form through reduction or loss of the shell and visceral hump. Each change has occurred independently several times in the course of gastropod evolution.

Prosobranch gastropods are the most primitive. One group, the Diotocardia, which retains two sets of mantle organs, is nearest the generalized gastropod in structure. Gradual loss of the right set of mantle organs occurs in the primitive archaeogastropod superfamilies Trochacea and Neritacea, thus providing a transition to the more highly developed order Monotocardia, with only one set of mantle organs. Among the numerous changes in the Monotocardia are fewer radular teeth and a shift from grazing on algae and fungi to predation and the consumption of larger sessile organisms. The two main divisions of the Monotocardia show different evolutionary patterns. Although most mesogastropods have remained coastal marine, several families moved into fresh water. Others crossed to land directly from the tidal zone, rather than passing through a freshwater transitional period. At the peak of prosobranch evolution is the predatory suborder Stenoglossa, all marine inhabitants, with highly modified radular teeth and often well-developed poison glands to aid in capturing prey. Reduction and loss of the right mantle organs are correlated with more efficient respiration and sensory apparatuses, in which a water current crosses over the sensory organs and gills on the left side, then out on the right side, together with excretory and fecal deposits.

Opisthobranchs probably arose from an unknown group of primitive prosobranchs and have evolved extensively into different lines showing a reduction of the visceral hump and shell. In certain forms the foot is shortened, and external cerata develop to provide a respiratory surface to replace the lost mantle-cavity surface. Such opisthobranch groups as the order Pyramidellacea contain a mixture of prosobranch and opisthobranch characteristics.

Pulmonates show varying degrees of adjustment to freshwater and land life, with increasing union of the male and female gonoducts characterizing the more advanced groups. Similarly, the highly advanced suborder Holopoda and superfamily Limacacea show complex accessory organs on the genitalia and a more sophisticated means of water conservation through development of a closed secondary ureter and resorption of water from the excretory products. More than a dozen different groups of pulmonates have become predators, usually upon other snails or earthworms.

The earliest gastropods

Fossil gastropods are known from Cambrian deposits. Since the shell is often very similar in unrelated families, fossil gastropods more than 350 million years old are not usually placed in the classification outlined below but instead are treated separately. Most stenoglossan prosobranchs appeared near the end of the Mesozoic (66.4 million years ago), and many groups of land snails are known from Eocene formations (57.8 to 36.6 million years old). Snails had their adaptive radiation early in geologic history. Living genera of marine, freshwater, and land snail families are known from Oligocene to Miocene deposits (36.6 to 5.3 million years old). Unlike mammals, who have undergone great evolutionary change in the last 50 million years, gastropods have shown little progressive evolution during that time.

CLASSIFICATION

Since the 1980s, gastropod classification has been the subject of extensive debate. Major revisions based on detailed information about traditional anatomy and shell features have been challenged by cladistic attempts to identify changes that have taken place once in the evolutionary history of a group and thus derive phylogenetic schemes, attempts to delineate the geneology of groups based primarily on neurological structures. Both traditional and cladistic classification schemes are being tested by data from molecular studies. Given the antiquity of the gastropods as a group, however, it is perhaps realistic to expect that most changes have occurred more than once. Graham gave an excellent review of anatomic and functional trends, concluding that many of the groups historically recognized as advanced are grades reached by several taxa independently, not monophyletic clades (groups with the same ancestor).

A conservative classification is presented below, basically using concepts from Vera Fretter and Alistair Graham (1962) for the prosobranchs, Louise Schmekel (1985) for the opisthobranchs, and Alan Solem (1978) for the pulmonates, with minor modifications from a number of sources. The remarkable radiation of primitive limpets associated with the hydrothermal vents was still under analysis in the late 1980s and is not included.

The pattern of change in the respiratory and nervous systems and in the mantle complex is fundamental. Among the major trends are the change from a streptoneurus (twisted) to a euthyneurus (straight) nerve loop, the progressive loss of the right part of the primitively paired mantle organs, the increasing sophistication of hermaphroditism, the tendency toward the reduction of the visceral hump and shell, the multiple changes from a herbivorous to a carnivorous diet, the shifts from marine to freshwater or land environments and occasionally the return from the land to the ocean, and the shifts in locomotor mechanics.

CLASS GASTROPODA (snails and slugs)
Snails typically with a calcareous shell, slugs with greatly reduced shell; length ranges from about 1 mm to 130 cm; about 65,000 species widely distributed in marine, freshwater, and land regions.

Subclass Prosobranchia
Streptoneurous (twisted) gastropods with an anteriorly located mantle cavity (space lined with epidermis); operculum (protective cover) generally present; sexes separate; shell can usually hold entire animal; primarily marine, several freshwater and terrestrial groups; about 33,000 species.

Order Diotocardia (Archaeogastropoda)
Heart usually with 2 auricles; 1 or 2 internal gills; no penis, siphon (organ used in food location), or proboscis (feeding organ); nervous system not concentrated; sex cells discharged by way of the right nephridium (kidney); about 3,000 species.

Superfamily Zeugobranchia (Pleurotomariacea). Slit shells (Pleurotomariidae) in deep ocean waters; abalones (Haliotidae) in shallow waters along rocky shores of western North America, Japan, Australia, and South Africa; keyhole limpets (Fissurellidae) in intertidal rocky areas.

Superfamily Patellacea (Docoglossa). Conical-shelled limpets, without slits or holes, found in rocky shallow waters (Acmaeidae and Patellidae).

Superfamily Trochacea. Small to large spiral shells in shallow to deep ocean waters, often brightly coloured, with or without heavy shell ornamentation; Trochidae (top shells), Turbinidae (turban shells), and Phasianellidae (pheasant shells).

Superfamily Neritacea. Small, generally intertidal marine shells (Neritidae), with some freshwater dwellers, particularly in Indonesia and the Philippines (Neritidae), and 2 groups of land dwellers: 1 sparsely distributed in the Old World (Hydrocenidae) and 1 widely distributed in both Old and New World tropics (Helicinidae).

Order Monotocardia
Heart with 1 auricle; 1 gill, often modified; siphon and chemoreception osphradium (sensory receptor) progressively more complex; penis present; head frequently modified into a proboscis; nervous system progressively more concentrated; about 30,000 species.

Suborder Mesogastropoda (Taenioglossa). Radula taenioglossate (with 7 denticles, or teeth) or reduced; most taxa herbivorous; a few families parasites or predators.

Superfamily Cyclophoracea. Land snails; particularly abundant in the West Indies and southern Asia to Melanesia.

Superfamily Viviparacea. Large, 2.5- to 5-cm globular pond and river snails of the Northern Hemisphere (Viviparidae) and tropical regions (Ampullariidae); frequently used in freshwater aquariums with tropical fish.

Superfamily Littorinacea. Periwinkles, on rocky shores (Littorinidae) of all oceans; land snails of the West Indies, part of Africa, and Europe (Pomatiasidae).

Superfamily Rissoacea. Small to minute, generally cylindrical, marine, freshwater and land snails found in most tropical and warm temperate regions of the world; about 17 families.

Superfamily Cerithiacea. Minute to large, generally elaborately sculptured shells, common in mud flats and mangroves, many species sand dwellers, with 1 group of families (Thiaridae, Pleuroceridae, Melanopsidae) especially abundant and varied in the Tennessee and Alabama river systems; 13 marine families, including worm shells (Vermetidae), horn shells (Potamididae), and button shells (Modulidae).

Superfamily Strombacea. Foot and operculum greatly modified and move with a lurching motion; feed on algae and plants; some species used for human food; conchs (Strombidae) of tropical oceans and the pelican's foot shells (Aporrhaidae) of near Arctic waters.

Superfamily Calyptraeacea. Cap shells (Capulidae) and slipper shells (Calyptraeidae) are limpets with irregularly shaped shells with a small internal cup or shelf; many species show sex reversal, becoming males early in life, then changing into females during old age; common on rocks and clamshells and in dead large snail shells in most oceans.

Superfamily Cypraeacea. Cowrie shells (Cypraeidae) and egg shells (Ovulidae) have highly polished and brilliantly coloured shells; mantle, which may cover the shell, is a totally different colour pattern; if touched, members of group suddenly withdraw, the change in colour serving to confuse predators; common in shallow tropical oceans, some species in cooler waters.

Superfamily Naticacea. Moon shells (Naticidae) medium-sized, globular predators on burrowing bivalves: bore a hole in the clamshell using acid secretions, then insert the radula to feed; common in most oceans.

Superfamily Ptenoglossa (Scalacea). Wentletraps (Epitoniidae) live in shallow to deep ocean waters; purple snails (Janthinidae) float on the ocean surface after building a raft of bubbles; large numbers of bubble shells occasionally blow ashore.

Superfamily Aglossa. Parasitic or predatory snails either with a reduced radula or with none, jaws often modified into a stylet-shaped structure; many occur on echinoderms; consists of several poorly known families.

Superfamily Doliacea (Tonnacea). Generally tropical predators on echinoderms; often burrow in sand; includes helmet shells (Cassidae), tun shells (Doliidae), frog shells (Bursidae), triton shells (Cymatiidae), and fig shells (Ficidae); frog and triton shells often live in rocky areas; most species large in size.

Suborder Stenoglossa (Neogastropoda). Carnivorous or scavengers with rachiglossate (with 3 denticles) or taxoglossate (with 2 denticles) radula; shell often with long siphonal canal; proboscis well developed and often extensible; shells generally large; all marine.

Superfamily Muricacea. Murex shells (Muricidae), rock shells (Purpuridae), and coral shells (Coralliophilidae) are common predators, often boring into shells of their prey; rock shells common in cooler waters, others mostly tropical.

Superfamily Buccineacea. Scavengers that have lost the mechanisms for boring; dove shells (Columbellidae), mud snails (Nassariidae), tulip shells (Fasciolariidae), whelks (Buccinidae), and crown conchs (Galeodidae) mainly cool-water species; but dove and tulip shells have many tropical representatives.

Superfamily Volutacea. Harp shells (Harpidae), olive shells (Olividae), mitre shells (Mitridae), volute shells (Volutidae), nutmeg shells (Cancellariidae), and marginellas (Marginellidae) generally have operculum reduced or lacking; most are tropical ocean dwellers, active predators or scavengers; many olive, volute, and marginella shells are highly polished and colourful.

Superfamily Toxoglossa. Auger shells (Terebridae), cone shells (Conidae) and turrid shells (Turridae) are carnivorous marine snails with poison glands attached to highly modified radular teeth; several cone shells have caused human deaths through poisoning and can catch and kill fish.

Subclass Opisthobranchia

Shell reduced or lacking, usually too small for withdrawal of animal; mantle cavity often lost, rotated to right side and facing anteriorly; hermaphroditic; operculum generally lost; nerve ganglia (clusters) very concentrated; marine except for 4 species; about 4,000 species.

Order Cephalaspidea

Shell present, often capable of containing whole body; head shield developed; Acteonidae with operculum; 14 families.

Order Pyramidellacea

Spiral shell; operculum present; gill and radula absent; long proboscis with stylet; ectoparasitic; in warm oceanic areas; generally minute.

Order Acochlidacea

Three families with visceral mass longer than foot; 4 species in fresh water; a few with sexes in separate animals; size minute.

Order Philinoglossacea

No head appendages; gill lacking; no external shell; 2 families.

Order Anaspidea

Shell reduced to flat plate; feed on large seaweed rather than microscopic algae; sea hares (Aplysiidae); 1 other small family.

Order Notaspidea

Shell and gill usually present; no parapodia (extensions of foot); sperm groove open; shell prominent, reduced, or hidden by mantle; 2 families.

Order Sacoglossa

One file of radular teeth; sperm duct a closed tube; shell reduced to bivalved (Juliidae); many feed by sucking juices out of algae; several families with uncertain limits.

Order Thecosomata

Shell present; pelagic ciliary feeders; no gill; 6 families.

Order Gymnosomata

Shell absent; no mantle cavity; complicated feeding mechanisms; pelagic carnivores; 7 families.

Order Nudibranchia

Sea slugs without shell, mantle cavity, osphradium, or internal gill; many feed on sessile animals; few swimmers (family Tethyidae); highly colourful, often conspicuous.

Subclass Pulmonata

Mantle cavity altered into a pulmonary sac; no gills or operculum; 1 auricle of heart anterior to ventricle; hermaphroditic; shell spiral to limpetlike, often reduced to a fragment hidden by mantle; mainly terrestrial or freshwater, few marine; about 28,000 species.

Superorder Systellommatophora

Mantle cavity absent; anal and usually nephridial opening at posterior; male gonopore behind right tentacle; female gonopore middle of right side; sole of foot narrow; no shell; 2 pairs of retractile, or invaginable, tentacles; marine (Onchidiidae), terrestrial and herbivorous (Veronicellidae), or terrestrial and carnivorous (Rathouisiidae); about 200 species.

Superorder Basommatophora

Mantle cavity present; eyes at base of 1 pair of tentacles; male and female gonopore separate, usually on right side of body; shell conical to patelliform; mostly freshwater but a few land and marine taxa; about 1,000 species. (No agreement exists concerning suprafamilial classification of the Basommatophora. The following superfamilies, though not grouped into formal orders and suborders, are listed in order of increasing specialization.)

Superfamily Patelliformia. Brackish water or marine limpets with (Siphonariidae) gill-like structures or with a lung (Gadinidae).

Superfamily Amphibolacea. Operculum present; shell conical; with pulmonary cavity; brackish water; burrow in sand; 1 family.

Superfamily Ellobiacea. Conical shells; pulmonary chamber; in tidal zone or salt flats, under rocks in spray zone, or completely terrestrial; 2 families.

Superfamily Lymnaeacea. Small to large, spiral-shelled snails of ponds, lakes, and rivers; 1 limpet group (Lancidae) and larger typical group (Lymnaeidae).

Superfamily Ancylacea. Limpets (Ancylidae), ramshorns (Planorbidae), and pond snails (Physidae); all restricted to freshwater habitats.

Superorder Stylommatophora

Mantle cavity a pulmonary sac; gonopores with common opening on right side or at most narrowly separated; shell conical to vestigial, heavily to weakly calcified; eyes at tips of upper (usually) tentacles; terrestrial; about 26,800 species.

Order Orthurethra

Pore of ureter opening into mantle cavity (part of the viscera) near anterior margin of lung after ureter passes forward from anterior kidney margin; about 6,000 species.

Superfamily Achatinellacea. Minute to medium-sized Pacific land snails with multicuspid radular denticles; many Hawaiian species highly coloured and variable.

Superfamilies Cionellacea and Pupillacea. Minute leaf-litter to arboreal snails, occasionally (Enidae) large; shells often with denticles in the aperture; 10 families.

Superfamily Partulacea. Small, generally arboreal snails found on high volcanic islands of Polynesia and Micronesia, a few in Melanesia.

Order Mesurethra

Ureter represented by lateral opening of very short kidney, pore of ureter opening near or behind middle of mantle cavity; about 1,500 species.

Superfamily Clausiliacea. Elongated shells of West Indian shore salt-spray zone (Cerionidae) or Andean mountains of South America and Eurasia (Clausiliidae).

Superfamily Strophocheilacea. Large helicoidal to elongated shells of South America (Strophocheilidae) or southwestern Africa (Dorcasiidae).

Order Sigmurethra

Ureter originates near anterior margin of kidney, follows backward to posterior end, then reflexes forward along hindgut to open alongside anus; position greatly altered in sluglike forms; about 18,000 species.

Suborder Holopodopes. A group of 4 superfamilies.

Superfamily Achatinacea. Besides the giant African snail, 4 families, including many species spread by commerce throughout the world.

Superfamilies Streptaxacea and Rhytidacea. Carnivorous snails and slugs (4 families) in most tropical areas, plus the herbivorous Acavidae of Australia, Sri Lanka, and Madagascar.

Superfamily Bulimulacea. Large, often arboreal snails of Melanesia and Neotropica (Bulimulidae); long, cylindrical snails of West Indies and Central America (Urocoptidae).

Suborder Aulacopoda. A group of 3 superfamilies.

Superfamily Succineacea. A problematic group including amber snails (Succineidae), which inhabit swamps and damp areas, and peculiar slugs from the South Pacific (Athoracophoridae).

Superfamily Arionacea. A group possessing marginal teeth of radula with squarish basal plates and 1 to several cusps; small litter or tree snails mainly in Southern Hemisphere (Endodontidae); slugs (Arionidae and Philomycidae) in the Northern Hemisphere.

Superfamily Limacacea. Marginal teeth of radula with narrow, lengthened basal plates, usually unicuspid; zonitid snails with smooth shells and many sluglike species, common in wet, tropical areas and in temperate regions; about 12 families, including limacid and milacid slugs.

Suborder Holopoda. A group of 3 superfamilies.

Superfamily Polygyracea. Common woodland snails of eastern North America (Polygyridae), plus a Neotropical group (Thysanophoridae) and a relict group of Asia (Corillidae).

Superfamily Oleacinacea. Carnivorous (Oleaciniidae) and herbivorous (Sagdidae) snails of the Neotropical region.

Superfamily Helicacea. Land snails without (Oreohelicidae and Camaenidae) or with (Bradybaenidae, Helminthoglyptidae, and Helicidae) accessory glands on the genitalia; dominant land snails in most regions, including the edible snails of Europe (Helicidae). (G.A.So.)

Bivalves (clams, oysters, mussels, and relatives)

The class Bivalvia, sometimes called Pelecypoda, is characterized by a shell that is divided from front to back into left and right valves. Enclosure in a shell has resulted in loss of the head. Similarly, the adoption of deposit-feeding using labial palps and, later, suspension feeding utilizing the respiratory gills modified into organs of filtration called ctenidia have resulted in loss of the radula from the mouth.

GENERAL FEATURES

Size range and diversity of structure. Bivalves range in size from about one millimetre (0.04 inch) in length to the giant clam of South Pacific coral reefs, *Tridacna gigas,* which may be more than 137 centimetres (54 inches) in length and weigh 264 kilograms (582 pounds). Such an animal may have a life span of about 40 years.

The shell forms are used in classification. In most surface-burrowing species (the hypothetical ancestral habit) the shells are small, spherical or oval, with equal left and right valves (Figure 8). In deeper-burrowing species the shells are laterally compressed, permitting more rapid movement through the sediments. The shells of the most efficient burrowers, the razor clams *Ensis* and *Solen,* are laterally compressed, smooth, and elongated. Surface-burrowing species may have an external shell sculpture of radial ribs and concentric lines, with projections that strengthen the shell against predators and damage.

From (Cerastoderma) W. de Haas and F. Knorr, *The Young Specialist Looks at Marine Life* (1966), Burke Publishing Co., London

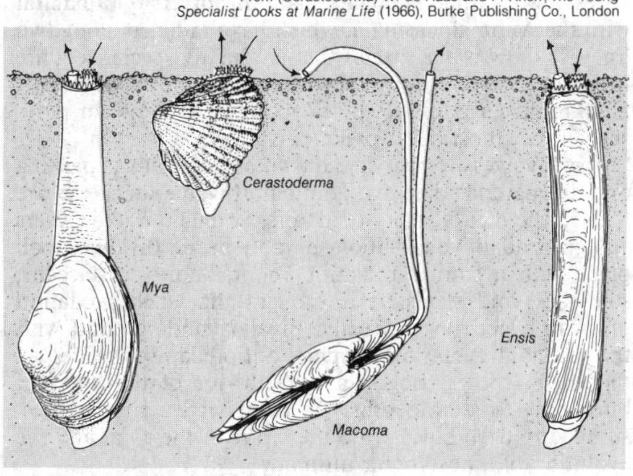

Figure 8: *Shallow- and deep-burrowing dimayrian bivalves.* *Cerastoderma* lives close to the sediment surface and has limited burrowing powers. When disturbed, *Mya* retracts its long siphons as does *Macoma,* but *Macoma* and *Ensis* can also dig deeper into the sediment using the muscular foot. Arrows indicate direction of current flow into the mantle cavity via the inhalant and exhalant siphons.

Endo-byssate and epibyssate

A triangular form, ventral flattening, and secure attachment to firm substrates by byssal threads (byssus; chitinous threads secreted by the foot) have allowed certain bivalves to colonize hard surfaces. This form, referred to as epibyssate for its byssal attachment to surfaces, has been adopted by many groups, most importantly the true mussels (family Mytilidae) of marine and estuarine shores and the family Dreissenidae of fresh and estuarine waters. Such a shell form and habit evolved first within sediments (endobyssate), where the byssus serves for anchorage and protection when formed into an enclosing nest. The byssus is a larval feature retained by some bivalve groups into adult life. The significance of this is crucial to an understanding of how bivalves have radiated. In addition to the triangular form, other bivalves have used the byssus to attach securely within crevices and thus to assume a laterally flattened, circular shape. The best example of this is the windowpane shell *Placuna.* This form has allowed the close attachment of one valve to a hard surface, and although some groups still retain byssal attachment (family Anomiidae), others have forsaken this for cementation, as in the true oysters (family Ostreidae), where the left valve is cemented to estuarine hard surfaces. Some scallops (family Pectinidae) are also cemented, but others lie on soft sediments in coastal waters and at abyssal depths. By limiting shell thickness to reduce weight, smoothing the shell contours to reduce drag, and assuming an aerofoil-like leading edge, such scallops can swim many metres.

Shell form in the bivalves is thus intimately related to habitat and the relative degree of exposure to predation. From the simple burrowing, equivalve ancestor, the various bivalve groups have repeatedly evolved an elongated, triangular or circular shell; thus, similar body adaptations have been responses to similar modes of life.

Distribution and abundance. Most bivalves are marine and occur at all depths in or upon virtually all substrates. In shallow seas, bivalves are often dominant on rocky and sandy coasts and are also important in offshore sediments. They occur at abyssal and hadal depths, either burrowing or surface-dwelling, and are important elements of the midoceanic rift fauna. In addition, bivalves bore into soft shales and compacted muds but may be important also in the bioerosion of corals. Bivalves thus occur at all latitudes and depths, although none are planktonic. There are also estuarine bivalves, and two important families, the Unionidae and Corbiculidae, are predominantly freshwater with complicated reproductive cycles. There are no terrestrial bivalves, although some high-intertidal and freshwater species can withstand drought conditions.

To be expected within a class comprising more than 8,000 living species, abundance varies considerably. Commensal and parasitic species are small, often highly host-specific, and comprise some of the rarest animals. Others, such as cockles and clams on soft shores and mussels and oysters on rocky coasts, can occur in densities high enough that they dominate entire habitats and assume important roles in nutrient cycles.

Economic importance

Importance. The total marine catch of mollusks is twice that of crustaceans, and the great majority of this is bivalve. Some three million metric tons (6,615,000,000 pounds) of bivalves are harvested throughout the world each year. Virtually all bivalves, with the possible exception of the thorny oyster *Spondylus,* are edible and fall into the main categories of oysters, mussels, scallops, and clams.

The most important edible oysters are representatives of the genus *Crassostrea,* notably *C. gigas* in the western Pacific, *C. virginica* in North America, and *C. angulata* in Portugal. Most mussels are cultivated on ropes suspended from floats. The European mussel *Mytilus edulis* has been introduced into the northern Pacific, and the practice now flourishes widely in Japan and China. Most scallops, *Pecten, Placopecten,* and *Amusium,* are caught by offshore trawlers, although cultivation is being attempted. A wide variety of clams are cultivated—*e.g., Mya arenaria* and *Mercenaria mercenaria* in the North Atlantic and *Venerupis japonica* and *Tapes philippinarum* in the Pacific. In some parts of the world, red tides, caused by large numbers of toxic protozoan dinoflagellates, are lethal to fish and certain invertebrates. Bivalves, by virtue of their filter-feeding apparatus, concentrate the toxin and, if eaten by humans, can cause paralysis or death.

Pearls

Bivalves of the genera *Pinctada* and *Pteria* have been collected in many tropical seas for the natural pearls they may contain, although in many countries, most notably Japan, pearl oyster fisheries have been developed. The windowpane oyster, *Placuna placenta,* has flat translucent valves that are used, primarily in the Philippines, in the manufacture of lampshades, trays, mats, and bowls, collectively called *tapis.* In developing countries, many kinds of bivalve shells are used in the manufacture of jewelry and ornaments.

Bivalves are important agents in bioerosion, most notably of calcium carbonate rocks and wood in the sea. Piddocks (family Pholadidae) bore into concrete jetties (particularly where the source of obtained lime is coral), timber, and plastics. Shipworms (family Teredinidae) bore softer woods. Date mussels (*Lithophaga*) bore into rocks and corals. Marine mussels (family Mytilidae) foul ships, buoys, and wharves; they may also block seawater intakes into the cooling systems of power stations.

Few bivalves are host to human parasitic infections. Industrial and agricultural effluents—notably trace metals, chlorophenothane (DDT), and chlorinated hydrocarbons—have contaminated bivalves, with subsequent concern over human health.

NATURAL HISTORY

Reproduction and life cycles. Although most bivalves are either male or female (dioecious), some produce both sperm and eggs (hermaphroditic); sexual dimorphism is rare. In dioecious species there is usually an equal division of the sexes. Some groups of bivalves, typically those occupying specialized habitats, have adopted hermaphroditism as a reproductive strategy, although expression of this condition may take various forms (simultaneous, consecutive, rhythmical consecutive, and alternative hemaphroditism). Simultaneous hermaphroditism occurs when sperm-producing tubules and egg-producing follicles intermingle in the gonads (as in the family Tridacnidae), or the gonads may be developed into a separate ovary and testis, as in all representatives of the subclass Anomalodesmata. In consecutive hermaphroditism, one sex develops first. Typically, this is the male phase (protandry), but in a few cases it is the female (protogyny). This is most clearly seen in the wood-boring family Teredinidae, where a young male becomes a female as it ages. Rhythmical consecutive hermaphroditism is best known in the European oyster, *Ostrea edulis,* in which each individual undergoes periodic changes of sex. Alternative hermaphroditism is characteristic of oysters of the genus *Crassostrea,* in which most young individuals are male. Later the sex ratio becomes about equal, and finally most older individuals become female.

Hermaphroditism

Bivalve sperm have two flagellae. Most eggs are small, and synchronized spawning results in the discharge of both types of gametes into the sea for external fertilization. Hermaphrodites either inhale sperm from another individual or fertilize their own eggs within the ctenidia; the eggs are then brooded, typically also within the ctenidia. There, the fertilized eggs, well endowed with yolk, develop directly (without a larval stage), and the young are released as miniature adults. Although ctenidial incubation is most common, there are other patterns: egg capsules are produced by *Turtonia minuta;* a brood chamber is plastered to the shell of the palaeotaxodont *Nucula delphinodonta;* and in members of the Carditidae the female shell is modified into a brood pouch.

Larval stage

For most marine species, however, the fertilized egg undergoes indirect development first into a swimming trochophore larva and then into a veliger larva in which the embryonic shell and rudiments of other organs are established. The veliger has a ciliated velum for swimming and also for trapping minute particles of food. Following a period in the plankton, the veliger settles to the seafloor, where metamorphosis into the adult takes place: the velum is lost, the foot develops and usually secretes one or two byssal threads for secure attachment, and the ctenidia develop.

In the freshwater Unionidae the released larva, called a glochidium, often has sharp spines projecting inward from each valve. The larva is attracted to fish and attaches to either their gills or fins, where it encysts, is temporarily parasitic, and eventually ruptures the cyst wall and falls to the lake floor. There it metamorphoses into an adult.

Ecology and habitats. The division and lateral compression of the shell into two valves is clearly related to the adoption of a burrowing mode of life, which is achieved by a muscular foot. Primitive forms were detritivorous, whereas modern bivalves are filter feeders that have modified the respiratory gills into complex structures called ctenidia. The burrowing, filter-feeding mode of life restricts bivalves to aquatic environments.

Retention of the larval anchoring byssus into adult life has freed many bivalves from soft substrates, allowing them to colonize hard surfaces. This has also been achieved by cementation, as, for example, in oysters.

There are no pelagic bivalves, except for *Planktomya hensoni,* which is still benthic as an adult but has an unusually long planktonic larval stage. Some bivalves can swim, albeit weakly, when removed from the sediment, as can some file shells. True swimming is, however, seen only in the family Pectinidae but is used mostly as an escape reaction.

Movement

Many representatives of the superfamily Galeommatoidea are commensal, a few are parasitic, and both have thus become miniaturized. Most bivalves are found in coastal seas, but their diversity is greatest on continental landmasses, where large rivers create suitable deltaic habitats and the continental shelf is broad. Except on tropical ones with coral reefs, few bivalves are found on islands.

Of the various subclasses, two are most important ecologically: the Heterodonta, which are modern burrowers that feed primarily on suspended material, and the Pteriomorphia, an older group that is epibyssate and dominates hard substrates. Some of their older representatives are endobyssate, exposing their evolutionary history. Most of these two classes occupy a wide diversity of subhabitats, with simple reproductive strategies, external fertilization, and planktonic larvae to effect wide dispersion. They apportion the shallow-water marine domain virtually everywhere. The Palaeoheterodonta are exclusively fresh water and infaunal although a few in South America are epifaunal, but all have significantly more complicated life cycles.

The Palaeotaxodonta are coastal and deepwater detrivores, always infaunal. They share this diversity of habitat with the Anomalodesmata, which have radiated along two lines: shallow-water species that are highly specialized, are hermaphroditic, occupy narrow niches, and have a short planktonic stage and deep-sea species that are even more specialized, most being predators.

Most bivalves are primary consumers, typically exploiting organic material. The two dominant bivalve subclasses are high in the diet of many predators. Some 60 million years ago great adaptive radiation, notably in the Bivalvia, took place with a similar radiation in predatory crustaceans, starfishes, and snails. It is thought that such predation pressure effectively drove the Bivalvia underground with the resultant evolution of many antipredation devices on the shell—spines, ridges, and teeth—or of the habit of burrowing to great depths. On coral reefs a similar pressure led to deep boring into the fabric of the coral and the evolution of a host–borer intimacy.

Locomotion. Unlike in other molluscan groups, locomotion in bivalves is used only when dislodgement occurs or as a means to escape predation.

The bivalve foot, unlike that of gastropods, does not have a flat creeping sole but is bladelike (laterally compressed) and pointed for digging. The muscles mainly responsible for movement of the foot are the anterior and posterior pedal retractors. They retract the foot and effect back-and-forth movements. The foot is extended as blood is pumped into it, and it is prevented from overinflating by concentric rings of circular, oblique, and longitudinal muscle fibres, which also help to direct pedal extension and permit fine mobility.

Burrowing

During burrowing, the foot is greatly extended anteriorly from between parted shell valves. Taking a grip on the substratum, typically by dilation of the tip, the pedal retractors pull the shell downward. This is accompanied by sharp adduction of the shell valves, forcing water out of the mantle cavity into the burrow, helping to fluidize the sediment, and making movement through it more efficient. So effective is this mechanism that fast burrowers, when removed from the sediment, can swim.

Food and feeding. The primitive bivalve was almost certainly a detritivore (consumer of loose organic materials), and the modern palaeotaxodonts still pursue this mode of life. The posterior leaflike gills serve principally for respiration; feeding is carried out by the palp proboscides, which collect surface detritus.

Evolution of the ctenidia

The vast majority of other bivalves feed on the plant detritus, bacteria, and algae that characterize the sediment surface or cloud coastal and fresh waters. The gills have gradually become adapted as filtering devices called ctenidia. The primitive posterior respiratory gills have enlarged and moved to lie lateral to the body as paired folds, or demibranchs. Further increases in surface area have been achieved by folding the platelike gill lamellae into plicae. Each lamella comprises vertical rows of filaments upon the outer head of which are complex arrays of cilia that create a flow of water through the gill, form a filtration barrier, and transport retained particles to food grooves in the dorsal axes or ventral margins of the ctenidia. Bound in mucus, the food is transported to the mouth via the labial palps, where further selection occurs (see below *Internal features*).

Two groups of bivalves have exploited other food sources. These are the shipworms (family Teredinidae) and giant clams (family Tridacnidae). Shipworms are wood borers and are both protected and nourished by the wood they inhabit. They possess ctenidia and are capable of filtering food from the sea. When elongating the burrow, they digest the wood as well. In the Tridacnidae, symbiotic zooxanthellae (minute algal cells) are contained within the inhalant siphon. The relationship between clam and algae is probably mutually beneficial, the algae having access to the dissolved waste products of the clam and the clam benefiting from the nutritional value of either culled zooxanthellae or their metabolic products.

A few bivalves are parasitic—*e.g.,* species of *Entovalva,* which live either in the esophagus or upon the body of sea cucumbers (Holothuroidea), and the larvae of freshwater Unionidae, which parasitize fish.

The most exotic adaptations of the basic bivalve feeding plan are found in two groups of deepwater bivalves. These are scallops of the genus *Propeamussium* and the various deepwater families of the Anomalodesmata. In *Propeamussium* what appear to be typical ctenidia are present in the mantle cavity, but on closer examination these prove to be wholly atypical in that the filament heads are internal. The ctenidia are incapable of filtering. The gut is minute, and detected prey is sucked into the mantle cavity by an inrush of water when the valves open. The food is then pushed into the mouth with the foot.

Many deepwater Anomalodesmata have modified the typical bivalve ctenidium into a septum—the "septibranch" ctenidium—that creates pressure changes within the mantle cavity and produces sudden inrushes of water, carrying prey into a funnellike inhalant siphon (*Cuspidaria*). Food is then pushed into the mouth by the palps and foot. Others evert the inhalant siphon, like a hood, over the prey (*Poromya* and *Lyonsiella*). Prey items include small bottom-dwelling crustaceans, polychaete worms, and larvae of other benthic animals.

Adaptations

Associations. The greatest affinity of bivalves is with coral reefs. Indo-Pacific, but not Caribbean, reefs are the habitat of giant clams, *Tridacna.* Dead corals are bored by representatives of the Gastrochaenidae, living corals by species of *Lithophaga.* A greater degree of intimacy between living coral and bivalve borer is now known, some species associating with a single coral.

Similarly with wood borers: piddocks (Pholadidae) are more common in hardwoods, while shipworms (Teredinidae) favour softwoods. In the degradation of wood in the sea, a variety of species may colonize it with time and with depth.

One group of bivalves, the superfamily Galeommatoidea, form highly intimate relationships with other marine invertebrates, particularly on soft shores and coral reefs. Typically less than 10 millimetres (0.4 inch) long, most are commensal; *i.e.,* they form an association in which there is no detriment to the host and exploit it for protection, food, and respiratory currents. On soft shores they share the burrows of polychaete worms and crustaceans, sometimes attaching to the body of the host.

FORM AND FUNCTION

General features. The bivalve body comprises a dorsal visceral mass and a ventral foot, which is enclosed within a thin mantle, or pallium. The mantle secretes from its outer surface a shell divided into left and right valves. Between the body and mantle is the mantle cavity, within which hang the left and right gills, or ctenidia. The ctenidia are divided into two demibranchs, inner and outer, each in turn comprising inner and outer lamellae. Anteriorly, the ctenidia unite with paired (left and right) labial palps, which are food-sorting organs. The mantle margin can be fused at various places leaving medial apertures anteriorly for the extension and retraction of the locomotory foot and, in most bivalves, posteriorly to create inhalant and exhalant apertures that may be formed into siphons of variable length according to habitat. Foot and siphons can be withdrawn between the shell valves into the mantle cavity for protection.

The shell

External features. The bivalves occupy a wide variety of habitats and, as a consequence, deviate widely from the basic body plan. The shell form is an obvious adaptation to the environment. Shells of many modern burrowers are ornamented and coloured, and those of near-surface-dwelling cockles are thick and radially ribbed. These adaptations stabilize the animal in the substrate and may confer some degree of protection against predators. Such bivalves are slow burrowers. In contrast, the shells of deep-burrowing species are thin and nonornamented. They are often brightly coloured, as in the Tellinidae. The shell is laterally compressed and thus more bladelike, but the adductor muscles are still of similar size (the isomyarian form). Such structural features adapt the animal for rapid movement through the sand; long siphons project to the surface above. Deep burrowing has been achieved by a different mechanism in the razor shells (e.g., the family Solenidae), where the anterior region of the shell is reduced and the posterior enormously elongate. Because of their short siphons, *Ensis* and *Solen* live close to the sediment surface, but, with the lateral compression of their polished shells, they are among the most proficient burrowers. Other bivalves—*e.g., Mya* (family Myidae)—live at great depths but do not burrow rapidly. The shell is largely unornamented and wider to accommodate the greatly elongated siphons, which can be retracted deeply within its borders.

Mechanical versus chemical borers

Rock and wood boring are also specialized consequences of burrowing—the evolution of borers proceeded from the habitation of stiff muds or from nestling within crevices. Mechanical borers tunnel anterior end first; that face of the shell having a sculpture of spines. Borers derived from a nestling epibyssate ancestor are chemical borers that produce a calcium carbonate chelating secretion from the mantle margin. In such cases the shell is typically smooth, although calcareous encrustations on the posterior shell protect the borer from aperture-attacking predators. Reduction of the anterior adductor (the anisomyarian form) creates a triangular-shaped shell, as in the buried fan shell *Pinna* (Pinnidae) and the mussels (Mytilidae) of rocky coasts. Although such bivalves lack ornamentation, the shell is typically thick and dark.

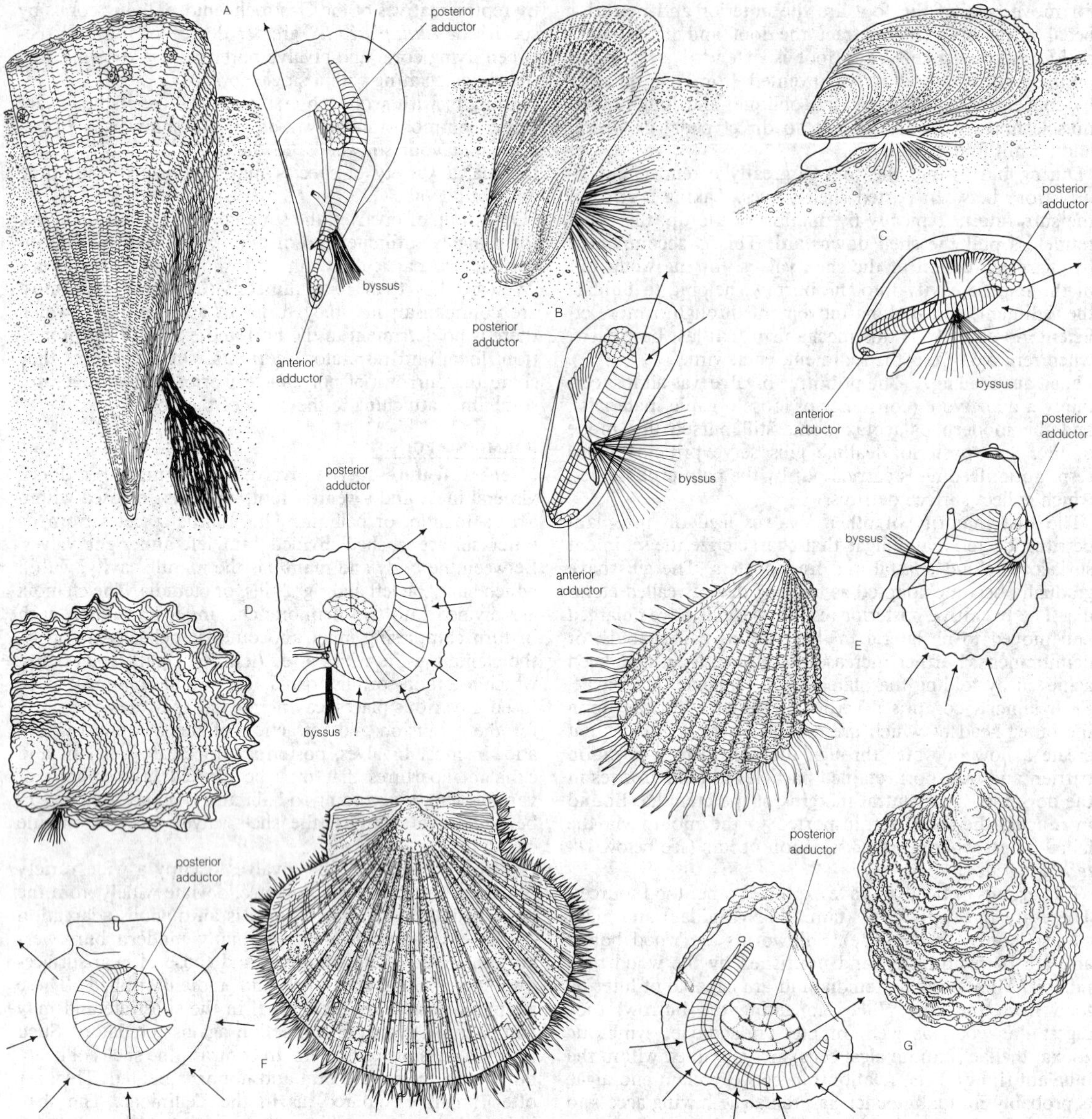

Figure 9: *Anisomyarian and monomyarian bivalves, with sketches of the internal gill and muscle arrangements.*
Arrows indicate inhalant and exhalant water currents. (A) *Pinna*, endobyssate with reduction of the anterior, and enlargement of the posterior, adductor. (B) *Geukensia*, endobyssate with reduction of the anterior, and enlargement of the posterior, adductor. (C) *Mytilus*, epibyssate with reduction of the anterior, and enlargement of the posterior, adductor. (D) *Pinctada*, epibyssate, laterally flattened, with loss of the anterior adductor. (E) *Lima*, epibyssate and monomyarian, with long tentacles and capable of limited swimming. (F) *Pecten*, with loss of the anterior adductor, byssus, foot, and associated musculature and capable of swimming. (G) *Ostrea*, cemented and with loss of the anterior adductor, byssus, foot, and associated musculature.
From (Geukensia) S.M. Stanley, *Relation of Shell Form to Life Habits of the Bivalvia (Mollusca)*, Geological Society of America Memoir no. 125 (1970); (*Mytilus, Pinctada, Lima*) R.C. Moore (ed.), *Treatise on Invertebrate Paleontology. Mollusca 6* (1969), Geological Society of America and University of Kansas Press; (Ostrea) W. de Haas and F. Knorr, *The Young Specialist Looks at Marine Life* (1966), Burke Publishing Co., London

Loss of the anterior adductor creates a shell with a circular outline, left and right valves being either equal or unequal. In some, lateral flattening and byssal attachment allows occupation of narrow crevices. Cementation by either valve is a further consequence of the loss of the anterior adductor muscle (the monomyarian form). Subsequent freedom from attachment, as in the scallops (Pectinidae), is associated with an almost circular outline, flat upper and cup-shaped lower valves, a deep radial sculpture, and, typically, bright coloration (*Pecten*).

Internal features. The general classification of the bivalves is typically based on shell structure and hinge and ligament organization (Figure 9). The internal anatomy is also a tool in classification, particularly the organs of the mantle cavity, the pattern of water movement through it, and the structure and functioning of the ctenidia and labial palps. Early anatomists established a correlation between shell and gill structure that is still often used as a basis for classification but which is now relegated to defining the evolutionary sequence from a deposit-feeding to a filter-feeding mode of life.

The primitive bivalve form

Nucula, from the subclass Protobranchia, reflects the primitive bivalve ancestor. Burrowing close to the sediment surface, *Nucula* is equivalve, anteriorly and posteriorly symmetrical, and isomyarian. The medial foot is wide. There are no mantle fusions ventrally, and the aerating water current passes through the mantle cavity from front to back, a feature not typical of most modern bivalves. The structure of the small gills (Figure 10), located posteriorly, is interpreted as being similar to the earliest mollusks—hence the name protobranch, or "first gills." The paired gills, separated by a central axis, are suspended from the mantle roof. Individual short gill filaments extend outward from either side of the axis, and cilia on their surfaces create an upward respiratory water current that passes from the mantle cavity below the gill (the

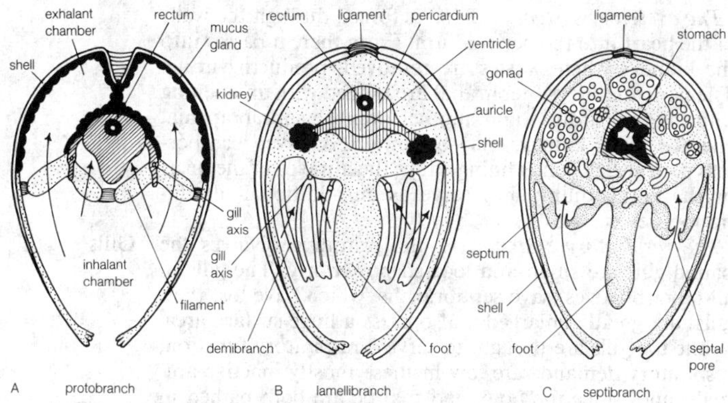

Figure 10: Transverse sections through the bodies of (A) *Nucula*, with a protobranch gill; (B) *Spisula*, with a lamellibranch gill; and (C) *Poromya*, with a septibranch gill. Arrows indicate the water currents through the gill for respiration but also for filter feeding in *Spisula*.

infrabranchial, or inhalant, chamber) to that area above it (the suprabranchial, or exhalant, chamber). The anus and the urogenital pores also open into the exhalant chamber so that all waste products exit the animal in the exhalant stream. The paired labial palps in the mantle cavity are used in feeding. The outer palp on each side bears a long, extensible proboscis with a ciliated groove that collects organic material, which is then sorted by the inner pair and outer pair of palps. Certain particles are transferred to the mouth by the ciliary currents of the inner pair of palps, while the remaining particles are sent by the outer palps into the mantle cavity as a mucus-bound mass known as pseudofeces, which are ejected by periodic contractions of the adductor muscles.

An important event in the evolution of the modern bivalve from the more primitive form illustrated above was the reorientation of the anterior inhalant stream to the posterior below the exhalant stream so that water both enters and exits the mantle cavity posteriorly. For burrowing bivalves, such a body organization allows deep burrowing in a vertical (head down) orientation, and thus escape from the sediment surface. These changes generally are associated with changes in the method of feeding and, as a consequence, the selective fusion of left and right mantle margins to exclude sediment from the mantle cavity.

Evolution of a new gill structure

The burrowing *Spisula* illustrates these changes. It, like *Nucula*, is equivalve and anteriorly and posteriorly symmetrical (isomyarian). The mantle margin is fused ventrally, allowing the foot to extend through an anterior pedal gape. The posterior inhalant and exhalant orifices are formed into tentacle-fringed siphons. The gills are here positioned on either side of the visceral mass. Gill filaments are greatly elongated and folded (forming the shape of a W) to increase their surface area. The central axis of the W joins it to the body, and the outermost arms unite with the visceral body on one side and the mantle on the other. A complex arrangement of cilia on the apex of each filament constituting the gill lamellae draws a water current through the gill, which provides oxygen, but more importantly now sieves food from this current and transfers such material along tracts in the gill axes or their ventral margins (bound in mucus) toward the labial palps. The palps process this food and eliminate the pseudofeces as in *Nucula*.

The modified gill is called a ctenidium, and its structure is best explained by the term lamellibranch. The lamellibranch structure may be further qualified as filibranch, pseudolamellibranch, or eulamellibranch. In filibranchs the filaments are only weakly united by cilia, and often the ctenidium retains some inherent sorting mechanism. Collection and sorting of potential food has not yet been definitively ascribed to gills and labial palps, respectively. In the pseudolamellibranch ctenidium, filaments and lamellae are more securely united, and an inherent sorting mechanism still exists in some. In many, however, the filaments are vertically aggregated into folds, or plicae, that greatly increase the total surface area. In the eulamellibranch ctenidium the filaments and lamellae are closely united, the selection function is lost, and gill structure varies widely. Most modern bivalves are filter feeders, and except in a few members the siphons suck in particles suspended in the water column.

In the deep seas, modification of the lamellibranch ctenidium has allowed the adoption of carnivory. The predatory bivalves of the subclass Anomalodesmata have an inhalant siphon that can be everted rapidly to form a capacious hood beneath which small crustaceans are trapped and brought into the mantle cavity. The eversion of the siphon is assisted by a horizontal septum across the mantle cavity, which is derived from the mantle and the greatly reduced ctenidium. This is the septibranch ctenidium.

Importance of the byssus

The release from a burrowing mode of life has been facilitated by the retention of a larval structure (the byssus) into adult life. The byssus, secreted by a gland in the foot, secures the animal to a hard surface in preparation for burrowing. Its retention and enlargement in the adult has provided a secure means of attachment to the open surfaces of rocks in the intertidal, estuarine, and fresh waters.

In the triangular mussels (Mytilidae) of such habitats the anterior is reduced, and the body and organs of the mantle cavity are contained in the expanded posterior regions of the shell. The reduction of the anterior adductor muscle is matched by a reduction in the size of the anterior pedal retractor muscles (and enlargement of the posterior equivalents). Since such muscles are less concerned with locomotion and more with pulling the shell down against the substrate, they are more correctly redefined as byssal retractors. The ctenidia and palps fulfil the same role as they do in burrowing lamellibranch bivalves, but, because of the triangular cross section of the shell, they come to lie largely underneath the visceral mass instead of beside it.

Further reduction of the anterior adductor, leading to its eventual loss, creates what is called the monomyarian condition. In bivalves with such a configuration, the anterior shell and mantle are confined to a small area; the foot, where present, is always greatly reduced and positioned anteriorly. The visceral mass and organs of the mantle cavity are arranged around the central posterior adductor muscle, and there is extreme reduction or loss of the anterior pedal/byssal retractor muscles. Shell valves may be so compressed that the space between them, as in *Placuna*, the windowpane oyster, is very narrow. Alternatively, as in oysters and scallops, one valve is cup-shaped, with the other fitting against it like a lid. In such a case, the body occupies the former valve, the left in oysters and generally the right in all others, such as the scallops. In these bivalves the bilateral symmetry of the shell and mantle is replaced by a radial symmetry from the midpoint of the hinge line. In these bivalves, too, the adductor muscle is more clearly demarcated into "quick" (striated) and "slow" (smooth) components for rapid and sustained adduction respectively. The capacity for work of the greatly enlarged quick component of the scallop muscle permits rapid adduction that facilitates swimming by directing jets of water out of the mantle cavity to each side of the hinge line characterized by shell auricles.

Shell structure

The shell. The bivalve shell is made of calcium carbonate embedded in an organic matrix secreted by the mantle. The periostracum, the outermost organic layer, is secreted by the inner surface of the outer mantle fold at the mantle margin. It is a substrate upon which calcium carbonate can be deposited by the outer surface of the outer mantle fold. The number of calcareous layers in the shell (in addition to the periostracum), the composition of those layers (aragonite or aragonite and calcite), and the arrangement of these deposits (*e.g.*, in sheets, or foliate) is characteristic for different groups of bivalves. Middorsally an elastic ligament creates the opening thrust that operates against the closing action of the adductor muscles. The ligament typically develops either externally (parivincular) or internally (alivincular) but comprises outer lamellar, and inner fibrous, layers secreted by the mantle crest. The ligament type is generally characteristic of each bivalve group. The hinge plate with ligament also possesses interlocking teeth to enforce valve alignment and locking, when closed, to prevent shear. Many variations in teeth structure occur.

The mantle and musculature. The mantle lobes secrete the shell valves; the mantle crest secretes the ligament and hinge teeth. Growth takes place at the margins, although increases in thickness take place everywhere. The mantle is withdrawn between the shell valves by mantle retractor muscles; their point of attachment to the shell being called the pallial line.

Muscula-ture

The musculature comprises two (dimyarian) primitively equal (isomyarian) adductor muscles; the anterior and the posterior. The anterior of these may be reduced (anisomyarian; heteromyarian) or lost (monomyarian). Only very rarely is the posterior lost and the anterior retained.

Internal to the adductors are paired anterior and posterior pedal retractor muscles. Where the anterior adductor muscle is reduced, so are the anterior pedal retractors. In highly active burrowers, paired anterior pedal protractors and pedal elevator muscles occur—for example, the family Trigonioidea.

In byssally attached bivalves, pedal retractors are reduced and byssal retractors serve to pull the animal down in closer opposition to the rock surface. In oysters, commensurate with the extreme reduction of the foot, pedal retractors are lost. This is also the case in swimming scallops.

The nervous system and organs of sensation. The nervous system is simple, reflecting the sedentary habit. In primitive bivalves (*e.g.,* Palaeotaxodonta) there are four pairs of ganglia—cerebral, pleural, pedal, and visceral. In all other bivalves the cerebral and pleural ganglia are fused into two cerebropleural ganglia, located above and on either side of the esophagus. The pedal ganglia are in the base of the foot, and the visceral ganglia are located under the posterior adductor muscle. Nerve fibres arising from the cerebropleural ganglia extend to the pedal and visceral ganglia. In some bivalves with long siphons, there are accessory siphonal ganglia, and in many swimming bivalves the visceral ganglia are much enlarged, presumably to coordinate complex swimming actions.

Again reflecting the sedentary life, sensory functions are largely taken over by the posterior mantle margins and typically comprise tentacles developed from the middle mantle folds that are mechanoreceptors and chemoreceptors. Scallops (family Pectinidae) have complex eyes with a lens and retina. In other bivalves, eyes are simple ciliated cups, although some variation is possible. In the predatory deepwater septibranchs the inhalant siphon, which captures food, is surrounded by tentacles that have vibration-sensitive papillae for detecting the movements of prey.

Statocysts

Situated close to the pedal ganglia but with direct connections to the cerebropleural ganglia are a pair of statocysts, which comprise a capsule of ciliated sense cells. In the lumen is either a single statolith or numerous crystalline statoconia. Their points of contact with the surrounding cilia yield information about the animal's orientation. Additionally, most bivalves with or without eyes have light-sensitive cells that respond to shadows. Below the posterior adductor muscle an osphradium has been identified in some bivalves that may monitor water flow and quality.

The digestive system and nutrition. The bivalve digestive system comprises a complex stomach and associated structures but an otherwise simple intestine. The various types of stomach have been used to erect an alternative classification. Digestion typically takes place in two phases: extracellular in the stomach and intracellular in the digestive diverticula, opening laterally from the stomach wall. Transport of food particles is effected by cilia, creating an array of tracts and sorting areas within the stomach. The principal organ of extracellular digestion is the crystalline style. It is rotated in its sac by cilia; the head, projecting into the stomach, grinds against a part of the stomach wall lined by a chitinous gastric shield. As it rotates, it dissolves, releasing enzymes and initiating primary extracellular digestion of the mucus-bound food. Products of this process are passed in a fluid suspension into large embayments and thence into the digestive diverticula, where intracellular digestion takes place. Waste material is consolidated in the midgut and rectum and expelled as firm fecal pellets from an anus opening into the exhalant stream. Feeding and digestion are highly coordinated, typically regulated by tidal and diurnal cycles.

The excretory system. Blood is forced through the walls of the heart into the pericardium. From there it passes into the kidneys where wastes are removed, producing urine. The paired kidneys (nephridia) are looped with an opening into the pericardium and another into the suprabranchial chamber. The kidneys may be united. Bivalves also possess pericardial glands lining either the auricles of the heart or the pericardium; they serve as an additional ultrafiltration device.

Gills

The respiratory system. In the primitive bivalves the paired gills are small and located posteriorly. The gills in all other bivalves (save septibranchs, which have lost their gills) are greatly enlarged and possess a huge surface area. While the gills are thought to serve a respiratory function, respiratory demands are low in these mostly inactive animals, and, since the body and mantle are both bathed in water, respiration probably takes place across these surfaces as well. Such a mechanism has been demonstrated for a few bivalves, most notably freshwater species that are exposed to occasional drought. In such species, drying induces slight shell gaping posteriorly, the mantle margins exposing themselves to air. For most intertidal bivalves (which are alternately exposed to wetting and drying), respiration all but ceases during the drying phase.

The vascular system. The heart, enclosed in a pericardium, comprises a medial ventricle with left and right auricles arising from it. Blood oxygenated within the ctenidia flows to the auricles and from there to the ventricle, where it is pumped into anterior and posterior aortas. The blood then enters hemocoelic spaces in the mantle and visceral mass and returns to the heart via the ctenidia or the kidneys. The blood serves both to transport oxygen and metabolic products to tissues deep within the body and as a hydrostatic skeleton (for example, in the extension of the foot during locomotion and siphons during feeding). There are amoeboid corpuscles but, except in a few bivalves, no respiratory pigment.

The reproductive system. The reproductive system is simple and comprises paired gonads. These gonads discharge into the renal duct in primitive bivalves but open by separate gonopores into the suprabranchial chamber in more modern bivalves. Typically, the sexes are separate, but various grades of hermaphroditism are not uncommon. Eggs and sperm are shed into the sea for external fertilization in most bivalves, but inhalation of sperm by a female permits a type of internal fertilization and brooding of young, usually within the ctenidia.

Significant adaptations

Features of defense and aggression. The most significant adaptation is the earliest division of the shell into two valves within which the animal was wholly contained. Slow components of the adductor muscle permit sustained adduction, while the interlocking hinge teeth prevent shear. In addition, the shell may be strongly ridged, forming an interlocking shell margin, and it may be concentrically ringed with spines or sharp ridges projecting outward. Posterior sense organs, including photophores and eyes, are developed around the siphons and mantle margins. Detection leads to withdrawal deep into the sediment by burrowing species. In such animals the shell is smooth and compressed. Scallops respond to predation by swimming; shallow-burrowing cockles can leap using the foot. In the razor clams the siphons can break off (autotomize) when bitten, to be regenerated later. Similarly, noxious secretions are produced by the similarly autotomizing long tentacles of the Limidae (file shells). The unique pallial organ of fan shells (family Pinnidae) produces a secretion of sulfuric acid when bitten.

Only the deepwater subclass Anomalodesmata (families Verticordiidae, Poromyidae, and Cuspidariidae) and the scallops are predators. Prey is captured either in the sudden rush of water into the mantle cavity or by the rapid eversion of the inhalant siphon.

EVOLUTION AND PALEONTOLOGY

Oldest bivalve

The oldest known bivalves are generally believed to be *Fordilla troyensis,* which is best preserved in the late Early Cambrian rocks of New York (about 550 million years ago), and *Pojetaia runnegari* from the Cambrian rocks of Australia. *Fordilla* is perhaps ancestral to the pteriomorph order Mytiloida, *Pojetaia* to the Palaeotazodonta order Nuculoida.

By the Ordovician period (505 to 438 million years ago) most modern subclasses were represented by definable ancestors. The oldest Ordovician bivalves are, however, the subclass Palaeotaxodonta, which are thought to have given rise to the Cryptodonta by elongation. Modern assessment of their shell structure and body form, notably with the possession of posterior protobranch gills and with palp proboscides for deposit feeding in the Palaeotaxodonta, generally supports this view. An extinct subclass Actinodontia also arose in the Ordovician period and may be represented today by the superfamily Trigonioidea (placed in the subclass Palaeoheterodonta), which are an aberrant group of the subclass Pteriomorphia. The remaining, more typical, members of the Pteriomorphia also arose at this time and persist today, still characteristically occupying a range of substrate types but with byssal attachment and a trend toward loss of the anterior adductor muscle. The common mussels (family Mytilidae) are thought to be derived from an extinct group, the family Modiomorphidae. The subclass Orthonotia also arose in the Ordovician period and are the probable ancestors of the deep-burrowing razor shells (Solenoidea). The origins of the subclass Anomalodesmata are less clear, but they too arose in the Ordovician period and may have links to the order Myoida, which presently includes deep-burrowing forms and borers. Representatives of the superfamily Lucinoidea are very different from all other bivalves, with an exhalant siphon only and an anterior inhalant stream. Some of these deposit feeders also possess, like the subclass Cryptodonta, sulfur-oxidizing bacteria in the ctenidia and are thought to have ancient origins, represented by the fossil *Babinka. Babinka* is itself interesting and is closely related either to *Fordilla,* one of the oldest bivalves or to the ancestors of the molluscan class Tryblidia. Today the superfamily Lucinoidea is generally placed within the subclass Heterodonta, which is a younger group that traces back to the Paleozoic era, when the first radiation of all bivalves took place.

The stamp of modernity was placed upon the Bivalvia in the Mesozoic era (245 to 66.4 million years ago), when virtually all families currently recognized were present. Throughout time, the fortunes of the subclasses have waxed and waned, with repeated modification of form allowing repeated diversification into different habitats. Similarity of habitat is matched by similarity in structure and form, allowing for various interpretations of the fossil record. It is clear, however, that most modern bivalves can trace their ancestry back a long way and that the inherent plasticity of the bivalve form is responsible for the success of a molluscan experiment in lateral compression of the shell.

CLASSIFICATION

No system of classification erected for the Bivalvia has been accepted by all. Paleontologists interpret bivalves on the basis of shell features, notably shell and ligament structure, arrangement of hinge teeth, and body form as interpreted from internal muscle scars.

Investigators of Recent (Holocene; 10,000 years ago to the present) forms use other anatomic features, such as adductor muscle arrangement, the ctenidia and their junction with the labial palps, the extent and complexity of mantle fusion, and stomach structure. Cluster analysis using many morphological features is effective with lower taxa but less so with higher taxonomic categories because of the many examples of parallel evolution from the basic bivalve plan. The triangular mussel form, for example, has evolved in representatives of virtually every subclass, resulting in similar morphologies. Shell microstructure and mineralogy evidence generally support paleontological conclusions that the class Bivalvia comprises six subclasses, recognizing, however, that some of these taxa may have more than one first ancestor (polyphyletic). In a group with a fossil history extending back to the Cambrian period and occupying a wide range of aquatic habitats, this is not unexpected, particularly since the basic bivalved form permits repeated modification.

Annotated classification.

CLASS BIVALVIA
Laterally symmetrical; left and right calcareous shell valves; dorsal elastic hinge ligament; anterior and posterior adductor muscles; lateral paired filtering ctenidia surrounding the visceral mass; primitively burrowing by means of a muscular foot, but some crawl, some attach to rocks by byssal threads from the foot, some are cemented, and some bore into soft rocks, corals, and wood; some commensal, a few parasitic, and some deepwater species predatory; microphagous feeding; mostly marine, at all depths, also estuarine and freshwater; about 8,000 extant species.

Subclass Palaeotaxodonta
Numerous similar teeth along the hinge plate; isomyarian; unique shell microstructure of aragonitic composite prisms and internal nacre; posterior ctenidia comprising 2 divergent rows of flat, short, filaments; protobranch respiratory gill; food collected by labial palps; mostly near-surface-dwelling marine detritivores; considered to be the most primitive of living bivalves, if not the most ancient.

Order Nuculoida
Equal shell valves with taxodont hinge teeth; isomyarian; posterior protobranch ctenidia; large labial palps usually with palp proboscides, which effect feeding; foot with flat sole; marine; unattached; infaunal.

Subclass Cryptodonta
Hinge either weakly taxodont or edentulous; distinctive shell structure of aragonitic simple prisms and nacre internally; large posterior protobranch ctenidia; small labial palps; of primitive and ancient lineage; marine; unattached; infaunal.

Order Solemyoida
Shell valves equal and elongate, lacking hinge teeth, covered by a shiny periostracum; dimyarian or monomyarian; some with protobranch ctenidia containing symbiotic sulfur-oxidizing bacteria; minute palps; minute or absent gut; foot with flat sole; marginally papillate; marine; deep-burrowing; infaunal.

Subclass Pteriomorphia
Highly variable shell form and structure; dimyarian, anisomyarian, or monomyarian; variable hinge dentition; lateral filibranch ctenidia comprise paired demibranchs of weakly united filaments; mostly marine; some cemented; most epibyssate; some infaunal; representative of the earliest filter-feeding bivalves.

Order Arcoida
Shell solid, elongate or circular-oval, often heavily ribbed; fibrous periostracum with simple crossed-lamellar outer layer and inner complex crossed-lamellar layer, thereby differing from all other pteriomorphs; dimyarian; hinge with vertical denticulations; ctenidia filibranch; mantle margin with uniquely divided outer fold; foot often byssate; marine; epibyssate; infaunal.

Order Trigonioida
Shell valves equal, trigonally oval, strongly ribbed; shell with outer aragonitic prismatic layer and inner nacre layers; strong hinge teeth transversely grooved; typically isomyarian, with pedal elevator and protractor muscles as well as retractors; ctenidia filibranch, without mantle fusions; powerful foot; marine; infaunal; living species confined to Australia.

Order Mytiloida (common mussels)
Shell equivalve, rounded, elongate or triangular depending on habits; anisomyarian tending toward monomyarian; hinge edentulous; shell microstructure of outer calcitic fibrous prisms and inner nacre; ctenidia filibranch; mantle margin lacking fusions; foot creeping; typically byssate; marine, estuarine, rarely freshwater; endobyssate and epibyssate.

Order Pterioida (pearl oysters and fan shells)
Shell equivalve, variably shaped; anisomyarian but often monomyarian; shell structure of outer simple calcitic prisms and inner nacre; ctenidia pseudolamellibranch, often plicate (deeply folded); mantle margin lacking fusions; foot reduced; marine; endobyssate or epibyssate.

Order Limoida
Shell equivalve, ovally elongate, ribbed, often thin and transparent, with outer foliated calcite and inner crossed-lamellar aragonitic layers; hinge short and edentulous; monomyarian; ctenidia pseudolamellibranch, encircling the adductor; palps small and lips of mouth variably fused; mantle margins unfused and often red, with long autotomizing tentacles; some swim weakly; marine; epibyssate with byssus sometimes formed into a nest.

Order Ostreoida (oysters and scallops)
Shell valves unequal, variable, typically lacking hinge teeth; shell structure of foliated calcite, upper valve with outer pris-

matic calcite; most scallops with inner crossed-lamellar layers; dimyarian but most monomyarian; ctenidia pseudolamellibranch; mantle fusions lacking; foot often lost in adult; scallops capable of swimming; some deepwater scallops predatory; marine; epibyssate; cemented by lower or left valve or free.

Subclass Palaeoheterodonta

Characterized by equal shell valves with a variable hinge dentition; aragonitic shell with outer prismatic and inner layers of nacre; most approximately isomyarian; ctenidia eulamellibranch; mantle fusions lacking, especially ventrally; complicated life cycles; wholly freshwater; nonbyssate; infaunal.

Order Unionoida

Large, equivalve, varying from round to elongate and with equally variable sculpture; shell of outer prismatic layer and inner layers of nacre; hinge schizodont; dimyarian; ctenidia eulamellibranch with either 1 or both demibranchs functioning as an incubatory marsupium; ovoviviparous; parasitically larviparous; freshwater; some cemented and oysterlike; mostly infaunal.

Subclass Heterodonta

Shell highly variable; hinge plate teeth may be reduced or absent; shell comprises crossed-lamellar, complex crossed-lamellar, or prismatic layers, but never nacreous; primitively isomyarian but with wide range of adductor muscle configurations; ctenidia eulamellibranch; mantle margins extensively fused, particularly posteriorly, often to form long inhalant and exhalant siphons; mostly marine but also estuarine and freshwater; some epibyssate, some bore soft rocks and wood; generally infaunal.

Order Veneroida

Shell typically equivalve and of outer crossed-lamellar and inner complex crossed-lamellar layers; hinge comprises radiating cardinal and lateral teeth, often weakly developed; adductor muscles of varying proportions according to habit; ctenidia eulamellibranch, mantle margins extensively fused, often developed into long siphons; most are active burrowers with a large foot; some epibyssate; mostly marine, some estuarine and freshwater; includes the poorly known miniature commensals and parasites; widely divergent, accounting for 50 percent of the extant bivalves.

Order Myoida

Shell typically thin, equivalve, comprising either 2 or 3 layers; hinge plate with cardinal dentition, often degenerate; approximately isomyarian but with much variation; boring forms develop accessory shell plates; ctenidia eulamellibranch, mantle margins extensively fused and covered in periostracum; small foot; marine deep burrowers with long siphons but also rock- and wood-boring.

Subclass Anomalodesmata

Characterized by highly variable shell, either equivalve or inequivalve, often gaping either posteriorly or anteriorly; hinge plate thickened and enrolled but generally edentulous; shell of two or three layers, the inner nacreous; typically isomyarian but with wide variation; ctenidia either eulamellibranch and plicate or septibranch; mantle margins extensively fused, often covered in periostracum; foot reduced; siphons of variable length; consistently hermaphroditic; marine; mostly burrowing; some epibyssate or cemented.

Order Pholadomyoida

Shell more or less equivalve but of widely divergent form; shell comprises aragonitic prisms and nacre or homogeneous structures; typically isomyarian; ctenidia eulamellibranch and plicate but many deepwater species are septibranch; extensive mantle fusions, reduced foot and pedal gape; siphons of variable length; shallow-water forms are burrowing, nestling, epibyssate, or cemented suspension feeders; some deepwater forms are predators with exotic modifications to the bivalve plan.

Critical appraisal. Generally, the classification scheme is accepted up to the level of family and even superfamily. The arrangement of higher categories is, however, still debated. Some authors, for example, combine the subclasses Palaeotaxodonta and Cryptodonta into a single group of primitive detrivores with protobranch gills. Differences in shell structure, however, argue against this. Similarly, the order Arcoida is separated by some from the subclass Pteriomorphia; shell structure again supports this, but other anatomic features do not. The order Trigonioida traditionally has been located within the subclass Palaeoheterodonta, but this has also been disputed, anatomic features suggesting instead an affinity with the subclass Pteriomorphia. This means that the subclass Palaeoheterodonta comprises only the order Unionoida, which has come to occupy the freshwater domain exclusively. Some authors would prefer to relocate the order Myoida from the subclass Heterodonta into the subclass Anomalodesmata, arguing that the edentulous shell, extensive mantle fusions, and deep-burrowing habit are characteristics shared with early ancestors of the order Pholadomyoida. The subclass Anomalodesmata, however, is itself possibly too narrowly demarcated, and some authorities would, for example, separate the deepwater carnivorous septibranchs from the shallow-water pholadomyoids into their own order, the Septibranchoida.

This lack of classificatory agreement is not unusual with regard to a group that has adopted a simple sedentary, filter-feeding mode of life. Simplification and parallel evolution will lead to similarity in form, structure, and function. Debate in creating classificatory trees and reconstructing the historical record is thus about the relative significance of the fossil shell record, as there is little information on tissue morphology, and the importance of morphological data obtained from living representatives. (Br.M.)

Cephalopods (octopuses, squids, cuttlefishes, and nautiluses)

Cephalopoda is a small class of highly advanced and organized, exclusively marine mollusks, of which the octopus, squid, cuttlefish, and chambered nautilus are familiar representatives. The extinct forms outnumber the living, the class having attained great diversity in late Paleozoic and Mesozoic times. The extinct cephalopods are the ammonites, belemnites, and nautiloids, except five living species of *Nautilus.*

GENERAL FEATURES AND IMPORTANCE TO HUMANS

The cephalopods agree with the rest of the Mollusca in basic structure, and the ancestors appear to have the closest affinity with the ancestors of the class Gastropoda. The best-known feature of the cephalopods is the possession of arms and tentacles, eight or 10 in most forms but about 90 in *Nautilus.* Except for the nautilus, all living members of the class show great modification and reduction of the characteristic molluscan shell.

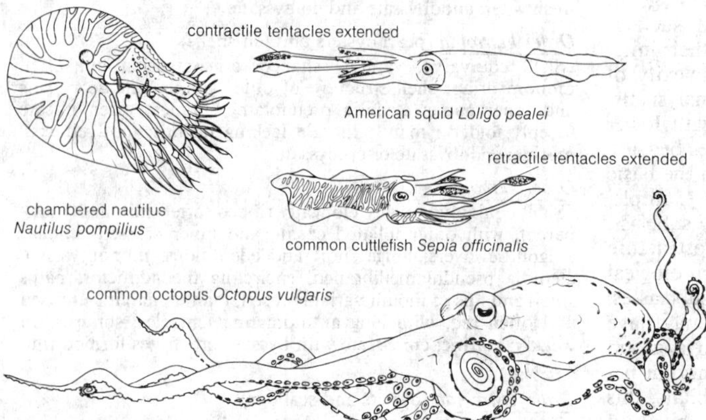

Figure 11: Body plans of typical cephalopods.

Size range

Cephalopods range greatly in size. The giant squids (*Architeuthis* species) are the largest living invertebrates; *A. dux* attains a length of more than 20 metres (60 feet), including the extended tentacles. The smallest cephalopod is the squid *Idiosepius,* rarely an inch in length. The average octopus usually has arms no longer than 30 centimetres (12 inches) and rarely longer than a metre (39 inches). But arm spans of up to nine metres (30 feet) have been reported in *Octopus dofleini.* The shell of the fossil ammonite *Pachydiscus seppenradensis* from the Cretaceous measures 205 centimetres (6 feet 8 inches) in diameter; it is considered to have been the largest shelled mollusk.

Cephalopods occur in large numbers and form one of the greatest potential food resources of the oceans. They are eaten in most parts of the world and have been accepted as part of the general diet in North America and northern Europe. They also are indirectly important to humans since they furnish a large part of the diet of sperm whales and smaller whales, seals, fishes, and seabirds.

NATURAL HISTORY

Reproduction and life cycles. The sexes are usually separate in the Cephalopoda. Sexual dimorphism is usually expressed in slight differences of size and in the proportions of various parts. In the argonaut and the blanket octopus (*Tremoctopus*) the males differ in appearance and size from the females.

Reproductive systems

The female reproductive system is simple, consisting of the posterior ovary and paired oviducts. Nidamental glands exist in species that lay eggs encased in heavy gelatinous capsules.

In males the reproductive system contains a series of chambers or sacs along the course of the vas deferens, which produce long tubes (spermatophores) to contain the spermatozoa. The final sac (Needham's organ) is used for storage of spermatophores. The spermatophores are complicated, containing sperm reservoir, cement body, cap, and a delicate triggering mechanism for releasing the tube and cementing it to the female's body, where the sperm are released when the eggs are mature and ready to be laid. Since spermatophores vary in appearance from species to species, they are important taxonomic characters.

During courtship the male deposits spermatophores in the female, either within the mantle cavity or on a pad below the mouth, by means of a specially modified arm, the hectocotylus. The hectocotylized arm of *Octopus* bears a deep groove on one side, ending in a spoonlike terminal organ. In *Argonauta* and *Tremoctopus* the arm is highly modified and in mating is autotomized (self-amputated) and left within the mantle cavity of the female. In the squids a much larger section of the arm may be modified; often the suckers are degenerate and the distal half of the arm bears rows of slender papillae, although special pouches and flaps may often be found. The modified arm of *Nautilus* is termed the spadix.

Cephalopod mating habits

Little is known about the mating habits of most cephalopods. In the common octopus the male and female remain some distance apart while the male caresses the female with the tip of the hectocotylized arm. The male then inserts the tip of the arm into the mantle cavity of the female, where it remains for more than an hour, during which time the spermatophores travel down the spermatophoral groove of the arm. In the cuttlefish (*Sepia*), according to the Dutch zoologist L. Tinbergen, the pair swims side by side, the male indulging in some courtship behaviour with its arms. Eventually, mating takes place by the pair intertwining their arms and remaining together while the spermatophores are placed on the inner side of the female's mouth membrane. In loliginid squids a somewhat similar type of mating occurs, except that it takes place en masse in schools of thousands of individuals.

Eggs may be laid shortly after mating or after a prolonged period of maturation during which time the sperm remain viable. In loliginids they are fertilized as they are ejected and before being fixed in the egg capsule. In the octopods they may be fertilized as they pass through oviductal glands near the end of the oviduct. In cuttlefishes the eggs are fertilized before the heavy capsule is formed. Egg laying in octopods is accomplished by the female individually fixing the eggs singly or in festoons by a short stalk or thread. In loliginids the eggs in fingerlike capsules often form immense moplike patches, the result of the communal spawning of perhaps hundreds of individuals. Spawning of oceanic squids is very poorly known. The number of eggs laid during a spawning period varies greatly; it may range from only a few dozen in octopuses with large eggs to more than 100,000 in the common octopus, laid over a period of about two weeks. In cuttlefishes the number of eggs is smaller, about 200 to 300 being laid in a season. In loliginids several thousand eggs may be laid by a single female, and the egg mop of the European common squid, resulting from the efforts of many individuals, may contain more than 40,000 eggs.

Egg laying

The eggs of most cephalopods are enclosed within a capsule that may be gelatinous and transparent (the squids of the genus *Loligo*) or opaque and leathery (*Octopus* and cuttlefishes). The eggs of oceanic species may be laid in large sausagelike gelatinous masses or singly. The eggs of most coastal species are laid inshore and are attached singly or in clusters, primarily to rocks and shells on the bottom. Parental care is exhibited by some octopuses, in which the female broods over the eggs in the den, and in the argonaut (*Argonauta*), in which the eggs are carried in a special shell secreted by the female. In most squids and cuttlefishes the eggs are left uncared-for. Squids that attach their eggs to the bottom engulf them in a gelatinous mass that protects them from disease and deters predators. Cuttlefishes squirt their eggs with ink when they are laid to camouflage the otherwise white eggs.

All cephalopod eggs have a remarkable amount of yolk, unlike that in the rest of the Mollusca, so that segmentation is incomplete and restricted to one end of the egg, where the embryo develops. The embryo of a cuttlefish (*Sepia*), squid (*Loligo*), or octopus (*Octopus*) has a yolk sac. In certain presumably archaic Teuthoidea there is less yolk, and the yolk sac is nearly absent. Development of the embryo is direct, without the distinctive larval stages and metamorphoses that occur in other mollusks.

Development

Incubation time varies, but in *Octopus* young hatch in about 50 days and in *Loligo* in about 40 days. At hatching, the young may closely resemble the adult and assume the adult habitat or they may differ from the adult and spend a considerable time in the plankton as part of the drifting life. The juveniles of many cephalopods were described as distinct genera before their juvenile status was discovered. In octopods with small eggs (*e.g., Octopus vulgaris*) the juveniles are planktonic, spending several weeks in the plankton; the "*Macrotritopus*" stage of *Scaeurgus* may greatly prolong its juvenile life until a favourable bottom substrate is found. In octopods with large eggs (*e.g., Octopus briareus*) the young resemble the adult and immediately assume a bottom-dwelling mode of life.

In the order Sepioidea (cuttlefishes and bottle-tailed squids) the young closely resemble the adults and are only briefly planktonic. In the Teuthoidea (squids), especially the Oegopsida, the larvae may differ widely from the adult and the juvenile period may be quite long.

Life span

Little is known about the life span of cephalopods. Studies have shown that in *Octopus joubini* raised from the egg in aquariums, sexual maturity and spawning were reached in five months; in a loliginid squid (*Sepioteuthis sepioidea*), likewise raised from the egg, sexual maturity and full growth were also attained in five months. It thus appears that the smaller inshore species may have a life span of no more than one year or, exceptionally, two or three. Nothing is known of the life span of the large oceanic squids, but it is presumed that giants such as *Architeuthis* attain their bulk only after a period of perhaps four to five years. In the smaller octopuses and squids, observational data indicate that many of the males die after mating and females after the first major spawning.

Behaviour. Cephalopods are unique among the invertebrates in the degree of cephalization and cerebralization attained. The uniting of the major ganglionic centres of the central nervous system constitutes a brain of considerable complexity. Studies undertaken at the Zoological Station in Naples by the British zoologists J.Z. Young, Martin J. Wells, and others have demonstrated that *Octopus* is capable of learning and has considerable intelligence. The behaviour of squids and octopuses differs considerably because of their different modes of life. Laboratory behavioral studies have dealt mainly with learning processes and have centred around food acceptance, reward and punishment, maze work, and shape discrimination. By means of surgical techniques it has been possible to determine the various functional centres of the brain of *Octopus* and the transmission and receiving pathways.

Research of a detailed nature has been concerned with colour change. Most cephalopods possess colour pigment cells (chromatophores) and reflecting cells (iridocytes) in the skin. The chromatophores are expanded by nerves controlled by the brain, and the colours are exposed (brown, black, red, yellow, or orange red). Colours and colour patterns are exhibited according to specific behavioral conditions—*e.g.,* attack on prey, camouflage, rest, and alarm or defense. Alarm patterns are the most readily recognized, consisting of strong contrasting light and dark areas, bars and peripheral dark outlines, or vivid displays of spots, like huge eyes.

Other behavioral patterns are found in changes in skin texture, including the erection of branched or spikelike papillae and curling of the arms. These actions often are attempts by cephalopods to conceal or camouflage themselves through imitating bottom objects such as sand, coral, or seaweed.

Discharge of ink

The ink of cephalopods is used for both defense and escape. In *Octopus* under attack by a moray eel, the cloud of ink seems to paralyze for some time the eel's senses of sight and smell. In squids the ink is ejected as a spindle-shaped mass about the size of the squid itself, the ink coagulating in the water. With this "dummy" left behind, the squid contracts its chromatophores, becomes nearly transparent, and jets away.

Many cephalopods (but not *Nautilus* and *Octopus*) possess special light organs (photophores), which emit chemical light or bioluminescence. Light is produced by the enzymatic reaction of luciferin and luciferase or, in bottle-tailed squids (sepiolids), indirectly, through cultures of luminescent bacteria. Photophores distributed over the body are employed at night or in the mid depths in various ways: mating play, recognition of the sexes, aid in schooling, attracting prey, defense, and camouflage. The light organs of the squid *Histioteuthis* are highly complicated, consisting of reflector, light source, directive muscles, lens, diaphragm, window, and colour screens.

Octopuses, squids, and cuttlefishes display considerable skill and cunning in hunting, stalking patiently, or luring prey within reach of their arms or tentacles. Both cuttlefishes and octopuses may use the tips of their arms as wormlike lures to attract small fishes, and octopuses have been reported to thrust stones between the valves of clams to prevent their closing. This has not been verified by later observers, but such intelligence is not beyond belief.

Locomotion. Cephalopods move by crawling, swimming, or jet propulsion, mainly the latter. The mantle, which has a passive role in the majority of mollusks, has become involved in locomotion in cephalopods, having almost entirely lost its rigid shell and become highly muscular. Its expansion and contraction produce a locomotory water current by drawing water into the mantle cavity and expelling it through the funnel. The rapid ejection of this jet of water enables the animal to execute quick backward and forward movements.

Jet propulsion

Water is drawn into the mantle cavity by the relaxation of the circular muscles and resultant expansion of the mantle. It enters around the neck region or aperture of the mantle (through the funnel in some deep-sea octopuses). In the oceanic squids the system is more efficient, with a nonreturn valve that prevents water from entering the wrong way through the funnel. When the mantle is contracted the aperture is closed by locking mechanisms and contraction of the anterior ring muscle, and the water is forced out through the funnel. This flexible tube is constructed similarly to a jet nozzle and may be turned in any direction, giving the animal great flexibility of motion for steering.

Squids also possess terminal or lateral fins used in slow movement or hovering. Locomotion is by the rapid undulation of the outer edges of the fins. Movement through the water is aided by lateral expansions (swimming keels) on the outer surface of the third pair of arms. Some squids (*Onychoteuthis, Thysanoteuthis*) are able to "fly" for several hundred feet, driven into the air by powerful thrusts from their jets and gliding on their expanded fins and arm keels. This normally occurs when the squids are pursued by predatory fishes and dolphins. When the squid jets rapidly through the water, the fins are often curled tightly around the mantle. Cuttlefishes, because of the large cuttlebone, are less active animals and spend most of their life lying on or hovering slightly above the bottom. Both jet and fins are used, the latter more frequently.

The benthic octopods are bottom crawlers, gliding about the bottom and in and out of crannies with amazing agility through the use of their eight arms and hundreds of suckers. Because of the extraordinary flexibility of the body, they are able to pass through openings hardly larger than the diameter of one eye. When disturbed, octopods swim rapidly by jet propulsion. Mass swimming migrations have been reported.

The finned octopods and the bottle-tailed squids have paddle-shaped fins that probably are most useful for hovering and slow swimming. The female argonaut (*Argonauta*) propels herself by jet propulsion while encased in her paper-thin shell. The chambered nautilus (*Nautilus*) is a less active swimmer, partly due to the inefficient funnel, which is composed of two flaps instead of a single fused tube, and to a reduced mantle cavity.

The active swimmers and most bottom dwellers apparently possess no hydrostatic organ. The cuttlefish, however, which swims or hovers above the bottom or rests on the bottom, adjusts its buoyancy through the amount of gases contained in the porous cuttlebone. *Nautilus,* which swims slowly above the bottom or in midwater, accomplishes this similarly, adjusting the gases in the chambered shell. Inactive oceanic squids, such as some cranchiids, concentrate ions lighter than seawater in the body chamber, while others, such as *Bathyteuthis,* concentrate buoyant oil in the chambers associated with the digestive gland.

Distribution

Ecology. The Cephalopoda are exclusively marine animals. There are numerous littoral species, but few have been reported from brackish water except for the squid *Lolliguncula brevis,* which occurs along the Florida coast in bays where the salinity is as low as 8.5 parts per thousand (about one-fourth that of the open ocean). Cephalopods are excluded from the Baltic Sea by lower salinities but have been found in areas of the Suez Canal where salinities are higher than in the oceans. There is some evidence that in parts of the open sea that differ only slightly in salinity there may be a varying cephalopod fauna. Grace E. Pickford, an American zoologist, has found that the vertical distribution of young in *Vampyroteuthis* is governed by water density, and, according to the American zoologist Clyde F.E. Roper, a similar situation exists in the deep-sea squid *Bathyteuthis.*

The Coleoidea are carnivorous and live principally on other cephalopods, crustaceans, mollusks, and small fishes. In the food cycle of the squid *Illex,* in which the adults feed upon young mackerel and the adult mackerel feed upon young squid. Squids also are cannibalistic. *Octopus* feeds upon bivalve mollusks and on decapod crustaceans, sometimes causing severe losses to the lobster fishery by entering the traps and eating the captive lobsters. The smaller oceanic squids probably feed primarily upon small fish, copepods, heteropods, and caridean shrimp. The Cirrata, which have reduced musculature and radula, indicating reduced activity and masticatory power, probably feed on bottom dwellers or small plankton.

The Cephalopoda are fed upon by many marine mammals, large fish, and seabirds. Sperm whales and other toothed whales feed primarily on squids.

Associations

The 19th-century French naturalist Alcide d'Orbigny asserted that the Cephalopoda are in general sociable, and this statement is certainly true of *Nautilus,* which are found together in large numbers. Some authorities, studying the Mediterranean cephalopods, have concluded that only certain pelagic cephalopods are gregarious (*Todaro-*

des, Ocythoe). Schools of the large oceanic squid *Thysanoteuthis rhombis* have been reported at Madeira. Although there is no proof that numbers constitute gregariousness, octopus colonies have been reported.

The breeding season has a marked effect on the local distribution of certain cephalopods. The common cuttlefish comes into shallow water in the spring and summer to breed, and similar migrations have been observed in some squids (*Loligo, Alloteuthis, Illex*).

The geographic distribution of cephalopods is incompletely known. Some open-ocean pelagic and bathypelagic forms are cosmopolitan in warm and temperate waters (*Onychoteuthis banksi, Cranchia scabra*). Others may be limited by genera to particular oceans or to continental waters. Even some species of bathypelagic habitat are limited to one ocean. The Octopoda, as a result of their bottom-dwelling habits, show stronger restrictions in their distribution, but *Octopus vulgaris* and *O. macropus,* both species with planktonic larvae, have gained worldwide distribution. In general, the pelagic and planktonic cephalopods conform in their distribution to other pelagic animals.

The vertical distribution is also incompletely known. *Nautilus* moves vertically through the water, living near the bottom, and has been obtained at a depth of about 550 metres (1,800 feet). It is fished in the Philippines when it comes into shallow water. Of the cuttlefishes, the Sepiidae are littoral, whereas the Sepiolidae dwell on or near the bottom, down to considerable depths. Among the squids the Myopsida are coastal forms, whereas the Oegopsida are oceanic, living from the surface to depths in excess of 5,000 metres (16,400 feet). The Octopoda occur from the surface of the open ocean (*Tremoctopus*) to the ocean floor (*Pareledone, Bentheledone, Cirroteuthis*) in excess of 5,000 metres (16,400 feet); most are bottom-dwelling forms restricted to the continental shelf and its slope.

FORM AND FUNCTION

Cephalopods vary from elongate, streamlined oceanic organisms to saccular, slow-moving bottom and drifting forms. Their body plan is indicative in many ways of the habitat in which they dwell and their mode of life.

The viscera of a generalized cephalopod are covered by a dome-shaped or elongated sheath of muscle, the mantle, which is connected with the head anteriorly. Ventrally, the mantle is free and encloses the mantle cavity, the space into which the gills project and the excretory and reproductive systems open.

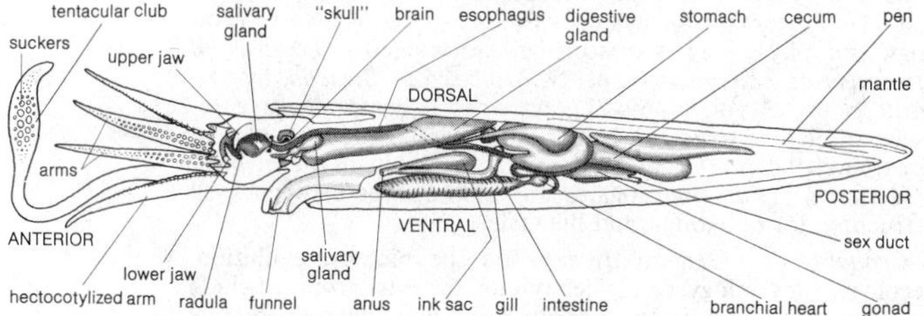

Figure 12: Internal structure of squid (*Loligo*). Left side of body, with four arms and one tentacle removed.

Number of arms and tentacles

Anterior to the mantle is the head-foot, which bears a ventral muscular tube, the funnel. Surrounding the mouth are eight long, prehensile arms, provided with suckers in octopuses and argonauts (order Octopoda), or eight arms and two tentacles, equipped with horny ringed suckers bearing teeth or hooks in squids and cuttlefishes (orders Teuthoidea and Sepioidea). The primitive *Nautilus* has about 90 small suckerless appendages.

The fossil nautiloids and ammonites (represented today only by *Nautilus*) were primitive, less-specialized forms, probably leading a rather inactive sluggish life. The modern octopuses, squids, and cuttlefishes have acquired an active, vigorous life that has led to marked departures in structure and function from the type represented by *Nautilus.* Modern forms are divided into three basic life-styles: the sluggish life in the great depths of the sea, a floating life in the midwaters, and a more active, aggressive existence near the surface. The nautiloids and ammonites were probably shallow-water animals living near the bottom and, like the slow-moving *Nautilus,* relied for protection on a coiled or curved calcareous external shell.

All cephalopods have an internal cartilaginous covering of the consolidated ganglia of the nervous system. In all except ammonites and nautiloids, it constitutes a cranium. Various other skeletal supports are found at the base of the fins and in the "neck," gills, and arms.

The alimentary system consists of a buccal mass with a pair of jaws (mandibles) and a rasping tongue (radula), esophagus, salivary glands, stomach, cecum, digestive gland ("liver"), intestine, and anus. In the Octopoda the esophagus may be expanded to form a crop, while in the deep-sea Cirrata the radula may be degenerate or lacking. Except in *Nautilus* and certain deep-sea Octopoda there is an ink sac located near the anus. This secretes a dark fluid, the sepia or ink, which is forcibly ejected through the funnel.

All members of the Coleoidea (octopuses, squids, and cuttlefishes) possess a closed circulatory system of blood vessels; in *Nautilus* it is partly lacunar (*i.e.,* made up of sinuses). The blood contains a blue respiratory pigment, hemocyanin (a copper compound), dissolved in the plasma. There are three hearts, the main systemic heart and the two branchial hearts, one at the base of each gill. The rhythmical contractions and expansions of the mantle cause a circulation of water over the gills where gas exchange takes place between the seawater and blood. The featherlike gills, consisting of a central axis with a row of lamellae on either side, are suspended in the mantle cavity from the mantle wall.

The excretion of nitrogenous wastes is carried out exclusively by the kidneys. There are four kidneys in *Nautilus* and two in the coleoids.

The central nervous system is highly developed, the major ganglionic centres being concentrated in the head. In some of the cuttlefishes (Sepioidea) the cerebral centres are subdivided for specialization, with the pedal ganglia divided into brachial and epipodal elements that innervate the arms and funnel respectively. In active squids the mantle is innervated by giant paired dorsal axons. Much of the present knowledge of mechanisms of nerve impulse conduction has come from the study of these giant axons. The sense organs of the cephalopods are eyes, rhinophores (olfactory organs), statocysts (organs of equilibrium), and tactile organs. In *Nautilus* the eyes are open pits without lenses. In the Coleoidea the eyes are complex and approach those of some lower vertebrates in efficiency.

EVOLUTION AND PALEONTOLOGY

The first cephalopods were probably provided with a simple, caplike shell. With elongation of the shell and the formation of septa or partitions, the nautiloid shell could be formed (Late Cambrian, 523 to 505 million years ago). The primitive elongate shell of *Orthoceras* became unmanageable and coiling resulted, as in the Gastropoda.

The Ammonoidea are usually considered to have evolved from Devonian (408 to 360 million years ago) straight-shelled forms (*Bactrites*) with certain nautiloid traits. Coiled ammonites appeared in the Late Devonian epoch (*Goniatites*). The subclass became extinct in the Cretaceous.

The shell

Modern cephalopods possess an internal and partly degenerate shell, straight except in *Spirula.* The state of the shell in modern forms is due to the progressive overgrowth of it by the mantle, probably accompanying the evolution of an active swimming life. The first evidence of the modification of the shell is in *Aulococeras* in the Triassic period (245 to 208 million years ago). The belemnites, with their modified, internal shell, gave rise to *Spirula* (coiled shell), to cuttlefishes (calcified phragmoconal septa, forming a thick shell), and to the squids (only the proostracum as a horny "pen"). These forms appeared in the Jurassic period (208 to 144 million years ago) and were probably derived from belemnite-like ancestors.

In the Octopoda the shell persists as cartilaginous stylets or fin supports. *Palaeoctopus newboldi,* the oldest known octopod, from the Cretaceous of Syria, was already too advanced to provide a clue to the derivation of the Octopoda. The Vampyromorpha are considered to be a possible connecting link between the Teuthoidea and the Octopoda.

CLASSIFICATION

Distinguishing taxonomic features. In fossil cephalopods, reliance is placed upon shell details (general shape, type of coiling, external sculpture, and sutures). In living forms, except for the Sepioidea, the shell is strongly degenerate or missing and the characters used consist of details of the soft parts: presence or absence of an eyelid, tentacles retractile or contractile or both, shape and size of fins, number of arms, number of sucker rows, presence or absence of teeth and hooks on arm and tentacular suckers, radular dentition, structure of funnel organ, spermatophores, details of the hectocotyles, number of gill lamellae, and the presence, patterns, and types of photophores.

Annotated classification. The following classification has gained considerable acceptance among modern specialists. Groups indicated by a dagger (†) are known only as fossils.

CLASS CEPHALOPODA
Mollusks in which typical molluscan foot surrounds head and forms arms and tentacles; mantle surrounds mantle cavity and is part of locomotory system; central nervous system highly developed, forming true brain encased in cartilaginous cranium; mouth contains pair of parrotlike jaws (or beak); body usually somewhat streamlined; eyes highly developed, most closely resembling in acuity those of some vertebrates; about 650 living species.

Subclass Nautiloidea (nautiloids)
Cambrian to present; now living only in the Indo-Pacific region, particularly East Indies; external coiled or straight chambered shell present, chambers connected by median siphuncle; smooth septa; sutures simple, little or no external sculpture; tentacles suckerless, adhesive; living and supposedly fossil forms with 4 gills; funnel formed of 2 nonfused flaps; about 5 living species, in genus *Nautilus*.

†Subclass Ammonoidea (ammonites)
Devonian to Cretaceous; fossils only; external, coiled or straight chambered shell with marginal siphuncle, last chamber protected by single horny plate or 2 calcareous plates; septa wrinkled; complex sutures; external sculpture.

Subclass Coleoidea (octopuses, squids, belemnites, cuttlefishes)
Triassic to present; shell internal, reduced, vestigial, or lacking; 2 sets of gills; 8 or 10 arms, having suckers or hooks.

†Order Belemnoidea (belemnites)
Triassic to Tertiary; fossils only; shell consisting of solid rostrum, small chambered phragmocone and anterior, broad proostracum; 6 to 10 arms bearing hooks in 1 or 2 rows; total length 5 to 210 cm.

Order Sepioidea (cuttlefishes and bottle-tailed squids)
Tertiary to present; worldwide with family exceptions; shell coiled and chambered (Spirulidae), straight with vestigial chambering (Sepiidae), vestigial, or lacking; eyes covered with transparent membrane; 8 sucker-bearing arms and 2 tentacles retractile into pockets; total length 2.5–90 cm.

Order Teuthoidea (squids)
Tertiary to present; shell thin, horny gladius; 8 arms, 2 tentacles, which are contractile only; worldwide; total length 1.5 to at least 1,800 cm (0.75 in. to 60+ ft).

Suborder Myopsida. Eye covered by transparent membrane; neritic, inshore animals.

Suborder Oegopsida. Eye open to water, completely surrounded by free eyelid; open-ocean animals living from the surface down to at least 3,000 m.

Order Vampyromorpha
Purplish-black gelatinous animals with 1 or 2 pairs of paddle-shaped fins at various stages of growth; 8 arms and 2 small retractile filaments not homologous with tentacles; deep web between the arms; worldwide; 1 species.

Order Octopoda (octopuses)
Cretaceous to present; shell lacking or vestigial, nonhomologous shell or egg case in female argonautids; fins absent or present; body generally saccular, with 8 mobile, highly contractile sucker-bearing arms; worldwide; total length 5–540 cm (2 in. to 18 ft); maximum arm spread to about 900 cm (30 ft).

Suborder Palaeoctopoda (finned octopod). Cretaceous, some living.

Suborder Cirrata (*Cirromorpha*). Holocene; soft-bodied, deep-webbed forms with cirri on arms and small to large paddle-shaped fins; primarily deep-sea.

Suborder Incirrata (common octopus). Holocene; compact, saccular to round bodied, finless forms with muscular, contractile arms; somewhat secretive; pelagic to deep-sea and shallow waters.

Critical appraisal. The elucidation of higher classification of the cephalopods is fraught with difficulties. Early specialists divided the living cephalopods into Octopoda and Decapoda without relation to their internal structure; these were both placed in the Dibranchia, in contrast to all fossil forms, which were considered as Tetrabranchia because *Nautilus* has four gills rather than two. This unnatural classification, accepted by the French zoologist Alcide d'Orbigny in 1838, was gradually modified through the efforts of the Swiss zoologist Adolph Naef and the German zoologist Georg Grimpe and later workers to the form given above. Phylogenetic linkages are still highly theoretical, but, with X-ray techniques that reveal soft parts in fossils and with new paleontological finds, the unfolding of the evolutionary history is in sight.

(G.L.V./C.F.E.R.)

BIBLIOGRAPHY

General: An extensive and updated treatment of molluscan structure, function, and evolution is KARL M. WILBUR (ed.), *The Mollusca,* 12 vol. (1983–88). The phylum is outlined in KENNETH J. BOSS, "Mollusca," in SYBIL P. PARKER (ed.), *Synopsis and Classification of Living Organisms,* vol. 1 (1982), pp. 945–1166; while J.E. MORTON, *Molluscs,* 5th ed. (1979), is a general discussion of their biology. LIBBIE HENRIETTA HYMAN, *The Invertebrates,* vol. 6, *Mollusca I* (1967), contains information on the lower groups and a classic summary of gastropods. Other overviews include ALAN SOLEM, *The Shell Makers: Introducing Mollusks* (1974); C.M. YONGE and T.E. THOMPSON, *Living Marine Molluscs* (1976); and, on three individual groups, LUITFRIED V. SALVINI-PLAWEN, *Schild- und Furchenfüsser (Caudofoveata und Solenogastres)* (1971); and PIET KASS and RICHARD A. VAN BELLE, *Monograph of Living Chitons* (1985–).

Gastropods: VERA FRETTER and ALASTAIR GRAHAM, *British Prosobranch Molluscs: Their Functional Anatomy and Ecology* (1962), is an essential reference. An introduction to land snail systematics and biology is found in M.P. KERNEY and R.A.D. CAMERON, *A Field Guide to the Land Snails of Britain and North-West Europe* (1979). W.F. PONDER (ed.), *Prosobranch Phylogeny* (1988), is a summary by a number of researchers. VERA FRETTER and J. PEAKE (eds.), *Pulmonates,* 2 vol. in 3 (1975–79), examines this subclass in detail—see especially the essay by A. SOLEM, "Classification of the Land Mollusca," in vol. 2A, pp. 49–97, which provides an outline of taxa. Another source is ROGER N. HUGHES, *A Functional Biology of Marine Gastropods* (1986).

Bivalves: R.D. PURCHON, *The Biology of the Mollusca,* 2nd ed. (1977), contains essays on various aspects of bivalve ecology and physiology. RAYMOND C. MOORE (ed.), *Treatise on Invertebrate Paleontology,* pt. N, *Mollusca 6: Bivalvia,* by L.R. COX *et al.,* 3 vol. (1969–71), provides a comprehensive review of bivalve structure, history, and classification. STEVEN M. STANLEY, *Relation of Shell Form to Life Habits in the Bivalvia (Mollusca)* (1970), investigates the relationships between shell structure, form, habitat, and life-style.

Cephalopods: General treatises on the biology, evolution, ecology, physiology, and behaviour of this group include MARION NIXON and J.B. MESSENGER (eds.), *The Biology of Cephalopods* (1977); P.R. BOYLE (ed.), *Cephalopod Life Cycles,* 2 vol. (1983–87); and CLYDE F.E. ROPER, MICHAEL J. SWEENEY, and CORNELIA E. NAUEN, *Cephalopods of the World: An Annotated and Illustrated Catalogue of Species of Interest to Fisheries* (1984), which also has an illustrated glossary and keys to identification of orders and families. K.N. NESIS, *Cephalopods of the World: Squids, Cuttlefishes, Octopuses, and Allies* (1987; originally published in Russian, 1982), is a review of anatomy, with keys to the identification of species. W. BRUCE SAUNDERS and NEIL H. LANDMAN (eds.), *Nautilus: The Biology and Paleobiology of a Living Fossil* (1987) is a comprehensive, scholarly treatise on the evolution, distribution, ecology, physiology, biology, shell structure, and aquarium maintenance of *Nautilus.* PETER DOUGLAS WARD, *The Natural History of Nautilus* (1987), compares the growth, buoyancy, physiology, and ecology of *Nautilus* with those of other living cephalopods. CLYDE F.E. ROPER and KENNETH J. BOSS, "The Giant Squid," *Scientific American,* 246(4):96–100, 104–105 (April 1982) is a nontechnical summary of current knowledge. M.J. WELLS, *Octopus: Physiology and Behaviour of an Advanced Invertebrate* (1978) is a highly technical but very readable review.

(L.v.S.-P./G.A.So./Br.M./G.L.V./C.F.E.R.)

Money

The subject of money has fascinated wise men from the time of Aristotle to the present day because it is so full of mystery and paradox. The piece of paper labelled one dollar or 100 francs or 10 kroner or 1,000 yen is little different, as paper, from a piece of the same size torn from a newspaper or magazine, yet it will enable its bearer to command some measure of food, drink, clothing, and the remaining goods of life while the other is fit only to light the fire. Whence the difference?

The easy answer, and the right one, is that people accept money as such because they know that others will. The pieces of paper are valuable because everyone thinks they are, and everyone thinks they are because in his experience they always have been. At bottom money is, then, a social convention, but a convention of uncommon strength that people will abide by even under extreme provocation. The strength of the convention is, of course, what enables governments to profit by inflating the currency. But it is not indestructible. When great variations occur in the quantity of these pieces of paper—as they have during and after wars—they may be seen to be, after all, no more than pieces of paper. People will then seek substitutes—like the cigarettes and cognac that for a time became the medium of exchange in Germany after World War II. As John Stuart Mill wrote:

> There cannot, in short, be intrinsically a more insignificant thing, in the economy of society, than money; except in the character of a contrivance for sparing time and labour. It is a machinery for doing quickly and commodiously, what would be done, though less quickly and commodiously, without it: and like many other kinds of machinery, it only exerts a distinct and independent influence of its own when it gets out of order. (*Principles of Political Economy,* W.J. Ashley [ed.], 1909, p. 488.)

Mill was perfectly correct, although one must add that there is hardly a contrivance man possesses that can do more damage to a society when it goes wrong.

This article is divided into the following sections:

FUNCTIONS OF MONEY

The basic function of money is to enable buying to be separated from selling, thus permitting trade to take place without the so-called double coincidence of barter. If a person has something to sell and wants something else in return, it is not necessary to search for someone able and willing to make the desired exchange of items. The person can sell the surplus item for general purchasing power—that is, "money"—to anyone who wants to buy it and then use the proceeds to buy the desired item from anyone who wants to sell it.

Barter and ease of exchange

The importance of this function of money is dramatically illustrated by the experience of Germany just after World War II, when paper money was rendered largely useless because, despite inflationary conditions, price controls were effectively enforced by the American, French, and British armies of occupation. People had to resort to barter or to inefficient money substitutes. The result was to cut total output of the economy in half. The German "economic miracle" just after 1948 reflected partly a currency reform by the occupation authorities, but some economists hold that it stemmed primarily from the German government's elimination of all price controls, thereby permitting a money economy to replace a barter economy.

Separation of the act of sale from the act of purchase requires the existence of something that will be generally accepted in payment—this is the "medium of exchange" function of money. But there must also be something that can serve as a temporary abode of purchasing power, in which the seller holds the proceeds in the interim between the first sale and the subsequent purchase, or from which the buyer can extract the general purchasing power with which to pay for what is bought. This is the "asset" function of money.

VARIETIES OF MONEY

Anything can serve as money that habit or social convention and successful experience endow with the quality of general acceptability, and a variety of items have so served—from the wampum (beads made from shells) of American Indians to cowries (brightly coloured shells) in India, to whales' teeth among the Fijians, to tobacco among early colonists in North America, to large stone disks on the Pacific island of Yap, to cigarettes and liquor in post-World War II Germany. The wide use of cattle as money in primitive times survives in the word pecuniary, which comes from the Latin *pecus,* meaning cattle.

Metallic money. The use of metals as money has occurred throughout history. As Aristotle observed,

> The various necessities of life are not easily carried about, and hence man agreed to employ in their dealings with each other something which was intrinsically useful and easily applicable to the purposes of life, for example, iron, silver, and the like. Of this the value was at first measured by size and weight, but in process of time they put a stamp upon it, to save the trouble of weighing and to mark the value.

The use of metal for money can be traced back to more than 2,000 years before the birth of Christ. But standardization and certification in the form of coinage, as referred to by Aristotle, did not occur except perhaps in isolated instances until the beginning of the 7th century BC. Historians generally assign to Lydia, a Greek state in Asia Minor, priority in using coined money. The first coins were made of electrum, a natural mixture of gold and silver, and were crude, bean-shaped ingots bearing a primitive punchmark certifying to either weight or fineness, or both.

Debasing the currency

The use of coins enabled payment to be by "tale," or count, rather than weight, greatly facilitating commerce. But this in turn encouraged clipping (shaving off tiny slivers from the sides or edges of coins) and sweating (shaking a bunch of coins together in a leather bag and collecting the dust that was thereby knocked off) in the hope of passing on the lighter coin at its face value. Gresham's law (that "bad money drives out good" when there is a fixed rate of exchange between them) came into operation, and heavy, good coins were held for their metallic value, while light coins were passed on. The coins became lighter and lighter, and prices higher and higher. Then payment by weight would be resumed for large transactions, and there would be pressure for recoinage. These particular defects were largely ended by the "milling" of coins (making serrations around the circumference of a coin), which began in the late 17th century.

A more serious matter was the attempt by the sovereign

to benefit from the monopoly of coinage. In this respect, Greek and Roman experience offers an interesting contrast. Though Solon, on taking office in Athens in 594 BC, did institute a partial debasement of the currency, for the next four centuries, until the absorption of Greece into the Roman Empire, the Athenian *drachma* had an almost constant silver content (67 grains of fine silver until Alexander, 65 grains thereafter) and became the standard coin of trade in Greece and in much of Asia and Europe as well. Even after the Roman conquest, the *drachma* continued to be minted and widely used.

The Roman experience was very different. Not long after the silver *denarius*, patterned after the Greek *drachma*, was introduced in 269 BC, the prior copper coinage (*aes*, or *libra*) began to be debased until, by the time the empire began, its weight had been reduced from one pound to half an ounce. The silver *denarius* and the gold *aureus* (introduced about 87 BC) suffered only minor debasement until the time of Nero (AD 54), when almost continuous tampering with the coinage began. The metal content of the gold and silver coins was reduced, and the proportion of alloy was increased to three-fourths or more of its weight. Debasement in Rome (as ever since) was a reflection of the state's inability or unwillingness to finance its expenditures through explicit taxes. But the debasement in turn worsened Rome's economic situation and undoubtedly contributed to the collapse of the empire.

Paper money. In the late 18th and early 19th centuries, paper money and bank notes spread widely. The bulk of the money in use came to consist not of actual gold or silver but of fiduciary money—promises to pay specified amounts of gold and silver. These promises were initially issued by individuals or companies as bank notes or as the transferrable book entries that came to be called deposits. But gradually the state assumed a role.

Fiat money

From fiduciary paper money promising to pay gold or silver, it is a short step to fiat paper money—that is, notes that are issued on the "fiat" of the sovereign, are specified to be so many dollars or francs or yen, and are legal tender but are not promises to pay something else. The first large-scale issue in a Western country occurred in France in the early 18th century (though there are reports of paper money in China many centuries earlier). Later, the French revolutionary government issued paper money in the form of assignats from 1789 to 1796. The American colonies and later the Continental Congress issued bills of credit that could be used in making payments. These early experiments gave fiat money a deservedly bad name. The money was overissued, and prices rose drastically until the money became worthless or was redeemed in metallic money (or promises to pay metallic money) at a small fraction of its initial value.

Subsequent issues of fiat money in the major countries during the 19th century were temporary departures from a metallic standard. In Great Britain, for example, payment of gold for the outstanding bank notes was "suspended" during the Napoleonic Wars (1797–1815). As a result, gold coin and bullion became more expensive in terms of paper. Similarly, in the United States during the Civil War, convertibility of Union currency (greenbacks) into specie was suspended, and resumption did not occur until 1879. At its peak, in 1864, the greenback price of gold, nominally equivalent to $100, reached more than $250.

STANDARDS OF VALUE

In the Middle Ages, when money consisted primarily of coins, silver and gold coins circulated simultaneously. As governments came increasingly to take over the coinage, and especially as fiduciary money was introduced, they tended to specify their nominal monetary units in terms of fixed weights of both silver and gold—to adopt a national bimetallic standard. Gresham's law, however, usually assured that the bimetallic standard degenerated into a monometallic standard: if the quantity of silver designated as the monetary equivalent of one ounce of gold was less than the quantity that could be purchased in the market for one ounce of gold (*i.e.*, if the mint overvalued silver), no one would bring gold to be coined. If one had gold, it was better to buy silver and bring it to be coined. Silver, the cheaper metal, "drove out" gold and became the standard. This happened in most of the countries of Europe, so that by the early 19th century all were effectively on a silver standard. In Britain, on the other hand, the ratio established in the 18th century at the advice of Sir Isaac Newton, then serving as master of the mint, overvalued gold and therefore led to an effective gold standard. In the United States a ratio of 15 ounces of silver to one ounce of gold was set in 1792. This ratio overvalued silver, so silver became the standard. In 1834 the ratio was altered to 16 to one, which overvalued gold, so gold became the standard.

The gold standard. The great gold discoveries in California and Australia in the 1840s and 1850s produced a temporary decline in the value of gold in terms of silver. This price change, plus the dominance of Britain in international finance, led to a widespread shift from a silver standard to a gold standard. Germany adopted gold in 1871–73, the Latin Monetary Union (France, Italy, Belgium, Switzerland) in 1873–74, the Scandinavian Union (Denmark, Norway, and Sweden) and The Netherlands in 1875–76. By the final decades of the century, silver remained dominant only in the Far East (China, in particular). Elsewhere the gold standard reigned.

The international gold standard

The early 20th century was the great era of the international gold standard. Gold coins circulated in most of the world; paper money, whether issued by private banks or by government, was convertible on demand into gold coins or gold bullion at an official price (with perhaps the addition of a small fee); and bank deposits were convertible into either gold coin or paper currency that was itself convertible into gold. In a few countries, a minor variant prevailed—the so-called gold-exchange standard, under which the currency was converted at a fixed price into the currency of another country (usually the British pound sterling) that was itself convertible into gold.

There was, in effect, a single world money called by different names in different countries. A U.S. dollar, for example, was defined as 23.22 grains of pure gold (25.8 grains of gold 0.9000 fineness). A British pound sterling was defined as 113.00 grains of pure gold (123.274 grains of gold 11/12th fine). Accordingly, one British pound equalled 4.8665 U.S. dollars (113.00/23.22) at the official parity. The actual exchange rate could deviate from this only by an amount that corresponded to the cost of shipping gold. If the price of the pound sterling in terms of dollars rose to a considerably higher value than this in the foreign exchange market, someone in New York City who had a debt to pay in London might find that, rather than buy the needed pounds on the market, it was cheaper to get gold for dollars at a bank or at the U.S. subtreasury, ship the gold to London, and get pounds for the gold from the Bank of England. This set an upper limit to the exchange rate. Similarly, the cost of shipping gold from Britain to the United States set a lower limit. These limits were known as the gold points.

Under such an international gold standard, the quantity of money in each country was determined by the specie-flow adjustment mechanism analyzed by 19th-century economists. If, for whatever reason, the quantity of money in a country rose unduly, this would tend to raise prices in that country relative to prices in other countries, discouraging exports and encouraging imports. The decreased supply of foreign currency from the sale of exports plus the increased demand for foreign currency to pay for imports would tend to raise the price of foreign currency in terms of domestic currency. As soon as this price hit the upper gold point, gold would be shipped out of the country to other countries. The decline in the amount of gold would produce in turn a reduction in the total amount of money—because banks and government institutions, seeing their gold reserves decline, would want to protect themselves against further demands by reducing the claims against gold that were outstanding. This would tend to lower prices at home. The influx of gold abroad would have the opposite effect, increasing the quantity of money there and raising prices. These adjustments would continue until the gold flow ceased or was reversed.

This is precisely the mechanism that operates within

a unified currency area, the mechanism that determines how much money there is in Illinois compared to how much there is in other states or how much there is in Wales compared to how much there is in other parts of the United Kingdom. In the early 20th century, most of the world was a unified currency area, so the gold standard functioned throughout the world. Its great advantage was that—if permitted to operate—it would greatly limit the power of any national government to engage in irresponsible monetary expansion. This was also its great disadvantage. In an era of big government and of full-employment policies, a real gold standard would tie the hands of governments in one of the most important areas of policy.

Managed gold-exchange standard

The decline of gold. World War I ended the real international gold standard. Most belligerents suspended the free convertibility of gold. The United States, even after its entry into the war, maintained convertibility but embargoed gold exports. For a few years after the end of the war, most nations had inconvertible national paper standards—inconvertible in that paper money was not convertible into gold or silver. The exchange rate between any two currencies was a market rate that fluctuated from time to time. During this period this was regarded as a temporary phenomenon, like the British suspension of gold payments during the Napoleonic era, and the U.S. suspension during the Civil War greenback period. The great aim was a restoration of the prewar gold standard.

This aim dominated monetary developments during the 1920s. Britain, still a major financial power, returned to gold in 1925. Winston Churchill, then chancellor of the Exchequer, decided to follow prevailing financial opinion and adopt the prewar parity (*i.e.,* to define a pound sterling once again as equal to 123.274 grains of gold 11/12th fine). This produced exchange rates that, at the existing prices in sterling, overvalued the pound and so tended to produce gold outflows, especially after France returned to gold in 1928 at a parity that undervalued the franc. By 1929 the important currencies of the world, and most of the less important ones, were again linked to gold.

The gold standard that was restored, however, was a far cry from the prewar gold standard. The establishment of the Federal Reserve System in the United States introduced an additional link in the international specie-flow mechanism. That mechanism no longer operated automatically. It operated only if the Federal Reserve chose to let it do so, and the Federal Reserve did not so choose; it took certain measures that prevented gold inflows from producing a corresponding expansion in the money supply. The United Kingdom had recurring difficulties in retaining its gold. It followed a restrictive monetary policy, but, because of rigidities in prices and particularly in wages, the result was unemployment rather than a lowering of prices. Unemployment reduced imports and stimulated exports, thus preventing gold losses. But this was not a tenable long-term position, as a lower price level might have been. Most other countries adopted a gold-exchange standard. Everywhere, central banks took scattered measures to loosen the connection between changes in the money supply and inflows or outflows of gold.

If the Great Depression had not occurred, this system might have grown and matured and improved. But the Depression brought the managed gold standards to a quick end. It originated in the United States, spread to all the countries linked by the gold exchange standard, and then reverberated back to the United States. Britain was the first major country to cut the link, leaving the gold standard in 1931. The United States followed in March 1933, restoring a fixed—but higher—dollar price for gold in January 1934, at $35 an ounce.

The dollar standard. The world's monetary system operated on a dollar standard from the end of World War II until 1971, when, in an attempt to control inflation, the United States unilaterally severed the connection between the dollar and gold. Under the dollar standard, the dollar was widely used in international trade, even in trade between countries other than the United States. It was the unit in terms of which the exchange rates of other currencies were expressed. Other countries maintained their "official" exchange rates by buying and selling U.S. dollars and held dollars as their primary reserve currency for that purpose. The existence of a dollar standard did not mean that other countries could not change their exchange rates—as Germany and France did in 1969—just as the gold standard did not mean that they could not "devalue" or "appreciate" in terms of gold. What it did mean was that the United States could not determine its own exchange rate or its balance of payments position. It also meant that U.S. monetary policy had a major effect on the world economy.

Since 1971 the world's monetary system has consisted of a collection of national fiat currencies linked by "floating" exchange rates set in the market. Frequent government interventions to affect exchange rates have been effective at most only temporarily. None of the numerous proposals to reform the system has come close to acceptance.

MODERN MONETARY SYSTEMS

Monetary systems are today very much alike in all the major countries of the world. They consist of three levels: (1) the holders of money (the "public")—individuals, businesses, governmental units; (2) commercial banks (privately or governmentally owned), which borrow from the public and make loans to individuals, firms, or governments; and (3) central banks, which have a monopoly on the issue of certain types of money, serve as the bankers for the central government and the commercial banks, and have the power to determine the quantity of money.

Currency and deposits

Public money holdings. The public holds its money as: (1) currency (including coin) and (2) bank deposits.

Currency. In most countries the bulk of the currency consists of notes issued by the central bank. In the United Kingdom these are Bank of England Notes; in the United States, Federal Reserve Notes; and so on. It is hard to say precisely what "issued by the central bank" means. In the United States, for example, the currency bears the words "Federal Reserve Note," but these notes are not obligations of the Federal Reserve Banks in any meaningful sense. The holder who presents them to a Federal Reserve Bank has no right to anything except other pieces of paper adding up to the same face value. The situation is much the same in most other countries.

The other major item of currency held by the public is coin. In almost all countries this is token coin, worth as metal much less than its face value.

Bank deposits. Bank deposits are counted also as part of the money holdings of the public. In the 19th century most economists regarded only currency and coin as "money," treating deposits only as claims to money. As deposits became more and more widely held, and as a larger fraction of transactions came to be effected by check, economists started to include not the checks, but the deposits they transferred, as money on a par with currency and coin.

The definition of money has been the subject of much dispute. The chief point at issue is which categories of bank deposits to call money and which to regard as near money. Many economists include as money only deposits transferable by check (demand deposits). Others include nonchecking deposits, such as "time deposits" or "current deposits" in commercial banks. Still others include deposits in other financial institutions, such as savings banks, savings and loan associations, and so on.

The term deposits is highly misleading. It connotes something deposited for safekeeping, like currency in a safe-deposit box. Bank deposits are not like that. When one brings currency to a bank for "deposit," the bank does not put the currency in a vault and keep it there. It may put a small fraction of the currency in the vault as "reserves," but it will lend most of it to someone else or buy an investment—that is, a bond or some other security. As part of the inducement to depositors to lend it money, it provides facilities for transferring demand deposits from one person to another by check.

The deposits of commercial banks are assets of their holders but liabilities of the banks. The assets of the banks consist of "reserves"—currency plus deposits at other banks—and "earning assets"—loans plus investments in the form of bonds and other securities. The reserves are only a small fraction of the aggregate deposits. Initially, in the history of banking, the amount of reserves held was determined by each bank separately in terms of its judgment of the likely demands on it. The growth of deposits enabled the total quantity of money (including deposits) to be larger than the total sum available to be held as reserves. A bank that received, say, $100 in gold might add $25 to its reserves and lend out $75. But the recipient of the $75 loan would spend it. Some of those who received gold this way would hold it as gold, but others would deposit it in this or in other banks. If, for example, two-thirds was redeposited, some bank or banks would find $50 added to deposits and to reserves and would repeat the process, adding $12½ to its reserves and lending out $37½. When this process worked itself out fully, total deposits would have increased by $200, bank reserves would have increased by $50, and $50 of the initial $100 deposited would have been retained as "currency outside banks." There would be $150 more money in total than before (deposits up by $200, currency outside banks down by $50). Although no individual bank created money, the system as a whole did. This multiple expansion process lies at the heart of the modern monetary system.

Central banking. An important part of the monetary system is the central bank. The Bank of England was the first modern central bank, serving as the model for many others. It was established as a private bank in 1694 but quickly came to be largely an agency of the government. The Bank of France was established as a governmental institution by Napoleon in 1800. In the United States, the 12 Federal Reserve Banks, which, together with the Board of Governors in Washington, D.C., constitute the Federal Reserve System, are technically owned by their member commercial banks, but this is a pure formality. Member banks get only a fixed annual percentage dividend on their stock and have essentially no real power. To all intents and purposes, the system is a governmental agency.

High-powered money

The notes issued by a central bank (or other governmental agency) plus deposits at the central bank are often called high-powered money, because when held as bank reserves each dollar or pound or franc may correspond to several dollars or pounds or francs of commercial bank deposits. Generally speaking, there is now no formal limit to the amount of notes and deposits that a central bank may have as liabilities.

The way in which a central bank increases or decreases the total amount of high-powered money is, typically, by making loans (discounting) or by buying and selling government securities (open-market operations). If, for example, the Federal Reserve System purchases $1,000,000 of government securities, it will pay for these securities by a check on itself, adding $1,000,000 to its assets and $1,000,000 to its liabilities. The seller can take the check to a Federal Reserve Bank, which will exchange for it $1,000,000 in Federal Reserve Notes. Or the seller may deposit the check at a commercial bank, and the bank will in turn present it to a Federal Reserve Bank, which will "pay" the check by making a book entry increasing that bank's deposits with it by $1,000,000. The bank may, in turn, transfer this sum to a borrower, who again will convert it into Federal Reserve Notes or deposit it.

The important point is that these bookkeeping operations simply record a process whereby the central bank has created, out of thin air as it were, additional high-powered money—the direct counterpart of printing Federal Reserve Notes. Similarly, if the central bank sells government securities, it destroys high-powered money. (See also GOVERNMENT FINANCE: *Tools of monetary policy.*)

In addition to the high-powered money of the central bank, the total quantity of money at any given time depends on the preferences of the public as to the relative amounts of money it wishes to hold as currency and as deposits and on the preferences of the banks as to the ratio they wish to maintain between their reserves and their deposits. (The reserve ratio is, of course, dominated by legal reserve requirements, where they exist, but may vary somewhat as banks think it prudent to keep a larger or smaller cushion in excess of required reserves.)

It follows that, by controlling the amount of high-powered money and by other, less important means, a central bank can vary the total quantity of money as it wishes within broad limits. The major problem of modern monetary policy is how the central bank should use this power.

MONETARY THEORIES

The relation between money and what it will buy has always been a central issue of monetary theory. Economists have generally held that the level of prices is determined by the quantity of money. But precisely how the quantity of money affects the level of prices, and what the effects are of changes in the quantity of money, have been conceptualized in different ways at different times. For an interval of two or three decades, from the mid-1930s to the mid-1960s, there was a widespread rejection of the quantity theory by professional economists. More recently, there has been something of a counterrevolution involving a partial return to and modification of earlier views. The following discussion of monetary theory will therefore deal first with the quantity theory of money, as it developed before the 1930s, then with the Keynesian revolution, and finally with the recent counterrevolution.

The quantity theory of money. In whatever way it has been formulated, the quantity theory of money has involved a distinction between the nominal quantity of money and the real quantity of money. The nominal quantity is that expressed in whatever units are used to designate money—talents, shekels, pounds, francs, lire, drachmas, dollars, yen, and so on. The real quantity is that expressed in terms of the volume of goods and services that the money will purchase. The quantity theory assumes that what ultimately matters to holders of money is the real rather than the nominal quantity. If this is so, then—whatever factors may determine the nominal quantity of money—it is the holders of money who determine the real quantity and, in the process, the price level.

Nominal and real quantities

The following may be considered a hypothetical example. In a certain community the quantity of money in existence is $1,000,000, and the total income of the community is $10,000,000 a year. On the average, each member of the community holds an amount of money equal in value to one-tenth of a year's income, or to 5.2 weeks' income. Put differently, the income velocity of circulation is equal to 10 per year; that is, each $1 on the average is paid out 10 times a year. For the sake of simplicity there are no business enterprises; the members of the community buy and sell services from and to one another.

The quantity of money is somehow then doubled, but in such a way that no one expects the quantity to change again. Each member of the community will regard himself as better off. Each now has 10.4 weeks' income in the form of cash instead of the previous 5.2 weeks'. If everyone were to hold onto the extra cash, nothing further would happen. But people will try to spend it. One person's spending, however, is another's receipts. All the people together cannot spend more than all the people receive. The attempt of each to do so is bound to be frustrated. In the attempt to spend more than they receive, people will simultaneously try to buy more of various services from each other and to sell less. To induce others to sell, they will offer higher prices; to induce others not to buy, they will ask higher prices. Whether the quantity sold goes up or down depends on whether the attempt to buy more is stronger or weaker than the attempt to sell less. But in either case total spending is sure to go up and so are total income and prices paid. When income has doubled, to $20,000,000, the amount of money in existence will again be equal in value to 5.2 weeks' income. The community will have succeeded in reducing its real cash balances to their former level, not by reducing nominal balances but by raising incomes and prices. The process of adjustment may not be smooth; spending may go too far and leave people with real balances that are too small, requiring a subsequent fall in the price level; but the final position will tend toward a doubling of prices, and the previous real flows of services will be resumed with no one any better off than before the new money was distributed.

This simple example embodies most of the basic principles of monetary theory: (1) the central distinction between the nominal and the real quantity of money; (2) the equally crucial contrast between the alternatives open to the individual and to the community as a whole. To each individual separately (in the hypothetical example and in the real world) it looks as if income is outside personal control, but each individual can determine how much cash to hold. To the community as a whole, the total amount of cash is fixed, but it is able to determine the size of its income in dollars; (3) the importance of attempts. The attempt of people as a whole to spend more than they receive, even though doomed to frustration, has the effect of raising total nominal expenditures and receipts.

Quantity equations. A useful device for clarifying the variables stressed in the quantity theory is the so-called quantity equation. The quantity equation has taken different forms according as quantity theorists have stressed different variables. The most famous is the so-called transactions version:

The transactions equation

$$MV = PT. \quad (1)$$

This version starts with the identity that any transaction has two sides: an amount of money paid and a corresponding quantity transferred at a certain price—for example, $20 paid for two books at $10 each. The left side of the equation sums up the amount of money paid out; the right side, the value of the transaction. Generalized to the whole economy, the left side of the equation becomes the amount of money in existence (M) multiplied by the average number of times per year (or other unit of time) that each dollar is used in effecting a transaction—the transaction velocity of circulation (V). The right side of the equation then becomes the product of an average price (P) times an aggregate quantity of goods (T).

In this version, all transactions of whatever kind are included—purchases of securities along with purchases of restaurant meals, purchases of the food ingredients by the restaurant as well as of the final meals. The inclusion of capital as well as current transactions, and of intermediate as well as final goods, makes the concepts of total transactions (T) and the "general price level" (P) highly ambiguous and difficult to handle statistically. The emergence of national income accounting in recent decades has led to the substitution of an income version of the quantity equation:

$$MV = Py. \quad (2)$$

In this equation y represents national income in constant prices (the total value at fixed prices of all final goods and services, including additions to the stock of capital), P is a price index, and V is the average number of times that the money stock is used for making income transactions (that is, payments for final goods and services, or alternately, for final productive services—services of labour, land, and so forth).

In both these equations the two sides are, by definition, precisely equal to one another—that is, each equation is an identity (like the equality of total assets and total liabilities on a double-entry balance sheet). In practice, the data on transactions or on income—the right sides of the equations—come from different statistical sources than do the data on the quantity of money, and only indirect data exist for velocity. As a consequence, when these equations are used to describe the real world, V is usually computed in such a way as to make the two sides equal, thus embodying all the statistical errors of the other terms.

These versions of the quantity equation emphasize the function of money as a medium of exchange—its use in making payments. But money also serves as a store of purchasing power in the interim between sale and purchase. This aspect is emphasized in the cash balance approach.

It has generally been supposed that the amount of money people will want to hold for this purpose bears some relation to their income. This leads to the equation

$$M = kPy, \quad (3)$$

in which M, P, and y are defined as in equation (2), and k is the ratio of money stock to income. Although equation (3) is simply a mathematical transformation of equation (2)—k being numerically equal to the reciprocal of V—it brings out the difference between the aspects of money stressed by the transactions approach and those stressed by the cash-balances approach.

In particular, the cash-balances approach fits in better with general economic analysis than does the transactions approach. Equation (3) can be regarded as describing the demand for money, with P and y being two of the variables on which the demand for money depends and with k symbolizing all the other variables. For completeness, the analysis requires another equation showing how the supply of money is determined. This approach provides a better bridge to the later Keynesian and more recent monetarist developments than does the transactions approach.

Uses of the equations. The purpose of the quantity equations is mainly to provide an analytical filing system to help sort out the forces at work. Their usefulness derives from the empirical hypothesis that each of the four main labels (M, V, P, and y for the income version) refers to a fairly distinct set of forces subject to influences that are different from those classified under another label.

Interpretation of the quantity equations

In its simplest form, the quantity theory regards output (y) as being determined by the productive opportunities of the community and its tastes and preferences; it regards the quantity of money (M) as being determined by the conditions of production of the monetary metal plus the characteristics of the financial and banking structure (for a commodity standard) or the decisions of the monetary authorities and the financial structure (for a fiat standard); it regards velocity (V) as being determined by payments practices, the financial and economic arrangements for effecting transactions, and the costs of and returns from holding money instead of other assets; and, finally, it regards the price level (P) as the variable that adjusts to reconcile the conditions of production determining y with the financial conditions determining M and V.

In the most rigid form of the quantity theory, velocity is seen as very stable. This view regards the level of prices as determined directly by changes in the quantity of money and as moving in strict proportion to the quantity of money. But the more sophisticated theorists never took this simplistic view. They all recognized that prices could not adjust instantaneously and fully and that, during so-called transition periods, changes in the quantity of money would affect output as well as prices. They also recognized that V was not a constant but itself a function of other variables, such as interest rates, and that it was subject to substantial random perturbations. As a result, they recognized that changes in output and prices could be produced in principle by independent changes in either V (the demand for money) or M (the supply of money).

On an analytical level the quantity theory of money is not the tautology of the equation; it is, rather, an analysis of the factors determining the quantity of money that the community wishes to hold. On an empirical level, it does not assume that V is constant; it holds that changes in the demand for money tend to proceed slowly and gradually or to be the result of events set in train by prior changes in supply, whereas, in contrast, substantial changes in the supply of nominal balances can and frequently do occur independently of any changes in demand. The conclusion is that substantial changes in prices or nominal income are almost invariably the result of changes in the nominal supply of money rather than of V.

An implication of the foregoing is that monetary policy—policy as to changes in the quantity of money—is the appropriate means for preventing inflation or deflation and for avoiding wide cyclical fluctuations.

The Keynesian critique. The groundwork for the Keynesian attack on the quantity theory was laid by two historical experiences. One was the British experience after the return to gold in 1925. In order to maintain the parity set for the pound in terms of gold, the Bank of England followed a consistently tight monetary policy. But prices did not move downward sufficiently, and there was persistent unemployment. This raised doubts about the allegedly classical postulate that money was only a veil, that total output was determined by real conditions, and that full employment was the "equilibrium," or normal, position. The second and even more dramatic experience was the Great Depression. Later study has shown that the severity of the Depression, certainly in the United States, can be attributed to bad monetary policy—a policy that permitted or forced the quantity of money to decline by one-third from 1929 to 1933. This was not known or understood at the time; on the contrary, the Federal Reserve authorities insisted that they were doing everything they could to offset the forces making for depression.

This stimulated the British economist John Maynard Keynes—who had been a highly sophisticated quantity theorist on strictly classical lines—to develop an alternative interpretation of the debacle after 1929 and an alternative prescription for policy. It also produced a sympathetic climate for his new theory, so that the Keynesian revolution swept the economics profession in a remarkably short time.

Keynes's interpretation. Keynes did not, of course, deny the validity of the quantity equation. What he maintained was very different: that the right-hand side—Py, or prices times output—was determined by forces largely independent of the left-hand side. P, he argued, was largely an institutional datum, linked to customary nominal rates of wages that were very resistant to change, or at least to decline. Real income or output, y, he argued, was determined by aggregate demand, which depended primarily on the amount of "autonomous spending"—that is, spending that was not linked directly to current income and that consisted mostly of investment expenditures by enterprises and spending by government. The rest of aggregate demand consisted mostly of consumption, which was linked closely to current income. On this view, the key factor determining the level of real income and output, and thereby the level of nominal income, was the strength of investment and of government spending.

How then could the quantity equation hold? Keynes's answer was that V was so pliable that it would adjust to keep the two sides equal. Let autonomous spending increase without a change in the quantity of money, and V would simply increase in response; let the quantity of money increase without an increase in autonomous spending, and V would decline to offset the increase in M.

In the extreme form of this approach—as much a caricature of Keynes's thinking as the attribution of a constant V is of his predecessors'—the quantity of money simply did not matter at all for the course of prices or real output but only for the movement of V.

Liquidity preference

How did Keynes explain the plasticity of V? He did so by means of a very special explanation of the demand for money, to which he applied the phrase "liquidity preference." He regarded the quantity of money demanded as divided into two parts, one part, M_1, "held to satisfy the transactions and precautionary-motives," the other, M_2, "held to satisfy the speculative-motive." He regarded M_1 as a roughly constant fraction of income, and with respect to this part he accepted a rather rigid form of the quantity theory. He regarded M_2, however, as largely independent of income and as highly sensitive to current interest rates and to the expectations of future interest rates. This explained the plasticity of V.

According to Keynes, if current interest rates are above the level many holders of money expect to prevail in the future, people will prefer to hold their speculative balances in bonds instead of money—because they expect a fall in interest rates, which means a rise in bond prices. Conversely, if current interest rates are below the level expected to prevail in the future, they will prefer to hold money. Over short periods, he argued, these expectations are widely and strongly held at about the same level. In the extreme, with everyone holding the same expectations and everyone sensitive, liquidity preference will become, as he termed it, absolute. Under such circumstances, let the monetary authorities try to increase the amount of money by buying bonds. This will tend to raise bond prices and lower interest rates, but even the slightest lowering will lead speculators to absorb the additional money and sell bonds. The result will be a lower V or a higher k for the community as a whole. The converse will hold if the authorities try to reduce the amount of money.

Alternatively, if nominal income rises, for whatever reason, without a change in the quantity of money, that will require an increase in M_1, but it can and will come out of M_2 without any further effects. The conclusion is that under circumstances of absolute liquidity preference income can change without a change in M or in interest rates, and M can change without a change in income or in interest rates. The holders of money are in metastable equilibrium, like a tumbler on its side on a flat surface; they will be satisfied with whatever the amount of money happens to be.

Liquidity and the interest rate

For the long run, Keynes regarded the size of M_2 as depending on the level of interest rates for a different reason. The interest rate measures the cost of holding money instead of bonds—it is the price, as Keynes put it, that the holder of money pays for retaining liquidity. If the interest rate is low, the cost of liquidity is low; hence people will hold a large fraction of their wealth in the form of money, and the fraction will be sensitive to small changes in the interest rate—liquidity preference being absolute in the long run as well as in the short run. If interest rates were high, and M_2 low—a condition that Keynes expected to hold only at times of full employment—then the quantity theory would "come into its own," in the double sense that velocity would be constant and that prices rather than output would respond to changes in the quantity of money.

Keynes himself regarded absolute liquidity preference as a strictly "limiting case"; while it "might become practically important in future," he knew "of no example . . . hitherto." In practice, however, he treated velocity as if its behaviour frequently approximated this limiting case, and his disciples went much further than he did.

If liquidity preference was not absolute, then in the Keynesian view a change in the quantity of money would first affect interest rates in order to induce the community to hold the changed quantity of money. This change in interest rates might in turn affect autonomous spending—a decline encouraging investment and a rise discouraging investment—and in this way aggregate demand, income, and employment. The more sensitive is the quantity of money demanded to interest rates, and the less sensitive is investment to interest rates, the smaller will be the final effect of changes in the quantity of money, and conversely.

Changing views. The Keynesian revolution swept the economics profession in the late 1930s and early 1940s; by the 1960s Keynesian ideas had become deeply embedded in the thinking of informed intellectuals. The course of events, however, did not follow the pattern that many had expected. Their analysis had predicted a great postwar depression if war spending was not replaced by other government spending. But government spending fell precipitously in the United States and elsewhere without ill effect. The analysis of the Keynesians had called for "cheap money" policies—that is, low interest rates—with a view to stimulating investment and thereby avoiding mass unemployment. Those policies proved in the main to be unnecessary; where they were adopted they were consistently followed by inflation that could be restrained only by abandoning the cheap-money policies. A reexamination of the Great Depression of the 1930s demonstrated that, contrary to general belief, it had been a tragic testament to the great power of monetary policy, not to its impotence. The U.S. Federal Reserve System could have prevented the decline of one-third in the quantity of money that occurred from 1929 to 1933. Had it done so, the evidence indicates, the Depression would have been far milder and briefer. Most important of all, extensive empirical research demonstrated that the velocity of circulation of money, far from moving to offset changes in the quantity of money, has generally moved in the same direction and reinforced the effect of these changes.

The monetarist view. The result has been a major change in the views of today's followers of Keynes. They attribute far more importance to the quantity of money than they earlier did, regarding the quantity of money demanded as less elastic with respect to interest rates, and investment as more elastic, than they did in the first flush of enthusiasm. Some economists have been waging a counterrevolution in the name of monetary policy, to which the name monetarism has become attached. This doctrine, although still probably a minority view among professional economists, has made significant gains and has influenced considerably the views even of those who still regard themselves as Keynesians.

No counterrevolution ever produces a return to the status quo. The monetarist doctrine has much in common with the quantity theory, but it has not expunged the Keynesian revolution. The Keynesian emphasis on the plasticity of velocity, for example, has led to extensive work on the stability of the demand for money, and in particular on the exploration of time lags between monetary changes and economic changes and on the separate effects of monetary changes on prices, output, and interest rates.

Key propositions. For the long run, monetarism accepts almost wholly the earlier quantity theory. Its main contribution to that theory is a much more detailed and sophisticated analysis of short-run effects and a more detailed set of empirical generalizations about these effects. The key propositions of monetarism are as follows:

1. The rate of growth of the quantity of money is consistently, though not precisely, related to the rate of growth of nominal income. That is, if the quantity of money grows rapidly, so will nominal income, and conversely. The velocity of circulation, though not constant, is fairly predictable.

2. This relation is not obvious, mainly because it takes time for changes in monetary growth to affect income.

The time factor in monetarist theory

3. On the average, a change in the rate of monetary growth produces a change in the rate of growth of nominal income six to nine months later. But this is an average.

4. If the rate of monetary growth is reduced, then about six to nine months later the rate of growth of nominal income and also of physical output will decline, but the rate of price rise will be affected very little. There will be downward pressure on prices only as a gap emerges between actual and potential output.

5. The effect on prices comes on the average about a year after the effect on nominal income and output, so that the total delay between a change in monetary growth and a change in the rate of inflation averages roughly two years.

6. The above relationships are not invariable. There is many a slip between the monetary change and the income change.

7. Monetary changes affect output only in the short run—though "short run" may mean five to 10 years. Over the longer run the earlier quantity theory seems to hold, and the rate of monetary growth affects only prices. What happens to output in the long run depends on such "real" factors as the enterprise, ingenuity, and industry of the people; the extent of thrift; the structure of industry and government; the relations among nations; and so on.

8. It follows that inflation is always and everywhere a monetary phenomenon, in the sense that it cannot occur without a more rapid increase in the quantity of money than in output. There are, of course, many possible reasons for monetary growth—gold discoveries, the manner in which government spending is financed, and even the manner in which private spending is financed.

9. Government spending may or may not be inflationary. It will be inflationary if it is financed by creating money—that is, by printing currency or creating bank deposits—and if the resultant rate of monetary growth exceeds the rate of growth of output. If it is financed by taxes or by borrowing from the public, the main effect is that the government spends the funds instead of someone else.

10. One of the most difficult things to explain is the way in which a change in the quantity of money affects income. Generally, the initial effect is not on income at all but on the prices of existing assets (bonds, equities, houses, and other physical capital). This is the liquidity effect stressed by Keynes; it occurs on the balance sheet, not on the income account. An increased rate of monetary growth raises the amount of cash people (or businesses) have relative to other assets. The holders of the excess cash will try to correct this imbalance by buying other assets. But one person's spending is another's receipts. All the people together cannot change the amount of cash all hold—only the monetary authorities can do that. Their attempts will tend, however, to raise the prices of assets and to reduce interest rates. These changes will in turn encourage spending to produce new assets. Thus the initial effect on balance sheets is translated into an effect on income and spending. In this connection the monetarists stress a far wider range of assets and interest rates than do the Keynesians; they emphasize such assets as durable consumer goods and other real property, and they regard market interest rates as only a small part of the whole complex of relevant rates.

11. One important feature of this mechanism is that a change in monetary growth affects interest rates in one direction at the outset and in the opposite direction later on. More rapid monetary growth at first tends to lower interest rates. But later on, as it raises spending and stimulates price inflation, it also produces a rise in the demand for loans that will tend to raise interest rates. Taking the opposite case, a slower rate of monetary growth at first raises interest rates, but later on, as it reduces spending and price inflation, it lowers interest rates. This inconsistent relation between the quantity of money and interest rates explains why monetarists insist that interest rates are not a good guide to monetary policy.

12. These propositions clearly imply that monetary policy is important and that what is important about monetary policy is its effect on the quantity of money, not on bank credit or total credit or interest rates. Wide swings in the rate of change of the quantity of money are evidently destabilizing and should be avoided. Beyond this, different monetarists draw different conclusions. Some conclude that the monetary authorities should make deliberate changes in the rate of monetary growth in order to offset other forces making for instability; these changes should be gradual and small and make allowance for the lags involved. Others maintain that not enough is known about the relations between changes in the quantity of money and in prices and output to assure that a discretionary monetary policy will do good rather than harm. They believe that a wiser policy would be simply to have the quantity of money grow at a steady rate over time.

Monetary prescriptions

Conclusion. No other subject in economics has been studied longer or more intensively than the subject of money. The result is a vast amount of documented experience and a well-developed body of theoretical analysis. The extent to which the students of monetary problems agree in their basic conclusions is concealed by the tendency of laymen to exaggerate their differences. But even among professional economists there remain important disagreements, centring mainly on empirical judgments about the stability and form of some of the relations between money and other economic magnitudes.

BIBLIOGRAPHY. Works on various aspects of monetary history include: PHILLIP CAGAN, "The Monetary Dynamics of Hyperinflation," in MILTON FRIEDMAN (ed.), *Studies in the Quantity Theory of Money* (1956); RUPERT J. EDERER, *The Evolution of Money* (1964); PAUL EINZIG, *Primitive Money in Its Ethnological, Historical, and Economic Aspects,* 2nd ed. rev. (1966); ALBERT E. FEAVEARYEAR, *The Pound Sterling: A History of English Money,* 2nd ed. (1963); MILTON FRIEDMAN and ANNA J. SCHWARTZ, *A Monetary History of the United States, 1867–1960* (1963, reissued 1971), and *Monetary Trends in the United States and the United Kingdom* (1982); ELGIN E. GROSECLOSE, *Money: The Human Conflict* (1934); EARL J. HAMILTON, *American Treasure and the Price Revolution in Spain, 1501–1650* (1934, reprinted 1977); HENRY C. WALLICH, *Monetary Policy and Practice* (1982), articles on a variety of monetary topics by a former member of the Board of Governors of the Federal Reserve System.

Useful readings in monetary theory, of varying levels of difficulty, include: WALTER EUCKEN, *This Unsuccessful Age* (1952); ROBERT J. GORDON (ed.), *Milton Friedman's Monetary Framework* (1974); JOHN G. GURLEY and EDWARD S. SHAW, *Money in a Theory of Finance* (1960); HARRY G. JOHNSON, *Essays in Monetary Economics,* 2nd ed. (1969); JOHN MAYNARD KEYNES, *A Treatise on Money,* 2 vol. (1930, reprinted 1976), and *The General Theory of Employment, Interest and Money* (1936, reprinted 1973); DON PATINKIN, *Money, Interest, and Prices: An Integration of Monetary and Value Theory,* 2nd ed. (1965); and DENNIS HOLME ROBERTSON, *Money,* 4th ed. (1956).

(M.Fr.)

Mongolia

Mongolia, the homeland of the Mongols, is now largely within the Mongolian People's Republic (Mongol: Bügd Nayramdah Mongol Ard Uls), although a large number of Mongols live in parts of China and the Soviet Union. The Mongolian People's Republic has an area of 604,000 square miles (1,565,000 square kilometres). Its shape is that of an elongated oval, measuring 1,486 miles (2,392 kilometres) from west to east and, at its maximum, 782 miles from north to south. Mongolia is bounded on the north by the Soviet Union, which accounts for about two-fifths of the total boundary, and on the south by China.

A landlocked country deep in the interior of eastern Asia, Mongolia has a marked continental climate, with long, cold winters and short, cool to hot summers. Its remarkable variety of scenery consists largely of upland steppes, semideserts, and deserts, although in the west and north forested, high mountain ranges alternate with dry, lake-dotted basins. Mongolia is highland country, with an average altitude of 5,200 feet (1,580 metres) above sea level. The highest peaks are in the Mongol Altai Mountains, of which Hüyten (Khuitun) Peak (also called Nayramdal Peak; 14,350 feet [4,374 metres]), at the western tip of the country, is Mongolia's highest point.

Nearly four-fifths of Mongolia's area consists of pasturelands, which support immense herds of grazing livestock; the remaining area is about equally divided between forests and barren deserts, with only a tiny fraction of the land in crops. Mongolia has one of the lowest population densities of any country in the world, although since the 1950s the country has had one of Asia's highest rates of natural increase.

The Mongols have a long prehistory and a most remarkable history. Their ancestors were the Huns, who lived in Central Asia from the 3rd to the 1st century BC. A single Mongolian feudal state eventually was formed in the early 13th century AD from nomadic tribal groupings. Its leader, Genghis Khan, and his successors in the 13th century controlled a vast empire that included much of China, Russia, and Central Asia. Because of its location between China and Russia, Mongolia subsequently was dominated first by one and then the other, but mainly by the Chinese (1691–1921). Damdiny Sühbaatar, modern Mongolia's national hero, was influenced by the October Revolution (1917) in Russia and later, with Soviet assistance, drove out both the White Russians and the Chinese. Sühbaatar's forces achieved power on July 11, 1921, traditionally the founding date of the present state. The Mongolian People's Republic was officially proclaimed on Nov. 26, 1924, with its capital at Ulaanbaatar ("Red Hero").

Since its independence from China in 1921, the Mongolian People's Republic has been closely allied with the Soviet Union. It has received technical, economic, and military assistance from the Soviet Union and other members of the Council for Mutual Economic Assistance (Comecon). Mongolia generally has followed Soviet guidance in political matters, both domestic and international. In 1990 the government agreed to several changes and reforms, including the holding of multiparty elections in July. These elections reaffirmed the position of the ruling Mongolian People's Revolutionary Party.

Although the Mongols traditionally have been nomadic herdsmen, they are becoming increasingly sedentary and even urban. By the late 20th century more than half the population lived in cities, one-fourth in Ulaanbaatar. Symbolic of profound changes in culture and society was the replacement in the 1940s of the traditional Mongolian alphabet by a new one based on the Cyrillic letters of the Russian alphabet. (C.D.H.)

This article is divided into the following sections:

Physical and human geography

THE LAND

Relief. Mongolia can be divided into three major topographic zones: the fingerlike mountain ridges that thrust into the northern and western areas, the basin areas that lie between and around them, and the enormous upland plateau belt that sweeps across the southern and eastern sectors. The entire country is prone to seismic movements, with some earthquakes reaching extreme limits of severity; their effects, however, are diminished by the low population density.

The mountains. The present relief is the result of geologically recent upheavals of the Alpine mountain-building period. There are three major mountain belts. The highest and the longest spine of mountains is the westernmost, the Altai, which sweeps in from the northwestern tip of the country and thrusts toward the southeast for 1,000 miles. The main range—the only one in the country where contemporary glaciation has developed—is the Mongolian Altai Mountains, and a lesser range splitting off to the southeast is known as the Gobi Altai Mountains. The southeastern extremities of the main range also split into a number of smaller hills, all following the same general trend, losing themselves in the expanses of the Gobi.

The three major mountain belts

The Hangayn (Khangai) Mountains, also trending northwest to southeast, form a solid mountain mass near the centre of the republic, with peaks towering to more than 12,000 feet. A characteristic feature is the gentle slopes and crests, often covered with fine pastures. The higher central portions are nevertheless rugged and precipitous. To the far north, the Hövsgöl (Khubsugal) Mountains, adjoining the vast Sayan Mountains of Siberia that curve away beyond the Soviet border, have a similar topography.

The third mountain block, the smaller and lower Hentiyn (Khentei) range, trends southwest to northeast of Ulaanbaatar; it reaches a maximum height of about 9,200 feet, but in general its elevation is between 6,000 and 8,000 feet. Ulaanbaatar lies at the southwestern base of the range. The enormous Greater Khingan Range rises along and beyond the eastern frontier with China.

The northern intermontane basins. Around and between the main ranges mentioned above lie an important series of basins. In the northwest of the country, tucked between the Altai, the Hangayn, and the mountains of the Soviet frontier, lies a scenic basin complex known as the Great Lakes region, in which are strewn more than 300 lakes. Another basin complex lies between the eastern slopes of the Hangayn Mountains and the western foothills of the Hentiyn Mountains. The southern portion (the basins of the Tuul and Orhon rivers) is a fertile region important in Mongolian history as the cradle of settled ways of life. Its landscapes are strewn with the ruins of numerous ancient communities.

Farther north, on the northern flanks of the Hangayn Mountains, lies the remarkable Khorgo region, in which as many as a dozen extinct volcanoes and numerous volcanic lakes are found in a small area. Swift and turbulent rivers have cut jagged gorges. The source stream of the Orhon River is in another volcanic region, with a cluster of lakes, deep volcanic vents, and hot springs, and there is a constant roar from the stream, almost invisible in its deep gorge. Near the northern border, Lake Hövsgöl is the focus of another rugged, lake-strewn region, noted for its huge subterranean caves.

The plateau and desert belt. The eastern part of Mongolia has a rolling topography of hilly steppe plains, supplanted in the extreme east by clusters of small, flat plains lying at altitudes of 2,000 to 2,300 feet. Here and there, small, stubby massifs contain the clearly discernible cones of extinct volcanoes. The Dariganga area of Mongolia's eastern tip contains some 220 such extinct volcanoes. Most of the southern part of the country is a vast rolling oasis-dotted plain, forming the northern fringe of the Gobi, which is predominantly stony. The flat relief is occasionally broken by low, heavily eroded ranges. Several spectacular natural features are found in the Gobi region. Huge, six-sided basalt columns, arranged in clusters resembling bundles of pencils, are found in the eastern and central regions. The southern Gobi contains three mountain ranges, known as the Gurvan Sayhan Mountains, and the scenic Yelyn Valley, now a national park, with deep gorges surrounded by towering rocky cliffs where condors have made their nests.

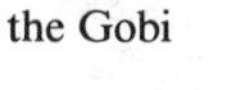
Features of the Gobi

Drainage. Mongolia lies on a continental divide: rivers in the north flow northward into the Arctic Ocean, and those in the northeast flow eastward into the Pacific. The western and southern two-thirds of the country consist of interior drainage basins, in which seasonal or intermittent streams end in salt lakes or disappear into the stones and sands of the desert. In the northern regions the turbulent mountain streams and small rivers merge into deep, well-developed rivers. In the southern areas—where there are only a few constantly flowing rivers—lakes, saltwater and freshwater springs, and wells draw on subterranean water supplies. The great divide, separating waters that flow into the oceans and into the interior basins, runs along the crest of the Hangayn Mountains. Mongolia's greatest river, the Selenge (Selenga), with its main tributary, the Orhon, drains northward across the Soviet border and into Lake Baikal; the Mongolian portion of the Selenge Valley is in the north-central portion of the country. Mongolia's other major rivers, the Onon and the Kerulen, run latitudinally across the eastern part of the country. The largest rivers draining into the interior are the Hovd (Kobdo), which rises from the glaciers of the Mongolian Altai Mountains, and the Dzavhan, which drains the southern slopes of the Hangayn Mountains; both flow into the Great Lakes region. A series of other rivers east of the Dzavhan run down from the southern flanks of the Hangayn, ending in salt lakes or disappearing in the Gobi expanses. Generally, the Mongolian rivers are swift and with a steep gradient, offering hydroelectric potential, as well as occasional flood dangers.

Mongolia has more than 3,000 lakes with areas of half a square mile or more. Many are salty, ephemeral, highly variable in area, and without outlets. The largest and deepest freshwater lake, Hövsgöl, occupies a structural depression in the northernmost part of the country. Other large lakes—all in the west—include the saline Lake Uvs, which is nearly 1,300 square miles in area, and the freshwater Lake Har Us, which drains into the saline Lake Hyargas. Many lakes are of volcanic origin, as is Lake Terhiyn Tsagaan on the Hangayn's northern slopes. A thick layer of lava once blocked the waters of the Terhiyn River to form this lake. A small island in the lake is a bird sanctuary. Mongolia also has a number of medicinal springs, one of the best known being associated with Hatan Hayrhan, a heart-shaped massif in the western Gobi. The spring flows from a crevice in the side of the formation and has, over the centuries, worn several deep basins that are known locally as the Kettles of Hatan Hayrhan.

Volcanic lakes

M. Koene/H. Armstrong Roberts

Orhon River, north-central Mongolia.

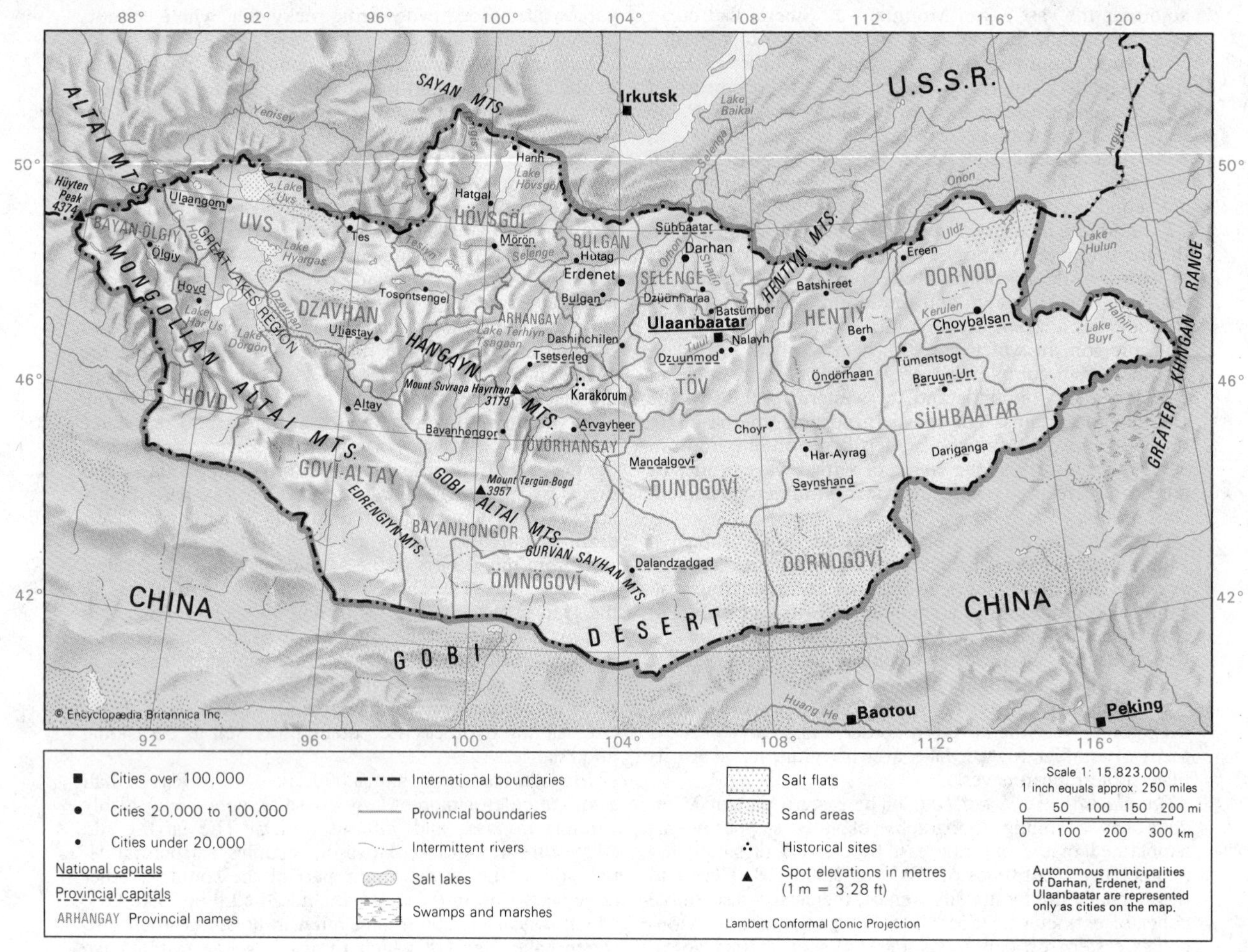

MAP INDEX

Political subdivisions

Arhangay . . . . . . 48 00 N 101 30 E
Bayan-Ölgiy . . . . 48 30 N 90 00 E
Bayanhongor . . . . 45 30 N 99 30 E
Bulgan . . . . 49 00 N 103 30 E
Darhan
  Municipality . . . . 49 29 N 105 55 E
Dornod . . . . 48 00 N 115 00 E
Dornogovi . . . . . . 44 30 N 110 00 E
Dundgovi . . . . . . 45 30 N 106 30 E
Dzavhan . . . . 48 00 N 96 00 E
Erdenet
  Municipality . . . . 49 02 N 104 05 E
Govi-Altay . . . . . . 45 00 N 96 00 E
Hentiy . . . . 48 00 N 110 30 E
Hovd . . . . 47 00 N 92 30 E
Hövsgöl . . . . 50 00 N 100 00 E
Ömnögovi . . . . . . 43 00 N 104 00 E
Övörhangay . . . . 46 00 N 102 30 E
Selenge . . . . 49 30 N 106 30 E
Sühbaatar . . . . . . 46 15 N 113 30 E
Töv . . . . 47 30 N 106 30 E
Ulaanbaatar
  Municipality . . . . 47 55 N 106 53 E
Uvs . . . . 49 30 N 93 00 E

Cities and towns

Altay . . . . 46 20 N 96 18 E
Arvayheer . . . . . . 46 15 N 102 48 E
Baruun-Urt . . . . . 46 42 N 113 15 E
Batshireet . . . . . . 48 40 N 110 08 E
Batsümber . . . . . 48 25 N 106 42 E
Bayan Tumen,
  see Choybalsan
Bayanhongor . . . . 46 08 N 100 43 E
Berh . . . . 47 45 N 111 07 E
Bulgan . . . . 48 45 N 103 34 E
Choybalsan
  (Bayan Tumen) . 48 04 N 114 30 E
Choyr . . . . 46 20 N 108 20 E
Dalandzadgad . . . 43 34 N 104 25 E
Darhan . . . . 49 29 N 105 55 E
Dariganga . . . . . . 45 18 N 113 52 E
Dashinchilen . . . . 47 51 N 104 03 E
Dzüünharaa . . . . . 48 52 N 106 28 E
Dzuunmod . . . . . 47 45 N 106 55 E
Erdenet . . . . 49 02 N 104 05 E
Ereen . . . . 49 15 N 112 29 E
Hanh . . . . 51 30 N 100 40 E
Har-Ayrag . . . . . . 45 49 N 109 17 E
Hatgal . . . . 50 26 N 100 09 E
Hovd (Jirgalanta) . 48 01 N 91 38 E
Hutag . . . . 49 23 N 102 43 E
Jirgalanta,
  see Hovd
Mandalgovi . . . . . 45 45 N 106 12 E
Mörön . . . . 49 38 N 100 10 E
Nalayh . . . . 47 45 N 107 16 E
Ölgiy . . . . 48 56 N 89 57 E
Öndörhaan
  (Tsetsen Khan) . 47 19 N 110 39 E
Saynshand . . . . . 44 52 N 110 09 E
Sühbaatar . . . . . . 50 15 N 106 12 E
Tes . . . . 49 41 N 95 48 E
Tosontsengel . . . 48 47 N 98 15 E
Tsetsen Khan,
  see Öndörhaan
Tsetserleg . . . . . 47 30 N 101 27 E
Tümentsogt . . . . 47 27 N 112 15 E
Ulaanbaatar . . . . 47 55 N 106 53 E
Ulaangom . . . . . . 49 58 N 92 02 E
Uliastay . . . . 47 45 N 96 49 E

Physical features and points of interest

Altai Mountains . . 50 00 N 90 00 E
Buyr, Lake . . . . . 47 48 N 117 42 E
Dörgön, Lake . . . 47 40 N 93 30 E
Dzavhan, *river* . . . 48 54 N 93 23 E
Edrengiyn
  Mountains . . . . . 44 15 N 97 45 E
Gobi Altai
  (Govi Altayn)
  Mountains . . . . 44 00 N 102 00 E
Gobi Desert . . . . 44 00 N 105 00 E
Great Lakes
  Region . . . . 48 00 N 93 00 E
Gurvan Sayhan
  Mountains . . . . . 43 50 N 103 30 E
Halhin, *river* . . . . . 47 55 N 117 47 E
Hangayn
  Mountains . . . . . 47 30 N 100 00 E
Har Horin,
  see Karakorum
Har Us, Lake . . . . 48 00 N 92 10 E
Hentiyn
  Mountains . . . . . 48 30 N 108 30 E
Hovd, *river* . . . . . 48 06 N 92 11 E
Hövsgöl, Lake . . . 51 00 N 100 30 E
Hüyten Peak
  (Nayramdal
  Peak) . . . . 49 09 N 87 47 E
Hyargas, Lake . . . 49 12 N 93 24 E
Karakorum (Har
  Horin), *historical
  site* . . . . 47 14 N 102 50 E
Kerulen, *river* . . . . 48 48 N 117 00 E
Mongolian Altai
  Mountains . . . . . 46 30 N 93 00 E
Nayramdal Peak,
  see Hüyten Peak
Onon, *river* . . . . . 51 42 N 115 50 E
Orhon, *river* . . . . . 50 21 N 106 05 E
Selenge
  (Selenga), *river* . 52 16 N 106 16 E
Sharin, *river* . . . . . 49 52 N 106 07 E
Suvraga
  Havrhan, Mount . 46 50 N 101 05 E
Tengis, *river* . . . . 51 27 N 99 02 E
Tergün-Bogd,
  Mount . . . . 44 55 N 100 18 E
Terhiyn Tsagaan,
  Lake . . . . 48 10 N 99 42 E
Tesiyn, *river* . . . . 50 28 N 93 04 E
Tuul, *river* . . . . . . 48 57 N 104 48 E
Uldz, *river* . . . . . . 49 56 N 115 31 E
Uvs, Lake . . . . . . 50 20 N 92 45 E

Climate. Mongolia is situated at high latitudes, far from the moderating influences of any ocean, and much of the land is at high altitude. As such, the country experiences a marked continental climate, with cold winters, cool to hot summers, considerable annual and diurnal ranges in temperature, and generally scanty rainfall. Weather is often unpredictable. Sudden downpours in the summer months can occasion severe flooding, and spring meltwater can also swell the rivers; the spring ice run on the Tengis River, which flows through the Hövsgöl area, is an awesome spectacle, with its thunderous cannonading of breaking ice swept down through gorges by the pressure of meltwater. Heavy snow occurs only in the mountain regions, but fierce blizzards of almost indescribable severity can sweep across the steppes, and even a thin coating of snow can prevent animals from getting at their pasture. Sand or hail storms may spring up almost without warning.

A remarkable feature of Mongolia's climate is the number of clear, sunny days, averaging between 220 and 260 each year; even more striking, however, are the great ranges of temperature that occur. The difference between the mean temperatures of January and July can reach 80° F (44° C), and temperature variations of as much as 55° F (30° C) can occur in a single day. Mean temperatures in the north generally are cooler than those in the south: the mean January and July temperatures for the Ulaanbaatar area are −15° F (−26° C) and 63° F (17° C), respectively, while the corresponding temperatures for the Gobi area are 0° F (−18° C) and 73° F (23° C).

Precipitation increases with altitude and latitude, with annual amounts ranging from less than four inches (100 millimetres) in some of the low-lying desert areas of the south and west to about 14 inches in the northern mountains; Ulaanbaatar receives about nine inches annually. The precipitation, which typically occurs as thunderstorms during the summer months, is highly variable in amount and timing and fluctuates considerably from year to year. (Sh.Ts./C.D.H.)

Plant and animal life. *Vegetation zones.* Climatic conditions are reflected in soil and vegetation patterns. Soils are predominantly of the chestnut or brown type, but with considerable salinization in desert and semidesert areas. Latitudinal and altitudinal belts of vegetation, often changing rapidly over a few miles, are probably the most obvious feature of the local Mongolian landscape. There are four basic divisions running in latitude from north to south and in altitude from the mountains to the basins and plains: forest–steppe, steppe, semidesert, and desert. In addition, the higher mountains have bands of coniferous forest (taiga) and higher yet an alpine zone. The steppes (grasslands) predominate, covering more than three-quarters of the national territory.

The importance of latitudinal and altitudinal belts

The mountain forest–steppe zone exhibits the richest diversity of plant and animal life. Forests grow thickest on the northern shady slopes, the most widely distributed tree being the Siberian larch, followed by the cedar, with a varying admixture of spruce, pine, and fir. Deciduous trees include the birch, aspen, and poplar. Steppe vegetation is found in the intermontane basins, the wide river valleys, and the sunny southern flanks of the mountains. These huge expanses of pastureland are covered with feather grass, couch grass, wormwood, and many fodder plant species. In summer the steppes are carpeted with a magnificent covering of bright violet, blue, red, and yellow flowers. On the highest mountain slopes the damp, dark taiga gives way to the thin grasses and occasional flowers of the alpine zone, merging into the bare rocks and rugged glaciers of the summit zone.

Semideserts are found in the Great Lakes intermontane depression in the west and over the Gobi in the south, giving way to true desert conditions near the southern border. Vegetation is scarce there but heavy enough to feed camels, goats, and sheep. Tracts of saxaul (xerophytic vegetation adapted to very dry conditions) and groves of elm and poplars cluster around springs or other underground water sources. The Gobi is a typical hammada, or rock-floored desert with gravel cover; only the extreme east has small areas of sandy desert.

Animal life. The varied natural conditions, the interior location, and the sparse human population of Mongolia all contribute to a rich and diverse wildlife that has attracted international attention and has great commercial importance. Lying on the borders of several distinct zoogeographic regions (the Tibetan, the Afghano-Turkistani, the Siberian, and the North-Chinese-Manchurian), the country has a fauna combining species from each of them. The northern forests harbour lynx, maral (Asiatic red deer), elk, roe deer, musk deer, brown bears, snow leopards, wolverines, wild boars, squirrels, and sables. The steppes are the home of, among others, the marmot—whose pelts are important economically—and the lithe Mongolian gazelle. Clustering around water holes in the semidesert and desert region may be found the wild sheep known as *argal,* Asiatic wild asses (*kulans*), wild horses (*takhs*), wild camels (*khavtgays*), and the Gobi bear (*mazalai*); some of these species are extremely rare and found nowhere else in Asia. Domesticated animals include sheep, camels, cattle, the hairy highland yak, goats, dogs, and the famous Mongolian horses. Bird life includes larks, partridges, cranes, pheasants, bustards, and falcons in the steppes; geese, ducks, gulls, pelicans, swans, and cormorants in the rivers and lakes; the snowy owl, the golden eagle, and the condor, which frequent some areas. The freshwater lakes and rivers harbour some 70 fish species, including salmon, trout, grayling, perch, and pike. Hunting and fishing, for sport and for commercial purposes, are important; but the government has introduced stringent hunting regulations and other conservationist measures, including the establishment of national parks and nature reserves. (D.Ba./O.Sh./C.D.H.)

Settlement patterns. The hand of man has long been in evidence in this part of what is sometimes called High Asia; and the ruins of long-abandoned cities, as well as archaeological remains dating back to the earliest days of prehistory, have attracted the attention of Mongolian and international scholars. Settlement in modern Mongolia is characterized by sharp regional contrasts: in the better-watered northern basins of the Orhon and Selenga rivers, densities of population may reach 10 persons per square mile (four per square kilometre), but some desert areas are devoid of inhabitants. The core of habitation lies in the north-central area between Ulaanbaatar and Sühbaatar. There are found the richest pastures, the main crop area, the largest cities, the most industrial establishments, and the best transportation.

Rural patterns. The huge rural areas of the country have their own charm. A feature distinctive of the countryside is the yurt, or *ger,* the traditional Mongolian dwelling. It is a cone-shaped, latticed structure, light, strong, and easy to assemble, transport, and reerect, which offers warmth in winter and coolness in summer. It is still used by herdsmen moving from pasture to pasture, and the clusters of white felt-and-canvas cones against a green background still dominate the landscape in many areas. As the nomadic population becomes more settled, however, the yurt clusters are becoming associated with

The yurt

M. Koene/H. Armstrong Roberts

Settlement of felt-and-canvas yurts, Mongolia.

cooperatives and state farms, often at centres with more permanent dwellings.

Urban patterns. It is in the cities, however, that Mongolia presents its modern aspect. Cities grew rapidly in the second half of the 20th century, increasing their proportion of the total population from about one-quarter in 1950 to one-half by 1980. Ulaanbaatar is by far the largest and most important urban centre. It lies on the banks of the Tuul River in the north-central portion of Mongolia. Formerly known among Europeans as Urga, it was originally a nomadic princely residence and became settled on the present site in 1639. The old city—which numbered some 60,000 people in 1921—consisted mainly of monasteries, a few adobe structures, and clusters of yurts. By the late 20th century, however, the "city of felt" had been transformed into a modern city, with broad avenues and streets, apartment complexes, and massive governmental, cultural, and educational buildings. The yurt areas and the fenced-off small houses had become a diminishing feature of the peripheral regions. Two other important cities, Darhan and Sühbaatar, lie between Ulaanbaatar and Mongolia's northern border. The city of Darhan is a spectacular example of planned urbanization. Its foundation stone was laid in 1961 in an existing settlement of about 1,500 people, and within 20 years the population exceeded 50,000. The new city became the centre of a major industrial complex, second only to Ulaanbaatar itself. Sühbaatar, founded in 1937, is a transportation and trade centre located at the confluence of the Orhon and Selenge rivers and on the Trans-Mongolian Railway near the Soviet border. Other industrial centres include Choybalsan, on the Kerulen River in the northeast, and Erdenet, located west of Darhan.

Growth of Darhan

THE PEOPLE

Ethnic and religious background. Anthropologically, the Mongols are quite homogeneous, belonging to the classic physical type to which they lent their name. Within the Mongolian People's Republic, Khalkha-speaking Mongols constitute almost four-fifths of the population. Other Mongolian groups—including Dörbed, Buryat, Bayad, and Dariganga—account for about one-eighth of the population. By tradition the Mongols have been Buddhists. Much of the rest of the population consists of Turkic-speaking peoples, mainly Kazakhs, who traditionally have been Muslims; located mainly in the western part of the country, they have been granted an autonomous area. A small but significant number of Russians live mainly in the cities. The Chinese, who were formerly important in cities, trade, and finance, have largely left the country.

At the time of the founding of the modern state, the social composition was strongly influenced by the then prevailing religious traditions of the lamas (monks), who followed tenets derived from Tibetan Buddhism, with a strong admixture of more primitive elements. Control lay in the hands of the head of the Mongolian Tibetan Buddhist Church (who was proclaimed the khan of all Mongolia), together with various local khans, hundreds of princes and noblemen, and the higher clergy. The new regime sought to replace feudal and religious structures with socialist and secular forms. During the 1930s the government closed monasteries, confiscated their livestock and landholdings, and induced large numbers of monks to renounce religious life. Many aspects of the national cultural traditions are preserved in museums, but it is the young, educated Mongol—often an urban worker—who is increasingly setting the pace of national life.

The theocratic background

Demography. After a period of stagnation, the population of Mongolia increased rapidly in the second half of the 20th century, as birth rates climbed and death rates dropped. Between 1952 and 1984 the total population more than doubled. Improved health, sanitation, and medical facilities played a major role in reducing mortality, especially infant mortality. Also important was the government policy of encouraging families to have more children. Mongolia's rate of natural increase reached a peak in 1960 and declined slowly thereafter. Thus, by the late 20th century Mongolia's main demographic trend was toward a youthful, fast-growing population; in addition, as mentioned above, the population has become increasingly urbanized. (B.Gu./C.D.H.)

Population growth

THE ECONOMY

Resources. Mongolia is rich in mineral resources. Geological surveys have confirmed the existence of large deposits of coal and iron, tin, copper, gold, and silver ore and a number of lesser known minerals. Mongolia's biologic resources consist largely of the great herds of livestock in the country. Overall livestock figures rose throughout most of the 20th century, providing a rich agricultural resource base that even enabled some exports of meat to be made. In addition, the northern rivers of Mongolia offer great potential for hydroelectric development, whereas the wildlife of the country offers potential for commercial exploitation.

Agriculture. Livestock raising—based on millions of head of sheep, goats, cattle, and horses, and including a large number of camels—accounts for about 70 percent of the value of agricultural production. Livestock are widely distributed throughout the entire country. The number of horses and cattle reach their greatest concentrations in the wetter north-central regions, whereas goats and camels are proportionately more numerous in the drier west and south. Most of the livestock belong to agricultural cooperatives. Although the earliest cooperatives were formed in the 1930s, the main government campaign to organize the livestock herders (*arats*) into giant cooperatives took place in the years 1955–59. Each of these cooperatives averages about 1,700 square miles in area.

Livestock production

Pastoral Mongols traditionally have abhorred crop tillage, and for many years they left it largely in the hands of Chinese or Russian settlers. With the departure of most Chinese after the establishment of the Mongolian People's Republic, crop production for several decades remained very low; but under Soviet guidance in the second half of the 20th century, the area in crops expanded greatly, increasing about 30-fold between 1941 and 1985. Crop production is largely limited to the moister northern parts of the country, particularly in the broad lower valleys of the Orhon and Selenge rivers but also along the Onon, Uldz, and Kerulen rivers in the northeast. Part of the cropland receives supplemental irrigation. Because of the long, cold winters only a single annual crop is possible. About four-fifths of the cropland is in grains—primarily in spring wheat but with some in barley or oats—and nearly all of the rest is in fodder crops (hay). Yields are relatively low and vary greatly from year to year. Potatoes and vegetables occupy only a tiny fraction of the crop area. About four-fifths of the cropland is in state farms, with the rest in cooperatives. The large state farms each average about 700 square miles in size and typically include some livestock production as well as crops.

Mining and industry. The chief minerals extracted are coal, primarily for domestic use, fluorite (fluorspar), and copper and molybdenum ores, both of which are exported to the Soviet Union. Some gold and tungsten deposits are also worked. The two main coal-mining districts are Sharïn Gol, southeast of Darhan, and Nalayh, just southeast of Ulaanbaatar. To the southwest of Darhan lies the gigantic Erdenet copper- and molybdenum-mining complex, which began operation in the late 1970s.

Although the government has devoted a great amount of effort to industrializing the nation, much of Mongolia's industrial capacity is still engaged in processing raw materials or meeting basic domestic consumer needs. Thus, the principal manufactured products are processed foods (meat, beverages, dairy products, and flour); articles of clothing and footwear made from wool, hides, skins, and furs; and lumber, paper, matches, and furniture. Also important are the operation at Erdenet that concentrates copper and molybdenum ores for shipment and the construction industry. About half of the industrial employment is in Ulaanbaatar, which is the centre of light industry. Heavy industry is concentrated in Darhan, and forest products are processed in Sühbaatar.

Industrial production

Trade. During the 1980s minerals and ore concentrates became Mongolia's principal export, surpassing the traditional exports of livestock and their by-products. The main imports are machinery and equipment; fuels, minerals, and metals; and manufactures, particularly consumer goods. More than three-fourths of Mongolia's trade is with the Soviet Union; most of the rest is with members of Comecon.

Transportation. Mongolia's most important transportation artery is the Trans-Mongolian Railway, which runs north–south through the central part of the country; it links Mongolia to the Soviet Union and to China and provides the shortest overland route between Moscow and Peking. The railway is divided into northern and southern sections. The northern section extends from the Soviet border to Ulaanbaatar, following several river valleys through the mountainous terrain. It connects Mongolia's main urban and industrial centres and carries a substantial portion of the country's freight. The southern section, from Ulaanbaatar to the Chinese border, runs through rolling steppe and semidesert country. It was built in the mid-1950s, during the period of close Sino-Soviet cooperation. Another railway connects Choybalsan and other urban centres in the northeast with the Soviet rail system.

The Trans-Mongolian Railway

Roads provide connections between Ulaanbaatar and the *aymag* (provincial) centres and among smaller settlements. Nearly all of the country's roads are unpaved. Trucks carry most of the rest of the nation's freight not carried by rail, particularly outside of the core area along the northern Trans-Mongolian Railway. Camels are still used in the sparsely populated desert areas of the south, and yaks and oxen still haul some goods in the rugged mountains of the west.

Air service is particularly suitable for passenger movement in Mongolia because distances between population centres are great, population density is low, and weather conditions generally are favourable for flying. Level, unobstructed terrain for landing strips is also widely available. Ulaanbaatar has an international airport, and the capital has regularly scheduled service to the *aymag* centres. Special medical and veterinary flights also are arranged.

(C.D.H.)

ADMINISTRATION AND SOCIAL CONDITIONS

Government. The Mongolian constitution adopted in 1960 states that the country is a Socialist state of workers, *arat*s organized in cooperatives, and working intellectuals, in the form of a people's democracy. The constitution secures for citizens the right to work, rest, and leisure; to old-age social security; and to education. There are also provisions for safeguarding rights of national minorities. In turn, the constitution enjoins the citizenry to observe the laws, to maintain labour discipline, and to defend the country.

According to the constitution, power is exercised through bodies known as the *khural*s (assemblies) of people's deputies. The People's Great Khural, or Parliament, is the supreme legislative body; its deputies are elected by universal adult suffrage for terms of five years. The deputies, in turn, elect a Presidium, which performs legislative functions when the larger body is not in session, and form a Council of Ministers, which is the assembly's executive body. The chairman of the Presidium is head of state.

Until the reforms of 1990, actual power resided exclusively in the Mongolian People's Revolutionary Party (MPRP), which was the country's only political party. The MPRP was officially characterized as the guiding and directing force of the state, and its structure and leadership closely paralleled the structure and leadership of the government. Party congresses were held every five years, at which time the members of the party's Central Committee were elected; in turn, the committee elected a Politburo, which was the most important decision-making body in the party, and a Secretariat, which ensured that party policies were carried out. The MPRP has traditionally had a number of auxiliary organizations, the most active being the Revolutionary Youth League, or Revsomol, and the Mongolian trade unions.

The country is divided administratively into 18 *aymag*s (provinces), with further local subdivisions into towns and *somon*s (counties). The cities of Ulaanbaatar, Darhan, and Erdenet have independent administrative status. The standing commissions of the *khural*s at every level, set up for every branch of the national economy and culture, take a direct and day-to-day part in their work.

Justice. Justice is administered through the Supreme Court, which is elected by the People's Great Khural, and through the *aymag* and town courts, which are elected by the corresponding *khural*s of people's deputies. The procurator of the republic, appointed by the People's Great Khural, and the procurators of *aymag*s and towns, appointed by the procurator of the republic, supervise the work of the courts.

Armed forces. The small Mongolian military forces have been equipped, supplied, and trained by the Soviet Union, but defense of the country has relied primarily on the presence of Soviet troops. In 1990 the two countries agreed that all Soviet troops would be withdrawn by 1992.

Education. From the foundation of the modern state, educational development has been regarded as one of the most important elements in the building of the new way of life. Until 1940 the main thrust was directed at eradicating illiteracy, establishing a free system of public education, and creating a trained intelligentsia. The beginnings were scarcely auspicious, for only a small percentage of the population was literate; the entire country, in 1921, contained but one general educational school and no public secondary school or institution of higher education. The creation of a network of schools was undertaken first. From the 1940s on, the main educational emphasis passed to establishing institutions of higher education and expanding elementary and secondary facilities. There are now several hundred general schools (offering primary and secondary education), many special vocational schools, and several higher education institutions—the Mongolian State University (established 1942), the Higher Party School, and teachers' training, medical, and agricultural institutes.

General schools

Most children attend school for at least eight years; those in larger urban centres receive 10 years of schooling. Illiteracy has been almost eradicated. The ratio of college students to the population is higher than in some developed countries. Mongolian students also study abroad, mostly in the Soviet Union. The Academy of Sciences coordinates research institutions, experimental stations, and other scientific establishments and supervises scholarly work.

Health and welfare. Health services were similarly expanded over the republic's first half century. Medical treatment is free, and the state also maintains a network of sanatoriums and holiday rest homes.

Among other social services, the provision of housing has been greatly emphasized. The yurt remains the main traditional dwelling in the countryside. Increasing urbanization, as well as the introduction of more settled ways in the country, has necessitated the building of modern apartment blocks in the cities and an increasing number of permanent rural structures. Motor-transport mail links date from 1924, shortwave communications from 1934–36, and national radio broadcasting from 1934. A trunk telephone–telegraph link connecting Ulaanbaatar with all the *aymag* centres was established in the late 1940s. In the 1960s, satellite communication systems were used, and television broadcasts began in 1967. (B.Sv./D.Dn./C.D.H.)

CULTURAL LIFE

Contemporary cultural life in Mongolia is a unique amalgam of traditional elements—the heritage of centuries—and a growing modern element. Official policy is to preserve what are regarded as the better elements of the old ways of life, thus avoiding, on the one hand, uncritical adulation, and, on the other, an equally uncritical total rejection of old values.

Traditional elements. Mongolian literature evolved a wealth of traditional genres: heroic epics, legends, tales, *yurol* (the poetry of good wishes), and *magtaal* (the poetry of praise), as well as a host of proverbial sayings. These genres are infused by what Mongols regard as a national characteristic—a good-humoured love of life, with particular fondness for witty sayings and jokes, particularly evident in the image of Dalan Khuldalchi, the hero of humorous folktales, and in the stories about the *badarchins,* clever but wily wandering monks. The *baatar*—the popular hero of folk legend—is also a symbolic figure. *Khurchins*—folk poets and singers—carried down the oral epics and ballads; and their mime and gesture gave rise to the popular trenchant satirical vaudevilles, *Sumya Noyon* and *Dunkher Da-Lam.* The religious mysteries, *tsam* and *maidari,* were formerly staged as mass spectacles. Other folk arts include the making of *shirdeg,* richly ornamented felt carpets noted as adorning the entrances to yurts by 13th-century European travelers. The Mongolian form of chess, *shatar,* with a stern khan for king, a dog—the cattle breeder's traditional honoured friend—as queen, and a camel as a bishop, has very deep roots and has produced some finely carved chess sets. The ancient faience decoration of glazed earthenware, with exquisite motifs, has been revived. A complicated and dignified ritual still accompanies the traditional offering and acceptance of hospitality in a country where traveling is all-important, and the seating arrangements in the yurt are likewise carefully arranged. When conversing, Mongolians traditionally place the right palm on that of the left hand, a symbol of mutual esteem, and the same gesture, together with a light bow, expresses gratitude, greeting, or farewell.

The Naadam festival of the Three Games of Men

The most famous celebration of traditional ways, however, is the annual Naadam festival of the Three Games of Men, beginning each year on July 11, National Day, and held in all *aymag*s and *somons.* The festival has recorded roots going back 2,300 years or more. The first sport is wrestling, prominent in ancient times at religious festivals, and the ritual entry into the arena of several hundred participants, clad in the bright colours of a special tight-fitting costume known as the Dzodog Shudag and simulating the flight of the mythical Garudi bird, is a spectacular sight. The contests themselves are also conducted with great ceremony. Titles awarded at the national Naadam festivals are those of Titan, Lion, Elephant, and Falcon. A three-time winner becomes a Darkhan Avraga ("Invincible Titan"). The second sport is archery; and bowmen vie for the title of Merghen, or "Supermarksman," in individual and group contests, shooting at a leather-covered target with weapons of ancient design. Exceptional winners are characterized as Miraculous Archer, Most Scrupulous Archer, and similar names. The third sport, horse racing, is in many ways the most spectacular because all of the competitors are children, ranging in age from seven to 12. They are highly skilled and wear fine ornamental dresses as they race for about 20 miles across country. National horse-riding competitions for all ages are held during January and February, the Mongolian New Year, and are claimed to date back to the Bronze Age. Marco Polo, visiting in the 13th century, described a gathering of not less than 10,000 white horses held at the behest of the Great Khan. The races are keenly competitive and the riders highly skillful.

Modern elements. Modern sports range from freestyle wrestling (introduced 1962) to motorcycling, rifle shooting, table tennis, boxing, and gymnastics. A growing number of economic enterprises cater to the various folk arts. The Palace Museum has a superb collection of folk art housed in the former winter palace of the khan, built in 1898. The architectural ensemble contains temples housing the famous sculptures of the goddess Tara made by the 17th-century artist Zanabazar. The State Central Museum and related exhibits portray the rich archaeological and paleontological remains of the country. Buddhist relics are exhibited in the Temple Museum, built 1903–05. The Erdene-Dzuu Monastery Museum on the site of Karakorum (Har Horin), Mongolia's ancient capital, is also noteworthy. Each *aymag* now has its own museum of regional studies. The State Public Library contains works of great variety and historical value.

In contemporary literature, the popular poems and short stories of Dashdorjiyn Natsagdorj became particularly significant in the 1930s. In the 1940s literature became more varied in theme and genre, and the autobiographical "Old Scribe's Story" by G. Navaannamzhil became popular. Younger writers in the 1950s and 1960s injected a more contemporary note, attempting to balance psychological and social imagery. The realistic epic novel continues in popularity.

The State Drama Theatre, founded 1931, shows both Mongolian and classical works, and the State Opera and Ballet Theatre has a deserved reputation. There is a puppet theatre in the capital and internationally known song and dance companies. Practically every community has its own amateur art group, and the State Circus is also very popular. The Mongolkino film studio in the late 20th century was making an increasing impact at international festivals: its productions are assisted by the magnificent landscapes and clear air of the country, which help the production of wide-screen epics. Mass radio and television services are of importance because of the great distances in the country and are now aided by satellite links. The vast majority of households have radio sets, and the ownership of television sets has spread. There are about a dozen central and nearly two dozen local newspapers. The leading newspapers are *Unen* ("Truth") and *Pionyeriyn Unen* ("Pioneers' Truth"). There are also several dozen popular and specialist periodicals. (Sh.Bi./C.D.H.)

For statistical data on the land and people of Mongolia, see the *Britannica World Data* section in the BRITANNICA WORLD DATA ANNUAL.

History

The Mongols constitute one of the principal ethnographic divisions of Asian, or Oriental, peoples. Their traditional homeland is centred in Mongolia, a vast plateau in Central Asia now divided politically into an autonomous region of the People's Republic of China (Inner Mongolia) and the Mongolian People's Republic (Outer Mongolia), which lies at the eastern end of what was a great corridor of migration between Northeast China (Manchuria) and Hungary throughout history. It is unfortunate, because confusing, that 19th-century physical anthropologists introduced the terms Mongol and Mongolian as descriptive of racial type. The Mongols exhibit a wide range of physical characteristics and should be considered not as a race but as a group of peoples bound together by a common language and a common nomadic tradition.

The geographic origin of the Mongols themselves is the northeast corner of the present Mongolian People's Republic. To the east, the ancient tribal history is mostly that of the Tungus peoples (including the ancestors of the Manchu) and to the west, that of the Hsiung-nu, or eastern Huns, and their Turkic-speaking successors, whom the Mongols eventually displaced and in part absorbed. As a result of later wars and migrations Mongols are now found in the Mongolian People's Republic; in the Kalmyk, Tuvinian, and Buryat Autonomous Soviet Socialist republics of the Soviet Union; in the Inner Mongolia Autonomous Region (which includes a large portion of Northeast China), the Hui Autonomous Region of Ningsia, the Uighur Autonomous Region of Sinkiang (Chinese Turkistan), and the northern part of the Tibet Autonomous Region of China; and in Afghanistan.

ETHNOGRAPHY AND EARLY TRIBAL HISTORY

All Mongols recognize their kinship to each other in varying degrees through legend, written history, and especially language. Dialects vary from east to west more than from north to south, but very few are unintelligible to other Mongols. Historical change in the language is indicated by the fact that reading *The Secret History of the Mongols* (mid-13th century), the oldest major document written in Mongol, is for the Mongols of today like reading the work of Chaucer for the modern English. Pan-Mongolism, the desire to reunite politically all the Mongols, was always more a romantic than a practical idea, and today it is a dead issue.

Nomadic tradition

The Mongols have always been nomads, though there has also always been some cultivation. But nomadism is the seasonal movement of livestock and camps from one pasture to another, not unfettered wandering. Nomads have a clear concept of the possession of territory, though they sometimes interpret this in socially conflicting ways. Legend and folklore show that among the premodern Mongols the common people considered livestock to be private property and land to be the collective property of the tribe, while the families of ruling chiefs tried to claim the land as well as individual subjects as their property.

Traditional society was based on blood relationship traced through the common male ancestor who gave his name to the clan, though evidence exists of a more ancient system of matrilineal descent. Marriage was forbidden between members of the same clan, giving rise to complicated marriage alliances (and also feuds) among the clans. As clans grew and merged into tribes (often inventing a fictitious common ancestor), the most successful families tended to arrogate to themselves claims to "real" ancestry and, at the same time, to control of the tribal territory, while lesser families could claim ancestry only in a vaguer, tribal sense. In this process weak clans fell to a subordinate but not servile status: they owned their own cattle and had their own headmen, but paid tribute to the ruling clan and moved, camped, pastured, and fought under its orders.

Political and military organization was matched to the family–clan–tribe pattern. Every man who could ride and bear arms was both a herdsman and a soldier according to the need of the moment. Raiding other tribes to capture cattle, women, and prisoners was a recognized method of property accumulation. When, however, a tribe rose to notable power, as in the time of Genghis (Chinggis) Khan in the 13th century, a decimal form of military organization was adopted, with units of 10, 100, 1,000, and 10,000. Commanders of large units were assigned territories from which they drew the tribute to the supreme khan and mustered their quotas of troops. Mongol history fluctuates between such periods of feudal concentration and those of tribal dispersion.

The first mention in the Chinese chronicles of tribes that can be identified with Mongolia goes back in a shadowy way to the 2nd millennium BC. The first inhabitants of whom there is certainty, however, are the Hsiung-nu, about the 5th or 4th century BC. It was once thought that they were Turks, or at least Turkic speaking, but the opinion has grown that they spoke a paleo-Asiatic language, represented today by the Ket dialects of the Yenisey Valley in Siberia. The Hsiung-nu created a great tribal empire in Mongolia while China was being unified as an imperial state under the Ch'in (221–206 BC) and Han (206 BC–AD 220) dynasties. After several centuries of war with the Chinese, complicated by civil wars among themselves, the Hsiung-nu confederation broke up. Some of the southern tribes surrendered to the Chinese and were settled within China, where they were eventually absorbed. Some of the northern tribes migrated westward, where descendants—together with the members of other tribes—appeared in Europe in the 5th century AD as the Huns of Attila. By then, of course, they were a very mixed people.

The Hsiung-nu

In Mongolia the Hsiung-nu were succeeded both by Turkic-speaking peoples and by others identified by some scholars as Mongols, or Mongol speaking. There is a lack of convincing archaeological or historical evidence that these groups came to Mongolia from some distant region to fill a void left by the Hsiung-nu departure. Probably they were there all the time as the subjects of the Hsiung-nu, until the breakup of that confederation gave them the opportunity to assert themselves. Among the peoples who have been considered possibly Mongol the most important tribal names are Sienpi (Hsien-pi), who may however have been Tungus (modern Evenk) rather than Mongol, recorded in Han dynasty annals, and the Juan-juan (Jou-jan, or Geougen) of the 4th to 6th centuries. The latter have been identified by some scholars with the Avars, who migrated into Europe along the plains of the Danube and were nearly annihilated in Hungary by Charlemagne in the late 8th century.

The Orhon Turks

According to a legend recorded by the Chinese, the Turks of Mongolia, whose name is recognizable under its Chinese transcription "T'u-chüeh," were a subject tribe ruled by the Juan-juan. The Turks overthrew their masters and soon were in control of all Mongolia, centring their power in the Orhon Valley in the northern part of the country. The Orhon (Orkhon) Turks were contemporaries of the T'ang dynasty (618–907) in China, and their fortunes rose and fell in counterpoint to periods of T'ang strength and weakness. Comparison of archaeological and historical data, moreover, shows that power in Mongolia was at this time not based simply on levies of nomad horsemen. The khans and great men had fixed headquarters, surrounded by cultivated land that enabled them to breed large, stable-fed horses capable of carrying a man in armour. This situation emphasized a class distinction between the aristocrat on his charger and the herdsman-warrior-archer on his smaller horse. Agriculture also became an element in the economy, and the Uighurs, who came to power after the fall of the Orhon Turks, enter history as an oasis-centred people.

In the welter of tribes the name Mongol first appears in a tribal list recorded under the T'ang dynasty. It then vanishes, to reappear only in the 11th century, when the Khitan (Khitai, from which comes the word Cathay) ruled in Northeast and North China, and controlled most of Mongolia. The Khitan, who established the Chinese dynasty of Liao (907–1125), were themselves a Mongol people, but their homeland was in Northeast China rather than in what is now Mongolia. Like other Chinese dynasties, the Liao exercised its power in Mongolia by playing off the tribes against one another. Liao sources record the existence of a rather shadowy tribal power known in Mongol tradition as Khamag Mongol Uls ("Nation of all the Mongols"), which did not, however, include all of the population who spoke the Mongol language.

When the Khitan fell, their power in China was taken

By courtesy of Asia House Gallery, New York

A Mongol encampment, showing a central yurt surrounded by felt screens, beside which stand three Mongolian horses. Detail from the "Wen Chi Scroll," a Chinese hand scroll of the Southern Sung period (1127–1279), which illustrates the story of Wen Chi, a Chinese lady captured by the steppe nomads. In a private collection.

over and extended by the Juchen (Jürched), a Tungus people based farther north in northeastern China. They took the Chinese name of Chin ("Golden"). In their tribal policy they switched their favour from "All the Mongols" to the Tatars (known in the West as Tartars, from a medieval pun on *tartarus,* Latin for "hell"). Though Mongols, the Tatars were not part of the tribal league of All the Mongols, centred in the Onon and Kerulen valleys in the eastern half of North Mongolia; the Tatars lived to the east and south of them.

On the whole, though chastened occasionally by punitive expeditions, All the Mongols had been transfrontier allies or auxiliaries of the Khitan-Liao. A contingent of 50,000 Mongols (large for that time) fought on the Khitan side in the last battles of the Khitan Empire. Presumably, this was one reason why the Juchen-Chin transferred their favour to the Tatars, nearer to their frontier. Such alternations, between using the more distant and using the nearer transfrontier and frontier tribes, were frequent in the policies of dynasties in China, and this one had the desired effect of creating a feud between Mongols and Tatars.

Before the era of Genghis Khan, a defeated Khitan army had migrated westward at the fall of their Liao dynasty. It was led by a prince of the Khitan imperial line but must have included heterogeneous tribal elements. Moving westward through Mongolia, it reached what is now Kazakhstan in the southeast of Soviet Asia and created a new and briefly powerful empire, the Karakitai. It ruled primarily over Turkic-speaking peoples, made up of nomads and city dwellers in the oases, and the Khitan nucleus had the opportunity to apply its knowledge of how to deal with nomads and its ability in the administration of a bureaucracy.

The Karakitai

THE RISE OF GENGHIS KHAN

Such was the setting in Mongolia when Genghis Khan (his given name was Temüjin) was born, about 1162 (the date accepted by contemporary Mongol scholars). Genghis was born into a clan that had a tradition of power and rule, being the great-grandson of Khabul (Qabul) Khan, who had been the greatest ruler of All the Mongols. Genghis inherited a feud against the Juchen-Chin dynasty and another against the Tatars, who had betrayed a collateral ancestor of his to the Juchen. His own father was poisoned by Tatars. He also inherited feuds among the ruling clans of All the Mongols, and a feud with the powerful Merkit (Mergid) tribe, from whom his father had stolen his mother.

Genghis was even more deeply a political man than a warrior, and he resorted to war only as an extension of policy by other means. He was orphaned in his teens; his family fell on bad times, and power among the Mongols passed to other clans. Even in such apparently primitive practices as camp raiding and horse thieving, he skillfully used ancient customs: marriage alliances; putting himself under the patronage of a stronger prince; making an alliance with Jamuka (later his dangerous rival) by the oath of *anda,* under which men became as if blood brothers; and recruiting *nökhör* (the modern Mongol term for "comrade"). Unlike the institution of *anda,* which created a fictitious kinship and harboured the possibility of deadly rivalry, a man who became a *nökhör* forswore all loyalties of kinship and tribe and declared himself solely "the man" of his chosen leader. Genghis later fell out with his *anda,* but he was never betrayed by a *nökhör,* and his most brilliant generals were *nökhör.*

Genghis broke alliances and betrayed loyalties, but only when he could seem to be acting in "the common cause." By 1206 his success in tribal warfare caused him to be proclaimed ruler of All the Mongols with the rank of khan and the title of Genghis (Chinggis)—a word deriving probably ultimately from the Turkic *tengiz,* meaning "a large body of water, the ocean"; although this explanation has not convinced all Mongol scholars, it is consistent with the belief that the ocean symbolized breadth and depth of wisdom, and later the equivalent Mongol word of *ta-le* (Anglicized as "dalai") was applied to the supreme lama of Tibet. Previous nomads had invaded China, but none had yet ruled the whole of it, chiefly because they had invaded prematurely, leaving other nomads on their flanks and in their rear. Genghis, however, first united all the "dwellers in felt-walled tents" (*tuurgatan*), probing far back, away from China, to make sure that he controlled all potential nomadic rivals.

Ruler of All the Mongols

His first move was to bring under control the major tribal groups to the west of him in Mongolia, the Naiman and Kereit (Kerait) with whom he had been alternately in alliance and rivalry, as well as the tribes fringing the northern Mongolia–Siberia frontier. He then turned toward China, where at this time the eastern half of North China, south almost to the Yangtze, was ruled by the Juchen-Chin. In the northwest corner of China and the western extension of Inner Mongolia there was a small state, that of the Hsi Hsia: its rulers were Tangut from Tibet, and under them there were Turkish and Sogdian merchants who exploited the caravan trade, the cultivators of the oases being Turks and Chinese. China south of the Yangtze was ruled by the Southern Sung dynasty (1127–1279). Although they had lost North China, the Southern Sung were expanding southward toward Indochina, bringing rich new land under cultivation. Among all of these states there was an interplay of diplomacy, alliances made and broken, and open warfare. The Mongols themselves, far from being ignorant barbarians, understood the game and played it skillfully.

Between 1207 and 1215 the armies of Genghis probed deep into North China. Genghis made good use of the Khitan in northern and northeastern China, whose Liao dynasty the Juchen-Chin had overthrown and who were now discontented subjects of the Chin. In 1215 the Chin capital Chung-tu (modern Peking), from which the Chin emperor had withdrawn southward, was taken and sacked. Realizing, however, that it was premature to commit his main strength to the conquest of China, Genghis withdrew to Mongolia, leaving one of his best generals, Mugali, to ravage and weaken the country. He himself turned westward. When he had defeated the Naiman, the last of the powerful tribes in Mongolia proper, the son of the last ruler of that tribe, Küchlüg, fled to Karakitai and married the daughter of its last ruler, whom he then overthrew. In that variegated kingdom, which included Semirechiya in Russian Turkistan and the Kashgarian Oases in Chinese Turkistan (Uighur Autonomous Region of Sinkiang), he favoured the Buddhist minority and persecuted Islām, the majority religion. This situation made it easy for the Mongols to defeat him. The Mongol general Jebe (Jeb) proclaimed freedom of religion and forbade massacre and plunder. This policy indicates that the Mongols did not massacre out of sheer savagery but only when they thought it necessary to break the power of an opponent.

Sack of Peking

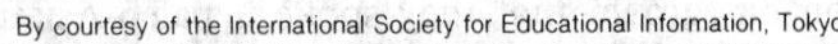
By courtesy of the International Society for Educational Information, Tokyo

The Japanese champion Takezaki attacking Mongol archers, a detail from the "Mongol Invasion Scroll," *c.* 1293. In the Imperial Household Collection, National Museum, Tokyo.

Taking over the lands of the Karakitai opened the way for Genghis to Khwārezm, the land of the oases along the Syr Darya and Amu Darya in northern Iran. For drawing on the resources of a higher civilization this gave him an alternative to China, and it also secured him against the danger of any other nomadic power organizing, on his flank and rear, a military striking force backed by agricultural and urban resources. This done, he turned back toward China, leaving further campaigning into Russia and the eastern fringes of Europe to his generals and sons. He would not, however, commit his main forces in China until he had dealt with the wealthy Tangut state of Hsi Hsia; it was on this successful campaign in 1227 that he died.

THE SUCCESSOR STATES OF THE MONGOL EMPIRE

Genghis had already dealt with the problem of succession. Each of his four sons was to hold a vassal kingdom: Jöchi, the eldest, was given the land from the Yenisey River and the Aral Sea westward "as far as the hooves of Mongol horses have reached"—a wording attributed to Genghis himself; the second son, Chagatai (Tsagadai), received Kashgaria (now the southern part of Sinkiang) and most of Mavrannakhar between the Amu Darya and Syr Darya; the third son, Ögödei (Ogadai), received western Mongolia and the region of Tarbagatai (now the northwestern corner of Sinkiang); the youngest, Tolui, inherited the ancient Mongol homeland of eastern Mongolia. Two years later, in 1229, a great Mongol assembly confirmed the succession of Ögödei as the great khan (khagan).

Tradition of succession

These dispositions made skillful use of ancient traditions. It was the custom among prosperous families that the eldest son, on reaching manhood, was given a wife and his share of the future inheritance; he then moved away and set up his own camp, independent but still allied to his family. The other brothers followed in due order, but each one nearer to the "home camp" than his next older brother. The youngest, as "guardian of the hearth and fire," remained with his parents until their death and received the residual heritage. It was convenient that Jöchi could in this way be placed at the greatest distance from the ancient homeland because he got on poorly with his brothers who considered him illegitimate, conceived while his mother was the captive of a hostile tribe. The election of Ögödei as great khan over the head of his elder brother Chagatai (Jöchi had already died) did not do violence to nomadic tradition; it was quite acceptable in wartime for the dying ruler to nominate as his successor the son who was considered ablest and most acceptable to his brothers.

With this first division, further fission was inevitable. Under Batu, the successor of Jöchi, there began the formation of the Golden Horde, which ruled, or rather, drew tribute from the city-states of Russia. In this khanate the Mongols were greatly outnumbered by Turks; the Turkish language soon displaced Mongol, and Islām became the prevailing religion. Because its reservoir of nomad power was in the Kipchak Steppe, the Golden Horde is sometimes known as the Kipchak khanate. By its methods of collecting taxes and tribute it contributed to the rise of the grand dukes of Muscovy; and it was eventually a Moscow-led alliance that broke the power of the Mongols (by then more frequently called Tatars), at the Battle of Kulikovo in 1380. Partly by treachery and partly by guile the Golden Horde was still able to take and sack Moscow two years later, but its power soon disintegrated—an important factor being attacks by Timur (Tamerlane), coming from Turkistan.

House of Chagatai

To the east were the khanates of the House of Chagatai and the Il-Khans of Iran (Persia). Like the rulers of the Golden Horde, the rulers of the House of Chagatai considered themselves senior, in genealogy, to the House of Ögödei; they were frequently at odds with the great khan, with each other, and with the Il-Khans. On the other hand, the Il-Khans (the title itself implies subordination) accepted and supported the authority of the great khans. Like the Golden Horde, again, the House of Chagatai controlled wide pastures and therefore retained a strong nomadic base, while the Il-Khans, like the great khans (especially after Kublai [Khubilai] moved his capital into China), were directly affected by the urban influences of an old, highly developed civilization with a rich literary tradition. As in China, this situation led rather rapidly to the passage of real administrative control from Mongol hands into the hands of their subjects. The greatest of the Il-Khans was Hülegü (Khulagu, Hulagu), a brother of Kublai Khan of Mongolia and China, who began the Il-Khan tradition of supporting Peking against the House of Chagatai and the Golden Horde.

This brief review of the outer khanates helps to explain the subsequent history of the Mongols in Mongolia and the Mongol dynasty in China. As great khan, Ögödei authorized the continuation of Mongol campaigns in Russia and the west and also in China, where the disintegration of the Juchen-Chin dynasty in 1234 had brought the Mongols face to face with the surviving Sung dynasty in the Yangtze Valley. Ögödei was also able to maintain a system of imperial representatives in the appanages of his imperial kinsmen in Central Asia and Iran but was less able to control the always insubordinate Golden Horde. He died in 1241 and was succeeded, after a stormy regency under his widow, Töregene, by his son Güyük (Kuyug) who had already quarreled with his cousin Batu of the Golden Horde. Güyük died at Samarkand in 1248, while preparing an attack on Batu.

A major change then occurred in the succession. At the next great assembly of the descendants of Genghis Khan, enlarged by the presence of powerful commanders and officials, the great khan chosen (again after much intrigue) was not a son of the House of Ögödei but Möngke (Mungke, Manga), a son of Tolui, the "guardian of the fire and hearth" of the Mongol homeland. This choice was favoured by Batu Khan, and Möngke responded by trying to stabilize and pacify relations among the khanates. Of his brothers he sent Kublai (later Great Khan) to continue the conquest of Sung China and Hülegü to subdue the Assassins (Nizārī Ismāʿīliyūn); on this campaign Hülegü also took Baghdad, a rich and powerful city and seat of the ʿAbbāsid caliphate. Möngke was aware of the desire of some of the crusaders for a Mongol alliance against the Saracens, but like Ögödei and Güyük he would not consider this except on terms of the submission of the European rulers and the pope. He himself campaigned deep into southwest China and there died of a fever in 1259.

Kublai Khan

The succession was then disputed between Möngke's second brother, Kublai, and his youngest brother, Arigböge (Ariböx, Arikböge). A third brother, Hülegü, supported Kublai. The dispute was more than a brawl over spoils

Adapted from *Muir's Historical Atlas; Medieval and Modern*, R.F. Treharne and H. Fullard (eds.), 9th ed. (1962); George Philip & Son Ltd., London

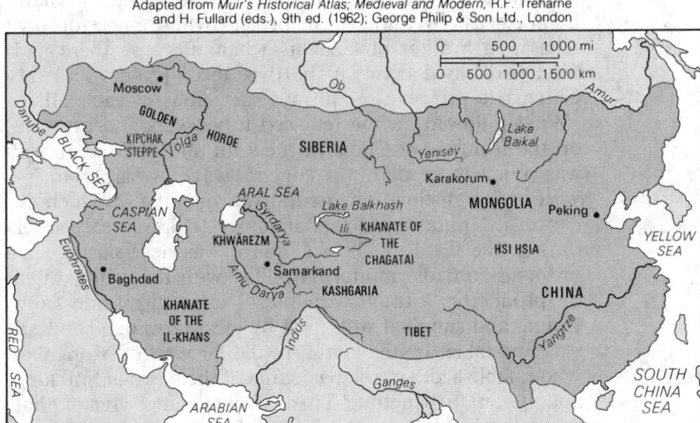

The Mongol Empire.

among barbarian warriors; ideology was involved. Genghis Khan's concept of conquest and rule had been clear: the "people of the felt-walled tents" should remain in the steppes and continue their ancient warrior way of life, drawing tribute from the world of farms, cities, and caravan trade. Kublai and Hülegü, however, favoured moving into the conquered countries and there becoming the new ruling class—even if this meant mingling with the remnants of the conquered ruling class.

In this respect Arigböge was closer to the concept of Genghis than was Kublai, but Kublai prevailed and Arigböge died in honourable captivity. Kublai had himself proclaimed great khan in Mongolia in 1260. Kublai's reign has been romanticized in the West ever since Marco Polo. Kublai Khan moved the capital from Karakorum (Kharakhorum), which had been built by Ögödei (not Genghis Khan, as is often said), to a new city that he had built on the site of Chung-tu, naming it Ta-tu ("Great Capital"). He used Mongolia as his base for ascendancy over the other Mongol khanates, but drew his main revenue directly from China. He used foreigners (including

Mongol warriors in cavalry pursuit wearing lamellar armour, which covers them from the neck to the elbow and to the lower leg. Miniature from *Jamiʿat-tawarikh* by Rashīd od-Dīn, 14th century. In the Topkapı Saray Museum, Istanbul.

By courtesy of the Topkapi Saray Museum, Istanbul

Marco Polo and his family) to lessen his dependence on Chinese bureaucrats, but the administrative structure was essentially on the Chinese model; and consequently the Mongols, because they no longer held the real keys to power, lost the throne to the native Chinese Ming dynasty in 1368, only a century after the accession of Kublai and within a decade or two of the end of the Golden Horde and the Il-Khanate.

Internecine strife. Although in the first vigour of reconquest the Chinese penetrated deeply into Mongolia and destroyed Karakorum, they never succeeded in establishing control. Mongol unity was shattered, but Mongols in different regions began to recover. Mongol fission followed several lines. In western Mongolia there arose new lines of chieftains who did not claim descent from Genghis Khan. As a group, these were the Oyrat (Oirat), but at times the names of subgroups or individual tribes, such as the Dzungar (Jüüngar) or the Dörbed (Dörböd), predominated. In the centre, both in Outer and Inner Mongolia, the ruling princes claimed descent from Genghis Khan. In northeastern China were princes whose ancestor was Khasar, a brother of Genghis Khan. Because there had been bad blood between the two, these princes and the Chingiside princes were always suspicious of each other.

The Oyrat

What followed, in the renewed tribal wars and pressure on the frontiers of China in the 15th and 16th centuries, was much more than a resurgent "wave of barbarian invasions." A distinct new period was opening in which all concerned understood that in order to have real power outside the Great Wall of China it was necessary to coordinate nomadic military mobility with towns inhabited by productive artisans, capable of attracting trade from China, and supplied with food by local farming. The lead was first taken by the Oyrat, in the far west of Mongolia, who established control over some of the oases of Sinkiang and began to penetrate Tibet. This advance meant that in the regions where the Imperial power and economic ascendancy of China under the Ming dynasty (1368–1644) were weakest, the Oyrat drew on new resources. Both the Tibetans and the Turkic-speaking oasis people were active merchants, had a literate class whose thinking was independent of the Chinese model, and could keep the records without which a state more advanced than a tribal league was impossible. This stage initiated the long-enduring cleavage between the Oyrat and the Khalkha, the main body of what was later to be Outer Mongolia.

Altan Khan

Ascendancy then passed to the Mongols of the Ordos, in the great loop of the Yellow River, under Altan Khan (reigned 1543–83). He exploited a geographic base that enabled him to develop agriculture and trade, to challenge the Oyrat in Tibet, and to pressure the Chinese. Meanwhile, the Mongols of the centre, Khalkhas in the north, and Chahars (Chakhars) in the south (there was as yet no "Outer" and "Inner" Mongolia) had lagged behind for lack of a suitably diversified geographic base. The best that they could achieve was a tribal league unification under Dayan Khan, a descendant of Kublai and grandfather of Altan Khan, who was proclaimed khan in 1470 at the age of five and died in 1543. After this, and after the death of Altan Khan, the supremacy over the Mongols of the centre passed to the south to another descendant of Dayan, Ligdan (Legdan, Lingdan) Khan of the Chahars. Using the geographic advantages of the modern Chinese frontier province of Chahar, close to the Great Wall, he tried during his reign (1604–34) to build up a power comparable to that which had been held by Altan Khan. He was too late, however, because of the rise of the Manchu.

Revival of Buddhism. During this period there was a second flowering of Buddhism among the Mongols. In the reign of Kublai, Buddhism in its Tibetan form had been fashionable at court and among some of the Mongol aristocracy, but the people as a whole had not been converted. The new entry of Buddhism was promoted by political considerations. A number of Mongol princes saw that for the kind of power that was now advantageous it was necessary to have not only a religious ethos higher than that of shamanism (whose priests used magic to cure the sick, to divine what was hidden, and to control events), but a literate class to provide a bureaucracy. To use the Chinese language meant the risk—as had been proved under the Mongol empire in China—of the absorption of the Mongol ruling class into the Chinese ruling class. Tibet was not strong enough to dominate Mongolia, and the Tibetan monastic system had already produced able clerical bureaucrats. Moreover, Tibetan alphabetic writing was easier to use than Chinese ideographs.

Establishment of the Dalai Lama

Thus it was that Altan Khan invited from Tibet a prelate who had claims to primacy in Tibet, but also rivals, and proclaimed him Dalai Lama. Moreover, a way was found to link church and state. A son of the line of the Tüshētü Khans of Khalkha was conveniently found to be the first "reincarnation" of the line of Jabtsandamba Khutagt (Khutukhtus) of Urga. The significance of this device is underlined by the fact that as soon as the Manchu controlled Mongolia, they ruled that no man of the lineage of Genghis Khan could be "discovered" to be a reincarnation or "living Buddha," and also that the Khutagt of Urga must always be discovered in Tibet. In their rule of Mongolia they thus separated church and state and used them against each other.

At the beginning of the revival of Buddhism in Mongolia there was a great burst of translation of the scriptures from Tibetan (and Sanskrit) into Mongol. The Mongols wanted to use Buddhism as a unifying principle in a new nationalism. When the Manchu won control, however, they threw their support to the use of Tibetan as the "Latin" of the church, further widening the cleavage between clerical and secular authority and bureaucracy. By the end of the Manchu regime there were many monks in Mongolia who were literate in Tibetan but not in their own language.

THE ASCENDANCY OF THE MANCHU

The rise of the Ch'ing, or Manchu dynasty, which had such profound effects on the fate of Mongolia, began long before 1644, the year a Manchu emperor was first seated on the throne in Peking. In the late 16th century it was becoming clear that a new barbarian conquest of China was again possible. In competition with the various Mongol princes and tribes already mentioned, the Manchu had the advantage that in the southern part of Northeast China

(Manchuria), but outside the Great Wall of China, there was a large Chinese population with a number of urban centres and a flourishing trade that, instead of passing by land through the Great Wall, went largely by sea to the Shantung Peninsula—to the rear, that is, of the rulers in Peking. These Chinese were somewhat alienated from other Chinese. They had for centuries been accustomed to trading with the barbarians and to farming under the patronage of barbarian princes, and they did not like Peking's periodic attempts to maintain a "closed frontier" along the Great Wall.

The Manchu not only subjugated these Chinese but also cultivated their loyalty and were soon heavily dependent on them, not only economically but for military manpower. To balance this dependence they built up a network of alliances with their other neighbours, the easternmost Mongols. Mongol troops took part in the conquest of China; and before they occupied Peking, the Manchu had control of the southern fringe of Mongolia. They organized it as part of their military reserve for the domination of China; this organization is the origin of the institutional and administrative concept of "Inner" Mongolia.

It took the Manchu about a century to add northern or "Outer" Mongolia to their empire, resulting in two Mongolias markedly different from each other, Inner Mongolia being much more closely integrated with China.

Attempt at Mongol revival

Meanwhile, the Oyrat, under their leading tribe, the Dzungar, made a belated effort to unite all the Mongols in rivalry with the Manchu. The Oyrat were strengthened by their control of a number of the Sinkiang oases but weakened by rivalries among their chiefs, by the diversion of much of their strength to adventures in Tibet, and by the reluctance of the Khalkha princes to accept the overlordship of princes not descended from Genghis Khan. Led by such warriors as Galdan (Dga'-ldan), the Oyrat made sweeping campaigns far to the east in Mongolia but were never quite able to consolidate their gains. In trying to make the Oyrat a recognizably distinct nation, the great religious leader, the Jaya Pandita, revised the Mongol alphabet, making it phonetically more accurate, and originated an independent literary tradition.

Unwilling to accept submission to the Oyrat as the price of unification, the Khalkha princes rallied more and more to the Manchu, who guaranteed their aristocratic privileges and titles in a great convention at Dolon Nor (To-lun), in Inner Mongolia, in 1691. With the added resources of Khalkha, the Manchu were then able to mount a long series of military campaigns in which they annihilated the Oyrat power with tremendous slaughter on the scale of genocide.

This conquest, however, was not completed until 1759, and it was complicated by many events, particularly a major revolt against Manchu rule in western Khalkha in the 1750s led by a noble named Chingunjav. Chingunjav was a coconspirator with an Oyrat leader named Amursana, who in turn had first submitted to the Manchu and then rebelled against them. But this was the last period of general warfare involving the Mongols, and it ended with a considerable redistribution of the tribes. Several Khalkha groups that had fled from the Oyrat into Inner Mongolia never returned; a few Chahars from Inner Mongolia were settled in Sinkiang as garrisons; numbers of the Oyrat group were included in the western part of Khalkha geographically but not within the tribal organization; some ended their migrations in Ala Shan, at the western end of Inner Mongolia, but not within the Inner Mongolian organization; and some ended theirs far away in the Kokonor-Tsaidam region of Tibet. The most distant Oyrat wanderers (mostly Torgut and Dörbed) migrated in the early 17th century from the Altai to the Volga, where they took service under the tsars and took part in the Russian conquest of the Caucasus. In 1771 about 70,000 families migrated all the way back to Sinkiang, where they were accepted under Manchu rule and allotted pastures for grazing. The descendants of those who remained on the Volga were known as the Kalmyk (Kalmuck).

Mongol dispersion

The ensuing period of peace degenerated into stagnation and economic decline. Chinese camp followers had accompanied the Manchu conquest, and from this grew Chinese control of the caravan trade and of a barter trade exploiting usurious terms of credit. Because Mongol troops were of decreasing use for the control of China, there was no incentive for the Manchu to protect, economically, this source of manpower, and the Manchu authorities relied increasingly on the potentates of the Lama Buddhist Church, who were themselves increasingly corrupt, for the control of Mongolia. Chinese colonization began to encroach on the pasturelands of Inner Mongolia, and at the end of the 19th century an attempt was made to plant a screen of Chinese colonists along the frontier between Siberia and Outer Mongolia.

THE 20TH CENTURY

In the Russo-Japanese War of 1904–05 both Russians and Japanese enlisted Mongol mercenaries as auxiliaries; from this time on there were Japanese army officers who dreamed of a new Mongol nationalism that could be used against both Russia and China. The Russians were more restrained and were satisfied with Buryatia (Buryat Mongolia). By secret treaties after the war Inner Mongolia east of the meridian of Peking was recognized by Russia as a Japanese sphere of interest.

By 1911, when the Chinese Revolution broke out, unrest was widespread in Mongolia. At the time, the Mongol language and Mongol sources being little known outside Mongolia, most observers thought of Mongolia only in terms of Russian and Japanese intrigue. But the rich documentation that later became available proved that the unrest was both social and political. The Mongols by this time identified the Manchu with the Chinese, the Chinese with usurious debt, and their own clerical and secular rulers as people who lived in luxury on Chinese loans and passed on the usurious interest to their subjects. The rulers, for their part, saw both the chance of a new government they could control and the danger that if they did not act, they would not be able to control the people.

Independence

Under the leadership of the Jabtsandamba Khutagt, the Mongols declared their independence. Uncertain of themselves in world politics, however, they sought to replace Manchu Imperial patronage with that of the tsar; but the Russians, because of the secret treaties with Japan and an understanding with Britain about Tibet and Mongolia (which, though not secret, could hardly be comprehended by the Mongols), would go no further than support of "autonomy," not "independence." This status was ratified after difficult negotiations between the Mongols, the Russians, and the new Republic of China. Union between Inner and Outer Mongolia was similarly frustrated. Some leaders in Inner Mongolia saw themselves as the future elite of a united Mongolia because they could draw on an intelligentsia with a knowledge of the language and politics of China, but for the same reason they were distrusted in Outer Mongolia as being too Chinese.

This uneasy situation endured with increasing economic distress and social unrest until the Russian Revolution. A Japanese-controlled clique in the Chinese government then sent a military expedition into Mongolia that forced the Mongols to sign a "request" to be taken over by the Chinese Republic. Almost immediately afterward, defeated anti-Bolshevik troops began to retreat into Mongolia. Their most important leader was Baron Roman von ("Mad Baron") Ungern-Sternberg, who defeated the Chinese occupation forces and treated the Mongols with unfeeling savagery.

In this period of terror and confusion two secret revolutionary groups, which later merged, were formed by Damdiny Sühbaatar, a former trooper and machine gunner in the Mongol forces disbanded by the Chinese, and Khorloghiyin Choibalsan, who had been a boy runaway from a monastery and later a student in Siberia. Choibalsan, though not the principal leader during the lifetime of Sühbaatar, was in touch with underground Bolsheviks—hiding there as refugees—later massacred by Ungern-Sternberg. Memoirs of the Mongol partisans enlisted by these two show that quite apart from Russian propaganda there was already in Mongolia a geographically widespread and socially embittered demand for radical social and political change. The traditional leaders had been discredited by their inability to handle either the Chinese intervention or the incursions of the anti-revolutionary Russians.

The revolutionaries took the initiative in going to the Bolsheviks for help, which was quickly granted. The remnants of the Chinese warlord forces were driven out and Ungern-Sternberg was handed over to the Bolsheviks for execution. Urga, the capital (now Ulaanbaatar), was taken by a joint Mongol-Russian column in July 1921, and this is now considered the date of the founding of the present republic, though the first measures of the revolutionary victors were surprisingly moderate. The Jabtsandamba Khutagt (the living Buddha of Urga) was continued in office, but as a "constitutional monarch," meaning he could sign only documents prepared for him by the new regime.

Sühbaatar died in 1923 and the Khutagt in 1924. In the Soviet Union Lenin also died in 1924, and in China Sun Yat-sen died in 1925. Mongolia was engaged in a revolutionary process also going forward at different rates of speed in the Soviet Union and in China. The problem of the Khutagt was easily solved; no successor was found, and on Nov. 26, 1924, Mongolia was proclaimed a People's Republic—using a wording that exactly follows the Chinese, not the Soviet model. The government, and the controlling People's Revolutionary Party, was a coalition of conservative and nationalistic revolutionary elements. Shifts between "rightist" and "leftist" policy ensued, closely affected by the rise of Joseph Stalin in the Soviet Union and by the defeat of the Chinese Communists (for the time being) by Chiang Kai-shek. Increasingly important, too, was the Japanese invasion of Northeast China (Manchuria) in 1931, followed by Japanese encroachment on Inner Mongolia and North China and all-out invasion of China in 1937.

Proclamation of the People's Republic

The uncertainty, both internal and external, engendered cliques and conspiracies—some real and others imagined—resulting in an atmosphere of suspicion and fear that cost many lives. The situation began to clear after 1939, when the Japanese, in a thrust toward Siberia, invaded the northeastern corner of Mongolia, testing the Soviet–Mongol alliance. The Mongol border troops fought ferociously, holding the heights of Nomynkhan (Nomonhan) and the line of the Khalkyn River until Soviet troops came up. The Japanese defeat was shattering, and it undoubtedly played a major part in their fateful decision not to honour the "Berlin–Tokyo Axis" with Hitler but to make their major effort in the Pacific and Southeast Asia. In Mongolia the victory dispelled fears that elements of the army might go over to the Japanese; on the contrary, many Inner Mongolian troops recruited by the Japanese went over to the Mongols. The military alliance with the Soviet Union was reconfirmed when the Mongols took part in the Soviet campaign in Inner Mongolia and Manchuria in the last two weeks of World War II.

At this time, refugees from Inner Mongolia swarmed into the Mongolian People's Republic. The Japanese had organized a puppet government of Inner Mongolia under Teh Wang (Prince Teh, Demchukdongrub). He had, however, tried to minimize Japanese control and to promote Mongol nationalism. When the Chinese Communists came to power in Inner Mongolia, he was condemned as a war criminal but later released.

Postwar plebiscite

Under an agreement made by U.S. President Franklin D. Roosevelt at the Yalta Conference (February 1945), Chiang Kai-shek consented to a plebiscite in Mongolia after the war. The result was overwhelmingly in favour of independence over "autonomy." Full diplomatic recognition did not follow, however, because of a border dispute. Mongolian membership in the United Nations was at first sponsored by Chiang Kai-shek but later opposed by him and by the United States, and it was not until 1961 that Mongolia gained membership. In the meantime, Inner Mongolia was reorganized as an autonomous region within the People's Republic of China.

For many years Mongolia's relations with China were strained because of Mongolia's unswerving loyalty to the Soviet alliance. Nevertheless, its long frontier with China was amicably redemarcated. Tensions eased considerably in the 1980s, leading to the establishment of diplomatic relations between the two countries in 1986. (O.La.)

For later developments in the history of Mongolia, see the *Britannica Book of the Year* section in the BRITANNICA WORLD DATA ANNUAL.

For coverage of related topics in the *Macropædia* and *Micropædia,* see the *Propædia,* sections 932, 933, and 975.

BIBLIOGRAPHY

Physical and human geography: A comprehensive general survey is provided in E.M. MURZAEV, *Die Mongolische Volksrepublik: Physisch-geographische Beschreibung* (1954; originally published in Russian, 2nd ed., 1952), which includes a substantial bibliography up to the time of the work's publication. ERICH THIEL, *Die Mongolei: Land, Volk, und Wirtschaft der Mongolischen Volksrepublik* (1958), is a detailed, illustrated account; and HELLMUTH BARTHEL, *Land zwischen Taiga und Wüste: 50 Jahre freie Mongolei* (1971), is a brief overview. *Mongolia* (bimonthly), published by the Mongolian State Committee for Information, Radio, and Television, is an illustrated magazine in English that provides features on different subjects, as well as statistical information. Economic developments of the first half of the 20th century are surveyed in B. SHIRENDYB, *By-passing Capitalism* (1968). For later developments, see *The 60th Anniversary of People's Mongolia* (1981); and *National Economy of the MPR for 65 Years* (1986), collections of essays published by Mongolian and Soviet information agencies. SECHIN JAGCHID and PAUL HYER, *Mongolia's Culture and Society* (1979), discusses the nomadic traditions, religion, arts, economy, and sociopolitical structure of the Mongols. UNESCO, *Cultural Policy in the Mongolian People's Republic: A Study* (1982), deals with contemporary tendencies. For a discussion of social and political structure from the Mongolian point of view, see OWEN LATTIMORE and FUJIKO ISONO, *The Diluv Khutagt: Memoirs and Autobiography of a Mongol Buddhist Reincarnation in Religion and Revolution* (1982). WALTHER HEISSIG, *The Religions of Mongolia* (1980; originally published in German, 1970), is a scholarly study from shamanism to Lamaism. See also PAUL HYER and SECHIN JAGCHID, *A Mongolian Living Buddha: Biography of the Kanjurwa Khutughtu* (1983). ALAN J.K. SANDERS, *Mongolia: Politics, Economics, and Society* (1987), is an interdisciplinary study.

History: For the Mongol conquests, empire, and succession states, see *The Secret History of the Mongols: For the First Time Done into English out of the Original Tongue and Provided with an Exegetical Commentary,* by FRANCIS WOODMAN CLEAVES (1982); DAVID MORGAN, *The Mongols* (1986); THOMAS T. ALLSEN, *Mongol Imperialism: The Policies of the Grand Qan Möngke in China, Russia, and the Islamic Lands, 1251–1259* (1987); MORRIS ROSSABI, *China and Inner Asia: From 1368 to the Present Day* (1975); and M. SANJDORJ, *Manchu Chinese Colonial Rule in Northern Mongolia,* trans. from Mongolian (1980). Comprehensive coverage of developments up to the 1960s is provided in B. SHIRENDYB *et al.* (eds.), *History of the Mongolian People's Republic* (1976; originally published in Mongolian, 1966); ROBERT A. RUPEN, *Mongols of the Twentieth Century,* 2 vol. (1964); and C.R. BAWDEN, *The Modern History of Mongolia* (1968). For later events, see ROBERT A. RUPEN, *How Mongolia Is Really Ruled: A Political History of the Mongolian People's Republic, 1900–1978* (1979). The opinion that the Mongolian revolution was largely made in the Soviet Union and exported to Mongolia is opposed in the studies of the social, economic, and political support for the revolution within Mongolia itself, and of genuine Mongolian leadership, as exemplified by URGUNGGE ONON and DERRICK PRITCHATT, *Asia's First Modern Revolution: Mongolia Proclaims Its Independence in 1911* (1987); OWEN LATTIMORE and URGUNGGE ONON, *Nationalism and Revolution in Mongolia* (1955), which includes a translation of a biography of the leader of the Mongolian revolution; and OWEN LATTIMORE, *Nomads and Commissars: Mongolia Revisited* (1962).

(C.D.H./O.La.)

Montaigne

Michel Eyquem de Montaigne wrote, in his *Essais* (*Essays*), one of the most captivating and intimate self-portraits ever written, on a par with Augustine's and Rousseau's. Living, as he did, in the second half of the 16th century, he bore witness to the decline of the intellectual optimism that had marked the Renaissance. The sense of immense human possibilities, stemming from the discoveries of the New World travelers, from the rediscovery of classical antiquity, and from the opening of scholarly horizons through the works of the humanists, was shattered in France when the advent of the Calvinistic Reformation was followed closely by religious persecution and by the Wars of Religion (1562–98). These conflicts, which tore the country asunder, were in fact political and civil as well as religious wars, marked by great excesses of fanaticism and cruelty. At once deeply critical of his time and deeply involved in its preoccupations and its struggles, Montaigne chose to write about himself—"I am myself the matter of my book," he says in his opening address to the reader—in order to arrive at certain possible truths concerning man and the human condition, in a period of ideological strife and division when all possibility of truth seemed illusory and treacherous.

Giraudon—Art Resource/EB Inc.

Montaigne, portrait by an unknown French artist, 16th century. In the Condé Museum, Chantilly, Fr.

Life. Born on Feb. 28, 1533, in the family domain of Montaigne, in Périgueux, southwestern France, Michel Eyquem spent most of his life at his château and in the city of Bordeaux, 30 miles to the west. The family fortune had been founded in commerce by Montaigne's great-grandfather, who acquired the estate and the title of nobility. His grandfather and his father expanded their activities to the realm of public service and established the family in the *noblesse de robe,* the administrative nobility of France. Montaigne's father, Pierre Eyquem, served as mayor of Bordeaux.

As a young child Montaigne was tutored at home according to his father's ideas of pedagogy, which included the creation of a cosseted ambience of gentle encouragement and the exclusive use of Latin, still the international language of educated people. As a result the boy did not learn French until he was six years old. He continued his education at the College of Guyenne, where he found the strict discipline abhorrent and the instruction only moderately interesting, and eventually at the University of Toulouse, where he studied law. Following in the public-service tradition begun by his grandfather, he entered into the magistrature, becoming a member of the Board of Excise, the new tax court of Périgueux, and, when that body was dissolved in 1557, of the Parliament of Bordeaux, one of the eight regional parliaments that constituted the French Parliament, the highest national court of justice. There, at the age of 24, he made the acquaintance of Étienne de la Boétie, a meeting that was one of the most significant events in Montaigne's life. Between the slightly older La Boétie (1530–63), an already distinguished civil servant, humanist scholar, and writer, and Montaigne an extraordinary friendship sprang up, based on a profound intellectual and emotional closeness and reciprocity. In his essay "On Friendship" Montaigne wrote in a very touching manner about his bond with La Boétie, which he called perfect and indivisible, vastly superior to all other human alliances. When La Boétie died of dysentery, he left a void in Montaigne's life that no other being was ever able to fill, and it is likely that Montaigne started on his writing career, six years after La Boétie's death, in order to fill the emptiness left by the loss of the irretrievable friend.

Étienne de la Boétie

In 1565 Montaigne was married, acting less out of love than out of a sense of familial and social duty, to Françoise de la Chassaigne, the daughter of one of his colleagues at the Parliament of Bordeaux. He fathered six daughters, five of whom died in infancy, whereas the sixth, Léonore, survived him.

In 1569 Montaigne published his first book, a French translation of the 15th-century *Natural Theology* by the Spanish monk Raymond Sebond. He had undertaken the task at the request of his father, who, however, died in 1568, before its publication, leaving to his oldest son the title and the domain of Montaigne.

In 1570 Montaigne sold his seat in the Bordeaux Parliament, signifying his departure from public life. After taking care of the posthumous publication of La Boétie's works, together with his own dedicatory letters, he retired in 1571 to the castle of Montaigne in order to devote his time to reading, meditating, and writing. His library, installed in the castle's tower, became his refuge. It was in this round room, lined with a thousand books and decorated with Greek and Latin inscriptions, that Montaigne set out to put on paper his *essais,* that is, the probings and testings of his mind. He spent the years from 1571 to 1580 composing the first two books of the *Essays,* which comprise respectively 57 and 37 chapters of greatly varying lengths; they were published in Bordeaux in 1580.

Although most of these years were dedicated to writing, Montaigne had to supervise the running of his estate as well, and he was obliged to leave his retreat from time to time, not only to travel to the court in Paris but also to intervene as mediator in several episodes of the religious conflicts in his region and beyond. Both the Roman Catholic king Henry III and the Protestant king Henry of Navarre—who as Henry IV would become king of France and convert to Roman Catholicism—honoured and respected Montaigne, but extremists on both sides criticized and harassed him.

After the 1580 publication, eager for new experiences and profoundly disgusted by the state of affairs in France, Montaigne set out to travel, and in the course of 15 months he visited areas of France, Germany, Switzerland, Austria, and Italy. Curious by nature, interested in the smallest details of dailiness, geography, and regional idiosyncrasies, Montaigne was a born traveler. He kept a record of his trip, his *Journal de voyage* (not intended for publication and not published until 1774), which is rich in picturesque episodes, encounters, evocations, and descriptions.

Journal de voyage

While still in Italy, in the fall of 1581, Montaigne received the news that he had been elected to the office his father had held, that of mayor of Bordeaux. Reluctant to accept, because of the dismal political situation in France and because of ill health (he suffered from kidney stones, which had also plagued him on his trip), he nevertheless assumed the position at the request of Henry III and held it for two terms, until July 1585. While the beginning of his tenure was relatively tranquil, his second term was marked by an acceleration of hostilities between the warring factions, and Montaigne played a crucial role in preserving the equilibrium between the Catholic majority and the important Protestant League representation in Bordeaux. Toward the end of his term the plague broke out in Bordeaux, soon raging out of control and killing one-third of the population.

Montaigne resumed his literary work by embarking on the third book of the *Essays.* After having been interrupted again, by a renewed outbreak of the plague in the area that forced Montaigne and his family to seek refuge elsewhere, by military activity close to his estate, and by diplomatic duties, when Catherine de Médicis appealed to his abilities as a negotiator to mediate between herself and Henry of Navarre—a mission that turned out to be unsuccessful—Montaigne was able to finish the work in 1587.

The year 1588 was marked by both political and literary events. During a trip to Paris Montaigne was twice arrested and briefly imprisoned by members of the Protestant League because of his loyalty to Henry III. During the same trip he supervised the publication of the fifth edition of the *Essays,* the first to contain the 13 chapters of Book III, as well as Books I and II, enriched with many additions. He also met Marie de Gournay, an ardent and devoted young admirer of his writings. De Gournay, a writer herself, is mentioned in the *Essays* as Montaigne's "covenant daughter" and was to become his literary executrix. After the assassination of Henry III in 1589, Montaigne helped to keep Bordeaux loyal to Henry IV. He spent the last years of his life at his château, continuing to read and to reflect and to work on the *Essays,* adding new passages, which signify not so much profound changes in his ideas as further explorations of his thought and experience. Different illnesses beset him during this period, and he died after an attack of quinsy, an inflammation of the tonsils, which had deprived him of speech. His death occurred while he was hearing mass in his room, on Sept. 13, 1592.

The Essays. Montaigne saw his age as one of dissimulation, corruption, violence, and hypocrisy, and it is therefore not surprising that the point of departure of the *Essays* is situated in negativity: the negativity of Montaigne's recognition of the rule of appearances and of the loss of connection with the truth of being. Montaigne's much-discussed skepticism results from that initial negativity, as he questions the possibility of all knowing and sees the human being as a creature of weakness and failure, of inconstancy and uncertainty, of incapacity and fragmentation, or, as he wrote in the first of the essays, as "a marvelously vain, diverse, and undulating thing." His skepticism is reflected in the French title of his work, *Essais,* or "Attempts," which implies not a transmission of proven knowledge or of confident opinion but a project of trial and error, of tentative exploration. Neither a reference to an established genre (for Montaigne's book inaugurated the term essay for the short prose composition treating a given subject in a rather informal and personal manner) nor an indication of a necessary internal unity and structure within the work, the title indicates an intellectual attitude of questioning and of continuous assessment.

Skepticism

Montaigne's skepticism does not, however, preclude a belief in the existence of truth but rather constitutes a defense against the danger of locating truth in false, unexamined, and externally imposed notions. His skepticism, combined with his desire for truth, drives him to the rejection of commonly accepted ideas and to a profound distrust of generalizations and abstractions; it also shows him the way to an exploration of the only realm that promises certainty: that of concrete phenomena and primarily the basic phenomenon of his own body-and-mind self. This self, with all its imperfections, constitutes the only possible site where the search for truth can start, and it is the reason Montaigne, from the beginning to the end of the *Essays,* does not cease to affirm that "I am myself the matter of my book." He finds that his identity, his "master form" as he calls it, cannot be defined in simple terms of a constant and stable self, since it is instead a changeable and fragmented thing, and that the valorization and acceptance of these traits is the only guarantee of authenticity and integrity, the only way of remaining faithful to the truth of one's being and one's nature rather than to alien semblances.

Yet, despite his insistence that the self guard its freedom toward outside influences and the tyranny of imposed customs and opinions, Montaigne believes in the value of reaching outside the self. Indeed, throughout his writings, as he did in his private and public life, he manifests the need to entertain ties with the world of other people and of events. For this necessary coming and going between the interiority of the self and the exteriority of the world, Montaigne uses the image of the back room: human beings have their front room, facing the street, where they meet and interact with others, but they need always to be able to retreat into the back room of the most private self, where they may reaffirm the freedom and strength of intimate identity and reflect upon the vagaries of experience. Given that always-available retreat, Montaigne encourages contact with others, from which one may learn much that is useful. In order to do so, he advocates travel, reading, especially of history books, and conversations with friends. These friends, for Montaigne, are necessarily men. While none can ever replace La Boétie, it is possible to have interesting and worthwhile exchanges with men of discernment and wit. As for his relations with women, Montaigne wrote about them with a frankness unusual for his time. The only uncomplicated bond is that of marriage, which reposes, for Montaigne, on reasons of family and posterity and in which one invests little of oneself. Love, on the other hand, with its emotional and erotic demands, comports the risk of enslavement and loss of freedom. Montaigne, often designated as a misogynist, does in fact recognize that men and women are fundamentally alike in their fears, desires, and attempts to find and affirm their own identity and that only custom and adherence to an antiquated status quo establish the apparent differences between the sexes, but he does not explore the possibility of overcoming that fundamental separation and of establishing an intellectual equality.

Friendship and love

Montaigne extends his curiosity about others to the inhabitants of the New World, with whom he had become acquainted through his lively interest in oral and written travel accounts and through his meeting in 1562 with three Brazilian Indians whom the explorer Nicolas Durand de Villegagnon had brought back to France. Giving an example of cultural relativism and tolerance, rare in his time, he finds these people, in their fidelity to their own nature and in their cultural and personal dignity and sense of beauty, greatly superior to the inhabitants of western Europe, who in the conquests of the New World and in their own internal wars have shown themselves to be the true barbarians. The suffering and humiliation imposed on the New World's natives by their conquerors provoke his indignation and compassion.

Involvement in public service is also a part of interaction with the world, and it should be seen as a duty to be honourably and loyally discharged but never allowed to become a consuming and autonomy-destroying occupation.

Montaigne applies and illustrates his ideas concerning the independence and freedom of the self and the importance of social and intellectual intercourse in all his writings and in particular in his essay on the education of children. There, as elsewhere, he advocates the value of concrete experience over abstract learning and of independent judgment over an accumulation of undigested notions uncritically accepted from others. He also stresses, throughout his work, the role of the body, as in his candid descriptions of his own bodily functions and in his extensive musings on the realities of illness, of aging, and of death. The presence of death pervades the *Essays,* as Montaigne wants to familiarize himself with the inevitability of dying and so to rid himself of the tyranny of fear, and he is able to accept death as part of nature's exigencies, inherent in life's expectations and limitations.

Montaigne seems to have been a loyal if not fervent Roman Catholic all his life, but he distrusted all human pretenses to knowledge of a spiritual experience which is not attached to a concretely lived reality. He declined to speculate on a transcendence that falls beyond human ken, believing in God but refusing to invoke him in necessarily presumptuous and reductive ways.

Although Montaigne certainly knew the classical philosophers, his ideas spring less out of their teaching than out of the completely original meditation on himself, which he extends to a description of the human being and to an ethics of authenticity, self-acceptance, and tolerance. The *Essays* are the record of his thoughts, presented not in artificially organized stages but as they occurred and reoccurred to him in different shapes throughout his thinking and writing activity. They are not the record of an intellectual evolution but of a continuous accretion, and he insists on the immediacy and the authenticity of their testimony. To denote their consubstantiality with his natural self, he describes them as his children, and, in an image of startling and completely nonpejorative earthiness, as the excrements of his mind. As he refuses to impose a false unity on the spontaneous workings of his thought, so he refuses to impose a false structure on his *Essays.* "As my mind roams, so does my style," he wrote, and the multiple digressions, the wandering developments, the savory, concrete vocabulary, all denote that fidelity to the freshness and the immediacy of the living thought. Throughout the text he sprinkles anecdotes taken from ancient as well as contemporary authors and from popular lore, which reinforce his critical analysis of reality; he also peppers his writing with quotes, yet another way of interacting with others, that is, with the authors of the past who surround him in his library. Neither anecdotes nor quotes impinge upon the autonomy of his own ideas, although they may spark or reinforce a train of thought, and they become an integral part of the book's fabric.

Form of the *Essays*

Montaigne's *Essays* thus incorporate a profound skepticism concerning the human being's dangerously inflated claims to knowledge and certainty but also assert that there is no greater achievement than the ability to accept one's being without either contempt or illusion, in the full realization of its limitations and its richness.

Readership. Throughout the ages the *Essays* have been widely and variously read, and their readers have tended to look to them, and into them, for answers to their own needs. Not all his contemporaries manifested the enthusiasm of Marie de Gournay, who fainted from excitement at her first reading. She did recognize in the book the full force of an unusual mind revealing itself, but most of the intellectuals of the period preferred to find in Montaigne a safe reincarnation of stoicism. Here started a misunderstanding that was to last a long time, save in the case of the exceptional reader. The *Essays* were to be perused as an anthology of philosophical maxims, a repository of consecrated wisdom, rather than as the complete expression of a highly individual thought and experience. That Montaigne could write about his most intimate reactions and feelings, that he could describe his own physical appearance and preferences, for instance, seemed shocking and irrelevant to many, just as the apparent confusion of his writing seemed a weakness to be deplored rather than a guarantee of authenticity.

In the 17th century, when an educated nobility set the tone, he was chiefly admired for his portrayal of the *honnête homme,* the well-educated, nonpedantic man of manners, as much at home in a salon as in his study, a gentleman of smiling wisdom and elegant, discreet disenchantment. In the same period, however, religious authors such as Francis of Sales and Blaise Pascal deplored his skepticism as anti-Christian and denounced what they interpreted as an immoral self-absorption. In the pre-Revolutionary 18th century the image of a dogmatically irreligious Montaigne continued to be dominant, and Voltaire and Denis Diderot saw in him a precursor of the free thought of the Enlightenment. For Jean-Jacques Rousseau, however, the encounter with the *Essays* was differently and fundamentally important, as he rightly considered Montaigne the master and the model of the self-portrait. Rousseau inaugurated the perception of the book as the entirely personal project of a human being in search of his identity and unafraid to talk without dissimulation about his profound nature. In the 19th century some of the old misunderstandings continued, but there was a growing understanding and appreciation of Montaigne not only as a master of ideas but also as the writer of the particular, the individual, the intimate—the writer as friend and familiar. Gustave Flaubert kept the *Essays* on his bedside table and recognized in Montaigne an alter ego, as would, in the 20th century, authors such as André Gide, Michel Butor, and Roland Barthes.

The *Essays* were first translated into English by John Florio in 1603, and Anglophone readers have included Francis Bacon, John Webster, William Shakespeare, Lord Byron, William Makepeace Thackeray, Ralph Waldo Emerson, Virginia Woolf, T.S. Eliot, and Aldous Huxley.

Today Montaigne continues to be studied in all aspects of his text by great numbers of scholars and to be read by people from all corners of the earth. In an age that may seem as violent and absurd as his own, his refusal of intolerance and fanaticism and his lucid awareness of the human potential for destruction, coupled with his belief in the human capacity for self-assessment, honesty, and compassion, appeal as convincingly as ever to the many who find in him a guide and a friend.

MAJOR WORKS

ESSAYS: *Essais de messire Michel Seigneur de Montaigne,* 2 vol. in 1 (1580); *Essais de messire Michel Seigneur de Montaigne; édition seconde, revue & augmentée* (1582); and *Essais de messire Michel Seigneur de Montaigne; cinquiesme édition, augmentée d'un troisième livre et de six cens additions aux deux premiers,* 3 vol. (1588).

OTHER WORKS: *Journal de voyage* (1774).

EARLY TRANSLATIONS: *The Essays; or, Morall, Politike, and Millitarie Discourses of Lo: Michaell de Montaigne,* trans. by John Florio (1603); and *The Diary of Montaigne's Journey to Italy in 1580 and 1581,* trans. by E.J. Trechmann (1929).

COLLECTED WORKS: *Œuvres complètes de Michel de Montaigne,* ed. by A. Armaingaud, 12 vol. (1924–41); *Œuvres complètes,* ed. by Albert Thibaudet and Maurice Rat, new ed. (1967); and *Complete Works: Essays, Travel Journal, Letters,* trans. and ed. by Donald M. Frame (1957).

RECOMMENDED EDITIONS: *Complete Essays* (1958, reprinted 1973), and *Selections from the Essays* (1973), both trans. and ed. by Donald M. Frame.

BIBLIOGRAPHY. DONALD M. FRAME, *Montaigne* (1965, reprinted 1984), is a detailed biography by an authority in the field. Interpretive approaches to reading Montaigne are collected in *Montaigne: Essays in Reading* (1983). PETER BURKE, *Montaigne* (1982), offers a very readable brief survey of the historical and philosophical context of Montaigne's life and creativity. Most other critical works focus on exploring the essays and their role in shaping the intellectual tradition: R.A. SAYCE, *The Essays of Montaigne* (1972); M.A. SCREECH, *Montaigne and Melancholy: The Wisdom of the Essays* (1983); JEAN STAROBINSKI, *Montaigne in Motion* (1985; originally published in French, 1982); and DOROTHY GABE COLEMAN, *Montaigne's Essays* (1987).

(T.A.Sa.)

Montreal

Montreal (French Montréal), the largest city of Quebec province and the second most populous city of Canada, is uniquely situated. The present city proper occupies about one-third of Île de Montréal (Montreal Island), the largest of the 234 islands of the Hochelaga Archipelago, one of three archipelagos near the confluence of the Ottawa and St. Lawrence rivers. The city was built around and up Mont-Royal, which rises 763 feet (233 metres) above sea level (some 660 feet above the island shores). The city proper occupies an area of 61 square miles (158 square kilometres); and several independent cities and towns comprise the 1,087-square-mile metropolitan area that covers Montreal and other islands, as well as both shores of the St. Lawrence. Montreal is the major seaport on the St. Lawrence River and Seaway, lying between the navigable waters of the open Atlantic Ocean to the east and of the Great Lakes to the west.

Along with New York City and San Francisco, Montreal is one of North America's most cosmopolitan cities. It is often said to be the second largest French-speaking city in the world (after Paris), a boast that is sometimes disputed. English and French are Canada's two official languages but, in accordance with a law passed for Quebec province in 1977, the use of English in schools and in government and commercial activity is restricted. Yet, in several areas of Montreal, one must still express oneself in English to be understood fully. This phenomenon reflects decades of dominance over Montreal's economic life by the English-speaking minority. With the advent to power in 1976 of the Parti Québécois—which advocates political independence from and economic association with the rest of Canada—"normal" tensions between French- and English-speaking communities have fluctuated.

In spite of politics and unrest, Montreal remains a city of great charm, of vivacity, and of gaiety, one of the most appealing in North America, as well as one of unquestioned modernity in its physical appearance and way of life. Thus it was chosen as the site of the International World Exposition in 1967—Expo 67. No great objections were raised when the event was perpetuated for the public each summer under the title Terre des Hommes (Man and His World).

The article is divided into the following sections:

Physical and human geography

THE LANDSCAPE

The city layout. The layout of Montreal has been affected throughout its history by the river and the natural rises of the terrain from it, including the slopes of Mont-Royal. These factors produced a general southwest–northeast pattern of growth, and since its incorporation the city has been divided by Boulevard Saint-Laurent (St. Lawrence Street) into western and eastern sections. Such designations as street, avenue, and boulevard are virtually interchangeable in Montreal, and the ensuing confusion is enhanced by the occurrence of the place-names of thoroughfares and other city and suburban sites in both French and English.

The city centre. Since about 1958 the centre of Montreal has been transformed significantly, abetted by post-World War II prosperity, by preparations for Expo 67 and the exposition itself, and by an administration intent upon grand designs. Built with the aid of U.S. capital and developers, Place Ville-Marie comprises a cruciform building more than 40 stories tall and many underground shops, restaurants, and theatres, linked to which are nearby skyscrapers with similar underground complexes. Together, this downtown area provides the Canadian metropolis with an answer to New York City's Rockefeller Center, with an underground commercial, culinary, and artistic life among the most advanced in the Western Hemisphere. Similar change has spread throughout the city, often obliterating historic landmarks, but the city has preserved the historic centre known as Vieux-Montréal (Old Montreal). There, seekers after nostalgia stroll amid reminiscences of the past that are in striking contrast to the city's overall momentum into the vanguard of urban modernity.

Modernization of the city

THE PEOPLE

The 1871 population of Montreal proper—about 133,000—increased 10-fold in the following century, and the pace of metropolitan planning promises ongoing growth in addition to annexation of adjacent areas. Immigration from abroad practically ceased during World War I, but a steady flow of people continued from other parts of Canada and from the United States. Although the birth rate among Canadians of French descent dropped markedly, immigration from the Continent reduced the percentage of Montrealers of British descent after World War II. French-speaking citizens account for about two-thirds of the population, with the English-speaking proportion increasingly eroded by immigrants from all over the world. Religious affiliations generally follow ethnic traditions, with Roman Catholicism by far the dominant faith.

On the other hand, newcomers to Montreal quickly learn that English is the more practical tongue, for in Montreal as in most of Canada—except Quebec city and smaller centres of Quebec province—English is the primary language of commerce and industry. The economic upper classes are mostly old Montreal-bred English-speaking families, with a sprinkling of French and others. The middle classes are more mixed, whereas the lower economic stratum continues to be made up mainly of French- and Irish-Canadians and of new immigrants. Thousands of blacks have immigrated from the United States, most of them settling in the lower part of Montréal-Ouest. The instabilities of Montreal and of Quebec province as a whole are largely the result of the continuing sociolinguistic separateness of and economic disparity between the two major ethnic groups. Majority political power has been achieved by the French community, but equivalent weight in other areas has been slower to arrive.

Social and political tensions

THE ECONOMY

Trade and industry. Montreal suffered in the 1970s from a "Go West" trend, to the benefit of Ontario and the western provinces rich in oil and natural gas. It remains, however, the headquarters of most of the largest Canadian banks, railroad lines, and insurance companies, as well as for the International Civil Aviation Organization, an agency, affiliated with the United Nations, that sets the rules and standards for international air traffic. The city is also an important shipping and industrial centre. The

Place Jacques-Cartier in the Vieux-Montréal (Old Montreal) section of Montreal.
Milt and Joan Mann—CAMERAMANN INTERNATIONAL

centuries-long colonial fur trade that penetrated the new continent to its westernmost territories formed the city's earliest commercial ventures, while soapmaking, brewing and distilling (among John Molson's main civic legacies), and wood and leather fabrication are longtime Montreal industries. Innumerable other products of a modern manufacturing economy emanate from the city's factories, along with millions of gallons of processed petroleum each day from Montréal-Est refineries.

Shopping areas abound throughout the city, in the more remote residential sections as well as throughout the supermodern underground city of streets and shops that has aided Montrealers to carry on in spite of the five to 10 feet of snow dumped on the city each winter. This deluge of snow from November through April is among the most significant factors in Montreal's life, costing the city millions of dollars annually to remove it from the streets.

Transportation. The perennial grumbling of Montrealers about municipal transportation is more an exercise of democratic rights than a reflection of reality. Compared with those in other large cities, bus and subway lines allow easy movement throughout the area at relatively low cost. The subway, called the Métro, has three lines running under the city and to Longueuil on the south shore of the St. Lawrence River. Each station is different in architectural design and artistic decor. Public transportation dates from 1847, and by 1868 buses mounted on sleighs replaced rail cars during the winter. By 1894 the entire system had been electrified and the last horsecars withdrawn from service. Montreal is also served by two airports: Montreal International (also called Dorval), which handles domestic and U.S. flights, and Mirabel International, which handles all other international flights.

The modern Métro

ADMINISTRATIVE AND SOCIAL CONDITIONS

Government. From the present city hall, sixth in the city's history, Montreal is governed by a mayor and a 56-member council, all elected for four years, and a six-member executive committee selected by the council. A Montreal Urban Community replaced the Montreal Metropolitan Corporation in 1969. Its responsibilities, for the whole of Montreal Island and Bizard Island to the north, include assessment and tax collection, traffic control, water and sewage services, police and fire protection, and antipollution activities. It is governed by a general council and an executive committee.

The metropolitan area embraces numerous cities (including Montreal), towns, villages, and parishes. The changes in the region's economic structure and increasing business and white-collar employment, intensified by the growing modernization of the city, have brought about some of the main administrative problems. The French-speaking majority, most of whom were relegated to blue-collar jobs for decades, reacted against this historical pattern with some success, attributable in part to legislation and to the goodwill of the more moderate elements of the two communities.

Education. As throughout Quebec, a dual school system for Roman Catholic and Protestant students is supported from the public treasury. The language of instruction—French or English, respectively—rigidly follows the religious division.

Montreal is probably the outstanding city of Canada in terms of higher education. McGill University (founded 1821) and Concordia University (1974; formed by the merger of Sir George Williams University, founded 1929, and Loyola College, founded 1899) offer mainly English-language instruction, whereas the Université de Montréal (1876) and the Université du Québec à Montréal (1968) serve the French-speaking population.

CULTURAL LIFE

With its Place des Arts, museums, public libraries, art galleries, bookshops in most European languages, symphony orchestra, publishing houses, theatre companies, and free public lectures at the universities, Montreal must be accounted a major culture centre.

The Place des Arts is a complex of concert and theatre halls in downtown Montreal. The nearby Place Desjardins is an exciting example of modern architecture; the complex, with its multilevel terraces, balconies, mezzanines, and sunken plaza, comprises three office towers, a public square, a hotel, and several restaurants and retail stores. Art instruction is given, among other places, at the Museum of Fine Arts. Besides a conservatory of music, faculties or schools of music offer instruction at the universities. The Terre des Hommes exhibition, which draws millions of visitors yearly, is the site of the Museum of Contemporary Art.

In the 1930s only a few bookshops existed, but today bookshops can be found in all districts and shopping centres; and "new Canadians," as new immigrants are called, can buy books, reviews, and magazines in their native languages. The Municipal Library has several branches, and special libraries are located throughout the city. Publishing houses, both English and French, prosper.

Montrealers are great sports enthusiasts. Hockey and baseball are foremost, but other indoor and outdoor sports

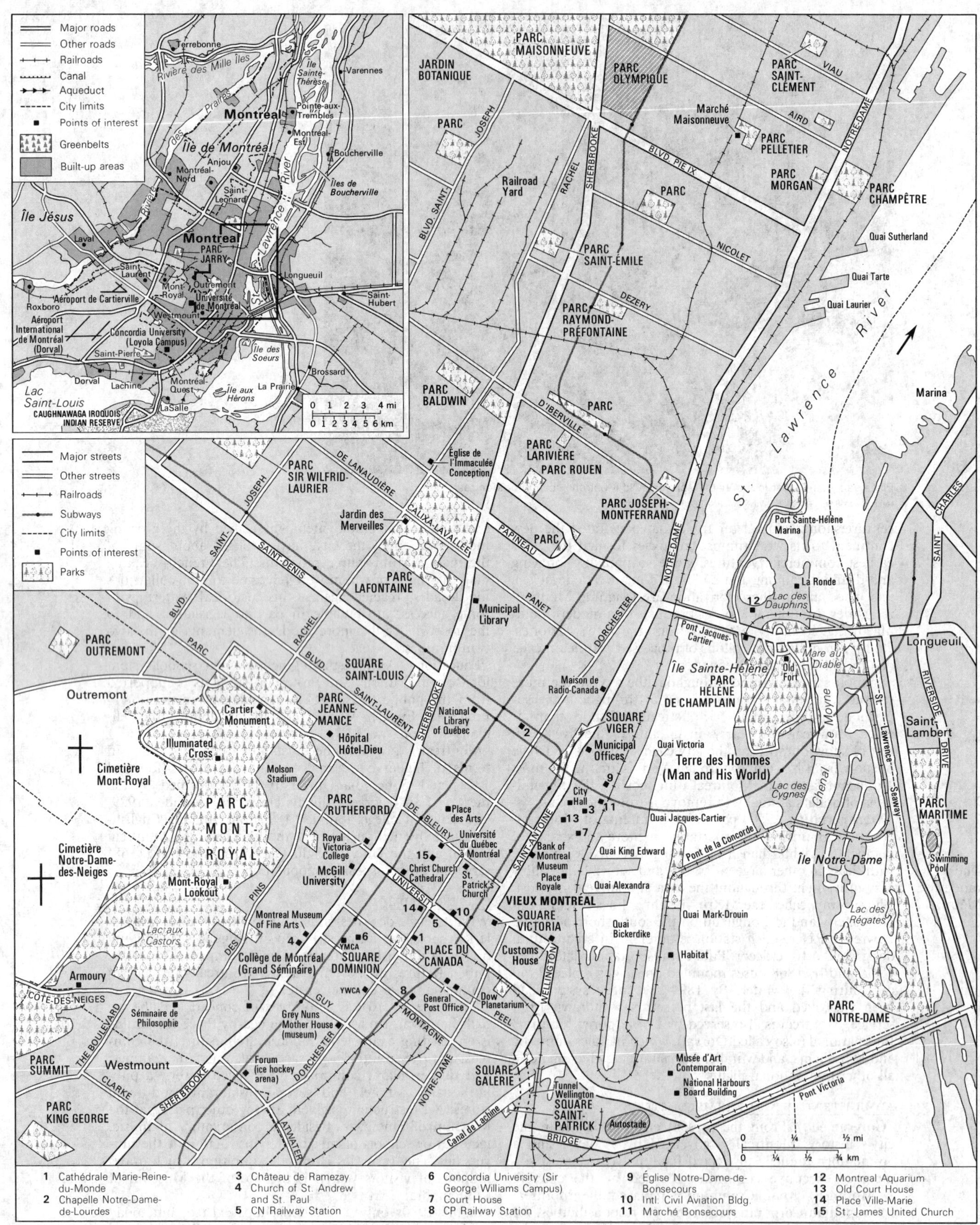

Central Montreal and (inset) its metropolitan area.

have many adherents. In winter the slopes of Mont-Royal are covered with skiers. Montreal also has two very popular racetracks and was the site of the international Summer Olympic Games, for which a sports stadium seating more than 70,000 and a complex containing six swimming pools were built.

History

EARLY SETTLEMENT

The site of Montreal was called Hochelaga by the Huron Indians when Jacques Cartier, a French navigator and explorer, visited it in 1535–36 on his second voyage to the New World. More than 1,000 Indians welcomed him on the slope of the mountain that he named Mont Réal, or Mont-Royal. More than 50 years elapsed before other Frenchmen returned, this time with Samuel de Champlain, the founder of Quebec city. Hochelaga had disappeared, replaced on the shores of the St. Lawrence by a settlement that Champlain called Place Royale.

The founding fathers

It was not until May 1642 that Paul de Chomedey, sieur de Maisonneuve, founded today's Montreal. He built dwellings, a chapel, a hospital, and other structures, protecting the settlement against Indian attack with a stockade. He named the aggregate Ville-Marie.

The community was granted its first civic charter by King Louis XIV in 1644, and Chomedey became its first governor. The first hospital, the Hôtel-Dieu, was founded in 1644 by Jeanne Mance and the first school for girls in 1653 by Marguerite Bourgeoys. Almost immediately a society of priests, Les Messieurs de Saint-Sulpice, took charge of education for boys.

The real development of Montreal began during the first half of the 18th century. Land grants were made, and farming was developed outside the original fortifications. Colonization was initiated under the French seigniorial system, in which a landowner leased portions of his holdings to numerous farming families. For many years, Montreal was a base for explorers and traders, and by the end of the 18th century outlying settlements—Saint-Henri and Lachine to the west and Longue-Pointe and Pointe-aux-Trembles to the east—had taken root, later to become part of the city or of the Montreal Urban Community.

By 1672 the population of Montreal had reached 1,500, but it did not obtain city status for another 120 years and was not incorporated until 1833. The city surrendered peacefully to British forces in 1760 and, with all of New France, became part of the British North American empire in 1763. In November 1775 Montreal was occupied by American Revolutionary forces, who retreated in the spring following the abortive siege of the city of Quebec by Benedict Arnold and thus failed to secure Canada for the new United States. In 1796 Canada's first public library was opened in Montreal, and in the following year daily postal service was established between Montreal and the United States.

EVOLUTION OF THE MODERN CITY

In 1809 John Molson—entrepreneur, brewer, banker, and carrier—linked Montreal and Quebec by water with the first Canadian steamship. Canada's first bank, the Bank of Montreal, was founded in 1817, and the Lachine Canal, forerunner of the St. Lawrence Seaway, was started in 1821. In 1825 Molson, the "Montrealer par excellence," provided his city with a splendid theatre, and gas lighting appeared by 1838. A Committee of Trade, forerunner of the Board of Trade (1842), was founded in 1822, and from 1844 to 1849 Montreal was the capital of Canada. On April 25, 1849, a mob put fire to the Parliament building, possibly on the ground that it had lost its vocation. In 1847 telegraph links were made with the cities of Quebec and New York; in 1853 a shipping service between Montreal, Liverpool, and the Continent was begun; in 1856 a railroad to Toronto opened; in 1858 a transatlantic cable to Europe was laid; and in 1861 the city's first horse-drawn tramways began operation.

Sequence of civic firsts

Fires destroyed hundreds of buildings in the early 1850s, and an economic slump provoked numerous bankruptcies in 1857. The Confederation of Canada was proclaimed in 1867, and 10 years later the city had its first labour strike and first telephone conversation with Quebec. It had its first electric lighting in 1882, electric tramways in 1892, and the first automobile along its streets and movie houses along its sidewalks in 1903.

By 1900 Montreal's population reached 270,000, and it began to annex several cities, towns, and villages on its outskirts. It purchased Île Sainte-Hélène (St. Helen's Island) in 1908, the site, with two neighbouring man-made islands, of Expo 67. Montreal's famous ice-hockey team, the Canadiens, was founded in 1909 (and has since won more world championships than any other professional team). In 1922 several mergers gave birth to the Canadian National Railways Company (CNR), which, like the Canadian Pacific in 1881, established its head office in Montreal.

The world wars gave impetus to the economic life of Montreal, as they did to most industrial centres of North America, and in January 1947 the U.S. Congress began to consider a joint venture with Canada for building the St. Lawrence Seaway. In 1959 the need for a Montreal Metropolitan Corporation was recognized by the Quebec provincial government (which, like others in Canada, has exclusive jurisdiction over municipalities). In 1960 the Metropolitan Boulevard, a throughway encircling Montreal, was opened. In 1962 construction was started on the Métro, supervised by engineers from the Paris Métro; the system was inaugurated six months before the opening of Expo 67. With the growing recognition of Montreal as a major world centre following this universally acclaimed exposition, it became the first non-U.S. city to be awarded a major-league baseball franchise. Its players first took the field in 1969 as the Montreal Expos.

BIBLIOGRAPHY. Firsthand accounts are the narrative journals of JACQUES CARTIER and SAMUEL DE CHAMPLAIN; and the *Histoire du Montréal* of FRANÇOIS DOLLIER DE CASSON (1672). Standard works include: WILLIAM H. ATHERTON, *Montreal,* 3 vol. (1914); STEPHEN LEACOCK, *Leacock's Montreal,* rev. ed. by JOHN CULLITON (1963); KATHLEEN JENKINS, *Montreal: Island City of the St. Lawrence* (1966); ROBERT RUMILLY, *Histoire de Montréal,* 5 vol. (1970–75); and GERALD CLARK, *Montreal: The New Cité* (1982). JOHN IRWIN COOPER, *Montreal: A Brief History* (1969), is a good summary although some interesting details are omitted. Also of interest is the article on Montreal in the *Encyclopedia Canadiana* (1977). The numerous publications of the MONTREAL ECONOMIC RESEARCH BUREAU, including the *Abridged History of Montreal,* rev. and enlarged (1970), are both informative and reliable. JEAN-CLAUDE MARSAN, *Montreal in Evolution* (1981), is a history of Montreal's architecture and urban development.

(C.Fe./W.J.C.)

Moscow

One of the world's great cities, Moscow (Russian Moskva) is the capital of the Soviet Union and also of its largest constituent unit, the Russian Soviet Federated Socialist Republic. As capital of the largest and one of the most powerful countries in the world, Moscow is a city of international significance. Since first mentioned in chronicles of 1147, Moscow has played a vital role in Russian history; indeed, the history of the city and of the state are closely interlinked. For more than 600 years Moscow has also been the spiritual centre of the Russian Orthodox Church.

Today Moscow is not only the political centre of the Soviet Union but also the country's leading city in population, in industrial output, and in cultural, scientific, and educational importance; the name Kremlin (Russian Kreml), the seat of government in Moscow, has become a synonym for Soviet authority.

Moscow covers an area of about 386 square miles (1,000 square kilometres), its outer limit being roughly delineated by the Moscow Ring Road. Most of the area beyond this highway has been designated as a Forest-Park Zone, or greenbelt, in which urban development is carefully controlled.

This article is divided into the following sections:

Physical and human geography

THE LANDSCAPE

Site and relief. Moscow stands on the Moskva River, a tributary of the Oka and thus of the Volga, in the centre of the vast plain of European Russia. The city and its surrounding area, the Moscow oblast (administrative region), are at the heart of what is called the Central Economic Region, which is the most highly developed and densely populated part of the Soviet Union. Moscow lies in the broad, extremely shallow valley of the Moskva and its tributaries. The valley itself overlies a deep syncline of the Russian Platform of very ancient crystalline rocks, a granitic basement more than a mile below the present-day surface. The trough in the platform has been filled through long geological time by sedimentary rocks, mostly of Devonian and Carboniferous age, with Jurassic series and some Cretaceous rocks nearest the surface. Hardly anywhere is the bedrock exposed on the surface.

The advances and retreats of Pleistocene glaciers deposited a thick mantle of boulder clays and morainic sands and gravels into which the sinuous Moskva River cut its wide valley in successive stages, marked by four corresponding levels. Geologically recent alluvial deposits cover their surfaces. Beside the river itself is a narrow belt of floodplain; a few feet above this is the first terrace, which yields to the successively higher second and third levels. The last of these terraces, rising up to 100–115 feet (30–35 metres) above the river, is the most extensive, and much of Moscow is built on it. Northward the third terrace merges imperceptibly with a plain of clays and sands, which slopes up very gradually to the Klin-Dmitrov morainic ridge some 40 miles (64 kilometres) north of the city. Eastward and southeastward the surface equally gradually merges into the vast, almost completely flat and very swampy clay plain of the Meshchera Lowland, which extends far beyond the city limits.

Almost everywhere surface relief is minor. The legend that Moscow is built on seven hills is an exaggeration, although there are a few small hills in and around the city centre. Only in the southwest of the city is there an upland area on Cretaceous rocks, covered by glacial morainic material. This is the Teplostanskaya Upland, which rises more than 400 feet above the Moskva River and on which is the highest elevation within Moscow's limits, 830 feet above sea level. One of the sweeping bends of the Moskva has cut into the edge of the Teplostanskaya Upland a steep cliff, the Lenin Hills (formerly the Sparrow Hills), from the top of which there are fine panoramic views of the city.

The human imprint. Long occupation has extensively altered the natural setting. The "cultural layer," consisting of debris of buildings demolished long ago and of other materials deposited by humans, is up to 50 feet deep in some parts of central Moscow. Almost all the small rivers and streams that once flowed into the Moskva through the city area have now been put into underground conduits or filled in. The only tributaries still visible are the Yauza on the left (northern) bank and, on the right bank, the Gorodnya and Kotlovka. The Yauza, the largest of these, and the Moskva itself are controlled by stone embank- Rivers

Novosti Press Agency

The Kremlin in Moscow, on the Moskva River, with the Water Tower in the foreground and (from the left) the Borovitskaya Tower, the Armoury Palace, the Kremlin Great Palace, and the Archangel Cathedral.

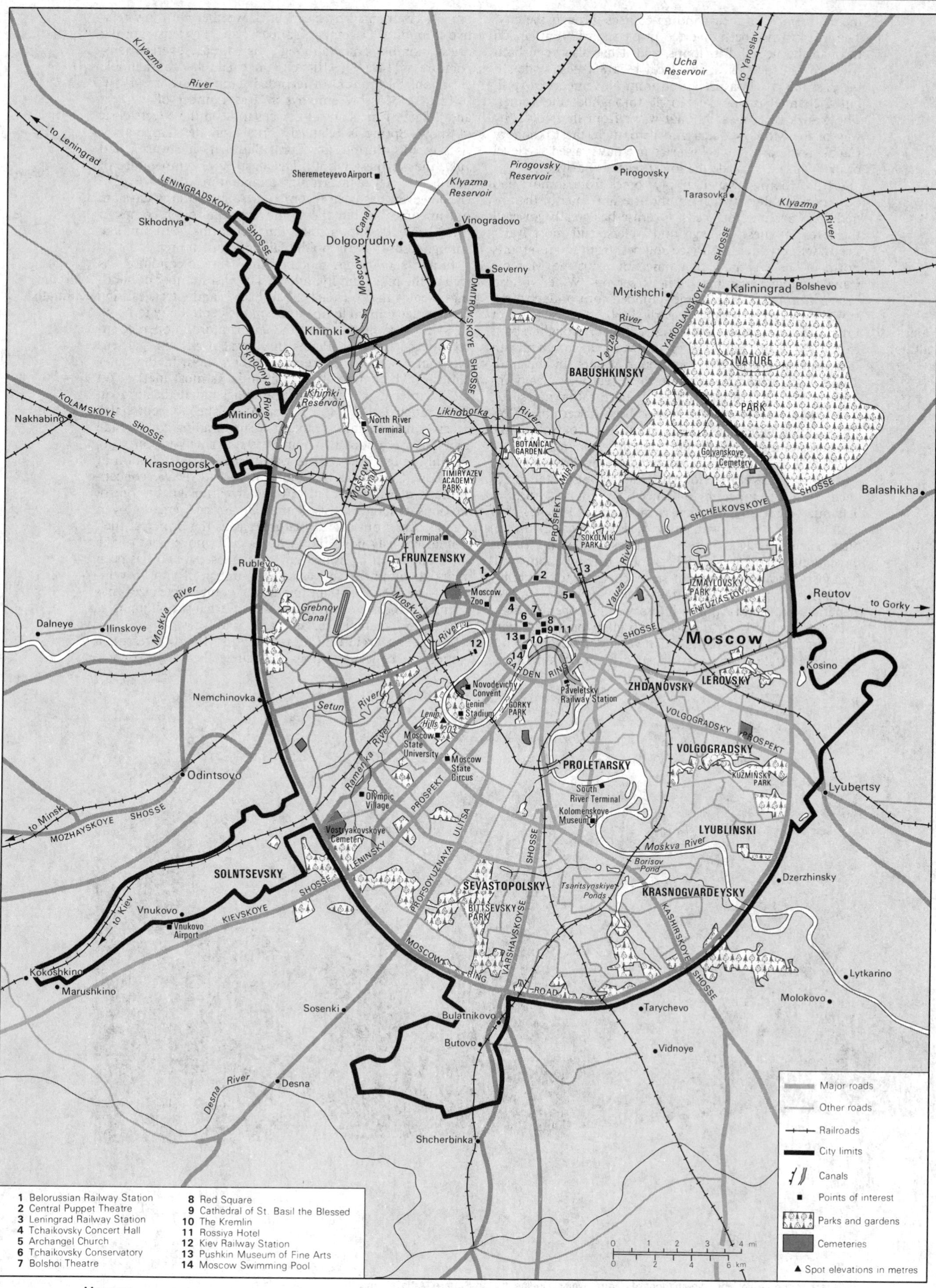
1 Belorussian Railway Station
2 Central Puppet Theatre
3 Leningrad Railway Station
4 Tchaikovsky Concert Hall
5 Archangel Church
6 Tchaikovsky Conservatory
7 Bolshoi Theatre
8 Red Square
9 Cathedral of St. Basil the Blessed
10 The Kremlin
11 Rossiya Hotel
12 Kiev Railway Station
13 Pushkin Museum of Fine Arts
14 Moscow Swimming Pool
Major roads
Other roads
Railroads
City limits
Canals
Points of interest
Parks and gardens
Cemeteries
▲ Spot elevations in metres
Moscow
FRUNZENSKY
BABUSHKINSKY
ZHDANOVSKY
LEROVSKY
VOLGOGRADSKY
PROLETARSKY
LYUBLINSKI
SEVASTOPOLSKY
KRASNOGVARDEYSKY
SOLNTSEVSKY
NATURE PARK
Ucha Reservoir
Pirogovsky Reservoir
Klyazma Reservoir
Khimki Reservoir
Sheremeteyevo Airport
Vnukovo Airport
to Leningrad
to Yaroslavl
to Gorky
to Minsk
to Kiev
GARDEN RING
MOSCOW RING ROAD

Moscow.

ments for most of their winding courses through the city. The Moskva has been diverted in places, with cuts made through the necks of its loops, and it has also been both widened and deepened; in places it is 800 feet wide. In the past the river was icebound from November to April, but a channel is now kept open throughout the winter. The Yauza receives additional water from the Volga, by way of the Moscow Canal and its branch, the Likhobory Canal. Two dams on its lower course have raised the level of the Yauza and made the lower reaches navigable.

Part of Moscow's water supply comes from some 1,000 deep bores in the city that tap the artesian water of the underlying Carboniferous beds. Overuse has greatly lowered the levels of these underground waters, and most water needs are now met by surface sources, from the reservoirs north of the city built in connection with the Moscow Canal, in particular the Ucha Reservoir. Water is also drawn from the Moskva and pumped into underground storage reservoirs. Until the early 1960s the discharge of untreated sewage and industrial effluents brought about extremely severe pollution of the Moskva, together with increasing pollution of underground waters. In the mid-1960s a major effort was made to correct it by heavy investment in antipollution and water purification measures. Since then great improvement has been discernible. Slow but steady progress has also been made in controlling the discharge of industrial effluents into the river and into bore wells, and the discharge of untreated sewage has ended.

Water pollution

Climate. The climate of Moscow is continental, modified by the temperate influence of westerly winds of Atlantic origin. Precipitation is moderate, 23 inches (581 millimetres) a year, with a marked summer maximum that reaches a peak in July. A considerable part of the precipitation falls as snow; beginning usually about mid-October—though permanent snow cover is not normally established before the beginning of November—it lasts generally until mid-April. Winters are thus long and dark, although southerly airstreams occasionally bring days with temperatures above freezing. Conversely, northerly winds from the Arctic bring very sharp drops in temperature, often accompanied by clear, brisk weather with low relative humidity. December, January, and February are the driest months. Thus, although the January average temperature is 14° F (−10° C), there can be considerable variation; the minimum recorded temperature is −44° F (−42° C). Moscow employs a large number of workers and a fleet of mechanical devices to keep the streets clear of snow. Spring is relatively brief, and the temperature rises rapidly during late April. Summers are warm, and July, the warmest month, has an average temperature of 65° F (18° C); a maximum temperature of 99° F (37° C), however, has been recorded in August. Rainy days are not uncommon, but the summer rainfall often comes in brief, heavy downpours and thunderstorms. Autumn, like spring, is short, with rapidly falling temperatures.

Human activity has modified the climatic conditions as well as the relief and hydrology. The vast number of buildings creates the so-called urban heat-island effect, causing the average annual temperature in the central city to be up to 3° F (2° C) higher than the temperature in open country outside the city. Plants in central parks and gardens blossom a week or more earlier than those in the outer suburbs. The temperature differential is most marked on clear winter nights, when the buildings radiate heat; it can be as much as 18° F (10° C) or more. The city centre also receives heavier rainfall than the surrounding countryside and averages about 100 hours less sunshine per year.

Urban climate

Until the late 1950s there was increasing air pollution in Moscow. Smog was common, often with heavy concentrations of sulfur dioxide. A major campaign to control noxious emissions was launched, assisted greatly by a changeover from coal to natural gas as the principal fuel. Some seriously polluting factories were moved out of the city. The resulting improvement in Moscow's air has been marked, although the growing number of motor vehicles—still far fewer than in cities of comparable size—has increased the concentrations of such exhaust pollutants as carbon monoxide in certain parts of Moscow.

Layout and architecture. A map of Moscow presents a pattern of concentric rings that circle the rough triangle

Nikolai Ignatiev

Visitors to the Lenin Mausoleum (right of centre) waiting in line in Red Square. At left is the Cathedral of St. Basil the Blessed; to the right, the east wall of the Kremlin.

of the Kremlin and its rectangular extension, the Kitay-gorod, with outwardly radiating spokes connecting the rings, the whole pattern being broken by the twisting, northwest–southeast-trending Moskva River. These rings and radials mark the historical stages of the city's growth: successive epochs of development are traced by the Boulevard Ring and the Garden Ring (both following the line of former fortifications), the Moscow Little Ring Railway (built in part along the line of the former Kamer-Kollezhsky customs barrier), and the Moscow Ring Road.

The Kremlin. The hub of the layout, and today as throughout its history the heart of Moscow, is the fortified enclosure of the Kremlin, the symbol of first Russian and later Soviet power and authority. Its crenellated red brick walls and 20 towers (19 with spires) were built at the end of the 15th century, when a host of Italian builders arrived in Moscow at the invitation of Ivan III the Great. Of the most important towers, the Saviour (Spasskaya) Tower leading to Red Square was built in 1491 by Pietro Solario, who designed most of the main towers; its belfry was added in 1624–25. The chimes of its clock are broadcast by radio as a time signal to the whole nation. Also on the Red Square front is the St. Nicholas (Nikolskaya) Tower, built originally in 1491 and rebuilt in 1806. The two other principal gate towers—the Trinity (Troitskaya) Tower, with a bridge and outer barbican (the Kutafya Tower), and the Borovitskaya Tower—lie on the western wall.

Kremlin gate towers

Within the walls is one of the most striking and beautiful architectural ensembles in the world: a combination of churches and palaces, which are open to the public and are among the city's most popular tourist attractions, and the highest offices of the Soviet state, which are surrounded by the strictest security. Around the central Cathedral Square (Sobornaya Ploshchad) are grouped three magnificent cathedrals, superb examples of Russian church architecture at its height in the late 15th and early 16th centuries. These and the other churches in the Kremlin ceased functioning as places of worship after the Revolution and are now museums. The white stone Cathedral of the Assumption (Uspensky Sobor) is the oldest, built in 1475–79 in the Italianate-Byzantine style. Its pure, simple, and beautifully proportioned lines and elegant arches are crowned by five golden domes. The Orthodox metropolitans and patriarchs of the 14th to the 18th century are buried there. Across the square is the Cathedral of the Annunciation (Blagoveshchensky Sobor), built in 1484–89 by craftsmen from Pskov; though burned in 1547, it was rebuilt in 1562–64. Its cluster of chapels is topped by golden roofs and domes. Inside are a number of early 15th-century icons attributed to Theophanes the Greek and to Andrey Rublyov, considered by many to be the greatest of all Russian icon painters. The third cathedral, the Archangel (Arkhangelsky), was rebuilt in 1505–08; in it are buried the princes of Moscow and tsars of Russia (except Boris Godunov) up to the founding of St. Petersburg (now Leningrad).

Just off the square stands the splendid, soaring white bell tower of Ivan the Great; built in the 16th century and damaged in 1812, it was restored a few years later. At its foot is the enormous Tsar Bell (Tsar-Kolokol), cast in 1733–35 but never rung. Nearby is the Tsar Cannon (Tsar-Pushka), cast in 1586. Beside the gun are the mid-17th-century Cathedral of the Twelve Apostles (Sobor Dvenadtsati Apostolov) and the adjoining Patriarchal Palace.

On the west of Cathedral Square is a group of palaces of various periods; the Palace of Facets (Granovitaya Palata)—so called from the exterior finish of faceted, white stone squares—was built in 1487–91. Behind it is the Terem Palace of 1635–36, which incorporates several older churches, including the Resurrection of Lazarus (Voskreseniye Lazarya), dating from 1393. Both became part of the Kremlin Great Palace, built as a royal residence in 1838–49 and now used for sessions of the Supreme Soviet of the U.S.S.R.; its long, yellow-washed facade dominates the riverfront. It is connected to the Armoury Palace (Oruzheynaya Palata), built in 1844–51 and now the Armoury Museum, housing a large collection of treasures of the tsars. Along the northeast wall of the Kremlin are the Arsenal (1702–36), the former Senate building (1776–88), now housing meetings of the Council of Ministers, and the School for Red Commanders (1932–34), now used by the Presidium of the Supreme Soviet. The only other Soviet-period building within the Kremlin is the Palace of Congresses (1960–61), with a vast auditorium used for Communist Party congresses and as a theatre.

Kremlin Great Palace

The Kitay-gorod. Along the east wall of the Kremlin lies Red Square (Krasnaya Ploshchad), the ceremonial centre of the capital and scene of the May Day and October Revolution parades. The modest Lenin Mausoleum, with its ever-present line of visitors, blends into the wall, which itself contains the graves of most of the Soviet Union's past leadership. At the southern end of Red Square is the Church of the Intercession (Pokrovsky Sobor), better known as the Cathedral of St. Basil the Blessed. Built in 1554–60 to commemorate the defeat of the Tatars (Mongols) of Kazan and Astrakhan by Ivan IV the Terrible, it is a unique and magnificent architectural fantasy, each of its 10 domes differing in design and colour. Along Red Square facing the Kremlin is the State Department Store, GUM, with its long aisles, iron bridges linking the upper floors, and great skylights; it is the best store in Moscow. The slightly earlier State Historical Museum (1875–83) closes off the northern end of the square.

GUM

Many old churches survive in the Kitay-gorod. Of particular note are the Church of the Trinity (1628–34) in Nikitniki, the 15th-century Church of St. Anne of the Conception, and the Epiphany Cathedral (1693–96). The Kitay-gorod was for centuries the commercial centre of Moscow, and its narrow, crowded streets still contain former banks, the stock-exchange building, and warehouses. Many of the old buildings near the river, however, were demolished in the 1960s to make room for the huge Rossiya Hotel. Along the northern front of the hotel is a row of preserved buildings, including the 16th-century house of the Romanov boyars and Old English Embassy and the 17th-century Monastery of the Sign.

The inner city. In the remainder of the central part of Moscow, within the Garden Ring (Sadovoye Koltso), are buildings representative of every period of Moscow's development from the 15th century to the present day. Scattered through the inner city are several fine examples of 17th-century church architecture, notably the Church of All Saints of Kulishki, built in the 1670s and '80s to replace a 14th-century edifice, and the Church of the Nativity of Putniki (1649–52). This was the period of development of the Moscow Baroque style; one of the best examples of this style, the Church of the Intercession at Fili (1693), is outside the city centre. Buildings of the classical period—beginning about the latter half of the 18th century and covering the rebuilding of Moscow after the fire of 1812—abound within the Garden Ring and the Boulevard Ring (Bulvarnoye Koltso), the latter forming a rough horseshoe north of the Moskva around the Kremlin and Kitay-gorod, and Zamoskvoreche, a largely residential district south of the Moskva. Notable examples are the old university and the former assembly of nobles with its Hall of Columns (now the House of Trade Unions), both built by Kazakov in the 1780s; the elegant Pashkov House (1785–86), now part of the Lenin State Library; the Lunin House (1818–23), now the Museum of Oriental Art; the Manezh (Riding School; 1817), which is now used as an exhibition hall; and the magnificent Bolshoi Theatre (1821–24), rebuilt in 1856 after a fire. Toward the end of the 19th century and continuing into the early 20th, buildings in the revivalist Old Russian style were built, including the State Tretyakov Gallery (1906) and—just outside of the Garden Ring—the Yaroslavl railway station (1902–04).

In the Soviet period many of the old buildings of the inner city have been replaced by large office and apartment buildings. Side by side with the old appeared new buildings in the modern, functional style of the 1920s, in the ponderous, often over-ornate style of the later Stalin period (1930s to '50s), and in the high-rise concrete and glass predominant since the 1960s. Cheek by jowl with the Pashkov House stands the main building of the Lenin State Library (1927–29). Among more imaginative examples of later architecture is the Taganka Theatre (1983).

In the Soviet period much more open space has been created, especially by constructing large squares such as the Square of the 50th Anniversary of October (formerly Manezhnaya Square). Many streets have also been widened, in particular Gorky Street (Gorkogo Ulitsa), now one of Moscow's principal radial roads, lined with large shops, hotels, and offices. The Garden Ring itself has been widened to form a broad highway with multiple lanes in each direction and with overpasses where it is intersected by the main radial routes. In the 1960s a new radial street, Prospekt Kalinina, was built through an area of older housing westward from the Kremlin to the Moskva River; it is lined by high-rise office and apartment buildings, linked at street and second-floor levels by a shopping mall. At its outer end rises the lofty, three-winged Comecon (Council for Mutual Economic Assistance) building overlooking the river. Yet, just next to this bustling thoroughfare is Arbat Street (also called Old Arbat), one of the most picturesque streets of Moscow and now closed to vehicular traffic. Most of the historic buildings of central Moscow have been preserved—since the 1960s much careful restoration and repair work has been undertaken—but some architectural monuments disappeared in the early Soviet period. Where before the Revolution the Cathedral of the Saviour stood, near the river just above the Kremlin, there is now a vast open-air swimming pool.

Prospekt Kalinina

Inner Moscow has the functions typical of a central business district. In this area are concentrated most of the government offices and administrative headquarters of state bodies, most of the hotels and larger shops, and the principal theatres, museums, and art galleries. But its function as a residential area has not been lost; the many large apartment buildings of modern times have ensured that a large population continues to live in the centre, and there are still many quiet residential neighbourhoods within the Garden Ring.

Nikolai Ignatiev

The interior of the State Department Store, GUM.

The middle zone. Beyond the Garden Ring and approximately as far as the Moscow Little Ring Railway lies a zone mostly of late 18th- and 19th-century development. Within it are many factories and the principal railway stations and freight yards. The Likhachyov Automobile Works, with its associated housing, occupies much of the southeastern sector. Enveloped within this zone are further examples of the best of classical Moscow, such as the 18th-century palace that now houses the Presidium of the Academy of Sciences of the U.S.S.R. on Leninsky Prospekt. Also to the southwest, on the banks of the Moskva, are the most important of the fortified monasteries, the 16th-century Novodevichy Convent, with its beautiful Smolensk Cathedral, whose tall bell tower (1690) dominates the churches and buildings within the crenellated walls and towers of the convent. The cathedral now houses the Novodevichy Convent Museum, and the complex includes a cemetery where, among other prominent Soviet citizens, Nikita Khrushchev is buried. Just south of Novodevichy, within the large loop of the Moskva and facing the Lenin Hills, is the sports complex known as Luzhniki Park, dominated by the huge Central Lenin Stadium (1955–56).

Novodevichy Convent

The middle zone has undergone the most urban renewal in Soviet times. Among the features of the present Moscow skyline are the ornate "wedding cake" skyscrapers along the Garden Ring, built in the late 1940s and early 1950s. In the same Stalin-period style are the Ukraina Hotel across the river and the gigantic building in the Moscow State University complex on the Lenin Hills. Most of the renewal that has taken place since 1960 consists of extensive neighbourhoods of wide streets lined with rows of apartment buildings. A number of areas still have narrow streets of 19th-century housing and smaller factories.

Outer Moscow. Beyond the Garden Ring is the zone of modern factory development and of extensive housing construction. Closer to the centre are the micro-regions, or neighbourhood housing units, of the Khrushchev period, typically five- to nine-story apartment buildings built predominantly of yellowish brick. Farther out, the neighbourhoods are characterized by high-rise buildings (20 or more stories), made of standardized, prefabricated concrete sections. Commonly the street levels of the buildings are occupied by shops. Streets are broad and tree-lined. Between the densely populated micro-regions are wedge-shaped areas of open land, notably the extensive Izmaylovsky Park in the east, Sokolniki Park and large forest tracts to the northeast, and on the north the grounds of the permanent Exhibition of National Economic Achievements. Nearby, in Dzerzhinsky Park at Ostankino, is the 1,758-foot television tower.

In the sea of new building, individual monuments of the past, such as the 17th-century Church of the Intercession in Medvedkovo, survive. Moscow's growth has engulfed a number of former country estates, the mansions of which date mostly from the period of classical architecture. On the east side of the city is Kuskovo, once the estate of the Sheremetyev family, its palace built in the 1770s, a church, hermitage, and Baroque grotto. To the south is the Uzkoe mansion, formerly belonging to the Trubetskoy family; to the north are the Petrovsky Palace (built by Kazakov in 1775–82) and, best known of all, the Ostankino Palace (1790–98). In the southeastern suburbs is the former village of Kolomenskoye, once a summer residence of the princes of Moscow. Its most remarkable architectural ensemble of buildings is dominated by the tower of the Church of the Ascension (1532). The Kazan Church and the gatehouse both date from the later 17th century. The surrounding park has a collection of examples of early Russian wooden architecture, brought from various parts of the country. In the nearby village of Dyakovo is the ornate Church of St. John the Baptist, built in 1557.

Beyond the newest suburbs are remaining areas of open land and forest within the Ring Road, together with the satellite industrial towns and dormitory suburbs that were included within the extended boundaries of the city of Moscow in 1960. The principal satellites are Babushkin to the north, with textile mills and a large number of commuters, Perovo to the east, with major marshaling

Satellite towns

yards and engineering and chemical factories, Lyublino to the southeast, Kuntsevo to the west, and Tushino to the northwest. In the mid-1980s several areas outside the Ring Road—including the suburban city of Solntsevo (now the Solntsevsky District [*rayon*]) to the southwest—were added to Moscow. Another part of Moscow, the new town of Zelenograd, established in 1963, is several miles north of the Ring Road.

THE PEOPLE

The inhabitants of Moscow are overwhelmingly of Russian nationality, the largest minority groups being Jews, Ukrainians, Belorussians, and Tatars. It is possible, however, to meet people on the streets of Moscow who belong to any of the numerous nationalities that make up the Soviet Union; these include Georgians and Armenians from the Caucasus Mountains; Uzbek, Turkmen, and Kazakhs from Central Asia; and Lithuanians, Estonians, and Latvians from the Baltic republics.

A considerable percentage of the residents were not born in Moscow but migrated there during the rapid growth of the city. Some of the older generation have lived through the Stalinist purges and the deprivations of World War II. There is no typical Muscovite, but to some visitors the residents seem guarded in their relations with others. With the coming of summer, however, this seems less true as people shed their winter clothes and mingle more freely. Among the more common scenes are those in the courtyards of apartment buildings where the children play, while their elders gossip on benches and play chess, and young people congregate to listen to music.

The great increase in the amount of housing since the late 1950s has brought a fundamental change in the Muscovites' way of life as many have moved farther from the central city. For most of them, living in the suburbs has involved lengthier travel to and from work. Gradually the subway system is being extended to the new housing districts, but most working Muscovites must spend at least two hours a day commuting. The new housing pattern has also inevitably led to the breakup of the close communities that existed in the old central areas, such as the so-called intelligentsia district around Kropotkinskaya and the Arbat. The degree of change has been marked: in 1926 more than one-third of the population lived within the Garden Ring, but by 1967 less than 9 percent of the people lived there. The population density of central Moscow, however, is still much higher than in the suburbs.

THE ECONOMY

Industry. Moscow is the largest industrial centre of the Soviet Union. The city is the focus of the Central Economic Region, an extensive area of industrial development that includes not only Moscow and its satellites but also many other textile and engineering towns linked with the capital. The principal industrial area of this region stretches east and northeast to the Volga between Yaroslavl and Gorky. Moscow's own industries are mainly of the kind that require a skilled and educated labour force but somewhat limited raw materials; they cause relatively little pollution. More than half of the city's labour force is composed of women, who form the vast majority of workers in the textile and food-processing industries. They also predominate in the teaching and medical professions.

Central Economic Region

At the time of the Revolution, Moscow's industry was dominated by textiles, but engineering and metalworking have become by far the most important, employing more than half of the industrial work force. There is significant production of automobiles and trucks. The largest plant in the city is the Likhachyov Automobile Works, followed by the Lenin Komsomol Automobile Plant. Closely linked with these two plants are a number of factories producing component parts, both elsewhere in Moscow and in other towns of the Central Economic Region, together with some as far away as the Urals. Ball bearings are manufactured both for the vehicle industry and for other purposes. The manufacture of machine tools is another major branch of engineering, particularly grinding lathes at the Red Proletariat Plant, precision cutting tools at the Stankoliniya Plant, and machinery for the textile industry. Precision engineering is highly developed and is Moscow's fastest growing industry; it is noted for measuring and other instruments (especially at the Kalibr and Frezer factories), as well as for watches and platinum needles. In addition, Moscow is a large centre of electrical, electronic, and radio engineering; the wide range of items made includes transformers, computers, radio and television sets, refrigerators, vacuum cleaners, and electric motors. Aviation engineering and bicycle manufacturing are also well established.

Precision engineering

Some of the specialized, high-grade steels required by this formidable array of engineering industries are made in the city at the Hammer and Sickle Steel Works; specialized steels also come from the satellite town of Elektrostal, 36 miles east of Moscow.

Moscow is the nation's leading textile centre, and the numerous branches of its textile industry are the city's second leading employer. All types of natural and synthetic cloth are manufactured.

Moscow's large chemical industry was originally geared to produce dyestuffs for the textile industry. The industry's product line has been expanded, however, to include synthetic industrial rubber and rubber tires, paints, plastics,

Chemical industry

Nikolai Ignatiev

Housing in southwestern Moscow.

pharmaceutical goods, and perfumes. Many of its chemical products are derived from Moscow's oil refinery, which processes petroleum piped from the Volga–Urals oil field.

A wide range of consumer goods industries serves the Moscow region primarily and also its wider hinterland. These include foodstuffs, especially confectionery and processed dairy and meat products. Footwear and pianos are specialties of Moscow. Furniture making is part of a varied timber-processing industry, which also makes pulp and paper. Some of the timber is used in the vast construction industry, the workers of which include not only the large numbers actually employed in building but also those engaged in making building materials, such as reinforced concrete sections, glass, and bricks. Printing and publishing is an industry of particular note in Moscow, which is the nation's largest printer of books, journals, and newspapers.

Moscow's general development plan called for a number of factories to be relocated outside the central city; especially cited were those factories that caused the most harm to the urban environment. At the same time the location of new industries in Moscow was prohibited. The pressures on industrial ministries to keep up and indeed to increase production year by year, however, have operated against the aims of the plan. The process of moving the industries did not proceed as quickly as expected, although some plants were relocated. Established factories were expanded and new industries brought in, among them the Khromotron Works, maker of colour television tubes. Many of Moscow's factories are not large, and many are long-established works that make highly specialized items.

Moscow draws on a wide area for its power supply. Electrical generating stations in the city are fired by natural gas, which is piped via a grid system from fields in Siberia and elsewhere. Large gas storage facilities have been constructed near Moscow, and a linking pipeline rings the city. Electrical power also comes from nuclear plants, the nearest of which is about 37 miles to the south, and from the hydroelectric stations on the Volga. Other sources are the large thermal stations at Konakovo to the northwest and Kashira to the south. A by-product of the power industry is hot water, which is piped from the district central stations to apartment buildings for heating and domestic use.

Commerce. As the capital and as the largest city of the Soviet Union, Moscow not surprisingly is the country's largest commercial centre. The headquarters of nationwide state insurance and state banking organizations are located there. The city's retailing facilities are heavily used, not only by the inhabitants of Moscow itself and its satellite towns but also by people throughout the Soviet Union. Its shops are better stocked with a wider range of goods than those of any other Soviet city and are always crowded with customers. Yet in comparison with major cities of western Europe and North America, Moscow is poorly provided with retail outlets, and waiting in lines to buy scarce items is a way of life for Muscovites. Many of the stores are fairly large, including some of the central food shops (*gastronomy*) and department stores (*univermagy*). The most important of the department stores are Children's World (Detsky Mir); the Central Department Store (TsUM); the Moskva, close to three main railway stations; and, best known and most heavily patronized, GUM. GUM, the direct descendant of the medieval trading rows, alone handles about one-tenth of Moscow's total retail trade in goods other than foodstuffs. Moscow does not have local shopping centres; generally, shops are widely dispersed on the ground-floor levels of apartment buildings, which tends to add to the time taken up by shopping. An important part of Moscow's retail trade is carried on at the collective farmers' markets, where collective farms and individual members of such farms bring fruit, vegetables, and meat for direct sale to the populace; though more expensive than the state shops, they tend to excel in quality and in the availability of produce.

Moscow has thousands of eating places, but most are canteens in places of work, which is where most of the cafés, buffets, and snack bars are also located.

Hotels

As a world-renowned capital, Moscow is a principal focus for foreign visitors. For many years, however, tourists outnumbered hotel beds. It was not until the 1980 Olympic Games were awarded to the city that several new large hotels were built. These included the Cosmos, the Inturist, and Mezhdunarodnaya 1 and 2 in the International Trade Centre.

Transportation. *Rail.* The Soviet Union is heavily dependent for freight transport on its railways. The hub of this network is the capital. Trunk lines radiate out from the city in all directions. The first in operation was the Leningrad line, opened in 1851. Others include the Savyolovo line, running north to the Volga and on as a secondary route to Leningrad; the Yaroslav line, which is connected by way of the Trans-Siberian route to Vladivostok; the Gorky line, linked to Kirov; the Kazan line, the most direct route to the Urals and Siberia; the Ryazan line, leading to Central Asia and the Caucasus; the Pavelets line, a secondary route to the European south and the Caucasus; the Kursk line, the main route south to the Crimea; the Kiev line to the southwest; the Smolensk line to Minsk, Warsaw, and Berlin; and the Riga line to the Baltic. The most heavily used of these lines are now electrified—notably those to Leningrad, Kiev, the Donbass, and the Trans-Siberian—as are all suburban-zone lines, which carry the heavy commuter traffic. To link the radial lines the Moscow Little Ring Railway was built in 1908 within the city; this has been supplemented by the Greater Moscow Ring Railway at a distance of some 25 to 40 miles from the city.

Moscow Canal

Waterways. Moscow is a major river port. The canalized Moskva can take only smaller craft, but the Moscow Canal, built by forced labour in 1932–37, can take ships of seagoing size. The canal runs from the Moskva, upstream of the city, northward to the Khimki and Ucha reservoirs and, continuing northward, through the Klin-Dmitrov Ridge to the Volga at Ivankovo. The Volga's various canal links open up Moscow to all the seas bordering European Russia. The capital has three large river ports mainly for freight and two terminals for passengers that are part of the urban transit system.

Air. Moscow is similarly the hub of the Soviet Union's airline network, and the number of passengers rises steadily each year. Four airports operate in the Moscow area. Sheremetyevo-2 to the north is the main airport for international flights, with direct links to most European capitals and to Havana, New York City, Montreal, Tokyo, and other foreign cities. Sheremetyevo-1 handles mostly domestic flights, as does Vnukovo, 15 miles to the southwest. Other domestic airports are Bykovo (closed to foreigners), 20 miles to the southeast, and Domodedovo, 28 miles to the south.

Intracity transport. Compared with other large cities in most developed countries, Moscow has few privately owned cars, although their number is steadily increasing. There are, however, a considerable number of officially owned cars, which have added to the increase in traffic congestion. At the same time there is heavy reliance on public transport, and in this respect Moscow is generally well served.

Subway system

The most important element in Moscow's city transport is the Metropolitan (Metro) subway. The system, begun in 1935, is renowned for the elaborate architecture of its stations, especially the older ones, which are highly decorated with marble, stained glass, statuary, and chandeliers. Trains usually arrive at three-minute intervals, although the interval is less during rush hours. The network copies the city street pattern, with a series of radial lines linked by a single ring subway. Although the lines extend to most parts of the city, the stations are spaced far apart so that it is usually necessary to use them in conjunction with bus, trolley, and streetcar lines.

The inflexibility of fixed-line forms of transport poses a potential problem as traffic gradually increases. Many streetcar lines, consequently, have been replaced by bus routes.

Although Moscow has for the most part a dense network of surface transport, new routes sometimes tend to lag behind housing construction, so that certain new suburbs are rather poorly served for some time after their completion.

On the positive side, fares on all forms of transport are very low regardless of distance.

ADMINISTRATION AND SOCIAL CONDITIONS

Government. In the period after the 1917 Revolution, Moscow was divided into 11 administrative districts, or wards. With the expansion of the municipal limits in 1960 the number of administrative units was increased to 17 *rayony* (districts; singular *rayon*). The subsequent huge building program and redistribution of population from central areas to the suburbs necessitated the creation of new divisions in 1968 and again in 1976, when the number reached 30. Further annexations caused an increase by the mid-1980s to 32 *rayony,* a figure that would rise as the city continued to grow. The *rayony* vary in population, the inner *rayony* usually being somewhat smaller in area and population than the outer. The *rayony* elect delegates to the Moscow City Soviet of Workers' Deputies (Mossovet), which has its headquarters on Gorky Street. The council handles the city's annual budget, which is chiefly derived from central government funds. Since Moscow is a "city of republic subordination," the City Council is responsible to the government of the Russian S.F.S.R. rather than to a smaller administrative unit.

Although the centre of national government is the Kremlin (which houses the meetings of the Presidium of the Supreme Soviet, the Politburo, and the Central Committee and congresses of the Communist Party), the buildings of various ministries and government departments are scattered fairly widely over the inner city. The Ministry of Foreign Affairs is in a skyscraper of the Stalin period on the Garden Ring. Several ministries are housed in the new tower buildings on Prospekt Kalinina, at the outer end of which stands the R.S.F.S.R. Council of Ministers building. A number of foreign embassies have been transferred to the southwestern suburbs on the Lenin Hills, although many are still located in the city centre. Moscow also serves as headquarters of most national bodies and organizations.

Education. Even considering its size and political importance, Moscow has an exceptionally large concentration of educational establishments. At the pre-university level, schools serving the city's own population include those for handicapped children, special foreign language schools, and boarding schools. For children below school age (six years old in the Soviet Union) there are nurseries and kindergartens; many are attached to individual places of employment, which permits parents more freedom to work. Moscow's higher educational institutions draw students from throughout the Soviet Union. A large percentage of the students are registered for correspondence courses. Although the students are predominantly Russians, they include representatives of almost every ethnic group in the Soviet Union, together with a number of overseas students.

Moscow M.V. Lomonosov State University

Higher education. The leading institution of higher learning is the Moscow M.V. Lomonosov State University, founded in 1755. Some of the humanities departments are still housed in the old university buildings facing the Square of the 50th Anniversary of October, near the Kremlin. Science departments are located in the complex of buildings on the Lenin Hills, which date from the early 1950s and are dominated by a 34-story skyscraper in the Stalin-period style; this building houses the central administration, the Museum of Earth Science, and accommodation for thousands of students. In 1970–78 two other humanities buildings were constructed on the Lenin Hills site. Moscow's second university, the Patrice Lumumba People's Friendship University, was founded in 1960 to serve students from the world's developing nations.

Among the specialist higher educational foundations are the Moscow Timiryazev Academy of Agriculture in the north of Moscow and the Moscow P.I. Tchaikovsky State Conservatory, where some of the world's finest musicians have received their training. Also important are the Moscow D.I. Mendeleyev Institute of Chemical Technology, the Moscow N.E. Bauman Higher Technical School, and the A.V. Lunacharsky State Institute of Dramatic Art. Many institutes, among them the Moscow Institute of Aviation Technology and the All-Union Extra-Mural Institute of Railway Engineers, produce specialists for particular industries.

Research. In addition to the large volume of research undertaken in the university and in other teaching establishments, there is a formidable array of scientific research institutions. Between them they constitute the second largest employer in Moscow after industry. More than one-third of all Soviet citizens holding the doctor of science degree are employed in Moscow. The main focus of research is the Academy of Sciences of the U.S.S.R., the Presidium of which is located in a building on Lenin Prospekt south of Gorky Park. There are also national academies of arts and medical, pedagogical, and agricultural sciences.

Many scientific institutes, such as the Experimental Research Institute of Metal-Cutting Machine Tools, are con-

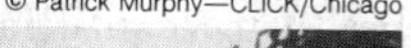

The State Academic Bolshoi (Great) Theatre.

cerned with highly specialized industrial research. These are often connected closely with Moscow's own industries, as in the case of the Central Research Institute of Automobile Engineering. Linked to the research bodies are the many design bureaus, such as the All-Union Planning, Surveying, and Scientific Research Institute, which designs hydroelectric power projects, and the State All-Union Institute for the Planning of Metallurgical Plants.

Lenin Library

Foremost among Moscow's libraries is the V.I. Lenin State Library of the U.S.S.R., one of the world's largest. There are also a number of specialty libraries in the arts and sciences and in other fields.

Health. The health of the Muscovites is attended to at the neighbourhood level by hundreds of clinics, giving medical, dental, and maternity services. Perhaps the most prominent of the city's numerous hospitals is the Botkinskaya, founded in 1911. Among specialist institutions are maternity, mental, and tuberculosis hospitals, supported by a number of specialist medical research institutions.

CULTURAL LIFE

Moscow has numerous theatres, headed by the renowned State Academic Bolshoi (Great) Theatre, which was founded in 1825, though its present splendid building facing Sverdlov Square dates from 1856. Also on Sverdlov Square is the Maly (Little) Theatre. The city's principal drama theatre, the Moscow Art Theatre, was founded in 1898 by the actor, director, and producer Konstantin Stanislavsky and the playwright-producer Vladimir Nemirovich-Danchenko; in its early days it was especially noted for its performances of the plays of Anton Chekhov. Also of worldwide fame are the State Central Puppet Theatre and the Moscow State Circus, which in 1971 acquired new quarters on the Lenin Hills. The repertory companies of these theatrical groups tour frequently both in the Soviet Union and abroad. There are several concert halls, notably the Tchaikovsky Concert Hall and the two halls of the Conservatory. The U.S.S.R. State Philharmonic Orchestra has won international repute, as have a number of Moscow-based folk dance and choral ensembles.

Motion pictures are a popular form of entertainment in Moscow, and the city's many cinemas are augmented by facilities for showing films in numerous clubs and cultural institutions. The October and Rossiya cinemas are the largest in the Soviet Union. Several studios in the city produce motion pictures, notable among which is Mosfilm. The television and radio broadcasting networks also have headquarters in Moscow; programs produced there are received throughout the Soviet Union.

Museums and galleries

The museums and art galleries in the capital include several of international rank. Foremost among these are the State Pushkin Museum of Fine Arts, with a fine international collection, and the State Tretyakov Gallery. The latter, which began in 1856 as the private collection of a connoisseur, Pavel Tretyakov, is noteworthy for its superb collection of icons, including several by Andrey Rublyov. Other notable museums are the Armoury Museum in the Kremlin, the State Historical Museum on Red Square, and the nearby Central Lenin Museum on Revolution Square.

Although many places of worship were closed, converted into museums, or destroyed after the Revolution, Moscow still has a number of functioning Russian Orthodox churches in addition to a few other Christian churches and Jewish and Muslim places of worship. The Russian Orthodox patriarch has a residence in Moscow.

The Luzhniki Park complex is the leading Moscow facility for sports and was one of the main arenas for the 1980 Olympic Games. The Central Lenin Stadium, accommodating 103,000, is flanked by a smaller arena, swimming pool, and the indoor Sports Palace. There are many stadiums and swimming pools in the area, including a large, heated, open-air pool that is in use all year round. In addition there are a large number of soccer fields, gymnasiums, and volleyball and basketball courts; most of these are attached to individual places of work or to sports clubs.

Parks

Outside the Garden Ring, Moscow is well provided with parks and open spaces. Gorky Central Park of Culture along the right bank of the Moskva is the closest to the centre and, with its amusement park, is very popular. A large green area, covering nearly 3,000 acres (1,200 hectares), is Izmaylovsky Park on the east side. To the northeast is the more formal Sokolniki Park, which leads to an extensive tract of forest called Moose Island. North of the city centre are the Botanical Gardens of the Academy of Sciences, one of several such gardens in the city, and the grounds of the Moscow Timiryazev Academy of Agriculture. Bittsevsky Park, also of considerable size, has been established adjacent to the Ring Road south of the city centre. The Moscow Zoo, one of the world's leading zoos, is a popular attraction west of the city centre. The Khimki Reservoir is used for boating and aquatic sports, but even more popular are the other reservoirs to the north, just outside Greater Moscow. The surrounding forest-park zone provides extensive space for recreation.

History

THE EARLY PERIOD

Foundation and medieval growth. The first documentary reference to Moscow is found in the early monastic chronicles under the year 1147, when on April 4 Yury Vladimirovich Dolgoruky, prince of Suzdal, was host at a "great banquet" for his ally the Prince of Novgorod-Seversky "in Moscow." This is the traditional date of Moscow's foundation, although archaeological evidence shows that a settlement had existed on the site since Neolithic times. Archaeological work has also revealed the remains of corduroy roads and evidence of iron and leather working dating from the 11th century. The disturbed times made defense essential, and in 1156 Prince Dolgoruky built the first fortifications—ditches and earthen ramparts topped by a wooden wall with blockhouses. This was the Kremlin. The origin of the word *kremlin* is disputed; some authorities suggest Greek words for "citadel" or "steepness," others the early Russian word *krem,* meaning a conifer providing timber suitable for building. The Kremlin was sited on the relatively high spit of land between the Moskva River and a small tributary, the Neglinnaya. The triangular piece of land between the rivers was protected on the eastern side by a moat joining them. The Neglinnaya now flows through an underground conduit, but part of its course is traced by a street of the same name.

First fortifications

Moscow soon developed as one of the more important towns of the principality of Vladimir-Suzdal. A trading settlement, or *posad,* grew up to the east of the Kremlin, along the Moskva in the area known as Zaradye. Like most other Russian towns, Moscow was captured and burned by the Mongols in their great invasion of 1236–40, and its princes had to accept Mongol suzerainty. It soon recovered, though the Mongols sacked it once again in 1293. Three years later the Kremlin was strengthened with a new earthen wall and oak palisade. Thereafter Moscow grew in importance, in trading and artisan activity, and in size, overtaking the older and previously more important centres of Suzdal and Vladimir. The town was fairly centrally placed in the system of rivers and portages that formed the trade routes across European Russia. The area east of Moscow between the Oka and Volga rivers moreover had rather better soils than most of northern Russia and formed a region of more developed agriculture and prosperous towns. Moscow's authority was greatly enhanced when in 1326 the metropolitan of the Russian Orthodox Church transferred his seat from Vladimir to Moscow. Thereafter the town was to remain the centre of Russian Orthodoxy, and after the fall of Constantinople to the Turks (1453) it claimed the title of the Third Rome. Under Ivan I Kalita the principality of Vladimir was incorporated into that of Moscow. Gradually the princes of Moscow extended their rule over the other surrounding Russian princedoms, and the town became the leader in the long struggle against Mongol hegemony.

Seat of the metropolitan

The struggle at first fluctuated. In 1378 a Muscovite army repulsed a Mongol attack on the Vozha River south of the town, and in 1380 Prince Dmitry of Moscow inflicted a crushing defeat on the Mongols under the great khan Mamai at Kulikovo on the Don River, for which victory he was thereafter known as Dmitry Donskoy ("of the Don"). The Kremlin had been enlarged and given walls and towers of white limestone in 1367, but the new fortifications were unable to withstand a renewed Mongol attack in 1382, when, despite a heroic defense, the khan Tokhtamysh captured and plundered Moscow. Yet another attack in 1408 under Khan Yedigei, however, was beaten off. Moscow grew steadily in size and importance as it continued to absorb the surrounding princedoms. Within the Kremlin the first stone cathedral, the Assumption, was built in 1326. Palaces for the prince and leading boyars, monasteries, and churches were erected. Outside the Kremlin walls, the trading and artisan quarter to the east grew in size and became known as the Kitay-gorod; this name, which originated in the 16th century, probably derives from the word *kita,* a binding of poles used in the fortifications before stone walls were built, and does not mean "Chinese City" as it is sometimes translated.

The rise of Moscow as capital. By the second half of the 15th century, especially after the annexation of Novgorod in 1478, Moscow had become the undisputed centre of a unified Russian state. During the reign of the grand prince of Moscow Ivan III the Great, the Kremlin was again enlarged and given brick walls more than a mile in length and in places up to 60 feet high. From this period also date the rebuilt Cathedral of the Assumption and the equally beautiful Annunciation and (also rebuilt) Archangel cathedrals, the Palace of Facets, and the bell tower of Ivan III. In 1534–38 the Kitay-gorod, previously protected only by earth banks and palisades, was also surrounded by a brick wall, with 12 towers. The town continued to grow and spread outside the walls to form what became known as the Bely Gorod ("White City") in a semicircle around the Kremlin and Kitay-gorod.

Despite its new fortifications, Moscow remained subject to disaster and attack. In 1547 two fires destroyed the greater part of the town. In the mid-16th century Ivan IV the Terrible conquered the Tatar (Mongol) khanates of Kazan (1552) and Astrakhan (1556), but in 1571 the Crimean Tatars succeeded in capturing Moscow, burning everything but the Kremlin. The annals record that only 30,000 of 200,000 inhabitants survived. A further attack was launched by the Crimean Tatars in 1591, but they failed to overcome Moscow's stubborn resistance. The defense was helped by the new walls, built between 1584 and 1591 to protect the Bely Gorod, made of stone and some five miles long. The line of these fortifications is marked today by the strip of parkland and tree-lined streets of the Boulevard Ring. In 1592 an outer earth rampart with 50 towers was thrown up around the city, including an area on the right bank of the Moskva. This encompassed a further extension of Moscow that had grown up beyond the Bely Gorod; known at first as Skorodom, this outer sector came to be called the Zemlyanoy Gorod, or Earthen City. The line of its fortifications is also traced today by the Garden Ring. As an outermost line of defense, a chain of strongly fortified monasteries was established beyond the ramparts to the south and east, principally the Novodevichy Convent and Donskoy (Don), Danilovsky, Simonov, Novospassky, and Andronikov monasteries, most of which survive today as museums.

Zemlyanoy Gorod

With much improved security, trade and craft manufacture flourished. Distinct quarters were occupied by particular trades; for example, the suburbs of Bronnaya by armour makers, Kuznetskaya by blacksmiths, and Kotelniki by kettle makers. Across the Moskva was the weavers' suburb. These artisan sectors are commonly commemorated today by street or quarter names. State workshops cast cannon and made weapons and gunpowder. The tsar's court and its attendant nobility provided patronage for luxury crafts. Increasingly the boyars took over the Kitay-gorod, with artisans and traders moving to the outer parts; the Kremlin became solely the seat of temporal and ecclesiastical authority. The centre of commercial activity was the market in Red Square between the Kremlin and the Kitay-gorod, where there were rows of stalls, each handling a specific variety of goods; the Russian word for "red" (*krasnaya*) also means "beautiful," which was the original name for the square. Trade with western Europe (especially England and Holland), as well as with Central Asia, Transcaucasia, Persia, and the Black Sea coast, was brisk, furs forming a major staple in this international commerce. Foreign merchants lived in the Nemetskaya Sloboda ("German suburb"), and a flourishing cultural life was marked by the growth of the book trade and the founding in 1553 of the first printing house.

At the turn of the 17th century Moscow, like the rest of Russia, suffered severely during the Time of Troubles. In the reign of Boris Godunov there were severe famines from 1601 to 1603. After Boris' death in 1605, the first False Dmitry seized Moscow with Polish help, and though he was killed in 1606 and the Poles were driven out, they reoccupied Moscow with a second False Dmitry in 1608–10. In May 1611 the Muscovites attacked the Poles, and the invaders retreated into the Kremlin. Under the energetic leadership of a boyar, Prince Dmitry Mikhaylovich Pozharsky, and a merchant, Kuzma Minin, the Russians forced the Poles to surrender in October 1612.

With the establishment in 1613 of the Romanov dynasty under Michael, relative peace returned to Moscow and with it further economic advance. Nevertheless the conditions of the poor of the town often led to riots and uprisings; such events were nothing new, having occurred also in 1382, 1445, and 1547. In 1648, as a result of an increase in the salt tax, and again in 1662 (the so-called Copper Riots) there were disturbances by artisans, labourers, and tradesmen. The great revolt of Stenka Razin in southern Russia (1667–71) was echoed by unrest in the capital, and in 1671 Razin was executed in Moscow as a warning to its inhabitants. The revolts were put down by the hereditary militia, the *streltsy,* who in 1698, early in the reign of Peter I the Great, themselves revolted and were suppressed only with great slaughter.

Riots and uprisings

Despite the frequent upheavals, however, culture flourished. Russia's first higher educational institution, the Slavonic-Greek-Latin Academy attached to the Zaikonospassky Monastery in the Kitay-gorod, dates from 1687. In 1701 Peter founded a School of Mathematics and Navigation. The first newspaper in Russia began publication in Moscow in 1703.

EVOLUTION OF THE MODERN CITY

The 18th and 19th centuries. In 1703 Peter I began constructing St. Petersburg (now Leningrad) on the Gulf of Finland, and in 1712 he transferred the capital to his new, "westernized," and outward-looking city. Members of the nobility were compelled to move to St. Petersburg; many merchants and artisans also moved. Both population growth and new building in Moscow languished for a time, but even during Peter's reign the city began to recover from the loss of capital status. Peter himself stimulated economic growth by establishing new industries, and private entrepreneurs followed suit. By 1725 there were some 32 new factories employing 5,500 workers; more than 20 of the factories were textile mills, including a crown enterprise making sailcloth. At the same period there were about 8,500 craft workers.

During the 18th century Moscow retained its major role in the cultural life of Russia. In 1755, on the initiative of the great man of letters and science Mikhail Vasilyevich Lomonosov, Moscow University (now Moscow M.V. Lomonosov State University) was founded, the first university in Russia; a medical and surgical college was opened in 1786. Although serious fires did much damage in 1737, 1748, and 1752, many splendid new buildings appeared, designed by such architects as Giacomo Quarenghi, Vasily Bazhenov, Matvey Kazakov, and Vasily Stasov. In 1741 Moscow was surrounded by a barricade 25 miles long, the Kamer-Kollezhsky barrier, at whose 16 gates customs tolls were collected; its line is traced today by a number of streets called *val* ("rampart") and by place-names such as Kaluga Zastava (Customs Gate). Industry flourished, and by the end of the 18th century there were about 300 factories in Moscow, more than half of them textile mills. The population had grown to 275,000 by 1811.

Moscow University

In 1812 Napoleon invaded Russia; after a bitter 15-hour battle on September 7 at Borodino on the approaches to Moscow, the Russian commander in chief, Gen. M.I. Kutuzov, evacuated troops and civilians from the city, which was occupied by the French a week later. A fire broke out and spread rapidly, eventually destroying more than two-thirds of all the buildings. Looting was rife. The lack of supplies and shelter and continual harassment by Russian skirmishing forces made it impossible for Napoleon to winter in Moscow, however, and on October 19 the French troops began their catastrophic retreat.

Rebuilding

In 1813 a Commission for the Construction of the City of Moscow was established. It launched a great program of rebuilding, which included a partial replanning of the city centre. Among many buildings constructed or reconstructed at this time were the Kremlin Great and Armoury palaces, the university, the Manezh (Riding School), and the Bolshoi Theatre. Industry also recovered rapidly and continued to develop through the 19th century. In 1837 the Moscow stock exchange was established. The emancipation of the serfs in 1861 and the beginning of the railway era with the opening of the line to St. Petersburg in 1851 greatly increased labour mobility, and large numbers of peasants from the villages began moving into Moscow. The population, which had reached 336,000 in 1835, had almost doubled, to 602,000, in 1871 and by 1897 had reached 978,000. Moscow became the hub of Russia's railways, with trunk lines to all parts of European Russia. A ring of main line termini was built, mostly on or near the Kamer-Kollezhsky barrier at the limits of the built-up area. Outside the barrier many new factories, particularly those concerned with textiles, began operation. In the 1890s heavy engineering and metalworking industries also developed. Between 1897 and 1915 Moscow yet again doubled in size, to a population of 1,983,700.

The later 19th century was a period of ostentatious building by public bodies and wealthy private persons, in various imitative "Old Russian" styles and the so-called modern style. From this period date the old Town Hall (meeting place of the Gorodskaya Duma, now the Central Lenin Museum), the State Historical Museum, and the Upper Trading Rows (now GUM).

The growth of an industrial proletariat in Moscow, together with the generally low living standards of the workers, brought growing unrest and strikes. Various revolutionary groups were active. In the Revolution of 1905 a small-scale insurrection took place in Moscow, and an attempt was made to seize the Nikolayev (now Leningrad) station; the revolt was ruthlessly crushed. In 1917, although a Council of Workers' and Soldiers' Deputies was set up in Moscow, the city remained relatively quiet until after the Bolshevik seizure of power in Petrograd (formerly St. Petersburg) on October 25 (November 7, new style), which was immediately followed by fighting in Moscow. Military cadets held out for a time in the Kremlin, but by November 3 (16, N.S.) they were overcome and Bolshevik power was firmly established.

The Bolshevik Revolution

Moscow in the Soviet period. In March 1918 Lenin and the Soviet government moved to Moscow, which thereby resumed its former status as capital. This status was formally ratified on Dec. 30, 1922, when the first All-Union Congress of Soviets met in the Bolshoi Theatre and passed the legislation setting up the Union of Soviet Socialist Republics. In the civil war period Moscow, like other Soviet cities, suffered greatly, with grave food shortages, loss of population (falling to 1,027,300 in 1920), and reduction of industry. In the years following the final establishment of Soviet power and peace, recovery was swift, and the beginning of the series of five-year plans in 1928 brought great industrial progress. The city's existing plant and labour force formed one of the main springboards for industrialization elsewhere in the Soviet Union. Between the censuses of 1926 and 1939, Moscow once more doubled its population, from 2,029,425 to 4,182,916 (within the 1959 boundaries). Priority in investment went to industry, and housing construction was very limited; in consequence, exceptional overcrowding of existing housing developed, with extremely high population densities. Living standards in all respects were low.

During World War II, the Germans in late 1941 reached the outskirts of Moscow, less than 25 miles from the Kremlin. Many factories were evacuated, together with much of the government. From October 20 the city was declared to be in a state of siege. Its remaining inhabitants built and manned antitank defenses, while the city was bombarded from the air. A desperate counterattack on December 6 threw the German forces back from the outskirts and saved Moscow. Recovery was quick after the war, with further growth of the city's economy. Two major events have marked the city's progress: in 1947, two years after the war's end, Moscow celebrated its 800th anniversary, and in 1980 it hosted the summer Olympic Games.

In the postwar period immigration to Moscow caused a housing shortage that reached grave proportions in the 1950s; the population density within the Garden Ring surpassed 132,000 persons per square mile (51,000 per square kilometre) by 1959. Under Khrushchev a major construction program was initiated. Much of the old housing, often single storied and made of wood, was cleared, and extensive new tracts of large apartment buildings sprang up around the historic core of the city. Considerable urban renewal has taken place in the central areas, and high-rise buildings now dominate the skyline.

In 1935 a far-reaching development plan for Moscow was formulated; but the plan devised in 1960, in which adjacent satellite towns were incorporated into the city, was even more ambitious than the earlier plan. Under this plan urban growth was to be contained within the Moscow Ring Road, and residential and industrial zones and greenbelts were carefully designated. Implementation of this plan was instrumental in alleviating housing shortages, reducing traffic congestion, and improving air quality in the city centre. By the late 1970s, however, urban growth had outstripped original predictions, and in the 1980s planned urban expansion was initiated beyond the Ring Road. (R.A.F./K.B.M.)

BIBLIOGRAPHY

General works: A comprehensive single-volume reference source is *Москва: энциклопедия* (1980), an encyclopaedia containing several topical articles with bibliographies and about 5,000 shorter entries, of which more than 1,000 are biographical. For statistical information, see *Москва в цифрах,* a yearbook of statistics. ПЕТР ВАСИЛЬЕВИЧ СЫТИН, *Из истории московских улиц,* 3rd ed. (1958), is a historical account of the topography of Moscow streets and squares. LEO GRULIOW, *Moscow* (1977); HENRI CARTIER-BRESSON, *The People of Moscow* (1955); JAN LUCAS, *Moscow: A Book of Photographs* (1964); and KAREL NEUBERT, *Portrait of Moscow* (1964), are pictorial works.

Geography and economics: LESLIE SYMONS *et al., The Soviet Union: A Systematic Geography* (1983), a work with useful bibliographies; Ю.Г. САУШКИН and В.Г. ГЛУШКОВА, *Москва среди городов мира* (1983), an analysis of economic geography, comparing Moscow to other major cities of the socialist world; YURI SAUSHKIN, *Moscow* (1966; originally published in Russian, 1964), a geographical-historical survey of the city; VLADIMIR PROMYSLOV, *Moscow in Construction: Industrialized Methods of Building* (1967; originally published in Russian, 1967); and А.П. ЦАРЕНКО and Е.А. ФЕДОРОВ, *Московский метрополитен имени В.И. Ленина* (1984), a reference work devoted entirely to the Moscow subway.

History: АКАДЕМИЯ НАУК СССР, *История Москвы,* 6 vol. in 7 (1952–59), is a comprehensive work, including detailed analyses, with illustrations, of the economy, culture, science, art, architecture, education, public health, and other aspects of Moscow in its historic development. Also see S.S. KHROMOV *et al.* (eds.), *History of Moscow: An Outline* (1981; originally published in Russian, 1974; 4th rev. ed., 1980). The following are special studies: ROBERT EUGENE JOHNSON, *Peasant and Proletariat: The Working Class of Moscow in the Late Nineteenth Century* (1979); LAURA ENGELSTEIN, *Moscow, 1905: Working-Class Organization and Political Conflict* (1982); and DIANE KOENKER, *Moscow Workers and the 1917 Revolution* (1981). The postrevolutionary period is presented in П.П. АНДРЕЕВ *et al., Москва за 50 лет Советской власти, 1917–1967* (1968), a survey of the first 50 years of Soviet power.

Architecture: KATHLEEN BERTON, *Moscow: An Architectural History* (1977), an illustrated survey; and А.В. ИКОННИКОВ, *Каменная летопись Москвы* (1978), a detailed architectural guide, with maps. M.A. IL'IN, *Moscow: Monuments of Architecture of the 14th–17th Centuries* (1973), and *Moscow: Monuments of Architecture 18th–the First Third of the 19th Century,* 2 vol. (1975); and E. KIRICHENKO, *Moscow: Architectural Monuments of the 1830–1910s* (1977), contain photographs with explanatory texts in both English and Russian. В.В. КИРИЛЛОВ, *Архитектура русского модерна* (1979); and А.В. ИКОННИКОВ, *Архитектура Москвы, XX век* (1984), analyze 20th-century architecture. M.B. ПОСОХИН *et al.* (eds.), *Памятники архитектуры Москвы: Кремлъ, Китай-город, центральные площади,* 2nd rev. ed. (1983), describes major historical architectural complexes, including the Kremlin; and O.A. SHVIDKOVSKY (ed.), *Building in the USSR, 1917–1932* (1971).

Culture: ARTHUR VOYCE, *The Moscow Kremlin: Its History, Architecture, and Art Treasures* (1954, reprinted 1971), and *Moscow and the Roots of Russian Culture* (1964, reissued 1972). БОРИС СЕРГЕЕВИЧ ЗЕМЕНКОВ, *Памятные места Москвы: страницы жизни деятелей науки и культуры* (1959), explores places of interest associated with notable figures of science and culture. Cultural treasures in the museums of the Moscow area are described in VLADIMIR CHERNOV and MARCEL GIRARD, *Splendours of Moscow and Its Surroundings,* trans. from French (1967); N.N. VORONIN (ed.), *Palaces and Churches of the Kremlin* (1966); BORIS A. RYBAKOV, *Treasures in the Kremlin* (1962); and DAVID DOUGLAS DUNCAN, *Great Treasures of the Kremlin,* rev. ed. (1968, reissued 1979).

Guidebooks: The following differ in the depth of coverage, but most include at least one informative map: EVAN MAWDSLEY and MARGARET MAWDSLEY (eds.), *Moscow and Leningrad* (1980), with a street atlas; *Moscow and Leningrad* (1985), from the Berlitz series; ЮРИЙ ФЕДОСЮК, *Москва в кольце Садовых* (1983); and *Baedeker's Moscow,* text by BERNHARD POLLMAN, trans. from German (1987), both of which provide detailed descriptions of the central parts of the city.

(K.B.M.)

Moses

Moses (Hebrew Moshe) was the gifted Hebrew leader who, in the 13th century BCE (before the Common Era, or BC), delivered his people from Egyptian slavery. In the Covenant ceremony at Mt. Sinai, where the Ten Commandments were promulgated, he founded the religious community known as Israel. As the interpreter of these Covenant stipulations, he was the organizer of the community's religious and civil traditions. In the Judaic tradition, he is revered as the greatest prophet and teacher, and Judaism has sometimes loosely been called Mosaism, or the Mosaic faith, in Western Christendom. His influence continues to be felt in the religious life, moral concerns, and social ethics of Western civilization, and therein lies his undying significance.

THE HISTORICAL PROBLEM

Historical views of Moses. Few historical figures have engendered such disparate interpretations as has Moses. Early Jewish and Christian traditions considered him the author of the Torah ("Law," or "Teaching"), also called the Pentateuch ("Five Books"), comprising the first five books of the Bible, and some conservative groups still believe in Mosaic authorship.

View of Martin Noth

Opposing this is the theory of the German scholar Martin Noth, who, while granting that Moses may have had something to do with the preparations for the conquest of Canaan, was very skeptical of the roles attributed to him by tradition. Although recognizing a historical core beneath the Exodus and Sinai traditions, Noth believed that two different groups experienced these events and transmitted the stories independently of each other. He contended that the biblical story tracing the Hebrews from Egypt to Canaan resulted from an editor's weaving separate themes and traditions around a main character Moses, actually an obscure person from Moab.

This article, following the lead of the biblical archaeologist and historian W.F. Albright, presents a point of view somewhere between these two extremes. While the essence of the biblical story (narrated between Exodus 1:8 and Deuteronomy 34:12) is accepted, it is recognized that during the centuries of oral and written transmission the account acquired layers of accretions. In general, the reconstruction of the documentary sources of the Pentateuch by literary critics is considered valid, but here the sources are viewed as varying versions of one series of events (see BIBLICAL LITERATURE). Other critical methods (studying the biblical text from the standpoint of literary form, oral tradition, style, redaction, and archaeology) are equally valid. The most accurate answer to a critical problem is thus likely to come from convergence of various lines of evidence. Despite the aid of critical scholarship, the sources are so sketchy that the man Moses can be pictured only in broad outline.

The date of Moses. According to the biblical account, Moses' parents were from the tribe of Levi, one of the groups in Egypt called Hebrews. Originally the term Hebrew had nothing to do with race or ethnic origin. It derived from Habiru, a variant spelling of Ḥapiru (Apiru), a designation of a class of people who made their living by hiring themselves out for various services. The biblical Hebrews had been in Egypt for generations, but apparently they became a threat, so one of the pharaohs enslaved them. Unfortunately, the personal name of the king is not given, and scholars have disagreed as to his identity and, hence, as to the date of the events of the narrative of Moses. One theory takes literally the statement in I Kings 6:1 that the Exodus from Egypt occurred 480 years before Solomon began building the Temple in Jerusalem. This occurred in the fourth year of his reign, about 960 BCE; therefore, the Exodus would date about 1440 BCE.

This conclusion, however, is at variance with most of the biblical and archaeological evidence. The storage cities Pithom and Rameses, built for the pharaoh by the Hebrews, were located in the northeastern part of the Egyptian delta, not far from Goshen, the district in which the Hebrews lived. It is implicit in the whole story that the pharaoh's palace and capital were in the area, but Thutmose III (the pharaoh in 1440) had his capital at Thebes, far to the south, and never conducted major building operations

By courtesy of Staatliche Museen Preussischer Kulturbesitz Gemaldegalerie, West Berlin

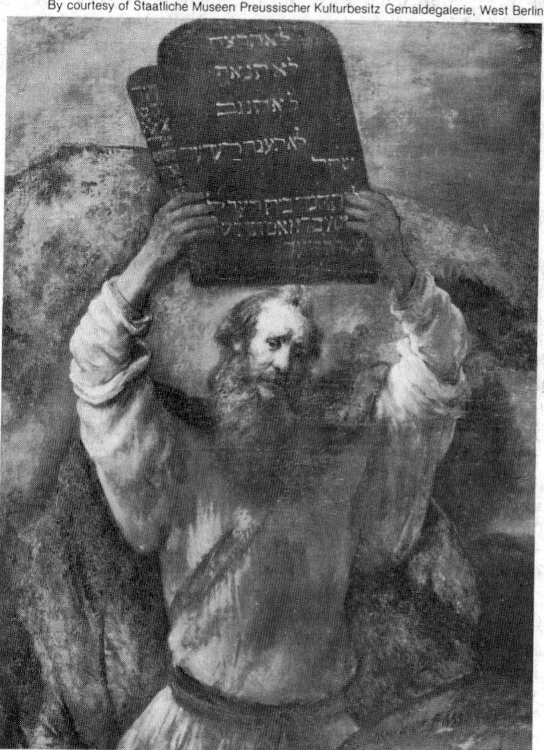

"Moses Showing the Tables of the Law to the People," oil painting by Rembrandt, 1659. In the Staatliche Museen Preussischer Kulturbesitz, Berlin.

in the delta region. Moreover, Edom and Moab, petty kingdoms in Transjordan that forced Moses to circle east of them, were not yet settled and organized. Finally, as excavations have shown, the destruction of the cities the Hebrews claimed to have captured occurred about 1250, not 1400.

Inasmuch as tradition figured about 12 generations from Moses to Solomon, the reference to 480 years is most likely an editorial comment allowing 40 years for each generation. Since an actual generation was nearer 25 years, the most probable date for the Exodus is about 1290 BCE. If this is true, then the oppressive pharaoh noted in Exodus (1:2–2:23) was Seti I (reigned 1318–04), and the pharaoh during the Exodus was Ramses II (*c.* 1304–*c.* 1237). In short, Moses was probably born in the late 14th century BCE.

YEARS AND DEEDS

The formative years. One of the measures taken by the Egyptians to restrict the growth of the Hebrews was to order the death of all newborn Hebrew males. According to tradition, Moses' parents, Amram and Jochebed (whose other children were Aaron and Miriam), hid him for three months and then set him afloat on the Nile in a reed basket daubed with pitch. The child, found by the pharaoh's daughter while bathing, was reared in the Egyptian court. While many doubt the authenticity of this tradition, the name Moses (Hebrew Moshe) is derived from Egyptian *mose* ("is born") and is found in such names as Thutmose ([The God] Thoth Is Born). Originally, it is inferred, Moses' name was longer, but the deity's name was dropped. This could have happened when Moses returned to his people or possibly even earlier, because the shortened form Mose was very popular at that time.

The young prince or courtier

Moses' years in the court are passed over in silence, but it is evident from his accomplishments later that he had instruction in religious, civil, and military matters. Since Egypt controlled Canaan (Palestine) and part of Syria and had contacts with other nations of the Fertile Crescent, Moses undoubtedly had general knowledge of life in the ancient Near East. During his education he learned somehow that he was a Hebrew, and his sense of concern and curiosity impelled him to visit his people. According to the biblical narrative, Moses lived 120 years and was 80 when he confronted Pharaoh, but there is no indication how old he was when he went to see the Hebrews. Later Jewish and Christian tradition assumed 40-year periods for his stay in the Egyptian court, his sojourn in Midian, and his wilderness wanderings.

Most likely Moses was about 25 when he took the inspection tour among his people. There he saw the oppressive measures under which they laboured. When he found an Egyptian taskmaster beating a Hebrew, probably to death, he could control his sense of justice no longer. After checking to make sure that no one was in sight, he killed the tough Egyptian overlord. As a prince in the court, Moses was probably in excellent physical condition, and apparently he knew the latest methods of combat.

The flush of victory pulled Moses back the next day. He had removed one threat to his people and was determined to assist them again. This time, however, he found two Hebrews fighting. After parting them, he questioned the offender in an attempt to mediate the disagreement. Two questions jolted him: "Who made you a prince and a judge over us? Do you intend to kill me as you killed the Egyptian?" The confidence of the self-appointed deliverer turned into fear. One of his own knew his "secret" and soon Pharaoh would, too. Realizing that he would have to flee, he went to Midian (mainly in northwest Arabia).

Moses in Midian. In noting the flight to Midian the narrative says nothing of the difficulties involved. Like Sinuhe, the Egyptian court official whose flight in about 1960 BCE was narrated in a famous story, Moses undoubtedly had to filter through the "Wall of the Ruler," a series of forts at the eastern border, approximately where the Suez Canal is now located. From there he made his way southeast through very desolate country. Unfortunately, the Bible does not specify the part of Midian in which Moses resided. Midian proper was east of the Gulf of Aqaba, in the northern section of Hejaz in Arabia, but there is evidence that some of the Midianite clans crossed over the Arabah (the great valley south of the Dead Sea) and settled in the eastern and southern sections of the Sinai Peninsula.

While Moses was resting at a well, according to the biblical account, seven daughters of the Midianite priest Jethro came to water their father's flocks. Other shepherds arrived and drove the girls away in order to water their own flocks. Again Moses showed his courage and prowess as a warrior because he took on the shepherds (perhaps with the girls' help) and routed them. Moses stayed on with Jethro and eventually married Zipporah, one of the daughters. In assuming the responsibility for Jethro's flocks, Moses roamed the wilderness looking for pasture.

The burning bush

One day at the base of a mountain, his attention was attracted by a flaming bush, but, oddly, it was not consumed. He had seen bushes brilliant with flamelike blossoms, but this phenomenon was different, and so he turned aside to investigate it. Before he could do so, he was warned to come no closer. Then he was ordered to remove his sandals because he was standing on holy ground.

Regardless of how one interprets the burning bush, the important fact is that Moses was conscious of an encounter with Deity. This God, who claimed to be the God of Abraham, Isaac, and Jacob, was calling him to deliver the Hebrews from Egypt. Although on his own he had previously been zealous to help his own people, now that he was being commissioned to deliver them he expressed doubt concerning his qualifications. The underlying reason was probably fear—he had fled from Seti I, and he did not relish confrontation with Ramses II. God reassured Moses that in the future he and the Hebrews would worship at this mountain. Then Moses asked to know the name of the Deity commissioning him. The God of the fathers had been known mostly as El ʿElyon (God Most High) or El Shaddai (God of the Mountain or Almighty God), but he identified himself to Moses as Yahweh and gave instructions that he was to be called by his new name from then on. As the causative form of the verb "to be," Yahweh means He Who Creates (Brings Into Being). This revelation enabled Moses to understand the God of the Hebrews as the sovereign Lord over nature and the nations of the world.

Even after further assurances, Moses was still reluctant to accept Yahweh's call; therefore, he pleaded for release because he was a stammerer. Yahweh acknowledged the defect but promised to help him express himself. Awed by his assignment, Moses made a final desperate plea, "Oh, my Lord, send, I pray, some other person." Although angry at Moses, Yahweh would not yield. Moses would still be Yahweh's representative, but his golden-tongued brother Aaron would be the spokesman. Apparently Moses was ready to play the role of God to Pharaoh providing Aaron would serve as his prophet. He returned to Jethro and requested permission to visit his people in Egypt, but he did not disclose that he had been commissioned by Yahweh.

Moses and Pharaoh. Ramses II became king as a teenager and reigned for 67 years. He aspired to defeat the Hittites and control all of Syria, but in the fifth year of his reign Ramses walked into a Hittite trap laid for him at Kadesh, on the Orontes River in Syria. By sheer determination he fought his way out, but in the light of his purpose the battle was an utter failure. Yet Ramses, like all the pharaohs, claimed to be divine; therefore, the defeat had to be interpreted as a marvellous victory in which he alone subdued the Hittites. His wounded ego expressed itself in massive building operations throughout Egypt, and before his reign ended the boast of his success literally filled acres of wall space.

Confrontation with Ramses

It was probably only a few years after the Kadesh incident that Moses and Aaron confronted Ramses with their demand, "Thus says the Lord, the God of Israel, 'Let my people go.' " As a god in human form Ramses was not accustomed to taking orders from lesser gods, let alone an unknown like Yahweh. "Who is the Lord," he inquired, "that I should heed his voice and let Israel go? I do not know the Lord, and moreover I will not let Israel go."

Thus the stage was set for a long struggle between a distrustful ruler with an outsize ego and a prophet with a new understanding of Yahweh and his power.

Ramses increased the oppression of the Hebrews by the fiendish plan of requiring them to gather the straw binder for the bricks and still produce the same quota each day. Some of the Hebrews rebuffed Moses, and in frustration he asked Yahweh, "Why didst thou ever send me?" Moses' doubt was allayed by Yahweh's promise to take action against Pharaoh. Scholars differ widely concerning the narrative about the plagues. Some claim that three sources have been combined, but more recent scholarship finds only the two traditions. While granting that some of the plagues had a core of historicity, older critics tended to discount the present accounts as fantastic stories with pious decorations. A recent school of research suggests that, notwithstanding some later additions, all the plagues probably had a historical core.

The basic cause, according to one interpretation, was an unusually high flooding of the Nile. The White Nile originates in the lake region of east central Africa, known today as Uganda. The flow is fairly even throughout the year because of consistent equatorial rains. The Blue Nile, on the other hand, originates in the headwaters of the Ethiopian highlands, and it varies from a small stream to a raging torrent. At the time Moses was bargaining with Ramses, excessively heavy summer rains in Ethiopia washed powdery, carmine-red soil from the slopes of the hills. Around the Lake Tana region the blood-red torrent picked up bright red algae (known as flagellates) and their bacteria. Since there were no dams at that time, the Nile flowed blood-red all the way to the Mediterranean. It probably reached the delta region in August. Thus, this rare natural event, it is held, set in motion a series of conditions that continued until the following March.

During these months Moses used the plagues of the frogs, gnats, mosquitoes, cattle murrain, boils, hail, locusts, and thick darkness to increase the pressure on Ramses. At first the King was adamant. The Hebrews were not the only disgruntled slaves, and, if he agreed to let them go, then other groups would want the same privilege. To protect his building program, he had to suppress the slave rebellion at its outset. Yet he could not discount the effect of the plagues, and grudgingly he began to acknowledge Yahweh's power. As an expedient attempt to restore order, he offered to let the Hebrews sacrifice in Goshen. When this failed, he suggested that they make offerings to Yahweh at the edge of the Egyptian border. Moses, however, insisted on a three-day journey into the wilderness. Pharaoh countered by allowing the Hebrew men to make the journey, but this, too, was rejected. As his final offer Pharaoh agreed to let the people go. He would keep the livestock, however, as the guarantee of their return. Moses spurned the condition, and in anger Pharaoh drove him out. After nine rounds with Pharaoh it appeared that the deliverance of the Hebrews was no nearer, but, in contrast to his earlier periods of doubt and frustration, Moses showed no despair. Apparently he had an inner assurance that Pharaoh would not have the last word.

From Goshen to Sinai. Chapters 11–14 of Exodus comprise an exceedingly complex section, and at times the traditions have contradictory statements. The drama is more blurred than usual, and scholars vary tremendously in their interpretation of the material. One tradition notes that Pharaoh was shaken when death took his son and that he ordered the Hebrews to leave. Another source indicates that Moses used the period of mourning for the first-born son as the occasion for fleeing secretly from the country. In either case, it is clear that Pharaoh finally had his forces pursue the Hebrews. Although tradition interpreted the Hebrew text to claim that about 2,000,000 people left Egypt, interpretation by critical methods reduces the number to 15,000 or so.

Yahweh's victory at the Reed Sea

The Egyptian army cornered them at the Sea of Reeds (papyrus), which barred their exit to the east. Later Jewish tradition understood the body of water to be the Red Sea, and this erroneous interpretation persists today, even in some of the most recent English translations of the Bible. Scholars disagree as to the precise location of the Reed Sea, but, since papyrus grows only in freshwater, it was most probably a shallow lake in the far northeastern corner of Egypt.

Hemmed in by the Egyptians, the people vented their complaints on Moses. According to one tradition, Moses shared their uneasiness, and he called to Yahweh for help. Another account claims that Moses confidently challenged them to be calm and watch for Yahweh's deliverance. A strong east wind blew all night, creating a dry corridor through the lake and permitting the Hebrews to cross. The pursuing Egyptians were destroyed when the waters returned. The timing of this natural event gave the final answer to Pharaoh's arrogant question, "Who is Yahweh?" Safely on the other side, Moses and his sister Miriam led the people in a victory song of praise to Yahweh (Ex. 15:1–21). The style of the poetry is similar to that of 14th-century Canaanite literature, and there is every reason to believe that the poem virtually preserves the original form of the song, with its refrain, "Sing to the Lord, for he has triumphed gloriously; the horse and his rider he has thrown into the sea."

The route of the Hebrews is contested by scholars, but the most likely possibility is the southern route to Jabal Mūsā, the traditional location of Mt. Sinai (Horeb), in the granite range at the southern tip of the Sinai Peninsula. The journey there traversed some very desolate country, and Moses had to contend with bitter complaints about the lack of water and food. Finally, however, he brought the people to "the mountain of God," where Yahweh had appeared to him in the burning bush.

The Covenant at Sinai. During the 14th century BCE the Hittites of Asia Minor made a number of treaties with neighbouring rulers who came under their control. The agreement was not between equals, but between the Hittite king (the suzerain) and a subordinate ruler (the vassal). In the prologue the Hittite ruler described himself as "the great king," the one granting the treaty. Then followed a historical survey of relationships between the Hittite suzerain and his vassal. Special attention to the kindnesses shown the underling by the overlord was intended to remind the vassal of his obligation to abide by the treaty stipulations. The basic requirement was an oath of loyalty. Since Egypt was involved with the Hittites in the international politics of the time, Moses probably learned about the Hittite treaty form during his years in the Egyptian court.

The revelation at Sinai: the Ten Commandments

The appearance of Yahweh in a terrific storm at Mt. Sinai, narrated in chapters 19 and 20 of Exodus, was a revelatory experience for Moses, just as the burning bush had been. Somehow he realized that the Hittite treaty was an accurate analogy of the relationship between Yahweh and the Hebrews. Yahweh had a claim upon them because he had delivered them. The only proper response to his love and care would be a pledge of obedience to his will. Scholars have tended to date the Ten Commandments, or Decalogue (contained in the revelation at Sinai), after the conquest of Canaan, but there is absolutely nothing in these guidelines to indicate their origin in an agricultural context. More likely they were the stipulations in the covenant ceremony at Mt. Sinai.

Because Yahweh was proclaimed the only true God, one of the first commands was appropriately a ban against all other gods. Authorities have debated whether or not this understanding was interpreted as monotheism. Most certainly it was not the philosophical monotheism of later periods, but it was a practical monotheism in that any gods recognized by other nations were under Yahweh's control. Inasmuch as he had brought them into being and authorized their presence in his council, he was Lord over all gods and nations.

Another early command has been taken to mean a ban on making images of other gods, but originally the prohibition applied to representations of Yahweh himself. Worship in the ancient world was unthinkable without some idol or image; therefore, the uniqueness of Moses' restriction is all the more evident. Yahweh is the unimageable Deity who cannot be represented in material forms. Since Yahweh had revealed the meaning of his name to Moses, it was fitting that the Decalogue should also prohibit any magical or unethical use of his name. Undoubtedly the ideas underlying the other commands came from the religious culture of his day, but they were raised to a significantly higher level because of the holy, righteous character of Yahweh. Moses realized that, if the Covenant people were to have a stable, just society, they would have to emulate their God. Concern for his creatures would mean respect for them as persons. Murder, adultery, theft, lying, and covetousness would never be legitimate because they lead to chaos and breakdown of the community. Moreover, inasmuch as Yahweh had been concerned to protect the powerless Hebrews in Egypt, they in turn would have to guarantee justice for the orphans, widows, resident aliens, and any other disadvantaged persons under their jurisdiction.

Interpretations and elaborations

On confirmation of the Covenant, Moses and the people faced the task of living by the stipulations. This called for interpretations of the commands, and so Moses began issuing ordinances for specific situations. Many of these he drew from the case law of his day, but insight as to their selection and application probably came in the "tent of meeting" (a simple sanctuary tent pitched outside the camp), where Yahweh spoke to Moses "face to face, as a man speaks to his friend." Breaches of the Covenant necessitated means of atonement, which in turn meant provision of a priesthood to function at sacrifices and in worship. In short, the rudiments of the whole Hebrew cult, according to tradition, originated at Sinai. At Jethro's suggestion Moses instituted a system of judges and hearings to regulate the civil aspects of the community. It was at Sinai, perhaps, where the people were organized into 12 tribes.

One of Moses' most remarkable characteristics was his concern for the Hebrews, in spite of their stubborn, rebellious ways. When they reverted to worshipping a young bull (probably made of limestone, instead of gold, as the biblical text says), Yahweh was ready to disown them and begin anew with Moses and his descendants. Moses rejected the offer, however, and later, when pleading for the forgiveness of the people, he even asked to have his own name blotted out of Yahweh's book of remembrance if the Lord would not forgive them.

From Sinai to Transjordan. After leaving Mt. Sinai, Moses faced increasing resistance and frustration, according to the narrative in the book of Numbers. Apparently his virility did not diminish during these years because he took a Cushite woman as his second wife. But Miriam, with the support of Aaron, opposed the marriage. At Kadesh-barnea the pessimistic majority report of the spies who had been sent out to reconnoitre thwarted Moses' desire to march north and conquer the land of Canaan. When he urged the people to reconsider their action they almost stoned him. But here again, according to tradition, Moses interceded for the people with Yahweh, who threatened to destroy them and raise up another and greater nation. In one instance, however, tradition recalled that Moses' anger overrode his compassion. At Meribah, probably in the area of Kadesh-barnea, Moses addressed the complaining people as rebels and struck a rock twice in anger, whereupon water flowed forth for the thirsty people. He had been angry before in defense of Yahweh's name, honour, and cause, but this time his anger stemmed from utter frustration with his contentious people. Although tradition interpreted this lapse as the reason why Yahweh would not permit Moses to enter Canaan, the remarkable fact is that Moses was able to bear up under such continuous pressure.

In Transjordan the new states of Edom and Moab, vassals of the Midianites, rejected Moses' request for passage. He wisely circled east of them and moved north to conquer Sihon, king of the Amorites, and Og, king of Bashan. After Moses permitted some of the tribes to settle in Transjordan, it evoked opposition from the Moabites and their Midianite overlords. They hired the Syrian diviner Balaam to put a curse on the Hebrews, but instead he pronounced a blessing. Some scholars interpret this as proof that Balaam was a convert to Yahwism. If this be true, he must have reverted later on, because the biblical tradition implies that Balaam incited his former employers to weaken the Hebrews by religious seduction. Moses responded to the enmity of the Midianites with a successful holy war against them shortly before his death.

Final conflict against the Midianites

As his last official act Moses renewed the Sinai Covenant with those who had survived the wilderness wanderings. From his camp in the Jordan Valley, Moses climbed to a vantage point on Mt. Pisgah. There he viewed the land of promise. The Hebrews never saw him again, and the circumstances of his death and burial remain shrouded in mystery. Tradition claimed that Yahweh buried him in the valley opposite Beth-peor, the shrine of the people's apostasy.

MOSES THE MAN

Although time undoubtedly enhanced the portrait of Moses, a basic picture emerges from the sources. Five times the narratives claim that Moses kept written records (Ex. 17:14; 24:4; 34:27–28; Num. 33:2; and Deut. 31:9, 24–26). Even with a generous interpretation of the extent of these writings, they do not amount to more than a fifth of the total Pentateuch; therefore, the traditional claim of Mosaic authorship of the whole Pentateuch is untenable. Moses formulated the Decalogue, mediated the Covenant, and began the process of rendering and codifying supplemental interpretations of the Covenant stipulations. Undoubtedly he kept some records, and they served as the core of the growing corpus of law and tradition. In a general sense, therefore, the first five books of the Hebrew Bible can be described as Mosaic. Without him there would have been no Israel and no collection known as Torah.

Moses was a gifted, well-trained person, but his true greatness was probably due to his personal experience of and relationship with Yahweh. This former stammering murderer understood his preservation and destiny as coming from the grace of a merciful Lord who had given him another chance. Moses had an understanding spirit and a forgiving heart because he knew how much Yahweh had forgiven him. He was truly humble because he recognized that his gifts and strength came from Yahweh.

The multiple roles of Moses

Because of the uniqueness of his situation, Moses had to function in a number of roles. As Yahweh's agent in the deliverance of the Hebrews, he was their prophet and leader. As mediator of the Covenant, he was the founder of the community. As interpreter of the Covenant, he was an organizer and legislator. As intercessor for the people, he was their priest. Moses had a special combination of gifts and graces that made it impossible to replace him. Although his successor, Joshua, and the priest Eleazar, the son of Aaron, tried to do so, together they did not measure up to him. Later prophets were great men who spoke out of the spirit that Moses had, but they were not called to function in so many roles. As tradition claimed, he was indeed the greatest of the prophets, and, as history shows, few of mankind's great personalities outrank him in influence. (D.M.Be.)

BIBLIOGRAPHY. WILLIAM F. ALBRIGHT, *From the Stone Age to Christianity*, 2nd ed. with new introduction (1957), classic synthesis of Israel's history and religion in the setting of the ancient Near East (see pp. 11–17, 200–272); *The Biblical Period from Abraham to Ezra* (1963), a popular historical survey (see pp. 1–23); *Yahweh and the Gods of Canaan* (1968), a technical analysis contrasting Israelite and Canaanite religion (see pp. 64–109, 153–182); ELIAS AUERBACH, *Moses* (1975; originally published in German, 1953), a search for the historic Moses; in ALBRECHT ALT, *Essays on Old Testament History and Religion* (1967; originally published in German, 1953–59), see the classic article, "The God of the Fathers," pp. 1–86; DEWEY M. BEEGLE, *Moses, the Servant of Yahweh* (1972, reissued 1979), a wide-ranging account for laymen and students; WALTER BEYERLIN, *Origins and History of the Oldest Sinaitic Traditions* (1965; originally published in German, 1961), a technical study of biblical sources in Exodus 19–20, 24, 32–34; JOHN BRIGHT, *A History of Israel*, 3rd ed. (1981), a standard work mediating scholarly extremes; MARTIN BUBER, *Moses, the Revelation and the Covenant* (1946), a sympathetic treatment with philosophical emphasis but weak in details of the ancient Near East; DANIEL J. SILVER, *Images of Moses* (1982), an examination of literary, artistic, and historical treatments of Moses; GEORGE W. COATS, *Rebellion in the Wilderness* (1968), a detailed critical study of the murmuring motif in the wilderness traditions; FRANK MOORE CROSS, JR., "Yahweh and the God of

Patriarchs," *Harvard Theological Review,* 55:225–259 (1962), a scholarly treatment of issues raised by Alt's classic article; DELBERT R. HILLERS, *Covenant: The History of a Biblical Idea* (1969), an excellent popular study; GRETA HORT, "The Plagues of Egypt," *Zeitschrift für die alttestamentliche Wissenschaft,* 69:84–103 (1957) and 70:48–59 (1958), the historical basis of the plagues; YEHEZKEL KAUFMANN, *The Religion of Israel,* trans. and abridged by MOSHE GREENBERG (1960), which considers Moses the founder of Israel and its religion but doubts details of the historical tradition and neglects much modern archaeological and linguistic research; GEORGE E. MENDENHALL, "The Mask of Yahweh," in *The Tenth Generation: Essays in Early Biblical History* (1972); MURRAY LEE NEWMANN, JR., *The People of the Covenant* (1962), a popular study of Israel from Moses to the monarchy (see pp. 13–101); MARTIN NOTH, *The History of Israel,* 2nd ed. rev. (1960; originally published in German, 1956), a basic study but with radical treatment of Hebrew history prior to the conquest (see pp. 110–138), and *A History of Pentateuchal Traditions* (1972, reissued 1981; originally published in German, 1948), a technical study of the biblical sources in the Pentateuch that doubts its accuracy (see pp. 156–188); HAROLD H. ROWLEY, *From Joseph to Joshua* (1950), an attempt to relate the data of biblical traditions to the findings of archaeology; MARY R. D'ANGELO, *Moses in the Letter to the Hebrews* (1979), a study of how Christology has influenced the interpretation of Moses; and J.J. STAMM and M.E. ANDREW, *The Ten Commandments in Recent Research,* 2nd ed. rev. (1967).
(D.M.Be./Ed.)

Moss Animals: Phylum Bryozoa

Bryozoa, also called Polyzoa or Ectoprocta, comprises a phylum in which there are probably more than 4,000 extant species. The bryozoans are a widely distributed, aquatic, invertebrate group of animals whose members form colonies composed of numerous units called zooids (hence the term Polyzoa, which means "many animals"). Until the mid-18th century, bryozoans, like corals, were regarded as plants; hence their name, which means "moss animals." Seventy-five years later, the bryozoans were distinguished from the cnidarians, and the characteristic structure of the zooid was first described.

Bryozoans are separated into three classes: Phylactolaemata (freshwater dwelling); Stenolaemata (marine); and Gymnolaemata (mostly marine). The order Cheilostomata (class Gymnolaemata), containing 600 genera, is the most successful bryozoan group.

For coverage of related topics in the *Macropædia* and *Micropædia,* see the *Propædia,* section 313.

This article is divided into the following sections:

GENERAL FEATURES

Distribution and abundance. Bryozoan colonies are found in both fresh and salt waters, most commonly as growths or crusts on other objects. Freshwater bryozoans live among vegetation in clear, quiet, or slowly flowing water. Marine species range from the shore to the ocean depths but are most plentiful in the shallow waters of the continental shelf. They cover seaweeds, form crusts on stones and shells, hang from boulders, or rise from the seabed. Bryozoans readily colonize submerged surfaces, including ship hulls and the insides of water pipes. A few form non-attached populations on sandy seabeds.

The zooid walls, which constitute the most permanent portion of the colony, generally are calcareous (*i.e.,* impregnated with calcium carbonate), giving bryozoans a fossil record that dates from the Ordovician onward (*i.e.,* from about 500,000,000 years ago).

Size range and diversity of structure. Bryozoan colonies vary in size. In the gymnolaemate genus *Monobryozoon,* which lives between marine sand particles, a colony consists of little more than a single feeding zooid less than one millimetre (0.04 inch) in height. Colonies of the coralline genus of European seas *Pentapora,* however, can reach one metre (3.3 feet) or more in circumference; a warm-water gymnolaemate genus, *Zoobotryon,* which hangs from harbour pilings, and the freshwater phylactolaemate *Pectinatella* each produce masses that may be one-half metre across. Colonies that form crusts generally cover only a few square centimetres; erect colonies may rise only two to five centimetres (0.8–2 inches).

The texture of the colonies is variable. Some colonies, especially those in fresh water and on seashores, are gelatinous or membranous; others are tufted, with flat fronds (leaflike structures) or whorls of slender branches, whose horny texture results from light deposits of lime in zooid walls. Still other colonies are hard and have calcified skeletons. Such colonies may form rough-surfaced patches or may rise in slender branching twigs (such as those that form a network in the beautiful lace corals; *e.g., Sertella*).

Colonies

The colonies, diverse and complex in structure, are composed of individual modules, or zooids, and each zooid effectively is a complete animal. A bryozoan colony usually has many zooids, which may be of one type or of types that differ both functionally and structurally. Neighbouring zooids are united and may communicate by tiny pores present in the zooids' walls. Zooids capable of feeding have a ring of slender tentacles at one end on which are found cilia (hairlike projections) that propel tiny particles of food toward the zooid mouth. The mouth opens into a digestive tract that is divided into several regions and terminates at an anus, which is outside (but near) the tentacles (hence the name Ectoprocta, meaning "outside anus"). If zooids are disturbed, they withdraw their tentacles inside the body cavity. Only if the zooids have transparent walls, such as in the gymnolaemates *Bowerbankia* and *Membranipora,* is the digestive tract visible. The internal living parts of each zooid—*i.e.,* the nervous and muscular systems, the tentacles, and the digestive tract—are called the polypide.

NATURAL HISTORY

Reproduction and life cycle. Many animals, bryozoans included, have a life cycle that incorporates phases of asexual and sexual reproduction (Figure 1). Asexual reproduction, in which gametes (sex cells) do not participate, produces genetically identical progeny (clones), which separate in larger animals (*e.g.,* sea anemones). In bryozoans, the progeny, called zooids, are produced by an asexual process called budding and almost invariably remain in intimate contact as a colony. As the colony continues to grow by budding, the zooids become sexually mature, producing eggs and spermatozoa. Sexual reproduction, by the production and subsequent fusion of gametes, generates the genetic variability necessary for a species to survive in a habitat that varies from place to place and from time to time. Fertilized eggs develop into larvae.

Some bryozoans also propagate colonies asexually. The

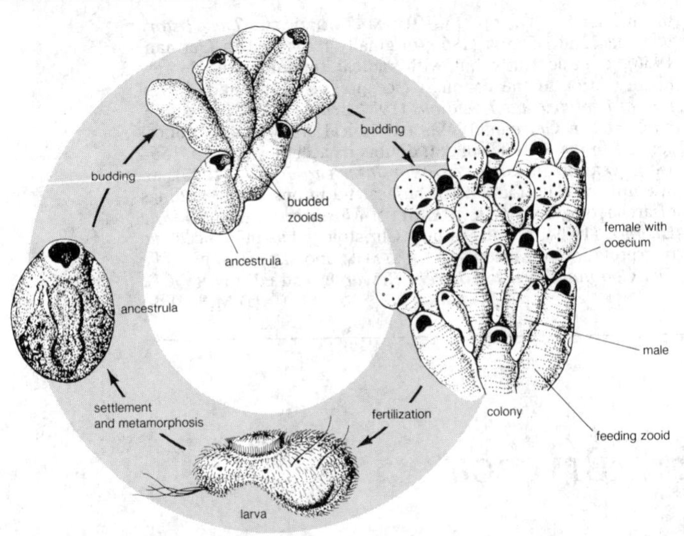

Figure 1: Life cycle in Bryozoa (*Celleporella*).

From (colony) E. Marcus, "Bryozoarios Marinhos Brasileiros," *Boletins da Faculdade de Philosophia, Sciencias e Letras* (1938), Universidade de Sao Paulo; (others) J.H. Barrois, *Recherches sur l'embryologie des bryozoaires*, pl. IX (1877), Six-Horemans, Lille

cheilostome *Discoporella* has small, nonattached, saucer-like colonies. Groups of zooids at the colony rim detach at special fracture zones and grow into new colonies. The statoblasts (dormant buds) of freshwater bryozoans are another asexual means of reproduction. Asexual reproduction, whether leading to a clone, a colony, or a clone of colonies, is a means of perpetuating and spreading a successful genetic constitution (genotype).

Primary zooid

Budding. The colony formed by asexual budding originates from either a primary zooid (or ancestrula) or a statoblast. The ancestrula is formed by the metamorphosis of a sexually produced larva (Figure 1). New zooids bud from the ancestrula to produce colonies of definite shape and growth habit. In the phylactolaemates, the primitive zooids are cylindrical in form, and the budding pattern results in a branched colony. In more highly evolved phylactolaemates, colonies are compact, and discrete zooids can be recognized only with difficulty. New polypides, which originate by ingrowth of the superficial cell layer, or epithelium, remain suspended within a common colonial coelom, or body cavity.

Among living members of the primitive (and mainly fossil) marine stenolaemates, the long and slender zooids have calcified tubular skeletons. A larva metamorphoses into a hemispherical primary disk (or proancestrula). A cylindrical extension grows from the proancestrula, and the matrix of the colony then is built up by repeated divisions of the zooidal walls. Internal walls of the colony are called septa. The growth and budding zones of the colony are found at its outer edges. Cells from the surface epithelium push inward to produce the polypide, and the septa create a chamber around it. The walled portion of a zooid is called the cystid.

In the gymnolaemates, in which the zooids frequently are flattened, budding occurs as transverse septa form and cut off parts of the primary zooid (or any other parent zooid). As each bud enlarges to become a zooid, a polypide forms inside. In the order Cheilostomata, budding usually produces rows of identical zooids that radiate from the primary zooid. The rows divide periodically to keep pace with the increasing circumference of the colony. Successive zooids in a row are separated by transverse septa, but adjoining rows are separated by double walls. Interzooidal pores are present both in the walls and in the septa.

Reproduction. Mature gymnolaemate and phylactolaemate zooids are generally hermaphroditic (*i.e.,* both male and female reproductive organs in the same zooid); small gonads are attached in clusters to the membrane that lines the body wall or the polypide. In a few species the individual zooids are of one sex only. In these circumstances, female zooids are usually larger (*e.g.,* the cheilostome *Reptadeonella*), male zooids may be simpler (*e.g.,* the cheilostome *Hippoporidra*), or female and male reproductive zooids each may be distinguishable from ordinary feeding zooids (*e.g.,* the cheilostome *Celleporella*). Among living stenolaemates most zooids contain only testes (male gonads). The few female zooids enlarge to form spacious brood chambers, which are called gonozooids. During development, a young embryo squeezes off groups of cells that form secondary embryos; these in turn may form tertiary embryos. In this way, many larvae can develop in a single brood chamber.

Brood chambers

Among the phylactolaemates, the fertilized egg develops in an internal embryo sac; a larva, which already contains the first polypide, is formed there, then liberated. Phylactolaemates also produce statoblasts, which develop on the funiculus, a cord of tissue that links the stomach to the lining of the body wall. As it grows, each statoblast is surrounded by a hard protective case that may also include an air-filled float and slender, hooked spines. Statoblasts usually develop in late summer and are liberated as the colony disintegrates with the approach of winter. Statoblasts survive dry and freezing conditions and can initiate a new colony when favourable climatic conditions recur.

In gymnolaemates one oocyte at a time usually enlarges and bursts from the ovary into the coelom. The oocyte then is fertilized and transferred to a brood chamber. This may be an undifferentiated part of a zooid; usually among the cheilostomes, however, each reproducing zooid develops a special globular or hooded ooecium in which the embryo grows. In most cheilostomes the egg at transfer has sufficient yolk to nourish its developing embryo, but in the cheilostomes *Bugula* and *Celleporella* the egg, which is small at transfer, establishes a pseudoplacenta with tissues of the mother zooid and receives nourishment as the embryo develops. The ciliated larvae, spherical and often about $^1/_4$ millimetre in diameter, are liberated when fully developed and may swim first toward the light and thus away from the parent colony; later, however, the larvae avoid light as they seek a place in which to settle. Metamorphosis of larvae to adults occurs within a few hours after larvae are liberated.

In certain genera (*e.g., Membranipora*) of the class Gymnolaemata, each zooid produces many tiny eggs, which are fertilized by sperm from another zooid as they are shed directly into the sea. The fertilized eggs develop into triangular, bivalved larvae, known as cyphonautes, which for several weeks live among, and feed on, plankton. Larvae from brood chambers and cyphonautes settle in a similar way; *i.e.,* both locate a suitable surface and explore it with sensory cilia. Attachment is achieved by flattening a sticky holdfast, which pulls the larva down on top of it. As metamorphosis proceeds, larval organization degenerates, and the first polypide develops inside a primary zooid.

Ecology. *Freshwater bryozoans.* Freshwater bryozoans live mainly on leaves, stems, and tree roots in shallow water. Before drinking water was filtered, they regularly polluted water supply pipes. Though not uncommon, freshwater bryozoans are inconspicuous in pools, lakes, or gently flowing rivers, especially in slightly alkaline water.

Marine bryozoans. The most familiar marine bryozoans are those that inhabit shores, though they occur in greater numbers below tidemarks. Dredge hauls of stones and shells yield colonies in abundance. Colonies also occur on the ocean bed, even at great depths, but the frequently muddy bottom of the oceanic abyss is an unfavourable habitat. A few species tolerate hypersaline or brackish waters. The predominantly marine Gymnolaemata have a few freshwater representatives; *e.g., Paludicella.*

Bryozoans along shores

Shallow, sheltered channels that have currents but are protected from severe waves are typical bryozoan habitats. Open coastlines support fewer species, but noncalcareous species occur abundantly on intertidal algae in temperate waters. A familiar genus is the lacy gymnolaemate *Membranipora,* which is found throughout the world and is well adapted to living on kelp weeds at, and just below, the low-water mark. Although the zooid walls of *Membranipora* colonies are calcified, they contain flexible joints, which allow the colony to bend as the alga sways in the waves. *Membranipora,* which may cover large areas with a million or more zooids, always grows predominantly toward the youngest part of an algal frond. Overhangs, which form when soft rock erodes along a shoreline, as well as the shaded pilings of jetties and piers are other favoured bryozoan habitats. Since they do not require light and can grow in dark places, bryozoans can avoid competition from algae that could smother them. Sea slugs and sea spiders appear to be the principal predators of bryozoans.

Food and feeding. Bryozoans feed on minute planktonic particles that are captured by the tentacles (from eight to about 30), which, in marine species, spread as a funnel with the mouth at its vertex (Figure 2). The beating of long lateral cilia draws water into the top of the funnel and propels it out between the tentacles. Particles are projected toward the mouth, and those that would leave the funnel between the tentacles appear to be flicked back into it by a reversal of the ciliary beat. Shorter cilia on the inner face of the tentacles carry food particles toward the mouth without the involvement of mucus; from there they are sucked into the pharynx. Diatom shell valves are separated or broken in the gizzard, when present. Digestion and absorption occur in the stomach, and indigestible remains are compacted by rotation and expelled as fecal pellets. Freshwater bryozoans have more tentacles, which are disposed in a crescent shape, the ends of which project behind the mouth.

FORM AND FUNCTION

Zooids. Although zooid appearance and structure vary considerably from class to class, all conform to a basic plan (Figure 2). Zooids are rarely longer than one millimetre; the most primitive are cylindrical, suggesting that the bryozoan ancestor was probably wormlike. The skeleton is external, ranging from a thin, cuticular cover to a thick, calcified layer. The tentacles, collectively termed the lophophore, are raised above the zooid on a slender extension of the body wall (the tentacle sheath, or introvert). When not spread for feeding the tentacles are withdrawn into the coelom in a movement that involves the inrolling of the tentacle sheath as the mouth and tentacles are pulled down within by the action of paired retractor muscles. Eversion of the tentacle sheath and tentacles is effected by raising the hydrostatic pressure of the body fluid. Phylactolaemates have a muscular and contractile body wall for this purpose; in gymnolaemates the wall is nonmuscular but in whole or in part flexible, so that it can be pulled inward by the body musculature associated with it (parietal muscles). In most extant bryozoans the zooids are not cylindrical but flat, with rigid side walls. The upward facing or frontal wall either remains flexible or has concealed below its calcified surface a membranous cavity, the ascus (sac), which can be inflated with seawater, thereby compressing the body fluid. At the free end of a cylindrical zooid or near the distal end of a flat zooid is an opening known as the orifice, through which the tentacle sheath and tentacles emerge; in cheilostome gymnolaemates the orifice has a closable lid, the operculum. Stenolaemate zooids are different, and the walls have the form of a slender calcareous tube, no part of which can be inflected to evert the tentacles; instead, body fluid is forced from one part of the zooid to another by muscles.

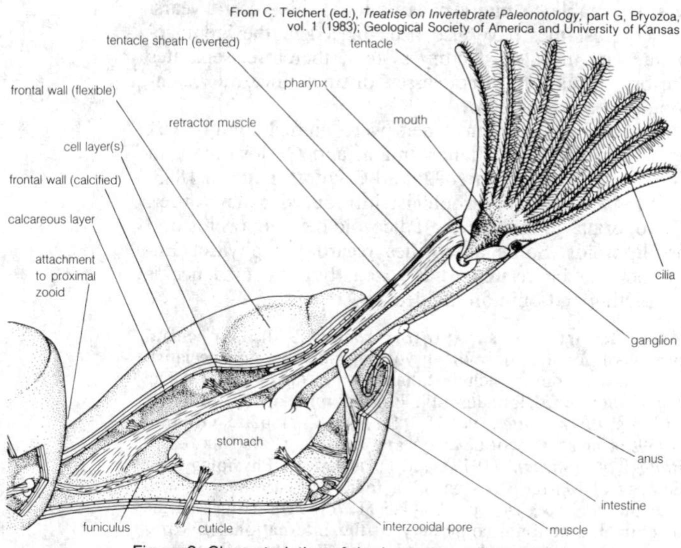

Figure 2: Characteristics of the bryozoan zooid with the lophophore protruded.

The digestive canal forms a deep loop; the pharynx descends to the stomach, the anterior part of which forms a gizzard in some genera, such as the gymnolaemate *Bowerbankia;* the rectum rises from the stomach, and the anus is situated just outside the lophophore. Respiratory, circulatory, and excretory systems are absent in bryozoans. The reproductive organs (ovary, testes) are sited on the lining of the body wall or on the funiculus, a cord of tissue that links the stomach to the lining of the body wall and distributes nutrients throughout the colony. The polypide degenerates periodically during the lifetime of a zooid, and a compact mass, called a brown body, frequently remains in its place. A new polypide soon differentiates from living cells of the cystid.

Zooid polymorphism in cheilostomes

Zooid polymorphism exists among the cheilostome colonies, and the operculum seems to have been significant in the evolution of the specialized zooids of this order. The avicularium type of zooid has a small body and a rudimentary polypide; the operculum, however, is proportionally larger, has strong adductor (closing) muscles, and has become, in effect, a jaw. Avicularia are found among normal zooids but usually are smaller and attached to normal zooids, as in the gymnolaemate *Schizoporella.* In the gymnolaemate *Bugula* the avicularia are movable on short stalks and closely resemble miniature birds' heads; hence the name avicularium. Another specialized form of zooid is the vibraculum, in which the operculum has become a whiplike seta (*i.e.,* hairlike projection). The functions of avicularia and vibracula are not clearly known, but both types of zooids may help to keep the colony free from particles and epizoites (*i.e.,* organisms that attach to the surface of the colony but do not parasitize it).

Colonies. Despite their ill-defined shape, colonies, at least in extant bryozoans, are not just aggregations of zooids but whole organisms having an integrated physiology and behaviour that appear to be coordinated to some extent. The agency for integration is the system of interzooidal pores (Figure 2) and the cells that traverse them. Most conspicuous are those of the funiculus, which in gymnolaemates becomes a colonial network capable of distributing nutrients to nonfeeding areas, such as the growing edge. The nervous system of bryozoans consists of a small ganglion (brain) positioned between the mouth and the anus that supplies nerves to the zooidal organs. In some bryozoans there is also a colonial network that unites the zooids through the interzooidal pores. A stimulus that causes the lophophore to withdraw in a zooid of the gymnolaemate *Membranipora* almost instantaneously evokes the same response nearby, and nerve impulses can at that time be recorded. Nevertheless, to a large extent the colony is not individualistic; for example, it usually has no definite shape, can grow in any direction, and can be partially destroyed without harm to the rest. It may live a few months or a couple of years, or it may be theoretically immortal, its life of continual budding terminated only by some catastrophe.

EVOLUTION AND PALEONTOLOGY

The Bryozoa have a long history. From the Lower Ordovician (500,000,000 to 430,000,000 years ago) onward, most limestone formations, especially those with shale alternations, are rich in bryozoan fossils. The skeletons of calcified bryozoans are easily preserved. Stenolaemates are abundant fossils; after their appearance in the Upper Jurassic (140,000,000 years ago), cheilostome fossils also are abundant. The soft-bodied phylactolaemates, on the other hand, have left no fossil record, and fossilized ctenostomes are rare but long antedate the cheilostomes.

Oldest bryozoan fossil

The most ancient bryozoans are stenolaemates from the Lower Ordovician of the United States and the Soviet Union (Arenig series, about 499,000,000 years old); both cystoporate and trepostome stenolaemates have been found. The ceramoporoids, a group belonging to the order Cystoporata, flourished during the Ordovician and evidently were the progenitors of a more advanced group, the fistuliporoids, which were successful until the end of the Permian (280,000,000 to 225,000,000 years ago).

Dominant among the early Paleozoic (570,000,000 to 225,000,000 years ago) stenolaemates, however, was the order Trepostomata, which evolved rapidly during the Ordovician and attained its peak during the upper part of the same period. The long, slender zooids of trepostomes grew together to form large, solid colonies. As a zooid grew longer and longer, diaphragms (or transverse partitions) were deposited. The trepostomes declined in importance after the Ordovician, perhaps as a result of competition from the cryptostomes, and were extinct by the close of the Permian (225,000,000 years ago).

Cryptostomes evolved rapidly during the Ordovician. They were similar to the trepostomes but evolved freely erect, leaflike, branching or lacy colonies in the ptilodictyoids, or branching in rhabdomesoids, and were the dominant bryozoans from the start of the Devonian until the Permian (395,000,000 to 225,000,000 years ago). For reasons not yet clear, the cryptostomes dwindled and became extinct soon after the end of the Paleozoic Era (225,000,000 years ago).

The Cyclostomata arose in the Paleozoic, flourished during the Jurassic (190,000,000 to 136,000,000 years ago) and Lower Cretaceous, and still survive.

The ctenostomes (class Gymnolaemata) have left a sparse fossil record. During the Late Jurassic Period they apparently gave rise to the complex and successful cheilostomes. The early cheilostomes had encrusting flat zooids similar to some of their contemporary ctenostomes, but with side walls that were calcified. This type of organization, termed anascan (meaning without an ascus), permitted inflexion of the front wall to evert the lophophore but seemed to offer little protection. The Ascophora (ascus bearers) evolved in the Late Cretaceous by calcifying the membranous front but preserving its hydrostatic function by a flexible infolding (ascus) below the wall. The parietal muscles attach to the ascus and pull its lower surface into the coelom to evert the lophophore, while the ascus itself fills with seawater.

CLASSIFICATION

Distinguishing taxonomic features. Although both colony type and zooid morphology are used to classify bryozoans, zooidal characters are more reliable. The cylindrical zooids are of rather uniform appearance in the stenolaemates, making classification difficult. Wall structure and the morphology of the embryo chambers are important taxonomic characters. In cheilostomes the skeletal features of the zooids, particularly the presence, extent, and structure of the frontal wall—together with shape of the orifice, type of ooecia, and zooid polymorphism—provide the most important distinguishing taxonomic criteria. Among ctenostomes and phylactolaemates, whose zooids lack skeletal features, colony form is more important. Statoblasts are of taxonomic value. Internal characters have been used less, but the presence or absence of a gizzard, number of tentacles, and colour of developing embryos are of taxonomic significance.

Annotated classification.

PHYLUM BRYOZOA

Sedentary, aquatic invertebrates; form colonies of zooids by budding; each zooid with circular or crescentic lophophore surrounding a mouth from which slender, ciliated tentacles arise; anterior part of body forms an introvert within which the lophophore can be withdrawn; alimentary canal deeply looped; anus opens near mouth but outside lophophore; excretory organs and a blood vascular system absent; each zooid secretes a rigid or gelatinous wall to support colony; over 4,000 extant species.

Class Phylactolaemata

Zooids basically cylindrical, with a crescentic lophophore and an epistome (hollow flap overhanging mouth); body wall noncalcareous, muscular, used for everting the lophophore; coelom continuous between zooids; new zooids arise by replication of polypides; special dormant buds (statoblasts) are produced; zooids monomorphic; exclusively freshwater; cosmopolitan; apparently primitive, but with no certain fossil record; about 12 genera.

Class Stenolaemata

Fossil except for some Cyclostomata; zooids cylindrical; body wall calcified, without muscle fibres; not used for everting the lophophore; zooids separated by septa; new zooids produced by division of septa; limited polymorphism; marine; Ordovician to present; about 550 genera.

Order Cyclostomata

Orifice of zooid circular; lophophore circular; no epistome; zooids interconnected by open pores; sexual reproduction involves polyembryony, usually in special reproductive zooids; all seas; Ordovician to present; about 250 genera.

Order Cystoporata

Zooid skeletons long and tubular, interconnected by pores and containing diaphragms (transverse partitions); cystopores (not pores but supporting structures between the zooid skeletons) present; Ordovician to Permian; about 80 genera.

Order Trepostomata

Colonies generally massive, composed of long tubular zooid skeletons with lamellate calcification; without interzooidal pores; orifices polygonal; sometimes with numerous diaphragms, zooid walls thin proximally, thicker distally; Ordovician to Permian; about 100 genera.

Order Cryptostomata

Colonies mostly with foliaceous or reticulate fronds or with branching stems; zooid skeletons tubular, shorter than in trepostomes; without pores; with diaphragms; proximal portions thin walled, distal portions funnellike and separated by extensive calcification; Ordovician to Triassic; about 130 genera.

Class Gymnolaemata

Zooids cylindrical or squat, with a circular lophophore; no epistome; body wall sometimes calcified; nonmuscular; eversion of lophophore dependent on deformation of body wall by extrinsic muscles; zooids separated by septa or duplex walls; pores in walls plugged with tissue; new zooids produced behind growing points by formation of transverse septa; zooids polymorphic; mainly marine; all seas; Jurassic to present, but presumed to have been established at least by the Ordovician; about 650 genera.

Order Ctenostomata

Zooids cylindrical to flat; walls not calcified; orifice terminal or nearly so, often closed by a pleated collar; no ooecia or avicularia; Jurassic to present, but presumed older; about 40 genera.

Order Cheilostomata

Zooids generally shaped like a flat box, walls calcified; orifice frontal, closed by a hinged operculum; specialized zooids, such as avicularia, commonly present; embryos often developing in ooecia (brood chambers). Upper Jurassic to present; about 600 genera.

Critical appraisal. Classification of bryozoans began in 1837 when the freshwater and marine Bryozoa were separated into the classes now known as Phylactolaemata and Gymnolaemata. Later a third class, the Stenolaemata, was separated from the Gymnolaemata. The cyclostomes and the fossil trepostomes were placed in the new class, which was acceptable to many paleontologists. In recent years, the cryptostomes have also been placed in the Stenolaemata. The most satisfactory system, therefore, separates the bryozoans into three classes, distinct since the beginning of the fossil record.

Most of the bryozoan orders were named many years ago: Cheilostomata, Ctenostomata, and Cyclostomata in 1852; Trepostomata in 1882; and Cryptostomata in 1883. In 1964 a Soviet bryozoologist introduced a new order, Cystoporata, to include the Paleozoic ceramoporoids and fistuliporoids. Some authorities regard the phylum Entoprocta to be related to Bryozoa, but the evidence is conflicting and opinion divided.

BIBLIOGRAPHY. J.S. RYLAND, *Bryozoans* (1970), is a general survey of fossil and living bryozoans for the nonspecialist. Advanced accounts include LIBBIE HENRIETTA HYMAN, "The Lophophorate Coelomates—Phylum Ectoprocta," ch. 20 in the author's *Invertebrates,* vol. 5, "Smaller Coelomate Groups" (1959); ROBERT M. WOOLLACOTT and RUSSELL L. ZIMMER (eds.), *Biology of Bryozoans* (1977); and J.S. RYLAND, "Physiology and Ecology of Marine Bryozoans," a review in *Advances in Marine Biology,* vol. 14, pp. 285–443 (1976). Proceedings of the seventh international conference of the International Bryozoology Association, held in 1986, resulted in the collection of current research in JUNE R.P. ROSS (ed.), *Bryozoa: Present and*

Past (1987). Other contributions to the subject are found in RICHARD S. BOARDMAN, ALAN H. CHEETHAM, and WILLIAM A. OLIVER, JR. (eds.), *Animal Colonies: Development and Function Through Time* (1973); G. LARWOOD and B.R. ROSEN (eds.), *Biology and Systematics of Colonial Organisms* (1979); JEREMY B.C. JACKSON, LEO W. BUSS, and ROBERT E. COOK (eds.), *Population Biology and Evolution of Clonal Organisms* (1985); and J.L. HARPER, B.R. ROSEN, and J. WHITE (eds.), *The Growth and Form of Modular Organisms* (1986). Well-illustrated surveys of the bryozoans may be found on pp. 667–677 of ch. 26, "Lophophorates," in VICKI PEARSE *et al., Living Invertebrates* (1987), and on pp. 238–242 of ch. 14, "Lesser Lights," in RALPH BUCHSBAUM *et al., Animals Without Backbones,* 3rd ed. (1987). Extensive introductions are offered in the four works belonging to the "Synopses of the British Fauna" series: J.S. RYLAND and P.J. HAYWARD, *British Anascan Bryozoans: Cheilostomata, Anasca: Keys and Notes for the Identification of the Species* (1977); P.J. HAYWARD and J.S. RYLAND, *British Ascophoran Bryozoans* (1979); P.J. HAYWARD, *Ctenostome Bryozoans* (1985); and P.J. HAYWARD and J.S. RYLAND, *Cyclostome Bryozoans* (1985). A classification of extant Bryozoa is provided by J.S. RYLAND, "Bryozoa," pp. 743–769, vol. 2, in SYBIL P. PARKER (ed.), *Synopsis and Classification of Living Organisms,* 2 vol. (1982).
(J.S.R.)

Motion Pictures

A remarkably effective medium in conveying drama and especially in the evocation of emotion, motion pictures consist of the projection of luminous moving images onto a screen. The art of motion pictures is exceedingly complex, requiring contributions from nearly all of the other arts as well as countless technical skills. Nonetheless, probably no other art has proliferated as much in the 20th century nor can any other equal it in popularity or influence.

The motion picture is the newest of the generally recognized "fine arts." It is the product of photographic and technological developments that culminated by 1900 in practical devices for the recording of a moving image and its projection onto a flat surface. During its early development, the motion picture was discounted by many critics for its subservience to commercial interests, the immediacy of its appeal to the uninstructed, its mechanical technique, and its apparent lack of an identifiable artist as its primary creator. After the middle of the 20th century, however, increasing attention was devoted to it as a form of artistic endeavour that is as legitimate as the theatre, literature, dance, music, or the visual arts. (R.St.)

This article traces the historical development of the motion picture, the art of film, and its technology. Other articles in which specialized aspects of the subject are treated include SOUND, PHOTOGRAPHY, and OPTICS, PRINCIPLES OF.

For coverage of related topics in the *Macropædia* and *Micropædia,* see the *Propædia,* sections 623 and 735.

The article is divided into the following sections:

History

EARLY YEARS: 1830–1910

Persistence of vision and the phi phenomenon

Origins. The illusion of motion pictures is based on the optical phenomena known as persistence of vision and the phi phenomenon. The first of these causes the brain to retain images cast upon the retina of the eye for a fraction of a second beyond their disappearance from the field of sight, while the latter creates apparent movement between images when they succeed each other rapidly. Together, these phenomena permit the succession of still frames on a motion-picture film strip to represent continuous movement when projected at the proper speed (usually 16 frames per second for silent films and 24 frames per second for sound films). Before the invention of photography, a variety of optical toys exploited this effect by mounting successive phase drawings of things in motion on the face of a twirling disk (the phenakistoscope, *c.* 1832) or inside of a rotating drum (the zoetrope, *c.* 1834). In 1839, however, Louis-Jacques-Mandé Daguerre perfected the positive photographic process known as daguerreotypy, and as negative photography was innovated and refined over the next few decades, it became possible to replace the phase drawings in the early devices with individually posed phase photographs, which was widely and popularly done.

There would be no true motion pictures, however, until live action could be photographed spontaneously and simultaneously as it occurred. This required a reduction in photographic exposure time from Daguerre's 15 minutes to William Henry Fox Talbot's one-hundredth (and, ultimately, one-thousandth) of a second in 1870, as well as the development of the technology of series photography by the British-American photographer Eadweard Muybridge between 1872 and 1877. During that time, Muybridge was employed by Governor Leland Stanford of California, a zealous racehorse breeder, to prove that at some point in its gallop a running horse lifts all four hooves off the ground at once. Conventions of 19th-century illustration suggested otherwise, and the movement itself occurred too rapidly for perception by the naked eye; so Muybridge experimented with multiple cameras to take successive photographs of horses in motion. Finally, in 1877, he set up a battery of 12 cameras along a Sacramento racecourse with wires stretched across the track to operate their shutters. As a horse strode down the track, its hooves tripped each shutter individually to expose a successive photograph of the gallop, confirming Stanford's belief. When Muybridge later mounted these images on a rotating disk and projected them on a screen through a magic lantern, they produced a "moving picture" of the horse at full gallop as it had actually occurred in life.

Series photography

The French physiologist Étienne-Jules Marey took the first series photographs with a single instrument in 1882; once again, the impetus was the analysis of motion too rapid for perception by the human eye. Marey invented the chronophotographic gun, a camera shaped like a rifle that recorded 12 successive photographs per second, in order to study the movement of birds in flight. These images were imprinted on a rotating glass plate (later, paper roll film), and Marey subsequently attempted to project them. Like Muybridge, however, Marey was interested in deconstructing movement rather than synthesizing it, and he did not carry his experiments much beyond the realm of high-speed, or instantaneous, series photography. Muybridge and Marey, in fact, conducted their work in the spirit of scientific inquiry; they extended and elaborated existing technologies in order to probe events that occurred beyond the threshold of human perception. Those who came after would return their discoveries to the realm of normal human vision and exploit them for profit.

In 1887 in Newark, N.J., an Episcopalian minister named Hannibal Goodwin first used celluloid roll film as a base for photographic emulsions, and within the year his idea had been appropriated by the industrialist George Eastman, who in 1888 began to mass-produce celluloid roll film for still photography at his plant in Rochester, N.Y. This event was crucial to the development of cinematography: series photography such as Marey's chronophotography could employ glass plates or paper strip film because it recorded events of short duration in a relatively small number of images, but cinematography would inevitably find its subjects in longer, more complicated events, requiring thousands of images and therefore just the kind of flexible but durable recording medium represented by celluloid. It remained for someone to combine the principles embodied in the apparatuses of Muybridge and Marey with celluloid strip film to arrive at a viable motion-picture camera—an innovation achieved by William Kennedy Laurie Dickson in the West Orange, N.J., laboratories of the Edison Company in 1888.

Edison and the Lumière brothers. Thomas Alva Edison invented the phonograph in 1877, and it had quickly become the most popular home entertainment device of the century. It was to provide a visual accompaniment to the phonograph that Edison commissioned Dickson, a young laboratory assistant, to invent a motion-picture camera in 1887. Dickson built upon the work of Muybridge and Marey, a fact that he readily acknowledged, but he was the first to combine the two final essentials of motion-picture camera and projection technology. These were a device, adapted from the escapement mechanism of a clock, to ensure the intermittent but regular motion of the film strip through the camera and a regularly perforated celluloid film strip to ensure precise synchronization between the film strip and the shutter. Dickson's camera was patented as the Kinetograph in 1893, and it initially imprinted up to 50 feet of celluloid film at the rate of about 40 frames per second.

The Kinetograph

Because Edison had originally conceived of motion pictures as an adjunct to his phonograph, he did not commission the invention of a projector. Rather, he had Dickson design a type of peep-show viewing device called the Kinetoscope in which a continuous 47-foot film loop ran on spools between an incandescent lamp and a shutter for individual viewing. Starting in 1894, Kinetoscopes were marketed commercially through the firm of Raff and Gammon for $250 to $300 apiece, and the Edison Company established its own Kinetograph studio (a single-room building called the "Black Maria" that rotated on tracks to follow the Sun) in West Orange, N.J., to supply films for the Kinetoscopes that Raff and Gammon were installing in penny arcades, hotel lobbies, amusement parks, and other such semipublic places. In April of that year the first Kinetoscope parlour was opened in a converted storefront in New York City. The parlour charged 25 cents for admission to a bank of five machines.

The syndicate of Maguire and Baucus acquired the foreign rights to the Kinetoscope in 1894 and began to market the machines. Edison had declined to file for international patents on either his camera or viewing device, and as a result, the machines were widely and legally copied throughout Europe, where they were modified and improved far beyond the American originals. In fact, it was a Kinetoscope exhibition in Paris that inspired the Lumière brothers, Auguste and Louis, to invent the first commercially viable projector. Their *cinématographe,* which also functioned as a camera and printer, ran at the economical speed of 16 frames per second. It was given its first commercial demonstration on Dec. 28, 1895.

Unlike the Kinetograph, which was battery-driven and weighed more than 1,000 pounds, the *cinématographe* was hand-cranked, lightweight (less than 20 pounds), and relatively portable. This naturally affected the kinds of films that were made with each machine: Edison films initially featured material such as circus or vaudeville acts that could be brought into a small studio and played out before an inert camera, while early Lumière films were mainly documentary views, or "actualities," shot outdoors on location. In both cases, however, the films themselves were composed of a single, unedited shot emphasizing lifelike movement; they contained little or no narrative content. (After a few years design changes in the machines made it possible for Edison and the Lumières to shoot the same

The *cinématographe*

By courtesy of the British Film Institute, London

An early series of photographs by Eadweard Muybridge (1887).

kinds of subjects.) In general, Lumière technology became the European standard during the early primitive era, and because the Lumières sent their cameramen all over the world in search of exotic subjects, the *cinématographe* became the founding instrument of such far-flung cinemas as the Russian, the Australian, and the Japanese. (It also, of course, is the source for the word cinema.)

In the United States, the Kinetoscope installation business had reached saturation point by the summer of 1895, although it was still quite profitable for Edison as a supplier of films. Raff and Gammon persuaded Edison to buy the rights to a state-of-the-art projector, developed by Thomas Armat of Washington, D.C., which incorporated a superior intermittent movement mechanism and a loop-forming device (known as the Latham loop, after its earliest promoters, Grey and Otway Latham) to reduce film breakage, and in early 1896 Edison began to manufacture and market this machine as his own invention. Given its first public demonstration on April 23, 1896, at Koster and Bial's Music Hall in New York City, the Edison Vitascope brought projection to the United States and established the format for American film exhibition for the next several years. It also encouraged the activities of such successful Edison rivals as the American Mutoscope and Biograph Company, which was formed in 1896 to exploit the Mutoscope peep-show device and the American Biograph camera and projector patented by W.K.L. Dickson in 1896. During this time, which has been characterized as the "novelty period," emphasis fell on the projection device itself, and films achieved their main popularity as self-contained vaudeville attractions. Vaudeville houses, among which there was intense competition at the turn of the century, headlined the name of the machines rather than the films (The Vitascope—Edison's Latest Marvel, The Amazing Cinématographe). The projectors came supplied from the producer, or manufacturer, with an operator and a program of shorts. These films, whether they were Edison-style theatrical variety shorts or Lumière-style actualities, were perceived by their original audiences not as motion pictures in the modern sense of the term but as "animated photographs" or "living pictures," emphasizing their continuity with more familiar media of the time.

The novelty period

During the novelty period, the film industry was autonomous and unitary, with production companies leasing a complete film service of projector, operator, and shorts to the vaudeville market as a single, self-contained act. Starting around 1897, however, manufacturers began to sell both projectors and films to itinerant exhibitors who traveled with their programs from one temporary location (vaudeville theatres, fairgrounds, circus tents, lyceums) to another as the novelty of their films wore off at a given site. This new mode of screening by circuit marked the first separation of exhibition from production and gave the exhibitors a large measure of control over early film form, since they were responsible for arranging the one-shot films purchased from the producers into audience-pleasing programs. The putting together of these programs—which often involved narration, sound effects, and music—was in effect a primitive form of editing, so that it is possible to regard the itinerant projectionists working between 1896 and 1904 as the earliest directors of motion pictures. Several of them, notably Edwin S. Porter, were, in fact, hired as directors by production companies after the industry had stabilized in the first decade of the 20th century.

By encouraging the practice of peripatetic exhibition, the U.S. producers' policy of outright sales inhibited the development of permanent film theatres in the United States until nearly a decade after their appearance in Europe, where England and France had taken an early lead in both production and exhibition. Britain's first projector, the theatrograph (later, the animatograph), had been demonstrated in 1896 by the scientific instrument maker Robert W. Paul. In 1899 Paul formed his own production company for the manufacture of actualities and trick films, and until 1905 Paul's Animatograph Works, Ltd., was England's largest producer, turning out an average of 50 films per year. Between 1896 and 1898, two Brighton photographers, George Albert Smith and James Williamson, constructed their own motion-picture cameras and began producing trick films featuring superimpositions (*The Corsican Brothers,* 1897) and interpolated close-ups (*Grandma's Reading Glass,* 1900; *The Big Swallow,* 1901). Smith subsequently developed the first commercially successful photographic colour process (Kinemacolor, *c.* 1906–08, with Charles Urban), while Williamson experimented with parallel editing as early as 1900 (*Attack on a Chinese Mission Station*) and became a pioneer of the chase film (*Stop Thief!,* 1901; *Fire!,* 1901). Both Smith and Williamson had built studios at Brighton by 1902 and, with their associates, came to be known as members of the "Brighton school," although they did not represent a coherent movement. Another important early British filmmaker was Cecil Hepworth, whose *Rescued by Rover* (1905) is regarded by many historians as the most skillfully edited narrative produced before the Biograph shorts of D.W. Griffith.

Méliès and Porter. The shift in consciousness away from films as animated photographs to films as stories, or narratives, began to take place around the turn of the century and is most evident in the work of the French filmmaker Georges Méliès. Méliès was a professional magician who had become interested in the illusionist possibilities of the *cinématographe;* when the Lumières refused to sell him one, he bought an animatograph projector from Paul in 1896 and reversed its mechanical principles to design his own camera. The following year he organized the Star Film company and constructed a small glass-enclosed studio on the grounds of his house at Montreuil, where he produced, directed, photographed, and acted in more than 500 films between 1896 and 1913.

Méliès' "trick" films

Initially, Méliès used stop-motion photography (the camera and action are stopped while something is added to or removed from the scene, then filming and action are continued) to make one-shot "trick" films in which objects disappeared and reappeared, or transformed themselves into other objects entirely. These films were widely imitated by producers in England and the United States. Soon, however, Méliès began to experiment with brief multi-scene films, such as *L'Affaire Dreyfus* (*The Dreyfus Affair;* his first, 1899), which followed the logic of linear temporality to establish causal sequences and tell simple stories. By 1902 he had produced the influential 30-scene narrative *Le Voyage dans la lune (A Trip to the Moon).* Adapted from a novel by Jules Verne, it was nearly one reel in length (about 825 feet, or 14 minutes).

By courtesy of the Museum of Modern Art/Film Stills Archive, New York City

Le Voyage dans la lune (1902), directed by Georges Méliès.

The first film to achieve international distribution (mainly through piracy), *Le Voyage dans la lune* was an enormous popular success. It helped to make Star Film one of the world's largest producers (an American branch was opened in 1903) and to establish the fiction film as the cinema's mainstream product. In both respects Méliès dethroned the Lumières' cinema of actuality. Despite his innovations, Méliès' productions remained essentially filmed stage plays. He conceived them quite literally as successions of living pictures or, as he termed them, "artificially arranged scenes." From his earliest trick films through his last successful fantasy, *La Conquête du pole* ("The Conquest of the Pole," 1912), Méliès treated the frame of the film as the proscenium arch of a theatre stage, never once moving his camera or changing its position within a scene. He ultimately lost his audience in the late 1910s to filmmakers with more sophisticated narrative techniques.

The origination of many such techniques is closely associated with the work of Edwin S. Porter, a free-lance projectionist and engineer who joined the Edison Company in 1900 as production head of its new skylight studio on East 21st Street in New York City. For the next few years, he served as director-cameraman for much of Edison's output, starting with simple one-shot films (*Kansas Saloon Smashers,* 1901) but progressing rapidly to trick films (*The Finish of Bridget McKeen,* 1901) and short multi-scene narratives based on political cartoons and contemporary events (*Sampson-Schley Controversy,* 1901; *Execution of Czolgosz, with Panorama of Auburn Prison,* 1901). Porter also filmed the extraordinary *Pan-American Exposition by Night* (1901), which used time-lapse photography to produce a circular panorama of the exposition's electrical illumination, and the 10-scene *Jack and the Beanstalk* (1902), a narrative that simulates the sequencing of lantern slides to achieve a logical, if elliptical, spatial continuity.

Continuity editing

It was probably Porter's experience as a projectionist at the Eden Musee theatre in 1898 that ultimately led him in the early 1900s to the practice of continuity editing. The process of selecting one-shot films and arranging them into a 15-minute program for screen presentation was very much like that of constructing a single film out of a series of separate shots. Porter, by his own admission, was also influenced by other filmmakers—especially Méliès, whose *Le Voyage dans la lune* he came to know well in the process of duplicating it for illegal distribution by Edison in October 1902. Years later, Porter claimed that the Méliès film had given him the notion of "telling a story in continuity form," which resulted in *The Life of an American Fireman* (about 400 feet, or six minutes, produced in late 1902 and released in January 1903). This film, which was also influenced by James Williamson's *Fire!,* combined archival footage with staged scenes to create a nine-shot narrative of a dramatic rescue from a burning building. It was for years the subject of controversy because in a later version the last two scenes were intercut, or crosscut, into a 14-shot parallel sequence. It is now generally believed that in the earliest version of the film these scenes, which repeat the same rescue operation from an interior and exterior point of view, were shown in their entirety, one after the other. This repetition, or overlapping continuity, which owes much to magic lantern shows, clearly defines the spatial relationships between scenes but leaves temporal relationships underdeveloped and, to modern sensibilities, confused. Contemporary audiences, however, were conditioned by lantern slide projections and even comic strips; they understood a sequence of motion-picture shots to be a series of individual moving photographs, each of which was self-contained within its frame. Spatial relationships were clear in such earlier narrative forms because their only medium was space.

Motion pictures, however, exist in time as well as space, and the major problem for early filmmakers was the establishment of temporal continuity from one shot to the next. Porter's *The Great Train Robbery* (1903) is widely acknowledged to be the first narrative film to achieve such continuity of action. Comprised of 14 separate shots of noncontinuous, nonoverlapping action, the film contains an early example of parallel editing, two credible back, or rear, projections (the projection from the rear of previously filmed action or scenery onto a translucent screen to provide the background for new action filmed in front of the screen), two camera pans, and several shots composed diagonally and staged in depth—a major departure from the frontally composed, theatrical staging of Méliès.

The Great Train Robbery

The industry's first spectacular box-office success, *The Great Train Robbery* is credited with establishing the realistic narrative, as opposed to Méliès-style fantasy, as the commercial cinema's dominant form. The film's popularity encouraged investors and led to the establishment of the first permanent film theatres, or nickelodeons, across the country. Running about 12 minutes, it also helped to

The Great Train Robbery (1903), directed by Edwin S. Porter.
By courtesy of the Museum of Modern Art/Film Stills Archive, New York City

boost standard film length toward one reel, or 1,000 feet (about 16 minutes at the average silent speed). Despite the film's success, Porter continued to practice overlapping action in such conventional narratives as *Uncle Tom's Cabin* (1903) and the social-justice dramas *The Ex-Convict* (1904) and *The Kleptomaniac* (1905). He experimented with model animation in *Dream of a Rarebit Fiend* (1906) and *The Teddy Bears* (1907) but lost interest in the creative aspects of filmmaking as the process became increasingly industrialized. He left Edison in 1909 to pursue a career as a producer and equipment manufacturer. Porter, like Méliès, could not adapt to the linear narrative modes and assembly-line production systems that were developing.

Industrialization of European cinema

Early growth of the film industry. Méliès' decline was assisted by the industrialization of the French and, for a time, the entire European cinema by the Pathé Frères company, founded in 1896 by the former phonograph importer Charles Pathé. Financed by some of France's largest corporations, Pathé acquired the Lumière patents in 1902 and commissioned the design of an improved studio camera that soon dominated the market on both sides of the Atlantic (it has been estimated that, before 1918, 60 percent of all films were shot with a Pathé). Pathé also manufactured his own film stock and in 1902 established a vast production facility at Vincennes where films were turned out on an assembly-line basis under the managing direction of Ferdinand Zecca. The following year, Pathé began to open foreign sales agencies, which would soon become full-blown production companies—Hispano Film (1906), Pathé-Rouss, Moscow (1907), Film d'Arte Italiano (1909), Pathé-Britannia, London (1909), and Pathé-America (1910). He acquired permanent exhibition sites, building the world's first luxury cinema (the Omnia-Pathé) in Paris in 1906. In 1911 Pathé became Méliès' distributor and helped to drive Star Film out of business.

Pathé's only serious rival on the Continent at this time was Gaumont Pictures, founded by the engineer-inventor Léon Gaumont in 1895. Though never more than a quarter the size of Pathé, Gaumont followed the same pattern of expansion, manufacturing its own equipment and mass-producing films under a supervising director (through 1906, Alice Guy, the cinema's first woman director; afterward, Louis Feuillade). Like Pathé, Gaumont opened foreign offices and acquired theatre chains. From 1905 to 1914 its studios at La Villette, Fr., were the largest in the world. Pathé and Gaumont dominated pre-World War I motion-picture production, exhibition, and sales in Europe, and they effectively brought to an end the artisanal mode of filmmaking practiced by Méliès and his British contemporaries.

The formation of film exchanges

In the United States a similar pattern was emerging through the formation of film exchanges and the consolidation of an industry-wide monopoly based on the pooling of patent rights. Around 1897 producers had adopted the practice of selling prints outright, which had the effect of promoting itinerant exhibition and discriminating against the owners of permanent sites. In 1903, in response to the needs of theatre owners, Harry J. and Herbert Miles opened a film exchange in San Francisco. The exchange functioned as a broker between producers and exhibitors, buying prints from the former and leasing them to the latter for 25 percent of the purchase price (in subsequent practice, rental fees were calculated on individual production costs and box-office receipts). The exchange system of distribution quickly caught on because it profited nearly everyone: the new middlemen made fortunes by collecting multiple revenues on the same prints; exhibitors were able to reduce their overheads and vary their programs without financial risk; and, ultimately, producers experienced a tremendous surge in demand for their product as exhibition and distribution boomed nationwide. (Between November 1906 and March 1907, for example, producers increased their weekly output from 10,000 to 28,000 feet and still could not meet demand.)

The most immediate effect of the rapid rise of the distribution sector was the nickelodeon boom, the exponential growth of permanent film theatres in the United States from a mere handful in 1904 to between 8,000 and 10,000 by 1908. Named for the Nickelodeon (ersatz Greek for "nickel theatre"), which opened in Pittsburgh in 1905, these theatres were makeshift facilities lodged in converted storefronts. They showed approximately an hour's worth of films for an admission price of five to 10 cents. Originally identified with working-class audiences, nickelodeons appealed increasingly to the middle class as the decade wore on, and they became associated with the rising popularity of the story film. Their spread also forced the standardization of film length at one reel, or 1,000 feet, to facilitate high-efficiency production and the trading of products within the industry.

By 1908 there were about 20 motion-picture production companies operating in the United States. They were constantly at war with one another over business practices and patent rights, and they had begun to fear that their fragmentation would cause them to lose control of the industry to the two new sectors of distribution and exhibition. The most powerful among them—Edison, Biograph, Vitagraph, Essanay, Kalem, Selig Polyscope, Lubin, the American branches of the French Star Film and Pathé Frères, and Kleine Optical, the largest domestic distributor of foreign films—therefore entered into a collusive trade agreement to ensure their continued dominance. On Sept. 9, 1908, these companies formed the Motion Picture Patents Company (MPPC), pooling the 16 most significant U.S. patents for motion-picture technology and entering into an exclusive contract with the Eastman Kodak Company for the supply of raw film stock.

The Motion Picture Patents Company

The MPPC, also known as the "Trust," sought to control every segment of the industry and therefore set up a system to issue licenses and assess royalties therefrom. The use of its patents was granted only to licensed equipment manufacturers; film stock could be sold only to licensed producers; licensed producers and importers were required to fix rental prices at a minimum level and to set quotas for foreign footage to reduce competition; Patents Company films could be sold only to licensed distributors, who could lease them only to licensed exhibitors; and only licensed exhibitors had the right to use Patents Company projectors and rent company films. To further ensure their control, in 1910—the same year in which motion-picture attendance in the United States rose to 26,000,000 persons a week—the MPPC formed the General Film Company, which integrated the licensed distributors into a single corporate entity. Although it was clearly monopolistic in practice and intent, the MPPC helped to stabilize the American film industry during a period of unprecedented growth and change by standardizing exhibition practice, increasing the efficiency of distribution, and regularizing pricing in all three sectors. Its collusive nature, however, provoked a reaction that ultimately destroyed it.

In a sense, the MPPC's iron-clad efforts to eliminate competition merely fostered it. Almost from the outset there was widespread resistance to the Patents Company on the part of independent distributors (numbering 10 or more in early 1909) and exhibitors (estimated at 2,000 to 2,500); and in January 1909 they formed their own trade association, the Independent Film Protective Association—reorganized that fall as the National Independent Moving Picture Alliance—to provide financial and legal support against the Trust. A more effective and powerful anti-Trust organization was the Motion Picture Distributing and Sales Company, which began operation in May 1910 (three weeks after the inception of General Film) and which eventually came to serve 47 exchanges in 27 cities. For nearly two years, independents were able to present a united front through the Sales Company, which finally split into two rival camps in the spring of 1912 (the Mutual Film Corporation and the Universal Film Manufacturing Company).

By imitating Patents Company practices of joining forces and licensing, the early independents were able to compete effectively against the Trust in its first three years of operation, netting about 40 percent of all American film business. In fact, their product, the one-reel short, and their mode of operation were initially fundamentally the same as the MPPC's. The independents later revolutionized the industry, however, by adopting the multiple-reel film as their basic product, a move that caused the MPPC to embrace the one-reeler with a vengeance, hastening its own demise.

THE SILENT FEATURE: 1910–27

Introduction of the feature film

Pre-World War I U.S. cinema. Multiple-reel films had appeared in the United States as early as 1907, when Adolph Zukor distributed Pathé's three-reel *Passion Play;* but when Vitagraph produced the five-reel *The Life of Moses* in 1909, the Patents Company forced it to be released in serial fashion at the rate of one reel a week. The multiple-reel film—which came to be called a "feature," in the vaudevillian sense of a headline attraction—achieved general acceptance with the smashing success of Louis Mercanton's three-and-one-half-reel *Les Amours de la Reine Elizabeth* (*Queen Elizabeth,* 1912), which starred Sarah Bernhardt and was imported by Adolph Zukor (who founded the independent Famous Players production company with its profits). In 1912 Enrico Guazzoni's nine-reel Italian super-spectacle *Quo Vadis?* was road-shown in legitimate theatres across the nation at a top admission price of one dollar, and the feature craze was on.

At first, there were difficulties in distributing features, because the exchanges associated with both the Patents Company and the independents were geared toward cheaply made one-reel shorts. Owing to their more elaborate production values, features had relatively higher negative costs. This was a disadvantage to distributors, who charged a uniform price per foot. By 1914, however, several national feature-distribution alliances that correlated pricing with a film's negative cost and box-office receipts were organized. These new exchanges demonstrated the economic advantage of multiple-reel films over shorts. Exhibitors quickly learned that features could command higher admission prices and longer runs; single title packages were also cheaper and easier to advertise than programs of multiple titles. As for manufacturing, producers found that the higher expenditure for features was readily amortized by high volume sales to distributors, who in turn were eager to share in the higher admission returns from the theatres. The whole industry soon reorganized itself around the economics of the multiple-reel film, and the effects of this restructuring did much to give motion pictures their characteristic modern form.

Feature films, for example, made motion pictures respectable for the middle class by providing a format that was analogous to that of the legitimate theatre and was suitable for the adaptation of middle-class novels and plays. This new audience had more demanding standards than the older lower-class one, and producers readily increased their budgets to provide high technical quality and elaborate productions. The new viewers also had a more refined sense of comfort, which exhibitors quickly accommodated by replacing their storefronts with large, elegantly appointed new theatres in the major urban centres (one of the first was Mitchell L. Marks's 3,300-seat Strand, which opened in the Broadway district of Manhattan in 1914). Known as "dream palaces" because of the fantastic luxuriance of their interiors, these houses had to show features rather than a program of shorts to attract large audiences at premium prices. By 1916 there were more than 21,000 movie palaces in the United States. Their advent marked the end of the nickelodeon era and foretold the rise of the Hollywood studio system, which dominated urban exhibition from the 1920s to the 1950s. Before the new studio-based monopoly could be established, however, the patents-based monopoly of the MPPC had to expire, and this it did as a result of its own basic assumptions in about 1914.

End of the nickelodeon era

As conceived by Edison, the basic operating principle of the Trust was to control the industry through patents pooling and licensing, an idea logical enough in theory but difficult to practice in the context of a dynamically changing marketplace. Specifically, the Trust's failure to anticipate the independents' widespread and aggressive resistance to its policies cost it a fortune in patent-infringement litigation. Furthermore, the Trust badly underestimated the importance of the feature film, permitting the independents to claim this popular new product as entirely their own. Another issue that the MPPC misjudged was the power of the marketing strategy known as the "star system." Borrowed from the theatre industry, this system involves the creation and management of publicity about key performers, or stars, to stimulate demand for their films. Trust company producers used this kind of publicity after 1910, when Carl Laemmle of Independent Motion Pictures (IMP) promoted Florence Lawrence into national stardom through a series of media stunts in St. Louis, Mo., but they never exploited the technique as forcefully or as imaginatively as the independents. Finally, and most decisively, in August 1912 the U.S. Justice Department brought suit against the MPPC for "restraint of trade" in violation of the Sherman Antitrust Act. Delayed by countersuits and by World War I, the government's case was finally won and the MPPC formally dissolved in 1918, although it had been functionally inoperative since 1914.

The rise and fall of the Patents Company was concurrent with the industry's move to southern California. As a result of the nickelodeon boom, exhibitors had begun to require as many as 20 to 30 new films per week, and it became necessary to put production on a systematic year-round schedule. Because most films were still shot outdoors in available light, such schedules could not be maintained in the vicinity of New York City or Chicago, where the industry had originally located itself in order to take advantage of trained theatrical labour pools. As early as 1907, production companies, such as Selig Polyscope, began to dispatch production units to warmer climates during winter. It was soon clear that what producers required was a new industrial centre—one with warm weather, a temperate climate, a variety of scenery, and other qualities (such as access to acting talent) essential to their highly unconventional form of manufacturing.

Various companies experimented with location shooting in Jacksonville, Fla., in San Antonio, Texas, in Santa Fe, N.M., and even in Cuba, but the ultimate site of the American film industry was a Los Angeles suburb (originally a small industrial town) called Hollywood. It is generally thought that Hollywood's distance from the MPPC's headquarters in New York City made it attractive to the independents, but Patents Company members such as Selig, Kalem, Biograph, and Essanay had also established facilities there by 1911 in response to a number of the region's attractions. These included the temperate climate required for year-round production (the U.S. Weather Bureau estimated that an average of 320 days per year were sunny and/or clear); a wide range of topography within a 50-mile radius of Hollywood, including mountains, valleys, forests, lakes, islands, seacoast, and desert; the status of Los Angeles as a professional theatrical centre; the existence of a low tax base; and the presence of cheap and plentiful labour and land. This latter factor enabled the newly arrived production companies to buy up tens of thousands of acres of prime real estate on which to locate their studios, standing sets, and backlots.

Hollywood

By 1915 approximately 15,000 workers were employed by the motion-picture industry in Hollywood, and more than 60 percent of American production was centred there. In that same year, the trade journal *Variety* reported that capital investment in American motion pictures—the business of artisanal craftsmen and fairground operators only a decade before—had exceeded $500,000,000. The most powerful companies in the new film capital were the independents, who were flush with cash from their conversion to feature production. These included the Famous Players-Lasky Corporation (later Paramount Pictures, *c.* 1927), which was formed by a merger of Adolph Zukor's Famous Players Company, Jesse L. Lasky's Feature Play Company, and the Paramount distribution exchange in 1916; Universal Pictures, founded by Carl Laemmle in 1912 by merging IMP with Powers, Rex, Nestor, Champion, and Bison; Goldwyn Picture Corporation, founded in 1916 by Samuel Goldfish (later Goldwyn) and Edgar Selwyn; Metro Picture Corporation and Louis B. Mayer Pictures, founded by Louis B. Mayer in 1915 and 1917, respectively; and the Fox Film Corporation (later 20th Century-Fox, 1935), founded by William Fox in 1915. After World War I, these companies were joined by Loew's, Inc. (parent corporation of MGM, by merger of Metro, Goldwyn, and Mayer companies cited above, 1924), a national exhibition chain organized by Marcus Loew and Nicholas Schenck in 1919; First National Pictures, Inc., a circuit of independent exhibitors who established their own production facilities at Burbank, Calif., in 1922; Warner Bros. Pictures, Inc., founded by Harry, Albert, Samuel, and Jack Warner in 1923; and Columbia Pictures, Inc., incorporated in 1924 by Harry and Jack Cohn.

These organizations became the backbone of the Hollywood studio system, and the men who controlled them shared several important traits. They were all independent exhibitors and distributors who had outwitted the Trust and earned their success by manipulating finances in the post-nickelodeon feature boom, merging production companies, organizing national distribution networks, and ultimately acquiring vast theatre chains. They saw their business as basically a retailing operation modeled on the practice of chain stores such as Woolworth's and Sears. Not incidentally, these men were all first- or second-generation Jewish immigrants from eastern Europe, most of them with little formal education, while the audience they served was 90 percent Protestant and Catholic. This circumstance would become an issue during the 1920s, when the movies became a mass medium that was part of the life of every American citizen and when Hollywood became the chief purveyor of American culture to the world.

Pre-World War I European cinema. Before World War I European cinema was dominated by France and Italy. At Pathé Frères, director-general Ferdinand Zecca perfected the *course comique,* a uniquely Gallic version of the chase film, which inspired Mack Sennett's Keystone Kops, while the immensely popular Max Linder created a comic persona that would deeply influence the work of Charlie Chaplin. The episodic crime film was pioneered by Victorin Jasset in the "Nick Carter" series, produced for the small Éclair Company, but it remained for Gaumont's Louis Feuillade to bring the genre to aesthetic perfection in the extremely successful serials *Fantômas* (1913–14), *Les Vampires* (1915–16), and *Judex* (1916).

Another influential phenomenon to appear from prewar France was the *film d'art* movement. It began with *L'Assassinat du duc de Guise* (1908), directed by Charles Le Bargy and André Calmettes of the Comédie Française for the Société Film d'Art, which was formed for the express purpose of transferring prestigious stage plays starring famous performers to the screen. *L'Assassinat*'s success inspired other companies to make similar films, which came to be known as *films d'art.* These films were long on intellectual pedigree and short on narrative sophistication. The directors simply filmed theatrical productions in toto, without adaptation. Their brief popularity nevertheless created a context for the lengthy treatment of serious material in motion pictures and was directly instrumental in the rise of the feature.

French *film d'art* movement

No country, however, was more responsible for the popularity of the feature than Italy. The Italian cinema's lavishly produced costume spectacles brought it international prominence in the years before the war. The prototypes of

Italian super-spectacles

the genre, by virtue of their epic material and lengths, were the Cines company's six-reel *Gli ultimi giorni di Pompei* (*The Last Days of Pompei*), directed by Luigi Maggi in 1908, and its 10-reel remake, directed by Ernesto Pasquali in 1913; but it was Cines' nine-reel *Quo vadis?* (1912), with its huge three-dimensional sets of ancient Rome and 5,000 extras, that established the standard for the superspectacle and briefly conquered the world market for Italian motion pictures. Its successor, the Italia company's 12-reel *Cabiria* (1914), was even more extravagant in its historical reconstruction of the Second Punic War, from the burning of the Roman fleet at Syracuse to Hannibal crossing the Alps and the sack of Carthage. The Italian superspectacle stimulated public demand for features and influenced such important directors as Cecil B. deMille, Ernst Lubitsch, and especially D.W. Griffith.

Griffith. There has been a tendency in modern film scholarship to view motion-picture narrative form as being governed by the operations of an overall production system. Although narrative film was and continues to be strongly influenced by a combination of economic, technological, and social factors, it also owes a great deal to the individual artists who viewed film as a medium of personal expression. Chief among these innovators was D.W. (David Wark) Griffith. It is true that Griffith's self-cultivated reputation as a Romantic artist—"the father of film technique," "the man who invented Hollywood," "the Shakespeare of the screen," and the like—is somewhat overblown. It is also true that by 1908 film narrative had already been systematically organized to accommodate the material conditions of production. Griffith's work nevertheless transformed that system from its primitive to its classical mode. He was the first filmmaker to realize that the motion-picture medium, properly vested with technical vitality and seriousness of theme, could exercise enormous persuasive power over an audience, or even a nation, without recourse to print or human speech.

Griffith began his film career in late 1907 as an actor. He was cast as the lead in the Edison Company's *Rescued from an Eagle's Nest* (1907) and also appeared in many Biograph films. He had already attempted to make a living as a stage actor and a playwright without much success, and his real goal in approaching the film companies seems to have been to sell them scripts. In June 1908 Biograph gave him an opportunity to replace its ailing director, George "Old Man" McCutcheon, on the chase film *The Adventures of Dollie.* With the advice of the company's two cameramen, G.W. "Billy" Bitzer (who would become Griffith's personal cinematographer for much of his career) and Arthur Marvin (who actually shot the film), Griffith turned in a fresh and exciting film. His work earned him a full-time director's contract at Biograph, where, over the next five years, he directed more than 450 one- and two-reel films.

In the Biograph films, Griffith experimented with all of the narrative techniques he would later use in the epics *The Birth of a Nation* (1915) and *Intolerance* (1916)—techniques that helped to formulate and stabilize Hollywood's classical narrative style. A few of these techniques were already in use when Griffith started; he simply refined them. Others were innovations Griffith devised to solve practical problems in the course of production. Still others resulted from his conscious analogy between film and literary narrative, chiefly Victorian novels and plays. In all cases, however, Griffith brought to the practice of filmmaking a seriousness of purpose and an intensity of vision, which, combined with his intuitive mastery of film technique, made him the first great artist of the cinema.

Griffith's innovations in editing

Griffith's first experiments were in the field of editing and involved varying the standard distance between the audience and the screen. In *Greaser's Gauntlet,* made one month after *Dollie,* he first used a "cut-in" from a long shot to a full shot to heighten the emotional intensity of a scene. In an elaboration of this practice, he was soon taking shots from multiple camera set-ups—long shots, full shots, medium shots, close shots, and, ultimately, close-ups—and combining their separate perspectives into single dramatic scenes. By October 1908, Griffith was practicing parallel editing between the dual narratives of *After Many Years,* and the following year he extended the technique to the representation of three simultaneous actions in *Lonely Villa,* cutting rapidly back and forth from a band of robbers breaking into a suburban villa, to a woman and her children barricaded within, to the husband rushing from town to the rescue. This type of crosscutting or intercutting came to be known as the "Griffith last-minute rescue" and was employed as a basic structural principle in both *The Birth of a Nation* and *Intolerance.* It not only employed the rapid alternation of shots but also called for the shots themselves to be held for shorter and shorter durations as the parallel lines of action converged; in its ability to create the illusion of simultaneous actions, the intercut chase sequence prefigured Soviet theories of montage by at least a decade, and it remains a basic component of narrative film form to this day.

Griffith's use of camera movement and placement

Another area of experiment for Griffith involved camera movement and placement, most of which had been purely functional before him. When Biograph started sending his production unit to southern California in 1910, Griffith began to practice panoramic panning shots not only to provide visual information but also to engage his audience in the total environment of his films. Later, he would prominently employ the tracking, or traveling, shot, in which the camera—and therefore the audience—participates in the dramatic action by moving with it. In California, Griffith discovered that camera angle could be used to comment upon the content of a shot or to heighten its dramatic emphasis in a way that the conventionally mandated head-on medium shot could not; and, at a time when convention dictated the flat and uniform illumination of every element in a scene, he pioneered the use of expressive lighting to create mood and atmosphere. Like so many of the other devices he brought into general use, these had all been employed by earlier directors, but Griffith was the first to practice them with the care of an artist and to rationalize them within the overall structure of his films.

Griffith's one-reelers grew increasingly complex between 1911 and 1912, and he began to realize that only a longer and more expansive format could contain his vision. At first he made such two-reel films as *Enoch Arden* (1911), *Man's Genesis* (1912), *The Massacre* (1912), and *The Mothering Heart* (1913), but these went virtually unnoticed by a public enthralled with such recent features from Europe as *Queen Elizabeth* and *Quo Vadis?*. Finally, Griffith determined to make an epic himself, based on the story of Judith and Holofernes from the Apocrypha. The result was the four-reel *Judith of Bethulia* (1913), filmed secretly on a 12-square-mile set in Chatsworth Park, Calif. In addition to its structurally complicated narrative, *Judith* contained massive sets and battle scenes unlike anything yet attempted in American film. It cost twice the amount Biograph had allocated for its budget. Company officials, stunned at Griffith's audacity and extravagance, tried to relieve the director of his creative responsibilities by promoting him to studio production chief. Griffith quit instead, publishing a full-page advertisement in *The New York Dramatic Mirror* (Dec. 3, 1913), in which he took credit for all of the Biograph films he had made from *The Adventures of Dollie* through *Judith,* as well as for the narrative innovations they contained. He then accepted an offer from Harry E. Aitken, the president of the recently formed Mutual Film Corporation, to head the feature production company Reliance-Majestic; he took Bitzer and most of his Biograph stock company with him.

Griffith's departure from Biograph

As part of his new contract, Griffith was allowed to make two independent features per year, and for his first project he chose to adapt *The Clansman,* a novel about the Civil War and Reconstruction by the Southern clergyman Thomas Dixon, Jr. (As a Kentuckian whose father had served as a Confederate officer, Griffith was deeply sympathetic to the material, which was highly sensational in its depiction of Reconstruction as a period in which mulatto carpetbaggers and their black henchmen had destroyed the social fabric of the South and given birth to a heroic Ku Klux Klan.) Shooting on the film began in secrecy in late 1914. Although a script existed, Griffith kept most of the continuity in his head—a remarkable feat considering that the completed film contained 1,544 separate shots at a time when the most elaborate of foreign spectacles boasted fewer than 100. When the film opened in March 1915, retitled *The Birth of a Nation,* it was immediately pronounced "epoch-making" and recognized as a remarkable artistic achievement. The complexity of its narrative and the epic sweep of its subject were unprecedented, but so too were its controversial manipulations of audience response, especially its blatant appeals to racism. Despite its brilliantly conceived battle sequences, its tender domestic scenes, and its dignified historical reconstructions, the film also contained shocking images of miscegenation and racial violence that provoked fear and disgust. As the film's popularity swept the nation, denunciations followed, and many who had originally praised it, such as President Woodrow Wilson, were forced to recant. Ultimately, after screenings of *The Birth of a Nation* had caused riots in several cities, it was banned in eight northern and midwestern states. (First Amendment protection was not extended to motion pictures in the United States until the late 1950s.) Such measures, however, did not prevent *The Birth of a Nation* from becoming the single most popular film in history to date; it achieved national distribution in the year of its release and was seen by nearly 3,000,000 people.

The Birth of a Nation

Although it is difficult to believe that the film's racism was unconscious, as some have claimed, it is easy to imagine that Griffith had not anticipated the power of his own images. He seems to have been genuinely stunned by the hostile public reaction to his masterpiece, and he fought back by publishing a pamphlet entitled *The Rise and Fall of Free Speech in America* (1915), which vilified the practice of censorship and especially intolerance. At the height of his notoriety and fame, Griffith decided to produce a spectacular cinematic polemic against this flaw in human character as it had endangered civilization throughout history. The result was the massive epic *Intolerance* (1916), which interweaves stories of martyrdom from four separate historical periods. The film was conceived on a scale so monumental as to dwarf all predecessors. Crosscutting freely between a contemporary tale of courtroom injustice, the fall of ancient Babylon to Cyrus the Great in 539 BC, the St. Bartholomew's Day Massacre in 16th-century France, and the Crucifixion of Christ, Griffith created an editing structure so abstract that contemporary audiences could not understand it. Even the extravagant sets and exciting battle sequences could not save *Intolerance* at the box-office. To reduce his losses, Griffith withdrew the film from distribution after 22 weeks; he subsequently cut into the negative and released the modern and the Babylonian stories as two separate features, *The Mother and the Law* and *The Fall of Babylon,* in 1919. (Although ignored by Americans, *Intolerance* was both popular and vastly influential in the Soviet Union, where filmmakers minutely analyzed Griffith's editing style and techniques.)

Intolerance

It would be fair to say that Griffith's career as an innovator of film form ended with *Intolerance,* but his career as a film artist certainly did not. He went on to direct another 26 features between 1916 and 1931, chief among them the World War I anti-German propaganda epic (financed, in part, by the British government) *Hearts of the World* (1918), the subtle and lyrical *Broken Blossoms* (1919), and the rousing melodrama *Way Down East* (1920). The financial success of the latter made it possible for Griffith to establish his own studio at Mamaroneck, N.Y., where he produced the epics *Orphans of the Storm* (1921) and *America* (1924), which focused on the French and American revolutions, respectively; both lost money. Griffith's next feature was the independent semidocumentary *Isn't Life Wonderful?* (1925), which was shot on location in Germany and is thought to have influenced both the "street" films of the German director G.W. Pabst and the post-World War II Italian Neorealist movement.

Griffith's last films, with the exception of *The Struggle* (1931), were all made for other producers. Not one could be called a success, although his first sound film, *Abraham Lincoln* (1930), was recognized as an effective essay in the new medium. The critical and financial failure of *The Struggle,* however, a version of Zola's *L'Assommoir* (*The Drunkard*), forced Griffith to retire.

It might be said of Griffith that, like Méliès and Porter, he outlived his genius, but that is not true. Griffith was fundamentally a 19th-century man who became one of the 20th-century's greatest artists. Transcending personal defects of vision, judgment, and taste, he developed the narrative language of film. He lost touch with his contemporaries because his subjects came to seem old-fashioned, but he remains peculiarly, uniquely in touch with the present because the techniques and structure he contributed to the motion-picture medium are still in use.

Post-World War I European cinema. Prior to World War I, the American cinema had lagged behind the film industries of Europe, particularly those of France and Italy, in such matters as feature production and the establishment of permanent theatres. During the war, however, European film production virtually ceased, in part because the same chemicals used in the production of celluloid were necessary for the manufacture of gun powder. The American cinema, meanwhile, experienced a period of unprecedented prosperity and growth. By the end of the war it exercised nearly total control of the international market: when the Treaty of Versailles was signed in 1919, 90 percent of all films screened in Europe, Africa, and Asia were American, and the figure for South America was (and remained through the 1950s) close to 100 percent. The main exception was Germany, which had been cut off from American films from 1914 until the end of the war.

Germany. Before World War I, the German motion-picture audience was largely uneducated and unemployed or from the working class. Most of the films exhibited were imported from other countries, particularly Denmark. The few German films produced were usually cheaply and crudely made. This impoverished state of the domestic industry became a matter of concern among military leaders during the war, when a flood of effective anti-German propaganda films began to pour into Germany from the Allied countries. Therefore, on Dec. 18, 1917, the German general Erich Ludendorff ordered the merger of the main German production, distribution, and exhibition companies into the government-subsidized conglomerate Universum Film Aktiengesellschaft. UFA's mission was to upgrade the quality of German films. The organization proved to be highly effective, and when the war ended in Germany's defeat in November 1918, the German film industry was prepared for the first time to compete in the international marketplace. Transferred to private control, UFA became the single largest studio in Europe and produced most of the films associated with the "golden age" of German cinema during the Weimar Republic (1919–33).

UFA

UFA's first peacetime productions were elaborate costume dramas (*Kostümfilme*) in the vein of the prewar Italian superspectacles, and the master of this form was Ernst Lubitsch, who directed such lavish and successful historical pageants as *Madame Dubarry* (released in the United

By courtesy of the Museum of Modern Art/Film Stills Archive, New York City

The temple of Babylon sequence from *Intolerance* (1916), directed by D.W. Griffith.

States as *Passion,* 1919), *Anna Boleyn* (*Deception,* 1920), and *Das Weib des Pharao* (*The Loves of Pharaoh,* 1921) before emigrating to the United States in 1922. These films earned the German cinema a foothold in the world market, but it was an Expressionist work, *Das Kabinett des Dr. Caligari* (*The Cabinet of Dr. Caligari,* 1919), that brought the industry its first great artistic acclaim. Based on a scenario by the Czech poet Hans Janowitz and the Austrian writer Carl Mayer, the film recounts a series of brutal murders that are committed in the north German town of Holstenwall by a somnambulist at the bidding of a demented mountebank, who believes himself to be the incarnation of a homicidal 18th-century hypnotist named Dr. Caligari. Erich Pommer, *Caligari's* producer at Decla-Bioskop (an independent production company that was to merge with UFA in 1921), added a scene to the original scenario so that the story appears to be narrated by a madman confined to an asylum of which the mountebank is director and head psychiatrist. To represent the narrator's tortured mental state, the director, Robert Wiene, hired three prominent Expressionist artists—Hermann Warm, Walter Röhrig, and Walter Reimann—to design sets that depicted exaggerated dimensions and deformed spatial relationships. To heighten this architectural stylization (and also to economize on electric power, which was rationed in postwar Germany), bizarre patterns of light and shadow were painted directly onto the scenery and even onto the characters' makeup.

German Expressionism

By courtesy of the Museum of Modern Art/Film Stills Archive, New York City

Werner Krauss in *The Cabinet of Dr. Caligari,* directed by Robert Wiene (1919).

In its effort to embody disturbed psychological states through decor, *Caligari* influenced enormously the UFA films that followed it and gave rise to the movement known as German Expressionism. The films of this movement were completely studio-made and often used distorted sets and lighting effects to create a highly subjective mood. They were primarily films of fantasy and terror that employed horrific plots to express the theme of the soul in search of itself. Most were photographed by one of the two great cinematographers of the Weimar period, Karl Freund and Fritz Arno Wagner. Representative works include F.W. Murnau's *Der Januskopf* (*Janus-Faced,* 1920), adapted from Robert Louis Stevenson's *Dr. Jekyll and Mr. Hyde;* Paul Wegener and Carl Boese's *Der Golem* (*The Golem,* 1920), adapted from a Jewish legend in which a gigantic clay statue becomes a raging monster; Arthur Robison's *Schatten* (*Warning Shadows,* 1922); Wiene's *Raskolnikow* (1923), based on Dostoyevsky's *Crime and Punishment;* Paul Leni's *Das Wachsfigurenkabinett* (*Waxworks,* 1924); and Henrik Galeen's *Der Student von Prag* (*The Student of Prague,* 1926), which combines the Faust legend with a doppelgänger, or double, motif. In addition to winning international prestige for German films, Expressionism produced two directors who would become major figures in world cinema, Fritz Lang and F.W. (Friedrich Wilhelm) Murnau.

Lang had already directed several successful serials, including *Die Spinnen* (*The Spiders,* 1919–20), when he collaborated with his future wife, the scriptwriter Thea von Harbou, to produce *Der müde Tod* ("The Weary Death"; English title: *Destiny,* 1921) for Decla-Bioscop. This episodic Romantic allegory of doomed lovers, set in several different historical periods, earned Lang acclaim for his dynamic compositions of architectural line and space. Lang's use of striking, stylized images is also demonstrated in the other films of his Expressionist period, notably the crime melodrama *Dr. Mabuse, der Spieler* (*Dr. Mabuse, the Gambler,* 1922), the Wagnerian diptych *Siegfried* (1922–24) and *Kriemhilds Rache* (*Kriemhild's Revenge,* 1922–23), and the stunningly futuristic *Metropolis* (1926), perhaps the greatest science-fiction film ever made. After directing the early sound masterpiece *M* (1931), based on child murders in Dusseldorf, Lang became increasingly estranged from German political life. He emigrated in 1933 to escape the Nazis and began a second career in the Hollywood studios the following year.

Murnau made several minor Expressionist films before directing one of the movement's classics, an (unauthorized) adaptation of Bram Stoker's novel *Dracula* entitled *Nosferatu—eine Symphonie des Grauens* ("Nosferatu, a Symphony of Horror," 1922), but it was *Der letzte Mann* ("The Last Man"; English title: *The Last Laugh,* 1924), a film in the genre of *Kammerspiel* ("intimate theatre"), that made him world famous. Scripted by Carl Mayer and produced by Erich Pommer for UFA, *Der letzte Mann* told the story of a hotel doorman who is humiliated by the loss of his job and—more important, apparently, in postwar German society—of his splendid paramilitary uniform. Murnau and Freund, his cameraman, gave this simple tale a complex narrative structure through their innovative use of camera movement and subjective point-of-view shots. In one famous example, Freund strapped a lightweight camera to his chest and stumbled drunkenly around the set of a bedroom to record the inebriated porter's point of view. In the absence of modern cranes and dollies, at various points in the filming Murnau and Freund placed the camera on moving bicycles, fire engine ladders, and overhead cables in order to achieve smooth, sustained movement. The total effect was a tapestry of subjectively involving movement and intense identification with the narrative.

Use of subjective camera movement in *The Last Laugh*

Der letzte Mann was universally hailed as a masterpiece and probably had more influence on Hollywood style than any other single foreign film in history. Its "unchained camera" technique (Mayer's phrase) spawned many imitations in Germany and elsewhere, the most significant being E.A. (Ewald André) Dupont's circus-tent melodrama *Variété* (1925). The film also brought Murnau a long-term Hollywood contract, which he began to fulfill in 1927 after completing two last super-productions, *Tartüff* (1925) and *Faust* (1926), for UFA.

In 1924 the German mark was stabilized by the so-called Dawes Plan, which financed the long-term payment of Germany's war reparations debt and curtailed all exports. This created an artificial prosperity in the economy at large, which lasted only until the stock market crash of 1929, but it was devastating to the film industry, the bulk of whose revenues came from foreign markets. Hollywood then seized the opportunity to cripple its only serious European rival, saturating Germany with American films and buying its independent theatre chains. As a result of these forays and its own internal mismanagement, UFA stood on the brink of bankruptcy by the end of 1925. It was saved by a $4,000,000 loan offered by two major American studios, Famous Players-Lasky (later Paramount) and Metro-Goldwyn-Mayer, in exchange for collaborative rights to UFA studios, theatres, and creative personnel. This arrangement resulted in the founding of the Parufamet (Paramount-UFA-Metro) Distribution Company in early 1926 and the almost immediate emigration of UFA film artists and technicians to Hollywood, where they worked for a variety of studios. This first Germanic migration was temporary. Many of the filmmakers returned to UFA disgusted at the assembly-line character of the American studio system, but many—such as Lubitsch, Freund, Murnau, and Kertész—stayed on to launch full-fledged Hollywood careers, and many more would come back during the 1930s to escape Adolf Hitler.

In the meantime, the new sensibility that had entered German intellectual life turned away from the morbid psychological themes of Expressionism toward an acceptance of "life as it is lived." Called *die neue Sachlichkeit* ("the new objectivity"), this spirit stemmed from the economic dislocations that beset German society in the wake of the war, particularly the impoverishment of the middle classes through raging inflation. In cinema, *die neue Sachlichkeit* translated into the grim social realism of the "street" films of the late 1920s, including G.W. Pabst's *Die freudlose Gasse* (*The Joyless Street,* 1925), Bruno Rhan's *Dirnentragödie* (*Tragedy of the Streets,* 1927), Joe May's *Asphalt* (1929), and Piel Jutzi's *Berlin-Alexanderplatz* (1931). Named for their prototype, Karl Grune's *Die Strasse* (*The Street,* 1923), these films focused on the disillusionment, cynicism, and ultimate resignation of ordinary German people whose lives were crippled during the postwar inflation.

The master of the form was G.W. (Georg Wilhelm) Pabst, whose work established conventions of continuity editing that would become essential to the sound film. In such important realist films as *Die freudlose Gasse, Die Liebe der Jeanne Ney* (*The Love of Jeanne Ney,* 1927), *Die Büchse der Pandora* (*Pandora's Box,* 1929), and *Tagebuch einer Verlorenen* (*Diary of a Lost One,* 1929), Pabst created complex continuity sequences using techniques that became key features of the Hollywood "invisible" editing style, such as cutting on action, cutting from a shot of a character's glance to one of what the character sees (motivated point-of-view shots), and cutting to a reverse angle shot (one in which the camera angle has changed 180 degrees; *e.g.,* in a scene in which a man and a woman face one another in conversation, the man is seen from the woman's point of view, then the woman is shown from the man's point of view). Pabst later became an important figure of the early sound period, contributing in his pacifist films *Westfront 1918* (1930) and *Kameradschaft* ("Comradeship," 1931) two significant works. A few years later, however, Pabst found himself making films for the Nazis, a condition that afflicted the entire German film industry after 1933.

Pabst's editing techniques

By March 1927, UFA was once again facing financial collapse, and it turned this time to the Prussian financier Alfred Hugenberg, a director of both the powerful Krupp industrial empire and the right-wing German National Party, who was sympathetic to the Nazis. Hugenberg bought out the American interests in UFA, acquiring a majority of the company's stock and directing the remainder into the hands of his political allies. As chairman of the UFA board, he quietly instituted a nationalistic production policy that gave increasing prominence to the Nazis and their cause and that enabled the Nazis to subvert the German film industry when Hitler came to power in 1933. German cinema then fell under the authority of Joseph Goebbels and his Ministry of Public Enlightenment and Propaganda. For the next 12 years every film made in the Third Reich had to be personally approved for release by Goebbels. Jews were officially banned from the industry, causing a vast wave of German film artists to emigrate to Hollywood. Los Angeles became known as "the new Weimar," and the German cinema was emptied of the talent and brilliance that had created its golden age.

German cinema under the Third Reich

The Soviet Union. Before the Bolshevik Revolution of October 1917, Russia for all practical purposes had no native film industry. In the industrialized nations of the West, motion pictures had first been accepted as a form of cheap recreation and leisure for the working class. From that base, they had reached out successfully to the middle class and gained wide popularity among all classes by about 1914. In prerevolutionary Russia, however, the working class was composed largely of serfs too poor to support a native industry, and the small movie business that did develop was dominated by foreign interests and foreign films—mainly French, German, and Danish.

The first native Russian company was not founded until 1908, and by the time of the Revolution, there were perhaps 20 more; but even these were small, importing all of their technical equipment and film stock from Germany and France. When Russia entered World War I in August 1914, foreign films could no longer be imported, and the tsarist government established the Skobelev Committee to stimulate domestic production and produce propaganda in support of the regime. The committee had little immediate effect, but when the Tsar fell in March 1917 the provisional Kerensky government reorganized it to produce antitsarist propaganda. When the Bolsheviks inherited the group eight months later, they transformed it into the Cinema Committee of the People's Commissariat of Education.

A minority party with approximately 200,000 members, the Bolsheviks had assumed the leadership of 160,000,000 people who were scattered across the largest continuous landmass in the world, spoke more than 100 separate languages, and were mostly illiterate. Vladimir Ilich Lenin and other Bolshevik leaders looked on the motion-picture medium as a means of unifying the huge, disparate nation. Lenin was the first political leader of the 20th century to recognize both the importance of film as propaganda and its power to communicate quickly and effectively. He understood that audiences did not require literacy to comprehend a film's meaning and that more people could be reached through mass-distributed motion pictures than through any other medium of the time. Lenin declared: "The cinema is for us the most important of the arts," and his government gave top priority to the rapid development of the Soviet film industry, which was nationalized in August 1919 and put under the direct authority of Lenin's wife, Nadezhda Krupskaya.

There was, however, little to build upon. Most of the prerevolutionary producers had fled to Europe, taking their equipment and film stock with them, wrecking their studios as they left. A foreign blockade prevented the importation of new equipment or stock (there were no domestic facilities for manufacturing them), and massive power shortages restricted the use of what limited resources remained. The Cinema Committee was not deterred however; its first act was to found a professional film school in Moscow to train directors, technicians, and actors for the cinema.

The Vsesoyuznyi Gosudarstvenyi Institut Kinematografii (VGIK; "All-Union State Institute of Cinematography") was the first such school in the world and is still among the most respected. Initially, it trained people in the production of *agitki,* existing newsreels reedited for the purpose of agitation and propaganda (agitprop). The *agitki* were transported on specially equipped agit-trains and agit-steamers to the provinces, where they were exhibited to generate support for the Revolution. (The state-controlled Cuban cinema used the same tactic after the revolution of 1959.) In fact, during the abysmal years of the Civil War (1918–20), nearly all Soviet films were *agitki* of some sort. Most of the great directors of the Soviet silent cinema were trained in that form, although, having very little technical equipment and no negative film stock, they were often required to make "films without celluloid."

Soviet *agitki*

Students at the VGIK were instructed to write, direct, and act out scenarios as if they were before cameras. Then—on paper—they assembled various "shots" into completed "films." The great teacher Lev Kuleshov obtained a print of Griffith's *Intolerance* and screened it for students in his "Kuleshov workshop" until they had memorized its shot structures and could rearrange its multilayered editing sequences on paper in hundreds of different combinations.

Kuleshov further experimented with editing by intercutting the same shot of a famous actor's expressionless face with several different shots of highly expressive content—a steaming bowl of soup, a dead woman in a coffin, and a little girl playing with a teddy bear. The invariable response of film school audiences when shown these sequences was that the actor's face assumed the emotion appropriate to the intercut object—hunger for the soup, sorrow for the dead woman, paternal affection for the little girl. Kuleshov reasoned from this phenomenon, known today as the "Kuleshov effect," that the shot in film always has two values: that which it carries in itself as a photographic image of reality, and that which it acquires when placed into juxtaposition with another shot. He reasoned further that the second value is more important to cinematic

The Kuleshov effect

signification than the first and that, therefore, time and space in the cinema must be subordinate to the process of editing, or montage (coined by the Soviets from the French verb *monter,* "to assemble"). Kuleshov ultimately conceived of montage as an expressive process whereby dissimilar images could be linked together to create nonliteral or symbolic meaning.

Although Kuleshov made several important films, including *By the Law* (1926), it was as a teacher and theorist that he most deeply influenced an entire generation of Soviet directors. Two of his most brilliant students were Sergey Eisenstein and Vsevolod Illarionovich Pudovkin.

Sergey Eisenstein

Eisenstein was, with Griffith, one of the great pioneering geniuses of the modern cinema, and like his predecessor he produced a handful of enduring masterworks. Griffith, however, had elaborated the structure of narrative editing intuitively, whereas Eisenstein was an intellectual who formulated a modernist theory of editing based on the psychology of perception and Marxist dialectic. Trained as a civil engineer, in 1920 he joined the Moscow Proletkult Theatre, where he fell under the influence of the stage director Vsevolod Meyerhold and directed a number of plays in the revolutionary style of Futurism. In the winter of 1922–23 Eisenstein studied under Kuleshov and was inspired to write his first theoretical manifesto, "The Montage of Attractions." Published in the radical journal *Lef,* the article advocated assaulting an audience with calculated emotional shocks for the purpose of agitation.

Eisenstein was invited to direct the Proletkult-sponsored film *Strike* in 1924, but, like Griffith, he knew little of the practical aspects of production. He therefore enlisted the aid of Eduard Tisse, a brilliant cinematographer at the state-owned Goskino studios, beginning a lifelong artistic collaboration. *Strike* is a semidocumentary representation of the brutal suppression of a strike by tsarist factory owners and police. In addition to being Eisenstein's first film, it was also the first revolutionary mass-film of the new Soviet state. Conceived as an extended montage of shock stimuli, the film concludes with the now famous sequence in which the massacre of the strikers and their families is intercut with shots of cattle being slaughtered in an abattoir.

Strike was an immediate success, and Eisenstein was next commissioned to direct a film celebrating the 20th anniversary of the failed 1905 revolution against tsarism. Originally intended to provide a panorama of the entire event, the project eventually came to focus on a single representative episode—the mutiny of the battleship *Potemkin* and the massacre of the citizens of the port of Odessa by tsarist troops. *Battleship Potemkin* (1925) emerged as one of the most important and influential films ever made, especially in Eisenstein's use of montage, which had improved far beyond the formulaic, if effective, juxtapositions of *Strike.*

Although agitational to the core, *Potemkin* is a work of extraordinary pictorial beauty and great elegance of form. It is symmetrically broken into five movements or acts, according to the structure of Greek tragedy. In the first of these, "Men and Maggots," the flagrant mistreatment of the sailors at the hands of their officers is demonstrated, while the second, "Drama on the Quarterdeck," presents the actual mutiny and the ship's arrival in Odessa. "Appeal from the Dead" establishes the solidarity of the citizens of Odessa with the mutineers, but it is the fourth sequence, "The Odessa Steps," which depicts the massacre of the citizens, that thrust Eisenstein and his film into the historical eminence that both occupy today. Its power is such that the film's conclusion, "Meeting the Squadron," in which the *Potemkin* in a show of brotherhood is allowed to pass through the squadron unharmed, is anticlimactic.

Eisenstein's theory of montage

Unquestionably the most famous sequence of its kind in film history, "The Odessa Steps" incarnates the theory of dialectical montage that Eisenstein later expounded in his collected writings, *The Film Sense* (1942) and *Film Form* (1949). Eisenstein believed that meaning in motion pictures is generated by the collision of opposing shots. Building on Kuleshov's ideas, Eisenstein reasoned that montage operates according to the Marxist view of history as a perpetual conflict in which a force (thesis) and a counterforce (antithesis) collide to produce a totally new and greater phenomenon (synthesis). He compared this dialectical process in film editing to "the series of explosions of an internal combustion engine, driving forward its automobile or tractor." The force of the Odessa steps sequence arises when the viewer's mind combines individual, independent shots and forms a new, distinct conceptual impression that far outweighs the shots' narrative significance. Through Eisenstein's accelerated manipulations of filmic time and space, the slaughter on the stone steps—where hundreds of citizens find themselves trapped between descending tsarist militia above and Cossacks below—acquires a powerful symbolic meaning. With the addition of a stirring revolutionary score by the German Marxist composer Edmund Meisel, the agitational appeal of *Potemkin* became nearly irresistible, and, when exported in early 1926, it made Eisenstein world famous.

Eisenstein's next project, *October* (1928), was commissioned by the Central Committee to commemorate the 10th anniversary of the Bolshevik Revolution. Accordingly, vast resources, including the Soviet Army and Navy, were placed at the director's disposal. Eisenstein based the shooting script on voluminous documentary material from the era and on John Reed's book *Ten Days That Shook the World.* When the film was completed in November 1927, it was just under four hours long. While Eisenstein was making *October,* however, Joseph Stalin had taken control of the Politburo from Leon Trotsky, and the director was forced to cut the print by one-third to eliminate references to the exiled Trotsky.

Eisenstein had consciously used *October* as a laboratory for experimenting with "intellectual" or "ideological" montage, an abstract type of editing in which the relationships established between shots are conceptual rather than visual or emotional. When the film was finally released, however, Stalinist critics attacked this alleged "formalist excess" (aestheticism or elitism). The same charge was leveled even more bitterly against Eisenstein's next film, *Old and New* (1929), which Stalinist bureaucrats completely disavowed. Stalin hated Eisenstein because he was an intellectual and a Jew, but the director's international stature was such that he could not be publicly purged. Instead, Stalin used the Soviet state-subsidy apparatus to foil Eisenstein's projects and attack his principles at every turn, a situation that resulted in the director's failure to complete another film until *Alexander Nevsky* was commissioned in 1938.

Eisenstein's nearest rival in the Soviet silent cinema was his fellow student Pudovkin. Like Eisenstein, Pudovkin developed a new theory of montage but one based on cognitive linkage rather than dialectical collision. He maintained that "the film is not shot, but built, built up from the separate strips of celluloid that are its raw material."

Pudovkin's use of montage

Pudovkin, like Griffith, most often used montage for narrative rather than symbolic purpose. His films are more personal than Eisenstein's; the epic drama that is the focus of Eisenstein's films exists in Pudovkin's films merely to

By courtesy of the Rosa Madell Film Library; photograph from the Museum of Modern Art/Film Stills Archive, New York City

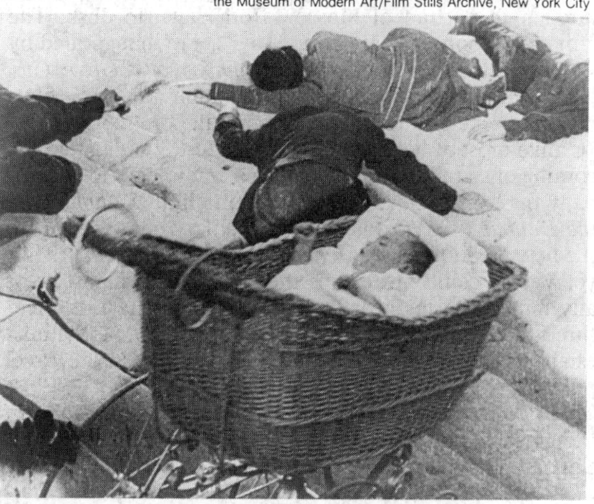

The descent of the baby carriage during the "Odessa Steps" sequence from *Battleship Potemkin,* Sergey Eisenstein (1925).

provide a backdrop for the interplay of human emotions.

Pudovkin's major work is *Mother* (1926), a tale of strikebreaking and terrorism in which a woman loses first her husband and then her son to the opposing sides of the 1905 Revolution. The film was internationally acclaimed for the revolutionary intensity of its montage, as well as for its emotion and lyricism. Pudovkin's later films include *The End of St. Petersburg* (1927), which, like Eisenstein's *October*, was commissioned to celebrate the 10th anniversary of the Bolshevik Revolution, and *The Heir to Genghis Khan* (1928; English title: *Storm over Asia*), which is set in Central Asia during the 1920 Civil War. Both mingle human drama with the epic and the symbolic as they tell a story of a politically naive person who is galvanized into action by tsarist tyranny. Although Pudovkin was never persecuted as severely by the Stalinists as Eisenstein, he too was publicly charged with formalism for his experimental sound film *A Simple Case* (1932) and was forced to release the film without its sound track. Pudovkin made several more sound films but remains best known for his silent work.

Two other seminal figures of the Soviet silent era were Aleksandr Dovzhenko and Dziga Vertov (original name Denis Kaufman). Dovzhenko, the son of Ukrainian peasants, had been a political cartoonist and painter before becoming a director at the state-controlled Odessa studios in 1926. After several minor works, he made *Zvenigora* (1928), a collection of boldly stylized tales about a hunt for an ancient Scythian treasure set during four different stages of Ukrainian history; *Arsenal* (1929), an epic film poem about the effects of revolution and civil war upon the Ukraine; and *Earth* (1930), which is considered to be his masterpiece. *Earth* tells the story of the conflict between a family of wealthy land-owning peasants (kulaks) and the young peasants of a collective farm in a small Ukrainian village, but the film is less a narrative than a lyric hymn to the cyclic recurrence of birth, life, love, and death in nature and in humankind. Although the film is acclaimed today, when it was released Stalinist critics denounced it as counterrevolutionary. Soon after, Dovzhenko entered a period of political eclipse, during which, however, he continued to make films.

Dziga Vertov (a pseudonym meaning "spinning top") was an artist of quite different talents. He began his career as an *agitki* photographer and newsreel editor and is now acknowledged as the father of *cinéma-vérité* (a self-consciously realistic documentary movement of the 1960s and '70s) for his development and practice of the theory of the *kino-glaz* ("cinema-eye"). Vertov articulated this doctrine in the early 1920s in a number of radical manifestos in which he denounced conventional narrative cinema as impotent and demanded that it be replaced with a cinema of actuality based on the "organization of camera-recorded documentary material." Between 1922 and 1925, he put his idea into practice in a series of 23 carefully crafted newsreel-documentaries entitled *Kino-Pravda* ("film truth") and *Goskinokalender*. Vertov's most famous film is *Man with a Movie Camera* (1929), a feature-length portrait of Moscow from dawn to dusk. The film plays upon the "city symphony" genre inaugurated by Walter Ruttman's *Berlin, the Symphony of a Great City* (1927), but Vertov repeatedly draws attention to the filmmaking process to create an autocritique of cinema itself.

Dziga Vertov's theory of the *kino-glaz*

Unlike most of his contemporaries, Vertov welcomed the coming of sound, envisioning it as a "radio-ear" to accompany the "cinema-eye." His first sound film, *Symphony of the Donbas* (1931), was an extraordinary contribution to the new medium, as was *Three Songs About Lenin* (1934), yet Vertov could not escape the charge of formalist error any more than his peers. Although he did make the feature film *Lullaby* in 1937, for the most part the Stalinist establishment reduced him to the status of a newsreel photographer after 1934.

Many other Soviet filmmakers played important roles in the great decade of experiment that followed the Revolution, among them Grigory Kozintsev and Leonid Trauberg (*The Overcoat*, 1926; *The New Babylon*, 1929), Boris Barnet (*The House on Trubnaya Square*, 1928), Yakov Protazanov (*Aelita*, 1924), Olga Preobrazhenskaya (*Women of Ryazan*, 1927), Abram Room (*Bed and Sofa*, 1927), and the documentarian Esther Shub (*The Fall of the Romanov Dynasty*, 1927). The period came to an abrupt end in 1929, when Stalin removed the state film trust (then called Sovkino) from the jurisdiction of the Commissariat of Education and placed it under the direct authority of the Supreme Council of the National Economy. Reorganized as Soyuzkino, the trust was turned over to the reactionary bureaucrat Boris Shumyatsky, a proponent of the narrowly ideological doctrine known as socialist realism. This policy, which came to dominate the Soviet arts, dictated that individual creativity be subordinated to the political aims of the party and the state. In practice, it militated against the symbolic, the experimental, and the avant-garde in favour of a literal-minded "people's art" that glorified representative Soviet heroes and idealized Soviet experience. The restraints imposed made it impossible for the great filmmakers of the postrevolutionary era to produce creative or innovative work, and the Soviet cinema went into decline.

Soviet socialist realism

Post-World War I U.S. cinema. During the 1920s in the United States, motion-picture production, distribution, and exhibition became a major national industry and movies perhaps the major national obsession. The salaries of stars reached monumental proportions, filmmaking practices and narrative formulas were standardized to accommodate mass production, and Wall Street began to invest heavily in every branch of the business. The growing industry was organized according to the studio system that, in many respects, the producer Thomas Harper Ince had developed at Inceville, his studio in the Santa Ynez Canyon near Hollywood, between 1914 and 1918. Ince functioned as the central authority over multiple production units, each headed by a director who was required to shoot an assigned film according to a detailed continuity script. Every project was carefully budgeted and tightly scheduled, and Ince himself supervised the final cut. This central producer system was the prototype for the studio system of the 1920s, and, with some modification, it prevailed as the dominant mode of Hollywood production for the next 40 years.

Virtually all of the major film genres evolved and were codified during the 1920s, but none was more characteristic of the period than the slapstick comedy. This form was originated by Mack Sennett, who, at his Keystone Studios, produced countless one- and two-reel shorts and features (*Tillie's Punctured Romance*, 1914; *The Surf Girl*, 1916; *Teddy at the Throttle*, 1917) whose narrative logic was subordinated to fantastic, purely visual humour. An anarchic mixture of circus, vaudeville, burlesque, pantomime, and the chase, Sennett's Keystone comedies created a world of inspired madness and mayhem, and they employed the talents of such future stars as Charlie Chaplin, Harry Langdon, Roscoe "Fatty" Arbuckle, Mabel Normand, and Harold Lloyd. When these performers achieved fame, many of them left Keystone, often to form their own production companies, a practice still (if briefly) possible in the early 1920s.

Charlie Chaplin

Chaplin, for example, who had developed the persona of the "little tramp" at Keystone, went on to direct and star in a series of shorts produced by Essanay in 1915 (*The Tramp*, *A Night in the Show*) and Mutual between 1916 and 1917 (*One A.M.*, *The Rink*, *Easy Street*). In 1917 he was offered an eight-film contract with First National that enabled him to establish his own studio. He directed his first feature there, the semiautobiographical *The Kid* (1921), but most of his First National films were two-reelers. In 1919 Chaplin, Griffith, Mary Pickford, and Douglas Fairbanks, the four most popular and powerful film artists of the time, jointly formed the United Artists Corporation in order to produce and distribute—and thereby retain artistic and financial control over—their own films. Chaplin directed three silent features for United Artists: *A Woman of Paris* (1923), his great comic epic *The Gold Rush* (1925), and *The Circus* (1928), which was released after the introduction of sound into motion pictures. He later made several sound films, but the two most successful—his first two, *City Lights* (1931) and *Modern Times* (1936)—were essentially silent films with musical scores.

Charlie Chaplin in *Modern Times* (1936).

© Roy Export Company Establishment; photograph, the Museum of Modern Art/Film Stills Archive, New York City

Buster Keaton

Buster Keaton possessed a very different kind of comic talent than Chaplin; but both men were wonderfully subtle actors with a keen sense of the tragic often contained within the comic, and both were major directors of their period. Keaton, like Chaplin, was born into a theatrical family and began performing in vaudeville skits at a young age. Intrigued by the new film medium, he left the stage and worked for two years as a supporting comedian for Arbuckle's production company. In 1919 Keaton formed his own production company, where, over the next four years, he made 20 shorts (*One Week,* 1920; *The Boat,* 1921; *Cops,* 1922; *The Balloonatic,* 1923) that represent, with Chaplin's Mutual films, the acme of American slapstick comedy. A Keaton trademark was the "trajectory gag," in which perfect timing of acting, directing, and editing propels his film character through a geometric progression of complicated sight gags that seem impossibly dangerous but are still dramatically logical. Such routines inform all of Keaton's major features—*Our Hospitality* (1923), *Sherlock Jr.* (1924), *The Navigator* (1924), *Seven Chances* (1925), and his masterpieces *The General* (1927) and *Steamboat Bill, Jr.* (1928). Keaton's greatest films, all made before his company was absorbed by MGM, have a reflexive quality that indicates his fascination with film as a medium. Although some of his MGM films were financially successful, the factory-like studio system stifled Keaton's creativity, and he was reduced to playing bit parts after the early 1930s.

Important but lesser silent comics were Lloyd, the team of Stan Laurel and Oliver Hardy, Langdon, and Arbuckle. Working at the Hal Roach Studios, Lloyd cultivated the persona of an earnest, sweet-tempered boy-next-door. He specialized in a variant of Keystone mayhem known as the "comedy of thrills," in which—as in Lloyd's most famous features, *Safety Last* (1923) and *The Freshman* (1925)—an innocent protagonist finds himself placed in physical danger. Laurel and Hardy also worked for Roach. They made 27 silent two-reelers, including *Putting Pants on Philip* (1927) and *Liberty* (1929), and became even more popular in the 1930s in such sound films as *Another Fine Mess* (1930) and *Sons of the Desert* (1933). Their comic characters were basically grown-up children whose relationship was sometimes disturbingly sadomasochistic. Langdon also traded on a childlike, even babylike, image in such popular features as *The Strong Man* (1926) and *Long Pants* (1927), both directed by Frank Capra. Arbuckle, however, in his few years of stardom, unfortunately created the character of a leering, sensual adult. Arbuckle's talent was limited, but his persona affected the course of American film history in a quite unexpected way.

By the early 1920s some 40,000,000 Americans—half of them minors—were attending the movies each week. The rapid spread of the medium and its easy accessibility had already caused mild public concern, especially since films had begun to feature increasingly risqué plots and situations. Concern increased as Hollywood became identified in the popular mind with the materialism, cynicism, and sexual license of the Jazz Age. Then, in September 1921 the popular Arbuckle was charged with the rape and manslaughter of a young starlet, and the concern turned into anger and rage. Arbuckle was eventually exonerated, but other Hollywood scandals surfaced—the murder of director William Desmond Taylor, the death from drug addiction of matinee idol Wallace Reid—and the tabloid press screamed for blood.

The Hays Office

In an attempt to stave off probable mass boycotts and government censorship, in March 1922 the studio heads formed a self-regulatory trade organization, the Motion Picture Producers and Distributors of America (MPPDA), and hired the U.S. postmaster general, Will H. Hays, to head it. In practice, the Hays Office, as the MPPDA was known, functioned as an advisory body and engaged in little actual censorship. It promulgated an unenforceable "Purity Code," which was facetiously called the "Don'ts and Be Carefuls," and it endorsed a policy of "compensating values," whereby all manner of screen vileness could be depicted so long as it was shown to be punished by the film's end. Throughout the 1920s, the Hays Office primarily (and successfully) served to mollify pressure groups and to manage public relations.

The leading practitioner of the compensating values formula was the flamboyant director Cecil B. deMille. He first became famous after World War I for a series of sophisticated comedies of manners that were aimed at Hollywood's new middle-class audience (*Old Wives for New,* 1918; *Forbidden Fruit,* 1921). When the Hays Office was established deMille turned to the sex- and violence-drenched religious spectacles that made him an international figure, notably *The Ten Commandments* (1923; remade 1956). DeMille's chief rival in the production of stylish sex comedies was the German émigré Ernst Lubitsch. An early master of the UFA *Kostümfilm,* Lubitsch excelled at sexual innuendo and understatement in such urbane essays as *The Marriage Circle* (1924). Also popular during the 1920s were the swashbuckling exploits of Douglas Fairbanks, whose lavish adventure spectacles, including *Robin Hood* (1922) and *The Thief of Bagdad* (1924), thrilled a generation, and the narrative documentaries of Robert Flaherty, whose *Nanook of the North* (1922) and *Moana* (1926) were unexpectedly successful with the public and with critics.

The most enigmatic and unconventional figure working in Hollywood at the time, however, was without a doubt the remarkable Viennese émigré Erich von Stroheim. Stroheim, who also acted, learned directing as an assistant to Griffith on *Intolerance* and *Hearts of the World.* His first three films—*Blind Husbands* (1918), *The Devil's Passkey* (1919), and *Foolish Wives* (1922)—constitute an obsessive trilogy of adultery; each features a sexual triangle in which an American wife is seduced by a Prussian army officer. Even though all three films were enormously popular, the great sums Stroheim was spending on the extravagant production design and costuming of his next project brought him into conflict with his Universal producers, and he was replaced.

Stroheim then signed a contract with Goldwyn Pictures and began work on a long-cherished project—an adaptation of Frank Norris' grim, naturalistic novel *McTeague.* Shot entirely on location in the streets and rooming houses of San Francisco, in Death Valley, and in the California hills, the film was conceived as a sentence-by-sentence translation of its source. Stroheim's original version ran approximately 10 hours. Realizing that the film was too long to be exhibited, he cut almost half of the footage. The film was still deemed too long, so Stroheim, with the help of director Rex Ingram, edited it down into a four-hour version that could be shown in two parts. By that time, however, Goldwyn Pictures had merged with Metro Pictures and Louis B. Mayer Pictures to become MGM. MGM took the negative from Stroheim and cut out another two hours, destroying the excised footage in the process. Released as *Greed* (1924), the film had enormous gaps in continuity, but it was still recognized as a work of genius in its rich psychological characterization and in its creation of a naturalistic analogue for the novel.

Stroheim made one more film for MGM, a darkly satiric

adaptation of the Franz Lehár operetta *The Merry Widow* (1925). He then went to Celebrity Pictures, where he directed *The Wedding March* (1928), a two-part spectacle of imperial Vienna, but his work was taken from him and recut into a single film when Celebrity was absorbed by Paramount. Stroheim's last directorial duties were on the botched *Queen Kelly* (1929) and *Walking Down Broadway* (1932), although he was removed from both films for various reasons. He made his living thereafter by writing screenplays and acting.

Decline of independent filmmaking

Although many of Stroheim's troubles with Hollywood were personal, he was also a casualty of the American film industry's transformation during the 1920s from a speculative entrepreneurial enterprise into a vertically and horizontally integrated oligopoly that had no tolerance for creative difference. His situation was not unique; many singular artists, including Griffith, Sennett, Chaplin, and Keaton, found it difficult to survive as filmmakers under the rigidly standardized studio system that had been established by the end of the decade. The industry's conversion to sound at that time reinforced its big-business tendencies and further discouraged independent filmmakers. The studios, which had borrowed huge sums of money on the very brink of the Great Depression in order to finance the conversion, were determined to reduce production costs and increase efficiency. They therefore became less and less willing to tolerate artistic innovation or eccentricity.

THE PRE-WORLD WAR II SOUND ERA

Introduction of sound. The idea of combining motion pictures and sound had been around since the invention of the cinema itself: Edison had commissioned the Kinetograph to provide visual images for his phonograph, and Dickson had actually synchronized the two machines in a device briefly marketed in the 1890s as the "Kinetophone." Léon Gaumont's Chronophone in France and Cecil Hepworth's Vivaphone system in England employed a similar technology, and each was used to produce hundreds of synchronized shorts between 1902 and 1912. In Germany, producer-director Oskar Messter began to release all of his films with recorded musical scores as early as 1908. By the time the feature had become the dominant film form in the West, producers regularly commissioned orchestral scores to accompany prestigious productions, and virtually all films were accompanied by cue sheets suggesting appropriate musical selections for performance during exhibition.

Actual recorded sound required amplification for sustained periods of use, however, which became possible only after Lee De Forest's perfection in 1907 of the Audion tube, a three-element, or triode, vacuum tube that magnified sound and drove it through speakers so that it could be heard by a large audience. In 1919 De Forest developed an optical sound-on-film process patented as Phonofilm, and between 1923 and 1927 he made more than 1,000 synchronized sound shorts for release to specially wired theatres. The public was widely interested in these films, but the major Hollywood producers, to whom De Forest vainly tried to sell his system, were not: they viewed "talking pictures" as an expensive novelty with little potential return.

By that time, Western Electric, the manufacturing subsidiary of American Telephone & Telegraph Company, had perfected a sophisticated sound-on-disc system called Vitaphone, which their representatives attempted to market to Hollywood in 1925. Like De Forest, they were rebuffed by the major studios, but Warner Bros., then a minor studio in the midst of aggressive expansion, bought both the system and the right to sublease it to other producers. Warner Bros. had no more faith in talking pictures than did the major studios but thought that the novelty could be exploited for short-term profits. The studio planned to use Vitaphone to provide synchronized orchestral accompaniment for all Warner films, thereby enhancing their marketability to second- and third-run exhibitors who could not afford to hire live orchestral accompaniment. After mounting a $3,000,000 promotion, Warners gave the system its debut on Aug. 6, 1926, in *Don Juan,* a lavish costume drama starring John Barrymore, directed by Alan Crosland, and with a score performed by the New York Philharmonic Orchestra. The response was enthusiastic; Warners announced that all of its films for 1927 would be released with synchronized musical accompaniment and then turned immediately to the production of its second Vitaphone feature. *The Jazz Singer* (1927), also directed by Crosland, included popular songs and incidental dialogue in addition to the orchestral score; its phenomenal success virtually ensured the industry's conversion to sound.

Success of Warners' first sound films

Sensing that Warners' gamble on sound might pay off, MGM, First National, Paramount, and others had asked the MPPDA to investigate competing sound systems in early 1927. There were several sound-on-film systems that were technologically superior to Vitaphone, but the rights to most of them were owned by William Fox, president of Fox Film Corporation. Fox, like the Warners, had seen sound as a way of cornering the market among smaller exhibitors. In the summer of 1926 he therefore acquired the rights to the Case-Sponable sound-on-film system (which was closely, and illegally, based upon De Forest's Phonofilm) and formed the Fox-Case Corporation to make shorts under the trade name Fox Movietone. Six months later, he secretly bought the American rights to the German Tri-Ergon process, whose flywheel mechanism was essential to the continuous reproduction of optical sound. To cover himself completely, Fox negotiated a reciprocal pact between Fox-Case and Vitaphone in which each licensed the other to use its sound systems, equipment, and personnel. The sound-on-film system eventually prevailed over sound-on-disc because it enabled image and sound to be recorded simultaneously in the same (photographic) medium, ensuring their precise and automatic synchronization.

Despite Warners' obvious success with its sound films, film industry leaders were not eager to lease sound equipment from a direct competitor. They banded together, and Warner Bros. was forced to give up its rights to the Vitaphone system in exchange for a share in any new royalties earned. The major film companies then wasted no time. By May 1928 virtually every studio in Hollywood, major and minor, was licensed by Western Electric's newly created marketing subsidiary, Electrical Research Products, Incorporated (ERPI), to use Western Electric equipment with the Movietone sound-on-film recording system. ERPI's monopoly did not please the Radio Corporation of America (RCA), which had tried to market a sound-on-film system that had been developed in the laboratories of its parent company, General Electric, and had been patented in 1925 as RCA Photophone. In October 1928, RCA therefore acquired the Keith-Albee-Orpheum vaudeville circuit and merged it with Joseph P. Kennedy's Film Booking Offices of America (FBO) to form RKO Radio Pictures for the express purpose of producing sound films using the Photophone system (which ultimately became the industry standard).

The wholesale conversion to sound of all three sectors of the American film industry took place in less than 15 months between late 1927 and 1929, and the profits of the major companies increased during that period by as much as 600 percent. Although the transition was fast, orderly, and profitable, it was also enormously expensive. The industrial system as it had evolved for the previous three decades needed to be completely overhauled; studios and theatres had to be totally reequipped and creative personnel retrained or fired. In order to fund the conversion, the film companies were forced to borrow in excess of $350,000,000, which placed them under the indirect control of the two major New York-based financial groups, the Morgan group and the Rockefeller group.

Furthermore, although cooperation among the film companies through such agencies as the the MPPDA, the Academy of Motion Picture Arts and Sciences, and the Society of Motion Picture Engineers (SMPE) ensured a smooth transition in corporate terms, inside the newly wired theatres and studio sound stages there was confusion and disruption. The three competing systems—Vitaphone, Movietone, and Photophone—were all initially incompatible, and their technologies were under such constant modification that equipment was sometimes obsolete before it was uncrated. Whatever system producers chose, exhibitors during the early transitional period were forced to maintain both sound-on-disc and sound-on-film reproduction equipment. Even as late as 1931, studios were still releasing films in both formats to accommodate theatres owned by sound-on-disc interests.

Production problems caused by conversion to sound

It was in the area of production, however, that the greatest problems arose. The statement that "the movies ceased to move when they began to talk" accurately described the films made during the earliest years of the transition, largely because of technical limitations. Early microphones, for example, had a very limited range. In addition, they were large, clumsy, and difficult to move, so that they were usually concealed in a single, stationary location on the set. The actors, who had to speak directly into the microphones to register on the sound track, were therefore forced to remain practically motionless while speaking dialogue. The microphones caused further problems because they were omnidirectional within their range and picked up every sound made near them on the set, especially the noisy whir of running cameras (which were motorized in 1929 to run at an even speed of 24 frames per second to ensure undistorted sound synchronization; silent cameras had been mainly hand-cranked at rates averaging 16 to 18 frames per second). To prevent the recording of camera noise, cameras and their operators were initially enclosed in soundproof glass-paneled booths that were only six feet long per side. The booths, which were facetiously called "ice-boxes" because they were uncomfortably hot and stuffy, literally imprisoned the camera. The filmmakers' inability to tilt or dolly the camera (although they could pan it by as much as 30 degrees on its tripod), combined with the actors' immobility, helps to account for the static nature of so many early sound films.

The impact of sound recording on editing was even more regressive because sound and image had to be recorded simultaneously to be synchronous. In sound-on-disc films, scenes were initially made to play for 10 minutes at a time in order to record dialogue continuously on 16-inch discs; such scenes were impossible to edit until the technology of rerecording was perfected in the early 1930s. Sound-on-film systems also militated against editing at first because optical sound tracks run approximately 20 frames in advance of their corresponding image tracks, making it extremely difficult to cut a composite print without eliminating portions of the relevant sound. As a result, no matter which system of sound recording was used, most of the editing in early sound films was purely functional. In general, cuts could only be made—and the camera moved—when no sound was being recorded on the set.

Most of these technical problems were resolved by 1933, although equilibrium was not fully restored to the production process until after the mid-1930s. Sound-on-disc filming, for example, was abandoned in 1930, and by 1931 all the studios had removed their cameras from the ice-boxes and converted to the use of lightweight, soundproof camera housings known as "blimps." Within several years, smaller, quieter, self-insulating cameras were produced, eliminating the need for external soundproofing altogether. It even became possible to move the camera again by using a wide range of boom cranes, camera supports, and steerable dollies. Microphones, too, became increasingly mobile as a variety of booms were developed for them from 1930 onward. These long radial arms suspended the microphone above the set, allowing it to follow the movements of actors and rendering the stationary microphones of the early years obsolete. Microphones also became more directional throughout the decade, and track noise suppression techniques came into use as early as 1931.

Postsynchronization

The technological development that most liberated the sound film, however, was the practice known variously as postsynchronization, rerecording, or dubbing, in which image and sound are printed on separate pieces of film so that they can be manipulated independently. Postsynchronization enabled filmmakers to edit images freely again. Because the overwhelming emphasis of the period from 1928 to 1931 had been on obtaining high-quality sound in production, however, the idea that the sound track could be modified after it was recorded took a while to catch on. Many motion-picture artists and technicians felt that sound should be reproduced in films exactly as it had originally been produced on the set; they believed that anything less than an absolute pairing of sound and image would confuse audiences.

For several years, both practice and ideology dictated that sound and image be recorded simultaneously, so that everything heard on the sound track would be seen on the screen, and vice versa. A vocal minority of film artists nevertheless viewed this practice of synchronous, "naturalistic," sound-recording as a threat to the cinema. In their 1928 manifesto "Sound and Image," the Soviet directors Eisenstein, Pudovkin, and Grigory Aleksandrov denounced synchronous sound in favour of asynchronous, contrapuntal sound—sound that would counterpoint the images it accompanied to become another dynamic element in the montage process. Like the practical editing problem, the theoretical debate over the appropriate use of sound was eventually resolved by the practice of postsynchronization.

Postsynchronization seems to have first been used by the American director King Vidor in the all-black musical *Hallelujah* (1929) for a sequence in which the hero is chased through Arkansas swamplands. Vidor shot the action on location without sound, using a freely moving camera. Later, in the studio, he added to the film a separately recorded sound track containing both naturalistic and impressionistic effects. In the following year Lewis Milestone's *All Quiet on the Western Front* and Pabst's *Westfront 1918* both used postsynchronization for their battle scenes. Lubitsch used dubbing in his first American sound films, the dynamic musicals *The Love Parade* (1929) and *Monte Carlo* (1930), as did the French director René Clair in *Sous les toits de Paris* (1930). In all of these early instances, sound was recorded and rerecorded on a single track, although some American directors, including Milestone and the Russian-born Armenian Rouben Mamoulian (*Applause,* 1929; *City Streets,* 1931), had experimented with multiple microphone setups and overlapping dialogue as early as 1929. Generally, through 1932, either dialogue or music dominated the sound track unless they had been simultaneously recorded on the set. In 1933, however, technology was introduced that allowed filmmakers to mix separately recorded tracks for background music, sound effects, and synchronized dialogue at the dubbing stage. By the late 1930s, postsynchronization and multiple-channel mixing had become standard industry procedure.

Other changes wrought by sound were more purely human. Directors, for example, could no longer literally direct their performers while the cameras were rolling and sound was being recorded. Actors and actresses were suddenly required to have pleasant voices and to act without the assistance of mood music or the director's shouted instructions through long dialogue takes. Many found that they could not learn lines; others tried and were defeated by heavy foreign accents (*e.g.,* Emil Jannings, Pola Negri, Vilma Banky, and Lya de Putti) or voices that did not match their screen image (*e.g.,* Colleen Moore, Corinne Griffith, Norma Talmadge, and John Gilbert). Numerous silent stars were supplanted during the transitional period by stage actors or film actors with stage experience. "Canned theatre," or literal transcriptions of stage hits, became a dominant Hollywood form between 1929 and 1931, which brought many Broadway players and directors into the film industry on a more or less permanent basis. In addition, to fulfill the unprecedented need for dialogue scripts, the studios imported hundreds of editors, critics, playwrights, and novelists, many of whom would make lasting contributions to the verbal sophistication of the American sound film.

Sound's effect on film genres

As sound demanded new filmmaking techniques and talents, it also created new genres and renovated old ones. The realism it permitted inspired the emergence of tough, socially pertinent films with urban settings. Crime epics such as Mervyn LeRoy's *Little Caesar* (1930), William Wellman's *Public Enemy* (1931), and Howard Hawks's *Scarface* (1932) used sound to exploit urban slang and the audible pyrotechnics of the recently invented Thompson submachine gun. Subgenres of the gangster film appeared in the prison film (*The Big House,* 1930; Hawks's *The Criminal Code,* 1931; LeRoy's *I Am a Fugitive from a Chain Gang,* 1932) and the newspaper picture (Milestone's *The Front Page;* LeRoy's *Five Star Final,* 1931; John Cromwell's *Scandal Sheet,* 1931; Frank Capra's *Platinum Blonde,* 1931), both of which relied on authentic-sounding vernacular speech.

The public's fascination with speech also accounted for the new popularity of historical biographies, or "biopics." These films were modeled on the UFA's silent *Kostümfilm,* but dialogue enhanced their verisimilitude. Several actors with impressive speaking voices were often associated with the genre, notably George Arliss (*Disraeli,* 1929; *The House of Rothschild,* 1934) and Paul Muni (*The Life of Emile Zola,* 1937; *Juarez,* 1939) in the United States and Charles Laughton (Alexander Korda's *The Private Life of Henry VIII,* 1933, and *Rembrandt,* 1936) in England.

In the realm of comedy, pure slapstick could not and did not survive, predicated as it was on purely visual humour. It was replaced by equally vital—but ultimately less surreal and abstract—sound comedies: the anarchic dialogue comedies of the Marx Brothers (*The Cocoanuts,* 1929; *Animal Crackers,* 1930; *Monkey Business,* 1931; *Horse Feathers,* 1932; *Duck Soup,* 1933) and W.C. Fields (*The Golf Specialist,* 1930; *The Dentist,* 1932; *Million Dollar Legs,* 1932) and the fast-paced wisecracking "screwball" comedies of directors like Frank Capra (*Lady for a Day,* 1933; *It Happened One Night,* 1934; *Mr. Deeds Goes to Town,* 1936), Howard Hawks (*Twentieth Century,* 1934; *Bringing Up Baby,* 1938), Gregory La Cava (*My Man Godfrey,* 1936), Mitchell Leisen (*Easy Living,* 1937), and Leo McCarey (*The Awful Truth,* 1937).

The horror-fantasy genre, traditionally rooted in German Expressionism, was greatly enhanced by sound, which not only permitted the addition of eerie sound effects but also restored the dimension of literary dialogue present in so many of the original sources. Appropriately, Universal Pictures' three great horror classics—Tod Browning's *Dracula* (1931), James Whale's *Frankenstein* (1931), and Karl Freund's *The Mummy* (1932)—were all early sound films.

One significant genre whose emergence was obviously contingent upon sound was the musical. Versions of Broadway musicals were among the first sound films made (including, of course, the catalyst for the conversion, Warner Bros.' *The Jazz Singer*), and by the early 1930s the movie musical had developed in formal sophistication to become perhaps the major American genre of the decade. Among the formidable artists who helped to achieve this sophistication were Lubitsch at Paramount (*The Love Parade,* 1929; *Monte Carlo,* 1930; *The Smiling Lieutenant,* 1931), dance director Busby Berkeley at Warners (*42nd Street,* 1933; *Gold Diggers of 1933,* 1933; *Footlight Parade,* 1933; *Dames,* 1934), and dancer-star Fred Astaire, who choreographed and directed his own integrated dance sequences at RKO (*The Gay Divorcee,* 1934; *Roberta,* 1935; *Top Hat,* 1935; *Swing Time,* 1936).

Walt Disney pioneered a genre that might be called the animated musical with *The Skeleton Dance* (1929), the first entry in his "Silly Symphony" series. Unburdened by the awkward logistics of live-action shooting, Disney was free to combine sound and image asynchronously or with perfect frame-by-frame synchronization in such classic cartoons as *Steamboat Willie* (1928—Mickey Mouse's debut) and *The Three Little Pigs* (1933). To enhance their fantasy-like appeal, both the musical and the animated film made early use of the photographic colour systems introduced by the Technicolor Corporation during the conversion to sound (two-colour imbibition, 1928; three-colour, three-strip imbibition, 1932), and the two genres quickly became associated with colour in the public mind.

Early colour effects

Introduction of colour. Photographic colour entered the cinema at approximately the same time as sound, although, as with sound, various colour effects had been used in films since the invention of the medium. Méliès, for example, employed 21 women at his Montreuil studio to hand-colour his films frame by frame, but hand-colouring was not cost-effective unless films were very short. In the mid-1900s, as films began to approach one reel in length and more prints of each film were sold, mechanized stenciling processes were introduced. In Pathé's Pathécolor system, for example, a stencil was cut for each colour desired (up to six) and aligned with the print; colour was then applied through the stencil frame by frame at high speeds. With the advent of the feature and the conversion of the industry to mass production during the 1910s, frame-by-frame stenciling was replaced by mechanized tinting and toning. Tinting coloured all the light areas of a picture and was achieved by immersing a black-and-white print in dye or by using coloured film base for printing. The toning process involved chemically treating film emulsion to colour the dark areas of the print. Each process produced monochrome images, the colour of which was usually chosen to correspond to the mood or setting of the scene. Occasionally, the two processes were combined to produce elaborate two-colour effects. By the early 1920s, nearly all American features included at least one coloured sequence; but after 1927, when it was discovered that tinting or toning film stock interfered with the transmission of optical sound, both practices were temporarily abandoned, leaving the market open to new systems of colour photography.

Walt Disney pioneered the use of sound and colour in motion pictures with such cartoon shorts as *The Three Little Pigs* (1933).

The Three Little Pigs, © 1933, The Walt Disney Company; photograph from the Museum of Modern Art/Film Stills Archive, New York City

Photographic colour can be produced in motion pictures using either an additive process or a subtractive one (see below *Technology: Introduction of colour*). The first systems to be developed and used were all additive ones, such as Charles Urban's Kinemacolor (*c.* 1906) and Gaumont's Chronochrome (*c.* 1912). They achieved varying degrees of popularity, but none was entirely successful, largely because all additive systems involve the use of both special cameras and projectors, which ultimately makes them too complicated and costly for widespread industrial use.

One of the first successful subtractive processes was a two-colour one introduced by Herbert Kalmus' Technicolor Corporation in 1922. It used a special camera and a complex procedure to produce two separate positive prints that were then cemented together into a single print. The final print needed careful handling but could be projected using ordinary equipment. This "cemented positive" process was used successfully in such features as *Toll of the Sea* (1922) and Douglas Fairbanks' *The Black Pirate* (1926). In 1928 Technicolor introduced an improved process in which two gelatin positives were used as relief matrices to "print" colour onto a single strip of film. This printing process, known as imbibition or dye-transfer, made it possible to mass-produce sturdy, high-quality prints. Its introduction resulted in a significant rise in Technicolor production between 1929 and 1932. Colour reproduction in the two-colour Technicolor process was good, but because only two of the three primary colours were used, it was still not completely lifelike. Its popularity began to decline sharply in 1932, and Technicolor replaced it with a three-colour system that employed the same basic principles but included all three primary colours.

Drawbacks of Technicolor's three-colour system

For the next 25 years almost every colour film made was produced using Technicolor's three-colour system. Although the quality of the system was excellent, there were drawbacks. The bulk of the camera made location shooting difficult. Furthermore, Technicolor's virtual monopoly gave it indirect control of the production companies, which were required to rent—at high rates—equipment, crew, consultants, and laboratory services from Technicolor every time they used the system. In the midst of the Depression, therefore, conversion to colour was slow and never really complete. After three-colour Technicolor was used successfully in Disney's cartoon short *The Three Little Pigs* (1933), the live-action short *La Cucaracha* (1934), and Rouben Mamoulian's live-action feature *Becky Sharp* (1935), however, it gradually worked its way into mainstream feature production (*The Garden of Allah,* 1936; *Snow White and the Seven Dwarfs,* 1937; *The Adventures of Robin Hood,* 1938; *The Wizard of Oz,* 1939; *Gone with the Wind,* 1939), although it remained strongly associated with fantasy and spectacle.

The Hollywood studio system. If the coming of sound changed the aesthetic dynamics of the filmmaking process, it altered the economic structure of the industry even more, precipitating some of the largest mergers in motion-picture history. Throughout the 1920s, Paramount, MGM, First National, and other studios had conducted ambitious campaigns of vertical integration by ruthlessly acquiring first-run theatre chains. It was primarily in response to these aggressive maneuvers that Warners and Fox sought to dominate smaller exhibitors by providing prerecorded musical accompaniment to their films. The unexpected success of their strategy forced the industry-wide conversion to sound and transformed Warners and Fox into major corporations. By 1929, Warners had acquired the Stanley theatre circuit, which controlled nearly all of the first-run houses in the mid-Atlantic states, and the production and distribution facilities of its former rival First National to become one of the largest studios in Hollywood. Fox went even further, building the multimillion-dollar Movietone City in Westwood, Calif., in 1928 and acquiring controlling shares of both Loew's, Inc., the parent corporation of MGM, and Gaumont British, England's largest producer-distributor-exhibitor. Its holdings were surpassed only by those of Paramount, which controlled an international distribution network and the vast Publix theatre chain. In an effort to become even more powerful, Paramount in 1929 acquired one-half of the newly formed Columbia Broadcasting System and proposed a merger with Warner Bros. It was then that the U.S. Department of Justice intervened, forbidding Paramount's merger with Warners and divorcing Fox from Loew's.

Without government interference, "Paramount-Vitaphone" and "Fox-Loew's" might have divided the entertainment industries of the entire English-speaking world between them. As it was, by 1930, 95 percent of all American production was concentrated in the hands of only eight studios—five vertically integrated major companies, which controlled production, distribution, and exhibition, and three horizontally integrated minor ones that controlled production and distribution. Distribution was conducted at both a national and an international level: since about 1925, foreign rentals had accounted for half of all American feature revenues, and they would continue to do so for the next two decades. Exhibition was controlled through the major studios' ownership of 2,600 first-run theatres, which represented l6 percent of the national total but generated three-fourths of the revenue. Film production throughout the 1930s and '40s consumed only 5 percent of total corporate assets, while distribution accounted for another 1 percent. The remaining 94 percent of the studios' investment went to the exhibition sector. In short, as film historian Douglas Gomery pointed out, the five major studios of the time can best be characterized as "diversified theater chains, producing features, shorts, cartoons, and newsreels to fill their houses."

The major studios

Each studio produced a distinctive style of entertainment, depending on its corporate economy and the personnel it had under contract. Metro-Goldwyn-Mayer, the largest and most powerful of the major studios, was also the most "American" and was given to the celebration of middle-class values in a visual style characterized by bright, even, high-key lighting and opulent production design. Paramount, with its legions of UFA-trained directors, art directors, and cameramen, was thought to be the most "European" of the studios. It produced the most sophisticated and visually baroque films of the era. Conditioned by its recent experience as a struggling minor studio, Warner Bros. was the most cost-conscious of the major companies. Its directors worked on a quota system, and a flat, low-key lighting style was decreed by the studio to conceal the cheapness of its sets. Warners' films were often targeted for working-class audiences. 20th Century-Fox was formed in 1935 by the merger of Fox Film Corporation and Joseph M. Schenck's 20th Century Pictures after William Fox was bankrupted through his financial manipulations. The studio acquired a reputation for its tight budget and production control, but its films were noted for their glossy attractiveness and state-of-the-art special effects. RKO Radio was the smallest of the major companies and never achieved complete financial stability during the studio era; it became prominent, however, as the producer of *King Kong* (1933), the Astaire-Rogers dance cycle, and Orson Welles's *Citizen Kane* (1941) and also as the distributor of Disney's features.

The minor studios were Carl Laemmle's Universal Pictures, which became justly famous for its horror films; Harry Cohn's Columbia Pictures, whose main assets were director Frank Capra and screenwriter Robert Riskin; and United Artists, which functioned as a distributor for independent American features and for Alexander Korda's London Film Productions. In terms of total assets, the five major studios were about four times as big as the three minor ones, with MGM, Paramount, Warners, and 20th Century-Fox all about the same size and RKO approximately 25 percent smaller than its peers. At the very bottom of the film industry hierarchy were a score of poorly capitalized studios, such as Republic, Monogram, and Grand National, that produced cheap, formulaic, hour-long "B-films" for the second half of double bills. The double feature, an attraction introduced in the early 1930s to counter the Depression-era box-office slump, was the standard form of exhibition for about 15 years. The larger studios were, for the most part, not interested in producing B-films for double bills because unlike the main feature, whose earnings were based on box-office receipts, the second feature rented at a flat rate, which meant that the profit it returned, though guaranteed, was fixed at a small amount. At their peak, the B-film studios produced 40–50 films per year and provided a training ground for such stars as John Wayne. The films were made as quickly as possible, and directors functioned as their own producers, with complete authority over their projects' minuscule budgets.

B-films

The Production Code

An important aspect of the studio system was the Production Code, which was implemented in 1934 in response to pressure from the Legion of Decency and public protest against the graphic violence and sexual suggestiveness of some sound films (the urban gangster films, for example, and the films of Mae West). The Legion had been established in 1933 by the American bishops of the Roman Catholic Church (armed with a mandate from the Vatican) to fight for better and more "moral" motion pictures. In April 1934, with the support of both Protestant and Jewish organizations, the Legion called for a nationwide boycott of movies it considered indecent. The studios, having lost millions of dollars in 1933 as the delayed effects of the Depression caught up with the box office, rushed to appease the protesters by authorizing the MPPDA to create the Production Code Administration. A prominent Catholic layman, Joseph I. Breen, was appointed to head the administration, and under Breen's auspices, Father Daniel A. Lord, a Jesuit priest, and Martin Quigley, a Catholic publisher, coauthored the code whose provisions would dictate the content of American motion pictures, without exception, for the next 20 years.

In a swing away from the excesses of the "new morality" of the Jazz Era, the Production Code was monumentally repressive, forbidding the depiction on screen of almost everything germane to the experience of normal human adults. It prohibited showing "scenes of passion," and adultery, illicit sex, seduction, and rape could not even be alluded to unless they were absolutely essential to the plot and severely punished by the film's end. The code demanded that the sanctity of marriage be upheld at all times, although sexual relations were not to be suggested between spouses. It forbade the use of profanity, vulgarity, and racial epithets; prostitution, miscegenation, sexual deviance, or drug addiction; nudity, sexually suggestive dancing or costumes, and "lustful kissing"; and excessive drinking, cruelty to animals or children, and the representation of surgical operations, especially childbirth, "in fact or silhouette." In the realm of violence, it was forbidden to display or to discuss contemporary weapons, to show the details of a crime, to show law enforcement officers dying at the hands of criminals, to suggest excessive brutality or slaughter, or to use murder or suicide except when crucial to the plot. Finally, the code required that all criminal activity be shown to be punished; under no circumstances could any crime be represented as justified. Studios were required to submit their scripts to Breen's office for approval before beginning filming, and completed films had to be screened for the office, and altered if necessary, in order to receive a Production Code Seal, without which no film could be distributed in the United States. Noncompliance with the code's restrictions brought a fine of $25,000, but the studios were so anxious to please that the fine was never levied in the 22-year lifetime of the code.

Studio acceptance of the code

The studio heads were willing not merely to accept but also to institutionalize this system of de facto censorship and prior restraint because they believed it was necessary for the continued success of their business. The economic threat of a national boycott during the worst years of the Depression was real, and the film industry, which depends on pleasing a mass audience, could not afford to ignore public opinion. Producers found, moreover, that they could use the code to increase the efficiency of production. By rigidly prescribing and proscribing the kinds of behaviour that could be shown or described on the screen, the code could be used as a scriptwriter's blueprint. A love story, for example, could only move in one direction (toward marriage), adultery and crime could have only one conclusion (disease or horrible death), dialogue in all situations had well-defined parameters, and so forth. The code, in other words, provided a framework for the construction of screenplays and enabled studios to streamline what had always been (and still is) one of the most difficult and yet most essential tasks in the production process—the creation of filmable continuity scripts. Finally, the Depression was a time of open political anti-Semitism in the United States and the men who controlled the American motion-picture industry were all Jewish; it was not a propitious moment for them to antagonize their predominantly non-Jewish audience.

Between 1930 and 1945, the studio system produced more than 7,500 features, every stage of which, from conception through exhibition, was carefully controlled. Among these assembly-line productions are some of the most important American films ever made, the work of gifted directors who managed to transcend the mechanistic nature of the system to produce work of unique personal vision. These directors include Josef von Sternberg, whose exotically stylized films starring Marlene Dietrich (*Shanghai Express,* 1932; *The Scarlet Empress,* 1934) constitute a kind of painting with light; John Ford, whose vision of history as moral truth produced such mythic works as *Stagecoach* (1939), *Young Mr. Lincoln* (1939), *The Grapes of Wrath* (1940), *My Darling Clementine* (1946), and *She Wore a Yellow Ribbon* (1949); Howard Hawks, a master of genres and the architect of a tough, functional "American" style of narrative exemplified in his films *Scarface* (1932), *Twentieth Century, Only Angels Have Wings* (1939), and *The Big Sleep* (1946); British émigré Alfred Hitchcock, whose films appealed to the popular audience as suspense melodramas but were in fact abstract visual psychodramas of guilt and spiritual terror (*Rebecca,* 1940; *Suspicion,* 1941; *Shadow of a Doubt,* 1943; *Notorious,* 1946); and Frank Capra, whose cheerful screwball comedies (*It Happened One Night*) and populist fantasies of good will (*Mr. Smith Goes to Washington,* 1939) sometimes gave way to darker warnings against losing faith and integrity (*It's a Wonderful Life,* 1946). Other significant directors with less consistent thematic or visual styles were William Wyler (*Wuthering Heights,* 1939; *The Little Foxes,* 1941), George Cukor (*Camille,* 1936; *The Philadelphia Story,* 1940), Leo McCarey (*The Awful Truth,* 1937; *Going My Way,* 1944), Preston Sturges (*Sullivan's Travels,* 1941; *The Miracle of Morgan's Creek,* 1944), and George Stevens (*Gunga Din,* 1939; *Woman of the Year,* 1942).

Lauren Bacall and Humphrey Bogart in Howard Hawks's *The Big Sleep* (1946), based on the Raymond Chandler novel and adapted for the screen by William Faulkner.

Welles's innovations in *Citizen Kane*

The most extraordinary film to emerge from the studio system, however, was Orson Welles's *Citizen Kane* (1941), whose controversial theme and experimental technique combined to make it a classic. The first of six films Welles had contracted to produce for RKO with his Mercury Theater radio ensemble company, *Citizen Kane* made radically innovative use of sound and deep-focus photography as it examined the life of Charles Foster Kane, a character based on the press baron William Randolph Hearst. The film employs a complicated flashback structure in which Kane's friends and associates give their accounts of the man after his death, paradoxically revealing not greatness or might but pathetic insecurity and emptiness. In creating this portrait of a powerful American who could bend international politics to his will but never fathom human love, Welles stretched the technology of image and sound recording beyond its contemporary limits. Using a newly available Eastman film stock with increased sensitivity to light, plastic-coated wide-angle lenses opened to smaller than normal apertures, and high-intensity arc lamps, cinematographer Gregg Toland achieved a photographic depth of field that approximated the perceptual range of the human eye and enabled Welles to place the film's characters in several different planes of depth within a single scene. These deep-focus sequence shots are complemented throughout the film by the techniques of ambient and directional sound that Welles had learned from radio. Most important of all, the resonance of the film's narrative matches the technical brilliance of its presentation, functioning on several levels at once, the historical, the psychological, and the mythic. Although recognized by many critics as a work of genius, *Citizen Kane* was a financial failure on its release, and Welles directed only three other films under his RKO contract. *Citizen Kane* remains, nevertheless, one of the most influential films ever made and is widely considered to be one of the greatest.

European conversion to sound

International cinema. Having created large new markets for their sound recording technologies in the United States, Western Electric and RCA were anxious to do the same abroad. Their objective coincided with the desire of the major American film studios to extend their control of the international motion-picture industry. Accordingly, the studios began to export sound films in late 1928, and ERPI and RCA began installing their equipment in European theatres at the same time. Exhibitors in the

United Kingdom converted the most rapidly, with 22 percent wired for sound in 1929 and 63 percent by the end of 1932. Continental exhibitors converted more slowly, largely because of a bitter patents war between the German cartel Tobis-Klangfilm, which controlled the European rights to sound-on-film technology, and Western Electric. The dispute was finally resolved at the 1930 German-American Film Conference in Paris, where Tobis, ERPI, and RCA agreed to pool their patents and divide the world market among themselves. The language problem also delayed the conversion to sound on the Continent. Because dubbing was all but impossible in the earliest years of the transition, films had to be shot in several different languages (sometimes featuring a different cast for each version) at the time of production in order to receive wide international distribution. Paramount therefore built a huge studio in the Paris suburb of Joinville in 1930 to mass-produce multilingual films. The other major American studios quickly followed suit, making the region a factory for the round-the-clock production of movies in as many as 15 separate languages. By the end of 1931, however, the technique of dubbing had been sufficiently perfected to replace multilingual production, and Joinville was converted into a dubbing centre for all of Europe.

Great Britain. Because of the lack of a language barrier, the United Kingdom became Hollywood's first major foreign market for sound films. The British motion-picture industry was protected from complete American domination, however, by the Cinematograph Films Act passed by Parliament in 1927. The act required that a certain minimum proportion of the films exhibited in British theatres be of domestic origin. Although most of the films made to fulfill this condition were low-budget, low-standard productions known as "quota quickies," the British cinema produced many important film artists (most of whom were soon lured to Hollywood). One of the first major British talents to emerge after the introduction of sound was Hitchcock, who directed a series of stylish thrillers for British International Pictures and Gaumont British, before he moved to Hollywood in 1939. His first sound film, *Blackmail* (1929), marked the effective beginning of sound production in England. The film was already in production as a silent when the director was ordered to make it as a "part-talkie." It was especially noted for the expressive use of both naturalistic and nonnaturalistic sound, which became a distinguishing feature of Hitchcock's later British triumphs (*The Man Who Knew Too Much,* 1934; *The Thirty-Nine Steps,* 1935; *Sabotage,* 1936), as well as of the films of his American career. Among the significant British filmmakers who remained based in London were the Hungarian-born brothers Alexander, Zoltán, and Vincent Korda, who founded London Films in 1932 and collaborated on some of England's most spectacular pre-World War II productions (*e.g., The Private Life of Henry VIII; Rembrandt; Elephant Boy,* 1937; *The Four Feathers,* 1939), and John Grierson, who produced such outstanding documentaries as Robert Flaherty's *Industrial Britain* (1933) and Basil Wright's *Song of Ceylon* (1935) for the Empire Marketing Board Film Unit and its successor, the General Post Office (GPO) Film Unit.

"Quota quickies"

France. In France during the 1920s, as a result of the post-World War I decline of the Pathé and Gaumont film companies, a large number of small studios had leased their facilities to independent companies, which were often formed to produce a single film. This method of film production had lent itself readily to experimentation, encouraging the development of the avant-garde film movement known as Impressionism (led by Germaine Dulac, Jean Epstein, Marcel L'Herbier, and Fernand Léger) and the innovative films of Abel Gance (*La Roue,* 1923; *Napoléon vu par Abel Gance,* 1927) and Dmitri Kirsanoff (*Ménilmontant,* 1926). Because the French film industry had evolved no marketable technology for sound recording, however, the coming of sound left producers and exhibitors alike vulnerable to the American production companies at Joinville and to the German Tobis-Klangfilm, which had been purchasing large studios in the Paris suburb of Epinay since 1929. In the face of this threat, the French industry attempted to regroup itself around what was left of the Pathé and Gaumont empires, forming two consortia—Pathé-Natan and Gaumont-Franco-Film-Aubert—for the production and distribution of sound films. Although neither group was financially successful, they seem to have created an unprecedented demand for French-language films about French subjects, reinvigorating the country's cinema. Between 1928 and 1938, French film production doubled from 66 to 122 features, and in terms of box-office receipts, the French audience was considered to be second only to the American one. By 1937–38 French cinema had become the most critically acclaimed in the world, leading export markets in every industrial nation in the West.

The rise of French cinema

Many filmmakers contributed to the prominence of French cinema during the 1930s, but the three most important were René Clair, Jean Vigo, and Jean Renoir. Clair was a former avant-gardist whose contributions to the aesthetics of sound, although not so crucial as Hitchcock's, were nevertheless significant. His *Sous les toits de Paris* (1930), frequently hailed as the first artistic triumph of the sound film, was a lively musical comedy that mixed asynchronous sound with a bare minimum of dialogue. Clair used the same technique in *Le Million* (1931), which employed a wide range of dynamic contrapuntal effects. *À nous la liberté* (*Liberty Is Ours,* 1931) was loosely based on the life of Charles Pathé and dealt with more serious themes of industrial alienation, although it still used the musical-comedy form. The film's intelligence, visual stylization, and brilliant use of asynchronous sound made it a classic of the transitional period.

Vigo completed only two features before his early death: *Zéro de conduite* (*Zero for Conduct,* 1933) and *L'Atalante* (1934). Both are lyrical films about individuals in revolt against social reality. Their intensely personal nature is thought to have influenced the style of poetic realism that characterized French cinema from 1934 to 1940 and that is exemplified by Jacques Feyder's *Pension mimosas* (1935), Julien Duvivier's *Pépé le Moko* (1937), and Marcel Carné's *Quai des brumes* (*Port of Shadows,* 1938) and *Le Jour se lève* (*Daybreak,* 1939). Darkly poetic, these films were characterized by a brooding pessimism that reflected the French public's despair over the failure of the Popular Front movement of 1935–37 and the seeming inevitability of war.

Jean Renoir, the son of the Impressionist painter Pierre-Auguste Renoir, made nine films before he directed the grimly realistic *La Chienne* (*The Bitch,* 1931) and *La Nuit du carrefour* (*Night at the Crossroads,* 1932), his first important essays in sound. Renoir subsequently demonstrated a spirit of increasing social concern in such films as *Boudu sauvé des eaux* (*Boudu Saved from Drowning,* 1932), a comic assault on bourgeois values; *Toni* (1934), a realistic story of Italian immigrant workers; *Le Crime de Monsieur Lange* (*The Crime of Monsieur Lange,* 1935), a political parable about the need for collective action against capitalist corruption; and *La Vie est à nous* (*Life Is Ours,* 1936), a propaganda film for the French Communist Party that contains both fictional and documentary footage. The strength of his commitment is most clearly expressed, however, by the eloquent appeal he makes for human understanding in his two pre-World War II masterworks. *La Grande Illusion* (*Grand Illusion,* 1937), set in a World War I prison camp, portrays a civilization on the brink of collapse due to national and class antagonisms; in its assertion of the primacy of human relationships and the utter futility of war (the "grand illusion"), the film stands as one of the greatest antiwar statements ever made. In *La Règle du jeu* (*Rules of the Game,* 1939), set in contemporary France, the breakdown of civilization has already occurred. European society is shown to be an elegant but brittle fabrication in which feeling and substance have been replaced by "manners," a world in which "the terrible thing," to quote the protagonist Octave (played by Renoir), "is that everyone has his reasons." In both films Renoir continued his earlier experiments with directional sound and deep-focus composition. His technical mastery came to influence the American cinema when he emigrated to the United States to escape the Nazis in 1940.

Renoir's social concern

Germany. Because of its ownership of the Tobis-Klang-

Early German sound films

film patents, the German film industry found itself in a position of relative strength in the early years of sound, and it produced several important films during that period, including Sternberg's *Der blaue Engel* (*The Blue Angel,* 1930), Pabst's two antiwar films, *Westfront 1918* (1930) and *Kameradschaft* (1931), and his adaptation of Bertolt Brecht's *Die Dreigroschenoper* (*The Threepenny Opera,* 1931). The most influential of the early German sound films, however, was Lang's *M* (1931), which utilized a dimension of aural imagery to counterpoint its visuals in the manner of Hitchcock's *Blackmail. M* has no musical score but makes expressive use of nonnaturalistic sound, as when the child murderer (played by Peter Lorre) is heard to whistle a recurring theme from Grieg's *Peer Gynt* before committing his crimes offscreen.

German cinema became moribund after Hitler took power in 1933, primarily because Goebbels encouraged filmmakers to produce trivial and escapist entertainment rather than more meaningful or thought-provoking fare. One director who did create films of undeniable artistic quality under Goebbels' regime was Leni Riefenstahl. She made striking use of asynchronous sound and montage in two propaganda epics commissioned by Hitler, *Triumph des Willens* (*Triumph of the Will,* 1935) and *Olympische Spiele 1936* (1938). A similar situation existed in Mussolini's Italy, where Fascist censorship mandated the production of *telefono bianco,* or "white telephone" films (lightweight romantic comedies with glamorous studio sets), and occasional nationalist propaganda, although Mussolini did establish a national film school (the Centro Sperimentale di Cinematografia, 1935) and a huge new studio complex (Cinecittà, 1937) in Rome.

Soviet Union. Although the Soviet engineers P.G. Tager and A.F. Shorin had designed optical sound systems as early as 1927, neither was workable until 1929. Sound was slow in coming to the Soviet Union: most Soviet transitional films were technically inferior to those of the West, and Soviet filmmakers continued to make silent films until the mid-30s. As in Germany and Italy, however, sound reemphasized film's propaganda value, and through the authoritarian government's policy of socialist realism the Soviet cinema became an instrument of mass indoctrination as never before. The filmmakers most affected by the new policy were the great montage artists of the 1920s. Each of them made admirable attempts to experiment with sound—Kuleshov's *The Great Consoler* (1933), Vertov's *Symphony of the Donbas* (1931) and *Three Songs About Lenin* (1934), Eisenstein's *Bezhin Meadow* (1935; terminated by Shumyatsky in mid-production), Pudovkin's *A Simple Case* (1932) and *Deserter* (1933), and Dovzhenko's *Ivan* (1932)—but their work was ultimately suppressed or defamed by the party bureaucracy. Only Eisenstein was powerful enough to reassert his genius: in the nationalistic epic *Alexander Nevsky* (1938), whose contrapuntal sound track is a classic of its kind, and in the operatically stylized *Ivan the Terrible, Parts I and II* (1944–46), a veiled critique of Stalin's autocracy. Most of the films produced at the time were propaganda glorifying national heroes (Sergey and Georgy Vasiliev's *Chapayev,* 1934; Vladimir Petrov's *Peter the First, Parts I and II,* 1937–39), literary adaptations (Mark Donskoy's Gorky trilogy: *The Childhood of Maxim Gorky,* 1938; *My Apprenticeship,* 1939; and *My Universities,* 1940), or escapist, Hollywood-style musicals (Grigory Aleksandrov's *Jazz Comedy,* 1934).

Japanese conversion to sound

Japan. In Japan, as in the Soviet Union, the conversion to sound was a slow process: in 1932 only 45 of 400 features were made with sound, and silent films continued to be produced in large numbers until 1937. The main reason for the slow conversion was that Japanese motion pictures had "talked" since their inception through the mediation of a *benshi,* a commentator who stood to the side of the screen and narrated the action for the audience in the manner of Kabuki theatre. The arrival of recorded sound liberated the Japanese cinema from its dependence on live narrators and was resisted by the *benshi,* many of whom were stars in their own right and possessed considerable box-office appeal. In the end, however, Japan's conversion to sound was complete.

As in the United States, the introduction of sound enabled the major Japanese film companies (Nikkatsu, founded 1912; Shochiku, 1920; and Toho, *c.* 1935) to acquire smaller companies and form vertical monopolies controlling production, distribution, and exhibition. Production procedures were standardized and structured for the mass production of motion pictures, and the studios increased their efficiency by specializing in either *jidai-geki,* period films set before 1868 (the year marking the beginning of the Meiji Restoration, 1868–1912, and the abolition of the feudal shogunate), or *gendai-geki,* films of contemporary life, set any time thereafter. Although, as a matter of geopolitical circumstance, there was hardly any export market for Japanese films prior to World War II, the domestic popularity of sound films enabled the Japanese motion-picture industry to become one of the most prolific in the world, releasing 400 films annually to the nation's 2,500 theatres. Most of these films had no purpose other than entertainment, but in the late 1930s, as the government became increasingly expansionist and militaristic, Japan's major directors turned to works of social criticism called "tendency" films, such as Ozu Yasujirō's *The Only Son* and Mizoguchi Kenji's *Osaka Elegy* and *Sisters of the Gion* (all 1936). In response the government imposed a strict code of censorship that was retained throughout the war.

India. In India, sound created a major industrial boom by reviving a popular 19th-century theatrical form: the folk-music drama based on centuries-old religious myths. Despite the fact that films had to be produced in as many as 10 regional languages, the popularity of these "all-talking, all-singing, all-dancing" mythologicals or historicals played an enormous role in winning acceptance for sound throughout the subcontinent and in encouraging the growth of the Indian film industry. An average of 230 features were released per year throughout the 1930s, almost all for domestic consumption.

THE WAR YEARS AND POST-WORLD WAR II TRENDS

Decline of the Hollywood studios. During the U.S. involvement in World War II, the Hollywood film industry cooperated closely with the government to support its war-aims information campaign. Following the declaration of war on Japan, the government created a Bureau of Motion Picture Affairs to coordinate the production of entertainment features with patriotic, morale-boosting themes and messages about the "American way of life," the nature of the enemy and the allies, civilian responsibility on the home front, and the fighting forces themselves. Initially unsophisticated vehicles for xenophobia and jingoism with titles like *The Devil with Hitler* and *Blondie for Victory* (both 1942), Hollywood's wartime films became increasingly serious as the war dragged on (Lang's *Hangmen Also Die,* Renoir's *This Land Is Mine,* Tay Garnett's *Bataan,* all 1943; Delmer Daves's *Destination Tokyo,* 1944; Hitchcock's *Lifeboat,* 1944; Milestone's *The Purple Heart,* 1944; *A Walk in the Sun,* 1946). In addition to commercial features, several Hollywood directors produced documentaries for government and military agencies. Among the best-known of these films, which were designed to explain the war to both servicemen and civilians, are Frank Capra's seven-part series *Why We Fight* (1942–44), William Wyler's *The Memphis Belle* (1944), John Ford's *The Battle of Midway* (1942), and John Huston's *The Battle of San Pietro* (1944). The last three were shot on location and were made especially effective by their immediacy.

When World War II ended, the American film industry seemed to be in an ideal position. Full-scale mobilization had ended the Depression domestically, and victory had opened vast, unchallenged markets in the war-torn economies of western Europe and Japan. Furthermore, from 1942 through 1945, Hollywood had experienced the most stable and lucrative three years in its history, and in 1946, when two-thirds of the American population went to the movies at least once a week, the studios earned record-breaking profits. The euphoria ended quickly, however, as inflation and labour unrest boosted domestic production costs and as important foreign markets, including Britain and Italy, were temporarily lost to protectionist quotas.

The Paramount decrees

The industry was more severely weakened in 1948, when a federal antitrust suit against the five major and three minor studios ended in the "Paramount decrees," which forced the studios to divest themselves of their theatre chains and mandated competition in the exhibition sector for the first time in 30 years. Finally, the advent of network television broadcasting in the 1940s provided Hollywood with its first real competition for American leisure time by offering consumers "movies in the home."

The American film industry's various problems and the nation's general postwar disillusionment generated several new film types in the late 1940s. Although the studios continued to produce traditional genre films, such as westerns and musicals, their financial difficulties encouraged them to make realistic, small-scale dramas rather than fantastic, lavish epics. Instead of depending on spectacle and special effects to create excitement, the new lower-budget films tried to develop thought-provoking or perverse stories reflecting the psychological and social problems besetting returning war veterans and and others adapting to postwar life. Some of the American cinema's grimmest and most naturalistic films were produced during this period, including those of the so-called social consciousness cycle, which attempted to deal realistically with such endemic problems as racism (Elia Kazan's *Gentleman's Agreement,* 1947; Alfred Werker's *Lost Boundaries,* 1949), alcoholism (Stuart Heisler's *Smash-Up,* 1947), and mental illness (Anatole Litvak's *The Snake Pit,* 1948); the semidocumentary melodrama, which reconstructed true criminal cases and were often shot on location (Kazan's *Boomerang,* 1947; Henry Hathaway's *Kiss of Death,* 1947); and the *film noir,* whose dark, fatalistic interpretations of contemporary American reality are unique in the industry's history (Tay Garnett's *The Postman Always Rings Twice,* 1946; Welles's *The Lady from Shanghai,* 1948; Jacques Tourneur's *Out of the Past,* 1947; Abraham Polonsky's *Force of Evil,* 1948).

Hollywood blacklisting

Film content was next influenced strongly by the fear of Communism that pervaded the United States during the late 1940s and early '50s. Anti-Communist "witch-hunts" began in Hollywood in 1947 when the House Un-American Activities Committee (HUAC) decided to investigate Communist influence in motion pictures. More than 100 witnesses, including many of Hollywood's most talented and popular artists, were called before the committee to answer questions about their own and their associates' alleged Communist affiliations. On Nov. 24, 1947, a group of eight screenwriters and two directors, later known as the Hollywood Ten, were sentenced to serve up to a year in prison for refusing to testify. That evening the members of the Association of Motion Picture Producers, which included the leading studio heads, published what became known as the Waldorf Declaration, in which they fired the members of the Hollywood Ten and expressed their support of HUAC. The studios, afraid to antagonize already shrinking audiences, then initiated an unofficial policy of blacklisting, refusing to employ any person even suspected of having Communist associations. Hundreds of people were fired from the industry, and many creative artists were never able to work in Hollywood again. Throughout the blacklisting era, filmmakers refrained from making any but the most conservative motion pictures; controversial topics or new ideas were carefully avoided. The resulting creative stagnation, combined with financial difficulties, contributed significantly to the demise of the studio system, although, paradoxically, the actions that the studios took between 1952 and 1965, including the practice of blacklisting, can be viewed as an attempt to halt the industry's decline.

The film industry's reaction to television

The film industry believed that the greatest threat to its continued success was posed by the television industry, especially in light of the Paramount decrees. The studios seemed to be losing their control of the nation's theatres at the same time that exhibitors were losing their audiences to television. The studios therefore attempted to diminish television's appeal by exploiting the two obvious advantages that film enjoyed over the new medium—the size of its images and, at a time when all television broadcasting was in black and white, the ability to produce photographic colour. (In the 1952–53 season, the ability to produce multiple-track stereophonic sound joined this list.) In the late 1940s, less than 12 percent of Hollywood features were produced in colour, primarily because of the expense of three-strip Technicolor filming. In 1950, however, a federal consent decree dissolved the Technicolor Corporation's de facto monopoly on the process, and Kodak simultaneously introduced a new multilayered film stock in which emulsions sensitive to the red, green, and blue parts of the spectrum were bonded together on a single roll. Patented as Eastmancolor, this "integral tripack" process offered excellent colour resolution at a low cost because it could be used with conventional cameras. Its availability hastened the industry's conversion to full colour production. By 1954 more than 50 percent of American features were made in colour, and the figure reached 94 percent by 1970.

The aspect ratio (the ratio of width to height) of the projected motion-picture image had been standardized at 1.33 to 1 since 1932, but as television eroded the film industry's domestic audience, the studios increased screen size as a way of attracting audiences back into theatres. For both optical and architectural reasons this change in size usually meant increased width, not increased height. Early experiments with multiple-camera wide-screen (Cinerama, 1952) and stereoscopic 3-D (Natural Vision, 1952) provoked audience interest, but it was an anamorphic process called CinemaScope that prompted the wide-screen revolution. Introduced by 20th Century-Fox in the biblical epic *The Robe* (1953), CinemaScope used an anamorphic lens to squeeze a wide-angle image onto conventional 35-millimetre film stock and a similar lens to restore the image's original width in projection. CinemaScope's aspect ratio was 2.55 to 1, and the system had the great advantage of requiring no special cameras, film stock, or projectors. By the end of 1954, every Hollywood studio but Paramount had leased a version of the process from Fox (Paramount adopted a nonanamorphic process called VistaVision that exposed double-frame images by running film through special cameras and projectors horizontally rather than vertically), and many studios were experimenting with wide-gauge film systems (*e.g.,* Todd-AO, 1955; Panavision-70, 1960) that required special equipment but eliminated the distortion inherent in the anamorphic process.

Like the coming of sound, the conversion to wide-screen formats produced an initial regression as filmmakers learned how to compose and edit their images for the new elongated frame. Sound had promoted the rise of aurally intensive genres such as the musical and the gangster film, and the wide-screen format similarly created a bias in favour of visually spectacular subjects and epic scale. The emergence of the three-to-four hour wide-screen "blockbuster" in such films as *War and Peace, Around the World in Eighty Days,* and *The Ten Commandments* in 1956 coincided with the era's affinity for safe and sanitized material. Given the political paranoia of the times, few subjects could be treated seriously, and the studios concentrated on presenting traditional genre fare—westerns, musicals, comedies, and blockbusters—suitable for wide-screen treatment. Only a director like Hitchcock, whose style was oblique and imagist, could prosper in such a climate. He produced his greatest work during the period, much of it in VistaVision (*Rear Window,* 1954; *The Man Who Knew Too Much,* 1956; *Vertigo,* 1958; *North by Northwest,* 1959; *Psycho,* 1960; *The Birds,* 1963).

In spite of the major film companies' elaborate strategies of defense, they continued to decline throughout the 1950s and '60s. Because they could no longer dominate the exhibition sector, they faced serious competition for the first time from independent and foreign filmmakers. "Runaway" productions (films made away from the studios, frequently abroad, to take advantage of lower costs) became common, and the Production Code was dissolved as a series of federal court decisions between 1952 and 1958 extended First Amendment protection to motion pictures. As their incomes shrank, the major companies' vast studios and backlots became liabilities that ultimately crippled them. The minor companies, however, owned modest studio facilities and had lost nothing by the Paramount decrees because they controlled no theatres. They were thus able to prosper during this era, eventually becoming major companies themselves in the 1970s.

Italian Neorealist movement

International cinema. *Italy.* World War II physically and economically devastated the film industries of the Soviet Union, Japan, and most of the European nations. Italy's early surrender, however, left its facilities relatively intact, enabling the Italian cinema to lead the post-World War II film renaissance with its development of the Neorealist movement. Although it had roots in both Soviet expressive realism and French poetic realism, Neorealism was decidedly national in focus, taking as its subject the day-to-day reality of a country traumatized by political upheaval and war.

Most of the major figures in the Neorealist movement had studied at Mussolini's Centro Sperimentale, but they vigorously rejected the stagy, artificial style associated with the *telefono bianco* films in favour of a Marxist aesthetic of everyday life. The first identifiable Neorealist film was Luchino Visconti's *Ossessione* (*Obsession,* 1942), a bleak contemporary melodrama shot on location in the countryside around Ferrara. It was suppressed by the Fascist censors, however, so that international audiences were first introduced to the movement through Roberto Rossellini's *Roma, città aperta* (*Open City,* 1945), which was shot on location in the streets of Rome only two months after Italy's surrender. The film featured both professional and nonprofessional actors and focused on ordinary people caught up in contemporary events. Its documentary texture, postrecorded sound track, and improvisational quality became the hallmark of the Neorealist movement. Rossellini followed it with *Paisà* (*Paisan,* 1946) and *Germania, anno zero* (*Germany, Year Zero,* 1947) to complete his "war trilogy." Visconti's second contribution to Neorealism was *La terra trema* (*The Earth Trembles,* 1948), an epic of peasant life that was shot on location in a Sicilian fishing village. In many respects it is more exemplary of the movement than *Ossessione* and is widely regarded as a masterpiece. Neorealism's third major director was Vittorio De Sica, who worked in close collaboration with scriptwriter Cesare Zavattini, the movement's major theorist and spokesman. De Sica's films sometimes tend toward sentimentality but in *Sciuscià* (*Shoeshine,* 1946), *Ladri di biciclette* (*Bicycle Thieves,* 1948), and *Umberto D.* (1952), he produced works central to the movement.

By courtesy of the Museum of Modern Art/Film Stills Archive, New York City

Lamberto Maggiorani and Enzo Staiola as the father and son in Vittorio De Sica's *Bicycle Thieves* (1948).

Influence of Neorealism

Neorealism was the first postwar cinema to reject Hollywood's narrative conventions and studio production techniques, and, as such, it had enormous influence on future movements like British "social realism," Brazilian *Cinema Nôvo,* and the French and Czech New Wave. It also heralded the practices of shooting on location using natural lighting and postsynchronizing sound that later became standard in the film industry. Despite its influence, in the 1950s Neorealism disappeared as a distinct national movement, together with the socioeconomic context that had produced it, as the the Marshall Plan began to work its "economic miracle" in Europe. Italian cinema remained prominent nevertheless through the films of several gifted directors who began their careers as Neorealists and went on to produce their major work during the 1960s and '70s.

Federico Fellini had worked as a scriptwriter for Rossellini before directing in the 1950s an impressive series of films whose form was Neorealist but whose content was allegorical (*I vitelloni* [*The Loafers*], 1953; *La strada* [*The Road*], 1954; *Le notti di Cabiria* [*Nights of Cabiria*], 1956). During the 1960s Fellini's work became increasingly surrealistic (*La dolce vita* [*The Sweet Life*], 1960; *Otto e mezzo* [$8^{1}/_{2}$], 1963; *Giulietta degli spiriti* [*Juliet of the Spirits*], 1965; *Fellini Satyricon,* 1969), and by the 1970s he was perceived to be a flamboyant ironic fantasist—a reputation that sustained him through such serious and successful films as *Fellini Roma* (1972), *Amarcord* (1974), and *E la nave va* (*And the Ship Sails On,* 1983).

Michelangelo Antonioni had also collaborated with Rossellini. Accordingly, his first films were Neorealist documentary shorts (*Gente del Po* [*People of the Po*], 1947), but during the 1950s he turned increasingly to an examination of the Italian bourgeoisie in such films as *Cronaca di un amore* (*Story of a Love Affair,* 1950), *La signora senza camelie* (*Camille Without Camellias,* 1953), and *Le amiche* (*The Girlfriends,* 1955), and in the early 1960s Antonioni produced a trilogy on the malaise of the middle class that made him internationally famous. In *L'avventura* (*The Adventure,* 1959), *La notte* (*The Night,* 1960), and *L'eclisse* (*The Eclipse,* 1962), he used long-take sequence shots equating film time with real time to create a vision of the reverberating emptiness of modern urban life. Antonioni then began to use colour expressionistically in *Deserto rosso* (*Red Desert,* 1964) and *Blow-Up* (1966) to convey alienation and abstraction from human feeling, and all of his later works in some way concerned the breakdown of personal relationships (*Zabriskie Point,* 1970; *Identificazione di una donna* [*Identification of a Woman*], 1982) and of identity itself (*The Passenger,* 1975).

While Fellini and Antonioni were putting Italy in the vanguard of modernist cinema, the country's second post-World War II generation of directors emerged. Ermanno Olmi (*Il posto* [*The Job*], 1961; *Un certo giorno* [*One Fine Day*], 1968; *L'albero degli zoccoli* [*The Tree of Wooden Clogs*], 1979) continued the Neorealist tradition in his tales of ordinary people caught up in systems beyond their comprehension. Pier Paolo Pasolini, who had worked as a scriptwriter for Fellini, achieved international recognition for *Il vangelo secondo Matteo* (*The Gospel According to St. Matthew,* 1964), a brilliant semidocumentary reconstruction of the life of Christ with Marxist overtones. Pasolini went on to direct a series of astonishing, often outrageous films that set forth a Marxist interpretation of history and myth—*Edipo re* (*Oedipus Rex,* 1967), *Teorema* (*Theorem,* 1968), *Porcile* (*Pigsty,* 1969), *Medea* (1969), *Salò* (1975)—before his murder in 1975. Like Pasolini, Bernardo Bertolucci is a Marxist intellectual whose films attempt to correlate sexuality, ideology, and history; his most successful films have been *Il conformista* (*The Conformist,* 1970), a striking dissection of the psychopathology of fascism, *Ultimo tango a Parigi* (*Last Tango in Paris,* 1972), a meditation on sex and death, and *Novecento* (*1900,* 1976), a six-hour epic covering 50 years of Italian class conflict. Other important Italian filmmakers have included Francesco Rosi (*Salvatore Giuliano,* 1962), Marco Bellocchio (*La Cina è vicina* [*China Is Near*], 1967), Marco Ferreri (*La Grande Bouffe* [*Blow-Out*], 1973), Ettore Scola (*Una giornata speciale* [*A Special Day*], 1977), Paolo and Vittorio Taviani (*Padre padrone* [*Father, Master*], 1977), Franco Brusati (*Dimenticare Venezia* [*To Forget Venice*], 1979), and Lina Wertmüller (*Pasqualino settebellezze* [*Seven Beauties*], 1976).

France. French cinema of the Occupation and postwar era produced many fine films (Marcel Carné's *Les Enfants du paradis* [*The Children of Paradise*], 1945; Jean Cocteau's *La Belle et la bête* [*Beauty and the Beast*], 1946; René Clément's *Jeux interdits* [*Forbidden Games*], 1952; Jacques Becker's *Casque d'or* [*Golden Helmet*], 1952; Henri-Georges Clouzot's *Le Salaire de la peur* [*The Wages of Fear*], 1953), but their mode of presentation relied heavily on script and was predominantly literary. There were exceptions in the austere classicism of Robert Bresson (*Le Journal d'un curé de campagne* [*The Diary of a Country Priest*], 1950; *Un Condamné à mort s'est échappé* [*A Man Escaped*], 1956), the absurdist comedy of Jacques Tati (*Les Vacances de M. Hulot* [*Mr. Hulot's Holiday*], 1953; *Mon oncle* [*My Uncle*], 1958), and the lush, magnificently stylized masterworks of the German émigré Max Ophüls, whose *La Ronde* (1950), *Le Plaisir* (1952), *Madame de . . .* (1953), and *Lola Montès* (1955) represent significant contributions to world cinema. An independent documentary movement, which produced such landmark nonfiction films as Georges Rouquier's *Farrebique* (1948), Georges Franju's *Le Sang des bêtes* (*The Blood of the Beasts,* 1949), and Alain Resnais's *Nuit et brouillard* (*Night and Fog,* 1956), also emerged at this time. It provided a training-ground for young directors outside the traditional industry system and influenced the independent production style of the movement that culminated the French postwar period of renewal—the *nouvelle vague,* or New Wave movement.

French New Wave movement

The most important source of the New Wave lay in the theoretical writings of Alexandre Astruc and, more prominently, of André Bazin, whose thought molded an entire generation of filmmakers, critics, and scholars. In 1948 Astruc formulated the concept of the *caméra-stylo* ("camera-pen"), in which film was regarded as a form of audiovisual language and the filmmaker, therefore, as a kind of writer in light. Bazin's influential journal *Cahiers du Cinéma,* founded in 1951, elaborated this notion and became the headquarters of a group of young *cinéphiles* ("film-lovers")—the critics François Truffaut, Jean-Luc Godard, Claude Chabrol, Jacques Rivette, and Eric Rohmer—who were to become the major directors of the New Wave. Bazin's basic principle was a rejection of montage aesthetics—both radical Eisensteinian cutting and Hollywood-style continuity, or invisible, editing—in favour of the long take and composition in depth, or what he called mise-en-scène. Borrowed from the theatre, this term literally means "the placing in the scene," but Bazin used it to designate such elements of filmic structure as camera placement and movement, the lighting of shots, and blocking of action—that is, everything that precedes the editing process.

The *Cahiers* critics embraced mise-en-scène aesthetics and borrowed the idea of authorship from Astruc. In proposing *la politique des auteurs* ("the policy of authors"), christened the auteur theory by the American critic Andrew Sarris, they maintained that film should be a medium of personal artistic expression and that the best films are those imprinted with their makers' individual signature. As a logical consequence of this premise, the *Cahiers* critics rejected mainstream French cinema and its "tradition of quality" in favour of the classical mise-en-scène tradition (exemplified in the films of Feuillade, Murnau, Stroheim, Renoir, Welles, Ophüls), Hollywood studio directors who had transcended the constraints of the system to make personal films (Hawks, Sternberg, Hitchcock, Ford), and the low-budget American B-film in which the director usually had total control over production.

The first films of the New Wave were independently produced dramatic shorts shot in 16-millimetre by the *Cahiers* critics in 1956–57, but 1959 was the year that brought the movement to international prominence, when each of its three major figures made their first features. Truffaut's *Les Quatre cents coups* (*The 400 Blows*), Alain Resnais's *Hiroshima, mon amour,* and Godard's *À bout de souffle* (*Breathless*) were all in their different ways paradigms of a fresh new style based on elliptical editing and location shooting with hand-held cameras. This style was both radically destructive of classical Hollywood continuity and pragmatically suited to the New Wave's need to make its films quickly and cheaply. Its ultimate effect was to deconstruct the narrative language that had evolved over the previous 60 years and to create a reflexive cinema, or meta-cinema, whose techniques provided a continuous comment on its own making.

Truffaut, Resnais, and Godard

The critical and commercial success of the first New Wave features produced an unprecedented creative explosion within the French industry. Between 1960 and 1964, literally hundreds of low-budget, stylistically experimental films were made by *cinéphiles* with little or no experience. Many of these ended in failure, and the New Wave as a collective phenomenon was over by 1965. But the three figures who had initiated the movement, and a small group of sophisticated but less spectacular talents—Claude Chabrol, Louis Malle, Eric Rohmer, Agnès Varda, Jacques Demy, and Jacques Rivette—continued to dominate French cinema until well into the 1970s.

By courtesy of Janus Films, Inc.; photograph, from the Museum of Modern Art/Film Stills Archive, New York City

Jean-Pierre Léaud as Antoine Doinel (centre) in *The 400 Blows* (1959), directed by François Truffaut.

Truffaut was the most commercially successful of the original New Wave group, and through such films as *Jules et Jim* (1961) and the autobiographical "Antoine Doinel" series, which began with *Les Quatre Cents Coups,* acquired a reputation as a romantic ironist. Truffaut's range also extended to parodies of Hollywood genres (*Tirez sur le pianiste* [*Shoot the Piano Player*], 1960), homages to Hitchcock (*La Mariée etait en noir* [*The Bride Wore Black*], 1967), historical reconstructions (*L'Enfant sauvage* [*The Wild Child*], 1970), reflexive narratives (*La Nuit américaine* [*Day for Night*], 1973), and literary adaptations (*L'Histoire d'Adèle H.* [*The Story of Adele H.*], 1975; *Le Dernier Métro* [*The Last Metro*], 1980).

Godard was the most stylistically and politically radical of the early New Wave directors. Some of his early films were parodies of Hollywood genres (*Une Femme est une femme* [*A Woman Is a Woman*], 1961; *Alphaville,* 1965; *Pierrot le fou,* 1965), but the majority treated political and social themes from a Marxist, and finally Maoist, perspective (*Le Petit Soldat* [*The Little Soldier*], 1960; *Vivre sa vie* [*My Life to Live*], 1962; *Les Carabiniers* [*The Riflemen*], 1963; *Bande à part* [*Band of Outsiders*], 1964; *Une Femme mariée* [*A Married Woman*], 1964). With *Masculin-féminin* (1966), Godard turned away from narrative toward the form of the *cinéma vérité*-style essay, and his later films became increasingly ideological and structurally random (*Made in U.S.A.,* 1966; *Deux ou trois choses que je sais d'elle* [*Two or Three Things I Know About Her*], 1967; *La Chinoise,* 1967; *Week-end,* 1967; *One Plus One,* 1968). During the 1970s, Godard made films for the radical Dziga Vertov production collective (*Pravda,* 1969; *Le Vent d'est* [*Wind from the East*], 1969; *Letter to Jane,* 1972) and experimented with combinations of film and videotape (*Numero deux* [*Number Two*], 1975; *La Communication,* 1976). In the 1980s Godard returned to theatrical filmmaking, purified of ideology but no less controversial for it, with such provocative features as *Sauve qui peut/La Vie* (*Every Man for Himself,* 1980), *Passion* (1982), and *Je vous salue, Mary* (*Hail Mary,* 1986).

Resnais was slightly older than the *Cahiers* group, but he identified with the New Wave through style and theme. His most famous film is the postmodern mystery *L'Année dernière à Marienbad* (*Last Year at Marienbad,* 1961), which questions the processes of thought and memory—central concerns in Resnais's work. *Muriel* (1963), *La Guerre est finie* (*The War Is Over,* 1966), *Stavisky* (1974), *Providence* (1977), and *Mon oncle d'Amérique* (*My Uncle in America,* 1978) are all in various ways concerned with the effects of time on human memory from both a historical and a personal perspective.

Other important New Wave figures who remain influential are Claude Chabrol, whose entire career can be seen as an extended homage to Hitchcock (*La Femme infidèle* [*Unfaithful Wife*], 1968; *Que la bête meure* [*This Man Must Die*], 1969; *Le Boucher* [*The Butcher*], 1970; *Violette Nozière,* 1978); Louis Malle, a master of film types who relocated in the United States (*Le Feu follet* [*The Fire Within*], 1963; *Le Souffle au coeur* [*Murmur of the Heart*], 1971; *Lacombe, Lucien,* 1973; *Pretty Baby,* 1978; *Atlantic City,* 1980); Eric Rohmer, whose "moral tales," including *Ma Nuit chez Maud* (*My Night at Maud's,* 1968) and *Le Genou de Claire* (*Claire's Knee,* 1970), established the ironic perspective on human passion that he maintained in such later films as *Pauline à la plage* (*Pauline at the Beach,* 1983); Agnès Varda, famed for her improvisational style (*Cléo de cinq à sept* [*Cleo from Five to Seven*], 1962; *Le Bonheur* [*Happiness*], 1965); Jacques Demy, whose best films are homages to the Hollywood musical (*Les Parapluies de Cherbourg* [*The Umbrellas of Cherbourg*], 1964; *Les Demoiselles de Rochefort* [*The Young Girls of Rochefort*], 1967); and Jaçques Rivette, the most austerely abstract and experimental of the *Cahiers* group (*La Religieuse* [*The Nun*], 1965; *L'Amour fou,* 1968; *Céline et Julie vont en bateau* [*Celine and Julie Go Boating*], 1974; *Duelle,* 1977).

Influence of the New Wave

Few national movements have influenced international cinema as strongly as the French New Wave. By promoting the concept of personal authorship, its directors demonstrated that film is an audiovisual language that can be crafted into "novels" and "essays"; and by deconstructing classical Hollywood conventions, they added dimensions to this language that made it capable of expressing a new range of internal and external states. In the process, the New Wave helped to reinvigorate such stylistically moribund cinemas as the British, West German, and American, and it created a current of "second waves" and "third waves" in the already flourishing Italian, Polish, Czech, Hungarian, and Japanese cinemas. Finally, the New Wave made France the leading centre of modernist and postmodern film and film theory, a position that it continues to hold.

Great Britain. In Great Britain the post-World War II cinema was even more literary than in France, relying heavily on the adaptation of classics in the work of such directors as Laurence Olivier (*Henry V,* 1944; *Hamlet,* 1948; *Richard III,* 1955), David Lean (*Great Expectations,* 1946; *Oliver Twist,* 1948), and Anthony Asquith (*The Importance of Being Earnest,* 1952). Even less conventional films had literary sources (Carol Reed's *Outcast of the Islands,* 1951; Michael Powell's and Emeric Pressberger's *The Red Shoes,* 1948, and *The Tales of Hoffman,* 1951). There were exceptions to this trend in a series of witty, irreverent comedies made for Michael Balcon's Ealing Studios (*The Lavender Hill Mob,* 1951; *The Man in the White Suit,* 1951; *Kind Hearts and Coronets,* 1949), most of them starring Alec Guinness, but on the whole British postwar cinema was elitist and culturally conservative.

In reaction, a younger generation of filmmakers led by Lindsay Anderson, Czechoslovak-born Karel Reisz, and Tony Richardson organized the Free Cinema movement in the mid-50s. Its purpose was to produce short, low-budget documentaries illuminating problems of contemporary life (Anderson's *O Dreamland,* 1953; Richardson's *Momma Don't Allow,* 1955). Grounded in the ideology and practice of Neorealism, Free Cinema emerged simultaneously with a larger social movement assailing the British class structure and calling for the replacement of bourgeois elitism with liberal working-class values. In the cinema this antiestablishment agitation resulted in the New Cinema or social realist movement signaled by Reisz's *Saturday Night and Sunday Morning* (1960), the first British postwar feature with a working-class protagonist and proletarian themes. Stylistically influenced by the New Wave, with which it was concurrent, the social realist film was generally shot in black and white on location in the industrial Midlands and cast with unknown young actors and actresses. Like the New Wave films, social

British social realist movement

Jean Simmons as Estella, Martita Hunt as Miss Havisham, and Anthony Wager as young Pip in David Lean's *Great Expectations* (1946).

By courtesy of the Museum of Modern Art/Film Stills Archive, New York City

realist films were independently produced on low budgets (many of them for Woodfall Film Productions, the company founded in 1958 by Richardson and playwright John Osborne to adapt the latter's *Look Back in Anger*), but their freshness of both content and form attracted an international audience. Some of the most famous were Richardson's *A Taste of Honey* (1961) and *The Loneliness of the Long Distance Runner* (1962), John Schlesinger's *A Kind of Loving* (1962) and *Billy Liar* (1963), Anderson's *This Sporting Life* (1963), and Reisz's *Morgan: A Suitable Case for Treatment* (1966).

These films and others like them brought such prestige to the British film industry that London briefly became the production capital of the Western world, delivering such homegrown international hits as Richardson's *Tom Jones* (1963), Schlesinger's *Darling* (1965), Richard Lester's two Beatles films, *A Hard Day's Night* (1964) and *Help!* (1965), Schlesinger's *Far from the Madding Crowd* (1967), and Anderson's *If. . .* (1968), as well as such foreign importations as Roman Polanski's *Repulsion* (1965) and *Cul-de-sac* (1966), Truffaut's *Farenheit 451* (1966), Antonioni's *Blow-Up* (1966), and Stanley Kubrick's *2001: A Space Odyssey* (1968) and *A Clockwork Orange* (1971). This activity inspired a new, more visually oriented generation of British filmmakers—Peter Yates, John Boorman, Ken Russell, Nicolas Roeg, and Ridley Scott—who would make their mark in the 1970s; but as England's economy began its precipitous decline during that decade, so too did its film industry. Many British directors and performers defected to Hollywood, while the English-language film market simultaneously experienced a vigorous and unprecedented challenge from Australia. In the 1980s, amid widespread speculation about the collapse of the film industry, British annual production reached an all-time low, although such works as Neil Jordan's *The Company of Wolves* (1984) and Terry Gilliam's *Brazil* (1985) demonstrated that uniquely individual films continued to be made there.

Germany. Germany's catastrophic defeat in World War II and the subsequent partitioning of the country virtually destroyed its film industry, which had already been corrupted by the Nazis. Rebuilt during the 1950s, the West German industry became the fifth largest producer in the world, but the majority of its output consisted of low-quality *Heimatfilme* ("homeland films") for the domestic market. When this market collapsed in the 1960s because of changing demographic patterns and the diffusion of television, the industry was forced to turn to the federal government for subsidies. In recognition of the crisis, 26 writers and filmmakers at the Oberhausen Film Festival in 1962 drafted a manifesto proclaiming the death of German cinema and demanding the establishment of a *junger deutscher Film,* a "young German cinema." The members of this Oberhausen group became the founders of *das neue Kino,* or New German Cinema, which was brought into being over the next decade through the establishment of the Kuratorium Junger Deutscher Film (1965; Young Ger-

New German Cinema

man Film Board, a grant agency drawing on the cultural budgets of the federal states), the Filmförderungsanstalt, or FFA (Film Subsidies Board, which makes production funds available by levying a federal tax on theatre tickets), and the independent distributing company Filmverlag der Autoren (1971; Authors' Film-Publishing Group), with additional funding from the two West German television networks.

These institutions made it possible for a new generation of German filmmakers to produce their first features and established a vital new cinema for West Germany that attempted to examine the nation's *unbewältige Vergangenheit,* or "unassimilated past." The first such films, which were deeply influenced by the New Wave, especially by the work of Godard, included Volker Schlöndorff's *Der junge Törless* (*Young Torless,* 1966) and Alexander Kluge's *Die Artisten in der Zirkuskuppel: ratlos* (*The Artists Under the Big Top: Disoriented,* 1968). In the 1970s, however, three major figures emerged as leaders of the movement—Rainer Werner Fassbinder, Werner Herzog, and Wim Wenders. Fassbinder was the most prolific, having made more than 40 features before he died in 1982. His films are also the most flamboyant. Nearly all of them take the form of extreme melodrama, ending in murder or suicide—*Warum läuft Herr R. amok?* (*Why Does Herr R. Run Amok?,* 1969), *Die bitteren Tränen der Petra von Kant* (*The Bitter Tears of Petra von Kant,* 1972), *Angst essen Seele auf* (*Fear Eats the Soul/Ali,* 1973)—and several are consciously focused on German wartime and postwar society (*Die Ehe der Maria Braun* [*The Marriage of Maria Braun*], 1979; *Lola,* 1981; *Veronika Voss,* 1982).

Herzog's films have tended more toward the mystical and the spiritual than the social, although there is nearly always some contemporary referent in his work—the image of idealism turned to barbarism in *Aguirre, der Zorn Gottes* (*Aguirre, the Wrath of God,* 1972); the hopeless inability of science to address the human condition in *Jeder für sich und Gott gegen alle* (*Every Man for Himself and God Against All/Kaspar Hauser,* 1974); the inherently destructive nature of technology in *Herz aus Glas* (*Heart of Glass,* 1977); the incomprehensible nature of pestilence in his remake of Murnau's *Nosferatu* (1979). Wenders, on the other hand, is profoundly postmodern in his contemplation of alienation through spatial metaphor. In such works of existential questing as *Die Angst des Tormanns beim Elfmeter* (*The Goalie's Anxiety at the Penalty Kick,* 1971) and *Im Lauf der Zeit* (*In the Course of Time/Kings of the Road,* 1976), he addressed the universal phenomena of dislocation and rootlessness that afflict modern society.

The state subsidy system has enabled hundreds of filmmakers, many of whom are women (*e.g.,* Margarethe von Trotta) or members of minorities, to participate in the New German Cinema. With the exception of the work of Fassbinder, Herzog, and Wenders, however, the New German Cinema has not found a large audience outside of West Germany. Yet in terms of exploring and extending the audio-language system of film, it has been to the 1970s and '80s very much what the New Wave was to the '60s, and its influence has been widely felt.

Japan. Although more than half of Japan's theatres were destroyed by American bombing during World War II, most of its studio facilities were left intact. Japan, therefore, continued to produce films in quantity during the Allied occupation (1945–52). Many traditional Japanese subjects were forbidden by the Allied Command as promoting feudalism, however, including all films classified as *jidai-geki.* Nevertheless, the film that first brought Japanese cinema to international attention belonged to that category: Kurosawa Akira's *Rashomon* (1950), which won the Golden Lion at the 1951 Venice Film Festival. The film, a meditation on the nature of truth set in the medieval past, marked the beginning of the Japanese cinema's unprecedented postwar renaissance. During this period, new export markets opened in the West, and Japanese filmmakers produced some of their finest work, winning festival awards throughout the world. Kurosawa, who was already well known in his homeland for a number of wartime and postwar genre films, became the most famous Japanese director in the West on the strength of his masterful samurai epics—*Seven Samurai* (1954), *The Throne of Blood* (1957), *The Hidden Fortress* (1958), *Yojimbo* (1961), and *Sanjuro* (1962)—which raised the *chambara,* or "sword-fight," film to the status of art. He made films in other genres, including literary adaptations (*The Idiot,* 1951; *The Lower Depths,* 1957), *gendai-geki* (*Ikiru* [*To Live/Living*], 1952; *Dodesukaden,* 1970), gangster films (*Stray Dog,* 1949; *The Bad Sleep Well,* 1960; *High and Low,* 1963), and period films that cannot be categorized at all (*Red Beard,* 1965; *Dersu Uzala,* 1975); but Kurosawa always returned to the samurai form for his most profound statements about life and art (*Kagemusha* [*The Shadow Warrior*], 1980; *Ran,* 1985).

Japanese cinema's postwar renaissance

By courtesy of Daiei Motion Picture Co.; photograph, the Museum of Modern Art/Film Stills Archive, New York City

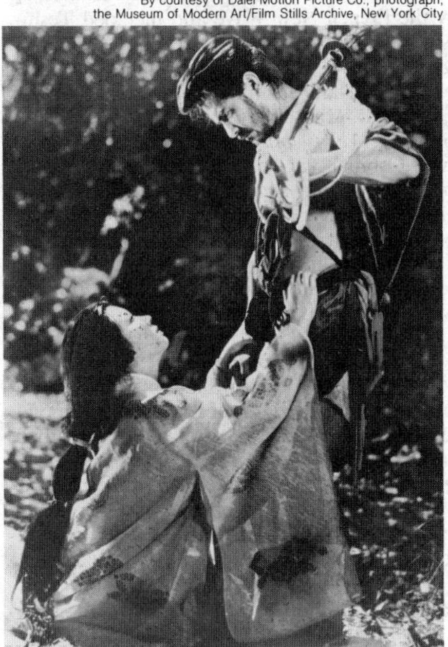

Rashomon (1950), directed by Kurosawa Akira.

Two other established directors who produced their greatest films in the postwar period were Mizoguchi Kenji and Ozu Yasujirō. Both had begun their careers in the silent era and were more traditionally Japanese in style and content than Kurosawa. Mizoguchi's films, whether period (*Sansho the Bailiff,* 1954; *Crucified Lovers,* 1954) or contemporary (*Women of the Night,* 1948; *Gion Festival Music,* 1953), were frequently critiques of feudalism that focused on the condition of women within the social order. His greatest postwar films are *The Life of Oharu* (1952), the biography of a 17th-century courtesan, and *Ugetsu* (1953), the story of two men who abandon their wives for fame and glory during the 16th-century civil wars. Both are masterworks that clearly demonstrate Mizoguchi's expressive use of luminous decor, extended long takes, and deep-focus composition. As one of the great mise-en-scène directors, Mizoguchi can be compared to Murnau, Ophüls, and Welles, but his transcendental visual style makes him unique in the history of cinema.

Ozu, too, was a stylist, but the majority of his 54 films are *shomin-geki,* a variety of *gendai* film dealing with the lives of lower-middle-class families (*The Only Son,* 1936; *There Was a Father,* 1942; *Late Spring,* 1949; *Early Summer,* 1951; *Tokyo Story,* 1953; *Early Spring,* 1956; *Tokyo Twilight,* 1957; *Equinox Flower,* 1958; *Floating Weeds,* 1959; *An Autumn Afternoon,* 1962). They are all very much alike and, in a sense, are all part of a single large film, whose subject is the ordinary lives of ordinary people and the sacred beauty therein. Ozu's minimalist style—originating in both Zen Buddhist aesthetics and the fact that most of his films were shot within the confines of a typical Japanese house—is based on his use of low-angle long takes in which the camera is positioned about three feet off the floor at the eye-level of a person seated on a tatami mat. This practice led Ozu to an especially imaginative use of offscreen space and "empty scenes."

The second postwar generation of Japanese filmmakers

was mainly composed of Kobayashi Masaki, Ichikawa Kon, and Shindo Kaneto. Kobayashi is best known for *The Human Condition* (1959–61), his three-part antiwar epic set during Japan's brutal occupation of Manchuria, the two graphic *jidai-geki Harakiri* (1962) and *Rebellion* (1967), and the beautiful ghost film *Kwaidan* (1964). Ichikawa's major works are the pacifist films *The Burmese Harp* (1956) and *Fires on the Plain* (1959) and his beautifully composed wide-screen films, *Conflagration* (1958), *The Key* (1959), and *Tokyo Olympiad* (1965). Shindo is best known for his poetic semidocumentary *The Island* (1960) and the bizarre, folkloristic *Onibaba* (1964).

The third generation of postwar directors was most active during the 1960s and '70s. The group was deeply influenced by the French New Wave and included Teshigahara Hiroshi (*Woman in the Dunes,* 1964), Masumura Yasuzo (*The Red Angel,* 1965), Imamura Shohei (*The Pornographer,* 1966), Hani Susumu (*The Inferno of First Love,* 1968), Shinoda Masahiro (*Double Suicide,* 1969), Yoshida Yoshishige (*Eros plus Massacre,* 1970), and, quintessentially, Oshima Nagisa (*The Man Who Left his Will on Film,* 1970; *In the Realm of the Senses,* 1976).

Decline of the Japanese film industry

In the mid-1960s, however, competition from multiple-channel colour television and from American distributors forced the Japanese film industry into economic decline. A decade later, two major studios were bankrupt, and film production was increasingly dominated by two domestic exploitation genres, the *yakuza-eiga,* or contemporary urban gangster film, and the semipornographic "eroduction" film, which mixed sex and sadism. During the 1980s, Japan continued to produce the highest annual volume of films of any nation in the world, but the studios remained in decline and most serious productions, such as Kurosawa's *Kagemusha,* were funded by foreign interests.

India. Serious postwar Indian cinema was for years associated with the work of Satyajit Ray, a director of singular talent who produced the great Apu trilogy (*Pather panchali* [*The Song of the Road*], 1955; *Aparajito* [*The Unvanquished*], 1956; *Apur sansar* [*The World of Apu*], 1959) under the influence of both Jean Renoir and Italian Neorealism. Ray continued to dominate the Indian cinema through the 1960s and '70s with such artful Bengali films as *Devi* (*The Goddess,* 1960), *Charulata* (*The Lonely Wife,* 1964), *Aranyer din ratri* (*Days and Nights in the Forest,* 1970), and *Ashanti sanket* (*Distant Thunder,* 1973). The Marxist intellectual Ritwik Ghatak received much less critical attention than his contemporary Ray, but through such films as *Ajantrik* (*Pathetic Fallacy,* 1958), he created a body of alternative cinema that greatly influenced the rising generation.

In 1961 the Indian government established the Film Institute of India to train aspiring directors. It also formed the Film Finance Commission (FFC) to help fund independent production (and, later, experimental films). The National Film Archive was founded in 1964. These organizations encouraged the production of such important first features as Mrinal Sen's *Bhuvan Shome* (*Mr. Shome,* 1969), Basu Chatterji's *Sara akaash* (*The Whole Sky,* 1979), Mani Kaul's *Uski roti* (*Daily Bread,* 1969), Kumar Shahani's *Maya darpan* (*Mirror of Illusion,* 1972), Avtar Kaul's *27 Down* (1973), and M.S. Sathyu's *Garam hawa* (*Scorching Wind,* 1973) and promoted the development of a nonstar "parallel cinema" centred in Bombay. A more traditional path was followed by Shyam Benegal, whose films (*Ankur* [*The Seedling*], 1974; *Nishant* [*Night's End*], 1975; *Manthan* [*The Churning*], 1976) have been relatively realistic in form and deeply committed in sociopolitical terms. During the 1970s the regional industries of the southwestern states—especially those of Kerala and Karnātaka—began to subsidize independent production, resulting in a "southern new wave" in the films of such diverse figures as G. Aravindan (*Kanchana sita* [*Golden Sita*], 1977), Adoor Gopalakrishnan (*Elipathayam* [*Rat-Trap*], 1981), and Girish Karnad (*Kaadu* [*The Forest*], 1973). Despite the international recognition these films have earned, the Indian government's efforts to raise the artistic level of the nation's cinema have been largely unsuccessful. India remains a land of some 700,000,000 people, most of them illiterate and poor, whose exclusive access to audiovisual entertainment is film; television is the medium of the rich and powerful middle class. The Indian film industry therefore continues to be the world's largest producer of low-quality films for domestic consumption, releasing 700 features per year in 16 languages.

Development of Australian cinema

Australia. Australia was a country virtually without a film industry until the late 1960s and early '70s, when the federal government established the Australian Film Development Corporation (after 1975, the Australian Film Commission) to subsidize the growth of an authentic national cinema, founded a national film school (the Australian Film and Television School, or AFTS) to train directors and other creative personnel, and initiated a system of lucrative tax incentives to attract foreign investment capital to the new industry. The result was a creative explosion unprecedented in the English-language cinema. Australia produced nearly 400 films between 1970 and 1985—more than had been made in all of its prior history.

With financing from the Film Commission and such semiofficial bodies as the New South Wales Film Corporation (by the end of the decade each of the federal states had its own funding agency), the first films began to appear in the early 1970s, and within the next few years several talented directors began to receive recognition, including Peter Weir (*Picnic at Hanging Rock,* 1975), Bruce Beresford (*The Getting of Wisdom,* 1977), Fred Schepisi (*The Chant of Jimmy Blacksmith,* 1978), George Miller (*Mad Max,* 1979), and the first AFTS graduates, Phillip Noyce (*Newsfront,* 1978) and Gillian Armstrong (*My Brilliant Career,* 1979). Unlike the productions financed with foreign capital by the Canadian Film Development Corporation during the same period, these new Australian films had indigenous casts and crews and treated distinctly national themes. By the end of the 1970s, Australian motion pictures were being prominently featured at the Cannes International Film Festival and competing strongly at the box office in Europe. In 1981 Australia penetrated the American market with two critical hits, Beresford's *Breaker Morant* (1980) and Weir's *Gallipoli* (1981), and the following year achieved a smashing commercial success with Miller's *Mad Max II* (1981; retitled *The Road Warrior,* 1982). In the 1980s, many Australian directors came to work for the American film industry, with varying degress of success (Schepisi—*Barbarossa,* 1982; Beresford—*Tender Mercies,* 1983; Armstrong—*Mrs. Soffel,* 1984; Weir—*Witness,* 1985; Miller—*The Witches of Eastwick,* 1987). Despite this temporary talent drain and a decline in government tax concessions, the Australian cinema remains one of the most influential and creatively vital in the world.

Soviet Union. After World War II the Soviet Union's film industry experienced greater stagnation than that of any other nation except Germany. The socialist realism doctrine imposed during Stalin's dictatorship caused film production to fall from 19 features in 1945 to five in 1952. Although Stalin died the following year, the situation did not improve until the late 1950s when such films as Mikhail Kalatozov's *The Cranes Are Flying* (1957) and Grigory Chukhrai's *Ballad of a Soldier* (1959) emerged to take prizes at international film festivals. Some impressive literary adaptations were produced during the 1960s (Grigory Kozintsev's *Hamlet,* 1964; Sergey Bondarchuk's *War and Peace,* 1965–67), but the most important phenomenon of the decade was the graduation of a whole new generation of Soviet directors from the VGIK, many of them from the non-Russian republics—the Ukraine (Yury Ilyenko, Larissa Shepitko), Georgia (Tengiz Abuladze, Georgy Danelia, Georgy and Eldar Shengelaya, Otar Yoseliani), Moldavia (Emil Lotyanu), Armenia (Sergey Paradzhanov), Lithuania (Vitautas Zhalekevichius), Kirgiziya (Bolotbek Shamshiev, Tolomush Okeyev), Uzbekistan (Elyor Ishmukhamedov, Ali Khamraev), Turkmenistan (Bulat Mansurov), and Kazakhstan (Abdulla Karsakbayev). By far the most brilliant of the new directors were Sergey Paradzhanov and Andrey Tarkovsky, who both were later persecuted for the unconventionality of their work. Paradzhanov's greatest film is *Shadows of Forgotten Ancestors* (1964), a hallucinatory retelling of a Ukrainian folk legend of ravishing formal beauty.

Tarkovsky created a body of work whose seriousness and symbolic resonance had a major impact on world cinema (*Ivan's Childhood,* 1962; *Andrey Rublev,* 1966; *Solaris,* 1971; *Mirror,* 1974; *Stalker,* 1979; *Nostalgia,* 1983; *The Sacrifice,* 1986), even though it was frequently tampered with by Soviet censors.

During the 1970s, the policy of socialist realism (euphemized as "pedagogic realism") was again put into practice, so that only two types of films could safely be made—literary adaptations (Andrey Mikhalkov-Konchalovsky's *Uncle Vanya,* 1970; Nikita Mikhalkov's *Oblomov,* 1980) and *bytovye,* or films of everyday life (Danelia's *Autumn Marathon,* 1979; Vladimir Menshov's *Moscow Does Not Believe in Tears,* 1980). The Soviet cinema then experienced a far-reaching liberalization under the regime of Party Secretary Mikhail Gorbachev, whose policy of *glasnost* ("openness") took control of the industry away from bureaucratic censors and placed it in the hands of the filmmakers themselves. The Soviet cinema began to be revitalized as formerly suppressed films, such as Elem Klimov's *Agoniya* (1975), were distributed for the first time, and films that dealt confrontationally with Stalinism, such as Abuladze's *Repentance* (1987) were made without government interference.

Liberalization of Soviet cinema

Eastern Europe. Of the eastern European nations that fell under Soviet control after World War II, all except East Germany and Albania have produced distinguished cinemas. Following the pattern set by the Soviets, these countries nationalized their film industries and established state film schools. They experienced a similar period of repressive government-imposed restrictions between 1945 and 1953, with a "thaw" during the late 1950s under premier Nikita Khrushchev. In Poland the loosening of ideological criteria gave rise to the so-called Polish School led by Jerzy Kawalerowicz (*Mother Joan of the Angels,* 1961), Andrzej Munk (*Eroica,* 1957; *Passenger,* 1963), and, preeminently, Andrzej Wajda (*A Generation,* 1954; *Canal,* 1956; *Ashes and Diamonds,* 1958). Wajda's reputation grew throughout the 1960s and '70s, when he was joined by a second generation of Polish filmmakers that included Roman Polanski (*Knife in the Water,* 1962), Jerzy Skolimowski (*Barrier,* 1966), and Krzysztof Zanussi (*Structure of Crystals,* 1969; *Illumination,* 1972). The Polish cinema expressed its support of the Solidarity trade union in the late 1970s through films by Wajda (*Man of Marble,* 1977; *Without Anesthesia,* 1978; *Man of Iron,* 1981), Zanussi (*Camouflage,* 1977; *The Constant Factor,* 1980), and such younger directors as Krysztof Kieslowski, Agnieszka Holland, and Feliks Falk.

Czech New Wave

The example of the Polish School encouraged the development of the Czech New Wave (1962–68), which became similarly entangled in politics. The Czechoslovak films that reached international audiences during this period were widely acclaimed for their freshness and formal experimentation, but they faced official disapproval at home and many were suppressed for being politically subversive. Among the directors who were most critical of President Antonín Novotný's hardline regime were Věra Chytilová (*Daisies,* 1966), Jaromil Jireš (*The Joke,* 1968), Ján Kadár (*The Shop on Main Street,* 1965), Miloš Forman (*Firemen's Ball,* 1967), Jiří Menzel (*Closely Watched Trains,* 1966), Evald Schorm (*Everyday Courage,* 1964), and Jan Němec (*The Party and the Guests,* 1966). When Alexander Dubček became president in January 1968, the Czechoslovak cinema eagerly participated in his brief attempt to give Socialism "a human face." After the Soviet invasion of August 1968, many New Wave films were banned, the Czechoslovak film industry was reorganized, and several prominent figures, including Forman and Němec, were forced into exile.

In Hungary, the abortive revolution of 1956 forestalled a postwar revival until the late 1960s, when the complex work of Miklos Jancsó (*The Round-Up,* 1965; *The Red and the White,* 1967; *Red Psalm,* 1972) began to be internationally recognized. The rigorous training given students at the Budapest Film Academy ensured that the younger generation of Hungarian filmmakers would rise to prominence, as has been the case for István Szábo (*Mephisto,* 1981), István Gaál (*Falcons,* 1970), Márta Mészáros (*Adoption,* 1975), and Pál Gábor (*Angi Vera,* 1978), many of whose films—as do Jancsó's—involve ideological interpretations of the national past.

Yugoslavia, Romania, and Bulgaria, unlike their more sophisticated Warsaw Pact allies, did not begin to develop film industries until after World War II. Yugoslavia was the most immediately successful and produced the countries' first internationally known director: the political avant-gardist Dušan Makavejev (*The Tragedy of the Switchboard Operator,* 1967; *W.R.—Mysteries of the Organism,* 1971). Makavejev belonged to the late-1960s movement known as *novi film* ("new film"), which also included such directors as Puriša Djordjević, Aleksandar Petrović, and Živojin Pavlović, all of whom were temporarily purged from the film industry during a reactionary period in the early 1970s. This dark period came to an end in 1976 when the filmmakers of the Prague school made their debuts. Goran Marković, Rajko Grlić, Srdjan Karanović, Lordan Zafranović, and Emir Kusturica were all graduates of the FAMU film school in Prague who had begun their careers working for Yugoslav television. Their offbeat, visually flamboyant social comedies brought a new breath of life into Yugoslav cinema and won a number of international prizes. Like Czechoslovakia, whose Jiři Trnka brought puppet animation to a state of perfection in the 1950s, Yugoslavia also became world famous for its animation, especially that of the "Zagreb School" founded by Vatroslav Mimica and Dušan Vukotić.

The Romanian and Bulgarian film industries did not begin to progress until the mid-1960s, but both countries now possess authentic national cinemas and boast a handful of directors well known on the festival circuit (*e.g.,* the Romanians Dan Piţa, Mircea Veroiu, and Mircea Daneliuc, and the Bulgarians Hristo Hristov, Eduard Zakhariev, Georgi Dyulgerov, and award-winning animator Todor Dinov).

Nationalism in Third World cinema

The Third World. As in eastern Europe, ideology pervades what has come to be known as Third World Cinema—an often militant alternative cinema emanating from Latin-American and African nations with long histories of colonial oppression. Modes of production vary depending on local political circumstance, but most Third World films are made outside the context of established industries and virtually all of them have as their goal the reclamation of an authentic national consciousness from imposed foreign values. Latin America led the Third World in the development of a distinct cinematic style during the 1960s. In postrevolutionary Cuba, the government-subsidized Instituto Cubano del Arte y Industria Cinematográficos (ICAIC) fostered a sophisticated cinema of ideological praxis (*cine liberación*) in the work of such talented directors as Tomás Gutiérrez Alea (*Memorias del subdesarrollo* [*Memories of Underdevelopment*], 1969), Humberto Solás (*Lucía,* 1969), and Sara Gómez (*De cierta manera* [*One Way or Another*], 1977). From Brazil, the indigenous *cinema nôvo* ("new cinema") movement founded by Glauber Rocha (*Terra em transe* [*Land in Anguish*], 1967; *Antonio das Mortes,* 1968) and Ruy Guerra (*Os fuzis* [*The Guns*], 1963) spread to Argentina (Fernando Solanas and Octavio Getina, *La hora de los hornos* [*The Hour of the Furnaces*], 1968), Bolivia (Jorge Sanjinés, *Yawar mallku* [*Blood of the Condor*], 1969), and Chile (Miguel Littín, *La tierra prometida* [*The Promised Land*], 1973). Although repressed in many Latin-American states by military dictatorships during the late 1960s and the 1970s, *cinema nôvo* provided the model for subsequent Third World film movements in Arab and black Africa, especially in Algeria (Mohamed Lakhdar-Hamina, *Chronique des années de braise* [*Chronical of the Years of Embers*], 1975) and Senegal (Sembène Ousmane, *Mandabi* [*The Money Order*], 1970; *Xala* [*The Curse*], 1974).

Buñuel's controversial satires

Spain and Mexico. Of the smaller film industries of the West, Spain's should be noted because it produced one of the world's greatest satirists in Luis Buñuel, and Mexico's should be commended because it allowed Buñuel to work after he was forced out of Spain by the Fascists. (Buñuel also worked frequently in France.) In a career that spanned most of film history, Buñuel directed scores of brilliantly sardonic films that assaulted the institutions of bourgeois Christian culture and Western civilization. Among his most successful are *Los olvidados* (*The Forgotten Ones,* 1950), *Él* (*Torment,* 1952), *Nazarín* (1958), *Viridiana* (1961), *El ángel exterminador* (*The Exterminating Angel,* 1962), *Belle de jour* (1967), *Le Charme discret de la bourgeoisie* (*The Discreet Charm of the Bourgeoisie,* 1973), and *Le Fantôme de la liberté* (*The Phantom of Liberty,* 1974). Buñuel deeply influenced Carlos Saura, another Spanish filmmaker whose work tends toward the grotesque and darkly comic (*La caza* [*The Hunt*], 1966; *La prima Angélica* [*Cousin Angelica*], 1974; *Bodas de sangre* [*Blood Wedding*], 1981), as well as an entire generation of younger directors who began to work after Spanish dictator Francisco Franco's death in 1975 (*e.g.,* Victor Erice, Manuel Gutiérrez Aragón, Jaime Chavarri, and Pilar Miró). Buñuel's presence in Mexico between 1946 and 1965 had little effect on the general mediocrity of that nation's film industry, however. The commercialism of the Mexican cinema was briefly mitigated by a group of idealistic young filmmakers in the late 1960s (Arturo Ripstein, Felipe Cazals, Jaime Humberto Hermosillo) but reappeared even more relentlessly in the following decade.

Sweden. The Scandinavian film industries are small, state-subsidized, and (since the introduction of sound) oriented largely toward the domestic market; however, the post-World War II Swedish cinema, like the Spanish, is noted for producing a single exceptional talent: Ingmar Bergman. Bergman first won international acclaim in the 1950s for his masterworks *The Seventh Seal* (1956), *Wild Strawberries* (1957), and *The Virgin Spring* (1960). His trilogies of the 1960s—*Through a Glass Darkly* (1961), *Winter Light* (1963), and *The Silence* (1963); *Persona* (1966), *Hour of the Wolf* (1968), and *Shame* (1968)—were marked by a deep spiritual and intellectual probing, and later films, such as *Cries and Whispers* (1972) and *Fanny and Alexander* (1984), confirmed that he is essentially a religious artist.

By courtesy of the Swedish Film Institute, *Fanny and Alexander,* ©1984 the Swedish Film Institute; photograph from the Museum of Modern Art/Film Stills Archive, New York City

Permilla Allwin as Fanny and Bertik Guve as Alexander in Ingmar Bergman's *Fanny and Alexander* (1984).

RECENT TRENDS IN U.S. CINEMA

In the United States, as elsewhere, the last half of the 1960s was a time of intense conflict between generations and of rapid social change. Deeply involved with its own financial crisis, Hollywood was slow to respond to this new environment, and the studios made increasingly desperate attempts to attract a demographically homogeneous audience that no longer existed. The stupendous failure of 20th Century-Fox's blockbuster *Cleopatra* (1963) was briefly offset by the unexpected success of its *The Sound of Music* (1965), but over the next few years one box-office disaster after another threatened the studios' independence until most were absorbed by conglomerates. RKO had been sold to the General Tire and Rubber Corporation in 1955, and Universal had been acquired by MCA (the Music Corporation of America) in 1962. Paramount was then taken over by Gulf and Western Industries, Inc., in 1966, United Artists by Transamerica Corporation in 1967, Warner Bros. by Kinney National Services, Inc. (later renamed Warner Communications), in 1969, and MGM by the Las Vegas financier Kirk Kerkorian in 1970. Continuing this trend, in 1981 20th Century-Fox was acquired by Denver oil tycoon Marvin Davis (who later shared ownership with publisher Rupert Murdoch), and Columbia was purchased by the Coca-Cola Company in 1982. United Artists merged with MGM in 1981 to form MGM/UA, which was subsequently acquired by Turner Broadcasting System, Inc., in 1986. The impact of such mergers was pronounced because they reduced filmmaking in the United States to a subordinate role; in the profit-making machinery of these multinational corporations film production was often less important than the production of such items as refined sugar, ball bearings, field ammunition, rubber tires, and soft drinks. Walt Disney Productions was the only studio-era survivor to remain in the hands of veteran (though not its original) industry management, while producer/distributor organizations, such as Orion Pictures Corporation and Tri-Star Pictures, Inc., abounded.

Corporate acquisition of Hollywood studios

Before conglomeration had completely restructured the industry, however, there was an exciting period of experiment as Hollywood tried various things to attract a new audience among the nation's youth. In an effort to lure members of the first "television generation" into movie theatres, the studios even recruited directors from the rival medium, such as Irvin Kershner (*A Fine Madness,* 1966), John Frankenheimer (*Seconds,* 1966), Sidney Lumet (*The Pawnbroker,* 1965), Robert Altman (*Countdown,* 1968), Arthur Penn (*Mickey One,* 1965), and Sam Peckinpah (*Major Dundee,* 1965). These directors collaborated with film-school-trained cinematographers (including Conrad Hall, Haskell Wexler, and William Fraker), as well as with the Hungarian-born cinematographers Laszlo Kovacs and Vilmos Zsigmond, to bring the heightened cinematic consciousness of the French New Wave to the American screen. Their films frequently exhibited unprecedented political and social consciousness as well.

Success of "youth-culture" motion pictures

The years 1967–69 marked a turning point in American film history as Penn's *Bonnie and Clyde* (1967), Stanley Kubrick's *2001: A Space Odyssey* (1968), Peckinpah's *The Wild Bunch* (1969), Wexler's *Medium Cool* (1969), and Dennis Hopper's *Easy Rider* (1969) attracted the youth market to theatres in record numbers. (Altman's *M*A*S*H* [1970] provided a novel comedic coda to the quintet.) The films were unequal aesthetically (the first three being major revisions of their genres, the latter two canny exploitations of the prevailing mood), but all shared a cynicism toward established values and a fascination with apocalyptic violence. There was a sense, however briefly, that such films might provide the catalyst for a cultural revolution. Artistically, the films domesticated New Wave camera and editing techniques, enabling once-radical practices to enter the mainstream narrative cinema. Financially, they were so successful (*Easy Rider,* for example, returned $50,000,000 on a $375,000 investment) that producers quickly saturated the market with low-budget youth-culture movies, only a few of which—Penn's *Alice's Restaurant* (1969), Michael Wadleigh's *Woodstock* (1970), and David and Albert Maysles' *Gimme Shelter* (1970)—achieved even limited distinction.

MPAA ratings system

Concurrent with the youth-cult boom was the new permissiveness toward sex made possible by the institution of the MPAA ratings system in 1968. Unlike the Production Code, this system of self-regulation did not proscribe the content of films but merely categorized them according to their appropriateness for young viewers. (G designates general audiences; PG recommends parental guidance for children under 17; PG-13 suggests parental guidance for children under 13; R indicates that the film is restricted for persons under 17, unless they are accompanied by a parent or guardian; and X signifies that no one under 17 may be admitted to the film. In practice, the X rating is usually given to unabashed pornography and the G rating to children's films, which had the effect of concentrating sexually explicit but serious films in the R category.) The introduction of the ratings system led immediately to the production of serious, nonexploitative adult films, such as John Schlesinger's *Midnight Cowboy* (1969) and Mike

Michael J. Pollard, Faye Dunaway, and Warren Beatty in a scene from Arthur Penn's *Bonnie and Clyde* (1967).

From the motion picture *Bonnie and Clyde*, Copyright © 1967 by Warner Bros.-Seven Arts, Inc.; photograph, from Pictorial Parade

Nichols' *Carnal Knowledge* (1971), in which sexuality was treated with a maturity and realism unprecedented on the American screen.

The revolution that some had predicted would overturn American cinema, as well as American society, during the late 1960s never took place. Conglomeration and inflation did occur, however, especially between 1972 and 1979, when the average cost per feature increased by more than 500 percent to reach $11,000,000 in 1980. Despite the increasing costs, the unprecedented popularity of a few films (Francis Ford Coppola's *The Godfather,* 1972; Steven Spielberg's *Jaws,* 1975; George Lucas' *Star Wars,* 1977) produced enormous financial profits and stimulated a wildcat mentality within the industry. In this environment, it was not uncommon for the major companies to invest their working capital in the production of only five or six films a year, hoping that one or two would be extremely successful. At one point, Columbia reputedly had all of its assets invested in Spielberg's *Close Encounters of the Third Kind* (1977), a gamble that paid off handsomely; United Artists' similar investment in Michael Cimino's financially disastrous *Heaven's Gate* (1980), however, caused the sale of the company and its virtual destruction as a corporate entity.

The new generation of directors that came to prominence at this time included many who had been trained in university film schools—Francis Ford Coppola and Paul Schrader at the University of California at Los Angeles, George Lucas and John Milius at the University of Southern California, Martin Scorsese and Brian De Palma at New York University, Steven Spielberg at California State College—as well as others who had been documentarians and critics before making their first features (Peter Bogdanovich, William Friedkin). These filmmakers brought to their work a technical sophistication and a sense of film history eminently suited to the new Hollywood, whose quest for enormously profitable films demanded slick professionalism and a thorough understanding of popular genres. The directors achieved success as highly skilled technicians in the production of cinematic thrills, although many were serious artists as well.

The graphic representation of violence and sex, which had been pioneered with risk by *Bonnie and Clyde, The Wild Bunch,* and *Midnight Cowboy* in the late 1960s, was exploited for its sensational effect during the '70s in such well-produced R-rated features as Coppola's *The Godfather,* Friedkin's *The Exorcist* (1973), Spielberg's *Jaws,* Scorsese's *Taxi Driver* (1976), De Palma's *Carrie* (1976), and scores of lesser films. The newly popular science-fiction/adventure genre was similarly supercharged through computer-enhanced special effects and Dolby sound, as the brooding philosophical musings of Kubrick's *2001* gave way to the cartoon-strip violence of Lucas' *Star Wars,* Spielberg's *Raiders of the Lost Ark* (1981), and their myriad sequels and copies. There was, however, originality in the continuing work of veterans Robert Altman (*McCabe and Mrs. Miller,* 1971; *Nashville,* 1975; *Three Women,* 1977) and Stanley Kubrick (*A Clockwork Orange,* 1971; *The Shining,* 1980), American Film Institute graduate Terrence Malick (*Badlands,* 1973; *Days of Heaven,* 1978), and controversial newcomer Michael Cimino (*The Deer-hunter,* 1978; *Heaven's Gate*). In addition, Coppola (*The Godfather; The Godfather, Part II,* 1974; *Apocalypse Now,* 1979) and Scorsese (*Mean Streets,* 1973; *Raging Bull,* 1980) created films of unassailable importance. Some of the strongest films of the era came from émigré directors working within the American industry—John Boorman's *Deliverance* (1972), Roman Polanski's *Chinatown* (1974), Miloš Forman's *One Flew over the Cuckoo's Nest* (1975), and Ridley Scott's *Alien* (1979). In general, however, Hollywood's new corporate managers lacked the judgment of industry veterans and tended to rely on the recently tried and true (producing an unprecedented number of high-budget sequels) and the viscerally sensational.

Growth of exploitation films

To this latter category belong the spate of "psycho-slasher" films that glutted the market in the wake of John Carpenter's highly successful, low-budget chiller, *Halloween* (1978). The formula for producing films of this type begins with the serial murder of teenagers by a ruthless psychotic and adds gratuitous sex and violence, with realistic gore provided by state-of-the-art makeup and special-effects artists. Its success was confirmed by the record-breaking receipts of the clumsily made *Friday the Thirteenth* (1980). There were precedents for psycho-killer violence in Hitchcock's *Psycho* (1960) and Tobe Hooper's *The Texas Chainsaw Massacre* (1974), but for decades the exploitation of gore had existed only at the periphery of the industry (in the "splatter" movies of Herschell Gordon Lewis, for example). The slasher films took the gore and violence into the mainstream of Hollywood films. In fact, the trade journal *Variety* reported 25 such films among the 50 top-grossing movies of 1981, a year in which the genre accounted for nearly 60 percent of all domestic releases. The wave of popularity peaked shortly thereafter, but slasher films remain a regular feature of the annual production schedule, and their blend of sex and violence has become an obligatory ingredient of many high-budget horror films (*The Hunger,* 1983; *Fright Night,* 1985; *Vamp,* 1986), science-fiction films (*Aliens,* 1986; David Cronenberg's *The Fly,* 1986), and thrillers (De Palma's *Body Double,* 1984; *Psycho III,* 1986). Slasher films also became an important staple of the videocassette and cable markets, in part because of the sheer numbers in which they were produced.

Influence of video technology

During the 1980s, the fortunes of the American film industry were increasingly shaped by new technologies of video delivery and imaging. Cable networks, direct-broadcast satellites, and half-inch videocassettes provided new means of motion-picture distribution, and computer-generated graphics provided new means of production, especially of special effects, forecasting the prospect of a fully automated "electronic cinema." Many studios, including Universal and Columbia, devote the majority of their schedules to the production of telefilms for the commercial television networks, and nearly all of the studios presell their theatrical features for cable and videocassette distribution. In fact, Tri-Star, one of Hollywood's major producer/distributors, is a joint venture of CBS Inc., Columbia Pictures, and Time-Life's premium cable service Home Box Office (HBO). HBO and Showtime both function as producer/distributors in their own right by directly financing films and entertainment specials for cable television. In 1985, for the first time since the 1910s, independent film producers released more motion pictures than the major studios, largely to satisfy the demands of the cable and home-video markets.

The strength of the cable and video industries led producers to seek properties with video or "televisual" features that would play well on the small television screen (*Flashdance,* 1983; *Footloose,* 1984), or to attempt to draw audiences into the theatres with the promise of spectacular 70-millimetre photography and multitrack Dolby sound (*Amadeus,* 1984; *Aliens*). Ironically, the long-standing 35-millimetre theatrical feature survived in the mid-1980s in such unexpected places as "kidpix" (a form originally created to exploit the PG-13 rating when it was instituted in 1984—*The Breakfast Club,* 1985; *Stand by Me,* 1986) and, more dramatically, the Vietnam combat film (Oliver Stone's *Platoon,* 1986; Coppola's *Gardens of Stone,* 1987; Kubrick's *Full Metal Jacket,* 1987). Responding to the political climate, the studios produced some of their most jingoistic films since the Korean War, endorsing the myth of political betrayal in Vietnam (*Rambo: First Blood, Part II,* 1985), fear of a Soviet invasion (*Red Dawn,* 1985), and military vigilantism (*Top Gun,* 1986). Films with a "literary" quality, many of them British-made, were also popular in the American market during the 1980s (*A Passage to India,* 1984; *A Room with a View,* 1985; *Out of Africa,* 1985).

Tom Berenger, Mark Moses, and Willem Dafoe as American soldiers in Vietnam in *Platoon* (1986), directed by Oliver Stone.

Rise of independent production

Independent producers regained strength under the new regime of video and created some of the most unconventional and interesting work the American cinema had seen in some time, including Joel and Ethan Coen's *Blood Simple* (1984) and *Raising Arizona* (1987), Jim Jarmusch's *Stranger Than Paradise* (1984) and *Down by Law* (1986), Oliver Stone's *Salvador* (1986) and *Platoon,* and David Lynch's *Blue Velvet* (1986). These films were too original to have been made in the studio era and too eccentric for the mass-market economies of the 1970s. They hark back to the vitality and integrity of the pre-studio age—to the work of Griffith, Keaton, Stroheim, and Chaplin—when anything was possible because everything was new.

(D.A.C.)

The art of film

ESSENTIAL CHARACTERISTICS OF MOTION PICTURES

In its short history, the art of motion pictures has frequently undergone changes that seemed fundamental, such as that resulting from the introduction of sound. It exists today in styles that differ significantly from country to country and in forms as diverse as the documentary created by one person with a hand-held camera and the multimillion-dollar "epic," involving hundreds of performers and technicians. Despite its diversity, however, an essential unchanging nature can be discerned in most of its manifestations.

A number of factors immediately come to mind in connection with the motion-picture experience. For one thing, there is something mildly hypnotic about the illusion of movement that holds the attention and may even lower critical resistance. The accuracy of the motion-picture image is compelling because it is made by a nonhuman, scientific process. In addition, the motion picture gives what has been called a strong sense of being present; the film image always appears to be in the present tense. There is also the concrete nature of film; it appears to show actual people and things.

No less important than any of the above are the conditions under which the motion picture ideally is seen, where everything helps to dominate the spectators. They are taken from their everyday environment, partially isolated from others, and comfortably seated in a dark auditorium. The darkness concentrates their attention and prevents comparison of the image on the screen with surrounding objects or people. For a while, spectators live in the world the motion picture unfolds before them.

Still, the escape into the world of the film is not complete. Only rarely does the audience react as if the events on the screen were real; for instance, by ducking before an onrushing locomotive in a special three-dimensional effect. Moreover, such effects are considered to be a relatively low form of the art of motion pictures. Much more often, viewers expect a film to be truer to certain unwritten conventions than to the real world. Although spectators may sometimes expect exact realism in details of dress or locale, just as often they expect the film to escape from the real world and make them exercise their imaginations, a demand made by great works of art in all forms.

The unwritten conventions

The sense of reality most films strive for results from a set of codes, or rules, that are implicitly accepted by viewers and confirmed through habitual filmgoing. The use of brownish lighting, filters, and props, for example, has come to signify the past in films about American life in the early 20th century (*The Godfather,* 1972; *Days of Heaven,* 1978). The brownish tinge that is associated with such films is a visual code (one that may have some basis in reality; brown was a leading decorative element in clothing and furniture of the time). Storytelling codes are even more conspicuous in their manipulation of actual reality to achieve an effect of reality. Audiences are prepared to skip over huge expanses of time in order to reach the dramatic moments of a story. *La battaglia di Algeri* (*The Battle of Algiers,* 1966), for example, begins in a torture chamber where a captured Algerian rebel has just given away the location of his cohorts. In a matter of seconds that location is attacked, and the drive of the search-and-destroy mission pushes the audience to believe in the fantastic speed and precision of the operation. Furthermore, the audience readily accepts shots from impossible points of view if other aspects of the film signal the shot as real. For example, the rebels in *The Battle of Algiers* are shown inside a walled-up hiding place, yet this unrealistic view seems authentic because the film's grainy photography plays on the spectator's unconscious association of poor black-and-white images with newsreels.

Fidelity in the reproduction of details is much less important than the appeal made by the story to an emotional response, an appeal based on innate characteristics of the motion-picture medium. These essential characteristics can be divided into those that pertain primarily to the motion-picture image, those that pertain to motion pictures as a unique medium for works of art, and those that derive from the experience of viewing motion pictures.

Qualities of the film image. The primary unit of expression in film is the image, or the single shot. The attribution of magical properties to images has a long history; this association is well documented among many primitive peoples, and it is even reflected in the term magic lantern as a synonym for the film projector. Any image taken out of the everyday world and projected onto a screen to some extent appears to become magically transmuted. This magical quality helps to explain the enthusiastic reception accorded such early films as *La Sortie des ouvriers de l'usine Lumière* ("Workers Leaving the Lumière Factory"), which were merely photographic records of commonplace scenes in France in the 1890s by the French film pioneers, the Lumière brothers.

Intensity, intimacy, ubiquity. The qualities of intensity, intimacy, and ubiquity have been singled out as the salient characteristics of the motion-picture image. Its intensity derives from its power to hold the complete attention of the spectator on whatever bit of reality is being shown. Outside the theatre, a person's attention is usually dispersed in the endless reality around him, except for sporadic moments of concentration on what he selects for closer scrutiny. In the cinema he is compelled to look at something that not he but the filmmaker has selected, for reasons that are not always immediately apparent. This quality of intensity becomes most noticeable when the camera remains fixed on something for a longer time than seems warranted,

Focusing the viewer's attention

and the spectator gradually becomes acutely conscious of his loss of volition over his own attention. This technique is not often used but is very effective when used well.

The intimacy of the film image is related to the camera's ability to see things in greater detail than the eye can. This ability is demonstrated in long-distance shots through a telephoto lens as well as in close-ups. At the beginning of the Japanese film *Woman in the Dunes* (1964), for example, a pervading theme of the film is indicated by shots of grains of sand many times enlarged.

The impression of ubiquity—being everywhere at once—is achieved in part by the camera's apparent freedom to move from place to place or to approach or withdraw instantaneously. No less important to this illusion of ubiquity is the effect achieved by editing, which allows countless images representing a long, elaborate action to be presented in a comparatively short film or sequence, such as that exemplified by the opening of *The Battle of Algiers*. The geographic and temporal authority of the image even permits credibility to be given to sequences representing the past, the future, and dreams.

Particularity. Other equally important characteristics of the film image may be singled out. One of these is its particularity. The language of words lends itself to generalization and abstraction. In themselves, words such as man or house do not suggest a particular man or a particular house but men and houses in general; and more abstract terms such as love or dishonesty have even less precise associations with specific things. Motion pictures, on the other hand, only show particular things—a particular man or a particular house. In this way a film image may be less ambiguous than the language of words but also less evocative, less likely to be enriched by imagination, association, or recollection. Despite its particularity, however, the motion-picture image may also be ambiguous in that it shows but does not explain. It does not in itself tell what it means, and people instinctively search for meanings in images. This is why commentary is thought to be essential in tying down precise meaning in educational films. On the other hand, many evocative documentaries, from Robert Flaherty's *Nanook of the North* (1922) to Frederick Wiseman's *High School* (1968), abjure commentary, thus forcing the spectator to take in the remarkable and untranslatable specific sights and sounds they collect. The particular insistence of given photographed objects also explains why the juxtapositions of montage are so effective—the spectator compulsively searches for the reason behind a particular sequence of images.

The mind and the eye

Neutrality. Another characteristic of the film image is its neutrality. The world people see around them is strongly influenced by their emotions and their interests. A plumber fixing pipes in a museum may not see the masterpieces around him, while an angry man may hear an insult where none was intended. The camera and the microphone, however, are thought to reproduce images and sounds without feeling. Although focus, directionality, and other technological factors limit what can be seen and heard, audiences are prepared to believe that the motion picture itself is nonhuman or even superhuman in its passive reception of information. Courts of law, for example, are more likely to accept film as evidence of an occurrence such as a bank robbery than they are to accept an artist's sketch or a journalist's report of the same incident. When a film appears to be charged with emotion, it is usually because the director has carefully manipulated the images to give this illusion. In everyday life, the eyes follow the mind; in the cinema, the mind follows the eyes.

Characteristics of the medium. Four characteristics may be stressed as factors that differentiate the motion-picture medium, either in degree or in kind, from other mediums for works of art: luminosity, movement, realism, and montage.

Luminosity. The intense brightness of the picture projected by powerful light onto a coated screen in itself transforms the most mundane element of reality. The appeal of a luminous picture is attested by efforts of advertisers to achieve luminous effects in posters and displays and in the popularity of viewing still photographs as transparencies rather than as ordinary prints. The luminosity of the motion-picture image also results in a considerable range of tone, between the brightest highlight and the deepest black. Both in black-and-white and in colour films, the most delicate gradations in the image are therefore possible.

Movement. As a feature of the motion picture, movement is so obvious that its central importance is sometimes forgotten. The motion picture has much in common with the graphic arts, but the added dimension of movement transforms it, allowing a narrative or a drama to unfold in time, in a way no other graphic art can. Both in filmmaking and in film appreciation, movement must constantly be borne in mind: composition in the motion picture is kinetic rather than static. It is not a single colour but the cumulative effect that matters, not a single situation but a developing plot. The composition within any frame, or exposure, of a motion picture is less important than the relationship of that frame to those that precede and follow it.

Realism. Another essential element of the motion-picture image is that it gives an impression of reality. Whether in a drama enacted expressly for the camera or in a documentary film of an event at which the camera just happened to be present, this feeling of realism deriving from motion-picture photography accounts for much of the force of motion pictures. Animated films, which lack this element of photographic realism, tend to be taken as fantasies.

The attempt of the motion picture to reproduce three-dimensional reality on a flat screen presents the same problems and opportunities that are encountered in still photography and in painting. The standard camera lens, in fact, is constructed to produce visual effects precisely similar to those achieved by painters using the principles of perspective that were developed during the Renaissance.

Cinematic realism is most fully heightened when the images are accompanied by synchronous sound, whereby a second sense, hearing, ratifies what the eyes see. Although reproduced sound can be manipulated with regard to distance, timbre, clarity, and duration, in combination with photographed moving images, it forcefully brings alive its subject as present in a way unavailable to the other arts of representation.

Montage. Perhaps the most essential characteristic of the motion picture is montage, from the French *monter*, "to assemble." Montage refers to the editing of the film, the cutting and piecing together of exposed film in a manner that best conveys the intent of the work. Montage is what distinguishes motion pictures from the performing arts, which exist only within a performance. The motion picture, by contrast, uses the performances as the raw material, which is built up as a novel or an essay or a painting, studiously put together piece by piece, with an allowance for trial and error, second thoughts, and, if necessary, reshooting. The order in which the segments of film are presented can have drastically different dramatic effects.

Kuleshov's experiment

Several major contributions to the theory of montage were made by Soviet directors. After the Russian Revolution of 1917, Soviet films were encouraged for their propaganda value, but film stocks were scarce. Soviet directors carefully studied the films of D.W. Griffith and other masters to make the most effective use of their own meagre resources. One of these early Russian directors, Lev Kuleshov, conducted an experiment involving identical shots of an actor's expressionless face. He inserted it in a film before a shot of a bowl of soup, again before a shot of a child playing, and still again before one of a dead old woman. An unsuspecting audience, which was asked to evaluate the actor's performance, praised his ability to express, respectively, hunger, tenderness, and grief.

Sergey Eisenstein, who excelled both as a director and as a teacher, based much of his theory of film on montage, which he compared to the compounding of characters in Japanese writing. The character for "dog" added to the character for "mouth," he noted, results not merely in "dog's mouth" but in the new concept of "bark"; similarly, film montage results in more than the sum of its parts. Still another great Russian director, Vsevolod I. Pudovkin, also stressed the importance of the carry-over in the spectator's mind. Only if an object is presented as part of a synthesis, he said, is it endowed with filmic life.

Three types of montage may be distinguished—narrative, graphic, and ideational. In narrative montage the multifarious images and scenes involve a single subject followed from point to point. In a fiction film, a character or location is explored from multiple angles while the audience builds a comprehensive image of the situation being explored or explained. Graphic montage occurs when shots are juxtaposed not on the basis of their subject matter but because of their physical appearance. Some avant-garde works depend on the spectator's ability to match the graphic relations of assorted images, such as the people, objects, and the shapes of numerical and alphabetical figures in Fernand Léger's *Le Ballet mécanique* (1924) or the torpedoes, swimming seals, and blimps in Bruce Conner's *A Movie* (1958). In graphic montage cutting usually occurs during shots of movement rather than ones of static action. This cutting on motion facilitates the smooth replacement of one image by the next. In ideational montage, two separate images are related to a third thing, an idea that they help to produce and by which they are governed. In *Strike* (1924), for example, the director Eisenstein, to whom the theory of ideational montage is credited, effectively conveys the idea of slaughter by intercutting a shot of cattle being butchered with shots of workers being cut down by cavalry.

These three types of montage seldom appear in their pure form. Most ideational montage proceeds on the basis of the graphic similarity of its components, as does narrative montage when relying on graphic cutting to cover its movement. Similarly, the graphic matches between torpedoes, seals, and blimps in *A Movie* ultimately construct an idea of movement toward explosion and destruction. Besides the complications brought about by the intermixing of these types, the addition of the sound track multiplies the possibilities and effects of montage. Eisenstein and Pudovkin referred to such possibilities as "vertical" montage, opposing it to the "horizontal" unrolling of shot after shot. Because sound permits the establishment of relations between what is seen and heard at each moment, the film image can no longer be said to be a self-contained unit; it interacts with the sound that accompanies it. Sound relations (including dialogue, music, and ambient noise or effects) may be built in constant rapport with the image track or may create a parallel organization and design that subtends what is seen. In all, montage appears to be the most extraordinary factor differentiating the motion picture from the other arts, and it is the one often singled out as the basis of the medium. Nevertheless, many films, including those of Mizoguchi Kenji of Japan, Roberto Rossellini of Italy, and Miklós Jancsó of Hungary, rely not on montage but on the medium's unique qualities of luminosity, movement, and realism to convey their power and beauty.

The motion-picture experience. Other distinguishing characteristics of the motion picture are more closely related to the conditions under which they are normally seen.

The Kinetoscope, a peep-show motion picture that could be seen by only one person at a time, became obsolete soon after it was introduced by Thomas A. Edison in 1894, because it could not compete with projected films, which could accommodate audiences. Since that time, an atmosphere of group entertainment has been associated with films. Even for films being seen on broadcast or cable television, this aspect of community viewing remains significant; although the audience before any particular set may be as small as a single individual, each spectator brings to it past associations of films seen in the theatre and the realization that millions of other people are watching the same broadcast.

Collective versus private film viewing

Since 1980, however, this tradition has been reversed and the peep show has returned in the guise of the videocassette. The proliferation of videocassette recorders (VCRs) and portable television sets demonstrates that films serve multiple functions in culture. The function usually deemed primary might be termed "concentrated entertainment." The private viewing conditions provided by the VCR can enhance this function and may be preferred by some viewers in the same way that a stereo recording of a Beethoven symphony is preferred by some to the concert hall experience. The less socially acceptable function of pornography, which has been represented in motion pictures since their inception, is also well served by the anonymity and privacy characteristic of VCR viewing. Other, more public, functions of motion pictures contribute to sociability. Although the movie theatre remains a key site for such activity, television serves a significant population that prefers to stay at home either because of convenience or because the more casual viewing conditions permit them to participate in additional activities. This latter quality is also found in older phenomena, such as the drive-in theatre, where families or small groups maintained their own cohesiveness while viewing a motion picture. Such epiphenomena as talking and eating, which were encouraged by the drive-in venue, are replicated in living rooms where movies are watched on cassettes. In sum, the motion picture raises questions of the privacy and sociability of artistic representations more insistently

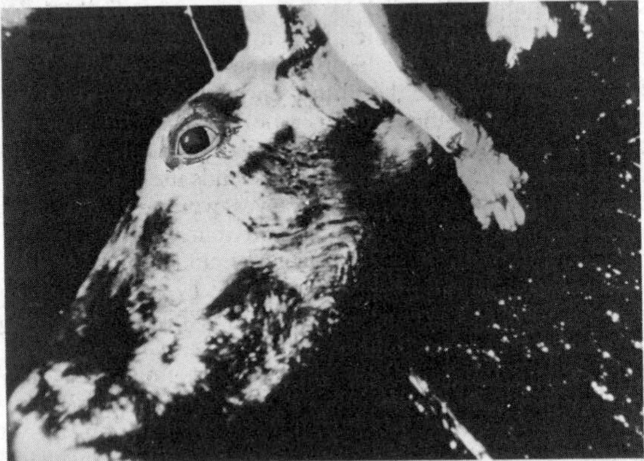

The concluding montage from *Strike!* (1924), directed by Sergey Eisenstein. (Top and bottom) Shots of the massacre of the strikers and their families are intercut with (centre) images of cattle being slaughtered.

Photographs from David Cook and the Museum of Modern Art/Film Stills Archive, New York City

than any other medium, but few generalizations about its "pure" state stand up. Different eras and different cultures use motion pictures in different ways. Its connection to both personal and collective vision is always relevant and is always affected by the site of its exhibition.

Although the motion-picture experience is most often a group experience, it is exceptional for its impersonal nature. In this respect the cinema is quite different from live theatre, for example, in which the audience feels the presence of the actors and the equally compelling presence of the audience. Whether at home in front of a television set or in a movie theatre, the film viewer feels less inhibited. People come and go as they please, generally unnoticed, in an easy, relaxing atmosphere. Especially in the heyday of the large movie palaces there was little feeling of association with the other members of the cinema audience, whereas at a ballet, opera, or play, members of the audience sense a collective ritual that is reinforced by intermissions during which they mingle with one another. The impersonality of the motion-picture experience enhances its private function, although the informality of the cinema has probably contributed to the tendency to regard it less seriously than other performing arts.

Another basic feature of motion pictures is their accessibility to an audience of vast size. A drama presented in a theatre can be attended by no more than a few hundred persons at a time. In a film, however, the same drama and the same performers may be seen throughout the world by millions of people almost simultaneously. Accessibility has been a determining characteristic of films. From the start, they were a sidewalk attraction, and with the advent of television in addition to cinemas, motion pictures are available almost anywhere at almost any time.

Effect of the mass audience

This mass audience allowed the motion-picture industry to develop vast production and distribution organizations, but it also limited the artistic development of films, since it was commercially safer to present the simplest and least demanding entertainment that would appeal to the widest audience. After television took over much of this mass audience in the 1950s, many motion pictures were taken more seriously by a more discriminating audience. Since the days of the *film d'art* movement in France (*c.* 1910), many films have claimed the status of art, but the "art films" that are shown in specialized art theatres are a product of this competition with television. After 1980 cable distribution as well as the videocassette market decentralized distribution, providing potential outlets targeting limited audiences. Despite these developments, the motion picture, and critical or artistic attitudes toward it, has been greatly shaped by its seemingly universal appeal.

EXPRESSIVE ELEMENTS OF MOTION PICTURES

Many observers have seen in films a means of expression comparable to a language. The French poet and filmmaker Jean Cocteau (1889–1963), for example, called the cinema "picture writing." The language of motion pictures, however, is not the language of words, even though spoken dialogue has been an integral part of motion pictures since the late 1920s and written captions were usually required to explain the action before that. It is primarily in the qualities of its images and sounds that the expressivity of the cinema must be sought. Certain basic traits of motion pictures may operate with the logic of natural language, but few theorists have held that cinematic expression follows rules like those of natural language. As Christian Metz, one of the foremost modern theorists, argued, it is not linguistics so much as poetics that should serve as a model for those interested in understanding or explaining how a film works; making and watching a film is far closer to writing or appreciating a novel or symphony than a sentence or discourse.

Various codes of expression have, nevertheless, been shown to operate naturally or to have been inculcated, and their effects can be calculated. Such codes and effects occur in all aspects of the medium and can most readily be categorized into those affecting cinematography, editing, sound, the script, acting, and design.

Cinematographic expression. The filmmaker has a number of ways of modifying the camera's neutrality and thereby the "reality" that is conveyed to the audience. It is largely by means of these devices that the motion picture becomes such an expressive medium. Several of these expressive techniques should be emphasized. First, there is framing; that is, carefully selecting what will be included within each frame of the film and what will be excluded. Second, there is scale, the size and placement of a particular object or a part of a scene in relation to the rest, a relationship that is determined by the placement of the camera. Third is camera movement, or the lack of it, during shooting. Fourth, there are the peculiar advantages of either colour or black-and-white photography that can be exploited. Finally, through the cinematographer's skill and knowledge of laboratory processes, other highly expressive techniques can be achieved. Each of these means of expression will be discussed below.

Framing. The process of framing is intended to eliminate what is unessential in the motion picture, to direct the spectator's attention to what is important, and to give it special meaning and force. Each frame of film, which corresponds in shape to the image projected on the screen, forms the basis for a graphic composition in the same way as the frame of a painting encloses the area in which the painting must be organized.

The aspect ratio

Several different ratios of frame width to frame height (called "aspect ratios") have been used in motion pictures. The most common, known as the Academy ratio, is 1.33 to 1, or 4 to 3, a ratio corresponding to the dimensions of the frame of 35-millimetre film. By using 70-millimetre film or a special CinemaScope lens, an image with wider horizontal and shorter vertical dimensions is achieved—a proportion of about 5 to 2, or between 2.2 to 1 and 2.65 to 1. A similar effect, called wide screen, was sometimes achieved without the expensive equipment required for CinemaScope by using 35-millimetre film and masking the top or bottom, or both, giving a ratio of 1.75 to 1, or 7 to 4. Although some theatres in the 1970s were enlarged and widened to accommodate 70-millimetre images, a trend toward smaller theatres fixed the image ratio close to 1.85 to 1 in the United States and 1.66 to 1 in Europe.

The moderate elongation provided by the Academy ratio has proved most versatile for achieving standard compositional effects. For example, an expansive feeling is easily rendered when small-scale figures in the foreground are shot against a towering sky, as in *Days of Heaven.* In the wide CinemaScope dimension, the tension established between the outward movement of the composition and the rectangle of the screen can readily be lost; nevertheless, early fears about wide screen's insensitivity to intimate love scenes proved to be unfounded, at least in the hands of careful cinematographers. A number of foreign directors, notably Kurosawa Akira (Japan), François Truffaut (France), and Miklós Jancsó (Hungary) achieved stunning effects in CinemaScope by overcoming the fear of moving the camera, as seen in, respectively, the battle scenes of *Seven Samurai* (1954), the bicycle ride in *Jules et Jim* (1961), and the nonstop camera dance of *Red Psalm* (1972). Wide screen calls for an altered aesthetic, because the spectator's eye is invited to roam the visual field, making connections that in the standard ratio are more tightly determined.

Regardless of its ratio, the frame may be divided to show two or more scenes at the same time. This technique is generally reserved for credit sequences, musical interludes, or moments when the presentation on a single screen of two or more simultaneous occurrences results in comic interrelationships.

Use of offscreen space

An effective use of framing consists of temporarily or permanently excluding a vital part of the action. Offscreen space may be said to function more actively in cinema than in painting or the theatre. For example, the camera may remain fixed on the hero while the villain is perceived only by a voice saying "Hands up!"; or in a science-fiction film, the camera may linger on the horror expressed by the victim before revealing the monster that is causing it.

Finally, very strong dramatic effects may be obtained by oblique framing; that is, by turning the camera sideways so that the image on the screen appears askew. This was done in the early Russian film *The Ghost That Never*

Returns (1929), in which a prison riot shown by oblique framing gives the impression that the building is being pushed over. Some directors, such as Britain's Carol Reed, have made this a trademark (*The Third Man,* 1949).

Scale. Since scale in the cinema constantly changes from shot to shot, the spectator can easily be deceived about the size of objects. When appearing next to enormous tables and chairs, for instance, the actors can be made to look like midgets or children, as in the Stan Laurel and Oliver Hardy comedy *Brats* (1930). By contrast, in *King Kong* (1933) a small-scale model of New York City was used to give the illusion of the actual city under attack by a giant gorilla. Scale may have a marked effect on the emotional tone of a scene. In the distance an actor may seem lonely, remote, helpless, pathetic; close up, he may appear powerful, threatening, bestial. The scale of shots for artistic purposes ranges from an extreme long shot (the widest view on the smallest scale), with houses or ships appearing as tiny dots on the horizon, through medium shots, two shots (*i.e.,* a shot of convenient size to include two actors) and others, to the close-up, with part of a face, an eye, or a fist filling the screen (the most restricted view on the largest scale). Telescopic or microscopic shots beyond these extremes are usually of scientific rather than of artistic interest.

Scale of shots

Different scales are occasionally juxtaposed in a single shot to produce an unmistakable dramatic or rhetorical effect. In Orson Welles's *Citizen Kane* (1941) significant characters are repeatedly framed in the right or left foreground while in the background an action takes place which disturbs that character or which that character somehow controls. The gigantic political poster of Kane that rises behind the podium on which he, in the foreground, makes a speech promising to ruin his rival, Gettys, becomes suddenly the size of a postage stamp when the shot changes to one in which Gettys is in the foreground looking down from a balcony on the insignificant speaker. Through this use of different scales, Gettys is shown to have power over the action.

By courtesy of RKO Radio Pictures, a division of RKO General; photograph from the Museum of Modern Art/Film Stills Archive, New York City

Orson Welles in *Citizen Kane* (1941).

As has been noted, the camera exaggerates perspective, and this exaggeration adds to the dramatic effect. It is most striking in an ordinary still photograph of an enormous hand or a sunbather's giant feet that were close to the camera lens. In cinematography, the director ordinarily minimizes the effect of this distortion, but occasionally he uses it in an extreme form. In *Easy Rider* (1969), for instance, it was used to give an atmosphere of hallucination and nightmare to a drug-taking session, and in *Brazil* (1985) it was used continuously to promote an atmosphere of paranoia and nightmare.

Finally, scale is affected by what precedes and follows. The close-up has its most dramatic impact coming after long or medium shots, and after many close-ups, it is a relief to escape to the middle or far distance.

Shooting angle and point of view. Another element in motion-picture language is shooting angle. In common language, the phrases "to look up to" and "to look down on" have connotations of admiration and condescension in addition to their obvious reference to physical viewpoint. In one sense or another, children, dogs, and beggars are often looked down upon, while the preacher in his pulpit, the judge on the bench, and the policeman on his horse are looked up to. Even a slight upward or downward angle of a camera is enough to express a mood of inferiority or superiority.

The camera's viewpoint

Upward or downward shooting angles lead to questions of objectivity and subjectivity. In most motion pictures, both for variety and for breadth of treatment, the camera's viewpoint switches from one character to another and sometimes is associated with none of the characters but merely looks on. The camera may take the viewpoint of the heroine, looking with dismay at the villain as he breaks into her room; in this case, an upward camera angle gives a subjective impression of her fear. Similar subjectivity may be seen in a shot of buildings reeling in the way they might appear to a drunken man, as in the German classic *The Last Laugh* (1924), or in a rapid camera movement from a window to the pavement below to express a thought of suicide, as in the Italian Neorealist film *Umberto D.* (1952). Occasionally, an entire motion picture may be shot from one person's point of view, often with a personal narration accompanying the images. Very rarely does this point of view literally take over the optical view of the character for an extended period. (One noted exception is the 1946 film directed by the actor Robert Montgomery, *Lady in the Lake,* in which the camera actually plays the main character. The entire film is seen from the camera/character's point of view so that the audience sees only what the camera/character sees. The movie is an interesting experiment in the use of subjective camera, but it is considered an artistic failure.) More often voice-over, music, or other elements are combined with shooting angle to render a particular character's feelings throughout a film. Alfred Hitchcock is generally considered the master of point of view, controlling (and even misguiding) viewer sympathy.

Extreme upward or downward angles are too far removed from ordinary experience to have many applications in motion pictures, but they may express exceptional situations—a sick man on his back, a baby's or a dog's point of view, a man in a pit or in a coffin, a spy covertly looking down on an enemy meeting. As with scale, the shots that precede and follow alter the effect of the shooting angle. Upward angles are stronger following a level or downward-looking camera, and vice versa.

Camera movement. Framing, scale, and shooting angle are all greatly modified by the use of camera movement. Filmmakers began experimenting with camera movement almost immediately after the motion-picture camera was developed. In 1897 photographers employed by Auguste and Louis Lumière floated a *cinématographe,* the combination camera/projector devised by the French brothers, in a gondola through Venice to give viewers all over the world a dynamic view of that much-painted city.

Panning and tracking

One of the simplest and most common movements is to turn, or pan (from the word panorama), the camera horizontally so that it sweeps around the scene. It can also be tilted up or down in a vertical panning shot, or in a diagonal pan, as when it follows an actor up a stairway. Panning was possible quite early in film history, but methods of physically conveying the camera itself through a scene developed more slowly. Initially, the camera was mounted on a dolly, truck, or other hand-propelled wheeled vehicle to facilitate smooth movement. Later, tracks were laid for the dolly or truck to ride on, providing even smoother, more effortless motion. Trucking, dollying, and tracking can even be combined with panning in a complex movement that may require the adjustment of focus or aperture en route. One such camera movement that is often used imitates the gaze of a traveler who turns in a moving automobile or train to focus on a stationary point of interest.

Often commercial vehicles, such as trolleys, automobiles, or airplanes, are used to transport the camera; the relatively jerky ride they supply simulates real movement more accurately than does the steady motion provided by a specially designed apparatus. Nevertheless, the film industry has long sought equipment that would allow the camera (and the viewer) to weave in and out of action in the most ethereal way. The crane, which facilitates aerial movement, was developed in the late 1920s, replacing the jerry-built movable platforms, the slings, and the sleds that ingenious directors, such as Abel Gance (for *Napoléon,* 1927) and Marcel L'Herbier (for *L'Argent,* 1929), both in France, had devised to achieve vertical or elevated swinging movements. A host of such special camera supports now exists, many of which were originally developed for use on medical and scientific films. The most advanced equipment can be operated from a distance with electronic viewfinders, allowing the camera to follow vigorous, continuous action with unprecedented ease and intimacy, as in the pre-credit sequence of *Raiders of the Lost Ark* (1981). The look and style of film art is constantly changing as technological advances increase the mobility of the camera and consequently the flexibility of the spectator's viewpoint.

Harrison Ford in the opening sequence of *Raiders of the Lost Ark* (1981), directed by Steven Spielberg.

Regardless of the state of technical capability, the effect of camera movement depends on the context and on the pace of movement. At a deliberate pace the camera can explore a scene and reveal significant details. If it is raised well above the ground, the movement has a dreamlike power, and, when combined with slow motion, it may give a somnolent impression or express recollection or hallucination. The camera movement may end dramatically on a dagger, on a gun half-hidden in an assailant's hand, or on a suspicious bulge in a pocket. It may link the hero walking in the garden and the heroine watching him with loving eyes from a window. It may bring a dramatic surprise, as in the American western *Stagecoach* (1939), when director John Ford had the camera, mounted high above a rocky defile, move slowly from the stagecoach below to reveal a band of Indians waiting in ambush. On the other hand, the camera may simply turn away from a scene to leave the remainder to the spectator's imagination, as when it withdraws from a torture scene or from a love scene. In filming a conversation, the director may turn the camera from one speaker to the other, thus animating the scene with movement and showing the expression of the speaker, or listener, more closely than would be possible with a static two shot. Camera movement can even be used to change the scene to a distant place, to a different period of time, or to an imaginary world.

Very rapid camera movements may express a sudden surge of emotion or a contemplated action, as in the suicide example from *Umberto D.* In *The Rains Came* (1939), as the heroine realizes with horror that she has drunk from a glass that may be contaminated with typhus, the camera rushes forward to a close-up on the fatal glass, shining in the darkness. These movements are often effected without physically moving the camera, by means of a zoom lens, a lens of variable focal length that simulates the effect of moving toward or away from a subject by increasing or decreasing the size of the subject as the focal length changes. Although a zoom shot is generally smoother than a tracking shot, it always results in pictorial distortion. To zoom in from a distance to a close-up, the focal length of the lens is changed from, for example, 18 millimetres to 125 millimetres. The former length curves the picture anamorphically on the sides, giving great depth to the background, while the latter tends to flatten the background. All objects within view are enlarged at the same rate. Tracking in from a distance to a close-up requires careful adjustment of focus, but depth and dimension appear more realistic.

Zooming

Camera movement is one of the key indicators of the presence of a narrator. When the camera moves independently of the action, the narrator can be thought of as hovering above the action, poetically reacting to it or commenting on it. When the camera moves instead to keep the action in view, to follow as many elements as possible, the narrator can be thought of as a reporter investigating but not commenting on what is seen. The documentary tradition, particularly since 1959 when lightweight cameras and tape recorders first permitted extended hand-held filming, represents this investigative function of cinema and of camera movement.

Montage versus mise-en-scène

Directorial styles may be cataloged on the basis of an overall predilection for linking elements in a scene via cuts (montage) or camera movement. Eisenstein has already been cited as a master of montage. One of the directors most acclaimed for the expressive use of camera movement is Japan's Mizoguchi Kenji. Although Mizoguchi was not beyond making strongly rhetorical points by juxtaposing shots, the overall impression his films convey derives from the use of a seemingly floating camera to join not only elements within a scene but also the scenes themselves. In *Ugetsu* (1953) the hero, seduced in a hot spring by a beautiful ghost woman, moves screen right to join her, while the camera pans left across the pool and then tracks along the ground. The shot dissolves imperceptibly into one in which the camera pans up to reframe the couple picnicking in an extreme long shot. The magical mixture of spaces and the conflation of time sensuously express the erotic imagination that both the hero and the audience have fallen prey to. Mizoguchi is known as a mise-en-scène director, one who is primarily concerned with the relationships within a shot rather than those between shots. He employs long takes, camera movement, and the expressive use of elements within the film frame to convey mood and emotion. The possibility of movement was so important to Mizoguchi that at the end of his career he invariably directed from a crane, even during static scenes.

Colour and black and white. A practical, accurate commercial system of colour cinematography was not perfected until Technicolor was introduced in Walt Disney's animated short *Flowers and Trees* (1932) and in the feature film *Becky Sharp* (1935). The introduction of colour was less revolutionary than the introduction of sound; the silent film soon disappeared, but even though most feature films made since the 1960s have been in colour, the black-and-white film has continued to be made. In fact, directors such as Woody Allen (*Manhattan,* 1980) and Martin Scorsese (*Raging Bull,* 1979) have chosen to film in black and white to give their movies a calculated tone.

Use of black and white for realism

A black-and-white motion picture is not merely a picture that lacks colour but rather is an artistic creation with positive qualities of its own. An ample range of effects can be obtained—from precise images in which every hair, every grain can be clearly seen, to a smudged charcoal effect. Oddly, black and white often gives a stronger impression of realism than colour does, perhaps because of associations with newsreels and newspaper photographs. Black and white may suggest the hard news of the daily paper, while colour may connote the fantasies of glossy fashion magazines, advertisements, and comic strips. In the cinema, black-and-white composition is often stronger and more dramatic than colour.

Nevertheless, colour introduced a new world into the cinema and steadily grew more effective. It can be used to produce a powerful dramatic impression. The German director Rainer Werner Fassbinder, for example, used garish colours in films such as *Despair* (1977) to lend a seductive but finally suffocating tone to his melodramas. The Italian director Michelangelo Antonioni claimed to have studied colour for years before venturing to make his first colour film, *The Red Desert* (1964). In that film he used disturbing yellows, pinks, grays, and greens, even going so far as to paint dump heaps and fruit gray for one scene, to express a neurotic woman's sensibility and the oppressiveness of her industrial environment. He changed film stock for a sequence in which the woman tells her child a story about a girl on the beach. The bright postcard colours seen in that sequence contrast dramatically with the sickly grays and greens of the rest of the film. Colour can be employed even more symbolically than this—in Eisenstein's *Ivan the Terrible, Part II* (1946), red turning to a bluish shade represents the fear of a pretender about to be assassinated.

Role of the cinematographer. Cinematographers remain virtually unknown outside the motion-picture industry even though their contribution sometimes matches that of the director in importance. Although the director has ultimate control over the visual image, the cinematographer actually records that image on film, translating the director's ideas and creating the atmosphere and the look of the film. The association between the cinematographers and the processing laboratory is also of highest importance because the cinematographer often spends hours there after shooting, checking the negative. On most feature films a camera team (often consisting of a director of photography, cameraman, and assistant cameraman) shares the responsibilities.

Cinematographers are responsible for exact framing, sometimes for screens of more than one type. They also must decide upon the use of masking, the choice of lens, the camera angle, and the control of camera movement. They must either keep the focus sharp or put all or part of the picture out of focus if this effect is required. Cinematographers also control slow motion or accelerated motion; with early hand-cranked cameras, the camera operator simply slowed down or cranked faster, but later special controls and cameras were developed. Trick photography was once effected by simple manipulation of the camera: magical transformations were made simply by stopping it and changing the scene; and the impression of backward motion was achieved by turning the camera upside down and reversing the film. More elaborate processes now at the cinematographer's command involve laboratory technicians as much as the camera crew. Many effects require the actors to perform against a background of previously prepared film. The cinematographer must be in command of all these processes. The best cinematographers give a motion picture a visual style that is peculiarly their own.

Editing. The process of trimming and piecing together lengths of film in order to make an artistically concise and complete motion picture is certainly the most obvious technique of film language and the one most often discussed. The terms editing, cutting, and montage are often applied interchangeably to the process. In montage the emphasis is on the juxtaposition of ideas resulting from this process, cutting stresses the physical work with the actual strips of film, and editing encompasses both.

Editing, cutting, and montage

A single shot (*i.e.,* the length of film exposed at one time, without interruption, by one camera), makes a visual and aural record of some segment of the physical world; by effective editing, this record can be taken apart, restructured, and shaped into an imaginative world or a discourse about the world. While all viewers presumably notice that a film is made up of a number of scenes, few realize that fiction films contain on the average approximately 600 cuts, one every 10 seconds. Editors strive to hide their work by cutting on action, so that the movement of a character's arm in one location flows into another such movement elsewhere, masking the change of shot. More important is the principle by which an editor anticipates the spectator's line of inquiry. By releasing information just as the spectator needs it, the editor constructs a natural drama whose seams are invisible.

Invisible editing

Probably the most common convention of this sort is the "accordion" sequence wherein, for example, a drawing room conversation between two people is introduced in an establishing shot of the setting and the actors. The editor will cut to a full shot of the actors once they begin their dialogue, because their speech gives them prominence over the setting. To help viewers understand the nuances of the dialogue, the editor will move in for a medium shot, showing both characters from the waist up. While many directors and editors stop here, Hollywood has traditionally gone in even closer, using alternating close-ups of each character (generally from over-the-shoulder shots) to convey innuendos and reactions. In the earlier days of cinema, an editor was likely to back out of the sequence in the reverse order, going from close-up to medium shot, to full shot, and finally to long shot, thus making the structure of the sequence resemble the in-and-out movement of an accordion. Most contemporary, faster-paced films skip some of these "logical" steps, but they nevertheless usually include other strategies that let the viewer glide into and out of the action unconsciously.

Unforgettable moments in films are often made possible through shocking juxtapositions. When an initially smooth progression is disrupted by a quick cut to a close-up, as in the *Halloween* cycle of horror films, the effect can be startling and frightening. In such cases the editor insists upon a strange or important connection in a scene.

Beyond rendering scenes in unobtrusive or striking ways, editing connects scenes into sequences and larger units. It serves as a system of punctuation. In the standard Hollywood film a straight cut between two scenes suggests that the scenes are close in space or time, whereas other more visible forms of transition signal more distant relations. The picture may fade out and fade in, the screen being left dark for a moment. Or it may dissolve, or mix, to a new scene, one image showing on top of the other for a moment. The filmmakers may use other devices, such as a wipe (*i.e.,* a line moving across the screen that wipes out the preceding image while introducing the next), irising (gradually reducing the old image from the edges to a pinpoint size and then expanding the new one in the reverse way), or a turnover (in which the entire screen seems to turn over, with the new image seeming to appear on what was the reverse side).

The director may introduce creative touches in cutting. The German-born director Max Ophüls, for example, connected the separate episodes of *La Ronde* (1950) by means of the musical leitmotiv of a hurdy-gurdy tune. In *Vivre sa vie* (1962), Jean-Luc Godard, one of the outstanding French New Wave directors of the late 1950s, introduced chapter headings marking the heroine's step-by-step involvement in prostitution and, ultimately, her murder, as if it were a didactic 19th-century novel. Alfred Hitchcock, probably the greatest director of suspense films, in his British film *The Thirty-nine Steps* (1935) cut from a woman's scream to the similar sound of a train whistle, an effect so dramatic that it was frequently imitated thereafter.

Illusions created by editing

Editing permits highly dramatic effects that could never be staged in a single shot. In the American western film *Butch Cassidy and the Sundance Kid* (1969), for example, the title characters are seen cornered by lawmen on a high cliff overlooking a river, into which they make an almost suicidal leap to their escape. Actually, the scenes involving the two leading actors on the cliff and those of the dives were shot weeks apart, and they involved different crews and even different rivers, yet the audience readily accepts the illusion created by the editing. *The Stunt Man* (1978) takes such editing as its very theme. The main character is engaged in the rigged dangers and tricks involved in making a movie, while the audience is fooled by the greater tricks of the film that it is watching. Editing opens up a bagful of ingenious tricks of substitution, tricks that allow a marvelous or tragic experience to appear as a natural occurrence in the filmed world.

The common illusionistic experience of motion pictures depends on editing for its force and excitement, but editing can play an even more important role in films that bypass or refuse the illusion of realism. The use of graphic and ideational montage demonstrates that some filmmakers purposely flaunt the fabrication involved in motion pictures. Many films incorporate extraneous material within their fictions in order to set the illusion of the story they tell against the hard reality of other types of images. In Warren Beatty's *Reds* (1981), for example, interviews with "witnesses" to the events portrayed in the film open, and occasionally interrupt, the story in order to validate the fiction being re-created as history. Editing permits the juxtaposition of very different kinds of material for a variety of rhetorical effects.

The editor's function. Like camera-work, editing is a function that is ordinarily hidden from the audience, but it is vital to the finished picture. It is the editor's job to judge the length of each shot, choosing the exact moment to cut. The length of a shot may depend upon the amount of detail it contains, its scale, its dramatic impact, or its context in relation to the shots that precede and follow it. Though the audience is unconscious of these judgments, the impact of the finished film depends on how well they are made.

The director generally views the day's rushes (*i.e.,* advance prints of the film shot that day) and, in consultation, selects what is to be used. Some directors spend a good deal of time in the cutting room; others spend none at all. Often, the editor is influential in rearranging shots, discarding them, or even ordering reshooting or additional shooting. An important factor in the work of the editor is the cutting ratio—the proportion of film shot to that used in the final film. Some directors shoot as little as three times as much as is required, while others may shoot 10 times as much or even more. In its widest sense, editing includes mixing the sounds and correlating them with the visual film.

Cutting ratio

Cinema time. The motion picture has been defined as a series of images of space that are arranged in time. The time of film language is quite different from that of reality and that conveyed by the other arts, such as drama and literature. Movement on the screen is produced by showing the spectator 24 frames, or still photographs, with dark intervals between them, every second. The movement seems to be at the same rate as that of ordinary life only if the pictures are taken and shown at the same speed. Slow motion may be achieved either by speeding up the camera or slowing down the projector, and accelerated motion is obtained in the opposite way. In common practice, the speed of the projector is constant, and the speed of the camera is varied to achieve these effects. Like extremes of scale, extremes of speed—such as in accelerated-motion films of plant growth or slow-motion films of bullets, explosions, or materials being broken—are of less interest to the art of motion pictures than to science. Moderate slow motion has been used, however, to give a mythic or legendary quality to scenes of destruction and violence, as in Arthur Penn's *Bonnie and Clyde* (1967) and the films of Sam Peckinpah. It can also be used to express dreams or ecstasy, while accelerated motion is often very effective in comedy. The cinema can give the illusion of reversing time by showing events happening backward, or of holding time still by showing the same image again and again.

Time conventions. Despite the possibilities for manipulating it, the time presented in a single shot of film is ordinarily the time of the real world. From shot to shot, however, the time is presented according to certain conventions. In most motion pictures, the story may be assumed to be presented in chronological order and in real time except when certain conventions are invoked, such as ellipsis, repetition for emphasis, flashbacks, or dream sequences.

The narrative may be advanced with immense speed and economy simply by the omission, or ellipsis, of what is not essential. A straight cut may be used between a shot of a girl dressing for a ball and a shot of her at the ball itself. To show a lapse of years, however, it may be necessary to fade one shot slowly from the screen and fade the next in, or to use a dissolve, or mix, which shows both shots superimposed as one supersedes the other.

To emphasize important scenes of short duration, repetition is an effective device. Such a scene may be shown from different angles, from a distance and then close up, and it may occupy much more time on the screen than would the actual event. By emphasizing what is important and eliminating the rest, a motion picture can give the illusion of covering a lifetime in only 90 minutes.

A flashback is an interruption of the actual chronology of a story to relate a significant event of an earlier time. The flash forward, a much less used device, interjects future events in the same way. These devices require special optical effects, such as fades, dissolves, or irising, to stress the break in continuity. The break can also be stressed by the use of a melody associated with the past, or by an unusual camera movement, as well as by the more obvious devices of using noticeably different period styles in the settings or having the actors made up to look much older or younger.

Flashback and flash forward

A thought or dream sequence requires similar emphasis on the departure from chronology of real time. Nearly all of *La Rivière de l'Hibou* (1962), a prize-winning French short film adapted from Ambrose Bierce's 1891 short story, *An Occurrence at Owl Creek Bridge,* consists of the fleeting last thoughts of a man about to be hanged. By not indicating a break between the actual events of the hanging and the fantasy of the condemned man, the film deceives the audience, until the very end, into thinking he is making an escape.

Tempo. The tempo or pace that an audience senses in a film may be influenced in three ways: by the actual speed and rhythm of movement and cuts within the film, by the accompanying music, and by the content of the story. For most people, time seems to pass quickly during moments of happiness, excitement, or exhilaration, and slowly during sadness or boredom. In films, it is possible to reverse this apparent cause-and-effect relationship and to induce a feeling of happiness, excitement, or exhilaration by making the picture seem to move quickly. Means of accomplishing this include lively music, quick cutting, or fast action. Conversely, a sense of sadness or boredom can be induced by solemn music or immobility of the images.

A feeling of suspense is unusual in combining excitement with a sense that time is passing slowly. Much of the suspense depends upon the audience's awareness of a danger unknown to the characters in the film. Conversely, the sense of serenity and wisdom achieved by directors such as India's Satyajit Ray or Japan's Ozu Yasujirō emanates from the deliberateness with which they pace even the most dramatic of actions.

Tempo is not necessarily related to the actual length of a motion picture. A poorly made short film may seem long, for example, while *Intolerance* (1916), D.W. Griffith's 3½-hour masterpiece, can command the full attention of connoisseurs.

Sound. Mechanical reproduction of sound was developed as early as the first motion pictures, but the problems of amplifying sound sufficiently for an audience and synchronizing it with the film image were not solved until the late 1920s. Although sound attracted crowds to the cinema to hear the new miracle, the artistic levels of the best silent pictures were not reached immediately. The new "talkies" were mostly poor imitations of theatrical plays, with dialogue and sound used indiscriminately. Sound equipment was cumbersome and imperfect. The mobile camera of the silent film lost its freedom, and the editing of film tied to a sound track became stodgy and slow.

Sound also resulted in great advantages, however. The cumbersome captions of the silent film could be dropped; certain strained methods of showing sound in pictures, such as shots of factory whistles, guns firing, or rows of clapping hands, became unnecessary. Music could be composed for a film and enjoyed in the humblest as well as the grandest cinema. Just as the visual image in the frame of a motion picture was elevated from the profusion of nature and could be seen fresh, so could sound be isolated for artistic purposes—the screech of automobile tires, the ticking of a watch, the baying of hounds, the whinny of a horse. The dramatic effect of sound could be tremendous. The rushing, crackling sound of a great fire in the last scene of Robert Bresson's *Trial of Joan of Arc* (1962) is as terrifying as any visual effect could be. In Hitchcock's *Torn Curtain* (1966) there is a desperate struggle in the

Dramatic effect of sound

kitchen of a lonely farmhouse; as the doomed man's head is held in an oven, and his hands (the only thing in the picture) convulsively twitch, the sound of hissing gas dominates the scene. The introduction of sound also made it possible to use silence with a dramatic effect that is more telling than either words or music.

Like images, sounds can be used to represent subjective thoughts, indicating not what the character is saying but what is in his mind. For example, in Hitchcock's *Blackmail* (1929), the first English sound film, the words "knife, knife, knife" are repeated in the thoughts of a frightened girl who thinks that she has committed a murder.

In terms of montage, sound, dialogue, and music are used in combination not only with one another but also with the visual image. They can overlap and vary in intensity in a flexible and complex pattern. The finished sound track may involve mixing together tracks of dialogue, background noises, and music recorded at different times; the tracks must be matched to one another and to the visual film. Though the audience may hear it simply as an accompaniment to what they see, the sound may be the most expensive and difficult part of a motion picture.

Music. The live music that accompanied silent films varied from a full orchestra to a honky-tonk piano, according to the size of the cinema. Music was effectively used on the film set to improve an actor's performance. With sound, music became an integral part of the picture on the screen. Early mood music was so expressive that often it now seems overblown. Conscientious filmmakers soon learned the virtue of restraint, using music less frequently but with more effect. Since the 1960s, electronic music, as in *Close Encounters of the Third Kind* (1977), has come to be commonly used.

Music often has an important function in emotional climaxes of motion pictures. It can be used effectively to relieve or sublimate intolerable intensity—of grief, pain, or ecstasy. *The Gospel According to St. Matthew* (1964) by the Italian director Pier Paolo Pasolini reveals how expressive periods of silence can be, and how great music can ennoble scenes like those of Christ's persecution and agony on the cross. Music may also be used symbolically. In *Léon Morin, prêtre* (*Leon Morin, Priest,* 1961), for example, a sequence of harsh chords represents the German occupation forces, and a dancing bugle motif represents the Italian troops. Organ music is used in scenes showing the heroine with the priest in church, and piano music when they are in his flat. Hurdy-gurdy music represents two gossiping spinsters, and in a climactic scene louder and louder electronic music represents the heroine's obsessive sexual feeling for the priest, until she reaches out to take his hand.

Sound engineering. It is the function of the sound engineer to select and modify sound as the cameraman selects visual images. Since the noise of crockery, cutlery, or paper or the chirping of crickets would be intolerable transferred in full volume to the screen, the sound engineer must tone them down. Treble and bass must be balanced. In other cases, in order to get the effect needed, sound has to be built up and orchestrated as if it were music. Again, sound need not correspond exactly with the visual images. Artistic use can be made of asynchronism; that is, contrasting the sound to the visual image. Motion-picture sound is capable of remarkable delicacy, richness, and variety. Sound libraries put most conceivable sounds readily at the disposal of filmmakers. Instruments and voices can be modified, overlapped, echoed, or given a resonance and volume that transform them. Dialogue can be crystal clear, bringing the audience far closer to an actor than in the theatre, or it may deliberately reproduce the careless enunciation of everyday speech.

The script. Although conventions vary from one country to another, the script usually develops over a number of distinct stages, from a synopsis of the original idea, through a "treatment" that contains an outline and considerably more detail, to a shooting script. Although the terms are used ambiguously, script, or screenplay, usually refers to the dialogue and the annotations necessary to understand the action; a script reads much like other printed forms of dramatic literature, while "shooting script" or "scenario" more often includes not only all of the dialogue but also extensive technical details regarding the setting, the camera work, and other factors. Moreover, a shooting script may have the scenes arranged in the order in which they will be shot, a radically different arrangement from that of the film itself since, for economy, all of the scenes involving the same actors and sets are ordinarily shot at the same time. Some scripts are subsequently modified into novels and distributed in book form, such as the U.S. best-seller *Love Story* (1970) by Erich Segal, and, in the instance of Dylan Thomas' *The Doctor and the Devils* (1953), a script became a literary work without ever having been made into a motion picture. Generally, more elaborate productions require more elaborate shooting scripts, while more personal films may be made without any form of written script. The script's importance can vary greatly, however, depending on the director. Griffith and other early directors, for example, often worked virtually without a script, while directors such as Hitchcock planned the script thoroughly and designed pictorial outlines, or storyboards, depicting specific scenes or shots before shooting any film.

Shooting script

Film adaptations of literary works

Adaptation from other art forms must take into account differences of complexity and scale in film. A film often must omit characters and incidents in the novel from which it is adapted, for example, and the pace usually must be accelerated. Ordinarily, only a fraction of a novel's dialogue can be included. In an adaptation of a play, the curtailment is less severe, but much dialogue still must be cut or expressed visually.

Well over half of all fiction films made since 1920 have been adapted from plays or novels, and it is understandable that certain formulas have been tacitly accepted to facilitate the remaking of literature into moving pictures. Adaptation has been thought of as an aesthetically inferior exercise, because most such films merely illustrate the classics or reshape a literary text until it conforms to standard cinematic practice. The particular qualities that made the original interesting are often lost in such a process. Certain films and filmmakers, however, have achieved an aesthetic premium by accepting the literariness of the original and then confronting this with the technology and methods of the cinema. Since the 1970s numerous directors have explored literature in an almost documentary manner. The artifice of the French director Eric Rohmer's *Die Marquise von O.* (1976), for example, aptly expresses the literary sensibility of Heinrich von Kleist's romantic, ironic work. On the other hand, less adventurous, big-budget adaptations continue to reshape the literary works they are based on into conventional "Hollywood" movies, as some critics complained about Sidney Pollack's *Out of Africa* (1985). The delicate and changing sensibility of the main character, evident in the prose of the original, was not reflected in the film's traditional, albeit grand, presentation.

Although many eminent literary authors, including F. Scott Fitzgerald and William Faulkner, have worked on film scripts, the ability to write a good original script, especially under strict studio conditions, frequently belongs to lesser-known scenarists with a strong visual sense. Some writers, particularly in France, have tried to narrow the gap between the written and cinematic modes of expression. Marguerite Duras and Alain Robbe-Grillet became leaders of a new kind of author who is able and willing to "write" directly on film. Both have directed their own films, which they see as equivalent to their novels and plays.

Motion-picture acting. Of all the artists involved in films, the actors and actresses are closest to the audience. The public more often goes to see a motion picture for its stars than for any other single reason. The divergent techniques of stage and film acting are well understood, and there are many leading players who excel in both. But the greatest film stars have a talent peculiar to the screen alone. This talent often seems to be related not to how well they act, but to the sort of person they appear to be.

Being oneself

Film acting requires restraint. "Don't act, think," was the advice of the eminent German director F.W. Murnau. While stage actors may be praised for a performance that is highly wrought, film stars usually must appear to be themselves. Close-ups accentuate the more intimate relationship the actor can establish with a film audience, an audience that has often followed the actual life of certain actors whom the industry promotes as "stars." The German theorist Walter Benjamin argued that the image of the star compensated the film audience for the loss of direct access to live performance. For this reason film actors from movie to movie are likely to be cast in similar roles, as the case of John Wayne makes clear.

Some actors, however, have deliberately tried to avoid being typecast. Robert De Niro, for example, is well known for the violent, obsessive characters he played in such films as *Taxi Driver* (1976) and *Raging Bull,* but he has been equally effective in more quiet, controlled roles, such as the charismatic hero in *The Deer Hunter* (1977) or the romantic movie producer in *The Last Tycoon* (1976). In his films, De Niro downplayed his own personality to "become" the characters he portrayed, even transforming himself physically by gaining excessive weight for his role in *Raging Bull.* Actors who have been strongly identified with one role have found it harder to change their image. Sean Connery, for example, has appeared in more than 40 films, playing such diverse characters as an eccentric poet in *A Fine Madness* (1966), an Arab chieftain in *The Wind and the Lion* (1975), a medieval monk in *The Name of the Rose* (1986), and a Prohibition-era Chicago policeman in *The Untouchables* (1987), but he remains most recognized for the seven films in which he starred as the sophisticated British secret agent James Bond.

A motion-picture performance can be synthesized bit by bit, by the joint efforts of the actor, the director, the cameraman, and others. The conditions of film production, however, are such that some actors find them trying. They may have to put up with long hours on the set and endless repetition, they must adapt to shooting scenes out of sequence, and in close-ups they often have to respond to the camera rather than to another actor. They require a talent different from, but equal to, that of theatrical performers.

Styles of acting

Throughout the history of the art, acting styles have frequently led to major revolutions in film style. Most of the shifts in acting have been toward what is deemed a more "realistic" approach. Often this realism is the result of the studied application of acting precepts, as when Marlon Brando brought to *On the Waterfront* (1954) the lessons he had digested at the Actors Studio (the professional workshop in New York City). In the 1960s several successful Czechoslovak films featured effective performances by what appeared to be average citizens; but in truth the players' long silences, their bumbling, and the foibles that seemed so natural were the result of lifelong practice and interminable rehearsals. Some films, however, have exploited the documentary power of the medium to reveal the behaviour of untrained but expressive individuals. Many of the masterpieces of the postwar Italian Neorealist movement relied on absolute amateurs, who were frequently picked up off the streets by the casting director.

Side by side with the never-ending quest for naturalness in acting, an opposite impulse has brought to the screen both stylized and histrionic performances of great power. Cinematic expressionism (largely identified with German films from the 1920s but also evident in Eisenstein's *Ivan*

Sean Connery and Kevin Costner in *The Untouchables* (1987), directed by Brian De Palma.

Marlon Brando and Eva Marie Saint in *On the Waterfront* (1954), directed by Elia Kazan.

the Terrible) depends on contorted bodily and facial gestures, which are amplified by decor and camera angle. Eminent actors, including Laurence Olivier and Orson Welles, have shown that some types of film thrive on expansive theatrical voicing and gesture.

Comedy requires other considerations. The impassive visages of the silent star Buster Keaton and the French comic Jacques Tati helped transform their bodies into expressive machines that interacted with the greater machine of the films they starred in. The Marx Brothers, on the other hand, depended on loose cinematic construction, dialogue, and zany, spontaneous action. In short, there can be no single theory of film acting.

Motion-picture design. Under the heading of design, all of the elements of a picture's setting may be included—art direction, scenic composition, set design, costume, and makeup. At its simplest and most naturalistic, the camera can choose and frame ordinary people in a real location. At its most elaborate, motion-picture production may involve the expenditure of vast sums to put up gigantic sets that require building houses, ships, churches, and monuments, or re-creating lost cities, bygone landscapes, or ancient battles, and dressing thousands of extras in period costumes. Thunderstorms, tornadoes, snowstorms, earthquakes, volcanic eruptions, and tidal waves may be simulated, or monsters, spaceships, and cities of the future created.

Film sets are constructed more solidly than stage scenery, but of the lightest, cheapest materials that will both look authentic and photograph well. Whether for black and white or for colour, their shades, proportions, and shapes are chosen for the camera rather than the eye. The camera can deceive the viewer about scale, however, and the model makers and special effects technicians can reproduce virtually anything in miniature, from the aurora borealis shining on an igloo to a tempest destroying the Spanish Armada. A whole series of film monsters have attracted goggle-eyed audiences since the French pioneer Georges Méliès' formidable man-in-the-moon of 1902. Miracles can be achieved in film, either in the colossal form of the crossing of the Red Sea by the children of Israel in Cecil B. deMille's epic *The Ten Commandments* (1956) or in the comparatively simple treatment of angels and miracles in Frank Capra's *It's a Wonderful Life* (1946) or Warren Beatty's *Heaven Can Wait* (1978). Film publicity makes much of the creations of epics such as *Cleopatra* (1963) or *Apocalypse Now,* but, even on a more

Use of sets to depict the bleak life of the future generation.
(Left) *Metropolis* (1926), directed by Fritz Lang; and (right) *Blade Runner* (1982), directed by Ridley Scott, with Harrison Ford as detective Rick Deckard.

By courtesy of Warner Brothers, Inc., *Blade Runner*, copyright © 1982 the Blade Runner Partnership, all rights reserved; photographs from the Museum of Modern Art/Film Stills Archive, New York City

modest scale, sets can contribute enormously to a motion picture, as in Ken Adam's sets for *Dr. Strangelove* (1964), *Sleuth* (1972), and the James Bond series.

The Expressionist influence on set design

The strongest single artistic influence in motion-picture set design was the German Expressionist cinema of the 1920s, which combined elements of Max Reinhardt's theatre, a Wagnerian philosophy of doom, and Expressionist painting and graphics. Expressionist films such as *The Cabinet of Dr. Caligari* (1919), *The Golem* (1920), *Nosferatu* (1922), and *Metropolis* (1926) created a world of fantasy and horror peopled with menacing, shadowy figures. In other German Expressionist motion pictures, such as *The Student of Prague* (1926) or *The Nibelungen* (1924), there was a baroque beauty of architectural, woodland, and floral settings. The influence of Expressionism can be seen in later cinema in the work of the directors Orson Welles and Carl Dreyer, and in many gangster movies.

Subject matter and how it is treated is reflected in all the elements of design in a motion picture. In the hectic atmosphere of a horror movie or a thriller, a studio set may pass unnoticed, even though it would seem disconcertingly artificial in another film. In a musical everything may look artificial: a chambermaid's bedroom may be a model of daintiness and taste. Some films, however, depend on realistic sets for dramatic effect. Accordingly, some directors, especially the French master Jean Renoir in his 1930s films, went to great lengths to be authentic, avoiding the use of rear screen projection, or process shots (*i.e.,* a shot in which new action is filmed in front of a screen on which previously filmed background footage is projected). All of the train sequences in Renoir's *La Bête humaine* (1938), for example, were shot on a moving engine, except the final scene, in which the hero, played by Jean Gabin, leaps to his death. Another French director of the same era, Marcel Pagnol, had his cast and crew construct the farmhouse for his masterpiece, *Angèle* (1934), not to save production money but to increase the naturalness of their behaviour on the set during shooting.

In historical epics, such as *A Passage to India* (1984), or science fiction films, such as *Blade Runner* (1982), settings vie with actors and story for the viewer's attention. In carefully constructed, intimate dramas, such as those by Robert Bresson (*L'Argent,* 1983) or Jim Jarmusch (*Stranger Than Paradise,* 1984), the setting can embody the tone of the film. Numerous stylistic options are attached to decor: its richness or sparseness; its naturalness or artificiality; its contemporaneity or period look; its cleverness or simplicity. Because all these factors are related to the full conception of the film, the set designer is one of the first artistic collaborators called in by the director in the quest for a strong, forceful production.

Lighting. In a medium consisting of the projection of impressions on a light-sensitive material, lighting is of special importance. Daylight is the readiest, cheapest, and strongest source of lighting. Hollywood was said to owe its preeminence as a motion-picture production centre to its sunny climate. Even in daylight shooting, however, artificial aids may be necessary to reduce the highlights or to lighten the shadows.

Lighting, a part of camera-work, is under the control of the chief cameraman or lighting cameraman. In black-and-white films, lighting is of paramount importance in giving the overall light or dark tone of the scene and in providing for dramatic contrasts or emphasis within the scene. In colour, the lighting works indirectly to bring out or modify the colour. Lighting in the cinema is a method of composition, used to complement and reinforce the dramatic situation. Generally, dark lighting is associated with tragedy and bright light with romance or comedy, but overlighting gives ghastly or unearthly effects, as in the memory sequence at the beginning of the Swedish director Ingmar Bergman's *Sawdust and Tinsel* (1953; also called *Naked Night*). Lighting an actor from above gives his face a spiritual effect; from below, an uncanny or evil appearance. Front lighting blurs faults but takes away character; side lighting gives relief and solidity but may show wrinkles and defects. Lighting from behind tends to idealize a subject and give it an ethereal quality.

Lighting as a method of composition

Fashions in film lighting have fluctuated through the years. Early films tended to be flat and uniform. Later, especially in German Expressionist films of the 1920s, strong contrasts of light and shade were favoured for their highly dramatic effect. Still later, this tendency was modified toward more balanced lighting. Even in dramatic scenes, the centre of interest now tends to be more discreetly emphasized.

Occasionally, different types of lighting are used for dramatic effect in a single film. For his Shakespearean adaptation *Henry V* (1944), Laurence Olivier employed uniform, bright light for the sequences modeled on medieval book illustrations, but in the contemplative sequences (Falstaff's death and Henry's solitude the night before the battle) he used single-source lighting from the side, which allows extensive gradation of light and shadows, making the images look like paintings by Rembrandt. The elegiac humanity of the latter scenes contrasts with the brittle, eternal quality of the former. More often, directors choose a single look. Stanley Kubrick's decision to film *Barry Lyndon* (1975) in candlelight is a notable example.

Related to lighting is the development of the print in the laboratory, where sections of film shot under different conditions can be modified to avoid a violent contrast where none is desired. Finally, the lighting of the projector that shows the picture and the brilliance of the screen are important. As light sources for the projector, both the traditional carbon arc and the modern Xenon lamp have advocates; what matters most is that the light be powerful, brilliant, and unvarying throughout the projection of the picture.

Settings. A salient feature of the cinema is its ability to reproduce natural scenery. From the earliest years filmmakers have mixed outdoor footage with scenes shot inside the studio to give audiences the impression that the carefully calculated dramas they are witnessing are faithful records of events that occurred spontaneously in the real world. Just after World War I the Swedish directors Mauritz Stiller and Victor Sjöström stunned audiences with their films featuring simple folktales set in the mountains. The seasons of the year, the weather, and the Swedish streams, lakes, and waterfalls were active participants in these tales. After the success of such documentary features as those by Robert Flaherty (*Nanook of the North*), even Hollywood made room for films in which the natural setting was clearly the main protagonist, with the fictional drama used as a way to convey the audience around the landscape. More often the landscape provides an alternative attraction, allowing viewers to see favourite stars in exotic locations, as in *Out of Africa*. Another trend has been the use of familiar surroundings as the sets for futuristic dramas. Jean-Luc Godard's *Alphaville* (1965) turned Paris into an oppressive metropolis on another planet, and *Blade Runner* made contemporary Los Angeles look like a city of the 21st century.

Location filming

With the invention of lighter, more portable equipment, filming on location—that is, in an actual setting like the one in which the story takes place rather than in a studio set—has become less difficult and expensive and more often used. As a result, many earlier motion pictures now look artificial, since no studio set can equal the authenticity of a real location. Nonetheless, films may have to be shot in a studio when natural settings are unavailable, as in historical films, or are too remote. On the other hand, the effect of certain films can be utterly lost when inauthentic locations are substituted for genuine ones. The 1948 British Technicolor epic *Scott of the Antarctic*, for example, was shot in the Swiss Alps, which facilitated filming but ruined the documentary aspect of the film. In some cases, rear screen projection can be used to provide a background setting against which the actors perform.

Costume. Actors in motion pictures have been dressed in noticeable and often significant ways since the beginning of film history. The Italian epics made before World War I displayed Roman and Egyptian styles that the public had come to expect from popular paintings and stage plays dealing with these ancient subjects. After World War I, Ernst Lubitsch gained fame directing historical dramas, such as *Madame Dubarry* (1919), that were termed "costume dramas" even in their own day. From the 1920s to the 1950s various national cinemas, but particularly those in France and the United States, vied with one another in using the cinema to promote fashion. Christian Dior's rise in the world of haute couture was accelerated by his experiments with, and his advertising of, costumes in motion pictures. In Hollywood a motion picture was often an opportunity for an actress to wear one gorgeous costume after another, and many screen designs initiated popular offscreen fashion trends. After World War II the Italian Neorealist movement proved that audiences could also be drawn by authenticity of dress. Since then, many films attempting to convey a realistic effect have been outfitted not from the costume shop but from secondhand clothing stores.

Costume and the actor's identity

Costume also once played a more important role in an actor's identity. Charlie Chaplin, Buster Keaton, Mae West, and other stars of the 1920s and '30s all created characters in which costume was an integral part of the total identity. Audiences were often able to discern the type of character an actor was portraying—hero, villain, comic foil, romantic rival—by the clothes that he was wearing.

Makeup. Film makeup differs significantly from that of the stage, where heavy lines are required to convey a characteristic expression to the audience. By means of the camera, the motion-picture audience can study the actor's face quite closely. The makeup must be flawless to stand up under such scrutiny, but since it need not be applied nightly for several months running, as in theatre, elaborate preparations are feasible. Many of the greatest filmmakers, such as Carl Dreyer and Robert Bresson, have favoured naturalism in makeup—the unadorned lines of old age or a face caked with dust, running with perspiration. Whatever the style of makeup, its purpose is to make the face a more photogenic object, whether monster or ingenue. The efforts of wig makers, dentists, and plastic surgeons, as well as cosmeticians, are aimed at a heightened reality.

The cosmetics industry grew up in the 1920s alongside motion pictures. Max Factor's fame owes much to the work his company did in modifying makeup to adjust to new types of film and lighting, including the shift to colour cinematography. With changing audience perceptions, caused by television and other factors, more natural makeup styles became just as popular as the "idealized" methods applied to the great studio stars. Sylvester Stallone is one actor whose makeup is exceedingly important in emphasizing his craggy, often sweating features. Ironically, the "natural look" is often the result of extensive makeup tests.

While makeup generally is meant to remain unnoticed or to play servant to the beauty of a face, in science fiction and horror films it may take centre stage. Although it is an art as old as society itself, makeup is, like the other aspects of cinema, subject to technological development. Advances in contact lenses, in prosthetics, and in chemistry have made possible such magnificent and startling displays as *2001: A Space Odyssey* (1968), *Planet of the Apes* (1968), *Time Bandits* (1981), and the never-ending flow of creatures that terrorize horror-film audiences.

(R.St./D.A.)

Peter Vaughan, in costume and makeup, for the role of Ogre in Terry Gilliam's *Time Bandits* (1981).

Authority of the director

Motion-picture directing. The modern motion-picture director is the person most responsible for the ultimate style, structure, and quality of a film. Cinema is an art of collaboration, and in some instances someone other than the director may come to dominate (for example, a producer with authority over the final cut, or an actor whose box-office popularity gives him the power to direct the director), but in general it is assumed that the person assigned to direct the picture must take the credit or blame for its form and content.

While the function the director serves has always been filled by someone, the priority of that function has not always been recognized. Georges Méliès, for example, thought of himself as a "producer" of films, and indeed from 1896 to 1912 he took care of all aspects of the making of the films bearing his name, including set design, acting, and camera-work. Charles Pathé, in turn-of-the-century France, was one of the first producers to assign an assistant (Ferdinand Zecca) specifically to direct the pictures of his rapidly expanding film empire. At France's Gaumont Pictures, Louis Feuillade and Alice Guy, the first woman to take on a key position in cinema, shared the task of directing, each specializing in separate genres. In the United States as in Europe, many of the first film directors were cameramen (Edwin S. Porter) or actors (D.W. Griffith) until circumstance compelled them to take on various directorial duties. The movie industry was growing rapidly, however, and by 1910 the number of films required to fill the many newly constructed movie theatres was such that production had to be delegated. The director's role was to work with the actors, designers, technicians, and others involved in the moviemaking process, coordinating and overseeing their efforts in order to rapidly turn out interesting and comprehensible movies within given financial and material strictures.

As early as the 1920s those who wrote seriously about motion pictures had no qualms about attributing successes and failures to the director. Some directors, notably F.W. Murnau and Fritz Lang in Germany and Victor Sjöström in Sweden, were virtually as famous as the stars who acted in their films. In 1926 William Fox paid Murnau $1,000,000 to relocate in Hollywood in the hopes that he would make the greatest movies the world had yet seen. The primary issue of this marriage of art and money, *Sunrise* (1927), remains an anomaly in the history of the film industry, for Murnau was given unusual control and virtually unlimited resources. The film still astounds critics, but it was not a commercial success and it stunted for a time the growing stature of the director. Erich von Stroheim's more dramatic encounters with producers such as Irving Thalberg further encouraged this businesslike attitude, which led to the practice of quickly typing directors as either workmanlike or difficult.

In the great age of the studio system (1927–48), strong directors vied with the factory conditions in which films were made. Those directors with powerful personalities (such as Frank Capra, Howard Hawks, John Ford, and Ernst Lubitsch) were given great freedom, but they still had to work with actors and actresses contracted to the studio, with union personnel following time-honoured routines, with scripts and scriptwriters selected by the studio, and with deadlines that discouraged experimentation.

The auteur theory

The "auteur theory," which was propagated by French film theorists in the 1950s, offered a powerful method for studying and evaluating the films of the studio era. The word "auteur" (literally "author" in French) had been employed in France in the 1930s in legal battles over the rights to artistic property. This legal struggle to determine whether a film "belonged" to its scriptwriter, director, or producer strengthened the belief held by many critics and theorists that it was the director alone who deserved credit for a film, just as an architect could be credited for a building even though it was built and used by other people. While this view made eminent sense when strong directors were concerned, it tended to ignore average filmmakers.

Auteurs are defined as directors with solid technique, a well-defined vision of the world, and a degree of control over their productions. Some directorial situations are easy to evaluate. Griffith and Chaplin had complete financial control over their major efforts; European art directors, such as Ingmar Bergman, enjoyed similar freedom. Indeed their films were often marketed as the expressions of important artistic personalities. The auteur theory, however, was developed to encourage the reevaluation of countless films by directors operating in the middle of suffocating studio situations. Directors such as Leo McCarey, Gregory La Cava, and Anthony Mann stylistically and thematically imbued their films, whatever the genre, with a consistent, personal aesthetic. Their output, even when unsuccessful, is deemed immeasurably more valuable than the undistinguished films of weaker directors who merely translated the words and actions indicated in a script into routine screen images. (Scriptwriters in the studio years worked mainly in teams. A single script often passed through the hands of several different writers so that most films are more recognizable as the product of a particular studio than of an individual writer.)

The tension between director and genre or studio is thought to be productive of films that appeal to the public while expressing the vision of an individual. Thus, through the auteur, the popular art of cinema is able to achieve the traditional goals of poetry and the fine arts, goals of authentic expression and of genius.

The auteur theory was especially influential in the 1960s and arguably was instrumental in creating not only the French New Wave but also similar movements in Britain and the United States. Directors such as Lindsay Anderson, Joseph Losey, Stanley Kubrick, John Cassavetes, Francis Ford Coppola, and Arthur Penn thought of themselves as budding auteurs and earned critical and popular acclaim for their distinctive styles and themes. With the fall of the studio system in the 1950s there was indeed room for a single personality to take control of a film and to market it on the basis of personal vision.

Artisanal format of filmmaking

After 1960 first-rank American motion-picture directors began to make films under conditions that had been in practice in Europe throughout the century. The insignificant studio system of France, for example, had enabled and encouraged individual entrepreneurs to put together film projects on a onetime basis. Such projects generally revolved around an *équipe,* or team of creative personnel, with the director at its head. The director could then truly shape the work of the designer, composer, and (most importantly) the scenarist, so that the film had a consistent and relatively personal style from beginning to end. In this artisanal format, a producer depends on the director to develop a distinctive way of handling scenes. The director may even be required to rewrite the scenario in order to achieve a particular effect. As a result of this personal commitment, the well-publicized arguments that occur during the production of many important films almost always involve the director.

Alfred Hitchcock was one director who disdained arguments. He kept the blueprint of his films in his head and provided detailed instructions for each shot, without any discussion. His producers were not given the opportunity to offer alternative suggestions or to recut the film. The scenes fit together in one way only, Hitchcock's way. While some critics have complained that the acting in a Hitchcock film is often stilted, that the sets are artificial, and that the rear-projection shots are obvious, the Hitchcock style is immediately recognizable. Most people admire the effectiveness of Hitchcock's direction, some even claiming that in his films can be found profound moral and metaphysical insight.

Major directors throughout the world have often enjoyed such respect. Among others, Mizoguchi Kenji and

North by Northwest, © 1959 Loew's Incorporated; photograph from the Museum of Modern Art/Film Stills Archive, New York City

Cary Grant in *North by Northwest* (1959), directed by Alfred Hitchcock.

Kurosawa Akira of Japan, Satyajit Ray of India, Federico Fellini of Italy, Luis Buñuel of Spain, and Carl Dreyer of Germany have been given rare opportunities to make individual artistic statements. Some have been treated as virtual national treasures whose films bring cultural glory to the countries within which they work.

Television versus film directing

Despite these exceptions, most directors labour under great restrictions, particularly in the age of the television industry. A conventional television series rotates directors episode after episode so that the producers, actors, and production crew, who work continuously on the show, have much greater control over the product. Each scene of a television program is typically filmed from three different camera setups. The director strives to get the best performances possible from the actors, confident that the crew is delivering appropriate images, and an editor later chooses the best shots to use to tell the story. In comparison, powerful film directors have often involved themselves deeply in editing and postproduction. The television industry has accentuated the assembly-line features of the studio system, while independent film production today often distinguishes itself by according the director dictatorial power.

Whether granted complete or restricted control, every director must approve the screenplay and then concentrate on the scene being filmed in its relation to the overall design of the film. The management unit (an assistant director and script girl) concerns itself with the details of organization so that the director can interact with the creative personnel on the set (cinematographers, lighting and sound crews, set decorators, and, of course, actors). As for postproduction, all directors look with the editor at daily rushes from the lab, but only some follow through and become involved with the editing, music, and mixing phases. In all cases, the director is the one person to maintain a complete view of the project, drawing the best from all the personnel, from writer through sound mixer, and shaping their efforts so that the film attains a consistent look and meaning.

Successful directing has much to do with intangible social relations, such as keeping harmony (or productive competition) alive on the set, drawing the best possible performances from actors, shaping a script into a form that takes advantage of the talents of the director of photography or of the main actor, or beseeching the producer for the money needed for a special shot. Beyond such routine expectations, the great director is identified for a unique or ingenious approach to the medium. Directors have earned praise for their audacious handling of stories. Refusing to be hemmed in by the standard requirements of a two-hour drama dealing with a few central characters, Francis Ford Coppola, for example, pieced together a truly epic fresco in his two-part masterpiece *The Godfather,* as did Robert Altman in such collage narratives as *Nashville* (1975). Italian directors have experimented with the epic form, as in Ermanno Olmi's *The Tree of Wooden Clogs* (1979) or Bernardo Bertolucci's *1900* (1976), and with narrative structure, as in Rossellini's *Paisà* (1946) and Ettore Scola's *Le Bal* (1983), which abandon traditional plot construction and a single story line in favour of separate short episodes that are thematically or historically linked.

Some directors gain more fame for their visual style than for their narrative acuity. Bertolucci's films, for example, are not always well received, but his fluid, saturated images and their "psychoanalytic" effect have made their mark in films such as *The Conformist* (1970) and *Luna* (1979). The same might be said for Federico Fellini, Andrey Tarkovsky, and Werner Herzog. Some critics feel that Coppola's *One from the Heart* (1982) projects an intense, personal vision, which is much more interesting from the directorial point of view than his more commercially successful efforts, including *The Godfather.* Although many directors credit their cinematographers for achieving such notable visions, most cinematographers claim merely to solve technical problems at the behest of the director.

The same can be said of effects achieved in postproduction. The incredibly dense aural ambience surrounding Coppola's *Apocalypse Now,* for example, resulted from the concatenation of scores of individual sound tracks mixed by a team of talented experts, but Coppola himself had already evinced a powerful understanding of the possibilities of sound in his much smaller film *The Conversation* (1974). Similarly, a good share of Robert Altman's fame must go to the engineers who coordinated the radio miking of as many as a dozen characters in a single scene in *Nashville.* It was, however, Altman who recognized the total effect that two hours of overlapping conversations would have on the spectator. Martin Scorsese's rugged editing in *Taxi Driver* and *Raging Bull* was a function not only of an editor's ingenuity but also of a total conception of script, acting style, camera-work (including harsh black-and-white tones for the latter film), and music.

The director as problem solver

A director might best be thought of as a problem solver. Seldom concerned with technology, the director takes the resources at hand (the technological capabilities and the conventions of filmmaking operating at the moment) and searches for effective solutions to dramatic or visual problems. A style emerges when these solutions, or "techniques," are applied consistently across a series of films. For example, Robert Bresson's penchant for employing off-camera sound to signal important events (a car wreck in *Au Hasard Balthasar,* 1966; a bank robbery in *L'Argent*) defies standard filmmaking conventions and reaches toward a peculiarly valuable way of understanding an interior or spiritual drama. Bresson's sound techniques have become part of his austere and evocative style.

Directors may be characterized by the solutions they regularly arrive at when a story or scene is presented to them. Murnau and Mizoguchi preferred the languorous tracking shot to editing a dramatic situation, so that the drama could be seen to arise in the midst of the shot. Antonioni let the camera continue to shoot well after the characters were out of range, so that the spectator could observe the way a dramatic scene disappeared or sense its smallness in the landscape that remained. Most American directors have employed hard-hitting, swift techniques to give power to the gritty stories that dominated world cinema after 1970. Close-up sound, pounding music, and abrupt editing keep the spectator interested and excited. Within this general American style, however, individual directors have found different methods to achieve similar effects, and they have discovered that using similar techniques does not guarantee similar results. It is generally acknowledged that the best directors are those who consistently contribute not only ingenious techniques but also an effective, coherent, personal style or theme to their films. Brian De Palma's use of point-of-view strategies, for example, gives a particular horror to such films as *Carrie* (1976) and *Body Double* (1984), and his technique has been compared to that of Hitchcock. Most critics agree, however, that Hitchcock is the more significant director because the rigorous point-of-view strategy that Hitchcock employed in such films as *Rear Window* (1954) was far more than a tour de force of moviemaking technique; it was an expression of the director's thoughts on vision and knowledge. (D.A.)

TYPES OF MOTION PICTURES

Film modes

Most connoisseurs of the art of motion pictures feel that the greatest films are the artistic and personal expression of strong directors. The cinema exists, however, for many social functions, and its "art" has served many types of film that do not set out to be artistic. In practical terms these functions divide films into what are usually termed modes, including the documentary, the experimental, and the fictional. The documentary mode incorporates those films relying primarily on cinema's power to relay events in the world automatically. The experimental includes the variety of approaches that have tested and played with the technological limits and capabilities of the medium, including animated (nonphotographic) and computer-generated images. The fictional is the mode most often thought of as simply "the movies." It has adopted the forms of storytelling that have always existed in culture, creating various cinematic languages to convey its tales. Each of these three modes can in turn be subdivided into genres (*i.e.,* commonly recognized types of stories or forms).

The documentary. The turn of the century witnessed

not only the invention of the motion picture but also tremendous growth of popular interest in journalism, picture postcards, lectures by travelers (frequently illustrated with slides), and so forth. The motion picture quickly came to serve society's need to learn about the geography and social conditions of the world at large. Some of the first motion pictures depicted exotic locations, contemporary events (battles, coronations), and unknown cultures. Indeed as late as 1908 such a major company as Biograph actually produced more nonfiction films than narratives. This would soon change, in part because the production of documentary films is dependent on world events and is therefore more haphazard and more difficult than the fully controlled process of making fiction films in studios. The decline of the nonfiction film has also been attributed to the belief that, after a decade, audiences were saturated with "views" and "actualities," as such films were called. Moviegoers were no longer drawn to the sheer recording ability of motion pictures; they demanded imaginative entertainment instead.

Travelogues and ethnographic films. One sort of film that has had continuous appeal, albeit for a specialized audience, has been the travel film. Much of the attraction of such films—from the crude pictures cranked out by Lumière cameramen in Japan, Africa, and the Arctic, to Robert Flaherty's films about the Eskimos, the South Sea Islands, and the wild western coast of Ireland, to National Geographic presentations on television—results simply from the thrill of seeing a foreign culture or a distant location. Flaherty proved, however, that there could also be tremendous artistry in such films. His unforgettable compositions matched the harmonious rhythm of his editing to render the lives of his subjects in a gloriously romantic tone.

Influence of travel films on fiction films

Both anthropologists and Hollywood producers immediately recognized the value of Flaherty's work, initiating several long-lived genres. In Hollywood *King Kong* (1933), one of the most famous monster movies ever made, was conceived by producer-director Merian C. Cooper, who was inspired by his experience shooting travel documentaries. The surprising success of *The Gods Must Be Crazy* (1981), a comedy about life in the Kalahari desert of Botswana, shows that audiences continue to enjoy the mixture of foreign locations and familiar dramas. The Bushmen (San) of the Kalahari are also the subject of an important ethnographic film, John Marshall's *The Hunters* (1958). Marshall's tradition dates to the 1930s and to the films the anthropologists Margaret Mead and Gregory Bateson made in the Pacific.

Most scholars prefer that all artistry be eliminated from ethnographic films so that the visual data recorded by the camera remains as fresh and uninterpreted as possible. The audience for these films typically consists of members of a university or museum community for whom entertainment is less significant than authenticity. When such films are prepared for mass television audiences, however, many concessions may be necessary, including the addition of extensive explanatory narration, musical accompaniment, and scenic photography.

Newsreels and documentaries. The argument over the role of art and artlessness in travelogues and ethnographic films is also pertinent to newsreels, where the standard principles governing journalism must apply. In the first years of cinema, reconstructions of such events as *The Dreyfus Affair* (Méliès, 1899) and *L'Assassinat de McKinley* (Pathé, 1901) were commonly accepted. Since then, viewers have required that newsreel material be neither prearranged nor fabricated, and they have become aware of the effects of the intrusiveness of the reporter and the limitations of point of view on the objectivity of any documentary film.

Newsfilms, more than any other type of motion picture, depend on their timeliness. Hence, for all of its ability to show the actual world, the motion picture failed to provide genuine news until it did so by means of television. Too stale and infrequent for day-to-day coverage, newsreels showed not news but parades, ceremonies, sporting events, bridge building, and similar events. *The March of Time,* inspired by *Time* magazine and produced by Louis

Scene from *Nanook of the North* (1922), documentary film directed by Robert Flaherty.

By courtesy of International Film Seminars, Inc.; photograph, the Museum of Modern Art/Film Stills Archive, New York City

de Rochemont from 1935 to 1951, was a series in which a topic of political or social importance was discussed in depth in a 30-minute film. The series was an immediate and continued success. It is television, however, that has developed the screen presentation of news, comment, and discussion beyond anything known before.

It is less in the straight presentation of reality than in its creative interpretation that the documentary has produced works of lasting value. Among the pioneers of the documentary besides Flaherty were the Russian theorist Dziga Vertov, whose films include *The Man with the Movie Camera* (1929), and the British director John Grierson, whose *Drifters* (1929) inspired a school of fine directors to produce a succession of memorable documentaries through the 1930s. With the outbreak of World War II, Humphrey Jennings' *Fires Were Started* (1943) and Harry Watt's *Target for Tonight* (1941), two among many outstanding British wartime documentaries, dramatized Britain's war effort better than fictional films could.

The British documentarists

In the United States, Pare Lorentz made dramatic documentaries about soil erosion and the dust bowl, such as *The Plow That Broke the Plains* (1936) and *The River* (1937) during the era of the Great Depression, and, during World War II, Frank Capra, who had been an outstanding director of Hollywood comedies, made a series of documentaries under the title *Why We Fight.* The later French movement, *cinéma vérité,* made films that are much closer to journalism than to the careful compositions of the English documentary school. Though often untidy, they are fresh and realistic. Television deeply affected the development of the documentary film in two major ways: by providing a training ground for documentary directors, and by building a supply of news film that could be adapted to documentary form. *Point of Order* (1964), a U.S. documentary film that ran successfully in motion-picture theatres, was made from television films of the U.S. Senate hearings on the charges and countercharges made by Senator Joseph McCarthy and the U.S. Army.

The Vietnam War gave rise to a plethora of documentary essays, some of them politically committed, some attempting a balanced exploration of the situation. American *cinéma vérité,* sometimes called "direct cinema," matured during the war, though not only in response to it. The first of the rock concert films, D.A. Pennebaker's portrait of Bob Dylan, *Don't Look Back,* first played theatrically in 1967, and that same year Frederick Wiseman's *Titicut Follies,* which exposed the horrendous conditions in a Massachusetts institution for the mentally ill, caused such an uproar that it was banned in that state. Excitement over public events and celebrations permitted this spate of documentaries to compete with fiction films for screens in larger cities. The films, which were often of inflammatory content, were kept off television but nonetheless influenced that medium tremendously. *Hearts and Minds* (Peter Davis, 1974), for example, a powerful, though one-sided, attack on U.S. Vietnam policy, had an enormous impact just because it could not be shown on television. Conversely, in the 1980s, many documentaries were increasingly seen on television rather than on movie-theatre screens. Claude Lanzmann's *Shoah* (1985), for example, a nine-and-a-half-hour examination of the Nazi concentration camps, received limited theatrical distribution in many areas because of its length but still managed to reach wide audiences through the distribution markets provided by the growing cable-television and videocassette industries.

By courtesy of New Yorker Films, *Shoah*, © 1985, Claude Lanzmann; photograph from the Museum of Modern Art/Film Stills Archive, New York City

Henrik Gawkowski, a Polish locomotive engineer in *Shoah* (1985), Claude Lanzmann's documentary of the Nazi concentration camps. The film uses no archival footage of the camps, relying on oral descriptions from eyewitnesses and participants to create its impact.

Propaganda. In presenting a background, an environment, and characters who behave in a certain way, every motion picture may be said to be propaganda. The term is usually restricted, however, to pictures made deliberately to influence opinion or to argue a point. The most powerful and most consistent use of the cinema for propaganda has been by the Soviet Union. After the 1917 revolution, Soviet films exploded on the screen with fervent conviction. Gradually, however, the pictures became lifeless, and in the 1930s and 1940s, during the Stalin regime, great directors such as Eisenstein and Aleksandr Dovzhenko worked under severe restraints. Nazi Germany produced its own brand of propaganda in the 1930s, the most striking being Leni Riefenstahl's *Triumph of the Will* (1936), a terrifying spectacle of a huge Nazi rally that had in effect been staged for the film made about it.

Few filmmakers would admit to making propaganda, although, in effect, many so-called educational films and all advertising or promotional shorts, whether featuring consumer products, vacation sites, or religious sects, may be seen as examples of propaganda. This form of film bears a stigma due to its undisguised aim: to influence ideas and change behaviour. Cinematic artistry serves merely as a tool in propaganda. (R.St./D.A.)

The experimental and animated film. Films of all kinds may be the results of experiments or may contain attempts to overturn traditional genres, but the mode of experimental film has always been reserved for those endeavours produced and exhibited with the aim of questioning or revolutionizing the medium itself. The mode is by definition limited, because no real traditions can develop that do not soon cease to be experimental.

The first significant experimental film movements emerged during the 1920s, when sophisticated artists began to play with the film medium and when film societies, specialized theatres, journals, and museum lectures began to cater to audiences wanting to be disturbed or surprised. In France at that time a true avant-garde led by painters such as Marcel Duchamp, Man Ray, Fernand Léger, and Salvador Dali scorned the mass market and sought exhibition in clubs and museums. French directors of the time, including Jean Epstein, Marcel L'Herbier, and Abel Gance, experimented with narrative structure in their films but were still involved in creating feature films for theatrical release. Although these films, especially Gance's *Napoléon* (1927), are full of experimental camera and editing techniques, they are not considered to be experimental films because of their exhibition histories.

Influence of fine arts and technology on experimental films

The experimental film has been forged out of two impulses. The first has stemmed from movements in the fine arts, such as Futurism, Constructivism, Dada, Surrealism, Minimalism, and Abstract Expressionism. Artists working in these movements have often shifted to cinema as new terrain for their ideas, radically rethinking the medium to make a personal or cultural point. The other impulse has been technological. The experimentalist, curious to see what the medium can do, has explored and expanded the basic processes and techniques involved in filmmaking. The early films of Méliès were precursors of this type of cinema.

The two impulses have rarely been seen separately. Luis Buñuel's scandalous *Un Chien andalou* (*The Andalusian Dog,* 1928) arose as much from his curiosity about film and narrative as it did from his association with the Surrealist movement. The same can be said of Maya Deren, founder of the American avant-garde during the 1940s. Other artists have rejected narrative altogether and linked up with traditions in poetry and the visual arts. During the 1950s and 1960s, the heyday of the American avant-garde, Stan Brakhage manipulated focus, lighting, and sequence in a range of distinctively personal and often mythic films. His most radical technical strategy was to eliminate photography altogether—by scratching directly on film, gluing particles on the emulsion, and even growing algae on the film before copying it—in an attempt to express himself without the mediation of character, plot, or objects. Like other filmmakers of the period, he called on the theories of action painting to justify his excesses.

Uses of animated films

Nonphotographic techniques can also be used to produce representational objects and even stories, as the experimentalist Len Lye proved with his short animated films of the 1930s. Laboriously drawing black-and-white (and later polychrome) figures on every film frame, he achieved a lightness of effect impossible in photography. Imaginative animation can also be used to demonstrate movements or changes that are difficult or impossible to photograph. It can produce striking, eye-catching effects or make a dull subject interesting and entertaining. In addition, information is often conveyed more quickly and clearly through animation than through live action. For these reasons, animated films are widely used for instructional and advertising or other promotional purposes. Animated films can, of course, exist simply to amuse, and the best-known works of animation are undoubtedly the cartoon comedies.

Whatever their length or purpose, animated films have a motion and characterization more succinct than live action. They can more freely contract or distort both time and space and defy the forces of gravity; they can be as realistic or as fantastic as their designers wish. The potentialities of animation have fascinated filmmakers since the earliest days of the motion picture.

The graphic style of early animated entertainments followed at first that of the cartoon strips of the period—hard outlines, little or no modeling, and the flat application of paint when colour was introduced. Walt Disney was responsible for improving the professionalism of the animated film and for getting it into the standard theatrical distribution system. He also helped to develop and popularize the animated feature film. Disney's feature-length *Snow White and the Seven Dwarfs* (1937) contained about 477,000 photographed drawings; it was the leading international box-office favourite of 1938, and its sound track was dubbed into 13 foreign languages.

Use of serious subject matter

The symbolic political fable *L'Idée* (1934), by the Austro-Hungarian animator Berthold Bartosch, represented a rare use of animation to present a serious, as distinct from a comic or legendary, subject; the approach was first achieved at feature length by the British husband-and-wife team of John Halas and Joy Batchelor in their adaptation of George Orwell's novel *Animal Farm* (1954). More recently, cartoons have been used on occasion in certain Communist countries to make social statements in the guise of highly stylized anecdotes or fables. Some of the most advanced, most inventive work of this kind has been done in such countries as Yugoslavia, Czechoslovakia, and Poland. In the United States, highly individual styles were pioneered in the 1940s by the United Productions

An illustration from the first animated feature film, *Snow White and the Seven Dwarfs* (1937).

Snow White and the Seven Dwarfs, © 1937, The Walt Disney Company; photograph from the Museum of Modern Art/Film Stills Archive, New York City

of America (UPA) group under the direction of Stephen Bosustow. Among their creations were the series that featured Mr. Magoo and Gerald McBoing Boing.

Later, various kinds of graphic fantasy found expression through animation, and the older style of cartooning associated with Walt Disney was completely overtaken by artists using a diversity of contemporary graphic styles, often extremely elaborate. The work of Jiří Trnka and Kařel Zeman exemplified the long-established Czech leadership in animated puppetry. Trnka's *Old Czech Legends* (1951) and *The Good Soldier Schweik* (1955) used stylized puppets in naturalistic settings to dramatize social satires, folk legends, and classics. Zeman's work used both puppets and live actors moving within real sets.

Since the 1950s, the experimental filmmakers Robert Breer and Norman McLaren, among others, have developed new styles and techniques of animation, including collage and pixilation (a technique that makes human movements look like those of animated automatons). In the 1960s the cartoon film appeared to lose ground as pure entertainment, except in the Communist countries, but it has steadily advanced in the fields of education and public relations. The growing use of computers in graphic design has further emphasized this use of animation.

(R.M./D.A.)

Fictional genres. Motion pictures are the most important narrative art form of the 20th century, having taken on the functions served earlier by dime novels, serial novels, staged melodramas, wax museum displays, epic paintings, and professional storytelling. These earlier forms continued into the century and were supplemented by comic books, radio, and television, but it is the motion picture that came to dominate them all. Still, most films can be seen as descendants and variants of types of stories and storytelling that predated the invention of the cinema.

Production advantages of genre films

Always plagued by the need for a constant flow of new product to satisfy patrons returning to the movies week after week, film companies quickly began to rely on genres to help regularize production and to help presell their motion pictures. A studio that decided to make half a dozen police thrillers in one year could organize its production schedule efficiently, saving time and money by reusing sets, costumes, and other items. More important, the studio could assign the same personnel to certain genres, allowing writers, directors, technical crew, and actors to establish a routine that often resulted in quicker and improved filmmaking from work to work. In addition, it was found that the initial success of a new film was frequently enhanced by the popularity of previous films in the same genre. Viewers knew, to a great extent, what to expect from a genre film; they recognized the stars, or at least the characters, in it; and they were sensitive to music, lighting, and plot devices because of long familiarity with the type of story being portrayed.

Although the movies have created their own genres, most have been derived from prototypes in the other arts, especially literature. The western, for example, has important precursors in popular painting, Wild West shows, and pulp fiction. It does not matter, however, if audiences are unfamiliar with these other media; viewers quickly learn the rules of the genre, acquiring the ability to recognize the hero from his costume, to anticipate the final shoot-out, and so forth. Genres epitomize the dilemma of the fiction film, in that they promise to deliver to a waiting audience something that is similar to what that audience has enjoyed in the past and yet something that is also quite new and different. Often the most highly acclaimed films are those that invoke the conventions of a genre only to break them down in the pursuit of ideas and visions never attained in that form before. Examples include John Ford's western *The Searchers* (1956), the comedies of Preston Sturges, Arthur Penn's gangster film *Bonnie and Clyde* (1967), and Robert Altman's comedy *M*A*S*H* (1970).

Well-formed genres typically characterize the production of highly centralized studio systems such as those of Hollywood, of Japan, or of India. They play a lesser role in countries where individual producers dominate. In France, for example, most films are treated as single-effort productions, a practice that can permit far more revolutionary films to develop, as was seen during the French New Wave of the late 1950s and early '60s. François Truffaut, Jean-Luc Godard, Claude Chabrol, Eric Rohmer, and other New Wave directors utterly overturned standards of storytelling and visualization to the delight of an international audience tired of old formulas. These directors were not oblivious to genres; rather they played with conventions, mixing comedy and pathos, suspense and spectacle. Their highly personal films confirmed the importance of genre to the fictional mode.

Hollywood genres. Most genres can be defined by their subject matter or setting—*e.g.,* the western, gangster film, police thriller, science-fiction film, and social problem film. Others are classified according to the type of narrative form they exhibit. The musical, for example, often has a show business setting or theme, but it is not so narrowly restricted; it can be about almost any subject. The melodrama also encompasses many subjects and styles; it has even been combined with other genres, for example, with the western in *Rancho Notorious* (1952) and with the problem film in *Ordinary People* (1980).

Evolution of genres

The evolution of genres can be used to trace the history of Hollywood cinema and 20th-century American popular culture. Different genres have achieved popular success in different periods. Some, termed "cycles," are short-lived (*e.g.,* the disaster cycle of the 1970s, which included *Earthquake* [1974] and *The Towering Inferno* [1974]); but even lasting genres go through phases of popularity. The western, for example, was well-established as a genre by the 1920s. It was particularly strong in the late 1940s and early 1950s but not during the '30s. It resurged in the 1960s but subsided later in the 1970s. Musicals came into prominence with the introduction of sound. They remained important until the late 1960s, when a number of expensive, overblown productions flooded theatres and met financial failure. Most film historians were ready to proclaim the genre dead, but several astounding successes in the late 1970s and early 1980s caused them to revise their view of the musical and the culture it addresses.

The internal mutation of a genre reflects the changing tastes and mores of the public. The modern musical (*All That Jazz,* 1979; *Fame,* 1980; *Coal Miner's Daughter,* 1980) is more socially conscious and more serious than the colourful, vividly stylized, self-conscious musicals of the 1940s and 1950s (*Singin' in the Rain,* 1952; *The Band Wagon,* 1953), which in turn are derived from, but upend, such early escapist masterpieces as *42nd Street* (1933) and *Top Hat* (1935). Each phase can be seen as a response to the prevailing political, social, and economic conditions of its time.

The western is the genre most scrutinized for this evolution. Its classical phase (*Stagecoach,* 1939) mutated after World War II into a variant capable of dealing with social problems (*High Noon,* 1952) or with tortured heroes (*Winchester 73,* 1950). In the 1960s, the Italian "spaghetti western" announced a decadent phase. *The Good, the Bad, and the Ugly* (1966) inverted character roles and culminated in a three-man gunfight. Audiences applauded

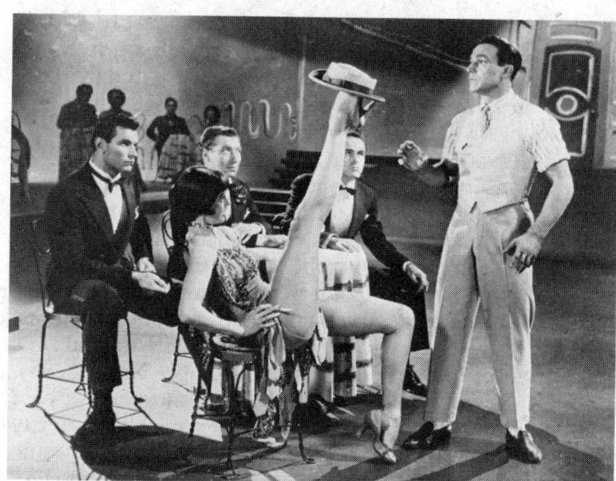

Cyd Charisse and Gene Kelly in a dance sequence from the musical film *Singin' in the Rain* (1952).

Singin' in the Rain, © 1952 Loew's Incorporated, renewed 1979, Metro-Goldwyn-Mayer, Inc; photograph from the Museum of Modern Art/Film Stills Archive, New York City

both the attenuated spectacle of these films and their ironic perversion of the codes operating in the standard genre. Some scholars, citing the *Star Wars* trilogy (1977, 1980, 1983) as an example, have argued that in the 1970s the mutation went so far as to leap across the boundary of subject matter toward science fiction. Although some science-fiction films may share fascinating properties with the western, it is unlikely that the production or reception of such films was consciously affected by westerns. Genres with strong, well-defined iconographies rarely consciously influence or combine with one another, even when they are clearly related. When Hollywood remade Kurosawa's *Seven Samurai* (1954) into the western *The Magnificent Seven* (1960), production personnel and audiences were far more conscious of the new film's relationship to previous westerns than of its similarities to Japanese samurai pictures.

The serial. While genres implicitly rely on an audience's interest in and familiarity with earlier movies of a certain kind, the serial is a type of movie that explicitly requires an audience to return episode after episode. Also called the chapter-play or cliff-hanger, the serial flourished in the days of silent films, when cinema going was a weekly habit. Perhaps the most famous were Louis Feuillade's *Fantômas* (1913–14) and *Judex* (1916) in France and the U.S. series of the same period with Pearl White, such as *The Perils of Pauline.* Old serials have been revived since the 1960s as period pieces of popular art, with their improbable plots, exaggerated acting, and old-fashioned decor appealing to modern, sophisticated audiences. The French director Georges Franju made a modern pastiche *Judex* in 1963. Since the late 1970s new serials have appeared in the form of multiepisode sagas shown on television. *Roots* (1977) in the United States had its counterpart in Rainer Werner Fassbinder's 16-hour *Berlin Alexanderplatz* (1980), which aired in installments on German television and then played as a serial in art house theatres around the world. (D.A.)

Interpretations

Films of art and the art cinema. For want of a better term, "interpretation" may be used to describe the type of motion picture in which a play, a ballet, an opera, or some other work of another art form is kept virtually intact and recorded by the camera and microphone. Adaptations of novels or plays re-create the work in motion-picture form, but interpretations merely give the performance a wider audience. The English director Tony Richardson's version of *Hamlet* (1970) is an example of such a filmed record of a theatrical performance. Most motion pictures of operas and ballets may be classed as interpretations. Public and cable television have become obvious sponsors and disseminators of this type of film, although some interpretations, including Joseph Losey's *Don Giovanni* (1979), and numerous films of rock concerts continue to thrive in theatrical distribution.

At one time the recording of an already established work of art was deemed "uncinematic" and thought to be a doubtful use of the medium. Such arguments were made as early as 1911 in response to the French Film d'Art company, which photographed high-class stage plays. Recently, however, imaginative and innovative cinematic techniques have been employed to record operas, ballets, and stage plays. The complexity of the resulting hybrid works, such as Arnold Schoenberg's *Moses and Aaron* as filmed by Jean-Marie Straub and Danièle Huillet (1975), have made the validity of the early generalizations questionable. Important filmmakers, including Robert Altman in the United States, Eric Rohmer in France, and Carlos Saura in Spain, have turned to the filming of works of other art forms as ways to open up the motion picture to new types of experiences.

Art films versus popular films

The motion-picture recording of the acknowledged artistic successes of other media raises the important issue of the artistic stature of the cinema. As early as 1920 an audience of film connoisseurs could be identified in Europe. Ever since that time it has been possible to divide the cinema audience of any nation into a mass audience that seeks entertainment and a smaller group that is consciously concerned with artistic values in the motion picture. The films that appeal to these two groups, however, vary from one nation to another and from one period to another. The Hollywood comedies of the 1920s by Charlie Chaplin, Buster Keaton, and others, for example, were originally popular entertainment, but they were later taken up by the art film audience. The comedies of Jerry Lewis received little serious critical attention in their native United States but a great deal in France. The low-budget thrillers of directors who were adopted by auteur critics met a similar experience. The distinction between popular entertainment and high art seems indisputable in most instances, but confusions of fashion and conflicts in artistic standards resulting from experiment and change make it difficult to generalize about them.

Although there may be disagreements over what constitutes cinematic art, certain institutions have developed that foster the art of film. In the United States after World War II, "art houses" catered to sophisticated audiences in large cities, screening primarily European films, such as those directed by Fellini, Bergman, Buñuel, and Antonioni. The distribution of 16-millimetre films to museums and college campuses sparked interest in avant-garde films as well. In one sense art films represent a genre; the audience that seeks them out has precise expectations which producers have been known to exploit. In 1951 Daiei films of Japan, for example, expressly aimed to conquer the export market by winning awards at international festivals. The company, which generally produced cheap domestic genre motion pictures, reserved a portion of its budget to make lavish historical spectacles, such as Mizoguchi's *Ugetsu* (1953), that would appeal to the art audience outside of Japan. The art film usually cannot be characterized in advance, however; it does not follow prescribed conventions but prides and sells itself on its uniqueness or distinctiveness.

THE STUDY AND APPRECIATION OF MOTION PICTURES

Film criticism

Criticism of motion pictures generally follows the pattern of the other arts, though it has some peculiar features. In the criticism of painting, music, theatre, and literature, some technical knowledge of the medium has generally been required. Motion-picture reviewers, however, rarely have any experience of filmmaking. A lack of experience in filmmaking is not necessarily a handicap. Film is such a complex medium that a technician is unlikely to be expert in every aspect of it and may well be overly conscious of his specialty. In addition, even though the technique is complex, the results are plain to view, and an intelligent critic may well appreciate such technicalities as fine camera-work, tight editing, authentic location shooting, or competent direction without knowing in detail how the result was achieved.

Film periodicals and books

Besides reviews in the daily and weekly press, there are specialized monthlies and quarterlies that engage scholars, students, and enthusiasts of the medium. In the United States *Film Quarterly, Wide Angle, Quarterly Review of Film Studies,* and *Cinema Journal* have great influence, just as *Screen* does in England and *Bianco e nero* in Italy.

As a country France has made cinema a central part of its culture. The French *Cahiers du Cinéma* sustains several times the circulation of the U.S. *Film Quarterly* and is rivaled by several other serious journals and countless magazines. Aiming at a less specialized but still avid film audience, glossy magazines such as *American Film* in the United States and *Sight and Sound* in England mix serious reviews, interviews, and features. There are similar publications in Poland and India. Popular magazines, which lure a large readership with their blend of pictures and gossip, have always been a part of movie culture, as have trade papers such as *Variety,* one of the most reliable and thorough sources of information about the international film business.

Books about the cinema range from serious studies of its economic, sociological, and technical aspects to light memoirs, ephemeral gossip, and innumerable biographies and autobiographies of actresses, actors, producers, and directors. Monumental film histories and theories written by Sergey Eisenstein, Vsevolod Pudovkin, André Bazin, Lewis Jacobs, Georges Sadoul, and others have triggered a remarkable industry of book publishing on these topics in many countries. The U.S.-based Society for Cinema Studies enrolls more than 500 teachers of film, who read these books and recommend titles to students. Most major university libraries now routinely collect film books and periodicals, although certain centres of research house the most complete collections. In the English-speaking world these include the British Film Institute, the special collections libraries at the University of California at Los Angeles and the University of Southern California, the Margaret Herrick Library of the Academy of Motion Picture Arts and Sciences in Beverly Hills, Calif., and the Lincoln Center Library in New York City. Other institutions house important documentation along with archives of films. The International Museum of Photography at George Eastman House in Rochester, N.Y., is particularly rich in material on the early cinema, while the Wisconsin Center for Film and Theater Research in Madison has gathered data pertaining to its collection of films produced by Warner Bros., RKO, and United Artists.

Preservation of film. The permanence of the motion-picture medium—the fact that films can be stored and reproduced indefinitely—not only makes it an enduring theatrical art but also a vivid record of past life. Despite the fact that motion pictures can theoretically last forever, relatively few have been preserved and many of these are in poor condition. One reason is that inflammable nitrate film stock, which was generally used until the 1940s, when it was replaced by acetate, is chemically unstable. Also, as film runs through a projector, it is eventually worn, scratched, or damaged. Still another factor is that commercial conditions of filmmaking discouraged preservation; the stress was on the present and the future, not on preservation of the past. Early motion pictures were best preserved when filmmakers such as Chaplin or Disney had control over their own work and a personal interest in preserving and representing it. During the 1960s and 1970s, however, there developed a tremendous interest in old movies. Revival houses sprang up in most major U.S. cities, and distribution companies were established solely for the reissue of old films.

Film preservation that allows access to old motion pictures is costly, requiring careful scientific control of storage conditions. Few private organizations or governments have been willing to spend the necessary funds. The earliest film archive was the Swedish Film History Collection begun in 1933. Archives in Paris, London, and New York City followed shortly afterward. An international federation (FIAF; Fédération Internationale des Archives du Film) was founded with headquarters in Paris in 1938.

Problems of the archivists

The archivists' problems are many: first, selecting the motion pictures to be preserved; second, acquiring copies (a negative or a fine-grain positive if possible) in good condition; third, storing them under the best possible conditions of temperature and humidity; fourth, cataloguing them and keeping some record of their contents; and fifth, allowing them to be viewed or letting stills or extracts be taken, without damaging the copies. The ideal solution to the problem of choice would be to preserve everything, but the cost would be prohibitive. Even with a limited selection, acquisition and storage are expensive and difficult, and nitrate film requires regular testing to see whether it has deteriorated enough to require copying.

The preservation of colour films has become perhaps the most serious problem. While Technicolor films (mostly made before 1953) can be reproduced faithfully and endlessly, virtually all colour films made since 1953 are subject to fading that can be arrested only by storing prints at very low temperatures. Video technology has been used to help preserve some colour motion pictures; computer-driven viewers are able to read the original tints of films and reproduce them on videotape. Nevertheless, until the development of a suitable and inexpensive base onto which colour films can be transferred, the majority of colour motion pictures made after 1953 will continue to deteriorate. (R.St./D.A.)

Film societies, film festivals, and awards. Predating and indispensable to the academic study of motion pictures are the linked phenomena of film societies and film festivals. These social institutions provided readership for film journals and serious film books, which eventually led to the acceptance of film study in universities. The first and most lasting function of film societies has been to foster the appreciation of the art of film. The second function has been to emphasize the social dimension of film in culture, sometimes using the film as a prop for the examination and propagation of moral and political ideas.

Functions of film societies

These two directions were evident by the 1920s. Louis Delluc and Ricciotto Canudo are credited with forming the first important *ciné-club* (as such societies are frequently called, especially when devoted to film art). The list of adherents to these clubs contains many luminaries from the film world (Epstein, Gance, L'Herbier, Germaine Dulac) and the other arts (Colette, André Gide). The Film Society of London, for example, was founded in 1925 by H.G. Wells, George Bernard Shaw, Augustus John, John Maynard Keynes, and other dignitaries who wanted to see French, German, and Soviet pictures that commercial exhibitors did not handle. The movement spread rapidly, and cinema was included in several international art forums, beginning with the 1925 Paris Exposition des Arts Décoratifs et Industriels Modernes that launched Art Deco. There, for several months, a history of cinema played in the Grand Palais and was accompanied by lectures on technique and appreciation of motion pictures.

Specialized theatres in major cities began to cater to *ciné-club* audiences. One of Jean Renoir's first films, *La Petite Marchande d'allumettes* (*The Little Match Girl,* 1928) was actually commissioned by a theatre and shot on its premises. *Ciné-clubs,* too, sponsored films made by their own members until the invention of sound made such amateur productions too expensive and technically intricate.

The political power of film societies was first recognized by Léon Moussinac, an official in Delluc's club who traveled to the Soviet Union in the 1920s and recognized immediately the importance of motion pictures in the education of the masses. Through his writing and organization, he was responsible for thousands of "average citizens" joining film clubs that featured controversial and sometimes revolutionary films. In 1928 Les Amis de Spartacus purportedly enrolled more than 75,000 subscribers. The mayor of Paris found it necessary to prohibit some of their meetings, the most important being a scheduled appearance by Sergey Eisenstein, whose *Battleship Potemkin* (1925) was officially banned in some countries.

In the 1930s enthusiasm for film societies waned, perhaps due to the Depression, although it was in this decade that the Roman Catholic Church developed networks of societies for the projection and discussion of exemplary films, particularly in parishes in Italy and France. After World War II, a resurgence of film societies occurred internationally. The French film theorist André Bazin was associated with both an artistic club headed by Jean Cocteau and a trade union club, indicating that the old split between "film art" and "film and social issues" remained. In the United States, clubs were devoted primarily to film art, fostering the American underground film movement. This postwar flourishing must be credited in part to the marketing of convenient 16-millimetre equipment.

Decline of film societies

The importance of such societies inevitably declined after universities and museums regularly began to include motion pictures as part of their collections, and in most countries film societies eventually attached themselves to universities. In the 1980s the availability of videocassettes further dissolved the strength of the *ciné-club* by allowing would-be members to select their own films for viewing at times convenient to them.

Film festivals provide a forum for promotion and recognition of artistic achievements of national film industries. The first festival was founded at Venice in 1932. It remained unique until after World War II, when the Cannes Festival was founded, and festivals began to assume their modern-day importance. Struggling nations, rebuilding their shattered film industries, saw in festivals a chance for world recognition. The growing interest everywhere in film imports made the festivals an international marketplace for distributors. Festivals were initiated at Berlin; Moscow; Karlovy Vary, Czech.; London; San Francisco; Chicago; and New York City. Through the early 1960s, the U.S. film industry remained wary of festivals; films that won festival awards did not necessarily do well at the box office, though a poor reaction at a festival might reduce the audience for a serious film. After 1965, however, distributor attitudes changed as investments increased in films for specialized audiences, particularly in "foreign" films backed by U.S. companies, and favourable critical acclaim became a vital promotional aid. Interest in the festivals persisted, and they continued to increase in number and in size. By the early 1980s there were more than 100 scheduled annually in some 25 different countries.

Functions of film festivals

Film festivals serve several functions. They provide an international marketplace where producers and distributors can exchange ideas, view films, and sign contracts. For example, the phenomenon of the international coproduction, so important to European cinema, arose at the Cannes festivals of the late 1940s. Festivals also provide an opportunity for fans to see popular stars and other celebrities. A further function of film festivals has been to provide a cultural rendezvous for those interested in the art and influence of the movies. Festivals often showcase new films or movements, as when the Venice festivals of the early 1950s introduced the stunning accomplishments of the Japanese film industry, which had been previously unknown in the West. At other times festivals are sites of artistic and political contention. At the Cannes festivals of 1958 and 1959, for example, advocates and opponents of the French New Wave heatedly exchanged diatribes and manifestos. A decade later several key New Wave directors, most notably François Truffaut and Jean-Luc Godard, helped close the festival to protest government policies during the events of May 1968. The Venice Film Festival, generally deemed more serious and less commercial than Cannes, ceased its juried competition from1969 to 1979 because of political strife.

Festivals are regulated by the Fédération Internationale des Associations de Producteurs de Films (FIAPF), which licenses those who want to award prizes. The competition that is associated with most festivals is in many instances, however, only a publicity device. Film screenings are often not even announced. The real purpose of the festival is to allow distributors to view and bid on the latest movies.

Academy Awards

The best known of all competitions, the Academy Awards, does not take place at a festival at all. The U.S. industry, with its overwhelming control of the world's screens, long had virtually no interest in film awards except for the awards voted each year since 1929 by the Academy of Motion Picture Arts and Sciences. The academy, which represents various artistic and technical disciplines, originally intended its annual awards as modest, peer-group citations within the tightly knit Hollywood industry. After media coverage created widespread interest, however, there was an increase in box-office revenues for winning films, and the Academy Awards, or "Oscars," became valuable in merchandising. The prestige of the academy's artistic judgments, however, has failed to keep pace with its economic power. Serious students of the film tend to place more credence in the awards of the New York Film Critics (founded in 1935), and the National Society of Film Critics (1966), as well as in the oldest U.S. reviewing organization, the National Board of Review of Motion Pictures (1909). (R.St./A.D.M./D.A.)

Technology

Motion-picture technology is a curious blend of the old and the new. In one piece of equipment state-of-the-art digital electronics may be working in tandem with a mechanical system invented in 1895. Furthermore, the technology of motion pictures is based not only on the prior invention of still photography but also on a combination of several more or less independent technologies; that is, camera and projector design, film manufacture and processing, sound recording and reproduction, and lighting and light measurement.

HISTORY

Motion-picture photography is based on the phenomenon that the human brain will perceive an illusion of continuous movement from a succession of still images exposed at a rate above 15 frames per second. Although posed sequential pictures had been taken as early as 1860, successive photography of actual movement was not achieved until 1877, when Eadweard Muybridge used 12 equally spaced cameras to demonstrate that at some time all four hooves of a galloping horse left the ground at once. In 1877–78 an associate of Muybridge devised a system of magnetic releases to trigger an expanded battery of 24 cameras.

Eadweard Muybridge

The Muybridge pictures were widely published in still form. They were also made up as strips for the popular parlour toy the zoetrope "wheel of life," a rotating drum that induced an illusion of movement from drawn or painted pictures (see Figure 1). Meanwhile, Émile Reynaud in France was projecting sequences of drawn pictures onto a screen using his Praxinoscope, in which revolving mirrors and an oil-lamp "magic lantern" were applied to a zoetrope-like drum, and by 1880 Muybridge was similarly projecting enlarged, illuminated views of his motion photographs using the Zoöpraxiscope, an adaptation of the zoetrope.

Although a contemporary observer of Muybridge's demonstration claimed to have seen "living, moving animals," such devices lacked several essentials of true motion pictures. The first was a mechanism to enable sequence photographs to be taken within a single camera at regular, rapid intervals, and the second was a medium capable of storing images for more than the second or so of movement possible from drums, wheels, or disks.

A motion-picture camera must be able to advance the medium rapidly enough to permit at least 16 separate exposures per second as well as bring each frame to a full stop to record a sharp image. The principal technology

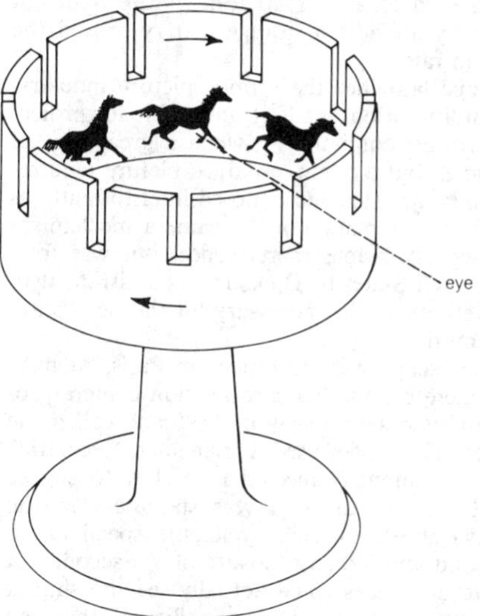

Figure 1: Zoetrope.

that creates this intermittent movement is the Geneva watch movement, in which a four-slotted star wheel, or "Maltese cross," converts the tension of the mainspring to the ticking of toothed gears. In 1882 Étienne-Jules Marey employed a similar "clockwork train" intermittent movement in a photographic "gun" used to "shoot" birds in flight. Twelve shots per second could be recorded onto a circular glass plate. Marey subsequently increased the frame rate, although for no more than about 30 images, and employed strips of sensitized paper (1887) and paper-backed celluloid (1889) instead of the fragile, bulky glass.

Étienne-Jules Marey

The transparent material trade-named celluloid was first manufactured commercially in 1872. It was derived from collodion, that is, nitrocellulose (gun cotton) dissolved in alcohol and dried. John Carbutt manufactured the first commercially successful celluloid photographic film in 1888, but it was too stiff for convenient use. By 1889 the George Eastman company had developed a roll film of celluloid coated with photographic emulsion for use in its Kodak still camera. This sturdy, flexible medium could transport a rapid succession of numerous images and was eventually adapted for motion pictures.

Thomas Edison is often credited with the invention of the motion picture in 1889. The claim is disputable, however, specifically because Edison's motion-picture operations were entrusted to an assistant, W.K.L. Dickson, and generally because there are several plausible pre-Edison claimants in England and France. Indeed, a U.S. Supreme Court decision of 1902 concluded that Edison had not invented the motion picture but had only combined the discoveries of others. His systems are important, nevertheless, because they prevailed commercially. The heart of Edison's patent claim was the intermittent movement provided by a Maltese cross synchronized with a shutter. The October 1892 version of Edison's Kinetograph camera employed the format essentially still in use today. The film, made by Eastman according to Edison's specifications, was 35 millimetres (mm) in width. Two rows of sprocket holes, each with four holes per frame, ran the length of the film and were used to advance it. The image was 1 inch wide by 3/4 inch high.

At first Edison's motion pictures were not projected. One viewer at a time could watch a film by looking through the eyepiece of a peep-show cabinet known as the Kinetoscope. This device was mechanically derived from the zoetrope in that the film was advanced by continuous movement, and action was "stopped" by a very brief exposure. In the zoetrope, a slit opposite the picture produced a stroboscopic effect; in the Kinetoscope the film traveled at the rate of 40 frames per second, and a slit in a 10-inch-diameter rotating shutter wheel afforded an exposure of 1/6,000 second. Illumination was provided by an electric bulb positioned directly beneath the film. The film ran over spools. Its ends were spliced together to form a continuous loop, which was initially 25 to 30 feet long but later was lengthened to almost 50 feet. A direct-current motor powered by an Edison storage battery moved the film at a uniform rate.

The Kinetoscope

The Kinetoscope launched the motion-picture industry, but its technical limitations made it unsuitable for projection. Films may run continuously when a great deal of light is not crucial, but a bright, enlarged picture requires that each frame be arrested and exposed intermittently as in the camera. The adaptation of the camera mechanism to projection seems obvious in retrospect but was frustrated in the United States by Dickson's establishment of a frame rate well above that necessary for the perception of continuous motion.

After the Kinetoscope was introduced in Paris, Auguste and Louis Lumière produced a combination camera/projector, first demonstrated publicly in 1895 and called the *cinématographe*. The device used a triangular "eccentric" (intermittent) movement connected to a claw to engage the sprocket holes. As the film was stationary in the aperture for two-thirds of each cycle, the speed of 16 frames per second allowed an exposure of 1/25 second. At this slower rate audiences could actually see the shutter blade crossing the screen, producing a "flicker" that had been absent from Edison's pictures. On the other hand, the hand-cranked *cinématographe* weighed less than 20 pounds (Edison's camera weighed 100 times as much). The Lumière units could therefore travel the world to shoot and screen their footage. The first American projectors employing intermittent movement were devised by Thomas Armat in 1895 with a Pitman arm or "beater" movement taken from a French camera of 1893. The following year Armat agreed to allow Edison to produce the projectors in quantity and to market them as Edison Vitascopes. In 1897 Armat patented the first projector with four-slot star and cam (as in the Edison camera).

The *cinémato-graphe*

One limitation of early motion-picture filming was the tearing of sprocket holes. The eventual solution to this problem was the addition to the film path of a slack-forming loop that restrained the inertia of the take-up reel. When this so-called Latham loop was applied to cameras and projectors with intermittent movement, the growth and shrinkage of the loops on either side of the shutter adjusted for the disparity between the stop-and-go motion at the aperture and the continuous movement of the reels (see Figure 6).

The Latham loop

When the art of projection was established, the importance of a bright screen picture was appreciated. Illumination was provided by carbon arc lamps, although flasks of ether and sticks of unslaked calcium ("limelight") were used for brief runs.

Introduction of sound. The popularity of the motion picture inspired many inventors to seek a method of reproducing accompanying sound. Two processes were involved: recording and reproducing. Further, the sound reproduction had to be presented in an auditorium and had to be quite good. This could not be achieved without a good amplifier of electrical signals. In 1907 Lee De Forest invented the Audion, a three-element vacuum tube, which provided the basis in the early 1920s for a feasible amplifier that produced an undistorted sound of sufficient loudness.

Next came the problem of synchronization of the sound with the picture. A major difficulty turned out to be the securing of constant speed in both the recorder and reproducer. Many ingenious ideas were tried. In 1918 in Germany, the use of a modulated glow lamp in photographically recording sound and a photocell for reproduction were studied. In Denmark in 1923, an oscillograph light modulator and selenium-cell reproducer were developed. De Forest tried a gas-filled glow discharge operated by a telephone transmitter to record a synchronized sound track on the film. For loudspeakers he experimented with a variety of devices but finally chose the speaker with horn. The operating signal was obtained from a light shining through the film sound track and detected by a light-sensitive device (photocell). These were used in a system called Phonofilm, which was tried experimentally in a number of theatres. In 1927 the Fox Film Corporation utilized some of these principles in the showing of Fox Movietone News.

Meanwhile, the Western Electric Company laboratories in the United States had been making extensive studies on the nature of speech and other sounds and on techniques for recording and reproducing such sounds. They experimented with recording on a phonograph disc and developed a 16-inch (40.6-centimetre) disc rotated at 33 1/3 revolutions per minute; they improved loudspeakers, introduced the moving-coil type of speaker, and generally improved the entire electronic amplification system. The Warner Bros. movie studio became interested in all these developments and formed the Vitaphone Corporation to market the complete system.

Vitaphone sound-on-disc recording

Warner Bros. premiered Vitaphone in 1926 with a program featuring short musical performances and a full-length picture, *Don Juan,* which had synchronized music and effects but no speech. In 1927 it brought out *The Jazz Singer,* which was essentially a silent picture with Vitaphone score and sporadic episodes of synchronized singing and speech. Warners presented the first "100-percent talkie," *The Lights of New York,* in 1928.

Although the Vitaphone system offered fidelity superior to sound-on-film systems at this stage, it became clear that recording on film would be much more convenient.

Among other disadvantages, it was extremely difficult with the wax discs to shoot outdoors or to edit sound. By 1931 Warner Bros. ceased production of sound-on-disc and adopted the sound-on-film option preferred by the other studios.

Sound-on-film, a system that in various guises had enjoyed several periods of popularity, underwent constant improvements in the 1910s and 1920s. Although a sound track on the picture negative was used for Movietone News, Fox's dramatic productions used a separate sound film on fine-grain print stock that could be edited apart from the picture yet in synchronism with it. One serious problem of sound-on-film systems had been the distortion of the signal introduced by the glow lamp when recording the sound track on film. The Western Electric Company devised a "double-string" light valve. A wire was looped around a post and parallel to itself. When speech current was applied to the wire in a magnetic field, the wire vibrated toward and away from itself according to the applied electrical waveform. A steady beam of white light shining through the loop was modulated in intensity by the varying gap between the wires; the modulated beam was photographed while masked by a slit perpendicular to the edge of the film. The resulting sound track appeared as darker or fainter parallel lines on the edge of the film. Known as the variable density system, this method of optically recording sound was originally used by all but one of the major Hollywood studios.

Variable area sound-on-film recording

The Radio-Keith-Orpheum Corporation (RKO) was created in 1928 to showcase the Radio Corporation of America (RCA) Photophone system of variable area recording. With this system, the sound recording was modulated by a rotating mirror and the slit was parallel to the edge of the film; reproduction employed the perpendicular slit of the variable density sound track. Minor problems of incompatibility between recording and reproduction were solved in late 1928 when the track was narrowed down to stay safely within the area scanned by the beam. Identical side-by-side tracks were employed to compensate for lateral misalignment. Initially inferior in quality, the variable area system gradually drew even with the quality of the density system and supplanted it altogether in the 1950s.

Whereas there was wide variation in the speed at which silent films were photographed and projected, sound necessitated standardization of the frame rate. In 1927 the speed was standardized at 24 frames per second, or 90 feet per minute for 35-mm film.

The development of sound technology in the first years of talking pictures focused on two areas. One involved the development of blimped cameras, directional microphones, microphone booms, and quieter lights, so that sound could be recorded more cleanly at the time of shooting. The other technologies involved the ability to add, edit, and mix sound separately from the time the picture was recorded. (P.Me./E.We./S.G.H.)

Introduction of colour. From their earliest days, silent films could be coloured using nonphotographic methods. One means was to hand-colour frames individually. Another method made it possible to use monochrome sections for mood (*e.g.,* blue for night scenes or red for passionate sequences). Monochrome stock was created by "tinting" the film base or "toning" the emulsion (by bathing the film in chemical salts).

The photography of colour was theorized decades before it was developed for motion pictures. In 1855 the British physicist James Clerk Maxwell argued that a full-colour photographic record of a scene could be made by filming three separate black-and-white negatives through filters coloured, respectively, red, green, and blue, the three primary colours. When converted to positives, the transparent exposed areas of the three films could pass light through the appropriate filter to produce three images, one red, one green, and one blue. Superimposing the three images would "rebuild" the image in its original colours.

Additive and subtractive systems of colour

In 1868 Louis Ducos du Hauron identified the additive and subtractive systems of colour. Both systems originate as red, green, and blue negative records. The difference occurs in the positive image, which may be composited from either the additive or subtractive primaries. The subtractive primaries—cyan, magenta, and yellow—are the complements of the additive primaries and can be obtained by subtracting, respectively, red, green, and blue from white. (Subtracting all three additive primaries yields black; adding all three yields white.)

In motion-picture prints, overlapping dye layers in the three subtractive primaries are simultaneously present on a clear, transparent base, and the image is projected with an exposure of white light. The dark areas of the cyan layer subtract all red colour, permitting only cyan (the mixture of blue and green) to pass through; the transparent areas pass all the white light. The magenta and yellow layers act similarly, and the original colour image is reproduced. The fineness of resolution is limited only by the structure of photographic grain or dye globules.

The first film colour systems were additive, but they were confronted by insurmountable limitations. In an additive system, the three colour records remain discrete and meet only as light rays on the screen. The best picture results when a separate film is made for each colour; however, each colour can occupy alternating frames or small, alternating portions of each frame of a single film. (A contemporary example of additive colour can be seen in projection television, in which red, green, and blue lenses converge to produce an image so enlarged that the separate colour areas, or dots, become discernible.)

The best known of the early additive processes was Kinemacolor (1906), which, for manageability, reduced the three colour records to two: red-orange and blue-green. A single black-and-white film was photographed and projected at 32 frames per second (twice the normal silent speed) through a rotating colour filter. The two colour records occupied alternate frames and were integrated by the retention characteristic of the human eye. As there were no separate red-orange and blue-green records for each image, displacement from frame to frame was visible during rapid movement, so that a horse might appear to have two tails. Inventors tried to increase the film speed, reduce the frame size, or combine two films with mirrored prisms, but additive systems continued to be plagued by excessive film consumption, poor resolution, loss of light, and registration problems.

The first subtractive process employing a single film strip in an ordinary projector without filters was Prizma Color in 1919. (Prizma Color had been introduced as an additive process but was soon revised.) The basis was an ingenious "duplitized" film with emulsion on both sides. One side was toned red-orange and the other blue-green. The stock long outlasted the Prizma company and was in use as late as the early 1950s in such low-cost systems as Cinecolor.

Similar enough to provoke litigation was an early (1922) process by Technicolor in which separate red and green films were cemented back-to-back, resulting in a thick and stiff print that scratched easily. Although only four two-colour Technicolor features were produced by the end of the silent era, Technicolor sequences were a highlight of several big-budget pictures in the mid-to-late 1920s, including *The Phantom of the Opera* (1923–25) and *Ben Hur* (1925). Technicolor devised the first of its dye-transfer, or imbibition, processes in 1928. Red and green dye images were printed onto the same side of clear film containing a black silver sound track.

Three-strip Technicolor

When Technicolor's appeal seemed on the wane, it devised a greatly improved three-register process (1932). The perfected Technicolor system used a prism/mirror beam-splitter behind a single lens to record the red, green, and blue components of each image on three strips of black-and-white film. Approximately one-third of the light was transmitted to the film behind a green filter in direct path of the lens; the film was sensitized to green light by special dyes. A partially silvered mirror (initially flecked with gold) directed the remainder of the light through a magenta (red plus blue) filter to a bi-pack of orthochromatic and panchromatic films with their emulsion surfaces in contact. The orthochromatic film became the blue record. As it was insensitive to red light, the orthochromatic film passed the red rays to the panchromatic film. A 1938 improvement added red-orange dye to the orthochromatic film so that only red light reached the panchromatic layer.

In 1941 Monopack Technicolor was introduced. This was a three-layer film from which separation negatives were made for the Technicolor dye-transfer printing process.

Using the dye-transfer method, it was necessary to make gelatin positives that contained the image in relief. Dye filled the recesses while the higher areas remained dry. Each gelatin matrix thus imprinted its complement onto the film base. As in the two-colour process, a black silver sound track was printed first on clear film. When magnetic sound became popular, the oxide strips were embossed after printing. Technicolor gave excellent results but was very expensive.

In 1936 Germany produced Agfacolor, a single-strip, three-layer negative film and accompanying print stock. After World War II Agfacolor appeared as Sovcolor in the Eastern bloc and as Anscocolor in the United States, where it was initially used for amateur filmmaking. The first serious rival to Technicolor was the single-strip Eastmancolor negative, which was introduced in 1952 by the Eastman Kodak Company but was often credited under a studio trademark (*e.g.,* Warnercolor). Eastmancolor did not require special camera or processing equipment and was cheaper than Technicolor. Producers naturally preferred the less expensive Eastmancolor, especially since they had, in response to the perceived threat of television, increased production of colour films. (After the 1960s black-and-white films were so rare that they cost more to print than colour films.) The 1950s vogue for CinemaScope and three-dimensional productions, both incompatible with the Technicolor camera, also hastened the demise of Technicolor photography.

Eastman-color

Dye-transfer printing remained cost-effective somewhat longer, but Technicolor was forced to abandon the process in the 1970s. This has created a significant problem for film preservationists because only Technicolor film permanently retains its original colours. Other colour prints fade to magenta within seven years, yet the hard gelatin dyes of a Technicolor print remain undimmed even after the film's nitrate base has begun to decompose.

In the 1980s computerized versions of the hand-stenciled colour films of the silent era were developed to rejuvenate old black-and-white films for video. (E.We./S.G.H.)

Wide-screen and stereoscopic pictures. Until the early 1950s, the screen shape, or aspect ratio (expressed as the ratio of frame width to frame height), was generally 1.33 to 1, or 4 to 3. In the mid-1950s the ratio became standardized at 1.85 to 1 in the United States and 1.66 or 1.75 to 1 in Europe. These slightly wider images were accomplished by using the same film but smaller aperture plates in the projector and by using shorter-focal-length lenses.

Many people have felt that, while vision at the extreme sides of the vision field does not usually contribute much information to the eyes, it does add substantially to the illusion of reality when it is present. Hence, there have been periods when film producers have attempted to introduce extremely wide formats. As early as 1929, Grandeur films were presented using 70-mm instead of the standard 35-mm film to give a wider field of view.

In 1952 a radical attack was made on wide-screen projection in the form of the Cinerama, which used three projectors and a curved screen. The expanded field of view gave a remarkable increase in the illusion of reality, especially with such exciting and spectacular subjects as a ride down a toboggan slide. There were technical problems, including the necessity of carrying three cameras bolted together at the correct angles on the toboggan or other carrier, synchronization of the three separate films, and matching of the image structure and brightness at the joining edges on the screen. After 1963 Cinerama replaced its three-film process with a 70-mm anamorphic system with an aspect ratio of 2.75 to 1.

Heighten-ing the illusion of reality

The use of anamorphic lenses for wide-screen projection was introduced by CinemaScope in 1953. An anamorphic optical system photographs with a different magnification horizontally than it does vertically. The lens seems to squeeze the image so that on the film itself figures appear tall and thin. A lens on the projector reverses the effect, so that the images on the screen reacquire normal proportions.

In 1955 Todd-AO introduced a wider film (photographed on a 65-mm negative and printed on a 70-mm positive for projection), with several sound tracks added. Like anamorphic systems, the wider format could be achieved with a single projector. The first two Todd-AO productions, *Oklahoma!* (1955) and *Around the World in 80 Days* (1956), were made at 30 frames per second for a nearly flicker-free image; 70-mm films are now photographed and projected at 24 frames per second.

Amusement parks and world's fairs have often featured 360-degree projection. The first system was presented at the Disneyland amusement park in 1955. At first, the projection involved 11 16-mm projectors and screens and, later, nine 35-mm projectors. The audience stood on a low platform in the middle. The result was extremely realistic. In one scene, showing the view from a cable car in San Francisco, the viewers were seen involuntarily to lean over on the curves, as if they were actually on the cable car. The format, however, has limited uses for general storytelling.

In the 1980s, efforts to improve picture quality took two routes: increase in frame rate (Showscan operates at 60 frames per second) or increase in overall picture size—height as well as width (IMAX and Futurevision). In these formats the sound tracks are usually printed on a separate, magnetic strip of film.

Another project intended to improve the illusion of reality in motion pictures has been stereoscopic, or three-dimensional, cinematography. "3-D" films use two cameras or one camera with two lenses. The centres of the lenses are spaced 2½ to 2¾ inches apart to replicate the displacement between a viewer's left and right eyes. Each lens records a slightly different view corresponding to the different view each eye sees in normal vision.

Stereo-scopic cinema-tography

Despite many efforts to create "3-D without glasses" (notably in the U.S.S.R., where a screen of vertical slats was used for many years), audience members have had to wear one of two types of special glasses to watch 3-D films. In the early anaglyph system, one lens of the glasses was red and the other green (later blue). The picture on the screen viewed without glasses appeared as two slightly displaced images, one with red lines, the other with green. Each lens of the glasses darkened its opposite colour so that each eye would see only the image intended for it.

The Polaroid system, used for commercial 3-D movies since the early 1950s, is based on a light-polarizing material developed by the American inventor Edwin H. Land in 1932. In this method, known as Natural Vision, two films are recorded with lenses that polarize light at different angles. The lenses on the glasses worn by spectators are similarly polarized so that each admits its corresponding view and blocks the other. Early versions of Polaroid 3-D used two interlocked projectors to synchronize the two pictures. A later system, revived in the 1970s and 1980s, stacked the left and right components vertically on half-frames two sprocket holes high. The images were converged by means of a mirror and/or prism.

PROFESSIONAL MOTION-PICTURE PRODUCTION

Cameras. The principles of operation of modern professional motion-picture cameras are much the same as those of earlier times, although the mechanisms have been refined. A film is exposed behind a lens and is moved intermittently, with a shutter to stop the light while the film is moving. In the process, the film is unrolled from a supply reel, through the intermittent to the gate where the exposure takes place, and then on to the take-up reel.

Principal parts. Lenses have gone through a continuous evolution in the last half century, for both still and motion-picture photography. The two major objectives have been to focus properly all the colours of the image at the film plane (*i.e.,* to make the lens achromatic) and to focus portions of a beam coming from different portions of the lens, the centre or the edges, at the same point on the film (*i.e.,* anastigmatic). Both objectives require solution for as large a lens opening as possible, in order to capture maximum light for the exposure, and for as wide a field of view as will be needed in the use of the lens. In order to solve these problems, lenses have been

Achro-matic and anastig-matic lenses

made with more and more components. Also, more types of glass have been discovered and developed, to give better achromatic performance. It was found, about 1939, that a special coating of the glass-to-air surface of a lens component could greatly diminish reflections from this surface without affecting other properties of the lens. The use of such coatings improved image contrast by reducing the stray rays that were produced by reflections in a multiple-component lens. Coatings also reduce loss of light by reflection in the desired rays. Coating developments have permitted the manufacture of lenses with many more components than had previously been possible.

Long experience with both motion-picture and still cameras has shown the need for a variety of focal lengths (ranging from ultrawide angle to telephoto) to photograph scenes under the best conditions. To make changing focal lengths more convenient, the lenses have sometimes been mounted on a turret, so that one out of a set of three lenses may be quickly selected. For motion pictures this would mean an interruption in the action depicted. A continuous change would be more desirable.

When two lenses are used in a tandem combination, the focal length of the combination varies according to the separation between the two components. For example, when two thin converging lenses are mounted close together, the combined focal length is shorter than when they are separated a certain distance. Thus, the focal length of the combination can be continuously varied over a range merely by changing the separation.

This observation led to the conception of camera lenses of variable focal length in which the variation is obtained by moving one or more elements. One simple design consists of two fixed convex (converging) lenses of unequal power with a movable concave (diverging) lens between them. When the central concave lens is located close to the front convex element, the combination focal length can be shorter (and the image therefore smaller) than when it is located close to the rear convex element. The design can be made such that, with the two convex elements remaining fixed, a distant view can remain almost in focus on the film as the middle element is moved. Exact focus for this arrangement, however, could not be attained. Thus, for lenses of this design, a cam device has in the past been provided to move the front convex element a short distance as the middle element is moved over its range, to keep the focus exact. This kind of lens has come to be called a zoom lens.

The zoom lens

By increasing the number of elements, the focus can be kept exact without the need of a correcting cam. Other improvements include increasing the range of focal lengths covered, increasing the effective lens aperture, increasing the angular field of view seen by the film, and improving the colour correction with radically new glass materials.

For a long time the change in focal lengths was carried out manually. More recently, the use of an electric motor drive has allowed a smoother change, with less distraction to the cameraman.

The general principles utilized in the film transport system have remained much the same over recent years, at least for the 35-mm film. The films are usually preloaded in lighttight reel cases (called magazines), with an exposed loop between the supply and take-up reels. This loop is quickly fitted into the camera mechanism when loading.

The intermittent is usually a claw-type mechanism, sometimes a "dual-fork" claw that pulls down four sprocket holes at a time. The fork protrudes and recedes to engage the sprocket holes. Some cameras are equipped with pin-registering mechanisms, which hold the film firmly in place in the exposure gate, with the pins engaging sprocket holes.

In the early days of sound films, the noise made by the intermittent and other moving parts in the camera was loud enough to interfere with the sound picked up by the microphone. Cameras were sheathed ("blimped") with outer, separate sound-absorbing materials. The sound insulation is now usually self-contained in the camera.

The film drive

Before the introduction of sound, the film and intermittent were driven by a crank operated by the cameraman. With sound, considerably more uniformity in the speed of the film drive became necessary. For this and other reasons, the film drive in modern cameras is provided by an accurately controlled electric motor, which maintains the standardized sound speed of 24 frames per second.

The shutter keeps light from striking the film while it is moving from one frame to the next. A variable shutter opening can also be used to reduce exposure when it is necessary or desirable to do this without reducing the lens aperture. The shutter is in most cases rotary and is synchronized with the intermittent.

Viewfinding for motion pictures is especially critical: whereas still photographs can be cropped during enlargement or printing, the film image must be framed as it will appear on the screen. Older cameras employed a mechanical "rack-over" that enabled the camera operator to sight directly through the aperture with the film transport out of the way. When an external viewfinder is used, the image seen through it is not exactly the same as that photographed. The viewfinder must be angled so that it and the taking lens both point at the centre of the subject. A system of cams in the focus mechanism of the camera keeps the viewfinder image free of parallax (viewpoint difference) by adjustment from infinity to the near-point of the lens with a separate cam for each focal length.

Most cameras used today are of the reflex type. A partially reflecting mirror (beam splitter) is positioned in the door of the camera body or built into the lens itself with a parallel viewing tube. The mirror diverts to the viewfinder some of the light rays coming through the lens. This method's major drawback is that it takes away part of the light that would otherwise be used for the exposure. A much-admired viewing system that allows the full amount of light to reach the film is the rotating mirror shutter employed in the Arriflex camera. Light is reflected into the viewfinder only when the shutter blade covers the film as it advances to the next frame. This arrangement, however, is not wholly free from objections. Chief among these is that the arrangement opens a return path for light from the viewer's eyepiece to reach the film. The eyepiece must fit snugly around the eye while the viewfinder is in use, and the finder must be closed completely while it is not in use. In addition, since the camera shutter is closed only once per frame, the image will be subject to a distinct flicker, to which the cameraman must adjust himself. Some cameras incorporate a "video assist" or "video tap" wherein the viewfinder image is electronically fed to a video monitor or video recorder, thus allowing evaluation of the take by videotape replay.

Focusing has also been a perennial problem for the motion-picture camera. On the camera the position of the lens is precisely indicated on a calibrated scale. The actor's location on the set was formerly marked on the floor and the exact distance to the camera measured with a tape. The actor moved to previously marked places, and an assistant to the cameraman, called a focus puller, or follow-focus assistant, kept the lens in adjustment. Various electrical devices have now been introduced for remote adjustment by the assistant. Where a through-the-lens finder is used, focusing can be done directly, using the viewfinder image. Also, experienced cameramen can estimate distances quite closely.

It is usual to generate some kind of signal in synchronism with the intermittent when an auxiliary, magnetic-tape sound recorder is used, so that the sound record can later be synchronized exactly with the picture. The sync-generator provides a record of the speed of the camera motor; each frame of picture causes 2.5 cycles of a 60-hertz pulse to be recorded on the sync-track of the sound tape. A newer system is based on the "time code" originally developed for videotape. A separate generator uses a digital audio signal to provide each frame of film with its own number. For each take the time code generator is set to zero; when the camera and film are running, the generator starts to emit numbers that represent "real-time" in hours, minutes, seconds, and frames. In one system, a light-emitting diode next to the camera aperture records the information as ordinary numbers that can be read by the eye; in others, the binary numbers are contained in a control surface of magnetic particles on the base side of the

Time-code numbers

film. One hundred feet of 35-mm film would be rendered in time code as 00:01:07:08, or one minute, seven seconds, eight frames. Corresponding information is recorded on the "address" track of the audio tape. The time code's last two digits, which represent frames, go up to either 24 or 30. Material intended for theatres is photographed at the international sound projection speed of 24 frames per second. Material filmed for American television is often shot at 30 frames per second (in countries with 50 hertz AC power, the rate is 25 frames per second).

The camera is often supplied with electric motors to perform miscellaneous functions, such as to provide smooth rotation (panning) of the camera or to change the magnification in a zoom lens (or change lenses in a turret). The camera is normally provided with footage indicators to indicate the amount of film left unexposed and with frame counters used when it is desired to superimpose a second exposure. There can also be an "inching knob" to reposition the film to a given frame for multiple exposures. When the camera is used at a speed different from standard, a tachometer may be provided to indicate the actual speed.

The cameras that have so far been described are for the standard 35-mm film. Cameras for 65-mm film are generally quite similar, though heavier. The 16-mm professional camera may differ from the 35-mm in the form of its case, in its use of a spring-operated film drive, and in its method of film loading, as a result of its development from a former amateur camera. On the other hand it may be a smaller version and have the same features as the 35-mm model by the same manufacturer.

Camera supports. The camera must be mounted on a substantial support to avoid extraneous movements while film is being exposed. In its simplest form this is a heavy tripod structure, with sturdy but smooth-moving adjustments and casters, so that the exact desired position can be quickly reached. Often a heavy dolly, holding both the camera and a seated cameraman, is used. This can be pushed or driven around the set. When shots from elevated positions are to be used, both camera and cameraman are carried on the end of a crane, also on a dolly. In some cases the assemblage is smoothly driven to follow the action being pictured, such as movement along a street. If the surface being traversed is not smooth, rails, resembling train tracks, must be laid on the floor or ground for the dolly. The camera may be freed from the tripod or dolly and carried by the operator by means of a body brace and gyroscope stabilizer. One such support is the Steadicam, which eliminates the tell-tale motions of the hand-held camera.

Film formats

Film. Film types are usually described by their gauge, or approximate width. The 65-mm format is used chiefly for special effects and for special systems such as IMAX and Showscan. It was formerly used for original photography in conjunction with 70-mm release prints; now 70-mm theatrical films are generally shot in 35-mm and blown up in printing. With some exceptions the 35-mm format is for theatrical use, 16-mm for institutional applications, and 8-mm for home movies. The more frequently encountered film formats are illustrated in Figure 2. There are some minor differences in the shape of the sprocket holes in 35-mm film between negative and positive film. The first 8-mm film was made by using 16-mm film, punched with twice as many sprocket holes of the same size and shape. One side, to the middle line, was exposed in one direction. The supply and take-up reels were then interchanged in the camera, and the other side was exposed in the other direction. After processing, the film was split into two strips, which were spliced into one. An improved version of 8-mm stock, called Super-8 film, was designed with the idea of reducing the sprocket-hole size and employing the space thus made available for a larger picture area.

Originally, the film base was some form of celluloid or cellulose nitrate. This material is highly flammable, and extensive precautions were required in projection rooms to avoid film ignition because of the proximity of the projector arc lamp to the film. In 1923, when 16-mm amateur film was introduced, cellulose acetate (or safety film), much less flammable than the nitrate, was used. It was not considered desirable to adopt it for professional 35-mm film, largely because it was inferior in strength and dimensional stability. By the late 1930s an improved cellulose acetate safety film was introduced, and by the early 1950s it had generally replaced the nitrate film. Since 1956 acetate has lost ground to polyester- or mylar-based film, which is thinner, less brittle, and more resistant to tearing.

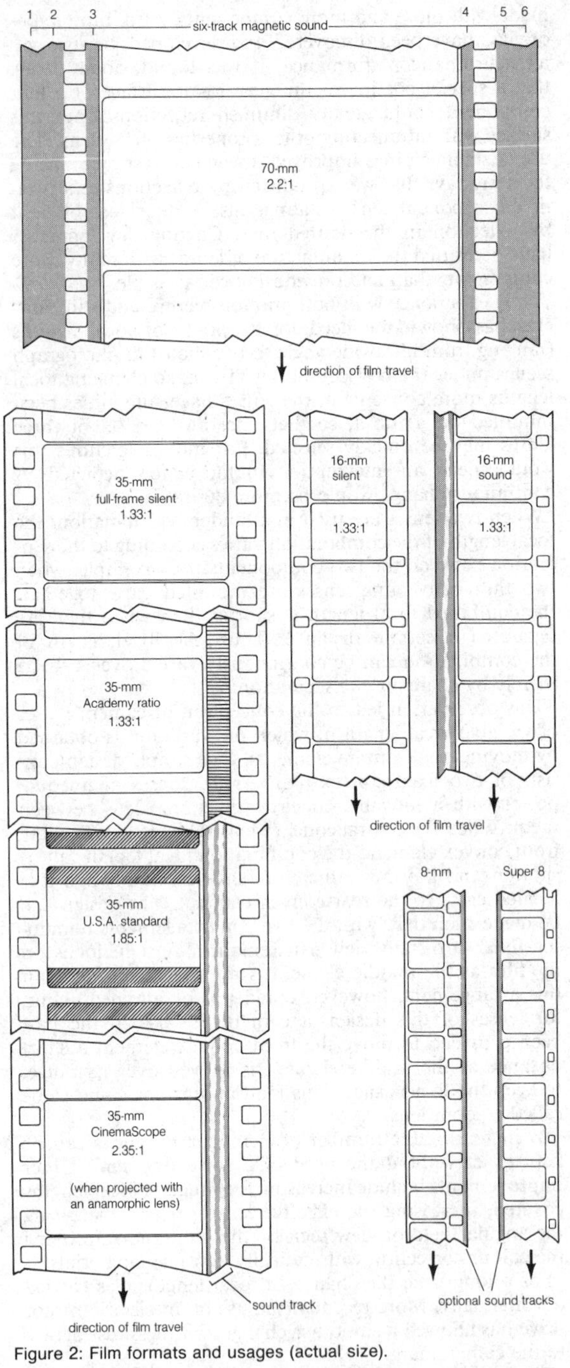

Figure 2: Film formats and usages (actual size).

Emulsions. The film base is coated with a light-sensitive layer of silver halide emulsion; multiple layers are used for colour film. Emulsion manufacture is quite complicated and delicate. The earlier emulsions were most sensitive to violet and blue light, as shown schematically in Figure 3, curve *a.* Toward the cyan and green, sensitivity drops rapidly. Such an emulsion is called natural, or ordinary. The result of such a characteristic is that in a natural scene reds and yellows appear black in the positive, and green appears too dark. As early as 1873 it was found that dyes introduced into the emulsion could increase the sensitivity in the yellow and green (Figure 3, curve *b*). The change increased the natural appearance of the reproduced picture, and the emulsion was called orthochromatic. Later (1904) dyes were found to prolong the sensitivity into

Orthochromatic and panchromatic film

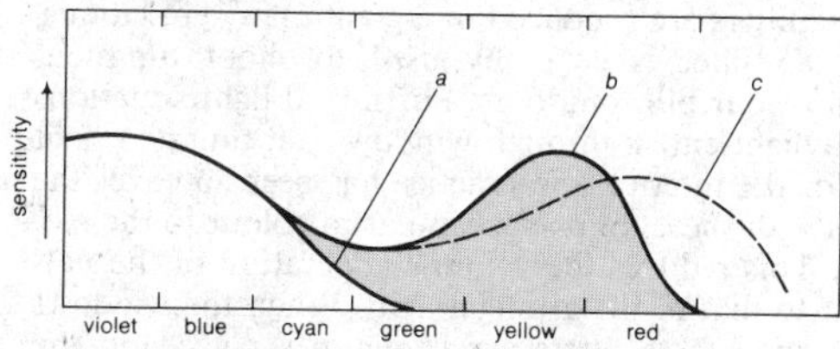

Figure 3: Sensitization of photographic emulsions (see text).

the red, and this emulsion is called panchromatic (Figure 3, curve *c*). The dates are fairly early for motion-picture application, but the development had importance in the general technology.

The overall sensitivity for picture taking has been increased greatly, from below about 10 ASA before 1930 to several hundred and even several thousand. The ASA (American Standards Association) scale is an arbitrary rating of film speed; that is, the sensitivity of the film to light. If everything else is kept constant, the required exposure time is inversely proportional to the ASA rating. Negative films designed for original picture exposure are usually faster (*i.e.*, have higher ASA ratings) than those for prints and are apt to be somewhat coarser grained.

Current technology has made use of a flatter crystal or "T-grain" that exposes more readily to light without an increase in the visible dimension of the grain. This enables use of very low light levels, especially when the film is "pushed" (given extended development) or "flashed" (prestruck with white light to accelerate exposure). When extreme sensitivity to light is not required, finer grain film may be used, particularly when it is intended to enlarge a 16-mm negative for 35-mm release or a 35-mm negative for 70-mm release.

The development of modern colour film

There are two major steps involved in making a dye image on motion-picture film. The first is to convert the negative silver image that is obtained from a normally exposed film into a positive dye image. The clue to how this can be done came from experience with a developer known as pyro (pyrogallol), once very popular with still photographers. A negative developed with pyro developer has not only a silver image but also a brown stain. Study of the process showed that the stain was caused by oxidation products given off locally by the developer in the development process. A substance in the developer reacts with these oxidation products to give an insoluble brown dye. The substance is called a dye coupler. Since the dye is not soluble, it does not wash off in the subsequent film treatment.

This suggested the possibility of bleaching to take away the silver image, leaving the dye image on the film. The first step was to find a developer and dye couplers that would produce the three dye colours that give a faithful three-colour picture rendering. The second step was to carry out the process in the film coating with three separate colours and keep them separate, all the way from exposure to the final three-colour image on the completed film.

The first portion of this second step is carried out by obtaining three emulsions that can be laid on top of one another and are sensitive, respectively, to the red, green, and blue of the exposing image without interfering with each other and that give corresponding silver layers that similarly do not interfere with each other.

It has been observed above that normal silver halide photographic emulsion is particularly sensitive to blue light and that one of the early problems was to obtain a more natural pictorial rendering by extending the sensitivity of the emulsion to green and finally to red light. The problem was solved by inserting appropriate dyes in the emulsion. The dye adds a peak of increased sensitivity, respectively, to green and red light, as in Figure 3. The triple-layer film then consists of, on the top, an ordinary blue-sensitive emulsion; below this, a yellow filter to cut off blue light; next below this, an emulsion with a sensitivity peak in the green, with the yellow filter cutting off blue sensitivity; and, finally, an emulsion with a peak sensitivity in the red, a valley in the green, and blue sensitivity cut off by the yellow filter. The sensitization can be chosen to locate and enhance the sensitivity peaks.

Thus, the blue layer responds to the blue light in the original, the green layer to the green light, and the red layer to the red light. These can be given a first development together, so that the individual responses will be indicated as silver deposits in the respective layers. The developer used is one which leaves no dye-coupler stains.

The nonsubstantive process

In what is called the nonsubstantive subsequent process, the dye couplers are introduced in a second development. Each colour layer is treated separately. Uniform red light is applied (from the bottom up) to expose the undeveloped silver halide in the red layer. It has no effect on the other layers because of their insensitivity to red. The film is processed with a developer containing a minus-red (or cyan) dye coupler. This leaves a silver and minus-red dye deposit wherever there was newly exposed silver halide in the red layer. Similarly, the blue layer, newly exposed with blue light from above and processed with a developer containing a minus-blue (or yellow) dye coupler, leaves a silver and minus-blue dye deposit wherever there was newly exposed silver halide in the blue layer. In the remaining green layer, a white-light exposure and development with a minus-green (or magenta) dye coupler converts the residual silver halide into a silver and minus-green dye deposit.

All the silver deposits and the yellow filter are finally bleached out. The remaining dye deposits serve to subtract from white light, in the manner that was described earlier, the correct part of the spectrum to leave the colour of the initial exposing light. For example, where this light was red, the final dyes absorb blue and green. Of the spectrum, this therefore leaves red light to go through the film.

The substantive process

In a modification called the substantive process, the appropriate dye couplers are suitably embedded in the emulsion in the appropriate colour layers to prevent their moving about during processing and contaminating the colours (an important problem). It is then possible to carry out the second exposure and development on all three layers in a single step with white light and with only one developer.

Nonsubstantive film is essentially an amateur medium that enables the camera original to be processed as a projection print. Commercial theatrical motion pictures are photographed on a colour negative stock containing dye couplers (*i.e.*, substantive type) from which prints can be made.

Lighting. The art of cinematography is, above all, the art of lighting, and the British term for the chief of the camera crew, lighting cameraman, comes closer to the matter than the Hollywood director of photography. In motion-picture photography, decisions about exposure are governed by the overall style of film, and light levels are set to expose the particular film stock at the desired f-stop.

Light sources. The earliest effective motion-picture lighting source was natural daylight, which meant that films at first had to be photographed outdoors, on open-roof stages, or in glass-enclosed studios. After 1903, artificial light was introduced in the form of mercury vapour tubes that produced a rather flat lighting. Ordinary tungsten (incandescent) lamps could not be used because the light rays they produced came predominantly from the red end of the spectrum, to which the orthochromatic film of the era was relatively insensitive. After about 1912, white flame carbon arc instruments, such as the Klieg light (made by Kliegl Brothers and used for stage shows) were adapted for motion pictures. After the industry converted to sound in 1927, however, the sputtering created by carbon arcs caused them to be replaced by incandescent lighting. Fresnel-lens spotlights then became the standard. Fresnel lenses concentrate the light beam somewhat and prevent excessive light loss around the sides. They can also, when suitably focused, give a relatively sharp beam. In the studio there are racks above and stands on the floor on which lamps can be mounted so that they direct the light where it is wanted. The advent of Technicolor led to a partial reversion to the carbon arc because incandescent light affected the colours recorded on the film. Around 1950, however, economic pressures caused Technicolor film to be rebalanced for incandescent light.

The modern era in lighting began in the late 1960s when

tungsten-halogen lamps with quartz envelopes came into wide use. The halogen compound is included inside the envelope, and its purpose is to combine with the tungsten evaporated from the hot filament. This forms a compound that is electrically attracted back to the tungsten filament. It thus prevents the evaporated tungsten from condensing on the envelope and darkening it, an effect that reduces the light output of ordinary gas-filled tungsten lamps. The return of the tungsten to the filament means that the incandescent lamp can be run with a long life at a higher filament temperature and, more important, remain at precisely the same colour temperature. These lamps are now sometimes provided with a special multilayered filter to give a bluish light that approaches the colour of daylight. Halogen lamps give brilliant light from a compact unit and are particularly well-suited to location filming.

Tungsten-halogen lamps

The principal light on a scene is called the key light. The position of the key light has often been conventionalized (*e.g.,* aimed at the actors at an angle 45 degrees off the camera-to-subject axis). Another school of cinematographers prefers source lighting, in the tradition of Renaissance and Old Master paintings; that is, a window or lamp in the scene governs the angle and intensity of light. A fill light is used to provide detail in the shadow areas created by the key light. The difference in lighting level between the key plus the fill light versus the fill light alone yields the lighting contrast ratio. The "latitude" of the film, or the spread between the greatest and least exposure that will produce an acceptable image, governs the lighting contrast ratio. For many years, the latitude of colour films was so restricted that it was thought necessary to have numerically low lighting ratios, typically 2 to 1 (a very flat lighting) and never more than 3 to 1. The introduction of Eastman 5254 colour negative in 1968 and the even more sophisticated 5247 in 1974 opened a new era in which colour film was exposed with higher ratios approaching the previous subtleties of black-and-white.

Light measurement. Precise control of exposure throughout filming is necessary to maintain consistent tones from shot to shot and to give an overall tenor of lighting that suits the pictorial style. To determine light levels in the studio and on interior locations, an incident light meter is primarily used. This type of meter is recognizable by a white plastic dome that collects light in a 180-degree pattern (the dome is an approximation of the shape of the human face). Because it measures the overall light (calibrated in footcandles) falling on the scene, it may be used without the actors present.

Reflected light readings measure the average light coming toward the camera from the scene being photographed. This works well for average subjects but gives wrong exposures if the background contains either many bright areas, as in a beach scene, or very dark areas, as in front of a dark building. In such cases the photocell must be held not at the camera but very close to the subject of interest, to eliminate the effect of the background. This is also the case when the scene contains a good deal of backlight. These shortcomings eventually led to the development of the spot meter.

Spot measurement readings measure the light coming toward the camera from selected spots in the subject being photographed. The meter for this purpose has an optical system that covers measurement of a spot of about one degree, making it extremely useful on exterior locations.

Colour temperature

Light is also measurable in terms of colour temperature. Light rich in red rays has a low reading in kelvins. Ordinary household light bulbs produce light of about 2,800 kelvins, while daylight, which is rich in rays from the blue end of the spectrum, may have readings from 5,000 to more than 20,000 K. The colour temperature meter uses a rotating filter to indicate a bias toward either red or blue; when red and blue rays are in balance, the needle does not move. Some meters also use red/blue and blue/green filters for fuller measurement.

The general practice has been to shoot the entire picture on stock balanced for artificial light at 3,200 K. Lights for filmmaking generally range between 3,200 K and 3,400 K. For daylight shooting, an orange filter is employed to counter the film's sensitivity to blue light. Although colour-correcting filters are produced in a great many gradations, the No. 85 filter is generally used to shoot tungsten-balanced colour film outdoors. For mixed-light situations where daylight enters through windows but tungsten light is used for the interior, the practice has been to cover the windows with sheets of plastic similar in colour to the No. 85 filter. This reduces the colour temperature of the natural light to that of the artificial light. When the windows are very large, blue filters are sometimes placed on the lights and the No. 85 orange filter is used on the lens, as if filming in exterior daylight. Yet another approach is to supplement natural daylight with metal halide (daylight-balanced) lights. With the increase in location shooting, daylight-balanced high-speed films have been introduced to allow shooting in mixed-light situations without light loss due to filters.

Film processing and printing. In the early days of motion pictures, films were processed by winding on flat racks and then dipping in tanks of solution. As films became longer, such methods proved to be too cumbersome. It was recognized that the processing system should have the following characteristics: it must run continuously; it must be lighttight and yet capable of being loaded in daylight; and it must be as compact as possible to provide a minimum air surface for the processing solutions. A general form evolved that is still in use.

Continuous method of film processing

For continuous operation the film must be passed continuously through the solutions and folded back over rollers that do not touch the emulsion surface. It must be handled very carefully, as the impregnation with solution weakens the support, and the sprocket holes should not be engaged. Drive should, therefore, be accomplished by a light friction force at the edges.

Splicing on a fresh film without affecting the motion of the part of the film being processed is handled by using a storage unit or reservoir. This reservoir has a variable capacity so that the output end can be giving out film while the input end is stationary as the new film is spliced. Lighttight gates prevent all but a short length of film being light-struck at the very beginning or end of the film (and leaders may be used). The take-up-reel case is fastened in a lighttight way to the storage unit so that after splicing, the film is unreeled into the storage and processing units until the other end is reached, ready for splicing to the next film after changing cases.

Many tank shapes have been tried. Long vertical tanks provide for several passes of the film through each tank. The spools are designed so as to hold the film at the edges by friction. There are a number of types of drive, but all function gently to avoid strain. Sometimes the spools have multistepped edges to accommodate various film widths. The lower spools (or "diabolos") are more or less free but guided in a loose fashion so that they will not jam or tangle. The long vertical tanks give a minimum of air surface to the solution. The motion of the film through the liquid can be sufficient for proper contact of the film with the solutions, but sometimes submerged sprays with small jets of fine nitrogen bubbles are provided to increase the agitation.

The last receptacle in the processing sequence is a drying oven. There are several designs, some of which generally resemble the tank but without solution and are provided with heating elements. This receptacle does not need to be lighttight.

The processing steps for the many different types of film are similar in principle, though there are variations in specific solutions and treatments. One variation is known as reversal processing. After partial development, the camera original is bleached and given a second exposure of uniform white light. This yields a positive rather than a negative image and thus saves the cost of an additional generation.

In laboratory parlance, the major functions are divided into "front end" and "release print" work and may be performed at different facilities. Front end work begins even before shooting with tests by the cinematographer on the same film stocks that will be used for the production. These will be used as a guide when takes from the camera negative that come in from each day's shooting are printed. A colour video analyzer reads the red, blue, and green records of the tests over a range of six f-stops to establish "printer lights." As desired, the work print may be "one light" (given uniform exposure) or "timed" (exposure corrected for scene-to-scene variations).

The original negative is stored until postproduction is finished. Positive work print is furnished in 1,000-foot rolls for editing. When all editing, including the insertion of optical effects and titles, is completed, the negative cutter matches the original camera film frame by frame at each editing point. The edited camera negative is combined with the synchronized sound track negative into a composite print called the answer print. (The first answer print is rarely the same as the final release print.) After all colour-correction and timing takes place, the information is recorded on perforated paper tape that serves to control both the exposure for each shot and the louvered filters that add red, green, and blue values.

The answer print

For theatrical distribution, exhibition release prints are not normally struck from the original camera negative. The original negative is used to make a master positive, sometimes known as the protection positive, from which a printing negative is then made to run off the release prints. Alternatively, a "dupe" negative can be made by copying the original camera negative through the reversal process. This yields a colour reversal intermediate (CRI) from which prints can be struck.

Printing takes a number of different forms. In contact printing, the master film (or negative) is pressed against the raw stock; this combination is exposed to light on the master film side. In optical printing, the master film is projected through a lens to expose the raw stock. In continuous printing, the master film and the raw stock both run continuously. Continuous printing is usually contact printing but can be optical, through a projected slit. In intermittent, or step-by-step, printing, each frame of the master film is exposed as a whole to a corresponding frame space on the raw film.

It is possible to print from one size master film to another size raw stock, such as 35-mm to 16-mm, or vice versa. In such cases the printing must, of course, be optical, and in the examples cited must be intermittent if there is a sound track. This is because 35-mm sound film has a spacing between frames and 16-mm does not. The sound track must be printed separately. The preferred method for making 16-mm versions of 35-mm films is to make a 16-mm negative by reduction from the 35-mm negative. Sometimes a 35-mm release print is reduced and printed by reversal, but this yields a coarser image. When 16-mm film is "blown up," the 16-mm negative is immersed in a solution that conceals scratches and grain as it is being rephotographed; this process is called wet-gate printing.

Film prints to be used for projection are given a coat of wax over the sprocket-hole areas. This eases the film passage between the pressure plates at the projection aperture.

Sound-recording techniques. The art of sound recording for motion pictures has developed dramatically. Most of the improvements fall into three areas: fidelity of recording; separation and then resynchronization of sound to picture; and ability to manipulate sound during the postproduction stage.

Optical recording. Until the early 1950s the normal recording medium was film. Sound waves were converted into light and recorded onto 35-mm film stock. Today the principal use of optical recording is to make a master optical negative for final exhibition prints after all editing and rerecording have been completed.

Magnetic recording. Magnetic recording offers better fidelity than optical sound, can be copied with less quality loss, and can be played back immediately without development. Magnetic tracks were first used by filmmakers in the late 1940s for recording music. The physical principles are the same as those of the standard tape recorder: the microphone output is fed to a magnet past which a tape coated with iron oxide runs at a constant speed. The changes in magnetic flux are recorded onto the tape as an invisible magnetic "picture" of the sound.

At first the sound was recorded onto 35-mm film that had a magnetic coating. Today sprocketed 35-mm magnetic tape is used during the editing stages. For onset recording, however, the film industry converted gradually to the same unperforated quarter-inch tape format widely used in broadcasting, the record industry, and even the home. Documentary and independent filmmakers were the first to develop and use the portable, more compact apparatus. Improvements in magnetic recording have paralleled those in the recording industry and include the development of multiple-track recording and Dolby noise reduction.

Double-system recording. Although it is possible to reproduce sound, either optically or magnetically, in the same camera that is photographing a scene (a procedure known as single-system recording), there is greater flexibility if the sound track is recorded by a different person and on a separate unit. The main professional use for single-system recording is in filming news, where there is little time to strive for optimal sound or image quality. Motion-picture sound recording customarily uses a double system in which the sound track remains physically separate from the image until the very last stages of postproduction.

Synchronizing sound and image recording

Double-system shooting requires a means of rematching corresponding sounds and images. The traditional solution is to mark the beginning of each take with a "clapper," or "clapstick," a set of wooden jaws about a foot long, snapped together in the picture field. The instant of clacking then is registered on both picture and sound tracks. Each new take number is identified visually by a number on the clapper board and aurally by voice. A newer version of the clapper is a digital slate that uses light-emitting diodes and an audio link to synchronize film and tape.

Precise synchronism must be maintained between camera and recorder so that sound can be kept perfectly matched to the visuals. (Lack of perfect synchronism is most conspicuous in close-up shots in which a speaker's lips do not match his voice.) On some occasions several cameras shoot a scene simultaneously from different points of view while only one sound recording is made, or several sound records may be taken of a single shot. Thus, to maintain synchronism, all sound and picture versions of a particular scene must be recorded at the same speed; the camera and the recorder cannot fluctuate in speed. One way to achieve this is to drive all cameras and recorders from a common power supply. Alternatively, synchronization may be achieved through the automatic, continual transmission from cameras to recorders of a sync-pulse signal sent by cable or wireless radio. More convenient yet is crystal sync, whereby the speed of both cameras and recorders is controlled through the use of the oscillation of crystals installed in each piece of equipment. The most advanced system uses a time-code generator to emit numbers in "real-time" on both film and tape.

The sound recordist. The main task of the recordist during live recording is to get "clean" dialogue that eliminates background noise and seems to correspond to the space between speaker and camera. Most of the nonsynchronous dialogue, sound effects, and music can be added and adjusted later. During shooting the sound recordist adjusts the sound by setting levels, altering microphone placement, and mixing (combining signals if there is more than one microphone). Major technical and aesthetic reshaping is left for the postproduction phase when overhead is lower, the facilities are more sophisticated, and alternative versions can be created. It is also the job of the sound personnel to record wild sound (important sound effects and nonsynchronous dialogue) and ambient sound (the inherent sound of the location). Ambient sound is added to the sound track during postproduction to maintain continuity between takes. Usually, wild sound and music are also adjusted and added then.

Choice of microphones

Microphones. Microphones of many different types have been used for sound recording. These may differ in sound quality, in directional characteristics, and in convenience of use. Conditions that may dictate the choice of a particular microphone include the presence of minor echoes from objects in the set or reproduction of speech in a small room, as distinct from that in a large hall. Painstaking adjustments are made by careful attention to the choice of microphones, by the arrangement and sound absorbency of walls and furniture on the set, and by the exact positioning of the actors. For recording a conversation indoors, the preferred microphone is sensitive in a particular direction in order to reduce extraneous noises from the side and rear. It is usually suspended from a polelike "boom" just beyond camera range in front of and above the actors so that it can be pivoted toward each actor as he speaks. Microphones can also be mounted on a variety of other stands. A second way to cut down background noise is to use a chest (or lavaliere) microphone hidden under the actor's clothing. For longer shots, radio microphones eliminate the wires connecting actors to recorders by using a miniature transistor radio to send sound to the mixer and recorder. (P.Me./E.We./S.G.H.)

Editing. The postproduction stage of professional filmmaking is likely to last longer than the shooting itself. During this stage, the picture and the sound tracks are edited; special effects, titles, and other optical effects are created; nonsynchronous sounds, sound effects, and music are selected and devised; and all these elements are combined.

Picture editing. The developed footage comes back from the laboratory with one or more duplicate copies. Editors work from these copies, known as work prints, so that the original camera footage can remain undamaged and clean until the final negative cut. The work prints reproduce not only the footage shot but also the edge numbers that were photographically imprinted on the raw film stock. These latent edge numbers, which are imprinted successively once per foot on the film border, enable the negative matcher to conform the assembled work print to the original footage.

Work prints

Before a day's work, or rushes, are viewed it is usual to synchronize those takes that were shot with dialogue or other major sounds. Principal sound is transferred from quarter-inch to sprocketed magnetic tape of the same gauge as the film (*i.e.*, 16-mm or 35-mm) so that once the start of each shot is matched, sound and image will advance at the same rate, even though they are on separate strips. Once synchronism is established, the sound and image tracks can be marked with identical ink "rubber" numbers so that synchronism can be maintained or quickly reestablished by sight.

The editor first assembles a rough cut, choosing with the director one version of each shot and providing one possible arrangement that largely preserves continuity and the major dialogue. The work print goes through many stages from rough to fine cut, as the editor juggles such factors for each shot and scene as camera placement, relation between sound and image, performance quality, and cutting rhythm. While the work print is being refined, decisions are made about additions or adjustments to the image that could not be created in the camera. These "opticals" range from titles to elaborate computer-generated special effects and are created in special laboratories.

Editing equipment. Rushes are first viewed in a screening room. Once individual shots and takes have been separated and logged, editing requires such equipment as viewers, sound readers, synchronizers, and splicers to reattach the separate pieces of film. Most work is done on a console that combines several of the above functions and enables the editor to run sound and picture synchronously, separately at sound speed, or at variable speeds. For decades the Hollywood standard was the Moviola, originally a vertical device with one or more sound heads and a small viewplate that preserves much of the image brightness without damaging the film. Many European editors, from the 1930s on, worked with flatbed machines, which use a rotating prism rather than intermittent motion to yield an image. Starting in the 1960s flatbeds such as the KEM and Steenbeck versions became more popular in the United States and Great Britain. These horizontal editing systems are identified by how many plates they provide; each supply plate and its corresponding take-up plate transports one image or sound track. Flatbeds provide larger viewing monitors, much quieter operation, better sound quality, and faster speeds than the vertical Moviola.

Electronic editing. Despite the replacement of the optical sound track by sprocketed magnetic film and the introduction of the flatbed, the mechanics of editing did not change fundamentally from the 1930s until the 1980s. Each production generated hundreds of thousands of feet of work print and sound track on expensive 35-mm film, much of it hanging in bins around the editing room. Assistants manually entered scene numbers, take numbers, and roll numbers into notebooks; cuts were marked in grease pencil and spliced with cement or tape. The recent application of computer and video technology to editing equipment, however, has had dramatic results.

The present generation of "random access" editing controllers makes it likely that physical cutting and splicing will become obsolete. In these systems, material originated on film is transferred to laser videodiscs. Videotape players may also be used, but the interactive disc has the advantage of speed. It enables editors to locate any single frame from 30 minutes of program material in three seconds or less. The log that lists each take is stored in the computer memory; the editor can call up the desired frame simply by punching a location code. The image is displayed without any distracting or obstructing numbers on a high-resolution video monitor. The editor uses a keypad to assemble various versions of a scene. There is neither actual cutting of film nor copying onto another tape or disc; computer numbers are merely rearranged. The end product is computer output in which the "edit decision" list exists as time code numbers (see above *Cameras*).

Electronic editing also simplifies the last stage in editing. Instead of assembling the camera negative with as many as 2,000 or more splices, an editor can match the time code information on a computer program against the latent edge numbers on the film. Intact camera rolls can then be assembled in order without cutting or splicing. Electronic editing equipment has been used primarily with material photographed at the standard television rate of 30 frames per second. Material shot at the motion-picture rate of 24 frames per second can be adapted for electronic editing by assigning each film frame three video fields, of which only two are used.

Special effects. Special effects embrace a wide array of photographic, mechanical, pyrotechnic, and model-making skills.

The most important resource of the special effects department is the optical printer, essentially a camera and projector operating in tandem, which makes it possible to photograph a photograph. In simplest form this apparatus is little more than a contact printer with motorized controls to execute simple transitions such as fades, dissolves, and wipes. A 24-frame dissolve can be accomplished by copying the end of one film scene and the beginning of another onto a third film so that diminished exposure of the first overlaps increased exposure of the second. Slow motion can be created by reprinting each frame two or three times. Conversely, printing every other frame (skip printing) speeds up action to create a comic effect or to double the speed when filming action such as collisions. A freeze frame is made by copying one frame repeatedly.

Optical printing

The optical printer can also be used to replace part of an image. For example, a high-angle long shot in a western may reveal what looks like an entire frontier town surrounded by wilderness. Rather than take the time and trouble to actually build and film on location for a shot that may last less than a minute, filmmakers can make the shot using standing sets on the studio backlot, with skyscrapers and freeway traffic visible in the distance. One frame of the original scene is then enlarged so that a matte artist can trace the outline of the offending area on paper. When the copy negative is made, the offending area is masked and remains unexposed. The negative can then be rewound to film a matte painting of suitable location scenery. In addition to combining artwork with live action, optical printing can combine two or more live-action shots.

In the aerial image optical printer, the camera is aimed straight down at a ground glass easel on which an image is projected from below. The large image allows the artist to make a very precise alignment of the artwork and live action so that they can be filmed in one pass.

Blue-screen photography

Optical printing can be combined with blue-screen photography to produce such effects as characters flying through the air. Ordinary superimposition cannot be used

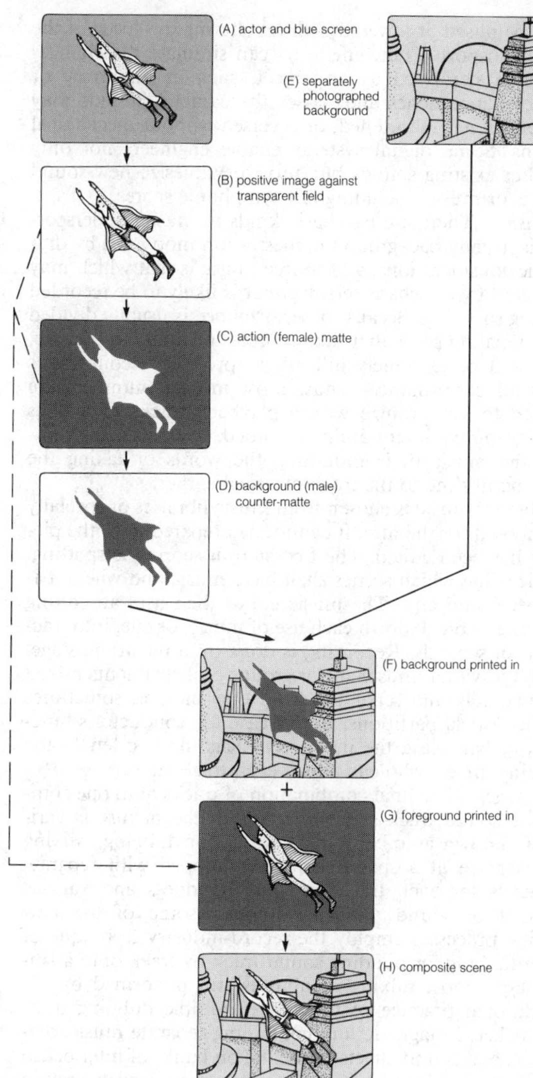

Figure 4: Steps in a blue-screen effect.

for this effect because the background will bleed through as the character moves. To create a traveling matte shot, it is necessary to obtain an opaque image of the foreground actors or objects against a transparent background. This is done by exploiting film's special sensitivity to blue light. In a traditional blue-screen process the actor is posed before a primary blue background, which, to avoid shadows, is illuminated from behind (see Figure 4A). Eastman No. 5247 colour negative is used to film the shot because its blue-sensitive layer yields a dense black-silver image in the area of the blue screen. On the positive print, the foreground action appears against a transparent field (see 4B). This image, printed with red light onto high-contrast panchromatic film, produces the action, or female, matte (see 4C). An additional generation yields a countermatte known as the background, or male, on which the action appears as an opaque silhouette (see 4D). This silhouette is placed with a separately photographed background (see 4E) in an optical printer. In the first pass through the optical printer, the background is "printed in" (see 4F). In the second pass, the actor and action matte are combined and the foreground is printed in (see 4G). All the elements are thus composited on one film (see 4H). There are many variations using more or fewer generations. In some systems the foreground is printed first. With a negative, or reverse, matte, the action matte is made from the camera negative and is opaque against a transparent background. The blue-screen process, in a form more complex than that described here, was used to create many spectacular effects in such films as *Star Wars* (1977) and *E.T.—The Extraterrestrial* (1982). The term blue-screen need not be taken literally. Blue-garbed Superman required a differentiated backing, and sodium vapour (yellow) light was used on the screen to yield a transparent background for the flight scenes in *Mary Poppins* (1964).

In the past two actors talking in a car were likely to be filmed in the studio using rear projection (process) shots; that is, the actors were photographed in front of a translucent screen through which previously filmed footage of passing scenery was projected. Location shooting and lightweight sound equipment have all but eliminated this formerly common practice in feature films, although it survives in television. When routine background replacement is still used in expensive productions, it is more likely to be done with blue-screen than with rear projection.

Front projection

The light loss and lack of sharpness (especially noticeable in colour) that made rear projection shots obvious has also inspired some interest in front projection. The camera is placed facing the screen, and the background projector is positioned in front of and to the side of the camera so that the beam it projects is perpendicular to the camera's line of sight. A semitransparent mirror is angled at 45 degrees between camera and projector; the camera photographs the scene through the glass while the mirror particles reflect the projection beam onto the screen. The screen is made of Scotchlite, the trade name for a material that was originally devised to make road signs that would reflect light from a car's headlight to the driver's eyes. Because camera and projector are in the same optical axis in the front projection process, the background illumination is reflected directly to the camera lens so brilliantly that it is not washed out by the lighting on the actors. The actors also mask their own shadows. Front projection was used to great effect in "The Dawn of Man" sequence in *2001* (1968) wherein a leopard's eyes lit up in facing the camera. Scotchlite screens have been used to reflect powerful lights that have been shone through tanks of dyed water to produce large-scale blue-screen effects.

To reduce the graininess that each generation of film adds to the original, concerns such as George Lucas' Industrial Light and Magic produce their effects on 65-mm film. Others, notably Albert Whitlock, have revived the old practice of making matte effects on the camera negative. In the silent film days, this was achieved using a glass shot in which the actors were photographed through a pane of glass on which the background had been painted. The Whitlock method employs a black matte in front of the camera. A hole is cut in the matte to expose the live action, which may account for only a small portion of the image. The partially exposed negative is rewound, and the background is photographed from a matte painting on glass on which the corresponding area of live action is absent.

Miniatures and models

Miniatures (scale models) are often used in special effects work because they are relatively inexpensive and easy to handle. Great care is needed to maintain smooth, proportionate movement to keep the miniatures from looking as small and insubstantial as they really are. Models may be filmed at speeds greater than 24 frames per second (*i.e.*, in slow motion) to achieve more realistic-looking changes in perspective and time scale. John Dykstra's Apogee, Inc., is a leader in the field of motion control, the use of computer-controlled motors to regulate the movement of models and camera in relation to one another, thereby improving the illusion of motion. The model aircraft or spacecraft can even be made to swoop and turn as they approach the camera.

Until recently it was difficult to introduce camera movement into special effects shots. Limited camera movement was achieved by moving the camera in the optical printer, thereby creating an optical zoom, but this method did not create a convincing illusion of three-dimensionality because the foreground and background elements, as well as the grain pattern in the film, were enlarged or reduced at the same rate. When a crane or dolly was used to shoot the live portion of the scene, the background had to be animated frame-by-frame, involving considerable expense in draftsmanship. Computer-enhanced animation has made it possible to store and recall the algorithms needed to model shapes and surfaces at varied perspectives.

The increased interface of film and video techniques has great implications in the effects area. The ease with which colour components can be separated and reformed makes the electronic medium especially well suited to blue-screen and similar image replacement techniques. The creation of mattes through computer graphics rather than the laborious process of laboratory development is an obvious area of cost savings. Digital image storage on laser videodiscs, as in the Abekas system, enables images to be manipulated with ease.

Sound editing. Less than 25 percent of the sound track of a feature film may have been recorded at the time of photography. Much of the dialogue and almost all of the sound effects and music are adjusted and added during postproduction. Most sound effects and music are kept on separate magnetic tracks and not combined until the rerecording session.

Dialogue. Because of drastic changes in microphone placement from one shot to another, excessively "live" acoustics, background noise, and other difficulties, part or all of the dialogue in a scene may have to be added during postproduction. Production sound is used as a cue or guide track for replacing dialogue, a procedure commonly known as dubbing, or looping. Looping involves cutting loops out of identical lengths of picture, sound track, and blank magnetic film. The actor listens to the cue track while watching the scene over and over. The actor rehearses the line so that it matches the wording and lip movements and then a recording is made. The cutting of loops has largely been replaced by automatic dialogue replacement (ADR). Picture and sound are interlocked on machines that can run forward or backward. In the 1980s digitalized systems were developed that could, with imperceptible changes in pitch, stretch or shrink the replacement dialogue to match the waveforms in the original for perfect lip sync.

Dubbing

Dubbing also refers to the process of substituting one language for another throughout the entire picture. If this is to be done credibly, it is necessary to make the speech in the second language fit the character and cadence of the original. If the actor's face is visible in the picture it is also necessary to fit the words of the translation so that the lip movements are not too disparate. In the United States and England pictures intended for foreign distribution are prepared in a version with an M&E (music and effects) track separate from the dialogue to facilitate dubbing. In certain other countries, notably Italy, most dialogue recorded during production is meant merely to serve as a guide track, and nearly all sound is added during postproduction. One last form of speech recorded separately from photography is narration or commentary. Although images may be edited to fit the commentary, as in a documentary using primarily archival footage, most narration is added as a separate track and mixed like sound effects and music.

Sound effects. All sounds other than speech, music, and the natural sounds generated by the actors in synchronous filming are considered sound effects, whether or not they are intended to be noticed by the audience. Although some sounds may be gathered at the time of shooting, the big studios and large independent services maintain vast libraries of effects. Still other effects may be generated by re-creating conditions or by finding or creating substitute noises that sound convincing.

An expedient way of generating mundane effects is the "foley" technique, which involves matching sound effects to picture. For footsteps, a foley artist chooses or creates an appropriate surface in a studio and records the sound of someone moving in place on it in time to the projected image. Foleying is the effects equivalent of looping dialogue.

Background noise (room tone or presence) from the original location must be added to all shots that were not recorded live so that there is continuity between synchronous and postsynchronized shots. Continuous noises, such as wind or waves, may be put on separate tracks that are looped (the beginning of a track is spliced to follow its end), so that the sound can be run continuously.

Sound effects can be manipulated with the use of digital technology known as audio signal processing (ASP). The sound waveform is analyzed 44,000 times per second and converted into binary information. The pitch of a sound may be raised or lowered without altering the speed of the tape transport. Thus, engineers can simulate the changes in pitch perceived as an object, such as an arrow or vehicle, approaches and passes the camera. Sounds may be lengthened, shortened, or reversed without mechanical means. Some digital systems enable engineers not only to alter existing sounds but also to synthesize new sound effects or music, including full symphonic scores.

Underscoring and source music

Music. There are two basic kinds of music; underscoring is usually background orchestration motivated by dramatic considerations, and source music is that which may be heard by the characters. Neither is likely to be recorded during shooting. Because a performance is usually divided into separate shots that take minutes or hours to prepare, it would be extremely difficult to produce a continuous musical performance. Thus, most musical numbers are filmed to synchronize with a playback track. The songs and accompaniment are prerecorded, so that during filming the musician is mouthing the words or faking the playing in time to the track recorded earlier.

Whether music is chosen from music libraries or specially composed for the film, it cannot be prepared until the picture has been edited. The first step in scoring is spotting, or deciding which scenes shall have music and where it is to begin and end. The music editor then uses an editing console to break down each use of music, or cue, into fractions of seconds. Recording is done on a recording stage, with individual musicians or groups of instruments miked individually and separated from one another, sometimes by acoustical partitions. In this case the conductor's function of balancing the instrumentalists may be left to the scoring mixer, who can adjust each track later.

Mixing. The final combination of tracks onto one composite sound track synchronous with the picture is variously known as mixing, rerecording, or dubbing. Mixing takes place at a special console equipped with separate controls for each track to adjust loudness and various aspects of sound quality. Although some of the new digital processes employ the record-industry technique of overdubbing, or building sound track-by-track onto a single tape, most mixing in films is still performed by the traditional practice of threading multiple dubbing units (sprocketed magnetic film containing separate music, dialogue, and sound effects elements) on banks of interlocked dubbers. The playback dubbers are connected by selsyn motors to one another, as well as to the rerecorders that produce the master, or parallel music/dialogue/effects (M/D/E), track on full-coat magnetic stock. Also in interlock are a projector that allows the mixer to work from the actual image and a footage counter that allows the mixer to follow cue sheets, or logs, which indicate by footage number when each track should be brought in and out.

The mixer strives to strike the right dramatic balance between dialogue, music, and effects and to avoid monotony. Mixing procedures vary widely. Some studios use one mixer for each of the three main tracks, in which case the effects tracks have probably been mixed down earlier onto one combined track. In the early days of magnetic recording, stopping the rerecording equipment produced an audible click on the track; if a mistake were made, mixing would have to be redone from the beginning of the tape reel. The advent of back-up recording in the 1960s eliminated the click, making it possible for mixers to work on smaller segments and to correct mistakes without starting over. This enables the mix to be controlled by one person, who may be combining as many as 24 tracks. An even greater advance is the computerized console that enables the mixer to go back and correct any one track without having to remix the others.

Back-up recording

For monaural release, a composite music/dialogue/effects master on full-coat 35-mm magnetic film is converted to an optical sound negative. For stereo, four-track submasters for M/D/E are mixed down to a two-track magnetic matrix encoded to contain four channels of sound information. Optical sound negatives are copied from the magnetic master, and they are then composited with the picture internegative so that they are in projection sync (on 35-mm prints the sound is placed 21 frames in advance of its corresponding image; on 16-mm prints the sound is 26 frames in advance of the picture).

Because of narrow track width, optical stereo sound tracks require a system of noise reduction such as Dolby Type A. The Dolby system works by responding to changing amplitudes in various regions of the frequency spectrum of an audio signal. The quieter passages are boosted to increase the spread between the signal (desired sound) and the unwanted ground noise. When played back, normal levels are restored, and the ground noise drops below the threshold of audibility.

Projection technology and theatre design. *Projectors.* The projector is the piece of motion-picture equipment that has changed the least. Manufacturers produce models virtually identical to those of the 1950s, and even the 1930 model Super Simplex is still in wide use. The essential mechanism is still the four-slot Maltese cross introduced in the 1890s. The Maltese cross provides the intermittent Geneva movement that stops each frame of the continuously moving film in front of the picture aperture, where it can be projected (or, in a camera, exposed). The movement starts with a continuously rotating gear and cam (see Figure 5, top). Each 360-degree rotation of the gear and cam causes a pin to engage one of the slots of the Maltese cross. The pin rotates the cross, which in turn rotates a shaft, one quarter turn. As the shaft rotates, four of the 16 teeth on the intermittent sprocket advance and engage the perforations (sprocket holes) on one frame of the film. The sprocket moves only when the pin is fully engaged in the Maltese cross slot (see Figure 5, bottom). This is the "pull-down" phase; in the other phases the curved surfaces of the cam and the cross are in contact and the movement is in the "dwell" position. The Geneva movement is also called a 3:1 movement because there are three quarter-cycles of dwell for every one quarter-cycle of pull-down.

Intermittent Geneva movement

Sound, unlike images, cannot be reproduced intermittently; sound must be continuous to be realistic. The optical-sound-reading equipment on a projector is therefore

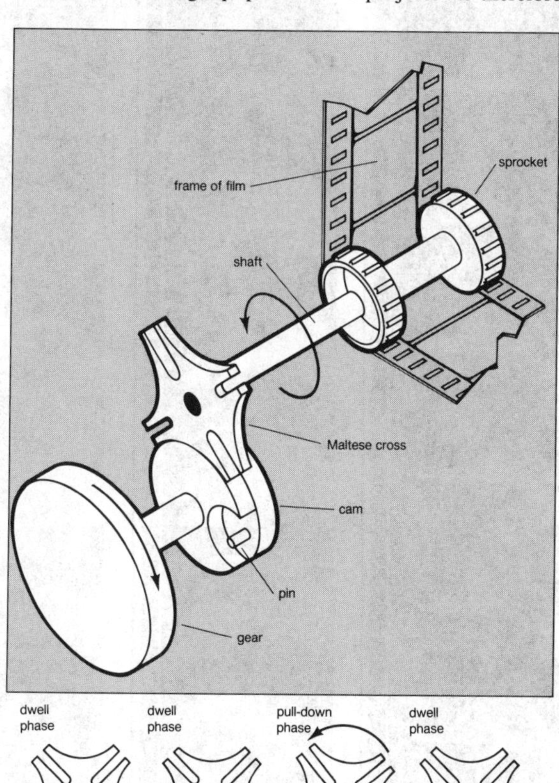

Figure 5: (Top) Intermittent Geneva movement. (Bottom) Successive positions of the Maltese cross.

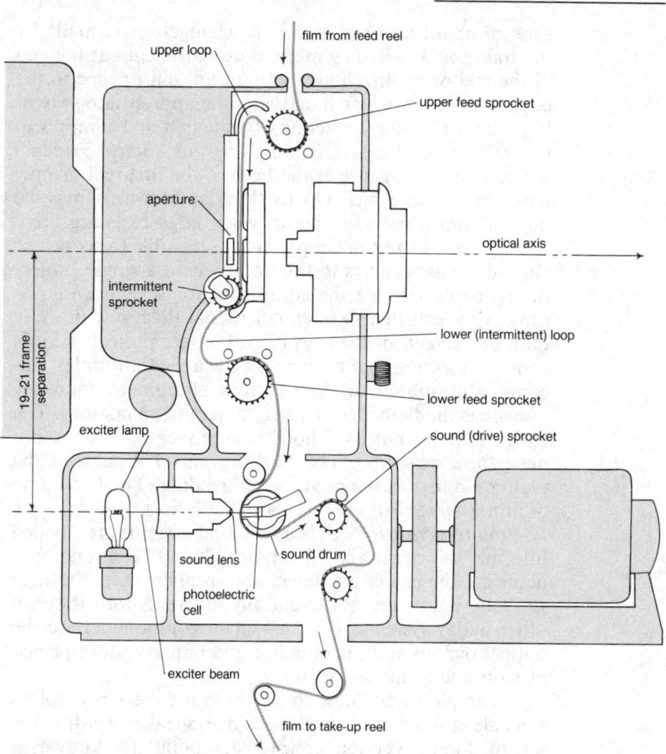

Figure 6: Film path in a typical 35-mm theatrical projector with optical sound reproducer (doors removed).

located below the picture aperture (see Figure 6), and the sound on an optical 35-mm print is located 21 frames ahead of its corresponding image. A light beam (supplied by a direct current for stability) is shone through a rectangular slit and focused by a lens to dimensions of .001 by .084 inch onto the sound track. The sound track's varying bands of light and dark then modulate the amount of light from the beam that is allowed to pass to the optical pickup. In older equipment this pickup was a photoelectric cell that changed electrical resistance under exposure to light. Newer designs employ a solar cell of photovoltaic material to convert light energy to electric energy.

An important element of picture quality on the screen is brightness. For decades the standard light source was the carbon-arc lamphouse, which used disposable electrodes (positive and negative carbon-clad rods) that would be moved together as they burned; the rods needed to be replaced every hour or so. Xenon lamps were introduced in West Germany in the 1950s, and carbon-arc projection is now found only in older theatres. Both carbon-arc and xenon lamps are run off a direct-current power supply in order to minimize brightness variations due to fluctuations in voltage. The xenon bulb replaces the positive and negative carbons with a tungsten anode and cathode in a quartz envelope filled with xenon gas under pressure. Light from xenon bulbs has a colour temperature closer to that of daylight than carbon-arc light does; that is, it is bluer and is therefore particularly well suited to colour films.

Carbon-arc and xenon lamps

Projection techniques. A 35-mm exhibition print is furnished to the theatre mounted on 2,000-foot (22-minute) reels. Thus, a typical feature film consists of five or six reels. For decades, the 2,000-foot reel was the basic unit of projection, and each screening required four or five changes of projector. Circular cue marks printed in the upper right corner of the picture indicated when each changeover should take place. Today the 2,000-foot reel is used primarily in single-screen theatres and in archival and repertory theatres that may present only a single screening of a film. Theatrical exhibition increasingly requires the film to be "made up"—that is, reels must be spliced together to enable the projectionist to make a single changeover between large reels or to use external transports that contain an entire feature without changeovers. For the former, a feature film of six 2,000-foot reels would be reassembled onto two 6,000-foot reels with a running

Changeovers

time of about an hour each. The changeover is made by the traditional switching method using the cues at the end of the reel or by attaching a strip of foil sensor tape to the edge of the film, where it activates the appropriate switching relays. Coming attractions ("trailers") and announcements ("snipes," *e.g.,* "No Smoking" or "Starts Friday") are spliced in sequence at the head of the first reel or may be on a separate reel. Up to three auditoriums may be served from a common booth when large reels are used.

The advent of xenon lamps made it possible to reduce or eliminate changeovers to the point where a single projectionist could operate the equipment for several auditoriums. Although there was an occasional theatre with more than one screen in the days of carbon-arc projection, it is xenon projection that truly began the age of multiplex cinemas. With more than three screens, equipment popularly known as the flatbed, or platter, system is mandatory. The entire film is shown without changeovers and does not need to be rewound. The most advanced version of the platter eliminates the need for rethreading. The last frame of film is spliced to the first, as in the Edison Kinetoscope.

Sound reproduction. Theatre sound systems are divided into the "A" chain and "B" chain. The "B" chain components are the power amplifiers and speakers that, although specially made, are not essentially different from those in other audio systems. The "A" chain components are the optical pickup and preamplifier and employ some principles unique to motion pictures.

The simplest and most common sound system employs a single amplifier channel and one speaker behind the screen. Stereo variable area (SVA), popularly known as Dolby, though in fact made by several manufacturers, employs a split optical pickup for two sets of wires for the left and right channels. Three stage speakers (left, right, and centre) are mounted behind the screen, and an array of speakers is spread along the side and rear of the auditorium for "surround" sound. Most feature films are prepared so that dialogue issues from the centre speaker, music and on-screen sound effects from the left and right, and off-screen sounds from the surrounds. A processor decodes the four channels from dual variable area tracks; information appearing on the left track is sent to the left speaker, on the right track to the right speaker, while information on both tracks is combined in the centre channel. The surround channel is derived from inversion phase relationships between the left and right tracks.

In monaural systems, a treble cut is employed in accordance with the Standard Electrical Characteristic of 1938, or Academy Curve, so that frequencies above 8,000 hertz (Hz) are "rolled off." This practice dates from an era when sound tracks had a large degree of ground noise and vacuum tube amplifiers produced an audible hiss concentrated in the upper frequencies. A treble boost is added during rerecording so that monaural sound tracks sound shrill and sibilant when played without the Academy filter. The introduction of Dolby noise reduction in conjunction with optical tracks made it possible for frequencies to range up to about 12,000 Hz. With the replacement of tube power amplifiers by solid state ones, large wattages are easily obtainable, and theatre sound is generally louder than it was formerly. The normal level for dialogue in a monaural film is 80 decibels (dB) in the centre of the auditorium; the normal Dolby level is 85 dB, or nearly double that.

SVA is a direct replacement for the four-track magnetic sound introduced in 1953 in conjunction with CinemaScope. Today, magnetic sound is used only with 70-mm prints where six tracks are contained in four stripes of magnetic oxide embossed on the film. The magnetic reproducer, called a penthouse, is mounted above the projector. On a magnetic print, the sound displacement is behind the picture (28 frames in 35 mm and 23 frames in 70 mm).

Until recently, theatre speakers were not capable of reproducing sounds below 80 Hz. The standard theatre speaker was a two-way system with a high-frequency horn mounted atop a cabinet containing a wide, shallow paper cone woofer. The impetus given to 70-mm six-track sound by the great success of *Star Wars* led to the development

THX system

of the THX system for exhibition. In the six-track system, five stage speakers are mounted in a flat baffle wall behind the screen; each has double 15-inch woofers for low-frequency reproduction down to 40 Hz. For frequencies down to 30 Hz sub-woofers are connected to a bass extension module that augments signals below 100 Hz on the tracks. At this level sound is not heard but felt as vibration in the viewer's diaphragm. The THX system delivers undistorted sound up to a level of 108 dB per channel.

(E.We./S.G.H.)

ANIMATION

The basis of all animation is the building up, frame by frame, of the moving picture by exact timing and choreography of both movement and sound. All film movement is achieved by projecting during every second of time a certain number of frames, normally 24, each a still photograph minutely varied from its predecessor, which record the successive phases of the subject's movement before the camera. The same motion, or a stylized or caricatured version of it, can be achieved by "stop-motion" or "stop-action" cinematography, the frame-by-frame photographing of a similarly phased series of drawings (see Figure 7) or the phased movement of such objects as puppets, marionettes, or commercial products. And, as in live filming, the camera itself can create movement by tracking into a scene or panning across it. The great majority of animated films are short and have always been so for obvious reasons. When each second of action requires, for the fullest animation, 24 adjustments of the image, a minute's action may call for many hundreds of drawings.

EB Inc

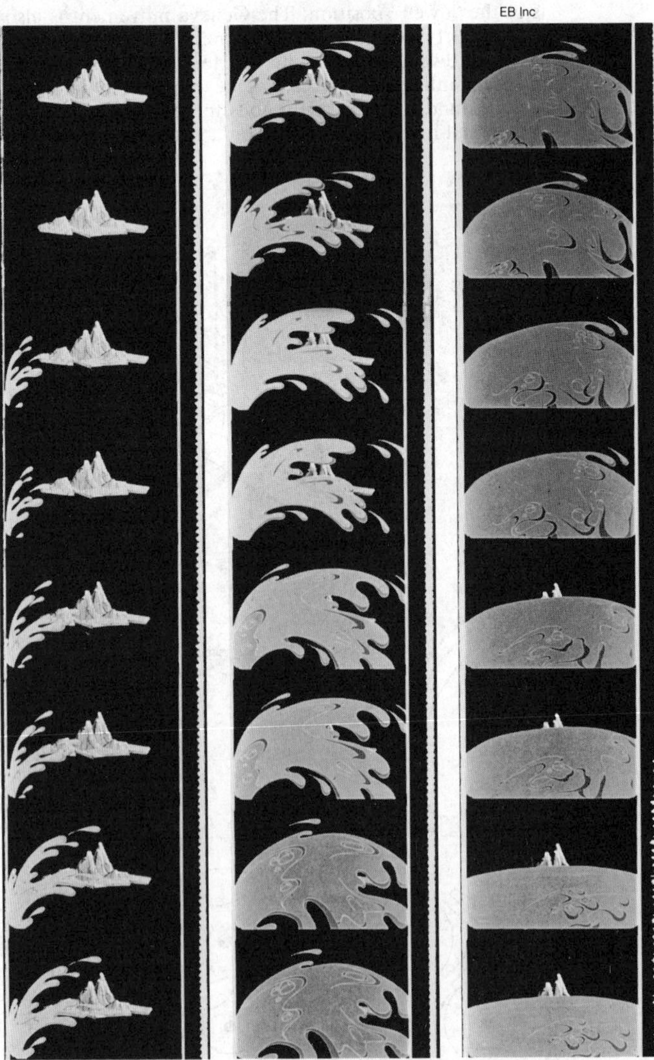

Figure 7: Twenty-four frames, the length of film projected each second, from *If You Could See the Earth*, an educational film. The jagged white line to the right of each frame is the sound track.

The range of techniques in animation production is broad. The basic form is the simple, outlined figure, however, that moves against a simple, outlined background.

Figural basis of animation. The development of cel (or cell) animation permitted the phased movements of the figures to be traced onto a succession of transparent celluloid sheets and superimposed, in turn, onto a single static drawing representing the background. With this technique the background could be drawn in somewhat greater detail and tonal qualities introduced through shading, while the figure itself became a black silhouette, blotting out the background when the cels were superimposed. Multiple cel animation—the superimposition of several cel layers, each carrying different figures or parts of figures requiring special care in animation—allowed increased complexity in the image with minimum work load for the artist-animators. With the more modern forms of colour film introduced in the early 1930s, opaque paints and coloured inks could be used on the cels. Cel animation required the use of a so-called rostrum camera, which photographs downward onto the background with its series of superimposed cel layers pegged into place to secure accurate registration.

Cel animation

Noncellular animation. Other forms of animation include silhouette animation, developed by Lotte Reiniger in Germany during the 1920s. It uses jointed, flat-figure marionettes whose poses are minutely readjusted for each photographic frame. Movement is similarly simulated in puppet animation, which photographs solid three-dimensional figures in miniature sets. The puppets are often made of a malleable yet stable material, such as clay, so that the carefully phased movements may be adjusted between the exposures of successive frames. Even people may be photographed frame by frame, as in the so-called pixilation process used by the Canadian filmmaker Norman McLaren in his short film *Neighbors* (1952), which makes human beings look like automatons.

Abstract animation

Although abstract animation can be realized through orthodox animation techniques (as in parts of *Fantasia,* 1940), it may also be inked or painted directly onto the film. This form of abstract animation was pioneered in the 1920s with the individual and collaborative work of the German Hans Richter and the Swede Viking Eggeling, and continued in the 1930s with the films of Len Lye, a New Zealander also known for his abstract sculpture. McLaren, too, experimented with a wide range of techniques for animating directly on film; he even created many of his scores by stenciling directly onto the sound track rather than recording in the traditional manner. Since the 1970s, computers have often been used to generate abstract or stylized patterns, and means were developed to circumvent photography by transferring the results directly to 35 mm.

Planning. The preparation of these films, whatever their length or form, follows a similar process. First comes the story, plot, action, or situational idea, which may be a written treatment with or without supporting sketches. It describes the continuity of what it is proposed should take place on the screen, the nature of the cartoon or puppet characters, the graphic stylization of the film as a whole, and similar considerations. Such a treatment, perhaps very brief, precedes any fuller scripting or other elaboration that may take place.

Since visual emphasis is the key to animation, and sound its close counterpart, the sooner ideas are translated into pictures the better. The "storyboard" provides the continuity of the action, which is worked out scene by scene simultaneously with the animation script. In the storyboard the story is told and to some extent graphically styled in a succession of key sketches with captions and fragments of dialogue, much like a cartoon strip but with much fuller treatment. A feature-length film could easily require a final continuity of several hundred such sketches.

Meanwhile, an animation director is also preparing modeling drawings for the principal characters and drawings establishing the backgrounds, or settings, for the film. These begin to indicate the general graphic style and, when colour is involved, the colour scheme and decor to be used. The modeling drawings must indicate the nature and temperament of the characters as well as their appearance when seen from a variety of angles and using a number of characteristic gestures. These will act as guides for the key animators, who with their assistants must bring the figures to dramatic life through the succession of final drawings created on the drawing board.

Sound synchronization

Animated films are, in effect, choreographed; since mobility involves time, the movements must be exactly timed and so deployed through the right number of successive drawings, like notes in music deployed through bars in a score. When the characters speak or sing, their lip movements must be synchronized with the words they appear to utter. When sound tracks, both dialogue and music, are prerecorded, the animators have an exact time scheme to follow; if the tracks are not prerecorded, then the "scoring" of the action will control the subsequent timing of the speech and music at recording stage. The timing in either case is predetermined on paper in a workbook, which grades the progression of the animators' drawings frame by frame with the same precision as a musical score. A similar control in the form of a time chart may be created by the director as a guide for the composer. A third control, the so-called dope sheet or camera exposure chart, guides the rostrum cameraman in the frame-by-frame setups and sequence of cels or backgrounds.

Execution. When the exacting labour of animation is under way, difficult moments in the choreography of the figures may be "line-tested," that is, outlined in pencil, photographed, and tested out on the screen for rhythm and characterization. The key, or senior, animators, draw, or "cartoon," the highlights, or salients, of the movement, perhaps the five or more drawings out of the 24 per second that will give the special edge of liveliness or characterization to the movements. Assistant animators, sometimes called in-betweeners, close the gaps by completing the intermediate drawings. The smaller the animation unit the greater the burden each artist has to bear in the preparation of final drawings. These drawings, the backgrounds of which remain on drawing paper, are transferred to the cels by specialized artists, who trace the animators' work and paint over it with opaque colouring. The work of tracing and painting can be saved when the animators draw directly on the cels with coloured chinagraph pencils, which they can rub out or correct without harm. When the picture track and the sound track with speech, sound effects, and music dubbed together are completed under the control of the director and the editor, a "married print" can be made, with the track recorded optically.

Newer techniques. Efforts to lessen the extraordinary labour and costs of animation have taken two basic directions: simplification and computerization. Inexpensive cartoons made for television have often resorted to "limited animation," in which each drawing is repeated anywhere from two to five times. The resultant movements are jerky, rather than smoothly gradated. Often only part of the body is animated, and the background and the remaining parts of the figure do not change at all. Another shortcut is "cycling," whereby only a limited number of phases of body movement are drawn and then repeated to create more complicated movements such as walking or talking.

Computer animation

Although computers can be used to create the limited animation described above, they can also be used in virtually every step of sophisticated animation. Computers have been used, for example, to automate the movement of the rostrum camera or to supply the in-between drawings for full animation. If a three-dimensional figure is translated into computer terms (*i.e.,* digitized), the computer can move or rotate the object convincingly through space. Hence, computer animation can demonstrate highly complex movements for medical or other scientific researchers. Animators who work with computers usually distinguish between computer-assisted animation, which uses computers to facilitate some stages of the laborious production process, and computer-generated animation, which creates imagery through mathematical or computer language rather than through photography or drawing. Finally, computers may be used to modify or enhance a drawing that has been initiated in the traditional manner.

(R.M./E.We.)

BIBLIOGRAPHY

General histories: ARTHUR KNIGHT, *The Liveliest Art: A Panoramic History of the Movies,* rev. ed. (1979), an influential history; PAUL ROTHA, with RICHARD GRIFFITH, *The Film till Now,* new ed. (1967), a substantial history, though now dimmed by age and a lack of critical perspective; PIERRE LEPROHON, *Histoire du cinéma,* 2 vol. (1961–63), a useful reference work of names, dates, titles, and events; GERALD MAST, *A Short History of the Movies,* 4th ed. (1986); DAVID A. COOK, *A History of Narrative Film* (1981), a wide-ranging historical survey of international film; ERIC RHODE, *A History of the Cinema from Its Origins to 1970* (1976, reprinted 1985), an international critical history, providing detailed though opinionated coverage; KENNETH MACGOWAN, *Behind the Screen: The History and Techniques of the Motion Picture* (1965), a dated but still valuable history by an industry insider; and EPHRAIM KATZ, *The Film Encyclopedia* (1979), an informative reference source.

Historical studies of specific periods: Early developments are studied in TERRY RAMSAYE, *A Million and One Nights: A History of the Motion Picture,* 2 vol. (1926, reissued in 1 vol., 1986), a romantic account covering the period to 1925, with emphasis on American film between 1890 and 1915; MICHAEL CHANAN, *The Dream That Kicks: The Prehistory and Early Years of Cinema in Britain* (1980), an extraordinary study of the cultural/ideological "site" of cinema at the moment of its birth; KEVIN BROWNLOW, *Hollywood, the Pioneers* (1979), a systematic treatment of the subject through the 1920s, copiously illustrated by JOHN KOBAL; JOHN FELL (ed.), *Film Before Griffith* (1983); and LARY MAY, *Screening Out the Past: The Birth of Mass Culture and the Motion Picture Industry* (1980, reprinted 1983).

Further developments are presented in GEORGES SADOUL, *Histoire générale du cinéma,* 6 vol. in varied editions (1973–75), a detailed study of the epoch of silent film; KEVIN BROWNLOW, *The Parade's Gone By* (1968), a well-illustrated study of American silent films and stars, based on interviews with survivors; JOHN KOBAL, *Hollywood: The Years of Innocence* (1985), a pictorial work on the period; GRAHAM PETRIE, *Hollywood Destinies: European Directors in America, 1922–1931* (1985); and BENJAMIN B. HAMPTON, *A History of the Movies* (1931, reissued as *History of the American Film Industry from Its Beginnings to 1931,* 1970). An excellent, well-researched account of the coming of sound is found in ALEXANDER WALKER, *The Shattered Silents: How the Talkies Came to Stay* (1978, reissued 1986); see also EVAN WILLIAM CAMERON (ed.), *Sound and the Cinema: The Coming of Sound to American Film* (1980), an anthology of scholarly essays and reminiscences; LEONARD QUART and ALBERT AUSTER, *American Films and Society Since 1945* (1984), a brief, penetrating study; and WILLIAM LUHR (ed.), *World Cinema Since 1945* (1987).

Historical and critical studies of national film movements: British filmmaking is the subject of ROY ARMES, *A Critical History of the British Cinema* (1978); RACHAEL LOW, *The History of the British Film,* 7 vol. (1948–79), a detailed study of the silent film; ERNEST BETTS, *The Film Business: A History of British Cinema, 1896–1972* (1973), a standard, compact history; ALEXANDER WALKER, *Hollywood UK: The British Film Industry in the Sixties* (1974; U.K. title, *Hollywood, England,* reprinted 1986); and GEORGE PERRY, *The Great British Picture Show,* rev. ed. (1985), a popular concise history. For France, see RICHARD ABEL, *French Cinema: The First Wave, 1915–1929* (1984), a definitive scholarly study of avant-garde and commercial cinema of the era, superbly illustrated; JAMES MONACO, *The New Wave: Truffaut, Godard, Chabrol, Rohmer, Rivette* (1976, reprinted 1980), an excellent critical study; GEORGES SADOUL, *French Film* (1953, reissued 1972); and ROY ARMES, *French Cinema* (1985). For Germany, see SIEGFRIED KRACAUER, *From Caligari to Hitler: A Psychological History of the German Film* (1947, reissued with additions, 1974), a psychological, sociological, and political analysis; DAVID STEWART HULL, *Film in the Third Reich: A Study of the German Cinema, 1933–1945* (1969, reissued 1973), an exploration of the cinema's role in Nazi propaganda; DAVID WELCH, *Propaganda and the German Cinema, 1933–1945* (1983); JULIAN PETLEY, *Capital and Culture: German Cinema, 1933–45* (1979), a discussion of the economic and social structure of the Nazi film industry; LOTTE H. EISNER, *The Haunted Screen: Expressionism in the German Cinema and the Influence of Max Reinhardt* (1969, reissued 1973; originally published in French, 1965; new enl. French ed., 1981), a study of the influence of the arts of painting, drama, and the novel on the cinema; and ERIC RENTSCHLER, *West German Film in the Course of Time: Reflections on the Twenty Years Since Oberhausen* (1984), a scholarly account of the New German Cinema and its historical-economic contexts.

Italian filmmaking is the subject of PIERRE LEPROHON, *The Italian Cinema* (1972; originally published in French, 1966); JAMES HAY, *Popular Film Culture in Fascist Italy: The Passing of the Rex* (1987); MIRA LIEHM, *Passion and Defiance: Film in Italy from 1942 to the Present* (1984), an informative though sometimes eccentric critical study; ROY ARMES, *Patterns of Realism* (1971, reprinted 1986), a standard study of the Neorealist cinema; and PETER BONDANELLA, *Italian Cinema: From Neorealism to the Present* (1983), a definitive scholarly analysis. Films from the Soviet Union and eastern European countries are the subject of JAY LEYDA, *Kino: A History of the Russian and Soviet Film,* 3rd ed. (1983), a broad, authoritative study of developments beginning with tsarist times; MIRA LIEHM and ANTONÍN J. LIEHM, *The Most Important Art: Eastern European Film After 1945* (1977), a survey of Soviet, Polish, Czechoslovak, Hungarian, Yugoslav, East German, Rumanian, and Bulgarian cinema, illustrated with many rare stills; RONALD HOLLOWAY, *The Bulgarian Cinema* (1986), a well-illustrated study; PETER HAMES, *The Czechoslovak New Wave* (1985); GRAHAM PETRIE, *History Must Answer to Man: The Contemporary Hungarian Cinema* (1978); and DANIEL J. GOULDING, *Liberated Cinema: The Yugoslav Experience* (1985), a critical history of the postwar period. For other European countries, see PETER COWIE, *Swedish Cinema* (1966) and *Swedish Cinema from Ingeborg Holm to Fanny and Alexander* (1985); and PETER BESAS, *Behind the Spanish Lens: Spanish Cinema Under Fascism and Democracy* (1985).

For the survey of Australian movies, see GRAHAM SHIRLEY and BRIAN ADAMS, *Australian Cinema, the First Eighty Years* (1983), a standard scholarly history, covering developments to 1975; and BRIAN MCFARLANE, *Australian Cinema 1970–1985* (1986), a valuable account of Australia's unprecedented film explosion. Filmmaking in Asian and African countries is discussed in NOËL BURCH, *To the Distant Observer: Form and Meaning in the Japanese Cinema,* revised and edited by ANNETTE MICHELSON (1979), a classical study of the film form and its misinterpretations in the West; TADAO SATO, *Currents in Japanese Cinema,* trans. from Japanese (1982), original essays with a filmography to 1981; AUDIE BOCK, *Japanese Film Directors* (1978, reprinted 1985), a scrupulously researched critical study of 10 directors spanning the history of the industry; JOSEPH L. ANDERSON and DONALD RICHIE, *The Japanese Film: Art and Industry,* expanded ed. (1982); JAY LEYDA, *Dianying: An Account of Films and the Film Audience in China* (1972); ERIK BARNOUW and S. KRISHNASWAMY, *Indian Film,* 2nd ed. (1980), an authoritative study; T.M. RAMACHANDRAN (ed.), *70 Years of Indian Cinema, 1913–1983* (1985), a well-illustrated, extended history; and ROY ARMES, *Third World Film Making and the West* (1987), a historical overview that also includes discussions of Latin-American cinema.

Book-length works on Latin America, Cuba, and Mexico include JORGE A. SCHNITMAN, *Film Industries in Latin America: Dependency and Development* (1984), an economic analysis from the silent era through the 1980s; RANDAL JOHNSON and ROBERT STAM (eds.), *Brazilian Cinema* (1982), a definitive English-language history; MICHAEL CHANAN, *The Cuban Image: Cinema and Cultural Politics in Cuba* (1985); and CARL J. MORA, *Mexican Cinema: Reflections of a Society, 1896–1980* (1982), a scholarly critical history. The cinema of the United States is the subject of ROBERT SKLAR, *Movie-Made America: A Social History of American Movies* (1975); LEWIS JACOBS, *The Rise of the American Film, a Critical History,* expanded ed. (1968, reissued 1974), a detailed study, with emphasis on trends and audience preference; DAVID BORDWELL, KRISTIN THOMPSON, and JANET STAIGER, *The Classical Hollywood Cinema: Film Style & Mode of Production to 1960* (1985); DOUGLAS GOMERY, *The Hollywood Studio System* (1985); ANDREW SARRIS, *The American Cinema: Directors and Directions, 1929–1968* (1968, reprinted 1985), a classic definition of the auteur theory and its critical application to American films and filmmakers; and TINO BALIO (ed.), *The American Film Industry,* rev. ed. (1985), an anthology of historical scholarship and primary documents from the origins to the 1980s.

Genre studies: THOMAS SCHATZ, *Hollywood Genres: Formulas, Filmmaking, and the Studio System* (1981), examines prevalent styles and forms. Nonfiction films are discussed in RICHARD MERAN BARSAM, *Nonfiction Film: A Critical History* (1973), which focuses on British and American documentaries; RICHARD MERAN BARSAM (ed.), *Nonfiction Film: Theory and Criticism* (1976); and ERIK BARNOUW, *Documentary: A History of the Non-Fiction Film,* rev. ed. (1983). War themes are explored in CRAIG W. CAMPBELL, *Reel America and World War I: A Comprehensive Filmography and History of Motion Pictures in the United States, 1914–1920* (1985); and JEANINE BASINGER, *The World War II Combat Film: Anatomy of a Genre* (1986).

Studies of the western, crime movies, and *film noir* include GEORGE N. FENIN and WILLIAM K. EVERSON, *The Western, from Silents to the Seventies* (1973, reprinted 1977); JIM KITSES, *Horizons West: Anthony Mann, Budd Boetticher, Sam Peckinpah: Studies of Authorship Within the Western* (1969); JON TUSKA, *The Filming of the West* (1976); LAWRENCE ALLOWAY, *Violent America: The Movies, 1946–1964* (1971); CARLOS CLARENS,

Crime Movies: From Griffith to The Godfather and Beyond (1980), a historical cross-genre survey; ALAIN SILVER and ELIZABETH WARD (eds.), *Film Noir: An Encyclopedic Reference to the American Style* (1979), a critical reference work; FOSTER HIRSCH, *The Dark Side of the Screen: Film Noir* (1981, reprinted 1983), an in-depth study; and JON TUSKA, *Dark Cinema: American Film Noir in Cultural Perspective* (1984). Experimental cinema is the subject of SHELDON RENAN, *An Introduction to the American Underground Film* (1967). The social-issue movie is explored in PETER ROFFMAN and JIM PURDY, *The Hollywood Social Problem Film: Madness, Despair, and Politics from the Depression to the Fifties* (1981). For feminist studies of Hollywood films, see MARY ANN DOANE, *The Desire to Desire: The Woman's Film of the 1940s* (1987); and E. ANN KAPLAN, *Women and Film: Both Sides of the Camera* (1983), which also covers independent films.

Two surveys of specific genres are KALTON C. LAHUE, *Continued Next Week: A History of the Moving Picture Serial* (1964) and *World of Laughter: The Motion Picture Comedy Short, 1910–1930* (1966, reprinted 1972). Other works on comedy include WALTER KERR, *The Silent Clowns* (1975); and GERALD MAST, *The Comic Mind: Comedy and the Movies*, 2nd ed. (1979), a thematic study of silent and sound comedies and the relationship between intellectual content and comic form. Musicals are discussed in JOHN KOBAL, *A History of Movie Musicals: Gotta Sing, Gotta Dance*, rev. ed. (1983), an extremely well-represented international survey; TED SENNETT, *Hollywood Musicals* (1981, reprinted 1985); JANE FEUER, *The Hollywood Musical* (1982); and RICK ALTMAN, *The American Film Musical* (1987), a definitive study of the structure of the genre. For an overview of animated films, see LEONARD MALTIN, *Of Mice and Magic: A History of American Animated Cartoons* (1980); DONALD CRAFTON, *Before Mickey: The Animated Film, 1898–1928* (1982), a scholarly discussion of pre-Disney works; and CHRISTOPHER FINCH, *The Art of Walt Disney: From Mickey Mouse to the Magic Kingdoms* (1973, reprinted 1983), a richly illustrated study.

(D.A.C.)

The art of film: There are numerous primers to film study, but the best systematic introductions are DAVID BORDWELL and KRISTIN THOMPSON, *Film Art*, 2nd ed. (1986); and BRUCE F. KAWIN, *How Movies Work* (1987). The essential and classical books concerned with the nature of the film include the following: SERGEI EISENSTEIN, *The Film Sense* (1947), and *Film Form* (1949), two essays in film theory, translated from Russian and available in various later editions of the author's theoretical essays; BÉLA BALÁZS, *Theory of the Film: Character and Growth of a New Art* (1952, reprinted 1972; originally published in Hungarian, 1948); RUDOLF ARNHEIM, *Film as Art* (1957, reprinted 1971; originally published in German, 1932); SIEGFRIED KRACAUER, *Nature of Film: The Redemption of Physical Reality* (1961, reissued as *Theory of Film*, 1974); ANDRÉ BAZIN, *What Is Cinema?*, 2 vol., trans. from French (1967–71); HUGO MÜNSTERBERG, *The Photoplay: A Psychological Study* (1916; reissued as *The Film, a Psychological Study: The Silent Photoplay in 1916*, 1970); PETER WOLLEN, *Signs and Meaning in the Cinema*, new ed. (1972); CHRISTIAN METZ, *Film Language: A Semiotics of the Cinema* (1974; originally published in French, 1968), and *The Imaginary Signifier: Psychoanalysis and the Cinema* (1982; originally published in French, 1977); and NÖEL BURCH, *Theory of Film Practice* (1973, reissued 1981; originally published in French, 1969). Of these Bazin and Eisenstein have proved the most fertile and lasting. An overview of classical theories can be found in J. DUDLEY ANDREW, *The Major Film Theories: An Introduction* (1976); for more recent ideas see his *Concepts in Film Theory* (1984). Several anthologies of essays stemming from the academic era of film study put the reader in touch with issues such as semiotics, psychoanalysis, feminism, ideology, and structuralism as they influence the cinema. See GERALD MAST and MARSHALL COHEN, *Film Theory and Criticism: Introductory Readings*, 3rd ed. (1985); BILL NICHOLS (ed.), *Movies and Methods: An Anthology*, 2 vol. (1976–85); and PHILIP ROSEN (ed.), *Narrative, Apparatus, Ideology: Film Theory Reader* (1986). Individual modern theories have been advanced in DAVID BORDWELL, *Narration in the Fiction Film* (1985); STEPHEN HEATH, *Questions of Cinema* (1981); BRUCE F. KAWIN, *Mindscreen: Bergman, Godard, and First-Person Film* (1978); and TERESA DE LAURETIS, *Alice Doesn't: Feminism, Semiotics, Cinema* (1984). The most thorough study of experimental cinema remains P. ADAMS SITNEY, *Visionary Film: The American Avant-Garde*, 2nd ed. (1979).

(D.A.)

Technology: *The Focal Encyclopedia of Film & Television Techniques* (1969), is a fairly complete reference source; RAYMOND FIELDING (comp.), *A Technological History of Motion Pictures and Television: An Anthology from the Pages of the Journal of the Society of Motion Picture and Television Engineers* (1967, reprinted 1983), provides a remarkable survey. The society's own invaluable publications include DON V. KLOEPFEL (ed.), *Motion-Picture Projection and Theatre Presentation Manual* (1969); FRANK P. CLARK, *Special Effects in Motion Pictures: Some Methods for Producing Mechanical Special Effects* (1966); and *Widescreen Motion-Picture Systems* (1965). See also RAYMOND FIELDING, *The Technique of Special Effects Cinematography*, 4th ed. (1985). Other works include BARRY SALT, *Film Style and Technology: History and Analysis* (1983), the evolution of film equipment; STEVE NEALE, *Cinema and Technology: Image, Sound, Colour* (1985), an economic and aesthetic context for the emergence of the motion-picture technologies; and R.W.G. HUNT, *The Reproduction of Colour*, 3rd ed. (1975), an extended discussion of specific technology. CHARLES G. CLARKE, *Professional Cinematography*, rev. ed. (1968), is an older but still valuable brief summary; and FRED H. DETMERS, *American Cinematographer Manual*, 6th ed. (1986), is a later informative handbook.

DOMINIC CASE, *Motion Picture Film Processing* (1985), is a definitive text on laboratory procedure; PAUL M. HONORÉ, *A Handbook of Sound Recording: A Text for Motion Picture and General Sound Recording* (1980), covers sound production; and GLEN BALLOU (ed.), *Handbook for Sound Engineers: The New Audio Cyclopedia* (1987), is an extended reference manual. Works on editing techniques include KAREL REISZ and GAVIN MILLAR, *The Technique of Film Editing*, 2nd enl. ed. (1968, reprinted 1982); WILLIAM B. ADAMS, *Handbook of Motion Picture Production* (1977); and ERNEST WALTER, *The Technique of the Film Cutting Room*, 2nd rev. ed. (1982). Detailed techniques in high-speed and scientific cinematography are discussed in J.S. COURTNEY-PRATT (ed.), *Proceedings of the Fifth International Congress on High-Speed Photography* (1962); and WILLIAM G. HYZER and WILLIAM G. CHACE (eds.), *Proceedings of the Ninth International Congress on High-Speed Photography* (1970). JOHN HALAS and ROGER MANVELL, *The Technique of Film Animation*, 4th ed. (1976), is the standard text on the subject; in *Art in Movement: New Directions in Animation* (1970), the same authors explore the link between animation and kinetic art forms. THOMAS W. HOFFER, *Animation, a Reference Guide* (1981), is a scholarly guide with many bibliographic essays. For information on computer graphics, see *Proceedings of the Conference of the National Computer Graphics Association* (annual). Information on state-of-the-art technologies is provided in the following monthly periodicals: *SMPTE Journal; BKSTS Journal; Millimeter; On Location;* and *American Cinematographer.*

(E.We./S.G.H./P.Me./R.M.)

Mozart

Wolfgang Amadeus Mozart is widely recognized as one of the greatest composers in the history of Western music. With Haydn and Beethoven he brought to its height the achievement of the Viennese Classical school. Unlike any other composer in musical history, he wrote in all the musical genres of his day and excelled in every one. His taste, his command of form, and his range of expression entitle him to be considered the most universal of all composers.

Early life and works. Mozart was born in Salzburg, now in Austria, then in church lands, on Jan. 27, 1756. Although baptized Joannes Chrysostomus Wolfgangus Theophilus, he most commonly called himself Wolfgang Amadè or Wolfgang Gottlieb. His father, Leopold, came from a family of good standing, which included architects and bookbinders, and was the author of a famous violin-playing manual; his mother, Anna Maria Pertl, was born of a middle-class family active in local administration. Mozart and his sister Maria Anna ("Nannerl") were the only two of their seven children to survive.

The boy's early talent for music was remarkable. At three he was picking out chords on the harpsichord, at four playing short pieces, at five composing. There are anecdotes about his precise memory of pitch, about his scribbling a concerto at the age of five, and about his gentleness and sensitivity (he was afraid of the trumpet). Just before he was six, his father took him and Nannerl, also highly talented, to Munich to play at the Bavarian court, and a few months later they went to Vienna and were heard at the imperial court and in noble houses.

"The miracle which God let be born in Salzburg" was Leopold's description of his son, and he was keenly conscious of his duty to God, as he saw it, to draw the miracle to the notice of the world (and incidentally to profit from doing so). In mid-1763 he obtained a leave of absence from his position as deputy Kapellmeister at the prince-archbishop's court at Salzburg, and the family set out on a prolonged tour. They went to what were all the main musical centres of western Europe—Munich, Augsburg, Stuttgart, Mannheim, Mainz, Frankfurt, Brussels, and Paris (where they remained for the winter), then London (where they spent 15 months), returning through The Hague, Amsterdam, Paris, Lyon, and Switzerland, and arriving back in Salzburg in November 1766. In most of these cities Mozart, and often his sister, played and improvised, sometimes at court, sometimes in public or in a church. Leopold's surviving letters to friends in Salzburg tell of the universal admiration that his son's achievements aroused. In Paris they met several German composers, and Mozart's first music was published (sonatas for keyboard and violin, dedicated to a royal princess); in London they met, among others, Johann Christian Bach, Johann Sebastian Bach's youngest son and a leading figure in the city's musical life, and under his influence Mozart composed his first symphonies—three survive (K 16, K 19, and K 19a—K signifying the work's place in the catalog of Ludwig von Köchel). Two more followed during a stay in The Hague on the return journey (K 22 and K 45a).

First European tour

After little more than nine months in Salzburg the Mozarts set out for Vienna in September 1767, where (apart from a 10-week break during a smallpox epidemic) they spent 15 months. Mozart wrote a one-act German singspiel, *Bastien und Bastienne,* which was given privately. Greater hopes were attached to his prospect of having an Italian opera buffa, *La finta semplice* ("The Feigned Simpleton"), done at the court theatre—hopes that were, however, frustrated, much to Leopold's indignation. But a substantial, festal mass setting (probably K 139/47a) was successfully given before the court at the dedication of the Orphanage Church. *La finta semplice* was given the following year, 1769, in the archbishop's palace in Salzburg. In October Mozart was appointed an honorary Konzertmeister at the Salzburg court.

La finta semplice

By courtesy of the Internationale Stiftung Mozarteum, Salzburg, Austria

Mozart, unfinished oil portrait by Joseph Lange, 1789. In the Internationale Stiftung Mozarteum, Salzburg, Austria.

Still only 13, Mozart had by now acquired considerable fluency in the musical language of his time. The early Paris and London sonatas, the autographs of which include Leopold's helping hand, show a childlike pleasure in patterns of notes and textures. But the London and The Hague symphonies attest to his quick and inventive response to the music he had encountered, as, with their enrichment of texture and fuller development, do those he produced in Vienna (such as K 43 and, especially, K 48). And his first Italian opera shows a ready grasp of the buffo style.

The Italian tours. Mastery of the Italian operatic style was a prerequisite for a successful international composing career, and the Austrian political dominion over northern Italy ensured that doors would be open there to Mozart. This time Mozart's mother and sister remained at home, and the family correspondence provides a full account of events. The first tour, begun on Dec. 13, 1769, and lasting 15 months, took them to all the main musical centres, but as usual they paused at any town where a concert could be given or a nobleman might want to hear Mozart play. In Verona Mozart was put through stringent tests at the Accademia Filarmonica, and in Milan, after tests of his capacities in dramatic music, he was commissioned to write the first opera for the carnival season. After a stop in Bologna, where they met the esteemed theorist Giovanni Battista Martini, they proceeded to Florence and on to Rome for Holy Week. There Mozart heard the Sistine Choir in the famous *Miserere* of Gregorio Allegri (1582–1652), which was considered the choir's exclusive preserve but which Mozart copied out from memory. They spent six weeks in Naples; returning through Rome, Mozart had a papal audience and was made a knight of the order of the Golden Spur. The summer was passed near Bologna, where Mozart passed the tests for admission to the Accademia Filarmonica. In mid-October he reached Milan and began work on the new opera, *Mitridate, rè di Ponto* ("Mithradates, King of Pontus"). He had to rewrite several numbers to satisfy the singers, but, after a series of rehearsals (Leopold's letters provide fascinating insights as to theatre procedures), the premiere at the Regio Ducal Teatro on December 26 was a notable success. Mozart, in the traditional way, directed the first three of the 22 performances. After a brief excursion to Venice he and his father returned to Salzburg.

Rome

Plans had already been laid for further journeys to Italy: for a theatrical serenata commissioned for a royal wedding in Milan in October 1771 and for a further opera, again for Milan, at carnival time in 1772–73. Mozart was also commissioned to write an oratorio for Padua; he composed *La Betulia liberata* during 1771, but there is no record of a performance. The second Italian visit, between August and December 1771, saw the premiere of his *Ascanio in Alba,* which, Leopold gleefully reported, "completely overshadowed" the other new work for the occasion, an opera (*Ruggiero*) by Johann Adolph Hasse, the most respected opera seria composer of the time. But hopes that Leopold had entertained of his son's securing an appointment in Milan were disappointed. Back in Salzburg, Mozart had a prolific spell: he wrote eight symphonies, four divertimentos, several substantial sacred works, and an allegorical serenata, *Il sogno di Scipione.* Probably intended as a tribute to the Salzburg prince-archbishop, Count Schrattenbach, this work may not have been given until the spring of 1772, and then for his successor Hieronymus, Count Colloredo; Schrattenbach, a tolerant employer generous in allowing leave, died at the end of 1771.

Third Italian journey

The third and last Italian journey lasted from October 1772 until March 1773. *Lucio Silla* ("Lucius Sulla"), the new opera, was given on Dec. 26, 1772, and after a difficult premiere (it began three hours late and lasted six) it proved even more successful than *Mitridate,* with 26 performances. This is the earliest indication of the dramatic composer Mozart was to become. He followed *Lucio Silla* with a solo motet written for its leading singer, the castrato and composer Venanzio Rauzzini, *Exsultate, jubilate* (K

165), an appealing three-movement piece culminating in a brilliant "Alleluia." The instrumental music of the period around the Italian journeys includes several symphonies; a few of them are done in a light, Italianate style (*e.g.*, K 95 and K 97), but others, notably the seven from 1772, tread new ground in form, orchestration, and scale (such as K 130, K 132, and the chamber musical K 134). There are also six string quartets (K 155–160) and three divertimentos (K 136–138), in a lively, extroverted vein.

Early maturity. More symphonies and divertimentos, as well as a mass, followed during the summer of 1773. Then Leopold, doubtless seeking again a better situation for his son than the Salzburg court (now under a much less sympathetic archbishop) was likely to offer, took him to Vienna. No position materialized, but Mozart's contact with the newest Viennese music seems to have had a considerable effect on him. He produced a set of six string quartets in the capital, showing in them his knowledge of Haydn's recent Opus 20 in his fuller textures and more intellectual approach to the medium. Soon after his return he wrote a group of symphonies, including two that represent a new level of achievement, the "Little" G Minor (K 183) and the A Major (K 201). Also dating from this time was Mozart's first true piano concerto (in D, K 175; earlier keyboard concertos were arrangements of movements by other composers).

The year 1774 saw the composition of more symphonies, concertos for bassoon and for two violins (in a style recalling J.C. Bach), serenades, and several sacred works. Mozart was now a salaried court Konzertmeister, and the sacred music in particular was intended for local use. Archbishop Colloredo, a progressive churchman, discouraged lavish music and set a severe time limit on mass settings, which Mozart objected to but was obliged to observe. At the end of the year he was commissioned to write an opera buffa, *La finta giardiniera* ("The Feigned Gardener Girl"), for the Munich carnival season, where it was duly successful. It shows Mozart, in his first comic opera since his childhood, finding ways of using the orchestra more expressively and of giving real personality to the pasteboard figures of Italian opera buffa.

La finta giardiniera

A period of two and a half years (from March 1775) began in which Mozart worked steadily in his Salzburg post. The work was for him undemanding and by no means compatible with his abilities. During this period he wrote only one dramatic work (the serenata-like *Il rè pastore,* "The Shepherd King," for an archducal visit), but he was productive in sacred and lighter instrumental music. His most impressive piece for the church was the *Litaniae de venerabili altaris sacramento* (K 243), which embraces a wide range of styles (fugues, choruses of considerable dramatic force, florid arias, and a plainchant setting). The instrumental works included divertimentos, concertos, and serenades, notably the *Haffner* (K 250), which in its use of instruments and its richness of working carried the serenade style into the symphonic without prejudicing its traditional warmth and high spirits. The five concertos for violin, all from this period (No. 1 may be slightly earlier), show a remarkable growth over a few months in confidence in handling the medium, with increasingly fanciful ideas and attractive and natural contexts for virtuoso display. The use of popular themes in the finales is typically south German. He also wrote a concerto for three pianos and three piano concertos, the last of them, K 271, showing a new level of maturity in technique and expressive range.

Mannheim and Paris. It must have been abundantly clear by this time to Mozart as well as his father that a small, provincial court like that at Salzburg was no place for a genius of his order. In 1777 he petitioned the archbishop for his release and, with his mother to watch over him, set out to find new opportunities. The correspondence with his father over the 16 months he was away not only gives information as to what he was doing but also casts a sharp light on their changing relationship; Mozart, now 21, increasingly felt the need to free himself from paternal domination, while Leopold's anxieties about their future assumed almost pathological dimensions.

They went first to Munich, where the elector politely declined to offer Mozart a post. Next they visited Augsburg, staying with relatives; there Mozart struck up a lively friendship with his cousin Maria Anna Thekla (they later had a correspondence involving much playful, obscene humour). At the end of October they arrived at Mannheim, where the court of the Elector Palatine was musically one of the most famous and progressive in Europe. Mozart stayed there for more than four months, although he soon learned that again no position was to be had. He became friendly with the Mannheim musicians, undertook some teaching and playing, accepted and partly fulfilled a commission for flute music from a German surgeon, and fell in love with Aloysia Weber, a soprano, the second of four daughters of a music copyist. He also composed several piano sonatas, some with violin. He put to his father a scheme for traveling to Italy with the Webers, which, naive and irresponsible, met with an angry response: "Off with you to Paris! and that soon, find your place among great people—aut Caesar aut nihil." The plan had been that he would go on alone, but now Leopold felt that he was not to be trusted and made the ill-fated decision that his mother should go too. They reached Paris late in March 1778, and Mozart soon found work. His most important achievement was the symphony (K 297) composed for the Concert Spirituel, a brilliant D Major work in which he met the taste of the Parisian public (and musicians) for orchestral display without sacrifice of integrity; indeed he exploited the devices they admired (such as the opening coup d'archet—a forceful, unanimous musical gesture) to new formal ends.

By the time of its premiere, on June 18, his mother was seriously ill, and on July 3 she died. Mozart handled the situation with consideration, first writing to his father of her grave illness, then asking an abbé friend in Salzburg to break the news. He went to stay with Friedrich Melchior, Baron von Grimm, a German friend. Soon after, Grimm wrote pessimistically to Leopold about his son's prospects in Paris, and Leopold negotiated a better post for him in Salzburg, where he would be court organist rather than violinist as before, though still nominally Konzertmeister. Summoned home, Mozart reluctantly obeyed, tarrying en route in Mannheim and in Munich—where the Mannheim musicians had now mostly moved and where he was coolly received by Aloysia Weber. He reached Salzburg in mid-January 1780.

Mother's death

Salzburg and Munich. Back in Salzburg, Mozart seems to have been eager to display his command of international styles: of the three symphonies he wrote in 1779–80, K 318 in G Major has a Parisian premier coup d'archet and crescendos of the type favoured in Mannheim, and K 338 in C Major shows many features of the brilliant Parisian manner. His outstanding orchestral work of this period was, however, the sinfonia concertante for violin and viola K 364; the genre was popular in both cities, and there are many features of the Mannheim style in the orchestral writing, but the character of the work, its ingenious instrumental interplay, and its depth of feeling are unmistakably Mozartian. Also from this time came the cheerful two-piano concerto and the two-piano sonata, as well as a number of sacred works, including the best-known of his complete masses, the *Coronation Mass.*

But it was dramatic music that attracted Mozart above all. He had lately written incidental music to a play by Tobias Philipp von Gebler, and during 1779–80 he composed much of a singspiel, known as *Zaide,* although with no sure prospects of performance. So Mozart must have been delighted, in the summer of 1780, to receive a commission to compose a serious Italian opera for Munich. The subject was to be Idomeneus, king of Crete, and the librettist the local cleric Giambattista Varesco, who was to follow a French text of 1712. Mozart could start work in Salzburg as he already knew the capacities of several of the singers, but he went to Munich some 10 weeks before the date set for the premiere. Leopold remained at home until close to the time of the premiere and acted as a link between Mozart and Varesco; their correspondence is accordingly richly informative about the process of composition. Four matters dominate Mozart's letters home. First, he was anxious, as always, to assure his father of the enthusiasm with which the singers received his music. Second, he was concerned about cuts: the libretto was far too long, and Mozart had set it spaciously, so that much trimming—of the recitative, of the choral scenes, and even of two arias in the final acts—was needed. Third, he was always eager to make modifications that rendered the action more natural and plausible. And fourth, he was much occupied with accommodating the music and the action to the needs and the limitations of the singers.

Idomeneo

In *Idomeneo, rè di Creta* Mozart depicted serious, heroic emotion with a richness unparalleled elsewhere in his operas. Though influenced by Christoph Gluck and by Niccolò Piccinni and others, it is not a "reform opera": it includes plain recitative and bravura singing, but always to a dramatic purpose, and, though the texture is more continuous than in Mozart's earlier operas, its plan, because of its French source, is essentially traditional. Given on Jan. 29, 1781, just after Mozart's 25th birthday, it met with due success. Mozart and his father were still in Munich when, on March 12, he was summoned to join the archbishop's retinue in Vienna, where the accession of Joseph II was being celebrated.

Vienna: the early years. Fresh from his triumphs in Munich, where he had mixed freely with noblemen, Mozart now found himself placed, at table in the lodgings for the archbishop's entourage, below the valets if above the cooks. Furthermore, the archbishop refused him permission to play at concerts (including one attended by the emperor at which Mozart could have earned half a year's salary in an evening). He was resentful and insulted. Matters came to a head at an interview with Archbishop Colloredo, who, according to Mozart, used unecclesiastical language; Mozart requested his discharge, which was eventually granted at a stormy meeting with the court steward on June 9, 1781.

Mozart, who now went to live with his old friends the Webers (Aloysia was married to a court actor and painter), set about earning a living in Vienna. Although eager for a court appointment, he for the moment was concerned to take on some pupils, to write music for publication, and to play in concerts (which in Vienna were more often in noblemen's houses than in public). He also embarked on an opera, *Die Entführung aus dem Serail* (*The Abduction from the Seraglio*). (Joseph II currently required that German opera, rather than the traditional Italian, be given at the court theatre.) In the summer of 1781, rumours began to circulate, as far as Salzburg, that Mozart was contemplating marriage with the third of the Weber daughters, Constanze; but he hotly denied them in a letter to his father: "I have never thought less of getting married . . . besides, I am not in love with her." He moved lodgings to scotch the gossip. But by December he was asking for his father's blessing on a marriage with Constanze, with whom he was now in love and to whom, probably through the machinations of her mother and her guardian, he was in some degree committed. Because Constanze later destroyed Leopold's letters, for reasons that are easy to imagine, only one side of the correspondence exists; Leopold's reactions can, however, be readily inferred, and it would seem that this period marked a low point in the relationship between father and son.

Die Entführung aus dem Serail

Musically, Mozart's main preoccupation was with *Die Entführung* in the early part of 1782. The opera, after various delays, reached the Burgtheater stage on July 16. The story of the emperor's saying "very many notes, my dear Mozart" may not be literally true, but the tale is symptomatic: the work does have far more notes than any other then in the German repertory, with fuller textures, more elaboration, and longer arias. Mozart's letters to his father give insight into his approach to dramatic composition, explaining, for example, his use of accompanying figures and key relationships to embody meaning. He also had the original text substantially modified to strengthen its drama and allow better opportunities for music. Noteworthy features are the Turkish colouring, created by "exotic" turns of phrase and chromaticisms as well as janissary instruments; the extended Act 2 finale, along the lines of those in opera buffa but lacking the dramatic propulsion of the Italian type; the expressive and powerful arias for the heroine (coincidentally called Constanze); and what Mozart called concessions to Viennese taste in the comic music, such as the duet "Vivat Bacchus."

Die Entführung enjoyed immediate and continuing success; it was quickly taken up by traveling and provincial companies—as *La finta giardiniera* had been, to a lesser degree—and carried Mozart's reputation widely around the German-speaking countries. Later in the year he worked on a set of three piano concertos and began a set of six string quartets. He also started work on a mass setting, in C Minor, which he had vowed to write on his marriage but of which only the first two sections, "Kyrie" and "Gloria," were completed. Among the influences on this music, besides the Austrian ecclesiastical tradition, was that of the Baroque music (Bach, Handel, and others) that Mozart had become acquainted with, probably for the first time, at the house of his patron Baron Gottfried van Swieten, a music collector and antiquarian. The Baroque influence is noticeable especially in the spare textures and austere lines of certain of the solo numbers, though others are squarely in the decorative, south German late Rococo manner (this interest in "old-fashioned" counterpoint can also be seen in some of Mozart's piano music of the time and in his string arrangements of music from Bach's *The Well-Tempered Clavier*). Mozart and his wife visited Salzburg in the summer and autumn of 1783, when the completed movements were performed, with (as always intended) Constanze singing one of the solo soprano parts, at St. Peter's Abbey. On the way back to Vienna Mozart paused at Linz, where he hastily wrote the symphony known by that city's name for a concert he gave there.

The Baroque influence

The central Viennese period. Back in Vienna Mozart entered on what was to be the most fruitful and successful period of his life. He had once written to his father that Vienna was "the land of the piano," and his greatest triumphs there were as a pianist-composer. During one spell of little more than five weeks he appeared at 22 concerts, mainly at the Esterházy and Galitzin houses but including five concerts of his own. In February 1784 he began to keep a catalog of his own music, which suggests a new awareness of posterity and his place in it (in fact his entries are sometimes misdated). At concerts he would normally play the piano, both existing pieces and improvisations; his fantasias—such as the fine C Minor one (K 475) of 1785—and his numerous sets of variations probably give some indication of the kind of music his audiences heard. He would also conduct performances of his symphonies (using earlier Salzburg works as well as the two written since he had settled in Vienna, the *Haffner* of 1782, composed for the Salzburg family, and the *Linz* [*Symphony No. 36 in C Major*]); but above all the piano concertos were the central products of his concert activity.

In 1782–83 Mozart wrote three piano concertos (K 413–415), which he published in 1785 with string and optional wind parts (so that they were suitable for domestic use) and described as "a happy medium between what is too easy and too difficult." Six more followed in 1784, three each in 1785 and 1786 and one each in 1788 and 1791. With the 1784 group he established a new level of piano concerto writing; these concertos are at once symphonic, melodically rich, and orchestrally ingenious, and they also blend the virtuoso element effectively into the musical and formal texture of the work. Much melodic material is assigned to the wind instruments, and a unique melodic style is developed that lends itself to patterns of dialogue and instrumental interplay. After the relatively homogeneous 1784 group (K 449, 450, 451, 453, 456, and 459), all of which begin with themes stated first by the orchestra and later taken up by the piano, Mozart moved on in the concertos of 1785 (K 466, 467, and 482) to make the piano solo a reinterpretation of the opening theme. These concertos are increasingly individual in character—one a stormy and romantic D Minor work, the next a closely argued concerto in C Major with a slow movement remarkable for its troubled beauty, and the third, in E-flat Major, notable for its military rhythms and wind colouring. The 1786 group begins with the refined but conservatively lyrical K 488, but then follow two concertos with a new level of symphonic unity and grandeur, that in C

Minor (K 491), using the largest orchestra Mozart had yet called for in the concert hall, and the imperious concerto in C Major (K 503). The two final concertos (K 537 and 595) represent no new departures.

Mozart's other important contributions of this time come in the fields of chamber and piano music. The outpouring of 1784 included the fine piano sonata K 457 and the piano and violin sonata K 454 (written for a visiting violin virtuoso, it was produced in such haste that Mozart could not write out the piano part and played from blank paper at the premiere). He also wrote, in a style close to that of the concertos, a quintet for piano and wind instruments (K 452), which he considered his finest work to date; it was first heard at a concert in the house of his pupil Barbara Ployer, for whom two of the 1784 concertos had been written (K 449 and 453). The six string quartets on which he had embarked in 1782 were finished in the first days of 1785 and published later that year, dedicated to Haydn, now a friend of Mozart's. In 1785 Haydn said to Leopold Mozart, on a visit to his son in Vienna, "Your son is the greatest composer known to me in person or by name; he has taste, and what is more the greatest knowledge of composition."

Haydn's praise

From Figaro to Don Giovanni. In spite of his success as a pianist and composer, Mozart had serious financial worries, and they worsened as the famously fickle Viennese found other idols. One may calculate his likely income during his last five years, 1786–91, as being far larger than that of most musicians though much below that of the section of society with which he wanted to be associated; Leopold's early advice to be aloof ("like an Englishman") with his fellow musicians but friendly with the aristocracy had its price. His sense of being as good a man as any privileged nobleman led him and his wife into tastes that for his actual station in life, and his income, were extravagant. He saw a court appointment as a possible source of salvation but knew that the Italian musical influence at court, under the Kapellmeister Antonio Salieri, was powerful and exclusive—even if he and Salieri were never on less than friendly terms personally.

Success in the court opera house was all-important. Joseph II had now reverted to Italian opera, and since 1783 Mozart had been seeking suitable librettos (he had even started work on two but broke off when he came to realize their feebleness for his purpose). He had become acquainted with Lorenzo da Ponte, an Italian abbé-adventurer of Jewish descent who was a talented poet and librettist to the court theatre. At Mozart's suggestion he wrote a libretto, *Le nozze di Figaro,* based on Beaumarchais's revolutionary comedy, *Le Mariage de Figaro,* but with most of the political sting removed. Nonetheless, the music of *Figaro* makes the social distinctions clear. *Figaro,* as well as the later opera *Don Giovanni,* treats the traditional figure of the licentious nobleman, but the earlier work does so on a more directly comic plane even though the undercurrents of social tension run stronger. Perhaps the central achievement of *Figaro* lies in its ensembles with their close link between music and dramatic meaning. The Act 3 Letter Duet, for instance, has a realistic representation of dictation with the reading back as a condensed recapitulation. The act finales, above all, show a broad, symphonic organization with each section worked out as a unit; for example, in the B-flat section of the Act 2 finale the tension of the count's examination of Figaro is paralleled in the tonal scheme, with its return to the tonic only when the final question is resolved: a telling conjunction of music and drama. These features, coupled with the elaborate commentary on character and action that is embodied in the orchestral writing, add depth to the situations and seriousness to their resolution and set the work apart from the generality of Italian opere buffe.

Le nozze di Figaro

Figaro reached the stage on May 1, 1786, and was warmly received. There were nine performances in 1786 and a further 26 when it was revived in 1789–90—a success, but a modest one compared with certain operas of Martín y Soler and Giovanni Paisiello (to whose *Il barbiere di Siviglia* it was a sequel, and planned in direct competition). The opera did, however, enjoy outstanding popularity in Prague, and at the end of the year Mozart was invited to go to the Bohemian capital; he went in January 1787, giving a new symphony there and accepting a further operatic commission. He returned to Vienna in February 1787.

Mozart's concert activities in Vienna were now on a modest scale. No Viennese appearances at all are recorded for 1787. In April he heard that his father was gravely ill. Mozart wrote him a letter of consolation putting forward a view of death ("this best and truest friend of mankind") based on the teachings of Freemasonry, which he had embraced at the end of 1784. Leopold died in May 1787.

Mozart's music from this time includes the two string quintets K 515–516, arguably his supreme chamber works. Clearly this genre, with the opportunities it offered for richness of sonority and patterns of symmetry, had a particular appeal for him. The quintet in C Major (K 515) is the most expansive and most richly developed of all his chamber works, while the G Minor (K 516) has always been recognized for its depth of feeling, which in the circumstances it is tempting to regard as elegiac. From this period come a number of short but appealing lieder and three instrumental works of note: the *Musikalischer Spass* (*Musical Joke*), a good-humoured parody of bad music, in a vein Leopold would have liked (it was thought to have been provoked by his death until it was found that it was begun much earlier); *Eine kleine Nachtmusik,* the exquisite and much-loved serenade, probably intended for solo strings and written for a purpose that remains unknown; and a fine piano and violin sonata, K 526.

But Mozart's chief occupation during 1787 was the composition of *Don Giovanni,* commissioned for production in Prague; it was given on October 29 and warmly received. *Don Giovanni* was Mozart's second opera based on a libretto by da Ponte, who used as his model a libretto by Giovanni Bertati, set by Giuseppe Gazzaniga for Venice earlier in 1787. Da Ponte rewrote the libretto, inserting new episodes into the one-act original, which explains certain structural features. A difference in Mozart's approach to the work—a *dramma giocoso* in the tradition of Carlo Goldoni that, because of its more serious treatment of character, had a greater expressive potential than an opera buffa—is seen in the extended spans of the score, with set-piece numbers often running into one another. As in *Figaro,* the two act finales are again remarkable: the first for the three stage bands that play dances for different social segments, the second for the supper scene in which the commendatore's statue consigns Giovanni to damnation, with trombones to suggest the supernatural and with hieratic dotted rhythms, extreme chromaticism, and wildly lurching harmony as Giovanni is overcome. But it remains a comic opera, as is made clear through the figure of Leporello, who from under a table offers the common man's wry or facetious observations; and at the end the surviving characters draw the moral in a cheerful sextet. The "demonic" character of the opera has caused it to exercise a special fascination for audiences, and it has given rise to a large critical, interpretative, and purely fanciful literature.

Don Giovanni

The last travels. On his return from Prague in mid-November 1787, Mozart was at last appointed to a court post, as *Kammermusicus,* in place of Gluck, who had died. It was largely a sinecure, the only requirement being that he should supply dance music for court balls, which he did, in abundance and with some distinction, over his remaining years. The salary of 800 gulden seems to have done little to relieve the Mozarts' chronic financial troubles. Their debts, however, were never large, and they were always able to continue employing servants and owning a carriage; their anxieties were more a matter of whether they could live as they wished than whether they would starve. In 1788 a series of letters begging loans from a fellow Freemason, Michael Puchberg, began; Puchberg usually obliged, and Mozart seems generally to have repaid him promptly. He was deeply depressed during the summer, writing of "black thoughts"; it has been suggested that he may have had a cyclothymic personality, linked with manic-depressive tendencies, which could explain not only his depression but also other aspects of his behaviour, including his spells of hectic creativity.

Financial difficulties

During the time of this depression Mozart was working on a series of three symphonies, in E-flat Major (K 543), G Minor (K 550), and C Major (the *Jupiter,* K 551), usually numbered 39, 40, and 41; these, with the work written for Prague (K 504), represent the summa of his orchestral output. It is not known why they were composed; possibly Mozart had a summer concert season in mind. The Prague work was a climax to his long series of brilliant D Major orchestral pieces, but the closely worked, even motivic form gives it a new power and unity. The E-flat Major work, scored with clarinets and more lyrical in temper, makes fewer departures, except in the intensity of its slow movement, where Mozart used a new palette of darker orchestral colours, and the epigrammatic wit of its finale. In the G Minor work the tone of passion and perhaps of pathos, in its constant falling figures, is still more pronounced. The *Jupiter* (the name dates from the early 19th century) summarized the series of C Major symphonies, with their atmosphere of military pomp and ceremony, but it went far beyond them in its assimilation of opera buffa style, profundity of expression (in its andante), and richness of working—especially in the finale, which incorporates fugal procedures and ends with a grand apotheosis in five-voice counterpoint.

Early in 1789 Mozart accepted an invitation to travel to Berlin with Prince Karl Lichnowsky; they paused in Prague, Dresden (where he played at court), and Leipzig (where he improvised on the Thomaskirche organ). He appeared at the Prussian court and probably was invited to compose piano sonatas for the princess and string quartets with a prominent cello part for King Friedrich Wilhelm II. He did in fact write three quartets, in parts of which he allowed the individual instruments (including the royal cello) special prominence, and there is one sonata (his last, K 576) that may have been intended for the Prussian princess. But it is unlikely that Mozart ever sent this music or was paid for it.

The summer saw the composition of the clarinet quintet, in which a true chamber style is warmly and gracefully reconciled with the solo writing. Thereafter Mozart concentrated on completing his next opera commission, the third of his da Ponte operas, *Così fan tutte,* which was given on Jan. 26, 1790; its run was interrupted after five performances when theatres closed because of the death of Joseph II, but a further five were given in the summer. This opera, the subtlest, most consistent, and most symmetrical of the three, was long reviled (from Beethoven onward) on account of its subject, female fickleness; but a more careful reading of it, especially in light of the emotional texture of the music, which gains complexity as the plot progresses, makes it clear that it is no frivolous piece but a penetrating essay on human feelings and their mature recognition. The music of Act 1 is essentially conventional in expression, and conventional feeling is tellingly parodied in certain of the arias; but the arias of Act 2 are on a deeper and more personal level. Features of the music of *Così fan tutte*—serenity, restraint, poise, irony—may be noted as markers of Mozart's late style, which had developed since 1787 and may be linked with his personal development and the circumstances of his life, including his Masonic associations, his professional and financial situation, and his marriage.

Così fan tutte

The year 1790 was difficult and unproductive: besides *Così fan tutte,* Mozart completed two of the "Prussian" quartets, arranged works by Handel for performance at van Swieten's house (he had similarly arranged *Messiah* in 1789), and wrote the first of his two fantasy-like pieces, in a variety of prelude-and-fugue form, for a mechanical organ (this imposing work, in F Minor [K 594], is now generally played on a normal organ). In the autumn, anxious to be noticed in court circles, he went to Frankfurt for the imperial coronation of Leopold II, but as an individual rather than a court musician. His concert, which included two piano concertos and possibly one of the new symphonies, was ill timed, poorly attended, and a financial failure. Anxieties about money were a recurrent theme in his letters home.

The last year. But 1791 promised to be a better year. Music was flowing again: for a concert in March Mozart completed a piano concerto (K 595) begun some years before, reeled off numerous dances for the Redoutensaal, and wrote two new string quintets, the one in D (K 593) being a work of particular refinement and subtlety. In April he applied successfully for the role of unpaid assistant to the elderly Kapellmeister of St. Stephen's Cathedral, Leopold Hofmann (with the expectation of being duly appointed his successor, but Hofmann was to live until 1793).

An old friend of Mozart's, Emanuel Schikaneder, had in 1789 set up a company to perform singspiels in a suburban theatre, and in 1791 he engaged Mozart to compose a score to his *Die Zauberflöte* (*The Magic Flute*); Mozart worked on it during the spring and early summer. Then he received another commission, anonymously delivered, for a requiem, to be composed under conditions of secrecy. In addition he was invited, probably in July, to write the opera to be given during Leopold II's coronation festivities in September. Constanze was away taking a cure at Baden during much of the summer and autumn; in July she gave birth to their sixth child, one of the two to survive (Carl Thomas, 1784–1858, and Franz Xaver Wolfgang, 1791–1844, a composer and pianist). Mozart's letters to her show that he worked first on *Die Zauberflöte,* although he must have written some of the Prague opera, *La clemenza di Tito* ("The Clemency of Titus"), before he left for the Bohemian capital near the end of August. Pressure of work, however, was such that he took with him to Prague, along with Constanze, his pupil Franz Xaver Süssmayr, who almost certainly composed the plain recitatives for the new opera. The work itself, to an old libretto by Pietro Metastasio, condensed and supplemented by the Dresden court poet Caterino Mazzolà, was long dismissed as a product of haste and a commission unwillingly undertaken; but in fact the spare scoring, the short arias, and the generally restrained style are better understood in terms of Mozart's reaction to the neoclassical thinking of the time and the known preferences of Leopold II. The opera was indifferently received by the court but quickly won over the Prague audiences and went on to become one of Mozart's most admired works over the ensuing decades.

Die Zauberflöte

Mozart was back in Vienna by the middle of September; his clarinet concerto was finished by September 29, and the next day *Die Zauberflöte* had its premiere. Again, early reactions were cautious, but soon the opera became the most loved of all of Mozart's works for the stage. Schikaneder took its plot from a collection of fairy tales by Christoph Martin Wieland but drew too on other literary sources and on current thinking about Freemasonry—all viewed in the context of Viennese popular theatre. Musically it is distinguished from contemporary singspiels not merely by the quality of its music but also by the serious ideas that lie below what may seem to be merely childish pantomime or low comedy, welding together the stylistically diverse elements.

Mozart had been ill during the weeks in Prague, but to judge by his letters to Constanze in October he was in good spirits and, with some cause, more optimistic about the future. He wrote a Masonic cantata for his lodge and directed a performance of it on November 18. He was also working steadily on the commissioned requiem. Later in November he was ill and confined to bed; some apparent improvement on December 3 was not sustained, and on Dec. 5, 1791, he died. "Severe miliary fever" was the certified cause; later, "rheumatic inflammatory fever" was named. Other diagnoses, taking account of Mozart's medical history, have been put forward, including Schönlein–Henoch syndrome. There is no evidence to support the tale that he was poisoned by Salieri (a colleague and friend, hardly a real rival) or anyone else. He was buried in a multiple grave, standard at the time in Vienna for a person of his social and financial situation; a small group of friends attended the funeral.

Constanze Mozart was anxious to have the requiem completed, as a fee was due; it had been commissioned, in memory of his wife, by Count von Walsegg-Stuppach to pass off as his own. She handed it first to Joseph Eybler, who supplied some orchestration but was reluctant to do more, and then to Süssmayr, who produced a complete version, writing several movements himself though pos-

Completion of the requiem

sibly basing them on Mozart's sketches or instructions. Although subject to criticism for its technical weaknesses, which editors have sought to remedy, this must remain the standard version by dint of its position as the only one with a source close to Mozart. The sombre grandeur of the work, with its restrained instrumental colouring and its noble choral writing, hints at what might have been had Mozart lived to take on the Kapellmeistership of St. Stephen's.

Mozart's place. At the time of his death Mozart was widely regarded not only as the greatest composer of the time but also as a bold and "difficult" one; *Don Giovanni* especially was seen as complex and dissonant, and his chamber music as calling for outstanding skill in its interpreters. His surviving manuscripts, which included many unpublished works, were mostly sold by Constanze to the firm of André in Offenbach, which issued editions during the 19th century. But Mozart's reputation was such that even before the end of the 18th century two firms had embarked on substantial collected editions of his music. Important biographies appeared in 1798 and 1828, the latter by Constanze's second husband; the first scholarly biography, by Otto Jahn, was issued on Mozart's centenary in 1856. The first edition of the Köchel catalog followed six years later, and the first complete edition of his music began in 1877.

First edition of the Köchel catalog

The works most secure in the repertory during the 19th century were the three operas least susceptible to changes in public taste—*Le nozze di Figaro, Don Giovanni,* and *Die Zauberflöte*—and the orchestral works closest in spirit to the Romantic era—the minor-key piano concertos (Beethoven wrote a set of cadenzas for the one in D Minor) and the last three symphonies. It was only in the 20th century that Mozart's music began to be reexamined more broadly. Although up to the middle of the century Mozart was still widely regarded as having been surpassed in most respects by Beethoven, with the increased historical perspective of the later 20th century he came to be seen as an artist of a formidable, indeed perhaps unequaled, expressive range. The traditional image of the child prodigy turned refined drawing-room composer, who could miraculously conceive an entire work in his head before setting pen to paper (always a distortion of the truth), gave way to the image of the serious and painstaking creative artist with acute human insight, whose complex psychology demanded exploration by writers, historians, and scholars. But regardless of such shifting currents of interpretation, in public esteem and affection Mozart's place more than equals that of any other composer.

MAJOR WORKS

Mozart's works are listed in the catalog of LUDWIG RITTER VON KÖCHEL, *Chronologisch-thematisches Verzeichniss sämtlicher Tonwerke Wolfgang Amade Mozarts* (1862). It was twice significantly revised and enlarged, namely, for the 3rd ed., edited by ALFRED EINSTEIN (1937), with suppl. (1947), and the 6th ed., edited by FRANZ GIEGLING, ALEXANDER WEINMANN, and GERD SIEVERS (1964, reprinted 1983).

The following list excludes works that are lost, of doubtful authenticity, or substantially incomplete.

Vocal works

SACRED WORKS: 7 long masses (1 incomplete); 7 short masses; *Requiem,* K 626, 1791 (incomplete); 4 litanies; 2 vespers; 22 motets and miscellaneous works (including *Exsultate, jubilate,* K 165, 1773); 17 church sonatas.

ORATORIOS AND CANTATAS: 2 oratorios; 1 act of a sacred drama; Passion cantata; 4 Masonic cantatas.

DRAMATIC WORKS: 15 operas (including *Idomeneo, rè di Creta,* K 366, 1781; *Die Entführung aus dem Serail,* K 384, 1782; *Le nozze di Figaro,* K 492, 1786; *Don Giovanni,* K 527, 1787; *Così fan tutte,* K 588, 1790; *Die Zauberflöte,* K 620, 1791; *La clemenza di Tito,* K 621, 1791); 2 serenatas; 1 ballet; 1 Latin intermezzo; incidental music.

MISCELLANEOUS VOCAL: 17 pieces for 2 to 4 voices with orchestra, ensemble, or piano; 48 songs and arias with orchestra (some for insertion into operas); 31 songs with piano; 15 vocal and 20 unspecified canons.

Instrumental works

SYMPHONIES: 56 symphonies, with some adapted from overtures and serenades (the traditional numbering up to 41 omits many and includes three not by Mozart), including *No. 38 in D Major* (*Prague*), K 504, 1786; *No. 39 in E-flat Major,* K 543, 1788; *No. 40 in G Minor,* K 550, 1788; *No. 41 in C Major* (*Jupiter*), K 551, 1788.

OTHER ORCHESTRAL AND ENSEMBLE MUSIC: 21 serenades (including *Serenata notturna,* K 239, 1776; *Serenade in D Major* [*Haffner*], K 250, 1776; *Serenade in D Major* [*Posthorn*], K 320, 1779; *Eine kleine Nachtmusik,* K 525, 1787), cassations, and divertimentos; 17 serenades and divertimentos for wind instruments; 13 marches, 105 minuets, 56 German dances, 47 contredanses.

CONCERTOS: For piano, 21, 7 arrangements of music by other composers, and 2 rondos (the traditional numbering includes 2 multiple concertos and 4 arrangements); 1 for 2 pianos; 1 for 3 pianos; 5 for violin; 1 *Concertone,* K 190, 1774, for two violins; 1 *Sinfonia concertante,* K 364, 1779, for violin and viola; 2 for flute; 1 for oboe; 1 for clarinet; 1 for bassoon; 3 and 1 incomplete for horn.

CHAMBER MUSIC: 6 string quintets; 26 string quartets and *Adagio and Fugue,* K 546, 1788; 2 string trios; 2 string duos; 1 duo for bassoon and cello; 4 flute quartets; 1 oboe quartet; 1 clarinet quintet; 1 horn quintet; 1 quintet for piano and winds; 2 piano quartets; 7 piano trios (1 with clarinet); adagio and rondo for glass harmonica, wind, and strings; 32 sonatas and 2 sets of variations for piano and violin.

KEYBOARD MUSIC: 19 piano sonatas; 5 sonatas for piano duet; 1 two-piano sonata; 16 sets of variations for piano; 1 set of variations for piano duet; 27 pieces for piano; fugue for 2 pianos; 3 pieces for mechanical organ; adagio for glass harmonica.

BIBLIOGRAPHY. The Mozart literature is vast. Sources and documents of his lifetime begin with his numerous letters that are available in a critical edition of the family correspondence, *Mozart, Briefe und Aufzeichnungen: Gesamtausgabe,* 7 vol., ed. by WILHELM A. BAUER and OTTO ERICH DEUTSCH (1962–75); and in WOLFGANG AMADEUS MOZART, *Briefe,* ed. by ALBRECHT GOES (1979). For the English translation of the correspondence, see EMILY ANDERSON (ed.), *The Letters of Mozart and His Family,* 3rd ed. (1985, rev. 1989).

A comprehensive bibliography of secondary sources appeared as the *Mozart-Jahrbuch 1975* and in 1976 was published as *Mozart-Bibliographie (bis 1970),* RUDOLPH ANGERMÜLLER and OTTO SCHNEIDER (comps.). These compilers have continued the bibliography in *Mozart-Bibliographie, 1971–1975* (1978), *Mozart-Bibliographie, 1976–1980* (1982), and *Mozart-Bibliographie, 1981–1985* (1987). More selective bibliographies are included in many of the biographical works cited here.

Basic secondary sources begin with a biography-obituary that appeared in the periodical *Nekrolog auf das Jahr 1791,* ed. by FRIEDRICH SCHLICHTEGROLL (1793), vol. 2, pp. 82–112, and supplement, 2, pp. 159ff. Other early biographies are FRANZ XAVER NIEMETSCHEK, *Life of Mozart* (1956, reprinted 1979; originally published in German, 1798); and GEORG NIKOLAUS VON NISSEN, *Biographie W.A. Mozarts* (1828, reprinted 1984). The first scholarly biography is OTTO JAHN, *Life of Mozart,* 3 vol. (1882, reissued 1970; originally published in German, 1856–59). This work was later thoroughly revised and greatly enlarged for the 5th edition by HERMANN ABERT (ed.), *W.A. Mozart,* 2 vol. (1919–21, reissued 1983), but this edition has not been translated into English. Documentary sources are compiled and annotated in OTTO ERICH DEUTSCH, *Mozart: A Documentary Biography,* 2nd ed. (1966; originally published in German, 1961); it is supplemented by JOSEPH HEINZ EIBL (comp.), *Mozart: Die Dokumente seines Lebens: Addenda und Corrigenda* (1978). MAXIMILIAN ZENGER and OTTO ERICH DEUTSCH, *Mozart and His World in Contemporary Pictures* (1961), is a pictorial account with parallel English and German text.

Other studies of the composer's life include ALFRED EINSTEIN, *Mozart, His Character, His Work,* trans. from German (1945, reissued 1971), a sympathetic and perceptive, if a little dated, work; ARTHUR HUTCHINGS, *Mozart, the Man, the Musician* (1976), a generously illustrated exploration of the life and the career; WOLFGANG HILDESHEIMER, *Mozart* (1982; originally published in German, 1977), a speculative psychological exploration; MICHAEL LEVEY, *The Life and Death of Mozart,* rev. ed. (1988), an attempt to discover new links between life and music; IVOR KEYS, *Mozart: His Music in His Life* (1980), a general introduction; STANLEY SADIE, "Wolfgang Amadeus Mozart," in *The New Grove Dictionary of Music and Musicians,* vol.12 (1980), pp. 680–752, a biography with an exhaustive list of Mozart's works, available also as a monograph; and H.C. ROBBINS LANDON, *1791, Mozart's Last Year* (1988), a new interpretation of documentary sources.

Discussions of Mozart's music include CHARLES ROSEN, *The Classical Style: Haydn, Mozart, Beethoven,* rev. ed. (1976), a study of both the technicalities and aesthetics of the music. H.C. ROBBINS LANDON and DONALD MITCHELL (eds.), *The Mozart Companion* (1956, reprinted 1981); and PAUL HENRY LANG (ed.), *The Creative World of Mozart* (1963), are collections of essays by specialists. Operas are surveyed in WILLIAM MANN,

The Operas of Mozart (1977), treating all of the composer's dramatic works; and CHARLES OSBORNE, *The Complete Operas of Mozart: A Critical Guide* (1978, reprinted 1986), an introductory guide. New standpoints on the operas are seen in FRITS NOSKE, *The Signifier and the Signified: Studies in the Operas of Mozart and Verdi* (1977); WYE JAMISON ALLANBROOK, *Rhythmic Gesture in Mozart: Le Nozze di Figaro & Don Giovanni* (1983); BRIGID BROPHY, *Mozart the Dramatist: The Value of His Operas to Him, to His Age, and to Us*, rev. ed. (1988), a psychoanalytical study; and ANDREW STEPTOE, *The Mozart-Da Ponte Operas: The Cultural and Musical Background to Le nozze di Figaro, Don Giovanni, and Così fan tutte* (1988). The "Cambridge Opera Handbooks" series offers valuable surveys of individual operas: JULIAN RUSHTON, *W.A. Mozart: Don Giovanni* (1981); TIM CARTER, *W.A. Mozart: Le Nozze di Figaro* (1987); and THOMAS BAUMAN, *W.A. Mozart: Die Entführung aus dem Serail* (1987).

For instrumental music, see ARTHUR HUTCHINGS, *A Companion to Mozart's Piano Concertos*, 2nd ed. (1950, reprinted 1980), an enthusiastic, personal survey; and the works from the useful "BBC Music Guides" series: A. HYATT KING, *Mozart Chamber Music* (1968, reprinted 1986), and *Mozart Wind and String Concertos* (1978, reprinted 1986); STANLEY SADIE, *Mozart Symphonies* (1986); and ERIK SMITH, *Mozart Serenades, Divertimenti, and Dances* (1982). ALAN TYSON, *Mozart: Studies of the Autograph Scores* (1987), offers fascinating glimpses into Mozart's creative workshop; while A. HYATT KING, *Mozart in Retrospect: Studies in Criticism and Bibliography* (1955, reprinted with revisions, 1976), looks at his changing image and reputation over the years. (S.Sa.)

Muscles and Muscle Systems

All animals must either move to find food or, if they are sedentary, have means of bringing food to themselves. Many invertebrates and all vertebrates depend upon contractile tissue called muscle to move themselves about. Muscles in turn are grouped into coordinated systems for greater efficiency.

This article consists of a comparative study of the muscle systems of various animals, including an explanation of the process of muscle contraction and an account of the human muscle system as it relates to upright posture. A brief survey of the diseases that affect human muscle is also included.

For coverage of related topics in the *Macropædia* and *Micropædia*, see the *Propædia*, sections 421 and 423, and the *Index*.

The article is divided into the following sections:

General features of muscle and movement

Muscle powers the movements of multicellular animals and maintains posture. Its gross appearance is familiar as meat or as the flesh of fish. Muscle is the most plentiful tissue in many animals; for example, it comprises 50 to 60 percent of the body mass in many fishes, and 40 to 50 percent in antelopes. Some muscles are under conscious control and are called voluntary muscles. Other muscles, called involuntary muscles, are not consciously controlled by the organism; for example, in vertebrates, muscles in the walls of the heart contract rhythmically, pumping blood around the body; muscles in the walls of the intestines move food along by peristalsis; and muscles in the walls of small blood vessels constrict or relax, controlling the flow of blood to different parts of the body. (The effects of muscle changes in the blood vessels are apparent in blushing and paling due to increased or decreased blood flow, respectively, to the skin.)

Non-muscular movement

Muscles are not the only means of movement in animals. Many protozoans (unicellular animals) move instead by using cilia or flagella (actively beating processes of the cell surface that propel the organism through water). Some unicellular animals are capable of amoeboid movement, in which the cell contents flow into extensions (pseudopodia) from the cell body. Some of the ciliated protozoans move by means of rods called myonemes, which are capable of shortening rapidly.

Cilia and other nonmuscular methods of movement are important for multicellular animals as well. Many microscopic animals, such as the larvae of mollusks and marine worms, swim by means of beating cilia. Some small mollusks and flatworms crawl using cilia on the underside of the body. Some invertebrates that feed by filtering small particles from water use cilia to create the necessary water currents. In higher animals, white cells use amoeboid movements, and cilia from cells lining the respiratory tract remove foreign particles from the delicate membranes.

Muscles consist of long, slender cells (fibres) each of which is a bundle of finer fibrils (Figure 1). Within each fibril are relatively thick filaments of the protein myosin and thin ones of actin and other proteins. When a muscle fibre lengthens or shortens, the filaments remain essentially constant in length but slide past each other as shown in Figure 2. Tension in active muscles is produced by cross bridges (*i.e.,* projections from the thick filaments that attach to the thin ones and exert forces on them). As the active muscle lengthens or shortens and the filaments slide past each other, the cross bridges repeatedly detach and reattach in new positions. Their action is similar to pulling a rope in hand over hand. Some muscle fibres are several centimetres long, but most other cells are only a fraction of a millimetre long. Because these long fibres cannot be served adequately by a single nucleus, numerous nuclei are distributed along their length.

From *Biological Science: Molecules to Man*, Houghton Mifflin Co., Boston, Mass., by permission of the Biological Sciences Curriculum Study

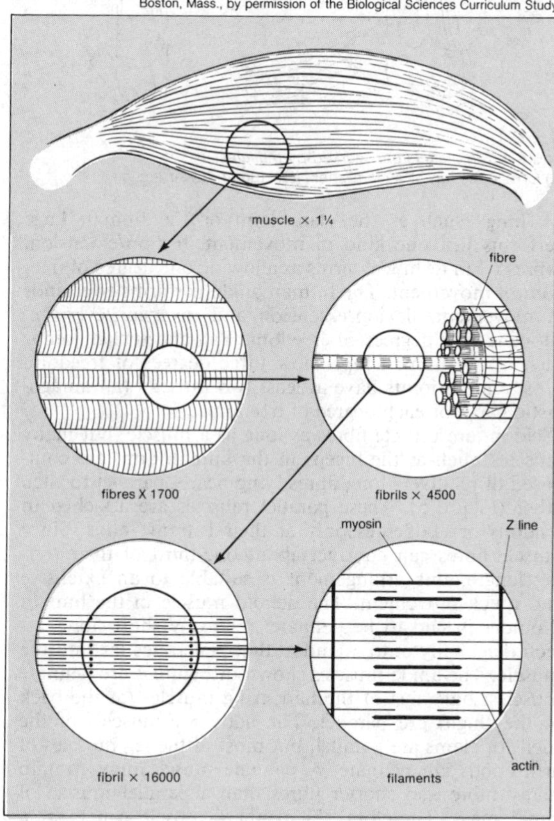

Figure 1: Striated muscle structure in increasingly magnified drawings.

Energy requirements

The work done by muscle requires chemical energy derived from the metabolism of food. When muscles shorten while exerting tension and performing mechanical work (such as lifting), some of the chemical energy is converted to work and some is lost as heat. When muscles lengthen while exerting tension (such as in slowly lowering a weight), the chemical energy that is used along with the mechanical energy absorbed by the action is converted to heat. Generation of heat is an important subsidiary function of muscle in homeothermic (warm-blooded) animals. Shivering is muscle activity that generates heat and warms the body. Similarly, some insects vibrate their wings for a while before flight, heating the muscles to the temperature at which they work best.

DIVERSITY OF MUSCLE

Muscle fibres differ from species to species of animal and between parts of the same animal. Apart from the distinction between voluntary and involuntary muscles, muscles differ in structure and activity.

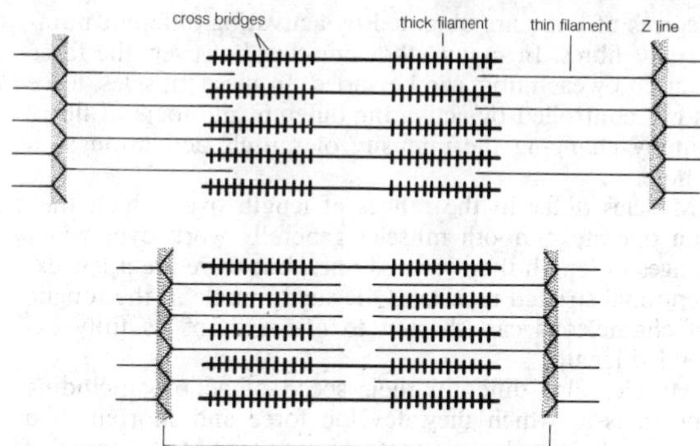

Figure 2: *The arrangement of the myofilaments in a striated muscle.*
The muscle is extended in the upper diagram and contracted in the lower one. The thick filaments are 1.6 micrometres (0.0016 millimetres) long in vertebrate striated muscle but up to six micrometres long in some arthropods.

Types of muscle fibres

Muscles differ in the arrangement of their myofilaments. The principal types of muscle are striated muscle, in which the filaments are organized in transverse bands as in Figure 2; obliquely striated muscle, in which the filaments are staggered, making the bands oblique (Figure 3); and smooth muscle, in which the filaments are arranged irregularly. In vertebrates, all voluntary muscles are striated and all involuntary muscles are smooth, except for cardiac muscle, which is involuntary but striated. Obliquely striated muscle is found only in some invertebrate groups (the nematodes, annelids, and mollusks), and has the protein paramyosin in the thick filaments as well as myosin.

Muscles differ in the stimuli required to activate them. In vertebrates, voluntary muscles require action potentials (electrical signals) in their nerves to initiate every contraction. Some involuntary muscles are spontaneously active, and the action potentials in their nerves only modify the natural rhythm of contraction. The leg muscles of all insects, and the wing muscles of many, require action potentials to initiate every contraction; however, the wing muscles of other insects consist of fibrillar muscle, which requires only occasional action potentials to maintain its rapid rhythmic contractions. The wings of these insects are attached to the body in such a way as to have a resonant frequency of vibration (like a guitar string that vibrates, when plucked, at its resonant frequency). When fibrillar muscles are active they contract so as to maintain the vibrations of the resonant system.

Stress

Muscles differ in the ability to exert stress. Muscles that exert large stresses have long thick filaments that carry larger numbers of cross bridges. The result is more cross bridges than in other muscles. This means that more force can be transmitted from each thick filament to the adjacent thin filaments, and larger stresses can be exerted. Less stress can be exerted when the fibres are shortening than when they are maintaining constant length, and more when they are being forcibly stretched.

Muscles differ in the manner in which their forces are controlled. Most of the fibres in the voluntary muscles of mammals can only be switched on or off, and different

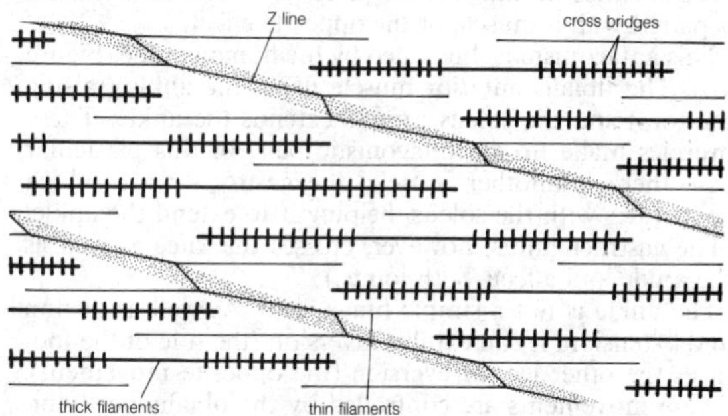

Figure 3: The arrangement of the myofilaments in obliquely striated muscle.

degrees of force are obtained by activating different numbers of fibres. In many other muscles, however, the force exerted by each fibre can be varied. In these muscles, force is not controlled by activating different numbers of fibres but by changing the intensity of muscle activation as a whole.

Muscles differ in the ranges of length over which they can operate. Smooth muscles generally work over wider ranges of length than striated ones, but there are a few exceptional striated muscles. One such muscle in the tongue of chameleons can shorten to one-sixth of its fully extended length.

Muscles also differ in their speed of action, including the rates at which they develop force and shorten. If a muscle shortens by one-tenth of its length in one-tenth of a second, its rate of shortening is one length per second. Maximum rates of shortening vary between species and between muscle fibres in a single animal. For example, two muscles in the limbs of mice have maximum shortening speeds (at 37° C) of 24 and 13 lengths per second.

Metabolism

Finally, muscles differ in their metabolism. The adenosine triphosphate (ATP) that they use as their immediate energy source may be produced either by oxidative reactions, in which food is oxidized to carbon dioxide and water, or by processes that do not require oxygen (anaerobic). Vertebrates and crabs use the anaerobic process of glycolysis, converting the carbohydrate glycogen to lactic acid, for short bursts of vigorous activity such as sprinting. The burst of activity is followed by a recovery period in which oxygen is used to oxidize some of the lactic acid, releasing the energy needed to convert the rest back to glycogen. The advantage of using anaerobic metabolism in this way is that the intensity of activity during the burst is not limited by the rate at which the blood can bring oxygen to the muscles.

In vertebrates, many muscle fibres perform only oxidative metabolism or only glycolysis, though some perform both. Oxidative fibres are commonly red, owing to the presence of the pigment myoglobin. Most fishes show an obvious distinction between the main bulk of white swimming muscle and a narrow strip of red muscle along the side of the body. Slow swimming is powered by the red (oxidative) muscle and bursts of fast swimming by the white (glycolytic) muscle. Red and white muscles are also easy to distinguish in the domestic chicken, in which the pale meat of the breast consists mainly of white fibres and the dark meat of the legs the red fibres. The breast muscles are the main muscles of the wings, which are used by chickens only for occasional short bursts of flight. Other birds that practice sustained flight (*e.g.,* hummingbirds) mainly have red breast muscles.

MUSCLES THAT WORK SKELETONS

Figure 4 shows a simple system, in which a skeleton is worked by muscles. The two rigid parts of the clam shell (Figure 4A) are hinged together. They can be closed to protect the animal within or allowed to open. A block of rubbery protein, the inner hinge ligament, lies just inside the hinge. When the adductor muscle contracts it closes the shell, but in so doing it compresses the inner hinge ligament. When it relaxes, the ligament recoils elastically, reopening the shell. This is an unusual system, in that it is worked by just one muscle. Most other skeletal systems need muscles in antagonistic pairs, in which each muscle is paired with a muscle of the opposite effect.

Human ankle joint

This antagonism is illustrated by the human ankle (Figure 4B). The tibialis anterior muscle flexes the ankle (raising the toes) and the soleus muscle extends the ankle. These muscles make up an antagonistic pair. In this particular case there is another muscle, the gastrocnemius, which cooperates with the soleus, helping it to extend the ankle. (The gastrocnemius, however, crosses the knee as well as the ankle and affects both joints.)

The ankle is not a simple hinge joint. As well as flexion and extension, it can exhibit inversion (the sole of the foot faces the other leg) or eversion (the opposite movement). These movements are controlled by the tibialis posterior, which inverts the ankle, and the peronaeus muscles, which are antagonistic and evert it (Figure 4B).

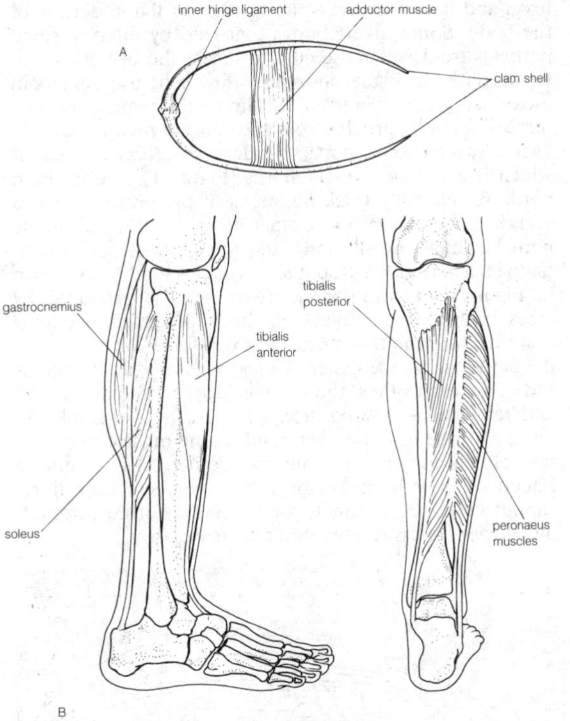

Figure 4: *Rigid skeletons worked by muscles.*
(A) Cross section of a clam shell. (B) Human lower leg.

A hinge such as the clam joint or the human knee performs just one kind of movement, flexion/extension, expressed in technical terms as allowing one degree of freedom of movement. The human ankle performs two kinds of movement, flexion/extension and inversion/eversion, allowing two degrees of freedom. Ball-and-socket joints, such as the human hip, allow three degrees of freedom. Most animal joints have at least two muscles (an antagonistic pair) for each degree of freedom.

Seldom are muscle fibres as long as a muscle, but many muscles, such as the biceps in the human arm, are composed of relatively long fibres lying nearly parallel to each other (Figure 5). These parallel muscles are attached to tendons or apodemes only at their extreme ends. Since muscle fibres can contract about one-third of their resting length, this arrangement is suitable to an extensive and quick movement. The deltoid muscle in the human shoulder is said to be pennate: relatively short fibres attach diagonally onto a tendon that penetrates far into the muscle. The ankle muscles shown in Figure 4 are pennate muscles, but most of the hamstring muscles (at the back of the thigh) are parallel. The adductor muscles of the shells of clams are parallel, but most of the leg muscles of arthropods are pennate. A pennate muscle may contain many more and shorter fibres than a parallel muscle of equal mass. Therefore, the pennate muscle can exert a greater force but cannot shorten a great deal; the parallel-fibred muscle can exert only a relatively small force but can shorten significantly. The presence of pennate muscle in a given structure may have the same effect as a longer lever arm. In the slender legs of arthropods, with insufficient space for bulky muscles or long lever arms, many of the muscles are pennate.

Pennate muscle

Tendons and apodemes (in arthropods, chitinous rods that serve as sites for muscle attachment) have elastic properties. Tendons in the legs of mammals serve as springs, reducing the energy cost of running: energy that is lost as the foot hits the ground and decelerates the body is stored as elastic strain energy in tendons and is subsequently returned in an elastic recoil. An apodeme in the hind legs of locusts is one of the important elastic elements in the catapult mechanism that powers jumping.

MUSCLE IN SOFT ANIMALS

Slugs, worms, and many other invertebrate animals have no skeleton, and thus movement is not produced by lever

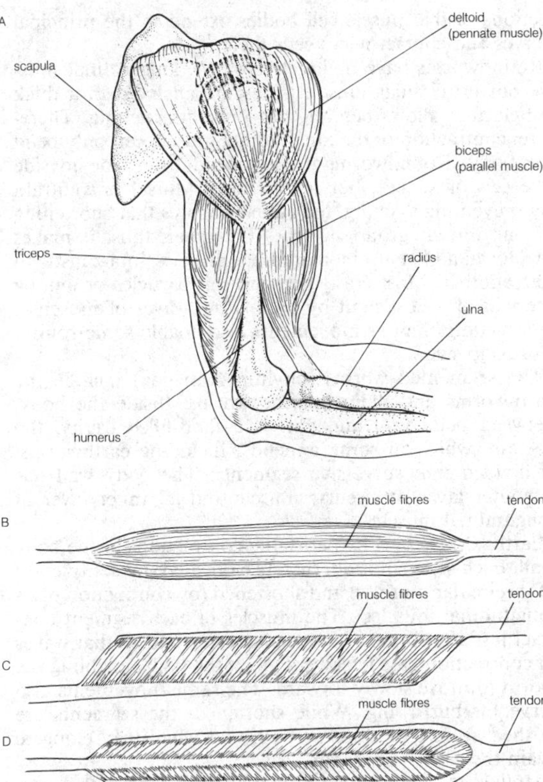

Figure 5: *Gross muscle structure.*
(A) Lateral view of some muscles in the human upper arm. (B) Parallel fibred muscle. (C,D) Two types of pennate muscles.
Adapted from *Melloni's Illustrated Medical Dictionary* (1978); reproduced by permission of Williams and Wilkins, Baltimore

action. Even vertebrates have parts of the body that have muscles but no skeletal component (for example, the tongue). Many soft-bodied animals have muscle systems based on the principle illustrated in Figure 6, which shows a simple wormlike animal. The longitudinal muscle fibres run lengthwise along the body and the circular fibres encircle it. The body contents are liquids or tissues that can be deformed into different shapes, but they maintain a constant volume. If longitudinal muscles contract and the body shortens, it must widen to accommodate its volume; if the circular muscles contract and the body thins, it must lengthen. Thus the longitudinal and circular muscles are antagonistic, and shortening of either extends the other.

Antagonism of muscles

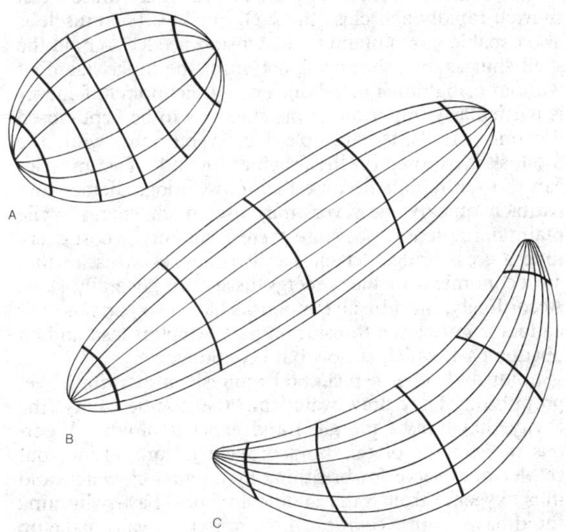

Figure 6: *Changes in body form in wormlike soft-bodied animals.*
(A) The longitudinal muscle contracting. (B) The circular muscle contracting. (C) The longitudinal muscle above contracting while the circular muscles maintain a constant length, stretching the longitudinal muscles below.

Further, if the length of a circular muscle remains constant while the longitudinal muscle of one side of the body shortens, the body bends and the longitudinal muscle of the other side is stretched. Thus the longitudinal muscles of the left and right sides can be antagonistic toward each other. In worms the body fluids render muscles antagonistic through hydrostatic forces. The principle involved is sometimes called the principle of the hydrostatic skeleton.

The principle of the hydrostatic skeleton can apply to individual muscles as well if their fibres run in several directions. For example, in a muscle that has some fibres running longitudinally and others running circularly and/or radially, when the longitudinal fibres shorten, the muscle becomes shorter and fatter; and when the circular and radial fibres shorten, it becomes longer and thinner. There are many examples of muscle structure like this in the mollusks. One such is the shell muscle of the abalone *Haliotis,* which connects the domed shell of the animal to its adhesive foot. When the muscle shortens, with the foot attached to a rock, the shell is pulled down over the animal to protect it. When the muscle lengthens (by contraction of circular and radial fibres) the shell is raised from the rock, allowing respiratory water currents to circulate.

Muscle systems

INVERTEBRATE MUSCLE SYSTEMS

Hydras and medusae

Cnidarians. The phylum Cnidaria includes the hydras, jellyfishes, and sea anemones. Cnidarians have two main body forms, the cylindrical tentacled polyp exemplified by the hydra and the sea anemone, and the bell-shaped (or inverted saucer-shaped) medusa. Hydras are some of the simplest multicellular animals to have muscle. They are hollow, cylindrical, freshwater creatures about 10 millimetres long. One end attaches to a plant or some other support, and the other end is free and has a mouth surrounded by tentacles. The body wall consists of two layers of cells with a middle gelatinous layer (mesoglea). In hydras and other two-layered animals one kind of cell serves as both muscle and epithelial cells. The compact body of each cell is packed closely with the adjacent cells to form an epithelium, and the base of each cell, where it meets the mesoglea, is drawn out into a long muscle fibre.

In the hydra the musculoepithelial cells that cover the outer surface of the body have longitudinal muscle fibres; those that line the gut cavity (the gastrodermis) have circular muscle fibres. Sea anemones have all of the muscle fibres in the gastrodermis, though some of the fibres are longitudinal and some are circular. When the mouth of the sea anemone is closed, the water in the gut cavity acts as a hydrostatic skeleton, permitting the animal to grow longer and thinner or shorter and fatter, or to bend in any direction. These changes result from the interaction of the longitudinal and circular muscles through movements that are not as simple as those of the schematic worm of Figure 6. The hydra can reduce its volume by using its muscles to squeeze water out of the gut cavity through the open mouth. It can reinflate using cilia to circulate water into the gut cavity. Its movements are also influenced by the viscoelastic properties of the mesogleal jelly.

Jellyfishes

The largest and most familiar medusae are the jellyfishes of the class Scyphozoa, some of which grow to a diameter of two metres. Though large, the scyphozoan jellyfishes have only a single layer of cells on the outer surface of the body and a single layer lining the gut cavity; most of the volume of the animal is occupied by the gelatinous mesoglea. The epidermis of the undersurface of the bell includes the musculoepithelial cells responsible for the animal's weak swimming movements. The muscle fibres contract, reducing the diameter of the bell and forcing out a stream of water. The bell then returns to its original shape by elastic recoil of the mesoglea. These movements are performed in a regular rhythm with a period of a few seconds, propelling the animal through the water. Medusae are among the simplest animals that use muscles to make rhythmic movements. In at least some medusae the circular muscles, which do most of the work of swimming, are striated. In contrast, most of the other muscles of cnidarians are smooth.

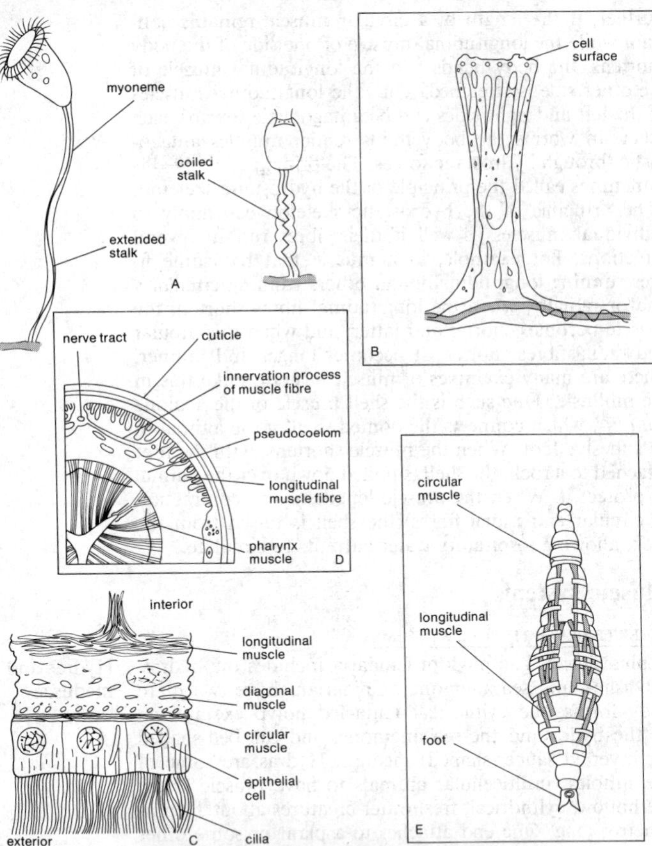

Figure 7: *Types of invertebrate contractile systems.* (A) Contractile stalk in protozoan *Vorticella.* (B) Epitheliomuscle cell of coelenterate *Hydra.* (C) Longitudinal section through ventral portion of body wall of freshwater flatworm. (D) Quadrant of cross section through a nematode (*Ascaris*) at level of pharynx. (E) Muscle bands in body wall of rotifer.

From (A) Parker and Haswell, *A Textbook of Zoology*, St Martin's Press, Inc., Macmillan & Co., Ltd., (B) W. Andrew, *Textbook of Comparative Histology* (1958), and (C,D,E) *Invertebrate Zoology* by Paul Meglitsch. Copyright © 1967 by Oxford University Press, Inc. Reprinted by permission

Multilayered animals. *Worms.* Although all worms have more than two layers of cells and most have long, slender bodies, the various groups of worms are different from each other in other respects.

The simplest worms are the flatworms (phylum Platyhelminthes), most of which have flattened shapes like leaves or ribbons. Although musculoepithelial cells have been found in some flatworms, the muscle cells in most are distinct from the epithelial cells. There is a layer of circular muscle fibres immediately under the epidermis, a layer of diagonal fibres, and a still deeper longitudinal layer (Figure 7C). There are also dorsoventral muscle fibres running from the upper to the lower epidermis of the flattened body. These sets of muscle fibres act in various combinations to make the body long and thin, short and fat, or bent to one side or the other. These muscles are also used by some of the larger flatworms to pass waves of muscular contraction along the body, enabling the worm to crawl in a snaillike fashion.

Many flatworms have a mouth opening connected to the pharynx, a muscular tube that conveys food from the mouth to the intestine. In some flatworms the pharynx is protruded and inserted into invertebrate prey, to digest and suck out the contents. The sucking is done by peristalsis, waves of muscular contraction that move along the tube from the mouth toward the gut. Although the muscle cells of flatworms are generally not musculoepithelial, their nuclei are found in large cell bodies. The muscle fibres of vertebrates and higher invertebrates, on the other hand, have no projecting cell body.

Roundworms

Roundworms (phylum Nematoda) also have large cell bodies on their muscle cells, but these muscle cells are unique in that nerve fibres do not travel to them as they do in the muscles of other animals. Instead, narrow projections of the muscle cell bodies extend to the principal nerves and contact nerve cells there.

Roundworms have obliquely striated, longitudinal muscle but no circular muscle. They are enclosed in a thick cuticle that allows bending but prevents swelling. Therefore, contraction of the longitudinal muscle can only bend the body. Roundworms do not bend from side to side like eels or snakes, but up or down (dorsal or ventral). By preventing swelling, the cuticle ensures that shortening of one muscle group stretches the other; thus, it makes the dorsal and ventral longitudinal muscles antagonistic to one another. Most crawl between soil particles or among the villi of a host's gut by undulating waves of muscular contraction. Similar movements also enable some roundworms to swim.

The segmented worms (phylum Annelida) include the earthworms and many marine worms. Inside the body, between body wall and gut, is a fluid-filled cavity, the coelom, which in some annelids, including earthworms, is divided into successive segments. The body wall has an outer layer of circular muscle and an inner layer of longitudinal muscle.

Earthworms crawl by peristaltic contractions of the body wall. Each segment is alternately elongated (by contraction of its circular muscles) and shortened (by contraction of its longitudinal muscles). The muscles of each segment contract just after those of the segment in front, so that waves of contraction pass backward along the body, enabling the worm to move slowly forward. The same movements also serve for burrowing. While shortened, the segments are pushed against the burrow wall, and when they elongate again the worm moves forward.

Mollusks. The phylum Mollusca includes the gastropods (snails, slugs, periwinkles), the bivalves (clams, oysters, mussels, and scallops), the cephalopods (octopods and squids), and other smaller classes. All mollusks, except the cephalopods, have a highly muscular organ called the foot, through which muscle fibres run in all directions. The foot of a gastropod is a flat structure used for crawling. Waves of muscular contraction travel along its length, moving the animal slowly over the ground. The foot of a bivalve mollusk is a bulbous or tonguelike organ that is used for burrowing in sand or mud. The foot pushes down into the substrate, then swells to anchor itself and pulls the rest of the animal down behind it.

In addition to the muscles of the foot, gastropod and bivalve mollusks have large muscles attached to their shells. The columellar (shell) muscles of gastropods pull the foot and other parts of the body into the shell. The adductor muscles of bivalves (Figure 4) shorten to close the shell or relax to allow the shell to spring open, enabling the mollusk to extend its foot or to feed. The adductor muscle can shorten rapidly and close the shell quickly. The muscle is also capable of maintaining the tension needed to hold the shell shut against the spring action of the hinge ligament without using much metabolic energy. Economy of energy is particularly important if the shell has to be kept closed for long periods; for example, for several hours while the mollusk is exposed on the beach at low tide. Fast muscles can shorten rapidly because their cross bridges detach and reattach quickly; however, they use much energy while maintaining tension because there is an energy cost every time a cross bridge detaches and reattaches. Muscles that are economical in their energy usage are generally slow. Accordingly, most bivalve mollusks have two parts to their adductor muscles, a translucent part, which is fast, and an opaque part, which is slow but economical.

Squids and cephalopods

Squids and other cephalopod mollusks also swim by jet propulsion. They draw water into the mantle cavity (the cavity that houses the gills) and expel it rapidly. Vigorous movements of this kind provide jet propulsion, but gentler ones serve for breathing by circulating water, and thus oxygen, through the mantle and gills. Fast-swimming squid have mantle cavities whose muscular walls make up as much as 35 percent of the mass of the body.

These walls mainly consist of circular muscle fibres that squeeze water out of the mantle cavity when they contract. Other fibres run radially through the thickness of the wall. These fibres make the wall thinner when they

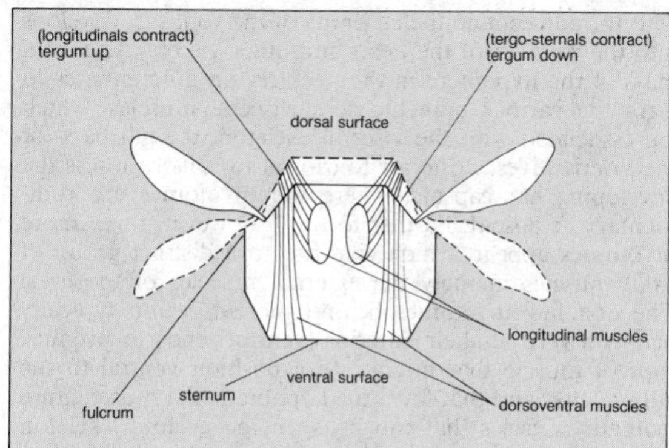

Figure 8: Muscles involved in insect flight (see text).
From C.A. Villee, W.F. Walker, and F.E. Smith, *General Zoology* (1963), W.B. Saunders Company

contract, stretching the circular muscle and enlarging the cavity again. Cephalopods do not have longitudinal muscle fibres; however, layers of collagen fibres on the outer and inner surfaces of the muscle prevent the animal from lengthening when the muscles contract. Thus the circular and radial muscle fibres are antagonistic. Enlargement of the cavity, however, is not solely due to the radial muscle fibres: the cavity tends to expand by elastic recoil of the tissues, when the circular muscles relax.

Though many mollusks have shells, most molluscan muscle systems depend on the principle of the hydrostatic skeleton. In some cases body fluids are involved, for example, in the feet of clams, which are extended and inflated by inflow of blood. In other cases the muscle itself serves as the incompressible element that must thicken as it shortens or become slender as it elongates, to maintain constant volume. Examples include the shell muscle of the abalone and the tentacles of squid, which are shortened by contraction of longitudinal muscle fibres and lengthened by circular and transverse ones.

Arthropods. Arthropoda is the largest phylum of invertebrate animals and comprises the crustaceans, insects, arachnids (spiders and scorpions), and other classes. Some arthropods have soft-bodied young stages in which the principle of the hydrostatic skeleton is important. Most adult arthropods are encased in a skeleton with jointed appendages formed from a stiff cuticle that is divided into separate plates to assist in movement. This skeleton, working as a system of levers, is largely responsible for making muscles antagonistic.

Insect wings

The wing muscles of dragonflies (Odonata) and those of some other insects are worked in simple, direct ways by pulling on the wing bases and making them pivot about their joints. More advanced insects, including flies (Diptera), work their wings indirectly by muscles that attach to other parts of the skeleton. Although the details of the mechanisms are complicated, the basic principle is simple. Each wing-bearing segment of the body is enclosed by two main plates of cuticle, a tergum above and a sternum below (Figure 8). These plates are flexible enough to be distorted by muscle action. Distortions of the tergum are particularly important in the wing mechanism.

The principal wing muscles are the dorsoventral muscles, which run vertically from the sternum to the tergum, and the longitudinal muscles, which run lengthwise along the segment. Contraction of the longitudinal muscles makes the tergum bow upward, and contraction of the dorsoventral muscles pulls it down again. The wings have joints connecting them to the tergum and to the sternum. Upward movement of the tergum (from contraction of the longitudinal muscles) lowers the wings and downward movement (from contraction of the dorsoventral muscles) raises them.

All arthropod muscles seem to be striated, not obliquely striated or smooth, and the sarcomeres are of varying lengths. In locusts the sarcomeres (the primary structural and functional unit responsible for contraction; see below *Striated muscle: The myofilament*) of wing muscles are 3.9 micrometres long, but the sarcomeres of leg muscles (which do not have to contract so quickly) are 8.5 micrometres long. Wing muscles in many other insects have shorter sarcomeres, often about the same length as those in mammalian muscle (about 2.5 micrometres).

The force exerted by the muscle is controlled by varying the frequency of action potentials in the axons (an extension of the nerve cell that conducts nerve impulses away from the cell body). The higher the frequency, the larger the force, within limits. In contrast, in vertebrates each muscle is served by many motor axons, each of which is connected to only a small group of muscle fibres. In the twitch muscles that predominate in vertebrates, each muscle fibre is either inactive or fully active and force is varied by recruiting different numbers of muscle fibres. Like those of other animals, most arthropod muscles require an action potential to initiate each contraction.

Fibrillar muscle

Fibrillar muscle is found in the sound-producing, or tymbal, muscles of some cicadas and in the wing muscles of several orders of insects including the Diptera (flies), Coleoptera (beetles), Hymenoptera (wasps), and Hemiptera (bugs). Most fibrillar muscles work at high frequencies, often of several hundred cycles per second, but they are kept working by action potentials arriving at much lower frequencies. They contract at the resonant frequency of the tymbal or of the wing system. Clipping the wings of an insect that has fibrillar wing muscles increases the frequency of the wing beat, because reduction of the vibrating mass increases the resonant frequency.

All insect wing muscles work aerobically and produce high power outputs. Consequently they need many mitochondria, which may occupy 40 percent or more of their volume both in fibrillar and in non-fibrillar muscles. Non-fibrillar muscles that work at high frequencies also need large sarcoplasmic reticulums, but fibrillar ones do not.

Although insect muscles seem always to work aerobically, some crustacean muscles can work anaerobically. The leg muscles that the crab *Callinectes* uses for swimming include two types of fibres. One type resembles the red muscle fibres of vertebrates in that it is deep pink and contains a high proportion of mitochondria. The other resembles vertebrate white fibres because it is white with far fewer mitochondria, and presumably works anaerobically. Similar differences occur in other crustacean muscles. Crabs use anaerobic metabolism for short bursts of violent activity in the way that vertebrates do.

Echinoderms. The phylum Echinodermata comprises the starfishes, sea urchins, and their relatives. Their internal skeletons are made of porous blocks of calcium carbonate and they have muscles to work their skeleton. Echinoderms also have a hydraulic system, the water-vascular system, with movable projections from the body called tube feet.

Tube feet

The details of the tube feet differ among the different groups of echinoderms, but Figure 9 shows the arrangement in sea urchins. Five double rows of tube feet project through the test, so that every part of the body surface has tube feet near it. The tube feet are slender tubes, with

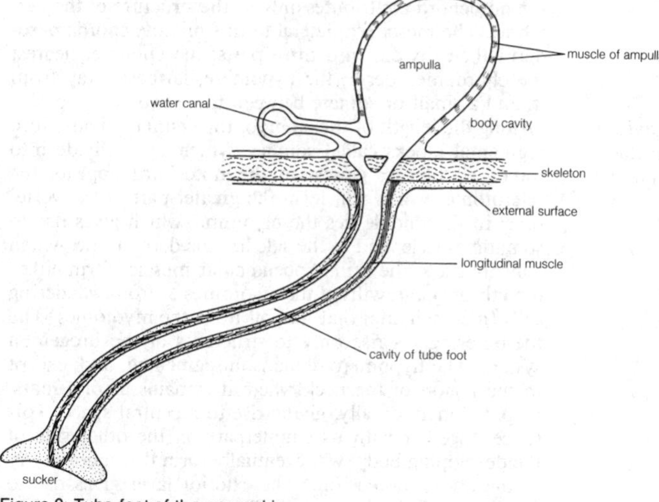

Figure 9: Tube foot of the sea urchin.

a sucker on the closed end. Muscles in the sucker enable it to attach to objects, so the tube feet can be used by the animal to anchor, to move, or to manipulate its prey. Connective tissue in the tube feet limits their diameter but allows them to lengthen, to shorten, and to bend. The tube feet have only longitudinal muscles, which extend the length of the cavity of the tube foot. They are extended by water that has been forced into them by muscles in the wall of the ampulla at their bases. (W.F.W./R.McN.A.)

VERTEBRATE MUSCLE SYSTEMS

Major types of vertebrate muscle. In terms of its microscopic structure, the musculature of vertebrates is usually divided into three types: striated, cardiac, and smooth muscle. Smooth and cardiac muscle are under the control of the involuntary, or autonomic, nervous system. Striated muscle, on the other hand, is mainly under the control of the voluntary, or central, nervous system. Smooth and cardiac muscle are also similar in their development, being generally associated with the yolk sac. Striated muscle develops directly from the middle of the three embryonic layers, arising largely from the mesodermal somites (see below). In the adult, smooth and cardiac muscle are associated with organs or tubes (viscera), and striated (skeletal) muscle with the bony or cartilaginous skeleton.

Although some evidence suggests that a twofold division of the musculature into visceral and skeletal muscle might be appropriate, one set of striated muscles is distinct in development and in innervation from all other striated muscle. In humans these include both the muscles of the jaw and some of the muscles of the shoulder and are called the branchiomeric, or branchial, muscles. Branchiomeric muscles, even in humans, are innervated by visceral nerve fibres as is the case with smooth and cardiac muscle, not the somatic nerve fibres (those that supply the outer body wall or soma), and thus are usually grouped with the smooth and cardiac muscles despite their striated nature.

Vertebrate muscle divisions

The two major divisions of the vertebrate musculature are thus the visceral musculature (smooth, cardiac, and branchiomeric) and the somatic musculature (the striated muscles of the body wall). Somatic musculature may be divided into appendicular, or limb, muscles and axial muscles. The axial muscles include the muscles of the tail, trunk, and eyeballs as well as a group of muscles called hypobranchial muscles, which separate and migrate from the others during development.

Basic pattern of development. The gastrula is the stage of embryonic development at which the embryo appears as three distinct layers of cells (the germ layers): the exterior ectoderm, the middle mesoderm, and the interior endoderm. The mesoderm differentiates to form most of the remaining tissues, structures, and organs of the body. As the embryo lengthens, the mesoderm lying along the midline differentiates to form the chordamesoderm, which gives rise to the notochord, a hollow, cartilaginous nerve tube and a major distinguishing feature of the vertebrates and their closest relatives, the protochordates. In the adult the notochord contributes only to the structure of the vertebrae. The mesoderm lateral to this midline chordamesoderm then divides into three parts: the epimere, nearest the chordamesoderm; the hypomere, farthest away from it; and a small mesomere between these two.

Division of the epimere

Along the length of the embryo, the epimere divides into segmental blocks called somites, which again divide into three cell blocks: closest to the notochord appears the sclerotome, which will form the greater part of the vertebrae; in the middle lies the myotome, which gives rise to somatic muscle; and to the side lies the dermatome, which contributes to the skin. Appendicular muscles form either directly as outgrowths of the myotomes or from wandering cells (mesenchyme) that bud off from the myotomes. The mesomere gives rise only to structures of the urogenital system. The hypomere remains unsegmented, and, except in the region of the neck where it remains a solid mass, it splits longitudinally, giving rise to a central space. This space, together with its counterpart on the other side of the developing body, will eventually form the major cavity of the body, the coelom. The exterior layer gives rise to the lining of the body wall. The interior layer, together with the adjacent epithelial lining of the yolk sac, develops into the muscles of the heart and other viscera. The solid mass of the hypomere in the neck region differentiates to form the various branchiomeric visceral muscles, which are associated with the visceral skeleton, the gill bars, or their derivatives. Posterior to (dorsal to) this region is the developing ear capsule, where the myotomes are rudimentary or absent. Farther forward, however, three more myotomes appear, which give rise to a distinct group of axial muscles, namely the external muscles of the eyes. The first few myotomes behind the ear region typically bend forward at their anterior (ventral) ends to produce slips of muscle that migrate to a position ventral to the gill pouches and that form the hypobranchial musculature (somatic muscles that run between the pectoral skeleton and the jaw).

Comparative anatomy. One problem in discussing the differences in arrangement of muscles between the various vertebrate groups is in deciding which muscles in each species are homologous; that is, which have the same evolutionary and developmental origin. The problem arises because the position and attachment of muscles change during evolution: a muscle lying in the same position and attached to the same bone or cartilage in one vertebrate may have different origins from those of another vertebrate species. Comparison of the development of muscles in the embryo of each species, and of their nerve supply, probably will give the best clues. No single method may be relied upon in all cases, and many different types of evidence are considered before the homology is decided upon.

Origin of muscle names

Vertebrate muscles are given names derived from Latin according to their attachments. In this system, the Latin names of the bony points of attachment are either joined, as in the human "sternocleidomastoid," which runs from the sternum and clavicle to the mastoid region of the skull, or they may be named for their form or their gross function. There are several standard terms that describe form and function. A muscle may have more than one point of origin: thus it may be described as having, for example, two "heads" as in "biceps femoris" (*bi* for two, *-ceps* for heads, *femoris* meaning "of the femur"). It may be long, "longus," or short, "brevis." It may run transversely across a body segment "transversus," or obliquely, "obliquus." It may lie close to the surface, "superficialis," or deep, "profundus." In describing function, flexors are muscles that tend to close the angle made by the two bones to which they are attached, extensors tend to increase the angle. Adductors pull a bone or cartilage closer to the axis of the body, or limb, while abductors pull away from the axis. Rotators turn one bone or cartilage with respect to another, or turn it with respect to the midline. Pronators turn the sole of the foot or the palm of the hand to face the ground, while the opposite function is performed by supinators. Constrictors and sphincters diminish the volume of spaces or the area of structures, and dilators increase them. Because human anatomy is better understood than that of other species, the names of muscles in humans often have been applied to grossly equivalent muscles in animals, a situation that often causes confusion.

Jawless fishes. The earliest known vertebrates were jawless fishes of the class Agnatha, and their only living representatives are the cyclostomes—the lampreys and the hagfishes. The modern agnathans retain much of the general organization of the ancestral vertebrates, and therefore, much of their musculature is relevant to an understanding of the evolution of muscles in more advanced vertebrates.

Cyclostomes

The cyclostomes are free-swimming animals with prominent axial somatic musculature, which during contraction produces undulating waves that propagate from head to tail to produce thrust. The axial muscles form a single segmented mass in which each embryonic myotome has given rise to a strip of muscle running vertically down the side of the fish. These muscle segments, known as myomeres, consist of relatively short fibres that insert into septa of connective tissue, the myocommata, between the adjacent myomeres. There is only a rudimentary axial skeleton and no appendicular skeleton, so there are no limb muscles. The eyes of cyclostomes are degenerate structures, and the six axially derived muscles normally found associated with vertebrate eyes are diminished or absent. The branchiomeric muscles in cyclostomes are represented by a sheet of constrictors that compresses the gill pouches and helps the pumping mechanism draw water through the pharynx to the gills. Other muscles of the branchiomeric series have been modified for specialized feeding functions.

Chondrichthyes

The branchiomeric musculature of more primitive jawless fishes would probably have been similar for each of the gill arches. The sharks and other cartilaginous fishes (the class Chondrichthyes) have modified the structure of the first two arches, the cartilages of the anterior arch forming the mandible and upper jaw (palatoquadrate), and modifications also having taken place in the second, hyoid arch. The posterior five gill arches of more primitive sharks, however, are a good model for the condition in the ancestral jawless fishes. Each arch has a visceral skeleton comprising five cartilages named, from dorsal to ventral, the pharyngobranchial, epibranchial, ceratobranchial, hypobranchial, and basibranchial. The cartilages are arranged at angles to each other. Each cartilaginous arch is provided with a set of branchial muscles, which receives separate, visceral innervation. Superficially, a thin sheet comprising dorsal and ventral constrictor muscles runs in the flap of skin that covers each gill slit and forms the gill septum. Most fibres attach, dorsally and ventrally, to connective tissue sheathing the body (fascia). Some of the deeper fibres attach to the gill bar and may run between adjacent bars. These thin, broad muscles squeeze the pharynx closed as part of the pumping action necessary for gill breathing. Dorsal and deep to this layer, a levator muscle runs from the sheathing fascia to the pharyngobranchial, and it can elevate the gill arch. In some sharks, however, the most posterior sets of levator muscles, whose fibres run diagonally down and back, may join adjacent levators, become enlarged, and attach to the pectoral girdle. This mass is known as the trapezius and evolves into the tetrapod muscle of the same name. Adductor muscles are positioned so as to close the angle between the epibranchial and ceratobranchial, and an interarcual muscle performs the same function for the angle between the pharyngobranchial and epibranchial cartilages.

Myomeres

Jawed fishes. In the jawed fishes, including the sharks, the axial musculature of the trunk and tail (a single block in cyclostomes) differentiates into dorsal and ventral components, which are separated by connective tissue. The dorsal block of muscle is known as the epaxial musculature, and the ventral block, the hypaxial (Figure 10A). The epaxial block runs from the back of the skull to the end of the tail, while the hypaxial block is not present any farther forward than the pectoral (shoulder) girdle (because of the presence of the branchial [gill] apparatus). The hypaxial musculature in the tail forms a solid block of muscle, while in the trunk it encloses the body cavity. Ribs develop in the horizontal septum separating the two blocks of muscle and usually lie in the myocommata, the fascial tissue separating each myomere (Figure 10B). In fishes, the ribs primarily serve to improve the leverage of the myomeres in producing the undulatory movements of swimming. The ribs are short in sharks but may develop to considerable length in bony fishes. Unlike the cyclostomes, where the myomeres form a series of essentially vertical strips of muscle, the myomeres of all jawed fishes are folded in a complex fashion. This development is related to the development of a more powerful swimming ability in the jawed fishes. The myomeres are folded in a zigzag pattern, projecting strongly forward halfway down the side of the fish, with a smaller, backward projection both dorsal and ventral to this point: the effect is of a W on its side. These projections become sharper and more cone-shaped deep to the surface of the fish and thus come both to be overlapped by the folds of several anterior myomeres and to overlap those of several more posterior myomeres. The folding and overlapping of myomeres has the effect that contraction of a single myomere produces curvature over a considerable part of the body of the fish. The fishes who swim faster thus tend to have a greater degree of folding and overlapping. In the tunny, for example, one myomere may have an overlap with 20 others. The undulations of the body and caudal (tail) fin produced by these axial muscles can produce much greater thrust than is produced by the beating of the appendicular fins. The latter are mostly used in slow "precision" swimming, as when a fish is investigating food, while undulations of the body are used for faster, powerful swimming. The axial musculature of fishes contributes up to half the weight of the fish, while the appendicular muscle contributes less than a fifth of the fish's mass.

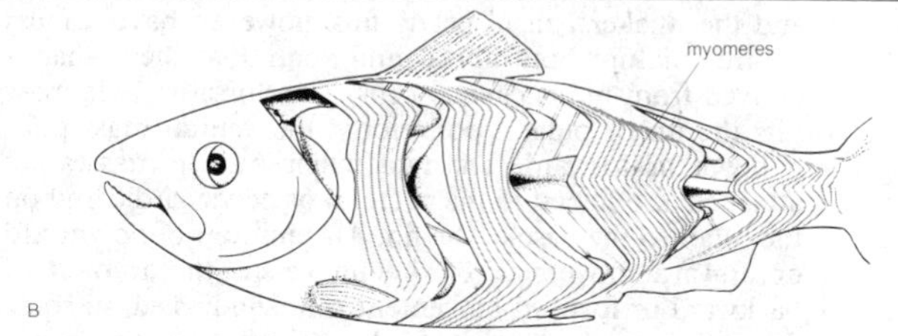

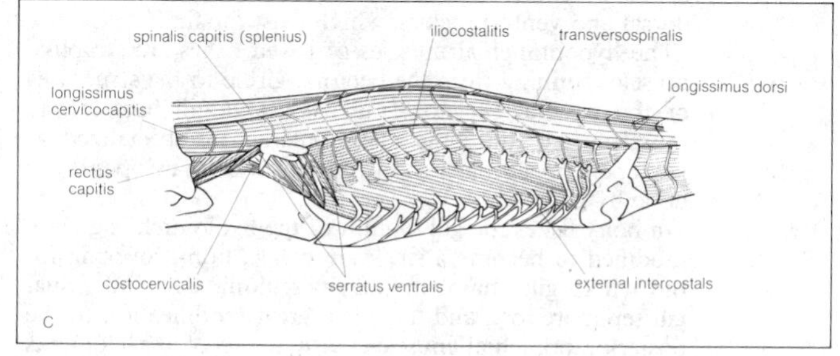

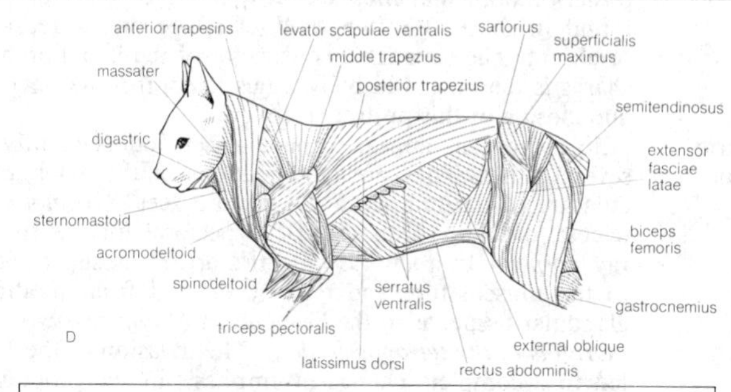

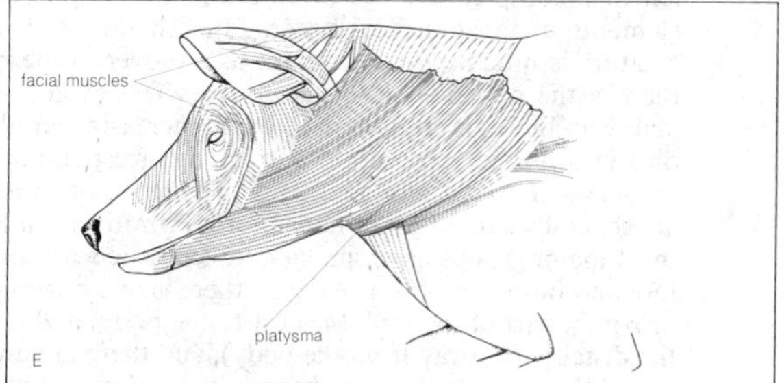

Figure 10: *Vertebrate trunk musculature.*
(A) Lateroventral view of anterior muscles of dogfish. (B) Lateral view of trunk muscles of salmon. (C) Axial muscles in lizard. (D) Lateral view of trunk muscles of a cat. (E) Lateral view of facial muscles of a dog.

From (A) W. Walker, *Vertebrate Dissection*, 4th ed. (1970); W.B. Saunders & Co., and (B,C,E) A. Romer, *The Vertebrate Body* (1964); W.B. Saunders & Co., and (D) *Chordate Anatomy* by H.V. Neal and H.W. Rank. Copyright © 1944 by McGraw-Hill Book Co. Used with permission of McGraw-Hill Book Company

Eye muscles

In all higher vertebrates the most anterior element in the axial musculature is the set of six eye muscles derived from the three pre-otic somites (those anterior to the ear region of the embryo). The rectus muscles move the eyes about the longitudinal axis of the body, that is superiorly (upward), or inferiorly (downward), or about a vertical axis, in other words, laterally (backward) or medially (forward), according to their position relative to the eyeball. They take appropriate names. The oblique muscles, superior and inferior, rotate the eyes about a transverse axis.

Jawed fishes have single midline fins and two sets of paired fins. The unpaired dorsal and anal fins of teleosts (advanced bony fishes) have axially derived muscle sheets on either side, which, when contracted, may change their angle and even fold the fins. The paired pectoral fins and the weaker pair of pelvic fins, however, have a mass of musculature both dorsal and ventral to them that is derived from mesenchymal cells. The dorsal muscle mass lifts the fin or pulls it posteriorly; the ventral mass pulls it down or forward. The two major muscle masses are attached at one end to the pectoral or pelvic girdle and on the other to the base of the fin. The amount of downward or upward movement of the fin versus the amount of backward or forward movement can be adjusted, in some fishes, by small slips of muscle derived from the major dorsal and ventral masses, which twist the fin.

The hypobranchial muscles of jawed fishes are straplike muscles running from the pectoral girdle to the structures of the visceral skeleton, the jaws, and gill bars. Some muscles, like the coracomandibularis, are specialized as jaw openers, although most of the work of jaw opening is done by gravity.

In bony fishes the gill septum of the hyoid arch is greatly modified to become a single, movable, bony covering for the whole gill chamber: the operculum. The individual gill septa are lost, and there is a great modification of the posterior branchial muscles, with many of the elements found in sharks (levators, adductors) becoming reduced or absent. The superficial constrictor of the hyoid arch in sharks is remodeled in bony fishes to control the opening and closing of this protective cover.

Electric organs

Electric organs appear to have arisen independently in several fishes. They are modifications of the axial musculature of the tail, as in the electric "eel" *Gymnotus,* a teleost, or of the muscles of the pectoral fins, as in the ray *Torpedo.* In a few cases electric organs lie superficially to the musculature and may be derived from modified glandular tissue, as in the Nile catfish *Malapterurus.*

Origins of the tetrapod limbs. The invasion of the land led to a complete change in emphasis in the propulsive elements of the muscular system. In fish the axial musculature is much more important as a mover of the body than is the appendicular musculature. The evolution of land vertebrates is characterized by an increasing emphasis on the limbs for propulsion and by a corresponding deemphasis on the axial musculature. The limbs of tetrapods are generally similar in overall pattern. Primitively, at least, most major groups have similar characteristic features: the fore and hind feet have five digits; there is one bone in the proximal part of the limb (nearest to the body) and two in the distal part (away from the body); and there are a wrist or ankle joint, an elbow or knee joint, and a shoulder or hip joint. Although most muscles have several roles, the major actions of tetrapod limb muscles are similar: some primarily resist the downward force of the body at hip and shoulder; others press the supporting fore or hind feet down onto the ground at wrist or ankle or pull back on the supporting limbs (at all three joints) to create thrust; others primarily pull the "swing" limbs forward into a new support position.

The limbs may originally have developed more as supportive struts. Structurally, the tetrapod limb can be derived from the pattern found in the paired fins of Sarcopterygii, a class of lobe-finned fishes. These were once a large radiation but largely have been replaced by the Actinopterygii, the class of ray-finned fishes. Today, the lobe-finned fishes are represented by *Latimeria,* the coelacanth, and the lungfishes, or *Dipnoi.* The lungfishes, denizens of shallow and seasonal waters, habitually use their fins as supports, but propulsion is largely achieved by undulations of the body as is the case with other fish.

Amphibians

Tetrapod musculature. In the living urodeles (the newts and salamanders) of the class Amphibia, the axial muscles are most important for propulsion. The limbs of urodeles are quite weak and tend to be carried forward passively with the undulations of the body. As the primary propulsive force is provided by the muscles of the trunk, urodeles retain large axial muscles. The axial muscles are still segmented, separated by myocommata, although the myomeres run vertically and without the elaborate folding seen in jawed fishes. The epaxial muscles, given the name "dorsalis trunci" in tetrapods, are little changed, although some modification has taken place to promote a facility for dorsoventral bending of the spine that occurs in tetrapods but rarely in fishes.

The anurans (frogs and toads) have rather similar, but considerably reduced, epaxial muscles. There is, however, a trend in tetrapods toward finer control of muscular action with increasing complexity. In the reptiles the epaxial muscles, although still retaining a semisegmental structure, are divided into several structural and functional units. The deepest set of muscles, the transversospinalis group, are short and run obliquely forward, over one to four vertebrae, from the transverse process of one vertebra to the lamina (the flat plate of bone at the base of the vertebral spine) of a more anterior vertebra (Figure 10C). The transversospinalis group is particularly responsible for rotatory movements of the spine. Superficial to transversospinalis lies longissimus, with much longer fibres, which is important in extension of the back. More superficially still, and lateral to these muscle blocks, iliocostalis is a flat, sheetlike muscle that runs from the pelvic girdle upward and laterally to attach to the ribs. It is particularly important in lateral flexion (bending) of the spine. This general pattern is further complicated in snakes, which have secondarily returned to the propulsive use of the axial muscles. In birds the vertebral column of the trunk region undergoes much fusion, and this complexity is reduced, as indeed it is in chelonians (turtles and tortoises). Mammals retain the broad pattern of the reptile epaxial musculature but (with the exception of the innervation of the musculature) have greatly reduced the segmentation that is present in reptiles (Figure 10D and 10E).

Trunk modifications

In the tails of urodeles the hypaxial muscles are also largely unchanged. As with all land vertebrates, however, the demands of support of the viscera when living in an air environment have brought about major modifications of the hypaxial musculature of the trunk. In typical tetrapods a strong series of ribs has developed for the same reason. Although urodeles have secondarily reduced their ribs, they show many of the typically tetrapod features of the hypaxial musculature. The muscles fall into three groups. A group of subvertebral muscles forms ventral to the vertebrae, in the region of their joints with the ribs at the transverse processes. It acts in ventral and lateral flexion (bending) of the spine. A rectus abdominis muscle runs longitudinally along the ventral aspect of the body wall between the pectoral and pelvic girdles, and laterally this is associated with the third group, the lateral hypaxial muscles. This consists of three major layers of muscle whose fibres are oriented in differing directions, a feature that gives additional strength to the body wall. Superficially lies the external oblique muscle, with fibres running longitudinally but somewhat ventrally; deep to this lies the internal oblique, with fibres running longitudinally and somewhat dorsally; and deepest lies the transversus muscle, whose fibres run dorsoventrally.

In the higher tetrapods the external and internal obliques tend to become further divided into layers in the abdominal region. The thoracic representatives of these muscles tend to become divided into discontinuous, rather thin muscle layers between the ribs (external and internal intercostals), superficial to the ribs (supercostals), and deep to the ribs (subcostals). While only the rectus abdominis tends to retain visible evidence of segmental origin, in its tendinous intersections (which are present even in humans) the segmental innervation of the hypaxial muscles is retained in all tetrapods.

Pectoral girdle

In tetrapods, unlike fishes, the pectoral girdle does not have a solid bony connection to the axial skeleton but rather is supported by a series of muscles derived from the outer layer of hypaxial trunk muscles. This is no doubt another adaptation to life in an air environment, where the cushioning effect of water has been lost. These muscular slings are not readily demonstrated in the living amphibians, which are either skeletally degenerate as in urodeles or highly specialized toward leaping, as in the anurans (frogs and toads). In more typical tetrapods, there are two major derivatives of the external oblique attaching the scapula (shoulder blade) to the body: first, the serratus, made up of numerous fingerlike slips running from the scapula to the neighbouring ribs; second, levator scapulae, which are fused with serratus along its caudal (tail-end) border. Levator scapulae consist of fibres running more anteriorly to ribs or transverse processes of the neck. Mammals, and some reptiles, have a third such muscle, attaching the pectoral girdle to the region of the spine, called rhomboideus. The mammals also have utilized part of the hypaxial musculature to form a muscular septum between the region of the lungs and heart (the thoracic cavity) and the region of the digestive and reproductive viscera (the abdominal cavity). This is the diaphragm, which is the most important respiratory muscle in the mammalian body.

Eye movements

The six axially derived eye muscles of fishes undergo only small modifications in tetrapods. Eye movements are changed, partly according to changes in the orientation of the orbit such as the trend toward orbital frontality that is typical in the primates. Additional eye muscles may be derived by splitting some of these six muscles. An example of this is the retractor bulbi muscle, which is derived from the lateral rectus muscle. In amphibians and some reptiles it pulls the eyeball deeper into the orbit for protection, and in amphibians it is an aid in swallowing. Another example is the levator palpebrae superioris, derived from the superior rectus, which elevates the upper eyelid to open the eye.

The limb muscles of typical tetrapods are derived from the dorsal and ventral muscle blocks of the paired fins of fishes. In tetrapod development, this pattern of derivation from dorsal and ventral muscle blocks is repeated. As a consequence, the homologies of the muscles of the typical tetrapod limb often can be traced by considering the source of innervation of each muscle from the nerves of the dorsal (or extensor) compartment or the ventral (or flexor) compartment.

Latissimus dorsi

In the pectoral limb, the dorsal, extensor group of muscles includes several that appear consistently and with similar roles. Beginning with the muscles that act on the humerus (the proximal bone of the limb), all tetrapods have a large, sheetlike muscle, known as the latissimus dorsi, which runs from the side of the trunk to the humerus. The latissimus dorsi muscle retracts the humerus and thus propels the body forward. Acting to rotate, flex, or adduct the humerus, depending on limb posture, is a muscle known as subcoracoscapularis in amphibians, reptiles, and birds and subscapularis in mammals. It runs from the deep surface of the shoulder girdle to the humerus. In amphibians, the dorsalis scapulae arise from the anterior edge of the scapula. The same muscle is known as the deltoideus in reptiles and mammals, and in the latter, part of its origin moves from the scapula to the clavicle (collar bone). It is a major abductor of the shoulder in most tetrapods. At the elbow joint, all tetrapods have a muscle called triceps as the major extensor. It arises in several heads from the shoulder girdle and humerus. There are always a variable number of extensor muscles for the wrist and digits (fingers and toes) arising from the region of the elbow joint, on the lateral aspect of the humerus.

On the ventral, flexor aspect of the pectoral limb, the pectoralis is found in all tetrapods. The pectoralis runs from the chest wall to the humerus, on which it acts to pull the humerus downward and backward. This muscle is not only important in providing forward thrust in quadrupedal locomotion but is the chief depressor of the forelimb in birds and bats. The major elevator of the wing in birds, supracoracoideus, is present in all tetrapods. In mammals, the supracoracoideus retains its attachment to the humerus, but its previous point of origin (the coracoid plate) disappears and the muscle now appears as two separate blocks of muscle arising on either side of the spine of the scapula as an abductor muscle (supraspinatus) and a rotator and flexor (infraspinatus). Coracobrachialis and (except in amphibians) biceps arise from the tip of the coracoid and act to flex the elbow. In this they are aided by the brachialis muscle, which arises from the humerus. As on the extensor aspect, there are always a number of flexors of the wrist and digits. These arise on the medial side of the distal humerus.

Effect of limb posture

The muscles of the pelvic limb cannot be readily compared beyond the reptiles and mammals. Even in these cases, changes in limb posture have led to major changes in the arrangement and function of muscles. On the dorsal aspect, a single, large muscle in reptiles, puboischiofemoralis, runs from the bones of the pelvis to the femur (the proximal bone of the hind limb). This reptilian muscle appears to be represented by three mammalian hip muscles: psoas, iliacus, and pectineus. Iliofemoralis acts as an abductor of the hip in reptiles and appears to be represented by the gluteal muscles in mammals, but the function of the gluteal muscles is different. More similar in reptiles and mammals is the quadriceps or quadratus femoris, which consists of multiple heads (four in mammals) that arise from the pelvic girdle and femur and insert by a common tendon into the tibia (the larger bone of the distal pectoral limb). It is the sole extensor of the knee joint in both the reptiles and the mammals. The extensors of the ankle and digits in both reptiles and mammals are not dissimilar to those of the pectoral limb and take origin from the lateral and anterior surfaces of the two distal bones of the pelvic limb. On the ventral aspect of the hind limb, small, deep muscles run from the internal and external pelvis to the head of the femur and help in adduction and rotation. Of these, the puboischiofemoralis externus of reptiles appears to be represented by the obturator externus of mammals, and similarly the ischiotrochantericus of reptiles appears to be the homologue of the obturator internus of mammals. Again, the major adductor of the hip of reptiles, adductor femoris, appears to be homologous with some of the muscles called the adductors in mammals.

Reptile and mammal homologies

There seem to be some homologies between the major flexors of the hip and thigh in reptiles, such as puboischiotibialis, and two deeper muscles, flexor tibialis externus and internus, and some functionally equivalent muscles in mammals: the gracilis, semimembranosus, and semitendinosus. In reptiles, the axial muscle of the tail is strong, and the caudifemoralis, a powerful flexor of the thigh which originates in the tail, is consequently large. The tail in mammals, although usually present, is much more gracile, and as a result caudofemoralis is represented by only a few small muscles. Another major change is in the flexors of ankle and digits. In reptiles, these insert by long tendons passing below the ankle joint, much as in the forelimb. In mammals, however, the equivalent long flexor, gastrocnemius, inserts on a new bony process, the calcaneal tuberosity or heel bone, which gives more efficient leverage.

The hypobranchial muscles of tetrapods are both reduced and modified in comparison with those of jawed fishes. In tetrapods these straplike muscles still arise from elements of the pectoral girdle but now pass to the new derivatives of the gill arches of fishes: the hyoid bone and laryngeal cartilages. They act primarily in the gross movements of these structures in swallowing and the production of sound—for example, as depressors of the hyoid (sternohyoid, omohyoid) or of the larynx (sternothyroid). Fibres of the hypobranchial muscles in the region of the hyoid are utilized to form the internal musculature of the tongue.

The branchial musculature is also modified in tetrapods from the condition seen in jawed fishes. The development of a shoulder muscle, the trapezius, from the levator muscles of the gill arches of fishes, as previously discussed, is taken further in tetrapods, by the separation of further slips of muscle to form muscles such as sternocleidomastoid, a muscle important for humans in movements of the head and in breathing. In mammals that lose the clavicle, these slips may further be modified to form muscles running from the head to the pectoral limb. Tetrapods, with the exception of mammals, utilize part of the constrictor muscle of the hyoid arch to form the depressor mandibulae, which replaces the hypobranchial muscles as the major jaw-opening muscle. The restructuring of the posterior jaw in mammals leads to the further replacement of this new muscle by the digastric, which is a compound muscle made up of parts of the constrictors of the first and second branchial arches. Thus it is partly innervated by the mandibular division of the fifth cranial nerve (as is the case with other jaw muscles and the tensor tympani, one of the muscles of the ear), and partly by the seventh cranial nerve, the facial nerve (which also supplies an ear muscle associated with the stapes, an ear bone derived from the hyoid arch). The levator palatoquadrati, which elevates the upper jaw in jawed fishes, is retained as a jaw muscle in birds and in some reptiles, as they share the ability of fishes to move the upper jaw. The adductor mandibulae is much altered in tetrapods, although its overall function is retained. During the course of tetrapod evolution it becomes a superficial muscle, and in mammals it splits into several functional units arising from the undersurface and side of the skull and attaching to various points on the mandible. These are: the lateral pterygoid, which pulls the jaw forward; the medial pterygoid and its partner, the masseter, which close the jaw and move it from side to side; and the temporalis, which closes the jaw and pulls it backward. All are innervated by the first-arch cranial nerve, the fifth nerve. The intermandibularis of jawed fishes is retained as the mylohyoid of tetrapods, which is an elevator of the tongue.

Restructuring of the mammal jaw

Finally, the constrictor muscle of the hyoid arch, which in bony fishes is used to control the operculum, is remodeled in tetrapods as a sheathing superficial muscle of the neck, the sphincter colli. It derives its innervation from the nerve of the hyoid arch, the seventh, or facial, nerve. This cranial nerve is named from the further adaptation of the sphincter colli muscle in mammals, particularly in higher primates, as the many small muscles of facial expression, which allow people to smile, laugh, and frown.

MODIFICATIONS FOR UPRIGHT POSTURE AND HUMAN MUSCULATURE

Human muscles

Human muscle can be divided into striated (or skeletal), smooth, and cardiac. With a very few exceptions, the arrangement of smooth and cardiac muscle has undergone little modification with the assumption of the upright posture. A discussion of the changes in the striated, or somatic, muscles follows.

Evolutionary context. The arrangement of striated muscle in modern humans conforms to the basic pronograde (horizontal) quadrupedal vertebrate and mammaliam plan that was outlined in an earlier section. The primates inherited the primitive quadrupedal stance and locomotion, but since their appearance in the Cretaceous Period, several groups have modified their locomotor system to concentrate on the use of the arms for propulsion through the trees. The most extreme expression of this skeletal adaptation in living primates is seen in the modern gibbon family. Their forelimbs are relatively elongated; they hold their trunk erect; and for the short periods that they spend on the ground they walk only on their hind limbs (in a bipedal fashion).

Modern humans are most closely related to the living great apes, the orangutan, chimpanzee, and gorilla. Their most distant relative in the group, the orangutan, has a locomotor system that is adapted for moving among the vertical tree trunks of the Asian rain forests. It grips these trunks equally well with both fore and hind limbs and was at one time aptly called quadrumanal, or "four-handed."

Human ancestor

There is little direct fossil evidence about the common ancestor of modern humans, chimpanzees, and gorillas, so inferences about its habitat and locomotion must be made. The ancestor was most likely a relatively generalized tree-dwelling animal that could walk quadrupedally along branches as well as climb between them. From such an ancestor, two locomotor trends were apparently derived. In one, which led to the gorillas and the chimpanzees, the forelimbs became elongated so that when these modern animals come to the ground they support their trunks by placing the knuckles of their outstretched forelimbs on the ground. The second trend involved shortening the trunk, relocating the shoulder blades, and, most importantly, steadily increasing the emphasis on hind limb support and truncal erectness. In other words, this trend saw the achievement of an upright bipedal, or orthograde, posture instead of a quadrupedal, or pronograde, one. The upright posture probably was quite well established by 3,000,000 to 3,500,000 years ago, as evidenced both by the form of the limb bones and by the preserved footprints of early hominids found from this time.

Muscles of the lower limb. The major muscular changes directly associated with the shift to bipedal locomotion are seen in the lower limb. The obvious skeletal changes are in the length of the hind limb, the development of the heel, and the change in the shape of the knee joint so that its surface is flat and not evenly rounded (Figures 11, 12, and 13). The hind limbs of modern humans are proportional to body size, while the hind limbs of the apes are relatively short for their body size. The changes that occur in the bones of the pelvis are not all directly related to the shift in locomotion, but they are a consequence of it. Bipedality, by freeing the hands from primary involvement with support and locomotion, enabled the development of manual dexterity, and thus the manufacture and use of tools, which has been linked to the development in human ancestors of language and other intellectual capacities. The result is a substantially enlarged brain. Large brains clearly

Effect of bipedality

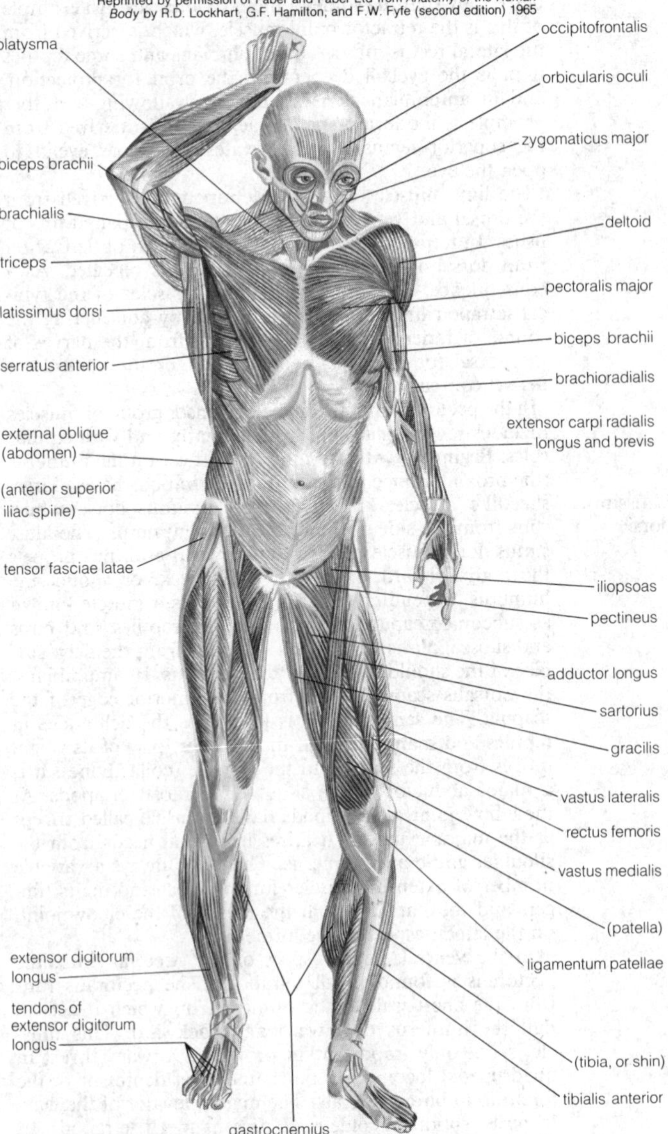

Figure 11: Anterior aspect of the human muscular system. Platysma removed on the left.

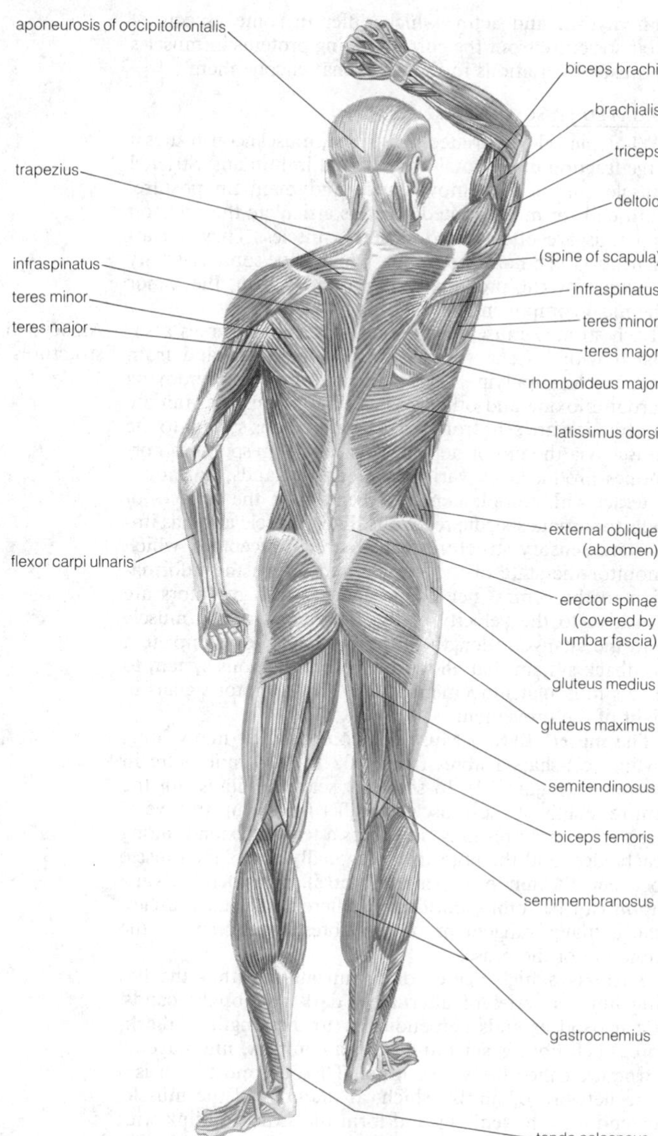

Figure 12: Posterior aspect of the human muscular system.

Reprinted by permission of Faber and Faber Ltd from *Anatomy of the Human Body* by R.D. Lockhart, G.F. Hamilton, and F.W. Fyfe (second edition) 1965

affect the form of the skull, and thus the musculature of the head and neck. A larger brain also has a direct effect on the pelvis because of the need for a wide pelvic inlet and outlet for the birth of relatively large-brained young. The larger pelvic cavity means that the hip joints have to be farther apart. Consequently, the hip joints are subjected to considerable forces when weight is taken on one leg, as it has to be in walking and running.

To counteract this, the muscles (gluteus minimus and gluteus medius) that are used by the chimpanzee to push the leg back (hip extensors) have shifted in modern humans in relation to the hip joint so that they now act as abductors to balance the trunk on the weight-bearing leg during walking. Part of a third climbing muscle (gluteus maximus) also assists in abduction as well as in maintaining the knee in extension during weight bearing. The gluteal muscles are also responsible for much of the rotation of the hip that has to accompany walking. When the right leg is swung forward and the right foot touches the ground, the hip joint of the same side externally rotates whereas that of the opposite side undergoes a similar amount of internal rotation. Both these movements are made possible by rearrangements of the muscles crossing the hip.

The bones of the trunk and the lower limb are so arranged in modern humans that to stand upright requires a minimum of muscle activity. Some muscles, however, are essential to maintaining balance, and the extensors of the knee have been rearranged and realigned, as have the muscles of the calf.

Human foot

The foot is often, but erroneously, considered to be a poor relation of the hand. Although the toes in modern humans are normally incapable of useful independent movement, the flexor muscles of the big toe (hallux) are developed to provide the final push-off in the walking cycle. Muscles of all three compartments of the modern human lower leg contribute to making the foot a stable platform, which nonetheless can adapt to walking over rough and sloping ground.

Muscles of the upper limb. The major changes in the musculature of the upper limb involve the secondary effects that result from freeing the forelimb from a major supportive or propulsive role. The hand of a chimpanzee is dexterous, but the proportions of the digits and the rearrangement and supplementation of muscles are the major reasons for the greater manipulative ability of modern humans. Most of these changes are concentrated on the thumb. For example, modern humans are the only living great apes to have a separate long thumb flexor, and the short muscle that swings the thumb over toward the palm is particularly well developed in humans. This contributes to the movement of opposition that is crucial for the so-called precision grip; *i.e.,* the bringing together of the tips of the thumb and forefinger.

Pronation and supination of the forearm, which allows the palm of the hand to rotate 180 degrees, is not peculiar to humans. This movement depends upon the possession of both a small disk in the wrist joint and on an arrangement of the muscles such that they can rotate the radius to and fro. Both the disk and the muscle arrangement are present in other great apes.

Muscles of the head and neck. The muscle group of the head and neck is most directly influenced by the change to an upright posture. This group constitutes the muscles of the back (nape) and side of the neck. Posture is not the only influence on these muscles, for the reduction in the size of the jaws in modern humans also contributes to the observed muscular differences. Generally, these involve the reduction in bulk of nuchal (or nape) muscles. In the upright posture the head is more evenly balanced on the top of the vertebral column, so less muscle force is needed, whereas in a pronograde animal with large jaws, the considerable torque developed at the base of the skull must be resisted by muscle force. The poise of the human head does pose other problems, and the detailed attachment and role of some neck muscles (*e.g.,* sternocleidomastoid) is different in humans than in the apes.

Muscles of the trunk. The consequences of an upright posture for the support of both the thoracic and abdominal viscera are profound, but the muscular modifications in the trunk are few. Whereas in pronograde animals the abdominal viscera are supported by the ventral abdominal wall, in the orthograde posture most support comes from the pelvis. This inevitably places greater strain on the passage through the muscles of the anterior abdominal wall, the inguinal canal, which marks the route taken by the descending testicle in the male. Weakness in the canal can result in herniation.

Differences are also seen in the musculature (the levator ani) that supports the floor of the pelvis and that also controls the passage of feces. The loss of a tail in all the apes has led to a major rearrangement of this muscle. There is more overlap and fusion between the various parts of the levator ani in modern humans than in the apes, and the muscular sling that comprises the puborectalis in humans is more substantial than in the apes. (B.Wo./R.H.C.)

Muscle types

PRIMITIVE CONTRACTILE SYSTEMS

Cilia and flagella. Unicellular organisms such as the paramecium, a protozoan that lives in freshwater ponds and streams, propel themselves by the action of cilia. Cilia occur in large numbers and move in a coordinated way. Ciliated cells within the vertebrate body propel fluid and mucus along interior passages, such as the lining of the respiratory tract.

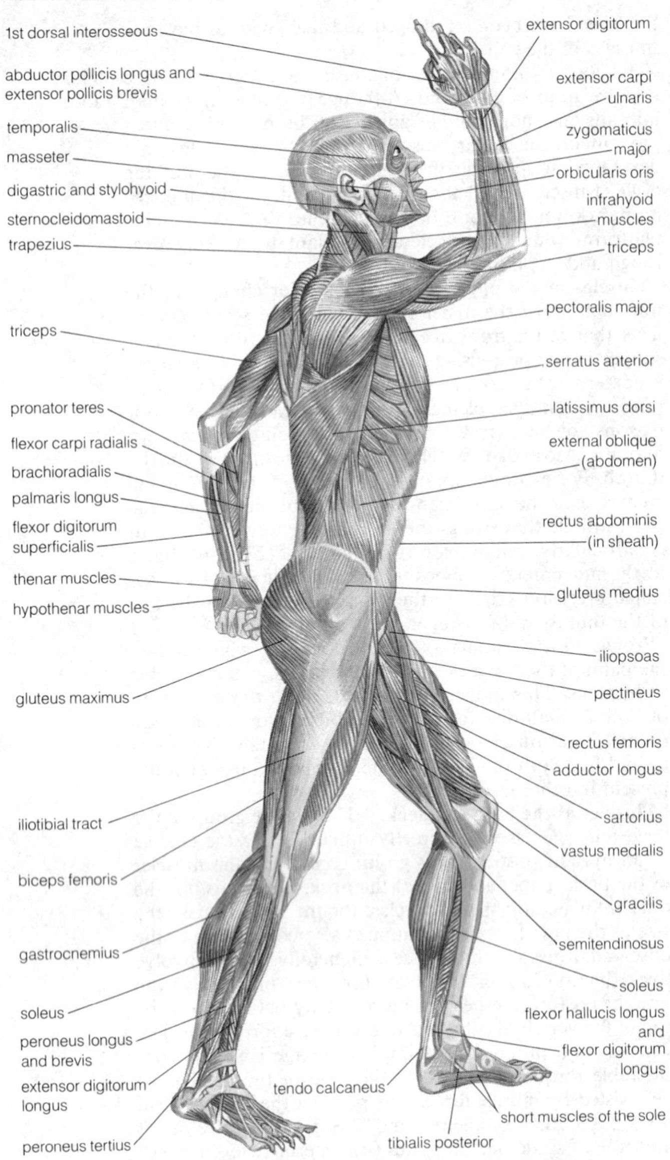

Figure 13: Lateral aspect of the human muscular system.

Reprinted by permission of Faber and Faber Ltd from *Anatomy of the Human Body* by R.D. Lockhart, G.F. Hamilton, and F.W. Fyfe (second edition) 1965

Flagella are structurally similar to cilia, except that they are longer (sometimes up to 50 times longer) than cilia and usually number only one or two per cell. Sperm cells of most higher organisms move using flagella. Many types of unicellular algae and protozoans use flagella in swimming through the water.

Pattern of tubules

Both cilia and flagella contain a regular pattern of tubules extending along their lengths; there is an outer ring of nine pairs of tubules surrounding a central pair of tubules. Each tubule is composed of filaments comprising a string of globular subunits. The movement of a cilium or a flagellum requires energy, which is obtained from the breakdown of adenosine triphosphate (ATP), catalyzed by a protein attached to the outer tubules, dynein.

Some types of bacteria have flagella whose motion seems to depend on a cellular particle called the basal body, to which the flagellum is attached. Such flagella derive their energy from a difference in hydrogen ion concentration across the cell membrane.

Amoeboid motion. Amoeboid movement occurs as an extension of the cytoplasm, called a pseudopod ("false foot"), flows outward, deforms the cell boundary, and is followed by the rest of the cell. Many pseudopodia may be formed at the same time, and their actions do not seem to be coordinated.

Although amoeboid motion is characteristic of the amoeba, a unicellular protozoan, it is also found in nonmuscle cells of multicellular organisms. These cells contain myosin and actin, which differ in some aspects of their structure from the corresponding proteins in muscles because of variations in the genes that encode them.

STRIATED MUSCLE

Whole muscle. Striated, or striped, muscle constitutes a large fraction of the total body weight in humans. Striated muscle contracts to move limbs and maintain posture. Both ends of most striated muscles articulate the skeleton and thus are often called skeletal muscles. They are attached to the bones by tendons, which have some elasticity provided by the proteins collagen and elastin, the major chemical components of tendons.

Associated structures

Each striated muscle has blood vessels and nerves associated with it. The vessels transport blood to and from the muscle, supplying oxygen and nutrients and removing carbon dioxide and other wastes. The signals that initiate contraction are sent from the central nervous system to the muscle via the motor nerves. Muscles also respond to hormones produced by various endocrine glands; hormones interact with complementary receptors on the surfaces of cells to initiate specific reactions. Each muscle also has important sensory structures called stretch receptors, which monitor the state of the muscle and return the information to the central nervous system. Stretch receptors are sensitive to the velocity of the movement of the muscle and the change in length of the muscle. They complete a feedback system that allows the central nervous system to assess muscular movement and to adjust motor signals in light of the movement.

The muscle fibre. Muscle is composed of many long, cylindrical-shaped fibres from 0.02 to 0.08 millimetre in diameter (Figure 14). In some muscles the fibres run the entire length of the muscle (parallel fibres), up to several tens of centimetres long. In others a tendon extends along each edge, and the fibres run diagonally across the muscle between the tendons (pennate fibres). Considerable variation can be found among the different skeletal muscles, the actual arrangement of the fibres depending on the function of the muscle.

There is a high degree of organization within the living fibre, a series of alternately dark and bright bands. Each band extends perpendicular to the length of the fibre. Each fibre is surrounded by a complex, multilayered structure called the sarcolemma. The outermost layer is a fine network of fibrils, which, at the ends of the muscle, extend into the tendons and form the structural link with them. The next layer of the sarcolemma is a foundation, or basement, membrane. The innermost layer is a plasma membrane similar to the ones that surround most cells. The plasma membrane consists of a lipid bilayer with proteins embedded in it. Some of the proteins are embedded entirely within the lipid layer; others extend to one or the other surface; still others span the whole width of the two layers. These proteins represent enzymes, receptors, and various channels (such as those involved in the movement of ions between the exterior and interior of the cell). The plasma membrane maintains the electrical potential, which plays a major role in stimulating muscle contraction.

Sarcoplasm

Sarcoplasm is the cytoplasm of a muscle fibre. It is a water solution containing ATP and phosphagens, as well as the enzymes and intermediate and product molecules involved in many metabolic reactions. The most abundant metal in the sarcoplasm is potassium. Sodium and magnesium are present in lower concentrations. Most of the calcium of muscle is bound to proteins or stored in the sarcoplasmic reticulum. Contraction is initiated by the release of calcium ions (Ca^{2+}) upon the depolarization of the membrane, which is induced by nerve impulses.

Each striated muscle cell, or fibre, contains many nuclei. This is the result of the fusion of singly nucleated cells that occurs during the embryological development of striated muscle. After fusion, the cells never again divide.

Mitochondria in the sarcoplasm of the muscle fibre contain the enzymes involved in the Krebs cycle and in oxidative phosphorylation. Granules in the sarcoplasm of muscle cells contain glycogen, the storage form of carbohydrate. The breakdown of glycogen and the metabolism of

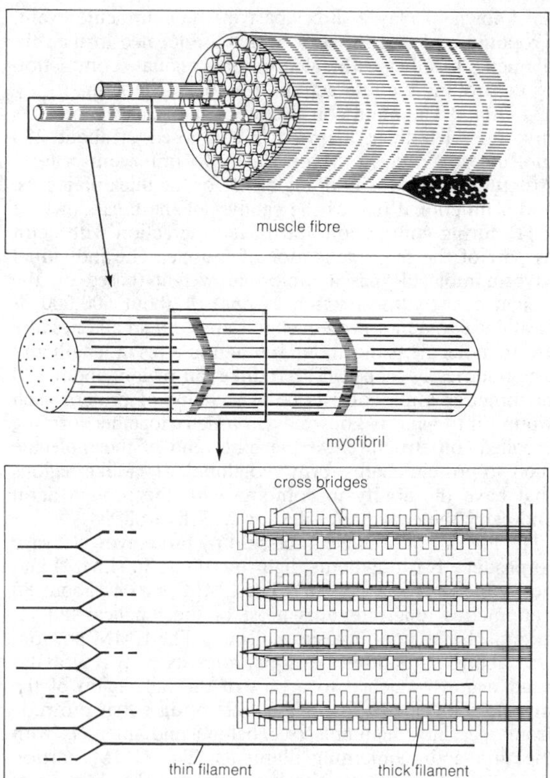

Figure 14: The spatial relationships of a striated muscle fibre, myofibrils, and sarcomeres (see text).
From E.P. Hammel, V.M.D., and K.M. Friedenberg, J. Vet. Med., M.R.C.V.S., in *Equine Medicine and Surgery*, ed. by E.J. Catcott (1972); American Veterinary Publications

the individual units of the resulting carbohydrate through glycolysis, the Krebs cycle, and oxidative phosphorylation are important sources of ATP, the immediate source of energy for muscle contraction. Muscles that contain many fibres that operate at a steady, low level of activity are red, owing to the presence of cytochromes (molecules involved in oxidative phosphorylation) and myoglobin (an oxygen-carrying molecule in the sarcoplasm). Muscles that work in bursts of activity contain fibres that have fewer mitochondria and fewer molecules of cytochromes or myoglobin, are white, and depend more heavily on reactions that do not require oxygen to make ATP.

The myofibril. Electron micrographs of thin sections of muscle fibres reveal groups of filaments oriented with their axes parallel to the length of the fibre. There are two sizes of filaments, thick and thin. Each array of filaments, called a myofibril, is shaped like a cylindrical column. Along the length of each myofibril alternate sets of thick and thin filaments (Figure 14) overlap, or interdigitate, presenting alternate bands of dark regions (with thick filaments and overlapping thin ones) and light regions (with only thin filaments). Within a fibre all the myofibrils are in register, so that the regions of similar density lie next to each other, giving the fibre the characteristic striated appearance it shows in the phase-contrast or polarized light microscope. Each light region is divided in two by a dark band. The unit between two dark bands is known as a sarcomere.

Each myofibril is about one or two micrometres (or microns; one micrometre = 10^{-6} metre) in diameter and extends the entire length of the muscle fibre. The number of myofibrils per fibre varies. At the end of the fibre the myofibrils are attached to the plasma membrane by the intervention of specialized proteins.

Forty to 80 nanometres usually separate adjacent myofibrils in a fibre. This space contains two distinct systems of membranes involved in the activation of muscle contraction (Figure 15). One system is a series of channels that open through the sarcolemma to the extra-fibre space.

Transverse tubules

These channels are called the transverse tubules because they run across the fibre. The transverse tubular system is a network of interconnecting rings, each of which surrounds a myofibril. It provides an important communication pathway between the outside of the fibre and the myofibrils, some of which are located deep inside the fibre. The exact spatial relationship of the tubules to the filaments in the myofibril depends on the species of animal.

The other membrane system that surrounds each myofibril is the sarcoplasmic reticulum, a series of closed saclike membranes. Each segment of the sarcoplasmic reticulum forms a cufflike structure surrounding a myofibril. The portion in contact with the T tubule forms an enlarged sac (terminal cisterna).

Associated cisternae

In most vertebrates each transverse tubule has two cisternae closely associated with it, forming a three-element complex called a triad. The number of triads per sarcomere depends on the species: in frog muscle there is one per triad; in mammalian muscle there are two. In fishes and crustaceans only one cisterna is associated with each transverse tubule, thus forming a dyad. The sarcoplasmic reticulum controls the level of calcium ions in the sarcoplasm. The terminal cisternae apparently are the sites from which the calcium ions are released when the muscle is stimulated, and the longitudinal tubules are the sites at which calcium ions are effectively removed from the sarcoplasm. The removal of calcium ions (Ca^{2+}) from the sarcoplasm is accomplished by a protein that catalyzes the breakdown of ATP making the free energy of hydrolysis available for the energy-requiring process of Ca^{2+} transport.

The myofilament. As mentioned earlier, the myofibril is a columnlike array of filaments. Figure 15 is a diagram of a longitudinal section through a group of myofibrils. In the centre of the I band (the light band, of low density) there is a prominent dense line called the Z line, though in reality, considering the three-dimensional structure of the myofibril, it is more appropriate to speak of Z disks. The area between two Z lines, a sarcomere, can be considered to be the primary structural and functional unit directly responsible for muscle contraction. The myofibril can thus be thought of as a stack of sarcomeres. The A band, which contains thick filaments partly overlapped with thin filaments, appears dark.

Cross bridges. At high magnification small bridgelike structures can be seen on the thick filaments extending toward the thin filaments in the overlap region (Figure 14). They are called cross bridges and are believed to be responsible for the movement and force developed during contraction (for the relation of cross bridges to the molecular architecture of thick filaments, see below). In the middle of the A band, where only thick filaments are present, is a region called the H zone; it looks somewhat

From *Journal of Cell Biology* (1965)

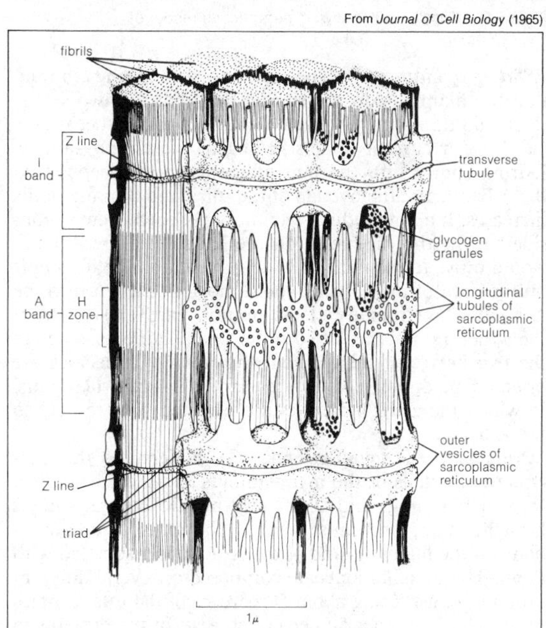

Figure 15: Ultrastructure of a group of myofibrils, showing the sarcoplasmic reticulum and transverse tubules, which constitute the two membrane systems within a muscle fibre.

lighter than the overlap region of the A band. Also in the A band is a narrow, lightly stained region that contains bare thick filaments without cross bridges and is called the pseudo-H zone. In the centre of the A band is a narrow, darkly stained region called the M band, in which occur fine bridges between the thick filaments. These bridges differ from the cross bridges between the thick and thin filaments and are in fact composed of an entirely different protein.

If cross sections of the myofibril at different levels of the sarcomere are examined in the electron microscope, the filaments can be seen end-on, and the three-dimensional nature of the lattice of filaments can be appreciated (Figure 16). The I band contains only thin filaments, with a diameter of six to eight nanometres. In the A band, in the overlap region, the thin filaments appear with thick ones (diameter of 12 nanometres) in an extremely regular pattern or lattice. In vertebrates the thick filaments are arranged in a hexagonal lattice and the thin ones are located at the centre of the equilateral triangles formed by the thick filaments. Sections through the H zone contain only thick filaments arranged in the same hexagonal pattern they form in the overlap region. In the M band the hexagonal array of thick filaments can be seen with M bridges running between them.

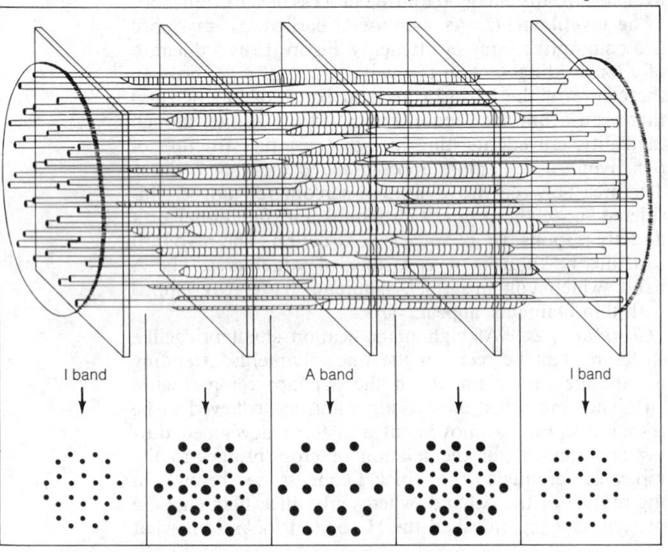

Figure 16: Muscle fibril, showing perspective model of the sarcomere.

Sliding of filaments. The discovery that during contraction the filaments do not shorten but that the two sets—thick and thin—merely move relative to each other is crucial for our current understanding of muscle physiology. During contraction the thin filaments move deeper into the A band, and the overlap of the thick and thin filaments increases. If a longitudinal section of the sarcomere is considered, the thin filaments on the left side of the A band would move to the right into the A band and the filaments on the right of the A band would move to the left into the A band. Directionality of the motion partly results from the structural polarity of both the thick filaments, since in the two halves of the filament the myosin molecules are oriented in opposite directions, and the actin filaments, in which the actin molecules are oriented with respect to the Z bands.

Filaments during contraction

Proteins of the myofilaments. To understand the finer structural details of the myofilaments and the mechanism by which sliding, and ultimately muscle contraction, is brought about one must turn to the molecular components of the filaments and of the structures associated with them. The myofilaments are composed of several different proteins, constituting about 50 percent of the total protein in muscle. The other 50 percent consists of the proteins in the Z line and M band, the enzymes in the sarcoplasm and mitochondria, collagen, and the proteins in membrane structures. Of the myofilament proteins, myosin and actin are known to play a direct part in the contractile event. Troponin and tropomyosin, which are located in the thin filaments together with calcium ions, regulate contraction by controlling the interaction of myosin and actin.

Myosin. The main constituent of the thick filaments is myosin. Each thick filament is composed of about 250 molecules of myosin. Myosin has two important roles: a structural one as the building block for the thick filaments; and a functional one as the catalyst of the breakdown of ATP during contraction and in its interaction with actin as part of the force generator of muscle. The individual myosin molecule has a molecular weight (based on the weight of a hydrogen atom as one) of about 500,000; it contains two major protein chains and four small ones, the entire molecule being about 160 nanometres in length and asymmetrically shaped. The rodlike tail region, about 120 nanometres long, consists of two chains of protein each wound into what is known as an α-helix together forming a coiled-coil structure. At the other end of the molecule the two protein chains form two globular headlike regions that have the ability to combine with the protein actin and carry the enzymatic sites for ATP hydrolysis.

Role of myosin

The myosin molecule can be split by proteolytic cleavage to produce two fragments, light meromyosin (LMM) and heavy meromyosin (HMM). The LMM portion, about 80 nanometres long, contains most of the α-helical tail region of the original myosin molecule. The HMM portion, also about 80 nanometres long, consists of two globular head regions attached to a part of the tail region of the myosin molecule. It forms the cross bridges that protrude from the thick filaments (see below) and interacts with the thin actin-containing filaments. The HMM portion contains the enzymatic site that catalyzes the splitting of ATP. Under appropriate conditions single myosin heads (subfragment-1, or S-1) and actin binding ability also can be obtained.

There are some structural differences in myosins isolated from different muscles within the same animal and from muscles at different stages of development. These so-called isoforms are products of genes belonging to a family. Some differences in corresponding protein components are due to different ways of processing the messenger RNA produced by the same gene. While the basic pattern of myosin structure is preserved, there are many differences in the sequence of amino acids (primary structure). Many other proteins involved in muscle contraction (*e.g.,* actin, troponin) also have isoforms characteristic of different types of muscle.

Isoforms

Thick filament assembly. In the middle portion of the thick filament the molecules are assembled in a tail-to-tail fashion. Along the rest of the filament they are arranged head to tail. The tail parts of the molecules form the core of the filament: the head portions project out from the filament. The cross bridges are actually the globular head regions of myosin molecules extending outward from the filament, and the smooth pseudo-H zone is the region of tail-to-tail aggregation in which there are only tails and no heads.

The precise three-dimensional arrangement of the cross bridges projecting from the thick filament cannot be seen easily in electron micrographs but can be determined from X-ray diffraction study of living muscle (Figure 17). The three bridges project 120 degrees from the opposite sides of the filament every 14.3 nanometres along the length of the filament. Each successive set of bridges is located in a position rotated 40 degrees farther around the filament. The pattern of nine bridges (three sets of three bridges) repeats itself every 42.9 nanometres along the thick filament. Some variation may exist from species to species and muscle to muscle.

Thin filament proteins. The thin filaments contain three different proteins—actin, tropomyosin, and troponin. The latter is actually a complex of three proteins.

Actin, which constitutes about 25 percent of the protein of myofilaments, is the major component of the thin filaments in muscle. An individual molecule of actin is a single protein chain coiled to form a roughly egg-shaped unit. Actin in this form, called globular actin or G-actin, has one calcium or magnesium ion and one molecule of

Actin

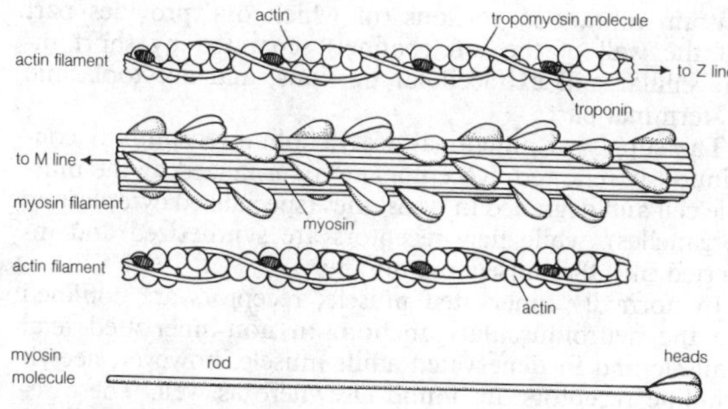

Figure 17: *The structure of actin and myosin filaments.* Actin filaments consist of globular (not strictly spherical) actin monomers, long strands of tropomyosin molecules, and the regulatory protein complex troponin. The myosin filament consists of a backbone made up of the rod parts of many myosin molecules (at bottom), with two myosin heads in each molecule projecting from the surface of the backbone.

Adapted from J.M. Squire, *Muscle: Design, Diversity, and Disease* (1986); The Benjamin/Cummings Publishing Co.

ATP bound to it. Under the proper conditions G-actin is transformed into the fibrous form, or F-actin, that exists in the thin filament in muscle. When the G-to-F transformation takes place, the ATP bound to G-actin breaks down, releasing inorganic phosphate (P_i) and leaving an adenosine diphosphate (ADP) molecule bound to each actin unit. Actin molecules repeat every 2.75 nanometres along the thin filament. They give rise to a helical structure that can be viewed as a double or single helix. The apparent half-pitch is about 40 nanometres long. Actin is believed to be directly involved in the process of contraction since the cross bridges can become attached to it.

Tropomyosin is a rod-shaped molecule about 40 nanometres long with a molecular weight of about 70,000. Two strands of tropomyosin molecules run diametrically opposed along the actin filaments. Tropomyosin has a structure similar to that of the myosin tail, being a coiled unit of two protein chains. Each tropomyosin molecule is in contact with seven actin units.

Troponin is a complex of three different protein subunits. One troponin complex is bound to every tropomyosin molecule. A troponin molecule is located approximately every 40 nanometres along the filament. Troponin and tropomyosin are both involved in the regulation of the contraction and relaxation of muscles. One of the subunits (TnC) is the receptor for Ca^{2+} released from the sarcoplasmic reticulum on activation of the muscle. It is thought that calcium-binding then causes further structural changes in the interaction of actin, tropomyosin, and another troponin subunit (TnI) that lead to contraction by activating the actin-myosin interaction.

Z lines and M bridges

The exact structure of the Z line has not yet been completely established, but it is thought that four filaments extend from the end of each thin filament to four different thin filaments on the other side of the Z line. This type of arrangement would give the Z line a three-dimensional structure resembling a series of pyramid-like units. The Z line contains proteins that form links with actin and establish lateral connections among Z disks (α-actinin, desmin) and establish connections between the Z disks and the cell membrane (*e.g.,* vinculin).

The fine M bridges are composed of proteins that have not yet been fully characterized. The M bridges run between sites on the thick filaments at which myosin molecules are joined tail to tail. It may be that the M bridges keep the filaments in register during contraction. A continuous network of filaments extending from Z disk to Z disk has also been identified; it contains some large proteins (titin, nebulin).

Actin-myosin interaction and its regulation. Mixtures of myosin and actin are used in the test tube to study the relationship between the ATP breakdown reaction and the interaction of myosin and actin. The ATPase reaction can be followed by measuring the change in the amount of phosphate present in the solution. The myosin-actin interaction also changes the physical properties of the mixture. If the concentration of ions in the solution is low, myosin molecules aggregate into filaments. As myosin and actin interact in the presence of ATP, they form a tight, compact gel mass; the process is called superprecipitation. Actin and myosin interaction can also be studied on muscle fibres whose membrane is destroyed by glycerol treatment; these fibres still develop tension when ATP is added. A form of ATP that is inactive unless irradiated with a laser beam has been found to be useful in the study of the precise time course underlying contraction.

Superprecipitation

If troponin and tropomyosin are also present, however, the actin and myosin do not interact, and ATP is not broken down. This inhibitory effect corresponds to the state of relaxation in the intact muscle. When calcium ions are added, they combine with troponin, inhibition is released, actin and myosin interact, and ATP is broken down. This corresponds to the state of contraction in intact muscle. The exact mechanism by which troponin, tropomyosin, and calcium ions regulate the myosin-actin interaction is not fully agreed upon. In the thin filament there is one troponin and one tropomyosin molecule for every seven actin units. According to one view Ca^{2+} binding to troponin, actually the TnC subunit, induces a change in the position of tropomyosin, moving it away from the site where myosin also binds (steric blocking). Alternatively, the calcium-induced movement of tropomyosin in turn induces changes in the structure of actin permitting its interaction with myosin (allosteric model). In smooth muscles Ca^{2+} activates an enzyme (kinase) that catalyzes the transfer of phosphate from ATP to myosin and the phosphorylated form is then activated by actin.

A somewhat different scheme of regulation operates in the muscle of mollusks. As in vertebrate muscles, calcium ions act as the initiator of contraction. The difference is that the component that binds calcium ions in the molluscan muscle is myosin rather than a component of the actin-containing thin filaments. The interaction of actin and myosin provides a basis for molecular models of force generation and contraction in living muscle.

(R.E.Da./N.A.C./J.G.)

The neuromuscular junction. The signal for a muscle to contract originates in the nervous system and is transmitted to the muscle at the neuromuscular junction, a point of contact between the motor nerve and the muscle. In higher organisms each muscle fibre is innervated by a single motor nerve fibre; in other species (*e.g.,* crustaceans) inhibitory fibres are also present. As the nerve approaches the muscle, it loses its myelin coat but remains partially covered by processes of the Schwann cells, which elsewhere surround the nerve and produce myelin. The nerve then branches several times, indenting the surface of the muscle to form the end plate that occupies only a small region of the total surface area of the muscle. The narrow (50 nanometres) synapse separates the nerve from the muscle and contains the basement membrane (basal lamina). In the subneural region the muscle membrane is deeply folded, forming secondary synaptic clefts into which the basement membrane penetrates.

Schwann cells

The neural signal is an electrical impulse that is conducted from the motor nerve cell body in the spinal cord along the nerve axon to its destination, the neuromuscular junction. No electrical continuity exists between the nerve and the muscle; the signal is transmitted by chemical means that require specialized presynaptic and postsynaptic structures.

Storage of acetylcholine in the nerve terminal. The nerve terminal contains many small vesicles (membrane-enclosed structures) about 50 nanometres in diameter, each of which contains 5,000–10,000 molecules of acetylcholine. Mitochondria are also present, providing a source of energy in the form of ATP. Acetylcholine is formed in the nerve terminal from choline and acetyl-CoA through the catalytic action of the enzyme choline acetyltransferase. Choline is obtained by the active uptake of extracellular choline, a breakdown product of previously released acetylcholine. Concentrations of acetylcholine (and ATP) in the cytoplasm are several hundredfold lower than in the vesicles. Packaging of the transmitter into the vesicles occurs within the nerve terminal and is an energy-requiring process.

Vesicles

Release of acetylcholine from the nerve terminal. The

vesicles cluster close to specialized regions of the nerve terminal membrane called the active zones. Freeze-fracture electron microscopy reveals an orderly array of small particles (about 10 nanometres in diameter) within these active zones, which are believed to represent voltage-gated calcium channels. The channels are opened by depolarization (increase in membrane potential) of the nerve terminal membrane and selectively allow the passage of calcium ions.

The nerve impulse is a wave of depolarization traveling along the axon of the motor nerve such that the resting membrane potential of about −70 millivolt is reversed, becoming briefly positive. At the nerve terminal the nerve impulse causes voltage-gated calcium channels at the active zones to open until depolarization subsides. This allows calcium ions to enter the nerve terminal along their concentration gradient. The region of raised calcium concentration within the nerve terminal is localized close to the active zones and, by a process that is not yet understood, causes vesicles in this region to fuse with the nerve terminal membrane and to open outward (exocytosis), thereby discharging their contents into the synaptic cleft. A nerve impulse causes the release of about 50–100 vesicles of acetylcholine in humans, and somewhat more in some other species.

Discharge of acetylcholine

At high rates of stimulation, sufficient to cause a smooth contraction (tetanus) of the muscle, the quantity of transmitter released per impulse declines for the first few impulses (synaptic depression), which may be due to a reduction in the number of vesicles ready for release.

Following the voltage-dependent influx of calcium into the nerve terminal, it is necessary for calcium to be removed to prevent continuous discharge of neurotransmitter. Mechanisms underlying this process are likely to involve sodium–calcium exchange across the nerve terminal membrane and possibly calcium uptake by mitochondria.

Acetylcholine is released from the nerve terminal by two other processes, independently of the nerve impulse. Neither of these processes leads to muscle contraction. The first occurs spontaneously when individual vesicles randomly fuse with the nerve terminal membrane and discharge their contents, generating a small potential change (about 0.5–1 millivolt), the miniature end plate potential. This potential is below the threshold at which an action potential is triggered in the muscle cell and thus does not lead to muscle contraction. The frequency of such events varies; in humans they occur at each end plate about once every five seconds. The second process of acetylcholine release occurs as a continuous "molecular leakage" of neurotransmitter from the nerve terminal rather than from vesicles. The overall amount released in resting muscle by this means greatly exceeds the spontaneous release of individual vesicles.

The acetylcholine molecules diffuse across the synaptic cleft and react with the acetylcholine receptors. The number of available acetylcholine binding sites greatly exceeds the number of acetylcholine molecules released. Acetylcholine is either rapidly broken down by the enzyme acetylcholinesterase, which is anchored in the basement membrane, or diffuses out of the primary cleft, thus preventing constant stimulation of acetylcholine receptors. Drugs that inactivate acetylcholinesterase and thereby prolong the presence of acetylcholine in the cleft can lead to repetitive firing of the muscle cell in response to a single nerve stimulus.

Acetylcholine receptors. Acetylcholine receptors are ion channels that span the postsynaptic membrane, and they have extracellular, intramembranous, and cytoplasmic portions. They are located principally over the peaks of the postsynaptic folds, where they are present at high density. They consist of five subunits arranged around the central ion channel. One of the subunits is represented twice. The different subunits are products of separate genes. This implies that the acetylcholine receptor has been highly conserved in evolution and suggests that the genes coding for the different subunits may have evolved from a single primeval acetylcholine receptor gene.

Structure

Models of acetylcholine receptors indicate that its structure contains an extracellular *N*-terminal portion, several intramembranous portions (of which one provides part of the wall of the ion channel) separated by short intracellular and extracellular portions, and a cytoplasmic *C*-terminal part.

The supply of junctional acetylcholine receptors is continuously renewed. Receptors are internalized by the muscle cell and degraded in lysosomes (specialized cytoplasmic organelles), while new receptors are synthesized and inserted into the muscle membrane.

In normally innervated muscle, receptors are confined to the neuromuscular junction. In non-innervated fetal muscle and in denervated adult muscle, however, acetylcholine receptors are found elsewhere as well. These receptors have slightly different properties from junctional receptors, notably a much higher rate of turnover.

Acetylcholine/acetylcholine receptor interaction. The resting membrane potential of the muscle cell is held at about −80 millivolt. Binding of acetylcholine to each of the two alpha subunits causes the receptor molecule to alter its configuration so that the ion channel is opened for about one millisecond (0.001 second). This permits the entry of small positive ions, mainly sodium. The resulting local depolarization (the end plate potential) causes voltage-gated sodium channels located around the end plate to open. At a critical point (the firing threshold for the muscle cell) a self-generating action potential is triggered, causing the membrane potential to reverse and become briefly positive. The action potential propagates over the muscle fibre membrane to activate the contractile process.

Firing threshold

The amplitude of the end plate potential is normally sufficient to bring the membrane potential of the muscle cell well above the critical firing threshold. The extent to which it does so represents a "safety factor" for neuromuscular transmission. The safety factor will be reduced by any event that, by interfering with presynaptic or postsynaptic function, reduces the size of the end plate potential. (J.M.N.-D.)

Mechanical properties. *The physical aspects.* Vertebrates are able to move about and to exert and bear forces because of the contraction of the striated muscles. These activities usually involve several structures operating in different ways. The skeleton to which the muscles are attached operates as a lever system. When a muscle shortens, it moves the joints that it spans. In addition, in coordinated movement usually several muscles contract in different ways. As some muscles shorten, others develop a force while at a fixed length, and still others may be lengthened by an external force even as they contract.

The force that a muscle develops is a "pulling" force, never a "pushing" force. If the load is small enough, the muscle can shorten and produce a pulling motion (an isotonic condition). If the load is just equal to the maximum force the muscle can develop, the length of the muscle will remain the same (an isometric condition). An even larger load will stretch the muscle.

The size and the rate of the mechanical responses to stimulation, whether by a nerve in the body or by direct electrical shocks of an isolated muscle, depend on the muscle and the temperature. In a frog sartorius muscle (of the leg) at 0° C (32° F), the action potential reaches its peak of depolarization about 1.5 milliseconds after the stimulus (Figure 18).

Time course of contraction

The very early tension changes require much more rapid and sensitive measuring and recording instruments than are necessary for studying other aspects of the contraction process. The latent period, the first seven milliseconds, is the amount of time needed for the electrical signal, which appears as an action potential at the surface membrane, to be translated and travel to the contractile apparatus within the muscle fibres. The explanation for latency relaxation (a four-millisecond period during which the tension drops slightly), however, is not so clear. It may be related to a change in shape of the sarcoplasmic reticulum, which releases a large amount of calcium ions at about the time latency relaxation occurs. The tension begins to rise after 15 milliseconds.

Twitch and tetanus responses. Skeletal muscles respond to a single electric shock of sufficient magnitude by rapid,

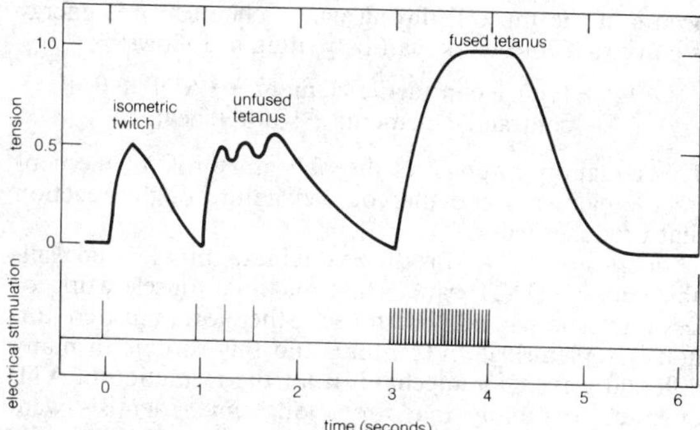

Figure 18: The effect of the rate of stimulation on the development of force in a frog muscle (at 0° C, or 32° F).

intense contractions called phasic contractions. If the ends of a frog sartorius muscle (at 0° C) are fixed to prevent shortening, the tension increases for about 200 milliseconds and then begins to decrease, at first rather rapidly and then more slowly. More happens during this mechanical response to a single stimulation, called a twitch, than the tension record suggests.

Absolute refractory period

The mechanical response to repeated stimulation depends on the rate of the stimulation. Muscle, like other excitable tissues, has a period following its action potential during which the membrane will not respond to stimulation regardless of the strength. This absolute refractory period in the frog sartorius at 0° C lasts about 10 milliseconds after stimulation. Therefore, a second pulse coming within that time span will not elicit any response. If, however, the pulses are 300 milliseconds apart, the muscle will be relaxing when the second pulse is given, and the tension will appear in waves in phase with the stimulation, causing an unfused tetanus. It is possible to stimulate the muscle at a frequency between these extremes so that the tension developed by the muscle remains constant. This latter type of contraction is called a fused tetanus, and the rate of stimulation that produces it is called the fusion frequency. The exact rate depends upon the particular muscle and the temperature.

Effects of series elasticity

Usually, the maximum tetanus tension is from 1.2 to 1.8 times greater than the maximum tension during a twitch. Within the muscle many elastic structures, connected in series with the contractile elements, are stretched during contraction. The attachment of the muscle fibres to the tendons at the end of the muscle and the attachment of the thin filaments to the Z line contribute to this elastic component. In single fibres, however, most of the elasticity of the series elastic elements is contributed by the actin-myosin cross bridges themselves. Full maximum tension is not apparent at the end of the muscle until the contractile elements have shortened enough to stretch the elastic elements—somewhat like taking up the slack in rope before a pull on one end can be felt at the other end. In a twitch, the activity of the muscle is so brief that the contractile elements cannot extend the elastic elements completely before relaxation begins; as a result, the tension at the ends of the muscle does not reach the maximum possible level. During a tetanus, on the other hand, the activity of the contractile elements is maintained, and they can eventually shorten enough to extend fully the series elastic elements. When this has been accomplished, the maximum tension is apparent at the ends of the muscle.

Length-tension relationship. The force developed by a muscle, whether it is contracting or resting, is strongly dependent on the length of the muscle (Figure 19). Resting skeletal muscle does not exert any force at lengths less than the normal length of the resting muscle in the body (l_o). When resting skeletal muscle is extended somewhat beyond l_o, however, a passive force begins to assert itself. The exact length at which this passive force occurs depends on the particular muscle. This force is characterized as passive because it is developed in noncontracting or inactive muscles by the elastic elements of the muscle.

Skeletal muscles do not develop any force when they are stimulated at lengths of less than about 50 percent l_o. The amount of force developed, however, increases during isometric contractions at lengths from 50 to 100 percent of l_o. Once beyond l_o, the passive force becomes a factor: the total force has two components, a passive one, resulting from elasticity, and an active one, resulting from contraction. For isometric contractions the active force developed during contraction decreases beyond l_o; at about 150 percent l_o, the muscle fails to develop any active force.

The structural basis for the dependence of the magnitude of active force on the length of skeletal muscle has been established in experiments with single fibres rather than whole muscles. The active force has been correlated with the relative position of thick and thin filaments during contraction at each sarcomere length. The tension increases as the sarcomere length shortens from 3.65 to 2.25 μ (Figure 19A, 1 and 2) because more sites for actin-myosin cross-bridge interaction become available as the overlap of the thick and thin filaments increases (19B, 1 and 2). The force is constant from sarcomere length 2.25 to 2.00 μ (19A, 2 and 3) as the thin filaments move over the bare region devoid of cross bridges in the centre of the thick filaments (19B, 2 and 3). As the sarcomeres shorten further, from 2.00 to 1.67 μ (19A, 3 to 5), the thin filaments overlap each other, preventing effective interaction with myosin in the thick filaments (19B, 3 and 5) and consequently diminishing the force. Finally, from sarcomere length 1.67 to 1.27 μ (19A, 5 to 6) the thick filaments run up against the Z lines (19B, 6), and internal resistance causes an even greater diminution of the force.

From *Journal of Physiology* (1966)

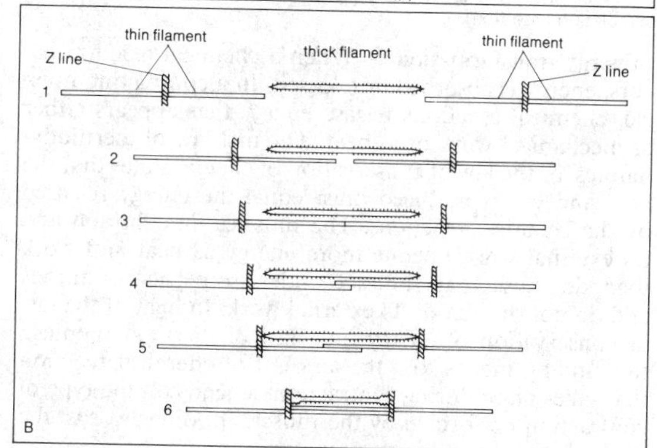

Figure 19: (A) The amount of force developed during an isometric tetanus of a single muscle fibre at various sarcomere lengths. (B) Relative positions of the thick and thin filaments at various sarcomere lengths.

Load–velocity relation. When a muscle is to lift a constant load (isotonic conditions) after stimulation starts, the force increases, just as in an isometric contraction, and, when the force is equal to the load, the muscle begins to shorten and lifts the load. When the activity of both the muscle and the force in it begin to decline, the load stretches the muscle back to its initial length. The tension in the muscle is equal to the load during the shortening and the lengthening of the muscle, except during brief periods of acceleration as the muscle begins to move. Only after the muscle has returned to its initial length does the tension begin to diminish. The size of the load also determines the velocity of shortening, and this relationship between load and velocity also applies to cardiac and smooth muscle. It can be mathematically described by Hill's equation:

$$V = \frac{(P_o - P)b}{P + a},$$

in which V is the velocity of shortening; P_o is the maximum force developed under isometric conditions; P is the force developed at a particular muscle length; and b and a are physical constants. A graphic interpretation of these values results in a rectilinear hyperbola called the force–velocity curve (Figure 20). From this curve can be determined both the velocity of shortening when the load is known and the force developed to overcome the load when the velocity is known.

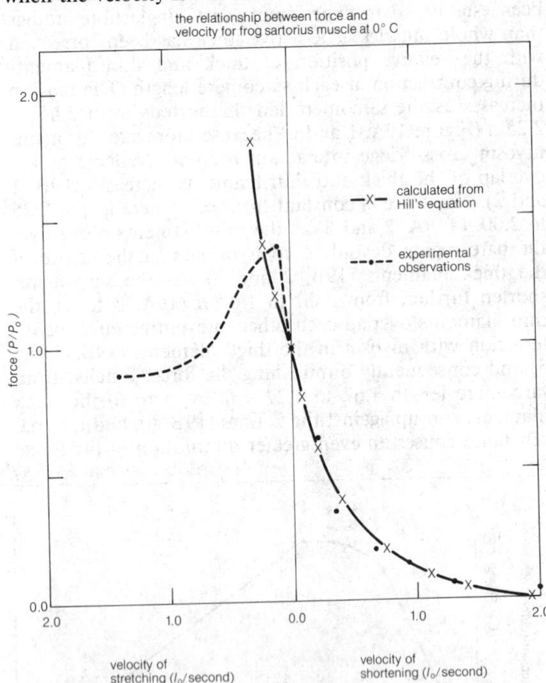

Figure 20: The force–velocity curve: relationship of the velocity of movement to the amount of force developed during tetanic stimulation (see text).

Energy transformations. When a chemical reaction occurs, energy is absorbed or released. In a contracting muscle, chemical reactions release energy that appears either as mechanical work or as heat. The first law of thermodynamics, or the law of conservation of energy, states that the heat and work produced must equal the energy released by the chemical reactions. The muscles that shorten and do external work liberate more energy as heat and work than do those that contract under isometric conditions and do not shorten or do external work. In light of the law of conservation of energy (first law of thermodynamics), this finding means that the amount of chemical reaction that takes place during contraction depends on the type of contraction performed by the muscle. In other words, the flow of energy is subject to regulation.

The mechanical work of muscles

The efficiency of the process of muscle contraction depends on the fate of the free energy released in chemical reactions; *i.e.*, whether it is converted primarily into work or degraded into heat. The second law of thermodynamics sets limits to the amount of energy that can be transformed into mechanical work. Although the production of heat can detract from the efficiency of working muscle, energy that appears as heat is not always wasted. In warm-blooded animals, for example, the heat released by muscles maintains a constant body temperature regardless of the environmental temperature. When an animal shivers in the cold a large amount of heat is generated in the muscles. The muscles alternately contract and relax, releasing energy chiefly as heat.

Source of energy for muscle work. Muscles use the free energy released by chemical reactions by coupling the chemical reaction to physical changes in the contractile proteins. The exact molecular details of this fundamental coupling process are not yet completely known. Of the reactions that have been identified, the splitting of ATP is the energy-yielding reaction nearest to the contractile event. Water participates in this reaction in which ATP is broken down to ADP and phosphate (P_i); the reaction that occurs in the muscle, during which chemical free energy is converted into work, can be written as follows:

$$\text{ATP} + \text{H}_2\text{O} + \text{contractile elements} \rightarrow \text{ADP} + \text{P}_i + \text{contractile elements} + \text{work} + \text{heat}.$$

This equation emphasizes the obligatory role of the contractile elements and the coupled nature of the reaction that produces work.

Energy stores. In a resting vertebrate muscle, the available supply of ATP can sustain maximal muscle work for less than one second. The muscle, therefore, must continuously replenish its ATP store, and this is done in many different ways. One mechanism for the formation of ATP operates so rapidly that for a long time scientists were unable to detect any change in the amount of ATP in the muscle as a result of contraction. This immediate rebuilding of ATP is accomplished by the reactions of compounds called phosphagens. All of them contain phosphorus in a chemical unit called a phosphoryl group, which they transfer to ADP to produce ATP (these compounds are also referred to as high-energy phosphates). Whereas different phosphagens occur in various animals, all of them contain two common chemical units—a guanidino group and a phosphoryl group.

Phosphagens

The reaction for the rebuilding of the ATP utilized during contraction in vertebrate muscle can be written as follows:

$$\text{ADP} + \text{PCr} \rightarrow \text{ATP} + \text{Cr}.$$

The phosphagen, phosphorylcreatine (PCr), gives rise to creatine (Cr) upon the formation of ATP. This reaction is catalyzed by the enzyme ADP : creatine phosphoryl transferase.

Resting skeletal muscle has about 10 times more phosphagen compound than ATP. During rapid and intense contraction, the phosphagen can be utilized to rebuild ATP rapidly and maintain its level as long as the phosphagen lasts, which in a maximally working human muscle is just a few seconds. After contraction ATP is utilized to form phosphagen (PCr) from creatine (Cr); ADP is also formed.

$$\text{ATP} + \text{Cr} \rightarrow \text{ADP} + \text{PCr}$$

This formation of PCr occurs at the same time that ATP is produced by various reactions that are described in a later section.

As mentioned earlier, changes in the ATP level during contraction are difficult to measure since it is rapidly re-formed from ADP and Cr. Such changes can be observed, however, when the muscle is treated with the chemical 2,4-dinitro–fluorobenzene (DNFB), which inhibits the enzyme ADP : creatine phosphoryl transferase. In DNFB-treated muscles, the ATP level decreases during contraction; the ADP and phosphate (P_i) levels increase, and phosphorylcreatine and creatine levels remain constant. The mechanical properties of DNFB-treated muscle during maximal contraction are the same as those of untreated muscles, except that DNFB-treated muscle runs out of ATP sooner and therefore contracts for a shorter time.

The amount of phosphagen is higher in skeletal muscle than it is in cardiac or smooth muscle. This correlates with the type of activity of the muscles. Skeletal muscle operates in bursts of activity, whereas cardiac and smooth muscle contract in a regular pattern. Skeletal muscle needs an immediate supply of a large amount of ATP, which is provided by the phosphagen reaction; cardiac and smooth muscle, which use ATP at a lower rate, rely on slower reactions to fill their energy requirements.

Metabolic pathways producing ATP. *ATP from glucose.* In skeletal muscle most of the ATP is produced in metabolic pathways involving reactions of the sugar glucose or some other carbohydrate derived from glucose. During contraction, for example, glucose is made available for these reactions by the breakdown of glycogen, the storage form of carbohydrate in animal cells. The concentration of Ca^{2+} is transiently increased on activation of muscle. The ions are also activators of the process of glycogen breakdown. During the recovery period the glycogen supply is replenished by synthesizing glycogen from glucose supplied to the muscle tissue by the blood.

The glycolytic pathway. In all but the most brief, intense contractions—during which phosphagen is utilized to form ATP—additional ATP is supplied by a set of chemical reactions called the glycolytic pathway, or the Embden–Meyerhof–Parnas pathway. These reactions are especially important when the muscle is doing work at a high rate. The enzymes that catalyze these reactions are located in the sarcoplasm, as is glucose, the major starting material. The glycolytic pathway can be summarized as follows: reactions of glucose to lactate are coupled to formation of ATP from ADP and phosphate.

$$\underset{\text{glucose}}{C_6H_{12}O_6} + 2ADP + 2P_i \rightarrow \underset{\text{lactate}}{2C_3H_6O_3} + 2ATP + 2H_2O$$

As already indicated, ATP is broken down in the contractile reaction to form ADP and P_i, which can then be recycled into the pathway. The lactate, a waste product, diffuses out of the muscle and is transported by the blood to the liver. The removal of lactate from the muscle is slower than its production; if the muscle contracts for an extended period, the accumulation of lactate in the muscle causes fatigue and ultimately muscle cramps.

Most of the lactate taken to the liver is converted to glucose, from which glycogen is formed in a series of reactions that require ATP to provide more ATP. About one-sixth of the lactate is oxidized to carbon dioxide by reactions that require oxygen (see below) after the exercise is done; a so-called oxygen debt accumulates during brief intense exercise. Animals breathe hard after intense exercise to supply the oxygen needed for the reconversion of lactate.

The relative speed of glycolysis

The glycolytic pathway can operate up to 1,000 times faster in a contracting muscle than it does in a resting muscle. Two regulatory mechanisms play roles in the increase in the rates of these reactions. First, reacting compounds (reactants) accumulate; for example, more glucose is available because glycogen breakdown increases during contraction, and ADP and P_i accumulate. The second type of regulation depends on the activity of the enzyme phosphofructokinase, which catalyzes one of the early steps in glycolysis. This enzyme can bind either ATP or adenosine monophosphate (AMP). When ATP is bound, the activity of the enzyme is low; that is, the reaction it catalyzes proceeds slowly. When AMP is bound, the enzyme has a high activity. During contraction the ATP level drops and that of ADP increases; ADP, in turn, produces AMP as well as ATP, in a reaction catalyzed by the enzyme adenylate kinase, or myokinase. The AMP then can bind with the phosphofructokinase, thereby accelerating glycolysis and the production of ATP. The formation of ATP in the myokinase reaction enables the muscle to use the energy in the ADP formed during contraction.

The oxidative pathways. A large amount of ATP is produced by the complete oxidation of carbon-containing compounds (*e.g.,* glucose) to carbon dioxide and water in reactions of the Krebs cycle and oxidative phosphorylation. These reactions take place inside the membrane-bound components of cells called mitochondria. Carbohydrate can enter the oxidative pathways at a branch point in the glycolytic pathway. At the branch point, two kinds of reaction can occur: pyruvate, a three-carbon compound, can either react to form lactate or lose a carbon dioxide molecule to form a two-carbon unit, which then enters the Krebs cycle. If the muscle is working hard and using ATP rapidly, lactate is formed. If it is working slowly, a larger fraction of the carbon enters the oxidative pathways.

During reactions of the Krebs cycle, carbon dioxide and hydrogen atoms are removed from the compounds that enter the cycle. The carbon dioxide diffuses out of the muscle and is carried by the blood to the lungs, where it is exhaled. The electrons from the hydrogen atoms are passed through an electron-transport chain consisting of the series of reactions involving cytochrome molecules. These events occur in the mitochondria, in which ADP is also combining with phosphate (P_i) to form ATP. In the last step of this reaction sequence, the hydrogen atoms combine with oxygen to form water. The net reaction for each glucose molecule that enters the glycolytic pathway and proceeds through the Krebs cycle and oxidative phosphorylation is summarized below.

$$\underset{\text{glucose}}{C_6H_{12}O_6} + 6O_2 + 36ADP + 36P_i \rightarrow 6CO_2 + 36ATP + 6H_2O$$

Efficiency of oxidative pathways

Although the oxidative pathways result in the formation of more ATP from each glucose molecule than does the glycolytic pathway, the complete process is much slower than glycolysis. The slowest steps are those involving the passage of the carbon-containing compounds from the sarcoplasm into the mitochondria and the delivery of oxygen, which ultimately comes from the air that is breathed. In red blood cells oxygen is combined with hemoglobin, a protein containing four identical subunits, during its transfer from the lungs to the muscles. Muscle contains myoglobin, which has a structure similar to a single subunit of hemoglobin. Myoglobin, which combines with and can store oxygen, is responsible for transporting much of the oxygen through the sarcoplasm to the mitochondria. Myoglobin is especially important in the heart and "red" muscles, which rely heavily on oxidative metabolism for the production of ATP.

During intense exercise of skeletal muscle, ATP is supplied almost entirely by carbohydrate metabolism. During rest or very light exercise, however, skeletal muscle depends largely on the oxidation of stored fats—actually of their breakdown products, fatty acids—for the production of ATP. Two-carbon units and hydrogen atoms are removed from fats in a stepwise fashion. The two-carbon units enter the Krebs cycle, as do the identical units derived from carbohydrates, as the compound acetyl coenzyme A. The hydrogen atoms from the breakdown of the fat and from the reactions of the Krebs cycle proceed through oxidative phosphorylation, and ATP is produced.

Heart muscle, which operates constantly but at a lower level of intensity than does skeletal muscle, depends on oxidative reactions for ATP. Most of the two-carbon units are derived from either fatty acids or ketones, components of fat, brought to the heart by the blood.

Molecular mechanisms of contraction. *Excitation–contraction coupling.* The nerve impulse that ultimately results in muscle contraction appears as an action potential at the sarcolemma, the membrane that surrounds the muscle fibre. This electrical signal is communicated to the myofilaments inside the fibre in the following way. When the action potential reaches the opening of the transverse tubules (channels that open through the sarcolemma to the space outside the fibre; see above *The myofibril*) in the surface of the fibre, it travels down into the fibre along the tubular membranes, which are continuous with the surface membrane, to within a fraction of a micrometre of each functional contractile unit (Figure 15). In frog muscle the transverse tubules surround the myofibril at the level of each Z line, and in mammalian muscles they are located at the edge of the A bands and I bands. At the triads (the three-element complex consisting of one transverse tubule and two cisternae, which are enlarged saclike membranes) the transverse tubule walls are close to the membranes of the terminal cisternae of the sarcoplasmic reticulum.

The effect of calcium ions

By some as yet unknown mechanism, the change in the electrical properties of the transverse tubule during an action potential causes the rapid release by the terminal cisternae of relatively large amounts of calcium ions into the sarcoplasm. As the concentration of calcium ions increases in the sarcoplasm, they become bound to the troponin in the thin filaments. This releases (or removes) the troponin–tropomyosin-mediated inhibition of the myosin-actin interaction. As the stimulation of the muscle continues, the terminal cisternae continue to release calcium ions. At the same time, however, some of the calcium ions are being removed from the sarcoplasm by another portion of the sarcoplasmic reticulum, the longitudinal tubules. Once the calcium ions are inside the lumen (cavity) of the longitudinal tubules, many of them slowly diffuse back to the terminal cisternae, where they are bound to a protein, calsequestrin, as a storage site. The removal of calcium ions from the sarcoplasm by the sarcoplasmic reticulum is energy requiring. The breakdown of ATP is the chemical reaction that supplies the energy, and two calcium ions are apparently removed from the sarcoplasm for each ATP molecule that is split.

The development of muscular force. In the early 1950s it became clear that there were two types of filaments in muscle and that neither extended the entire length of the muscle (see Figure 14). Furthermore, it was found that the overall length of the filaments did not change during contraction. Those findings ruled out most of the then existing theories about the mechanism of muscle contraction and, based on shape or length changes in structural elements, provided the basis for the now widely accepted sliding-filament theory.

Sliding-filament theory

Shortening of the entire muscle occurs as the thin filaments on both sides of the A band slide further into the A band. As the sliding progresses, the areas of the sarcomere containing only one type of filament—that is, the I band and the H zone—decrease in size because more and more of the thin and thick filaments overlap each other. On the other hand, the A band remains the same length because the thick filaments do not change in length except in extreme shortening. The distance from the Z line to the edge of the H zone also remains virtually the same length because that distance is determined by the length of the thin filaments. The sliding-filament theory must be expanded to explain certain aspects of contraction: how the force that moves the filaments past each other is generated; how ATP takes part in the process of contraction.

Cross-bridge theories

The sliding of the filaments is thought to result from the interaction of the cross bridges with the thin filaments during contraction. Each time a bridge links to a thin filament and operates in a specific way (see below), it causes a small movement of the thin filament along the thick filament. Since muscles are able to shorten considerably, requiring sliding of the filaments through large distances, there must be repeated cycles of interaction between a given cross bridge and successive sites on the thin filament.

The myosin heads attached to the actin filament are thought to change their angle with respect to the thin filaments. This change leads to force development, the elastic element residing in some part of the cross bridge (*i.e.,* the portion of myosin connecting the core of the thick filaments to actin) or in the actin-myosin junction itself. The precise connection between various chemical steps in the hydrolysis of ATP and force generation is still under investigation. Similarly, the precise nature of the structural change that corresponds to force generation is not fully understood—instead of the rotation of the whole myosin head about the point of contact between actin and myosin, a bending motion may take place within the head. Some theories suggest purely electrostatic interactions between thick and thin filaments without specific interaction between actin and the myosin heads. The many similarities, however, between factors that affect actin and myosin interactions in solution and those that modulate the behaviour of whole muscle fibres make models of contraction and force development based on specific protein–protein interaction more fruitful. (R.E.Da./N.A.C./J.G.)

CARDIAC MUSCLE

The heart is the pump that keeps blood circulating throughout the body and thereby transports nutrients, breakdown products, antibodies, hormones, and gases to and from the tissues. The heart consists mostly of muscle, the myocardial cells (collectively termed the myocardium), arranged in ways that set it apart from other types of muscle. The outstanding characteristics of the action of the heart are its contractility, which is the basis for its pumping action, and the rhythmicity of the contraction.

Contractility and rhythmicity

Heart muscle differs from its counterpart, skeletal muscle, in that it exhibits rhythmic contractions. The amount of blood pumped by the heart per minute (the cardiac output) varies to meet the metabolic needs of the peripheral tissues (muscle, kidney, brain, skin, liver, heart, gastrointestinal tract). The cardiac output is determined by the contractile force developed by the muscle cells of the heart (myocytes; Figure 21) as well as the frequency at which they are activated (rhythmicity). The factors affecting the frequency and force of heart muscle contraction are critical in determining the normal pumping performance of the heart and its response to changes in demand.

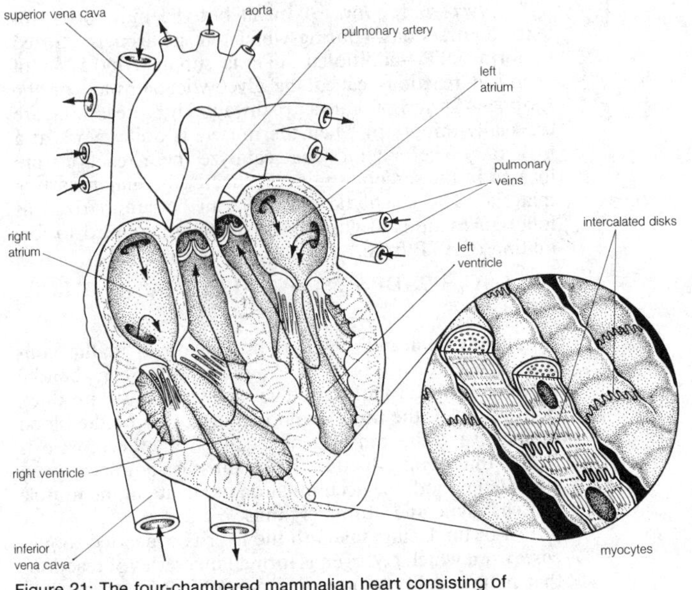

Structure and organization. The heart is a network of highly branched cardiac cells 110 micrometres in length and 15 micrometres in width, which are connected end to end by intercalated disks (Figure 21). The cells are organized into layers of myocardial tissue that are wrapped around the chambers of the heart. The contraction of the individual heart cells produces force and shortening in these bands of muscle with a resultant decrease in the heart chamber size and the consequent ejection of the blood into the pulmonary and systemic vessels. Important components of each heart cell (Figure 21) involved in excitation and metabolic recovery processes are the plasma membrane and transverse tubules in registration with the Z lines, the longitudinal sarcoplasmic reticulum and terminal cisternae, and the mitochondria. The thick (myosin) and thin (actin, troponin, and tropomyosin) protein filaments are arranged into contractile units (*i.e.,* the sarcomere extending from Z line to Z line) that have a characteristic cross-striated pattern similar to that seen in skeletal muscle.

Myocyte excitation and recovery

Figure 21: The four-chambered mammalian heart consisting of the right and left atria and the right and left ventricles. Blood enters the right atrium from the superior and inferior venae cavae, passes from the right atrium to the right ventricle, and then is pumped to the lungs through the pulmonary artery. The blood is returned to the left atrium from the lungs through the pulmonary veins, passes to the left ventricle, and then is pumped to the peripheral tissues through the aorta. Inset shows the heart muscle cells (myocytes).

After Frank H. Netter, M.D., *The CIBA Collection of Medical Illustrations;*

The frequency of contraction. The rate at which the heart contracts and the synchronization of atrial and ventricular contraction required for the efficient pumping of blood depend on the electrical properties of the myocardial cells and on the conduction of electrical information from one region of the heart to another. The action potential (activation of the muscle) is divided into five phases (0–4) and is graphed in Figure 22. Each of the phases of the action potential is caused by time-dependent changes in the permeability of the plasma membrane to potassium ions (K^+), sodium ions (Na^+), and calcium ions (Ca^{2+}). The resting potential of the myocytes of the ventricle (phase 4) begins with the outside of the cell being positive; *i.e.,* having a greater concentration of positive ions. Atrial and ventricular myocytes are normally quiescent (nonrhythmic), however, when the resting membrane potential is depolarized to a critical potential (E_{crit}), a self-generating action potential follows, leading to muscle contraction. Phase 0, the upstroke, is associated with a sudden increase in membrane permeability to Na^+. Phases 1, 2, and 3 result from changes in membrane permeability and conductance to Na^+, K^+, and Ca^{2+}.

The electrical activity of heart muscle cells differs substantially from that of skeletal muscle cells in that phases 1, 2, and 3 are considerably prolonged (200 milliseconds versus five milliseconds, respectively). Another significant

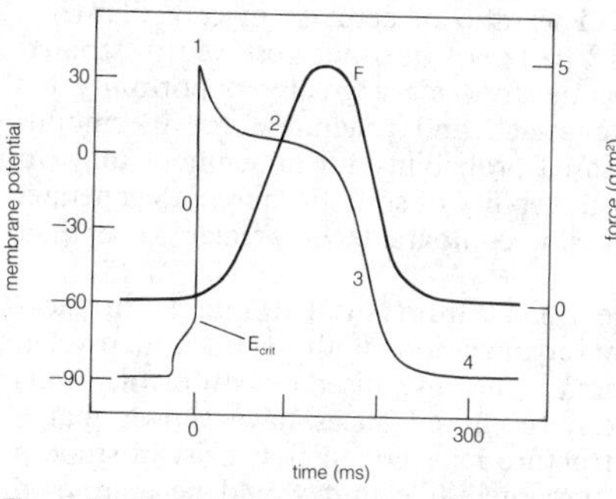

Figure 22: The time course of each of the phases of the ventricular action potential (0–4) and the isometric force (F) developed by an isolated heart muscle bundle.

difference in excitability is that heart muscle cannot be tetanized (*i.e.,* induced to spasm) by the application of repetitive stimuli (see above *Striated muscle*), thus ensuring the completion of the contraction/relaxation cycle and the effective pumping of blood.

Sources of myocyte excitation

Because atrial and ventricular cells are normally quiescent, exhibiting action potentials only after the muscle is depolarized to the critical membrane potential (E_{crit}), the source of the rhythmic contractions of the heart must be sought elsewhere. In contrast to atrial and ventricular myocytes, the myocytes of the sinoatrial (SA) node, the atrioventricular (AV) node, the bundle branches, and the Purkinje fibre system are made up of specialized cardiac muscle cells that exhibit a spontaneous upward drift in the resting potential toward E_{crit}, resulting in the generation of the action potential with all of its phases. The normal rhythmicity of cells from each of these regions depends on the rate at which spontaneous depolarization occurs and the resting membrane potential from which it starts. The region with the fastest intrinsic rate, the SA node, sets the pace for the whole heart. The pacemaker activity is propagated to the rest of the heart by means of the low electrical resistance pathways through the muscle cells (*e.g.,* intercalated disks) and the presence of specialized conducting tissue (bundle branches, Purkinje system). The time course of activation and the shape of the action potentials in different parts of the heart are responsible for the synchronous activation and contraction of the muscles of the atrium followed by those of the ventricle.

The normal rhythm of the heart (*i.e.,* the heart rate) can be altered by neural activity. The heart is innervated by sympathetic and parasympathetic nerves, which have a profound effect on the resting potential and the rate of diastolic depolarization in the SA nodal region. The activity of the sympathetic nervous system may be increased by the activation of the sympathetic nerves innervating the heart or by the secretion of epinephrine and norepinephrine from the adrenal gland. This decreases the resting potential of the myocytes of the SA node while increasing the rate of diastolic depolarization. The result is an increase in the heart rate. Conversely, stimulating the parasympathetic nervous system (vagal nerves to the heart) increases the resting potential and decreases the rate of diastolic depolarization; under these circumstances the heart rate slows. The sympathetic nervous system is activated under conditions of fright or vigorous activity (the so-called "fight or flight" reaction), where the increase in force and rate of heart contraction are easily felt; the parasympathetic system exerts its influence during periods of rest.

Excitation/contraction coupling. Immediately following depolarization of the plasma membrane and the ensuing action potential, the heart muscle develops force and then relaxes. The surface action potential is transmitted to the interior of the muscle by means of the T tubular system. Calcium ions enter the muscle cell during the plateau phase of the action potential (phase 2), triggering the release of calcium from the terminal cisternae of the sarcoplasmic reticulum. Calcium diffuses to the myofilaments and combines with the troponin-tropomyosin system (associated with the thin actin filaments), producing a conformational change that allows actin and myosin to interact. This interaction in the presence of ATP results in cross-bridge cycling and ATP hydrolysis. The force developed in the whole muscle is the sum of all the forces developed by each of the millions of cycling cross bridges of the muscle. The free calcium ions in the cytosol are removed by an energy-dependent calcium uptake system involving calcium ion pumps located in the longitudinal sarcoplasmic reticulum. These calcium pumps lower the concentration of free calcium in the cytosol, resulting in the dissociation (release) of calcium from the troponin-tropomyosin system. The troponin-tropomyosin system is then transformed back to its original state, preventing myosin and actin from interacting and thus causing relaxation of the muscle. At the same time calcium is extruded from the cell into the surrounding medium.

Cross-bridge cycling

Force and velocity of contraction. There are a number of factors that change the force developed by heart muscle cells. In a manner similar to that seen in skeletal muscle, there is a relationship between the muscle length and the isometric force developed. As the muscle length is increased, the active force developed reaches a maximum and then decreases. This maximum point is the length at which the heart normally functions. As with skeletal muscle, changes in length alter the active force by varying the degree of overlap of the thick myosin and thin actin filaments. The force developed by heart muscle also depends on the frequency at which the muscle is stimulated. As the stimulus frequency is increased, the force is increased until the maximum is reached, at which point it begins to decrease. An increase in the level of circulating epinephrine and norepinephrine from the sympathetic nervous system also increases the force of contraction. All of these factors can combine to allow the heart to develop more force when required. At any given length the velocity of contraction is a function of the load lifted, with the velocity decreasing as the load is increased. The force–velocity relationship is similar to that of skeletal muscle and takes the shape of a rectangular hyperbola. When force–velocity curves are measured at different lengths, there is a change in maximum force while the maximum velocity of shortening (V_{max}) remains unchanged. Under conditions where there is an increase in inotropic performance of the muscle (frequency, epinephrine or norepinephrine) there is a shift in both the maximum velocity and maximum force developed.

Response of the heart to stress. Demands on the heart vary from moment to moment and from day to day. In moving from rest to exercise the cardiac output may be increased tenfold. Other increases in demand are seen when the heart must pump blood against a high pressure such as that seen in hypertensive heart disease. Each of these stresses requires special adjustments. Short-term increases in demand on the heart (*e.g.,* exercise) are met by increases in the force and frequency of contraction. These changes are mediated by increases in sympathetic nervous system activity, an increase in the frequency of contraction, and changes in muscle length. The response to long-term stress (hypertension, thyrotoxicosis) results in an increase in the mass of the heart (hypertrophy) providing more heart muscle to pump the blood, which helps meet the increase in demand. In addition, subtle intracellular changes affect the performance of the muscle cells. In the pressure overload type hypertrophy (hypertensive heart disease) the pumping system of the sarcoplasmic reticulum responsible for calcium removal is slowed while the contractile protein myosin shifts toward slower cross-bridge cycling. The outcome is a slower, more economical heart that can meet the demand for pumping against an increase in pressure. At the molecular level the slowing of calcium uptake is caused by a reduction in the number of calcium pumps in the sarcoplasmic reticulum. The change in V_{max} and economy of force development occur because each myosin cross-bridge head cycles more slowly and remains in the attached force-producing state for a longer period of time. In the thyrotoxic type of hypertrophy, calcium is removed more quickly while there is a shift in myosin. At the molecular level there are more sarcoplasmic reticular calcium pumps, while the myosin cross-bridge head cycles

Short- and long-term stress

more rapidly and remains attached in the force-producing state for a shorter period of time. The result is a heart that contracts much faster but less economically than normal and can meet the peripheral need for large volumes of blood at normal pressures.

SMOOTH MUSCLE

Because vertebrate smooth muscle is located in the walls of many hollow organs (Figure 23), the normal functioning of the cardiovascular, respiratory, gastrointestinal, and reproductive systems depends on the constrictive capabilities of smooth muscle cells. Smooth muscle is distinguished from the striated muscles of the skeleton and heart by its structure and its functional capabilities.

Characteristics of smooth muscle

As the name implies, smooth muscle presents a uniform appearance that lacks the obvious striping characteristic of striated muscle. Vascular smooth muscle shortens 50 times slower than fast skeletal muscle but generates comparable force using 300 times less chemical energy in the process. These differences in the mechanical properties of smooth versus striated muscle relate to differences in the basic mechanism responsible for muscle shortening and force production. As in striated muscle, smooth muscle contraction results from the cyclic interaction of the contractile protein myosin (*i.e.,* the myosin cross bridge) with the contractile protein actin. The arrangement of these contractile proteins and the nature of their cyclic interaction account for the unique contractile capabilities of smooth muscle.

Structure and organization. Smooth muscle contains spindle shaped (Figure 23) cells 50 to 250 micrometres in length by five to 10 micrometres in diameter. These cells possess a single, central nucleus. Surrounding the nucleus and throughout most of the cytoplasm are the thick (myosin) and thin (actin) filaments. Tiny projections that originate from the myosin filament are believed to be cross bridges. The ratio of actin to myosin filaments (approximately 12 to 1) is twice that observed in striated muscle and thus may provide a greater opportunity for a cross bridge to attach and generate force in smooth muscle. An increased probability for attachment may, in part, account for the ability of smooth muscle to generate, with far less myosin, comparable or greater force than striated muscle.

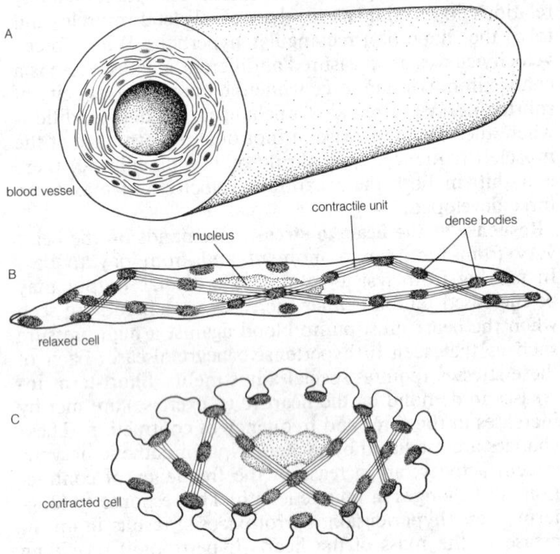

Figure 23: *The artery wall and the ultrastructure of the smooth muscle cells within it.*
(A) Smooth muscle cells are circumferentially oriented and interconnected within the wall by a dense connective tissue matrix. (B) A relaxed smooth muscle cell with a smooth membrane boundary and central nucleus. Contractile units traverse the cell interior. (C) A contracted smooth muscle cell with large membrane blebs formed as the contractile proteins generate force and pull at the dense amorphous plaques on the cell membrane. (D) Attachment sites (dense bodies) for the contractile proteins, actin filaments are located in the cytoplasm and on the membrane. Thick myosin filaments interdigitate with the thin actin filaments.

Smooth muscle differs from striated muscle in lacking any apparent organization of the actin and myosin contractile filaments into the discrete contractile units called sarcomeres. Recent advances have shown that a sarcomere-like structure may nonetheless exist in smooth muscle. Such a sarcomere-like unit would be composed of the actin filaments that are anchored to dense, amorphous bodies in the cytoplasm as well as dense plaques on the cell membrane (Figure 23). These dense areas are composed of α-actinin, a protein, found in the Z lines of striated muscle, to which actin filaments are known to be attached. Thus, force generated by myosin cross bridges attached to actin is transmitted through actin filaments to dense bodies and then through neighbouring contractile units, which ultimately terminate on the cell membrane.

Changes with contraction

Relaxed smooth muscle cells possess a smooth cell membrane appearance, but upon contraction, large membrane blebs (or eruptions) form as a result of inwardly directed contractile forces that are applied at discrete points on the muscle membrane (Figure 23). These points are presumably the dense plaques on the cell membrane to which the actin filaments attach. As an isolated cell shortens it does so in a corkscrewlike manner. It has been hypothesized that, in order for a single cell to shorten in such a unique fashion, the contractile proteins in smooth muscle are helically oriented within the muscle cell. This helical arrangement agrees with earlier speculation that the contractile apparatus in smooth muscle may be arranged at slight angles relative to the long axis of the cell. Such an arrangement of contractile proteins could contribute to the slower shortening velocity and enhanced force-generating ability of smooth muscle.

The contractile proteins interact to generate a force that must be transmitted to the tissue in which the individual smooth muscle cells are embedded. Smooth muscle cells do not have the tendons present in striated muscles, which allow for transfer of muscular force to operate the skeleton. Smooth muscles, however, are generally embedded in a dense connective tissue matrix that connects the smooth muscle cells within the tissue into a larger functional unit (Figure 23).

Mitochondria

Other organelles of the cell interior are related to energy production and calcium storage. Mitochondria are located most frequently near the cell nucleus and at the periphery of the cell. As in striated muscles, these mitochondria are linked to ATP production. The sarcoplasmic reticulum is involved in the storage of intracellular calcium. As in striated muscle, this intracellular membrane system plays an important role in determining whether or not contraction occurs by regulating the concentration of intracellular calcium.

Initiation of contraction. Smooth muscle cells contract in response to neuronal or hormonal stimulation, either of which results in an increase in intracellular calcium as calcium enters through membrane channels or is released from intracellular storage sites. The elevated level of calcium in the cell cytoplasm results in force generation. The rise in the level of intracellular calcium, however, initiates contraction through a mechanism that differs substantially from that in striated muscle. In striated muscle, myosin cross bridges are prevented from attaching to actin by the presence of the troponin-tropomyosin system molecules on the actin filament (see above *Striated muscle*). In smooth muscle, although tropomyosin is present, troponin is not, which means that an entirely different regulatory scheme operates in smooth muscle. Regulation of the contractile system in smooth muscle is linked to the myosin filament; regulation in striated muscle is linked to the actin filament.

In order for the smooth-muscle myosin cross bridge to interact cyclically with actin, a small protein on the myosin molecule, called the light chain, must be phosphorylated (receive a phosphate group). This phosphorylation is the result of a series of interdependent biochemical reactions that are initiated by the rise in intracellular calcium. For the cell to relax, the concentration of intracellular calcium falls, thus inactivating these biochemical processes associated with light chain phosphorylation. The phosphate molecule that was added in the previous steps, however, still must be removed from the light chain so that attachment of the cross bridge to actin is prevented. Phosphatases are enzymes in the muscle cell that cleave the phosphate group from the myosin light chain.

Release of chemical energy

Cross-bridge cycle and ATP breakdown. Smooth-muscle contraction requires the release of chemical energy stored in ATP molecules. The release of this chemical energy by the myosin cross bridge and the resultant mechanical work is commonly referred to as the cross-bridge cycle, which in smooth muscle is believed to be a multistep process similar to that in striated muscle. Therefore, the mechanical properties of smooth muscle, as of striated muscles, are intimately linked to this multistate cross-bridge cycle. For instance, there is a correlation between the rate at which the cross bridges cycle and the maximum shortening velocity of the muscle. Since the actomyosin ATPase cross-bridge cycle in smooth muscle is considerably slower than that in striated muscle, the slower shortening velocity in smooth muscle must be due, in part, to the reduced turnover rate of the cross bridge. The slower cycling rate could also account for the high economy of ATP utilization that characterizes smooth-muscle force production, since fewer cycles are required and less energy is consumed in the generation of force.

Mechanical properties. The relationship between smooth muscle's ability to shorten and to generate force is characterized by the force–velocity relationship. The form of this relationship is qualitatively similar to that in striated muscle; however, the smooth-muscle force–velocity relationship differs from that of striated muscle in having a slower maximum shortening velocity (V_{max}) and greater force per cross-sectional area of muscle (F_{max}). As mentioned above, the slower shortening velocity may relate to the slower cycling rate of the cross bridge as well as the orientation of the contractile proteins within the muscle cell.

Force-generating capabilities

The force-generating capabilities of smooth muscle are greater than those of striated muscle despite the fact that there is considerably less myosin in smooth muscle. Possible explanations for this relate to the arrangement of the contractile apparatus within the cell, which gives rise to more cross bridges effectively operating in conjunction with one another. Second, enhanced force production could be related to the greater amount of time that the cross bridge spends in the attached, high force-producing state (*i.e.,* duty cycle). Evidence for such an increase in the duty cycle does exist in smooth muscle.

When fully contracted, the amount of force that smooth muscle can generate depends on the muscle length. Therefore, as in striated muscle, an optimal length for force production exists, with force being reduced at both lesser and greater lengths (for an explanation of underlying mechanism, see above *Striated muscle*). The similarity in shape for both the force–velocity and length–tension relationships between smooth and striated muscle suggests that in smooth muscle both a cross-bridge mechanism and sliding of contractile filaments must occur.

Constant force

Smooth muscle cells often must generate constant force for prolonged periods of time. In order to do this without depleting the muscle's energy supply, smooth muscle appears to have adapted by altering the cross-bridge cycling rate during the time course of a single contraction. If shortening velocity is a reasonable indicator of cross-bridge cycling, then the observed reduction in shortening velocity with time of contraction suggests that the cross-bridge cycling rate must be slowing with contraction. At present it is not clear whether the cycling rate of the entire cross-bridge population slows with duration of contraction or whether a subset of slowly cycling cross bridges (*i.e.,* latch bridges) appears with a contraction time that hinders the action of the normally cycling bridges. Regardless of the mechanism, the modulation of cross-bridge cycling rate represents a highly economical means of generating force in a muscle that often exists in a tonic state of contraction.

Smooth muscle in disease states. Smooth muscle cells lining the artery walls have been implicated in cardiovascular diseases such as atherosclerosis and hypertension (high blood pressure). In hypertension an increase in the size of the individual cells (hypertrophy) and of their number (*i.e.,* hyperplasia) has been hypothesized. The increased quantity of smooth muscle in the artery wall could increase the constrictive ability of the artery or the artery wall thickness, either of which could constrict the lumen of the artery, thus reducing blood flow through the vessel. To compensate for this resistance to blood flow, the cardiovascular system responds by elevating blood pressure to assure that the various tissues of the body are adequately supplied with blood. A consequence of the need to raise blood pressure, however, is a greater workload for the heart, and thus individuals who are diagnosed with high blood pressure are at a higher risk of heart attack or stroke. Drugs that relax smooth muscle in an effort to lower blood pressure have been successful in reducing the risk of cardiovascular complications. (N.R.A./D.M.W.)

Diseases and disorders of muscle

Muscle diseases and disorders that result from direct abnormalities of the muscles are called primary muscle diseases; those that can be traced as symptoms or manifestations of disorders of nerves or other systems are not properly classified as primary muscle diseases. Because muscles and nerves (neurons) supplying muscle operate as a functional unit, disease of both systems results in muscular atrophy (wasting) and paralysis.

INDICATIONS OF MUSCLE DISEASE

Muscular atrophy and weakness are among the most common indications of muscular disease (see below *Muscle weakness*). Though the degree of weakness is not necessarily proportional to the amount of wasting, it usually is so if there is specific involvement of nerve or muscle. Persistent weakness exacerbated by exercise is the primary characteristic of myasthenia gravis.

Pain is ordinarily present in muscle disease because of defects in blood circulation or injury or inflammation of the muscle. Pain is rare, except as a result of abnormal posture or fatigue, in muscular dystrophy—a familial disease characterized by progressive wasting of the muscles. Cramps may occur with disease of the motor or sensory neurons; with certain biochemical disorders (*e.g.,* hypocalcemia, a condition in which the blood level of calcium is abnormally low); when the muscle tissues are affected by some form of poisoning; from disease of the blood vessels; and with exercise, particularly when cold.

Muscle enlargement—muscular hypertrophy—occurs naturally in athletes. Hypertrophy not associated with exercise occurs in two unusual forms of muscular dystrophy, known as myotonia congenita and hypertrophia musculorum vera. (The latter condition combines increased muscle size with strength; in the former, muscle cramping is an additional feature.) Pseudohypertrophy, muscular enlargement through deposition of fat rather than muscle fibre, occurs in other forms of muscular dystrophy, particularly the Duchenne type.

Tetany, tetanus, and fasciculation

Tetany is the occurrence of intermittent spasms, or involuntary contractions, of muscles, particularly of the arms and legs and the larynx, or voice box; it results from low levels of calcium in the blood and from alkalosis, an increased alkalinity of the blood and tissues. Tetanus, also called lockjaw, is a state of continued muscle spasm, particularly of the jaw muscles, caused by toxins produced by a particular bacillus, *Clostridium tetani.*

The twitching of muscle fibres controlled by a single motor nerve cell, a process called fasciculation, may occur in a normal person but may indicate that muscular atrophy is due to disease of motor nerve cells in the spinal cord. Fasciculation is seen most clearly in muscles close to the surface of the skin.

Glycogen is a storage form of carbohydrate, and its breakdown is a source of energy. Muscle weakness is found in a rare but important group of hereditary diseases, the so-called glycogen-storage diseases, in which various enzyme defects prevent the release of energy by the normal breakdown of glycogen in muscles. As a result, abnormal amounts of glycogen are stored in the muscles and other organs. The best-known type clinically affecting muscles is McArdle's disease, in which the muscles are unable to degrade glycogen to lactic acid on exertion because of the absence of the enzyme phosphorylase. Abnormal accumulations of glycogen are distributed within muscle cells. Features of the condition include pain, stiffness, and weakness in the muscles on exertion. McArdle's disease usually begins in childhood. No specific treatment is available, and persons affected are usually required to restrict exertion to tolerable limits. The condition does not appear to become steadily worse, but there are threats to continuing activity and to life when the muscle protein myoglobin is excreted in the urine. Other glycogen-storage diseases result from deficiency of the enzymes phosphofructokinase or acid maltase. With acid maltase deficiency both heart and voluntary muscles are affected, and death occurs within a year or so of birth as a rule.

McArdle's disease

MUSCLE WEAKNESS

Signs and symptoms. Weakness is a failure of the muscle to develop an expected force. Weakness may affect all muscles or only a few, and the pattern of muscle weakness is an indication of the type of muscle disease. Often associated with muscle weakness is the wasting of affected muscle groups. The many reasons why a muscle is not fully activated in weakness may include less than maximal voluntary effort; disease of the brain, spinal cord, or peripheral nerves that interferes with proper electrical stimulation of the muscle fibres; or a defect in the muscle itself. Only when all causes have been considered can weakness be attributed to failure of the contractile machinery (*i.e.*, the anatomy) of the muscle cell.

The effect of weakness in a particular muscle group depends on the normal functional role of the muscle and the degree to which force fails to develop. A weakness in muscles that are near the ends of the limbs usually results in a tendency to drop things if the upper limb is affected or in foot drop if the lower limbs are affected. The overall disability is not as great as weakness of more proximal (closer to the body) muscles controlling the pelvic or shoulder girdles, which hold large components of the total body mass against the force of gravity. Weakness of the proximal muscles that control the shoulder blade (or scapula), for example, results in "winging" (*i.e.*, when the sharp inner border protrudes backward) as the arms are held outstretched. If the weakness is severe, the arms cannot be raised at all.

Clinical presentation

Assessment. Muscle disease may be detected by assessing whether the muscle groups can withhold or overcome the efforts of the examiner to pull or push, or by observing the individual carrying out isolated voluntary movements against gravity, or more complex and integrated activities such as walking. The weakness of individual muscles or groups of muscles can be quantified by using a myometer, which measures force based on a hydraulic or electronic principle. The recording of contraction force repeatedly over a period of time is valuable in determining whether the weakness is improving or worsening.

Assessment of muscle weakness

The assessment of muscle weakness (and wasting) is directed toward discovering evidence of muscle inflammation or damage. These changes are discerned by blood tests or by measuring alterations of the electrical properties of contracting muscles. Another investigative tool is the muscle biopsy, which provides muscle specimens for pathological diagnosis and biochemical analysis. Muscle biopsies can be taken by a needle or by a surgical procedure.

Classification of muscle weakness. Muscle contraction results from a chain of events that begins with a nerve impulse traveling in the upper motor neuron from the cerebral cortex in the brain to the spinal cord. The nerve impulse then travels in the lower motor neuron from the spinal cord to the neuromuscular junction, where the neurotransmitter acetylcholine is released. Acetylcholine diffuses across the neuromuscular junction, stimulating acetylcholine receptors to depolarize the muscle membrane. The result is the contraction of the muscle fibre. Contraction depends on the integrity of each of these parts; disease or disorder in any part causes muscle weakness.

Upper motor neuron disease. Muscle weakness typical of upper motor neuron disease is seen in stroke (cerebrovascular accident), producing weakness of one side of the body. The arm is typically flexed, the leg is extended, and the limbs have increased tone. Some movement may be preserved, though the use of the hand is particularly limited. In comparison with muscle weakness due to disease of the lower motor neuron or muscle, in the upper motor neuron weakness the muscle bulk is usually well preserved. Other causes of upper motor neuron disorders include multiple sclerosis, tumours, and spinal cord injury.

Lower motor neuron disease. Degeneration of the lower neuron produces a flaccid muscle weakness. Muscle wasting is a prominent feature because the shrinkage and eventual death of neurons leads to denervation of the muscle. Diseases of the motor neurons lying in the spinal cord are termed motor neuron diseases. The most common is motor neuron disease itself, termed in the United States amyotrophic lateral sclerosis and generally known as Lou Gehrig's disease. Patients are generally between 50 and 70 years of age and have upper and lower motor neuron weakness. Paralysis progresses rapidly, and death often results within three years. The spinal muscular atrophies are a group of disorders affecting infants, juveniles, and young adults, often with an autosomal recessive mode of inheritance (*i.e.*, requiring the gene from both parents for expression). The infantile type is fatal within one year, but the older cases tend to be less severe. No cause is yet known for any of these diseases, and no cure is available.

Lou Gehrig's disease

Diseases of the peripheral nerves (peripheral neuropathies, or polyneuropathies) can produce symptoms and signs similar to the motor neuron diseases. Sensory disturbance due to involvement of the nerve fibres carrying sensory impulses is usually also involved. Symptoms usually begin in the hands and feet and progress toward the body. Peripheral neuropathies can cause degeneration of the axons, the core of the nerve fibres. The axons can regenerate but only at a rate of one to two millimetres per day. Thus, after injury to a nerve at the elbow, the hand will not recover for six to nine months. Toxins and damage to blood vessels tend to cause axonal types of neuropathy.

Peripheral neuropathy also can be caused by degeneration of the myelin sheaths, the insulation around the axons. These are termed demyelinating neuropathies. Symptoms are similar to neuropathies with axonal degeneration, but since the axons remain intact, the muscles rarely atrophy. Recovery from demyelinating neuropathies can be rapid. Diphtheria and the autoimmune diseases like Guillain-Barré syndrome cause demyelinating neuropathies. Other causes of peripheral neuropathy include diabetes mellitus, nerve trauma, inherited factors, and chronic renal failure.

Neuromuscular junction disorders. Diseases of the neuromuscular junction typically involve the generation of an end-plate potential that is too low to propagate an action potential in the muscle fibre. These diseases are associated with weakness and fatigability with exercise. Diseases of neuromuscular transmission may be acquired or inherited and may be the result of an autoimmune disorder such as myasthenia gravis (see below *Primary diseases and disorders*), a congenital disorder, or a toxin such as in botulism and some drug-induced disorders.

General causes

PRIMARY DISEASES AND DISORDERS

It appears that the maintenance of muscle mass and function depends on its use. For example, weight lifters and sprinters have muscle fibres with a greater capacity for glycolysis (and thus ATP production) and sudden force generation. Striated muscles can regenerate after damage and can adapt to the loads they carry. Thus, in a muscle biopsy from an individual with any of the muscular dystrophies, there is likely to be a mixture of the cellular changes associated with damage and those associated with regeneration and growth (hypertrophy).

Muscular activities in which the muscle resists an extending force (eccentric contractions) cause more damage to the muscle cells than contraction of the muscle at constant length (isometric contraction) or where shortening occurs (concentric contractions). The greater damage with eccentric contraction occurs despite the fact that the metabolic rate may be one-sixth of that of an equivalent concentric or isometric contraction.

Muscles that are immobilized, as by a plaster cast following fracture of a long bone, tend to waste rapidly through shrinkage of the muscle fibres. A consistent finding is that the oxidative capacity of the muscle is reduced. These changes are reversible with muscle-strengthening exercises. In animals with inherited muscle diseases, the progress of the disease is slowed by immobilizing the limb. Recent evidence in human muscular dystrophy, however, suggests that exercise can strengthen the muscle.

The muscular dystrophies. The muscular dystrophies are a group of hereditary disorders characterized by progressive muscular atrophy and weakness. In most varieties the muscles of the limb girdles—the pelvic and shoulder muscles—are involved.

Measurement of the activity of serum creatine kinase, analysis of a muscle biopsy, and recordings from an electromyograph frequently establish that the muscle weakness is due to primary degeneration of the muscles. Creatine kinase is an enzyme of muscle fibres that is released into the bloodstream when the fibres degenerate as in the muscular dystrophies. Muscle biopsies reveal the characteristic degeneration and necrosis of muscle fibres, as well as the phagocytic actions of wandering macrophages and the attempted regeneration of damaged fibres. Electromyography shows electrical patterns that are characteristic of normal muscle, myopathy, or chronic denervation, such as in the spinal muscular atrophies.

Duchenne type muscular dystrophy

In contrast to the several varieties of muscular dystrophy that are relatively benign, the Duchenne type predominately affects boys. It causes difficulty in walking at about the age of four years, loss of the ability to walk at about the age of 11, and death at about the age of 18 or later, usually due to respiratory failure. There is paradoxical increase in the size of the calf muscles giving rise to the term pseudohypertrophic muscular dystrophy (because the increase in size is the result of replacement with fat and fibrous tissue rather than growth of fibres, as in true hypertrophy). Duchenne type muscular dystrophy is an X-linked condition; a defect of a large gene on the X chromosome is responsible for the disease. Females do not manifest the disease but transmit the gene for the disease to half of their sons and half of their daughters (who themselves become carriers). Muscle degeneration appears to be due to lack of a large protein called dystrophin, which causes a disruption of the membrane covering the muscle fibre; the result is the entry of excess amounts of calcium ions into the cell and cell degeneration.

Other muscular dystrophies

Becker's muscular dystrophy is similar to Duchenne type muscular dystrophy except that Becker's appears later in life and is more benign. It is due to different damage to the same gene on the X chromosome that causes Duchenne type muscular dystrophy.

Facioscapulohumeral muscular dystrophy starts in the face, the muscles around the shoulder blades, and the upper arms. It is more slowly progressive than Duchenne type muscular dystrophy, and most patients have a normal life span. The leg weakness frequently causes "drop foot" and a waddling gait. Facioscapulohumeral muscular dystrophy is inherited in an autosomal dominant fashion; thus the individual will receive the gene from one parent, and will pass the disease to approximately half the children.

Limb-girdle muscular dystrophy is similar to facioscapulohumeral muscular dystrophy, but the face is not involved. Where inheritance is observed, it is usually autosomal recessive; *i.e.,* both parents must donate the affected gene for expression of the disease.

There are a number of other muscular dystrophies, each characterized by an individual pattern of muscle weakness and inheritance. Ocular muscular dystrophy, or myopathy, predominantly affects muscles moving the eyes. Oculopharyngeal muscular dystrophy affects not only the eye muscles but also those of the throat and is usually dominant with onset in the later years of life. Distal myopathy particularly affects the muscles of the feet and hands.

Remedial devices and measures, including physical therapy, spinal supports, and splints for the limbs, may be useful. Prevention of obesity is considered important, especially in Duchenne type muscular dystrophy, and infections are promptly treated. The identification of carriers of the trait and genetic counseling represent the best hope of reducing the incidence of this group of diseases.

Underlying causes

Myasthenia gravis. Myasthenia gravis is an acquired autoimmune disorder that involves a failure in the transmission of nerve impulses to the muscles and is characterized by persistent muscular weakness and a tendency of muscles to be easily fatigued. Individuals affected have weakness, particularly of the face, limbs, and neck. Symptoms include double vision, difficulty swallowing and breathing, and excessive muscle fatigue during exercise with partial recovery after rest.

Autoimmune antibodies (those produced against the body's own cells) cause the destruction of acetylcholine receptors of the neuromuscular junction. Removal of the thymus, treatment with high doses of corticosteroids (which depress the immune response), and blood exchange to remove the autoimmune antibodies are frequently effective in controlling this potentially fatal disease.

Toxic myopathies. Striated muscle may be damaged by a number of drugs and toxins. Some, such as intramuscular injection of bupivicaine, cause damage to the muscle fibres by disrupting the membrane and allowing calcium to enter and destroy the cell. Other drugs, such as chloroquine, emetine, and vincristine, seem to disrupt the internal biochemistry of the muscle fibre. Still others, such as corticosteroids, affect the muscle metabolism; this is particularly true of the fluoro-substituted corticosteroids, which cause increased catabolism and thereby produce proximal muscle weakness especially of the upper limbs. Finally, other drugs, such as hydralazine, produce an autoimmune lupuslike disorder and are associated with dermatomyositis or polymyositis.

There are rare individuals who suffer a potentially lethal attack of muscle rigidity and hyperthermia when exposed to general anesthetic agents such as succinyl choline and halothane. During or after induction of the anesthesia, the patient develops rigidity and an increase in central body temperature. Death may occur in five to 15 minutes when the central temperature reaches above 110° F (43° C). There is a 60 percent death rate in such attacks; should the patient recover, there will be recurrences with future exposures to these drugs. The condition tends to run in families and it may be inherited as an autosomal dominant trait. The cause is not completely known but apparently relates to an abnormality in the chemistry of calcium in the muscle fibre. Excess calcium is released into the sarcoplasm during exposure to the general anesthetic agents, stimulating the mitochondria to burn glycogen and thereby produce heat. The excess calcium also causes the muscle fibres to contract and become rigid. Drugs that prevent calcium release in the muscle appear to prevent the attack and are given at the first sign of attack. After the onset of the attack the anesthetic agent should be removed and the patient cooled.

Common pathogens

Inflammatory myopathies. Bacterial myositis, inflammation of muscle tissues as the result of infection with bacteria, is commonly localized and is the aftermath of injury. *Staphylococcus* and *Streptococcus* organisms are usually responsible. General indications of infection, such as fever and increased numbers of white blood cells, are accompanied by local signs of inflammation, such as reddening, swelling, and warmth. Abscess formation is rare, except in the tropics. In general, bacterial myositis responds to treatment with antibiotics and with minor surgery.

Viral myositis may also occur. The best example of this is Bornholm disease, also called epidemic myalgia, devil's grip, and epidemic pleurodynia, caused by the Coxsackie virus. Affected persons recover completely after a brief period of intense muscular pain and fever.

In addition to bacteria and viruses, the muscles may be invaded by animal organisms, including protozoa and helminths, or worms. Trichinosis is an infection with the roundworm *Trichinella spiralis.* It results from eating infested pork that has not been thoroughly cooked. Reproduction of the worm takes place in the intestines. Larvae migrate from the intestinal walls and bury themselves in muscle tissue. Fever, muscular pains, and sometimes weakness result from the invasion of the muscles. Most persons recover after about two months, but death can result from invasion of the heart muscle.

Autoimmune diseases

The autoimmune diseases of muscle, grouped together under the term polymyositis, frequently are associated with inflammation of the skin in a characteristic distribution. The eyelids, cheeks, knuckles, elbows, knees, and backs of the hands are frequently involved. The combination of polymyositis and the typical dermatitis is classified as dermatomyositis. Muscle weakness can be proximal or diffuse. Frequently swallowing is difficult and the neck is weak. The disease can develop acutely within a few days or chronically over years. The muscle biopsy shows infiltration of the striated muscle by white blood cells, mainly lymphocytes. These collect between the muscle fibres and around small blood vessels and appear to damage the muscle fibres. Vascular damage is a major feature, particularly in the childhood form of dermatomyositis.

The cause of the autoimmune reaction to the striated muscle is not known. The disease frequently occurs in association with other autoimmune diseases, such as rheumatoid arthritis and progressive systemic sclerosis, and it can be associated with carcinoma in a significant proportion of older patients, particularly those with dermatomyositis.

High-dose corticosteroid treatment, often combined with a cytotoxic immunosuppressant drug (*i.e.,* one that destroys the cells and suppresses the immune system), such as cyclophosphamide, frequently is successful in suppressing the disease and allowing destroyed muscles to regenerate.

Endocrine and metabolic myopathies. *Hormones.* Striated muscle is directly or indirectly affected in most disorders caused by the underproduction or overproduction of hormones. This is true because the rates of synthesis or breakdown of the proteins of muscle are affected. If the thyroid gland is overactive (thyrotoxicosis, hyperthyroidism), there is muscle wasting of both type 1 fibres (oxidative-rich fibres responsible for endurance) and type 2 fibres (glycogen-rich fibres responsible for rapid, sprint-type muscle contraction). If the thyroid exhibits underactivity (myxedema, hypothyroidism), there is a predominance of type 1 fibres and sometimes a decrease in type 2 fibre size. If the adrenal gland is overactive (Cushing's syndrome), there is selective atrophy of the type 2 fibres. This pattern is seen as well in prolonged treatment with corticosteroid drugs (such as prednisolone for asthma), which can result in profound wasting and weakness of proximal muscles.

Osteomalacia

Vitamin D deficiency. A similar mechanism underlies the wasting and weakness associated with lack of vitamin D (osteomalacia) in which marked atrophy of type 2 fibres may be seen. The actions of vitamin D in muscle are not fully understood, but it appears that at least one of its metabolites, 25-hydroxycholecalciferol, may influence the resting energy state of the muscle and also protein turnover. Unlike the inherited diseases of muscle, endocrine causes of disease may be eminently treatable.

Mitochondrial myopathies. The mitochondria are the cellular structures in which biochemical processes produce energy (in the form of heat and work) from the oxidation of fuels such as glucose and fat. The first observation of a mitochondrial myopathy was in a patient with unregulated mitochondrial oxidative metabolism, resulting in excessive heat production. Since then a number of biochemical defects in mitochondria have been discovered. There is no single entity that can be diagnosed as a "mitochondrial myopathy." In those mitochondrial defects in which a defective oxidative metabolism exists, a common result is a tendency for the muscles to generate large amounts of lactic acid. This is a consequence of needing to provide energy from the nonoxidative breakdown of the glycogen stored in the muscle.

Glycogenoses. In 1951 Brian McArdle recognized a disorder of muscle that gave cramplike pains yet was not associated with the normal production of lactic acid from exercise. The defect was identified later as an absence of phosphorylase, the enzyme involved in the first step in the cascade (the splitting off of the glucose-1-phosphate units from glycogen). Since blood-borne glucose could still be used to make glycogen, this disorder is classified among the 10 glycogen storage diseases (glycogenoses).

Glycogen storage diseases

Lipid storage myopathies. Lipid storage myopathy is a potentially confusing term because the more severe forms of muscle disease (*e.g.,* muscular dystrophy) are often associated with the replacement of the lost muscle fibres with fat cells. In the lipid storage myopathies the fat, or triglyceride, is deposited as tiny droplets within the cytoplasm of the muscle fibre. Normal type 1 muscle fibres have a greater amount of lipid droplets than type 2 muscle fibres.

In the early 1970s two disorders of muscle fat metabolism were discovered to affect a component of the shuttle system transporting free fatty acids into mitochondria for subsequent oxidation. This shuttle requires the fatty acid (acyl) molecule to attach to the carrier molecule, carnitine, in the presence of the enzyme acylcarnitine transferase. The acylcarnitine that is formed crosses the outer and inner mitochondrial membranes and then is split in the presence of another form of the enzyme acyltransferase to give carnitine and the acyl molecule, which is then oxidized. A deficiency of carnitine results in the storage of fats in the cytoplasm. Deficiency of acylcarnitine transferase results in muscle damage on severe exertion. Recognition is important because the conditions are potentially treatable.

Myotonic diseases. Myotonia is a difficulty in relaxing a muscle after contraction; it may manifest as difficulty in relaxing the hand after a handshake. Though slow relaxation may be due to delayed disengagement of the thick and thin filaments of myosin and actin, most cases of myotonia are due to continuing electrical activity of the sarcolemma. In this most common type of myotonia, a single nerve action potential causes multiple firing of the sarcolemma, thereby continuing muscular contraction. The cause of this problem lies in abnormal ion channels or ion pumps in the sarcolemma, although the exact cause is not known. In many forms of myotonia, cold exacerbates the problem. Weakness is a problem in the myotonic syndromes; it tends to be more pronounced after inactivity, with a rapid "warm up" on commencing exercise.

Symptoms of myotonia

Myotonic dystrophy, or dystrophia myotonica of Steinert, is the most common of the myotonic disorders. It is an autosomal dominant disorder affecting many systems of the body in addition to muscle. There is premature balding, cataract formation, mental impairment, gonadal atrophy, endocrine deficiencies, gastrointestinal tract dysfunction, and muscle fibre degeneration. While the disease has manifested itself by the age of 25 years in most cases, some patients or family members may escape developing significant symptoms throughout their lives.

Myotonia congenita of Thomsen is also an autosomal dominant disorder, but it is not associated with any dystrophic features. The onset is at birth, usually with severe difficulty in relaxing the muscle after a forced contraction, such as a sneeze. Myotonia can occur in a number of other conditions including the periodic paralyses.

Drugs that suppress the extent of the myotonia, such as quinine, procainamide, and phenytoin, have had variable success on the weakness. No cure of these diseases is yet available.

THE PERIODIC PARALYSES

Patients with periodic paralysis suffer from recurrent attacks of muscle paralysis that may last from half an hour to 24 hours. Attacks particularly affect the legs and to a lesser extent the arms and trunk muscles. During an attack the muscles may be slightly swollen and tender. Attacks frequently occur with rest after vigorous exercise.

Types of periodic paralysis

There are two types of periodic paralysis. In hypokalemic periodic paralysis, the serum potassium falls during the attack, which also can be precipitated by anything that tends to lower the serum potassium. Hyperkalemic periodic paralysis, on the other hand, is associated with an increase in serum potassium. An attack may be precipitated by oral therapy with potassium.

Both periodic paralyses are autosomal dominant disorders. Though neither is likely to lead to fatal muscle weakness, the temporary incapacity and embarrassment are severe. In the attack, the muscle fibres lose their electrical potential (become depolarized) and thereby become incapable of excitation. The disease appears to be due to changes in the movements of ions through membranes of the skeletal muscle. Potassium appears to be one of the ions responsible for the condition. Abnormal ion channels or ion pumps in the membrane may be the cause. Treatment by drugs appropriately altering the serum potassium can be effective, and acetazolamide, which affects the acidity of the blood and cells, is often effective.

FATIGUE

Fatigue is a failure of the muscle to sustain force in a prolonged contraction or to reattain force in repeated contractions. The mechanisms underlying fatigue share several features with those underlying weakness: electrical excitation of the muscle cell; electromechanical coupling; and the major processes supplying energy for contraction, work, and heat production.

The action potential that is conducted along the length of the muscle cell has its origin in a depolarization of the postsynaptic membrane of the neuromuscular junction caused by the release of acetylcholine from the presynaptic nerve terminal. The synapse is thus potentially a key control point in the chain of command for muscular contraction. Complete failure of neuromuscular transmission occurs from poisoning with curare or botulinum toxin and results in complete paralysis. Incomplete or variable neuromuscular transmission is a feature of myasthenia gravis, the diagnosis of which can be confirmed by finding evidence of fatigue in response to electrical stimulation of the nerve supplying the muscle. This behaviour is a consequence of the immunologic damage to the postsynaptic membrane of the synapse by antibodies to the acetylcholine receptor.

Curare poisoning

Electrical stimulation of a muscle via its nerve is a means by which some of the mechanisms underlying human muscle fatigue can be analyzed. By stimulating the nerve at a range of frequencies and measuring the force of the contractions produced, it is possible to plot the frequency : force curve. Failure of force at high stimulation frequencies is seen with myasthenia gravis. In conditions in which normal muscle is cooled or lacks blood supply, there is also a high frequency fatigue.

After severe exercise a form of fatigue may persist that is characterized by a lower force production at the lower stimulation frequencies with no decrease in the amplitude of the evoked action potential recorded from the muscle. This type of fatigue would be expected with the failure of excitation-contraction coupling, the inward spread of the action potential by the transverse tubular system, resulting in the release of intracellular calcium, which activates the actin-myosin interaction and subsequent contraction.

There is a relationship between the development of fatigue and the depletion of energy stores in exercising muscle. In prolonged exercise, such as marathon running, fatigue is associated with glycogen depletion due to oxidative glycolysis. Intense exercise that lasts only a few minutes is associated with the accumulation of lactate and an intracellular acidosis due to anaerobic (nonoxidative) glycolysis. In both types of exercise there is a reduction of phosphocreatine, although no appreciable depletion of ATP. In contrast, in patients with myopathies, more striking changes are seen with only low total work or power output. Fatigue in patients with McArdle's disease, in whom there is absent glycogenolysis, is not associated with the usual acidosis. Pronounced acidosis is a finding in patients with defective mitochondrial metabolism in whom there may be a slow resynthesis of phosphocreatine after exercise. (R.A.He./R.H.T.E./W.G.Br.)

BIBLIOGRAPHY

General features of muscles and muscle systems: Basic information at various levels of difficulty may be found in GEOFFREY H. BOURNE (ed.), *The Structure and Function of Muscle,* 2nd ed., 4 vol. (1972–73), a collection of important articles on most aspects and types of muscles; GRAHAM HOYLE, *Muscles and Their Neural Control* (1983), which includes a survey of the diverse kinds of muscle found in different animals; THOMAS A. MCMAHON, *Muscles, Reflexes, and Locomotion* (1984), a book that ranges from basic muscle mechanics to the mechanics of walking and running; R.B. STEIN, *Nerve and Muscle: Membranes, Cells and Systems* (1980), a comprehensive treatment of the biophysics of muscles; and "Design and Performance of Muscular Systems," *Journal of Experimental Biology,* 115:1–412 (1985), an entire volume devoted to the proceedings of an important conference.

Invertebrate muscle systems: R. MCNEILL ALEXANDER, *The Invertebrates* (1979), is a survey that emphasizes the mechanics of movement. E.R. TRUEMAN, *The Locomotion of Soft-Bodied Animals* (1975), is mainly about worms and mollusks.

Vertebrate muscle systems: Sources include ALFRED SHERWOOD ROMER and THOMAS S. PARSONS, *The Vertebrate Body,* 6th ed. (1986), a textbook of comparative anatomy that describes the embryonic development and evolution of the vertebrate muscular system; and WARREN F. WALKER, *Vertebrate Dissection,* 7th ed. (1986), a laboratory manual for comparative anatomy that gives a thorough description of the muscular systems of the dogfish, mud puppy, cat, and rabbit. MILTON HILDEBRAND, *Analysis of Vertebrate Structure,* 3rd ed. (1988); and ALFRED SHERWOOD ROMER, *The Vertebrate Story,* 4th ed. (1959, reprinted 1971), are reference texts on vertebrate muscle.

Human muscle systems: Information on the unique human musculature can be found in ERNST HUBER, *Evolution of Facial Musculature and Facial Expression* (1931, reprinted in *Evolution of Facial Expression,* 1972), detailed presentations of the evolution of two important groups of muscles; ARTHUR KEITH, "Man's Posture: Its Evolution and Disorders," *British Medical Journal,* 1:451–454, 499–502, 545–548, 587–590, 624–626, 669–672 (March 17–April 21, 1923), a classic summary of the adaptation of musculature to upright posture; and PAUL E. KLOPSTEG *et al.* (eds.), *Human Limbs and Their Substitutes* (1954, reprinted 1968), a comprehensive review of normal human limbs and their artificial replacements.

Muscle types: (*Striated*): BERNARD KATZ, *Nerve, Muscle, and Synapse* (1966), is an excellent brief work. GERALD H. POLLACK, "The Cross-Bridge Theory," *Physiology Reviews,* 63(3):1049–1113 (July 1983), is a good summary of minority views suggesting alternatives to the cross-bridge theory. See also ERIC R. KANDEL and JAMES H. SCHWARTZ, *Principles of Neural Science,* 2nd ed. (1985).

Works on muscle contraction include J.R. BENDALL, *Muscles, Molecules and Movement: An Essay in the Contraction of Muscles* (1969), with numerous references to original papers; GRAHAM HOYLE, *Comparative Physiology of the Nervous Control of Muscular Contraction* (1957), a review of the literature for the general reader of biology; ANDREW HUXLEY, *Reflections on Muscle* (1980), rich in history and in identifying unsolved problems; and JOHN SQUIRE, *The Structural Basis of Muscular Contraction* (1981). Several useful journal articles are found in *Scientific American:* CAROLYN COHEN, "The Protein Switch of Muscle Contraction," 223(3):36–45 (November 1975); GRAHAM HOYLE, "How Is Muscle Turned On and Off?" 222(4):84–93 (April 1970); H.E. HUXLEY, "The Mechanism of Muscular Contraction," 213(6):18–27 (December 1965); KEITH R. PORTER and CLARA FRANZINI-ARMSTRONG, "The Sarcoplasmic Reticulum," 212(3):73–80 (March 1965); and DAVID S. SMITH, "The Flight Muscles of Insects," 212(6):76–88 (1965).

(*Cardiac*): Diseases of the heart are discussed in NORMAN R. ALPERT (ed.), *Myocardial Hypertrophy and Failure* (1983); EUGENE BRAUNWALD, JOHN ROSS, JR., and EDMUND H. SONNENBLICK, *Mechanisms of Contraction of the Normal and Failing Heart,* 2nd ed. (1976), information on structure, metabolism of heart muscle, operation of the heart, and heart failure; and HARRY A. FOZZARD *et al., The Heart and Cardiovascular System: Scientific Foundations,* 2 vol. (1986).

(*Smooth*): Studies of smooth muscle include DAVID F. BOHR, ANDREW P. SOMLYO, and HARVEY V. SPARKS, JR. (eds.), *Vascular Smooth Muscle,* vol. 2 in *Handbook of Physiology: A Critical, Comprehensive Presentation of Physiological Knowledge and Concepts,* section 2, *The Cardiovascular System* (1980); and MARION J. SIEGMAN, ANDREW SOMLYO, and NEWMAN L. STEPHENS (eds.), *Regulation and Contraction of Smooth Muscle* (1987).

Muscle disease: A comprehensive modern review of the myopathies will be found in JOHN WALTON (ed.), *Disorders of Voluntary Muscle,* 5th ed. (1988); this work also contains chapters on the anatomy and physiology of muscle. MICHAEL H. BROOKE, *A Clinician's View of Neuromuscular Diseases,* 2nd ed. (1986), is a good, brief review of muscle disease. STIRLING CARPENTER and GEORGE KARPATI, *Pathology of Skeletal Muscle* (1984); and ANDREW G. ENGEL and BETTY Q. BANKER, *Myology: Basic and Clinical,* 2 vol. (1986), are extensive treatments.

(W.F.W./R.McN.A./J.G./B.Wo./J.M.N.-D./N.R.A./D.M.W./W.G.Br.)

Museums

As institutions, museums may reveal remarkable diversity in form, content, and even function, but all museums have as common goals the preservation and interpretation of material aspects of society's cultural consciousness. Traditionally, and in the normally accepted sense of the term, a museum holds the primary tangible evidence of aspects of man and his environment. In this it differs markedly from the library, with which it is often associated, because the items housed in museums are mainly unique and constitute the raw materials of study and research. In the museum the object, which in many cases has been removed in time, place, and circumstance from its original context, communicates itself in a way not possible through other interpretive media.

Museums have been founded and developed for a variety of purposes: as recreational facilities, as educational resources, or as means of contributing to the quality of life of an area; or to attract tourism to a region, to promote civic pride or nationalistic endeavour, or even to transmit overtly ideological concepts.

This article is divided into the following sections:

History of museums

The word *museum* has classical origins. In its Greek form, *mouseion,* it meant "seat of the Muses" and designated a philosophical institution or a place of contemplation. Use of the Latin derivation, *museum,* appears to have been restricted in Roman times mainly to places of philosophical discussion. Thus the great museum at Alexandria, founded by Ptolemy I Soter late in the 3rd century BC, with its college of scholars and its library, was more a prototype university than an institution to preserve and interpret material aspects of the heritage. The word *museum* was revived in 15th-century Europe to describe the collection of Lorenzo de' Medici in Florence, but the term conveyed the concept of comprehensiveness rather than denoting a building. During the Enlightenment the term carried an encyclopaedic connotation in book titles to indicate comprehensiveness of coverage. By the 17th century *museum* was being used in Europe to describe collections of curiosities. Ole Worm's collection in Copenhagen was so called, and in England visitors to John Tradescant's collection in Lambeth (now a London borough) called the array there a museum; the catalog of this collection, published in 1656, was titled *Musaeum Tradescantianum.* In 1675 the collection, having become the property of Elias Ashmole, was transferred to the University of Oxford, and the building constructed to receive it, opened to the public in 1683, became known as the Ashmolean Museum. Although there is some ambivalence in the use of *museum* in the legislation, drafted in 1753, founding the British Museum, nevertheless the idea of an institution called a museum and established to preserve and display a collection owned by and opened to the public was fairly common in the 18th century. Indeed, Denis Diderot outlined a detailed scheme for a national museum for France in the ninth volume of his *Encyclopédie,* published in 1765.

Use of the word *museum* during the 19th and most of the 20th century denoted a building housing cultural material to which the public had access. Later, as museums continued to respond to the societies that created them, the emphasis on the building itself became less dominant. Open-air museums, comprising a series of buildings preserved as objects, and ecomuseums, comprising large outdoor environments, were introduced as new ways to display objects, cultures, and concepts.

Along with the identification of a clear role for museums in society there gradually developed a body of theory, the study of which is known as museology. For many reasons the development of this theory was not rapid. Museum personnel were nearly always experienced and trained in a discipline related to a particular collection, and therefore had little understanding of the museum as a whole, its operation, and its role in society. As a result the emphasis of their work tended toward the individual disciplines, and the practical aspects of museum work, such as conservation and display, were achieved through borrowing from other disciplines and techniques, whether or not they particularly met the requirements of the museum and its public.

Museology and museography

Thus not only was the development of theory slow, but the theory's practical applications—known as museography—fell far short of expectations. Museums suffered from a conflict of purpose, with a resulting lack of clear identity. Further, the apprenticeship method of training for museum work gave little opportunity for the introduction of new ideas. This situation prevailed until other organizations began to coordinate, develop, and promote museums. In some cases, museums came to be organized partly or totally as a government service; in others, professional associations were formed, while an added impetus arose where universities and colleges took on responsibilities for museum training and research.

The words derived from *museum* have a respectable, if confused, history. Emanuel Mendes da Costa, in his *Elements of Conchology,* published in 1776, referred to "museographists," and a *Zeitschrift für Museologie und Antiquitätenkunde* appeared in Dresden in 1881. But the terms *museology* and *museography* have been used indiscriminately in the literature, and there is a tendency, particularly in English-speaking countries, to use *museol-*

ogy or *museum studies* to embrace both the theory and practice of museums.

THE PRECURSORS OF MUSEUMS

The origins of the twin concepts of preservation and interpretation, which form the basis of the museum, lie in the human propensity to inquire and acquire. Collections of objects have been found in Paleolithic burials, while evidence of inquiry into the environment, and communication of the findings, can be seen in the cave and mobiliary art of the same period. A development toward the idea of the museum certainly occurred early in the 2nd millennium BC at Larsa, in Mesopotamia, where copies of old inscriptions were made for use in the schools. But the idea also involves the interpretation of original material. The criteria were met by Sir Leonard Woolley's discoveries in the 6th-century-BC levels of the Babylonian city of Ur. His findings indicated that the Babylonian kings Nebuchadrezzar and Nabonidus certainly collected antiquities in their day. In addition, in a room next to the unearthed temple school was found not only a collection of antiquities but also a tablet describing 21st-century-BC inscriptions. Woolley interpreted the tablet as a museum label. This discovery seems to suggest that Ennigaldi-Nanna, Nabonidus' daughter and a priestess who ran the school, had a small educational museum there.

Classical collecting. The archaeological and historical records, however, do not provide evidence that the museum as it is known today developed in such early times; nor does the word *museum* support this, despite its classical origin. Nevertheless, the collection of things that might have religious, magical, economic, aesthetic, or historical value, or that simply might be curiosities, was undertaken worldwide by groups as well as by individuals. In the Greek and Roman empires the votive offerings housed in the temples, sometimes in specially built treasuries, are but one example: they included works of art and natural curiosities, as well as exotic items brought from far-flung parts of the empires, and were normally open to the public, often upon payment of a small fee. Closer to the concept of a museum was the Greek *pinakotheke,* such as that established in the 5th century BC on the Acropolis at Athens, which housed paintings honouring the gods. Nor was there a lack of public interest in art at Rome. Indeed art abounded in the public places of Rome, but there was no museum. The inaccessibility of the collection of more than one Roman emperor was the subject of public comment, and Agrippa, a deputy of Augustus, commented in the 1st century BC to the effect that paintings and statues should be available to the people.

The Greek *pinakotheke*

The veneration of the past and of its personalities in Oriental countries also led to the collection of objects. Paintings and calligraphs graced the Imperial palaces of China in the 2nd and 3rd centuries AD. In the 8th century AD at Nara, Japan, was built the Tōdai-ji, the temple that houses the Great Buddha (Daibutsu), a colossal seated bronze statue. The temple's treasures still can be seen in the Shōsō-in, or repository, at Nara. At about the same time Islāmic communities were making collections of relics at the tombs of early Muslim martyrs. The idea of *waqf,* formalized by Muḥammad himself, whereby property was given for the public good and for religious purposes, also resulted in the formation of collections.

In medieval Europe collections were mainly the prerogative of princely houses and the church. Indeed there was often a close link between the two, as in the case of the fine treasures of the emperor Charlemagne, which were divided among a number of religious houses early in the 9th century. Such treasures had an economic importance and were used to finance wars and other state expenses. Other collections took the form of alleged relics of Christendom, in which there was a considerable trade. At this time Europe's maritime links with the rest of the world were largely through the northern Mediterranean ports of Lombardy and Tuscany, which, together with the ecclesiastical significance of Rome, brought considerable contact between the Italian peninsula and the Continent. There is evidence of the movement of antiquities, and of a developing trade, from the 12th century. Henry of Blois, bishop of Winchester, is reported to have bought ancient statues during a visit to Rome in 1151 and to have dispatched them to England on a journey of about one month's duration. The movement of antiquities was not confined to those of Italy. Exotic material from other areas entering the ports soon found its way into royal collections, while the Venetian involvement in the Fourth Crusade early in the 13th century resulted in the transfer of the famous bronze horses from Constantinople to St. Mark's Basilica in Venice.

Collections in the Renaissance. The influences that led to the European Renaissance were already at work in Italy, and as a result the first great collections began to form. A reawakening of interest in Italy's classical heritage, and the rise of new merchant and banking families at this northern Mediterranean gateway to the Continent, produced impressive collections of antiquities, as well as considerable patronage of the arts. Outstanding among the collections was that formed by Cosimo de' Medici in Florence in the 15th century. The collection was developed by his descendants until it was bequeathed to the state in 1743, to be accessible "to the people of Tuscany and to all nations." It was to display some of the Medici paintings that the upper floor of the Uffizi Palace, designed to hold offices (*uffizi*), was converted and opened to the public in 1582. Indeed many of the palaces holding such collections were open to visitors and were listed in the tourist guides of the period.

The Medici collections

Royal collections. Elsewhere in Europe royal collections were developed. King Matthias I (Matthias Corvinus) of Hungary maintained his paintings at Buda and kept Roman antiquities at Szombathely Castle during the 15th century. Maximilian I of Austria acquired a collection for his castle in Vienna. Samples of both scientific material and art were featured in the "green vaults" of the Dresden palace of Augustus of Saxony, while the archduke Ferdinand of Tirol housed a varied collection that included Benin ivories and Chinese paintings at Ambras Castle near Innsbruck (now in Austria). Other notable central European collections included those of the Holy Roman emperor Rudolf II at Prague and of Albert V, duke of Bavaria, who in 1569–71 had a building designed and erected to house his collection in Munich. The collection of the Polish king Sigismund II Augustus was housed at Wawel Castle, Kraków.

Royal patronage was crucial to the encouraging of the arts at this time. Rudolf II sponsored astrologers and alchemists as well as artists. Francis I of France invited famed French and Italian craftsmen and artists to rebuild and embellish his château at Fontainebleau, and there he kept his outstanding collection of art. In England, Henry VIII gave his attention to music and thus did not form a collection of significance. He was responsible, however, for the appointment in 1533 of a King's Antiquary, whose task was to list and describe the antiquities of the country. Similar appointments were made subsequently by the Habsburg monarchs and by King Gustav II Adolf of Sweden.

Specialized personal collections. The developing interest in human as well as natural history led to the creation of specialized collections by the intelligentsia of the day. In Italy alone, more than 250 natural history collections are recorded for the 16th century, including the fine herbarium of Luca Ghini at Padua and the more eclectic collection of Ulisse Aldrovandi at Bologna. Other notable natural history collections of the time elsewhere in Europe were those of Conrad Gesner, Félix Platter, and, a little later, the John Tradescants, father and son. Among the specialized historical collections were those of portraits of great men assembled by Paolo Giovio at Como, the archaeological collection of the Grimani family of Venice, and the fine collection of illuminated manuscripts made by Sir Robert Cotton in England. A number of the latter had been acquired from monasteries closed during the Reformation, and during that period material was also transferred from ecclesiastical establishments to the Zürich municipal authority in Switzerland. In due time these various collections were to find their way into museums. So were the collections of Ferrante Imperato of Naples,

Bernard Paludanus (Berant ten Broecke) of Amsterdam, and Ole Worm of Copenhagen.

Cabinet, Kammer, and *gallery*

These collections were normally known as *cabinets* in 16th-century England and France, while in German-speaking Europe the equivalents *Kammer* or *Kabinett* were used. Greater precision was sometimes applied, the terms *Kunstkammer* and *Rüstkammer*, for example, referring respectively to collections of art and collections of historical objects or armour. Natural specimens were to be found in a *Wunderkammer* or *Naturalienkabinett.* In England the term *gallery*, borrowed from Italian *galleria*, referred to a place where paintings and sculpture were exhibited. One Italian collection of natural specimens was called a *museo naturale.*

In 1565 Samuel van Quicheberg published a work on the nature of collections, advocating that they represent a systematic classification of all materials in the universe. His view reflects the spirit of system and rational inquiry and the encyclopaedic approach to knowledge that had begun to emerge in Europe. Collections of natural and artificial objects were to play an important part in this movement. This can be seen in antiquarian studies, in the work of Nicolas-Claude Fabri de Peiresc at Aix-en-Provence in France early in the 17th century, for example, or in the classification of the plant and animal kingdoms by Carolus Linnaeus (Carl von Linné) a century later. For the less specialized collector works such as *Museographia*, by Casper F. Neickel (pseudonym of Kaspar Friedrich Jenequel), published at Leipzig in 1727, were generally available to aid in classification, care of a collection, and the identification of potential sources from which collections might be developed.

Collections of learned societies. Another product of the age was the learned society, many of which were established to promote corporate discussion, experimentation, and collecting. Some commenced as early as the 16th century. Better known societies, however, date from somewhat later years; examples are the Accademia del Cimento in Florence (1657), the Royal Society of London (1660), and the Académie des Sciences in Paris (1666). By the turn of the century organizations covering other subject areas were being established, among them the Society of Antiquaries of London (1707); and learned societies were also appearing in provincial towns. This was the beginning of a movement that, through the collections formed and the promotion of their subjects, contributed much to the formation of museums.

THE ESTABLISHING OF MUSEUMS

If many of the collections formed during the Renaissance were symbols of social prestige and served as an important element in the traditions of the nobility and the ruling families, the subsequent developing spirit of inquiry brought to collecting a different meaning and purpose as well as a much wider group of practitioners. These new collectors, concerned with enjoyment and study and the advancement of knowledge, while equally concerned with the continuity of their collections, had no such guarantee of succession. If this guarantee could not be found in the family unit then the route of succession had to be found elsewhere, and the corporate unit provided greater security. Furthermore, if knowledge were to have lasting significance, it had to be transmitted in the public domain.

Public collections. The earliest recorded instance of a public body receiving a private collection occurs in the 16th century with the bequests of the brothers Cardinal Domenico Grimani and Antonio Grimani to the Venetian Republic in 1523, to be supplemented in 1583 with a further bequest from the family. The motivation seems to have been both to promote scholarship and to grace the seat of government. In the following century, as already noted, the Zürich municipal authority was the recipient of ecclesiastical collections. The city of Basel, concerned that the fine cabinet of Basilius Amerbach might be exported, purchased it in 1662 and nine years later arranged for its display in the university library. In 1694 the head abbot of Saint-Vincent de Besançon in France bequeathed his collection of paintings and medallions to the abbey to form a public collection. To some extent the emerging learned societies also were becoming repositories for such collections, in addition to developing their own. In the case of Ole Worm's collection, as in other cases, lack of interest among the owner's family after his death resulted in the transfer of the collection in 1655 to the royal cabinet in Copenhagen.

The Ashmolean Museum

The first public museums. The first of the corporate bodies to receive such a collection, erect a building to house it, and make it publicly available was the University of Oxford. The building was its Ashmolean Museum, opened in 1683. (The Ashmolean later moved to another new building nearby, and its original building was occupied by the Museum of the History of Science.)

The 18th century saw the flowering of the Enlightenment and the encyclopaedic spirit, as well as a growing taste for the exotic. These influences, encouraged by increasing world exploration, by trade centred on northwestern Europe, and by developing industrialization, are evident in the opening of two of Europe's outstanding museums, the British Museum, in London, in 1759 and the Louvre, in Paris, in 1793. The British Museum was formed as the result of the government's acceptance of responsibility to preserve and maintain three collections "not only for the inspection and entertainment of the learned and the curious, but for the general use and benefit of the public." These were housed in Montagu House, in Bloomsbury, specially purchased for this purpose. The collections had been made by Sir Robert Cotton; Robert Harley, 1st earl of Oxford; and Sir Hans Sloane. The Cotton and Oxford collections were composed mainly of manuscripts. The Sloane collection, however, included his specimens of natural history from Jamaica and classical, ethnographic, numismatic, and art material, as well as the cabinet of William Courten, comprising some 100,000 items in all, which Sloane had acquired. Although public access to the British Museum was free of charge from the outset, for many years admission was by application for one of the limited number of tickets issued daily. Despite this, François de la Rochefoucauld, visiting from France in 1784, observed with approval that the museum was expressly "for the instruction and gratification of the public."

It was a matter of public concern in France that the royal collections were inaccessible to the populace, and eventually a selection of paintings was exhibited at the Palais du Luxembourg in 1750 by Louis XV. Continuing pressure, including Diderot's proposal of a national museum, led to arrangements for more of the royal collection to be displayed to the public in the Grande Galerie of the Louvre palace. The Grande Galerie was opened to the public in 1793, by decree of the Revolutionary government, as the Muséum Central des Arts. There were, however, many difficulties, and the museum was not fully accessible until 1801.

The different nature of the British and French collections and perhaps different cultural characteristics of the two nations resulted in different approaches in the presentation of their collections. At the British Museum the trend was to promote the historical and scientific; at the Louvre the aesthetic was emphasized. The collection at the Louvre grew rapidly, not least because the Convention Nationale instructed Napoleon to appropriate works of art during his European campaigns; as a result many royal and noble collections were transported to Paris to be shown at what became known as the Musée Napoléon. The return to its owners of this looted material was required by the Congress of Vienna in 1815. Nevertheless the Napoleonic episode awakened a new interest in art and provided the impetus that made a number of collections available to the public.

The extensive collections of the Vatican also saw considerable reorganization during the 18th century. The Capitoline Museum was formed in 1734, and the Palazzo dei Conservatori was converted to a picture gallery in 1749. The Museo Pio-Clementino opened in 1772 to house an extensive collection of antiquities. This building's Neoclassical architecture set a standard that was emulated in a number of European countries for half a century.

Before the end of the 18th century the phenomenon of the museum had spread to other parts of the world. In

1773 the Charleston Library Society of South Carolina announced its intention of forming a museum. Its purpose was to promote the better understanding of agriculture and herbal medicine in the area. Another early institution in America, known as the Peale Museum, was founded privately in 1786 in Philadelphia by the painter Charles Willson Peale. The collections rapidly outgrew the space available in his home and were displayed for a time at Independence Hall. After a number of vicissitudes the collections were finally dispersed in the middle of the 19th century, but not before the fine Chinese collection had formed a major exhibition in London.

Early museums in America

European colonial influence was responsible for the appearance of museums elsewhere. In Jakarta the collection of the Batavia Society of Arts and Science was begun in 1778, eventually to become the Central Museum of Indonesian Culture. The origins of the Indian Museum in Calcutta were similar, being based on the collections of the Asiatic Society of Bengal, which commenced in 1784. In South America a number of the national museums originated in the early 19th century: the Argentine Museum of Natural Sciences in Buenos Aires was founded in 1812; and Brazil's National Museum in Rio de Janeiro owed its origin to a selection of paintings presented by the King of Portugal and opened to the public in 1818. Among others were the National Museum, Bogotá, Colom. (1824), and the national museums of natural history in Santiago, Chile (1830), and Montevideo, Uruguay (1837). In Canada the zoological collection of the Pictou Academy in Nova Scotia was probably opened to the public by 1822. In South Africa a museum based on the zoological collection of Andrew (later Sir Andrew) Smith was founded in Cape Town in 1825. It is likely that an amateur naturalist and diplomat, Alexander Macleay, was responsible for the initiatives that led to the opening in 1827 of what was to become the Australian Museum in Sydney.

By this time a number of new collections were available to the public in Europe. Many of these resulted from royal and noble patronage, while others were created on the initiative of public authorities. The Prado in Madrid dates from 1787, when Charles III commissioned the erection of a new building to serve as a museum of natural science. Construction was interrupted by the Napoleonic Wars, and when the building opened in 1819 it instead housed an art gallery to display part of the royal collection. In Germany, Frederick William III had a picture gallery built in Berlin to house some of his collection, and the gallery was opened to the public in 1830. This was the beginning of a remarkable complex that developed over the next century to house various portions of the national collection on a single site, now known as the Museuminsel. Another development in Germany was the erection of the Alte Pinakothek (1836) at Munich to display the painting collections of the dukes of Wittelsbach. This building was designed to exacting standards by Leo von Klenze, who was also responsible for the New Hermitage, one of the five buildings of the Hermitage museum in Leningrad, where in 1852 Nicholas I made available to the public the major collection of the Russian tsars. The Musées Royaux in Brussels originated by royal warrant in 1835 in the interests of historical study and the arts. In the Netherlands a national art gallery was opened at the Huis ten Bosch in 1800; it was later moved to Amsterdam and eventually became the Rijksmuseum. The National Gallery in London, founded on the personal collection of the merchant and philanthropist John Julius Angerstein, opened on Trafalgar Square in 1838.

Museums and national identity. A developing national consciousness, particularly in central Europe, contributed to the establishment of museums at this time. The Hungarian Assembly founded a national museum in 1802 at Pest from the collections of Count Ferenc Széchenyi; in Prague the natural history collections of the counts of Sternberg and other noble families were formed into a museum in 1818 with the intention of promoting national identity. The Moravské Múzeum ("Moravian Museum") in Brno opened in 1818, and others followed at Zagreb and Ljubljana in 1821. At the centre of the Austro-Hungarian Empire, in Vienna, the imperial collections acted as the national museum; regional museums were formed at Graz, Innsbruck, and Salzburg during the period 1811–34. In Nürnberg the Germanisches Nationalmuseum was directed by a proponent of a unified Germany, Hans von Aufsess, and most of the Germanic states had a museum by mid-century. Further north, in Poland, a national museum, although conceived in 1775, was not established until 1862, but the princess Czartoryska had a museum in the castle park at Puławy, near Warsaw, for eight years at the beginning of the 19th century, and two private collections were opened to the public at about the same time in Wilanów and Warsaw.

Increasing interest in antiquities led to the excavation of local archaeological sites and had an impact on museum development. To the north of the Black Sea four archaeological museums were opened, at Feodosiya, Kerch, Nikolayev, and Odessa, in the years 1806–26. The Museum for de nordiske Oldsager ("Museum of Northern Antiquities") was opened in Copenhagen in 1807 (it was there that its first director, Christian Jürgensen Thomsen, developed the three-part system of classifying prehistory into the Stone, Bronze, and Iron ages). This museum was merged with three others (of ethnography, antiquities, and numismatics) in 1892 to form the Danmarks Nationalmuseum. In France the Musée des Antiquités Nationales opened at Saint-Germain-en-Laye late in the 18th century. The Statens Historiska Museum in Stockholm houses Sweden's archaeological material, some of which was recovered as early as the 17th century. The national archaeological museum in Greece was started at Aeginia in 1829; and Yugoslavia's national archaeological museum was founded in Belgrade in 1844. Certain European countries, however, England and Germany for example, do not have well-developed national collections of antiquities, and as a result regional museums in those countries are the richer.

Archaeological museums

The mid-19th century. In Britain, social reforms to overcome problems resulting from industrialization contributed to the development of municipal museums. The support of museums by local authorities was seen as a means of providing instruction and entertainment to the increasingly urbanized population and was the subject of special legislation in 1845. Museums were also viewed as a vehicle for promoting industrial design and scientific and technical achievement. Such promotion was the motivation behind the precursor of the Victoria and Albert Museum (for decorative arts) and the Science Museum, both in London; the founding collections were acquired from the Great Exhibition of 1851—the first of the world's fairs. International exhibitions have contributed to the formation of a number of museums since then, including the Technisches Museum in Vienna and the Palais de la Découverte ("Palace of Discovery") in Paris.

The Smithsonian Institution, in Washington, D.C., came into existence through the remarkable bequest of nearly one-half million dollars from James Smithson, an Englishman. He wished to see established in the United States an institution "for the increase and diffusion of knowledge among men." In 1846 the U.S. Congress accepted his bequest and passed legislation establishing the Smithsonian as an institution charged with representing "all objects of art and curious research . . . natural history, plants, [and] geological and mineralogical specimens" belonging to the United States. The U.S. National Museum opened in 1858 as part of the Smithsonian's scientific program and formed the first of its many museums, most of which stand along the Mall in Washington, D.C.

The Smithsonian Institution

The first of the historic house museums, a type characteristic of the United States, was Hasbrouck House, at Newburgh, N.Y., which served as the final headquarters of George Washington in the Revolutionary War. The purchase of the house by the State of New York in 1850 established another precedent, whereby public authorities provide and maintain museum buildings while a body of trustees assumes responsibility for the collections and staff. Two other well-known museums, both in New York City, provide examples of this system: the American Museum of Natural History, founded in 1869, and the Metropolitan Museum of Art, opened in 1870.

The middle of the 19th century saw the establishment of a number of other well-known museums. The collection of the National Museum of Canada commenced in 1843 as part of the Geological Survey (it moved to Ottawa in 1880), while the precursor of the Royal Ontario Museum in Toronto, the Ontario Provincial Museum, was founded in 1855. The National Museum of Victoria was established at Melbourne, in Victoria, Australia, in 1854 and was followed by the National Gallery of Victoria in 1861 and the Science Museum of Victoria in 1870. In Cairo the Egyptian Museum was established in 1858. These all followed the European model, and even in South America art collections tended to be predominately of European origin, to the neglect of indigenous works of art.

The first museum boom. It was during the second half of the 19th century that museums began to proliferate in Europe. About 100 opened in Britain in the 1870s and '80s, while 50 museums were established in Germany in the five years from 1876 to 1880. This was also a period of innovation. The Liverpool Museums in England, for example, began circulating specimens to schools for educational purposes; panoramas and habitat groups were used to facilitate interpretation. As first gas lighting and then electric lighting became available, museums extended their hours into the evenings to provide service to those unable to visit during the day.

The museum boom in South America

The increase in the number of museums was not, however, a peculiarity of Europe or North America. In South America particularly, new museums were founded both in the capital cities and in the provinces. Some of these were provided by universities, as in the case of the Geological Museum in Lima (1891) or the Geographical and Geological Museum at São Paulo, Brazil (1895). Others were created by provincial bodies: the regional museums at Córdoba (1887) and Gualeguaychu (1898), both in Argentina, and at Ouro Prêto (1876), Brazil; the Hualpen Museum (1882), Chile; or the Municipal Museum and Library at Guayaquil (1862), Ecuador. New specialist national museums also appeared in certain countries, while at Tigre, in Argentina, a maritime museum was founded in 1892. Early in the following century memorial museums were created, including those dedicated to Bartolomé Mitre, a former president of Argentina, in Buenos Aires (1906) and to Simón Bolívar in Caracas (1911).

By this time the Indian Museum, in Calcutta, and the Central Museum of Indonesian Culture, Jakarta, were well-established institutions in Asia, but a number of new museums were appearing as well. In Japan a museum to encourage industry and the development of natural resources was opened in 1872; this provided the basis for the modern-day Tokyo National Museum and National Science Museum. Although some learned-society museums existed in China in the late 19th century, the first museum in the strict sense of the word was the Nan-t'ung (Nantong) Museum in Kiangsu (Jiang-su) Province, founded in 1905, to be followed within a decade by the Museum of the History of China in Peking (Beijing) and the Northern Territory Museum in Tientsin (Tianjin). The collections established in the Grand Palace at Bangkok in 1874 became, about 60 years later, the National Museum of Thailand. The National Museum in Ceylon (now Sri Lanka) opened to the public in 1877; the Sarawak Museum opened in 1891; and the Peshāwar Museum, in Peshāwar, Pak., in 1906.

In central and southern Africa museums were founded early in the century. Zimbabwe's national museums at Bulawayo and Harare (formerly Salisbury) were founded in 1901, the Uganda Museum originated in 1908 from collections assembled by the British District Commissioners, and the National Museum of Kenya in Nairobi was commenced by the East Africa and Uganda Natural History Society in 1909. Mozambique's first museum, the Dr. Alvaro de Castro Museum in Maputo, was founded in 1913. Meanwhile in North Africa the Egyptian Museum in Cairo had been relocated to its new building in 1902, and certain of the collections had been transferred to form two new institutions: the Museum of Islāmic Art (1903) and the Coptic Museum (1908). In South Africa there was steady museum development in a number of the provinces, for example in Grahamstown (1837), Port Elizabeth (1856), Bloemfontein (1877), Durban (1887), Pretoria (1893), and Pietermaritzburg (1903).

A period of reassessment. The first half of the 20th century saw the profound social consequences of two world wars, the Russian Revolution, and periods of economic recession. For museums in Europe this was a period of major reassessment. Governments, professional associations, and other organizations reviewed the role of museums in a changing society and made a number of suggestions to improve their service to the public. In some countries new approaches were developed; in others new museums continued to reflect their diverse ancestry, but some decades were to pass before resources generally became available for the implementation of major changes.

In the Soviet Union, collections and museums were brought under state control following the Revolution. Lenin's belief that culture was for the people and his efforts to preserve the country's cultural heritage led to a trebling of the number of museums in the 20 years' time. Not only was much of the country's artistic, historic, and scientific heritage brought together in museums, but other types of museums emerged as well. Among these were the memorial museums housing the personal effects of well-known figures. Particular attention was given to amassing material related to Russia's three revolutions, and in 1924 the Central Order of Lenin Museum of the Revolution in Moscow was created to house the collection. Museums also were seen as an important means of communicating political propaganda, and the V.I. Lenin Central Museum in Moscow, opened in 1936, served this purpose.

In Germany a large number of regional museums were established after World War I to promote the history and important figures of the homeland, and they undoubtedly encouraged nationalism.

The national museum service in France was eventually extended, following World War II, to provide financial and other assistance to a number of the provincial museums. For the most part, however, museums were not well organized to meet the changing social conditions. In Britain there was a diversity of providers: national and local government, universities, societies, companies, and individuals. In central Europe associations attempted to develop and run individual museums but were unable to provide the necessary resources. In the United States, however, the need to establish a coherent past was widely encouraged through private patronage.

Preservation of historical sites and customs

In the industrialized world new types of museums appeared. Some nations made conscious attempts to preserve and display structures and customs of their more recent past. Examples, following Sweden's pioneering reerection of significant buildings, include the open-air museums at Arnhem in The Netherlands (the Openluchtmuseum, opened in 1912) and at Cardiff, Wales (the Welsh Folk Museum, opened in 1947). The preservation and restoration of buildings or entire settlements in situ also began; particularly well known is Colonial Williamsburg, founded in Virginia in 1926. A new type of science museum also emerged in which static displays of scientific instruments and equipment were replaced with demonstrations of the applications of science. London's Science Museum, founded in 1857, eventually was moved to specially built premises in 1919. Similarly the Deutsches Museum in Munich was transferred to new premises in 1925. Both established worldwide reputations for excellence in interpreting science and technology for the general public.

New developments and new roles. The years immediately following World War II were a period of remarkable achievement for museums. This was reflected both in international and national policy and in the individual museums as they responded to a rapidly changing, better educated society. Museums became an educational facility, a source of leisure activity, and a medium of communication. Their strength lay in the fact that they were repositories of the "real thing," which, unlike the surrounding world of plastics and reproduced images, and a deteriorating natural and human environment, could inspire and invoke a sense of wonder, reality, stability, and even nostalgia.

Postwar renovation and reconstruction

In Europe particularly there was a period of postwar reconstruction. Many art treasures had been removed to places of safety during the war, and they now had to be recovered and redisplayed; buildings had to be refurbished. In some cases museums and their collections had been destroyed. This reconstruction provided opportunities for the realization of some of the ideas that had been advanced earlier in the century. A new approach emerged in which curators in the larger museums became members of a team comprising scientists as conservators, designers to assist in exhibition work, educators to develop facilities for both students and the public, information scientists to handle the scientific data inherent in collections, and even marketing managers to promote the museum and its work. There was a perceptible shift from serving the scholar, as befits an institution holding much of the primary evidence of the material world, to providing for a lay public as well.

Attendance figures give an indication of the new popularity of museums. One report from the United States in the 1970s, for example, estimated that more than 300,000,000 visits a year had been made to some 1,800 of the country's museums, and during the same period the Soviet Union's state museums alone recorded about 140,000,000 visits annually. Certainly some of the oldest established museums in Europe, such as the British Museum, the Louvre, and the Hermitage, each regularly attract more than 3,000,000 visitors a year, and some of the science and technology museums are even more popular. Many of the visitors are tourists, and governments, particularly in certain European countries, recognize the value of museums in attracting foreign visitors and acknowledge the museums' contribution to the economy.

Among other factors that have contributed to the development of museums is an increased awareness of the environment and the need to preserve it. Many sites of scientific significance have been preserved and interpreted, sometimes under the aegis of a national park service, and historic sites and buildings have been restored and used as museums. This has led to the development of historic and natural landscapes as museums, such as the renovation of Mystic Seaport in Connecticut as a maritime museum, the use of Ironbridge Gorge as a museum to interpret the cradle of the Industrial Revolution in England, and the restoration of the walled medieval cities at Suzdal and Vladimir in the Soviet Union. In Australia the heyday of the gold rush has been re-created in the form of the Sovereign Hill Historical Park, at the gold-mining town of Ballarat. Gorée, a small island off the Senegal coast that served as a major entrepôt for the Atlantic slave trade, has been restored as a historic site with a number of supporting museums. Another related development was the ecomuseum, such as the Musée de l'Homme et de l'Industrie at Le Creusot–Montceau-les-Mines in France. Here a bold experiment involves the community as a whole, rather than specialists, in interpreting the human and natural environment, thereby generating a better understanding among its inhabitants of the reasons for cultural, social, and environmental change. Some of these projects have involved the acquisition and preservation of massive artifacts, but perhaps no undertaking has been as spectacular as the recovery from the seabed of ships such as the *Vasa,* the Song dynasty ship from Quanzhou, the *Mary Rose,* or the Hanseatic cog from Bremerhaven, now preserved in museums in Sweden, China, England, and West Germany, respectively.

A feature of contemporary museum development has been the initiative taken by local groups and individuals in their concern to preserve the past of their communities. This movement can be found in both the East and the West and in the Northern and Southern hemispheres. Public concern, however, does not mean that governments have been inactive. Many of the older museums have been refitted and extended to meet more exacting requirements for the preservation of cultural property and to provide better facilities for visitors. A number of new major museums have also been built. Australia opened its National Gallery of Art in Canberra in 1982; and the National Gallery of Victoria has been developed as part of Melbourne's arts complex. In Paris the Centre National d'Art et de Culture Georges Pompidou (Centre Beaubourg) combines a gallery of modern art and special exhibition galleries with other cultural activities. The Museum of London, amalgamating the collections of two previous museums, has been built to tell the story of the capital and its immediate environs. The magnificent Museo Nacional de Antropología, just one of a fine complex of museums in Mexico City, displays the country's archaeological richness, while additions to the Smithsonian's museums in Washington, D.C., have included the National Air and Space Museum and the Hirshhorn Museum and Sculpture Garden. In the Soviet Union the State Historical Museum of the Uzbek S.S.R. in Tashkent and the V.I. Lenin House and Museum, Ulyanovsk, are but two of many newer museum buildings. Many buildings of historical significance also have been adapted to house museums. Among these is the Gare d'Orsay, formerly a major railroad station, in Paris, redeveloped as a national museum of the 19th century.

Modern Masters: Manet to Matisse, a traveling exhibit organized by the Museum of Modern Art, New York City, on display in the National Gallery of Victoria, Melbourne, in an area especially designed for temporary shows.

By courtesy of the National Gallery of Victoria, Melbourne

Nor have developments been restricted to the industrialized countries. A desire to preserve their local history has led many Caribbean islands to establish small museums. Several African nations also have given high priority to the provision of museums. Museums have been established in the principal cities of Nigeria by its National Museums and Monuments Commission to assist in developing cultural identity and promoting national unity. The Jos Museum, one of the earliest of these, also administers a museum of traditional buildings, while others have developed workshops where traditional crafts can be demonstrated. Crafts are also a feature of the National Museum in Niamey, Niger, and products of these workshops are exported to Europe and North America.

Types of museums

With their diverse origins, varying philosophies, and differing roles in society, museums do not lend themselves to rigid classification. Nevertheless it is convenient, for a variety of purposes, to group them; and the classification can be based either on source of funding or on the nature of collections. Classifying museums by source of funding, however, fails to indicate the character of their collections. For example, institutions funded by the national government—national museums—may hold outstanding international collections, as do the British Museum, the Hermitage, and the Louvre; may hold special collections, as do a number of the national museums of antiquities on the European continent; or may have an essentially local character, as does the Smithsonian's Anacostia Neighborhood Museum in Washington, D.C. An analysis of museums based on the nature of their collections, on the other hand, although it fails to indicate the wide disparities of scale and quality, does have the merit of distinguishing between the general and the specialized museum. The most common classification scheme distinguishes among general, art, history, and science museums.

GENERAL MUSEUMS

Many of the general museums were founded in the 18th, 19th, or early 20th century. Most originated in earlier private collections and reflected the encyclopaedic spirit of the times. Certain general museums reflect the influence of cultural contact made through trade. Some museums hold a number of important specialized collections that would qualify them to be grouped in more than one category of specialization. This is true particularly of many of the large general museums, which may have collections in one or more fields equal to if not exceeding both the quantity and quality of material exhibited in a specialized museum. Some national museums display general collections within their main building; indeed many commenced in this fashion, but the necessity of finding additional space later caused a division of the collections and encouraged the growth of specialized museums. Although this is a logical division to make, particularly in an institution that emphasizes scholarly work in the traditional disciplines, it can result in arbitrary decisions, particularly with multivalent artifacts that may contribute, for example, to historic, technological, and aesthetic understanding.

Regional and local general museums

Most common among general museums are those that serve a region or a locality. Many of these owe their foundation to civic pride and a desire to promote knowledge of the area. They are widespread in eastern and western Europe and are found as well in India, Australia, New Zealand, and North and South America. Their prime responsibility is to reflect the natural and human history, traditions, and creative spirit of the area. In many cases the community thus served is culturally homogeneous, but where it is not, the museum may develop specific programs to foster mutual understanding among the diverse peoples. In cities that have a sizable immigrant population, such as, for example, Bradford or Leicester in England, the regional museum has engaged actively in such work. Where the regional museums form part of a state museum network, and sometimes also in separately administered regional museums, special exhibitions prepared by the national museum or other agencies provide opportunities for the community to appreciate the wider aspects of the national or even international heritage.

The general museum, particularly at the regional or local level, faces severe problems because of the high cost of employing the large numbers of specialists necessary to care for the variety of collections involved, particularly if a strong research program is maintained. In some museums research has diversified as curators, particularly in archaeology, history, and the natural sciences, have agreed to advise planners and developers considering projects for sites of historical interest. Other general museums have maintained their more traditional roles but have concentrated their efforts on public services, as at the Kanazawa Bunko Museum, Yokohama, Japan, where a multidisciplinary approach is apparent in its exhibitions. Among other developments fostered by many regional and local museums are the erection of on-site museums to interpret archaeological or natural features; the provision of heritage centres, particularly in urban areas, to tell the story of an aspect of the historic environment; or, as an extramural activity of the museum, the development of town landmark trails and nature trails.

Certain museums provide for a particular audience, often acquiring general collections to suit the purpose. One of these is the children's museum (also well attended by adults), well-known examples of which are the Brooklyn Children's Museum, New York City; the Children's Museum, Boston; the National Children's Museum of New Delhi; and the Mont Riant Children's Museum of Algiers.

ART MUSEUMS

The art museum (called an art gallery in some places) is concerned primarily with the object as a means of unaided communication with its visitors. Aesthetic value is therefore a major consideration in accepting items for the collection. Traditionally these collections have comprised paintings, sculpture, and the decorative arts. A number of art museums have included the industrial arts since the 19th century, when they were introduced, particularly to encourage good industrial design. The collection of so-called primitive art is of more recent origin and has had a profound influence on certain forms of 20th-century art, but it can be argued that aesthetics have subordinated function and association to such an extent that primitive pieces are often presented in a totally alien context. In some countries this criticism applies to archaeological material as well.

The display of works of art

The display of works of art presents the curator with certain problems. Works of art are exhibited to convey a visual message. While other disciplines tend to adopt didactic methods of display, as in a history panorama or a demonstration of technique, the art curator is concerned particularly with unimpeded presentation of a given work. The ambience of the work is enhanced by highlighting its form and colour with proper lighting and background. Artificial light was at one time preferred for paintings, both to create an effect and to prevent exposure to harmful elements in natural light, but it sometimes provides an unnecessarily theatrical presentation or creates an artificiality that can inhibit the visitor's appreciation or enjoyment of the work. Much greater use is now made of

Leonard Freed—Magnum

Spectator viewing Femmes d'un Jour, an exhibit of shopwindow mannequins at the Musée National d'Art Moderne in the Centre Beaubourg, Paris.

indirect natural light or, as at the Tate Gallery, London, of a controlled mixture of daylight and simulated daylight. Some art museums have returned to the earlier custom of hanging paintings in a tiered arrangement in order to exhibit more of their works.

The search for context has led to the design of period settings in which to present certain art objects, to the development of furnished period-house museums, and to the preservation of country houses and other appropriate properties, together with their contents, in situ. In a specialized context, the restoration of the Moscow Kremlin, particularly the Great Palace and the churches with their fine murals and icons, provides an example of this approach. Some of the churches are open to the public as museums. Some art museums have introduced other visual and performing arts—music, film, video, or theatre—to facilitate or enhance interpretation; others operate artist-in-residence programs for the same purpose.

Another factor in the display of art objects concerns their continued preservation. Because of the sensitivity of some of the materials used in their creation it is necessary to control within narrow limits the temperature, humidity, and lighting to which they are exposed. In addition, sophisticated security precautions are necessary for items of high value.

The display of modern art

In many cases modern art is displayed in a separate institution. The role of such museums is to confront the public with art in the process of development, and their work has a considerable experimental component. This is particularly so at the Centre Beaubourg in Paris, the Stedelijk Museum ("Municipal Museum") in Amsterdam, or the museums of modern art in Stockholm and New York City, where other contemporary art forms besides painting are also presented. Because of the experimental nature of modern art and the high cost involved in purchases, temporary exhibitions normally play a major role in such museums and in some cases are their principal activity. Contemporary sculpture is often exhibited outdoors, as at the Hirshhorn in Washington, D.C.; the Open-Air Museum in Hakone, Japan; or the Billy Rose Art Garden in Jerusalem.

Another form of art museum is the portrait gallery. The pictures displayed there have been created to communicate an image. The approach, however, is more akin to that of a specialized history museum, and aesthetic considerations generally are secondary in forming the collections. Although the idea of a portrait gallery is of some antiquity—a large collection of portraits of the kings of France and their statesmen was exhibited in Paul Ardier's gallery at the Château de Beauregard, near Blois, in the 1620s, for example—the national portrait gallery as a public institution is a later development.

HISTORY MUSEUMS

The term history museum is often used for a wide variety of museums where collections are amassed and, in most cases, are presented to give a chronological perspective. Because of the encompassing nature of history, museums of this type may well hold so many objects of art and science that they would more properly be called general museums (see above).

Museums of general history are rare at the national level. An example, however, is the Museo Nacional de Historia in Chapultepec Castle, Mexico City. At the local level there are many examples, of which the Museum of London and the city museums of Amsterdam, Dresden, New York City, Stockholm, and Warsaw are but a few. In many cases, if artifacts are not available or are inappropriate, curators use reconstructions, models, and graphics to maintain chronological continuity and to increase the opportunity for interpretation within their essentially didactic approach.

While such history museums may include archaeological material, there is nevertheless a distinctive type, the antiquities museum. Such collections of relics of the ancient world can be found in national museums in a number of cities, for example, Amman, Jordan; Athens; Cairo; Copenhagen; Edinburgh; and Madrid. The antiquities museum is particularly common in Europe and Asia.

Specialized archaeology museums also are found in areas of rich antiquity or as on-site museums. The archaeology museum is concerned mainly with historical evidence recovered from the ground and in many cases provides information on a period for which the written record can make little or no contribution.

Another specialized form of the history museum collects and exhibits material from an ethnographic viewpoint. As the term suggests, emphasis is placed on culture rather than chronology in the presentation of the collections. The ethnography museum is common among newer nation-states of Africa and Oceania, where it is seen as a means of contributing to national unity among different cultural groups. Among the industrialized nations, and particularly in countries that have been involved in colonization, the ethnography museum is a museum of the cultures of other peoples. Many of these institutions have been established in the capital cities, which at the height of colonization were the nation's window on a world otherwise distant and unknown. Thus were founded the Musée de l'Homme, Paris; the Museum of Mankind (a branch of the British Museum), London; and the Tropenmuseum (Museum of the Royal Tropical Institute), Amsterdam. Specialized ethnography museums are also to be found in provincial cities with links to other cultures: the Übersee-Museum ("Overseas Museum") in Bremen resulted from the city's proximity to a major international port, as did the fine ethnology collection in the general museum at Liverpool. In many cases the collections reflect the country's trade or colonial connections.

The ethnography museum

There are other forms of the cultural history museum. Particularly prolific are museums concerned with preserving urban and rural traditions; these have rapidly increased in number with the pace of technological progress. Indeed, some history museums are involved in documenting various material aspects of contemporary life and in the selective collection of artifacts. Artur Hazilius developed the first museum of traditional life at the Nordiska Museet ("Nordic Museum"), Stockholm, in 1872, to be followed by the first open-air museum, at Skansen. Museums of both types soon appeared in other countries. The Musée National des Arts et Traditions Populaires in Paris exemplifies a national approach within a museum building. Outdoor museums preserving traditional architecture, sometimes in situ, and often demonstrating the activities associated with them, are to be found in many parts of the world: the National Museum of Niamey, Niger, or

By courtesy of Nordiska Museet, Stockholm

Tower of Seglora Kyrka, an 18th-century wooden church from Västergötland, Swed., which now is among many historic buildings preserved at Skansen, the first open-air museum, in Stockholm.

the Museum of Traditional Architecture in Jos, Nigeria; the Muzeul Satului ("Village Museum") of Bucharest; Upper Canada Village, Morrisburg, Ont.; or the Novgorod State Museum Preserve in the Soviet Union. Individual historic houses have been preserved as museums, in some cases because they are typical of the period and in other cases because of their associations. Among the latter are the memorial museums, such as the cottage of Tu Fu (Du Fu) at Ch'eng-tu (Chengdu), in the Chinese province of Szechwan (Sichuan), and the Leo Tolstoy Museum, Moscow (both of which could also be regarded as literature museums), or Mount Vernon, George Washington's home in Virginia.

Military and maritime museums

Other museums commemorate events, as do the Australian War Memorial in Canberra or the Imperial War Museum, London; both are military museums, members of a category that grew after World War I. Another development in the 20th-century history museum has been the maritime museum. Like other types of museums, they may be housed in historic buildings, as at the National Maritime Museum at Greenwich, Eng.; in new premises, as in the case of the Deutsches Schiffahrtsmuseum ("German Ship Museum") at Bremerhaven, W.Ger.; or in a restored waterfront environment, as at South Street, New York City.

SCIENCE MUSEUMS

The origins of the science museum lie in the cabinets of curiosities and the spirit of the Enlightenment in Europe. They are concerned with the natural or applied sciences, or sometimes with both. Some approach their collections historically, as do museums of natural history or museums of the history of science and technology, the latter being concerned with scientific ideas and instrumentation and the technology developing from them. Such museums have an important role in preserving the material evidence of scientific and technological endeavour. Other science and technology museums may be more concerned with demonstrating science and its applications, and in these museums the preservation of processes is emphasized over the preservation of objects.

Specimens from natural science were included, albeit as part of an encyclopaedic collection, in some of the earliest museums: the Ashmolean, the British Museum (the specimens were later separated from the larger collection and relocated at the British Museum [Natural History]), and the Muséum National d'Histoire Naturelle in Paris. With the development of the natural sciences in the 19th century these museums flourished and their number multiplied. In the United States and Latin America their collections often included physical and social anthropology as well as natural science. More recently, natural science museums have responded to new trends in nature conservation and broader environmental matters. Other museums have established programs for recording biological data for the area they serve, to facilitate environmental planning (often in conjunction with local planning authorities) and to provide information to assist in the interpretation of ecological displays. Major museums such as the British Museum (Natural History), the Smithsonian's National Museum of Natural History, and the American Museum of Natural History in New York City continue to be international centres of taxonomic work that sustain large amounts of research.

Museums of the applied sciences and technical museums are popular with children and adults alike and often provide opportunities for their visitors to participate through models and displays. Well-known examples of these are at the Deutsches Museum, Munich; the Science Museum, London; and, of a more specialized nature, the Smithsonian's National Air and Space Museum, Washington, D.C. Developing countries see an important role for museums of science and technology in education, and in India museums of this type have been established at Calcutta, Bangalore, Pilani, and elsewhere. Others are of a more technical nature, such as the very popular Museum of Science and Industry of Chicago or the Museo Tecnológico in Mexico City. Industry often directly or indirectly sponsors these museums. Occasionally industries or individual companies have founded their own museums to preserve their heritage and promote their work. Museums and science centres devoted to modern science also provide demonstrations of scientific theory. Other more specialized institutions of this type include transport museums.

Reproduced by courtesy of the trustees of the British Museum (Natural History)

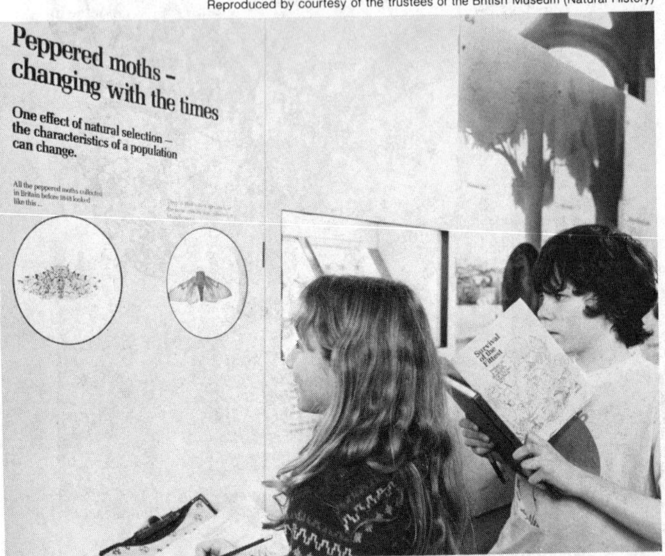

Students availing themselves of the information provided by an educational display on natural selection at the British Museum (Natural History).

The museum operation

THE ORGANIZATION OF MUSEUMS

Unesco's role

On an international level, the United Nations Educational, Scientific and Cultural Organization (Unesco) forms an important link between governments for museum collaboration. Since its inception in 1946 it has been responsible for an increasing body of legislation to protect the world's cultural property. Unesco has aided in the return of cultural property to its country of origin and also has initiated campaigns to ensure the protection of major world heritage sites. It has provided financial assistance for the renovation of older museums and the establishment of new ones, particularly in developing countries. Some of its member states were responsible for the creation of the International Centre for the Study of the Preservation and the Restoration of Cultural Property (ICCROM) in Rome.

A number of regional governmental bodies also have an interest in museum provision. For example, the Organization of African Unity was instrumental in the creation of the Organization for Museums, Monuments and Sites of Africa to promote the better protection of the continent's heritage. In western Europe the Council of Europe has promoted legislation for the protection of the archaeological heritage, undertaken a number of studies on museum provision, and promoted an award for museums. The European Communities promotes exchanges between museums, encourages the development of "European rooms" in certain museums of its member states, and has contributed to the capital costs of museum development.

The organization of museums varies from one country to the next. For example, France and the Soviet Union exercise considerable state control. In other countries a few museums in the capital cities may be financed by the government, as in Britain, Canada, and the United States, although not necessarily under direct government control; the majority of the museums in these countries, however, are provided by other agencies. Although there has been a marked increase in the number of private museums, even in the Soviet Union, in general private patronage has declined, making probable an increase in the need for corporate patronage or government funding.

The first organized international cooperation at a professional level arose through the League of Nations Committee of Intellectual Cooperation, which established an International Museums Office. The office initiated a number of studies and publications during its existence from 1922 to 1946. In the latter year the International Council of Museums (ICOM) was created as a nongovernmental, international forum for museum professionals. The organization is the recognized adviser on museum matters to the Social and Economic Council of the United Nations and to Unesco. In some countries the national committees of ICOM fulfill the role of professional associations, but a number of countries now have nongovernmental associations for museum personnel.

LEGAL ARRANGEMENTS

Legislation concerning the preservation of cultural property is to be found at both the national and the international level and has a considerable history. Indeed, as early as 1162, the Roman Senate decreed that Trajan's Column in Rome be protected as a monument in honour of the Roman people, and in 1624 an edict of Cardinal Aldobrandini prohibited unauthorized excavation of the city's sites and required that any finds of historic interest be reported within 24 hours of discovery. Today statutes embracing both historic and natural heritage are widespread at the national level, and in certain countries tax incentives are available to encourage the availability of the heritage. The pattern of legislation providing for museums to house movable cultural property, however, is far from consistent. Museums may be either privately or publicly administered, and the former have grown considerably in number. Some of these have corporate standing under general legislation and receive public moneys. Generally, however, they remain independent of public policy. Certain countries, notably France, some countries in eastern Europe, and some developing nations, have centralized public museum systems that may also have responsibility for monuments and sites.

Patterns of legislation

In France, under legislation of 1945, not only are there national museums in a number of locations outside Paris, but considerable technical control of the country's municipal museums is exercised by a central administration. In contrast, the public museums of the United Kingdom have considerable autonomy. A government-funded museum, usually located in a capital city, has its own legislation that empowers a board of trustees, independent of government, to administer the funds allocated and guide the museum's policies. The municipal museums, however, are provided for under general legislation, and by law local government representatives form the management committees. This pattern can be found elsewhere in Europe and in many other English-speaking countries. In the United States only the dependent museums of the Smithsonian Institution and the National Park Service have national statutes.

Similarly there is no consistent pattern for the general administration of public museums. At the national level they may be overseen by any of several authorities: offices of education, tourism, defense, environment, culture, or leisure, for example. The position can be even more complicated at a local level. This reflects in part the diversity of museum collections but also an ambivalence in understanding their roles: as guardians and interpreters of the heritage, as repositories and scientific institutions for the study of the primary evidence relating to human and natural history, as social instruments in community development, or as facilities for leisure and recreation.

The lack of well-defined legislation to outline objectives concerning the museum's function and its administration, and the variety of interpretation of the museum's role by policymakers, has led a number of professional associations to attempt self-regulation through codes of ethics and professional practice. While the codes are not normally mandatory, they have contributed toward more consistent professional standards among museums.

MUSEUM MANAGEMENT

Most museums, except for unincorporated privately owned institutions, operate under some form of governing body. This body defines the general policy and provides and controls the necessary resources. The appointment of the director and perhaps of other staff members usually is among its responsibilities. The director of a museum governed by this type of body is responsible for the formulation and implementation of policy and for the day-to-day running of the institution and generally provides the link between the governing body, the staff, and the museum's clientele.

The operation of a museum involves a wide variety of skills, which can be divided into those related to the museum's two principal functions. The first involves specialists in subjects relevant to museum collections (normally designated curators or keepers), information scientists involved in the documentation of collections and related scientific information (sometimes known as registrars), and conservators concerned with the scientific examination and treatment of collections to prevent deterioration. The other group is involved more actively with the public functioning of the museum. These include specialists in education, communication and interpretation specialists, designers, the security staff, and marketing and public relations personnel, as well as administrative, maintenance, and other support workers. Such diversity leads to complex staff structures. Many of the larger, older established museums with encyclopaedic collections have a large number of senior specialized personnel. In museums where the emphasis is on providing services for the general public and the collections are less wide-ranging, there are likely to be fewer curatorial and more service personnel. Nevertheless, museums are labour-intensive and, as with other academic-related institutions, the extent to which new technologies can alleviate the need for labour is limited. In all types of museums the operation is based on teamwork, and this has important implications for the management structures adopted as well as for the training of museum staffs.

Staff structures

Organized training for museum personnel is of relatively recent origin and is by no means widely available. By 1910 three courses were being provided in the United States. The following decade, however, saw the commencement of further courses, some in the United States at Harvard University's Fogg Art Museum and at the Newark Museum, New Jersey, and others in Europe. One of these was the well-known École du Louvre, created to train curators for the French museums. Museology was also introduced in the curriculum of Purkyně University in Brno, Moravia (now in Czechoslovakia), in 1921. The first validation for museum training, organized on an in-service basis, appears to have been the diploma of the Museums Association introduced in Britain in 1930. There the University of London also introduced postgraduate courses in art history and archaeology intended to train specialist curators.

It was not until after World War II, however, that university faculties or departments of museology—museum studies, as it is more commonly known in the English-speaking countries—were created with a specific emphasis on the theory and practice of museums, as opposed to an emphasis on the subjects represented in their collections. Programs at the postgraduate level are particularly representative of this approach. In certain countries, notably Japan and some Latin-American nations, curators are required by law to have been graduated in museology before they can practice. Such courses, where available, normally provide some training in museum management.

The financial management of museums changed in the mid-1970s. Until then, public funds constituted the major source for public museums and in many cases contributed a considerable percentage of the income of those operated privately. With increasing restrictions on expenditure of public moneys, however, funding from multiple sources has become far more commonplace, particularly for specific activities and capital works. In developing countries this can be crucial to the formation and continued maintenance of a museum service.

Funding of museums

The main source of funds for museums in the public sector remains the local or national government. This can result in a lack of flexibility in the use of such moneys, because the funds usually are subject to government policies that have little bearing on the particular requirements of museums. In addition, these museums are required to compete for funds against such traditional public expenditures as education, social services, defense, and law and order, and in consequence museums often are given low priority.

Many museums were founded through private benefaction, and a few have endowments that help to support their routine operation. Others may have received bequests, many of which are designated to be used only for the purchase of objects. Such sources, although they may seem appropriate when secured, can suffer from changes in economic circumstances and may have attached to them conditions that are incompatible with requirements of the modern museum.

Today museums, particularly in the industrialized nations, are becoming increasingly involved in fund-raising, in seeking commercial sponsorship, and in their own trading activities. Fund-raising may be undertaken by the museum, by a commissioned organization, or by a support body such as the many "friends of the museum" organizations now in existence. Fund-raising and sponsorship are normally directed toward a specific project or development.

Many museums charge entrance fees to help finance operations, but some countries, such as the United Kingdom, have a strong tradition of free entry to museums. Some museums charge admission fees only for major exhibitions. Others have introduced a system of voluntary donations by visitors on entry to supplement their income, but the results of this approach generally have been disappointing.

Commercial activities have become a significant feature of many museums. These may take the form of restaurants or shops that provide a service to visitors as well as income to the museum. Some museums have separate trading companies that act as publishers or engage in mail-order business, the profits from which are directed to the museum for general purposes. In this way the museum retains its charitable status, is not exposed to the direct dangers that would follow commercial failure, and also circumnavigates any requirements that direct income be returned to the public purse.

Museum buildings and plants also require management by specialists. The popular concept of the public museum originating in the Greek temple has led to the monumental character of many museum buildings. These buildings, which by no means are restricted to museums of art, are generally inefficient in use of space and in environmental control. The majority of museums created since the beginning of the 19th century, however, have been housed in historic buildings that present problems of adaptation for a specialized use. It is rare, therefore, that a museum's premises meet the conflicting needs of utilization and preservation, of providing both public access and security.

COLLECTION

The history of museums and their precursors indicates the influence that the existence of a collection has had on the founding of museums and therefore on the nature of their original holdings. Before the 20th century few museums were established with the goal of making a collection; instead, they were created to receive an existing collection. With the existing collection as its base, the museum proceeded to collect to fill gaps or to extend its activity into other, usually related, fields. For this reason many museums have heterogeneous collections, at best accumulated under an "encyclopaedic" philosophy (which has rarely been successful unless major resources were available to achieve it), and at worst continuing a "cabinet of curiosities" (which may amuse and entertain the clientele but have little scientific validity). Often the collections made depended on the expertise or whim of the curator and were sure to change when that curator was succeeded by someone with different interests. This method has produced some outstanding special collections, but these have resulted from circumstance rather than long-term planning.

Collection policies

Explicit collection policies have become more common. Indeed where national codes of practice exist a strong recommendation is normally to be found on the need for a clear statement of collecting activity. This has arisen for a number of reasons. Not only should a public institution's policies be available for scrutiny, but the cost of maintaining collections of ever-increasing size must be justified, a factor highlighted at times of economic pressure. Further, although a museum may have arisen from circumstance, an assessment of its available resources, the clientele it attracts or intends to attract, and the role it can serve in society generally must be matched against its primary resource, its collections.

Every museum is responsible for ensuring the legality of its acquisitions. Many nations have ratified the Unesco convention of 1970 on the illicit import, export, and transfer of ownership of cultural property. Other similar regional legislation also exists. In 1976 the Organization of American States adopted the San Salvador Convention on the protection of the archaeological, historical, and artistic heritage of the American nations, while the Council of Europe's 1969 convention on the protection of the archaeological heritage has a similar purpose.

Indeed, it is unlikely that a museum with clearly stated academic objectives will acquire illicit material. Methods of collection reflect the fact that a museum is concerned not only with collections per se but also with the information inherent in or associated with them. Where applicable, direct acquisition through fieldwork is much preferred. This involves collecting material through archaeological excavation, ethnological expeditions, or natural science fieldwork, and the collecting either is undertaken by the staff of the museum or is sponsored by it. Indirect acquisition is handled through purchases, gifts, bequests, and loans of objects.

The collecting activities of the industrialized world and those available to the developing nations are markedly different. In some instances the significant cultural property of entire nations has been dispersed to private collections and museums in different parts of the world, leaving the developing museums to rely on casts and replicas to convey the area's cultural achievements. The international community has had only limited success in encouraging the return, through exchange or loan, of such material to its country of origin.

The true significance of cultural property, collectively the universal heritage of mankind, places on museums a considerable responsibility. The acceptance of objects or collections into their care implies a permanence not associated with the acceptance of other types of property. Some museum legislation acknowledges this, declaring such collections inalienable. The disposal of museum collections in part, or in full, therefore normally only occurs in cases where items no longer serve a useful scholarly or interpretative purpose. The case for deaccessioning, as it is known in North America, can only otherwise have any validity where it is done to correct the imbalances of earlier indiscriminate collecting, and in that case the material concerned should first be made available to other suitable museums before being disposed of.

CONSERVATION

A museum's prime responsibility must be to maintain its collections and to do all possible to delay the natural laws of deterioration. The acquisition of an item almost certainly brings it into a new and potentially alien environment. Material that has been recovered from the ground through archaeological excavation may need immediate treatment to stabilize it, and in many cases it is important that some attention be given to this before it reaches the museum. Many of the materials from which objects are made are inherently unstable and undergo chemical or structural change as they age. A new or shifting environment can accelerate these changes, and temperature, light, humidity, human, and other biological factors all need to be controlled. In addition, conservation involves the treatment and, where feasible and acceptable, the restoration of objects as nearly as possible to their former condition.

Conservation laboratories

Most large museums have their own laboratories where preservation and restoration work is carried out, and some take on projects for other museums as well. In some cases, as at the British Museum, a separate research laboratory supports the museum's academic and conservation work, providing advanced scientific equipment for the analysis, dating, and identification of materials. Some museums are served by independent conservation laboratories, an example of which is the Canadian Conservation Institute, in Ottawa, which uses a fleet of mobile laboratories to attend to museum collections in many parts of the country. (For further discussion of conservation, see ART CONSERVATION AND RESTORATION.)

DOCUMENTATION

Documentation is a significant function of any museum, whether it holds only a few hundred objects or, as in the case of the largest institutions, many millions of items. Quite apart from the need for records to maintain adequate control of its collections, a museum's documentation system provides an indispensable record of the information associated with the objects for research. It may also include records, indirectly associated with the collections, to facilitate the museum's interpretative and other work.

The form of a museum's documentation system may vary considerably, but to meet these requirements it should provide the fullest possible information about each item and its history. There are no generally accepted classification schemes for museum objects, although certain subjects have developed schemes with numeric or alphanumeric notations to facilitate the ordering and retrieval of information. For the natural sciences, taxonomic names are normally used.

With the advent of information technology, a number of museums have developed computerized documentation systems, some on-line but others relying on machine-generated indexes, periodically updated. In certain countries the potential offered by computers to exchange data among museums has been exploited.

RESEARCH

Because they hold the primary material evidence for a number of subjects concerned with an understanding of man and his environment, museums clearly have an important role in research. The museum's research program is related to its objectives as an institution. A program may be concerned directly with the public services provided, in preparing exhibitions, catalogs, and other publications; or with promoting a better understanding of the region it serves. In large museums, and in university museums in particular, pure and applied research may be of national or international significance and may be associated with fieldwork or study visits. Active research and publication on a given topic, apart from contributing to the academic standing of the institution, may attract further collections relevant to the topic.

Many museums provide facilities, apart from those used by casual visitors, for researchers to study collections and associated documentation. These may include study rooms with a supporting library and equipment to assist in the examination of collections. Certain museums have accommodations for visiting foreign scholars; this is particularly helpful at on-site museums that are difficult to reach.

EXHIBITION

Many museums have abandoned the traditional approach to exhibition, by which storage and display are ends in themselves, in favour of an approach that enhances the setting of the object or collection. Museums have sought the expertise of a number of specialist designers, educators, sociologists, and interpreters to improve communication through objects. The result has been a remarkable transformation in the presentation of information, both in permanent collections and in special exhibits. Far greater use is made of colour and light (within the bounds prescribed by conservation requirements), in the way material is interpreted through a variety of mediums (sound, video, interaction between visitor and exhibit, as well as more traditional methods), and in the provision of a more relaxing environment in which to enjoy the exhibits. A result of museums' increased awareness of the needs of their visitors has been a considerable increase in museum attendance.

As the museum's cultural role has developed, so its exhibition work has diversified. Large international exhibitions have been organized by cooperating nations and have

Facsimile of the Apollo Lunar Module on exhibit in Space Hall, the National Air and Space Museum, Washington, D.C.

By courtesy of the National Air and Space Museum, Washington, D.C.

been shown in the major museums of the participating countries. Exhibitions organized for national circulation are also increasingly common. Museums concerned with a particular region have arranged topical exhibitions to tour the area, and in places without suitable premises for display, or in sparsely populated areas, exhibitions have toured in specially adapted buses or trains. Some countries have developed multipurpose cultural centres, and collaboration with museums has resulted in exhibition programs successfully reaching a wide audience.

The marked increase of interest in the historic and natural environment globally has involved museums in the preservation and interpretation of sites, monuments, and landscapes. A museum responsible for a historic property has the opportunity to reenact events associated with the property, such as period battle scenes and banquets, to demonstrate industrial or craft techniques, or to use theatre and son et lumière performances to interpret the site.

EDUCATIONAL SERVICES

The contribution that museums can make to education, both formally and informally, is widely acknowledged. The majority of their clientele learn by looking at exhibitions and displays. There has been, however, a long association among museums and schools, and many museums provide services specifically designed to meet schools' needs. Services include facilities for use both in the museum and at the school, many of which are administered by separate departments of museum education employing teachers for the purpose.

Facilities for education

Special rooms equipped for teaching and for handling specimens are provided in many museums. By allowing the study and handling of objects from its collections, the museum can give substance and form to the bare facts of art, history, and science. Some museums build special collections for this purpose. Teaching may be undertaken by the museum's educational staff or, more often, by the schoolteacher, who will have been advised and instructed by the staff. Apart from such facilities, schools and colleges also make use of public displays to teach specific topics. For advanced studies, particularly in subjects like archaeology and geology, the availability of museum collections can be indispensable.

Although opinion differs as to the value of school loan collections, many museums do provide small exhibit cases or kits that may be borrowed by the school for a limited period for classroom teaching. Unlike libraries, museums

A guide at the Museo Nacional de Antropología, Mexico City, explaining a piece of pre-Columbian pottery to schoolgirls who are visiting the museum as part of their schoolwork.

are not able to provide extensive loan services (which would conflict with their prime purpose), but for rural schools unable to visit the museum such a facility, albeit limited, meets a need. In some areas museums include the larger community schools within their traveling exhibition schedules.

As a better educated adult population with increased leisure time seeks purposeful outlets, museums are well placed to provide activities. Many museums have adult programs such as lectures, courses, demonstrations, and field excursions, some of which are planned as family events.

INFORMATION SERVICES

A museum acts as an information centre for its community. In addition to its displays and exhibitions, its data banks and publications, it has a staff of specialists, who in most cases are available by appointment to provide information on request. Together they constitute an important source of information.

Museum publications may be educational or cultural or may be designed for a popular market. They may take the form of periodicals, handbooks, catalogs, research papers, or general guides to aspects of the museum and are an important medium for disseminating information to the lay public and scholar alike. Many museums also offer an opinion on items brought to them for identification. This can be of value to both the inquirer and the museum because it provides an awareness of local discoveries and holdings that aids the museum's efforts to define its area of responsibility. At the same time it provides an informed opinion as a public service. Museums rarely provide valuations, however, and some, to avoid conflicts of interest, decline to have any connection with the antiques trade.

OTHER SERVICES

A number of museums have support organizations, sometimes known as friends of the museum. These groups engage in such activities as fund raising and provide voluntary assistance in a number of ways, and they can provide a powerful lobby for the museum's cause. The museum's volunteers may form a separate organization. The museum usually acts as host to such organizations for their various activities. In some countries a national coordinating body provides advice and assistance, and the World Federation of Friends of Museums was founded in 1975 to encourage worldwide cooperation among such societies.

BIBLIOGRAPHY. The information relating to museums is scattered in specialized publications, and there are few detailed monographic studies. The following list identifies some of the available sources. General periodicals include the quarterly *Museum,* published by Unesco; and the quarterlies *ICOM News* (published by the International Council of Museums), *Curator, International Journal of Museum Management and Curatorship,* and *Museums Journal.* The American Association of Museums publishes *Museum News* (bimonthly). For bibliographic information, see the *International Museological Bibliography* (annual), published under the auspices of ICOM, as well as FREDERICK L. RATH, JR., and MERRILYN ROGERS O'CONNELL (eds.), *A Bibliography on Historical Organization Practices,* 6 vol. (1975–84). See also CANADIAN MUSEUM ASSOCIATION, *Bibliography* (1976–), continued in irregular supplements; and *Art and Archaeology Technical Abstracts,* published irregularly by the International Institute for Conservation of Historic and Artistic Works.

Directories of museums include *Museums of the World,* 3rd rev. ed. (1981); KENNETH HUDSON and ANN NICHOLLS (eds.), *The Directory of Museums and Living Displays,* 3rd ed. (1985); and *Directory of African Museums* (1981) and *Directory of Asian Museums* (1983), prepared by the Unesco-ICOM Documentation Centre. ICOM also publishes some directories of specialized museums. Information on national museums can be found in the Museum Association of the United Kingdom, *Museums Yearbook,* and in *The Official Museum Directory* (annual), published by the American Association of Museums. BILL TRUESDELL (comp. and ed.), *Directory of Unique Museums,* enlarged ed. (1985), describes more than 300 specialized museums in the United States and Canada.

General works about museums and their operation include EDWARD P. ALEXANDER, *Museums in Motion: An Introduction to the History and Functions of Museums* (1979); G. ELLIS BURCAW, *Introduction to Museum Work,* 2nd rev. ed. (1983); RALPH H. LEWIS, *Manual for Museums* (1976); KENNETH HUDSON, *Museums for the 1980s: A Survey of World Trends* (1977); JOHN M.A. THOMPSON *et al.* (eds.), *The Manual of Curatorship: A Guide to Museum Practice* (1984); and ALMA S. WITTLIN, *Museums: In Search of a Usable Future* (1970). For a national position statement, see AMERICAN ASSOCIATION OF MUSEUMS, *Museums for a New Century; A Report of the Commission on Museums for a New Century* (1984). History of museums and collecting is explored in EDWARD P. ALEXANDER, *Museum Masters* (1983); GERMAIN BAZIN, *The Museum Age,* trans. from the French (1967); OLIVER IMPEY and ARTHUR MACGREGOR (eds.), *The Origins of Museums* (1985); FRANCIS HENRY TAYLOR, *The Taste of Angels: A History of Art Collecting from Rameses to Napoleon* (1948); HUGH TREVOR-ROPER, *Princes and Artists: Patronage and Ideology at Four Habsburg Courts, 1517–1633* (1976); and NIELS VON HOLST, *Creators, Collectors, and Connoisseurs: The Anatomy of Artistic Taste from Antiquity to the Present Day* (1967; originally published in German, 1960).

The legal arrangements concerning museums are closely related to those of the preservation of cultural property, and the following are helpful: BONNIE BURNHAM, *The Protection of Cultural Property: Handbook of National Legislations* (1974); LYNDEL V. PROTT and P.J. O'KEEFE, *Law and the Cultural Heritage* (1984); *The Protection of Movable Cultural Property: Compendium of Legislative Texts,* 2 vol. (1984), prepared by Unesco; SHARON A. WILLIAMS, *The International and National Protection of Movable Cultural Property* (1978); MARIE C. MALARO, *A Legal Primer on Managing Museum Collections* (1985); and MARILYN PHELAN, *Museums and the Law* (1982).

Specific works on aspects of museum operation include H.J. PLENDERLEITH and A.E.A. WERNER, *The Conservation of Antiquities and Works of Art: Treatment, Repair, and Restoration,* 2nd ed. (1971); GARRY THOMSON, *The Museum Environment* (1978); ROBERT G. TILLOTSON, *Museum Security* (1977); D. ANDREW ROBERTS, *Planning the Documentation of Museum Collections* (1985); DOROTHY H. DUDLEY *et al., Museum Registration Methods,* 3rd rev. ed. (1979); JIŘI NEUSTUPNÝ, *Museum and Research,* trans. from Czech (1968). Interpretative functions of museums are treated in ROYAL ONTARIO MUSEUM, *Communicating with the Museum Visitor: Guidelines for Planning* (1976); R.S. MILES *et al.* (comps.), *The Design of Educational Exhibits* (1982); UNESCO, *Museums, Imagination, and Education* (1973); BARBARA Y. NEWSOM and ADELE Z. SILVER (eds.), *The Art Museum as Educator* (1978); ULLA KEDING OLOFSSON (ed.), *Museums and Children* (1979); HANS L. ZETTERBERG, *Museums and Adult Education* (1968); G. DONALD ADAMS, *Museum Public Relations* (1983); and ICOM, *Training of Museum Personnel* (1970).

(G.D.L.)

The Art of Music

The word music comes from the Greek *mousike* by way of the Latin adaptation *musica.* The Greek word is itself derived from *mousa,* "muse," and hence was applied to all branches of art over which the Muses were supposed to preside. In the instruction of the young, *mousike* was roughly equivalent to what in modern times would be called a liberal education, as opposed to *gymnastike,* which was concerned with the development of the body (the modern "gymnastics"). This conception survived in the Roman world, so that *ars musica* could mean either music or poetry; but it did not prevent "music" from being used in the specific sense now given to it. The use of a comprehensive term of this kind implied particularly a close connection between music and poetry that has survived to the present day. It is characteristic that St. Augustine's treatise *De musica,* in the form in which it has come down, is concerned almost entirely with metrics.

This article is divided into four main sections. Music's nature and significance includes the philosophical and theoretical basis and is followed by the elements of musical sound. Composition is discussed in sections on rhythm, scale, mode, harmony, and counterpoint as well as those on notation, the history of compositional technique, and instrumentation. Modern recording covers types of mechanical and electronic reproduction and their effects on composition, criticism, and music appreciation.

The article is divided into the following sections:

The nature and significance of music

HISTORICAL CONCEPTIONS

Music is everywhere to be heard. But what *is* music? Commentators have spoken of "the relationship of music to the human senses and intellect," thus affirming a world of human discourse as the necessary setting for the art. A definition of music itself will take longer. As Aristotle said, "It is not easy to determine the nature of music or why anyone should have a knowledge of it."

Early in the 20th century, it was regarded as a commonplace that a musical tone was characterized by the regularity of its vibrations; this uniformity gave it a fixed pitch and distinguished its sounds from "noise." Although the view may be supported by traditional music, it would be an unacceptable yardstick in the latter half of the 20th century, when "noise" itself may be treated as an element in composition, to say nothing of the random sounds incorporated (without prior knowledge of what they will be) by modern composers, such as the American John Cage, and others in works having aleatory (chance) or impromptu features. Tone, moreover, is only one component in music, others being rhythm, timbre (tone colour), and texture. Electronic machinery has enabled some composers to create works in which the traditional role of the interpreter is abolished and to record, directly on tape, sounds that were formerly beyond human ability to produce, if not to imagine.

The non-Western world. From historical accounts, it is clear that the power to move men has always been attributed to music; its ecstatic possibilities have been recognized in all cultures and have usually been admitted in practice under particular conditions, sometimes stringent ones. In the civilization of India, music was put into the service of religion from earliest times; Vedic hymns stand at the beginning of the record. As the art developed over many centuries into a music of profound melodic and rhythmic intricacy, the discipline of a religious text or the guideline of a story determined the structure. Even today the narrator is central in most performances of Indian music, and the virtuosity of a skillful singer rivals that of the instrumentalists. There is very little concept of vocal or instrumental idiom in the Western sense. The vertical dimension of chord structure—that is, the effects created by sounding tones simultaneously—has never been developed in South Asian music; the divisions of an octave (intervals) are more numerous than in Western music, and melodic complexity in Oriental music goes far beyond that of Western practice. Moreover, an element of improvisation is retained that is vital to the success of a performance. The spontaneous imitation carried on between an instrumentalist and narrator, against the insistent rhythmic subtleties of the drums, can be a source of the greatest excitement, which in large measure is because of the faithful adherence to the rigid rules that govern the rendition of ragas—the ancient melodic patterns of Indian music.

Indian music in religion

Confucius and music in China

Chinese music, like the music of India, has traditionally been an adjunct to ceremony or narrative. Confucius (551–479 BC) assigned an important place to music in the service of a well-ordered moral universe. He saw music and government as reflecting one another and believed that only the superior man who can understand music is equipped to govern. Music, he thought, reveals character through the six emotions that it can portray: sorrow, satisfaction, joy, anger, piety, love. According to Confucius, great music is in harmony with the universe, restoring order to the physical world through that harmony. Music, as a true mirror of character, makes pretense or deception impossible.

Ancient Greek ideas. Although music was important in the life of ancient Greece, it is not now known how that music actually sounded. Only a few notated fragments have survived, and no key exists for restoring even these. The Greeks were given to theoretical speculation about music; they had a system of notation, and they "practiced music," as Socrates himself, in a vision, had been enjoined to do. But the Greek term from which the word music is derived was a generic one, referring to any art or science practiced under the aegis of the Muses. Music, therefore, as distinct from gymnastics, was all encompassing. (Much speculation, however, was clearly directed toward that more restricted meaning with which we are familiar.) Music was virtually a department of mathematics for the philosopher Pythagoras (*c.* 550 BC), who was the first musical numerologist and who laid the foundations for acoustics. In acoustics, the Greeks discovered the correspondence between the pitch of a note and the length of a string. But they did not progress to a calculation of pitch on the basis of vibrations, though an attempt was made to connect sounds with underlying motions.

Plato (428–348/347 BC), like Confucius, looked on music as a department of ethics. And like Confucius he was anxious to regulate the use of particular modes (*i.e.,* arrangements of notes, like scales) because of their supposed effects on men. Plato was a stern musical disciplinarian; he saw a correspondence between the character of a man and the music that represented him. Straightforward simplicity was best. In the *Laws,* Plato declared that rhythmic and melodic complexities were to be avoided because they led to depression and disorder. Music echoes divine harmony; rhythm and melody imitate the movements of heavenly bodies, thus delineating the music of the spheres and reflecting the moral order of the universe. Earthly music, however, is suspect; Plato distrusted its emotional power. Music must therefore be of the right sort; the sensuous qualities of certain modes are dangerous, and a strong censorship must be imposed. Music and gymnastics in the correct balance would constitute the desirable curriculum in education. Plato admitted and valued music in its ethically approved forms; his concern was primarily with the effects of music, and he therefore regarded it as a psychosociological phenomenon.

Yet Plato, in treating earthly music as a shadow of the Ideal, saw a symbolic significance in the art. Aristotle carried forward the concept of the art as imitation, but music could express the universal as well. His idea that works of art could contain a measure of truth in themselves—an idea voiced more explicitly by Plotinus in the third century AD—gave added strength to the symbolic view. Aristotle, following Plato, thought that music has power to mold human character, but he would admit all the modes, recognizing happiness and pleasure as values to both the individual and the state. He advocated a rich musical diet. Aristotle made a distinction between those who have only theoretical knowledge and those who produce music, maintaining that persons who do not perform cannot be good judges of the performances of others.

Aristotle's view

Aristoxenus, a pupil of Aristotle, gave considerable credit to the human listener, his importance and his powers of perception. He denigrated the dominance of mathematical and acoustical considerations. For Aristoxenus, music was emotional and fulfilled a functional role, for which both the hearing and the intellect of the listener were essential. Individual tones were to be understood in their relations to one another and in the context of larger formal units. The Epicureans and Stoics adopted a more naturalistic view of music and its function, which they accepted as an adjunct to the good life. They gave more emphasis to sensation than did Plato, but they nevertheless placed music in the service of moderation and virtue. A dissenting 3rd-century voice was that of Empiricus, who said that music was an art of tones and rhythms only that meant nothing outside itself.

The Platonic influence in musical thought was to be dominant for at least a millennium. Following that period of unquestioned philosophic allegiance, there were times of rededication to Greek concepts, accompanied by reverent and insistent homage (*e.g.,* the group of late 16th-century Florentines, known as the Camerata, who were instrumental in the development of opera). Such returns to simplicity, directness, and the primacy of the word have been made periodically, out of loyalty to Platonic imperatives, however much these "neo" practices may have differed from those of the Greeks themselves.

In the 20th century, the effects of Greek thought are still strongly evident in the belief that music influences the ethical life; in the idea that music can be explained in terms of some component such as number (that may itself be only a reflection of another, higher source); in the view that music has specific effects and functions that can be appropriately labelled; and in the recurrent observation that music is connected with human emotion. In every historical period there have been defectors from one or more of these views, and there are, of course, differences of emphasis.

Music in Christianity. Much of the Platonic–Aristotelian teaching, as restated by the Roman philosopher Boethius (*c.* 480–524), was well suited to the needs of the church; the conservative aspects of that philosophy, with its fear of innovation, were conducive to the maintenance of order. The role of music as accessory to words is nowhere more clearly illustrated than in the history of Christianity, where the primacy of the text has always been emphasized and sometimes, as in Roman Catholic doctrine, made an article of faith. In the varieties of plainchant, melody was used for textual illumination; the configurations of sound took their cue from the words. St. Augustine (AD 354–430), who was attracted by music and valued its utility to religion, was fearful of its sensuous element and anxious that the melody never take precedence over the words. These had been Plato's concerns also. Still echoing the Greeks, Augustine, whose beliefs were reiterated by St. Thomas Aquinas (*c.* 1225–74), held the basis of music to be mathematical; music reflects celestial movement and order.

Martin Luther (1483–1546) was a musical liberal and reformer. But the uses he envisioned for music, despite his innovations, were in the mainstream of tradition; Luther insisted that music must be simple, direct, accessible, an aid to piety. His assignment of particular qualities to a given mode is reminiscent of Plato and Confucius. John Calvin (1509–64) took a more cautious and fearful view of music than did Luther, warning against voluptuous, effeminate, or disorderly music and insisting upon the supremacy of the text.

Music as mathematics

17th- and 18th-century Western conceptions. In reviewing the accounts of music that have characterized musical and intellectual history, it is clear that the Pythagoreans are reborn from age to age. The German astronomer Johannes Kepler (1571–1630) perpetuated, in effect, the idea of the harmony of the spheres, attempting to relate music to planetary movement. René Descartes (1596–1650), too, saw the basis of music as mathematical. He was a faithful Platonist in his prescription of temperate rhythms and simple melodies so that music would not produce imaginative, exciting, and hence immoral, effects. For another philosopher–mathematician, the German Gottfried von Leibniz (1646–1716), music reflected a universal rhythm and mirrored a reality that was fundamentally mathematical, to be experienced in the mind as a subconscious apprehension of numerical relationships.

Immanuel Kant (1724–1804) ranked music as lowest in his hierarchy of the arts. What he distrusted most about music was its wordlessness; he considered it useful for enjoyment but negligible in the service of culture. Allied with poetry, however, it may acquire conceptual value. Georg Wilhelm Friedrich Hegel (1770–1831) also extolled the discursive faculties, saying that art, though it expresses the divine, must yield to philosophy. He acknowledged the peculiar power of music to express many nuances of the emotions. Like Kant, Hegel preferred vocal music to instrumental, deprecating wordless music as subjective and indefinite. The essence of music he held to be rhythm, which finds its counterpart in man's innermost self. What is original in Hegel's view is his claim that music, unlike the other arts, has no independent existence in space, is not "objective" in that sense; the fundamental rhythm of music (again an aspect of number) is experienced within the hearer.

Subjectivism in Hegel

After the 18th century, speculations upon the intrinsic nature of music became more numerous and profound. The elements necessary for a more comprehensive theory of its function and meaning became discernible. But philosophers whose views have been summarized thus far were not speaking as philosophers of music. Music interested them in terms extrinsic to itself, in its observable effects; in its connections with dance, religious ritual, or festive rites; because of its alliance with words; or for some other extramusical consideration. The only common denominator to be found, aside from the recognition of different types of music, is the acknowledgment of its connection with the emotional life; and here, to be sure, is that problematic power of the art to move men. Various extramusical preoccupations are today the raison d'être of "contextualist" explanations of music, which are concerned with its relation to the human environment. The history of music itself is largely an account of its adjunctive function in rituals and ceremonies of all kinds—religious, military, courtly—and in musical theatre. The protean character of music that enables it to form such easy alliances with literature and drama (as in folk song, art song, opera, "background" music) and with the dance (tribal, ethnic, "social," ballet) appears to confirm the wide range and influence that the Greeks assigned to it.

MODERN THEORIES OF MUSICAL MEANING

Musical theorists

Before the 19th century, musicians themselves seldom were theorists, if theorist is defined as one who explicates meaning. Musical theory, when it was something other than the exposition of a prevalent or emerging style, was likely to be a technical manual guiding vocal or instrumental performance, a set of directions for meeting current exigencies in church or theatre practice, or a missive advocating reforms. Prolific masters, such as Johann Sebastian Bach, produced not learned treatises but monuments of art.

The 19th century saw the emergence of composer–critics (Carl Maria von Weber, Robert Schumann, Hector Berlioz, Franz Liszt), versatile artists with literary proclivities who were not, to be sure, propounding comprehensive theories or systems of thought. Richard Wagner, an active theorizer, presaged a new species, the composer–author. But he did little to advance musical theory. He proposed a unity of music and drama (*Gesamtkunstwerk*)—a reflection of the "programmatic" preoccupations of 19th-century composers—but its multiplicity of musical and extramusical elements only added to the confusion of musical thought. The distinctly musical character of Wagner's genius, clearly discernible in *The Ring,* is in no way explained by his discursive credos. Igor Stravinsky, Arnold Schoenberg, and other composer–authors of the 20th century were to be somewhat more successful in elucidating their techniques and aims.

The concept of dynamism. Present-day ideas of music as a symbolism owe much to two German philosophers, Arthur Schopenhauer (1788–1860) and Friedrich Nietzsche (1844–1900), who brought to the theory of music a new concept, articulated by each in different ways and in divergent terms but faithful to the same principle—dynamism. Both saw in music an art that is not "spatialized" (hence not "objective") in the way that other arts are by the very conditions of their manifestation. Music is closer to the inner dynamism of process; there are fewer technical (and no concrete) impediments to immediate apprehension, for an entire dimension of the empirical world has been bypassed.

Schopenhauer looked upon Platonic Ideas as objectifying will, but music is

> by no means like the other arts, the copy of the Ideas, but the *copy of the will itself.* This is why the effect of music is so much more powerful and penetrating than that of the other arts, for they speak only of shadows, but it speaks of the thing itself.

In contrast to Kant he accords a special efficacy to music:

> The effect of music is stronger, quicker, more necessary and infallible. Men have practiced music in all ages without being able to account for this; content to understand it directly, they renounce all claim to an abstract conception of this direct understanding itself.

Schopenhauer acknowledged a connection between human feeling and music, which "restores to us all the emotions of our inmost nature, but entirely without reality and far removed from their pain." Music, which he is presenting an as analogue of the emotional life, is a copy or symbol of the will.

Nietzsche posed an Apollonian–Dionysian dichotomy, the former representing form and rationality and the latter drunkenness and ecstasy. For Nietzsche, music was the Dionysian art *par excellence.* In *The Birth of Tragedy from the Spirit of Music,* Nietzsche anticipated the 20th-century discovery that symbol making (whether in dreams, myth, or art) is a necessary and to some extent even automatic human activity. The rich suggestiveness and prescience of his insights embraced the concept of the "symbolical analogue"—the artistic function of ordering and heightening the ingredients of the actual world—and the polarities of experience symbolized in the Apollonian–Dionysian conflict itself, which Igor Stravinsky also explored. Nietzsche gave short shrift to mathematical aspects of music, and like Schopenhauer he deprecated blatantly programmatic music that abounds in obvious imitations of natural sounds. Discerning a power in music to create myths, he looked upon mere "tone painting" as the antithesis of its essential character.

Efforts of theorists to account for the universal appeal of music and to explain its effects have, since the 19th century, been various, contradictory, and highly controversial. In pointing out the chief points of view that have emerged, it must be emphasized that there are no completely isolated categories, and there is usually considerable overlapping; a single spokesman, the 19th-century English psychologist Edmund Gurney, for example, may incorporate formalist, symbolist, expressionist, and psychological elements, in varying proportions, to explain the phenomenon of music. Although some disagreements are more apparent than real because of the inherent problems of terminology and definition, diametrically opposing views are also held and tenaciously defended.

Referentialists and Nonreferentialists. Among those who seek and propound theories of musical meaning, the most persistent disagreement is between the referentialists (or "heteronomists"), who hold that music can and does refer to meanings outside itself, and the nonreferentialists (who are sometimes called formalists or absolutists), who maintain that the art is autonomous and "means itself." The Austrian critic Eduard Hanslick, in his *The Beautiful in Music* (German edition published 1854), was a strong proponent of music as an art of intrinsic principles and ideas; yet even Hanslick, ardent formalist though he was, struggled with the problem of emotion in music. Hanslick's views have been classified as a modified heteronomous theory.

One looks in vain for an extremist of either persuasion, referentialist or nonreferentialist. Igor Stravinsky first achieved fame as a composer of ballet music, and his works throughout his career were rich in extramusical associations. It would be a comfortable simplification to ally referentialism with "program" music and nonreferentialism with "absolute" music. But the problem cannot be resolved by such a choice, if only, first of all, because extramusical referents can vary in complexity from a mere descriptive title to the convolutions of the Wagnerian leitmotiv, in which a particular musical phrase is consistently associated with a particular person, place, or thing. The referentialist does not require an explicit program (which may, when present, be altogether too meagre by his canons), and the nonreferentialist does not necessarily denigrate program music, though he makes a point of distinguishing between the extramusical program and the musical meaning. The contemporary U.S. theorist Leonard Meyer, in his *Emotion and Meaning in Music* (1956), speaks of "designative" and "embodied" meanings; he recognizes both kinds in music but appears to give equal weight to the extrinsic and intrinsic.

If there is intrinsic, or embodied, meaning, one may well ask what meaning is embodied and how it is to be apprehended. An extreme formalist would say that the acoustic pattern itself and nothing more is the sense of music; Hanslick, indeed, said this, though he did not hold consistently to the view. But most nonreferentialists regard music as, in one way or another, emotionally meaningful or expressive. Referentialists, too, find expressive content in music, though this emotional content may be extramusical (even if not explicit) in origin, according to the American theorists John Hospers in *Meaning and Truth in the Arts* (1946) and Donald Ferguson in *Music as Metaphor* (1960). Meyer has made the observation that while most referentialists are expressionists, not all expressionists are referentialists. He makes the useful distinction between absolute expressionists and referential expressionists and identifies his own position as "formalist–absolute expressionist." In acknowledging that music can and does express referential (designative) meanings as well as nonreferential ones, Meyer exhibits an eclectic and certainly permissive view. But he has been criticized for failing to make clear the *modus operandi* of this referential meaning in music.

Intuition and intellect. Most theorists agree that music is an auditory phenomenon and that hearing is the beginning of understanding. Beyond this there is little agreement. There is bad blood especially between proponents of intuition, like Benedetto Croce, and champions of intellectual cognition, like Hospers. Gurney was constrained to postulate a special musical faculty that need not reside exclusively either in the mind or the heart. The main problem for theorists arises from the inveterate tendency to dichotomize thought and feeling. Henri Bergson (1859–1941) broke with this tradition when he spoke for "an intellectual act of intuition." Recently, a reawakened philosophic and artistic concern for the concept of organic unity has revealed strong affinities among such disparate works as Gurney's *The Power of Sound* (1880); the U.S. philosopher Susanne K. Langer's *Philosophy in a New Key* (1942) and her later works; John Dewey's classic *Art as Experience* (1934); and the U.S. composer Roger Sessions' *The Musical Experience* (1950).

It is apparent that music is connected in some way with the emotional life of man, but the "how" continues to be elusive. Sessions (echoing Aristotle) states the problem fairly:

> No one denies that music arouses emotions, nor do most people deny that the values of music are both qualitatively and quantitatively connected with the emotions it arouses. Yet it is not easy to say just what this connection is.

The language analogy

It was long fashionable to speak of the "language" of music, or of music as the "language of the emotions," but since a precise semantics is wanting in music, the analogy breaks down. Two or more listeners may derive very different "meanings" from the same piece of music, and since written and spoken language cannot render these musical "meanings," whatever they may be, in consistent and commonly recognizable terms, verbal explication often seems to raise more questions than it settles. Philosophic analysts who hold that all meaning is capable of rendition in language therefore pronounce music—unless it can be saved by the referentialists—without meaning, confronting the thoughtful listener, thereby, with a proposition that seems clearly to contradict (and trivialize) his own experience. The difficulty, of course, is a semantic one and explains why some theorists substitute such terms as import, significance, pattern, or gestalt for meaning. Recognizing an incompatibility between the modalities of nonverbal arts and their treatment by discursive thought, it is hardly surprising that musical aestheticians have been few.

Symbolist contributions. Significant contributions to musical theory have been made in the 20th century by several investigators who may be classified as symbolists, though most of them exhibit formalist, expressionist, and psychological elements as well. The most influential (and controversial) work has been done by Langer. Her most adamant critics (such as John Hospers) have objected to her use of the term symbol that must, in their lexica, stand for something definite; she takes pains to ascribe this more limited usage to the term signal. The more general use of the term symbol that she endorses has a long history, notably in such 19th-century figures as Goethe, Carlyle, and the French Symbolist poets. Langer is accused of having somewhat weakened her argument through a vacillating terminology, and she has described the musical symbol as "unconsummated" because of its ambiguity. But the validity of her theory does not depend upon the term symbol; her thought, indeed, has much in common with that of Edmund Gurney, who does not employ the term and whose "ideal motion," if substituted for symbol, would remove most of her critics' objections. Her use of symbol is nevertheless defensible; she construes art as a "symbolic analogue of emotive life," rendering the "forms of sentient being" into intelligible configurations. She is a naturalist; she sees art as organic in origin, and she echoes the view, long held among symbolists, that artistic form and content compose an indissoluble unity that each art manifests according to its peculiar conditions. The symbolism of music is therefore tonal (or, at its broadest, auditory) in character and can be realized only in time; in psychological experience, time assumes an ideal guise. (Painting and sculpture, in their distinctive modalities, embody ideal space.) Langer embraces all the arts in her purview. The U.S. musical theorist Gordon

Epperson's *The Musical Symbol* (1967) is an application of her concepts, with modifications, intensively to music.

Contextualist theories. In moving from symbolic to contextualist explanations of music, it is well to note that a source of great confusion, in the former, is the fact that tone painting (with explicit signals that yield, when the code is understood, designative meanings) is widely regarded as musical symbolism. An example of such tone painting is Bach's introduction of musical notes, corresponding to the letters of his own name, as a theme in the unfinished final fugue of the *Art of the Fugue.* And surely it may be argued that this qualifies on one level. But the contention that there is an intrinsic symbolism in the musical meaning itself is a claim that referentialists are generally unwilling to honour. Yet many theorists, whose concern is with the sociological or psychological effects of music, are not so much opposed to the idea of inner or profound meaning as indifferent to such meaning per se. Even an absolutist, however, is unable to examine music in isolation from its human environment. Meyer deliberately eschews logical and philosophical problems of music and makes "no attempt to decide whether music is a language or whether musical stimuli are signs or symbols." (He does not defend the inference that such concerns are irrelevant to meaning.) Musical meaning and communication, he maintains, cannot exist in the absence of the cultural context. The statement is hardly open to dispute; a theorist is classified according to his proximity to the referential or nonreferential pole. If a referentialist emphasizes explicit aims and associations of a particular work (as in varieties of *Gebrauchsmusik*, or "utility" music, written for specific social or educational purposes), the formalist can maintain that there is also an intrinsic, or embodied, meaning to which he attaches the greater aesthetic value.

Among contextualists, however, a simple referential view is the exception rather than the rule. Any theorist who examines musical perception is making a study of a complex human activity. He is dealing with the psychology of music, in which certain elements—*e.g.,* music, listener, mode of apprehension, cultural context—are indispensable and in which characteristic processes recur. Specialists will emphasize one element or another: formalists the music itself, sociologists the listener and his milieu, psychologists the how of perception. Though psychology could survey the whole field, in practice psychologists, according to their persuasions, investigate the perception of measurable acoustic phenomena, the physical-mental effects of musical sound, or—more rarely—the functional role of music in human experience; and pragmatists and analysts alike may leave something out of account. But it remains for the comprehensive theorist, probably one who, like Langer, is equipped to discern relationships among many departments of thought, to construct a valid hierarchical structure of musical meaning in all its ramifications.

Psychological approaches

Deryck Cooke, the British musicologist and the author of *The Language of Music* (1959), who may be classified as a referential expressionist, has offered a sophisticated argument for the notion of music as language. Concepts, however, may not be rendered by this language, only feelings. Cooke reaffirms the possibility, long disputed by many theorists, that such feelings may be recognized, identified, and even classified. But he confines his investigation to the last few hundred years of the Western tradition.

Information theory. The French theorist Abraham Moles's *Information Theory and Esthetic Perception* (1966) brings the new science of information theory to bear on musical perception, emphasizing that the concept of form is the essential thing; the "sonic message," whose dimensions vary from one composition to another, is a whole. Information theory thus proves to be a novel ally for organicists. The message, which is subjected to "atomistic" study of its components, is (thanks to recording) concrete; there is a temporal sonic material, a *materia musica.* Moles gives reinforcement to the aesthetic theory of distance:

> The esthetic procedure of isolating sonic objects is analogous to the sculptor's or decorator's isolating a marble work against a black velvet draping: This procedure directs attention to it, alone and not as one element among many in a complex framework.

Information theory, which Leonard Meyer also discusses, begins its investigations without the help of traditional theory, which it finds to be untenable for its procedures. Musical messages discerned through information theory are not referential, yet Moles chooses to term the measurable elements in the sonic repertoire symbols: "each definable temporal stage represents a 'symbol' analogous to a phoneme in language." According to Moles, music must, as an art, obey rules; the role of aesthetics is to enumerate universally valid rules, not to perpetuate the arbitrary or merely traditional. He foresees experimentation with a much richer repertoire of sounds, transcending musical instruments and drawing on whatever sources—certainly electronic ones—are available for realizing the "most general orchestra." A host of composers have set out to fulfill this desideratum. In order to increase the compass of possible sounds, various electronic synthesizers were constructed. In electronically synthesized music, the medium itself is indistinguishable from its message.

The quest for some distillation of musical meaning may be foredoomed to failure. Meanings, intrinsic and extrinsic, abound; meanings of all kinds, moreover, are revealed in and through the social setting. Church, theatre, and broadcasting affect music in characteristic ways. The modern concert is a device whereby formal, autonomous meanings are emphasized; further, the scope and available repertoire of the concert have been enormously increased through recordings, for any suitably equipped room may become, at the turn of a switch, a recital hall.

Considerations related to performance practice. Listening to music for its own sake, apart from ritual or storytelling, is a recent historical development. There have always been impromptu song and dance; and performances of music in home, church, and theatrical productions have a long history. But there was no public opera house until 1637 when the first one opened in Venice; the first public concerts for which admission was charged appeared in London in 1672. During the next 50 years there were beginnings in Germany and France also, but the modern concert was not a significant feature of musical life until the late 18th century.

Of the forms that have characterized distinct periods of musical history, it is sufficient to remark here that the chief Renaissance forms—mass, motet, the polyphonic chanson, and madrigal—were allied to texts that strongly influenced their structure. Instrumental music was for the most part in the service of the voice, though instrumental church compositions, dances, and chansons arranged for organ were not uncommon. A strong alliance between voices and instruments has continued into the present, with musical theatre, the art song, and religious music. Instrumental music as a separate genre emerged in the 16th century, gaining considerable momentum in the 17th through a variety of idiomatic pieces. Increased attention to technical fluency was accompanied by greater complexity and sophistication in the instruments themselves. In response to stylistic demands for greater resonance and power, the modern forms of the violin appeared in the late 16th century, only gradually supplanting the earlier viols. The harpsichord did not finally yield to the pianoforte until the 18th century. The once-prevalent idea that early stringed and keyboard instruments were primitive precursors of their modern counterparts has been effectually demolished by research in medieval and Renaissance music and by dedicated performers, who seek to restore the sounds and spirit of those eras.

The development of opera, oratorio, and the cantata gave a prominence to vocal music throughout the Baroque era (*c.* 1600–1750) that made it equal in importance to instrumental music, with which these forms were closely allied. But instrumental chamber and independent orchestral ensembles, as they exist today, also had their beginnings during this period. A highly significant development of the late 18th century was the definitive appearance of the modern sonata (whether in the form of the solo and duo sonata, piano trio, string quartet, concerto, or symphony) with the Viennese classicists Haydn and Mozart and, later, Beethoven.

Since a vocal text is likely to be confused with intrinsic

musical meaning, or at least to divert attention from a preoccupation with it, it is not surprising that modern aesthetic theory followed on the emergence of an autonomous instrumental music requiring greater concentration on the sound itself, its colour and intensity, and the intelligibility (in terms of tonal organization alone) of a composition. Moreover, the very concept of listening as an attentive (and sometimes rigorous), serious, and necessary activity of the music lover gained acceptance only slowly, following the inauguration of public concerts, and is still vigorously resisted. The expectation that the art should provide enjoyment without effort is, indeed, widespread and accounts for much of the opposition to new and demanding idioms. But even for the well-disciplined and eager listener there is the problem of quantity: he must cope as best he can with what Langer has called "the madhouse of too much art." If more effort is required, more discrimination is also needed. In music education, articulate voices ask that teaching be centred more upon qualitative aspects of the art ("aesthetic education"), less upon music making as an activity. This concern for musical value appears to reflect a more intensive search for meaning, which is not likely to be the exclusive property of a particular style or era; nor is it to be sought in an indiscriminate acceptance or rejection of novelty per se. A pronounced pedagogical interest developed in such contemporary popular music as "rock," "soul," and similar folk idioms with great numbers of followers, especially among the young, whose gigantic festivals generated feelings of religious exaltation. The texts of the songs are highly emotional and often deal with "protest" themes; accompaniments are provided by guitars, keyboard and percussion instruments, and are electronically amplified. Music educators became attracted by the intrinsic structural values of this music, especially its distinctive rhythmic and modal characteristics, its texts, and the qualitative levels that may be distinguished. A music so vital and widespread, moreover, was deemed by many to be worth studying in school. The "rock" movement became a musical–sociological phenomenon of large proportions.

Music and world view. Again, music proves its protean susceptibilities in the service of disparate world views. Among humanist psychologists (such as the Americans Gordon Allport and Abraham Maslow) music may be one among other means toward self-fulfillment, integration, self-actualization; for aesthetic Existentialists (such as the philosopher Jean-Paul Sartre) it is yet another crucial department of choice and freedom; for spiritual Existentialists (such as the philosophers Karl Jaspers and Martin Buber) it transmits transcendent overtones. For expressionists (such as the composers Schoenberg, Ernst Krenek, and René Leibowitz) music carries austere, and sometimes doctrinaire, moral imperatives. Theodor Adorno, a composer–philosopher and pupil of Alban Berg, writes powerfully of these and speaks for an awareness of dazzling lucidity, but the tone, notwithstanding his humour, is one of obligation. Only the expressionists, among those mentioned here, are committed primarily to music, though Adorno, in particular, considers music and musicians always in interaction with their environments. The aesthetic concept of play is virtually absent, except among such humanists as Maslow. With Sartre, no less a humanist, the tone is one of responsibility. Many educators long held the explicit aim (at least in part because of a misinterpretation of John Dewey) of presenting the content of a discipline as "fun"; the present concern for aesthetic education, an area of great interest to Dewey himself, eschews this trivial view. But play, in the aesthetic sense, follows rules, as information theory has demonstrated; even "controlled aleatory" composition observes some limits. And the play may be very serious indeed, as in the important 20th-century atonal style known as "12-tone technique," practiced by the Viennese expressionists and their successors.

Tonality and meaning. The most troublesome problem not only for the untutored listener but also for the professional musician has been, in much contemporary work, the loss of explicit tonality; and this accounts for the tardy popular response to Schoenberg and his school: the vocabulary is esoteric. Nineteenth-century compositions did, indeed, stretch the tonal system to its outer limits; but it is now clear that Wagner and Richard Strauss, and even the early Schoenberg, had not broken from it. As for Debussy, his use of "exoticisms" was filigree upon a secure tonal base. So were such practices as the juxtaposition of keys by Stravinsky. This is not to say that the tonality of the Western world, fecund though it has been, is superior or more natural than other systems. Ethnomusicology and comparative musicology have proved this to be a parochial view, though there are still those who champion harmonic practices based on the physical laws governing overtones—as Western tonality is—as the only "natural" source of development. It should not be irrelevant, however, to inquire if any folk music has been discovered that exhibits atonal characteristics.

Tonality in Western music, though a significant aspect, cannot be considered the crux of musical meaning. The tone rows that are used in the 12-tone compositions of Schoenberg, like major–minor tonality in earlier music, are a technical substratum and must be no more explicit in the finished work than the chemical makeup of pigments in the "Mona Lisa." The devices selected may affect the comprehensibility or accessibility of the work, but they are not, per se, the determinants of its worth or quality. Similarly with musical colour, or timbre; the 19th century produced a great profusion of compositions, particularly in the orchestral repertoire (*e.g.,* works by Liszt and Berlioz) that exploited the unique sonorities of instruments; control of volume was, in itself, a rich source of colour. Works with literary or other extramusical associations were excellent vehicles for sonorous effects, but colour, like tonality, must be evaluated in musical context. Langer, among present-day aestheticians, regards words themselves as musical, rather than discursive, ingredients; they are "assimilated" by the song. (G.E./Ed.)

CRITICISM

Musical criticism, properly considered, is a branch of philosophy—more exactly, of aesthetics. It is chiefly concerned with making value judgments, either about composition or about performance, or both. This section reviews the history and fundamental issues of music criticism.

Unfortunately, it is difficult to show that a value judgment can stand for anything that is even remotely true about music, as opposed to standing for something that is merely a personal whim on the part of the critic, since there is, as yet, no such thing as an organized body of knowledge called "musical criticism." The entire history of musical criticism can be summed up as a vain struggle to forge itself into a suitable tool for coming to grips with the art of music.

Historical development. The criticism of music first gained serious hold in the 17th and 18th centuries. Among the first writer-musicians to make systematic contributions to criticism were Jean-Jacques Rousseau in France, Johann Mattheson in Germany, and Charles Avison and Charles Burney in England. Their work coincided with the emergence of periodicals and newspapers all over Europe. The first journal devoted entirely to music criticism was *Critica Musica,* founded by Johann Mattheson in 1722. Mattheson had a number of successors, notably the Leipzig composer Johann Adolph Scheibe, who brought out his weekly *Der critische Musicus* between the years 1737 and 1740 and whose chief claim to notoriety was his scurrilous attack on Bach. Generally speaking, the criticism of the time was characterized by an obsessive interest in the rules of music, and it tended to judge practice in the light of theory—a fatal philosophy. Mattheson, for instance, castigated Bach for ignoring certain rules of word setting in his cantatas.

Mattheson's contribution to musical criticism

At the turn of the century, the age of academicism dissolved into the age of description. Schumann, Liszt, and Berlioz, the leaders of the Romantic era, frequently saw in music the embodiment of some poetic or literary idea. They composed program symphonies, symphonic poems, and lesser pieces bearing such titles as "novellette," "ballade," and "romance." Their literary outlook naturally influenced criticism, the more so as they themselves frequently wrote it. In his pamphlet *On John Field's Noc-*

turnes (1859), Liszt wrote, in the purple prose of the time, of their "balmy freshness, seeming to exhale copious perfumes; soothing as the slow, measured rocking of a boat or the swinging of a hammock, amid whose smoothly placid oscillations we seem to hear the dying murmur of melting caresses." Most of the Romantics were guilty of this type of descriptive criticism. Its weakness is that, unless the music is already known, the criticism is meaningless; and once the music is known, the criticism is redundant, since the music itself says it all far more effectively.

Schumann and Hanslick

The most influential critic of the age was Schumann. In 1834 he founded the periodical *Neue Zeitschrift für Musik* ("New Journal for Music") and remained its editor in chief for 10 years. Its pages are full of the most perceptive insights into music and music makers. The first major article Schumann wrote was a laudatory essay on the young Chopin, "Hats off, gentlemen, a genius" (1834), and the last, called "New Paths" (1853), introduced to the world the young Brahms.

During the second half of the 19th century, the critical scene was dominated by the Viennese critic Eduard Hanslick, who is rightly regarded as the father of modern musical criticism. He was a prolific writer, and his book *Vom Musikalisch-Schönen* (1854: *The Beautiful in Music*) is a milestone in the history of criticism. It took an anti-Romantic stand, stressing the autonomy of music and its basic independence of the other arts, and it encouraged a more analytical, less descriptive approach toward criticism. The book was continually reprinted until 1895, appearing in many languages.

Inspired by Hanslick's example, critics in the 20th century rejected the age of description for the age of analysis. Scientific materialism created a climate of rationalism from which music did not remain immune. Critics spoke of "structure," "thematicism," "tonality"—a far cry from Liszt's "dying murmur of melting caresses." A group of musician–thinkers arose who questioned the very basis of musical aesthetics. They included Hugo Riemann, Heinrich Schenker, Sir Henry Hadow, Sir Donald Tovey, Ernest Newman, and, above all, Arnold Schoenberg, whose theoretical writings show him to be one of the most radical thinkers of the age. Criticism itself was criticized, its basic weakness clearly diagnosed. The search was on to discover the criteria for the evaluation of music. This quest—made ever more urgent by the rapidly changing language of music in the late 20th century—has dominated the work of serious critics ever since.

Criticism always seems to founder on the same small handful of basic problems. These problems are essentially philosophical. They appear to be insoluble. They are aggravated not only by the esoteric nature of music but also by the psychological mystery surrounding the very act of criticism. Are there any "standards" in criticism? If so, can they be defined? Are they objective or subjective? If the latter, can they possibly be true? These questions are fundamental. They disclose the full range of the philosophy of criticism.

The practice of criticism. Musical criticism has a primary aim: the evaluation of music. How does the critic set about this difficult task? The scientific school of criticism holds that he apply certain standards to the work in question. His evaluation is the result of testing music against his critical yardsticks and observing how far short it falls. According to this view, a value judgment is like a prize to be won by careful, objective, intelligent effort. This is an attractive notion, particularly among critics. It fosters the view that the critic is in a position of authority, and that he possesses the means to arbitrate over the creative artist. Unfortunately for criticism, there is nothing to suggest that this is anything but an illusion.

The intuitive nature of value judgments

If one reflects on the way in which one listens to music, a basic fact is apparent. Music's value is inherent; it resides in the work of art itself. A value judgment is something that comes across as part of musical communication. Paradoxically, a value judgment appears to be necessary before the critical process can start. The consequences of this observation are far-reaching. Rather than critics with standards, there appear to be only works with standards, which critics observe. It is not necessary to prove that Mozart's *Jupiter Symphony* is a masterpiece in order to be certain that it *is* a masterpiece. Its mastery is self-evident. Critics did not bestow value on Mozart; they perceived it in him.

Music as an autonomous communication. Music is autonomous. It refers to nothing outside itself. This sets it apart from the other arts, which rely upon the outside world for their images. A hat, a man, or an apple tree may all turn up in a painting, a sculpture, or a play. Indeed, they may be part of the very language of visual art and therefore essential to its understanding. Music has no such aids toward comprehension. It is completely lacking in conceptual crutches. It develops according to its own laws. It is a purely musical truth that is comprehended on a purely musical level. The purity of musical communication is what the German philosopher Arthur Schopenhauer was admiring when he said that all of art aspires toward the condition of music.

The inexplicability of musical experience

The totally musical nature of musical experience raises a difficulty for the critic. Such experience is virtually impossible for him to describe. Consequently, the critic can hardly be called "the man in the middle," a role frequently assigned to him. Music is not like a foreign language that requires an expert to translate it for a lay audience. It is a universal tongue. It either speaks to each listener directly, or it does not speak to him at all. If it speaks, the critic's words are already redundant. If it does not speak, a problem exists that his words cannot solve.

Two important consequences flow from these views. They are among the axioms of criticism. First: since music is autonomous, all knowledge about it must spring from experience of it; practice, in short, precedes theory. Second: because of the purely private and personal nature of musical communication, a work's mastery can only be demonstrated to those listeners who already know about it, who have already experienced it—and they hardly require the demonstration. To those listeners who have not experienced it, a work's mastery is not demonstrable. If it were demonstrable, it goes without saying that critical differences would cease to exist: there would be nothing to prevent those who had experienced it from converting those who had not. Yet critical differences remain.

Objectivity versus subjectivity. A difficulty confronting all critics concerns the subjectivity of their observations. Since music is perceived subjectively, so the argument runs, does this not reduce criticism to mere personal opinion? And if this is so, what makes one critic's opinions any truer than another's? This objection can be disposed of, first, on the broadest philosophical level. Since all things perceivable are perceived subjectively, the charge of subjectivity must either be levelled against every other human endeavour, or it must be withdrawn from criticism. Second, and more to the point, what would be said of a performer who proclaimed to all the world his objectivity, his noninvolvement with music? As for the composer, he would be thought strange indeed if he managed to avoid subjective entanglement with his creations. Why is it considered virtuous for performers and composers to enjoy an inner participation with music and not critics? Quite clearly, there is a contradiction here.

The crucial question facing every critic is how to demonstrate the truth of his reaction. Yet all critics cannot be right; many are diametrically opposed to one another. It is no wonder that musical criticism has been described as stuck at the litmus paper stage: critics take a dip into music, and one sees what colour they turn. Plainly, criticism remains indistinguishable from mere speculation until the critic develops the means of confirming the truth of his views. If he wishes to develop such means, it is to the theory of criticism that he must turn.

A definition of criticism

Meanwhile, a definition of musical criticism emerges: Criticism is the rationalization of intuitive musical understanding.

Issues in the theory of criticism. If the practice of criticism, as has been noted, can be reduced to one thing—expressing value judgments—the theory of criticism is essentially one thing, too—explaining them. It is not enough for critics to assert that one work is a masterpiece, another a mediocrity. An attempt must be made to explain why, and this may lead to a central discovery. A masterpiece is not a matter of chance, nor is a mediocrity. Both are symptomatic of deep, far-reaching principles.

Unity. When Rudolph Reti, the Viennese critic, was a young man studying music at the Vienna Conservatory, he once stood up in the middle of a composition class and put the following question to his professor: "Why can't we take the themes of one work and substitute the themes of another?" Reti did not receive a very convincing reply and was therefore stimulated to think about the problem for himself. Forty years later, he worked out an answer in his book *The Thematic Process in Music* (1951). Briefly, it was that masterpieces diversify a unity. They grow from an all-embracing idea. Their contrasting themes hang together because each of them represents a different aspect of a single basic thought. This observation was not new. Schoenberg had made it years earlier. So, too, had Heinrich Schenker, who used it as the basis for a major theory of aesthetics in his monumental *Das Meisterwerk in der Musik*, 3 vol. (1926–29; "The Masterpiece in Music"). Reti sharpened the concept. He made the critics think again about what, precisely, they mean when they talk about the integrity of a musical structure.

Diversity in unity

Reti's thesis can be vividly demonstrated by taking an existing masterpiece and substituting random themes from another. Even if such themes preserve a semblance of continuity (matching the key, metre, and mood of the themes they displace), they lose the deep sense of unity communicated by the original.

Not all musicians accept this theory. They argue that many composers, notably Bach, have put together works by borrowing materials from other sources. They fail to realize, however, that the act of borrowing is so highly selective that it, too, must be regarded as part of the creative process. The question then becomes: Why was that particular theme or movement borrowed?

Medium. Another question is why a composition expresses itself through its particular medium? Why that medium rather than another?

If a masterpiece is transferred from the instrumental medium for which it was conceived to some other, alien medium, it undergoes a curious distortion. Such distortion offers the clearest proof that a musical law is operating in the original: an identity of the idea with its medium. A master's inner inspiration adapts to his outer terms of reference. Individual instruments lay down individual limitations. If a composer ignores this fact, he can never be certain that his creative aims will ever coincide with the musical results.

Occasionally, a great composer deliberately engineers a collision between the idea and the medium for a special musical purpose. The fugue in Beethoven's *Hammerklavier Sonata*, for example, is one of the most physically awkward works to play in the entire piano repertoire. It has been composed against, rather than for, the instrument. Some bars are strictly unplayable, and Beethoven knew it; they contribute to the sense of struggle that is an essential part of musical communication, which is present even in the greatest performance. The orchestration of this fugue by the Austrian composer and conductor Felix Weingartner does a major service to musical aesthetics by providing an alternative musical experience of the same work; but by rendering the difficult easy, his orchestral version robs the music of its basic characteristics. It is a splendid illustration of the way in which, in Beethoven's original, a creative aim has been identified with a physical limitation.

Collision of idea and medium

Thematic chronology. A further question is why the chronology of the themes of a masterpiece cannot be changed. Why does one thematic chronology sound good, another bad? If the movements of a great sonata or a symphony are switched around, the result will be musically inferior. If the themes of one movement are mixed with those from the same work's companion movements, the result may even be an artistic disaster.

An illuminating exercise in criticism is to "reconstruct" a masterpiece so that its thematic running order is altered; that is, to transfer the first movement's second subject to the position occupied by the finale's second subject, and vice versa. Any musician can carry out this simple experiment for himself. Nothing is better calculated to reveal to him the presence of a creative principle of contrast distribution in the original. Given the thousands of different directions in which the material of a work could be unfolded, a master chooses the "right" one, the one that maintains structural tension—and, hence, musical interest. The themes of a masterpiece cannot assume one another's functions. They are born to fulfill specific roles. They develop out of each other because they create a musical need for each other.

The creative principle of contrast distribution

Economy. Composers through the ages have hinted at a law of economy toward which all great music strives. Brahms, in a characteristic piece of understatement, once said of composing that "the essential thing is that every note should be in its place." Beethoven expressed the same truth another way. Once, after he had heard the "Funeral March" from the opera *Achille* by the Italian composer Ferdinand Paer, he observed: "I must compose that!" To "fix" the idea, to define it, to pin it down—both composers felt that this was of the essence. Notes are redundant that do not stand for precisely those musical thoughts they are supposed to express. To have more notes, or less, than are actually required to communicate musical meaning must render such meaning correspondingly obscure. This law may be divided into three subsidiary principles.

First is the principle of identity between the idea and its utterance. There is a concrete musical difference between what a composer intends (the idea) and what he actually says (the utterance). Some musicians contend that the distinction is merely theoretical, that in practice it cannot be made. Fortunately, composers have left ample evidence to the contrary. Consider the act of revision. Revision is an acknowledgment by the composer himself that what he actually wrote was not, on reflection, what he actually meant. Revision is self-criticism. The very word implies that a composer has a re-vision of the work, that he returns to the utterance and modifies it in order to be truer to the idea. Revision can sometimes result in criticism on a grand, creative level. Composers occasionally revise the work of other composers with such effective results that the original composition may be eclipsed by the new version, the "criticism," often succeeding where the original work failed. Bach's arrangement (in A minor) for four harpsichords of Vivaldi's *Violin Concerto in B Minor,* for example, is more than an adaptation from one medium to another. It is an act of musical criticism *par excellence.* Vivaldi created the idea. But it was left to Bach to give it complete utterance.

Revision as self-criticism

Second is the relation of form and content. Why does music unfold a particular structure? Why that kind of structure rather than another? The textbooks on form remain silent. Yet this is a profound question. It is surely of paramount interest to know why music unrolls in one direction rather than another. Inspired music appears to carry within itself its own blueprint, according to which it propels itself across precise distances and in precise directions. If it is prematurely halted, diverted, or too long continued—all hallmarks of creative immaturity—it loses the sense of punctuality, the feeling of arriving "on time," the knowledge of being in the right place at the right moment, which characterizes each stage of an emerging structure masterfully handled.

The importance of structure

Some musicians have observed that the distinction between form and content is a false one. They rightly argue that no one hears one without the other, that the one is an organic result of the other. Therefore, why not abolish the distinction? They are right in regard to good forms, forms that arise inevitably from the musical material, in which case there is indeed no distinction to abolish. But bad forms, those that are not true to their content, produce a symptomatic division between the inner direction the music was born to follow and the outer direction it was made to follow.

The third subsidiary principle is audibility. The objective of all compositions is to make a total aural impact. There have been some famous miscalculations, intrinsically inaudible passages, which even the most illustrious performance could not render audible. A striking case of inaudibility occurs toward the end of Grieg's *Piano Con-*

certo in A Minor, in which the "big tune" of the finale returns in full orchestral splendour and obliterates the part of the solo pianist. In the concert hall, it is an extraordinary sight to see the soloist racing up and down the keyboard, fortissimo, without producing any sound. The observation is beyond all question and may be checked every time the work is played in public.

In 1937 Schoenberg completed an orchestration of Brahms's *Piano Quartet in G Minor,* Opus 25. As a young man, he had regularly participated in performances of the quartet. Time and again, he was bothered by its intermittent inaudibility: the piano tended to swamp the strings. Schoenberg's orchestration, as he himself claimed, attempted to put matters right. It remains an exercise in musical audibility—one master helping another to communicate. It constitutes an act of criticism on the highest creative level.

Other principles could be formulated to show that a theory of criticism is also a theory of composition. A search for these principles is really a search for the ultimate justification of the feelings of value inspired by great music.

Criticism and performance. Since music does not exist until it is brought to life by the player, two basic requirements are demanded of the critic: a knowledge of the work and a knowledge of the instrument. Many critics talk loosely about "the work" and "the performance" as though they were separate aspects of musical experience. They are, in fact, different aspects of a total musical experience, and it can be misleading to split them. Much bad criticism results from trying to do so. The Polish-American pianist Leopold Godowsky used to survey his audience before commencing his recitals in an endeavour to discover how many "detectives" there were in the house. Being such a superb pianist, he attracted all those critics exclusively interested in keyboard gymnastics. On the other hand, those interested exclusively in the composition may be equally biassed. In this age of authenticity, when the urtext is the thing, many a promising career has been blighted through what, in the profession, is called a "departure from the text." It is not always appreciated that at least a part of the total musical experience is created by the performer, who has a twofold artistic duty: first, to the fundamental character of the work he interprets; and, second, to his own artistic conscience, which tells him how the work should unfold. The two are not necessarily mutually exclusive.

The performer's duty

The criticism of performance is the most public, and publicized, aspect of a critic's function. It is also the least important. Unfortunately, what particular critics think of particular artists accounts for most contemporary music criticism. This is due rather to arbitrary factors than to the critic's sense of priority. Most newspapers insist that a musical event be reported the following day. The critic, consequently, is forced to telephone his review to his newspaper immediately after the concert, limiting himself to a strictly prescribed number of words. Under these conditions, it is not surprising that most criticism consists of predictable accounts of what was played, who played it, and how it was played. Nevertheless, performing artists are obliged to rely on these critical notices if they are to secure further work, even though neither critics nor artists like it. The box-office economics of performance are so delicate that bad publicity, or no publicity, can wreck artists and management alike.

(A.W./Ed.)

PERFORMANCE

Musical performance is that step in the musical process during which musical ideas are realized and transmitted to a listener. In Western music, performance is most commonly viewed as an interpretive art, though it is not always merely that. A performer to some degree determines aspects of any music he plays. Issues of tempo, phrasing, dynamics, and, in some types of music, pitches and instrumentation are subject to a performer's discretion. In this section, the various aspects and traditions of musical performance in Western and non-Western civilization are treated and their development traced.

Because the pleasure people derive from sounds has always been closely related to the pleasure they derive from making the sounds themselves, it is difficult to conceive of the origin of music as separate from an act of musical performance. Models for the establishment of rhythm may be found in heartbeat and breathing, and in the inflections of speech and cries of grief, pleasure, and desire are found the source of what became song.

The earliest visual manifestations of musical performance are found in rock paintings and excavated objects. While the interrelationship of music and ritual is clear, there is evidence that music was performed for dancing, in various work activities, and primitive games as well. Flutelike instruments of many sizes, made from bones and wood, and elaborate percussion instruments figure prominently in all primitive cultures, in which these instruments often were assigned symbolic significance associated with forces of the supernatural.

Singing is most probably the oldest musical activity. Even in the most primitive cultures the singer has had a special, defined position. In primitive singing there are three classes of sound: the first is called logogenic, in which words form the basis for the wavering musical incantation; the second, called pathogenic, consists of harsh, forceful, percussive, nonverbal sounds emitted to express strong feeling; in the third category, called melogenic, the sounds of the two previous categories combine to form a contour of pitches that pursue a course seemingly dictated by the weight of tensions inherent in the sequence of pitches and hence melodic in effect.

Primitive antiphony

Primitive societies evolved several means to relieve the monotony of one person's singing. A principle device is called antiphony, which involved two groups that sang in alternation or a leader who sang and was answered by a group of singers. In the latter may be seen the origin of responsorial singing, which continues today and which may be the point of origin for several types of musical phrase structures. Polyphony was also anticipated in primitive musical performance. It appeared through haphazard rather than intentional manifestations, such as the singing of the same melody with the parts starting on different pitches or at different times.

This section deals primarily with Western musical performance and its history but also deals briefly with non-Western traditions.

Aspects of Western musical performance. *The performer as interpreter.* Music as an interpretive art is a relatively recent phenomenon. In primitive societies, music plays a ritual role based on an oral tradition, and each performer in a sense interprets the tradition, but, more importantly, he renews it and transforms it through his own performance.

The development of the performer's role as interpreter coincided with the development of musical notation. Because composers for so many centuries were in a position to supervise the performances of their music, certain aspects of performance were not notated. Notation has grown increasingly complex as the dissemination of printed music has become more widespread. Ultimately, the degree of judgment a performer may exercise is determined by the period in which the music was composed. For music of certain periods, even though their notational systems are incomplete and give few indications of how the music should sound beyond pitch and rhythm, musical scholarship has amassed much information concerning proper instrumentation, ornamentation, improvisation, and other traditional performing practices that determine to a large degree the sound and stylistic character of the music. A performer as interpreter operates within a range of limitations imposed upon him by his understanding of the printed page, whatever knowledge may be available concerning the tradition that surrounds the music he is playing, and the extent to which his personal tastes coincide with this information. Certain aspects of the musical taste of the past sometimes cease to be expressive and gradually disappear from usage. Just as often, with the passage of time, performers tend to reassess the literature of previous ages and find renewed interest in practices that an earlier generation may have set aside. In any case, the performer as interpreter speaks to and with the tastes of his own time. And his task, no different from that of the performer in primitive music, is to renew, to refine, and to enrich the materials and traditions he inherits.

Mediums of performance. The mediums for musical performance are extraordinarily various. Western technology has had a tremendous impact on the development of musical instruments and has thereby greatly expanded the means whereby music is made. Performance may be vocal, instrumental, or electronic. Vocal performance is the oldest and the primary influence for the development of all subsequent musical gestures and materials. Instrumental music began with the development of percussion instruments and crude horns; stringed instruments came later. Electronic music is a 20th-century development involving the reproduction of traditional performance mediums through electronic means, at the same time that it is also evolving composition and performance of its own. At first it reproduced natural sounds by electronic means; later, composers and technicians began to invent electronic sounds and to discover new sound relationships.

Vocal, instrumental, and electronic performance

In all musical mediums the solo performance is the most spectacular. The power of music to compel attention and to stir emotions lends to the solo performer an especially fascinating aura. This is the domain of the virtuoso, that musical performing phenomenon of prodigious technical mastery, invention, and charisma. Most solo literature includes another instrument or group of instruments, and the literature varies from one medium to another according to the expressive range and technical capabilities of the solo instrument.

The largest solo literature for a single instrument is for keyboard instruments. Vocal solo literature is very important and extensive, and the stringed instruments also have a distinguished solo repertoire. The wind, brass, and percussion solo literature is more restricted.

In vocal and instrumental chamber ensemble performance, the performing groups are divided into duets, trios, quartets, quintets, sextets, septets, and octets, which exist for every medium and combination. Of particular importance is a string quartet consisting of two violins, viola, and violoncello. Dating from the 18th century, this instrumental ensemble is analogous to the vocal ensemble consisting of soprano, alto, tenor, and bass.

Beginning of symphonic music

Symphonic music dates from the 17th century. With the rise of the middle class and its aspirations for culture, music as an art required performing situations that would accommodate more people. Larger halls required ensembles acoustically suited to the expanded performing areas. The primary result of this development was the symphony orchestra with its multiple stringed, wind, brass, and percussion instruments.

Ensemble performance places a special responsibility on the concentration of the performer, who must attend not only to his own playing but also to that of all the others in the ensemble. All aspects of the performance depend on this mutual awareness. The leader of most small ensembles is one of the performers, the first violinist, a keyboard player, or one of the singers who indicates tempi, entrances, and musical character and supervises rehearsals. As ensembles grew in size and complexity and their problems of coordination increased, the leader set aside his instrument and devoted his efforts to the beating of time and the communication through clear hand signals of his indications for entrances, tempo changes, dynamic accents, and the shaping of phrases. This leader is called a conductor. The conductor often occupies a position analogous to that of a soloist in the attention of an audience, though the conductor himself makes no musical sound. As they are chiefly responsible for the music orchestras play, both in terms of choice and execution, conductors have had considerable impact on the development of music.

Opera, the marriage of music and drama, is the most complex performance situation. It entails much more than a single performer or group of performers, their instruments, and a hall in which to play. Text, decor, costumes, histrionic projection, preparation time, as well as singers, instrumentalists, and a bevy of extramusical technicians, must all be brought together and coordinated into the final production.

Artistic temperament. Many forces interact in developing those traits that distinguish various performing traditions and individual performers. Personality and temperament fundamentally affect the manner in which a performer works, as does his cultural milieu. There are performers who use music as a vehicle for display and others for whom performance is only a means to illuminate the music. Nor does performance necessarily mean public performance. For some people musical performance is essentially private, requiring no confirmation in the form of audience approval. The musical pleasure of such people rests solely on performing, either alone or with other musicians. Much chamber music is played under these private circumstances, and much music has been written for such situations. This used to be the primary realm of the musical amateur, that skilled but nonprofessional music lover whose ranks are diminishing in the era of the phonograph.

The type of performing situation at the opposite end of the spectrum is one directed to securing audience attention and affection. The need for audience approval has led to innovations as well as some decadence in its impact on the musical scene: innovation, if the performer is led to discover imaginative and fresh means of attracting public acclaim; decadence, if the devices for audience attraction become cheap and thinly spectacular, when the performer may distract the audience from more deserving work and debase its taste.

Intuition versus intellect

Intuition and intellect figure prominently in the temperament of a musical performer. Intuition is the capacity to do the musically "right" thing without instruction or special consideration of the alternatives. Intellect is the means whereby a musician enlarges the range of his instincts through the pursuit of new information, reflection, and analysis of the musical material at hand. Each element informs and completes the other.

Many musicians depend heavily on intuition in solving performance problems. Their solutions are often imaginative and fresh and their performances exciting. Others pursue a methodical path as they examine minutely relevant musical details. They analyze thoroughly the scores they perform, comparing manuscript facsimiles and various printed editions, and attempt to discover new musical relationships, new ways of delineating these relationships in performance, and, in short, new ideas as to how the music might best be played and how it should sound. Art, poetry, biography, cultural history, and any material relating to the period of the piece of music being studied for performance may be sources of musical insight for the performer.

National characteristics. At various times in history, national origin has been considered an important delineating characteristic in musical performance. This is partly the result of certain consistent emphases and features in the music written by composers of different nationalities. The Italians' interest in the voice has evolved a special singing (bel canto) quality in their music, which has carried over into their music for instruments (the stringed instruments especially), and into the general texture of Italian music, which has always given melody special prominence.

The English have had a highly developed and sophisticated musical performance tradition. Amateur improvisation figured importantly in its early history. While this has perhaps tended toward a conservative musical atmosphere, it has also produced a high standard for performance. The French have maintained a strong sense of national identity in their performing arts. In music their concerns for orderly design, delicate expressiveness, simplicity, naturalness, and beauty of sound extend back for centuries. Articulate philosophical and structural considerations have played important roles in developing nationalistic traits in the German tradition of musical performance.

The rich folklorist traditions of Spain, Hungary, and Russia have influenced rhythm, melody, and sonority in Western musical performing traditions. The Russian schools of string and piano technique have greatly advanced the performance resources of these instruments in the past 100 years. The United States, younger and more heterogeneous, has had a shorter musical history but an abundance of great symphony orchestras and solo artists, who are in demand because of their precise execution, versatility, and breadth of repertoire.

Historical stylistic developments. In antiquity the Sumerians, Egyptians, Greeks, and Romans evolved the first aesthetic theories and musical systems relevant to the music of the modern Western world. Unfortunately, few actual musical examples survive because of primitive notational practices and the gradual erosion of oral traditions. What is known is derived from the writings of the period and iconography—depictions of performing musicians, instruments, and musical events in sculpture and in wall and vase paintings.

In the Middle Ages traditions of musical performance were kept alive by the church and in the music sung and played by wandering minstrels.

In the Renaissance, polyphony (combining several simultaneous voice parts) and the early precursors of modern tonality (organization of music around a focal tone) were developed. The smooth flow of Renaissance liturgical counterpoint (polyphony) and the perky rhythms of secular Renaissance dance music remain as models of taste and musical technique even into the 20th century.

Developments in the Baroque

The performer emerged as a central figure in the focus of musical attention and purpose during the Baroque period. The heightening of the role of the individual performing artist and the invention of increasingly dramatic gestures to demonstrate performers' skills combined with a steady refinement in the construction of musical instruments. The reduction of musical materials to two modes (scale and melody patterns), in this case the major and minor scales, and the initial efforts to compose with large musical forms (opera, oratorio, sonata, and concerto) took place in this period. It is notable that in the Baroque era the equal-temperament system for tuning the strings or pipes of keyboard instruments evolved—a development that has had profound effect on the nature of musical language.

In the Rococo or Classical period that followed, the elaborate contrapuntal texture of Baroque music gave way to music of subtle dynamic differentiation, often based on simple folk materials (rhythms and melodies). The relationships between tonal materials and large musical forms achieved their highest state in the sonata and in opera.

The Romantic age was a period of refinement and intensification of Rococo principles with heavy literary overtones. It was the true age of the star virtuoso; that is, the age in which the role, person, and effect of the virtuoso was most dramatized and glamourized. The symphony orchestra in this period achieved its maximum development. Italian opera under Verdi found its noblest expression and German opera with Wagner expanded into the *Gesamtkunstwerk* ("complete art work").

Modern music dates from an era beginning roughly around World War I. Concert life has remained more or less what the 19th century established; the virtuoso conductor and performer dominate the musical establishment. More chamber, symphony, and opera programs are performed in more parts of the world than ever before, but musical progress has ceased to occur in established organizations and is found instead in the combo: jazz, rock, improvisational, experimental, live electronic, and multimedia groups that have sprung up in the 20th century.

The development of Western musical performance. *Antiquity.* The civilizations of antiquity expanded the role assigned to music in primitive cultures. The Sumerians established the foundations for the tradition of liturgical music. Some of the prayers that they sang have survived. From various artifacts of this civilization something is known about Sumerian musical instruments and some of the situations in which music was played. Such instruments as the lyre, harp, sistra, pipes, timbrels, and various drums figured importantly. Particular instruments were identified as accompaniment with specific types of religious poetry, and indeed the development of different poetic genres seems to have been considerably influenced by the nature of these instruments. While its primary purpose was religious, music also had something of a secular role in Sumerian culture and was played in processions, at banquets, and during primitive sporting events. Music as a profession first developed in Sumerian culture. Both men and women participated as singers and instrumentalists and held priestlike positions with specific functions and ranks of authority.

The musical culture of ancient Egypt, which apparently emerged from the same primitive sources as Sumer, resembles that earlier culture in many aspects: the close relationship between music and religion, the presence of a musical profession, some secular musical activity, and similar musical instruments. Of special interest in Egyptian music is the development of chironomy, the use of hand signals to indicate to instrumentalists what they should play. The singer in this manner guided instrumentalists through melodies with which the singer was seemingly more familiar than the players.

In these ancient cultures there was no notational system or codified theory of musical practice. Different musical traditions were exchanged in the process of trade, migration, military conquest, and intermarriage to form that common body of practices that is the basis of Western music.

Importance of Greek music

Of the early civilizations, Greece provided the musical culture of greatest significance for the development of Western music. The system of scales and modes, as well as a large part of the general philosophy concerning the nature and effect of musical sounds, has been inherited from the Greeks. It was also the Greeks who developed the theory of ethos, which defines the character of psychological and emotional response to different musical stimuli. Building on the ancient religions and magical accoutrements of music, the Greeks assigned specific mental and emotional states to specific pitch arrangements and instrumental combinations. Music infused with this motivating power stood at the centre of the social order.

Though a major part of Western musical terminology, basic music theory and philosophy, basic notational practices, and the foundations of acoustical physics derive from the ancient Greeks, very little of their music has survived. The great ethical significance of music in Greek society caused performing mastery to be an essential aspect of education. Everyone was taught to sing and to play instruments. For a major part of the period all music was a setting of words with instrumental accompaniment, for the most part doubling the voice at the interval of octaves, fourths, or fifths. It was only in the later part of the period, after the age of Pericles (late 5th century BC), that instruments began to play independently of singers.

Music, in the later stages of the Hellenic period, became an increasingly important part of public spectacles. As musical performance became increasingly secularized and became the property of the masses, the upper classes withdrew to esoteric considerations of the art and reflections on its past. It was perhaps at this point that music was divided into two fairly artificial categories: the contemplation of music's nature and history and practical musical performance.

Assuming the artistic mantle of ancient Greece, the Romans disseminated Greek music throughout the known world. The essential role of music in the Roman Empire remained unchanged. Rome's principal contribution consisted in serving as a catalyst for the mixing of Hebraic and Hellenic traditions of musical performance, which, preserved by the Christian Church for a thousand years, emerged again in the Renaissance into the first flowering of modern musical practices in the West.

Although not in the mainstream of Western musical performance, Islāmic (North African and Near Eastern) classical music closely approaches the orchestral tradition of European music in one respect: large choruses and orchestras—consisting of tambourines, pot drums, recorder-flutes, *ʿūds* (plucked lutes), bowed lutes, and dulcimers—are assembled to perform "suites" consisting of a series of instrumental solos and orchestral selections interspersed with unison choral songs or solo recitatives based on classical poetry. But while these suites are perfectly suited to performance in formal concert halls, they may also be heard in much less regulated settings, such as cafés. Here the listener is free either to concentrate intellectually on the progress and development of the musical ideas or to converse and eat, relaxing in the beauty of the general musical design. The more "oriental" side of Islāmic musical performance is more improvisatory, either in solo performance on a recorder-flute, fiddle, *ʿūd,* or dulcimer or by any of these in combination with the voice—the instrumentalist then elaborating on the singer's improvisation. Here, too, the relationship of audience to performer is much less formal than in the performance of European music.

"Oriental" side of Islāmic musical performance

The Middle Ages. The tradition of sung prayers and psalms extends into the shadows of early civilization. Such sacred singing was often accompanied by instruments, and its rhythmic character was marked. In the synagogue, however, the sung prayers were often unaccompanied. Ritual dance was excluded from the synagogue as the rhythmic character of sacred music surrendered its more sensual aspects. Even in the prayers themselves, rhythmic verse gave way to prose. The exclusion of women, the elevation of unison singing, and the exclusion of instruments served to establish a clear differentiation between musical performance in the synagogue and that of the street.

The musical performance tradition of the Christian Church grew out of the liturgical tradition of Judaism. The melodic formulas for the singing of psalms and the sung recitation of other scriptural passages are clearly based on Hebraic models.

Music in the Roman Catholic liturgy was performed mainly for the mass. Originally, the music was performed by the priest and the congregation, until, in time, there emerged from the congregation a special group of singers, called the choir, who assumed the musical role of answering and contrasting the solo singing of the priest. Women participated actively in musical performances in the ancient Christian Church until 578, when older Hebraic practices excluding them were restored. From that time until the 20th century, Roman Catholic Church choirs were composed solely of men and boys.

First codification of church music

The first codification of early church music was reputedly made by Pope Gregory I during his reign (590–604). Gregory's collection was selected from chants already in use. His codification assigned these chants to particular services in the liturgical calendar. In general it reinforced the simple, spiritual, aesthetic quality of liturgical music. The music in this collection serves as a model of melodic design even in the 20th century and is regarded as one of the monuments of Western musical literature. This school of unison liturgical singing is called plainchant, plainsong, or Gregorian chant. Specific details concerning the manner in which chant was performed have been lost. There are speculations that the quality of sound the singers employed was somewhat thinner and more nasal than that used by contemporary singers. The authentic rhythmic style of chant cannot be ascertained. There is a theory, however, that the basic rhythmic units had the same durational value and were grouped in irregularly alternating groups of twos and threes. Pitch levels and tempos apparently varied somewhat according to the occasion. There are preserved manuscript notations reminding singers to be careful and modest in their work, indicating that temptations of inattention and excessive vocal display existed for even the earliest liturgical musicians.

While modern musical traditions in the West are based to a large extent on the principles of antiquity preserved in the notated music of the early church, a secular musical practice did exist; but because of the pervasive influence of the church, the dividing line between sacred and secular aspects was thin throughout a good part of the medieval period.

Several types of later secular song have survived. The musical notations are for the most part inadequate to give an accurate impression of the music, but it is known that it retained the essential monophonic character of liturgical music. One curious type of secular song, conductus, originated in the church itself. This song did not use traditional liturgical melodies or texts but was composed to be sung in the liturgical dramas or for processions. For this reason it dealt occasionally with subjects not religious in character. The goliard songs dating from the 11th century are among the oldest examples of secular music. They were the often bawdy Latin songs of itinerant theological students who roamed rather disreputably from school to school in the period preceding the founding of the great university centres in the 13th century.

Several other groups of medieval performers developed literary and musical genres based on vernacular texts: the jongleurs, a group of travelling entertainers in western Europe who sang, did tricks, and danced to earn their living; the troubadours in the south of France and the trouvères in the north; and the minnesingers, a class of artist-knights who wrote and sang love songs tinged with religious fervour.

Instruments, such as the *vielle,* harp, psaltery, flute, shawm, bagpipe, and drums were all used during the Middle Ages to accompany dances and singing. Trumpets and horns were used by nobility, and organs, both portative (movable) and positive (stationary), appeared in the larger churches. In general, little is known of secular instrumental music before the 13th century. It is doubtful that it had a role of any importance apart from accompaniment. Yet the possibility of accompanied liturgical music has not been eliminated by modern scholars.

Medieval polyphony

The medieval musical development with the furthest-reaching consequences for musical performance was that of polyphony, a development directly related, as indicated above, to the experience of performing liturgical chant. For performers and performance, perhaps the most important developments in the wake of polyphony were refinements of rhythmic notation necessary to keep independent melodic lines synchronous. At first the obvious visual method of vertical alignment was used; later, as upper voices became more elaborate in comparison with the (chant-derived) lower ones, and writing in score thus wasted space, more symbolic methods of notating rhythm developed, most importantly in and around the new cathedral of Notre-Dame in Paris.

In the 14th century, partly because of the declining political strength of the church, the setting for new developments in music shifted from the sacred field to the secular, from the church to the court. This shift led in turn to a new emphasis on instrumental music and performance. Already the lower voices began to be performed on instruments—both because their long notes made them difficult to sing and because their texts (of only a few syllables) became senseless outside their original liturgical positions. Now, as secular princes became increasingly important patrons of composers and performers—a situation that would continue well into the 18th century—secular and instrumental music flourished. The polyphonic music of the church merged with the poetic art of the troubadours, and the two most important composers of the age were the blind Florentine organist Francesco Landini and the French poet Guillaume de Machaut, canon of Reims.

Most of the music of these composers seems to have been intended for combined vocal-instrumental performance, although this is seldom expressly indicated in the manuscripts. Medieval composers probably had no rigid expectations about performance media. Until the 17th century, and even through the 19th in the case of domestic performance, choice of instruments was likely to be dependent as much on available performers as on anything else. Many sources do, however, indicate that medieval musicians tended to separate instruments into two groups, loud and soft (*haut* and *bas,* or, very generally, wind and string), and to prefer contrasting sonorities within those groups for maximum differentiation of the individual parts. Outdoor or ceremonial music would be performed with loud instruments (shawm, bombard, trombone, organ); room music, with soft ones (lute, viol, recorder, harp). Paintings and manuscript illuminations of the period show that much secular performance included both a wide variety of bells, drums, and other percussion instruments and instruments with drones—bagpipes, fiddles, double recorders, hurdy-gurdies. The parts for these instruments are never found in the musical sources and must be reconstructed for modern performance.

The notation of medieval music often is misleading for the modern performer. Accidentals (sharps and flats, called then musica ficta) were often omitted as being understood.

Notation of medieval music

Further, it seems likely that variation, embellishment, and improvisation were very important elements of medieval performance. It is known that sections of some 15th-century two-part vocal music were enhanced by an extempore third part, in a technique called fauxbourdon; the notation of the 15th-century *basse danse* consisted of only a single line of unmeasured long notes, evidently used by the performing group of three instrumentalists for improvisation, much as a modern jazz combo's chart.

The Renaissance. The very concept of improvisation as a mere subcategory within performance practice could arise only after the invention of music printing, which had at first little discernible effect on performance. Extemporized ornamentation of polyphonic music continued and increased during the 16th century in instrumental, vocal, and combined performance, both secular and sacred. Later in the century, liturgical music again became less extravagant in the wake of the Council of Trent (1545–63), which ordered that masses be sung "clearly and at the right speed" and that singing "be constituted not to give empty pleasure to the ear, but in such a way that the words may be clearly understood by all." Music printing was at first too expensive to alter seriously the social structure of musical performance; the traditions of ostentation and exclusiveness embodied in music written by Guillaume Dufay for the early 15th-century Burgundian court were continued in the magnificent musical establishments of the Italian Renaissance princes and popes. Detailed records exist of the elaborate musical festivities arranged for weddings and baptisms of the powerful Florentine family, the Medici. Printing increased the dissemination as well as the survival of these works; but, like the earlier Burgundian chanson and unlike the contemporary Parisian chanson, which was cast in a more popular mould, they were nonetheless primarily intended for a select group of discriminating performers.

Printing, both of music and of books, does document the ever increasing development and sophistication of instrumental music during the 16th century. Printed descriptions of instruments date from the 16th century. Their discussions of tuning and technique supplied the needs of professional and nonprofessional musicians alike. There was a growing tendency to construct instruments in families (whole consorts of homogeneous timbre, high, middle, and low), a tendency perhaps related to recent expansion at both ends of the musical scale: with more space available, contrapuntal parts no longer crossed so frequently and no longer needed the differentiation provided by the markedly contrasting timbres of the medieval "broken consort."

The 17th and 18th centuries. After printing, the next significant influence on music performance was the gradual emergence of the audience, for the relationship between participants in the musical experience—between performer and listener—became polarized. The first evidence for this shift was the rise of the professional vocal virtuoso about the last quarter of the 16th century, and this development soon had a profound influence on musical style. Italian composer-singers, such as Giulio Caccini and Jacopo Peri, reacted quickly to their audiences' desire for more expressive and passionate vocalism, and the music they wrote for themselves eventually was imitated and refined by other composers, such as the Italian Claudio Monteverdi, whose nine successive books of madrigals document the changes in style from music composed for four to six essentially equal voices to music in which the interest lay primarily at the extremes of the texture. The technical underpinning for this new monodic style was the basso continuo, or thorough bass, played by one or more polyphonic solo instruments "realizing" a "figured bass": that is to say, improvising chords above a single line of music provided with numbers and other symbols to indicate the other notes of the chords. In the 17th century a wide variety of continuo instruments was used, including lute, theorbo, harp, harpsichord, and organ. By the 18th century the practice was more standardized: the bass line would be realized on a keyboard instrument and reinforced by a monophonic bass instrument, such as a lute, viola da gamba, violoncello, or bassoon. The continuo player not only completed the harmony but could also control rhythm and tempo to suit the particular conditions of a performance.

Rise of the vocal virtuoso

The development of monody was itself a necessary precondition for that most expensive of all performance institutions, opera. Beginning in Florence at the very end of the 16th century, opera soon spread over Italy: through Rome, where its initially pastoral nature matured into full-blown spectacle, to Venice, where the first public opera theatre opened in 1637. There, although audiences were still aristocratic, opera was dependent upon the sale of admissions rather than royal patronage, and musical performance began to find an entirely new method of economic support.

In the realm of purely instrumental music, the new economy of performance was slower to emerge, but there were many other new developments. By far the most popular Renaissance instrument had been the versatile lute; it served all levels from the merchant's daughter learning the simplest dance melody to the virtuoso. In the 17th century the lute began to yield to keyboard instruments, but the intimate music of the French *clavecinistes* (harpsichordists) was still a clear outgrowth of the precious and evanescent performance style of the lutenist Denis Gaultier (1597/1603–1672). Later, keyboard ornamentation began to be codified in tables of agrément-symbols published with each new collection of music. In Italy composers also were attempting to provide performers with more explicit directions. Contemporary keyboard fingering systems, which used the thumb much less than modern ones, also served contemporary preference for subtlety and unevenness of rhythm. As the century progressed and national styles drew further apart, there evolved a specifically French tradition of *inégalité:* performing certain evenly written notes unequally, with alternately longer and shorter values.

Predominance of keyboard instruments

A more lasting French development was the first instance of instrumental music consistently performed by more than one player to a part. In 1656, Jean-Baptiste Lully made his orchestra, the Petits Violons ("Little Violins"), abandon the old tradition of free embellishment and drilled them in a disciplined and rhythmically pointed precision that was widely imitated. Simultaneously, the violin and its family, because of their passionate brilliance and versatility, replaced viols as the standard ensemble instruments—especially quickly in Italy, where performance was less sophisticated, less mannered, and less restrained than in France.

In the 18th century, national performance styles tended again to merge, except in the case of opera. French opera, which had reached its first height under Lully and had counted among its star performers Louis XIV himself, continued to emphasize ballet and correct declamation more than pure vocalism. In other areas, standardization and codification were the trend. The place of improvised embellishment and variation was further circumscribed, limited in general to such recognized spots as repeated sections in binary and da capo forms, slow movements of sonatas and concertos, and cadences. Instrumental tutors by famous performers were important and widespread.

The foundation of public concerts increased, and orchestras all over Europe followed the pattern set by the famous ensemble maintained by the Elector of the Palatine at Mannheim, with its standard size (about 25) and new style of performance with dramatic dynamic effects and orchestral devices (*e.g.,* crescendos, tremolos, grand pauses). The Mannheim composers also hastened the decline of the improvised thorough bass by writing out harmonic filler parts for the violas; conducting from the keyboard nevertheless remained standard practice into the 19th century. Meanwhile, entrepreneurial speculation was finally supplanting aristocratic patronage as the economic base for concert activity. Haydn, who had already spent one full career in Austria, in the service of the House of Esterházy, in 1791 began another and more lucrative one in association with the concert manager Johann Peter Salomon—conducting his London symphonies from the piano.

Foundation of public concerts

The 19th century. The heyday of the concert artist began before Haydn's first journey to London, and it still shows few signs of ending. It reached its zenith and was the primary factor in all music performance in the 19th century. Mozart and Beethoven were famous concert pianists before they were famous composers, and succeeding generations saw a large number of piano virtuosos travelling over Europe and, later, North and South America. Some were composers of works for themselves; others were more important as interpreters of other composers' works. The tradition of the star singer was of course much older, and it continued; one new development was that of the claquer, paid by the star for his applause. The independent conductor, as distinct from the first violinist or the continuo player, emerged from the body of the orchestra during the first half of the 19th century, and his development toward the lionized figures of the 20th century was swift. Parallel with this rise came the establishment of many of today's major orchestras: New York Philharmonic (1842), Vienna Philharmonic (1842), Boston Symphony (1881), Berlin Philharmonic (1882), Amsterdam Concertgebouw (1883), Chicago Symphony (1891), and London Symphony (1904).

Establishment of major orchestras

The result of the enormous widening of concert activity and of the increasingly international reputations of performers was an even further standardization of performance practice. Eighteenth-century concern with appropriateness and taste in embellishment yielded to emphasis on clarity and evenness of touch, purity of intonation, and accuracy of execution. As composers' scores became increasingly precise, the performers' interpretative decisions were increasingly limited to matters of technique, tempo, rhythmic and dynamic nuance and personality—a subjectivism justified by the cult of Romantic genius prevalent in 19th-century artistic life. Real improvisation in music would not re-emerge until the 20th century—in jazz. The addition of such mechanical aids and improvements as chin rests and end pins to stringed instruments (which permitted a wider and more constant vibrato without tiring); valves and extra keys to brass and woodwind instruments (making scales more even and intonation more secure); and double-escapement action, iron frames, and cross-stringing to the piano (which facilitated crisper and surer attack and made both tone and tuning last longer) all had profound influence not only on performance techniques but also on the very sound of the instruments. The most successful new instrumental and vocal teaching methods emphasized virtuosity, brilliance, evenness, and wide range, reflecting a desire to make music more effective for large audiences.

Technical advances in instruments

The rise of the concert artist was seconded by the appearance of the professional music critic, whose influence on performance has been, and is, difficult to assess. At first critics tended to be primarily practicing musicians; later this was less the case. A more tangible residue of 19th-century music performance and one that illustrates how little its basic social structures have changed since then is the large number of concert halls and opera theatres that were built and are still used today.

One final development, the import of which would not be fully realized until the present century, was that of historicism: the active revival of old music. This incipient recognition of the validity of other styles of composition and performance is dated conventionally from the German composer Felix Mendelssohn's 1829 performance of parts of Bach's *St. Matthew Passion,* but it was preceded in a sense by the Concerts of Antient Music (1776–1848) in London. The stated policy of this musical group was not to perform music less than 20 years old (but they often updated the compositions with added brass parts). The revival of interest in the music of Palestrina and Bach, while at first expressed only in terms of 19th-century Romanticism, would pave the way for 20th-century advances and retrenchments in both style and performance.

The 20th century. The major performing institutions of the 19th century have continued into the 20th century with only minimum structural change, except for a rather belated movement toward unionization of personnel; this development has of course improved the performers' lot greatly, while increasing the costs of performance. Unquestionably, the major new influence on 20th-century music performance has been electronics. Broadcasting and recording have widened even further the potential audience for concert artists, at the same time as they have tended to decrease the physical necessity for large new public performance arenas. Electronic instruments have appeared, both amplified versions of older ones (guitar, piano, and even some woodwinds) and instruments with fundamentally electronic means of tone production (electronic pianos and organs, the theremin and Ondes Martenot, and sound synthesizers). Other new compositional and performance possibilities have also developed; for example, film, tape, stereophonism, and computers. Even before the phonograph (invented *c.* 1875) had begun to be regarded as more than a toy, serious research into the authentic performance of older music had produced an awareness of possibilities that pointed the way out of the seeming dead end of late Romantic gigantism and subjectivism. From the very beginning of the century, the chamber concerts given by Arnold Dolmetsch and his family, on reconstructions of old gambas and recorders, attracted attention to small ensembles and different sonorities and encouraged the activities of other artists.

Appearance of electronic instruments

The true end of the Romantic era and the beginning of the modern era can be dated from the second decade of the 20th century, the time of the composition of two masterpieces that more than any others mark the departure from 19th-century performance ideas: the German composer Arnold Schoenberg's *Pierrot Lunaire* (1912) and the Russian composer Igor Stravinsky's *Histoire du soldat* (*The Soldier's Tale,* 1918). These are chamber works, but their instrumental makeup is a unique mixture of instruments that do not necessarily blend and that seem further to repudiate the orchestra as a performing medium. *Pierrot* is a series of songs which repudiate the 19th-century lied: the voice does not sing but produces a kind of pitched speech (*Sprechstimme*). *Histoire* repudiates both orchestra and opera as previously understood: it is specifically (and inexpensively) designed for performance on a portable stage by three dancers, a narrator, and seven instrumentalists. For these works a new kind of performer is required, and these works in turn have helped to train the new performer—who might be called the group-virtuoso. Teams or groups of such performers have sprung up everywhere. Often they are centred on a living composer or the university where he teaches, where they function as partners to his composition, realizing the work rather than interpreting it. The performer is very much involved in the creative act, the product of which reflects his particular skills and personality, and the dynamics of the working situation.

In the second half of the 20th century the established performance situation moved from the formal, ritualized event of the past to a more informal and spontaneous type of gathering. The interaction of various media has led to new art forms and circumstances. Many artists attempt to create performance situations that actively involve as participants all those in attendance. The roles of composer, performer, and listener are consolidated in a single participant, who in interaction with others arrives at an art work, which all have invented, realized and perceived, and which can never take place again. On the other hand, the growing use of technology intensifies the problem of evaluating the meaning and effect of electronically produced and assembled performances that, in their totality, never took place at all and possibly never could.

Increasing spontaneity of performance situations

The electronic media continue to improve so that anyone may be able to select chamber, concert, opera, and other new types of performance from anywhere in the world, experiencing them through nearly lifelike reproduction facilities. Vast numbers of people may study performance skills via two-way transmission with great artists. The number of actual public performing events may decrease as private musical performance increases. Already there is the phenomenon of the widespread dissemination of great performers' recordings, which has forced the standards of quality for a live performance to almost inhuman heights and has increased interest in the performance of older as well as contemporary music.

Non-Western musical performance traditions. *South Asia.* Although the classical South Asian or Indian musician usually performs in a concert situation quite analogous to that of a typical Western artist, his audience responds to him quite differently: he is not judged on how faithfully he reproduces the music the composer imagined but on how well he creates his own music within certain wide bounds set by the composer and by the general practice of Indian music. Since Indian musical performance is based on improvisation, Indian musical pedagogy is therefore a more personal procedure, in which an aspiring musician will "apprentice" himself to a guru, with whom he thereafter identifies himself; in the West this kind of organization is reflected in the rise of the group-virtuoso discussed above. Similarly, Western development away from large performing groups such as the full orchestra reflects—or at least parallels—the more intimate character of Indian music, the basic texture of which usually involves a quite small group of performers: one player to provide rhythm on a drum such as the double-headed, pitched tabla; one to provide a basic drone, often on the lute-like tamboura; and a central performer on the sitar (technically also a plucked lute but one with melodic capability, unlike the tamboura). The players often engage in a kind of competition not unlike that of Western jazz groups. If there is singing, the style of performance is low and soft, in contrast to that of Indonesian classical vocalism.

Intimate character of Indian music

Southeast Asia. The gamelan is at the center of the art-music tradition of Indonesia. It may range in size from a few to over 75 instruments. The basic melodic instrument is the *saron* (bronze xylophone), accompanied by various gongs, a kind of violin, a recorder-flute and/or a zither; the group is led by a drummer. As in medieval Western music, there are two kinds of gamelan playing, one emphasizing the bronze instruments (comparable to medieval *haut*, or loud, consorts) and the other the wind and stringed instruments (*bas*, or soft, groups). A similar differentiation exists in Indochinese music in the contrast between the percussion-dominated *pi phat* band of Thailand and the string-dominated *mahori* bands of Thailand and Cambodia. Gamelan playing, particularly of the softer type, often accompanies solo and unison choral singing of classical poetry (music is connected with most of Indonesian literature). Southeast Asian vocal performance—like that of a great deal of non-Western art music—is characterized by tense, high, often nasal voice production; this is one of many alternatives being explored by the more experimental 20th-century Western composers and performers.

China and Japan. The most extensively developed and most important Chinese and Japanese traditions of musical performance are closely tied to theatrical styles and traditions. Perhaps the most spectacular of non-Western performance traditions is Chinese opera, in which singers, acrobats, costumes, scenery, and instruments are combined in the creation of a highly varied work of art. Peking opera uses two basic kinds of instrumentation: for military scenes a battery of drums, gongs, and cymbals with a kind of oboe playing the melody; for the more frequent domestic scenes a wider variety based on a drum (*pan ku*) with a peculiarly sharp, cracking sound for keeping time, and a number of two-stringed, bowed lutes played with the bow passing between the strings. Plucked lutes and flutes also appear at times. All of the melody instruments play heterophonically with the singers, whose vocal style, as in the West, is highly artificial. Heroines are usually portrayed (sometimes by female impersonators) in a high, thin voice; heroes use a raucous, rasping tone quite foreign to traditionally oriented Western ears—but, again, not unlike some of the vocal techniques required by 20th-century Western avant-garde composers.

A performance tradition peculiarly Japanese is the emphasis on the visual aspects of making music: custom directs that *gagaku* (court orchestra) instruments must be played as gracefully as possible. (L.Fo./J.Th./B.A.C.)

Musical sound

That some sounds are intrinsically musical, while others are not, is an oversimplification. From the tinkle of a bell to the slam of a door, any sound is a potential ingredient for the kinds of sound organization called music. The choices of sounds for music making have been severely limited in all places and periods by a diversity of physical, aesthetic, and cultural considerations. This section will analyze those involved in Western musical traditions.

General characteristics. The fundamental distinction usually made has been between tone and noise, a distinction best clarified by referring to the physical characteristics of sound. Tone differs from noise mainly in that it possesses features that enable it to be regarded as autonomous. Noises are most readily identified, not by their character but by their sources; *e.g.*, the noise of the dripping faucet, the grating chalk, or the squeaking gate. Although tones too are commonly linked with their sources (violin tone, flute tone, etc.), they more readily achieve autonomy because they possess controlled pitch, loudness, timbre, and duration, attributes that make them amenable to musical organization. Instruments that yield musical sounds, or tones, are those that produce periodic vibrations. Their periodicity is their controllable (*i.e.*, musical) basis.

The strings of the violin, the lips of the trumpet player, the reed of a saxophone, and the wooden slabs of a xylophone are all, in their unique ways, producers of periodic vibrations. The pitch, or high-low aspect, created by each of these vibrating bodies is most directly a product of vibrational frequency. Timbre (tone colour) is a product of the total complement of simultaneous motions enacted by any medium during its vibration. Loudness is a product of the intensity of that motion. Duration is the length of time that a tone persists.

Each of these attributes is revealed in the wave form of a tone. The pattern may be visualized as an elastic reed—like that of a clarinet—fixed at one end, moving like a pendulum in a to-and-fro pattern when set into motion. Clearly, this reed's motion will be in proportion to the applied force. Its arc of movement will be lesser or greater depending upon the degree of pressure used to set it into motion. Once moving, it will oscillate until friction and its own inertia cause it to return to its original state of rest. As it moves through its arc the reed passes through a periodic number of cycles per time unit, although its speed is not constant. With these conditions prevailing, its motion through time could be charted by placing a carbon stylus on its moving head, then pulling a strip of paper beneath it at a uniform rate. The reed's displacement to-and-fro diminishes in a smooth fashion as time passes (decreasing intensity). Each cycle of its arc is equally spaced

The vibrating reed

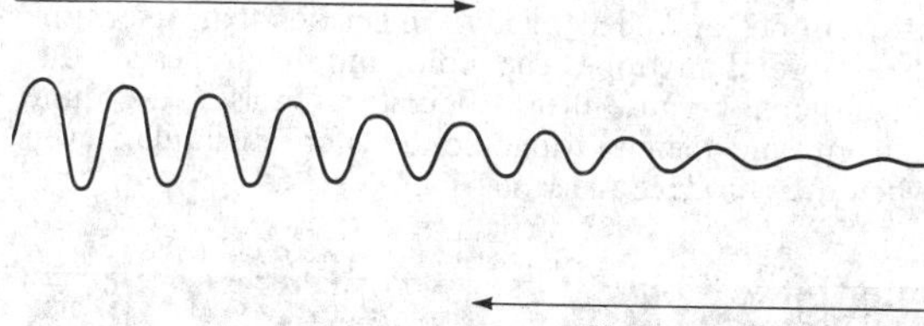

Visual representation of a reed's vibration.

(uniform frequency). Each period of the motion forms the same arc pattern (uniform wave content). If this vibratory motion were audible, it could be described as follows: it grows weaker from the beginning (diminishing loudness) until it becomes inaudible; it remains at a stable level of highness (steady pitch); and it is of unvarying tonal quality (uniform timbre). If the reed were a part of a clarinet and the player continued blowing it with unvaried pressure, loudness, pitch, and timbre would appear as constants.

TONE

Most musical tones differ from the demonstration tone (above) in that they consist of more than a single wave form. Any material undergoing vibratory motion imposes its own characteristic oscillations on the fundamental vibration. The reed probably would vibrate in parts as well as a whole, thus creating partial wave forms in addition to the fundamental wave form. These partials are not fortuitous. They bear harmonic relationships to the fundamental motion that are expressible as frequency ratios of 1:2, 3:4, etc. This means that the reed (or string or air column as well) is vibrating in halves and thirds and fourths as well as a whole. Another way of expressing this is that half the body is vibrating at a frequency twice as great as the whole; a third is vibrating at a frequency three times greater; etc.

Overtone series These numerical relationships also are expressible by pitch relationships as the harmonic, or overtone, series, which is merely a representation of numerical ratios in terms of pitch equivalents. Depending upon its shape and substance, a vibrating mass performs motions that are the equivalents of these partial vibrations, whether it be the mass of a string, reed, woodblock, or air column. This means that most tones are composites: they consist of partial vibrations of the vibrating body as well as the vibrations of the whole mass. Although one can develop the acuity required to hear some of these overtones within a musical tone, the ear normally ignores them as separate parts, recognizing only a more or less rich tone quality within the fundamental pitch.

Although pure tones, or tones lacking other than a fundamental frequency, sometimes occur in music, most musical tones are composites. A typical violin tone is

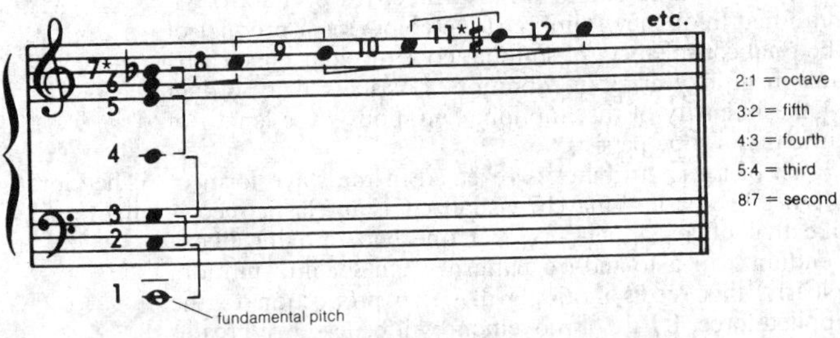

Overtone series.

relatively rich in overtones while a flute tone sometimes approaches a pure tone. What the listener recognizes as "a violin tone" or "a trumpet tone" also is a product of the noise content that accompanies the articulation of any sound on the particular instrument. The friction of the bow as it is set into motion across the string, the eddies of air pressure within a horn's mouthpiece, or the hammer's impact on a piano string all add an extra dimension, a significant "noise factor," to any manually produced tone. After articulation, however, it is the presence or absence of overtones and their relative intensities that determine the timbre of any tone. The violin and flute tones are distinguishable because their articulatory "noises" are quite different and their overtone contents are dissimilar, even when they produce the same pitch.

From C. Culver, *Musical Acoustics*. Copyright 1956. Used with permission of McGraw-Hill Book Company

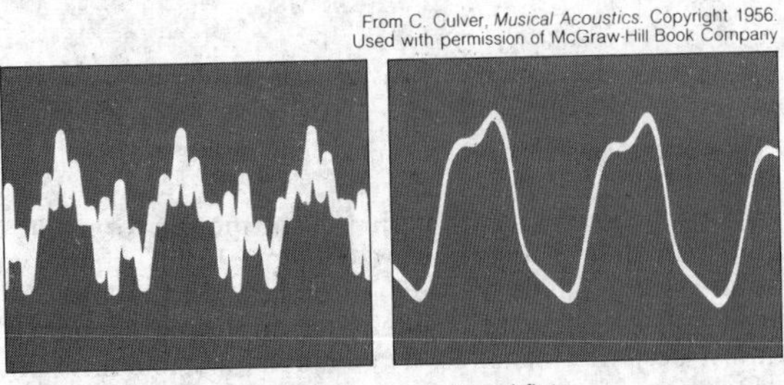
Comparison of (left) violin wave form, d′, and flute wave form, d′.

Electronic sound Musical tones of determined harmonic content can be produced by electronic vacuum tubes or transistors as well as by traditional manual instruments. Some electronic organs, for example, use single vacuum tubes whose frequency output can be varied through control of an adjustable transformer. Through ingenious mixing circuits a compound tone consisting of any predetermined overtone content can be produced, thereby imitating the sound of any traditional instrument. Composers of electronic music have utilized this capability to synthesize tones quite different from any available on traditional instruments, as well as tones similar to natural sounds. Electronic computers are capable of complete imitation of such sounds; the tone is broken down into its component parts, then synthesized through an auditory output circuit.

MOVEMENT

Once an audible oscillation is produced by a vibrating body, it moves away from its source as a spherical pressure wave. Its rate of passage through any medium is determined by the medium's density and elasticity; the denser the medium, the slower the transmission; the greater the elasticity, the faster. In air at around 60° F, sound moves at approximately 1,120 feet per second, the rate increasing by 1.1 feet per second per degree of rise in temperature.

Sound waves move as a succession of compressions through the air. The wavelength is determined by frequency; the higher the pitch, the shorter the wavelength. A pitch of 263 cycles per second (middle C of the piano) is borne as a wavelength of around 4.3 feet (speed of sound ÷ frequency = wavelength).

By the time a wave has moved some distance, it has changed in some of its characteristics. The journey has robbed it of intensity, which is inversely proportional to the square of the distance. Its timbre has been altered slightly by objects within its path that disrupted an equitable distribution of frequencies, particularly the high-frequency waves, which, unlike the low, move in relatively straight paths from their sources.

Resonance The area within which a sound occurs can have considerable effect upon what is heard. Just as a string or reed or air column has a natural resonance period (or rate of vibration), any enclosure—whether an audio speaker cabinet or the nave of a cathedral—imposes its resonance characteristics on a sound wave within it. Any tone that approximates in frequency the characteristic resonance period of an enclosure will be reinforced through the sympathetic response, or natural resonance, of the air within the enclosure. This means that tones of frequencies differing from the resonance of the enclosure will be less intense than those that agree, thereby creating an inequity of sound intensities.

Fortunately, most rooms where music is performed are large enough (wall lengths greater than about 30 feet) so that their natural resonance periods are too slow to fall within the range of pitches of the lowest musical tones (usually no lower than 27 cycles per second, although some organs have pipes that extend to 15 cycles per second). Smaller rooms can produce disturbing sympathetic resonance unless obstructions or absorbent materials are added to minimize that effect. (Bathroom singers revel in this phenomenon because the band of resonance sometimes lies close enough to the pitches of the male voice to support it, making it appear richer and more powerful.)

Reverberation period In addition to resonance, any enclosure possesses a reverberation period, a unit of time measured from the instant a sound fills the enclosure (steady state) until that sound has decayed to one-millionth of its initial intensity. Anyone who has spoken or clapped his hands inside a large, empty room has experienced prolonged reverberation. There are two reasons for such protracted reverberation: first, the space between the surfaces of the enclosure is so great that reflected sound waves travel extended distances before decaying; and, second, the absence of highly absorbent materials precludes appreciable loss of intensity of the wave during its movement.

The reverberation period is a crucial factor in rooms where sounds must be heard with considerable fidelity. If the period is too long in a room where speech must be understood, spoken syllables will blend into each other and the words will be mumbled confusion. If, on the other hand, the reverberation period is too brief in a room where human "presence" and music each contribute to the acoustics, only a "cold" and "dull" feeling will persist, because no reverberative support of the prevailing sounds can be provided by the enclosure itself. (See also ENGINEERING: *Acoustical engineering.*)

Although all sound waves, regardless of their pitch, travel at the same rate of speed through a particular medium, low tones mushroom out in a broad trajectory while high tones move in straight paths. For this reason listeners in any room should be within a direct path of sound propagation. Seats far to the side at the front of an auditorium offer occupants a potentially distorted version of sound from its source. Thus the high-frequency speakers (tweeters) in good audio reproduction systems are angled toward the sides of the room, ensuring wider coverage for high-frequency components of all sounds.

Sites of musical performance in the open demand quite different acoustical arrangements, of course, since sound reflection from ceilings and walls cannot occur and reverberation cannot provide the desirable support that would be available within a room. A reflective shell placed behind the sound source can provide a boost in transmission of sounds toward listeners. Such a reflector must be designed so that relatively uniform wave propagation will reach all locations where listening will occur. The shell form serves that purpose admirably since its curved shape avoids the right angles that might set up continuous reflections, or echoing. Furthermore, sound waves are reflected more uniformly over a wide area than with any other shape, diffusing them equally over the path of propagations. (The needs here are similar to those of the photographer who wishes to flood a scene uniformly with flat light rather than focus with a spotlight on a small area.)

PITCH AND TIMBRE

Just as various denominations of coins combine to form the larger units of a monetary system, so musical tones combine to form larger units of musical experience. Although pitch, loudness, duration, and timbre act as fourfold coordinates in the structuring of these units, pitch has been favoured as the dominating attribute by most Western theorists. The history of music theory has to a great degree consisted of a commentary on the ways pitches are combined to make musical patterns, leaving loudness and timbre more as the "understood" parameters of the musical palette.

Music terminology, for example, recognizes loudnesses in music in terms of an eight-level continuum of nuances from "extremely soft" (ppp, or pianississimo) to "extremely loud" (fff or fortississimo). (The musical dominance of Italy from the late 16th to the 18th century—when these Italian terms first were applied—explains their retention today.)

The timbres of music enjoy an even less explicit and formalized ranking; other than the vague classifications "shrill," "mellow," "full," and so on, there is no standard taxonomy of tone quality. Musicians for the most part are content to denote a particular timbre by the name of the instrument that produced it.

Divisions of the pitch spectrum

Pitch is another matter. A highly developed musical culture demands a precise standardization of pitch, and Western theory has been occupied with this task from as early as Aristoxenus (4th century BC). Especially since the Renaissance, when instruments emerged as the principal vehicles of the musical impulse, problems of pitch location (tuning) and representation (notation) have challenged the practicing musician. When at least two instrumentalists sit down to play a duet, there must be some agreement about pitch, or only frustration will result. Although the standardization of the pitch name a′ (within the middle of the piano keyboard) at 440 cycles per second has been adopted by most of the professional music world, there was a day—even during the mid-18th century of Bach—when pitch uniformity was unknown.

Man's perception of pitch is confined within a span of roughly 15 to 18,000 cycles per second. This upper limit varies with the age and ear structure of the individual, the upper limit normally attenuating with advancing age. The pitch spectrum is divided into octaves, a name derived from the scale theories of earlier times when only eight (Latin *octo*) notes within this breadth were codified. Today the octave is considered in Western music to define the boundaries for the pitches of the chromatic scale.

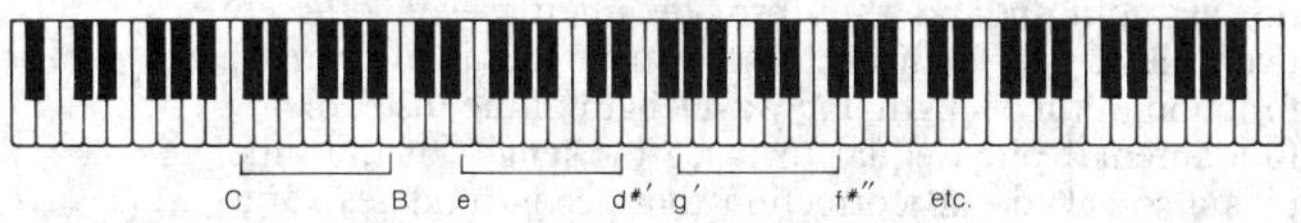

Piano keyboard.

The piano keyboard is a useful visual representation of this 12-unit division of the octave. Beginning on any key, there are 12 different keys (and thus 12 different pitches), counting the beginning key, before a key occupying the same position in the pattern recurs.

One must keep in mind that the chromatic scale, within the various octave registers of man's hearing, is merely a conventional standard of pitch tuning. Performers like singers, trombone and string players, who can alter the pitches they produce, frequently make use of pitches that do not correspond precisely to this set of norms. The music of many non-Western cultures also utilizes distinct divisions of the octave. Furthermore, some contemporary music makes use of pitch placements that divide the octave into units smaller than the half-step. This music, called microtonal, has not become standard fare in Western cultures, in spite of its advocates (Alois Hába, Julian Carillo, Karlheinz Stockhausen) and even its special instruments that provide a means for consistent performance.

Western music history is dotted with systems formulated for the precise tuning of pitches within the octave. From a modern viewpoint all suffer from one of two mutually exclusive faults: either they lack relationships (intervals) of uniform size, or they are incapable of providing chords that are acceptable to the ear. Pythagorean tuning provides uniformity but not the chords. Just tuning, based on the simpler ratios of the overtone series, provides the chords but suffers from inequality of intervals. Meantone tuning provides equal intervals but gives rise to several objectionable chords, even in simple music. All three of these systems fail to provide the pitch wherewithal for the 12 musical keys found in the standard repertoire (see below *Tuning and temperament*).

The compromise tuning system most widely accepted since the mid-19th century is called "equal temperament." Based on the division of the octave into 12 equal half-steps, or semitones, this method provides precisely equal intervals and a full set of chords that, although not as euphonious as those of the overtone series, are not offensive to the listener.

The semitone is the smallest acknowledged interval of the Western pitch system. The sizes of all remaining intervals can be calculated by determining how many semitones each contains. The names of these intervals are derived from musical notation through a simple counting of lines

Generic names of pitch intervals.

Consonance and dissonance

and spaces of the staff. Just as the overtone content of a single tone determines timbre, the relationship of the constituent pitches of an interval determines its quality, or sonance. There is a long history of speculations in this area, but the subjectivity of the data indicates that little verifiable fact can be sorted from it.

Until the 20th century, music theorists were prone to concoct tables that showed an "objective" classification of intervals into the two opposing camps of consonant and dissonant. But only the person who utters these terms can know with assurance what he means by them, although many attempts have been made to link consonant with pleasant, smooth, stable, beautiful and dissonant with unpleasant, grating, unstable, and ugly. These adjectives may be reasonably meaningful in musical contexts, but difficulty arises if one attempts to pin a singular evaluation on a particular interval per se.

Theorists have noted that the character of an interval is altered considerably by the sounds that surround it. Thus the naked interval that sounds "grating," "unstable," and lacking in fusion might within a particular context create an altogether different effect, and vice versa.

Recognition of the power of context in shaping a response to the individual pitch interval has led some music theorists to think more in terms of a continuum of sonance that extends from more consonant to more dissonant, tearing down the artificial fence once presumed to separate the two in experience.

Helmholtz theory

The explanation of consonance and dissonance offered by Hermann von Helmholtz in *On the Sensations of Tone* (1863) is perhaps as helpful as any. An initial theory was based on the notion that dissonance is a product of beats, which result from simultaneous tones or their upper overtones of slightly differing frequencies. Another explanation, offered later by Helmholtz, held that two tones are consonant if they have one or more overtones (excluding the seventh and ninth) in common.

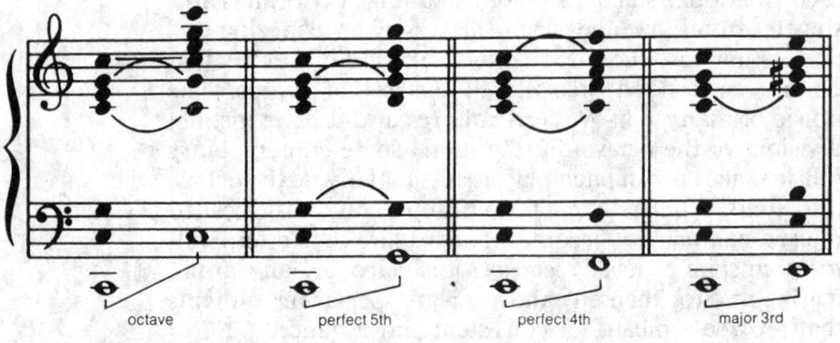

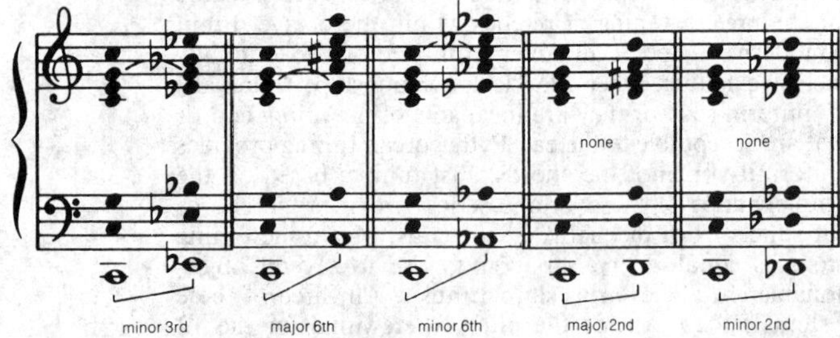

Common overtones (incomplete series, excluding the seventh) at various pitch intervals.

Music in which a high degree of dissonance occurs has rekindled interest in this old problem of psychoacoustics. The German composer Paul Hindemith (1895–1963) provided one explanation of harmonic tension and relaxation that depends upon the intervals found within chords. According to his view a chord is more dissonant than another if it contains a greater number of intervals that, as separate entities, are dissonant. Although Hindemith's reasonings and conclusions have not been widely accepted, the absence of any more convincing explanation and classification often leads musicians to use his ideas implicitly.

Although the complete pitch spectrum can be tuned in a way that provides 12 pitches per octave (as the chromatic scale), pitch organization in music usually is discussed in terms of less inclusive kinds of scale patterns. The most important scales in traditional Western theory are seventone (heptatonic), which, like the chromatic, operate within the octave. These scales are different from one another only in the intervals formed by their constituent pitches. The major scale, for instance, consists of seven pitches arranged in the intervallic order: tone–tone–semitone–tone–tone–tone–semitone.

Called major because of the large (or major) third that separates the first and third pitches, this scale differs from the minor scale mainly in that the latter contains a small (or minor) third in this location. Since three variants of the minor scale are recognized in the music of the Western repertoire, it is important to note that they share this small interval between their first and third pitches.

Scales and modes

Major and minor scales formed the primary pitch ingredients of music written between 1650 and 1900, although this is a sweeping generalization for which exceptions are not rare. Other scales, called modes, possess greater representational power for music of earlier times and for much of the repertoire of Western folk music. These too are heptatonic patterns, their uniqueness produced solely by the differing pitch relationships formed by their members. Each of the modes can most easily be reproduced by playing successive white keys at the piano.

The modes and the major and minor scales best represent the pitch structure of Western music, though they do not utilize the total complement of 12 chromatic pitches per octave. They are abstractions that are meaningful for tonal music; *i.e.,* music in which a particular pitch acts as a focal point of perception, establishing a sense of repose or tonality to which the remaining six pitches relate. Major and minor scale tonality was basic to Western music until it began to disintegrate in the art music of the late 19th century. It was replaced in part by the methods of Arnold Schoenberg (1874–1951), which used all 12 notes as basic material. Since that revolution of the early 1920s, the raw pitch materials of Western music have frequently been drawn from the complete chromatic potential. By contrast, the music of several Eastern cultures, a number of children's songs, and occasional Western folk songs incorporate pitch materials best classified as *pentatonic* (a five-pitch scale).

SOUND PRODUCTION OF MUSICAL INSTRUMENTS

Classification of musical instruments

Excluding electronic tone synthesizers, which employ vacuum tubes or transistors to produce tones, musical instruments can be classified within three groups: (1) chordophones, or strings; (2) aerophones, or winds; and (3) idiophones and membranophones, nearly all of which are percussion instruments. Each category is further divisible into groups according to the way the vibrating medium is set into motion.

Chordophones. Three means of eliciting sounds determine three categories within the family of chordophones. They are bowing, plucking, and striking. Most common of the first category are the violin, viola, violoncello, and double bass of the orchestra, all of which use a horsehair bow for setting their strings into motion. Essentially a resonant box bearing strings of four different fundamental frequencies, members of this group have not changed appreciably in construction since the 17th century, except for the 20th-century advent of the electrified bass, which is in fact a close cousin of the amplified guitar.

Violins and the larger members of its group are sounded by plucking (pizzicato) on occasion, which provides a brittle tone of extremely brief duration. The harp is the best known orchestral instrument whose tone depends upon the noise components added by plucking. Other plucked instruments are the guitar, banjo, mandolin, ukelele, zither, lyre, lute, and the harpsichord. The latter differs from the piano in that its strings are actuated by the plucking action of a tiny plectrum.

The piano is most notable of the struck stringed instruments, employing a hammer mechanism linked with the keyboard for producing its wide range of sounds. Other instruments of this group are the clavichord and the dulcimer.

For all chordophones pitch is proportional to string tension and inversely proportional to length, thickness, and density. Since string length is the most readily altered of these factors, all chordophones provide a means for altering the resonating length of strings (as with the violin and guitar) or a set of many string lengths and masses (as with the piano and harp) for producing a variety of pitches.

Aerophones. This category covers everything from the piccolo to the pipe organ and is best understood by consistent reference to the nature of the air column employed in the various types of instruments, as well as the way this air column is set into motion.

Brass instruments consist of a long tube whose cross section is proportionately small. Coupled with a mouthpiece that, in response to vibrations of the performer's lips, helps to create eddies of air pressure that set an enclosed air column into motion, these instruments produce a range of pitches corresponding to the overtone series. The bugle is a primitive kind of brass instrument in that it is limited to only one overtone series, while the modern trumpet, cornet, French horn, trombone, tuba, flügelhorn, and various kinds of euphoniums utilize valves or a slide to lengthen the air column and thus provide up to seven different overtone series. Pitch on these instruments is primarily a function of tube length, the wavelength of the instrument's fundamental pitch equal to twice the length of the tube, plus a so-called end correction that accommodates variations of bore. Timbre is a product of mouthpiece shape, bore (whether cylindrical or conical), and material, aside from the important role performed by the player himself in obtaining desired overtones.

Woodwinds prior to the 20th century were made for the most part of wood. Today the flutes and clarinets are classified in this group only because of this heritage, while the saxophones, always built of metal, share only the reed mouthpiece and similar fingering technique with the clarinet. All are, nonetheless, called woodwinds, and they consist of an air column set into motion by one of two means: (1) through high pressure eddies produced by the wind of the performer blown directly into the instrument (as with a recorder or whistle) or over it (as with the flute and piccolo), or (2) by means of a vibrating reed that is set into motion by air pressure from the performer. The clarinets and saxophones utilize a single reed fixed at one end, while the oboe, English horn, and bassoon use two thin reeds that are connected laterally and vibrate jointly. For all of these instruments, either keys or the fingers of the performer directly open holes, with the effect of shortening the enclosed air column of the instrument and thereby producing higher fundamental pitches. Through overblowing and various fingering procedures, the overtone series provides the wealth of pitches available on these instruments.

Free reed instruments utilize a single, freely vibrating reed, different in nature from that of a woodwind. The category includes the accordion, harmonica, and harmonium and their relatives. In these instruments the reed vibrates, causing periodic vibrations in the air; but the reed's size, rather than the air enclosed by the instrument, determines the pitch.

Pipe organs are of the aerophone (wind) category, too, although their keyboard mechanism and literature link them closely with the piano and harpsichord. Like a grand synthesis of woodwinds and brasses, organs produce their tones by means of tuned air columns that are formed with pipes of varied length, cross section, and shape (called flue pipes) or by means of a vibrating brass reed actuated by forced air (called reed pipes). Flue pipes range in length from under an inch to 32 feet.

Idiophones and membranophones. Idiophones are instruments whose bodies vibrate to produce sound. The class contains most of the pitched percussion instruments. These include instruments made of wood or other organic material, such as xylophones. They also include pitched percussion instruments that are struck or plucked and are made of metal or other inorganic material (triangle, glockenspiel, vibraphone, celesta, tubular bell, gong, steel drum, cymbal, glass harmonica, etc.). Idiophones without pitch consist of such instruments as the percussion board, castanets, and rattles, all of which are made of wood or other organic material and are struck, scraped, rubbed, brushed, or shaken.

Membranophones produce sound by a vibrating membrane. The group consists most notably of the timpani, or kettledrums, which can be tuned by increasing or decreasing the tension of the membranes that form the heads of the enclosed cavities. Other membranophones consist of drums without fixed pitch, such as side drums, bongos, and various non-Western types of fixed and indefinite pitch. Tone quality and character are the result of the player's skill in controlling intensity and overtone character of the sound.

(W.E.T.)

TUNING AND TEMPERAMENT

Musical sound largely depends on the organization of pitch, the high or low quality of sound; and the determination of acceptable pitch plays a large part in both the theory and practice of music. The adjustment of one sound source—such as a voice, a string, or a column of air enclosed in a wind instrument—to produce a desired pitch in relation to a given pitch is called tuning. Two concepts fundamental to the theory of tuning are those of frequency ratio and of consonance and dissonance. A given musical pitch is determined by the frequency of vibration of the sound wave that produces it, as a′ = 440 cycles per second. An interval, or distance between two pitches, can thus be mathematically described as the ratio of the frequency of the first pitch to the frequency of the second. Various frequency ratios can be reduced to the same basic relationship; for example, 440:220 and 30:15 and 750:375 can all be reduced to the ratio 2:1.

Consonance and dissonance

When two tones are sounded together the subjective reaction may be anything from one of perfect consonance to one of extreme dissonance. Dissonance is produced by beats (interference between pulsations of sound waves), and it is found that maximum dissonance occurs when the rate of beats between the two tones is about 33 per second. Consonance results from the absence of beats, which occurs only when the ratio between the frequencies of the two tones is numerically simple. When the two tones are tuned to the same pitch, they are said to be in unison (ratio 1:1) and their consonance is absolute. Next in order of consonance comes the octave (2:1), the interval between c and c′ (encompassing eight notes of the piano keyboard); another highly consonant interval is the fifth (3:2, as from c to g). When a unison, octave, or fifth is slightly mistuned, the resulting combination is markedly dissonant and is judged "out of tune." The slight mistunings that occur in systems of tempered tuning are necessary for reasons that will be discussed later in this article.

The problems of tuning. So long as music consists of melody without harmony, consonance plays little part in the determination of successive pitches in a scale. Many primitive scales are sung, not played, and are variable in the exact pitches of their notes. When instruments are made, it is often necessary to determine precise pitches. The tendency is either to make the steps in the scale sound equal in size or to place them in simple arithmetic relationship to one another. The fundamental unit is the octave, which has the unique property that its two notes are felt in some indefinable way to be the same, though in pitch level they are recognizably different. For this reason, high and low voices naturally sing the same tune an octave apart. In nearly all musical cultures the octave is subdivided into a number of steps, each a simple fraction of an octave. In the diatonic, or seven-note scale, for example, which is the basis of Western music and is represented by the white notes on the piano keyboard, there are five steps of one-sixth of an octave and two of one-twelfth. In contrast to these uncomplicated fractions, the frequency ratios of these intervals are actually the irrational numbers: $\sqrt[6]{2}$:1 and $\sqrt[12]{2}$:1. As has been noted, consonance is related to simple frequency ratios such as 2:1. Consequently, the arithmetic subdivision of the octave can never produce perfectly consonant intervals. This unavoidable fact underlies many of the problems in the history of tuning. Insignificant when notes are heard melodically, it becomes highly important when notes of different pitch are heard simultaneously. The complex development of harmony has been the most striking peculiarity of Western music, and it has brought with it a host of tuning problems.

Conflict of scale and consonance

Apart from the octave, which presents no problem, there are really only three distinct intervals in the diatonic scale the consonance of which is important. These are the fifth (3:2, as C–G), the major third (5:4, as C–E), and the major sixth (5:3, as C–A). The other three consonant intervals are the fourth (4:3, as C–F), the minor sixth (8:5, as C–A♭), and the minor third (6:5, as C–E♭). The intervals of this second group are not truly distinct, for they can be derived from the first three by inversion—*i.e.*, by transposing the lower note of the interval up an octave. Thus, inverting the fifth c–g yields the fourth g–c′. Inverting the major third c–e yields the minor sixth e–c′, and inverting the major sixth c–a yields the minor third a–c′. Because of the phenomenon of inversion, if the fifths in a scale are in tune, the fourths also will be in tune. For each of these six intervals the tuning expressed by the above simple frequency ratios sounds "right"; if modified slightly in either direction it sounds seriously out of tune. The same cannot be said of other intervals of the diatonic scale. The major and minor seventh (as c–b and d–c′) and the diminished fifth (as b–f′), with their inversions, sound dissonant in any case; they have no one tuning that is clearly more acceptable than another. Hence the harmonic merits of any tuning system depend on the way fifths, major thirds, and

Inversion of intervals

Table 1: Melodic Comparison of the Four Principal Tuning Systems*

diatonic scale

note	step	Pythagorean tuning	"just intonation"	mean-tone temperament	equal temperament
C					
	semitone	90	112	117	100
B					
	whole tone	204	204	193	200
A					
	whole tone	204	182	193	200
G					
	whole tone	204	204	193	200
F					
	semitone	90	112	117	100
E					
	whole tone	204	182	193	200
D					
	whole tone	204	204	193	200
C					

chromatic scale (semitones)

note	Pythagorean tuning	"just intonation"	mean-tone temperament	equal temperament
C				
	90	112	117	100
B				
	114	92	76	100
B♭				
	90	112	117	100
A				
	90	90	117	100
G♯				
	114	92	76	100
G				
	90	112	117	100
F♯				
	114	92	76	100
F				
	90	112	117	100
E				
	114	92	76	100
E♭				
	90	90	117	100
D				
	90	112	117	100
C♯				
	114	92	76	100
C				

*The sizes of successive steps in the diatonic and chromatic scales are shown for each of the four systems, in cents. Black notes of the chromatic scale are indicated by bold lines.

major sixths are tuned. In the diatonic scale (indefinitely extended through several octaves) there are six perfect fifths (F–C, C–G, G–D, D–A, A–E, E–B), three major thirds (F–A, C–E, G–B), and four major sixths (F–D, C–A, G–E, D–B). It is impossible to tune the seven notes of the scale so that each of these 13 intervals is maximally consonant. This is the second inescapable obstacle to perfection in the tuning of the diatonic scale.

Classic tuning systems. Of the two ancient Greek systems that were used chiefly in the Middle Ages, one,

The Pythagorean system

Pythagorean tuning, makes all the fifths perfectly consonant. As a result, all the major thirds and major sixths are sharp (too wide) by 22 cents (a cent is 1/1200 of an octave) or by the ratio of 81:80. This amount is called a comma of Didymus, and it makes intervals severely dissonant when their notes are sounded simultaneously. Within the gamut, the pitch range in use during the Middle Ages, a major third or sixth mistuned by a comma beats between 6 and 32 times a second. Melodically, the Pythagorean system is satisfactory. (Table 1 compares whole tone and semitone sizes in the four main tuning systems.) Pythagorean tuning makes all five whole tones (the larger steps in the diatonic scale) equal at 9:8 (204 cents), and the two semitones (the smaller steps) equal at 256:243 (90 cents). The semitones are considerably less than half the whole tones in size, but this is not particularly objectionable in a melody.

Just intonation

Ptolemaic tuning, often misleadingly named just intonation, sacrifices one of the fifths (D–A), which is altered to 40:27 from the simpler ratio 3:2, making it flat (too narrow) by a comma. The advantage of this system is that all the major thirds are true, or "in tune," as are all the major sixths except F–D, which is tuned to the ratio 27:16, as in the Pythagorean tuning (instead of to 5:3). The triad D–F–A is quite unusable, although the other triads used are perfectly in tune. (A triad is a chord built of two thirds.) For melody the system has the drawback of employing two different sizes of whole tones: C–D, F–G, and A–B are major tones (9:8, or 204 cents), and D–E and G–A are minor tones (10:9, or 182 cents). The difference is noticeable without being great enough to suggest that they are two purposely distinct intervals. To sing the first phrase of "Three Blind Mice" with the middle note perceptibly too high can hardly have seemed satisfactory at any period.

Although just intonation occupied the attention of many theorists, its disadvantages are so great that it is doubtful whether the system was ever strictly applied to harmonized music. Some kind of temperament may have been practiced empirically long before it was described in writing. The addition over several centuries of the five chromatic notes (the black notes of the piano), giving the full chromatic scale, certainly does nothing to improve either the Pythagorean or the Ptolemaic tuning (see Table 2, which shows the deviation of the four main tuning systems from the ideal tuning of the principal intervals). To either system the use of the chromatic notes adds more true fifths but also more untrue thirds and sixths. The advantages of just intonation over Pythagorean tuning are experienced only

Table 2: Harmonic Comparison of the Four Principal Tuning Systems*

	diatonic scale						added black notes					enharmonic intervals			
Perfect fifths	F-C	C-G	G-D	D-A	A-E	E-B	E♭-B♭	B♭-F	B-F♯	F♯-C♯	C♯-G♯	G♯-E♭			
Pythagorean tuning	0	0	0	0	0	0	0	0	0	0	0	−24			
"just intonation"	0	0	0	−22	0	0	0	0	0	0	0	−2			
mean-tone temperament	−5	−5	−5	−5	−5	−5	−5	−5	−5	−5	−5	+35			
equal temperament	−2	−2	−2	−2	−2	−2	−2	−2	−2	−2	−2	−2			
Major thirds	F-A	C-E	G-B				E♭-G	B♭-D	D-F♯	A-C♯	E-G♯	B-E♭	F♯-B♭	C♯-F	G♯-C
Pythagorean tuning	+22	+22	+22				+22	+22	+22	+22	+22	−2	−2	−2	−2
"just intonation"	0	0	0				+22	+22	+22	+22	+22	+20	+20	+20	+20
mean-tone temperament	0	0	0				0	0	0	0	0	+42	+42	+42	+42
equal temperament	+14	+14	+14				+14	+14	+14	+14	+14	+14	+14	+14	+14
Major sixths	F-D	C-A	G-E	D-B			E♭-C	B♭-G	A-F♯	E-C♯	B-G♯	F♯-E♭	C♯-B♭	G♯-F	
Pythagorean tuning	+22	+22	+22	+22			+22	+22	+22	+22	+22	−2	−2	−2	
"just intonation"	+22	0	0	0			+22	+22	+22	+22	+22	+20	+20	+20	
mean-tone temperament	+6	+6	+6	+6			+6	+6	+6	+6	+6	+49	+49	+49	
equal temperament	+16	+16	+16	+16			+16	+16	+16	+16	+16	+16	+16	+16	

*The tuning of each of the three basic intervals is analyzed for each system. Deviations from the "true" intervals are given in cents. 100 cents = 1 equal-tempered semitone. The sizes of the "true" intervals are as follows: perfect fifth, 702 cents; major third, 386 cents; major sixth, 884 cents.

in chords made up of white notes. With the development of harmony and the increased use of chromatic notes, both tuning systems became increasingly unsatisfactory.

Mean-tone temperament

Temperament. The first mention of temperament is found in 1496 in the treatise *Practica musica* by the Italian theorist Franchino Gafori, who stated that organists flatten fifths by a small, indefinite amount. This practice tends to spread out the mistuning of the fifth D–A over several fifths, so that all are tolerable although none is perfect. This principle was systematized as mean-tone temperament, first described in 1523. Under this scheme, all the major thirds of the scale are made perfect (*i.e.*, are tuned in the simple ratio 5:4); it results in an imperfection in the tuning of fifths that is spread out evenly over the entire cycle. Specifically, the interval of two octaves and a major third is tuned perfectly and divided into four fifths (C–G–d–a–e′), each of which has the ratio $\sqrt[4]{5}:1$ (compared to 3:2 for a perfectly tuned fifth). The fifths are flat by a quarter of a comma, which is much less dissonant than a comma: it gives a beat rate of 0.9 to 4 per second for fifths that fall within the compass of the medieval gamut. All major sixths are sharp by the same amount. Melodically, the scale resulting from mean-tone temperament is superior to the Ptolemaic (just intonation) scale, for all the whole tones are equal in size, being exactly half a true major third, or 193 cents. This is the source of the system's name: the mean, or average, whole tone. The semitones of the diatonic scale are relatively large, at 117 cents.

Mean-tone temperament, which was specifically designed for keyboard instruments, was an acceptable compromise so long as the black notes used in a composition did not extend beyond E♭ and G♯. As soon as D♯ was needed as well as E♭, the system collapsed. The keyboard provided only one key for E♭ and D♯. This key was tuned as E♭ and with no reference to the G♯ below it. The enharmonic fifth G♯–E♭ (in which E♭ is treated as equal to D♯) is nearly two commas out of tune in the mean-tone system. Worse even than the mistuned fifth of just intonation, it was often given the name "the wolf." Organs were occasionally built with split black keys so that E♭ and D♯ could be differently tuned and also A♭ and G♯. This expedient slightly extended the range of usable harmonies, but a more drastic remedy was soon needed. By spreading out the mistuning of the "wolf" fifth among its neighbours, in the same way that their predecessors had spread out the mistuning of the fifth D–A, musicians of the 17th century moved imperceptibly away from mean-tone temperament, in which the fifths are tuned unequally, toward the system of equal temperament, in which all fifths are equally flat.

Equal-tempered tuning

In equal temperament, all intervals are made up of semitone units, each of which is set exactly at a 12th of an octave, or 100 cents. A fifth is built of seven semitones; in relation to a pure fifth, it is 2 cents flat. A major third is four semitones and is 14 cents sharp; a major sixth is nine semitones and is 16 cents sharp. Because in equal temperament the intervals are identical in all parts of the chromatic scale, the system is the only one that can accommodate the expanded range of harmonies of 19th- and 20th-century music. Melodically, it fulfills the ideal of equal steps. The price for these great advantages is the total disappearance of perfectly tuned intervals, save only the octave. For the piano and the harpsichord this is scarcely a drawback: the characteristic tone of these instruments is, in any case, rich in dissonant components. Indeed, it has been found that piano tuners systematically set octaves and even unison strings out of tune. But on the organ, with its purer and more sustained tone, the disadvantages of equal temperament are considered by many to outweigh its blessings. In England such musicians as the organist and composer Samuel Sebastian Wesley continued to oppose it even as late as the mid-19th century.

On fretted instruments—such as lutes, guitars, and viols—the frets extend across the fingerboard, producing at any one point divisions of equal lengths on strings of different pitch. Unless equal temperament is used, the positioning of the frets results in mistuned octaves and unisons when the same note is played on different strings. For this reason equal temperament was applied at least as early as the 16th century in the construction of fretted instruments.

It has often been stated that singers and players on instruments of undetermined tuning, such as violins and trombones, naturally use just intonation when performing together. Experimental evidence does not support this theory. In such circumstances musicians tend either to play in equal temperament, or, if anything, to distort intervals away from perfect consonance. Most probably this is the result of generations of conditioning. Moreover, it has been found that few musicians can distinguish melodically between just intonation and equal temperament and that those who can do so prefer the latter.

Tuning and musical history. It is seldom realized what an important effect tuning practices have had on the development of harmony and tonality. From the 10th to the 13th century thirds and sixths—now considered consonant—were treated as dissonances simply because, according to then-current tuning methods, they *were* dissonances. In Pythagorean tuning, only the bare fifth and octave could provide a tolerable point of repose in music accompanied by the organ. Although just intonation permitted some harmony based on triads, the use of sharpened leading notes (the last note of the scale, leading upward into the first), which by the 16th century had caused the older system of modes to disintegrate, was made acceptable only by the use of some kind of temperament. At a later date it was the existence of lutes tuned in equal temperament that made possible the more extreme experiments in chromaticism of composers such as Luca Marenzio and Don Carlo Gesualdo. The formation of a unified orchestra was probably delayed by the simultaneous practice of two incompatible tuning systems—mean-tone for keyboard instruments, equal temperament for lutes and viols. The decline of viols and their replacement by the violin family may have been hastened by the inability of viols to play with the organ. The modern orchestra began with the Vingt-quatre Violons du Roi (Twenty-four Violins of the King) of Louis XIV, and most later Baroque music is based on a keyboard instrument with from one to 30 members of the violin family playing in mean-tone temperament. The cycle of six related keys, established in the operas of Alessandro Scarlatti and the sonatas of Arcangelo Corelli and followed closely in most of the music of J.S. Bach and George Frideric Handel, is probably a direct outcome of mean-tone temperament. Within the limits of mean-tone temperament, the six keys exhaust the chromatic compass available. On the other hand, "wolf" chords may have been deliberately introduced by Domenico Scarlatti, François Couperin, and other composers to give an added piquancy to certain harpsichord passages. Many harpsichord players, including Bach, would retune a few notes of their instruments to prepare to play a piece in a new key, shifting the "wolf" fifth to part of the scale where it would do no harm. But in organ works such temporary retuning was hardly possible. Bach's organ tuning must have been as close to equal temperament as modern instruments are, although it is known that he was opposed to a strictly mathematical equality of intervals. By his title *Well-Tempered Clavier* he probably meant a kind of modified mean-tone temperament.

Enharmonic modulation

Enharmonic modulation, in which one note (say B♭) is treated as identical to another (say A♯) that actually has the same pitch only in equal temperament, was an exceptional device in Baroque music. But as orchestras became free of keyboard instruments and as keyboard instruments increasingly adopted equal temperament, it became a normal stock-in-trade, allowing the use of a series of key changes in one direction that eventually returns to the original key. Thus, it is not unusual for Mozart to complete the cycle of 12 keys in the course of a movement. Equal temperament permitted 19th-century composers to use the 12 notes of the chromatic scale with the utmost freedom. It also fixed those 12 notes so immutably in the Western musical consciousness that the revolutionary developments of 20th-century music, far from undermining them, have tended to perpetuate them.

(N.T.)

Elements of musical composition

At its most fundamental level the act of composition involves the ordering of pitched sounds in musical time and space. Pitch relationships are referred to as intervals; their specific occurrence in musical time is determined by rhythm, a concept that embraces all durational aspects of music. Rhythm in turn may or may not be regulated by metre. In metrically organized rhythm, recurring patterns of accented and unaccented "beats" furnish a durational substructure that necessarily affects all the other elements of composition, including the nature of melody, harmony, and texture. Metrical rhythm is nearly always present in dance music because its patterning is largely analogous to that of bodily motions and step figurations. But logogenic, or word-determined, music also often employs metrical patterns, corresponding as a rule to those of the poetic text. The first large corpus of logogenic compositions transmitted through the ages is that of medieval plainchant, consisting of monophonic settings (limited to a single melodic line) of liturgical texts for the entire year, based on a system of eight church modes, diatonic scales abstracted from the melodic motives utilized by medieval singers. Modality—whether referring to a melodic or a rhythmic framework—furnishes compositional frames of reference in a wide variety of essentially monophonic musical styles, especially in Asia. Asian influences upon early European music cannot be ruled out, whether by way of ancient Judaea, Greece, Byzantium, or the medieval Arab invasions. But unlike their Asian counterparts, Europeans at first limited modality to melody, through pitch arrangements. The rhythmic properties of plainchant have largely remained a matter of conjecture, for no systematic discussion of plainchant rhythm survives, and the notation used was noncommittal with respect to rhythm. By the same token, plainchant no doubt owed much of its amazing vitality to the absence of an all-encompassing notation, which made possible the flexibility of performance and regional variation inherent in a partly written, partly oral tradition.

Music like medieval plainchant, in which the lengths of individual tones tend to be rather uniform, is often referred to as nonrhythmic or rhythmless. Such careless terminology denies the very essence of music as a temporal art, which implies by definition the omnipresence of rhythm as "order in musical time." Actually, the relative presence or lack of rhythmic differentiation in the duration of tones can act as a decisive stylistic determinant. Thus the rhythmic equanimity of the monophonic plainchant, at least in the interpretation set forth by the 19th-century Benedictine monks of Solesmes, France, and recognized as authoritative by the Roman Catholic Church, effectively symbolizes an atmosphere of faith and inner peace. By contrast, the strictly metrical organization of rhythm in most 18th-century music reflects the thinking of an age of reason, favouring mathematically definable, hence "natural," structures in its music.

The smallest melodic-rhythmic unit (minimally two separately perceived sounds) is the motive. Pitched sounds are, however, not of the essence: drum motives are so effective rhythmically precisely because they lack pitch definition. By and large, rhythmic motives are used to endow pitch relationships with identifiable durational characteristics. And consequently rhythmic identity often serves to establish motive connections between different intervals. A famous case in point is the opening short–short–short–long motif of Beethoven's *Symphony No. 5 in C Minor*, Opus 67, which serves as an effective element of structural cohesion in this large-scale work.

Types of melody owe their aesthetic associations in many instances to their motivic peculiarities. In Western music motivic contrast has been identified with emotional conflict since at least the mid-16th century, when composers of madrigals (Italian polyphonic secular songs) began to set dramatic texts. The opening of Mozart's *Symphony No. 35 in D Major*, K 385 (the *Haffner Symphony*), offers an excellent example. Analogous in its motivic structure to a section of the first act of Mozart's opera *Don Giovanni*, the opening of the symphony engenders emotional contrasts similar to those inherent in the opera's dramatic action when Donna Anna, under the double impact of attempted rape and her father's violent death at the Don's hands, impulsively rejects Don Ottavio's sympathy until, realizing that she has no one else to rely on for help, she reverses herself and induces him to swear revenge. Conversely, melodic lyricism correlates with a high degree of motive affinity.

This section will examine the process of musical composition in the Western tradition from its basic elements to its history as an art.

RHYTHM

In its most general sense rhythm (Greek *rhythmos*, derived from *rhein*, "to flow") is an ordered alternation of contrasting elements. The notion of rhythm occurs in music and in other arts (*e.g.*, poetry, painting, sculpture, and architecture) as well as in nature (*e.g.*, biological rhythms).

Attempts to define rhythm in music have produced much disagreement, partly because rhythm has often been identified with one or more of its constituent, but not wholly separate, elements, such as accent, metre, and tempo. As in the closely related subjects of verse and metre, opinions differ widely, at least among poets and linguists, on the nature and movement of rhythm. Theories requiring "periodicity" as the *sine qua non* of rhythm are opposed by theories that include in it even nonrecurrent configurations of movement, as in prose or plainchant.

Elements of rhythm. Unlike a painting or a piece of sculpture, which are compositions in space, a musical work is a composition dependent upon time. Rhythm is music's pattern in time. Whatever other elements a given piece of music may have (*e.g.*, patterns in pitch or timbre), rhythm is the one indispensable element of all music. Rhythm can exist without melody, as in the drumbeats of primitive music, but melody cannot exist without rhythm. In music that has both harmony and melody, the rhythmic structure cannot be separated from them. Plato's observation that rhythm is "an order of movement" provides a convenient analytical starting point.

Beat. The unit division of musical time is called a beat. Just as one is aware of the body's steady pulse, or heartbeat, so in composing, performing, or listening to music one is aware of a periodic succession of beats.

Tempo. The pace of the fundamental beat is called tempo (Italian "time"). The expressions slow tempo and quick tempo suggest the existence of a tempo that is neither slow nor fast. his "moderate" tempo is often assumed to be that of a natural walking pace (76 to 80 paces per minute) or of a heartbeat (72 per minute). The tempo of a piece of music indicated by a composer is, however, neither absolute nor final. In performance it is likely to vary according to the performer's interpretative ideas or to such considerations as the size and reverberation of the hall, the size of the ensemble, and, to a lesser extent, the sonority of the instruments. A change within such limits does not affect the rhythmic structure of a work.

Rubato. The tempo of a work is never inflexibly mathematical. It is impossible to adhere in a musical manner to the metronomic beat for any length of time. In a loosely knit passage a tautening of tempo may be required; in a crowded passage a slackening may be needed. Such modifications of tempo, known as *tempo rubato*—*i.e.*, "robbed time"—are part of the music's character. Rubato needs the framework of an inflexible beat from which it can depart and to which it must return.

Time. The mind apparently seeks some organizing principle in the perception of music, and if a grouping of sounds is not objectively present it imposes one of its own. Experiments show that the mind instinctively groups regular and identical sounds into twos and threes, stressing every second or third beat, and thus creates from an otherwise monotonous series a succession of strong and weak beats.

In music such grouping is achieved by actual stress; *i.e.*, by periodically making one note stronger than the others. When the stress occurs at regular intervals, the beats fall into natural time measures. Although in European music the concept of time measures reaches back to a remote age, only since the 15th century have they been indicated by means of bar lines. Thus, the terms measure and bar are often used interchangeably.

Time signatures

The time measure is indicated at the opening of a piece by a time signature; *e.g.,* $\frac{2}{4}$, $\frac{4}{8}$, $\frac{3}{4}$, $\frac{6}{8}$. The length of each beat in a measure may be a time unit of short or long duration:

The signature $\frac{4}{1}$ (above) means that the whole note (1) is the unit in each measure, and there are four (4) of them to each measure. In the second illustration, $\frac{4}{2}$, the half note (2) is the unit of measurement, with four of them (4) to each measure, etc.

The two basic types of time measure have either two or three beats and admit of many different notations.

2/4 or 2/2, etc.: "two time"

3/4 or 3/8, etc.: "three time"

"Four time," or "common time," is really a species of duple time allied to "two time," as it can hardly be thought of without a subsidiary stress at the half measure; *i.e.,* on the third beat; thus:

4/4 : "four time"

Duple, triple, and quadruple time measures—*i.e.,* those in which there are two, three, and four beats to a measure—are known as simple time. The division of each of the component beats into three produces compound time:

6/4 compound duple

9/4 compound triple

12/4 compound quadruple

More complex times, such as the quintuple, $\frac{5}{4}$, usually fall into groups of 3 + 2, as in "Mars" from Gustav Holst's suite *The Planets* and in the second movement of Tchaikovsky's *Sixth Symphony.* Rimsky-Korsakov, in *Sadko,* and Stravinsky, in *Le Sacre du printemps,* use 11 as a unit. Ravel's piano trio opens with a signature of $\frac{8}{8}$ with the internal organization 3 + 2 + 3. Folk song and folk dance, particularly from eastern Europe, influenced the use of asymmetrical time measures, as in the "Bulgarian Rhythm" pieces in $\frac{7}{8}$ and $\frac{5}{8}$ in Bartók's *Mikrokosmos.*

Metre. The combinations of long (—) and short (◡) syllables are known in prosody as feet. The system of notating the musical equivalents of feet derives from the application of prosody to music. The foundations for European music were laid in ancient Greece, where classical music and poetry were regarded as parts of a single art. These principles were adopted by the Romans and were transmitted, by way of Latin poetry, to medieval Europe. The feet of classical poetry and their equivalents in music are shown in Table 3. And in late antiquity St. Augustine (354–430), in *De musica,* added more.

Prosody applied to music

Table 3: Classical Poetic Metre

	metrical foot	poetic syllables	musical notation	groups of beats	equivalent time signatures
duple	dactyl	— ◡◡		2 + 2	$\frac{2}{4}$
	anapest	◡◡—		2 + 2	$\frac{2}{4}$
triple	trochee	— ◡		2 + 1	$\frac{3}{8}$
	iamb	◡—		1 + 2	$\frac{3}{8}$

Rhythmic metre. Until the 12th century, church music was virtually limited to unadorned plainchant. The early composers found that polyphony required a rhythmical organization to keep the parts together; so rhythmic metre was adopted (see Table 4). Compared with a hypothetical flow of beats equal in stress, metre adds significance to what was merely a forward flow in time—though the continuation of a metrical pattern may itself become monotonous. Thus, metre, though "rhythmic" by comparison with pulse, is not the whole of rhythm. The 13th-century musicians often varied the rhythmic modes by combining several of them simultaneously in different parts of polyphonic composition.

Table 4: Classification of Rhythmic Metre

poetry	metrical foot	musical notation
— ◡	trochee	
◡—	iamb	
— ◡◡	dactyl	
◡◡—	anapest	
— —	spondee	
◡◡◡	tribrach	

Polyphonic metre. Theoretically, metre appears to be without stress accent, and certainly much polyphonic music of a later period, such as the masses of Palestrina, has an almost stressless flow. Yet these works reveal a subtle rhythmical organization. At a later period metre and time measure cannot be wholly separated. In their "purest" forms they may be extremes, but in music predominantly of one type, the other element is rarely wholly absent, though on an instrument such as the organ, actual dynamic stress is impossible. After all, metres like the spondee, ♩♩, and the dispondee, ♩♩♩♩, need an accent on the first beat to keep their identity. Notwithstanding the opposite tendencies of metrical organization and stress accent, however, some metre is obviously subject to stress, so that metre and time measure become very closely linked, as in the scherzo of Beethoven's *Ninth Symphony,* where a measure has a strong first beat and at the same time follows a metre.

Organic rhythm. In broad terms, the time framework of music is composed of tempo, time measure, metre, and period; and its rhythmical life hangs on rubato, musical motif (which may already include cross accent), and metrical variation, as well as on asymmetry and balance of phrase. Whereas the former are more or less measured and rational, the latter are organically inspired and numerically irrational—the very life of the music.

Rational and irrational features

Prose rhythms and plainsong. Rhythm is, therefore, not any one of these rational or formal features, nor is it composed solely of a combination of these factors. Yet rhythm requires the background of a rational framework in order that it may be fully perceived, but this framework need not embrace all the rational factors described above.

Thus plainchant, as it is known in modern times, makes no use at all of measure or of regular metre but is supremely rhythmical in conception; its "free" rhythms are felt. Whereas so much music has for its framework a regular repetition of underlying accent, whether stress or durational, the framework of plainchant is irregular. Its rhythm belongs to the Latin tongue and springs from the correct accentuation of the text and the dynamic quality inherent in the word grouping.

Rhythm, melody, and harmony. Thus far, music's structure in time has been examined separately from its structure in tone, but no such separation is really possible. Melody and rhythm are intimately connected. Moreover, various styles of music tend to standardize their melodic cadences and, with them, their time divisions (*e.g.,* Mozart's melodic rhythm is much more regular than Prokofiev's).

In music employing harmony, the rhythmic structure is inseparable from harmonic considerations. The time pattern controlling the change of harmonies is called harmonic rhythm. In 17th- and 18th-century music, harmony tends to limit rhythmic subtleties and flexibility of the melodic elements (as well as determining the basic type of melody) in regard to stress accents. It is, therefore, no accident that the polyphonic music of Indonesia and Southeast Asia, like much European music, exhibits certain four-square melodic tendencies. By contrast, the music of India and the Perso-Arab world employs a melody instrument or voice performing in a given metre offset by a drum playing cross rhythms or (in the Arab world) a quite different metre; with no harmony (except a drone) to impede its flow, the rhythm can reach a structure of great subtlety and complexity.

Diversity from conceptual differences

Rhythm, structure, and style. In European music the great variety of styles derives its relation to melody from different concepts of rhythm. They include the strict rhythmic modes of the 13th century; the free oratorical speech-rhythms of the Renaissance; the almost stressless flow of Renaissance polyphony; the strong body rhythms of the Baroque; the freedom of the late Romantics; and the primitivistic rhythms of the 20th century with composite and ever changing time signatures.

Thus, study of musical history shows a varying attitude toward rhythm, sometimes closer to strict rule, sometimes to "freedom," as the temper of the times and the relative influence of poetry, dance, and folk music decree. Plato's definition of rhythm as "an order of movement" might, therefore, be expanded. As a determining factor in the vitality of music, rhythm may be described as "an inspired, organic order of movement," communicating intelligibly to the senses. From the analytical viewpoint, it operates in the rational framework described, which it varies in terms of rubato, motif, etc. Ultimately, rhythm is the organic process of music in time; it is music's direction in time. The quality of rhythm is the quality of life; however vitally the composer conceives his music, he must depend upon the performer to recreate it rhythmically. (P.C.-H.)

SCALE

A theoretical description of pitch relationships that exist in music is called a musical scale. The specific selection of different tones in any piece of music generally reveals a pattern of relationships among its pitches that can be expressed as a series of fixed distances (intervals) from one pitch to another within the span of an octave. The interval relationships among pitches of a scale are its essential feature, and a particular pattern of intervals defines every scale. Other aspects of pitch usage in music, such as range (distance from the highest pitch used to the lowest), emphasis placed on certain pitches, or the simultaneous (harmonic) and successive (melodic) occurrence of tones, do not alter the identity of the scale, although they may be essential in describing its function.

Although the number of different scales that can be formulated is theoretically nearly infinite, particular scales tend to become conventionalized within any given culture or musical tradition. The scale of a single piece of music may therefore be characteristic of the tone system of a whole culture. In general, the simplest scales can be found in very old music and in the music of nonliterate cultures, while the most complex scales occur in the world's most advanced cultures.

Non-explicit scales

Scale and melody. Scales have proven to be important in the analysis of folk music and the music of nonliterate cultures, but scholars have been obliged to deduce the scales through a study of the actual music, since the creators of the music were not cognizant of scales as theoretical concepts. By contrast, music of the most highly developed cultures (variously described as classical music, art music, cultivated music, and high-culture music) is created in full awareness of rules or conventions pertaining to scale usage.

In view of the wide range of possibilities, a surprisingly small number of scale types predominate throughout the world. The intervals found in non-Western music often approximate rather closely the basic whole-step and half-step intervals that are used in Western music. Variations from Western intervals are often expressed as measurements in cents (100 cents = one half step in equal temperament, the pattern of 12 equal half steps used in Western music; see above *Tuning and temperament*). The task of identifying scales in non-Western music is complicated further by the occasional appearance of highly variable intervals or by singing techniques that produce sounds whose pitches cannot be specified accurately through conventional notation, like the "tumbling strains" (falling melodies) described by musicologist Curt Sachs in the singing of Aboriginal Australians.

Although music performed only on one pitch does exist, the study of scales properly begins with the occurrence of at least two different pitches. Scales consisting of only one or two intervals (*i.e.,* two or three pitches) can be found throughout the world in monophonic music (that consisting of a single unharmonized melodic line), though they are perhaps most numerous in Ceylon, eastern Siberia, California Indian cultures, and in regions near the Ural Mountains. Such scales commonly display a narrow range in which the pitches are separated by a half step, a whole step, or a minor third (one and one-half steps, as, C–E♭). Larger skips in two- and three-note scales do occur but are less frequent. Some simple scales have probably acquired additional pitches through a tendency to fill in large skips with intervening pitches. Another process by which scales may have expanded is the transposition within a single melody of one characteristic melodic motive (identifiable fragment) to a different pitch level, thus creating additional scale degrees, as in the melody of the Makurap Indians shown below.

From F. Blume (ed.), *Die Musik in Geschichte und Gegenwart;* Barenreiter-Verlag Kassel, Basel

Occasionally, primitive melodies apparently generated by motivic transposition also contain evidence of emphasis on particular pitches. As an example, the skips in the following Osage Indian melody are arranged so that the pitches G and C are consistently reiterated.

From F. Blume (ed.), *Die Musik in Geschichte und Gegenwart;* Barenreiter-Verlag Kassel, Basel

The melodic "weight" given to those two pitches could not have been achieved by the simple transposition of motives. Further, weighted scales may also give prominence to certain pitches by using them as range limits or by placing a particular pitch at the ends of sections or the end of a piece.

Explicit scale systems

Scales function somewhat differently in the art-music traditions of highly sophisticated cultures, since they are not only a means of description and analysis but are also pre-existent assumptions for the composer or performer. Within those cultures, knowledge of the characteristics and requirements of various scales is often perpetuated by written treatises on music theory as well as by oral communication from generation to generation. The existence of professional composers and performers also encourages continuity in musical knowledge, even though some cultures, like those of the Western world, advocate continuous change in musical practices within acceptable limits. Through gradual evolutionary processes, the nature of scales and their functions may change radically over a period of several centuries.

Highly developed, complex systems governing the use of scales exist in a variety of cultures, principally in the Far East, India, Iran, the Muslim world, and the West. The differences in musical styles among those cultures are indeed great, yet there are some similarities in the manner in which scales function in each instance. Each culture has a number of basic scales (interval patterns), called *grāma* in India, *dastgah* in Iran, *maqām* in Muslim cultures. Generally, a basic scale is used to produce a number of different modes, or bases for melodic construction, in which the intervallic structure of the scale remains intact while primary and secondary melodic importance is attached to different pitch degrees (see below, *Mode*). This hierarchy in which modes are generated by basic scale types consequently produces a greater number of modes than there are basic scales. The terms *maqām* and *dastgah* also are used to refer to such modes; the corresponding Indian term is *jāti.* In some art-music traditions the modes serve as the basis for an even larger number of specific melody types, which may again be elaborated further by improvisation in performance. In India the basic melodies are called *rāgas*; in Iran they are *gūsheh.* Although Western art music has a system of scales and modes, the melody types are not used as systematically or as consciously as they are in some of the non-Western traditions.

Common scale types. Pentatonic (five-note) scales are used more widely than any other scale formation. In fact, Western art music is one of the few traditions in which pentatonic scales do not predominate. Their frequency is especially notable in the Far East and in European folk music. The most common varieties of pentatonic scales use major seconds and minor thirds, with no half steps (anhemitonic). A representative type could be spelled C–D–E–G–A, for example. The pentatonic scale is so pervasive that melodies exhibiting tetratonic (four-note) scales often appear to be pentationic with one pitch omitted. Hexatonic (six-note) scales appear rather rarely in folk music and nonliterate cultures. Examples that are known often seem to be fragments of the seven-note Western diatonic scale.

Heptatonic scales are especially prominent in the world's art-music traditions. The tone systems of India, Iran, and the West are entirely heptatonic, and seven-note scales are also present in the art music of some cultures that do not use such scales exclusively (*e.g.,* the *ritsu* scale in Japan and the *pelog* scale in Java).

The diatonic scale

With some exceptions in both the distant and the recent past, Western art music has been based largely on one heptatonic scale, known as the diatonic scale. The origins of this scale can be traced to ancient Greece, and it has been formulated to some extent according to acoustical principles. Since the octave in Western music is normally divided into 12 equal half steps, the characteristic intervals of the diatonic scale can be constructed upon any one of the 12 pitches. Such transpositions of the scale are known as keys.

Before the 17th century, as many as 12 different mode permutations of the diatonic scale were in common use (see below *Mode*), but only two modes—now called major and minor—have been in general use during most of the past 300 years. The diatonic scale itself consists of five whole steps (W) and two half steps (H), with the half steps dividing the whole steps into groups of two or three. The major scale uses the sequence W–W–H–W–W–W–H, as shown in the first of the following examples, while the intervals in the minor scale are W–H–W–W–H–W–W, as in the second.

In actual music the minor scale is usually altered in one of two ways to create greater emphasis on particular pitches. In the harmonic minor scale (the third example shown) the seventh note is raised one half step, and in the melodic minor scale (the fourth example) both the sixth and seventh notes are raised by one half step in ascending patterns while they are left unaltered in descending patterns (the fifth example).

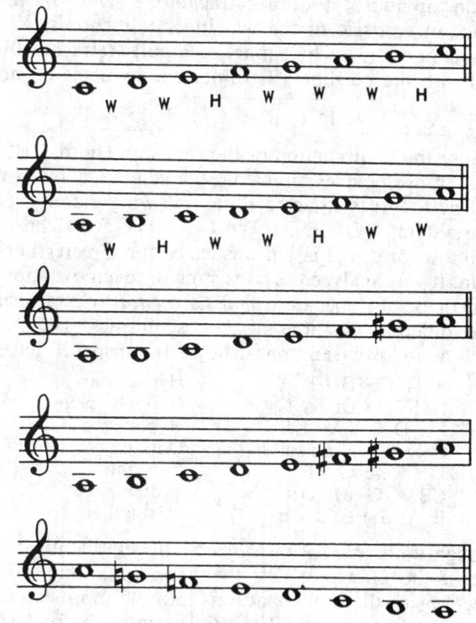

Chromatic, whole-tone, and microtonal scales

In the 19th and 20th centuries, composers have made increasing use of pitches lying outside the diatonic scale, and that tendency has stimulated a variety of novel scale systems, developed as alternatives to the diatonic scale. Principles for composition within the chromatic scale (consisting of all of the 12 half steps within the octave) were first articulated by the Austrian-born composer Arnold Schoenberg early in the 20th century. Other scales have also been employed on an experimental basis. The whole-tone scale (comprising six whole steps) was used prominently by the French composer Claude Debussy and others, especially in France and England. Microtonal scales requiring intervals smaller than the conventional half step have also appeared sporadically in the 20th century. Among microtonal structures the most important, perhaps, have been scales calling for quarter tones (equal to half the distance of a half step).

Other uses of the term scale. The word scale is sometimes used to describe musical passages consisting of a succession of consecutive scale degrees in ascending or descending patterns. It is also used to describe scalelike exercises that are practiced for the development of technical proficiency on a musical instrument. "Scale" can refer in rare instances to the ordering of some musical element other than pitch. An example is the term *Klangfarbenmelodie* used in some recent music to denote a carefully arranged succession of different tone colours. (J.C.Gr.)

MODE

In musical theory and analysis, the word mode has been employed in a variety of more or less correlated meanings. Mode designates particular aspects of melodic construction; its meaning ranges from strictly defined scales whose identity stems from the position of given intervals (distances between notes) in the sequence of tones to broadly delineated melody types and constellations of motivic figures (brief, identifiable melodic fragments) that may serve as bases for improvised or written compositions.

Ancient Greek modes. The modes of Greek antiquity were placed by theorists in orderly fashion within a larger context. Although the modes were a series of seven-note diatonic scales (*i.e.,* containing five whole tones and two semitones), the nucleus of the tone system was the tetrachord—a group of four consecutive notes (as, from C to F on the piano) comprising the interval of a fourth. Except in late antiquity, the notes were always arranged in a descending order, the basic tetrachord consisting of two whole tones and one semitone: E–D–C–B. Two such tetrachords, separated from one another by a whole tone, formed the so-called Greek Dorian mode: E–D–C–B A–G–F–E. The Dorian mode was taken as a basis for the construction of the larger system. Its single-octave range was extended by the addition of a third tetrachord, A–G–F–E, on top and of a fourth tetrachord, E–D–C–B, at the bottom. In contrast to the two inner tetrachords, which were separated by a whole tone, each outer tetrachord was linked with the neighbouring inner one by a shared note:

A G F E D C B A G F E D C B.

The Greater Perfect System

Because the combination of the four tetrachords yielded a range of two octaves minus one whole tone, a low A was added by theorists to achieve the following diatonic two-octave system: A G F E D C B A G F E D C B A. This two-octave row, or disdiapason, was called the Greater Perfect System. It was analyzed as consisting of seven overlapping scales, or octave species, called *harmoniai,* characterized by the different positions of their semitones. They were termed as follows (semitones shown by unspaced letters):

A G FE D CB A	Hypodorian
G FE D CB A G	Hypophrygian
FE D CB A G F	Hypolydian
E D CB A G FE	Dorian
D CB A G FE D	Phrygian
CB A G FE D C	Lydian
B A G FE D CB	Mixolydian

Although the names of the *harmoniai* were identical with those of the Greek modes, the *harmoniai* were instead projections of the modal patterns into the more extensive Greater Perfect System. The modes proper were termed *tonoi,* their essence being their interval pattern. On the kithara or *lyra* (the two basic plucked stringed instruments of ancient Greece) the *tonoi* were produced either by the basic tuning or by the raising or lowering of one or more of the strings by a semitone. Thus, the seven *tonoi* would sound within the octave E–E as follows (black notes indicate changes from the Dorian tuning):

Greek theory distinguished three different genera of tetrachords, producing an additional variety of modes. The previously described tetrachord (two descending whole tones plus one semitone) was called diatonic. There were also chromatic and enharmonic genera. The two tones bounding the tetrachord were fixed and always formed a perfect fourth; the two inner tones were movable. The chromatic tetrachord consisted of a minor third (encompassing 1½ whole tones) plus two semitones, the enharmonic tetrachord of a major third (encompassing two whole tones) plus two approximate quarter tones:

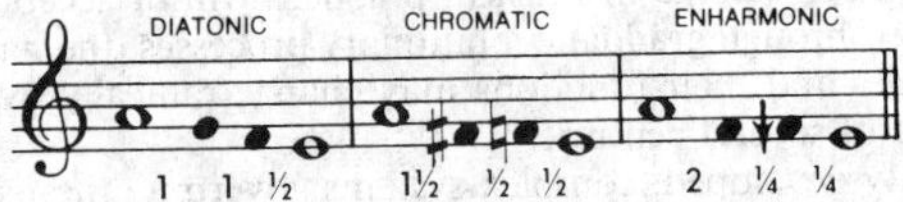

Also prominent in Greek music was the concept of ethos, which ascribed certain ethical characteristics to the different modes. The Dorian mode was preferred because of its strong and virile character; the Phrygian mode was ecstatic and emotional, the Lydian mode intimate and lascivious. In *The Republic* Plato stressed the educational values of the Dorian mode and warned against the softening influence of the Lydian ode.

In early Greek antiquity a system of modal categories developed, referred to as *nomoi* (singular, *nomos,* "law"). The *nomoi* represented modes in that they were characterized by distinctive melodic formulas suited to different song types. The performers were free to improvise within the boundaries of these modal formulas.

Jewish and Eastern Christian chant. Ancient Hebrew music followed well-established modal patterns. According to Abraham Zevi Idelsohn, a musicologist whose comparative research conducted during the early decades of the 20th century established modern understanding of the Hebrew modes,

> A mode . . . is composed of a number of motives (*i.e.,* short music figures or groups of tones) within a certain scale. The motives have different functions. There are beginning and concluding motives, and motives of conjunctive and disjunctive [*i.e.,* convergent and divergent] character. The composer operates with the material of these traditional folk motives within a certain mode for his creations. His composition is nothing but his arrangement and combination of this limited number of motives. His "freedom" of creation consists further in embellishments and in modulations from one mode to the other.

The modal Hebrew music strongly influenced early Christian chant. This correlation can be illustrated by comparing a plainchant Kyrie, in the third mode, with a Babylonian Jewish melody for a phrase from Exodus:

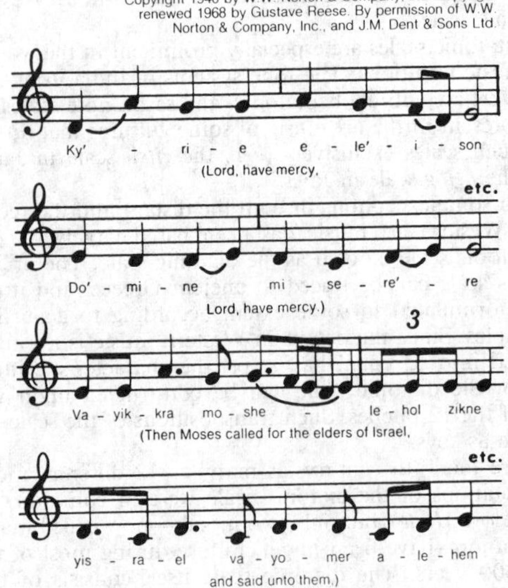

Syria played an important part in developing early Christian chant by integrating both Hellenistic and Hebrew elements. The Syrians devised a musical system called *oktōēchos,* a term suggesting a classification into eight *ēchoi.* The Syrian *ēchoi* are modes, although there is no consensus on whether they represented modes in a specifically technical sense, comparable to the Greek *tonoi,* or melodic formulas, comparable to the Greek *nomoi.*

Byzantine chant molded the features of early Christianity with Hellenic and Oriental traits, including the Syrian *oktōēchos,* and achieved a brilliant and distinctive style that served as a prototype for the chant of the Greek Orthodox Church. The eight *ēchoi* of the Byzantine *oktōēchos* were divided into four authentic and four plagal (derived) forms. The most common classification of the Byzantine modes was in terms of typical initial and final notes of melodies in a given mode, with the characteristic distinctions as follows (the orderly progression of notes in each series should be observed).

	Ēchos	Initial Note	Terminal Note
Authentic	I	a′	a′ or d′
	II	b′ or g′	e′ or b′
	III	c″ or a′	f′ or c″
	IV	d″ or g′	g′ or d″
Plagal	I	d′ or g′	d′
	II	e′ or g′	e′
	III	f′ or a′	f′
	IV	g′, a′, or c″	g′

The above classification reflects only two of various characteristics (not all completely clarified by modern scholars) that gave the modes their identity.

Even before the foundation of the Byzantine Empire, Armenia adopted Christianity as a state religion (AD 303). Although the early Armenian chant did not survive, the arrangement of the hymns of the Armenian Church in the comprehensive collection, known as the *Sharakan,* indicates that Armenian chant used an *oktōēchos* classification the modal characteristics of which seem to have been defined by melodic formulas rather than by scalar distinctions.

Another variety of the *oktōēchos* occurs in Russian Church chant. Although a concept of eight *ēchoi* points to the Byzantine system, the Russian *ēchoi* show a different structure. The melodic motives characteristic of the *ēchoi* are called *popievki;* but similar *popievki* could be employed in more than one *ēchos.* The use of some *popievki* is limited to the beginning, the middle, or the end of a chant. Occasionally, two *popievki* are merged into a compound *popievka.*

Plainchant. Plainchant, or plainsong, is also known as Gregorian chant and forms the core of the musical repertoire of the Roman Catholic Church. It consists of about 3,000 melodies collected and organized during the reigns of several 6th- and 7th-century popes. Most instrumental in codifying these chants was Pope Gregory I.

Melodically, Gregorian chants are based on eight different modes, often called church modes. Seven of them were given names identical with those used in the musical theory of ancient Greece: Dorian, Hypodorian, Phrygian, Hypophrygian, Lydian, Hypolydian, and Mixolydian, while the name of the eighth mode, Hypomixolydian, was adapted from the Greek. Each mode comprises a diatonic scale with the compass of one octave. The modes are classified by their *finalis,* the usual final note of a melody in that mode. Each of the four notes of the tetrachord D–E–F–G serves as the *finalis* of an "authentic" mode (see chart below).

Structure of Gregorian modes

An authentic mode consists of a pentachord (a succession of five diatonic notes) followed by a conjunct tetrachord, for example:

D E F G A B C D.

But the tetrachord may be added below rather than above the pentachord, thus generating a "plagal" mode:

A B C D E F G A.

In either case the *finalis* falls on the lowest note of its pentachord. Each authentic mode has a correlated plagal mode, which is identified by the prefix *Hypo.* In the following chart of the eight church modes, the *finalis* is marked by a capital letter:

1. Dorian		D e f g a b c d
2. Hypodorian	a b c	D e f g a
3. Phrygian		E f g a b c d e
4. Hypophrygian	b c d	E f g a b
5. Lydian		F g a b c d e f
6. Hypolydian	c d e	F g a b c
7. Mixolydian		G a b c d e f g
8. Hypomixolydian	d e f	G a b c d

The tones of the Hypomixolydian mode are identical with those of the Dorian, but the two modes differ in the location of their *finalis.* The character of the church modes was further determined by a number of distinctive melodic formulas, and sometimes a particular ethos was attributed to the different modes.

Contrary to the Byzantine classification, which lists first the four authentic and then the four plagal modes, the Roman classification alternates the authentic and plagal modes, so modes with the same *finalis* follow each other. This principle underlies the medieval fourfold system of the so-called *maneriae* (Latin: "manners"), a division of the modes into four pairs. The first pair, or *protus maneria,* includes the Dorian and Hypodorian modes; the second, or *deuterus,* the Phrygian and Hypophrygian; the third, or *tritus,* the Lydian and Hypolydian; and the fourth, or *tetrardus,* the Mixolydian and Hypomixolydian.

Although Greek names were sometimes applied to the church modes and the principle of diatonic octave scales is found in both systems, certain significant discrepancies seem to belie any direct historical connection. Most conspicuous is the different meaning attributed to the names of the Greek octave species and of the church modes. Comparing the two systems provides a plausible explanation: medieval theorists apparently assumed wrongly that the Greek octave species were named in ascending rather than descending order. The Greek octave species Dorian (E–E), Phrygian (D–D), Lydian (C–C), and Mixolydian (B–B) thus appeared in the church modes as Dorian (D–D), Phrygian (E–E), Lydian (F–F), and Mixolydian (G–G).

Gradual emergence of major and minor tonality

The strict consistency of the system of church modes was gradually weakened by the appearance of B♭ in addition to B♮, although the two notes never occurred in succession. The main reason for the use of a tone not included in the basic scale pattern was that medieval musicians sought to avoid the tritone F–B. The tritone (so called because it includes three whole tones) was considered an undesirable interval sharply contrasting with the perfect fourth F–B♭. The substitution of B♭ for B♮ changed the character of a mode. For example, the Lydian mode with a flattened B was identical with the modern major mode, specifically, with the F-major scale (F G A B♭ C D E F); and the Dorian mode with a flattened B generated a minor mode corresponding to the natural D minor scale (D E F G A B♭ C D).

Nevertheless, for centuries medieval theorists considered these alterations as special forms of the Lydian or Dorian mode rather than as new modes. The reluctance to acknowledge the existence of additional modes is reflected in the so-called musica ficta. According to this practice, musical notation appears to conform strictly to the system of church modes but presupposes that the performer makes certain adjustments by raising or lowering a note through the insertion of a sharp or flat.

Two different developments occurring between the 12th and the 16th centuries resulted in a radical change in modal theory: an infiltration of folk music into the ecclesiastical and secular art forms and the steadily evolving fabric of harmony destined to unify the growing complexity of polyphonic (many-voiced) musical texture. Finally, a theorist, Heinrich Loris, commonly known by his assumed name Henricus Glareanus, sanctioned the coexistence between the old church modes and the emerging major and minor modes. In his *Dodecachordon* (1547; from Greek *dōdeka,* "twelve," and *chordē,* "string"), perhaps the most significant musical treatise of the time, Glareanus enlarged the system of the eight church modes by adding the following four:

9. Aeolian A b c d e f g a
10. Hypoaeolian e f g A b c d e
11. Ionian C d e f g a b c
12. Hypoionian g a b C d e f g

The Ionian and Hypoionian modes correspond to the major mode, the Aeolian and Hypoaeolian modes to the "natural" minor mode. The 12 modes of the *Dodecachordon* comprise authentic and plagal structures with tonal centres on the notes C, D, E, F, G, and A, without recourse to sharpened or flatted tones. Glareanus mentions another two modes: the Locrian and the Hypolocrian, having B as their tonal centre. But because in these two modes B and the fifth degree above it, F, form a "false" (*i.e.,* diminished, or flattened) fifth (another form of the forbidden tritone), Glareanus states that for practical purposes only 12 modes are available.

The growing complexity of polyphonic music caused the distinction between authentic and plagal modes to become more and more irrelevant, and, as a result, the number of modes was virtually reduced to only six. The further development of art music in the Western Hemisphere is characterized by the gradual abandonment of the old ecclesiastical modes in favour of the dual major-minor system that dominated 18th- and 19th-century harmony. This system is often termed tonal, in contradistinction to that of the church modes; in fact, some 20th-century works reviving the patterns of the old church modes, as well as folksongs that occasionally use them, are often termed modal. Nevertheless, major and minor scale patterns have all essential characteristics of modes and should therefore be evaluated as such.

Non-Western modes and melody types. Modal concepts permeate all manifestations of Oriental art music. They represent a synthesis of well-established systems both of scalar construction and of a variety of melodic formulas and motivic configurations. The amalgamation of these elements yields specific melody types that are imbued with ethical, emotional, and cosmological connotations and form the basis of musical creation. Whereas the Western composer strives for originality and individual expression, his Eastern counterpart submits to the limitations of existing melody types, seeking to excel in an exploitation of their potentials.

The *rāga* and the *maqām*

The most elaborate modal concepts are those of the Indian *rāga* and of the Arabian-Persian *maqām.* They correspond to the Javanese *patet,* the Jewish *nigun,* and the aforementioned Greek *nomos.* The Oriental musician first exposes the characteristic features of a particular melody type in a free, improvisatory prelude leading to the more formalized section of the composition. These improvised introductions developed into a specific art form, called in India *ālāpa* ("conversation"), in Java *bebooka* ("guide"), in Iran *mukhtaṣarī* ("summary"), in Egypt and Turkey *taqsīm* ("dissection, analysis"), and in northwestern Africa *istahbar* ("information"). The following example (recorded by G. Schünemann, transcribed by R. Lachmann)—the first of four phrases constituting an introduction to a Tunisian art song composed in the *maqām raṣd ad-dīl*—illustrates this aspect of modal exposure.

From Robert Lachmann, *Musik des Orients* (1929); Ferdinand Hirt

Rāgas and *maqāmāt* embrace a wide variety of emotional content. They can be courageous, amorous, melancholy, cheerful, soothing, or ecstatic and are capable of conveying these qualities to the listener. Some melody types are supposed to influence illnesses, calm storms, tame wild animals, and increase the fertility of the soil. Others have pernicious power; for example, a certain *maqām* attracts evil spirits, while a certain *rāga* may cause fire. According to an ancient legend, a singer who performed such a *rāga* under the reign of Emperor Akbar (1556–1605) was reduced to ashes, although as a precaution he had submerged his body in the Ganges River. Cosmological connotations have caused melody types to be assigned to different parts of the day; for example, a mid-morning *rāga* may not be performed during the evening. The Westernized younger generation, however, tends to disregard these traditional restrictions.

The music of many tribal societies shows well-organized scalar and modal patterns, but they have not been explicitly formulated and systematized by the peoples involved. A comparative analysis reveals that, in spite of a great structural diversity, scalar and modal correlations exist not only among culturally unrelated tribal societies but also among tribal, Western folk, and Eastern art music. Modal systems and their unconscious counterparts thus may be said to have contributed substantially to the structure of a vast amount of the world's music.

(M.Ko.)

HARMONY

In music, harmony can be broadly defined as the sound of two or more notes heard simultaneously. In practice, this broad definition can also include some instances of notes sounded one after the other. If the consecutively sounded notes call to mind the notes of a familiar chord (a group of notes sounded together), the ear creates its own simultaneity in the same way that the eye perceives movement in a motion picture. In such cases the ear perceives the harmony that would result if the notes had sounded together. In a narrower sense, harmony refers to the extensively developed system of chords and the rules that allow or forbid relations between chords that characterizes Western music.

Musical sound may be regarded as having both horizontal and vertical components. The horizontal aspects are those that proceed during time such as melody, counterpoint (or the interweaving of simultaneous melodies), and rhythm. The vertical aspect comprises the sum total of what is happening at any given moment: the result either of notes that sound against each other in counterpoint, or, as in the case of a melody and accompaniment, of the underpinning of chords that the composer gives the principal notes of the melody. In this analogy, harmony is primarily a vertical phenomenon. It also has a horizontal aspect, however, since the composer not only creates a harmonic sound at any given moment but also joins these sounds in a succession of harmonies that gives the music its distinctive personality.

Non-harmonic music

Melody and rhythm can exist without harmony. By far the greatest part of the world's music is nonharmonic. Many highly sophisticated musical styles, such as those of India and China, consist basically of unharmonized melodic lines and their rhythmic organization. In only a few instances of folk and primitive music are simple chords specifically cultivated. Harmony in the Western sense is a comparatively recent invention having a rather limited geographic spread. It arose less than a millennium ago in the music of western Europe and is embraced today only in those musical cultures that trace their origins to that area.

The concept of harmony and harmonic relationships is not an arbitrary creation. It is based on certain relationships among musical tones that the human ear accepts almost reflexively and that are also expressible through elementary scientific investigation. These relationships were first demonstrated by the Greek philosopher Pythagoras in the 6th century BC. In one of his most famous experiments, a stretched string was divided by simple arithmetical ratios (1:2, 2:3, 3:4, . . .) and plucked. By this means he demonstrated that the intervals, or distances between tones, that the string sounded before and after it was divided are the most fundamental intervals the ear perceives. These intervals, which occur in the music of nearly all cultures, either in melody or in harmony, are the octave, the fifth, and the fourth. (An octave, as from C to the C above it, encompasses eight white notes on a piano keyboard, or a comparable mixture of white and black notes. A fifth, as from C to G, encompasses five white notes; a fourth, as from C to F, four white notes.) In Pythagoras' experiment, for example, a string sounding C when cut in half sounds C, or the note an octave above it. In other words, a string divided in the ratio 1:2 yields the octave (c) of its fundamental note (C). Likewise the ratio 2:3 (or two-thirds of its length) yields the fifth, and the ratio 3:4, the fourth. These notes—the fundamental and the notes a fourth, fifth, and

octave 2:1 | fifth 3:2 | fourth 4:3

octave above it—form the primary musical intervals, the cornerstones on which Western harmony is built.

The roots of harmony. The organized system of Western harmony as practiced from *c.* 1650 to *c.* 1900 evolved from earlier musical practices: from the polyphony—music in several voices, or parts—of the late Middle Ages and the Renaissance and, ultimately, from the strictly melodic music of the Middle Ages that gave rise to polyphony. The organization of medieval music, in turn, derives from the medieval theorists' fragmented knowledge of ancient Greek music.

Although the music of ancient Greece consisted entirely of melodies sung in unison or, in the case of voices of unequal range, at the octave, the term harmony occurs frequently in the writings on music at the time. Leading theorists such as Aristoxenus (fl. 4th century BC) provide a clear picture of a musical style consisting of a wide choice of "harmonies," and Plato and Aristotle discuss the ethical and moral value of one "harmony" over another.

Greek scales

In Greek music a "harmony" was the succession of tones within an octave—in modern usage, a scale. The Greek system embraced seven "harmonies," or scale types, distinguished from one another by their particular order of succession of tones and semitones (*i.e.,* whole steps and half steps). These "harmonies" were later erroneously called modes, a broader term involving the characteristic contours of a melody, as well as the scale it used (see above *Mode*).

Harmony before the common practice period. By the 9th century the practice arose in many churches of performing portions of plainchant melodies with an added, harmonizing voice—possibly as a means of greater emphasis, or of reinforcing the sound to carry through the larger churches that were being built at the time. This harmonizing technique, called organum, is the first true example of harmony. The first instances were extremely simple, consisting of adding a voice that exactly paralleled the original melody at the interval of a fourth or fifth

From the booklet edited by Gerald Abraham accompanying *The History of Music in Sound* (booklet published by Oxford University Press); examples reprinted with permission of the publisher

Sit glo - ri - a Do - mi - ni in sae - cu - la

(parallel organum). Within a short time the new technique was explored in far greater diversity. Added harmonic lines took on melodic independence, often moving in opposite, or contrary, motion to the given melody. This style was called free organum. In such cases it was impossible to maintain at all times the accepted harmonies of fourth, fifth, and octave. These intervals were considered consonances—*i.e.,* intervals that because of their clear sonority, implied repose, or resolution of tension. In free organum they were used at the principal points of articulation: the beginnings and ends of phrases and at key words in the text. In between occurred other intervals that were relatively dissonant; *i.e.,* they implied less repose and more tension. In the following example of free organum, dissonances are marked by asterisks. Free organum is an early example of harmonic motion from repose to tension to repose, basic to Western harmony. The emphasis on con-

From the booklet edited by Gerald Abraham accompanying *The History of Music in Sound* (booklet published by Oxford University Press); examples reprinted by permission of the publisher

sonances at the end of compositions set the final points of arrival in strong relief and reinforced the idea of the cadence, or the finality of the keynote of a mode (on which pieces normally ended).

Until the late 14th century the attitude toward consonance, especially among continental composers, adhered largely to the Pythagorean ideal, which accepted as consonances only intervals expressible in the simplest numerical ratios—fourths, fifths, and octaves. But in England the interval of the third (as from C to E) had been in common use for some time, although it is not expressible as such a simple ratio. A kind of English organum known as gymel, in which the voices move parallel to each other at the interval of a third, existed in the late 12th century; and in the famous *Sumer is icumen in* canon of the 13th century, a remarkably elaborate piece for the time, the harmonic style is almost entirely centred on thirds. The sixth (as from E to C), an interval closely related to the third, was also common in English music. These two intervals sounded much sweeter than did the hollow-sounding fourths, fifths, and octaves.

Rise of the intervals of the third and the sixth

By the early 15th century, in part because of the visits of the illustrious English composer John Dunstable to the courts of northern France, the third and sixth became accepted in European music as consonant intervals (prior to this time they were considered mildly dissonant). The result was an enrichment of the harmony in musical compositions.

This was a time, too, of a developing awareness of tonality, the concept of developing a composition with a definite keynote used as a point of departure at the beginning and as a point of arrival at the final cadence.

At this time there also began the tendency by composers to think of harmony as a "vertical" phenomenon, to regard the sound of notes heard simultaneously as a definite entity. Although the basic style of composition was primarily linear—*i.e.,* concerned with counterpoint—the chords that emerged from the coincidences of notes in contrapuntal lines took on a personality of their own. One phenomenon that bears out this development is fauxbourdon (French: "false bass"), or, in England, faburden. The following example illustrates English faburden of about 1300. This was a musical style in which three voices move

From the booklet edited by Gerald Abraham accompanying *The History of Music in Sound* (booklet published by Oxford University Press); examples reprinted with permission of the publisher

parallel to each other; the middle voice consisted of a succession of notes in parallel organum a fourth below the top voice; the lowest voice paralleled the sequence a third below the middle voice, producing a chord such as G–B–E, known as a $^6_3$, or first inversion, chord. This was originally an English development adopted in the 15th century by continental composers seeking to enrich their harmonies. It combined the continental fondness for "pure" intervals such as the fourth (here, B–E) with the English taste for parallel thirds (here, G–B) and sixths (here, G–E).

A final phenomenon in early 15th-century harmonic

The weakening of the modes

practice clearly foreshadowed the end of the ancient modal system in favour of the major and minor modes of the later common practice period. The old modes were used by composers of the time, and they persisted to some extent until the end of the 16th century. But their purity became undermined by a growing tendency to introduce additional notes outside the mode. This was achieved by writing either a flat or sharp sign into the manuscript, or by leaving the performer to understand that he was expected to improvise accordingly. The effect of this musica ficta (Latin: "invented music"), as the technique of introducing nonmodal notes was called, was to break down the distinction between modes. A mode owes its distinctive character to its specific pattern of whole and half steps. Introducing sharps and flats upsets the mode's normal pattern by placing half steps at unusual points. In many cases the resulting change made one mode resemble another. For example, adding an F♯ to the medieval Mixolydian mode (from G to G on the white keys of the piano) made that mode's intervals identical with those of the Ionian

Mixolydian modal scale

Mixolydian scale with added F♯ identical with G major scale

mode (from C to C on the white keys), which in turn is identical with the modern major scale. Likewise, adding a B♭ to the Dorian mode (from D to D) made its intervals equivalent to those of the Aeolian (A to A) mode, which is identical with one form of the modern minor scale. As this practice became increasingly prevalent, the major and minor modes gradually became predominant over the medieval church modes. The process is especially observable in the music of the late Renaissance.

New uses of dissonance

At the same time there emerged a more sophisticated attitude toward dissonance, favouring its use for expressive purposes. By the time of the Flemish Josquin des Prez, the leading composer of the Renaissance, contrapuntal music had assumed a more resonant texture through the use of four-, five-, and six-part writing instead of the older three-part scoring. The increased number of voices led to further enrichment of the harmony. A typical Josquin device using harmony for expressive purposes was the suspension, a type of dissonant harmony that resolved to a consonance. Suspensions arose from the chords occurring in contrapuntal music. In a suspension one note of a chord is sustained while the other voices change to a new chord. In the new chord the sustained, or "suspended," note is dissonant. One or two beats later the suspended voice changes pitch so that it resolves into, or becomes consonant with, the chord of the remaining

*suspended note
†dissonance
‡resolution

voices. The following illustration from Jean d'Okeghem's *Missa prolationum* shows a suspension at the cadence. The suspension, which became a standard musical device, creates tension because the expected harmony is delayed until the suspended voice resolves. Its use as the next to last chord of a cadence, or stopping point, was favoured by composers as a way to enhance, through dissonance resolving to consonance, the sense of completeness of the final chord. The use of suspensions indicates a growing awareness of chords as entities, rather than coincidences, that have expressive potential and of the concept that harmony moves through individual chords toward a goal. This concept was developed in the harmony of the common practice period.

At the end of the 16th century there was an upheaval in musical style. Contrapuntal writing was frequently abandoned, and composers sought out a style that placed greater emphasis on an expressive melodic line accompanied, or supported, by harmonies. This style, called monody, brought about no marked changes in the harmonic language (the particular chords used), although such composers as the Italian Claudio Monteverdi did experiment with a heightened use of dissonance toward expressive ends. The major change at this time was in the conception of harmony. The bass line became the generating force upon which harmonies were built. It was often written out with figures below it to represent the harmonies to be built upon it. From this single line—plus figures, known variously as figured bass, basso continuo, or thorough bass—the accompanying instrumentalists were expected to improvise, or "realize," a full harmonic underpinning for the melody of the topmost voice or voices. In the example below, from the continuo madrigal *Amarilli* by Giulio Caccini, the second line shows the harmonies supplied by the keyboard player. There was, thus, a polarization between

From W.J. Starr and G.F. Devine, *Music Scores Omnibus*, Part 1 (© 1964); Prentice-Hall, Inc.

the melodic and bass lines, with everything in the middle regarded as harmonic filling-in. This contrasts markedly with the older concept, in which all voices were regarded as of equal importance, with the harmony resulting from the interweaving of all parts.

Classical Western harmony. The approach to harmony according to which chords are purposely built up from their bass note marked the beginning of the common practice period of Western harmony. The transition began around 1600 and was nearly complete by 1650. Certain new concepts became important. These had their roots in the harmonic practices of the late Middle Ages and Renaissance and in the medieval modal system. They include the concepts of key, of functional harmony, and of modulation.

A key is a group of related notes belonging to either a major or minor scale, plus the chords that are formed from those notes, and the hierarchy of relationships among those chords. In a key the tonic, or keynote, such as C in the key of C—and thus the chord built on the keynote—is a focal point toward which all chords and notes in the key gravitate. This is a further development of the idea of a harmonic goal that appeared in the music of the late Renaissance and that ultimately developed from the medieval idea that modes have characteristic final notes.

In the new system keys further assumed relationships to one another. The larger organizational system embracing keys, key relationships, chord relationships, and harmonic goals was called tonality, or the major-minor system of tonality, because the keys were built on major and minor scales. In the tonal system, given chords assumed specific functions in moving toward or away from harmonic goals, and the system assigning goals to all chords was called functional harmony. The main goal was the keynote, or tonic, of the principal, or tonic, key. Modulation, or change of key, became an important factor in composition because it allowed the composer to exploit the listener's ability to sense the relations between keys.

Rameau's theories of chords

The approach to harmony that emerged about 1650 (the bass-note approach) was soon formalized in one of the most important musical treatises of the common practice period, *Traité de l'harmonie* (1722), by the French composer Jean-Philippe Rameau. The crux of Rameau's theory is the argument that all harmony is based on the "root" or fundamental note of a chord; for example, D. Other notes are placed a third (as D–F or D–F♯) and a fifth (as D–A) above the root. A chord formed in this way is a triad (as D–F–A or D–F♯–A), the basic chord type of the common practice period. The third and fifth above the triad can be placed within the same octave as the root (close position) or can be spread out over several octaves (open position) in compound intervals such as an octave plus a third or two octaves plus a fifth. A triad can exist in its basic, or root position, with the root as the lowest, or bass, note (as D–F♯–A). It can also exist in inversions or rearrangements of its notes placing the third or fifth in the bass, as F♯–A–D (first inversion) and A–D–F♯′ (second inversion). Theorists after Rameau observed that inverted

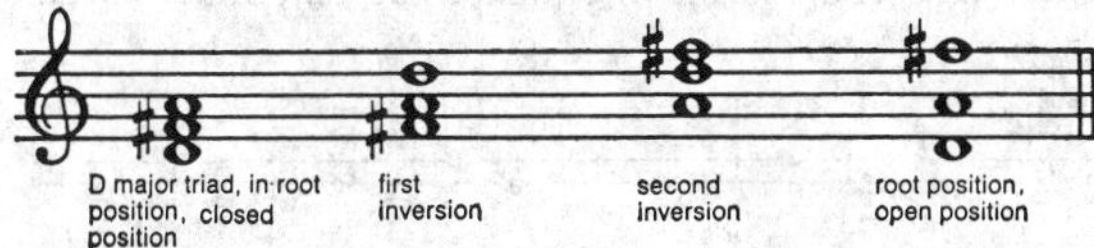

chords are less stable than chords in root position; at the end of a composition, for example, they do not have sufficient finality. Although Rameau's monumental work contains certain elements that later practices tended to disprove, his writing remains the basis for the study of common-practice harmony.

By Rameau's time no vestige remained of the ancient modal system, which was replaced by 12 major and 12 minor keys beginning on each of the 12 notes of the piano keyboard (C, C♯, D, . . . A♯, B). The invention in the late 17th century of equal temperament (see above *Tuning and temperament*) made it possible to play keyboard and other instrumental music in all 24 keys of the chromatic system, the system embracing all possible notes of the 24 scales. Such a work as J.S. Bach's *Well-Tempered Clavier* was, among many things, a set of exercises to acquaint keyboard players with this newfound freedom. Equal temperament also made it possible for a composer to modulate freely from one key to another to obtain contrast in works of an extended nature. Modulation was no new invention, but it now became of prime importance.

In normal, or functional, harmony, the succession of chords is analyzed by the distance, or interval, between their roots. The most common movement from chord to chord is through "strong" intervals: fourths (as C to F), fifths (as C to G), and seconds (as C to D). A movement from one chord to another having this root relation is strong because the two chords have the fewest notes in common and therefore contrast more with each other. Movement by "weak" intervals—thirds (as C to E) and sixths (as C to the A above it)—is weaker, or less pronounced, because the two chords in this case usually share two out of their three notes; for example, C–E–G and E–G–B, or C–E–G and A–C–E. Similarly, modulation from one key to another in the course of a piece was most characteristically from one key to another whose keynote is a strong interval apart from that of the first key, as from C to G. Usually the modulation was to the key built on the fifth note, or dominant, of the original scale. A work in C major, for example, tended to move toward the area of G. In works in a minor key, the modulation might be to the dominant minor key (A minor to E minor, for example); or it might be to the relative major key (the key that shares the same scale notes as the minor scale but arranging them in major scale order rather than minor scale order [A minor and C major, for example]). In the second case the contrast of major and minor mode appeared to compensate for the weak modulation (A and C are a third apart).

By the early 18th century these modulatory principles were well established and were made use of in musical form. In the keyboard sonatas of Domenico Scarlatti, for example, or the instrumental dance movements in Bach's partitas, the opening key is well established at the beginning of the piece. There then begins a movement to a new key, normally the dominant key. This is characteristically achieved by an emphasis on chords common to both keys (known as "pivots"), plus a strong musical statement in the new key leading to a cadence in that key. After the modulation there is a process of return to the initial key. During this process the harmonic motion tends to be more rapid, passing quickly through many chords and often including momentary diversions into many new keys, thus lending greater impact to the eventual return to the original key. Such a composition is said to be in "binary form." In binary form compositions in a minor key, there occasionally occurred an exception to the rule of return to the home key. The composer could at his option return to the tonic major, the major key built on the same keynote, or tonic, as the original minor key—A major from A minor, for example. But even in this case the harmonic goal toward the tonic note (A in this case) remained the same.

Harmony and modulation in the 18th century

This basic modulatory scheme from tonic key to dominant key back to tonic key formed the basis of the large-scale musical forms that developed during the 18th century and persisted well into the 19th. The sonata forms of Mozart and Haydn, with their exposition, development, and recapitulation, adhere closely to this plan, often greatly expanded. Here the movement from the tonic to the dominant key or to the relative major key made up the exposition; the rapid harmonic movement en route back to the tonic made up the development; and the return to the tonic key—usually reinforced by a return of the initial thematic (melodic) material—signalled the start of the recapitulation. An optional final coda, or concluding section, further strengthened the sense of the tonal journey's having come to an end. In the large, multi-movement works from this period, there was usually a further contrast achieved by having one of the inner movements in another key, but the final movement almost invariably was once again in the same key as the first movement.

Romantic changes in classical harmony

This clear and logical system of organization seemed highly consistent with an age that took its cues from the clarity and balance of ancient classical architecture. It was not so consistent, however, with the ideals of the ensuing era of Romanticism. Already in the mature works of Beethoven, there is the beginnings of a breaking-down of the classic modulatory scheme; the opening movement of the *Waldstein Sonata,* Opus 53 (completed, 1804), for example, is built on a modulation from the tonic, C major, to the sharply contrasting key of E major, instead of the expected key of G. Much of the individual harmonic language of Franz Schubert is based on his purposeful disavowal of modulation via the smooth succession of pivot chords and his fondness, instead, for dropping suddenly into unrelated, and therefore unexpected, keys, as C major to E flat major in the opening movement of the *String Quintet in C Major,* Opus 163 (1828); C major to E minor in the opening movement of the *Symphony No. 9 in C Major* (1828), known as the *Great Symphony.*

Throughout the 19th century there was also a great increase in the use of chromatic tones—tones not belonging to the scale of a given key and that formed "foreign," sometimes dissonant, harmonies with the notes of that key. In addition to the triad, the typical chord of functional harmony, other more complex chords were used, the harmonic functions of which were extremely ambiguous to the listener. As a result the sense of clearly established tonality created by traditional harmonies began to vanish from the musical language—doubtless in line with composers' greater obsession with music and all arts as something mysterious and personalized.

By the time of the German composer Richard Wagner, the sense of tonality as the unifying musical force showed definite signs of disintegration. For one thing, Wagner's idea of the "endless melody" led him in his late works to abjure almost completely, except at the end of acts, the full cadence that establishes tonality. A seeming approach to a cadence in *Tristan und Isolde* or the *Ring des Nibe-*

lungen tetralogy is more often than not thwarted by a quick and unprepared switch to a sharply contrasting key and a continuation of the music in that new area. For another, Wagner's passion for complex chords subject to more than one functional interpretation made the tonality of even short passages difficult to assess.

Post-Wagnerian developments

Although Wagner's specific harmonic concepts were not universally accepted, during his time or afterward, the blurring of the tonal sense by one means or another became prevalent throughout Western music by the last decades of the 19th century. Even in the works of the Italian Giuseppe Verdi, whose music was regarded as the opposite pole from Wagnerian techniques, this abandonment of clear tonal outlines may be noted: the sudden changes to unrelated keys, the piling up of dissonances that leave the sense of key obscured for minutes at a time, the emergence in his late works of a continuous melodic style that avoided regular, key-defining cadences. In France, the blurring of clear outlines characteristic of Impressionist painters found its musical counterpart in the music of Claude Debussy, who employed such devices as the scale consisting entirely of whole tones as a means of sidestepping the tonal feeling created by traditional scales. In the music of later French composers, especially the members of the post-World War I group known as "Les Six," a common practice was polytonality, or the sounding of two tonalities simultaneously, each defined with relative clarity but neither dominating the other. Similar polytonal methods also occur in the works of the Hungarian-born Béla Bartók and the Russian émigré Igor Stravinsky.

Schoenberg's 12-tone row

The Wagnerian influence continued most directly, via the music of Gustav Mahler, into the serial techniques developed in the 1920s by Arnold Schoenberg and his Viennese school. In Schoenberg's serialism the 12 notes of the chromatic scale are arranged into an arbitrary series, or 12-tone row, that becomes the basis for the melodies, counterpoint, and harmonies of the composition. Of these 12 notes no single note is allowed to predominate. This

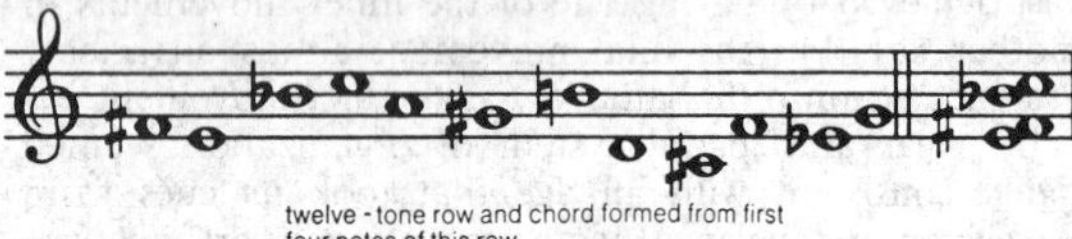
twelve-tone row and chord formed from first four notes of this row

is in complete contrast to the predominance of the tonic, or keynote, in the music of the late Renaissance and the common practice period. Serialism thus completely and systematically obliterated traditional harmonic organization. With no single note serving as a musical goal, tonality—at least as it was known from the 15th century—ceased to be a unifying musical force. Other elements, including serialization of rhythms and tone colours as well as of notes, came to prevail.

Chromaticism in harmony. Although the preceding paragraphs represent a brief outline of composers' attitudes toward harmony and tonality from the late Middle Ages to the 20th century, there is the danger that the broad outlines may be taken as a rigid statement of standard practices by composers at any period in musical history. Actually, although these outlines remained the general framework in which composers worked, they frequently diverged from it to some extent, particularly in their use of chromatic notes (notes outside the scale of the basic key of the composition) and chromatic chords (chords containing chromatic notes).

The capacity of chromatic tones to add harmonic colour, expressiveness, and interest was apparent to composers from the beginnings of standard harmonic practice. J.S. Bach, for example, in a striking passage at the end of the "Crucifixus" of the *Mass in B Minor,* lent poignance to the verbal description of the burial of Christ by the musical device of a sudden modulation from B minor to a sharply contrasting new key, G major, that contained notes chromatic to the basic key. Mozart, too, derived much of the drive of his harmonic style from a constant use of chromaticism. A characteristic device of Mozart, for example, is his frequent use of secondary dominants to intensify harmonic movement. A secondary dominant is a chord related to the dominant; specifically, it is the dominant of the dominant. If the key is C, the dominant is G and the secondary dominant is D. Secondary dominant chords by their nature contain a note that is chromatic to the basic key. In Mozart's music a harmonic progression from tonic chord (I) to dominant chord (V) will often pass through the dominant of the dominant (V-of-V): from I to V-of-V to V. By using the secondary dominant, he expanded the harmonic range of the composition by introducing chromaticism. In his later works Mozart also came to rely more and more on the dissonant value of suspensions to create harmonic interest. The slow introduction of his *String Quartet in C Major,* K. 465 (the *Dissonance Quartet*; 1785), consists of a string of long-delayed suspensions so that the harmonic definition at any given instant is as blurred as anything in Wagner.

Increased use of chromaticism

Although the harmonic style of the common practice period remained a basic framework, the history of music from Mozart's time to the present shows a constant increase in harmonic density, or the amount of chromaticism and frequent chord changes present. The opening bars of Beethoven's *Eroica Symphony* demonstrate the power of chromaticism to enhance the emotional effect.

The first eight notes of the are resolutely normal in their outline, the triad of E flat major, the tonic chord of the movement. But the ensuing two notes lead violently away from this harmonic stability, with the 10th note a totally unrelated C sharp. This completely upsets the harmonic structure and gives unmistakable notice that a long, complex movement will be necessary to right the imbalance. Not until the coda of the movement, 15 minutes later, is this opening theme allowed to follow the expected harmonic outline dictated by the style of the times.

Throughout the 19th century, composers remained rooted in the basic concept of tonality while at the same time doing everything in their power to complicate or obscure the tonal sense for the listener. Even in the 20th century, the large, varied, and important group of composers who are called conservative—among them, Samuel Barber, Aaron Copland, Sir William Walton, Dmitri Shostakovitch, Gian Carlo Menotti, Benjamin Britten—adhered to the concept of tonality only as a challenge. Tonality in their works exists, in the sense that there are extended stable areas that give the impression of being in some definable key. But the intense chromaticism of 20th-century composition, be it conservative or radical, makes it nearly impossible for the listener to grasp the unity of a work in terms of its adherence to a clear tonal plan. Unity is achieved, rather, by melodic means, the organization of rhythms, or even of tone colour. For all practical purposes, the function of tonality as the prime unifying force in musical structures, known from the 15th through the 19th century, is a thing of the past.

Dissonance in harmony. The very foundation of harmonic music has been the interplay of consonance and dissonance. Consonance can be defined as the normal range of tone combinations accepted by theorists and composers of any given time as implying repose; dissonance, therefore, refers to any sounds outside that range. From the 19th century on, as writers increasingly explored the exact effect of music on the emotions, these two terms took on the aspect of value judgments. There is a tendency to confuse consonance with concord, or sweet sound, dissonance with discord, or clashing sound. This has led to a certain amount of confusion.

Dissonance is in fact the prime element in the harmony that creates movement, and this has been recognized by composers from the dawn of the harmonic millennium. When the human ear recognizes a certain harmony as unstable within the context of a composition, it demands that this instability be rectified by the resolution to a stable harmony. Dissonance, therefore, has never been forbidden in music, for without it music would be hopelessly static.

What has been clearly defined in each era has been, rather, the treatment of dissonance, the approach toward it and away from it in a smooth and logical manner so that the musical flow is of a continual tension and relaxation.

The regulation of dissonance. The notion of which specific chords and intervals constitute consonance and dissonance has altered violently from the beginning of harmony. In the earliest harmonic writing, the parallel organum of the 9th century, the accepted intervals were the perfect consonances, or those of the simplest harmonic ratios: the fourth, the fifth, and the octave. As contrapuntal movement among voices became freer, certain other combinations necessarily occurred: thirds and sixths and, in some cases, seconds (as C–D) and sevenths (as C–B). These combinations were regarded as dissonances and were to be confined to weak beats of the musical metre; they were to be resolved, for the most part, by stepwise movement downward to the adjacent consonance. Another interval that the musicians of the modal era took great pains to avoid was the augmented fourth (the tritone, or "devil in music"), an interval containing three whole steps, as between F and B—the whole steps F–G, G–A, and A–B. This interval was considered intolerably dissonant. Primarily to avoid the forbidden, unstable harmonic relationship of the tritone, the use of accidentals (sharps, flats, natural signs) entered music and introduced chromatic tones into a mode.

Chords with a pull to cadence

By the time of Rameau, the concept of the dissonance had altered markedly. The basis of the harmony had changed, as noted above, from the perfect intervals (unison, fourth, fifth, octave) to the triad, or chord such as C–E–G, built of thirds above a root, or bass note. The tonic, or keynote, triad became the point of departure and of arrival for an entire composition and also for melodic phrases and larger sections within that composition. The harmonic movement to the cadence, a prime means of establishing points of articulation, became by the mid-18th century a more or less standard progression of harmonies subject to variation according to the composer's own powers of imagination. Preceding the tonic chord in these cadences, and pushing toward it, was the chord built on the dominant, or fifth note of the scale. This convention developed because of the nature of the dominant chord. In a dominant chord, the note a third above the root (as B in the chord G–B–D—considering the G chord the dominant and the basic key C) is the seventh note of the scale (C, D, E . . . B). This note has a strong leading tendency toward the tonic, or keynote (here, C), because it is only a half step away from the tonic, and is thus called the leading note. Because the leading note is a member of the dominant chord, this chord also has a strong pull toward the tonic chord.

By Rameau's time it was also a common practice to enhance the pull of the dominant chord to the cadence by adding to it the note a seventh above the root of the chord (as F, in the chord G–B–D–F), that note being the fourth note of the scale (C, D, E, F). Such a chord, a dominant seventh chord (V_7) contains two leading notes: the seventh of the scale, here B, with its strong pull toward the tonic, and the fourth of the scale, here F, which has a strong pull toward another of the notes of the tonic chord (in this case toward E in the chord C–E–G), being a half step away from that note. In this way two notes of the dominant seventh chord pulled strongly toward two notes of the tonic chord. Another reason for the strong pull of the seventh chord toward the tonic is that that chord contains a tritone (in this case B–F). Although the tritone was less intolerable by that time than it was to medieval ears, it was still considered a particularly strong dissonance that demanded resolution. This resolution occurred when the dominant seventh chord moved to the tonic chord. In the example below a dominant seventh chord (V_7) moves to a tonic chord (I) in the key of C major. Arrows show the resolution of the tritone dissonance. The dominant seventh chord thus became one of the basic chords in functional harmony. In addition, because it contained two dissonances (a seventh, as G–F in the chord G–B–D–F, and a tritone, as B–F in the same chord), it was the first instance of incorporating dissonance into a

system built on the basically consonant triad. Throughout the common practice period dissonances were continually added to the basic harmonic language, so that the range of harmony and use of dissonance in late 19th-century music had expanded considerably beyond that of the early 17th century.

Music using the system of functional harmony has a flow of harmonic movement through contrasting chords and through passages from consonant to dissonant to consonant chords. If the change of chords is frequent in relation to the musical rhythm, there is said to be a rapid harmonic rhythm. Similarly, a leisurely pace of chord change is a slow harmonic rhythm. The slow or fast harmonic rhythm of a composition helps define its musical character, and by varying the harmonic rhythm within a piece a composer can create contrast, thereby defining sections of musical form.

Modulation and dissonance in the common practice period

Modulation. Modulation, or change of key, was, like dissonance, increasingly explored during the common practice period. In the sonata forms that emerged as the primary musical forms of the mid-18th century, modulation from the tonic to other keys as a means of obtaining contrast became of prime importance. This musical esthetic involved not only the necessity of modulation itself but also drew much of its strength from the varying rate of modulation. Thus, the exposition, or first section, of the "normal" sonata form involves a modulation from the tonic to a nearby related key—usually the dominant, or in works in a minor key, the relative major. The development, or second section, on the other hand, depended on a rapid series of modulations, the purpose being to cast the return to the tonic in as strong a dramatic light as possible by having the stability of the tonic contrast with the instability of rapid modulation that preceded it.

The process of modulation to many keys involved the addition of dissonant, often chromatic, notes to the basic harmonic outline of a composition. A common way of preparing for the appearance of the dominant key area in a sonata exposition was for the composer to overshoot his mark, moving temporarily to the dominant of the dominant, thereby using chromatic chords. Thus, in the transition from tonic key (C major) to dominant key (G major) in the first movement of *Symphony No. 1 in C Major,* Opus 21 (1800), of Beethoven, there is considerable emphasis on the chords of D, both major and minor, establishing D as a dominant leading to a cadence on G, the point of arrival. Much of the dissonance in music of the late classic composers is traceable to this use of secondary dominants. The tendency to move quickly through extended sequences (musical patterns repeated at higher or lower pitch) based on secondary dominant chords became a highly sophisticated technique in the mature works of Haydn and Mozart (as, for example, the extraordinary sequence in the slow movement of Haydn's *Symphony No. 104 in D Major,* the *London Symphony*).

Functional harmony was based on chords built from the diatonic (seven-note) major and minor scales; chromatic notes and chords were integrated into the functional system. Although composers of this period proved remarkably adventurous in straying beyond the limits of purely diatonic harmony, their use of dissonance and chromatism was at all times both rational and functional. Chords, even though complex, normally resolved sooner or later into the chords toward which they tended, even when the composer, as in the Haydn passage cited, added unstable elements to the chord of resolution and therefore occasioned further resolution.

Use of dissonance for harmonic colour. By the early

19th century, composers became aware that harmony could also serve another purpose: it could exist outside of a purely functional context as a means of enhancing the pure harmonic colour of a composition. The opening of the *Quintet in C Major* of Schubert provides a simple and quite early example of chords used for the sheer effect of their sound. The C major triad of the first two bars seems to swell in the ensuing two bars into a diminished seventh chord, a chord functioning much like a dominant chord in its pull to its tonic but built instead with a leading note as its root, as, for example, F♯, the leading note of G, on which is built a chord such as F♯–A–C–E♭. (The top and bottom notes of such a chord, here F♯–E♭, encompass the interval of a diminished seventh, giving the chord its name.) In Schubert's quintet the particular diminished seventh chord used would normally resolve to a chord on G. Instead it simply subsides back to the C major triad of the preceding bars, so that there occurs no real harmonic movement in the opening six bars.

Nineteenth-century harmonic usage, therefore, tended to expand not only the chordal vocabulary itself but also the function of chords. In the former respect there was an increase in the use of chords the particular type of dissonance of which lent them an unstable and a functionally ambiguous quality; for example, a chord that became of prime importance as a means of thickening the harmonic sound and of blurring the exact tonality of a musical passage was the augmented sixth chord. This is an altered chord, or one built by taking a chord normally occurring in its key and chromatically altering it. In this case, two of its notes are changed by a half step. Specifically, an augmented sixth chord is built on the first inversion of a triad, as, for example, A–C–F, the first inversion of the triad F–A–C. Taking the first inversion (A–C–F), the A is flatted and the F is sharpened, resulting in a chord (A♭–C–F♯) that is both dissonant and ambiguous in harmonic function. The ambiguity of sound is partly due to the nature of enharmonic chords, chords that sound identical but in musical notation use different notes (as G♭, identical in sound with F♯). Thus the chord A♭–C–F♯ may move smoothly to a chord built on G, but the identical sounding chord A♭–C–G♭ will progress to a vastly different chord,

on D♭. Composers can thus use such ambiguous chords to achieve unusual or expressive harmonies that blur the listener's expectations and therefore his ability to perceive key and tonality.

The opening of Wagner's music drama *Tristan und Isolde,* famous for its ambiguous sense of tonality, is an augmented sixth chord that resolves by way of a second

dissonance to the dominant seventh chord of the key of A. This sequence is repeated at a higher pitch, here resolving to the dominant seventh chord of the key of C. Although this passage can be explained in terms of normal harmonic analysis, it was in itself strikingly abnormal for its time. The passage occurs at the beginning of the composition, the point where a composer normally would be expected to establish his basic tonality. In addition, there is considerable doubt as to the exact nature of the resolution. The dominant seventh chord (here the chord of resolution) is itself dissonant, although less so than the augmented sixth chord. The tonality of the passage is obscured, for it is impossible to tell whether the passage is in A minor or A major. Since the notes of the scale that would give this information to the listener are missing from the passage, it is clear that Wagner does not want the listener to be sure. He wants the passage, rather, to stand for the substance of the opera itself: unrequited passion is equal to unresolved harmonies.

Dissonance and emotion in Wagner's music

Other composers, too, sought out harmonic as well as melodic and rhythmic means to underscore the content of passion, restlessness, mystery, or tragedy in their scores. The unstable, ambiguous chord of the diminished seventh accompanies the appearances of the evil Samiel and his seven supernatural bullets in the opera *Der Freischütz (The Freeshooter)* by Carl Maria von Weber. Long strings of this chord, moving rapidly up and down the scale for purely colouristic purposes, also appear in climactic passages of the tone poem *Les Préludes,* by Franz Liszt, expressing the struggle of the soul against supernatural forces. The highly embroidered piano style of Frédéric Chopin, touched, in passing, on showers of dissonant, often chromatic tones—again used not for any exploitation of their functional value but as a spray of colour used as an overlay for a basically diatonic (nonchromatic) style, well-hidden underneath and recognizable only at the cadence.

Until the genuinely revolutionary *Tristan und Isolde* of 1865, the increase in the amount of chromaticism in the musical language of the Romantic composers was largely an enhancement of expressive detail. The diatonic (nonchromatic) basis of 18th-century functional harmony was in the main respected, as was the orderly process of modulation as a means for giving structure to large musical forms. With *Tristan,* and even more markedly with Wagner's music drama *Parsifal,* one can discern the beginnings of a gradual but unmistakable dissolution of the diatonic system on which traditional harmony was based. The analysis of *Tristan's* harmony by Rameau's principles, although possible, is simply unimportant. What matters more is the constant flow of chromaticism, of Wagner's wide variety of means—altered chords, chains of secondary dominants, and resolutions to chords that themselves prove unstable—for blurring any sense of functional harmony. Doubtless impelled by the dramatic substance of this music drama, he succeeded in evading the cadence, or coming to rest, that traditionally defined harmonic direction.

The impact of this step became apparent in the directions taken by harmony by the end of the 19th century. After Wagner, dissonance, particularly dissonance caused by chromaticism, largely ceased to function as it had in traditional harmony, and composers created their own individual, often experimental, usage of dissonance. No composer, whether he accepted *Tristan* as a masterpiece or dismissed it as madness, was left untouched by its implications.

Dissonance after Wagner. In France, where musical culture stood in some ways the direct antithesis to Wagnerism, Claude Debussy evolved his own style that succeeded, as Wagner's had, in beclouding the harmonic basis of a work either altogether or for extended periods. Debussy was influenced by a number of sources: the Impressionist painters, who were involved with the renunciation of clear perspectives and outlines in favour of the play of light across surfaces and the effect of images only half seen; exotic music, particularly that of Indonesia; and folk music, especially the modal scales of Russia. All of these led him to a partial abandonment of functional tonality. Among the devices he used toward this end is a scale composed

Debussy's sources

entirely of whole tones (as C–D–E–F♯–G♯–A♯–C). Such a scale lacks the distribution of whole and half steps that define the character of the major and minor scales of the common practice period. Chords built from the whole tone scale are by normal harmonic analysis unstable: all possible triads are augmented (the top note is altered by being sharpened; for example, C–E–G♯ instead of C–E–G) and as a result are dissonant. The perfect fourth and fifth, the ancient cornerstones of harmony, do not exist. Because the chords to which dissonances traditionally resolve are impossible with this scale, a work built upon it—*e.g.,* "Voiles" ("Sails"), from the first book of preludes for piano—can be said to exist without harmonic resolution and, therefore, without traditional tonality. Other Debussian devices include the regarding of the seventh chord (*e.g.,* dominant seventh, diminished seventh) as a self-sufficient harmony instead of as a dissonance that must resolve; sequences of sevenths moving parallel to each other giving the effect, in his music, of lines of harmony plus a dissonant descant (a countermelody in the highest part, or voice) blurring any real sense of traditional harmonic movement. This use of self-sufficient seventh chords was also much exploited by Maurice Ravel and came, through his great appeal, into a great deal of the popular music of western Europe and America from the 1920s onward.

Again, as with Wagner, Debussy's methods cast their shadow over composers both influenced by and hostile to his musical style. Igor Stravinsky, who was a little of both, first mirrored some of Debussy's harmonic usage in *Le Sacre du printemps* (*The Rite of Spring;* 1913). In *Le Sacre,* chords appear, as they often do in Debussy, purely for their colouristic value, related to each other only by virtue of the rhythmic insistence in the music's patterns. Much of Stravinsky's harmonic style, however, is actually derived from much simpler elements than Debussy's. His complex chord structures often break apart to reveal two unrelated and dissonant diatonic chords sounded simultaneously. In the works of his Neoclassical period, Stravinsky reverts to a clear harmonic language reminiscent, at least as regards individual chords, of the 18th century; but in harmonic movement from chord to chord there is a noticeable difference from earlier styles. Stravinsky, even in this clear compositional style that occupied him in the 1920s and into the 1930s, tends to use these classical harmonies in isolation, for the chords move freely one to the other without their classical function.

Chord structures of Stravinsky

Polytonality. Similar in a sense to Stravinsky's pandiatonicism, or use of diatonic chords without the limitations of classical harmonic function, is the tendency toward polytonality in the works of the post-World War I group of French composers known as "Les Six." These composers, notably Darius Milhaud, worked for a time with simple, diatonic chords piled upon each other in a way that suggested a clash between simultaneous tonal areas, almost a kind of counterpoint of tonalities—again leading to the dissolution of any sense of a single, central key area. Some traces of polytonality also occur in the early works of Bartók, who was much taken with French influences early in his career. But Bartók did not pursue this device to any great extent later on. He turned instead to an exploration of the folk styles of eastern Europe—Hungarian and Romanian, predominantly. His music, though harmonically dense and complex, remained rooted in tonality, with an admixture of harmonies gleaned from the modal scales of folk music.

Certain other composers, similarly obsessed with the desire to expand the harmonic vocabulary but loath to abandon the tonal system entirely, experimented with some success with synthetic scales of their own devising and with chords built of intervals other than the third. The Russian mystic Aleksandr Scriabin and the German Paul Hindemith both worked extensively with chords built out of fourths (as C–F–B♭). Scriabin employed these sounds primarily in a quasi-Impressionist way, using their unusual sounds as sonorous self-sufficient units. His "mystic" chord, shown below, formed the entire basis for many of his later works. Hindemith, whose orientation was toward the Neoclassical, dealt with these chords by devising his own system of harmonic function, creating a quite success-

ful reincarnation of the dissonance–consonance tensions of earlier composers.

The direct influence of Wagner's methods, however, was felt within the German–Austrian orbit. The restless, unresolved chromaticism of *Tristan* was directly reflected in the late works of Gustav Mahler. In such a work as the long, slow movement that ends Mahler's *Ninth Symphony,* one feels the *Tristan* influence quite directly: the long, lyric lines move freely through a systematic evasion of cadences and through a widening range of tonalities, often reaching tonal regions far removed from the starting point. Yet Mahler, too, remained a tonal composer, as did Richard Strauss, whose overlays of dissonance in such works as *Elektra* are easily separable from a basically tonal harmonic movement.

Schoenberg's relationship to Wagner

Early scores by the Viennese composer Arnold Schoenberg—such as the string sextet *Verklärte Nacht* (*Transfigured Night;* 1899), the *Chamber Symphony in E Major,* Opus 9 (1906), and the first two string quartets—are direct outgrowths of *Tristan's* chromaticism, masking but not obliterating the tonal basis. But by 1912 Schoenberg began actively to question tonality as a musical inevitability and to accept the broader implications of Wagner's style. From then on the pileup of dissonance in Schoenberg's music became so pronounced as to make the concept of dissonance itself meaningless. In such a seminal work as the chamber cantata *Pierrot Lunaire* (1912), tonality has been put aside. In this work it is no longer possible to discuss consonance and dissonance, for these concepts relate to the structure of a composition according to the harmonic principles of tonality.

Schoenberg's far-reaching musical philosophies, which were epitomized in his invention of the technique of serialism, have had a potent impact on the music of the decades following his own writing. They have also been resisted by large numbers of composers who are conveniently, if not always accurately, described as conservative. The conflict between tonality and atonality (*i.e.,* nontonality) has provided a dynamic dualism for musical styles ever since.

Harmony and melody. As noted above, melody and harmony were synonymous in classical Greek theory; the term harmony referred not to notes sounded simultaneously, but to the succession of notes, or the scale, out of which melody was formed. During classical antiquity and the European Middle Ages melodies were written that had an inner logic in terms of their scale, or mode, its important notes, and the melodic patterns associated with it. This is also true of many non-Western melodies. After the gradual evolution in Europe, through the polyphony of the late Middle Ages and the Renaissance, of the common practice, or classical, system of Western harmony, the inner logic of melodies was strongly affected by harmony. Because the ear can perceive harmonic patterns in certain groups of notes, even when sounded successively rather than simultaneously, melodies began to carry a strong implication of underlying harmonies. During this period there arose the conception that melody was the surface of harmony. Thus, for example, the partitas for unaccompanied violin by J.S. Bach, despite their melodic basis and lack of outright harmonic underpinning, clearly set forth their basic tonality and harmonic direction. This is achieved by a melodic style that includes frequent scale passages and arpeggiated chords (chord notes played successively, in melodic fashion, rather than simultaneously, as in a chord) that make clear to the listener the scales, harmonies, and keys belonging to the tonality of the composition. Through the 18th century and well into the 19th, melodies tended to be the bearers of their own harmonic implications. The above noted opening of Bee-

Melody as the harmonic surface

thoven's *Eroica Symphony* represents this practice at both its height and at the beginnings of its dissolution. The opening eight notes outline an unmistakable E♭ triad, and would do so even if they were sounded unharmonized; the ensuing plunge to the unexpected C♯ likewise indicates by its mere melodic shape the harmonic unrest arising at this juncture.

Nevertheless, melody in the hands of a composer seeking a genuine expressiveness must function with some degree of independence from its harmonic underpinning. The long, expressive dissonances in the vocal lines of Romantic composers not only heighten the passion sought after in the music but also specifically represent a seeking for a heightened independence of melody from harmony.

The shift of harmonic usage in the 20th century can be viewed partly as a marked change in relationships between melody and harmony. In Schoenberg's techniques, the generating force is the 12-tone row, which is primarily a melodic sequence out of which harmonies, as well as themes, are generated. Thus, it is possible to detect a reversal of the traditional relationship, whereby harmony has become the surface—or at least the final result—of melody.

Harmony in musical form. The chief problem of composition, in any style from ancient times to the present, is the creation of a form, or structure in which the principles of unity and contrast operate in some kind of equilibrium. The listener enters into this process by the use of his powers of recognition and of memory.

In purely melodic, modal music the form often derives from the inner logic of the melody in terms of the important notes and melodic patterns of the mode. In polyphonic music before the common practice period, musical form depended partly on the unity achieved by setting a piece in a given mode, partly on the use of musical themes, and partly on creating harmonic movement and tension toward stopping points, or cadences. During the common practice period—from Bach to Debussy—much of the creation of musical form took place through the organization of harmonies into keys and relationships between keys. Thus, the sonata forms of the 18th and early 19th centuries depended as much on the statement of a key, the movement to other key areas, and the eventual return to the same key as they did on themes and other melodic devices. The composer was likely, of course, to employ the two principles of melody and harmony simultaneously; the return to the tonic key late in the course of a movement was usually reinforced by a restatement of the initial themes. In certain works of Haydn and Mozart, the listener was often thrown off course purposely by the premature return of initial themes in an unexpected key; such devices served further to enhance the drama of the genuine recapitulation, or return to the main key.

By the 19th century, however, the power of harmony to suggest clear formal structures was greatly undermined by freer use of dissonance, which broke down the clarity with which a key was defined. Other customary procedures were also abandoned. Many of Schumann's songs do not return to the tonic, or home key, for the final cadence. The extended length of Wagner's music dramas, and their wide-ranging modulation, make it impossible to regard key as a unifying force. Mahler's *Ninth Symphony*, the first movement of which is in D major, ends with a movement in D flat major, and since the symphony lasts nearly 90 minutes, there seemed to Mahler to be no reason to pay any closer lip service to classical practices of unity of key. Such necessities, by the time of this symphony, had vanished from the musical language.

Avant-garde conceptions of harmony. The course of harmony after Wagner followed three distinct paths. (1) Within the broad outlines of tonality, composers explored the potential of chords of far greater complexity than the traditional triad. In doing so they often allowed unstable chords such as dominant sevenths to stand as self-sufficient entities, and they greatly increased the use of ambiguous chords such as augmented sixths and diminished sevenths to thicken or occasionally to blur the sense of a stable tonality. (2) Composers broke away from the classical system of tonality by using chords that, although clearly recognizable as derived from earlier harmonic practices, resolved in other than the expected direction. Some also went further afield by substituting for the major and minor scales unusual scales such as whole tone and Gypsy folk music scales, by using chords built out of fourths, and by utilizing polytonality. (3) Composers systematically abandoned tonality through Schoenberg's technique of granting equal importance to all 12 chromatic tones, rather than allowing one tone to predominate as tonic. When this was done, the concept of a single, predominant key centre vanished entirely in favour of atonality. In such cases, the traditional duality of consonance and dissonance also disappeared.

New ways of creating harmony

Among most "progressive" composers of the 20th century, atonality has been extensively explored. By far the greatest concern among avant-garde composers has been to revive contrapuntal writing, or composition stressing the combination of independent melodic lines. This was partly a reaction against the lush harmonies and lyricism of the Romantic period. During the common practice period any counterpoint that occurred was subordinated to the principles of traditional harmony. The 20th-century obsession with counterpoint tended to sweep aside concern with harmonic relationships beyond the incidental fact that clusters of notes in counterpoint are indeed heard simultaneously. In the music of the American Charles Ives, for example, many skeins of fully developed atonal, contrapuntal writing pass by simultaneously, producing momentary sonorities. Such sonorities may occasionally, and quite accidentally, be identical with recognizable harmonies; but these accidental sonorities have little to do with traditional harmonic organization. Similarly, the "tone-cluster" writing of another American innovator, Henry Cowell, whereby a pianist's forearm sounds every note it can depress at once, can hardly be analyzed as functional harmony in any sense.

Other developments, too, point to the dissolution of traditional attitudes toward harmony. The aleatory, or indeterminacy, experiments of John Cage, Earle Brown, and others assign part of the composer's melodic, harmonic, and rhythmic events to a specific performer at a specific instance. In such music any discussion of harmonic direction is irrelevant. Most importantly, the rise of electronic music, which breaks away from any traditional scales such as might be produced on "normal" instruments, can only with the greatest stretch of the imagination lend itself to considerations of harmony.

Yet, there is a possible analogy with traditional harmony in electronic music as its musical styles and languages take shape. In the works of Karlheinz Stockhausen, one of the electronic pioneers and a composer of enormous influence among his younger colleagues, there are organizational systems that point to a clear control and regulation of musical elements. The strict control of musical factors such as densities of sonority, rates of rhythmic change and of change in phrase structure, rates of change in the spread of sound in an auditorium through the use of carefully positioned and modulated loudspeakers point toward a new musical system that may possibly be analyzed in terms of a new, fundamentally different harmony.

Search for a new order

The dissolution of harmony in the "progressive" music of the 20th century was not a matter of anarchy replacing order. Actually, the common practice period is of relatively short duration against the entire history of harmony. Before Bach other rules existed. Such rules, in contrast to the later system of traditional harmony, depended not on the contrast of keys but on harmonic unity brought about by the use of a given mode. Since Debussy, similarly, harmonic styles have been dictated by new rules or by the desire of many composers to seek out new rules. And, as both the modal and the common practice systems of harmony evolved only after centuries, so is it also safe to predict that the seeming anarchy of much of 20th-century music represents a state of movement toward new harmonic precepts. The question at hand, moreover, is not one of the dissolution of harmony itself, for any notes sounded simultaneously produce a harmony—whether the notes be from traditional scales or from the infinity of musical pitches produceable through electronic means. The matter is, rather, the question of the uses to which these harmonies are put and the changing relations of harmony to musical structure.

An awareness of the value of harmony as pure, expressive sound persists among all composers of the present time. Some have pursued the atonal principles toward the point where harmonic sounds are totally dissonant (which is the same as saying that they are all consonant, because the contrast between consonance and dissonance disappears). Others have written works that consist of almost nothing but static, unadorned harmony—not necessarily harmoniousness. Such a work as Terry Riley's *In C,* for example, consists basically of a sustained triad on C (lasting, at the performer's option, anywhere from 30 minutes to several hours), over which fleeting dissonances are occasionally sounded, seldom more revolutionary than an F sharp or B flat. Here again, although one is more conscious of harmony in this work than of any other musical element, the harmony itself does not move or progress in the traditional sense; the sound exists, but not its function. Here one can discuss the work as pure consonance—which is the same, for lack of harmonic contrast, as pure dissonance.

Thus, in the 20th century the concepts basic to traditional harmony began to lose their importance. In counterpoint harmonies became the incidental result of the combination of melodic lines. New experiments with unusual harmonies (such as tone clusters, functionless in the traditional sense), the lessening of the tension between consonance and dissonance, and the creation of unprecedented harmonies by the use of computers have been the result of a search for new methods of musical organization. This in turn was the natural outgrowth of the blurring and final dissolution of the harmonic system that had prevailed for over two centuries in Western music. (A.Ri.)

COUNTERPOINT

A peculiarly Western phenomenon, counterpoint is the art of combining different melodic lines in a musical composition. It is the most characteristic element in Western music and a major distinguishing feature between the music of the West and that of the Orient and of primitive peoples.

Counterpoint and polyphony distinguished

The word counterpoint is frequently used interchangeably with polyphony. This is not properly correct since polyphony refers generally to music consisting of two or more distinct melodic lines, while counterpoint refers to the compositional technique involved in the handling of these melodic lines. Good counterpoint requires two qualities: (1) a meaningful or harmonious relationship between the lines (a "vertical" consideration—*i.e.,* dealing with harmony), and (2) some degree of independence or individuality within the lines themselves (a "horizontal" consideration, dealing with melody). Musical theorists have tended to emphasize the vertical aspects of counterpoint, defining the combinations of notes that are consonances and dissonances, and prescribing where consonances and dissonances should occur in the strong and weak beats of musical metre. In contrast, composers, especially the great ones, have shown more interest in the horizontal aspects: the movement of the individual melodic lines and long-range relationships of musical design and texture, the balance between vertical and horizontal forces, existing between these lines. The freedoms taken by composers have in turn influenced theorists to revise their laws.

The word counterpoint is occasionally used by ethnomusicologists to describe aspects of heterophony—duplication of a basic melodic line, with certain differences of detail or of decoration, by the various performers. This usage is not entirely appropriate, for such instances as the singing of a single melody at parallel intervals (*e.g.,* one performer beginning on C, the other on G) lack the truly distinct or separate voice parts found in true polyphony and in counterpoint. Finally, contemporary theorists generally use the word counterpoint in a narrow sense for musical styles resembling those of Palestrina or Bach and emphasizing clear melodic relationships (*e.g.,* melodic imitation) between the voice parts.

Counterpoint can be considered more broadly, however, as an essential element in many styles within Western music. Composers in different periods have used counterpoint differently: in the Middle Ages they used it for the superimposing of different rhythmic groupings; in the Renaissance for melodic imitation; in the Baroque for contrasts between groups of instruments or voices; in the Classical period in conjunction with tonality, the organization of music in terms of key; in the Romantic in the combining of leitmotifs, or short melodic fragments; and in 20th-century music in the arrangement of isolated components of sound.

Counterpoint in the Middle Ages. The earliest examples of actual written counterpoint appear in the late 9th-century treatise *Musica enchiriadis.* Here a plainchant

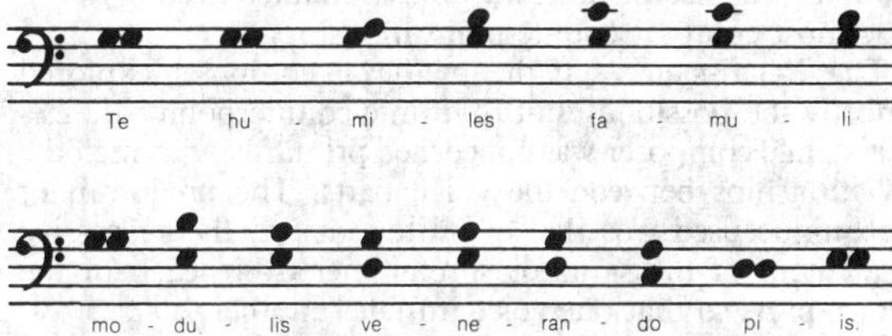

Early organum; from *Musica enchiriadis* (*c.* 859).

Organum: the earliest counterpoint

melody, or "principal voice" (*vox principalis*), is combined with another part, "organal voice" (*vox organalis*), singing the same melody in parallel motion a perfect fourth or fifth below (*e.g.,* G or F below C). Such music was called organum, probably because it resembled the sound of contemporary organs. In the early 11th century the teacher and theorist Guido of Arezzo in his *Micrologus* described a variety of organum in which the accompanying or organal voice had become more individualized. In addition to moving parallel to the main voice, it included oblique (diverging or converging) motion and contrary (opposite) motion. In this era the organal voice remains melodically awkward and subservient to the chant voice, as though it were composed one note at a time simply to colour or ornament each note of the chant. Early organum is thus not far removed from heterophony. Until the end of the 11th century organum was written entirely in note-against-note style, described, in 1336, as *punctus contra punctum* (point against point—*i.e.,* note against note), hence the name counterpoint.

In the 12th century true polyphony comes into being; the melodic lines become individualized mostly by being given different rhythms. There emerges a hierarchy between the voice parts. The emphasis is upon the chant voice, which now becomes the lower part. Its notes are prolonged, or "held," and this part is now called the tenor, from the Latin *tenere,* to hold. The contrapuntal genius of the Middle Ages realizes itself mostly through the use of rhythmic contrasts between the different voice parts, and such contrasts gradually increase in complexity from *c.* 1100 to *c.* 1400. Around 1200 Pérotin, composer at Notre Dame in Paris who wrote some of the earliest music in three and four parts, superimposed different rhythmic modes (short fixed rhythmic patterns) in the voice parts. In his three-part *Alleluia Nativitas,* the voices are in different rhythmic modes, and they are also distinguished

Medieval rhythmic complexity

From *Alleluia Nativitas* by Pérotin.

by different phrase lengths, consisting of more or fewer repetitions of the rhythmic pattern. During the 13th century such contrasts were carried still further in the motet, a musical form usually in three voice parts, each in a different rhythmic mode. The theorist Franco of Cologne advocated the use of consonance at the beginning of each measure; such consonances (usually a chord made up of the unison, fifth, and octave, such as C–G–C) served as fixed pillars in terms of which the horizontal extensions of different rhythmic lengths were like soaring arches of sound. The tenor voice part in the motets of the 14th and early 15th centuries was organized by huge rhythmic recurrences known as isorhythm (*i.e.,* the return throughout the piece of a complex rhythmic pattern, not necessarily in conjunction with the same pitches of the melody). During the 14th century, particularly in the works of Guillaume de Machaut, the upper voice part was sometimes displaced by a beat or more in respect to the other parts, giving it further rhythmic independence. In the late 14th century complicated syncopations (displaced accents) and the simultaneous use of different metres characterized some of the most complex counterpoint in history.

The Renaissance. If the medieval composer explored mostly the possibilities of rhythmic counterpoint, the Renaissance composer was concerned primarily with melodic relationships between the voice parts. The predominant technique used was that of imitation; *i.e.,* the successive statement of the same or similar melody in each of the voice parts so that one voice imitates another.

Imitation had appeared earlier in the Italian caccia and French *chace,* roundlike vocal forms of the 14th century, and in England in the 13th-century round, *Sumer is icumen in.* These compositions anticipate the Renaissance and also emphasize the rhythmic relationships typical of medieval counterpoint.

During the Renaissance the technique of imitation contributed to a new unity between the voices, as opposed to the hierarchy found in medieval counterpoint. Renaissance composers strove also for clear melodic relationships between voices; consequently imitations usually began on the same beat of a measure and were separated in pitch by simple intervals such as the fifth (as, C–G) or octave (as, C–C). The Renaissance theorists, among them Johannes Tinctoris and Gioseffo Zarlino, categorized dissonances according to type and governed each type by definite rhythmic and melodic restrictions.

Golden age of melodic counterpoint

What is often proclaimed as the "golden age" of counterpoint—meaning melodic counterpoint—stretches from the late 15th to the late 16th century, from the Flemish master Jean d'Okeghem to the Spanish Tomás Luis de Victoria and the Elizabethan William Byrd. Its leading masters were Josquin des Prez, Giovanni Pierluigi da Palestrina, and Orlando di Lasso. The northern composers in particular showed a penchant for complex melodic relationships. Okeghem's *Missa prolationum* (*Prolation Mass*), for example, involves simultaneous canons in two pairs of voices. (In a canon, one melody is derived from another. It may be identical, as in a round, or it may be given various alterations, as of speed, or metre or omission of certain notes.) The most versatile craftsman of the Renaissance was Josquin, whose music displays a continual variety of contrapuntal ingenuities, including melodic imitation. His use of successive imitation in several voices, as in his *Missa da pacem* based on the chant melody "Da pacem" ("give peace"), is coupled with melodic smoothness and

San- (ctus)

From *Missa da Pacem* by Josquin des Prez.

rhythmic vitality. The imitative style came to its fullest flowering in the late 16th century not only in the masses and motets of di Lasso and Palestrina but also in secular songs such as the French chanson and Italian madrigal. It also flourished in instrumental music in such contrapuntal forms as fantasias, canzonas, and ricercari.

The Baroque period. During the 17th and early 18th centuries the pure linear—*i.e.,* melodic—counterpoint of the Renaissance, now called the first practice, was retained alongside the newer type of counterpoint known as the second practice. This latter type was characterized by a freer treatment of dissonances and a richer employment of tone colour. The new liberties with dissonance disturbed the conservative theorists of the time; but they were justified by their proponents on the ground that they allowed a more expressive treatment of the text. Still more distinct was a new use of tone colour. Although the individual melodic lines often resembled those of the Renaissance, they were intensified and made to stand out through differences of scoring or instrumentation. In figured bass compositions (in which a keyboard instrument improvised the harmonies over a given bass melody) the counterpoint was between the upper melody and the bass line. These stood out clearly from one another because of their differences of instrumental or vocal tone colour. Also significant at this time was the development of concerto-like scoring. In a concerto a soloist or group of instruments is contrasted with the entire orchestra. Hence concerto style emphasized contrasts between the numbers of performers, the high and low registers, and the tone colours of two or more performing groups. This was anticipated in some of the madrigals (Italian part-songs) of the late Renaissance, especially those of Luca Marenzio and Don Carlo Gesualdo, in which two or three voice parts in a high or low register were immediately answered by parts in a contrasting register. Giovanni Gabrieli of Venice expanded this principle in his *Symphoniae Sacrae* (*Sacred Symphonies*) by setting off choirs of voices or instruments, thus achieving a counterpoint of contrasting sonorities. Such concerto-like effects became an essential part of the later madrigals and operas of Claudio Monteverdi. In his madrigal *Lament of the Nymph,* a single soprano voice is pitted against three male voices, and both in turn against

Influence of the concerto

From *Lament of the Nymph* by Claudio Monteverdi.

an instrumental continuo (figured bass played, for example, by cello and harpsichord) in the background. This type of counterpoint was ideal for emphasizing dramatic contrasts in the new forms of the opera and the oratorio. In these forms soloists, ensembles, and instrumental parts were opposed and combined in a great variety of ways by composers like Heinrich Schütz, Giacomo Carissimi, and Henry Purcell. In the late Baroque Arcangelo Corelli and Antonio Vivaldi added this style of dramatic contrasts to the purely instrumental contrasts of the concerto. The Baroque concerto culminated in the *Brandenburg Concertos* of J.S. Bach, which are characterized by a remarkable fusion of contrapuntal lines and instrumental colours.

Bach's counterpoint has a retrospective side, which uses a mainly melodic approach. The fugue, a composition using the technique of melodic imitation, became highly developed in Bach's hands—*e.g.,* the fugues of the *Well-*

From *Brandenburg Concerto No. 5* by J.S. Bach.

Tempered Clavier and his final compendium of contrapuntal devices, *The Art of the Fugue.* A similar melodic, rather than tone-colour, approach occurs in works such as the *Inventions* and in the canons of the *Musical Offering.* These works are akin to "the first practice," the melodic counterpoint of the Renaissance, although in their use of dissonance and harmony they go considerably beyond Renaissance convention.

The Classical period. The turn from the Baroque to the Classical period in music was marked by the change from a luxuriant polyphonic to a relatively simple homophonic texture—*i.e.*, a texture of a single melodic line plus chordal accompaniment. Composers of the early Classical period (*c.* 1730–70) largely eschewed counterpoint altogether, drawing on it only when preparing church music in the "learned style," as the Renaissance style was then called. Many of the keyboard sonatas of Domenico Scarlatti and Carl Philipp Emanuel Bach, despite a basically homophonic approach, reveal a skillful interplay between the main melody and accompaniment. In the late Classical period (*c.* 1770–1820), especially in the music of the Viennese school of Haydn, Mozart, and Beethoven, there was an ever-increasing penetration of counterpoint into musical forms based on this homophonic style and its contrasts of tonality, or key (see above *Harmony*). This counterpoint in turn was tempered by the Classical style and musical forms. For example, although combined melodic lines are heard as counterpoint, together they can also be heard as a series of harmonies. In this way they form unified phrases in the homophonic style. This satisfied demands for symmetrical phrase lengths and clear-cut cadences, or stopping points, necessary to mark the sections of Classical forms such as the sonata.

Use of counterpoint by Haydn, Mozart, and Beethoven

Haydn underwent his contrapuntal "crisis," or movement toward counterpoint, during the 1770s, the period of *Sturm und Drang* ("Storm and Stress") in German literature, which had a deepening effect on other arts as well. Three of his *Sun Quartets* (1772) had fugues as final movements, and in the *Russian Quartets* (1781) Haydn proclaimed "an entirely new manner," in which the thematic material was to be more equally shared by all of the stringed instruments instead of being given to a single principal melody instrument. Haydn heard Handel's oratorios in London, which inspired him to write his own richly contrapuntal late oratorios, *The Creation* and *The Seasons.*

Mozart's discovery of the contrapuntal art of Bach and Handel impressed him so deeply that almost all of his later works were affected. The ensembles of the operas—*e.g., Don Giovanni* and *Così fan tutte*—with their clear delineation of several characters through their vocal lines, only became possible because of his new feeling for counterpoint. And at one point in his *Jupiter Symphony* five different themes are stated simultaneously, singly, or in combination. Nevertheless the counterpoint is kept entirely subservient to the harmonies of the symphony's tonal design, or its use of keys. Each voice is also governed by an underlying phrase structure applied to all of them, so that the combined parts form unified musical phrases.

Beethoven began his career in Vienna under the tutelage of the noted contrapuntal theorist Johann Albrechtsberger, and this, coupled with his admiration for Handel, probably accounts for his lifetime interest in counterpoint. He drew upon counterpoint to create musical intensity, especially in the development section of sonata form (the form prominent in Classical symphonies and chamber music), as in the first movement of the *Razumovsky Quartet,* Opus 59, No. 1, for example. In his late sonatas and quartets, except for obvious fugal works such as the first movement of Opus 131, or the *Great Fugue,* Opus 133, almost every movement shows the interpenetration of the principles of counterpoint, which deals with melodic lines, and tonality, which deals with harmonies.

The Romantic period. Counterpoint in the 19th century had a retrospective side in addition to a characteristically Romantic style. Richard Wagner admired the counterpoint of Palestrina, and Johannes Brahms revered the Baroque masters. Felix Mendelssohn revived Bach's *St. Matthew Passion* in 1829, and this led to numerous Bach-like works, such as the organ sonatas of Mendelssohn and numerous organ works by Max Reger, as well as arrangements of Bach's works by Franz Liszt. Yet the true bent of Romantic composers was toward combinations of motives (small melodic fragments), use of motivic accompaniments against themes, and, later, of the combination of leitmotifs, or motives with significance beyond the music itself.

Combinations of motives and leitmotifs

The lieder (songs) of Franz Schubert were highly innovative because of their motivic accompaniments, which balance in interest the vocal part itself and contrapuntally interact with it. This technique is still more pronounced in the songs of Robert Schumann and Hugo Wolf. It is also the tendency in 19th-century opera. In the later operas of Giuseppe Verdi the voices often have a parlante character (imitating speech through music) while the orchestra defines the dramatic substance. This, too, is the principle of the Wagner music dramas, with their "speech-song" (*Sprechgesang*) in the voice balanced contrapuntally by the leitmotifs of the accompaniment. In *Tristan und Isolde* Wagner set the leitmotifs in counterpoint against one another. Similarly, in the Prelude to

From *Siegfried* (Act III) by Richard Wagner.

Act III of *Siegfried,* a motive known as the "Need of the Gods" is cast against one associated with the "Valkyries." This results in a "counterpoint" of connotations and of emotions as well as in a musical counterpoint. In purely instrumental music a similar joining of motives previously heard separately is encountered in the finale of Hector Berlioz's *Symphonie fantastique* when the plainchant melody "Dies Irae" ("Day of Wrath") is heard together with the theme called "Round of Sabbath." Richard Strauss, in his tone poem *Ein Heldenleben* (*A Hero's Life*), skillfully combines several themes taken from his earlier tone poems. And in the late symphonies of Gustav Mahler there is sometimes a complex of interwoven motives, each of which stands out contrapuntally through its presentation by a solo instrument.

In the 20th century Arnold Schoenberg carried this technique further, especially in his 12-tone works, which are based on a 12-tone row, or specific ordering of the 12 notes of the chromatic scale, arranged in such a way as to avoid a sense of tonality. In some 12-tone operas—*e.g., Moses und Aron* by Schoenberg and *Lulu* by Alban Berg—there is but one tone row used in the entire work; nonetheless, several hours of music are spun out of it through a continual variety of thematic shapes and contrapuntal combinations.

The 20th century. The 20th century, like the 19th, has had its counterpoint inspired by earlier music. Anton Webern, for example, advocated a return to the forms of counterpoint used by Renaissance composers such as Heinrich Isaac, and in numerous of his own works (*e.g., Symphonie*) he makes use of Renaissance contrapuntal devices such as simultaneous canons and retrograde movement between the voice parts—*i.e.,* one voice using the other's melody but with the notes in reverse order. Out of a similar return to Baroque forms came musical works such as the double fugue (a fugue based on two themes) that forms the second movement of the *Symphony of Psalms* by Igor Stravinsky.

Counterpoint of polytonality and tone colours

But the use of older musical forms is no more of the essence of 20th-century counterpoint than it was of the 19th. A basic characteristic of 20th-century counterpoint is the separation of the voice parts into isolated entities of sound that are of themselves rather static. This may take the form of polytonality (the simultaneous use of two or more keys), using as static entities the notes of each key. It may also take the form of contrast of individual tone colour effects, rather than of melodies, found in much electronic music. (This use extends beyond the original definition of counterpoint simply as the combination of melodies.)

Richard Strauss's *Elektra* (1909) was one of the earliest works to make use of polytonality; in certain passages the instruments and voice parts are grouped into layers, each of which defines a different tonality, or key, although in this case all of the keys can also be interpreted as complicated aspects of the basic key. Stravinsky's *Three Pieces for String Quartet* (No. 1) suggests four keys at the same time: G, B, D, and A♭. In this particular work each instrument is limited throughout the piece to a few notes assigned to

From *Three Pieces for String Quartet* (No. 1) by Igor Stravinsky.

it. Thus each part is absolutely individual and, except for the viola, consists of an ostinato melodic and rhythmic pattern. The coming together of these ostinato patterns at different times and in continually shifting arrangements suggests the effect of a mobile.Béla Bartók carried out a similar procedure in many of the short piano pieces of his *Mikrokosmos,* and in his *Fourth Quartet* (1928) he set apart tone clusters (chords built up in seconds, as C–D–E–F–G) in this way.

Turning now to a counterpoint purely of tone colours, *Intégrales* (1925) by Edgard Varèse presents 11-note "sound-clouds" in the wind instruments in opposition to the sounds of a large battery of percussion instruments. This approach probably grew directly out of earlier experiments with polytonality, but here tone colours, rather than keys or tones, are differentiated. Elliott Carter in his *Double Concerto* (1961) set apart two groups of instruments, one around a piano, another around a harpsichord, each with its distinctive tone colours and its own distinctive harmonic intervals or note combinations. In György Ligeti's *Atmospheres* every instrument in a symphony orchestra, including every string part, plays its own unique, melodic pattern; all of these parts coalesce into gigantic bands, or spectra, of tone colour that contrast with one another. In later experiments, the sound-producing groups are further set off by visual or spatial contrasts in the physical placement of performers; *e.g.,* Ramon Zupko's *Third Planet from the Sun,* 1970.

The literature of counterpoint. Most of the writings on counterpoint have sought to increase the student's skill in musical composition. From the 18th century onward, textbooks of counterpoint have recommended as a model usually Palestrina or Bach, and in some recent cases 20th-century composers. Medieval and Renaissance treatises also were originally intended for student guidance and reflect the taste and attitudes of their own time. Several 20th-century studies deal with the contrapuntal technique of a particular composer or group of composers.

(R.J.J.)

NOTATION

Broadly defined, musical notation is a visual record of heard or imagined musical sound, or a set of visual instructions for performance of music. It usually takes written or printed form and is a conscious, comparatively laborious process. Its use is occasioned by one of two motives: as an aid to memory or as communication. By extension of the former, it helps the shaping of a composition to a level of sophistication that is impossible in a purely oral tradition. By extension of the latter, it serves as a means of preserving music (although incompletely and imperfectly) over long periods of time, facilitates performance by others, and presents music in a form suitable for study and analysis.

The primary elements of musical sound are pitch, or the location of musical sound on the scale (hence interval, or distance, between notes); duration (hence rhythm, metre, tempo); timbre or tone colour; and volume (hence stress, attack). In practice, no notation can handle all of these elements with precision. Most cope with a selection of them in varying degrees of refinement. Some handle only a single pattern—*e.g.,* a melody, a rhythm; others handle several simultaneous patterns.

General principles of Western staff notation. The position of staff notation as the first notational system to be described in this article acknowledges its international acceptance in the 20th century. As an indirect result of colonization, of missionary activity, and of ethnomusicological research—not because of any innate superiority—it has become a common language among many musical cultures.

Pitch and duration. Staff notation, as it has developed, is essentially a graph. Its vertical axis is pitch, its horizontal axis, time; and note heads are dots plotting the graph's curve. The five horizontal lines of a musical staff function like horizontal rulings of graph paper, bar lines like vertical rulings. In practice, the system is far more complex and sophisticated than this. The vertical axis of pitch operates to represent melodic contour in music for a single instrument or voice; but when several staves are combined to form a score, the principle breaks down, each staff being a self-contained vertical system. Representation of time (duration) by horizontal spacing is used only in a very limited way. It is in reality made almost redundant because the symbol for a note gives the necessary information itself: not its absolute duration but its duration in relation to the notes around it. These symbols are as follows; each has half the duration of its neighbour to the left:

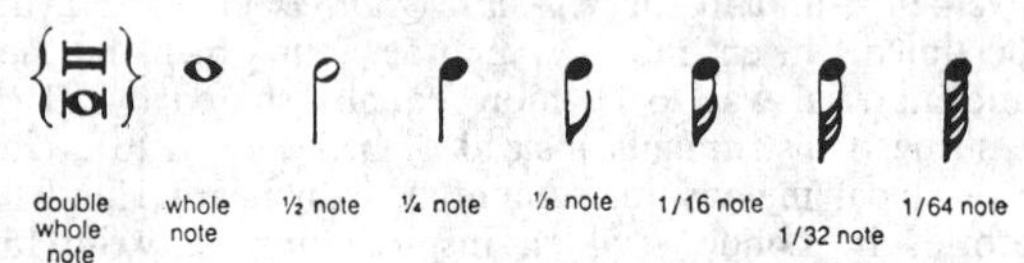

A system of "rests" measures silence in the same way:

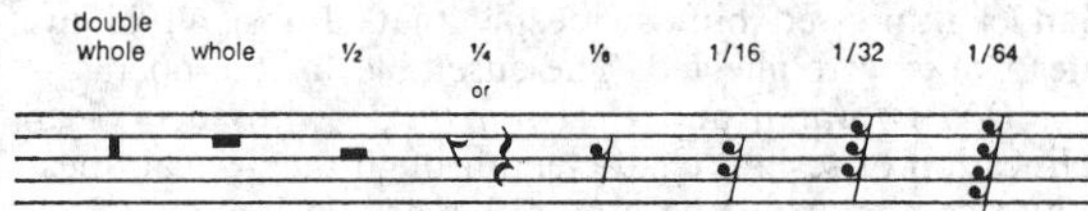

A dot placed to the right of a note head increases by half the duration of that note. Such symbols when placed on a staff may indicate relative pitch and relative duration. In the grid, lines represent alternate notes of the scale and the spaces the intervening notes. Pitch and duration may be fixed by supplying two further indications: a clef and a tempo mark. The clef assigns a definite pitch to a given line of the staff; the first clef fixes the second line up as the G (g′) above middle C (c′):

Tempo and duration. The tempo mark is a sign that lies outside the staff. It appears above and may be a precise fixing of one duration ("♩ = 120 MM" means that the quarter note lasts 1/120 of a minute, or one-half second), or it may be an approximate verbal indication setting tempo by reference to accepted conventions (allegro, or quickly; moderato, or moderate speed; etc.).

Staff notation is well adapted to two fundamental aspects of Western music: harmony and rhythm. For harmony, note symbols can easily be placed vertically together on a single stem, and these notes need not be all of the same duration; or more than one stem may be used to indicate multiple melodic lines in the musical texture. For rhythm, the existence of an underlying regular pulse, or stress, must be indicated. This is achieved by two devices: the bar line and the time signature. The bar line primarily indicates a point of main stress. Bar lines are usually equally spaced as to duration, though there are numerous exceptions. A time signature indicates, first, the duration of the space between two bar lines (a measure, or bar); and, second, the subsidiary stress patterns within that space. A supplementary system for indicating stress is the device of linking successive notes together by beaming, or stroking. Two eighth notes may be linked together as shown in (a); four sixteenth notes (b); or a mixed group of values (c):

The function of a time signature

(a) (b) (c)

The implication of such grouping is generally that the first note carries a stress. Beaming thus may be used either to reinforce the stress patterns of the time signature (the metre) or to contradict it and set up a cross rhythm.

Accidentals. Staff notation rests firmly on the Western system of scales, within which all notes are assumed to be natural unless accidentals precede them or a key signature is in use. An accidental (♭, or flat; ♯, or sharp) is a temporary lowering or raising of pitch by a semitone; a key signature is the use of the same signs on a more permanent basis, valid to the end of a piece or until countermanded by a new signature. Another accidental, the natural (♮), cancels a previously indicated flat or sharp and may be used to alter one note or in a key signature to emphasize a key change. Any combination of sharps or flats is theoretically possible in a key signature, but the actual combinations are usually governed by the Western system of keys, or groups of interrelated notes and chords.

Auxiliary signs. Timbre and volume are specified through a variety of additional signs: symbols such as > (stress) and —— (increase in volume), and verbal instructions (frequently in Italian) such as forte (loud) and col legno (with the wood of the bow) placed above or below the staff wherever space permits. Additional symbols may also provide information about pitch and duration: the dot for staccato, the fermata, or hold sign (𝄐), the phrase mark, indications of amount of vibrato, and so forth. Other verbal instructions indicate the general manner of performance (pesante, "heavy"; cantabile, "songlike"; etc.) or expression (con dolore, "with suffering"; giocoso, "playfully"; etc.). Further, there are for each type of instrument certain technical signs, as for bowing, breathing, tonguing, or use of mutes.

Types of musical "shorthand"

Other auxiliary signs are a kind of shorthand. Most important are symbols indicating notes not shown on the staff. An ornament sign may call for additional notes to be played within the value of a note. It may even delay the sounding of the main note. The precise meaning of such an ornament varies from one style of music to another and must be interpreted according to the conventions governing a particular style.

Comparable to the use of "shorthand" signs for ornaments is the system of placing arabic numerals beneath a bass line in keyboard music of the 17th and 18th centuries. A numeral, or "figure," signifies a harmonic (*i.e.,* a vertical) interval; thus a "6" indicates a note six degrees of the scale above a given bass note (A above C, for example). It is in itself an imprecise measurement, specifying neither whether the interval is major or minor nor in which octave register that upper note should be played. But the figures are governed by the same prevailing key signature as notes on the staff and can, like notes, carry their own accidentals. They are thus not an independent type of notation but a hybrid representation of interval/pitch that works in conjunction with staff notation. Its purpose is to indicate the harmonies implied by a bass line (even absence of figuring has a meaning) while at the same time leaving the player free to choose the precise notes to be played. The systems of letters and figures used by jazz musicians have this same imprecision; they are less dependent upon conjunction with staff notation but lack clear rhythmic significance unless allied to staff notation in at least a simplified form. They operate by defining a harmony in relation to the tonic chord (the chord built on the key note, or tonic) rather than by interval or pitch.

Evolution of Western staff notation. *Neumes.* Staff notation has its roots in the neumatic notations of plainchant and secular song of the 9th–12th century. Neumes were graphic signs indicating essentially the rise and fall of the voice. Their origin lies probably 1,000 years earlier in signs devised by Greek and Roman grammarians to guide declamation, such as ⁄ *acutus* (high voice), ∖ *gravis* (low), and ∧ *circumflexus* (falling). The musical adaptations of these signs took many different regional forms. Unlike note symbols in staff notation, neumes, with two exceptions, comprised two, three, four, or more notes each and indicated their approximate relative pitches. Each comprised the notes belonging to a single syllable of text, though in florid chant the notes of a single syllable might be split up into several neumes:

Neumes were only a memory aid to singers who knew words and melody by heart. Between the 10th and 12th centuries, however, there occurred significant developments toward a notation that could be sight-read. "Heighted," or "diastematic," neumes were spaced on the page in relation to each other, so that an entire line of them formed a continuous graph of pitch over the words of text:

Sight-reading developments

Eventually, precision of pitch was further achieved by using horizontal scratched lines as a grid on which to space the neumes, so that degrees of the scale fell alternately on a line or in a space, and by colouring one line red to signify the pitch F and possibly another yellow to signify C—or by placing a letter F or C at the beginning of the appropriate line. Together, the two devices fixed the relative pitches of all notes by indicating where the semitones of the scale occurred (that is, immediately below the marked lines: E–F or B♮–C). In the 11th century two signs from a quite different system of notation (alphabetical notation; see below) were incorporated as accidentals before the pitch "B": b, the ancestor of ♭; ♮, the ancestor of ♮ and ♯, and also of the German "h," which refers to b♮. These two signs were progressively applied to other pitches in the following centuries. By the 13th century a four-line staff ruled entirely in black or red had become established, using stylized forms of the letters *f, c,* and *g* (ancestors of the modern 𝄢, 𝄡, and 𝄞) as clefs. For polyphonic music a five-line staff became standard by the 14th century, but keyboard music in some countries used six- or seven-line staves as late as the mid-17th century.

Adoption of the five-line staff

During the 12th century, in northern and northeastern France the thin, curved lines of neumes were drawn more thickly at the points corresponding to the separate notes within them. In time, a firmly rectilinear notation of heavy horizonal pen strokes, diamond-shaped dots, and hairline vertical strokes emerged, whose groups of notes are called "ligatures":

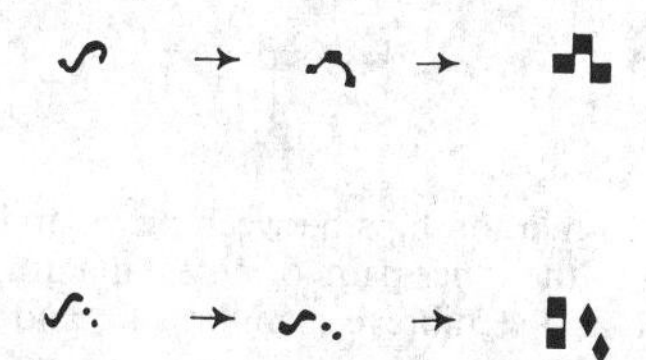

This was the notation of the troubadours' and trouvères' songs; also of plainchant from the 13th century to the present day. It was also used in 12th-century polyphony for the upper voices, which were without text. Freed from syllabic considerations, the grouping of notes into ligatures took on rhythmic significance, specific groupings representing short, repeated patterns called rhythmic modes:

A = 6/8 (trochaic metre)

B = 6/8 (iambic metre)

A ligature did not yet have a single, unvarying meaning. Its rhythmic pattern depended upon context.

Mensural notation. The freeing of ligatures from considerations of context occurred during the early 13th century. Time values for ligatures, single notes, and rests were codified around 1260 by the influential theorist Franco of Cologne. The notes then in use included the duple long, later called maxima ( ); long ( ); breve (■); and semibreve (◆). In French music a shorter note value was created: the minim ( ).

These note symbols provided the basis for notation from the late 13th to the late 15th century. This system, called mensural notation, was based on several fundamental principles that determined the value of a note relative to that of its neighbours. In the terminology of mensural notation a given note might be either perfect—*i.e.,* divided into three notes of the next lesser time value; or imperfect—*i.e.,* divided into two notes of the next lesser value. Thus, as in part (a) of the example below, a long might be perfect, containing three breves; or imperfect, containing two breves.

(a) imperfect = + ; perfect = + +

To determine which note symbols were perfect and imperfect for a given piece, special symbols were devised: , , , , , $\frac{3}{2}$, $\frac{3}{1}$, $\frac{4}{3}$, etc. (Of these C and ¢ survive, together with fractions such as $\frac{3}{2}$, as modern time signatures.)

Specific rules provided for lengthening or shortening the value of notes in certain instances. To "imperfect" a long meant to shorten it by one-third of its value; this occurred when the long was preceded or followed by a breve or by notes equalling a breve in value, as shown in part (b) of the example below (for purposes of illustration, numbers have been placed under the notes showing their time value relative to the shortest note). Part (c) of the example shows another common alteration of time value: in a composition in which the long is perfect, a breve (brevis) preceding it may be doubled in value under certain conditions.

(b) 3 but 2 - 1 or 1 - 2

(c) 1 - 2 - 3

The time-value relationships between breve and long similarly applied to the other pairs of notes: maxima and long (longa); breve and semibreve (semibrevis); and semibreve and minim (minima).

As the system of mensural notation evolved, another device, coloration, came into use. If a composer wished to render a potentially perfect note imperfect, he could write it in red or as a hollow note (as , , or); these two devices had, however, various other, less common meanings. About 1400, hollow note shapes were adopted where full black notes had hitherto been used, and full black served as coloration. The notes then current and their corresponding rests were as follows:

Transition to modern staff notation. In 16th-century manuscripts and, later, in printed music, the diamond-headed notes became rounded. Ligatures were used less often in the later 15th century. The principles of perfection and imperfection gave way to the modern relationship of 2 to 1 between adjacent note values, with the dot adding an extra half value to give a 3 to 1 relationship.

Shorter note values were also introduced, and the old, longer ones became obsolete. Yet, because of a paradoxical survival from 15th-century practice, slow music has tended to be written in short values (*e.g.*, Beethoven's slow movements) and fast music in long values.

Introduction of the bar line

The bar line as a measure of metre arose first in 15th-century tablatures (notation showing playing position rather than pitch, as for lute). Barring entered staff notation in the 17th century, but regularly spaced barring became a practice only in the 18th century. Separate tempo indications, arising first in the 17th century, were verbally expressed; for example, adagio, largo, presto. The range of these terms greatly increased during the 18th and 19th centuries, and the metronome mark, an absolute indication of tempo, has never superseded them since its arrival in Beethoven's day. The bulk of the shorthand devices emerged during the 17th century, figured bass early in the century, the majority of ornamental signs later. Indications for loud and soft arose early in the century, expressed as words (forte, mezzoforte, piano) and later as abbreviations (*f, mf, p*). Graphic signs for dynamic and attack (staccato dot, crescendo mark, for example, and also phrase marking) appeared in the 18th century. A great proliferation of dynamic instructions and signs occurred in the late 19th and early 20th centuries.

20th-century notation. Two developments in musical style in the 20th century have placed great strain upon staff notation: integral serialism—in which the music is controlled by a mathematical system—and indeterminacy, or chance music. In the former, every note in a texture may have its individual dynamic marking and type of attack (for example, in Olivier Messiaen's *Mode de valeurs et d'intensités* and in parts of *Structures I* and *II* of Pierre Boulez). There may also be extensive use of unconventional playing techniques. Since staff notation indicates volume, attack, and technical effects in a comparatively clumsy manner, the written page becomes cluttered and unclear. In indeterminate and aleatory music (the latter type allowing the performer a limited degree of freedom), the notation must offer choices to the performer or be deliberately imprecise. Staff notation is for these purposes often too specific. In addition, electronic music, composed with such devices as graphs, mathematical symbols, and diagrams, is not easily translated into a readable "score" for publication.

Notation that offers the performer a choice

New systems. Notation, in face of this, has moved in two directions: toward adaptation of staff notation and

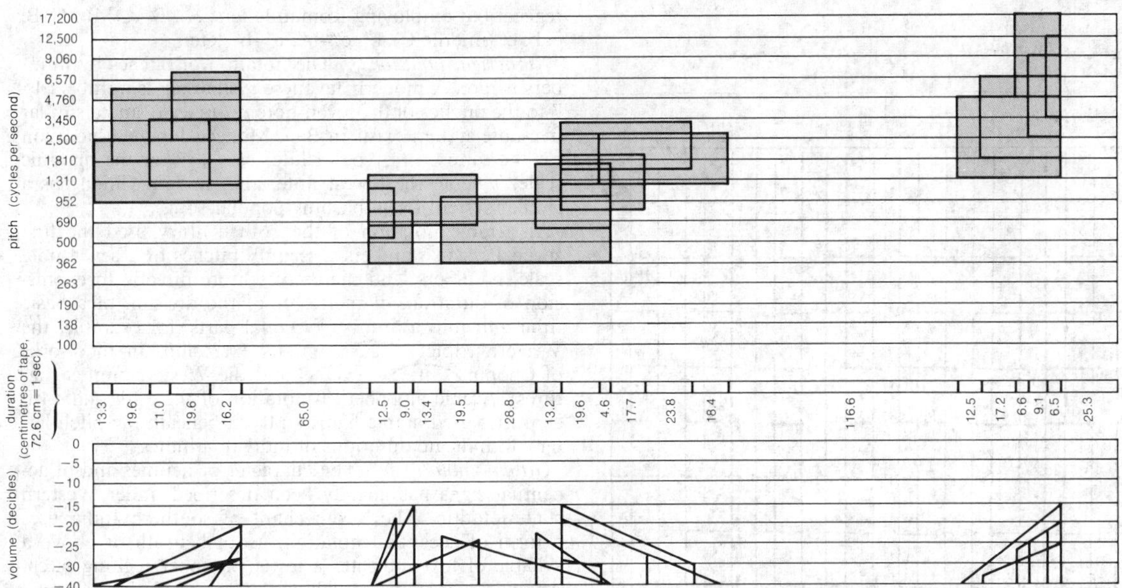

Page from the score of Stockhausen's *Electronic Study No. 2.*

toward the devising of new notational systems. Music using microtonal intervals (less than a semitone) has tended to adapt by modifying the standard accidental signs—meaning one-third sharp, two-thirds sharp, and so on (*e.g.,* in Krzysztof Penderecki's *Anaklasis*). So-called space time notation is a further adaptation that reasserts the graphic nature of staff notation. It abandons symbolic indication of note values and replaces it by the spacing of note heads horizontally on the staff, accompanied by an instruction such as "1 inch = 1 second." The principle may then be amplified by using different note heads (○, □, ◇, etc.) to signify short, medium, and long sustaining of a note, thus obviating the use of rests, and by beaming together notes to be performed in one breath or bow (*e.g.,* Witold Lutosławski's *Trois poèmes d'Henri Michaux* and John Cage's *Music of Changes*).

Indeterminacy. Indeterminate music requires constant experimentation with notation. A composer may offer directions for one element of the music—as rhythm or pitch contour—and leave the performer to improvise the remaining elements. Or he may simply describe the general character of a passage by resorting to a specially designed symbol, a verbal description, or even an impressionistic drawing (as in Earle Brown's *Hodograph*). At the extreme, John Cage supplies "materials" (lines, dots, shapes) and leaves the performer to attach musical significance to them. For electronic music, published scores have so far adopted either strict graph form (Karlheinz Stockhausen, *Electronic Study II*) or pictorial form, using patterned drawings to represent different timbres (as in Henri Pousseur's *Electre* and Stockhausen's *Kontakte*).

Cage's "materials"

Page from the score of *Electre* by Henri Pousseur.

Adaptation to non-European music. Notations evolve with the musical styles they serve, and they reflect the underlying aesthetics of their own cultures. Thus staff notation is ill-equipped to cope with non-Western scales and tunings, with music to which the idea of the "note" (a stable, sustained pitch) is foreign, or with music whose subtlety lies as much in delicate gradations of volume or timbre as in pitch and rhythm. Ethnomusicologists have developed a range of supplementary symbols—*e.g.,* for notes of uncertain pitch, glissandi (slides), slight lengthening of a value, half-voiced notes, and other sounds. They have also experimented with staves of fewer or more lines. The Western system of proportional note values (for example, quarter note = half of a half note) does not easily cope with fine fluctuations of value; instead, constant changes of metronome tempo mark may be necessary. Among the most complex uses of staff notation in ethnomusicology are the transcriptions of Serbo-Croatian and Romanian folk song by the Hungarian composer Béla Bartók. Other transcribers have used graph paper to draw a curve of pitch against time. Many significant mechanical methods of transcription have been devised. The two most notable are the melograph, invented by the ethnomusicologist Charles Seeger, which traces a pitch/time graph immediately above a volume/time graph, and a device developed by Dahlbeck, which produces two similar graphs by means of a cathode-ray tube. These methods can reveal a level of interpretation by the performer that aural transcription into staff notation fails to bring out.

Other systems of notation. Written notations are to be found in the musical cultures of the Far East, Southeast Asia, South Asia, the Middle East, and the West. Early examples survive from Ancient Egypt and Greece. Notation may be classified into two broad categories: phonetic symbols—words, syllables, abbreviations of these, letters, and numbers; and graphic signs—accentual signs for the rise and fall of the voice (developing into neumelike "ecphonetic" signs), curves, lines, dots, and other symbols, perhaps originally depicting hand signs, and neumes. Symbols in both categories may denote simple sounds or stand for groups of successive sounds. In the West they are read in lines from left to right, whereas in the Orient many are read from right to left or vertically, in columns.

Major categories of notational systems

A second fundamental distinction is that between representational notations, which depict the sound of the music—leaving the player to produce that sound as he wishes—and tablatures, which instruct a player as to the technical means of producing a sound. Phonetic symbols play an important role in both types of notation, while graphic signs contribute mainly to representational nota-

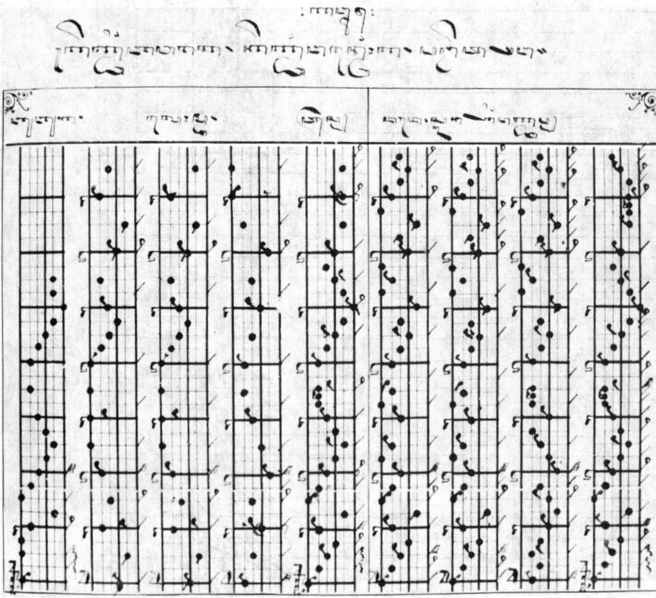

Javanese *kraton* notation.

From Mantle Hood, "Music the Unknown" in Harrison, Hood, and Palisca *Musicology* (1963); reproduced by permission of Prentice-Hall, Inc.

tions. A prime example of non-Western representational notation is the *kraton* notation used in music for the Javanese gamelan orchestra, its grid using the "graph" principle found also in Western staff notation but oriented at a 90° angle relative to the latter.

Verbal and syllabic notations. In oral traditions of music, solmization (the naming of each degree of a basic scale with a word or syllable) plays an important role. The modern European sol-fa method ("do," "re," "mi," etc., representing the notes of the rising major scale at any pitch transposition) is such a system. The Indian syllables *ṣa, ṛi, ga, ma, pa, dha, ni* are similar; as are the Balinese *ding, dong, deng, dung, dang*; the ancient five-note Chinese scale *kung, shang, chiao, chih, yü*; and the Korean *tŭng, tung, tang, tong, ting.* Slightly different are the 12 chromatic Chinese *lü* syllables: each pitch bears the name of a bell—as *huang chung* ("yellow bell"), *ling chung* ("forest bell")—and its name is reduced to a syllable—*huang, ling, t'ai,* etc. Though primarily for reciting or singing as a melody is being learned, these syllables can be used to write down the notes of a melodic line (each appearing as a single ideogram in the Chinese examples) and thus form a simple syllabic pitch notation. Of the five Balinese syllables, only their vowels are used in written form—*i, o, e, u, a*—so that a letter notation results; this is still essentially an abbreviated syllabic notation, not an alphabetical notation.

Notation for duration

Words and syllables are not only applied to pitch. In Western plainchant, abbreviated words were used to indicate duration (for example, *c* = *cito* or *celeriter* = "short" value) and direction of melodic movement (*l* = *levare,* and *s* = *sursum* = "upward"). In the notation of early Ethiopian church music a single letter or a pair of letters (short for a passage of text) signified a group of notes, even a complete melodic phrase. The drum syllables of North Indian music are a solmization of timbre (as *na, ta, dhin*) and often also of rhythmic patterns (as *tirikita, dhagina*) and can be written down to make a notation.

Alphabetical notations. Alphabets are historically a phenomenon of the Middle East, Europe, and the Indian subcontinent. Their ordering of letters provides a convenient reference system for the notes of musical scales in ascending or descending order. Alphabetical notations are among the most ancient musical scripts. Two Greek notations were of this type, the earlier using an archaic alphabet and the latter using the Classical Greek alphabet. Many comparable notations arose in the Middle Ages, and the modern note names, A to G, are an outgrowth of these.

The clefs of staff notations are a formalized survival. The system of pitch notation devised by the 19th-century German philosopher and scientist Hermann Helmholtz was derived from the Greek system, using dashes for octave register but employing Roman letters: A,,, B,,, C,–B,, C–B, c–b, c′ (middle C)–b′, c″–b″, c‴–b‴, etc.

Numerical notations. The notation of pitches by numbers is rare. A modern Javanese system allots numbers 1–7 to the pitches of the seven-note *pelog* scale, and a similar five-note system exists in Bali. Modern Japanese notation for the samisen (a type of lute) uses 1–7 for the diatonic scale, 7 being the lowest note; and modern China has a similar system for publishing popular songs.

From William P. Malm, *Japanese Music*; reproduced by permission of Charles E. Tuttle Co., Inc., Tokyo

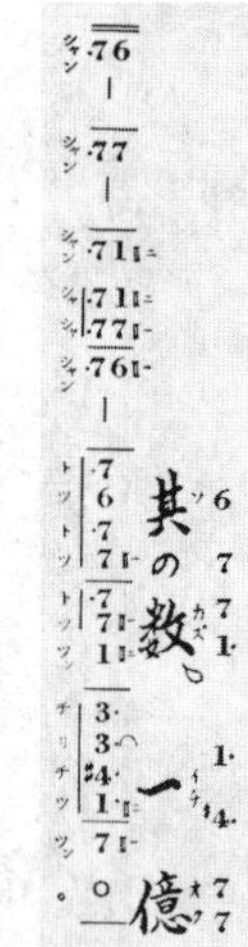

Notation for Japanese samisen from the piece *Tsuru kame.*

An Arabic notation of the 16th century used the first seven Persian numbers to signify pitches of a seven-note scale. Numbers lend themselves more directly to expression of duration, of metre, or of the division of a basic time unit into a number of equal parts (for example, the Western triplet 3 and its extensions in the works of Chopin 11 21; and the Western time signatures). Arabic alphabetical notation of the 13th and 14th centuries used arabic figures, placed beneath the pitch letters, to indicate durations of individual notes.

Graphic notations. The character of neumes and of accentual signs has already been described under Western staff notation. The Vedic chant of southern India uses a form of accentual notation: a dot beneath or above a syllable of text indicates a lower or upper reciting pitch. Analogous systems, involving dots and dashes, formed a notation for ancient Jewish cantillation and for early Syrian Christian chanting. Such signs are really only an extension of punctuation. A more developed form ("ecphonetic" notation) was used for recitation of Byzantine liturgical chants. In addition to simple signs for vocal inflection, it had also more elaborate, compound signs, such as

capable of signifying degrees of loudness and changes of voice production. The Western phrase mark and crescendo and decrescendo symbols are graphic signs of this type.

The dividing line between compound ecphonetic signs and neumes is slender. Neumes are concerned not with inflection of the voice between high, medium, and low but with groups of sung pitches rising and falling over a quite narrow range: a neume may represent a given pattern of intervals whether it lies high or low in the voice's compass. Neumes made up of curves, hooks, lines, and dots are found in Tibetan Buddhist chant books; in vocal notations for Japanese Buddhist chant, Nō plays, and *gagaku* (court music); and, in simplified form, they are used in Chinese notation in conjunction with pitch syllables.

From W. Kaufmann, *Musical Notations of the Orient* (© 1967); reproduced by permission of Indiana University Press

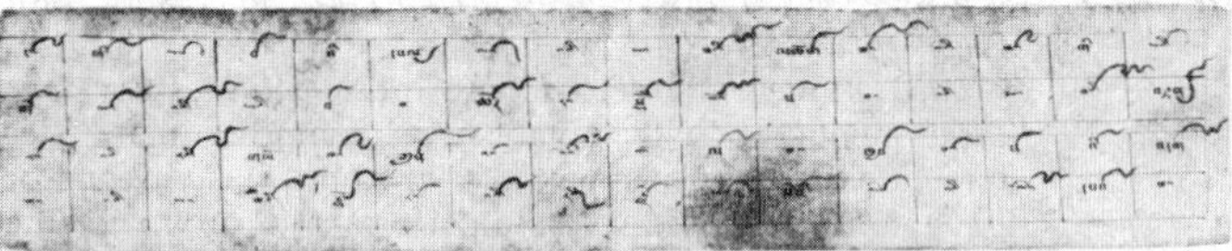

Neumes for a Tibetan Buddhist chant.

Tablatures. A tablature notates music as a series of playing positions. Hence a tablature for a plucked stringed instrument guides the player's fingers to the string he

By courtesy of Todaiji, Nara, Japan

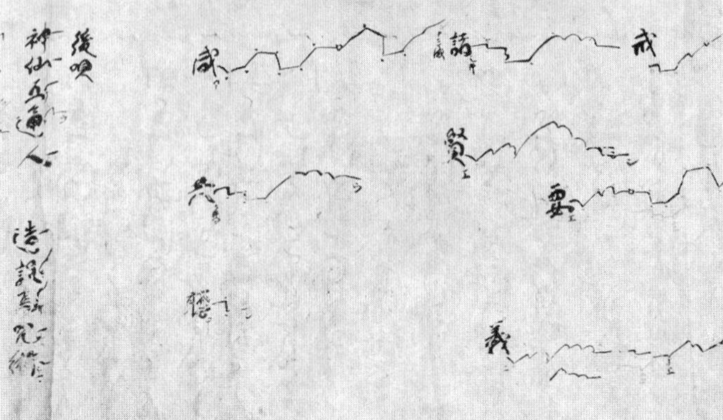

Neume notation from the third part of the psalm of Upāli.

must pluck and to the fret at which the string should be stopped. Similarly, a tablature for a wind instrument guides a player's fingers to cover certain holes, and a tablature for percussion directs a player as to which drum to strike, which hand and stick to use, and what type of stroke to execute. Each single instruction in a tablature corresponds to one action by the performer. The order of his actions is automatically prescribed, and more precise rhythmic indication can be given quite easily as the length of time between successive actions—rests are unnecessary. Thus, a tablature for a plucked instrument requires signs for: each string, each fret, and possibly also each right-hand plucking finger, direction of stroke, and ancillary techniques such as harmonics, vibrato, and left-hand plucking. To indicate these, the tablature may use letters, numbers, and graphic signs. Thus 16th-century French lute tablatures indicate the strings (more properly the "courses") graphically as parallel horizontal lines, frets as letters, and right-hand fingering by dots:

From Francis Pilkington, Brian Jeffrey (ed.), *Complete Works for Solo Lute* (1970); by permission of Oxford University Press, London

Italian lute tablatures use numbers in place of letters.

The tablature for the Japanese koto zither is simpler in that its 13 strings are not stopped. The pitch of each string is indicated at the beginning of a tablature, and thereafter the strings are represented by numbers combined with graphic signs for special technical effects. The tablature for the Chinese *ch'in,* a zither whose strings are stopped, uses a combination of numbers (for strings and for stopping points) and ideograms (for other technical details). These are grouped close together in composite symbols. One composite symbol may contain an ideogram for the left-hand finger; a number for the stopping-point; another number for the string itself; an ideogram for the right-hand finger; and possibly an ideogram indicating loudness, legato, glissando, etc. German 16th-century lute tablature achieved economy of space by indicating string and fret as a single letter (as, k = first string stopped at third fret). No grid of lines was necessary. (I.Be.)

From Mantle Hood, "Music the Unknown" in Harrison, Hood, and Palisca, *Musicology* (1963); reproduced by permission of Prentice-Hall, Inc.

Tablature for the Chinese *ch'in.*

HISTORY OF WESTERN COMPOSITIONAL TECHNIQUES

Societal perspectives. Whether referring to the process or to the completed work, composition implies the creation of a unique musical event that may or may not be based on original musical materials. At certain cultural levels and in many non-Western societies, unique performance characteristics tend to assume greater significance than composition itself. In oral traditions, related variants of common origin often take the place of unalterable musical entities, so that tune families rather than single autonomous tunes form the collective repertoire. Where certain patterns of musical structure have gained broad recognition (as the ragas, or melody types, of India), musicians will as a rule rework such patterns extemporaneously though in accordance with prevailing conventions.

Oral tradition

European music was communicated orally well into the Middle Ages and received important stimuli from a variety of oral traditions even after musical notation had developed to a high degree of precision. Indeed, the lower population strata, especially in rural areas, never abandoned the relative freedom that comes from reliance on the ear alone, and the sophisticated music of the upper strata, throughout its rapid evolution, rarely severed its connection with folk music altogether. Ultimately, the process of composition, as seen by the American musicologist Alan P. Merriam, does "not seem to differ radically between literate and non-literate peoples save in the question of writing." As a conscious act of social communication it always "involves learning, is subject to public acceptance and rejection, and is therefore a part of the broad learning process which contributes, in turn, to the processes of stability and change." Whether explicitly or not, composition is thus subject to rules that represent the stylistic consensus of a specific segment of society at a given stage of cultural development. During the Middle Ages, when man's natural instincts were held in particularly low esteem, musical compositions were often judged primarily in terms of their adherence to the rules. Hence, the supreme authority in matters musical was the *musicus* as theorist; only he was considered sufficiently conversant with musical science to vouchsafe its continued existence as the sonorous embodiment of universal truths. And it was because the metaphysical properties of numbers were allegedly embedded in the rules of composition that music, on a par with arithmetic, geometry, and astronomy, attained and retained an honorable place as a constituent member of the quadrivium, the more exalted of the two divisions of the seven liberal arts. Characteristically, music was not classified with grammar, rhetoric, and logic, the "rhetorical arts" gathered in the trivium. About 1300, musical composition as a mere craft was ranked by Johannes de Grocheo, a shrewd observer of the Parisian musical scene, with shoemaking and tanning.

Development of composition in the Middle Ages. The European written tradition, largely because it evolved under church auspices, de-emphasized rhythmic distinctiveness long after multipart music had superseded the monophonic plainchant. But multipart music might never have gone beyond the most primitive stages of counterpoint (see above *Counterpoint*) had it not been for the application of organized rhythm to musical structure in the late Middle Ages. This era witnessed the emergence of basic polyphonic concepts identified with European art music ever since. The precise measurement of musical time was simply an indispensable prerequisite for compositions in which separate, yet simultaneously sounded, melodic entities were combined in accordance with the medieval theorists' rules of consonance (specifying the proper intervals to be used between voice parts, especially at points of musical repose). Toward the end of the 1st millennium of the Christian Era, church singers had grown accustomed to enhancing their chants through organum (see above *Harmony*). "Parallel" organum was followed, in turn, by "free" organum, which allowed the synchronized voice parts to utilize contrary melodic motion.

The decisive relationship between text and melody in early European music led to stylistic distinctions that have survived the ages. Thus, "syllabic" denotes a setting where one syllable corresponds to one note; "melismatic" refers to a phrase or composition employing several distinct pitches for the vocalization of a single syllable. Late medieval composers made clever use of these distinctions, including an intermediate "neumatic" style (Greek *pneuma,* "breath") to create ever more extensive polyphonic pieces. By the 12th century musicians at Notre-Dame in Paris, led by Léonin, the first polyphonic composer known by name, cultivated a type of melismatic organum that featured a highly florid upper part above a slow moving cantus firmus taken from a suitable plainchant melody. The melismatic sections alternated with strictly measured, or "discant," sections. This very effective procedure possibly was inspired by Middle Eastern practices with which the crusaders must have been well acquainted. In Eastern music, the rhythmically measured portions following the virtuoso singer's florid "outpouring of the soul" are nearly always played or at least supported by instruments. In the 13th century the clausula, a short, textless composition in discant style, tended to be dancelike in its systematic sectionalization, strongly suggesting instrumental derivation if not necessarily actual performance. The motet, a major genre of the medieval and Renaissance eras, was in its 13th-century form essentially a texted clausula, frequently employing two or three different texts in as many languages. This fact merely reinforces the suspicion that little distinction was made between vocal and instrumental composition in an era that so blithely based dancelike settings of erotic, in a few instances outright obscene, texts on a chant-derived cantus firmus. The point is not without its broader ramifications. For, brought up largely on 19th-century notions about the "purity" of church music, one easily overlooks the fact that even Bach and Mozart had few compunctions about the use of secular—in their cases mostly operatic—styles and specific tunes in church music. Over the centuries, the church has been the most important employer of composers and has offered far greater outlets for newly created music than any other social institution or category. Thus, composers of sacred music have had to satisfy the aesthetic needs and expectations of its highly differentiated "public." The church in turn repeatedly permitted the adaptation of promising secular types of composition, even though instrumental music, because of its more lascivious associations, remained suspect well into the 17th century.

Rhythmic contrast as a structural device

In accordance with medieval tendencies generally, Gothic polyphonic music was conceived in loosely connected separate layers. Thus, two-part motets could be converted into three-part motets, and Léonin's successor Pérotin expanded the organum to three and four parts. Inevitably, as their compositions gained in length and depth, musicians began to search for new integrative procedures. A system of six rhythmic modes (short, repeated rhythmic patterns) evolved rapidly. Pérotin used a single rhythmic mode for the multiple upper parts of his organums so that, separated from their cantus firmus, they resembled the conductus, a syllabic setting of a sacred text for two or three voices sharing the same basic rhythm. Finally, as organum faded into history, conductus-type motets were composed outright. Most prominent among the devices used to achieve structural integration in the 13th century were *color,* or melodic repetition without regard to rhythmic organization; *talea,* or rhythmic repetition without regard to pitch organization; and ostinato, or repetition of a relatively brief melodic-rhythmic pattern. Exchanges of melodic phrases between two or more parts in turn led to canon, a form in which all voice parts are derived from one tune—either by strict imitation of the basic melody or by manipulations stipulated in often quite sophisticated verbal instructions (canon = law). For instance, the canon *Ma fin est mon commencement (My End Is My Beginning*), by Guillaume de Machaut, the leading French composer of the 14th century, demands the simultaneous performance of a melody and its retrograde version (the notes are sung in reverse order). French musicians of the 14th century were particularly partial tomisorhythm, which refers to repetition of the rhythmic organization of all the voices in a given compositional segment. It enjoyed considerable popularity for more than 100 years.

Melodic and rhythmic manipulation

Meanwhile, though somewhat eclipsed historically by the increasingly abstract nature of polyphony, the primacy of poetry was safeguarded in 13th-century music by the troubadours of southern France and their northern counterparts, the trouv̀gres, as well as the German Minnesingers. These noble poet-composers created a rich tradition of purely monophonic secular song that furnished convenient points of departure for much of the secular polyphonic music in both 14th-century France and 15th-century Germany. By the beginning of the 15th century, European music had also begun to feel the impact of English music. The English emphasis on the rich sonorities of the third and sixth provided welcome relief from the aesthetic consequences of the earlier continental dedication to the "perfect" intervals of the octave, fourth, and fifth. Because the perfect intervals were also those formed by the lowest pitches of the harmonic overtone series, their "naturalness" had long been an unassailable theoretical axiom.

Impact of English music

Late 14th-century French secular music literally lost itself in rhythmic complexities without any substantive changes in the basic compositional approach, which continued to favour relatively brief three-part settings of lyrical poetry. But in the ensuing 15th century the simpler melodic and rhythmic ideas associated with the rich harmonies of the English style were eagerly embraced; often melodies were outright triadic in contour; *i.e.,* they outlined the intervals of the triad, an increasingly important chord composed of two linked thirds (*e.g.,* C-E-G). But the truly amazing stylistic development from the influential English composer John Dunstable to Josquin des Prez, the Flemish composer who stands at the apex of his era, was equally indebted to the flowing cantilenas, or lyric melodies, that characterized the top parts of Italian trecento music. If the French music of the waning Middle Ages was structured essentially from the bottom up, with relatively angular melodic and rhythmic patterns above the two-dimensional substructure of tenor and countertenor, its Italian counterparts were quite often monodically conceived; *i.e.,* a highly singable tune was sparingly yet effectively supported by a single lower voice. Indeed, the passion for melody, if need be to the detriment of other musical elements, has been a constant of Italian music. It sparked the *nuove musiche,* or "new music," of about 1600 and is exemplified in innumerable works of composers as diverse as Claudio Monteverdi (1567–1643) and Luigi Dallapiccola (1904–75). But it found its first major artistic expression in the city-states of northern Italy during the lifetimes of such 14th-century literary figures as Giovanni Boccaccio and Petrarch.

Composition in the Renaissance. During the latter part of the 15th century, French rhythmic sophistication, Italian cantilena, and English harmony finally found common ground in the style of Renaissance polyphony that, under the aegis of Flemish musicians, dominated Europe for nearly two centuries. Often referred to as modal because it retained the medieval system of melodic modes, Flemish polyphony was characterized by a highly developed sense of structure and textural integration. Although the older cantus firmus technique was never totally abandoned, Renaissance polyphony is identified above all with imitative part writing, inspired no doubt by earlier canonic procedures but devoid of their structural limitations. After a canonic or freely imitational beginning, each of the subunits of such a polyphonic piece proceeds unfettered by canonic restrictions, yet preserves the fundamental equality of the melodic lines in accordance with contrapuntal rules amply discussed by various 15th- and 16th-century theorists and ultimately codified by the Italian theorist

Gioseffo Zarlino. Through the works of Giovanni da Palestrina, the model composer of the Catholic Counter-Reformation, Renaissance modal counterpoint has influenced the teaching of musical composition to the present, suggesting the near perfection with which it conveys some fundamental aspects of the historic European ideal of composition as the art of lasting musical structures.

Whereas imitative polyphony affected virtually all 16th-century music, modal counterpoint was paramount in sacred pieces, specifically the motet and mass, probably because of its close kinship with the traditional modality of liturgical plainchant. In contrast, the beginnings of functional harmony (chordal relationships governed by primary and secondary tonal centres) manifested themselves first in the polyphonic French chanson; its Italian counterpart, the madrigal; and related secular types. Under the influence of less sophisticated music, such as that of the Italian frottola, a popular vocal genre, these secular polyphonic genres favoured rather simple bass lines highlighting a limited number of related harmonies. Thus, undisturbed by the theoretical writings from the pens of church-employed musicians, secular musical practice in the later Renaissance laid the foundations for the harmonic notions that were to dominate three centuries of Western art music. The increasing emotionalism of texts taken from the leading Italian poet of the 16th century, Torquato Tasso, and his immediate successors acted as a further stimulant, as Italian composers, searching for appropriate musical symbols, discovered the expressive possibilities of chordal progressions.

Changing conceptions of harmony

The Baroque period. Inevitably, the strong desire for heightened expression through harmony led at first to new, mostly chromatic, chord progressions. Eventually it precipitated the total abandonment of traditional polyphony about 1600 in the monodic experiments of the Florentine Camerata, a group of aristocratic connoisseurs seeking to emulate the Greek drama of antiquity. The accompaniment for these passionate and heroic solo recitations is based on a simple basso continuo. Only the bass part was written down; it was played by low, sustaining instruments bowed or blown, while plucked or keyboard instruments supplied the chords suggested by the bass and melody lines. The small figures used to indicate the proper harmonies gave the system the alternative name figured bass. Monody had its historical antecedents in mid-16th-century solo lute songs and in the plentiful arrangements of polyphonic vocal compositions for single voices accompanied by plucked instruments and for solo keyboard instruments. But it was the attempt to resurrect the spirit of antique drama in the late Renaissance that created the textural revolution that has been equated with the beginnings of modern music: the monodic style with its polarity of bass and melody lines and emphasis on chords superseded the equal-voiced polyphonic texture of Renaissance music. Monteverdi, the undisputed master of the monodic style, recognized the possibility of two basic approaches to composition: the first, or polyphonic, "practice" and the second, or monodic, "practice." Thus, with penetrating analytical insight he formulated the basic stylistic dialectic that has since governed the course of Western music.

Aesthetic and technical reorientation

The emergence of an essentially nonpolyphonic style went hand-in-hand with the rise of a variety of specifically instrumental idioms. Not only did accompanied vocal music offer instrumentalists various opportunities for improvisation; the basically chordal style also facilitated the emergence of virtuosity in the modern sense of the term, especially among keyboard artists. But as the singer and composer Giulio Caccini demonstrated in the preface to his influential collection *Le nuove musiche* (*The New Music;* 1602), singers, too, put their newly found freedom to good improvisational and ornamentational use. In short, after two centuries dominated by the highly structured, rationalistic polyphony of the Renaissance, the performing musician reiterated his creative rights. Inevitably, under such forceful pressures, the teaching of composition, previously tied to the laws of modal counterpoint, quickly shifted to the harmonic challenges of the figured bass.

Because the bass-oriented music of the 17th century relied primarily on chord progressions as fixed by the bass notes, it was structurally quite open-ended; *i.e.,* the new technique suited any number of formal patterns. Even so, the incipient rationalism that was to reach its peak in the 18th century soon led to the consolidation of broadly accepted structural types. Indeed, the very concept of musical "form," as generally understood from the late 17th century on, was intimately tied to the growing importance of instrumental music, which, in the absence of a text, had nothing to rely upon save its own organically developed laws. At least for a while, vocal music, which had been so largely responsible for the monodic revolution, continued to adhere to the Monteverdian principle that the words must act as "the mistress of harmony." Both melody and harmony, therefore, reflected often minute affective textual differentiations. And as late as the early 18th century similar musico-rhetorical considerations led to *Affektenlehre,* the theory of musical affects (emotions, feelings), developed primarily in Germany. Following this theory, German musicians dealt with composition systematically in terms of a specific but broadly adopted expressive vocabulary of melodic, rhythmic, and harmonic figures. Meanwhile, the Italians laid the foundations for such lasting categories of instrumental music as the symphony, the sonata, and the concerto. In each instance the structural outline was harmonically determined through juxtapositions of principal key areas acting as focal centres of tonality. As for tempo, the earliest 17th-century solo sonatas had relied on drastic short-range changes in accordance with a general predilection for "instant sensations." Subsequently, as musical composition fell in line with the prevailing rationalistic trend, tempo served above all as a means of differentiation between the various movements, or self-contained sections, that constituted the large-scale works of the Italian string school and of French and German instrumental composers as well. Texture, too, was used to provide contrast, particularly within a given movement, as in the concerto grosso with its alternation between small and large groups of players (concertino and tutti).

Emotional expressiveness

Interrelated with the spectacular rise and amazing vitality of instrumental music was its unprecedented variety. By the early 18th century, composers drew freely upon everything from contrapuntal forms like the fugue (an adaptation of the imitative techniques of the Renaissance motet within the context of functional harmony) to stylized popular dances, such as those that make up the suites and partitas of J.S. Bach. The figured bass era took full advantage of the possibilities of variety and contrast through judicious manipulations of all elements of composition. Whereas accompanied solo music pitted bass against treble (the latter often split up into two parts, as in the trio sonata), composers generally liked to juxtapose figured bass and polyphonic textures. Melodically, the far-flung phrases of Italian bel canto, the florid singing style characteristic of opera seria (17th- and 18th-century tragic opera), had little in common with the concise, symmetrically balanced phrases found in music of popular inspiration, whether in opera buffa (Italian comic opera) or the many types of dances. As for the latter, their impact on sophisticated 18th-century music is evident not only in many dance-inspired arias and concerto movements but also in certain polyphonic compositions. Both the chaconne and passacaglia, related polyphonic types, were based on dancelike ostinato patterns, often with specific harmonic implications. Perhaps the most famous example is Bach's "Chaconne" for solo violin, which concludes the *Partita in D Minor.*

Even though the Baroque preoccupation with style worked somewhat to the detriment of structural definition, certain closed forms did gradually emerge. The da capo aria distinguished clearly between an initial section (A), a contrasting section (B), and the repeat (da capo) of the initial section, as a rule with improvised vocal embellishment. In instrumental music, the French opera overture began with a slow, stately introduction followed by a fast, often fugal movement, whereas its Italian counterpart had a tripartite fast-slow-fast scheme. Dance-based suite movements were binary in outline: the first of the two sections, each separately repeated, moved to the dom-

Major structural developments of the Baroque

inant key (a fifth above the tonic or principal key) or to the relative key (*i.e.*, a minor third above the tonic in the case of a minor key); the second section, after some modulatory activity (*i.e.*, passing through several key areas), returned to the central key. Even more decisive in its far-reaching historical consequences was the structural organization of a number of the keyboard "sonatas" of the composer Domenico Scarlatti. These works consisted of single, essentially binary movements, the first section of which differentiated not only between two key areas but two contrasting thematic ideas as well.

The Classical period. The Classical era in music is compositionally defined by the balanced eclecticism of the late 18th- and early 19th-century Viennese "school" of Haydn, Mozart, Beethoven, and Schubert, who completely absorbed and individually fused or transformed the vast array of 18th-century textures and formal types. Expansion of the tripartite Italian overture had produced the basic three-movement scheme of the symphony even before the 18th century reached midpoint. Shortly thereafter, the minuet, borrowed from the dance suite, was inserted with increasing frequency as a fourth movement between the slow movement and the fast finale. The French opera overture in turn lent its slow introduction where needed for structural variety. Texturally, homophony (chordal texture) and polyphony soon assumed rather specific roles, with polyphonic writing usually reserved for the central or development section of the classical first-movement form.

Integration of homophony and polyphony

The organic fusion of a number of stylistic traits previously associated with strong and immediate contrast is exemplified by the obbligato accompaniment, the texture most typical of Viennese classicism. Here the relative equality of all the melodic parts in a given composition is ensured without denying the melodic supremacy of the treble and the harmonically decisive role of the bass. The evolution of this characteristic texture can be traced in the string quartets of Haydn. At first, following earlier 18th-century custom, Haydn wrote strictly treble-dominated compositions with a simplified bass (as compared with the more varied basso continuo); then, with the six *Sun Quartets*, Opus 20, dating from the early 1770s, he defied precedent and concluded each work with a fugue in the "learned style" of Handel. Finally, in his *Russian Quartets,* Opus 33, written, in his own words, "in a new manner," Haydn achieved the fusion of elements of both the learned and the treble-dominated styles. The result was a harmonically oriented, yet polyphonically animated, texture that was to affect both instrumental and vocal ensemble music for generations. It was also at this point, when compositional procedures reached a degree of stability and universality unmatched since Renaissance polyphony, that composition began to be taken seriously as a separate musicianly discipline. Johann Joseph Fux's famous *Gradus ad Parnassum* (*Steps to Parnassus*), published first in Latin in 1725 and subsequently in every important modern language, was still basically a didactic treatise on counterpoint abstracted from 16th-century practice. As such it served its purpose throughout the 18th century, while harmony continued to be taught as the art of accompaniment—*i.e.*, the improvised realization of a figured bass. But eventually the general fascination with comprehensive knowledge, sparked by the French *Encyclopédie,* inspired at first sporadic, then ever more numerous, volumes dealing progressively with all aspects of composition. During the ensuing 19th century the rapid institutionalization of musical education in the image of the National Conservatory of Music in Paris, created while the French Revolution was still raging, added further to the academic systematization of all musical studies along lines that have essentially remained in force. Thus the teaching of musical composition reflects to this day the biases of the 19th century, specifically its concern with functional harmony as the principal generative force in music—a doctrine first proclaimed in the 1720s in the name of nature (as being consistent with the harmonic overtone series) by the composer and theorist Jean-Philippe Rameau.

Composition as an academic discipline

The Romantic period. With the onset of the Romantic era in the wake of the French Revolution, composers began to view their own role in society as well as the social function of their work, and hence also its aesthetic prerequisites, in a radically different light. With respect to social function, Beethoven was actually the first musician of stature to achieve emancipation in the sense that his work reflected, with relatively few exceptions, purely personal artistic concerns. He simply took it for granted that patrons would supply funds sufficient for him to pursue his creative career unfettered by financial worries. This attitude represents a total reversal of the basic assumptions of the preceding century, when composers were hired by and large to satisfy the musical needs of specific individuals or institutions.

The view of the composer as artist also changed. If during the Middle Ages the craft of musical composition had been evaluated largely in terms of its strict adherence to established rules, instinctiveness and spontaneity had remained suspect well into the Italian Renaissance. For a 15th-century composer-theorist like Johannes Tinctoris, the value of a musical composition depended on learned judgment as well as spontaneous reaction. Thus his admiration for certain composers of his time stemmed both from the happiness and from the enlightenment that he found in examining their music. But the Swiss theorist Henricus Glareanus, writing 70 years later, explicitly preferred natural talent to the most exquisite craftsmanship. The Renaissance was the first epoch in European intellectual history to recognize that the greatness of a composer rests upon his inherent talent and unique personal style, and that genius supersedes both experience and the observance of theoretical precepts. Likewise, it was the first era in which the process of composition was viewed as linked to powerful internal impulses. The rising tide of academicism notwithstanding, this basic attitude on the whole dominated the European scene more or less consistently from then on. According to E.T.A. Hoffmann, the early 19th-century poet, critic, and composer, "effective composition is nothing but the art of capturing with a higher strength, and fixing in the hieroglyphs of tones, what was received in the mind's unconscious *ecstasis.*" And Romantic composers from Schumann and Chopin to Hugo Wolf and Gustav Mahler did in fact produce much of their very best creative work in precisely such a state of exaltation, in a few tragic instances (*e.g.*, Schumann and Wolf) to the ultimate detriment of their sanity.

The composer as genius

The aesthetic effects of this drastic change in conception of the composer's task and potential were immediate and far reaching. For one, every large-scale composition assumed artistic significance of a type previously accorded only a whole series of works, sometimes a composer's entire output. And, concomitantly, many leading composers of the 19th century wrote in considerably smaller quantities than their predecessors. But in exchange they revelled in idiomatic and structural peculiarities even in works that nominally fell into the same formal category. Thus, although "characteristic" symphonies alluding to nonmusical ideas occurred occasionally in the late 18th century, virtually every symphonic composition postdating Beethoven's *Symphony No. 3 in E Flat Major,* Opus 55 (*Eroica;* completed 1804), could be so designated. "Characteristic" works like Beethoven's *Symphony No. 6 in F Major,* Opus 68 (*Pastoral;* 1808), or his overture to Goethe's drama *Egmont* are but one step removed from the kind of characteristic scenes that make up the *Symphonie fantastique* of the French composer Hector Berlioz or, for that matter, Felix Mendelssohn's *Hebrides* (also known as *Fingal's Cave*), an overture unrelated to any particular drama, spoken or sung. Franz Liszt, in the freewheeling forms of his symphonic poems, simply pursued the individualistic line to its ultimate consequences, severing whatever tenuous ties to traditional structures the works of his immediate predecessors had still maintained. The Romantic composer viewed himself basically as a poet who manipulated musical sounds instead of words. But if the composers catered to poetry, writing Lieder (German songs) and attempting to retell stories in instrumental works, the poets looked with awe and envy upon the composers' use of a language so utterly dissociated from material existence. "All art aspires to the condition of music," said Wordsworth. It is thus hardly surprising

Nonmusical allusions

that opera, whose extramusical connotations had in the past been responsible for some of the most daring stylistic innovations, rapidly incurred the disfavour of progressive composers. Although some, like Berlioz, Mendelssohn, and Schumann, tried their hands at an occasional opera, others, including Chopin, Liszt, and Brahms, felt no inclination whatever to compose for the stage. Instead, each developed personal idioms capable of a depth of expression that words could not match. Mendelssohn spoke indeed for many when he remarked that, as far as he was concerned, music was more precise in meaning than words.

As in the late Renaissance, harmony once again furnished the primary expressive means. In defining musical structure, too, harmonic and modulatory procedures predominated at the expense of the contrapuntal interplay of motives. Numerous Romantic composers excelled in concise forms of strong melodic-harmonic import, variously entitled Impromptu, Nocturne, Song Without Words, Ballade, Capriccio, Prelude, Étude, etc. The form of these works was nearly always tripartite, with a literal or modified repeat of the first part following a melodically and harmonically contrasting middle section. Works of larger scope often consisted of a series of relatively autonomous subunits tied together either by the same tune presented in different guises (as in variation sets) or by fairly literal recurrences of an initial musical idea (the rondo principle). Compositions of the Classical sonata-allegro type, to which motivic-contrapuntal development was essential, inevitably suffered from the Romantic love for pure, harmonically defined melody. Thus Tchaikovsky frankly admitted in 1878 that, although he could not complain of poverty of imagination or lack of inventive power, his lack of structural skill had frequently caused his "seams" to show: "there was no organic union between my individual episodes." Composers such as Tchaikovsky were indeed particularly successful with chainlike formations like the serenade or the ballet suite, which comprised a well-calculated number of carefully wrought smaller entities.

Inter-relation of aesthetic, technique, and form

In the context of functional harmony, the Classical motivic-contrapuntal approach had no doubt been exploited in the last sonatas and string quartets of Beethoven to the very limits of its potential to define musical structure. The heroic image of Beethoven as one who had overcome every possible personal and artistic difficulty to achieve the highest aims of the art assumed well-nigh traumatic proportions among 19th-century musicians. Not only did composers ill equipped both by training and artistic temperament try to emulate him, but theorists from Adolf Bernhard Marx to Vincent d'Indy based treatises on his works. Thus, unwittingly the Classical Beethovenian inheritance turned into something of an aesthetic liability for Romantic composers swayed by the image of Beethoven and unable or unwilling to face the fact that their particular talents were totally unsuited for any further capitalization of his basic compositional procedures. Confronted with the task of writing in the Beethovenian manner, a great master like Schumann, who had created the near-perfect, totally Romantic suite *Carnaval,* Opus 9 (1835), was clearly out of his element: the development of his *Symphony No. 1 in B Flat Major,* Opus 38 (*Spring;* 1841), offers a prime example of the "rhythmic paralysis" that affected so many large-scale 19th-century works. That this symphony managed nevertheless to maintain itself in the concert repertoire, on the other hand, demonstrates the extent to which the best among the German composers compensated for obvious weaknesses in handling motivic development by sustaining above all constant harmonic interest. For their part, the French, always coloristically inclined, turned instrumentation into a principal compositional resource, so that in an unadorned piano transcription Berlioz' *Symphonie fantastique* retains little more than its basic contours. That by the end of the century virtuoso instrumentation had become universal practice is attested by any work of Richard Strauss or Gustav Mahler.

Characteristically, the most unique compositional achievement of the 19th century, that of Richard Wagner, was also the most eclectic. Wagner represents the apotheosis of Romanticism in music precisely because he fused into musico-poetic structures of unprecedented proportions virtually every musical resource that went before him. Seen in this light it may be more than mere coincidence that *Tristan und Isolde,* perhaps Wagner's most perfect music drama, begins with the same four notes that make up the motivic substance of four of Beethoven's string quartets (Opuses 130–133). Unlike most instrumental composers after Beethoven, the dramatist Wagner fully assimilated the motivic-contrapuntal process, even though his texture is principally determined by strong harmonic tensions and by a masterful use of instrumental colour in the vein of Berlioz and French grand opera. Just as he integrated diverse compositional techniques, Wagner also achieved a balance of musical and poetic elements so perfect that critics, both favourable and unfavourable, have never ceased to be puzzled by its aesthetic implications. How consciously Wagner proceeded is attested not only by his numerous theoretical writings but also by compositional sketches pointing in some instances to several stages of mutual adjustments involving music and text.

Wagner's fusion of counterpoint with late Romantic harmony

The 20th century. Wagner's highly expressive harmonic bequest could not but drive chromaticism eventually beyond the retaining confines of the idea of a central key, for the extensive use of chromatic chords tends to blur the listener's ability to perceive the basic harmonic relationships that define a key. In their nontonal compositional procedures, Arnold Schoenberg and his 20th-century second Viennese school abandoned the concept of key, using all notes freely without relating them to the system of functional harmony. They thus represent not so much a reaction to as a logical extension of Wagnerian principles. Wagner's compelling artistic personality certainly exercised near-magic powers over many of his younger contemporaries and successors, exceeding even Beethoven's spell. But others, too, contributed to "the music of the future." As Schoenberg was to point out in one of his remarkable essays, even Brahms, who looked upon himself as a conservative in the best sense of the term, was, historically speaking, a true "progressive," especially in his propensity for irregular phrasing and complex motivic manipulations.

The growth of political nationalism in the "peripheral" countries of Europe also had significant repercussions in musical composition. In the last half of the 19th century distinctive folk-music elements, previously totally unheeded by Europe's elitist musical cultures, found enthusiastic response in sophisticated circles, exerting an "exotic" attraction similar to that which had accounted earlier in the century for the Romantic infatuation with Eastern civilizations. Thus at a time when the exhaustion of Europe's "civilized" compositional resources appeared imminent, the "untutored" harmonies of the Russian composer Modest Mussorgsky—steeped in the spirit of Russian folk music and based on chord progressions alien to the standard harmonic usage of his day—helped breathe new life into a harmonic language about to succumb to redundant overdoses of functional chromaticism. Mussorgsky thus paved the way for the later whole-tone and pentatonic (five-note scale) experiments of Claude Debussy and Béla Bartók.

What was being questioned publicly in many quarters at the dawn of the 20th century was the evolutionistic view of Western art music as man's ultimate achievement in the realm of sound and its logical consequent that 19th-century harmony represented in turn music's most advanced stage of development. This increasing skepticism, given by the nature of late 19th-century music itself, was strongly reinforced by the growing awareness of historical compositional techniques that resulted from the mushrooming discoveries of musicological scholarship. Before long, all manner of pre-19th-century textures and structural principles were seized upon to counteract the type of self-defeating post-Wagnerianism—so tragically exemplified in several of the most ambitious works of Max Reger. The 20th-century search for fresh, flexible techniques extended far beyond the nontonal second Viennese school of Schoenberg. In historical perspective, Anton Webern's fascination with 15th-century canonic techniques, Paul Hindemith's predilection for both modal and early-18th-century polyphony, Igor Stravinsky's emulation of

Re-application of older techniques

Domenico Scarlatti, and, for that matter, Kurt Weill's reinterpretation of John Gay's *Beggar's Opera* (1728) represent but various individual and culturally conditioned manifestations of the same determination: to put the burden of history to positive use in a concerted effort to revitalize an art that seemed moribund by the time World War I changed the socio-economic and political physiognomy of Europe.

Historically, Schoenberg's formulation of the laws of composition with 12 tones—involving the consistent melodic and harmonic use of a specifically arranged sequence of the 12 notes of the chromatic scale—sprang in the early 1920s from the same obsession with textural and structural clarity that marked the postwar Neoclassical syndrome as a whole. Schoenberg himself may have considered his most fundamental contribution to musical history to be "the emancipation of dissonance"—a relativistic conception of intervals and chords that disregarded the careful regulation of dissonance characteristic of functional harmony. Actually, the 12-tone procedures he developed so consistently served to restore, to an extent far beyond that which Mahler had been able to achieve within the traditional harmonic framework, the primacy of motivic-contrapuntal development as a musical resource. Thus it was that the profusion of simultaneous melodies that animates Mahler's *Symphony No. 4 in G Major* (completed 1900) found its ultimate potential realized in Schoenberg's most uncompromising polyphonic work, the *Wind Quintet* (1924).

Possibly the most successful attempt to regenerate Beethovenian procedures without the total abandonment of functional tonality is represented by the string quartets and certain other instrumental compositions of Bartók. Drawing upon the rhythmic-melodic properties of Hungarian and Romanian folk music, Bartók produced a unique type of functionally extended harmony determined largely by the contrapuntal interaction of motives. Others, such as Charles Ives in the United States and, under the impact of South American popular music, Darius Milhaud in France, transcended traditional tonality by writing polytonally (in two or three keys simultaneously).

Whatever their specific approach, progressive 20th-century composers everywhere clearly gave precedence to melodic-rhythmic energies. Even instrumental colour was pressed into the service of melodic definition. Years before World War I Schoenberg had advocated in practice (*Five Orchestral Pieces*) and in theory (*Harmonielehre,* 1911; *Theory of Harmony,* 1947 [the English edition omits the pertinent chapter]) the idea of tone-colour melody, or *Klangfarbenmelodie.* But it was his pupil Webern who, in his mature works, divided the individual components of melodic phrases over several instruments as an imaginatively coloristic reinforcement of the complex polyphony that characterized his style. After World War II Webern's procedures were adopted enthusiastically by composers on both sides of the Atlantic. Living in increasingly automated societies, the post-Webern composers soon discovered total serialism, a manner of composition in which all musical parameters follow numerical rules laid down in the course of what has been called the precompositional process. Whereas Schoenberg's row technique merely fixed the sequence of the 12 pitches of the chromatic scale in accordance with the motivic context of a given piece, Webern had indeed begun to serialize rhythm and to some extent instrumentation, possibly under the influence of medieval isorhythmic techniques. But total serialization, as practiced by the post-Webernians, left little, if anything, to spontaneous inspiration, and the 1950s thus witnessed the closing of a creative circle initiated during the early Middle Ages when spontaneous inspiration was manifestly suspect. Perhaps inevitably, such a hermetically closed system of composition provoked reactions that moved the aesthetic pendulum violently to the extreme opposite position. Spur-of-the-moment action became the watchword in music as well as in life generally. Aleatory (chance-music) composition in its more radical manifestations provides only minimal guidelines for performers who are told to improvise freely within certain temporal or spatial limitations, or both.

Serialization of all elements

Thus, with the 20th century in its final quarter, Western man has returned, insofar as is possible, to the pretypographical stage when musical tradition was essentially oral. More than that, the relatively recent replacement of "the public," once essentially the cultural elite, by a whole host of publics to whom mutually exclusive types of composers cater with great solicitude, suggests that the private musical life of Western man in the immediate past is in the process of being transplanted by experiences serving, among other things, the identification of special group interests and needs. At the same time, novelty rather than originality has become the order of the day. Musical compositions, electronically recorded—more recently also electronically produced—and distributed as salable items by mass-oriented corporations, have attained the status of physical objects that are easily discarded and replaced. Still, there are those who try to transform the burdens of history into significant new forms of composition. A new eclecticism is in the making, destined perhaps to preserve a long tradition that has been among Western man's proudest achievements. (A.L.R./Ed.)

INSTRUMENTATION

Most authorities make little distinction between the words instrumentation and orchestration. Both deal with musical instruments and their capabilities of producing various timbres or colours. Orchestration is somewhat the narrower term since it is frequently used to describe the art of instrumentation as related to the symphony orchestra. Instrumentation, therefore, is the art of combining instruments in any sort of musical composition, including such diverse elements as the numerous combinations used in chamber groups, jazz bands, rock ensembles, ensembles employing chorus, symphonic bands, and, of course, the symphony orchestra. Included under this designation are the various instrumental groups that play non-Western music, such as the gamelan orchestras of Bali and Java and the traditional ensembles of India, Africa, the Far East, and the Middle East.

In Western music there are many standard or traditional groups. The modern symphony orchestra usually comprises the following instruments, although they are not necessarily used in every composition:

Constituents of the orchestra

1. Woodwinds: four flutes (one doubling, or duplicating the part of the piccolo), four oboes, English horn (cor anglais), three clarinets, bass clarinet, three bassoons, contrabassoon (double bassoon);
2. Brass: four trumpets, four or five French horns, three trombones, tuba;
3. Strings: two harps, first and second violins, violas, violoncellos, double basses;
4. Percussion; four timpani (played by one player) and at least three general percussion players.

The orchestra has arrived at this complement through centuries of evolution; the present size is needed to perform repertoire from the Baroque, Classical, Romantic, and Impressionistic periods, as well as the repertoire of the 20th century.

The various sections, with the exception of percussion, divide themselves in somewhat the same manner as a choir. The woodwinds, for example, divide into flutes (sopranos), oboes (altos), clarinets (tenors), and bassoons (basses), although this distinction must be greatly qualified. Instrumental range is larger than vocal range, and the clarinets of an orchestra may play higher than the flutes in a woodwind passage.

The standard instrumental groups of Western chamber music include the string quartet (two violins, viola, and violoncello), the woodwind quintet (flute, oboe, clarinet, French horn, and bassoon), the combinations employed in sonatas (one wind or stringed instrument with piano), and the brass quintet (frequently two trumpets, French horn, trombone, and tuba). In addition to these standard groups there are, however, hundreds of other possible combinations.

Other groups that deserve mention are those used in the popular music of the 20th century. The dance band, popular in the 1930s and 1940s, consisted of five saxophones, four trumpets, four trombones, double bass, piano, guitar, and drums. The basic rock ensemble consists of two electric guitars, electric bass, electronic organ (doubling electric piano), drums, and frequently one or more singers. The concert band, which is particularly popular in North America, consists of mixed wind and percussion players totalling from about 40 to well beyond 100 players.

The music of the non-Western world is most frequently performed by groups of chamber music size. In this category would fall the music played by the Javanese gamelan orchestra (consisting mainly of tuned gongs and other metal instruments), Japanese *gagaku* music (performed on flutes, mouth organs, lutes, drums, and gongs), and Chinese music (with a traceable history of about 4,000 years) consisting of sacred, folk, chamber, and operatic music.

Types of instrumentation. The approach to the art of instrumentation is naturally greatly influenced by the type of group for which the composer is writing. He cannot treat a string quartet or a group of brass instruments in the same manner as he would a symphony orchestra. In general, the larger and more diverse the instrumental group, the more coloristic possibilities it presents to the composer. The smaller instrumental groups often have a sound character of their own, and the composer is challenged to find new and interesting ways to deal with this limitation.

The symphony orchestra has had definite traditions in relation to orchestration. The composer of the 18th century was likely to use the orchestral instruments at least part of the time in the following manner: the flutes doubling the same part as the first violins (frequently the melody); the oboes doubling the second violins or the first violins in octaves; the clarinets (by the end of the century) doubling the violas; and the bassoons doubling the violoncellos and double basses. French horns were often used as harmonic "filler" and in conjunction with every section of the orchestra because of their ability to blend easily with both stringed and wind instruments.

Development of wind instruments

These traditional doublings were not so often used in the orchestration of the 19th and 20th centuries because of the great improvement in the making of wind instruments and their consequent ability to function in a solo capacity. Wind instruments became used more and more for colouring; the flutes, for instance, were noted for their bright tone quality and great technical agility, the clarinets for all the aforementioned qualities, and the bassoons for their special tone quality. Brass instruments had to await the development of valves, which increased greatly the musical proficiency of brass players and overcame previous typecasting of these instruments as bugles and hunting horns.

String techniques. The string quartet has long been considered one of the greatest challenges to the composer because the contrast to be achieved by changing from one type of instrument when writing for a full orchestra is simply not available. The composer has had to rely on varying timbres to be arrived at by different playing techniques, such as pizzicato (plucking the strings), tremolo (the quick reiteration of the same tone), sul ponticello (bowing near the bridge of the instrument), sul tasto (bowing on the fingerboard), the use of harmonics (dividing the string in such a way as to produce a high flutelike tone), col legno (striking the strings with the wood of the bow), and many special bowing techniques.

Wind techniques. Special playing techniques also can alter the timbres of wind instruments. For instance, on many, tremolos can be played on two different notes.

Some wind instruments—and the flute is particularly agile in this respect—can produce harmonics. Flutter tonguing (produced by a rapid rolling movement of the tongue) is possible on most wind instruments; so are many other tonguing techniques that affect the quality of sound in orchestration.

Muting. The string mute is a device that softens the tone of the instrument. Muting is also used by brass instruments, particularly the trumpet and trombone, a development that took place in 20th-century popular music and then came into common use in all types of music.

Mutes—of which there are various kinds—provide the trumpet and trombone with a different tone colour. Mutes on woodwind instruments have been experimented with, but the results have not been satisfactory.

Percussion instrumentation. Percussion instruments have become a favourite source of colour for the 20th-century composer, both in the concert and popular fields. Instruments from all over the world are now commonly available and are divided into two categories: of definite and of indefinite pitch. The former include the xylophone, marimba, vibraphone, glockenspiel, timpani, and chimes. Instruments of indefinite pitch exist by the hundreds. Some of the more common ones are the snare drum, tenor drum, tom-tom, bass drum, bongos, Latin American *timbales,* many types of cymbals, maracas, claves, triangles, gongs, and temple blocks.

The availability of these instruments and the great improvement in percussion playing has resulted in an enormous increase in the number of compositions for percussion instruments. The percussion ensemble, a group of from four to eight players, is a chamber group that has existed only in the 20th century, particularly since the late 1940s. One of the interesting features of such an ensemble is that each player in it is capable of playing many instruments. An ensemble of four players, for instance, can easily handle 25 or 30 instruments, once again showing the rich palette available in a single composition.

Keyboard instrumentation. Since the 17th century, keyboard instruments have played an important role in orchestration. Those commonly available today are the harpsichord, celesta, organ (both pipe and electronic), and electric piano, in addition to the instrument for which most of the standard literature has been written—the piano. Keybord instruments vary greatly in the manner in which they produce a sound: the harpsichord has quills that pluck the strings; the piano has hammers that strike the strings; the celesta has hammers that strike a metal bar; the pipe organ sends air through a pipe; the electronic organ employs electronic oscillators to produce its sound. The resulting colours are naturally very different.

The piano, with its wide range (more than seven octaves), has been used in conjunction with virtually every instrument and instrumental combination. In the 18th century it gradually replaced the harpsichord as the common keyboard instrument because of the piano's ability to alter dynamics rapidly and its ability to sustain sounds. There is a vast amount of literature for the piano as the accompanying instrument in sonatas, partly because the piano can function as a "one-man orchestra." Many composers of the 20th century have discovered facets of the piano that had been previously ignored. The inside of the grand piano is a harplike body that has presented many new possibilities to the composer, such as the "prepared" piano. To prepare a piano, objects such as bolts, pennies, and erasers are inserted between the strings, thus producing many different sounds. The piano strings can be plucked or played with percussion mallets and can produce harmonics in the manner of non-keyboard stringed instruments, much to the dismay of piano tuners and traditional pianists.

The "prepared" piano

Electronic instrumentation. The electric piano is one of a number of instruments that have gained in popularity in recent times. These instruments either produce sound by means of electronic oscillators or are amplified acoustic instruments. The sound produced by ensembles playing this type of instrument is distinctive. The rock ensemble is the best known, but rock musicians are by no means the only instrumentalists to employ electric instruments. For the composer, amplified or electric instruments pose certain problems. Balances can be achieved or ruined simply by turning an amplifier up or down. The timbres produced by rock ensembles and other groups employing electronics are unusual for a number of reasons. The electric guitar has such devices as reverberation controls, "wa-wa" pedals, and filters that enable the performer to change timbre radically in the middle of a performance. Composers since the early 1960s, being much concerned with coloristic possibilities of instruments, have found the electronic ones most attractive.

Vocal instrumentation. The largest quantity of literature in Western music has been written for the chorus.

The choir, an instrument capable of great subtleties of colour, has been a favourite of composers for centuries. The range of most individual singing voices is rather limited. Choral singers, who usually have a limited amount of training, are capable of a range of about an octave and a fifth, which is considerably smaller than the range of individual instruments. Singers are usually not capable of singing wide leaps, that is to say, notes that are far apart in range. Great skill is required in the musical setting of the text in a choral work. Attention must be paid to the vocal qualities of vowel sounds as well as to the way in which the consonants are treated.

For centuries composers have been intrigued with the combination of voices and instruments, and many of the most important compositions in Western music have been written for chorus and orchestra. Almost every major composer of the past three centuries has written for choir and large instrumental ensembles.

The development of Western instrumentation. The development of the art of using instruments for their individual properties did not really begin in Western music until about 1600. The known history of musical instruments, however, has been traced back 40,000 years, although nothing is known about the music these early instruments produced. The Greeks left mostly musical theories and only a small amount of extant music. The Romans used instruments particularly in military bands, but, again, little is known of their specific use. The music of the Middle Ages and Renaissance was primarily vocal, although instruments were frequently used in compositions to accompany or reinforce the individual vocal line. Stringed, brass, woodwind, and percussion instruments were added not so much for their coloristic potential but because of their availability. Another practice in the Middle Ages was to make literal instrumental versions of vocal compositions, which, of course, has rather little in common with the modern art of instrumentation.

The Baroque period. Orchestration in a modern sense probably began in the 16th century with Giovanni Gabrieli, organist of St. Mark's in Venice. He was the first composer to sometimes designate specific instruments for each part in a composition, as in his *Sacrae symphoniae* (1597). Claudio Monteverdi made important contributions to the art of orchestration. His opera *Orfeo* was first performed at Mantua (now Mantova, Italy) in 1607 with an orchestra of about 40 instruments, including flutes, cornetts, trumpets, trombones, strings, and keyboard instruments. For the first time, a composer, in order to heighten certain dramatic moments, specified exactly which instruments were to be used.

Monteverdi's orchestra

The century after the first performance of *Orfeo* was characterized by a rise in the use of stringed instruments that were similar to the modern ones. Although that trend helped set the stage for the modern orchestra, it was not a period that made great strides in the art of orchestration: the prevalent practice of writing out only the melody and the bass line of a composition did not lend itself easily to creative scoring. By the end of the 17th century, however, the groundwork had been laid for new developments. Instruments and instrumentalists had improved steadily. Johann Sebastian Bach created works that occasionally exploited the coloristic capabilities of instruments but in a rather limited way. In some of Bach's music the stringed instruments are played pizzicato, although this practice had already been employed by Monteverdi. Bach also wrote for muted strings. Wind instruments were treated occasionally for their special sounds, although more frequently they were simply employed on a musical line that their range happened to fit.

Handel, whose life covered the same period as Bach's, had a keener sense of orchestral effect. He introduced the clarinet into his orchestra, although it was not to become standard until the 19th century, and in his operas Handel often used instrumental colour in a way that did not become common practice until much later. Jean-Philippe Rameau, the leading French composer of the 18th century, also contributed much to the development of orchestration. Rameau, like Handel, was principally famous as an opera composer, and the overtures and dances of his operas represent the most advanced uses of instruments during that period. Rameau was probably the first composer to treat each instrument of the orchestra as a separate entity, and he introduced interesting and unexpected passages for flutes, oboes, and bassoons.

By the middle of the 18th century the symphony orchestra was beginning to resemble the modern instrumental group, yet it was still considerably smaller. The orchestra at the court of Mannheim, Germany, consisted of 20 violins, four violas, four cellos, two double basses, two flutes, two oboes, two bassoons, four French horns, one trumpet, and kettledrums. Baroque composers frequently could not count on a fixed orchestra and therefore had to write the various parts so that they could be played on more than one instrument. The contrapuntal style that prevailed from the time of Monteverdi until the mid-18th century usually meant simply assigning instruments to each line in a composition; the basic consideration was whether that line stayed within the range of the chosen instrument. The fixed personnel of such orchestras as the Mannheim group, therefore, freed the composers to experiment with the capabilities of the instruments within the group. Musical style was also changing, the contrapuntal style of the Baroque giving way to a style that relied more heavily on melodic invention supported by harmony.

The court orchestra in Mannheim

One of the more important composers of the period between the Baroque and Classical eras was Johann Sebastian's son, Carl Philipp Emanuel Bach. In C.P.E. Bach's symphonies the strings become melodic instruments, and the winds—two flutes, two oboes, one or two bassoons, two horns—fill out chords and provide body to the orchestration.

The Classical period. The Classical era, which covers roughly the second half of the 18th century, is one of the most significant periods in the development of orchestration. The most talented composers of this period were Mozart and Haydn. Many important developments took place during this time. The orchestra became standardized. The Classical orchestra came to consist of strings (first and second violins, violas, violoncellos, and double basses), two flutes, two oboes, two clarinets, two bassoons, two or four French horns, two trumpets, and two timpani. Toward the end of his career, in the *London Symphonies,* Haydn introduced clarinets as part of the woodwind section, a change that was to be permanent. Haydn also introduced the following innovations: trumpets were used independently instead of always doubling the horns, cellos became separated from the double basses, and woodwind instruments were often given the main melodic line. In the *Military Symphony (No. 100)* Haydn introduced some percussion instruments not normally used in the orchestras of this time, namely, triangle, hand cymbals, and bass drum; and, what is still more unusual, they are employed in the second movement, which in the Classical tradition is normally the slow movement.

Standardization of the orchestra

In Haydn's music a method of composition appeared that had a bearing on orchestration. This consisted of the conscious use of musical motives; motive is defined in the *Harvard Dictionary of Music* as: "The briefest intelligible and self-contained fragment of a musical theme or subject." Perhaps the best known musical motive in Western music is the four-note group with which Beethoven's *Fifth Symphony* begins. These musical cells became the musical building blocks of the Classical period, particularly in the middle or development section of a movement, with the composer moving the musical motive from instrument to instrument and section to section, giving a new facet to the orchestration. The art of orchestration was thus becoming a major factor in the artistic quality of the music.

Mozart, too, was responsible for great strides in the creative use of instruments. His last two symphonies (*Nos. 40,* K. 550, and *41,* K. 551) are among the most beautifully orchestrated works of this or any period. For his 17 piano concertos, Mozart exhaustively explored the combination of piano and orchestra.

Mozart's special contribution

The Romantic period. Beethoven began his career under the influence of the Classical composers, particularly Haydn, but during his lifetime he transformed this heritage into the foundation of a new musical practice that was to become known as Romanticism. The Classical composers for the most part attempted to orchestrate with a sense of grace and beauty. Beethoven occasionally made deliberate use of new, intense, often even harsh orchestral sounds. He also, in his later symphonies, augmented the orchestra with a piccolo, contrabassoon, and third and fourth horn. The *Ninth Symphony* has one passage calling for triangle, cymbals, and bass drum, a combination identified with the imitations of Turkish Janissary music in vogue in previous years, and the final movement calls for four vocal soloists and full chorus.

The Romantic era was characterized by great strides in the art of instrumentation, and, in fact, the use of instrumental colour became one of the most salient features of this music. The piano really came into its own as a source of interesting sonorities; the orchestra expanded in size and scope; new instruments were added; and old instruments were improved and made more versatile. The Romantic period saw the appearance of the first textbook on the subject of orchestration. It was the French composer Hector Berlioz' *Traité d'instrumentation et d'orchestration modernes* (1844; *Treatise on Instrumentation and Orchestration,* 1856). Berlioz was one of the most individual orchestrators in the history of music, and his *Symphonie fantastique* (1830) is one of the most remarkable pieces of music to come out of this era. Berlioz made use of colour to depict or suggest events in his music, which was frequently programmatic in character. He called on large forces to express his musical ideas, an idea that persisted throughout the 19th century and into the 20th. Berlioz' *Grande Messe des morts* (*Requiem,* 1837) calls for four flutes, two oboes, two English horns, four clarinets, 12 French horns, eight bassoons, 25 first violins, 25 second violins, 20 violas, 20 violoncellos, 18 double basses, eight pairs of timpani, four tam-tams (a type of gong), bass drum, and 10 pairs of cymbals; four brass choirs placed in various parts of the hall, each consisting of four trumpets, four trombones, two tubas, and four ophicleides (a large, now obsolete brass instrument); and a chorus of 80 sopranos, 80 altos, 60 tenors, and 70 basses. The coloristic ideas in Berlioz' music were carried on in various ways by other important 19th-century composers and reached a culmination in the music of the German composer Richard Strauss and the Austrian Gustav Mahler—both of whom demanded a virtuoso orchestra—and were orchestrated in a complex fashion, although Mahler was capable of very delicate effects.

First treatise on orchestration

Post-Romanticism and the 20th century. Claude Debussy in France was probably the most important composer of the Impressionistic era, which lasted roughly from 1880 until the turn of the century. The Impressionist composers attempted to describe scenes and evoke moods by the use of rich harmonies and a wide palette of timbre. No composer ever handled the colours of the orchestra with greater subtlety. Naturally, this is also dependent on his use of harmony, melody, and rhythm, but the dominant impression of a Debussy work is focussed on his use of orchestral instruments to create light and shadows. Works that exemplify his techniques are *Prélude à l'après-midi d'un faune* (*Prelude to the Afternoon of a Faun;* 1894), *Nocturnes* (1899), and *La Mer* (*The Sea;* 1905). In *Nocturnes* he uses a wordless women's chorus as a section of the orchestra, functioning as another source of timbre rather than as the transmitter of a text.

The Impressionist school

Many of the composers who followed Debussy and Mahler brought about radical changes in the use of the orchestra. A good example of some of these changes is in *The Rite of Spring* (1913), by the Russian-born composer Igor Stravinsky. The strings frequently do not assume a dominant role but, rather, often play music that is subservient to the brass or woodwinds. Percussion instruments greatly increased in importance and have continued to do so. In 1931, Edgard Varèse composed an important work, *Ionisation,* for 13 percussion players, a landmark in the emergence of percussion instruments as equal partners in music.

The period between World War I and World War II was dominated by two main schools of composers with vastly differing results for orchestration. One was responsible for the Neoclassical style; the other, gathered around the Austrian composer Arnold Schoenberg, drew heavily on the Romantic movement for its direction. The Neoclassical composers sought to free music from the influence of Impressionism. Whereas the Impressionist and Romantic composers had frequently employed the instrumental forces at hand to create a deliberate sense of vagueness, the Neoclassical composers, beginning in about 1917 with a group in France known as Les Six, attempted to recreate the clarity of the Classical period by turning to models found in the popular music of the period, the music of the dance halls and cabarets. The Neoclassical composers also turned away somewhat from the orchestra as a medium, finding the forces of chamber music more suitable for their ideals. Neoclassical music returned to a clearer concept of "sections" in orchestration. The music of a composer such as Paul Hindemith in Germany is closer to the music of Mozart in its sense of instrumentation than it is to Romanticism or Impressionism.

The music of Schoenberg and his fellow Austrian Alban Berg drew heavily on the Romantic movement and eventually became known as Expressionism, which stressed inner experience. Emphasis on the inner man produced a music that was thick, dark, and intense.

In the first half of the 20th century electronic music emerged, although it did not become important until after 1950. The principal reasons for the inclusion here of electronic music are that electronic sounds, either taped or live, frequently are included in a composition combined with traditional instruments, and it has had a decided influence on orchestration. (For a treatment of historical and compositional aspects of electronic music, see MUSICAL FORMS AND GENRES: *Electronic music.*) By the 1960s many composers were writing works for electronic sounds and instruments. The electronic sounds provide a dimension to instrumentation never before possible. A number of things are noteworthy. Electronic sounds are capable of incredibly subtle changes of timbre, pitch, and mode of attack. When combined with traditional instruments they add a rich new spectrum of colour. This in turn has influenced the composer to attempt to produce "electronic" sounds with standard instruments. The result has been a great extension of the sound possibilities of Western instruments.

Importance of electronic music

Another 20th-century trend was away from large orchestras and toward chamber ensembles, often of nontraditional combinations. Compositions for such ensembles may excel in economy of means and explore individual instrumental timbres. To achieve this, unusual playing techniques may be required.

Non-Western instrumentation. Much of music outside the West has entirely different aesthetic aims; the music of the Hindu world, best known to the West through the classical music of India, provides an example. Indian music always has had strong ties with mythology and religion and thus produced an art that is as different from Western music as Hinduism is from Christianity. It achieves unity through similarity rather than through change and is based on a more purely sensual approach. Hindu music is divided, for example, into ragas, or melody types. The word raga means colour or mood. Combined with the ragas are *tālas,* or rhythmic patterns. The possible combinations of *tālas* and ragas are many, producing a music that is wonderfully subtle.

The instruments for this music consist of various drums made of terra-cotta, wood, or metal; cymbals also serve as percussion instruments. Probably the instrument best known to Western audiences is the tabla, a two-drum set capable of very subtle changes in sound. The two best known stringed instruments are the sitar (plucked) and the tamboura, a four-stringed instrument that provides the omnipresent drone accompaniment. In addition, there are various wind instruments, such as the bamboo flute and the *sheh'nai* (oboe).

Instruments of Indian and Balinese music

Balinese and Javanese music is centred on the gamelan orchestra, the instruments of which include the *saron* and *gender* metallophones (like xylophones but with metal, not wooden, keys), the *gambang kayu* xylophone, tuned gongs, flutes, and the *rebab,* a violin-like instrument with two strings. All the instruments follow the same nuclear melody but elaborate it in different ways. The heavy reliance on tuned percussion instruments has given this music a brilliant quality that Western audiences have found extremely attractive. The gamelan orchestra, for instance, influenced Debussy, who first heard the music at the Paris Exposition in 1889.

The approach to instrumentation in the music of India and Bali is quite different from that of Western music. The concept of contrast created through the various "choirs" of the Western orchestra is not a primary concern. In Indian music a sameness of colour is created through the use of the drone played on the tamboura. This is not to say that this music is uncolourful but that a specific timbre is established for an entire composition. Since the time of Debussy, Western composers have come increasingly into contact with, in particular, the music of India, Bali, and Japan. A comparison of Balinese gamelan music with the *Sonatas and Interludes* for prepared piano by the 20th-century American composer John Cage shows how profound this influence can be.

Arrangement and transcription. A practice that has been much employed in the 20th century, although by no means confined to it, has been the writing of arrangements and transcriptions. Though little distinction is made between the two, there are, at least in current practice, differences. A transcription is essentially the adaptation of a composition for an instrument or instruments other than those for which it was originally written. An arrangement is a similar procedure, although the arranger often feels free to take musical liberties with elements of the original score. This is especially true of arrangements for jazz or rock groups and arrangements of popular compositions or songs from musical comedies.

In the 18th and 19th centuries, chamber and orchestral music was transcribed, or "arranged," for the piano for the purpose of study and, of course, for the pleasure of playing at home the music that had been heard at a concert. This practice has continued. Piano versions of many 18th- and 19th-century orchestral works exist in two- and four-hand arrangements. Another common practice is to reduce the orchestral parts of concertos to a keyboard version to enable students to study and play these works without an orchestra.

Piano versions of orchestral works

The symphonic band, despite its popularity in Great Britain and North America, was faced with a dearth of repertoire written specifically for it. In the past, one answer was to transcribe orchestral works for band, substituting particularly the clarinets, with their wide pitch range, for the strings of the symphony orchestra. The necessity for that substitution is no longer so great because in recent times composers have written much more music specifically for the symphonic band.

The dance band predominant in the 1930s and 1940s is treated roughly in the following way by arrangers: the saxophones carry the melody more frequently than the other sections; the trumpets provide embellishment or figures that work around the melody; the trombones either are combined with the trumpets or serve as a melodic instrument; the piano and guitar provide harmonic filler; and the double bass and drums set the rhythm.

The jazz or rock arranger has done much more than simply transcribe the keyboard version of a song. All forms of popular music in the 20th century have been involved in the art of improvising. Musicians working in this field almost always embellish the music as they perform it. The jazz or rock arranger in a sense improvises on manuscript paper. In making an arrangement for a group of musicians the arranger will embellish both the harmonic structure and the melody of the composition; or the arrangement will be worked out in rehearsal and memorized or written down later. Usually, the arranger keeps enough of the original material to enable the listener to recognize the source. His skill depends on how well he can manipulate the materials of the original and on his originality in scoring the composition for the group at his disposal. The men who work in this field are frequently composers of popular music themselves.

(D.Er.)

The recording of music

TYPES OF REPRODUCTION

The physical reproduction of music has been accomplished in three major ways, which can be designated the mechanical, the acoustical, and the electrical. In the mechanical, an automatic instrument, such as the barrel organ, plays music that has been built, or programmed, into the mechanism by the designer; the resulting sound is that of the apparatus. In the acoustical and electrical methods of reproduction, sonic vibrations themselves are captured in performance and reproduced—by purely mechanical means in the acoustical method and by the use of vacuum tubes, transistors, and other such devices in the electrical. In both cases, the resulting sound is expected to be that of the independent performance.

Mechanical, acoustical, and electrical methods

Until the end of the 19th century, music was reproduced primarily by means of the mechanical method. There are reports of other methods, probably based on the action of wind or forced air, dating as far back as about 1500 BC, in the 18th dynasty of ancient Egypt, when a colossal statue of the god Memnon at Thebes made some sort of sounds to greet his mother, the goddess of the dawn. (Toppled by an earthquake in the year 27, the statue seems to have lost this ability upon reconstruction.) Friar Roger Bacon is reported to have invented some sort of talking head in the Middle Ages, and Josef Faber created in Vienna in 1860 a talking man with ivory reeds for vocal cords, a rubber tongue and lips, and with a keyboard that altered the mouth cavity to control word formation. The most common technique, however, called for a human hand or clockwork to turn a cylinder embedded with pins that would strike or otherwise operate some sound-producing apparatus, such as the metal teeth of a music-box comb; the hammers, quills, or pipes of a keyboard instrument; or the clappers of a set of bells. Automatic carillons are known from the 1300s; automatic harpsichords and organs, from the 1500s. King Henry VIII of England owned an automatic virginal; his daughter Queen Elizabeth I in 1593 sent the sultan of Turkey an elaborate musical clock. Every six hours it played a tune on 16 chimes, followed by a two-trumpet tantara, then by an organ tune and performance by "a holly bushe full of birds and thrushes, which at the end of the musick did singe and shake theire winges." In the 19th century Queen Victoria of Great Britain owned a bustle that would play "God Save the Queen" when she sat down.

Some of the most illustrious composers in the history of music wrote for mechanical devices. Haydn wrote tunes for musical (pipe organ) clocks; Mozart wrote several pieces for mechanical organ; and Beethoven wrote his *Wellington's Victory* (or *Battle Symphony*) for the panharmonicon, a full mechanical orchestra invented by Johann Nepomuk Maelzel (Mälzel), a German musician who perfected the metronome.

At the end of the 19th century two inventions superseded the barrel-and-pin mechanism. One was the player piano, which used a perforated cardboard roll to control a stream of air that activated the piano's hammers. This had the advantage of enabling pianists to record their performances for future playback, and many virtuosos and composers took advantage of this device, among them Ignacy Paderewski, Edvard Grieg, Claude Debussy, and Sergey Rachmaninoff. Some composers, including Igor Stravinsky and Paul Hindemith, wrote music especially for the piano roll, using devices such as combinations of as many as 30 notes played simultaneously; while impossible for two hands, such chords could readily be played by the perforated paper.

The player piano

The second invention, which was to make obsolete all previous music-reproducing apparatuses (except in toys and cuckoo clocks), was the phonograph. (For the technology of musical reproduction, see SOUND: *Sound recording and reproduction*.)

THE INFLUENCE OF RECORDING

Composition. In 1967 a survey of hundreds of American composers indicated that they were almost unanimous in regarding the recordings of their works as being more important than either printed publication or live performances. Through recordings, composers gained not only an easy familiarity with the music of others but also a new medium for their own works.

The contemporary American composer and teacher Milton Babbitt, in a conversation in 1965 with the Canadian pianist Glenn Gould (who maintained his own reputation largely by means of records and broadcasts, rather than by concert performances), said:

> We have all been affected as composers, as teachers, as musicians by recordings to an extent that cannot possibly be calculated as yet. . . . I don't think one can possibly exaggerate the extent to which the climate of music today is determined by the fact that the total Webern is available on records, that the total Schoenberg is becoming available.

The use of the record as a medium had superficial beginnings as early as 1904 in Ruggero Leoncavallo's song "Mattinata," specifically written for the record according to the label. Later, in 1925, Stravinsky composed a piano piece, *Serenade in A Major,* expressly for the record medium, though it is also perfectly capable of being performed live. Ottorino Respighi's *Pines of Rome* (1924) incorporates a recording of a nightingale's song in its third movement. Much more important use of recording as a medium occurred toward mid-century in works fundamentally relying on recorded tape, such as Edgard Varèse's *Poème électronique,* an 11-channel tape played through 425 speakers at the 1958 Brussels World Fair, and Morton Subotnick's *Silver Apples of the Moon* (1967), an electronic work playable only as a recording.

Teaching. In music education the phonograph was early adopted as a tool in teaching both serious students and laymen. Teachers who could not adequately illustrate musical examples at the piano found in records a means of demonstration. They could also bring entire orchestras into the classroom by means of the phonograph.

Recorded histories of music

In 1930 the *Columbia History of Music by Ear and Eye,* a phonographic survey that became popular in music history classes, enabled many students—as well as many of their teachers—to hear for the first time such instruments as viols, lutes, virginals, clavichords, and harpsichords together with the then little-known music written for them. A half dozen years later another educational recorded project, *L'Anthologie sonore,* added impetus to this specialized field. By the 1960s the Baroque music of the 17th and 18th centuries—as well as the earlier music of the Renaissance and medieval era—increasingly was recorded in performances using the instruments for which it was written. Such music found a wide audience beyond educational institutions; this audience was developed in large part by the phonograph.

By the late 20th century many conservatories, colleges, and universities, and even some secondary schools, had constructed recording studios to enable students to analyze their own performances or to rehear their own compositions.

Criticism. Records also enabled music critics to expand their knowledge and perspective of music and performance practices. Unfortunately, a record collection also allows reviewers to write on superficial differences between performances with very little expenditure of intellectual energy. New music has suffered especially from the resulting loss of the ability of many critics to expostulate on music for their readers.

Concerts. The impact of recordings on the concert hall has also been enormous, both for classical and for popular performances. Performers today can hardly hope to attract a concert audience if they have not produced distinguished recordings; usually, their audiences, both at home and abroad, consist of persons who know the performers' work through recordings. In the popular music field especially, many performers cannot compete in live appearances with recordings in which they depend heavily on technical aid. There are some who feel that the phonograph may cause the demise of live performance in the concert hall, which, if it survives at all, will do so for social rather than musical reasons. A possible indication of this trend is the disappearance of independent, nonacademic, nonprofessional classical music magazines in America; instead, there are record magazines. Their name changes are significant: *The American Record Guide,* established in 1935 as *The American Music Lover; High Fidelity,* established in 1951; and *Stereo Review,* established in 1958 as *Hi Fi/Music Review.* The record magazine is not a peculiarly American phenomenon; England has *The Gramophone* and *Records and Recording;* France, *Diapason* and *Harmonie;* Germany, *HiFi Stereophonie* and *Fono Forum;* Italy, *Discoteca Hi Fi;* Holland, *Luister;* Belgium, *Hi-Fi Musique;* Sweden, *Musikrevy;* and Japan, *Record Art/Record Geijutsu,* among many other periodical publications.

Musicology. The entire field of comparative musicology—*i.e.,* the study of the relationships between Western, non-Western, and primitive music—depends upon disc and tape recordings. Although the discipline may be traced to the 18th century, it did not emerge from a primitive state until it acquired phonographic tools. Primitive music is generally transmitted orally rather than through a written tradition, and as such its performance practices—certainly in rhythm and intonation—cannot be accurately transcribed into Western notation. Since World War II anthropologists and musicologists have visited the most remote parts of the world with tape machines to record aboriginal music before it was either tainted or wiped out by Western civilization. The most recent studies have been conducted as a race against time or more specifically against the transistor radio, a ubiquitous commodity that is homogenizing the world's musics.

THE ROLE OF THE PRODUCER

Although the record producer has at times become an equal partner with the musicians in creating the recorded performance of classical music, in the popular field he is frequently in total command. Here, in fact, the sounds produced by the musicians may simply be the raw material for the producer to work with; artificial sounds, overlays of sound upon sound, electronically introduced reverberation, multichannel effects with directional interplay and moving instruments, all may serve as vital ingredients of the recording. Paradoxically, as technological advancement brought the recording beyond the mere imitation of live performances, popular musicians began to bring complex electronic equipment into the concert halls to imitate the sounds of their recordings.

In productions of classical music, serious thought is given to whether the recording should faithfully capture the performance as heard from the optimum position in the concert hall or studio or whether the recording setup should be used to "enhance" the performance. Few question any longer the common practice of correcting actual mistakes. Ever since magnetic tape made detailed editing possible, extra takes have been made of sections in which musical problems are evident. The best taping of each section is spliced into a master tape. Even in recordings made during an actual concert, performers sometimes return to the hall afterward to emend any blemishes. The improvements in recorded performances made possible by tape splicing, however, often mislead audiences into anticipating the same perfection in live performances. Also, although tape editing facilitates the excision of poor passages that, while acceptable in the heat of a concert, would become irritating upon repeated hearings, it also has been said to hamper the continuity of the performance. It is unlikely, however, that a listener can spot the rare movement that has required no splicing from the majority that have. This alleged lack of continuity, however, was much worse when music had to be recorded in five-minute segments, for recordings at 78 revolutions per minute (rpm).

Microphone placement

Microphone placement has been perhaps the major criterion in separating the "natural" or "re-creative" from the "creative" technique of large-scale classical recordings. In a natural setup microphones are placed in the optimum positions in the hall—often directly over the conductor—in order to re-create the concert-hall or opera-house effect. In the natural arrangement the conductor is responsible for instrumental and vocal balances.

Some record-producing companies prefer to put microphones closer to the performers—this is called close-miking technique. Here the record producer—generally with the final approval of the conductor or leader—is responsible for balances, for bringing out particular instrumental or vocal lines; in other words, the producer participates in the interpretation. Studio-made popular recordings—other than those of a lush semiclassical nature—have generally used the close-miking technique; in some cases, each performer in a small musical group is assigned his own microphone. In a close-miked symphonic recording session, as many as 18 microphones may be used: three for violins; one for cellos and basses (sometimes one for each); one each for woodwinds, brasses, timpani, snare drum and triangle, bass drum and cymbals, celesta or harp, and soloist; and from three to six for a chorus. Several separate recordings, or "tracks," each comprising the inputs of several microphones, generally are made at the same time, and the producer must balance the strength of these various inputs during the recording session. Until about 1960 two-track machines were ordinarily used; by 1970 eight-track recorders were in use, allowing much more subtle mixing of channels during the editing sessions subsequent to the actual recording. For popular music sessions 16-track recorders are sometimes used. For stereophony all the recording tracks must be edited and mixed to make the final two channels. The record producer also determines the degree of separation between those two channels, and during a dramatic recording—an opera, for example—he may function as stage director in guiding the performers around the aural stage.

In quadraphony (quadriphony), which has four channels and which, in disc format, unsuccessfully tried to find a market in the early 1970s, the controversy between natural and close-miked recordings persisted. In classical music, when the two rear channels were used mainly for hall ambience, the arguments centred on the placement of the two front channels. Some companies, however, began to use the four channels as equal partners even in the classics. Columbia, for example, sometimes placed the conductor in the middle of the orchestra, which was seated for optimum quadraphonic array rather than for optimum concert-hall effect. In the early 1970s several quadraphonic disc systems competed for prominence, most notably Columbia's SQ, Japan Victor Company's CD-4 (RCA's Quadradisc in the United States), and Sansui's RM (also called QS). Since they were incompatible systems, confused consumers, waiting for one to become standard, withheld their votes from all, and by the end of the decade the aural and aesthetic benefits of quadraphony had all but disappeared from the marketplace.

THE DEVELOPMENT OF MUSICAL RECORDING

In 1877 the U.S. inventor Thomas Alva Edison heard "Mary had a little lamb" emanate from a machine into which he had just spoken the ditty. It was the first time a recording of the human voice had been reproduced, and the event signalled the birth of the phonograph. There was, to be sure, a long gestation period.

Edison sent representatives, machines, and cylinders to Europe almost as soon as he had invented the phonograph, and between 1888 and 1894 recordings were made by such notables as Alfred, Lord Tennyson, Robert Browning, and even Johannes Brahms, who played a Hungarian rhapsody. The first "celebrity" recording, however, was made in Edison's West Orange, New Jersey, laboratories when the pianist Josef Hofmann, then a 12-year-old prodigy, paid a visit to Edison's studio in 1888. Hans von Bülow followed shortly after with a recording of a Chopin mazurka on the piano.

The first "celebrity" recordings

In 1894 Charles and Émile Pathé built a small phonograph factory in a suburb of Paris and began to record singers as eminent as Mary Garden. Within a decade their catalog boasted some 12,000 items, and their name became almost synonymous with the cylinder phonograph in Europe. Meanwhile, Emile Berliner, a German immigrant living in Washington, D.C., had filed a patent in 1887 for a "Gramophone," using a disc rather than a cylinder, and he began manufacturing Gramophones and discs in 1894. The disc had the commercial advantage of being more easily manufactured than the cylinders. One of his representatives established a branch in London, the Gramophone Company (in 1898), a branch in Berlin, Deutsche Grammophon AG, and one in France, the Compagnie Français du Gramophone, while Berliner's brother set up a disc-pressing facility in Hamburg. Most of Europe's recording industry thus was started by Berliner's representatives, and in the United States the small Berliner organization was to turn into the giant Victor company.

By the beginning of the 20th century, recording industries had been established in Germany, Austria, Russia, and Spain. Much of the managerial and technical talent, not to mention equipment, had been imported from America. (By 1970, the positions would be reversed, with Europe in command of most of the American market.)

During the 1890s recordings had become popular primarily through coin-in-the-slot phonographs in public places. Talent was incidental to the novelty of the apparatus; most of the recordings were of whistlers, bands, comic numbers, ditties, ethnic routines, and the like. In the first years of the 20th century, Victor and its affiliates raised cultural expectations with its Red Seal series (Red Label in Europe), particularly with discs made, beginning in 1902, by Enrico Caruso. By 1910 the vast majority of record sales—some estimates are as high as 85 percent—were classical.

The Red Label had been initiated in 1901 in Russia with some of the first 10-inch disc recordings made, and the basso Fyodor Chaliapin was among the first artists to record on the new Russian Red Label.

In 1902 Victor and another major label, Columbia, decided to help the development of the new industry by pooling their patents. Victor was thereby legally able to record on wax (which would then be electroplated) for the first time, and the new wax discs were then used in recording Caruso in Milan. Caruso's discs were a major catalyst in transforming the amusing gadget of a phonograph into a respected cultural phenomenon. That same year the new series received London-made recordings by stars of the Covent Garden opera house, primarily through the efforts of the Gramophone Company's music director, Landon Ronald, a bona fide serious musician and conductor who was able to convince his colleagues of the musical worth of the Gramophone. One instrumentalist also appeared in the new Red Label series, the violinist Jan Kubelík.

In the United States, Columbia followed suit in 1903 with its 10-inch Grand Opera Records, recording Metropolitan Opera stars. Shortly after, Victor began its own celebrity recording sessions of opera stars and others on $3^1/_2$-minute 12-inch discs. Victor also made many of its associated European companies' Red Label recordings—which included Mary Garden singing music by Debussy with the composer at the piano—available in the United States on its Red Seal series. Columbia soon dropped its opera series when the recordings did not sell as well as songs and marches, but Victor saw an institutional value in the celebrity recordings. The prestige of the Red Seal influenced Victor's other products: "Victrola" became, in the popular mind, almost a generic term for the (disc) phonograph, and the company practically monopolized the quality-minded market for many years. Indeed, the total Western Hemisphere record market became virtually monopolized by Victor and Columbia, while their London affiliates controlled the rest of the world. The first major break did not come until World War I, when ties were severed with Deutsche Grammophon, which emerged after the war as the independent Deutsche Grammophon Gesellschaft (DGG).

Between 1907 and 1910 Columbia tried to approach Victor's cultural prominence by releasing records from Europe and later by reinstating its own recording sessions with operatic singers. Columbia also began issuing double-sided discs, as had already been done in Europe. Victor did not do so until 1923.

During the early days of recording, both the cylinder and the disc were produced acoustically rather than electronically. A singer would sing into a horn, and the accompanist behind him played a piano placed on a platform so that the rear of the instrument—with the back removed—would also be level with the horn. With the development of a sound box to be placed on violins and violas, small orchestras could be used as accompaniment, but bassoons were required to play the cello part and a tuba the double bass part. It was an event worthy of a London newspaper announcement in 1904 when Kubelík made two records with his own Stradivarius, rather than on a violin with the sound box. When symphonic recordings came to be made, the wind and brass instruments still played or doubled the parts written for the lower strings, which could not be reproduced adequately. Although acoustical recordings were improved by the 1920s, the problems were not overcome until the introduction of the microphone and the consequent electrical recording process around 1925.

Birth of a mass medium

In the decade 1910–20, the phonograph became a truly mass medium for popular music, and recordings of large-scale orchestral works and other classical instrumental music proliferated. The rise of the popular record coincided in the United States with the new ragtime, popularized by Scott Joplin's rags at the turn of the century and sensationalized by Irving Berlin's "Alexander's Ragtime Band," written in 1910, which swept the country the following year. It stimulated an unprecedented dance craze at a time when the phonograph was becoming increasingly available. As the fad spread to millions who had never danced before, phonographs were sold to people who had never owned records before. Between 1914 and 1919 phonograph sales increased more than fivefold. In 1917 Victor issued the first jazz recordings, by the Original Dixieland Jass (sic) Band, but few major jazz releases appeared before the 1920s.

The first large-scale symphonic recording, Tchaikovsky's *Nutcracker Suite,* was issued in 1909 in England. The first attempt to record a concerto came the following year, also in London, when Wilhelm Backhaus recorded a cut version of the first movement of Grieg's *Piano Concerto.* In 1913 the first complete symphonies, Beethoven's *Fifth* and *Sixth,* were recorded in Germany under an anonymous conductor; later that year, a celebrity conductor, Arthur Nikisch, led a full-scale symphony for the first time, again the Beethoven *Fifth.* Solo instrumentalists vied with the opera singers for the record-buying public's affection, mainly by recording tidbits. In 1917 Victor began to record with a combination that was to prove its star classical music attraction for decades: Leopold Stokowski and the Philadelphia Orchestra.

The serious recording of serious music became a growing phenomenon as the phonograph matured during the early 1920s. Tidbits and orchestral snatches gave way to a spate of uncut symphonies, sonatas, quartets, and concerti; the music itself came to mean as much as its star performers, and the electrical recording process, from 1925 on, raised the quality of the recordings as well. But in the mid-1920s radio, which provided free music, developed, and this new factor, plus the worldwide economic depression of the 1930s, threw the phonograph industry into serious decline.

The companies realigned themselves. In 1929 the Radio Corporation of America (RCA) bought Victor. Later that year, Edison left the phonograph business he had created. In 1931 the English Columbia Graphophone Company divested itself of its near-defunct American progenitor and joined the Gramophone Company to form Electric and Musical Industries, Ltd. (EMI), bringing into the merger nearly every important European firm except DGG and its export label, Polydor. American Columbia was revived by its purchase, in 1938, by the Columbia Broadcasting System.

During the 1930s, as the American companies relied mainly on dance records in jukeboxes to satisfy a dwindled market, Europe supplied a slow but steady trickle of classical recordings. In 1931 the His Master's Voice (HMV) label in Great Britain began its "Society" issues: a limited public was asked to subscribe in advance to then esoteric releases—the complete Beethoven piano sonatas played by Artur Schnabel or Pablo Casals performing the Bach unaccompanied cello suites. A new British company, Decca, organized in 1929, also began to issue serious recordings. In the United States, Columbia began to record a number of distinguished orchestras, including those of New York City, Chicago, Cleveland, and Minneapolis. RCA retained its leadership, however, with the Philadelphia Orchestra under Eugene Ormandy, the Boston Symphony Orchestra under Serge Koussevitzky, and—perhaps the greatest orchestral combination ever assembled—the NBC Symphony under Arturo Toscanini, as well as with the violinist Jascha Heifetz and the pianist Vladimir Horowitz.

British Decca had a far-reaching role to play after World War II when its ffrr—full frequency range recording—became internationally known. The frequency range of discs had been dramatically extended, and Ernest Ansermet's recording of Stravinsky's *Petrushka* in the new process was to awaken the unsuspecting ears of many record collectors in 1946 to the future high fidelity, or "hi-fi," possibilities of the phonograph.

Two other developments in the late 1940s combined with the extended frequency range to produce a radical change in the development of recordings: magnetic recording and the first commercially successful long-playing (LP) record. In 1948 Columbia Records demonstrated 12-inch unbreakable vinyl discs that could play about 25 minutes of music per side. The standard shellac disc had revolved at 78 rpm, and a 12-inch disc had to be changed, automatically or manually, every five minutes, thus breaking up the continuity of longer works; the 12-inch LP, revolving at 33⅓ rpm, could hold the average symphony, sonata, or quartet on a single side. And the vinyl discs had quieter surfaces than the shellac. Victor soon countered with its own microgroove records: seven-inch vinyl discs at 45 rpm. Each contained approximately as much music as a 12-inch 78-rpm disc, but the package was smaller. By 1950, a pattern had been set: 12-inch LPs for classical works and popular albums, 45s for individual popular songs. Extended-play 45s also were developed and successfully marketed. The LP opened up an entirely new market—not only newcomers but older record collectors who could see the advantage of the new technology and were willing to repurchase their collections as LPs. The 78-rpm shellac disc followed the cylinder into oblivion.

Tape had a major impact on recording starting in the late 1940s: anyone with a good recorder and microphone could become a record producer. Small companies sprang up in areas of music ignored by the giants: the esoteric and the avant-garde, the music of the periods before and after the highly popular Romantic classics of the 19th century. Chamber music, as well as Baroque works of the 18th century and earlier, which required paying fewer musicians than an entire symphony orchestra, flooded record stores and resulted in an unprecedented Baroque revival among music lovers. All-Vivaldi concerts were sold out, and Bach became a best-seller. Orchestral recordings of less familiar works—produced in a Europe that had been ravaged by World War II, where musicians' fees were minimal—crested the flood. New companies recorded for the first time many symphonies, quartets, masses, little-known operas, and many other once esoteric works, some of which were now available in competing versions. The more popular standard works, the symphonies of Beethoven, Brahms, and Tchaikovsky, became duplicated by the dozens. By the mid-1950s it seemed that most of the worthwhile musical output of Western civilization—and much from Asia and Africa—had been made available to the average home.

The stereo revolution

For a few owners of some deluxe tape recorders, a new listening experience was available by 1956: stereophonic tape recordings. Within two years stereo discs made their commercial appearance; every major U.S. company began issuing stereo discs by the end of 1958.

Now a new flood of records hit the market: notably popular were those that displayed the spectacular effects possible with stereo. It was again Decca/London that convinced the serious music lover of the musical benefits of stereo with the release in 1959 of Wagner's *Das Rheingold,* conducted by Georg (later Sir Georg) Solti, a pioneer work in the "creative" school of classical record production. Within a decade two complete recordings of Wagner's *Ring* cycle, comprising four complete operas on 19 discs, were available. Again, as with the advent of the LP, a technical advance spurred the record industry into recording an even greater repertoire than was available previously. By the late 1960s most American record companies had discontinued their monaural recordings, except for "historical reissues."

The 1950s saw a rearrangement of record company alliances, as Europe began its strong invasion of America. By the 1970s not only did Europe own a sizable chunk of the American record industry, but it had taken over the recording, for the first time, of many of the most prestigious U.S. orchestras.

Another far-reaching phenomenon of the 1950s was Elvis Presley, a popular U.S. singer who inspired a new, militantly youth-oriented style of music: rock and roll. It generated a multitude of solo singers and groups as well as a teenage and subteen culture of rabid record buyers. The success of the British rock group the Beatles helped stimulate record sales in the 1960s to an all-time high. The sales of classical records, however, represented a declining portion of the total. It seemed that most people who wanted the standard classics had already bought them and that few new standard works of any length were being written. Rather than new classical recordings, re-releases were issued in new packages (*e.g.,* "Debussy's Greatest Hits") and in the new medium of tape. During the mid-1960s two small and conveniently packaged tape formats began a steady rise to popularity: the continuous-loop one-reel cartridge and the two-reel cassette. Each obviated the need for threading tape in order to play it. The cartridge first achieved consumer acceptance as an automobile accessory and was designed primarily as a playback-only format; the cassette configuration was first introduced in an inexpensive portable recorder player.

Cartridges, cassettes, and videotape

Cassettes had the advantage over continuous-loop cartridges in being rewindable and thus easier to control for selective "spotting" and for amateur recording. For nonselective music or music in which it is not necessary to start at the beginning—background music, for instance—the continuous-loop cartridge had the advantage of not having to be rewound at all. By the end of 1982 sales of recorded music on cassettes had overtaken those of LP discs in the United States.

Meanwhile, a new recording technique that boasted, among other things, a wider dynamic range had begun to revolutionize the market for quality recordings: the music was taped "digitally," via pulse-code modulation. Pioneered by the Denon label in Japan, it was most enthusiastically adopted by Cleveland-based Telarc Records in the late 1970s. Another small company, Sheffield Lab, had already been producing impressive-sounding results by recording directly onto disc, foregoing the tape stage entirely. These and other "audiophile" companies began to corner the quality market, while charging two to three times the price of standard discs for their products; by 1983 this had led more than 40 companies, including the major labels, to adopt audiophile, primarily digital, techniques for at least their new classical releases. The first true digital discs, called Compact Discs, played back with a laser as the "stylus," became available in Japan in 1982 and in Europe and the United States in 1983.

Video has continued to be used to record musical performances via several incompatible disc and tape formats. The first years of the medium demonstrated that the grafting of images onto music would become viable only with the emergence of genius comparable to that of the great composers themselves. (L.M.M.)

BIBLIOGRAPHY

Modern theories of musical meaning: ARTHUR SCHOPENHAUER, *Die Welt als Wille und Vorstellung* (1883; Eng. trans., *The World as Will and Idea,* 1961); and FRIEDRICH NIETZSCHE, "The Birth of Tragedy from the Spirit of Music," trans. by CLIFTON P. FADIMAN in *The Philosophy of Nietzsche* (1954). EDUARD HANSLICK, *Vom musikalisch Schönen* (1854; Eng. trans., *The Beautiful in Music,* 1957), remains the best single exposition of the formalist (or nonreferentialist) position in musical aesthetics. EDMUND GURNEY, *The Power of Sound* (1880, reprinted 1966), maintains a similar point of view but with considerably greater amplitude and subtlety. For background of the contemporary symbolist views of musical meaning, see ALFRED NORTH WHITEHEAD, *Symbolism* (1959); SUSANNE K. LANGER, "On Significance in Music," in *Philosophy in a New Key,* 2nd ed. (1951), and *Feeling and Form* (1953). LEONARD B. MEYER has made an important contribution to the aesthetics of music. His interest in the relevance of information theory to music has been evidenced in two articles: "Meaning in Music and Information Theory," *Journal of Aesthetics and Art Criticism,* 14:412–424 (1957), and "Some Remarks on Value and Greatness in Music," *ibid.,* 17:486–500 (1959), reprinted in his *Music, The Arts, and Ideas: Patterns and Predictions in Twentieth-Century Culture* (1967). JOHN DEWEY, *Art as Experience* (1934, reprinted 1959); and KARL JASPERS, *Von der Wahrheit* (1947; Eng. trans., *Truth and Symbol,* 1959), have given reinforcement to organic and symbolic theses, respectively. PETER LE HURAY and JAMES DAY (eds.), *Music and Aesthetics in the Eighteenth and Early-Nineteenth Centuries* (1981), expounds theories of musical aesthetics from the pre- and early-Romantic period. PETER KIVY, *The Corded Shell* (1981), is a study of the emotional expressivity of music.

Performance practice, styles, and musical forms: The best historical accounts of musical forms, styles, and performance practice are to be found in DONALD J. GROUT, *A History of Western Music* (1960); GUSTAVE REESE, *Music in the Middle Ages* (1940), and *Music in the Renaissance,* rev. ed. (1959); MANFRED F. BUKOFZER, *Music in the Baroque Era* (1947); ALFRED EINSTEIN, *Music in the Romantic Era* (1947); and WILLIAM W. AUSTIN, *Music in the 20th Century, from Debussy to Stravinsky* (1966). SIR DONALD FRANCIS TOVEY, *The Forms of Music* (1956), contains informative and engaging short pieces. ROBERT SCHUMANN, *On Music and Musicians,* ed. by KONRAD WOLFF (Eng. trans. 1947), is an example of the work by a 19th-century precursor of the phenomenon of the present-day composer-authors who have contributed to aesthetic theory by elucidating their own works and commentating on other composers and on the scene in general. See also IGOR STRAVINSKY, *Poetics of Music in the Form of Six Lessons* (1947); PAUL HINDEMITH, *A Composer's World* (1952); AARON COPLAND, *Music and Imagination* (1952). Discussion of music and film may be found in LEWIS JACOBS (ed.), *The Emergence of Film Art* (1969). Twelve-tone technique and varieties of serialism deriving from it are treated in ARNOLD SCHOENBERG, *Style and Idea* (1950); and RENÉ LEIBOWITZ, *Schoenberg, et son école* (1947; Eng. trans., *Schoenberg and His School,* 1949). Short pieces on electronic music appear often in periodical literature. HAROLD C. SCHONBERG, *Facing the Music* (1981), is a collection of performance-oriented articles. See also CAROL MACCLINTOCK (ed.), *Readings in the History of Music in Performance* (1979).

Musical sound: WILLEM A. VAN BERGEIJK, J.R. PIERCE, and E.A. DAVID, *Waves and the Ear* (1960); ARTHUR H. BENADE, *Horns, Strings and Harmony* (1960); CHARLES A. CULVER, *Musical Acoustics,* 4th ed. (1956); JOHN BACKUS, *The Acoustical Foundations of Music* (1969); JOHN MILLS, *A Fugue in Cycles and Bels* (1935); MAX F. MEYER, *How We Hear: How Tones Make Music* (1950); LLEWELYN S. LLOYD, *The Musical Ear* (1940); ALEXANDER WOOD, *The Physics of Music,* 6th ed. (1962); RENÉ DESCARTES, *Musicae compendium* (1650; Eng. trans., *Compendium of Music,* 1961); CORNELIS J. NEDERVEEN, *Acoustical Aspects of Woodwind Instruments* (1969).

Works on tuning and temperament include HERMANN VON HELMHOLTZ, *Die Lehre von den Tonempfindungen als physiologische Grundlage für die Theorie der Musik* (1862; Eng. trans. by ALEXANDER J. ELLIS, *On the Sensations of Tone,* 1875), still the classic treatment of the subject, with useful additional observations by the translator; J. MURRAY BARBOUR, *Tuning and Temperament: A Historical Survey* (1951), a comprehensive study of the theoretical aspects of the subject, with a good bibliography; LLEWELYN S. LLOYD and HUGH BOYLE, *Intervals, Scales and Temperaments* (1963), designed for the musician; PAUL C. GREENE, "Violin Intonation," *Journal of the Acoustical Society of America,* 9:43–44 (1937), disposes of the theory that violinists naturally play in just intonation; ROGER E. KIRK, "Tuning Preferences for Piano Unison Groups," *ibid.,* 31:1644–48 (1959), shows that musicians prefer groups of unison strings on the piano to be mistuned; D.W. MARTIN and W.D. WARD, "Subjective Evaluation of Musical Scale Temperament in Pianos," *ibid.,* 33:582–585 (1961), shows that musicians do not prefer just intonation to equal temperament; FRITZ A. KUTTNER and J. MURRAY BARBOUR, *The Theory of Classical Greek Music; Meantone Temperament in Theory and Practice;* and *The Theory and Practice of Just Intonation,* Musurgia Records, Theory Series A, No. 1–3, an opportunity to hear the three major tuning systems that preceded equal temperament, both in scales and chords and in actual music.

Criticism: The foundation for most of the subsequent developments in musical criticism was laid by SIR HENRY HADOW in his influential essay, "Music and Musical Criticism—A Discourse on Method," *Studies in Modern Music* (1892). This essay cleared the ground for two major inquiries into musical criticism: M.D. CLAVOCORESSI, *The Principles and Methods of Musical Criticism* (1923); and ERNEST NEWMAN, *A Musical Critic's Holiday* (1925). All these books consider the problem of criteria that now dominates the field of musical aesthetics.

Further contributions to the problem have been made by PAUL HINDEMITH in *A Composer's World* (1952); and by ARNOLD SCHOENBERG in *Style and Idea* (1950), containing a key essay, "Criteria for the Evaluation of Music." A later book that challenges the philosophical premises on which criticism is based is ALAN WALKER, *An Anatomy of Musical Criticism* (1966), an attempt to relate aesthetics to psychology. Important supplementary reading exists in the related field of musical analysis. The more significant books include: SIR DONALD FRANCIS TOVEY, *Essays in Musical Analysis*, 6 vol. (1935–39); HEINRICH SCHENKER, *Das Meisterwerk in der Musik*, 3 vol. (1926–29); DERYCK COOKE, *The Language of Music* (1959); and the analytical essay, "Mozart's Chamber Music" by HANS KELLER, in *The Mozart Companion*, ed. by H.C.R. LANDON and DONALD MITCHELL (1956). PAUL GRIFFITHS, *Modern Music: The Avant Garde Since 1945* (1981), is a history and criticism.

Performance: The best direct and concise account of the issues of performance is THURSTON DART, *The Interpretation of Music* (1954). Other general views of the subject are FREDERICK DORIAN, *The History of Music in Performance: The Art of Musical Interpretation from the Renaissance to Our Day* (1942, reprinted 1981); and ROBERT DONINGTON, *The Interpretation of Early Music*, 2nd ed. (1965), which, like Dart, includes a bibliography of sources. What bibliographic aids to individual performers exist are given in "Dictionaries and Encyclopedias of Musical Instruments, Makers, and Performers," in VINCENT H. DUCKLES, *Music References and Research Materials: An Annotated Bibliography*, 2nd ed., pp. 40–50 (1967). Certainly the most extensive bibliography ever published on the subject is KARY VINQUIST and NEAL ZASLAV (eds.), *Performance Practice: A Bibliography* 1971. Some book-length studies of particular aspects of musical performance are listed below: P. ALDRICH, *Rhythm in Seventeenth-Century Italian Monady* (1966); F.T. ARNOLD, *The Art of Accompaniment from a Thorough-Bass As Practised in the XVIIth and XVIIIth Centuries* (1931); J.H. BARBOUR, *Tuning and Temperament* (1951); D.D. BOYDEN, *The History of Violin Playing, from Its Origins to 1761 and Its Relationship to the Violin and Violin Music* (1965); WALTER EMERY, *Bach's Ornaments* (1953); R.E.M. HARDING, *Origins of Musical Time and Expression* (1938); WILFRID H. MELLERS, "Theory and Practice," in *François Couperin and the French Classical Tradition* (1950); FRITZ ROTHSCHILD, *The Lost Tradition in Music: Rhythm and Tempo in J.S. Bach's Time* (1953) and *Musical Performance in the Times of Mozart and Beethoven: The Lost Tradition in Music, Part II* (1961); DENIS W. STEVENS (ed.), *The Art of Ornamentation in the Renaissance and Baroque* (1967), a stereophonic record; HENRY PLEASANTS, *The Great Singers: From the Dawn of Opera to Our Own Time* (1966); and WILLIAM P. MALM, *Music Cultures of the Pacific, the Near East, and Asia* (1967).

Rhythm: CURT SACHS, *Rhythm and Tempo* (1953), the most comprehensive work on rhythm in music, ranges over many non-Western cultures as well as over the successive periods of Western musical history. Detailed rhythmical analyses of Western music since the 17th century appear in GROSVENOR W. COOPER and LEONARD B. MEYER, *The Rhythmic Structure of Music* (1960). Studies of special periods are available in CHARLES F. ABDY WILLIAMS, *The Aristoxenian Theory of Musical Rhythm* (1911); W.F. JACKSON KNIGHT, *St. Augustine's De Musica: A Synopsis* (1949); WILLIAM G. WAITE, *The Rhythm of Twelfth-Century Polyphony, Its Theory and Practice* (1954); PHILIP F. RADCLIFFE, "The Relation of Rhythm and Tonality in the Sixteenth Century," *Proc. R. Musical Assn.*, 57:73–97 (1931); and HENRY D. COWELL, *New Musical Resources* (1930, reprinted 1969). Particular applications of rhythm have been studied in CHARLES F. ABDY WILLIAMS, *The Rhythm of Song* (1925); and WILLIAM THOMSON, *The Rhythm of Speech* (1923). Aesthetic aspects are considered in MARGARET GLYN, *The Rhythmic Conception of Music* (1907); and MATHIS LUSSY, *Le Rythme musical*, 3rd ed. rev. (1897; abridged Eng. trans., *A Short Treatise on Musical Rhythm*, 1909). ÉMILE JAQUES-DALCROZE, *Le Rythme, la musique et l'éducation* (1920; Eng. trans., *Rhythm, Music and Education*, 1921), is the pioneer work in its aspect of the field; musical rhythm has been put in wider perspective by ELSIE FOGERTY in *Rhythm* (1937).

Scale: CURT SACHS, *The Wellsprings of Music*, ed. by JAAP KUNST (1965), a systematic study of rudimentary scale types throughout the world and their evolution; BRUNO NETTL, *Music in Primitive Culture* (1956), a concise and authoritative introduction to scale types and their geographical distribution; WILLIAM P. MALM, *Music Cultures of the Pacific, the Near East, and Asia* (1967), lucid summaries of scale systems in non-Western art-music traditions; JOHN L. DUNK, *The Structure of the Musical Scale* (1940), a thorough description of the diatonic scale; ANTOINE AUDA, *Les Gammes musicales* (1947), a classic, comprehensive study of the history of scales in Western art music.

Mode: GUSTAVE REESE, *Music in the Middle Ages* (1940), provides a competent account and critique of a wide variety of modal concepts prevailing during the Western Middle Ages and discusses their origins and repercussions. WILLI APEL, "The Tonality," in *Gregorian Chant*, ch. 3 (1958), describes thoroughly the system of church modes. EGON WELLESZ, *Eastern Elements in Western Chant: Studies in the Early History of Ecclesiastical Music* (1947, reprinted 1967), discusses the modal structure of the melodies of Byzantine hymns and compares them with those of the Western Church. ABRAHAM Z. IDELSOHN, *Jewish Music in Its Historical Development* (1929, reprinted 1967), an authoritative work on Jewish music, contains chapters on "The Modes of the Bible" and "The Modes of the Prayers." EGON WELLESZ (ed.), *The New Oxford History of Music*, vol. 1 (1957), includes the following chapters discussing modes: ARNOLD BAKE, "The Music of India," CARL H. KRAELING and LUCETTA MOWRY, "Music in the Bible," ERIC WERNER, "The Music of Post-Biblical Judaism," ISOBEL HENDERSON, "Ancient Greek Music," and HENRY G. FARMER, "The Music of Islam." MIECZYSLAW KOLINSKI, "Classification of Tonal Structures, Illustrated by a Comparative Chart of American Indian, African Negro, Afro-American and English-American Structures," *Studies in Ethnomusicology*, 1:38–76 (1961), comprises a new system of modal classification accommodating a wide range of Western and non-Western modal patterns. ROBERT LACHMANN, *Musik des Orients* (1929, reprinted 1966), is the first scholarly survey of the music of Eastern cultures.

Harmony: Two works by 20th-century composers that give considerable insight into the role of all musical elements in composition are PAUL HINDEMITH, *Unterweisung im Tonsatz* (1937–39; Eng. trans., *The Craft of Musical Composition*, 2 bks., 1941–42); and ARNOLD SCHOENBERG, *Harmonielehre*, 3rd ed. (1922; abridged Eng. translation, *Theory of Harmony*, 1948). Schoenberg's formulation of his 12-tone theories may be found in his *Style and Idea* (1950). Other theoretical works that trace the fluid state of harmony since the later 19th century are ELLIOTT ZUCKERMAN, *The First Hundred Years of Wagner's "Tristan"* (1964); HENRY COWELL, *New Musical Resources* (1930, reprinted 1968); and GEORGE PERLE, *Serial Composition and Atonality*, 2nd. ed. (1968). Standard textbooks based on the theories of Rameau are WALTER PISTON, *Harmony*, 3rd ed. (1962); and ROGER SESSIONS, *Harmonic Practice* (1951).

Counterpoint: General studies of the subject include HUGO RIEMANN, *History of Music Theory*, trans. by RAYMOND HAGGH (1962), rather outdated but still the most thorough summary of medieval and Renaissance theoretical studies on counterpoint; KNUD JEPPESEN, "Outline History of Contrapuntal Theory," in *Counterpoint*, pp. 3–53 (1939), the main theoretical views on the subject; GUSTAVE REESE, *Fourscore Classics of Music Literature* (1957), a synopsis of 80 theoretical sources, many of which deal with counterpoint; OLIVER STRUNK, *Source Readings in Music History* (1950), numerous excerpts from musical theorists on the subject of counterpoint.

Historical treatises on counterpoint include JOHANNES TINCTORIS, *Liber de arte contrapuncti* (1477; trans. by ALBERT SEAY, *The Art of Counterpoint*, 1961), a famous landmark, the first extensive outline of contrapuntal principles; GIOSEFFO ZARLINO, *Le istitutioni harmoniche* (1558; pt. 3 trans. by GUY MARCO and CLAUDE PALISCA as *The Art of Counterpoint*, 1968); THOMAS MORLEY, "Treating of Descant," *A Plain and Easy Introduction to Practical Music*, pt. 2 (1597; new ed. by R. ALEC HARMAN, 1952), a pupil-master discussion that offers firsthand information concerning the 16th-century approach to counterpoint; LODOVICO ZACCONI, *Prattica di musica*, pt. 2 (1622), one of the first presentations of the five species as a means of teaching counterpoint; JOHANN FUX, *Gradus ad Parnassum* (1725; trans. by ALFRED MANN and JOHN EDMUNDS, *Steps to Parnassus*, 1943), probably the most celebrated of all books on this subject; mainly concerned with the problems encountered in writing counterpoint.

Notation: WILLI APEL, *The Notation of Polyphonic Music, 900–1600*, 5th ed. (1961), a standard textbook, including staff notation and tablatures, and many facsimiles used as exercises for transcription; ERHARD KAŘKOSCHKA, *Das Schriftbild der neuen Musik* (1966), an excellently documented study of contemporary notation; WALTER KAUFMANN, *Musical Notations of the Orient: Notational Systems of Continental East, South and Central Asia* (1967); CARL PARRISH, *The Notation of Medieval Music* (1957), excellent facsimiles; EMANUEL WINTERNITZ, *Musical Autographs from Monteverdi to Hindemith* (1955), a study of musical handwriting, with many facsimiles.

Western compositional technique: Because most writings on musical composition were conceived as didactic treatises for would-be composers, their content has virtually no bearing on a better understanding of crucial aesthetic attitudes and mental processes. Instead, depending on the era from which they hail as well as the specific outlook of their authors, such treatises deal for the most part with contrapuntal rules, harmonic laws, and the like. While numerous books of this type appeared through the ages, it was only with the creation of the educational institutions known as conservatories of music, following the lead of the National Conservatory of France established in the last years of the 18th century, that composition became a discipline formally taught and hence requiring comprehensive textbooks, including the theory of form and instrumentation. This profitable need was satisfied by the voluminous activities of 19th-century writers from J.J. Momigny and Anton Reicha to Vincent d'Indy in France and from Heinrich Christoph Koch to Hugo Riemann in Germany. Few of these books were translated into English, and they are of primary interest to the specialist. The following is a selection of easily accessible monographs and documentary collections with emphasis on firsthand testimonies of the creative artists themselves.

JACQUES BARZUN (ed.), *Pleasures of Music* (1951), a collection of writings about music, including many from the pens of men of literature; LEONARD BERNSTEIN, *The Joy of Music* (1959), contains Bernstein's seven "Omnibus" television scripts, including his excellent comments on sketch materials relating to Beethoven's *Fifth Symphony* and its ultimate realization; FREDERICK DORIAN, *The Musical Workshop* (1947), a discussion of various aspects of musical composition, including comments on creative procedures; HANNS EISLER, *Composing for the Films* (1947), rare insights into the problems of cinematographic music from a composer who, during his Hollywood years, tried to turn music into an integral aspect of film art; MAX GRAF, *From Beethoven to Shostakovich* (1947, reprinted 1969), a popular study of psychological processes involved in composition; MICHAEL HAMBURGER (ed. and trans.), *Beethoven: Letters, Journals and Conversations* (1960), a concise but well-chosen selection of Beethoven's own words concerning both specific compositions and the problems of the composer in general; LEJAREN A. HILLER, JR., and LEONARD M. ISAACSON, *Experimental Music* (1959), the first and still basic monograph dealing with the philosophy, procedures, and techniques of composition with an electronic computer; PAUL HINDEMITH, *A Composer's World* (1961), a leading 20th-century composer looks at various facets of the composer's world, including questions of musical perception, inspiration, technique, performance, and education; IRVING KOLODIN (ed.), *The Composer as Listener: A Guide to Music* (1958), excerpts from pertinent writings, including letters mostly by important composers of the 19th and early 20th centuries; EDWARD E. LOWINSKY, "Musical Genius: Evolution and Origins of a Concept," *Musical Quarterly*, 50:321–340, 476–495 (1964), excellent documentation of the evolution of a concept that has been associated through the ages more consistently with music than with any other form of artistic production; ALAN P. MERRIAM, *The Anthropology of Music* (1964), a comprehensive treatment of music in relation to culture, drawing upon fieldwork on every continent and at all social levels (see especially ch. 9, "The Process of Composition"); SAM MORGENSTERN (ed.), *Composers on Music: An Anthology of Composers' Writings from Palestrina to Copland* (1956), an excellent collection, mostly of letters, dealing with general and specific aspects of the composer's work; ERNEST NEWMAN, *The Unconscious Beethoven*, rev. ed. (1970), a fascinating, if not unproblematic, study of the successive stages of Beethoven's work as revealed in his sketches by one of Britain's most famous critics; GERTRUDE NORMAN and MIRIAM LUBELL SHRIFTE (eds.), *Letters of Composers: An Anthology, 1603–1945* (1946), one of the most comprehensive of several collections of composers' letters available in paperback; JOSEF RUFER, *Die Komposition mit zwölf Tönen* (1952, 2nd ed. 1966; Eng. trans., *Composition with Twelve Notes Related to One Another*, 1965), a cogent introduction to dodecaphonic aesthetics and technique by a dedicated Schoenberg disciple; WILLIAM RUSSO, *Jazz Composition and Orchestration* (1968), one of the very few serious treatments of a type of composition that has gained respectability only in recent years; ARNOLD SCHOENBERG, *Style and Idea* (1950), a discussion of Schoenberg's artistic motivation and procedures as well as those of the composers he admired most, including Brahms and Mahler; ROGER SESSIONS, *The Musical Experience of Composer, Performer, Listener* (1962), a discussion of fundamental musical problems by America's senior living composer; WILLIAM OLIVER STRUNK (ed.), *Source Readings in Music History from Classical Antiquity Through the Romantic Era* (1950), an indispensable collection of relevant excerpts from the writings of philosophers, musical theorists, and composers from Plato to Richard Wagner; DONALD FRANCIS TOVEY, *The Mainstream of Music, and Other Essays* (1961), a paperback reprint of some of the finest essays by the great British critic who discusses basic compositional issues. See also ERICH LEINSDORF, *The Composer's Advocate* (1981).

Instrumentation: WILLI APEL, *Harvard Dictionary of Music*, 2nd ed. rev. (1969), a good source on any musical subject; DONALD JAY GROUT, *A History of Western Music* (1960), the best general history of music to date; ADAM CARSE, *The History of Orchestration* (1925, reprinted 1964), a detailed look at the evolution of the orchestra and musical instruments; NICOLAS RIMSKY-KORSAKOV, *Principles of Orchestration, with Musical Examples Drawn from His Own Works*, ed. by MAXIMILIAN STEINBERG, 1 vol. (1964; orig. pub. in Russian, 1910), still one of the best texts for the serious student; ROMAIN GOLDRON, *Ancient and Oriental Music* (1968), examples of non-Western music and instruments.

Recording of music: ROLAND GELATT, *The Fabulous Phonograph*, 2nd rev. ed. (1977), a general history of the phonograph, particularly good on the complex corporate developments; OLIVER READ and WALTER L. WELCH, *From Tin Foil to Stereo*, 2nd ed. (1976), a scholarly and detailed phonographic history with much elucidation of technical matters; FREDERIC W. WILE, *Emile Berliner: Maker of the Microphone* (1926, reprinted 1974), an adulatory, but worthwhile, biography; FRED GAISBERG, *The Music Goes Round* (1942, reprinted 1977), an autobiographical account of the history of the phonograph by a man associated with Berliner from the earliest days (a valuable source despite many inaccuracies); MATTHEW JOSEPHSON, *Edison* (1959), a thoroughly researched biography of the inventor of the phonograph; JOSEPH BATTEN, *Joe Batten's Book: The Story of Sound Recording* (1956), another personal documentation of early phonographic history, not as far-ranging as Gaisberg's but with much unduplicated material. RUSSELL MILLER and ROGER BOAR, *The Incredible Music Machine* (1982), is a popular history.

The History of Western Music

All ancient civilizations entered historical times with a flourishing musical culture. That the earliest writers explained it in terms of legend and myth is evidence of the remote beginnings of the art of sound. Among the speculations about its origin, the more plausible are that it began as a primitive form of communication, that it grew out of a device to expedite communal labour, or that it originated as a powerful adjunct to religious ceremonies. While such theories must necessarily remain speculative, it is clear, despite the prehistoric musical artifacts found in central Europe, that the cradle of Western music was the fertile crescent cupping the eastern end of the Mediterranean Sea. There the Mesopotamian, Egyptian, and Hebrew nations, among others, evolved political, social cultures that were absorbed by the conquering Greeks and, in turn, by the Romans, who transported a relatively sophisticated art form back to western Europe.

In all of these early cultures the social functions of music were essentially the same since their climate, geographic location, cultural pace, and mutual influences produced many more social similarities than differences. The primary function of music was apparently religious, ranging from heightening the effect of "magic" to ennobling liturgies. The other musical occasions depicted in both pictures and written accounts were equally functional: stirring incitements to military zeal, soothing accompaniments to communal or solitary labour, heightening aids to dramatic spectacles, and enlivening backgrounds to social gatherings that involved either singing or dancing or both. In every case musical sounds were an adjunct either to bodily movement (dance, march, game, or work) or to song. Many centuries were to pass before pleasure in euphonious sound became an end in itself.

This article is divided into the following sections:

The establishment of Western musical traditions

ROOTS IN ANTIQUITY

Ancient Middle East and Egypt. The inhabitants of the Mesopotamian region around the Tigris and Euphrates rivers (the Sumerians, the Babylonians, and the Assyrians) flourished from *c.* 3500 to *c.* 500 BC. Their pictures and the few surviving artifacts indicate that they had instruments of every basic type—idiophones, whose sound is made by resonating as a whole; aerophones, which resonate a column of blown air; chordophones, with strings to be plucked or struck; and membranophones, made of stretched skins over a resonating body. An undecipherable hymn engraved in stone, dating from *c.* 800 BC, is evidence of a primitive system of musical notation.

The Egyptians, entering historical times about 500 years later than the Mesopotamians, enjoyed all of the same types of activities and instruments, as may be deduced from numerous written references to music as well as seen on many artifacts, especially the pictures preserved on pottery utensils.

The musical culture of the Hebrew peoples, recorded from about 2000 BC and documented primarily in the Old Testament, was more directly influential in the West because of its adoption and adaptation into the Christian liturgy. Because of the prohibition of Jewish religious law against the making of "graven images," there are very few surviving artifacts or pictures. Among the established practices of the temple service still current in the synagogue are the extensive use of the shofar (a ritualistic ram's-horn trumpet) and the singing of passages from the Pentateuch (the first five books of the Old Testament), prayers, and songs of praise.

Ancient Greece. Of the eastern Mediterranean cultures, it was undoubtedly that of the Greeks that furnished the most direct link with musical development in western Europe, by way of the Romans, who defeated them but adopted much of Greek culture intact. Entering historical times relatively late, *c.* 1000 BC, the Greeks soon dominated their neighbours and absorbed many elements of earlier cultures, which they modified and combined into an enlightened and sophisticated civilization. The two basic Greek religious cults—one devoted to Apollo, the other to Dionysus—became the prototypes for the two aesthetic poles, classical and romantic, that have contended throughout Western cultural history. The Apollonians were characterized by objectivity of expression, simplicity, and clarity, and their favoured instrument was the kithara, a type of lyre. The Dionysians, on the other hand, preferred the reed-blown aulos and were identified by subjectivity, emotional abandon, and sensuality.

Apollonian and Dionysiac expression

The prevailing doctrine of ethos, as explained by ancient Greek philosophers such as Plato and Aristotle, was based on the belief that music has a direct effect upon the soul and actions of mankind. As a result, the Greek political and social systems were intertwined with music, which had a primary role in the dramas of Aeschylus, Sophocles, Euripides, and Aristophanes. And the Grecian educational system was focussed upon *musica* and *gymnastica,* the former referring to all cultural and intellectual studies, as distinguished from those related to physical training.

To support its fundamental role in society, an intricate scientific rationale of music evolved, encompassing tuning, instruments, modes (melodic formulas based on certain scales), and rhythms. The 6th-century-BC philosopher and mathematician Pythagoras was the first to record the vibratory ratios that established the series of notes still used in Western music. From the total gamut of notes used were derived the various modes bearing the names of Grecian tribes—Dorian, Phrygian, Lydian, etc. The rhythmic system, deriving from poetry, was based on long-short relationships rather than strong-weak accentual metre. After Pythagoras, Aristoxenus was the major historian and theoretician of Greek music.

Origin of musical modes

Ancient Rome. When the musical culture of the eastern Mediterranean was transplanted into the western Mediterranean by the returning Roman legions, it was inevitably modified by local tastes and traditions. In most cases, the resulting practices were more limited than their models. The diatonic (seven-note) scale, for example, became the standard, displacing the chromatic and enharmonic structures of the Grecian system. Of particular consequence was the new concept of metre as a series of equal durations, with emphasis being determined by accent (stress) rather than by duration.

An inventory of the musical heritage transplanted from the ancient East (particularly Greece) to Rome reveals the rich treasure inherited: an acoustical theory that accounted for the identification and classification of tones; a concept of tonal organization resulting in the system of modes; principles of rhythmic organization; basic principles of instrument construction; a system of notation that conveyed all necessary indications of pitch and duration; and a large repertory of melodies to serve as models for further composition.

THE MIDDLE AGES

Monophonic liturgical chant. With the decline of the Roman Empire, the institution destined to perpetuate and expand the musical heritage of antiquity was the Christian Church, but it was not a unified process. Many of the cultural centres of the Western church developed distinctive characteristics while sharing the common heritage of the Hebrew liturgy and Greek culture. In Milan, for example, metrical hymnody, as distinguished from the earlier practice of unmetred psalmody, was cultivated, particularly under the influence of the 4th-century Bishop Ambrose, who first attempted to codify the growing repertory of chants. This body of Milanese church music, therefore, came to be called Ambrosian chant. Somewhat later a unique style and repertory known as Mozarabic chant evolved in Spain, and in France the Gallican style prevailed.

But the mainstream of church music was the type of chant practiced in Rome. Beginning in the late 6th century, according to tradition, with Pope Gregory I, the vast number of traditional melodies that became the foundation for the later development of Western art music were codified and organized. A systematic organization of tonal materials also was gradually accomplished, resulting in the eight church modes. Each melody was assigned a specific function in the services of the liturgical year—some for the mass and some for the divine offices such as Matins, Vespers, and Compline. After a period of assimilation, the Gregorian chant repertory began a process of expansion in the 9th century, when the practice of troping originated. A trope is either a text or a melodic section added to a preexisting melody or a combination of text and music incorporated into existing liturgical music. It is not surprising that church musicians, after years of singing traditional chants, should want to express themselves by adding words to vocalized melodies. Perhaps the motive was more functional: the added syllables would make the long textless passages easier to remember. Tuotilo (died 915), a monk of St. Gall in Switzerland, is credited with the invention of tropes. Notker Balbulus (died 912) is notable for his association with the sequence, a long hymn that originated as a trope added to the final syllable of the Alleluia of the mass.

Gregorian chant

Development of polyphony. At the same time that the Gregorian repertory was being expanded by the interpolation of tropes and sequences, it was being further enriched by a revolutionary concept destined to give a new direction to the art of sound for hundreds of years. This concept was polyphony, or the simultaneous sounding of two or more melodic lines. The practice emerged gradually during the Dark Ages, and the lack of definite knowledge regarding its origin has brought forward several plausible theories: it resulted from singers with different natural vocal ranges singing at their most comfortable pitch levels; it was a practice of organists adopted by singers; or it came about when the repetition of a melody at a different pitch level was sung simultaneously with the original statement of the melody. Whatever motivated this dramatic departure from traditional monophony (music consisting of a single voice part), it was an established practice when it was described in *Musica enchiriadis* (*c.* 900), a manual for singers and one of the major musical documents of the Middle Ages. To a given plainsong, or *vox principalis,* a second voice (*vox organalis*) could be added at the interval (distance between notes) of a fourth or fifth (four or five steps) below. Music so performed was known as organum. While it may be assumed that the first attempts at polyphony involved only parallel motion at a set interval, the *Musica enchiriadis* describes and gives examples of two-part singing in similar (but not exactly parallel) and contrary movement—evidence that a considerable process of evolution had already taken place.

The beginnings of polyphony

The next major source of information was the *Micrologus,* written in the early 11th century by the Italian monk and musical theorist Guido of Arezzo. This work documented principles that were crucial to the further development of polyphony. Rhythmic independence was added to melodic independence, and the added voice might sing two or more tones to one in the original plainsong. During the half century after Guido's death, developments came more rapidly as the plainsong chant became the lower rather than the upper voice. After the emancipation of the organal part, *vox organalis,* its ultimate freedom was reached in the organums of the monastery of Saint-Martial in Limoges, France, where the plainsong part was reduced to the role of sustaining each tone while the organal part indulged in free melismata (groups of notes sung to a single syllable), either improvised or composed. This new style was called *organum purum.*

The Notre-Dame school. Early in the 12th century the centre of musical activity shifted to the church of Notre-Dame in Paris, where the French composer Léonin recorded in the *Magnus Liber Organi* ("Great Book of Organum") a collection of two-part organums for the entire church year. A generation later his successor, Pérotin, edited and revised the *Magnus Liber,* incorporating the rhythmic patterns already well-known in secular music and adding more than one part to the cantus firmus (the "given" or preexisting plainsong melody). When metre was applied to the original plainsong as well as to the *vox organalis,* the resulting form was called a clausula. Then, when words were provided for the added part or parts, a clausula became a motet. At first the words given to the motet were a commentary in Latin on the text of the original plainsong tenor (the voice part "holding" the cantus firmus; from Latin *tenere,* "to hold"). Later in the 13th century the added words were in French and secular in nature. Finally, each added part was given its own text, resulting in the classic Paris motet: a three-part composition consisting of a portion of plainchant (tenor) overlaid with two faster moving parts, each with its own secular text in French. At the same time another polyphonic form, the conductus, was flourishing. It differed from a motet in that its basic part was not plainsong and that all parts sang the same Latin text in note-against-note style. The conductus gradually disappeared with the rise of the motet, which apparently served both liturgical and secular functions.

The beginnings of the motet

Ars Nova. When the influential treatise *Ars Nova* ("New Art") by the composer Philippe de Vitry appeared early in the 14th century, the preceding epoch acquired its designation of Ars Antiqua (Old Art), for it was only in retrospect that the rapid developments of the century and a half from *c.* 1150 to *c.* 1300 could appear as antiquated. De Vitry recorded the innovations of his day, particularly in the areas of metre and harmony. While 13th-century music had been organized around the triple "modal" rhythms derived from secular music and a harmonic vocabulary based on "perfect" consonances (unison, fourth, fifth, octave), the New Art of the 14th century used duple as well as triple divisions of the basic pulse and brought about a taste for harmonious intervals of thirds and sixths.

The musical centre of 14th-century Italy was Florence, where a blind organist, Francisco Landini, and his predecessors and contemporaries Giovanni da Cascia, Jacopo da Bologna, and Lorenzo and Ghirardello da Firenze were the leading composers of several new forms: madrigals (contrapuntal compositions for several voices), ballatas (similar to the French virelai), and caccias (three-voice songs using melodic imitation).

Monophonic secular song. Secular music undoubtedly flourished during the early Middle Ages, but, aside from sporadic references, the earliest accounts of such music in the Western world described the music of the goliards; these people were itinerant minor clerics and students who, from the 7th century on, roamed the land singing and playing topical songs dealing with love, war, famine, and other issues of the day. The emergence in France of a fully developed secular-musical tradition about the beginning of the 12th century is evidence that the art had been evolving continuously before that time. Partially motivated by the attitude of chivalry engendered by the Crusades, a new life-style began among the nobility of southern France. Calling themselves troubadours, they circulated among the leading courts of the region, devoting themselves to writing and singing poetry in the vernacular. The troubadour movement flourished in Provence during the 12th and 13th centuries. About the middle of the 12th century, noblemen of northern France, most notably Adam de La Halle, took up the pastime, calling themselves trouvères. In Germany a similar group known as Minnesingers, represented by Walther von der Vogelweide, began their activities about 1150 and continued for almost a century after their French counterparts had ceased composing. Late in the 13th century the burgher class in Germany began imitating the aristocratic Minnesingers. Calling themselves Meistersingers, they flourished for more than 500 years, organizing themselves into fraternities and following strict rules of poetry, music, and performance. The most famous of them, Hans Sachs, was immortalized in the 19th century in Richard Wagner's opera *Die Meistersinger von Nürnberg.* Relatively little is known of similar secular-musical activities in Italy, Spain, and England. Closely associated with the entertainments of the aristocratic dilettantes were the professional musicians of the peasant class called jongleurs and minstrels in France, *Gaukler* in Germany, and scops and gleemen in England.

Troubadours and Meistersingers

The musical style that had been established by the troubadours—which was monophonic, of limited range, and sectional in structure—was adopted by each of the succeeding groups. Of particular significance in view of its influence on polyphonic music was the metric system, which is based on six rhythmic modes. Supposedly derived from Greek poetic metres such as trochaic (long–short) and iambic (short–long), these modes brought about a prevailing triple metre in French music, while German poetry produced duple as well as triple metre. A great variety of formal patterns evolved, in which musical structure and poetic structure were closely related. The most characteristic was the ballade, which was called *Bar* form in Germany, with an AAB structure. This type, along with the rondeau (song for solo voice with choral refrain) and the similar virelai (an analogue of the Italian ballata), was destined to become a favoured form employed by composers of polyphony such as Guillaume de Machaut, the universally acknowledged master of French music of the Ars Nova period. Machaut also continued the composition of motets, organizing them around recurrent rhythmic patterns (isorhythm), a major structural technique of the age. The beginnings of an independent instrumental repertory during the 13th century are represented by the estampie, a monophonic dance form almost identical in style to the vocal secular music.

THE RENAISSANCE PERIOD

The term Renaissance, in spite of its various connotations, is difficult to apply to music. Borrowed from the visual arts and literature, the term is meaningful primarily as a chronological designation. Some historians date the beginning of the musical Renaissance at about 1400, some with the rise of imitative counterpoint, about 1450. Others relate it to the musical association with Humanistic poetry at the beginning of the 16th century, and still others reserve the term for the conscious attempt to recreate and imitate supposedly classical models that took place about 1600.

The court of Burgundy. No one line of demarcation is completely satisfactory, but, adhering to commonly accepted usage, one may conveniently accept as the beginning of the musical Renaissance the flourishing and secularization of music at the beginning of the 15th century, particularly at the court of Burgundy. Certainly many manifestations of a cultural renaissance were evident at the time: interest in preserving artifacts and literature of classical antiquity, the waning authority and influence of the church, the waxing Humanism, the burgeoning of urban centres and universities, and the growing economic affluence of the states of western Europe.

As one manifestation of their cultivation of elegant living, the aristocracy of both church and state vied with one another in maintaining resident musicians who could serve both chapel and banqueting hall. The frequent interchange of these musicians accounts for the rapid dissemination of new musical techniques and tastes. Partly because of economic advantages, Burgundy and its capital, Dijon, became the centre of European activity in music as well as the intellectual and artistic focus of northern Europe during the first half of the 15th century. Comprising most of eastern France and the Low Countries, the courts of Philip the Good and Charles the Bold attracted the leading musicians of western Europe. Prime among them was Guillaume Dufay, who had spent some time in Rome and Florence before settling in Cambrai about 1440. An important contemporary of Dufay was Gilles Binchois, who served at Dijon from about 1430 until 1460. The alliance of Burgundy with England accounted for the presence on the Continent of the English composer John Dunstable, who had a profound influence on Dufay. While the contributions of the English to the mainstream of continental music are sparsely documented, the differences in style between Dufay and his predecessor Machaut are partially accounted for by the new techniques and, especially, the richer harmonies adopted by the Burgundian composers from their English allies.

Rivalry between church and state in musical patronage

New religious musical forms. The social circumstances of the age determined that composers would devote their efforts to the mass, the motet, and the chanson (secular French song). During the first half of the 15th century, the mass became established as a unified polyphonic setting of the five main parts of the Ordinary of the mass (Kyrie, Gloria, Credo, Sanctus, Agnus Dei), with each movement based on either the relevant portion of plainsong or, reflecting the dawning Renaissance, a secular song such as the popular "L'Homme armé" ("The Armed Man") and "Se la face ay pale." Still reflecting medieval practices, the preexisting melody (or cantus firmus) was usually in the tenor (or lowest) part and in long, sustained tones, while the upper parts provided free elaboration. Dufay's nine complete settings of the mass, compared with Machaut's single setting, give a clear indication of the growing importance of the mass as a musical form. The motet became simply a setting of a Latin text from Scriptures or the liturgy in the prevailing polyphonic style of the time. It was no longer necessarily anchored to a plainsong tenor; the composer could give free reign to his invention, although some did, of course, resort to older techniques.

Importance of the mass

Secular music. It was in secular music that giant strides took place. While their chansons continued the tradition of rondeaux, virelais, and ballades, Dufay and his contemporaries added free forms divorced from the ordered patterns of the Ars Antiqua and Ars Nova periods.

Among the distinctive features of Burgundian musical style was the prevailing three-part texture, with melodic and rhythmic interest centred in the top part. Because it was so typical of secular songs, this texture is commonly referred to as "ballade style" whether it appears in mass, motet, or chanson. Its possible stylistic implication is that a solo voice sang the upper melody, accompanied by instruments playing the lower parts, although no documents remain to establish exactly how the music was performed. There was probably no standard performing medium: all parts may have been sung; some or all may have been doubled by instruments; or there may have been one vocal part supported by instrumental accompaniment.

The Franco-Flemish school. A watershed in the history of music occurred about the middle of the 15th century. The fall of Constantinople in 1453 and the end of the Hundred Years' War at about the same time increased commerce from the East and affluence in the West. Most significant musically was the pervasive influence of musicians from the Low Countries, whose domination of the musical scene during the last half of the 15th century is reflected in the period designations the Netherlands school and the Franco-Flemish school. These musicians travelled and resided throughout Europe in response to their great demand at princely courts, including those of the Medici family in Florence and the Sforzas in Milan. Further dissemination of knowledge resulted from the invention and development of printing.

Travelling musicians at courts

The leading composers, whose patrons were now members of the civil aristocracy as well as princes of the church, were Jean d'Okeghem, Jakob Obrecht, and, especially, Josquin des Prez. D'Okeghem, born and trained in Flanders, spent most of his life in the service of the kings of France and was recognized by his contemporaries as the "Prince of Music." Obrecht remained near his birthplace in the Netherlands, going occasionally to Italy in the retinue of Duca Ercole I (Duke Hercules I) of Ferrara. More typical of the peripatetic Netherlanders was the career of Josquin, the most influential composer of the period. After training at St. Quentin, he served the Sforza family in Milan, the papal choir in Rome, Ercole I, and King Louis XII of France before returning to his native Flanders in 1516. These three composers and several contemporaries hastened the development of the musical techniques that became the basis of 16th-century practice and influenced succeeding developments.

Rather than the three parts typical of most Burgundian music, four parts became standard for vocal polyphony in the late 15th century. The fourth part was added below the tenor, increasing the total range and resulting in greater breadth of sound. The presence of the four parts also allowed for contrasts of texture such as the "duet style" so characteristic of Josquin, when the two upper parts might sing a passage alone and be echoed by the two lower parts alone. The emergence of the technique of imitation (one voice repeating recognizably a figure heard first in another voice) as the chief form-generating principle brought about more equality of parts. At the same time "familiar style," in which all parts move together in chords, provided a means of textural contrast. The great variety of rhythmic techniques that evolved during the 14th and early 15th centuries made possible a wide range of expression—from quiet tranquillity for sacred music to lively and spirited secular music. Knowledge of the musical practices comes not only from the thousands of surviving compositions but from informative treatises such as the 12 by the composer Johannes Tinctoris (1436–1511), one of which, *Terminorum musicae diffinitorium* (*c.* 1475), is the earliest printed dictionary of musical terms.

Wider range of expression through rhythmic developments

The chief forms of vocal music continued to be the mass, the motet, and the chanson, to which must be added other national types that developed during the 15th century—the villancico (secular poetry set for voice and lute or for three or four voices) in Spain and the frottola (a simple, chordal setting in three or four parts of an Italian text) in Italy. The emergence of the frottola in northern Italy led to the development of the Renaissance madrigal, which impelled that country to musical supremacy in Europe.

Instrumental music. At the same time, an independent instrumental idiom was evolving. While instruments had been in common usage throughout the Middle Ages, their function was primarily to double or to substitute for voices in vocal polyphonic music or to provide music for dancing. Techniques unsuitable for voices were doubtless part of an instrumentalist's musical vocabulary, but most such music was improvised rather than being written. Although there are a few sources of instrumental music dating from the 13th and 14th centuries, the earliest relatively extensive documentation comes from the 15th century, particularly from German sources, such as the *Buxheimer Orgelbuch* and Conrad Paumann's *Fundamentum organisandi* (*Fundamentals of Organ Playing*). The compositions in both collections are of two basic types, arrangements of vocal works and keyboard pieces entitled *Praeambulum* (*Prelude*).

During the course of the 16th century, instrumental music burgeoned rapidly, along with the continually developing idiomatically instrumental techniques, such as strongly accented rhythms, rapid repeated tones and figures, angular melodic lines involving wide intervallic skips, wide ranges, long, sustained tones and phrases, and much melodic ornamentation.

Musical forms. Dance forms, a continuation of a tradition unbroken since the beginnings of recorded music history, were most characteristically composed in pairs, although single dances as well as embryonic suites of three or more dances appeared. The pairs usually consisted of pieces in contrasting tempo and metre that often were unified by sharing a common melody. Common dance pairs included the pavane and galliard, the allemande and courante, and the basse danse and tourdion.

Preludes continued as a major form of organ music and were joined by the fantasia, the *intonazione,* and the toccata in a category frequently referred to as "free forms" because of the inconsistency and unpredictability of their structure and musical content—sections in imitative counterpoint, sections of sustained chords, sections in virtuoso figuration. If a distinction must be made, it might be said in very general terms that the fantasia tended to be more contrapuntal while the toccata (or "touch piece") featured passages designed to demonstrate the performer's agility, although the designations were freely interchangeable. To the same category belong the descriptive pieces such as *The King's Hunt,* which featured naive musical representations of natural sounds.

Fantasias and toccatas

The ricercar and the canzona, generally referred to as fugal forms because of their relationship to the principle of the fugue (that of melodic imitation), arose out of the growing understanding of and dependence on imitation as a unifying structural technique. Although these designations were applied to a great variety of pieces—some identical in style to the fantasia or prelude—the classic ricercar of the 16th century was virtually an instrumental motet, slow and churchlike in character and consisting of a number of sections, each utilizing imitation. The canzona followed the same structural principle but was a lively counterpart to the chanson, with the sections sometimes in contrasting tempo and metre. Cantus firmus compositions were based upon preexisting melody. During the 16th century most were designed for liturgical usage but were based upon both secular melodies and plainsong. In most cases the cantus firmus was sounded in long, sustained tones while the other part or parts added decorative contrapuntal lines. The organ mass, in which the choir and the organ alternated lines of the liturgical text, was a popular practice.

Variations also often used a preexisting melody but differed from cantus firmus compositions in that the melody was much shorter and was repeated a number of times, each time with different accompanying parts. The two basic types during the Renaissance were the plain, or melodic, variations and the ground. In the former, the chosen melody usually appeared in the top part and was varied in each repetition with ornamentation and melodic figuration or with changing accompaniments. The ground, or ground bass, was a simple melodic pattern sounded in the lowest part, which served as a foundation for imaginative figuration in the upper parts.

Solo and ensemble instruments. The four major vehicles for instrumental music of the period were the lute, the organ, stringed keyboard instruments, and instrumental ensembles. Most popular by far was the lute, which could produce the major elements of instrumental style except for long, sustained tones. Noteworthy composers of lute music included Luis Milán in Spain, Arnold Schlick in Germany, and John Dowland in England. The organ, because of its close association with liturgical music, continued to be an important instrument, and its literature includes all of the formal types except dances. Among the leading organ composers were the Germans Paumann, Schlick, and Paul Hofhaimer, the Italians Claudio Merulo and Andrea and Giovanni Gabrieli, the Spaniard Antonio de Cabezón, and the Englishman John Bull.

The two basic classes of stringed keyboard instruments were the harpsichord (virginals, spinet, clavecin, clavicembalo), with quill-plucked strings, and the clavichord, with strings struck by thin metal tongues. Keyboard instruments were highly capable of idiomatically instrumental effects and flourished, particularly in England, from the last half of the 16th century onward, thanks to the composers William Byrd, John Bull, and Orlando Gibbons. A major manuscript source of the keyboard works of these masters is the famous *Fitzwilliam Virginal Book* of the 17th century.

Instrumental ensembles of the Renaissance were not standardized, although consorts (groups) of viols, of woodwind instruments such as recorders and shawms (loud oboes), or of brass-family instruments such as the cornet and sackbut (early trombone) were common. More common, however, were mixed consorts of various types of instruments, depending on the players available. All types of instrumental forms were performed by ensembles except for the prelude and the toccata, which were essentially keyboard works. Representative composers included the Gabrielis and Gibbons.

Vocal music in the 16th century. At the beginning of the 16th century the style of vocal music was generally uniform because of the pervading influence of Netherlanders during the preceding half century. That uniformity persisted well into the late Renaissance but was gradually superseded by emerging national differences, new forms, and the increasing importance of Italy as a musical centre during the last half of the 16th century.

The rapid accumulation of new musical techniques and resources produced a wide vocabulary of artistic expression, and the invention of music printing helped the rapid dispersal of new techniques. In an age in which music was an essential social grace, composers wrote more secular music, in which fewer technical restrictions were in force and experimentation and novelty were applauded. Advances were particularly apparent in venturesome harmonies as chromaticism (the use of notes not belonging to the mode of the composition) sounded the death knell of the modal system.

Harmonic experiment

Liturgical practice dictated that the mass and the motet remain the chief forms of sacred vocal music. Compared with secular music, their style was conservative, but inevitably some of the newer secular techniques crept in and figured effectively in the music of the Counter-Reformation within the Roman Catholic Church.

Four distinct types of mass settings were established during the century. Two types were continuations of earlier practice: the tenor mass, in which the same cantus firmus served for all five portions of the Ordinary of the mass, and the plainsong mass, in which the cantus firmus (usually a corresponding section of plainsong) differed for each portion. Reflecting the more liberal attitudes of the Renaissance were the free mass, with no borrowed materials, and the parody mass, in which the entire polyphonic web was freely adapted from a motet or a secular composition. In all cases when a cantus firmus was used, the preexistent melody might appear in its original form or in paraphrased version, with tones added, omitted, or altered. As a result of the upheaval in the church caused by the Reformation, new forms derived from established models appeared in Protestant worship: the German Lutheran chorale (hymn tune, arranged from plainsong or a secular melody), the chorale motet, English anthems (Anglican form of motet) and services, and the psalm tunes in Calvinist areas.

Italy. While not young in a chronological sense, the musical life of Italy was reborn at the beginning of the 16th century after a century of relative dormancy. The frottola remained the prevailing secular form in northern Italy for the first three decades of the century.

When the humanistic poets, seeking a more refined expression, and the Netherlanders and composers trained by them, applying a more sophisticated musical technique, turned their efforts to the frottola, the result was the madrigal. The name was borrowed from the 14th-century form, but there was no resemblance in poetic or musical structure. Compared to the frottola, the earliest Renaissance madrigals, dating from about 1530, were characterized by quiet and restrained expression. Usually written for three or four voices, they were mostly homophonic (melody supported by chords) with occasional bits of imitation. Among the early madrigal composers were several Flemish composers resident in Italy, among them Adriaan Willaert, Jacques Arcadelt, and Philippe Verdelot. About 1560 the normal number of parts increased to five or six, and the texture became more consistently polyphonic. At the same time, more attention was given to expressive settings of the text, notably in the madrigals of Cipriano de Rore, Philippe de Monte, and the Gabrielis. During the last two decades of the century and continuing until the middle of the 17th century, the musical style of the madrigal changed appreciably. The late madrigals were of a very dramatic nature, featuring colouristic effects, vivid word-painting, and extensive chromaticism. Their declamatory character dictated a return to a more homophonic style. Noteworthy among the many composers of the late madrigal were Luca Marenzio, Don Carlo Gesualdo, and Claudio Monteverdi.

Birth of the madrigal

During the course of the century simpler secular forms, such as the villanella, the canzonetta, and the balletto, appeared in Italy, largely as a reaction against the refinement, complication, and sophistication of the madrigal. They reverted to the chordal style of the frottola, often with intentionally parodistic lyrics. The balletto was particularly distinguished by a refrain of nonsense syllables such as "fa la la."

England. Most of the Italian forms, along with their designations, were adopted by Elizabethan England during the last half of the 16th century. Most leading English composers, from William Byrd and Thomas Morley to John Wilbye, Thomas Weelkes, and Orlando Gibbons, contributed to the vast treasury of English secular music. Morley is particularly important as the editor of the most significant collection of English madrigals, the *Triumphes of Oriana,* published in 1603 and dedicated to Queen Elizabeth I (Oriana). These pieces correspond in style roughly to the middle-period Italian madrigal. English counterparts of the canzonetta and balletto were the canzonet and ballett. A late 16th-century innovation in both Italy and England was the ayre (air), a simple, chordal setting especially suitable for a solo voice with a lute or a consort of instruments playing the other parts. John Dowland and Thomas Campion were notable composers of ayres.

France. The French counterpart of Italian and English madrigals was the polyphonic chanson, a continuation of the chief medieval and early Renaissance form of secular music. Revitalized by composers such as Josquin, Clément Janequin, and Claudin de Sermisy, the chanson developed several distinctive features: a clearly delineated sectional structure with some repetition of sections, much vivid programmatic writing, and occasional use of irregular metric organization. The irregular metric structure, called *musique mesurée,* was used for maintaining faithfully the accentuation of the poetry and reflects the traditional primacy of textual over musical considerations in French music.

The chanson

Germany. The lied, or song, continued its 15th-century role as the chief secular form in Germanic areas, but it did not develop to the same extent as the madrigal and the chanson. Throughout the Renaissance it was relatively conservative in its adherence to the cantus firmus principle and its tendency toward chordal over contrapuntal texture. Following Heinrich Isaac in the 15th century, the major 16th-century lieder composers were Ludwig Senfl, Hans Leo Hassler, and Johann Hermann Schein. To all national schools of the 16th century must be added the name of the Flemish composer Orlando di Lasso, who wrote in French, Italian, or German, depending on his current employment. The Spanish villancico was a flourishing popular form, but there was no Iberian equivalent to the madrigal, the chanson, or the lied.

The tonal era and after: 1600 to the present

The beginning of the 17th century was one of the most dramatic turning points in the history of music, even more so than the beginning of the Ars Nova and almost as revolutionary as the beginning of the 20th century. The winds of change had been felt several decades earlier, and the establishment of the new style required several decades after the turn of the century, but the year 1600 saw the performance of several works destined to change the course of music.

THE BAROQUE ERA

The spirit of the Baroque

Originally used in a derogatory sense of referring to something bizarre, degenerate, and abnormal, the term Baroque gradually acquired a positive connotation for the grandiose, dramatic, energetic spirit in art that prevailed during the period from about 1600 to about 1750. The new spirit required a vastly expanded musical vocabulary, and a rapid evolution of new techniques occurred, particularly in vocal music. Two distinct musical styles were recognized. One, the *prima prattica* (or *stile antico*), was the universal style of the 16th century, the culmination of two centuries of adherence to Flemish models. The other, called *seconda prattica,* or *stile moderno,* referred to the new theatrical style emanating from Italy.

The expanded vocabulary allowed for a clearer distinction between sacred and secular music as well as between vocal and instrumental idioms, and national differences became more pronounced. The tonal organization of music evolved also, as the medieval modes that had previously served as the basis of melody and harmony were gradually replaced, during the 17th century, by the system of tonality dominating Western music until about 1900: a system based on contrasting keys, or sets of interrelated notes and chords deriving from a major or minor scale. Viewing the period as a whole, two additional innovations most clearly distinguish it from the preceding Renaissance: concertato, or the contrast, combination, and alternation of voices and instruments, and basso continuo (thorough bass, figured bass), an accompaniment consisting of a low-pitched instrument, such as a violoncello or a bassoon, combined with a keyboard instrument or lute capable of harmonic elaboration.

Opera. Most typical of the emerging style were the dramatic productions of the Camerata, a group in Florence who were dedicated to recreating and imitating the musical ideals and practices of classical antiquity—in a sense, the musical manifestation of the Renaissance. Their guiding philosophy was the preeminence of textual over musical considerations; their belief was that the function of music was to heighten the dramatic impact of words. The musical result was monody: originally recitative (solo singing reflecting speech rhythms), later also arioso (more lyric than recitative) and aria (more elaborate song), accompanied by a basso continuo that could provide an innocuous background to a solo voice. Among the major figures in this revolutionary movement were Giulio Caccini and Jacopo Peri, both of whom composed operas based on the legend of Orpheus and Eurydice. Caccini also provided the name for the new movement with his publication of *Le nuove musiche,* a collection of solo songs with continuo accompaniment. The ideas and techniques conceived by the Camerata spread rapidly over Italy and, subsequently, all over Europe.

17th-century developments in Rome

Early Italian operatic schools. During the 1620s and 1630s the centre of operatic activity shifted from Florence to Rome, where several distinctive features developed: a chorus was used extensively, dancing was incorporated into the dramatic spectacle, and an overture in the style of a canzona became the accepted norm. A flourishing operatic activity developed a decade later in Venice, where the first public opera house was opened in 1637. Public taste began to influence operatic composition, and, as a result, several innovations, such as the extensive use of popular tunes, spectacular staging, and short, fanfare-like overtures, were introduced. The audience's desire for tuneful songs also contributed to the clear distinction between recitative and aria, which began with the Venetian school. Foremost among contemporary composers was Monteverdi, who had known of the activities of the Florentine Camerata while serving as musical director to the Gonzaga family in nearby Mantua. He adopted the new style for his later madrigals and wrote two operas, *Orfeo* (1607) and *L'Arianna* (1608), before moving to Venice in 1613. Francesco Cavalli and Antonio Cesti became the leading Venetian operatic composers after Monteverdi's death in 1643.

Neapolitan opera. The last major operatic centre to develop in Italy began its activities in the 1670s in Naples. Neapolitan opera seria, or serious opera, with characters from classical history or mythology, dominated Europe for a century. It was essentially a series of recitatives and arias, the latter mostly of the da capo type (ABA, the A section given improvised embellishment on its repetition) characterized by florid virtuosic singing. Other features were, first, the distinction between recitativo secco (dry recitative), accompanied by the continuo, and recitativo accompagnato, or stromentato, accompanied by the orchestra, and, second, the establishment of the Italian overture. Called a sinfonia, the overture in three parts (fast–slow–fast) evolved into the symphony during the 18th century. Alessandro Scarlatti was the most influential of the early Neapolitan operatic composers.

The joining of the French and Italian forms

France. During the same period, opera was introduced at courtly functions outside Italy. After Luigi Rossi's *Orfeo* was performed in Paris in 1647, the Italian form was gradually merged with the major French dramatic form, the ballet; the importance of dancing in French operas thereafter is not surprising. Another distinguishing feature was the French overture (a slow movement, a fast movement, and, occasionally, a return to the opening slow section), which, like the Italian overture, later had an independent life. The masters of French opera during the Baroque period were Jean-Baptiste Lully and his successor Jean-Philippe Rameau. Because of the social and political upheaval of the Thirty Years' War, there was less operatic activity in Germany than in France, and the activity that did occur was more completely dominated by the Italian style. Hamburg, Munich, Dresden, and Vienna were the major centres, with Reinhard Keiser and Georg Philipp Telemann as the most prolific composers.

England. The situation in England resembled that in France, since the English also had a flourishing musico-dramatic form, the masque, which gradually merged with Italian opera. Henry Purcell and John Blow were the chief composers of opera in English before Italian domination of serious opera became almost complete during the 18th century.

Cantata and oratorio. The leading Neapolitan opera composers also helped to establish the Baroque successor to the madrigal—the cantata—which originated as a secular form for solo voice with instrumental accompaniment. Giacomo Carissimi standardized the form as a short drama in verse consisting of two or more arias with their preceding recitatives. The cantata was introduced into France by one of Carissimi's students, Marc-Antoine Charpentier; Louis Nicolas Clérambault continued the tradition in the late Baroque period. With the fading stylistic distinction between sacred and secular music, the cantata was quickly converted to church purposes, particularly in Germany, where it became the chief decorative service music for the Lutheran Church. Dietrich Buxtehude and Johann Kuhnau were two of the leading composers of such church cantatas.

While the new concertato techniques were being applied to established forms of church music, such as the mass, service, motet, anthem, and chorale, new forms emerged that were clear departures from Renaissance styles and types. The oratorio and settings of the Passion story developed simultaneously with opera and on almost identical lines, consisting of recitatives, arias, vocal ensembles, instrumental interludes, and choruses. Emilio del Cavaliere was the "founder" of the oratorio with his *La rappresentazione di anima e di corpo* (*The Representation of the Soul and the Body*). Produced in Rome in 1600, this work, unlike true oratorio, used actors and costumes. Carissimi and Alessandro Scarlatti were the chief Italian Baroque composers of oratorio, and Heinrich Schütz, a pupil of both Giovanni Gabrieli and Monteverdi in Venice, was the leading 17th-century German composer in this field.

Instrumental music. The new techniques of *Le nuove musiche* were to be heard in music for instruments, especially now that they participated in genres formerly written for unaccompanied voices (*e.g.,* the motet). The forms and mediums of instrumental music remained essentially the same but with considerably different emphasis. The lute, for example, lost status quickly with the rise of the harpsichord as the most common instrument for continuo accompaniment of dramatic productions. The organ, as the traditional church instrument, retained its position and assimilated the evolving forms.

Continuo instruments

Modification and expansion of older forms. Dance pairs of the Renaissance grew, about the middle of the 17th century, into dance suites consisting basically of four dances: allemande, courante, saraband, and gigue, with optional dances such as the gavotte, the bourrée, and the minuet sometimes inserted before the final movement. Variation forms—the chaconne (in which a set of harmonies or a bass theme is continuously repeated), the passacaglia (in which the theme is repeated but not necessarily in the bass), along with the ground bass and variations on well-known melodies—continued to be popular. Free forms also continued in the patterns of their Renaissance antecedents, while growing in dimension and inventiveness. The toccata, prelude, and fantasia were expanded into multisectional forms using the three basic instrumental textures—imitative counterpoint, chordal homophony, and virtuosic passage work—in combination, alternation, and contrast. The Renaissance fugal forms, chiefly the canzona and the ricercar, gradually evolved into the late Baroque fugue, and cantus firmus compositions continued to flourish as a result of their liturgical function.

The sonata and concerto. The major new categories of instrumental music during the Baroque period were the sonata and the concerto. Originally applied to instrumental ensemble pieces derived from the canzona, the term sonata became the designation for a form that was to dominate instrumental music from the mid-18th until the 20th century. In its keyboard manifestation, it was a binary (two-part) structure similar to a dance-suite movement. For small ensemble, it evolved into a series of independent movements (usually in a slow–fast–slow–fast arrangement) called a *sonata da chiesa* ("church sonata") or a dance suite called a *sonata da camera* ("chamber sonata"). Especially prominent was the trio sonata, for two violins (or flutes or oboes) and cello with continuo. Eventually, similar forms were adopted for orchestra (sinfonia or concerto), for orchestra with a small group of featured instruments (concerto grosso), or for a solo instrument with orchestra (solo concerto). The fundamental principle of the concerto was that of contrast of instrumental groups and musical textures.

Throughout the period, keyboard music flourished, notably in the hands of Jan Pieterszoon Sweelinck in the Netherlands, Johann Pachelbel and Johann Froberger in Germany, Girolamo Frescobaldi in Italy, and Domenico Scarlatti in Spain; in France the chief exponents included Rameau and François Couperin.

Instrumental ensemble music, both chamber and orchestral, was dominated by Italians, chiefly from Bologna, the Bolognese school producing such composers as Arcangelo Corelli, Antonio Vivaldi, and Giuseppe Tartini. Purcell in England and Couperin and Jean-Marie Leclair in France are representative of the many composers in other nations who were influenced by Italian models of instrumental ensemble music.

The late Baroque. The Baroque era reached its zenith in the work of Johann Sebastian Bach (1685–1750) and George Frideric Handel (1685–1759). Both were born in the same part of Germany; both were reared in the Lutheran Church; and both were primarily organists; but because of different environmental circumstances each became a master of different musical forms. Handel, because of his conditioning in Italy, was primarily a dramatic composer, writing opera, oratorio, and secular cantatas, mostly after he reached England. He also wrote quite extensively for orchestra and instrumental ensemble. Bach, by contrast, was influenced by his lifelong employment in the church and by his dedication as a teacher; his works thus include Passions, cantatas for church services, liturgical organ pieces, and harpsichord compositions, many instructional in purpose.

The primacy of Bach and Handel

In the works of both Handel and Bach changes in technique reached a culmination with the clear establishment of the tonal system, allowing for modulation from one key centre to another, primarily as a device for formal organization. Rich, chromatic harmonic language was both reason and result of such a change. The fusion of contrapuntal technique with homophonic style resulted in a distinctive hybrid texture that employed figured bass (homophony) as a foundation for two or more independent melodic lines (polyphony).

THE CLASSICAL PERIOD

As in the case of the Renaissance, difficulties with terminology again arise with the label classical. Does it refer to a period of time, a distinctive musical style, an aesthetic attitude, an ideal standard, or an established norm? Again, the term was borrowed from the visual arts of the same epoch and is awkward when applied to music in that there were no known models from classical antiquity for composers to imitate. A full understanding of the term depends on a clear conception of the term romantic, for the two stand at opposite poles. Each represents a set of artistic ideals that has been in opposition to the other since both were recognized by early Grecian writers. As has been noted, the ancient Greek followers of Apollo established the ideal of classicism, whereas the cult of Dionysus produced the prototype of romanticism. A mixture of the two qualities has prevailed throughout recorded history, with first one and then the other in the ascendancy. Thus, there have been many "classic" and many "romantic" eras, but the labels have come to refer most specifically to the last half of the 18th century and the 19th century, respectively, because those periods represent most vividly the two tempers.

The term classical

The social and political scene during the late 18th century was hardly a setting for a quiet, composed "classical" age in view of the prevailing revolutionary spirit and colonial rivalry. The revolutionary movement did have a direct effect on music in that "music for the masses" became a new ideal—music directly appealing to a large number of unsophisticated people who had previously been excluded from courtly entertainments.

Precursors of the Classical style. *The Rococo style galant.* As the pendulum swung from the predominantly romantic Baroque period toward the Classical period, there was an inevitable overlapping of the old and the new. While Bach was composing his intricate and erudite polyphony, his sons were reflecting a new ideal, the Rococo. Fostered by the court of the French king Louis XV, whose life-style was far less formal than that of his illustrious great grandfather, the Rococo ideal was artistic expression dedicated to elegance, frivolity, and gracefulness; a work of art must be delicate, playful, entertaining, and immediately appealing. The result was often artificial and unrealistic, but it succeeded in capturing the discreetly sentimental and hedonistic attitudes of the times. Powdered wigs, lace cuffs, and perfumed handkerchiefs for both sexes were other manifestations of the same playful spirit that produced music in the *style galant.*

The empfindsamer Stil. The German counterpart of the essentially French Rococo was the *empfindsamer Stil,* or "sentimental style," which flourished in the 1750s and 1760s. Its leading exponent was one of J.S. Bach's sons, Carl Philip Emanuel Bach, who served for a time at the court of Frederick the Great in Berlin. The distinguishing feature of this German reaction against Baroque profundity was its concern with emotional feeling in the music itself, on the part of the performers and, hopefully, in the reaction of the audience. The French obsession with lightness, gracefulness, and decoration was countered by the German determination to affect sensibilities that were often more attuned to tears than to laughter. A late and less reserved manifestation of *Empfindsamkeit* was the *Sturm und Drang* ("storm and stress") movement in the arts during the 1770s and 1780s. The inclination toward the more intense personal expression of that movement was a harbinger of the coming Romantic period.

Consolidation of the Classical style. The fundamental changes in musical style that distinguished Classical from Baroque were inspired by Rococo ideals and refined and stabilized by the Classicists, particularly Joseph Haydn, Wolfgang Amadeus Mozart, Christoph Willibald Gluck, and the young Ludwig van Beethoven.

Stylistic elements. For the first time in the history of music, instrumental music became more important than vocal music. The orchestra and chamber groups, such as the string quartet, trio, and quintet, and the piano trio became standardized and replaced the heterogeneous trio sonata and other ensembles of the Baroque period. The basic duple and triple organization of metre remained unchanged, but rhythmic patterns tending toward more regularity and simplicity became the rule, producing the "tyranny of the bar line" that was to prevail for more than a century.

Central role of instrumental music

Melody was inclined to be more motivistic, tuneful, and epigrammatic, in contrast to the extended, figurative style of many Baroque melodies. Harmony was second only to melody as a focal element. Harmonic patterns that clearly established the tonal centre were the rule of the day.

As a reaction against the intricate polyphony of the later Baroque period, homophonic texture dominated by melody became the norm, but the accompanying patterns were different from those of the early Baroque, when monody supported by sustained chords was the prevailing style. In the late 18th century, figurations such as the Alberti bass (form of accompanying figure consisting of broken chords) and rhythmically enlivened repeated chords formed the typical textural patterns. Counterpoint was retained in some forms, however, and regained status particularly in development sections of works in sonata form.

Formal structure, a definitive aspect of classical style, was characterized by simplicity and clarity. Sectional forms (created by contrast and repetition of thematic materials, tonalities, and textures), variations, and the new principle of development (fragmentation, expansion, and modification of themes) were the established norms. Phrases of musical material became shorter and more clearly demarcated as well as more balanced and regular. A new concept of dynamic contrast also contributed to formal clarity. Shading from loud to soft or vice versa provided a dramatic means of building toward an expressive climax. Orchestration and instrumentation were closely allied to dynamic variation, and much more colour contrast and variety appeared in orchestral music, even though the ensemble was more standardized than formerly.

Sonata form. The pattern that served as the structural basis for most instrumental music of the classical period was the sonata. A large-scale work in several movements, it evolved from several Baroque predecessors, chiefly the Italian overture, the *sonata da chiesa,* and the concerto grosso. Depending on the medium of performance for which it was intended, it would be called, for example, a symphony, a concerto, a string quartet, a sextet, a trio. The designation sonata was reserved for a solo instrument or for an instrument accompanied by harpsichord or piano. Originally in three movements, the sonata became standardized as a four-movement form when a minuet was incorporated in the following sequence: (1) a serious allegro, (2) a slow, lyrical movement (andante or adagio), (3) a minuet and trio, and (4) a brilliant, vivacious finale. The internal structure of the first movement was so uniform that it acquired the designation sonata-allegro form; that is, the form employed in the allegro movement of a sonata, consisting basically of exposition, development, and recapitulation. The slower second movement is less structurally predictable. It is frequently a sectional form (for example, ABA, AABA, ABCA) or a set of variations. It may, even though in a slow tempo, be a sonata-allegro form, illustrating again the inconsistency of musical terminology. The third movement, usually omitted in the concerto and sometimes in other forms, is either a graceful minuet or a scherzo, a lively rhythmic form derived from the minuet. The structural pattern of the minuet had been fixed when it was established as the official court dance by Louis XIV in the mid-17th century. The last movement is frequently a rondo form, in which the principal theme recurs regularly between subordinate themes.

Instrumental music. *The symphony.* The most important and influential manifestation of the sonata form was that played by an orchestra—the symphony. During the 17th century the term sinfonia had been used for various kinds of instrumental music. "Sonata" was equally ambiguous. Late in the century, the designation sinfonia began to be confined to the Italian opera overture—a three-movement arrangement, fast–slow–fast. By the mid-18th century, opera overtures were being played independently in concerts. The insertion of the minuet between the last two movements resulted in the prototype of the Classical symphony.

During the waning Baroque period, vigorous advocates of the burgeoning Rococo and *Empfindsamkeit* ideals were active in Milan, Vienna, and Mannheim. In Milan, Giovanni Battista Sammartini began writing his symphonies, some 25 of them, in the 1730s. While employing the continuo of his models, Corelli and Giuseppe Torelli, the bithematic plan for his opening movements foreshadowed the exposition of the Classical symphonies. At about the same time, young composers in Vienna were experimenting with the new genre, thus laying the foundation for the later Viennese masters. The most famous and probably the most influential group was active in Mannheim in the court orchestra of Karl Theodor, the elector of the Palatinate. Their activity began in the 1740s, when Johann Stamitz became leader of the orchestra. His experiments with dynamic techniques—crescendo (increasing in loudness), diminuendo (decreasing in loudness), sforzando (special emphasis)—with homophonic textures featuring the first violins in virtuoso passages and with tremolo and other dramatic effects, became the hallmarks of the Mannheim style and served as models for his son Karl Stamitz and for composers in Vienna. Thanks to the fortuitous presence of certain instrumentalists as well as to benevolent patronage, the basic ensemble of the modern symphony orchestra was gradually established: violins, violas, violoncellos, and double basses; two flutes, two oboes, and two bassoons; two French horns and two tympani. Trumpets were added for festive occasions.

The Mannheim school

The concerto. Unlike the symphony, which had its origins in other forms, the Classical concerto grew directly out of the Baroque solo concerto and resembles it in that it is based on exchange of musical material between solo instrument or instruments and orchestra. While directly derived from the ritornello principle of the Baroque concerto (that of a recurrent musical passage when the soloists are silent), the internal structure of the first movement assimilated the developmental principle of sonata-allegro form. Pietro Locatelli and Giuseppe Tartini are especially notable for their numerous late-Baroque violin concerti.

Chamber music. While music for small instrumental ensembles had flourished for over 200 years previously, the late 18th century witnessed the establishment of chamber music in the modern sense of the term: music in sonata form for a small group of instruments with one player for each part. Replacing the trio sonata of the Baroque period, the most popular classical ensemble was a group of four stringed instruments—two violins, a viola, and a violoncello. Both the group itself and a sonata written for the group were called a string quartet. Among other popular ensembles were the string trio (violin, viola, and violoncello; or two violins and a violoncello) and the piano trio (violin, violoncello, and piano).

The keyboard sonata. The solo keyboard sonata was one of the most vital forms of the period, partly because of the great increase in amateur performers resulting from the newly affluent middle class. The sonatas of Domenico Paradisi, of J.S. Bach's sons, and of Haydn and Mozart reflect the evolution from the one-movement, binary form of the Baroque period to the standard classical three-movement form. A four-movement form did not become popular until the time of Beethoven. A celebrated contemporary of Mozart, Muzio Clementi, composed more than 60 sonatas for the piano alone and half again as many for piano and violin or flute and strongly influenced the style of piano writing.

Clementi's 60 sonatas

Other instrumental forms. While the sonata was unquestionably the most important form of instrumental music during the period, several other types were cultivated. For orchestra and chamber ensemble, a suitelike work called variously divertimento, serenade, cassation, or notturno was popular for light entertainment, differing from the more serious symphonies, concerti, and sonatas (which were intended for attentive listening) in that the ensemble of instruments was inconsistent, unpredictable, and often unspecified. The number, types, and arrangements of movements were equally flexible, ranging from three to 10 or more, some in dance forms and others in forms suitable for a sonata. While nonsonata forms for solo instruments (particularly keyboard) occasionally bear these designations, the most popular smaller solo forms were sets of variations, individual dances or marches, fantasies, and small pieces that would have been appropriate as movements of sonatas. For some reason, composition for the organ dwindled drastically after the death of J.S. Bach, in 1750.

Vocal music. *Opera.* There was less distinction between Baroque and Classical opera than between instrumental styles of the two periods because opera, with musical interest centred on a solo voice, had been largely melodic-homophonic since its inception. Another reason for the continuity of operatic style throughout the 18th century was the universal domination by the Neapolitan opera seria. Even in Paris, where the Lully-Rameau tradition maintained its vitality, there was an Italian opera theatre. While there was some effective reform of certain aspects of Neapolitan style that had become decadent and some nationalistic reaction in the field of comic opera, nothing in the nature of serious opera challenged Neapolitan supremacy. As a result, the late 18th century was a period of great vitality in operatic composition.

Domination of opera seria

The distinguishing characteristics of Neapolitan opera seria reveal why it is little known and rarely heard today. It was a very conventionalized form, with artificial and overcomplex plots. There were usually six main characters representing three of each sex, with some of the male and female parts sung by castrati (emasculated male sopranos and contraltos). Each character was allotted a standardized number of arias in fairly standardized succession. Obviously, with such constant interruption of the action, dramatic truth received little if any consideration. The singers and the arias were the focus of the entire production, with little of musical interest in the parlando recitatives (*i.e.,* using speech rhythms), little use of chorus, and little function for the orchestra aside from providing a subordinate accompaniment.

Objections to the decadence and artificiality of the Neapolitan style, which had begun to appear as early as the 1720s, would have been fruitless had not a champion appeared to put suggestions and theories for reform into actual practice. Culminating the movement for reform was Christoph Willibald Gluck, who began his career in the 1740s by writing about 20 operas in the prevailing style. Then, beginning with *Orfeo ed Euridice* in 1762, he attempted to enhance both the dramatic and musical components of opera. Superfluous virtuosity and vocal display were drastically curtailed if not eliminated by providing music that reflected the emotional or dramatic situation. As a result of Gluck's reforms, opera moved toward a classical simplicity of style of which his and Mozart's works were the culmination.

Comic opera

A second challenge to established Neapolitan opera was emerging through comic opera in which the subject matter was light, sentimental, often topical, and satirical, reflecting both the social changes of the period and ridicule of serious opera. The music was engagingly tuneful, easy to perform and to comprehend. Comic opera had appeared during the 17th century but began its independent existence during the first half of the 18th century in Italy, where it was called the opera buffa. The French opéra comique evolved during the same period and was given new impetus by the *guerre des bouffons* ("war of the buffoons") of the early 1750s, when support of the Italian opera buffa company then performing in Paris exceeded that of the French heroic opera of Rameau. In England, ballad opera, beginning with *The Beggar's Opera* in 1728, followed a course of development similar in both period and style to that of the opéra comique. German singspiel grew out of translations and imitations of English ballad opera. Models that centred on Vienna adhered to the Italian style and culminated in Mozart's *The Abduction from the Seraglio* and *The Magic Flute.* Yet Mozart also brought the old Italian style to its zenith in *Le Nozze di Figaro* (*The Marriage of Figaro*), *Così fan tutte* (*Thus Do They All*), and *Don Giovanni.*

Other vocal music. Aside from opera, secular vocal music was composed for solo voice and chorus. But the production of solo songs and cantatas in other countries could not compare with the growing interest in the German lied, which flourished under C.P.E. Bach and later composers. The most extensive development of secular part-songs took place in England, where numerous catches and glees were written.

Large-scale sacred choral music of the period was strongly influenced by the prevailing operatic style. Except for the text, some passages from oratorios and passions are indistinguishable from an operatic excerpt. But the Handelian tradition combined with the Neapolitan style and culminated in Haydn's two noble oratorios, *The Creation* and *The Seasons.* Liturgical music, such as masses, motets, litanies, psalms, and canticles, also demonstrated that the same composers were writing for both church and theatre. In many instances the style was uniform for the two types, although the chorus naturally played a much greater role in church music.

THE ROMANTIC PERIOD

The beginning of the 19th century witnessed a change of both musical style and aesthetic attitude that has become identified as Romantic. The term romantic originated in German literature of the late 18th century, illustrating once again the overlapping of classical and romantic attitudes and ideals. The Franco-Swiss writer Mme de Staël articulated the new ideals of the movement in 1813 as original, modern, national, popular, derived from the soil, religion, and prevailing social institutions. Obviously, some of these proclaimed romantic ideals and purposes were the same as those of the 18th-century Classicists.

Establishment of the Romantic idiom. In defining classicism, it was suggested that the distinctive elements of musical romanticism embrace emotionalism, subjectivity, individualism, nationalism, and a preference for a certain type of subject matter. Emotionalism is reflected in the revelation of intensely personal feelings, indeed, the sentimentality that pervades 19th-century music. Subjectivity replaces the formalism of the Classical period, in that impulse and inspiration play a major role in the motivation of both composer and performer, and the listener's response is expected to be more sensory than intellectual. Closely related to subjectivity is the individualism reflected in the highly self-centred expression of composers of the period, as well as by the conviction that a composer's most personal thoughts and feelings are the ultimate artistic message. In contrast to the universality of musical style that prevailed during the 18th century, much 19th-century music is identifiable in terms of national origin. Nationalism—the consciousness of the distinctive features of a nation and the intent to reveal, emphasize, and glorify those features—played a prominent part in Romantic music, partly as a result of social and political developments. The subject matter favoured by Romantic composers is most apparent in vocal music, where words can convey the explicit theme, but instrumental music was also affected

Personal aspect of romanticism

by the Romantic attraction to national identification and to remoteness, strangeness, and fantasy, particularly to the fantastic aspects of medieval tales and legends.

Stylistic traits. During the 19th century, musical techniques and materials were rapidly enriched by new resources, all devoted to the ideal of emotional or dramatic expressiveness. The orchestra, the piano, the solo voice with piano accompaniment, and the opera were the four predominating mediums; chamber and choral music occupied a less central position. Duple and triple divisions of the measure remained the basis of metre, but there were occasional experiments with metric irregularity, and rhythm was recognized as one of the most effective agents of expressiveness in music. Strong rhythmic energy, frequently produced by dotted patterns, provided a vigorous force that could be enhanced by faster and faster tempi. Flaccid patterns in slower tempi provided for the requisite pensive or sorrowful moods.

Melodic style was determined on one hand by the vocal ideal of song, with long, lyric lines. On the other hand, the new idiomatic possibilities of instruments were being exploited. In either case, expressiveness was the governing ideal. Harmonic and tonal elements were gradually expanded during the century, with more chromaticism, enriched sonorities (seventh and ninth chords), and more nonharmonic tones resulting in a more flexible tonal scheme. Tonic and dominant chords (those based on the first and fifth notes of the key), were no longer the secure poles of tonal movement; frequent and remote modulations (changes from one key to another) contributed to the restlessness of key centres. Because musical interest was centred in melody and harmony, texture remained prevailingly homophonic, though counterpoint played a prominent role in developmental sections. Fugues and other imitative forms occurred as a result of studied archaism or for special effect, but the composers' preoccupation with direct and immediate expression led them to neglect the traditional polyphonic forms, with their inherent traditions and restraints.

Increasing importance of modulation

The Romantic abhorrence of formalism has frequently been exaggerated for the purposes of distinguishing between Classical and Romantic attitudes. Established patterns such as the sonata-allegro and rondo forms were subjected to many modifications and extensions, but musical coherence demands a judicious balance of unity and variety, so most compositions of the 19th century are still fairly clear-cut sectional, variational, or developmental forms. The distinctive new features are largely in the area of emphasis and dimension—symphonies lasting over an hour in contrast to the 20- to 30-minute standard of the Classical period. Instrumental colour and variety, as another aspect of expressiveness, was made possible by a greatly enlarged orchestra and figured prominently in the new sound ideal.

Beethoven as a transitional figure. The Janus-like figure who marked the transition from the Classical to the Romantic style was Beethoven, the first composer whose personality and character made a purposeful impact on the types and style of music he composed. Inspired by the revolutionary forces prevailing at the time, he declared himself a free artistic agent, with neither allegiance nor responsibility to any patron. His early works reflected the 18th-century acceptance of providing music on demand, and he applied his craftsmanship to supplying compositions in hope of financial reward. But in his later works, from about 1820 on, he declared his personal independence and wrote only what his imagination and inspiration dictated, thus establishing individuality, subjectivity, and emotional expression as the standard for Romantic composers. Yet the body of music he produced reflects the tastes of the 18th rather than the 19th century, in that he was attracted more by the absolute forms of instrumental music than by the dramatic and lyrical forms cultivated by the Romanticists. Symphonies, chamber music (particularly string quartets), and piano pieces (including 32 sonatas) far outweigh his one opera, one oratorio, one major mass, and assorted songs and part-songs. His lack of interest in dramatic vocal music reflects the classical side of his nature, though the expressive changes apparent in his instrumental works are evidence of his being the springboard to the Romantic epoch.

Opera. The opera remained a flourishing medium throughout the 19th century, and Italian opera continued as the dominant type during the first half of the century in the hands of Gioacchino Rossini, Vincenzo Bellini, and Gaetano Donizetti. The reforms instigated by Gluck were discernible, but enough of the genre's indigenous Italianate character remained to distinguish it from other national types. The man who, more than any other, personifies Italian opera of the period is Giuseppe Verdi (1813–1901), whose works are still among the most performed. Late in the century, the tendency toward even more realistic and topical subject matter produced the *verismo* ("realism") school of Ruggiero Leoncavallo, Pietro Mascagni, and Giacomo Puccini.

Meanwhile, German opera developed into the epitome of romantic subject matter and expressiveness, beginning in 1821 with the performance of *Der Freischütz* (*The Freeshooter*), by Carl Maria von Weber. Plots based on tales from Teutonic mythology and medieval legend that emphasized the mystical aspects of nature were a distinctive feature of Germanic operas and distinguished them from the more mundane Italianate plots. Richard Wagner (1813–83) crystallized the German Romantic ideal into the music drama, in which all aspects of the production—drama, music, design, performance—were intended to fuse into a manifestation of pure artistic expression in which no one element predominated over the others, as singing still tended to do in Italian opera. There was no development in Germany after Wagner comparable with the post-Verdi *verismo* group in Italy. Wagner's innovations—once again a readjustment of dramatic versus musical forces in musical theatre—were the point of departure for most German opera since his time, from Richard Strauss to the present.

Wagner's music drama

In Paris, the operatic centre of the world from late in the 18th century until well into the 19th, native composers were quick to sense the Gluckian changes in Italian opera as well as the new directions in Germany. Beginning with Rossini's *Guillaume Tell* in 1829 and crystallizing in the operas of Giacomo Meyerbeer in the 1830s and 1840s, French grand opera emerged as the most opulent and grandiose musico-dramatic spectacle of the first half of the century. During the later 19th century, opéra comique and grand opera merged to produce the prevailing French lyric opera. At the same time, opéra comique branched off in another direction to produce operettas, which developed into the musical comedies of the 20th century. Indigenous opera appeared in other regions, especially in Russia, Bohemia, and Scandinavia, as a result of nationalistic fervour.

Orchestral music. Reaching both a culmination and a turning point in the nine symphonies of Beethoven, orchestral music developed in two directions during the 19th century. On the one hand were composers who, because of their training and temperament, adhered primarily to Classical forms and ideals of absolute music. On the other hand were the composers seeking new realms of dramatic content, colour, and expressiveness. Even for the more conservative group, both the forms and the orchestra itself were greatly expanded during the century, but the total output of works was much smaller than in the Classical period. Romantic musical vocabulary replaced the Classical language in symphonies, of course, and programmatic content (*i.e.,* an extramusical image or story) was a frequent element.

New orchestral forms. The more progressive composers cultivated new musical types that represented the tastes and ideals of the Romantic period—the concert overture, the symphonic poem (later called tone poem), the symphonic suite, and symphonic variations. The concert overture, a direct development of overtures to dramatic works, was an attempt to reconcile the old classical demands for form with Romantic desire for programmatic content. It was usually a sonata-allegro form with picturesque themes designed to suggest (with the help of the title) characters, locations, or dramatic situations. Felix Mendelssohn's *Hebrides* overture and Brahms's *Tragic Overture* (completed 1880) are representatives of the genre. The symphonic

Programmatic and picturesque works

poem, foreshadowed in Hector Berlioz' *Symphonie fantastique* (completed 1830), was originated by Franz Liszt at midcentury as an orchestral work, usually in one movement, based on an extramusical idea such as a poem or a narrative. The futility of attempting to depict explicit events and attitudes in purely musical terms resulted in the demise of the form early in the 20th century after the many tone poems of Richard Strauss. The symphonic suite was one of three distinct types: (1) an outgrowth of 18th-century dance suites, divertimentos, or serenades, (2) the extension of the symphonic poem into a composite work of several movements of related programmatic nature, or (3) a group of selections from a dramatic work such as a ballet. Rimsky-Korsakov's *Scheherazade* represents the second type, and Tchaikovsky's *Nutcracker Suite* is typical of the third. While variations had appeared as movements of symphonies and concerti since the mid-18th century, they became an independent orchestral form during the last quarter of the 19th century. César Franck's *Variations symphoniques* (1885) is a good example of the type. Popular orchestral pieces, such as the waltzes of Johann Strauss, also flourished.

The mainstream of composers whose orchestral music reflected most clearly their allegiance to Classical forms and models—though conditioned by Romanticism, of course—is represented by Beethoven, Franz Schubert, Robert Schumann, Johannes Brahms, and Anton Bruckner. The more overtly Romantic contingent was centred around Berlioz, Liszt, Gustav Mahler, and Richard Strauss.

The movement toward national expression. A third group, chiefly nationalists who were reacting against Germanic domination of instrumental music as well as reflecting the sociopolitical developments of the era, combined features of both conservative and progressive camps, to which they added national characteristics. While there were manifestations of the movement in countries such as Hungary, Poland, Spain, and England, the most productive and outstanding of those who sought to reflect national distinctiveness were the Russian "Five"—César Cui, Mily Balakirev, Aleksandr Borodin, Modest Mussorgsky, and Nikolay Rimsky-Korsakov—the Bohemians Bedřich Smetana and Antonín Dvořák, and the Scandinavians Edvard Grieg, Carl Nielsen, and Jean Sibelius. French composers such as Camille Saint-Saëns, César Franck, and Vincent d'Indy were motivated by the same impulse of independence, but they could hardly be categorized as nationalists in the same sense as their eastern European colleagues, since there was less distinctive folk material from which to draw colourful materials and since they had been in the mainstream of musical development all along.

Piano music. One of the most popular media of the Romantic era, thanks to the rapid technical development of the instrument, was piano music. Another reason for the popularity of the piano was the growing demand for recreation and entertainment on the part of the newly affluent middle class. In tune with the taste of the times, small pieces of distinctive expressive character (hence, "character pieces") were the most popular type, either as single pieces or as parts of composite works. Stylized dances continued to be popular, but nationalistic types such as the polonaise and mazurka and the novel waltz replaced the staid minuets of the previous era. Sonatas continued to occupy serious composers, and sets of variations continued to flourish. The virtuosity of the violinist Niccolò Paganini and his contemporaries led to many studies, or études, designed to exhibit the performer's dexterity as well as the invention of the composer. Chopin, Schumann, Liszt, and Brahms were the major composers of piano music after Beethoven, but practically all composers of the time contributed to the literature.

Songs. The vocal counterpart of the keyboard character piece was the solo song with piano accompaniment. With the rise of the German romantic poetry of Goethe, Schiller, Heine, and others, about the beginning of the 19th century, the German lied ("song") flourished. After 1850, composers of other nations, especially France and Russia, also produced a song literature of universal appeal. A pioneer and certainly the most prolific composer of lieder was Schubert, who in his short life wrote more than 600 songs. His chief successors, in chronological order, were Karl Loewe, Mendelssohn, Schumann, Brahms, Hugo Wolf, and Richard Strauss.

Schubert's 600 lieder

Chamber and choral music. The great Viennese tradition of chamber music reached its zenith in the works of Beethoven and with the death of Schubert came temporarily to a close. The conciseness, unity, and balance that were basic to the Classical ideal were incompatible with the essence of musical Romanticism. When writing for instruments, the typical Romantic composer was inclined toward the colouristic effects and expressive possibilities of the orchestra. Chamber music continued to be written and performed, of course, but nowhere was it one of the primary interests of composers as it had been during the 18th century. Predictably, the more conservative composers, such as Mendelssohn, Schumann, and Brahms, were the chief composers of chamber music.

While the same musical vocabulary and style had served both church and opera house since the rise of dramatic music, the 19th century witnessed a separation of musical idioms according to function—sacred or secular. Music for use in church was generally conservative, especially after the "rediscovery" of Palestrina and systematic research into the reform of Gregorian chant. On the other hand, cantatas and popular part-songs produced for the many amateur choral societies incorporated as many of the new techniques as could be managed by the singers. There was some fusion of the two idioms in oratorios and in settings of liturgical texts for the concert hall or for special occasions. The requiem mass, with its vividly dramatic content, was attractive to Romantic composers, and Berlioz's and Verdi's settings remain as emotionally telling today as most operas of the period.

MODERN PERIOD

Diversity of styles. The striking changes in musical style that occurred about 1900 were a turning point in the history of Western music comparable to the dramatic transformation of the early 14th and early 17th centuries. But never before had the change been so rapid, and never before had there been such a diversity of resulting styles. The last decades of the 19th century witnessed what might be termed the diffusion of Romanticism, when significant departures from the current musical vocabulary appeared in the works of some nationalist composers and especially in the Impressionistic style represented in France by Claude Debussy and Maurice Ravel. The amorphous rhythmic patterns, the whole-tone scale, the concept of free relationship of adjacent harmonies, and the kaleidoscopic textures of musical Impressionism were musical manifestations of the aesthetic movements current in painting and literature.

The experimental works of Arnold Schoenberg and Igor Stravinsky about 1910 heralded a new epoch in music. Schoenberg was the pioneer when his adoption of the ideals of the Expressionist movement—like Impressionism an aesthetic development shared by other art forms—resulted in his discarding traditional harmonic concepts of consonance and dissonance and led to the development of atonality and 12-tone technique (in which all 12 tones of the octave are serialized, or given an ordered relationship). Stravinsky's revolutionary style, variously labelled "dynamism," "barbarism," or "primitivism," concentrated on metric imbalance and percussive dissonance and introduced a decade of extreme experimentation that coincided with World War I, a period of major social and political upheaval.

Stravinsky's innovations and experiments in Neoclassicism

In contrast with Schoenberg's and Stravinsky's experiments during the second decade of the century, another line of demarcation appeared about 1920 with a general return to the aesthetic ideals of the late 18th century. Following the leadership of Stravinsky, Paul Hindemith, Béla Bartók, and Sergey Prokofiev, among others, most prominent composers entered a Neoclassical period characterized by restraint of emotional content; simplification of materials, structures, and textures; a greater attention to craftsmanship; and a revival of concern for linear counterpoint rather than instrumental or harmonic colour. Baroque emphasis on counterpoint and Classical formalism were now clothed in 20th-century melodic, harmonic, rhythmic, tonal, and orchestral idioms. The Expressionist followers of Schoenberg, most notably Alban Berg, continued in their preoccupation with serial techniques.

Neoclassicism continued as the dominant trend throughout the period from about 1920 until World War II, while many of the experimental techniques introduced during the revolutionary second decade of the century were gradually refined, modified, and assimilated into the accepted musical vocabulary. At the same time, experimentation continued alongside a tenacious conservatism that echoed Romantic ideals and styles. Nationalism also continued to flourish, reaching a level in some countries never achieved during the 19th century.

After World War II the two leading artistic attitudes tended to merge when the followers of Anton von Webern carried serial composition to such a rigorous extreme that its craftsmanship and intellectual orientation suggested Classicism rather than Expressionism. Shortly afterward, Stravinsky, the doyen of the Neoclassical group, began experimenting with serialism. Avant-garde music since that time has begun to employ the techniques made possible by technological developments in electronics.

Advent of electronic composition. Beginning about 1950, two leading groups began experimenting with electronic music, one in Cologne and the other in Paris. The product of the latter group was referred to as *musique concrète* in acknowledgement of the principle that preexisting, or "concrete," recorded sounds serve as the basis of all sonorities in the finished work. The basic sounds, which may be derived from any source—musical, natural, or mechanical—are modified electronically and arranged in any combination and succession suitable to the composer's purpose. The German group, led by Karlheinz Stockhausen, was concerned with a purer form of the medium in that its basic sounds are electrically generated instead of being recorded from sources external to the electronic apparatus. The two approaches share one connecting link with music of the past: all sounds have pitch, intensity, duration, and quality. All other concepts of musical organization have been discarded, including the necessity of a performer. Electronic compositions exist on a tape (or disc), and can be made audible by a speaker system.

Computer music

The dehumanizing of music has been carried several steps further by the use of mathematics and even of computers to determine the nature of sound materials—either electronic or that produced by more conventional means—and their organization. At the other extreme is aleatoric music, in which the performer is allowed to choose the manner and order of presentation of materials specified or simply suggested by the composer.

Popular music. Another result of advances in electronics has been the tremendous growth of popular music during the 20th century. New techniques have made possible high-fidelity reproduction of sound and its widespread and rapid dissemination through radio, phonograph, tape recorder, and television. In addition, some of the instruments used in popular music have incorporated electronic amplification as well as sound production. While there has been a popular music as long as mankind has turned to singing and dancing for diversion and recreation, much of it was folk music and existed only as an oral tradition. But popular music in the modern sense originated in the late 18th century, when ballads made popular in ballad opera and dance music received wide circulation. The same types flourished throughout the 19th century and into the 20th, when a new direction was prompted by the emergence of jazz among blacks in the southern United States. After the original ragtime came jazz proper, swing, bebop, and rock in its numerous manifestations—punk, new wave, etc. Early in the century, the novelty of jazz rhythms and dominance of brass, woodwind, and percussion instruments over strings attracted some serious composers who occasionally incorporated suitable jazz idioms into their works. Since about 1930, the influence has worked in both directions, and popular music has gradually adopted techniques that originated in serious music. Regardless of the interaction of popular and serious music, the popularity of the former is one of the most significant musical developments of the 20th century, especially in view of the widening gulf between the serious composer and the potential audience.

Interaction of serious and popular idioms

It is impossible to arrive at a complete and objective description of a revolutionary movement while it is in progress; only a period of time can provide the necessary perspective. It can be acknowledged, however, that music has never before passed through a more anarchic phase than in the 20th century. The tremendous number and diversity of stylistic distinctions has precluded a characteristic designation for the first half of the century, but one must be forthcoming, for musicians of the future will need the terms modern and contemporary for their own times.

Despite the disproportionate publicity given to the most radical experiments, the majority of leading composers continue along the moderate path established in the late 1920s and 1930s. And, if one can rely on the lessons of history, the mainstream of music will continue to absorb those new techniques that contribute to expressiveness and communication while discarding the merely novel and sensational, so that music history will remain an evolutionary rather than a revolutionary process.

BIBLIOGRAPHY

Reference works: WILLI APEL (ed.), *Harvard Dictionary of Music,* 2nd rev. ed. (1969, reprinted 1977); THEODORE BAKER, *Biographical Dictionary of Musicians,* 7th ed., rev. by NICOLAS SLONIMSKY (1984); STANLEY SADIE (ed.), *The New Grove Dictionary of Music and Musicians,* 20 vol. (1980); FRIEDRICH BLUME (ed.), *Die Musik in Geschichte und Gegenwart,* 16 vol. (1949–79).

Survey histories: DONALD JAY GROUT and CLAUDE V. PALISCA, *A History of Western Music,* 3rd ed. (1980); RICHARD L. CROCKER, *A History of Musical Style* (1966); PAUL HENRY LÁNG, *Music in Western Civilization* (1941, reprinted 1969); *New Oxford History of Music* (1954–), by 1982 with eight of the projected 11 volumes published, some of them revised since the inception of the project; HOMER ULRICH and PAUL A. PISK, *A History of Music and Musical Style* (1963).

Period monographs: CURT SACHS, *The Rise of Music in the Ancient World, East and West* (1943); GUSTAVE REESE, *Music in the Middle Ages* (1940, reprinted 1968), *Music in the Renaissance,* rev. ed. (1959); MANFRED F. BUKOFZER, *Music in the Baroque Era, from Monteverdi to Bach* (1947); ALFRED EINSTEIN, *Music in the Romantic Era* (1947, reprinted 1975); WILLIAM W. AUSTIN, *Music in the Twentieth Century, from Debussy Through Stravinsky* (1966); ERIC SALZMAN, *Twentieth-Century Music,* 2nd ed. (1974).

(R.T.D.)

Musical Forms and Genres

The term used to refer to the structure or shape of a musical composition is musical form. In writing on music the word form is regularly used in two senses: to denote a standard type, genre, or species (*e.g.,* symphony, sonata); and to denote the procedures in a particular work. The situation is complicated by the fact that nomenclature for the various musical formal types is determined in different ways—by, for instance, the medium of performance (string quartet, trio sonata), the technique of composition (fugue, variation), or function (prelude, overture, offertory).

The article is divided into the following sections:

Development of musical form

PRINCIPLES OF MUSICAL FORM

Music exists in time; as an aesthetician, Susanne K. Langer, put it in *Feeling and Form,* "music is time made audible." The proper perception of a musical work depends in the main on the ability to associate what is happening in the present with what has happened in the past and with what one expects will happen in the future. The frustration or fulfillment of such expectations and the resulting tensions and releases are basic to most musical works.

Musical form depends, therefore, on the disposition of certain structural units successively in time. The basic principles can be discerned from a brief consideration of melody, which may be defined as an organized succession of musical tones. This succession of tones consists of component parts, structural units, the principal of which is the phrase—a complete musical utterance, roughly corresponding to what can be sung or played in one breath

Melody

or played with a single stroke of the bow. A melody, then, ordinarily consists of a succession of phrases, in which there may occur repetition (the same phrase repeated), contrast (a completely different phrase), or variation (the phrase altered, but in such a way that its identity remains perceptible). The relation between these component phrases is important for form. There may, for instance, be a complementary grouping of phrases as antecedent and consequent or "question and answer." The phrases may or may not be equal in length. Some writers, pressing the analogy between music and language, also distinguish larger groupings of phrases: into periods, sentences, paragraphs, and the like. Most musical forms are thus not only additive but also hierarchical: phrases are conjoined to produce a melody, which in turn may be a constituent part of a larger work. A melodic entity that functions as an element in a larger whole is called a theme.

Coherence may be produced by the use of a motive or figure, *i.e.,* short elements consisting ordinarily of two to four notes. But whereas the motive is usually characterized by a striking interval or rhythmic arrangement, the figure consists of entirely conventional elements (a scale segment, notes of a chord, etc.). Finally, coherence may also be achieved by the consistent use of a rhythmic pattern.

A few examples will serve to illustrate these points. The various phrases have been identified by slurs (phrase marks) and by lowercase letters (the exponential numbers designate variations), whereas larger groupings are designated by capital letters. In the hymn tune "Bethany," by Lowell Mason, shown below, the eight phrases may be grouped in pairs to produce the scheme:

a b a b^{1} c c^{1} a b^{1}
A A^{1} B A^{1} .

This four-phase arrangement with statement, repetition (here with variation at the cadence), contrast, and restatement is extremely common in the traditional and art music of the West.

Other schemes based on repetition and contrast abound. The famous "Largo" from Antonín Dvořák's *New World Symphony,* Opus 95, goes like this:

Here the scheme is:

a a^{1} b b a a^{2}
A B A^{1}

This common arrangement is known as three-part form. Coherence is provided by the use of a rhythmic motive, (marked "x" in the second example).

A common device is melodic sequence, in which the phrase is repeated but in transposition, as in the refrain of the Christmas carol "O Come All Ye Faithful."

Different from the above procedures is an English traditional song, "How Should I Your True Love Know" (example follows). The phrase structure here is a b c d, so that there is no repetitive plan. Such a melody is said to be through-composed. In some through-composed melodies a rhythmic pattern may appear throughout to promote coherence.

Other elements contribute to formal organization in music. Among those having solely to do with pitch are range or register—whether most of the activity is high, low, or in the middle, or combinations of these, and whether the range of pitches used is large or small; types of melodic motion, whether conjunct (*i.e.,* by step along the scale) or

Function of pitch

disjunct (by leaps); and the use of different types of scales or modes. Factors included in music's temporal aspect include tempo, whether fast or slow, as well as duration; *i.e.,* whether individual notes are long or short (the gradually increasing use of constantly shorter note values, for instance, is associated with acceleration and accumulation, thus with increasing intensity). Among the harmonic aspects, there is key, or tonality (set of interrelated notes and chords, based on a major or minor scale), whereby the reassertion of a key following the intervention of other keys may produce an effect akin to the restatement of a phrase after a contrasting one has been heard; in this respect, cadences (sections giving the impression of conclusion) are of crucial importance in defining key. Still other factors include the use of dynamics (loud and soft); timbre, or tone colour, especially in the employment of unusual instruments or combinations of instruments; texture, whether monophonic (consisting of a single melodic line) or polyphonic (many-voiced), be it contrapuntal (having simultaneous independent melodic lines) or homophonic (one voice leading melodically, supported by chordal procedures); and, in vocal music, whether the text is set syllabically (one note to a syllable) or melismatically (many notes to a syllable).

FORMAL TYPES

Four basic types of musical forms are distinguished in ethnomusicology: iterative, the same phrase repeated over and over; reverting, with the restatement of a phrase after a contrasting one; strophic, a larger melodic entity repeated over and over to different strophes (stanzas) of a poetic text; and progressive, in which new melodic material is continuously presented (thus synonymous with through-composed). The following discussion deals first with Western and then with non-Western music.

Iterative and reverting types. Iterative types, not common in Western music, may be found in the recitation tones of Gregorian chant, in which, for example, each line of a psalm is sung to the same melodic formula. Far more common, however, are reverting types. In the Middle Ages there existed the fixed forms used in songs, such as the French ballade (a a b), virelai (A b b a A), and rondeau (A B a A a b A B), the Italian ballata (A b b a A) and the German bar form (a a b), where the patterns of repetition and contrast correspond to poetic forms. (In the representations of the reverting types in songs, lowercase letters refer to the same music set to different words, while capital letters indicate that both text and music are the same.) Since the Baroque period (*c.* 1600–*c.* 1750) there has been binary, or two-part form, such as a b. A variety of binary form particularly prominent in the dances of the 18th century is the rounded binary form, the two sections of which are a and b a (*i.e.,* with a final return to original material in the second section), each of which is repeated, part one being heard twice before part two begins: ‖ : a : ‖ ‖ : b a : ‖ (‖ : and : ‖ indicate the enclosed material is to be repeated).

Binary. The rounded binary form took on great importance in the late 18th century, when it was expanded and elaborated into what is known as sonata form (also called sonata-allegro or first movement form), which may be represented thus: ‖ : exposition : ‖ ‖ : development recapitulation : ‖, whereby the kinship to the ‖ : a : ‖ ‖ : b a: ‖ structure of rounded binary form is clear. Ordinarily, in the exposition the principal musical themes are stated; in the development they are subjected to a process of working out and variation; and, finally, in the recapitulation they are restated. Sometimes the scheme is enlarged by adding a slow introduction before the exposition or a coda (concluding passage) at the end, or both. This formal principle, usually treated with a certain freedom, has been of basic importance in Western instrumental music since the mid-18th century.

Sonata form

Ternary. Another basic reverting type is ternary (three-part) form, a b a, also known as "song form" because of its frequent use in that genre, as well as in character pieces for piano. The form dominates the aria in late Baroque opera (the da capo aria, in which the final statement of a is not written out, but the performers simply follow the written instruction da capo, meaning "from the beginning," and repeat the first part). The da capo principle also appears in the instrumental minuet and scherzo with trio.

Rondo. On a larger scale are refrain schemes, in which contrasting episodes appear between statements of the refrain. In instrumental music this is found most often in a five-part arrangement, the rondo, frequently a b a c a b a; but many departures from the form occur, most common being the replacement of c by a development passage, usually based on the rondo theme. This important variant, known as the sonata-rondo, is particularly associated with Joseph Haydn. The refrain principle also appears in the rondeau of 18th-century French harpsichord music, in which there is no set limit to the number of episodes. The third movements of concertos, with the reversions of the tutti or ritornello (passage for full orchestra) and the intervening episodes for the solo instrument or instruments, are also of this type, as occasionally are large operatic arias.

Strophic types. The strophic type is seen in hymns and traditional ballads, in which different poetic strophes are set to the same melody. Thus, while the melody of a single stanza may accord with one of the reverting types, the hymn or ballad as a whole is strophic; this also applies to the fixed forms of medieval music and to many other types of song, simple and complex.

Theme and variation

The instrumental equivalent of the strophic type is variation (or theme and variation) form, in which a musical theme, often a complete melody with a harmonic accompaniment, is stated and then repeated a number of times, but with variations. A clear example of the relation between variation and strophic form is the chorale-partita of the Baroque era, a keyboard piece based on a hymn, with each varied statement of the hymn tune corresponding to a strophe of the hymn text. But the structure is more common in independent instrumental compositions, often of considerable dimensions (*e.g.,* Beethoven's *Diabelli Variations* for piano). In the Baroque a common type was the ostinato, or variations on a ground, in which the composition was built on a recurring melodic or harmonic pattern, generally in the bass, the accompanying parts being varied with each statement of the pattern, as in Bach's *Passacaglia and Fugue in C Minor* for organ or his "Chaconne" from the *Partita in D Minor* for unaccompanied violin. This procedure is also found in early operatic arias in the strophic variation form, in which each statement of the ostinato corresponds to a strophe of the aria's text. In the 19th century Brahms made impressive use of the ostinato (finales of the *Variations on a Theme by Haydn* and the *Symphony No. 4 in E Minor*).

Progressive types. The progressive type is common in songs and instrumental pieces of the 19th and 20th centuries but is also found in earlier music (*e.g.,* in the melodies used for the Gloria and Credo of the mass in plainchant) and in the prose, or sequence (*c.* 9th–*c.* 12th centuries), the phrases of which are arranged in pairs (a a b b c c d d, etc.), and its instrumental equivalent, the estampie. Polyphonic forms using a cantus firmus or basic melody (often a plainchant excerpt) also belong to the progressive type and include the liturgical organum, the early motet, and the conductus from the medieval era, as well as many chorale-preludes for organ of the Baroque. If, however, the cantus firmus itself is in one of the reverting forms, then the polyphonic setting will frequently follow suit.

The most important forms of Renaissance polyphony also belong to the progressive type, since the characteristic procedure was to give each line of the text its own musical phrase, as in the Renaissance motet and other types of secular polyphonic music. The same applies to the instrumental contrapuntal forms of the late Renaissance and Baroque: the ricercare, canzona, invention, and fugue. Other progressive types include intonations, preludes, toccatas and fantasias for lute and keyboard of the 16th, 17th, and early 18th centuries, in which the thematic material consists primarily of figurative elements (scale passages, arpeggiated chords, trills, turns, and the like); in larger works of this kind—by Bach for instance—passages in fugal style are often also present. Finally, there is simple binary form (a b), often found in early dances and in large operatic arias of the Classical period (Mozart and Beethoven).

WESTERN COMPOUND FORMS

Early history. With the larger forms of instrumental music there are extended musical pieces, usually called movements, which in their succession and totality make up a larger whole. An important unifying factor is key: a single key often dominates the work, others being used for contrast. This idea goes back at least to the Baroque, when two formal types were established: the first is the *sonata da camera,* or chamber sonata, consisting of a series of dances in the same key (also known as partita and, later, suite). By J.S. Bach's time (1685–1750) a set arrangement of dances was common: allemande (moderate slow triple time), courante or corrente (fast triple time), saraband (slow triple time), and gigue (fast triple time), usually with some other dance inserted between the saraband and the gigue. The other type is the *sonata da chiesa,* or church sonata, which consists of four movements, again all in the same key, in a slow–fast–slow–fast succession. The distinction between the two types is explicit in Bach's sonatas and partitas for unaccompanied violin: the sonatas are in the "church" form, whereas the partitas are suites. Other large forms of Baroque music are the two types of overture: the French, in two parts, the first slow and stately, the second fast and fugal; and the Italian, in three movements in the succession fast–slow–fast, the middle movement usually in a different key. The instrumental concerto after 1700 usually employed the same scheme as the Italian overture.

The sonata. Around 1750 a combination of these types produced the forms most common in the standard repertory of concert music. The sonata became a piece for either a keyboard instrument or a solo instrument accompanied by keyboard. It ordinarily consisted either of three movements in the arrangement fast–slow–fast or of four, with a minuet inserted between the slow movement and the finale; but there are examples of two-movement sonatas, notably by Beethoven, and even of one-movement sonatas (*e.g.,* by Domenico Scarlatti, the Italian-born composer to the Spanish court). Usually all movements except the slow one (and sometimes the trio, as well) are in the same key. The first movement typically is cast in the sonata form, the slow movement in one of the reverting schemes (often ternary), and the finale either in sonata or rondo form; but variation form may appear in any of these movements.

This large form is also used in chamber music, particularly the string quartet, and in the large form of orchestral music, the symphony, both of which ordinarily have four movements. Notable exceptions to this are the late quartets of Beethoven as well as those of the 20th-century composer Béla Bartók, the latter in two instances using what is called the "arch form," a large reverting arrangement, A B C B A, each element being a separate movement; needless to say, there are innumerable other exceptions. The concerto, on the other hand, adheres more to the older three-movement form. The various kinds of late 18th-century entertainment music (cassation, divertimento, nocturne, serenade, and the like) may employ any of a number of arrangements, ranging from three movements all the way to six or more.

Exceptions to sonata form

Cyclic form. Some authorities believe that since the 18th century such sonata-form compositions have been organized by the use of a few musical thematic motives, often submitted to considerable variation throughout. Compositions organized in such a way are said to be in cyclic form. While this becomes important in the 19th century, the extent to which it characterizes the Classical period is a matter of some controversy at present.

Fantasias and program music. Simultaneously a much freer form was cultivated, beginning in the late 18th century, the fantasia, primarily for keyboard, notably in the hands of Carl Philipp Emanuel Bach. Consisting of an indefinite number of highly contrasting sections, surprise and expression were of prime significance.

The fantasia, along with the overture to a play or opera, was the precursor of the large forms of orchestral program music of the 19th century, in which an extramusical content (usually a narrative of some kind), called the program, is expressed in the composition. There are two main types: the program symphony, associated with Hector Berlioz, in which the norms of symphonic form are for the most part preserved, and the symphonic poem, associated with Franz Liszt and Richard Strauss, in which the composer allows the extramusical subject matter to determine the structure of the composition. Some 19th-century concert overtures by German composers such as Felix Mendelssohn and Robert Schumann belong to this type of composition. Important here is the association of musical themes with aspects of the program, the themes being used throughout the work, often in varied forms.

The symphonic poem

Another arrangement is called the suite, which no longer consists exclusively of dances but also of instrumental pieces of all kinds. Usually some common element runs throughout: a cyclic theme may be used, as in Schumann's *Carnaval* or the Russian composer Modest Mussorgsky's *Pictures from an Exhibition,* or the music may originally have been intended for use with a play (Mendelssohn's music to *A Midsummer Night's Dream* or the Norwegian Edvard Grieg's for Henrik Ibsen's *Peer Gynt*).

Opera and oratorio. Among the large forms of vocal music, opera and oratorio are the most significant. Both are extended works in which a narrative is set to music. While an opera is performed in a theatre, an oratorio is a concert piece. Both may be either sacred or secular. A special type of oratorio is the Passion, the setting of New Testament accounts of Christ's crucifixion. The cantata may be regarded as a smaller form of oratorio.

Operas and oratorios ordinarily consist of several musical genres: recitative (imitating the manner of speech), aria, ensemble and choral pieces, often with instrumental interludes and an overture (most overtures of the late 18th and 19th centuries being cast in sonata form). Opera often includes ballets and large sectional finales at the ends of acts. With respect to the oratorio, Handel greatly increased the role of the chorus in his work with this genre (especially *Israel in Egypt*), an example seized upon by his successors. Oratorios also differ from operas in that they frequently make use of a *testo* (narrator), who relates the events of the action, usually set in recitative style. Stravinsky's *Oedipus Rex* (1927) combines the two traditions.

Whereas operas are usually composed as a series of enclosed musical forms, the German composer Richard Wagner devised a special kind, known as music drama, in which the music is continuous and in which the distinction between recitative, aria, and ensemble is largely eliminated. Instead, Wagner used a flexible melodic line which he referred to as "tone speech." Wagner also greatly increased the role of the orchestra, stressing the technique of thematic development and transformation borrowed from instrumental music and further associating each theme with an aspect of the operatic plot, such themes being known as leitmotivs ("leading motifs").

Wagner's new operatic form

The mass. Another large vocal form is the mass, the earliest polyphonic settings of which date from the 14th century. At first the mass was set in cantus firmus style, each movement built on the appropriate Gregorian chant melody, as in the mass of the French composer Guillaume de Machaut. In the 15th century a Burgundian composer, Guillaume Dufay, and his contemporaries developed the cyclic mass, in which a single cantus firmus was employed throughout. This idea was extended in the parody mass, built by elaborating thematic material taken from an existing polyphonic work, usually a motet or chanson; most 16th-century masses are of this kind. In the Baroque mass, each segment of the text is treated as an independent composition (aria, duet, chorus), similar to the procedure in a cantata or oratorio, except that no recitatives are used. J.S. Bach's *Mass in B Minor* is of this type.

In the 16th and 17th centuries, Monteverdi and others grouped madrigals into a kind of cycle around a particular subject; should a dramatic text be involved, the form is known as a madrigal comedy. In the 19th century and after, similarly grouped songs with piano accompaniment are known as a song cycle (*e.g.,* those by Beethoven, Schubert, and Schumann).

20th-century modifications. In the 20th century many composers have continued to use the traditional forms, although in other respects their work makes significant departures from what had been established. Others have virtually discarded them. Radically new elements have been introduced to serve as structural units: instead of the traditional phrases and motives, composers have come to employ what they call "sound events," combinations of textures, types of timbre, aggregates of different simultaneously sounding pittches, and the like. An early example is afforded by the notion of the melody of timbres—the *Klangfarbenmelodie* of Arnold Schoenberg and Anton von Webern. The broadest possible range is included in the conception of a sound event: not merely tones but also noises; in fact, sounds of all kinds. These sound events have been arranged in a complex manner. An important principle of organization has been serialism, originally applied only to pitch, so that the pitch content of the work is decided by reiterations of a series (set or row) of pitches that has been determined in advance (*e.g.,* in the 12-tone compositions of Schoenberg and Webern). Since 1945 the serial principle has been extended to other aspects of music as well: durations, dynamics, and types of attack and tempi, as in the music of the French composer Olivier Messiaen and the German Karlheinz Stockhausen. Other composers, including Stockhausen and the Greek Yannis Xenakis, have used numerical relationships to determine the structure of compositions mathematically. Still others have conceived of form as a dynamic interaction between contrasting and continually evolving sound events—the French composer Edgard Varèse and the American Elliott Carter. Simultaneously, there are works, such as those of the American John Cage, in which the form is not predetermined by the composer but left to chance, such pieces being called indeterminate or aleatoric. These statements apply particularly to electronic music.

"Sound events"

NON-WESTERN FORMS

Elements of structure. In many non-Western civilized cultures, such as those of India and Middle Eastern Islāmic countries, music for the most part is not written down in advance of the performance but improvised upon framework-like patterns. In effect a composition exists only in its performance. Problems are presented by the different scales and intervals, rhythmic patterns, timbres, inflections, and the like. Or, again, a type of polyphony known as heterophony may result from the discrepancies that occur when several different singers or players simultaneously vary the same melodic line. In Japanese *gagaku* music, in which improvisation is not a factor, the beats often vary in duration, producing what is known as "elastic rhythms," akin to the Western tempo rubato. Much non-Western music is functional: each piece has a specific purpose and is associated with certain events, actions, or situations, which often determine the musical structure.

Important elements of form in non-Western music are melody types and rhythmic patterns. By melody type is meant a melodic formula using a recognized scale, stressing particular tones and using specific configurations of intervals, which can provide the basis for a larger piece. In a given society or culture there ordinarily exists a large repertory of these melody types from which the musician, following convention, selects those for use in his rendition. The use of rhythmic patterns for form is seen, for instance, in colotomic structure, in which the composition is marked off in temporal entities by the differing but regularly recurring entrances of particular musical instruments in a set order.

Rhythmic patterns used for form

In the music of nonliterate cultures, simple iterative and strophic structures predominate. These are characterized by short phrases and the frequent use of alternation between a soloist and the group (the "call-and-response" pattern). Such pieces, often associated with dancing, usually belong to specific rituals of one kind or another.

In literate cultures comprehensive theoretical music systems often exist, with elaborate musical forms. Nonetheless, the conception of propriety, that each musical piece has a certain function, is dominant. While strophic forms continue to be important, as in the Indian *gat,* the *umui* religious chants of the Ryukyu Islands (both of which also use variation), and in the popular music of most cultures, there are also such large musical forms as those related to the Indian *rāgas,* the Arabic *maqāmāt* (melody types), and the music of the *gamelan* (gong and percussion ensembles) of Java and Bali.

Specific formal patterns. The term *rāga,* meaning colour or passion, refers not only to a scale but also to the melody type. It has given rise to several musical forms, among them the ancient northern *dhurpad* and the shorter type known as *khyāl* in the North and *kīrtana* in the South. These may be vocal, instrumental, or both, the main performer or performers being accompanied by a drone played by a bass lute and by the reiteration of an extended rhythmic pattern (the *tāla*) by a drum. While much variety is possible, a typical formal arrangement includes a prelude which states the *rāga* (scale and melody type) in its simplest form and continues with a number of contrasting sections that differ in the degree of elaboration of the *rāga,* the register exploited, and the rapidity of the notes and figuration, usually reaching a climax near the end, in which daring variations on the *rāga* in the uppermost register are played or sung in very rapid tempo; the performance may conclude with a return to the character of the prelude. Interludes or linking passages, related to the prelude, are often present, so that an irregular reverting scheme results.

The Arabic *maqām,* roughly equivalent to the *rāga,* provides the basis, among others, for the *bashraf,* a reverting type not unlike the Western rondo, and the *nawba,* an extended multisectional performance with some resemblance to the suite. In Java and Bali particularly noteworthy is the *gending* (musical composition) for the *gamelan,* which may take one of several progressive sectional forms in which the colotomic principle is important: the large *gending agen,* usually bipartite, a slow movement followed by a fast one, and the shorter *gending gangsaran,* used as preludes and interludes. (F.E.Ki.)

Instrumental music

CHAMBER MUSIC

In its original sense chamber music refers to music composed for the home, as opposed to that written for the theatre or church; since the "home"—whether it be drawing room, reception hall, or palace chamber—may be assumed to be of limited size, the music is most often composed for a small ensemble, traditionally dispenses with a conductor, and permits no more than one player to a part. Music written for combinations of stringed or wind instruments, often with a keyboard (piano or harpsichord) as well, and music for voices with or without accompaniment have historically been included in the term.

An essential characteristic of chamber music results from the limited size of the performing group employed: it is intimate music, suited to the expression of subtle and refined musical ideas. Rich displays of varied instrumental colour, and striking effects produced by sheer sonority, play little part in chamber music. In place of those effects are refinement, economy of resources, and flawless acoustical balance.

This section discusses instrumental ensemble music written for groups of two to eight players with one player to a part, and in which stringed instruments and piano (or harpsichord) supply the principal interest.

Historical development. Instrumental music designed

for home use has existed since about the middle of the 15th century. It became customary in Germany to supply folk-song melodies with two or three countermelodies, to expand and elaborate the whole, and to arrange the result for groups of instruments; original melodies were given similar treatment. The instruments were not often specified, but on the basis of many paintings of the time one may assume that groups of viols of various sizes predominated.

A more important source of later chamber music is to be found in the arrangements of 16th-century chansons (songs of French origin composed usually for four voices on a variety of secular texts), some for voices and lute, others for lute alone. The typical chanson was characterized by contrasts in musical texture and often in metre; the effect of the whole was that of a short composition in several even shorter sections. That sectional form retained in the arrangements later became a striking feature.

The chanson travelled to Italy about 1525, became known as canzona, and was transcribed for organ. The earliest transcriptions differed from the French arrangements in treating the original chanson with greater freedom, adding ornaments and flourishes, and sometimes inserting new material. Soon original canzonas for organ, modelled on the transcriptions, and for small instrumental ensembles, were composed. One such type, characterized by elaborate figurations and ornamented melodies, became influential in England late in the 17th century and played a role in the works of Henry Purcell.

Development from dance suites

Parallel to the developments that led from the vocal chanson, in France, to the instrumental canzona, primarily in Italy, was the development of the dance suite. Early 16th-century dance tunes in all countries of western Europe usually had appeared in pairs: one was slow, stately in mood, and in duple metre (*i.e.,* with two beats to the measure); the other fast, lively in mood, usually in triple metre, and often melodically similar to the first. Through much of the 16th century, composers in the several countries sought to expand the dance pair into a unified dance suite. Suites based on variations of one movement appeared in England; suites in which each of four dances had its own rhythmic character, melodically based on the first dance, were written in Germany; sets of dances with no internal relationships to each other were common in Italy. The most influential steps were taken in France by composers for the lute or the clavecin (harpsichord). Consisting essentially of four dance forms that were then popular—the allemande, courante, sarabande, and gigue—the suites they composed were based on contrasting tempos, metres, and rhythmic patterns. The French version of the dance suite became the prototype for later chamber-music forms.

Toward the middle of the 17th century the two types of composition—one derived from the canzona and composed in sectional form, the other derived from the dance suite and consisting of several movements—appeared as works for small instrumental ensembles. In Italy small groups of stringed instruments were often employed in Roman Catholic churches to perform appropriate music; thus canzonas came to be widely used for church purposes. For church use the dance movements were omitted, and what came to be called a church sonata (*sonata da chiesa*) resulted. And a set of *sonate da chiesa* composed in 1667 by Giovanni Battista Vitali marked the beginning of the form as a separate entity.

Rosenmüller's chamber sonatas

In the same year Johann Rosenmüller, a German composer working in Venice, published a set of *Sonate da camera cioè Sinfonie . . .* (*Chamber Sonatas, that is, Symphonies . . .*), each consisting of four to six dance movements with an introductory movement (sinfonia) not in dance style. The development of chamber music for the remainder of the century centred upon these two types, *sonata da chiesa* and *sonata da camera.*

The first half of the 17th century was marked by considerable variety in the constitution of chamber-music groups. Compositions were commonly for one to four viols, or for combinations of viols and woodwind instruments, most often with a figured-bass accompaniment, a kind of musical shorthand, employed in virtually all music of the period about 1600 to 1750, in which the composer wrote a bass line and inserted figures and other symbols under certain notes. The figures indicated the nature of the desired chord to be improvised over the note—whether major or minor, whether in normal or in inverted position, and so on—and the figured-bass line was designed to be "realized" or played by a harmony instrument (such as a lute, organ, or harpsichord), often with a melody instrument (bass, cello, or bassoon) to reinforce the bass line. The bass line with its figures and the two instruments performing it were called basso continuo or simply continuo.

As early as 1622, the Italian composer Salomone Rossi had begun to specify two violins and *chittarone* (a large lute) in his dance sets; and soon similar combinations were adopted generally. A work written for two violins and bass (continuo) became known as a *sonata a tre* or "trio sonata"—even though four instruments (the three strings and the lute or harpsichord) were usually involved in the performance. Later in the 17th century works for one instrument and continuo appeared also and were called variously solo sonatas, duos, or *sonate a due.* The combinations of violin and continuo or cello and continuo were favoured, and sonatas for those combinations took regular places in the chamber-music field.

Works for two violins and continuo (with harpsichord and bass understood) virtually dominated the field until the middle of the 18th century. About that time the custom of serenading became popular; small groups of instrumentalists strolled the streets of Austrian and Italian cities, performing serenades and divertimenti. The keyboard instrument realizing the continuo proved unwieldy and was soon abandoned. To the three remaining strings a viola was added to fill out the harmonies, the bass was replaced by a cello, and the string quartet emerged. This new combination of two violins, viola, and cello was then adopted by composers of serious music, and from about 1750 the string quartet took its place as the principal medium for chamber music. Owing its development largely to the Austrian composer Joseph Haydn, it has reigned supreme to the present day. About 1760, other combinations for strings alone began to play important but relatively smaller roles in the field: the string trio (violin, viola, cello), string quintet (quartet plus a second viola), and string sextet (quintet plus a second cello) are chief among them.

Function of the harpsichord

Meanwhile, as the continuo principle gradually approached obsolescence, the harpsichord (which was superseded by the piano about 1770) took on a new function in chamber music. In works with continuo it had been an accompanying instrument, improvising its part according to the directions indicated in the figured bass; now the keyboard instrument became dominant in new combinations that included one to four strings. The most important of these is the piano trio (piano, violin, cello), the repertory of which includes works from Haydn to the present. Various combinations of piano and one instrument loom almost as large. Toward the end of the 18th century and extending through the 19th, the combinations of piano quartet (piano trio plus viola) and piano quintet (piano and string quartet) give rise to a small but significant repertory ornamented by composers such as Mozart, Beethoven, Brahms, and many others.

Finally, works for individual combinations exist in considerable number after about the 1780s. Representative compositions of that nonstandard group include the clarinet quintets (string quartet and clarinet) by Mozart (K. 581) and Brahms (Opus 115); the *Septet,* Opus 20 (violin, viola, cello, bass, clarinet, bassoon, and horn), by Beethoven; the *Octet,* Opus 166 (as in the septet plus a second violin), the *Trout Quintet,* Opus 114 (violin, viola, cello, bass, and piano), and the *String Quintet in C Major,* Opus 163 (two violins, viola, and two cellos), all by Schubert; and the *Horn Trio,* Opus 40 (violin, horn, and piano), by Brahms. Composers of the 20th century have written works for instrumental groups to which a voice is added.

Late Baroque period, c. 1675–1750. The work of Arcangelo Corelli (1653–1713) in standardizing the two major sonata types of his time had tremendous impact on chamber music. Corelli was of considerable influence on Henry

Purcell (*c.* 1659–95), the most important English composer of his time. Purcell's works include 22 trio sonatas closely allied to the *chiesa* type, and over a dozen "fancies" (that is, fantasies), works of a single movement largely in contrapuntal style for groups of three to seven viols. Another Italian Baroque composer of widespread influence, Antonio Vivaldi (1678–1741), in addition to several hundred concertos for various instruments and orchestra, composed some 75 chamber-music works. Of these, 12 trio sonatas, 16 sonatas for violin and continuo, and about 16 for various other instruments have entered the repertory.

Bach's contributions

The contributions of Johann Sebastian Bach (1685–1750) to development of chamber music were noteworthy. In all, Bach's chamber works include 18 sonatas for one instrument (nine for violin, three for viola da gamba, six for flute) and harpsichord, two separate trio sonatas, and two late works of an unusual nature; *Das musikalisches Opfer* (*The Musical Offering*) and *Die Kunst der Fuge* (*The Art of the Fugue*). Half of the sonatas require figured bass; the other half, with written-out keyboard parts, are essentially in three-voice counterpoint: one voice in the solo instrument and two in the keyboard part. *The Musical Offering* consists of 12 canons and fugues for various combinations of two to six instruments and a four-movement trio sonata; the whole is based on a theme given to Bach by Frederick the Great in 1747, upon which Bach improvised in the presence of the King, and which he later elaborated to constitute this "offering." The work reveals Bach's enormous technical skill and is filled with emotional intensity. *The Art of the Fugue,* Bach's last work, is a set of 19 fugues (the last unfinished) for two to four unspecified instruments. The work is based on one theme that is transformed in systematic fashion in successive movements, and employs two additional themes on occasion. The whole summarizes the contrapuntal practices of the past, contains profound spiritual symbolism, and is unique in music.

The 40-odd chamber works of George Frideric Handel (1685–1759), representing both *chiesa* and *camera* types, contain a wealth of melody and carefully worked-out fugal movements and are filled with the rhythmic drive that represents Handel at his best. Of these about 18 are solo sonatas (with continuo) for various instruments, and some 22 are trio sonatas.

Haydn's 83 quartets

Classical period, c. 1750–1825. The 83 string quartets (of which seven are single-movement arrangements of orchestral pieces titled *The Seven Words of Our Saviour on the Cross* and known as *The Seven Last Words*) by Joseph Haydn (1732–1809) constitute a series in which virtually the entire history of the string quartet is represented. Most of them appeared in sets of six, each under a separate opus number. The earliest sets, Opus 1 and 2, express merely the superficial and diverting elements of Rococo style—the fanciful, ornamental style that was prevalent in the 18th century. From Opus 3 onward the four-movement form is regularized, and in Opus 9 thematic materials begin to reveal details that point to the future. Opus 17 discloses a virtuosic element in its first-violin parts, and lower voices are given only a small share in the thematic work. The latter process comes to full expression in Opus 20, for now cello and viola are entrusted with thematic statements and the quartet style is close at hand.

After a nine-year interval (1772–81) Haydn introduced a "new manner" (his phrase) in the quartets of Opus 33; this resulted in the establishment of the principle of thematic development. Motive manipulation is basic to the texture, and the fully developed sonata form appears. Also in Opus 33 Haydn introduced the scherzo in place of the minuet, but did not continue that practice in later quartets.

The 33 quartets from Opus 50 onward (excepting Opus 51, *The Seven Last Words*) include the masterworks on which Haydn's reputation is so firmly founded. Of them 18 (Opus 50, 54, 55, 64) were composed during the time (*c.* 1786–90) Haydn was in close contact with Mozart and are characterized by an increasing use of chromaticism to produce poignant effects. The 15 quartets written after Mozart's death (Opus 71, 74, 76, 77, 103) return to the optimistic style that was innate, and they reveal an ever-increasing expressiveness and mastery of detail.

Haydn also composed more than 30 piano trios, eight violin sonatas, and over 60 string trios. While those works contain attractive melodies, they represent a minor aspect of the composer's activity.

Of the 26 string quartets written by Wolfgang Amadeus Mozart (1756–91) the qualities of the last 10 are such that they have virtually overshadowed the 16 earlier works. Six of the 10 reflect Mozart's first attempts to work in Haydn's "new manner" and reveal how successfully he adopted the principle. The last three, dedicated to King Frederick William II of Prussia, a competent cellist, show Mozart's ability to adapt to the interests of his potential patrons. Here the cello parts reveal something of the virtuosity required of the first violin. Taken together, the last 10 quartets are among Mozart's masterpieces.

Of Mozart's eight string quintets, three rise to supremacy. The *String Quintet in C Major,* K. 515 (K. stands for Köchel, a cataloger of Mozart's works), is a model of strength and delicacy, filled with moods reflecting grace and good humour, but also high dramatic tension. Its companion in G minor, K. 516, is characterized by the same strength but is the embodiment of anguish. Two years later Mozart composed the *Clarinet Quintet,* K. 581; now moods of grace, humour, and cheer prevail. The addition of the woodwind instrument enabled Mozart to achieve a high level of brilliance and colour throughout; the *Clarinet Quintet* is one of the monuments of the literature.

Exactly half of Mozart's 32 violin sonatas were composed before his 10th birthday; in them the violin parts do little more than accompany the piano. The last 16 move gradually to a true ensemble texture, which is fully attained in K. 454, K. 481, and K. 526. Two piano quartets, contrasting greatly in mood, are alike in containing a balance between piano and strings. His seven piano trios are somewhat like the violin sonatas in gradually reaching a true ensemble texture. Of the seven, one in B flat major (K. 502), one in E major (K. 542), and one in E flat major for clarinet, viola, and piano (K. 498) rise to greatness in variety of moods, balanced forms, and perfection of detail.

The backbone of the repertory

In the works of Ludwig van Beethoven (1770–1827) chamber-music composition takes a central place. His 17 string quartets constitute the backbone of the repertory. The first six take points of departure from the quartet style of Haydn's later works, but far exceed them in strength, occasional boisterousness, and variety of material. Five quartets of Beethoven's middle period represent a great increase in size, depth of expression, and formal freedom. The six last quartets include works that transcend conventional forms and textures. Development techniques and contrapuntal devices play more important roles here; forms are imaginative and fluid, movements are often thematically related, and a range of expression that uncovers new depths of the soul is here disclosed.

Beethoven's other chamber music, like the quartets, reveals a gradual increase in the power of the motive to generate thematic sections. This is especially true in the *Three Piano Trios,* Opus 1; the *String Trio in C Major,* Opus 9, No. 3; and the *String Quintet in C Major,* Opus 29. Particularly in the scherzo movements, which Beethoven employs in place of minuets, he generally begins with a one-measure motive, from which most of the thematic material is derived. The *Septet,* Opus 20, together with many of the violin sonatas, the cello sonatas, and a few miscellaneous works, occupy an intermediate stage in this development. Some are based on long melodies that are developed, others on short motives that are manipulated. In virtually every case, however, a masterpiece results.

Early Romantic period, c. 1825–55. Franz Schubert (1797–1828), in about 28 chamber-music works, at first modelled his compositions on those of the Classical period. His restless search for instrumental and harmonic colour soon took him beyond the bounds of Classical style and aligned him with the prophets of Romanticism. Of the eight works in which his mature mastery is so clearly revealed, all but one were composed after 1824. They include the last three string quartets, the *Trout Quintet* for piano and strings, an *Octet* for strings and winds, two piano trios, and the *String Quintet in C Major* with second cello added to the usual quartet.

Schubert's melodic flow

Less concerned with traditional formal structure than other composers of his stature, Schubert relied on unceasing melodic flow coupled with rare harmonic imagination. Typically a melodic section is repeated with changed harmonies, ranging far beyond the usual; the finale of the *Piano Trio in E Flat Major,* Opus 100, is an extreme example. But Schubert also had a keen sense of drama, as the *String Quartet No. 14 in D Minor* (*Death and the Maiden*) exhibits eloquently. Such characteristics (lyrical melody, harmonic variety, and drama) are wonderfully combined in Schubert's last large composition, the *String Quintet in C Major* with two cellos—probably the most perfect work of this composer's short life.

With Felix Mendelssohn (1809–47) a return to Classical ideals of form is seen, coupled, however, with Romantic enthusiasm. Of his about 24 chamber-music works, eight represent the composer at his best; these include five string quartets, two piano trios, and an *Octet* for eight strings. Mendelssohn's contributions include primarily a new kind of light and deft music, heard especially in his scherzos; a rich melodiousness that embraces all sections of the sonata-form movements (hence removing the element of thematic contrast on which musical conflict depends); and scrupulous attention to detail. The scherzo of the *String Quartet No. 4 in E Minor,* Opus 44, No. 2; that of the *String Octet in E Flat Major,* Opus 20; and the finale of the *String Quartet No. 3 in D Major,* Opus 44, No. 1, are among the finest representatives of Mendelssohn's enchanting style.

Robert Schumann (1810–56) represents the best aspects of early Romanticism; these include an interest in tone colour, melodiousness, a free approach to details of form, and subjective expression in which enthusiasm plays a large part. Twelve chamber-music works reflect those aspects in varying degrees. A set of pieces entitled *Märchenerzählungen* (*Fairy Tales*) for piano, clarinet, and viola illustrates the search for new tone colours; the *Piano Quintet,* in which the piano is combined with two violins, viola, and cello (possibly for the first time in the 19th century), does likewise. Three string quartets are melodious, dramatic, brusque, and dreamy in turn. In three piano trios, as in one piano quartet, Schumann's tendency to let the piano dominate the strings is sometimes seen. And in all those works his characteristic impulsiveness and tendency to alternate between forthright and moody expression is characteristic.

Late Romantic period, c. 1855–1900. In chamber music of the last half of the 19th century, only a few dozen works by composers other than Brahms survive in the repertory of the period. A piano quintet, one string quartet, and a single violin sonata by César Franck reveal that composer's fondness for cyclical form, in which successive movements are thematically linked, and for a structural scheme that is based on harmonic manipulation rather than melodic development. Bedřich Smetana (1824–84), in two string quartets and one piano trio, tended toward autobiographical expression in which Czech folk dances played a part. His first quartet, *Z mého života* (*From My Life*), is supplied with a program.

The work of Antonín Dvořák (1841–1904) represents a combination of the finest Romantic writing with a decidedly nationalistic flavour. Of about 30 works of chamber music, nine held an important place in the repertory; these include two string sextets, three quartets, two piano trios, a piano quartet, and a piano quintet. One of the string quartets, the *American,* Opus 96, purports to express Dvořák's impressions of American (including Indian) music. Another work, the *Piano Quintet,* Opus 81, marks a high point in the composer's use of attractive melody and rhythmic vitality; it, too, has Czech overtones. And the *Dumky Trio,* Opus 90, contains six dumky (a dumka being a Ukranian folk music form with moods alternating between melancholy and wild abandon); here the element of contrast is stressed to the utmost.

Aleksandr Borodin (1833–87), in the second of his two quartets, combined traces of Russian nationalism with expressions of pure lyricism. Peter Ilich Tchaikovsky (1840–93), with three string quartets (one of them containing the famous "Andante cantabile"), a string sextet, and a big-scale piano trio, often brought moments of orchestral sonority into his chamber music. The *Piano Trio,* Opus 50, is a virtuosic work in two movements—one a lengthy sonata form, and the other a set of brilliant variations—and is primarily elegiac in mood.

Preeminence of Brahms

It was Johannes Brahms (1833–97), however, who dominated the period. All of Brahms's 24 chamber-music works are highly successful; in all these works Brahms's characteristic balance of emotional and intellectual expression is clearly revealed. Rich sonorities, thick textures, and rhythmic complexity are present everywhere, and the forms are those of the Classical period, somewhat modified in the light of Brahms's temperament and expressive requirements.

Eloquent melodic writing is most characteristic of his earlier works, notably the *String Sextet No. 1 in B Flat Major,* Opus 18; the *Piano Quartet in G Minor,* Opus 25; and large portions of the *Piano Quintet,* Opus 34. Later works, by contrast, reveal Brahms's increasing concern with motivic and rhythmic development; as a consequence, lyricism plays a smaller role in such works as the two string quartets Opus 51, and the four late works with clarinet, namely the *Clarinet Trio,* Opus 114, the *Clarinet Quintet,* Opus 115, and the two sonatas Opus 120.

The 20th century. As in all times of stylistic change, considerable overlapping of styles occurred at the turn of the 20th century. In chamber music, several composers born in the 19th century carried the modified Late-Romantic style into the 20th. Among the French composers were Gabriel Fauré (1845–1924), who, with 10 works, is remembered primarily for a refined and controlled style that is rhythmically subtle; and Vincent d'Indy (1851–1931), represented by about eight works, who reflected the style of César Franck. Likewise the Hungarian Ernő Dohnányi (1877–1960) revealed the strong influence of Brahms in about six works noted for their outspoken melodiousness and contrapuntal excellence. The German Max Reger (1873–1916), with about 36 works, was primarily an exponent of chromatic writing in forms that are derived essentially from the 19th century.

The first step toward the new styles of the 20th century were taken in France by Claude Debussy (1862–1918); his one string quartet (1893) and three sonatas (late works) represent the Impressionistic style based on whole-tone harmony, of which he was an exponent. Somewhat similar are the string quartet and piano trio by Maurice Ravel (1875–1937), with a rich array of tremolos, forms based on repetition of melodic fragments, and many astringent harmonies. In England, on a different path are a string quartet and piano quintet by Sir Edward Elgar (1857–1934) and two string quartets, a string quintet, and a song cycle (*On Wenlock Edge:* for tenor, string quartet, and piano) by Ralph Vaughan Williams (1872–1958). Elgar reveals an intensely personal style; Vaughan Williams uses English folk song, elusive harmonies, and strong rhythms.

Three major influences

The musical styles that have dominated the later 20th century are largely the work of three composers and their respective followers. The most influential was Arnold Schoenberg with his development of the "12-tone style"; but his earlier works were not yet representative of that style. A string sextet, *Verklärte Nacht* (*Transfigured Night*), transferred the form and content of the symphonic poem to the field of chamber music; two string quartets, Opus 7 and 10, are similarly post-Romantic in style, and the second includes a part for soprano voice. A set of 21 short poems for quasi-reciting voice and five instruments, *Pierrot Lunaire,* marked an intermediate stage; and four later works, including the third string quartet, saw the full development of the 12-tone style. In a fourth quartet and a few smaller works the system was carried to completion.

In the *Lyric Suite* for string quartet (1927) Alban Berg (1885–1935), also an Austrian and one of Schoenberg's pupils, brought elements of Romantic expression into the system. And another Austrian pupil, Anton von Webern (1883–1945), sought to develop utmost refinement and consistency, along with brevity. A string quartet, a quartet for violin, clarinet, saxophone, and piano, and a chamber concerto for nine instruments are the principal works that illustrate his methods of extreme economy in the use of all materials. Webern's approach has been of maximum influence on many composers of the present day, and has led to the development of serial writing.

A completely different path was taken by the Hungarian Béla Bartók in six string quartets and a trio, *Contrasts,* for piano, violin, and clarinet. In those works the main thrust has been on harmony (including acrid dissonances that border on atonality), greatly rhythmic drive with many irregular rhythmic patterns (some of them based on eastern European folk song, in which field Bartók was an avid worker), and the development of new instrumental effects. Coupled with such technical elements are fervent expressiveness and, in the slow movements, great repose. The Bartók quartets are among the major chamber-music works of the 20th century.

The third principal influence, that of the Russian-born Igor Stravinsky (1882–1971), was felt perhaps less in chamber music than in orchestral, for Stravinsky composed fewer than a dozen works in the field. Five song cycles for voice and small groups of instruments, several short pieces for string quartet, and a pantomime, *The Soldier's Tale,* for narrator and seven instruments are varied in content and style. An *Octet* for wind instruments (1923) represents a deliberately impersonal style that requires no subjective interpretation on the part of the performers. And a *Septet* for three winds, three strings, and piano (1952) marks Stravinsky's adoption of serial writing, a style that he had consciously rejected earlier.

Other major contributions

The German Paul Hindemith (1895–1963), with seven string quartets and more than two dozen sonatas and other works, favoured polyphonic textures, an expanded harmonic scheme, and great rhythmic drive. His style in later works became less dissonant, more lyric, and was characterized by a general lightening of the thick counterpoint that had distinguished his work of the 1940s. His seven works called *Kammermusik* are for larger groups and so do not come within the scope of this article. The French composer Darius Milhaud, in about 18 string quartets, four quintets for various combinations, and a number of other works, for a time espoused the principles of polytonality, the device of employing several keys simultaneously. Characterized by moods that are often pungent, humorous, and even satirical, his works reveal a mixture of dissonant counterpoint, rhythmic flexibility, and graceful expression. His 14th and 15th quartets, independent works in their own right, may be performed simultaneously to form an octet.

Two Russian composers, Sergey Prokofiev (1891–1953) and Dmitry Shostakovich, are represented in the repertory by about 20 works adhering, in the main, to the forms and textures of the 19th century. Both men embrace the new harmonic techniques without departing entirely from Romantic expressiveness. Many of their compositions reveal a sense of humour. Of British composers, Sir William Walton, Lennox Berkeley, Alan Rawsthorne, and Benjamin Britten have made significant contributions to the medium.

American composers

The chamber music by American composers has in general reflected the international styles mentioned above. One exception is seen in two quartets, a piano trio, and several violin sonatas by Charles Ives (1874–1954), who maintained a style of great originality through his long lifetime. Another exception may be noted in the work of Ernest Bloch (1880–1959), Swiss by birth, but identified with the United States since about 1917. In five string quartets, two piano quintets, and a few smaller works, Bloch brought his Jewish heritage to expression in styles that are robust and varied.

Among the more prominent American composers, a few may be singled out for their notable contributions. Walter Piston, with four string quartets, a piano trio, a quintet for flute and strings, and a piano quintet, is perhaps the most eclectic; his works are basically Neoclassical and are distinguished by elegance and vitality. Roger Sessions, represented principally by two string quartets and a string quintet, has written in an austere, reserved, and strongly dissonant style. Quincy Porter (1897–1966) composed 10 string quartets, several quintets for various combinations, and smaller works; they are characterized by warm expressiveness achieved in textures that employ considerable repetition of short motives. The works of Roy Harris are distinguished by forms that depart from 19th-century models; three string quartets and a piano quintet are among his most significant works.

Aaron Copland may be mentioned for a piano trio; a sextet for clarinet, piano, and strings; a piano quartet; and a violin sonata. Those works include variously nationalistic allusions (including Jewish and Latin American), unresolved dissonance, and elements of serial style. William Schuman in four string quartets and smaller works discloses a strongly dissonant style that remains, nevertheless, within the tonal system; his works are rhythmically vital and express great energy.

Elliott Carter, Jr., is best represented by a cello sonata and two string quartets. He employs elements of serial writing, composes in a virtually free rhythmic manner, and employs new instrumental effects in the manner of Bartók; yet his style is a completely individual expression. Leon Kirchner has composed two string quartets, a violin sonata, and a piano trio; unmetrical rhythm is a striking characteristic of his style, along with a variety of harmonies ranging from purely diatonic to atonal, and warm expressiveness is usually present.

Latin-American composers

Among composers representing the countries of Central and South America, three have risen to international prominence. Heitor Villa-Lobos (1887–1959) was the outstanding exponent of Brazilian national idioms, including those of the indigenous Indians. In his many chamber-music works (10 string quartets, several piano trios, and a few sonatas are representative) Villa-Lobos gave expression to those idioms. Carlos Chávez (1899–1978) worked similarly with the idioms of Mexican Indians, but in several of his relatively few chamber-music works, Neoclassical style elements are prominent. Alberto Ginastera (1916–83), representing Argentina, stressed the element of rhythm to a high degree in a style that is thoroughly contemporary.

Structural elements. *Form.* A major distinction must be drawn between the prevailing musical forms of the period before about 1750 and those after that date. The earlier forms included primarily the *sonata da chiesa,* which emerged from the instrumental canzona, and the *sonata da camera,* which owed its origin to the dance suite. In the first of these, the several sections that had been taken over from the canzona were gradually extended, cadences (harmonic devices analogous to punctuation marks in prose) were confined largely to ends of sections, and the single-movement form soon dissolved into a set of movements of varying length, tempo, and metre. Toward the 1640s a tendency arose to standardize the number of movements and regularize the contrasts between them; soon a pattern of four movements arranged in slow–fast–slow–fast sequence, with textures based to a large extent on imitative or fugal writing, emerged. The Italian violinist-composer Arcangelo Corelli, with about 38 *sonate da chiesa,* was the most consistent in employing that pattern after about 1680.

Chamber and church sonatas

The other form, *sonata da camera,* remained less regular. Its parent, the dance suite, had most often contained four movements, but works of three to eight or more movements exist also. When the dance suite adopted the trio-sonata instrumentation and gradually became the *sonata da camera,* it at first maintained that irregularity. Soon, however, it was altered to include a nondance first movement (prelude, preamble, or *intrada*), after which a number of idealized dance forms followed. In keeping with its origin, the *sonata da camera* revealed a relationship to dance rhythms in its several movements (except the first), and homophonic style (*i.e.,* with a single melodic line supported by chords) dominated. The work of Corelli, embodied in 34 *sonate da camera,* again served as a model for later composers.

Toward the end of the 17th century the two forms began mutually to influence each other. The *sonata da chiesa,* with its serious moods set usually in contrapuntal texture (*i.e.,* employing counterpoint, the intertwining of independent melodic lines), adopted some of the lighter and more rhythmic aspects of its rival. Likewise, the *sonata da cam-*

era, light in its total mood and based on dance rhythms, often embodied contrapuntal devices and contained movements that were essentially imitative or fugal in texture and serious in mood. By the end of the 17th century the distinctions between the two types tended to disappear; soon the terms *chiesa* and *camera* were dropped, and the term *sonata a tre* or "trio sonata" prevailed to about 1750. The situation in regard to solo sonatas (for violin and continuo, for example) was similar; they, too, took on common characteristics derived from the contrasting trio-sonata types, and contained both dance metres and contrapuntal textures.

Pattern of the string quartet

The post-1750 forms, on the other hand, were based on different patterns. A standard pattern of a string quartet consisted of four movements, the first of which was most often cast in sonata form—three-part form containing an exposition of two contrasting melodic ideas, a transition (later elaborated to create a "development section"), and a recapitulation of the first part with changed harmonies. The second movement was generally in slow tempo and could represent one of several forms: another sonata form, a set consisting of theme and variations, or the like. Then followed a movement in triple metre (at first a minuet and later a faster version of that dance called a "scherzo") derived from the dance field and consisting actually of two such idealized dances; the second, called a "trio," usually lighter in texture, was followed by a recapitulation of the first dance. The last movement was a rondo (consisting of a regular alternation of two or more musical ideas, in the form A B A B A or A B A C A), or a set of variations, or even another sonata form. The whole represents a compound form called a "sonata," although post-1750 and pre-1750 sonatas have few structural elements in common.

The term sonata (in the post-1750 version) can be applied to most of the forms within the field of chamber music as well as to several outside that field. As seen in the compositions of a line of composers from Haydn in the late 18th century to Brahms in the late 19th and beyond, the piano trio, violin sonata, string quintet, and the others are all based essentially on the pattern that characterizes, above all, the string quartet. Even the symphony and the concerto of the post-1750 period are, in effect, sonatas for orchestra. Internal differences exist, of course; the piano trio and the violin sonata, for example, do not always include a dance-derived third movement, which the string quartet and symphony generally do. Conversely, the exposition of the symphony's first movement often contains more than two contrasting themes, and is often preceded by a massive introduction; and the recapitulation is often followed by a large concluding section or coda (literally, "tail"). Similarly, the first movement of a concerto (for piano and orchestra, say) is generally characterized by two expositions—one for the orchestra, the other for the solo instrument. In most other respects, the majority of the larger instrumental forms of the post-1750 period are closely related in their total structure.

Melody. The years about 1600, marking roughly the date when chamber music emerged as a separate branch, also mark one of the major turning points in the evolution of music. Virtually all the factors of music were affected by the developments of the time. A new system of melodic organization (the tonal system, with its major and minor scales) soon assumed a preeminent position; the principles of harmony were expanded and systematized; a texture based on the polarity between melody and bass (as opposed to one that had been largely the result of writing intertwined and independent melodies) came to the fore; and the figured bass or continuo was invented (albeit, a few decades earlier) to deal with the new texture. In those new developments all the musical factors continued to be mutually related; but they are considered separately here for the sake of clarity.

The melodies of the canzona, or sonata, at first continued to imitate vocal melodies; easily sung intervals, relatively slow tempos, and undulating stepwise contours were characteristic. Gradually composers began to consider the nature of the instruments they were using and to write melodies appropriate to those instruments. Soon the concept of instrumental idioms was developed; each instrument was given melodies appropriate to its structure. That development is seen most clearly in the many trio sonatas written by Corelli after about 1680.

Harmony as a system

With the emergence of systematized harmony, in which specific functions were given to chords according to their relationships to the tonic (the basic, or root, tone of a given scale), melodies became harmonically directed, moved from one harmonic goal to another, and began to take on regular periodic structure (in units of four measures, eight measures, and so on). Slow movements often adopted elements of vocal style, in which sharp contours were avoided, and the melody followed purely musical or aesthetic laws rather than the laws of textual declamation. The ever-increasing use of harmonic dissonance was reflected in melodic writing through the 18th and 19th centuries. Extreme leaps, angular contours, irregular rhythmic shapes—such characteristics became the common property of all composers.

Influence of tonality

Harmony. The complex of chords gradually evolved into the system of tonality. Central to that system is the idea that the triad on the first tone of the scale (*i.e.*, the tonic and the third and fifth intervals above it) determines the key or tonality (C major, D minor, and so on) around which other chords are grouped. Modulations (shifts to other key centres) became regularized: those to the dominant (the fifth note of the scale) and subdominant (an interval of a fifth below, or the fourth note of the scale) became the most important. In the period immediately before and after 1800, especially in the works of Beethoven and Schubert, modulations to the mediant and submediant (an interval of a third above and below the tonic, respectively) became characteristic. And throughout the 19th century, modulation to ever more remote keys was practiced assiduously. Further, chromatic tones—tones not related to the key centre (F sharp or D flat in a C major context, for example)—appeared in increasing numbers; and tones not part of the chord at a given moment (F in a triad on C, for example) were treated more freely. The consequence was a system in which tonality became so ambiguous that it ceased to serve any real function through long passages in the music. Chromatic harmony dominated much music of the late 19th century, and the steps from chromaticism to the atonal and serial systems of the 20th century, in which tonality was entirely abandoned, followed as a matter of course.

Texture. Similarly, the element of texture underwent a series of changes. Much music was composed in homophonic style, with a melody supported only by a few chords built above the continuo. Gradually, especially in the trio sonatas, an inner part came to imitate the upper melody to some extent; bits of figuration gave the two upper melodies a degree of independence, and eventually polyphonic texture, composed of two or more intertwining melodies, was restored. That texture reflected the harmonic developments of the time and came under the control of the tonal system with its dissonances, modulations, chromatic embellishments, and all the rest. Mixed textures, partly homophonic and partly polyphonic, became common also; but in general the uppermost melody dominated the structure well past the middle of the 18th century.

Toward the 1770s, with the string quartet an established grouping, increasing attention was given to the inner and lower parts. Viola and cello were occasionally given thematic material, the violins at times played accompanying parts, and detailed writing for all four instruments compensated for the absence of the continuo. The practice of improvising harmonies at the keyboard came to an end, and all parts were obbligati (that is, obligatory). Continued refinement in the writing and equal distribution of musical responsibility to all four instruments resulted in the so-called quartet style, in which the distinction between melody and accompaniment disappeared and no instrument dominated the others. From that point forward, the idea of a soloist in chamber music lost whatever validity it had had earlier; the performers in a chamber-music work became members of a group of equals.

Style. In style, too, there has been a continuing series

of changes. "Style" may be defined in this context as the sum of the devices—melodic, structural, harmonic, and all the rest—that a composer consistently employs, that a class of works regularly exhibits, or that a particular age finds most useful for its aesthetic purposes.

In this sense, the majority of chamber-music works composed before 1750 are monothematic in style; those after about 1750 are polythematic. The typical fast movement of a trio sonata, say, consists of a series of phrases largely similar in contour and mood and differentiated primarily by harmonic considerations; whereas the typical sonata-form movement is characterized by having two or more themes embodying sharp contrasts of mood and shape, and further contrasted by means of texture, instrumentation, and harmonic colour. Alternation of dramatic and lyric moods, further, is most often characteristic of post-1750 chamber music.

With the emergence of the string quartet and sonata form toward the middle of the 18th century, thematic materials most often took the shape of relatively long melodies—whatever their contour or mood. Those melodies were then manipulated or repeated in accord with harmonic principles and constituted sections in tonic, dominant, and so on. In the 1780s, and specifically in the quartets Opus 33 by Haydn, certain melodies were so constructed that they could, in effect, be broken apart into fragments or motives, each motive with its own distinctive shape. In the appropriate sections of sonata-form movements—namely, those that connected one thematic section with another, and the large transition that comprised the midsection of the form—the motives were treated separately, manipulated, combined in new ways, served to suggest yet other ideas to the composer; in short, they were "developed."

Thematic development

Such treatment of the motives led to the principle of thematic development and to the practice of motive manipulation. Begun by Haydn, carried forward notably by Beethoven and Brahms, and employed by virtually every other instrumental composer of the 19th century, the principle of thematic development is one of the chief distinguishing marks of late Classical and Romantic instrumental music. Beethoven, however, and after him many other major composers, employed the process somewhat differently from Haydn; he often began with a melodic or rhythmic motive, then let the themes themselves grow out of the motive manipulation.

The repertory of works for piano and strings also grew considerably from the late 18th century onward, and there was considerable modification in the role of the piano in that repertory. The keyboard instrument had entered the field, it will be remembered, after having played a century-long role as the improvising member of the continuo team, in which it provided accompaniments to the other instruments. When it emerged in its new role with written-out parts to play, it at first assumed a dominant position—in violin or cello sonatas and in piano trios alike. Many of the piano trios by Haydn are essentially sonatas for solo piano with accompaniments furnished by violin and cello; the latter often do little more than double the parts given to the pianist's right and left hands, respectively.

Evolution of role of piano

Gradually the string parts acquired a degree of independence and became obbligato parts. The final steps toward complete equality were taken across the interval from about 1790 to 1840, especially in the piano trios and quartets of Mozart and Beethoven and in Schumann's *Piano Quintet,* Opus 44 of 1842. In many of those works, particularly the later ones, the piano emerged as one-half of the tonal body with the two, three, or four stringed instruments providing the other half. Again, as in the string quartets, the concept of soloist versus accompanist has no validity in chamber music with piano. A keyboard player does not "accompany" the strings; he is an equal partner in the ensemble—which marks a major change from the role he played in the 17th and the first half of the 18th centuries.

Chamber music in the later 19th century became ever more affected by developments in the orchestral field. The rise of professional quartets in the time of Beethoven had the effect of moving chamber music from the confines of the home to the public concert stage. Composers took advantage of the virtuosic attainments of the best performers and wrote music with which the nonprofessional performer could not always cope. Effects requiring consummate technical ability became common; true virtuosity became a general requirement. Further, orchestral effects depending upon sheer volume of sound were often employed; the string quartets and piano trio of Tchaikovsky are examples. And with the rise of descriptive or program music in the orchestral field, extramusical or nationalistic elements sometimes entered chamber-music works; Smetana's autobiographical string quartet, *Z mého života* (*From My Life*), and certain of Dvořák's compositions containing Czech folk idioms and representing the Czech spirit are typical.

The overwhelming majority of chamber music composed before about 1900 consists of works that employ instruments in conventional ways. Tones are limited to the pitches in the chromatic scale (*i.e.,* a scale consisting of half steps, C, C sharp, D, D sharp, E, and so through all 12 tones), stringed instruments are used in the traditional manner, and the piano likewise. A few notable exceptions may be mentioned: in the *Piano Trio No. 1 in D Minor,* Opus 63, by Schumann the strings play a short passage *sul ponticello* ("against the bridge")—that is, play closer to the bridge of the instruments than usual in order to produce the higher overtones and give the pitches an ethereal or veiled quality; in the same composer's *Piano Quartet in E Flat Major,* Opus 47, the cello must retune its lowest string downward a whole step in order to supply a longheld tone beyond the normal range of the instrument. And, in a few works of the time, harmonics are called for: a string is touched lightly at its midpoint or at one of the other nodal positions at one-third or one-quarter of its length, and the harmonic (overtone) thus produced adds a distinctive quality to the music. Such effects, plus the traditional pizzicato (in which the string is plucked rather than set in motion by the bow) are virtually the only exceptions to normal writing.

In 20th-century chamber music, however, the number of purely instrumental effects has been increased; the Hungarian composer Béla Bartók in several of his quartets became the leading exponent of such devices. In his *String Quartet No. 4* (1928), for example, glissandi are required; in such cases the player slides his finger up or down the string to cover the span of an octave or more, and produces a wailing effect. Pizzicati are directed to be performed so that the string slaps back against the fingerboard, to add a percussive effect to the pitch. In works by other composers employing the clarinet, the performer is required to blow through the instrument with its mouthpiece removed while opening and closing the keys at random; this produces the effect of a high-pitched whistling wind along with a semblance of pitch changes. Or again, in the case of brass instruments, the composer's directives call for the player to tap his hand against the mouthpiece, to create a hollow percussive sound.

Pitches themselves are altered on occasion, for tones lying between those of the chromatic scale are sometimes employed; among early exponents of the quarter-tone practice, the contemporary composer Ernest Bloch may be mentioned. In his *Piano Quintet,* and elsewhere, the string performers are required to play certain tones a quarter step higher or lower than written, thereby departing from the scales that had served music for many centuries. Other composers carried the quarter-tone practice further and developed a kind of microtonal music that employs intervals even smaller than quarter-tones.

Use of quarter-tones

All such developments give evidence that 20th-century composers continue to seek new means of expression and expand their available resources—thus continuing a practice characteristic of composers in all periods. Two further aspects of that search remain to be considered: the development of new systems of tonal organization and the increasing use of instruments that embody the results of contemporary technology.

Early in the 20th century a number of composers led by Arnold Schoenberg experimented to reach beyond the confines of the tonal system. In a series of chamber music and other works, Schoenberg gradually arrived at a system in which all 12 tones of the chromatic scale are used as independent entities; concepts of tonic and dominant, of major and minor, and of key centres themselves no longer apply in those works. The 12 tones are arranged in a self-determined series called a "tone row"; certain sections of that row, used vertically, form the chords that supply the harmonic material; the row may be manipulated in accord with self-imposed rules; and the row may be arranged differently for each composition. The system of composing with 12 tones, as Schoenberg referred to his invention, has been modified and enlarged by later composers, the relevant principles have been applied to other elements of music (notably the rhythmic factor); and under a new term, "serial composition," the system has become one of the most influential of the present day.

Electronic synthesizers

The other aspect concerns the use of various electronic sound-generating devices called "electronic synthesizers," and of magnetic tape recorders to transmit the results. The composer working with a synthesizer has virtually complete control over the shape and sound of the tones he wishes to produce. He can select tones with characteristics unlike those produced by conventional instruments, noises (that is, sounds with irregular vibration rates) to which a semblance of pitch has been given, or rapid changes in pitch, loudness, duration, and quality beyond the ability of any human mechanism. The new tonal materials, then, can be combined with voices and conventional instruments, or can be used alone. Devices such as the synthesizer have given the composer access to a new world of tonal resources; he still faces the problems of selection, combination, organization, and expressive purpose that have plagued composers since music began. Since his medium of performance is a tape recorder, since human participation in the performance may not be required, and since his composition may contain a few strands or a hundred strands of tone, it becomes impossible to make distinctions between chamber music, orchestral music, or any other genre. Electronic music is, thus, on the way to becoming a completely new type to which traditional classifications do not apply (see below *Electronic music*).

Audiences. For well over a century after its inception about 1600, chamber music was supported primarily by the nobility. Aristocratic establishments customarily employed groups of musicians who served as composers, conductors, and performers of a variety of operatic, orchestral, and chamber music; and traditionally the audiences were restricted to the patrons and their guests. Chamber-music concerts were instituted in London in 1672, and seem to have been exceptional for their time, for regularly established professional chamber-music groups did not emerge until about 1810, apparently first in Vienna.

Meanwhile, primarily at certain German university towns in the 1700s, the establishment of collegia musica (music societies) marked the beginning of a movement that brought nonprofessional participation in its wake. Eminent musicians directed those societies in many cases; the Collegium Musicum at Leipzig, for example, was founded by Georg Philipp Telemann and had Bach as its director for a decade after 1729. Audiences were at first restricted to university students; later the general public was admitted, and the rise of the modern chamber-music audience began.

Famous quartets

Since the mid-19th century, chamber-music concerts have been a staple of musical life. Many of the best known string quartets (for example, the Joachim Quartet from 1869 to 1907, the Kneisel from 1885 to 1917, the Flonzaley from 1902 to about 1928, the London from 1908 to 1935, the Budapest from 1918 to 1968, and the Juilliard, Paganini, Amadeus, and Fine Arts quartets of the present day) have travelled to countries around the world performing the standard and contemporary repertories of their day.

Parallel to this has been the continuing activity of informal, nonprofessional groups in virtually all musical centres of the Western world. An international association of amateur chamber-music players exists, whose members grade themselves (in a directory) according to technical ability and experience. The colleges and universities of the United States often stress ensemble activity in their music curricula, and many schools of music are centres of activity in the field.

The sheer amount of music being composed makes it virtually inevitable that chamber music will continue to receive the attention of major composers—especially in view of the economic factors that make performance of new orchestral works hazardous at best. One may hope that chamber music will play as vital and significant a role in the future as it has played in the last three and a half centuries. (H.U.)

FUGUE

Although the statement is debatable, it is often said that the fugue is the most complex and highly developed type of composition in Western music. The term fugue, derived from *fuga,* the Latin word for "flight," was first used about 1330 by Jacques de Liège, the author of *Speculum musicae,* an important medieval treatise. At that time it referred to a technique of musical writing based on strict imitation. Later, after its emergence as an independent musical form in the 17th century, the fugue became a composition in counterpoint based on a generating theme, in which different parts, or voices, enter successively in imitation, as if in pursuit of each other. The heir of all the compositional techniques that had developed earlier, it differs from its ancestors (the motet, the ricercare, the canzona) in having a more specifically tonal character, unity of form, and a greater economy.

The fugue is written in counterpoint, two or more lines that sound simultaneously. Counterpoint's laws and techniques have developed from the 10th century to the Renaissance, a period during which Western music was essentially polyphonic. One of the main problems was the harmonic aspect of the meeting of the voices, and the rules of counterpoint are always precise regarding the use of consonance and dissonance. Counterpoint deals also with movement between the parts. It includes various techniques of development, among which imitation is probably the most remarkable feature of polyphonic music. There are many kinds of imitations. The strictest is the canon, in which the melody stated by the first voice is later reproduced by the second voice. A good example is the song "Frère Jacques." Other common types of imitation include inversion of all the intervals, augmentation (in which the rhythmic values are doubled), diminution (in which they are reduced), or even retrograde imitation, in which the last note of one voice becomes the first note of the next. All these techniques are used in fugal composition, which is characterized more by its "language" than by its form.

Types of imitation

Elements of the fugue. The fugue is written for a certain number of voices, or instrumental parts. The most frequent are fugues for three or four voices, but there are also fugues for two, five, or more voices. Although the fugal form varies from composer to composer, there are certain common elements.

The subject is the theme of the fugue. It is stated alone by the first voice before being taken up by the others. In the course of the fugue, it will be stated in different keys, and it will be sometimes slightly modified or inverted. Some of its elements may be developed separately.

The second voice brings in the answer, generally stated in the key of the dominant (the fifth degree of the major or minor scale). If it reproduces the subject exactly, it is called a real answer. But in most cases, in order to preserve the tonal unity of the fugue, the answer has to undergo a "mutation" that alters some of its melodic intervals and makes the modulation to the dominant key smoother. This is called the tonal answer.

The countersubject accompanies the answer. If it is maintained throughout the fugue, it is called sustained or obbligato countersubject and will follow the subject like its shadow for each new statement. Subject and countersubject are the two principal "actors" of the fugue, and theoretically all the musical substance must be derived from them.

The first part of the fugue, which includes the successive entrance of the voices, in subject–answer alternation, is called exposition. This progressive enrichment of the polyphonic web is one of the most striking traits of the fugue. In some fugues, after the exposition, the composer brings in the answer followed by the subject. This is called counterexposition.

An episode is any passage, developed or not, that links two statements of the subject. It is characteristically written in imitative style. Generally it uses a motive from the subject or the countersubject, but sometimes a new element is introduced. There is a great variety of episodes.

When the subject overlaps the answer (or the answer the subject), it is called a stretto. This device, whereby the entries are drawn more closely together, is often used at the end of the fugue, where it achieves spectacular effects.

Once past the exposition, the plan of the fugue depends on the will of the composer and the resources of its thematic elements. For instance, the Danish composer Dietrich Buxtehude (died 1707) often presents the subject and the answer only in the principal and in the dominant keys, in short expositions linked by small episodes. With J.S. Bach, the tonal plan becomes more elaborate and includes a journey to the principal neighbouring keys. Since the composer adapts his plan to the character and to the potential of his themes, the itinerary is always different. That is why in his hands the fugue becomes the most versatile of musical forms; each fugue of Bach brings a new solution to the problem of the relation between form and content.

Versatility of the fugue

Theorists created an ideal plan of the fugue and gradually perfected it, in the 19th century, as fewer and fewer real fugues were being written. They devised a tripartite form consisting of the exposition, the development, and the stretto.

Varieties of fugue. The simple fugue is monothematic, without a maintained countersubject (such as the *Fugue in D Major* of Bach's work *The Well-Tempered Clavier,* Book I, No. 5). More elaborate fugues use one or more countersubjects. In a counterfugue, the answer imitates the subject by inversion. There are beautiful examples of this technique in Bach's work *The Art of the Fugue,* numbers 5 to 7.

There are two ways of writing a double fugue; either the two subjects may be presented simultaneously, in which case the fugue is not very different from a fugue with countersubject (Bach, *Fugue in B Minor on a Theme of Corelli,* BWV 579), or else the second subject has a special exposition. The latter yields, in general, a tripartite scheme: exposition and development of the first subject, exposition and development of the second subject, and finally combination of the two elements, which are devised so that they can be superimposed. A splendid example is given by Bach's *Toccata and Fugue in F Major* for organ, BWV 540. The same principles apply to a triple or quadruple fugue.

The fughetta is a miniature fugue but strictly written, whereas the fugato starts like a fugue but gives up its discipline once past the exposition.

The choral fugue plays a considerable role in works for chorus and orchestra. Generally the chorus sings in strict counterpoint, while the instruments play an expressive or decorative accompaniment. The composition techniques of the fugue can also be used in forms as universal as the prelude, the aria, the chorus, the overture, the concerto, and others.

Literature of the fugue. Since vocal polyphony was based on a text that had to be sung by each of the parts (either simultaneously or, more frequently, in imitation), it was not very much concerned with the problem of form. That is why theorists and musicians concentrated on questions of texture.

At first the term *fuga* applied to strict imitations (which would now be called canons); the concept evolved in a more general sense when it was realized that a freer use of all kinds of imitations offered much more stimulating opportunities. Besides the purely vocal polyphony, the first independent forms of keyboard music (the ricercar, the canzona, the capriccio, the fantasia) testify to the remarkable development of what can be called the fugal style of the 16th and 17th centuries. In this evolution, the role of the Italian composer Andrea Gabrieli and of the English virginalists was preponderant. The two great precursors of the fugue proper were the Dutch composer J.P. Sweelinck (died 1643). Both greatly influenced the keyboard music of the 17th century, in particular through their students Samuel Scheidt and Johann Jakob Froberger. In Germany, a generation of musicians dominated by Buxtehude gave the fugue its modern form by putting it in a tonal perspective and abandoning the fragmentary style of their predecessors. Almost all the composers of the 17th century contributed to the history of the fugue.

The genius of J.S. Bach found particular expression in the fugue, perhaps because it allies the strictest economy of language to a relative freedom of form. Each of his fugues amazes by the freshness of its inspiration, the wonders of its writing, or by its gigantic proportions, all marvellously represented in the two volumes of *The Well-Tempered Clavier* (1722–44), two sets of 24 preludes and fugues going through the cycle of the 24 major and minor keys. Some of his organ fugues tend toward development, some toward symmetry, and some toward virtuosity; others take the form of double fugues.

His last work, *The Art of the Fugue,* is a collection of 14 fugues and four canons, all based on a theme in D minor and its inversion. All the resources and procedures of the fugue are demonstrated in what constitutes the most inspiring treatise on fugue, a treatise without words, in which music speaks alone. After being long slighted as a purely theoretical work, *The Art of the Fugue* has won a high place in the hearts of music lovers, who see it as Bach's musical testament. Bach's cantatas, passions, and oratorios abound in admirable fugues.

Bach's *Art of the Fugue*

Handel's fugues are less erudite than those of Bach and sometimes employ looser counterpoint, but they touch the listener by their vitality and their harmonious proportions. The great fugal sections of his oratorios are more important than his keyboard fugues.

After Bach the fugue lost much of its importance. With the appearance of the sonata, the musical taste changed, and composers tended to consider counterpoint as an archaic discipline. Nonetheless, the fugue retained a place in choral works, and fugal methods were kept in the sonata form, particularly in the development section.

A great passion for the music of Bach led Mozart (died 1791) to a more contrapuntal style. This influence is obvious in the *Fugue in C Minor,* for two pianos, K. 426, which, though pure Mozart, is nonetheless a homage to Bach. In ingenuity and mastery, Mozart rivalled the greatest contrapuntists in, for instance, the great choruses of the *Mass in C Minor,* K. 427, or in the final development of the *Jupiter Symphony.*

Beethoven resorted more and more to fugal technique in his last works. He confessed that he wrote his fugues with the greatest difficulty, and it is true that his counterpoint gives an impression of effort. Most of the fugal passages integrated into his last sonatas and quartets create a dramatic tension. Far from being a scholastic technique, the fugue was for Beethoven a means to reach the expressive limits of an idea. He used this language in particular circumstances. The strange and desolate atmosphere of the opening fugue of the *String Quartet in C Sharp Minor,* Opus 131, brings to mind the 20th-century fugue in the first section of the *Music for Strings, Percussion and Celesta* of Béla Bartók. The Promethean side of Beethoven asserts itself particularly in the *Great Fugue* from the *String Quartet in B Flat Major,* Opus 130, and the noble fugal section of the *Missa Solemnis.* Unlike Mozart's classical fugues, Beethoven's are rather irrational in form but are justified by their creative power alone.

Compared with the fugues of Beethoven, those of Felix Mendelssohn defer to traditional rules. Critics sense in them a nostalgia for Bach, sometimes weakened by a touch of sentimentalism. A more authentic romantic breath animates the fugues of Robert Schumann on B.A.C.H. (the German letters for the notes B♭–A–C–B♮), but the fugue is not his natural language. The genre is more suited to César Franck, as may be seen in his *Prélude, fugue et variation,* or in his *Prélude, chorale et fugue.* His harmonic sensitivity enriches a contrapuntal technique while not breaking with tradition. The fugues of Franz Liszt are entirely different: once past the exposition, he cannot renounce symphonic developments. There is an original use of the fugato before the re-exposition in his *Piano Sonata in B Minor.* The fugal style was used to varying degree by the major composers of the 19th century, including Brahms in his *German Requiem,* Richard Wagner in his opera *Die Meistersinger,* and Verdi in his *Requiem* and at the end of his last opera, *Falstaff.*

Among the post-Romantics, who cultivated their own exaggerated form of counterpoint, mention must be made of Max Reger, whose admirers took him as the heir of J.S. Bach. Though that appears to be going too far, his counterpoint does possess vitality in works such as the *Variations and Fugue on a Theme by Mozart,* for orchestra, or the fugue on the chorale melody "Wachet auf, ruft uns die Stimme," for organ.

Bartók's use of fugue

As an autonomous form, the fugue played only a modest role in the first half of the 20th century. The most beautiful example is the already mentioned fugue of the *Music for Strings, Percussion and Celesta* of Béla Bartók, a born contrapuntist. This is a true model of fugal treatment in a post-tonal style. The methods of the fugue are also found in his *Sonata for Two Pianos and Percussion* and in his admirable quartets.

Stravinsky, though influenced by the composers of the 17th and 18th centuries, showed no particular interest in the fugue. Although the second part of his *Symphony of Psalms* can be considered a double fugue, it does not strike the listener as such.

In his collection of interludes and fugues, called *Ludus Tonalis,* Paul Hindemith seems to have drawn his inspiration from Bach's *Well-Tempered Clavier.* Although an interesting work, it did not herald a rebirth of the fugue. A new conception of counterpoint appeared in the works of Arnold Schoenberg and Anton von Webern. The serial techniques of composers like Pierre Boulez can, to a certain extent, claim some kind of kinship with fugal language, and a work such as the *Passion According to St. Luke* of Krzysztof Penderecki testifies to the permanence of a musical form the history of which is probably unfinished. (L.A.R.)

SYMPHONY

The term symphony (literally, "sounding together"), though it has many meanings in musical literature, is commonly understood to refer to a lengthy composition for orchestra, often employing a sonata form (see below) in one or more large sections called "movements." Symphonies of this sort began to be composed during the so-called Classical era in European music history, *c.* 1740–1820 (the early part of this period and the decade immediately preceding it are sometimes called pre-Classical, as are the symphonies written before about 1750). During the 19th century, which included the Romantic era, symphonies grew longer, and composers concerned themselves with ways of unifying the movements; extramusical programs and new approaches toward tonality (the major–minor system of chord progressions) were among the solutions to the problems of large-scale symphonic form. Late in the century, symphonies—and orchestras—had grown to such an extent that reaction set in, culminating in the Neoclassical movement of the early 20th century, in which composers turned again toward principles of balance and formal discipline, using new techniques to achieve dynamic coherence. Economic considerations forced a reduction in the size of orchestras and amount of rehearsal time available to mid-20th-century composers, further justifying a return to less extravagant symphonic thinking. But throughout the 19th century a number of outstanding symphonists were able to reconcile the demands of fashion with strict musical logic; these composers represent the mainstream of symphonic activity, and their works remain models for much 20th-century activity in the genre. Throughout the following section two concerns predominate: a survey of the chief symphonic works and composers and consideration of the evolution of symphonic thought.

The concept of symphony before c. 1750. The word *symphōnia* was used by the Greeks in reference to notes sounding together in harmony and by extension meant an "ensemble" or "band" rather than a musical form. The word implies a pleasant concord of different notes and has been used in fields other than music to denote a pleasing combination of various elements. In the New Testament Gospel According to Luke (King James Version), *symphōnia* is translated as "musick," as distinct from *choroi,* "dancing." In the Middle Ages the name was given to several musical instruments, among them a double-headed drum, bowed stringed instruments, a large hurdy-gurdy, and bagpipes. Mention is made in 1582 of *eine Symphonie,* evidently a stringed keyboard instrument.

Vocal and instrumental works

From the mid-16th century, symphonia (and related spellings) is a term often found in titles in which it simply indicated ensemble music, whether for instruments with voices or either alone. A collection of madrigals published in Antwerp in 1585 is entitled *Symphonia angelica . . . raccolta per Huberto Waelrant.* Later notable examples are the *Sacrae symphoniae* of the Venetian composer Giovanni Gabrieli (Book I, 1597; Book II, 1615), collections of elaborate vocal and instrumental music, often for multiple choirs; and the *Symphoniae sacrae* of his celebrated German pupil, Heinrich Schütz (1629, 1647, 1650). Schütz's collection reveals his debt to the colourful and brilliantly orchestrated Italian style in works ranging from several voices to large polychoral compositions with solo parts and instruments. His countryman Samuel Scheidt's 70 *Symphonien auff Concerten-Manir* (1644) likewise combine instrumental and vocal ensembles to enrich the texture and heighten the drama of his music.

Symphonies for instruments alone during the early Baroque era (*c.* 1600–30) occur as independent pieces and as introductions or interludes in theatrical productions. The Italian Biagio Marini's Sinfonia *"La Orlandia"* (1617) is a duet for violin or cornetto (a wind instrument with finger holes and cup-shaped mouthpiece) and continuo in five brief contiguous sections, distinguished by contrasting metres and new melodic material in each section. (The continuo is a harmonic accompaniment improvised over the written bass line, usually played on a keyboard instrument and a bass viol or other bass melody instrument.) Early operas often include instrumental symphonies. Jacopo Peri's *Euridice* (first performed 1600) includes a sinfonia for three flutes; Claudio Monteverdi's lavish musical drama *Orfeo* (1607) is punctuated with five richly scored sinfonias, while a *sinfonia da guerra* ("sinfonia of war") accompanies a staged battle in his *Il ritorno d'Ulisse in patria* (*The Return of Ulysses to his Country*; 1641). Each act of Stefano Landi's opera *Il Sant' Alessio* (1632) opens with a sectional sinfonia. Many other opera and oratorio composers used short descriptive or introductory sinfonias, often of sectional form with contrasting metres and tempos.

Characteristics of Italian and French overtures

It remained for a Neapolitan, Alessandro Scarlatti (1660–1725), to formalize the overture to his operas as a fast–slow–fast *sinfonia avanti l'opera,* as in his opera *Dal male il bene* (*Good from Evil*; 1681). The so-called Italian overture of this and later works, scored for strings and continuo, has been widely considered to contain the germ of the later three-movement symphony. In contrast with the more contrapuntal French overture, which begins with a pompous slow movement and continues in a fugal section (involving imitation of a melody among several voices), the Italian style is immediately tuneful and predominantly homophonic (chordal) in texture. The first fast movement may be trivial; its symmetrical phrasing is unexpressive. The contrasting second movement may be more lyrical, perhaps anticipating tunes heard later in the opera. The last movement, sometimes a minuet, is an exuberant curtain raiser. This format spread quickly outside Italy, even to France. Jean-Philippe Rameau's *Zoroastre* (1749), for example, includes such a fast–slow–fast overture. Rameau, indeed, was considered an exponent of the Italian style, particularly in his lucid harmonic treatment. This late-Baroque concern with tonal clarity prefigured the attitudes of early Classical symphonists. Among the devices used to assure clarity are melodies constructed of arpeggiated ("harplike," or broken) chords and passages in unison or in parallel thirds or sixths (sequences of harmonies formed by thirds, such as C–E or D–F, or sixths, such as C–A or D–B). These features are not common in Baroque music that is strictly contrapuntal (based on interwoven melodic lines) in texture.

While the opera overture settled into a form that eventually inspired early symphonists, the term sinfonia, or symphony, as yet had no formal definition. As late as 1771 *Encyclopædia Britannica,* reflecting ancient Greek usage, defined symphony merely as ". . . a consonance or concert of several sounds agreeable to the ear, whether vocal or instrumental, called also harmony." Sinfonia was used interchangeably with concerto, consort, overture, suite, and so on. Commonly a brief instrumental interlude, as in a song, was called a symphony, even into the 19th century. In the late Baroque era (*c.* 1700–50) the term was applied to such dissimilar pieces as J.S. Bach's didactic *Three-Part Inventions* for keyboard, called *Sinfonien* in the 1723 copy, and the orchestral "Pastoral Symphony," a quasi-descriptive interlude in Handel's *Messiah* (composed 1741), said to have been based on an Italian shepherd bagpipe tune and very much in the tradition of earlier descriptive symphonies in opera.

Bach's *Sinfonia VII in E minor* and *Sinfonia XI in G minor* are interesting in that in each piece the opening material recurs at the end. In *VII* this repetition is merely suggested, but in *XI* the last eight measures of the piece virtually duplicate the first eight. The whole intermediate body of these pieces develops the motivic material presented at the beginning, and the initial material is transformed contrapuntally and harmonically. In the closing bars the tension thus aroused resolves and the rhythmic drive reins in. This suggestion of an expository unit moving from the home key to a different key, followed by an extended development that explores still more remote keys and the motivic and contrapuntal implications of the beginning, concluding with a recapitulation in which the energy of the development is somewhat dissipated by a return to the opening material, prefigures the sonata form of the Classical symphonists. Bach uses this technique in some of his instrumental concerto movements; the concertos have other elements in common with early symphonies, especially in the mood of their lyric slow movements and fast duple-metre finales.

Exploitation of key relationships

The word sinfonia was applied to a trio sonata for flute, oboe, and continuo in Johann Joseph Fux's *Concentus Musico-instrumentalis* (1701), a collection of suites each comprising a number (as many as 15) of bipartite (two-section) dances and descriptive pieces. An intellectual and influential Viennese court composer, Fux departed in this sinfonia from the typical 17th-century suite, which is merely a collection of contrasting dances in the same key. The work falls into two major divisions, both comprising three short movements; the key scheme is F major, D minor, F major—F major, D minor, F major, and the last three movements have programmatic titles. Here is not merely a collection of various dances but a conscious attempt to relate movements tonally and thereby create larger hierarchic units. F major and D minor are closely related keys, and it would not be possible to omit a single movement without destroying the symmetry of the whole (not that either group of three, or even each dance, does not sound good by itself). By means of this simple, balanced harmonic structuring Fux advanced beyond the looser architecture of the typical suite; and by framing a minor-key movement between two movements in the same related major key he anticipated the overall form of many early symphonies.

Importance of tonal harmony

Both Fux and Bach were products of the evolution of tonal harmony, a system of key relations which brought with it the possibility of basing large-scale forms not only on melodic variation or counterpoint, as earlier, but on harmonic tension and modulation. (Modulation, unlike simple change of key, implies the establishment of a new tonic, or tonal centre, by means of progression through a number of related keys.) The wide-ranging modulations and affective harmonic progressions of German Baroque composers depended on equal temperament, a system that permits exploration of keys distant from the tonic without the necessity of retuning to accommodate the remote harmonies. Bach exploited this system to the utmost, as did many of his North German contemporaries; but their rich harmonic palette was foreign to the south, where many important symphonists arose. Concerned less with powerful emotions (*Affekten*) and more with clarity, the southerners avoided intricate counterpoint and convoluted harmonic progressions, preferring a restricted chord vocabulary and clear-cut symmetrical phrasing dominated by tuneful melody.

Besides the suite and opera overture, the short humorous intermezzo, which originated in Naples and flourished *c.* 1685–1750, strongly influenced pre-Classical symphonists. Neapolitan composers, headed by Alessandro Scarlatti, concerned themselves in the intermezzo with dramatic, comic interplay between two singers in two or three short acts made up of arias, recitatives, and duets. Because the texts demanded clear articulation and careful declamation, they influenced the melodic phrase structure, giving rise to repeated-note figures and brief rhythmic or melodic motives. These phrases normally fall into two-measure units. Counterpoint was abandoned, for it tended to obscure the text; and harmonies became simple and slow-moving. Intermezzo melodies abound in ornaments, sudden accents, syncopation (displaced accents), and playful leaps reflecting the text declamation and lack the broad, spunout arch and driving rhythm of typical Baroque melodies. Rather, they are made up of short motives joined one to another and give rise to frequently articulated phrase groups. This word-derived idiom furnished the melodic impulse of the early symphonies.

The symphony proper. *Early Classical period.* Chord-generated melodies (those arising from arpeggiated triads) abound in 18th-century symphonies, among which a number of stereotyped "theme families" can be distinguished. These furnished raw material for further development. In fact, a composer's originality found expression not so much in his original theme as in his realization of the implications of the theme later in the composition. Certain tunes are by nature not highly implicative; they are perfect closed units that cannot be easily developed and so are superficially inappropriate for symphonic use. Such, for example, are many folk tunes; and this explains why great symphonists rarely use folk tunes without at least distorting them so as to open them to development. On the other hand, motivic melodies, such as those in the intermezzi, coupled with slow harmonic motion, lend themselves well to fragmentation, recombination, extension, elision, reharmonization, and other developmental techniques. By the 1740s, Italian symphonists had learned to sustain interest by these means and to obtain contrast by dramatically apposing tunes of different character in different keys (usually the tonic, or home key, and the dominant, located five tones above the tonic, or related major or minor keys).

Early uses of sonata form

Among Italians influenced by these factors was Tomaso Albinoni (significantly, a composer of 48 operas). The third movement of his *Sinfonia in D Major,* fifth of the *Sei sinfonie a quattro* (1735), displays a simple sonata form (also known as "first movement form," though not so limited). Sonata form, crucial in the symphony's evolution, is based on the dramatic apposition and eventual reconciliation of contrasting keys. In essence it consists of an exposition in which one or more themes are presented, the first (often forceful in character) in the tonic key and the second (often lyric) in the dominant. Sometimes a third, closing theme follows in the dominant. The two key areas contrast not only harmonically and melodically but often in instrumentation, loudness, and texture. So-called monothematic sonata movements lack a contrasting second melody; indeed, it is not so much the character of the tunes but the dynamism of the opposed key areas that is essential to the dramatic structure. The transition between tonic and dominant areas was to become a focus of interest to later composers, but in early symphonies the transitions were brief and simple.

The exposition, often marked to be repeated, comes to a close on a key other than the tonic (usually the dominant) and is followed by a development section, beginning on the dominant, in which themes previously heard are re-harmonized, fragmented, or otherwise reshaped. Again it is not melodies so much as harmonies that arouse tension in the development. The composer confronts the problem of returning to the tonic via more distant chords, and this is sometimes accomplished by modulations that bear no thematic relation to the exposition. In early symphonies this process is only tentatively exploited, and developments are brief, sometimes involving merely transposition of the original first theme to a new key. Later the development assumed the character of the meat in the sandwich, as it were.

Following the development comes a recapitulation of the exposition, this time all in the tonic key (before *c.* 1770 the recapitulation sometimes retained the key scheme of the exposition, except for the closing bars), resolving the harmonic tension of the development. The recapitulation may be simply a virtual repetition of the exposition, with appropriate key changes, or may be truncated, expanded, or otherwise varied so as to continue developmental processes. Many early symphonies take advantage of the implications of a varied recapitulation, literal repetition being abhorrent to imaginative composers. It will be observed that when both themes appear recapitulated in the tonic, the function of the transition between themes differs from that in the exposition, in which it leads from one key to another. After the 1750s, however, the first theme was often omitted in the recapitulation. Obviously, the recapitulation's tonal scheme allows extended treatment of the tonic, but sometimes a coda (tail) is added after the recapitulation to consolidate further the focal nature of the tonic.

It is important to understand that sonata form was subject to great variation and deviation from "textbook" norms throughout the symphony's history. Ideas of a "typical" sonata form did not evolve until *c.* 1830. Nevertheless, the vocabulary of exposition, development, recapitulation, transition, and so on is capable of wide application and will simplify the remainder of the present section.

Albinoni's *Sinfonia in D Major* as a whole is forward-looking. The orchestra lacks a continuo, harmonic orientation replaces counterpoint, and the movements are of larger scale than typical Baroque dance movements. The central minuet-and-trio movement, surprisingly modern-sounding, contrasts lightheartedly with the sonata form. Minuets and song-form movements relieve the dramatic tension of sonata movements; and from this time on minuets appeared frequently in symphonies. Gradually losing dance character, they moved from the last or middle position to penultimate place when, later, a fast fourth movement appeared as finale.

The symphonies of Sammartini

A leading early symphonist, the Italian Giovanni Battista Sammartini, is known from some 77 extant symphonies, some of them available in modern editions. A prolific composer of instrumental chamber music, his use of incipient sonata form, restricted harmonic vocabulary, and motivic, not highly ornamented melodies pointed to the future. Though dependent on Baroque models for inspiration during his first period of activity (to *c.* 1740), he had abandoned the continuo by about 1760, filling the harmony instead with horns or trumpets—which, however, were restricted in their ability to play in certain keys and therefore operated to constrict the available harmonic vocabulary. More than many contemporaries, Sammartini infused inner parts with contrapuntal life, especially in earlier works, although he rarely used extended imitation. His rhythmic energy was appreciated by operawriting contemporaries, from whom (especially the Italians Niccolò Jommelli and Rinaldo di Capua) he perhaps drew inspiration for the long, expressive cantabile (singing) phrases that, along with a firm grasp of modulation, characterize his later works. His slow movements are especially rich. Another late characteristic is the extended role of wind instruments, which are given independent, idiomatic parts. Sammartini wrote for oboes, flutes, and bassoons among the woodwinds (bassoons doubling the bass line); clarinets were also in use at this time, usually interchangeably with oboes. Significantly, Mozart heard Sammartini's music during a visit to Milan.

A third Italian, Padre Giovanni Battista Martini, renowned as a teacher and music historian, left 24 symphonies dating roughly between 1736 and 1777. There is remarkable consistency among this corpus. All but one are in the then-normal three movements (Sammartini wrote a number in four), and all have outer movements in a major key, whereas the middle slow movements are nearly always minor. Music of the Classical period greatly favours major keys; according to one investigator all but about 2 percent of 18th-century symphonies are major (excepting their expressive slow movements). Martini, although trained in counterpoint, avoided it in these works, favouring instead a treble-dominated texture over a simple, slow-moving bass. His chord vocabulary was restricted, his orchestration elementary. His melodies reflect a number of banal formulas in current use, but his manipulation and development of these formulas was skillful. Mozart visited Martini several times in Bologna in 1770.

In the hands of these and other Italian composers, symphonic style evolved considerably by 1740, and there was continued fruitful experimentation through the 1750s. That Italians influenced contemporary and later German and, especially, Austrian symphonists cannot be doubted; but the extent of indebtedness and mutual influence cannot now be fully determined because of the scarcity of available scores. Relatively few of the surviving early symphonies have appeared in reliable modern editions, and those known to survive in manuscript represent but a fraction of the thousands composed. The early history of the symphony remains, therefore, a matter of speculation and debate, despite the enormous progress in research and publication in the mid-20th century.

The Mannheim composers

Germany and Austria were important centres of symphonic composition after about 1740. In Mannheim, Germany, the Bohemian Johann Wenzel Stamitz developed a remarkably well-trained orchestra that by 1756 comprised (in addition to 30 strings) four horns, pairs of flutes, oboes, clarinets, bassoons, trumpets, and timpani. With this ensemble, independent wind writing and creative orchestration flourished. Stamitz—himself a violinist and composer of more than 70 symphonies, chiefly mature works—and his contemporary Ignaz Holzbauer evolved a bold style born of the confluence of Italian melody and German seriousness. Counterpoint is abandoned; expression arises from orchestral crescendos and diminuendos (anticipated by Jommelli), characteristic melodic effects such as sighing appoggiaturas (falling figures) and rocketing arpeggiated (broken) chords, and strong dynamic, thematic, and textural contrasts. This style degenerated into mannerism with Stamitz's son Karl (composer of about 80 symphonies) and Johann Christian Cannabich, who enlarged the Mannheim orchestra.

Mannheimers paid special attention to their development sections, which have been described as a "mosaic of fragments." They tended toward incomplete recapitulations, wrote tender slow movements, extended the number of movements to four: allegro (lively), andante (slow), minuet, and presto (rapid). Insisting on disciplined and precise performance, they wrote all parts out in full instead of leaving some to be realized by the players. With the rise of independent wind parts after *c.* 1770, the continuo became redundant and was abandoned; in outdoor music and in huge orchestras it had become inaudible anyway. Musical textures, which in early works were equally appropriate for string quartet or orchestra, became truly symphonic. Holzbauer occasionally features bassoon solos (as in the *Symphony in E Flat Major,* Opus 4, No. 3), liberating that instrument from simply doubling the bass. The elder Stamitz and Holzbauer were particularly highly regarded in Paris and strongly influenced symphonic activity there.

In Berlin and northern Germany another school arose, dominated by Carl Philipp Emanuel Bach (a son of J.S. Bach), Johann Gottlieb Graun, and other musicians reared in a tradition of rigorous counterpoint and formal conservatism. Retaining three-movement format and avoiding strongly contrasting themes, they maintained contrapuntal interplay in the prevailingly homophonic texture. Even more than the Mannheimers, they concerned themselves with melodic development and oramentation and with emotional expressiveness—an aesthetic approach they termed *Empfindsamkeit* (sensitivity). C.P.E. Bach's set of six symphonies commissioned by Baron Gottfried Bernhard van Swieten (completed 1773) aroused enthusiasm for their humour, technical challenge, and novelty of harmonic invention. Even more intensely passionate are the late *Orchestral Symphonies for Twelve Obbligato Parts* (1780), with their clever instrumentation and affective harmonies punctuated by unison passages. Reflecting the literary *Sturm und Drang* (storm and stress) movement, the Berliners powerfully influenced Haydn and Mozart and even Beethoven.

Another son of J.S. Bach, Johann Christian, the so-called London Bach, was perhaps yet more important for the future, influencing Mozart, who met him in London (1764) and again in Paris (1778). His 50 or so symphonies lack the passionate gestures of the Berliners' but are finely wrought and sophisticated in melody and orchestration. The *Sinfonias for Double Orchestra,* Opus 18, reflect in their *style galant* tunes the influence of his study with Martini in Italy, as well as French and Mannheim characteristics (*galant* was the 18th-century term for modern, light, elegant style). Numbers two and three of the set served as opera overtures. Simple in form, complex in texture, J.C. Bach's works are now considered to epitomize elegant, fashionable chamber music.

The Viennese school

The style most influential on Haydn, Mozart, and Beethoven was that of the Viennese school, headed by Georg Matthias Monn and Fux's pupil Georg Christoph Wagenseil. The Viennese experimented further with orchestration and tone colour, emphasized the violin's melodic role, and displayed popular influence in their playful minuets. Monn, though perfectly at ease with counterpoint, ignored it in his symphonies. His four-movement *Symphony in E Flat Major* for pairs of oboes and horns, strings, and continuo is noteworthy for its wide dynamic range and gracious melody so characteristic of Viennese music. The first movement's first theme recurs in the recapitulation transformed into a virtuoso horn duet, reflecting the skill of the players at his disposal and the liberation of horns from a mere harmony-filling role. Elsewhere in the movement are found the slow, repeated-note bass and inconsequential viola part common in early symphonies. As yet the development is quite short and thematically limited, and the movement's scale is small—only a little more than three minutes. But as is often the case, the first movement is the most extended of the four, first movements having gained importance beyond the first movements of opera overtures. In later works Monn dropped the continuo and extended the role of the winds. Together with Johann Stamitz he has been considered highly influential in establishing modern symphonic style, although perhaps Wagenseil, an experienced keyboard player and opera composer, was a more successful composer, especially notable for skillful thematic construction and manipulation, working ornamentation into structure. Also active in Vienna was Haydn's friend Karl Ditters von Dittersdorf, who contributed no fewer than 115 symphonies.

The Viennese style became widely disseminated in Europe. As many as 25 Viennese composers migrated to Paris; others moved to Dresden, Mannheim, and Munich and even as far as Dublin, St. Petersburg, and North America. Their style thus became truly international, and the innovations of these minor masters paved the way for the fully developed symphonic style of Haydn and Mozart. The music of the Viennese composers, mainly intended for elite entertainment, reflects the virtuosic attainments of many private orchestras and the cultured taste of aristocrats who commissioned a constant stream of symphonies and lighter chamber music.

The mature Classical period. Joseph Haydn, despite his isolation from urban musical centres for much of his life, was revered throughout Europe, beloved by Mozart and Beethoven, and widely published and copied—so much so that the authenticity of many works attributed to him remains in question. One hundred and eight symphonies are thought to have been written by him; one of these is lost. Few composers show such remarkable growth as Haydn; from his insignificant youthful pieces, entirely dominated by the style of his pre-Classical elders, to the towering achievement of his last works, his symphonies display an evolution in form and content that had tremendous effect on his followers.

Viennese in style, some of his early symphonies display originality in the use of nonstandard phrase lengths and in their monothematic tendencies. *Symphonies Nos. 1* and *2* are in three movements, lacking a minuet. These works require a continuo (the slow movement in *No. 2* consists only of a bass and treble part), and horns and oboes are as yet not independent. *Symphony No. 3* and others incorporate contrapuntal movements. The sonata recapitulations are subtly altered; but unlike Stamitz', they are generally complete. Melodically, Haydn drew on folk music for inspiration, especially in minuets but also on *galant* and operatic styles. His work reveals a gradual growth in appreciation of the idiomatic qualities of wind instruments, especially in trios of minuets (*e.g., Symphony No. 22, Symphony No. 40*); in *Symphony No. 5* he included winds in the slow movement, unusual at this time, and in *Nos. 6–8* he wrote independent wind solos, recalling the instrumental dialogue found in the Baroque concerto grosso. *Symphonies Nos. 6* and *11* begin with slow introductions, a characteristic which became common in Haydn's symphonies after *No. 84*.

Haydn's later works

With his appointment to the service of Prince Esterházy in 1761, Haydn's individuality began to emerge, partly because of his opportunity to experiment with the Esterházy orchestra. The bulk of his symphonic production dates from these years before 1771. Although humour and good nature pervade these works, stronger emotions and tension also begin to appear, as in the minor-key *Symphonies Nos. 26, 39,* and *49.* The *Farewell Symphony (No. 45),* with its adagio (slow) coda, displays Haydn's wit and is one of the best of his symphonies from the decade before 1780. This transitional period shows him striking out into more remote keys, introducing new themes in development sections, and growing more confident in formal craftsmanship and orchestration. Powerful and concentrated, the symphonies of the so-called *Sturm und Drang* period recall the *Empfindsamkeit* of C.P.E. Bach. By turns rigorously contrapuntal and lucidly witty, the vitality evident in the forms reflects Haydn's overflowing adventurousness. Contredanse (country dance) melodies may have inspired some of his themes, for example in the finale of *Symphony No. 88.*

The late *London* and *Paris Symphonies* reflect the influence of Mozart and show Haydn at the height of his power. No two movements are alike; the "mosaic" of theme elements pervades even transition sections and codas; each instrument shares in the melodic development; minuets grow in fire or dignity while finales exploit varieties of rondo form (see below). His slow movements, often straightforward sets of variations, engage in artful modulations prefiguring the romantic aspect of Beethoven. *Symphony No. 103* is especially thematically economical, and its movements are related by thematic resemblances, foreshadowing the cyclic nature of many 19th-century symphonies.

Haydn, though by no means the "father of the symphony," contributed enormously to a definition of the harmonic basis of Classical form, the dramatic role of key relationships, and the expressive capabilities of the winds. Major–minor contrasts, wide-ranging modulations, and reconciliation between counterpoint and homophony underlie his unambiguous moods, so different from those of Mozart. An eclectic architect, he amalgamated all the styles of his time in uniquely free and expressive shapes.

Use of rondo-form movements

Rondo form (in which a recurrent theme alternates with other material, as A B A C A) had been found especially in Italian opera and French instrumental music before *c.* 1770; in the 1770s and '80s it became second only to sonata form in symphonic importance. Exploited already by C.P.E. Bach, Stamitz, and others, rondos became a favourite last-movement form with Haydn and Mozart after about 1773. Haydn wrote a number of slow movements as rondos (*Symphonies Nos. 73, 74, 76*) and employed rondos 12 times in his last 17 symphonies. Mozart avoided the rondo in his last symphonies, perhaps because of the light nature of the form. Its vogue seems to have been brought about by the public's demand for structural simplicity and repetitive tunefulness. In the hands of Haydn and Mozart, however, the rondo increased in complexity, demonstrating in the so-called sonata-rondo the characteristics of sonata form, such as developments of earlier-stated material by means of fragmentation and modulation.

Wolfgang Amadeus Mozart raised the symphony to heights never surpassed. Of his 50-odd symphonies, produced between 1764 and 1788, the earliest ones are conventional but precocious, reflecting influences of J.C. Bach, Sammartini, and Haydn. An invigorating first movement predominates, followed by a light cantabile movement and a fast finale or minuet (minuets in his symphonies date mostly after 1767). The *Symphony in B Flat Major,* K. 22 (1765; Köchel numbers are the standard way of identifying Mozart's works) contains a lovely chromatic slow movement in the key of G minor.

Mozart's synthesis of Italian and German structures

Mozart's exposure to Europe's main musical currents led him to synthesize the playful Italian homophonic and operatic style with serious German polyphony. This is evident in the agitated *Symphony in G Minor,* K. 183 (1773)—a *Sturm und Drang* work and his first minor-key symphony—and in the cheerful *Symphony in A Major,* K. 201 (1774). In these works the balance of interest shifts to the last movement. The addition of codas ("tails," extended closing sections reaffirming the tonic), the increased length and scope of slow movements and minuets, and a growing orchestral sensitivity all point toward maturity. In contrast with those of Haydn, Mozart's slow movements lean toward the sonata form with its inherent drama.

Mozart, unlike Haydn, was not a formal experimenter; he re-used successful structural formulations in later works. It was his treatment of melody that set him apart. He preferred to ignore monothematic structure; and his first and second themes, neither folklike nor mosaic-like, contrast strongly. His harmonic range is narrow compared with Haydn's, but within his range he constantly transformed thematic material. Development sections expand with the introduction of new thematic material and modulations over a wider tonal field. His recapitulations tend to be straightforward. In this mature period, Mozart's symphonies became unified thematically and expressively, using fuller imitation, more singing figuration, freer instrumentation (the *Paris Symphony,* K. 297, in D major, introduces clarinets). Mozart rejected Mannheim gesture in favour of better integrated dynamics.

Mozart's last 10 years saw him further exposed to Haydn's influence and very aware of J.S. Bach's music. The monumental last six symphonies reflect his experience as an opera and chamber music composer. The *Symphony in C Major,* K. 425, has a rare, slow chromatic introduction, while K. 504 in D major (*Prague Symphony*) dispenses with the minuet, has all three movements in sonata form, and uses canonic development (development by means of exact imitation). The last three symphonies (K. 543, in E flat major; K. 550, in G minor; K. 551, in C major, or the *Jupiter Symphony*), summits of the Classical genre, are bold in their harmonies and counterpoint; the serious minuet of K. 550 foreshadows the scherzo of Beethoven's *Fifth Symphony.* (The scherzo is a rapid, rhythmic, minuet-derived form.)

Mozart was no revolutionary. Receptive to the influence of others, he rejected more than he assimilated, transforming all into a uniquely personal idiom. Several of his symphonies were used as opera overtures, but the best ones are so complete in themselves as to make their use as incidental music unthinkable to modern taste. Mozart's and Haydn's mature symphonies are comprehensive in mood and design. The various movements balance one another so well that those who are accustomed to hearing them would find it difficult to accept the substitution of other movements. This tendency toward intimate relation among the standard four movements reflects the urge of these composers to seek unity on the highest hierarchic level—a trend foreign to most of their lesser contemporaries but a basic factor in the symphony's evolution throughout the next two centuries.

With Ludwig van Beethoven the symphony became no longer entertainment music but an expression of monumental intellect and innermost feeling, as in Haydn's and Mozart's late works. The *Symphony No. 1 in C Major* (completed 1800) is Haydnesque, particularly in the opening theme of the finale (comparable to the finale of Haydn's *Symphony No. 88*), but full of originality. Its four classically structured movements reflect Beethoven's concern with expressive woodwind writing and dynamics. The third movement (Menuetto) is prophetic of Beethoven's later whirling scherzos. The slow introduction to the first movement is remarkable for its avoidance of the tonic, a technique used often in later works to arouse tension.

The *Eroica* symphony

The *Symphony No. 2 in D Major* (1802) is transitional and, like the *Symphony No. 1,* somewhat diffuse. A long introduction announces a work of grand dimensions. The lyric slow movement is rich in themes that are organically unified. A dynamic scherzo, only slightly dancelike, and an expanded sonata finale (with an enormous coda introducing a new theme) point toward the revolutionary length and structure of the *Symphony No. 3 in E Flat Major* (*Eroica;* completed 1804), a work that many consider to herald the dawn of musical Romanticism. The *Eroica* (Beethoven's title) no longer aims at an elite audience. Its first movement employs a multitude of themes, again drawn together into a cohesive organism and developed in a context of great harmonic tension. The tonic, E♭, is avoided near the beginning for 14 measures. A pathetic funeral march, replacing the ordinary slow movement, is followed by a vigorous scherzo; this leads to a variation finale, based on a theme from his *Creatures of Prometheus* ballet and full of contrapuntal development. The symphony marked a new fusion of old formal structures with Beethoven's dynamic outlook.

The cheerful *Symphony No. 4 in B Flat Major* (1806) and fateful *Symphony No. 5 in C Minor* (1808), so unalike in character, were composed side by side. The *Fifth,* like the *Third,* a visionary work, is unified by the famous four-note motive that permeates all four movements in one form or another. The scherzo and finale are joined, and an explosion of C major in the last movement is celerated with three trombones (possibly their first use in a symphony), piccolo, and contrabassoon. This grandiose edifice is constructed with relentless logic and rhythmic drive, hallmarks of Beethoven's mature style.

The *Symphony No. 6 in F Major* (1808), called the *Pastoral,* is in five movements, the first two and last in sonata form, each, according to Beethoven, expressing an aspect of rustic life. The whole has a unity of character that reflects a deeper rhythmic unity. A descriptive "Storm" movement links the scherzo ("Merrymaking of the Peasants") with a calm "Thanksgiving after the Storm" finale, which, incidentally, incorporates a Swiss yodel tune. The relaxed human and poetic qualities of the *Sixth* set it apart from the *Fifth* and from the demoniac *Symphony No. 7 in A Major* (1812), with its expanded scherzo and trio, blazing finale, and spirited first movement preceded by a long modulatory introduction.

The small scale of the first three movements of the *Symphony No. 8 in F Major* (1812) leaves one unprepared for its breathtaking finale. Its minuet is a subtle parody of the classical minuet of Mozart and Haydn.

The *Symphony No. 9 in D Minor (Choral)* found Beethoven deaf at its first performance in 1824. It marked a turning point in music history, not only for its novel inclusion of chorus and vocal soloists in the last movement and the extraordinarily variegated sonata form of that movement—incorporating a Turkish march, double exposition, double fugues, strophic (stanzaic) variations—but for the scope of the whole, a summary of Beethoven's ethical and symphonic achievements.

In his development of motifs and variation of entire themes Beethoven went unchallenged. He expanded the limits of Classical form, particularly in his finales, and increased the length of the symphonic process to more than four times the 15 or so minutes required for a pre-Classical symphony. Further, his orchestral sensitivity allowed all instruments a structural role while simultaneously making new demands on player and listener alike. Besides widening the scope of the orchestra with extra winds and percussion, he made it more than ever a cohesive single instrument, bequeathing to the 19th century a standard against which composers measured the effectiveness of their own orchestrations. Finally, through the immense concentration of his symphonies he made it impossible for his followers to equal the sheer quantity of production of the Classical composers; far too much effort went into creating a symphony to allow pouring them out by dozens.

So overwhelming was the impact of Beethoven's symphonies, along with that of Mozart's and Haydn's mature ones, on later generations that they utterly obscure the productions of many other worthy symphonists. François Joseph Gossec, an early French symphonist, and Pierre van Maldere came to grips successfully with the dominating German–Italian idiom and were important among the Parisians influenced by Stamitz and his school. Van Maldere was eulogized for his imaginative thematic structures as well as for the unusually serious nature of his compositions, which strongly contrasted with the more lighthearted style characteristic of the Mannheimers.

An English composer, William Boyce, eclipsed by the London Bach, wrote eight sinfonias that betray in design the strong influence of theatre music. Basically merely overtures in French or Italian styles, they show none of the modern characteristics being formulated at the time in Germany; England, in general, was not quick to adopt the new symphonic style.

Revolutionary composers of Eastern Europe

Eastern Europe produced revolutionary composers of whom until recently little has been known. Stamitz, Bohemian by birth, overshadowed such competent composers as Jiří Benda. Benda's symphonies, dating mostly between 1750 and 1765, are generally brief, in three movements, and close to the Italian overture in form and feeling. The sonata form is not exploited, although characteristics such as contrasting themes and contrast within a single theme (a technique used also by Mozart) suggest a Mannheim influence or at least a revolt against Baroque conventions.

Luigi Boccherini, Giovanni Giuseppi Cambini, Michael Haydn (Joseph's brother), Leopold Mozart (father of Wolfgang), and many other important chamber music composers contributed numerous symphonies well worth performance. Later composers included the conservative Swede Franz Berwald and a brilliant but short-lived Spaniard, Juan Crisóstomo Arriaga, influential mostly in their own countries; and Muzio Clementi, Luigi Cherubini, Louis Spohr, and Carl Maria von Weber, who, although better known for work in other genres, were nevertheless popular symphonists. Spohr wrote a number of highly pictorial programmatic symphonies, going well beyond Beethoven's *Sixth.*

The Romantic era. Among 19th-century symphonists several trends can be distinguished. Concerned to some extent with self-conscious emotional expression, they often tended to use looser forms and slower paces than the Classical composers. Sometimes this led to lax discipline but not in the case of the finest composers, among them Schumann, Brahms, and Dvořák, who were all very conscious of their debt to Beethoven, Mozart, and Haydn. With later composers, such as Anton Bruckner, Peter Ilich Tchaikovsky, and Gustav Mahler, the normal balance of form was sometimes upset in favour of romantic license, but they too derived their basic goals from the Classical composers, with a more or less heavy admixture of the influence of Richard Wagner.

Schubert

Franz Schubert is known primarily as a songwriter. His nine symphonies stand in the shadow of Beethoven's but are revolutionary and Romantic in a way utterly different from Beethoven's. Whereas Beethoven wrestled with melodic problems, Schubert was a born melodist and consequently concerned himself more with the harmonic basis of form. He was likewise the more sensitive orchestrator, and in the last three symphonies he greatly expanded the role of the brasses.

His *Symphony No. 1 in D Major* (1813) and *Symphony No. 2 in B Flat Major* (1815) illustrate Schubert's departure from Classical models. Although the first movements are in sonata form, their pace is slower than the ordinary Classical allegro and is supported by long nonthematic passages that expand the harmonic arch. In the youthful sonata-form movements the second theme group is often set in an unexpected key before the music turns to the dominant at the end of the exposition. In recapitulations, too, Schubert shies away from harmonic simplicity and Classical expectation; his phrasing also is often irregular. Schubert's slow movements, scherzos, and minuets are not as strikingly original. Clear references to movements and themes of Beethoven occur in these early works, and in key scheme and major–minor contrast Schubert often betrayed his indebtedness to Beethoven. He was unembarrassed to borrow melodic material, which he transformed in an utterly personal way. This is particularly the case in the *Symphony No. 4 in C Minor* (the *Tragic;* 1816). The *Symphony No. 5 in B Flat Major* (1816), scored for a smaller orchestra, more strongly recalls Mozart and Haydn. The highly emotional *No. 6 in C Major* (1818) is of larger scale, based as usual more on rhythmic and harmonic impetus than melodic development. The incomplete draft of the *Symphony in E Minor-Major* (1821) has inspired attempts at completion. But it is the last two (the *Symphony in B Minor* or *Unfinished,* 1822, and *Symphony in C Major,* or *Great,* 1828) that raise Schubert to high rank among symphonists. Composed for large orchestras, they nevertheless reflect Schubert's experience in writing for voice and piano.

Schubert's *Unfinished* and *Great* symphonies

The *Unfinished* consists of two complete movements in $\frac{3}{4}$ and $\frac{3}{8}$ time and a sketch for a scherzo. The complete movements form a convincing unity; masterful in harmonic organization and orchestration, they are expressive without being diffuse, a criticism often levelled against passages in Schubert's earlier works. The *Great* is of Beethovenian scale, partly because of extensive repetition. The scherzo and related slow movement, no longer simply rustic pieces, are both sonatas. Irregular phrases, modulatory schemes, and rhythmic force give evidence of Schubert's concern with form based on slowed-down and far-reaching harmonic motion. His rhythmic manipulation was un-Classical, his themes personal and of more than Classical significance.

With the first group of symphonists born in the 19th century the Romantic style was fully fledged. The French composer Hector Berlioz and the Hungarian Franz Liszt contributed large symphonic works that to some extent departed in form from the Classical sonata-centred model. The literary program to Berlioz' *Symphonie fantastique: Épisode de la vie d'un artiste* (1830) was not written until the music was well along toward completion. The symphony was thoroughly planned out thematically and formally and stands as a musical unity without regard to the program, which Berlioz himself eventually withdrew. A very personal expression nevertheless, the *Fantastique* introduces a structural *idée fixe,* a theme (representing his mistress?) recurring throughout the five movements in various rhythmic forms, serving to unite the "scenes" musically as well as dramatically.

Harold en Italie (1834; after Byron's poem), like the *Fantastique,* makes use of preexistent material and is unified not only by a program but by a recurrent theme, a viola solo representing Harold. This theme is not subject to the kind of variation given the *idée fixe* in the *Fantastique;* yet from it springs much of the melodic inspiration of the whole work. Berlioz' third symphonic work, *Roméo et Juliette* (1839), rarely heard in its entirety, incorporates chorus and vocal soloists into its five large sections, which are programmatically derived from episodes of Shakespeare's drama. Not coincidentally, Berlioz was a great admirer of Beethoven. Beethoven's unity of moods, thematic development, and dramatic orchestration were models for Berlioz to extend, although he did so outside the formal confines of the sonata and with even more explicit passion.

Liszt owed much to Berlioz, both in his handling of enlarged orchestral forces and in thematic transformation (as opposed to development). The three movements of his *Faust Symphony* (1854) bear the names of Goethe's characters: Faust, Gretchen, and Mephistopheles; and the final movement parodies themes of the first two in a satisfyingly diabolical manner. Characters aside, the music is highly effective and balanced; Liszt revised the score over several decades. The score is dedicated to Berlioz.

Liszt's other symphonic work, the *Symphony to Dante's Divina Commedia* (1856), depicts the Inferno, Purgatory, and Paradise. Liszt, at times a devout Catholic, portrayed Dante's scenes with great imagination and passion, cleverly suiting his melody—sometimes simple and tranquil, sometimes chromatic and writhing—and harmony to the special characters of the three levels. The symphony is dedicated to Wagner, who suggested the third-movement setting of the Magnificat for female chorus and orchestra. As do many operas of Wagner, Liszt's work uses the leitmotiv, an extension of Berlioz' *idée fixe*.

If Berlioz and Liszt represented a trend toward freedom and extramusical content in symphonic writing, Schumann and Mendelssohn were more conservative though not strictly comparable. All four were deeply concerned with formal discipline, but Schumann and Mendelssohn departed less widely from Classical norms and made less point of extramusical associations.

Mendelssohn's symphonic works

Felix Mendelssohn wrote 16 symphonies and a symphony-cantata. Twelve of the symphonies are immature works; but the remainder fairly exemplify his style: facile, full of light melody and brilliant orchestration, occasionally oversentimental, according to some critics. He is best known for his *Symphonies No. 3* (*Scottish*) and *No. 4* (*Italian*), both in A major–minor. The *Scottish* (also called *Scotch*), completed in 1842, although not programmatic, is expressive of Mendelssohn's poetic nature. Its beginning was sketched during a visit to Scotland in 1829. In structure the work consists of four movements played without pause, with a slow introduction. Its fairylike scherzo, which incorporates part of a Scottish folk song, exemplifies the delicate moods that Mendelssohn excelled in creating. The other movements are well developed, the many contrasting themes integrated contrapuntally and extended with interesting modulations. But although it is full of good music, the symphony is less powerful than its companion, the *Italian* (finished 1833). This happy work, inspired by visits to Rome and Naples, is particularly colourfully orchestrated. It ends with a dance movement incorporating three themes; the minor tonality does not detract from its vivacity. The first movement, too, has three themes, the third introduced in the development section. The second movement, recalling a religious procession, and the third, a quasi-minuet and trio, are picturesque without being descriptive and represent Mendelssohn at his finest—uncomplicated, lush, and vigorous.

Robert Schumann, like Mendelssohn and Mozart, wrote his symphonies at an age when most longer-lived composers are just beginning to mature and wrote only a few truly great ones. Like many first-generation Romantic composers Schumann was essentially a miniaturist, most at home in songs and short piano works. His orchestral style reflects these qualities; rhythmically restless, often repetitive, not sensitively scored, they have been praised more for their harmonic subtleties and wonderful lyric melodies than for development of these ideas.

Schumann's miniaturist style

The *Symphony No. 1 in B Flat Major* (*Spring*, 1841), based on a poem by Adolph Böttger, originally had titles given each movement; these were soon rejected by Schumann and indeed are irrelevant to the music. The first movement, opening with a slow introduction (a tradition since the days of Haydn), incorporates three contrasting themes (the third introduced toward the conclusion of the movement) as well as the opening dramatic figure of the introduction. The slow movement and unusual scherzo (it has two different trios, rather than one) are linked thematically and played without a pause between them. The impulsive progress of the finale is interrupted before the recapitulation by slower passages for flute and hunting horns, perhaps intended by Schumann to be descriptive.

The *Symphony No. 2 in C Major* (1846) is tightly organized and owes something in design to Beethoven. It has been overshadowed by more frequent performances of the last two symphonies, *No. 3 in E Flat Major* (*Rhenish*; 1850) and *No. 4 in D Minor* (1841, rev. 1851). The five-movement *Rhenish* is less "classical" than the *Symphony No. 2.* Inspired by a ceremony at Cologne Cathedral as well as by the appearance of the cathedral itself, the polyphonic grandeur and harmonic richness, especially of the fourth movement, are tempered by the relaxed pace and rustic character of the scherzo and following short, quiet slow movement. The outer movements are related both thematically and in mood, and the last two movements also share material, forming a large cohesive structure.

Even more cohesive is the plan of the *Fourth Symphony* in which all four movements are played, as in Mendelssohn's *Scottish Symphony,* without pause. A single theme recurs in various guises in all four movements; this thematic transformation is a hallmark of Schumann's style, as of Berlioz' and Liszt's. The last movement introduces new material but without destroying the cyclic nature of the whole work. Cyclic structure, which relates separate movements by means of re-use of thematic material, is a feature of much symphonic writing after Beethoven. As composers gradually departed from repetitive forms, cyclic construction became a chief mode of achieving unity over a large time span and greatly enlarged harmonic vocabulary. An advanced form of cyclic construction may be seen in the Belgian composer César Franck's influential single *Symphony in D Minor* (1888).

Although Johannes Brahms's four symphonies are popularly considered to be no less important than the greatest earlier symphonies, the contribution of his contemporary Anton Bruckner is controversial. Bruckner, a devout Catholic whose church music is among the finest of his generation, is noteworthy not only for the excessive length and heavy orchestration of many late movements but for his Wagnerian harmonies, large-scale repetitions, and (at its best) monumental conceptions of form. Bruckner gathered much from studying late Beethoven and Schubert. Yet his style evolved little in the course of nine symphonies (he was over 40 when he wrote his first symphonies; two other unnumbered early ones are never heard, and his last was incomplete at his death). Entirely personal in expression, his symphonies underwent frequent revision. They are in four movements and are basically unprogrammatic, even conservative. Despite his devotion to Wagner and Beethoven, Bruckner remained provincial; his technique was grounded on traditional studies, and his movement types seem to follow a set of typical formulas that derived from Classical patterns, especially the sonata. Within these formal types he develops themes powerful in their simplicity and monolithic in harmonic expanse. Chords reminiscent of German chorale (hymn melody harmonizations) and tremolo or pizzicato (plucked) accompaniments occur along with organ-like counterpoint and pedal tones (sustained notes against changing harmonies). Hardly imbued with youthful vigour, some scherzos still have roots in the fertile Austrian popular music that nourished Haydn and Beethoven. These movements, however, are not sufficient to lighten the overall impression of density. Unlike those of Brahms, Bruckner's symphonies are not immediately rewarding; yet connoisseurs, including Mahler, respect Bruckner's heroic finales, in which themes from earlier movements are sometimes combined. *Symphony No. 4 in E Flat Major* (1874, first performance of revision, 1881), with a Beethovenian andante and scherzo recalling the hunt, is noteworthy for the use of four themes in the first movement. *No. 7 in E Major* (1881–83, rev. 1885), well received at first hearing, is Wagnerian in orchestration (Wagner tubas play in the adagio) and makes use of contrapuntal techniques developed in the Renaissance. In the last two symphonies the adagio movements occur after the scherzos rather than before.

Traits of Bruckner's symphonic style

The symphonies of Brahms, each highly individual, appealing on first hearing, and rewarding to rehear, could hardly be more different from Bruckner's. Yet Brahms, his technique grounded on thorough study of Classical and Baroque works, was no less essentially conservative. He retained the four-movement format and familiar methods of thematic development and rigorous contrapuntal craftsmanship, avoided programmatic content, and was always concerned with aural effect. These concerns are reflected in his orchestration, which is never merely flashy, never astonishing. His entire remarkable skill and attention to detail served the lyrical, spontaneous flow of his melody.

Individuality of Brahms's symphonies

His tunes, Romantic as Schubert's, are developed with consistency, refinement, and a harmonic interest foreign to many lesser contemporaries (especially those seduced by Berlioz and Liszt but without understanding their talent). Brahms is a master of understatement. Finished in 1876, 20 years after it was begun, his *Symphony No. 1 in C Minor* was the fruit of a mature man's experience. It carried on where Beethoven left off, drawing inspiration especially from Beethoven's *Fifth.* The triumph of major over minor, epitomized in the finale, underlies the whole. The key scheme of the movements is cyclic, based on a succession of rising major thirds: C minor, E major, A♭ (=G♯) major, C minor–major. The third movement, formally a scherzo with trio, slackens tension as though to prepare for the marvellously developed finale, which is preceded by a broad introduction (as is the first movement) that sets harmonic and thematic goals for the remainder.

Clear goal orientation also characterizes the *Symphony No. 2 in D Major* (1877). Unlike the *First* in mood, it is pervaded in all movements by optimistic calm. The first and last share a three-note motive that is joined by other serene themes in the first movement, which includes a long horn solo near the end. The second movement begins in B major, a third lower than the first, and the fast third movement begins a lower third still, in G major; the finale returns to D. This third-based tonal scheme, like that of the *First,* marks Brahms as a true Romantic, as do the tempo changes within movements, the sensuous modulations that circumscribe harmonic goals, and the intense major–minor conflicts.

Modal tension—major versus minor—characterizes the cyclic *Symphony No. 3 in F Major* (1883), the movements of which are related by material derived from Brahms's "motto" motive, FAF, *frei aber froh* ("free but joyful"). Winds are prominently featured, particularly clarinet and horn, as elsewhere in these symphonies. Brahms retained Classical outlines as usual; but, as in the *First,* the scherzo with trio serves to throw the vigorous, stormy finale into relief. The first movement plunges to the heart of things from the opening chords, harmonizing the motto; there is no introduction, no coyness in exposing the main themes. Chromatic harmony and contrapuntal development are fully exploited.

Brahms's architectural skill is nowhere more in evidence than in the finale of the *Symphony No. 4 in E Minor* (1884–85), an extended chaconne, or set of variations over an (eight-bar) repeated bass melody. This movement is almost Baroque; and elsewhere in the work Brahms employs Baroque contrapuntal techniques, chromatic labyrinths, and modal melody that hovers between major and minor but is neither. In this work particularly, but throughout the symphonies, Brahms epitomized the tendency of the later Romantics to seek a balance between the expressive forms of the early 19th century and older traditional technique, to apply to the wealth of available harmonic and orchestral colour constructive methods consciously founded upon study of Beethoven (particularly *Symphonies No. 4, No. 7,* and *No. 8*), Handel, and other models. These disciplined composers (including Schumann and Mendelssohn) reacted partly against what they felt to be the extramusical emphasis and compositional excesses of Berlioz, Liszt, and lesser figures, who took as their point of departure the less conventional Beethoven of *Symphonies No. 5, No. 6,* and *No. 9.*

Dvořák and Tchaikovsky

Both trends found reflection in the symphonies of Dvořák and Tchaikovsky, composers who were products of growing nationalistic tendencies in music. Antonin Dvořák continued a distinguished line of Bohemian symphonists stretching back to Stamitz. Conscious of his musical heritage, Dvořák infused his music with folk-derived elements, particularly dances; his last symphony, *No. 9 in E Minor* (*From the New World,* 1893), even incorporates American tunes; but these are almost incidental to the strong Slavonic character of the work. An early devotee of Wagnerian sonorities, Dvořák in his later symphonies returned to the more conservative models and orchestrations of Beethoven and Brahms. It is these later works, through which Dvořák is known today, that have led detractors to call him a "second-rate Brahms." In fact, Dvořák's melodic invention, often based on irregular folklike scale forms, and his captivating irregularity of phrase length, surprising variety of orchestration, and impetuous rhythms are entirely personal.

Peter Ilich Tchaikovsky, on the other hand, was not comfortable working with preestablished formal models but was at his best in ballets and tone poems in which his somewhat extravagant nature found fuller scope for expression. Of his eight symphonies, only *No. 4 in F Minor* (1877), *No. 5 in E Minor* (1888), and *No. 6 in B minor* (*Pathétique,* 1893), actually fourth, sixth, and eighth in order of composition, are well-known. These are controversial works, partly because their novel structures are not easily analyzed (or heard) in standard formal ways. Some feel that Tchaikovsky's freedom and tendency to musical autobiography were inimical to purely abstract musical expression and that understanding of his music depends on knowledge of his state of mind at various times or upon some extramusical imagery or program. This attitude conflicts with an essential determinant of symphonic idiom, which is that the establishment and working-out of tensions in the piece are primarily occasioned by purely musical, formal means; and that extramusical data, interesting though they may be, are not directly relevant to apprehension and appreciation of the symphonic process. If Tchaikovsky's symphonies are to be considered successful as symphonies, they must make purely musical sense—and the three mentioned fulfill this condition.

Tchaikovsky's kind of musical logic, however, is quite different from that exemplified by the main-line German symphonists. Isolated in his formative years from the influence of Brahms and Wagner, he learned instead by hearing Mozart and Italian opera, characteristics of which he fused with elements of non-European melody, harmony, rhythm, and colour; in this he followed Aleksandr Borodin and other Russians. He strongly favoured the minor mode, no doubt partly because of its inherent instability. This unique confluence of stylistic sources produced a new model for later symphonists, particularly in regard to orchestration and a reevaluation of sonata form based on a fresh conception of tonal harmony.

Mahler as the culmination of the Viennese tradition

With Gustav Mahler, the central path, if not the culmination, of Viennese symphony was regained. In importance Mahler's nine completed symphonies (a 10th was left unfinished at his death) stand equal to any corpus since Beethoven's. That this has been so recently recognized may have something to do with historical perspective but is more probably a matter of relevance of his music to the mood of the mid-20th century. Nowhere else in music is found such explicit cynicism, such deliberate distortion of the familiar; by the same token no symphonist exceeds him in desire for reconciliation. Mahler's melodies and harmonies are strongly goal oriented; that his goals are so frequently frustrated or beset with obstacles reflects a truly contemporary outlook.

Mahler's symphonies, like those of Tchaikovsky and Berlioz, suffer from being too often considered solely in the light of extramusical associations. Mahler himself suppressed the programs of his early symphonies and subjected their music to frequent revision. Structurally, the symphonies are entirely logical, even simple, beneath the multitude of themes and wealth of colouristic detail. Mahler was a fastidious and brilliant orchestrator. The seeming superfluity of orchestral resource he called for, especially in the later symphonies, is handled with restraint and sensitivity—Mahler was a conductor as well as a composer and knew well the capabilities of the instruments.

Enormous in time scale, Mahler's symphonies contain sufficient variety and contrast to maintain interest. Underlying this stylistic multiplicity—including parodies of folk song, waltzes, fanfares, marches, text painting (four symphonies include voices), chorales, borrowings from other composers as well as his own songs—was a leaning toward cyclic structure, with themes or motives shared among movements, as in his song cycles and those of Schubert and Schumann. Mahler also experimented with tonal structure to the extent of combining movements in unrelated keys, so that the ear never tires of a single tonal area. *Symphonies No. 5, No. 6,* and *No. 7,* themselves a huge cycle, show him coming to grips with Classical sonata form, greatly expanded though it is. Unity on a lower level is achieved through extensive counterpoint. These later works show an economy of structure that is foreign to Bruckner, from whom Mahler nevertheless learned much.

Nielsen and Sibelius

The 20th century. Important symphonists of the early 20th century include many non-Germans. Carl Nielsen and Jean Sibelius, the former Danish, the latter Finnish, both owe much to the Viennese symphonists but acquired individual styles that resulted in new conceptions of symphonic form. Nielsen's six symphonies display a kind of unity based on "progressive" or "emergent" harmony, one key moving on to the next in such fashion that the gamut of harmonies in a single symphony (or movement) does not totally relate to a single tonic. His harmonies sometimes fluctuate between two or more goals and incorporate chromatic and modal features. This untraditional harmonic tension is an aspect of the breakdown of normal Classical ways of establishing tonality, for which the 19th century (and Wagner in particular) is largely responsible. (Nielsen, however, was an anti-Wagnerian.) This "destructive" impulse, elements of which may already be heard in Haydn, led to constant re-evaluation of the basis of sonata form and hence of the symphony as a whole. As the traditional harmonic foundation weakened—partly because the enlarged time scale makes long-term harmonic relationships hard to hear—symphonists sought new unifying techniques, among them cyclic forms, extramusical plots, progressive harmony, etc. None of these is incompatible with dramatic sonata form, taken in its broadest sense. Nielsen retained and emphasized key conflict as a dynamic force and experimented with counterpoint and conflicting rhythms (*e.g., Symphony No. 4, The Inextinguishable,* 1916; and *Symphony No. 5,* 1922), joined movements, and the rest.

Sibelius wrote his seven symphonies between 1899 and 1925. Like Nielsen's, they departed from Classical models (notably Beethoven's *Fifth*) and reflected especially the advances of Brahms and Bruckner. Sibelius was a restrained orchestrator, a non-Wagnerian. Although nationalistic, he used no folk songs and incorporated no programs. He had little immediate influence, isolated as he was after World War I, but is highly regarded presently in his native country, and in England and the United States. Sibelius, like Nielsen, is not tied to Classical tonic-dominant opposition. He sometimes introduces modal scales and polar harmonic goals between which the music oscillates. A chief unifying device is a repeated bass line or sustained pedal tone. His themes are often groups of melodic fragments, meaningless when out of context, that are capable of being combined in various ways. The gradual integration of these motifs is an important means of development. In this Sibelius resembles Borodin; the effect is quite unlike that of Mahler's long melodies. Structurally Sibelius is terse and simple. He eliminated transitions and introductions, avoided simple recapitulation, and kept harmonies static or ambiguous over long stretches. Rarely was he merely playful. He was fond of low, dark sounds. Sibelius is hardly unemotional but certainly is not effusively romantic. His symphonies represent a great contrast with Mahler's, and he strikes a new path away from the sonata.

Elsewhere in the early 20th century important symphonic contributions were being made by the Frenchman Albert Roussel, whose four symphonies are elegant and classical in form; the American Charles Ives, who quotes well-known tunes in his highly dissonant four symphonies; and the Englishmen Sir Edward Elgar and Ralph Vaughan Williams. Their works are not often heard outside their native countries, and the extent of their influence on the growth of symphonic thinking remains to be determined. A more important innovator, the Viennese Arnold Schoenberg, considered his *Chamber Symphony,* Opus 9 (1906), "the climax of my first period." Basically still sonata-oriented and tonal, this work departed from the gargantuan orchestrations of Mahler and Richard Strauss and is scored for 15 soloists, 10 of whom play winds. The idiom is highly dissonant and motivic, straining at the limits of traditional tonality and pointing to Schoenberg's formulation of dodecaphony, or 12-tone serialism (deriving melody and harmony from the composer's ordering of the 12 tones of the chromatic scale).

Stravinsky's imaginative force

Igor Stravinsky likewise inherited a living tradition and transformed it with great imaginative force. Like Schoenberg, he was not primarily a symphonist; his early *Symphony in E Flat Major* (1905–07) is no more original than anything of other Russians such as Borodin or Aleksandr Glazunov. But the *Symphony in C* (1940) and *Symphony in Three Movements* (1942–45) are unique. The former, a Neoclassical work, reinterprets in Stravinsky's language the thematic construction and sonata form of the Classical era. The result, far from a simple parody of Classical style (such as in Sergey Prokofiev's *Symphony No. 1 in D Major* or *Classical Symphony* of 1917), was an altogether fresh and revealing insight into the implications of Haydn's work. The *Symphony in Three Movements,* inspired by wartime impressions, is independent of models, yet in outward form the movements appear traditional. Two other of Stravinsky's works deserve mention here: the *Symphonies of Wind Instruments* (1920, rev. 1947) and the *Symphony of Psalms* (1930), which includes chorus. These works are symphonies only in the 17th-century sense of ensemble pieces; in both form and structure they are dissimilar from the other symphonies.

Chief among other Russians are, besides Prokofiev (seven symphonies), Nicolay Myaskovsky (also seven) and Dmitry Shostakovich (15). Shostakovich's large corpus marks him as one of the most important and prolific modern symphonists. His works are uneven in quality. A number are programmatic, dealing with Russian political and social upheavals. Shostakovich at times concerns himself with incorporating popular and folk tunes, giving expression to national feelings, and, more basically, with problems of achieving cyclic unity by such means as leitmotivs and thematic recurrences and joining movements without pause.

The mainstream of American symphonic production resides with Roy Harris, Walter Piston, William Schuman, and Roger Sessions. Important as teachers, these men have influenced younger symphonists such as Easley Blackwood and helped create a distinctive style of composition that resulted in the first important symphonic output in the Western Hemisphere. Although many younger composers on both sides of the Atlantic are turning to avant-garde techniques, including experiments in formlessness, and to small instrumental and vocal ensembles as well as to electronic sources, the future of the symphony seems secure. Extremely large orchestrations are not widely favoured, partly because of the difficulty and expense of mounting a performance; yet Blackwood has written one symphony for an orchestra larger than Mahler's as well as one for chamber orchestra. Audiences tend to favour works in familiar forms. Prizes and commissions assure a steady output of symphonies and many have been written for college and university orchestras. Flourishing amateur orchestras also furnish outlets for the young composer. As regards the masters of the 18th and 19th centuries, there seems no possibility that their symphonies will become museum pieces in the foreseeable future. On the contrary, the recording and broadcasting industry has brought about renewed interest in even the lesser known symphonists. Scholars and public alike have now almost unlimited access to the treasures of three centuries of symphonic production. (La.L.)

SONATA

Deriving from the past participle of the Italian verb *sonare,* "to sound," the term sonata originally denoted a composition played on instruments, as opposed to one that was *cantata,* or "sung," by voices. Its first such use was in 1561, when it was applied to a suite of dances for lute. The term has since acquired other meanings that can easily cause confusion. It can mean a composition in two or more movements, or separate sections, played by a small group of instruments, having no more than three independent parts. Most frequently it refers to such a piece for one or two instruments. By extension, sonata can also refer to a composition for a larger instrumental group having more than two or three parts, such as a string quartet or an orchestra, provided that the composition is based on principles of musical form that from the mid-18th century were used in sonatas for small instrumental groups. The term has been more loosely applied to 20th-century works, whether or not they rely on 18th-century principles.

Sonata and sonata form

Quite distinct from all of the preceding, however, is the use of the term in "sonata form." This denotes a particular form or method of musical organization normally used within instrumental sonatas, string quartets, and other chamber music, and symphonies written since the beginning of the Classical period (the period of Mozart, Haydn, and Beethoven) in the mid-18th century.

The first concern of this section will be to establish the principles of musical form often associated with sonatas for small and large groups of instruments. They will be approached through an examination of the principle of musical structure called "sonata form." A historical account of the origins and development both of the instrumental sonata and of sonata form will then endeavour to throw light on other meanings of the term. In conclusion, some estimate will be offered of the present and possible future roles of the sonata in musical life.

Structure of the Classical sonata. Sonata form denotes a particularly fertile manner of organizing the musical structure of a single movement. It commonly occurs within the larger context of a multimovement scheme. Maturing in the second half of the 18th century, it provided the instrumental vehicle for much of the most profound musical thought until about the middle of the 19th century, and has continued to figure largely in the methods of composers down to the present day.

The basic elements of sonata form are three: exposition, development, and recapitulation, in which the musical subject matter is stated, explored or expanded, and restated. There may also be an introduction, usually in slow tempo, and a coda, or tailpiece, but these optional sections do not affect the basic structure. Although sonata form is sometimes called first-movement form, the first movements of multimovement works are not always in sonata form, nor does the form occur only in first movements. Likewise, another name for it, sonata-allegro form, is misleading, for it need not be in a quick tempo such as allegro.

At first glance sonata form may appear to be a species of three-part, or ternary, form. The three parts of ternary form are a first section (A), followed by a contrasting section (B), followed by a repetition of the first section (that is, A B A). The parts are interrelated not in terms of basic structure but by purely lyrical or character contrast. Actually, the three parts of sonata form developed out of the binary, or two-part, form prominent in the music of the 17th and early 18th centuries. In binary form the structure depends on the interrelationship not only of themes but also of tonalities, or keys, the particular sets of notes and chords used in each part. Thus, the initial part, which is repeated, leads directly into the second part by ending in the new key in which the second part begins. The second, also repeated, moves from the new key back to the original key, in which it ends. The second part thus completes the first.

Binary form

In sonata form the exposition corresponds to the first part of binary form, the development and recapitulation to the second. The exposition moves from the original key to a new key; the development passes through several keys and the recapitulation returns to the original key. This echoes the motion, in binary form, away from and back to the original key. In relation to binary form, sonata form is complex. It offers, in the exposition, contrasting musical statements. In the development these are treated dialectically; that is, they are combined, broken up, recombined, and otherwise brought into change and conflict. In the recapitulation they are restated in a new light. This organic relationship between parts marks the sonata form as a higher, more complex, type than the ternary form. The occasional designation of sonata form as compound binary form is useful in that it stresses its origins in the earlier form, but notes its added complexity.

The emphasis on contrast, even conflict, is the element that distinguishes the exposition of a sonata-form movement from the first section of an earlier binary form. The first section of a binary movement in a Baroque suite or instrumental sonata, for example, might contain two clearly differentiated themes, but the stress is on continuity and on uniformity of musical texture rather than on contrast. In sonata form the emphasis is more dynamic; there is a stronger sense of contrast within the movement. The terms usually given the contrasting areas are "first subject/second subject" or "principal group/subsidiary group." These are misleading terms, for they imply a simple contrast of themes.

Thematic and tonal contrast

In reality it is contrast of key, or tonal contrast, that characterizes the sonata exposition. Usually the opening of the exposition is firmly rooted in the tonic, or "home," key of the work. The later segments of the exposition move decisively to a closely related but distinct key. The second key chosen is almost invariably one of the two keys most closely related to the home key. If the home key was a major key, the dominant key is chosen; if the home key was minor, the relative major is chosen. (The dominant key is the one whose keynote is five tones above that of the tonic, as C–G; the relative major has a keynote three tones above the relative minor, as A minor–C major.) The exposition thus creates an opposition of tonalities or key areas that the rest of the movement—the development and recapitulation—will strive to reconcile. Compared with the contrast of keys, the question of how many themes the movement possesses is of minor structural significance. Very often, a movement in sonata form has two clearly defined main themes, for example the first movement of Mozart's *Symphony No. 41 in C Major.* It may also have only one, like the first movement of Haydn's *Symphony No. 85 in B Flat Major.* Or it may have more than a half dozen strongly characterized themes, as does the first movement of Brahms's *Fourth Symphony.*

The thematic organization of a movement in sonata form may affect the character of the exposition, and thus of the whole movement, in two specific respects. When two themes or groups of themes are clearly differentiated, their distribution may help the listener to assimilate the cardinal points of the tonal design (that is, the arrangement of keys) of the movement. When, on the other hand, such differentiation between themes is obscured or set at variance with the organization of tonalities, the very tension between thematic design and tonal scheme may greatly enhance the subtlety and interest of the form. Such tension may produce not merely an interplay of melody and key within the movement but an interplay between two interplays. One fairly simple way of achieving this is shown in the first movement of Haydn's *Symphony No. 99 in E Flat Major.* Here, as in *No. 85,* the first theme is restated in the dominant key. This restatement could appear at first to be the second subject. But later it is followed by another distinct motive that, in terms of themes, is the real second subject. At the same time the neat, almost epigrammatic character of the second subject makes it similar to a codetta theme, which is often used to round off the exposition after both main subjects have been stated.

In the first movement of Mozart's *Symphony No. 35 in D Major (Haffner)* this interplay of interplays reaches a higher level of subtlety. The second theme, against which the first persists as a counterpoint, is stated "on" rather than "in" the dominant; that is, its harmonies suggest the dominant key, but remain part of the home, or tonic, key. The second theme is thus heard as a new perspective on the tonic. Later, when the dominant key is firmly established in its own right, Mozart introduces a new subject whose tune is closely related to the first theme. In this richly ambiguous structure, the newly introduced motive would be regarded by the criterion of key, as the second subject; in purely thematic terms, it might almost be said to constitute the beginning of the codetta, or concluding section.

The functions of the other two main sections follow naturally from what has been established in the exposition. Their purpose is to discuss and resolve the conflicts of tonality and theme that the exposition has raised. The development is an area of tonal flux—it usually modulates, or changes key, frequently, and any keys it settles

Modulation and thematic alteration

in are likely to be only distantly related to the keys found in the exposition. It frequently proceeds by breaking the principal themes down into smaller elements and bringing these elements into new tonal or contrapuntal relations with each other. That is, themes or fragments of themes may appear in new keys; they may be combined to form apparently new melodies; they may be played against each other as counterpoint, or countermelody. One of the finest illustrations of the methods of development used in the Classical period occurs in the first movement of Mozart's *Symphony No. 38 in D Major (Prague).* Another resource of development is to seize on an apparently minor feature of the exposition and, by developing it extensively, to demonstrate its hidden importance. Another is to introduce entirely new material. This may provide a moment of relief in the course of a rigorous argument (as in the last movement of Mozart's *Piano Sonata in C Major,* K. 330); or it may allow the composer to expand the scope of a large-scale movement (as in the first movement of Beethoven's *Symphony No. 3 in E Flat Major,* the *Eroica*).

Sometimes such a theme may only *seem* to be new. In the first movement of Beethoven's *Symphony No. 4 in B Flat Major,* for instance, the theme in the development that is usually described as "new" is really a decorated version of a motive already heard in the exposition.

One common tactic in the Classical development is to begin the section with the codetta theme that ended the exposition. The first movement of Beethoven's *Cello Sonata No. 2 in G Minor,* Opus 5, No. 2, is an example.

The impact of this device, and of the development section as a whole, is often obscured by the common tendency among modern performers to ignore the composer's instruction, present in almost all sonata form movements of the Classical period, to repeat the entire exposition. When this repetition is omitted, the thematic balance of the movement is upset and the dramatic effect of the development's sudden departure from an established regularity can be ruined. Music is an art to which the controlled use of time is basic. The temporal structure of a movement cannot be altered without seriously changing the proportions of the whole.

Tension and recapitulation

Like the beginning of the development section, the point at which development passes into recapitulation is one of the most important psychological moments in the entire sonata structure. It marks the end of the main argument and the beginning of the final synthesis for which that argument has prepared the listener's mind. The Classical masters differ in their handling of this juncture. All usually prepare for it with a long passage of gathering tension. In Mozart the return of the tonic key and subject is managed with understated punctuality, the actual moment of recapitulation gliding in almost unnoticed. Haydn and Beethoven tend to celebrate its advent with panoply.

The recapitulation presents the principal subject matter of the movement in a new state of equilibrium. The main subjects of the exposition are heard almost always in the same order as before, but now both subjects are typically in the tonic key, whereas in the exposition the first was in the tonic, the second in the dominant key. As a result of the musical events in the development, the listener perceives the subjects in a new relationship—rather like a traveller who glimpses the constituent parts of a valley separately as he climbs a hill and then, when he reaches the summit, sees the entire landscape for the first time as a whole. The recapitulation can vary greatly in the literalness with which it repeats the elements of the exposition. Sometimes, as in the first movement of Mozart's *Sonata in B Flat Major,* K. 570, a tiny modification in the transition that originally led from the tonic to the dominant key is enough to effect the necessary change of key perspective and keep the second subject in the tonic key. In other cases (the first movement of Beethoven's *Eroica Symphony,* for instance, and many of Haydn's symphonic movements) far-reaching modifications and reshufflings of the original material are made in the recapitulation. As in any living manifestation of a principle of musical form, the methods differ vastly from work to work; but the effect is always to bring about the reconciliation of opposites that is essential to sonata form.

A large-scale sonata movement often creates conflicts of key and theme that cannot be completely settled even by the full process of recapitulation. In this case, the movement may be rounded off with a coda, or concluding section. Beethoven often extends the coda so greatly that it becomes almost a second development section, as in his *Appassionata* piano sonata. But this is no more an essential element of sonata form than the introduction that may precede the main movement.

The form described above is that exemplified in most first movements of sonatas, and of sonata-style compositions, in the Classical period. There are usually two, three, or four movements in the entire work. Two-movement and, more particularly, three-movement schemes are most common in sonatas for one or two instruments. Symphonies and string quartets almost always have four movements, and Beethoven, particularly in his earlier period, sometimes expanded the scheme of the instrumental sonata to four movements too.

The first movement in all of these patterns is usually fast; the second commonly provides the contrast of a slower tempo; and the last in most cases is again fast. When there are four movements, a simpler, dance-style movement of the type also found in the suite is included. This is usually placed between the slow second movement and the finale; in some cases it stands second and the slow movement third.

The forms of these other movements vary much more than that of the first, which in Classical examples is almost invariably the weightiest. Since their function is to complement the experience of the first movement through a new but related range of contrasts, their scope and manner depend on the point to which the issues of the work have already been taken. Simple ternary (A B A) form and variation form (*i.e.,* theme and variations) are among the most common patterns for the slow movement, but rondo and sonata forms are also used. In rondo form a recurring theme is contrasted with a number of intervening themes, as A B A C A. When sonata form is used in slow tempos, the demands of overall proportion frequently cause the omission of the development section. Sonata form, rondo, and, less often, variation form are also used for the final movement. In final movements, also, the simple rondo pattern (A B A C A) is often expanded into A B A-development-B A, with B in the dominant key at its first appearance and in the tonic key at its second. The result is a hybrid form known as sonata-rondo.

The dance movement

In the first part of the Classical period, the dance movement, when it appeared, usually consisted of a minuet in fairly simple binary form (the two-part form from which sonata form evolved). This was followed by a second minuet known as the trio, which tended in orchestral works to be more lightly scored. The first minuet was then repeated, normally without its own internal repeats. The minuet-trio-minuet structure forms an overall ternary pattern. Haydn frequently, and Beethoven still more often, chose to speed the traditional minuet up to the point at which it lost its dance character and became a scherzo, a quick, light movement usually related to the minuet in form. In some extreme cases, such as the ninth symphonies of both Beethoven and Schubert, the binary structures of both scherzo and trio were expanded into small but complete sonata-form structures. In this way, as with the sonata-rondo, the principles of thematic development and key contrast spread during the Classical period as the sonata form began to influence other movements.

Such are the outlines of the most fertile form in Western instrumental music since 1750. Before discussing its origins, growth, and later modification, there should be a warning against phrases like "true sonata form." If sonata form as described is considered the sole "true sonata form," the implication is that instrumental sonatas written in forms other than sonata form are not genuine.

Actually, the principle exemplified in sonata form represents one way of organizing the passage of sound through time. Its scope is enormous; it was the basis for some of the greatest works of Western music; and it still contains the seeds of potential further development. But it is only one episode in a complex chronicle of styles and principles of musical organization. In contrast to earlier forms, it emphasizes conflict instead of continuity and derives its impact from the explosive power of tonal organization instead of the smoother influence of melody.

History of the sonata. The sonata in all its manifestations has roots that go back long before the first uses of the actual name. Its ultimate sources are in the choral polyphony of the late Renaissance (music having several equal melodic lines, or voices). This in turn drew at times on both liturgical and secular sources—on the ancient system of tones or modes of Gregorian chant, and on medieval European folk music. These two lines were constantly interweaving. Popular tunes, for example, were used as the starting point for masses and other religious compositions from the 15th to the early 17th centuries. Sacred and secular elements influenced the development of both the sonata and the partita (or suite) of the Baroque period.

Earliest origins

The specific musical procedures that were eventually to be characteristic of the sonata began to emerge clearly in works by the Venetian composers of the late 16th century, notably Andrea Gabrieli (*c.* 1520–86) and Giovanni Gabrieli (1556–1612). These composers built instrumental pieces in short sections of contrasted tempo, a scheme that represents in embryo the division into movements of the later sonata. This approach is found not only in works entitled "sonata," such as Giovanni Gabrieli's *Sonata pian' e forte* (*Soft and Loud Sonata*) of 1597, which was one of the first works to specify instrumentation in detail; the instrumental fantasia and the canzone, an instrumental form derived from the chanson or secular French part-song, display a similar sectional structure. Like early sonatas, they were often contrapuntal (*i.e.,* built by counterpoint, or the interweaving of melodic lines in the different voices, or parts). At this stage sonatas, fantasias, and canzoni were often indistinguishable from each other, and from the fuguelike ricercare, though this form is generally more serious in character and more strictly contrapuntal in technique.

In the 17th century stringed instruments eclipsed the winds, which had played an at least equally important role in the sonatas and canzoni composed by the Gabrielis for the spacious galleries of St. Mark's Cathedral, Venice. Claudio Monteverdi (1567–1643) devoted more of his energies to vocal than to instrumental composition. The development of instrumental writing—and of instrumental musical forms—was carried on more and more by virtuoso violinists. One of these was Carlo Farina (flourished *c.* 1630), who spent part of his life in the service of the court of Dresden, and there published a set of sonatas in 1626. But the crowning figure in this early school of violinist-composers was Arcangelo Corelli (1653–1713), whose published sonatas, beginning in 1681, sum up Italian work in the field to this date.

Apart from their influence on the development of violin technique, reflected in the works of such later violinist-composers as Giuseppe Torelli (1658–1709), Antonio Vivaldi (1678–1741), Francesco Maria Veracini (1690–*c.* 1750), Giuseppe Tartini (1692–1770), and Pietro Locatelli (1695–1764), Corelli's sonatas are important for the way they clarify and help to define the two directions the sonata was to take. At this point the *sonata da chiesa,* or church sonata, and the *sonata da camera,* or chamber sonata, emerged as complementary but distinct lines of development.

Church and chamber sonatas

The *sonata da chiesa* usually consists of four movements, in the order slow–fast–slow–fast. The first fast movement tends to be loosely fugal in style (*i.e.,* using contrapuntal melodic imitation), and thus reflects, most clearly of the four, the sonata's roots in the fantasia and canzone. The last movement, by contrast, is simpler and lighter, often differing from the dance style typical of the *sonata da camera* only in that its sections are not repeated. The *sonata da camera* is altogether less serious and less contrapuntal than the *sonata da chiesa,* and it tends to consist of a larger number of shorter movements in dance style. If the *sonata da chiesa* was the source from which the Classical sonata was to develop, its courtly cousin was the direct ancestor of the suite, or partita, a succession of short dance pieces; and in the 18th century, the terms suite and partita were practically synonymous with *sonata da camera.* The two streams represented by church and chamber sonatas are the manifestation, in early Baroque terms, of the liturgical and secular sources found in Renaissance music. The Baroque style flourished in music from about 1600 to about 1750. Down to the middle of the 18th century the two influences maintained a high degree of independence; yet the injection of dance movements into the lighter examples of the *sonata da chiesa* and the penetration of counterpoint into the more serious suites and *sonate da camera* show that there was always some cross-fertilization.

Another characteristic of the Baroque sonata that Corelli's work helped to stabilize was its instrumentation. Around 1600 the musical revolution that began in Italy had shifted emphasis from the equal-voiced polyphony of the Renaissance and placed it instead on the concept of monody, or solo lines with subordinate accompaniments. The comparatively static influence of the old church modes was superseded by the more dramatic organizing principle of the major–minor key system with its use of contrast of keys. Although counterpoint continued to play a central role in musical structure for another hundred years and more, it became a counterpoint that took careful account of the implications of harmony and of chords within the framework of the major and minor keys.

The continuo part

In this context the continuo, or thorough bass, assumed primary importance. The composer that used a continuo part wrote out in full only the parts of the upper melody instruments. The accompaniment, which was the continuo part, was given in the form of a bass line, sometimes supplemented with numbers, or figures, to indicate main details of harmony, whence the term "figured bass." The continuo was "realized," or given its performed form, by a low melody instrument (viola da gamba, violone, or later cello or bassoon) in collaboration with an organ, harpsichord, or lute. The collaborating instrument improvised the harmonies indicated by the figures or implied by the other parts and so filled the gap between the treble and bass lines.

In Corelli's work, "solo" sonatas, for one violin with continuo, are found alongside others for two violins and continuo described as sonatas *a tre* (*i.e.,* for three), early examples of the trio sonata that was the principal chamber-music form until about 1750. The use of "trio" for sonatas played by four instruments is only superficially paradoxical: although trio sonatas were played by four instruments, they were considered to be in three parts—two violins and continuo. Moreover, specific instrumentation at this period was largely a matter of choice and circumstance. Flutes or oboes might play the violin parts, and if either harpsichord or cello or their substitutes were unavailable, the piece could be played with only one of them representing the continuo. But a complete continuo was preferred.

Corelli's importance is as much historical as musical. Perhaps because a vigorous line of Italian composers of violin music followed him, he is commonly accorded the main credit for late 17th-century developments in sonata style. But his undeniably vital contribution should not distract attention from equally important work that was done around the same time outside Italy.

Early development outside Italy

In France Jean-Baptiste Lully's lucrative monopoly of music at the royal court and the immense popularity of spectacular ballets used as courtly entertainments naturally led, through François Couperin (1668–1733), to a concentration on the smaller dance forms found in the ballet and courtly social dance. This concentration gave the French school its preeminence as producer and influencer of the 18th-century dance suite. The French, thus occupied with dance music, had little effect on the growth of the *sonata da chiesa.* But in Germany, where in 1619 Michael Praetorius (1571–1621) published some of the earliest sonatas, the sonata developed from an originally close relation to the suite into a more ambitious blend. As it evolved it combined the suitelike multisectional structure of the *sonata da camera* with the contrapuntal workmanship and emotional intensity of the Italian *sonata da chiesa* form.

One of the first contributors to this development of

the Italian influence was the Austrian composer Johann Heinrich Schmelzer (*c.* 1623–80). In Nürnberg in 1659 he published a set of trio sonatas for strings, following it in 1662 with a set for mixed strings and wind instruments, and in 1664 with what may have been the first set of sonatas for unaccompanied violin. The German composer Johann Rosenmüller (*c.* 1620–84) spent several years in Italy; his *Sonate da camera cioè sinfonie* (*i.e.*, suites or symphonies), published in Venice in 1667, are essentially dance compositions. But 12 years later, in Nürnberg, he issued a set of sonatas in two, three, four, and five parts that vividly illustrate the German trend toward more abstract musical structure and expressive counterpoint. During this period even pieces with dance titles began to lose their danceable character and became compositions meant only for listening.

Meanwhile, the greatest member of this school, Heinrich Ignaz Franz von Biber (1644–1704), published several sets of sonatas—some for violin and continuo, others in three, four, and five parts. In these, from 1676 onward, he took a penchant for expressiveness to extremes of sometimes bizarre but often gripping profundity that contrast sharply with the bland, polished style of Corelli. The titles of some of Biber's sets of sonatas specifically indicate his aim of reconciling church and chamber styles. The 1676 publication, for instance, is entitled *Sonatae tam aris quam aulis servientes* (*Sonatas for the Altar as Well as the Hall*). And being himself, like Corelli, a violinist of extraordinary powers, Biber made a valuable contribution to the development of instrumental technique in a set of sonatas for unaccompanied violin in which the practice of *scordatura* (adjustment of tuning to secure special effects) is ingeniously exploited.

Contribution of English polyphony

The English composers were achieving a comparable intensification of expression during the 17th century, though in their case the technical starting point was different. In accordance with the characteristic time-lag of the English in the adoption of new European musical methods, the English continued to work with polyphony in the Renaissance manner, while the Italians were perfecting monody and the Germans fruitfully uniting monody with their own contrapuntal tradition. English polyphony in the 17th century attained a remarkable level of technical finish and emotional grandeur. Thomas Tomkins (1572–1656), Orlando Gibbons (1583–1625), John Jenkins (1592–1678), and William Lawes (1602–45) were the chief agents of this refining process. They and their predecessors, notably John Coperario (*c.* 1575–1626), made a gradual transition from the string fantasia bequeathed by William Byrd and other composers during the reign of Elizabeth I (1558–1603) and approached the new kind of musical form associated with the Baroque sonata; but they always stayed closer than their continental colleagues to the spirit of polyphony.

When Henry Purcell (*c.* 1659–95), in his three-part and four-part sonatas, submitted this rich English tradition to the belated impact of French and Italian influence, he produced a fusion of styles that was the highest point of musical inspiration yet reached by the emergent sonata form.

The Baroque era. The years from the end of the 17th century to the middle of the 18th represent a moment of equilibrium in the interaction of counterpoint and monody that had created the Baroque sonata. The continuo device, as long as it endured, was a sign that the balance still held—and it did endure as long as the trio sonata kept its central position as a chamber-music medium. During the first half of the 18th century the later Italian violinists, most notably Vivaldi, were prolific creators of trio sonatas. Sometimes they leaned to a three-movement pattern (fast–slow–fast), influenced by the direction the Italian operatic sinfonia, or overture, was taking. More often the old four-movement pattern was preserved. In this well-tested shape, too, Georg Philipp Telemann (1681–1767) produced hundreds of examples that maintained a remarkably consistent standard of musical interest, George Frideric Handel (1685–1759), working for most of his life in England, composed some trio sonatas, and also some valuable sonatas for solo instrument with continuo. In France, Joseph Bodin de Boismortier (1691–1755) and the violinist Jean-Marie Leclair the elder (1697–1764) cultivated both solo and trio genres with charm although with less profundity.

Rise of tonal consciousness

Yet even while the sonata with continuo flourished, the forces of tonality, or organization in terms of keys, developed intensely toward a use of key contrast that would eventually drive the trio sonata from the scene. The continuo itself was being undermined by the growth of interest in instrumental colour, and the figured bass could not long survive the tendency toward scoring for specific instruments and exhaustive detailed musical notation.

Beginning in 1695 Johann Kuhnau (1660–1722) had published the first sonatas for keyboard instrument alone, some of them programmatic pieces on biblical subjects. J.S. Bach (1685–1750), the greatest composer of Baroque sonatas, continued the move away from the treatment of the keyboard in the subordinate, "filling-in" capacity that was its role in the continuo. He wrote a small number of trio sonatas after the traditional scheme, and also a few violin and flute sonatas with continuo; but at the same time he produced the first violin sonatas with obbligato harpsichord parts (that is, obligatory and fully written out, rather than improvised), others for flute or viola da gamba with obbligato harpsichord, and three sonatas (along with three partitas) for unaccompanied violin.

In these works, as in some of Telemann's later sonatas, the power of key or tonality to articulate sections of musical structure, and its ability to provide a harmonically derived eventfulness—a sense of expectation succeeded by fulfillment—began to make itself felt. These powers of key are the seed from which the Classical sonata form originated. But at this point the dualism engendered by tonal and thematic contrast had not yet supplanted the more continuous, unitary processes at work in a composition based on counterpoint. Nor was the consciousness of tonality any more advanced in the otherwise forward-looking work of Domenico Scarlatti (1685–1757). His harpsichord sonatas—555 movements survive, many designed to be played in pairs or in groups of three—are often original to the point of idiosyncrasy in expression. They introduced a valuable new flexibility in the treatment of binary form, and they had a powerful effect on the development of keyboard writing. But in formal terms they still belong in the old world of unity—even their strongest contrasts have an air of being suspended in time, quite unlike the far-ranging effects of conflict through time that are the basis of the Classical sonata.

Transition from Baroque to Classical

A later generation of composers completed the transition from Baroque to Classical sonata. One of J.S. Bach's sons, Carl Philipp Emmanuel Bach (1714–88), plunged enthusiastically into the new resource of dramatic contrast. In about 70 harpsichord sonatas, and in other works for chamber ensembles and for orchestra, he placed a new stress on key contrast not only between but, more important, within movements. Correspondingly, he emphasized the art of transition.

In the development of sonata form in orchestral music, particular value attaches to the work of the Austrians Georg Matthias Monn (1717–50) and Georg Christoph Wagenseil (1715–77) and of the Italian Giovanni Battista Sammartini (1701–75). All three played vital roles in shaping the symphony, which assumed an importance equal to that of the solo or small-ensemble sonata. Their symphonies further stressed the individual characterization of themes and, in particular, the use of the second subject to shape form. Another of Bach's sons, Wilhelm Friedemann Bach (1710–84), made sporadic but interesting contributions to this development, and a third, Johann Christian Bach (1732–82), who settled in London, exploited a vein of melodic charm that influenced Mozart.

The Classical era and later. By about 1770 most of the specific changes that dictated the shift from Baroque sonata to Classical sonata were firmly established. Through the work of the Neapolitan school of opera led by Domenico Scarlatti's father Alessandro (1660–1725), the operatic sinfonia, or overture, had streamlined the traditional *sonata da chiesa.* It omitted the opening slow movement and abandoned the fugal manner that was the first allegro's link with the past. In the new three-movement pattern, a minuet sometimes replaced the fast, abstract finale. In other cases, the inclusion of both minuet and finale brought the number of movements back to four. The south German Mannheim school of composers —most notably Johann Wenzel Stamitz (1717–57) and his son Karl (1745–1801)—developed the technique of the orchestra, whose resources now provided an ideal laboratory for experimentation with the dramatic effects of tonal contrast.

By this time the Classical sonata proper (*i.e.,* with at least one movement in sonata form), whether in the medium of sonata, trio, quartet, quintet, or symphony, could provide a vehicle for consolidating the process begun nearly two centuries earlier by the revolution from equal-voiced polyphony to monody, with its emphasis on melody and harmony. The Rococo style of the mid-18th century, generally known as *style galant,* had attained a halfway stage in which counterpoint had been virtually dropped and tunes had occupied the forefront of interest. But now, in the mature Classical style of Haydn and Mozart, superficial melodic interest was in turn subordinated. In this style the value of tunes lay in their role as functions of tonality. Key by this time had had assumed a central role as the fundamental articulator of form. As a corollary, musical themes were often, though not always, reduced to the status of mere motives, or tags. The theme's harmonic implications, which contribute to the feeling of key, took precedence over its attractiveness as melody.

Subordination of melody to tonality

The new musical principle—that of contrast of key—reached full expression in Haydn and Mozart through their use of sonata form as a principle of musical organization. Haydn's most valuable work in the sonata form is found in his series of over 80 string quartets, over 100 symphonies, 52 keyboard sonatas, and 31 trios for piano, violin, and cello. Unlike Haydn, Mozart was at his greatest in the fields of opera and of the solo concerto. (The latter, though it shared with sonata form such elements as the central principle of key contrast, was a medium that evolved, through the Baroque concerto grosso, from the fundamentally different source of the solo vocal aria and the vocal-instrumental concerto.) But in the last six symphonies, the last 10 string quartets, about a dozen keyboard sonatas, and several trios, quartets, quintets, and serenades, Mozart achieved outstanding examples of sonata structures. The formerly prominent sonata for violin plays a relatively minor part in both men's output: the violin had been eclipsed by the rise of interest in keyboard instruments. It was reintroduced almost surreptitiously as a distinctly subordinate partner and regained a leading role only toward the end of the 18th century in Mozart's later violin sonatas and then in Beethoven's.

The strikingly individual details in Haydn's and Mozart's handling of sonata form are all features consonant with the general outlines of the form. Examples of different approaches include Haydn's taste for combining dualistic key schemes with monistic thematic material (that is, the use of the same basic theme in both keys). He also frequently set slow movements in keys only distantly related to the key of the first movement. Mozart preferred strongly differentiated themes, and he often reshaped his second subjects drastically when they reappeared in the recapitulation. Beethoven, in his sonata compositions (preeminently, the 32 piano sonatas, the 16 string quartets, the trios, the 9 symphonies, and the sonatas for violin and for cello), retained the basic sonata form. But he vastly extended its scale; *e.g.,* by increasing the importance of the coda, or concluding section, and by using unusual keys in the exposition, which was greatly increased in length. He also introduced extramusical implications of a profound philosophical nature. In his later sonatas and quartets he began to move away from the dualistic sonata principle and back to the monistic approach exemplified in variation form and fugue.

The case of Franz Schubert (1797–1828) is quite different. The first movement of the *Symphony No. 5 in B Flat Major* (written when he was 19) is one among several places that illustrates a changing attitude to sonata principles. In the recapitulation of this movement, the first theme is given in the subdominant key (the key whose keynote is five tones below that of the tonic, or home key, as F–C, just as the tonic's keynote is five tones below that of the dominant key, as C–G). This device enables Schubert to place the second theme in the tonic key (the goal of the recapitulation) without altering the transition between the two themes; for the same passage that, in the exposition, took the music from the tonic to the dominant serves, in the recapitulation, to take it from the subdominant to the tonic. This essentially labour-saving procedure is evidence of a certain lack of patience with the workings of sonata form as hitherto practiced. Up to this time, sonata form, first treated as a textbook study after Schubert's death, was not a set of rules codified by theorists and followed by composers. Rather, it was a principle of composition that grew out of earlier forms and that can be generalized from an examination of the actual work of Haydn, Mozart, Beethoven, and their contemporaries.

19th-century trends

Schubert's interests lay in new directions, and the first steps in two such directions are to be found in the greatest of his instrumental works. His later sonata-form compositions in all media—when they follow the rough traditional scheme of exposition, development, and recapitulation—modify it substantially. He frequently expanded the number of tonal centres (central keys) in the exposition, and sometimes also the number of basic themes, from two to three. This tendency to expansion affects the whole subsequent course of the Austro-German symphonic tradition. It is the direct ancestor of the expositions of Anton Bruckner (1824–96), with their three distinct thematic groups, and of the vastly extended sonata structures of Gustav Mahler (1860–1911). At the same time, Schubert's *Fantasy in C Major (Wanderer)* for piano (1822) exemplifies an opposite 19th-century trend toward contraction, through the fusion of the sonata's formerly separate movements in one closely integrated whole: the four movements of the fantasy are based on transformed versions of a single theme. Similarly, in France, Hector Berlioz (1803–69) in his *Symphonie fantastique* transformed the theme representing the artist's beloved (the *idée fixe,* or fixed idea) so that it took different forms in each movement. In this case the transformation was affected by the program or "plot" of the symphony. This was a departure from the abstract, or plotless, character of the Classical sonata. The tendency to fusion—that is, to thematic unity between movements—was the source of the thematic transformations used in symphonic poems, such as those of Franz Liszt (1811–86), as a basic principle of musical structure. But in these works the program rather than any abstract musical form suggests the particular course of the transformation of the themes. For this reason their specific form does not depend, as did that of the Classical sonata, on the exposition–development–recapitulation principle of contrast, conflict, and reconciliation of keys. A corresponding evolution away from the Classical form of the sonata for one instrument occurs in Liszt's one-movement *Piano Sonata in B Minor* (1853). In this work he used a single extended movement with subdivisions analogous to the sections of sonata form. But the specific use of his four themes, which are transformed and combined in free fashion, departs from the usual order of the classical Sonata.

The influence of program music

Robert Schumann (1810–56) likewise experimented fruitfully, especially in his *Symphony No. 4 in D Minor,* with the Schubertian idea of fusing movements together. The tendency to use thematic transformation in a manner that moved away from the Classical sonata form was complemented by César Franck, who adhered to the basic form but from 1841 utilized a "cyclic" approach; that is, one of fusion, or thematic relationships between movements. Brahms, on the other hand, carried the more familiar Classical sonata form to its highest point of complexity. In addition to making valuable innovations in rhythmic structure, he gave the role of counterpoint a new lease of vigour and interest and used the concept of thematic relationships between movements in a particularly subtle way. Chopin's three piano sonatas are concerned more with lyrical expression than with innovative formal methods. Similarly, the sonata compositions of Carl Maria von Weber (1786–1826) and Felix Mendelssohn (1809–47), which generally followed the patterns of their Classical predecessors and were highly regarded in their day, contributed little to the evolution of sonata form away from its Classical state. This evolution, illustrated by the works of Berlioz and Liszt, was carried forward by Mahler. In his symphonies expansion, through inclusion of more than two tonal centres and groups of themes, and fusion, or the creation of unity between movements, are combined. This gives rise to expansive compositions held together by complex interrelationships between themes. Arnold Schoenberg (1874–1951), in such works as his *First String Quartet* (1904), carried the idea of fusion of movements to its logical conclusion: this is a one-movement work with contrasting sections in which all the themes used are derived from a few basic motives.

Weakening of the Classical sonata form

Two important 19th-century developments tended to weaken the effectiveness of the Classical sonata form as an organizing principle. One, exemplified by Richard Wagner (1813–83), was an increasing use of chromaticism; that is, of notes and chords foreign to the key in which a passage of music is written. Chromaticism, when used extensively, broke down key feeling. Instead of being heard as a contrast to, or special modification of, the key, it became so prominent that the key itself was not heard strongly enough to establish itself in the listener's mind. Secondly, Liszt and his followers weakened the sonata form by using in their symphonic poems musical organizations based on program rather than on contrast of keys. But although the effectiveness of key as a basis for musical organization was weakened by the late 19th century, Mahler and Carl Nielsen (1865–1931) provided a modification of the sonata form that made use of tonality in a new way. This innovation, progressive tonality, used the home key as a goal to be worked toward from more or less distant key regions, so that a work ends in a different key from the one in which it began. Mahler and Nielsen arrived at the same notion independently at the same time. Nielsen's *First Symphony* and Mahler's *Second Symphony* (both 1894) are the first to use progressive tonality, and both composers forged highly individual new forms from it.

Most compositions written in sonata form after Wagner's era, however, lack a certain sense of vitality. Frequently, because the effectiveness of key or tonality has been weakened, such compositions centre on melody without the strong contrast of tonality that underlay the Classical sonata. Some composers made stylistic compromises. Schoenberg's *Fourth String Quartet* used his 12-tone (dodecaphonic) approach to composition, an approach that began with a "row," or series, of the 12 tones of the chromatic scale, chosen by the composer to serve as the melodic and harmonic basis for the composition. In this work he fits the 12-tone style into the outlines of sonata form. The result is based on contrasting themes, rather than on the Classical sonata principle of key contrast, because 12-tone music, being atonal, deliberately avoids the creation of a sense of key. In a comparable way, though in the context of a different style, some of the sonatas of Sergey Prokofiev (1891–1953) use the outward formal divisions of the classical sonata form but stress the interest of melody as such, leaving tonality—still present in this case—to play a decorative rather than a structural role.

New principles

Other modern composers developed new principles of musical form. Although these principles appear in genres traditionally associated with the sonata, such as instrumental sonatas, string quartets, and orchestral works, they vary in the degree to which they are or are not related to the Classical sonata form.

One of the more useful of such principles has been the technique of constructing large-scale compositions from transformations and developments of a single germinal motive, often merely two or three notes. Like Schoenberg's approach, in which a 12-tone row is transformed, this is actually the application at a more radical and consistent level of the 19th-century principle of thematic transformation. The symphonies of Jean Sibelius (1865–1957) are based on this method. So are those of Ralph Vaughan Williams (1872–1958), who also used some of the features of sonata form but imaginatively reshaped them and transformed their proportions to suit his purpose. In the nonsonata works of Schoenberg and his pupils Alban Berg (1885–1935) and Anton Webern (1883–1945), the 12-tone method produced legitimate new forms of the highest historical importance; but when forced into an uncomfortable liaison with earlier schemes of organization such as the sonata, its effectiveness diminished. In the works of Béla Bartók (1881–1945), passages built on folk music scales, rather than on the major and minor scales of 18th- and 19th-century keys or tonalities, are used alongside atonal passages. His musical structure frequently takes the form of a combination of elements of sonata form with a simple "archlike" structure such as A B C B A. Paul Hindemith (1895–1963) contributed copiously to the sonata medium with works for almost every known instrument, but as far as the form was concerned his innovations were of minor significance. Sir Michael Tippett in his *Second Symphony* and sonatas (*e.g.,* for piano; for four horns) uses tonality in a fresh and valid way, and he has effected a stimulating rapprochement of the sonata form with the equal-voice polyphony characteristic of the English fantasia and madrigal (a genre of part-song) of Elizabethan and Jacobean times. The *Second Symphony* of Wilfred Josephs shows yet another potentially valuable reinterpretation of the fused-movement approach to the sonata: its long first movement serves the function of exposition, three intermediate movements act on one level as development and on another level as a combination of slow movement and scherzo, and a brief finale serves as a kind of recapitulation.

Other musical approaches use metre and instrumental tone colour to mark important musical points much as traditional sonata form used contrast of keys. Elliott Carter has combined a use of germinal motifs with a new rhythmic technique known as "metric modulation," a controlled change of metre foreshadowed in Brahms by such passages as the end of the *Second Piano Concerto.* Carter's *Sonata for Cello and Piano* is an example of this use of metre. Carter also uses the idea of sharply differentiating the musical subject matter given to the individual instruments of an ensemble—a resource found earlier in the *Second String Quartet* of Charles Ives (1874–1954). Some of the many styles of Igor Stravinsky (1882–1971), particularly after his late adoption of the 12-tone approach, make ingenious use of germinal motifs; but his music really bases its structure on the juxtaposition of large blocks of distinct musical character, rather than on "development" in the sense traditionally associated with the sonata.

Music in the latter half of the 20th century is too various in form, medium, esthetic attitude, and social function to allow any confident predictions. But all of these examples suggest that the sonata, and its special manifestation, the sonata form, can still provide composers with fertile areas of activity. As in the time of Haydn, Mozart, and Beethoven, success will continue to reward those who develop musical forms that grow naturally from the specific principles of composition used in their works, much as the sonata form grew out of the principle of contrast, conflict, and resolution of tonalities that characterized the sonatas, symphonies, and chamber music of the 18th and 19th centuries. (B.Ja.)

CONCERTO

Since about 1750 the term concerto has been applied primarily to the solo concerto; *i.e.,* a musical composition for instruments alone in which an orchestra and a soloist interrelate by alternating, competing, or combining on a more or less equal footing. In this sense the concerto, like the symphony or the string quartet, may be seen as a special case of the generic musical form embraced by the term sonata. Like the sonata and symphony, the concerto is typically a cycle of several contrasting movements integrated tonally and often thematically. The individual movements are usually based on certain recognized designs, including sonata form, A B A (the letters refer to large distinct musical sections), variations, and rondo (such as A B A C A).

But the concerto tends to differ from the sonata, too, in certain ways that set it apart. Thus, in the sonata form of the concerto's first movement, the exposition often remains in the tonic key while played by the entire orchestra the first time through. The expected departure to a nearly related key and the introduction of the soloist are reserved to a characteristically more elaborate repetition of the exposition. Moreover, to meet a felt need for a more brilliant ending in the same movement, the concerto provides or at least invites an improvised cadenza near the end of the movement—an extended, free flourish that may go on for as long as several minutes. A shorter cadenza may also occur at a strategic point in one or more of the other movements. In addition, the concerto has followed much more consistently than the sonata the plan of three movements, in the order fast–slow–fast. The second movement leads, often without pause, into the finale, or last movement, and the finale has shown a more consistent preference for the rondo design. But, importantly, all of these distinctions of musical form are secondary to the dialogue inherent in the concerto's interrelationship of soloist and orchestra. This dialogue influences the very nature of the solo part by almost forcing the soloist into a virtuoso's role so that he can compete on an equal footing with his adversary, the orchestra. The dialogue, furthermore, influences not only the construction of individual musical phrases but also the musical textures chosen. In addition, it affects the ways of developing musical material (*e.g.,* themes, rhythms) according to the logic of musical form, and even the broader blocking off of sections within forms, as in the concerto's repeated exposition, with its sections for full orchestra (tutti) and soloist.

Dialogue between soloist and orchestra

The literature of the concerto since 1750 is extensive in all categories, although the standard repertoire is limited to scarcely more than a few works for each main solo instrument. Being a prime ingredient of popular concert fare, the concerto is subject, much as is opera, to the exigencies of the box office. The film and phonograph industries have helped further to give disproportionate promience to a few highly successful and undeniably effective examples like those for piano by the Norwegian Edvard Grieg (in A minor) and the Russians Peter Ilich Tchaikovsky (in B flat minor) and Sergey Rachmaninoff (in C minor).

Taking music's commonly accepted eras for its framework, this examination of the concerto starts in the late Renaissance (16th century), with the origins and first uses of the term. It proceeds to the Baroque era (about 1580 to 1750), which was the first main era of the concerto, including the vocal-instrumental concerto in the late 16th and 17th centuries and, especially, the concerto grosso in the late 17th and early 18th centuries. The discussion progresses next to the Classical era (about 1730 to 1830) and the Romantic era (about 1790 to 1915), which mark successive though dissimilar heydays of the solo concerto partially discussed above. Lastly it reaches the modern era (from about 1890), which has witnessed further vitality in the solo concerto and a renaissance of the older concerto grosso principle of contrasting instrumental groups. Within each era examined, the prime considerations of the discussion are the meanings of "concerto" as then current; the concerto's place in the social life of the time; its scoring, or particular use of musical instruments and voices; its means of achieving opposition and contrast (if any); its musical structure; and its output by chief regions and masters.

Origins of the concerto. The word concerto has given trouble to music historians concerned with word origins because within a century after its first known applications to music, in the early 1500s, it had acquired two meanings that would seem to be mutually exclusive. One meaning still current in Italian is that of "agreement," or, as in English, of being "in concert." The other is that of "competing" or "contesting," from the Latin *concerto, -are, -atus* ("to contend"). Probably derived from the same Latin word are such related terms as the Italian *conserto, concertato,* and *concertante;* the Spanish *concierto;* the French *concert* and *concertant;* and the English consort. Yet it is this dual meaning itself that offers the most tangible thread of unity throughout the four-century history of the concerto in its various forms. In other words, the concerto, in whatever guise it assumes, reveals a continuing need to resolve the antithetical ideas of concord and contest. The balance between contest and concord is the concerto's particular solution to the problem of variety within unity that must be resolved in all dynamic art forms.

Original dual meaning of concerto

In the 16th century the word concerto embodied several meanings. As early as 1519 in Rome it referred simply to a vocal or instrumental group (*un concerto di voci in musica*). By 1551 it was used with implications of musical texture, specifically of the contrast of soprano voice with bass and alto ("soprano in concerto col basso & alto"). By 1565 the cognate word concertato was being used in reference to both voices and instruments. And by 1584 a Venetian title, *Musica . . . per cantar e sonar in concerti,* brought forth the meaning of group presentations or concerts.

Although in 1578 "concerti" was used to mean the music itself, for both voices and instruments (rather than performers or concerts), the first formal musical title of this sort appeared in 1587. This was the *Concerti . . . a 6–16 voci* (*Concertos . . . in 6 to 16 Parts*), a collection of vocal and instrumental music by the Venetian composer Andrea Gabrieli and his nephew Giovanni Gabrieli. No formal title concerto is known to be given to strictly instrumental music before 1621, and then the word means both "concerted" or "playing together" and "technically [or even 'virtuosically'] elaborated." This title, with significant implications of a new style—that of the virtuoso soloist—is the *Sonate concertate in stilo moderno* (*Concerted Sonatas in the Modern Style*), by an Italian, Dario Castello, a collection for a violin and for a bassoon that elaborates on the basso continuo part. (The basso continuo, a constant device of Baroque music, calls for a low, sustained-tone instrument—*e.g.,* cello, viola da gamba, bassoon—playing the bass line, plus one or more chordal instruments—*e.g.,* harpsichord, organ, lute—that improvise harmonies above the bass line. Small numbers, or figures, are often placed above the bass line music as a guide to the harmonies, hence the term figured bass.)

In these early, loosely titled collections by the Gabrielis and by Castello, there can be found at least five of the means of contention or opposition that later became closely identified with the *stile concertato* or concerto. Listed in their approximate order of evolution, they include opposition between voices and instruments; between one choir and another (whether of voices or instruments); between the essential basso continuo and its melodic elaboration; between simple, straightforward parts and more decorative, virtuoso parts; and between two or more voices or instrumental parts engaged in imitative or motivic interplay.

Means of contrast

Within the span of a century and a half the Baroque era saw the word concerto change from a broad general term applied on several musical levels to a fairly specific term whose meaning had two senses: that of an instrumental group and that of a musical structure or process. Thus in the Gabrielis' early Baroque "Concerti" the title referred to a collection consisting of church motets (Latin choral compositions) and madrigals (similar Italian compositions) for six to 12 voices in one or two choruses, without and with instruments; a piece for eight voices imitating a battle; and a "Ricercar per sonar" for eight instruments (a ricercar is a piece often based on melodic imitation; *sonar* means to play instrumentally). By contrast the more than 460 late-Baroque "Concerti" composed by the Italian Antonio Vivaldi from the first half of the 18th century are purely instrumental works, mostly three-movement cycles (fast–slow–fast) for one to four soloists and strings with or without other orchestral instruments.

The same century and a half saw a similar narrowing of definition in two closely allied terms: sonata and sinfonia. Before sonata, sinfonia, and concerto became clearly defined and attained a degree of mutual exclusion, they often overlapped and were sometimes even equated in meaning. The full title on one musical manuscript by the Italian Alessandro Stradella, for example, reads, *Sonata di viole, cioé per concerto grosso di viole, concertino di due violino e leuto* (*Sonata for Viols, that is, for Full Complement* [*concerto grosso*] *of Viols, and Small Group* [*concertino*] *of Two: Violin and Lute*). Another reads, *Sinfonia per violini*

Sonata, symphony, and concerto

e bassi a due concertini distinti (*Sinfonia for Violins and Basses in Two Distinct Groups*). Many so-called trumpet sonatas of the same period, especially those by Domenico Gabrielli and Giuseppe Jacchini, simply equate the three terms without distinction. When Tommaso Antonio Vitali entitled his Opus 4 *Concerto di sonate* . . . (published 1701), he evidently meant no more than "A Collection of Sonatas," for there was only a violin part, a basso continuo part, and the *concertate* cello part that so often elaborated on the basso continuo. But later, when "Concerto" was crossed off a harpsichord solo by the German composer Johann David Heinichen, copied posthumously in 1731, and "Sonata" was entered in its place, the intention was probably to choose a title more identified with the performing instrument, although the work may well have been transcribed from a concerto.

Cross-influences

It is no wonder, then, that even the traits most basically identified with the concerto can be found in works of other titles. G. Gabrieli wrote works for as many as five opposed choirs of instruments under the title of "Sonata." The "sonatas" of the German composers Johann Joseph Fux and Georg Muffat have passages actually marked "T." and "S." for tutti and soli (soloists) groupings, and, indeed, the tutti–soli principle of contrast still operates strongly in the classical symphonies of Haydn and Mozart. These cross-influences are important reminders that any full history of the concerto idea must take into account not only the concerti in the literature but many works with other titles. Yet in a more concise, encyclopaedic summary it is necessary to stay close to the evolution of the term concerto itself, and there is a real significance in observing how the word acquired definition. The evolution of the word in effect reveals the composers' own developing concepts of it. Concerto was the last of the three terms (sonata, sinfonia, concerto) to attain clear definition. In part this was because the word first had to grow free of its original association with music for both voices and instruments.

The Baroque vocal-instrumental concerto (c. 1585–1650). As already suggested, the first category of music to be associated significantly with the term concerto was that of the vocal-instrumental concerto. If this category is sometimes incorporated only incidentally into overall accounts of the concerto, the reasons lie, first, in its lack of clear identification with any one type of musical form and, second, in the longer, more vivid association of all later categories of the concerto with music exclusively for instruments.

Both the early association of the word with vocal-instrumental combinations and the lack of a clear, identifiable musical form are apparent in the important discussion of the concerto in 1619 by the German composer and theorist Michael Praetorius in his *Syntagma Musicum* ("Writings on Music"). Praetorius classified the concerto, along with the motet and the *falsobordone* (or simple harmonization of a liturgical reciting tone), among vocal pieces that have a sacred or serious secular text. He recognized the two general, and related, types that were to prevail in the vocal-instrumental concerto. The multivoice type was in more than four parts and typically subdivided into opposing choirs, especially low versus high choirs. The few-voice type was for one to four parts; often solo parts, and basso continuo; according to Praetorius, this type, which permitted the text to be understood better, was then replacing the madrigal in Italy. Aside from implications of modernism and greater appeal in the concerto and conservatism and greater weightiness in the motet, Praetorius found no distinction between *concert, concertos ecclesiasticos, sacras cantiones, sacros concentus,* and *motettas.*

Praetorius found that the concerto was performed especially in the church and, particularly the few-voiced type, in the monastery. Today one surmises from titles and prefaces to published concerti, from contemporary paintings, and even from the kinds of instruments specified, that the main social breeding ground for the vocal-instrumental concerto was the chapel, above all the court chapel, and the chapel's resources of musicians and instruments were in fact largely those called for by the concerti of the time.

The distinction that Praetorius drew between the multi-voice, polychoir concerto and the few-voice, soloistic concerto proved to be the most significant distinction throughout the course of the vocal-instrumental concerto. Yet the two types were not independent of each other but were interrelated in their common derivation from the late-Renaissance, polyphonic madrigal and motet. Moreover, they were interdependent. On the one hand, the few-voiced concerto thrived not only on the desire to make the text more understandable and hence more appealing but also on a practical need, in the smaller, less fortunate chapels, to reduce the larger vocal and instrumental groupings to such resources as were available locally (as, for example, during the economizations in Germany brought on by the Thirty Years' War, 1618–48). On the other hand, the polychoir and other larger groupings thrived not only on the desire for more massive, imposing sound but on the opportunity that larger, better staffed chapels provided to expand compositions written for the smaller groupings, whether by adopting alternative scorings that the composer might provide or by improvising other dispositions to suit the immediate place and occasion.

Freedom in use of singers and instruments

There is a clear instance of expanding the scoring in one Gabriele Fattorini's . . . *Sacri concerti a due voci* . . . (. . . *Sacred Concerts for Two Voices* . . .). This work appeared originally in 1600 merely "with a basso continuo for the greater convenience of organists" and only two years later was republished "with a new addition of some four-part ripieni [or *tutti* groupings] to sing in two [opposed] choirs." A good hint of the improvisatory practices is offered in the *Vezzo di perle musicali* (1610; *Necklace of Musical Pearls*), by Adriano Banchieri. Banchieri explains that his pieces are arranged so that "the same concerto can be altered in six ways over the *basso seguente* [a composite bass line taken from the lowest notes in whatever parts], with one or more parts, whether vocal or instrumental."

The natural consequence of this much interdependence and interrelationship of the two types, multivoice and few-voice, was their fusion in vocal-instrumental concerti that provided the massive oppositions of the larger groups, the subjective intensity of the soloists, and the opposition between group and soloist. This fusion, especially in Protestant Germany, often with the incorporation of a Protestant chorale, or hymn, substantially influenced the subsequent development of the German cantata, which was frequently based on a chorale and, like the vocal-instrumental concerto, included vocal soloists, choir, and instruments.

Influences of the Protestant chorale

A more specific idea of the Baroque vocal-instrumental concerto might best be given by a brief description of the scoring and nature of six successive, representative examples, running from shortly after the pioneer collection by the Gabrielis in 1587 to a late collection (1650) by the German composer Heinrich Schütz. Banchieri's *Concerti ecclesiastici,* published in Venice in 1595, consists entirely of eight-part motets for double chorus, with a "score" added for organ. This "score" for this double-chorus collection consisted of the soprano and partially figured bass parts of the first chorus only—a partial score enabling the keyboard player to orient himself. Unlike the Gabrieli collection of concerti, Banchieri's is composed exclusively of sacred texts. By contrast, Lodovico da Viadana's popular and influential *Cento concerti ecclesiastici a 1, a 2, a 3, e a 4 voci, con il basso continuo per sonar nell'organo* (*100 Ecclesiastical Concertos* [*i.e.,* motets] *for One, Two, Three, and Four Voices, with the Basso Continuo to be Played on the Organ;* Venice, 1602) exploits the new style, simpler and more intimate, yet florid and expressive, and including actual monody (solo vocal melody accompanied by expressive harmonies, a type of music new with the Baroque Era). These "concerti" achieve opposition mainly through the polarity of upper part(s) and bass, including such dispositions as two tenors and bass, tenor and two trombones, or two sopranos and two basses. In an important preface, especially treating of the organ part, Viadana argued that the reduction from the multivoice type of motet to these new few-voice "concerti" was made possible by the device of the basso continuo and its realization (*i.e.,* the improvised harmonies), which serve as a filler in lieu of the missing parts. Similar oppositions of high and low parts, but with secular texts and still greater variety, appeared in the *Concerto, Settimo libro de madrigali a 1, 2, 3, 4, & 6 voci, con altri generi de canti* (*Concerto* [*i.e.,* ensemble or concert consisting of the], *Seventh Book of Madrigals in 1, 2, 3, 4, & 6 Voices* [plus basso continuo], *with Other Kinds of Songs;* Venice, 1619), by the celebrated composer Claudio Monteverdi. Along with two pieces in homophonic, or chordal, style, labelled "Sinfonia," for five unnamed instruments, the book contains both compositions for smaller groups with virtuosic tendencies in the vocal parts and large pieces employing melodic imitation and suggesting Renaissance polyphony, with its independent melodic lines. An example of the larger type is *Con che soavità* [*With What Gentleness*], *concertato a una voce e 9 instrumenti* (making up three choirs of instruments specified for the viola family and a corpus of bass and filler instruments).

German developments

In the same year (1619), in Wolfenbüttel, Germany, there appeared one of several pertinent collections by Praetorius, *Polyhymnia caduceatrix & panegyrica* (named after the muse Polyhymnia), "containing 40 concertos of solemn peace and joy" for one to 21 or "more voices, arranged in" two to six choirs, "to be performed and used with all sorts of instruments and human voices, also trumpets and kettledrums." As Praetorius made clear in his detailed, prefatory instructions and in broader remarks about his concerti in his *Syntagma Musicum,* his concerti comprise a virtual compendium of the vocal-instrumental concerto in all its uses of voices and instruments and styles of opposition and in all its applications of the Protestant chorale, as well. The German composer Johann Hermann Schein acknowledged the influence of Viadana's more intimate concerti in the first set of his "sacred concertos," *Opella nova I* (1618; *Little New Opus*). But in his second set (Leipzig, 1626), he turned more to the larger scale styles of Praetorius for three to six voices and basso continuo. Representative is No. 12, *Hosianna dem Sohne David* (*Hosannah to the Son of David*), for two sopranos, two tenors, two basses, three *bombardi* (bass shawms), and basso continuo, with alternating sections of instrumental episodes, tutti in chordal style, and melodic imitation. In addition there are passages for three instrumental or vocal soloists, a combination often already encountered in the popular Baroque trio setting of two high parts over a low part. The last main landmarks of the vocal-instrumental concerto were the three sets of Schütz's *Symphoniae sacrae,* or *Sacred Symphonies* (Venice, 1629; Dresden, 1647 and 1650), works that reveal all the variety of treatment to be found in Schein's sacred concerti, except for Schein's interest in the chorale. The first two of Schütz's sets consisted of few-voice settings, mostly one to three voices with one or two obbligato (required solo) instruments and basso continuo. The third set extended to as many as eight parts (some of them optional) and basso continuo; in style it showed a considerable return to the concept of oppositions between choirs, chiefly between vocal and instrumental choirs.

The composers cited here were the main exponents and the Italian and German chapels were the main centres of the early-Baroque, vocal-instrumental concerto. After giving birth to the genre, Italy soon turned to opera, oratorio, and more independent instrumental forms. The Germans, whose derivation from the Italians was direct and unequivocal, developed the idea further and longer before it largely gave way to the Protestant cantata around the mid-17th century. Yet echoes of the vocal-instrumental concerto are still strong in the cantatas of J.S. Bach and his predecessor Dietrich Buxtehude.

The Baroque concerto grosso (c. 1675–1750). Late in the 17th century, within a generation after the vocal-instrumental concerto had last flourished in Germany, the concerto grosso began to assume a clear identity of its own in Italy and soon after in Germany and beyond. Its main ingredients have been noted earlier—the opposition of choirs or choir and soloists, the exchanges of melodic imitation, the trio setting of soloists, and even the use of "concertate" in a title of a purely instrumental work (by Castello). Other purely instrumental precedents of the mature concerto grosso exist in the considerable literature of music for opposing instrumental choirs in numerous "sonatas," "sinfonias," and "canzone" (instrumental pieces in several sections), starting with the works of Giovanni Gabrieli. Such anticipations, including the *Sinfonia à 8* (*i.e.,* in eight parts; 1618) of one Francesco Usper—a fortuitous, miniature concerto grosso in all but the name—accumulated during the 17th century. Good examples are the orchestral "trumpet sonatas" written in Bologna, Italy, during the second half. But not until the 1670s did the term concerto grosso itself come into general use. It indicated the larger of two contrasting instrumental groups within a composition, and in this sense the term was opposed to concertino (the smaller group), and signified the relation of full orchestra to one or more soloists. By 1698 it appeared as an actual title itself, in the published *Concerti grossi . . . ,* by an Italian, Lorenzo Gregori. That this title did indicate a composite concept (*i.e.,* of opposing instrumental groups) is evidenced by frequent distinctions in prefaces and tables of contents between it (or its shorter equivalent, "Concerti") and the sinfonia or sonata. As one example, the *Sinfonie a tre e concerti a quattro* (*Sinfonias in Three Parts and Concertos in Four Parts,* Opus 5; 1692), by the Italian violinist and composer Giuseppe Torelli makes a distinction not only in the number of parts but in the style: between a dense, polyphonic, older style in the sinfonias, often performed with only one player to a part, and a newer, more open style in the concerti, suitable to multiple (orchestral) performance of the parts. As another example, whereas the German Georg Muffat had already called attention to the tuttisoli dispositions in his five orchestral "Sonate" of 1682, when he republished these in 1701 with revisions he changed the title of each to "Concerto."

Early examples of concerti grossi

Place in society

The social function of the concerto grosso was explicitly stated in 1701 by Muffat, who was as articulate about the secular concerto grosso and its performance as Praetorius had been about the sacred vocal-instrumental concerto:

> These concertos [in his *Ausserlesene . . . Instrumental-Music* or, *Selected . . . Instrumental Music*], suited neither to the church (because of the ballet airs and airs of other sorts which they include) nor for dancing (because of other interwoven conceits, now slow and serious, now gay and nimble, and composed only for the express refreshment of the ear), may be performed most appropriately in connection with entertainments given by great princes and lords, for receptions of distinguished guests, and at state banquets, serenades, and assemblies of musical amateurs and virtuosi. (As translated in Oliver Strunk's *Source Readings in Music History,* W.W. Norton and Company, Inc., New York, 1950, p. 449.)

The breeding ground of the concerto, therefore, was no longer the chapel but the court. From the standpoint of the local court administrator the concerto grosso offered certain economic as well as functional advantages, advantages that might even help to account for its predominance in Baroque instrumental music. The opposition of a full orchestra, playing relatively simple parts, to a few soli, playing more difficult, even virtuosic parts, made it possible to entrust the full-orchestra parts to relative novices in the court entourage, often to servants who could play in addition to their other duties. Thus, only a few solo parts had to be played by experts hired primarily as professional musicians. This practical advantage can be argued only while the distinction between simple and difficult parts prevailed. The distinction became less clear as the concerto matured, at least in works with one or more soloists.

Fundamental not only to the scoring but to the style, and even the musical structure of the Baroque concerto, was the opposition between the full orchestra, or *concerto grosso* (also called tutti, or *ripieno*), and the *concertino* (also called soli, or *principale*). A full complement of strings, usually two to four on a part, often sufficed for the "full orchestra," in addition to the one to three instruments needed to play and realize the basso continuo. Usually at least a low melody instrument, bowed or blown, and a chordal instrument, plucked or keyed, were used for the basso continuo. The same trio setting that had been popular from the start of the century, typically two violins and a cello, often served as the concertino. When the concertino was not playing soli passages it figured as part of the *concerto grosso.* Illustrative of these typical settings is the celebrated *Christmas Concerto* (Opus 6, No. 8; 1714), by the Italian violinist and composer Arcangelo Corelli. The basso continuo sometimes rested while the concertino played (a frequent procedure in Vivaldi's concerti). One significant consequence of the tutti–soli relationship and its opposition of weighty and light masses of sound was a tendency to sharpen the contrast with the popular Baroque device of "terrace dynamics," or blocks of contrasting loud and soft sound. This occurred especially in the echo effect of a soli passage played piano after a tutti passage played forte. To this dynamic contrast might be added the rhythmic contrast between steady, solid beats in the tutti and more intricate, quicker figures in the soli, growing out of that same tendency toward simplicity, on the one hand, and virtuosity, on the other. Furthermore, not only all of the melodic ornamentation but also most of the passagework were ordinarily given to the soli rather than the tutti. When the tutti strings were augmented by wind instruments and the concertino was reduced to two players or only one (resulting in the first solo concerti), all these oppositions became that much more pronounced. Attention may be called, too, to the artful highlighting of the contrasts through different spacing—that is, through varied alternations of the two groups, now frequent, now less frequent after longer passages.

Opposition and contrast

These several means of contrast provided by motive interplay hardly exhaust the sources of variety to be found in the Baroque concerto grosso. Much variety is achieved in another of its basic kinds of opposition or competition. This is the motivic (or imitative) interplay between parts that is so characteristic of the *stile concertato,* or concerted style.

Such interplay may occur either between tutti and soli choirs or entirely within a succession of single instrumental parts in the full orchestra. In fact, there are numerous Baroque "concerti" that thrive primarily on the latter style of continuity, without any tutti–soli designations at all (for example, Bach's *Brandenburg Concerto No. 3*). The employment of motivic interplay offers certain inherent contrasts of its own. These include shifts from one high or low range to another within a texture of interwoven melodies: rhythmic conflicts based on patterns that do not necessarily coincide with the regular musical metre; and an almost continuous change of key. The last is achieved by rapid successions of modulations (bridges from key to key) and drives to the cadence; *i.e.,* building up of tension in the harmonies used, culminating and relaxing in the cadence, or stopping point. In fast movements, when the propelling force is not such motivic interplay, it is likely to be a force achieved by outright statements of musical figures based on chords and scales. Or it may be an unfolding succession of figures together with the harmonic drive to the cadence. In slow movements it is likely to be compelling progressions of chords, enhanced by melodic ornamentation and enlivened by continual suspensions, dissonances, and resolutions (*i.e.,* by suspending single notes while the harmony around them changes; this creates dissonance, the tension of harmonies that seem to clash; the tension is "resolved" when the harmonies change again).

In spite of all this variety there are consistencies of style in the scoring and musical textures just described. In addition, certain additional rhythmic and melodic traits help further to bring a sense of overall unity to the concerto grosso. With regard to rhythmic traits, a steady motoric pulse is likely to prevail throughout the fast movements. Also, true to the nature of the ever-present basso continuo, a steady running bass line is likely to underlie both the slow and the fast movements. With regard to melodic traits, one cannot ordinarily speak of "main and contrasting themes" as in the classical and later concerto. One reason is the lack of individuality in the main thematic ideas. Corelli's and Vivaldi's themes, vigorous as they may be rhythmically, hardly stand out melodically from the remaining music. Like the musical context in which they occur, the themes themselves are likely to consist of chord notes, scales, or simple repeated notes. Frequently they are announced in unison (all parts playing the same notes) and thus lack a strong initial association with the harmonies of an accompaniment. Bach is exceptional for the individuality of his themes, especially in the finales, where they are usually out-and-out tunes, memorable and fetching (as in his *Violin Concerto No. 2 in E Major,* BWV 1042). The less a melodic idea stands out, the less it functions as a true "theme" or unifier when it recurs and the less it can contrast with any of the other melodic ideas.

Concerto grosso themes

Such relatively neutral themes and motives, which unfold more as supplements than as contrasts, seem to have satisfied most Baroque, especially North German, tastes, including the express preference for limiting any one piece or movement to but one "Affekt" (or characteristic emotion). In addition, and more important for musical continuity, the themes, such as they are, do tend to recur, not only at the more local level of melodic imitation and motivic interplay but also at certain strategic points in the musical structure. Their recurrence, most often at the three or four main tonal landmarks, imparts at least a vague overall outline of formal musical structure. In fact, these strategic recurrences, plus the melodic imitations, the passagework, and the adjunct musical themes that separate them, produce in a loose way the most prevalent structural principle of the fast movements. This is the rondo principle, which is based on the alternation of a refrain, or "ritornello," with contrasting musical passages. In the more tuneful finales, or final movements, the sense of a rondo "ritornello" is most distinct (as in Handel's Opus 6, No. 11). Generally, the alternations of refrains and intervening episodes tally with alternations of the tutti and soli groups, respectively.

Recurring melodic ideas account for two other of the most frequent principles of musical structure in the concerto grosso, those of fugue and of variation. A fugue is based on the polyphonic treatment (through extensive melodic imitation) of a recurring subject, or theme. In fugal sections of a concerto grosso, tutti and soli unite as one group or alternate in expositions (statements of the subject) and episodes (passages in which the subject appears only fragmentarily, if at all). The fugal style occurs largely in fast movements and varies from loose applications, especially among the Italians, to strict ones, especially among the Germans. The variation process depends on continual variation of a constant factor, such as a theme or a group of harmonies. In the concerto grosso it occurs largely in slow movements; its constant factor is a simple, freely recurring bass line, or ostinato (a short, repeated motive or melody). The ostinato often sounds alone in the tutti and may be played in unison at the beginning and end of the movement. It serves as a foil for the soli parts, which sometimes enter successively on long tones and gradually unfold into decorative, expressive passages (as in Bach's *Violin Concerto No. 2.*) When the ostinato's recurrences are free enough and the bass line and treble melody of the tutti stand out enough, the effect is that of an expressive aria (solo song, as in an opera) with a firm prelude and postlude (as in Vivaldi's Opus 3, No. 8), providing one of the many hints of operatic influences in the concerto grosso. To these structural types—rondo, fugue, and variation—may be added especially the binary design, with each half repeated, that prevails in Baroque dances. In binary form, the music of the first half moves from the tonic key to a closely related key. The second half begins in the new key and progresses back to the original key. Dances abound in concerti grossi, not only in those that are primarily orchestral suites or groups of related dance pieces (as are many by Handel) but in others as well. For instance, the finale of Corelli's Opus 6, No. 3, although headed only "Allegro," is a fine example of a binary gigue (a courtly dance ultimately derived from the jig).

Fugue and variation

The number of movements in the concerto grosso varies more than in the later solo concerto or in the sinfonia, symphony, and sonata at any time after the concerto grosso's emergence. But the average may be put at from three to five. Corelli and other Italian pioneers had led off with more movements (insofar as separate movements can be distinguished from mere sectional changes in their concerti). Vivaldi reduced the number, mostly by omitting an initial slow movement that his predecessors had probably derived from the French overture. Instead, Vivaldi largely settled on and, in fact, standardized the cycle at three movements in fast–slow–fast order. He may have been influenced by the same cycle in the Italian opera sinfonia (or overture). The Germans seem to have varied the number more, with the most movements likely to be made up of relatively short dances. Bach's six *Brandenburg Concertos* do follow the fast–slow–fast plan except that Number 1 adds two dances and No. 3 leaves out the slow movement, simply substituting in its place two slow chords that create a feeling of suspension. Handel's *Twelve Grand Concertos* in Opus 6 contain four to six movements that vary considerably in order and type.

Unity among movements

As usual in tonal music (music based on the system of major and minor keys), additional variety within unity is achieved in the cycle of concerto grosso movements through departure from and return to the home key. Much more often than in the suite, a slow inner movement is placed in a nearly related key. In the shortest, freest slow movements the tonality, or key orientation, sometimes remains uncertain and in flux, giving the sense of a bridge from the previous to the following movement (as in Vivaldi's Opus 3, No. 10). Unlike the Baroque suite and sonata, in the concerto the use of interrelated musical themes is not a frequent means of linking the movements. But the concerto grosso is like these other cycles in its dynamic tendency to progress from the more serious to the lighter movements. Infrequently a "program"—a story or nonmusical image—lends further unity to the cycle, as it does in the four concerti of Vivaldi's Opus 8 that are known collectively as *The Four Seasons.* Each of these concerti is tied closely to a sonnet describing one of the seasons. More often a special unity results from some unusual trait of musical style or use of an instrument. An example is the brilliant solo part given, exceptionally, to the "cembalo concertato" (*i.e.,* a harpsichord that participates with the other instruments in the melodic discourse rather than, as is normal, confining itself to the realization of the basso continuo) in Bach's *Brandenburg Concerto No. 5.*

Like the vocal-instrumental concerto before it, the concerto grosso originated and reached a first peak in Italy, then attained a further peak in Germany. French and English centres responded more than they contributed to it. Again, some of the main landmarks may be briefly noted. The 12 concerti grossi in Opus 6 by Corelli were not first published until 1714, the year after he died. Although they were preceded in print by other pioneer examples, like those of Torelli (from 1698), Tomaso Albinoni (from 1700), and even Vivaldi (from 1712), some of them may have been among the "several concertos" by Corelli that Muffat had already heard in Rome by 1682. Corelli still made the loose distinction, best known in the 17th-century sonata, between *da chiesa* and *da camera*—that is, church and court-style, or serious and light. The first eight of his concerti grossi are *da chiesa* (church-style), in four to seven movements, the last four *da camera* (court-style), in five movements. A trio setting of two violins and cello is specified for the *concertino,* and two violins, viola, and bass for the *concerto grosso,* "which may be doubled as desired." Between the two groups the opposition is not an antiphony of musical ideas but only a change of musical texture and sonority in the continuous unfolding of the short, tasteful, well-proportioned movements.

Vivaldi's more than 460 "Concerti" (written from about 1710 to 1740) bring the Italian contribution to full maturity, and they rank Vivaldi with his contemporaries Bach and Handel among the greatest masters of the concerto grosso. The maturity is marked by larger forms and broader musical architecture, including tighter organization of the rondo principle, and by more distinctive, energetic musical themes, at least rhythmically if not melodically. There is also greater brilliance and exploitation of idiomatic instrumental techniques, including *bariolage* (quick shifts from string to string) and broken chords for the solo violin. Another characteristic is the standardization, as noted earlier, of the three-movement cycle, fast–slow–fast. But if the cycle becomes standardized, with only infrequent exceptions, very little else is predictable about Vivaldi's imaginative, resourceful concerti. Least predictable of all is the scoring, which makes highly varied combinations of string and wind instruments—for example, a tutti of strings with cello and bassoon as the soli; or two oboes, two horns, bassoon, and violin as the soli; or viola d'amore (a violin-like instrument) and lute as the soli.

Starting with Muffat's concerti done under Corelli's immediate guidance, the spread of the instrumental concerto from Italy to Germany was as direct and wide as that of the vocal-instrumental concerto had been. French influences in Germany were considerable, too, especially where the suite touched the concerto. This was often true in the large, resourceful, and highly varied output of the German Georg Philipp Telemann. In Bach's approximately 25 concerti (about 1720–35) Italian influences are especially evident, quite apart from his unusual setting for harpsichord alone specifically entitled *Concerto in the Italian Style.* Again, Italian influence is reflected in the many concerti by Vivaldi and others that Bach transcribed and reworked for harpsichord or for organ. A rare opportunity to learn what mattered most to Bach in concerto structure is provided by a study of his changes in the Vivaldi models. Such changes include themes sharpened melodically and musical textures enriched by the addition of new melodic entries to contrapuntal passages or by more intensive interplay of musical motives. The designs of the musical forms themselves are pointed up by insertions of new musical material, deletions, and altered timing of phrases and entries. Bach summed up the Baroque concerto as he did the cantata, fugue, and other Baroque genres. Besides the transcriptions and the magnificent six *Brandenburg Concertos,* with all their own varieties of scoring, he left concerti in which the solo requirements are one violin; two violins; flute, violin, and harpsichord; violin and oboe; one harpsichord; two harpsichords; three harpsichords; and four harpsichords. The majority of the harpsichord concerti are further transcriptions and reworkings, some not yet tracked to their sources. For example, two of seven solo harpsichord concerti come from Bach's own solo violin concerti, and the concerto for four harpsichords comes from Vivaldi's Opus 3, No. 10, for four violins. These concerti, like the *Brandenburg Concerto No. 5* already noted, emphasize Bach's priority in giving the harpsichord prominence as a concerto solo instrument.

Bach's concerti grossi

Handel's concerto style

Handel left around 35 concerti in all (about 1715–50), including three sets of organ concerti with oboe and strings; one set for strings and winds (Opus 3); one set in the tutti–soli setting for strings alone (Opus 6) that Corelli had used; and several concerti not in sets. Among the last are two works more properly classified in his day as trio sonatas (works usually for two violins and basso continuo but sometimes for orchestra). Transcriptions and reworkings figure in many of Handel's concerti, as in Bach's. Handel's concerto style, like that of his chief contemporary in England, the Italian violinist-composer Francesco Geminiani, is more progressive than Bach's in its frequent French dance influences and in its more open, less complex musical textures. Although imposing fugues can be found, the prevailing atmosphere in Handel's concerti is more often that of light, wide-spaced chamber music. Thanks to his unmatched skill, imagination, good timing, and almost childlike enthusiasm, there is also a feeling of extraordinary vitality, robustness, and breadth in the concerti, especially in the finest of the sets, the *Twelve Grand Concertos* (that is, concerti grossi as translated then), Opus 6. The exploitation of the tutti–soli opposition is less in Opus 3, although the instrumental scoring is more restricted in Opus 6. But in both sets the variety of instrumental combinations is exceptional, even from movement to movement. In Opus 3, No. 2, for example, the soli change from two oboes and two violins to solo oboe, then to two oboes doubling two violins and a viola, further to two oboes and two violins not doubled, and finally to two oboes and cello. Much as Bach had transcribed concerti for organ alone to serve as introductions to cantatas, so Handel played his own original and transcribed concerti for organ and orchestra as introductions and entr'actes in his oratorios. These organ concerti were widely copied by minor followers of Handel in England. Nothing in France close to Handel's level can be pointed to until near the end of the era, when a violinist and composer, Jean-Marie Leclair, produced his solo concerti.

In the opening of this section "concerto" was defined as

it is thought of first today—that is, in the sense that has prevailed since about 1750. Essential to that definition is the interrelation of orchestra and soloist, not soli. Whereas a *concertino* of soli had been the norm before 1750, with a single soloist being a variant or reduction of the concertino idea, the single soloist became the norm after 1750. As a result two or more soloists became the exception in what has since become known as "double concerto," "triple concerto," and so on. Because the concerto since 1750 has been likened to the sonata (again, as in the opening definition), it is often distinguished as the "sonata concerto," although the same could have been done with at least as much justification, especially because of the confusions of terms noted earlier, for the concerto before 1750. More justified, in spite of all the exceptions, might be the designations "solo concerto" for the later type and "orchestral concerto" (or concerto grosso) for the earlier type. The concerto grosso may be said to have dissolved into the solo concerto and the sinfonia concertante. The second term was Mozart's designation for certain concerti with more than one soloist, but it has also been used for symphonies that still reveal the imitative interplay of the concerto grosso or that employ the tutti–soli rondo principle. There are differences between the earlier solo part, which was a minimal concertino, and the later solo part, which was a self-sufficient adversary to the orchestra. There is also a difference in scoring between the two types of concerto, for at the time that the concerto grosso was being replaced by the solo concerto the basso continuo was falling into disuse. In addition there is a difference of degree, with a sharp increase of independence and virtuosity in the soloist's part in the later form of the concerto.

The Classical concerto (c. 1750–1830). Since 1750 the concerto has found its chief place in society not in church or at court but in the concert hall. Some of the excitement it could arouse in classical musical life is recaptured in the Mozart family letters. Mozart's introduction of a new piano concerto (K. 456?) in a Vienna theatre concert was reported by his father on February 16, 1785:

The solo concerto

> . . . your brother played a glorious concerto, . . . I was sitting [close] . . . and had the great pleasure of hearing so clearly all the interplay of the instruments that for sheer delight tears came into my eyes. When your brother left the platform the Emperor waved his hat and called out "Bravo, Mozart!" And when he came on to play there was a great deal of clapping. (As translated by Emily Anderson, *The Letters of Mozart and His Family,* 2d. ed. The Macmillan Co., New York, 1966.)

The solo concerto was the main concert vehicle for composer-performers such as Mozart and for itinerant virtuosos like the Italian violinist Antonio Lolli, whose incessant crisscrossing of all Europe scarcely can be reconciled with the incredibly bad travel conditions that still prevailed. A secondary place for the solo concerto has been in the realm of musical instruction. Although the category of "student concerto" to which certain works have been relegated seems largely to associate with the 19th century, a good many classical concerti evidently served that purpose too. Thus, Mozart, who wrote his latest, finest, and most difficult concerti for his own concert appearances, earlier wrote easier ones to be used mainly in teaching. The concerto also had an occasional place in the theatre, as evidenced by the fact that the Italian composer Francesco Maria Veracini played concerto movements as entr'actes during operatic performances.

The strings remained the nucleus, though less often the whole, of the tutti in the solo concerto. But now the more equivoice setting of the string quartet gradually superseded the polarity of the basso continuo and the melody or concertante parts. Moreover, the tutti was no longer reinforced by the solo instrument in the tutti passages, as it had been in the concerto grosso, for the solo became exclusively a solo part. Though optional instrumentation disappeared insofar as the choice of instruments for the old basso continuo was concerned, the free use of what instruments were available still applied to the wind parts of the usual concerto tutti throughout most of the 18th century. The instrumental colour of solo concerti, up to Mozart's mature works, was therefore relatively neutral, without particular refinement or individuality caused by specifically exploiting the tone colours of the instruments. On the other hand, the solo part became increasingly individualized in the solo concerto as a result of the further exploitation of spectacular playing techniques. Accordingly, the music of the solo part became highly idiomatic for the chosen instrument; that is, it was calculated to take most advantage of the characteristic sound and techniques particular to that instrument. Solo violin parts in particular had already reached heights of virtuosity during the overlap between the Baroque and Classical eras. Such works were scarcely surpassed before the most brilliant writing of the violin virtuoso Niccolò Paganini and his successors in the Romantic era. Examples may be found in abundance in the solo violin concerti of Leclair and the Italians Pietro Locatelli, Veracini, and Giuseppe Tartini. Most of these works, especially Tartini's, have real musical distinction, rooted as they are in an important heritage from Torelli, Albinoni, and Vivaldi in Italy and Johann Georg Pisendel, Telemann, and Bach in Germany.

The rise of the piano

Yet, from the 1780s and the peak of the Classical era, and despite a continuing if limited output of concerti for the cello, flute, oboe, clarinet, bassoon, and horn, it was no longer the violin or any of these instruments that ranked first among solo instruments of the concerto. Rather it was the newly emerging piano, which was rapidly superseding the harpsichord and clavichord. Mozart, who with the London-centred, Italian-born Muzio Clementi was one of the first great pianists, wrote not only some of the first but some of the greatest concerti the instrument has yet known. Two generations earlier, Bach's more limited exploitation of the keyboard in his harpsichord concerti had already shown what a stalwart adversary a keyboard instrument could be in the concerto contest. Now, with the greater independence of the solo part and the greater self-sufficiency of a keyboard part, both the drama and the variety of the tutti–solo opposition could be increased considerably. As for the variety, either orchestra or soloist might perform alone, either might carry the theme while the other accompanied, or the two might share in the theme by doubling, by antiphony (alternating with each other in playing phrases of the theme), or by more rapid interchange and alternation. Thus, Mozart's popular *Concerto in A Major,* K. 488, begins with an extended orchestral tutti without soloist, after which the solo piano enters on a restatement of the main theme, lightly and intermittently accompanied by the strings alone. Another tutti, this time short, leads into a modulatory (key-changing) bridge consisting of rapid piano scales that elaborate on harmonies given in simpler notes in the tutti. The piano now enters alone on a second theme, then decorates snatches of the theme as the orchestra restates it an octave higher. So the work unfolds in a kaleidoscope of ingenious, fresh settings.

Movement cycles and forms

The standard cycle of three movements, fast–slow–fast, became even more standardized in the Classical era. It occurred without notable exception in the concerti of that era's three greatest masters, Haydn, Mozart, and Beethoven. Furthermore, the outer movements are generally predictable, too, at least in their overall plans. "Sonata form" is approximated in the opening movements. In the finales, apart from an occasional minuet (a dance form) in Haydn's concerti, the prevalent forms are rondo and sonata-rondo (which combines the recurrent refrain of the rondo with the exposition-development principle of the sonata). The middle movements are only a little less predictable, with A B A design being far in the majority (as in Mozart's *Concerto in D Minor,* K. 466). Forms such as the dialogue-like fantasy in Beethoven's *Piano Concerto No. 4 in G Major,* Opus 58, or the free variations in his *Violin Concerto* are late-Classical or pre-Romantic exceptions. But, of course, these masterworks are no stereotypes. They find their variety and distinctions in the details and working out of the forms. At most, "sonata form" in the Classical era was not yet the conscious concept or crystallized design that later textbooks have made it out to be. Its thematic organization in particular was still fluid and certainly not bound to any fixed number of themes or any fixed dualism of "masculine" and "feminine" themes. Textbook discussions of the solo concerto say that the tutti plays the exposition first, all in the tonic key, after which the soloist joins to repeat it, this time more elaborately and with the contrasting theme in a nearly related key. But that concept of the strict "double exposition" is honoured as much in the breach as the observance.

Actually, the application of "sonata form" was likely to be freer, even looser, in the concerto than in the symphony or string quartet. In part this was because of the extensive passagework that is inherent in the virtuosity and idiomatic treatment of the solo instrument. This passagework and the loose treatment of the musical form reach their extreme in a terminal cadenza of the first movement, more so than in the shorter cadenzas likely to be found at one or more focal points in the other movements. The cadenza had already been introduced in late-Baroque violin concerti, undoubtedly influenced by singers' florid, improvised embellishments of arias in current opera, although early instrumental precedents exist, too. The concerto's cadenza was generally improvised by the performer until Beethoven insisted on the use of his own short cadenzas as supplied in *Piano Concerto No. 5 in E Flat Major,* Opus 73. Many later performers have found too little opportunity for technical display in other cadenzas that the masters previously had left for optional performance in some of their own concerti. The dissatisfied performers often substituted more brilliant cadenzas in such cases. But the structural looseness of the cadenza becomes less tolerable when the virtuoso performer goes to later sources or composes new cadenzas that are anachronistic in their technical and harmonic style, out of proportion in length, and inadequately related to the musical themes of the movement.

Improvised and written cadenzas

As with both the vocal and the instrumental concerto of the Baroque era, the starting point for the solo concerto in the Classical era lies in Italian music. But this time more weight must be attached to the evolution of the concerto in Germany and Austria. In these countries, there lies the more significant development, that of the piano concerto, as cultivated by the chief Classical masters.

The transition to the lighter texture and more fragmented musical thoughts of the pre-Classical "gallant style" may be credited in part to the Italian string concerti, notably those of Tartini, Giovanni Battista Sammartini, Luigi Boccherini, and Giovanni Battista Viotti. But the one piano concerto that Boccherini may have left about 1768, along with several cello concerti, and the very few concerti that Clementi in England supposedly converted to solo piano sonatas hardly make any niche for Italian composers in the history of the piano concerto. The full exploitation of the piano in the concerto and the creation of more substantial, consequential concerti for it must be credited primarily to two of J.S. Bach's sons and to the high-Classical Viennese triumvirate of Haydn, Mozart, and Beethoven. Whereas Wilhelm Friedemann Bach had largely followed his father in his half dozen concerti for harpsichord, strings, and basso continuo, Carl Philipp Emanuel Bach opened new paths in about 50 keyboard concerti, as well as some violin concerti and flute concerti. This is especially true of his later concerti intended for the piano (1772) rather than the harpsichord. Original instrumentation, dialogue between piano and orchestra, bold flights and expressive recitatives, are among the characteristics of Emanuel's concerti. So also are final movements that resemble in character the lively musical and dramatic development at the end of an act of opera buffa (Italian comic opera).

By contrast, Johann Christian Bach's 37 harpsichord or piano concerti from the same period are lighter, more fluent, easier works aimed at amateur skills and tastes. Most of them, like his sonatas but unlike most of his 31 sinfonie concertante, have only two movements, the finale often being a minuet or set of variations. The anticipations of Mozart's style are unmistakable.

Haydn left 36 concerti that can be verified, spanning the years from about 1755 to 1796; for violin (four); cello (five); bass; horn (four); hurdy-gurdy, or wheel fiddle (five); trumpet; flute; oboe; baryton, a cello-like instrument (three); and keyboard (11, whether for organ, harpsichord, or piano). In 1792 he also wrote a sinfonia concertante for violin, oboe, cello, bassoon, and full orchestra that returns to the tutti–soli relationships of the concerto grosso. The keyboard concerti bear witness in their unenterprising, sometimes pedestrian handling of the solo part that Haydn was no distinguished keyboardist. Even the best known of them, the *Piano Concerto in D Major* (1784), is heard today more in education than in concert circles, in spite of its musical strengths, especially in the "Rondo all'Ungherese" ("Rondo in the Hungarian style"). The one concerto by Haydn that is widely performed in today's concert world is an admirable, sonorous work for cello, in D major (1783, once attributed to the German cellist Anton Kraft). Cast in the usual three movements, with clear thematic ties between them and accompanied only by the usual orchestra in eight parts (four strings, two oboes, two horns), this work is variously songful, brilliant to a taxing degree, and dancelike. Another important contribution by Haydn was his last concerto (1796), a resourceful and difficult work in E-flat major that exploited the new keyed trumpet, which unlike earlier trumpets was capable of playing diatonic (seven-note) and chromatic (12-note) scales.

Haydn's concerti

During his short career, Mozart left about 45 verifiable concerti dating from 1773 to his last year, 1791. These do not include five early piano concerti arranged from concerto or sonata movements written by Emanuel and Christian Bach and two lesser composers. Out of the total, there are 21 for piano, six for violin, five for horn, two for flute, and one each for oboe, clarinet, bassoon, flute, and harp, two pianos, three pianos, and two violins (called *Concertone*). Two further examples, entitled "Sinfonia concertante," are for violin and viola, and for a concertino of oboe, clarinet, horn, and bassoon. Best known and most played are five of the last eight solo piano concerti (K. 466, 467, 488, 491, and 595), which rank among the finest of his works and the best of the genre. Highly valued and often played, too, are the *Sinfonia concertante in E Flat Major for Violin, Viola and Orchestra,* K. 364, E. 320d, and the *Concerto for Two Pianos,* K. 365, E. 316a. Two of the violin concerti are well-known (K. 218 in D major and K. 219 in A major), although more so to students than to concertgoers. Among those five solo piano concerti, that in D minor (K. 466) reveals a new urgency and compactness in Mozart's writing, reflecting the atmosphere of the *Sturm und Drang* ("Storm and Stress") period in German art, except in the naïvely charming "Romance" that is the middle movement. One among many instances of the striking tutti–solo contrasts in this work is the reservation of certain material, including the soloist's initial theme, for the soloist alone. The *Concerto in C Major,* K. 467, is a more cheerful work, broad and stately in its opening ideas, bubbling with intriguing melodic figuration, and capped by one of Mozart's most delectable rondos. The *Concerto in A Major,* K. 488, is rich in wistful songlike melodies. The spun-out line of the middle movement, in the rhythm of the siciliano (an Italian dance), makes an ideal foil for the gay, tuneful "Presto" that follows. Like the D-minor concerto, that in C minor (K. 491) is an intense work, more extended but even more driving. Mozart's last concerto for solo piano, that in B-flat major (K. 595), is another masterpiece, ever fresh in its ideas, yet with an air of sweet resignation in its almost neoclassical simplicity.

The concerti of Mozart

The much smaller output of concerti by Beethoven, anticipating the still smaller outputs by his 19th-century successors, is not surprising in view of the wider range of expression, further exploration of instrumental resorces, and greater size of his concerti. There are nine complete works in all. These include seven with piano—the so-called standard five (1795–1809) plus one more from his boyhood and another, using chorus as well as orchestra, that is seldom performed, oddly constructed, and almost unclassifiable (*Choral Fantasia,* Opus 80, first performed 1808). Further, there is the *Violin Concerto in D major* (1806) and a worthy, but much less successful, *Triple Concerto in C Major for Piano, Violin, and Cello,* Opus 56 (1804). One could hardly find a wider range of expression than that between the third, fourth, and fifth (*Emperor*) piano concerti. Reduced to capsule, subjective terms, the third, in C minor, must be characterized as compelling drama, hushed serenity, and feverish drive in its respective

Beethoven's concerti

movements; the fourth as joyous lyricism, stark tragedy, and scintillating gaiety; and the fifth as heroic grandeur, noble dignity, and victorious rejoicing. The opening tutti sections may be taken as samples of the wide variety of musical structure in these same three concerti. In the third, the tutti extends the exposition of the themes by developing or discussing each after it is first stated. The solo enters almost at once, with only a short flourish, on the main theme. In the fourth concerto, the piano begins alone with a short, refreshingly simple pronouncement of the main theme, followed immediately by a surprising, tangential entrance of the orchestra. There unfolds a full exposition that discusses each theme even more than in the third concerto. This time the solo enters for the repeated exposition only after a more extended flourish, lasting 15 measures. In the last concerto, the soloist begins by embellishing each of the three primary harmonies in the orchestra with a separate cadenza. Only after this opening does there begin a complete tutti exposition that, in its discussion of the themes, is still more developed than in the fourth concerto. Not until the orchestral exposition is ended does the solo enter again to begin its highly virtuosic elaboration in a repeated exposition. It is such development throughout all parts of the musical forms, and not only in the "development sections," that accounts for the great lengths of *Piano Concerto No. 5* and the *Violin Concerto.* Notable are the exceptional technical difficulties in these two peerless masterpieces, which grow as much out of their musical complexities as out of the composer's evident desire to reveal new ways to utilize his solo instruments (especially the rapidly advancing piano, with its wider range, heavier action, and bigger tone).

The Romantic era (c. 1790–1915). Between the Romantic and the Classical concerto there occurred no such marked, relatively abrupt changes in form or style as were observed earlier here between the Classical and the Baroque concerto. The onset of the Romantic era was not signalled by any shift in the concerto's musical structure. Thus there was no stylistic change equivalent to the shift from the polyphonic interplay of short motives in the concerto grosso to the solo concerto's grouping of longer musical phrases in homophonic style (based on chords). Nor was there any shift in instrumental texture equivalent to that from the polarity of basso continuo and melody parts to a more equal distribution of voices or parts. Nor again was there any shift from the piano to another instrument as the preferred solo vehicle.

Gradual evolution of the genre

As with much other Romantic music, the Romantic concerto was marked by an extension or expansion of those same Classical trends in all directions. This development led eventually to their exaggeration and ultimately to their extremes or breaking points. The concerto as a genre became more than ever the ideal showpiece at public concerts, doing much for the composer's profit, the performer's triumph, and the listener's delectation. Indeed, Franz Liszt, the dominant composer-pianist of his time, distinguished between the concerto and the sonata, calling the first a public showpiece and the second a private, personal expression (in 1838, while questioning a publisher's title, *Concerto Without Orchestra,* for the Opus 14 of Robert Schumann, a title changed to *Piano Sonata No. 3 in F Minor*). Over the century, several 19th-century concerti won more popularity than was accorded to any earlier concerti. Time has influenced that preference but little, to judge from a listing, in order of popularity, of the 15 piano concerti most played in major U.S. concerts in the late 1960s: Beethoven No. 5, Tchaikovsky No. 1, Brahms No. 2, Beethoven No. 3, (Prokofiev No. 3, Modern era), Schumann, Rachmaninoff No. 2, Mozart K. 595, Grieg, Beethoven No. 4, Camille Saint-Saëns No. 2, Brahms No. 1, Chopin No. 2, Beethoven No. 1, and Liszt No. 1 (from statistics compiled by Broadcast Music Industries).

Concerto orchestration

Another expansion of Classical trends is seen in the concerto orchestra, with the larger number, greater variety, and more discriminating use of its instruments. It is true that only the thinnest possible "support" for the soloist sufficed for composer-performers such as the pianist Chopin, the violinist Paganini, and others whose musical thinking ranged but little beyond the spheres of their own instruments. But the orchestra developed the status of a genuine if not superior adversary of the soloist in newly resourceful orchestrations by composers of wider instrumental perspective. Examples of this exploitation of the orchestra include *Harold en Italie* (1834), a symphony with solo viola, by the French composer Hector Berlioz; *Piano Concerto No. 1 in E Flat Major* (published 1857), by Liszt; and *Burleske* (completed 1885) for piano and orchestra, by the German Richard Strauss. At the same time, the piano, as the ideal Romantic instrument, secured ever more firmly its Classical preeminence as the preferred solo vehicle of the concerto. Although the total output of violin concerti in particular was very great, there was a decided preponderance of piano concerti among all concerti that appeared on printed public concert programs. In turn, the use of the piano in concerti was one main incentive for further advances in piano construction. By the mid-19th century the instrument reached a peak very close to the sonorous, seven-octave, triple-strung, cast-iron framed behemoth that is the modern "concert grand." With its perfection came also the extension of keyboard technique to the last reaches of athletic dexterity. Evidence of such technical development includes the unreasonably difficult requirements of the three etudes ("studies") that comprise the huge unaccompanied *Concerto,* Opus 39, Nos. 8–10, by the French pianist-composer Alkan (Charles-Henri Morhange). It is also apparent in the more reasonable but no less difficult requirements in Rachmaninoff's *Piano Concerto No. 3 in D Minor,* Opus 30 (1909). The wind instruments used in concerto solos underwent mechanical advances, too, and both they and the stringed instruments enjoyed analogous exploitations of their technical possibilities in this century of virtuosos—not only of Liszt (and so many more) on the piano but of others such as Paganini on the violin, Alfredo Piatti on the cello, and Domenico Dragonetti on the double bass.

Romantic innovations

The most significant extension or expansion of the concerto principle in the Romantic era might in one sense be called a contraction, for it concerns a continuing effort to consolidate, interrelate, and fuse the over-all cycle, both within and between the movements. Certain composers, mostly forgotten perfunctories, yet including as important and successful a figure as Chopin, were satisfied to pour new wine into old bottles. Thus many concerti accepted without question the movement forms and cycle that by then had become self-conscious stereotypes, especially "sonata form" in the first movement. Brahms largely preferred to accept the traditional cycle and forms, too, but with the masterful individuality, flexibility, and logic that were needed to revitalize them. On the other hand, most of the Romantics whose concerti are still played sought to modernize and advance the traditional structural principles. These changes may be summed up in six categories.

First, there is the elimination, in the opening movement, of the long initial tutti section. This innovation corresponded to the elimination in the sonata of the previously customary repeat of the exposition, a change that had begun in Beethoven's late sonatas and had soon become general. Such is the pattern in Schumann's *Piano Concerto in A Minor,* Opus 54 (1845), in which the soloist enters at the outset and proceeds promptly to an almost constant interrelationship with the orchestra as the exposition unfolds but once.

Second, there is the interlocking of the movements, achieved by leading not only from one movement to the next without appreciable pause in time or sound but also without either a definitive cadence (stopping point made clear by the harmonies) or full break in the continuity of harmonies or tonality. Thus in the *Violin Concerto in E Minor,* Opus 64 (1844), of Felix Mendelssohn, a lone bassoon suspends one note of the final chord of the first movement. Preventing a pause in time or sound, it leads directly into the middle movement. Again, between the middle and final movements a brief interlude, midway in tempo, mood, and intensity, supplies the continuity and avoids any full break.

A third Romantic innovation is the effort to bind the cycle more positively through the use of related themes and motives in the successive movements. Such themes and motives can be only melodic nuclei, as in the so-called basic motive employed by Brahms. Or they may be more extended melodic thoughts, such as are subjected to "thematic metamorphosis" by Liszt or "cyclical" treatment by the Belgian César Franck. (Both terms refer to the practice of transforming a theme melodically and rhythmically in various ways throughout the cycle of movements.) Among well-known examples is the tight thematic organization, with its final retrospective summary, in the four interconnected movements of Liszt's *Piano Concerto No. 1* (*Triangle Concerto,* published 1857), a work Liszt himself claimed to be innovational on this account.

Fourth, there are certain other, more incidental, yet effective means of unifying the cycle. These include the sense of culminating joy or triumph in those many concerti that change from a minor home key to its tonic major (for example, from A minor to A major) for the finale; or the consistency of musical textures caused by making all the movements similar in weight and style; or the stronger sense of return achieved by a finale that follows a middle movement characterized by a marked sense of departure or contrast.

"Program" concerti and fusion of movements

The remaining two categories of changes concern Romantic developments that go somewhat beyond expansions (or contractions) of Classical concerto traditions. As a fifth category, there is the extramusical unification of the cycle by means of a program—that is, a story or image. Unlike the Romantic sonata, the Romantic concerto abounds in examples. One of the earliest such examples is the image that the German composer Carl Maria von Weber identified with his *Konzertstück* (*Concert Piece*) for piano and orchestra (1821). Its four interconnected movements are said to describe a medieval lady's longing for her absent knight, her agonized fears for his safety, the excitement of his impending return, and the joys of reunion and love.

Sixth and last, there are numerous efforts to contract or consolidate the concerto cycle still more drastically, by fusion of movements. Four different solutions may be cited as representative. Tchaikovsky's *Piano Concerto No. 1 in B Flat Minor* (1875) follows a number of symphonies and sonatas of the period by integrating the slow movement with the scherzo (a lively movement that had become a rather frequent additional item in the cycle). Liszt's *Piano Concerto No. 2 in A Major* (published 1863) is a pioneer among the several concerti that reduce the separate movements to sharply contrasting sections within a single movement. Franck's *Variations symphoniques* for piano and orchestra (first performed 1885) substitute for the cycle a single movement based on a single principle of musical structure (in contrast to the distinct structures of distinct movements). And the Russian Nikolay Medtner's *Piano Concerto in G Minor* is a single, experimental variation of "sonata form." It consists, as he himself explains,

> of an exposition, [a short, transitional cadenza,] a series of [nine] variations on the two chief themes, constituting the development [section], and then the recapitulation.

Still other changes from the Classical to the Romantic concerto are concerned less with overall plans than with language and idiom: the characteristic harmonies, melodic styles, and manner of musical development. But such changes were not limited to the concerto. They touched all of Romantic music. Among them are fuller, more varied textures, greater use of the high and low extremes of instruments' ranges, and more sonorous, widespread spacing of sounds. Indicative of the third development was the significant change in piano writing from the Alberti bass in close position to the "um-pah-pah" bass and free arpeggiations in open position.

Romantic harmonies and nationalistic colour

In addition there was a marked new preference for minor keys as being almost indispensable to the intensity of Romantic feeling. There was also an increased use of chromatic harmonies (chords whose notes do not all belong to the key of the composition and that frequently seem to have a more expressive character). Similarly characteristic of the era were brief, temporary modulations whose functions were more colouristic than structural (*i.e.,* they were introduced more for the harmonic colour they embody rather than strictly as a means of changing keys). Another new development was the late-Romantic turn to nationalistic colours, introducing folk melodies or allowing folk music to influence melodies, harmonies, and rhythms. An example is the *Symphonie espagnole* for violin and orchestra (1875), by the French composer Édouard Lalo.

From beginning to end in the Romantic era, Germany reigned supreme in the concerto, both as leader and producer, as with all the major instrumental forms. The majority of the non-Germans whose concerti were more or less successful in their day were at least trained in Germany. Here, in one loose chronology, may be mentioned the most important of the Romantics from both in and out of Germany, along with their most important concerti, which generally are those with the best chance still of being heard today. The once successful piano concerti of the Czech Jan Ladislav Dussek and the Germans Johann Nepomuk Hummel and Ignaz Moscheles—all renowned virtuoso pianists—have given way to other early Romantic works. These include the *Konzertstücke* of Weber, two concerti by Mendelssohn, and, especially, two by Chopin and the one by Schumann. Mendelssohn's two piano concerti are rapidly slipping into the status of "student concerti" today, but his *Violin Concerto in E Minor* continues to hold top position in its class, along with the violin concerti of Beethoven, Brahms, and Tchaikovsky. These works followed and eclipsed the successes of Viotti, Paganini, the German Ludwig Spohr, and other violinist composers. Schumann left one of the era's few most played cello concerti, two others being the later ones by Saint-Saëns and the Czech Antonín Dvořák. As noted, Liszt was a pathbreaker with his two piano concerti. His other, more programmatic works for piano and orchestra are less played today, but they also exercised a variety of influences on such different late-Romantics as Grieg, Franck, the American Edward MacDowell, Rachmaninoff, Richard Strauss, and the Hungarian Ernő Dohnányi. Brahms's concerti, every one a highly popular masterpiece today, mark a peak for the era on the conservative side. They include besides the two piano concerti in D minor and B-flat major, the *Violin Concerto in D Major* and the *Double Concerto in A Minor* (with violin and cello as the solo instruments). Among later romantic concerti, though those onetime favourites for violin by Henri Vieuxtemps, Henryk Wieniawski, Max Bruch, Karl Goldmark, Aleksandr Glazunov, and Sir Edward Elgar have recently lost much ground in the concert hall, those of Dvořák, Saint-Saëns, the Finnish composer Jean Sibelius, and, especially, Tchaikovsky still hold strong. Similarly, while the piano concerti of the famed piano virtuoso Anton Rubinstein are all but forgotten, two (in G minor and C minor) out of the five by Saint-Saëns and the *Concerto No. 2 in D Minor* by MacDowell get occasional hearings, and those already mentioned by Tchaikovsky and Rachmaninoff remain among the most successful. Certain concerti are less likely to be heard at least partly because they are written for less usual solo instruments. These include works for bassoon by Weber; for clarinet by Spohr, Weber, and Ferruccio Busoni; and for horn by Weber and Richard Strauss.

The modern era (from about 1915). By and large, and up to about 1950, the concerto of the modern era has kept pace with the language and idiom of modern music. There has been little introduction of new principles, or new trends, or even further extensions of the structural changes that have been noted here in the Romantic era. If anything, it has turned back on itself. It has sloughed off the advances, if such they be, of the Romantic era and has reverted to styles and forms of the Baroque and Classical concerto. In so doing it has provided some of the most telling examples of the neo-Baroque and Neoclassical trends in modern music.

More explicitly, the modern concerto has kept pace with the breakdown in traditional tonality and various efforts to revitalize, bypass, or replace that comfortably secure system. It has shared in the modern erosion of the contrast between chords traditionally considered consonant (*i.e.,* bearing musical repose) and dissonant (*i.e.,* bearing musical tension), thus contributing to the release of endless new chord forms and progressions. And it has joined in perhaps the most basic trend; *i.e.,* the return from the

Romantic and Classical tendency of groups of melodic phrases in predominantly homophonic textures to the Baroque ideal of interplay of melodic motives in predominantly polyphonic textures. But at the same time, the modern concerto has abandoned the gigantic orchestra, the massive technical requirements and extreme opposition of the solo part, and the decided preference for the piano as the ideal solo instrument. Similarly, it has abandoned the intensive effort to interconnect, consolidate, and contract the musical forms and has turned away from the frequent concern with extramusical programmatic content. The downgrading of virtuosity for its own sake has caused the soloist to become more a part of the orchestra again. Some modern works, such as *Piano Concerto No. 3 in C Major,* Opus 26 (1921), by Prokofiev, do continue to offer some of the formidable difficulties, glittering passagework, and soaring lyricism of the late Romantic concerto in the solo part. But even in these, the nature of the modern musical language permits the soloist generally to blend with the orchestra rather than to "do battle" with it, as has been said regarding Tchaikovsky's *Piano Concerto No. 1* and similar concert favourites of the Romantic era.

Changes in the soloist's role

From the present limited perspective, no one country appears yet to have dominated the cultivation of the modern concerto. The total output has continued to be high, with nearly every composer of renown having contributed to it. Among representative German works that have won widest public endorsement—which, in the very nature of the solo concerto, must continue to be a main criterion—may be cited numerous concerti (mostly called "Chamber Music") that Paul Hindemith seems systematically to have written for almost every standard instrument as a solo, and for a variety of combinations. Both the Austrians Arnold Schoenberg and his disciple Alban Berg left 12-tone concerti for violin and Schoenberg left one for piano. (Twelve-tone music is based on a series or "row" of the 12 notes of the chromatic scale, chosen by the composer to serve as the melodic and harmonic basis for the composition.)

From France may be cited works by Claude Debussy for piano (*Fantaisie*) and for saxophone (*Rapsodie*); by Maurice Ravel for piano (two, of which one is for left hand alone) and for violin; and by Darius Milhaud for various instruments, even mouth organ, and various instrumental combinations, including percussion. From England there is a double concerto for violin and cello by Frederick Delius and there are various works by Sir Arnold Bax, Sir Arthur Bliss, Ralph Vaughan Williams, Sir William Walton, and Benjamin Britten. Among examples from the United States are successful concerti by George Gershwin, including *Rhapsody in Blue* for piano and jazz orchestra, and by Aaron Copland, whose *Piano Concerto* (1926) also exploits jazz. Of major importance have been solo or duo concerti by Prokofiev (five for piano, two for violin, and one for cello), the Russian-born Igor Stravinsky (two for horn, one for violin, one for oboe, and one for clarinet and bassoon), and the Hungarian Béla Bartók (four for piano and three for violin). Attention also should be called to the neo-Baroque *Harpsichord Concerto* (1926), by the Spaniard Manuel de Falla.

A special indication of neo-Baroque interest may be seen in the return on the part of a number of composers to the tutti–soli grouping, the motoric pulse, and the interplay of motives of the concerto grosso. Notable examples have been left by Bartók, Stravinsky, the German Max Reger, the Swiss-born Ernest Bloch, and the Austrian-born Ernst Krenek.

The present discussion of the modern era has concerned developments largely ending by about 1950, although occasional returns to what might already be called the "traditional (solo) concerto" have occurred since, as by John Cage, Leon Kirchner, and Elliott Carter in the United States; by the Argentine Alberto Ginastera; the French composer Olivier Messiaen; the Greek Yannis Xenakis; and the Russian Dmitry Shostakovich. In the main, from 1950 on, the pronounced swing of the avant-garde to electronic, computerized, and aleatoric, or chance music, has tended to do away with everything traditionally identified with "concerto," including the title itself. The only identifiable characteristic to remain is the basic idea of the group–solo relationship, as in several works by Karlheinz Stockhausen and Lukas Foss. That basic idea is essential not only to the concerto but to much other music. Whether it alone will survive in a way that still can be related to the venerable career of the concerto remains to be seen. (W.S.N.)

ELECTRONIC MUSIC

Although any music produced or modified by electrical, electromechanical, or electronic means can be called electronic music, it is more precise to say that for a piece of music to be electronic its composer must anticipate the electronic processing subsequently applied to his musical concept, so that the final product reflects in some way his interaction with the medium. This is no different from saying that a composer should have in mind an orchestra when he composes a symphony and a piano when he composes a piano sonata. A conventional piece of popular music does not become electronic music by being played on an electronically amplified guitar, nor does a Bach fugue become electronic music if played on an electronic organ instead of a pipe organ. Some experimental compositions, often containing chance elements and perhaps of indeterminate scoring, permit but do not necessarily demand electronic realization, but this is a specialized situation.

Definition and nature of electronic music

Electronic music is produced from a wide variety of sound resources—from sounds picked up by microphones to those produced by electronic oscillators (generating basic acoustical wave forms such as sine waves, square waves, and sawtooth waves), complex computer installations, and microprocessors—that are recorded on tape and then edited into a permanent form. Generally, except for one type of performed music that has come to be called "live electronic music" (see below), electronic music is played back through loudspeakers either alone or in combination with ordinary musical instruments.

This section covers both early experimentation with electronic sound-producing devices and composers' subsequent exploitation of electronic equipment as a technique of composition. Throughout the discussion it should be clear that electronic music is not a style but rather a technique yielding diverse results in the hands of different composers.

Historically, electronic music is one aspect of the larger development of 20th-century music strongly characterized by a search for new technical resources and modes of expression. Before 1945 composers sought to liberate themselves from the main Classical–Romantic tradition of tonal thinking and to reconstruct their thinking along new lines, for the most part either Neoclassical or atonal and 12-tone, in which a composition is built up entirely from a tone row consisting of all 12 notes of the ordinary chromatic scale.

This pre-World War II period was accompanied by substantial experimentation with electrical and electronic devices. The most important outcome for the composer was the development of a number of electronic musical instruments (such as the Hammond organ and the theremin) that provided new timbres and that laid the technical foundations for the future development of electronic music proper from about 1948 onward. The rapid development of computer technology has had its effect in music, too, so much so that the term computer music is replacing electronic music as the more accurate description of the most significant interaction between the composer and the electronic medium.

Electronic music is represented not only by a wide variety of 20th-century works, and not only by serious concert pieces, but also by a substantial literature of theatre, film, and television scores and by multimedia works that use all types of audiovisual techniques. Electronic music for theatre and films seems an especially appropriate replacement for a disembodied, nonexistent orchestra heard from a tape or a sound track. Electronic popular music has also won adherents. This mostly has consisted of arrangements of standard popular music for electronic synthesizers, the tentative use of electronic alterations by some of the more ambitious and experimental rock groups, and the preparation of recordings by innovative studio techniques.

History and stylistic development. *Beginnings.* During the 19th century attempts were made to produce and record sounds mechanically or electromechanically. For example, the German scientist Hermann von Helmholtz traced wave forms of regular sounds to check results of his acoustical researches. An important event was the invention of the phonograph by Thomas Edison and Emile Berliner, independently, in the 1870s and 1880s. This invention not only marked the beginning of the recording industry but also showed that all the acoustical content of musical sounds could be captured (in principle, if not in actuality at that time) and be faithfully retained for future use.

Cahill's pioneer work

The first major effort to generate musical sounds electrically was carried out over many years by an American, Thaddeus Cahill, who built a formidable assembly of rotary generators and telephone receivers to convert electrical signals into sound. Cahill called his remarkable invention the telharmonium, which he started to build about 1895 and continued to improve for years thereafter. The instrument failed because it was complex, impractical, and could not produce sounds of any magnitude since amplifiers and loudspeakers had not yet been invented. Nevertheless, Cahill's concepts were basically sound. He was a visionary who lived ahead of his time, and his instrument was the ancestor of present-day electronic music synthesizers.

The Italian Futurist painter Luigi Russolo was another early exponent of synthesized music. As early as 1913 Russolo proposed that all music be destroyed and that new instruments reflecting current technology be built to perform a music expressive of industrialized society. Russolo subsequently did build a number of mechanically activated *intonarumori* (noise instruments) that grated, hissed, scratched, rumbled, and shrieked. Russolo's instruments and most of his music apparently vanished during World War II.

Between World War I and World War II developments occurred that led more directly to modern electronic music, although most of them were technically, rather than musically, important. First was the development of audio-frequency technology. By the early 1920s basic circuits for sine-, square-, and sawtooth-wave generators had been invented, as had amplifiers, filter circuits, and, most importantly, loudspeakers. (Sine waves are signals consisting of "pure tones"—*i.e.,* without overtones; sawtooth waves comprise fundamental tones and all related overtones; square waves consist only of the odd-numbered partials, or component tones, of the natural harmonic series.) Also, mechanical acoustical recording was replaced by electrical recording in the late 1920s.

Invention of the electronic organ

Second was the development of electromechanical and electronic musical instruments designed to replace existing musical instruments—specifically, the invention of electronic organs. This was a remarkable achievement and one that absorbed the attention of many ingenious inventors and circuit designers. It should be stressed, however, that it was the objective of these organ builders to simulate and replace pipe organs and harmoniums, not to provide novel instruments that would stimulate the imaginations of avant-garde composers.

Most electromechanical and electronic organs employ subtractive synthesis, as do pipe organs. Signals rich in harmonic partials (such as sawtooth waves) are selected by the performer at the keyboard and combined and shaped acoustically by filter circuits that simulate the formant, or resonant-frequency, spectra—*i.e.,* the acoustical components—of conventional organ stops. The formant depends on the filter circuit and does not relate to the frequency of a tone being produced. A low tone shaped by a given formant (a given stop) is normally rich in harmonics, while a high tone normally is poor in them. Psychologically, one expects this from all musical instruments, not only organs but also orchestral instruments.

Some electronic organs operate on the opposing principle of additive synthesis, whereby individually generated sine waves are added together in varying proportions to yield a complex wave form. The most successful of these is the Hammond organ, patented by Laurens Hammond in 1934. The Hammond organ has odd qualities because the richness of its harmonic content does not diminish as the player goes up the keyboard. The German composer Karlheinz Stockhausen (in *Momente,* 1961–62), the Norwegian composer Arne Nordheim (in *Colorazione,* 1968), and a few others have scored specifically for this instrument.

New instruments in the 1920s

Third was the development of novel electronic musical instruments designed to supply timbres not provided by ordinary musical instruments. During the 1920s there was a burst of interest in building an extraordinary variety of such instruments, ranging from practical to absurd. The most successful of these were relatively few in number, were monophonic (*i.e.,* could play only one melodic line at a time), and survive chiefly because some important music has been scored for them. These are the theremin, invented in 1920 by a Russian scientist, Leon Theremin; the Ondes Martenot, first built in 1928 by a French musician and scientist, Maurice Martenot; and the trautonium, designed by a German, Friedrich Trautwein, in 1930.

The theremin is a beat-frequency audio oscillator (sine-wave generator) that has two condensers placed not inside the circuit chassis but, rather, outside, as antennas. Because these antennas respond to the presence of nearby objects, the pitch and amplitude of the output signal of the theremin can be controlled by the manner in which a performer moves his hands in its vicinity. A skilled performer can produce all sorts of effects, including scales, glissandi, and flutters. A number of compositions have been written for this instrument since the 1920s.

The Ondes Martenot consists of a touch-sensitive keyboard and a slide-wire glissando generator that are both controlled by the performer's right hand, as well as some stops controlled by the left hand. These, in turn, activate a sawtooth-wave generator that delivers a signal to one or more output transducers. The instrument has been used extensively by several French composers, including Olivier Messiaen and Pierre Boulez, and by the French-American composer Edgard Varèse.

The trautonium, like the Ondes Martenot, uses a sawtooth-wave generator as its signal source and a keyboard of novel design that permits not just ordinary tuning but unusual scales as well. Most of the music composed for this instrument is of German origin, an example being the *Concertino for Trautonium and Strings* (1931) by Paul Hindemith. In about 1950 a polyphonic version (capable of playing several voices, or parts, simultaneously) of this instrument was built by Oskar Sala, a former student of Trautwein and Hindemith, for preparing sound tracks in a Berlin film studio. These instruments have become virtually obsolete, however, because all the sounds they produce can easily be duplicated by electronic music synthesizers.

Tape music. With tape music the history of electronic music in the narrower sense begins. This history seems split into three main periods: an early (by now classical) period lasting from the commercial introduction of the tape recorder immediately following World War II until about 1960; a second period that featured the introduction of electronic music synthesizers and the acceptance of the electronic medium as a legitimate compositional activity; and the third period, in which computer technology is rapidly becoming both the dominant resource and the dominant concern.

Invention of the tape recorder

The invention of the tape recorder gave composers of the 1950s an exciting new musical instrument to use for new musical experiences. Fascination with the thing itself was the dominant motivation for composing electronic tape music. Musically, the 1950s, in contrast to the 1960s, were relatively introverted years: in all kinds of music, the focus of interest was technique and style, especially with the avant-garde. In time, the medium became fairly well understood, the techniques for handling it became increasingly standardized, and a repertory of characteristic and historically important compositions came into being. The burning issues were whether tape would replace live musicians; whether the composer was at last freed from the humiliations so often endured to get his music into the concert hall; and whether a new medium of expression had been created, quite different from and independent of instrumental music, analogous, say, to photography as opposed to traditional painting.

It became increasingly evident, however, that there was no reason to think that the electronic tape medium would eliminate instrumental performance by live musicians. Tape was increasingly regarded as something that could be—but did not need to be—treated as a unique medium. Thus the notion that the tape recorder could function as one instrument in an ensemble grew more and more popular. This conception obviated the visual monotony of an evening in an auditorium with nothing to look at but a loudspeaker. To this has been added a further stage of evolution, namely, live electronic music, in which the tape recorder and its tape is eliminated or greatly restricted in function, and transformations of the sounds of musical instruments are effected at the concert with electronic equipment. Not infrequently, this kind of performance environment also involves scores in which aleatory (chance, or random), improvisatory, or quasi-improvisatory musical guidelines for the manipulation of such equipment are supplied by a composer who prefers to let what happens just happen. Actually, it is open to question whether live electronic music is really an advance or a reversion to a more primitive state of the art, in the sense that it is the enhancement of the timbres of familiar instruments, rather than music conceived totally in terms of electronic media per se.

The first period of development was certainly one into which Europeans put the most consistent work. Tape music quickly gained recognition and financial support, and, before long, a number of well-equipped electronic music studios were established, primarily in government-supported broadcast facilities. Some important work was also done in the United States, but this was much more fragmentary, and not until after 1958 did Americans begin to catch up, either technically or artistically.

Establishment of electronic studios

In 1948 two French composers, Pierre Schaeffer and Pierre Henry, and their associates at Radiodiffusion et Télévision Française in Paris began to produce tape collages (analogous to collages in the visual arts), which they called *musique concrète.* All the materials they processed on tape were recorded sounds—sound effects, musical fragments, vocalizings, and other sounds and noises produced by man, his environment, and his artifacts. Such sounds were considered "concrete," hence the term *musique concrète.* To this Paris group certainly belongs the credit both for originating the concept of tape music as such and for demonstrating how effective certain types of tape manipulation can be in transforming sounds. These transformations included speed alteration, variable speed control, playing tapes backward, and signal feedback loops. Schaeffer however, opposed the use of electronic oscillators as sound sources, claiming that these were not "concrete" sound sources, not "real," and hence artificial and anti-humanistic.

Two of the most successful and best known *musique concrète* compositions of this early period are Schaeffer and Henry's *Symphonie pour un homme seul* (1950; *Symphony for One Man Only*) and Henry's *Orphée* (1953), a ballet score written for the Belgian dancer Maurice Béjart. These and similar works created a sensation when first presented to the public. *Symphonie pour un homme seul,* a descriptive suite about man and his activities, is an extended composition in 11 movements. *Orphée* is concerned with the descent of Orpheus into Hades.

The second event of significance was the formation of an electronic music studio in Cologne by Herbert Eimert, a composer working for Nordwestdeutscher Rundfunk (now Westdeutscher Rundfunk), who was advised in turn by Werner Meyer-Eppler, an acoustician from the University of Bonn. Eimert was soon joined by Karlheinz Stockhausen, who composed the first really important tape composition from this studio, the now-famous *Gesang der Jünglinge* (1956; *Song of Youth*). The Cologne studio soon became a focal point of the reemergence of Germany as a dominant force in new music.

Stockhausen's first tape composition

At Cologne emphasis was immediately placed on electronically generated sounds rather than concrete sounds and on electronic sound modifications such as filtering and modulating rather than tape manipulation. Eimert and Stockhausen also published a journal, *Die Reihe* ("The Row"), in which appeared articles emphasizing the "purity" of electronic sounds and the necessity of coupling electronic music to serial composing (using ordered groups of pitches, rhythms, and other musical elements as compositional bases), which made no more sense than the Paris group's insistence on using only nonelectronic, nonserial material. This activity was part of the campaign of the 1950s that brought about the collapse of Neoclassicism (a style that drew equally on 20th-century musical idioms and earlier, formal types); the emergence of the Austrian composer Anton von Webern as the father figure of the new music; the development of total serialism, pointillism (a style making use of individual tones placed in a very sparse texture), and intellectualism; and an emphasis on technique. The examples set by these two studios were soon widely imitated in Europe. This trend continued in the 1960s, with many more studios, from modest to elaborate, being set up in almost every major urban centre in Europe. As time passed, the techniques and equipment in the newer studios became more standardized and reliable, and the rather peculiar issue of concrete versus electronic sounds ceased to concern anyone.

In the United States the production of electronic music, until 1958, was much more sporadic. The only continuing effort of this sort was the project undertaken by two composers at Columbia University, Otto Luening and Vladimir Ussachevsky, to create a professional tape studio and to compose music illustrating the musical possibilities of the tape medium. Luening and Ussachevsky often collaborated on joint compositions. They gained particular attention for the composition of several concerto-like works for tape recorder and orchestra. In 1959 Luening and Ussachevsky joined with another U.S. composer, Milton Babbitt, to organize, on a much larger scale, the Columbia–Princeton Electronic Music Center, in which an impressive number of composers of professional repute have worked.

Varèse's *Déserts*

Other tape compositions in the early 1950s in the United States were largely those of individual composers working as best they could under improvised circumstances. One major composer who did so was Varèse, who completed *Déserts,* for tape and instrumental ensemble, in 1954, and *Poème électronique,* for the Philips Pavilion at the 1958 Brussels World's Fair. Another was John Cage, who completed *Williams Mix* in 1952 and *Fontana Mix* in 1958. Both Varèse and Cage had anticipated the electronic medium; Cage's *Imaginary Landscape No. 1* (1939) for RCA test records and percussion can well be regarded as a forerunner of current live electronic music.

With the establishment of the Experimental Music Studio at the University of Illinois in 1958 by Lejaren Hiller and the University of Toronto studio in 1959 by Myron Schaeffer, the formation of facilities for both production and teaching began to move forward. The number of studios in university music departments grew rapidly, and they soon became established as essential in teaching as well as composing.

The individual components may vary in a well-designed "classic" studio, but basically the equipment may be divided into five categories: sound sources (sine-wave, square-wave, sawtooth-wave, and white-noise generators; and microphones for picking up concrete sounds); routing and control circuitry (patch panels, switching boards, and mixers for coupling components together; amplifiers; and output connections); signal modifiers (modulators, frequency shifters, artificial reverberators, filters, variable-speed tape recorders, and time compression–expansion devices); monitors and quality-control equipment (frequency counter, spectrum analyzer, VU metres that monitor recording levels, oscilloscope, power amplifiers with loudspeakers and headsets, and workshop facilities); and recording and playback equipment, including high-quality tape recorders.

With this equipment the composer records sounds, both electronic and microphoned; modifies them singly or in montages by operations such as modulation, reverberation, and filtering; and finally re-records them in increasingly complex patterns. Inevitably, a major part of the composer's effort is tape editing, unless he is satisfied with the crudest string of effects merely linked together in sequence. As in any other kind of music, the aesthetic merit of an electronic music composition seems to depend not only on musical ideas as such but also on the way in which they relate to one another and how they are used to build up a musical structure.

Integration of live instruments and recorder with performance ensembles

The integration of the tape has become a rather popular form of chamber music, if not of symphonic music. Varèse's *Déserts* is an early example of this. It is scored for a group of 15 musicians and a two-channel tape and consists of four instrumental episodes interrupted by three tape interludes. In other works the tape recorder is "performed" together with the remaining instruments rather than merely in contrast to them. The problems of coordination, however, can become overriding, for it is difficult for a group of performers to follow a tape exactly. Obviously, the tape dominates the situation, remorselessly moving along no matter what happens in the rest of the group.

Thousands of electronic tape compositions were in existence by the early 1970s, many of ephemeral interest. It is relatively rare for a composer to have established a reputation solely as a composer of tape music. Pierre Henry perhaps is an example, but in general the important names in instrumental music of the 1950s and 1960s are the significant contributors in electronic music, too.

Stockhausen remained in the forefront of electronic music composers with several important pieces following *Gesang der Jünglinge.* These included *Kontakte* (1959–60; *Contacts*), for tape, piano, and percussion, and *Telemusik* (1966), for tape alone. Luciano Berio and Bruno Maderna, both Italians, worked for a while at the Radio Audizioni Italia (now Radiotelevisione Italiana) studio in Milan. Besides *Différences* (1958–60), a composition for tape and chamber group, Berio's tape pieces include *Thema-Omaggio a Joyce* (1958; *Homage to Joyce*) and *Visage* (1961), which exploited the unusual voice of the American singer Cathy Berberian.

In the United States the Columbia–Princeton Electronic Music Center has had the greatest output, a long list of composers besides Luening and Ussachevsky having used its facilities. Tape music from the University of Illinois studio includes Salvatore Martirano's *L's GA* (1967), a savage political satire for tape, films, helium bomb, and gas-masked politico. The University of Toronto studio, in spite of its technical excellence, has not been well represented on discs. One Canadian piece that is very amusing, however, is Hugh LeCaine's *Dripsody* (1955), all the sounds of which are derived from the splash of a single drop of water.

Music synthesizers. Composing tape music by the classic method was neither easy nor free of technical pitfalls. A complex piece had to be assembled from hundreds or even thousands of fragments of tape. Splicing these sounds together consumed a vast amount of time and could also lead to an accumulation of errors and deterioration of the sound. Consequently, substantial efforts were expended to reduce this work load and at the same time improve quality. Music synthesizers were the first product of these efforts. They cannot, however, be regarded as more than an intermediate technological development because of later computer technology (see below).

In contrast to Cahill's period, by the 1950s the means finally existed to construct full-scale music synthesizers, starting with the RCA Electronic Music Synthesizers, designed by Harry Olson and Herbert Belar, research scientists working at the RCA Laboratories at Princeton, New Jersey. The first machine was introduced in 1955; a second, improved model was turned over to the Columbia–Princeton Electronic Music Center in 1959.

The basic advance of the RCA synthesizer was an information input mechanism, a device for punching sets of instructions into a wide roll of punched paper tape. The composer could at any time during the programming process interrupt this activity to listen to what had been punched, to make corrections, and to edit the material before making a final paper tape that then constituted the "master score" of the composition.

The composer whose name became particularly associated with the RCA synthesizer was Milton Babbitt. He had developed a precisely defined compositional technique involving total serialization (*i.e.,* of every musical element). When he became aware of the synthesizer, he was anxious to use it, because it gave him the opportunity to realize his music more precisely than had hitherto been the case. Among Babbitt's compositions created with this machine were *Composition for Synthesizer* (1961), *Vision and Prayer* (1961), *Ensembles for Synthesizer* (1963), *Philomel* (1964), and *Phonemena* (1974).

In about 1960 a new circuit, the voltage-controlled oscillator (VCO), attracted the attention of engineers interested in electronic music because the frequency of its output signal is proportional to an independently generated input voltage rather than being internally set. The response is immediate because no mechanical couplings or controls are required. Robert Moog was the first to design several types of compact synthesizers of moderate price that supplied an extended range of possibilities for sound manipulation. In addition to VCO's, which produce sine, square, sawtooth, and triangular waves, the Moog synthesizer contained white-noise generators, attack and decay generators (controlling a sound's onset and fading), voltage-controlled amplifiers, and band-pass filters and sequencers.

Design of the Moog synthesizer

One major advance in sound manipulation provided by VCO's is frequency modulation; if the input is a periodic function, the output frequency will vary periodically to provide tremolos, trills, and warble tones. Moog's synthesizer soon had to compete with several other synthesizers of essentially the same design, the Buchla Electronic Music Box, the ARP, and the later, more sophisticated Prophet 10.

These popular synthesizers eliminate much of the drudgery of tape splicing, but at a price. The range of timbres and processes is more limited because they operate by subtractive synthesis and impose transients that affect all partials (component vibrations) of a complex wave identically. An advantage of a harmonic tone generator built in 1962 by James Beauchamp at the University of Illinois, also from VCO's, was that it used additive synthesis—*i.e.,* it created sound by combining signals for pure tones (sine waves)—instead of removing partials from a complex signal. It was designed so that each partial of a sound could have its own entry point, its own rise time, and its own decay time. The improvement in tone quality was enormous, because the ear normally expects nuances such as higher partials that decay faster than lower ones. Salvatore Martirano's *Underworld* (1965) is a good example of music in which the tape was made largely by additive synthesis.

A composer closely associated with synthesizers is Morton Subotnik, who has produced a series of extended electronic music compositions, starting with *Silver Apples of the Moon* (1967). These pieces were created on the Buchla synthesizer, and any one of them demonstrates in relatively unmodified form the types of sounds one may obtain with these instruments.

The success of *Switched-on Bach*

A word should be said about realizations of instrumental music through synthesizers, notably an early, commercially successful album called *Switched-on Bach* (1968), arrangements made by Walter (later Wendy) Carlos on a Moog synthesizer. The record displayed technical excellence in the sounds created and made the electronic synthesis of music more intelligible to the general listening public. This is useful so long as it is realized that the materials on the record are arrangements of familiar music, not original compositions. (Carlos later created an original electronic score for the science fiction film *Tron.*)

Computer music. Perhaps the most important development in electronic music is the use of digital computers. The kinds of computers employed range from large mainframe, general-purpose machines to special-purpose digital circuits expressly designed for musical uses. Musical applications of digital computers can be grouped into five basic categories: data processing and information retrieval, including library applications and abstracting; processing of music notation and music printing; acoustical, theoretical, and musicological research; music composition; and sound synthesis. In all these fields considerable research and experimentation is being carried out, with sound synthesis perhaps being the most widespread and advanced activity. Dramatic illustrations of the growth of this work include the appearance of the periodical *Computer Music Journal,* the formation of the Computer Music Association, made up of hundreds of members, and the holding each year of the International Computer Music Conference. The 1982 conference dominated the Venice Biennale—one of the major festivals of contemporary music.

Computer composition. Composition and sound synthesis are complementary processes because the first may lead to the second. A composer may elect to use a set of compositional programs to produce a composition. He may then stop using a computer and print his results for transcription to instrumental performance. Alternatively, he may transfer his results directly into electronic sounds by means of a second set of programs for sound synthesis. Finally, he may desire only to convert an already composed score into sound. When he does this, he translates his score into a form that can be entered into a computer and uses the computer essentially as a data translator.

The first point to understand about computer composition is that, like electronic music, it is not a style but a technique. In principle, any kind of music, from traditional to completely novel, can be written by these machines. For a composer, however, the main appeal consists not in duplicating known styles of music, but, rather, in seeking new modes of musical expression that are uniquely the result of interaction between man and this new type of instrument.

At present, composers above all need a compiling language comprised of musical or quasi-musical statements and a comprehensive library of basic compositional operations written as closed subroutines—in effect, a user's system analogous to computer languages (such as Fortran) used by mathematicians. Two major obstacles stand in the way of building up an effective musical computer language. The first is the obvious one of allocation of sufficient time, money, and other resources. The second is defining what goes into the subroutine library; *i.e.,* of stating with precision the smallest units of activity or decision making that enter into the process of musical composition. Unlike mathematics, in which traditional modes of thinking prepared the way for such a definition of subroutines, in music the defining of "modules" of composition leaves even sophisticated thinkers much more at sea.

Earliest example of computer-composed music

The earliest example of computer-composed music is the *Illiac Suite for String Quartet* (1957) by two Americans, the composer Lejaren Hiller and the mathematician Leonard Isaacson. It was a set of four experiments in which the computer was programmed to generate random integers representing various musical elements, such as pitches, rhythms, and dynamics, which were subsequently screened through programmed rules of composition.

Two very different compositions, *ST/10-1,080262* (1962), by Yannis Xenakis, and *HPSCHD* (1968), by John Cage and Hiller, are illustrative of two later approaches to computer composition. *ST/10-1,080262* is one of a number of works realized by Xenakis from a Fortran program he wrote in 1961 for an IBM 7090 computer. Several years earlier, Xenakis had composed a work called *Achorripsis* by employing statistical calculations and a Poisson distribution to assign pitches, durations, and playing instructions to the various instruments in his score. He redid the work with the computer, retitled it, and at the same time produced a number of other, similar compositions. *HPSCHD,* by contrast, is a multimedia work of indeterminate length scored for one to seven harpsichords and one to 51 tape recorders. For *HPSCHD* the composers wrote three sets of computer programs. The first, for the harpsichord solos, solved Mozart's *Musical Dice Game* (K. 294d), an early chance composition in which successive bars of the music are selected by rolling dice, and modified it with other compositions chosen with a program based on the Chinese oracle *I Ching* (*Book of Changes*). The second set of programs generated the 51 sound tracks on tape. These contained monophonic lines in microtone tunings based upon speculations by the composers regarding Mozart's melodic writing. The third program generated sheets of instructions to the purchasers of a record of the composition.

Hiller has continued to develop compositional programming techniques in order to complete a two-hour cycle of works entitled *Algorithms I, Algorithms II, and Algorithms III.* Otherwise, interest in computer composition gradually has continued to grow. For example, Gottfried Michael Koenig, director of the Instituut voor Sonologie of the University of Utrecht in The Netherlands, has after a lapse of several years written new computer music such as *Segmente 99-105* (1982) for violin and piano. Related to Koenig's work is an extensive literature on theoretical models for music composition developed by the American composer Otto Laske. Charles Ames, another American, has written several works for piano or small ensemble that are less statistical and more deterministic in approach than most of the above. Clarence Barlow has written a prize-winning composition, *Çoğluatobüsíşletmesí* (1978), that exists in two versions—for piano or for solo tape. A different, but nevertheless important, example of computer music composition is Larry Austin's *Phantasmagoria: Fantasies on Ives' Universe Symphony* (1977). This is a realization, heavily dependent on computer processing, of Charles Ives's last and most ambitious major composition, which he left in a diverse assortment of some 45 sketch pages and fragments.

The borderline between composition and sound synthesis is becoming increasingly blurred as sound synthesis becomes more sophisticated and as composers begin to experiment with compositional structures that are less related to traditional musical syntax. An example of this is *Androgeny,* written for tape in 1978 by the Canadian composer Barry Truax.

Computer sound synthesis. The production of electronic sounds by digital techniques is rapidly replacing the use of oscillators, synthesizers, and other audio components (now commonly called analogue hardware) that have been the standard resources of the composer of electronic music. Not only is digital circuitry and digital programming much more versatile and accurate, but it is also much cheaper. The advantages of digital processing are manifest even to the commercial recording industry, where digital recording is replacing long-established audio technology.

Basic techniques for producing sounds with a computer

The three basic techniques for producing sounds with a computer are sign-bit extraction, digital-to-analogue conversion, and the use of hybrid digital–analogue systems. Of these, however, only the second process is of more than historical interest. Sign-bit extraction was occasionally used for compositions of serious musical intent—for example, in *Computer Cantata* (1963), by Hiller and Robert Baker, and in *Sonoriferous Loops* (1965), by Herbert Brün. Some interest persists in building hybrid digital-analogue facilities, perhaps because some types of signal processing, such as reverberation and filtering, are time-consuming even in the fastest of computers.

Digital-to-analogue conversion has become the standard technique for computer sound synthesis. This process was originally developed in the United States by Max Mathews and his colleagues at Bell Telephone Laboratories in the early 1960s. The best known version of the programming that activated the process was called Music 5.

Digital-to-analogue conversion (and the reverse process, analogue-to-digital conversion, which is used to put sounds into a computer rather than getting them out) depends on the sampling theorem. This states that a wave form should be sampled at a rate twice the bandwidth of the system if the samples are to be free of quantizing noise (a high-pitched whine to the ear). Because the auditory bandwidth is 20–20,000 hertz (Hz), this specifies a sampling rate of 40,000 samples per second though, practically, 30,000 is sufficient, because tape recorders seldom record anything significant above 15,000 Hz. Also, instantaneous amplitudes must be specified to at least 12 bits so that the jumps from one amplitude to the next are low enough for the signal-to-noise ratio to exceed commercial standards (55 to 70 decibels).

Music 5 was more than simply a software system, because it embodied an "orchestration" program that simulated many of the processes employed in the classical electronic music studio. It specified unit generators for the standard wave forms, adders, modulators, filters, reverberators, and so on. It was sufficiently generalized that a user could freely define his own generators. Music 5 became the software prototype for installations the world over.

One of the best of these was designed by Barry Vercoe at the Massachusetts Institute of Technology during the 1970s. This program, called Music 11, runs on a PDP-11 computer and is a tightly designed system that incorporates many new features, including graphic score input and output. Vercoe's instructional program has trained virtually a whole generation of young composers in computer sound manipulation. Another important advance, discovered by John Chowning of Stanford University in 1973, was the use of digital FM (frequency modulation) as a source of musical timbre. The use of graphical input and output, even of musical notation, has been considerably developed, notably by Mathews at Bell Telephone Laboratories, by Leland Smith at Stanford University, and by William Buxton at the University of Toronto.

There are also other approaches to digital sound manipulation. For example, there is a growing interest in analogue-to-digital conversion as a compositional tool. This technique allows concrete and recorded sounds to be subjected to digital processing, and this, of course, includes the human voice. Charles Dodge, a composer at Brooklyn College, has composed a number of scores that incorporate vocal sounds, including *Cascando* (1978), based on the radio play of Samuel Beckett, and *Any Resemblance Is Purely Coincidental* (1980), for computer-altered voice and tape. The classic *musique concrète* studio founded by Pierre Schaeffer has become a digital installation, under François Bayle. Its main emphasis is still on the manipulation of concrete sounds. Mention also should be made of an entirely different model for sound synthesis first investigated in 1971 by Hiller and Pierre Ruiz; they programmed differential equations that define vibrating objects such as strings, plates, membranes, and tubes. This technique, though forbidding mathematically and time-consuming in the computer, nevertheless is potentially attractive because it depends neither upon concepts reminiscent of analogue hardware nor upon acoustical research data.

Another important development is the production of specialized digital machines for use in live performance. All such instruments depend on newer types of microprocessors and often on some specialized circuitry. Because these instruments require real-time computation and conversion, however, they are restricted in versatility and variety of timbres. Without question, though, these instruments will be rapidly improved because there is a commercial market for them, including popular music and music education, that far exceeds the small world of avant-garde composers.

Some of these performance instruments are specialized in design to meet the needs of a particular composer—an example being Salvatore Martirano's *Sal-Mar Construction* (1970). Most of them, however, are intended to replace analogue synthesizers and therefore are equipped with conventional keyboards. One of the earliest of such instruments was the "Egg" synthesizer built by Michael Manthey at the University of Århus in Denmark. The Synclavier later was put on the market as a commercially produced instrument that uses digital hardware and logic. It represents for the 1980s the digital equivalent of the Moog synthesizer of the 1960s.

The most advanced digital sound synthesis, however, is still done in large institutional installations. Most of these are in U.S. universities, but European facilities are being built in increasing numbers. The Instituut voor Sonologie in Utrecht and LIMB (Laboratorio Permanente per l'Informatica Musicale) at the University of Padua in Italy resemble U.S. facilities because of their academic affiliation. Rather different, however, is IRCAM (Institut de Recherche et de Coordination Acoustique/Musique), part of the Centre Georges Pompidou in Paris. IRCAM, headed by Pierre Boulez, is an elaborate facility for research in and the performance of music. Increasingly, attention there has been given to all aspects of computer processing of music, including composition, sound analysis and synthesis, graphics, and the design of new electronic instruments for performance and pedagogy. It is a spectacular demonstration that electronic and computer music has come of age and has entered the mainstream of music history.

In conclusion, science has brought about a tremendous expansion of musical resources by making available to the composer a spectrum of sounds ranging from pure tones at one extreme to random noise at the other. It has made possible the rhythmic organization of music to a degree of subtlety and complexity hitherto unattainable. It has brought about the acceptance of the definition of music as "organized sound." It has permitted the composer, if he chooses, to have complete control over his own work. It permits him, if he desires, to eliminate the performer as an intermediary between himself and his audience. It has placed the critic in a problematic situation, because his analysis of what he hears must frequently be carried out solely by ear, unaided by any written score. (L.Hi.)

Vocal music

Music for voices encompasses a broad variety of genres for solo voice and voices in combination, with or without instrumental accompaniment. It includes monophonic music (having a single line of melody) and polyphonic music (consisting of more than one simultaneous melody). This section deals with Western art music preserved in staff notation, either for a single solo voice or for voices in unison, and briefly discusses the differences between Western and non-Western traditions. It excludes the complex forms of opera, oratorio, cantata, mass, and requiem, in which solo singing is frequently combined with choral music. The earliest written examples date from the 10th century, prior to which music was transmitted principally by oral tradition.

GENRES OF VOCAL MUSIC

Medieval and Renaissance periods. The chant most important for Western music is the so-called Gregorian repertory, earliest preserved in French manuscripts beginning from *c.* 900. Music for other major early medieval Latin repertories either has not survived (old Frankish, or Gallican, chant), is indecipherable (Mozarabic chant from Spain), or did not serve as the basis for later musical development (Ambrosian chant from Milan).

French development of Gregorian chant

From *c.* 750 to 850, music and musicians moved freely between the north and south with the intention of transferring Roman chant to France, but the methods and the extent of the process cannot be documented. The French greatly expanded their repertory until *c.* 1150 through the addition of both melodies and texts. Particularly important for future developments in vocal music were the new hymns, sequences, and other poetic settings, which were organized into regular stanzas with rhymes and metrical patterns. Gregorian chants not only served a liturgical function but also provided source material for much of the polyphonic music of the Middle Ages and Renaissance.

The degree of elaboration in a particular chant melody generally relates to its function within the liturgy. In chants that serve for recitations, such as psalms, lessons, or prayers, the music is secondary to a clear projection of the text; these settings are predominately syllabic (*i.e.,* only one note per syllable) and use relatively few pitches. Somewhat more ornate are melodies that accompany a liturgical action (such as processionals or communions in the mass), while chants completely independent of these functions, such as mass graduals and alleluias, tend to become the most elaborate. In these last two types, settings vary from neumatic (two to five notes per syllable) to highly melismatic (many notes per syllable).

Unlike the Gregorian repertory, the medieval chants of the major Eastern churches no longer continue as living traditions. The Byzantine liturgy, codified by the 11th century, has been subject to continual change since the fall of Constantinople in 1453. The early chants, preserved in manuscripts from the 11th to the 15th centuries, show fascinating parallels with the Gregorian repertory, suggesting close relationships or common origins between the two liturgies. Other Eastern churches developed independent chant repertories: Coptic (Egyptian), Abyssinian, and

Armenian; but written sources for these chants are either nonexistent or presently indecipherable. Russian (*znamenny*) chant evolved from the Byzantine liturgy imported in the 10th century and reached a classical stage in the 15th–17th centuries; but the only legible manuscripts date from the end of this period.

Latin songs by wandering scholars as early as the 7th century survive in a musical notation now unreadable. But the largest repertories of monophonic songs come from the troubadours in southern France (late 11th to early 13th centuries), the trouvères in northern France (mid-12th through 13th centuries), and the German minnesingers (mid-12th to late 15th centuries). These musicians and poets from all classes of society composed and performed for the nobility until well into the 13th century, after which patronage gradually shifted to the bourgeoisie and prosperous clergy. Their texts most frequently treat the ideals of chivalry and courtly love, using polished and often obscure language; at times similar poems offer praise to the Blessed Virgin. Service songs, called *sirventes* in southern France (*Spruch* in German), deal with didactic, political, or personal matters, perhaps in a satirical fashion. Other texts record events of the court, such as marriages, deaths, or participation in crusades. Among the more traditional songs from northern France are the *chansons de geste,* extended narratives glorifying earlier heroes or saints.

Poetic form and music

The poetic texts inherited strophic (stanzaic) design, rhyming, and metrical schemes from earlier medieval Latin. To these devices the trouvères added the idea of a refrain, varying in length from a single word to several poetic lines and placed at any position within the stanza. Eventually certain arrangements became fixed forms: the *ballade* or German *Bar* form (a a B), the *rondeau* (A B a A a b A B), and the *virelai* (A b b a A). In the diagrams, identical letters indicate same rhymes, and capitals show the refrain; as a rule, two sections of music are repeated according to the design of the poem. Shown here in their simplest structures, the forms were regularly expanded or varied in detail. Less standard designs were the *lai* in northern France (*Leich* in German), with irregular groupings of couplets, and the lengthy *chansons de geste,* probably repeating a simple melodic formula for each text line.

Many monophonic songs resemble Gregorian chant, although without lengthy melismas. Others present a more modern sound through the use of the major scale and organization in short symmetrical phrases. Most of the earlier songs (before 1200) have no written indications of metre. Recent scholarship suggests a free rendition for songs with irregular phrasing and embellishments but more regulated rhythms for the simple dancelike tunes. Improvised accompaniments are often appropriate, although not indicated in the original manuscripts.

Vernacular songs spread to the courts of England, Spain, and Italy, although the surviving examples from these regions are primarily religious. The monophonic art eventually declined during the 14th century for three principal reasons: the rise of interest in polyphonic composition, the loss of aristocratic patronage, and the substitution of theoretical rules for creative instinct. The last phenomenon is best illustrated in the works of the German middle class meistersingers from the 15th and 16th centuries.

Polyphonic settings of fixed-form songs

The most characteristic and persistent type of early polyphonic song is the French chanson, in the form of a *rondeau, ballade,* or *virelai.* Chanson composers included the most outstanding musicians of the 14th and 15th centuries, among them Guillaume de Machaut, Guillaume Dufay, Gilles Binchois, Antoine Busnois, and Jean d'Okeghem. Their activities centred in the courts of France and Burgundy, although many travelled to other areas, particularly Italy and northern Spain. Indigenous forms developed in the 14th century in Italy (*madrigal, ballata,* and *caccia*), and in the 15th century in Spain (*villancico* and *romance*), England (carol), and German (*Bar*); but these types shared many features of the Franco-Burgundian compositions. The chanson consists of two principal sections of music, with no text repetition except as required by the poetic structure. Three contrasting voices are standard: cantus, tenor, and contratenor. The cantus typically moves in a high tenor or alto range, in counterpoint with the lower tenor. To this two-part framework is added the contratenor, at times following the style and range of the cantus but at other times that of the tenor. Although most performances undoubtedly combined the voice(s) with instruments, it is by no means certain how the parts were distributed. Evidence suggests that performances were quite flexible, depending upon the singers or instruments available and upon the style of the individual song.

During the later 15th century new ideals for vocal composition arose that were incompatible with the earlier fixed-form songs. The different voice parts, now at least four in number, tended toward more equalization in style. All voices were underlain with a text, or were potentially singable; they either imitated the same melody or had similar rhythmic and melodic characteristics. Poetic structure was now obscured by a continuous overlapping of sections, and the words of the text were often blurred by the activity of the various voices. Native Italian partsongs (*frottole,* carnival songs, and *villanelle*) generally presented texts with clearer declamation, but, as the century advanced, even these simpler types gave way to the more complex Renaissance madrigal, with frequent use of melodic imitation. Musicians regularly arranged these polyphonic works for solo performance with instrumental accompaniment. But no significant part of this artistic repertory, with the possible exception of Spanish *vihuela* songs, was designed exclusively for the solo singer.

Transition to a new style

The advent of the modern art song depended upon a rejection of two prevailing attitudes found in mid-16th-century polyphony: the principle that a piece of vocal music was performable in any conceivable medium (for solo, for ensemble of voices, or even for instruments alone) and the idea that the text needed only be the servant of the music. An increasing concern for textual interpretation and declamation began to appear in late 16th-century polyphonic compositions. Texts were often delivered in a speechlike recitation; emotionally charged words were emphasized through special rhythms, unexpected harmonic progressions, chromaticism (use of notes foreign to the song's mode), and coloratura (florid ornamentation); and simultaneous rhythms in the different voices made possible a clearer projection of the words. Of more temporary influence were the French experiments with quantitative metre in poetry and music (*musique mesurée*). But the final step in the transfer of these various techniques from part music to genuine solo music came at the end of the century, notably in Italian monody (expressive melody with chordal accompaniment) and English lute songs.

The 17th–20th centuries. The art song of the 17th through 20th centuries always reflects the mutual influences of music and literature, and most enduring masterpieces show an extraordinary sensitivity of the composer to the individual words, to the prosody, or simply to the overall character of his text. The poet Goethe felt that the simpler the musical setting, the more likely it was to reflect the original nature of the poem; any extensive musical elaborations often reinterpreted the message or character of the poem and were therefore undesirable. But the more imaginative composers, particularly those of the 19th and 20th centuries, used the full resources of their art to embellish the text or even to realize potentials that were not explicit in the original.

Song cycles

Ages producing great poetry have often prompted a flourishing of important song writing, as Elizabethan England, 19th-century Germany and Austria, and late 19th-through early 20th-century France. Since the early 19th century, composers have frequently selected a group of poems by a particular author or on a single topic by different authors to produce a collection of related songs. Some of these cycles are undoubtedly designed to be performed as integrated compositions. As examples, Beethoven's *An die ferne Geliebte* (*To the Distant Beloved*) musically relates the opening with the closing of the cycle and joins each song to the next without interruption; individual songs in Schumann's *Frauenliebe und Leben* (*Woman's Love and Life*) and Brahms's *Magelone* present lyrical moments within a continuous narrative.

Three methods are possible for setting strophic poetry.

Methods for strophic setting

Simple-strophic setting consists of a single piece of music to be repeated for all stanzas. Modified-strophic setting retains the same musical framework for each stanza but with changing details in the voice and accompaniment to suit the progressing text. Through-composed setting proceeds to a different musical plan for each new stanza. The simple-strophic approach is effective if the entire poem suggests a central mood that can be captured in the music or if the composer creates a neutral setting that avoids detailed text illustration. Prosody and syntax must follow a regular pattern in each stanza if the result is to be satisfactory. Thus in Franz Schubert's "Das Wandern" ("Wandering) from the cycle *Die schöne Müllerin* (*The Miller's Beautiful Daughter*), the accompaniment suggests the continual flow of the millstream, while the energetic vocal melody reflects the enthusiasm of the young traveller. The singer's rhythm is easily adaptable to each stanza of text.

Either the modified-strophic or the through-composed method is more likely to be successful for poems that contain widely differing moods in each stanza, progress to a dramatic climax, or follow irregular prosodic patterns. In the modified-strophic setting of "Der Lindenbaum" ("The Linden Tree"), from the cycle *Winterreise* (*Winter Journey*), Schubert changes from major to minor for the stanza suggesting bitter recollections, gives a more dramatic interpretation to both the voice and piano for references to the chilling winter wind, and, finally, repeats the music for the opening stanza but with modifications in the piano when the thoughts return to pleasant memories. The through-composed approach does not necessarily require new musical ideas for all parts of the song; the crucial distinction is the lack of any structural correspondence between the stanzas of text and the sections of music. Although the vocal lines in each stanza of Claude Debussy's "C'est l'extase langoureuse" ("This Is Langorous Ecstasy") are entirely different, the piano unifies the setting by frequently returning to its opening motive. The art song since the late 19th century and simple strophic works from earlier periods normally provide a straightforward setting that avoids any word repetitions. The frequent text repetitions in many art songs from the 17th through mid-19th centuries generally indicate a predominance of musical over textual considerations, a feature also important in the operatic or concert aria.

Speech rhythms and prosody

In setting a text to a vocal melody, the composer may choose to present his interpretation of the natural speech patterns in the poem; in his solution, the rhythmic complexity, the melodic range of tones, and variations in volume will depend ultimately upon his own musical language. Also open to the composer's interpretation is the versification of the poem. The music may reflect whatever prosodic principles are present in the language: poetic feet, qualitative or quantitative accent, or mere count of syllables. Although some vocal settings show a complete preoccupation with speech inflections (strict recitatives of the 17th century) or with prosody (*musique mesurée* experiments in the late 16th and early 17th centuries), most successful songs incorporate either or both of these considerations into a melodic line that is satisfying because of musical qualities as well. Hugo Wolf's "Kennst du das Land" ("Do You Know the Land") faithfully reflects the iambic feet (⏑′) of Goethe's poem, but this prosodic awareness is combined with a sensitivity to the important words in the text. Furthermore, the melody progresses to a musical climax, as Wolf prepares for his setting of the high point of the poem. Even in works in which the text is obviously the servant of the music, a neutral treatment of rhythm and pitch usually avoids glaring distortions of the words. In the final portion of Arnold Schoenberg's "Sommermüd ("Weary of Summer") Opus 48, the pitches in the vocal melody are entirely determined by the 12-tone row (composer's ordering of the 12 notes of the chromatic scale) chosen for the whole song; yet the rhythm generally follows that of the poem.

Continuo accompaniment

The nature and role of the accompaniment has undergone many changes since the earliest art songs. In the repertory of the 17th and 18th centuries, the singer is the prime interpreter of the text. As a rule, the accompanying part of these songs consists only of a figured bass (the basso continuo), in which the notation for the bass melody also indicates the harmonies to be improvised on the harpsichord, lute, or some other chord instrument. Except for an occasional imitation or anticipation of the voice or for interludes between the stanzas, the continuo accompaniment provides little commentary on the poem. Even when these early songs call for additional instruments, such as a flute or violin, or when the harmony is fully written out, as in 17th-century lute songs, the accompaniment only supports or imitates the voice. Complete piano parts regularly appear first in the late 18th century, replacing the abbreviated continuo. Although some piano accompaniments continue a subservient relationship to the voice, the trend in the 19th and 20th centuries has been toward greater participation in the interpretation. The piano may reinforce the emotional states of the poem; *e.g.,* underlying anxiety in Wolf's "In der Frühe" ("In the Early Morning"); represent external details in the setting, as the spinning wheel in Schubert's "Gretchen am Spinnrade" ("Gretchen at the Spinning Wheel"); or assist in building dramatic climaxes, as in Wolf's "Kennst du das Land." It may provide extensive preludes, as in Richard Strauss's "Morgen" ("Morning"), interludes or postludes, as in Schumann's "Alten, bösen Lieder" ("Old, Evil Songs") from *Dichterliebe* (*Poet's Love*), or complete the phrasing in the voice; *e.g.,* Schumann's "Nussbaum" ("Nut Tree"). In the present century, the piano frequently follows its independent ideas, freeing the voice for more expressive declamation, as in Maurice Ravel's *Histoires naturelles,* in which the instrument effectively portrays the various animals in the texts. Many songs from the 19th and 20th centuries, particularly the period *c.* 1880–1920, have either alternative or original accompaniments for orchestra (*e.g.,* by Gustav Mahler, Strauss, Schoenberg, Alban Berg, Anton Webern, Ravel, and many others). Such settings enrich the texture and make possible a much greater range of colouristic effects. Other 20th-century songs require small chamber ensembles. The instruments may provide interpretative details, as in Ravel's *Chansons madécasses* (*Madagascan Songs*) or simply complement the musical ideas of the voice, as in Webern's chamber songs for various combinations.

Role of the piano

The concert aria, primarily an 18th-century composition with orchestral accompaniment, was originally intended either as an independent showpiece, as a substitute aria for an operatic production, or as a special number, called *licenza,* to follow a performance. Usually composed for a specific singer, the aria was generally more concerned with displaying vocal qualities than with interpreting the literary details of the text. Consequently, the poems are concise, with each verse typically repeated many times throughout a setting. The structure follows the same designs of the operatic aria. Most characteristic is the *da capo* plan, consisting of two contrasting sections of music: after the second section, the performers repeat the first, this time with more elaborate embellishments improvised by the singer. Another plan, popular in the later 18th century, is the composite design, consisting of several different sections with contrasting moods, usually with a brilliant conclusion. In both the *da capo* and composite forms, the composer represents a minimum of stereotyped emotional states, generally one for each section of music. A single tempo and metre are maintained for each section. If the aria is preceded by a recitative, the entire composition becomes a dramatic scene (*scena*).

The concert aria's influence

The concert aria was so influential a form that many continuo songs followed its structure and style. Henry Purcell's "Ye Gentle Spirits of the Air, Appear" (published posthumously in 1702) is in *da capo* structure, with textual repetitions and difficult coloratura, but it is also an objective musical portrayal of the words "repeat" and "trembling." Such text painting, characteristic of the earlier madrigal genre and sometimes found in arias, is exceptional in the general literature of the art song.

The solo voice has at times been used within works that are primarily instrumental, as an imposing climax to a symphonic composition (the finales of Beethoven, *Symphony No. 9;* Mahler, *Symphonies Nos. 2* and *3;* and Franz Liszt, *Faust Symphony*—each example using a chorus as well); as an incidental commentary to introduce completely instrumental movements (Hector Berlioz, *Roméo et Juliette*); as the primary participant in a song movement with a symphonic or chamber work (Mahler, *Symphonies Nos. 2–4*; Schoenberg, *Quartet No. 2* and *Serenade,* Opus 24); and as an inconspicuous member of an otherwise instrumental ensemble, as in the finale of Pierre Boulez's *Marteau sans maître* (*The Hammer Without a Master*), where the voice generally has a humming part. Two other of Mahler's symphonic compositions have more extensive vocal participation: *Das Lied von der Erde* (*The Song of the Earth*), labelled "A Symphony for Tenor, Contralto (or Baritone), and Orchestra," where one or the other soloist is heard in each movement, and *Symphony No. 8,* employing voices (solo or choral) throughout; the finale of the latter work has the spirit of an oratorio.

Vocal compositions with no articulated text are called vocalises (*vocalizzi* in Italian). Although such works have been traditionally used as exercises, many 20th-century composers have written concert vocalises as well, among them Ravel, Sergey Rachmaninoff, and Igor Stravinsky. Vocalises are particularly suitable for chamber compositions, since the voice without text is easily adapted to the level of the other instruments.

THE REPERTORY SINCE 1600

Continuo Lieder and concert arias

Art songs in German, French, and English. The most important German songs (Lieder) of the 17th century were continuo Lieder used for informal entertainment, notable composers being Heinrich Albert and Adam Krieger. With the rising prestige of opera in the later 17th century, these simple Lieder declined in favour of extended virtuoso songs and concert arias, such as Handel's nine *Deutsche Arien* (*German Arias*) of *c.* 1729. The concert aria eventually reached a peak in the late 18th-century works of Mozart and Haydn. At the same time, three counterdevelopments pointed toward the future for the German Lied: a reaction against the superficialities of the operatic aria, the availability of a new repertory of lyric poetry, and an increasing use of the keyboard (eventually the piano) as an expressive accompaniment. First to reflect these directions were north German composers (Carl Philipp Emmanuel Bach, Johann Friedrich Reichardt, Karl Friedrich Zelter, and Johann Rudolf Zumsteeg), particularly in their settings of devotional poetry by Christian Gellert, Julius Sturm, and Friedrich Klopstock. The keyboard part was often fully written out, yet generally subordinate to the voice. Beethoven eventually expanded the role of the accompaniment in his finest songs, including settings of Goethe and Gellert, and the cycle *An die ferne Geliebte.*

At the head of distinguished 19th-century Lied composers stands Schubert, whose masterpieces combine a natural feeling for musical design with an extraordinary sensitivity to the essentials of the text. More than 600 in number, his Lieder encompass a wide range of poets, forms, and moods. Schumann's approximately 250 songs draw from outstanding German lyricists: Heinrich Heine, Goethe, Friedrich Rückert, Joseph Eichendorff, Justinus Kerner, and Adelbert von Chamisso. His accompaniments are closely linked with the voice through doubling, imitation, or completion of musical ideas. Brahms, more like Schubert than Schumann, assigned prime importance to the voice but at times sacrificed text declamation for balance in musical phrasing. Among his approximately 300 solo works are numerous harmonizations of folk tunes (many altered according to his musical taste), a cycle of 15 romances from Ludwig Tieck's *Magelone,* and the extensive *Vier ernste Gesänge* (*Four Serious Songs*) of his last years. Wolf, in sharp contrast to Brahms, gave scrupulous attention to literary details, frequently requiring changes of pace and vocal styles within a single song. The best songs of Richard Strauss, like Wolf's, combine an expressive vocal line with a rich accompaniment, often in alternative versions for piano or orchestra.

The 20th century

Early 20th-century Lieder either develop further the possibilities of the orchestral song (Mahler, Schoenberg, Berg, Webern), explore revolutionary techniques in works using chamber ensemble or piano (Schoenberg, Webern), or merely continue late 19th-century traditions (Max Reger, Joseph Marx). Mahler's songs—*e.g., Lieder eines fahrenden Gesellen* (*Songs of a Wayfarer*), settings from *Des Knaben Wunderhorn* (*The Youth's Magic Horn*), *Kindertotenlieder* (*Songs on the Death of Children*), *Das Lied von der Erde*—deal with the sorrows and aspirations of man, the consoling powers of nature, and childlike visions of heaven; the vocal lines range from folklike simplicity to soaring lyricism. Of central importance in their composers' careers are Schoenberg's *Buch der hängenden Gärten* (*Book of the Hanging Gardens*) and his 12-tone *Drei Lieder,* Opus 48; Webern's aphoristic yet highly contrapuntal chamber songs (Opuses 13–19) and later settings of Hildegard Jone; and Berg's more lyrical *Altenberg Lieder* and concert aria *Der Wein* (*Wine*). Continuing later into the century, Paul Hindemith's skillful songs in German, French, and English incorporate various accompaniments and styles.

Airs de cour

French publishers issued numerous books of *airs de cour,* or "courtly airs," during the early 17th century. Some airs treat serious secular topics. Others, called *voix de ville,* have jovial texts, which are often set to dance rhythms. *Récits* concentrate on textual declamation, since they usually originated as commentaries within the *ballets de cour,* or "courtly ballets"; but they have little of the passion found in Italian recitatives of the same time. Still other airs are settings from the Huguenot psalter. France was nevertheless slow in developing compositions designed only for the solo singer. Aside from the *récits* and psalm settings, the airs were either arrangements of polyphonic chansons or were easily singable as part-songs. In the late 17th and 18th centuries, most vocal writing was for the large forms of opera, cantata, and motet. But a demand for songs returned with the "back to nature" movement in the mid-18th century and with the French Revolution, giving rise to *romances,* or simple, rustic tunes with folkish texts, and to patriotic songs, including "La Marseillaise."

Many 19th-century composers continued writing *romances,* some of more extended scope. But the most important type of song was the new *mélodie,* which concentrated on subtle nuances of the text and provided a substantial accompaniment, as in Hector Berlioz' cycle *Les Nuits d'été* (*Summer Nights*; to poems by Théophile Gautier), with accompaniment for orchestra or piano. The *mélodie* flourished with the rich developments in French poetry during the later 19th century. Gabriel Fauré, in his cycle *La Bonne Chanson* (*The Good Song*), set nine love poems of Paul Verlaine; the lyrical voice soars above continuous figurations in the piano. Henri Duparc's *mélodies,* only 14 in number, have long been considered masterful settings of Charles Baudelaire, Charles Leconte de Lisle, Armand Silvestre, and others. Debussy's 57 published songs use poems of his contemporaries (especially Verlaine) but also three by the 15th-century François Villon. His vocal lines freely mix a declamatory style with more lyricism at points of climax. The piano emphasizes contours of the poem and imparts unity through recurring motives. Among the most colourful song composers of the early 20th century is Ravel. His *Shéhérazade* has orchestral accompaniment, while *Trois Poèmes de Stéphane Mallarmé* and the *Chansons Madécasses* use chamber ensembles. Originally for voice and piano (although some are also orchestrated) are his folk-tune harmonizations; *Don Quichotte à Dulcinée,* dance-inspired songs intended as movie music; and the *Histories naturelles.*

Darius Milhaud treated both humorous and serious poems from all periods, while Francis Poulenc's most characteristic texts are by the Surrealists. Among the more recent French composers, Olivier Messiaen, André Jolivet, and Boulez employed advanced vocal techniques with various instrumental combinations.

Lute ayres

England's first art songs are the lute ayres published in large numbers from 1597 to 1622; the principal composers are John Dowland, John Daniel, and Thomas Campion. Of high literary quality, the strophic texts are generally anonymous, except those by the composers themselves. Many ayres resemble dance music, using standard rhythms and symmetrical phrasing. The finest songs place the voice and lute in full partnership. The ayres of the early 17th century gradually gave way to declamatory songs, usually through-composed, many of which were originally written for masques or the theatre. In the simplified accompaniment, the complete lute part was eventually replaced by a single basso-continuo line. Late 17th-century continuo songs reached a high point in the works of Purcell. His earliest songs emphasize textual prosody, but his more representative works become brilliant concert pieces.

In the 18th and 19th centuries, many songs continued to reflect the influence of opera and operetta. But more characteristic of the two centuries are less pretentious strophic works, many originating in popular concerts in the London Gardens. In the late 18th century, the turn toward simplicity resulted in collections of Scottish, Irish, and Welsh folk music; the Scottish publisher George Thomson commissioned folk-song arrangements from Haydn, Beethoven, and others.

Since the late 19th century, England has revived interest in the art song. Texts are often from the best contemporary poets, as well as from earlier classics. Musical styles have drawn on folk-music tradition as well as on advanced 20th-century musical idioms. Although the piano remains the principal accompanying instrument, orchestral or chamber-ensemble accompaniments are also prominent. Among the more significant song composers have been Sir Hubert Parry and Sir Charles Villiers Stanford; Frederick Delius, largely influenced by continental and Scandinavian music; Gustav Holst and Ralph Vaughan Williams, both with a strong interest in folk music; Peter Warlock (real name, Philip Heseltine); John Ireland; Benjamin Britten; and Sir Michael Tippett.

In the United States, songs composed before the mid-19th century were primarily by amateur musicians, and intended for singing instruction, devotion, or entertainment. Minstrel shows of the early 19th century provided the source for the stage songs of Daniel Decatur Emmett, Stephen Foster, and others. Songs of late 19th-century composers such as George Chadwick, George Foote, Horatio Parker, and Edward MacDowell were influenced by conservative trends in European Romanticism. Early 20th-century songs show the effects of French Impressionism (John Alden Carpenter, Charles Loeffler, Charles Griffes) or follow more individual directions. Sidney Homer's songs focus on a smooth vocal melody, while those of Charles Ives often vigorously represent textual details. After a lull during the 1930s and early 1940s, composers returned to the art song, often setting contemporary American literature. Some of the better known are Theodore Ward Chanler, Virgil Thomson, Samuel Barber, David Diamond, Aaron Copland, Ben Weber, Miriam Gideon, and Milton Babbitt.

Art songs in other countries. The Russian art song dates primarily from the 19th and 20th centuries, although the period of Catherine the Great (reigned 1762–96) supplies a substantial background in its imitations of French *romances* (either in French or Russian), editions of Russian folk tunes (or pseudo-folk tunes), ballads, and pseudo-Oriental songs. The chief pioneers of the 19th-century song were Mikhail Glinka and Aleksandr Dargomyzhsky, the latter brilliant for his depiction of realistic peasant scenes. The "Russian Five" (César Cui, Mily Balakirev, Aleksandr Borodin, Modest Mussorgsky, and Nikolay Rimsky-Korsakov) contributed the most significant repertory in the second half of the 19th century. Their songs present a remarkable variety of moods and styles, perhaps best illustrated in the works of Borodin and Mussorgsky. In contrast to "The Five," the conservatory musicians (chiefly Anton Rubinstein and Peter Ilich Tchaikovsky) were governed more by Western influences than by native styles. Among other pre-Revolutionary song composers, Aleksandr Grechaninov, Sergey Rachmaninoff, and Nikolay Medtner provided polished masterpieces, but no significant technical advances; more forward-looking are the early songs of Stravinsky and Sergey Prokofiev. Soviet composers have avoided the radical musical developments elsewhere. As a rule, songs since the Revolution are objective settings of Soviet poetry or traditional Russian literature (especially works by the poet Pushkin).

The art songs of Italy begin with the numerous books of monodies (continuo songs) from the first third of the 17th century by such composers as Giulio Caccini, Jacopo Peri, and Sigismondo d'India (a more significant composer). Although originally labelled with various titles, the songs fall into two general types: madrigals and strophic arias. Some madrigals are strict recitatives, although the vocal style is more frequently a smooth-flowing arioso (*i.e.,* freely expressive and lyrical). Arias tend toward symmetrical phrasing and standard rhythmical patterns, sometimes dancelike, but at times approach madrigalesque style. Many arias repeat the same music for each stanza, but others have a through-composed vocal line over the same bass (strophic-bass arias). As a rule, the accompaniments are entirely subordinated to the voice, which in the more expressive songs introduces ornaments for emphasizing important words or punctuating poetic lines. The early monodies eventually expanded into longer, more musically oriented compositions called cantatas.

Early Baroque monody

Opera was so dominant in the 18th and 19th centuries that song composition became a lost art. A return to song writing in the early 20th century, for composers such as Ottorino Respighi, Alfredo Casella, and Gian Francsco Malipiero, was inspired by the ideals and accomplishments of Italy's past, especially the Middle Ages and Renaissance. Other outstanding recent song composers are Mario Castelnuovo-Tedesco (settings of all Shakespeare's songs), Luigi Dallapiccola (using 12-tone techniques), Ildebrando Pizzetti, and Goffredo Petrassi.

Spanish and Latin American songs

Spanish songs from the 17th through 19th centuries are primarily related to theatrical productions: either the older and more enduring *zarzuelas* or the lighter *tonadillas* (*c.* 1750–1810). The vocal style is simple, often with rhythmic and ornamental clichés; the accompaniment frequently consists only of the composer's sketches to be filled out in performance. In the repertory of serious modern art songs the way was led by Felipe Pedrell, who composed folk-inspired melodies and published works of older Spanish masters. Among his better known successors are Enrique Granados, Manuel de Falla, Joaquín Turina, and Federico Mompou.

Latin America has produced a rich and varied repertory of art songs, but mostly during the present century. A great number of these compositions depict regional colour through their texts, melodies, and rhythms. Other works eschew native influences in favour of an international style. Among 20th-century Latin-American composers, the Brazilian Heitor Villa-Lobos and the Argentine Alberto Ginastera achieved worldwide fame.

The most outstanding Norwegian song composer was Edvard Grieg, whose song style blends folklike simplicity with imaginative musical ideas. As is usual with Scandinavian composers, the texts are drawn from several languages (German, Danish, Norwegian), but his finest works are in his native Norwegian. The Finn Jean Sibelius concentrated primarily on Swedish literature, interpreting a wide range of moods in a highly distinctive musical language.

Hungary's principal contributions come from Béla Bartók and Zoltán Kodály, whose songs reflect their lifelong interest in collecting native peasant tunes. For both composers folk-song arrangement became a refined art. Many songs faithfully set a traditional tune to a simple accompaniment, while more elaborate works blend native elements with advanced contemporary idioms.

In Czechoslovakia, strong ties with German culture long prevented the development of native art songs. Nineteenth-century nationalism inspired some composers to turn to Czech texts, although part of their output continued in German: Jaroslav Tomášek, Bedřich Smetana, Anton Dvořák, and the younger Leos Janáček. Poland shows a similar pattern: during the 19th century many composers turned to their native literature (especially the poetry of Adam Mickiewicz), the most important being Joseph Elsner, Frédéric Chopin, Stanislaw Moniuszko, and Karol Szymanowski. Belgium, the Netherlands, and Switzerland have also produced sizable repertories of art songs, particularly in the 19th and 20th centuries.

WESTERN AND NON-WESTERN CONCEPTIONS

In the relationship between poet, composer, and performer—and especially in the importance assigned to the composer—Western vocal music has arrived at a stage during the past few centuries that is basically unlike that of any other world culture. By the 19th century composers were recording in musical notation virtually all the essentials in their interpretations of the text: pitch, rhythm, and tempo, as well as indications for dynamics and articulation. Although the performers must bring the composer's notation to life, particularly through subtle nuances and appropriate vocal sounds, this process is primarily one of reinterpreting a previously established work of art. Comparative research in the present century has revealed certain general parallels in the vocal art of other civilizations, but no culture other than Western has placed such a premium on individual compositions from the past, and consequently nowhere else is there preserved such an extensive history of vocal literature. Aside from certain types of ritualistic music, where the slightest change in tradition is viewed as a desecration, the non-Westerner has relied primarily upon the creative role of the performer. Although the singer at times begins with a preexistent "work" notated with some pitches, rhythms, or even other indications for performance, this notation merely functions as a suggested framework. The performer contributes new details for the voice and the accompaniment, so that the composition is actually re-created rather than reinterpreted. Because of this process of creative performance, most non-Western vocal art before the advent of 20th-century recordings has been irretrievably lost.

Performer's role

During the present century, Western concepts of art song have strongly influenced the vocal music in non-Western cultures, unfortunately threatening the continued existence of many indigenous practices. The influence has at times gone in the other direction: recent examples of Western avant-gardism give the singer many improvisatory options within broader limits prescribed by the composer. It can be expected that future vocal music will continue to show intercultural exchanges of ideas and techniques without requiring the complete sacrifice of any heritage.

(W.V.P.)

CHORAL MUSIC

Music sung by a choir, known as choral music, ranks as one of several musical genres subject to misunderstanding because of false historical perspectives or misinterpretation caused by the confusion engendered by unsolved semantic problems. Choral, chorale, choir, and chorus stand in obvious relationship to one another and are in some respects used interchangeably when a body of singers, for example, is referred to as a choir, a chorus (Latin noun derived from the Greek word *choros*), or a chorale, which properly is a Lutheran hymn tune. The adjective choral may therefore be applied in a general way (choral music, choral technique) or in a specific way (such as Beethoven's *Choral Symphony* and *Choral Fantasia*). The nouns chorale, choir, and chorus are frequently used as adjectives in such expressions as chorale prelude ("choral prelude" is incorrect), choir organ, or chorus part.

The definition of choral music has by circumstance and usage been forced to comprise a far wider area than a comparable definition of an instrumental genre. It is unusual, to say the least, to perform a symphony with only a single instrument to each part, even though the opposite has occasionally happened when a string quartet movement is played by the massed strings of an orchestra. Much music now performed by choirs, however, was originally intended for soloists; and, while the lack of historical authenticity may here be deplored, it is evident that a choral performance of a madrigal (equivalent to an orchestral performance of a string quartet movement) permits many amateur musicians to enjoy, as members of a team, music that might otherwise escape their knowledge.

If a choral performance of genres for several solo voices, such as the madrigal, ballett, villanella, and part-song, results in a more neutral sound and a less personal intensity of expression, it is nevertheless true that the reverse sometimes offers unsuspected advantages, as when a work written for choir alone is performed by a group of soloists. In certain cases the work may take on a new and enhanced aspect because each strand of melody within the texture carries a personal rather than a group expression.

Variation in size of choirs

In defining choral music, some attention should also be paid to the enormous variation in the size of choirs. A chamber choir need contain only a dozen voices, certainly not more than 20; whereas a choir assembled for the Handel Festivals in the 19th century or for the Berlioz *concerts monstres* in Paris during the same epoch, might have numbered thousands. Modern traces of such massive choral effects may be found in the *Symphony No. 8 in E Flat Major* (sometimes called *Symphony of a Thousand*) of the Austrian composer Gustav Mahler. This work calls for a large double choir and a separate boys' choir, in addition to a large orchestra and eight soloists. On the other hand, numerous modern choral works, because of their difficulty and complexity, seem to have been composed with a chamber choir in mind, as in the case of *Cinq rechants* (1949) by the French composer Olivier Messiaen.

If there is more than one voice to each part—*i.e.,* to each line of polyphony (music of several voice parts) or strand of melody—the performance is choral, even though the actual sonority may not seem choral in the accepted sense until there are more than five or six voices to a part. Both types of singing may also coexist, since a choir may contain several capable soloists who may at certain points sing as a group without the choir or with the choir as a background. This feature is the choral equivalent of the orchestral concerto grosso, in which a small group of solo instruments alternate or combine with the main body of players. Examples of this may be found in choral music of all types and ages. The medieval rondeau was usually performed by a soloist who sang the verses, with a small choir for the refrain. When the mass became a vehicle for choral performance in the 15th century, the Christe Eleison, certain parts of the Gloria and the Credo, the Benedictus, and the Agnus Dei were frequently assigned to a group of soloists within the choir. *The Eton Choirbook* motets demand similar treatment since red and black text is used to differentiate between those sections intended for soloists and those for full choir. Comparable effects may be found in music written for special occasions, oratorios, verse anthems, and settings of the Passion.

Emergence of the choral tradition

Although choirs existed throughout Europe in the Middle Ages, their role was restricted to unison singing of plainchant. Polyphony was the exclusive preserve of soloists. This state of affairs was gradually modified for several reasons. Early forms of musical notation were not precise enough to allow choral performance of even the simplest two-part polyphony. As time went on, improved accuracy in notating pitch and time values permitted some degree of experiment in choral performance.

Knowledge of the subtleties of mensural (precisely measured) music was at first the prerogative of a small number of initiates. The ordinary member of the plainchant choir, or schola, was not expected to understand the notation or to perform music using it. But the teaching of musical theory spread rapidly in the 14th century, and singers became better equipped and educated than they had been at any previous time. The ever-growing wealth of the church also acted to encourage choral performance, since abbeys, cathedrals, parish and collegiate churches, and court chapels vied with each other in the opulence and perfection of their choral establishments. Laws were passed enabling royal chapels to impress (that is, to seek out and enroll) eligible provincial choirboys for the great central establishments, and in consequence every boy was a soloist in his own right, just as were the countertenors, tenors, and basses. Finally, the rapidity with which composers took advantage of this situation, evolving new techniques and adapting old ones, created a tremendous surge of choral activity and composition, which the new art of music printing was to aid even further in the early years of the 16th century. From that time until the present, there has been no abatement of interest in choral music, which is performed at amateur and professional levels throughout the entire world.

Sacred music. *The mass.* The ordinary of the mass (consisting of the Kyrie, Gloria, Credo, Sanctus and Benedictus, Agnus Dei, and in some medieval masses also the

"Ite, missa est") has been a focal point of choral music for more than 600 years. The earliest masses, such as the four-part setting by the 14th-century French composer Guillaume de Machaut, were intended for soloists; remarkable both in musical texture and structure, they are often performed chorally today. In the 15th century this tradition, in which architectonic considerations still held sway, was carried on in the masses of the English composer John Dunstable and his Burgundian contemporary, Guillaume Dufay. The use of a plainchant cantus firmus, or dominating tenor theme, knit together the movements even though they were separated during the liturgy. Modern concert performances and recordings obscure this feature, sometimes to the disadvantage of even the greatest masterpieces, which, with all movements in immediate sequence may sound too concentrated. The Renaissance saw the highest development of the cantus firmus mass, using as the central melodic support not only plainchant but even secular songs, as Josquin's *L'Homme armé* (printed in 1502) or folk songs, as John Taverner's mass, *The Western Wynde* (*c.* 1520).

Hundreds of composers wrote settings of the ordinary of the mass at this time; some, like the Italian composer Giovanni da Palestrina, wrote more than 100 masses. The Spaniards Cristóbal de Morales and Tomás Luis de Victoria and the Englishmen William Byrd and Thomas Tallis all avoided secular melodies, even though these would have been largely obscured by the texture of the voices. On the other hand, the Netherlanders Orlando di Lasso and Philippe de Monte did not hesitate to draw upon themes of diverse origins. Byrd and his Flemish contemporary Heinrich Isaac also set a considerable amount of the proper of the mass (that part of the liturgy liable to change according to the feast), but such settings remained comparatively rare.

The parody mass found many advocates, since it was possible by this means to base a long work on all voice parts of a shorter one, such as a motet or a hymn, and by beginning with familiar and recognizable material, to progress gradually into inventive independence. This particular technique may have owed as much to convenience as to a desire to pay homage to another composer.

Addition of instruments

The 16th- and 17th-century Venetian school, especially Giovanni Gabrieli and Claudio Monteverdi, added an instrumental element to the basically choral foundation of the mass. They also occasionally employed two or more choirs to create massive antiphonal effects. Further development of the orchestral mass occurred in the 17th century in the works of the Italian composers Francesco Cavalli and Alessandro Scarlatti and the French composer Marc-Antoine Charpentier, while the polychoral element was brought to a colossal and almost unmanageable pitch by Orazio Benevoli in his mass for the dedication of the Salzburg cathedral (1628) in 53 parts.

In the 18th century, Haydn's early masses, notably the *Missa Sanctae Caeciliae,* lean toward Italian models. His choral writing is robust and sonorous, even though four-part writing is the norm. His later masses emphasize soloists and orchestra but without diminishing the interest of the choral writing. Mozart's early masses tend to be brief (because of the taste and dictates of his archbishop patron), yet the fugal choruses sometimes dispel this impression by their very excellence, as in the *Mass in C Major,* K. 317 (1779; *Coronation Mass*). The unfinished *Mass in C Minor,* K. 427, abounds in magnificent choral music.

Remote in style and function from the Classical Viennese works, J.S. Bach's *Mass in B Minor* (1733–38) was a monument of the preceding Baroque era. It was never intended to be performed as a whole within the liturgy, and its various movements date from different periods of Bach's life. Five-part choral writing is most in evidence, the two soprano lines adding brilliance and edge to a richly contrapuntal (interwoven melody) texture. In the "Sanctus," Bach branches into six-part polyphony, and in the "Osanna" he calls for an eight-voice double choir apt for antiphonal writing.

Beethoven's *Mass in C Major,* Opus 86 (1807), and *Missa Solemnis,* Opus 123 (1823), written in the maturity of the Classical era, are not liturgical, yet they stem from an inner need to carry on a great tradition and to set to music a text of central importance. The role of the choir is central to the work. The composer uses it to produce effects ranging from breathtaking mystery to the utterly grandiose. The masses of the 19th-century Austrian composers Franz Schubert and Anton Bruckner worthily continue the same tradition in their individual ways. The *Petite Messe solennelle* (*Little Solemn Mass;* 1864) of Italian composer Gioacchino Rossini was originally written for soloists, chorus, and an accompaniment of two pianos and harmonium, but it was later scored for full orchestra.

Outstanding among 20th-century masses are those of the English composer Ralph Vaughan Williams, the Czech composer Leoš Janáček (*Glagolitic Mass,* setting an Orthodox text in Old Slavonic), and the Russo-American composer Igor Stravinsky, who is said to have derived his inspiration from Mozart, although some of the effects created by the mixed chorus and wind instruments are more reminiscent of medieval music.

The Missa pro Defunctis ("Mass for the Dead"), or Requiem Mass (often simply called Requiem) also stimulated numerous choral masterpieces, beginning with Jean d'Ockeghem in the late 15th century and continuing through Victoria, Felice Anerio, Scarlatti, Mozart, Luigi Cherubini, Hector Berlioz, Giuseppe Verdi, and Gabriel Fauré to the present century. Johannes Brahms' *Ein deutsches Requiem* (*German Requiem,* 1857–68) is based on the composer's own selection of Biblical texts. The *Requiem* (1914–16) of the early 20th-century British composer Frederick Delius derives its libretto from the 19th-century German philosopher and poet Friedrich Nietzsche. The *War Requiem,* Opus 66 (first performed, 1962), of the British composer Benjamin Britten makes skillful and impressive use of liturgical texts but also contains secular poetry by Wilfred Owen, killed in World War I. The work as a whole is thus linked with the senseless suffering of war and the idea of sacrifice induced by false patriotism. The choral effects are rich in novelty, originality, and forcefulness. One of the most successful of 20th-century masses for unaccompanied chorus is the *Mass in G Major* (1937) by Francis Poulenc.

Vespers and Anglican services

In the Middle Ages, the service of greatest musical importance, after the mass, was Vespers. Its component antiphons, psalms, hymn, and Magnificat have given rise to much noble choral music, from the time of the Flemish composer Adriaan Willaert in the 16th century, through Monteverdi, Scarlatti, and Mozart. In the Anglican Church, service settings embrace Holy Communion and Morning and Evening Prayer and have been continuously written since the time of Byrd and Tallis. These early services for choir and organ were followed by "verse services," in which solo voices played an important part, combining or alternating with the choir. By the time of the 17th-century British composer Henry Purcell, instruments were accepted as a means to fuller accompaniment, notably in the Chapel Royal, London. But modern composers, except in works for ceremonial use, tend to return to scoring their services for choir and organ.

Motets. Choral music has been enriched for centuries by the composition of motets, which were originally settings of liturgical or biblical texts. Responsories (liturgical texts originally performed responsively) were of major importance until the great monastic institutions lost their influence in the early years of the 16th century. Subsequently, the choral motet was mainly cultivated in royal and collegiate chapels. Settings of votive antiphons (verses preceding psalms and canticles), frequently, though not exclusively, texts in honour of the Virgin Mary, were popular in the late 15th and early 16th centuries. Many of these compositions demanded a high degree of skill and virtuosity from the choir and its soloists; a noble example is the British composer John Browne's *Stabat Mater,* from *The Eton Choirbook.* An Italian contemporary, Giovanni Spataro, displays a more simple and restrained style in his four-part *Virgo prudentissima,* which nevertheless belongs to the same category of motet.

During the 16th and 17th centuries, the term motet was used in looser connotation, sometimes linked with a few verses of a psalm, sometimes a complete psalm including Gloria Patri (lesser doxology). Many of these longer settings, by 16th-century composers such as Josquin, Willaert, and Lasso, attain the level of symphonic choral writing through their high degree of formal organization and their imaginative vocal scoring. The concertato motet (using contrasting groups of singers and instruments), as developed and perfected in the 17th century by Gabrieli, Monteverdi, Heinrich Schütz, and Scarlatti, added the vivid colours of the orchestral palette to the already highly malleable vocal textures. Pergolesi's *Stabat Mater,* although sometimes performed as a choral work, was originally written with solo voices in mind. Bach's motets, of which *Jesu meine Freude* (*Jesus My Joy; c.* 1723) is a typical and splendid example, return to the a cappella manner of performance. Contrary to one popular conception, this often included instrumental doubling of the voice parts and the use of an organ continuo, an improvised part. Subsequently little used in the Protestant Church, the motet continued to be cultivated by the Catholic composers of Europe and the Americas. Especially worthy of note are the motets and psalm settings of Anton Bruckner, whose *Te Deum* (composed 1881, revised 1883–84) is one of his choral masterpieces. Conservative tastes in much religious music somewhat discouraged the greatest talents from contributing fully to this genre. Stravinsky's *Threni* (on the Lamentations of Jeremiah), for instance, is more frequently heard in the concert hall than in church, as are also Poulenc's *Stabat Mater* (1951) and other liturgical motets of his.

Anthems. The use of the vernacular after the Reformation in England made it necessary for composers to forge a new style of choral music. The elaborate melodic tracery of Robert Fayrfax and John Taverner gave way to a completely unelaborate kind of choral counterpoint designed to allow the English words to be clearly heard. Both Thomas Tallis and William Byrd made outstanding contributions to the development of the anthem. Tallis perfected a style of contrapuntally animated homophony that ensured clarity of declamation, while Byrd experimented with more elaborate textures both in full anthems (for choir alone) and in verse anthems, in which the choir was supported by the organ and sometimes other instruments, allowing solo voices to detach themselves from the main body of singers. Among Byrd's finest verse anthems are *Christ rising again* (for Easter) and *O God that guides the cheerful sun.* Orlando Gibbons carried to a further stage the use of a consort of viols, which accompanies with a rich but discreet body of sound the countertenor and bass soloists in *Glorious and powerful god.* One of the most effective of his full anthems is the seven-part *Hosanna to the Son of David* for Palm Sunday. Thomas Tomkins displays a mastery of 12-part polyphony in his full anthem *O praise the Lord, all ye heathen,* but for quiet expressive intimacy of thought there is little to surpass *When David heard that Absalom was slain.* Among a considerable number of verse anthems by Tomkins, two of the most inspiring are *My Shepherd is the living Lord* and *Thou art my King, O God,* both of which can be accompanied by organ alone or by organ and string ensemble.

When the monarchy was restored in 1660, Matthew Locke contributed a number of fine anthems to the repertory of the revived Chapel Royal, among them the double-choir setting of *Not unto us, O Lord* and the grandiose, almost Venetian *The king shall rejoice,* scored for three four-part choirs and orchestra. Another eminent musician of the time was Pelham Humfrey, whose verse anthem *By the waters of Babylon* is one of the best examples of its kind. For chromatically expressive music Michael Wise provides an admirable pattern in his *The ways of Sion do mourn,* as does Daniel Roseingrave in his *Lord, thou art become gracious.*

The verse anthem with instruments reached its zenith in the late 17th century in the music of Henry Purcell and John Blow. Much of their music was performed in the Chapel Royal, the choir and consorts of which had improved markedly. Among the most memorable of Purcell's full anthems are the eight-part *Hear my prayer, O Lord* and the five-part *Remember not, Lord, our offences.* His most successful verse anthems frequently make use of short, impressive passages for choir alone, as in the evocation of the turtle's voice in *My beloved spake* and the moving harmonies of "O worship the Lord" toward the end of *O sing unto the Lord.* Blow excels in the antiphony of verse soloists and full choir in *I beheld, and lo, a great multitude.* In his full anthems, such as *God is our hope and strength* and *O Lord God of my salvation,* he sometimes almost equals Purcell in the richness and resource of his eight-part writing.

Of the succeeding generation of composers, William Croft seems most at ease in his full anthems, notably *Put me not to rebuke* and *O Lord, rebuke me not,* two distinct and different works in spite of the similarity of text. Maurice Greene excelled in this style in works such as *God is our hope and strength* and *Acquaint thyself with God.* William Boyce carried on the tradition of sensitive word setting in such works as *I have surely built thee an house* and *O where shall wisdom be found?.*

Although the late 18th and early 19th centuries did not exactly overflow with masterpieces, a trio of composers proved themselves competent craftsmen. *O Lord, look down from heaven* will assure Jonathan Battishill a place in the history of the genre, while the Epiphany anthem *O God, who by the leading of a star* speaks eloquently for Thomas Attwood. Although Samuel Wesley, converted to Catholicism, chose Latin for the greater number of his church compositions, one of these is sometimes sung to its English text, *Sing aloud with gladness.*

Samuel Sebastian Wesley attempted, often with considerable success, to raise up the anthem to a new level of artistry and accomplishment, extending it so as to form a kind of cantata giving freer rein to soloists than was customary in the older type of verse anthem. His finest contributions are perhaps *The Wilderness; Ascribe unto The Lord;* and *O Lord, Thou art my God.* Also noteworthy from this epoch are Sir John Goss's setting of *The Wilderness,* Thomas Attwood Walmisley's *O give thanks,* and the double-choir anthem *O Saviour of the world* by Sir Frederick Gore Ouseley.

Sir Joseph Barnby, Sir John Stainer, and Sir Arthur Sullivan wrote anthems of fair quality, but not until Sir Hubert Parry demonstrated the need for a return to conscientious word setting did new spirit begin to pervade English church music in works such as Parry's double-choir anthem *Lord let me know mine end,* Sir Charles Stanford's similarly scored *Jesus Christ is risen today,* and Charles Wood's *O thou the central orb.* In the 20th century, T.T. Noble's *The souls of the righteous* and John Ireland's *Greater love hath no man* are typical of the earlier period, while *O pray for the peace of Jerusalem* by Herbert Howells and Benjamin Britten's *Hymn to St. Peter* successfully continue a long tradition.

Cantata and oratorio. The cantata, as developed in northern Germany in the 17th century, often relied only upon soloists and a small group of instruments, although the role of the chorus gradually became more important. In more than 200 church cantatas written by J.S. Bach, the chorus often occupies a prominent place and is given music of challenging complexity—frequently on a par with the music of the accompanying instrumental forces. The cantatas use the chorus again in the closing chorale, which is usually a special setting of a hymn tune with orchestral doubling or accompaniment.

Bach's 200 church cantatas

In Italy, the oratorio achieved what was beyond the motet's capabilities by projecting through verse and music a story of Biblical origin that the public could enjoy while learning. Giacomo Carissimi, whose *Jephtha* is still an established classic, led the way to the oratorios of Antonio Vivaldi (*Juditha triumphans,* first performed 1716), Handel (a long series of oratorios written for London, all dramatic in form except for *Israel in Egypt* of 1739 and the *Messiah* of 1741), and Haydn, whose greatest oratorio is *Die Schöpfung* (1798; *The Creation*). The choral contribution to 19th-century oratorios remained at a remarkably high level, enhancing such works as Beethoven's *Christus Am Ölberg* (1803; *Christ on the Mount of Olives*), the perennially popular *Elijah* (1846) of Mendelssohn, Franz Liszt's *Die Legende von der heiligen Elisabeth* (*The Leg-*

end of St. Elizabeth), Berlioz's *L'Enfance du Christ,* Opus 25 (1854), and a series of compositions by the British composer Edward Elgar, culminating in *The Dream of Gerontius* (1900). The oratorio tradition, because of its links with choral bodies, has shown constant renewal and growth in the 20th century. Among outstanding 20th-century oratorios are Frank Martin's *Golgotha* (1949), Arthur Honegger's *Le Roi David* (*King David;* 1921), Sir William Walton's *Belshazzar's Feast* (1931), and Bernard Rogers' *The Passion* (1944). A work in oratorio style, though in a class of its own, is Ernest Bloch's *Avodath Hakodesh* (*Sacred Service*) composed 1930–33 and scored for baritone solo, chorus, and orchestra.

Occasional music. In addition to sacred and secular works, a very considerable number of compositions, many of them choral, were written for great occasions of state. These include motets and cantatas based on special texts, suitable for performance in a palace, outdoors on a platform or rampart, in a private chapel, or wherever the occasion demanded. The signing of a peace treaty, a royal marriage, ducal obsequies, consecration, election of a doge—all these and many similar events called for music written to order; since composers have always been happy to receive a commission, the number of occasional works is virtually incalculable.

Soon after St. Mark's, Venice, inaugurated in 1403 a choir of boys from the city, their master Antonio Romano was invited to compose a festive work in honour of the doge. When Francesco Foscari was elected doge in 1423, Christoforo de Monte introduced the choral parts of his motet with brass fanfares. Dufay, asked to produce a stirring work for the consecration of a new cathedral at Patras (now Pátrai) in Greece, scored his *Apostolo glorioso-Cum tua doctrina-Andreas* (1426) for wind ensemble and mixed chorus; but, although the work was undoubtedly performed in the cathedral, the use of an Italian rather than a Latin text places it firmly in the category of occasional music. An equally impressive work by the same composer, *Supremum est mortalibus bonum pax* (*The Supreme Gift for Mortals Is Peace*), was written expressly for the signing of the Treaty of Viterbo in 1433, when Pope Eugenius IV and King Sigismund of Bohemia were both present at the ceremony. Toward the end of the motet, the choir sings, in successive block chords, the names of Pope and King, syllable by syllable. Another peace treaty celebrated in music is that of Bagnolo, Italy, when the Franco-Flemish composer Loyset Compère was commissioned to write the motet *Quis numerare queat* (1484). Imaginative use is made of the chorus throughout this work, even to the extent of the composer's choice of tessitura (high or low part of the voice range): when the chorus sings of the lamentations of the people over the terrors of war, the words are sung by the dark-hued combination of tenors, baritones, and basses in their middle or lower register. A further example of choral writing so disposed as to represent a state of mind is the "Amen" of Isaac's *Optime pastor* (written in 1513 in honour of the newly elected Pope Leo X), where the opulent six-part polyphony suggests the wealth and substance of the Emperor Maximilian I and his desire to impress listeners with a show of temporal power at least the equivalent of the Pope's spiritual power.

Occasional music is sometimes considered of less value than sacred or secular music, even when it stems from a composer of high reputation. Since the work could by definition receive only one formal performance and since it might have been written in a hurry, the theory is that the music must be inferior. There are, however, examples of such works whose music was used for more than one occasion, thanks to the simple but effective process of stripping away the original text and substituting another, or even substituting one name for another. A study of the text of Taverner's motet *Christe Jesu pastor bone* (*Jesus Christ, Good Shepherd*) shows that it must have been intended first as a votive antiphon for St. William of York, then as a paraliturgical prayer for Cardinal Wolsey (Taverner being at one time organist and master of the choristers at Cardinal's College, now Christ Church, at Oxford), and finally as a prayer for Henry VIII. Similarly, the anthem *O Lord, make thy servant Elizabeth our Queen,* written by William Byrd for Queen Elizabeth I, remained in the repertoire of the Chapel Royal for several decades, the name being changed first to James and then to Charles.

Repetition of occasional works

Most events of importance were planned months in advance, and the composer could usually count on being given adequate warning of a new commission. The meeting of Louis XII of France and Ferdinand V the Catholic of Castile at Savona in 1507, for which the French composer Antoine de Févin wrote a superb choral work, *Gaude Francorum regia corona,* was certainly not decided upon at short notice. Nor was the visit of Cardinal Ippolito de' Medici to Venice the result of a sudden decision, for Willaert had ample time to pen his solemn and sonorous motet *Adriacos numero* just as he did in the case of *Haud aliter pugnans,* in honour of King Ferdinand.

A later Ferdinand, who became Holy Roman Emperor Ferdinand III in 1637, commissioned two outstanding choral works by Monteverdi, both of which were published in his *Madrigali guerrieri et amorosi* (*Madrigals of War and Love,* 1638). *Altri canti d'amor* (*Let Others Sing of Love*) is a choral cantata for six voices, bass solo, and instrumental ensemble. The Emperor's military prowess is recounted in considerable detail, with choral imitations of swords clashing and guns firing. His qualities as a leader are also referred to in the ballet *Movete al mio bel suon* (*Move to my Beautiful Sound*), which extols him also as a just and equitable monarch in time of peace—although the Thirty Years' War did not in fact come to an end for several years. The text used by Monteverdi was a reworking of a poem which his friend the Italian poet Ottavio Rinuccini had originally written for Henry IV of France.

Purcell's odes

Purcell, a composer of occasional music who was also a brilliant choral writer, enriched the history of music with a series of odes and welcome songs beginning in 1680 (*Welcome, vicegerent of the mighty King*) and extending until the year of his death, 1695, which saw the production of the ode for the Duke of Gloucester's birthday, *Who can from joy refrain?* Among the finest of the series, and especially notable for the noble vigour of the choruses, are the odes for Queen Mary's birthday and for the St. Cecilia's Day celebration, 1692.

In France scores of comparable proportions were being written for such occasions as the baptism of the Dauphin (1688), for which Jean-Baptiste Lully set Pierre Perrin's *Plaude laetare* for double chorus and orchestra. Numerous court ceremonies or rejoicings called for large-scale performances of the Te Deum, Marc-Antoine Charpentier and Michel-Richard de Lalande, as well as Lully, providing music of the requisite pomp and proportions. Handel wrote two festive settings of the Te Deum for the Treaty of Utrecht (1713) and the British victory at Dettingen (1743). His royal odes worthily continue the Purcellian tradition, especially in the *Ode for the Queen's Birthday* (1713) for Queen Anne and in two wedding anthems, *This is the Day* (1734) for Princess Anne and *Sing unto God* (1736) for the Prince of Wales.

Although J.S. Bach did not disdain to write occasional music, he followed Handel's practice in the *Occasional Oratorio* (a patriotic piece given in 1746) without ever knowing Handel, by reworking this kind of music to a new text. One of the cantatas Bach supplied for the election of the Leipzig town councillors was deftly changed into a cantata for the 12th Sunday after Trinity; another, destined for the same annual event, *Preise, Jerusalem, den Herrn* (*Praise the Lord, O Jerusalem*), BWV 119 (1723), has been reedited in modern times with a new text, in imitation of the composer's own practice.

Haydn, in spite of his considerable duties as court conductor and composer, found time to write occasional works of considerable proportions, such as the two-hour birthday cantata, *Applausus* (1768), intended for the Abbot of Zwettl Stadt, Austria. His masses, even though they are liturgical, sometimes border also on the occasional because of their close ties with contemporary events, such as the *Missa St. Bernardi de Offida* (1796) written to celebrate the recent canonization of a Capuchin monk from Offida in Italy. An occasional choral composition of Beethoven's is his *Kantate auf den Tod Kaiser Josephs*

II (1790; *Cantata on the Death of the Emperor Joseph II*).

Berlioz, who had toyed with the idea of a large-scale choral and orchestral work to honour Napoleon, eventually had to abandon it but salvaged certain movements and incorporated them into his *Te Deum* (1849). His contemporary, Liszt, was more deliberately productive in this area, enjoying consistently enthusiastic receptions for his choral works of an occasional nature, such as the St. Cecilia antiphon *Cantantibus organis* (for a Palestrina festival in Rome in 1880), the *Missa solennis zur Einweihung der Basilika in Gran* (1855; *Mass for the Dedication of the Basilica at Gran*); the *Hungarian Coronation Mass* for Emperor Francis Joseph I (1867), and a unique composition for male chorus and organ accompaniment, *Slavimo Slavno Slaveni!,* written in 1863 for the millenary of SS. Cyril and Methodius. Also noteworthy are his two cantatas in honour of Beethoven.

The Czech composer Josef Förster achieved widespread recognition in his own country as a master of choral style, and a telling example of this may be heard in the cantata *Mortuis fratribus,* written as a kind of requiem after the end of World War I. In Hungary, Zoltán Kodály went to texts of a 16th-century Hungarian poet, Michael Veg, for his *Psalmus Hungaricus* (first performed, 1923) celebrating the 50th anniversary of the union of the cities Buda and Pest. For the Paris Exhibition of 1937, the French composer Florent Schmitt composed one of his finest choral works, the *Fête de la lumière* (*Festival of Light*).

Modern English occasional music

In 20th-century England the royal odes appeared less frequently than in the time of Purcell and Handel, yet there are a few choral works worthy of mention—Charles Stanford's *Welcome Song* for the opening of the Franco-British Exhibition (1908), and Sir Arthur Bliss's *Song of Welcome* (1954) for the homecoming of Queen Elizabeth II. Britten's cantata *St. Nicolas,* for tenor solo, mixed chorus, strings, piano, organ, and percussion, was written for the centenary of Lancing College in 1948, and 12 years later he supplied a *Cantata Academica* for the quincentenary of the University of Basel. The score of this work has parts where alternative words may be used for celebrations at other institutions of learning.

Secular music. Since the vast majority of secular vocal works of the Middle Ages and the Renaissance were written with soloists in mind rather than a chorus, this repertory will be dealt with in a later section of this article. A truly secular choral tradition does not really emerge until the 17th century, apart from dramatic works, which are mainly dealt with in the section on opera. Choruses were, however, supplied by way of incidental music to plays in the late 16th century; outstanding examples include the music written in 1585 by Andrea Gabrieli for the *Oedipus Tyrannus* of Sophocles and that of Giovanni Giacomo Gastoldi for Battista Guarini's play *Il pastor fido* (1590; *The Faithful Shepherd*). Choruses appear in 17th-century drama from time to time, as well as in masques and comparable extravaganzas. In the age of Lully, Marc-Antoine Charpentier, Purcell, and Matthew Locke, their position is clearly established. Secular cantatas tended for the most part to rely on solo voices, and when the chorus does make its appearance it sometimes consists only of three-part writing, as in Purcell's setting of Abraham Cowley's poem "If ever I more riches did desire."

The majority of Bach's secular cantatas call for solo voices only, in addition to the orchestra. Among those that do make full use of the chorus are *Phoebus and Pan* (*Geschwinde, geschwinde, ihr wirbelnden Winde,* BWV 201; 1731), the *Birthday Cantata* (*Schleicht, spielende Wellen,* BWV 206; 1733), and the *Hunt Cantata* (*Was mir behagt, ist nur die muntre Jagd,* BWV 208; 1716). The choral writing in Handel's secular cantatas and odes tends to be as massive and dignified as in the best of his oratorios, yet they are on the whole less frequently performed in the 20th century; as a group they do not fit easily into any single category. *Athalia* (1733) draws its inspiration and plot from the drama by the 17th-century French playwright Jean Racine; *Il trionfo del tempo e del disinganno* (1708; *The Triumph of Time and Truth*) is an allegory deriving from two of the composer's youthful Italianate compositions; *Alexander's Feast* (1736) and the *Ode for St. Cecilia's Day* (1739) both have texts by the 17th-century English poet Dryden; and the trilogy *L'allegro, Il penseroso, ed il moderato* (1740) is based on the poetry of another Englishman, John Milton.

Those powerful and opposite poles, church and opera, monopolized choral writing for many years, and apart from isolated works of an occasional nature there is little in the truly secular field until Beethoven's *Choral Fantasia* (1808), an unusual work in nine movements, the first seven of which are a set of variations for piano and orchestra. Voices are introduced only in the eighth movement—solo voices at first, singing verses in praise of music by a minor German poet of the early 19th century named Christoph Kuffner, then the choir, so that the previously dominant instrumental texture is gradually and effectively modified to include richly deployed vocal sonorities that assist the work to a climax in the same way as in the later *Choral Symphony.*

Beethoven's "Choral" symphony

This gigantic work, the ninth and last symphony by Beethoven, is planned in such a way that the choral finale is the only proper and logical way for it to end, although performances have been given where the finale has been omitted (using the scherzo as ending). The choral finale of the *Ninth Symphony* grows from the fertile soil of its predecessors and becomes a structural, thematic, and aesthetic necessity. It is notoriously difficult to perform, as Beethoven often seems to treat the singers like instruments.

The influence of his *Ninth Symphony* on later symphonic literature was considerable. Beethoven's bravura choral writing sent its echoes to the outer limits of the Romantic era, and there were many subsequent essays in the integration of choral and orchestral forces. In *La Damnation de Faust,* Opus 24 (1846), Berlioz uses the weight of massed voices in an imaginative and dramatic way; in contrast, in his *Roméo et Juliette* symphony the voices tend to serve as an extra dash of colour to the orchestral palette. Brahms made skillful use of the chorus in his *Rhapsodie* (1869) and *Schicksalslied* (*Song of Destiny;* 1871), and Schumann relied upon it throughout his *Das Paradies und die Peri* (*Paradise and the Peri;* 1843), a kind of secular oratorio based on the long poem *Lalla Rookh* (1817) by the Irish poet Thomas Moore. The best of both composers, chorally speaking, is to be found in their many settings of contemporaneous poems for mixed voices, male voice choir, or female choir. Much of this remains little known outside Germany, to the detriment of choral programs that would gain interest from one of Schumann's finely constructed double-choir compositions or from one of Brahm's sensitive settings of the poetry of Ludwig Uhland or Goethe.

The technical demands of the choral sections in Antonín Dvořák's *Svatební košile* (*The Spectre's Bride*), a cantata written for the Birmingham Festival of 1885, are within the capabilities of the amateur choral societies for which it was intended, and in general his treatment of voices shows consideration as well as ingenuity. The macabre plot of this work is a narrative poem by a learned countryman of the composer's, the Czech poet Karel Erben, who achieved fame as a collector of folklore. Czech folk songs and tales exercised a powerful attraction for Dvořák throughout his life, and some of his best choral music consists of settings such as *V přírodě* (*Amid Nature,* 1882) and *Tři sborg* (*Three Slovak Folksongs,* 1877). Czech poetry gave rise to many remarkable compositions among the choral works of Janáček, perhaps the most memorable being the three male-voice choruses written between 1906 and 1909 that were based on poems by Petr Bezruč: *Kantor Halfar* (*Teacher Halfar*), *Maryčka Magdanova,* and *Sedmdesát tisíc* (*The Seventy Thousand*).

In modern Germany and Austria, the most far-reaching attempt to bring together choral and orchestral forces in symphonic literature was that of Gustav Mahler. Unable for three years to find the solution to the problem of a finale for his second symphony, Mahler heard at the funeral of the eminent conductor-pianist Hans von Bülow the *Resurrection* Ode by the 18th-century German poet Friedrich Gottlieb Klopstock. He decided to use this poem as a basis for a choral finale in the *Symphony No. 2 in C*

Minor (1894). The use of massed voices for unaccompanied passages, such as the beginning of the ode, and later on with orchestral accompaniment and the collaboration of soprano and contralto soloists, affords ample evidence of Mahler's deep understanding of choral effects and techniques. The role of the choir is considerably less in his *Symphony No. 3 in D Minor* (1896), but it is nonetheless highly artistic and imaginative in the setting of the old popular verses *Es sungen drei Engel* ("Three angels were singing"). The *Eighth Symphony* (1906–07) marks the high point of symphonic choral music not only in Mahler's own output but in the entire history of the symphony as an art form. Instead of saving the chorus for climactic effects in the finale, as in his *Second Symphony* (and as in Beethoven's *Ninth*), Mahler integrates it from the very beginning into the complex and many-hued vocal and instrumental colours—eight soloists, a boys' choir, two large choirs of mixed voices able to project powerful antiphonal effects with orchestra and organ. This *Symphony of a Thousand,* as it is generally called, presents two texts of a complementary and opposing nature: the hymn *Veni creator spiritus* and the closing scene of Goethe's *Faust.* Mahler's inspired use of his colossal forces to enhance, explain, and endow with added meaning the divine and human aspects of the two texts is without parallel. His achievement has not since been matched for sheer virtuosity and impact.

The importance of Mahler

It is true that Arnold Schoenberg's *Gurrelieder* (1900–11) calls for even larger orchestral forces than Mahler's *Eighth Symphony,* although it has never enjoyed as much success. Choirs have preferred other early works of Schoenberg or those of Anton von Webern.

At the opposite end of the scale are the robust, tonal, and extrovert compositions of Paul Hindemith and also of Carl Orff, whose particular genius for setting classical and medieval texts may be seen in his *Catulli Carmina* (1943) and *Carmina Burana* (1937). Modern American choral music has been much enlivened by the contributions of Charles Ives (*An Election* composed in 1920), Randall Thompson, Roger Sessions, and many other eminent composers. Igor Stravinsky, who spent the latter part of his life in the United States, retained his interest in choral writing and constantly sought new ways of presenting the sonorities of a massed group of voices. To his earlier *Les Noces* (1923; *The Wedding*), and *Symphony of Psalms* (1930) for chorus and orchestra, he added the *Cantata on Old English Texts* (1952) on anonymous English poems of the 15th and 16th centuries and *A Sermon, A Narrative, and a Prayer* (1961) which is not a liturgical work, though its text is taken from the New Testament.

Twentieth-century English choral music for secular use finds one of its best advocates in Ralph Vaughan Williams, whose early setting of *Toward the Unknown Region* (first performed 1907) by the 19th-century American poet Walt Whitman was followed by *A Sea Symphony* (1910) based on material by the same poet. Frederick Delius also drew upon Whitman for his *Sea Drift* (1903) and upon the poems of the contemporary British poet Arthur Symons for his *Songs of Sunset* (1907). Britten's genius for word setting is evident in his *Hymn to St. Cecilia* (1942) and *A Ceremony of Carols* (1942) and in the handling of the boys' choir and mixed chorus in his *Spring Symphony* (1949), which ends with a choral waltz combining syllabic effects and the Old English lyric *Sumer is icumen in.* Outstanding among contemporary Polish choral works are three compositions by Krzysztof Penderecki: *Dimensions of Time and Silence* for chorus and chamber orchestra (published 1961); *Stabat Mater* for three choirs (1962); and *Psalms of David* for choir and percussion (1958).

Madrigals and related forms. A considerable amount of music sung by choirs in the 20th century is not really choral music at all, since it was conceived for performance by small groups of soloists and attains its fullest expression only through the individually projected personality of the solo voice. Assignment of these solo lines to a body of singers tends to neutralize this effect of personality, producing instead a weight of tone and an impression of superimposed dynamics and expression which, however carefully cultivated and disciplined, cannot surpass the kind of performance originally envisaged by the composer; yet a reasonable multiplication of voices does no harm to the texture as such, since the harmonies, the interweaving of parts, and the vocal spacing all remain constant. It is also true that a madrigal sung by 50 instead of by only five musicians will be more readily and rapidly understood by those directly involved because a massed performance of a five-part madrigal with 10 singers on each line is a more practical proposition than forming 10 separate consorts of five soloists. Individual voices, especially in amateur groups, may not possess the technique, the stamina, or the confidence to sustain a part on their own, but if they sing as a member of a group the likelihood is that they will achieve good results.

Choral performance of madrigals

Madrigals were originally published for professional singers and for amateur singers of high standard. They were issued not in score, as is the 20th-century custom, but in the form of part books, each one of which contained only the music necessary for one line—soprano, alto, tenor, bass, or any intermediate voice. The quantity printed of each edition was generally modest, with the result that prices were high, and choral performance was ruled out for economic reasons as well as artistic ones. The development of modern methods of engraving and printing music, allied to the creation of a worldwide market for choral works, has brought about a situation directly opposed to that of the Middle Ages and the Renaissance, whereby each singer now has a full score (or vocal score) that is less expensive than the part books printed in earlier times. In consequence, the choral performance of madrigals and related forms has become an economic possibility.

One of the most important predecessors of the madrigal proper was the frottola, which flourished in Italy between 1490 and 1520. In its early stages, the frottola was a song with instrumental accompaniment, with the main melody and text in the uppermost part (usually in the soprano or alto range) and supporting harmonies below. These harmonies were so simple and functional that an entire line could be dispensed with when intabulations for voice and lute were made. Four-part harmony was thus reduced to three, though without any serious loss since the polyphonic element tended to be of minimal importance. In later collections of frottolas, however, a different technique appears: instead of the upper line alone being supplied with text, all four parts join in. These completely texted frottolas were certainly intended to be sung by four singers, possibly, though not necessarily, doubled by instruments; and they could even have been sung by a small chorus.

Contemporary with the frottola were cognate forms such as the German lied, the French chanson, the Spanish villancico, and the English songs for voice and viols. All these began as accompanied songs, and all eventually followed the Italian fashion by dropping the instruments and substituting voices. This process was at first an obvious makeshift and can be detected as such because of the characteristically instrumental nature of the lower three parts, with numerous unvocal skips and contours. Words can be added to lines such as these, but they are often uncomfortable to sing because of the lack of conjunct movement and the paucity of breathing spaces. Occasionally, the added words appear only in one source, often a manuscript copy rather than a printed edition, the earlier sources on the other hand retaining the instrumental nature and function of the alto, tenor, and bass. The songs of Isaac provide clear examples of this gradual change, by which *Tenorlieder* (songs with the tune in the tenor) were transformed into part-songs by the addition of text to the instrumental lines. Some German composers, however, favoured the purely vocal or choral type of performance and made certain that all parts were texted.

Similar tendencies can be seen in France, in Spain, and in England, where many of the court songs written during Henry VIII's reign have text in all voice parts. One of the best known of these, *Passetyme with good cumpanye,* is a part-song for three male voices, written in all probability by the monarch himself. As the century progressed, amateurs began to take an interest in the part-song, which was generally for four voices, and several composers helped

Henry VIII's part-song

to lay the foundation for the English madrigal school. It is worthy of note that Byrd, in his *Psalmes, Sonets, & songs of Sadnes and pietie* (published, 1588), underlaid text to every part but mentioned in his preface that the songs were "originally made for Instruments to expresse the harmonie, and one voyce to pronounce the dittie."

The early development of the Italian madrigal was fostered as much by foreigners as by natives, and the considerable contributions made by the 16th-century Flemish composers Jacques Arcadelt, Philippe Verdelot, and Adriaan Willaert should not be underestimated. Although Willaert's settings of the works of the 14th-century Italian poet Petrarch and other serious Renaissance poets maintain an invariably high contrapuntal interest and are frequently suitable for choral performance, his compositions in the lighter, more homophonic vein, are well worth acquaintance.

Cipriano de Rore, another Netherlander adopted by Italy, felt Willaert's influence strongly yet contrived to set new standards in the interpretation of poetry through music and also to encourage an artistic fusion of the contrapuntal and homophonic styles, using them alternately in one and the same composition according to the dictates of the poem. Even his early madrigals show a deep concern for intensity of expression, as in the Petrarch setting for five voices *Hor che'l ciel e la terra.* One of his finest four-part madrigals, *Ancor che col partire,* sets off pairs of voices one against the other. New heights of expression are reached in his descriptive madrigal *Quando lieta sperai* (text by the woman poet Emilia Anguissola), in which a sudden and disappointing change in the weather is perfectly mirrored in the music. The four-part *Datemi pace,* based on a Petrarch sonnet, favours homophony and looks eagerly forward to the bold chromaticism of Pomponio Nenna and Don Carlo Gesualdo. In his maturity, Rore produced a number of remarkably intense madrigals for the court of Parma. One of the finest is his setting of *Dalle belle contrade,* full of powerful contrasts of mood and colour underlining the interplay of direct and indirect speech.

Further experiments in chromaticism were carried out by Nicola Vicentino, whose dramatic setting of *O messaggi del cor,* by the Renaissance poet Ludovico Ariosto, makes highly effective use of a mounting modulatory scheme (changes of key) to enhance the insistent repetition of the opening exclamations. His early madrigals exploit a more classical vein, without ignoring illustrative possibilities. His most typical and fascinating work is nevertheless to be found in such madrigals as *Poichè il mio largo pianto* or *L'aura che il verde lauro* in which Petrarch's verbal puns are suitably matched by Vicentino's harmonic ambiguities. Even more extreme is the Neapolitan composer Pomponio Nenna, whose striking and original harmonies must have made an indelible impression on his pupil Gesualdo. But whereas Gesualdo's chromaticism is often wayward and illogical, that of Nenna tends toward reason and reality. Several of the master's madrigals can be usefully compared with those of his noble pupil that were set to identical texts. *Mercè, grido piangendo,* for example, is treated by Nenna with an enviable intensity of expression heightened by tremendous contrasts of timbre and dynamic; and, although this pattern is followed in Gesualdo's setting (*Book V,* 1611), perhaps with even greater violence, the most favourable musical impression comes from Nenna. His four-part madrigal *La mia doglia s'avvanza* is startling by any standards, for the opening four bars move rapidly from G minor to F-sharp major, D minor, and C-sharp major.

Gesualdo's extraordinary range

Gesualdo's preoccupation with poems containing diametrically opposed ideas and concepts finds its outlet in his last two books of madrigals (V and VI, both 1611). *Itene, O miei sospiri* not only looks forward in its manneristic treatment of vocal texture and harmony; it looks backward to classical procedures such as the interpolation of rests at the word *sospiri* (sighs), invented much earlier when the quarter-note rest was called *suspirium.* It would be wrong, however, to classify Gesualdo as an extremist on every occasion, for he could often write melting phrases of unforgettable beauty. He can even be witty at times, as in the madrigal about a venturesome mosquito (*Ardita zanzaretta*), which is somewhat in the vein of a vocal scherzo.

Luca Marenzio, one of the most prolific among late 16th-century Italian madrigalists, achieved his high reputation not through experiment but rather through his remarkable sensitivity to words, both as single entities and as the basic elements of a poetic phrase. His balance between the two opposing claims of general mood and particular effect is always perfect, and the mastery of his vocal spacing is probably unrivalled, no matter whether four, five, or six parts are involved.

At the court of Mantua (now Mantova, Italy), two important composers were active toward the very end of the 16th century—Giaches de Wert and Giovanni Giacomo Gastoldi. Each of them, in his own particular way, helped to renew and transform madrigal techniques even though the countless admirers of Marenzio felt that the pinnacles of perfection had already been reached. De Wert's contribution to the new madrigal was in some ways unusual and unexpected, for he approached the dramatic madrigal-poetry in a way that combined realism with clarity. He returned, in fact, to homophonic writing when it was necessary to emphasize a point, allowing the highest voice part to project the melody in what was essentially a kind of "choral recitative." His pupil Monteverdi published nine books of madrigals. From the sixth book onward continuo support becomes obligatory, and in consequence solo voices emerge from a choral background with tremendous dramatic effect, especially in the later works. The ballet *Tirsi e Clori* is rich in five-part choral writing of considerable elegance and resource, and the same is true (though in six-part texture) of *Altri canti di Marte. Vago augelletto* contrasts solo and choral writing until the last tutti, when all singers combine in a sonorous statement. Perhaps the greatest Monteverdi work of all is *Hor che'l ciel e la terra,* a six-part madrigal in two sections, with many solos and choral sections accompanied by violins and continuo. Monteverdi rarely surpassed the heights of emotional expressiveness found in this product of his maturity.

Monteverdi's mastery of the madrigal

At the time of the Italian madrigal's fullest flowering, German composers derived much inspiration from the south while still contriving to retain something of their earlier heritage. The result was often a kind of international style, greatly influenced by Orlando di Lasso, who was as much at home writing Italian madrigals as he was with French chanson and German lieder. His pupils, the Austrian Leonhard Lechner and the German Johann Eccard, developed this style still further, as may be seen in the former's setting of *Wohl kommt der Mai* (*Welcome May*), a lively and optimistic May song full of expressive harmonic colour. The setting by Lasso of the same text is calmer, more homophonic; yet its apparent simplicity and unostentatiousness hides a subtle and skillful mastery of vocal art.

In his five-part lieder, Lasso makes the most of contrasting duets and trios very frequently, as in *Es jagt ein Jäger* a hunting song which serves as an excuse for lightly concealed amatory dalliance. Hans Leo Hassler was obviously fired by Lasso's lead in the sheer variety and latent possibilities of secular vocal style, and much of his best work was done in the dialogue form. A peak of brilliance and energy is reached in his eight-part dialogue for two opposing choral bodies, *Mein Lieb will mit mir kriegen* (*My Love Wants to Wage a War*), which might be described as a musically stylized battle of the sexes, with blows given and taken freely until the two groups combine to sing of final reconciliation and contentment.

Dialogues in this vein were also cultivated successfully by Christoph Demantius, whose anthology of 1609 contains examples of memorable beauty and charm. In his *Jungfrew, ich het ein' Bitt' an euch* (*Maiden, I have a Request for You*), Demantius allows one four-part choir to represent the girl and the other the boy in a conversation full of innocent affection and honest courtship, the two groups joining at the end to sing goodnight. In his five-part lieder, Demantius sometimes displays a learned touch in his imitative counterpoint, although the general impression is one of Italianate elegance rather than of studious endeavour. It is worthy of note that many of his lieder are strophically conceived, and in consequence he printed the verses complete in each voice part, a feature which has been unfortunately obscured in the modern edition of his works. One of the finest of his lieder is *Lieblich ich hörte singen,* which tells of the Sirens' song and reproduces its allegedly hypnotic effect by means of flowing melismata in the upper voices.

The dialogue, considered as an art form of the Renaissance and Baroque eras, contains many choral elements. In its earliest form, as exemplified by the dialogues of Willaert, seven voices is the norm, and the texture is not yet clearly separated into two groups. Instead there is a kaleidoscopic impression caused by the skillful deployment of varied groupings. By the time of Andrea Gabrieli, a dialogue such as the popular and erotic *Tirsi morir volea* calls for a trio of high voices representing the girl and a quartet of deeper voices for the man. The amorous interchanges are carefully allocated to the individual groups, and there is no attempt to join them together until the very end. But in a typical dialogue by the younger Gabrieli, *Dormiva dolcemente,* there is no relationship between direct and indirect speech as far as the music is concerned. The setting is in this sense abstract, and the beauty of the dialogue lies in its purely musical architecture and expression.

The dialogues of Lasso

One of the greatest masters of the French dialogue was Orlando di Lasso, who set two poems of the 16th-century French poet Pierre de Ronsard in eight-part, double-choir compositions of exceptional quality. *Que dis-tu, que fais-tu?* (1576; *What Are You Saying, What Are You Doing?*) plays off one group against another in a series of sympathetic exchanges culminating in a final chorus praising the constancy of the lovebirds. Another masterpiece of this kind is *O doux parler* (1571), in which the interlocutors are human and the approach of both poet and composer more intensely passionate.

The French chanson, one of the most popular secular vocal genres in the 16th century, is essentially in miniature form. Unlike the Italian madrigals, which were sometimes composed in sequences of three, four, or more sections, French chansons tend to remain individual in the sense that they are self-contained, epigrammatic, and brief. It is partly for this reason that they have been less explored by 20th-century choral groups, although the language factor must also be taken into consideration.

English madrigals, because of their relatively innocuous texts and their moderate degree of difficulty, have always been a staple diet of choral societies and to an even greater extent of chamber choruses. The 16th- and 17th-century madrigals of William Byrd, Thomas Weelkes, John Wilbye, Thomas Morley, and their contemporaries and successors are too well-known to need elaborate description and too numerous to permit individual discussion. It is nevertheless true that although this repertory may today be considered as generally choral, certain madrigals are better reserved for performance by soloists. The criterion for making such a choice lies often with the text rather than with the music, for a certain degree of personal intensity in the words demands a corresponding projection of individual lines and their message. On the other hand, others are eminently suitable for choral performance.

After the vogue of the madrigal had disappeared, that of the glee eventually took its place, flourishing from the early 18th century to the middle of the 19th. Like the madrigal, the glee was originally intended for solo voices, but choral performances were by no means infrequent. The word glee, derived from the Anglo-Saxon word for music (*gligge*) does not necessarily imply a composition of a cheerful nature, and many of the best glees in fact express solemn or poetic themes. Samuel Webbe's *Glorious Apollo* and R.J.S. Stevens's *Ye spotted snakes* provide very different, though typical, examples of this vocal genre. Tonality is for the most part simple and unaffected, harmony is robust, and the span of musical thought necessarily brief. (D.W.S.)

Theatre music

Music as an art of the theatre has its roots in primitive ritual and ceremony and its branches in every modern means of theatrical presentation. Its functions are as varied as the forms require and range from being the primary reason for performance, as in opera, to mere noise, filling a vacuum in imagination for some screen and stage presentations. The more significant and universal aspects of theatrical music are considered in this section; opera is the subject of a separate section.

Theatre music is all music composed to govern, enhance, or support a theatrical conception. Music composed for theatrical purposes obeys different laws than does the music for concert performance or conventional opera. Whereas in opera the music dictates the form in which the dramatic visual imagery is presented and governs its development, in other kinds of theatre the music is, at best, an equal partner among its principal elements. In concert, of course, the music is the sole factor that determines the experience.

In the West, the concept of music as an intellectual experience for its own sake emerged only in the second half of the 18th century. Theatrical music is variously related to something other than itself, whether as an enrichment of words (as in operetta), a factor in structure and mood (ballet), or an intensification of situation and feeling (as in incidental music for plays and films).

In some instances music is dominant, in some it is subservient, and in operetta or stage musical the emphasis alternates between speech, song, and dance. In opera and spoken drama, in which words are wholly sung or spoken, a convention once set is consistently sustained and thereby creates its own kind of reality. The constant change of focus in operetta and musical, from music to speech and back again, emphasizes the artificiality of the illusion they seek to create.

The classical mainstream of theatre music in the West extends from the mid-17th century to the 1930s, and the instances of drama and music meeting on an equal level of imagination are relatively few. More frequently great music was lavished on weak or corrupt theatre, or great drama was embellished with indifferent music. From the early 20th century new dramatic developments were seldom directly matched in music. A German-Italian composer, Ferruccio Busoni, wrote in 1906:

> The greater part of modern theatre music suffers from the mistake of seeking to repeat the scenes passing on the stage, instead of fulfilling its own proper mission of interpreting the attitudes of the persons represented.

The German composer Kurt Weill's score for *Der Silbersee* (1933; *The Silver Sea*) was the last major musical contribution to a serious play requiring a full orchestra and chorus. Thereafter, for economic reasons, the dramatic theatre had to equip itself with small-group music or prerecorded tapes. The orchestra and chorus became the prerogative of stage musicals and films. The more these were commercially debased the more they came to rely heavily on the clichés of 19th-century music, to the exclusion of newer musical developments.

Producers of stage musicals, the choreographers of dance, and the directors of drama need to be wary of the properties of music. It is more demanding of attention than is often thought, and its use should ideally be confined to circumstances where it can provide something that none of the other theatrical elements can offer. The more its qualities are understood and respected, the better it can be guided to an effective theatrical purpose.

MUSIC FOR BALLET

During the 20th century the element of music in all forms of ballet has changed and developed its significance to an unprecedented extent. It has acquired the status of an equal partner with the choreography, where once it was entirely the servant of the ballet master. In the 19th century he asked little more than that the music should decorate his ballets prettily and give rhythmic support to the movements of the dancers. His modern successors have been made aware that the highest level of balletic achievement now requires the music and choreography to become extensions of each other, to be heard and seen on equal levels of perception.

The partnership of choreography and music

The finest modern choreographers are not content simply

to ride the surface of their chosen music, whether it is specially written, borrowed, or adapted. They seek to exploit the relationship of eye and ear, recognizing that the effect of any danced step can be changed by the stress of the musical rhythm, the degree of loud or soft in its dynamics, the nature of its harmonic character, and the expressive quality of its instrumental timbre. All these factors can make a positive contribution to the ballectic image, and they give coherence to the sequence of movement as they merge into its continuous momentum.

Until the end of the 19th century each new ballet customarily had music specially composed for it, but it was rare for any composer of distinction to write ballet music, unless it was part of an opera. There were exceptions—such as Beethoven's score for *Die Geschöpfe des Prometheus* (1801; *The Creatures of Prometheus*), originally a ballet by an Italian choreographer, Salvatore Viganò—but the great era of Romantic ballet from about 1830 was seldom enhanced by music of intrinsic worth. When ballet gained a musical interest the difference was soon apparent; it has been well said that Léo Delibes gave ballet music a heart, Peter Tchaikovsky gave it a soul, and Igor Stravinsky made an honest woman of it.

Stravinsky's influence on music for ballet

Stravinsky was the dominating figure for nearly half a century (beginning in 1910) in composing music for ballet. He gained international acclaim with the first products of his collaboration with the Ballets Russes of the Russian impresario Sergey Diaghilev: *The Firebird* (1910), *Petrushka* (1911), and *The Rite of Spring* (1913). The first two continue to be performed in their original choreography by Michel Fokine, also a Russian, each with a narrative basis illustrated in music notable for its expressive colour and harmonic innovations. *The Rite of Spring* provoked one of the most notorious scandals in theatre history when Vaslav Nijinsky's original ballet reduced its first Paris audience to verbal insult and physical assault; its rhythmic audacity has since remained a recurring challenge to other choreographers.

Largely as a result of the standard set by Diaghilev's flair and artistic success, most leading composers in the 20th century have contributed something to the art of dance. Diaghilev directly commissioned two outstanding examples in the French composer Maurice Ravel's *Daphnis et Chloé* (1912), which the composer defined as a "poème choréographique," and *The Three-cornered Hat* (1919) by the Spanish composer Manuel de Falla. Distinctive original scores for ballet continued usually to be the outcome of specific commissions. Composers do not yet normally think in terms of dance (as they do in terms of song), although in Great Britain the composer Peter Maxwell Davies incorporated an integral role for solo dancer in his otherwise instrumental work, *Vesalii icones* (1969).

Contrary to what is still sometimes thought by musicians and a section of the public, music for ballet is not necessarily written to be "interpreted" in dance. Stravinsky has emphasized:

> Choreography must realise its own form, one independent of the musical form though measured to the musical unit. Its construction will be based on whatever correspondences the choreographer may invent, but it must not seek merely to duplicate the line and beat of the music.

Stravinsky's collaboration with Balanchine

The composer was writing from the experience of a long collaboration with a Russian-born choreographer, George Balanchine, mainly for what is now the New York City Ballet. Their partnership began in 1928 with *Apollo,* reached a peak in 1957 with *Agon,* and was to the 20th century what the collaboration of Tchaikovsky with choreographers Marius Petipa from France and Lev Ivanov from Russia was to the 19th.

In the Soviet Union a post-revolutionary equivalent to the classical three-act narrative ballet has continued to be in demand. This form has been furnished by many composers of ballets that have not been performed beyond the U.S.S.R., but it has been chiefly distinguished by the work of Sergey Prokofiev. His full-length scores for *Romeo and Juliet* (1940), *Cinderella* (1948), and *The Stone Flower* (posthumously staged in 1954) have variously succeeded in reconciling an older classical form to new expressive demands. Its offshoots in western Europe have included, in Great Britain, Benjamin Britten's music for *The Prince of the Pagodas* (staged by the Royal Ballet, 1957) and Hans Werner Henze's music for *Ondine* (Royal Ballet, 1958).

The stronger emphasis in western Europe and the United States in the late 20th century was on one-act ballets, varying from about 15 minutes to more than one hour's duration. Composers continue to show some reluctance to write music specifically for dancing, partly because they are seldom closely involved with the art, and also because they have relatively less control over the finished performance than in opera and in most other forms of musical theatre. Apart from works already mentioned, however, the ballet repertory has been enriched by such scores as the French composer Erik Satie's *Parade* for Diaghilev in 1917; the British composer Vaughan Williams' *Job* (1931) and the English composer Sir Arthur Bliss's *Checkmate* (1937) for the British choreographer Ninette de Valois, in Britain; and the U.S. composer Aaron Copland's *Appalachian Spring* (1944) and the American composer Samuel Barber's *The Serpent Heart* (1946; later revised as *Cave of the Heart,* 1947) for the choreographer Martha Graham, in the United States.

Creation of modern ballets to existing scores

Nevertheless, the greater proportion of new ballets in the West during the last half-century have been created to pre-existing music, and it is evident that choreographers have felt a greater freedom to experiment visually in the use of such music. The practice dates principally from the first orchestration (by the Russian composer Aleksandr Glazunov, 1894) of an arbitrary suite of piano music by Frédéric Chopin to which Fokine created *Chopiniana* (1908)—a title retained by Soviet ballet companies for what Diaghilev renamed *Les Sylphides* (1909). More than 60 years later, another arbitrary suite by Chopin, although retained in its piano form, proved to be no less fruitful for the U.S. choreographer Jerome Robbins in *Dances at a Gathering* (1969).

Almost every category of music—from medieval music to advanced electronics and from symphonic compositions to the simplest pop tunes—has now been used for choreographic purposes. The function of music in a dance context has varied almost as much—staining the ballet's surroundings as a kind of aural decor at one extreme, as with the soundscapes of John Cage for Merce Cunningham's dance works in the United States, to the mutual absorption of music and choreography phrase by phrase in such works as the British choreographer Sir Frederick Ashton's *Symphonic Variations* to the music of César Franck (Royal Ballet, 1946), and the Balanchine-Stravinsky *Agon* (1957) and *Movements* (New York City Ballet, 1963).

Sometimes the same music has been used for several different ballets within a short time by various choreographers. An outstanding example is the *Sinfonia* by an Italian composer, Luciano Berio, written originally in 1968 as a concert work. By the end of 1971 it had been taken over for at least eight separate ballets in almost as many countries in western Europe alone.

Ballet concerned with musical associations

Another trend in ballet in the second half of the 20th century has been to make ballets apparently more concerned with musical associations than with human personality. Instances include Balanchine's *Agon* and *Movements,* already mentioned, and the British choreographer Kenneth (later Sir Kenneth) MacMillan's *The Song of the Earth* (1965) to the song-symphony by the Austrian composer Gustav Mahler. The dancers seem required to assume the "personality," or expressive character, of the musical instruments they parallel, as if the choreographers were moving toward a form of "ideal" dance once postulated by a French poet, Stéphane Mallarmé, who envisaged music and dance not only as equals but also equally devoid of human personality.

In the view of most ballet critics, the antidote lies in the continuing appeal of narrative dance-dramas with their illustrative music, although the success or otherwise of any ballets that engage preexisting music is basically governed by a single crucial principle: the level of choreographic imagination should never be less than that of the music. A ballet can be better than its music, but it can never afford to be worse. There will always be ballets dependent on music for no more than expressive colour and supporting rhythm, but the "perfect analogous concord between what we see and what we hear," recommended as the ideal nearly 150 years ago by Carlo Blasis, a great Italian teacher, still remains the most desirable aspiration for every kind of ballet music.

STAGE MUSICALS

When, in the 1930s and 1940s, dancing became an integral element in a genre governed chiefly by song—instead of being merely a diversion—the "musical" established itself as the legitimate theatrical heir to "musical comedy" and a form of popular theatre art that dominated the latter half of the 20th century. It has lately been challenged by the newer "rock musical," using a variation of the common musical vernacular and techniques related more to the recording studio than to the theatre, the effect of which is not yet determined. Meanwhile, what originally started as a democratic counterpart to aristocratic opera reached its fruition as the theatrical association of sentiment with illusion.

The sentiment is usually dispensed by the narrative; the illusion is created by the music. The most potent narratives in stage musicals have often been adaptations of classical drama and literature—for example, *Romeo and Juliet* transformed into *West Side Story; The Taming of the Shrew* into *Kiss Me, Kate; Don Quixote* into *Man of La Mancha;* and *Oliver Twist* into *Oliver*—or the many variations on the *Cinderella–Pygmalion* legend by which rags are transformed into riches (from *The Shop Girl* in 1894 to *My Fair Lady* in 1956). A distinction was at one time drawn between the frivolous musical comedy and the "musical play," denoting a dramatically serious or even tragic narrative, but both are now equally defined as musicals.

Their specifically musical character is born from a marriage of convenience between first and second generation descendants of European operetta and music-hall variety, on the one hand, and American jazz and American music hall, on the other—plus the romantic balladry of both continents. An English musicologist, Wilfred Mellers, asserts that although most successful stage songs contain subtleties unappreciated by the non-musical listener, they all reflect "an illusion that we can live on the surface of our emotions" and that "the world of musical comedy never gets beyond, or wants to get beyond, this illusion."

First musical comedy

The first musical comedy so to be called was *A Gaiety Girl,* staged in 1893 by George Edwardes at the Gaiety Theatre, London. A romantic farce, adorned by the songs of Sidney Jones, it was successfully exported to New York in the same year. John Hollingshead (Edwardes' predecessor at the Gaiety Theatre) wrote in 1903:

> The invention or discovery of musical comedy was a happy inspiration of Mr. George Edwardes's. It provided a new form of entertainment for playgoers who go to a theatre for amusement and recreation, which was more elastic in plot or story than the old burlesque . . . [It] exhibited a little of the old burletta and vaudeville, most of the best elements of farce, a dash of the French revue . . . and much that would not have been out of place in Parisian *opéra-bouffe.*

Some 50 years of development in musical theatre is reflected in the contrast between the foregoing remarks and the following comment in 1952 by Jack Burton, U.S. theatre historian, on *Oklahoma!* (1943), an epoch-making musical by Richard Rodgers and Oscar Hammerstein:

> This phenomenal production set a new pattern in which every line, every song, every dance routine is an indispensable part of a closely-knit whole. It was a show that had dramatic substance and never ran off the plot track, and so real, so simple, so engrossing was its story that its narrative could be safely entrusted to other than big-name stars.

The years embraced by these comments set up a dominant axis of theatrical exchange between New York and London. Success in this field is governed more by economic than artistic considerations, with longer and longer runs of each production becoming necessary to recover increasingly heavy expenditures before profits can be made. The primary requirements for the composer are, therefore, quick assimilation combined with durability. His music should also be easily adaptable to other media such as motion pictures and phonograph or tape reproduction, whereby it becomes a commonplace of experience to a mass audience far beyond the reach of the original theatrical context.

Although musical theatre of this kind has developed toward a closer integration of music and story, its primary feature has remained the individual song. Lehman Engel, a leading conductor of stage musicals in the United States, has defined five types of song basic to the stage musical: ballad—usually but not exclusively romantic in feeling; rhythm song—varied in emotional character but primarily propelled by a prominent musical beat; comedy song—enhancing verbal humour and divided into "short joke" and "long joke"; charm song—generally delicate, optimistic, and lightly rhythmic; and musical scene—in which a song may form part of a continuous dramatic episode. Engel further asserts that the successful impact of any song in the first instance is generally governed by the following considerations: the tempo, the mood of the scene, the song's position in relation to the whole production, the inherent value of the song itself, and the relative importance of the character who delivers it. It will be noted that integral musical quality is subordinate on this scale, although it is specifically the musical appeal that establishes success in the first place, disseminates that success through other media, and may later lead to revival in the country of origin and to reproduction in other countries.

Success of *My Fair Lady*

Probably the most successful specimen to date is *My Fair Lady,* with music by Frederick Loewe, Viennese-born U.S. composer. This musical had first runs of 2,717 performances in New York (from 1956) and 2,281 in London (from 1958), and it has since been staged in translation in most European countries and in the Soviet Union. It is rare for the English-language dominance of the musical-comedy genre to be breached by other countries, as France did with *Irma la Douce* (1956) or pre-Nazi Germany did with *Die Dreigroschenoper* (*Threepenny Opera,* 1928) and *Im weissen Rossl* (1930; *White Horse Inn*); but in most European countries except Britain the line between musical and operetta (see below) is less distinctly marked.

In Italy such lighter forms of musical theatre are submerged in an already popular taste for the broadest range of opera, while in Spain they manifest themselves in the category of zarzuela (discussed below in conjunction with operetta). Differences of idiom are often more the outcome of theatrical or other conditions in their respective countries than of theatrical or musical distinctions in the work itself. In the Soviet Union, according to Andrey Olkhovsky, a Russian-born musicologist,

> the numerous attempts which have been made to create a Soviet repertory have led to no results. At best the plots of comedies are based on episodes from Soviet life, but musically they are still imitations of the pre-Revolution operettas.

Stage musical comedies in the Western sense have produced their own original talents among composers—notably Jerome Kern, Irving Berlin, George Gershwin, Cole Porter, and Richard Rodgers in the United States; and Noel Coward, Vivian Ellis, Ivor Novello, Lionel Bart, and Sandy Wilson in Great Britain. They have also had occasional recourse to adaptations from classical composers, including Franz Schubert and Edvard Grieg, who are dramatically characterized respectively in *Lilac Time* (originally *Das Dreimäderlhaus;* 1916) and *The Song of Norway* (1944); Georges Bizet, whose music became the basis of *Carmen Jones* (1943); and Aleksandr Borodin, for *Kismet* (1953).

The arrival of the rock musical

Musicals ought to be adaptable to varied instrumentation, because theatre orchestras can vary considerably in size and composition from place to place. Paradoxically, the looser form of the new rock musical is propelled by a much more rigid instrumentation derived from the ensemble used in pop-music recording, itself determined by studio techniques. In *Jesus Christ Superstar* (1971) the covering of the orchestra pit, the permanent amplification of instruments, and the use of voices entirely dependent on microphones amounts to a replacement of the illusion of theatre in any traditional sense with the actuality of a modern recording studio made visible.

MUSIC FOR MOTION PICTURES

Many successful stage musicals have become additionally popular through the medium of motion pictures, but music as a basic element in filmmaking has only gained recognition since midcentury as something more than a means to heighten local colour or intensify emotional expression. In the early silent films, all kinds of music were recorded, classified, and adapted to fit different moods (Beethoven overtures for cowboy–Indian chases, for instance). Several talented hacks also wrote short descriptive pieces. A few bigger films, such as *The Birth of a Nation,* had special scores fitted to them. Since the 1960s it has turned a full circle of the wheel back to extensive musical quotation from classical resources for similar ends but in different ways.

Russian film makers first gave serious consideration to the contribution music could make. V.I. Pudovkin, a Russian musicologist, defined a theory and practice of film music in the early 1930s, advocating a close and contrapuntal relationship between sound and sight. The Russian film director Sergey Eisenstein described his careful collaboration with Prokofiev in making *Alexander Nevsky* (1938). His perceptive observations on the potential link between cinematic rhythm and musical rhythm suggested a technique that has influenced others, such as the British composer Sir William Walton in his score for *Hamlet.*

Hanns Eisler's theories of film music

Hanns Eisler, a German-born composer, formed his own theories of film music, based on empirical experience composing in this medium. His published findings recommended: short musical forms in a film context; the composer's conscious awareness of the film's realistic sound element (the "where" and "when" of its location); and music that could suggest an objective, universal character for the film's emotions, rather than being introspective on its own account. Eisler also supported Pudovkin in maintaining that film music should create its own sense of line independently of, although related to, the film narrative.

Film music has travelled through five broad phases: an initial borrowing from existing conventional sources; the use of musical-cliché catalogs, which enabled any musician of modest ability to assemble an emotional or dramatic sequence and which served as the basis for most later background music in films; the active interest of major composers in writing original scores; a subsequent reaction of either near silence or advanced techniques of electronic sound generation and transformation; and the borrowing from classical sources for new purposes.

In the Soviet Union and France, in particular, the regular participation of leading composers in film music has been the rule rather than the exception. The opposite holds true in the United States and Great Britain, although most composers of distinction in both countries between the mid-1930s and the mid-1950s made some original contributions to motion-picture medium. In the United States these included Aaron Copland, Marc Blitzstein, and Virgil Thomson, who received the first Pulitzer Prize awarded to film music—for *Louisiana Story* (1948); in Great Britain, Ralph Vaughan Williams, Benjamin Britten, Sir William Walton, Alan Rawsthorne, and Richard Rodney Bennett.

Isolated experiments to marry films to specific classical music have been made from time to time. These include the Austrian director Max Reinhardt's film of Shakespeare's *A Midsummer Night's Dream* (1935), which varied the cinematic structure to incorporate the complete suite of Mendelssohn's incidental music originally written for the play. The U.S. film maker Walt Disney's celebrated *Fantasia* (1940) adapted the technique of the animated cartoon to illustrate a sequence of musical classics, outraging some people because the visual relationships were held to be irrelevant to the music but continuing to the present to entertain audiences, especially young ones, on an international scale.

When the making of motion pictures became an industry more than a craft, a situation developed in which music was recognized as desirable by the manufacturers, who nevertheless made no claim to "understand" music in the way they would be expected to understand motion-picture techniques. A parallel attitude among musicians unfortunately came to regard the skilled provision of a score tailored to the demands of script and camera as a spiritually impoverished relation of aspiring symphonic or operatic works.

Renewed use of concert music

In the late 1960s original film composition tended to decline in favour of renewed and often extensive borrowing from existing concert music. The slow movement from a Mozart piano concerto served to express the passage of time as well as for emotional mood in *Elvira Madigan.* The U.S. film director Stanley Kubrick's *2001: A Space Odyssey* (1968) led an audience's imagination outward into space by a transition from the diatonic (using the natural scale of five tones and two semitones) C major of the introduction to Richard Strauss's tone-poem *Also sprach Zarathustra,* to the polytonal Kyrie from the *Requiem* by the contemporary Hungarian-born composer György Ligeti. In the Italian film director Luchino Visconti's *Death in Venice,* four repetitions of a long passage from the Adagietto movement of Gustav Mahler's *Symphony No. 5* achieved a different expressive purpose in association with the visual scene each time it was heard.

Examples like these achieved an even greater impact than many original scores because they formed an organic part of the filmmaker's conception. Conversely, even scores distinguished by their own merits—such as Copland's for *Of Mice and Men* (1939), or Walton's for *Henry V* (1944)—were added only after the film itself was more or less finished. The major hope for the future of this medium lies in what Vaughan Williams urged: the composition of original scores but prepared in conjunction with the director from the film's inception. Film music might then be turned to more constructive instead of merely decorative purposes, without the dramatic license of the British film director Ken Russell's treatment of extensive passages from Tchaikovsky's music in his film *The Music Lovers* (1971).

MUSIC FOR TELEVISION

The screen medium's first law, that the visual element must come first, has been intensified by television. On the home screen, the experience of music performed for its own sake customarily operates under a double disadvantage. First, it runs the risk of being swamped by its visual presentation, which may range in character from the matching of nonmusical images in varying degrees of relevance to the technique of using close-ups of musicians in action. Secondly, it suffers the continuing handicap of inadequate reproduction by the average television receiver.

Limited repertory of television music

Apart from rare exceptions—such as an occasional "television opera," a dance-film, or Stravinsky's mixed media *The Flood* (1962)—original music to television is chiefly confined to the provision of theme passages or supporting music hopefully intended to enhance verbal or dramatic presentation. Like the cinema pianist who played for silent films, television music has a limited repertory of conventional gestures. Even when these are given a more contemporary harmonic or instrumental garb, they remain basically governed by the 19th-century mode of musical thought, to which it is assumed that mass audiences will most easily react.

Programs about rather than of music have obtained a modicum of television success. While the occasional theme quotation has perhaps introduced a famous musical classic to millions who would not otherwise have heard it, the "workshop" program, showing how music and musicians go about their business, has broken down barriers of technique and exposed the raw materials of music in a way that has probably helped to foster a wider interest in the finished product. Television cannot otherwise be accepted as a musical medium, until sets have a higher standard of musical reproduction.

INCIDENTAL MUSIC FOR THE THEATRE

Incidental music in the theatre, whatever its idiom or degree of stylistic emancipation, justifies itself through its exclusive concern with a specific play or theatrical presentation. Its three main uses involve songs, intensified dramatic effect, and interlude filling, and these have been clearly defined in Western theatre since Renaissance drama freed itself from the church in the 16th century.

A major modification of its character since the 1920s has been brought about largely by the wider use of mechanical techniques of amplification and recorded music. This has encouraged short musical fragments rather than fully composed pieces, except where the latter are specifically called for. Examples of this technique were heard in modern times in the musical productions of the National Theatre and the Royal Shakespeare Company in Great Britain. Such carefully planned but more informal use of incidental music has replaced the elaborate suites customary in the 19th and early 20th centuries, which presupposed the complete performance of each piece and required the stage drama to be produced so that the music could be accommodated in it (a characteristic example is Mendelssohn's music for *A Midsummer Night's Dream* at Potsdam, Germany, in 1843).

Informal incidental music

Economic conditions are now the principal factor governing the provision of incidental music. Theatres not concerned with opera or ballet can no longer afford to hire musicians for a pit band. Trade-union restrictions in the musical profession also limit the public use of recorded music in many countries. The trend is consequently for spoken drama either to dispense with music, to restrict it to one or two musicians with a singer, or to make increasingly fruitful use of electronic sounds on prerecorded tape.

Some famous 19th-century suites of incidental music were brought into being by conditions that favoured resident musicians at court theatres in Germany or lavish orchestral resources in Tsarist Russia. The music has since acquired independent status on its own merits and has become part of the classical concert repertory, such as the Mendelssohn just mentioned and Beethoven's music for Goethe's *Egmont* (1810); Schubert's for the German playwright Helmina von Chézy's *Rosamunde* (1823); Schumann's for Lord Byron's *Manfred* (1852); and Grieg's for Henrik Ibsen's *Peer Gynt* (1876).

Earlier theatre music was often, for long periods of time, governed by measures of censorship and legal restrictions that varied greatly from one country to another. In England, for instance, the monopoly of spoken drama was vested by King Charles II in the Theatres Royal in the 17th century, and this continued until 1843. Other theatres that opened during this time—including those catering to a new working class—were licensed only on condition that plays included five musical items in each act or a "musical accompaniment." The latter condition was sometimes held to be satisfied by no more than a chord struck at intervals on a piano during the performance. Such conditions inevitably brought about a profusion of inferior music, which in turn gave rise to the traditions of music hall and burlesque.

The renaissance of secular theatre, from the 17th century onward, led in Italy to the evolution of the predominantly musical forms of opera and oratorio, in France to the court ballet, and in England and Spain to the cultivation of spoken plays with incidental music. The unparalleled achievements of secular drama in the latter two countries are the roots of present-day musical theatre and help to explain why opera failed to flourish in competition. The drama in England expanded into the allied form of masque and involved the participation of such composers of distinction as Henry Purcell.

The masque in relation to its own period might well have been defined as "mixed media." This term has now come to stand for theatre presentations in a line of descent from Stravinsky's *Histoire du Soldat* (1918; *The Soldier's Tale*), which combines speech, song, mime, dance, and instrumental music with pictorial design. These elements have since been supplemented by the mechanical techniques of film or photographic projection, and of electronic sounds, in almost infinite permutations, together with a free form of expression no longer necessarily shaped by a narrative content.

The masque

Most of these manifestations incorporated two different kinds of musical contribution. One has been defined by a 20th-century German composer, Bernd Alois Zimmermann:

> All elements of the theatre of movement, including film, sound, speech, electronic music, must be mobilized into one great time-space structure, whose arrangement will be constituted by music as the most general form of temporal order.

Zimmermann's ideas were embodied in his opera, *Die Soldaten* (The Soldiers). The alternative is described by another composer, John Cage, as "Single sounds or groups of sounds which are not supported by harmonies but resound within a space of silence" and are added more or less at random to the other elements. It remains to be discovered whether the future of theatre music in drama or mixed media lies primarily with the highly organized patterns of interaction postulated by Zimmermann or with Cage's arbitrary combination of simple, disparate activities into a complex whole.

OPERETTA AND ALLIED FORMS

It seems unlikely that any future exists for operetta except as part of a "museum" repertory, because the contemporary musical has taken its place in musical theatre. Operetta in the usual sense of a work of lesser musical pretensions than opera, with spoken dialogue linking the musical episodes, was a direct descendant of comic opera, overlapping this category, on one hand, and early musical comedy, on the other. It was born as a democratic expression of popular wit and social satire, flourished for almost exactly a century (*c.* 1840–1940), and died from a surfeit of sentiment.

Offenbach. The satirical, romantic operetta emerged primarily in Paris in the mid-19th century with the French composer Jacques Offenbach; two of his works are still widely staged: *Orphée aux enfers* (1858; *Orpheus in the Underworld*) and *La Belle Hélène* (1864; *Beautiful Helen*). The character of Offenbach's operettas established several musical precedents, including the burlesque of Italian opera, the romantic ballad in $\frac{3}{8}$ or $\frac{6}{8}$ metre, and the drinking song and the *ensemble de perplexité* ("ensemble of confusion"). In England, Arthur Sullivan followed in Offenbach's wake with his fruitful partnership with the author W.S. Gilbert, bequeathing a commentary on aspects of Victorian society through music of popular and enduring, if somewhat relentless, charm.

Viennese operetta. Charm is the main ingredient of the more sentimental Viennese operetta, and it usually submerges the rarer shaft of social comment. The younger Johann Strauss made operetta an international entertainment by an expert blend of charm and craft, and his *Die Fledermaus* (1874; *The Bat*) remains a classic of its kind. A second generation in this tradition was chiefly distinguished by Franz Lehár, whose *Die lustige Witwe* (1905; *The Merry Widow*) represents the genre at its peak of romantic elegance, demonstrating a style and craftsmanship that seems in serious danger of being lost altogether.

Johann Strauss's contribution to operetta

Such operettas remain current in today's musical theatre mainly as an indulgence of musical and emotional nostalgia. Their popular style enabled them to take root and flourish far from their native territories, including transplantation to the United States. The indigenous tradition of the U.S. stage musical, already mentioned, first had to compete with European-style operetta. That the latter keeps a tenacious hold on popular affections is demonstrated by figures listing Rudolf Friml's *Rose Marie* (1924) and Sigmund Romberg's *The Desert Song* (1926) as the most frequently performed works in U.S. musical theatre, in terms of both amateur and professional performances.

Zarzuela. Spain was a prominent exception to the wide dissemination of operetta, preferring instead the flourishing native variety of zarzuela. This form customarily incorporates regional songs and dances, sometimes with traditional rather than original music. It continues to some extent as a staple fare in Spanish musical theatre, although the general contemporary trend toward a more universal style of musical expression has meant that the younger Spanish composer has shown much less interest in the zarzuela form as an outlet for his musical imagination.

The Romantic zarzuela has little resemblance to the aristocratic and courtly character of its 17th-century namesake and emerged with French and Viennese operetta during the 19th century. It divided into two forms—the *zarzuela grande* in three acts, equivalent to romantic operetta, and the *género chico* in one act, invariably comic, usually satirical, employing the broadest musical vernacular, and verging on revue. In the former category, the names of Francisco Barbieri, Amadeo Vives, and Federico Moreno Torroba are probably the most significant representatives of their respective generations.

The Spanish character and language of the Romantic zarzuelas made them exportable to Central and South America, where they became a model for the limited indigenous musical theatre. The South American centres are otherwise dominated by imports or imitations of the Italian opera tradition or used as transit bases for the latest North American stage musical on its theatrical circumnavigation. Certain examples of the Spanish zarzuela, such as Moreno Torroba's *Luisa Fernanda* (1932), have achieved popular success in Latin American countries, where local contributions to the genre have notably been made by Juan Bautista Massa in Argentina, Andrés Martínez Montoya in Colombia, Luis Delgadillo in Nicaragua, and Teodoro Valcárcel in Peru.

ORIENTAL MUSICAL THEATRE

Theatre music generally serves different purposes in non-Western idioms—usually adding dimension and perspective to song and dance, indicating symbolic associations, suggesting mood, and even inducing a desired response in an audience. Most Oriental streams of music divide between popular music of a folk character and a more sophisticated style for a cultured elite. The distinction is often less clearly defined than in Western music and is now not so firmly maintained in the wake of recent political and social changes.

China. The classical Peking opera (*ching-hsi*) in China is a form of musical theatre in which music is one among several elements rather than a governing factor, as in Western opera. The vocal writing alternates between styles broadly equivalent to recitative and song, distinguished by a forced high falsetto tone required from the male singers. A less stylized variety is the all-female *yüeh ch'ü*, in which natural singing voices perform musical plays in realistic and decorative scenery, and the Manchurian *P'ing Hsi*, which has developed into an operetta-like equivalent, with traditions and subjects derived from strolling players and folk legends.

Since 1964 the performance of classical Peking opera in Communist China has been mainly restricted to festival occasions (although state-sponsored schools continue to train performers especially for it). More emphasis has been put on entertainments closer to Western musicals, involving contemporary dialogue, everyday dress, and less stylized music. As a popular form of musical theatre it has been turned to political and social advantage with a new and adapted repertory of dramatic ballets and musical plays, bearing such titles as *Taking Tiger Mountain by Strategy* and *The Red Detachment of Women*.

Political overtones of modern Chinese opera

Japan. Music is as much a regular part of theatre performance in Japan as it is in China. The highly formal tradition of Japanese Nō drama incorporates music as an integral feature, usually performed by flute, a variety of stringed instrument called the samisen, drums, and singers. The music varies in content and character with the subject of the play and obeys detailed melodic rules—especially in the central dance episode designed to reveal the spirit of the play's principal character. A less formal counterpart, the Kabuki theatre, has almost as impressive an ancestry as the Nō and continues to be widely performed, with music used to indicate period, place, time, or mood and often functioning by phrase association like the principle of leading motives in Richard Wagner.

India. Japanese theatre also incorporates music dramas of Indian origin, and the Indian theatre tradition is a full combination of poetry, music, dance, and symbolism. The music is often interpolated rather than specially composed and is likely to be drawn from the repertory of widely known songs without aiming at a high classical standard. The close association of music with drama in Indian culture has been carried over into Indian film, which cannot hope to enjoy wide success among its modern audiences unless it is liberally embellished with songs and other forms of music.

THE HISTORY OF THEATRICAL MUSIC

Formative period. What is thought to be the oldest document of musical history depicts a man wearing an animal mask, manipulating what is possibly a form of musical bow, and dancing in the wake of a herd of reindeer. This is a prehistoric cave painting dating from the Stone Age, discovered at Ariège in France. Masks are tangible signs of that transfer of personality on which every form of theatre is based and in which song and dance have participated since the dawn of communication and animated ritual. Music in dramatic entertainment reached early peaks of development in European and Oriental cultures in, respectively, the ancient Greece of Homer and, some centuries later, the Chinese classical drama.

Descriptive evidence of the earliest Greek theatre indicates that music, mostly sung by a chorus, was essential but not continuous. At drama festivals the poet wrote his own music (as well as being actor, producer, and choreographer), probably based on some kind of traditional repeated formula. Later Greek theatre, after the fall of Athens (404 BC), initiated both the repertory system and a category of musicians trained more highly than the populace. Amateur and professional became separated for the first time, and increasing sophistication brought about its counterpart in popular pantomime expressed in song and dance, often satirical or bawdy in character.

Early Greek and Roman theatrical music

The Roman musical theatre derived directly from the Greek, ousting a short-lived native form with Etruscan actors who also danced to pipe music. Latin versions of the Greek theatre with music were supplemented by a Roman variant of the pantomime as a dramatic solo dance with chorus and orchestra. It implied some prior knowledge on the audience's part of the subject and the dance vocabulary. Amphitheatre shows of gladiatorial contests were regularly accompanied by music, sometimes involving up to 100 horn blowers and 200 pipers, as well as such extra devices as water organs.

About the time the Roman theatre flourished, an Oriental equivalent emerged in China from ritual ceremonies that came to be repeated for their entertainment value. The puppet theatre was a significant intermediate stage in this process, and the forms evolved into different styles of entertainment for courtier and commoner. Strings, flute, and handbells accompanied the songs and dances in upper-class entertainments; a form of mouth organ replaced the bells in shows for the common people. By the time of the Sung dynasty (AD 960–1279), from which the earliest written music survives, a type of musical variety theatre, the *tzarjiuh*, was widely popular.

The Chinese classical opera tradition has already been mentioned as a modern form of musical theatre. It first developed during the Yüan dynasty (1206–1368) and reached its peak of style and classical form in the Ming period (1368–1644). Its evolution was accompanied by a less formal counterpart based on the dramatization of folk songs linked by a thin narrative plot (*Chueichang*). The full-scale opera and its regional variants remained the most significant form of Oriental musical theatre until the modern post-revolutionary times, but throughout the Far East the indigenous forms of music have always played a prominent part in theatrical presentations.

In Europe the vestiges of Greco-Roman culture were submerged by the early Christian Church. By the 6th century the church had suppressed drama and adapted pagan rituals to its own liturgical puposes. A small flame of musical theatre was left burning only in the form of religious ceremonial (for example, in the mass). Festive religious celebrations eventually expanded into the liturgical music drama that slowly developed from about the 10th century. This brought in its wake the equally religious "mysteries" and miracle plays of the Middle Ages in Europe, which were performed in the vernacular instead of in Latin, had a strong musical element, and, in due course, developed a secular counterpart.

Musical elements of the miracle plays

In a pattern that was to repeat itself after the birth of opera 200 years later, the secular theatre in the Middle

Ages established itself either as lighthearted interludes in serious moralities or as deliberate parody tolerated by the church as a safety valve to consistent piety. The annual Feast of Fools in 15th-century Paris, for instance, incorporated an obscene parody of the mass performed in song and dance within the church. By the year 1400 numerous comedies and farces had appeared, usually performed on festive occasions in aristocratic houses or on open stages in municipal squares.

These plays often employed musical forces comparable to those of the religious plays and used them for similar purposes. Choirboys from the church sometimes took part, but surviving texts suggest that there was little choral music as such. The individual actors incorporated parts of songs chanted monophonically to embellish or heighten the dramatic effect, and dancing to specific instrumental music also had a regular place in the entertainment. Professional musicians might be hired and might also be required to act; the constituent parts of the entertainment varied widely from place to place.

The fact that, except for songs, documents of the period contain almost no music directly linked with the theatre is thought to indicate that very little original instrumental music was written for theatrical purposes at this time. Whatever was suitable for weddings, banquets, and other feasts perhaps served a theatrical purpose just as well. Musicians probably had little or no acquaintance with musical notation and played pieces from their regular repertory. These seem to have included arrangements of vocal melodies as well as dance tunes, among which the play texts most frequently identify *basses-dances* and branles.

The Renaissance and Baroque periods. When Catherine de Médicis married King Henry II of France in 1533, she brought from Italy a taste for entertainments in which dancing was prominent. Her encouragement established the court ballet (*ballet de cour*) as the foundation of classical ballet, the source of a new theatrical identity for music and a precursor of French opera. As a unified blend of poetry, music, and movement, the court ballet dates from the performance of the *Ballet comique de la reine* at a court wedding in 1581. The form comprised an optional number of scenes in mime and dance, prefaced by explanatory verses that were either spoken or sung; the scenes were accompanied by solo and choral songs with lute, and instrumental ensemble pieces for strings.

The French court ballet

In about 1605 a more mannered style of singing had become customary, and by 1620 the court ballet was more a vehicle for display than drama. Unified dramatic plots were restored by the poet Isaac de Benserade in midcentury, and Jean-Baptiste Lully, who entered the service of King Louis XIV in 1652, endowed the music with fresh distinction. He favoured dramatic musical expression with the use of larger choral and orchestral forms and formulated such dances as the minuet, first danced by Louis as "Le Roi soleil" (the sun king), the gavotte, rigaudon, bourrée, passepied, and loure—each with its particular rhythmic metre.

Lully collaborated with the playwright Molière in a famous succession of comedy-ballets, of which *Le Bourgeois Gentilhomme* (1670) is probably the best known. Thereafter the character of Lully's work became essentially operatic, and music in the French theatre was left to function in a more subsidiary role. The dramatist Pierre Corneille, for instance, wrote "I have employed music only to satisfy the ear while the eyes are occupied with looking at the machines." In another category, the pastoral comedies derived from Italian models were liberally embellished with songs loosely strung together and alternating with spoken verses.

The French court ballet exerted an influence on the English masque, which took its name and some of its early character from the medieval Italian *mascherate* (masquerades) in carnival entertainment. At a time of distinctive English literary achievement, the masque reached a high artistic level, performed mainly as an aristocratic entertainment. It combined instrumental and vocal music, mixed with dancing and acting, in the representation of mythological and allegorical subjects. At the same time, the first public theatres in London came into being. They date from 1576 (61 years before the first public Venetian opera house); the earliest public plays are known to have incorporated some form of music.

The English masque

Cues for music recur throughout Shakespeare's plays, usually for simple songs or dances. Music between the acts of public plays was customary by 1600, with the audience often calling for the tunes they wanted played. Instrumental music was employed for supernatural effects and to heighten dramatic tension; it was usually performed behind, at the side of, or even under the stage. After the suppression of playhouses during the Civil War, the restoration of the English monarchy with King Charles II brought an even richer flowering of theatre music, led by Henry Purcell.

Besides those works of Purcell that are nearer to masque than drama, such as the Shakespeare adaptations for *The Fairy Queen* (1692) and *The Tempest* (1695), he composed suites of incidental music for more than 40 plays. These generally comprised overtures, "act-tunes" (interludes), dances, and songs. Rather than growing out of the verbal drama, however, they are often so arbitrarily interpolated into it that only the quality of the music can justify most of them. After Purcell's death, English theatrical music ceased to contribute significantly to the theatre, but Thomas Arne, who wrote numerous masques and ballad operas such as *Love in a Village* (1762), was very popular in the mid-18th century, and his simplicity of expression has a certain direct appeal.

The flourishing tradition of Spanish Renaissance drama precluded much opera from taking root in Spain, but the music for plays had generally less distinction than the English equivalent. The early zarzuela (not to be confused with the later Romantic version already mentioned) originated in the 17th century as a court entertainment. It was the Spanish counterpart to the court ballet and acquired a strong Italian influence on its musical character. Spanish music and musicians travelled to the Western Hemisphere with the early explorers, and by the late 17th century the Peruvian capital of Lima had become musically important. The composer José Diaz worked there and wrote much incidental music to the plays of Calderón de la Barca.

Renaissance theatre in Italy bred the *intermedio,* which consisted of songs and instrumental music added before or after the acts of a play. The words of the songs were generally relevant to the action of the drama, and this development—together with more extended musical settings in pastoral plays—became the direct precursor of Italian opera. As a new form of "drama in music" which rapidly acquired serious artistic pretensions, the opera inevitably brought in its train a less aristocratic variety of musical theatre variously termed opera buffa (comic opera), vaudeville, ballad opera, singspiel (literally, song-play), or *tonadilla,* always performed in the vernacular of its audience and often in dialect.

The Italian *intermedio*

These depicted current events instead of historical or mythological subjects, involved elements of parody and social satire, and usually depended on modest musical resources for economic reasons. They began as interludes performed between the acts of serious opera and comprise an essential link in the history of musical theatre. By about 1700 the scenes (usually two) had acquired a linked plot, and by 1740 they were performed apart from the opera as a genuinely popular entertainment. Eventually they responded to the demands of the rising middle classes by raising their own standards into the category of comic opera.

Classical developments. The Italian commedia dell'arte entertainment of strolling players in mainly improvised comedy had left its mark on French fairground theatre, although the performers were expelled from France in 1697 for having ventured their satire too close to court topics. Ten years later French satirical comedies were also banned, whereupon the resourceful performers found a new way round by employing monologue, mime, and music. They thereby developed a new form of popular entertainment to contrast with the aristocratic *opéra-ballets,* which were soon to be dominated by the spectacular productions with Jean-Philippe Rameau as composer, and in 1713 two theatrical managements in

Paris were given license to perform "Le nouvel Opéra-comique."

Opéra-comique was a contraction of *opéra rendu comique* ("opera made comic"), signifying parody and satire at the expense primarily of serious opera. The entertainment soon came to veer either toward *comédie vaudeville,* mostly made up of bawdy satire or simply songs of disparaging social comment, or to the alternative *comédie à ariette,* involving a generally more decorous musical parody at the expense of Italian styles. The *Guerre des Bouffons* ("war of the comedians") between partisans of French and Italian theatrical styles was eventually resolved by the emergence of the opéra bouffe (literally, "comic opera")—the French variety of operetta. It is usually dated to the Paris production in 1753 of *Les Troqueurs* ("The Barterers"), based on a fable by Jean de La Fontaine and having original music by a court violinist, Antoine Dauvergne.

Ballet was declining about this time from courtly heroics to simple diversion unrelated to any dramatic point. Apart from the *opéra-ballets* of Rameau, little significant music was composed for the dance until the German composer Christoph Willibald Gluck, who initiated the major reform of serious opera during the century, first turned his attention to a move for balletic reform involving a more dramatic style. In 1761 Gluck composed the music for *Don Juan,* a ballet by Gasparo Angiolini, the Italian ballet master at Vienna, who maintained that dancing should be self-expressive without recourse to verbal explanations.

Gluck's contribution to ballet music

Gluck's vividly descriptive score contains 31 musical pieces, alternating between formal dance and narrative drama. It made the music a foreground element in the ballet instead of a background accompaniment and could have brought about—if its example had been followed up—a revitalization of ballet music almost as significant as the operatic reform Gluck launched in *Orfeo ed Euridice* a year later. In the ballet, the fight scene near the beginning and the dance of the Furies at the end (itself later incorporated into *Orfeo*) have a concentrated intensity of musical expression, and the graveyard scene has a degree of imaginative orchestration that is unsurpassed in any other music at that date.

For reasons that belong more properly to the history of ballet, Gluck's influence on its future course was less fruitful than in opera. Perhaps his example, nevertheless, encouraged the participation of such composers as Mozart with *Les Petits Riens* (1778; "Sweet Nothings") and Beethoven in *The Creatures of Prometheus* (1801). It was, otherwise, an era theatrically dominated by opera of various kinds, so that there was at first little call for music in relation to spoken drama. Haydn, however, composed some music (1796) for an early German translation of Alexander Bicknell's *The Patriot King, or Alfred and Elvida,* and Mozart contributed a suite of superior choral and orchestral music for *Thamos, König in Ägypten* (1773; *Thamos, King of Egypt*), which was never used for the play in his lifetime but which has survived where the play has long been forgotten.

Eighteenth-century opera nourished musical developments in the theatre chiefly through establishing regular orchestras of some quality. Outside of cities with more than one theatre, such as Vienna, Prague, Paris, and London, the numerous court theatres needed to keep a resident and costly orchestra reasonably occupied, with interest divided between opera and drama. It therefore became customary either to commission incidental music for existing plays whenever possible (especially the historical classics, as more and more of them were translated from one language to another) or to commission new plays that would incorporate ample provision for orchestral and sometimes choral music.

Romantic expansion. Examples of commissioned incidental music have previously been cited in Beethoven's music for *Egmont,* which belongs to the first category just mentioned, and Schubert's for *Rosamunde,* which is in the second. The practice spread as a matter of rivalry and prestige to cities without a court but which maintained a municipal theatre (for example, Hamburg and Leipzig) and to other countries with a thriving theatrical interest and ample funds. In Russia, for instance, Mikhail Glinka composed music to *Prince Kholmsky* (1840), an otherwise obscure drama by Count Kukolnik, and the Shakespeare repertory brought the collaboration of such composers as Mily Balakirev (*King Lear,* 1861) and Tchaikovsky (*Hamlet,* 1891).

France and England, having different systems of patronage, produced different results during the 19th century. English theatre music was confined for most of its course to a taste for crude melodrama and burlesque at a low level, apart from a sporadic interest in mostly imported opera and ballet. Arthur Sullivan, however, provided incidental music for Shakespeare plays as well as cultivating, in his collaboration with the author W.S. Gilbert, a native variety of operetta derived from the French model. France fared somewhat better with the popularity of opéra bouffe, and the birth of romantic ballet in Paris also kindled a new kind of theatre interest, even though its musical quality was usually secondary.

Gilbert and Sullivan operetta

Music for Romantic ballet developed in two directions. From the time of the French composer Adolphe Adam's score for *Giselle* (1841), ballet composers made rudimentary attempts to express mood and scene, to create dramatic tension, and to characterize personality in music. The general level was somewhat raised by the French composer Léo Delibes in his music for *Coppélia* (1870) and more especially for *Sylvia* (1876); the latter was a score that Tchaikovsky came to know and admire. The second feature in many ballet scores of the period was the attempt to compose suitably flavoured music to match the new growth of interest in national and regional dances, which were regularly incorporated into the ballets.

Music in 19th-century ballet reached its peak of achievement with Tchaikovsky, whose instinct for the theatre was probably stronger than his talent for the subtleties of symphonic argument. He treated the art of ballet as worthy of real musical imagination and told a colleague who adversely likened some of his *Symphony No. 4* to ballet music: "I cannot understand why the term should be associated with something reprehensible. There is such a thing as good ballet music." Tchaikovsky demonstrated its possibilities in three original scores for ballet that enjoy continuing universal popularity in the theatre: *Swan Lake* (first performed 1877); *The Sleeping Beauty* (1890); and *The Nutcracker* (1892).

Swan Lake achieved lasting success only after the composer's death—a fact which accounts for the recurring problems of the relationship of music to choreography, because some of the original musical sequence was changed for the 1895 production at St. Petersburg (now Leningrad), from which most current versions of the ballet are descended. The two later scores benefitted from detailed choreographic specifications. According to Stravinsky, *The Sleeping Beauty* is "the convincing example of Tchaikovsky's great creative power," and *The Nutcracker* in its theatre context has a narrative vividness much beyond the limited charm of the concert suite that Tchaikovsky arranged from it.

Adolphe Adam's contribution to the development of ballet music had its parallel in the sphere of romantic operetta. By incorporating a measure of frivolous vaudeville into the otherwise conventional comedy of *Le Châlet* (1834), Adam stimulated a popular taste for what became the mainstream of operetta. Its source was in Paris, and it flowed in turn principally to Vienna, to London and thence to North America, submerging the German singspiel and its Scandinavian offshoots but leaving the Spanish zarzuela to cultivate its own regional idiom.

Adam's enterprise in opening a theatre in 1847 to stage his own works and those of other young composers disdained by the operatic establishment in Paris was brought to a premature end by the political uprising a year later, but Offenbach was poised to take advantage of the subsequent situation. He opened his Bouffes-Parisiens theatre in 1855, whence travelled such immediate hits as *Orpheus in the Underworld, La Belle Hélène, La Grande-Duchesse de Gérolstein,* and *La Périchole* over almost all of Europe. The Parisian operetta was principally continued to the end of the century by Charles Lecocq and André Messager.

Offenbach's influence in Europe

Offenbach meanwhile had paid several visits to Vienna

from 1858, when Franz von Suppé was quick to turn the French model to local advantage, notably with *Die schöne Galatea* (1865; *The Beautiful Galatea*). The younger Johann Strauss was eventually persuaded to follow this trend by turning the Viennese craze for his waltzes, polkas, and other social dances to theatrical purpose. With the aid of an unusually good libretto, Strauss created the supreme example of Viennese operetta in *Die Fledermaus.* The Viennese tradition was continued in turn by Franz Lehár and Emmerich Kálmán.

Offenbach's influence extended southward to Bohemia, where the composer Bedřich Smetana compared his first song-and-dialogue version of *The Bartered Bride* (1866) to an Offenbach operetta, and Antonín Dvořák composed an outstanding but little-known example in *The Peasant a Rogue* (1878). Otherwise, no particularly distinguished composer of operetta emerged in southeastern Europe, nor in Poland or Russia, where there were only occasional contacts with forms of musical theatre other than full-scale opera and ballet for the moneyed classes.

The northward spread of the Offenbach model reached England, where it influenced the character of Sullivan's first operetta, *Cox and Box* (1867). It led in due course to the success of *H.M.S. Pinafore* (1878), in collaboration with Gilbert, and the subsequent line of "Savoy operettas" (their collective nickname derived from the London theatre where they were first performed by the D'Oyly Carte Opera Company, Ltd.). England made no other contributions of comparable musical interest to the operetta repertory until it was overtaken in due course by the trend to musical comedy in the 20th century.

English operetta represented by Gilbert and Sullivan nevertheless put down fresh roots in North America after the D'Oyly Carte company first travelled there in 1879, in the wake of a pirated version of *H.M.S. Pinafore.* The impact of Sullivan's music in New York and Boston was comparable to that of Offenbach in Vienna. Instead of stimulating an American equivalent, it first opened the way to 20 years or so of European imports to the American stage. The composers Reginald De Koven and Victor Herbert later established a short-lived local counterpart to European operetta, before it was overtaken by the indigenous idiom of American musical theatre noted earlier.

The language of ragtime and early jazz, with its rhythmic syncopation and varying degrees of harmonic innovation within a common musical vernacular, brought the first new element to the idiom of musical theatre (in musical comedy) since the emergence of national folk characteristics in 19th-century Europe. As the trends already described succeeded one another during the 20th century, in and out of fashion, and the musical theatre tried to reconcile the nostalgia for its past heritage with the need to experiment in search of a viable future, the immediate present can be seen to represent only one turn of a larger wheel across seven or eight centuries. The religious rock musical of the contemporary musical scene is but a variant of the mysteries and miracle plays that initiated all our modern forms of musical theatre when Western civilization first groped its way out of the Dark Ages.

(N.Go.)

Opera

The English word opera is an abbreviation of the Italian phrase *opera in musica* ("work in music"). It names a theatrical form consisting of a dramatic text (libretto, or "little book") combined with music, usually singing with instrumental accompaniment. Besides solo, ensemble, and choral singers and a group of instrumentalists, the forces performing opera since its inception have often included dancers. A complex, often costly variety of musicodramatic entertainment, opera has attracted audiences for nearly five centuries. Although its supporters have greatly outnumbered its detractors, it has been the target of intense adverse criticism.

Charles de Saint-Évremond, a French man of letters in the 17th century, called it "a bizarre thing consisting of poetry in music, in which the poet and the composer, equally standing in each other's way, go to endless trouble to produce a wretched result." The 18th-century English statesman and writer Lord Chesterfield wrote to his son: "As for operas, they are essentially too absurd and extravagant to mention. I look upon them as a magic scene contrived to please the eyes and the ears at the expense of the understanding." At the opposite extreme of reaction to opera, it has been said that the mere existence of such a masterpiece as Mozart's *Le nozze di Figaro* (*The Marriage of Figaro*) suffices to justify Western civilization.

The unique characteristics of opera

Although the characteristic of opera that most clearly separates it from other theatrical forms is that its principals sing rather than speak their lines, to approach it or criticize it as simply one variety of the musical art is to misjudge it. Its multiple creators almost always have intended an opera to be a lofty and eloquent form of theatrical performance. What commonly differentiates it from other varieties of musicodramatic theatre such as operetta (literally "small opera") and musical comedy is sobriety of workmanship, density of texture, and (even in operas with comic and farcical librettos) accompanying seriousness of musical tone. On the other hand, some lighter works—by Jacques Offenbach, Johann Strauss the Younger, Gilbert and Sullivan, Kurt Weill, George Gershwin, and a few others—make neat categorization impossible.

In the preparation of an opera performance, many individual artists and artisans, sometimes spread out across a century and more, necessarily are or have been involved. The first, unintentional recruit is likely to have been the writer of the original story. Then comes the librettist, who puts the story or play into a form suitable for musical setting and singing, and the composer, who sets that libretto to music. Architects and acousticians have built an opera house suited or adaptable to performances that demand a sizable stage, a pit to house an ensemble of instrumentalists, and a reasonably large audience. A producer-director has to specify the work of designers, scene painters, costumers, and lighting experts. The producer, conductor, and musical staff have to work for long periods with chorus, dancers, orchestra, and extras as well as the principal singers to prepare the performance—work that may last anywhere from a few days to many months. All this does not even take into account the part played by the administrative staff.

Once the complete operatic score—the final libretto and music—is available, what must rule all of those involved is dedication to fulfilling the wishes of the librettist and the composer. Overemphasis or underemphasis of any larger component of an operatic performance can be as damaging to it as off-pitch singing or false entries by instrumentalists. More than one desirable balance among the constituents of performance is often possible. What is certain is that one or another of them must be decided upon, worked toward, and achieved.

THE EARLY HISTORY

Italian origins. Works in antiquity had combined poetic drama and music. The plays of the ancient Greek dramatists Aeschylus, Sophocles, and Euripides employed choral music in a manner that certainly reflected related usages in earlier times. During the Middle Ages, biblical dramas were commonly accompanied by some music, being known under various labels, including mystery and miracle plays. These and other related musicodramatic forms may or may not have become collateral ancestors of opera: their descent seems most certain in some 17th-century operas on religious subjects performed in Rome and at several places in Germany. Musical historians and musicologists continue to debate opera's ancestry. The earliest universally accepted direct ancestors of opera appeared in 16th-century Italy. Purely nonreligious works of edifying drama with music, they included intermezzos and *intermedii* played between the acts of spoken dramas, with which their purported subject matter often claimed a tenuous connection, and staged ballet. The latter, Italian by birth, achieved a complex, quasi-operatic state in the court ballet (*ballet de cour*) danced in France late in the 16th century and throughout the 17th: it approached ever closer to opera in the *comédie-ballet* evolved by Molière and Jean-Baptiste Lully in the 1660s, beginning with *Le*

Mariage forcé (*The Enforced Marriage,* first performed 1664).

Musicians, singers, poets, playwrights, and enthusiasts of the literary, musical, and theatrical arts had long cherished a desire for some more formally constituted and more stable form of drama with music, especially in Italy. One response to that expressed desire was the 16th-century "madrigal comedy," the singing of dramatic or semidramatic lines (often farcical, and most often with story and characters borrowed from the traditional commedia dell'arte as it had become formalized during the 16th century) in a linked series of more or less discrete madrigals and other varieties of polyphonic song.

16th-century "madrigal comedy"

But polyphony—the musical texture created by simultaneous, largely unaccompanied singing of interwoven melodies—was by nature alien to theatrical drama: it made extremely difficult, when not impossible, the delineation of individual characters through clearly understandable text words. This is noticeable even in the most celebrated of the madrigal comedies, Orazio Vecchi's paean to the "double Parnassus" of poetry and music, *L'Amfiparnaso* (Modena, 1594).

The gestation of opera required the simultaneous availability of a dramatic literary style and a musical texture suitable for incorporation into a new theatrical unity. The essential literary materials had begun to appear in Italy in such chivalresque epics as Lodovico Ariosto's *Orlando furioso* (published complete in 1532) and Torquato Tasso's *Gerusalemme liberata* (1575), both of which were to be mined for subjects by innumerable opera librettists. More immediately decisive in setting the first direction of opera was one sort of poetic drama: the shorter pastoral writings of 16th-century Italian poets, notably Tasso's *Aminta* (1573) and Giovanni Battista Guarini's *Pastor fido* (*The Faithful Shepherd,* completed in 1590). Idylls or eclogues that had sprung up in the 15th century, like the *Orfeo* of the Italian poet Poliziano (Politian) with music by Germi (one of the earliest examples, which was staged at Mantua in 1472, with solo song, chorus, and spoken dialogue), were seized on, adapted, and imitated by the men who had begun to evolve the musical texture essential to the birth of opera and who found apt subjects in the loves, joys, and sorrows of Arcadian shepherds and shepherdesses, often with the intervention of gods, demigods, and heroes.

Until the 1950s it was generally accepted that opera originated with a *camerata* (a sort of humanistic discussion group) that met in the late 1570s and early 1580s in the Florentine palace of Giovanni Bardi, count of Vernio. In 1953, however, the Roman musicologist Nino Pirrotta showed that the Bardi Camerata, far from having furthered innovation or interested itself in musical drama, was predominantly conservative, often acted in defense of the polyphonic madrigal, and showed no sympathy with the new combinations that would shortly produce opera. In fact, that literary-musical texture was evolved at Florence, but largely among a group of intellectuals, artists, and dilettantes who met informally in the palace of the theatrical theoretician Jacopo Corsi during the 1590s. This latter group also included Emilio del Cavaliere, the composer, impresario, and choreographer who was to write what is often called the first oratorio, *La rappresentazione di anima e di corpo* (*The Representation of Soul and Body,* an acted form unlike later oratorios); the singer-composer Jacopo Peri; and—although they attended infrequently—both the poet Tasso and the composer Claudio Monteverdi. Still active at the time, though a little out of favour, was the singer-composer Giulio Caccini. Corsi and his friends were by no means the first creators of solo vocal lines with instrumental accompaniment, and they shaped their musicotheatrical creations partly in the mistaken belief that their performances were reviving ancient Greek procedures. What, in fact, they did was to take hints from the French court ballet and simultaneously discard polyphony in favour of monody (or homophony)—accompanied singing or recitation on musical tones (recitativo) of one melody at a time. Thus, they insured both the relative comprehensibility of the words (which to them seemed much more important than the accompanying music) and the use of at least some instrumental support.

Florentines who "created" opera

An important "manifesto" of the monodic innovators was a collection of short vocal pieces with thorough-bass accompaniment (instrumental chords in sequence as accompaniment to melody) by Caccini, published in 1602: *Le nuove musiche,* a title that often has been extended to cover the novel musical texture itself. The interaction of these and other Italians with the texture of monody was what finally led, after some false starts, to the emergence not only of opera more or less as it is known today but also of the cantata and the oratorio.

The honour of being deemed "the first opera" usually is given to a setting by Peri of *Dafne* by the Renaissance pastoral poet Ottavio Rinuccini. It was staged at the Palazzo Corsi in Florence during the pre-Lenten Carnival of 1597–98. The text, divided into a prologue and six scenes, was published in 1600 and therefore survives, but neither Peri's music (the prologue and one aria excepted) nor that of an almost contemporary setting of the same text by Caccini can now be recovered. The earliest surviving opera is also Peri's: a setting of Rinuccini's pastoral *Euridice,* likewise in a prologue and six scenes, which was performed at the Palazzo Pitti in Florence on October 6, 1600. More unusual, the musical score also was issued in 1601 and reprinted several times thereafter.

However significant historically, the pioneering operas of Peri and Caccini were tentative in both style and structure; further, neither of the founding fathers of opera seems to have possessed notable dramatic talent.

Within 10 years of the premiere of Peri's *Dafne* at Florence, Mantua heard an opera that is a masterpiece and still is staged frequently. This was *La favola d'Orfeo* (*The Fable of Orpheus*), a setting by Monteverdi of a poetic text by Alessandro Striggio the Younger. Presented during the Carnival of 1607 (the libretto was published then, the score in 1609), it soon was presented elsewhere in Italy. In *Orfeo,* the accompanying instruments come into their own as a dramatic element: the score contains more than two dozen pieces for increased (though not precisely determinable) numbers of instruments. It not only introduces, as a preluding toccata, the idea of the operatic overture but also achieves some sectional unity by repeating brief instrumental numbers (ritornellos). More important, Monteverdi uses recitative expressively and gives it an organizational function by repetitions and developments in predetermined patterns.

Monteverdi's *Orfeo*

Monteverdi continued to compose operas for more than 35 years; meanwhile, the new manner of musicodramatic entertainment spread to other Italian cities. Rome probably first heard an opera as early as 1606, Bologna before 1610. Continuing to employ librettos based on Italian interpretations of Greek and Roman myth, legend, and pseudo-history, literary men and composers rapidly swelled the number of operas heard. At Venice in 1642, the 75-year-old Monteverdi created his masterpiece *L'incoronazione di Poppea* (*The Coronation of Poppea*). Gian Francesco Busenello's superior libretto carried a new note of realism into opera, particularly in the development of human character; it was to have a prolonged, important line of descent, and Monteverdi translated it blazingly into music. Throughout that first period of operatic history, the importance given by composers to emotional drama, to instrumental music, and to structural stability increased along with the capabilities (and pretensions) of singers and the magnificence and complexity of stage settings, stage machinery, and costuming.

The inauguration early in 1637 of the first opera house open to the general public, the Tron family's Teatro di San Cassiano at Venice, was another decisive factor in establishing opera. That action removed opera from the exclusive hands of royalty and nobility and placed it within reach of all but the poorest sectors of the Italian urban population.

The first opera house

A pupil of Monteverdi, Pier Francesco Caletti-Bruni, known as Francesco Cavalli (1602–76), became the most popular opera composer of his era by furnishing the opera houses of Venice with some 40 operas between 1639 and 1669. A highly talented but not always fastidious composer, Cavalli reacted to the librettos he used with dramatic force and directness. The most renowned of his operas was *Giasone* (*Jason,* 1649), whose libretto by Giacinto Andrea Cocignini included farcical episodes. His chief Venetian rival and successor was Pietro Antonio (often called Marc' Antonio) Cesti (1623–69), about a dozen of whose nearly 100 operas have survived. Some notion of the extravagance to which imitation of Louis XIV's spectacles at Versailles had driven the production of opera elsewhere can be gained from descriptions of the Cesti opera *Il pomo d'oro* (*The Golden Apple,* 1667), composed for the wedding of Emperor Leopold I and Margarita Teresa of Spain in Vienna. Constructed in a prologue and five acts (the third and fifth of which have been lost), with 48 characters, it contained 66 scenes requiring 24 stage settings making use of complex stage machinery. Ballets occurred in every act, and a grand triple ballet brought the opera to its conclusion. *Il pomo d'oro* provided numerous purely instrumental introductions and interludes, gave relatively little importance to the chorus, skipped rapidly over the essential storytelling recitative, and concentrated on arias and duets that often were most sensuous and almost feminine in allure.

Opera in Venice and Rome

Venetian opera continued to flourish in the works of such greatly talented theatrical composers as Cavalli, Cesti, and Giovanni Legrenzi (1626–90). In some details, these Venetian operas reflected the pressures exerted by the tastes and wishes of the paying audiences for which they were designed. Not so lavish with choral interpolations as their Roman contemporaries, the Venetians demanded and received complex, strong librettos calling for large casts and special lavishness in staging. They also began to develop the sensuous melodic profiles that have come to be thought of as particularly "Italian." Furthermore, they all but separated the solo aria from the surrounding recitative. They also frequently prefaced and followed solos with purely instrumental music, so continuing the orchestra's elevation from a purely accompanying role. After the middle of the 17th century, the Venetian operatic style began to decline. Among the later Venetian operatic composers of talent and fame were Antonio Lotti (*c.* 1667–1740), Carlo Francesco Pollaroli (1653–1722), Antonio Vivaldi (*c.* 1678–1741), and Baldassare Galuppi (1706–85), who is often referred to somewhat loosely as "the father of opera buffa."

Several Italian cities soon developed recognizably indigenous operatic styles. At Rome, for example, a group of composers tended toward unified structure, gave ensemble and choral song expanded roles, and increased the difference between the solo (aria) and the Florentine type of continuous recitative by allowing arias to interrupt dramatic progress in order to express or comment upon emotional moods. Less emphatic about stage magnificence than their Venetian counterparts, such Roman composers as Stefano Landi (*c.* 1590–*c.* 1655), Domenico Mazzocchi (1592–1655), Luigi Rossi (1597–1653), and Michelangelo Rossi (1600?–70) also permitted comic episodes to lighten prevailingly tragic stories. They concentrated attention productively on instrumental overtures and on overture-like pieces preceding acts or sections of acts. Two Roman composers—Domenico Mazzocchi's brother Virgilio (1597–1646) and Marco Marazzoli (1619–62)—often are cited as having created the first completely comic opera, *Chi soffe speri* (*He Who Suffers, Hopes,* 1639). Its libretto was written by Cardinal Giulio Rospigliosi, who was to be elevated to the papacy in 1667 as Clement IX. The invited guests at its first performance, in the Palazzo Barberini, included the English poet John Milton and Giulio Mazarini, the future Cardinal Mazarin, statesman to Louis XIV.

With the 18th century the centre of Italian opera shifted to Naples, where so great a variety of styles evolved that the term Neapolitan opera eventually covered operas that dominated most of Italy and many foreign centres of operatic activity. With some exceptions, the earliest unmistakably Neapolitan operas changed their focus back from the music to the words. Two of its instigators were dramatic poets: Apostolo Zeno (1668–1750), born a Venetian, and the Roman Pietro Trapassi, known as Metastasio (1698–1782)—perhaps the greatest of the 18th-century librettists. Continuing the custom of basing librettos on Greco-Roman legend and pseudo-history (but dispensing almost entirely with classical mythology), Zeno and Metastasio wrote texts of formal beauty and linguistic clarity, preferring solemn, usually tragic subjects (opera seria) in three acts to comic episodes and characters. The aria came to dominate, and the use of chorus declined.

Contributions of Zeno and Metastasio

The term Neapolitan opera also came to indicate harmonically naïve, melodious lighter operas in the gallant tone of the Rococo style; the rich development of the bel canto styles (where beautiful singing *per se* was predominant), signifying supreme vocal agility and smoothness that was supplied first by castratos, men who had been castrated before puberty in order to preserve the high ranges of their boyish voices; and the appearance of the *centone* or pasticcio, a libretto set to a score made up of music borrowed either from scores (then uncopyrighted or otherwise legally protected) of several composers or from several operas by a single composer. The use of the orchestra also became limited. But perhaps the most discussed, and often senselessly maligned, feature that particularly designated Neapolitan opera was the aria da capo, an aria in three sections, the third part repeating the first. It had appeared in northern Italy early in the 17th century but was employed with comparative infrequency there. Some Neapolitan operas, however, consisted of up to 20 da capo arias separated by a minimum of story-advancing recitativo secco (narrative passages in which voice is accompanied only by a thorough bass).

Domination of the aria da capo

A masterly operatic composer of the transitional style who bridged the era between the Baroque and the pre-Classical Neapolitan style was Alessandro Scarlatti (1660–1725). In his many operas Scarlatti triumphed, by the strength of musical imagination, over librettos intended to provide vehicles for phenomenally trained singers in the prevailing pattern and the consequent reduction of dramatic interest to a narrow minimum. Talented and influential among Scarlatti's contemporaries were such composers as Nicola Antonio Porpora (1686–1768), Leonardo Vinci (1690–1730), and Leonardo Leo (1694–1744).

In 1720 the Venetian composer-poet-statesman Benedetto Marcello (1686–1739) published a mordant satire on the increasingly rigid and undramatic conventions that had taken hold of opera seria: *Il teatro alla moda, o sia metodo sicuro e facile per ben comporre ed eseguire opere italiane in musica* ("The Theater à la Mode, or The Secure and Easy Method of Composing and Performing Italian Operas"). The distress that it and other criticisms brought resulted in an improved genre, still in effect opera seria but showing attempts at reform of its mannerisms. The principal operas against which that reform later evolved were the often melodically seductive works of Gaetano Latilla (1711–88), Giuseppe Sarti (1729–1802), Antonio Sacchini (1730–86), Johann Christian Bach (1735–82), Antonio Salieri (1750–1825), and Mozart's *Idomeneo, rè di Creta* (1781) and *La clemenza di Tito* (*The Clemency of Titus,* 1791). Representative composers within the short "reform" movement itself were Niccolò Jommelli (1714–74) and Tommaso Traetta (1727–79). A more intellectually rigorous reformation was undertaken consciously by Christoph Willibald Gluck in collaboration with the librettist Ranieri de' Calzabigi, beginning with *Orfeo ed Euridice* (1762).

Comic opera. Comic opera meanwhile had expanded from its shadowy existence within and between the acts of opera seria. From the early, tentative efforts of several 17th-century Roman and Florentine composers, it had moved into a bustling, rude, independent vitality of its own, often in the form of satirical opera buffa (Italian: "comic opera"), generally shaped in two acts rather than the usual three of opera seria. Expelled from the precincts of opera seria by the librettos of Zeno and Metastasio, the comic spirit had taken refuge in such an expanded intermezzo as *La serva padrona* (*The Maid Mistress,* 1733), by Giovanni Battista Pergolesi. When it matured, the style borrowed back some of the more serious emotional qualities of opera seria, often including "serious" roles among those of the comedians. This led to a hybrid nature in many operas, including two works using librettos derived from the plays of Pierre de Beaumarchais—*Il barbiere di Siviglia* (*The Barber of Seville,* 1782), by Giovanni

Paisiello, and Mozart's *Le nozze di Figaro* (1786)—as well as *Il matrimonio segreto* (*The Secret Marriage,* 1792), by Domenico Cimarosa.

One of the determining characteristics of this mixed style was the elaboration of ensemble numbers concluding acts. These operas dispensed almost entirely with the magnificent display and grandeur of staging increasingly required of opera seria. Another of the drawbacks of the mixed style was well summed up by the 20th-century Italian musicologist Andrea Della Corte:

> With few exceptions among the great composers dedicated to instrumental music or to teaching, almost all the serious composers also collaborated in the comic theatre. Not so the literary men. The best dramatists were not equally tempted by this tendency.

The natural result was that the large majority of opera buffa librettos remained inferior to the serious texts by Metastasio and his imitators and successors, though not necessarily less workable in their own way.

Early opera in France. Opera was imported into France from Italy before 1650, but it long failed to take firm hold there with royal and other audiences, at first having to compete on unequal terms with the spoken drama (often with musical interludes) and the ballet. The *Pomone* (1671) of Robert Cambert, to a pastoral libretto by Pierre Perrin, is commonly called the first French opera. Its premiere almost certainly inaugurated the Académie Royale de Musique (now the Paris Académie de Musique or Paris Opéra) on March 3, 1671. Only fragments of the music of *Pomone* still exist.

Lully's important role

Opera really did not become a French art until the time of Jean-Baptiste Lully (1632–87). This highly talented, very shrewd, and dictatorial man borrowed freely from both the spoken French drama and the court ballet. Though himself an Italian, he played down the extended, formalized Italian aria in favour of shorter, more instantly captivating "airs." He formed recitative after the declamatory manner of the Comédie-Française theatre company and also evolved the "French overture" (one movement with a slow and a fast section) as distinct from the "Italian overture" (one movement with a fast, slow, and another fast section). His operas and those of his imitators and followers assigned great importance to dancing, choruses, instrumental interludes, and a dazzlingly complex stage setting. Lully became the virtual dictator of music in France partly because of the strengths of his literary collaborators: first the dramatist Molière (1662–73) in *comédie-ballet,* then the exceedingly able librettist Philippe Quinault (1635–88).

The pervasive Lullyan style, altered surprisingly little except in the direction of still more imposing grandeur, attained its culmination in the magnificent operas of Jean-Philippe Rameau (1683–1764), especially in his *Hippolyte et Aricie* (1733; libretto by Simon-Joseph de Pellegrin), *Les Indes galantes* (*The Courtly Indies,* 1735; libretto by Louis Fuzelier), and particularly *Castor et Pollux* (1737; libretto by Pierre-Joseph-Justin Bernard), which was performed at the Paris Opéra 254 times in 48 years. Except for the special instance of *Les Indes galantes,* which was billed as a *ballet héroïque,* Rameau's chief operas were each divided into a prologue and five acts, a pattern that many later French composers favoured. Rameau confirmed the still-enduring insistence of French operatic composers on setting their language to music with such probity and clarity that it can be understood properly when sung. His operatic works are regarded widely as the apogee of 18th-century French opera.

Early opera in Germany and Austria. Although Heinrich Schütz composed *Dafne,* the first known opera with a German text, and heard it played at Torgau on April 23, 1627, the active history of opera in Germany began with the Italian composers residing there. A remarkable Venetian composer-diplomatist-ecclesiastic, the Abbé Agostino Steffani, carried much of his native city's early operatic manner to Munich, Hanover, and other German centres, beginning his operatic production with *Marco Aurelio* (Munich, 1681), and continued thereafter to compose operas for 28 years. In his use of both Italian and French procedures, particularly in handling overture and recitative, Steffani evolved a sort of international Italian style that clearly influenced other "transplanted" composers.

For the next 100 years the influence of Italian opera was so pervasive that even native German composers adopted the Italian operatic style and used texts in Italian.

The German word *Singspiel* was originally used for all sorts of opera. The earliest known entertainments so designated were composed by a pupil of Heinrich Schütz, Johann Theile (1646–1724). One of them, *Adam und Eva,* eminently "serious" as to story, inaugurated the Hamburg Opera in 1678. During the mid-18th century the term singspiel came to be reserved for what the English called "ballad opera," the French *opéra-comique:* light, usually comic operas including spoken dialogue. The comic singspiel of the 18th century was born with *The Devil to Pay* (London, 1731) and its sequel, *The Merry Cobbler* (London, 1735), English ballad operas with texts by Charles Coffey. These had pasticcio scores capitalizing, not very successfully, on the great popularity of *The Beggar's Opera* (1728), which had a text by John Gay and an assembled (pasticcio) score brought together by John Christopher Pepusch. The Coffey texts having been translated into German, scores were composed to them by J.C. Standfuss (died 1759?) as *Der Teufel ist los* (Leipzig, 1752) and *Der lustige Schuster* (Lübeck, 1759); they later were restaged as arranged by Johann Adam Hiller (1728–1804), who also composed several other singspiels and brought to culmination the so-called Leipzig School. Both Berlin and Vienna inevitably took up the singspiel, examples of which, composed in those cities and elsewhere, included *Der neue krumme Teufel* (Vienna, 1752, music lost), by Joseph Haydn; Mozart's *Die Entführung aus dem Serail* (*The Abduction from the Seraglio,* Vienna, 1782) and *Die Zauberflöte* (*The Magic Flute,* Vienna, 1791); *Doktor und Apotheker* (Vienna, 1786), by Karl Ditters von Dittersdorf; Beethoven's *Fidelio* (Vienna, 1805), which, like *Die Zauberflöte,* immeasurably transcends the common artistic scope of the singspiel; and *Die Zwillingsbrüder* (*The Twin Brothers,* Vienna, 1820), by Schubert.

Popularity of *The Beggar's Opera*

The most important opere serie composed in Germany during the early 18th century were created for the Hamburg Opera, at which both Reinhard Keiser (1674–1739) and, for a brief interval, the young George Frideric Handel worked. Keiser composed more than 125 operas, mostly to German texts. Of Handel's large operatic output, only two works with Italian texts—*Almira* and *Nero* (both 1705, the second now lost)—were staged during his Hamburg stay. Keiser doggedly tried to attract the widest possible public. His operas often succeeded in charming audiences, but most of them have vanished, and those that survive appear to possess only superficial allure, although they are historically of interest for their skillful exploitation of the orchestra and of solo instruments tellingly used during arias.

Handel went from Italy to England in 1710. In London, with the opera *Rinaldo* (1711), he began 30 years of stubborn dedication to the by then moribund (but still dominant) traditions of Neapolitan opera seria. He created, however, a dozen or more of the most inspired operas of the first half of the century, including *Giulio Cesare* (*Julius Caesar,* 1724), *Tamerlano* (1724), *Rodelinda* (1725), *Sosarme* (1732), *Orlando* (1733), *Ariodante* (1735), and *Alcina* (1735). Handel transcended the formal style of opera seria by his melodic inspiration and harmonic daring. He even managed an immense variety of characterization within the cramped style with which he had to comply.

Handel's operatic style

German by birth, but almost wholly Italianate by disposition, Johann Adolph Hasse (1699–1783) successfully carried on the Metastasian traditions of opera seria in a plethora of operas to Italian texts. The intensely Italian sensuousness of his best melodies, supported by some attractive adventurousness in harmonic placement and in instrumentation, did almost as much as Handel's operas to prolong past its true prime the glory of the Neapolitan style.

FROM THE "REFORM" TO GRAND OPERA

The "reform." Christoph Willibald Gluck (1714–87) has become an ambivalent figure in the evolution of opera:

he has been loosely and often incorrectly categorized, and both praised and condemned, for mistaken reasons. His operas to Italian texts that he composed up to about 1756 were conventional settings of Metastasian librettos. After settling in Vienna in 1750, though not abandoning the composition of traditional opere serie in Italian, Gluck began to react to the French operatic styles popular there. At first he merely added a few new numbers to trivial one-act opéras-comiques brought to Vienna from Paris, which he arranged and conducted for the court at Schönbrunn and Laxenburg. Then he began to compose similar operas in French.

Thanks to the enthusiasm of the superintendent of the imperial Vienna theatres, Conte Giacomo Durazzo, Gluck had been absorbing the example of the outstanding French dancer-choreographer Jean-Georges Noverre (1727–1810). Seminal in Noverre's call for reform was the insistence that a ballet should not be left as a simple collection of unconnected episodes but should be shaped into a mimed dance drama. Gluck then composed the ballet *Don Juan* (1761), the earliest of his scores to place him among the great composers. In the same year a very talented poet-librettist-adventurer, Ranieri Calzabigi, reached Vienna from Paris. Falling in with the anti-Metastasian intellectuals spearheaded by Durazzo, Calzabigi thereafter brought his acquaintance with Rameau's stately operas to the writing of three librettos for Gluck, for whose signature he also drew up the renowned preface to the publication of the Calzabigi–Gluck *Alceste* in 1769. That dedication is the central document of "operatic reform," summing up one side of the unending debate between supporters of the primacy of the opera libretto and supporters of the primacy of the music. The *Alceste* preface emphasized that superfluous, florid da capo arias were to be dispensed with: simplicity of expression and emotional truth were to take their place.

The influence of *Alceste*

Although some of the most accomplished composers of opera certainly would not have agreed that, as Calzabigi–Gluck stated, the "true office" of music is "serving poetry," and though a strict obedience to all the precepts of the *Alceste* dedication would have impoverished much of the richest operatic music (Gluck himself did not follow them with iron strictness), the pronouncement unquestionably summoned opera back temporarily to its best condition: as musicotheatrical drama. The most obvious, as well as the greatest, results of the attitudes it expressed were the magnificent Calzabigi–Gluck operas first staged in Vienna: *Orfeo ed Euridice* (1762), *Alceste* (1767), and *Paride ed Elena* (*Paris and Helen,* 1770). The two earliest of these became even more stately and Rameau-like when Gluck reconstituted them to French librettos for Parisian audiences.

A little below *Orphée* and the French *Alceste* in austere dramatic force stands the somewhat mixed, only partially "reformed" *Armide* (Paris, 1777). But Gluck was to produce his best results in *Iphigénie en Aulide* (*Iphigenia in Aulis,* 1774; libretto adapted from Racine's tragedy by Bailli du Roullet) and in his masterpiece, *Iphigénie en Tauride* (*Iphigenia in Tauris,* 1779; libretto adapted from Euripides by Nicholas-François Guillard).

Gluck's extraordinary power at his best derives from a reasonable, pliable adherence to the precepts of the *Alceste* dedication; a lean sparseness of means, particularly of harmonic density, with the result that the smallest shifts arrive with great power; and the ability to make the most of the dramatic strengths of the often excellent librettos he used. Yet Gluck did not really "reform" opera, for opera is an incorrigible art form. Its mood and manners shift with changes in society, dramaturgy, techniques of composition, and taste.

Followers and imitators of the Gluck reform

Gluck had some immediate followers and imitators, notably Antonio Salieri, who gave lessons to Beethoven, Schubert, and Liszt, was friendly with both Haydn and Rossini, and was ridiculously accused of having poisoned Mozart. Another, belated, Gluckian was Gluck's onetime "rival" in a Parisian polemic "war," Niccolò Piccinni (1728–1800), whose masterpiece, *Didon* (*Dido,* 1783; libretto by Jean-François Marmontel, Fontainbleau), joined a peculiarly Italianate melodiousness to Rameau-like solemnity and the massive simplicities of Gluck's style. Finally, there was Antonio Sacchini, remembered chiefly for his *Oedipe à Colone* (*Oedipus at Colonus,* 1786; libretto by Nicolas-François Guillard). On the highest level, however, the Gluckian "reform" produced only his own masterpieces, although it led indirectly to certain of the "international," though very French, operas of Gasparo Spontini (1774–1851), particularly *La Vestale* (*The Vestal Virgin;* Paris, 1807), and Luigi Cherubini, particularly *Médée* (1797). In part, Gluck also influenced the vast masterwork of Hector Berlioz, *Les Troyens* (*The Trojans,* composed 1856–58).

Opera in England. Just as immediate acceptance of opera had been made difficult in France by the entrenched ballet and the 17th-century drama of Jean Racine and Pierre Corneille, so it was delayed in England by the court masque, an aristocratic 16th- and 17th-century entertainment derived largely from ballet. Most often dealing with allegorical and mythical subjects, the masque mixed poetic text, instrumental and vocal music, dancing, and acting. The most familiar masque is *Comus* (text by John Milton and music by Henry Lawes), which was staged at Ludlow Castle in 1634. Many other embryonic operas were produced in the middle decades of the 17th century, often being more like plays with incidental music. The first (and, in the view of many, still the finest) English opera, *Dido and Aeneas,* by Henry Purcell (*c.* 1659–95), was originally sung about 1689 by the pupils at a girls' school in London. This musical masterpiece, with libretto by a future poet laureate, Nahum Tate, contains the earliest operatic aria (apart from "Lasciatemi morire" from Monteverdi's *Arianna*) still frequently heard: Dido's lament "When I am laid in earth." In this opera, Purcell succeeded in writing a real, albeit brief, music drama, breaking down the formal barriers between recitative and song.

The first English opera

England, however, was not ready for opera. Although later Purcell works, including *The Fairy Queen* (1692), *The Indian Queen,* and *King Arthur* (1691), have been called operas, they were actually suites of incidental music for plays. No other composer in England of Purcell's genius turned his attention to opera, and before many decades had passed after the scarcely noticed performance of *Dido and Aeneas,* the rage for Italian opera (particularly when the singers included a good castrato) barred that road to English composers. The arrival of Handel from Italy in 1710 decided the direction of opera in London for many decades. Beginning in 1711 with *Rinaldo* (libretto by Giacomo Rossi, indirectly derived from Tasso's epic *Gerusalemme liberata*) and continuing intermittently until *Deidamia* (libretto by Paolo Rolli) in 1741, Handel provided English audiences with his own remarkable variant of Neapolitan opera seria, acting as both composer and, most often, impresario. The greatest composer of opera in his age, Handel eventually outlasted his popularity in London's opera houses and turned to the creation of a magnificent series of oratorios set to English texts. His operatic reign was challenged at its height only by a faction that set up the very gifted Modenese composer Giovanni Bononcini in an unequal battle against him. Handel's operas all but vanished from the repertory in the 19th century, but after a burst of German interest in them in the 1920s, they began to be increasingly revived by some major opera houses, smaller opera companies, students, musicologists, and recording companies.

An event that contributed to the defeat of Handel as an opera impresario was the London production in 1728 of *The Beggar's Opera.* That bawdy, rollicking satire in English became phenomenally popular and spawned a family of imitations that finally accustomed audiences in London and elsewhere in the British Isles to hearing a staged play sung in the vernacular.

Viennese masters. Italian opera buffa strongly attracted Viennese audiences, and Austrian composers were naturally influenced by it. Perhaps the most interesting of the Vienna-born composers of 18th-century comic opera was Karl Ditters von Dittersdorf, whose Italianate *Doktor und Apotheker* (1786; libretto by Gottlieb Stephanie), though successful and lively, was overshadowed by the contemporary works of Mozart.

Haydn, who lacked a strong theatrical bent, nonetheless

composed about 20 musicodramatic scores: a singspiel, five short operas for marionettes, and several very Italianate opere buffe and opere serie for private performance in the Eisenstadt palace theatre of his employer-patrons, the Esterhazy princes. Several of Haydn's dramatically undistinguished operas have had modern revivals, including *Il mondo della luna* (*The World on the Moon,* 1777; libretto by Carlo Goldoni), *L'isola disabitata* (*The Deserted Island,* 1779; libretto by Metastasio), and *La fedeltà premiata* (*Faithfulness Rewarded,* 1780; libretto by Giovanni Battista Lorenzi).

Vienna, however, was to be one of the centres of the operatic career of Mozart, one of the greatest masters of opera. Mozart began to write theatrical music when only 10 years old and brought out the first of his important operas at Munich in 1781, when only 25. This was *Idomeneo.* Its libretto, by Giambattista Varesco, is an imitation of Metastasio's style. But Mozart rose above the conventional operatic patterns and filled them with richly expressive music so that the result is scarcely recognizable as an opera seria. As a work of musical (though not of dramatic) art, *Idomeneo* is as fine as Gluck's *Iphigénie en Tauride* and ranks as the supreme Italian opera seria of the late 18th century.

One year after *Idomeneo,* Mozart, with the versatility of his unique genius, wrote a masterly, charming singspiel to a German text: *Die Entführung aus dem Serail* (libretto by Christoph Friedrich Bretzner as edited by Gottlieb Stephanie). A sentimental farce full of immediately attractive music and graced with a fine part for a comic bass (Osmin), *Die Entführung* also contains in "Martern aller Arten," a soprano aria so extensive in plan and difficult to sing that it has challenged the foremost sopranos down to the present. The opera has been called the greatest of all truly comic singspiele, and it is notable for the seriousness with which it treats the relationship between its two principal characters and for the human nobility of its "moral."

Production of *Figaro* at Vienna

Mozart's next completed opera—except for *Der Schauspieldirektor* (*The Impresario,* 1786), a trifling one-act comedy—is one of the treasures of Western civilization, the greatest of all seriocomic operas, *Le nozze di Figaro* (libretto by Lorenzo da Ponte, after Pierre de Beaumarchais's *Le Mariage de Figaro,* 1786), produced at Vienna. In addition to its purely musical beauty, this work shows Mozart to be a creator of individual characters of almost Shakespearean calibre; he goes far beyond the opportunities offered by his able librettist and creates, by musical means, believable, rounded human beings, often employed in ensembles as well as in solos and in elaborately constructed finales.

In 1787 Mozart's next opera, written for Prague, was *Don Giovanni* (libretto by da Ponte, based on earlier Don Juan librettos and other writings related to plays by Tirso de Molina, Thomas Corneille, and others). The 19th century tended to regard *Don Giovanni* as the greatest opera ever composed, in part because musical elements in it foretold operatic romanticism. Aspects of da Ponte's libretto disturb some 20th-century critics—particularly the grim, morally justifiable ending of what up to then has been a comedy, followed by the "vaudeville" postlude, during which the singers step out of character to underline the "moral," in line with a then long-established convention. Musically, *Don Giovanni* shares many of the supreme virtues of *Le nozze di Figaro,* in beauty, in characterization, and in dramatic power.

In his last collaboration with Da Ponte, Mozart created another opera buffa, *Così fan tutte* (1790). Most musical opinion today considers it to be an opera of flawless workmanship reconciled with the dramatic claims of a seemingly artificial and cynical libretto, which in fact exposes the foibles of mankind. Farcical productions too often destroy its knife-edge balance between artificiality and reality. Too richly scored, too erotic, and too intense for Viennese taste of the time, it was not a success with the easy-going Viennese, but it now ranks as one of Mozart's greatest stage works.

In 1791, returning to the singspiel in German, Mozart composed *Die Zauberflöte* (libretto by Emanuel Schikaneder), an allegorical and Masonic opera with a seemingly nonsensical but in fact elaborately significant libretto in strong contrast with *Così fan tutte's* cynicism about women. Here, Mozart created some of the most radiantly beautiful music ever composed, assigning it lavishly to both the serious and the comic, both the admirable and the vicious characters. George Bernard Shaw once said that the two arias given to the benevolent Sarastro in *Die Zauberflöte* were the only music he knew that would not sound out of place in the mouth of God—and they are but two of many numbers in this opera that have helped to place Mozart's theatrical works, together with his concertos, at the very apex of his astonishing and endlessly varied output.

Also in 1791 Mozart composed, to a Metastasio libretto slightly revised, another outdated opera seria, *La clemenza di Tito.* Created in 18 days for festivities surrounding the coronation of Emperor Leopold II as king of Bohemia in Prague, *La clemenza* provides numerous examples of Mozart's musical mastery, none of his mastery of dramatic creation through music.

Like *Die Zauberflöte,* Beethoven's *Fidelio* (1805, revised 1806 and 1814) rose above the limitations of the singspiel pattern, becoming something bigger and grander. In most of this, his only opera, Beethoven is musically at nearly his greatest. The libretto has never satisfied anyone entirely; also, some of the writing for the voices is instrumental rather than truly vocal. Beethoven lacked Mozart's theatrical sensibility and his ability to mix the comic-frivolous with the solemn and near tragic, as the text required. Yet the grandeur of much of the *Fidelio* music and the noble humanity of the central character (a wife, Leonore, who disguises herself as a young man, Fidelio, in order to rescue her husband, at terrible risk, from political incarceration in a dungeon) irradiates the opera from the moment of Leonore's first appearance. Its theme of the triumph of the human spirit over oppression has helped to place *Fidelio* among the world's most popular operas.

The *Guerre des Bouffons*

France, 1752–1825. Political changes and that intensity of intellectual discussion that has always played a role in determining the nature of artistic production in Paris led, in the early 1750s, to one of those polemic "wars"—this one called the *Guerre* (or *Querelle*) *des Bouffons* (War of the Buffoons)—that delight the French. This was a mainly literary confronation of the solemn past of opera seria and *tragédie lyrique* with the farce and sentiment of opera buffa, though many of the writers saw it in nationalistic terms. It had a happy outcome: the subsequent composition by both French composers and resident foreigners of excellent examples of opéra comique, which became a French amalgam of the English ballad opera, the German singspiel, and the Italian opera buffa.

In 1752, the year of the first battles of the *Guerre des Bouffons,* Jean-Jacques Rousseau staged at Fontainebleau his one-act comic opera *Le Devin du village* (*The Village Soothsayer*). The libretto was his own. In the score he had brought together, in the pasticcio manner, melodies reflecting the very popular romances and vaudevilles being heard at the Paris fairs. It pleased battlers on both sides of the operatic war, being very French in manner and sentiment but Italian in being through-composed (continuously set) and employing recitative. Rousseau hoped to establish this combination as a standard for French comic opera, but his plan was not immediately successful. In 1755, however, a Naples-trained Italian, Egidio Duni, settled in Paris and began to compose (or perhaps, at first, merely to assemble) recognizably Rousseauesque opéras comiques. French and Belgian composers gladly adapted the new variety of opéra comique (not always with comic subject matter) and soon established its reign in the Paris and provincial theatres (nearly all of them simultaneously composed other sorts of musicodramatic works as well). Among them, several names stand out, together with the finest or most renowned of their operas. One of the most interesting of these opéra comique composers was François-André Danican (1726–95), called Philidor, also a famous chess player, who wrote about 20 works in the evolving manner.

More sentimental—in fact, tending toward the tenderly tearful—was Pierre Alexandre Monsigny (1729–1817), never thoroughly trained in music but endowed with the ability to create winning melodies and to exploit for dramatic purpose the timbres of individual instruments. Probably the finest of the 18th-century composers of opéra comique was a Belgian, André Grétry (1741–1813), who most happily balanced the French and Italian styles. He was a very original and extremely productive composer over a 30-year period spanning the French Revolution.

Étienne-Nicolas Méhul (1763–1817), who used opéra comique conventions including the retention of spoken dialogue, also had a career spanning the Revolution. A devoted Gluckian, Méhul had composed numerous works in many genres when, in 1807, he produced his masterpiece, *Joseph,* which is a rarity among operas in several ways: its libretto by Alexandre Duval is derived from the Bible, a source of drama usually reserved for the oratorio; it has no female characters; and it mixes the most solemn classicism with the sentiment of the popular romances.

Boieldieu's immense success

Early in the 19th century, French opéra comique achieved a new equilibrium of classical tint in the best works of François-Adrien Boieldieu (1775–1834). He won truly astonishing and, to several composers (Berlioz included), maddening popularity with *La Dame blanche* (*The White Lady,* 1825; libretto by Eugène Scribe, based upon Sir Walter Scott's novels *Guy Mannering* and *The Monastery*). There were 1,669 performances of this work at the Opéra-Comique, Paris, between 1825 and 1926.

Le Pré aux clercs (*The Field of Honour,* 1832; libretto by François de Planard), the most accomplished opera of Louis-Joseph-Ferdinand Hérold (1791–1833), all but equalled the popularity of *La Dame blanche;* it had received 1,600 performances at the Paris Opéra-Comique by 1939. Hérold's other outstanding success was *Zampa* (1831; libretto by Anne-Honeré Mélesville), so much like the work of Carl Maria von Weber that it became vastly popular in Germany. An extraordinarily prolix composer, Hérold never succeeded in working out a dependable, unified manner of his own, with the result that his French operas are structurally weak. Opéra comique after Boieldieu became more Italianized, reflecting very largely Rossini's influence.

Italy in the first half of the 19th century. The splendid musical achievements of the classicial Viennese style during the late 18th century and early 19th threatened to leave Italy, opera's native home, to one side of the operatic highroad. Two accidents—one the voluntary expatriation to northern Italy of a German, Johann Simon Mayr, the other the unpredictable eruption of a genius, Gioacchino Rossini—saved the day for Italian opera in Italy and outside it.

Mayr, known in Italy as Giovanni Simone Mayr, composed nearly 70 operas in Italian between his first (1794) and his last (1815). He appears to have been influenced deeply by Mozart, and his intensely keen dramatic sense, together with the extraordinary pliability with which he employed the conventions of opera seria and his varied use of the orchestra (particularly of solo woodwinds and horns within it), would have made him a major composer of opera had he not lacked major gifts as a melodist. Many of his operas were for a long time extremely popular throughout Italy, and his immediate influence was beneficial, particularly on the practice of his most famous pupil, Gaetano Donizetti, and on another, less talented, but still admirable operatic composer, Saverio Mercadante.

The operas of Nicola Zingarelli (1752–1837) and of Ferdinando Paer (1771–1839) were transitional, between Classical and grand opera in mode and manner. Zingarelli's conventional opere buffe displayed a genuine humour and some liveliness of musical imagination; his most enduringly performed work, however, was an opera seria, *Giulietta e Romeo* (1796; libretto by Giuseppe Maria Foppa). He is now remembered chiefly as a teacher of Vincenzo Bellini. Paer, who composed more than 40 operas, worked mostly in Vienna, Dresden, and Paris; his musical style changed with his surroundings.

The production at Venice in 1810 of the first performed opera of Rossini, *La cambiale di matrimonio* (*The Bill of Marriage;* libretto by Gaetano Rossi), announced a new operatic genius. Into the genteel, often charming atmosphere of lingering 18th-century operatic manners, Rossini brought genuine originality marked by rude wit and humour and an entire willingness to sacrifice all "rules" of musical and operatic decorum. Both his opere buffe and his now sadly neglected opere serie soon became so popular throughout Italy and then throughout the Western world that they all but blotted out his unfortunate contemporaries—Donizetti and Bellini excepted.

Rossini's originality and wit

Rossini's dazzling career marked the zenith of the bel canto style, a singer-dominated manner of composition (and at times improvisation) that played to audiences' delight in vocal agility, smoothness of voice, and long, florid phrasing. From the period of Rossini's greatest Italian triumphs (he had a second career in Paris) and of Donizetti and Bellini come the names of now legendary voices such as Isabella Colbran (Rossini's first wife), Giuditta Pasta, Maria Malibran, Giovanni David, Giovanni Battista Rubini, Domenico Donzelli, Antonio Tamburini, and Luigi Lablache. For appearances by these singers, composers altered their scores; when they sang, they interpolated extraneous arias that displayed their prowess. Rossini tried to insist that his operas be sung as he himself composed or revised them, but it was a losing battle. The polished artistry and extreme technical training and technique of such singers, as well as their extraordinarily wide ranges, have left performance of the bel canto operas bristling with nearly insoluble problems for latter-day singers.

Rossini's most famous opera is *Il barbiere di Siviglia* (*The Barber of Seville,* 1816; based on the libretto by Cesare Sterbini after the 18th-century play by Beaumarchais), the most nearly flawless of all opere buffe. Several others among his comedies rank only a little lower in musical invention, genuine comic brio, and opportunities for trained singers of vocal display and for farcical characterization: *L'Italiana in Algeri* (*The Italian Girl in Algiers,* 1813; libretto by Angelo Anelli), *Il Turco in Italia* (*The Turk in Italy,* 1814; libretto by Felice Romani); *La cenerentola* (*Cinderella,* 1817; libretto by Jacopo Ferretti), and the half Italian opera buffa and half French opéra comique *Le Comte Ory* (*Count Ory,* 1828; libretto by Scribe and Charles-Gaspard Delestre-Poirson). Rossini prefaced several of these operas with swift, witty overtures that have held a place in the repertory of symphony orchestras.

Perfection of Rossini's comic operas

His style began to have a more serious bent with *Otello* (*Othello,* 1816; libretto by Francesco di Salsa), the opera semiseria (a serious opera with a happy ending), *La gazza ladra* (*The Thieving Magpie,* 1817; libretto by Giovanni Gherardini), and *Armida* (1817; libretto by Giovanni Schmidt), all of which show the composer adapting his florid style to more dramatic, and often eloquent, purposes. But it was only in his Parisian pieces, such as *Semiramide* (1823; libretto by Gaetano Rossi), *Le Siège de Corinthe* (*The Siege of Corinth,* 1826; a revision of the earlier opera, *Maometto II* [1820]; libretto by Alexandre Soumet and Luigi Balocchi), and *Guillaume Tell* (*William Tell,* 1829; libretto by Étienne de Jouy and Hippolyte Bis), his last opera, that his talent for works on a bigger scale, presaging Parisian grand opera, found its full flowering. Some of these later operas owe their revival in the middle of the 20th century to the appearance of a few singers able to project meaningfully their difficult vocal lines.

Gaetano Donizetti first composed a series of very Rossinian, well-made, and largely undistinguished operas but gradually developed dramatic strength, a latent gift for memorable melody, and a forceful deployment of the orchestra for theatrical drama. In 1830, the year after Rossini's farewell to operatic composition, Donizetti produced at Milan the first of his forward-tending, less Rossinian, dramatically remarkable operas: *Anna Bolena* (*Anne Boleyn*), with a libretto by Felice Romani, who worked with so many opera composers of the time. It immediately placed him with Bellini as an inevitable successor to Rossini. What became clear only in retrospect was that it also showed him to be the most important immediate predecessor—in some sense, teacher—of Giuseppe Verdi. Donizetti clung to the long, legato (smoothly flowing) melodies and the ornamented vocal lines of bel canto, but he also unmistakably foreshadowed Verdi's dramatic vigour and many of the younger man's compositional methods. Several unconscious borrowings from Donizetti have been noted by students of Verdi's operas.

Like Rossini, but unlike Bellini, Donizetti moved freely back and forth between serious and comic subjects. He composed about 70 stage works in 25 years. After the success of *Anna Bolena,* with speed and facility that remain astonishing, he composed numerous operas of enduring quality. They include the sentimental comedy *L'elisir d'amore* (*The Elixir of Love,* 1832; libretto by Felice Romani); *Lucrezia Borgia* (1833; libretto by Romani) and *Maria Stuarda* (*Mary Stuart,* 1834; libretto by Giuseppe Bardari); the popular *Lucia di Lammermoor* (1835; libretto by Salvatore Cammarano was derived from Sir Walter Scott's *The Bride of Lammermoor*)—an opera that reflects Donizetti's acquaintance with the music of Bellini; *Roberto d'Evereux* (1837; libretto by Cammarano); the delightful opéra comique *La Fille du régiment* (*The Daughter of the Regiment,* 1840; libretto by Jules-Henri Vernoy de Saint-Georges and Jean-François-Alfred Bayard); the grand opera *La Favorite* (1840; libretto by Alphonse Royer, Gustave Vaëz, and perhaps Scribe); the opera semiseria *Linda di Chamounix* (1842; libretto by Gaetano Rossi); and—judged by many to be Donizetti's masterwork—the ever fresh and vivid opera buffa, *Don Pasquale* (1843; libretto by Giacomo Ruffini and Donizetti).

Altogether different from either Rossini or Donizetti was Vincenzo Bellini. His operas have come to seem the natural habitat of bel canto, of the unchallenged supremacy of vocal melody in amazingly long-breathed and highly decorated lines. Only his first student opera contains even a trace of humour. He and his librettists filled their collaborations with intensely amorous and other subjective emotion, ethical confrontations, and usually tragic involvements (of the seven finest among his 10 operas, only two—*La sonnambula* and *I puritani*—conclude happily for the principal characters). Bellini cultivated with meticulous care his unrivalled, native gift for convincingly melancholy melody, especially in arias and duets; he gave much less attention to ensembles, choruses, and the expressive potentialities of the orchestra. His orchestra, in fact, might have been what it was had Haydn, Mozart, Mayr, and Rossini never existed.

Bellini's innate gift of melody

Beginning in 1827 with *Il pirata* (*The Pirate,* libretto by Felice Romani, who thereafter supplied all of Bellini's librettos except that for *I puritani*), Bellini made his presence felt throughout Italy and then gradually throughout Europe and the Americas. In 1831 two of Bellini's enduring masterworks were produced: the pastoral opera semiseria *La sonnambula* (*The Sleepwalker*) and the heroic tragedy *Norma.* Bellini's previously faithful public temporarily deserted him when, in 1833, he gave it *Beatrice di Tenda.* In the year of his death after his final removal to Paris, he won another triumph with an opera very loosely connected with Cromwellian times in England, *I puritani* (*The Puritans;* libretto by conte Carlo Pepoli).

Unlike Rossini and Donizetti, Bellini exercised little or no influence upon the style of his successors: the most noticeable of his compositional means, his exclusively personal sort of melody, could only be debased in imitation by others. With these three men, both the late period of bel canto and the second period of opera buffa drew to a close. After the onset of Donizetti's crippling illness in 1847, the Italian opera houses in Italy, Paris, London, and elsewhere could look to Giuseppe Verdi.

GRAND OPERA AND BEYOND

French grand opera. Nineteenth-century Paris was to foster and witness the birth of "grand opera," an international style of large-scale operatic spectacle employing historical or pseudohistorical librettos and filling the stage with elaborate scenery and costumes, ballets, and phalanxes of supernumeraries. Dispensing almost entirely with the delicacies of bel canto, it vastly enlarged both the orchestra itself and its role in the dramatic happenings. Grand opera naturally had roots in the past, particularly in the Venetian "machine operas" of the 17th century, such as Cesti's *Il pomo d'oro,* as well as in the stately scores of Rameau and Gluck. But the immediate drive toward this new style of opera was instituted in Paris by Italian expatriates: Luigi Cherubini, who spent the last 54 years of his life in France, and Gasparo Spontini, whose most impressive operas were designed for Paris.

Cherubini was a greatly learned composer in almost all musical forms who won the admiration of Beethoven. His two most imposing operas were the embryonic grand opera *Médée* (1797; libretto by François-Benoît Hoffman) and a *comédie lyrique, Les Deux Journées* (*The Two Days,* 1800; libretto by Jean-Nicolas Bouilly). *Les Deux Journées* became something like a national German opera under its German title, *Der Wasserträger* (*The Water Carrier*). Spontini, in his French operas, ranged far beyond Cherubini and his other contemporaries in his demands for complex staging, finally reaching a sort of splendid megalomania. Daniel-François-Esprit Auber brought out a nearly total grand opera; *La Muette de Portici* (*The Mute Girl of Portici,* also known as *Masaniello,* 1828; libretto by Scribe). The popularity of *La Muette* became phenomenal in both France and Germany. This opera remains unique on several counts. Its title character neither sings nor speaks, the role being performed by a mime. A performance of it at Brussels on August 25, 1830, set off disorders that led to the separation of Belgium from The Netherlands. Eighteen months after the premiere of Auber's opera, the appearance of Rossini's *Guillaume Tell* showed that master of opera buffa and bel canto responding to the new genre. Auber's later operas include several charming comedies, among them *Fra Diavolo* (1830; libretto by Scribe).

The final, official birth of grand opera occurred in 1831, with the first French opera of another Parisian expatriate, the German Giacomo Meyerbeer: *Robert le Diable* (libretto by Scribe and Germain Delavigne). The popularity of this work became a sort of frenzy (by August 1893 it had been sung 751 times at the Paris Opéra). Although Meyerbeer's operas are rarely performed in the late 20th century, he remains a controversial figure. Using an expanded, powerful orchestra, with much emphasis placed on individual instrumental colours, requiring almost every kind of singing, filling huge stages with dazzling pageantry, employing characters who pretend to be actual figures from history, four of his operas held their leading positions even through the Wagnerian revolution and into the early 20th century. Besides *Robert le Diable,* they were *Les Huguenots* (1836; libretto by Scribe with the collaboration of Émile Deschamps), *Le Prophète* (1849; libretto by Scribe), and the posthumously staged *L'Africaine* (libretto by Scribe). The author of all of these, Eugène Scribe, was the most phenomenally productive librettist of his time, writing (with the help of various collaborators) a huge number of librettos for many composers, including Auber, Boieldieu, Cherubini, Donizetti, Gounod, Halévy, Meyerbeer, Rossini, and Verdi. He was, in fact, a major force in the evolution of French grand opera.

Imitators of Meyerbeer's successes naturally sprang up immediately. Later, numerous men totally unlike him stylistically—including Berlioz, Wagner, and Verdi—were influenced unwittingly by his practices. The first of the imitators was Fromental Halévy, whose works included at least one grand opera that could almost be mistaken for Meyerbeer's: *La Juive* (*The Jewess,* 1835; libretto by Scribe). After the times of Meyerbeer and Halévy, grand opera began to respond to new musical and intellectual currents, evolving into a variety of mixed forms.

Like most of Hector Berlioz's other compositions, his three operas stand apart from the mainstream of historical evolution. When first staged at the Paris Opéra in the shadow of *Robert le Diable* and *La Dame blanche,* his first opera, *Benvenuto Cellini* (1838; libretto by Léon de Wailly and Auguste Barbier), was a complete failure. The second, the lighthearted *Béatrice et Bénédict* (his own libretto, based upon Shakespeare's *Much Ado About Nothing*), finally was given its premiere at Baden-Baden in 1862 by Franz Liszt. And Berlioz's masterpiece, *Les Troyens* (his own libretto), is based on Virgil's *Aeneid* and divided into *La Prise de Troie* (*The Capture of Troy*), two acts, and *Les Troyens à Carthage* (*The Trojans at Carthage*), three acts. It was not performed complete during his lifetime: he

Modern revival of *Les Troyens*

heard only the second part as staged in Paris in 1863. Mid-20th-century complete (or very nearly complete) performances of *Les Troyens,* notably in London, showed it to be a great, noble, idiosyncratic work not without traces of grand opera, but in seriousness and scope much closer to the Wagner of *Der Ring des Nibelungen.* Berlioz's operas, like his other music, are distinguished by the individual arch of his melody, his revolutionary orchestration, and the dramatic thrust of the whole.

Even more popular than Auber as a purveyer of light operatic comedy was Jacques Offenbach, a German émigré to Paris who supplied the Second Empire and the early years of the Third Republic with a long series of very tuneful, witty, and satiric operettas of deliberate frivolity. Remembered among them are *Orphée aux enfers* (*Orpheus in the Underworld,* 1858; libretto by Hector Crémieux and Ludovic Halévy), *La Belle Hélène* (*Beautiful Helen,* 1864; libretto by Henri Meilhac and Halévy), *Barbe-Bleue* (*Bluebeard,* 1866; libretto by Meilhac and Halévy), *La Vie Parisienne* (*Parisian Life,* 1866; libretto by Meilhac and Halévy), *La Grande-Duchesse de Gérolstein* (1867; libretto by Meilhac and Halévy), and *La Périchole* (1868; libretto by Meilhac and Halévy). Left incomplete at Offenbach's death was his major serious opera, *Les Contes d'Hoffmann* (*The Tales of Hoffmann;* libretto by Jules Barbier and Michel Carré, after their play of the same name based on tales by the German Romantic writer E.T.A. Hoffmann). Recitatives replacing the original dialogue were provided by Ernst Guiraud, and the opera was staged posthumously in 1881. This fantasy involving supernatural interventions rapidly became a worldwide favourite.

German Romantic opera. Romanticism, part philosophical, part literary, part aesthetic, made one of its first appearances, and certainly its earliest overt appearance, in opera, in three works composed between 1821 and 1826 by Carl Maria von Weber. Beginning with his masterpiece, *Der Freischütz* (*The Freeshooter,* 1821; libretto by Friedrich Kind), Weber successfully challenged the outdated dictatorship of Spontini at Berlin. For the Italian's stiff grandeurs he substituted, in singspiel form, tender sentiment, grisly horrors, manly choruses, moral nicety, and music of extraordinary instrumental and vocal allure. *Der Freischutz* illustrates the German Romantic writers' love for dark forests, the echoes of hunters' horns, the threatening supernatural, the frustrations of pure young love. Its popularity in Germany and elsewhere was enormous.

Elements of German Romanticism

Weber smarted under the anti-Romantic criticism of *Der Freischütz* as a mere singspiel (a work with spoken dialogue) rather than a musically continuous opera. His next major composition, *Euryanthe* (1823; libretto by Helmina von Chézy), was something like a proto-grand opera and therefore contained no spoken dialogue. Almost since its premiere, writers have attacked the remarkable silliness (on paper) of its libretto, but most of them have never witnessed the work in performance and therefore cannot judge how the libretto works on stage with Weber's fine score. His last opera, *Oberon,* or *The Elf King's Oath* (1826; libretto, in English, by James Robinson Planché), returns to the singspiel form. Like *Euryanthe,* it has not held the stage, and again the libretto has been blamed. The overtures to all three of these operas are still played frequently, and whatever future opinion of the operas themselves may be, *Der Freischütz* opened the floodgates of musical Romanticism in Germany.

Louis Spohr (1784–1859), a violinist, conductor, and composer of instrumental music, sounds pallidly Romantic if compared with Weber, but certain of his harmonic innovations taught something to Wagner, of whose early operas he was a defender. Heinrich August Marschner (1795–1861), more Romantic by nature than Spohr, borrowed sufficiently from Weber's style to serve as one bridge to Wagner. He displayed talent as orchestrator and melodist, and he applied his gifts to intensely Romantic and equally Teutonic librettos. The finest of his now unheard operas is *Hans Heiling* (1833; libretto by Eduard Devrient).

The other German-language composers of opera active during the Weber–Spohr–Marschner period were less important. Albert Lortzing composed several operas that have been likened to genre painting. He travelled in the direction of operetta in his popular sentimental comedies, such as *Zar und Zimmermann* (*Tsar and Carpenter,* 1837; his own libretto) and *Der Waffenschmied* (*The Armourer,* 1846; his own libretto). The same direction was taken by Friedrich, Freiherr von Flotow, whose operetta-like *Martha* (1847; libretto by Friedrich Wilhelm Reise) continues to be performed frequently. This trend toward operetta as a less intense variety of Romanticism continued in *Die lustigen Weiber von Windsor* (1849; libretto by Salomon Hermann Mosenthal, based on Shakespeare's *Merry Wives of Windsor*), the major success of Otto Nicolai, and in the extremely popular works of Franz von Suppé, a Dalmatian of Belgian ancestry. It culminated in operetta on the highest level of musical accomplishment in the masterworks of Johann Strauss the Younger. Many of Strauss's operettas are known now only by their overtures and waltzes, but one of them, *Die Fledermaus* (1874; libretto by Carl Haffner and Richard Genée), has never left the stage for long. Only the finest opéras comiques and opéras bouffes of Auber and Jacques Offenbach match Strauss's elegance, wit, humour, musical invention, and scrupulous workmanship.

Strauss's operettas

Verdi. When, in 1839, an opera called *Oberto, conte di San Bonifacio* (libretto by Antonio Piazza, revised by Bartolomeo Merelli and Temistocle Solera) was staged at the leading Italian opera house, the Teatro alla Scala (La Scala) at Milan, its first audiences received it reasonably well. Rossini had not offered a new opera for 10 years, Bellini was dead, and Donizetti was composing for Paris, so the debut of a new talent was welcome. Those early audiences, however, could not know that *Oberto* had opened the active career of the greatest of all later Italian composers of opera, Giuseppe Verdi. Verdi's second opera, *Un giorno di regno* (*King for a Day,* 1840; libretto by Felice Romani), was a failure and was to remain his only comedy for 53 years. It was followed by *Nabucodonosor,* known as *Nabucco* (1842; libretto by Solera), which displayed the emergence of a musical dramatist of enormous vigour and rich melodic invention.

Verdi long suffered from his inability to obtain librettos worthy of his special talents, but each of the six operas that he wrote between *Nabucco* (1842) and *Macbeth* (1847) includes scenes and numbers of great power and immediately winning, memorable melody. Even *Macbeth* (libretto by Francesco Maria Piave, revised in 1865 by Verdi to a libretto in French), although it is marked both dramatically and musically by passages of astonishing vitality, has structural weaknesses.

Another period of lesser achievement by Verdi stretched from 1847 to 1851, the best of his five operas of those years having been *Luisa Miller* (1849; libretto by Salvatore Cammarano). Meanwhile, Verdi was on the way to becoming a public symbol of the risorgimento, the Italian movement of rebellion against foreign domination and toward political unification, both because of the patriotic emphasis in several of his librettos and because of his staunchly liberal public character (he was eventually to become a true national hero).

Beginning in 1851, Verdi produced three masterpieces, having found three librettos that fired aspects of his genius. The first of them was *Rigoletto* (libretto by Piave), in which his abundant creation of melody was at the service of his gift for musical characterization. *Rigoletto* was followed, less than two years later, by *Il trovatore* (*The Troubadour,* 1853; libretto by Cammarano), perhaps unmatched among his operas for its profusion of strong and memorable melodies.

Less than two months after the premiere of *Il trovatore* came *La traviata* (1853; libretto by Piave, after Alexandre Dumas *fils*'s *La Dame aux camélias*). At first a failure, it later came to be accepted as a masterpiece. It also established a composer's right to set librettos dealing with contemporary life and with characters not of exalted station. By comparison with the thunderous melodrama of *Il trovatore, La traviata* seems an intimate, quiet, almost chamber-music opera. The musical portrait of Violetta, the tubercular courtesan heroine, remains extraordinary for its depiction of the effects of love and sorrow on her character.

Production of *La traviata*

After *La traviata* came a comparative failure, a grand opera composed in French for Paris, *Les Vêpres siciliennes* (*The Sicilian Vespers,* 1855; libretto by Scribe and Charles Duveyrier). It was succeeded only two years later by *Simon Boccanegra* (1857; revised 1881), a gloomy opera of great power. Then came *Un ballo in maschera* (*A Masked Ball,* 1859; libretto by Antonio Somma, after Scribe's libretto for Auber's 1833 opera *Gustave III, ou Le Bal Masqué*), no less gloomy and powerful but including, in the page Oscar (sung by a soprano), a ray of light and youthful humour, and *La forza del destino* (*The Force of Destiny,* 1862; libretto by Piave), a kaleidoscopic mixture of the tragic and the farcical, with touches of matter not far from operetta and opera buffa.

For Paris, and again to a libretto in French, Verdi next composed *Don Carlos* (1867; libretto by François-Joseph Méry and Camille du Locle, revised by Verdi in 1884 to an Italian translation and again in 1887). This long opera, and particularly its fourth act, is majestic and subtle, its various musical confrontations—many of them duets—displaying a depth of characterization hitherto unknown in Italian or French opera, in spite of faults in the libretto.

By 1869 Verdi's fame had become so international that the Khedive of Egypt invited him to compose an opera for Cairo to mark the opening of the new Cairo Opera House (and possibly the opening of the Suez Canal). In fact, the canal began to operate in 1869, but the opera received its premiere at Cairo only in 1871. This was *Aida* (libretto by Antonio Ghislanzoni, based on a scenario by Auguste Mariette, the French Egyptologist, and Camille du Locle, with the collaboration of Verdi). The masterly libretto and its four well-delineated principal characters evoked from Verdi a Meyerbeerian opera of such unfailing melodic, orchestral, and dramatic richness that many have called *Aida* his masterpiece. For pageantry, combined as it is with harmonic, melodic, and instrumental skills and convincing, if generalized, characterization, it remains unrivalled—and probably has been sung more often than any other opera.

Verdi's Shakespearean operas

In 1869 the public and the writers on opera assumed that Verdi would continue to produce a new opera every few years. But 16 elapsed before the premiere of his next opera, *Otello* (1887; libretto by Arrigo Boito). Verdi's varied, intensely dynamic, compressed, and tragic score was the result not only of his ripened genius but also of nearly 50 years of operatic practice. Many critics consider it the finest tragic opera ever composed.

In the following six years, rumours grew that the aged Verdi not only was composing still another opera but that it was to be a comedy. The comic masterpiece *Falstaff* (libretto by Boito, derived largely from Shakespeare's *Merry Wives of Windsor* and *Henry IV*) was performed in 1893 at La Scala, where Verdi's first opera had been staged more than 53 years before. An opera buffa with serious overtones, *Falstaff* always has been praised by critics and enthusiasts, but it has never become a true popular favourite.

Arrigo Boito not only wrote the librettos of Verdi's last two operas but was also himself a composer, as well as a poet, polemicist, and man of letters. He completed only one opera, *Mefistofele* (1868; his own libretto, derived from Goethe's *Faust*). It was at first a failure and then became more popular. His command of technical musical resources was vast. Unfortunately, he placed them at the service of lofty but diffuse philosophical concepts and ideals mostly beyond his range of expressiveness. *Mefistofele,* for instance, is more impressive and admirable than theatrically convincing.

Wagner and his successors. Richard Wagner (1813–83) is a unique figure in the history of both opera and music. A concentrated egoist gifted with a powerful, tenacious, and at times stubbornly confused intellect, he wrote both the music and librettos of his operas. He began his career, except for a youthful attempt, *Die Feen* (*The Fairies,* completed, 1834; first performed, 1888), with two grand operas mixing the influences of Meyerbeer, Marschner, and Weber: *Das Liebesverbot* (*The Ban on Love,* 1836) and *Rienzi* (1842). In 1843, with *Der fliegende Holländer* (*The Flying Dutchman*), he began to develop what was to become an extremely personal, powerful manner of operatic construction. Turning to mythic legend for his subjects and making unacknowledged bows to the operas of Weber and Marschner, while dispensing with the trappings of grand opera, he composed an intensely German, Romantic opera. In it he instituted the use of brief melodic and other motifs as materials for evolving a more-or-less continuous web of music in which the separate numbers of earlier opera appeared only when the libretto demanded them. Already, at the age of 30, he was giving harmony, in very unclassical guise, a central constructive role in the creation of both drama and characterization.

Wagner's personal operatic style

Patiently and challengingly elaborating a vast, interlocked system of theories in many published books and essays, Wagner continued the ripening of his style in two large, transitional operas, *Tannhäuser* (1845) and *Lohengrin* (1850). *Tannhäuser* again displays some grand-opera characteristics (particularly in the revision of it that Wagner prepared for the 1861 Paris performance); *Lohengrin,* the last of Wagner's serious operas peopled by human beings of recognizable dimensions, has been called the Romantic opera par excellence.

The earliest example of what Wagner called "music drama" (a term he preferred to "opera") was the monumental *Tristan und Isolde* (1865), the libretto of which illustrates his obsession with the idea of man's redemption through woman's love. *Tristan und Isolde* advances harmonic language. The score is woven in a harmonic idiom so advanced chromatically that it speeded the destruction of orthodox concepts of harmony. *Tristan* requires singers possessed of powerful voices capable of penetrating a vastly enlarged orchestra. It came to be regarded as the greatest German opera of the late 19th century, and its influence upon compositional methods and techniques continued into the 20th century.

In *Die Meistersinger von Nürnberg* (*The Mastersingers of Nürnberg,* 1868) he partly deserted his most "advanced" style because central episodes in the libretto required self-contained numbers. Warmhearted, overflowing with young love and the bitter wisdom of age, *Die Meistersinger* ranks with Verdi's *Falstaff* among late-19th-century comic operas. From 1853 until 1874 Wagner worked intermittently on the four poems and the scores of *Der Ring des Nibelungen.* It is an epic, based on Teutonic myths, of such proportions and implications that it cannot be summarized. Musically, Wagner uses leitmotivs—constantly recurring fragments—and weaves them into a large, elaborate pattern. Performed in its entirety, and without intermissions, the *Ring* would last about 12 hours; many listeners, almost bewitched, would have been and now would be willing to attend such a continuous performance, so compelling is the musical power of this unique, all but inhuman, masterpiece.

The last of Wagner's operas, *Parsifal* (1882), introduced few structural elements not used in *Tristan und Isolde* and *Der Ring des Nibelungen.* Wagner called it *Ein Bühnenweihfestspiel*—a sacred festival drama—and it is heavy with religious and ethical messages. It perfectly illustrated both his musicodramatic theories and the unsmiling solemnity with which he approached operatic composition and demanded, successfully, that his audience absorb the results. *Parsifal* closed a career unparalleled in its aggressive demands on society and on operagoers, a career that would have seemed a form of madness if it had not produced some of the most lastingly impressive of all operatic creations and many pages of music of the greatest beauty.

Operatic composers influenced by Wagner

Curiously, Wagner's influence has been felt more in the evolution of post-Romantic harmony than in the constructive practices of later operatic composers. An adaptation of his leitmotiv usage marked the delightful fairytale opera *Hänsel und Gretel* (1893; based upon the tale by the Brothers Grimm), by Engelbert Humperdinck. Wagner's early theories about both libretto and music played a constructive part in the excellent comic opera *Der Barbier von Bagdad* (*The Barber of Bagdad,* 1858), by Peter Cornelius, and his mature style was wholly adopted in *Guntram* (1894), the first opera of Richard Strauss. Otherwise, the Wagnerian revolutions (in contrast with his at times unrevolutionary practice) are clearly seen in the operas of some ardent French Wagnerians such as Ernest Reyer and Vincent d'Indy.

Later opera in France. The history of French opera contemporary with and later than Berlioz includes many talented composers and stageworthy works, but it degenerates quickly into a catalog of pieces of considerable charm and some originality seldom made arresting by the appearance of operas unmistakably of the first rank. Charles Gounod, who composed many operas, had a unique gift for sentimental melody but an uncertain sense of what is theatrically viable. In his ever-popular *Faust* (1859; libretto by Jules Barbier and Michel Carré), his talents were most creatively gathered together, but *Faust* took no place in the steady evolution of operatic styles. Among Gounod's other operas, the best, mixing in different proportions the virtues and flaws of *Faust,* are probably *Mireille* (1864; libretto by Carré, derived from Frédéric Mistral's Provençal poem *Mirèio*) and *Roméo et Juliette* (1867; libretto by Barbier and Carré).

The works of Georges Bizet are on a higher level in both their vigour and variety. He began to display his considerable ability with *Les Pêcheurs de perles* (*The Pearl Fishers,* 1863; libretto by Eugène and Carré) and *La Jolie Fille de Perth,* (1867; libretto by Jules-Henry Vernoy de Saint-Georges and Jules Adenis, based on Sir Walter Scott's *Fair Maid of Perth*). In 1875 Bizet produced his masterpiece, *Carmen* (libretto by Henri Meilhac and Ludovic Halévy, after a tale by Prosper Mérimée). Its then savage realism, broad but convincing characterization, and dazzling pseudo-Spanish ambience shocked its first audiences and strongly influenced Italian *verismo.* A lonely masterpiece, *Carmen* remains one of the steady props of operatic repertory everywhere.

Production of *Carmen*

Ambroise Thomas, as prolific as Gounod but not as gifted in emotional or musical persuasion, had composed many operas when Paris first welcomed his *Mignon* (1866; libretto by Barbier and Carré), probably his best opera. Two years later he composed *Hamlet* (1868; libretto by Barbier and Carré). Thomas, like Gounod, interlarded his operas with florid, often essentially undramatic and "showy" arias for a new type of lyric-coloratura soprano. One of the most frequently heard of such vacuous arias is the "Bell Song" from Léo Delibes' *Lakmé* (1883; libretto by Edmond Gondinet and Philippe Gille). Although Camille Saint-Saëns composed numerous operas, the only work by him to remain in the repertory is *Samson et Dalila* (libretto by Ferdinand Lemaire), originally sung under Franz Liszt's aegis in 1877 in German. It is lusciously melodic but so lacking in drama as to seem half oratorio.

Phenomenally popular when first composed were many of the operas of Jules Massenet, who had a surer sense of the stageworthy than Saint-Saëns but often made saccharine what to many had seemed too sweet in the earlier French opera of the 19th century. At his best however, Massenet was something better than "the daughter of Gounod": in *Manon* (1884) he produced not only one of the most enduringly popular of operas but also a stylistically unflawed reflection of the tragicosentimental 18th-century novel by the Abbé Prévost on which Henri Meilhac and Philippe Gille had based the libretto. Much the same qualities have kept alive Massenet's *Werther* (1892; libretto by Édouard Blau, Paul Milliet, and Georges Hartmann, derived from Goethe's *Leiden des jungen Werthers*), first performed at Vienna in a German translation. Some other operas by Massenet, particularly *Thaïs* (1894; libretto by Louis Gallet, after the novel by Anatole France), are important for their sensuous portrayals of seductive female characters.

Gustave Charpentier's *Louise* (1900; libretto by the composer) has remained in opera house repertories because of its loving, romanticized portrait of "Bohemian" Paris, the sentiment and surface allure, and the popularity of Louise's hymn to love, "Depuis le jour."

Claude Debussy, the greatest French composer after Berlioz and a decisive influence upon 20th-century music, completed only one opera: *Pelléas et Mélisande* (1902), an almost verbatim setting of Maurice Maeterlinck's play. Like *Tristan und Isolde*—which, having helped to shape Maeterlinck's drama, inevitably and against Debussy's will also shaped some of his compositional procedures—*Pelléas* remains unique. Listeners immune to the attraction of its aristocratic sensuality often find it monotonous. Nonetheless, it is a masterwork in its wholly apt amalgamation of text and score, the inescapable rightness for its quiet dramatic purposes of Debussy's individual harmonies, the marvelous manner with which he made the sounds of Maeterlinck's French an integral element in a shimmering orchestral web. In *Pelléas,* the Wagnerian ideal of continuous music without separate numbers was attained. Although *Pelléas* remains one of the handful of important operas composed in the 20th century, it has had few descendants. One of those few is Paul Dukas' *Ariane et Barbe-Bleue* (*Ariadne and Bluebeard,* 1907)—like *Pelléas,* an almost verbatim setting of a Maeterlinck play. It, however, is notably noisy where *Pelléas* is quiet, and it lacks Debussy's thematic invention.

The achievement of *Pelléas*

Maurice Ravel wrote one opera, *L'Heure espagnole* (*The Spanish Hour,* 1911; libretto by Maurice Legrand), and a *fantaisie lyrique* (really a ballet-pantomime-opera), *L'Enfant et les sortilèges* (*The Child and the Enchantments,* 1925; text by Colette). The former is opéra bouffe in Spanish dance rhythms overlaid with vocal lines that seem indebted to the works of Richard Strauss. The latter reverses the orchestra's domination over the voices in *L'Heure espagnole.* It is an edifying and hilarious fantasy about a child being punished for his mistreatment of his toys and other objects. Perhaps only its uncomfortable mixture of genres has kept it from widespread performance.

Of the professedly anti-Debussyan, anti-Impressionist group known as Les Six, three have places in the history of opera: Arthur Honegger, Darius Milhaud, and Francis Poulenc. Honegger, a Swiss, employed a somewhat Teutonic "neoclassical modern" idiom in thickly dissonant, heavily percussive operas that have failed to hold the stage. Milhaud's once sensational *opéras-minutes* (1927–28), three brief one-act compositions, were first staged in German translation in Germany. They parody Greek myths and have music composed in a jazz manner that inevitably has lost effectiveness with the passing decades. Milhaud also composed large modern versions of grand opera, but his persistently undramatic and often busily indecisive musical style have kept them from popularity. Poulenc composed one comic monodrama and one serious opera that seem likely to endure. The first, *Les Mamelles de Tirésias* (1947), is a wildly nonsensical opéra bouffe, the sardonic music of which is humorously appropriate to the text by the French poet Guillaume Apollinaire. The second, *La Voix humaine* (*The Human Voice,* 1959; text by Jean Cocteau), has as its only visible character a distraught young woman conversing by telephone with her lover. Poulenc's only large serious opera, *Dialogues des Carmélites* (*Dialogues of the Carmelites,* 1957; libretto by Georges Bernanos), appears to be the most impressive French opera since *Pelléas et Mélisande.* It makes telling operatic use of Poulenc's instantly identifiable style of melody, harmony (only very gently dissonant), and rhythm to tell a moving and tragic story of nuns martyred during the French Revolution.

Tragic and sardonic themes

Later opera in Italy. Viewed broadly, the story of Italian opera contemporary with and following Verdi parallels that of French opera after Berlioz, in the appearance of talented composers and stageworthy operas as well as in quickly becoming a tally of pieces of considerable charm and some degree of originality responding to shifting musical techniques and manners. It includes only two or three composers of the first rank.

Amilcare Ponchielli, shining clearly in light reflected from Verdi, composed one opera that remains in the international "standard" repertory—*La Gioconda* (1876; libretto by Arrigo Boito). The general turn toward realism began on a Roman stage in 1890 with Pietro Mascagni's dazzlingly successful one-act opera *Cavalleria rusticana* (*Rustic Chivalry;* libretto by Guido Menasci and Giovanni Targioni-Tozzetti). It soon evoked the descriptive term *verismo* (realism) and set a vogue for raw, violent, melodramatic librettos matched to music clearly descended from the middle-period operas of Verdi. Mascagni went on composing operas for 50 years after *Cavalleria,* but none won a permanent place on the stage. The best of them is *L'Amico Fritz* (*Friend Fritz,* 1891; libretto by Nicolo Despure). And two years after the premiere of *Cavalleria rusticana,* an equally successful product of *verismo* was staged in Milan: *I pagliacci* (*The Clowns,* 1892; libretto by the composer), by Ruggero Leoncavallo, who had no more staying power than Mascagni, though he produced operas for the remainder of his life.

The Italian counterpart of Massenet in France made his first important contribution to the operatic stage the year after *I pagliacci.* He was Giacomo Puccini, whose work is characterized by emotional directness of appeal and colourful, rich orchestration; the opera was *Manon Lescaut* (1893), based on the novel by the Abbé Prévost from which the libretto of Massenet's *Manon* had been derived. Puccini established himself unmistakably as the most important post-Verdian Italian operatic composer with *La Bohème* (1896; libretto by Giuseppe Giacosa and Luigi Illica, after Henri Murger's *Scènes de la vie de bohème*). It, too, remains "standard," as do *Tosca* (1900; libretto by Giacosa and Illica) and *Madama Butterfly* (1904; libretto by Giacosa and Illica), which again capitalized upon Puccini's attraction to, and ability to characterize in music, sorrowing, attractive young women. Returning closer to violent *verismo,* Puccini (who always had to struggle to find librettos germane to his purposes) next composed an opera of the American "Wild West," *La fanciulla del west* (*The Girl of the Golden West,* 1910; libretto by Guelfo Civinini and Carlo Zangarini).

Establishment of Puccini's reputation with *La Bohème*

Fumbling for apposite literary materials, Puccini next proposed to write an operetta for Vienna; the outcome was a mixed, uncertain operetta-like piece, *La Rondine* (1917; libretto by Giuseppe Adami), produced by Monte Carlo, instead of Vienna, because of World War I. It was followed by a trio of one-act operas given its premiere at the Metropolitan, in 1918. *Il trittico* (*The Triptych*) consisted of the veristic and powerful *Il tabarro* (*The Cloak;* libretto by Adami), the sweetly sad, all-female *Suor Angelica* (*Sister Angelica;* libretto by Giovacchino Forzano) and the opera buffa of medieval Florence, *Gianni Schicchi* (libretto by Forzano). *Gianni Schicchi,* in its sarcastic humour and musical vitality, is the finest Italian operatic comedy after *Falstaff.*

Puccini died before finishing *Turandot* (libretto by Adami and Renato Simoni based on the Italian writer Carlo Gozzi's fable of the same name). It was produced posthumously in 1926. *Turandot* shows Puccini taking note of the then-recent developments in harmony, while giving them an Eastern flavour. The bloodthirsty story with a happy ending (for the two characters who least deserve it) alienates some operagoers, but many of those who accept *Turandot* as the brilliant, extremely melodious, highly pictorial representation of a legend consider it the finest of Puccini's operas. The music of *Turandot* was completed after the composer's death by the Italian composer Franco Alfano.

The other Italian operatic composers of the late 19th century and early 20th displayed neither the brash originality of the young Mascagni and Leoncavallo nor the varied theatrical genius of Puccini. They included Alfredo Catalani, whose best known opera, shaped with extreme melodic refinement and mildly interesting orchestral commentary, is *La Wally* (1892; libretto by Luigi Illica). Another of these minor men was Umberto Giordano (1867–1948), whose bombastic *Andrea Chenier* (1896; libretto by Illica) and *Fedora* (1898; libretto by Arturo Colautti) are still staged. Francesco Cilea overtly copied the more sentimental aspects of Puccini in his biggest success, *Adriana Lecouvreur* (1902; libretto by Colautti). The 20th-century music critic Donald Jay Grout made an accurate description of nearly all of the post-Verdian Italian operas except *Cavalleria rusticana, I pagliacci,* and the best of Puccini when he wrote of *Adriana Lecouvreur* as "expertly contrived music of a lyrical-tragic sort . . . unadventurous harmonically or rhythmically, but good theatre and grateful for the singers."

Of much greater interest (though not of equal popularity) were two contrasted half-Italian, half-German composers active early in this century: Ferruccio Busoni and Ermanno Wolf-Ferrari. Busoni, a learned musician, wrote, in a then-advanced harmonic idiom and using his own librettos, four operas that have had scattered enthusiasts but no large public: *Die Brautwahl* (*Choice of a Bride,* 1912); two commedia dell'arte parodies—*Turandot* (1917; libretto after Gozzi) and the equally short *Arlecchino* (*Harlequin,* 1917)—and his major work, *Doktor Faust,* left incomplete at his death and completed by Philipp Jarnach (1925). Busoni's operas, and *Doktor Faust* in particular, are notable for their intellectual mastery, spiritual elevation, and other operatically peripheral virtues, but their almost total lack of dramatic cogency and musical allure have probably kept them from frequent performance.

At the other end of the operatic spectrum, Wolf-Ferrari possessed a fine talent for opera buffa of an especially light, airy sort, and also composed one of the rawest later examples of *verismo.* There is enormous charm in his comedies *Le donne curiose* (*The Curious Women,* 1903; libretto by Luigi Sugana), *I quattro rusteghi* (*The Four Ruffians,* 1906; libretto by Giuseppe Pizzolato), and *Il segreto di Susanna* (*The Secret of Susanna,* 1909; libretto by Enrico Golisciani). All three were first given in German translation. The melodrama *I gioielli della Madonna* (*The Jewels of the Madonna,* 1911; by Golisciani and Zangarini) has been well described as Donizetti plus *verismo.*

The "big three" Italian composers of the 1920s and 1930s—Ottorino Respighi, Gian Francesco Malipiero, and Alfredo Casella—all composed operas and operalike works of considerable musical interest but little theatrical vitality. What historical influence they have had has operated largely outside the opera house.

Russian opera. After long subjection to imported Italian, French, and German composers, opera in Russia by Russians asserted itself in two well-known works by Mikhail Ivanovich Glinka (1804–57): *Zhizn za tsarya* (*A Life for the Tsar*), also known as *Ivan Susanin* (1836; libretto by Baron Georgy Fyodorovich Rosen), and *Ruslan i Lyudmila* (*Ruslan and Lyudmila,* 1842; libretto by Valeryan Fyodorovich Shirkov and others). Basically old-fashioned Italianate operas, they—*Ruslan* in particular—determined the nature of much future Russian music because of Glinka's approximations of Slavic folk music, his pre-Wagnerian use of a tentative leitmotiv technique, and the clarity and shifting colours of his orchestration. Glinka's operas, weakened by evidence of his lifelong dilettantism, remain in the repertory only in the Soviet Union, but their stylistic importance was decisive.

Glinka as father of Russian nationalism

Almost as influential as Glinka in shaping future Russian opera was his much less successful disciple Aleksandr Sergeyevich Dargomyzhsky. His *Rusalka* (1856; his libretto, after a fairy tale by Pushkin) illustrated his strong emphasis on a declamation midway between recitative and aria, as well as his musical amateurism. Even more influential, although left incomplete at Dargomyzhsky's death, was *Kamenny gost* (*The Stone Guest,* an integral setting of Pushkin's short Don Juan play; completed by César Antonovich Cui and Nikolay Rimsky-Korsakov and staged posthumously in 1872). It is couched in what were then advanced harmonic terms, powerful in characterization, but musically all but sterile. Dargomyzhsky remains more interesting to historians than to opera goers.

The operas of Aleksandr Borodin, Rimsky-Korsakov, and Modest Mussorgsky are still performed. Borodin's incomplete *Knyaz Igor* (*Prince Igor,* his own libretto; completed and edited by Rimsky-Korsakov and Aleksandr Glazunov) was staged posthumously in 1890. It is dramatically shapeless but is splashed with Slavic and Oriental colours. Most of Rimsky-Korsakov's numerous fairy-tale operas have the nature of brilliantly illustrated books, but what may be his finest work is "the Russian *Parsifal,*" *Skazaniye o nevidimom grade Kitezhe i deve Fevroni* (*The Legend of the Invisible City of Kitezh,* 1907; libretto by Vladimir Ivanovich), a work of marked emotional strength. Of his lighter works, the best known are *Snegurochka* (*The Snow Maiden,* 1882; his own libretto), *Sadko* (1898; libretto by the composer and Byelsky), and the fantastic opera buffa, *Zolotoy petushok* (*Le Coq d'or,* or *The Golden Cockerel,* 1909; libretto by Byelsky, after Pushkin). Like *Prince Igor,* Rimsky-Korsakov's operas contributed largely to what many music lovers came to consider typically "Russian" music, though the splashily coloured world they create was in reality Rimsky-Korsakov's own invention.

Mussorgsky composed all or part of several operas. Among them, *Khovanshchina* (to his own libretto; the score completed and orchestrated by Rimsky-Korsakov; posthumous premiere in 1886) bears a family resemblance to *Prince Igor,* particularly in its employment of real and simulated Orientalism, but is more serious and much more confident in tone. Mussorgsky's greatest achievement, and the most worthwhile Russian opera, is *Boris Godunov* (1874; his own libretto, based upon Pushkin's drama and a history of Russia by Nikolay Mikhailovich Karamzin). Boris, the guilty usurper of the throne, dominates this glittering but dour pageant in which the Russian people are present in remarkably forceful choral writing. Mussorgsky's ability to transmit textual points in very condensed music has possibly never been matched. Except at a few weak moments, he made a virtue out of amateurishness and naïveté, fearlessly extracting intense power and theatrical effectiveness from his newly developed techniques. The influence of *Boris Godunov* has been strong on numerous composers of opera both in Russia and elsewhere.

Greatness of *Boris Godunov*

The operatic practice of Peter Ilich Tchaikovsky was very different. For dramatic vigour he substituted clear characterization expressed lyrically, creating, among others, two highly idiosyncratic operas: *Eugene Onegin* (1879; libretto by the composer and Konstantin S. Shilovsky, after Pushkin) and the stronger melodrama *Pikovaya dama* (*The Queen of Spades,* 1890; libretto by Modest Ilich Tchaikovsky, after Pushkin). The personal emotion and the characterization of hero and heroine in *Eugene Onegin* are vivid. In all of Tchaikovsky's operas the highly subjective emotion that long made him the most often performed of orchestral composers is tellingly present. Many consider his other operas, containing much fine music, all unjustly neglected.

Igor Stravinsky turned to opera three times during his long composing career, to near-opera more often. First came *Solovey* (*The Nightingale,* 1914; libretto by the composer and Stepan Nikolayevich Mitusov, after Hans Christian Andersen), which clearly reveals the influence of Rimsky-Korsakov, who had been Stravinsky's teacher. Next among his true operas came *Mavra* (1922; libretto by Boris Kochno, derived from Pushkin), an opera buffa in the unmistakable musical style that made Stravinsky the foremost composer of his era. Then a long period, marked by several near-operas (among them the urgent opera-oratorio *Oedipus Rex,* 1927) elapsed before the appearance of Stravinsky's full-length opera in English, *The Rake's Progress* (libretto by the poets W.H. Auden and Chester Kallman, after Hogarth's engravings, 1951), a neoclassical, austere, but compassionate work.

Sergey Prokofiev composed numerous operas both in his "modern" musical manner and in a harmonically less advanced "socialist realist" style after his return to the Soviet Union in 1934. Among the former, the best and most often staged are the opera buffa, *L'Amour des trois oranges* (*The Love for Three Oranges,* Chicago, 1921; his own libretto), in a musical style that might be called Rimsky-Korsakov updated, and the lurid opera of hallucination, *Angel of Fire* or *The Fiery Angel* (radio premiere 1954; his own libretto after a story by Valery Yakovlevich Bryusov). Of Prokofiev's Soviet operas, the most winning is the gay *Betrothal in a Monastery,* also known as *The Duenna* (1946; libretto by Mira Mendelson based on a play of that name by the 18th-century Irish-born dramatist Richard Brinsley Sheridan). The most ambitious is the massive *War and Peace* (1946; revised, condensed version, 1955; libretto by the composer and Mira Mendelson).

Prokofiev's Soviet operas

The best known Soviet opera outside its homeland, however, is a grim tale of sexual repression and violence by Dmitry Shostakovich originally called *Ledi Makbet Mtsenskogo Uyezda* (*Lady Macbeth of the Mzensk District,* 1934; libretto by the composer and Y. Priess, after a story by Leskov), later revised, after a long period of eclipse caused by government disapproval, as *Katerina Ismaylova* (1963). Numerous other Soviet operas have not been staged outside the Soviet Union or have proved substantially unexportable when so staged.

Later opera in Germany and Austria. Richard Strauss was greeted as the obvious "heir to Wagner" (and Liszt). His worldwide reputation was being established by his orchestral music and lieder (songs) before he turned to opera for the first time. But his pre-eminence among non-Italian composers of opera was established by two "shocking" one-act operas: *Salome* (1905; libretto taken from Oscar Wilde's drama, translated into German by Hedwig Lachmann) and *Elektra* (1909). With the latter work Strauss began a long and fruitful association with the poet and dramatist Hugo von Hofmannsthal as his librettist. Couched in a violent harmonic idiom, requiring huge orchestral forces and leading singers of great vocal power and stamina, *Salome* and *Elektra* seemed to many critics to be Straussian tone poems with added voices, but they soon became, and have remained, part of the standard repertory. They were followed by an altogether different sort of opera, *Der Rosenkavalier* (1911), again with a libretto by Hofmannsthal, a bittersweet comedy notable for the superb musical creation of the central character (the Marschallin) and for three-quarter rhythms that placed this Strauss alongside Johann the Younger as a composer of Viennese waltzes. It marks Strauss's invention of a subtle *parlando* (conversational) style all his own, which he also used to great effect in his later opera.

Strauss's collaboration with Hofmannsthal

Strauss composed 10 operas after *Der Rosenkavalier.* All but one or two of them won wide popularity; none of them displays any constructive or musical characteristics not present in his earlier works. The most successful have been the "chamber opera" *Ariadne auf Naxos* (*Ariadne on Naxos,* 1912; revised 1916); the giant allegory *Die Frau ohne Schatten* (*The Woman Without a Shadow,* 1919), which some writers have called Strauss's masterpiece, whereas others denounce it as confused, even megalomaniac; and *Arabella* (1933), which closely resembles *Der Rosenkavalier* in many details. *Capriccio* (1942), his last opera, is an absorbing characterization of the old argument as to whether words or music should take precedence in opera.

Several harmonically conservative German composers active during and just after Strauss's long career were much less gifted and also less successful. Probably the most notable of them were Hans Pfitzner and Paul Hindemith. The antimodern Pfitzner, partly a belated Wagnerian, composed several operas of melodically long-lined, subjective, at times mystical content which have not reached beyond the German-speaking countries. The best-known is *Palestrina* (1917; his own libretto), dealing with the great Italian composer, in which the austerities of 16th-century counterpoint are oddly mixed with Pfitzner's often abrupt dissonances.

Hindemith damagingly lacked theatrical insight, but was admired for his technical wizardry and lofty aims. He composed some satirical comedies, but came to be heard in opera houses only with the serious *Cardillac* (1926, revised 1952; libretto by Ferdinand Lion, after a tale by E.T.A. Hoffmann) and *Mathis der Maler* (*Mathias the Painter,* 1938; his own libretto on the life of Matthias Grünewald).

If "modernism" seems to be struggling toward birth in the operas of Strauss, Pfitzner, Hindemith, and some others, it sprang fully armed from the music of three Viennese composers: Arnold Schoenberg, Alban Berg, and Anton von Webern, propagators and chief practitioners of what came to be called atonality and 12-tone composition. Webern composed no operas. Schoenberg's first theatrical works—the one-act *Erwartung* (*Expectation,* composed in 1909, performed in 1924; single-character libretto by Marie Pappenheim) and the one-act *"Drama mit Musik" Die glückliche Hand* (*The Hand of Fate,* 1924; his own libretto)—are extremely discordant, thickly and earnestly romantic, even expressionistic, and occasionally use *Sprechstimme,* a variety of vocal emission between speech and song that Schoenberg himself described as "the voice rising and falling relative to the indicated intervals, and everything being bound together with the time and rhythm of the music except where a pause is indicated." Their harmony is unremittingly chromatic.

Schoenberg's first theatrical works

Schoenberg's only comedy, the one-act *Von Heute auf*

Morgen (*From Today to Tomorrow,* 1930; libretto by Max Blonda), is in strictly construed 12-tone texture; following the theories attending that technique, it therefore returned to separate-number construction. Schoenberg's largest opera, left incomplete at his death, was the powerful, oratorio-like *Moses und Aron* (1957; his own libretto). (H.We.)

The two operas of Alban Berg—*Wozzeck* (1925; libretto by the composer, after Georg Büchner's play *Woyzeck*) and *Lulu* (1937; libretto by the composer after Frank Wedekind's plays *Erdgeist* [*Earth-spirit*] and *Die Büchse der Pandora* [*Pandora's Box*])—are among the most powerful, effective music dramas of the 20th century. Well described as "expressionistic, morbid, neurotic, hysterical" as to story, *Wozzeck* seamlessly joins an intensely learned and appropriate score to a melodrama of a poor soldier's helplessness at the hands of his fate. *Wozzeck* is such an intense work that audiences who might be expected to be alienated by its extreme dissonance and "tunelessness" have accepted it as the great opera it is. *Lulu,* virtually finished at the time of Berg's death and later completed by others, is a part-tragic, part-comic drama; it adds film clips and spoken dialogue to the means employed in *Wozzeck.* Although Berg's score was elaborated from a single "tone-row" (arrangement of the 12 tones of a chromatic scale) and though the resultant tonal clashing is not bilked, many passages in *Lulu* appear to show Berg tending toward less dissonance.

Intensity of *Wozzeck*

The most appreciable Germanic musicodramatic composer outside the Viennese orbit has appeared to be Carl Orff (1895–1982), who has juggled many varieties of almost-operatic forms. Best known for his absorption of bawdy medieval student songs into a "scenic oratorio," *Carmina Burana* (1937), Orff worked that singular exploitation of repetitive rhythms, bare harmonies, *ostinati,* and crying vocal colours into a trilogy called *Trionfi* by adding to it *Catulli Carmina* (1943) and *Il Trionfo d'Afrodite* (1953). More conventionally operatic is his one-act comedy *Die Kluge* (*The Clever Girl,* 1943; his own libretto, after a tale by the Brothers Grimm). Probably his major effort in musical drama is another trilogy, consisting of *Antigonae* (1949), *Oedipus der Tyrann* (1959), and *Prometheus* (1968). In it a texture of spoken and declaimed texts is spaced out with incidental music of almost brutal force. Bernd Alois Zimmermann's opera *Die Soldaten* (*The Soldiers,* 1969) is the most successful of the multi-media operas.

Hans Werner Henze is the most recent major operatic composer to come out of Germany. His best-known works are *Elegy for Young Lovers,* his first collaboration with the poets W.H. Auden and Chester Kallman, and *Der junge Lord* (*The Young Lord*), which satirizes German provincial life. He has experimented with other forms of musicodramatic experiment.

Czechoslovakia. The specifically Russian operas of Glinka, Dargomyzhsky, and the Five have parallels in other countries. In what is now Czechoslovakia, the national school effectively began with Bedřich Smetana, best known outside his homeland for the vigorous, highly coloured folk comedy *Prodaná nevěsta* (*The Bartered Bride,* 1866; libretto by Karel Sabina), which determined many aspects of future Czech musical usage as clearly as Borodin and Mussorgsky had set Russian styles. Several of Smetana's other operas, both comic and tragic, remain on Czech stages—most notably the overtly patriotic *Dalibor* (1868) and *Libuše* (1881), both to librettos in Czech translation of originally German texts by Joseph Wenzig, and his comedy *Hubička* (*The Kiss,* 1876). The other leading Czech composer of Smetana's period, Antonín Dvořák, wrote nine operas but remained preponderantly an instrumental composer, never matching the older composer's stage success. Of Dvořák's mature operas, the best known outside Czechoslovakia is the melancholy fairy tale *Rusalka* (libretto by Jaroslav Kvapil), made attractive by his considerable melodic and harmonic gifts.

Production of *The Bartered Bride*

Leoš Janáček was specifically Moravian in musical background, far more harmonically advanced than Smetana and Dvořák, though less adroit technically. He was clearly a 20th-century composer, whose highly individual music, typified by a short-phrased melodic idiom used to catch the speech-rhythm of his native language, was rediscovered after World War II. A follower of Mussorgsky, whose much-discussed "dilettantism" his closely resembles, Janáček is now represented intermittently in non-Czech opera houses chiefly by *Její pastorkyňa* (*Her Foster Daughter,* 1904; changed to *Jenufa* for Janáček's 1916 revision; his libretto derived from a story by Gabriela Preissová), *Kát'a Kabanová* (1921; libretto by Vincenc Červinky), *Příhody lišky bystroušky* (*The Cunning Little Vixen,* 1924; libretto by the composer), and *Věc Makropulos* (*The Makropoulos Case,* 1926; libretto by the composer), each of which has a character and milieu of its own while preserving the peculiarly individual setting of the Czech language.

Hungary and Poland. The most important Hungarian operas of the early 20th century, neither of them representing its composer at his finest, are the one-act *Duke Bluebeard's Castle* (1918; libretto by Béla Balázs), by Béla Bartók, and the ballad opera *Háry János,* by Zoltán Kodály (1926; libretto by Béla Paulini and Zsolt Harsányi), both of which have become more familiar in concert performance or excerpts than in staged productions. The most influential and popular of Polish nationalist operas, *Halka* (1854; libretto by Włodzimierz Wolski), was composed by Stanisław Moniuszko; he also wrote an admirable comedy, *The Haunted Manor* (1865; libretto by Jan Chichiński). Of 20th-century Polish operas, perhaps the most substantial is the much less popular *Król Roger* (*King Roger,* 1926; libretto by Jarosław Iwakiewicz) by Karol Szymanowski.

Spain. Spanish operatic nationalism began with Felipe Pedrell, more influential as teacher-propagandist than as producing composer. Of his 10 operas, the most imposing were to have been contained in a trilogy, based on a Catalan libretto by Victor Balaguer, but only the first two sections, *Los Pirineos* (*The Pyrenees*) and *La Celestina,* were completed and only the first was staged (1902). Of the more familiar Spanish composers, both Isaac Albéniz and Enrique Granados composed operas of strongly Spanish colour that have lapsed from the repertory—Albéniz particularly in the comic one-act *Pepita Jiménez* (1896), Granados in the semi-veristic *Goyescas* (1916; libretto by Fernando Periquet y Zuaznabar), the score of which clearly reveals its origin in a suite of piano pieces. The best results of Spanish operatic nationalism (possibly because more than a little tinged with internationalism) are two very different operas by Manuel de Falla: the specifically Andalusian *La vida breve* (*Brief Life;* libretto by Carlos Fernández Shaw; first staged in French translation, 1913) and the one-act *El retablo de Maese Pedro* (*Master Peter's Puppet Show,* 1923; text by the composer, after a scene in *Don Quixote*), in effect a chamber opera for marionettes. (H.We./Ed.)

England. English opera, which had languished for centuries, was revitalized by the theatrical talent of the eclectic Benjamin Britten, whose stage works show a remarkable sympathy for the human predicament expressed in readily accessible, deeply felt music. His masterpiece is the gloomy, forceful *Peter Grimes* (1945; libretto by Montague Slater). Among Britten's other operas to win widespread stagings are the chamber operas *The Rape of Lucretia* (1946; libretto by Ronald Duncan) and *Albert Herring* (1947; libretto by Eric Crozier), the all-male *Billy Budd* (1951; libretto by E.M. Forster and Crozier; based upon Herman Melville's story), the eerily effective *Turn of the Screw* (1954; libretto by Myfanwy Piper, after the Henry James story), *A Midsummer Night's Dream* (1960; libretto by Britten and Peter Pears, from Shakespeare), three church operas to librettos by William Plomer (1964–68), and *Owen Wingrave* (1971; libretto by Myfanwy Piper). So far, less popular outside England are the idiosyncratic operas, to his own complex librettos, of Sir Michael Tippett: *The Midsummer Marriage* (1955), *King Priam* (1962), and *The Knot Garden* (1970).

Benjamin Britten's works

United States. American contributions to international opera, after a 19th-century desert of imitation German and French operas, became much more numerous after World War II. It is possible here to mention only one composer and a few isolated operas that have evoked enduring resonance. The most often performed of contemporary operatic composers has been the Italo-American Gian Carlo Menotti. Using his own librettos, he has produced, in a variety of structural styles, a series of Puccini-derived melodramas and sentimental tragedies of considerable popular appeal, among them *The Medium* (1946), *The Consul* (1950), *Amahl and the Night Visitors* (composed for television performance, 1951), and *The Saint of Bleecker Street* (1954). He also wrote the libretto for the first, mildly successful, opera of Samuel Barber, *Vanessa* (1958; awarded 1958 Pulitzer Prize). Barber's second large opera, *Antony and Cleopatra* (1966; libretto derived from Shakespeare by Franco Zeffirelli), commissioned to inaugurate the second Metropolitan Opera House in New York, was a failure and vanished quickly from performance.

Menotti's works

A unique niche is occupied by the two operas that Virgil Thomson composed to texts by Gertrude Stein arranged by Maurice Grosser: the Spanish-tinted *Four Saints in Three Acts* (1934) and *The Mother of Us All* (1947), a delicious flow of invention around the figure of Susan B. Anthony. Their fragile but real durability has resulted from Thomson's singable, apt folk-based setting of texts that alternate among the apparently nonsensical, the satiric, and the emotionally moving. Perhaps the most important national opera consistently in repertory is George Gershwin's *Porgy and Bess* (1935; libretto by DuBose Heyward and Ira Gershwin), a blending of folk opera and American musical comedy, which has had no recognizable descendant of high quality. Within the United States—not to count the "workshop operas" and simplified semi-folk near-operas that many American composers recently have favoured—two of the most frequently performed recent American operas are the folklike "Western" *Ballad of Baby Doe* (libretto by John Latouche, 1956), by Douglas Moore (1893–1969) and the melodramatic, "Southern" *Susannah* (libretto by the composer, 1955) by Carlisle Floyd.

THE FUTURE OF OPERA

The existing audience for the standard repertory operas throughout the world is enormous. If to it be added the large number of people attending workshop, college and university, music school, amateur, and semi-amateur performances—both of the same repertory and of operas created for those special purposes—the statistics suggest that all is well with opera. Yet by the late 20th century the art of opera had become largely a museum art. Constant repetitions of a relatively small group of operas of the past far exceed creation of new works that can be categorized with the finest of those mentioned in this article. What, then, are the future prospects for this art, now nearing four centuries of fertile existence?

The prospects for the creation of major new operas are poor. How could they be better when the two major components of opera—dramatic literature and music—are both in a period of fundamental crisis? Outside the opera house, audiences for the spoken theatre and for concert and recital have been oscillating widely while economic problems have multiplied swiftly. Some writers have seen the future of opera in new varieties of semioperatic "happenings" and other mixed forms, others in the numerous pieces written and composed specifically for workshop and school staging. For the large paying audience, however, opera continues to mean more or less traditional performances of the operas of Mozart, Verdi, Wagner, Puccini, Richard Strauss, and a few others.

Revivals of long-neglected operas have meanwhile attracted audiences in many opera houses (notably, to speak only of the United States, with such companies as the New York City Opera and those in Chicago, Dallas, San Francisco, and Santa Fe). That trend, which freshens the repertory in the absence of new operas, has brought back most noticeably some of the bel canto masterpieces of Rossini, Donizetti, and Bellini. These revivals, in turn, have affected the otherwise tradition-bound activities of record-publishing companies, whose reluctance to issue operas in any idiom more recent than that of Britten has reflected general public taste. Ballet, which flowered during the period between the two world wars, has fallen heir to what might, under different conditions, have become a large audience for operas employing "advanced" harmonic and melodic idioms.

The bel canto revival

Until the harmonic and melodic idioms of contemporary composers and the taste of the large paying audience converge, until the crises in style and subject matter no longer prevent librettists from writing meaningfully for that same audience, the present situation in opera houses can be expected to continue with only an occasional foray into less immediately hospitable territory. Predictions about future developments in any art are especially hazardous, and the fact that opera has survived more than three and a half centuries of social, political, literary, musical, and other changes without losing either its audience or its particular glamour strongly suggests that it will evolve ways out of its current predicaments. What remains true is that if this greatest of musicodramatic forms is to approach its absorbing best, it must, in one of numerous possible ways, be what Livia Miragoli (1924) defined it as being:

> a work of unique art, then, in which the value of the literary element is higher or lower as it is better or less well adapted to being combined with music, the musical element as it is a better or a less good response to the contents of the text.

(H.We.)

Jazz

Jazz has not been defined in technical terms. It diverges widely, even violently, from all previous canons of musical composition and performance and is immediately distinguishable. Certainly, it is the most enigmatic of musical forms, never respecting any of the received truths about itself. It is generally accepted, for instance, that all jazz is improvised, which is untrue; that jazz is synonymous with syncopation, which is even more untrue; that jazz owes its idiosyncratic nature to the ingenious subtleties of its rhythmic pulse, whereas for at least the first half of the 20th century the precise opposite was true, its rhythmic conception being extremely rigid and formalized. As jazz is neither purely composed music nor purely extemporized music and as it cannot be accurately notated, a logical positivist would have no difficulty demonstrating that, like the beach of the German philosopher Hegel, which was neither sea nor land, jazz does not exist at all. As jazz is essentially the musical experience of a passing moment, which cannot be repeated in quite the same way, in a sense the most important figure in all its history was Thomas A. Edison, who invented the phonograph.

A loose definition that has served well enough for most of jazz history is that it is a music where the performer plays melodic variations on a given harmonic base against a regular rhythmic pulse; in the latter half of the 20th century even this definition became unacceptable, because the avant-garde movement dispensed with prearranged harmonic signals, indeed, with any kind of form. Difficulties of definition are aggravated by the fact that the terminology of jazz retains its validity only within the jazz context, so that to describe, say, the leading figures of the harmonic revolution of the 1940s as "Modernists" is to beg the question of Modernism as a movement in the music world at large that has been flourishing throughout the present century. An example is the chord of the minor seventh (for instance, C–E♭–G–B♭), which the standard-bearers of jazz Modernism held aloft like a banner but which in a "classical" music context had long become venerable through the French composer Claude Debussy and the school of musical Impressionists. Indeed, much earlier still, in 1858, the Russian author Ivan Turgenev could make one of his heroes sit at the piano "entranced over minor sevenths." In the same way, other terms, such as traditional, progressive, and classical, have very specialized meanings within the jazz world.

Because of the oddly eccentric nature of its whole being, jazz has enjoyed the questionable benefits of definitions that are either tautological—"Jazz music is any music played by jazz musicians"—or confusing to the layman—"Jazz is a matter of lip-technique." What can be said with confidence is that, whereas in more conventional musical areas the artist is fundamentally an executant expressing the findings of the creative mind of the composer, in jazz

The executant as the composer

the performer is usually his own composer. Within the strict meaning of the term, there can be no such thing as a jazz theme, although of course some themes will lend themselves to the jazz idiom more readily than others. The customer unable to acquire the recording of Brahms's *Fourth Symphony* conducted by Herbert von Karajan would probably settle for someone else's recording of that work, but the buyer thwarted in his attempt to buy the jazz musician Duke Ellington's version of "Caravan" might well accept as a substitute anything else played by Ellington. That is why, in jazz, there is at least one truism that has always applied: the performer playing a theme always tries to make it sound not like itself but like himself.

ORIGINS

The birth pangs of jazz are perhaps of more concern to the musicologist, the social historian, and even the anthropologist than the musician. The multiracial origins of jazz are clear enough. Had it not been for the traffic in slaves from West Africa to the United States, jazz would never have evolved, either in the United States or Africa, for jazz is the expression in music of the African native who is isolated both socially and geographically from his natural environment.

Among the West African tribes supplying victims for the slave trade, music, and especially vocal and percussive music, had developed in a way quite unknown to the academic Western ear. Scales and harmony were purely intuitive, and music was deployed less as an abstract aesthetic gesture than as a specific language conveying subtle shades of meaning and emotion. By varying the pitch of a note or changing the inflection of the voice while uttering a musical sound, the performer could convey far more concrete messages than his sophisticated Western counterpart. If his art was cruder, his function was more practicable. Although most of the prehistory of jazz is speculative, the flexibility of this musical language, unfettered either by conventional ideas of correctness or by precedent, resulted in the unwitting development of a scale utterly original so far as the West was concerned. This scale, in which the third (E in the key of C), or mediant, and the seventh (B in the key of C), or leading tone, were flattened and thereby turned into what are sometimes referred to as "blue notes," became the basis of the language that eventually emerged as jazz. The transfer of these West African tribal traditions to the slave fields, railways, and rivers of the southern U.S. was of advantage to oppressed and oppressor alike, the slave obviously taking solace in the cultural memory of his own collective past, the slaveowner encouraging work songs in the same spirit as an infantry general might approve of military bands—for the stimulus they gave to work rate. Many of the early examples of primitive vocal jazz relate closely to the labours being performed, and the content of the lyrics is a reminder that not only the cotton plantations but also the levees and railroads of the Deep South were created and maintained by slave labour. Joe "King" Oliver's "Lift 'Em Up Joe" and many of the songs of Huddie Ledbetter (Leadbelly) are examples of the work-song convention surviving as art long after its original functional need had declined.

The jazz scale

There was another major influence on the evolution of Afro-American vocal style. If the slave could derive no comfort from the laissez-faire philosophy of his owners, at least he could draw spiritual consolation from their religion. Until the beginning of the 19th century, the established church, by performing a series of comically dishonest intellectual cartwheels, had managed to reconcile Christianity with the possession of slaves, the argument being that, although one Christian must not enslave another, it was acceptable for him to enslave a savage. This meant that the work of the missionary was actually rendered sacrilegious, and throughout the 18th century the absurdity of such an attitude became more and more exposed, until about 1790 the Methodist movement began to address itself to the redemption of the souls of men who until now had not been thought to have possessed any. This missionary campaign flourished for almost 100 years and had one of the most astounding outcomes of any evangelizing crusade in history, one that the Christian Church could never have anticipated. By attempting to convert the slaves to Christianity, the missionaries achieved the Africanization of their own hymnbooks.

By adapting his own ritual music to the liturgy of the Christian Church, by contributing, as a member of a congregation, to the creation of new tunes, or by making his own variations on the existing ones, the slave and his emancipated descendants developed the spiritual to the point where, in the form of hymns, ring shouts, revival chants, camp songs, and funeral songs, it gradually merged into a semi-secular tradition. Significantly, ragtime, that coarse yet disarming bridge between the old songs of slavery and emergent jazz, figured unmistakably in the accompaniment of hymns such as "Good Lord'll Help Me on my Way" several years before ragtime music was published officially under its own name. This vast influence of Africanized church music on the development of jazz underlines one more fallacy about the music, which is that it was always linked irrevocably to the lowlife. Its connections with the brothels of Louisiana and the saloons of Chicago tell only half the story, for jazz has been concerned with sanctity as well as with sin, has been a sacred music as well as a profane one. Its links with Christianity and particularly with the act of worship and the rituals of birth, marriage, and death have proved so durable that they remain unbroken to this day, not only in the person of gospel singers, such as the late Mahalia Jackson and Sister Rosetta Tharpe, but also in more secular figures who insist on the church as their primary source of musical inspiration.

Development of the spiritual

Not all of the early Africanized church music was vocal, although, naturally, any instrumental playing was bound to be crude in conception, execution, and instrumentation. The slave generations obviously had access neither to conventional musical education nor to legitimate orchestral instruments, and, even after the liberation that followed the War between the States, such things as education and conventional musical instruments remained, if not impossible, at least difficult to acquire. The New Orleans pioneer drummer Warren "Baby" Dodds is said to have made his first pair of drumsticks from the legs of a kitchen chair, and the semilegendary cornet player Charles "Buddy" Bolden was seen at times to thrust half a coconut shell, a bathroom plunger, and an old derby hat into the bell of his instrument to do service as mutes. The early jazz artists, it would seem, improvised not only the music they played but also the instruments with which they played it.

Improvised instruments of the early days

A key figure, because he personifies the antipathetic traditions of religious piety and worldly musical wit and also the tensions created by the unorthodoxies of musical education of so many of the pioneer jazz figures, is the pianist-composer-singer Thomas "Fats" Waller. Waller was born into a religious family the head of which was a minister of the Abyssinian Baptist Church who regarded jazz, to quote his son, "as music from the devil's workshop." Waller, a brilliant natural musician (see below), taught himself the piano and soon developed an outstanding gift for composition. His commercial as well as artistic success was enormous, but it seems reasonable to conclude, both from Waller's own occasional remarks and from the evidence of his love for the organ and the presence in his repertory of Bach, Liszt, and Rimsky-Korsakov, that Waller was a formal musician manqué.

The generation of men such as Bolden created the earliest jazz traditions. Liberated but not freed, cast on to the open labour market for the first time, and endowed with a musical tradition self-formed but speedily secularized, the men of Bolden's time had two problems to face, no less daunting simply because they were mere subconscious anxieties. How were they to arrive at some code of artistic behaviour when making communal music and for whom were they to play the music? Clearly, if jazz were to shed its religious connotations, it must become a functional music, and, equally clearly, if formal music offered neither any precedents for procedure nor even a polite interest, then jazz would have to create its own.

The latter third of the 19th century was a crucial point in the prehistory of jazz—a time when jazz was interacting with church music, with the white commercial world of dances, soirées, drawing-room ballads, and concerts, with opera, with the theatre, with vague occasional wisps from the European tradition, and a time when the Southern black was learning how to live with uneasy freedom; during this period the traditions of jazz were slowly forged. It is a period and a process impossible to document with any accuracy, for obvious reasons, and about which even the most basic terms have remained in contention. The institution of ragtime piano playing, for instance, is regarded by many as no more than a subdivision of emerging jazz piano styles, but, by many others, it is regarded as a distinct, separate form, marked out from jazz because its repertory consisted largely of formal, composed works rather than slight themes for improvisation. There also exist several abstruse theories about regional variations in jazz styles. Nobody has ever decided to the satisfaction of anyone else where the "folk" music of, say, the itinerant guitarists of the Southwest ends and jazz proper begins. But, indisputably, by the beginning of the 20th century, a few jazz forms had begun to combine into a recognizable tradition, and the hub of this development was located at the Louisiana seaport of New Orleans, where the dominant form among jazz musicians was the blues.

The blues. Much of the confusion over the identity of the blues has been caused by the word itself, which has had to perform a dual purpose. It has been used for at least 200 years by writers as a synonym for a depressed mood and, more strictly, as a specific musical term, so that misconceptions have been perpetuated that all blues music must by definition be concerned with depressed subjects and even that only depressed musicians play it. Another belief about the blues, that it is the acid test of a performer's improvising ability, is more accurate for reasons intimately connected with its harmonic structure.

The blues as a test of a jazz performer

In jazz, a blues sequence extends over 12 bars, containing three harmonic crisis points, and only these give the improviser hints as to where his melodic variations should go and what kind of musical mood they should imply. The paradox is that, sparse though these are, they have a vast emotional potential for the gifted player to discover, so that, ever since the beginnings of instrumental jazz, a player's ability with a blues sequence has been a guide to his true talent. Perhaps the most extraordinary thing about the blues has been its durability; it has retained its attraction for soloists of all eras and schools, changing with new approaches and movements but remaining intrinsically itself. The black composer William Christopher ("W.C.") Handy was an important figure in the development of the blues. He was fundamentally a kind of folklorist-orchestrator who took his themes from the blues performers he heard around him, wrote them down, and harmonized them. Some blues was published before Handy's, but, as a result of his disseminating work, jazz players by the late 1920s were freely improvising and spontaneously inventing melodies on blues chord sequences. His most important compositions were the "Memphis Blues" (1911) and "St. Louis Blues" (1914).

Exploration and improvisation. A close textual analysis of the harmonies employed in the blues since the beginnings of recorded jazz reveals the process of ceaseless embellishment of the original sequence, and this process may stand as a symbol for the whole of jazz history. In effect, the story of jazz has been a saga of harmonic exploration. Most of the jazz pioneers were men without musical schooling or formal knowledge who had to evolve a musical language and harmonic vocabulary by trial and error. They were artists intent on hammering out some formality of procedure, some kind of convention that would reconcile the individual freedom of each player to express himself with the adherence to the demands of the ensemble without which all performances would disintegrate. This is the crowning paradox of the art of jazz: it is at once the art of the individual musician and an almost exclusively communal exercise.

Although jazz criticism has divided the music into three equal categories—traditional, mainstream, and modern—harmonic exploration and the growth of melodic vocabulary have comprised a constant, continuing process in jazz history. New labels have been attached to new styles not when some dramatic advance has been made but when the cumulative weight of several years' findings has caused people to realize that the music has steadily been changing its personality. The three compartments are useful as an approximation, not an arbitrary judgment. As the harmonic vocabulary of the jazz musician has been extended and as the degree of technical sophistication has increased accordingly, so have new conventions been forged, although it is not true that, as one style established itself, others have been superseded. Uniquely and because of the very fast pace of its evolution (covering an advance from primitivism to neoclassicism in little more than half a century), several schools of jazz have existed concurrently.

EARLY JAZZ STYLES

The New Orleans style. The rigid convention of collective improvisation, based on a specific instrumentation, flourished in Louisiana in the early years of the 20th century, and two powerful factors dictating the formulation of the convention were probably the social and the functional. In the social life of the black, community music played a more prominent part than perhaps can now be easily comprehended. There was almost no social activity in New Orleans then that did not imply a musical corollary. There was live music for births, weddings, christenings, funerals, picnics, parades, marches, and all kinds of celebrations. A great deal of this music was naturally played outdoors, which may explain the unchallenged dominance of the trumpet over all other instruments. All the early leaders of New Orleans jazz were trumpeters, with the line of succession passing from Bolden, through historically documented musicians such as Freddie Keppard and Joe "King" Oliver, and down to Louis Armstrong. New Orleans also produced brilliant players on other instruments, particularly a school of musicians who effected a limpid, highly attractive clarinet style, but leadership was almost exclusively the preserve of trumpeters like Bolden and Oliver.

Roles of the instruments in New Orleans jazz

In the classic New Orleans style, the trumpet's duty is to state and embellish the melodic line of the theme. The trombone stresses the harmonic root notes, providing also a solidity of resonance on which the other performers may build. Above the trumpet soars the clarinet voice, weaving further variations on the same harmonies. Thus, the three voices, linked yet independent, are able to compile between them the simple triads (chords consisting of a root and the third and fifth tone above it) that were the basis of all jazz harmony at this period of its development. And, as all three were playing together throughout the performance, the band, though small, was able to maintain a surprising degree of volume.

There was a vital reason why the ensemble convention was adhered to so faithfully. In New Orleans or, indeed, anywhere else at that time, there were few musicians capable of playing an extended solo, even had the rules of their game permitted them to do so. Apart from a handful of virtuosos, the idea that a jazz performance should consist of a succession of solos would have been unthinkable for the simple reason that there was no such thing as a succession of soloists. But the musicians were developing at an astonishing rate, and, in retrospect, it can be seen that the classic New Orleans style, rigid as it had to be, was doomed by its very nature: there was no question that, in time, a player or group of players would emerge for whom the constriction of the ensemble was intolerable. When this player arrived, then the whole New Orleans conception of tightly integrated ensemble improvisation would become obsolete. Another reason why the frailty of the New Orleans tradition is more apparent now than in the heyday of that style is the fact that jazz as a musical lubricant to oil the social machine was restricted largely to the New Orleans lowlife. Although the myth-making process has drawn a picture of jazz limited strictly to the brothels and sporting houses of Storyville, the town's bordello district, there were, of course, many instances of the music splashing over into the life of the city at large. Nonetheless, jazz, linked to the black performer and the social events of black life in the city, retained a connotation of sin and dissipation for many years after the New Orleans pioneers were forgotten. The saxophonist Sidney Bechet, one of the most gifted of all the New Orleans musicians, insisted in his autobiography that the word jazz in its original form of jass was local slang for sexual intercourse, and the evidence in favour of Bechet's assertion seems overwhelming.

Supposed origin of the word jazz

These brothels were thus a link in the jazz musician's economic chain, for many employed bands or, at the very least, a house pianist whose job was to thump out ragtime rhythms against a background of red plush and gilt. The collapse of the Storyville economy was naturally disastrous for the working musician. In 1917 the United States secretary of the Navy decreed that, in view of the repeated fighting and violence involving seamen on leave in the city, the New Orleans red-light district must be closed down. The sense of outrage and the disarming worldliness of the city are reflected in the official statement by the then mayor, Martin Behrman:

> Preterpermitting the pros and cons of legislative recognition of prostitution as a necessary evil in a seaport the size of New Orleans, our city government has believed that the situation could be administered more easily and satisfactorily by confining it within a prescribed area. Our experience has taught us that the reasons for this are unanswerable, but the Navy Department of the Federal Government has decided otherwise.

The theory that the closing of Storyville brought the heyday of New Orleans jazz to an abrupt end is one of those critical platitudes excused by the fact that it is largely true. Jazz did not, however, immediately stop in New Orleans, nor was the migration north of the musicians sudden or absolute, nor had jazz until then been unknown in the North. As early as 1917, the year of the Storyville edict, the Original Dixieland Jass Band, a group of white Southerners with a comically inflated sense of their own importance as musical innovators, had introduced jazz to the patrons of Reisenweber's restaurant in New York and recorded two compositions.

One potent evangelizing factor was the riverboat, which would ply up and down the Mississippi, often with a jazz band aboard. More than one white middle-class jazz pioneer has testified that the first jazz he ever heard came floating across the water from one of these boats as they approached the levee of some Southern port of call. The accessibility of Europe was also a factor at a surprisingly early point in the music's history. In 1919 the Southern Syncopated Orchestra, with Sidney Bechet as its star performer, played in London, there attracting the notice of a Swiss conductor, Ernest Ansermet, who was the first distinguished figure of formal music to react favourably to jazz and to discern in it uniquely vital qualities.

The spread of jazz to Europe

The main force pushing the New Orleans musician north was his need to find employment, and perhaps the most significant sequence of events after the closing of Storyville was that involving Joe "King" Oliver. Early in 1918 Oliver, acknowledged trumpet champion of New Orleans, migrated north to Chicago. By 1920 he had become a popular bandleader there, and two years later, wanting to increase the size of his band, he sent to New Orleans for the most brilliant of his disciples and, indeed, of all the jazz musicians who came out of the city, Louis Daniel Armstrong. From this point on, jazz evolved from a local musical dialect into an international language, proliferating in geographical range and in stylistic variation to a degree that astonished those of the New Orleans founding fathers who lived long enough to watch the process for themselves.

The Louis Armstrong style. Armstrong may partly stand as a representative symbol of the history of the music itself. A trumpeter of freakish gifts, he performed at least three feats—two aesthetic, one sociological—for which he will be remembered as the most influential jazz musician of all time. He took the classic style of his native city and split it at the seams through his limitless ability as an imaginative soloist. The moment his style began to mature, the convention of ensemble playing was outmoded, and he established the primacy of the improvising soloist. Then, having liberated the player from an exclusively team performance, he unwittingly codified the vocabulary of the soloist in a series of famous recordings between 1925 and 1928. These recordings, featuring his groups the Hot Five and the Hot Seven, emphasize the enormous gulf between Armstrong and even the best of his contemporaries. They also show how he summarized all that had gone before and enriched the jazz tradition with a whole range of melodic effects relevant ever after.

The Hot Five and Hot Seven recordings

Several of the performances of the Hot Five and Hot Seven are traditional blues, successively asserting the power of the idiom in a way not to be equalled for at least a generation, until the rise of Charlie Parker. Still more important was Armstrong's success as an evangelist for the jazz cause. By the late 1920s, quickly graduating from the strictly specialist environment of his formative years into being a Broadway and nightclub star, he was the first jazz personality to become a national and then an international figure. Many with no particular interest in jazz were utterly beguiled by his genius. His sense of comedy, his career in Hollywood, his spectacular physical appearance and mannerisms, and, above all, his extraordinary vocal style, all contributed to this process. By using his voice in the same way that other musicians used their instruments, Armstrong, usually dispensing with words and substituting for them an odd, wholly idiosyncratic language of sounds, popularized scat singing. Had he not drifted into the world of entertainment at large, jazz might never have won the widespread currency it did. From 1930 on, he never really found himself outflanked by others and so never developed his musicianship more fully, his vitality enabling him to retain a hold on his art almost to the end of his life in 1971.

In his failure to develop, Armstrong was typical of most jazz musicians, who have generally become reconciled to the style formulated at a comparatively early time of life. Although the music itself seems to evolve, individuals hardly ever do so. The recorded evidence to support this theory is there, but it is usually overlooked in the hunt for fresh effects and styles. Although Armstrong was to improve vastly in the years following his decision to join Oliver in Chicago, his classic style was already becoming permanent before he had ever left his home town.

Chicago style. Armstrong's arrival in Chicago, added to the burgeoning of the speakeasies of the Prohibition era (the illegal drinking establishment became the 1920s equivalent, so far as the jazz musician was concerned, of the Louisiana brothels of the previous decade), made that city the new centre of jazz. By the mid-1920s it was becoming clear that young, white, imitative musicians were quickly learning the lessons taught by men such as Armstrong. One of the better derivative groups of white musicians was the New Orleans Rhythm Kings, but the real flowering of white talent began a little later, farther north, in time causing the rise of a new style of playing jazz, which was a compromise between the ensemble tradition of New Orleans and Armstrong's solo power. In Chicago style, the triumvirate of trumpet, trombone, and clarinet was retained, though the saxophone was becoming much more common by the end of the decade. Although performances usually began and ended with a rousing ensemble variation of the theme, the central part of the performance usually consisted of a string of solos.

Flowering of white talent

Because the term Chicago style is neither strictly geographically accurate nor musicologically precise, its umbrella usually covers stylists of widely contrasting or even antipathetic talents. The leading player of the style was Leon Bismarck "Bix" Beiderbecke, a self-taught cornetist and pianist whose pure tone and introspective curiosity about harmonic theory mark him as the exact opposite of Armstrong, whose intuitive style was rooted in a radically different racial background (Bix was middle class, the son of German immigrants).

Beiderbecke, whose recordings of "I'm Coming Virginia," "Way Down Yonder in New Orleans," and "Singin' the Blues" have become classics of the genre, was also responsible for one of the most remarkable and apocalyptic of all jazz recordings, the piano solo of his own composition, "In a Mist." In this fragment are strangely fused the honky-tonk beginnings of Bix's early musical life and the subtler overtones of those modern classical composers

Beiderbecke's significance

whose recitals he attended and whose comparatively complex harmony caused him to ask the question: "Why should the jazzman be limited to the simplest triads when his conservatory-trained fellow musician has recourse to so many more variegated effects?" Although this has remained the most vital of all the questions posed by jazz, Beiderbecke did not live long enough to see it answered. He was still a young man when he died, technically of pneumonia, actually of frustration, self-neglect, disenchantment—ailments that can destroy any creative artist whose sensibilities far outstrip his technical equipment. Beiderbecke, the first patron saint of jazz, has remained the archetypal figure of the playing fool, the instinctive creator who operated against the frenetic background of illicit stills and gang warfare.

Racial segregation was long the rule in the recording studios, so posterity has tended to have a false view of the mingling of musicians in the 1920s. These players were by no means unaware of each other, as a glance at the recording catalogs of the period might suggest. Armstrong and Beiderbecke, for instance, admired each other's playing. The traffic in ideas was generally one-way, from black to white, but the white musician was occasionally something more than a plagiarist. One of these was the Texan trombonist Jack Teagarden, a musician of remarkable fluency and assurance even at the start of his career in the middle 1920s. After being associated largely with the Chicago-style groups of his first years in the North, Teagarden often worked with Armstrong, to whose All-Stars he belonged during 1947–51. Like Armstrong, he used his voice as a useful second instrument, and, like Armstrong, he retained his creative ability throughout his life. In retrospect, the recordings he made with the young white musicians of the late 1920s and early 1930s show an amazing poise and maturity. The other white Chicagoan who affected the course of jazz history was the clarinetist Benny Goodman. Born in Chicago, he was a child prodigy, a master of Chicago idiom while still in his teens, and destined to lead jazz into new areas.

Strictly speaking, Goodman's clarinet style was hardly original, consisting as it did of a brilliantly executed synthesis of all that had gone before, with particular reference to the limpid fluency of the New Orleans player Jimmie Noone; but Goodman brought to the playing of jazz a technical expertise, an academic intelligence, a speed of thought not heard before. In time his classically based style became ossified, and Goodman himself came to turn more and more frequently to playing Brahms and Mozart; but he remained the most prolific, technically accomplished, and melodically resourceful of the white musicians generally designated as the Chicagoans, though he was later dismissed by some as a peripheral rather than a central figure in jazz history.

LATER DEVELOPMENTS

The emergence of the virtuoso. Throughout the 1920s, techniques were steadily becoming more efficient, thinking more sophisticated, harmonic exploration gradually more daring, so that many styles that were to flower during the soloist's golden age of the 1930s were already being shaped. One of the most gifted of all the musicians in jazz history, Coleman Hawkins, a tenor saxophonist, virtually single-handedly raised the status of that instrument. His work was characterized by a deep, passionate tone, which may be taken as the working definition of "hot" music, by sequences of ingeniously related arpeggios and, above all, by an indefinable sense of form that enabled him to transmute successions of fragmentary phrases into a corporate whole. This sense of form, unteachable but unmistakable when encountered, had already distinguished the truly gifted improviser from the merely talented, and Hawkins, particularly in slower ballads, possessed this gift to a remarkable degree. His outstanding recordings are scattered over five decades. Especially noteworthy are his version of "One Hour," made in 1929, one of the very first recordings by a racially mixed group and one of the very first on which the tenor saxophone in jazz approaches maturity; his famous recording of "Body and Soul" in 1939, a performance so finely constructed that it has long since come to acquire the standing of formal composition; and some sides he made with a cosmopolitan band in Paris in 1937, of which "Out of Nowhere" was a remarkable exposition of the art of romantic extemporization. From 1934 to 1939 Hawkins travelled in Europe, inspiring European musicians to attain fluency in what was at that time an essentially alien art.

Hawkins' development of saxophone technique

The development of jazz piano. There have been deviations of style and approach on all instruments throughout jazz history, giving rise to rival "schools" the differing precepts of which were sometimes the centre of bitter debate, but the case of the piano in jazz is unique in the way that two antipathetic styles emerged and, at least for a time, developed concurrently but independently. These two approaches, embodying contrasting philosophies, were "stride" and "trumpet-style" piano playing. The stride style, whose roots in the early jazz past are obvious enough, is based on the premise that any instrument that makes it possible for the performer to play two or more notes simultaneously and therefore to create a harmonic as well as melodic effect ought to deploy those possibilities as far as is practicable. At their best, the stride pianists have produced work teeming with an orchestral richness, yet they have rarely been the kind of players to produce a single melodic line that might conceivably be transposed to a different instrument. The best stride exponents, pounding out 10-note chords, stressing the rhythmic pulse with great muscularity in the left hand, have been men whose music is full of harmonic possibilities and enchanting rhythmic variation.

Probably the most important stride pianist was James P. Johnson, one of the most resourceful figures in jazz history and a rare personality among the pioneers in that his musical accomplishments enabled him to compose and orchestrate at a period when such abilities were rare. Apart from his purely jazz activities, Johnson wrote some early film music, a tone poem, and a ballet; he also enjoyed great success as a songwriter, producing the "One Hour" that Hawkins (and also Louis Armstrong) recorded so finely and "Runnin' Wild."

Johnson presided over what came to be known as the Harlem group of pianists, whose stride playing in the 1920s made them virtually one-man jazz bands. Johnson's great friend and rival was Willie "The Lion" Smith, and their two unofficial pupils were Thomas "Fats" Waller and Edward Kennedy "Duke" Ellington. In both cases, the stride style underwent the most astonishing changes. Waller is perhaps the only example in all jazz of the pupil outstripping his masters. Apart from the irresistible strength and wit of his piano playing and his gifts as a composer ("Honeysuckle Rose," "Ain't Misbehavin'," "Blue Turning Grey Over You," and literally hundreds of others), Waller, like Armstrong, was a natural buffoon and stage extrovert, capitalizing on these gifts to become a popular as well as a jazz figure. Ellington's subsequent career (reviewed below) was even more remarkable, and both he and Waller acknowledged their stylistic debt to Johnson and Smith. Ironically, although the stride school avoided the dogmatic melodic statement in favour of the implied harmonic one, at least three of its greatest practitioners—Johnson, Waller, and Ellington—were also successful songwriters.

Events eventually overtook the stride school, and its eclipse may be dated from the moment in the late 1920s when Earl "Fatha" Hines, yet another outstanding jazz pianist, who augmented his income by working as a songwriter, saw that, in addition to stating the harmony in the left hand, the pianist might well emulate the single-note instruments, such as the trumpet, in creating with the right hand linear improvisation producing melodic single-note variations on the melody. Probably the two great influences on Hines that helped crystallize his style were the pianist Teddy Weatherford, to whom Hines acknowledged a debt of inspiration, and Louis Armstrong, with whom Hines worked during the Hot Five and Hot Seven period. Armstrong's apparently limitless powers of invention must have shown Hines how the same kind of melodic aphorisms could be produced by a pianist.

Hines's right-hand improvisations

Hines, a pianist of amazing technical command and tireless energy, had a profound influence on the development of jazz piano. His findings eventually led to the eclipse of the stride style, especially when in the early 1940s the new Modernism preferred the pianist with the ability to create right-hand, single-note lines. In the 1930s the most accomplished follower of Hines was Teddy Wilson, after which time the work of pioneer Modernists such as Bud Powell and, later, the Canadian Oscar Peterson showed at least to some degree a corroboration of Hines's methods.

Tatum's unorthodox technique

Art Tatum, one of the greatest and most controversial of jazz musicians and pianists, had a style too personal to be categorized. For him, stride and trumpet-style were not so much approaches to piano playing as incidents in the course of a single casual chorus, just two of many effects that Tatum had at his fingertips. Almost totally blind, Tatum developed a technique as unorthodox as it was infallible, so that he became the despair of his fellow musicians. Because of the rococo flourish of his style, Tatum was hardly ever able to integrate his piano playing into the texture of a group and was therefore almost always heard either at the head of a trio or as a solo pianist. Although he began about the time Hines was formulating the principles of trumpet-style piano and lived on to know the violent disputes of the postwar Modernist movement and after, Tatum remained a constant. Toward the end of his life, his playing became, if anything, more florid than ever, but it hardly evolved at all, so complete and subjective was his music. Because of the technical problems presented by Tatum's all-embracing style, he has had virtually no imitators, with the notable exception of Peterson, whose work grew increasingly closer to Tatum's in spirit as the years went by.

The era of the big bands and swing. In the first years of its history, jazz was confined almost exclusively to small-group collective improvisation, and such a conception as orchestral effect was a refinement that, for obvious reasons in a world populated by musicians illiterate at least in the conventional sense, had to come later. The first musician to make a serious attempt to organize a group of players who might keep, at least in part, to a plan was Ferdinand "Jelly Roll" Morton. Although his career has been more heavily documented and annotated than that of any other jazz musician, his recorded legacy was not large enough to decide whether he was a pioneer or a charlatan. Certainly, his announcement that he "invented jazz in 1902" did nothing to help.

Henderson's contribution to orchestral effects

The first indisputable figure in the evolution of orchestral jazz was Fletcher Henderson, an unremarkable pianist whose contribution to jazz lies in his pioneering of methods later universally adopted. Henderson, far better educated than most black musicians of his day, formed his own orchestra in 1923, and it became the first to gain wide fame by playing jazz. For several years after, his band employed the best black jazz talents, among them, at various times, Louis Armstrong (this was the last time in his life Armstrong was ever hired by a bandleader) and Coleman Hawkins. Despite an embarrassment of riches in the solo department, the Henderson band is unique for the way in which its leader experimented with orchestral effects. According to many purists, orchestral jazz is a contradiction in terms, for, if it is true that jazz is improvised music, then it follows that a jazz orchestra cannot exist. Henderson was among the first to see that it is not necessarily improvisation that lends jazz its fierce vitality but the preservation of its spirit. If musicians could play written parts with the same sense of self-discovery as a solo, then the effects need not be anticlimatic, and their solo talents could shape an ensemble into the contours of a jazz performance.

Henderson also contributed the concept of sections of instruments, comprising three or four voices, playing responses to the solo voice in harmony. The soloist, used to the accompanying figures provided for him, could often space his own improvisation, shape it, and adjust its dynamics to this scored accompaniment. Henderson's harmonic vocabulary and orchestral technique, profound in the jazz context of their period, were naïve in the broader musical sense, and, by an irony of fortune, his most revolutionary success happened in the end to somebody else (see below).

Many other bands of merit more or less followed Henderson's example, notably Chick Webb's band from 1926, Jimmie Lunceford's from 1927, and Bennie Moten, whose move from Kansas City eastward in 1926 coincided with the increase in the size of his group. Although none of these orchestras won the national and, in a few cases, the international fame that attended the touring orchestras of the 1930s, they were at least as good, if not much better, than their more exalted contemporaries. One of the main barriers to their being heard on a truly national scale was their colour.

As bands such as Henderson's, Webb's, and Lunceford's moved into the 1930s, the growing complexity of their harmony and technique combined with a more general process of advancing musical curiosity to produce a golden age of solo virtuosity. Some of the virtuosos remained in an orchestral setting, others were in the proliferating small groups. One of the greatest of these soloists was the tenor saxophonist Lester Young, who was associated for many years with one of the finest of all jazz orchestras, the Kansas City-based Count Basie band, which had evolved from Bennie Moten's group after the leader's death. Basie, a stride pianist, amended his style from a flow of harmony to a great plain of silence dotted with exquisite melodic epigrams neatly executed and gathered together a large orchestra that preserved the buoyancy of an improvised act by literally improvising. Many of his most effective orchestrations, such as "One O'Clock Jump," were, in effect, not orchestrations at all but "head arrangements"—that is to say, fragments of improvised music put together by the musicians in a process of trial and error, conned by rote, then gradually becoming a predictable performance. The Basie band, stressing four beats to a bar and retaining, long after others had abandoned it, the four-man rhythm section of piano, double bass, drums, and guitar, set unsurpassed standards of vigour and precision, and in this setting Young, a remarkable soloist, thrived.

Lester Young's contribution

Young's contribution to the solo art was twofold. First, he displayed and popularized a peculiar sensibility that paved the way for the Modernists of the following generation. Young is often credited with being the first Modernist, but, strictly speaking, he was a man of his era who did nothing to corrupt the harmonic innocence of his day. His tone, revolutionary in the 1930s in the way it distilled the hot breath of Hawkins' romanticism into something far more sinuous and oblique, set the style for saxophonists for a generation to come. In this way he contributed an alternative approach to the instrument: ever after, an apprentice could follow either Young or Hawkins, but not both. Jazz saxophone playing was thus immeasurably enriched. His other achievement was to demonstrate a new way of building an improvised solo, by using little-used chords, such as the minor sixth, by showing how silence could help a solo, by breaking down an arpeggio so that unusual intervals could express conventional harmonies, and by perfecting an ingenious series of false fingerings so that the player could produce different densities of sound on the same note. While the Modernists of a later age added to the jazz language by their increased harmonic scope, Young created a new vocabulary for the soloist within the conventional apparatus.

Many imponderables contributed to the astonishing upsurge of popularity of the big bands in the 1930s. The end of Prohibition in 1933 was a large factor; it altered the social habits of a nation and deprived jazz musicians of their biggest potential source of employment. By 1934 jazz had to find a new audience, and by a happy coincidence it reached a stage of sophistication that made the capture of a new audience possible. Benny Goodman formed his first organized orchestra in 1934, and, after an unsuccessful beginning touring the nation's dance halls, stumbled on the truth that others were soon quick to discover: that a new generation of young people was ready to patronize jazz-oriented dance bands. Jazz, though admittedly in a somewhat bowdlerized form, took to the ballrooms of the day.

Goodman and the swing age

In 1935 at the Palomar Ballroom in Hollywood, Goodman found all the factors of the swing age: massed audiences, fans clustered around the bandstand, enthusiasm for individual musicians, pressures changing bandleaders into brand names. Soon, Goodman was the "King of Swing," a Hollywood film star, a millionaire, an international celebrity. Naturally, others followed, among them a rival clarinetist, Artie Shaw, also Tommy and Jimmy Dorsey. Goodman ensured his success by recruiting the semi-retired Fletcher Henderson as chief arranger and by incorporating within his large group a smaller one (at first, a trio, later, a quartet), comprising the first racially mixed group ever to tour nationally in the United States—Goodman and drummer Gene Krupa being white, pianist Teddy Wilson and vibraphonist Lionel Hampton being black.

The swing age culminated in Goodman's 1938 concert at Carnegie Hall. Then, with orchestras hit by the wartime draft and running costs rising all the time, it petered out, losing its jazz connotations. By 1941, with the hysterical career of Glenn Miller, it ran into the quicksands of commercialism. Perhaps the jazz purist would commend Goodman's career as a bandleader for discovering a hitherto obscure Midwestern guitarist, Charlie Christian, the first guitar virtuoso to use electrically amplified equipment, although others had pioneered this method. He was one of the few stars of the swing era psychologically and musically equipped to make the leap into the Modernist era of the 1940s; his early death ended a brilliant career.

Until this time, jazz had been more or less diatonic (adhering to the natural scale), restricting itself, for the most part, to cycles of resolving dominant seventh chords. The Modernist movement of the 1940s thrust it forward into unexplored realms of chromaticism (use of harmonies built on notes not in the key of the piece), which split players and devotees into for-or-against armies and caused the advanced spirits to forgo the allegiance of mass audiences, which was never recovered.

Modernism. The origins of the Modernism of the 1940s, or "bebop," as it was then onomatopoetically known, are confused. One of its leaders, John Birks "Dizzy" Gillespie, said it was a device to shake off white plagiarists, but its most gifted practitioner, Charlie Parker (known to many as Bird), explained it in strictly technical terms. By evolving a system of substituted chords superimposed on the original ones and by playing in double the time of the tempo being asserted by the rhythm section, Parker, an alto saxophonist of extraordinary gifts, changed the face of jazz. His early death was symbolic of the tragic involvement of many jazz musicians of his generation with drug addiction. Although technically he made jazz more complex, emotionally he cleansed it, and his famous blues recordings looked back to Armstrong's achievements with the Hot Five, in spirit, if not in method. Parker could not have realized it, but he was making, on behalf of jazz, the last great appropriation of musical territory. To use an American pioneer analogy, after jazz had moved harmonically westward for a half a century, Parker took it to the sea. This caused heart-searching among those who inherited Parker's findings. Among his disciples was the trumpeter Miles Davis, who in 1956 made the first coherent attempt to escape from the cage of "discord to resolution," a method so persistently explored that the men of Davis' generation felt its usefulness to be ended. In an album called *Kind of Blue,* Davis substituted modal (scales not based on the major and minor) patterns for the more conventional harmonic ones, the first step in a process that was to characterize jazz thereafter. The theories of men such as Davis seemed to be negatively proved by the tenor saxophonists John Coltrane and Sonny Rollins, for, in the playing of both these men, the number of harmonic changes being crammed into each theme was so big that the music was in danger of being choked to death. One possible solution came from the alto saxophonist Ornette Coleman, who abandoned all rules of discord and resolution, time signatures, and keys, in his formulation of "Free Form," which in effect was no form at all. That jazz was not yet reduced to such extremes was suggested by a few of Ornette Coleman's contemporaries, who continued to raise the technical and inventive standards of jazz. These included the pianist Oscar Peterson, the drummer Buddy Rich, the tenor saxophonist Stan Getz, and the guitarist Wes Montgomery, all of whom attained high standards of performance.

Charlie Parker's influence

Much avant-garde jazz of the 1960s was committed art, in the sense that its creators insisted vigorously on their music as an artistic expression of racial protest, but all that their polemic suggested was that, in accusing society of anarchic tendencies, they had induced those tendencies in their own music and that art committed to a good cause is not necessarily good art.

The role of Duke Ellington

Throughout its history jazz has been abstract, in the sense that, subconsciously informed though it may be by race memory, it has been guided less by concrete or living factors than by the mathematical precision of the march from discord to resolution, the soloist being like a man working out an algebraic equation. For this reason Duke Ellington was unique, in that he moved toward that ideal where authentic jazz performances may reflect the nuances of personality of some outside object or person. Ellington thus attempted to make his music measure up to a constant dual standard, for he intended it to be not only fine jazz but also intelligible program music.

Nothing comparable has been attempted in jazz by anyone else, although the work of "progressive" jazz musicians such as Thelonious Monk and the Modern Jazz Quartet in the 1950s and 1960s hinted at extramusical connotations through the relentless Europeanization of its theme titles; and the Dave Brubeck Quartet made occasional gestures of a similar nature. Ellington attempted to make his jazz mirror the people and places that led him to the extreme sophistication of his old age. After his graduation from the Harlem group of pianists and his recruitment of a quintet, the Washingtonians, he moved steadily forward to orchestral mastery, increasing the size of his group as his palette became broader. In 1939 he recruited an orchestral assistant, Billy Strayhorn, but by this time he was already far along the road to a technique enabling him to embrace a far wider range of sound than jazz musicians normally aspire to.

By using his orchestra as an instrument on which to perform his feats of orchestrating brilliance and by assimilating the talents of each individual member of that organization as a saxophonist might acquaint himself with the workings of every key on his instrument, Ellington welded together a group inimitable by any standards. The rich impressionism of his early works, in the late 1920s, slowly evolved into the thumbnail sketches of the 1930s. In 1943 came *Black, Brown and Beige,* a musical history of blacks in the United States, after which Ellington scarcely stopped pouring out fresh works—some whole, some mere fragments, all of them informed by the romanticism of his view of the world.

Among his most remarkable achievements were many popular songs, such as "Sophisticated Lady" and "Mood Indigo," whose instrumental structure has not prevented them from becoming world famous. Of his more ambitious projects, he composed *Perfume Suite,* the sound track for the film *Anatomy of a Murder,* jazz versions of Tchaikovsky's *The Nutcracker* and Grieg's *Peer Gynt, Liberian Suite, The Far East Suite,* and, possibly his masterpiece, *Such Sweet Thunder* (1957), a series of 12 Shakespearean vignettes that demonstrate Ellington's working method. By settling on the stylistic idiosyncrasies of each soloist, Ellington attempted, in this work, to express his own idea of a dramatic character; thus, the elegiac fervour of his greatest soloist, the saxophonist Johnny Hodges, became the voice of Cleopatra, the stratospheric range of trumpeter William "Cat" Anderson the dementia of Hamlet, the cold academic hauteur of clarinetist Jimmy Hamilton's tone the patrician disdain of Caesar.

Vocal jazz. Although the essence of jazz is instrumental, one or two artists have shown that the human voice can express the spirit of the music. Apart from instrumentalists such as Armstrong and Teagarden, whose singing was an adjunct to instrumental expression, there have been two main groups of jazz singers, one rooted firmly in the folk-oriented communal past of the Southern U.S. black, the other committed to the world of commercial music and the fringes of show business. The male blues singers of the South, often men who earned their livelihood at some menial task, sang of life close to the bone, in terms whose graphic candour reflected the earthiness of the life

Blues singers

they had known. Outstanding were Huddie Ledbetter, Big Bill Broonzy, Blind Lemon Jefferson, Sleepy John Estes, and Peetie Wheatstraw. Their female counterparts, much more closely linked to the professional world of vaudeville and cabaret, include Gertrude "Ma" Rainey, her young protégé Bessie Smith, Mamie Smith, and Bertha "Chippie" Hill. By far the greatest was Bessie Smith, whose vast recorded output has preserved a style outstanding for its integrity, honesty to life, and immense technical skill. Less traditional male singers have included Count Basie's robust blues shouter James Rushing and Joe Turner, whose 1938 recordings with pianist Pete Johnson coincided with Johnson's short-lived but freakishly popular boogie-woogie piano style, a variation of blues playing whose hypnotic, reiterated rhythmic patterns won a world following and whose other notable exponents included Albert Ammons and Meade "Lux" Lewis. The most important female singers of this later period include Mildred Bailey, Ella Fitzgerald, and Sarah Vaughan, but by far the finest singer of modern times and, with the possible exception of Bessie Smith, the most gifted vocalist of either sex that jazz has so far produced, was Billie Holiday. Whereas Bessie Smith was incomparable as an interpreter of the poetry of the blues, Billie Holiday achieved the same intensity with the far less substantial repertory of Tin Pan Alley. Many of her small-group recordings from 1935 to 1942, prized classics of the art of impromptu composition, reflect in musical terms the close personal relationship between the singer and saxophonist Lester Young. An interesting departure of the 1950s was tried by the Dave Lambert-Jon Hendricks-Annie Ross Trio, which sang lyrics composed to transcribed instrumental jazz solos.

JAZZ AS A SOCIAL FORCE

The question of the extent to which jazz reflects the society that has nurtured it has seldom been asked. The 1960s saw a belated acknowledgment of its powerful ability to evoke the urban ambience. Duke Ellington's music for *Anatomy of a Murder* (1959) was the first movie score ever composed by a jazz writer. Since then, the jazz language has overrun all spheres of popular musical expression. One of the most intriguing things about its career has been the way in which advancing technique has run concurrently with social improvement, so that, while the crude emergent music of early New Orleans was brothel music and its more polished descendant in the 1920s the music of the ginmill, the suave orchestral felicities of the swing age became the wholly respectable background music for the innocent romances of its college audiences. Finally, with the advance to chromaticism, jazz invaded the concert hall and installed itself at festivals all over the world.

For the most part, jazz has remained the province of the urban U.S. black, who has contributed almost every viable new idea that has helped jazz along its path to literacy and self-confidence. Although there have been astonishing advances by European musicians in the past 30 years, there remains only one non-U.S. figure in the entire history of jazz who had something original and also valid to contribute. This was the Basque guitarist Django Reinhardt, whose best work was achieved in the 1930s, before he succumbed to the blandishments of amplification.

The source of the musician's repertory has also changed radically over the years. While the blues has retained its primacy throughout jazz history, the players of the swing era, harmonically cultured, turned to the urbanities of the best musical-comedy writers, so that names such as George Gershwin and Jerome Kern occur repeatedly on recordings of all kinds. Indeed, Gershwin, with "I Got Rhythm," created a harmonic pattern whose popularity with improvisers stands second only to the blues. In recent years, however, there has been a tendency among the younger, more revolutionary players to write their own material, which has made it more difficult than ever for the onlooker to distinguish genuine inventiveness from mere charlatanism.

The influence of jazz on other music

Jazz, in watered-down form, has strongly influenced various other kinds of music, many of them commercially more viable, such as "pop" songs, rock 'n' roll, skiffle, rhythm and blues, Broadway musicals. Some critics include these in the history of jazz; others consider that anything other than original Dixieland, which had a revival in the 1950s and 1960s, cannot be considered as pure jazz. Another form, Afro-Cuban music, which has some affinities with jazz, in fact had different ethnic roots, but some jazz musicians, such as Gillespie, incorporated its rhythms in their music making.

By and large, attempts to wed jazz with more formal methods of music making and composition have not been successful, although attempts to create a "third stream," involving musician-composers such as William Russo and Gunther Schuller, have not been without virtues to commend them. The oddest work in this direction remains Igor Stravinsky's *Ebony Concerto,* composed in 1945 for Woody Herman's orchestra. Although not in the specialist sense a jazz composition, it underlined the inherent contradictions in a marriage between the two forms of music. There appears to be a distinct possibility that jazz, faced at last with the challenge that its room to expand is finite, may eventually be merged into the world of music at large, to become an orchestral effect in a more general context. On the other hand, the tradition as represented by such artists as Armstrong, Ellington, Hawkins, Young, Tatum, Parker, and Holiday seems almost too fiery ever to be extinguished altogether. (B.Gr.)

BIBLIOGRAPHY. Comprehensive treatments of form in Western music are HUGO LEICHTENTRITT, *Musikalische Formenlehre,* 3rd ed. (1927; Eng. trans., *Musical Form,* 1951); and R.E. TYNDALL, *Musical Form* (1964); a shorter treatment in GROSVENOR COOPER, *Learning to Listen* (1957). For form in traditional and non-Western music, see BRUNO NETTL, *Folk and Traditional Music of the Western Continents* (1965); and *Music in Primitive Culture* (1956); and WILLIAM P. MALM, *Music Cultures of the Pacific, the Near East and Asia* (1967). See also, generally, the relevant articles in WILLI APEL, *Harvard Dictionary of Music,* 2nd ed. rev. (1969), a good source on any musical subject; DONALD JAY GROUT, *A History of Western Music* (1960), the best general history of music to date; ADAM CARSE, *The History of Orchestration* (1925, reprinted 1964), a detailed look at the evolution of the orchestra and musical instruments; NICOLAS RIMSKY-KORSAKOV, *Principles of Orchestration, with Musical Examples Drawn from His Own Works,* ed. by MAXIMILIAN STEINBERG, 1 vol. (1964; originally published in Russian, 1910), still one of the best texts for the serious student; ROMAIN GOLDRON, *Ancient and Oriental Music* (1968), examples of non-Western music and instruments. Later monographs include DAVID EPSTEIN, *Beyond Orpheus: Studies in Musical Structure* (1979); and ETHAN MORDDEN, *A Guide to Orchestral Music: The Handbook for Non-Musicians* (1980).

Chamber music: WALTER W. COBBETT, *Cobbett's Cyclopedic Survey of Chamber Music,* 2nd ed. by COLIN MASON, 3 vol. (1963), an invaluable and comprehensive work containing analyses and descriptions of works and topics in the field; EDWIN EVANS, *Handbook to Brahms,* vol. 2 and 3, *Chamber and Orchestral Music* (1933–35), contains detailed analyses and comparisons of all of Brahms's chamber-music works, with a general overview of his style; ERNST MEYER, *English Chamber Music* (1946, reprinted 1951), a specialized study devoted primarily to the works of Elizabethan and later 17th-century composers; DONALD FRANCIS TOVEY, *Essays in Musical Analysis: Chamber Music* (1944), a standard work that covers, in nontechnical language, large areas of the repertory; HOMER ULRICH, *Chamber Music,* 2nd ed. (1966), an historical account of the field before Haydn, with descriptive analyses and history of the repertory since 1750.

Fugue: Major historical treatises on the study of the fugal style include: N. VINCENTINO, *L'Antica Musica ridotta alla moderna prattica* (1555); GIOSEFFO ZARLINO, *Institutioni harmoniche* (1558; Eng. trans. of part 3, *The Art of Counterpoint,* 1968); THOMAS MORLEY, *A Plaine and Easie Introduction to Practicall Musicke* (1597; new ed. by R.A. HARMAN, 1952); JAN PIETERSZOON SWEELINCK, *Kompositionslehre* (1670, reissued 1891); JOHANN JOSEPH FUX, *Gradus ad parnassum,* 2 vol. (1725; Eng. trans., *Steps to Parnassus,* 1943), part of this work ed. and trans. by ALFRED MANN as "The Study of Fugue," in *Musical Quarterly,* vol. 36–37 (1950–51); JEAN PHILIPPE RAMEAU, *Traité de l'harmonie* (1772); FRIEDRICH WILHELM MARPURG, *Abhandlung von der Fuge,* 2 vol. (1753–54); G. MARTINI, *Esemplare, o sia saggio fondamentale pratico di contrappunto sopra il canto fermo,* vol. 2 (1775, reissued 1965); and JOHANN GEORG ALBRECHTSBERGER, *Gründliche Anweisung zur Komposition* (1790).

Academic works treating the fugue as a pure fiction include: LUIGI CHERUBINI, *Cours de contrepoint et de fugue,* ed.

by JACQUES HALEVY (1835; Eng. trans., *A Course of Counterpoint and Fugue,* 1837); E.F. RICHTER, *Lehrbuch der Fuge* (1859; Eng. trans., *A Treatise on Fugue,* 1878); S. JADASSOHN, *Lehre vom Canon und der Fugé* (1884; Eng. trans., *A Course of Instruction on Canon and Fugue,* 1904); H. RIEMANN, *Katechismus der Fuge* (1890–91); and T. DUBOIS, *Traité de contrepoint et de fugue* (1901). Modern academic works marking a return to Bach are: ANDRE GEDALGE, *Traité de la fugue* (1901; Eng. trans., *Treatise on Fugue,* 1964); E. PROUT, *Fugue* (1891); C.H. KITSON, *Studies in Fugue* (1922); and GEORGE OLDROYD, *The Technique and Spirit of the Fugue* (1948).

Modern studies on style include: KNUD JEPPESEN, *Kontrapunkt* (1930; Eng. trans., *Counterpoint,* 1939); ALFRED MANN, *The Study of Fugue* (1958); and WARREN KIRKENDALE, *Fugue and Fugato in Rococo and Classical Chamber Music,* 2nd rev. and enl. ed. (1979; originally published in German, 1966).

Concerto: ABRAHAM VEINUS, *The Concerto,* rev. ed. (1964), the only broad survey in English, with good knowledge of the subject but generally not well documented; DAVID BOYDEN, "When Is a Concerto Not a Concerto?" in the *Musical Quarterly,* 43:220–232 (1957), an essential clarification of the word itself; ARNOLD SCHERING, *Geschichte des Instrumentalkonzerts bis auf die Gegenwart,* 2nd ed. (1927), the principal survey in any language, although now somewhat outdated and inadequate; HANS ENGEL, *Die Entwicklung des deutschen Klavierkonzerts von Mozart bis Liszt,* 2 parts (1927), the main survey of its topic, completed by THEOPHIL STENGEL, *Die Entwicklung des Klavierkonzerts von Liszt bis zur Gegenwart* (1931); NORMAN CARRELL, *Bach's Brandenburg Concertos* (1963), an analytic discussion, well illustrated by examples and cuts; C.M. GIRDLESTONE, *Mozart's Piano Concertos* (1948), separate analytic chapters on each of the main concerti; RALPH HILL (ed.), *The Concerto* (1961), an anthology of 29 articles primarily on the Romantic and Modern concerto; A.J.B. HUTCHINGS, *The Baroque Concerto* (1961), inadequately documented and organized, but keen and authoritative in its observations; PIPPA DRUMMOND, *The German Concerto: Five Eighteenth-Century Studies* (1980), a summary of current research on five composers.

Symphony: FRIEDRICH BLUME *et al.,* "Symphonie," in *Musik in Geschichte und Gegenwart,* vol. 12, col. 1803–99 (1965), important historical and regional surveys of symphonic production, with extensive bibliography; NATHAN BRODER, "The Wind-Instruments in Mozart's Symphonies," *Musical Quarterly (MQ),* 19:238–259 (1933), a study of the changing role of winds in 18th-century orchestration; HOWARD BROFSKY, "The Symphonies of Padre Martini," *MQ,* 51:649–673 (1965), a discussion of Martini's pre-Classical symphonic style; BARRY S. BROOK, *La Symphonie française dans la seconde moitié du XVIII*[e] *siècle,* 3 vol. (1962), an important survey of over 1,200 works by 150 composers; ADAM CARSE, *Eighteenth-Century Symphonies: A Short History . . .* (1951), with emphasis on pre-Classical and early Classical forms and the overture; MALCOLM S. COLE, "The Vogue of the Instrumental Rondo in the Late 18th Century," *Journal of the American Musicological Society* (*JAMS*), 22:425–455 (1969), evidence for the rise and passing of a formal fashion; CHARLES L. CUDWORTH, "The English Symphonists of the Eighteenth Century," *Proceedings of the Royal Musical Association,* 78:31–51 (1951–52), a survey of a neglected national school; PHILIP G. DOWNS, "Beethoven's 'New Way' and the *Eroica,*" *MQ,* 56:585–604 (1970), an examination of the symphony in the light of a crisis in Beethoven's life; FRANK E. KIRBY, "Beethoven's Pastoral Symphony as a *Sinfonia caracteristica,*" *MQ,* 56:605–623 (1970), traditional pastoral elements related to Beethoven's symphonic form and content; H.C.R. LANDON, *The Symphonies of Joseph Haydn* (1955, suppl. 1961), a thorough analysis of Haydn's evolution toward greatness; JAN LARUE, "Major and Minor Mysteries of Identification in the 18th-Century Symphony," *JAMS,* 13:181–196 (1960), on problems of authenticity and attribution, mostly among minor masters; and "Significant and Coincidental Resemblance Between Classical Themes," *JAMS,* 14:222–234 (1961), discusses and illustrates "theme families" and elements of melodic formation; GORDANA LAZAREVICH, "The Neapolitan Intermezzo and Its Influence on the Symphonic Idiom," *MQ,* 57:294–313 (1971), an examination of a strong determinant of early symphonic style; ERNEST SANDERS, "Form and Content in the Finale of Beethoven's Ninth Symphony," *MQ,* 50:59–76 (1964), a study of the structure of this famous movement; ROBERT SIMPSON (ed.), *The Symphony:* vol. 1, *Haydn to Dvořák* (1966) and vol. 2, *Elgar to the Present Day* (1967), a collection of essays surveying the production of important symphonists; NICHOLAS TEMPERLEY, "The *Symphonie fantastique* and Its Program," *MQ,* 57:593–608 (1971), on Berlioz' music as related to its extramusical "plot"; DONALD F. TOVEY, *Essays in Musical Analysis,* vol. 1, *Symphonies* (1935), old but perceptive and well-written discussions of chief works; HOMER ULRICH, *Symphonic Music: Its Evolution Since the Renaissance* (1961), one of the few wide-ranging histories available in English. Origins of the symphony are explored in CLIVE UNGER-HAMILTON (ed.), *The Great Symphonies* (1983).

Sonata: E. BORREL, *La Sonate* (1951), a general modern study; W. MELLERS, "The Sonata Principle from c. 1750," in *Man and His Music* (1957), a description of stylistic trends that led from the Baroque to the Classical attitude; M. BUKOFZER, *Music in the Baroque Era, from Monteverdi to Bach* (1947), a general survey covering the period of the pre-Classical sonata; D.F. TOVEY, "Sonata Forms," in *The Forms of Music* (1956), a brilliant study, *Essays in Musical Analysis,* vol. 1–2 (1935), perceptive program notes on specific symphonic works, *Essays and Lectures on Music* (1949), important studies of Haydn, Beethoven, Schubert, and Brahms, and *A Companion to Beethoven's Pianoforte Sonatas* (1931); F.H. MARKS, *The Sonata: Its Form and Meaning in Piano Sonatas by Mozart* (n.d.); H. KELLER, "Wolfgang Amadeus Mozart," in R. SIMPSON (ed.), *The Symphony,* vol. 1 (1966), an imaginative and learned application of modern analytical principles to Mozart's symphonies; H.C. ROBBINS LANDON, *The Symphonies of Joseph Haydn* (1955), a monumental, detailed study of one of the central areas of sonata-form history; CHARLES ROSEN, *Sonata Forms* (1980), an exploration of the musical form in the context of social conditions.

Electronic music: The history of electronic music through the 1950s is covered in ABRAHAM A. MOLES, *Les Musiques expérimentales* (1960); and FRED K. PRIEBERG, *Musica ex Machina: Über das Verhältnis von Musik und Technik* (1960). Later books with an emphasis on history or the music itself include HERBERT RUSSCOL, *The Liberation of Sound: An Introduction to Electronic Music* (1972); ELLIOTT SCHWARTZ, *Electronic Music: A Listener's Guide,* rev. ed. (1975); JON H. APPLETON and RONALD C. PERERA (eds.), *The Development and Practice of Electronic Music* (1975); and DAVID ERNST, *The Evolution of Electronic Music* (1977). Many how-to books and manuals have been published, most of them emphasizing the use of synthesizers. Typical examples include GILBERT TRYTHALL, *Principles and Practices of Electronic Music* (1973); and ALLEN STRANGE, *Electronic Music: Systems, Techniques and Controls,* 2nd ed. (1983). A French publication, MICHEL CHION and GUY REIBEL, *Les Musiques électroacoustiques* (1976), is valuable because its emphasis is on European rather than American practice. Books that deal primarily with relevant aesthetic problems include JOHN CAGE, *Silence* (1961, reissued 1973); LUIGI RUSSOLO, *The Art of Noises* (1967; originally published in Italian, 1913); KARLHEINZ STOCKHAUSEN, *Texte zur elektronischen und instrumentalen Musik,* 2 vol. (1963–64); and IANNIS XENAKIS, *Formalized Music* (1971). Electronic musical instruments and their components, many of which were at one time used for electronic music, are discussed in RICHARD H. DORF, *Electronic Musical Instruments,* 3rd ed. (1968); ALAN L. DOUGLAS, *The Electronic Musical Instrument Manual: A Guide to Theory and Design,* 6th ed. (1976), and *The Electrical Production of Music* (1957); and WERNER MEYER-EPPLER, *Elektrische Klangerzeugung* (1949). Discussions of computer music may be found in HERBERT BRÜN, *Über Musik und zum Computer* (1971); HEINZ VON FOERSTER and JAMES W. BEAUCHAMP (eds.), *Music by Computers* (1969); LEJAREN A. HILLER, *Informationstheorie und Computermusik* (1964), and, with L.M. ISAACSON, *Experimental Music* (1959, reprinted 1979); HARRY B. LINCOLN (ed.), *The Computer and Music* (1970); MAX V. MATHEWS *et al., The Technology of Computer Music* (1969, reissued 1974); HUBERT S. HOWE, *Electronic Music Synthesis* (1975); CHRISTOPHER P. MORGAN (ed.), *The Byte Book of Computer Music* (1979); WAYNE BATEMAN, *Introduction to Computer Music* (1978, reissued 1980); and HAL CHAMBERLIN, *Musical Applications of Microprocessors* (1980). For current articles see *Source, Perspectives of New Music,* and *Journal of Music Theory* (all semiannual); *Audio Engineering Society Journal* (monthly); and *Computer Music Journal* and *Interface* (both quarterly). For recordings of electronic and computer music, the reader is referred to HUGH DAVIES (comp.), *International Electronic Music Catalog* (1968); *Schwann-1: Record and Tape Guide* and *Schwann-2* supplements; and ERNST (cited above). SANDRA L. TJEPKEMA, *A Bibliography of Computer Music* (1981), is a valuable reference tool.

Vocal music: For a general survey of song literature, see DENIS STEVENS (ed.), *A History of Song* (1960); and "Song," in *Grove's Dictionary of Music and Musicians,* 5th ed., vol. 7 (1954); for discussions of early chants and songs to 1640, with bibliographies and editions: *The New Oxford History of Music,* vol. 2–4 (1954–68); for problems in text setting: the introductions to *An Elizabethan Song Book,* ed. by NOAH GREENBERG, W.H. AUDEN, and CHESTER KALLMAN (1955); *The Ring of Words: An Anthology of Song Texts,* ed. by PHILIP L. MILLER (1963); and *The Penguin Book of Lieder,* ed. by S.S. PRAWER (1964); also ARCHIBALD T. DAVISON, *Words and Music* (1954); VINCENT DUCKLES and FRANKLIN B. ZIMMERMAN, *Words to Music* (1967); NORTHROP FRYE (ed.), *Sound and Poetry* (1957), esp. ch. 1, "Words into Music: The Composer's Approach to the Text," by EDWARD T. CONE; and JACK STEIN, "Was Goethe Wrong About the Nineteenth-Century Lied?" *PMLA*, 77:232–239 (1962). For a discussion of the concert aria, see PAUL HAMBURGER, "The Concert Arias," in *The Mozart Companion*, ed. by H.C. ROBBINS LANDON and DONALD MITCHELL (1956). MANFRED F. BUKOFZER, *Studies in Medieval and Renaissance Music* (1950) and *Music in the Baroque Era* (1947), are both well-established classics, the first volume being of particular importance since it discusses the beginnings of choral music. ALFRED EINSTEIN, *The Italian Madrigal*, 3 vol. (1949, reprinted 1971), is a detailed account of the entire history of the Italian madrigal. The third volume contains hitherto unpublished compositions. EDMUND H. FELLOWES, *English Cathedral Music from Edward VI to Edward VII*, 2nd ed. rev. (1945), and *The English Madrigal Composers*, 2nd ed. (1948), are regarded as classics and are well suited to the general reader as well as to the professional musician. FRANK L. HARRISON, *Music in Medieval Britain* (1958), is the most thorough account of church music in Britain from the earliest times up to the middle of the 16th century. PETER LE HURAY, *Music and the Reformation in England, 1549–1660* (1967), provides especially good coverage for this period. GUSTAVE REESE, *Music in the Renaissance*, rev. ed. (1959), is the finest single-volume study of music from the time of Dufay up to that of Byrd. DENIS W. STEVENS, *Tudor Church Music* (1961), is a study of forms and styles in 16th-century church music. See also NICHOLAS TEMPERLEY, *The Music of the English Parish Church*, 2 vol. (1979); and STEPHEN DAW, *The Music of Johann Sebastian Bach, the Choral Works* (1981).

Theatre music and opera: MARK LUBBOCK, *The Complete Book of Light Opera*, with an American section by DAVID EWEN (1962), gives synopses and background dates of numerous European and American operettas and musicals. GERVASE HUGHES, *Composers of Operetta* (1962), is a reliable critical and historical account of classical operetta. STANLEY GREEN, *The World of Musical Comedy*, rev. ed. (1969), gives a comprehensive account of the American musical in terms of its composers; and an informed discussion of its character and constituents is in LEHMAN ENGEL, *The American Musical Theatre* (1967). IVOR GUEST, *The Romantic Ballet in Paris* (1966), contains much little known background on music of its period; and NATALIA ROSLAVLEVA, *Era of the Russian Ballet Music* (1966), performs a similar but less well-documented service for its own subject. ROGER FISKE, *Ballet Music* (1958), is the only musically informed analysis to date of certain major ballet classics. HANNS EISLER, *Composing for the Films* (1947), remains a useful account of applied research. The wider historical aspects of theatrical music as a whole are included in the various volumes of the *New Oxford History of Music*, projected 11 vol. (1957-); and are comprehensively summarized in the excellent 1-vol. *Man and His Music* by ALEC HARMAN and WILFRID MELLERS (1962). Books on all aspects of opera are overwhelmingly numerous, particularly in Italian, German, French, and English. The following suggested list is confined to books written in English, a few indicative titles excepted. Unique in its coverage of opera (as well as of the spoken theatre, ballet, the cinema, and the circus) is the 12-vol. Italian *Enciclopedia dello Spettacolo* (1954–68). Among books on opera in general, useful basic information and informed opinion may be found in: WALLACE BROCKWAY and HERBERT WEINSTOCK, *The World of Opera* (1962); EDWARD J. DENT, *Opera* (1940); DONALD JAY GROUT, *A Short History of Opera*, 2nd ed. (1965); JOSEPH KERMAN, *Opera As Drama* (1956); GUSTAV KOBBE, *Complete Opera Book*, rev. and enlarged by the EARL OF HAREWOOD (1954), particularly useful for its libretto stories; ALFRED LOEWENBERG (comp.), *Annals of Opera, 1597–1940*, 2nd ed., 2 vol. (1955), the basic source for data on premieres and the dates and places of important later productions; and ERNEST NEWMAN (ed.), *Stories of the Great Operas* (1927, reprinted 1948), *More Stories of Famous Operas* (1943), and *Seventeen Famous Operas* (1954), which extensively analyze both libretto and music. Later monographs include GERALD BORDMAN, *American Operetta: From H.M.S. Pinafore to Sweeney Todd* (1981), and *American Musical Comedy: From Adonis to Dreamgirls* (1982); and MILTON CROSS and KARL KOHRS, *The New Milton Cross' More Stories of Great Operas*, rev. ed. (1980).

Among books treating opera in individual cities and opera houses, reliable data may be found in: (German) ANTON BAUER, *Opern und Operetten in Wien* (1955); ARTHUR J. BLOOMFIELD, *The San Francisco Opera, 1923–1961* (1961); JOHN FREDERICK CONE, *Oscar Hammerstein's Manhattan Opera Company* (1966); RONALD L. DAVIS, *Opera in Chicago* (1966); QUAINTANCE EATON, *The Boston Opera Company* (1965); (Italian) CARLO GATTI, *Il Teatro alla Scala (1778–1963)*, 2 vol., the second, compiled by GIAMPIERO TINTORI, being a detailed chronology of operatic and other performances (1964); IRVING KOLODIN, *The Metropolitan Opera, 1883–1966* (1966); MARCEL PRAWY, *The Vienna Opera* (1970); HAROLD D. ROSENTHAL, *Two Centuries of Opera at Covent Garden* (1958); WILLIAM H. SELTSAM (comp.), *Metropolitan Opera Annals: A Chronicle of Artists and Performances* (1947; also two supplements, 1957, 1968); and (French) STEPHANIE WOLFF, *Un Demi-siècle d'opéra-comique, 1900–1950* (1953) and *L'Opéra au Palais Garnier, 1875–1962* (1962).

A 122-page bibliography, including periodical and monographic articles of importance, may be found in vol. 2 of the first, 2-vol., edition of DONALD JAY GROUT, *A Short History of Opera* (1947). A prime source of operatic events since 1950 is the volumes (with annual index) of the London periodical *Opera*. History of opera is well covered in *The Concise Oxford Dictionary of Opera*, ed. by HAROLD ROSENTHAL and JOHN WARRACK, 2nd ed. (1979); ROBERT DONINGTON, *The Rise of Opera* (1981); and JOHN D. DRUMMOND, *Opera in Perspective* (1980).

Jazz: HUGUES PANASSIE, *Le Jazz hot* (1934; Eng. trans., *Hot Jazz*, 1936); WILDER HOBSON, *American Jazz Music* (1939); and FREDERIC RAMSEY, JR., and C.E. SMITH (eds.), *Jazzmen* (1939), although tainted by early naïveté, are indispensable pioneer attempts to formulate a critical method. ANDRE HODEIR, *Hommes et problèmes du jazz* (1954; Eng. trans., *Jazz: Its Evolution and Essence*, 1956), is an erudite attempt at close textual analysis. Among biographies, ALAN LOMAX, *Mister Jelly Roll* (1950), is outstanding for its graphic style and priceless sociological importance. BILLIE HOLIDAY with WILLIAM DUFTY, *Lady Sings the Blues* (1956); and WILLIE SMITH with GEORGE HOEFER, *Music on My Mind* (1964), successfully survive the ghosting process. STANLEY DANCE, *The World of Duke Ellington* (1970), presents a partial view of an extraordinary man. ARTIE SHAW, *The Trouble with Cinderella* (1952), is the only jazz autobiography with any real literary pretensions. NAT SHAPIRO and NAT HENTOFF (ed.), *Hear Me Talkin' to Ya* (1955), is a brilliant use of the spoken word to build a picture of jazz history. The best attempts at more general critical analysis include FRANCIS NEWTON, *The Jazz Scene* (1959); BENNY GREEN, *The Reluctant Art* (1962); and HENRY PLEASANTS, *Serious Music, and All That Jazz* (1969). MARSHALL W. STEARNS, *The Story of Jazz* (1956), has the charm of modesty. WHITNEY BALLIETT, *The Sound of Surprise* (1959), is an interesting if impressionistic collection of short reviews. PAUL OLIVER, *Blues Fell This Morning* (1960), is an outstanding specialist work. LEONARD G. FEATHER, *Encyclopedia of Jazz*, rev. ed. (1960) and the *Encyclopedia of Jazz in the Sixties* (1967); and G.T. SIMON, *The Big Bands* (1967), are indispensable works of reference. PAUL OLIVER *et al.*, *Jazz on Record* (1968), is useful but partisan. DONALD KENNINGTON, *The Literature of Jazz* (1970), is the first serious attempt to annotate all jazz literature. Interesting information can be found in EDDIE S. MEADOWS, *Jazz Reference and Research Materials: A Bibliography* (1981); CHARLES EUGENE CLAGHORN, *Biographical Dictionary of Jazz* (1983); SALLY PLACKSIN, *American Women in Jazz: 1900 to the Present* (1982); GARY GIDDINS, *Riding on a Blue Note: Jazz and American Pop* (1981); MARK MILLER, *Jazz in Canada: Fourteen Lives* (1982); and S. FREDERICK STARR, *Red and Hot: The Fate of Jazz in the Soviet Union, 1917–1980* (1983).

(F.E.Ki./D.Er./H.U./L.A.R./W.S.N./La.L./B.Ja./L.Hi./W.V.P./D.W.S./ N.Go./H.We./B.Gr.)

Musical Instruments

A device that produces musical sounds is a musical instrument, whether it is used for ritual or ceremonial purposes, for entertainment, or for private enjoyment. The fact that a number of instruments produce sounds of no definite pitch does not exclude them from this definition, since rhythm is an essential element in all music. The beat of a drum can be as important in a composition as a melody played by violins. Many instruments seem to have developed from the imaginative use of objects originally designed for other purposes. The drum has its origin in the pot and the pitcher; the rattle was used to mark the steps of a dance and also as a charm against evil spirits. Composers of recent times have used other objects not normally associated with music. Stage properties such as the wind machine and the thunder machine have been called for in works of a dramatic character. Iron chains, typewriters, and milk bottles are not unknown in 20th-century music. None of these, however, has established itself in normal use; and to extend the definition of musical instruments to include such objects would involve admitting any object or device that can make a sound when struck or manipulated.

The material of which an instrument is made does not necessarily affect the sound that it produces. In the case of instruments that are struck with some kind of beater, the difference may be very marked. Wood and metal when struck produce quite different sounds. On the other hand, a flute made of metal does not produce a substantially different sound from one made of wood, as in this case the vibrations are in the column of air in the instrument. Oboes have been made of ivory, clarinets of ebonite. The characteristic timbre of wind instruments depends on other factors, notably the length and shape of the tube and the means by which the air column is set in motion. The length of the tube not only determines the pitch but also affects the timbre: the piccolo, being half the size of the flute, has a shriller sound. The shape of the tube determines the presence or absence of the "upper partials" (harmonic or nonharmonic overtones), which give colour to the single note.

The volume of sound produced by an instrument depends on resonance, whether created by a vibrating air column or by a solid body vibrating in sympathy. In bowed string instruments the hollow box over which the strings are stretched vibrates in sympathy when the bow is drawn across the strings. Similarly, the volume of sound produced on the piano depends on the vibrations of the soundboard, without which the impact of the hammers on the strings would produce little effect.

The article is divided into the following sections:

General characteristics

The use of instruments purely for entertainment is a development of civilized societies. In primitive societies instruments were used as an adjunct to dancing and labour, and they also had magical properties that could serve in religion and medicine. These functions naturally overlapped. Bells or flutes could be used to attract the opposite sex and also to ward off evil spirits. It is also significant that most instruments were assigned to men. As an element in magic, instruments could be used equally to repel evil or to invoke a deity. The use of instruments for religious ceremonies has continued down to the present day, though at various times they have been suspect because of their secular associations. The many references to instruments in the Old Testament are evidence of the fact that they played an important part in Jewish worship until for doctrinal reasons they were excluded. It is also clear that the early Christians in the eastern Mediterranean used instruments in their services, since the practice was severely condemned by ecclesiastics, who insisted that the references to instruments in the Psalms were to be interpreted symbolically. As a result of this official attitude the music of the Christian Church became for several centuries restricted to voices. The organ, which seems to have been developed in Alexandria in the 3rd century BC, was a purely secular instrument in the Greco-Roman world. It remained so at Byzantium after the official acceptance of Christianity: it was used for ceremonial occasions such as banquets and chariot races but not for church services. The use of the organ in church in western Europe appears to date from the 8th century AD, when the Frankish monarch Pepin III installed at Compiègne an instrument he had received as a present from Byzantium.

The invention of the organ

Belief in the magical properties of instruments is found in many societies. The Jewish *shofar* (a ram's horn), which is still blown on Rosh Hashana (New Year) and Yom Kippur (Day of Atonement), must be heard by the congregation. The power of the *shofar* is illustrated by the story of Joshua at the siege of Jericho: when the priests blew their shofars seven times the walls of the city fell flat. In India, according to legend, when the deity Krishna (Kṛṣṇa) played the flute, the rivers stopped flowing and the birds came down to listen. The birds are said to have done the same in 14th-century Italy when the composer Francesco Landini played his organetto, or portative organ. In China, instruments were identified with the points of the compass, with the seasons, and with natural phenomena. The Melanesian bamboo flute was a charm for rebirth. Many primitive instruments were phallic symbols.

Most of the instruments used in the West in medieval times came from the Near East. Trumpets, long associated with military operations, had a ceremonial function in the establishment of kings and nobles and were, in fact, regarded as a sign of nobility. In the later Middle Ages and for long afterward, they were associated with kettledrums (known originally as nakers, after their Arab name, *naqqārah*), which were often played on horseback, as they still are in some mounted regiments. Trumpet fanfares, heard on ceremonial occasions in the modern world, are a survival of medieval practice. In the 17th century, trumpets and kettledrums were introduced into opera and orchestral music of a festal character. In the same way, horns, originally hunting instruments, became normal members of the orchestra in the 18th century.

TECHNOLOGICAL DEVELOPMENTS

The earliest instruments appear to have been natural objects capable of producing sound; for example, the conch (marine shell) and the bone pipe. The conch and the primitive trumpet at first served only as a means of amplifying the human voice. The discovery that tubes possessed acoustic properties that enabled them, by vibration of the lips, to sound more than one note was a later development. From using natural objects, it was an obvious step to construct instruments that would serve a similar purpose, using wood or terra-cotta or any other available material.

Another development of natural resources was the discovery that a stretched string could produce a musical note. This resulted in the construction of the musical bow, the ancestor of all plucked string instruments. Its shape is similar to that of the hunter's bow, but it seems to have had an independent origin. Since the sound of the simple string is feeble, it is reinforced by means of a resonator—either a pot placed on the ground beneath the instrument or a gourd attached to it or the player's mouth. The string can either be struck with a stick or be plucked with the fingers. In the former case it could be regarded as the forerunner of the Persian dulcimer, in which numerous strings are struck with a stick, and ultimately of the piano.

Development of string instruments

The construction of all but the simplest instruments requires skill and craftsmanship: the piercing of a tube to a uniform or expanding width, the flaring of the bell of a wind instrument to increase sonority, the measurement of the bars of a xylophone or glockenspiel, the curvature of the back of a lute, the internal and external structure of the body of a violin. All of these involve accurate workmanship from experts in wood and metal and, from present-day designers, a knowledge of the mathematics of sound. The latter is particularly true in the case of woodwind instruments, where the holes must be accurately pierced in order to produce a scale that is in tune. Of all instruments, the organ demands the fullest cooperation from workers in different skills: in the construction of pipes in metal and wood, in fashioning them to the right length, in securing uniformity of tone throughout a single row, and in adjusting the great variety of sounds so that they blend happily together; in the provision of leather pallets to allow the passage of air; in providing direct and immediate contact between the keyboard and the pipes; and in constructing a blowing apparatus that will be adequate for the pressure required.

The first step in the building of any instrument is the selection of material. Wood, whether cocus, rosewood, or maple (to mention three that are favoured for woodwind instruments) or pine, used for string instruments, needs to be seasoned. This applies equally to the reeds of oboes, clarinets, and bassoons, which are cut from the plant *Arundo donax,* now grown for this purpose, particularly in the south of France. Climate is also an important consideration. The moist, damp climate of tropical countries has often proved disastrous to instruments built for use in Europe.

Woods used for making instruments

Our knowledge of medieval instruments is derived almost entirely from pictorial illustrations, and the men who made them remain anonymous. Their skill, like that of the cabinetmaker and the silversmith, was developed by long practice, and the principles that determine both tone and intonation were discovered by trial and error. The growth of instrumental playing in the 16th century stimulated the production of instruments to be used not merely for ceremonial and official entertainment but also for social occasions and private pleasure. From this time we begin to know the names of makers, many of whom established family businesses that lasted for several generations. These include, for example, Andrea Amati (16th century), violin maker in Cremona; Hans Ruckers (late 16th century), harpsichord maker in Antwerp; and Johann Haas (1649–1723), trumpet maker in Nürnberg.

Modern technology has in many cases simplified or improved the construction of instruments. In the past, for example, the tubes of horns and trumpets were made from a sheet of brass cut to the right width, which was rolled into shape, leaving the edges to be joined by brazing. In modern manufacture the tube is drawn in one piece, and there is no seam. Evolution of design has been particularly notable in the construction of wind instruments: in the case of woodwind instruments, not only in the fixing of the metal keys and the mechanism that controls them but also in the piercing of holes in such a way that they are both acoustically correct and under the direct control of the fingers. This achievement, which dates from the first half of the 19th century, was due mainly to the pioneering work of Theobald Böhm (1794–1881). His system, designed for the flute, was also applied to the clarinet, and some of its mechanical principles were adapted for the oboe and bassoon. The early 19th century also saw a revolution in the manufacture of brass instruments: the

Modern changes in design

addition of pieces of tubing of different lengths through which the air could be directed by the depression of valves (or pistons), enabling an instrument to produce all 12 notes of the chromatic scale, in place of its earlier limitation to the notes of the natural harmonic (overtone) series.

The discovery of plastics in the 20th century has also influenced the manufacturers of instruments; for example, plastic has been used instead of quill or leather for the plectra that pluck the strings of the harpsichord, and plastic recorders have been built. Mechanization has made possible the mass production of instruments of all kinds. Insofar as this makes it possible for people to acquire an instrument at a moderate price, mass production is a good thing, and in education it has been beneficial to schools working on a small budget. A natural development has been the provision of kits consisting of the separate parts of an instrument, which can then be assembled by the purchaser. It remains true, however, that the production of an instrument of the finest quality still demands the highest degree of individual skill. A violin glued together from mass-produced parts cannot be the equal of one that has been meticulously constructed from the first by an individual craftsman who will not be satisfied with his work until every detail of it has been tested.

Importance of craftsmen

Technology has been of service to music by providing composers with instruments they have asked for, by eliminating the defects of instruments and facilitating the work of performers, and by making instruments more widely available to the community in general. Richard Wagner suggested the heckelphone, a double-reed instrument akin to the oboe, and ordered a special type of tuba for use in his music drama tetralogy *Der Ring des Nibelungen.* Not all the improvements in construction have been wholly advantageous. It is easier to play in tune on a modern woodwind instrument, but the older examples, being less cluttered with metal fittings, had a purer tone. Similarly, the modern horn, which is virtually two instruments in one, is inferior in tone quality to its 18th-century predecessor. Only the trombone and the string instruments have remained, apart from minor modifications, unchanged in structure over the centuries, though the substitution of wire strings for gut has materially altered the tone of the violin.

The older makers of instruments were craftsmen who took delight in the appearance of their work. Pictures were painted on the inside of harpsichord lids; delicate inlay and carved heads adorned string instruments. Rings of ivory concealed the joints in woodwind instruments; the bells of trumpets were richly chased. Sometimes there was extravagance—for instance, making the bell of a wind instrument in the shape of a dragon's head. Modern taste in most cases rejects ornamentation. The coats of arms painted on military bass drums are there principally to indicate their regimental function. But overall design and finish are as important as they have always been. If instruments were not meant for use, those that are produced today would deserve, on aesthetic grounds, to find a place in museums, side by side with the musical treasures of the past that lead a beautiful but generally silent existence there.

CLASSIFICATION OF INSTRUMENTS

Instruments have been classified in various ways, some of which overlap. The Chinese divide them according to the material of which they are made—as stone, wood, silk, and metal. Although applicable to Chinese instruments, this system will not do as a classification of instruments in general. To take a simple example, a saxophone is made of metal, but its method of tone production associates it with the clarinet, which is, at least in origin, a wooden instrument. Writers in the Greco-Roman world distinguished three main types of instruments: wind, string, and percussion. This classification was retained in the Middle Ages and persisted for several centuries: it is the one preferred by some writers, with the addition of electronic instruments, at the present day. Some 16th-century writers excluded certain instruments from this classification; the musical theorist Ludovico Zacconi (1555–1627) went so far as to exclude all percussion instruments and established a fourfold division of his own—wind, keyed, bowed, and plucked. A different fourfold classification was accepted by the Hindus at least as early as the 1st century BC: they recognized string instruments, wind instruments, percussion instruments of wood or metal, and percussion instruments with skin heads (that is to say, drums). This ancient system—based on the material producing sound—was adopted by the Belgian instrument maker and acoustician Victor-Charles Mahillon (1841–1924), who named his four main classes autophones, or instruments made of a sonorous material that vibrates to produce sound (*e.g.,* bells, rattles); membranophones, in which a stretched skin is caused to vibrate (*e.g.,* drums); aerophones, in which the sound is produced by a vibrating column of air (wind instruments); and chordophones, or string instruments. In their highly influential studies of musical instruments, the Austrian musicologist Erich von Hornbostel (1877–1935) and his German colleague Curt Sachs (1881–1959) accepted and expanded Mahillon's basic division, creating the classification now used in most systematic studies of instruments. The name idiophones was substituted for autophones, and each class was subdivided according to a method similar to that used by botanists. A fifth class, electrophones, in which vibration is produced by oscillating electric circuits, was added later. The Table gives examples of instruments that come within the various categories.

Systems based on the material sounded

Classification and Examples of Some Musical Instruments

Idiophones	
Struck	against each other: cymbals, castanets
	with a beater: triangle, glockenspiel, xylophone, slit drums
Shaken	rattle, jingles
Scraped	scraper
Plucked	jew's harp, music box
Rubbed	musical glasses
Membranophones	
Struck	tambourine, side drum, bass drum, timpani
Rubbed	friction drum
Blown	mirliton (or kazoo)
Chordophones	
Plucked	without keyboard: harp, lute, violin, zither, lyre
	with keyboard: harpsichord
Struck	without keyboard: dulcimer
	with keyboard: clavichord, piano
Rubbed (with a bow)	viol and violin families
Aerophones	
Flues	without keyboard: recorder, flute
	with keyboard: organ
Reeds	without keyboard: single reed—clarinet, saxophone
	double reed—shawm, crumhorn, oboe, bassoon, sarrusophone
	with keyboard: harmonium, American organ (melodion)
Lipped	horn, cornet, trumpet, trombone, tuba, serpent
Electrophones	
Monophonic	producing a single line of melody: theremin, trautonium, Ondes Martenot
Polyphonic	producing harmony and simultaneous melodic lines: Hammond organ

The classification shown in the Table is convenient, but it is not completely logical. Some instruments may belong to more than one class or more than one subdivision. The tambourine is a membranophone in so far as it has a skin head which is struck; but, if it is only shaken so that its jingles sound, it should be classed as an idiophone, for in this operation the skin head is irrelevant. Flue pipes are the foundation of organ tone, but the instrument also has a number of reed pipes, so that the organ belongs equally to the first and second order of aerophones. The violin is undoubtedly a chordophone, but if the strings are struck with the wooden part of the bow it belongs to the second order of this class, not the third. Modern composers not infrequently require players to slap their instruments instead of playing them in the normal way. A slapped guitar or a slapped trombone is technically an idiophone. The classification according to the source of vibrations also ignores common elements in means of production.

It is normal practice to speak of keyboard instruments as a group, including piano, harpsichord, organ, and so on; but in the Hornbostel–Sachs classification these are either chordophones or aerophones, and, if the keyed glockenspiel is included, there is an idiophone as well.

HISTORY AND EVOLUTION

Men have speculated about the origin of instruments since antiquity. Older writers were generally content to rely on Greek mythology or Old Testament legends. In the 19th century there was an attempt at a more scientific approach, partly as a result of theories of evolution put forward by Darwin and Herbert Spencer. The British writer John Frederick Rowbotham argued that there was originally a drum stage, followed by a pipe stage, and finally a lyre stage. The Austrian writer Richard Wallaschek, on the other hand, maintained that, although rhythm was the primal element, the pipe came first, followed by song, and the drum last. Sachs, instead of relying on anthropological evidence, based his chronology on archaeological excavation and the geographical distribution of the instruments found in them. Following this method, he established three main strata. The first, of wide distribution, consists mainly of noisemakers, such as the rattle and the bullroarer. The second, found in several continents but not universally, includes drums, trumpets, and plucked strings. The third, occurring only in certain areas, includes more advanced instruments, such as the xylophone and the flute. That percussion instruments should appear at an early stage is not surprising. From stamping out a rhythm with his feet, primitive man learned to do the same with an implement: these implements became more elaborate as time went on and were followed by further experiments in extracting sound from sonorous objects.

The development of musical instruments among ancient high civilizations appears to have been most substantial in Asia and North Africa. By contrast, instrumental performance remained confined to winds and percussion in Central and South America. It is not always easy to say whether instruments are indigenous to a particular area, since their cultivation may well have spread from one country to another through trade or migration. The harp was used from early times in Mesopotamia, Egypt, and India but was not imported into China before the end of the 4th century AD. In Greece it was regarded as a foreign instrument: the standard plucked instrument was the lyre, known in its fully developed form as the kithara (or cithara). Apart from the trumpet, the only wind instrument in normal use in Greece was the aulos, a double-reed instrument akin to the modern oboe. The Egyptians used wind instruments not only with double reeds but also with single reeds and thus may be said to have anticipated the clarinet. Peculiar to China was the *sheng*, or mouth organ; the Chinese also used as an artistic instrument the panpipes (*hsiao*), which in Greece had merely a rustic function.

Early use of the harp

The most notable development in western Europe was the practice, originating apparently in the 15th century, of building instruments in families, from the smallest to the largest size. A typical family was that of the shawms, which were powerful double-reed instruments. A distinction was made between *haut* (loud) and *bas* (soft) instruments, the former being suitable for performance out of doors and the latter for more intimate occasions. Hence, the shawm came to be known as the *hautbois* (loud wood), and this name was transferred to its more delicately toned descendant, the 17th-century oboe: the Italian name was a phonetic transliteration of the original French. By the beginning of the 17th century the German musical writer and composer Michael Praetorius, in his *Syntagma Musicum* ("Musical Treatise"), was able to give a detaied account of families of instruments of all kinds—recorders, flutes, shawms, trombones, viols, and violins.

Stringed instruments. The idea of playing a string instrument with a bow appears, from the available evidence, to have originated in Persia in the 9th century AD. The medieval fiddle, like its Eastern prototype, was originally a folk instrument and existed in various forms: by the 16th century these had settled down into two distinct types—the viol, known in Italy as viola da gamba (leg fiddle), and the violin, or viola da braccio (arm fiddle). The two types differ in several respects. The viol has a flat back and sloping shoulders, the violin a rounded back and rounded shoulders. The viol has six or seven strings, the violin four. The viol, unlike the violin, has frets—pieces of gut wound at intervals around the fingerboard—which make every stopped note (*i.e.,* the string being pressed by the finger to produce a higher pitch) sound like an open (unstopped) string. The violin, being the smallest member of the family, came to be known by the diminutive violino: the tenor of the family was called simply viola (in France *alto;* in Germany *Bratsche,* a corruption of Italian *braccio,* "arm"), while the bass acquired the name violoncello, a diminutive of violone ("big fiddle").

Origin of viols and violins

Keyboard instruments. Of all instruments, the organ showed the most remarkable development from the early Middle Ages to the 17th century. Originally, sound was admitted to the pipes by withdrawing sliders or depressing levers. Both of these methods were clumsy: they gave way to a reduction in the size of the levers, which eventually could be depressed by the fingers, while the larger pipes were controlled by pedals. A further development was to separate the various rows of pipes, so that each row could be brought into action or suppressed by means of a draw stop. Once a manageable keyboard had been produced, it could be applied to the portable organ, carried by the player, which was already in use by the 12th century. Scientific experiments with the monochord, a stretched string that could be divided into various lengths by means of a metal tangent, were followed by the construction of an instrument with a whole range of strings and a keyboard similar to that of the organ—the clavichord. A similar adaptation of the plucking of string instruments led to the harpsichord, the ingenious mechanism of which had been perfected by the 16th century. It is curious that a similar method was not applied to the dulcimer, which was struck with hammers, until the early 18th century, when the Italian maker Bartolomeo Cristofori constructed the first pianoforte, so-called because, unlike the harpsichord, it could vary the tone from soft (*piano*) to loud (*forte*).

The clavichord, harpsichord, and piano

The effect of the orchestra. The establishment of orchestras, as opposed to chamber groups, in the early 17th century favoured the violin family at the expense of the viols. The latter gradually dropped out of use, with the exception of the bass viol, which was still used in the first half of the 18th century as a solo instrument and as the bass of an accompaniment. It was not until the end of the 19th century that the viols were revived, in order to play the music written for them in the past. Other instruments besides the viols fell into temporary oblivion. The medieval crumhorn, a double-reed instrument with the reed inside a pierced cap, barely survived the 16th century. Another old instrument, the cornett, consisting of a wooden tube with finger holes and played with a cup-shaped mouthpiece, dropped out of use in the 17th century, except in Germany, where it was still played by *Stadtpfeifer,* or "town musicians," in the 18th century. Both Bach and Handel wrote for this instrument, but its tone was too weak for later orchestral music, and it had to wait until the 20th century for a full-scale revival.

Wind instruments. The practice of constructing instruments in families continued from the 17th century onward. English composers wrote for the tenor hautbois, which in various forms was known as oboe da caccia ("hunting oboe," possibly from its curved shape) or cor anglais ("English horn"). There was also an intermediate instrument called oboe d'amore. The bass, or baritone, oboe originated in the 18th century but was not perfected until the 19th. The clarinet (the name means "little trumpet") emerged at the end of the 17th century and, like the oboe, developed into a family extending to a contrabass clarinet in the 19th century and later a subcontrabass. It established itself only gradually in the orchestra in the course of the 18th century.

The improvement of brass instruments by the addition of valves in the early 19th century led to the creation of others. A pioneer in this field was the Belgian instrument maker Antoine Joseph Sax, who in 1845 built a family

The work of Sax

of valve instruments called saxhorns, using the bugle as the basis for his invention. Similar instruments were soon being manufactured all over Europe. They were widely adopted in military and brass bands, but only the bass, under the name bass tuba, became a normal member of the orchestra, replacing the older ophicleide and serpent. Sax also invented the saxophone, a single-reed instrument like the clarinet but with a conical tube. This, too, was made in various sizes, which came to be used both in military bands and in jazz ensembles. The saxophone never became a normal member of the orchestra, but the alto and the tenor have been used by composers, largely as solo instruments, and occasionally a complete quartet of four different sizes has appeared in an orchestral work.

Electrically powered instruments. The development of electricity led not only to its use for mechanical purposes—for example, to control the key action and wind flow in the organ—but also as a means of amplification (*e.g.,* in the vibraphone) and as a source of vibrations that can be converted into sound. In the Hammond organ (1935), the player, by selecting the appropriate harmonics that comprise their timbres (tone colours), can produce a tolerable imitation of a variety of orchestral instruments and of certain organ stops, though the tone is not likely to be confused with the sound produced by pipes. Many keyboard instruments working on similar principles have been produced in the course of the 20th century. The use of electronic equipment such as sound synthesizers and tapes to produce and combine sound unrelated to the musical scale has become common. (J.A.W.)

Percussion instruments

Two distinct groups of musical instruments, namely, idiophones and membranophones, comprise the large classification known as percussion instruments, which along with the stringed and wind instruments forms the third section of the Western orchestra. Idiophones are instruments whose own substance vibrates to produce sound (as opposed to the strings of a guitar or the air column of a flute); examples include bells, clappers, and rattles. Membranophones emit sound by the vibration of a stretched membrane; the prime examples are drums. Although many idiophones and some membranophones are tunable and hence may be melody instruments, both groups serve typically to delineate or emphasize rhythm. The term percussion instruments goes back to the German composer and organologist Michael Praetorius, who in 1619 wrote of *percussa, klopfende Instrument* (German *klopfen,* "to beat") as any struck instrument, including struck chordophones (stringed instruments). The same combination, including pre-bow chordophones, constituted the *divisio rhythmica* in the 7th-century *Etymologiae* of Isidore, archbishop of Seville.

IDIOPHONES

The following classification of idiophones provides some idea of the diversity of this large group of disparate instruments. Concussion instruments, consisting of two similar components struck together, include clappers, concussion stones, castanets, and cymbals. Percussion idiophones, which are instruments struck by a nonsonorous striker, form a large subgroup including triangles and simple percussion sticks; percussion beams, such as the *semanterion;* percussion disks and plaques, single and in sets; xylophones, lithophones (sonorous stones), and metallophones (sets of tuned metal bars); percussion tubes, such as stamping tubes, slit drums, and tubular chimes; and percussion vessels varying from struck gourds and pots to gongs, kettle gongs, steel drums, bells, and musical cups.

Types of idiophones

Shaken idiophones, or rattles, include vessels filled with rattling material, such as pellet bells, gourd, basketry, and hollow-ring rattles; strung rattles, such as dancers' leg rattles or anklets; stick rattles, including the sistrum, originally a forked stick with crossbars on which rattling shells, etc., were strung; pendant rattles with suspended rattling objects; and sliding rattles.

Other categories include scraped idiophones, comprising scrapers and cog rattles; split idiophones made of split hollow cane, including the Southeast Asian "tuning fork" idiophones and the chopstick; plucked idiophones, or linguaphones (so named because of their plucked tongues), such as the Jew's harp, sansa, and music box; friction idiophones, including friction sticks, simple or combined, and musical glasses; and blown idiophones, such as the 19th-century *Äolsklavier* and *piano chanteur.*

In Europe. Europe received most of its idiophones either directly or indirectly from the high cultures of the ancient East or from Egypt, a country regarded by the Greeks and Romans as forming part of Asia rather than of Africa.

Antiquity. European antiquity knew many idiophones. Dancers' clappers, held pairwise in the hands of maenads (women participants in Dionysian rites) and other female dancers, often stressed the rhythm of accompanying *auloi* (the ancient Greek reed pipes). The time-beating foot clappers of chorus leaders, attached to the right foot like a sandal, were known in Greece as *kroupezai,* or *kroupala,* and adopted by Rome as the *scabella.* Other idiophones included bells, cymbals, the unidentified *ēcheion,* and an instrument simply called "the bronze" (*chalkos*), probably a metal percussion disk. When the cult of Isis spread to Greece and Rome, her sistrum followed, always in the hands of priest or—rarely—priestess.

With the exception of clappers, all these instruments were of bronze; as such they were credited with the apotropaic powers (the special protective powers against evil) accorded this metal in the East. Not only among primitive Asian islanders but in Greece itself was it customary to "sound the *chalkos* at eclipses of the moon," for example, "because it has power to purify and to drive off pollutions" (a scholiast, writing on Theocritus). According to the Roman poet Ovid, the annual visit of ghosts of the dead to their former homes was terminated by requests to depart emphasized by the clanging of a bronze plate. Thin, bronze percussion disks have been excavated at Volci, Etruria, and at Pompeii, affixed to metal handles; one from Pompeii is even garnished with pellet bells. Bells of bronze do not emit the clear, ringing tone associated with modern ones of bell metal; those of antiquity were small and made a clanging rather than ringing sound. They warded off evil spirits, averted the evil eye, served as sentinels' and watchmen's signal instruments, or were attached to the handle of a Greek warrior's shield in order to terrify the enemy by their clamour. Anklets adorned with small bells were frequently worn by jesters, dancers, and courtesans, particularly in Hellenistic times. In Rome, *tintinnabulae* ("bells") served as signal instruments or were suspended from the necks of herd animals—again to ward off evil.

Use of bronze

Cymbals were sounded in religious rites, also at secular dances; deeply cupped, they may be seen on Greek and Roman art objects played together with a frame drum. Forked cymbals known as *crotala* travelled from Egypt to Greece and Rome, and finger cymbals were introduced from the East, chiefly for dancers, a pair being attached to thumb and middle finger of each hand.

Among the oldest instruments of mankind, rattles originally combined the functions of prophylactic amulets and children's toys; both functions coexisted as late as Roman times when *crepundia* ("rattles") served both as charms against evil and as children's toys. A number of existing Roman pellet bells (often misnamed jingles) are notable for their exquisite workmanship.

The Middle Ages. Greek and Roman idiophones were passed on to postclassical Europe, their distribution undoubtedly aided by wandering *joculatores,* or minstrels. Whereas prior to the adoption of Christianity most were ritual instruments, their function in medieval times—with the notable exception of the bell—was strictly secular.

Clappers called *tabulae,* made of bone, are mentioned by Amalarius of Metz (9th century AD) as being in the hands of church cantors during liturgical services; possibly they were similar to the flat clappers played by jongleurs in the late Middle Ages and by lepers who sounded them as a warning of their approach. A three-piece clapper was used for this purpose in Spain, the *tablillas de San Lázaro* (*lazarus* being a Late Latin synonym of leper).

Lepers' warning clappers

Dancers' castanets, hollow clappers in bivalve form, were

played in Spain throughout the Middle Ages; they are illustrated from the 11th century on. Already in Roman times, dancers of Cádiz are known to have played metal castanets, but those of sonorous hardwoods have been preferred since. Forked cymbals are portrayed on ivory and in miniatures of the Carolingian period. Small, cup-shaped cymbals called *acetabulae,* made of brass or silver, are mentioned by Cassiodorus (died *c.* 580) and Isidore of Seville. Interestingly, the modern practice of striking a single cymbal with a stick was anticipated by Isidore and by the *Suda* lexicon (late 10th century). Nonetheless, larger cymbals continued to be played pairwise and—at least in the later Middle Ages—were found among the "loud" instruments that accompanied dancing and were played at seigneurial festivities. Gongs appear intermittently from the 15th century on, first in the soup-plate form associated in Asia with gong chimes.

Symbolic importance of bells

Bells were still thought to possess apotropaic powers; with their adoption, the Christian Church took over the belief that ghosts and demons could be put to flight by the sound of metal, a power henceforth augmented by the protection afforded by association with the divine cult and, more specifically, by baptism. The rite of baptizing bells is first recorded in a capitulary (civil ordinance) of Charlemagne of 789. Exorcizing celebrants sounded handbells or wore bells on their garments. St. John Chrysostom (died 407) felt compelled to protest against the custom of attaching bells to the clothing or bracelets of children in order to preserve them against demons, yet small bells or pellet bells continued to adorn the vestments of priests, a practice inherited from the ancient Near East: 51 bells ornamented the cope of Lanfranc, 11th-century archbishop of Canterbury. The tolling of passing bells in England, already recorded by Bede (died 735), was intended to ward off evil spirits from dying persons. Church bells announced the time of day, summoned the faithful to worship, sounded alarms, fought off lightning, broadcast the news of peace or the birth of a princeling, and praised God. In secular life handbells were played in mixed instrumental ensembles, usually one bell in each of the player's hands.

Tuned bells are strung together to form chimes. Early chimes are generally represented as clapperless, hemispheric bells—inverted resting bells, in fact—struck on the outside by a hammer; less frequently, they are shown as clapper bells sounded by pulling on long cords attached to the clapper. From the 13th century, chimes were connected to clockwork and struck mechanically. As bells grew larger and the compass of the chime was extended, it became known as a carillon. The distinction today is merely one of compass, any set exceeding 1½ or two octaves in compass being considered a carillon.

In secular life, pellet bells were suspended from ladies' belts or worn by jesters. Before the introduction of bells in the Greek Orthodox Church in the 11th century, the *semanterion,* a percussion beam sounded by a striker, summoned the congregation, and in the Roman Catholic Church it has been used as a substitute for bells during Easter Week. Triangles first appear in the 14th century; originally a number of loose, rattling rings were threaded on the lower portion, as though the ancient sistrum had projected itself through the centuries. Scraped idiophones, known in Europe since Paleolithic times, are encountered as scraped pots intermittently from the 12th century on; such noisemakers were played—to judge by a 14th-century miniature—with other percussive instruments for merrymaking. Few instruments are as suitable for personal music making as the Jew's harp; coming from the East, it passed through Rome, but there is no evidence of its presence in the West before the mid-14th century, although it is unlikely to have disappeared completely during the intervening centuries.

Noise-making and musical improvisation

Most of the above idiophones are nontonal; with the exception of bells and percussion beams, they form part of the *musica irregularis* decried by writers such as the German organologist Sebastian Virdung in 1511 and as such were restricted to popular entertainment or signalling. Written music of this period does not help to determine whether, or how, idiophones were played with voices or with other instruments.

Modern times. Additional idiophones came into use from the Renaissance on. The xylophone was introduced from Indonesia; curiously enough, its first appearance was as the name of an organ stop in 1506, when it was termed a new stop. Virdung and the blind organist Arnold Schlick were the first to write of it, both in 1511. It remained little exploited until the Flemish carillonneurs combined it with a keyboard and transformed it into a practice instrument in the first half of the 17th century. The older form remained a folk instrument, chiefly in and east of Germany. An Austrian violinist, Ignaz Schweigl (died 1803), wrote concert pieces for it during his last years, and Saint-Saëns revived it in his *Danse macabre* of 1874. Lately, Afro-American marimbas have been incorporated into Western rhythm bands. Lithophones, stone imitations of xylophones, enjoyed a certain vogue in the 19th century; among these short-lived curiosities, the English stonemason Richardson's "rock harmonicon," with its tuned basalt bars, is best known.

Gongs were always considered alien instruments, as indeed they are: although the word gong was known in the 16th century, its use is not further recorded until the late 18th century. Since then, gongs of indefinite pitch have been included in orchestral scores for arresting effect. For generations both flat and bossed (knobbed) gongs also performed the lowly task of summoning the family to meals.

Cymbals were apparently forgotten during the Renaissance; they reappear in the German composer Nicolaus Adam Strungk's opera *Esther* (1680) to provide local colour and are reintroduced through "Turkish music" (imitating the Turkish Janissary bands) to opera from 1770 on; soon afterward they acquired a permanent position in the orchestra. As folk instruments they have been played for centuries in Provence in France, probably as a continuation of an older ritual tradition.

In 16th-century Spain the saraband was usually danced to castanets or to a guitar; castanets have remained dancers' instruments ever since, either clicked together rhythmically or in sustained rolls. Modern rhythm bands now include one or two single castanets or a pair attached to a long handle for ease in clicking (the traditional manner of playing in the hand is difficult to master).

Bells grew larger until the largest ever produced, the Tsar Kolokol (Emperor Bell; 1733–35) of Moscow, weighing 433,200 pounds (196,500 kilograms), proved too cumbersome and heavy for hanging. The hemispherical form was abandoned early as chimes became larger, culminating in tower-borne carillons brought into existence by progress in casting methods and mechanization. Chime bells were connected to town clocks and then hung in separate bell towers. In carillons of the Low Countries and northern France the bells' external hammers were automatically released by iron pegs set in a large wooden barrel (later, a metal cylinder) revolved by weight and pulley, permitting whole tunes to be played. Chorales and other melodies preludized the announcements of time on the European continent, while in Britain "chimes," or short sequences, fulfilled the office of timekeeper. Furthermore, instead of automatically playing melodies, British tower bells are rung in "changes"—a series of mathematical permutations—on bells hung dead. The role of small bells has become negligible, although handbell ringing is still a hobby in England.

Metallophones reached northern Europe from Indonesia in the second half of the 17th century and, like the xylophones, were promptly adopted by carillonneurs. In both the Low Countries and the regions to which such instruments spread from there, steel was the metal employed for bars. Provided with a keyboard, one served as "carillon" in Handel's oratorio *Saul;* another, struck with a beater, served as *strumento d'acciaio* (literally, "steel instrument") in Mozart's *Die Zauberflöte* (*The Magic Flute*). The modern glockenspiel (from the German *Glockenspiel,* "bell chime") was originally a bell chime, as its name indicates. Its transformation into a metallophone was in response to the need for a portable instrument; for marching bands the bars were hung in a lyre-shaped frame and called bell lyre. Symphony and opera orchestras—and today rhythm bands as well—make use of a larger, horizontal glocken-

The celesta

spiel to which resonators have been added since 1935. Graduated steel bars struck from a keyboard by piano hammers form the celesta, patented in 1886 by Auguste and Alphonse Mustel of Paris; this has been scored in both symphony and opera and is a favourite of light orchestras. Its descendant, the vibraharp (called vibraphone in England), has characteristic tubular metal resonators that sustain the tone while imparting vibrato. These last two instruments are successfully exploited for their special tone colour in 20th-century music. Late 18th-century experiments with graduated sets of tuning forks struck by hammers from a keyboard produced the 19th-century "tuning-fork pianos," the most noteworthy of which were different models of Victor Mustel of Paris (from 1865 on).

Tubular bells are European adaptations of Southeast Asian bamboo chimes. Bells have always been both expensive and cumbersome, and substitutes started appearing in the 19th century, first in the form of steel bars, then hollow bronze cylinders, and finally brass tubes struck with wooden mallets. For use in churches, tubular bells can be played directly from the manual of an organ and the tone picked up, amplified, and fed into a system of loudspeakers in the tower.

Pellet bells and other rattles today play a very minor role, the former chiefly as horse or mule bells. In the present century the gourd-shaped maraca rattle has been added to the complement of rhythm band idiophones. Scrapers have all but disappeared from Europe: Virdung illustrated the scraped pot, now defunct, but other forms survive, mostly as carnival noisemakers. More sophisticated were the giant cog rattles with diameters up to 6½ feet installed in or outside church towers in the Iberian Peninsula, substitutes since the 15th century for bells during Easter Week. Scraped gourds are now part of the professional percussionists's equipment.

Jew's harps were part of the regular stock-in-trade of instrument dealers in the 16th and 17th centuries, and in the mid-18th century the playing of multiple Jew's harps is mentioned. Several of these little instruments combined in a single frame were played by virtuosos in the late 18th and 19th centuries and enjoyed enormous popularity. Miniaturization of musical clocks in the latter part of the 18th century resulted in the creation of the music box, a linguaphone provided with a metal-comb mechanism made from about 1770 on, chiefly in Switzerland. In its heyday—1810 to 1910—it was an immensely popular household instrument with a repertory of opera arias, folk songs, popular tunes of the day, and waltzes (after the midcentury). In the late 19th century it was transformed into a free-reed wind instrument (aerophone) by the substitution of free reeds for the metal comb, but neither comb nor free reed could resist the impact of the phonograph, which rendered both forms obsolete.

Experimental instruments

During the 18th century several friction idiophones were introduced, among them the nail violin of Johann Wilde (*c.* 1740) with its tuned nails bowed by a violin bow. More characteristic of the period were the friction-bar instruments arising as a result of the German acoustician Ernst Chladni's late 18th-century experiments, particularly those concerned with the transmission of vibrations by friction. Chladni's own instrument, the euphone of 1790, and the aiuton of Charles Claggett of about the same time were first in a series of models, some with piano keyboard and horizontal friction cylinder or cone acting on upright bars and others with bars stroked by the player's fingers or bowed by a continuous bow.

Musical glasses are considerably older: the tuned metal cups or bowls of the East were transformed in Europe into tuned glasses and are first seen in the *Musica theoretica* (1492) of the Italian musical theorist, Franchino Gafori. One hears of them intermittently thereafter until they come to the fore in the mid-18th century as concert instruments. The rims of glasses of graduated sizes containing enough water to tune them were rubbed by the player's moistened fingers. By the 1760s they had attracted the attention of the American scientist and philosopher Benjamin Franklin, who proceeded to convert them into a more efficient and, above all, a polyphonic (many-voiced) instrument, which he called armonica—now known as the glass harmonica. Its popularity was immediate. Mozart's *Adagio und Rondo* K. 617 was written for it, as was his *Adagio für Harmonika* K. 356, both performed in 1791. Efforts to combine it with a keyboard were successful from 1784 on but enjoyed only a passing vogue. Among the last to write for it was the French composer Hector Berlioz in his *Fantasia on The Tempest* of 1830; a decade later it was replaced by the growing family of free reeds.

The foregoing reveals the trend in Western musical culture to make diminishing use of nontonal idiophones. Those that succeeded in gaining access to the orchestra are used sparingly, often only as special effects (gongs) or indications of local colour (castanets). This trend is reversed in popular music of the 20th century, in which idiophones, both traditional and alien, play a basic part. On the other hand, tonal idiophones have assumed increasing importance. Those inherited from the Middle Ages, such as xylophones and Jew's harps, were expanded to the limit of their potential; others were imported and modified to meet local requirements. The new idiophones that came into being—for example, the music box and the friction-bar idiophones—proved ephemeral. Influenced by the great popularity of the piano, keyboards were adapted to numerous 19th-century idiophones in an attempt to render hitherto monophonic (single-voiced) instruments polyphonic.

In Asia. Still preserved today are actual clappers from Sumer of about 3000 BC and ancient Egyptian clappers, some of which took the form of a pair of hands. Their use seems never to have died out in Egypt. Copts still ritually strike clappers of a type that has probably been in existence since the 3rd or even 4th millennium BC. Modern Vietnam also retains clappers—often artifacts of great beauty—in its religious observances. On the Indian subcontinent circular wooden clappers, one held in each hand, are played by beggars and fakirs in some regions and are used as rhythm instruments in others. In the Far East they have a role in the theatre, as signal instruments, at funerals, or, as in the Ryukyu Islands, accompanying traditional dances. Castanets probably originated in ancient Phoenicia; they appear in Egypt in the 24th dynasty (*c.* 730–709 BC) and are typical dancers' instruments.

Ritual, social, and musical uses of clappers

Cymbals are indigenous to Asia; ancient Assyria had a unique form, funnel-shaped with long necks serving as handles. Known in ancient Israel from *c.* 1100 BC on, cymbals were the only permanent idiophones of the Temple orchestra. Egypt did not have true metal cymbals until the 24th dynasty. Today they remain in ritual use in northern India, Japan, Tibet, and Vietnam. They appear in the 5th century AD in India, where they are now also played at secular festivities. In China they play a prominent part in the theatre. Turkey, in contrast, has traditionally connected cymbals with military usage. In some part of Southeast Asia their ancient metal-connected function of dispelling evil spirits still prevails.

Xylophones reach their highest development in Southeast Asia. They vary in form from the most primitive log type to the highly developed orchestral instruments found in Indonesia. Trough xylophones were depicted in Java in the 14th century but are not restricted to Southeast Asia; those of Japan, for instance, are rhythm rather than melody instruments, and in Burma they are associated with royalty. Xylophones of the Indonesian gamelan, or percussion orchestra (and some mainland ensembles), have various complementary compasses.

Stone chimes (lithophones) of two types occur: oblong bars like xylophone keys resting horizontally, found in Vietnam only, and vertically suspended plaques. In China their generic name is *ch'ing;* there, single sculpted musical stones and also 16-stone chimes are suspended from ornate frames. Stones forming a chime are carved in a typical L-form and struck with a mallet on their larger portion. The L-shape is very ancient; a chime of this form dating from the late Shang era (*c.* 1401–*c.* 1123 BC) was excavated at An-yang, in northeast China. Both in China and Korea, where the oldest chime goes back to the 14th century, the lithophone is a Confucian ritual instrument. Single stones and chimes are still in use in rural Annam (Vietnam).

Use of chimes in Confucian ritual

Metallophones occur in the same two forms as lithophones, those in the horizontal position being the more common. Indonesia and Indochina have metallophones constructed like xylophones, of which they are indeed metal counterparts. But in China the *fang-hsiang* with its 16 bars is a metal imitation of the lithophone. Among important components of the gamelan is the *saron,* a trough metallophone depicted as early as *c.* 800 AD on the Borobuḍur *stūpa* (Buddhist monument), Java, and the frame metallophone *gender,* now usually supplied with tubular resonators, which has been known from the 12th century on. Introduced to China by a Turkic people in the 7th century, the horizontal type of metallophone reached Korea in the 12th century and is still occasionally played there. In Japan it is a Buddhist ritual instrument.

The slit-drum is an instrument made by hollowing a log or wood block through a slit. Those of east Asia and Indonesia are of great antiquity and of a high degree of development. The Chinese *mu yü* (traditionally fish-shaped) is a Buddhist and Taoist ritual slit-drum. Its Korean and Japanese counterparts are likewise ritual time markers, while in Vietnam the slit-drum is both a temple and a watchmen's instrument. On Java slit-drums can be traced to the Hindu–Javanese period (1st–9th century AD). Small models are generally suspended vertically, whereas larger ones rest horizontally; some underscore dance rhythms; others are signal instruments.

Southeast Asia is the home of tubular chimes; resonant, tuned bamboo tubes are united to form a chime in rural Annam and Java. In western Java up to 16 tubes are strung in ladder formation and suspended from a house or a tree and played with padded beaters.

Western Asia is believed to be the home of the gong, which reached China in the 6th century, Java by the 8th. Originally, it seems to have afforded protection against evil spirits, and even today the Iban people of Borneo beat gongs during a storm. Chinese gongs are both bossed (knobbed) and flat, those of Indonesia are bossed, while those of India are flat. Chinese gongs serve a whole gamut of purposes: as signal instruments of the army, as rhythm makers to accompany a song and, in the case of the bossless *lo,* as a Buddhist ritual instrument. In Japan the employment of the gong varies from temple to theatre to folk festival.

Gong chimes in Indonesian orchestras

In Indonesia and eastern Asia tuned gongs are united to form gong chimes. The Chinese upright *yung lo* is a Buddhist and Confucian cult chime and was formerly also played at court. Better known are the horizontal gong chimes of Indonesia (called *bonang* in Java), outstanding components of Southeast Asian orchestras and known from the 10th or 11th century on. Individual gongs comprising a *bonang* are often referred to as "bonang kettles," from their sharply bossed and deeply rimmed form. Frames of Thai gong chimes arch upward at both ends to form an upright semicircle. Ancient kettle gongs, products of Bronze Age culture, are found only in China, Indochina, and Indonesia. They are hung so that the striking surface is vertical and are struck in the centre of this surface (the head). Kettle gongs were cult instruments connected with rainmaking; those of the Dong Son culture area of North Vietnam may be dated from the 5th to the 3rd centuries BC.

Bells of bronze dating from about 1000 BC have been excavated in India, from the 22nd dynasty (945–730) in Egypt, and from *c.* 700 in Assyria. An intimate connection existed in ancient India between bell sound and mystic experience, and today a handbell is still rung in temple ceremonies in India and other areas of Buddhist influence. The Chinese differentiate between clapper bells (*ling*) and clapperless ones (*chung*); their temple bells, like those of Japan, are always of the *chung* type. Temple bells usually assume the form of chimes in China; one from the 6th century has 13 bells, but more modern chimes consist of 16 bells hung in two rows of a frame. In addition to metal bells of the high-culture domains, rural areas still use primitive wooden bells with single or multiple clappers.

The sistrum in its earliest form, that of a U, is seen in Sumer in the mid-3rd millennium BC, and a little later, about 2100/2000, a rectangular form appears in Horoz tepe, Anatolia (modern Turkey). Egyptian sistrums are characterized by being closed at the top: the *sesheshet* was shaped like a temple, the *iba* like a closed horseshoe. Sacred to the Egyptian goddess Hathor, the *iba* was played only by women, and after Hathor's metamorphosis into Isis it remained sacred to Isis.

A sliding rattle called *angklung,* found only in Indonesia, consists of several tuned bamboo tubes with cut-back tongues, inserted into a frame; they slide back and forth when the frame is shaken. When the *angklung* is constructed as a chime, each player shakes his frame when it is his turn to sound it.

Scraped idiophones are Confucian ritual instruments in east Asia. The "tiger" of China is a vessel scraper of wood with a series of notches cut along its back; known as early as the Chou dynasty (*c.* 1122–221 BC), it is scraped with a split bamboo stick. Split idiophones (made of hollow cane split between nodes) are slapped against the player's wrist or thigh in south China and Southeast Asia, producing a fixed-pitch buzz.

Jew's harps have idioglott tongues (cut from the same material as the frame) in Indonesia, while both idioglott and heteroglott (the tongue made separately and attached to the frame) forms occur in China and on the Indian subcontinent. In southwest Yunnan (in southern China), three separate idioglott, tuned Jew's harps may be united by young people for the purpose of exchanging messages; such instruments are of bamboo and have the older, clothespin form. More recent are those of metal having the outline of an onion. In the Philippines and some other areas Jew's harps are important adjuncts to courtship.

Musical cups

Musical cups, the forerunners of musical glasses, are depicted on the Borobuḍur *stūpa* of *c.* 800; the Indian *rastrarang* can be played either with small sticks by percussion or by rubbing wetted fingers along the rims—the cups do not contain water. But the *jaltarang,* also of India, makes use of water for fine tuning and for the playing of *gamakas* (ornaments) by carefully bringing the sticks into contact with the surface of the water. Similar musical cups are played in Japan in Buddhist temples and in the music of the Kabuki theatre.

In Africa and Afro-America. Idiophones of Muslim Africa are mainly those of the Near East or derivations thereof. Outsize hollow clappers shaped like a dumbbell sliced lengthwise are clicked by Moroccan singers, who hold a pair in each hand. A percussion bowl, an inverted bowl set afloat in a larger, water-filled bowl, is beaten with a single stick by the Saharan Tuareg as their substitute for the West African water gourd. Finger cymbals are worn pairwise on finger and thumb of each hand by dancers. Basically, however, the percussion of this area is executed by drums. Idiophones do not participate in art music.

Black Africa. In contrast, Black Africa has an almost bewildering variety of idiophones. Clappers, generally of wood, are played from coast to coast. Simple percussion sticks are known in East and West Africa.

Xylophone ensembles

Xylophones vary from the primitive pit xylophone, with few wooden bars placed over a pit or trench and isolated from the ground by bundles of grass or by wooden members, to the leg xylophone, with a couple of bars placed on the outstretched legs of a woman player, to the large instruments with independent framework and tuned keys graduated in size. African xylophones are usually provided with a gourd resonator suspended from each key, often containing a mirliton device that adds a characteristic buzzing quality to the tone. Ensemble playing of several xylophones, reported by 17th-century travellers, is still practiced. In some areas xylophones form small orchestras with several players to one larger instrument. Unmistakable similarities of form, playing technique, tuning, and even of the music performed confirm the African xylophone's Southeast Asian origin.

Slit-drums occur in the Western "Bend" (of the Niger River, in modern Mali) and Congo Basin. They may be cylindrical, boat-, wedge-, or crescent-shaped, and zoomorphic with dorsal slit. Possibly related to the drummed tube zither, a cylindrical slit-drum with from two to five slits is encountered in West Africa; the Kissi people of Guinea not only strike the slats formed by the multiple slits but the ends of the slit-drum as well.

Bells occur in a large variety: metal and wooden, single or double, clapperless and with single or multiple clappers, played as rhythm or signal instruments. The apotropaic qualities of metal bells are recognized in Africa also, where such bells may be associated with chieftainship. Double bells, usually of metal, share a common handle: if this is straight, a dumbbell form results, but if bent, the bells lie cheek by jowl. Those of a pair differ in length or in diameter and, consequently, always in pitch. Metal double bells are devoid of clappers and are often made of sheet iron soldered down the side, whereas double bells of wood often have multiple clappers.

Water gourds—half gourds floated open side down in a pan of water and struck rhythmically with small sticks—are played in West Africa; in Dahomey their chief use is at funeral rites.

Construction of rattles

Rattles are the instruments *par excellence* of dancers, although they can also be worn on the leg simply to provide walking rhythm. Strung and gourd rattles are common, with the latter often serving in religious cults or magic rites in the Congo Basin area. In West Africa a variety of rattle sounded by external percussion was developed: the surface of a gourd is covered by a network of dried fruit seeds threaded on a cord. Sistrum-like forked sticks strung with threaded pairs of calabash fragments have an important part in fertility and initiation rites among the Mali of West Africa. The ancient horseshoe and rectangular forms of sistrum are still played in Ethiopia in the Monophysite Christian Church.

Scrapers in both solid and vessel form are widespread; a notched calabash, the *quilando,* was described by Girolamo Merolla in 1692.

The African linguaphone is known to the West by the native name sansa (zanza) or the Bantu name *mbira* and in English additionally by the misnomers "kaffir piano" and "thumb piano"; it consists of a varying number of cane or metal tongues fitted to a wooden board or resonator so as to permit one end of the tongues to swing freely; their different lengths determine the pitch. Sansas show affinity of tuning with xylophones that cannot be considered accidental, and thus they may be considered as small, portable versions of the latter.

Afro-America. West African idiophones introduced into the Americas with the slave trade are still flourishing. Clappers originating among the Yoruba (a Nigerian people) are played in Cuba; the claves, or pair of cylindrical percussion sticks of Haiti and Cuba, are now standard equipment in Western rhythm bands. The xylophone may already have entered America in pre-Columbian times. Known chiefly as marimba, one of its African names, it has been accepted in Western musical culture. Bells frequently figure as voodoo cult instruments in Caribbean and Afro-Brazilian communities. In Cuba water gourds are played at funeral rites for Afro-Cubans.

Steel drums

Steel drums originated in Trinidad during World War II and have become vehicles for popular music in the U.S. since. Actually a single "drum" forms a chime, as one head of an ordinary oil drum is divided into sections of different sizes by punched grooves, each section then being tuned to its own pitch. Today only a greater or lesser rim, depending upon the range required, is left but originally the oil drum was left intact.

Rattles play an important part in African cults of the New World, both gourd rattles with internal and external percussion and a distinct variety consisting of two metal cones joined at their widest part. (The maraca gourd rattle is probably indigenous to South America.)

Scrapers are highly popular. The notched gourd with natural handle, called guiro, is another Afro-American instrument taken over by the West. Notched turtle carapaces are scraped in the Caribbean. The jawbone of a horse, mule, or donkey, with its teeth left in, is played in both North and South America and in the Caribbean; its use among coastal Negroes of Peru goes back to the 18th century. In the United States it is still encountered in Louisiana and the Carolinas.

Sansas in the Caribbean and in South America bear such names as *marimbula* (Cuba) and *marimbao* (Brazil), clearly indicating their origin.

In America. A wide assortment of idiophones is available to American Indians, but many of these are restricted to nonmusical uses. Concussion sticks, for instance, serve as game calls in North America, while concussion stones are invariably ritual: they are clashed to make thunder. Small, conical bells of metal and multiclapper bells of wood were known in ancient Peru.

Slit-drums have been played in Central and South America since pre-Columbian times, but their occurrence in South America is now rare. Characteristic of the well-known *teponaztli* is the form of its slits, cut to form an H with tongues of different thicknesses, thus allowing it to emit two sounds. Formerly, Zapotec warriors of Ixtepeji, Mexico, went into battle carrying an idol and singing to the accompaniment of the *teponaztli,* while Indians of 16th-century Hispaniola danced to their slit-drums.

Strung rattles are worn as leggings to emphasize a dancer's movements, but when the strung material consists of a dead enemy's teeth, as among the Brazilian Mundurucú, the rattle becomes a source of magic strength to the wearer; elsewhere, strung deer or caribou hooves attract game during the hunt. Vessel rattles of gourd and pottery imitations of gourds have been in use since Aztec times. Cult instruments in prehistoric America, they are still used by medicine men during their incantations. Hollow, seed-filled staffs were ceremonial rattles of Aztec and Maya, and descendants of these instruments are still played in North America.

Scrapers are seen on the 8th- or 9th-century frescoes of the temple at Bonampak in Chivas State, Mexico, played in a procession. Today among the Pima Indians of Arizona, scrapers play an important part in rainmaking ceremonies. Elsewhere in North America they serve as time markers. Scraped sticks of animal or human bone or of antler, with a series of notches practiced along one side, were sounded at sacrificial or memorial ceremonies of the Aztec Empire. In modern times they have been played in North America by medicine men. Split idiophones were employed in western coastal areas of North America chiefly for ceremonial purposes; some tribes slapped them against their chests, others against their palms. Finally, a curious friction-instrument vessel of Central and South America, the rubbed tortoise carapace, is a ritual instrument and taboo to the noninitiated; the instrument is rubbed with the fingers, not scraped.

In the Pacific. The different cultures of this wide area where singing and dancing form so prominent a part of the muscal life include a number of primitive idiophones, some of which are played with considerable sophistication. Concussion sticks are clashed by an Aboriginal Australian singer to lend emphasis. The Maori breathe words of a song onto a carved stick held between their teeth while tapping it with a second stick. In Hawaii concussion stones were held pairwise by dancers who clicked them together like castanets. In New Britain and Papua primitive log xylophones are played, consisting of two banana stems or other logs placed on the ground with a few keys placed across them.

Aboriginal concussion sticks

A percussion gourd of New Guinea has an hourglass form, open at both ends; when plunged in and out of water, it is said to emit the sounds "uh-ah-uh-ah". Split-bamboo percussion tubes, doubling as rattles, are indigenous to the same area, while the percussion board *o-le-polotu* of Samoan and Tongan chiefs accompanies solo songs. Slit-drums can be huge. Made from a tree trunk, living slit-drums in Vanuatu (the New Hebrides) are carved with the faces of ancestors, and in New Guinea roofed drum houses are built over large, horizontal slit-drums to protect them from the weather. The Maori, one of the relatively few peoples who have no membrane drums, use their slit-drums as signal instruments. Related to these is a percussion tube of Fiji, partly hollowed and tapering at the ends and struck with two sticks on the side opposite the slit.

Slit-drums

Idioglott Jew's harps of bamboo are the major tonal idiophones of the area; here the tongue is vibrated either by the player's finger or by jerking it with a cord. A friction vessel of New Ireland consists of a rounded and hollowed block of wood, its upper portion carved into three tongues of different lengths and hence emitting as many pitches. Already rare nowadays and taboo to women and children, it is played at death commemoration rites by a male performer who rubs well-oiled hands over the tongues.

MEMBRANOPHONES

Musical instruments in which the sound-producing medium is a vibrating membrane fall into four main groups: kettledrums and bowl-shaped drums; tubular drums—whether cylindrical, barrel, conical, double conical, hourglass, goblet, or shallow—and rattle drums, the membranes of which are set in motion by enclosed pellets or by knotted ends of a thong or cord; friction drums, with membranes caused to vibrate by friction; and mirlitons, musical auxiliaries with membranes set in motion by directing the vibrating air column of an instrument or voice against them.

Kettledrums and tubular drums occur in both tunable and nontunable forms; friction drums and mirlitons are not tunable. The membranes of the first two groups are either glued, nailed, lapped, or laced to the body, or shell; if they are glued or nailed, the pitch can be modified by exposure to heat. Lapped and laced heads are readily tunable by tightening the lacings or screws, and wooden wedges may be inserted between the shell and lacings to further increase the membrane's tension and thus raise the pitch. The membranes of such instruments and of friction drums are set in vibration by percussion, while those of mirlitons vibrate by impact of sound waves. In all groups the shell plays a subordinate acoustical part, acting as resonator only. The greater the diameter of a head, the deeper is its sound; and the greater its tension, the higher is the pitch. In Western culture the only drums tuned to a definite pitch are kettledrums (the orchestral timpani).

Methods of striking drums

Kettledrums and tubular drums may be struck by the hands, with beaters, or both combined or by the knotted ends of a thong or cord. Beaters can be cylindrical, club-shaped, straight, curved, or angled, with or without knobs or padding, or may take the form of a switch or wire brush. Friction drums are sounded by rubbing the membrane with a piece of hide or by the more usual method of working an inserted friction stick or cord up and down or by rubbing the membrane with a player's wet fingers. Acoustically, they are subject to the same laws as other membranophones, but the speed of friction is an influencing factor. They occur in Africa, America, Europe, Asia (India and Japan), and Hawaii. Mirlitons are not true musical instruments but always voice modifiers, be it a human or an instrumental voice (as when affixed, *e.g.,* to African xylophone resonators); as such they have no pitch of their own.

Primitive ground drums, consisting in their simplest form of an animal skin stretched over the opening of a pit, are still found in many parts of the world. A skin may also be held taut by several players, each beating it with a stick. These and similar ground drums are played by women in Africa and Australia, in North America usually by men. By their very nature ground drums are nonportable; when need arose for a smaller "drum," a skin was stretched over the opening of a gourd, clay pot, or other object. Among the Swazi of South Africa such skins are not attached but held taut. Whether the skin is attached to or held taut over a pot, etc., such instruments are known as pot drums. They are found in Asia, Africa, and America—in Africa and America often in connection with exorcism.

In Europe. Only a few kinds of drum, none indigenous, were known to antiquity. The frame drum came from the East at an early date. The barrel drum was possibly known in Hellenistic times, for it appears in the Greco-Indian culture of Kushan. A shallow drum is depicted on a Greco-Scythian metal *gorytus,* or bow and arrow case, of the 4th century BC, but there again no evidence exists of its having been known to Greece. Frame drums, traditionally women's instruments in the Near East, remained in the hands of female players and dancers in Greece, and the Eastern playing technique was maintained: held upright on edge in the palm of one hand, the drum was tapped with the fingers of the other. Probably introduced into Greece in the 6th century BC with the cult of the great mother-goddess Cybele, the frame drum is depicted as being played by maenads and was also a cult instrument in rites of the Orphic religion. From Greece the frame drum passed into Rome, where it was also associated with Cybele. Romans also had double-headed drums and spread them as far north as the Isle of Wight, in Britain, where one is represented on a mosaic pavement as a dancing girl's instrument. In the late days of the Roman Empire, frame drums became instruments of street musicians and *joculatores;* the latter are sometimes portrayed throwing them up in the air and catching them again and are probably responsible for spreading them beyond the Italian Peninsula.

The frame drum

The Middle Ages. Frame drums were described by Isidore of Seville in the 7th century, but they seem to have played a negligible role in medieval Europe until reintroduced by the crusaders, after which they appear both in round and square form in the hands of both men and women. Jingles and pellet bells, frequently attached from the 14th century on, enliven the sound. French medieval poems place the instrument in the hands of female dancers, and in the 14th century Boccaccio writes of it as accompanying the voice.

Double-headed drums served as time beaters from the 6th century on. From the 7th century dates the first evidence of their being played with drumsticks, a technique adopted from Asia. Hourglass drums appear in southern Europe by the 10th century, only to die out in the late Middle Ages. The small cylinder drum known as the tabor was provided with a snare (material stretched across the head to produce a rattling sound) and struck with a stick right on the snare. Played together with the three-holed pipe, it formed a lively one-man ensemble, the companion of country dances throughout western Europe for centuries; it is still in use in some areas.

The naker

With the Crusades the small kettledrum called naker, always paired, entered Europe, reaching Russia in the 11th century and the West at the turn of the 12th and 13th century. A pair of nakers would be attached by a belt to the player's waist or suspended from the shoulder, each struck alternately as the heads sounded at different pitches. Not until the mid-15th century do the wide-diameter horse-borne kettledrums reach the West. Henceforth, they were to be paired with trumpets and associated with royalty and the cavalry, whereas the marching of infantry was regulated by plebeian fife and *Landsknecht's* (lansquenet's) drum, a cylinder drum of considerable proportions slung to the player's left. As mercenary soldiers from the late 15th century on, Swiss drummers and fifers popularized such ensembles throughout western Europe. The shallow drum, presumably of Turkish derivation, is seen in the late 14th century. Its two heads were at first nailed in Oriental fashion, but by the mid-15th century the instrument was suitably Occidentalized by the use of laced heads.

The less common friction drum first appears in the late 12th-century sculpture of the archbishop's palace at Santiago de Compostela, in Spain, complete with friction rod. Although it undoubtedly continued in existence, it is not known to be either pictured or mentioned again until the 17th century.

Modern times. By the Renaissance, Europe had a variety of drums performing specialized functions: frame drums and small tabors accompanied dance and song; larger tabors served as time beaters in small mixed ensembles; great cylinder drums with fifes were placed at the disposal of foot troops; large kettledrums and trumpets were restricted to cavalry and ceremonial music. Frame drums remained popular in the south, particularly in Spain, as dancers' instruments; from Spain they travelled to Hispaniola by the mid-16th century.

Admission of kettle-drums to the orchestra

Before the late 17th century, drums in the West served principally at court or other ceremonial functions and increasingly as military instruments, although smaller models filled social needs of everyday life. The 17th-century French composer Jean-Baptiste Lully appears to have been the first to admit drums and kettledrums to the opera and even, according to Titon du Tillet, 18th-century French writer and courtier, into church music. In the year of Lully's death (1687), Daniel Speer, a contemporary German musician, commented that echo effects could be obtained on kettledrums by playing softly close to the rim and striking hard at the centre; with such new techniques, modified drumstick heads, and the possibility of notating their music (hitherto prohibited by the rules of secrecy imposed upon guild members), kettledrums, henceforth called timpani, triumphantly entered orchestra, opera and church.

"Turkish" drums, descendants of the shallow drum, were admitted to the orchestra and military band in the 18th century. The composer Christoph Willibald Gluck was an early writer for this instrument in his opéra comique *Les Pélerins de la Mecque* (*The Pilgrims of Mecca,* 1764); also known as *La Rencontre imprévue*), and Mozart scored for it in his *Die Entführung aus dem Serail* (*The Abduction from the Seraglio,* 1782). Still called "Turkish" drum in 1823 by the French musicologist Guillaume-André Villoteau, a member of Napoleon's scientific mission to Egypt, it began to be known as the bass drum around this time. Another type sometimes called bass drum is the long drum, a military instrument of Turkish origin. Great, battle-scarred specimens of the 18th and 19th centuries in museums attest its continued use in Europe in its original form. The old *Landsknecht's* side drum became too unwieldy and was cut down to the proportions of the modern side or snare drum. It may also have been the ancestor of the tenor drum, the original function of which was to play rolls and which was gradually eased out of military bands in most countries in the 19th century in favour of the far lighter side drum. The long drum continues in use as a folk instrument in the Balkans.

The northern frame drum, or tambourine, was given the status of a salon instrument by 18th-century French society, and, combined with harp or keyboard instrument, it could be heard at fashionable soirees. Although it is rarely written for, Weber uses one for local colour in his opera *Preciosa* (1820), Berlioz in his overture *Carnaval romain* (*Roman Carnival,* 1844).

Friction drums have maintained an existence to this day in various parts of Europe, where they are played at Christmas, during the carnival season, or to greet the New Year in less industrialized areas.

Mirlitons, with their ability of amplifying and colouring tone, have been known in Europe since the 16th century, possibly earlier, but did not gain popularity until the early 19th century. From 1883 on, a French toy maker named Bigot brought out a series of bigotphones shaped like orchestral instruments, and as late as 1910 gatherings of "bigotphonists" took place in Paris. Popular in mid-20th century was the tubular kazoo.

Changes in drumming technique

Drumming in the 20th century gained an important place outside its traditional preserves of orchestra and military band: rhythm bands and experimental music opened hitherto unexplored fields. The latter was preoccupied with rhythmic stress and also exploited drum tone for its own sake as a source of independent sound and tone colour. Playing techniques consequently became freer, players striking either the membrane or the shell, using bare hands or a large range of beaters varying from stiff to flexible and hard to soft; wire "brushes" were frequently substituted for sticks in rhythm bands. The drum was treated as a solo instrument amid a group of its peers. On the popular level, rhythm may be stressed or punctuated, often by the clarity and opposing pitches of a pair of Afro-American drums (usually referred to as Latin-American drums).

In Asia. Unlike the drums of Western musical tradition, those found in ancient (and parts of modern) Asia are primarily cult and ceremonial instruments. Most, if not all, Western drums are their descendants, and west Central Asia may well be their common homeland. Babylonia already had a variety of forms: cylinder, hourglass, goblet, and bowl-shaped, all of terra-cotta and all beaten with bare hands. Assyrians also carried in procession a large, conical drum played in the same manner.

Babylonian drums

Temple drums were of considerable proportions: huge frame drums existed from the 3rd millennium on in Mesopotamia, and the waist-high *lilissu* had a goblet form—a bowl on a stand—and may have been the ancestor to the kettledrum. All these were played by men, but the smaller frame drums appearing in Sumer in about 2000 BC are depicted in the hands of women. An early Sumerian text informs us that the king's granddaughter was appointed player of the *balag di* in the Temple of the Moon at Ur around 2400 BC. Ever since, frame drums have been predominantly women's instruments. The Bible says that in ancient Israel "Miriam, the prophetess, the sister of Aaron, took a timbrel in her hand; and all the women went out after her with timbrels and dancing." They are still played throughout the Near East, in some areas in art music ensembles, in others only in popular and folk music.

Wherever the Muslim presence has made itself felt, large and small kettledrums are encountered. In Turkey classical monophonic singing is accompanied solely by a small kettledrum, played either in the centre of the head or close to the rim, depending upon whether clear or muffled beats are desired.

Association of drums with thunder

In many regions of the ancient and modern East drums were believed to create or imitate thunder. Sets of thunder drums are depicted on East Turkistan art objects from the 9th century to the 11th century. In China, Lei Kung, duke of Thunder, is traditionally surrounded by numerous drums on which he creates thunder, and in Japan thundering drums were even automated by attaching a number of them to the outer circumference of a wheel that, when revolved, caused them to rattle—an early application of the rattledrum principle. As in Africa and America, cult drums of Asia have been associated with human sacrifice; thus the Chinese *Tso Chuan* ("The Commentary of Tso," one of the classics of Confucian literature) mentions the consecration of drums in the 7th and 6th centuries BC by smearing them with the blood of a sacrificial human, usually a war captive.

Rattle drums, either containing in their cavities objects that rattle when the drum is twirled by a handle or with attached cords having knotted ends that strike the heads, can be traced back to the Shang dynasty (*c.* 1766–*c.* 1122 BC) and are now in use from Tibet and India to Japan. Still a cult drum in some areas—it is an attribute of Śiva (Shiva), the third member of the Hindu trinity—in others the rattle drum has degenerated to a mere toy. On the giant *stūpa* of Borobuḍur, Java, an archetypal image of the known cosmos, are sculpted the musical instruments in use at the time of its erection (*c.* 800). These include cylinder, conical, hourglass, and pot drums—all Indian instruments. Yet, today's Indonesian orchestra, the gamelan, virtually ignores drums in favour of metallophones. Drumming is exclusively a man's business on some islands of the Malay archipelago, where drums are kept in the men's house, out of sight of women.

Drums played an important part in early court orchestras of China and Korea, judging by their surviving elements in *gagaku,* court orchestral music of Japan. Here, the leader beats time on a drum, either cylindrical or hourglass-shaped, having projecting heads, a characteristic feature of Japanese hooped drums. Larger barrel-shaped drums with nailed heads are suspended from elaborate frames. On the Indian subcontinent a variety of membranophones participate in art music ensembles or accompany dances, while small kettledrums are played pairwise in processions; large, single kettledrums are temple instruments or may be mounted on elephants' backs in outdoor ceremonies. Many smaller drums have laced and wedged heads, the skin being further tensed by an application of tuning paste.

Drum chimes

In Burma, Thailand, and south Nias Island (Indonesia) a number of tuned barrel drums of varying sizes are suspended in a low circular pen to form drum chimes; such a chime may consist of from 16 to 24 drums, all played by a single musician with his fingers and palms, occasionally with a drumstick. These chimes form part of the theatre orchestra and are even played in processions.

In East and Southeast Asia a mirliton device is applied to many woodwinds in order to obtain a characteristic modification of tone quality. To this end an additional aperture is cut in the tube and covered with a thin membrane. A different application of this principle is encountered in India, where a pair of short, wooden mirliton "trumpets" are placed against the throat of a humming performer.

During the 1950s a similar technique was employed by the United States recording industry for the obtaining of anthropomorphic effects.

In Africa and Afro-America. Drumming tradition in the Muslim north centres on smaller, portable drums, such as frame, goblet, and small kettledrums. Frame drums are made in a number of forms: circular with single membrane, square, even diamond-shaped (ancient Egypt had circular, square, and rectangular ones). Islāmic cult admits no musical instruments, and the human voice is the preponderant instrument here, hence the frame drum's important role as vocal accompaniment. It also lends rhythm for dancing and is the basic percussion instrument of Muslim art-music ensembles. In Morocco groups of women may sing to the accompaniment of a frame drum supplied with jingles, a spike fiddle (one in which the handle traverses the body and emerges at the lower end to form a spike), small cymbals, and a pair of kettledrums, each playing her own instrument.

Black Africa. Black Africa makes perhaps wider use of its membranophones than does any other culture. Numerous variant forms of drums and lacings make classification difficult; indeed, a study of types remains to be established. Some drums are played as musical instruments, others transmit messages ("talking" drums), some are restricted to cult and funerals and others—partly desacralized—to royalty, while yet others participate in everyday life. Ethiopia admits drums to the church, while West African cult drums may not be seen by the uninitiated. Drums are beaten with bare hands or with rectangled or knobbed sticks. Footed drums (*i.e.,* with a base prolonged to form "feet") attain a height of ten feet in the Loango area of west Central Africa (coastal areas of modern Congo, Cabinda province of Angola, and Zaire) and must be tilted to bring the head within the performer's reach. The playing head of hourglass drums may be struck with one hand and with a stick alternately. Kettledrums are royal, ritual, or ceremonial, and unlike their North African counterparts they are of wood, often with sculpted shells. Their traditional pairing with trumpets reaches as far as south of the Congo.

"Talking" drums

That portion of West Africa known as "the Bend" (of the Niger River in modern Mali) is the area of "talking" drums, by means of which messages are conveyed for up to 20 miles, to be relayed by another drummer. Languages of this area are characterized by pronounced high and low pitch tones (tone languages), a quality exploited when two drums—a lower pitched, or male drum, and a higher pitched, or female one—transmit low and high tones respectively. Accent, number, and pitch of the syllables are transmittable. Among the Yoruba a "talking" drum set consists of four hourglass drums and a kettledrum; the leather lacings of the former are gripped by its player, enabling him to change the pitch as he exerts more or less pressure on them; the chief drum of the set is capable of an octave range and, in addition to tones, produces also the typical Yoruba glides by manipulation of the lacings.

East African drum chimes, of Asian heritage, are tuned to specific pitches; these instruments attained royal status in Uganda, where the largest chime consists of 15 drums requiring six musicians to play them.

Friction drums of the lower Congo area were once exclusively cult instruments but are now becoming desacralized. Whereas in Central Africa they are played only by men, women of the South African Pedi play them at female initiation rites.

African mirlitons can be most imaginative: standard material is a spider's egg membrane, and this may be added to apertures pierced in the bottom of xylophone resonators or applied to one end of an independent cane tube that is inserted into a nostril, as among the Fang (Fan) of Gabon.

Afro-America. West Africans reconstructed their native drums in the New World, preponderantly as cult instruments. Small sets of two or, more often, three drums of graded sizes form an integral part of Afro-American rituals and, in the Caribbean, also of voodoo dances. Only the skins of sacrificial animals may be used for membranes among Afro-Bahians in Brazil, who baptize their new drums, preferably with "holy" water obtained from a Catholic church. Drums in Haiti are sacred objects and may even represent the deity itself: as such they receive libations. One type of bongo drum—there exist at least four of these—has been adopted by Western rhythm bands, as has the conga.

In America. Pre-Columbian drums of Central America appear to have been played without sticks, regardless of their size, and to have been devoid of lacings, whether they were small pottery drums, such as those excavated in Costa Rica, or the large footed drums of Mexico. Slender pottery drums of the Guatemala highlands, open top and bottom, can be dated to the late classical period (*c.* 700–1000). Skeletons of wooden cylinder drums, very shallow, have been found in Peru. In shape but not in structure they are identical to the shallow drums played by North American Indians today.

The North American shallow drums are "medicine" (magic) and dance drums, having a heavy hide head struck by a hard beater and emitting a loud, staccato sound. Larger models are suspended and struck simultaneously by up to ten drummers seated in a surrounding circle. The "dream-dance" drum, a tub-shaped shallow drum, is elaborately decorated and has a bell suspended in its interior; it is credited with great medicine power.

Cylinder drums, made of a hollowed log of cottonwood, traditionally war and dance drums of tribes of the Southwestern United States, are now sold in tourist shops. Pottery drums, either potbellied, bowl-shaped, or footed, were formerly common among the eastern and southern tribes of the United States; the potbellied type remains in use among the Pueblo Indians of the Southwest.

American Indian frame drums are usually circular; square shapes are rare, but rectangular frame drums are found in California, Mexico, and Bolivia and octagonal ones among the Cherokee of the Southeastern United States. All were war drums, regardless of whether they had one or two membranes. By adding a rattling device, a frame drum is converted into a medicine drum. The Eskimo frame drum, a shaman's instrument, is distributed over Greenland, northern Siberia, North America, and among the Lapps of northern Scandinavia and differs from other frame drums in that it has a fixed handle and is struck on the hoop, not on the membrane. It may be circular, oval, or fan-shaped.

Eskimo shaman's drum

Friction drums are rare; in Venezuela one is formed from a small barrel over which a piece of leather is stretched, with central perforation to admit a friction stick.

In the Pacific. Two forms of drum are distributed over this huge area. Elongated hourglass drums, usually with wooden handles of a piece with the drum shell, often beautifully carved and ranging up to six feet in height, are commonly in the hands of dancers and singers and are said to symbolize the transition from earth to heaven. Among the Wapenamundu of New Guinea they lack handles and are war drums. Such hourglass drums are not found in Polynesia. The other form is a conical, footed drum made of a tree trunk, reaching great dimension. Those of Polynesia are sometimes eight feet high and have elaborately carved pedestals. They are usually made of breadfruit tree wood or hollowed coconut palm, with a single, sharkskin head. Throughout the area drums are beaten with bare hands.

Whirled friction drums are met with in Hawaii, where a large nut or a calabash is furnished with a friction cord and swung through the air. (S.Ma.)

Stringed instruments

All stringed instruments, or chordophones, produce sound by the vibration of strings, which may be made of vegetable fibre, metal, animal gut, or plastic. In nearly all stringed instruments the sound of the vibrating string is amplified by the use of a resonating chamber or soundboard. The string may be struck, plucked, or rubbed (bowed); in each case the effect is to displace the string from its normal position of rest and to cause it to vibrate in complex patterns.

Since most stringed instruments are made from wood or other easily perishable materials, their history before written documentation is almost unknown, and contemporary knowledge of "early" instruments is limited to the ancient cultures of the Far East, India, the Mediterranean, and Mesopotamia; but even for these places historians must depend largely on iconographic sources rather than surviving specimens.

Chordophones seem to have spread rapidly from one society to another across the length and breadth of Eurasia by means of great population shifts, invasions and counter-invasions, trade, and, presumably, through sheer cultural curiosity. In the Middle Ages the Crusades stimulated Europe in the adoption of a whole set of new instruments; similarly, the Chinese accepted many new instruments from their Central Asian invaders. Indeed, the only world area that did not echo to the sound of strings was pre-Columbian America.

No system of classification can adequately categorize the interactions of natural material, craftsmanship, and man's exuberant imagination that produced an endless variety of stringed instruments. The most widely accepted system of classification is one devised in 1914 by the writer-musicologists Erich Moritz von Hornbostel and Curt Sachs, a method based on the type of material that is set into vibration to produce the original sound. Thus, stringed instruments are identified as chordophones; that is to say, instruments in which the sound is produced by the vibration of chords, or strings. This main category is then further divided into four subtypes arranged according to the manner in which the strings are positioned in relation to the body of the instrument. Within these categories, the descriptive nomenclature of an instrument is given in terms of parts of the human body: for example, the belly (front), back, sides, and neck. Instruments are not necessarily related only to others in the same classification. Transformations continually occur, and "hybrids," according to the Sachs–Hornbostel system, may in fact represent altogether viable subtypes of their own. The instrument maker, who usually has been a forgotten link in the musical chain, has always represented a blend of conservatism with the ability to quickly seize on and use a new constructional technique, a new tool, or a new material. The instrument maker's contribution to both the history of music and the history of musical instruments has been enormous and little appreciated.

The role of the instrument maker

THE PRODUCTION OF SOUND

The ear, because of its own structure, adds to and subtracts from the outside sound. It is, for instance, relatively insensitive to low-frequency sound pressure but is extremely sensitive to fine degrees of pitch change. At the same time it can accept a great number of pitch and tuning systems. On a worldwide basis, there is a large and varied number of tonal systems. The oldest known of these in the West is the so-called Pythagorean system; others include mean-tone tuning, just intonation, and the even-tempered system, methods of tuning calculation that vary slightly in the exact size they assign to the intervals within an octave. All of these systems represent theoretical mathematical concepts to some degree, and their origins must be sought in arcane numerological systems rather than in practical musicianship. Thus, "tuning" and "playing in tune" do not necessarily refer to the same thing; players and tuners make constant adjustments to any basic mathematically determined framework according to their judgment and experience. Again, a given "scientific" tuning system outlines scales and modes; the instrumentalist who plays an instrument with great pitch flexibility (the violin, for instance) spends much time in the spaces between the notes assigned in the given scale. Again, the Japanese zither, koto, can be tuned according to a number of fixed systems, and, even so, its player produces many microtonal variations on these fixed pitches by manipulation of the strings. Even in such a technological society as that of the modern West, the well-tempered scale is honoured more in the breach than in the observance: a piano tuner would not think of tuning altogether according to its dictates and uses a so-called stretched tuning, in which he imperceptibly sharpens (raises) pitches as he ascends, thus making the highest notes relatively sharper than the lowest ones. Again, investigation has disclosed that string players tend to play in the Pythagorean rather than the well-tempered system.

Inconsistencies, then, are inherent in all tuning systems; makers of fretted lutes (the guitar or the Greek lute, *laghouta,* for example) operate according to a combination of ear and rule of thumb when they insert frets (note-position markers—*e.g.,* of gut or wire) in the fingerboard. Such instruments are fretted according to the "rule of the eighteenth," in which the first fret is placed at one-eighteenth of the distance from the top to the bottom of the string, the second, one-eighteenth of the distance from the first fret to the bottom, and so on. Even if this method produced an acoustically perfect scale (which it does not), the player would not be able to reproduce this exactly, for as he presses the string to the fingerboard, the string is stretched and is thus slightly lengthened. That is why the act of stopping a string at its exact centre gives a note slightly sharper than the expected octave above the open string. Despite all of this, the search for an acoustically perfect tuning system goes on.

Though constructional methods differ widely from one area and instrument to another, there are a limited number of basic problems to be overcome by the maker of stringed instruments. The very principle that makes it possible for chordophones to sound is string tension; at the same time, tension is destructive to the instrument since it tends literally to pull it apart. So the body of an instrument must be made of strong material; it must be reinforced, and at the same time it must not be so rigid that it cannot easily resonate; *i.e.,* produce a supplementary vibration intensifying that of the string. The challenge of reconciling these opposite needs is the central one for the chordophone maker. Climate, too, has a marked effect on musical instruments: humidity expands a wooden instrument, and dryness contracts it. Of these factors, dryness is the most harmful, since the contraction of the wood actually pulls the instrument apart. Much energy has been expended over the centuries in investigations of various varnishes, shellacs, glues, and sealers. Many makers prefer to make their instruments in dry conditions, for the expansion caused by humidity is unlikely to prove as harmful as the contraction caused by dryness.

Effect of climate on instruments

However common the practice may have been in the past, wooden instruments are not now usually gouged out of one piece of wood (though the Japanese lute, *biwa,* portions of the koto, and often the Puerto Rican lute, *cuatro,* are thus fashioned); it is too painstaking and time-consuming for the maker. Instead, the instrument is built up of many pieces of wood glued together; the shaping of curved pieces is accomplished by gouging and planing (as in the belly of the violin) or by heating and pressing in a frame (the sides of the violin or guitar). Soundboards, the most important part of the resonance system of stringed instruments, are carefully planed to close tolerances. Mass-production methods are unsuitable for the production of high-quality chordophones because no two pieces of wood are precisely alike in their acoustical qualities; each piece of wood requires special judgment and treatment. Ideally, therefore, stringed instruments of the highest quality must be individually made. Piano manufacture is a partial exception to this rule, but even in a piano factory, individual treatment and craftsmanship are allowed full sway. The modern piano is a product of several different factories. The cast-iron frames are made by specialized foundries—the steel strings, the keyboards, and the actions by specialized firms. Each of these processes requires experienced craftsmen; and the work of assembly, polishing, tuning, and tone regulation calls for hours of individual attention to each instrument.

Making of modern pianos

The construction and maintenance of stringed instruments has been complicated over the centuries by a continual rise in standard pitch, requiring strings to be tightened. Older instruments (such as a Stradivarius violin) have been subjected to additional physical strain and therefore needed heavier bass-bars (braces under the belly).

As already stated, the three possible methods of sound production on a stringed instrument are plucking, striking, and bowing. A string vibrates in a complex way: the entire string vibrates in one segment (producing the fundamental pitch), and various segments at the same time vibrate independently to produce overtones. The resulting sound is weak indeed unless the instrument is provided with a resonator to amplify the sound. The shape of the resonator varies greatly. It has been influenced by the materials, tools, and technology available in the society, the symbolic meaning of the shape, and the sound desired by the culture. The last factor seems to be governed by the first three: that is to say, the prescribed shape of the resonator affects the overtone structure of the instrument, producing a certain timbre, which the society in question then defines as attractive sounding.

Importance of the shape of the resonator

One of the clearest illustrations of the basic importance of the shape of the resonator to a musical instrument is the African mouth bow (a musical bow in which the player inserts the bow in his or her mouth). By varying the size and shape of the oral cavity while striking or plucking the single, unfingered string, the player produces a clearly perceptible, if quiet, melody that exists only because the changes in the mouth emphasize various overtones. On stringed instruments with permanently fixed resonators, the size, dimensions, shape of apertures, thickness, and bracing of the resonating surfaces largely determine which overtones will be emphasized and, thus, what the instrument will sound like. On a good violin, for example, the resonances of the body of air enclosed in the body of the instrument and of the belly should be close in pitch to the two strings A and D, thus amplifying and colouring these pitches and their overtones. The sound quality of a stringed instrument is also influenced by the thickness and material of the strings; primarily, however, it is the size and shape of the resonating body and especially the material, density, and thickness of the soundboard that determine the sound of an instrument. A well-known Spanish guitar maker, in a successful attempt to prove the importance of the belly of the guitar, once constructed an instrument—an excellent one—from the acoustically dead material papier-mâché, except for a carefully chosen and wrought wooden soundboard. Makers, then, devote a large part of their skill and knowledge to the choice of material for the soundboard; the maker of wood-bellied instruments prefers old wood because it is dry and well seasoned.

The Puerto Rican *cuatro* maker uses wood obtained from old houses; some guitar makers find the soundboards of discarded pianos unusually suitable for their purposes; makers of the classical Chinese zither, *ch'in*, preferred old coffins.

The timbre of a struck or plucked stringed instrument is also affected by the manner of setting the string into motion. A string plucked with a sharp point (the player's fingernail or a plastic plectrum) emphasizes the higher overtones, thus creating a "bright" tone quality. By contrast, a soft pad, such as that on a piano hammer, emphasizes the fundamental pitch. The relative hardness of the hammer on the piano is thus of critical importance to the sound of the instrument, and the final process in piano manufacture is voicing. A skilled worker adjusts the timbre of the instrument by the simple expedient of pricking the felt hammers with needles until he achieves a unified quality throughout the range of the instrument. The tone of an instrument is markedly affected by the place where the string is struck. The permanently fixed striking place on keyboard instruments has to be chosen with a combination of concern for the timbre and the mechanical requirements of the instrument. On all other stringed instruments the player varies the tone quality by choosing to pluck, strike, or bow at various places along the length of the string.

"Voicing" a piano

Another way in which musicians and musical instrument makers influence the sound of their instruments is by the use of sympathetically vibrating strings. On the piano, for example, when the so-called damper pedal is raised, thus leaving the strings free to vibrate, the act of striking one note causes all closely related pitches to vibrate in sympathy, thus modifying the loudness and tone of the struck note. This effect (which is encountered also on the zither and harp) is not a central feature of these instruments, but there are a number of Eurasian chordophones on which the principle is of fundamental importance. The North Indian plucked instruments, sarod and sitar, each possess about a dozen sympathetic strings tuned according to the notes of the mode being played. The Indian fiddle, sarangi, has from 35 to 40 sympathetic strings; the Norwegian Hardanger fiddle (*Hardangerfele*) has four sympathetic strings, the viola d'amore six or more. Sympathetic strings are generally made of thin brass or steel, and their vibration reinforces the upper harmonics, thus producing a bright, silvery sound.

TYPES OF INSTRUMENTS

Lutes. Probably the most widely distributed type of stringed instrument in the world is the lute (the word is used here to designate the family and not solely the lute of Renaissance Europe). The characteristic structure consists of an enclosed sound chamber, or resonator, with strings passing over all or part of it, and a neck along which the strings are stretched. The player moves his fingers up and down the neck, thus shortening the strings and producing various pitches.

In the lute the part of the resonating chamber over which the strings pass is called the belly and the other side of the resonator is called the back. The portion between the back and belly is the side, or rib. A lute may be plucked with the fingers or a plectrum or may be bowed, but the means of sound production do not affect the essential morphological identity of plucked, struck, and bowed lutes.

Lutes may be subdivided into those with skin and those with wood bellies; in most Eurasian cultures examples of both types exist side by side. In Japan the wood-bellied lute is the *biwa,* the skin-bellied one the samisen; in the Near East the wood-bellied one is the *ʿūd* and the skin-bellied, the *tār;* in the United States it is the guitar and the banjo, respectively. The two different varieties of lute are distinct in sound and structure; and methods of construction, timbre, history, and symbolic associations differ markedly. A second subdivision concerns the shape of the instrument; for instance, the lute proper has a round back, the guitar a flat one. These two basic constructional principles (the shape of the resonator and whether the belly is constructed from wood or skin) constantly interact, producing all sorts of combinations.

The string vibrations of the lute are transferred to the resonating chamber by a bridge; the resonator magnifies them and transmits them to the air. Makers lavish great attention on the choice and fashioning of material for the belly: if it is of wood, it must be selected and aged with much care and planed to a prescribed thickness; if it is of skin, it must be made only from certain materials. (The belly of the Japanese samisen is preferably made from the skin of a female cat; the wooden belly of the Puerto Rican *cuatro* is best constructed from wood of the female *jagrumo* tree.)

Lute strings

The lute strings themselves have traditionally been made of animal intestines (gut) or metal or silk, though nylon has now replaced these older materials all over the world. Whatever the material, each string must be of equal thickness throughout its length. Some lutes have only a single string, but the great majority have three, four, or more. Very often there are sets, or courses, of two strings to a pitch, so that an instrument that produces four pitches with open strings actually has eight strings arranged in pairs.

In the tunings of lutes, though fourths and fifths (intervals the size of four and five tones of a Western seven-note scale, as C–F and C–G) predominate in many places, any given instrument is likely to be tuned differently from one location, piece, or player to another. Functionally more important is the question of whether a lute is fretted or unfretted. It is clearly easy to change from one pitch to another on an unfretted instrument by sliding the finger along the string, but it is also possible to do this on an instrument with extremely high frets (Japanese *biwa,* Indian *vina*) by pressing—hence stretching—the string into the cavity between two frets. Instruments with low frets (the guitar, banjo, European lute, viola da gamba) are in use mainly in Europe, where a limited and clearly defined tonal system is in use and where significant microtonal changes in pitch are not necessary.

The fiddle can be distinguished from other lutes only by the manner in which it is played—with a horsehair bow. The practice of rubbing the strings with this implement is of uncertain age and origin, but it seems to have appeared almost simultaneously (9th–10th centuries AD) in China, Java, the Arab world, Byzantium, and Europe. As with the other lutes, there is a fundamental division between skin and wood-bellied instruments. (The former are far more common on the fiddle than the latter, which occur mainly in Europe.) Musically more significant, however, is the division between the stick fiddle, in which the player's finger does not actually press the string to a fingerboard (but rather slides up and down the string itself), and the fiddle with a fingerboard (for example, the violin). On fiddles without fingerboard (including the Chinese *erh-hu,* the Javanese and Arab *rabāb,* various African fiddles, and the East Indian *sarangi*), the player's left hand is able to move with extreme flexibility up and down the string, thus making the subtlest kind of inflection possible.

As with other lutes, fiddles may have only one string (the Tuareg *imzhad*) or as many as 40 (the *sarangi*); on the latter, sympathetic strings are not directly touched or sounded by the player but vibrate sympathetically when other strings are set into motion, thus giving a fuller resonance. Examples, in addition to the *sarangi,* include the Norwegian *Hardangerfele,* the Swedish *nyckelharpa,* and the viola d'amore.

The fiddle bow

The fiddle bow itself generally is constructed so that the player can tighten or loosen the hair at will; on most stringed instruments the player is able to make immediate changes by manipulating his hand on the bow hair while playing, thus producing various tone qualities. The modern Tourte bow of the violin has a screw mechanism that cannot be changed while playing. Most bows, again, are actually bow shaped, but the Tourte bow is made in a compound curve to which considerable tension can be applied, making it possible to apply much pressure to the strings.

The bowing principle has been applied to non-lutes from time to time: the old Icelandic *fidla* was a bowed zither; the Scandinavian *talharpa* was a bowed lyre.

Zithers. Instruments of the zither family, in which the strings lie parallel to and are of the same length as the resonator, are widely distributed in Eurasia, the Americas, and Africa. There are two important subdivisions of this category. The so-called long-zither family is found only in the Far East; its characteristic resonating chamber is slightly convex, as much as six feet (180 centimetres) long, and about a foot (30 centimetres) wide; there is a varying number of strings frequently provided with movable bridges. These instruments, of which the best known example is the koto, seem to devolve ultimately from zithers made directly from lengths of bamboo. The bamboo prototypes are said to be idiochordic because their strings, part of the bamboo itself, are worked loose from the tough surface of the tube, to which they remain attached at either end. The maker then inserts small bridges at the extremes of the strings. (Various modifications and transformations of this principle exist, as the bamboo-tube *valiha* of Madagascar and Malaya, in which wire strings replace the idiochordic ones). All long-bodied, curved-surfaced Far Eastern of koto type may owe something to this idiochordic principle. In Eastern tradition the most ancient zither is the seven-stringed *ch'in,* which seems to have originated in the Shang dynasty (*c.* 1400 BC). The Japanese *wagon* and koto, the Korean *kayagum,* and the Chinese *cheng* fit into this general category. All these ancient instruments are rich in symbolic associations.

The flat zither

The other important subdivision of the zither family is the flat zither; in Africa it is made either from a hollowed plank over which strings are fastened (board zither) or from individual narrow canes lashed together, each having one idiochordic string (raft zither). The box zither, which seems to be native to the Middle East, is a rectangular- or more often trapezoid-shaped hollow box the strings of which are either struck with light hammers or plucked. Examples of the former are the Persian *sanṭūr* and its modern Chinese derivative, the *yang ch'in* ("foreign zither"), the cimbalom of east central Europe, and the piano (which is a sort of cimbalom with keyboard). The most prominent plucked box zither is the Arab *qānūn* and its various derivatives, including the harpsichord (a plucked zither controlled by a keyboard). In Europe a variety of plucked zithers developed having a fretted fingerboard under one or a few of the strings.

Struck zithers are occasionally termed dulcimers, unfretted plucked ones psalteries, after European instruments using those names.

Lyres. The lyre family, though it was of great importance in the ancient centres of Babylonia, Egypt, and Greece, is now found only in a few areas of East Africa. A lyre is made from an oval, round, or rectangular sound chamber (usually skin bellied); from this resonator two arms protrude; they are joined at the top by a crosspiece; the strings extend from this crosspiece over the belly, with which they are connected by a bridge. These strings are not normally stopped but are allowed to vibrate throughout their entire length when plucked by the performer.

The *begenna* and the *krar*

In Ethiopia, where the lyre remains in extensive use, there are two distinctive types, as there were in ancient Greece. The 10-string *begenna* (which corresponds to the ancient Greek kithara) is a large, heavy, rectangular-shaped instrument that is considered by the Christian Ethiopians to be a God-given instrument that came to them from King David; it is used, of course, for sacred music. The smaller lyre, *krar* (the ancient Greek *lyra*), is emphatically secular in its use and connotations; indeed, Ethiopians think of it as the instrument of Satan. The construction of this five-stringed instrument illustrates the sort of change that is of wide occurrence in contemporary instrument making everywhere, for though the traditional *krar* was made from wood, the resonator of the present-day instrument is made of an easily available metal pan. The *krar* can be played in two ways: in the first (called muting) the left hand mutes the unwanted strings while the right hand strums with a plectrum; in the second, the fingers of the left hand pluck while the right hand plucks a drone on tonic strings tuned to the tonic, or focal note, of the melody.

The lyres of medieval western Europe (4th–12th centuries) had from five to seven strings and, to judge from iconographic evidence, were played in a way that closely resembled the muting technique of Ethiopia. Northern European shapes are considerably varied, but both the rectangular kithara-like shape and the rounded *lyra* shape apparently existed.

Harps. The harp family exhibits an extraordinary variety of constructions, but in all harps the strings are of unequal lengths and are fastened at either end to a frame that lies in the same plane as the strings. The least complex, and prototypical, harp type of instrument is the musical bow, shaped very much like a hunter's bow. The single string is tapped or struck, and the pitch can be varied by varying the tension of the string or by using the player's mouth as a resonator and varying its size and shape, thus emphasizing different harmonics. It is a favourite instrument in equatorial Africa.

The arched, or bow-shaped, harp, known in Egypt as early as 3000–4000 BC, is a multistringed version of this musical bow; its player kneels or stands, supporting the harp on the shoulder. Harps of this type may be found in West and Central Africa, where they are often provided with elaborate anthropomorphic carvings and skin-covered resonators. The bow harp, then, is a traditional African form that has been in use in that continent for at least 5,000 years.

On an angle harp the bowlike support is replaced with two crosspieces at right angles to one another; the strings are stretched between these at an angle of 45°. This type seems to have originated in Assyria, though occasionally it is found in Egypt and Greece.

The closed, or frame, harp is characteristic of both medieval and modern Europe; the shape of its frame is more or less triangular, the frame being strengthened by a pillar that encloses the strings in a kind of tripartite structure. It is to this category that the modern orchestral harp of Europe and the old Irish and Scottish harps belong. In all of these instruments the crosspiece held nearest the player is a hollow resonating chamber. The so-called Brian Boru harp (14th century), now at Trinity College, Dublin, is 32 inches (81 centimetres) high, with 36 brass strings; the sound box is carved from a single piece of willow, and the harp was plucked by the fingernails.

THE MUSIC OF STRINGED INSTRUMENTS

Solo uses. Music for a solo instrument is often, though not always, used to accompany dancing or is derived from dance music. In Europe and America, the violin is widely used to play dance music; for instance, the Norwegian Hardanger fiddle player performs rhythmically complex polyphonic music (*i.e.,* composed of several simultaneous melodic strands) to accompany the *halling, gangar,* or *springar.* In Scotland, Ireland, and rural North America, the violin is favoured for accompanying country dances. It is known that a single fiddler played for dancing among the upper classes in medieval Europe and also probably among the common people, with whom the fiddle was popular. In all areas, the fiddler has an additional repertory not for dancing, which shows off his compositional and improvisational ability as well as his virtuosity. A skillful medieval fiddler constantly improvised new pieces. It is no coincidence that the violin solo sonatas and partitas of Bach, like their country cousins, are polyphonic compositions having a liberal sprinkling of stylized dance movements.

A second genre of solo piece is the descriptive composition. In such diverse places as Ireland, West Africa, and the United States are found fiddle pieces picturing the hunt, in which the player delights in the depiction of such realistic sounds as the baying of the hounds, the sound of hooves, and the groans of the exhausted animal. In China there is a genre of highly realistic descriptive compositions for *p'i-p'a*—including some that depict famous battles from start to finish. Among numerous descriptive pieces in Renaissance and Baroque Europe, a well-known example is a sonata for viola da gamba, by the French virtuoso gamba player Marin Marais (1656–1728), that graphically and in detail describes a gallstone operation in the days before anesthetics.

Solo music of the Middle Ages and Renaissance

In the European Middle Ages and Renaissance, an important type of composition for solo stringed instruments was the transcription of polyphonic songs; in the medieval period fiddle and hurdy-gurdy players frequently rendered elaborated versions of well-known strophic songs. In northern Europe, songs intended to accompany dance could also be played on the fiddle, and in Spain the *vihuela de arco* filled a similar function. In the Renaissance, a string player was expected to have the ability to perform highly elaborated versions of pre-existent melodies on the viol, lute, or keyboard; and many manuals provided the player with exercises designed to teach him to elaborate the basic melody in a stylistically correct manner. Similar techniques continued to be practiced during the Baroque period and even into the 19th century.

For accompaniment. All over the world, stringed instruments have as one of their central functions the accompaniment of bards, who sing tales of heroes and otherwise reflect the preoccupations of their societies. The example of Homer and his lyre is of course the best known, and even today in the Balkans, bards, self-accompanied on the fiddles, *gusla,* or *lira,* play preludes and interludes while they sing tales of heroes in the wars against the Turks. The harpers of Celtic Ireland and Scotland devoted their skills to the accompaniment of learned bards; the *azmari* of Ethiopia sings lengthy historical epics and strophic love songs to his own accompaniment on the fiddle or lyre. In Japan, blind *biwa* players chant a narrative style of music known as *katarimono,* and here again the *biwa* is used only between verses, as it performs interludes and commentaries. A similar technique is in use among the minstrels of North Africa: the lute, *gunbrī,* is played only between verses of the story, as a descriptive comment. Again, the 19th-century European art song for solo voice and piano belongs to this genre.

Ensembles. Musical ensembles everywhere have their own internal social structure, mirroring that of their society at large in the degree of authoritarianism, the type of leadership, amount of freedom available to the individual players, and so on. The audience for a given ensemble also tends to be socially stratified. Large, authoritatively ruled ensembles tend to be found in societies that have a complex bureaucratic and pyramidal social order. Such groups are most typically to be found clustered around the royal or princely courts of China, Japan, and Korea, of Java and Bali, of North Africa, and in the court-derived music of Europe and America. In all of these instances a more or less fixed and archaic repertory remains in use. In Japan, Korea, and, to an extent, Southeast Asia, the court music has derived from an archaic (and no longer extant) court music of China. The two types of stringed instruments in use in Japan are the zithers, koto and *wagon,* and the lute, *biwa.* The koto has 13 strings and the *biwa* four.

The gamelan orchestras of Indonesia employ but two chordophones in ensembles, which are otherwise dominated by struck metallophones, or metal instruments, such as tuned gong sets and xylophone-like instruments with metal bars. The bowed *rebab* probably entered the orchestra from the Near East, where it was called *rabāb,* ancestor of the European rebec, when Java was converted from the Hindu religion to Islām. It plays in sliding fashion around the fixed pitches of the orchestra; its player is thought of by Javanese as the "rajah" of the gamelan, with the drummer as his "prime minister."

In Islāmic countries and in Europe, stringed instruments predominate numerically in the orchestra; the classical ensembles of the Maghrib, which mainly perform the ancient Andalusian suites, typically consist of about one dozen musicians. The instrumentalists include a number of violin or viola players, a *rabāb* player, lute players, drummers, and sometimes flutists, cellists, and a pianist. All of the string players play the melody together but not in unison, for they are expected to vary it individually with ornaments and improvised passages. A true unison, therefore, is neither expected nor desirable. The ensemble is normally led by an *ʿūd* player who indicates the pitch, mode, mood, the changes of tempo, and so on.

Orchestral stringed instruments

In Europe as in North Africa, the greater number of stringed instruments in use in the orchestra are bowed; Europe, however, is distinctive in that these bowed chordophones exist and are played in families of graduated size (violin, viola, cello, bass), and this phenomenon derives from the extent to which European musicians have been preoccupied with harmony and multipart composition. In the development of the European orchestra two great—but gradual—changes have occurred over the centuries: first, stringed instruments have increased dramatically in number in the orchestra; and second, higher and higher notes and hence finger positions have been demanded of string players. Socially and musially, the role of the player in an early 18th-century symphony (in which there would be no more than two or three players to each part) is very different from the anonymous function allowed the violinist in a symphony by Berlioz, say, or Mahler. The symphonic orchestra seems to represent the merger of two functionally and aesthetically different groups that medieval Europe probably derived from Arab civilization. One of these, used for outdoor ceremonial music, consisted originally of shawms (oboes), drums, and trumpets; the other, for indoor (chamber) use, was made up of stringed instruments, quiet percussion instruments, and flutes. The modern orchestra preserves vestiges of these two ensembles in its seating arrangements, orchestration, and leadership.

The European concept of chamber music is nowadays thought of as being entirely distinct from orchestral music; in the 17th and early 18th centuries, however, the distinction would have been difficult to draw, since there was no clear difference either in the music, the size, or the sociological position of the two types of ensembles. The symphonic orchestra arose because of middle class demand for public concerts and from the desire of composers after the French Revolution to provide democratic music for the masses; thus, mass audiences demanded large orchestras, and the striking multiplication of instrumentalists affected the strings above all others.

Modern Japan cherishes a number of traditional chamber-music ensembles; of these, the commonest one consists of the koto, the samisen, and the flute, *shakuhachi.* The *jiuta* is a common form played by this group; here, the koto plays the principal melody, and the samisen and *shakuhachi* simultaneously produce a variant of it. The Japanese picturesquely describe this ensemble by saying that the koto is the bone, the samisen the flesh, and the *shakuhachi* the skin.

Basic elements of Indian ensembles

The basic ensemble in South Indian music consists of a drone instrument (usually the tamboura), a tuned drum (mridanga), a violin, and a singer. The group is often augmented to include a number of other instruments, but the basic elements must be present. The violinist is an accompanist to the singer; he must be able to play in unison with him in fixed pieces and to follow him in immensely complicated improvisational sections, maintaining all the while the correct raga (melodic mode) and *tāla* (rhythmic mode). An analogous group in North India might include the sitar or sarod as solo instrument, with the accompaniment of the drums, tabla, and a drone. Often the fiddle, *sarangi* (with three main strings and 35–40 sympathetic ones), accompanies a singer.

Rather similar principles apply in the eastern Mediterranean: a chamber-music ensemble must include instruments—usually strings—to play the melody and to improvise in the introductory sections known as *taqsīm* and percussion instruments to deal with the rhythmic modes, known as *īqā'āt.* To these, in modern Greek music, the element of harmony has been added so that a solo instrument (clarinet or violin) plays the highly ornamented melody and another instrument (guitar, or *laghouta*) plays the chordal background and maintains the reiterated rhythmic pattern. Similar ensembles are found in the Americas and in Africa.

In Puerto Rican traditional music a guitar plays the harmony, the five double-stringed lute, *cuatro,* plays the melody with the singer, and the scraper, guiro, and drums, *timbales,* produce the rhythmic part. Among the Berbers of North Africa, groups of itinerant professional musicians typically play one or two lutes, *gunbrī,* a one-stringed fiddle (rendering a highly adorned melody), and percussion. In Senegal, lutes similar to the *gunbrī* are played by the musicians known as *griots,* often in ensembles of three or four flutes, drums, and rattles. The so-called Bluegrass style of Appalachian North America largely conforms to this Mediterranean and African pattern; the ensemble typically includes only bowed and plucked strings and singers.

Rock groups also adhere to these general principles: they also represent a blend of African and European traditions. The typical rock ensembles use plucked electric stringed instruments, electric keyboard instruments, voice, and drums. The electric guitar plays the melody, and the electric bass renders the bass part. In the American blend of Mediterranean, African, European, and indigenous tradition, the African element includes the percussion instruments and the skin-bellied lute (banjo); the Mediterranean element includes the wood-bellied guitar and *cuatro.* The bass parts are derived from Europe, the scraper from the American Indians, and the singing style from various of the four traditions.

SOCIAL AND CULTURAL ASSOCIATIONS

Throughout the world, particular instruments are associated with particular functions, social levels, areas, ages, and sexes. Certain instruments preserve the same function all over the world: the bard (a singer-poet) recounts tales of heroes, recites the genealogies of the great, and preserves and disseminates the precious traditions of a given society; this bard everywhere accompanies himself on a stringed instrument. An early example would be the blind Homer, who, presumably accompanied by his lyre, sang of gods and heroes. Similar traditions survive even today in Greece and the Balkans, but the instrument of the modern "singer of tales" is the fiddle. In Ethiopia, where so many traditions are reminiscent of Greece, the *azmari* accompany themselves with a lyre or fiddle. In North Africa and West Africa *griots* sing and play skin-bellied lutes called *gunbrī* or *halam;* in Morocco they play and sing alone in the squares of the towns for coppers; in Senegal (where they perform in groups) they are employed by the wealthy. The Japanese *biwa* (often, again, played by blind bards) was used to accompany epic narratives, the texts of which usually concern the adventures and battles of the samurai: the *biwa* is used also to accompany Buddhist chanting. In medieval Europe, minstrels, self-accompanied on the *vielle* (fiddle), sang of the heroism of such as Charlemagne.

Very often, stringed instruments are identified with a certain social class, either in the sense that the player himself occupies a particular caste position or in that the instrument is the prerogative of a particular rank in society.

A well-known example is that of the Irish and Scottish harp of the periods during which the Celtic kingdoms flourished; harpers, who were highly respected members of society, were employed in the households of only the very wealthy and the high nobility. By the same token, harpers were regarded with great suspicion by English officials in Ireland, for they were suspected of spreading sedition. In sharp contrast is the attitude of respectable members of medieval Arab society toward lute players; their status was low indeed (certain judges even held that the lute was an unlawful possession which could be destroyed at will). Paradoxically, the *'ūd* player's skill and imagination was highly valued by the courts. These attitudes are old indeed in the Mediterranean; Aristotle regarded professional kithara players as low caste and of questionable morals. In his view (and this is still prevalent in the West) the highborn should learn to play as an accomplishment but not professionally. In the 17th century, members of the English upper class were swept with a craze for playing consort music for ensembles of various sizes of viola da gamba ("leg viols," held, cello-fashion, between the knees). It was a common—and much valued—accomplishment to be able to play a part in a viol consort, and, as Samuel Pepys recorded in his diary, servants were often chosen because of their ability as violists.

The violin family in Europe has had two very different social connotations. In the string quartet and orchestra the instrument has been associated with the entertainment of the upper class and the bourgeoisie, and this represents the continuity of the medieval tradition under which the fiddle was highly regarded by the upper class. Alfonso X, the Wise, king of Leon and Castile, was one of many rulers who supported a group of fiddlers at his court.

The aural technique of the country fiddler

In opposition to this, the violin has long had great popularity among the folk. In almost every country in Europe and the Americas the rural fiddler has provided the music for dances and entertainments. This country fiddler is distinguished from his urban colleague by his nonstandardized technique, playing position, and tunings and by his learning process, which is totally aural. His virtuosity may be of a high order. The pleasures of the common folk have long been associated with the fiddle, though the medieval fiddler usually played the bagipes, sang, juggled, and told jokes as well.

The role of musical instruments in religious and healing practice is complex: at one time or another Judaism and Islām and Christianity have been generally hostile to the use of instruments in places of worship. The Church Fathers made frequent allegorical and symbolic reference to instruments, and it is common to find depictions of angels, cherubs, or of King David playing on the very instruments that were not permitted to sound in Christian worship. The Hindu attitude toward stringed instruments is very different. Though Vedic chanting is the oldest known music of India, the Ṛgveda nevertheless mentions the use of such chordophones as the *karkari* and a number of vinas.

Caste and symbolic associations of the *ch'ins*

The Chinese scholars' zither, *ch'in,* had definite caste and symbolic associations. No scholar would have been without one, for it restrained licentiousness and purified the heart; it compelled man to return to his divine origin and restrain his passions. Thus, the *ch'in* could not be played when drunk or after sexual intercourse; it could not be played for a courtesan, a merchant, or a barbarian. The *ch'in* was often played by Buddhist monks; complex cosmological and symbolic meanings existed for every aspect of its shape, constructional material, tone, and playing technique. The *ch'in,* therefore, was involved with healing, religion, and philosophy; and of these three, its therapeutic function was perhaps the most pervasive; this instrument harmonizes the blood circulation and regulates breathing; it leads to health and long life. It cures melancholy and can, it is claimed, even make a devoted player immortal.

The function of stringed instruments in the healing process is very often an indirect one: a healing specialist may sing his powerful songs to the accompaniment of a lute (the *gunbrī* of the North African Gnāwa) or a fiddle (Central Asia). Beyond this relatively prosaic association, stringed instruments have symbolic meanings that transcend their technological, sound-producing function. The horse-headed fiddle of the Mongols is directly a part of the Mongol system of belief in the horse as a symbol of fecundity and rebirth; the winged horse that the shaman is believed to ride in his quest for enlightenment and healing power is equivalent symbolically to the fiddle.

This close connection of stringed instruments with ideas of birth and rebirth explains why so often a particular instrument is typically played, or even listened to, by members of one sex only; in certain instances instrumentalists, whether they were Greek kitharodists or Arab *ʿūd* players, were slaves with a low moral reputation. The playing of many stringed instruments by women has been either a low-caste occupation or an accomplishment to be savoured in the confines of the home. In India during the Vedic period there seem to have been stringed instruments (such as the *kāṇḍa-vīṇā*) that were played only by women; and Chinese tradition has it that the long zither, *cheng,* was invented by a woman. In the Western continents, instrument makers seem usually to be men, since in most societies the manipulation of woodworking tools has been a male occupation. In medieval Europe, and in some places (such as Puerto Rico) today, minstrels made their own instruments. Since the making and playing of instruments have until recently been mainly in male hands, women have not had available to them this particular link to musical instruments through manufacture.

STRINGED INSTRUMENTS AS OBJECTS OF ART

There is no reason to suppose that the shape of an instrument is governed by acoustical requirements; it seems rather to be the other way around: the symbolically appropriate shape preferred by a given culture produces a particular tone quality, which then becomes the desirable one. Available materials, manufacturing techniques, and complex historical, symbolic, and artistic considerations guide the craftsman who creates musical instruments. Transformations occur as old meanings are lost: the scroll surmounting the pegbox of the violin may well be a faint visual echo of the horse's-head carving that surmounts the fiddle in its ancestral lands in Central Asia. Craftsmen are well aware that the soundboard of an instrument is responsible for the best part of its resonance; they are aware that other portions can be considerably altered without making much change in the sound quality. Instrument makers have long delighted in producing modifications of existing designs and in experimenting with new materials. In all this they are limited only by the essential technological requirment of a chordophone—ability to withstand the constant strain imposed by the tension of the strings and proper resonation.

A limited number of basic woodworking techniques are used almost the world over in the production of stringed instruments. In lute construction the entire sound box (and sometimes the neck as well) can be hewn from one block of wood. Instruments that are often made in this fashion are the Japanese *biwa,* the North African *gunbrī,* and the Puerto Rican *cuatro.* Existing side by side with this technique is another, in which the lute is made out of a kind of composite box in which any bent portions are fashioned by heating the wood and putting it into a mold. (Common examples include the violin and the guitar.) Again, the resonator can be made of pre-existent natural materials, as in the case of the Malagasy *valiha* zither (bamboo), the South Indian *vina* (gourd), or the lyre invented by Apollo (tortoiseshell).

Though occasionally (as in the case of many harpsichords and virginals) instruments with pictures painted upon them are encountered, this decorative technique is most unusual—probably because it requires a separate craftsman—and most instrument makers prefer to show their skill by the choice of woods, by complex inlays, and by carving.

Anthropomorphic and zoomorphic shapes surmount many of the harps and lyres of ancient Mesopotamia and Egypt. The anthropomorphic harp of ancient Egypt and modern Africa represents another example of this visually symbolic approach to instrument making, which has been described as producing "sounding statues." In Europe, anthropomorphic and zoomorphic carving exists side by side. Notable examples are the Irish Brian Boru harp (at Trinity College, Dublin), which exhibits a profuse variety of animal shapes; the Norwegian *Hardanger* fiddle, surmounted with a dragon's head; and the viola d'amore, which often is surmounted with the head of a blindfolded woman. The Balkan fiddle, *gusla,* and the Central Asian horse fiddle are usually crowned with a carved horse's head, and the South Indian *vina* possesses a carving of a dragon. These shapes are not mere decoration or fancy; they represent important symbols in the society from which the instruments come.

The anthropomorphic harp

In East Asia the craftsman's emphasis is on beauty of wood, excellence of finishing, and apparent simplicity of construction. Occasionally, on instruments such as the *ch'in,* one finds pictures painted or calligraphy inscribed. The proper material is extremely important: the belly of a good Japanese samisen should be made from the skin of a female cat; a *ch'in* should be made of wood taken from an old tree that had nestled next to a bubbling stream. Phoenix-bird symbolism of rebirth is abundant in the nomenclature of Far Eastern instruments, and this fact serves to point up a profoundly important truth about musical instruments everywhere: they are intimately connected in folktale, myth, and legend to local symbols of rebirth. Thus, legend relates that Apollo made the first lute from a turtle carapace; similarly, the first Arab lute was modelled after the body of a beloved male child; the Finnish culture hero, Väinämöinen, made the first zither, kantele, from the body of a giant pike; the Celts made their first legendary harp from whalebones. In each case, the symbolically significant creature is "reborn" as an instrument which "sings" as well as appears in a shape reminiscent of the creature modelled.

THE DEVELOPMENT OF STRINGED INSTRUMENTS

Little or no evidence is available concerning the chordophones of prehistoric times: the earliest iconographic evidence and the oldest surviving specimens come from Mesopotamia and Egypt, and evidence concerning instruments earlier than these can be gleaned only from myth and legend.

The harp. The harp clearly evolves from the musical bow, which must have been in existence prior to the establishment of Mesopotamian and Egyptian civilizations. Since this instrument is identical in shape with the simple hunter's bow, it has been assumed that the musical bow derives from the hunter's implement. There is, however, no evidence for this; quite the opposite: the musical bow is very often played by women, who do not usually hunt, and, further, there is absolutely no way of knowing whether or not man hunted with a bow-shaped implement before he made musical sound with a bow. The three early harps found in the burial chambers at Ur were bow-shaped instruments with 12 to 15 strings; nearly identical instruments were played in Egypt at roughly the same time. Iconographic evidence suggests that both in Egypt and Mesopotamia the harp, often played by women, was used in secular, erotic entertainments, although it had sacred uses as well.

Although the harp family is known to exist in Burma and to have been in use in China and India, it is not characteristic of these areas; it is, rather, musically important in equatorial regions of Africa, in Europe, and in the Americas. In Africa it clearly is related to the Egyptian harps, and again it is associated with women.

The harp has maintained and increased its importance in Europe. It is omnipresent in folktales and legends; it is the national symbol of Ireland. The Celtic harp must have been in use as early as the 10th century, and fragments of one were found in the 7th-century Sutton Hoo burial ship unearthed at Suffolk, England. In Gaul, Ireland, Wales, and Scotland, the harp was an important and favoured symbol; it was said that there were but three things necessary to a comfortable household—a virtuous wife, a chair cushion, and a harp. By the end of the 18th century the harp had almost gone out of use in the Celtic realms, but by then the large orchestral harp had made its appearance in other places in Europe.

The Celtic harp

This basic instrument (with the addition of a set of pedals for instantaneously altering the pitch of a note) is found—often still played by a woman—in the modern symphony orchestra; but the older European harp tradition flourishes best in Mexico and South America, where the harp is a component of various folk ensembles.

The lyre. Greek legend credits the invention of the lyre to Apollo, who had stolen Zeus's cows and, in order to atone for his transgression, presented the great god with the lyre, which he had accidentally discovered when he had brushed against a turtle carapace that lay on the ground and, as he did so, heard its sinews begin to vibrate. The tale is interesting for two reasons: first, the turtle shell *was* frequently used as the resonator of the Greek *lyra;* and second, the tale makes an explicit relationship between the lyre and cattle. Similarly, in Mesopotamia the lyre was surmounted with a carved bull's head, and in modern East Africa the lyre is most frequently encountered in cattle cultures.

A famous lyre from Ur (now at the University Museum, Philadelphia) is one of nine dug up at the burial ground; these and similar instruments seem to have been used both to accompany bardic recitations and for religious purposes. The "harp" that the Hebrews hung in the tree in their Babylonian captivity was actually a lyre, as was the instrument used by Homer (*phorminx*). In view of the importance of the bull in the worship ceremonies of Crete and Mycenae, it is not surprising to find lyres among the stringed instruments of these peoples. In Celtic society, depictions of lyres are found on the coins of pre-Christian Gaul. These instruments, which were U-shaped, may have come to western Europe from Southwest Asia with groups of Indo-European peoples who spread across Europe. Other types of lyres were found in Europe, too, and it is possible that these variously shaped but still related instruments might be analogous to the various Indo-European languages in that they are basically closely related but quite different in detail.

In medieval Germany and Scandinavia long, narrow lyres with four to seven strings were played, and similar lyres (the Finnish *jouhikantele,* the Swedish *talharpa,* the Welsh crwth) were played with a bow in parts of Europe until recent years. Today the lyre flourishes only in Ethiopia, in the Sudan, among the fishermen of the Persian Gulf, and in restricted areas of East Africa.

The zither. Several different types of instruments are classified as zithers; they are used today in all continents. The long zithers of China, Japan, and Korea are venerable indeed. Their curved surface and long, narrow shape betrays their affinity with the prototypical idiochordic bamboo zithers of the Pacific, Southeast Asia, and southeast Africa. The importance of bamboo to music in the Orient is literally legendary; in Java, music is thought to have been first produced by the accidental admission of air into a bamboo tube. In China, the source of Far Eastern civilization, musical instruments are classified according to their constructional material; one of the eight substances in the system is bamboo, which the Chinese relate to the direction East, the season Spring, and the phenomenon Mountain. The Chinese zither *cheng* includes the radical meaning "bamboo" in its ideograph. The ideographs of the older zithers, *ch'in* and *se,* are more difficult to interpret; but the narrow, curved shapes of the instruments themselves betray their affinity with the ancient principle. Zithers of this type are known to have existed in the Shang period (*c.* 1766–*c.* 1122 BC); the *cheng,* with either 13 or 16 strings, came into use during the Ch'in period (221–206 BC). By the 18th century, interest in this instrument had waned in China, but at an early date it was introduced to Japan, where, as the 13-string koto, it flourishes today. The koto, like the *cheng,* is played frequently by women.

Bamboo zithers

A relative newcomer to the spectrum of Chinese zithers is the *yang ch'in* (foreign zither), which reached China from Persia a number of centuries ago; it is the only representative of the box zither in the East. The history of this type of chordophone is obscure indeed, but two instruments of this general shape that may be very old are the African raft and board zithers. The raft zither is constructed on the idiochordic principle, but it uses a number of canes about half an inch in diameter; each of these has one string raised out of its own surface, and all of the canes are then lashed together. The board zither is made from a hollowed-out board over which a number of strings are attached. This latter instrument is found only in restricted areas of East Africa; it is possible that its principle of construction was carried to the Middle East by traders. Medieval Arab authors (including Ibn Khaldūn) mention the plucked trapezoidal zither, *qānūn* (derived from Latin *canon,* "rule"). Nowadays, the instrument has a range of three chromatic octaves with three strings to each pitch, and a complex system of levers by which its many strings may be finely and quickly retuned to the various Arab scales. Closely related is the Persian-derived *santūr,* another trapezoidal zither that is struck by two light hammers. Versions of this zither are found in China (*yang ch'in*), Greece (*santouri*), and Eastern Europe (cimbalom). These two zithers are the prototypes for the later keyboard instruments of western Europe: the *qānūn,* which is played with two plectrums, became, with the addition of a keyboard, the harpsichord; the cimbalom, with the addition of a keyboard, became the piano. In the Middle Ages, the keyboard was attached to a number of instruments, including the lute, the hurdy-gurdy, and the various Scandinavian keyed fiddles, of which the Swedish *nyckelharpa* survives. The experiment was truly successful, however, only on the clavichord, harpsichord, and later the piano; on the fiddle, it always remained of peripheral importance.

The lute. The first surviving evidence of the existence of the lute comes from Mesopotamia and Egypt. One of the earliest Babylonian delineations (*c.* 2500 BC) shows a shepherd with a long-necked, small-bodied lute; this instrument, which was doubtless skin bellied, had a rounded back that might well have been made from a turtle carapace (as in modern North Africa) or a gourd (as in Puerto Rico). A similar instrument is also found in Egypt, and from specimens surviving from ancient times it is known that the stick forming the neck passed through the body of the instrument, ending at the sound hole, where it served as a fastener for the ends of the strings. This instrument, like the harp, survives in West Africa and in North Africa (as the *gunbrī* or *halam*).

Earliest known lutes

The Greeks of old seem to have made rather sparing use of the lute, but it was commonly encountered in Rome. Though the skin-bellied lute predominated in the ancient Mediterranean, the wood-bellied lute has been more typical of Europe; indeed (with the exception of the African-derived banjo) more recently, all currently used European lutes and fiddles have wood bellies. The most important model for the European lute was the classical Arab lute, *al-ʿūd* ("the wood"), which has been the most important instrument of classical Arab music for 1,000 years. Not only the instrument itself, with its characteristically curved back, but also its name entered Europe, probably through a number of different gateways, including Sicily, Andalusia, and Palestine with the crusaders.

Though European and Arab lutes are very similar in general construction, the Arab lute is not fretted as is the European lute, and the European lute little by little acquired additional courses of strings during the Renaissance, when it became a standard instrument for solo playing and the accompaniment of singers. The many courses of strings caused numerous problems: "When a lute-player is 80 years old," wrote the 18th-century German theorist Johann Mattheson sarcastically, "he has spent 60 years tuning his instruments."

The many lutelike instruments of modern India (tambura, *vina*, sitar, and sarod) are, technically speaking, lute-zithers, since their fingerboards are hollow; in appearance and playing technique, however, they are indistinguishable from lutes. They seem to represent a special, and quite recent, subfamily of chordophones. In the Far East, again, the lute family exists only in a comparatively recent manifestation, but both in wood-bellied form (Chinese *p'i-p'a,* Japanese *biwa*) and skin-bellied version (Chinese *san-hsien,* Japanese samisen). In Japan, these instruments existed in the year 752, and the Imperial Treasury at Nara preserves three *biwas* used at a great concert held in that year. The *biwa-p'i–p'a* family can be traced ultimately to Persia, where, as the *barbat,* it influenced the music of Afghanistan and Turkestan on its way to China and Japan. The skin-bellied lute, *san-hsien,* can be traced in China only to the 13th century; from there it was taken to the Ryukyu Islands and thence to Japan (mid-16th century), where it still plays an important musical role as the samisen.

Lutes of the Far East

Bowed instruments. The principle of bowing is nearly always applied to stringed instruments of the lute class, though one occasionally finds it used with zithers or lyres. It is difficult, if not impossible, to make a clear-cut distinction between plucking with a plectrum and bowing, since plucking sometimes involves rubbing the string. But bowing, defined as the use of the almost universally encountered horsehair bow, can be traced as far back as the Islāmic civilization of the 10th century. The stroked *rabāb* evidently possessed a long neck and up to four strings. There is no iconographic evidence of such instruments before the 13th century in Islām itself, though an illustration (*c.* 930) from Christian Spain delineates a bowed instrument with three strings. In Byzantium, too, the bowed *lira* existed by this time, and it seems likely that the principle of bowing originated among the horse cultures of Central Asia, whence it spread quickly through Islām and the East, so that by 1000 it had almost simultaneously reached China, Java, North Africa, the Near East and Balkans, and Europe. Modern scholarship has shown that a word meaning "horse" is given to the bridge of the fiddle throughout Eurasia, from Japan (*koma*) to western Norway (*hest*). In China the fiddle is acknowledged to have come from the "barbarians" of Central Asia; in those days it was in China an instrument of the people; later, at the time of Kublai Khan, it began to be used in court music. In Africa, the fiddle seems to have entered the continent with Islām.

The bowed instrument in Europe

In Europe the bow appears first in Spain and shortly thereafter in Italy, and it is suspected that it entered through Muslim Spain and Sicily, though it is possible that other fiddles entered Europe through the Balkans, Hungary, and Scandinavia. Even in early illustrations, evidence is found of the uniquely European method of holding the fiddle against the shoulder. (Everywhere else in the world, the fiddle is held vertically.) At the same time, other European fiddles were held vertically, in the Oriental manner. Early European fiddles were made (by their players) in only two parts: the belly was a thin piece of spruce or fir wood, and the back was hollowed out of one piece of hardwood. These medieval fiddles divide into two types, one of which has a clearly discernible neck; the other possesses a neck that merges imperceptibly into the body; second type, exemplified by the rebec, is equivalent to the North African *rabāb* and the Byzantine–Greek *lira.* As the centuries passed, Europe continued to have two distinct types of fiddles: one, relatively square shaped, held in the arms, became known as the viola da braccia ("arm viol") family and evolved into the violin; the other, with sloping shoulders and held between the knees, was the viola da gamba ("leg viol") group. The gambas, which were important and elegant instruments during the Renaissance, lost ground to the louder (and originally less aristocratic) braccia-violin family. (T.Gr.)

THE VIOLIN FAMILY

The violin family includes the violin, viola, violoncello, and double bass and forms the basis of the modern orchestra. The family takes its name from its smallest member, which is perhaps the best known and most widely distributed musical instrument in the world.

The violin is a descendant of the horizontally held arm viols of the Middle Ages by a process of evolution and metamorphosis. Its immediate precursor is the *lira da braccio,* an elaborate instrument of the Renaissance, whose form foreshadows the physical essentials of the violin body: the arched modelling of the belly and back, and the shallow ribs. This shallow arched form probably encouraged or suggested another important detail: the use of a short vertical stick to prop the front and back apart and prevent the collapse of the belly arch under pressure of the strings. This device, the sound post, is peculiar to the violin; although it was later used on the viols, it is the acoustic effect of the sound post that imparts to the violin its lively response and generous singing tone, for it couples and coordinates the vibrations of the body as a whole, under the influence of the strings.

Although the generic name for the family is the Italian *viola* (whence violino, "small viola"; violone, "large viola"; violoncello, "small violone"), the treble instrument very soon became its most important member, from which the others took their main characteristics. Unlike the smaller viols, whose tone was reticent and impersonal, the violin was always recognized both for its superior cantabile and for its inherent sprightliness and smart attack, especially in Italy, its birthplace, where the earliest makers Gasparo da Salò, Andrea Amati, and Giovanni Paolo Maggini had settled its average proportions before the end of the 16th century. Thus the violin arrived at exactly the right time to lend impetus and conviction to the innovations of the Florentine school of composers, whose preoccupation with the expressive qualities of the solo voice marked a breakaway from the older polyphony. To this movement, the violin, the first treble instrument to achieve an innate lyricism, formed the perfect instrumental counterpart.

Two other features contributed to the character of the violin, the first being the tuning of the strings in fifths and their numerical limitation to four. This wide regular tuning was ideal in furnishing a uniform diatonic fingering technique, reducing the amount of string-crossing the bow has to do, generally freeing the bridge from too many strings and permitting better clearance on each string for bowing. The second additional feature is the unfretted fingerboard, in which the violin followed the *lira da braccio.* No doubt frets, if they were ever used, were removed from the arm viols because they impeded the use of the hand in supporting the instrument and in fingering. It is also true that the direct stopping of the strings by the fleshy part of the fingertips produces a tone quality that, although slightly damped, in consequence is more satisfying and easier to listen to than the pure open-string tone obtained from the use of frets, as on the viols, besides being more completely under the control of the player. Moreover, it leaves the player free to temper intonation as much as he pleases, since this is no longer dominated by the fixed tuning of the frets. It is perhaps this capacity for the mutual adjustment of intonation that led to the use of the violin family in a way that was entirely new in instrumental music—*i.e.*, as a massed "choir" in which the several parts were doubled at unison by instruments of like kind. This string ensemble, so different in its effect from the chamber music of the preceding "golden age," owes its first organization, if not its invention, to the French at the court of Louis XIV, whose *vingt-quaire violons du Roi* was the model for Europe of the embryo orchestra-to-be.

Tuning. The viola stands one fifth lower than the violin, its upper three strings being tuned to the same notes as the lower three of the smaller instrument. The tuning of the violoncello is one octave below the viola, while the normal double bass approximately covers the suboctave of the violoncello. There is some evidence for the former existence of a fifth member, the so-called true tenor violin, standing in pitch one octave below the treble instrument.

Playing positions. The violin and viola are played in the horizontal position—*i.e.*, "under the chin." The cello (customary abbreviation of violoncello) and double bass both stand vertically on the floor, the first resting on a long steel rod called the end pin, with the player holding the instrument between his knees while seated. For the double bass the player stands or rests on a high stool. As is done with every other necked stringed instrument, the player's left hand fingers the instrument, the bow being held in the right. The highest string is to the right, viewing the instrument from the front, the lowest to the left. Therefore, on the violin and viola, the bow attacks from the top-string side, and on the bass instruments from the bottom-string side. This makes scarcely any difference to the bowing technique except perhaps to give freer control of the upper strings of the smaller instruments and lower strings of the larger, a useful bias in view of their respective functions, at least in earlier times.

Violin. In structure and appearance, violins of all sizes are quite unmistakable. The body consists of a belly of pine and a back of sycamore, maple, or a similar hardwood, spaced apart by shallow ribs (sides) of the same material. The arching of the belly and back, already mentioned, is both transverse and longitudinal, so that when viewed from the side the effect is of a central bulge, flattening off in all directions to the edges, the undersides of which are plane where they meet the ribs. In most cases the "modelling" of the bulge changes from convexity to concavity as it approaches the edges, which are given a slight upward curl. The arching is worked from solid wood of suitable thickness, and the plate is dug out on its undersurface to a curve that follows the general contour of the outward modelling but not exactly, for the finished thickness is graduated in all directions, being thinnest in the margins of the outline just inside the ribs. The adjustment of these thicknesses is one of the prime skills in the craft of violinmaking. The wood used in both back and belly is usually, though not always, cut "on the quarter"—*i.e.*, in wedge-shaped segmental planks from the centre to the outside of the log. To form a plate, two wedges are glued "back to back" with the thin edges outward. This not only provides the basis for the modelling but also ensures that the annular rings of the tree are evenly disposed about the centre line of the plate, the oldest growth being on the outside edges.

The familiar, and deceptively simple, outline of the violin body is aesthetically satisfying, perhaps because its balance and proportion are largely functional. Its master makers have evolved a form based on an artistic unity of opposed curves that allows free play to individual nuance with scarcely any measurable deviation from the norm. The rounded ends of the body, called the upper and lower bouts, are separated by the indented waist, or middle bout, which provides clearance for the bow on the outer strings. The middle bout meets the upper and lower to form outturned corners, where the ribs are brought together and glued firmly to corner blocks within the instrument. Other blocks, called end blocks, are mounted top and bottom centre to provide firm bearings for the neck and end pin, which between them have to resist the tension of the strings. The ribs are slightly inset from the outline of the belly and back, so that the edge overhangs all around. The internal corners between the ribs and the plates are strengthened by a narrow fillet of pine, called the linings, which runs between the blocks. Despite the very considerable stresses to which it is subject, the violin body is held together by simple flush glued joints, which can in emergency be opened up, without damaging the instrument, for repairs.

The arched belly or soundboard of the violin is supported in a curiously unorthodox and individual way, quite different from the regular barring of instruments with flat soundboards. The sound post has already been mentioned. It is a loose stick of pine, carefully cut to size, that is wedged between the plates of the finished instrument under, but a little behind, the top-string side of the bridge. It is not a fixture because its position is critical and must be adjusted with great care for the best tonal result. This adjustment is made through the sound holes in the belly. The other side of the bridge is supported by a bar glued under the belly and running lengthways along the grain of the wood. This bar, called the bass bar, is deepest under the bridge, but tapers to nothing at either end, since it fits into the internal curvature of the belly. Externally, the plates are finished off with a narrow inlay of laminated woods, the purfling, which follows the outline close to the edges. Even this, the only decoration normally permitted, has the function of preventing incipient splits from running.

The neck and head are cut from a solid block of sycamore wood. The lower end is formed into a shoulder that abuts against the ribs at the top of the body and, in fact, passes through them into a shallow mortise cut in the end block within. The back end of this shoulder is covered by a projection of the wood at the top of the back, known as the button. The head or pegbox carries the four tuning pegs, two on each side. It is slotted to the front to receive the strings. The pegs are tapered and pass through two holes in the cheeks of the head. At the top of the head is the scroll, again a typical embellishment of the violin, its austere purity of line and curve being both the challenge and the sign manual of the master craftsman. The front face of the neck is flat, and to this is glued the fingerboard, which projects beyond the shoulder and over the belly toward the bridge. At the top of the neck is the nut, which is grooved to take the strings, keeping them correctly spaced apart and slightly raised over the fingerboard. The neck is raked back at an angle with the plane of the belly, so that the fingerboard rises with the strings toward the bridge. The bridge is high and arched because of the bowed technique. It is formed with two feet that are carefully cut to fit the transverse arch of the belly and is given a conventional perforated or fretted design, which is said to aid its free vibration. In section it is wedge-shaped, tapering to the thin, notched edge over which the strings pass. It is not a fixture but is kept in position only by the pressure of the strings. Its correct position is between the sound holes and just above the lower corners of the middle bout. The sound holes are of italic *f* form, sweeping outward and downward from the waist to the lower corners. A line joining the crosses of the *f*s marks the approximate position of the bridge. The lower ends of the strings are held by the long tailpiece below the bridge, whose function is to reduce the length of unused string behind the bridge and to keep the strings pulling radially inward on its top edge. The lower end of the tailpiece is anchored by a loop of gut to an end peg set in a hole in the lower end block. A small ebony button takes the pull of the tailgut off the edge of the belly.

During its history the violin has been subject to modifications that have progressively adapted it to its evolving musical functions. In general, the more primitive types have been more deeply arched in the plates, and the more modern, following the innovations of Antonio Stradivari (1644–1737), have been shallower and more virile, which has affected the over-all tonal characteristics. The stresses to which the instrument is subjected under working conditions have increased not only because of the rise in pitch from the 17th century onward but also because of certain changes in physical design from about the beginning of the 19th century. Before that time the height of the bridge and its arching were lower, the neck thicker and wider, and the bass bar shallower and shorter. These, with the type of bow then in use and the lower pitch, produced the small, delicate tone that served composers up to the time of Mozart. With the advent of larger auditoriums and the development of the violin virtuoso, however, greater power was demanded, and this demand was met by raising the height of the bridge, lengthening and slimming the neck slightly and setting it back at a greater angle, and putting in a stronger bass bar. The sum effect of these alterations was to develop the optimum sonority of which the instrument was capable, and the long experience of makers and players has shown that the Stradivari type with its shallower arching has stood up best to this metamorphosis. All fine violins now in use have been thus modified to bring them into line with modern technique and modern conditions.

Viola. This instrument, standing a fifth lower than the violin, is similar to it in every essential, but, owing to its larger size, it has never been completely standardized in its main dimensions, since, whatever these are, they are bound to tax the human frame and fingers when the instrument is played. A compromise has to be effected between what is the ideal size for the best tonal results and what is practicable to the player in handling. Too large an instrument is simply unplayable; too small an instrument is weakest where it is most wanted—on the lower strings. The problem has never been solved to everyone's satisfaction, but it has produced a viola tone that is darker, more weighty, and more sombre than the violin and without which the string ensemble cannot now be imagined. Violas have been made at various times with a body length (the most convenient measure of their manoeuvrability) of 15 to 18 inches (38 to 46 centimetres); probably the majority of the most manageable and successful instruments are midway between these extremes. However desirable it may appear in theory, too big a body, whether in length or depth, tends to develop a "tubby," aggressive, unmanageable tone that lacks the blending qualities of the traditional instrument.

Violoncello, or cello. The true bass of the violin, and the member of the family most nearly approaching it in character, is the violoncello, or cello. In build it differs somewhat, the ribs being proportionately much deeper and the much higher bridge standing on legs rather than feet. The neck is raked back at a sharper angle to allow for the height of the bridge. The instrument is held between the knees while it rests on an end pin, which is telescoped through the tailpin and can be clamped in any position to adjust the height of the instrument above the floor. This playing position leaves both arms exceptionally free; in particular, the left-hand technique is more fluid and covers a wider range than in any other stringed instrument. This is strikingly shown by the ease with which a good cellist commands the brilliant solo register of the top (A) string, high above the normal tessitura of the instrument.

Double bass. Because of its great size, the double bass has always shown less regularity of form, stringing, tuning, and technique than the other members of the violin family. Double basses have been in use for as long as the parent instrument, but they are not yet completely standardized in number of strings, tuning, shape, or body size. The bass is sometimes made with the blunt corners and flat back of the viol and, on that account, has been called a hybrid instrument. But true double bass violins, with arched back and outturned corners, have existed since the early 17th century and are still in the majority. It is immaterial whether the back is flat or arched, except that the flat back is both more convenient for the player and more economical to make. It is the fitting and adjustment of the bass, which follows that of the cello, that makes it what it is—a double bass violin. The tuning in fourths, which is almost universal, has been adopted on the bass owing to the great length of the strings (42½ inches, or 108 centimetres), which makes the whole-tone interval in the fingering so large that it can be covered only by the span of the first and fourth fingers. The closer tuning therefore brings the technique of fingering more into line with what is possible on the smaller instruments, namely a scalewise (diatonic) fingering that reduces hand movements to a minimum. The normal turning, E–A–D–G, means that the bass cannot descend an octave below the cello's bottom string, and it is for this reason that the low fifth string is sometimes added, tuned to 16-foot C. The note commonly occurs in symphonic works from the classical period onward and is being more specificially demanded by modern composers. Conversely, the high fifth C string, tuned a fourth above the normal top string, is occasionally used in dance bands, where it simplifies the fingering of high pizzicato (plucked) notes.

Another method of obtaining 16-foot C is to fit an attachment mechanism that lengthens the existing E string (which is carried up to the top of the head on an extension bar) when these low notes are wanted. This has the advantage that it preserves the normal four strings and their normal tuning for all ordinary purposes and imposes no extra load on the bridge, as does the fifth string. On the double bass the pegs are replaced by a "machine head," such as is commonly used on guitars and other plucked instruments, each tuning peg being fitted with a worm-and-wheel screw adjuster. The pegs themselves are made of solid brass. The "tailgut" of the smaller instruments is also replaced by metal, usually a thick copper wire but preferably a stranded steel cable. An extending end pin, similar to the pin used on the cello, is now in universal use. On most basses the ribs are not of equal depth all around but are cut away at the top so that the back slants toward the shoulder of the neck in its upper part. This enables the player to bring the neck and upper portion of the body closer to him and makes for ease of handling. The normal size of the bass, around six feet high, is about as large as the average person can manage for modern technical requirements. This size has been known since the early 17th century, but larger and smaller basses have been made at all times, and in the late 20th century the small electronic bass has become common in popular bands and orchestras.

The bow. The violin bow consists of a strong, light, flexible wooden stick, sprung so that a ribbon of horsehairs can be stretched between its ends. The hair is drawn across a solid cake of resin and rubs off a small quantity in powder form; this supplies the frictional element that is necessary to make the string vibrate. Proper design is as important in a violin bow as in the violin itself, for it must give the player a feeling of complete control over the tone he is producing and must respond to every nuance of pressure and attack imposed upon it. The modern bow, which is really the culmination of a long line of evolution, was perfected late in the 18th century by François Tourte, of Paris. The light tapering stick now is made of brazilwood (Pernambuco wood) with a hatchet-shaped head formed at the thinner end. At the other end is a movable frog, which has a threaded eye projecting into a mortise or groove cut in the stick and runs on a screw that can be turned at the lower end of the stick. The hank of hair is stretched between the head and frog, and its tension is adjusted by the screw. The hair is retained as a flat ribbon by passing through a specially shaped ferrule and a shallow channel in the frog before it is wedged into a socket farther along. The hair is usually concealed in the channel by a small sliding panel of mother-of-pearl. The hair is similarly wedged in the head, the front of which is faced either with ivory or silver to protect it from damage. When the screw is slackened off, the stick curves toward the hair. When the hair is tightened, the stick straightens out, or rather, the curve flattens somewhat. It is the correct setting of this curve, which is put into the stick by bending under dry heat, and the exact shaping of the tapering section of the stick that give a good bow its desired qualities.

The earlier type of violin bow, which was used almost everywhere from the beginning of the 17th century until the end of the 18th century, was shorter and had a lighter head and a narrower ribbon of hair. Its chief characteristic, however, was the shape of the stick, which bent outward from the hair under working tension. This design would not stand up to modern ideas of bowing technique, where, on occasion, optimum sonority must be developed from the instrument, but it was suited to the smaller scale and neat articulations of Baroque and early Classical violin music.

The larger instruments have followed the violin in bow design, adapting it to their special purposes by adjustments of dimension and weight. For a long time the double bass lagged behind, and during the first half of the 19th century this instrument was still being played with a broad, heavy version of the earlier outcurved bow. This was supplanted in France, and in other countries under French influence, by the violin-type bow and in Austria and German-speaking countries generally, a little later, by the Simandl bow, named after a contemporary professor of the Vienna Academy. This bow is really an adaptation of the older type but with an incurved stick, wide frog, and narrow head. (E.Hy.)

Keyboard instruments

The large and important group of keyboard instruments includes all musical instruments on which different notes may be sounded by pressing a series of push buttons or parallel levers. This group has assumed its great importance because the keyboard enables a performer to sound as many notes as he has fingers, either at once or in close succession. This unique capability enables him to play a reasonable approximation of any work in the entire literature of Western music, whether it involves complex harmonies or the interplay of independent contrapuntal parts. Moreover, the capabilities of keyboard instruments have influenced the composition of music for other media, because virtually every major composer from William Byrd (*c.* 1543–1623) to Béla Bartók (1881–1945) and beyond has been at least an accomplished keyboard performer, if not a renowned virtuoso.

In its broadest sense, the term keyboard instruments may be applied to any instrument with a keyboard and thus may refer to accordions, percussion instruments such as the celesta and the carillon, and many electronic instruments—for example, the Moog synthesizer and the Ondes Martenot. In a narrower sense it is restricted to instruments in which sound is produced from strings, whether by plucking, striking, or rubbing.

DEVELOPMENT OF THE KEYBOARD

Evolution from early forms. Long before the appearance of the first stringed keyboard instruments in the 14th century, the keyboard was developed and applied to the organ. A keyboard of the kind familiar today—a series of parallel levers balanced or pivoted so that they can be pushed down by the fingers—first appeared on the hydraulis, an organ used by the Romans at least as early as the 1st entury AD. This type of keyboard seems to have disappeared after the fall of Rome, and the organs of the early Middle Ages generally had sliders that were pulled out to sound different notes; some may have had keys that turned like the key for a lock. Keys of the last type were certainly used on the organistrum, a large medieval hurdy-gurdy operated by two players: one turned a crank rotating a wheel that rubbed against one or more strings to make them sound, while the other produced different notes by turning the key-shaped levers that stopped the strings at various points (much as guitar strings are stopped against the fingerboard).

Key arrangements and colours

Some small portable organs had push buttons instead of keys as late as the 1440s, but a keyboard very similar to the modern type existed in the 14th century, although the arrangement of naturals and sharps (corresponding to the white and black keys on the modern piano) was only gradually standardized. The arrangement of the keys depended in part on the music played and partly on the current state of musical theory. Thus, early keyboards are reported with only a single raised key in each octave (B♭), and there were organs that had both B and B♭ as "natural" keys, with C♯, D♯, F♯, and G♯ as raised keys. The colours of the keys—white for naturals and black for sharps—became standardized much later, *c.* 1800, depending on fashion or on the relative cost of ivory and ebony. Flemish instruments had bone naturals and black sharps by 1580; English instruments generally had either brown boxwood naturals and black sharps or ebony naturals and ivory sharps until *c.* 1720; French and German instruments had ebony naturals and ivory sharps until the 1790s.

Special key arrangements. *The short octave.* Even after the present arrangement of five raised keys and seven natural keys per octave had become standard in the 15th century, two special exceptions existed. The first of these—the "short octave"—concerned only the lowest octave at the bass end of the keyboard. In the short octave, not all keys actually sounded notes of the expected pitch; their respective strings were tuned to lower notes. In the earlier form (Figure 1A), the keyboard apparently started on E, but the string for this key note was tuned to the C below. The apparent F♯ was tuned to D and the G♯ to E, so that the notes of the entire octave from C to c were encompassed within an apparent key span of only E to c. With this arrangement C♯, E♭, F♯, and G♯ were not available in the bass octave, but these notes were rarely required in the bass in music of this period. When the missing F♯ and G♯ later became necessary, short-octave keyboards were made with these keys divided into two parts, the fronts sounding D and E and the back parts sounding F♯ and G♯. Later still, a second short octave was developed (Figure 1B) in which the keyboard apparently began on low B. This key

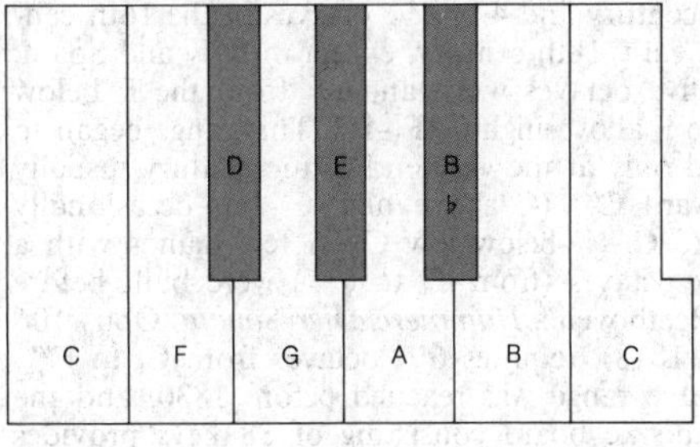

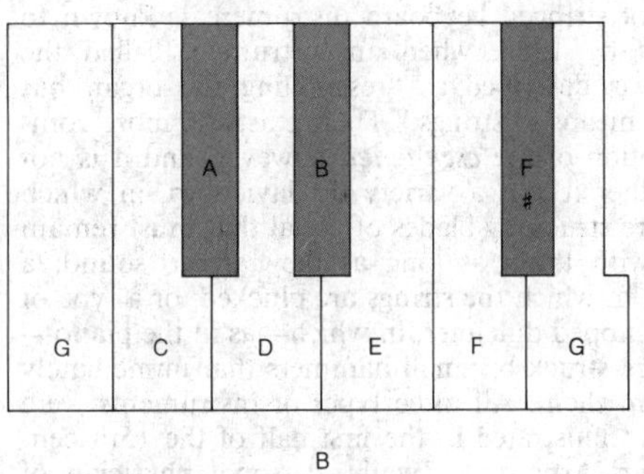

Figure 1: *Special key arrangements.*
Short octave (A) beginning on C and (B) beginning on G (see text).

actually sounded the G below, and the apparent C♯ and E♭ were tuned to A and B (or B♭). Eventually, as musical styles changed, the two retuned sharps were divided in this arrangement as well, providing C♯ (or sometimes B♭) and E♭ at the back of these keys while retaining A and B at the front.

Divided sharps. The second type of exceptional keyboard arrangement was originally required by the so-called meantone tuning system generally used in the 16th–18th centuries. Meantone tuning provided significantly purer tuning for a relatively small number of tonalities than does the system of equal temperament now in use (in which all tonalities are somewhat out of tune; see MUSIC, THE ART OF: *Tuning and temperament*), but only at the expense of making it virtually impossible to use any of the remaining tonalities. This characteristic arose because in meantone tuning each of the raised keys could be used in only one way: for example, if the key between D and E was tuned to E♭, it could not be used as D♯ without retuning. One solution was to build keyboards with the raised keys divided, the front half of the key sounding the appropriate sharp while the back half sounded the equivalent flat. The keys most commonly divided were A♭/G♯, E♭/D♯, and B♭/A♯. Instruments with up to three divided keys in each octave were commonly made in the 16th and 17th centuries, especially in Italy. Since the 1590s still more complicated keyboards have been built, permitting even more refined tunings; some in the 19th century had more than 50 keys per octave. Instruments have also been made with the octave divided into 24 rather than 12 equal parts to permit playing music utilizing quarter-tone intervals.

Impact of tuning systems

Keyboard size and range. Although some early organs had very wide keys that could be played only with the fists, stringed keyboard instruments seem always to have had natural keys no more than an inch wide, yielding an octave span of seven inches (17.8 centimetres). The octave span on the modern piano is about 6$^1/_2$ inches, much the same as on Flemish and Italian harpsichords of the 16th–18th centuries, whereas that of English keyboards was generally 6$^3/_8$ inches (16.2 centimetres). On most French and German instruments of the 18th century, the octave span was even narrower (6$^1/_4$ inches [15.9 centimetres]), permitting the playing of tenths—such as C to the second E above—by a hand of average size.

The range of the keyboard gradually expanded from a single octave for some early organs to 2$^1/_2$ or 3 octaves in the 15th century and 4 or 4½ octaves in the 16th century. By the early 18th century, except in Italy and Spain, a range of five octaves was standard: from the F below low C to the F above high C (F_1–f'''). This range began to be expanded only at the very end of the century, usually upward toward C'''' (C above high C) but occasionally downward to C_1 (C below low C). A few pianos with a range of six octaves (from C_1 to C'''') were built before 1800, and Beethoven's *Hammerclavier Sonata,* Opus 106 (completed, 1818), requires 6½ octaves from C_1 to F''''. A seven-octave range was reached before 1830, and the modern piano keyboard consisting of 88 keys provides the only slightly greater range seven octaves and a third, from A_2 to C''.

THE CLAVICHORD

Some kind of stringed keyboard instrument is known to have existed by 1385, when an instrument called the *eschiquier* was described as "resembling the organ but sounding by means of strings." There exists no more complete description of the *eschiquier,* however, and it is not known whether it was a variety of clavichord, in which the strings are struck by blades of metal that must remain in contact with them as long as they are to sound; a harpsichord, in which the strings are plucked; or a type of keyboard-equipped dulcimer, in which—as in the piano—the strings are struck by small hammers that immediately rebound from them. All three types of instruments were described and illustrated in the first half of the 15th century by Henri Arnaut of Zwolle, personal physician of Philip the Good, duke of Burgundy.

Despite the uncertainty regarding the *eschiquier,* it seems probable that the clavichord was the earliest stringed instrument having keys that could be pushed down by the fingers. Its principle of operation resembles that of the medieval organistrum, and it is apparently closely related to the monochord, an instrument consisting of a shallow closed box over which one or two strings were stretched. The monochord was in continuous use by theorists from ancient Greece onward as a tool for explaining and measuring musical intervals. Monochords were also used as performing instruments at least as early as the 13th century, and the kinship of the clavichord to the monochord was so close that, as late as the 16th century, clavichords were often called *monocordia.*

Principle of operation. The clavichord is rectangular in shape, and its strings run from left to right across the keys, which are placed along one of the longer sides of the rectangle. The soundboard of the instrument is at the right-hand end of the case, and the vibrations of the strings are communicated to it by a bridge on which the strings rest. The soundboard amplifies the sound of the strings by permitting them to set a large mass of air into vibration rather than the very small mass of air that can actually be in contact with the string itself. (This is the same principle that makes a tuning fork sound louder when its stem is held in contact with a tabletop.)

Shape and layout

The clavichord's principle of operation is extremely simple. A brass blade rather like the end of a screwdriver is driven into the top surface of each key near the back of the key (Figure 2); a smaller piece of wood, whalebone, or horn is driven into the back end of the key. (This piece fits into a fixed slot behind the key and prevents the key from moving from side to side as it moves up and down.) When the front end of the key is pushed down by the finger, the back end rises, and the brass blade, called a tangent, strikes the strings (which in most clavichords are arranged in pairs), causing them to vibrate. To the left of the tangent a strip of cloth is woven between the strings. When the key is struck, only the portion of the strings to the right of the tangent—*i.e.,* between the tangent and the bridge—sounds; the cloth prevents the string section to the left of the tangent from sounding. As soon as the key is released, the tangent falls away from the strings, which are then entirely silenced by the cloth. Because the sounding portion of each string is the segment between tangent and bridge, the tangent serves not only to set the strings in vibration but also to determine their sounding length. Thus, a series of tangents striking a given pair of strings at different points will produce a series of different notes, and all the earliest clavichords were designed to take advantage of this fact. Arnaut of Zwolle's clavichord used only nine or 10 pairs of strings to produce all the 37 notes of its three-octave keyboard, and the clavichord represented in an Italian intarsia (picture in wood inlay) of about 1480 (Palazzo Ducale, Urbino) used only 17 pairs of strings to produce 47 notes in a four-octave range.

From N. Bessaraboff, *Ancient European Musical Instruments* (1941); Harvard University Press

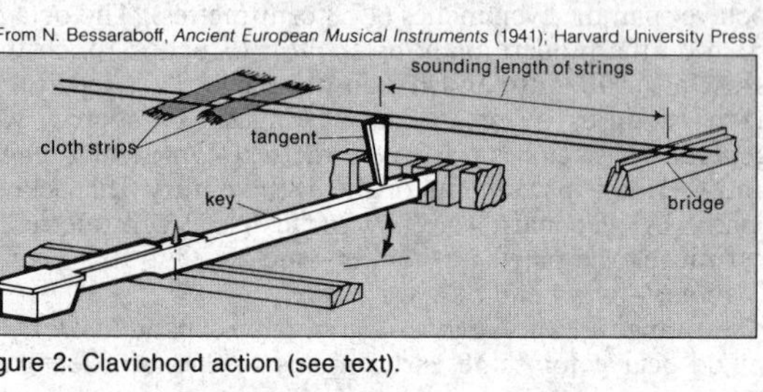

Figure 2: Clavichord action (see text).

Making a single pair of strings serve several keys had two important disadvantages. Because each pair of strings can sound only one note at a time, it is impossible to play any two notes sounded from the same strings simultaneously, making it impossible to play certain chords. Furthermore, an unpleasant clanking sound is likely to result if the performer attempts legato playing of successive notes sounded from the same strings, making it necessary to play in a semidetached fashion.

As early as the time of Arnaut of Zwolle, the first of these disadvantages was minimized by allowing no more than four keys to sound from the same pair of strings and by carefully choosing the points at which such groups of four keys were placed, so that only dissonant chords would be unplayable. The second problem could be solved only when a maximum of two keys were served by the same strings, so that each natural key shared its strings only with the sharp or flat next to it. G, for example, was paired with G♯, and in the normal music of the period the two notes were never needed at the same time or in immediate succession. Of course, if one wanted to use the G♯ key as an A♭, the problem would reassert itself; but, as long as meantone tuning was in use, the G♯ could not serve as A♭ in any case.

Eventually, however, it was felt necessary to be able to play in all tonalities without restrictions either of style of playing or in the use of dissonant chords, and clavichords began to be built with one pair of strings for each key. Such clavichords are called "unfretted," in contrast to those having several keys for each pair of strings, which are called "fretted." Although the unfretted clavichord was apparently known before 1700, fretted clavichords were being made well into the 1780s; they had fewer strings to go out of tune, and the smaller number of strings permitted all the keys to be shorter and more equal in length, giving the instrument a superior touch. In addition, the smaller number of strings imposed a smaller downward force on the soundboard, resulting in a brighter, clearer tone.

Fretted and unfretted clavichords

Tone quality. The greatest disadvantage of the clavichord is its extremely soft tone. Because it arises directly from the way in which the sound of the instrument is produced, this disadvantage cannot readily be overcome. It is impossible to impart very much energy to a string by striking it at one end (it is for this reason that a guitarist makes less sound when he strikes the strings against the fingerboard with his left hand than when he plucks them with his right, even though the pitches produced are the same). In compensation, the clavichordist alone of all keyboard-instrument players has control over a note once it has been struck. As long as a note is sounding, he has contact with the string through the tangent and key, and by changing his pressure on the key he can vary the pitch of the note, produce a controlled vibrato, or even create the illusion of prolonging or swelling the tone. Although the maximum loudness of which a clavichord is capable is not great, its softest pianissimo is very soft indeed, and the clavichordist has complete control over an enormous number of gradations in loudness between these two extremes. As a result of this touch sensitivity, the clavichord was highly valued as a teaching and practice instrument.

In addition, its relative cheapness made it the normal domestic keyboard instrument in Germany and Scandinavia.

The soft tone of the clavichord made it impossible to use the instrument for any kind of ensemble music, except for providing a very discreet accompaniment for a single singer. Although much of the solo keyboard music of the 16th–18th centuries can be played on the clavichord, it cannot be stated that any of it before the latter part of the 18th century was especially composed with the clavichord in mind. At that time, however, the clavichord experienced a great revival in Germany, and music composed with its singing tone and unique capabilities of dynamic shading and vibrato was written for it by such masters as Carl Philip Emanuel Bach (1714–88).

Clavichords in the 19th century

Clavichords continued to be made in Germany and Scandinavia well into the 19th century, long after the piano was both well known and popular. Indeed, many instrument makers built both clavichords and pianos (and harpsichords as well). The continued demand for the older instruments may have been a consequence—among other things—of musicians' recognition of the three instruments' differing capabilities.

The clavichord owes its modest modern revival largely to the efforts of Arnold Dolmetsch in England, who began building clavichords and performing on them in public in the 1890s. Both his style of playing the clavichord and the design of his instruments have remained a strong influence today. Only German makers, however, are presently producing clavichords in any great numbers.

THE HARPSICHORD

Principle of operation. *Plucking mechanism.* The sound of the wing-shaped harpsichord and its smaller rectangular, triangular, or polygonal relatives, the spinet and virginal, is produced by plucking their strings. The mechanism that accomplishes this is called a jack (Figure 3). It rests on the key and consists of a narrow slip of wood with two slots cut into it. The larger slot holds a pivoted tongue from which protrudes the quill, plastic, or leather plectrum that does the actual plucking; the smaller slot holds a piece of cloth that rests on the string and silences it when the key is not depressed. When the harpsichordist pushes down on a key, the back end rises, lifting the jack and forcing the plectrum past the string, plucking it. When he releases the key, the jack falls, and when the plectrum reaches the string on the way down, it forces the pivoted tongue backward so that the plectrum can get past the string again without plucking it. Once the plectrum has passed the string, a light spring made of bristle, plastic, or metal pushes the tongue forward again. Finally, when the key is completely at rest, the cloth damper touches the string, silencing it. A wooden bar covered with felt on its underside is placed over the jacks. The purpose of this wooden bar is to prevent the jacks from flying out of the instrument and to limit the depth to which the keys can be depressed.

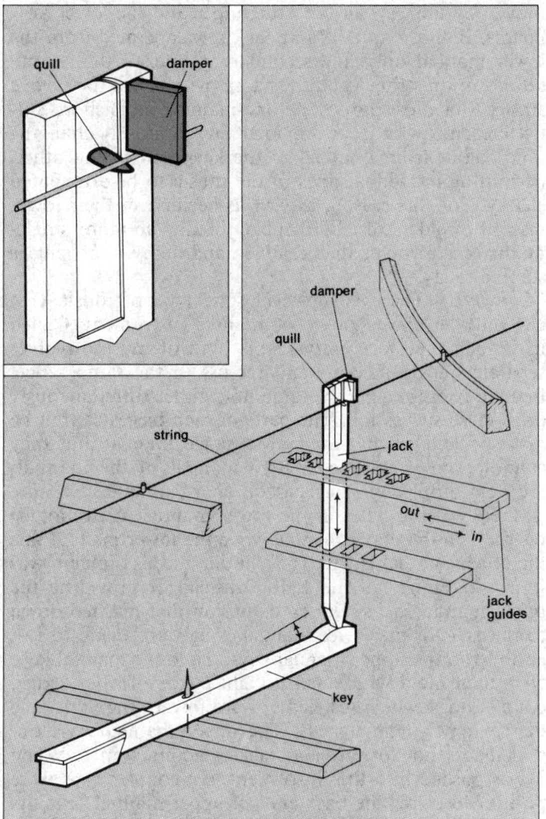

Figure 3: Harpsichord action (see text).

From N. Bessaraboff, *Ancient European Musical Instruments* (1941); Harvard University Press

Variations in loudness and timbre

Although minor variations in loudness and timbre, or tone colour, can be obtained by differences in the firmness with which the harpsichordist depresses the keys, no great differences in loudness and no sustained crescendos are obtainable by the action of the fingers alone. For this reason, most harpsichords made since about 1550 have had at least two strings and two jacks for each key. Each can be engaged or disengaged at will by a slight shift of the uppermost of two slotted guides through which the jacks pass. Moving the guide in one direction brings the entire row of jacks close enough to the strings for the quills to pluck them; moving the guide in the opposite direction takes the jacks far enough from the strings so that the quills cannot reach them. Two rows of jacks can provide three different levels of loudness or three differing tone colours, depending on whether the performer uses each row separately or both together.

Two-manual instruments. Even given two rows of jacks, it would not ordinarily be possible to produce the rapid changes in loudness required for pieces in echo style, for example, or to play loudly with one hand while providing a soft accompaniment with the other. To accomplish this, it is necessary to have two keyboards or "manuals," one of which operates a single row of jacks while the other operates two or more. It then becomes possible to play loudly on one keyboard and softly on the other, either simultaneously or in rapid alternation. Two-manual harpsichords of this kind were invented at some point before 1620 in Flanders and gradually became known throughout the rest of Europe during the 17th century. These instruments had three sets of strings, two unison strings at normal pitch (called 8′ pitch because the low C at this pitch is produced by an organ pipe eight feet long) and a third set of shorter strings tuned an octave higher, or at 4′ pitch; this shorter set passed over its own bridge and was fastened to pins driven through the soundboard into a rail fixed to its underside. There were three rows of jacks (Figure 4). The front row plucked one set of unison strings and was made in such a way that it would be

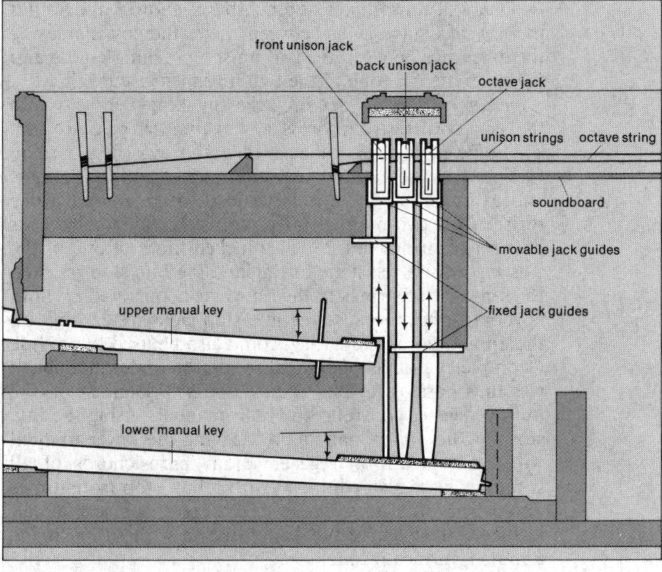

Figure 4: Flemish two-manual harpsichord action (see text).

moved by the keys of both the upper and the lower keyboards. Both the middle and back rows operated from the lower manual only; the second row plucked the second set of unison strings, and the back row plucked the octave strings. For most purposes a one-manual harpsichord sufficed: each row of jacks provided a continuously changing tone colour from one end of the keyboard to the other, permitting individual lines in the music to be articulated clearly. For this reason, as well as because of their lower price, the old harpsichord makers built far more single-manual instruments than doubles, and many more singles survive today.

Couplers. There is, however, one type of music that can only be played on a two-manual instrument. Called in French the *pièce croisée,* this kind of music involves separate lines that cross and recross in the same range, frequently employing the same note either simultaneously or in close succession. The parts in such pieces cannot be distinguished when played on a single manual and they cannot even be played on two manuals if the manuals are not completely independent. (For example, if a note is already being held on the lower manual, it cannot be restruck on the upper manual when the lower manual lifts the upper-manual jacks.) The solution to this problem was found in France in the 1640s. Instead of providing the upper-manual jacks with an extension that reached down to the keys of the lower manual, they were made to rest entirely on the upper-manual keys; the lower-manual keys were then fitted with small upright pieces of wood called coupler dogs, which reached upward toward the underside of the upper-manual keys. The upper manual was constructed to slide forward and back by about 1/4 inch. When it was pushed into the instrument, the coupler dogs were positioned below the back ends of upper-manual keys. As a result, when any lower-manual key was pushed down and its back end rose, the coupler dog would push up on the underside of the corresponding upper-manual key, lifting its jack as well. When one wished to uncouple the two keyboards in order to play *pièces croisées,* one could do so by pulling the upper manual outward. The coupler dogs then passed slightly beyond the ends of the upper-manual keys, so that they were not lifted when the lower-manual keys were depressed.

Music played on the two-manual instrument

Two-manual harpsichords of this kind permit one to exploit the difference in the tone colours produced by the two rows, or "registers," of unison jacks. This difference depends on the distance along the string at which it is plucked. The closer the plucking point is to the end of a string, the brighter and more nasal the sound; the farther away from the end that a string is plucked, the fuller and rounder the tone becomes, until one approaches the centre; plucking near the centre of a string produces a sweet, flutey, but somewhat hollow sound. In order to emphasize the difference in tone colours produced by the two rows of unison jacks French harpsichord builders put the row of octave jacks between them, thereby increasing the difference between the two unison plucking points and the difference in tone of the two unison registers.

Special effects. A set of jacks plucking very close to the end of the string yields a very brassy, nasal sound. This type of register, called a lute stop, was first used in Germany in the 16th century and later spread to Flanders and to England, where it was added to the normal three registers on two-manual instruments. It did not have its own set of strings but, rather, plucked those of one of the existing unison registers. In England the lute stop plucked the same set of strings as the set of jacks operated by both keyboards; but, because the lute-stop jacks rested only on the upper-manual keys, they could also be used to provide a completely independent register on the upper manual. It was thus possible to play *pièces croisées* by taking off the unison register controlled by both manuals, using the lute stop for the upper manual and leaving the lower manual with its own unison register. Many harpsichords of all countries were also equipped with a buff stop (sometimes also called a lute stop), a device that presses pieces of soft leather against one of the sets of unison strings, producing a muted, pizzicato tone.

In Germany in the 18th century, harpsichords were made with still more strings and jacks for each key. Some had three unison strings in addition to an octave string; some had two unisons, an octave, and a suboctave (or 16′) register; and some even had a 2′ register, with very short strings tuned two octaves above the unisons. Harpsichords with three keyboards were apparently built throughout the 17th and 18th centuries, although only one authentic three-manual harpsichord is known today.

Resources of the 18th-century harpsichord

It should be emphasized, however, that the harpsichord of the 16th–18th centuries normally had only one or two keyboards and only two or three sets of strings and jacks per note. In the 16th and early 17th centuries, one-manual instruments usually had only two registers (either two unisons or a unison and an octave) with or without a buff stop; in the second half of the 17th century a second unison register became common, increasing the number of jacks and strings to three per note. Two-manual instruments, likewise, had no more than three sets of strings (two unisons and an octave) and three sets of jacks throughout the 17th century. In the 18th century, a fourth row of jacks was sometimes added. In England and Flanders, this row was the close-plucking lute stop; in France, if a fourth row was added, it was placed behind the other three and equipped with plectra of soft buff leather that provided a gentle, flutey tone, which was highly prized in the rather decadent period of the harpsichord's decline. Until the last half of the 18th century, it was possible to change registers only by moving knobs at the side of the instrument or above the keyboards, which could be done only when one hand or the other was not playing. This fact and the surviving written evidence suggests that the harpsichordists of earlier times changed registers relatively infrequently, preventing monotony of sound by relying on variations of touch and the changes of texture and pitch level written into the music.

History. The harpsichord was described by Arnaut of Zwolle in the mid-15th century and was apparently known throughout Europe by the end of the century, although no 15th-century examples have survived. The harpsichords depicted in sculptures, paintings, and miniatures of the period all appear to be shorter and to have thicker cases than the earliest surviving 16th-century examples, all of which are Italian and are constructed of very thin cypress.

Italy. The thin-cased style of harpsichord construction appears to have been developed in Italy about 1500, and it rapidly influenced the design of harpsichords throughout the rest of Europe. The strings of the Italian harpsichords were rather short, with the strings for c″ (C above middle C) generally being about 10 inches (25 centimetres) long on instruments tuned to what is today considered normal pitch. On some Italian harpsichords, however, the strings for c″ are about 14 inches (36 centimetres) long; it is thought that these were tuned to a pitch a fourth below that of the shorter-strung ones, the key for C sounding what today would be the G below. The comparatively short strings imposed a relatively low tension on the case of the Italian harpsichord, allowing it to hold up with so light a structure.

In general, Italian harpischords had only one keyboard with two rows of jacks and two strings tuned in unison, although many of the instruments thought to have been tuned to a lower pitch had one unison and one octave string. The fragile Italian instruments were normally housed in thick softwood cases, which were either painted or covered with stamped leather. The cases, in turn, rested on separate legs or elaborate stands. The tone of these lightly constructed instruments is surprisingly loud and penetrating, making them ideal as accompanying instruments in an orchestra and suiting them perfectly to the rattling scale passages typical of Italian harpsichord music.

Flanders. As the new Italian design spread northward, first into Germany and then to Flanders, France, and England, it was modified to the extent that the 16th- and 17th-century northern European instruments had somewhat longer strings (11 1/2 to 12 1/2 inches [29 to 32 centimetres] for c″) and thicker cases (3/16 to 1/4 inch [5 to 6 millimetres] in contrast to the 1/8 inch [3 millimetres] found on Italian instruments). In the 1560s in Flanders, however, this type of instrument was replaced by still another design, which ultimately dominated all northern European harpsichord making. These instruments had long strings (about 14 inches for c″ at normal pitch) and thick cases with substantial internal bracing to withstand the greater tension imposed by the greater string length. Because the longer strings made it unfeasible to double the string length for each octave below middle C, harpsichords of the newer Flemish design have less gracefully curved bentsides and wider tails than either Italian harpsichords or the intermediate instruments built elsewhere north of the Alps.

Harpsichord building of the Ruckers family

The name most often associated with Flemish harpsichord building is that of the Ruckers family, which for four generations (from about 1580 to 1680) dominated Flemish harpsichord making and whose instruments were exported to all parts of Europe—one was even shipped as far as Peru. At first sight, Ruckers harpsichords appear to be rather crude compared to their Italian counterparts, and their thick softwood cases give the impression of being clumsily cobbled together on the inside. Nonetheless, the tone of unaltered or properly restored examples is extraordinarily good, and it is easy to see why Ruckers instruments were so highly prized that a lively business in making forgeries of them flourished in the 18th century.

In addition to a wide variety of virginals (discussed below), the Ruckers family made several different harpsichord models. The most popular was apparently six feet long, having a four-octave keyboard from C to c‴, with a short octave in the bass; one unison and one octave register; and, occasionally, a buff stop on the unison. They were typically painted in imitation of marble on the outside and decorated on the inside with block-printed paper on which a Latin motto was painted. The soundboard was usually decorated with paintings of flowers, leaves, and birds. (This decoration should be contrasted with that of the Italian harpsichords, which was generally lavished on the outer case, leaving the instrument unadorned except for finely profiled top and bottom moldings.) Flemish harpsichords were set directly on any of various types of fairly massive stands, examples of which may be seen in the numerous Dutch paintings of musical groups of the period. Similar harpsichords were made in smaller sizes tuned a fifth or an octave above normal pitch (the key c′ sounding either g′ or c″). By the mid-17th century, some single-manual instruments had a range of $4\frac{1}{2}$ octaves from F_1 or G_1 in the bass to c‴.

The Ruckers family appear to have been the first to make two-manual harpsichords. These were of two types: in one (which may have been the earlier type and was not built after *c.* 1650), both keyboards were served by a single set of unison and octave strings and were not meant to be played at the same time. Instead, the keyboards were so arranged that c‴ on the upper keyboard was placed over f‴ on the lower keyboard, which meant that playing a piece on the lower keyboard automatically transposed it to a pitch a fourth below that of the upper keyboard. Whether this arrangement was used to facilitate routine transpositions or whether it was intended to provide in a single instrument the same resources as those available from both an Italian instrument with a 10-inch c″ and one with a 14-inch c″ is still a subject for controversy. The second type of two-manual harpsichord built by the Ruckers family was basically the type one finds today, with keyboards aligned over one another and intended to provide contrasts in loudness. Because the only set of upper-manual jacks was also played directly from the lower manual, it was not possible to play *pièces croisées.*

France. During the 17th century, instruments of the Ruckers type gradually influenced those being built throughout northern Europe; and by the early 18th century France, England, and Germany all had developed their own national variations on the thick-cased Ruckers design, replacing the thinner cased and shorter strung instruments of their earlier native schools. The sound of a typical 18th-century French harpsichord is delicate and sweet compared to the rather more astringent sound of a Ruckers. Those examples by the Blanchet family and their heir Pascal Taskin (1723–93) are noted for their extraordinarily high level of craftsmanship and the lightness and evenness of their touch. Eighteenth-century French harpsichords were almost always painted and rest on elaborate carved and gilded cabriole (curved-leg) stands. As with Flemish harpsichords, the French soundboards are decorated with painted flowers and birds, and the maker's mark appears in the form of a cast ornament in the sound hole. In the 1760s, Taskin added a fourth row of jacks with soft plectra of buff leather as a special solo stop and also devised a highly ingenious system of knee levers that permitted the harpsichordist to play crescendos and decrescendos and to change registers without taking his hands from the keyboard. By the time of these inventions, however, the great Baroque composers of harpsichord music, such as François Couperin, J.S. Bach, Jean-Philippe Rameau, and Domenico Scarlatti, were dead, and these devices have no relevance to the historically accurate performance of virtually any of the harpsichord music one is likely to hear today.

Blanchet and Taskin harpsichords

England. In England the making of harpsichords in the 18th century was dominated by two London families, the Kirkmans and the Shudis. Both families made instruments for several generations and eventually moved on from harpsichord building to piano building. Their harpsichords are very similar, and the two-manual instruments all have a close-plucking lute stop in addition to the usual two unisons and octave. They are invariably veneered in walnut or mahogany and rest on simple stands, usually with straight or tapered legs. The tone of a Kirkman or Shudi harpsichord is both more robust and more brilliant than that of a French or Flemish instrument, making it a superb instrument for filling in the harmonies in the orchestral music as well as for the performance of the solo harpsichord literature.

Germany. Two German schools appear to have existed in the 18th century. One in the southern part of the country has left very few surviving instruments, which is unfortunate because these are the kind probably played by J.S. Bach. As far as is known, the southern German instruments were fairly plain, veneered ones, having only three registers and a rather darker tone than either French or Flemish instruments. The second German school was centred in the city of Hamburg and is best represented by the work of the Hass family. The Hass instruments are among the most elaborate ever made, both in decoration and complexity. They are the only 18th-century harpsichords with 16′ and 2′ registers, and some have lute stops as well. Their tone does not, unfortunately, live up to the quality of their craftsmanship or the ingenuity of their design, seeming overly brilliant and too thick in all of the surviving examples that have been restored to playing condition.

Hass family instruments

Decline of the harpsichord. Although many of the finest surviving harpsichords date from after 1750, few composers of the first rank were writing for the instrument by that time. Furthermore, the emergence of a newer, lighter style of music and an increased interest in crescendo and decrescendo effects led to the addition of various new devices foreign to the essential nature of the instrument. These include the knee- and foot-operated contrivances for the rapid changing of registers or for producing crescendos and decrescendos. Such devices represent the harpsichord builders' response to the same musical needs that eventually caused the harpsichord's replacement by the piano; but they were created before the real rise in the piano's popularity and must not be thought of as attempts to stave off the competition of the newer instrument.

As with the clavichord, builders continued to make harpsichords side by side with pianos. In England, Shudi's son-in-law, John Broadwood (see below), continued to make harpsichords until after 1800 (although in decreasing quantity), producing at the same time an ever-increasing number of pianos. There is even a small but interesting group of compositions by English, German, and French composers calling for both instruments.

Modern revival. The harpsichord had all but vanished except as a curiosity or in very rare historical concerts when the modern revival began in the 1890s with the building of new harpsichords by the piano firms of Érard and Pleyel in Paris. Almost immediately, the full brunt of 19th-century piano technology was applied to the manufacture of the revived instruments, and they became increasingly massively strung and framed as time passed. Pedals for changing registers were included from the beginning, and Pleyel first added the 16′ stop in 1911. The Pleyel's sound, as preserved in the recordings of the Polish virtuoso Wanda Landowska and her numerous pupils, typified the harpsichord for most music-lovers until the 1950s, and it is for a heavy, metal-framed instrument of this type, with pedals for changing registers and a 16′ stop, that most of the 20th-century harpsichord music has been composed.

Pleyel instruments

In 1905 modern harpsichord building was begun in Germany, initially taking the new Pleyel and Érard instruments as inspiration. Subsequent German building has produced a highly characteristic instrument somewhat reminiscent of the harpsichords of the 18th-century Hamburg school in sound. Taking as their model an improperly restored instrument falsely said to have belonged to Bach, these instruments generally have the unhistorical stop arrangement of one 8′ and the 4′ on the upper manual, with the second 8′ and a 16′ on the lower manual.

Arnold Dolmetsch, who began the modern revival of the clavichord, also built harpsichords, working in Paris and Boston as well as in England. He deserves to be considered the "godfather" of not only the present British school of harpsichord making but also of the flourishing U.S. school, most of whose members are, however, building a very different and far more historically based instrument than any that Dolmetsch made after about 1910.

Harpsichords specifically intended for electronic amplification have been built since the 1960s. Although some were meant for the performance of Baroque concertos with modern orchestras and in large halls, such instruments have had their greatest success among the other amplified instruments used by rock groups.

The virginal, spinet, and clavicytherium. The virginal, spinet, and clavicytherium are all varieties of harpsichord that differ from it primarily in size, shape, and musical resources. Virginals and spinets usually have only a single set of strings and a single row of jacks. The clavicytherium is basically a harpsichord set upright so that its soundboard is vertical. Instruments of this form were made from the 15th through the 18th centuries. Generally, their mechanism must be fairly complicated because the jacks must move horizontally rather than vertically and cannot therefore return to their rest position solely by the action of gravity. As a consequence of this complexity of its mechanism, the touch of the clavicytherium tends to be heavy, although the instrument takes up less space, and it is claimed that the vertical soundboard projects the sound outward far more effectively than the horizontal soundboard of the conventional harpsichord.

The virginal and spinet are small varieties of harpsichord, but the precise usage of the terms differs. Some writers reserve the term virginal for rectangular instruments and call all small triangular or polygonal instruments spinets. Others apply the term virginal to all plucked-stringed keyboard instruments whose strings run more or less from left to right across the keys (a usage followed in this article), reserving the term spinet for instruments in which the strings run obliquely away from the player. The terminological question is complicated by the fact that the word virginal in 16th- and 17th-century England referred to all plucked stringed keyboard instruments, including harpsichords and spinets as well as those today termed virginals. The term *épinette* ("spinet") had a similarly broad usage in France.

Italian builders of the 16th and 17th centuries made virginals and spinets employing a thin-cased construction similar to that of their harpsichords, and, like Italian harpsichords, these smaller instruments were kept in stout outer cases. The typical Italian virginal was either rectangular or polygonal in shape, with its keyboard projecting from the front of the case, and many of the surviving examples are sumptuously decorated with inlay or intarsia. Most Italian spinets are constructed as an irregular quadrilateral, but in the 17th century a new form was developed that more closely resembles a small harpsichord in having a bentside at the player's right and a long straight back slanting away from him. The new form was copied throughout Europe and became the standard domestic keyboard instrument in England in the late 17th century.

In Flanders, early virginals were polygonal and resembled Italian ones except that their keyboards were inset rather than projecting. In the 1560s, at the same time as the thick-cased harpsichord is believed to have emerged, thick-cased rectangular virginals made their appearance. By the end of the 16th century, two distinct types existed. They can readily be distinguished by the position of their keyboards: off-centre either to the left or to the right in one of the long sides of the rectangular case. Virginals with the keyboard at the right were far more common. They produce a characteristic flutey tone because the placement of the keyboard causes the strings to be plucked near their centre for most of the instrument's range. In virginals with the keyboard at the left, the strings are plucked off-centre except in the extreme treble, and the tone changes gradually from reedy in the bass, through full in the middle register, to flutey in the treble, much as on a harpsichord. Flemish builders produced virginals of both types in several sizes, the smaller ones being tuned to higher than normal pitches. They also made "double" virginals, consisting of a large virginal at normal pitch and a smaller one tuned an octave higher, which could be stored in a recess next to the keyboard of the larger instrument. The two virginals could be coupled together by placing the smaller instrument on top of the larger one.

Types of Flemish virginals

The virginals made in England were of the left-keyboard type. Those made elsewhere in Europe (some having the keyboard centred) were also built with strings plucking off-centre.

THE PIANO

Principle of operation. Although the basic principles of the piano's mechanism are simple, the refinements required in developing the powerful yet sensitive modern piano make it also the most complex of all instruments except the organ. The strings of the piano are struck by a felt-covered hammer that must rebound from the strings instantaneously or it will dampen their vibrations in the very act of initiating them. The hammer must thus be thrown toward the strings and allowed to fly freely. For the pianist to retain maximum control of loudness and softness, the distance of the hammer's free flight must be as small as possible; but, if the distance is too small, the hammer will bounce back and forth between the strings and the part of the mechanism that pushed it, producing a stuttering sound whenever the keys are struck firmly. As a consequence, all truly simple piano mechanisms—those in which, say, a rigid rod at the back of the key simply pushes the hammer upward until the key is stopped by a rail and the hammer flies free—must be adjusted to provide a large distance for free flight and can therefore give the pianist only limited dynamic range and control.

History. *Invention.* Piano mechanisms as unsophisticated as that described above continued to be devised and built throughout the 18th century. Nevertheless, the first successful piano—made in Italy by Bartolomeo Cristofori—solved the problems inherent in such simple mechanisms, as well as nearly every other problem facing piano builders until well into the 19th century. Cristofori reportedly started experiments on a "harpsichord with hammers" in 1698. By 1700 one of these instruments, together with six of his harpsichords and spinets, was included in an inventory of instruments belonging to the Medici family in Florence. In 1711 the instrument was described in detail in the Venetian *Giornale de' letterati d'Italia* by Scipione Maffei, who called Cristofori's invention *gravicembalo col piano e forte* ("harpsichord with soft and loud")—whence the present names pianoforte and piano.

In the three surviving examples of Cristofori's pianos, which date from the 1720s, the mechanism, or "action," differs somewhat from that described and pictured by Maffei; however, rather than merely representing an earlier phase of Cristofori's work, Maffei's diagram may be in error. In the surviving instruments a pivoted piece of wood is set into the key (Figure 5). The pivoted piece

Cristofori's pianos

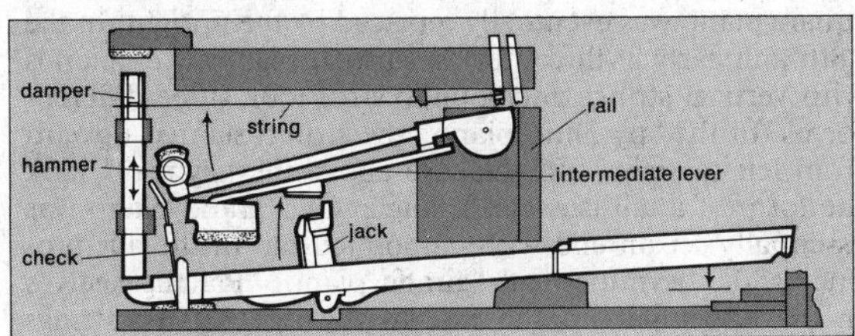

Figure 5: Cristofori's piano action (see text).
From R.E.M. Harding, *The Piano-Forte* (1933); published by Cambridge University Press

(which in a modern piano would be called a jack and should not be confused with the jack in a harpsichord) lifts an intermediate lever when the key is depressed. The lever, in turn, pushes upward on the hammer shaft near the hammer's point of attachment to a rail fixed above the keys. When the key is pressed completely down, the jack tilts and disengages itself from the intermediate lever, which then falls back, permitting the hammer to fall most of the way back to its rest position, even while the key is still depressed. This feature, called an escapement, is the heart of Cristofori's invention; it makes possible a short free flight for the hammer, after which the hammer falls so far away from the string that it cannot rebound against it, even when the keys are struck firmly. Cristofori provided a check (a pad rising from the back of the key) to catch and hold the falling hammer. At the end of the key he included a separate slip of wood, resembling a harpsichord jack, to carry the dampers that silence the string when the key is at rest.

Utilizing an intermediate lever to act on the hammer near one end of its shaft provides an enormous velocity advantage, and the hammer flies upward toward the string much faster than the front end of the key descends under the pianist's finger, adding to the crispness and sensitivity of Cristofori's action. The sound of his instruments is strongly reminiscent of the harpsichord, owing to the thinness of the strings and to the hardness of the hammers. The dynamic range is surprisingly wide, but it should be emphasized that the instrument's loudest sounds are softer than those of a firmly quilled Italian harpsichord and do not begin to approach the loudness of a modern piano.

German and Austrian pianos. After Cristofori's death, piano making in Italy appears to have languished, but word of his invention became known in Germany through a translation of Maffei's account published in 1725. Before 1720 there had been independent attempts in France as well as in Germany to devise hammer mechanisms, although none was comparable to Cristofori's in sophistication or practicality. In the 1730s Gottfried Silbermann, of Freiberg in eastern Germany, a builder of organs, harpsichords, and clavichords, began constructing pianos patterned on Cristofori's. The surviving ones, probably from the 1740s, appear to have been directly copied from an instrument imported into Germany rather than derived from Maffei's description, but the ones he made earlier (and of which Bach is said to have disapproved in 1736) may have owed their failure to an attempt to follow Maffei's diagram exactly. By 1747 Silbermann had sold several of his pianos to King Frederick the Great of Prussia, and one of these is reported to have met with Bach's approval in 1747.

Gottfried Silbermann's instruments

Subsequent German piano building did not follow the path charted by Silbermann. Instead, various German builders attempted to devise actions that were simpler than Cristofori's, generally adapting them to the clavichord-shaped instruments now called "square" pianos. In the most characteristic German actions, the hammers point toward, rather than away from, the player, and, instead of being hinged to a rail passing over all the keys, they are attached individually to their respective keys. As the front of the key is depressed, the back rises, carrying the hammer with it. A projecting point at the rear of the hammer shank catches on a fixed rail above the back of the keys, so that the hammers are flipped upward as the keys are stopped by a second rail set just above them. This action had no escapement, and (on the evidence of a letter of 1777 from Mozart to his father) many German instruments of the 1770s still lacked this highly important feature.

A pupil of Silbermann, Johann Andreas Stein of Augsburg in southern Germany, is generally credited with devising the first German action to include an escapement. As a replacement for the fixed rail that caught the projecting points at the rear of the hammer shanks, Stein provided an individually hinged and sprung piece for each key (Figure 6). As the back of the key reaches its highest point, this piece (the escapement) tilts backward

From R.E.M. Harding, *The Piano-Forte* (1933); published by Cambridge University Press

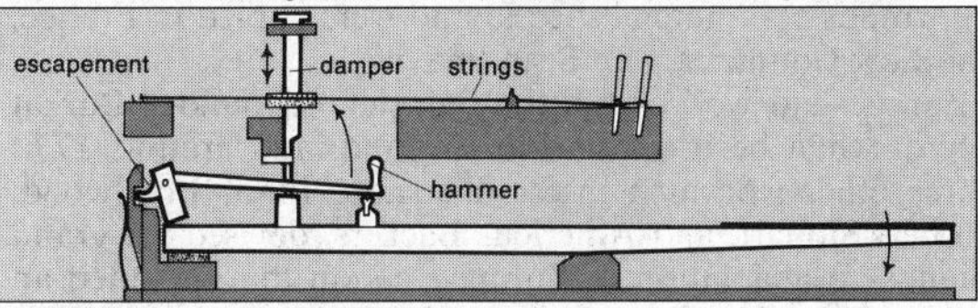

Figure 6: The German action (see text).

on its hinge and releases the point at the back of the hammer shank. The hammer is then free to fall back to rest position even when the key is still depressed. This is often called the "Viennese" action because it was used by all the important 18th- and early-19th-century piano makers in Vienna, including Stein's daughter and son-in-law, Nannette and Johann Andreas Streicher; Anton Walter, Mozart's favourite piano builder; and Conrad Graf, maker of Beethoven's last piano. It was used in German-speaking countries until the mid-19th century, when it was replaced by mechanisms derived from a Cristofori-based action developed in England.

Although the tone of a piano by Stein or Walter is not loud, it is very sweet, with a singing treble and a clear tenor and bass that blend superbly with the sound of stringed instruments. The touch is extremely light and shallow: the force required to depress a key is only one-fourth that required on a modern piano, and the key need only be depressed half as far. In their sensitivity to the finest differences in touch and their singing tone, the Viennese pianos suggest the tone of a clavichord, although producing a louder sound.

Austrian and German pianos of the late 18th and early 19th centuries often feature a great array of pedals. Only one of Cristofori's surviving pianos has any special effects: levers on the underside of the instrument permit the player to shift the action sideways so that the hammers strike only one of the two strings provided for each note. By the time Silbermann built his pianos for Frederick the Great, a second special effect had been introduced—a mechanism to lift the dampers from the strings so that they could vibrate freely whether or not the keys were depressed. (These two effects, the sideways sliding of the action—to produce a softer sound and different tone colour—and the lifting of the dampers—to produce a louder, more sustained sound and another variation in tone colour—are the only ones found on all modern grand pianos.) Silbermann's pianos had hand levers for raising the treble and bass dampers separately and an additional hand lever for muting the strings. Stein's pianos normally had two knee levers for raising the treble and bass dampers and a third knee lever that interposed a strip of cloth between the hammers and the strings to produce a velvety pianissimo. Later instruments might have five or more pedals that, for example, pressed a roll of parchment against the bass strings to produce a buzzing sound or rang small bells and banged on the underside of the soundboard in imitation of the cymbals and drums of the then-fashionable "Turkish" music.

Special effects

The English action. In the late 1750s a number of

From R.E.M. Harding, *The Piano-Forte* (1933); published by Cambridge University Press

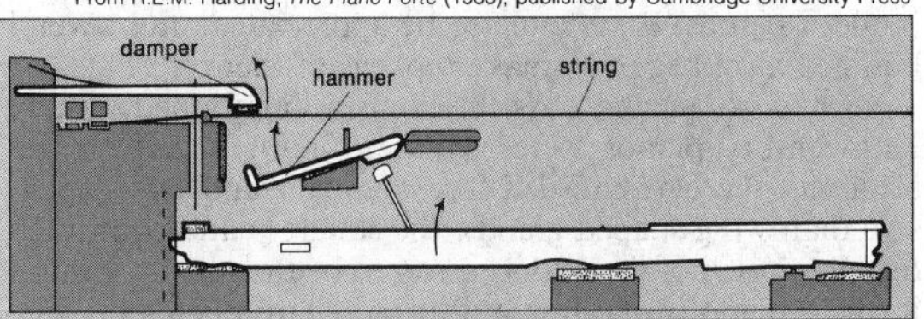

Figure 7: Zumpe's square-piano action (see text).

German piano builders emigrated to England, and one, Johann Christoph Zumpe, invented an extremely simple action for the square pianos he began building in the mid-1760s. Zumpe's action goes back to the Cristofori–Silbermann system in which the hammers point away from the player and are hinged to a rail over the keys. A metal rod tipped with a padded button is driven into the back of the key (Figure 7). When the key is depressed, the rod pushes the hammer upward; and the key is stopped by a padded rail over its back end, and the hammer flies freely. Despite the lack of an escapement, Zumpe's square pianos were an enormous commercial success and were copied in France, the Low Countries, and Scandinavia.

Zumpe had worked for the harpsichord builder Burkat Shudi when he first came to England, and around 1770 three other workmen in Shudi's shop, John Broadwood, Robert Stodart, and Americus Backers, devised for grand pianos an adaptation of Zumpe's action that included an escapement. This important development made London a major centre of piano building and created a characteristic English piano of fuller and louder sound than the Viennese piano but with a heavier, deeper touch and a consequent inability to play repeated notes as rapidly. In the English grand-piano action (Figure 8), the fixed rod of Zumpe's square-piano action was replaced by a pivoted jack, similar to that in Cristofori's action. The upper end of the jack fits into a notch at the base of the hammer shank, slipping out of the notch as the back of the key reaches its highest point; the hammer then flies free, strikes the string, and falls back to be caught by a hammer check even when the front of the key is still held down by the pianist. The tone of a typical 18th-century English grand piano is surprisingly reminiscent of the tone of an English harpsichord, suggesting that the English piano makers were, like Cristofori, seeking to make an expressive harpsichord, unlike the German builders who, in effect, appear to have been trying to build a louder clavichord.

From R.E.M. Harding, *The Piano-Forte* (1933); published by Cambridge University Press

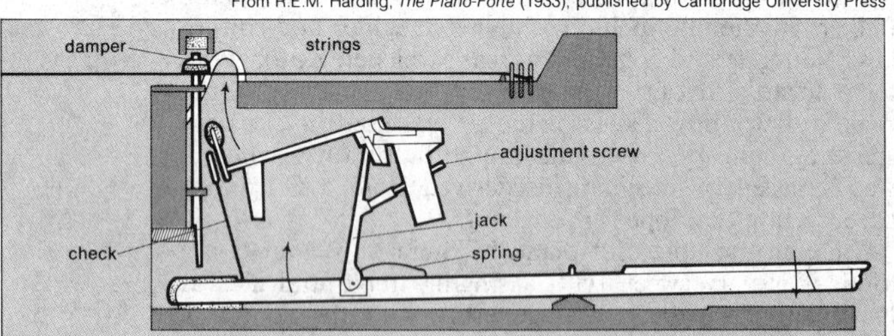

Figure 8: The English action (see text).

Unlike their Austrian and German counterparts, English pianos had two or, at most, three pedals. One of the two ordinary pedals shifted the keyboard sideways so that the hammers struck two or only one of the three strings provided for each note. The second pedal raised all the dampers. It was sometimes replaced by two pedals—one for the treble dampers, the other for the bass dampers—or, occasionally, by a single damper pedal divided into two parts that could be depressed separately or together with one foot, as on the piano presented by Broadwood to Beethoven in 1817.

Although the pianos of the late 18th and early 19th centuries were perfected instruments ideally suited to the music of their period, the increasing popularity of public concerts in large halls and concertos with large orchestras stimulated attempts by piano builders to produce an instrument of greater brilliance and loudness. Their efforts gradually created today's vastly different piano. In recent years, the special merits of the earlier instruments (sometimes called "fortepianos" to distinguish them from modern pianos) have come to be appreciated, and several builders have begun to make replicas of them.

Other early forms. As previously mentioned, many 18th-century pianos were "squares," built in a form resembling the clavichord. More compact and less expensive than wing-shaped grands, the square piano continued through much of the 19th century to be the most common form of piano in the home. But as square pianos became larger and larger, these advantages diminished, and the square piano was eventually replaced by the upright. In the 18th and early 19th centuries, upright pianos (*i.e.,* pianos with vertical strings and soundboard) took three different forms. In the "pyramid piano" the strings slanted upward from left to right, and the case above the keyboard took the form of a tall isosceles triangle. Or a grand piano was essentially set on end with its pointed tail in the air, producing the asymmetrical "giraffe piano." Placing shelves in the upper part of the case to the right of the strings yielded the tall rectangular "cabinet piano." Because the lower end of the strings, which ran nearly vertically, was about at the level of the keyboard, all such instruments were very tall. Although there were attempts to construct lower instruments by, in effect, positioning a square piano on its side, the American builder John Isaac Hawkins made the first truly successful low uprights in 1800 by placing the lower end of the strings near floor level. Robert Wornum in England built similar small uprights in 1811, and in 1842 he devised for them his "tape check" action, the direct forerunner of the modern upright action.

Pyramid, giraffe, and cabinet pianos

Development of the modern piano. In the early 19th century, piano makers were principally concerned with two problems whose solutions led to the modern piano. These were the relatively small volume of sound that could be produced from the thin strings then in use and the difficulty of producing a structure that could withstand the tension even of such light strings once the range of the instrument exceeded 5½ octaves.

Bracing and frame. Like 18th-century harpsichords, the pianos of the 18th and early 19th centuries were constructed entirely of wood, with the case (supported by a structure of internal wooden braces) sustaining the entire stress exerted by the strings. The only metal bracing in such instruments appears in the form of flat pieces bridging the gap through which the hammers rise to strike the strings. These braces eventually proved insufficient when the walls of the case itself and the pinblock (the long piece of wood into which all the tuning pins were driven) were incapable of withstanding the increasing tensions placed upon them. For this reason, ever-increasing quantities of metal bracing came into use, first in the form of individual bars running parallel to the strings from the side of the case to the pinblock but finally in the form of a single massive casting that took the entire tension of the strings upon itself. The one-piece cast-iron frame was first applied to square pianos by Alpheus Babcock of Boston in 1825, and in 1843 another Bostonian, Jonas Chickering, patented a one-piece frame for grands. With the adoption of such frames, the tension exerted by each string (about 24 pounds [10.9 kilograms] for an English piano of 1800) rose to an average of approximately 170 pounds (77 kilograms) in modern instruments, the frame bearing a total tension of 18 tons.

Babcock and Chickering pianos

Overstringing. The strings in early pianos, like those in harpsichords or clavichords, ran parallel to one another, causing the grand pianos of the 18th and early 19th centuries to retain much of the graceful shape of the harpsichord. In the 1830s it was realized that the bass strings could be made longer and their layout improved if they were made to fan out over the treble strings. This idea was first applied to square pianos, but in 1855 Steinway & Sons built a grand piano with a complete cast-iron frame embodying this "overstrung" plan, in which the strings of the treble and the middle registers fan out over most of the soundboard and the bass strings cross over them, forming a separate fan at a higher level. Because the bass strings fan out, the tail of the modern grand piano is far wider than that of the earlier "straight-strung" instruments.

Modifications in the action. The gradual strengthening of the piano's structure to permit the use of heavier strings eventually gave rise to hitherto unforeseen problems. The thicker strings could yield the louder sound of which they were capable only if they were struck by heavier hammers; because of the great velocity advantage provided by the early piano actions, any increase in the weight of the hammer required a manyfold increase in the force required to depress the keys. This difficulty was present to a minor extent even in the 18th-century English grand-piano action, and the touch on these instruments was both deeper and heavier than on Viennese pianos. Moreover, the deeper touch meant that it took longer for a key to return to rest position so that a note could be restruck. Consequently, English pianos were not capable of the rapid repetition of Viennese instruments. This problem became quite severe as the hammers grew heavier and as musicians wished increasingly to use tremolo effects in imitation of orchestral music.

The double-escapement action of Érard

What was necessary was an action that would permit a note to be restruck before the key returned to rest position. The first successful action of this type was devised by the Frenchman Sébastien Érard, who as a young man had built a harpsichord with a particularly elaborate system of pedals and knee levers and in 1810 devised the system of pedals still in use on the harp. Érard's first "repetition" or "double-escapement" action was patented in 1808, and an improved version that is the basis of the modern action was patented in 1821.

A further consequence of the use of thicker strings was that, if the sound of the instrument were not to become unduly harsh, the hammers had to be softer than those used on 18th-century instruments—light slips of wood covered with a few layers of thin leather. Felt-covered hammers were patented by the Parisian builder Jean-Henri Pape, who also contributed a number of other ingenious and important improvements, but the use of felt instead of leather did not become universal until after 1855.

With the adoption of the one-piece cast-iron frame, overstringing, and felt hammers, the piano achieved its modern form in all but a few details. One was the invention in 1862 by Claude Montal of Paris of a pedal that kept the dampers off the strings only for notes already held down. Individual notes could thus be sustained without the overall blurring caused by raising all the dampers by the ordinary damper pedal. This device is not generally found on European pianos, but it is included in American instruments as the middle pedal with the damper ("loud") pedal at the right and the action-shifting (una corda, or "soft") pedal at the left.

Types of modern piano. Since the abandonment of the square piano, only upright and grand pianos are manufactured. The grands range in length from a minimum of about 5 feet (150 centimetres) for a "baby" grand to a maximum of about 9 feet (270 centimetres) for a "concert" grand, although both shorter and longer instruments have been constructed. Among upright pianos, the models over 4 feet (120 centimetres) tall—which frequently had an excellent tone because of their relatively long bass strings—have largely been superseded by the lower models, the "console" (about 40 inches [100 centimetres] high) and the "spinet" (about 36 inches [90 centimetres high]), which look less bulky in the smaller rooms of present-day homes. Because the spinet's case rises such a small distance above the keyboard, it usually has "drop" action, most of which lies below the level of the keys.

Console and spinet models

Modern piano actions. In 1636 Marin Mersenne, the author of the treatise *Harmonie universelle,* quoted a remark that the harpsichord of his time contained 1,500 different parts. The modern piano contains 12,000, most of which are found in the action. The modern grand-piano action (Figure 9) is a simplified version of Érard's double-escapement action of 1821, and, although different manufacturers' actions differ in detail, they all work in much the same way. When the key is depressed, its back end rises, lifting the wippen. The wippen raises a pivoted L-shaped jack that pushes the hammer upward by means of a small roller attached to the underside of the hammer shank. The hammer flies free when the back of the L-shaped jack touches the adjustable regulating button. At the same time, the upper end of the repetition lever—through which the upright arm of the jack passes—rises until it is stopped by the drop screw. When the hammer rebounds from the string, the roller falls back until it is stopped by the intermediate lever, enabling the tip of the jack to return to position beneath the roller, even if the key is still partially depressed. The jack is then ready to raise the hammer again should the player restrike the key before it returns to rest position. In the meantime, the hammer is prevented from bouncing back up toward the strings by the padded hammer check, and the damper is raised above the strings by a separate lever lifted by the extreme end of the key.

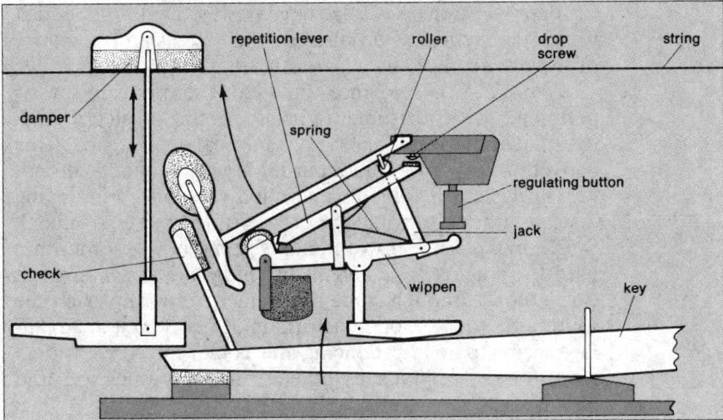

Figure 9: Modern grand-piano action (see text).
From E.Q. Norton, *Tuning and Care of the Pianoforte*

Action of the modern upright piano

In the modern upright-piano action (Figure 10), depressing the key also lifts a wippen, which in turn carries an L-shaped jack like that in the grand action. The tip of the jack engages a notch in the hammer butt, thrusting it forward until the regulating button causes the jack to pivot and escape from the notch. Rapid repetition is ensured by the bridle, a strip of cloth that tightens as the hammer moves toward the strings and helps to bring the hammer back to rest position. The dampers are moved away from the strings by a small metal pin, or "spoon," at the back of the wippen.

From E.Q. Norton, *Tuning and Care of the Pianoforte*

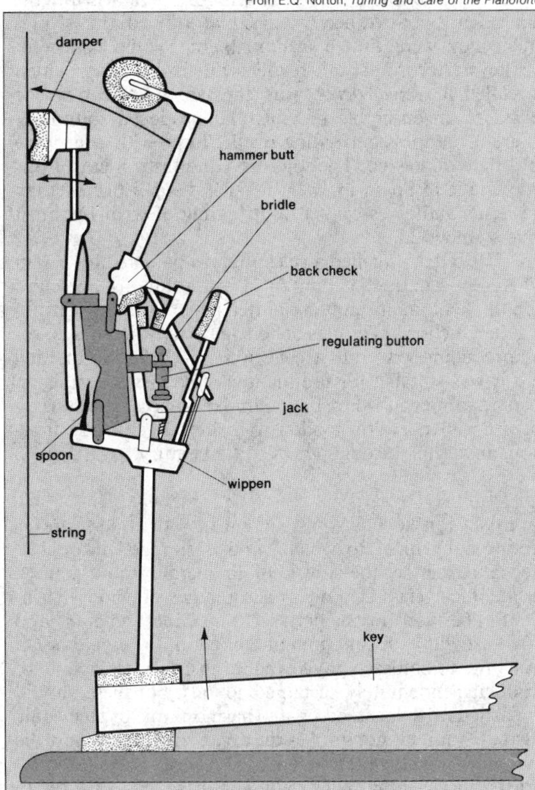

Figure 10: Modern upright-piano action (see text).

Player pianos. The history of automatically playing keyboard instruments dates at least to the 16th century. The inventory of musical instruments owned by King Henry VIII at his death in 1547 included "an instrument that goethe with a whele without playing upon," and three spinets equipped with a pinned barrel like that of a music box or barrel organ survive from the workshop of the Augsburg builder Samuel Bidermann (1540–1622). The most common type of player piano operates by means of a roll of punched paper that controls a pneumatic system for depressing the keys. Its heyday was the 1930s, and it was largely rendered obsolete by the increasing popularity of the phonograph and the radio.

Electronic pianos. Since the 1920s there have been experiments with instruments using electric or electromagnetic pickups, amplifiers, and loudspeakers instead of the conventional piano soundboard. Many such pianos do not use strings at all for the generation of sound, employing instead either electronic circuits or tuned pieces of metal. Small, inexpensive instruments of this type are sometimes used for practice, the student listening to himself through earphones. Although some electronic pianos approach the sound of a conventional instrument, their principal advantage seems to lie in producing effects that the conventional piano cannot, by means of electronic prolongation and alteration of their tone.

RELATED STRINGED KEYBOARD INSTRUMENTS

Stringed keyboard instruments have as their principal defects an inability, first, to sustain a tone indefinitely and, secondly, to alter the tone's loudness once a key has been depressed. There have been various attempts to build stringed instruments sounded by other means than plucking or striking—including vibrating the strings by blowing a current of air past them, as in the *piano éolien* of 1837. The most successful of these other instruments in one way or another adopted the principle of the hurdy-gurdy: *i.e.,* vibrating the strings by friction.

An instrument of this kind appears in several diagrams in the notebooks of Leonardo da Vinci (1452–1519). Some apparently highly successful ones (none of which, unfortunately, have survived) were made by the Nürnberg builder Hans Heyden, who described them at length in pamphlets published in 1605 and 1610. These instruments had a series of rosined wheels that rubbed the strings when they were drawn against them by the action of the keys. According to Heyden, the instrument, which he called a *Geigenwerck,* was capable of recreating the sound of an ensemble of viols and produced sounds of different loudness depending on the force with which the keys were depressed. The sole surviving instrument of this type, made in Spain in 1625, is far less sophisticated than Heyden's and gives only a faint inkling of what his must have sounded like.

Heyden's *Geigenwerck*

In 1772 a device called a celestina was patented by Adam Walker of London; it employed a continuous horsehair ribbon (kept in motion by a treadle) to rub the strings of a harpsichord. Thomas Jefferson, who ordered a harpsichord equipped with a celestina in 1786, commented that it was suitable for use in slow movements and as an accompaniment to the voice. Similar devices, some using rosined rollers, were applied to pianos by various ingenious inventors throughout the 19th century. (E.M.R.)

THE ORGAN

An organ is a keyboard instrument in which the sound is produced by pipes to which wind is supplied through a mechanism under the control of an operator (an organist). Its technical classification is aerophone, or wind instrument. The word organ derives from Greek *organon* and Latin *organum,* an instrument. By common usage, organ has come to embrace any keyboard instrument capable of producing indefinitely sustained sounds, but these should be particularized as reed organ (harmonium) or electronic organ. Organ, alone, implies an organ with pipes, and the term pipe organ is tautologous.

Parts, mechanism, and production of sound. An organ is divided into three main parts. At one end of the instrument are the keyboards, or manuals, and other controls that collectively are called the console. At the other end are the pipes that produce the tone. Between these two is the mechanism, or action, that accounts for a large part of the bulk and cost of any organ. The simplest type of organ has one keyboard and one pipe to each note. The pipes stand in a row on an airtight box or chest that is supplied with wind, through a trunk, from bellows. Under each pipe is a valve, or pallet, connected by a system of cranks and levers to its respective key of the keyboard. A reservoir is interposed between the bellows and the wind-chest, appropriately weighted to keep the supply of wind at a constant pressure. This reservoir has a blowoff valve that comes into operation when the reservoir is full. Although the bellows may resemble basically the familiar domestic type that is operated by hand or feet, wind is normally supplied from an electrically driven rotary blower.

Elements of simple organs

The pitch of each note is determined by the length of the pipe; the longest pipe makes the deepest note, the shortest pipe the highest note. If two comparable pipes sound an octave apart, the effective length of the higher-pitched pipe is exactly half that of the lower-pitched.

Since the tone of a pipe sounding on a constant pressure of wind is immutable, both as to quality and quantity, the uses of an organ with only one pipe to each note are strictly limited. Even the smallest organs, therefore, have at least three pipes to each note, and organs of cathedral size commonly have as many as 100 to each note. These sets, or ranks, of pipes are arranged in parallel rows on the wind-chest. The pallet controlled from each note admits wind to all the pipes belonging to that note; but, in order that the organist may be able to use at will all, none, or any of the sets of pipes, an intermediate mechanism is provided by which he may stop off any set or sets of pipes. From this function the control at the console by whose operation the pipes are stopped off has come to be known in English as a stop, a term also used loosely for each rank of pipes.

Mechanism. The operative part of the stop mechanism lies between the pallet and the footholes of the pipes. It normally consists of a strip of wood or plastic running the full length of the set of pipes, or stop. In it is drilled a series of holes. One hole registers exactly with each pipe. The strip of wood is placed in a close-fitting guide in which it may be moved; when it is moved longitudinally a short distance, so that its holes no longer register with the pipes, wind will no longer reach that set of pipes, even when the organist opens the pallets. These strips are therefore called sliders, and wind-chests in which the stops are operated in this way are called slider chests. There are other ways of working the stops, both ancient and modern, which will be referred to later; but the slider chest was in almost universal use before the 20th century, and many modern organ builders consider it the best. The slider is connected to the console by a system of levers and cranks, and it terminates in a knob that the organist pulls outward to bring the stop into play or pushes in to silence it.

It often happens that the organist needs either to play polyphonic music (*i.e.,* with interweaving of several voices) in two or more contrasted parts, to give prominence to a melody against a softer accompaniment, or to play loud and soft passages in rapid succession. None of these effects can be achieved on an organ with one keyboard, or manual, as so far described. Loud and soft passages can be played to some extent, but to change the stops between each alternation takes time, which is not always available. For this reason, organs of more than about seven or eight stops usually have two manuals, each controlling its separate wind-chest and stops. Each manual department is self-contained, so that the organ is really a composite instrument. By pre-arranging the stops on the manuals, the organist may perform in any of the three ways mentioned above. The organist, therefore, may vary the sounds produced in one or both of two ways: by changing the stops on the manuals being played or by leaving the stops as they are and changing from one manual to another.

The importance of two manuals

Since the 18th century organists have had yet a third way of controlling the volume of sound. The pipes of one or more manuals are usually placed in a box, one side of which consists of hinged and movable shutters (similar to vertical Venetian blinds) that are connected to a pedal at the console. By opening and closing the shutters, the sound from the stops of the manual concerned is made louder or softer. Such boxes are called swell boxes.

Since the 14th century, one department of the organ has commonly been played from a keyboard, or more properly a pedalboard, controlled by the organist's feet. The pedal department is basically like the manual departments but controls the longer pipes.

The organist sometimes wishes to combine the stops of

two different manuals or to couple one or more of the manuals to the pedals. This is effected by a simple mechanism, called a coupler, that is controlled by a stop knob at the console (stops that control a set of pipes are called speaking stops).

Certain combinations of stops on each manual are more commonly needed than others; in order that these combinations may be readily available, the console is provided with a number of short pedals disposed above the pedalboard. Each of these pedals is connected to one commonly needed combination of stops. When a pedal is depressed, the stops connected to it are drawn on, and any others that are already drawn are pushed off. These pedals are called combination (or composition) pedals.

In the simplest mechanical action, the connection from key to pallet is by a series of cranks and levers. The overall distance may be considerable, and the main distance is bridged by trackers, slender strips of wood, metal, or plastic, which are kept in constant tension.

The trackers

The mechanism of the organ as described so far is entirely mechanical, and such organs are said to have tracker action. Tracker action is used in many modern organs, especially in Germany, The Netherlands, Scandinavia, and increasingly in the United States and Canada; many organists prefer it to all other forms because it is so direct and sensitive in response. Organs may, however, have pneumatic, direct electric, or electropneumatic action, although these actions result in a loss of touch and responsiveness. In very large organs with tracker action, considerable strength may be necessary to depress the keys. Also, where the layout of the building is inconvenient and the departments of the organ have to be widely separated, tracker action is not practicable. To overcome these difficulties, especially with the object of lightening the touch, other forms of action were devised.

The Barker lever

The first effective system was developed (after a device invented by David Hamilton of Edinburgh in 1833) by Charles Spackman Barker, an Englishman. It consisted of a series of small, high-pressure pneumatic bellows or motors, one attached to each note of the main manual at the console. When a note was depressed, compressed air was admitted to the motor, which, in turn, operated the tracker action. Lacking encouragement at home, Barker went to France, where the great French builder Aristide Cavaillé-Coll employed the Barker lever almost exclusively from 1840 on.

Later, the trackers were supplanted by lead tubes, and the connection from key to pallet was solely by compressed air travelling through these tubes. This system was called tubular pneumatic action. At its best, it was remarkably effective, being reliable, long-lived, reasonably silent in action, and perfectly prompt in operation. At anything but its best, it was none of these things, and its worst fault usually lay in sluggish operation. Tubular pneumatic action is almost never used in modern times.

As early as 1860, electric action was used experimentally, and in 1888 it was employed by the English builder Henry Willis at Canterbury Cathedral. His action remained in satisfactory use there for 50 years before it needed to be replaced. The modern type of electric action was pioneered by Robert Hope-Jones in Britain at the end of the 19th century. Direct electric action may be used, but a combination of electric and pneumatic mechanism is more general. In this system the depression of a key completes an electrical circuit, which energizes an electromagnet, allowing wind to enter a pneumatic motor attached to the wind-chest, and this motor opens the pallet. The stops may be operated in exactly the same way, but, where they are operated electrically, the sliders are often replaced by a series of valves, one to each pipe. The organ is then said to have a sliderless chest, and the most usual type is the pitman chest, so called because it contains a type of floating valve called a pitman. This action is commonly known as electropneumatic.

The pitman chest

The combination pedals can also be operated electropneumatically. They are usually supplemented by a series of buttons, or pistons, piaced in the keyslips on each manual, where they are conveniently operated by the organist's thumbs. The pistons may easily be made adjustable so that the organist can quickly alter the combination of stops controlled by each one.

No electric action has yet lasted more than 50 years without needing a comprehensive rebuilding, and many have lasted for much shorter periods. But, with improvements in design and standardization of parts, it may be anticipated that rebuilding will become less frequent and expensive. On the other hand, there are small tracker-action organs working satisfactorily after 300 years, and even large ones have continued to operate for more than a century, despite almost total neglect.

Electric auxiliaries to tracker action

A compromise has been used successfully with tracker action for each department, with the coupler action operated electrically. This arrangement has considerable merit, since the coupling together of three or four manuals with tracker action results in a very heavy touch. Electric stop action may also be combined with tracker key action, enabling the use of electric (including solid-state) combinations—an invaluable aid, especially in larger instruments.

Tone production. The pipes are the most important part of an organ. There are two main categories: flue pipes and reed pipes. Flue pipes (made either of wood or metal; their construction is basically similar in principle) account for about four-fifths of the stops of an average organ. Figure 11 shows a front view and a vertical section of the most typical sort of metal flue pipe. The pipe consists of three main parts: the foot, the mouth, and the speaking length.

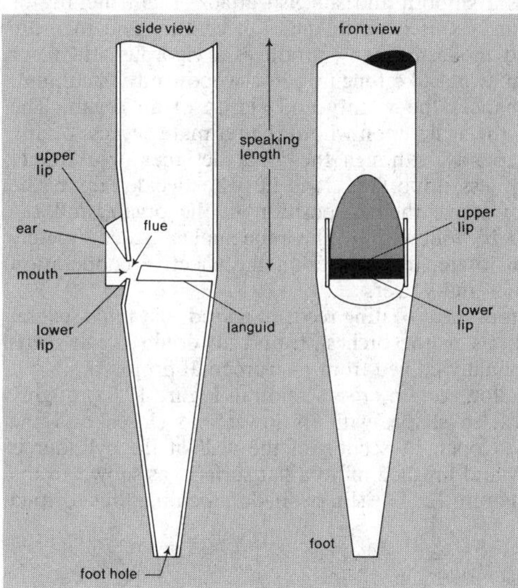

Figure 11: Typical flue pipe (principal).

The pipe stands vertically on the wind-chest, and wind enters at the foothole. The foot is divided from the speaking length by the languid, a flat plate; the only airway connection between the foot and the speaking length is a narrow slit called the flue. The wind emerges through the flue and strikes the upper lip, producing an audible frequency, the pitch of which is determined by and amplified in resonance by the speaking length of the pipe. A pipe of this kind is, in fact, identical in principle with a recorder or a tin whistle; but, whereas they have holes along the speaking length, which the player covers and uncovers with his fingers to secure the notes of the musical scale, in an organ there is a separate pipe for each note.

The tone of a pipe is determined by many factors, including the pressure of the wind supply, size of foothole, width of flue, height and width of mouth, and the scale, or diameter, of the pipe relative to its speaking length. The material of which the pipe is made also exerts an influence; it may be metal (*i.e.*, an alloy of lead and tin), wood, or, more rarely, pure tin or copper, and for the bass pipes zinc. The pipes may also vary in shape, a common variant being an upward taper in which the pipe is smaller in diameter at the top than at the mouth. Or, the top of the pipe may be completely closed by a stopper. Such a pipe is said to be stopped; a stopped pipe sounds an octave lower in pitch than an open pipe of the same speaking length.

Open pipes of large diameter are said to be of "large scale," and open pipes of small diameter are said to be of "small scale." Large-scale pipes produce a dull or foundational quality of tone that is free from the higher harmonics (the numbered series of partials, or component tones). Small-scale pipes produce a bright quality of tone that is rich in harmonics. Stopped pipes can be particularly foundational in tone, and they favour the odd-numbered at the expense of the even-numbered partials. Tapered pipes are somewhere between stopped and open pipes in tone quality.

Tuning and voicing

Flue pipes are tuned by increasing or decreasing the speaking length. In the past, several methods of tuning were employed, but in modern times this is often done by fitting a cylindrical slide over the free end of the speaking length and sliding it up and down, lengthening or shortening the pipe as required. In stopped pipes the stopper is pushed farther down to sharpen the pitch or is pulled upward to lower it.

The pipe maker thus broadly fixes the type of tone that a pipe will produce; but this is further controlled within fairly wide limits by the wind pressure and, finally, by the voicer, who adjusts the tone of each pipe by manipulating the foothole, flue, and upper and lower lips. The attack of the note may also be greatly influenced by cutting a series of small nicks in the edge of the languid. Heavy nicking, so commonly practiced in the early 20th century, produces a smooth and sluggish attack. Light nicking or no nicking, as used up to the 18th century and in more advanced modern organs, produces a vigorous attack, or chiff, somewhat like tonguing in a woodwind instrument. This enhances the vitality and clarity of an organ. The voicer is the artist upon whom the ultimate success of any organ depends, although the tonal designer or architect is hardly less important. It is he who decides upon the choice of stops, their disposition in the organ, and the scales to be followed by the pipe maker. A completely successful organ depends upon the effective cooperation of designer and voicer.

Reed stops have beating reeds of a kind that finds several counterparts in the orchestra, and no doubt organ reeds were originally copied from instrumental prototypes.

The shallot, seen in cross section in Figure 12, is roughly cylindrical in shape, with its lower end closed and the upper end open. A section of the wall of the cylinder is cut away and finished off to a flat surface, as shown in the inset to Figure 12. The slit, or shallot opening, thus formed

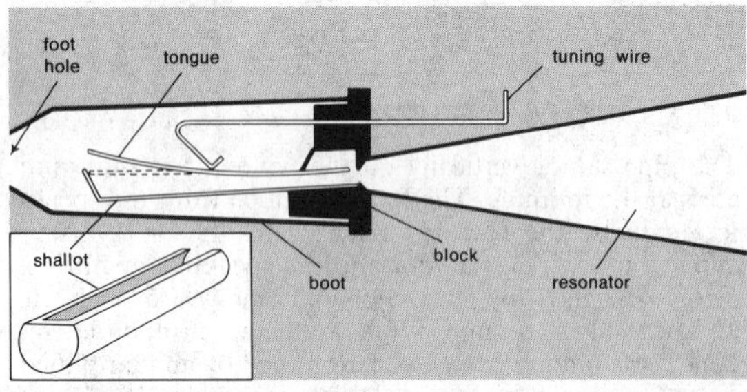

Figure 12: Section through a reed pipe (trumpet).

is covered by a thin brass tongue that is fixed to the upper end of the shallot. The tongue is curved and normally only partially covers the shallot opening. But, when wind enters the boot, the pressure of the wind momentarily forces the tongue against the shallot, completely closing the opening. Immediately, the elasticity of the brass asserts itself, and the tongue reverts to its curved shape, thus uncovering the opening. This process is repeated rapidly. The frequency of the pulsations of air that enter the shallot is determined by the effective length of the reed and, in turn, determines the pitch of the note. Thence, the pulsations pass out into the tube, or resonator, which further stabilizes the pitch and decides the quality of the note. Most reed resonators have a flared shape, as shown in Figure 12. As in flue pipes, a wide scale favours a fundamental tone, and a narrow scale favours a bright tone. Cylindrical resonators produce an effect similar to that of stopped flue pipes, the note being an octave lower than the equivalent flared pipe and the tone favouring the odd partials. Some reed pipes, such as the Vox humana, have very short resonators of quarter or eighth length. Pipes the resonators of which have no mathematical relationship to the pitch are known as regals; regal stops were very popular in the 17th century, particularly with the North German school, and their use has been revived in modern times. Their short resonators have varying and peculiar shapes, which produce a highly characteristic snarling tone; they can be difficult to keep in tune.

Reed length and pitch

Reed pipes are tuned by moving the tuning wire, thus shortening or lengthening the tongue (Figure 12). As in flue pipes, the scale and shape of the resonator largely determine the quality of tone to be produced; but the wind pressure, shape and size of the shallot, and thickness and curvature of the tongue also have important influence. The tongues may also be weighted with brass or felt; this weighting produces a smoother quality of tone, especially in the bass notes.

Organ reeds have been referred to as beating reeds because the tongue is larger than the shallot opening and therefore beats against it. In a free reed, on the other hand, the tongue is smaller than the opening and so vibrates through rather than against it. Harmoniums and harmonicas have free reeds, which are almost never used in organs.

Diapasons, or principals

It has already been explained that the pitch of any pipe is proportional to its length. Most modern organs have a manual compass of five octaves, from the second C below middle C to the third C above; an open pipe sounding the low C is about eight feet (2.5 metres) in speaking length (64 vibrations per second). The shortest pipe in the same rank is thus about three inches (eight centimetres) long (2,048 vibrations per second). The most characteristic tone of the organ is produced by its diapason, or principal, stops. These are of medium scale (usually about 6-in. scale at the 8-ft open pipe) and moderate harmonic development—*i.e.*, neither particularly dull nor bright. Such a tone quality becomes boring if heard for a long time. Also, when greater power is required, there is a distinct limit to what can be done by adding more stops of unison pitch. From the earliest times, stops, especially the principals, were arranged in choruses, and the principal chorus is the very backbone of any organ; without a complete principal chorus, an organ is hardly worthy of the name.

A chorus consists of stops of roughly similar quality and power but at a great variety of pitches. A unison principal is known as Principal 8 ft because of its longest (8-ft) pipe, and the figure 8 appears on the stop knob or tablet (rocking tablets are often used in place of knobs with electric action) at the console to give an indication of its pitch. The first step toward a chorus is to add a stop sounding an octave above 8-ft ranks (*i.e.*, at octave pitch), the largest pipe of which is therefore four feet long. Next comes a 2-ft stop, while in the other direction the suboctave pitch may be represented by a 16-ft stop. The top pipe of a 2-ft stop has a speaking length of only three-quarters of an inch, and this is about the practical upper limit. Nevertheless, an organ with nothing higher in pitch than a 2-ft stop would be lacking in brilliance, especially in the lower parts of the compass.

Mixtures and mutations

From the earliest times, organs have, therefore, been supplied with what are known generically as mixture stops, which have several high-pitched pipes to each note. But, since, for example, a 1-ft rank could not be carried right up to the top note, it breaks back an octave at some convenient point in the compass. Ranks pitched even higher will break back more than once. Thus, in the bass, a mixture adds definition to the slow-speaking, low-pitched pipes; in the treble, where the small pipes tend to be lacking in power, it duplicates the unison and octave ranks. A mixture, therefore, helps to maintain a balance of power between bass and treble, while adding harmonious power of a kind that is completely peculiar to the organ and can be produced in no other way.

Mixture stops also contain ranks sounding at pitches other than in octaves with the 8-ft principal. In chorus mixtures these sound at a fifth above the unison (*e.g.*, G above C), although ranks sounding at a third above and even at a flat seventh (*e.g.*, E and B♭ above C) and their respective octaves are also found; but these are best restricted to mixtures intended for somewhat special effects. The theoretical justification for these quint- (fifth) and third-sounding ranks is that they reinforce the natural upper partials of the harmonic series, but they were included in organs long before this was understood. The fact is that they were found to sound well, and any attempts to build organs without mixtures and off-unison ranks have been completely unsuccessful. The colourfulness and vitality of any organ depend largely upon copious, artistically voiced mixtures.

Off-unison ranks are also available as separate stops, mostly sounding at an interval of a 12th (an octave and a fifth; 2⅔ ft), 17th (two octaves and a third; 1⅗ ft), or 19th (two octaves and a fifth; 1⅓ ft) above the unison. These are used melodically to colour the unison and octave stops, and they may be wide or narrow in scale. Such stops are known as mutation stops, as opposed to the mixtures, or chorus stops. Their use is essential for the historically (and therefore artistically) correct performance of organ music written before 1800 and of much modern music as well. After a period of disuse throughout the 19th century, they are again included in all modern organs that have any pretensions to being artistically competent.

History of the organ to 1800. The earliest history of the organ is so buried in antiquity as to be mere speculation. The earliest surviving record is of the Greek engineer Ctesibius, who lived in Alexandria in the 3rd century BC. He is credited with the invention of an organ very much on the lines of the single-manual, slider-chest organ already described, except for its wind supply, which made use of a principle that was most ingenious, though applicable only to a very small instrument. A piston pump supplied air through an ordinary clack valve to a reservoir; at its upper end, this reservoir communicated directly with the wind-chest. The reservoir, cyclindrical in shape and with no bottom, was placed in a large drum-shaped container that was partly filled with water. As the reservoir became filled with air, the air would escape around its lower edge. In this way a more or less equal pressure of air was maintained inside the reservoir. Because of this arrangement the instrument was known as a hydraulis. A clay model of a hydraulis was discovered in 1885 in the ruins of Carthage (near modern Tunis, Tunisia), and the remains of an actual instrument were found in 1931 at Aquincum, near Budapest, Hungary.

The hydraulis

The development of the organ during the early Middle Ages is obscure, but by the 8th or 9th century it was being used in Christian churches. In the 10th century the famous instrument in the cathedral at Winchester, England, was constructed, of which the monk Wulfstan left a much quoted but manifestly garbled description ending: "the music of the pipes is heard throughout the town and the flying fame thereof is gone out over the whole country."

The artistic history of the organ begins with the development of the chromatic keyboard (*i.e.*, having 12 keys per octave) in the late 12th and early 13th centuries. By 1361 the cathedral organ at Halberstadt, Germany, had three chromatic keyboards and pedals; the keys, however, were much wider than those of the modern keyboard. The modern size of keys was fairly generally established by the end of the 15th century. Although the Halberstadt organ had three manuals, it had no stop mechanism. The main keyboard controlled a huge mixture stop, and the other keyboards controlled reduced groups of stops.

Ctesibius' slider arrangement was probably rediscovered some time in the early 15th century, and it became common soon after 1450. Reed stops began to appear at the same time, and by 1500 the organ had reached a stage in northern Germany in which all the important features of the modern organ were present. Each department had separate choruses; stopped, tapered, and open flue pipes; mutation stops; and reeds. The North German organ builders continued to be pre-eminent until about 1700, when the southern German builders took the lead.

During the Middle Ages and the Renaissance, three diminutive forms of the organ were widely used. These were, first, the positive (in which category are included most chamber organs of the period), a small organ capable of being moved, usually by two men, either on carrying poles or on a cart. The second type, the portative, was smaller still, with only one set of pipes and a manual of very short compass. It was carried by the player and was supported by a strap around his neck. He worked the bellows with one hand and played the keys with the other. Such instruments were used in processions and possibly in concerted instrumental ensembles. In between the last two in size was the third type, the regal, which usually had only one reed stop, a regal, as previously described.

Portable organs

Since national styles of organ building vary widely and it is necessary to know something about them before the music of each nation can be performed intelligently, the more important styles must next be considered briefly. Of the basic medieval organ, prior to the development of national styles, little if any material survives, except in the old cathedral at Sion in Switzerland, where a large proportion of the seven-stop organ appears to date from about 1400. Although voiced on very low wind pressure, the tone of the chorus is brilliant, colourful, and amazingly powerful. Not much is known about the precise uses of church organs in the Middle Ages. The organ hardly began to possess a literature of its own before the last portion of the 15th century.

Italy. Italy is mentioned first because its organs developed to their maturity soon after 1500 and remained relatively unaltered until about 1800. The Italian organ had one manual and usually only an octave of pedal keys, which had no pipes of its own (except an occasional independent 16-ft *contrabasso*) but was coupled permanently to the manual. The manual chorus (*ripieno*) had the peculiarity that there was no collective mixture; all the ranks were drawn by separate stops. Each rank broke back an octave as it reached the 1½-in. pipe. In addition, there were flute stops of 4-ft, 2⅔-ft, and 2-ft pitch and a register called the *fiffaro* or *voce umana* (not to be confused with the French *voix humaine* or German *Vox humana,* which are regals), a principal rank found only in the treble and tuned sharp so that when it is played together with the *principale* one hears an audible beat. It was the forerunner of the similarly constructed *voix céleste* stop popular in the 19th-century romantic organ. The scale of the classic Italian *principale* was not much different from its counterpart in the north, but its mouth was narrower, its voicing more delicate, and there was a notable lack of chiff. Reeds were not found until late in the 16th century and were never considered essential. There are well-preserved 16th-century instruments surviving, especially in Brescia and Bologna.

These simple resources were adequate for the performance of the keyboard works of Andrea (*c.* 1520–86) and Giovanni (*c.* 1556–1612) Gabrieli and Girolamo Frescobaldi (1583–1643). Organ music of these men and their contemporaries was not clearly differentiated from that for harpsichord, as indicated by the collections "*per organo o cembalo.*" The organ enjoyed some popularity: in Rome, according to Baini, no less than 30,000 people flocked to the square of St. Peter's hoping to find entrance to the cathedral to hear Frescobaldi's magic organ playing.

Spain and Portugal. The Iberian organ followed the Italian tradition, but, later, many reeds were added, most notably the *trompetas reales* ("royal trumpets") and other horizontal (*en chamada*) reeds arrayed in fanlike projections from highly ornamental cases. These reeds were on extremely low wind pressure and achieved amazingly full sounds that filled the huge edifices.

Like their Italian counterparts, Spanish and Portuguese organs had only a few rudimentary pedals. The manuals, however, were divided, with notes up to middle C controlled by a draw knob to the left and notes up from C sharp by a draw knob to the right. This enabled the playing of a solo voice against an accompaniment on the same manual.

The divided manuals of Iberian organs

A unique feature of Iberian churches was the presence of several separate and distinct instruments. The 13th-century Toledo Cathedral, for example, houses three organs: one over the Lion's Gate (south transept), known as the Emperor's organ (*c.* 1543), in an elaborate stone case that now houses a later 18th-century instrument; on both sides of the choir are separate organs—the Epistle organ from 1758 and the Gospel organ completed by the builder José Verdalonga in 1791. These two instruments have horizontal reeds projecting from both sides: into the choir and into the side aisles, enabling interesting uses of antiphony, or contrasting masses of sound. Toledo's three are surpassed in number at Mafra, Portugal, by the six organs in the monastic church, located in a sumptuous building considered Portugal's national monument. The reasons for multiple instruments have never been entirely clear. The use in services of different altars may have dictated the course, or perhaps when one instrument fell into disrepair it may have seemed simpler to add another; at least numerous organs have not been in playable condition for many years.

The leading composers of this era wrote for the instruments at hand. Their music is exciting on these instruments but is seldom effective elsewhere. Likewise, northern European literature is not satisfactory on the Iberian instrument.

In Spanish cathedrals the custom prevailed of alternating verses between organ and singers at the liturgical offices (Matins, Lauds, and Vespers) as well as for the ordinary (Kyrie, Gloria, Sanctus, and Agnus Dei) of the mass. The organ verses were invariably improvised, and the organist could change his registration during the choir verses between. Because improvisation was the norm, comparatively little written music exists from this period.

Antonio de Cabezón (1510–66) is the most illustrious of the historic Spanish composers. Others include Sebastián Aguilera de Heredia (1570–?) and Juan Cabanilles (1644–1712). Carlos Seixas (1704–42) is known as the Portuguese Bach.

Germany. From 1500 to 1800 Germany led the world in organ building and the composition of organ music. The organ builders reached the peak of their achievement about 1700 in the work of Arp Schnitger. His was the organ of the high Baroque; but his countrymen Andreas and Gottfried Silbermann were equally the masters of the slightly later, more sophisticated style of the mid-18th century.

The Schnitger organs

Schnitger made organs with four manuals, pedals, and as many as 60 speaking stops, but he made some instruments with less than 30 speaking stops that are capable of dealing with the whole pre-Romantic repertory. The finest surviving examples in this size are at Steinkirchen, near Hamburg, and at Cappel, near Cuxhaven. Two great larger examples are at Zwolle and Alkmaar, The Netherlands, both restored to excellent condition in the mid-20th century.

Seventeenth- and 18th-century German organs were usually constructed on *Werk*-principle lines: each department of the instrument, or *Werk,* was separately cased, the Hauptwerk (main manual) in front of and above the player, with the Pedals at each side and the Positiv (auxiliary manual) behind on the gallery railing. Each department, including the Pedal, had its own principal chorus, complete up to at least one mixture. All departments were roughly equal in power but varied in pitch, having, respectively, a 16-ft, 8-ft, and 4-ft preponderance (and 32-ft and 2-ft as well in larger instruments). Each manual department had a set of flutes and mutations that could be combined in a variety of ways to provide accompaniment and melody or the balanced but contrasting tone qualities essential for duet and trio passages. Although the pedal department consisted mainly of its principal chorus, it could be coloured for solo and obbligato passages by 2-ft flute and reed stops. The reeds were not much louder than the flue stops, and the Pedal 16-ft and 8-ft reeds were frequently drawn with the principal chorus for improved definition. When used in this way, they by no means caused the Pedal to overwhelm the Hauptwerk. Such an instrument could deal with the requirements of all 15th-through 18th-century organ music, although its limited supply of manual reeds placed it at some disadvantage in French music of the period.

The earliest organ music consisted of simple arrangements of vocal and instrumental music. A significant development in ornamented versions of such compositions for other mediums is the *Fundamentum organisandi* (*Fundamentals of Organ Playing;* Nürnberg, 1452) by Conrad Paumann, organist at the court of Bavaria. By the end of the 15th century, the polyphonic style was establishing itself in an independent form for the organ as a separate and distinct instrument. Pedal notes were ideally suited for a long-note cantus firmus ("fixed song," a basic melody chosen, for example, from a hymn) against manual counterpoint. The great Amsterdam organist Jan Pieterszoon Sweelinck (1562–1621), having studied in Venice (a tradition already established from northern Europe), developed a notable school of organ playing and composition that dominated a significant part of the musical world for almost two centuries, culminating in the genius of J.S. Bach (1685–1750). Among its composers were one of Sweelinck's greatest pupils, Samuel Scheidt of Halle; in the direct line from Sweelinck to Bach, Johann Adam Reinken of Hamburg; and the greatest composer of the high Baroque and one of the chief influences on Bach, Dietrich Buxtehude of Lübeck. In Austria and south Germany, a pupil of Frescobaldi, Johann Jakob Froberger of Vienna, was noted for his improvisational style. Johann Pachelbel of Nürnberg was the agent by which Italian and south German influences were again transported to northern Germany. By the time of Bach, the written *Choral-Vorspiel,* or chorale prelude (as opposed to the improvised prelude to the chorale within the Lutheran service), prelude and fugue, toccata, passacaglia, chaconne, and trio were firmly established forms for the organ—probably never again to be surpassed. A musical critic said of Bach: "He is the spectator of all musical time and existence, to whom it is not of the smallest importance whether a thing be new or old, so long as it is true."

Sweelinck and his successors

France. As far as the manual departments are concerned, French organs differed little from the German type, but the principal choruses were generally larger in scale. The separate, large-scaled Tierce ($1\frac{3}{5}$ ft) was also universal, and there were many cornet stops. These mixture stops consisted of five pipes to each note: a stopped unison (8 ft) and large-scale open 4 ft, $2\frac{2}{3}$ ft, 3 ft, and $1\frac{3}{5}$ ft. They extended only from middle C upward and were largely melodic in use. They were never drawn with the principal chorus (Plein Jeu) but generally were used with the reed chorus (Grand Jeu). Apart from this, the Plein Jeu, Grand Jeu, and Jeux de Mutation were seldom or never intermixed in French music.

The cantus firmus pedal

The pedal department of the French organ prior to 1700 was regarded largely as a sort of solo cantus firmus section that consisted usually of only 8- and 4-ft flutes and 8- and 4-ft trumpets. Only in the largest 18th-century organs were 16-ft stops included, although there were often as many as three on the Grand Orgue (the manual analogous to the German Hauptwerk and the English Great Organ). When French organs had more than two manuals (Grand Orgue and Positif), the others (Récit and Écho) were usually of short compass; but if, as sometimes, there was a fifth manual, it was a Clavier de Bombardes, consisting of 16-, 8-, and 4-ft trumpets and a cornet. Unlike its German counterpart, the main case housed all divisions except the Positif, which was in its usual location on the gallery railing.

French organs were notable for their reeds, and the highly stylized French music of the 17th and 18th centuries calls for their frequent use. Surviving specimens in good order are rare; but unaltered, late 18th-century, four-manual organs survive at Poitiers Cathedral (by the noted builder François-Henri Clicquot) and at Saint-Maximin, Provence (by Jean-Esprit Isnard).

Jean Titelouze (1563–1633) of Rouen may be considered the father of organ music in France. Nearly four centuries later the musicologist André Pirro and the composer Alexandre Guilmant say of his *Hymnes de l'église* (*Hymns of the Church;* 1623) in their preface to Guilmant's edition of the works of Titelouze, "He writes continued dissonances in the modes' natural scales and his use of sevenths gives, sometimes, a quite modern character to his modulations." A great tradition of playing and composing developed with a single dynasty presiding at a single church, Saint-Gervais in Paris, for more than 150 years:

the Couperin family, including Louis, François, Charles, and culminating in François le Grand (1668–1733), whose two famous masses are repertory staples even today. Contemporaries included the Paris organist Nicolas Lebègue and his pupil Nicolas de Grigny of Reims, whose mass and hymn verses Bach copied in his own hand; Louis Clérambault, known for two modal suites (*i.e.*, using the tonal structure of the old church modes rather than that of major and minor keys); and Louis-Claude Daquin, a great favourite in Paris who played his popular *Noëls* at the royal chapel.

Great Britain. British organs before the Commonwealth (1649–60) seem to have been very immature. Only a very few had two manuals, and none had pedals. Mixtures and reeds seem to have been unknown, and mutations were restricted to a single 12th.

After 1660 a new school rapidly grew up, and, although the two principal builders had both been abroad during the Commonwealth (Bernard Smith in Germany or Holland and Renatus Harris in France), their British work owed little to foreign influence. Only the Great Organ had a complete diapason chorus, and the Choir, or Chayre, organ usually extended upward only to a single 2 ft. Almost every organ had a Cornet, and the reeds in common use were Trumpet, Vox humana, and Cremona, or Krummhorn, with half-length, cylindrical resonators. There were no pedals, but the manual compass almost invariably extended to the third G below middle C. If there was a third manual, it consisted of a short-compass Echo department in which all the pipes were shut up in a box to produce the echo effect. In 1712 the builder Abraham Jordan first fitted the echo box with shutters that were controlled by a pedal at the console; this arrangement produced what Jordan described as the swelling organ, but it was not to reach its full development until 150 years later; no 18th-century organ music demands a swell box. There are hardly any surviving examples of British instruments of this period in original condition, and the only one of any size is the 14-stop, two-manual organ at Adlington Hall, near Macclesfield, dating from the last quarter of the 17th century. It is possibly the work of Bernard Smith. It is entirely original and was restored to perfect order in 1959.

Such instruments were adequate for the music of John Lugge, John Blow, Henry Purcell, George Frideric Handel, John Stanley, and even early 19th-century composers, such as Samuel Wesley.

Developments after 1800. Because of the increasing interest in orchestral and operatic music, the organ fell out of favour during the 18th century, and by 1800 it survived only as an ecclesiastical drudge. From the middle of the 19th century, however, a revival took place under the leadership of two great builders, Aristide Cavaillé-Coll of France and Henry ("Father") Willis of England. The German Edmund Schulze, who brought to England an organ built by his father's firm in central Germany, was also influential, especially in his flue choruses. In Britain during the first half of the 19th century, the introduction of pedals under the influence of Henry John Gauntlett made it possible for the first time to play the organ music of Bach and his German contemporaries and predecessors. While retaining respectable vestiges of the classical chorus, Cavaillé-Coll and Willis developed the solo stops, especially reeds, and Willis, in particular, provided new aids to registration.

Influence of Cavaillé-Coll

The work of Cavaillé-Coll was directly responsible for a new school of organ composition in France: César Franck (1822–90) composed chromatic and grandly Romantic works, culminating in his *Trois Chorals* (*Three Chorales*); also notable, although of less exalted stature, were Camille Saint-Saëns (*Three Rhapsodies on Breton Themes* and an important organ part in his *Symphony No. 3 in C Minor*), Alexandre Guilmant (numerous sonatas and small "service" pieces), and Charles-Marie Widor and Louis Vierne, both of whom wrote a number of large-scale "sonata suites" they entitled *Symphonies.* A successor of Franck at his post at Sainte-Clotilde in Paris was the great improviser Charles Tournemire, who left a highly individual collection of improvisatory-like modal pieces entitled *L'Orgue mystique.* Jean Langlais (born 1907) continued the modal tradition in many descriptive pieces for liturgical use, and Olivier Messiaen (born 1908) has perpetuated the mystical qualities in suites of great originality (*La Nativité du Seigneur, L'Ascension,* and others). Another prominent organist-improviser-composer-teacher in this largely Romantic mold was Marcel Dupré. Francis Poulenc contributed a popular *Concerto in G Minor for Organ, String Orchestra, and Timpani.*

Parallel to the French movement, German-born Felix Mendelssohn (1809–47), though working primarily in England, revived an interest in the works of Bach and composed sonatas and preludes and fugues for the organ. Franz Liszt and the German Julius Reubke added to the repertory several flamboyant, pianistic pieces. Johannes Brahms wrote chorale preludes and several preludes and fugues. A composer of monumental chromatic fantasies and fugues, as well as simple chorale preludes, was Max Reger (1873–1916).

Organists found that they could play effective arrangements of orchestral music on the new romantic style organ. Since orchestral music was popular and respectable orchestras very rare and other forms of public entertainment even more so, the organ suddenly regained an immense popularity hardly rivalled by that of the 17th and 18th centuries, when it was the acknowledged "king of instruments." Organ builders naturally responded by making their instruments increasingly orchestral in character, culminating at the end of the 19th century in the work of the English builder Robert Hope-Jones, who entirely abandoned the chorus and mutation stops and relied instead upon diapasons of vast scale on heavy-pressure wind, with reeds to match, backed up by huge-scaled flutes, tiny-scaled string stops (with keen-sounding flue pipes), and powerful stops of his own invention called diaphones. Hope-Jones emigrated to the United States, and, although a semblance of classical design returned to England soon after 1900, his influence continued to be felt throughout the first half of the 20th century. This discredited the organ as a musical instrument in the eyes of serious musicians and composers.

First instruments in the Colonies

The first organs in America had been imported from England beginning about 1700. This was the period of the English Commonwealth, and the Puritan view of the "unsuitability" of an organ in church was inherited by the colonies. Only parishes of the Church of England (later known as Protestant Episcopal Church) and Lutheran and Moravian churches in Pennsylvania would admit instruments. Another century elapsed before the New England Puritans did likewise. The only builder of note was the German-American David Tannenberg. A U.S. school of builders began to emerge in the early 1800s with such names as Henry Erben, Elias and George Hook, George Jardine, William A. Johnson, J.H. and C.S. Odell, and Hilborne and Frank Roosevelt. Perhaps the inevitable end of the U.S. "romantic" era was reached in Ernest M. Skinner, who lived until the middle of the 20th century. In Canada, Joseph Casavant built his first organ in Quebec province in 1837. Two of his sons visited France in 1878–79 and brought back to North America the Cavaillé-Coll tradition.

Although no significant school of organ composers has emerged in North America, two names, or at least two pieces, stand out: although neglected for years, Charles Ives in 1891 improvised (and later wrote down) *Variations on America;* this piece was remarkably ahead of its time and suits the U.S. organ at the turn of the century most admirably. Healey Willan, though British born, was for many years Canada's leading composer; his greatest work for the organ is probably *Introduction, Passacaglia and Fugue* (published 1919).

Organ revival. Albert Schweitzer, organist, philosopher, and later medical missionary, wrote a booklet, *Deutsche und französische Orgelbaukunst und Orgelkunst* ("The Art of German and French Organ Builders and Players"), in 1906 outlining the inadequacies of the 19th-century organ for the performance of Bach and his contemporaries. It was not until 1926, however, with Karl Straube, that the revival began. Straube, organist at Bach's Thomaskirche in Leipzig and noted recitalist, teacher, editor of Baroque organ works, and leading exponent of the very Romantic works of Reger, renounced his whole approach to the organ and called for a return to the instrument of Schnitger and the high Baroque. Since then, the movement has spread among such organ builders as Karl Kemper, Rudolph von Beckerath, and Johannes Klais in Germany; Victor Gonzalez in France; Sybrand J. Zachariassen and Th. Frobenius in Denmark; Dirk A. Flentrop in The Netherlands; Th. Kuhn in Switzerland; and Walter Holtkamp, G. Donald Harrison, and Herman Schlicker in the United States. Many organists interested in fine phrasing and articulation feel that these qualities are only realizable through the medium of tracker action, where there is a direct connection between player and pallet. This neoclassical movement has inspired a few, but significant, composers to write for the organ: Willem Vogel of The Netherlands; Finn Viderø of Denmark; the Germans Paul Hindemith (three sonatas and two concerti), Hugo Distler, Hermann Schroeder, and Helmut Walcha; and the Americans Daniel Pinkham and Alan Stout.

Exemplary modern builders

The revival in France, the United States, and Britain strove to produce an instrument that could do equal justice to all legitimate organ music of whatever period. This was not easy, but it was possible. Undoubtedly, the most successful exponent up to about 1950 was G. Donald Harrison (British born but associated with the Aeolian-Skinner Organ Co. in Boston)—*e.g.*, the instrument in the Mormon Tabernacle in Salt Lake City, Utah. In England, successful examples are the London organs of the Royal Festival Hall and St. Giles Cripplegate. (C.Cl.)

Wind instruments

Prominent in the music of all cultures from prehistoric times to the present, wind instruments comprise a variety of forms so wide that their only common denominator is their use of air as a primary vibrating medium for the production of sound. In a scientific terminology developed in the 20th century by an Austrian musicologist, Erich Moritz von Hornbostel, and his German colleague, Curt Sachs, such instruments are called aerophones in contrast to idiophones, membranophones, chordophones, and electrophones, in which, respectively, the instrument itself, a membrane, a string, or an electronic speaker, is the primary sound producer.

Some aerophones have remained essentially the same over millennia, but others have been extensively altered. When instruments became unsatisfactory, remedies were attempted. With such changes often closely linked to developments in tools and technology, wind instruments have been altered and sometimes new instruments have been invented in the course of inter-action between musical demands and technological progress.

GENERAL CONSIDERATIONS

Types of wind instruments. A system of classification of musical instruments must reflect and categorize the relationships and the differences between the many varieties. The study of types and their relationship can show the genetic and cultural links that bring understanding both to the instruments themselves and the societies that use them.

Common terminology divides wind instruments into brasses and woodwinds, but that classification is not always accurate in dealing with materials used and, furthermore, fails to recognize the significant factor of tone production. The system of Hornbostel and Sachs—developed in 1914 and itself an extension of the ideas of a Belgian instrument maker and museum curator of the late 19th century—has been criticized, changed in detail, but never supplanted. Wind instruments are recognized as aerophones because the air itself is the vibrating medium. The primary division, then, is between free aerophones, in which the air is not contained, and wind instruments proper, in which the vibrating air is within the instrument itself.

The classification system of Hornbostel and Sachs

The free reeds include a variety of primitive instruments as well as such sophisticated devices as reed stops in organs (see *Organ* above). The bull-roarer exemplifies the primitive. A board carved in the shape of a fish is attached to a rope, which is in turn attached to a stick. The instrument is whirled around in the air, producing sound by its disturbance of the air itself. For primitive man, the sound together with the symbolism of the fish was pure magic.

The reeds of the mouth organ, accordian, reed organ, and the reed stops of the pipe organ all produce sound in a similar manner. The reed vibrating above or through a slot sets the air into pulsations, the pitch being determined by the thickness and length of the vibrating reed.

The category of wind instruments proper includes woodwinds and brasses, but the next step in classification in the Hornbostel–Sachs system is in the manner of tone production. Consequently, edge instruments becomes a descriptive term for flutes, in which a stream of air is directed against a sharp edge, where it divides, sending the air within the instrument into regular pulsations. Many edge instruments have no duct. In the *shakuhachi* of Japan, the player covers part of the end of the wide bamboo tube with his lower lip and blows a stream of air across to a sharpened edge. Panpipes are also ductless, as is the side-blown flute with fingerholes, which is the most familiar in Western civilization. In the other subclassification, the air stream is blown through a duct to a sharp edge. Examples of these flutes are the recorder, the ocarina, and the open flue stops of the organ.

A second major division of wind instruments proper is reed pipes, a category in which the column of air is activated by the vibrations of either a double or a single reed alternately closing and opening the orifice. All double reeds are classified as oboes; and the single reeds, as clarinets. Thus, generically, the bassoon is an oboe; the saxophone a clarinet.

Reed pipes

The third division is trumpets, used generically to include all lip-vibrated aerophones, including horns. Trumpets are divided between the natural and chromatic. Consequently, natural trumpets include both the conch shell and the trumpet of J.S. Bach. Various subcategories separate the end blown from the side blown and those without mouthpieces from those with. Chromatic trumpets are divided into those with fingerholes, those with slides, and those with valves.

Perhaps a fourth major division, the human voice, should be added to the Hornbostel–Sachs list, for it may be classified as a double-reed aerophone in which the vocal chords act as a double reed and the cavities of the throat, mouth, sinuses, and nose form the resonant area. Indeed, a British musicologist, Robert Donington, has called the voice a throat instrument.

With the scientific classification well in mind, the common terminology can be used with the understanding that the term woodwinds refers to pipes (and globular flutes) and the term brasses to lip-vibrated aerophones.

The production of sound. Tubes used to produce a musical sound may be cylindrical, conical, or some combination of the two. They may also be straight or curved. Regardless of the material used, their interior surface must be smooth for best results. The relation of tube length to diameter varies widely but must remain within certain practical limits in order to produce musical pitches. The air contained within the tube is set into vibration by the breath, or in some cases a bellows, acting upon a sound-generating device. The pressure exerted against the molecules of air in the tube causes the particles to move forward along the tube until they bump into others, setting them in motion while the first bounce back. This process creates regular pulsations producing sound waves. Throughout the sounding length of the tube, the entire wave moves at the speed of sound. The air itself moves only slowly, and the phenomenon has been compared to the starting of a freight train, in which the first burst of energy from the engine jerks the car behind, which in turn passes the impulse of the car behind it, and so on throughout the length of the train. The impact of the cars also produces a reverse pressure as it moves along. Similarly, at the sounding length of the tube, the waves are reflected back upon themselves, creating a counter pressure that forms nodes and antinodes. The node results from interference between the forward and the reverse forces creating a static point; the antinode, on the other

Donington's freight-train analogy

hand, is the point of freest vibration in the sound wave. Antinodes always occur at the open ends of a tube, and it must be remembered that the end where the sound generates is also an open end, except in the clarinet types. In its simplest form, a node (N) is created at the exact middle between the two antinodes (A) at each end of the vibrating length.

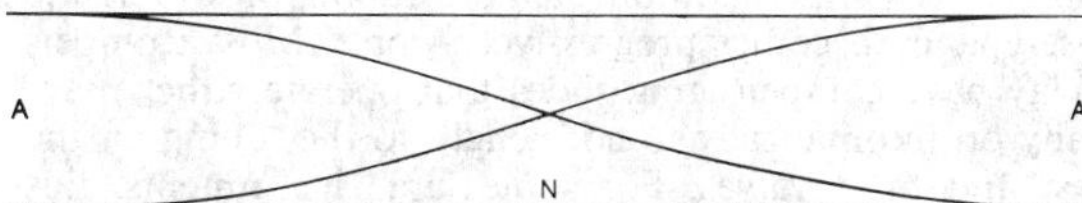

The note produced by this basic wave form is called the fundamental. If the generating vibration is quickened sufficiently, the sound waves divide in half, producing an antinode in the exact middle with consequent nodes between the three antinodes, producing a pattern consisting of A-N-A-N-A instead of A-N-A.

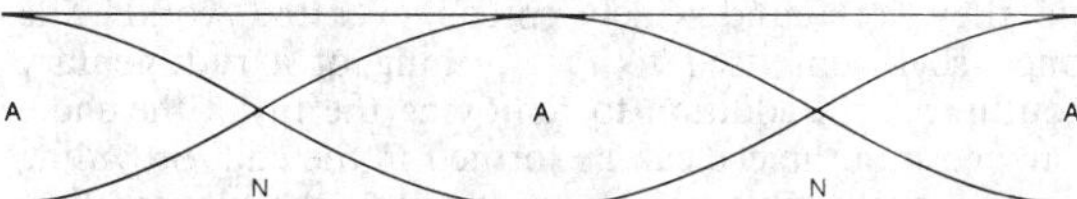

Similarly, with further increase in the generating speed, the column may be further divided into thirds, fourths, fifths, and so on. The process is known as overblowing. Pitches resulting from these divisions are called overtones, and their frequency, the speed of the waves, increases in proportion to the division of the air column—that is, 1:2, 1:3, 1:4, etc. If the fundamental is C at a frequency of 128 vibrations per second, the second partial will be C at 256 vibrations per second, the third will be g at 384, and the fourth will be c′ at 512. The successive pitches created by the vibration of the air column as a whole (the fundamental) and its various divisions (the series of harmonic overtones) create the harmonic series, theoretically obtainable *in toto* on any tube with the appropriate increase in the vibrating speed of the generator and theoretically extending to infinity. In addition to the successive individual pitches created by overblowing, a column (or any divison of a column) of air simultaneously vibrates in its parts. Consequently, the pitches of the harmonic series are usually present in some strength with the primary pitch heard as the fundamental. For this reason, the pitches of the harmonic series are known as partials and numbered in the order in which they appear. The following example shows the harmonic series for the fundamental pitch C. (Asterisked notes are noticeably out of tune with the tempered chromatic scale, which contains 12 equal semitones.)

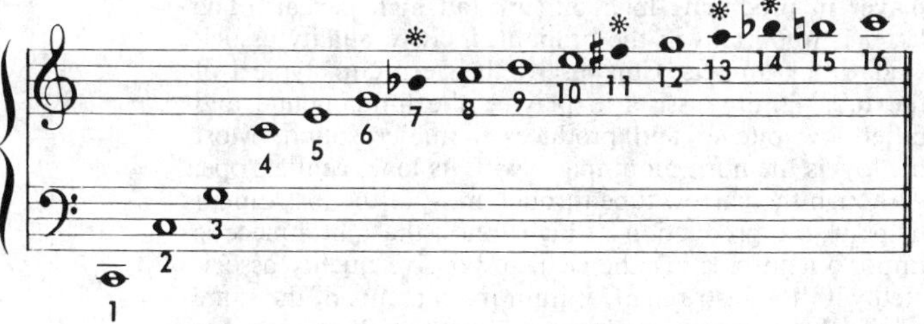

The relative strength of the various partials, which is controlled largely by the shape of the tube and the type of generator, is responsible for the timbre or colour of the pitch. It is this feature that allows the ear to distinguish between the quality of various tones.

It is notable that each successive interval of the harmonic series grows smaller, the number of partials doubles in each octave, and diatonic pitches of the major (*i.e.*, whole and half steps) scale become available in the fourth octave. The series is particularly significant among the natural brasses (*i.e.*, those lacking valves, fingerholes, keys, or slides), for the pitches that could be played are limited to a range of one to about 16 notes from this series without some device to alter the fundamental.

A pipe stopped at one end will have the static point of its air column there, consequently producing a node (N) at the open end and an antinode (A) at the other.

Stopped and unstopped pipes

Because of the closed end, the column cannot be divided in half nor into any even-numbered multiples, for such divisions would require an antinode at the closed end. Thus, all even-numbered partials are unavailable in the sound spectrum, and the instrument overblows only to the odd-numbered partials. The following is an illustration of overblowing at the third partial:

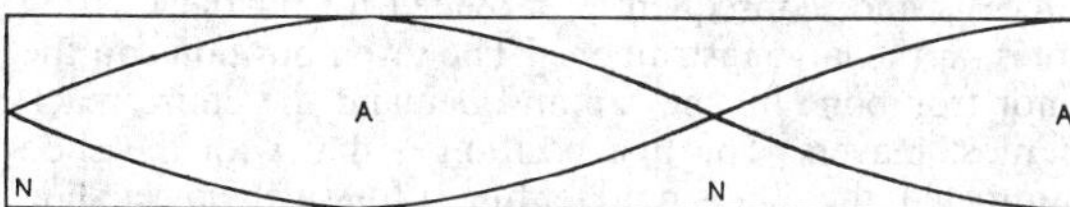

The clarinet family and stopped flue pipes in the organ are the most commonly known instruments of this type.

Pulsating air within a tube in turn initiates pulses in the free air, creating sound waves very roughly similar in a single dimension to the waves created on still water if a stone is dropped into it. Because free wind instruments must create such eddies in the air directly, the capabilities of these instruments are extremely limited. Even organ reeds, which belong to this class, are capable of sophisticated music merely because of their number. Each reed produces only the pitch to which it is tuned, and the pipe, if present, does not determine pitch but serves only as a resonator for the reed.

Differentiation between brass instruments and other winds

Brass instruments. The difference between brass instruments and other winds is actually the lip reed, which generates the tone. Cup-mouthpiece instrument is also a generally accurate and commonly used term, but the most precise reference is lip-vibrated aerophone. For the most part, the tube is long in relation to its width. The majority of cup-mouthpiece instruments, particularly in Western civilization and especially in historic times, have been made from metal: predominately of the alloy brass, which has lent its name in common parlance to the vast majority of the genre. Among brasses, a differentiation is made between trumpets and horns in that the trumpet is usually formed from a narrow, largely cylindrical bore, although some expansion in the final third of the instrument frequently leads to the typically relatively small bell. Such a configuration in conjunction with a shallow-cupped mouthpiece favours the production of high partials and results in a brilliant tone, particularly in the high register. Horns, on the other hand, have a relatively widely expanding bore through all or part of their length and normally end in a large bell. Aided by a deep-cupped or cone-shaped mouthpiece, these instruments favour low partials. Consequently, they produce a characteristically mellow tone and function efficiently in their lower range. The problem with this differentiation is that it works only in the most obvious examples, for no criteria exist to define the dividing line between the two; some writers prefer to call horns those instruments known or believed to have descended from the primitive instruments made from animal horns or tusks, terming the remaining lip-vibrated instruments trumpets. Lip-vibrated instruments may also be differentiated on the basis of whether or not the fundamental can be sounded. Those wide enough to sound the fundamental are called whole-tube instruments; those too narrow are half tube, and this criterion is used further to separate instruments that can overblow into the third and fourth octave. By far the greatest majority of modern lip-vibrated instruments have a relatively long tube for their width and, consequently, overblow into the third or fourth octave. Such overblowing provides only about 16 notes for the best of players. Evidence of the effectiveness of the Western trumpet and the French horn, for instance, even with this limitation, is a magnificent repertory over the centuries and continued idiomatic use of the basic pitch materials of the harmonic series even today.

The trumpet featured a device for filling in some tones as early as the 15th century. Late Gothic and Renaissance paintings occasionally show a trumpet with the player holding the mouthpiece to the lips. Later evidence shows that this playing position infers the *tromba da tirarsi*, an Italian term for a slide trumpet that moves on a mouthpiece with an extremely long shank.

Such a slide was awkward, however, and possibly the idea of bending the slide back upon itself was adopted soon after or even before the single slide was invented. It would have been essential for the longer trumpets. The long shank was held by a brace to the body of the instrument; and with the application of the double slide, a trombone, differing little from that used today, was formed. The trombone slide halved the movement necessary to descend intervals and, consequently, provided for all the missing notes on the large instruments. The seven positions on the tenor trombone fill the gap and demand the entire reach of most players. The first position is that with the slide contracted, the others representing successively lower slide positions. Each new position lengthens the tubing enough to lower the fundamental pitch a semitone and thus makes available the notes of another harmonic series.

Toward the end of the 17th century, the French hunting horn was undergoing the changes that inspired its development as an orchestral instrument in Germany and Bohemia in the 18th century. By 1718 crooks, or insertable pieces of additional tubing, were used to change the total length of tubing and the corresponding key of the horn. About mid-century, one Anton Hampel of Dresden introduced the use of the hand in the bell, which allowed the pitch to be lowered one-half step when the hand was cupped to form an extension to the air column. Despite the significant enlargement of pitches in the third and fourth octave, experiments continued to provide more pitches. A Bohemian horn player invented a keyed horn around 1770, which was a failure. The same device was, nevertheless, a reasonable success on the bugle. About 1815, however, either Heinrich Stölzel or Friedrich Blühmel, both of Berlin, invented the valve and applied it first to the horn. Both piston and rotary valves were in use early in the century. Both were devices that deflected the air stream into extra tubing when the valve was depressed but cut off the extra tubing when the valve was released. The first valve added tubing to lower the pitch one step; the second added only enough for the one-half step. The two together added one and a half steps. Eventually, a third valve was added to lower pitch another step and a half. With these valves and their combinations, the instrument became completely chromatic above the second partial. The illustration below shows the harmonic series made available by the depression of different valves and combinations of valves. Notes shown in black are slightly out of tune with the tempered scale.

Invention of the valve

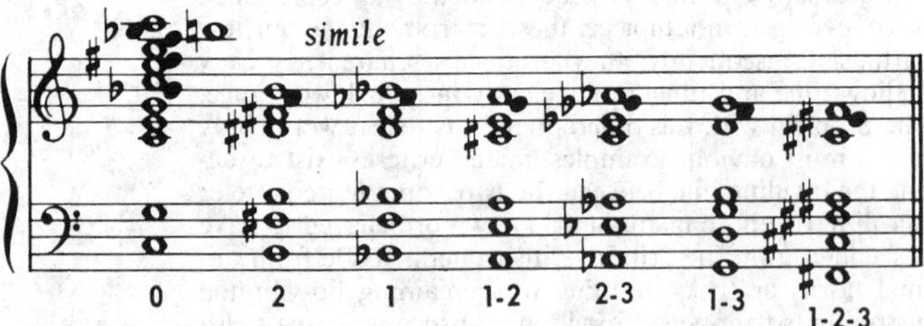

Perhaps because the natural horn had more notes available than did natural trumpets of that period and also because the valve system, particularly on the early horns, affected the purity of tone, valve horns were accepted slowly. Even when they were established, composers at first tended to use valves as if they were faster and more convenient crooks whose main effect was to make modulation (change of key) instantly available. In bands and in other ensembles playing light music, brass players adopted the valved instruments soon. In those mediums, the cornet, essentially a small horn fitted with valves, became a standard melody instrument.

The valve mechanism possesses an inherent defect in that the valves open a fixed amount of tubing. If the first valve is depressed to lower the pitch from C to B♭ the instrument becomes in effect B♭. As a result, using the second valve designed for a C instrument to lower the B♭ instrument a half-step would require slightly more tubing than needed to lower a C instrument one-half step. The discrepancy in this instance is so slight that players can "lip it down"; a slight decrease in the speed of the lip vibration will flatten the pitch without destroying the tone quality. With the addition of more tubing, however, the discrepancy becomes progressively worse. Most trumpets today have compensating slides that operate either manually or automatically to add length to the tubing on the first and third valves. For some large instruments, this device is impractical, and extra valves may be added.

Important in generating the sound is the mouthpiece or, in primitive instruments, the mouth hole. African animal horns, for instance, frequently have a hole on the side near the small end of a tusk. The rim of the hole supports the lips as the breath sets them into motion to produce the few notes available. Most horns are end blown, however, and they are found widely spread over the world. The conch shell lent itself to the forming of a rudimentary mouthpiece. In addition to removing the tip of the shell, a shaped mouthpiece can be formed in the end, providing a more comfortable and effective aid to the player's lips.

From A. Carse, *Musical Wind Instruments;* by permission of Macmillan, London and Basingstoke

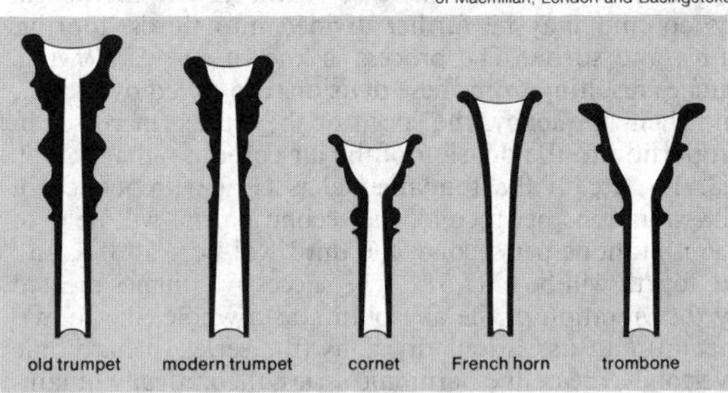

Figure 13: Mouthpieces of wind instruments.

On the metal cup-mouthpieced instruments and occasionally on those made of ivory or wood separate mouthpieces are made. They differ widely in shape and exert an important influence over the tone and technical capacity of the instrument. The wide end of the device is placed against the lips of the player and outlines the area that vibrates. Beyond the rim is a cup-shaped hollow usually constricting at the bottom, then expanding slightly into the shank as it directs the air stream into the instrument. French horn mouthpieces are cone shaped. Trumpets of East Asia typically have extremely shallow and broad-rimmed mouthpieces. The shallow mouthpiece aids the player in producing high pitches and high partials. The latter is important in the brilliant, incisive quality associated with trumpets. Conversely, the deep cup, typical of the tuba family, assists in playing the fundamental and other low pitches and produces a milder sound. Most mellow is the horn mouthpiece with its long, gentle slope. Although the narrow tube through most of the instrument helps in the production of high tones, the mouthpiece is important in creating the rich, responsive quality associated with the instrument. Within instruments of the same pitch, the trumpet, the cornet, and the flügelhorn are respectively more conical in bore and have increasingly deeper cup mouthpieces, the mouthpiece of the flügelhorn approaching that of the French horn. The quality of the instruments changes accordingly.

Relation of mouthpiece shape to timbre

Woodwind instruments. In contrast to most brasses, the typical woodwind is short in relation to its width. Consequently, most woodwinds not only sound their fundamental but also respond best to the pitches low in the harmonic series, which means that few pitches are available on instruments without finger holes. The player generates sound by blowing a stream of air across a sharp edge or by activating either a double or a single reed. A few instruments, most notably the organ, use bellows to produce the air stream.

Flutes without finger holes stem from the earliest civilizations, in which their limited pitches were used to lure birds or animals or to fulfill ritual or magical functions.

Most are end blown. Few reed instruments are found without finger holes.

The six-hole system of fingering

It is not surprising that fingering systems developed early. Typical of Western civilization is the six-hole system, most easily observed on the 18th-century prototypes of modern instruments. Oboes and transverse (side-blown) flutes in the 17th century, both pitched in D, had three holes each for the first, second, and third finger of the two hands. (The finger numbering does not include the thumb.) By the mid-18th century, the left hand always took the high position on the pipe. Holes were numbered one to six beginning with the highest and were indicated on fingering charts in contemporaneous methods as solid circles for those covered by a finger and by open circles for holes uncovered. Lifting fingers beginning with the lowest shortened the sounding length of the instrument with each successive opening and produced e, f♯, g, a, b, and c♯—the remaining notes of the D-major scale. Other pitches could be obtained by cross-fingering. The lowest open hole may reveal a definite pitch but is not large enough to cancel the influence of the remainder of the pipe. When the first finger of the right hand uncovers the fourth hole and the fifth hole remains covered, the result is f′ rather than f♯. With the first and third fingers of the right hand looking vaguely like the tines of a fork, the fingering became known as a fork fingering. Similarly, other chromatic pitches could be obtained by closing one or more holes below an open hole, but purists refer only to those made with the first and third fingers as fork fingerings. Cross-fingering can be used as a general term to describe all such arrangements.

From A. Carse, *Musical Wind Instruments;* by permission of Macmillan, London and Basingstoke

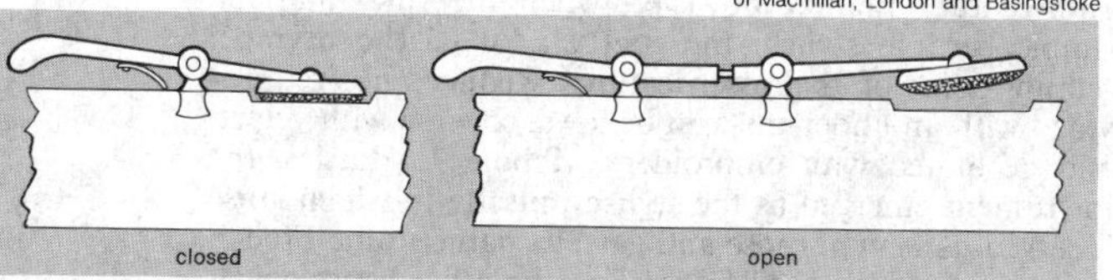

Figure 14: Typical woodwind instrument keys.

No cross-fingering could produce e♭, however, for there was no hole to cover beyond d. Consequently, a seventh hole was soon bored between the sixth and the end of the instrument and covered by a key.

Increasing lip tension in order to overblow will produce overtones on most woodwinds by making the generating pulsations too fast to stimulate the fundamental or, if still faster, to eliminate other low partials. With woodwinds, however, overblowing is not generally as easy as with brasses. Both the oboe and the clarinet are provided with special speaker keys to assist the lip in making the notes of the upper register emerge clearly and instantaneously. On flutes and bassoons, the first hole is opened on certain pitches to serve the same function. In the last decades of the 18th century, many keys were added to solve various difficulties. After the first quarter of the 19th century, however, more drastic changes were needed if certain problems were to be overcome. In earlier instruments, a ring was left in the original turning from which the axle of a key could be mounted. As keys proliferated, the ring was reduced to leave only the actual wooden mounting. First used on the bassoon and then on other woodwinds was a brass saddle that included the key mount. Finally, all of these devices were gradually replaced by metal pillars screwed directly into the wood. Reformers, notably Theobald Böhm, made basic changes, including all variable elements (discussed below). The constantly expanding key system caused changes in tone quality, as the valves did to the brasses. Though some consider the changes regrettable, they have made possible technical dexterity in all keys.

Sound is generated in woodwinds by three methods. Already mentioned is the device that defines flutes, a sharp edge against which a stream of air is directed. Other woodwinds generate the sound with reeds, which may be double or single. In either case, they are made from a cane called *Arundo donax,* which grows wild in marshes or on river banks in most temperate or tropical climates. The best appears to be that grown on the Mediterranean coasts of Spain, France, and Italy, where, in fact, it is now cultivated and harvested for reed making. Seasoned over a period of years after harvesting, it is periodically turned to insure even drying. Drying may also be speeded by ovens, and now even plastic is sometimes used to avoid the entire tortuous process; but cane is still generally preferred. Reed making at its best must still be done by craftsmen who are usually players of the instrument. They may be bought in finished form, but fine players often do the final stages and sometimes the entire process themselves.

The use of cane for reeds

Double reeds, used in Western music by the oboe and the bassoon, are made by bending a piece of cane back upon itself with appropriate trimming and scraping before and after bending. The final process involves binding the ends, clipping off the area of the best portion to produce two curved edges, and trimming to produce two strong, thin, complementary laminae. On the modern oboe and bassoon, the double reed is held by the tension of lips drawn in over the teeth, and the opening between the two laminae alternately opens and closes with the pressure of the breath to generate the pulsations in the tube. Lip control allows the player to increase tension for overblowing. Early and non-Western double reed instruments are more frequently uncontrolled and, consequently do not overblow.

The air in the tube of instruments of the clarinet family is activated by a single reed, which fits against a flat surface called the lay of the mouthpiece. The air column begins in a wide opening beneath the reed. The column of air is cylindrical, and when the reed is activated the air column acts as a closed pipe. The pitch is an octave lower than an open pipe of the same length, and it overblows at the 12th rather than the octave; the tonal spectrum—the fundamental plus the overtones in their various strengths—includes only the odd partials. When the single reed pulsates on the saxophone, which has a conical bore, the tube is open, the instrument overblows at the octave, and the spectrum contains even-numbered as well as odd-numbered partials.

Social aspects of wind instruments. Primitive man was superstitious. Endowed with few devices for self-preservation, he survived by his wits, and his wits found the supernatural everywhere. His world, inhabited by spirits, good and evil, was dangerous; and noises of the natural world, from ear-splitting thunder to the gentle snap of a breaking twig, were frequently interpreted as voices from the object or the spirit world. Primitive man responded with sounds that could frighten evil spirits and placate his gods.

Music and magic were closely intertwined. A voice was

Reprinted from *Woodwind Instruments and Their History* by Anthony Baines. Copyright 1957 by W.W. Norton & Company, Inc. By permission of W.W. Norton & Company, Inc. and Faber & Faber, Ltd.

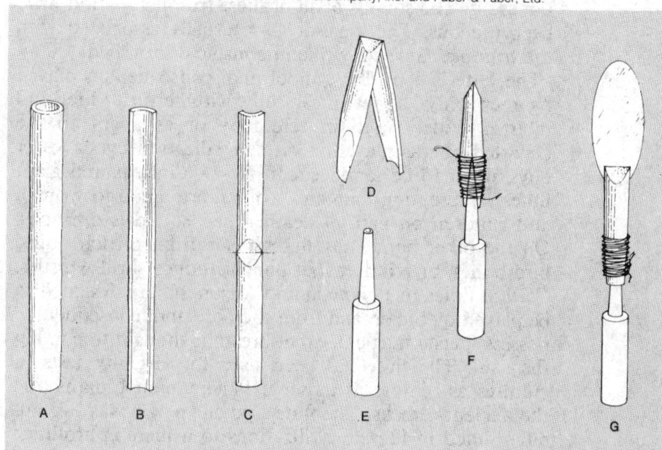

Figure 15: *Stages in the making of oboe reeds.*
(A) Cane is cut to desired length and (B) split in thirds, lengthwise, (C) nicked in the centre, and (D) folded over and cut in the desired shape. The folded cane is mounted on (E) the oboe's staple and (F) is tied, and (G) the tips of the reed are separated by a thin metal tongue.

found in a dead bone, a cut plant, or a marine shell; and these voices were used to deal with both the mysteries of life and the constant dangers in the environment. The function of the sexes was dramatized in innumerable ways. Musical instruments that were long and straight were played by men only; and, if they were coloured red, the magic was more powerful, for red was the color of blood and represented life. Most instruments reserved for males produced sound that was loud, harsh, ugly, aggressive, and frightening. Musical instruments that were round or curved or associated with the Moon or water were reserved for women. Water responded to tides, and tides, to the Moon; and the Moon measured the menstrual cycle of women. Women's instruments were usually muffled in quality. Beauty of tone was no object; the purposes of magic were better served by other characteristics. Occasionally, the almost universal symbolism became confused, as when the conch shell, for instance, was turned into a trumpet or a globular object became a flute. In such cases, cultures differ in their assignment of the instrument to the sexes.

Sexual symbolism in primitive instruments

The bull-roarer is a man's instrument. The fish shape represents fertility because of the copious roe in the fish, and its frequent red colour indicates male vigour. Whirling the instrument is presumed to suggest fertilizing power and to signify procreation—all endowing the instrument with the appropriate magic for adolescent rites. The woman who sees the instrument along with the man who shows it to her must die. In a later stage, the fish represents water, and the sound, the wind. Man whirls it to make rain, but the magical powers evaporate when Malaysians today employ the bull-roarer to frighten elephants away from their plantations.

The trumpet was first a megaphone that could distort the magician's voice and frighten evil spirits. As a musical instrument it has been used for circumcision ceremonies, for funerals, and for rites at sunset—in other words, for manhood, life, and rebirth. The conch shell, which began its long musical history as a megaphone, was used as well to call the dead from the tomb. In less dramatic circumstances, it proved to be an effective signalling instrument; but, in societies in which the conch trumpet was interpreted as a woman's instrument, it was kept from men.

The shamans of Tibet use a short trumpet made of a human leg bone and prefer that of a criminal as being more closely related to (and consequently more potent in dealing with) the many Tibetan devils. The troops of Joshua in biblical times blew the *shofar,* "and the walls came a'tumbling down"; and, in order to summon Yahweh when burnt offerings were prepared, the ancient Jews blew the two silver trumpets kept in the temple. As a remnant of the old superstition, a wooden trumpet blown at Advent in the south of Holland is hidden in a well for the remainder of the year, where women and children will not see it. The sounds of all of these trumpets would have been raucous. The majestic tone usually associated with the trumpet came only when its magic diminished.

The flute is a phallic symbol and, consequently, played by men only. It dealt magically with fertility, life, and rebirth. Widely used in ceremony or as a gift to the departed, it was played in Aztec civilization by slaves or boys about to be sacrificed. In New Guinea paired giant flutes representing man and woman are taboo to women and children on pain of death. Their sound is ominous. On the other hand, tiny flutes made from ostrich quills, bird bones, or reindeer foot bones produce shrill whistles. Certain flutes in Polynesia and Melanesia are designed to be played by breath and from the nose and, consequently, possess special magic, for that breath is thought to contain the soul. The flute has been used for virginity tests in cultures as remote as those of Panamanian Indians and the ancient Greeks. The flute's potent magic was eventually diluted in literate civilizations to a mere aphrodisiac power over women, and in this sense it has been used symbolically in art through the ages and still maintains vestiges of its tradition in some Western cultures.

The reed undoubtedly originated from the simple device of blowing across a stretched grass blade to make a sound, a trick known to children across the world and presumably for thousands of years. In primitive civilizations certain grasses are believed capable of making rain and hail and of keeping the women away from the initiated boys. Reed instruments became male instruments and possessed magical powers similar to trumpets and flutes.

That the tradition persisted into ancient Greece is clear from a fascinating legend: none other than the goddess Athena invented the aulos, the ancient foreunner of the oboe, and she proudly played it at a banquet of the gods on Mt. Olympus. Although many expressed delight and approval, Athena noticed Hera and Aphrodite exchanging glances. Athena rushed to the woods to play the aulos over the smooth mirror of the pond. When she saw her puffed-out cheeks and the facial distortion accompanying the difficult exertion of activating the reed, she pronounced a curse upon it and threw it away, an act that in turn inspired a legend of a contest between Apollo on the kithara with Marsyas on the pipes; for Marsyas retrieved the aulos that Athena had thrown away.

The legend of the ancient Greek aulos

The contest represents the dichotomy that the Greeks created between the two instruments, the stringed instrument having the virtues of the Apollonian cult, whereas the aulos represented the Dionysian. The aulos was, consequently, associated with the passionate, the orgiastic, and the intemperate and became the instrument of the theatre. Either the tone quality or the association has preserved at least some vestige of these qualities in our present ethos.

Another association with reed pipes remains. The bagpipe was pastoral in origin, and, although played by many town musicians in the Middle Ages, when its penetrating tone colour and its lusty drones were appropriate, it largely remained rustic. During a back-to-nature movement in 18th-century France, however, when the rural and the simple became stylish, the gentry adopted the bagpipe, refining some of its grosser features. Reduced in size, provided with an under-the-arm bellows, covered with velvet, and decorated with embroidery, ribbons, or tassles, the instrument emerged as the stylish musette in which guise it served its new purpose and gave its name to the French dance of the period. The Scots, on the other hand, developed the bagpipe into a loud military instrument, which remains a part of pageantry in Great Britain.

The trumpet, freed from primitive rites, remained as a signalling instrument. It was reserved for princes and potentates in the East, and the crusaders carried the traditions into Europe along with the trumpet. Because the impecunious Emperor Sigismund in the early 15th century allowed the city of Augsburg to maintain trumpeters for a price, municipalities then began to share its prestige. In Germany particularly, trumpeters gained exclusive legal rights that made them pre-eminent over any musician, and this privilege died only with the demise of the clarin trumpet in the mid-18th century.

The development of the music drama nurtured extramusical associations. Probably beginning with the emergence of miracle plays in the 10th century, trumpets were associated with royalty, trombones with other important personages, and both flutes and reed pipes with shepherds or pastoral scenes. In cantatas, in operas, and in program music these connections still remain.

Extra-musical associations

Society has always valued wind instruments, from their earliest uses in primitive ceremony down to the marching band of today. The many depictions in the *Cantigas de Santa Maria,* the books of King Alfonso the Wise of Spain (1252–84), now found in the library of El Escorial near Madrid, indicate the importance of wind instruments in that environment, while records of medieval processions show wind instruments in significant numbers. Although numerous papal instructions forbade the use of instrumental music in liturgical service, instruments were undoubtedly used or the instructions would not have been repeated so often. It is difficult to explain the profusion of carvings of musicians playing instruments at Beverley, in Humberside, England, for instance, unless it be assumed that the actual musicians had been welcome in the minster.

Within the course of the Renaissance and Baroque, princes used extravagant musical events to demonstrate their power and wealth. Such records as those of the wedding of Cosimo I, duke of Florence, to Leanor de Toledo in 1539 and "The Triumphal Procession of Emperor Maximillian," depicted in woodcuts by Hans Burgkmair the Elder and others, give ample evidence of the popularity of winds. Silent evidence remains in the inventories of many palaces and great houses: Count Georg Raymund Fugger of Augsburg, for instance, listed around 400 instruments, 111 of which were flutes. In England, 272 of Heny VIII's 381 recorded instruments were winds. Wind instruments reached a peak of popularity at the end of the Renaissance.

Establishment of the *Stadtpfeiffer* and *Grande Écurie*

Professionalism was nourished in Germany by the *Stadtpfeiffer,* a municipal organization of wind-instrument players who performed for town ceremonies and also for weddings and the more elaborately scored church music. In France during the reign of Louis XIV, the *Grande Écurie* cultivated wind instruments and contained within their group the finest players and wind-instrument makers. The *Grande Écurie* furnished wind music for royal occasions and also provided players for other ensembles. At a different level, amateur musicians included the famous English diarist Samuel Pepys, whose love of the recorder was matched only by his devotion to his viol and lute. As public concerts began, contemporaneously with Pepys, the middle classes became further involved in music. Among the amateurs of note was Frederick II the Great of Prussia, who hired the German musician and composer Johann Joachim Quantz to teach him the flute. Folk music was still supplied with its share of wind instruments, and in its own milieu many instruments of earlier times are still preserved.

With the passing of patronage from royal establishments to the public, art music simply found a broader base for support, while amateur music thrived at its own level. The 20th century marks another high point in the cultivation of wind instruments; the quantity of instruments is greater than ever, and technical development has reached new heights, while never before have so many become competent performers.

Craftsmanship in wind instruments. The value placed upon musical instruments has usually been reflected in the application of the best craftsmanship of the time to the instrument. Whereas instruments of a primitive society may be decorated with symbolic design or perhaps red colouring, more advanced cultures may provide elaborate inlay and elegant carving.

The Chinese *so-na*

Form itself may be highly decorative in winds. The *so-na,* the Chinese shawm, possesses the same grace and symmetry of a pagoda, the brass bell on the end of the tube visually supporting the conical shaft. The tube is gracefully indented for each finger hole, leaving a series of diminishing concentric circles between the finger holes, which are fittingly capped by the small brass pirouette and a short reed. The related *sūrnāy* of Persia, simply a symmetrical shape ending in a bell, may be decorated with inlay. As an import to Europe in the Middle Ages, the oliphant, an animal horn made from an elephant's tusk, was highly prized not only for the ivory itself but for its fabulous carvings. Such carvings, which cannot harm the tone of a wind instrument, are found sporadically throughout the history of winds. The typical profile of baroque woodwinds was lovely without decoration, the bulges at the sockets serving both a utilitarian and an artistic purpose. The addition of ivory rings at the joints added to their beauty. Among the more fantastic and ingenious specimens of woodwinds are certain flutes and clarinets of the late 18th century made as functional walking sticks.

Undecorated brass instruments with their graceful curves demand little additional garnishment; yet even these graceful instruments were frequently embellished on the rim of the bell or on the bell itself, particularly by the famous Nürnberg makers of the 17th and 18th centuries. Seams in brass were often reinforced by sleeves or balls to make them highly decorative. The most elaborate and grotesque decorations, however, emerged in the Renaissance, possibly inspired by the Chinese. Instruments were built especially for ostentatious, festive dramatic performances for royalty and their guests. Trumpets have been found shaped like dragons, the bell transformed into the dragon's head. At times a tongue was even inserted to vibrate when the instrument was blown, and scales were painted on the outside. Such extravagances appeared sporadically in the following centuries.

Elaborate key mechanism has inhibited decoration in woodwinds in the 20th century, and makers of brasses have generally been satisfied with the pure beauty of the functional design of their instruments.

THE HISTORY OF WIND INSTRUMENTS

In the study of musical instruments the name of Curt Sachs looms so large that, despite the studies made since his death in 1959, no one has yet achieved his eminence in the field of musical instruments. The origins of musical instruments extends to prehistoric times, and frequently only fantastic legends survive; yet, by combining information from anthropology, history, and linguistics, Sachs made discoveries, developed theories, and drew conclusions that have stimulated much research in and given purpose to the entire field. Much of the following material leans on his research and perception.

Early history. The sources of information are often nebulous. In a few instances, actual instruments have been preserved for thousands of years. Many depictions of instruments remain, but few give accurate detail. Legend and written records reveal other facts. Finally, among the instruments of contemporary primitive civilizations, those of exotic cultures, and those of folk cultures are some that have not changed basically in thousands of years. The study of what information is available reveals many facts and allows much plausible speculation when facts are obscure.

There are many conjectures concerning the origin of wind instruments, and, since they are found widely scattered over the face of the Earth, it is quite likely that the process of vibrating the lips against a hole in a branch, a bone, a shell, an animal horn, or a tusk may have been discovered independently in many primitive cultures. Their origin may, in fact have transcended even the first lip buzzing. Many primitive cultures employ these same mediums as masks with which to disguise the voice in magical or religious rites; their use as musical instruments appears to have been an afterthought. Such megaphones are still used today in as widely dissimilar cultures as those of Switzerland and the Brazilian Indians. The conch shell, the most frequent of marine shells used to produce sound, probably began its service to music as a voice distorter, later to become an effective trumpet.

Trumpets. Bamboo, cane, and the limbs or trunks of trees form other materials for primitive trumpets. The Australian didgeridoo, for instance, can be made either from cane or, more frequently, a eucalyptus branch, often hollowed out by termites. Sounding only one or two pitches, the possibilities of varying tone qualities are exploited to produce various rhythmic and colourful backgrounds for a singer. From the New Kingdom of Egypt in the tomb of King Tutankhamen (died *c.* 1350 BC) was found the earliest specimen of a silver trumpet. Later the *salpinx,* also a straight trumpet, was known in Greece. A beautiful specimen made of 13 fitted sections of ivory with a bronze bell (Boston Museum of Fine Arts) is ascribed to the 5th century BC. The Roman equivalent, the tuba, was bronze and reached Rome from the Etruscans.

The earliest silver trumpet

Another Roman trumpet was the *lituus,* a J-shaped instrument whose immediate origin was also Etruscan. Its inspiration, visible in its earliest examples, was a simple hollow cane with a cow horn for a bell. Similar instruments are also found in China, where the *cha chiao* adds a shallow and flat Oriental mouthpiece to the same basic design. Another long trumpet of Rome was the cornu, which was curved to a G-shape for portability and braced crosswise for carrying over the shoulder.

Horns. As ancient as the trumpet is the natural horn, which was derived from an animal horn or a tusk. With the multifarious species of horned animals, the African countries achieved a rich variety of shapes, sizes, and pitches. The earliest and the most progressive horns were end blown, but many side-blown horns remain in use even today, particularly in Africa. Such horns are sometimes dyed with blood, carved, or left in their original state. In medieval Europe the possession of an oliphant, a horn carved from an elephant tusk, was an important status symbol among the nobility. Even today the cow's horn is made into a signalling instrument in Europe and is frequently embellished with metal mountings.

The *shofar*

The *shofar* deserves special mention, for it has served the Jewish religion since the beginning of historic times and is now retained for New Year's and Yom Kippur (Day of Atonement) in most congregations. The instrument is merely a goat's or ram's horn, flattened and bent in a steaming process. The various ritual blasts use the second and third partial only, and its mighty sound was considered efficacious in reaching the ear of Yahweh.

The Roman version of the animal horn was the *buccina,* whose recent ancestry was merely the ox horn, sometimes supplied with a mouthpiece. Although ostensibly the *buccina* was a shepherd's instrument, its bronze counterpart was suitably decorated for use in the Roman army.

More impressive, however, were the *lurer* (singular *lur*), the early bronze horns of the Scandinavians. Conical and shaped in pairs, like the curves of mammoth tusks, they have a funnel-shaped mouthpiece and end in a flat studded disk. Although their origin was once thought to have been as early as 3000 BC, 1600 to 1000 BC now appears more likely. The line of development would appear to have passed from metal-studded animal horns to the impressive bronze pieces, many of which have been excavated in Denmark. The effective mouthpiece allowed production of tones to the 11th or 12th partial, but it appears unlikely that these unusual instruments had much influence on later European horns.

Flutes. Flutes are ubiquitous in primitive civilizations and in early depictions are sometimes confused with reed pipes. Their most primitive forms have already been mentioned. In early historical periods they were known in Sumer and Egypt, and in the latter country specimens have been found in tombs, excellently preserved through the centuries by the arid climate. The flute is vertical, about a yard long and a half-inch wide, and is easily end blown because of its narrow embouchure. Near the lower end there are two to six finger holes. The instruments exist today and are known by the Persian name *nāy.* In Greece panpipes, undoubtedly derived from the more sophisticated Chinese instruments, were shepherds' instruments. A series of graduated closed-end tubes were bound like a raft and end blown.

Egypt also made clarinets, instruments composed of two canes with three sides of a rectangle cut obliquely in the upper end of the two single reeds. The term idioglottic is used to describe a reed cut from the tube itself. From four to six equidistant finger holes are cut in each cane, and blowing with the entire reed engulfed in the mouth cavity produces a pungent, tremulous sound. The slight deviation of pitch between the two tubes creates the beats that cause the tremolo. The device was to be rediscovered or copied in organ pipes late in the 15th century in Germany. Sachs saw a double clarinet on a relief dated 2700 BC in the Egyptian Museum in Cairo. The same instrument is known today as *zummārah* wherever Islāmic civilization flourished; and closely related instruments—the *arghūl* of the Near East, which has one long drone pipe and one short fingered pipe, and the *launeddas* of Sardinia, which consists of three pipes—also preserve the same shrill, reedy sound that must have been characteristic four centuries ago.

The New Kingdom (1567–1085 BC) reveals the Egyptian oboe, known only as *mat,* the generic name of pipes. Like the flute, the oboes were made of narrow cane but were about two feet long; and, like the clarinet, they were blown in pairs, the left playing a drone while the right fingered a melody. Such instruments with their rich, penetrating sound have been known through the ages under various names and various shapes. Their effect has always been intoxicating. The Greek version of the double reed, the aulos, has been referred to. The two divergent narrow pipes activated by a large reed would create a loud, pungent sound highly prized by the Greeks. Probably no wind instrument has received as much praise over such an extended period of time.

The ancient Egyptian oboe

The idea of the hydraulis, a water organ, may have stemmed from the multitubed panpipe. Its main development appears to have been around Alexandria from the 3rd century BC. Air under hydraulic pressure activated the pipes as controlled by an elementary keyboard. The tone was reported to be loud and penetrating. Despite the invention of pneumatic power, the hydraulis lasted at least through the 5th century AD.

Developments in the Middle Ages. Western society in the Middle Ages went through crises that created decisive changes in music and musical instruments. Except for the *tibia,* which was the Roman equivalent of the aulos, Rome showed little interest in Greek instruments, preferring the more powerful brasses that could be heard in such spectacular events as those given at the Colosseum. So Greek music dissolved, and its instruments dispersed to the countryside. The invasions of migratory tribes began in AD 150, culminating in the fall of Rome in AD 476 and continuing long past that date. With Greek and Roman culture in decline, the migratory peoples might have established their own music; but they brought few musical instruments. The Christians, who controlled the Roman Empire after the conversion of the emperor Constantine (AD 312), had little love for the musical instruments associated with earlier persecutions. Folk instruments, of course, remained, and such documents as the Utrecht Psalter (*c.* 830; Utrecht, Bibliotheek der Reiksuniversiteit) contain drawings showing instruments, but there is little to indicate a flourishing musical culture. The great centres of learning in general as well as the cultivation of music and the playing of instruments remained in the Near East.

Influence of Islām on medieval musical instruments

The most significant movement affecting the history of medieval musical instruments was the spread of Islām in the 7th and the first half of the 8th centuries, by which time it had arrived at its maximum expansion—west across Africa as far as Southern Spain, south down the coast of eastern Africa to Madagascar, and east through Persia, northern India, and Indochina to Indonesia and the southernmost Philippine Islands. The Christians began pushing back the Muslims in the 9th and 10th centuries in Spain, Sicily, and Sardinia. In addition to this most obvious contact, the trade routes brought continuous Muslim products into the European cities engaged in Eastern commerce, especially Venice, Genoa, and Pisa; and from the late 11th to the early 13th centuries the Crusades took Christians to Muslim homelands, where they further absorbed Near Eastern ideas and customs. Finally, a slower, less dramatic route existed across the Balkans and to the north, by which musical instruments drifted from the Near East or Byzantium into the countries of northern Europe and on west to Iceland. Neither the Christians nor the Muslims attained their political or religious objectives in their conflicts, but the stimulation of the progressive civilization of the Muslims nevertheless had a profound effect in Europe.

In the manuscript of the *Cantigas de Santa María,* illuminations depict Muslims in their own costumes playing their instruments next to Christians, who are playing closely related specimens. If the West had not had strength and some tradition, Western music today would be Oriental. Instead, the West modified the instruments and developed them in special ways. The Eastern melody and drone, combined with rhythm, were retained through the period and, indeed, to this day in much of Western folk music. The development of polyphony forced changes in many musical instruments. With voice parts covering much the same general range, each instrument had to possess a distinctive colour and a power of penetration to delineate its musical part.

Among the earlier primitive instruments, the animal horn remained, often decorated and even provided with holes to allow the production of melody but leaving little evidence that it contributed to cultured music. The trumpet in the 13th and 14th centuries was bent back upon itself in the shape of a very flat S, making it easier to hold and carry, but the peculiar idiom of the trumpet limited it to fanfares and signals. It could not join with lesser instruments.

Woodwinds of the Gothic period

As with the trumpet, the important woodwind instruments of the medieval period did not appear until the Gothic period. The vertical flute, single and double, came from the Near East and remains today in the Balkans. A single short pipe, always associated with the drum (tabor), still persists in the Basque regions of Spain and France. Too narrow to sound the fundamental, the pipe needs only two finger holes and a thumb hole to complete its scale, and it can thus be played with the left hand alone, freeing the right hand to beat the tabor and leaving the legs free to dance. The transverse flute moved from the Byzantine Empire to Germany in the late Middle Ages. Although associated with the fiddle during the minnesinger period of the 12th and 13th centuries, it soon became linked with the drum and military music in the form of the fife.

A folk clarinet, often double, used a cow horn for a bell and occasionally a second cow horn to provide a wind chamber around the reed. Known as the hornpipe in England, the instrument is called by various names from Wales along the Mediterranean to India. The instrument may also appear with the reeds enclosed in a calabash (*magudi* or *pungi* of India) or in sheep's bladder (bladder pipe).

Origin of the bagpipe

Ostensibly, the bagpipe appears to have been a development of the simpler enclosed reed instruments, but actually the bagpipe was known to Rome (Latin *utriculus*), where it was presumably a recent import from Asia in the 1st century AD. The bag was formed originally from the entire hide of a sheep or goat, with the chanter, the pipe with finger holes, fitted into a wooden stock at the neck. When drones are present, they emerge from stocks in the forelegs. A blowpipe is necessary to fill the bag with air, and an arm over the bag provides pressure to activate the pipes. The chanter has seven holes in front and a thumbhole behind.

The pneumatic organ appeared around the 2nd century AD as a portative variety—that is, an organ small enough to be carried. These organs consisted of one or more ranks of flue pipes controlled by a keyboard. To aid portability, the ususal two octaves had only the essential chromatic notes. From the Gothic period, portatives were frequently found both in pictures of processions and in seated ensembles. Depictions show the player operating a bellows with his left hand while manipulating the keys with the second and third fingers of his right hand. Various references show the presence of organs of many sizes throughout the Middle Ages. By the 10th century the nonportable positive organ began its distinguished career as the earliest form of church organ.

The Renaissance. The major accomplishment of music in the Renaissance was the emancipation of instrumental from vocal music. As polyphony developed, the two- and three-part music of the 13th century expanded to a norm of four parts in the art music of the late 15th century and to five or six parts by the middle of the 16th. Early in this vertical expansion the voice parts were differentiated in range, forming a texture extending to approximately three to three and a half octaves. Apart from the organ, no winds possessed a diatonic range of that size. Furthermore, as the voice parts spread, the penetrating and contrasting quality so advantageous for the crossing parts in medieval music became less desirable. The music of the time then demanded the building of instruments in different sizes for the various parts in order to secure a smooth blend throughout the texture. Such ensembles were called consorts. Wind instruments flourished. At no time in the history of music was the choice of available timbres greater, and within the 16th century as many instruments as possible were built in families. The common sizes, built a fifth apart, were called the treble, tenor, and bass, usually with corresponding pitches in winds of a, d, and G. Flutes and recorders were an octave higher. A descant and a great bass were introduced for music that exceeded the combined range of the standard instruments. Woodwinds, in general, were made in one piece in a plain design, and Venice appears to have been the centre of wind-instrument manufacture.

Common sizes of Renaissance woodwinds

The new concept of blending tone quality was applied to the flutes and recorders. Both were made with a relatively large cylindrical bore, which emphasized the low partials. As a result, the upper range was limited, but the effective octave and a half that remained was sufficient for Renaissance music. Since the transverse flute adapted less well to various sizes, it was more often used with other instruments.

Double reeds were particularly numerous, and in many species the reeds were capped. The best known of these was the crumhorn (German *Krummhorn*), an instrument of narrow cylindrical bore whose intriguing J shape complemented its pungent, buzzy tone. The reed cap may have been inspired by bladder pipes or bagpipes in which the reed is activated without lip contact. The cap protected the large reed within so the instrument could not be overblown. Its seven finger holes, one thumbhole, and one upper key gave a range of only nine notes. Nevertheless, the crumhorn consort made an excellent ensemble, and some fine early sets of instruments still survive as testimony.

Other soft-toned capped double reeds, known largely from written descriptions and pictorial sources, are the Italian *cornamusa,* probably little more than a crumhorn without the nonfunctional curved area, and the *dolzaina,* appearing much the same as the *cornamusa.* A loud capped reed was the schryari, made in the three principal sizes. The outer shape was inverse conical, but, since no specimens remain, the contour of the bore is unknown.

Double-reed instruments

Shawms were a particularly important family of loud double reeds, with related instruments spread across all of Asia. Their wide conical bore, large double reed, and seven front finger holes provided them with a loud, reedy tone, reminiscent of Near Eastern shawms of today. The player could rest his lips on a wooden pirouette into which the reed was inserted and activate the reed without contact in the wind chamber formed in his mouth. Nevertheless, the reed could be controlled if desired, and the instrument was overblown partly through the second octave. Shawms were made in progressive sizes from the small descant in a′ to the great bass in GG or FF, the latter attaining a length of eight to nine feet (about 2½ metres). The power of the shawms enabled them to consort with trombones and to carry well in the outdoor tower music of central European cities.

The more gentle curtal (German *Dulzian;* Italian *fagotto;* French *basson*) was a noncapped double reed with its conical bore doubled back within the same block and ending in a small bell. It was activated by a long, carefully trimmed double reed connected with the instrument proper by a short tube called the *bocal.* Six front finger holes, two thumbholes, and two keys gave it a range of two octaves and a second. First mentioned in 1540, its bass (sometimes called the double curtal in England and the *Choristfagott* in Germany) soon became the most important size, particularly at the beginning of the Baroque period, when it was needed for a bass whenever higher winds were scored. German church composers of the 17th century normally used the *Choristfagott* as a bass for violins and violas as well. The double reeds with doubled back cylindrical bores were an interesting development. The *sordone* (French *courtaut*) was such an instrument, its narrow bore terminating in a side vent near the *bocal.* Most extraordinary was the racket, whose narrow bore went through a cylinder of ivory or wood as many as nine times to make a double-bass instrument from a cylinder length of a few inches. The instrument plays an octave below notation and forms the lowest of the Renaissance winds. The Renaissance reeds that were not adaptable to outdoor music vanished early in the 17th century, except for the curtal. The shawm survived somewhat longer.

The *cornetto*

Another important woodwind was the *cornetto* (an Italian name sometimes anglicized as cornett; also known under its German name, *Zink*), the descendant of the medieval cow's horn with finger holes. The treble *cornetto* in d′ was made from two pieces of wood, hollowed out and glued together to create a mildly conical tube, usually octagonal and most often curved in the shape of its prototype. A covering of leather, protecting the surface and sealing any leaks, was frequently decorated at the upper end. The *cor-*

netto was made in larger sizes, but only the descant was widely used.

The trumpet maintained its usefulness as a ceremonial instrument and developed in the direction more fully described in the next section. The trombone blended nicely in consort with cornetts as the treble instrument or in the loud consort in the company of shawms.

Baroque and Classical period. Dramatic events in music around 1600 in Italy profoundly affected the music of Europe during the Baroque era. A group of literary men and musicians who called themselves the Camerata gathered in the home of Count Giovanni Bardi in the last decade of the 16th century to experiment with a type of drama that would use music as an adjunct to poetry. The musical result was the negation of polyphony, the reduction of melody to a positon subservient to the text, and the creation of a bass line with improvised accompanying harmony to support the drama in the singing voice, altogether a direct repudiation of the ideals of the Renaissance. A 17th-century Italian composer, Claudio Monteverdi, referred to the style as *seconda prattica* and within his lifetime developed it into a much finer medium than the experimental style he inherited.

The new style affected instruments drastically. All those that could not produce expressive sounds and that could not imitate the passions as represented by the skilled singers were relegated to the middle or lower register of the ensemble, where they could serve either as an inconspicuous background or as a contrasting support for the predominately expressive melody. If the Renaissance was the era of woodwinds, the Baroque was the era of strings, and the violin family assumed a dominant position throughout both Baroque and Classical periods. Nevertheless, the winds were not forgotten, and before the end of the period they were altered in order to compete with the strings. In the meantime, the winds were useful for dance music and municipal music (*i.e.*, for town ceremonies). Particularly in Germany, the loud winds of the Renaissance continued to be used. They maintained their 16th-century functions of being played regularly from towers, and they were always available for music in churches and palaces.

Despite the revolutionary character of the Camerata and the other advanced movements of the time, tradition remained strong in Italy, France, England, and Germany, and Renaissance winds continued for a time. By the early 1730s, when Bach and Handel were producing many of their great works, reaction set in against the presumed pretentiousness of the elaborate Baroque style, and a premium was placed on simplicity and clarity. The importance of the bass line diminished, and the counterpoint, reborn in the 18th-century style, was again abandoned. By mid-century the sentimental style of an ornamented simple melody over an uncomplicated texture of basic tonal harmony had taken over, and it was on this foundation that Haydn and Mozart based their composition of a mature Classical style. The winds of the Renaissance were then preserved only in rural areas or as folk instruments; and the new winds, developed in the 18th century, challenged but never quite captured the supremacy of the strings.

Brass in Baroque opera

The Baroque opera demanded the depiction of the grand and majestic; so, obviously, the trumpet was important. The instrument of the Middle Ages was now compactly folded once to reduce seven feet of tube to only a little over two feet of length. The normal keys of the period were D or C, a crook lowering the D instrument when C was desired. The leading trumpeter played in the high or *clarino* range, which included the pitches of the fourth octave, where the tone was particularly magnificent and where the available diatonic notes permitted the playing of melodies, trills, and various ornaments. Other trumpets played successively lower pitches until one played only the fundamental. The trombone (German *Posaune;* English sackbut; French *saquebute;* Spanish *sacabuche*) was used in opera and church orchestras. By the Baroque period it was made in three sizes—f alto, B♭ tenor, and F bass—sizes that remained in use in Germany through much of the 19th century. The treble *cornetto* gained a new use in the Baroque. Since its range equalled that normally used by the violins in the 17th century, it could substitute for them or contrast them and also effectively contrast the soprano voice. Consequently, it was useful in Monteverdi's opera *Orfeo* (first performed 1607) and in many German church cantatas, as well as instrumental ensembles. Difficult to play, it was extremely treacherous, and to be played with sufficient control it needed not only a good musician but also one with luck. The names of the Renaissance winds are familiar to many music lovers since the Baroque organ adapted so many stops imitating the colour of these instruments. The beating reed adapted in the Renaissance regal was brought into the organ proper and formed a variety of useful colours.

Woodwind instruments were far too valuable for their individual tone colours to remain subservient to the ubiquitous violins; and in Paris the musician and instrument builder Jean Hotteterre, his family and associates all skilled wood turners, redesigned first the oboe and later the recorder, transverse flute, and bassoon—all in the last half of the 17th century. With the advent of these instruments, Renaissance woodwinds gradually vanished. The new instruments were turned in short sections, peculiarly with a broken profile—that is, an unevenly expanding or contracting bore between sections—a feature not long retained.

The oboe. The oboe (French *hautbois*) was first to compete with the violin. The upper register, difficult and incomplete in the shawms, had to be developed. Hotteterre narrowed the bore of the treble shawm, reduced the size of the finger holes, and considerably narrowed the reed, which was attached to a staple and inserted directly into the top section as in the musette. With the pirouette abandoned, the more delicate reed could be carefully controlled by the player and pinched between the lips to produce fast enough vibrations for overblowing. Hotteterre also lowered the customary d′ pitch in descant to c′ by fitting a "butterfly" key at the end; *i.e.*, in two-winged shape to accommodate the little finger of either hand. The oboe was immediately successful; in fact, it became the most favoured woodwind in the 18th century. Its tone was rich and expressive, and its better players could imitate all subtleties and expressive characteristics of highly trained operatic sopranos. A tenor form and a rare bass were not cultivated in art music. After the Renaissance, families of instruments were no longer necessary, and expressive playing was largely in demand in the soprano range. The English horn, or the alto oboe, was adopted around 1720 but made no great impact. The instrument was curved as a horn in its early form and covered with leather. Bach called it *oboe da caccia* and used it occasionally for its dark, smooth tone colour; the Classical composers generally ignored it.

Success of the oboe

The bassoon. The bassoon underwent far less radical changes in the hands of Hotteterre than the oboe. The curtal was simply built in four sections and lengthened to produce BB♭. Its introduction into the orchestra is uncertain since the double-reed instrument in the bass range was frequently taken for granted; but a French composer, Jean-Baptiste Lully, scored specifically for it in 1674. The standard bassoon for most of the 18th century had four keys, but six were common by the end of the century. The range was a remarkable three octaves, although the top b♭′ was available on few bassoons. As with the curtal, whose sound was mellow and obtrusive, the bassoon was praised for its tone and compared to the human voice, the ultimate in contemporaneous praise. Such comments testified to its success in playing expressively; and a considerable solo literature, rare among low-pitched instruments, bears further witness to its flexible melodic capabilities. Its service as a wind bass was indispensable. Some small bassoons, *tenoroons* and *fagottini,* were built in the century but remained obscure. More important was the contrabassoon, whose sporadic appearance in score probably reflected on its rarity more than its usefulness.

Developments in the recorder

The flute. The Renaissance recorder blended well in consort but was weak in its upper register and needed modification to meet the demand for an expressive melodic style. The very nature of the instrument, with its lack of lip control, prevented much command of forte and piano; but the Baroque changes nevertheless went far toward producing an expressive instrument. It is to be remembered that throughout the Baroque period the Italian term *flauto* referred to the recorder; the cross flute was normally called transverso or *flauto traverso* and was so indicated on scores. Although many ambiguous cases exist, the recorder was the type of flute called for in much of Baroque music. The redesigned recorder was built in three sections with an inverse conical bore in the middle and foot. Although the full consort sizes and many others were made, the treble recorder (with a bottom written note of f′) was the principal instrument used for solos and orchestral performance.

The transverse flute was also built in three sections with an inverse conical bore; and this flute as well as the recorder spoke better in the upper register. The E♭ key, as mentioned earlier, was soon added to make the instrument completely chromatic throughout its range (d′ to b♭‴). Intonation on the flute was nevertheless difficult. The necessary cross-fingerings caused a somewhat muffled quality. Consequently, the flute sounded best, and its technique was most facile in the key of D. Little flute music ventured far from the keys in one, two, or three sharps. To alleviate some of these problems and to adapt to the varying pitches at that time, after 1720 the middle section was often divided. Then the flute could be provided with from three to six different lengths for the upper of these sections. In spite of these difficulties, the one-keyed flute had a lovely tone, softer than the modern flute but pure and sweet. The addition of keys was inevitable. By 1760 some London makers added keys for f′, g♯, and b♭′, solving the usual cross-fingerings in the first octave. By the end of the 18th century, the flute was lengthened and the keys added for c′ and c♯′, thus matching the range of the oboe. The quality of the instrument changed little and its versatility improved.

The military fife, which retained the one-piece construction of the Renaissance, remained useful for its limited repertory, and the piccolo in B♭ or C was only occasionally used.

The clarinet. One of the most significant contributions to Western art music in the 18th century was the addition of the clarinet. The various cane instruments with a single reed and stemming from antiquity still remained in the area around the Mediterranean as folk instruments. Furthermore, the bagpipe had adapted the single-reed pipe as its chanter. The chalumeau, one of these single-reed folk instruments, occasionally emerged into art music, when the two oboists of the orchestra would use chalumeaus to imitate the sound of toy trumpets. Johann Christoph Denner, the renowned 16th-century recorder maker from Nürnberg, saw the possibilities of the instrument. He made them of boxwood, gave them an attached reed, and doubled their length, achieving a chalumeau register, as it is still called, from f to b♭′. Using the back key as a speaker, the instrument overblows at the 12th, making a *clarino* register from c′ to f″. Soon keys for b′, c♯″, and e♭″ were added, completing the classical clarinet. These extra keys also produced e, f♯, and a♭ in the chalumeau register, providing a total usable range of three octaves and one note. The clarinet had then emerged. Again, those describing the instrument compared its virtues to the human voice, and the instrument was adopted wherever players were available. Compared to the instruments of today, the cylindrical bore was narrow and the reed smaller to fit the long, narrow mouthpiece. Furthermore, the mouthpiece was inserted so that the reed, attached with cord, was on the upper side of the instrument.

Adaptation of the chalumeau

Early clarinets were made largely in C or B♭, sometimes with an A section to use on the B♭ instrument. Small F clarinets were available for use in bands; but, as with the other woodwinds of the time, a pair of treble clarinets were sufficient for the orchestra.

The basset horn

A more important auxiliary instrument was the basset horn, which provided an extension of the bore to take the chalumeau range down to c. The untimely demise of the basset horn in the 19th century has been regretted by many, for modern experimentation has shown it to be vastly superior to the alto clarinet in E♭ commonly used in bands.

The French horn. Another major contribution in the 18th century was the emergence of the French horn as an orchestral instrument. Early in the century the tone of the horn was appropriate for its use in signalling during the hunt. By midcentury, the mouthpiece had been altered and the hand inserted in the bell to provide the warm, mellow quality in midrange that Classical composers found so useful. Consequently, much experimentation to increase its usefulness ensued, resulting in the crooks and in hand stopping. Even with its severe limitations, the horn of the Classical period became an essential colour.

The trumpet. After the mid-18th century, high melodic parts in the trumpet appeared less necessary to an aesthetic that spurned the majestic for a simpler style. Trumpets were built in many keys, but for the most part trumpets in F replaced those in D and C; and the notes of the fourth octave, which were most difficult on the shorter instrument, were abandoned. In short, the complete *clarino* style disappeared along with those players of the privileged guild who had learned to master that treacherous range. The F trumpet remained standard in Europe through the 19th century.

Romantic period. In the 19th century the pendulum swung from the restraint of the classic to the emotionally expressive. The aesthetic demanded an emphasis on the personal, on the dramatic, and on the passionate. Music responded with modulation to remote keys and required instruments in increased range, more facile technique, and wider dynamic contrast. Obviously, instruments had to be adjusted. Families of instruments again became important, and new tone colours were introduced.

The entire period has sometimes appropriately been called the age of mechanization. Around the first quarter of the century, the period of Beethoven's major orchestral works, more keys were added to existing woodwinds, and evidence from one passage in Beethoven's *Ninth Symphony* infers that the fourth horn player already had one valve on his instrument. Almost immediately afterward more drastic changes were necessary in order to fulfill the demands of the composers.

The central figure in the changes in woodwinds was a Munich flutist and instrument builder, Theobald Böhm. Profiting by the experiments of many others, Böhm devised the long axle to allow control of holes from some distance and then proceeded to redesign the flute on acoustical principles. Böhm made the holes in his flute as large as possible and changed all closed keys to open keys to allow full venting. He then placed all holes in an acoustically correct position, providing for comfort in fingering by using ring keys on the long axle to close holes that players could not reach easily. At this stage the Böhm conical flute of 1832 appeared. By 1847 Böhm had become convinced that only a cylindrical bore would solve certain problems in intonation, and by using covered finger holes he could make them even larger. The Böhm experiments changed the character of the flute considerably, producing more volume and a more brilliant tone; but with his improvements, along with the subsequent minor changes, the flute became one of the most versatile instruments of the orchestra, performing superbly in all keys.

Böhm's innovations in instrument building

Similar changes were made over the midcentury in other woodwinds, the Böhm system (1843) adaptations to the clarinet finally conquering other key arrangements except in Germany. Charles Triébert and his son modified the oboe, finally adding some features from the Böhm flute to produce the "conservatory system." Certain improvements were made in the bassoon in 1825 by Carl Almanräder, a chamber musician of Biebrich. Since the improvements were accompanied by deficiencies in tone, the French preferred to develop the classic bassoon. Although the Heckel family (Johann Adam Heckel and Wilhelm, his son and successor), also of Biebrich, eventually corrected the faults, the difference between the French and the German bassoon still remains, the former having a reedier, more individual tone, the latter with its comparative richness blending better. First the Americans and finally the British accepted the German instrument.

The classic orchestra reached a certain perfection in balance between strings, woodwinds, and brass, which was distorted at the beginning of the 19th century by the addition of two horns and three trombones. From there on, the orchestra grew, and families of instruments again became important for additional colour and for balance. In his *Osnovy orkestrovki* (1913; *Principles of Orchestration,* written 1896–1908), the Russian composer Nikolay Rimsky-Korsakov developed the theory that the four basic woodwinds had a vast range of expression. At each end of the entire range were areas useful for their individual colour, and the instruments of smaller and larger sizes intensified those colour effects. This theory formed the basis of his orchestration and had profound effects on the art music of the early 20th century, even to the popular hotel dance bands of the 1930s in America.

Woodwinds of the 19th-century orchestra

The piccolo was accepted early, carrying upward and intensifying the brilliance of the top octave of the flute. It remained for the 20th century to exploit the low tones of the piccolo. By the end of the 19th century the alto flute, a weak instrument dynamically, joined the orchestra but was exploited most effectively by the French Impressionist composers of the early 20th century—for example, Claude Debussy. The oboe developed no satisfactory descant, but the English horn, first used notably in Hector Berlioz's *Roman Carnival Overture* (1844), became increasingly useful for its peculiar dark and melancholy expression. A small clarinet in D (E♭ in wind bands) proved effective for bright, strident effects, while the bass clarinet added a mysterious piquancy as an extension of the dark and colourful chalumeau register. The contrabassoon gained importance as the most effective wind double bass and the lowest instrument of the orchestra.

Little needs to be added about the trumpet and French horn. By midcentury, valves were established for horns and trumpets, but even through the early works of the 20th-century German composer Richard Strauss these were considered largely as a means for instant transposition of the instrument. At the same time, however, the full chromatic possibilities were exploited by such composers as the Frenchman César Franck and the Russian Tchaikovsky.

Since 1590 a wooden cup-mouthpieced instrument, the serpent, had been built to support boys' voices in French choirs; but by the mid-18th century it was serving as a double bass for the woodwind choir. The serpent and its derivatives, the Russian bassoon and the bass horn, were eventually replaced by the contrabassoon. The ophicleide, the bass of the keyed bugle, was prominent in the second quarter of the 19th century as a brass double bass.

The invention of the bass tuba by a German instrument builder named Johann Gottfried Moritz in 1835 provided a more reliable and more even brass bass. Tuned in F or E♭, its range was, respectively, BB♭–e♭′ and C–f′. Later a BB♭ contrabass became available. The tuba was distinguished by a wide conical bore and a deep cup mouthpiece, both of which favoured the fundamental and lower partials. It was built in many sizes to provide a rich and mellow brass choir for the wind band, of which the cornet of similar proportions was the lead melodic instrument, in contrast to the more penetrating trumpet of the orchestra. The flügelhorn, slightly more conical than the cornet, is also an appropriate treble for the tuba family. The tubing of the various instruments could be and was bent in many different shapes. Some even had bells pointing backward in order to send the sound toward marching soldiers in a parade. When the bass instrument was bent into an over-the-shoulder model, it was called a helicon. Later, the American bandmaster John Philip Sousa established his own variation of the helicon, and it became known as the sousaphone.

The Wagner tubas

Also noteworthy are the Wagner tubas, especially built for Richard Wagner's operas *Der Ring des Nibelungen* (*The Ring of the Nibelung*). Narrower in bore than the baritone horn, they are supplied with a funnel-shaped mouthpiece in order to form a tone intermediate between the French horn and the tuba. Built in tenor and bass ranges, the instruments fulfill their purpose admirably.

The 19th century gave rise to families of reed instruments. The Belgian instrument maker Adolphe Sax patented the saxophone in 1846, combining a wide conical bore with a large single reed and producing an instrument that overblows at the octave and covers a written range of b♭ to f‴. Sax's patent covered instruments in 14 different sizes, and others were added later. Intended for the military band, the saxophone has found only occasional use in the orchestra. It has been used most familiarly in America in dance orchestras of the 1930s and 1940s.

The Chinese *sheng,* which had reached Europe in the late 18th century, inspired the invention of three distinct musical instruments in the West: the mouth organ, the accordion, and the reed organ. It is a mouth organ consisting of free-reed pipes vibrating under wind pressure from a globular wind chamber blown into by the player. The pitch is determined by the reed itself, which activates vibrations in the surrounding air.

The Western mouth organ, invented *c.* 1825, has two reeds of the same pitch, one of which vibrates as the player exhales, the other, as he inhales. The slotted edge that the player puts in his mouth directs air to and from the reeds. Tones are eliminated by covering the slots, so that a skillful player can produce a single pleasant tone at a time. Although a few players have developed a skilled technique, the instrument is normally completely diatonic and is largely confined to folk and popular music.

Invented in 1822 by Friedrich Buschmann of Germany, one of the mouth-organ patenters, and operating on the same principle was the accordion, in which a bellows substitutes for the breath and buttons or keys open channels to free reeds. Melody is controlled by the right hand, the bass and accompanying chords, by the left. Although originally a diatonic instrument, by midcentury it became chromatic. Accordions with keyboard for the right hand have also become popular.

Invention of the reed organ

The reed organ dates from as early as 1810. It was a free-reed instrument with a foot-operated bellows providing wind pressure to vibrate reeds whose access was controlled by a keyboard. Provided with an assortment of Greek-derived trade names, the harmonium appears to be most prominent for those organs operating on the principle of pressure bellows. From about 1836, an instrument operating on sucker bellows was invented in France and taken to America, where it became the prototype for many American reed organs. In the 19th century the reed organ, mellow in tone and inexpensive, became an important instrument in homes and small churches.

The 20th century. The 20th century began with few radically new ideas in instruments. Many people were still debating the merits of Wagner and Brahms while Richard Strauss, the Impressionists, and the Russian nationalists were each continuing the exploitations of the tone colour and technical capacities of the expanded orchestra. Challenged by these works, instrument makers continued to make minor alterations to solve fingering problems or to produce even tone. For a time the standards of increased size and greater technical capacity were most important, but eventually such works as Arnold Schoenberg's *Pierrot Lunaire* (1912) and Anton von Webern's *Five Pieces for Orchestra* (1911–13) disturbed the overripe late Romanticism, and the emphasis on bigness evaporated. The entire aesthetic became confused. In general, after the first quarter of the century, ensembles became smaller and an anti-Romantic if not a purely Classical trend was discernible. In instruments, two diverse directions became apparent: (1) a return to the historically accurate sounds for the music of the repertory and (2) the application of electrical power to do everything from duplicating known tone colours with artificial amplification to the creation of entirely new instruments. Since the second trend has little concern with wind instruments, it can be disregarded. The first trend, however, produced important effects.

Revival of Baroque woodwinds

Most revolutionary was the reproduction of early brasses and woodwinds. Around 1925 an English musician and instrument builder named Arnold Dolmetsch began reproducing the Baroque recorder, which had been in eclipse for over 100 years and which again became one of the most widely played wind instruments. More recently, reproductions of other historical instruments became available, including crumhorns, shawms, *Rauschpfife,* Renaissance flutes and recorders, Baroque transverse flutes, Baroque oboes, and Baroque trombones. The Baroque trumpet was again made, although few trumpeters returned to the valveless eight-foot D trumpet of the period; with a discreet use of narrow bores, shallow mouthpieces, and valves, they obtained trumpets that give the range and character of the clarin trumpet.

In the United States and Canada, a tremendous number of schoolchildren began to learn wind instruments in order to play in school bands, and the quality of performance rose continually. Younger people have produced better music each year on better wind instruments. (R.A.Wa.)

THE MUSIC OF WIND INSTRUMENTS

In the West. Although medieval manuscript illustrations suggest that wind instruments were commonly used during the Middle Ages, no repertory of their music has been preserved. They were probably used in consort with string and percussion instruments to accompany voices or even in lieu of voices to perform secular music. According to illustrations from the 14th and 15th centuries, certain loud instruments, such as trumpets, sackbuts, shawms, and bagpipes were used to perform outdoors or for particularly noisy events indoors. Other, softer instruments, such as recorders, transverse flutes, and crumhorns, were used primarily indoors. In the performance of both the sacred motet and the secular chanson, winds frequently were used in broken consort with bowed or plucked string instruments and voices. The tenor part of a mass or motet was often performed by a wind instrument such as the trombone.

The 16th-century preference for homogenous tone colour bred a large repertory of music for matched consorts of recorders, crumhorns, and brasses. Most of this consort music consisted either of dance pieces or of transcriptions of vocal madrigals, chansons, or motets. The first music written specifically for wind instruments was composed during the 16th century. The Italian composer Silvestro Ganassi's *Fontegara* (1535) for the flute is the earliest known method of instruction for a wind instrument; and one of the first compositions for winds to designate precise instrumentation is Giovanni Gabrieli's *Sonata pian'e forte* (1597) for cornetto, six trombones, and violin. Heinrich Schütz, a German pupil of Gabrieli, followed his master's style in the use of wind instruments. Many of Schütz's sacred vocal works specify cornetti, trombones, bassoons, or, occasionally, trumpets.

First music composed specifically for winds

Several composers continued to write for consorts of similar wind instruments well into the 17th century. Johann Christoph Pezel, a German, was widely known as a composer of *turmsonaten,* music written for a brass choir to play from the tower of the city hall or a church. Municipal musicians, or *Stadtpfeifer,* were employed by many German towns to perform at weddings, funerals, and civic celebrations.

The Baroque era. Claudio Monteverdi's first operatic masterpiece, *Orfeo,* specified a splendid array of wind instruments, including two wooden pipe organs, four trombones, a reed organ, two cornetti, two soprano recorders, a clarin trumpet, and three additional muted trumpets. These wind instruments contrasted vividly with a large complement of bowed and plucked strings. Although opera orchestras after the middle of the 17th century were dominated by an ensemble of strings, winds were featured in certain operatic scores, both in Italy and in France. The operas of the Italians Marc' Antonio Cesti and Francesco Cavalli most often displayed trumpets, less frequently employed recorders and bassoons, and occasionally used cornetti and trombones. Jean-Baptiste Lully, court composer of Louis XIV, prepared a sizable repertory of military marches for ensembles of double-reed instruments. The ready availability of oboists may explain the appearance of oboe parts in all of Lully's operatic scores.

During the early 18th century, transverse flutes gradually gained favour over recorders. The Baroque aesthetic favoured competition between instruments of contrasting tone colour, so that composers of orchestral music frequently pitted the basic core of strings against the brighter sound of solo or paired trumpets, oboes, or flutes. Since these wind passages normally imitated the thematic material assigned to strings, a high level of technical facility was demanded. Instrumental technique was facilitated by superior wind instruments made by the famous master craftsmen of the early 18th century.

The later Baroque era boasts a large corpus of solo music for winds, both in the concerto repertory and in chamber music. Especially notable are the trumpet concertos of the Italian Giuseppe Torelli, the flute concertos of the German Georg Philipp Telemann and the Italian Antonio Vivaldi, and the oboe concertos of George Frideric Handel. J.S. Bach features wind instruments in four of his *Brandenburg Concertos.*

Baroque solo music for winds

The chamber repertory for wind instruments during this period consists primarily of solo sonatas accompanied by figured bass and trio sonatas for two treble winds accompanied by figured bass. Although most of these sonatas use flute, recorder, or oboe as solo instrument, a bassoon frequently doubles the figured bass line realized by a keyboard instrument. Many of Handel's 15 solo sonatas from Opus 1 are suitable for flute, recorder, or oboe. In addition to his six early trio sonatas for two oboes, many of his 16 trio sonatas from Opus 2 and Opus 5 are suitable for flutes or oboes. Prominent among Bach's chamber music are three sonatas for flute and figured bass and a suite for unaccompanied flute.

The Classical era. At the time of Bach's death, the most fashionable type of orchestral music was the new classical symphony. Most symphonies composed at midcentury called for a small wind section: two oboes or flutes and two horns, with bassoon doubling the bass line. But by the end of the 18th century many symphonic scores required pairs of flutes, oboes, clarinets, bassoons, and trumpets, as well as from two to four horns.

The style of orchestral writing for winds changed drastically from the time of the Baroque concerto grosso to that of the classical symphony. Composers began to write passages idiomatic to brass or woodwind instruments rather than figuration imitating violin technique. Improvements in key mechanisms during the 18th century greatly improved both the technical potential and the intonation of woodwind instruments. Among the outstanding composers of the classical era who contributed solo concerti for wind instruments are C.P.E. Bach (four for flute and two for oboe), Johann Stamitz (eight for flute and one each for clarinet and oboe), Joseph Haydn (two each for horn and flute and one each for trumpet and oboe), and Mozart (three for flute, four for horn, and one each for bassoon, oboe, and clarinet).

The wind concerti of Classical composers

Although composers in the early classical era continued to compose sonatas for flute with continuo realized either by harpsichord or by the new piano, later classical composers did not develop a significant repertory of solo wind sonatas with piano accompaniment. At the same time, wind instruments enjoyed popularity in chamber music, both in combination with piano or strings and in concert with other winds. Both Mozart and Beethoven wrote quintets for oboe, clarinet, bassoon, horn, and piano. Particularly successful are the six quintets for flute, oboe, and strings of Johann Christian Bach; the horn quintet and the clarinet quintet of Mozart; and the septet for clarinet, horn, bassoon, and strings of Beethoven.

Among many divertimenti for winds by Mozart and Haydn, the favourite combination of instruments was a sextet: two oboes, two horns, and two bassoons. Another popular ensemble, sometimes called a *harmonie,* added two clarinets to become an octet, the same ensemble used by Beethoven for his *Octet,* Opus 103, and his *Rondino,* Opus 146. Although the 18th-century bands of Frederick the Great used this same basic instrumentation, military bands at the end of the century adopted enough percussion instruments to satisfy the rage for Turkish Janissary music. An impressive repertory of military marches includes works by J.C. Bach, Haydn, and Beethoven.

The Romantic era. Despite the countless technical improvements that wind instruments underwent during the 19th century, many performers were reluctant to use the latest inventions, and the inevitable revolution in technical performance was not fully apparent until the end of the century. An early advocate of the improved wind instruments was Berlioz, whose *Traité d'instrumentation et*

Berlioz' treatise on orchestration

d'orchestration modernes (1844; *Treatise on Instrumentation and Orchestration* (dealt with the ranges, mechanical problems, and sound qualities of all wind instruments and even anticipated problems in combining winds with other instruments and voices. Typical of Berlioz' own compositions, the *Te Deum,* Opus 22, requires a greatly expanded wind section with four flutes, four oboes, four clarinets, four horns, four bassoons, alto saxhorn, two trumpets, two cornets, six trombones, and two tubas. Although the more conservative Romantics, such as Mendelssohn and Brahms, used a smaller mass of winds in their orchestral music, Wagner even augmented the wind forces used by Berlioz. The size of the wind section in orchestral music reached its zenith at the turn of the 20th century with the tone poems of Strauss and the *Gurrelieder* of Arnold Schoenberg. Many of the same composers who increased the number of orchestral wind instruments also increased the technical difficulty and thematic significance of the music assigned to winds.

The 19th century produced remarkably few concerti for solo winds and orchestra. The romantic era saw a similar decrease in chamber music for winds. Among the few composers of music for solo winds with piano are the Italian Gaetano Donizetti, the Germans Carl Maria von Weber, Robert Schumann, Brahms, and the Frenchman Camille Saint-Saëns. Some outstanding chamber works for winds and strings are Brahms's trio for violin, horn, and piano; trio for clarinet, 'cello, and piano; and clarinet quintet; and Franz Schubert's octet for clarinet, horn, bassoon, and strings. Among the earliest woodwind quintets are the 24 works for flute, oboe, clarinet, bassoon, and horn by Anton Reicha, a teacher of both Berlioz and Franz Liszt. Gioacchino Rossini wrote six quartets for flute, clarinet, horn, and bassoon; whereas Rimsky-Korsakov added piano to the same combination for his *Quintet in B Flat Major.*

Although most of the music performed by the countless military and municipal bands in Europe and America was of a popular nature during the 19th century, an increasing number of master composers wrote important works for large wind ensembles. Early works by Schubert and Mendelssohn were joined by Berlioz' monumental *Symphonie funèbre et triomphale* in 1840. Particularly interesting are the three solo works by Rimsky-Korsakov for oboe, trombone, and clarinet, each accompanied by wind band. One of the finest compositions for winds from the 19th century is the Austrian Anton Bruckner's Mass No. 2 in E Minor for mixed chorus and wind band. Bruckner's music for voices and winds culminated a tradition established by Berlioz and Liszt.

The 20th century. Although the huge symphony orchestra, with a large proportion of strings, continued to be accommodated in the early 20th century by such composers as Gustav Mahler and Igor Stravinsky, two important trends in instrumental music emerged after World War I. One of these was a growing interest by composers in ensembles consisting predominantly of wind instruments. Stravinsky, for example, composed his *Symphonies of Wind Instruments* in 1920, a *Concerto for Piano and Wind Instruments* in 1923–24, and in 1930 the *Symphony of Psalms,* which is scored with neither violins nor violas. The other important trend was a relative increase in the proportion of new music for chamber ensembles, especially those with wind instruments. Although the symphony orchestra enjoyed a resurgence in the 1930s and 1940s, it never regained a dominant position.

Stravinsky's use of winds

The catalog of wind chamber music composed in the 20th century is impressive both in quantity and in quality. In much recent chamber music, composers have greatly extended the level of technique and the range of special effects demanded of wind players. Outstanding among the works for unaccompanied winds are the *Syrinx* (1912) for flute by Claude Debussy and the *Three Pieces for Clarinet* (1919) by Stravinsky.

The literature for small wind ensembles is equally impressive. Important chamber works include Stravinsky's *Octet* and *Dumbarton Oaks* for 16 winds; the German Paul Hindemith's *Septet* for winds and *Sonata for Four Horns;* the Austrian Anton von Webern's *Five Canons on Latin Texts* for voice, clarinet, and bass clarinet; the American Elliott Carter's *Eight Etudes and a Fantasy* for woodwind quartet; and the German Karlheinz Stockhausen's *Zeitmasse* for wind quintet.

An American, John Philip Sousa, is well-known for his marches from around the turn of the 20th century. He has been joined by a host of modern composers. In addition to the previously mentioned works of Stravinsky, the band medium boasts Schoenberg's *Theme and Variations for Band* (1943), as well as Hindemith's *Symphony in B Flat Major* for concert band (1951).

Throughout the 20th century, jazz has provided one of the most vital sources of American wind music. An early type of jazz ensemble to feature wind instruments was the Dixieland band, which used trumpet, clarinet, and trombone soloists and which flourished in the 1920s. The following decade was the principal era of the "big bands," which Benny Goodman brought to public acceptance. Among the best known "big bands" were those led by Duke Ellington and Count Basie. During the 1930s and 1940s the wind sections of such groups grew from six (three reeds, two trumpets, and trombone) to a standard of 13 (five reeds, four trumpets, and four trombones). After World War II, the "big bands" gradually were supplanted by smaller "progressive" or "bebop" bands, many of which included trumpet and saxophone.

Winds of the Dixieland band

In the East. Wind instruments occupy a prominent place in the music of several Oriental cultures. The wedding songs, which are important in pan-Islāmic culture, for example, are frequently accompanied by a double-reed instrument known as the *zukrah* or *zamr* in the Maghrib or as the *sūrnāy* in Persian. The ensemble used to accompany classical dances of South India sometimes includes a native flute or a Western clarinet. Certain wind instruments normally appear in several of the typical ensembles of Southeast Asia. The *pi-nai* oboe, for example, is the only nonpercussive instrument in the *pi phat* bands of Thailand, Kampuchea (Cambodia), and Laos; a recorder-like *khlui* frequently participates in the *mahori* orchestras of Thailand; and *khen* mouth organs (related to the *sheng*) performing in groups constitute the best known wind ensemble of Southeast Asia. Certain winds help to accompany the Peking opera (*ching-hsi*) of China. The double-reed *so-na* joins a battery of percussion instruments to accompany battle scenes and military entrances; and the *ti-tzu* flute and the *sheng* mouth organ occasionally help to accompany civil and domestic scenes. The basic melodic instrument in the Japanese court orchestra is the double-reed *hichiriki,* which frequently is joined by flutes, a mouth organ, and percussion. In both the Nō and the Kabuki drama of Japan, accompaniment often is provided by a *hayashi* ensemble of three drums and a flute.

The double-reed *hichiriki*

In folk traditions. Wind instruments also play an important role in the folk music of many cultures. Most folk music for winds imitates a vocal model, such as the folk music for harmonica played by both black and white Americans, the love songs for flute played by North American Indian men, and the bagpipe music of eastern Europe, which usually consists of richly ornamented versions of local folksongs. But a few types of folk music are idiomatic to wind instruments. Both the Yugoslavian *dvojnice,* a double recorder, and the Sardinian *launeddas,* a triple clarinet, play highly idiomatic melodies with drone accompaniment. In the Basque region of northern Spain and southwestern France, dances and processions are often accompanied by a single musician who plays a three-holed flute with one hand and a six-stringed dulcimer with the other. In certain instrumental ensembles of black Africa, percussion instruments sometimes are joined by teams of flute or horn players, each of whom plays a single note whenever it appears in the melody. The Mbuti Pygmies of the Congo Basin often use up to six flutes, each playing variations of a different ostinato pattern. (E.J.E.)

Electronic instruments

HISTORY AND EVOLUTION OF ELECTRONIC INSTRUMENTS

Electricity was applied to the mechanism of musical instruments as early as 1761, when J.B. Delaborde of

Paris invented an electric harpsichord. Experimental instruments continued to be invented throughout the 19th century. The earliest instrument to generate sound electrically, however, was Thaddeus Cahill's Telharmonium, introduced in Mount Holyoke, Massachusetts, in 1906. This machine employed rotary generators and telephone receivers to convert electrical impulses into sound. Complex, bulky, and impractical, it was nevertheless the forerunner of the Hammond organ and the more recent music synthesizers. The invention of the three electrode tube by Lee de Forest (also in 1906) was significant for electronic music insofar as the tube made possible the later invention of smaller, more practical machines.

The earliest stage of development occurred from about 1920 until the beginning of World War II. This period was marked by the invention of a number of electronic instruments designed for performance in the conventional sense. These may be classified as follows:

1. Instruments that produce vibrations in familiar mechanical ways—the striking of strings with hammers, the bowing or plucking of strings, the activation of reeds—but with the conventional resonating agent, such as a sounding board, replaced by a pickup system, an amplifier, and a loudspeaker, which enable the performer to modify both the quality and the intensity of the tone. These instruments include electric pianos; electric organs employing vibrating reeds; electric violins, violas, cellos, and basses; and electric guitars, banjos, and mandolins.

2. Instruments that produce vibrations by means of oscillating electric circuits at set frequencies. The oscillations are amplified and heard through a loudspeaker. This group of instruments, which is a large one, can be further subdivided into those designed to simulate existing timbres, notably the electric organs, and—of particular interest to composers—those designed to produce new timbres. Among the latter, Leon Theremin's theremin (1920), Maurice Martenot's Ondes Martenot (1928), and Friedrich Trautwein's trautonium have been widely used; composers of the stature of Richard Strauss, Hindemith, Honegger, Milhaud, Messiaen, Jolivet, Varèse, and Martinů have written for one or more of these instruments. Among the electric organs, three basic systems of tone-generation are noteworthy: the use of rotating electromagnetic generators, as in the Hammond organ, the use of rotating electrostatic generators, and the transformation of light into sound by means of a photoelectric cell.

DEVELOPMENT

Tape music. The next stage of development in electronic instruments dates from the discovery of magnetic tape recording techniques and their refinement, especially during and after World War II. These techniques enable the composer to record any sounds whatever on tape and then to manipulate the tape to achieve desired effects. Recorded sounds can be superimposed upon each other (mixed), altered in timbre by means of filters, or reverberated. Dynamic levels can be changed. Repeated sound-patterns can be created by means of circular strands of tape (tape loops). By changing the speed of the tape, extreme variations in register can be effected, and with certain equipment tape speed can be changed without altering pitch. Attack-and-decay patterns of recorded sounds can likewise by altered. (The term attack and decay, or envelope, refers to the rate at which a sound grows to a peak of intensity and declines. This pattern is determined by the nature of the sound-producing mechanism and the way it is sounded. It is a fundamental attribute, distinguishing one type of sound from another.) By playing the tape backward, attack-and-decay patterns can be reversed. Splicing can also be employed to alter these patterns (*e.g.*, by reducing attack to zero) as well as to achieve striking juxtapositions of sounds. Thus the composer can exercise precise control over every aspect of his original sound material.

Although Hindemith, Toch, and others had experimented with it previously, the development of tape music began in earnest in 1948 with the work of Pierre Schaeffer and his associates at the Club d'Essai in Paris, under the auspices of Radio-diffusion et Télévision Française. They called their creations *musique concrète*—a term emphasizing their choice of a variety of natural sounds as raw material. These sounds were put together (or composed), altered, or distorted so as to form a unified artistic whole. The *Symphonie pour un homme seul* (Symphony for One Man Only), composed by Schaeffer and his collaborator, Pierre Henry, is one of the landmarks of *musique concrète*, for it laid the technical and aesthetic foundations for much of the later tape music.

In 1951 a studio for *elektronische Musik* was founded at Cologne by Herbert Eimert, Werner Meyer-Eppler, and others, under the auspices of the Nordwest Deutsche Rundfunk (Northwest German Broadcasting Studio). While the composers associated with this studio used many of the same techniques of tape manipulation as did the French group, they favoured synthetic rather than natural sound sources. In particular, they utilized simple sine-wave signals or pure tones (*i.e.*, tones without overtones), as raw material for the formation of complex tones. Certain compositions of Karlheinz Stockhausen, such as the *Gesang der Jünglinge* (*Song of Youth*), are illustrative of the resources available in the Cologne studio.

The music synthesizer. Further advances in electronic instruments were marked by the construction of the RCA Electronic Music Synthesizer by Harry Olson and Herbert Belar at the RCA Laboratories at Princeton, New Jersey. This machine was introduced in 1955; an enlarged and modified version (Mark II) was constructed and installed in the Columbia–Princeton Electronic Music Center in New York in 1959. The Mark II, which outwardly resembles a large computer, has a comprehensive assembly of signal generators, modulators, filters, and other components familiar from the electronic music studio plus a few special circuits of its own, such as a glide generator. Its basic advance was an information input mechanism.

The synthesizer is capable of producing, by electronic means, tones of any desired frequency, intensity, duration, rate of attack and decay, timbre, or degree of vibrato. Such tones can be "played" by the machine at any rate of speed or in any desired rhythmic patterns, including those which would be physically impossible for a human performer. Besides additive synthesis—the method employed earlier at Cologne and elsewhere, wherein complex tones are built up by the superimposition of sine-wave signals—the synthesizer is also capable of subtractive synthesis, wherein sawtooth-wave signals (those containing fundamentals and all their related overtones) are generated and modified by resonation or attenuation to achieve the desired tone-spectrum. Noise, or aperiodic sounds of any kind, can also be produced by the generation and modification of "white noise." (White noise is sound containing all audible frequencies. These are not simultaneously present; rather, each frequency is "sensibly constant," being heard at random intervals over a period of time.) Furthermore, prerecorded sounds can be fed into the machine and modified, as in *musique concrète*. The composer specifies the properties of the desired sounds through programming input, in the form of binary code instructions punched on paper tape. At any time during the programming process the composer may aurally test any sound, before permanently coding it, by calling for production of the sound and then listening to it over a loudspeaker. When programmed, the machine then plays the specified sounds by recording them directly on magnetic tape for future performance through amplifiers.

The music synthesizer is capable of producing virtually any sound or combination of sounds; it is limited only by the composer's ability to specify such sounds in terms of the coded input and, more significantly, by the thresholds of aural perception. Theoretically it could duplicate with perfect precision the sounds of conventional instruments, but in practice it has been employed chiefly for new effects not possible of achievement by any other means. The works of Milton Babbitt and several others, composed on this machine, are among the important contributions to the expanding repertoire of electronic music. Engineers continue to improve on the synthesizer; since 1960, the voltage-controlled oscillator and several types of compact synthesizer (such as the Moog synthesizer) have been introduced.

Computers as musical instruments. The direct synthesis of sound by computers was first described in 1963 by M. V. Mathews and co-workers at the Bell Telephone Laboratories (BTL). The BTL system, employing an IBM 7094 computer, involved the representation of each complex sound as a sound pressure-wave (a single-valued function of pressure versus time); the translation of the pressure-wave into a series of numbers representing the amplitudes of the wave over very small intervals of time, at a sampling rate of up to 10,000 samples per second; the transfer of these sample point numbers, in digital form, to magnetic tape; the conversion of each sample point number to a voltage proportional to that number by means of a digital-to-analogue converter; the "smoothing" of the resulting signal (which consists of a series of discrete pulses) by means of a low-pass filter; and, finally, the transformation of the smoothed analogue signal from its electromagnetic form into sound by means of an amplifier and loudspeaker. The program ("score") for music produced in this way consists of a deck of punched cards. For more information see MUSICAL FORMS AND GENRES: *Electronic music.*

ASSESSMENT

Electronic instruments have contributed to a tremendous expansion of musical resources. Their increasing sophistication has made available to the composer a spectrum of sounds ranging from pure tones at one extreme to the most complex noises at the other in addition to making possible the rhythmic organization of music to a degree of subtlety and complexity previously unattainable. One consequence of the use of electronic instruments has been the wide acceptance of a new definition of music as organized sound. Electronic instruments also allow the composer direct control over the composition; except for compositions that are designed for performers with an electronic accompaniment, most electronic works eliminate the need for the performer as an interpreter and intermediary between the composer and his audience. The "performance" is accomplished by loudspeakers carefully distributed throughout the hall for optimum stereophonic effect: for example, Edgard Varèse's *Poème électronique,* commissioned for performance at the 1958 Brussels World's Fair, utilized 400 loudspeakers. The absence of performers places the audience in a new and unaccustomed relationship to the composer and his music. The usual absence, moreover, of any classically rendered notation system places the critic in an unusual position, since his analysis of what he hears must be carried out solely by ear, unaided by any written symbols.

Some observers have felt that the elimination of the performer as interpreter, while it may enable the composer to realize perfectly his intentions, is nevertheless a serious loss. Performance, it is argued, is a creative discipline complementary to that of composition itself, and varieties of interpretation add richness to the musical experience; moreover, the physical presence of the performer infuses drama into what would be otherwise a purely aural, intellectual, and, by implication, somewhat lifeless event. But in fact certain developments in 20th-century music, such as jazz and the so-called aleatory (or chance) techniques of composition for traditional instruments, have given to the performer a role of freedom and responsibility unprecedented in Western musical tradition.

The most urgent problems arising from recent advances in electronic music lie in the field of psychoacoustics. These have to do with determining the limits of aural perception.

(Ca.G./Ed.)

BIBLIOGRAPHY

General. ANTHONY BAINES, *European and American Musical Instruments* (1966), a comprehensive summary, with 824 illustrations; and (ed.), *Musical Instruments Through the Ages,* rev. ed. (1966), chapters on individual instruments written by experts and numerous illustrations and figures in the text; NICHOLAS BESSARABOFF, *Ancient European Musical Instruments* (1941), a detailed account of the instruments in the Boston Museum of Fine Arts (some illustrations); ALEXANDER BUCHNER, *Les Instruments de musique à travers les âges* (1957; Eng. trans., *Musical Instruments Through the Ages,* 1961), a brief history followed by 323 illustrations, some in colour; ROBERT DONINGTON, *The Instruments of Music,* 3rd ed. (1970), a short account of the acoustics and history of European instruments (some illustrations); FRANCIS W. GALPIN, *A Textbook of European Musical Instruments* (1937), a summary history by categories, covering a wide field in a moderate space; KARL GEIRINGER, *Musical Instruments: Their History in Western Culture from the Stone Age to the Present Day,* 2nd ed. (1959), similar in scope to the preceding; FRANK L. HARRISON and JOAN RIMMER, *European Musical Instruments* (1964), a brief account, with 248 illustrations; CURT SACHS, *The History of Musical Instruments* (1940), the most comprehensive work of its kind (some illustrations); EMANUEL WINTERNITZ, *Musical Instruments of the Western World* (1967), a lavishly illustrated anthology of instruments, with an introduction and critical descriptions (251 plates, many in colour); BENJAMIN HADLEY (ed.), *Britannica Book of Music* (1980), brief descriptions of individual instruments, well illustrated. A comprehensive survey of musical instruments of the Western world is given in JEREMY MONTAGU, *The World of Medieval and Renaissance Musical Instruments* (1976), *The World of Baroque and Classical Musical Instruments* (1979), and *The World of Romantic and Modern Musical Instruments* (1981). PHILLIP T. YOUNG, *The Look of Music: Rare Musical Instruments* (1980), is a catalog of an exhibit of 305 musical instruments, with excellent photographs. REINHOLD BANEK and JON SCOVILLE, *Sound Designs: A Handbook of Musical Instrument Building* (1980), is also well illustrated. SUSAN CAUST FARRELL, *Directory of Contemporary American Musical Instrument Makers* (1981), presents complete information supplemented with a bibliography on the topic. JAMES COOVER, *Musical Instrument Collections: Catalogs and Cognate Literature* (1981), is another informative index and bibliography.

Percussion instruments. JAMES BLADES, *Percussion Instruments and Their History* (1971), world-wide survey with details on playing techniques, by a professional percussionist; CURT SACHS, *The History of Musical Instruments* (1940), the classic of its field including important synoptic coverage of both idiophones and membranophones; SIBYL MARCUSE, *Musical Instruments: A Comprehensive Dictionary* (1964), contains short articles on individual instruments. See also JAMES BLADES and JEREMY MONTAGU, *Early Percussion Instruments: From the Middle Ages to the Baroque* (1976); and JAMES HOLLAND, *Percussion* (1981).

Stringed instruments. The standard history of instruments is CURT SACHS, *The History of Musical Instruments* (1940). A recent book that traces bowing on a global scale is WERNER BACHMANN, *Die Anfänge des Streichinstrumentent spiels,* 2nd ed. (1966; Eng. trans., *The Origins of Bowing,* 1969). Articles on the symbolic meaning of musical instruments are THEODORE GRAME, "Bamboo and Music: A New Approach to Organology," *Ethnomusicology,* 6:8–14 (1962), "The Symbolism of the ʿŪd," *Asian Music,* 2:25–34 (1972), and with GENICHI TSUGE, "Steed Symbolism on Musical Instruments," *Musical Quarterly,* 63:57–66 (1972). Two standard books on African instruments are PERCIVAL R. KIRBY, *The Musical Instruments of the Native Races of South Africa* (1934); and MARGARET TROWELL and K.P. WACHSMANN, *Tribal Crafts of Uganda* (1953). Instruments of Mesopotamia are discussed in H.G. FARMER, "The Music of Ancient Egypt," and "The Music of Ancient Mesopotamia," in EGON WELLESZ (ed.), *The New Oxford History of Music,* vol. 1 (1957); and F.W. GALPIN, *The Music of the Sumerians and Their Immediate Successors, the Babylonians and Assyrians* (1937). Articles on various African instruments are collected in H.G. FARMER, *Studies in Oriental Musical Instruments* (1931). An excellent work on the history and symbolism of the Chinese ch'in is ROBERT VAN GULIK, *The Lore of the Chinese Lute,* rev. ed. (1969). NICHOLAS BESSARABOFF, *Ancient European Musical Instruments* (1941), is a full and complete treatment of European instruments through the 18th century; HORTENSE PANUM, *Middelalderens Strengeinstrumenter og deres forløbere i oldtiden* (1915; Eng. trans., *The Stringed Instruments of the Middle Ages,* 1939), is an older but still useful work on European chordophones and their analogues; IRVING SLOANE, *Classical Guitar Construction* (1966), is an illustrated practical account of the process of guitar making. Two important Scandinavian instruments are fully treated in OTTO ANDERSSON, *The Bowed Harp* (1930); and JAN LING, *Nyckelharpan* (1967), with summary in English; Celtic harps are discussed in JOAN RIMMER, *The Irish Harp* (1969); and FRANCIS COLLINSON, *The Traditional and National Music of Scotland* (1966). *Ellenika Laika Mousika Organa* (1965), is an illustrated catalog of modern Greek instruments; and S. KRISHNASWAMI, *Musical Instruments of India* (1965), is a similar work on the instruments of the Indian subcontinent. Two standard works on Japanese music and instruments are SHIGEO KISHIBE, *The Traditional Music of Japan* (1966); and WILLIAM P. MALM, *Japanese Music and Musical Instruments* (1959). The standard work on Javanese instruments is JAAP KUNST, *Music in Java,* 2nd rev. ed., 2 vol. (1949), while a specialized study of the Javanese fiddle is found in M. HOOD, "The Javanese Rebab," in *Music, Libraries and Instruments* (1961). JOHN H. FELIX, LESLIE MUNES, and PETER F. SENECAL, *The Ukulele: A Portuguese Gift to Hawaii* (1980), is a brief study of the instrument; HENRY RASOF, *The Folk, Country, and Bluegrass Musician's Catalogue* (1982), is a reference tool giving good coverage of 11 stringed folk instruments.

Keyboard instruments. *Development of the keyboard, the clavichord, and the harpsichord:* FRANK HUBBARD, *Three Centuries of Harpsichord Making* (1965), the only book on the subject to clarify the history of the instrument and the techniques of earlier harpsichord makers; RAYMOND RUSSELL, *The Harpsichord and Clavichord,* 2nd ed. (1973), a general history, less technical than Hubbard's, illustrated with excellent photographs; DONALD H. BOALCH, *Makers of the Harpsichord and Clavichord, 1440–1840* (1956), known data on all makers whose names have survived as well as the locations of their extant instruments; EDWIN M. RIPIN (ed.), *Keyboard Instruments* (1971), a collection of 10 articles on specialized topics, including Italian, Flemish, and English harpsichords, 15th-century instruments, and the *Geigenwerck;* HANNS NEUPERT, *Das Klavichord* (1956; Eng. trans., 1965) and *Das Cembalo,* 3rd ed. (1956; Eng. trans., *Harpsichord Manual,* 1960), elementary treatises with emphasis on modern instruments—much of the historical information has now been superseded; FRANZ J. HIRT, *Masterwerk des Klavierbaus* (1955; Eng. trans., *Stringed Keyboard Instruments,* 1968), a splendid picture book with interesting but somewhat unreliable supporting text; EMANUEL WINTERNITZ, *Keyboard Instruments in the Metropolitan Museum of Art* (1961), a useful, small, and inexpensive picture book with a fair text; WOLFGANG J. ZUCKERMANN, *The Modern Harpsichord* (1969), the standard work on modern harpsichords and their makers, although unreliable for historical information and technical aspects of instrument design and building; WILLI APEL, "Early History of the Organ," *Speculum,* 23:191–216 (1948), an excellent account, especially useful for the details it gives on the evolution of the keyboard; EDWIN M. RIPIN, "The Early Clavichord," *Musical Quarterly,* 53:518–538 (1967); "A Reassessment of the Fretted Clavichord," *Galpin Society Journal,* 23:40–48 (1970); "The Two-Manual Harpsichord in Flanders Before 1650," *ibid.,* 21:33–39 (1968); and "Expressive Devices Applied to the Eighteenth-Century Harpsichord," *The Organ Yearbook,* 1:65–80 (1970), a series of articles presenting new information or interpretations not available in book form; RAYMOND RUSSELL, "The Harpsichord Since 1800," *Proceedings of the Royal Musical Association,* 82:61-74 (1955–56), an account of the early period in the modern revival of the harpsichord that fills some of the gaps in Zuckermann's work. Later monographs include HOWARD SCHOTT, *Playing the Harpsichord* (1979); EVAN J. KERN, *Harpsichord Design and Construction* (1980); JOHN PAUL, *Modern Harpsichord Makers* (1981).

The piano: R.E.M. HARDING, *The Piano-Forte: Its History Traced to the Great Exhibition of 1851,* 2nd ed. (1978), the standard work in the field—the diagrams are excellent, but the text yields its information only reluctantly; ALFRED J. HIPKINS, *A Description and History of the Pianoforte and of the Older Keyboard Stringed Instruments* (1896), a classic that has never been superseded as a brief account of the subject, includes discussion of all stringed keyboard instruments; ARTHUR LOESSER, *Men, Women and Pianos* (1954), a lively account of all keyboard instruments, their music, and their place in society—the author's bias in favour of the modern piano makes the book unreliable for details on instruments before 1840; WILLIAM L. SUMNER, *The Pianoforte* (1966), an acceptable elementary history; DANIEL SPILLANE, *History of the American Pianoforte* (1890, reprinted 1969), still the standard work on American piano building; WILLIAM B. WHITE, *Piano Tuning and Allied Arts,* 5th ed. rev. (1946), the standard technician's manual in America; A.W.J.G. ORD-HUME, *Player Piano* (1970), an excellent history as well as a technical manual; THEODORE E. STEINWAY, *People and Pianos* (1953), contains interesting details and human-interest material; HUGH GOUGH, "The Classical Grand Pianoforte, 1770–1830," *Proceedings of the Royal Musical Association,* 77:41–50 (1950–51), a good discussion of the musical and technical aspects of the instruments, especially valuable for its comparison of English and German pianos. See also JAMES R. GAINES (ed.), *The Lives of the Piano* (1981); EDWIN M. GOOD, *Giraffes, Black Dragons, and Other Pianos: A Technological History from Cristofori to the Modern Concert Grand* (1982); and DOMINICK GILL (ed.), *The Book of the Piano* (1981).

The organ: AUSTIN NILAND, *Introduction to the Organ* (1968), is, as its name implies, a good introduction to the subject from a contemporary British point of view; in a similar vein, very practical, but from a continental approach, is HANS KLOTZ, *Das Buch von der Orgel* (1938; 7th ed., 1965; Eng. trans., *The Organ Handbook,* 1969). The classic work on the subject in English is EDWARD J. HOPKINS and EDWARD F. RIMBAULT, *The Organ,* 3rd ed. (1877, reprinted 1965); less complete, but general, more contemporary coverage is given in WILLIAM LESLIE SUMNER, *The Organ,* 4th rev. ed. (1973, reprinted 1981). Primarily historical is an extremely detailed work by JEAN PERROT: *L'Orgue de ses origines hellenistiques à la fin du XIIIe siècle* (1965; Eng. trans., *The Organ from Its Invention in the Hellenistic Period to the End of the Thirteenth Century,* 1971). PETER WILLIAMS, *The European Organ, 1450–1850* (1966), is a thorough history of continental organs. POUL-GERHARD ANDERSEN, *Orgelbogen* (1956; Eng. trans., *Organ Building and Design,* 1969), emphasizes architecture and the organ's relation to it. National schools are discussed in CECIL CLUTTON and AUSTIN NILAND, *The British Organ* (1963), post-revival; NOEL A. BONAVIA-HUNT, *The Modern British Organ* (1947), pre-revival; FENNER DOUGLAS, *The Language of the Classical French Organ* (1969); and WILLIAM HARRISON BARNES, *The Contemporary American Organ,* 8th ed. (1965), heavy on mechanics with drawings. JOSEPH EDWIN BLANTON, *The Organ in Church Design* (1957), very extensive and aimed primarily at architects; and *The Revival of the Organ Case* (1965), are primarily pictorial works on organ cases. See also the classic pen and ink drawings of ARTHUR G. HILL, *The Organ Cases and Organs of the Middle Ages and Renaissance* (1883, reprinted 1966; German trans., *Vierzig Orgelgehäuse-Zeichnungen,* 2nd ed., 1964)—many of these drawings appear in the other books listed. A fascinating book on portatives, positives, and regals is MICHAEL WILSON, *The English Chamber Organ: History and Development, 1650–1850* (1968). PETER WILLIAMS, *A New History of the Organ from the Greeks to the Present Day* (1980), covers development of the instrument in all countries and over 2,000 years. Other informative monographs include HERBERT NORMAN and H. JOHN NORMAN, *The Organ Today* (1980); HOMER D. BLANCHARD (ed.), *Organs of Our Time,* rev. ed., 2 vol. (1981–82); BARBARA OWEN, *The Organ in New England: An Account of Its Use and Manufacture to the End of the Nineteenth Century* (1979); CHARLES W. LINDOW (comp.), *Historic Organs in France: A Guide to Their Composition, Condition, and Location, with Synoptic and Statistical Analyses and Aids to the Traveller,* trans. from the French (1980); ROBERT B. WHITING (comp.), *Estey Reed Organs on Parade: A Pictorial Review* (1981); and JOHN ALLEN FERGUSON, *Walter Holtkamp, American Organ Builder* (1979).

Wind instruments. ANTHONY BAINES, *European and American Musical Instruments* (1966), 824 pictures of actual instruments designed to help with identification; *Woodwind Instruments and Their History,* 3rd ed. (1967), the most authoritative book in its field; and (ed.), *Musical Instruments Through the Ages* (1961), an excellent introduction to instruments written by various authorities in their respective fields; NICOLAS BESSARABOFF, *Ancient European Musical Instruments* (1941), a significant organological study, based on the collection of the Boston Museum of Fine Arts; ADAM CARSE, *The History of Orchestration* (1925, reprinted 1964), an outline of the use of wind instruments in orchestral music from the 17th through the early-20th centuries; *Musical Wind Instruments* (1939, reprinted 1965), still the best volume of its type; ROBERT DONINGTON, *The Instruments of Music,* 2nd ed. rev. (1951), an elementary but informative general book; KARL GEIRINGER, *Musical Instruments: Their History in Western Culture from the Stone Age to the Present Day,* 2nd ed. (1959); RICHARD FRANKO GOLDMAN, *The Wind Band: Its Literature and Technique* (1961), a survey of the history and literature of the military and the concert band; LYNDESAY LANGWILL, *An Index of Musical Wind-Instrument Makers,* 3rd ed. (1972), an invaluable aid to locating specimens, their makers, and their dates of production; WILLIAM P. MALM, *Music Cultures of the Pacific, the Near East, and Asia* (1967), a discussion of instrumental music in each of the most important Oriental cultures; SIBIL MARCUSE, *Musical Instruments: A Comprehensive Dictionary* (1964); BRUNO NETTL, *Folk and Traditional Music of the Western Continents* (1965), includes useful discussions of instrumental music in several ethnic cultures from Europe, Africa, and the Americas; CURT SACHS, *The History of Musical Instruments* (1940), a standard text important for theories and relations between East and West; ERICH M. VON HORNBOSTEL and CURT SACHS, "Classification of Musical Instruments," *Galpin Society Journal,* 14:3–29 (1961); DAVID WHITWELL, a series of 30 articles that appeared in *The Instrumentalist* (October 1965–March 1969), bibliographies and discussion of the wind music of 127 major composers; EMANUEL WINTERNITZ, *Musical Instruments of the Western World* (1967), a series of artistic pictures stressing instruments "pleasing to the eye and ear alike" along with location and commentary. Relevant information is found in KENNETH A. MELLER, *Complete Guide to the Maintenance and Repair of Band Instruments* (1982).

On individual instruments: PHILLIP BATE, *The Oboe* (1956), *The Flute* (1969), and *The Trumpet and Trombone* (1966); THEOBALD BOEHM, *Die Flöte und das Flötenspiel* (1871; Eng. trans., *The Flute and Flute-Playing,* 2nd rev. ed., 1922, reprinted 1964); EDGAR HUNT, *The Recorder and Its Music* (1962); LYNDESAY LANGWILL, *The Bassoon and Contrabassoon* (1965); WERNER MENKE, *History of the Trumpet of Bach and Handel* (1934); R. MORLEY-PEGGE, *The French Horn* (1960); F. GEOFFREY RENDALL, *The Clarinet,* 2nd rev. ed. (1957); WILLIAM H. STUBBINS, *The Art of Clarinetistry* (1965). MICHAEL SEYFRIT (comp.), *Recorders, Fifes, and Simple System Transverse Flutes of One Key* (1982), is a catalog in a series on musical instruments in the Library of Congress and contains a wealth of useful information.

Electronic instruments. Many books and manuals emphasize the use of synthesizers. Examples include GILBERT TRYTHALL, *Principles and Practices of Electronic Music* (1973); and ALLEN STRANGE, *Electronic Music: Systems, Techniques and Controls,* 2nd ed. (1983). MICHEL CHION and GUY REIBEL, *Les Musiques électroacoustiques* (1976), deals with European rather than American practice. Electronic musical instruments and their components are discussed in RICHARD H. DORF, *Electronic Musical Instruments,* 3rd ed. (1968); ALAN L. DOUGLAS, *The Electronic Musical Instrument Manual: A Guide to Theory and Design,* 6th ed. (1976), and *The Electrical Production of Music* (1957); WERNER MEYER-EPPLER, *Elektrische Klangerzeugung* (1949); PAUL GRIFFITHS, *A Guide to Electronic Music* (1979); DELTON T. HORN, *Electronic Music Synthesizers* (1980); and DEVARAHI, *The Complete Guide to Synthesizers* (1982). SANDRA L. TJEPKEMA, *A Bibliography of Computer Music* (1981), is a valuable reference tool.

Instrumentation: WILLI APEL, *Harvard Dictionary of Music,* 2nd ed. rev. (1969), a good source on any musical subject; DONALD JAY GROUT, *A History of Western Music* (1960), the best general history of music to date; ADAM CARSE, *The History of Orchestration* (1925, reprinted 1964), a detailed look at the evolution of the orchestra and musical instruments; NICOLAS RIMSKY-KORSAKOV, *Principles of Orchestration, with Musical Examples Drawn from His Own Works,* ed. by MAXIMILIAN STEINBERG, 1 vol. (1964; originally published in Russian, 1910), still one of the best texts for the serious student; ROMAIN GOLDRON, *Ancient and Oriental Music* (1968), examples of non-Western music and instruments. Interesting information can be found in MADEAU STEWART, *The Music Lover's Guide to the Instruments of the Orchestra* (1980); MICHAEL HURD, *The Orchestra* (1980); TONY BACON (ed.), *Rock Hardware: The Instruments, Equipment, and Technology of Rock* (1981); and DENNIS WARING, *Folk Instruments* (1979, reissued 1981).

Mystery Religions

Mystery religions were secret cults of the Greco-Roman world that offered to individuals a way to feel religious experiences not provided by the official public religions. They originated in tribal ceremonies that were performed by primitive peoples in many parts of the world. But, whereas in these tribal communities almost every member of the clan or the village was initiated, initiation in Greece became a matter of personal choice. The mystery religions reached their peak of popularity in the first three centuries AD; at that time an individual could choose among many religions of this type. Their origin, however, goes back to the earlier centuries of Greek history.

Etymologically, the word mystery is derived from the Greek verb *myein* ("to close"), referring to the lips and the eyes. Mysteries were always secret cults into which a person had to be "initiated" (taken in). The initiate was called *mystēs,* the introducing person *mystagōgos* (leader of the *mystēs*). The leaders of the cults included the *hierophantēs* ("revealer of holy things") and the *dadouchos* ("torchbearer"). The constitutive features of a mystery society were common meals, dances, and ceremonies, especially initiation rites. These common experiences strengthened the bonds of each cult.

This article is divided into the following sections:

HISTORY

Hellenic roots. *Dionysiac.* In every Greek city the god Dionysus was worshipped by fraternities and sororities and also by mixed communities. Dionysus was a god of fruitfulness and vegetation but especially of wine. The Dionysiac festivals provided an opportunity for stepping outside of the daily routine. The festivals included not only drinking wine and engaging in sexual activity but also participating in such significant features of Greek civilization as choral singing and mimes. In many cases, only the initiated could participate in the ceremonies. As almost every Greek did join in, initiation into the Dionysiac cult might be compared to tribal initiations. It seems that initiation into the Dionysiac Mysteries was accompanied by initiation into sexual life. The act of producing offspring, however, could never be wholly separated from the thought of death, so that the worshippers of Dionysus were aware of a mystic communion among the ancestors, the living generation, and the future members of the community.

Eleusinian. The most important sanctuary of Demeter (Ceres), the goddess of grain, and her daughter Kore (Persephone) was in the city of Eleusis in Attica, between Athens and Megara. Famous religious agricultural festivals—known as the Greater and the Lesser Eleusinian Mysteries—celebrating the sowing, sprouting, and reaping of the grain, were reenacted in this city. The cycle of the grain, pictured in the myth of Kore (Persephone), was thought to be parallel to the cycle of man. The myth, as told in the Homeric hymn to Demeter, tells how Hades (Pluto, or Pluton), god of the netherworld, wanted a wife and how he carried off Kore into the depths of the earth. Her mother, Demeter, through long days of searching, during which she came to Eleusis, refused to make the grain grow. Finally, Hades was bidden to send Kore back to earth. She came back to light as the grain maiden and gave birth to her son Plutus (Kore, "the maiden"; Pluton, "the rich one"; Plutus, "wealth," especially in grain). But, because Kore had eaten a pomegranate seed, a symbol of death and birth, she could not be completely released, and a compromise was reached by which she spent one-third of the year with her husband, the rest with her mother. Satisfied with this, Demeter caused grain to grow again and taught the Eleusinians her rites. The entire story of Demeter and Kore was elaborately reenacted in the Eleusinian ceremony. Just as in the myth Kore was carried away to marry Hades and to give birth to Plutus, so was grain thrown into the field and buried in the earth to bring forth new life. Just as grain came up out of the ground and was reaped to yield man's bread and to be

The myth of Kore

used as seed, so was a girl taken from her parents and her virginity "killed" to bring forth new offspring. And when a man died, he was buried in the earth to partake mystically in the cyclic renewal of life. This was the message of Eleusis: out of every grave new life grows—for the initiates there are "good hopes" for a glorious immortality in the afterlife.

Although there were festivals of Demeter throughout Greece, the true Eleusinian Mysteries were celebrated at Eleusis only. At first, the cult of Demeter was local and initiation was tribal rather than personal. By participating in the mysteries, a man became a full member of the civic body. This was changed when Eleusis was annexed to the Athenian territory about 600 BC. Initiation lost its importance as a means of conferring civic status; it became a purely religious ceremony. Every Athenian was admitted to the Eleusinian Mysteries, and soon the mysteries were open to every Greek, so that the ceremonies received an "international" character. Whoever wished to be initiated, however, had to go to Eleusis. It was a day's journey from Athens, a longer distance from most of the other Greek cities. The mystery rite became no longer a tribal ceremony. Each person had to decide for himself whether or not he wanted to be initiated. This development was possible only because Athens had become a large city with a differentiated culture that gave the individual ample choice of a way of life, including religion.

Meaning of the Dionysiac and Eleusinian mysteries

Both Dionysiac and Eleusinian mysteries had a wide range of meaning. Their essence was not contained in any written record but only in the festivals themselves—the holy days of the community. Many participants appreciated only the superficial level of the ceremonies and considered them as an opportunity for having a good time—good company, good food, intoxication, and sometimes (in the Dionysiac cult) sexual pleasures. The ceremonies were open to a deeper understanding, however, that was not made explicit by any theology or by any set of creeds but by the religious action itself, which contained the meaning and conveyed it to the participants without the interposition of words. Therefore, it was not possible to disclose to the noninitiated the mysteries by words, but it was treachery to reveal the secret dances.

Secular mystery communities. A society of initiates could drop its religious connections and become merely a social club. But because secrecy, common meals, and common drinking were implied, the Greeks and Romans regarded such clubs as mystery societies; they did not differentiate between religious associations and private clubs. The role of aristocratic clubs in Athenian politics was very important. In 415 BC the famous mystery scandal occurred. Several aristocratic societies conspired to overthrow the Athenian democracy. In order to pledge all members, a common crime was committed in which each member had to participate. One night the members of the social clubs took hammers and removed the genitals of the many Hermes statues in the city. Whoever would desert the common political cause would be denounced by his former friends for having committed a crime against religion, and many witnesses against him would be at hand. The people of Athens immediately understood that a conspiracy was developing. By a series of severe trials, the conspirators were traced and exiled. The speech of the orator Andocides, one of the conspirators, delivered in his defense in 400 or 399 BC, when the old affair was again taken up in a trial, still survives. The title of the oration is "On the Mysteries."

The secular mystery clubs continued throughout Greek and Roman history, and it was often difficult to distinguish them from religious associations. The Romans were especially distrustful of secret societies. This suspicion was justified in the case of Catiline, who led a conspiracy that attempted to overthrow the government in 63 BC. But Trajan, the Roman emperor from AD 98 to 117, did not allow the citizens of Nicomedia (modern İzmit, Turkey) to form a club that planned to provide a fire brigade, and he only reluctantly allowed the citizens of Amisus (modern Samsun, Turkey) to establish an association for charitable purposes.

Orphic. Besides community initiations, there were ceremonies for individual persons of deeper religious longing. Such persons were called Orphics after Orpheus, the Greek hero with superhuman musical skills who was supposedly the author of sacred writings; these writings were called the Orphic rhapsodies and they dealt with such subjects as purification and the afterlife. It is possible to reconstruct a common pattern for these initiations of individuals, although an Orphic "church" never existed, and the doctrines of the many small communities of individualists varied on a broad scale.

The Orphic sense of sin

Many Orphics seem to have had a strong feeling of sin and guilt. They believed that there was a divine part in man—his soul—but it was wrapped up in the body, and man's task was to liberate the soul from the body. This could be achieved by living an Orphic life, which included abstinence from meat, wine, and sexual intercourse. After death the soul would be judged. If a man had lived a righteous life, his soul would be sent to the meadows of the blessed in Elysium; but, if he had committed misdeeds, his soul would be punished in various ways and perhaps sent to hell. Following a period of reward or punishment, the soul would be incarnated in a new body. Only a soul that had lived a pious life three times could be liberated from the cycle.

Pythagoreans. The Orphic creeds were the basis of the Pythagorean brotherhood, which flourished in southern Italy beginning in the 6th century BC. The Pythagoreans were aristocratic fraternities that sometimes had a political scope. Their main achievements, however, lay in the fields of music, geometry, and astronomy. They discovered that these subjects could be explained by numbers and ratios. Combining Orphic eschatology (the study of the last things, especially death and afterlife) with their discoveries, they invested music, geometry, and astronomy with religious values. According to their doctrine, the original home of the soul was in the stars. From there it fell down to earth and associated with the body. Thus, man was a stranger on the earth, and he had to strive to liberate himself from the ties of the flesh and return to the soul's celestial home.

Platonists. The philosophy of Plato (*c.* 428–348 or 347 BC) by no means resulted from connections with a mystery cult. Yet Plato did take up many ideas from earlier Greek religion, especially from the Pythagorean brotherhood and from the Eleusinian communities, and often described his philosophy in terms derived from the mysteries. For example, the notion of searching and finding, so important in Eleusis, became an important notion in Plato's philosophy: the philosopher should never cease or relax in his quest for truth. A value was thus attached to the very act of searching. Later mystery religions, in their turn, borrowed freely from the rich imagery of Plato's dialogues and are thus deeply tinged with Platonism.

Plato's theory of the soul

In the *Timaeus,* which is an exposition of his theory of the universe, Plato also developed his theory of the soul. The earth is surrounded by the spheres of the seven planets; the eighth sphere is that of the fixed stars. Beyond the eighth sphere is the realm of the divine. The sphere of the fixed stars, moved by the divine, continuously turns to the right at an even speed. This clockwise rotation affects the spheres of the planets, although they have their proper movement, which runs to the left, or counterclockwise. The sphere of mortality begins with the planets. The original home of each soul is in one of the fixed stars. As a result of the movement of the spheres, the soul falls through the planetary spheres to earth, where it is united with the body. The soul must then try to liberate itself from the body and ascend to the fixed star from which it fell. In later generations this picture was vividly worked out. The soul, in the course of its fall through the planetary spheres, was thought to acquire the qualities of the planets: sloth from Saturn, combativeness from Mars, lust for power from Jupiter, voluptuousness from Venus, greed from Mercury. After death, when the soul returned to the fixed star, it discarded these qualities, just as the *mystēs,* in certain initiations, discarded his everyday garment before entering the sacred place.

Many other traditional religious images were taken over by Plato, including the music of the spheres, the migration of the soul, the soul's remembrance of its celestial origin, and the idea of rewards for the righteous and punishment for the wicked. Later mystery associations adopted these concepts, which Plato had expressed so beautifully, and were deeply influenced by Plato's explanations.

The Hellenistic period. When Alexander the Great conquered the Asiatic kingdoms as far east as the Indus River, the Greek world was extended immensely. The religious ideas in Greece itself and the western part of the Alexandrian Empire, however, changed very slowly, because the Greeks, now masters of the world, felt no need for change.

In the Messenian town of Andania mysteries were celebrated in honour of the goddesses Demeter and Kore. A long inscription of 92 BC gives elaborate directions for the conduct of the rites, although, naturally, it gives no details of what went on during initiation. The mysteries in honour of the Cabeiri (gods of fertility) on the island of Samothrace attracted great attention in this period. These gods were thought to be helpers of the seafarers, and initiation into their mysteries was looked upon as a general safeguard against all misfortune but particularly against shipwreck. The Dionysiac Mysteries, with their revels and merriment, continued throughout the whole of Greek history. Together with most of the elements of Greek civilization, this cult was transferred to Italy. In 186 BC a scandal about the Bacchanalia—the Latin name for the Hellenistic Dionysiac Mysteries—so upset the Romans that a decree of the Senate prohibited them throughout Italy, except in certain special cases. These mysteries were celebrated in a lower middle class milieu and involved gross sex parties and violence conducted under the cover of mystery secrecy.

Hellenistic Mysteries in the Greek Orient

The important developments in the mystery rites during the Hellenistic period took place in the Greek Orient, where elements from the Greek and Oriental religions were blended. Contact with Greek civilization completely changed life in the Orient, where the knowledge of writing had been confined to a few priests and scribes. Society first disintegrated after the conquest of Alexander and then developed along new lines. Changes in religion were inevitable, and some influence of Oriental traditions upon the Greeks was bound to follow. But the process was a slow one and became manifest only a few centuries later.

With regard to the institution of kingship, however, syncretism worked quickly. Ancient Near Eastern kingship was originally sacral. The Syrian and Egyptian inhabitants of the newly created Greek kingdoms inevitably regarded the Greco-Macedonian kings as semidivine beings. The Greeks themselves soon submitted to this mixture of politics and religion. Such a mixture was perfectly natural to the Egyptians and Syrians, who did not perceive the structure of society as an abstraction, such as "the state" or "the nation," but saw the unity of the body politic in the person of the king. He was the symbol of the security and help that man derives from an orderly society. Mystery rituals, called royal mysteries, were developed especially in Egypt. According to traditional Egyptian religion, the ruling pharaoh was an incarnation of Horus (the sun-god), his mother or wife an incarnation of Isis (the heavenly queen), and his deceased father an incarnation of Osiris (the god of fertility). In Hellenistic times, Osiris was commonly known by the name Sarapis. These gods became equated with Greek gods: Isis with Demeter and Aphrodite; Horus with Apollo and Helios; Sarapis with Zeus, Dionysus, and Hades (Pluto). Both Greek and Egyptian myths were adopted for these divinities.

One of the suburbs of Alexandria, the newly constructed Greek capital of Egypt, was called Eleusis after the city of Demeter in Greece, and the Eleusinian Mysteries were instituted in a Greco-Egyptian adaptation. Dionysiac Mysteries were introduced on an even greater scale, so that the royal court was temporarily thrown into turmoil by the number of Bacchic ceremonies in which the king was considered to be a reincarnation of Dionysus. The Pythagorean concept of the migration of the soul was also taken over and was blended with the Egyptian belief in the reincarnation of the sun-god Horus in the reigning king.

The cult of rulers thus introduced ideas from the Greek Orient into Greek communities. But the mixture of religion and politics was a great obstacle for the propagation of the Greco-Oriental mysteries in the Mediterranean world. Even the numerous Greeks who lived in Egypt and Syria maintained the traditional Greek concept of the separation of god and man, and it was only after the political aspect of the mysteries was discarded that the religious elements could gain a life of their own. Inscriptions discovered on the Greek island of Delos demonstrate this well. The worship of Sarapis was introduced at Delos during the time the island was temporarily a naval base of the Greco-Egyptian kings. When the Egyptian influence on the island receded, the cult of Sarapis not only remained but reached new heights. The Romans later used Delos as a free port for the eastern part of the Mediterranean, and from there the worship of Sarapis and Isis spread to most of the harbours of the Greek world and to the cities in the Bay of Naples, whence it was brought by Italian merchants to Rome.

The combination of mystery elements with ruler worship is also evident in the kingdom of Commagene (eastern Turkey and northern Syria). Here, the kings assigned large funds to construct throughout the country gigantic sanctuaries, where festivals of the gods and the royal ancestors were celebrated annually on the kings' anniversary days. Long inscriptions discovered in the remains of these sanctuaries bear striking similarities to the language of the mysteries. The ceremonies, however, seem to have contained little true religion.

Roman imperial times. The great period of the mystery religions began when the Romans imposed peace upon the Mediterranean world. The Dionysiac, or Bacchic, societies flourished in the whole empire—in Greece proper, on the Greek islands, in Asia Minor, along the Danube River, and especially in Italy and at Rome. Hundreds of inscriptions attest to Bacchic Mysteries. In some circles, Orphic and Dionysiac ideas were blended, as in the community that met in the underground basilica near the Porta Maggiore (Major Gate) at Rome. There was also a blend of ideas in the community for which the Orphic hymns were written. The members of this community (probably in Asia Minor) assembled at night in a clubhouse and held their services by the light of torches. Their rite consisted of a bloodless sacrifice and included the use of incense, prayer, and hymns. In addition to the mystery cults that were familiar from earlier times, the national religions of the peoples of the Greek Orient in their Hellenized versions began to spread. A faintly exotic flavour surrounded these religions and made them particularly attractive to the Greeks and Romans. The most popular of the Oriental mysteries was the cult of Isis. It was already in vogue at Rome in the time of the emperor Augustus, at the beginning of the Christian era. The Emperor, who wanted to restore the genuine Roman religious traditions, disliked the Oriental influences. But men of reputation, such as Messalla, a general and patron of writers, were strongly inclined toward the Isis Mysteries. Isis, the goddess of love, was the patroness of many of the elegant Roman courtesans. The religion of Isis became widespread in Italy during the 1st and 2nd centuries AD. To a certain extent, the expansion of Judaism and Christianity over the Roman world coincided with the expansion of the Egyptian cults.

Mysteries from Asia Minor

Far less important was the influence of cults from Asia Minor. By 200 BC the Great Mother of the Gods (Magna Mater) and her consort Attis were introduced into the Roman pantheon and were considered as Roman gods. Their cult seems to have been encouraged especially under Emperor Claudius about AD 50. The Great Mother was characterized by her universal motherhood, especially over wild nature. The mysteries symbolized, through her relationship to Attis, the relations of Mother Earth to her children and were intended to impress upon the *mystēs* the subjective certainty of having been united in a special way with the goddess. There was a strong element of hope for an afterlife in this cult. The Persian god Mithra (Mithras), the god of light, was introduced much later, probably not before the 2nd century. The cult of Mithra was concerned with the origin of life from a sacred bull that was caught and then sacrificed by Mithra. According to Persian sources, the bull by its death gave birth to the sky, the planets, the earth, the animals, and the plants; thus Mithra became the creator of life. From Syria came the worship of several deities, of which Jupiter Heliopolitanus (the local god of Heliopolis; modern Baʿlabakk, Lebanon) and Jupiter Dolichenus (the local god of Doliche in Commagene; modern Dülük, Turkey) were the most important. Adonis (a god of vegetation) of Byblos (in modern Lebanon) had long been familiar to the Greeks and was often considered to be closely related to Osiris; the myths and rituals of the two gods were similar. Adonis' female partner was Atargatis (Astarte), whom the Greeks identified with Aphrodite. At the time of Emperor Marcus Aurelius, in the latter half of the 2nd century AD, a pseudo-prophet named Alexander the Paphlagonian devised a great mystery spectacle centred around a holy snake called Glycon and had great success during his lifetime.

The height of Syrian influence was in the 3rd century AD when Sol, the Syrian sun god, was on the verge of becoming the chief god of the Roman Empire. He was introduced into Rome by the emperor Elagabalus (Heliogabalus) in about AD 220, and by about AD 240 Pythian Games (*i.e.,* festivals of the sun god Apollo Helios) were instituted in many cities of the empire. The emperor Aurelian (270–275) elevated Sol to the highest rank among the gods. Sanctuaries of Sol and the gods of other planets (*septizonium*) were constructed. Even the emperor Constantine the Great, some 50 years later, wavered between Sol and Christ. For some time his religious policy was devised so as to allow the coexistence of both religions. Finally, Christianity was accepted as the official religion.

The different mystery religions were not exclusive of one another, but they appealed to different sociological groups. The middle class of the Greek and Roman cities preferred the Dionysiac societies, the festivals of which were a cult of beauty and merriment. Isis was worshipped by lower middle class people in the seaports and trading towns. The followers of the Great Mother in Italy were principally craftsmen. Mithra was the god of soldiers and of imperial officials and freedmen. There were no special societies for slaves; but they were usually admitted to the societies, and, during the time of the festival, all men were considered equal.

BELIEFS AND PRACTICES

Common features in Roman imperial times. For the first three centuries of the Christian Era, the different mystery religions existed side-by-side in the Roman Empire. They had all developed out of local and national cults and later became cosmopolitan and international. The mystery religions would never have developed and expanded as they did, however, without the new social conditions brought about by the unification of the Mediterranean world by the Romans. In the large cities and seaports, men from the remotest parts of the empire flocked together. Many people were removed from their accustomed surroundings and suffered from loneliness. They longed for new acquaintances and for assimilation, and they needed the assurance that only the knowledge of belonging to a community can give. Economic and political conditions in the Roman Empire also accelerated the growth of the mysteries. Members of a mystery society helped one another. For a lawyer, a craftsman, or a contractor, membership in a club could be the road to success. Furthermore, there is less opportunity for private initiative in a society ruled by a monarch than in a democratic society. The individual who felt that his initiative was frustrated by the preponderance of the imperial structure might well turn to a community that offered him the hope of a better future. The mystery societies, thus, commonly satisfied both a taste for individualism and a longing for brotherhood. At least in principle, the members of the communities were considered equal: one man was the other man's brother, irrespective of his origin, social rank, or nationality.

Mysteries fostered by new social conditions in the Roman Empire

Because membership in each of the mystery communities was a matter of personal choice, propaganda and missionary work were inevitable. In the religions of Isis and Mithra, missionary zeal was particularly obvious. The followers of Isis and Mithra considered Rome to be the centre of their worship, and the city was called *sacrosancta civitas* ("sacred city") in an Isis romance written in the 2nd century AD by the Latin author Apuleius.

Priesthood. The organization of the mystery religions was rather loose. The priests of Dionysus were wealthy laymen, as the priests in Greece always were. The Roman community of the Great Mother had a large group of priests (the *galli*), headed by a chief priest (the *Archigallus*). They were eunuchs who wore female garb, who kept their hair long and perfumed with ointment, and who celebrated the goddess' rites with wild music and dancing until their frenzied excitement found its culmination in self-scourging, self-laceration, or exhaustion. Besides the priests there were priestesses and many minor officials. The followers were organized according to their function in the ritual procession as bearers of the tree (*dendrophori*) or bearers of the reed (*cannophori*). The men who carried the statue in the rites of Jupiter Dolichenus were called the sedan-chair men (*lecticarii*).

The higher grades of the Isis Mysteries were reserved to persons born of the priest caste of Egypt. To be born into this caste was more important than talent or skill. This limited the quality of the priests and was a serious disadvantage in the community's competition with other religions. But a second way of advancement within the religious group was devised for men of Greek or Roman origin. In Egypt, there was a group of elevated laymen—the porters of the holy shrine (*pastophori*). They were inferior in rank to everyone of the priest caste; but in Greek and Roman countries the rank of the *pastophori* became a surrogate for the native priest caste of Egypt. The *pastophori* were, in fact, the religious leaders of the communities.

Rites and festivals. A period of preparation preceded the initiation in each of the mysteries. In the Isis religion, for example, a period of 11 days of fasting, including abstinence from meat, wine, and sexual activity, was required before the ceremony. The candidates were segregated from the common folk in special apartments in the holy precinct of the community centre; they were called "the chastely living ones" (*hagneuontes*).

In all the mystery religions the candidates swore an oath of secrecy; the oath of the Isis Mysteries is preserved on papyrus. Before initiation, a confession of sins was expected. The candidate sometimes told at length the story of the faults of his life up to the point of his baptism, which was commonly a part of the initiation ceremony, and the community of devotees listened to the confession. It was believed that the rite of baptism would wash away all the candidate's sins, and, from that point on, his life would be changed for the better, because he had enrolled himself in the service of the saviour god.

In the Mithraic ceremonies, there were seven degrees of initiations: Corax (Raven), Nymphus (Bridegroom), Miles (Soldier), Leo (Lion), Perses (Persian), Heliodromus (Courier of the Sun), and Pater (Father). Those in the lowest ranks, certainly the Corax, were the servants of the community during the sacred meal of bread and water that formed part of the rite.

Initiation ceremonies

The initiation ceremonies usually mimed death and resurrection. This was done in the most extravagant manner. In some ceremonies, candidates were buried or shut up in a sarcophagus; they were even symbolically deprived of their entrails and mummified (an animal's belly with entrails was prepared for the ceremony). Alternatively, the candidates were symbolically drowned or decapitated. In imitation of the Orphic myth of Dionysus Zagreus, a rite was held in which the heart of a victim, supposedly a human child, was roasted and distributed among the participants to be eaten.

The baptism could be either by water or by fire, and the rites often included actions that had an exotic flavour. Sulfur torches were used during the baptism ceremony; they were dipped into water and then—contrary to the expectations of the observers—burned when drawn out of the water. In a dark room a script would suddenly become visible on a wall that had been prepared accordingly. Instructions still exist for producing a nimbus effect—the appearance of light around the head of a priest. The priest's head was shaved and prepared with a protective ointment; then a circular metal receptacle for alcohol was fixed on his head; it was set aflame in a dark room and would shine for some seconds. In the Dionysus and Isis mysteries, the initiation was sometimes accomplished by a "sacred marriage," a sacral copulation. Two cases are known in which a priest speaking from the statue of the god ordered a credulous woman to come to the temple and be the god's concubine, the part of the god being enacted by the priest.

The initiation ceremonies were usually accompanied by music and dance and often included a large cast of actors. In the Dionysiac societies, especially elaborate provisions were made for mimic representations. The names of the sacred roles varied from place to place; among the roles were: Dionysus and Ariadne (a vegetation goddess and wife of Dionysus), Palaemon (a marine deity), Aphrodite (the goddess of love and beauty), Proteurhythmos (the inventor of elegant rhythm), the "foster-father of Dionysus," Kore, Demeter, Asclepius (the god of medicine), Pan (the god of flocks and shepherds), Curetes (long-haired youths), nymphs (minor nature goddesses), shepherds, sileni and satyrs (creatures of the wild, part man and part beast), maenads (female attendants who shared in the nocturnal orgiastic rites of Dionysus), the "guardian of the grotto," and centaurs (a race of beings half man and half horse).

The ceremonies always contained a prayer for the welfare of the emperor and for the good fortune of the whole Roman Empire. In fact, the amalgamation of religion and politics was sometimes so close that the designation "imperial mysteries" is used. The pattern of imperial mystery ceremonies could vary widely. This was especially true of the Dionysiac rites. In the clubs of the upper middle class and wealthy, for example, the festivals were chiefly social events. But the members of these communities were grateful for the security and peace and for the opportunity to make a good living that the emperor guaranteed to them. They felt loyalty toward the Roman Empire and expressed this by ceremonies of the imperial mysteries.

Dionysus was the patron god of the important international society of actors, and their reunions were celebrated in the mode of Dionysiac Mysteries. When an emperor travelled in the empire, responsibility for dignified receptions of him was handed over to the society of actors. Because his route was known beforehand, a voyage of the emperor was turned into a series of pompous festivals that were organized in a manner closely resembling mystery ceremonies.

The meetings of the mystery clubs were often named after the common meal. The Dionysiac meetings were called *stibas* ("straw") because the participants ate their dinner sitting on straw. The meals of the followers of Sarapis and Attis were called *klinē* ("couch"), because the diners lay on couches.

Festivals connected with agriculture

Seasonal festivals. The religions of Dionysus and Demeter and of Isis and the Great Mother had something of an ecclesiastical year. The seasonal festivals were inherited from old tribal ceremonies that had been closely associated with the sowing and reaping of corn and with the production of wine. The dates varied greatly according to the geographical conditions and the emphasis of the seasonal rites in the country in which the mysteries had originated. Dionysiac festivals were held in all four seasons; vintage and tasting of the new wine were the most important occasions. But the religion of Dionysus was closely associated with that of Demeter, and, thus, sowing and reaping were also celebrated in Dionysiac festivals. In the religion of the Great Mother, a hilarious spring festival celebrating the renewal of life was enacted in Rome.

The festivals of the Isis religion were connected with the three Egyptian seasons caused by the cycle of the Nile River (inundation, sowing, and reaping). About July 19, when the whole country was almost desiccated by the heat and the drought, the high waters of the new flood miraculously arrived from Ethiopia. On that day, just before sunrise, Sirius (the Dog Star, or the star of Isis) would make its first appearance of the season on the horizon. This was the sacred New Year's Day for the Egyptians, and the festival of the Nile flood was their greatest festival. There were, in addition, the festivals of sowing and reaping. But because the Egyptian year was a solar year of 365 days without intercalation (leap years), the seasonal festivals that were fixed upon a particular date were retarded by one day every four years and complete confusion resulted. The Romans fixed the calendar of Egypt by introducing an intercalary day every fourth year. In Roman times, important Isis festivals were held on December 25, January 6, and March 5. The March festival, as it was celebrated in Corinth, is described at length in Apuleius' *Metamorphoses,* or *The Golden Ass.* It was a spring festival that celebrated the beginning of the seafaring season. A ship was carried on a cart (*carrus navalis*) through the city. It was followed by a procession of choruses, candidates, *mystai* in bright clothes wearing masks, and priests carrying the insignia of the goddess. The ship was let into the sea, and the participants returned to the temple, where initiation ceremonies, banquets, and dances were held.

In the religion of Sol, the festivals were determined by astronomy. The greatest festival was held on December 24–25, at the time of the winter solstice. Because from this date the length of the day began to increase, it was regarded as the day of the rebirth of the god and of the renovation of life.

Literature. The mystery communities had religious hymns, but almost nothing of them has been preserved. The initial words of some hymns from the Sta. Prisca Mithraeum in Rome are known, and some Isiac poems exist. More important is a text of 40 sentences in which the goddess Isis reveals herself; it was found at four different and geographically distant places and was probably exhibited in every Isis sanctuary. Narratives of the miracles wrought by the gods were preserved in many temple libraries; examples of these narratives, on papyrus and on stone, have been found. According to a recent theory, the literary genre of the romance was developed from these narratives. The last part of the *Metamorphoses* of Apuleius is an Isis text and narrates in detail the initiation into the Egyptian mysteries.

Hermetic writings and *Chaldean Oracles*

Hermes Trismegistos, the Greek name for the Egyptian god Thoth, was the reputed author of treatises that have been preserved. Thoth was the scribe of the gods, the inventor of writing, and the patron of all the arts dependent upon writing; he was sometimes thought of as an attendant of Isis and sometimes as the repository of all wisdom. These treatises are not exactly mystery texts, but they are works of revelation on occult subjects and on theology. Because the pagan mysteries had no official creed, each congregation of initiates was free to construct a theology of its own and to change it again. The Hermetic writings were attempts to provide a theology for a particular community. Although no authorized interpretation could exist for a doctrine that was in constant fluctuation and although none of the Hermetic treatises could claim to be the correct interpretation of the pagan mysteries, nevertheless, the texts give an instructive picture of spiritual life in mystery communities.

There are some contemporary texts that shed light on the mystery communities. Plutarch, the Greek biographer, wrote the philosophical treatise "About Isis and Osiris," which gives an interpretation of the Isis Mysteries. Arnobius, a 3rd-century Christian apologist, described an interesting semiphilosophical, semireligious mystery community known as the *viri novi* ("the new men"). Arnobius seems to have lived among them in North Africa for a time before his conversion to Christianity. They had a religious doctrine of the soul, with marked affinities to the teachings of the Neoplatonic thinkers Plotinus and Porphyry.

Only fragments are preserved of the *Chaldean Oracles,* a theosophical text in verse that was composed by Julianus the Theurgist and his son late in the 2nd century AD and had great influence on the Neoplatonists. The work combined Platonic elements with Persian or Babylonian creeds and was regarded by the later Neoplatonists as their basic religious book, something of a heathen bible. The doctrine of the *Chaldean Oracles* was associated with esoteric fire rituals. Julianus and his followers were called theurgists—*i.e.,* men who could perform divine operations. Their religion was partly one of meditation about the hidden and wondrous magical processes within the cosmos.

Theology. The creeds of the mystery religions were never worked out to the same extent that the Christian creeds were. Nevertheless, the doctrines of the mysteries may be called a theology. One of the central subjects in mystery writings was cosmogony—the theory of the origin or creation of the world. In the Hermetic treatises, in the *Chaldean Oracles,* and in the little known writings of Mithraism, the cosmogony was modelled after Plato's *Timaeus,* and it always dealt with the creation of the soul and with the soul's subsequent fate.

The myth of the soul

The theological doctrine of the soul and the myth about its celestial home, its fall, and its redemption were inseparable. The sequence is beautifully told in the "Hymn of the Soul," preserved in the *Acts of Thomas,* an apocryphal account of the journeys and death of the apostle. The hero of the hymn, who represents the soul of man, is born in the Eastern (the yonder) Kingdom; immediately after his birth, he is sent by his parents on a pilgrimage into the world with instructions to take a pearl from the mouth of a dragon in the sea. Instead of wearing his heavenly garment, he dresses in earthly clothes, eats earthly food, and forgets his task. Then his parents send a letter to rouse him. As soon as he has read the letter, he awakes and remembers his task, takes the pearl, and begins the homeward journey. On the way, his brother (the Redeemer) comes to accompany him and leads him back home to his father's palace in the east. This myth is a figurative representation of the theological doctrine of the soul's fall and its return to heaven.

Many of the questions that were the subject of later Christian theological discussions were already eagerly debated in the mystery religions. In a Hermetic treatise, for example, the existence of God was proved from the evident order of the world. This argument, which had first been formulated by Zoroaster, a 7th-century Iranian prophet, was expressed in the form of questions: Who could have created the heavens and the stars, the sun and the moon, except God? Who could have made wind, water, fire, and earth (the elements), the seasons of the year, the crops, the animals, and man, except God?

Passionate debates were held about the question of whether man was subject to blind fate. The Stoics (proponents of a Greek and Roman school of philosophy holding that men should be free from passion and calmly accept all occurrences as unavoidable) had adopted the doctrine that all events are determined by the stars. Thus, for many Greeks and Romans astrology became the only sensible method of studying man's life and fortune. But, for others, the idea that man could achieve nothing by his own will was frightening, and they wanted to be liberated from this fear; the mystery religions promised to liberate them. The theology of the mystery religions admitted that the stars ruled the world and especially that the planets had evil influences. But the highest god of the religion (for example, Sarapis in the Isis Mysteries) stood far above the stars and was their master. A man who decided to become a servant of this god stepped out of the circle of determination and entered into the sphere of liberty. The god could suspend determination, because he ruled over the stars; he could unravel the threads of the Moirai (the three spinners of fate); he could save his servant from illness and prolong his life, even against the will of fate. In the Isis Mysteries there was a theology of grace foreshadowing Christian doctrine.

In many of the mystery cults, there was a marked tendency toward henotheism—the worship of one god without denying the existence of other gods. Thus, Isis was the essence of all pagan goddesses; Sarapis was the name uniting the gods Zeus, Pluto, Dionysus, Asclepius, Helios, and even the Jewish god YHWH (Yahweh). In the religion of Sol, an elaborate syncretistic theology was developed to show that all known gods of all nations were nothing but provisional names for the sun god.

RELIGIOUS ART AND ICONOGRAPHY

Much of Greco-Roman art was executed for use in the mystery communities. The Dionysiac monuments are by far superior to all others in artistic quality. This is to be expected, because the worship of Dionysus often took the form of a worship of beauty. Nevertheless, the other communities also produced a great number of art objects.

Architecture. The mystery religions developed different types of edifices for their purposes. Every Greek city had temples and precincts of Dionysus. The Isis Mysteries adopted the Greek temples, frequently adding a cupola. Many Isis temples were modest in size, but the temple at Pergamum (modern Bergama, Turkey) was a great basilica with a vaulted roof and strong towers, in the fashion of the best Roman architecture. The Isis temple that the emperor Domitian erected on the Campus Martius (the Field of Mars) in Rome at the end of the 1st century AD was a stately building, and the Temple of Sarapis (the Sarapeum) at Alexandria was a huge construction. The subterranean basilica near Porta Maggiore in Rome (used by an Orphic or Pythagorean society) was a strong and magnificent structure, hidden in a large garden. The Mithraic sanctuaries were artificial caves illuminated from above by light shafts. They were built for communities of from 50 to 100 persons.

The buildings were designed to be functional for the religious ceremonies. The Mithraeum under the church of S. Clemente at Rome contained a system of underground galleries for initiation ceremonies. Beneath the temple of the Egyptian gods at Pergamum, subterranean passages existed for the use of the priests. One of the paths led into the huge, hollow statue of the god, so that the priest could speak from the mouth of the statue. By another secret way, an officiant could climb the huge corner towers of the temple to make announcements from there. The Sarapeum at Alexandria was directed toward the east; on a certain day of the year, at a certain time, sunbeams directly struck the head of the god's statue. This same temple was so arranged that those waiting to be initiated could hire rooms in an adjacent building during the time of preparation before the ceremony.

Because the use of water was such an important element in most of the mystery rites, the location of the temples was often determined by the availability of water; Mithraic sanctuaries were always erected on the spot at which a fountain had its source. In the temples of Isis, a cistern for the holy water was required; in Delos and in a house at Pompeii in Italy, a system of water basins could imitate the flood of the Nile. The Dionysus temple at Corinth had an underground system of tubes and barrels that could be operated by buttons from the outside. The priest showed the worshippers of the god a barrel filled with water. They left the temple together, and the door was sealed from without. By pressing the buttons, the water was let out of the barrel, and wine was poured in. The following day, when the seal was removed, the spectator witnessed the Dionysiac miracle of water turned into wine.

On the ground floor of the Mithraic sanctuaries at Ostia, mosaic pavements showed the seven grades of the initiation and their symbols together with the ladder of the seven steps that led to religious salvation. In initiation ceremonies the mosaic was perhaps used to indicate the place where the different participants were to take their places.

Statuary. A great many statues were exhibited in the temples and shrines of the mystery gods. They were usually executed in the traditional Greek style. In the sanctuary of Isis and Sarapis at Thessalonica (modern Thessaloníki), in northern Greece, there were statues of a whole series of Greek goddesses, each of whom was identified with Isis in one way or another to show that the Egyptian goddess was the essence and synthesis of Greek religion. In the 4th century BC, the sculptor Bryaxis created a famous colossal statue of Sarapis in the temple at Alexandria. It represented the god—as a combination of the Greek gods Zeus (the father of the gods), Hades, and Dionysus—seated upon a throne, with Cerberus, the three-headed monster, beside him. An interesting statuette found at Cyrene (modern Shaḥḥāt, Libya) shows a female initiate of Isis. The woman is wrapped from feet to waist like a mummy; but the upper part of her body is free, and she is wearing the crown of Isis on her head. The statue thus showed how an initiate would first die and subsequently resurrect in triumph during the ceremony. Many terra-cotta statues of Isis and her son Horus have survived from

Roman Egypt; they are similar to the later statues of the Christian Madonna and Child. Syrian statues of Jupiter Heliopolitanus represent the god in a rigid attitude, like a pillar. In the base of some of these statues are holes, into which sticks could be inserted for the purpose of carrying the statue in procession. In Mithraic sanctuaries a great number of statues, especially of the gods of the planets, were exhibited. Statues of the Mithraic time god were also frequent; they were often hollow and were constructed so that they could spit fire.

Reliefs. The Dionysiac reliefs are numerous. They show symbols of the religion, such as the shepherd's staff, the winnow (an ancient device for separating chaff from grain), and the phallus; they depict the gay life of satyrs and maenads, shepherds and shepherdesses; and they represent the "golden age" of the gods with tame and wild animals enjoying a peace that the god had instituted. A great, silver dish, dating from about the 4th century AD and found at Mildenhall, England, shows the swift and elegant dance of the maenads. Dionysiac sarcophagi represented Bacchic revels and the pastime of the Erotes and Psyches in afterlife. Many reliefs of the Isis Mysteries also survive. They display the mystical cista (a receptacle for carrying sacred objects) with the snake of Horus, the priest carrying the holy water in a procession, female attendants with a ladle, and a man in a dog's mask, who represents Anubis (the guardian god). Other Isiac reliefs show Isis riding on a dog, symbolic of her position as goddess of Sirius (the Dog Star).

In Mithraic caverns there was always a relief depicting the god sacrificing the bull. Representations of the sacramental meal were also frequent; a relief recently discovered in Konjic, Yugoslavia, shows the initiates at a banquet wearing masks, among them a lion, a raven, a soldier, and a Persian. Two reliefs—at Rome (now at Modena, Italy) and at Housesteads, England (the best preserved fort along Hadrian's Wall)—depict the creation of the world out of an initial egg; in this case, Orphic and Mithraic ideas were amalgamated. Other episodes of Mithraic mythology that were commonly displayed include the birth of Mithra from a rock with the shepherds who welcome him and his dealings with the sun god.

The stucco reliefs in the subterranean basilica near Porta Maggiore are of outstanding quality. In the central episode, Sappho—an early Greek poetess who supposedly killed herself in a "lover's leap" from the island of Leucas into the Ionian Sea—is shown leaping toward Apollo, the god of the sun; this symbolized the soul's transcendence into more favourable existence. Many of the reliefs in the basilica allegorize episodes from Greek mythology in the fashion of the Pythagoreans, who found a hidden religious or philosophical meaning behind the mythical tales of the Greek tradition.

Painting. There are few paintings from the temples of the mystery religions that have been preserved; nevertheless, some of these deserve comment. The superb Dionysiac frescoes of the Villa of the Mysteries (Villa dei Misteri) at Pompeii show the initiation of a girl into the Bacchic Mysteries: in one fresco she is lifting the cover of a sacred casket; in a second scene three followers of Dionysus are practicing lecanomancy (divination by the inspection of a bowl filled with water); in a third scene the girl is unveiling an erect phallus and because of this she is being flagellated; finally, she is seen dancing in happy bliss. A number of Isiac frescoes, preserved in the temple of Isis at Pompeii, show the sacred dance of the initiates, the presentation of an urn filled with the ritual holy water to the initiates, the coffin of Osiris and his resurrection, and episodes from the cycle of Io, a Greek heroine equated with Isis. Isiac frescoes dating from the time of the emperor Caligula in the 1st century AD are also found in the ruins on the Palatine at Rome. In the Mithraeum under Sta. Prisca in Rome, two layers of frescoes were found that show the procession of the initiates toward ritual sacrifice of a bull, called Suovetaurilia, and the sacred meal of the sun god and Mithra. Sometimes a fresco replaced the relief of the sacrifice of the bull. The initiation ceremonies are shown in the Mithraic sanctuary at Capua (in western Italy): the candidate, accompanied by the *mystagōgos,* is blindfolded, kneels down, and lies prostrate. At Rome, in the tomb of Vincentius and Vibia, who worshipped the god Sabazius (a Thracian form of Dionysus), frescoes show how Vibia was carried away by Death, as Kore had been carried away by Hades, how she was judged and acquitted, and how she was introduced by a "good angel" to the sacred meal of the blessed.

Mosaics. A mosaic at Antioch represents the Phoenix—the solar bird who died and resurrected from its own ashes and who was its own father and son at the same time—with sunrays encircling its head. A Dionysus mosaic at Cologne, Germany, depicts in several panels the life of satyrs and maenads and also Bacchic symbols such as the winnow (an implement of purification) and the oyster (which has to be liberated from the shell as the soul from the body). The room evidently was used for banquets and Dionysiac merrymaking.

MYSTERY RELIGIONS AND CHRISTIANITY

Christianity originated during the time of the Roman Empire, which was also the time at which the mysteries reached their height of popularity. This was by no means an accident. The Christian theologian Origen wrote in the 3rd century that it was part of the divine plan that Christ was born under the emperor Augustus: the whole Mediterranean world was united by the Romans, and the conditions for missionary work were more favourable than ever before. The simultaneousness of the propagation of the mystery religions and of Christianity and the striking similarities between them, however, demand some explanation of their relationship. The hypothesis of a mutual dependence has been proposed by scholars—especially a dependence of Christianity upon the mysteries—but such theories have been discarded. The similarities must rather be explained by parallel developments from similar origins. In both cases, national religions of a ritualistic type were transformed, and the transformation followed similar lines: from national to ecumenical religion, from ritualistic ceremonies and taboos to spiritual doctrines set down in books, from the idea of inherited tradition to the idea of revelation. The parallel development was fostered by the new conditions prevailing in the Roman Empire, in which the old political units were dissolved, and the whole civilized world was ruled by one monarch. People were free to move from one country to another and became cosmopolitan. The ideas of Greek philosophy penetrated everywhere in this society. Thus, under identical conditions, new forms of religious communities sprang from similar roots. The mystery religions and Christianity had many similar features—*e.g.,* a time of preparation before initiation and periods of fasting; baptism and banquets; vigils and early-morning ceremonies; pilgrimages and new names for the initiates. The purity demanded in the worship of Sol and in the Chaldean fire rites was similar to Christian standards. The first Christian communities resembled the mystery communities in big cities and seaports by providing social security and the feeling of brotherhood. In the Christian congregations of the first two centuries, the variety of rites and creeds was almost as great as in the mystery communities; few of the early Christian congregations could have been called orthodox according to later standards. The date of Christmas was purposely fixed on December 25 to push into the background the great festival of the sun god, and Epiphany on January 6 to supplant an Egyptian festival of the same day. The Easter ceremonies rivalled the pagan spring festivals. The religious art of the Christians continued the pagan art of the preceding generations. The Christian representations of the Madonna and child are clearly the continuation of the representations of Isis and her son suckling her breast. The statue of the Good Shepherd carrying his lost sheep and the pastoral themes on Christian sarcophagi were also taken over from pagan craftsmanship.

Similarities between mysteries and Christianity

In theology the differences between early Christians, Gnostics (members—often Christian—of dualistic sects of the 2nd century AD), and pagan Hermetists were slight. In the large Gnostic library discovered at Najʿ Ḥammādī, in upper Egypt, in 1945, Hermetic writings were found side-by-side with Christian Gnostic texts. The doctrine of the soul taught in Gnostic communities was almost identical to that taught in the mysteries: the soul emanated from the Father, fell into the body, and had to return to its former home. The Greeks interpreted the national religions of the Greek Orient chiefly in terms of the philosophical and religious concepts elaborated by Plato. Interpretation in Platonic concepts was also the means by which the Judeo-Christian set of creeds was thoroughly assimilated to Greek ideas by the early Christian thinkers Clement of Alexandria and Origen. Thus, the religions had a common conceptual framework. The doctrinal similarity is exemplified in the case of the pagan writer and philosopher Synesius. When the people of Cyrene wanted the most able man of the city to be their bishop, they chose him, and he was able to accept the election without sacrificing his intellectual honesty. In his pagan period he wrote hymns that closely follow the fire theology of the *Chaldean Oracles;* later he wrote hymns to Christ. The doctrine is almost identical.

The similarity of the religious vocabulary is also great. Greek life was characterized by such things as democratic institutions, seafaring, gymnasium and athletic games, theatre, and philosophy. The mystery religions adopted many expressions from these domains: they spoke of the assembly (*ekklēsia*) of the *mystai;* the voyage of life; the ship, the anchor, and the port of religion; and the wreath of the initiate; life was a stage and man the actor. The Christians took over the entire terminology; but many pagan words were strangely twisted in order to fit into the Christian world: the service of the state (*leitourgia*) became the ritual, or liturgy, of the church; the decree of the assembly and the opinions of the philosophers (*dogma*) became the fixed doctrine of Christianity; the correct opinion (*orthē doxa*) about things became orthodoxy.

Differences between mysteries and Christianity

There are also great differences between Christianity and the mysteries. Mystery religions, as a rule, can be traced back to tribal origins, Christianity to a historical person. The holy stories of the mysteries were myths; the Gospels of the New Testament, however, relate historical events. The books that the mystery communities used in Roman times cannot possibly be compared to the New Testament. The essential features of Christianity were fixed once and for all in this book; the mystery doctrines, however, always remained in a much greater state of fluidity. The theology of the mysteries was developed to a far lesser degree than the Christian theology. There are no parallels in Christianity to the sexual rites in the Dionysiac and Isiac religion, with the exception of a few aberrant Gnostic communities. The cult of rulers in the manner of the imperial mysteries was impossible in Jewish and Christian worship.

The mysteries declined quickly when the emperor Constantine raised Christianity to the status of the state religion. After a short period of toleration, the pagan religions were prohibited. The property of the pagan gods was confiscated, and the temples were destroyed. The precious metal from which Constantine's gold pieces were coined was taken from heathen temple treasuries. To show the beginning of a new era, the capital of the empire was transferred to the new Christian city of Constantinople. The centres of pagan resistance were Rome and Alexandria: in Rome the old aristocracy clung to the mysteries, and in Alexandria the pagan Neoplatonist philosophers expounded the mystery doctrines. When Julian the Apostate, Roman emperor from AD 361 to 363, tried to reestablish pagan worship, he found allies at Rome and Alexandria. After his death, the pagan opposition to Christianity continued for one more generation. The Roman aristocrats multiplied their efforts to maintain the piety of the mysteries, and the pagan philosophers tried to refine their theology by oversubtle interpretations. In 391, however, the Sarapeum at Alexandria was demolished, and in 394 the opposition of the Roman aristocracy was crushed in the battle at the Frigidus River (modern stream of Vipacco, Italy; stream of Vipava, Yugoslavia).

Only remnants of the mystery doctrines, amalgamated with Platonism, were transmitted by a few philosophers and individualists to the religious thinkers of the Byzantine Empire. The mystery religions exerted some influence on the thinkers of the Middle Ages and the philosophers of the Italian Renaissance.

BIBLIOGRAPHY

General: JAMES G. FRAZER, *The Golden Bough,* 3rd ed. (1911–15, reissued 1980), a famous and influential treatise on ancient religion, especially on Adonis, Attis, Osiris, Dionysus, and Demeter; MARTIN P. NILSSON, *A History of the Greek Religion,* 2nd ed. (1964; trans. of 2nd German ed., 1955), an excellent handbook; JOSCELYN GODWIN, *Mystery Religions in the Ancient World* (1981), an illustrated, popular overview of mystery religions in the Roman Empire.

Greek mysteries: ERWIN ROHDE, *Psyche* (1925, reissued 1972; originally published in German, 1894), by the first author to understand the religion of Dionysus; LOUIS R. FARNELL, *The Cults of the Greek States,* 5 vol. (1896–1909, reissued 1977), a careful and conscientious collection and interpretation of the sources for Demeter and Dionysus; JANE E. HARRISON, *Prolegomena to the Study of the Greek Religion,* 3rd ed. (1922, reprinted 1975), original accounts about Demeter, Dionysus, and Orpheus; ERIC R. DODDS, *The Greeks and the Irrational* (1951), relevant especially for Dionysiac and Orphic religion.

Mysteries in the Roman Empire: FRANZ CUMONT, *Oriental Religions in Roman Paganism* (1911, reprinted 1956; trans. of 2nd French ed., 1909), an excellent general account; A.D. NOCK, *Conversion* (1933, reissued 1972), a well-written and original study of the relation of Oriental cults and Christianity; *Early Gentile Christianity and Its Hellenistic Background* (1964), a learned collection of articles; MARTIN P. NILSSON, *The Dionysiac Mysteries of the Hellenistic and Roman Age* (1957, reprinted 1975), a clear and scholarly survey of the religion of Dionysus in later times; REINHOLD MERKELBACH, *Roman und Mysterium in der Antike* (1962), on the ancient romances as mystery texts; *Isisfeste in griechischrömischer Zeit* (1963), treats the Isis festivals and their relationship to Christian festivals; and RAMSAY MACMULLEN, *Paganism in the Roman Empire* (1981).

(R.Me.)

Myth and Mythology

Myth is a collective term denoting a kind of communication, specifically a symbolic narrative in religion, as distinguished from symbolic behaviour (cult, ritual) and symbolic places or objects (temples, icons). Myths are specific accounts of gods or superhuman beings involved in extraordinary events or circumstances in a time that is unspecified but which is understood as existing apart from ordinary human experience. As with all religious symbolism, there is no attempt to justify mythic narratives or render them plausible. Every myth presents itself as an authoritative, factual account, no matter how much the narrated events are at variance with ordinary experience. By extension from this primary religious meaning, the word myth may also be used more loosely to refer to an ideological belief when that belief is the object of a quasi-religious faith; an example would be the Marxist eschatological myth of the withering away of the state.

While the outline of myths from a past period or from a society other than one's own can usually be seen quite clearly, to recognize the myths that are dominant in one's own time and society is always difficult. This is hardly surprising, because a myth has its authority not by proving itself but by presenting itself. In this sense the authority of a myth indeed "goes without saying," and the myth can be outlined in detail only when its authority is no longer unquestioned but has been rejected or overcome in some manner by another, more comprehensive myth.

The word myth derives from the Greek *mythos,* which has a range of meanings from "word," through "saying" and "story," to "fiction"; the unquestioned validity of *mythos* can be contrasted with *logos,* the word whose validity or truth can be argued and demonstrated. Because myths narrate fantastic events with no attempt at substantiation, people have sometimes assumed that they are simply stories with no factual basis and thus have made the word myth a synonym for falsehood or, at best, misconception. In the study of religion, however, it is important to make a distinction between myths and stories that are merely untrue.

The term mythology denotes both the study of myth and the body of myths belonging to a particular religious tradition. The first part of this article discusses the nature, study, functions, cultural impact, and types of myth, taking into account the various approaches to the subject offered by modern branches of knowledge. In the second part, the specialized topic of the role of animals and plants in myth is examined in some detail.

For coverage of related topics in the *Macropædia* and *Micropædia,* see the *Propædia,* section 811.

The article is divided into the following sections:

The nature, functions, and types of myth

Myth has existed in every society. Indeed, it would seem to be a basic constituent of human culture. Because the variety is so great, it is difficult to generalize about the nature of myths. But it is clear that in their general characteristics and in their details a people's myths reflect, express, and explore the people's self-image. The study of myth is thus of central importance in the study both of individual societies and of human culture as a whole.

RELATION OF MYTHS TO OTHER NARRATIVE FORMS

In Western culture there are a number of literary or narrative genres that scholars have related in different ways to myths. Examples are fables, fairy tales, folktales, sagas, epics, legends, and etiologic tales (which refer to causes or explain why a thing is the way it is). Another form of tale, the parable, differs from myth in its purpose and character. Even in the West, however, there is no agreed definition of any of these genres, and some scholars question whether multiplying categories of narrative is helpful at all, as opposed to working with a very general concept such as the traditional tale. Non-Western cultures apply classifications that are different both from the Western categories and from one another. Most, however, make a basic distinction between "true" and "fictitious" narratives, with "true" ones corresponding to what in the West would be called myths.

If it is accepted that the category of traditional tale should be subdivided, one way of doing so is to regard the various subdivisions as comparable to bands of colour in a spectrum. Within this figurative spectrum there will be similarities and analogies between myth and folktale, or myth and legend, or fairy tale and folktale. In the section that follows it is assumed that useful distinctions can be drawn between different categories. It should, however, be remembered throughout that these classifications are far from rigid and that in many cases a given tale might be plausibly assigned to more than one category.

Fables. The word fable derives from the Latin word *fabula,* which originally meant about the same as the Greek *mythos;* like *mythos,* it came to mean a fictitious or untrue story. Myths, in contrast, are not presented as fictitious or untrue.

Fables, like some myths, feature personified animals or natural objects as characters. Unlike myths, however, fables almost always end with an explicit moral message, and this highlights the characteristic feature of fables—namely, that they are instructive tales that teach morals about human social behaviour. Myths, by contrast, tend to lack this directly didactic aspect, and the sacred narratives that they embody are often hard to translate into direct prescriptions for action in everyday human terms. Another difference between fables and myths relates to a feature of the narratives that they present. The context of a typical fable will be unspecific as to time and space; *e.g.,* "A fox and a goose met at a pool." A typical myth, on the other hand, will be likely to identify by name the god or hero concerned in a given exploit and to specify details of geography and genealogy; *e.g.,* "Oedipus was the son of Laius, the king of Thebes."

Fairy tales. The term fairy tale, if taken literally, should refer only to stories about fairies, a class of supernatural and sometimes malevolent beings, often believed to be of diminutive size, who were thought by people in medieval and postmedieval Europe to inhabit a kingdom of their own; a literary expression of this belief can be found in Shakespeare's *A Midsummer Night's Dream.* The term fairy tale, however, is normally used to refer to a much wider class of narrative, namely stories (directed above all at an audience of children) about an individual, almost always young, who confronts strange or magical events: examples are Jack and the beanstalk, Cinderella, and Snow White and the seven dwarfs. The modern concept of the fairy tale seems not to be found earlier than the 18th century in Europe, but the narratives themselves have earlier analogues much farther afield, notably in the Indian *Kathā-saritsāgara* (*The Ocean of Story*) and in *The Thousand and One Nights.*

Like myths, fairy tales present extraordinary beings and events. Unlike myths—but like fables—fairy tales tend to be placed in a setting that is geographically and temporally vague. A typical fairy tale might begin with the words "Once upon a time there was a handsome prince . . ."; a myth about a prince, by contrast, would be likely to name him and to specify his lineage, since such details might be of collective importance (for example, with reference to issues of property inheritance or the relative status of different families) to the social group among which the myth was told.

Folktales. There is much disagreement among scholars as to how to define the folktale; consequently, there is disagreement about the relation between folktale and myth. One view of the problem is that of the American folklorist Stith Thompson, who regarded myths as one type of folktale; according to this approach, the particular characteristic of myth is that its narratives deal with sacred events that happened "in the beginning." Other scholars either consider folktale a subdivision of myth or regard the two categories as distinct but overlapping. The latter view is taken by the British classicist Geoffrey S. Kirk, who in *Myth: Its Meaning and Functions in Ancient and Other Cultures* (1970) uses the term myth to denote stories with an underlying purpose beyond that of simple storytelling and the term folktale to denote stories that reflect simple social situations and play on ordinary fears and desires. Examples of folktale motifs are encounters between ordinary, often humble, human beings and supernatural adversaries such as witches, giants, or ogres; contests to win a bride; attempts to overcome a wicked stepmother or jealous sisters. But these typical folktale themes occur also in stories normally classified as myths, and there must always be a strong element of arbitrariness in assigning a motif to a particular category.

Relation of myth and folktale

A different and important aspect of the problem of defining a folktale relates to the historical origin of the concept. As with the notion of folklore, the notion of folktale has its roots in the late 18th century. From that period until the middle of the 19th century, many European thinkers of a nationalist persuasion argued that stories told by ordinary people constituted a continuous tradition reaching back into the nation's past. Thus, stories such as the *Märchen* ("Tales") collected by the Grimm brothers in Germany are folktales because they were told by the people rather than by an aristocratic elite. This definition of folktale introduces a new criterion for distinguishing between myth and folktale—namely, what class of person tells the story—but it by no means removes all the problems of classification. Just as the distinction between folk and aristocracy cannot be transferred from medieval Europe to tribal Africa or classical Greece without risk of distortion, so the importing of a distinction between myth and folktale on the later European model is extremely problematic.

Sagas and epics. The word saga is often used in a generalized and loose way to refer to any extended narrative re-creation of historical events. A distinction is thus sometimes drawn between myths (set in a semidivine world) and sagas (more realistic and more firmly grounded in a specific historical setting). This rather vague use of saga is best avoided, however, since the word can more usefully retain the precise connotation of its original context. The word saga is Old Norse and means "what is said." The sagas are a group of medieval Icelandic prose narratives; the principal sagas date from the 13th century and relate the deeds of Icelandic heroes who lived during the 10th and 11th centuries. If the word saga is restricted to this Icelandic context, at least one of the possible terminological confusions over words for traditional tales is avoided.

While saga in its original sense is a narrative type confined to a particular time and place, epics are found worldwide. Examples can be found in the ancient world (the *Iliad* and *Odyssey* of Homer), in medieval Europe (the *Nibelungenlied*), and in modern times (the Yugoslav epic poetry recorded in the 1930s). Among the many non-European examples are the Indian *Mahābhārata* and the Tibetan Gesar epic. Epic is similar to saga in that both narrative forms look back to an age of heroic endeavour, but it differs from saga in that epics are almost always composed in poetry (with a few exceptions such as Kazakh epic and the Turkish *Book of Dede Korkut*). The relation between epic and myth is not easy to pin down, but it is in general true that epics characteristically incorporate mythical events and persons. An example is the ancient Mesopotamian epic of Gilgamesh, which includes, among many mythical episodes, an account of the meeting between the hero Gilgamesh and Utnapishtim, the only man to have attained immortality and sole survivor (with his wife) of the flood sent by the gods. Myth is thus a prime source of the material on which epic draws.

Legends. In common usage the word legend usually characterizes a traditional tale thought to have a historical basis, as in the legends of King Arthur or Robin Hood. In this view, a distinction may be drawn between myth (which refers to the supernatural and the sacred) and legend (which is grounded in historical fact). Thus, some writers on the *Iliad* would distinguish between the legendary aspects (*e.g.,* heroes performing actions possible for ordinary humans) and the mythical aspects (*e.g.,* episodes involving the gods). But the distinction between myth and legend must be used with care. In particular, because of the assumed link between legend and historical fact, there may be a tendency to refer to narratives that correspond to one's own beliefs as legends, while exactly comparable stories from other traditions may be classified as myths; hence a Christian might refer to stories about the miraculous deeds of a saint as legends, while similar stories about a pagan healer might be called myths. As in other cases, it must be remembered that the boundaries between terms for traditional narratives are fluid, and that different writers employ them in quite different ways.

Parables. The term myth is not normally applied to narratives that have as their explicit purpose the illustration of a doctrine or standard of conduct. Instead, the term parable, or illustrative tale, is used. Familiar examples of such narratives are the parables of the New Testament. Parables have a considerable role also in Ṣūfism (Islāmic mysticism), rabbinic (Jewish biblical interpretive) literature, Ḥasidism (Jewish pietism), and Zen Buddhism. That parables are essentially non-mythological is clear because the point made by the parable is known or supposed to be known from another source. Parables have a more subservient function than myths. They may clarify something to an individual or a group but do not take on the revelatory character of myth.

Etiologic tales. Etiologic tales are very close to myth, and some scholars regard them as a particular type of myth rather than as a separate category. In modern usage the term etiology is used to refer to the description or assignment of causes (Greek *aitia*). Accordingly, an etiologic tale explains the origin of a custom, state of affairs, or natural feature in the human or divine world. Many tales explain the origin of a particular rock or mountain. Others explain iconographic features, such as the Hindu narrative ascribing the blue neck of the god Śiva to a poison he drank in primordial times. The etiologic theme often seems to be added to a mythical narrative as an afterthought. In other words, the etiology is not the distinctive characteristic of myth.

APPROACHES TO THE STUDY OF MYTH AND MYTHOLOGY

The importance of studying myth to provide a key to a human society is a matter of historical record. In the middle of the 19th century, for instance, a newly appointed British governor of New Zealand, Sir George Grey, was confronted by the problem of how to come to terms with the Maori, who were hostile to the British. He learned their language, but that proved insufficient for an understanding of the way in which they reasoned and argued. In order to be able to conduct negotiations satisfactorily, he found it necessary to study the Maori's mythology, to which they made frequent reference. Other government officials and Christian missionaries of the 19th and 20th centuries made similar efforts to understand the mythologies of nations or tribes so as to facilitate communication. Such studies were more than a means to an end, whether efficient administration or conversion; they amounted to the discovery that myths present a model or charter for man's behaviour and that the world of myth provides guidance for crucial elements in human existence—war and peace, life and death, truth and falsehood, good and evil. In addition to such practically motivated attempts to understand myth, theorists and scholars from many disciplines have interested themselves in the study of the subject. A close study of myth has developed in the West, especially since the 18th century. Much of its material has come from the study of the Greek and Roman classics, from which it has also derived some of its methods of interpretation.

Myths as a model of human behaviour

The growth of philosophy in ancient Greece furthered allegorical interpretations of myth—*i.e.,* finding other or supposedly deeper meanings hidden below the surface of mythical texts. Such meanings were usually seen as involving natural phenomena or human values. Related to this was a tendency toward rationalism, especially when those who studied myths employed false etymologies. Rationalism in this context connotes the scrutiny of myths in such a way as to make sense of the statements contained in them without taking literally their references to gods, monsters, or the supernatural. Thus, the ancient writer Palaiphatos interpreted the story of Europa (carried off to Crete on the back of a handsome bull, which was actually Zeus in disguise) as that of a woman abducted by a Cretan called Tauros, the Greek word for bull; and Skylla, the bestial and cannibalistic creature who attacked Odysseus' ship according to Homer's *Odyssey,* was by the same process of rationalizing interpreted as simply the name of a pirate ship. Of special and long-lasting influence in the history of the interpretation of myth was Euhemerism (named after Euhemerus, a Greek writer who flourished about 300 BC), according to which certain gods were originally great people venerated because of their benefactions to mankind.

Influence of Euhemerism

The early Church Fathers adopted an attitude of modified Euhemerism, according to which classical mythology was to be explained in terms of mere men who had been raised to superhuman, demonic status because of their deeds. By this means, Christians were able to incorporate myths from the culturally authoritative pagan past into a Christian framework while defusing their religious significance—the gods became ordinary humans. The Middle Ages did not develop new theoretical perspectives on myth, nor, despite some elaborate works of historical and etymological erudition, did the Renaissance. In both periods, interpretations in terms of allegory and Euhemerism tended to predominate.

In early 18th-century Italy, Giambattista Vico, a thinker now considered the forerunner of all writers on ethnology, or the study of culture in human societies, built on traditional scholarship—especially in law and philosophy—to make the first clear case for the role of man's creative imagination in the formation of distinct myths at successive cultural stages. His work, which was most notably expressed in his *Scienza nuova* (1725; *The New Science of Giambattista Vico*), had no influence in his own century. Instead, the notion that pagan myths were distortions of the biblical revelation (first expressed in the Renaissance) continued to find favour. Nevertheless, Enlightenment philosophy, reports from voyages of discovery, and missionary reports (especially the Jesuits' accounts of North American Indians) contributed to scholarship and fostered greater objectivity. Bernhard Le Bovier de Fontenelle, a French scholar, compared Greek and American Indian myths and suggested that there was a universal human predisposition toward mythology. In *De l'origine des fables* (1724; "On the Origin of Fables") he attributed the absurdities (as he saw them) of myths to the fact that the stories grew up among an earlier, more primitive human society. About 1800 the Romantics' growing fascination with language, the postulation of an Indo-European language family, the study of Sanskrit, and the growth of comparative studies, especially in history and philology, were all part of a trend that included the study of myth.

The relevance of Indo-European studies to an understanding of Greek and Roman mythology was carried to an extreme in the work of Friedrich Max Müller, a German Orientalist who moved to Britain and undertook important research on comparative linguistics. In his view, expressed in such works as *Comparative Mythology* (1856), the mythology of the original Indo-European peoples had consisted of allegorical stories about the workings of nature, in particular such features as the sky, the Sun, and the dawn. In the course of time, though, these original meanings had been lost (through, in Müller's notorious phrasing, a "disease of language"), so that the myths no longer told in a "rationally intelligible" way of phenomena in the natural world but instead appeared to describe the "irrational" activities of gods, heroes, nymphs, and others. For instance, one Greek myth related the pursuit of the nymph Daphne by the god Phoebus Apollo. Since—in Müller's interpretation of the evidence of comparative linguistics—"Daphne" originally meant "dawn," and "Phoibos" meant "morning sun," the original story was rationally intelligible as "the dawn is put to flight by the morning sun." One of the problems with this view is, of course, that it fails to account for the fact that the Greeks continued to tell this and similar stories long after their supposed meanings had been forgotten; and they did so,

Müller's study of myth and linguistics

moreover, in the manifest belief that the stories referred, not to nature, but precisely to gods, heroes, and other mythical beings.

Interest in myth was greatly stimulated in Germany by Friedrich von Schelling's philosophy of mythology, which argued that myth was a form of expression, characteristic of a particular stage in human development, through which men imagine the Absolute (for Schelling an all-embracing unity in which all differences are reconciled). Scholarly interest in myth has continued into the 20th century. Many scholars have adopted a psychological approach because of interest aroused by the theories of Sigmund Freud. Subsequently, new approaches in sociology and anthropology have continued to encourage the study of myth.

Allegorical. An example of an allegorical interpretation would be that given by an ancient commentator for the *Iliad,* book 20, verse 67. Referring to an episode in which the gods fight each other, the commentator cites critics who have explained the hostilities between the gods allegorically as an opposition between elements—dry against wet, hot against cold, light against heavy. Thus, the gods Apollo, Helios, and Hephaestus represent fire, and the god Poseidon and the river Scamander represent water. Similarly, the goddess Athena is interpreted as wisdom/sense, the god Ares as the absence of that quality, the goddess Aphrodite as desire, and the god Hermes as reason. An allegorical interpretation of a myth could be said to posit a one-to-one correspondence between mythical "clothing" and the ideas being so clothed. This approach tends to limit the meaning of a myth, whereas that meaning may in reality be multiple, operating on several levels.

Romantic. In the late 18th century artists and intellectuals came increasingly to emphasize the role of the emotions in human life and, correspondingly, to play down the importance of reason (which had been regarded as supremely important by thinkers of the Enlightenment). Those involved in the new movement were known as Romantics. The Romantic movement had profound implications for the study of myth. Myths—both the stories from Greek and Roman antiquity and contemporary folktales—were regarded by the Romantics as repositories of experience far more vital and powerful than those obtainable from what was felt to be the artificial art and poetry of the aristocratic civilization of contemporary Europe.

Myths as natural expressions of human experience

This new attitude is illustrated in a work of the German critic and philosopher Johann Gottfried von Herder entitled "Auszug aus einem Briefwechsel über Ossian und die Lieder alter Völker" (1773; "Extract from a Correspondence on Ossian and the Songs of Ancient Peoples"). Ossian is the name of an Irish warrior-poet whose Gaelic songs were supposedly translated and presented to the world by James Macpherson in the 1760s. Although largely the work of Macpherson himself, these songs made a colossal impact when they were published. Herder believed that the more "savage," that is, the more "alive" and "freedom-loving" a people (*ein Volk*) was, the more alive and free its songs would be. In opposition to the culture of the educated, Herder exalted the *Kultur des Volkes* ("culture of the people"). In 1769 Herder abandoned his job as a schoolteacher and took a boat from Riga, on the Baltic, to Nantes, on the Atlantic coast of France. In *Journal meiner Reise im Jahre 1769* (1769; *Journal of My Travels in the Year 1769*), a description of the experience, he wrote:

> In everything [on board ship] there is experience to illuminate the original era of the myths. *Then* [*i.e.,* in antiquity] every man, ignorant of nature, listened for signs and *had* to listen for them .... *Then,* Jupiter's lightning was terrifying—as indeed it *is* [*i.e.,* now] on the Ocean .... There are a thousand new and more natural explanations of mythology ... if one reads, say, Orpheus, Homer, Pindar ... on board ship.

In other words, for Herder ancient myths were the natural expressions of the concerns that would have confronted the ancients; and those concerns were the very ones that, according to Herder, still confronted the *Volk—e.g.,* ordinary sailors—in Herder's own day.

Comparative. Since the Romantic movement, all study of myth has been comparative, although comparative attempts were made earlier. The prevalence of the comparative approach has meant that since the 19th century even the most specialized studies have made generalizations about more than one tradition or at the very least have had to take comparative works by others into account. Indeed, for there to be any philosophical inquiry into the nature and function of myth at all, there must exist a body of data about myths across a range of societies. Such data would not exist without a comparative approach.

Folkloric. The classic folklore approach is that of Wilhelm Mannhardt, a German scholar, who attempted to collect data on the "lower mythology," which he considered to be more or less homogeneous in ancient and popular peasant traditions and basic to all formation of myth. Mannhardt saw sufficient analogies and similarities between the ancient and modern data to permit use of the latter in interpreting the former. Like Herder, he saw the source of mythology in the traditions passed on among the *Volk.* He collected information not only about popular stories but also about popular customs. He interpreted ancient Greek rituals by relating them to customs of the agricultural peoples of northern Europe, proposing this link in his book *Antike Wald- und Feldkulte* (1877; "Ancient Wood and Field Cults"). Other people who examined myth from the folklore standpoint included Sir James Frazer, the British anthropologist, the brothers Grimm (Jacob, who influenced Mannhardt, and Wilhelm), who are well-known for their collections of folklore, and Stith Thompson, who is notable for his classification of folk literature, particularly his massive *Motif-Index of Folk-Literature* (1955). The Grimms shared Herder's passion for the poetry and stories of the *Volk.* Their importance stems in part from the academic diligence and meticulousness that they brought to the recording and study of popular tradition. In addition to their collection of *Märchen* ("Tales"), they published volumes of *Deutsche Sagen* ("German Legends"). These were tales that purported to record actual events and that were ostensibly set in a specific place and period, as opposed to the "once-upon-a-time-in-the-forest" setting characteristic of the *Märchen.* Collecting and classifying mythological themes have remained the principal activities of the folklore approach.

Myth as a folk tradition

Functionalist. One of the leading exponents of the functionalist approach to myth was the French sociologist Marcel Mauss, who used the phrase "total social facts" in reference to religious symbols and myths and their irreducibility in terms of other functions. In his *Essai sur le don* (1925; *The Gift*), Mauss referred to a system of gift giving to be found in traditional, preindustrial societies. Observing that there was a mass of complex data on the subject, Mauss continued: in these "early" societies, social phenomena

> are not discrete; each phenomenon contains all the threads of which the social fabric is composed. In these *total* social phenomena, as we propose to call them, all kinds of institutions find simultaneous expression: religious, legal, moral, and economic.

In his introduction to the English edition Edward Evans-Pritchard commented on that passage:

> "Total" is the key word of the *Essay.* The exchanges of archaic societies which he examines are total social movements or activities. They are at the same time economic, juridical, moral, aesthetic, religious, mythological ... phenomena..... Their meaning can therefore only be grasped if they are viewed as a complex concrete reality.

Functionalism is primarily associated with the anthropologists Bronisław Malinowski and A.R. Radcliffe-Brown, however. Both ask not what the origin of any given social behaviour may be but how it contributes to maintaining the system of which it is a part. In this view, in all types of society, every aspect of life—every custom, belief, or idea—makes its own special contribution to the continued effective working of the whole society. Functionalism has had a wide appeal to anthropologists in Britain and the United States, especially as an interpretation of myth as integrated with other aspects of society and as supporting existing social relationships.

Structuralist. Structuralist approaches to myth are based on the analogy of myth to language. Just as a language is composed of significant oppositions (*e.g.*, between phonemes, the constituent sounds of the language), so myths are formed out of significant oppositions between certain terms and categories. Structuralist analysis aims at uncovering what it sees as the logic of myth. It is argued that supposedly primitive thought is logically consistent but that the terms of this logic are not those with which modern Western culture is familiar. Instead they are terms related to items of the everyday world in which the "primitive" culture exists. This logic is usually based on empirical categories (*e.g.*, raw/cooked, upstream/downstream, bush/village) or empirical objects (*e.g.*, buffalo, river, gold, eagle). Some structuralists, such as the French anthropologist Claude Lévi-Strauss, have emphasized the presence of the same logical patterns in myths throughout the world.

The logic of myth

In earlier anthropology, "primitive mentality" was characterized by the inability to make distinctions, by a sense of "mystic participation" or identity between man, his cosmos, and all other beings. Beginning with complex kinship systems and later exploring other taxonomies, structuralists argue to the opposite conclusion: the supposedly primitive man is, if anything, obsessed with the making of distinctions; his taxonomies reveal a complexity and sophistication that rival those of modern man.

Formalist. In contrast to the structuralists' search for the underlying structure of myths, the 20th-century Russian folklorist Vladimir Propp investigated folktales by dividing the surface of their narratives into a number of basic elements. These elements correspond to different types of action that, in Propp's analysis, always occur in the same sequence. Examples of the types of action isolated by Propp are "An interdiction is addressed to the hero"; "The interdiction is violated"; "The false hero or villain is exposed"; and "The hero is married and ascends the throne."

An important development of Propp's approach was made in the late 20th century by the German historian of religion Walter Burkert. Burkert detected certain recurrent patterns in the actions described in Greek myths, and he related these patterns (and their counterparts in Greek ritual) to basic biologic or cultural "programs of action." An example of this relation is given in Burkert's *Structure and History in Greek Mythology and Ritual* (1979). Burkert shows how certain Greek myths have a recurring pattern that he calls "the girl's tragedy." According to this pattern, a girl first leaves home; after a period of seclusion, she is raped by a god; there follows a time of tribulation, during which she is threatened by parents or relatives; eventually, having given birth to a baby boy, the girl is rescued, and the boy's glorious future is assured. The reason for the frequency and persistence of this pattern is, in Burkert's view, the fact that it reflects a basic biologic sequence or "program of action"; puberty, defloration, pregnancy, delivery. Another pattern Burkert explains in a similar way is found in myths about the driving out of the scapegoat. This pattern, Burkert argues, stems from a real situation that must often have occurred in early human or primate history; a group of men, or a group of apes, when pursued by carnivores, were able to save themselves through the sacrifice of one member of the group. The persistence of these patterns through time is explained, according to Burkert, by the fact that they are grounded in basic human needs—above all, the need to survive.

FUNCTIONS OF MYTH AND MYTHOLOGY

Explanation. The most obvious function of myths is the explanation of facts, whether natural or cultural. One North American Indian (Abnaki [Wabanaki]) myth, for example, explains the origin of corn (maize): a lonely man meets a beautiful woman with long, fair hair; she promises to remain with him if he follows her instructions; she tells him in detail how to make a fire and, after he has done so, she orders him to drag her over the burned ground; as a result of these actions, he will see her silken hair (viz., the cornstalk) reappear, and thereafter he will have corn seeds for his use. Henceforth, whenever Abnaki Indians see corn (the woman's hair), they know that she remembers them. Obviously, a myth such as this one functions as an explanation, but the narrative form distinguishes it from a straightforward answer to an intellectual question about causes. The function of explanation and the narrative form go together, since the imaginative power of the myth lends credibility to the explanation and crystallizes it into a memorable and enduring form. Hence myths play an important part in many traditional systems of education.

Justification or validation. Many myths explain ritual and cultic customs. According to myths from the island of Ceram (in Indonesia), in the beginning life was not complete, or not yet "human": vegetation and animals did not exist, and there was neither death nor sexuality. In a mysterious manner Hainuwele, a girl with extraordinary gift-bestowing powers, appeared. The people killed her at the end of their great annual celebration, and her dismembered body was planted in the earth. Among the species that sprang up after this act of planting were tubers—the staple diet of the people telling the myth. With a certain circularity frequent in mythology, the myth validates the very cultic celebration mentioned in the myth. The cult can be understood as a commemoration of those first events. Hence, the myth can be said to validate life itself together with the cultic celebration. Comparable myths are told in a number of societies where the main means of food production is the cultivation of root crops; the myths reflect the fact that tubers must be cut up and buried in the earth for propagation to take place.

Cultic or ritual validation

Ritual sacrifices are typical of traditional peasant cultures. In most cases such customs are related to mythical events. Among important themes are the necessity of death (*e.g.*, the grain "dies" and is buried, only to yield a subsequent harvest), a society's cyclic renewal of itself (*e.g.*, New Year's celebrations), and the significance of women and sexuality. New Year's celebrations, often accompanied by a temporary abandonment of all rules, may be related to or justified by mythical themes concerning a return to chaos and a return of the dead.

In every mythological tradition one myth or cluster of myths tends to be central. The subject of the central mythology is often cosmogony (origin of the cosmos). In many of those ceremonies that each society has developed as a symbol of what is necessary to its well-being, references are made to the beginning of the world. Examples include the enthronements of kings, which in some traditions (as in Fiji or ancient India) are associated with a creation or re-creation of the world. Analogously, in ancient Mesopotamia the creation epic *Enuma elish*, which was read each New Year at Babylon, celebrated the progress of the cosmos from initial anarchy to government by the kingship of Marduk; hence the authority of earthly rulers, and of earthly monarchy in general, was implicitly supported and justified.

Ruling families in ancient civilizations frequently justified their position by invoking myths—for example, that they had divine origins. Examples are known from Imperial China, pharaonic Egypt, the Hittite Empire, Polynesia, the Inca Empire, and India. Elites have also based their claims to privilege on myths. The French historian of ancient religion Georges Dumézil was the pioneer in suggesting that the priestly, warrior, and producing classes in ancient Indo-European societies regarded themselves as having been ordained to particular tasks by virtue of their mythological origins. And in every known cultural tradition there exists some mythological foundation that is referred to when defending marriage and funerary customs.

Description. Inasmuch as myths deal with the origin of the world, the end of the world, or a paradisiacal state, they are capable of describing what people can never "see for themselves" however rational and observant they are. It may be that the educational value of myths is even more bound up with the descriptions they provide than with the explanations. In traditional, preindustrial societies myths form perhaps the most important available model of instruction, since no separate philosophical system of inquiry exists.

Instruction through myths

Healing, renewal, and inspiration. Creation myths play a significant role in healing the sick; they are recited (*e.g.*, among the Navajo Indians of North America) when an individual's world—that is to say, his life—is in jeopardy.

Thus, healing through recitation of a cosmogony is one example of the use of myth as a magical incantation. Another example is the case of Icelandic poets, who, in singing of the episode in old Norse mythology in which the god Odin wins for gods and men the "mead of song" (a drink containing the power of poetic inspiration), can be said to be celebrating the origins of their own art and hence renewing it.

The poetic aspect of myths in archaic and primitive traditions is considerable. Societies in which artistic endeavour is not yet specialized tend to rely on mythical themes and images as a source of all self-expression. Mythology has also exerted an aesthetic influence in more modern societies. An example is the prevalence of themes from Greek and Roman classical mythology in Western painting, sculpture, and literature.

MYTH IN CULTURE

Myth and psychology. One of the most celebrated writers about myth from a psychological standpoint was Sigmund Freud. In his *Die Traumdeutung* (1899; *The Interpretation of Dreams*) he posited a phenomenon called the Oedipus complex, that is, the male child's repressed desire for his mother and a corresponding wish to supplant his father. (The equivalent for girls was the Electra complex.) According to Freud, this phenomenon was detectable in dreams and myths, fairy tales, folktales—even jokes. Later, in *Totem und Tabu* (1913; *Totem and Taboo*), Freud suggested that myth was the distorted wish-dreams of entire peoples. More than that, however, he saw the Oedipus complex as a memory of a real episode that had occurred in what he termed the "primal horde," when sons oppressed by their father had revolted, had driven out or killed him, and had taken his wives for themselves. That subsequent generations refrained from doing so was, Freud suggested, due to a collective bad conscience. The relevance of Freud's investigations to the study of myth lies in his view that the formation of mythic concepts does not depend on cultural history. Instead, Freud's analysis of the psyche posited an independent, trans-historical mechanism, based on a highly personal biologic conception of man. His anthropological theories have since been refuted (*e.g.,* totemic [symbolic animal] sacrifice as the earliest ritual custom, which he related to the first parricide), but his analysis is still regarded with interest by some reputable social scientists. Criticism, however, has been leveled against the explanation of myths in terms of only one theme and in terms of the "repression" of conscious ideas.

Freud's creation of a trans-historical method

Another theorist preoccupied with psychological aspects of myth was the Swiss psychoanalyst Carl Jung, who, like Freud, was stimulated by a theory that no longer has much support—*i.e.,* the theory of Lucien Lévy-Bruhl, a French philosopher, associating myth with prelogical mentality. This, according to Lévy-Bruhl, was a type of thought that had been common to archaic mankind, that was still common to primitives, and in which people supposedly experienced some form of "mystical participation" with the objects of their thought, rather than a separation of subject and object. Jung's theory of the "collective unconscious," which bears a certain resemblance to Lévy-Bruhl's theory, enabled him to regard the foundation of mythical images as positive and creative, in contrast with Freud's more negative view of mythology. Jung evolved a theory of archetypes. Broadly similar images and symbols occur in myths, fairy tales, and dreams because the human psyche has an inbuilt tendency to dwell on certain inherited motifs (archetypes), the basic pattern of which persists, however much details may vary. But critics of Jung have hesitated to accept his theory of archetypes as an account of mythology. Among objections raised, two may be mentioned. First, the archetypal symbols identified by Jung are static, representing personal types that conflate aspects of the personality: they do not help to illuminate—in the way that the analyses of Propp and Burkert do—the patterns of action that myths narrate. Second, Jungian analysis is essentially aimed at relating myth to the individual psyche, whereas myth is above all a social phenomenon, embedded in society and requiring explanation with reference to social structures and social functions.

Myth and science. Attention has sometimes focused on changes occurring in the way the real world is apprehended by different peoples and how these changes in "reality" are reflected in myths. This reality changes continually throughout history, and these changes have especially occupied philosophers and historians of science, for a sense of reality in a culture is basic to any scientific pursuit by that culture, beginning with the earliest philosophical inquiries into the nature of the world. Though it would perhaps be going too far to identify the images and concepts that make up a culture's scientific sense of reality with myth, parallels between science and myth, as well as the presence of a mythological dimension to science, are generally reckoned to exist.

Scientific models as paradigms

The function of models in physics, biology, medicine, and other sciences resembles that of myths as paradigms, or patterns, of the human world. In medicine, for instance, the human body is sometimes likened to a machine or the human brain to a computer, and such models are easily understood. Once a model has gained acceptance, it is difficult to replace, and in this respect it resembles myth, while at the same time, just as in myth, there may be a great variety of interpretations. In the 17th century it was assumed that the universe could be explained entirely in terms of minute corpuscles, their motion and interaction, and that no entities of any other sort existed. To the extent that many models in the history of science have partaken of this somewhat absolutist character, science can be said to resemble myth. There are, however, important differences. Despite the relative infrequency with which models in science have been replaced, replacement does occur, and a strong awareness of the limitations of models has developed in modern science. In contrast, a myth is not as a rule regarded by the community in which it functions as open to replacement, although an outside observer might record changes and even the substitution of a new myth for an old one. Moreover, in spite of the broad cultural impact of theories and models such as those of Newton and Einstein, it is in general true to say that models in science have their principal value for the scientists concerned. Hence, they function most strongly for a relatively small segment of society, even though, for instance, a medical theory held in academic circles in one century can filter down into folk medicine in the next. As a rule, myth has a much wider impact.

Modern science did not evolve in its entirety as a rebellion against myth, nor at its birth did it suddenly throw off the shackles of myth. In ancient Greece the naturalists of Ionia (western Asia Minor), long regarded as the originators of science, developed views of the universe that were in fact very close to the creation myths of their time. Those who laid the foundations of modern science, such as Nicholas of Cusa, Johannes Kepler, Sir Isaac Newton, and Gottfried Leibniz, were absorbed by metaphysical problems of which the traditional, indeed mythological, character is evident. Among these problems were the nature of infinity and the question of the omnipotence of God. The influence of mythological views is seen in the English physician William Harvey's association of the circulation of the blood with the planetary movements and Darwin's explanation of woman's menstrual cycles by the tides of the ocean.

Several thinkers (*e.g.,* the theologian Paul Tillich and the philosopher Karl Jaspers) have argued convincingly for a mythological dimension to all science. Myth, in this view, is that which is taken for granted when thought begins. It is at the same time the limit reached in the course of scientific analysis, when it is found that no further progress in definition can be made after certain fundamental principles have been reached. In recent scientific researches, especially in astronomy and biology, questions of teleology (final ends) have gained in importance, as distinct from earlier concerns with questions of origin. These recent concerns stimulate discussion about the limits of what can be scientifically explained, and they reveal anew a mythological dimension to human knowledge.

Myth and religion. The place of myth in various religious traditions differs.

Ritual and other practices. The idea that the principal

function of a myth is to provide a justification for a ritual was adopted without any great attempt to make a case for it. At the beginning of the 20th century many scholars thought of myths in their earliest forms as accounts of social customs and values. According to Sir James Frazer, myths and rituals together provided evidence for man's earliest preoccupation, namely, fertility. Human society developed in stages—from the magical through the religious to the scientific—and myths and rituals (which survived even into the scientific stage) bore witness to archaic modes of thought that were otherwise difficult to reconstruct. As for the relationship between myth and ritual, Frazer argued that myths were intended to explain otherwise unintelligible rituals. Thus, in *Adonis, Attis, Osiris* (1906) he stated that the mythical story of Attis' self-castration was designed to explain the fact that the priests of Attis' cult castrated themselves at his festival.

The Myth and Ritual school

In a much more articulate way, biblical scholars stressed the necessity to look for the situation in life and custom (the "Sitz im Leben") that mythical texts originally possessed. A number of scholars, mainly in Britain and the Scandinavian countries and usually referred to as the Myth and Ritual school (of which the best-known member is the British biblical scholar S.H. Hooke), have concentrated on the ritual purposes of myths. Their work has centred on the philological study of the ancient Middle East both before and since the rise of Islām and has focused almost exclusively on rituals connected with sacred kingship and New Year's celebrations. Of particular importance was the discovery that the creation epic *Enuma elish* was recited at the Babylonian New Year's festival: the myth was, it was argued, expressing in language that which the ritual was enacting through action. Classical scholars have subsequently investigated the relations between myth and ritual in ancient Greece. Particularly influential has been the study of sacrifice by Walter Burkert entitled *Homo Necans: The Anthropology of Ancient Greek Sacrificial Ritual and Myth* (1983).

Connections between myths and cult behaviour certainly exist, but there is no solid ground for the suggestion, following Frazer, that, in general, ritual came first and myth was then formulated as a subsequent explanation. If it is only the subsequent myth that has made the sense of the earlier ritual explicit, the meaning of the ritual may remain a riddle. There is in fact no unanimous opinion about which originated first. Modern scholars are inclined to turn away from the question of temporal priority and to concentrate instead on the diversity of the relationship between myth and ritual. While it is clear that some myths are linked to rituals, so that it makes sense to say that the myth is expressing in the language of narrative that which the ritual expresses through the symbolism of action, in the case of other myths no such ritual exists.

The content of important myths concerning the origin of the world usually reflects the dominant cultural form of a tradition. The myths of hunter-gatherer societies tell of the origin of game animals and hunting customs; agricultural civilizations tend to give weight to agricultural practices in their myths; pastoral cultures to pastoral practices; and so on. Thus, many myths present models of acts and organizations central to the society's way of life and relate these to primordial times. Myths in specific traditions deal with matters such as harvest customs, initiation ceremonies, and the customs of secret societies.

Religious symbolism and iconography. Sacred objects are found in all religious traditions, and sacred images in most. They are the material counterparts of myth inasmuch as they represent sacred realities of figures, as myths do in narrative form. Representing does not entail faithful copying of natural or human forms, and in this respect religious symbolism is again like myth in that both depict the extraordinary rather than the ordinary. Many symbolic representations have their sources in myths. Representations in human form, especially "natural" human form, are rare. The sculptures of divine figures in classical Greece (by sculptors such as Phidias and Praxiteles) are the exception. Usually the degree of representation occurring in cult practices and the depiction of mythical themes has been considerably less humanistic. An example is the way geometric and animal figures abound in the history of religions. Another example is the use of sacred masks, as in the mysteries of Dionysus, an ecstatic cult in the Aegean world of classical antiquity, and the indigenous traditions of Australia, America, prehistoric Europe, and elsewhere.

Biblical and Qur'ānic criticism of myth

Sacred texts. The Old Testament is usually regarded as embodying much material that anthropologists would regard as containing mythical themes in just the same way as the practices of the ancient Greeks, Chinese, or Abnaki Indians are bound up with myths. Yet the religion of Israel was in many respects critical of myths (in the sense of noncanonical, approved narratives). Similarly, it rejected any representation of God in natural forms. Antimythological tendencies exist in the religions that have their roots in Israel. The New Testament of Christianity in some instances derogates myths by describing them as "godless" and "silly." Islām's emphasis on the transcendence of God, as attested in the Qur'ān, similarly allows little room for mythological stories. The activities of the supernatural beings known as *jinn,* however, are acknowledged even by official Islām, besides being prominent in popular belief (as in *The Thousand and One Nights*); and other mythological themes, for example motifs relating to the end of time (eschatology), also figure in Islāmic religion, above all in its Shī'ite form. Orthodox Shī'ite Muslims believe in the existence of 12 *imāms*, semidivine descendants of the Prophet Muḥammad through his son-in-law 'Alī. Toward the end of time, according to the beliefs of Shī'ism, the 12th *imām* will return to bring truth and justice to mankind.

Other traditions with sacred scriptures are more tolerant of myth, for example Hinduism and Buddhism. Running through certain central texts of the Hindu sacred tradition is the theme of the contrast between the One and the Many. Thus, the philosophical poem known as the *Bhagavadgītā* contrasts the person who sees Infinity within the ordinary finite world with the person who merely sees the diversity of appearances. Yet this ascetic and abstract view by no means excludes a rich and extraordinarily diverse mythology, which is reflected in the tremendous variety of Indian religious statuary and which mirrors the religious complexity of Indian society. A justification for the coexistence of an ideal of unity with a pluralistic reality is found in the *Rigveda,* where it is written that although God is One the sages give him many names. Buddhism also finds room for exuberant mythology as well as for the plainer truths of sacred doctrine. Buddhism embraces not only the teachings of the Buddha about the pursuit of the path to Enlightenment and Nirvāṇa but also the exotic mythical figures of Yamantaka, who wears a necklace of skulls, and the grossly fat god of wealth Jambhala.

Myth and the arts. *Oral traditions and written literature.* Myths in ancient civilizations are known only by virtue of the fact that they became part of a written tradition. In the case of Greece, virtually all myths are "literature" in the form in which they have survived, the oldest source being the works ascribed to the Greek poets Homer and Hesiod (usually dated, in written form, to the 8th century BC). Literary forms such as the epic have frequently served as vehicles for transmitting myths inasmuch as they present an authoritative account. The Homeric epics were both an example and an exploration of heroic values, and the poems became the basis of education in classical Greece. The great epics of India (*Mahābhārata* and *Rāmāyaṇa*) came to function as encyclopaedias of knowledge and provided models for all human existence.

Mythological aspects of architecture

Visual arts. In principle, the sort of relationship that exists between myth and literature exists also with respect to the other arts. In the case of architecture and sculpture, archaeological discoveries confirm the primacy of mythical representations. Among the earliest known three-dimensional objects built by man are prehistoric megalithic and sepulchral structures. Mythological details cannot actually be discerned, but it is generally believed that such structures express mythological concerns and that mythical images dictated the shape. An especially intriguing example is the stone circle at Stonehenge in southern England. Axes of this construction are aligned with significant risings and settings of the Sun and Moon, but the idea that the circle was built for a religious purpose must remain likely rather than certain.

Grave monuments of rulers are among the most important remains of ancient civilizations (*e.g.,* the Egyptian pyramids; and the sepulchral structures of Chinese rulers since the Chou period, *c.* 1111–255 BC). There is worldwide evidence that in archaic cultures man considered the points of the compass to have mythological affiliations (*e.g.,* the West and death or the East and a new beginning). Mythological views even influenced building activity. One architectural feature that can have mythological significance is the column. In a number of popular traditions the sky is believed to be supported by one or more columns. The relatively strict separation between religious and civil architecture that modern man is perhaps inclined to take for granted has not existed in most cultures and periods and perhaps is not universal even in modern times.

Even when art ceases to represent mythological matters outright, it is still usually far from representational. That art has ceased to represent mythology is challenged by some theorists, who argue that what seems to be abandonment of mythological forms is really only a change in mythology. The opposing arguments are analogous to the favourable or unfavourable attitudes toward myth that religions have developed.

Myth as a source of the drama and the dance

Performing arts. Myth is one of the principal roots of drama. This is particularly obvious in the earliest Western drama, the tragedies of classical Greece, not only because of the many mythological subjects treated and the plays' performance at the festival of Dionysus but also because of the playwrights' mythlike presentation of events and facts. An example of such presentation is the story pattern, notably the way retribution follows transgression. Another feature of Greek drama that is relevant to the subject of myth is the fact that the role of the chorus was taken by a group of ordinary citizens. In Greek tragedy the heroic past was presented and explored by a chorus of nonheroic individuals; hence the meaning of the inherited myths was examined by a collectivity that can be seen as standing for the wider collectivity (more than 10,000 in number) that constituted the audience at the plays. In its songs the chorus frequently had recourse to expressions of a proverbial kind, using the distilled wisdom of the community to account for the strange and often disturbing events represented in the plays. The origins of drama are obscure, but Theodor Gaster, an American historian of religion, has suggested that in the ancient eastern Mediterranean world the interrelationship of myth and ritual created drama. Elsewhere, dramatic presentations (as in Japanese Nō plays and the Javanese *wayang*) are similarly rooted in myth.

Dance has been a medium for the expression of mythological themes throughout the world and in all periods for which there is evidence. Especially common are dances aimed at ensuring the continuity of fertility or the success of hunting, at curing the sick, or at achieving shamanistic trance states. An aspect of the decay of ritual in the modern West is the tendency for dance to lose its close and direct connection with the life of the community. A further consequence is that the role of dance in embodying and exploring a community's myths has often been overlooked, and dance may have become further removed from myth than any other form of art in the Western world. There are important and significant exceptions, however. One of the most notable is the work of the American choreographer Martha Graham, who frequently used mythical themes—often drawn from Greek antiquity—as the inspiration for her ballets.

Music. Myth and music are linked in many cultures and in various ways. For example, numerous stories ascribe the origins of music to a figure, usually divine, who lived in the mythical past. Thus, in ancient Greece the lyre was said to have been invented by the god Hermes, who handed it on to his brother Apollo as part of a bargain. From then on Apollo played the lyre at the banquets of the gods, while the Muses sang to his accompaniment. An ancient Chinese myth tells of the discovery of the "foundation tone," which, in addition to being a musical note of specific pitch, also had political implications, since each dynasty was thought to have its own "proper pitch." The foundation tone was produced when Ling Lun, a scholar, went to the western mountain area of China and cut a bamboo pipe in such a way that it produced the correct sound.

Throughout the world music is played at religious ceremonies to increase the efficacy and appeal of prayers, hymns, and invocations to divinities. The power of music to charm the gods is movingly expressed in the Greek story of Orpheus. This mythical figure goes to the underworld to try to have his dead wife, Eurydice, restored to life. By means of his lyre playing and singing he is able to win over even the god of death, so that Eurydice is allowed to leave the underworld. The continuing potency of the myth (including its tragic conclusion—Orpheus is forbidden to look back at his wife but does so and thus loses her again) is shown by the fact that it has been retold in Europe by numerous composers of opera since the early 17th century.

Lévi-Strauss's view of myth and music

That a particularly close connection exists between myth and music has been argued by Claude Lévi-Strauss. In an analysis of the myths of certain South American Indians (*Le Cru et le cuit,* 1964; *The Raw and the Cooked*) he explains that his procedure is "to treat the sequences of each myth, and the myths themselves in respect of their reciprocal interrelations, like the instrumental parts of a musical work and to study them as one studies a symphony." His treatment is divided into such subsections as "The 'Good Manners' Sonata," "Fugue of the Five Senses," and "The Opossum's Cantata." In *Myth and Meaning* (1978) Lévi-Strauss returned to the link between myth and music, which had proved difficult for his readers to understand. To make his point clearer Lévi-Strauss took the example of a theme from an opera by Richard Wagner. Each time the theme is repeated its overall meaning grows clearer, as each instance is superimposed on the others in the series, so that it becomes possible to see what the different occurrences of the theme have in common. Analogously, the meaning of a myth is found not simply by reading its narrative in sequence, but by superimposing upon one another similar mythical events from one narrative and boiling down each resulting "bundle" to a common denominator. It is the relationship between these bundles that constitutes the logic of the myth.

The use of music for religious ends has declined in modern Western societies, but mythical themes (*e.g.,* in opera and oratorio) are still used with genuine artistic effect. The repertoires of late 20th-century opera companies may include, for example, Giacomo Puccini's *Turandot,* about a princess who asks her suitors three riddles and beheads them if they fail to answer correctly and a prince who will die if his name is discovered; Richard Strauss's *Die Frau ohne Schatten* ("The Woman Without a Shadow"), about a princess who must gain a shadow or her husband will be turned to stone; and Wagner's *Tannhäuser, Lohengrin, Der Ring des Nibelungen,* and *Parsifal,* all loosely based on tales from medieval Germanic mythology.

Myth and history. Myth and history represent alternative ways of looking at the past. Defining history is hardly easier than defining myth, but a historical approach necessarily involves both establishing a chronological framework for events and comparing and contrasting rival traditions in order to produce a coherent account. The latter process, in particular, requires the presence of writing in order that conflicting versions of the past may be recorded and evaluated. Where writing is absent, or where literacy is restricted, traditions embedded in myths through oral transmission may constitute the principal sources of authority for the past. Hence, myths may be cited when a situation in the present is materially affected by what version of the past is accepted. For instance, if a dispute arises among the Iatmul of Papua New Guinea over the rights of different clans to possess land, the contending parties take part in oral contests involving the recitation of long lists of mythological names and other details from the myths. Since each clan's view of the mythic past has implications for the ownership of estates by persons living in the present, victory in these contests is a matter of direct practical importance to the participants.

Myth, history, and tradition

Even in societies where literacy is widespread and where

a considerable body of professional historians is at work, it may still be the case that a majority of the population form their views of the past on the basis of inherited mythlike traditions. Examples from the 20th century in Europe would be the polarized communities (Protestant and Roman Catholic) of Northern Ireland, or pro- and anti-Communist sympathizers in Greece. In the former case, the two communities have different and irreconcilable pictures of the events related to the partition of Ireland. In the latter case, the course of the civil war (after the end of World War II) is viewed quite differently by the two groups. These rival traditions may be described as mythlike because they are narratives with a strong validating function—the function of justifying current enmities and current loyalties—and they are believed with a quasi-religious faith against which objective historical testing is all but powerless.

Finally, similarities to myths may be present even in the work of those who are justifiably described as historians. A clear instance of this is the ancient Greek writer Herodotus, the so-called "father of history." He had the radically original idea of writing an account of the struggle between the Greek world and its "barbarian" neighbours during the Persian Wars, an account that combined and evaluated a range of disparate and often conflicting pieces of information. On these grounds he should certainly be described as a historian. Yet, his work is full of themes and story patterns that also occur in Greek myths—for example, transgression against the gods leads to retribution; again, people who live at the margins of the Greek world are imagined as having customs that are the exact inverse of their Greek equivalents. In the work of Herodotus there is no incompatibility between myth and history; both historical events and the patterns into which such happenings are perceived as falling form part of his overall enterprise: namely, to conduct an inquiry (the meaning of the Greek word *historia*) into the past. As with the distinction between myth and science, then, that between myth and history is by no means a straightforward one.

MAJOR TYPES OF MYTH

Myths of origin. Cosmogony and creation myth are used as synonyms, yet properly speaking, cosmogony is a preferable term because it refers to the origin of the world in a neutral fashion, whereas "creation myth" implies a creator and something created, an implication unsuited to a number of myths that, for example, speak of the origin of the world as a growth or emanation, rather than an act. Even the term origin should be used with caution for cosmogonic events (as well as for other myths purporting to describe the beginning of things), because the origin of the world hardly ever seems the focal point of a mythological narrative—as a mythological narrative is not a matter of inquiry into the first cause of things. Instead, cosmogonic myths are concerned with origins in the sense of the foundation or validity of the world as it is. Creation stories in both primitive and advanced cultures frequently speak of the act of creation as a fashioning of the earth out of raw material that was already present. In African cosmogonies, especially, the earth is preexistent. A creation out of nothing occurs as a theme much less frequently, for all that such creation myths are more satisfying to the philosophical mind. Philosophical questions, however, are less important in the justificatory systems set up by myth.

Water, though important everywhere as a source of life and image of endless potentiality, has a special role in Asia and North America, where the creator (often an animal) is assisted by another figure, who dives for earth in the primordial ocean. The earth-diver helper sometimes develops into an opponent, or Satan-like character, in other areas—*e.g.,* those touched by Zoroastrianism, an ancient Persian dualistic religion. Though hardly an explanation in the ordinary sense of the word, the theme accounts for the fact that evil is constitutive of the cosmos without holding the creator responsible for it. Other widely diffused motifs are: the cosmogonic egg, found in the Pacific world, parts of Europe and southern Asia (*e.g.,* in Hinduism); the world parents (usually in the image of sky and earth); and creation through sacrifice or through a primordial battle. Creation through the word of the creator also occurs outside the Old Testament account (in Polynesia).

Cosmogony sets the pattern for everything else in most traditions; other myths are related to it or derived from it. Because man's inhabitable world, the cosmos, is the crucial issue, no matter how various the contents may be and how different from one period to another, cosmogony probably is the clearest expression of man's basic mythological propensity. All cosmogonic accounts have certain formal features in common. They speak of irreconcilable opposites (*e.g.,* heaven and earth, darkness and light) and, at the same time, of events or things totally outside the common range of perception and reason (*e.g.,* a "time" in which heaven and earth were not yet separated and darkness and light intermingled). In other words, the basic ingredients of man's world and orientation are presupposed yet are realized, constituted, or brought about anew in the narration. The narrative can arrive at such a reconstitution only by transcending the limits of ordinary perception and reason.

Common features in cosmogonic and creation myths

The origin of man is usually linked immediately to the cosmogony. Man, for instance, is placed on the earth by God, or in some other way his origin is from heaven. Nevertheless, it is only in mythologies influenced by philosophical reflections that the place of man becomes the conspicuous centre of the cosmogony (*e.g.,* Pythagoreanism, a Greek mystical philosophical system; Orphism, a Greek mystical religious movement; Gnosticism, a Christian dualistic and esoteric movement; and Tantrism, a Hindu and Buddhist esoteric meditation system). Man is sometimes said to have ascended from the depths of the earth (as with the Zuni, an American Indian people) or from a certain rock or tree of cultic significance. These images are often related to the idea of a realm of ancestors as the origin of newborn children. Man is also said to be fashioned from the dust of the ground (as in Genesis) or from a mixture of clay and blood (as in the Babylonian creation myth). In all cases, however, man has a particular place (because of his duties to the gods, because of his limitations, or even because of his gifts), even though—especially in many hunters' civilizations (*e.g.,* the African San peoples and many North American Indian tribes)—the harmony of man and other forms of nature is emphasized.

In most cosmogonic traditions the final or culminating act is the creation of man. The condition of the cosmos prior to man's arrival is viewed as separate and distinct from the alterations that result from the beginning of the human cultural world. Creation is thus seen as a process of periods or stages, frequently in a three-stage model. The first stage consists of the world of gods or primordial beings; the second stage is the world of the ancestors of man; and the third stage is the world of man. The three stages are sometimes seen as interrelated; for example, the gods may be the creators of man or the ancestors of man, or ancestors may undergo a transformation to become men.

Among innumerable tales of origin, one of the most common types is related to the origins of institutions. Certain initiation ceremonies or ritual acts are said to have originated in the beginning, in mythical times, this primeval moment of inception constituting their validity.

Myths of eschatology and destruction. Myths of eschatology deal with "the end." The end is conceived of as the opposite of the cosmogony; it means first and foremost the origin of death but also, in a wider sense, the end of the world. Special forms of eschatology are prevalent in messianism (belief in a future salvation figure) and millenarianism (belief in a 1,000-year reign of the elect).

The origin of death

Myths about the origin of death, for which an added explanation has to be found in the sense that death is not seen as automatically the end of life, are probably as widely diffused as creation stories. One of the most common types of such myths speaks of a primordial time in which death did not exist and explains that it arose as the result of an error, as a punishment, or simply because the creator decided the earth would get too crowded otherwise. One example of a myth about the origin of death may be regarded as characteristic; it occurs, with variations, in many parts of the world. Among the Zulus the story is told that the supreme being Unkulunkulu instructed the chameleon to take a message to mankind, saying that they would be immortal. But the chameleon moved slowly, since he stopped to have something to eat (or, according to a variant, basked in the sun and fell asleep). In due course the supreme being changed his mind and sent a lizard to men, telling them that they would die. The lizard arrived and delivered his message. When the chameleon eventually arrived, his message conflicted with what mankind had already been told by the lizard. The chameleon was not believed, and men were mortal from then on.

Expectations of a cataclysmic end of the world are also expressed by myths. A universal conflagration with a final battle and defeat of the gods is part of Germanic mythology and has parallels in other examples of Indo-European eschatological imagery. In many "primitive" religions specific expectations about the end of the world do occur, but until recently they have not received much scholarly attention. An example of such a belief about the end of the world is found among the Pawnee Indians. In their view, there will come a time when everything will disappear and the star of death will govern the world. The Moon will turn red, the Sun will be extinguished, and men will be turned into stars flying along the route to heaven now taken by the dead.

Messianic and millenarian myths. The hope of a new world surges up from time to time in many civilizations. Many such religious movements have flourished in the 20th century in Melanesia, Africa, South America, and Siberia. Christian elements are usually detectable, but the basic element in virtually all cases is indigenous. These cults and movements centre on prophetic leaders, often emphasize the return of the dead at the renewal to come, and are convinced of a catastrophic end of the present world. In many cases, the culture hero is expected to return and lead believers in battle against the evil forces. In the history of Judaism and Christianity, as in many primitive millenarian and messianic movements, there is an expectation of a new heaven and a new earth.

Myths of culture heroes and soteriological myths. A great many nonliterate traditions have myths about a culture hero (most notably one who brings new techniques or technology to mankind—*e.g.,* Prometheus, who supplies fire to mankind in Greek mythology). A culture hero is generally not the person responsible for the creation but the one who completes the world and makes it fit for human life; in short, he creates culture. Another example of a culture hero is Maui in Polynesia, who brought islands to the surface from the bottom of the sea, captured and harnessed the Sun, lifted the sky to allow man more room, and, like Prometheus, gave fire to mankind.

The bringer of culture is often also the bringer of health. Thus, the culture hero of the Woodlands and Plains Indians in North America is at the same time related to the foundation of the medicine society. A comparable figure occurs in many traditions of classical antiquity or the Mediterranean basin generally as the "good son"—*e.g.,* Horus, the son of the god Osiris in Egypt, or the figure of the king in the Psalms. Health and (spiritual) salvation are synonymous, and this is implied in the Greek word *sōtēr,* which can mean both "saviour" and "preserver from ill health." Related to soteriological myths in many cases is the hope for a final and total salvation in which the "good" powers will triumph, such as through Saoshyant, the saviour in Zoroastrianism. In fact, Zoroastrianism shared with the Judeo-Christian tradition the notion of a Last Judgment followed by the ultimate salvation of the world. According to Zoroastrian belief, as the end approached heroes from the past would come to life and help in the struggle of good against evil. Saviours, the Saoshyants, would work toward the triumph of virtue and the spreading of heavenly light over all creation.

Myths of time and eternity. The apparent regularity of the heavenly bodies long impressed every society. The sky was seized as the very image of transcendence, and what seemed to be the orderly course of Sun, Moon, and stars suggested a time that transcended man's—in short, eternity. Many myths and mythological images concern themselves with the relationship between eternity and time on earth. The number four for the number of world ages figures most frequently. The Zoroastrians of ancient Persia knew of a complete world age of 12,000 years, divided into four periods of 3,000 each, at the end of which Ormazd (Wise Lord) would conquer Ahriman (Destructive Spirit). Similarly, the Book of Daniel (in the Old Testament) mentions four kingdoms—of gold, silver, bronze, and a mixture of iron and clay, respectively—after which God will establish an everlasting kingdom. The notion of four world ages, sometimes associated with metals, occurs also in the works of classical writers and in later speculative writings on human history. Judaism developed the view of a 1,000-year period between the four world ages and the everlasting kingdom (hence the words millennium and millenarian). Although other numbers occur (three, six, seven, 12, and 72), four is dominant. In ancient Mexico this world was held to be preceded by four other worlds. India, in both Hindu and Buddhist texts, has developed the most complex system of world ages and worlds that arise and come to an end. Here, too, the number four is important—*e.g.,* the four ages (*yugas*) of decreasing length and increasing evil. Many writings, often with large numbers, reflect exact astronomical observations and calculations. Some mythologies—*e.g.,* those of the Maya in Central America—have developed sophisticated views interrelating time and space. Mythological accounts of repetitions of worlds after their destruction occur not only in India but also elsewhere, such as in Orphism and in the Stoic philosophy that flourished in classical antiquity.

The ages of the world

Myths of providence and destiny. In attitudes to the idea of a link between human activity and the stars, the most familiar example of which is probably astrology, there is a broad range of mythical motifs between astrological calculations (in the sense of an attempt at an intellectualized account of what is happening) and devotional self-surrender. There are many occasions at which a man may be filled with doubt about his own fate or the fate of his community. In some myths divine supremacy is marked by a god's mastery over fate. Marduk, the patron god of Babylon, acquires the "tablets of fate" in his primordial battle preceding the creation. There is no doubt about Zeus's supremacy in the Greek poet Hesiod's genealogical account of the gods, yet in the works of Homer, Zeus is powerless to defy fate and save the life of his son Sarpedon. Mythological views of providence, destiny, or fate are given precise shades of meaning vis-à-vis dominant views in a tradition concerning justice and divine law, the philosophical problem of determinism, the theological problems of theodicy (justification of a good god with observable facts of evil), and predestination. An important difference in mythological accounts of providence exists between those traditions that speak of the creation of the world as a result of God's will (as in Judaism, Christianity, and Islām) and those that attribute worldly phenomena to causation by a lesser being (as Buddhism does).

Myths of rebirth and renewal. Myths of archaic traditions generally imply a conception of the world, nature, and man in terms of cyclic time. According to Australian Aboriginal myth, man is reincarnated into profane life at the moment of his birth. At his initiation he reenters sacred time, and through his burial ceremony he returns to his original "spirit" state. Similar beliefs are held by many tribal peoples, and their myths are expressed in terms of cosmic cycles. Special myths are narrated in many places in preparation for initiation procedures. In agricultural societies, in addition to the themes of cosmic renewal, renewal through birth, and rebirth through initiation ceremonies at the attainment of manhood and womanhood, the theme of seasonal renewal is of great importance. The cyclic concept of time in all these traditions is present in many of the great religious and philosophical systems, such as Brahmanism (a Hindu system), Buddhism, and Platonism, and to some extent it is at variance with the idea of linear time typical of Judaism, Christianity, and Islām. But no culture, not even that of Jews, Christians, or Muslims, completely disregards the cyclic patterns of the seasons, work, festivities, or existence. Such patterns seem to be engraved on man's perception of the world.

Cyclic time

Myths of memory and forgetting. Some of the North American medicine men claim to remember their prenatal existence. Such memory, according to their mythology, is lost in ordinary people. Similar myths of memory and forgetting are related to the hierarchy that exists in all archaic societies. The fundamental knowledge of the world, transcending ordinary consciousness, is not equally attainable by everyone. Myths of memory can take the form of collective nostalgia. In South America the Yaruros, whose material existence was so simple that they lacked the skills of the agricultural and pastoral life, were one of the many tribes that in the face of modern Western cultural expansion gave up the struggle for their own social and cultural identity, becoming assimilated into a more complex society. As the Yaruros ceased to struggle for the preservation of their tribal identity, they expressed a yearning to return to the Great Mother ruling the land of the dead and awaiting them in her paradise. Mythologies of memory and forgetting have a role in many traditions. They are of great significance in traditions where the idea of rebirth or reincarnation exists. Some people have claimed to remember previous existences, and a few (among them the Buddha) the very first. The veil of *māyā* ("illusion") in many Indian stories prevents a man from remembering his true origin and goal. In Gnosticism there is talk of a similar forgetfulness, which must be resisted. In ancient Greek myth, Mnemosyne (Memory), the mother of the Muses, is said to know everything, past, present, and future. She is the Memory that is the basis of all life and creativity. Forgetting the true order and origin of things is often tantamount to death (as in the case of Lethe, the river of death in Greek mythology, which destroys memory). Anamnesis, "commemoration" or "recollection," is one of the crucial parts of the Christian celebration of the Communion. Through the anamnesis, the passion and death of the Lord is "applied" to the congregation. In philosophy, the imagery of forgetting and remembering occurs in the thought of Śaṅkara, a medieval Indian philosopher, and of Plato in connection with the paramount calling of the thinker and the difficulty of living up to that calling.

Myths of high beings and celestial gods. Supreme celestial deities occur in many mythologies, with various qualities and attributes, in many shapes, and with great diversity in cultic significance. A cardinal distinction exists between the supreme being in many archaic or polytheistic traditions and the God of the great monotheistic systems (Judaism, Christianity, and Islām). Even though certain qualities seem alike in many cases (*e.g.,* transcendence, omniscience), the God of the latter arose historically in a reaction to polytheistic views and practices and demonstrates his supremacy accordingly, whereas the more archaic types of supreme beings nowhere show that aggressive aspect in their mythologies. The exalted status of archaic supreme beings and celestial gods does not necessarily involve exclusion of other supreme beings. Outstanding examples are Vishnu, Śiva, and the great goddess in Hindu literature, who are each described as supreme yet do not reduce the "reality" of the others. "Supremacy" is not as unambiguous and general a term as it seems, and in Hinduism it refers first and foremost to the *perfection* (*i.e.,* the idea that a deity is supremely perfect) of a deity in himself.

Distinction between high gods and one unique God

The sky seen as a sacred entity is an all but universal belief. It is often related to or identical with the highest divinity. Nevertheless, supreme beings are always more than what can be explained from celestial phenomena alone, for they are often called creators of the world, founders of the order of the world, and protectors of law; and they are praised for their eternity and goodness. Often, the supreme being that created the world does not—or has ceased to—receive attention in the cult, although he may still be invoked in moments of great crisis. In a good many ancient agricultural societies, the idea of a great goddess prevailed instead of a male creator-god. The great goddess (as in the ancient Middle East and India) is venerated principally because of her omnipotence, especially her power over life. The sky god-creator sometimes cedes to a divinity who is also related to the sky but apparently is experienced more concretely because of his activity. Such a divinity (especially in pastoral cultures) can be a god of atmospheric phenomena (storm, rain, thunder, or lightning), whose power for the good of the people is extolled. In spite of his power, however, he is one of several gods, and in some cases (Yahweh in ancient Israel and Allāh in Islām) one such god retains the full creative function of early creator gods, and in him all "true" divinity is concentrated. In addition, a divinity related to the Sun rather than the heavens can assume preeminence; this has happened in some ancient imperial traditions (*e.g.,* Egypt, Inca Empire). Among sky gods who remained important in the mythologies of ancient civilizations are Zeus in Greece, Jupiter in Rome, and T'ien in China.

Myths concerning founders of religions and other religious figures. Although the founders of great religions (Confucius, Zoroaster, the Buddha, Moses, Jesus, Mani, Muḥammad) are generally conceded to have had actual existence, information about them is couched in legendary terms that have many mythological features. The same is true of many other religious figures (prophets, saints, or gurus [Hindu spiritual teachers]). Those traditions that have preserved the memory of their founders have, as a rule, carefully emphasized the elements that function most mythologically, in the sense that they state categorically realities that could not be known in any ordinary fashion or that raise the founder above ordinary historical conditions. Examples are the account of Jesus' prayer in Gethsemane, which no one heard according to the text itself, his statement that he was before Abraham, and his prophecies. Buddhist texts state that the Buddha not merely surpassed all yogis in knowledge of previous existences but, in fact, had conquered time. Well known too are his predictions concerning the course and decline of Buddhism and (in Mahāyāna texts) his promises as to the future spiritual attainments of the bodhisattvas. Other examples are Muḥammad's eschatological teachings in the Qur'ān and those of Zoroaster.

Mythological features in records of historical figures

Myths of kings and ascetics. Genuine myths concerning kings are found only in traditions that know a form of sacred kingship. Temple records from ancient Babylon mention offerings to kings who were considered divine. Hymns addressed to them make references to the king's union with a goddess—*i.e.,* the mythological motif of the "sacred marriage." One of the epithets for the king in ancient Egypt was "endowed with life" or "imparting life." The twofold meaning of the epithet is significant and can serve to make the mythology of sacred kingship understandable in other places as well, because the function of the king is in fact double. He mediates between the divine world and the world of man, representing each to the other. Hence, in Egypt a sacrifice by an individual was understood as offered to the king and at the same time by the king. The king's role of mediator and protector brings royal mythologies close to myths of culture heroes. Solemn procedures in which kings become divinities occur relatively late in history. An early and most conspicuous case of such an apotheosis (becoming divine) is that of Alexander the Great, who was called a god in his lifetime. Later, apotheosis took place for Roman emperors, although there are no cases of an emperor being accorded divine honours in his lifetime. A great many legends have accumulated around the figures of kings (*e.g.,* around King Aśoka of India and King Arthur in Britain). Stories about the Holy Roman emperor Frederick I Barbarossa and Charlemagne have a somewhat eschatological mythical flavour, because they are said to dwell each in his mountain (in the Kyffhäuser and the Untersberg, respectively) until they appear again to act as saviours in a crisis.

Most narratives about great ascetics, as well as other saints, could be regarded as legends rather than myths. There are, however, instances of saints or ascetics who are presented as a more than worldly model, so that a case can be made for the mythological function of their legends (*e.g.,* al-Hallāj in Islām and St. Francis in Christianity). In the case of traditions that have asceticism as an integral part, certain figures and the legends around them do indeed function as exemplars.

Myths of transformation. Countless stories exist concerning the origin of peculiar rocks, properties of animals, plants, stars, or other features in the world. In addition to such etiologic tales there are several myths that speak of cosmic changes brought about at the end of primordial times. An altogether different and extensive mythology exists concerning initiation rites and other "rites of passage" that involve transformation of man's being.

Cosmic transformation may concern an original world, without proper human means of existence and without death, that was transformed through a certain event (*e.g.,* the death of Hainuwele, a type of primal being known as a dema, or ancestral, deity) into the world known to mankind, a truly inhabitable world with vegetation, animals, and other features that had not existed before.

On a wider scale are myths that could be appendages to cosmogonic myths but that have not turned into mere etiologies. Many myths akin to the type of the dema deity (like Hainuwele) and to the culture-hero type (like Prometheus) account for events—such as the invention of agriculture, domestication of animals, and the use of fire—that have transformed the world for the benefit of man. Many others are just as closely related to cosmogonic accounts but tell of "setbacks" in primordial times. In agricultural societies, for example, myths have been collected that ascribe the unevenness of land or the formation of mountains to an ancient mishap or evil force.

Realization of the contents of myths

In rites of passage (*e.g.,* rites accompanying birth, attainment of maturity, marriage, death) the contents of myths are acted out. In each case the intention behind the rites is that man's mode of being be affected, indeed transformed. Through the birth ceremony the child "becomes" a person, and through initiation an adolescent "becomes" an adult, a member of a sodality, or a warrior. There is a great variety of customs in different communities and traditions, but everywhere these rites dramatize graphically the cosmic processes and realities expressed in language in myths. In many traditions the myths of the community are conveyed to the novice at the time of his initiation. Even in the major world religions rites of passage are still performed, as evidenced in such ceremonies as circumcision, Baptism, weddings, and mortuary rites. In all instances, the rites derive their meaning from the core of the tradition, and for that reason man's existence is regarded as transformed. In some cases the transformation derived from the dominant myth is far-reaching. The initiated shaman is able to transcend the ordinary human condition and overcome dangers that would cause the death of a noninitiate. Through his initiation he is believed to have gone through death and thus conquered it. In certain Hermetic (an occult magical tradition) and Gnostic texts the certainty of attaining divine being is clearly expressed.

MYTH IN MODERN SOCIETY

Secularization of myth and mythology. Deciding the extent to which there has actually been any secularization of myth involves a problem of definition. If myth is seen as the product of a past era, it is difficult to determine at what actual moment that era ended. Thus, it is virtually impossible to state precisely when a certain mythical theme becomes a mere literary theme or to determine in general when myths are no longer being created. It is more fruitful to recognize that symbols, myths, and rituals are all subject to change over time. Nor is secularization an irreversible process. It is instead a process that takes place time and again. Secularization movements and movements toward "mythification" of a phenomenon, narrative, or idea are aspects of the same historical processes. There have also been many types of secularization; the one brought about in Western society since the Middle Ages is only a single example. Another instance was the development in archaic and classical Greece (sometimes referred to—with great oversimplification—as a movement "from myth to reason") whereby fundamental questions about the nature of the universe came increasingly to receive answers in terms of philosophical, as opposed to mythical, reasoning.

On the other hand, although the secularization of modern times is not a unique phenomenon, it is a new and complex type, to which many factors have contributed. Scientific, particularly astronomical, discoveries of the late medieval and Renaissance periods were accompanied by a new trust in cosmic laws and an increasingly abstract notion of God. More or less Euhemeristic historical accounts that were common in the Middle Ages and were a symptom of a certain secularization process themselves gave way to history writing, focusing on psychological, social, and economic facts. In philosophy, naturalism of various sorts opposed notions of transcendence that earlier systems had taken for granted. The most common tendency in modern society has been to regard the characters and events in mythical accounts as not real or as by-products of realities that are not transcendent but rather immanent.

Secularization with mythification

This secularization in modern society, like earlier secularization processes, is accompanied by a process whereby new myths are formed (see below *Political and social uses of myth*).

Demythologization of major religious traditions. Demythologization should be distinguished from secularization. Every living mythology must come to terms with the world in which it is transmitted and to that extent inevitably goes through processes of secularization. Demythologization, however, refers to the conscious efforts people make to purify a religious tradition of its mythological elements. The term demythologization (*Entmythologisierung*) was coined by Rudolf Bultmann, a German theologian and New Testament scholar. In the strict sense of the word, demythologizing efforts have been limited to theological discussions in 20th-century Christianity.

Even after secularization has taken place a certain mythological residue may persist. Edward B. Tylor, one of the founders of anthropology as an academic discipline in the 19th century, coined the use of the word survival for customs and beliefs that continued to be adhered to long after the context in which they had had their meaning had ceased to exist. Because such customs and beliefs may be regarded as mere superstitions, the word survival usually has a slightly derogatory overtone. There are many survivals of myth in this sense. The myth of "the noble savage," well-known from the 18th-century writer Jean-Jacques Rousseau, can be understood as a survival of a paradisiacal mythology: Western man expecting to find evidence of paradise on earth.

The secularization process in modern times has affected symbolic behaviour (cult, ritual, liturgy) and symbolic objects (sacred places) more than myth, however. Nevertheless, commonly accepted forms of mythology in modern society do not permeate all parts of society or fulfill all needs. (In all likelihood, no society has ever been perfectly homogeneous in its myths.) At the same time there exist profound mythological needs in modern society, and some are filled by myths borrowed from submerged or alien traditions. Modern society's neglect of cosmic symbolism (which in contrast was widespread in archaic tradition) has provoked certain reactions, such as the continuing interest in astrology, which may even be seen as an attempt to present a coherent account of the cosmos. And the huge scientific advances of the 20th century have given rise to a literature, science fiction, that resembles myth, even down to an eschatological element.

Political and social uses of myth. In the industrialized Western society of the 20th century, myths and related types of tales continue to be told. Urban folklorists collect stories that have much in common with the tales collected by the Grimm brothers, except that in the modern narratives the lone traveler is likely to be threatened, not by a werewolf, but by a phantom hitchhiker, and the location of his danger may be a freeway rather than a forest. Computer games use sophisticated technology to represent quests involving dragons to be slain and princesses to be saved and married. The myth of Superman, the superhuman hero who saves the world and preserves "the American way," is a notable image embodying modern Americans' confidence in the moral values that their culture espouses. Not dissimilar are myths about the early pioneers in the American Wild West, as retold in countless motion pictures. Such stories often reinforce stereotypical attitudes about the moral superiority of the settlers to the native Indians, although sometimes such attitudes are called into question in other movies that attempt to demythologize the Wild West.

A particular illustration of the power that myths continue to exert was provided as late as the 1940s by the belief in the existence of an Aryan racial group, separate from and superior to the Semitic group. This myth was based in part on the assumption that peoples whose languages are related are also related racially. The fact that this assumption is spurious did not prevent the Aryan myth from gaining wide acceptance in Europe from the 18th century onward, and it was eventually to provide a supposed intellectual justification for the persecution of the Semitic Jews by their Aryan Germanic "superiors" during the period of Nazi domination. This episode suggests that, in politics, a myth will take hold if it serves the interests and focuses the aspirations of a particular group; the truth or falsity of the myth is irrelevant. In a sense, of course, this function is merely an extension of its more general role in religion, where a myth, as well as addressing questions such as a society's place in the cosmos, may serve to justify a particular kind of governmental organization.

Although politics is often regarded as having taken over the role once played by religion or myth in Western society, the situation is more complex than such a generalization would imply. Just as myth has always had a strong social and political element, so political movements and theories have mythical dimensions. For instance, a mythological component has always been important in keeping political units together, from villages to nations. Recently, however, this mythical dimension has gained prominence with the rise of competing mythlike ideologies such as capitalism and communism; the word ideology might indeed be replaced, in much contemporary discussion about politics, by the term mythology. Finally, crucial terms in modern sociopolitical discussion, such as freedom and equality, although they have a long and complex philosophical history, are often posited in a manner analogous to the function of myth presenting its own authority.

Myths and ideologies

(K.W.Bo./R.G.A.B.)

Animals and plants in myth

Animals and plants have played important roles in the oral traditions and the recorded myths of the peoples of the world, both ancient and modern. This section of the article is concerned with the variety of relationships noted between man and animals and plants in myths and popular folk traditions and in so-called primitive and popular systems of classification.

Man has always been intrigued by the problem of boundaries: what distinguishes him from another man; what marks off his culture from another; what the dividing lines are between man and plants, man and animals, or man and his gods. At times he has maintained a rigid sense of separation and viewed the breaking of distinctions as transgression. At other times he has sought to cross the boundaries in order to gain power or knowledge. In some myths, he has glorified an age when distinct categories had not yet come into existence, and he has yearned for a return to this paradisiacal condition. In other traditions, he has viewed with horror the monsters that result when different spheres of being are mixed.

According to a view prevalent in many traditional societies, man was formed by the gods. His history is given in the myths of the primordial establishment of things, and his solemn responsibility, along with every other living thing, is to fit himself within this given world. This does not mean that people living in such traditional societies lack distinctions. Among the African Lele, for example, animals are distinguished from man by their lack of manners, their immense fecundity, and by their sticking to their own sphere and avoiding contact with humans. Animals that violate this third characteristic are understood to be human-animals, the product of sorcery or metempsychosis (transmigration of souls).

Man's relationship to nature and the divine

The Great Chain of Being that dominated Western thought throughout the Middle Ages made man both the highest of the animals and the lowest of the gods. Man's body was like that of the animals: corporeal, sensate, and mortal. Man's spirit or intellect resembled the gods: incorporeal, rational, and immortal. The great surge of ethnological and biologic data and theories from the 16th century on tended to undermine this point of view. New forms of men were encountered (*e.g.,* the "savage") who seemed to their first describers closely akin to the brute; new biologies were proposed that placed man wholly within the animal kingdom, merely as one species among many, and postulated man's descent from animals. More recently, psychology and ethology have emphasized the irrational (or brutish) elements in man and suggested close analogies between animal and human behaviour. Since the 18th century man has been defined in a new, nonbiological way: as a cultural being rather than as the inhabitant of a natural realm. There have been many forms of this dichotomy: man is the only being who has a language, uses symbols, employs tools, freely plays, is self-conscious, or possesses a history. Man, in short, creates himself as a cultural being in distinction to the animal or plant, which is created by its environment or heredity. These questions of man's identity and the way he resembles or differs from other sentient beings may be found in every culture and during every age.

Man is a creature who tends to draw boundaries, both conceptually and practically. Not only does his being demand that he find a position in a complex system of relationships but also his social life and his biologic survival depend on the making of distinctions. To speak with the gods, have relations with another human, take possession of another's territory, or eat this or that plant or animal involves man in a host of decisions upon which his existence depends. One of his chief resources for answering such questions is that of the myths and legends mapping the world in which he dwells.

Myths and legends concerning animals and plants employ a wide variety of motifs but express a limited number of relationships. Man, animals, and plants may stand in a relationship of (1) opposition or difference, (2) descent, (3) mixture, (4) transformation, (5) identity, or (6) similarity. These are determined by and expressive of the total worldview of a people. The hunter, for example, has a different understanding of the animal from that of the agriculturalist or pastoralist; the tuber planter has a different view of plants from that of the cultivator of grains. Even within these broad categories sharp differences occur. The Kalahari San of southern Africa, who, alone, naked, and crawling on the ground, blends in with his environment in order to kill an animal for food, reveals a way of looking at man's relation to nature different from that of the Masai tribesman of eastern Africa, who, costumed and walking upright as part of a line of chanting hunters in order to slay a lion as a symbol of his manhood, stands forth visibly as the ruler of the world through which he moves. The Cretan bull dancer of ancient Mediterranean culture, playing with the animal by somersaulting over his back, expresses a conception of man's relation to this powerful animal and the forces of fecundity and death that it symbolizes different from that of the Spanish bullfighter who slays the beast.

Relationships between man, animals, and plants

RELATIONSHIPS OF OPPOSITION OR DIFFERENCE

The fundamental religious boundary is that between the sacred and the profane, the sacred being conceived of as a sphere of power superior to or opposed to the mundane. That which is sacred may be either creatively or chaotically powerful. If the former, it is primarily expressed in creation myths; if the latter, in demonic traditions.

Cosmogonies. The notion of a creator deity in animal or plant form is comparatively rare. There are stories of animals, birds, or insects creating the world and of creators with animal attributes or animal companions, but these are isolated traditions. Even in the widespread motif of the birth of the world from a cosmic egg there is rarely the notion of a bird laying or incubating the egg (the most notable exception is the world egg laid by a beautiful bird in the beginning of the *Kalevala,* the national epic of Finland). There are, however, a number of cosmogonic (origin of the world) motifs that employ a fundamental animal or plant symbolism: the cosmic tree that supports and nourishes the world; the earth surrounded by a serpent or supported on a turtle or on some other animal's back; the features of the present world created by the actions of some primeval animal—*e.g.,* lakes and rivers caused by the digging of an animal or hills raised by the flapping wings of a bird. Sacrificial motifs abound, such as the world being formed from the cut-up parts of an animal or restored by its primordial sacrifice.

Animals in opposition to creation

A number of important traditions associated with animals occur in dualistic creation accounts in which animals oppose creation, acting as a foil to the creator, or creation is accomplished by combat between the creator and animal monsters representative of chaos who must be slain or bound before the world can be established. The widely distributed earth-diver myth is the most familiar example of dualistic creation (see above *Myths of origin*).

Other oppositions occur with respect to the creation of man (see below *Relationships of descent*). Perhaps the most frequent myth of the origin of death is that of the "perverted message" or "two messengers." In one, an animal is sent with a message from the creator that man is immortal, but the animal alters the message to state that man must die. In the other, two animals are sent, one with the word that man is immortal, one with the message that man will die. A mishap occurs to the first, and only the fatal message reaches man.

Union of disparate features expressing a creative totality

In some traditions, there is a union of disparate features or opposites in a given mythic being. This does not express a chaotic hybrid but rather a creative totality (the "coincidence of opposites"). Though most frequently expressed by androgyny (having both male and female characteristics), either in traditions of an androgynous creator or first man, the theme is present in some animal and plant traditions as well (*e.g.*, the emergence of man from the androgynous *rīvās* plant in Iranian mythology). Although it occurs in cosmogonic settings (*e.g.*, the tree that unites heaven and earth), motifs of the reconciliation of animal and plant opposites more usually occur in paradisiacal imagery that promises the harmonious mingling of realms (*e.g.*, the "peaceable kingdom" of Isaiah 11:6–8 or Virgil's Eclogue IV).

Animal and plant deities. Belief in sacred plants or animals is widespread. Common to all of these is the notion that the plant or animal is a manifestation of the sacred and thus possesses the dual attributes of beneficence (in healing, hunting, or agricultural magic) or danger (as expressed in taboos against their destruction or consumption). More rarely, gods are believed to have animal (theriomorphic) or plant (phytomorphic) forms. Influenced by ancient Greek disparagement of contemporary Egyptian religion and Judeo-Christian antipathy to "idolatry," Western scholars have tended to speak of such traditions as "animal worship," although it is usually not the animal itself but rather the sacred power revealed by the animal that is being revered. Other deities possess animal or plant attributes or are incarnations associated with particular animals or plants. Here the animals or plants possess a symbolic function. Certain qualities are associated with certain species (*e.g.*, wisdom with the owl, strength with the lion, immortality with the eagle, inspiration with the grape), and the god's possession of these qualities is indicated by his being identified with the appropriate animal or plant. In other traditions, natural phenomena are associated with the actions of certain species (*e.g.*, wind as a bird, lightning as a snake), and the god who controls such phenomena is identified with the species. At times, the animal or plant achieves a divine identity of its own—*e.g.*, the thunderbird or the earthquake monster.

Western attitudes toward animals and plants as manifestations of the sacred

Hunting and agricultural deities. In the traditions of archaic hunting peoples there is frequently a figure whom scholars term the master of the animals or the protector of game. He is the ruler of the forest, of all animal species, or of only one particular species (usually a large game animal—*e.g.*, the northern master of the caribou). The master controls all game animals (frequently by penning them up). He dispenses a certain number to man as food and can be invoked by a shaman when he withholds game. He guides the hunter and, in some traditions, avenges the spirits of slain animals, whose souls return to his enclosures when they die. He is sometimes pictured in human form, on occasion having animal attributes or riding an animal; in other traditions, he is a giant animal or can assume animal form.

In a related complex, a deity in animal form demonstrates to man the art of hunting, serving as the first victim (a motif found in some of the American Indian bear mother or buffalo woman tales). Or the deity appears among men as an animal who must be slain and eaten so that he may return to his heavenly home (*e.g.*, the Ainu Iyomante feast in Japan).

A similar pattern is found among archaic agricultural peoples. An ancestral (*dema*) goddess, at times in plant form, produces food asexually from her body. She is slain by the tribe, and from the dismembered portions of her body crops appear.

The archaic pattern of the *dema* deity needs to be distinguished from the widespread tradition among technically more sophisticated agricultural peoples of the bountiful mother earth or the god or goddess of vegetation or special crops. In the latter case, the deity, frequently depicted or associated with the appropriate animal and vegetative characteristics, is the principle of inexhaustible vitality. The god frequently has a human consort who participates in a sacred marriage in order to gain fecundity for man (this happens in ancient Mesopotamian religions, for instance).

The functions of the culture hero

Culture heroes. The master of the animals or corn mother is frequently found in association with animal culture heroes. An animal or trickster who can assume animal form secures for man the various attributes of culture (acting either in consort with or opposition to the gods). These traditions are found in etiologic stories about how man first learned to hunt, discovered tobacco, and accomplished other things. The most frequent motif is that of the animal who stole fire from the gods for man. Frequently, such traditions lie behind etiologies of specific animal or plant characteristics; *e.g.*, the bat is black and blind because it stole fire and was singed by the flames and blinded by the smoke. In other tales, the animals oppose the acquisition of culture by man and must be overcome by a human culture hero.

A closely related theme is the myth of a life-giving tree or other healing magical plant, growing in paradise or some other inaccessible place, to which the culture hero must travel in order to gain a boon for mankind. He is frequently assisted by or has to overcome supernatural animals. This is an especially widespread type of myth, with numerous instances found throughout the world.

Demonic plants and animals. Opposed to these positive conceptions of the creative powers of plants and animals is the notion that their sacred power is chaotic or demonic. Rather than aiding man, they are destructive. The most common examples are monstrous plants and animals, which figure especially in heroic quests as guardians of boons or threats to be overcome; mythical animals associated with destructive natural phenomena, such as the earthquake monster or the monster who according to some traditions causes eclipses by devouring the Sun or Moon; and personifications of evil powers such as death or disease (*e.g.*, the hound of hell) or chaos beasts (such as dragons) whose release marks the end of the world or who will be slain in a final battle by a saviour deity. A universal phenomenon is the association of certain species of animals with sorcerers and witches. The most frequent form of this belief is that of the familiar—an animal whose soul is bound up with that of the sorcerer, whose form the sorcerer can assume, and who may be commanded to serve his evil master.

Dragons and familiars

Some species (*e.g.*, animals such as the serpent and various narcotic plants) exhibit the ambivalence of the sacred—they are conceived as being both beneficent and dangerous. This reflects a crucial aspect of the sacred—that it is a region of power. As was stated above this power is ambivalent—*i.e.*, it can act for mankind's benefit or detriment—and is perceived therefore as the location either of creativity or of chaos.

RELATIONSHIPS OF DESCENT

One of the major ways man has of organizing his world is through genealogy or relations of descent. In theogonies, or tales of the origin of gods (*e.g.*, that by Hesiod), or in legendary lists of human offspring (such as the genealogies in the Old Testament), relations of descent and the association of characteristics, territories, and spheres of influence with descendants provide a means of mapping the cosmos and the human world. In traditions concerning animals and plants, relations of descent are most prominent in myths of the origin of man and in totemic (animal-clan relational) materials. Central to both is the figure of the plant or animal ancestor.

Creation of man from plants or animals. A widespread motif, especially among archaic peoples, concerns man's supposed descent from plants or animals. These descent traditions usually name a particular species as man's ancestor, and the tribe frequently takes its name from the plant or animal.

In some myths, an asexual mode of creation is implied; a child, for example, appears from the bud of a tree or from a split fruit, or man is a featherless bird sent from the sky. Even the motif of the birth of man from an egg is predominantly an asexual motif inasmuch as no preliminary coition is mentioned. Other traditions, particularly agricultural ones, see man as the product of the mating of a plant or animal species. In some myths, fabrication rather than descent is emphasized. Man is fashioned from a plant or animal by the gods, or his parts are modeled after other species. In these descent traditions, the primal man who results is usually the progenitor of a particular people. Other peoples are created from different or less favourable species. These traditions persist in folkloric accounts of the birth of individuals from plants or animals. Such myths express a close relationship between man and the animal and plant world. Man does not represent a new type of being but rather a new manifestation or form.

The widely distributed notion of animal or plant ancestors places considerable emphasis on transformation (see below *Relationships of transformation*). The ancestral myths describe a primeval time of creation (or successive creations) followed by a decisive alteration in the conditions of life in the shift from the ancestral to the present human mode of being. Compared with the "fixed" characteristics of the present period, the ancestral era is represented as having been one of flux, lacking definite boundaries. In it animals, plants, and men are much the same: they can speak with each other, have sexual relations with each other, and engage in other relationships. The ancestors are polymorphic (many formed) and are frequently depicted as emerging from the ground. In such cases their movement toward the surface is represented as an increasing differentiation, away from compound hybrids and toward forms somewhat resembling present species. But even on the surface, the ancestors remain relatively fluid: some resemble plants, others animals or men, and all have shared characteristics and the power to change their form at will.

The ancestral era

The ancestors are depicted as primordially powerful beings, but due to a variety of causes their world becomes transformed, and the present order of things comes into existence. Human culture and the decisive features of the world as man now knows it are established during the transformation: man's labour, sexuality, and death are due to some action of the ancestors; the topography of the land is the "tracks" left by the ancestors; men, animals, and plants are depicted as having received their present form after the ancestral age.

Totemism. The relations to an animal or plant ancestor are frequently associated with the complex phenomenon of totemism. Totemism is primarily a social relationship. It expresses the belief that there is a connection between a group of persons, on the one hand, and a species of animal or plant, on the other. The relationship to the totem (animal or plant symbol) occurs in a variety of forms; associated phenomena (*e.g.*, exogamy, or marriage outside the clan, and taboos against killing the totem species) may or may not be present. The myths associated with such traditions narrate the origin of a social group and the discovery of its totem. It was commonly believed in the 19th century that there was a stage in the development of human thought that could be called "totemic," a stage at which primitive peoples perceived a mystical connection between particular social groups and the animals or plants that were their totems. Totemism apparently covered a bewilderingly wide range of phenomena: the list of totems among the Nuer, for instance, includes lion, waterbuck, tortoise, papyrus, rafters, and certain diseases. Utilitarian explanations for the choices of totems—"good to eat," "useful," etc.—do not fit the ethnographic data, and to say that the totems are chosen because they have some special mystical significance is merely to rephrase the problem, without identifying why only certain items have mystical significance. In *Le Totémisme aujourd'hui* (1962; *Totemism*) Lévi-Strauss advocated a different approach. He suggested that totemism, far from being a special stage in human development, was merely an instance of the use, within so-called primitive systems of classification, of objects and categories from the world of everyday experience to divide and order that experience.

A phenomenon that has, at times, been confused with the social relations of totemism is that of the individual guardian. It involves a relationship between a particular person and a particular species, usually revealed to the individual in a vision, such as in the vision quests among the North American Plains Indians. These guardians become a source of knowledge and good fortune for the individual. To these traditions, other folkloric motifs may be related, such as the birth of various individuals from intercourse between humans and animals or plants; the animal wife; animal nurses; or the ability of certain persons to understand or converse with animals or plants.

Hierarchy. The fluidity of boundaries characteristic of relations of descent raises important questions as to the status of man or of culture in relation to nature. Are animals and plants more like men than not? Is the human world superior to or inferior to the natural sphere? Such questions lie behind a variety of motifs associated with descent traditions: that the first men were undeveloped, amorphous, or resembled animals; that animals resisted the creation of man; and that the primordial man is the ruler of the natural world. The characteristic fluidity of the descent traditions persists in traditions such as the wild man and in relations of transformation and identity (see below).

The status of man and culture in relation to nature

RELATIONSHIPS OF MIXTURE

For some societies boundaries and the maintenance of distinctions guarantee the continued existence of the cosmos as an integrated totality. There are rituals that periodically reenact the original process whereby the cosmos was divided up and established in its present form. In such cases a new beginning, for example New Year's celebrations as carried out in modern Western society, re-create the original beginnings of things as they are today. Other rituals foster remembrance of the decisive deeds of the ancestors in fixing the present state of things; ritualized social structures (such as the caste structure of India) maintain a complex system of distinctions; and religious ideologies (such as astrology) foster the notion of spheres of power that control all members of a class, be they gods, planets, animals, plants, minerals, or men. In such societies, to be real is to affirm and repeat the structures of the cosmos. Each being is called upon to dwell in a limited world in which everything has its given place and role to fulfill. To be sacred is to remain in place. To break out, to cross boundaries, is to open the world to the threat of chaos, to commit transgression. Associated with this worldview is the notion that the mixing of realms is the result of evil influence and leads to monsters, hybrids, and uncleanliness. An alternative view in the history of religions sees positive sacred power to be gained from the violation of the given boundaries of the world. Each being, in such a view, is called upon to challenge its limits; to break them and to create new possibilities for existence, to achieve freedom. Associated with this view is either the necessity for a periodic loosening of restraint or the celebration of gods or sacred persons who have achieved freedom. Religiously expressed, for the one view, the sacred is the ordinary, that which remains in place; for the other, the sacred is the extraordinary, that which is not restricted to its allotted place.

These two points of view—*i.e.,* that power comes from

conformity to class or freedom from class—may be illustrated by the widespread category of taboo. Research in the second half of the 20th century has led to the conclusion that taboo is primarily a taxonomic (classificatory) system. Those things that are forbidden involve the crossing of boundaries or are beings that fall between classes. Thus, one may not with impunity enter other spheres (*e.g.,* the realms of the gods) or touch sacred objects, transport an object from one realm to another, cross sexual or class lines, or have relations with a being not of one's class. Many food taboos have been shown to reflect taxonomic anomalies. An animal such as the bat is tabooed because it has fur like a mammal but flies like a bird; it has wings like a bird but has fur rather than feathers—and therefore is neither mammal nor bird and must be shunned. On the other hand, the consumption of forbidden foods or engaging in forbidden sexual practices (including homosexuality and bestiality) is part of the ritual of transcendence in many cultures. If an individual can survive the crossing of boundaries, he will obtain extraordinary sacred power (*e.g.,* adherents of Tantrism, a system of esoteric practices performed in both Buddhism and Hinduism, who violate both eating and sexual taboos; the Jewish magicians mentioned in the Old Testament Book of Isaiah, chapter 65, who eat the forbidden swine and say ". . . do not come near me, for I am holy").

Proscriptions against crossing boundaries

From the earliest times man has shown a readiness to be fascinated by monsters. Monsters are chaos beasts, lurking at the interstices of order, be they conceived as mythical creatures who preceded creation, survivals from an archaic era, creatures who dwell in dangerous lands remote from human habitation, or beings who appear in nightmares. Though the forms and types of monsters are numberless, a single principle holds good for the majority of them: a monster is out of place, conforming to no class or violating existing classes. This is most frequently expressed by the monster's having hybrid form (the result of a mixture of species, attributes, sexes, and other categories), being the result of a transformation, or having dislocated or superfluous parts. Because modes of locomotion and other bodily characteristics are prime modes of classification, the superfluity or lack of organs removes the monster from the ordinary taxonomic divisions. The dragon, for example—perhaps the most widespread monster in myth and folklore—is born through a mixture of species: it is a serpent born asexually from a rooster's egg incubated in manure; by the transformation of an animal; or by the joint generation of a man or worm and a metal. Its form is a compound of species: the body of a serpent or crocodile with the scales of a fish; feet, wings, and occasionally the head of a bird; the forelimbs and occasionally the head of a lion; or, in another dominant type, the ears of an ox, the feet of a tiger, the claws of an eagle, the horns of a deer, the head of a camel, the eyes of a demon, the neck of a snake, the belly of a mollusk, and the scales of a fish. In other types of dragons, organs or attributes of the snake, lizard, fish, mollusk, toad, elephant, horse, pig, ram, deer, eagle, falcon, octopus, or whale predominate. In many traditions, the dragon has the power to transform itself at will. Its possession of superfluous organs is most frequently expressed by its being many headed, and it has both subterranean and aerial characteristics and habits.

Generation of the dragon

The most common hybrid monster generally mixes differing species—*e.g.,* the Centaur (horse-man), the Minotaur (bull-man), Echidna (snake-woman), Pegasus (horse-bird), Sphinx (woman-lion-bird), Siren (bird-woman), and Empusa (animal-metal) of Greek mythology and the griffin (lion-eagle), mermaid (woman-fish), vegetable lamb (plant-animal), barnacle goose (mollusk-bird), and mandrake (plant-man). In other instances, the characteristics are juxtapositions of different species—*e.g.,* the tree that bears human heads as fruit; horses born from eggs; flesh-eating mares; milk-producing birds.

The most extreme form of the fluidity that is characteristic of monsters is the Protean figure who can change into any form or combination of forms at will. In all of these monstrous forms, the central notion appears to be the danger associated with beings that are out of place or are fluid. But some contemporary anthropologists have argued the opposite conclusion; *i.e.,* rather than being threats to the classificatory system, monsters, through their startling combinations and juxtapositions, force men to think more clearly about and distinguish more sharply between the different boundaries of their world. In this interpretation, the monsters are ultimately supportive of order rather than a destructive threat to it.

RELATIONSHIPS OF TRANSFORMATION

One of the largest groups of animal and plant traditions in folklore and religious material is that of transformation. Familiar stories—such as Beauty and the Beast; the transformation of a man into an ass in the *Metamorphoses* by Apuleius, a Roman writer of the 2nd century AD; the frog king or the swan maiden, as well as such well-known traditions as that of the werewolf, the vampire, or leopard man—testify to the wide dissemination of this theme. Every permutation and combination exists: man into mammal, bird, fish, insect, reptile, amphibian, or plant; animal into man or plant; animal into another species of animal; or plant into animal. There are also partial transformations resulting in hybrid forms as well as alternating transformations—*e.g.,* animal, man, or tree by day and the reverse at night. Another great series of transformations concerns the dead, who either transmigrate into or return in animal and plant forms.

The power to compel another to change form, or to cross boundaries oneself at will, may be judged good or evil depending on the assessment of order in the worldview of the particular culture. In the majority of instances of transformation of another, the transformation is considered to be the result of evil magical powers, and most tales conclude with the disenchantment of the subject, his release from the evil power, and his return to his original form. Many of the instances of self-transformation are for the positive purpose of transcendence.

Several of the motifs present in the folklore of transformation suggest cultic procedures (*e.g.,* transformation into an animal by putting on its skin). Cultic practices probably lie behind and lend credibility to many such tales.

In many societies, ritual change involves a transition period in which boundaries are broken and chaos rules, only to be overcome as order is restored. This is common in festivals in which the social order is temporarily suspended or reversed (as in the ancient Roman Saturnalia and the carnival celebrated in many Roman Catholic countries) and in rites of passage (such as initiation). Animal and plant transformations play a significant role in such ceremonies, both as negative symbols of chaos (*e.g.,* return of the dead in animal form to mingle with the living; ritualized combats against the primordial dragon) and as positive symbols of the breaking through of bounds and the release of the forces of life (*e.g.,* the presence in many of these ceremonies of young males dressed as animals who engage in sacred sexual intercourse). Prominent in such Saturnalian traditions are deities such as the Greek god Dionysus, who can assume vegetable, animal, or human forms at will, who is a god of sudden, dramatic epiphanies (manifestations) and license, and whose devotees, through orgiastic rituals, participate in his freedom to break all bounds in order to recover the boundless vitality and fecundity of primordial chaos. A new life for the cosmos, society, and the individual is supposedly obtained through the abolition of the order of the old.

Ritualized moments of transition

Initiation ceremonies make use of transformations to a somewhat different end. The initiant receives new birth by the dying of his old self after a series of ordeals. Antagonists, frequently in masked animal form, torment him, and his "death" and rebirth are analogous to the hero's successful fight against monsters. Alternatively, the culmination of initiation is frequently the narration of the myths of the ancestors and the vision of them. Masked men, in mixed animal and plant forms, appear to the initiant to remind him of his true origin as opposed to his biologic origin as a product of his parents. (Other ritual uses of masks achieve the same effect: the ritual transformation of the "actor" into the sacred animal, plant, or deity.)

Frequently, although the nomenclature for plants and animals is learned by a child from birth, the logic of the system is revealed only at initiation, at which point the initiant, as an adult, becomes responsible for the proper observance of all the boundaries required by his society (*e.g.*, among the Senufo of Africa, 58 figurines are presented to the initiant in a carefully prescribed order that provides an inventory of the basic classes of animals, men and human activities, and social distinctions).

The role of the shaman

Within many cultures there are religious specialists in the breaking of bounds. Perhaps the most widespread example is that of the shaman who is deemed able to journey at will to heaven or the underworld, mingling with both the gods and the dead. His journey occurs through magical flight (frequently in the form of a bird) with animal psychopomps (soul conductors) or guardians or by ascending the sacred tree that connects heaven and earth. The shaman may transform himself into an animal and know how to converse with animals. Another similar phenomenon is the existence of leopard societies in Africa. In these a practitioner is believed to be able to transform himself into an animal frequently considered to be his incarnate "second self."

RELATIONSHIPS OF IDENTITY

Works on the supposedly primitive mentality published in the 19th and early 20th century usually presumed that primitive man could not distinguish between plants, animals, and men. This "hazy vision," as it was often called, was believed to lie at the root of religious phenomena such as animism (belief that inanimate objects and natural phenomena have souls) and totemism. More recent studies have demonstrated the presence of complex taxonomies among peoples sometimes described as "primitive," although they do not usually employ the criteria of a modern biologist. Relations of identity, when compared with the other forms of relationship already described, are comparatively rare, occurring most frequently in traditions about the soul. Relations of similarity are more common, usually in literary settings, such as plant or animal fables. The most common expression of identity relates the soul of man to that of animals or plants.

Soul-stuff. Although man tends to associate the soul with personal survival or continuity after death, there is an equally ancient view that emphasizes the continuity of life. This view, to which the Dutch anthropologist Albertus Christiaan Kruyt gave the term soul-stuff (a term he contrasted with the postmortem soul), is chiefly found among the rice cultivators of the Indonesian culture area, although it is also witnessed elsewhere. Central to this belief is the circulation of vitality throughout different levels of existence. The soul-stuff is created by the deity as an indestructible reservoir of life. It is eternally reborn—either by returning to its creator, who will redistribute it, or by transmigrating into an embryonic human, animal, or plant. Whatever form it assumes, the same "stuff" is common to all beings.

Death, or postmortem, soul. The majority of traditions concerns the postmortem soul, which leaves the body or comes into existence only after death. A number of motifs reflecting different assessments of the nature of life and death occur. The soul may assume an animal or plant form or there may be animal psychopomps, most frequently a winged creature such as a bird or butterfly. The soul may transmigrate into or be reincarnated as an animal or plant. These traditions need to be distinguished from those concerning spirits of the dead who reappear in animal form. Related to these are traditions about the separable soul, which is capable of removing itself or being removed from a person while still living. This most usually occurs in sleep. While detached it may be placed in or assume the form of an animal or, more rarely, a plant. In general, where the notion of soul-stuff predominates, relations of identity are prevalent; where the notion of a death soul is present, the traditions are more closely akin to relations of transformation (see above).

Psychic interrelations

Plural souls. A more complex pattern, of wide distribution, is that of the plurality of souls. Man's vitality and personality are viewed as the result of a complex set of psychic interrelations. A classic example is that of the Apapocuva-Guaraní of Brazil, as described by the anthropologist Curt Nimuendajú: a gentle vegetable soul comes, fully formed, from the dwelling place of the gods and joins with the infant at the moment of birth. To this is joined, shortly after birth, a vigorous animal soul. The type of animal decisively influences the recipient's personality: a gentle person has received a butterfly's soul; a cruel and violent man, that of a jaguar. Upon death, the vegetable soul enters paradise; the animal soul becomes a fierce ghost that plagues the living. The plurality of souls provides a complex taxonomy accounting for and relating the distinctive character traits of plants, animals, and men.

The alter ego, or life index. Other religious and folkloric traditions view the life of man as bound up with that of a plant or animal: if one is destroyed the other dies as well. In some traditions, this is confined to the familiar or guardian of a witch or shaman; in others, it is an individual relationship possible for any man. An example of the latter relationship is nagualism, a phenomenon found among the Indians of Guatemala and Honduras in Central America. Nagualism is the belief that there exists a nagual—an object or, more often, an animal—that stands in a parallel relationship to a person. If a man's nagual suffers harm or death, the man suffers harm or death as well. According to one story, during the initial hostile encounters between the Indians and the Spaniards, the Indians' naguals fought on their side against the invaders. When the nagual of the Indian chief—which was in the form of a bird—was speared and killed by the Spanish general, the Indian chief died at the same moment.

Nagualism relates the life of each individual to the life of an animal or other object. More rarely, there is a relation between an entire tribe and a particular plant or animal. In some societies, a ritual of identification is performed, usually at birth (*e.g.*, planting a tree or burying the placenta at the roots of a tree). In others, an individual has a vision or undertakes a vision quest to identify his alter ego.

RELATIONSHIPS OF SIMILARITY

Relations of similarity between human beings and plants or animals usually depend upon the perception of an attribute or aggregate of attributes that they have in common. This process is apparent in colloquial expressions such as when someone is called a "cool cat," a "bitch," a "clumsy ox," a "greedy pig," or "foxy." A similar process appears to lie behind many of the so-called totemic names or theriophoric or phytophoric personal names (*e.g.*, Swift Deer, Bold Eagle) and is concealed in a number of familiar Western names (*e.g.*, Leo, "the lion"; Deborah, "the bee"; and Jonah, "the dove"). The reverse process, the giving of human names to plants or animals, also depends in a majority of instances on the discernment of character similarities. Care must be used, however, in the interpretation of proper names. Every plant or animal name does not necessarily reveal the perception of similarity. For example, the Seminole Indians combine a character name with a shape and animal name in an arbitrary fashion that appears to pay no attention to their meaning, resulting in unusual combinations such as that of a well-known Seminole medicine man whose name translates as "crazy, spherical puma."

Function of fables

The same process is at work in the universal literary form of plant and animal fables. The fable depends for its point upon the association made by the reader or listener between himself and one of a limited number of characteristics possessed by each animal or plant. More complex forms, verging on allegories, such as the beast epic and the debates between various plants and animals as to which are superior, also exist. The popular *Physiologus* ("Naturalist"), a Greek work from the 2nd century AD, and the medieval bestiary traditions draw morals particularly from monstrous or wondrous animals and plants. Both the fable and the bestiary traditions contributed to the formation of the stereotyped bird, beast, and flower emblems that figure in heraldry and religious iconography.

The process of discovering similarities of personality between plants and animals, on the one hand, and human beings, on the other, also plays a significant role in certain archaic sciences. Physiognomy, which claims to find correspondences between bodily features and psychological characteristics, often makes use of such supposed similarities. The earliest Western systematic treatise, the Aristotelian *Physiognomonica,* maintains that people with facial characteristics resembling certain animals have the temperaments ascribed to those animals (*e.g.*, persons who have noses with slight notches resemble the crow and are impudent just as the crow is). These views persist in popular figures of speech, such as "bulldog jaw." The same structure underlies the use of plants and animals in archaic healing practices, alchemy, and astrological tables in which animals, plants, and minerals, as well as human personality traits, are associated with the birth signs of the zodiac or planets. (J.Z.S./R.G.A.B.)

BIBLIOGRAPHY. KEES W. BOLLE, "Secularization as a Problem for the History of Religions," *Comparative Studies in Society and History,* 12(3):242–259 (July 1970), a comparative study of secularization processes in various cultures and periods; PETER BURKE, *Popular Culture in Early Modern Europe* (1978), especially ch. 1, "The Discovery of the People," pp. 3–22, a discussion of the development of the study of folklore; WALTER BURKERT, *Structure and History in Greek Mythology and Ritual* (1979, reprinted 1982), an attempt to relate myths to the biologic "programs of action" that lie behind them, and *Homo Necans: The Anthropology of Ancient Greek Sacrificial Ritual and Myth* (1983; originally published in German, 1972), an account of Greek myths and rituals of sacrifice; JOSEPH CAMPBELL, *The Masks of God,* vol. 1, *Primitive Mythology,* rev. ed. (1969, reissued 1982), neo-Romantic and Jungian in interpretation, and *The Way of the Animal Powers,* vol. 1 of the *Historical Atlas of World Mythology* (1983), continuing a discussion of myths and culture; HENRY CORBIN *et al., Man and Time* (1957, reissued 1983), excellent contributions on mythologies concerning time in early Christianity, Islām, Mazdakism, and the Book of Changes; FRIEDRICH CREUZER, *Symbolik und Mythologie der alten Völker, besonders der Griechen,* 3rd rev. ed., 4 vol. (1836–42, reprinted 1973), a classic work; MARCEL DETIENNE, *The Creation of Mythology* (1986; originally published in French, 1981), an analysis of *mythos* and the concept of mythology among the Greeks; GEORGES DUMÉZIL, *The Destiny of the Warrior* (1970; originally published in French, 1969), on the problem of myth and epic in Indo-European studies; ALAN DUNDES (ed.), *Sacred Narrative: Readings in the Theory of Myth* (1984), treatments of the concept of myth by scholars from various disciplines; MIRCEA ELIADE, *Birth and Rebirth: The Religious Meanings of Initiation in Human Culture,* trans. from French (1958, reissued 1975 with title *Rites and Symbols of Initiation: The Mysteries of Birth and Rebirth*), indispensable for an understanding of myth in its relation to initiation ceremonies, *From Primitives to Zen: A Thematic Sourcebook of the History of Religions* (1967, reprinted 1977), containing a wide selection of mythological materials, *Myths, Dreams, and Mysteries: The Encounter Between Contemporary Faiths and Archaic Realities* (1960, reissued 1975; originally published in French, 1957), of special interest for the study of myth in modern society, especially nostalgia for paradise and the function of psychoanalysis, *Myth and Reality,* trans. from French (1963, reprinted 1975), a collection of essays on myth, including an appendix on myths and fairy tales, an essay on the structure of myths, and a number of important observations on the continuation of myths in modern times, and *The Myth of the Eternal Return,* rev. ed. (1965, reprinted 1974; also published as *Cosmos and History: The Myth of the Eternal Return,* 1959, reprinted 1985; originally published in French, 1949), a discussion of cosmically and historically oriented myths; BURTON FELDMAN and ROBERT D. RICHARDSON (comps.), *The Rise of Modern Mythology, 1680–1860* (1972, reprinted 1975), an excellent anthology with commentary and bibliography; H. FRANKFORT *et al., The Intellectual Adventure of Ancient Man* (1951), a discussion of the "mytho-poetic age"—neo-Romantic but still stimulating; THEODOR H. GASTER, *Thespis: Ritual, Myth, and Drama in the Ancient Near East,* rev. ed. (1961, reissued 1977), a persuasive study on the historical relation between cult and drama (folkloric in character); JACK GOODY, *The Domestication of the Savage Mind* (1977), a critique of Lévi-Strauss's views as expressed in *The Savage Mind;* FRITZ GRAF, *Griechische Mythologie: Eine Einführung* (1985), an excellent modern analysis of Greek mythology; LOUIS HERBERT GRAY (ed.), *The Mythology of All Races,* 13 vol. (1916–33, reissued 1964), perhaps the best collection and discussion of myths ever published in English; S.H. HOOKE (ed.), *Myth and Ritual: Essays on the Myth and Ritual of the Hebrews in Relation to the Culture Pattern of the Ancient East* (1933), the "manifesto" of the Myth-Ritual school, and *Myth, Ritual, and Kingship: Essays on the Theory and Practice of Kingship in the Ancient Near East and in Israel* (1958, reprinted 1960), containing information on the myth of divine kingship; WERNER JAEGER, *The Theology of the Early Greek Philosophers,* trans. from German (1947, reprinted 1980), a discussion of the historical problem of the relationship between myth and philosophy; KARL JASPERS and RUDOLF BULTMANN, *Myth and Christianity: An Inquiry into the Possibility of Religion Without Myth* (1958; originally published in German, 1954), a discussion between the two authors on demythologization; ADOLF E. JENSEN, *Myth and Cult Among Primitive Peoples* (1963; originally published in German, 1951), important for the mythology of demi-deities and theoretical questions concerning myth and sacrifice; C.G. JUNG and C. KERÉNYI, *Essays on a Science of Mythology,* rev. ed. (1963, reissued 1969; originally published in German, 1949), the basic introduction to the Jungian approach to myth; G.S. KIRK, *Myth: Its Meaning and Functions in Ancient and Other Cultures* (1970, reprinted 1974), a discussion of the major modern theories of myth; SAMUEL NOAH KRAMER (ed.), *Mythologies of the Ancient World* (1961); WALTER KRICKEBERG *et al., Pre-Columbian American Religions* (1968; originally published in German, 1961); EDMUND LEACH (ed.), *The Structural Study of Myth and Totemism* (1967), a discussion of structuralism; G. VAN DER LEEUW, *Sacred and Profane Beauty: The Holy in Art,* trans. from German (1963), an elaborate and imaginative work on the relations between religion and art in dance, drama, literature, plastic art, architecture, and music; CLAUDE LÉVI-STRAUSS, *The Savage Mind* (1966, reissued 1972), a fundamental analysis of "primitive" thought written from a structuralist point of view, and his 4 vol. study of the science of mythology, *The Raw and the Cooked* (1969, reissued 1986; originally published in French, 1964), *From Honey to Ashes* (1973, reprinted 1983; originally published in French, 1966), *The Origin of Table Manners* (1978; originally published in French, 1968), *The Naked Man* (1981; originally published in French, 1971), and *Myth and Meaning* (1978), reflections on some of the principal theoretical issues that have occupied the author; CHARLES H. LONG, *Alpha: The Myths of Creation* (1963, reprinted 1983), the best and most available anthology of creation myths in English; BRONISŁAW MALINOWSKI, *Magic, Science and Religion, and Other Essays* (1948, reissued 1984), containing the influential essay "Myth in Primitive Psychology"; JOHN MIDDLETON (ed.), *Myth and Cosmos: Readings in Mythology and Symbolism* (1967, reprinted 1980), in which 18 well-known anthropologists present their views on myth, most of them on the basis of their own findings in a variety of nonliterate societies; ISIDORE OKPEWHO, *Myth in Africa: A Study of Its Aesthetic and Cultural Relevance* (1983); WALTER F. OTTO, *The Homeric Gods: The Spiritual Significance of Greek Religion* (1954, reprinted 1979; originally published in German, 3rd ed., 1947), mainly a treatise on the significance of Homeric mythology; RAFFAELE PETTAZZONI, *Miti e leggende,* 4 vol. (1948–63, reprinted 4 vol. in 2, 1978), a classic containing an unsurpassed collection of myths and exhaustive bibliographies; MAC LINSCOTT RICKETTS, "The North American Indian Trickster," *History of Religions,* 5(2):327–350 (Winter 1966), an excellent essay on a puzzling character of North American Indian mythology; J.W. ROGERSON, *Anthropology and the Old Testament* (1978, reissued 1984), on the relevance of 20th-century anthropology for the study of myth and ritual in the Bible; H.H. ROWLEY (ed.), *The Old Testament and Modern Study: A Generation of Discovery and Research* (1951, reprinted 1967), important for the problem of myth, directly and by implication; K.K. RUTHVEN, *Myth* (1976), a brief account of modern views of myth, especially the relation of myth to literature; H. SCHÄRER, *Ngaju Religion: The Conception of God Among a South Borneo People* (1963; originally published in German, 1946); THOMAS A. SEBEOK (ed.), *Myth: A Symposium* (1955, reprinted 1974), in which nine specialists present their basic views of myths, fascinating because of the diversity; STITH THOMPSON (ed.), *Tales of the North American Indians* (1929, reprinted 1971), a readily available collection of North American Indian and other stories; RUTH M. UNDERHILL, *Red Man's Religion: Beliefs and Practices of the Indians North of Mexico* (1965, reprinted 1974), an introduction to North American Indian mythology, with superb bibliographies; and JAN DE VRIES, *Forschungsgeschichte der Mythologie* (1961), the standard work on the history of scholarship devoted to myth, *Heroic Song and Heroic Legend* (1963, reprinted 1978; originally published in Dutch, 1961), especially important for the relation between myth and epic (or saga), and *The Study of Religion: A Historical Approach* (1967; originally published in Dutch, 1961), a historical survey of scholarship devoted to religious phenomena, in which mythology is prominent.

(K.W.Bo./J.Z.S./R.G.A.B.)

Names

A name is a word or group of words used to refer to an individual entity (real or imaginary); the name singles out this entity by directly pointing to it, not by specifying it as a member of a class. For instance, it is possible to refer to the same entity, in this case a river, in two distinct ways: (1) "The Colorado is a beautiful river," and (2) "The river that flows through Austin is beautiful." Because there is only one river that flows through Austin, Texas, the subject of sentence (2) is unambiguously identified, and the reference of the sentence is fully individual. The subject of sentence (2), however, is not a name but rather a nominal (noun) phrase that specifies one member of the whole class of rivers by indicating a unique property of it. The word Colorado in sentence (1), on the other hand, is a name, because it directly points to the specific river. The fact that there is more than one river called Colorado, and that more specific information is sometimes needed to identify the one being discussed (*e.g.*, "I prefer the Texan Colorado to the California one"), does not change the status of "Colorado" as a name, because each of the two rivers is referred to in the way required by the definition.

The article is divided into the following sections:

NAMES AND APPELLATIVES

A general appellative (*i.e.*, a common noun) capable of being used in reference to a whole class of entities can also be used with an individual reference. For instance, if an inhabitant of Austin, Texas, says, "Let's go swimming today, not in the pool but in the river," there is no doubt that the word river has a unique, individual reference to one single river, namely, the Colorado. This fact, however, does not make a name out of it; "river" is here a common noun, but its reference is specified by the extralinguistic context of the situation in which the sentence was said. Some names seem to belong more to the category of appellatives than to the category of names like Colorado in "the Colorado River." For example, names like Big River, Red River, Stony Brook, and Cedar Hill may have their origin in a specific use of a general noun. If a sentence like "After five days of marching, we had to cross a river, the big one, not one of the smaller ones" is used very often, the name Big River may result. Such names are more frequently given as directly descriptive names. The similarity of names of this type with expressions like those exemplified in sentence (2) above is deceptive. There is, after all, more than one big river, so that the specification "the big river" is not complete. The full identification of one single river as the reference is given by the context. Therefore, apart from certain special expressions (like "the big one, not one of the smaller ones"), names like Big River, Red River, and so on have the same status as names like Colorado.

In some languages, a name is differentiated from an appellative (common noun) by formal means. The difference is sometimes indicated by the script; *e.g.*, languages using alphabets such as the Latin, Greek, Cyrillic, Armenian, and Georgian use a capital letter at the beginning of a name. (But, on the contrary, in German all nouns, not only names, are written with an initial capital.) There are examples of a purely grammatical differentiation of names as well, such as the usual absence of the articles "a" or "an" in English; *e.g.*, "Yesterday I saw an archer practicing his art" and "Yesterday I saw (Bill) Archer practicing his art."

Formal means for marking names

The distinction between names and appellatives (common nouns) is generally clear: names are used in individual reference, appellatives can be used in reference to all members of a class or to any number of them (*e.g.*, river, hill, man, girl, car, table, virtue, and so on). Nevertheless, there are some borderline cases. For instance, a nation can be conceived as an individualized entity, so that "Americans," "Englishmen," and "Spaniards" are names; on the other hand, it is clear that other groups of people are not conceived in this way, so that expressions like "soldiers," "sailors," and "clergy" are not names. It is difficult to decide on the status of expressions like the "Baptists," "Adventists," and "spiritists." In a similar way, if all vehicles produced by Henry Ford are Fords and if one can buy an individual Ford as well, is "Ford" a name? It probably is, or approaches that status; but names of this type frequently lose the character of names and develop into common nouns. Expressions like "the Roman Catholic Church," "the Ministry of Education" (of a specific state) also have a dubious position as to their status as real names. The uncertainty in this respect is indicated by the vacillation in the use of capital letters in various languages. This overlapping has a long history and is reflected in modern terminology. The Greeks used the term noun (*onoma*) for both the common noun and the name; when they wished to make a distinction, they specified the name as a proper noun (*onoma kyrion*). It is in this tradition that the term proper noun, or proper name, is used for a name, and noun, general noun, or common noun, for an appellative.

THE SCIENCE OF ONOMASTICS

Categories of names. The science that studies names in all their aspects is called onomastics (or onomatology—an obsolete word). The subject of this science is broad because almost everything can have a name and because the study of names theoretically encompasses all languages, all geographical and cultural regions, and all historical epochs. For practical purposes, some divisions of the subject are necessary; *e.g.*, by language (as the study of Kiowa or Provençal names) or by geographical, historical, or similar partitions (the study of the names in India, of the Levant at the time of the Crusades, and so forth). Another division (usually combined with the preceding ones) is given by the character of the names themselves; in a very broad categorization, names of persons, or personal names, are discerned on the one hand, and names of places, or place-names, on the other. In the most precise terminology, a set of personal names is called anthroponymy and their study is called anthroponomastics. A set of place-names is called toponymy, and their study is called toponomastics. In a looser usage, however, the term onomastics is used for personal names and their study, and the term toponymy is used for place-names and their study. The term toponymy itself can be understood in two ways, even in the exact terminology: either it is taken in the broadest possible way as including inhabited places, buildings, roads, countries, mountains, rivers, lakes, oceans, stars, and so on, or it is restricted to inhabited places (cities, towns, villages, hamlets). If the latter alternative is the understanding of the term toponymy, then the uninhabited places (*e.g.*, fields, small parts of forests) are called microtoponymy; names of streets, roads, and the like are

Divisions within onomastics

called hodonymy; names of bodies of water, hydronymy; names of mountains, oronymy. Additional terms are not generally used (though one occasionally hears words like chrematonymy—names of things).

In any case, different categories of names frequently must be studied together, because there are transitions. For instance, many place-names are derived from personal names (*e.g.,* Washington), many names of planets and stars are derived from the names of mythological characters (*e.g.,* Venus, Mars, Alpha Centauri), and many personal names are derived from place-names, names of nations, and other such names (*e.g.,* Austerlitz, Napoleon's battlefield; French; Scott). There is also a division of names into primary and secondary ones. Neptune is primarily the name of a Roman god; transferred to the name of a planet, it is a secondary name.

Forms of personal names. There are many subdivisions and terms within the category of personal names. Originally, one name was given to a person at an early period of life—in Europe (and later in America), normally at Baptism. This is called either simply the name, the baptismal or Christian name, or the forename; in the United States and Canada it is usually called the first or given name. Because many people received the same name (given name), they were differentiated by surnames (of the type John Redhead, John Hunter, John Scott). Many of these surnames became fixed and hereditary in individual families. These are called either surnames or family names, and in the United States and Canada they are frequently known as last names. Thus the basic pattern is given + family name, together called the name or the personal name. There are exceptions concerning this sequence. Among the Chinese and Hungarians, for example, the family name precedes the given name: Mao Tse-tung, Nagy István. The Hungarians usually switch the order when they write English; thus, Nagy István becomes István (or Stephen) Nagy. The Chinese, however, maintain the order of family name first.

Surnames and family names

There are variations in the basic pattern. In the United States and Canada the usual practice is to insert another name (frequently expressed in writing only by the initial letter) between the given and the family name. This is the second, or middle, name. It may be the original family name of a married woman inserted between her first name and the last name of her husband, the maiden name of one's mother, as well as other names. In Europe, such a second name is less common and is usually acquired at Baptism (or, eventually, at Confirmation). In most European countries, the first baptismal name is the important one, and the second one (third, and so forth) can be omitted. In German usage, however, the baptismal name immediately preceding the family name is the most important one. For example, if one of the baptismal names in Johann Sebastian Bach or Johann Wolfgang von Goethe is to be omitted, it would be Johann. (But in a sequence like Johann Nepomucenus Nestroy, the shorter form is Johann Nestroy, because Nepomucenus is only an attribute discerning one of the numerous saints who had the name Johann.) British usage varies in this respect, but sometimes follows the German pattern—*e.g.,* W. Sidney Allen.

Use of patronymics

In a few areas, above all in the Slavic part of the Soviet Union, the so-called patronymic (*i.e.,* a name derived from the given name of the father) is inserted between the given and the family name. In Russian, if the father's name is Ivan Krylov, then the son's name, for example, will be Pyotr (given) Ivanovich (patronymic) Krylov (family), and the daughter's name will be, for example, Varvara Ivanovna Krylova. The usual form of address in Russian—among acquaintances, neighbours, colleagues at work, and inclusive superiors—is by the given name and the patronymic. In Iceland the given name is used with the patronymic, the use of family names being discouraged. In Spain the family name of an individual consists of the family names of father and mother, the first being the most important one.

The terms maiden name and girl's name are sometimes used for the original family name of a married woman. Nickname is used in reference to surnames (which have not developed into family names), mainly of the jocose type; *e.g.,* a thickish Mr. John Smith is called Fatty. A surname, also called a byname or to-name (obsolete), can be used to differentiate persons with the same family names if they belong to different families and if given names are not used among them. In a village, there may be several families with the name Jones; if they are not called or referred to by first names, they may be known as Jones at the Pond, Jones the Redhead, and so forth. Hypocoristic forms of names are those that are used in familiar, friendly, or intimate situations (usually shortened or otherwise modified); *e.g.,* Tom for Thomas, Jim for James. Some of these forms are also used as given names, particularly in the United States.

THE NAMING PROCESS

One of the most important elements of the naming process concerns the meaning and associations of the name. In this case the term meaning is radically different from that in the case of common nouns, in which the "meaning" is their ability to be used in reference to a class of entities, to denote or designate them. As was noted above, the absence of this ability to refer to a class of entities is typical of a name. If the meaning of a typical common noun, such as automobile, is considered, it can be seen that it denotes a certain type of vehicle. On the other hand, if the word automobile itself is considered, one can see that it consists of a Greek element, *auto* "self," and a Latin one, *mobilis* "movable," so that the sum of the meanings of the constituent parts of the word suggests a gloss like "self-movable," "self-mover." The meaning of a name involves that which the constituent parts suggest. In this sense, the meaning of a name like Red River is obvious. To get a meaning of a name like Philip, however, one must go back to its original Greek version, Philippos, which means "lover of horses." This meaning of names frequently gets lost, however. There are several causes for this, one being that the name may be accepted into another language, as were the Indian place-names in America (*e.g.,* Oshkosh, Chicago, Kankakee), and the Greek and other names transferred to Europe and America via Christianity. In addition, names may cease to be understood as a result of language change; *e.g.,* the place-name Birmingham was understandable in Old English as "habitation of Biorma's people," and the originally Germanic name Gerard was once understood as "strong spear" (*Ger-hardo*). Names also changed by shortening (*e.g.,* Los Angeles, from El Pueblo de la Reyna de los Angeles, "Town of the Queen of the Angels," the town named in honour of the Virgin Mary) and by scribal error (*e.g.,* Pria in France, a misread medieval abbreviation of Pradaria, "meadow"). Another cause of the loss of meaning in names is that the meaning simply fades out by constant use of the word as a name. No one thinks of the meaning "ford for oxen" when speaking about Oxford, and no one realizes a discrepancy if Mr. White has a dark complexion. Finally, it sometimes happens that a name has no meaning from the beginning. For instance, the place-name Tonolo and the family name Bréal were created from random sequences of sounds.

Loss of original meaning of names

Choice of personal names. Names that have no meaning (above all not for the person who chooses the name) still can have associations. Although "Mary" and "John" may have no specific meaning, they were the names of important persons in the Christian religion and therefore have been used very frequently. An association may be so strong that it overwhelms the meaning of a name, even a disagreeable meaning; *e.g.,* the association with the cult of St. Demetrios made the name Demetrios one of the most popular in the Greek Orthodox Church, though its meaning is "belonging to [the pagan goddess] Demeter." On the other hand, such an association may more or less completely fade out and be combined with or replaced by other associations, such as a national tradition (Patrick in Ireland, Yves in Brittany, István in Hungary, Ivan in Russia) or with a family tradition (Louis in the Bourbon family, Wilhelm among the Hohenzollerns, Henry in the Ford family). On a less elevated level, there is the example of a rich uncle making a given name more than eligible. A name can be associated, correctly or not, with various prestige factors, or its choice may be influenced simply by fashion. Another source of names, often extraordinary ones, was the occasional habit in Roman Catholic countries of giving a child the name of the patron saint whose day of celebration coincides with the child's day of birth (or Baptism); many names like Hyacinthus X, or Narcissus Y, were produced in this way.

"Good" and "bad" names

In the majority of cases, children are given "good," likable, and propitious names. In some cultures (*e.g.*, in some parts of sub-Saharan Africa, formerly in China, and sporadically in ancient Greece), however, the children are (or were) sometimes given "bad" names with meanings like "ugly," "disagreeable," or "crippled." The purpose of such names, which are called apotropaic names, is to make the child undesirable to demons.

The choosing of a given name is a highly private and individual matter. All the circumstances just mentioned can be motives for the choice, in addition to many other personal reasons, such as a consideration for the relatives' names or a simple liking of the phonetic shape of a given name. This wish to give a likable name may go so far that a sequence of sounds is chosen that sounds pleasant to the person who makes the choice but that has no relation to the existing stock of names or to the words of the language; *e.g.*, "Golly" was invented as a name of a girl and has no "meaning" or associations. This phenomenon is relatively common in the United States.

Choice of place-names. Place-names are less personal, less intimate, and a matter of public concern. The usual pattern is that the national Ministry of the Interior (or its equivalent) keeps an official list of place-names, particularly of place-names that form administrative units, together with lists of districts, counties, and the like. This function may also be performed by the ministry or agency that supervises the postal service. Bodies endowed with authority provide or choose new place-names if there is a need to create them on a greater scale; *e.g.*, the U.S. Board on Geographic Names.

International cooperation (performed above all by the Universal Postal Union) is necessary, because names of identical places may vary from language to language. Particularly difficult are place-names originally written in scripts other than the Latin (Roman) one (the official script of the Universal Postal Union), such as Arabic, Chinese, Cyrillic, and the Indic writing systems. But even within the Latin script, there are two basic types of difficulties. First, one place can have different names (or modifications of a name) in various languages—*e.g.*, French Nice and Italian Nizza; German München, English and French Munich, and Italian Monaco. A very difficult situation arises when a place is generally better known by its international name than by its original one; *e.g.*, Dublin is Baile Átha Cliath in Irish. Confusion may also be caused by names that are translated; *e.g.*, the Rocky Mountains are in German Felsengebirge and in Russian Skalistye Gory. There are also names with the same written form but with varying pronunciations; *e.g.*, for Paris, the accent, pronunciation of vowels, and pronunciation of consonants change from French to German to English.

The second difficulty involves the actual printing of all the letters with diacritical marks that are necessary for different alphabets of the Latin script. Because many printing firms lack the various marks, some possibly confusing omissions or modifications can hardly be avoided; *e.g.*, the dot over the *I* in Turkish İstanbul, and the bar through the *l* in Polish Kołobrzeg are frequently omitted. International cooperation is also necessary and is developing in connection with the choice of place-names in outer space, particularly on the surface of the Moon.

HISTORICAL AND CROSS-CULTURAL DEVELOPMENT OF NAMES

Legal aspects of naming. While place-names are considered a public matter, personal names also seem to be getting more regimented by various laws and regulations. The United Kingdom and the United States are practically the only countries that adhere to the principle of Roman law that a person has the right to use and change his name as he pleases, except for fraudulent purposes. The first important regulation concerning given names was the decision of the Council of Trent (1563), which specified that the Roman Catholic priest administering Baptism should make certain that children are given names of Catholic saints; if the parents were to insist on another name, the priest should administer Baptism in that name but add the name of a saint as the second baptismal name. This regulation, still a valid part of Canon Law, was directed against the Protestant custom (spreading at that time) of giving children names of important persons from the Old Testament otherwise unconnected with Christianity (*e.g.*, Abraham, Samuel, Rachel). In this respect the regulation was successful in Catholic countries, but it did not succeed in stopping the use of given (baptismal) names like Cesare in Italy (from Latin Caesar).

Naming regulations of the Council of Trent

The next important law was passed in France. The French Revolution first gave complete freedom in naming; the result was some very fanciful given names like Mort aux Aristocrates, Racine de la Liberté, or even Cafě Billard. To stop this, a law was passed in 1803 that restricted given names to "names of persons known from ancient history" and "names used in various calendars." Again, the law was successful in its main intention; in addition, it prevented the spread of controversial given names such as Marat and Robespierre and of literary names such as Aramis, d'Artagnan, and Romeo. Very reasonably, the law never was interpreted too narrowly, so that feminine given names such as Jeanette and Henriette, for example, have been admitted, though they were not legal because no calendar contains them. This law is still valid in France.

Similar laws were passed, at various times, in the states of eastern Europe, where the given name can be chosen only from names known and established as such, the exact formulation varying from country to country. One of the results of this legislation is that the repertory of Russian given names today is more or less exactly the same as that of the pre-Soviet period, when the Orthodox Church was paramount. In non-Russian areas of the Soviet Union, Catholic (in Lithuania), Muslim (in the Uzbek and Tadzhik S.S.R., etc.), and other names are used, sometimes without any ecclesiastical association whatsoever. In the Caucasus, for example, there are given names such as Soslan and Dzerassa, drawn from Caucasian mythology.

In regard to family names, the most important regulation was made at the Council of Trent (1563); it was decreed that every parish must keep complete registers of baptisms, with the names of the child and those of his parents and grandparents. This had been done before, but not so systematically. The new practice (soon followed in Protestant parishes) helped to establish the family names. There is not much legislation concerning family names, because two basic assumptions are made: that the bride will accept the bridegroom's family name by marriage and that their children will automatically have the family name of the parents.

Parish registers

Combined names—as under the West German law permitting the bride to add her original family name to her new one in a hyphenated form (Inka Schmidt, when married to Karl Neumann, may become Inka Neumann-Schmidt) or the practice in outstanding British families of combining the family names of the married couple in a hyphenated form (Beatrix Curzon and Frederic Cholmondeley become Beatrix and Frederic Cholmondeley-Curzon)—are rather rare.

In the majority of cases, the law is concerned with family names mainly in cases of divorce, adoption, and illegitimacy. After a divorce, the wife is usually eventually allowed to reassume her maiden name and in Germany, for example, can be forced to do so if she is judged to be the guilty party and her former husband so desires. In adoption procedures, either the family name of the adopting persons is accepted or a hyphenated form is created. An illegitimate child usually receives the family name of its mother.

In many parts of Europe, legislation or habit have changed the basic assumptions concerning the family name, and a different situation has developed. When a Czech woman, Anna Klímová, for example, marries a Josef Novák, both may retain their original family names, or the wife may become Anna Nováková or, more remarkably, the husband may become Josef Klíma, accepting the wife's family name. This must be decided by mutual agreement, and their children's names also are agreed upon in this way. The purported reason for this legislation is the full equality of women. (There is, however, one loophole in the system, namely, the Russian patronymic: this is automatically derived from the father's name, whereas equality understood in this way would demand a choice between the father's or the mother's name.) In Spain the married woman normally retains her maiden name.

Personal names. *European patterns of naming.* The development of personal names was complicated. In the old Indo-European system, a person had one name, which could be one of two types: a compound or a noncompound substantive. Noncompound names may originally have been given to inferior members of the tribe and their children. The compound names frequently associated the bearer with a god (they are called theophoric names) or attested to his virtues, abilities, skills, possessions, and so forth. The association of the meanings of the parts of the compound was sometimes only loose, as is particularly observable in German anthroponymy (see below). Examples of compound names include the Sanskrit Viṣṇuputra "son of Vishnu," Devadatta "given by god," Devarāja "god-king." From Iran come the Avestan name Hōrmizāfrīd "benediction of Ahura Mazdā" and the Old Persian name Mithradates "given by Mithra" (two Iranian gods).

Compound and noncompound names

Among Greek names there are also many theophoric names, such as Herodotos "given by Hera," Isidoros "given by Isis" (modern Isidore), or Theodoros (modern Theodore) and Dorotheos (modern only in the feminine form, Dorothy), both "given by god." There are many other similar Greek names; *e.g.,* Astyanax "lord of the city," Pericles "very famous," and Demosthenes "strength of the people." Plato "broad (in shoulders)" is a noncompound Greek name.

The compound names of the Celts include Vercingetorix "great king of warriors," Orgetorix "king of killers," Rextugenos "son of justice." Noncompound Celtic names included, for example, Artos "bear" and Galba "big." Examples of Germanic compound names include Heriberhto "army + resplendent" (modern Herbert), Huguberhto "resplendent by thought" (modern Hubert), Godofrido "divine peace" (modern Gottfried and Geoffrey), Frideriko "peace + powerful" (modern Frederic and Friedrich), and Theodobaldo "people + valiant." Among the noncompound Germanic names is Karl (or Charles), in the Latin form Carolus, meaning "man."

Typical Slavic compound names are Vladimir "governs the world," Vladislav "rule + glory," and Miroslav "world + glory."

The Latin system of personal names was quite different and probably developed under Etruscan influence. In the earliest times the Romans seemingly had only one name; *e.g.,* Romulus, Remus, Manius. From the beginning of historical times, however, the Roman personal name consisted of a praenomen (given name, forename) and a nomen (or *nomen gentile*). Only intimates used the praenomen, and its choice was restricted to fewer than 20 names, among them Gaius, Gnaeus, Marcus, Quintus, Publius, Tiberius, and Titus. The nomen that followed was hereditary in each gens (a related group of families, like the Scottish clan); examples include Antonius, Aurelius, Claudius, Cornelius, Fabius, Horatius, Julius, Lucius, Maccius, Tullius, and some others. Because the choice of both the praenomen and the nomen was restricted, the patrician families and later all families started using a hereditary name, called a cognomen.

These cognomina developed from original surnames; *e.g.,* Cicero "bean," Pictor "painter," Plautus "flat foot," Tacitus "silent." Thus the Roman name eventually consisted of three parts: Marcus Tullius Cicero, Gaius Julius Caesar. In addition, a person might acquire an individual surname, called an agnomen: Publius Cornelius Scipio Africanus was so named because of his successful war in Africa.

This system of naming was used during the whole republican period and later in the empire. Toward the end of the empire, however, the naming pattern began to change and subsequently was lost. One reason was that more persons used names lacking any real relation to themselves. For instance, a slave (and then his children) used the praenomen and the nomen of the master who set him free; *e.g.,* had Marcus Tullius Cicero freed a Syrian slave, the name of the latter might have been Marcus Tullius Syrus.

The number of freed slaves grew constantly, particularly after the victory of the Christian religion. Also, a free inhabitant of the empire who was granted Roman citizenship acquired the praenomen and nomen of the magistrate who made him a citizen, and in AD 212, when all free noncitizens were given citizenship by the emperor Caracalla, hundreds of thousands of persons prefixed Marcus Aurelius to their names, whether Greek, Syrian, African, or any other. In this way, Roman names lost their significance.

Another change was introduced by the Christians, who belonged to social classes that were not particularly concerned with the habits of the Roman higher class and who preferred names connected with their own religion; *e.g.,* from its founders (Petrus, Paulus, Joannes, Maria, Timotheus) or from the new martyrs, frequently persons with simple Latin or Greek surname-like names such as Stephanos "wreath" (modern Stephen), Laurentius "laurel" (modern Lawrence), and Sidonius "coming from Sidon [in Phoenicia]" (modern Sidney). Simple names like these were sometimes called *signum.* The Christians, however, soon started creating their own names; *e.g.,* Benedictus "blessed," Desiderius "desiring [salvation]," Renatus "reborn [by Baptism]," (modern René).

Christian names

With the spread of Christianity, this stock of names spread into territories that did not belong to the Roman Empire, but the diffusion was slow. In both the Germanic and the Slavic sphere (half of which came under the influence of the Eastern Church), the use of many of the original non-Christian names was continued, partly by tradition and partly because some of the bearers of these names became saints themselves. In this way, the repertory of given names was set, in general, somewhere around the 12th century. A notable addition to it was the influx of Old Testament names brought by the Reformation (Adlai, Benjamin, and so on). Certain names have left no trace of their ephemeral existence—*e.g.,* Puritan names such as Humility, Be Faithful, Kill Sin; French revolutionary names; and Russian postrevolutionary names such as Mels (an acronym containing the initial letters of Marx, Engels, Lenin, and Stalin). American fanciful given names for girls, such as Claretta, Elizene, Gwyned, and Marilla, are also relatively insignificant in impact, though the group is growing.

Christian and non-Christian given names

Family names. Family names came into use in the later Middle Ages (beginning roughly in the 11th century); the process was completed by the end of the 16th century. The use of family names seems to have originated in aristocratic families and in big cities, where they developed from original individual surnames when the latter became hereditary. Whereas a surname varies from father to son, and can even be changed within the life span of a person, a hereditary surname that develops into a family name better preserves the continuation of the family, be it for prestige or for the easier handling of official property records and other matters. Family names frequently developed (via surnames) from hypocoristic forms of given names; *e.g.,* from Henry came Harry, Harris, Hal, Halkin; from Gilbert came Gibbs, Gibbons, Gibbin, Gipps, Gilbye, Gilpin; and from Gregory there developed Gregg, Grigg, Greggs, Griggs, Greig. Other sources of family names are original nicknames—Biggs, Little, Grant (grand, large), Greathead, Cruikshank, Beaver, Hogg, Partridge; occupations—Archer, Clark, Clerk, Clarkson (son of a clerk), Bond, Bonds, Bound, Bundy (bondman); and place-names—Wallace (man from Wales), Allington, Murray, Hardes, Whitney (places in England), Fields, Holmes, Brookes, Woods (from microtoponyms).

A great number of family names come from patronymic surnames; in English, they are usually formed by the suffixation of "-son." Patronymic surnames can be formed from the father's given name or from any of its variants. Therefore, there is not only the form Richardson, but also Dickson, Dixon, Dickinson; and Henryson, Harrison, Henderson; Gilbertson, Gibson; and Gregson, Grigson. Some English patronymics, particularly in old families, are formed with a prefixed "Fitz-" (*e.g.,* Fitzgerald), which goes back to Norman French *fis* "son." In contradistinction to English, the Scottish patronymics are formed by a prefixed "Mac" or "Mc" (McGregor), the Irish with "O" (O'Brien) or "Mc" or "Mac," and the Welsh with "P-" (Powell "son of Howel"). In Modern Greek, patronymics are formed by suffixation; *e.g.,* Dimitriopoulos "son of Dimitrios."

French family names

The development of family names is similar in all of Europe. For example, French names such as Jaquet, Jacquot, Jacotot, Jacotin, Cottet, Cottin, Cotin, Jacquin, Jacquinet, Jacquinot, Jacquart, Jacquier all derive from Jacques; Davignon, Decaen, Derennes, and Beauvais developed from the place-names Avignon, Caen, and so forth; Breton, Lebreton, Lenormand come from the names of districts; Clerk, Leclerc, Duclerc, Auclerk, Clergue (*cf.* English Clark), Boucher, Boulanger, Masson designate professions ("butcher," "baker," "mason"); and Roux, Leroux, Roussel, Rousseau, Lerouge, Roujon are all variants of "red" (*i.e.,* red hair). Roughly the same scheme exists everywhere in Europe. Some family names can be traced to nicknames that must have their origin in incidents and attitudes that cannot be understood now; *e.g.,* Czech family names such as Nejezchleba "Don't eat bread!" and Skočdopole "Jump into the field!"

The development is slighty different among Jews. While living in ghettos, they used only given names. After the end of the 18th and the beginning of the 19th century, they chose or were given family names. Many of these names (which vary in the individual languages) are derived from religious vocations: Cantor, Canterini, Kantorowicz (lower priest); Kohn, Cohen, Cahen, Kaan, Kahane (priest); Levi, Halévy, Löwy (name of the tribe of priests). Many are derived from place-names—Morpurgo (Marburg)—or from nicknames—Hirsch ("deer" in German). Frequently, particularly in Austria, the Jews were given derisory family names, such as Eberstark "strong as boar," Rosenduft "fragrance of roses," and Hitzig "hot," from Itzick, a mocking form of Isaac.

The only outstanding exception to this European pattern of naming occurs with the names of kings, who use one of their given names. Some royal families have what could be called family names; *e.g.,* the Hohenzollerns (more correctly, Hohenzollers) of Prussia. The British royal family accepted the name Windsor only in 1917 (this was changed to Mountbatten-Windsor for the future members of the family who will not enjoy princely status). The pope of the Roman Catholic Church abandons his personal name after his election and chooses a single name, sometimes associated with his intentions; *e.g.,* Pope Paul VI chose the name Paulus because of St. Paul's missionary activities and travels.

Other patterns of naming. Names and naming practices in other cultural areas show a strong similarity in the basic trends. Among the ancient Assyrian and Babylonian names are theophoric designations such as Ashurbanipal, meaning "Ashur [a god] created son," and Nabukudurriusur (Nebuchadrezzar of the Bible), translated as "Nabu [a god] protected the estate." The Phoenician (Carthaginian) name Hannibal means "grace of Baal" (a god). The Hebrew Yehonatan, Yonatan (*i.e.,* Jonathan) means "God gave"; Rafa'el (Rafael) is translated as "God cured." There are also nontheophoric names such as Laban (from Hebrew *lavan* "white"). The Aramaic surname of the fisherman Simon, Kepha, meaning "stone," became famous in the New Testament as Petros (Peter), the Greek translation of the name (*petra* "rock, stone").

Theophoric names

The more complicated structure of Arabic society brought an independent development similar to the European one. Given names such as Muḥammad, Ibrāhīm (= Abraham), Manṣur "victor," ʿAli "exalted," ʿAbd Allāh "slave of Allāh" are differentiated by surnames such as Ibn ʿAbbās "son of ʿAbbās," al-Baghdādī "from Baghdad," al-Ghazālī "the spinner." The Caucasian (*e.g.,* Ossetic) personal name consists of a given name preceded by the name of the tribe (gens) in the genitive plural; the name of the father may be inserted, thus giving Gaglojty Soslany fyrt Nafi "Nafi, son of Soslan, of [the gens of] Gaglo." Chinese society has had the institution of hereditary family names since the 4th century BC, but the number of these names has been reduced to some 200. Examples include Chan, Mao, and Lu. The choice of the given name was formerly much freer, but legislation seems to have restricted it. In a similar way, there are not more than 300 Korean family names, but only three of them—Kim, Pak, and Yi—belong to the great majority of families in Korea. The given name is chosen, but its choice is limited by the practice that one of the two syllables of the name should be identical within a family for a generation; the whole given name should have an auspicious meaning.

By the 20th century, the originally European pattern of given name + family name had been introduced practically everywhere. Black Africa (*e.g.,* among the Yoruba) now has the "normal" pattern of personal names, but both the given and the family names are of vernacular stock. There are given names such as Olúṣolá "god [non-Christian] made greatness," Ọ̀ṣunbúnmi "Osun [a river] gave me," and Adeyẹmí "crown befits me," and family names like Ajólore "who [is] a kind doer." Among the American Indians there are, surprisingly, practically no theophoric names. Instead, the Indians used names related to the totem, to animals indicated by omens or dreams, and to successful incidents in life. Those North American Indians who did not accept English names now use the English translation of their names as last names (which sometimes are not hereditary); *e.g.,* John Sleeping Owl, Mary Little Bear.

Place-names. *Descriptive and commemorative place-names.* If the "meanings" of place-names and the motives for their choice are examined, several broad types may be discerned. Descriptive names indicate a characteristic feature of the entity; *e.g.,* Rocky Mountains, North Sea, Newcastle. The chosen feature is sometimes only illusory or observed by chance, as in the case of the Pacific Ocean (only a small part of it was calm, or pacific, when seen and named). Honorific and commemorative names are another broad category. Examples include Constantinople (formerly called Byzantium, renamed Konstantinoupolis "city of Constantine" because that emperor made it the capital of the Roman Empire); Aphrodisias "[the town of] Aphrodite" (in Asia Minor), changed into Stauropolis "city of the cross" with the advent of Christianity; Cartagena, transferred to Colombia (South America) in commemoration of Cartagena in Spain (Cartagena in Spain was in turn developed from Latin Carthago Nova, a translation of the name given to the town by the Phoenician settlers in commemoration of Carthage, the Phoenician rival of Rome); Nieuw-Amsterdam, commemorative of the Dutch capital, changed to New York (honorific for the Duke of York). Among the numerous benedictory, wishful names are the Russian Vladivostok "govern the East!" (founded and named by Russians as their main base on the Pacific coast), Cape of Good Hope (a renaming of a more descriptive Cape of Tempests), and Greek Pontus Euxinus (now the Black Sea) "hospitable sea" (a renaming of Pontus Axeinos "inhospitable sea"). In most cases, however, place-names do not have a "meaning" at all, particularly not for the general user.

Types of place-names

Place-names reflecting historical influences. Place-names are frequently accepted into the language of a new population. The toponymy of the United States illustrates this well. Spanish names are numerous in the South and Southwest; *e.g.,* Florida, San Antonio, Santa Fe, and San Diego, all of which are Spanish names of Roman Catholic saints or holidays. French names occur frequently in the Southeast and the central United States (*e.g.,* La Nouvelle Orléans, changed into New Orleans; Baton Rouge; St. Louis; Louisiana); Dutch names are found in the East (Haarlem changed into Harlem); Indian names are interspersed everywhere; and, finally, English names are superimposed over all the rest. An examination of all these names, which are now used by a mostly English-speaking population, could not fail to yield some information about the colonization of the United States, even if the history were not known.

In the same way, the place-names of Britain reflect its

history. Above all, there are Celtic names; *e.g.,* Eboracum (named for a tree), partly translated as Eoforwic, which changed into York. Roman names are also numerous; *e.g.,* Castra "military camp," changed into Chester, and Lindum Colonia "Colony Lindum" (which itself is Celtic, *linne* + *dunom* "town at the lake") is now Lincoln. There are, in addition, Anglo-Saxon names (*e.g.,* Whittingham "habitation of Hwita's people"), a few Scandinavian names (*e.g.,* Badby, in which *-by* is the Scandinavian element instead of English *-bury* "castle"), and Norman names (*e.g.,* Richmond, from a personal name consisting of *rīki* "rich, powerful" + *mond* "world").

Changes in place-names

Any country's toponymy consists of various layers. In France there are Celtic names such as Lucodunos "shining town" that became Latinized into Lugdunum and changed into the modern form Lyon; Greek names such as Agathe (Tyche) "good (luck)," which has become Agde; Roman names such as Forum Julii "marketplace of Julius," modern Fréjus; and old Germanic names such as Clarbec "clear brook" (*klar* + *Bach* in German). Most important is the fact that place-names can be used as a source of information themselves, even if other forms of evidence are lacking; for instance, because Moskva (= Moscow) is a Finnish name (Finnish *kva* "water"), and other Finnish toponyms are present in the central Soviet Union, the prehistoric presence of Finnish tribes in that location can be presumed. Names of rivers are particularly important for this purpose, because they are very conservative and usually are taken over by a new population. A considerable number of river names in western and central Europe show remarkable similarity (*e.g.,* Esera in Spain, Isère in France, Yser in Belgium, Isar in Bavaria, Jizera in Czechoslovakia) and are the only evidence of a pre-Celtic Indo-European population of those regions.

In a similar way, names are also indicative of cultural and political trends. Singapore (Sanskrit Siṃhapura "castle of lions"), for example, testifies to the cultural influence of India in the area. Particularly significant in this respect are deliberate changes of names caused by changes in political power, ideology, and so forth. Changes such as Nieuw-Amsterdam becoming New York, or Léopoldville (named after the king of Belgium who acquired the Congo) becoming Kinshasa, are very common. Some cases of renaming do not lack humour: La Roche-sur-Yon in France was rebuilt by Napoleon and renamed Napoléon-Vendée, which was changed to Bourbon-Vendée under the Restoration; during the 100 days of Napoleon's return from Elba and in the subsequent second Restoration, the cycle was repeated once more, and only the Third Republic restored the old name. Renaming also shows examples of cynicism: Lyon, which had rebelled against the revolutionary covenant, was punished by systematic demolition and a massacre of its inhabitants; the ruins of the city were renamed Commune-Affranchie "Liberated Commune." Changes of place-names are sometimes made systematically; when the territory called Alto Adige in Italian and Südtirol (South Tirol) in German became part of Italy after World War I, for instance, a systematic effort was made to give or to return to these territories the Italian character in both place-names and personal names. The Russian Revolution brought a change of names that were reminiscent of the old regime and ideology; *e.g.,* St. Petersburg (changed into a more Slavic Petrograd by the tsar during the war) became Leningrad, Tsaritsyn (from *tsar* "emperor") became Stalingrad (and then Volgograd in the late 1950s), Yekaterinodar (from Yekaterina [= Catherine], an empress) became Krasnodar (from *krasny* "red"), but Arkhangelsk "Town of Archangels" somehow escaped notice.

BIBLIOGRAPHY

Dictionaries: ELSDON C. SMITH, *New Dictionary of American Family Names* (1973); P.H. REANEY, *A Dictionary of British Surnames,* 2nd ed. (1976); CHARLES WAREING BARDSLEY, *A Dictionary of English and Welsh Surnames: With Special American Instances* (1901, reprinted 1967); C. L'ESTRANGE EWEN, *A History of Surnames of the British Isles* (1931, reprinted 1968), contains rich information and a bibliography; E.G. WITHYCOMBE (comp.), *Oxford Dictionary of English Christian Names,* 3rd ed. (1977, reprinted 1982), indicates the provenience of names listed; EILERT EKWALL, *Concise Oxford Dictionary of English Place-Names,* 4th ed. (1960), includes the provenience of place-names.

Narratives: L.G. PINE, *The Story of Surnames* (1965), readable and well informed; H.L. MENCKEN, *American Language,* suppl. 2 (1948), a survey of American naming, also available as part of the abridged 4th edition, ed. by RAVEN I. MCDAVID (1963, reprinted 1977); EDWARD MACLYSAGHT, *The Surnames of Ireland,* 5th ed. (1980), a general history; P.W. JOYCE, *Origin and History of Irish Names of Places,* 3 vol. (vol. 1–2, 1869–71; vol. 3, 1913), partly antiquated but still of great value; W.F.H. NICOLAISEN, *Scottish Place-Names* (1976); GEORGE R. STEWART, *Names on the Land,* 3rd ed. (1967), a readable and instructive study of the origin of American place-names, and *Names on the Globe* (1975), on the theory of place-naming around the world; ERNST PULGRAM, *Theory of Names* (1954), treats theoretical problems, such as the distinction between names and common nouns.

Journal: Names, quarterly journal of the American Name Society, publishes articles and research materials in the field of onomatology. Its June 1984 special issue, vol. 32, no. 2, contains *Symposium on Names and the Law,* ed. by RALPH SLOVENKO.

The study of names is plagued with imaginative and fantastic, but unfounded and unscholarly, publications; therefore, caution should be exercised in the choice of sources.

(L.Zg.)

Nanking

Nanking (Wade–Giles romanization Nan-ching, Pinyin Nanjing), capital of Kiangsu Province in central eastern China, is a port on the Yangtze River and a major industrial and communications centre. Rich in history, it served seven times as the capital of regional empires, twice as the seat of revolutionary governments, once (during World War II) as the site of a puppet regime, and twice as the capital of a united China (the second time from 1928 to 1937). The name Nanking ("Southern Capital") was introduced in 1421 during the Ming dynasty.

This article is divided into the following sections:

Physical and human geography

THE LANDSCAPE

The city site. Nanking is situated on the southeastern bank of the Yangtze, some 160 miles (260 kilometres) from Shanghai (215 miles by water, 193 miles by rail). The city proper comprises the area encircled by a gigantic wall constructed during the Ming dynasty (1368–1644) and adjacent suburbs. The city wall—of which about two-thirds is still standing—is 21 miles long, has an average height of 40 feet (12 metres), and contains 13 gates. The municipality (*shih*) of Nanking includes territory extending to the border of Anhwei Province on the north, west, and south and to the borders of Yang-chou and Cheng-chiang municipalities on the east. Included in the municipality, which has an area of about 2,516 square miles (6,516 square kilometres), are counties on either side of the Yangtze and both urban and rural districts.

The city wall

Climate. The four seasons are clearly distinguishable. The hot summer months are from July to September, while winter lasts from December until March. Spring and autumn are both mild and pleasant. January and July mean temperatures are about 37° F (3° C) and 82° F (28° C), respectively. The average annual rainfall is 39 inches (990 millimetres), the bulk of it falling between June and August.

The city layout. The city of Nanking, encircled by hills and rivers, resembles a gourd, with its tip pointing northwest, toward suburban Hsia-kuan, on the south bank of the Yangtze. Hsia-kuan and P'u-k'ou, which is opposite it on the north bank, house the harbour facilities of the huge Nanking River Port. On the west and south Nanking is bordered by the Ch'in-huai Ho (Ch'in-huai River), which runs along the outside of the city wall and is a tributary of the Yangtze. On the east are the foothills of the Tzu-chin Shan (Purple-Gold Mountains), and at the city's southern tip is the Chin-liang Shan ("Quite-Cool Mountain"). Outside of the city wall to the northeast is the extensive Hsüan-wu Hu ("Mystic Martial Lake"), containing five islets linked by embankments, and on the other side of the Ch'in-huai Ho to the southwest is Mo-ch'ou Hu ("Lake of No Sorrow"); both lake areas are city parks. The skyline suggests spaciousness and grandeur. Blue-glazed tiles adorning the old city gates, parklike scenery along the boulevards, lotus blossoms and tea pavilions on the lakes, and temples half hidden in the green hills are all characteristic sights in Nanking.

The city comprises four districts. The north district, from I-chiang Men (a city gate) to the Ku Lou (Drum Tower; built in 1382), traversed by Chung-shan Avenue as its axis, contains such landmarks as Pei-chi Ko ("North Pole Pavilion") and Chi-ming Ssu ("Cockcrow Temple"), as

The city's four districts

Ewing Galloway

Sun Yat-sen Mausoleum at Nanking.

well as government offices, Nanking University (founded in 1902), and modern residential quarters. The central district, surrounding Hsin Chieh-k'ou ("New Crossroads"), is the business centre of the city, and to the south is situated the populous old city—traditionally famous for entertainment. The east district, a centre of culture, contains the ruins of the former Ming palace as well as the Nanking Museum, with its exhibits on Chinese history, and scientific institutions.

Forming an integral part of the life of the city are its immediate outskirts. To the south is the Yü-hua T'ai ("Terrace of the Rain of Flowers"), noted for its five-colour pebbles and a Communist martyrs' memorial. In the eastern outskirts, on the magnificent forested Tzu-chin Shan range, are the Ming emperor Hung-wu's mausoleum, its approach noted for pairs of large stone animals; the blue-tile-roofed mausoleum of Sun Yat-sen; the Ling-ko Ssu ("Temple of the Valley of Spirits") and the nearby 200-foot-high pagoda; and the Tzu-chin Shan Astronomical Observatory. Other scenic spots include Yen-tzu Chi ("Swallow's Bluff") in the north and Ch'i-hsia Shan ("Abode of Clouds Mountain") farther to the northeast. Two industrial districts extend northeastward and southwestward from the city.

THE PEOPLE

Despite much industrial growth, the city of Nanking retains a traditional feature—the existence of a substantial rural population within the boundaries of the municipality. The people speak Mandarin with a marked local accent. The city has small communities of Christians, Buddhists, and Muslims.

THE ECONOMY

Agriculture. Much of the land in the municipality's rural districts is under cultivation; the major agricultural products are rice, wheat, peanuts (groundnuts), and fruits and vegetables. In and around the many lakes and ponds *pai-ho* (lily bulbs), water chestnuts, lotus roots, and other aquatic plants are grown. Both freshwater fishery and pig farming are important. Along the canals and creeks, farmers raise large flocks of ducks; the Nanking duck, preserved in salt and pressed, is one of China's food delicacies.

Industry. Before 1949, Nanking was noted chiefly for its traditional handicraft products, such as satins, velvets, and brocades. The city's major industrial expansion has taken place since then, and Nanking has become an important industrial centre. Hundreds of factories have been built to produce iron and steel, machine tools, motor vehicles, bicycles, clocks and watches, optical instruments, and building materials. Textiles, food processing, and other light industries are also important. In the suburban districts coal, iron ore, limestone, dolomite, lead, and zinc are mined. Petrochemical and electronic plants, however, mark the city's greatest progress in industrial development.

Major industries

Transportation. Nanking's major avenue of commerce is the Yangtze River, which connects the city with the Yangtze Delta and with central China. Nanking is connected by rail to Shanghai and to major Chinese cities to the north. Another railroad leading south extends to T'ung-ling in Anhwei Province; a loop line through the eastern suburbs links it with the Shanghai–Nanking line. In 1968 the rail ferry between P'u-k'ou and Hsia-kuan was replaced by the Yangtze bridge, more than 20,000 feet in length, with a double-track railroad on its lower deck and a four-lane highway on the upper deck.

Bicycles and buses are the principal means of transport within the city. Major highways fan out from Nanking to Shanghai and other cities in Kiangsu, Chekiang, and Anhwei provinces. Nanking airport, located in a southern suburb, has regular flights to other major cities in China.

ADMINISTRATION AND SOCIAL CONDITIONS

Government. Nanking's municipal government is part of the hierarchical structure of the Chinese government—and the parallel structure of the Chinese Communist Party—that extends from the national organization, through the provincial apparatus, to the municipal and, ultimately, neighbourhood levels. The principal responsibilities of the Nanking Municipal People's Congress, the major decision-making body, include issuing administrative orders, collecting taxes, determining the budget, and implementing economic plans. A standing committee selected from its members recommends policy decisions and oversees the operation of municipal government. Executive authority rests with the Nanking People's Government, the officers of which are elected by the congress; it consists of a mayor, vice mayors, and numerous bureaus in charge of public security, the judicial system, and other civil, economic, social, and cultural affairs.

Administratively, the city is divided into districts (*ch'ü*). Below the district, police substations supervise the population, while street mayoralties handle civil affairs in their areas. Neighbourhood associations help mediate disputes, carry out literacy campaigns, and promote sanitation, welfare, and family planning.

Health. Nanking made great progress in public health and medicine during the Nationalist period. Health conditions have continued to improve under the Communist government, which has placed great emphasis on public health education. There are many general and specialized hospitals in Nanking, and clinics and health stations are maintained by neighbourhood associations, factories, and schools. Nanking is also a noted centre for training doctors in traditional Chinese medicine.

Education. Nanking inherited from Nationalist days an excellent school system that in 1949 included 300 primary and middle schools and some of the best universities and colleges in China. Since the 1950s there has been a considerable increase in the number of primary, middle, and technical secondary schools.

In addition, much attention has been given to adult education, and many spare-time schools, university extensions, and other institutions that provide training in technical fields have been established. Nanking University and Nanking Institute of Technology are among the leading institutions of higher education in the country, and colleges of hydraulic engineering, aeronautical engineering, and meteorology are also of national significance.

Adult and higher education

CULTURAL LIFE

Nanking's long history as a cultural centre is reflected in its many surviving monuments and buildings of historical significance. The Nanking Museum, Museum of the Heavenly Kingdom of Great Peace (Taiping Museum), and the Kiangsu Provincial Museum are all housed in buildings constructed in traditional Chinese style. Among the city's numerous research agencies and scientific societies is the Kiangsu Academy of Science, a branch of the Chinese Academy of Sciences.

Some of the leading artists of China have worked in the Kiangsu College of Traditional Painting. Troupes of Peking opera and various Kiangsu operas give performances of both traditional theatrical pieces and modern plays in the city. Sports grounds are found in all parts of Nanking and its suburbs. The well-equipped Wu-t'ai Shan Stadium, in the centre of the city, is used for major sports events. The public at large, however, finds its recreation in the many beautiful parks and resorts.

History

THE EARLY EMPIRES

Nanking's recorded history dates to the Spring and Autumn (770–476 BC) and the Warring States (475–221 BC) periods, when a castle near Yü-hua T'ai was constructed by the Yüeh state in 472 BC. After the Yüeh territory was taken over by the Ch'u state, another castle under the name of Chin-ling was built on Chin-liang Shan to control the traffic between the Yangtze and the Ch'in-huai. Under the Ch'in (221–206 BC) and Han (206 BC–AD 220) dynasties, Nanking was successively under the jurisdiction of Mo-ling County (*hsien*) and Tan-yan County.

Nanking—under the name of Chien-yeh—emerged as the political and cultural centre of Southeast China during the period of the Three Kingdoms, when Sun Chien and his son Sun Ch'üan made it the capital of the kingdom of Wu from 229 to 280. In 317 the Eastern Chin dynasty

(317–420), fleeing foreign invaders in North China, again chose the city as a capital. Renamed Chien-k'ang, Nanking became a haven for northern families in exile. After the fall of the Eastern Chin, Nanking, under four successive dynasties—Liu-Sung (420–479); Southern Ch'i (479–502); Southern Liang (502–557); and Southern Ch'en (557–589)—was the seat of government of the regional empires south of the Yangtze.

These regimes were dominated by military men whose rivalries weakened the government. But in Nanking progress was made in areas other than politics, and its population grew to 1,000,000 during the Southern Liang. Bountiful harvests, coupled with tea, silk, papermaking, and pottery industries, supported a booming economy. Culturally, the Six Dynasties—as the dynasties that ruled from 220 to 589 are called—produced a galaxy of scholars, poets, artists, and philosophers. The works of Wang Hsi-chih and Ku K'ai-chih set the canons of calligraphy and painting, respectively. The publication of *Wen hsüan* ("Literary Selections") and of *Wen-hsin tiao-lung* (a classic in literary criticism), the evolution of what has come to be known as the Six Dynasties essay style (a blending of poetry and prose), and the invention by Shen-yüeh (a 6th-century courtier) of the system of determining the four tones of the Chinese language were achievements of this period. In philosophy, the so-called *ch'ing-t'an* ("pure discourse") movement, spiritually akin to a form of Taoism, found many adherents who held themselves aloof from politics. Hundreds of Buddhist temples were built. Voluminous Buddhist scriptures were edited and transcribed, and thousands, including the emperor Wu Ti, founder of the Southern Liang dynasty, took monastic vows.

The Six Dynasties

From 581 to 1368, under the successive unified empires of the Sui, T'ang, Sung, and Yüan dynasties, Nanking reverted to the status of a prefectural city. Various names were given the city: Chiang-chou and Tan-yang under the Sui; Chiang-chou, Chin-ling, and Pai-hsia in early T'ang; Sheng-chou in late T'ang; and Chin-ling again under the Five Dynasties in the 10th century; Chien-k'ang under the Sung; and Chi-ch'ing under the Yüan. When the Southern T'ang briefly maintained a regional regime in the city from 937 to 975, Nanking enjoyed much intellectual creativity (the ruler Hou-chu himself being a poet of consummate skill) and was the scene of new construction, notably, the octagonal stone pagoda of the Ch'i-hsia Temple and the crosstown channel of the Ch'in-huai Ho. Another period of prominence occurred during the Southern Sung dynasty (1127–1279), when Yüeh Fei used the city as his base for resistance against the Juchen in North China.

In 1368 the emperor Hung-wu, founder of the Ming dynasty, made Nanking the capital of a united China. Naming the city Ying-t'ien-fu ("Responding to Heaven"), he built a grand Imperial palace and the city wall. In addition, earth ramparts were prepared to form the basis for a larger outer wall. In 1421, however, Hung-wu's son, the Yung-lo emperor, moved the capital to Peking. The city became a subsidiary capital and was renamed Nanking.

The growth of trade and industry, however, brought new wealth to Nanking, especially to Hsia-kuan. Weaving, pottery, printing, and brocade making were the leading industries. Oceangoing vessels used by Cheng Ho in his famous 15th-century expeditions to the South Seas were built in the shipyards to the northwest of the city. An Imperial college—the Kuo-tzu chien—attracted students from all over the empire, as well as from Japan, Korea, Okinawa, and Thailand. The scholars of this college helped compile the *Yung-lo ta-tien* ("Yung-lo Emperor's Encyclopaedia"); its printing plant issued fine editions of many classics, as well as such works as *Pen-ts'ao kang-mu* ("Great Pharmacopoeia") by Li Shih-chen and *Yüan-shih* ("History of the Yüan Dynasty") by Sung Lien.

In the Ch'ing (Manchu) dynasty (1644–1911/12), Nanking, renamed Chiang-ning, became the government seat of the viceroy of Kiang-nan (who governed the provinces of Kiangsu, Kiangsi, and Anhwei). In 1842 the treaty ending the Opium War was signed there. A decade later, in 1853, the city was taken by the Taiping revolutionary forces under the leadership of Hung Hsiu-ch'üan. As the capital of T'ai-p'ing T'ien-kuo (Heavenly Kingdom of Great Peace), Nanking became a commune practicing universal brotherhood, equality of the sexes, and communal ownership of property. Numerous palaces for Hung and his lieutenants were built. When the Taipings were overthrown in 1864, there was widespread destruction of public buildings, of temples, and of the city wall by Ch'ing troops, and the city was left nearly prostrate.

The Taiping capital

THE MODERN CITY

Recovery took decades. Although it was sanctioned by the treaties of Tientsin concluded with France in 1858, foreign trade did not begin until 1899. By that time, modern industry and communication had reached the city. In 1908 the Shanghai–Nanking railroad was opened, followed four years later by a railroad from the port city of Tientsin in Hopeh Province to P'u-k'ou. Such economic growth, however, was overshadowed by the revolution of 1911. After the uprising had begun upstream at Wu-ch'ang in Hupeh Province, the revolutionary leaders proclaimed Nanking the seat of the provisional government of the Republic of China, and the democratic constitution of 1912 was adopted there before the first president, Yüan Shih-k'ai, moved the capital to Peking.

Under the infant Republic of China, Nanking was governed by warlords for more than a decade. Sun Yat-sen, leader of the Kuomintang (Nationalist Party), embittered by politicians' intrigues centred in Peking, vowed to make Nanking the Nationalist capital. Accordingly, when his follower Chiang Kai-shek achieved unified control of the country in 1928, the Nationalist government made Nanking once more the capital of a united China. Progress was made in developing communications, industries, and natural resources. Physically, too, the city acquired a new look; modern boulevards and government buildings were constructed; new railroad stations and airfields were built; and the Sun Yat-sen Mausoleum was erected.

Such achievements were, however, cut short by the war against Japan. Nanking fell in 1937. In the sack of the city that followed, between 40,000 and 300,000 civilians were slaughtered. The city was then ruled by puppet governments until Japan's defeat in 1945. From 1946 to 1949 Nanking resumed its status as the capital of Chiang Kai-shek's Nationalist government, but Chinese Communist forces took the city in 1949. When the People's Republic of China was proclaimed on Oct. 1, 1949, Nanking was once again abandoned in favour of Peking as the national capital. In 1952 it was made the provincial capital of Kiangsu. Nanking was transformed into a modern industrialized city. Despite the hardships suffered during the Great Leap Forward (1958–60) and the Cultural Revolution (1966–76)—especially during the latter, when many cultural and historical relics were damaged—the city has generally prospered during the Communist period and has remained a major tourist destination.

BIBLIOGRAPHY. Comprehensive general references are FREDRIC KAPLAN, JULIAN SOBIN, and ARNE DE KEIJZER, *The China Guidebook*, 6th ed. (1985); and NAGEL PUBLISHERS, *China*, English version by ANNE L. DESTENAY, 4th ed. (1982). More detailed information is contained in CHINA TRAVEL AND TOURISM PRESS, *Nanjing* (1983); CAROLINE COURTAULD, *Nanjing, Suzhou and Wuxi* (1981); and *Fifteen Cities in China*, published by CHINA RECONSTRUCTS MAGAZINE. For geography, see GEORGE BABCOCK CRESSEY, *China's Geographic Foundations: A Survey of the Land and Its People* (1934); and for an economic geography, see T.R. TREGEAR, *China, A Geographical Survey* (1980). FREDERICA M. BUNGE and RINN-SUP SHINN (eds.), *China, a Country Study*, 3rd ed. (1981), discusses several aspects of Nanking's industry, trade, and transportation. CHI TSUI, *A Short History of Chinese Civilization* (1942, reissued 1945); and IMMANUAL C.Y. HSÜ, *The Rise of Modern China*, 3rd ed. (1983), contain general references to Nanking's history. For accounts of specific epochs, see AUGUSTUS F. LINDLEY, *Ti-ping Tien-kwoh: The History of the Ti-ping Revolution*, 2 vol. (1866, reprinted in 1 vol., 1970); YU-WEN JEN (YU-WEN CHIEN), *The Taiping Revolutionary Movement* (1973); PAUL M.A. LINEBARGER, *The China of Chiang K'ai-shek* (1941, reprinted 1973); and HAROLD J. TIMPERLEY (ed.), *The Japanese Terror in China* (1938, reprinted 1969; U.K. title, *What War Means: The Japanese Terror in China*). Language, culture, and food in Nanking are discussed in LEO J. MOSER, *The Chinese Mosaic: The Peoples and Provinces of China* (1985).

(P.-c.K./Z.Z.)

Naples

Naples (Italian: Napoli) lies on the west coast of the Italian Peninsula, 120 miles (190 kilometres) southeast of Rome, in the fertile region of Campania. On its celebrated bay—flanked to the west by the smaller Gulf of Pozzuoli and, to the southeast, by the more extended indentation of the Gulf of Salerno—the city is situated between two areas of volcanic activity: Mount Vesuvius to the east and the Campi Flegrei (Phlegraean Fields) to the northwest. The most recent eruption of Vesuvius occurred in 1944. In 1980 an earthquake damaged Naples and its outlying towns.

Naples is located near the midpoint of the arc of hills that, commencing in the north at the promontory of Posillipo and terminating in the south with the Sorrentine peninsula, form the central focus of the Bay of Naples. To the south of the bay's entrance to the Tyrrhenian Sea, the island of Capri forms a partial breakwater, visible from the city in clear weather and at times of impending storm, but increasingly is screened by polluted air from the industrial zone developed, since World War II, between central Naples and the Vesuvian slopes. Pollution also afflicts the waters of the port, obliging the more scrupulous practitioners of the immemorial Neapolitan fishing industry to withdraw ever farther from their native shore.

While Naples' importance as the principal port of southern Italy is at last in decline, the city remains the centre of the nation's meridional commerce and culture, beset by inveterate difficulties, and distinguished by an adroit and original spirit that retains many suggestions of the classical past and of assimilated historical experience. Of all the cities of southern Italy with Greek origins, Naples presents the most striking example of a lively continuity. It is also perhaps the last great metropolis of western Europe whose monuments, albeit often in decay, may still be seen in their popular context, without distractions of tourism or self-conscious commercialism.

Since World War II, during which Naples suffered severe bombardment, modernization has increasingly altered the city's setting and character; and a measure of long-deferred but often speculative prosperity is reflected in new suburbs now proliferating in once-rural surroundings. However, Naples remains arcane and compelling, a city whose richness requires from the visitor time, accessibility, and some knowledge of the Neapolitan past.

This article is divided into the following sections:

Physical and human geography

THE LANDSCAPE

Description and climate. Generations of observers have described Naples as a vast popular theatre, a designation applying as much to the city's aspect of a tiered arena as to its animated street life. It may also be characterized as an immense *presepio,* in evocation of the populous scene of the traditional Neapolitan Christmas crèche—the expansive natural setting being countered, within the town itself, by a congested vitality. In the shadow of Vesuvius, within the sweep of the bay, the Neapolitan decor is still predominantly one of moldering palaces in red or ochre and ancient churches in stone or stucco. Although the narrow old streets, teeming and traffic-ridden, clamber up hillsides topped by new constructions, few buildings in central Naples as yet rise more than 10 stories. Three fortified castles—two of them on the seafront and one on a central eminence—still define the city's heart. At the picturesque, pale Castel dell'Ovo, the shoreline divides into two natural crescents.

The blond, volcanic tuff, or tufa, of the region is much used in construction, as is the dark Vesuvian lava that paves the older streets. Magisterial use was also made, in past centuries, of the dark southern stone *piperno,* seen at its most imposing at the Castel Nuovo. The city's aspect of southern colours interspersed with evergreen groves of ilex, palm, camellia, and umbrella pine reflects a climate in which balconies are in use most of the year. High temperatures in July and August often exceed 90° F (32° C), while the damp, chilly winter is alleviated by many brilliant days. Winter temperatures rarely fall to freezing, and the snow occasionally appearing on Vesuvius is seldom seen in the town itself. The south wind, the sand-laden sirocco, intermittently brings a burdensome humidity, terminating in rain. Temperatures

Layout and architecture. Suburban Naples incorporates the headland of Posillipo, which joins the city at the yachting port of Mergellina. The nearby church of Santa Maria di Piedigrotta is steeply overlooked by a small park encompassing the entrance to the Roman grotto called the Crypta Neapolitana. This poignant place also contains the Roman columbarium known as the Tomb of Virgil, and the sepulchre of the Romantic poet Giacomo Leopardi, who died at Naples in 1837.

From Mergellina, the seaside sweep of Via Francesco Caracciolo is flanked by the long, public park called Villa Comunale, sheltering the Zoological Station and the Aquarium (the oldest in Europe), both founded in 1872. Along the inland border of the park runs the Riviera di Chiaia, marking what was once the shoreline. Still for the most part lined with handsome old palazzi, the Riviera di Chiaia was a favourite residential area for foreign visitors in the 18th and 19th centuries. The Neoclassical Villa Pignatelli, constructed for Sir Ferdinand Acton in the 1820s, is now, with its period furnishings, a museum. Recessed in contiguous streets, the churches of Santa Maria in Portico and the Ascensione a Chiaia contain works of the prolific 17th- and 18th-century Neapolitan painters.

Above this busy littoral, the panoramic Corso Vittorio Emanuele unfurls northeastward around the lower slopes of the town, toward the labyrinthine zone of Rione Mater Dei. Higher still, the prosperous Vomero district is served, like other upper areas of the city, by spiraling roads and a funicular railway. Among the modern blocks of the Vomero, the early 19th-century Villa Floridiana—housing the national museum Duca di Martina, with a fine collection of European and Oriental porcelain and ceramics—is easily distinguished in its extensive park.

Piazza della Vittoria—whose titular church commemorates the Battle of Lepanto (1571)—closes the sweep of Villa Comunale and leads inland to the fashionable shops of Piazza dei Martiri, Via Chiaia, and Via dei Mille. The waterfront road, becoming Via Partenope, passes along the ancient quarter of Santa Lucia—much altered since the late 19th century by land reclamation and monotonous construction and bordered on the seafront by some of the city's best hotels. Beneath the spur of the Pizzofalcone quarter—the remaining fragment of the defunct volcano

The Bay of Naples with the view south toward Mount Vesuvius.
Leo de Wys, Inc./F. Damm

Echia and once the site of a villa of the Roman general Lucius Licinius Lucullus—a brief causeway leads to the seagirt Castel dell'Ovo, its ancient origins incorporated in a medieval fortress. On the bay's second crescent, the eastbound road passes below the long, red flank of the Royal Palace and arrives at the foot of the mighty Castel Nuovo, which, with its round towers, dominates the main port on the one hand and, on the other, the large Piazza del Municipio.

The Castel Nuovo

The Castel Nuovo, so called to distinguish it from the older Castel dell'Ovo, was founded in 1279 by Charles I of Naples (Charles of Anjou). One of many Neapolitan landmarks to bear interchangeable names, it is known locally as the Maschio Angioino. There, in the 14th century, the brilliant court of King Robert welcomed Petrarch and Boccaccio, and Giotto was summoned to execute frescoes (now lost). The castle was embellished by Alfonso V of Aragon (Alfonso I of Naples), whose triumphal entry into Naples in 1443 supplies the theme of magnificent Renaissance sculptures over the west entrance. The castle, containing important late medieval and Renaissance decoration, now houses municipal bodies and an institute of Neapolitan history with an important library. At the west end of Piazza del Municipio, the Naples city hall incorporates, in a handsome structure of the 1820s, a 16th-century church.

The waterfront road continues past docklands, skirting on its inner side the popular church of Santa Maria del Carmine. The nearby Piazza del Mercato, a lively scene of morning markets, was also, in past centuries, a place of execution. Bombardment of the port of Naples during World War II obliterated much of the character of this section of shoreline, and the road itself diverges in the industrial zone of San Giovanni a Teduccio. Visible history resumes in the approach to Portici and the Vesuvian shore.

Inland above Piazza del Municipio, San Martino Hill is surmounted by a former Carthusian monastery—now an important museum of paintings and objects concerned with the history of Naples—and by the massive abutment of Castel Sant'Elmo. Both are of Angevin origins. The castle, founded in 1329 by Robert of Anjou, was re-created in the 16th century, under the Spanish viceroys, in the form of a six-pointed star. Within the complex of the former San Martino monastery, the church itself is rich in paintings and marble decoration of the Neapolitan Baroque.

The Royal Palace

South of Piazza del Municipio, beyond the Castel Nuovo, stands the red complex of the Royal Palace, whose northeast wing, set in a small park, houses the great collections of the National Library of Naples. The main facade of the Royal Palace grandly faces, southwest across the vast Piazza del Plebiscito, the basilica of San Francesco di Paola, which—erected in royal thanksgiving for the restoration of Bourbon rule (1815)—is modeled on the Pantheon of Rome. The palace, created by Domenico Fontana early in the 17th century, now houses government offices and a notable picture gallery.

Adjacent to the palace on the north is the San Carlo opera house, which has heard and inspired most of the great artists of bel canto. Although the prodigious musical creativity of 18th-century Naples has no modern parallel, the San Carlo remains an important element of Europe's musical life. Across the busy intersection from the San Carlo, the late 19th-century arcades of the cruciform Galleria Umberto I serve, under their glass cupola, as an ornate meeting place; the arcades were familiar ground to Allied servicemen in the closing phase of World War II—a dramatic period recalled in such writings as John Horne Burns's *The Gallery* (1947) and the macabre *La pelle* (1949; *The Skin* [1952]), by the politically volatile Curzio Malaparte. Immediately south, on Piazza Trieste e Trento, the 17th-century church of San Ferdinando has traditionally given the *Stabat Mater* of Giovanni Battista Pergolesi—composed in 1736 for this confraternity—during Easter Week.

Via Toledo

From Piazza Trieste e Trento, the teeming thoroughfare of Via Toledo—named for the Spanish viceroy Don Pedro di Toledo, who laid it out in 1536—passes north into the dense centre of Naples. Its innumerable shops interspersed with grand churches, Via Toledo is banked with 17th- and 18th-century palazzi whose former magnificence has been turned to commercial or municipal use or—as in the case of the mighty Palazzo Maddaloni—has been allowed to lapse into residential decay. On the slope above Via Toledo, steep alleys climb toward San Martino through a zone that, preserving its labyrinthine 17th-century structure, is still known as the Spanish Quarter. The lower line of Via Toledo is interrupted at Piazza Carità by structures built during the Fascist and postwar eras.

Debouching into the Neoclassical hemicycle of Piazza Dante, Via Toledo resumes its route under other names, skirting the western flank of the National Archaeological Museum in its ascent toward Capodimonte.

Piazza Dante forms part of the western boundary to the district that, lying along three principal *decumani* (streets of orientation) of the Greek and Roman town, has comprised the city's heart since ancient times. Beyond the picturesque Alba Gate this district is introduced, at the western extreme of Via Tribunali, by the historic Naples Conservatory of Music and its great adjoining Gothic church of San Pietro a Maiella. Via Tribunali, the *decumanus maior* of Greco-Roman Naples, extends east for approximately one mile, terminating at the law courts near the old Capuana Gate. At its western end, the Renaissance Pontano Chapel (in decay) recalls the humanist Giovanni Pontano, who lived in Naples under Aragonese rule, while the older origins of the contiguous Baroque church of Santa Maria Maggiore are apparent in a Romanesque campanile.

Spaccanápoli

Parallel to Via Tribunali, the upper, briefer Via Anticaglia conserves, within subsequent structures, evident remains of Roman public buildings. The lower parallel—the street that, bearing interim names, becomes Via San Biagio dei Librai—delineates the so-called Spaccanápoli ("Split of Naples"), a designation more loosely applied to all of this ancient centre.

From Piazza del Municipio, Spaccanápoli is approached along the north-northwest trajectory formed by Via Medina and Via Monteoliveto—a route that passes, to the east of Via Monteoliveto, the recessed Renaissance and Baroque complex of Santa Maria la Nova; and, to the west, in a small square, the church of Monteoliveto, or Sant'Anna dei Lombardi, supreme in Naples for its abundance and quality of Renaissance sculpture. From Via Monteoliveto, the short slope called Calata Trinità Maggiore rises to Piazza del Gesù Nuovo, a principal means of access to Spaccanápoli.

Santa Chiara

Overlooked from the west by Palazzo Pignatelli (where the painter Edgar Degas resided while in Naples) and with the 18th-century ornate Neapolitan obelisk Guglia dell'Immacolata at its centre, this square is dominated by the church of Gesù Nuovo, its gem-cut facade masking a sumptuous Baroque interior. Opposite rises the medieval complex of Santa Chiara, erected for the Franciscan order in the 14th century. The vast church, transformed internally in the 18th century and now restored (following tragic bombardment in 1943) to its original Gothic form, houses a damaged splendour of royal tombs and early frescoes. At its rear the large cloister decorated in 18th-century majolica tiles is one of the loveliest in Naples.

From this square the line of Spaccanápoli runs due east. The profusion of important monuments there, the mingling of eras, and the exuberance of the human setting are of inexhaustible fascination. Near the Gesù Nuovo, Palazzo Filomarino houses the Italian Institute for Historical Studies, founded by the philosopher Benedetto Croce. (Another celebrated Neapolitan philosopher, Giambattista Vico, was born, two centuries before Croce, in a house also preserved in this street.) Flanked by great palazzi, the basilica of San Domenico Maggiore, its Gothic form merged into the structures of later centuries, is a treasury of painting and sculpture. In 1272–74, St. Thomas Aquinas taught in the adjoining monastery. Where the intersecting Via Mezzocannone turns south toward the University of Naples, the church of Sant'Angelo a Nilo contains a lofty tomb sculptured by Donatello and Michelozzo.

In the upward transverse of Via San Gregorio Armeno, the church of this name exemplifies the Neapolitan Rococo. In this street, in slotlike shops, figures are made for the innumerable Neapolitan family crèches—culminating each Christmas in a scene of indescribable liveliness and charm. Via San Gregorio Armeno terminates, at its junction with Via Tribunali, in the little Piazza San Gaetano, which overlies the site of the Greek agora and Roman forum. Bounded by the two great churches of San Lorenzo Maggiore and San Paolo Maggiore, and in close proximity to a third—the Gerolomini—this busy space remains a focus of Neapolitan continuity.

The splendid Gothic church of San Lorenzo Maggiore stands on layers of antiquities. Beneath its cloister, which contains exposed remains from Roman times, a large excavation from the Greek and Roman eras of Naples constitutes—with antiquities discovered below the nearby Duomo—a considerable segment of the ancient city centre. At San Lorenzo Maggiore, in 1334, Boccaccio claimed to have first seen Fiammetta; and there, in November 1345, Petrarch, then lodging in the adjacent monastery, prayed—as he recounts in a memorable letter—for the city's deliverance from a catastrophic storm. San Paolo Maggiore, on the site of a Roman temple, features antiquities incorporated into its handsome exterior and into the adjacent cloister. The great complex of the Gerolomini embraces a magnificent library and a small gallery of Neapolitan pictures. Its entrance on Via del Duomo faces the cathedral (Duomo) of Naples.

The Duomo

The Duomo is dedicated to the city's patron, St. Januarius (San Gennaro), the liquefaction of whose congealed blood is the stimulus for two popular festivals each year. The rich chapel (or treasury) of St. Januarius forms part of an interior whose abundance of antique columns, painting, sculpture, and fine objects constitutes, not least in its incongruity, a history of Naples. The present church gives access to the early basilica of Santa Restituta and the adjoining baptistery, with 5th-century mosaics, of San Giovanni in Fonte. Near the upper (southern) flank of the cathedral, the 14th-century church of Santa Maria Donnaregina is, in its interior decoration, among the most interesting and beautiful medieval monuments of Naples, while the nearby Santi Apostoli, on the site of a Roman temple, provides a prodigious display of 17th-century Neapolitan painting.

To the east, the formidable Castel Capuano—site of law courts since the 16th century—rises near the round towers of the Capuana Gate, which in turn overshadow the Renaissance church of Santa Caterina a Formiello. Renaissance also is the decoration, by Giuliano da Maiano, of the exterior arch of this Aragonese city gate. Beyond the Capuana Gate, the northwest–southeast diagonal of Via Carbonara follows the line of demolished city walls. Marked, on its upper slope, by the monumental church of San Giovanni a Carbonara—containing the statuary tomb of King Ladislas and other capital late Gothic and early Renaissance works—Via Carbonara descends, with a change of name, to Piazza Garibaldi and the railway station.

Toward the end of the 19th century, precipitate change was wrought, from Piazza del Municipio to the railway station, by the slum clearance, or *risanamento,* that, following a calamitous epidemic of cholera in 1884, drove the straight, ugly Corso Umberto I (also called the Rettifilo) through that historic quarter. The stolid Rettifilo conceals, in small recesses, many historic buildings—beginning with the church of San Pietro Martire and concluding, at Piazza Garibaldi, with that of San Pietro ad Aram and its paleo-Christian crypt. Near Piazza Garibaldi, the Aragonese Nolana Gate is an enclave of busy markets.

Museums. Naples possesses two of the world's great museums, both founded under Bourbon rule. The National Archaeological Museum houses unsurpassed collections of Greco-Roman antiquities, comprising many of the finest works—in marble, bronze, mosaic, fresco, and ceramic—from Herculaneum, Pompeii, and other Campanian sites and the Farnese marbles, a Bourbon inheritance. The museum also possesses significant Egyptian antiquities.

Capodimonte

Overlooking Naples on the north from its handsome park, the National Museum and Gallery of Capodimonte contains, together with important tapestries and porcelain, a splendid collection of paintings, including masterworks by Simone Martini, Masaccio, Botticelli, Colantonio, Lotto, Parmigianino, Correggio, Titian, El Greco, and Pieter Bruegel the Elder, and fine examples of the Neapolitan 17th- and 18th-century painters. Following the earthquake of 1980, works by Caravaggio and Titian were removed to Capodimonte from their traditional settings in the city.

In addition to museums already noted, the civic Filangieri Museum houses, in a Renaissance building on Via del Duomo, a collection of paintings and objects, many of them related to Neapolitan history. At the nearby State Archives, documents of great historic importance are installed in the former Benedictine monastery of SS. Severo and Sossio—a vast complex including, in the Platano cloister, celebrated frescoes by Antonio Solario.

THE PEOPLE

Travelers in Italy accustomed to great public squares where visitors may at leisure observe the monuments and manners of the town are often puzzled by Naples' apparent lack of such focal points—not because great piazzas do not exist there, but because they are often used as mere traffic arteries and because the city's life is not so much concentrated in such places as diffused around them. The city's heart will rather be discovered in the small, populous enclaves—animated in the mornings, dormant by afternoon, revived at evening—which, each with distinctive character, make up the town's traditional districts. Intimacy with such a city is necessarily gradual, requiring a state of mind amounting to a revelation.

Decline in tourism

Naples, which, following the 18th-century discoveries of the buried cities of Vesuvius, long remained essential to cultivated travel, now serves visitors mainly as a wayside halt to neighbouring sites and resorts. Already in decline, tourism at Naples was sharply reduced by the effects of World War II, which left the city a shambles, and by the cessation of regular sea travel, which no longer brought visitors to the port of Naples. Many of the city's monuments were, moreover, embedded in what modern travelers often viewed as uninviting squalor; and random street crime—making it unsafe to carry items of value—compounded the disadvantages. A new touristic emphasis on brevity, velocity, and large numbers imposed, in turn, requirements that Naples could not meet—the city's riches of ancient continuity and of a slowly unfolding charm being unsuited to a hasty or systematic approach.

Bypassed by the foreign influx, Naples has thus preserved much authenticity and some skepticism toward modern tenets. Goethe's generalization that Neapolitans "wish even their work to be a recreation" is still valid, however incompatible with economic and administrative realities. While Goethe himself could not resist the northern cliché that Neapolitans are childlike, the tolerant penetration of motive, the graceful absence of envy, belligerence, or nationalism, and above all the civilizing Neapolitan sense of mortality, seem indicative, rather, of a long transmitted comprehension in human affairs.

Intellectual life in Naples, which is mainly centred around scholars concerned with the classical and Neapolitan past, is marked by high distinction and strong animosities; and it generates an important and varied literature. Despite the growth of a middle class and a notable advance in the status of women, emphatic divisions persist between prosperous and poor, while, in all classes, history has fatally extinguished—with rare exceptions—the flame of civic spirit. Government corruption and neglect are intensified by bureaucratic confusion and by the violent interventions of the Camorra, an illicit Neapolitan association analogous to the Sicilian Mafia. Nevertheless, with infinite adaptation, a sense of identity is maintained. Many festivals have fallen victim to traffic, and the old Neapolitan songs—now electronically diffused—have no successors. But fervour and fireworks still greet saints and soccer players alike. The ironic Neapolitan dialect holds its own. Individuality and family loyalty remain strong, as does a capacity not only for pleasure but for joy.

THE ECONOMY

Early economic development

Industry. Naples is the industrial centre of southern Italy. Under the Bourbons the city had an early start in manufacturing, with foundation of the porcelain factory at the royal palace of Capodimonte in 1740 and the development of silk and other textile production soon thereafter. The textile industry has remained important. Other traditional industries of continuing importance are food processing and winemaking. The first steel mill opened at the end of the 19th century, but the industry did not add significantly to national production until the 1970s. Among the newer industries in the region are electronics manufacturing, petroleum refining, and automobile assembly. The tourist industry continues to be important to the regional economy.

Industrial development was aided considerably after World War II by the concerted action of state planning and fiscal agencies and of companies either owned or controlled by the national government. Local enterprise was associated with the programs. The region's infrastructure was upgraded extensively and its energy production expanded. Nevertheless, Naples and the whole of southern Italy lags well behind the north.

Transportation. In 1818 the first steamboat on the Mediterranean was launched at the royal shipyards in Naples. Remodeling of the ancient harbour and its early medieval additions—now mostly filled in—was begun in 1826. Port facilities were badly damaged during World War II, but the subsequent reconstruction and modernization of its facilities have made Naples one of the chief Mediterranean ports. In 1839 Italy's first railway traversed the five miles from Naples to the royal residence of Portici. The first funicular railway on the peninsula was opened to the heights of Vomero in 1880. Naples developed into an important railway centre, being the main junction between Rome and southern Italy.

History

THE EARLY PERIOD

Greek origins

Naples was founded in about 600 BC as Neapolis ("New City"), close to the more ancient Palaepolis, which had itself absorbed the name of the siren Parthenope. Both towns originated as Greek settlements, extensions almost certainly of Greek colonies established, during the 7th and 6th centuries BC, on the nearby island of Pithecusa (now Ischia) and at Cumae on the adjacent mainland where remarkable Greek ruins may be visited today. Ancient Neapolis, as Gibbon says, "long cherished the language and manners of a Grecian colony; and the choice of Virgil had ennobled this elegant retreat, which attracted the lovers of repose and study from the noise, the smoke, and the laborious opulence of Rome." Horace (here paraphrased by Gibbon), Virgil, and the Neapolitan poet Statius are among numerous classical writers who attest the Hellenism of Naples. The Greek language was preserved throughout the city's first millennium, surviving submission, in the 4th century BC, to the dominion of Rome.

Under the empire, Naples and its environs served as a centre of Greek culture and erudition and as a pleasure resort for a succession of emperors and wealthy Romans, whose coastal villas extended from Misenum on the Gulf of Pozzuoli (the ancient Puteoli) to the Sorrentine peninsula. The amenity of these dwellings, depicted in recovered Vesuvian frescoes, is confirmed in such remains as Tiberius' Villa Jovis on Capri, the villa of Oplontis at Torre Annunziata, and the ruins of Villa Pausilypon, which gave its Greek name—meaning "a pause from care"—to the headland of Posillipo. Near Herculaneum, the buried private establishment known as the Villa of the Papyri yielded, in the mid-18th century, a treasure of antique sculpture and a group of papyrus scrolls presumed to belong to an ancient library. These scrolls, many of them deciphered, are conserved in the National Library at Naples. The villa was never excavated, and its 18th-century tunnels of approach were reopened only in 1987. A floor plan drawn up in the 18th century was the basis for the J. Paul Getty Museum at Malibu, Calif.

In Roman times Naples was adorned with temples and baths, and with arenas similar to those surviving at Pozzuoli and Pompeii. Principal Roman roads connected the city to the capital, and aqueducts supplied fresh water. The gulfs of Naples and Pozzuoli were linked by galleries pierced through the yellow tufa of lower Posillipo. Of these, an evocative example may be visited at Mergellina, at the Crypta Neapolitana, beside the Roman tumulus long venerated as the Tomb of Virgil, in tribute to the Mantuan poet who celebrated the Neapolitan ambience in the sixth book of his *Aeneid* and composed the *Georgics* there between 37 and 30 BC.

Eruption of Vesuvius in AD 79

In AD 79 the great eruption of Vesuvius buried the seaside towns of Pompeii, Herculaneum, and Stabiae, engulfing also many villas confidently constructed on the slopes of a mountain that had not erupted for more than seven centuries. A contemporary account of this event remains to us in two letters addressed to the historian Tacitus by Pliny the Younger, who describes the doomed attempt of his uncle, the polymathic elder Pliny, to rescue survivors by sea. More than 16 centuries later, in 1738, systematic excavation of the buried towns was inaugurated at Herculaneum, under the aegis of the Neapolitan Bourbons—initiating discoveries that would profoundly influence Western aesthetic and scientific concepts and transform our knowledge of the ancient world.

Early tribulations of Christians at Naples are exemplified in the martyrdom of the city's patron, St. Januarius. The Catacombs of St. Januarius, on the Capodimonte slope, antedate in their earliest section the saint's legendary decapitation in AD 305 and are extremely interesting historically and for paleo-Christian decoration. Other early Christian sites include the baptistery incorporated in the Duomo, the ancient apse at the nearby church of San Giorgio Maggiore, and the Catacombs of San Gaudioso below the great church of Santa Maria della Sanità in one of the city's most colourful districts.

During the decline of the Roman Empire, Naples suffered with all the Italian Peninsula, and, having espoused the Gothic cause, drew, in 536, the vengeance of the Roman commander Belisarius. In the division of the late empire the city remained, with some vacillation, under the Exarchate of Ravenna until the 8th century when, rebelling against the Eastern emperors, Naples established a form of republican government that secured embattled independence for more than three centuries. Succumbing at last to the Lombard power established at Capua and Benevento, Naples saw the Lombards dispossessed, in turn, by the Norman conquests that swept southern Italy in the 12th century. While including Naples in that turbulent subjugation, Norman—and, subsequently, Swabian—dominion elevated the metropolis to a regional and cultural capital, a position Naples would retain under diverse rulers until the 19th century. Although maintaining his court at Palermo, the Holy Roman emperor Frederick II fortified Naples, founded the university there in 1224, and nurtured, in a rebellious ambience, the city's intellectual life.

NAPLES FROM THE ANGEVINS TO THE RISORGIMENTO

Renewal of the city's importance

In 1266 establishment of the Angevin dynasty in Naples renewed the city's importance—formidably proclaimed by erection of the Castel Nuovo and the Sant'Elmo fortress. The Angevin kings and their Aragonese successors attracted to Naples great figures of Italian thought and literature and the northern architects and artists whose genius survives in many Gothic and Renaissance monuments. Under Alfonso V of Aragon culture at Naples transcended warfare. In 1453 fugitives from the fall of Constantinople brought an infusion of Byzantine arts.

In 1503 Naples entered the possession of the Spanish Habsburgs, whose viceroys presided with autocratic severity for more than two centuries. Great churches, convents, and private palaces from this period testify to a concentration of power against which an oppressed populace might periodically but ineffectually rebel—as in the ill-fated revolt led by Masaniello (Tomaso Aniello) in 1647–48. This harsh viceregal power was terminated by Austrian conquest (1707). And, in 1734, Naples became, under the Spanish Bourbons, the capital of a large independent southern kingdom, Don Carlos (the future Charles III of Spain) assuming the old and all but impenetrable title of "king of the Two Sicilies."

Naples now burgeoned as a potent European capital, its implacable divisions of wealth and poverty thrown in relief by 18th-century illumination. Scholars and statesmen from this era—such as Giambattista Vico, Pietro Giannone, Bernardo Tanucci, Ferdinando Galiani, and Gaetano Filangieri—are of universal rather than exclusively Neapolitan distinction. Another period of prolific construction is commemorated in Bourbon public edifices—including the royal palaces of Portici and Caserta—and in private mansions. The Vesuvian littoral again became a site of busy communities and of the elegant Ville Vesuviane, today mostly in disrepair. The excavations at Herculaneum and Pompeii attracted foreign visitors, while, in a climate of Neoclassicism and incipient Romanticism, artists, writers, and scholars arrived to experience the Neapolitan ambience. Depictions of the city and its surroundings—and of its presiding volcano, slighted by earlier painters—now found their way around the world.

Ferdinand IV and Maria Carolina

At the court of Ferdinand IV (Ferdinand I of the Two Sicilies) and his masterful queen, Maria Carolina, the cultivated British envoy Sir William Hamilton forged an Anglo-Neapolitan bond that lingers today. Maria Carolina's repressive tendencies were traumatically intensified by the execution in 1793 of her sister Marie Antoinette, queen of France. With the irruption of Napoleon into Italy (1798), the royal family withdrew in panic to Palermo aboard Admiral Horatio Nelson's British ships. The Neapolitan educated classes proclaimed a republic; while the Neapolitan poor, the *lazzaroni,* abandoned by their sovereign, remained vigorously if incomprehensibly monarchist. The nobly conceived Parthenopean Republic collapsed in a welter of blood. A punitive return by the Bourbons and the execution or exile of the republicans make the year 1799 a tragic epoch in the Neapolitan story.

In 1805 the court fled anew to Palermo, and, until 1815, the Kingdom of Naples was ruled, with legislative reforms, by Napoleon's brother Joseph Bonaparte and, subsequently, by Joachim Murat. Following the fall of Napoleon, the Bourbons reentered Naples with Austrian assistance. However, the weakness and corruption of succeeding Bourbon monarchs and their ruthless suppression of progressive ideas set the scene for Giuseppe Garibaldi's triumphant entry into the city in 1860 and for absorption of Naples into the Kingdom of Italy.

THE MODERN CITY

Deprived of territorial power, the city of Naples has, since the late 19th century, increasingly sought survival in an elusive and temperamentally incompatible degree of industrialization and in the ingenuity of her citizens, whose gifts for improvization have been called forth no less by modern bureaucratic riddles than by the indifference of past monarchies. The cholera epidemic of 1884 aroused a transient spirit of reform, reflected in slum clearance, modernization of water and transport systems, and other public works. The optimism of the *risanamento* was blighted by the onset of World War I.

The rise of Fascism in Italy, compounded by the Great Depression of the 1930s, darkened the interval between the wars—from which, at Naples, the philosopher Benedetto Croce and other enlightened figures stand forth in defense of humanity and reason. While Naples shared with all Italy the degradation of Fascism, few Italian cities suffered so heavily in World War II or made so painful and incomplete a recovery. That the city survived the postwar period without complete economic and social collapse can be attributed almost exclusively to the vitality and philosophy of its populace and to the Neapolitan ability to combine strong passions with a resilient endurance.

BIBLIOGRAPHY

General: SIR WILLIAM HAMILTON, *Campi Phlegraei* (1776), offers illustrated observations on the area of volcanic activity that influences the environment of Naples. Other relevant historic writings include JOHANN WOLFGANG VON GOETHE, *Italian Journey, 1786–1788,* trans. from German by W.H. AUDEN and ELIZABETH MAYER (1962, reprinted 1982), a travel diary, completed in 1816–17, with celebrated chapters on Naples; and NORMAN DOUGLAS, *Siren Land* (1911, reprinted 1982), an illuminating discussion of the ancient Neapolitan setting, Capri, and Sorrento. DESMOND SEWARD (ed.), *Naples, a Travellers' Companion* (1984), is an anthology of writings on Naples by authors from the 13th to the mid-19th century. PETER GUNN, *The Companion Guide to Southern Italy* (1969); and H.V. MORTON, *A Traveller in Southern Italy* (1969, reprinted 1987), are descriptive guidebooks. Essential information is collected in the detailed guidebook *Napoli e dintorni,* 5th ed. (1976). Social conditions, the poor, and especially children, are the topic of MARIA CARMELA BARBIERO (ed.), *Gli eredi della povertà: stabilità e mutamento nel sottoproletariato nepoletano* (1981); JUDITH CHUBB, *Patronage, Power, and Poverty in Southern Italy: A Tale of Two Cities* (1982); and THOMAS BELMONTE, *The Broken Fountain* (1979). For an analysis of political developments, see P.A. ALLUM, *Politics and Society in Post-War Naples* (1973).

History: A fundamental encyclopaedic work, dealing authoritatively with every aspect of Neapolitan history, is *Storia di Napoli,* 11 vol. in 14 (1967–78), published by the Società Editrice Storia di Napoli. JOHN H. D'ARMS, *Romans on the Bay of Naples: A Social and Cultural Study of the Villas and Their Owners from 150 B.C. to A.D. 400* (1970), traces the life and culture through the analysis of the remains of important constructions; MARTIN FREDERIKSEN, *Campania* (1984), is a history of the region beginning with antiquity. GIOVANNI PUGLIESE CARRATELLI *et al., Megale Hellas: storia e civiltà della Magna Grecia* (1983), provides a comprehensive scholarly history of Greek civilization in southern Italy.

Works on later historical periods include GINO DORIA, *Storia di una capitale: Napoli dalle origini al 1860,* 6th rev. ed. (1975), covering the period up to the absorption of Naples into the Kingdom of Italy; VINCENZO CUOCO, *Saggio storico sulla rivoluzione napoletana del 1799,* new ed. (1929, reissued 1980), on the Parthinopean Republic and the revolution; HAROLD ACTON, *The Bourbons of Naples, 1734–1825* (1956, reprinted 1974), and *The Last Bourbons of Naples, 1825–1861* (1961); and PIETRO COLLETTA, *History of the Kingdom of Naples, 1734–1825,* 2 vol. (1858; originally published in Italian, 1834), on Bourbon rule in Naples. An essential comprehensive survey is provided in BENEDETTO CROCE, *Storia del regno di Napoli,* 5th ed. (1984).

For the modern period, see PETER GUNN, *Naples: A Palimpsest* (1961), a popular history including modern developments; GIANCARLO ALISIO, *Napoli e il risanamento: recupero di una struttura urbana* (1980), a study of urban renewal after the cholera epidemic of 1884.

Arts and architecture: ROBERTO PANE, *Il Rinascimento nell'Italia meridionale,* 2 vol. (1975), is a pioneering work on Renaissance art and architecture in Naples. PIERLUIGI LEONE DE CASTRIS, *Arte di corte nella Napoli angiona* (1986), treats the arts and art patronage under Angevin rule. Other works include RUDOLF WITTKOWER, *Art and Architecture in Italy, 1600 to 1750,* 3rd ed. (1973, reprinted with corrections and augmented bibliography, 1980); SACHEVERELL SITWELL, *Southern Baroque Art: A Study of Painting, Architecture, and Music in Italy and Spain of the 17th & 18th Centuries* (1924, reprinted 1971); ANTHONY BLUNT, *Neapolitan Baroque & Rococo Architecture* (1975); ROBERTO PANE *et al., Ville vesuviane del settecento* (1959); BENEDETTO CROCE, *I teatri di Napoli: dal Rinascimento alla fine del secolo decimotavo,* 5th ed. (1966), on the theatre from the Renaissance to the end of the 18th century; and MICHAEL F. ROBINSON, *Naples and Neapolitan Opera* (1972, reprinted 1984), a careful historical study.

(Sh.Ha.)

Napoleon

Napoleon Bonaparte (original Italian, Napoleone Buonaparte), a French general, was first consul and then emperor of the French and carried out many reforms that left a lasting mark on the institutions of France and of much of western Europe. But his driving passion was the military expansion of French dominion, and, though at his fall he left France smaller than it had been at the outbreak of the Revolution in 1789, he was almost unanimously revered during his lifetime and until the end of the Second Empire under his nephew Napoleon III as one of history's great heroes.

Napoleon was born at Ajaccio on the island of Corsica on August 15, 1769, shortly after the cession of Corsica to France by the Genoese. He was the fourth, and second surviving, child of Carlo Buonaparte, a lawyer, and his wife, Letizia Ramolino. His father's family, of ancient Tuscan nobility, had emigrated to Corsica in the 16th century.

Carlo Buonaparte had married the beautiful and strong-willed Letizia when she was only 14 years old; they eventually had eight children to bring up in very difficult times. The French occupation of their native country was resisted by a number of Corsicans led by Pasquale Paoli. Carlo Buonaparte joined Paoli's party, but when Paoli had to flee, Buonaparte came to terms with the French. Winning the protection of the governor of Corsica, he was appointed assessor for the judicial district of Ajaccio in 1771. In 1778 he obtained the admission of his two eldest sons, Joseph and Napoleon, to the Collège d'Autun.

Early years and education in France

A Corsican by birth, heredity, and childhood associations, Napoleon continued for some time after his arrival in Continental France to regard himself a foreigner; yet from the age of nine he was educated in France as other Frenchmen were. While the tendency to see in Napoleon a reincarnation of some 14th-century Italian *condottiere* is an overemphasis on one aspect of his character, he did, in fact, share neither the traditions nor the prejudices of his new country: remaining a Corsican in temperament, he was first and foremost, through both his education and his reading, a man of the 18th century.

By courtesy of the National Gallery of Art, Washington, D.C., the Samuel H. Kress Collection; photograph, Giraudon—Art Resource

"Napoleon in His Study" by Jacques-Louis David, 1812. In the National Gallery of Art, Washington, D.C.

Napoleon was educated at three schools: briefly at Autun, for five years at the military college of Brienne, and finally for one year at the military academy in Paris. It was during Napoleon's year in Paris that his father died of a stomach cancer in February 1785, leaving his family in straitened circumstances. Napoleon, although not the eldest son, assumed the position of head of the family before he was 16. In September he graduated from the military academy, ranking 42nd in a class of 58.

He was made second lieutenant of artillery in the regiment of La Fère, a kind of training school for young artillery officers. Garrisoned at Valence, Napoleon continued his education, reading much, in particular works on strategy and tactics. He also wrote *Lettres sur la Corse,* in which he reveals his feeling for his native island. He went back to Corsica in September 1786 and did not rejoin his regiment until June 1788. By that time the agitation that was to culminate in the French Revolution had already begun. A reader of Voltaire and of Rousseau, Napoleon believed that a political change was imperative, but as a career officer he seems not to have seen any need for radical social reforms.

THE REVOLUTIONARY PERIOD

The Jacobin years. When in 1789 the National Assembly, which had convened to establish a constitutional monarchy, allowed Paoli to return to Corsica, Napoleon asked for leave and in September joined Paoli's group. But Paoli had no sympathy for the young man, whose father had deserted his cause and whom he considered to be a foreigner. Disappointed, Napoleon returned to France; and in April 1791 he was appointed first lieutenant to the 4th regiment of artillery, garrisoned at Valence. He at once joined the Jacobin club, a debating society initially favouring a constitutional monarchy, and soon became its president, making speeches against nobles, monks, and bishops. In September 1791 he got leave to go back to Corsica again for three months. Elected lieutenant colonel in the national guard, he soon fell out with Paoli, its commander in chief. When he failed to return to France, he was listed as a deserter in January 1792. But in April France declared war against Austria and his offense was forgiven.

Apparently through patronage, Napoleon was promoted to the rank of captain but did not rejoin his regiment. Instead he returned to Corsica in October 1792, where Paoli was exercising dictatorial powers and preparing to separate Corsica from France. Napoleon, however, joined the Corsican Jacobins, who opposed Paoli's policy. When civil war broke out in Corsica in April 1793, Paoli had the Buonaparte family condemned to "perpetual execration and infamy," whereupon they all fled to France.

Napoleon Bonaparte, as he may henceforth be called (though the family did not drop the spelling Buonaparte until after 1796), rejoined his regiment at Nice in June 1793. In his *Souper de Beaucaire,* written at this time, he argued vigorously for united action by all republicans rallied round the Jacobins, who were becoming progressively more radical, and the National Convention, the revolutionary assembly that in the preceding fall had abolished the monarchy. At the end of August 1793, the National Convention's troops had taken Marseille but were halted before Toulon, where the royalists had called in British forces. With the commander of the National Convention's artillery wounded, Bonaparte got the post through the commissioner to the army, Antoine Saliceti, who was a Corsican deputy and a friend of Napoleon's family. Bonaparte was promoted to major in September and adjutant

Capture of Toulon

general in October. He received a bayonet wound on December 16, but on the next day the British troops, harassed by his artillery, evacuated Toulon. On December 22 Bonaparte, aged 24, was promoted to brigadier general in recognition of his decisive part in the capture of the town.

Augustin de Robespierre, the commissioner to the army, wrote to his brother Maximilien, by then virtual head of the government and one of the leading figures of the Reign of Terror, praising the "transcendent merit" of the young republican officer. In February 1794 Bonaparte was appointed commandant of the artillery in the French Army of Italy. Robespierre fell from power in Paris on 9 Thermidor (July 27, 1794). When the news reached Nice, Bonaparte, regarded as a protégé of Robespierre, was arrested on a charge of conspiracy and treason. He was freed in September but was not restored to his command. The following March he refused an offer to command the artillery in the Army of the West, which was fighting the counter-revolution in the Vendée. The post seemed to hold no future for him, and he went to Paris to justify himself. Life was difficult on half pay, especially as he was carrying on an affair with Désirée Clary, daughter of a rich Marseille businessman and sister of Julie, the bride of his elder brother, Joseph. Despite his efforts in Paris, Napoleon was unable to obtain a satisfactory command because he was feared for his intense ambition and for his relations with the "Montagnards," the more radical members of the National Convention. He then considered offering his services to the sultan of Turkey.

The Directory. Bonaparte was still in Paris in May 1795 when the National Convention, on the eve of its dispersal, submitted the new constitution of the year III of the First Republic to a referendum, together with decrees according to which two-thirds of the members of the National Convention were to be re-elected to the new legislative assemblies. The royalists, hoping that they would soon be able to restore the monarchy, instigated a revolt in Paris to prevent these measures from being put into effect. Vicomte Paul de Barras, who had been entrusted with dictatorial powers by the National Convention, was unwilling to rely on the commander of the troops of the interior; instead, knowing of Bonaparte's services at Toulon, he appointed him second in command. Thus, it was Napoleon who shot down the columns of rebels marching against the National Convention (13 Vendémiaire, year IV; October 5, 1795), thereby saving the National Convention and the republic.

Bonaparte became commander of the army of the interior and, consequently, was henceforth aware of every political development in France. He also became the respected adviser on military matters to the new government, the Directory. Lastly, he came to know an attractive Creole, Joséphine Tascher de La Pagerie, the widow of Gen. Alexandre de Beauharnais (guillotined during the Reign of Terror), the mother of two children, and a woman of many love affairs.

From every point of view, a new life was opening for Bonaparte. Having proved his loyalty to the Directory by dissolving a communistic group led by François Babeuf and an Italian, Filippo Buonarroti, whom Bonaparte had known in Corsica, he was appointed commander in chief of the Army of Italy in March 1796. He had been trying to obtain that post for several weeks so that he could personally conduct part of the plan of campaign adopted by the Directory on his advice. He married Joséphine on March 9 and left for the army two days later.

Commander in chief of Army of Italy

Arriving at his headquarters in Nice, Bonaparte found that his army, which on paper consisted of 43,000 men, numbered scarcely 30,000 ill-fed, ill-paid, and ill-equipped men. On March 28, 1796, he made his first proclamation to his troops:

> Soldiers, you are naked, badly fed.... Rich provinces and great towns will be in your power, and in them you will find honour, glory, wealth. Soldiers of Italy, will you be wanting in courage and steadfastness?

He took the offensive on April 12 and successively defeated and separated the Austrian and the Sardinian armies and then marched on Turin. King Victor Amadeus III of Sardinia asked for an armistice; and, at the peace treaty in Paris on May 15, Nice and Savoy, occupied by the French since 1792, were annexed to France. Bonaparte continued the war against the Austrians and occupied Milan but was held up at Mantua. While his army was besieging this great fortress, he signed armistices with the duke of Parma, the duke of Modena, and finally with Pope Pius VI.

At the same time, he took an interest in the political organization of Italy. A plan for its "republicanization" by a group of Italian "patriots" led by Buonarroti had to be shelved when Buonarroti was arrested for complicity in Babeuf's conspiracy against the Directory. Thereafter, Bonaparte, without discarding the Italian patriots altogether, restricted their freedom of action. He set up a republican regime in Lombardy but kept a close watch on its leaders, and in October 1796 he created the Cisalpine Republic by merging Modena and Reggio nell'Emilia with the papal states of Bologna and Ferrara occupied by the French Army. Finally he sent an expedition to recover Corsica, which the British had evacuated.

Austrian armies advanced four times from the Alps to relieve Mantua but were defeated each time by Bonaparte. After the last Austrian defeat, at Rivoli in January 1797, Mantua capitulated. Next, he marched on Vienna. He was about 60 miles (100 kilometres) from that capital when the Austrians sued for an armistice. By the preliminaries of peace, Austria ceded the southern Netherlands to France and recognized the Lombard republic but received in exchange some territory belonging to the old Republic of Venice, which was partitioned between Austria, France, and Lombardy. Bonaparte then consolidated and reorganized the north Italian republics and encouraged Jacobin—radical republican—propaganda in Venetia. Some Italian patriots hoped that these developments would soon lead to the formation of a single and indivisible "Italian Republic" modelled on the French.

Defeat of the Austrians and peace terms

Meanwhile, Bonaparte grew uneasy at the successes of the royalists in the French elections in the spring of 1797 and advised the Directory to oppose them, if necessary, by force. In July it attempted a coup d'etat against the royalists and failed; thereupon Bonaparte sent Gen. Pierre Augereau to Paris, along with several officers and men. Augereau's successful coup d'etat of 18 Fructidor (September 4, 1797) eliminated the royalists' friends from the government and legislative councils and also enhanced Bonaparte's prestige. Thus, Bonaparte could conclude the peace Treaty of Campo Formio with Austria as he thought best. The Directory was displeased, however, because the Treaty had ceded Venice to the Austrians and did not secure the left bank of the Rhine for France. On the other hand, it raised Bonaparte's popularity to its peak, for he had gained victory for France after five years of war on the Continent.

Only the war at sea, against the British, continued. The directors, who wanted to launch an invasion of the British Isles, appointed Bonaparte to command the army assembled for this purpose along the English Channel. After a rapid inspection in February 1798, he announced that the operation could not be undertaken until France had command of the sea. Instead, he suggested that France strike at the sources of Great Britain's wealth by occupying Egypt and threatening the route to India. This proposal, seconded by Talleyrand, the foreign minister, was accepted by the directors, who were glad to get rid of their ambitious young general.

The expedition, thanks to some fortunate coincidences, was at first a great success: Malta, the great fortress of the Knights Hospitallers of St. John of Jerusalem, was occupied on June 10, 1798, Alexandria taken by storm on July 1, and all the delta of the Nile rapidly overrun. On August 1, however, the French squadron at anchor in Abū Qīr Bay was completely destroyed by Adm. Horatio Nelson's fleet in the Battle of the Nile, so that Napoleon found himself confined to the land that he had conquered. He proceeded to introduce Western political institutions, administration, and technical skills in Egypt; but Turkey, nominally suzerain over Egypt, declared war on France in September. To prevent a Turkish invasion of Egypt and also perhaps to attempt a return to France by way of Anatolia, Bonaparte marched into Syria in February 1799. His progress northwest was halted at Acre, where

Failures in Egypt

the British withstood a siege, and in May Bonaparte began a disastrous retreat to Egypt.

The Battle of the Nile showed Europe that Bonaparte was not invincible, and Great Britain, Austria, Russia, and Turkey formed a new coalition against France. The French armies in Italy were defeated in the spring of 1799 and had to abandon the greater part of the peninsula. These defeats led to disturbances in France itself. The coup d'etat of 30 Prairial (June 18, 1799) expelled the men of moderate views from the Directory and brought into it men who were considered Jacobins. Yet the situation remained confused, and one of the new directors, Emmanuel Sieyès, was convinced that only military dictatorship could prevent a restoration of the monarchy: "I am looking for a sabre," he said. Bonaparte did not take long to make up his mind. He would leave his army and return to France—in order to save the republic, of course, but also to take advantage of the new circumstances and to seize power. The Directory had, in fact, ordered his return, but he had not received the order, so that it was actually in disregard of his instructions that he left Egypt with a few companions on August 22, 1799. Their two frigates surprisingly escaped interception by the British, and Bonaparte arrived in Paris on October 14.

By this time French victories in Switzerland and Holland had averted the danger of invasion, and the counter-revolutionary risings within France had more or less failed. A coup d'etat could therefore no longer be justified by any need to save the republic. Sieyès, however, had not given up his project, and now he had his "sabre." From the end of October he and Bonaparte were in league together planning the coup, and on 18–19 Brumaire, Year VIII (November 9–10, 1799), it was carried out: the directors were forced to resign, the members of the legislative councils were dispersed, and a new government, the Consulate, was set up. The three consuls were Bonaparte and two of the directors who had resigned, Sieyès and Pierre-Roger Ducos. But it was Bonaparte who was henceforth the master of France.

The coup of 18–19 Brumaire

THE CONSULATE

Consolidation of power. Bonaparte, now 30 years old, was thin and short and wore his hair cut close—*le petit tondu,* the "little crop-head," as he was called. Not much was known about his personality, but people had confidence in a man who had always been victorious (the Nile and Acre were forgotten) and who had managed to negotiate the brilliant Treaty of Campo Formio. He was expected to bring back peace, to end disorder, and to consolidate the political and social "conquests" of the Revolution. He was indeed exceptionally intelligent, prompt to make decisions, and indefatigably hardworking, but also insatiably ambitious. He seemed to be the man of the Revolution because it was due to the Revolution that he had climbed at so early an age to the highest place in the state. He was not to forget it: but more than a man of the Revolution, he was a man of the 18th century, the most enlightened of the enlightened despots, a true son of Voltaire. He did not believe in the sovereignty of the people, in the popular will, or in parliamentary debate. Yet he put his confidence more in reasoning than in reason and may be said to have preferred "men of talent"—mathematicians, jurists, and statesmen, for instance, however cynical or mercenary they might be—to "technicians" in the true sense of the word. He believed that an enlightened and firm will could do anything if it had the support of bayonets; he despised and feared the masses; and, as for public opinion, he considered that he could mold and direct it as he pleased. He has been called the most "civilian" of generals, but essentially he never ceased to be a soldier.

The military dictatorship

Bonaparte imposed a military dictatorship on France, but its true character was at first disguised by the Constitution of the Year VIII (4 Nivôse; December 25, 1799), drawn up by Sieyès. This constitution did not guarantee the "rights of man" or make any mention of "liberty, equality, and fraternity," but it did reassure the partisans of the Revolution by proclaiming the irrevocability of the sale of national property and by upholding the legislation against the émigrés. It gave immense powers to the first consul, leaving only a nominal role to his two colleagues. The first consul—namely, Bonaparte—was to appoint ministers, generals, civil servants, magistrates, and the members of the Council of State and even was to have an overwhelming influence in the choice of members for the three legislative assemblies, though their members were theoretically to be chosen by universal suffrage. Submitted to a plebiscite, the constitution won by an overwhelming majority in February 1800.

Program of reforms. The Consulate's work of administrative reform, undertaken at Bonaparte's instigation, was to be more lasting than the constitution and so more important for France. At the head of the government was the Council of State, created by the first consul and often effectively presided over by him; it was to play an important part both as the source of the new legislation and as an administrative tribunal. At the head of the administration of the *départements* were the prefects, who carried on the tradition of the intendants of the *ancien régime,* supervising the application of the laws and acting as the instruments of centralization. The judicial system was profoundly changed: whereas from the beginning of the Revolution judges had been elected, henceforth they were to be nominated by the government, their independence assured by their irremovability from office. The police organization was greatly strengthened. The financial administration was considerably improved: instead of the municipalities, special officials were entrusted with the collecting of direct taxes; the franc was stabilized; and the Banque de France, owned partly by shareholders and partly by the state, was created. Education was transformed into a major public service; secondary education was given a semi-military organization, and the university faculties were re-established. Primary education, however, was still neglected.

Bonaparte shared Voltaire's belief that the people needed a religion. Personally, he was indifferent to religion: in Egypt he had said that he wanted to become a Muslim. Yet he considered that religious peace had to be restored to France. As early as 1796, when he was concluding the armistice in Italy with Pope Pius VI, he had tried to persuade the Pope to retract his briefs against the French priests who had accepted the Civil Constitution of the Clergy, which in practice nationalized the church. Pius VII, who succeeded Pius VI in March 1800, was more accommodating than his predecessor, and ten months after negotiations were opened with him a concordat was signed reconciling the church and the Revolution. The Pope recognized the French Republic and called for the resignation of all former bishops; new prelates were to be designated by the First Consul and instituted by the Pope; and the sale of the property of the clergy was officially recognized by Rome. The concordat, in fact, admitted freedom of worship and the lay character of the state.

Religious peace and concordat with Rome

The codification of the civil law, first undertaken in 1790, was at last completed under the Consulate. The code promulgated on March 21, 1804, and later known as the Code Napoléon, gave permanent form to the great gains of the Revolution: individual liberty, freedom of work, freedom of conscience, the lay character of the state, and equality before the law; but, at the same time, it protected landed property, gave greater liberty to employers, and showed little concern for employees. It maintained divorce but granted only limited legal rights to women.

The army received the most careful attention. The First Consul retained in outline the system instituted by the Revolution: recruitment by forced conscription but with the possibility of replacement by substitutes; the mixing of the conscripts with old soldiers; and the eligibility of all for promotion to the highest ranks. Nevertheless, the creation of the Academy of Saint-Cyr to produce infantry officers made it easier for the sons of bourgeois families to pursue a military career. Moreover, the École Polytechnique, founded by the National Convention, was militarized in order to provide officers for the artillery and engineers. Yet Bonaparte was not concerned about introducing new technical inventions into his army. He put his trust in the "legs of his soldiers": his basic strategic idea was a fast-moving army.

Military campaigns and uneasy peace. The First Consul spent the winter and spring of 1799–1800 reorganizing the army and preparing for an attack on Austria alone, Russia having withdrawn from the anti-French coalition. With his usual quick assessment of the situation, he saw the strategic importance of the Swiss Confederation, from which he would be free to outflank the Austrian armies either in Germany or in Italy as he might see fit. His past successes made him choose Italy. Taking his army across the Great St. Bernard Pass before the snow had melted, he appeared unexpectedly behind the Austrian army besieging Genoa. The Battle of Marengo in June gave the French command of the Po Valley as far as the Adige; and in December another French army defeated the Austrians in Germany. Austria was forced to sign the Treaty of Lunéville of February 1801, whereby France's right to the natural frontiers that Julius Caesar had given to Gaul, namely, the Rhine, the Alps, and the Pyrenees, was recognized.

Great Britain alone remained at war with France, but it soon tired of the struggle. Preliminaries of peace, concluded in London in October 1801, put an end to hostilities, and peace was signed at Amiens on March 27, 1802.

General peace was re-established in Europe. The first Consul's prestige increased still more; and his friends—at his suggestion—proposed that a "token of national gratitude" should be offered to him. In May 1802 it was decided that the French people should vote in referendum on the following question: "Shall Napoleon Bonaparte be consul for life?" In August an overwhelming vote granted him the prolongation of his consulate as well as the right to designate his successor.

Consul for life

Bonaparte's conception of international peace differed from that of the British, for whom the Treaty of Amiens represented an absolute limit beyond which they were under no circumstances prepared to go. The British even hoped to take back some of the concessions they had been forced to make. For Bonaparte, on the other hand, the Treaty of Amiens marked the starting point for a new French ascendancy. He was, first of all, intent on reserving half of Europe as a market for France without lowering customs duties—to the indignation of British merchants. To revive France's expansion overseas, he also intended to recover San Domingo (now Hispaniola, which had rebelled), to occupy Louisiana (ceded to France by Spain in 1800), perhaps to reconquer Egypt, and at any rate to extend French influence in the Mediterranean and in the Indian Ocean. Finally, on the Continent of Europe, he advanced beyond France's natural frontiers: incorporating Piedmont into France; imposing a more democratic, decentralized government on the Swiss Confederation; and in Germany compensating the princes dispossessed of territory on the Rhine under the Treaty of Lunéville with shares of the secularized ecclesiastical states.

Great Britain was alarmed by this expansion of France in peacetime and found it scarcely tolerable that one state should command the coastline of the Continent from Genoa to Antwerp. The immediate occasion of Franco-British rupture, however, was the problem of Malta. According to the Treaty of Amiens, the British, who had taken the island on the collapse of the French occupation, should have restored it to the Knights Hospitallers; but the British, on the pretext that the French had not yet evacuated certain Neapolitan ports, refused to leave the island. Franco-British relations became strained, and in May 1803 the British declared war.

THE EMPIRE

The peace settlement had brought about the life consulate; the return of war was to stimulate the formation of the empire. The British government, which would have been glad to see Bonaparte deposed or removed by assassination, renewed its subsidies to the French royalists, who resumed their agitation and plotting. When a British-financed assassination plot was uncovered in 1804, Bonaparte decided to react vigorously enough to deter his opponents from any more such attempts. The police believed that the real head of the conspiracy was the young Duc d'Enghien, a scion of the royal house of Bourbon, who was residing in Germany, a few miles across the frontier. Accordingly, with the agreement of Talleyrand and the police chief Joseph Fouché, the Duc was kidnapped on neutral soil and brought to Vincennes, where he was tried and shot (March 21). This action provoked a resurgence of opposition among the old aristocracy but enhanced the influence of Fouché.

British-financed assassination plot

Founding the empire. In the hope of consolidating his own position, Fouché now suggested to Bonaparte that the best way to discourage conspiracy would be to transform the life consulate into a hereditary empire, which, because of the fact that there would be an heir, would remove all hope of changing the regime by assassination. Bonaparte readily accepted the suggestion, and on May 28, 1804, the empire was proclaimed.

Though there was little change in the organization of the government of France, Napoleon as emperor revived a number of institutions similar to those of the *ancien régime.* In the first place, he wanted to be consecrated by the pope himself, so that his coronation should be even more impressive than that of the kings of France. Pius VII agreed to come to Paris, and the ceremony, which seemed equally outrageous to royalists and to the old soldiers of the Revolution, took place in Notre-Dame on December 2, 1804. At the last moment, the Emperor took the crown from the Pope and set it on his own head himself.

The imperial regime also instituted its symbols and titles. Princely titles were brought back for the members of Napoleon's family in 1804, and an imperial nobility was created in 1808. As opposition was still lively, Napoleon intensified his propaganda and imposed an increasingly strict censorship on the press. A dictatorial regime allowed him to carry on his wars for years without worrying about French public opinion. Having been president of the Italian Republic (as the Cisalpine Republic was renamed) since January 1802, Napoleon in March 1805 was proclaimed king of Italy and crowned in Milan in May.

War with Britain. From 1803 to 1805 Napoleon had only the British to fight; and again France could hope for victory only by landing an army in the British Isles, whereas the British could defeat Napoleon only by forming a continental coalition against him. Napoleon began to prepare an invasion again, this time with greater conviction and on a larger scale. He gathered nearly 2,000 ships between Brest and Antwerp and concentrated his Grande Armée in the camp at Boulogne (1803). Even so, the problem was the same as in 1798: to cross the Channel, the French had to have control of the sea.

Still far inferior to the British Navy, the French fleet needed the help of the Spanish; and even then the two fleets together could not hope to defeat more than one of the British squadrons. Spain was induced to declare war on Great Britain in December 1804, and it was decided that French and Spanish squadrons massed in the Antilles should lure a British squadron into these waters and defeat it, thus making the balance roughly equal between the Franco-Spanish navy and the British. A battle in the entrance to the Channel could then be fought with some chance of success.

Franco-Spanish naval strategy

The plan failed. The French squadron from the Mediterranean, under Adm. Pierre de Villeneuve, found itself alone at the appointed meeting place in the Antilles. Pursued by Nelson and not daring to attack him, it turned back toward Europe and took refuge in Cádiz in July 1805; there the British blockaded it. Accused of cowardice by the angry Napoleon, Villeneuve resolved to run the blockade, with the support of a Spanish squadron; but on October 21, 1805, he was attacked by Nelson off Cape Trafalgar. Nelson was killed in the battle, but the Franco-Spanish fleet was totally destroyed. The British had won a decisive victory, which eliminated the danger of invasion and gave them freedom of movement at sea.

They had also succeeded in organizing a new anti-French coalition consisting of Austria, Russia, Sweden, and Naples. On July 24, 1805, three months before Trafalgar, Napoleon had ordered the Grande Armée from Boulogne to the Danube (thus ruling out an invasion of England even if the French had won at Trafalgar). In the week preceding Trafalgar, the Grande Armée won an outstanding victory over the Austrians at Ulm, and on November 13 Napoleon entered Vienna. On December 2, 1805, in his greatest victory he defeated the combined Austrian and Russian armies in the Battle of Austerlitz. By the Treaty of Pressburg, Austria renounced all influence in Italy and ceded Venetia and Dalmatia to Napoleon, as well as extensive territory in Germany to his protégés Bavaria, Württemberg, and Baden. The French then proceeded to dethrone the Bourbons in the kingdom of Naples, which was bestowed on Napoleon's brother Joseph. In July 1806 the Confederation of the Rhine was founded—soon to embrace all western Germany in a union under French protection.

Victories in Europe

In September 1806 Prussia entered the war against France, and on October 14 the Prussian armies were defeated at Jena and at Auerstädt. The Russians put up a better resistance at Eylau in February 1807 but were routed at Friedland in June. In Warsaw Napoleon fell in love with Countess Marie Walewska, a Polish patriot who hoped that Napoleon would resurrect her country. Napoleon had a son by her.

The Russian emperor Alexander I could have continued the struggle, but he was tired of the alliance with the British. He met Napoleon at Tilsit, in northern Prussia near the Russian frontier. There, on a raft anchored in the middle of the Niemen River, they signed treaties that created the Grand Duchy of Warsaw from the Polish provinces detached from Prussia and, in effect, divided control of Europe between the emperors, Napoleon taking the west and Alexander the east. Alexander even made a vague promise of a land attack against the British possessions in India.

Blockade and the peninsular campaign. As Napoleon could no longer think of invading England, he tried to induce capitulation by stifling the British economy. By closing all of Europe to British merchandise, he hoped to bring about a revolt of the British unemployed that could force the government to sue for peace. He forbade all trade with the British Isles, ordered the confiscation of all goods coming from English factories or from the British colonies, and condemned as fair prize not only every British ship but also every ship that had touched the coasts of England or its colonies.

For the blockade to succeed, it had to be enforced rigorously throughout Europe. But from the beginning, England's old ally Portugal showed itself reluctant to comply, for the blockade would mean its commercial ruin. Napoleon decided to break down Portuguese opposition by force. Charles IV of Spain let the French troops cross his kingdom, and they occupied Lisbon; but the prolonged presence of Napoleon's soldiers in the north of Spain led to insurrection. When Charles IV abdicated in favour of his son Ferdinand VII, Napoleon, seeing the opportunity to rid Europe of its last Bourbon rulers, summoned the Spanish royal family to Bayonne in April 1808 and obtained the abdication of both Charles and Ferdinand; they were interned in Talleyrand's château. After the bloody suppression of an uprising in Madrid, insurrection spread across the whole country, for the Spaniards would not accept Joseph Bonaparte, king of Naples, as their new king.

Defeats in Spain and Portugal

The subsequent defeat of his forces in Spain and Portugal were sensational blows to Napoleon's prestige. Soon the Iberian Peninsula, up in arms, became a bridgehead on the Continent for the British. Under the energetic Arthur Wellesley (later 1st duke of Wellington), in command from 1809, the Anglo-Spanish-Portuguese forces were to achieve decisive successes.

At the Congress of Erfurt (September–October 1808), a conference with Alexander I, Napoleon assembled a great concourse of princes to impress the Russian emperor in an attempt to extract promises of help. Whether impressed or not, Alexander would make no definite commitment. Alexander's refusal, furthermore, was partly prompted by Talleyrand, who had become dismayed by Napoleon's policies and was already negotiating with the Russian emperor behind his master's back.

By early 1809, however, with most of the Grande Armée thrown into Spain, Napoleon seemed on the point of overcoming the revolt. Then, in April, Austria launched an attack in Bavaria in the hope of rousing all Germany against the French. Napoleon once again defeated the Habsburgs (July 6) and by the Treaty of Schönbrunn (October 14, 1809) obtained the Illyrian Provinces, thus rounding out the continental system.

Consolidation of empire. In 1810 Napoleon's fortunes were at their zenith, despite some failures in Spain and Portugal. He considered himself Charlemagne's heir. He repudiated Joséphine, who had not given him a child, so that he could marry Marie-Louise, daughter of the Austrian emperor Francis I. The birth of a son, the king of Rome, in March 1811 seemed to assure the future of his empire—now at its greatest extent, including not only the Illyrian Provinces but also Etruria (Tuscany), some of the Papal States, Holland, and the German states bordering the North Sea. The empire was surrounded by a ring of vassal states ruled over by the Emperor's relatives: the Kingdom of Westphalia (Jérôme Bonaparte); the Kingdom of Spain (Joseph Bonaparte); the Kingdom of Italy (with Eugène de Beauharnais, Joséphine's son, as viceroy); the Kingdom of Naples (Joachim Murat, Napoleon's brother-in-law); and the Principality of Lucca and Piombino (Félix Bacciochi, another brother-in-law). Finally, other territories were closely bound to the empire by treaties: the Swiss Confederation (of which Napoleon was the mediator), the Confederation of the Rhine, and the Grand Duchy of Warsaw. Even Austria seemed bound to France by Napoleon's marriage to Marie-Louise.

European unity and the roots of new nationalisms

The political map of Europe, which had been so complicated before 1796, was now greatly simplified. Yet the frontiers did not coincide either with geographical features or with "nationalities." Whatever he may later have said, Napoleon, while he was in power, was not interested in realizing either German or Italian unity. Yet by reducing the number of states, by pushing the frontiers about, by amalgamating populations, and by propagating institutions like those that the Revolution and nationalism had created in France, he prepared the ground for German and Italian unification. National feeling in Europe, stirred by French ideas and by contact with Frenchmen, in turn gave rise to the first resistance against French domination. From 1809 onward Spanish guerrillas, supported by British troops, were harassing the French, and the national Cortes, convened at Cádiz by the insurrectionaries, in 1812, promulgated a constitution inspired by the ideas of the French Revolution of 1789 and by British institutions.

Disaster in Russia and its aftermath. Since the Congress of Erfurt, the Russian emperor had shown himself less and less inclined to deal with Napoleon as a trusted partner. In the spring of 1812, therefore, Napoleon massed his forces in Poland to intimidate Alexander. After some last attempts at agreement, in late June his Grande Armée—about 453,000 men, including contingents extorted from Prussia and from Austria—began to cross the Niemen River. The Russians retreated, adopting a "scorched earth" policy. Napoleon's army did not reach the approaches to Moscow until the beginning of September. The Russian commander in chief, Mikhail I. Kutuzov, engaged it at Borodino on September 7. The fight was savage, bloody, and indecisive, but a week later Napoleon entered Moscow, which the Russians had abandoned. On that same day, a huge fire broke out, destroying the greater part of the town. Moreover, Alexander unexpectedly refused to treat with Napoleon. Withdrawal was necessary, and the premature onset of winter made it disastrous. After the difficult crossing of the Berezina River in November, fewer than 10,000 men fit for combat remained with Napoleon's main force.

This catastrophe heartened all the peoples of Europe to defy Napoleon. In Germany the news unleashed an outbreak of anti-French demonstrations. The Prussian contingents deserted the Grande Armée in December and turned against the French. The Austrians also withdrew their troops and adopted an increasingly hostile attitude, and in Italy the people began to turn their backs on Napoleon.

Attempted coup d'etat in Paris

Even in France, signs of discontent with the regime were becoming more frequent. In Paris a malcontent general nearly succeeded in carrying out a coup d'etat after announcing, on October 23, 1812, that Napoleon had died in Russia. This incident was a major factor in Napoleon's decision to hasten back to France ahead of the Grande Armée. Arriving in Paris on December 18, he proceeded to stiffen the dictatorship, to raise money by various expedients, and to levy new troops.

Thus, in 1813 the forces arrayed against France were no longer armies of mercenaries but were those of nations fighting for their freedom as the French had fought for theirs in 1792 and 1793; and the French themselves, for all their courage, had lost their former enthusiasm. The Emperor's ideal of conquest was no longer that of the nation.

In May 1813 Napoleon won some successes against the Russians and Prussians at the battles of Lützen and Bautzen, but his decimated army needed reinforcements. The armed mediation of Austria induced Napoleon to agree to an armistice, during which a congress was held at Prague. There, Austria proposed very favourable conditions: the French Empire was to return to its natural limits; the Grand Duchy of Warsaw and the Confederation of the Rhine were to be dissolved; and Prussia was to return to its frontiers of 1805. Napoleon made the mistake of hesitating too long. The congress closed on August 10 before his reply arrived, and Austria declared war.

The French were even worse off than in the spring. The allies were gaining new troops every day, as one German contingent after another left Napoleon to go over to the other side. The greatest debacle since Napoleon came to power was the Battle of Leipzig, or "Battle of the Nations" (October 16–19, 1813), in which the Grande Armée was torn to shreds. That defeat degenerated fast into collapse. The French armies in Spain, forced to retreat, had been defeated in June; and by October the British were attacking their defenses north of the Pyrenees. In Italy the Austrians took the offensive, crossed the Adige River, and occupied Romagna. Murat, now openly a traitor to the Emperor who had made him king of Naples, entered into negotiations with the Viennese court. The Dutch and the Belgians demonstrated against Napoleon.

Downfall and abdication. In January 1814 France was being attacked on all its frontiers. The allies cleverly announced that they were fighting not against the French people but against Napoleon alone, since in November 1813 he had rejected the terms offered by the Austrian foreign minister Metternich, which would have preserved the natural frontiers of France. The extraordinary strategic feats achieved by the Emperor during the first three months of 1814 with the army of young conscripts were not enough; he could neither defeat the allies, with their overwhelming numerical superiority, nor arouse the majority of French people from their resentful torpor. The Legislative Assembly and the Senate, formerly so docile, were now asking for peace and for civil and political liberties.

Four-nation pact against Napoleon

By the Treaty of Chaumont of March 1814, Austria, Russia, Prussia, and Great Britain bound themselves together for 20 years, undertook not to negotiate separately, and promised to continue the struggle until Napoleon was overthrown. When the allied armies arrived before Paris on March 30, Napoleon had moved east to attack their rear guard. The Parisian authorities, no longer overawed by the Emperor, lost no time in treating with the allies. As president of the provisional government, Talleyrand proclaimed the deposition of the Emperor and, without consulting the French people, began to negotiate with Louis XVIII, the brother of the executed Louis XVI. Napoleon had only reached Fontainebleau when he heard that Paris had capitulated. Persuaded that further resistance was useless, he finally abdicated on April 6.

By the Treaty of Fontainebleau, the allies granted him the island of Elba as a sovereign principality with an annual income of 2,000,000 francs to be provided by France and a guard of 400 volunteers; also, he retained the title of emperor. After unsuccessfully trying to poison himself, Napoleon spoke his farewell to his "Old Guard," and after a hazardous journey, during which he narrowly escaped assassination, he arrived at Elba on May 4.

ELBA AND THE HUNDRED DAYS

"I want from now on to live like a justice of the peace," Napoleon declared on his little island. But a man of such energy and imagination could hardly be expected to resign himself to defeat at the age of 45.

In France, moreover, the Bourbon Restoration was soon exposed to criticism. Though in 1814 the majority of the French people were tired of the Emperor, they had expressed no wish for the return of the Bourbons. They were strongly attached to the essential achievements of the Revolution, and Louis XVIII had come back "in the baggage train of the foreigners" with the last surviving émigrés who had "learnt nothing and forgotten nothing" and whose influence seemed to threaten most of the Revolution's achievements. The apathy of April 1814 quickly gave way to mistrust. Old hatreds were revived, resistance organized, and conspiracies formed.

From Elba, Napoleon kept a close watch on the Continent. He knew that some of the diplomats at Vienna, where a congress was deciding the fate of Europe, considered Elba, between Corsica and Italy, too close to France and to Italy and wanted to banish him to a distant island in the Atlantic. Also, he accused Austria of preventing Marie Louise and his son from coming to join him (in fact, she had taken a lover and had no intention of going to live with her husband). Finally, the French government refused to pay Napoleon's allowance so that he was in danger of being reduced to penury.

Napoleon's return to France

All these considerations drove Napoleon to action. Decisive as ever, he returned to France like a thunderbolt. On March 1, 1815, he landed at Cannes with a detachment of his guard. As he crossed the Alps, the republican peasants rallied round him, and near Grenoble he won over the soldiers dispatched to arrest him. On March 20 he was in Paris.

Napoleon was brought back to power as the embodiment of the spirit of the Revolution rather than as the emperor who had fallen a year before. To rally the mass of Frenchmen to his cause he should have allied himself with the Jacobins; but this he dared not do. Unable to escape from the bourgeoisie whose predominance he himself had assured and who feared above all else a revival of the socialist experiments of 1793 and 1794, he could only set up a political regime scarcely distinguishable from that of Louis XVIII. Enthusiasm ebbed fast, and the Napoleonic adventure seemed a dead end.

To oppose the allied troops massing on the frontiers, Napoleon mustered an army with which he marched into Belgium and defeated the Prussians at Ligny on June 16, 1815. Two days later, at Waterloo, he met the British under Wellington, the victor of the Peninsular War. A savage battle followed. Napoleon was in sight of victory when the Prussians under Gebhard Blücher arrived to reinforce the British, and soon, despite the heroism of the Old Guard, Napoleon was overthrown.

Back in Paris, Parliament forced Napoleon to abdicate; he did so, in favour of his son, on June 22, 1815. On July 3 he was at Rochefort, intending to take ship for the United States, but a British squadron prevented any French vessel from leaving the port. Napoleon then decided to appeal to the British government for protection. His request granted, he boarded the "Bellerophon" on July 15. The allies were agreed on one point: Napoleon was not to go back to Elba. Nor did they like the idea of his going off to America. It would have suited them if he had fallen a victim to the "White Terror" of the returned counter-revolutionaries or if Louis XVIII had had him summarily tried and executed. Great Britain had no choice but to send him to detention in a far-off island. The British government announced that the island of Saint Helena in the southern Atlantic had been chosen for his residence; because of its remote position Napoleon would enjoy much greater freedom than would be possible elsewhere. Napoleon protested eloquently: "I appeal to history!"

EXILE ON SAINT HELENA

On October 15, 1815, Napoleon disembarked in Saint Helena with those followers who were voluntarily accompanying him into exile: Gen. Henri-Gratien Bertrand, grand marshal of the palace, and his wife; the comte Charles de Montholon, aide-de-camp, and his wife; Gen. Gaspard Gourgaud; Emmanuel Las Cases, the former chamberlain;

and several servants. After a short stay at the house of a wealthy English merchant, they moved to Longwood, originally built for the lieutenant governor.

Daily life at St. Helena

Napoleon settled down to a life of routine. He got up late, breakfasting about 10 AM, but seldom went out. He was free to go anywhere on the island so long as he was accompanied by an English officer, but he soon refused to comply with this condition and so shut himself up in the grounds of Longwood. He wrote and talked much. At first Las Cases acted as his secretary, compiling what was later to be the *Mémorial de Sainte-Hélène* (first published in 1823). From 7 to 8 PM Napoleon had dinner, after which a part of the evening was spent in reading aloud—Napoleon liked to hear the classics. Then they played cards. About midnight Napoleon went to bed. Some of his time was devoted to learning English, and he eventually began reading English newspapers; but he also had a large number of French books sent from Europe, which he read attentively and annotated.

Saint Helena has a healthful climate, and Napoleon's food was good, carefully prepared, and plentiful. His inactivity undoubtedly contributed to the deterioration of his health. The man who for 20 years had played so great a role in the world and who had marched north, south, east, and west across Europe could hardly be expected to endure the monotony of existence on a little island, aggravated by a self-imposed life of a recluse. He had also more intimate reasons for unhappiness: Marie-Louise sent no word to him, and he may have learned of her liaison with the Austrian officer appointed to watch over her, Graf Adam von Neipperg (whom she eventually married in secret without waiting for Napoleon's death); nor did he have any news of his son, the former king of Rome, who was now living in Vienna with the title of duke of Reichstadt. Finally, though the severity of Sir Hudson Lowe has been much exaggerated, it is certain that this "jailer," who arrived as governor of Saint Helena in April 1816, did nothing to make Napoleon's life easier. Napoleon from the start disliked him as the former commander of the Corsican rangers, a band of volunteers largely composed of enemies of the Bonaparte family. Always anxious to carry out his instructions exactly, Lowe came into conflict with Las Cases. He saw Las Cases as Napoleon's confidant and had him arrested and expelled. Thenceforward, relations between the governor and Napoleon were limited strictly to those stipulated by the regulations.

First signs of illness

Napoleon showed the first signs of illness at the end of 1817; he seems to have had an ulcer or a cancer of the stomach. The Irish doctor Barry O'Meara, having asked in vain for a change in the conditions under which Napoleon lived, was dismissed; so also was his successor John Stokoe, who was likewise thought to be well-disposed toward Napoleon. The undistinguished Corsican doctor who took their place, Francesco Antommarchi, prescribed a treatment that could do nothing to cure his patient. It is uncertain, however, whether Napoleon's disease was curable at all, even by 20th-century methods.

From the beginning of 1821, the illness became rapidly worse. From March, Napoleon was confined to bed. In April he dictated his last will:

> I wish my ashes to rest on the banks of the Seine, in the midst of that French people which I have loved so much. . . . I die before my time, killed by the English oligarchy and its hired assassins.

On May 5 he spoke a few coherent phrases: "My God . . . The French nation . . . my son . . . head of the army. . . . " He died at 5:49 PM on that day, not yet 52 years old. His body was dressed in his favourite uniform, that of the Chasseurs de la Garde, covered by the gray overcoat that he had worn at Marengo. The funeral was conducted simply, but with due propriety, in the Rupert Valley, where Napoleon had sometimes walked, beside a stream in which two willows were reflected. The stone covering his tomb bore no name, only the words *"Ci-Gît"* ("Here Lies").

THE NAPOLEONIC LEGEND

Napoleon's fall had set loose a torrent of hostile books designed to sully his reputation. One of the least violent of these was the pamphlet *De Buonaparte, des Bourbons, et de la nécessité de se rallier à nos princes légitimes* (1814; *On Buonaparte and the Bourbons, and the Necessity of Rallying Around Our Legitimate Princes, for the Safety of France and of Europe*) by François de Chateaubriand, a well-known writer of royalist sympathies. But this anti-Napoleonic literature soon died down, while the task of defending Napoleon was taken up. Lord Byron had published his "Ode to Napoleon Buonaparte" as early as 1814; the German poet Heinrich Heine wrote his ballad "Die Grenadiere"; and in 1817 the French novelist Stendhal began his biography *Vie de Napoléon*. At the same time, the Emperor's most faithful supporters were working toward his rehabilitation, talking about him, and distributing reminders of him, including engravings. They idealized his life ("What a novel my life is!" he himself had said) and began to create the Napoleonic legend.

Early memoirs and chronicles

As soon as the Emperor was dead, the legend grew rapidly. Memoirs, notes, and narratives by those who had followed him into exile contributed substantially to it. In 1822 Dr. O'Meara, in London, had his *Napoleon in Exile, or a Voice from Saint Helena* published; in 1823 the publication of the *Mémoires pour servir à l'histoire de France sous Napoléon, écrits à Sainte-Hélène sous sa dictée* (*Memoirs of the History of France during the Reign of Napoleon, Dictated by the Emperor at St. Helena*) by Montholon and Gourgaud, began; Las Cases, in his famous *Mémorial*, presented the Emperor as a republican opposed to war who had fought only when Europe forced him to fight in defense of freedom; and in 1825 Antommarchi published his *Derniers moments de Napoléon*. Thereafter the number of works in Napoleon's honour increased continually; among them were Victor Hugo's "Ode à la Colonne," the 28 volumes of the *Victoires et conquêtes des Français*, and Sir Walter Scott's *Life of Napoleon Buonaparte, Emperor of the French*. Neither police action nor prosecutions could prevent books, pictures, and objects evoking the imperial saga from multiplying in France.

After the July Revolution of 1830, which created the bourgeois monarchy under Louis-Philippe, thousands of tricolour flags appeared in windows, and the government had not only to tolerate the growth of the legend but even to promote it. In 1833 the statue of Napoleon was put back on the top of the column in the Place Vendôme in Paris; and in 1840 the King's son François, prince de Joinville, was sent in a warship to fetch the Emperor's remains from Saint Helena to the banks of the Seine in accordance with his last wishes. A magnificent funeral was held in Paris in December 1840, and Napoleon's body was conveyed through the Arc de Triomphe in the Place de l'Étoile to entombment under the dome of the Invalides.

Napoleon's nephew Louis-Napoleon exploited the legend in order to seize power in France. Though his attempts at Strasbourg in 1836 and at Boulogne in 1840 were failures, it was chiefly because of the growth of the legend that he won election to the presidency of the Second Republic with an overwhelming majority in 1848 and was able to carry out the coup d'etat of December 1851 and make himself emperor in 1852.

The disastrous end of the Second Empire in 1870 damaged the Napoleonic legend and gave rise to a new anti-Napoleonic literature, best represented by Hippolyte Taine's *Origines de la France contemporaine* (1876–94). World Wars I and II, however, together with the experience of the 20th-century dictatorships, made it possible to judge Napoleon more fairly. Any comparison with Stalin or Hitler, for instance, can only be to Napoleon's advantage.

Assessment and legacy

He was tolerant, he released the Jews from the ghettoes, and he showed respect for human life. Brought up on the rationalist *Encyclopédie* and on the writings of the Philosophes of the Enlightenment, he remained above all a man of the 18th century, the last of the "enlightened despots." One of the gravest accusations made against Napoleon is that he was the "Corsican ogre" who sacrificed millions of men to his ambition. Precise calculations show that the Napoleonic Wars of 1800–15 cost France itself about 500,000 men; *i.e.,* about one-sixtieth of the population. The loss of these young men, furthermore, seems to have had a notably adverse effect on the birth rate.

The social structure of France changed little under the First Empire. It remained roughly what the Revolution had made it: a great mass of peasants comprising three quarters of the population—about half of them working owners of their farms or sharecroppers and the other half with too little land for their own subsistence and hiring themselves out as labourers. Industry, stimulated by the war and the blockade of English goods, made remarkable progress in northern and eastern France, whence exports could be sent to central Europe; but it declined in the south and west because of the closing of the Mediterranean and the Atlantic. The great migrations from rural areas toward industry in the towns began only after 1815. The nobility would probably have declined more swiftly if Napoleon had not restored it; but it could never recover its former privileges.

Above all, Napoleon left durable institutions, the "granite masses" on which modern France has been built up: the administrative system of the prefects, the Code Napoléon, the judicial system, the Banque de France and the country's financial organization, the universities, and the military academies. Napoleon changed the history of France and of the world. (J.Go.)

BIBLIOGRAPHY

Sources: An enormous mass of documents is dispersed throughout the archives of Europe, but the essential source is *Correspondance de Napoléon I*, 32 vol. (1858–69, reprinted in 1974), published on command of Napoleon III, with the *Oeuvres de Napoléon à Sainte-Hélène*, 4 vol. (1870). In 1967 the *Oeuvres littéraires et écrits militaires* of Napoleon were published in 3 volumes. In English are *The Bonaparte Letters and Dispatches . . . from the Originals in His Private Cabinet*, 2 vol. (1846); *The Confidential Correspondence of Napoleon Bonaparte with His Brother Joseph . . .*, 2 vol. (1855); and the *Unpublished Correspondence of Napoleon I, Preserved in the War Archives*, 3 vol. (1913). The principal ideas of Napoleon may be found in the following works: R.M. JOHNSTON (comp.), *The Corsican: A Diary of Napoleon's Life in His Own Words* (1910); JAMES M. THOMPSON, *Napoleon Self-Revealed* (1934); J. CHRISTOPHER HEROLD (ed.), *The Mind of Napoleon* (1955); ANDRÉ PALLUEL (ed.), *Dictionnaire de l'Empereur* (1969); and *Pensées politiques et sociales de Napoléon*, ed. by ADRIEN DANSETTE (1969). For Napoleon's itinerary, see ALBERT SCHUERMANS, *Itinéraire général de Napoléon Ier* (1906); and LOUIS GARRES, *Itinéraire de Napoléon Bonaparte* (1947).

General biographies: PIERRE LANFREY, *The History of Napoleon the First*, 2nd ed. (1886, reprinted 1973; originally published in French, 1867–75), a hostile work written at the end of the Second Empire; AUGUST FOURNIER, *Napoleon I* (1911; originally published in German, 1886), an impartial study written by an Austrian historian; FRÉDÉRIC MASSON, *Napoléon et sa famille*, 13 vol. (1897–1919), which furnishes numerous details on the everyday life of Napoleon and his relationships with his relatives; J. HOLLAND ROSE, *The Life of Napoleon I*, 2 vol. (1902), an apologetic work; JAMES M. THOMPSON, *Napoleon Bonaparte: His Rise and Fall* (1952), an excellent rectification; E.V. TARLE, *Bonaparte* (trans. from Russian, 1937), the point of view of a Soviet historian; FELIX MARKHAM, *Napoleon* (1963), an objective study; JEAN MISTLER, *Napoléon et l'Empire* (1968, reissued 1979), a magnificently illustrated work, each chapter written by a specialist; ANDRÉ CASTELOT, *Napoléon* (1971; originally published in French, 1968), a vulgarized book that realized great success in France; JACQUES GODECHOT, *Napoléon* (1969), an essay and an empirical study (in French).

Specialized biographies: On Napoleon's youth, a basic work is that of ARTHUR CHUQUET, *La Jeunesse de Napoléon*, 3 vol. (1897–99). On the more intimate life of Napoleon, see ARTHUR LÉVY, *Napoléon intime*, 7th ed. (1932); and FRÉDÉRIC MASSON, *Napoleon at Home*, 2 vol. (1894; originally published in French, 1894). On Napoleon's health, see JAMES KEMBLE, *Napoleon Immortal* (1959).

Specialized studies: MABEL BROOKES, *St. Helena Story* (1960); NORMAN MACKENZIE, *The Escape from Elba: The Fall and Flight of Napoleon, 1814–1815* (1982), a popular account of his 10 months on Elba; JEAN LUCAS-DUBRETON, *Le Culte de Napoléon, 1815–1848* (1960), a definitive study of the Napoleonic legend; HUGH RAGSDALE, *Détente in the Napoleonic Era: Bonaparte and the Russians* (1980); and EDWARD A. WHITCOMB, *Napoleon's Diplomatic Service* (1979).

Films: Many films have been produced on the life of Napoleon. The best, *Napoléon* (1925) and *Austerlitz* (1960), are by ABEL GANCE. The film *War and Peace* (1967), adapted from the novel by Tolstoy and produced by the Soviet director SERGEI BONDARTCHUK, gives a valid reconstruction of the imperial era.

Navigation

Navigation, a word derived from the Latin *navis,* "ship," and *agere,* "to drive," originally denoted the art of ship driving, including steering and setting the sails. The skill itself is even more ancient than the word, and it has evolved over the course of many centuries into a science and a technology that encompasses the planning and execution of safe, timely, and economical operation of watercraft, aircraft, and spacecraft.

Many animals can find their way home from considerable distances by remembering what they saw or smelled along the way. A honeybee returning to its hive with food performs a dance to communicate to its fellows the direction (relative to the Sun) and distance (as far as six miles [10 kilometres]) they should fly to reach the source of the food. Many birds migrate thousands of miles, orienting themselves by the Sun and stars. Such pathfinding feats, which are treated in the article BEHAVIOUR, ANIMAL: *Migratory behaviour,* have undoubtedly been performed since long before human sailors first ventured out of sight of land, but detailed investigation of these activities has made no direct contribution to the analogous skills that have been perfected by human navigators.

Early mariners who embarked on voyages of exploration gradually developed systematic methods of observing and recording their position, the distances and directions they traveled, the currents of wind and water, and the hazards and havens they encountered. The facts accumulated in their journals made it possible for them to find their way home and for them or their successors to repeat and extend their exploits. Each new landfall became a signpost along a route that could be retraced and integrated into a growing body of reliable information.

For these pathfinders, the danger of running into another vessel was of negligible concern, but as heavy traffic developed along established routes, collision avoidance became a serious matter. In all fields of navigation, emphasis shifted from finding the way to maintaining an appropriate distance between craft moving in various directions at different speeds. The larger a ship is, the easier it is to see, but, by the same token, the larger a ship is, the more time it requires to change its speed or direction. When many ships are in a small area, an action taken by one to avoid colliding with another may endanger a third. This problem has been alleviated near busy seaports by confining incoming and outgoing ships to separate lanes, which are clearly marked and divided by the greatest practical distance. Airplanes travel so fast that even though two pilots may see one another in time to initiate evasive action, their maneuvers may be nullified if either one incorrectly predicts the other's move. Ground-based air traffic controllers are charged with the responsibility for assigning aircraft to selected paths that minimize the likelihood of collision. Civil air navigation is profoundly influenced by the requirements of following the instructions of these controllers.

The advent of steam-powered ships during the first half of the 19th century added the problem of fuel consumption to the navigator's duties. In the air as well as at sea, the need to carry large amounts of fuel for long trips reduces the cargo capacity; even if plenty of fuel is on board, economy requires that its consumption be kept to a minimum. In spaceflight, fuel is a major navigational consideration. The route to be followed and even the moment for lift-off must be chosen to keep the fuel requirements as small as possible.

Adherence to a predetermined schedule, a matter of vital importance in space navigation in connection with fuel consumption, has become important in sea and air navigation for a different reason. Today each voyage or flight is a single link in a coordinated network of transport that carries people and goods from any starting place to any chosen destination. The efficient operation of the whole system depends upon assurance that each journey will begin and end at the specified times.

Modern navigation, in short, has to do with the whole of a preconceived passage, from start to finish, and is concerned with four basics: selecting the course (and staying on it); avoiding collision with other moving ships and crashing into fixed obstacles; minimizing fuel consumption; and conforming to a timetable. (E.W.A./Ed.)

This article deals with the methods and devices integral to the science of navigation. It also provides a brief historical survey of their development. For additional information about these instruments and systems, see the articles MEASUREMENT AND OBSERVATION, PRINCIPLES, METHODS, AND INSTRUMENTS OF: *Radar;* TRANSPORTATION; AUTOMATION; EXPLORATION: *Space exploration;* and COMPUTERS.

The article is divided into the following sections:

DEVELOPMENT OF MARINE NAVIGATION

The earliest navigators probably learned to steer their ships between distant ports by familiarizing themselves with the sequences of intervening landmarks. Keeping these reference points in view required them to stay quite close to shore, but they made the transition to ocean voyages well out of sight of land thousands of years ago in various parts of the world. Regular trade was carried on between the island of Crete and Egypt, a distance of approximately 300 miles (500 kilometres), more than 25 centuries before the Christian Era. A passage in the *Odyssey* describes such a voyage from Crete: running before a north wind, sailing ships reached the mouth of the Nile in five days. Longer and longer routes became established by later sailors. By 600 BC the Phoenicians were routinely importing tin from Cornwall. Well before the 10th century AD, Irish seafarers successively reached the Shetland Islands, the Faeroe Islands, and Iceland, crossing 200 to 300 miles of the North Atlantic at each stage. The Vikings repeated those passages and ventured even farther, settling Greenland and visiting North America. In about AD 400, Polynesian navigators had reached Hawaii from the Marquesas Islands, 2,300 miles (3,700 kilometres) across the open Pacific.

Ancient sea voyages

Direction finding. The details of how these voyagers found their way are not known, but the use of the Sun and stars as guides is mentioned in many sources, including the works of Homer and Herodotus, the Bible, and the Norse sagas.

East and west are traditionally synonymous with the directions of sunrise and sunset; north and south are determined by the directions of shadows cast by the noonday Sun. By night the stars rise in the east and set in the west, and in the Northern Hemisphere their apparent rotation around the Pole Star has long been a fact of the navigator's life.

For many centuries practical navigators oriented themselves by relying just as strongly on meteorological clues (the directions from which steady winds blew) as on astronomical ones (the positions and apparent motions of the Sun and stars). The Mediterranean sailor could confidently distinguish the cold north wind from the warm south wind. Names were assigned to eight principal winds, and the directions of these winds became the eight equally

Wind rose

spaced points of the wind rose (*rosa ventorum*) of the classical mariner. The wind rose may have been devised by the Etruscans, whose power reached its peak around the 6th century BC; it certainly antedates the octagonal Tower of the Winds built in Athens by Andronicus of Cyrrhus in about 100 BC. From Roman times through the Middle Ages, an alternative 12-point wind rose was used by some navigators, but it was discarded in the 15th century when the Portuguese, at the opening of the great age of discovery, subdivided the eight points of the ancients and introduced a 16-point system.

Sailing instructions. The first written aid to coastal navigation was the pilot book, or periplus, in which the courses to be steered between ports were set forth in terms of wind directions. These books, of which examples survive from the 4th century BC, described routes, headlands, landmarks, anchorages, currents, and port entrances. No doubt the same information had formerly been passed along by word of mouth, as it still is in some parts of the world. It seems improbable that any sort of sea chart was used with these sailing guides, even though Herodotus' map of the known world, drawn in the 5th century BC, delineated the Mediterranean shoreline quite accurately. Reliable sea charts were not introduced until the advent of the magnetic compass (see below) and of methods for determining latitude and longitude.

Distance and speed measurements. Distances were cited in the early pilot books in units of a day's sail. Later, distances were deduced from estimates of the ship's speed and the lengths of time over which these speeds were

Maritime logs

maintained. Probably the oldest method of determining the speed is the so-called Dutchman's log, in which a floating object, the log, was dropped overboard from the bow of the ship; the time elapsing before it passed the stern was counted off by the navigator, who kept it in sight while walking the length of the vessel. This technique was eventually replaced by that in which the log, attached to a reel of light line, was dropped from the stern; as the ship moved away from the log, the length of line paid out during the emptying of a sandglass was the measure of the speed. In 1637 the English navigator Richard Norwood recommended the use of a line knotted at intervals of 47¼ feet (14.3 metres) and a 28-second sandglass; if the first knot appeared as the sand ran out, the ship's speed was 6,076 feet (1,852 metres [one nautical mile]) per hour, or one knot. As early as 1688 an English instrument maker, Humphry Cole, invented the so-called patent log, in which a vaned rotor was towed from the stern, and its revolutions were counted on a register. Logs of this kind did not become common until the mid-19th century, when the register was mounted on the taffrail, where it could be read at any time; another Englishman, Thomas Walker, introduced successive refinements of the patent log beginning in 1861. This form of log is still in use. (M.W.Ri.)

The magnetic compass. *Development.* It is not known where or when it was discovered that the lodestone (a mineral composed of an iron oxide) aligns itself in a north–south direction, as will a piece of iron that has been magnetized by contact with a lodestone. Neither is it known where or when marine navigators first availed themselves of these discoveries. Plausible records indicate that the Chinese were using the magnetic compass around AD 1100, western Europeans by 1187, Arabs by 1220, and Scandinavians by 1300. The device could have originated in each of these groups, or it could have been passed from one to the others. All of them had been making long voyages, relying on steady winds to guide them and sightings of the Sun or a familiar star to inform them of any change. When the magnetic compass was introduced, it probably was used merely to check the direction of the wind when clouds obscured the sky.

The first mariner's compass may have consisted of a magnetized needle attached to a wooden splinter or a reed floating on water in a bowl. In a later version the needle was pivoted on a pin fixed to the bottom of the bowl. By the 13th century a card bearing a painted wind rose was mounted on the needle; the navigator could then simply read his heading from the card. So familiar has this combination become that it is called the compass, although that word originally signified the division of the horizon. The suspension of the compass bowl in gimbals (originally used to keep lamps upright on tossing ships) was first mentioned in 1537.

On early compass cards the north point was emphasized by a broad spearhead and the letter *T* for tramontana, the name given to the north wind. About 1490 a combination of these evolved into the fleur-de-lis, still almost universally used. The east point, pointing toward the Holy Land, was marked with a cross; the ornament into which this cross developed continued on British compass cards well into the 19th century (see Figure 1). The use of 32 points by sailors of northern Europe, usually attributed to Flemish compass makers, is mentioned by Geoffrey Chaucer in his *Treatise on the Astrolabe* (written in 1391). It also has been said that the navigators of Amalfi, Italy, first expanded the number of compass points to 32, and they may have been the first to attach the card to the needle.

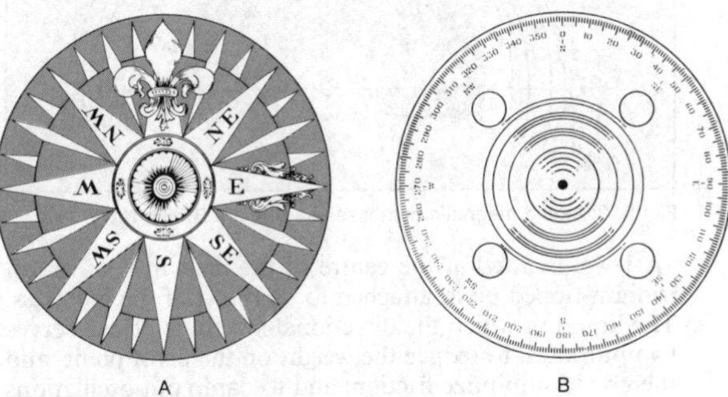

Figure 1: *Compass cards.*
(A) Eighteenth-century compass card divided into points and having ornamentation at the east point. (B) U.S. Navy compass card made of metal with graduations perforated through it.

During the 15th century it became apparent that the compass needle did not point true north from all locations but made an angle with the local meridian. This phenomenon was originally called by seamen the northeasting of the needle but is now called the variation or declination. For a time, compass makers in northern countries mounted the needle askew on the card so that when the needle pointed to magnetic north the fleur-de-lis indicated true north. This practice died out about 1700 because it succeeded only for short voyages near the place where the compass was made; it caused confusion and difficulty on longer trips, especially in crossing the Atlantic to the American coast, where the declination was west instead of east as in Europe. The declination in a given location varies over time. For example, in northern Europe in the 16th century the magnetic north pole was east of true geographic north; in subsequent centuries it has drifted to the west.

Compass variation

Despite its acknowledged value, the magnetic compass long remained a fragile, troublesome, and unreliable instrument, subject to mysterious disturbances. The introduction of iron and then steel for hulls and engines in the 19th century caused further concern because it was well known that nearby ironwork would deflect the compass needle. In 1837 the British Admiralty set up a committee to seek rational methods of ensuring the accuracy of compasses installed on iron ships. In 1840 the committee introduced a new design that proved so successful that it was promptly adopted by all of the principal navies of the world. Further refinements, aimed at reducing the effects of engine vibration and the shock of gunfire, continued throughout the century.

The modern magnetic compass. The liquid magnetic compass (see Figure 2), now almost universally used, is commonly accompanied by an azimuth instrument for taking bearings of distant objects. The compass consists of a set of steel needles with a compass card, attached to a float, in a bowl of water and alcohol. In modern instruments, the magnetic element is often in the form of a ring magnet, fitted within the float. The card is usually of mica or plastic with photographically printed graduations; metal cards with perforated graduations also are used. Cards are usually graduated clockwise from 0° at north to 359°, with the eight principal points indicated.

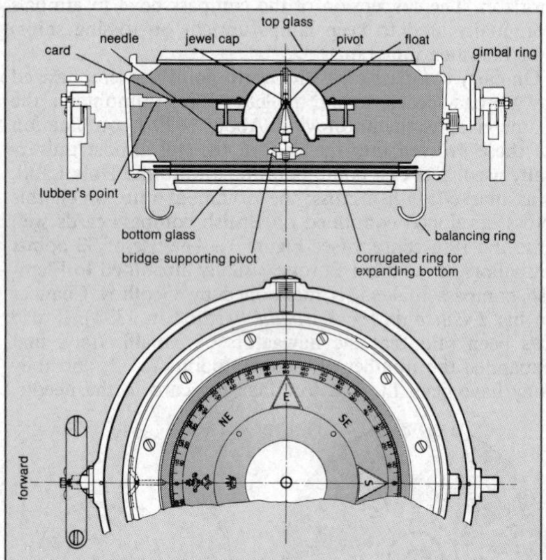

Figure 2: Liquid magnetic compass used by the British Navy.

A jewel is fitted at the centre of the float to bear on an iridium-tipped pivot attached to the bowl of the compass. The liquid in which the directional system is placed serves two purposes: to reduce the weight on the pivot point, and thereby to minimize friction; and to damp out oscillations from the ship's motion. The bowl is closed on the top and bottom by glass, the bottom glass permitting illumination from below, and is mounted in gimbals. A flexible diaphragm or bellows attached to the bowl accommodates the change in volume of the liquid caused by temperature changes. The ship's heading is read with the aid of the lubber's point, at the forward part of the compass, which indicates the direction of the ship's centre line.

When the ship alters course, liquid at the side of the bowl tends to displace slightly, deflecting the card and causing what is known as swirl error. To minimize swirl error the card is often made considerably smaller in diameter than the bowl. The directional system is made sufficiently bottom-heavy (pendulous) to counteract the downward pull of the vertical component of the Earth's magnetic field, which would otherwise cause the system to tilt.

The simplest, and probably earliest, azimuth instrument consisted of two sights on opposite sides of the compass bowl connected by a thread. The assembly could be rotated to permit sighting on the distant object. Because it was impossible to sight through the instrument and look at the compass card simultaneously, a prism (mirror) was positioned to reflect an image of the card, which was given a second set of graduations with reversed figures. Modern azimuth instruments embody a number of refinements, but the principle remains unchanged.

The binnacle

The binnacle, formerly called the bittacle, is the receptacle in which the compass is mounted. Originally constructed in the form of a cupboard, it is now usually a cylindrical pedestal with provision for illuminating the compass card, usually from below. It contains various correctors to reduce the deviations of the compass caused by the magnetism of the ship. These usually consist of properly placed magnets, a pair of soft iron spheres (or small strips close to the compass), and a vertical soft iron bar called the Flinders bar, which originated in recommendations made by the English navigator Matthew Flinders.

Binnacles are sometimes constructed so that an image of part of the compass card can be projected or reflected through a tube onto a viewing screen on the deck below. This arrangement can make it unnecessary to provide a second compass for the helmsman and may allow the binnacle to be placed in a position less susceptible to magnetic disturbances. (W.E.M./J.L.H./Ed.)

Marine charts. *The portolano.* During the course of 15 centuries or more the coastal pilot book of classical times evolved into the portolano, the harbour-finding manual of the Middle Ages. An early portolano for the whole Mediterranean Sea, *Lo Compasso da Navigare* (1296), gives directions in terms of half points, that is, halves of the angles defined by the 32-point compass. From such works, accumulated over generations and collected during the 13th century into a single volume for the entire Mediterranean, the first marine charts were drawn. On these charts, most of which were compiled in Genoa, Venice, and Majorca, north was at the top, rather than east, as was the practice on most land maps of the time. They carried a scale of distances and a pattern of rhumb lines (each of constant bearing) in different colours. To set a course between two ports, the pilot would join the corresponding points on the chart with a straight line, find the rhumb line most nearly parallel to it, and trace the rhumb line back to its parent wind rose, from which he obtained the required heading. As long as the ship's location was to be found by dead reckoning (keeping a running record of the distances and directions traveled), the Mediterranean chart was entirely adequate. Questions of latitude, longitude, compass variation, and curvature of the Earth's surface could be safely ignored.

Rhumb lines

The Mercator chart. When the Portuguese, under the leadership of Prince Henry the Navigator, ventured farther south along the west coast of Africa, they encountered navigational difficulties by assuming that the charts used in the Mediterranean could simply be extended. Over long distances the rhumb lines could not be taken as straight, and the charts bore no relation to the new methods of checking the dead reckoning that Portuguese astronomers and mathematicians had devised. These methods required a chart on which positions were expressed as latitudes and longitudes rather than bearings and distances. Such a chart had to embody a practical method of representing the curved meridians and parallels on a flat surface. Even for an area as large as the Mediterranean, this can be done without grossly falsifying either distances or directions, but for larger regions some distortions are inevitable, and a choice has to be made between alternative mapping techniques. On certain types of charts, distances can be shown accurately, but directions cannot; on other types, directions are reliably presented, but the scale of distance varies greatly between different parts of the chart. The navigator accepts the second type because the risk of lengthening the voyage is preferable to that of missing the target.

Map distortions

In 1569 the Flemish cartographer Gerardus Mercator published a world map that he had composed using a "projection suitable for navigation," the details of which he did not disclose. (The Mercator and other projections are treated in the article MAPPING AND SURVEYING.) On a Mercator chart the meridians of longitude are represented by equally spaced vertical lines, and the parallels of latitude are represented by horizontal lines that are closer together near the Equator than near the poles. The uneven spacing of the parallels compensates for the increasing exaggeration of the east–west distance between adjacent meridians at higher latitudes; this distance decreases on the Earth but remains the same on the chart. In 1599 the English mathematician Edward Wright supplied a rational explanation of Mercator's projection and provided tables by which the distorted distances could be corrected.

Latitude measurements. Portuguese seamen determined latitude by observing the altitude of the Pole Star, that is, the angle between its direction and the horizontal. They knew from astronomical studies that the star does not lie exactly on the extension of the Earth's axis, so that it appears to move daily in a small circle around the celestial pole, but the necessary correction (as much as 3½° in the 15th century) could be applied by noting the position of the nearby star Kochab. When the navigators got close to the Equator, these stars fell below the horizon; there it became necessary to rely on observing the altitude of the noonday Sun and calculating latitude with the aid of an almanac.

The first instruments used at sea for altitude measurements seem to have been the quadrant and the astrolabe, long known to astronomers. For both devices the reference direction was the vertical, rather than the horizontal, but conversion of the readings was an elementary matter. The mariner's astrolabe, however, was less widely used than its 16th-century successor, the cross-staff, a simple device consisting of a staff about three feet long fitted with a sliding crosspiece. The navigator, holding the staff to one eye, would move the crosspiece until its lower end coincided with the horizon and its upper end with the Pole Star (see Figure 3). The desired altitude could then

The cross-staff

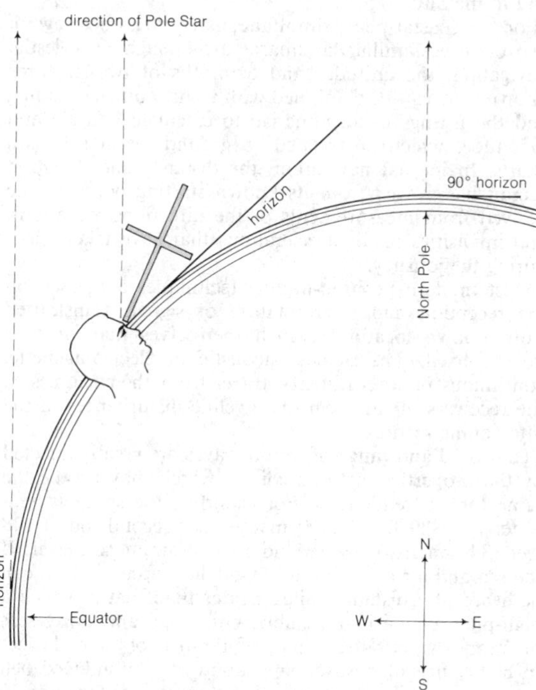

Figure 3: Altitude of Pole Star and latitude.

be read from the intersection of the crosspiece with the staff, on which a scale was marked in degrees. The cross-staff remained in use until the 18th century despite several drawbacks, the most serious being that it required the observer to look directly into the Sun. Coloured shades were fitted to the crosspiece, but the decisive improvement was made in 1594 by the English navigator John Davis. His instrument, called the backstaff because it was used with the observer's back to the Sun, remained common even after 1731 when the octant (an early form of the modern sextant) was demonstrated independently by John Hadley of England and Thomas Godfrey of Philadelphia. In the octant and the sextant, two mirrors—one fixed, the other movable—bring the image of the Sun into coincidence with the horizon. In the hands of the practiced observer, the modern sextant can be used to measure altitudes with an accuracy of 10 seconds of arc, that is, closely enough to determine a ship's north–south position within a few hundred metres.

Longitude measurements. *Almanacs and tables.* One of the earliest tabulations of the day-to-day positions of the heavenly bodies was *Ephemerides,* compiled by the German astronomer Regiomontanus and published by him in Nürnberg in 1474. This work also set forth the principle of determining longitude by the method of lunar distances, that is, the angular displacement of the Moon from other celestial objects. This method, which was destined to become the standard for a time during the 19th century, remained impracticable for more than three centuries because of the inaccuracy of the existing lunar tables, and because special knowledge and tedious computations were necessary in its use. Meanwhile, during the 16th and 17th centuries, working from translations of Portuguese and Spanish manuals, a flourishing school of instrument makers, chart makers, and teachers grew in England. This group rapidly improved the theory of navigation and compiled tables of increasing accuracy. In 1675 the Royal Observatory was established at Greenwich with the specific object of providing the sailor with astronomical data of the required precision. At Paris the *Connaissance des temps,* the first national almanac, was founded in 1679; it contained tables for the crude determination of longitude from observations of the eclipses of Jupiter's satellites, first seen by Galileo in 1610. (Galileo himself had advocated the preparation of such tables for this purpose, but the method, though sound in principle, could not be made practical.) In 1755 Johann Tobias Mayer, a German astronomer, published remarkably accurate tables of the motion of the Moon. To make them useful to navigators, however, it was necessary to prepare from them an ephemeris of the Moon for every noon and midnight. The English astronomer royal, Nevil Maskelyne, supervised this task; the results were published in the annual *Nautical Almanac,* which was inaugurated in 1766.

Mayer's lunar tables

The marine chronometer. Latitude could be determined by measuring the altitude of the Sun at noon or the altitude of any tabulated star when it crossed the local meridian, but the determination of longitude at sea remained a serious problem. By the Middle Ages, astronomers knew that the local time of an eclipse depended on the longitude, and in the 16th century they pointed out the principle of determining longitude by comparing the local time with the reading of a clock that reliably kept the time of a known meridian. No such clock was then available, but in 1714 the British Parliament offered a prize of £20,000 to anyone who could discover a method of finding the longitude within 30 miles during a sea voyage. The English inventor John Harrison eventually was awarded the prize for a chronometer tested in 1761–62. His success heralded the practice of making timed observations of heavenly bodies at sea. (M.W.Ri./Ed.)

Other aids to navigation. An Egyptian temple decoration dating from about 1600 BC shows a ship on which a member of the crew is measuring the depth of the water with a long pole. The Viking sailor took soundings with a lead weight on a line, hauling in the line and measuring it by the span of his arms. Depths are still cited in six-foot (1.8-metre) intervals called fathoms from the Old Norse word *fathmr* ("outstretched arms"). The weight was commonly given a hollow bottom filled with tallow to pick up a sample of the seabed for comparison with the composition indicated on the chart. Distance from a cliff could be estimated by timing the echoes of shouts or drumbeats.

Running lights

To reduce the risk of collision, a ship under way at night displayed running lights by which sailors on nearby vessels could judge its course and speed. The traditional coloured lights, red to port and green to starboard, were augmented on steamships with a white light at the head of the foremast. In foggy weather, gongs, bells, or explosives were used to produce loud warning sounds; eventually these devices were replaced by foghorns. Rules that specified what lights must be shown, what signals must be given, and how ships must navigate in respect of each other were formulated for British mariners in 1862. These rules formed the basis of the International Regulations for Preventing Collisions at Sea, which were adopted by nearly all maritime nations after a conference held in 1889. Collision avoidance also was fostered by general acceptance of the recommendation—separate lanes for eastbound and westbound steamers in the heavily traveled North Atlantic—appearing in *Sailing Directions* (1855), prepared by the

U.S. naval officer Matthew F. Maury. The danger of running aground was lessened by a worldwide system of lighthouses, lightships, buoys, bells, and channel markers; the development of these aids to navigation is treated in the article PUBLIC WORKS: *Lighthouses.*

20TH-CENTURY NAVIGATION

Navigation, in sharp distinction from aimless sailing or flying, presupposes a specific objective and may be subdivided into three stages. The first stage is the selection of the route along which the craft is to move and, ordinarily, a schedule that specifies the times at which the craft leaves its starting point, passes intermediate points, and reaches its destination. The route consists of a continuous succession of points, either on the surface of the sea or below it, in the air, on land, or in space. The second stage is the execution of the planned movement of the craft by driving it in the directions defined by the course at the speeds necessary to conform to the schedule. The third stage is the application of various accelerations at appropriate times and places. These accelerations are changes in velocity; they include increases and decreases in speed as required by the timetable or as dictated by external conditions along with alteration of direction as required to stay on the chosen course.

As the craft proceeds, the navigator regularly finds its position, comparing the progress with the predetermined route. If a deviation is detected, the navigator amends the route, adjusting speed and direction as needed to restore the craft to the proper path. Progress along the amended route is checked again by finding further positions, and further corrections are undertaken as required. The repetitive process of assessing progress and taking appropriate action is known as a closed loop.

Closed-loop navigation

Closed loops are seldom simple but consist of a series of loops one inside the other like the skins of an onion. Inside the outer position-finding loop there is an inner course and speed loop. In this loop, the course to be steered and the speed to be maintained are checked by compass and speedometer or log. Within the inner course and speed loop, there is also an innermost driving loop that relies on instruments to measure accelerations or, alternatively, on the judgment of the navigator. Finding the way thus involves three loops. Of these, the outer position-finding loop is used only at intervals, the course and speed loop is corrected more frequently, and the innermost driving loop is continually in action. A motor vehicle driver, by analogy, looks only occasionally at signposts, more frequently at the speedometer, but always keeps one or both hands on the steering wheel.

The aids that are employed in the outer position-finding loop cannot effectively be adapted to measure course and speed. For example, in the case of an aid that tells the distance to the destination, a minor irregularity, which momentarily diminishes this distance, would be translated as a complete reversal of speed, giving a completely false picture.

The reverse process is, however, quite possible. It has already been shown how, by dead reckoning, course, speed, and time can be used to find position. Similarly, devices used for driving may be adapted to give useful course and speed information and even position. To avoid collision, an outer position loop is used that relies on separation; for example, by one-way traffic lanes. There is also an inner course and speed loop that enables vehicles to avoid more imminent collision with each other by changing course or speed. (E.W.A./Ed.)

By the end of the 19th century, marine navigation had evolved into a fully systematic technique, combining the simplicity and reliability required by its practitioners with the rigour and accuracy founded in the skills and knowledge of astronomers, mathematicians, cartographers, and instrument makers. Accurate and detailed sea charts and books of sailing directions were available for the planning of any proposed voyage. At any stage during the voyage, dependable almanacs, sextants, and chronometers made it possible to ascertain the ship's position with great precision through observation of the altitudes and azimuths of a few familiar stars. Routine trigonometric procedures for making the needed computations had been introduced by Thomas H. Sumner of the United States in 1837 and Marcq St. Hilaire of France in 1875. These astronomical determinations were supplemented by dead reckoning, which had been made more trustworthy by the continued development of compasses and logs.

The navigational principles, techniques, and devices in use around 1900 formed a secure foundation upon which to superimpose the changes brought about during the 20th century. The advent of air travel and then space travel made it necessary to modify some of the concepts that had been developed for the period in which voyages had been restricted to the surface of the Earth. Many of the new problems, however, were solved by the application of technological innovations, notably radio communication and electronic instrumentation and computation. (Ed.)

Position finding. To find the position of a craft on the surface of the Earth, it is necessary to measure or estimate distances or directions, or both, in relation to one or more ground features at known locations. For vessels that travel above or below the surface, information about their altitude or depth also is needed; for those that move beyond the Earth's gravitational field, the reference points may be transferred to features of the Moon or to the predictable positions of the planets in relation to each other and to the Sun.

For the coastal pilot, simultaneous compass bearings of two or three familiar landmarks are enough. In celestial navigation, the altitudes and azimuths of two or three known stars can be combined with a chronometer reading and the listings in an almanac to calculate latitude and longitude, which are related to ground features by sea charts. In inertial navigation, the distance and direction a craft has moved from its known starting point can be derived from measurements of the directions, durations, and intensities of the accelerations that have taken place during the journey.

Transmission of signals

Most modern position-finding techniques are based on the reception and interpretation of signals transmitted from known locations, which themselves may or may not be fixed. The signals—acoustic or electromagnetic, continuous or intermittent—travel from their sources to the receivers in the form of wavelike disturbances in the intervening medium.

The speed and range of sound waves are greatly affected by the properties of the medium, which may not be the same for all frequencies. For example, the speed in seawater is 4,889 feet (1,490 metres) per second, but 1,128 feet (344 metres) per second in dry air at sea level. If the sea and air are calm, a low-pitched siren or horn can be heard at a distance miles greater than that at which a high-pitched one is detectable, but rough and noisy seas or strong winds affect the useful range of such devices in highly irregular ways. The sound of a submerged bell can be detected in a steel-hulled ship at a distance of 20 miles or more.

Electromagnetic radiation, including light and radio waves, travels very fast: about 186,000 statute miles (162,000 nautical miles; 300,000 kilometres) per second through empty space. This speed varies somewhat, depending on whether the waves are passing through space, air, water, the ground, or a telegraph wire; the wavelengths are inversely proportional to the speeds, but the frequencies remain unchanged. Frequency intervals, therefore, ordinarily are used to designate the bands into which the broad electromagnetic spectrum is divided for various purposes. In many microwave radar systems, for example, the frequencies of the waves lie in the so-called superhigh frequency band, between three and 30 gigahertz; the corresponding wavelengths are between one and 10 centimetres. The classification of these bands and their applications are treated in the article BROADCASTING: *Radio systems and equipment.*

At altitudes of tens to hundreds of kilometres above the Earth's surface, ionizing radiation from the Sun produces high concentrations of electrically charged particles in certain layers of the upper atmosphere. In the lower layers of this region, which is called the ionosphere, the charged particles revert to their neutral forms during the night.

Low-frequency waves reaching the ionized layers bounce back toward the Earth; such waves also are transmitted long distances through the ground and the oceans. High-frequency waves that strike the ionosphere at glancing angles also are reflected, but those incident at large angles (perpendicular or nearly so) pass through into outer space. High-frequency ground waves do not travel very far, so there is a gap, or dead space, between the range at which the ground wave dies out and that at which the waves reflected from the ionosphere (called sky waves) are first detectable.

Electromagnetic waves with frequencies greater than 30 gigahertz have wavelengths less than one centimetre. They are strongly scattered or reflected by raindrops, mist, fog, and snowflakes; for this reason, they are of no value for long-distance communication.

Speed measurement. The classical methods of measuring speed through the water have already been described. In the mid-18th century the French hydraulic engineer Henri Pitot, studying the flow of water in rivers and canals, invented a device—now called the Pitot tube—for measuring the speed of the flow past a given point. The Pitot tube has been applied to the measurement of wind speed; it is equally useful as a log for ships or aircraft. A typical Pitot marine log consists of a pair of thin-walled tubes projecting through the bottom of the ship and bent so as to face the direction of motion. One tube is open at the forward end; the opening is called the dynamic-pressure orifice. The second tube is closed at the end but has openings at right angles to its length; these are the static-pressure orifices. When the ship is dead in the water, the pressure is the same in the dynamic and static connections, but, when the vessel moves ahead, the dynamic pressure exceeds the static pressure by an amount that varies as the square of the ship's speed. Another part of the log consists of a centrifugal water pump driven by a variable-speed electric motor. The dynamic pressure produced by such a pump varies as the square of the speed of the motor. The pressure produced by the motion of the ship is exerted against one face of a diaphragm; that produced by the pump is exerted against the other. Movement of the diaphragm operates the speed control of the motor so as to equalize the two pressures and thereby make the speed of the motor directly proportional to the speed of the ship. A magneto attached to the shaft of the motor generates a voltage proportional to the speed, and on the ship's bridge a voltmeter calibrated in knots provides a continuous indication of the progress of the vessel. Analogous Pitot logs, with less bulky attachments for translating air pressure differentials to speed readings, are almost universally installed in aircraft. (M.R.Da./Ed.)

Pitot tube

In ships, a modern form of log incorporates a pair of electroacoustic transducers. One of these launches a sound wave from a point close to the keel; the second, a few metres ahead or astern, detects this wave and measures the time required for it to traverse the known distance. Motion of the ship relative to the water changes this interval in a way directly related to the speed of the ship. The speed of sound through water is slightly affected by temperature and salinity; even so, the electroacoustic log is much more accurate than its mechanical forerunners, and it is much less susceptible to fouling by barnacles or weeds.

Electroacoustic log

The Doppler effect—the familiar shift in the pitch of the sound of an automobile engine as it passes a stationary listener—also can be exploited to measure the speed of a ship or an aircraft. The effect can be accurately measured in either sound waves or electromagnetic waves emitted from a moving craft and reflected from a fixed object. Its use in navigation is treated in the sections *Sonar* and *Radar* of the article MEASUREMENT AND OBSERVATION, PRINCIPLES, METHODS, AND INSTRUMENTS OF. (S.S.D.J.)

Dead reckoning. *Correction for drift.* Starting from a known point, the mariner with a compass could draw a line on the chart to represent a vessel's course, then mark off the distance given by the log. The calculation of a new position was known as dead reckoning. In addition to errors in the compass and in the log, dead reckoning suffered from errors due to the drift of the water. When ocean currents were first marked on charts of the open sea, and tidal streams appeared on coastal charts, navigators could make allowance for drift. Fortunately, the currents were seldom fast and, on long voyages, often tended to cancel out each other. The situation in the air, however, was quite different. Early airplanes flew at around 100 knots, and the air that supported them was blown over the ground by the wind at speeds of up to 40 knots. It was therefore necessary to determine the velocity of the aircraft through the air and the velocity of the air over the ground in order to find the true velocity of the aircraft with respect to the ground. This was achieved by the triangle of velocities as shown in Figure 4. A line was drawn to show the direction in which the aircraft was heading,

Calculating aircraft velocity

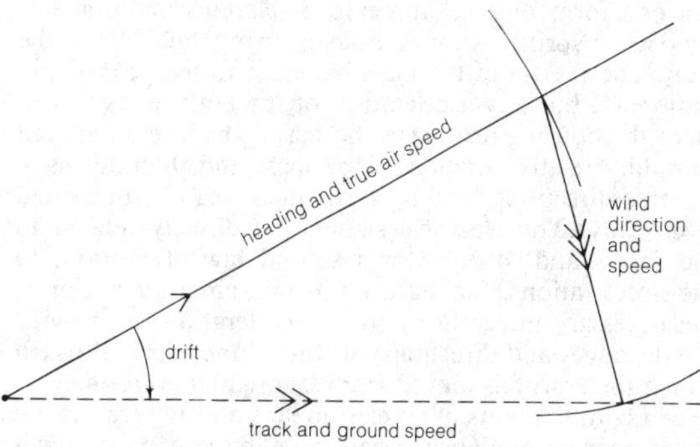

Figure 4: Triangle of velocities.

the length of the line representing the distance the aircraft would travel through still air in one hour, in other words, the true air speed. Such a line represents a vector; *i.e.,* a quantity that embodies both magnitude and direction. From the end of this line, a second line or vector was drawn in the direction toward which the wind was blowing, the length of this second line being determined by the wind speed. Finally, a third line drawn from the starting point of the first line to the end of the second line showed the path that the aircraft was following over the ground, the length of this line representing the true ground speed. Stated mathematically, the true ground speed was the vector sum of the craft's air velocity and the wind velocity.

The angle between the heading of the aircraft and its track along the ground was known as the drift because it resulted from the drifting effect of the wind. Early aircraft were fitted with drift sights through which the aviator visually aligned a grid with the moving ground below and so determined the drift. The plotting of triangles of velocity was simplified by using graphic instruments called computers before that term was appropriated for much more complex devices.

Paradoxically, higher aircraft speeds failed to eliminate the problem of wind drift because jet aircraft fly higher as well as faster, and, above 20,000 feet (6,100 metres), very narrow belts of wind—known as jet streams, which travel at speeds of 100 or 200 knots—occur under certain meteorological conditions.

Sea navigators did not follow the practice of air navigators and allow for ocean currents and tidal drifts in their initial calculations. Dead reckoning, long established as a navigational technique, continued to be used; an estimate for ocean current or tidal drift was added afterward. This practice continues today.

By dead reckoning, the navigator can quickly find a position that can often be checked by a landmark. On the other hand, the errors that are inherent in dead reckoning accumulate; when a position has been checked, the reckoning is therefore generally restarted from that position.

Importance of dead reckoning

Dead reckoning enables the navigator to plot not only where the craft is but also where it will be, provided the planned course and speed are maintained. It also makes it possible for the navigator to plan the whole journey, including the time of arrival at the destination. Planning is a part of all navigation; the preparation of a complete flight plan is mandatory before taking off in a civil aircraft. Space navigation is based even more completely on flight planning, and the time of splashdown is calculated to within minutes many weeks before lift-off.

Inertial guidance systems. By established principles of mathematical physics, the velocity of an object is defined as the rate of change of its position, and the acceleration is defined as the rate of change of the velocity. These relations can be applied to the navigational problem of position finding if an instrument can be devised to measure acceleration and then to convert it successively to velocity and to position. In the terminology of the calculus, velocity is the first derivative of distance (hence, position) with respect to time, and acceleration is the first derivative of velocity (the second derivative of distance). The process of evaluating a variable quantity (in this case, the distance) when its derivatives (velocity and acceleration) are known is called integration.

Accelerometers

In one form of accelerometer, a reference mass is suspended on springs within a housing firmly attached to the craft. The inertia of the mass causes it to tend to remain stationary, but any acceleration of the craft tends to displace the housing relative to the mass. The forces required to nullify relative motion of the mass and the housing—in three directions fixed by gyroscopes—can be measured electrically. The electrical signals are directly related to the forces and, by Newton's second law of motion, to the accelerations. Standard electronic circuitry performs the necessary integrations of the accelerations to provide the distances and directions, in three dimensions, through which the craft has moved from its original position.

Such combinations of accelerometers and integrators are called inertial guidance systems; in the context of navigation they amount to sophisticated dead-reckoning devices. Since their introduction, starting in 1950, they have proved extremely valuable in controlling the courses of submarines and spacecraft. Their errors, like those of any other dead-reckoning system, are cumulative with time, but nuclear-powered submarines have traveled under the north polar ice cap, guided solely by inertial systems, with errors of less than a mile per week.

Dead reckoning by computer. In modern craft, computers have proved well suited to processing the streams of data—directions, speeds, and times—involved in keeping track of position. In military land vehicles, computers are fed by compasses and signals taken from the wheels. Navigators aboard ships depend on the gyrocompass and the log; those in aircraft rely on the gyromagnetic compass and Doppler-effect speed measurements. The computers can be programmed to print periodically updated positional information. Generally, inertial guidance systems provide dead-reckoning information only, though compass and Doppler data can be included with inertial outputs. Information from radio fixing systems can be added to the dead reckoning; each item of information can be automatically compared with the others.

Radio fixing systems that can provide continuous indication of position are eliminating the distinction between position fixing and dead reckoning. Navigation is effected by supplying both the classical dead-reckoning data (speed and direction) and the continuously updated position to a computer, which determines the speed, heading, and rate of climb or descent that must be maintained to execute the flight plan. Many computers apply the technique called Kalman filtering, which weights each of the several supplied data according to its expected quality.

Instead of being mapped on a chart, position may be continuously displayed on a moving map. If the route is known beforehand, the map may be prepared in the form of a strip driven by rollers with a pointer moving to and fro to indicate exact position. When greater flexibility of route is essential, a series of maps covering a very wide area may be printed on film and projected on a ground glass screen on the bridge or in the cockpit.

Dead reckoning plays an important role in air traffic control. Not only does every air navigator have to file a complete flight plan showing courses and timings, but, during the flight, air traffic controllers keep what is virtually a dead-reckoning check on each aircraft. The flight plans are split into sections, and flight strips are prepared showing height, speed, and timings of each aircraft in a section. The air traffic controller responsible for that section can thus see which aircraft will be arriving and in what sequence.

Flight strips

These flight strips are continually updated by reports sent by radio from the aircraft and also by changes in height and course ordered by the air traffic controller to maintain adequate separation. In modern systems, automatic flight strips are displayed on cathode-ray tubes.

Radio navigation. *Direction finders.* To avoid the hazards marked on the charts, a mariner needs to know the vessel's exact position. By means of a sight fitted to the compass, the direction of any visible landmark or buoy can be measured. This direction, called a bearing, can be marked on the chart as a line passing through the identified reference point. A similar line corresponding to a second bearing will intersect the first and fix the position of the vessel, as shown in Figure 5.

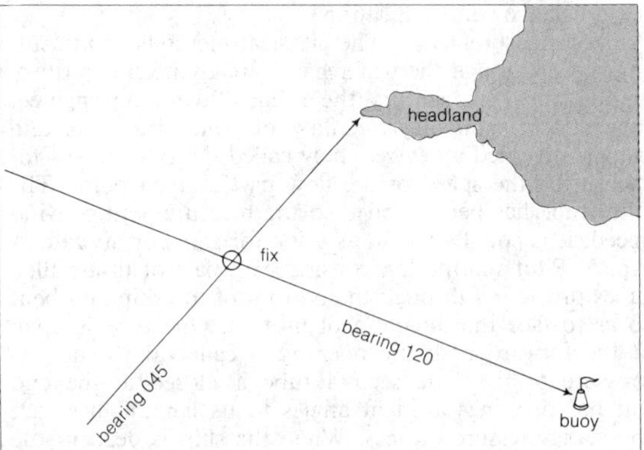

Figure 5: Determining position by intersection of compass bearings to known points.

The invention of radio transmission and reception led to an improvement in this navigational technique, making it possible to obtain bearings from reference points obscured by fog or darkness. The signals picked up by a loop antenna are weakest when the plane of the loop is perpendicular to the direction in which the radio waves are traveling. If the receiver is tuned to the frequency of a particular transmitter and the loop is rotated for minimum signal pickup, the direction to the transmitter can be found and plotted. A second position line then fixes the navigator's position, as before.

Loop antennas

Soon after ships were first equipped with radio, direction-finding stations were placed on shore at strategic points along navigational routes and near harbour approaches. Upon receiving a request by radio from a ship, two or more shore stations determined the directions from which the ship's signal arrived and transmitted this information to the vessel. The navigator then could fix his position. The limitation of this service to one vessel at a time, however, was a serious drawback in bad weather, when demands were heavy. Beginning in 1921, continuously operating transmitters were placed ashore and the direction finder on the ship to eliminate the possibility of overloading the system and to give the navigator two further advantages: that of taking continuous or frequent bearings on any shore beacon and that of taking bearings of any receivable signal, such as transmissions from commercial broadcasting stations and from other vessels. This change in the system was roughly coincident with the initial growth of aviation, and the airborne direction finder immediately became a valuable aid to air navigation.

Under ideal conditions a well-designed direction finder will provide bearings within 1° or 2° of the true value. The uncertainty can be considerably increased, however, if the direction of the radio waves is altered by reflection from the ionosphere or refraction in the atmosphere.

The loop-antenna radio direction finder, almost as old as radio itself, developed into a device in which a motor turned the loop, and electronic circuitry identified the direction of the source of the signals. This instrument, originally called a radio compass, could guide the navigator toward any detectable transmitter. It was often linked to a compass so as to display not merely the direction of the radio station compared to the heading of the craft but the actual direction as plotted on a chart.

Radio-beam systems. The directional selectivity of loop antennas when they are used as receivers is duplicated when they are used as transmitters. Such an antenna can be oriented so that it radiates strong signals to the north and south but practically none to the east or west. Pathway-defining ground stations for aircraft were developed during the 1920s and '30s. They were equipped with loop antennas in pairs at right angles, arranged so that one antenna broadcast the International Morse Code character *A* (dot–dash), and the other broadcast the character *N* (dash–dot). Midway between the directions in which only *A* or only *N* could be heard, the characters interleaved to produce a steady tone; these four intermediate directions were the preferred courses, called beams. Only a slight deviation of the receiver from a beam disrupted the steady tone, and the direction in which the craft was off the beam was indicated by the predominance of one Morse character or the other. The pilot flew in one of the four directions toward or away from the transmitting beacon, which was called a four-course beacon or a radio range.

The distance at which the signals could be detected was limited, and the four-course beacons were replaced by VOR (very-high-frequency omnidirectional radio range), the beacons of which operated on an entirely different principle. At each beacon, one antenna sent out waves that had the same intensity in all directions. A second antenna rotated and sent out a narrow beam of waves that, when directed north, coincided in phase with those of the first antenna; that is, the peaks of the waves from the two antennas reached the receiver at the same instant. When the rotating beam pointed east, the two sets of waves were out of phase by 90° (one quarter of a wavelength); when the beam pointed south, the phase difference was 180°; and so on. A receiver in the aircraft measured the phase difference and displayed the bearing of the VOR beacon along with the heading of the aircraft.

VOR beacons

From the radio range, with its so-called beams, true beam systems have developed. In these the loops are replaced by improved antennas that concentrate the radio waves into narrow beams a few degrees wide; the dots and dashes are replaced by more sophisticated patterns or modulations. In the instrument landing system (ILS), used to help aircraft approach and land on an airfield, the two antennas transmit waves about three metres long. This wavelength, though shorter than those employed in earlier systems, necessitates antenna structures about 100 feet (30 metres) long on the ground. Such installations make it possible for suitably equipped aircraft to land in conditions of practically zero visibility. The beams point in almost the same direction, and, once the aircraft has entered the beams, a receiver can measure the angular displacement from the centre line and display this displacement on an instrument or use it to guide the aircraft along a line toward the point of landing. In addition to the steering beams, which make up the localizer element of the ILS, there are two similar but even narrower beams transmitted in the vertical plane that guide the aircraft down the correct slope toward the point of touchdown.

Instrument landing systems have been made highly reliable, but further development with wavelengths of a metre or more is limited by the interference resulting from reflections of these waves from hills, buildings, and other aircraft. Systems based on microwaves (about one centimetre in length) are less susceptible to such interference.

Distance measurement. The echo sounder, already mentioned, measures the time that elapses between the transmission of a sharp acoustic "ping" from the keel of a ship and the return of the echo from the sea bottom. A radar altimeter similarly measures the distance between an aircraft and the ground by timing the reflection of short pulses of radio waves. A more common form of radio altimeter, better suited for measuring rate of change of altitude, transmits waves continuously and derives the height from the phase difference between the transmitted signal and that reflected from the ground. An observed phase difference is, in fact, consistent with a large set of discrete altitudes, but in practice such radio altimeters are used in connection with instrument landing systems for measuring altitude and rate of descent during the last few seconds before touchdown. At this stage, the lowest altitude consistent with the observed phase difference is the correct one. When the aircraft reaches a height of about 65 feet (20 metres) the landing system initiates a programmed reduction in rate of descent to ensure a firm but safe touchdown.

In the usage of navigation, distance-measuring equipment (DME) denotes a specific system, defined by internationally accepted standards. Aircraft fitted with DME transmit radio pulses at one of 126 designated frequencies; arrival of these pulses at a DME beacon on the ground causes the beacon—after a 50-microsecond delay—to transmit responding pulses at another frequency. The time elapsing between the aircraft's transmission and its reception of the response is measured by a clock accurate to a few nanoseconds and converted into the distance, which is displayed in digital form. The position of the aircraft can be determined by combining the distance indicated by the DME with the direction from a VOR beacon at the same site as the DME beacon. Alternatively, position can be established by triangulation, using the distances between the aircraft and two well-separated DME beacons.

Position hyperbolas. If a gun at position M in Figure 6 were fired, a listener 1,100 feet (340 metres) away in any direction—that is, anywhere on the smallest circle centred at M—would hear the sound one second later; a listener 2,200 feet away, on the second circle, two seconds later;

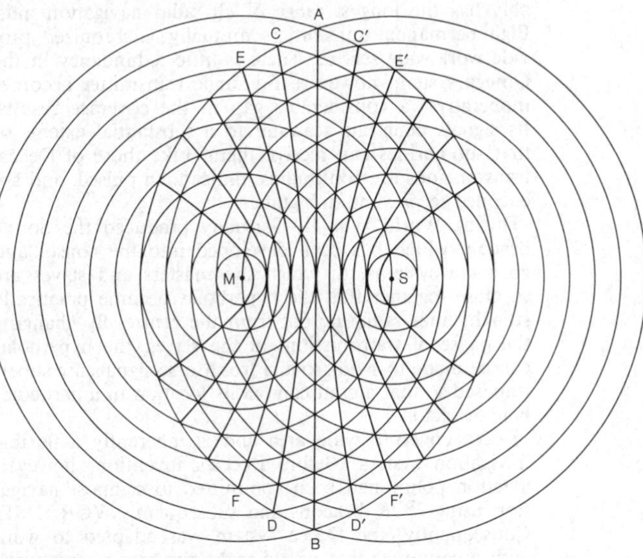

Figure 6: Hyperbolic position lines (see text).

and so on. If guns at M and S were fired simultaneously, a listener anywhere on AB, equidistant from M and S, would hear them at the same time. On a craft closer to one gun than the other, the sound of the nearer gun would be detected first. If gun M were heard one second before gun S, the craft would lie on CD, one of the two branches of a hyperbola; at a craft on C′D′, the other branch of the same hyperbola, gun S would be heard one second earlier than gun M. At a craft 2,200 feet closer to gun M, that gun would be heard two seconds before gun S, and the craft would lie on EF. Hence, by timing the interval to the nearest second, it is possible to find nearest which hyperbola the observer is located; knowledge of which gun was fired first makes it possible to choose between the two branches.

Signals from two sources

For navigation, the firing of guns is replaced by radio transmissions. A family of hyperbolas as shown in Figure 6 may be printed on a chart. A second family of hyperbolas, referring to a second pair of stations, can be printed on the same chart; the position of a craft is determined by the unique intersection of two curves. In radio systems, one of the two stations in a pair (the master) controls the other (the slave) to ensure accurate synchronization of the signals. In some systems, two or three slaves are distributed around a single master, and two or three families of hyperbolas are printed on the appropriate chart.

Loran

Systems of this kind are called loran, an acronym for long-range navigation.

Loran in its original form (now called loran A) was introduced during World War II; it operated at frequencies near two megahertz, but interference with and by other services and unreliable performance at night and over land led to its replacement by loran C. Loran C transmitters operate at the frequency of 100 kilohertz, and the signals are useful at distances of 1,800 nautical miles or more.

Decca, named for the British company that introduced it in 1946, is a hyperbolic system related to loran. Its master and slave transmitters broadcast different harmonics of a common frequency as continuous waves, rather than pulses. The hyperbolic position lines for any pair of transmitters are determined by the phase difference between the signals received, rather than the difference in arrival times of pulses. This arrangement provides a remarkably accurate and reliable system covering a range of 100–300 miles (160–480 kilometres) from the master station. Decca equipment is widely installed on ships and enjoys particular favour among fishermen, who can use it to return to specific shoals with great precision. Aircraft installations are less common than those of VOR/DME, the internationally accepted system for position finding. Decca is very well suited to navigation of helicopters, however, which usually operate at altitudes well below those at which VOR/DME is most effective.

Omega is a very-long-wave hyperbolic system that probably has the longest range of all radio navigation aids. Eight permanent transmitters, mutually synchronized, provide worldwide service. There is little redundancy in the Omega system, however; if a single transmitter becomes inoperative, a considerable gap in the coverage results. Its signals penetrate seawater to a substantial extent, so that submarines can receive them. Like those of Decca, transmissions are continuous, rather than pulsed, and are encoded to prevent ambiguities.

During World War II, Germany produced the Sonne beacon, which has been developed into the consol and consolan systems, in which the masters and slaves are so close together that the hyperbolas become practically straight lines radiating out from the centre. By changing the phase of transmissions of the slaves, the hyperbolas can be made to swing to and fro. Morse signals are superimposed so that a craft can tell its location in a particular lane or sector.

Decca covers a wide area and is inherently a flexible navigation system. Before Decca's invention, however, aviation policy had been committed to signpost navigation using VOR beacons and subsequently VOR/DME. Consequently, the Decca system was adapted to work with a computer that would make the area system work as if there were beacons placed anywhere the navigator wished. Thus Decca could work as a signpost or point navigation system.

The point navigation philosophy has since run into difficulties. As air traffic builds up, more and more routes are needed; thus more and more signposts must be set up. VOR/DME computers, however, have been developed so an aircraft can follow any track irrespective of the position of the VOR/DME. Thus the computer has restored to the point navigation system the flexibility originally possessed only by the area navigation system, a flexibility increasingly needed to ensure adequate separation between aircraft.

The computer has already become part of the inertial navigator; it is used also in automatic dead reckoning. Originally, analog computers were used in navigation systems, and calculations of a relatively simple nature involving inputs from various electrical sources were continuously performed. Today, digital computers are employed for performing the necessary calculations.

Use of the digital computer

The digital computer works so fast that for navigational purposes it can be considered virtually instantaneous and can therefore provide continuous information for control purposes. It has a memory to store information for use when needed. It is built from electronic modules that are mass-produced at low cost. It has only one disadvantage. Conversion of analog information into digital form is costly. Hence, although far superior to the analog computer, it is less economical whenever a large number of electrical signals must be combined in relatively simple ways without any need for memory. Such situations still apply to control systems in many craft. (E.W.A./S.S.D.J./Ed.)

Satellites as navigation aids. Artificial satellites can be equipped to transmit electromagnetic radiation at precisely controlled times and frequencies. The frequencies are chosen to avoid interference with other services, to minimize attenuation or delay as the signals penetrate the ionosphere, and to minimize the power needed by the satellite for broadcasting the signals. The practical range of frequencies corresponds to wavelengths between 10 and 100 centimetres.

Transit satellites

During the early 1960s a series of satellites named Transit was launched by the U.S. Navy to provide a worldwide navigation system. These satellites circled the Earth about every 90 minutes, moving in polar orbits about 600 miles (1,000 kilometres) above the Earth's surface. They radiated continuous signals modulated to indicate departures from the nominal frequencies and orbits. A receiver on the surface or in a submarine could compare the frequency received with that known to be transmitted and identify its own location by measuring both the magnitude and the rate of change of the Doppler shift. The calculations, which were performed by a small digital computer, were accurate to about 180 yards (160 metres).

Movement of the user modifies the Doppler shift and introduces an error unless it is taken into account. An uncertainty of one metre per second (two knots) in the velocity of the user causes an uncertainty of one kilometre in the deduced position. Such an error is of no great consequence in the case of ships, but it disqualifies the Transit system for the navigation of aircraft.

NavStar

A global position system suitable for aircraft navigation was initiated by the U.S. Air Force in 1978, when the first two of the series of NavStar satellites were launched. These move in circular orbits inclined at 63° to the equatorial plane at an altitude of about 12,500 miles (20,200 kilometres); their period is 12 hours. Eighteen of these satellites can provide continuous worldwide coverage adequate for determining latitude and longitude within about 10 metres and, in many places, altitude with the same accuracy. A system of 24 NavStar satellites would give worldwide three-dimensional coverage.

The NavStar system does not depend on the Doppler effect. The satellites transmit their signals on a time schedule precisely controlled by atomic clocks. The receivers automatically select the three (or four, if possible) satellites most favourably located and relay their signals into a computer, which calculates the position of the receiver by solving three or four simultaneous algebraic equations. The variables in these equations are the desired two or three position coordinates and a time-dependent quantity. The system is related to the hyperbolic systems loran and Decca, but the hyperbolas (two-dimensional figures) are replaced by hyperboloids of revolution (three-dimensional) that are moving rapidly in relation to the Earth. The complexity of the calculations makes the use of a fast digital computer essential. (S.S.D.J./Ed.)

Improved compasses. In the early days of aviation, it was soon learned that a liquid-filled mariner's compass could not operate satisfactorily in a rapidly accelerating and sharply turning aircraft. Spring-mounted bowls and cards of extremely small diameter alleviated the problem, but tilting still occurred, bringing the system frequently under the influence of the vertical component of the Earth's magnetic field and causing erroneous readings. The most important of such effects, called northerly turning error, caused the compass to indicate a greater or smaller angle than was actually being turned through. Other problems were the difficulty of obtaining stable magnetic conditions in the cockpit, with its array of metal and electrical equipment, and the need for the compass reading to be fed to other navigational aids. In the end, the direct-reading magnetic compass was reduced to a secondary role, its place being taken for most purposes by the gyromagnetic compass (see below).

The inductor compass. Whereas the pivoted-needle magnetic compass indicates direction by aligning itself with the horizontal component of the Earth's magnetic field, the inductor compass measures, in effect, the strength of this horizontal component and indicates the direction in which the strength is greatest. One such instrument, the saturable-inductor compass, makes use of magnetic materials that are easily saturated—that is, materials in which it is easy to build up the maximum number of lines of magnetic flow, or flux. The amount of flux through such a material depends on its orientation in the Earth's field, being greatest when it is aligned in the magnetic north–south direction. By means of suitable electronic circuitry, it is possible to determine the exact orientation of a bar of such material and thus indicate precisely the direction of magnetic north. Compasses of this type require no rotating parts. Several can be installed at various points aboard a craft and their outputs combined electronically.

Saturable-inductor compasses

The gyromagnetic compass. The errors that occur in aircraft and small, fast vessels during alterations of course or speed can be avoided by mounting the compass on a platform kept horizontal by a gyroscope. The directive element must be nonpendulous. The vertical pin supporting the compass needle can be pivoted at both ends, or an inductor element can be employed. In one such arrangement, a saturable inductor is mounted on a gyroscope, but this is not always convenient from the point of view of size and weight. (W.E.M./J.L.H.)

Another system has a means of comparison between the gyroscope heading and that of the magnetic element. The gyroscope maintains a specific directional line in space with a possible error caused by drift of two or three degrees in each half hour that the gyroscope is left free. The utility of this instrument may appear to be very limited, but it happens to complement the magnetic compass very well. By itself, neither is satisfactory as a directional reference, but a combination of the directional gyroscope with a magnetic compass gives the pilot complete and stable directional information. The magnetic compass is useful in an airplane only so long as the airplane continues on a straight course in smooth air. While the airplane is making banked turns, the magnetic compass may err by 90° or more. Therefore, if the pilot desires to change course by a definite number of degrees, the magnetic compass will be of little use. On the other hand, the directional gyroscope is not affected by banked turns or rough air. It accordingly gives a reliable and stable indication of the exact number of degrees of turn that the airplane makes. The relatively slow drift of the directional gyroscope from its heading may be corrected manually from time to time when the airplane is in level and straight flight.

Complementary compasses

(R.E.Gi./A.L.Ra./R.J.S./Ed.)

The gyrocompass. The gyrocompass is independent of the magnetic field of the Earth and depends upon the properties of the gyroscope and upon the rotation of the Earth.

The axis of a free gyroscope will describe a circle around the pole of the heavens. To convert it into a gyrocompass, a control must be introduced that, when the axis tilts, will operate to precess (turn) it toward the meridian. The case of the gyroscope is made pendulous, or a liquid is arranged to flow from side to side. Either will convert the path traced by the axis into an ellipse. By delaying the flow of the liquid or by making eccentric the point of action of the control, a damping factor is introduced that converts the ellipse into a spiral so that the gyrocompass finally settles pointing true north (see Figure 7).

(W.E.M./J.L.H.)

Instruments. The tactical management of a craft demands, for steering, continuous indication of heading and speed through the water or air and, for the propulsion system, information—either continuous or on demand—on engine speed, temperatures at critical regions, fuel flow, and fuel supply. In a modern aircraft, continuous monitoring by the crew of the numerous variables is impractical; instead, each instrument that indicates the value of a critical variable is designed so that any departure beyond specified limits is brought to the attention of the crew by warning lights, audible signals, or in the particular case of airspeed, "stick shake"; that is, artificially induced vibration of the control column in the event that indicated airspeed falls close to stalling speed.

Alarm systems

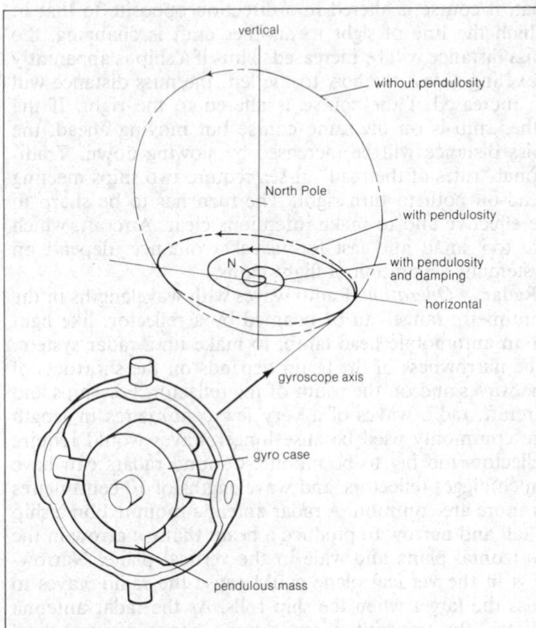

Figure 7: *Gyrocompass operation.*
Circular line shows the apparent motion of the axis of a gyroscope around the Pole Star in the absence of a pendulous mass. The addition of the pendulous mass (lower drawing) converts the circular motion into an ellipse; the ellipse can then be damped out and the gyroscope becomes a gyrocompass pointing to true north.

Rate of climb and, particularly, rate of descent must be indicated continuously because of their vital safety connotations. Rate of turn also is important in aircraft, and it is sometimes indicated in ships.

Airspeed is correctly indicated by the Pitot apparatus only if the air has the density typical at sea level at 15° C. Altitude has a major effect on air density, and temperature a minor one; in modern aircraft, indicated airspeed, altitude, and temperature are combined by a computer that indicates true airspeed and Mach number. Similarly, the independently operating compass, artificial horizon (an instrument that shows the degree of pitch and roll), and other instruments have been integrated into a so-called attitude and heading reference system.

The combination of daylight-visible optical displays with systems for storage and retrieval of digital data simplifies the design of aircraft cockpits and ship bridges by allowing the presentation of essential information on demand, relieving the navigator of the task of interpreting the readings of numerous separate indicators. (S.S.D.J./Ed.)

Collision avoidance. Figure 4 illustrates the calculation of an airplane's true ground velocity. A similar procedure can be used to calculate the course an airplane must avoid to prevent collision with another aircraft. In Figure 4 the wind is replaced by the course and speed of the other craft drawn in the opposite direction. What was track and ground speed in Figure 4 becomes the line of sight to the craft to be intercepted and the speed at which the two planes are approaching each other. If both planes maintain the speeds and directions indicated in Figure 4, a collision will occur.

Interception theory is based on a development of the way in which one animal hunts another. The predator runs toward its prey, and, as the prey tries to escape, the pursuer changes direction so that it is always running straight toward its target. Thus the hunter changes course at the same rate as its line of sight to its prey changes direction. Missiles that have to intercept ships or aircraft do a little better than this; they alter course faster than the direction of the line of sight changes, moving toward a predicted position rather than the present one.

Modern collision-avoidance theory depends on the fact

that, if course is altered in a direction opposite to that in which the line of sight to another craft is changing, the miss distance will be increased. Thus if a ship is apparently traveling across the bow to the left, the miss distance will be increased if the course is altered to the right. If the other ship is on the same course but moving ahead, the miss distance will be increased by slowing down. Traditional "rules of the road" at sea require two ships meeting head-on both to turn right. The turn has to be sharp to be effective and to make intentions clear. Aircraft, which are too small and fast for visual avoidance, depend on systematic separation of flight paths.

Radar. *Operation.* Radio waves with wavelengths in the centimetre range can be beamed by a reflector, like light in an automobile head lamp, to make up a radar system. The narrowness of the beam depends on the shortness of the waves and on the width of the reflector. For ships and aircraft, radio waves of a very few centimetres in length are commonly used because longer waves would require reflectors too big to be mobile. Ground radars can have much bigger reflectors, and wavelengths of 10 centimetres or more are common. A radar antenna mounted on a ship is tall and narrow to produce a beam that is narrow in the horizontal plane and wide in the vertical plane. Narrowness in the vertical plane could cause the radio waves to miss the target when the ship rolls. As the radar antenna rotates, the transmitter sends out a series of very short pulses every degree or so. When the pulse strikes an object, it is reflected back to the radar aerial and thence passed to the radar receiver. The pulse is displayed on a cathode-ray tube. Electronic lines are drawn from the centre outward, each starting as the pulse starts from the transmitter. When an echo returns, the image on the tube brightens. Thus a spot of light appears on the cathode-ray tube at a distance from the centre proportional to the time the pulse takes to go out and back and in a direction the same as that in which the pulse was transmitted. Hence, on the cathode-ray tube a faint ray of light rotates around the screen like a searchlight, following the rotation of the antenna, and paints in the positions of any reflecting objects as if they were on a map. The face of the cathode-ray tube is coated with a persistent phosphor—that is, one that continues to glow for several seconds after it is excited—thus allowing the viewer time to study and analyze the image.

Antenna shapes and sizes

The strength of the return signals will vary depending on the reflectivity of the surface of the reflecting object and on its distance. There will be little reflection from water unless it is very rough. From cliffs, ships at sea, and buildings, there will be strong reflections from the vertical surfaces. From the ground, there will be only scattered reflections, generally stronger in wooded country. Nevertheless, because the shortest radar waves are so much longer than light waves, the picture painted by radar shows little detail and requires careful interpretation.

Applications. Although radar can produce a map, its main use is in avoiding collision. Using radar, the navigator of a ship can see other vessels irrespective of light conditions. It is therefore safe for a craft to proceed—though slowly—even in thick fog, whereas without radar it would be necessary to heave to or anchor. Since the radar picture is imperfect, collision avoidance requires great skill in interpretation. In particular, it is not easy to see the direction in which other vessels are traveling, and the navigator has to make particularly bold alterations of course to make certain that other navigators do not misinterpret them.

Use of radar to avoid collision

With radar, air traffic controllers can watch the progress of aircraft in a large area. As each one approaches and lands, one radar follows it in the vertical plane and another in the horizontal plane. If necessary, the aircraft can be "talked down" (told exactly how to land) by the radar operator on the ground.

Special systems. For military purposes, infrared waves may be used; these are midway in frequency between radio and light waves. An infrared detector can distinguish between objects of different temperatures and can identify a ship on the water or a man hidden in undergrowth. Infrared radiation needs only a very small transmitter or receiver and therefore has been used to guide small missiles launched from aircraft to strike at enemy planes. The detectors, however, are distracted by other sources of infrared radiation, including the Sun and the engines of friendly aircraft.

Use of infrared waves

Lasers can also be adapted to produce radar-like devices of extreme precision. In addition, there is increased interest in simple television cameras; when equipped with light intensifiers, they can "see" in almost total darkness. Finally, for underwater detection of either submarines or shoals of fish, sonar systems have been developed.

Automation. The computer has already been mentioned in connection with point and area navigation systems, the use of satellites, and the mixing of various aids with inertial navigators. Automation is needed because craft speeds are increasing to meet demands for quick delivery of passengers and cargo and to lower operating costs. A jet aircraft with a crew of fewer than 10 can carry more passengers across the Atlantic than an ocean liner with a crew of hundreds, because its greater speed enables it to make many more trips a year.

Automation can also reduce crew sizes by taking over tasks that machines can do more reliably and more consistently. On the other hand, because engineers must design machines years before they are used, they cannot foresee some situations that arise. The first landing of astronauts on the Moon involved events not anticipated by the designers of the landing module. Had a human crew not been in the spacecraft, it would have crashed. Therefore the human navigator will doubtless be required in many types of craft well into the foreseeable future. Although the machine can manipulate, it cannot manage except insofar as it is programmed.

The navigator, although becoming more and more a manager of systems, is still required to undertake certain manipulative tasks because there is no substitute for human judgment in dealing with the occasional unexpected situation. (E.W.A.)

BIBLIOGRAPHY. General works include E.W. ANDERSON, *The Principles of Navigation* (1966); NATHANIEL BOWDITCH, *American Practical Navigator,* rev. ed. (1977, reissued 1982); ELBERT S. MALONEY (ed.), *Dutton's Navigation and Piloting,* 13th ed. (1978, reissued 1983), a standard text; BRUCE FRASER, *Weekend Navigator* (1981), a good introduction; ALTON B. MOODY, *Navigation Afloat: A Manual for the Seaman* (1981); and U.S. NAVAL OCEANOGRAPHIC OFFICE, *Navigation Dictionary,* 2nd ed. (1969). Works treating celestial navigation include JOHN SEYMOUR, *Self-Contained Celestial Navigation with H.O. 208* (1977); MARY BLEWITT, *Celestial Navigation for Yachtsmen,* 8th ed. (1980); MORTIMER ROGOFF, *Calculator Navigation* (1979); and CHARLES H. COTTER, *The Elements of Navigation and Nautical Astronomy* (1977). For mapping, see CHARLES H. DEETZ and O.S. ADAMS, *Elements of Map Projection,* 5th rev. ed. (1945, reprinted 1969); and DAVID GREENHOOD, *Mapping* (1964). Navigation in nature is addressed in G.V.T. MATTHEWS, *Bird Navigation,* 2nd ed. (1968); and HAROLD GATTY, *Nature Is Your Guide* (1958, reprinted 1983). Works treating control factors include BENJAMIN C. KUO, *Automatic Control Systems,* 4th ed. (1982); R.A.B. ARDLEY, *Harbor Pilotage and the Handling and Mooring of Ships* (1944); MALCOLM C. ARMSTRONG, *Practical Ship-Handling* (1981); A.I. MEES, *Dynamics of Feedback Systems* (1981); ANTHONY C. MCDONALD and H. LOWE, *Feedback and Control Systems* (1981), requiring some mathematics; CHARLES S. DRAPER, W. WRIGLEY, and J. HOVORKA, *Inertial Guidance* (1960); ROBERT BATESON, *Introduction to Control System Technology,* 2nd ed. (1980); and VAN VALKENBURGH, NOOGER AND NEVILLE INC., *Basic Synchros and Servomechanisms,* 2 vol. (1955). Works on guidance, including position finding and radar, include W. DENNE, *Magnetic Compass Deviation and Correction,* 3rd ed. rev. by A.N. COCKCROFT (1979); H.L. HITCHINS and W.E. MAY, *From Lodestone to Gyro-Compass* (1952); JOSEPH W. HORTON, *Fundamentals of Sonar,* 2nd ed. (1959, reissued 1965); F.J. WYLIE (ed.), *The Use of Radar at Sea,* 5th rev. ed. (1978); and EDWARD L. SAFFORD, *Modern Radar: Theory, Operation and Maintenance,* 2nd ed. (1981). See also *Guidance and Control* (annual). *Navigation,* vol. 25, no. 2 (1978), is a special issue dedicated solely to the NavStar global position system. The fundamentals of the timing technique, the basis of NavStar and of increasing importance in navigation systems, are introduced in R.C. DIXON, *Spread Spectrum Systems,* 2nd ed. (1984). See also F.S. STRINGER, "The Development of Flight Deck Display," *J. of Navigation,* vol. 37, no. 2 (1984).

(E.W.A./W.E.M./J.L.H./S.S.D.J./Ed.)

Nebula

Nebula (Latin: "mist") is a term formerly used in astronomy to denote any object situated beyond the solar system that is seen as a bright or dark area, in contrast to the pointlike images of stars. This definition, adopted at a time when very distant objects could not be resolved into great detail, unfortunately includes two unrelated classes of objects: the extragalactic nebulae, now called galaxies, which are enormous collections of stars and gas; and the galactic nebulae, which are much smaller masses of gas (with traces of solid particles) within a single galaxy. Today, the term nebula is restricted to the latter class of objects. The galactic nebulae collectively amount to only a few percent of the total mass of their galaxy, the rest being made up by the stars within the system. Galactic nebulae are also sometimes called gaseous nebulae. The present article is concerned only with the galactic nebulae. For additional information about the star systems in which they occur, see GALAXIES and COSMOS.

This article is divided into the following sections:

CLASSES OF NEBULAE

The galactic nebulae are divided into two subclasses on the basis of their appearance: (1) dark nebulae appear as black patches in the sky that are usually very irregular in shape, blotting out the light of the stars beyond them; (2) bright nebulae appear as faintly luminous, glowing surfaces, either emitting their own light or reflecting the light of nearby stars.

The bright nebulae can be subdivided into four classes on the basis of their origin and the details of their appearance: (*a*) diffuse nebulae, which are usually faint and irregular in shape and produce the radiation they emit; (*b*) reflection nebulae, which reflect light from a nearby bright star; (*c*) planetary nebulae, which typically appear as rather symmetrical round disks or rings of fairly high surface brightness (the name arises from the fact that many of them appear rather like out-of-focus images of planets seen through a telescope of poor resolution); and (*d*) supernova remnants, which are clouds of gas expanding away from the site of a stellar explosion called a supernova that disrupts the star and ejects most of its mass at speeds of thousands of kilometres per second.

The diffuse nebulae, reflection nebulae, and dark nebulae are basically the same type of physical entity, seen under different conditions. All are irregular clouds of gas, typically several light-years across but with a density of approximately 10 atoms per cubic centimetre (160 atoms per cubic inch), which is substantially less dense than an excellent laboratory vacuum. About 1 percent of their mass is in the form of "dust," or small, solid particles that are efficient in absorbing and scattering starlight. When the gas cloud happens to be near one of the massive, hot O-type stars or very close to a slightly cooler B star, it glows because these stars, with temperatures five to 10 times that of the Sun, emit enough ultraviolet radiation to ionize the gas in the cloud; the ionized gas then emits the radiation seen in the visible part of the spectrum. If the nebula is close to a cooler star that does not emit enough ultraviolet radiation to ionize the gas, the starlight may still be partially reflected from the dust grains, and the cloud is then seen as a reflection nebula. Finally, if the cloud lies between the observer and more distant stars, the dust either scatters the starlight into other directions or absorbs it, in either case reducing the amount of starlight that comes to the observer directly. Therefore, the starlight is dimmed, and, when the cloud is extensive enough, it is seen as a gap in the star field; that is, as a dark nebula. Thus, the same cloud could appear to hypothetical observers at different points in space as a reflection nebula (if viewed with a star near to it but in front of or beside it) or a dark nebula (if viewed with the same star behind it, so that it blocks the starlight).

Densities in nebulae

Nebulae differ greatly in size. The only one easily visible to the naked eye is the beautiful Orion Nebula (see Plate 2), which is seen as the central star in Orion's sword. It is the brightest and most thoroughly studied diffuse nebula. Some nebulae are extremely large; the largest, the Gum Nebula (named after its discoverer, the Australian astronomer Colin S. Gum), measures 40° in angular diameter. The whole constellation of Orion is embedded in extremely faint diffuse nebulosity that cannot be detected by the eye. Such large nebulae are so faint that they require special techniques (see below *Advances brought by photography and spectroscopy*) to detect them. Most supernova remnants are similar to these large, faint diffuse nebulae.

Sizes of nebulae

The planetary nebulae are all telescopic objects. The largest known, the Helix Nebula, in the constellation Aquarius, subtends an angle of about 20′ of arc—two-thirds of the angular size of the Full Moon; such large nebulae, however, have very low surface brightness and are not easily observed. The majority of bright planetary nebulae are less than 0.5′ of arc in size—*i.e.,* only 0.02 of the angular diameter of the Moon. The Crab Nebula, the best known supernova remnant, is slightly larger—approximately 3′ of arc.

PRE-20TH-CENTURY OBSERVATIONS OF NEBULAE

Naked-eye observations of "cloudy stars" were mentioned by the Greek astronomers Hipparchus (*c.* 190–125 BC) and Ptolemy (*c.* AD 138), but these objects are known to have been compact clusters of stars. In 1610, two years after the invention of the telescope, the Orion Nebula, which looks like a star to the naked eye, was discovered by the French scholar and naturalist Nicolas-Claude Fabri de Peiresc. In 1656 Christiaan Huygens, the Dutch scholar and scientist, using his own greatly superior instruments, was the first to describe the bright inner region of the nebula and to determine that its inner star is not single but a compact quadruple system—the well-known "Trapezium." The inner regions of the nebula are still referred to by his name.

Early 18th-century observational astronomers gave high priority to comet seeking. A by-product of their search was the discovery of many bright nebulae. Several catalogs of special objects were compiled by comet researchers; by far the best known is that of the Frenchman Charles Messier, who, in 1781, compiled a catalog of 103 nebulous, or extended, objects to avoid their confusion with comets. Most are clusters of stars, 35 are galaxies, and 11 are nebulae. Even today many of these objects are commonly referred to by their Messier catalog number: M20, for instance, is the great Trifid Nebula, in the constellation Sagittarius.

The work of the Herschels. By far the greatest observers of the early and middle 19th century were the English astronomers William Herschel and his son John. Between 1786 and 1802 William Herschel, aided by his sister Caroline, compiled three catalogs totalling about 2,500 clusters, nebulae, and galaxies. John Herschel later added to the catalogs 1,700 other nebulous objects in the southern sky visible from the Cape Observatory in South Africa but not from London and 500 more objects in the northern sky visible from England.

The origin of NGC and IC numbers

The catalogs of the Herschels formed the basis for the great *New General Catalogue* (NGC) of J.L. Dreyer, published in 1888. It contains the location and a brief description of 7,840 nebulae, galaxies, and clusters. In 1895 and 1908 it was supplemented by two *Index Catalogues* (IC) of 5,386 additional objects. The list still included galaxies as well as true nebulae, for they were often at this time still indistinguishable. Most of the brighter galaxies are still identified by their NGC or IC numbers according to their listing in the *New General Catalogue* or *Index Catalogues.*

Advances brought by photography and spectroscopy. The advent of photography, which allows the recording of faint details invisible to the naked eye and provides a permanent record of the observation for study of fine details at leisure, caused a revolution in the understanding of nebulae. In 1880 the first photograph of the Orion Nebula was made, but really good ones were not obtained until 1883. These early photographs showed a wealth of detail extending out to distances unsuspected by visual observers.

Much can be learned about the physical nature of an astronomical object by studying its spectrum—*i.e.,* the resolution of its light into different wavelengths (or colours). Study of the spectrum of a cloudy-looking object provides a decisive test as to whether it is composed of unresolved stars (as are galaxies) or glowing gas, because the natures of the spectra of stars and of gas are quite different. According to the laws of radiation as stated by the chemist Robert Bunsen and the physicist Gustav Kirchhoff, both German, in 1859, opaque, hot bodies (such as stars) should radiate continuously at all wavelengths, with perhaps dark absorption lines superimposed, while hot, transparent gas clouds should radiate only emission lines at certain wavelengths, or colours, characteristic of their constituent gases. In 1864 observation of the spectrum of the Orion Nebula showed bright emission lines of glowing gases, with conspicuous hydrogen lines and some green lines even brighter. The spectrum of galaxies was found to be stellar, so that a distinction between galaxies and nebulae—that nebulae are gaseous and galaxies are stellar—was appreciated at this time, although the true sizes and distances of galaxies were not demonstrated until the 20th century.

Early spectroscopic studies

20TH-CENTURY DISCOVERIES

The 20th century has witnessed enormous advances in observational techniques. In 1930 a German optical worker named Bernhard Schmidt invented an extremely fast, wide-angle camera that made possible the detection of large, faint nebulae. The development of ever more sensitive photographic plates has also led to improved observational capacity. Moreover, since about 1960, photoelectric devices more than 100 times as efficient as photography in light detection have been produced. At present, such devices are used almost exclusively. Most importantly, new wavelength regions have been made accessible to observation. The use of space satellites has permitted the study of the ultraviolet and X-ray portions of the spectrum that would otherwise be absorbed by the Earth's atmosphere. New detectors, some carried by aircraft and satellites, have enabled investigators to observe infrared radiation. Large radio telescopes developed since the late 1970s are capable of the same angular resolution as optical telescopes (namely, one arc second), enabling astronomers to obtain sharp images of distant cosmic radio sources that cannot be detected with optical instruments.

During the 20th century scientists have been able to acquire a reasonably good theoretical understanding of nebulae, although challenging and exciting problems still remain. In the 1920s astrophysics received added impetus from the detailed quantum-mechanical study of atoms (their emission and absorption processes and spectra), and this was applied to the study of nebulae. During the 1930s

By courtesy of © National Geographic Society—Palomar Observatory Sky Survey

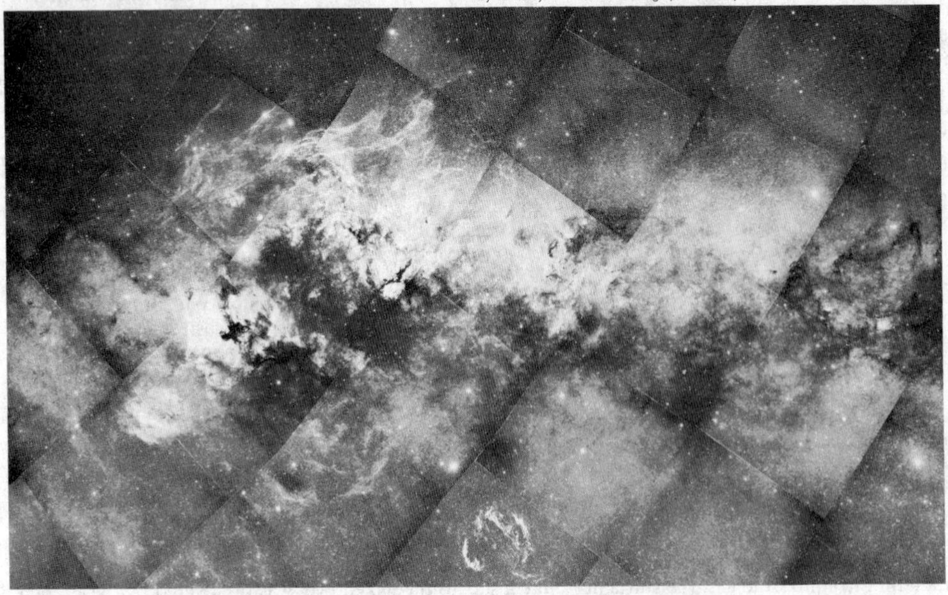

Red-light photomosaic shows many star clouds, glowing gas, and dark dust in the Milky Way, near the galactic plane. The brightest object (centre left) is the North American Nebula; the loop-shaped object (bottom) is the Cygnus Loop. The rich pattern of bright and dark nebulae, stars, and star clouds is due to the direction of the line of sight, in this region nearly parallel to the outer spiral arms of the Galaxy. (Photo taken by 122-centimetre [48-inch] Schmidt telescope; photograph, Palomar Observatory.)

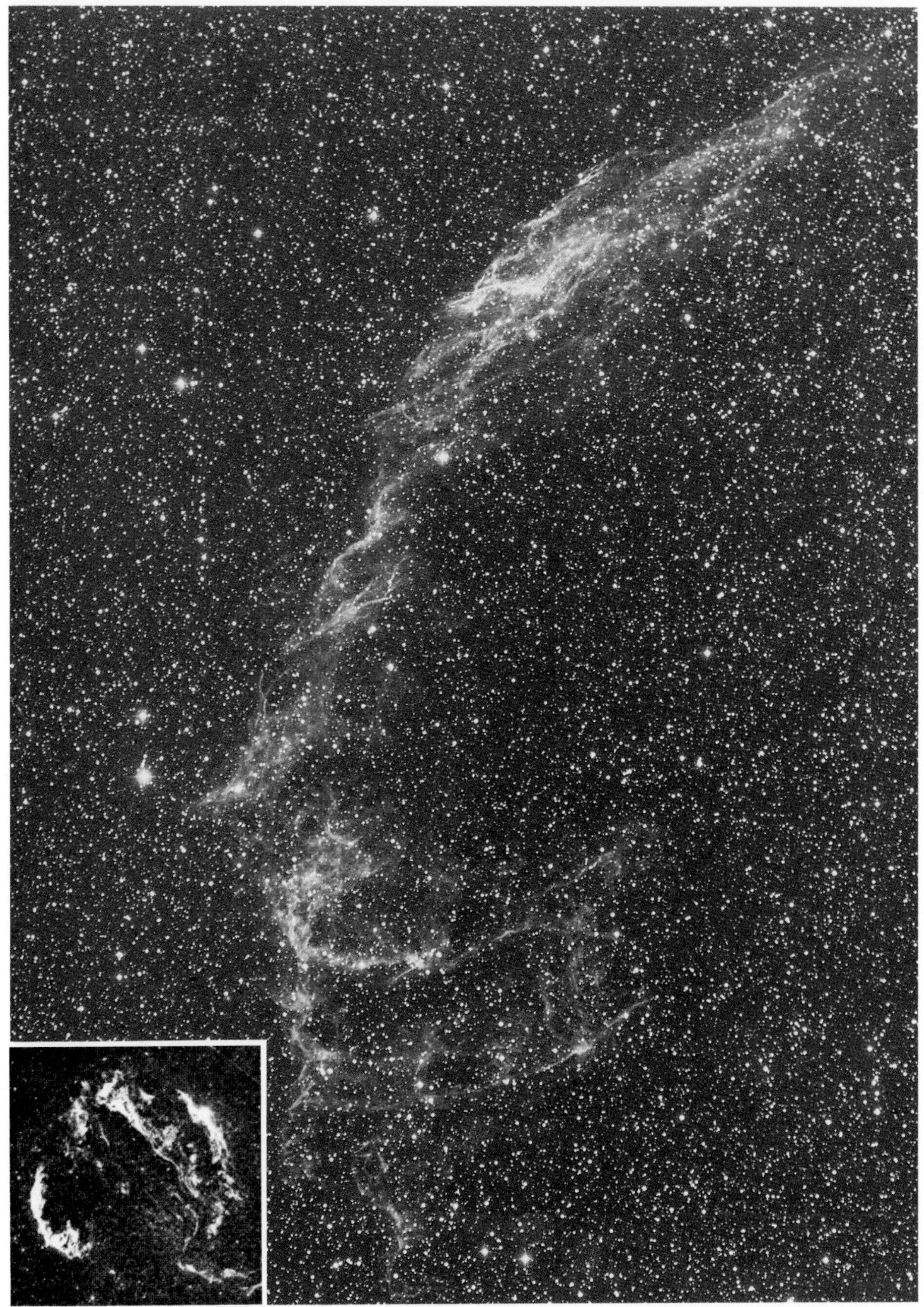

Veil Nebula (NGC 6992 and 6995) in the northern constellation Cygnus, which is part of a much larger spherical supernova remnant (inset). The nebula glows as it collides with dust and gas in interstellar space. Blue light is emitted from the hot leading edge of the nebula, where the most energetic collisions occur; the red glow is from hydrogen in the cooler gas.

Crab Nebula (M1, NGC 1952) in the constellation Taurus, a gaseous remnant of the galactic supernova of AD 1054, 6,000 light-years away, expanding at 700 miles/second.

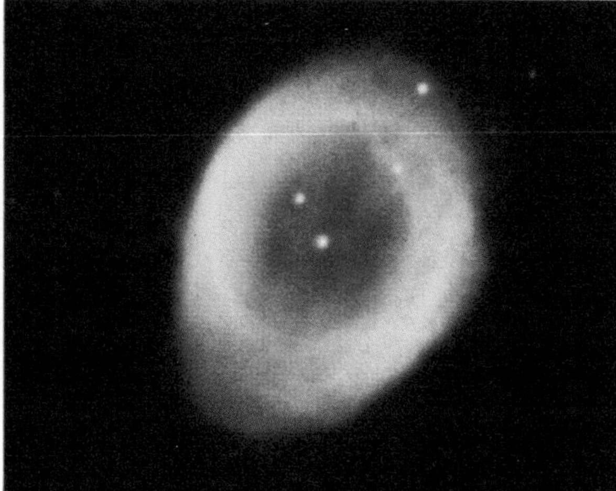

Ring Nebula (M57, NGC 6720) in the constellation Lyra, a planetary nebula consisting mainly of gases thrown off by the star in the centre.

(Above) The inner part of the 30 Doradus Nebula, the most luminous nebula in the entire Local Group of galaxies. It is located in the Large Magellanic Cloud.

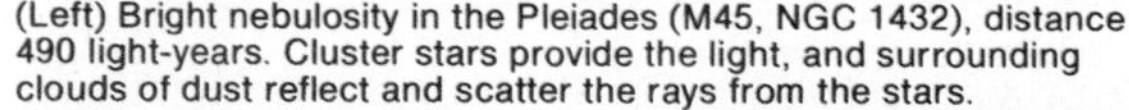

(Left) Bright nebulosity in the Pleiades (M45, NGC 1432), distance 490 light-years. Cluster stars provide the light, and surrounding clouds of dust reflect and scatter the rays from the stars.

Great Nebula in the constellation Orion (M42, NGC 1976), surrounded by glowing gas cloud, one of the largest gas-dust complexes in the Galaxy. Radiation from stars excites atoms of gas, causing them to emit the fluorescent light visible here.

Lagoon Nebula (M8, NGC 6523), in the constellation Sagittarius. This bright diffuse nebula is so large that light from the involved stars does not penetrate its boundaries and the bright nebula appears to be seen against a larger darker one.

Plate 2: By courtesy of (all except centre right) Hale Observatories; photographs, (centre right) National Optical Astronomy Observatories, (others) © California Institute of Technology (top left and right, bottom left) 1959, (centre left, bottom right) 1961

and 1940s the ionization and heating of nebulae were studied on the assumption that motions are negligible. During the 1950s problems of gas dynamics were considered, and since the early 1960s the use of high-speed digital computers has made it possible to take accurate account of ionization processes, heating and cooling, and even the dynamics of the resultant nebular motion. The agreement of these models with observations is encouraging.

Physical conditions in nebulae. There are several different types of nonreflecting bright nebulae (diffuse, planetary, supernovae remnants), but all of their basic physical processes are similar. These processes must be understood in order to understand the physical nature of the nebulae (for individual characteristics, as well as the origin and evolution of each nebular type, see below).

The composition of cosmic matter

Analysis of cosmic matter shows almost a uniform chemical composition, regardless of the object. This material is predominantly hydrogen (about 65 percent by weight, or 90 percent by number of atoms). There is about 2 percent by weight of heavy elements—*i.e.,* of all elements heavier than hydrogen and helium. By number of atoms these heavy elements make up only 0.1 percent of the atoms. The rest—about 30 percent by weight, 10 percent by number of atoms—is the noble gas helium, which on Earth is one of the rarer gases.

The diffuse nebulae, planetary nebulae, or supernovae remnants consist of such material in which nearly every atom has been ionized; that is, had one or more electrons stripped from it. The other types of nebulae—dark and reflection—are composed of almost completely neutral, or non-ionized, gases. The reason for this separation into two classes, one almost completely ionized and the other almost completely neutral, can be seen from consideration of a pure hydrogen cloud, because the basic idea applies equally well to a real nebula. The hydrogen in the cloud can be ionized by ultraviolet light at a wavelength of less than 912 angstroms or, equivalently, a photon energy of more than 13.6 electron volts. Such radiation, if produced by a star inside a cloud of gas, will ionize a region around the star. At a typical point within the ionized region, only one hydrogen atom in 10,000 is neutral. Since only neutral hydrogen can absorb the radiation, the absorption, once the gas has been ionized, is rather low, just enough to offset the "recombinations" (or captures of a free electron by an ion, resulting again in a neutral atom that must eventually be re-ionized). The intensity of ionizing radiation decreases with distance from the source, and the fraction of neutral material therefore increases. But the increasing fraction of neutral material absorbs the remaining radiation: when the fraction of neutral atoms has increased to 1 percent, the absorption is 100 times as large as it was when the matter was only 0.01 percent neutral. The remaining radiation is very quickly absorbed. Thus, the edge to the ionized region is very sharp, and one can divide the gas into almost completely ionized or almost completely neutral regions.

When several species of atoms are present, it is still found that the ionized region has a sharp boundary, because hydrogen and helium behave similarly and together make up 99.9 percent of the atoms of cosmic bodies. There is, in a sense, a competition for the ultraviolet radiation among the various species of ions and atoms, and a balance is quickly reached in which each stage of ionization is destroyed at the same rate as it is produced. A given stage of ionization is produced by (1) recombination (electron capture) from the next higher stage of ionization and (2) ionization (by absorption of radiation) of the next lower stage of ionization. It is destroyed by either the capture of an electron or the absorption of a photon so that the ionization goes a step further. The exact composition of the gas, for a given radiation field, is completely determined by the balance of these processes.

Physics of the nebular spectrum. The simplest atom, hydrogen, consists of a positively charged nucleus encircled by a negatively charged electron. The electron is attracted to the nucleus because of its opposite charge and therefore has a binding energy. One of the rather astonishing results of quantum mechanics, or the laws of atomic behaviour, is that only certain energies characteristic of the type of atom are available to the bound electron. The levels of hydrogen are designated by a quantum number, n. The higher levels are much more closely spaced than the lower ones. The lowest energy level is called the ground level; higher levels are said to be excited. An atom can change its level; if it radiates energy, it emits a quantum or photon of light and drops to a lower energy level, such that the photon energy exactly matches the difference in energy of the initial and final atomic levels. According to Planck's law of radiation, the energy of the photon is related to its wavelength, so that when an atom drops from one level to another a photon of a characteristic wavelength is emitted. Hα, the red hydrogen line at 6563 angstroms, corresponds to a transition from level 3 to level 2; the blue-green Hβ, 4 to 2. All of the hydrogen transitions ending on level 2 are called the Balmer series and are the only hydrogen lines in the visible region of the spectrum. The Lyman lines ending on the ground level, $n = 1$, are stronger but are all at short wavelengths (1215 angstroms or less) in the ultraviolet spectral region absorbed by the Earth's atmosphere.

Energy levels of atoms

Not all changes in energy levels are downward to lower energies: an atom can absorb a photon, using the photon's energy to move the electron into a larger orbit. If the absorbed photon is energetic enough, the electron may even be removed completely, and the atom is ionized. The energy required to ionize the ground level is called the ionization potential of the atom.

Besides emitting and absorbing photons, the atom can change its energy because of its close approach to another atom, ion, or electron when an exchange of energy may take place. Most such "collisions" do not change the energy level of either particle and are "elastic"; that is, the particles have the same kinetic energy after the collision that they did before. Occasionally, however, the collision can either raise the energy of the atom to a higher energy level, at the expense of the kinetic energy (an inelastic collision), or cause the atom to drop to a lower energy level, increasing the kinetic energy (a superelastic collision).

Collisions between atoms and other particles

The spectrum of the nebula can be understood in terms of such transitions between the energy levels of the atoms in the nebula.

Recombination. The hydrogen emission lines in nebulae are produced by the hydrogen nucleus (proton) passing near enough to an electron to recapture it into some bound energy level, emitting a photon in the process. Since the free electron can have any energy above the ionization energy, the photon produced can have any energy, from the ionization energy of the level upward. This gives rise to a continuum of radiation. Another process by which atoms can gain an electron is through an encounter with a neutral hydrogen or helium atom. An electron is then exchanged or transferred from the hydrogen or helium atom to the ion.

The atom is left neutral but, in general, is in an excited state after the recapture. It then drops down to lower energy levels, remaining for only a few hundred-millionths of a second in each level. Most of the nebulae are transparent to the emitted photons except those corresponding to transitions to the lowest, or ground, level; hence, the emitted photon usually escapes. The nebula is opaque to photons matching transitions of the Lyman series ($n = 1$) of hydrogen because almost all of the neutral atoms are in the ground level (they cascade down into it from excited states almost instantaneously), and the photon has exactly the right energy to be absorbed by that level. The result is that the photon can rarely escape, and the nebula is opaque to the Lyman-series lines. The probability of the hydrogen atom emitting the various lines can be calculated from atomic theory; the results agree very well with the observations of actual nebulae.

After an atom has regained its electrons through recombination and cascaded down to the ground state, it remains in the ground state until it absorbs another ionizing photon and is re-ionized. In a typical diffuse nebula this takes about one year. It then remains ionized for about 10,000 years, on the average, before recombining again. During the time it is ionized, the ion undergoes elastic encounters with electrons every few hours as it wanders through the vast spaces of the nebula at a speed of 10 kilometres (seven miles) per second.

All elements undergo recombination and ionization, but, of course, the strength of the lines emitted varies with the atomic abundance. Since hydrogen dominates the atomic abundances, it has by far the strongest recombination lines. The helium lines, however, are easily observed. There are weak recombination lines of carbon and oxygen detected.

Collisionally excited lines. The strongest lines in most nebulae are green lines; they are not emitted from hydrogen and are never observed in the laboratory. When first discovered, they were attributed to a hypothetical element, "nebulium," but it was known that there was no place for another element in the periodic table and that nebulium must be a known element in an unusual state of ionization or excitation. In 1927 the U.S. astronomer Ira Sprague Bowen identified nebulium as doubly ionized oxygen, which can be produced in the laboratory. The green nebular lines are not observed terrestrially because they are "forbidden"; that is, the transition from the upper level to the lower level that produces the emission requires a long time to take place. In the laboratory the excited atom hits another particle or the container walls before it emits the photon. In the nebulae the atom remains undisturbed long enough to emit the photon.

"Forbidden" lines

The doubly ionized oxygen ion enters the upper level of the transition through collisions with electrons, typically undergone about once every year for each ion. This is a comparatively rapid rate. In comparison, ionized hydrogen takes about 10,000 years to recombine and emit a photon at a hydrogen-line wavelength. The "rapid" rate of collisional excitation of the oxygen more than makes up for the fact that its abundance is lower than hydrogen by a factor of about 1,000.

The hydrogen lines are not produced by collisions, because the energy-level spacing is different in hydrogen and doubly ionized oxygen. Practically no electrons have enough energy to excite the hydrogen atom. In contrast, doubly ionized oxygen and many other heavy ions have low-lying levels that can be excited by the electrons. Many ions have energy levels only slightly above the ground level. The lines emitted from these levels have wavelengths of several micrometres (or microns). They are important because they can pass through cosmic dust without being absorbed.

In nebulae the forbidden lines provide an important means of measuring density and temperature. The rate at which collisions excite the upper levels depends on the temperature, which can be determined by comparing the strengths of lines arising from different upper levels of the same atom. The derived values are 6,000–9,000 K (0 K = −273° C or −460° F) for diffuse nebulae and 7,000–17,000 K for planetary nebulae. Similarly, for high-density objects the densities can be found by comparing two forbidden lines that are collisionally de-excited at different rates. The strongest lines of singly ionized oxygen, at 3726 and 3729 angstroms, are usually used for this purpose. The densities derived for the centre of the Orion Nebula are about 10,000 atoms per cubic centimetre.

The nebular continuum. In addition to the emission lines, there is a faint continuous background spectrum. It was noted above that recombination to a bound level can give rise to some of it. Another cause is the bremsstrahlung, radiation emitted by free electrons as they are accelerated by passing near ions. This is the strongest source of nebular continuous radiation in the radio-wavelength region. For short radio wavelengths the radiation escapes from the nebula, but for longer wavelengths the nebula absorbs the radiation, and only the radiation emitted close enough to the edge to escape can be observed.

Major source of continuous radio radiation

In the diffuse nebulae there is also a continuum contribution from starlight reflected from dust grains within the nebula. Thus, a diffuse nebula may have a weak reflection component, but its own line emission greatly dominates the light produced.

The temperature of nebulae. Nebulae differ from one another by factors of hundreds in mass, size, and density; their sources of ionization vary from stars whose temperatures are 30,000 K (B-type stars, for some diffuse nebulae) to the central stars of small, peculiar planetary nebulae that may be as high as perhaps 150,000 K. Yet practically all nebular temperatures fall in the range from about 6,000 to about 12,000 K. The temperature is kept within such a narrow range because the cooling processes (emission of optical or infrared forbidden lines that escape the nebula) are quite inefficient below 5,000 K. Hence, only a small amount of heating—mainly from the excess energy of a stellar photon after it ionizes a hydrogen or helium atom—suffices to bring the temperature up to this level. Above this value the cooling increases very rapidly, and a great deal of heating is needed to bring the temperature much above 10,000 K. The heavy ions of the nebula act as a thermostat set on the rather formidable temperature of 8,000 K.

DIFFUSE, DARK, AND REFLECTION NEBULAE

Forms taken by diffuse nebulae. Most nebulae are diffuse in appearance, having no regular structure or sharp boundaries (see illustration). In the case of the particular class of nebulae designated diffuse, however, the term is used in a more restricted sense, referring specifically to clouds of gas and dust, ionized by one or more young, massive stars (the "exciting" stars) within or near them. Their sizes and masses vary enormously; there is really no lower limit to their size, since a very faint nebula must exist around almost every star, while the largest diffuse nebulae are about 200 light-years across and contain about 100,000 solar masses of ionized gas. A typical diffuse nebula is about 30 light-years across and has a density of roughly 10 atoms per cubic centimetre. In spite of this low density, the total mass of gas in such a nebula would be several times that of the Sun. The density distribution is chaotic and irregular, and the obscuration caused by the dust within and in front of the nebula makes it difficult to get an accurate idea of the gas distribution by optical means. Radio waves penetrate the dust unhindered, and observations of radio emission from the ionized gas reveal that on a large scale diffuse nebulae are more regular than their photographs would suggest. For instance, the Trapezium, a group of bright stars exciting the Orion Nebula, appears in visible light near the edge of the nebula (see Plate 2). The radio contours indicate that the nebula is really rather symmetrical about the Trapezium; there is a dark cloud that acts as a curtain in front of about half of it.

Low density of diffuse nebulae

High-resolution studies of diffuse nebulae reveal one of the surprises that make the study of astrophysics delightful. Instead of the smooth structure that might be expected of a gas, a delicate tracery of luminous filaments can be detected, down to the smallest scale that can be resolved. In the Orion Nebula this is about 10 times the diameter of the orbit of Pluto, the outermost known planet, about the Sun. Even finer detail may exist, and there is evidence from spectra that much of the matter may be gathered into dense condensations, or knots, the rest of the space being comparatively empty. The time it would take unrestrained gas to fill a vacuum between the visible filaments is only about 200 years, much less time than the age of the nebula. The nebular gas is presumably restrained from expansion by the pressure of tenuous material pervading much of the space in the Galaxy. This material consists of hot gas having a temperature of a few million kelvins. Its pressure, however, is comparable to that in the visible "warm" (8,000 K) gas of the diffuse nebula. Hence, the density of the hot material is several hundred times lower, which effectively prevents it from radiating. Moreover, the material is invisible except in low-energy X rays. The space throughout the plane of the Galaxy is largely filled with this hot component, mainly produced and heated from supernovae. In diffuse nebulae, it also arises from the "wind" blown off the atmospheres of the exciting stars at speeds of up to 3,000 kilometres per second. This stellar wind creates a large cavity or bubble in the denser, cooler gas originally surrounding such a star. In the interior of the bubble, the radially flowing stellar wind passes through a transition in which its radial motion is converted into heat. The hot gas then fills most of the cavity (perhaps 90 percent or more) and serves to separate the filaments of the warm, comparatively dense diffuse nebula. Within the

Luminous filaments

condensations of visible plasma, there are neutral globules in which the gas is quite cold (about 100 K) and dense enough (typically, 10,000 atoms per cubic centimetre) to have about the same pressure as the hot and warm materials. In short, a diffuse nebula is much more complicated than its visual radiation would suggest.

The most energetic diffuse nebulae in the Galaxy are revealed only by radio telescope—they are so heavily obscured by dust that they are inconspicuous optically. These nebulae have over 100 times more ionizations per second than does the Orion Nebula, too many to be provided by a single star (unless there are stars more luminous than any known within the Galaxy; see below). Indeed, very high resolution images of the most luminous nebulae show there are clumps of ionized gas—probably ionized by tight groupings of single stars—embedded in rather diffuse gas that emit most of the radio radiation. Similar objects, about 200 light-years in diameter, can be detected in other galaxies; if they were located at the Orion Nebula, they would cover the entire constellation of Orion with brightly glowing gas. These supergiant nebulae are more than 10 times as luminous as any in the Galaxy. The entire Local Group—the cluster of galaxies consisting of the Galaxy, the great spiral galaxy in Andromeda, the smaller spiral in Triangulum, and more than 20 other stellar assemblages—contains but one supergiant nebula: the object called 30 Doradus, in the Large Magellanic Cloud (see Plate 2). This nebula requires over 1,000 times more ionizations per second than the Orion Nebula. It contains an object called R136, which may be the source of most of the energy radiated by the nebula. The nature of R136 remains controversial. It certainly appears to be a tight grouping of very luminous stars, with a bright core that may contain one or two stars, each having perhaps 500 solar masses—*i.e.,* approximately five times as massive as any known object in the Galaxy. Alternatively, R136 may be a grouping of about 10 of the most massive known stars of the Galaxy, all packed into a volume only a thousandth of a typical stellar spacing in size. How such a cluster could form, in either case, is a fascinating puzzle. There are other supergiant nebulae outside of the Local Group, some of which radiate 10 times the energy of 30 Doradus.

Cold, neutral clouds of matter

Forms taken by dark nebulae. Intimately associated with the diffuse nebulae are cold, neutral clouds of material that show up as dark nebulae because of the obscuring dust they contain. (The word cloud is used for convenience; actually there is probably some material everywhere, and cloud is used to mean a region with a local increase in density.) Sometimes the dark nebulae project as long, serpentine shapes seen against a background of stars beyond them; more typically, their borders are not sharp or obvious. A few dark nebulae are very opaque, allowing only $^1/_{1,000}$ of the incident light or less to pass through them, but more usually they absorb half of it or less. Most (perhaps 90 percent) of the mass of gas in the Galaxy is in this neutral material and can be seen as dark nebulae only when concentrated in dense clouds. On the average, the galactic material absorbs half of the light in a distance of about 3,000 light-years.

The dark nebulae are neutral and cold because not enough ultraviolet radiation is available in the regions they occupy to cause any appreciable ionization of hydrogen or helium (although the X rays and cosmic rays in the Galaxy will always provide at least some ionization, about 1 percent or less). Such a lack of radiation energy is very important to the physical state of the gas.

Absorption is a major difficulty for astronomers studying stars, since it dims the starlight being examined, but it does provide the means for studying the nature of the particles that cause the absorption. In general, these particles are a few micrometres in size, spaced about 90 metres apart. A significant fraction of them is carbon in a form similar to soot. There are particles of rocklike materials (silicates), silicon carbide, and other materials as well. An individual particle may possibly consist of a matrix of several different constituents. Ordinary water ice does not exist in large quantities on the particles.

The origin of the particles is an interesting theoretical problem. While they are probably composed of common substances, solid grains cannot form from a completely gaseous, dilute medium, such as interstellar clouds. Nuclei of a few hundred atoms must somehow first stick together into a tiny "seed" particle; until the grain is large enough to radiate away the energy gained by a collision with an approaching atom, the atom will simply rebound instead of sticking. Such grains may form in the outer atmospheres of cool supergiant stars where the gas density is comparatively high (perhaps 10^9 times what it is in the nebula). The grains are then blown out of the atmosphere by radiation pressure (the mechanical force of the light they absorb and scatter). Calculations indicate that refracting materials, such as the constituents of the grains proposed above, should condense in this way.

The formation of stars

In the inner regions of dark nebulae important events take place: the formation of stars. The discussion that follows will be slightly oversimplified by the assumption that the nebula has very little net rotation. Since the density in a star is immensely greater than that in a nebula, star formation must occur through condensation. The force of gravity in the nebula constantly pulls it together, working against the disruptive collisions of any one nebula or cloud with its neighbours. But, even if gravity can hold the cloud together against other forces, the cloud cannot collapse unless it can cool; gravitational energy is released in a contraction and would heat the gas cloud, thus increasing the outward pressure and preventing further collapse. The dust grains are efficient emitters of infrared radiation, which escapes, removing the energy from the nebula. A cloud, therefore, contracts under its own gravity, radiating away half of the gravitational energy of the contraction, the other half going into heating the gas. As it contracts, the density and gravitational binding increase, and finally the cloud's gravity so dominates the internal pressure that the material rushes inward in almost a free fall.

While the entire cloud has been collapsing, it does not have a smooth density distribution but rather consists of a chaotic jumble of smaller clouds. These cloudlets pull themselves together by their own gravity into "protostars," each of which is destined to be an individual stellar system. Most of these protostars are smaller than one solar mass, but a very few may be several (up to about 100) times as massive as the Sun. These few massive stars have a profound influence in the evolution of the nebula.

Origin of planetary systems

Each protostar collapses very quickly; its gas falls inward in free fall. A protostar can collapse from a size equal to the outer diameter of the solar system to about 30 times the Sun's size (the size of Mercury's orbit) in about six months. After it reaches that size, the material becomes so hot it has become a star; that is, an opaque body radiating energy only from its surface. Around it is a whirling ring of cold, dusty material, which will also break up into even smaller fragments, the "protoplanets." It is now believed that planetary systems are made out of this dusty chaos.

Many such newly formed stars continue to contract, becoming hotter but less luminous in the process, until they start to produce heat by converting hydrogen into helium rather than by contracting. Such a star would then pour forth this energy from thermonuclear reactions into the dark clouds around it and begin to ionize the nebular material, producing a bright nebula around it.

These ideas are given encouraging confirmation by observations of dark nebulae in very long wavelength infrared radiation. Some of the brightest infrared sources are associated with such dark dust clouds; a good example is the class of T Tauri variables, named for their prototype star in the constellation Taurus. The T Tauri stars are known for a variety of reasons to be extremely young. The variables are always found in or near dark nebulae; they are often also powerful sources of infrared radiation, corresponding to warm clouds of dust heated by the T Tauri star to a few hundred kelvins. There are some strong infrared sources (especially in the constellation of Orion) that have no visible stars with them; these are presumably "cocoon stars" completely hidden by their veils of dust.

Formation of reflection nebulae. In 1912 it was discovered that the bright nebula in the Pleiades star cluster has a spectrum like that of the nearby stars rather than a typical nebular spectrum of bright emission lines. The interpre-

Distinguishing characteristics of reflection nebulae

tation is clear; the nebula is shining by starlight reflected from the dust particles rather than by any emission of the gas itself. The star illuminating such a reflection nebula is almost always a bright star of type B2 (temperature about 20,000 K) or cooler; hotter stars would ionize the gas and cause nebular emission lines. Studies of the angular sizes of the reflection nebulae led to the conclusion that about 60 percent of the light incident upon the dust is reflected (scattered) rather than absorbed, showing that the material is almost as reflective as snow. Calculations show that even graphite, which, of course, is black in bulk, can produce this effect when dispersed into tiny particles.

According to present theories, the fate of the gas remaining in a cloud after star formation depends critically on the kind of star formed; most stars can be created in the interior of the cloud without much influence on the gas (other than to use it up in their formation). The situation changes abruptly when one or more of the rare, massive hot stars, called O stars, form. These stars produce ultraviolet radiation that ionizes the gas, heating it from perhaps 50 to 8,000 K in the process. The pressure in the gas is consequently increased by about 300 times. The ionized gas expands into the surrounding neutral, cold gas like a giant piston, compressing it tremendously. Just as in an explosion, a shock front is formed between the compressed gas and the quiet, undisturbed material ahead of it. Rapid star formation may occur in the compressed region, producing an expanding group of young stars. Such groups, the so-called O Associations (with O stars) or T Associations (with T Tauri stars), have been observed. The component stars simultaneously generate very fast outflows from their atmospheres (see above). These winds create regions of hot, tenuous gas surrounding the association. Eventually the massive stars in the association explode as supernovae, which further disturb the surrounding gas.

Stellar associations

This picture of the evolution of diffuse and dark nebulae is one of constant turmoil, a few transient O stars serving to keep the material stirred, in constant motion, constantly producing new stars and churning clouds of gas and dust. In this way the thermonuclear energy of stars is converted into kinetic energy of interstellar gas.

Location of diffuse and dark nebulae in the Galaxy. One of the remarkable features of the diffuse and dark nebulae is their extreme concentration in the spiral arms in the plane of the Galaxy. While there is no rigid boundary to the arms, which have irregularities and bifurcations (or "spurs"), the nebulae in other spiral galaxies are strung out along these narrow lanes and form a beautifully symmetric system when viewed from another galaxy. The nebulae are remarkably close to the galactic plane; most are within 300 light-years, only 1 percent of the distance of the Sun from the centre. The details of the explanation of why the gas is largely confined to the spiral arms is beyond the scope of this article (see GALAXIES). Briefly, the higher density of the stars in the arms produces sufficient gravity to hold the gas to them.

The question may be asked: why doesn't the gas simply condense into stars and disappear? The present rate of star formation is about one solar mass per year in the entire Galaxy, which contains something like two times 10^9 solar masses of gas. Clearly, if the gas received no return of material from stars, it would be depleted in roughly two times 10^9 years, about one-fifth the present age of the Galaxy. Several processes by which gas is returned to the interstellar medium from stars have been observed. Possibly the most important is the ejection of planetary nebula shells, discussed below; other processes are ejection of material from massive O- and B-type normal stars or from cool M giants and supergiants. This rate of gas ejection is roughly equal to the rate of star formation, so that the mass of free gas is declining very slowly.

This cycling of the gas through stars presumably has had one major effect: the chemical composition of the gas has been changed by the nuclear reactions inside the stars. There is excellent evidence that the Galaxy originally consisted of almost pure hydrogen with some helium and that all of the heavier elements have been produced inside stars by being subjected to the exceedingly high temperatures in the central regions. Thus, most of the atoms and molecules on the Earth, as well as in human bodies, owe their very existence to processes that occur within stars.

Original composition of the Galaxy

Chemical composition of diffuse nebulae. The composition of diffuse nebulae can be estimated by relating the strengths of the emission lines found in their spectra to the numbers of atoms producing them, and great strides have been made in calculating the necessary atomic properties. The principal difficulties in determining the abundances of elements from nebular emission lines are (1) the estimation of the nebular temperature, which is necessary because line emission for a given abundance increases rapidly with increasing temperature; and (2) the estimation of the abundances of stages of ionization of the element, if these stages do not have any observable lines. There are at least two reliable indicators of nebular temperatures. The first utilizes the relative strengths of forbidden lines of the same ions arising from two or more upper levels reasonably different in energy. The ratio of line strengths depends sensitively on the electron temperature. Unfortunately, there are not many such diagnostic line pairs. The most frequently available pair is that of doubly ionized oxygen. The line from the upper level, at a wavelength of 4363 angstroms, is very faint, often less than 1 percent of the strong green line at 5007 angstroms. If there are fluctuations of temperature within a nebula, this method estimates the temperature to be too high. The second method of determining nebular temperature is based on the strengths of emission lines of hydrogen in very high quantum states, such as the transition between the 110 and 109 levels. Because the higher levels are closely spaced, the transitions between two higher levels have low energies and correspondingly long wavelengths: six centimetres, in this case. This radio wavelength implies that the line can be observed through large amounts of dust. There is some action originating in nebulae to amplify the emission by means of a mechanism fundamental to the laser and maser—namely, stimulated emission. The strength of a radio line depends on the nebular temperature. If there are regions of various temperatures within a nebula, such radio lines, in contrast to the forbidden lines, give an estimate that is lower than the true average. The two methods of estimating nebular temperature give gratifyingly similar results when they are applied to the same object. This fact indicates that temperature fluctuations within a nebula are not a serious problem.

All abundant chemical elements have some stages of ionization that are associated with observable emission lines from which the abundance of a given ion can be determined after the temperature has been estimated in the manner discussed above. The primary interest, though, is in the total abundance of the element and not simply that of an individual stage of ionization. Ions that have no observable lines are accounted for by theoretical calculations. Elaborate computer calculations predict the ionization structure of gas ionized by a hot star; the temperature of the star is determined by matching the observed stages of ionization with the computer model. The calculations then provide predictions of the abundances of the invisible ions. The correction for unobserved stages is of little significance for some elements (oxygen) but absolutely crucial for others (argon and carbon). The final estimates for—in order of decreasing reliability—oxygen, sulfur, nitrogen, and neon abundances in diffuse nebulae are probably more accurate than determinations of stellar composition. Those for carbon and argon, however, are more problematic. The well-established abundances have uncertainties of about 30 percent. Such determinations apply only to the portions of the elements in the gas phase. Solids (dust grains) do not produce emission lines.

In the nearby Orion Nebula, by far the most thoroughly studied diffuse nebula, the abundances of elements other than hydrogen are (in atoms per million hydrogen atoms) as follows: helium, 80,000; oxygen, 400; carbon, 320; neon, 70; nitrogen, 50; sulfur, 12; and argon, 4. One of the most enigmatic results of the Orion investigations is that the oxygen abundance in the nebula is only about 0.6 that in the Sun. This finding is most unexpected because supernovae presumably have been adding oxygen to the interstellar gas ever since the Sun formed some 5,000,000,000 years ago. Grains are probably not responsible for the "missing" oxygen in the Orion Nebula because the inner part of the nebula seems to be free of dust. Furthermore, nitrogen and neon, both unlikely to be found in dust grains, also are deficient in Orion in exactly the same proportion as oxygen. One possibility is that there are chemical inhomogeneities within the Galaxy and that the Sun formed from material richer than average in heavy elements.

It is, in fact, clear that the Galaxy is not chemically homogeneous at the present time. Observations of radio recombination lines show that there is a gradient, or variation, in the temperature of nebulae throughout the Galaxy. This gradient almost surely implies a variation in the principal coolant, oxygen, and presumably in other heavy elements as well. The oxygen abundance is perhaps twice the solar value at one-third the Sun's distance from the galactic centre, and down to two-thirds of the solar abundance at the most distant points for which reliable determinations can be made (about 1.5 times the Sun's distance, or 45,000 light-years). These differences in heavy-element content reflect varying amounts of nucleosynthesis by massive stars. Similar gradients are found in other galaxies.

Determining the compositions of nebulae outside the Galaxy

The composition of nebulae in other galaxies can be determined by direct optical observations of emission lines. This method is not practical throughout the Milky Way because of the obscuration of dust. The Large Magellanic Cloud has compositions that are uniformly about one-half those of the Orion Nebula for oxygen, neon, argon, and sulfur and are one-quarter those of Orion for carbon and nitrogen. It appears that the first group of elements must be manufactured together, presumably in massive stars, and ejected together into the interstellar gas that is currently observable. Stars of a different mass (probably lower) must produce carbon and nitrogen. Planetary nebulae (discussed below) also suggest the same scenario.

The abundance of helium in nebulae has received considerable attention because the helium content of the oldest objects provides clues to the origin of the universe. The value cited above for the Orion Nebula is in agreement with the predictions of the Big Bang model, the prevailing cosmological theory according to which the universe began with an enormous explosion involving rapid expansion from a highly compressed primordial state. In order to determine the precise nature of this so-called Big Bang, a more precise estimate of helium abundance is needed than can be presently derived from nebulae.

THE PLANETARY NEBULAE

There are about 20,000 objects called planetary nebulae in the Galaxy. Such nebulae represent gas that has been expelled relatively recently from stars very late in their evolutionary cycles. By contrast, diffuse and dark nebulae are clouds of gas from which young stars form. Because of the obscuration of dust in the Galaxy, only about 1,000 planetary nebulae have been cataloged.

Forms and structure. Compared to the diffuse nebulae, planetary nebulae are small objects, having a radius, typically, of one light-year and containing a mass of gas equivalent to about 0.3 solar mass. They are considerably denser than most diffuse nebulae, typically containing 1,000–10,000 atoms per cubic centimetre within their dense regions, and are 1,000 times as luminous. Many are so far away that they appear stellar when photographed directly, but the conspicuous examples measure up to 20′ of arc across, 10″–30″ being usual. Those that show a bright disk have much more regular forms than the chaotic diffuse nebulae, but there are still usually some brightness fluctuations over the disk. The planetaries generally have regular, sharp outer boundaries; often they have a relatively regular inner boundary as well, giving them an appearance like a ring. Many have two lobes of bright material, resembling arcs of a circle, connected by a bridge—somewhat resembling the letter Z.

The central star

Most planetaries show a central star, called the nucleus, which provides the ultraviolet radiation required for ionizing the gas in the ring or shell surrounding it. Those stars are among the hottest known and are in a state of comparatively rapid evolution.

As with diffuse nebulae, the overall structural regularity conceals large-scale fluctuations in density. High-resolution photographs of a planetary nebula usually reveal tiny knots and filaments down to the resolution limit of the photograph. The spectrum of the planetary nebula is basically the same as that of the diffuse nebula; it contains bright lines from hydrogen and helium recombinations and the forbidden lines (defined above) of other ions. In general, the spectra of planetaries differ from those of diffuse nebulae in that they show much higher degrees of ionization. In some planetaries most of the helium is doubly ionized, and appreciable amounts of five-times-ionized oxygen and argon and four-times-ionized neon exist. In diffuse nebulae helium is mainly once ionized and neon and argon only once or twice. This difference in the states of the atoms results from the temperature of the planetary nucleus (up to about 150,000 K), which is much higher than that of the exciting star of the diffuse nebula (less than 60,000 K for an O star, the hottest). One of the conspicuous features of planetaries is that the high stages of ionization are found close to the central star. The rare heavy ions, rather than hydrogen, absorb the photons of several hundred volts' energy. Beyond a certain distance from the central star, all the photons of energy sufficient to ionize a given species of ion have been absorbed, and that species therefore cannot exist farther out. Detailed theoretical calculations have rather successfully predicted the spectra of the best observed nebulae.

Expansion of planetaries

The spectra of planetary nebulae reveal another interesting general fact: they are expanding from the central star at speeds of 24 to 56 kilometres per second. The gravitational pull of the star is quite small at the distance of the shell from the star, so the shell will continue its expansion until it finally merges with the interstellar gas around it. The expansion is proportional to the distance from the central star, consistent with the entire mass of gas having been ejected at one brief period from the star in some sort of instability.

The distances of planetary nebulae. Not a single planetary nebula is close enough to the Sun to allow a direct determination of its distance; the nearest, reasonably bright one (NGC 7293) is about 300 light-years away. It is necessary, therefore, to use indirect methods to find the distances. One method is to estimate the true rate of emission of one of the hydrogen lines from the nebula (from the gas density and temperature) and compare this with the observed brightness. From the intrinsic and apparent brightness the distance can be found. One planetary, NGC 246, has a normal G star as a companion and its distance can be estimated if it is assumed that the companion is similar in intrinsic brightness to nearby G stars of similar type. Once the distance is known, other quantities (such as size and mass) can easily be found. Unfortunately, different methods of estimating distances give results differing by factors of more than two. A more reliable way of estimating distance is to consider the planetaries found in the nearest external galaxies, such as the Andromeda Galaxy or the Magellanic Clouds. The distances to the galaxies are known from their other stars, such as the Cepheid variables. Even the most luminous planetary nebulae are very faint in other galaxies, and so only the few brightest and atypically massive nebulae can be studied.

From the best available average distance determination, the true size of any nebula can be found, within the limits of error, from its angular size; typically, planetary nebulae are found to be a few tenths of a light-year in radius. If this distance is divided by the expansion speed, the age of the nebula since ejection is obtained, with values up to roughly 30,000 years.

Chemical composition. The chemical composition of planetaries can be found from their spectra in the way discussed above for diffuse nebulae. The problem of correcting for unobserved stages of ionization of the various elements in planetaries is much more complicated than in diffuse nebulae because the hotter central stars produce a wider range of ionization. Many stages of ionization are observable only through ultraviolet emission lines arising from highly excited levels, and the ionic abundances determined from these lines are very dependent on nebular temperature, which is either calculated or measured. Some clear trends arise from abundance studies of the planetary nebulae. They definitely show signs of chemical enrichment from elements produced by nuclear processing within the central star. Some nebulae are carbon-rich, with twice as much carbon as oxygen, while the opposite is true for the Sun. Others are overabundant in nitrogen; the most luminous ones, observed in external galaxies, are conspicuous examples. Helium is modestly enhanced, up to a factor of two over the solar value. There is one object that contains almost no hydrogen; it is as if the gas had been ejected from the object at the very end of the nuclear-burning process. Planetary nebulae also show a clear indication of the general heavy-element abundance gradient in the Galaxy, presumably a reflection of the original composition of the stars that gave rise to the present nebulae.

Presence of cosmic dust

Some, but not all, planetary nebulae contain internal dust. In general, this dust cannot be seen directly but can be detected from the infrared radiation it emits after being heated by nebular and stellar radiation. The presence of dust implies that planetary nebulae are even richer in heavy elements than gas-phase abundance studies suggest.

Among nebulae so far discovered, two are particularly deviant in chemical composition: one is in the globular cluster M15 and the other in the "halo" (tenuous outer regions) of the Galaxy. Both have very low heavy-element content (down from normal by factors of about 50) but normal helium. Both objects are very old, and this result suggests that, while the primeval gas in the Galaxy had a low heavy-element content, it did have helium. The origin of helium in the Galaxy was probably the initial explosion of the universe itself.

Positions in the Galaxy. One of the best indicators of the average age of astronomical objects is their position and motion in the Galaxy. The youngest are in the spiral arms, near the gas from which they have formed; the oldest are not concentrated to the plane of the Galaxy, nor are they found within the spiral arms. By these criteria, the planetaries reveal themselves to be rather middle-aged; they are moderately but not strongly concentrated to the plane; rather, they are concentrated toward the galactic centre, as the older objects are. Their motions in the Galaxy follow elliptical paths, whereas circular orbits are characteristic of younger stars. They belong to the type of distribution often called a "disk population," to distinguish them from Population II (very old) and Population I (young) objects of U.S. astronomer Walter Baade. It is likely that there is a wide variation in the ages of planetaries and that some are very young objects.

Stellar populations

Evolution of planetary nebulae. A description of the evolution of a planetary nebula begins before the ejection of the nebula itself. As will be discussed below, the central star is a red giant before the ejection. In such a phase it experiences a rapid loss of mass, up to 0.01 Earth mass per day, in the form of a comparatively slowly expanding stellar wind. At this stage the red giant might be heavily obscured by dust, which forms from the heavy elements in the wind. Eventually the nature of both the star and its wind changes. The star becomes hotter because its hot core is exposed by the loss of the overlying atmosphere. The inner gas is ionized by radiation from the hot star. The ionization zone moves steadily outward through the slowly moving material of what was formerly the stellar wind. The expansion speed of the gas is typically 50 kilometres per second. Nebulae in this stage are bright but have starlike images as seen from the Earth, because they are too small to show a disk. The gas is at a relatively high density—about 1,000,000 atoms per cubic centimetre—but becomes more dilute as the gas expands. During this stage the nebula is surrounded by neutral hydrogen. It appears to expand faster than the individual atoms of gas in it are moving; the ionized shell is "eating into" the neutral material as the density falls.

The middle stage of evolution occurs when the density has dropped to the point where the entire mass of gas is ionized. After this stage is reached, some of the ultraviolet radiation escapes into space, and the expansion of the nebula is caused entirely by the motion of the gas. Most planetaries are now in this middle stage. Finally the central star becomes less luminous and can no longer provide enough ultraviolet radiation to keep even the dilute nebula ionized. Once again the outer regions of the nebula become neutral and therefore invisible. Eventually the gas is mingled with the general interstellar gas.

Faint outer rings

A curious feature of several planetaries is that faint rings surrounding the bright, inner nebula can be observed. Possibly the outer rings are the remnants of a previous shell ejected earlier by the star. Alternately, they might be at the outer edge of the expanding neutral (and invisible) gas, which is ramming into quiescent interstellar gas originally present when the planetary ejection occurred. There would be a strong shock wave at this interface, and the shocked matter would be heated to several thousand degrees, causing the emission. The matter would quickly radiate its heat and become cold and invisible again. The key to the choice of those alternatives would be the spectrum of the faint ring, if it could be determined.

The central stars. The central stars are known from their spectra to be very hot. A common type of spectrum has very broad emission lines of carbon or nitrogen, as well as of ionized helium, superimposed upon a bluish continuum. These spectra are indistinguishable from those from the very bright rare stars known as Wolf-Rayet stars, but the planetary nuclei are about 100 times fainter than true Wolf-Rayet objects. The stars appear to be losing some mass at the present time, though evidently not enough to contribute appreciably to the shell.

The presence of the nebula allows a fairly precise determination of the central star's evolution. The temperature of the star can be estimated from the nebula from the amounts of emission of ionized helium and hydrogen by a method devised by the Dutch astronomer H. Zanstra. The amount of ionized-helium radiation is determined by the number of photons of more than 54 volts' energy, while hydrogen is ionized by photons of over 13.6 volts. The relative numbers of photons in the two groups depend strongly on temperature, since the spectrum shifts dramatically to higher energies as the temperature of the star increases. Hence, the temperature can be found from the observed strengths of the hydrogen and helium lines. The rate of evolution of the stars can be found from the sizes of their nebulae, as the time since ejection of the shell is the radius of the nebula divided by the expansion rate. The energy output, or luminosity, of the central star can be estimated from the brightness of the nebula, because the nebula is converting the star's invisible ultraviolet radiation (which contains the greater part of the star's luminous energy) into visible radiation.

The resulting theoretical description of the star's evolution is quite interesting. While there seem to be real differences in stars at a given stage, the trends are quite clear. The central stars in the youngest planetary nebulae are about as hot as the massive O and B stars—35,000–40,000 K—but roughly 10 times fainter. They have half the diameter of the Sun but are 1,000 times as luminous. As the nebula expands, the star increases its brightness and temperature, but its radius decreases steadily. It reaches a maximum energy output, when it is roughly 10,000 times as luminous as the Sun, about 5,000 years after the initial expansion. This is an amazingly small fraction of the star's age of several times 10^9 years; it represents a period equivalent to about half an hour in a human life. From this point on the star becomes fainter, but for some time the temperature continues to increase while the shrinkage of the star continues. At its hottest the star is perhaps 200,000 K, almost five times hotter than the hottest of most of the stars. It then cools and after about 10,000 years becomes a very dense white dwarf star, hardly larger than the Earth but with a density of thousands of kilograms per cubic centimetre. From this point it cools very slowly, becoming redder and fainter indefinitely.

Final stages of central star's evolution

While there is not yet a very detailed theoretical picture of this contraction, a few results have emerged rather clearly: (1) white dwarf stars must obtain almost all of their energy from the contraction noted above, not from nuclear sources; therefore, (2) they must contain practically no hydrogen or helium, except perhaps in a very thin shell on their surfaces. These conditions would have to be met for the evolution to take place so quickly.

The absence of hydrogen in the star's interior is quite surprising; the planetary nebulae are all found to have a normal hydrogen abundance of about 1,000 times as many hydrogen atoms as heavy elements, such as oxygen. Thus, the mechanism of expulsion of the envelope must be very efficient at ejecting the hydrogen-rich outer layers of a star while leaving heavy-element-rich material behind.

The nature of the progenitor stars. The progenitor must have mass not much in excess of a solar mass because of the distribution of the planetaries in the Galaxy. Very massive stars are young and more closely confined than are nebulae to the galactic plane. Also, the mass of the nebula is roughly 0.3 solar mass, and the mass of a typical white dwarf (the final state of the central star) is roughly 0.7 solar mass. Next, the expansion velocity of the nebula is probably comparable with the velocity of escape from its progenitor, which implies that the progenitor was a red giant star, large and cool, completely unlike the small, hot, blue, nuclear star remaining after the ejection. Likely candidates are members of the class of Long-Period Variable stars, which have about the right size and mass and are known to be unstable. Symbiotic stars (*i.e.,* stars with characteristics of both cool giants and very hot stars) are also candidates. Novae, stars that brighten temporarily while ejecting a shell explosively, are definitely not candidates; the nova shell is expanding at hundreds of kilometres per second.

Red giant stars as probable progenitors

The cause of the ejection is the outward force of radiation on the outer layers of red giant stars. The ejection is triggered by a rapid variation in the nuclear luminosity in the interior of the giant, caused by instability in the helium-burning shell. The ejection takes place during more than one phase of the giant's evolution. Nitrogen-rich nebulae develop during an early episode when convection inside the star carries nitrogen, produced from carbon in a series of nuclear reactions (*i.e.,* the carbon–nitrogen cycle of hydrogen-burning), to the surface. A later ejection takes place with an enrichment of both nitrogen and helium, which is also produced by hydrogen-burning. A still later phase occurs when convection carries carbon, the product of helium-burning, to the surface.

FILAMENTARY BRIGHT NEBULAE: SUPERNOVA REMNANTS

The supernova phenomenon is a spectacular explosion in which a star ejects most of its mass in a violently expanding cloud of debris that soon becomes a remarkable nebula. At the brightest phase of the explosion, the expanding cloud radiates as much energy in a day as the Sun has done in the last 3,000,000 years. Such explosions occur roughly every 50 years within a galaxy. They have been observed less frequently in the Galaxy because most of them have been hidden by the obscuring clouds of dust. The most recent known galactic supernovae were observed in 1006 in Lupus, in 1054 in Taurus, in 1572 in Cassiopeia (Tycho's nova, named after Tycho Brahe, its observer), and finally in 1604 in Serpens, called Kepler's nova. The stars became bright enough to be visible in the daytime.

Known galactic supernovae

In spite of the rarity of supernovae in the Galaxy, they have been found in large numbers in other galaxies. For a few days the brightness of the supernova is comparable to that of the entire galaxy, and it is easy to detect a supernova within a not-too-distant galaxy. Hundreds have been photographed and studied spectroscopically. At the site of Kepler's and Tycho's novae, there are heavy obscuring clouds, and the optical objects remaining are now inconspicuous knots of glowing gas. Near Tycho's nova, in Cassiopeia, there are similar optically insignificant wisps that appear to be remnants of yet another supernova explosion. To a radio telescope, however, the situation is spectacularly different: the Cassiopeia remnant is the strongest radio source in the entire sky (easily outshining the Sun, although the Sun is almost 10^9 times closer). Study of this remnant, called Cassiopeia A, reveals that a supernova explosion occurred there in approximately 1680, missed by observers because of the obscuring dust.

The Crab Nebula. At the site of the 1054 supernova is one of the most remarkable objects in the sky, the Crab Nebula. Photographed in colour (Plate 2), it is revealed as a beautiful red, lacy network of long and sinuous, glowing hydrogen filaments surrounding a bluish, structureless region whose light is strongly polarized. The filaments emit the spectrum characteristic of a diffuse nebula. The gas is expanding at 1,100 kilometres per second—but still slower than the 6,400 kilometres per second in the shells of new supernovae in other galaxies.

The bluish, amorphous inner region of the Crab Nebula is even more remarkable. The glow is produced by the so-called synchrotron radiation—*i.e.,* from electrons spiralling about a magnetic field at almost the speed of light. This radiation is dramatically different from what it would be if it were emitted from electrons moving at low speeds: it becomes (1) strongly concentrated in the forward direction, like the beam of a searchlight, (2) spread out over a broad range of frequencies but with the average frequency increasing with the electron's energy, and (3) highly polarized. Electrons of many different energies produce radiation in a large range of wavelengths: radio, infrared, optical, and ultraviolet. Even X rays are emitted copiously by the Crab, which is the second-brightest X-ray source in the sky, indicating that the electrons must have energies in the cosmic-ray range. After almost 1,000 years, the nebula is still losing 100,000 times as much energy per second as the Sun.

Synchrotron radiation

On the basis of this huge outpouring of energy, it is easy to calculate how long the nebula can shine without a new supply of energy. The electrons emitting the X rays should decay, or drop to lower energies, in about 30 years—far less than the age of the nebula. The source of energy within the Crab Nebula supplying energy to the electrons that emit the X rays was discovered in 1969 to be the pulsar NP 0532, the remains of the star that exploded to form the nebula (see COSMOS).

Source of energy for the Crab Nebula

In the case of the Crab Nebula, the pulsar has been found to flash optically as well as at radio wavelengths, blinking on and off with the same period, believed to be a result of rotation: 0.033099324 second (on June 28, 1969). This period is slowly increasing (at the rate of 0.0012 second per century), which implies the pulsar is slowing down and thereby losing its energy to the nebula. The corresponding rate of energy loss is about equal to the nebula's rate of energy loss, convincing evidence that a tiny, extremely dense pulsar can supply the energy to the nebula, which is about four light-years across.

The Crab Nebula is unique in being a young supernova remnant and relatively free from obscuration, while Tycho's and Kepler's supernovae are conspicuous radio sources, apparently radiating by synchrotron emission; in neither case has a detectable pulsar been found. The failure to detect pulsars at the sites of Kepler's and Tycho's novae, or Cassiopeia A, does not mean that they are not there; the radiation from the pulsar is probably strongly beamed, and the Earth may not be located in the direction to which the pulsars are sending their energy.

The Crab Nebula is still in a stage of violent expansion, and it is interesting to consider how it will appear a few thousand years hence. The gas will continue to expand and the pulsar lose energy until the nebula enters a second stage: one in which the pulsar can no longer put much energy into the nebula, and the nebula expands like a hot bubble of gas into the cold, surrounding interstellar gas. As the hot gas rams into the cold much faster than its speed of sound, a strong shock wave results. The cold gas is heated to several million kelvins as it is hit by the shock wave and then cools by radiating forbidden and recombination lines. Almost all of the mass inside the shocked "bubble" will consist of this interstellar material swept up by the expanding shock wave.

The Cygnus Loop. As a general mechanism this picture seems well confirmed. The best observed old supernova remnant is the Cygnus Loop (or the Veil Nebula; see Plate 1), a beautiful, filamentary object roughly in the form of a circular arc in Cygnus. Its patchiness is striking: the loop consists of a series of wisps rather than a continuous cloud

The Veil Nebula

of gas. The most likely interpretation of this patchiness is that the interstellar medium into which the shock wave is propagating contains small clouds of denser material; many lines of reasoning from other evidence lead to the same result. The present speed of the filaments is about 100 kilometres per second; the approximate age of the Cygnus Loop is about 50,000 years.

Other supernova remnants. Many other such old supernova remnants in the Galaxy are recognized, because they are also sources of radio emission from synchrotron radiation. Optically, in general, they show a wispy appearance similar to that of the Cygnus Loop.

The eventual fate of many of these supernova remnants is to cool down, stop expanding, and finally merge with the interstellar medium. In the process they have modified the interstellar medium in two important ways: (1) They leave behind the elements that have been made in the presupernova star by a long process of heating and thermonuclear processing. Some very heavy elements are made in the extremely high temperatures right after the explosion. These elements are ejected into the supernova nebula and are finally merged with the interstellar medium. In this way the heavy-element content of the interstellar medium is increased. There is observational confirmation of this; both the Crab Nebula and the remnant of Tycho's supernova seem heavy-element rich. (2) They have provided kinetic energy to the surrounding gas by violent expansion, heating and accelerating the interstellar gas clouds. In addition, the original explosion emitted large quantities of very high energy particles that probably are cosmic rays. These cosmic rays, as well as the X rays emitted by the remnant, heat the interstellar gas. Some supernovae explode within the hot phase of the interstellar medium that has remained from previous supernovae and from stellar winds. In this case, the violently expanding shock reheats the tenuous gas that fills most of the volume of space in a galaxy but comprises very little of its mass. Thus, supernovae serve to maintain a hot component of gas, which is only revealed in X rays. It seems that supernovae play a very important role in the history of a galaxy, just as remarkable individuals shape the course of human history.

BIBLIOGRAPHY. Works appropriate for the lay reader include LYMAN SPITZER, JR., *Searching Between the Stars* (1982), written by one of the most authoritative figures in the field; J.E. DYSON and D.A. WILLIAMS, *Physics of the Interstellar Medium* (1980); and numerous articles written at a semitechnical level in the journals *Scientific American* (monthly); *Mercury* (bimonthly), published by the Astronomical Society of the Pacific; *Astronomy* (monthly); and *Sky and Telescope* (monthly). Readers with a thorough knowledge of physics may wish to consult LYMAN SPITZER, JR., *Physical Processes in the Interstellar Medium* (1978), very comprehensive and very terse; DONALD E. OSTERBROCK, *Astrophysics of Gaseous Nebulae* (1974); S.R. POTTASCH, *Planetary Nebulae* (1984); and JOHN DANZIGER and PAUL GORENSTEIN (eds.), *Supernova Remnants and Their X-Ray Emission* (1983), proceedings of the 1982 symposium of the International Astronomical Union.

(J.S.M.)

Nepal

The Kingdom of Nepal (Nepālī: Nepāl Adhirājya), lying along the southern slopes of the Himalayan mountain ranges, is a landlocked country located between India to the east, south, and west and the Tibet Autonomous Region of China to the north. Its territory, which has an area of 56,827 square miles (147,181 square kilometres), extends roughly 500 miles (800 kilometres) from east to west and 90 to 150 miles from north to south. Nepal, long under the rule of hereditary prime ministers favouring a policy of isolation, remained closed to the outside world until a palace revolt in 1950 restored the king to his position of authority in 1951; the country gained admission to the United Nations in 1955.

Wedged between two giants, India and China, Nepal seeks to keep a balance between the two countries in its foreign policy—and thus to remain independent. A factor that contributes immensely to the geopolitical importance of the country is the fact that a strong Nepal can deny China access to the rich Gangetic Plain; Nepal thus marks the southern boundary of the Chinese sphere north of the Himalayas in Asia.

As a result of its years of geographic and self-imposed isolation, Nepal is one of the least developed nations of the world. In recent years many countries, including India, China, the United States, the United Kingdom, Japan, Denmark, West Germany, Canada, the Soviet Union, and Switzerland, have provided economic assistance to Nepal. The extent of foreign aid to Nepal has been influenced to a considerable degree by the strategic position of the country between India and China.

This article is divided into the following sections:

Physical and human geography

THE LAND

Relief. Nepal contains some of the most rugged and difficult mountain terrain in the world. Roughly 75 percent of the country is covered by mountains. From the south to the north, Nepal can be divided into four main physical belts, each of which extends east to west across the country. These are, first, the Tarai, a low, flat, fertile land adjacent to the border of India; second, the forested Churia foothills and the Inner Tarai zone, rising from the Tarai plain to the rugged Mahābhārat Range; third, the mid-mountain region between the Mahābhārat Range and the Great Himalayas; and fourth, the Great Himalaya Range, rising to more than 29,000 feet (some 8,850 metres).

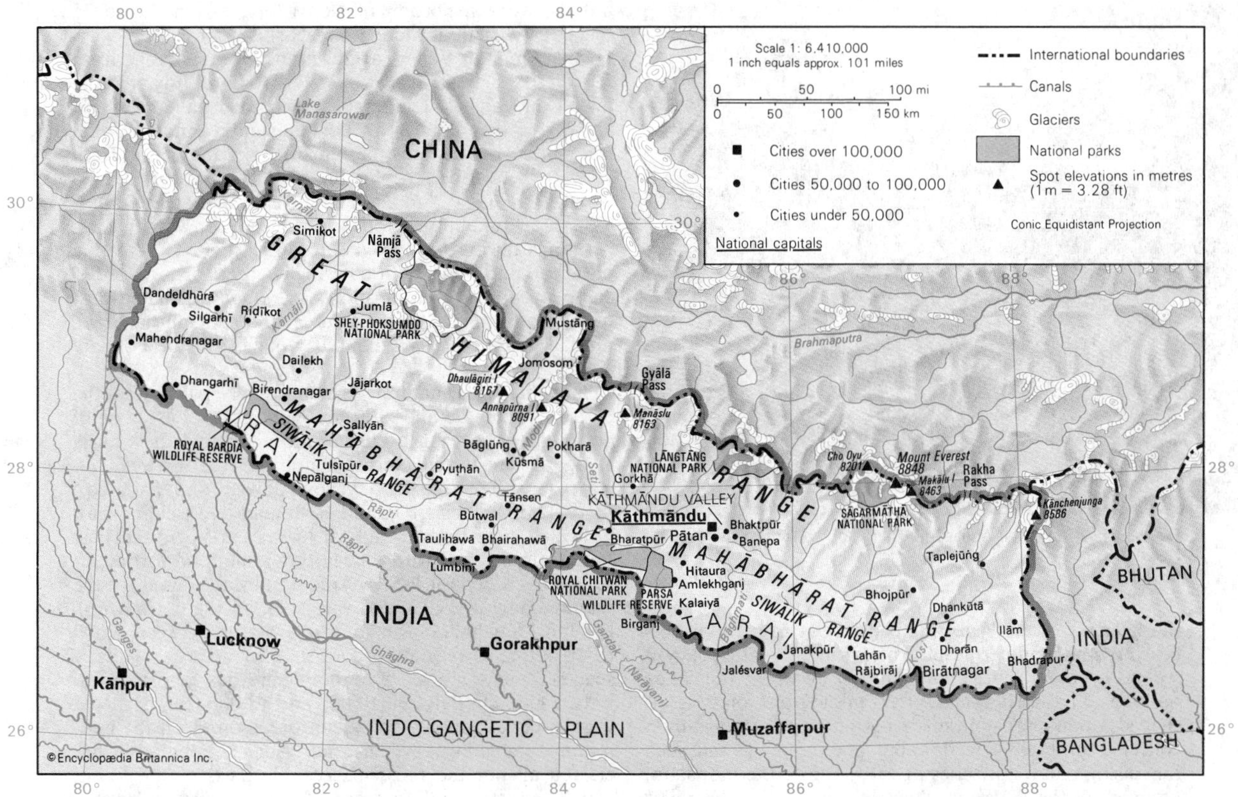

MAP INDEX

Cities and towns
Amlekhganj . . . . . . 27 17 N 84 59 E
Bāglūṅg . . . . 28 16 N 83 36 E
Banepa . . . . 27 38 N 85 31 E
Bhādgāon,
 see Bhaktpūr
Bhadrapur . . . . 26 33 N 88 05 E
Bhairahawā . . . . . . 27 30 N 83 27 E
Bhaktpūr
 (Bhādgāon) . . . . . 27 41 N 85 25 E
Bharatpūr . . . . 27 41 N 84 26 E
Bhojpūr . . . . 27 10 N 87 03 E
Birātnagar . . . . 26 29 N 87 17 E
Birendranagar . . . . 28 46 N 81 38 E
Birganj . . . . 27 00 N 84 52 E
Būtwal . . . . 27 42 N 83 27 E
Dailekh . . . . 28 50 N 81 44 E
Dandeldhūrā . . . . . 29 18 N 80 35 E
Dhangarhī . . . . 28 41 N 80 36 E
Dhankūtā . . . . 26 59 N 87 20 E
Dharān . . . . 26 49 N 87 17 E
Gorkhā . . . . 28 00 N 84 38 E
Hitaura . . . . 27 25 N 85 02 E
Ilām . . . . 26 54 N 87 56 E
Jājarkot . . . . 28 42 N 82 12 E
Jalésvar . . . . 26 38 N 85 48 E
Janakpūr . . . . 26 42 N 85 55 E
Jomosom . . . . 28 47 N 83 44 E
Jumlā . . . . 29 17 N 82 10 E
Kalaiyā . . . . 27 02 N 85 00 E
Kāthmāndu . . . . . . 27 43 N 85 19 E
Kūsmā . . . . 28 14 N 83 41 E
Lahān . . . . 26 43 N 86 29 E
Lalitpur,
 see Pātan
Lumbinī,
 (Rummin-dei) . . . . 27 29 N 83 17 E
Mahendranagar . . . 28 55 N 80 20 E
Mustāng . . . . 29 11 N 83 58 E
Nepālganj . . . . 28 03 N 81 37 E
Pātan (Lalitpur) . . . 27 40 N 85 20 E
Pokharā . . . . 28 14 N 83 59 E
Pyuṭhān . . . . 28 06 N 82 52 E
Rājbirāj . . . . 26 32 N 86 45 E
Riḍikot . . . . 29 13 N 81 13 E
Rummin-dei,
 see Lumbinī
Sallyān . . . . 28 22 N 82 10 E
Silgarhī . . . . 29 16 N 80 59 E
Simikot . . . . 29 58 N 81 50 E
Tānsen . . . . 27 52 N 83 33 E
Taplejūṅg . . . . 27 21 N 87 40 E
Taulihawā . . . . 27 32 N 83 03 E
Tulsīpūr . . . . 28 08 N 82 18 E

Physical features and points of interest
Annapūrna I,
 peak . . . . 28 36 N 83 49 E
Bāghmati, *river* . . . 27 00 N 85 50 E
Cho Oyu, *peak* . . . 28 06 N 86 40 E
Churia Range,
 see Siwālik Range
Dhaulāgiri I, *peak* . 28 42 N 83 30 E
Everest, Mount . . . 27 59 N 86 56 E
Gandak,
 see Nārāyani
Great Himalaya
 Range . . . . 29 00 N 83 00 E
Gyālā Pass . . . . . . 28 45 N 84 37 E
Kānchenjunga,
 peak . . . . 27 42 N 88 09 E
Karnāli, *river* . . . . . 28 45 N 81 16 E
Kāthmāndu
 Valley . . . . 27 30 N 85 20 E
Kosi, *river* . . . . 26 50 N 87 00 E
Lāngtāng
 National Park . . . . 28 15 N 85 35 E
Mahābhārat
 Range . . . . 28 45 N 83 30 E
Makālu I, *peak* . . . . 27 53 N 87 05 E
Manāslu, *peak* . . . . 28 33 N 84 34 E
Modi, *river* . . . . 28 14 N 83 40 E
Nāmjā Pass . . . . . . 29 58 N 82 34 E
Nārāyani
 (Gandak), *river* . . 27 00 N 84 15 E
Parsa Wildlife
 Reserve . . . . 27 20 N 84 50 E
Rakha Pass . . . . . . 27 53 N 87 32 E
Rāpti, *river* . . . . . . 27 50 N 82 41 E
Royal Bardīa
 Wildlife Reserve . . 28 25 N 81 30 E
Royal Chitwan
 National Park . . . . 27 30 N 84 20 E
Sāgarmāthā
 National Park . . . . 28 00 N 86 40 E
Seti, *river* . . . . 27 48 N 84 28 E
Shey-Phoksumdo
 National Park . . . . 29 30 N 82 55 E
Siwālik Range
 (Churia Range) . . 28 30 N 82 00 E
Tarai, *region* . . . . . 28 30 N 81 10 E

The Tarai forms the northern extension of the Gangetic Plain and varies in width from less than 16 to more than 20 miles, narrowing considerably in several places. A 10-mile-wide belt of rich agricultural land stretches along the southern part of the Tarai; the northern section, adjoining the foothills, is a marshy region in which wild animals abound and malaria is endemic.

The Churia Range, which is sparsely populated, rises in almost perpendicular escarpments to an altitude of more than 4,000 feet. Between the Churia Range to the south and the Mahābhārat Range to the north, there are broad basins from 2,000 to 3,000 feet high, about 10 miles wide, and 20 to 40 miles long; these basins are often referred to as the Inner Tarai. In many places they have been cleared of the forests and savanna grass to provide timber and areas for cultivation.

A complex system of mountain ranges, some 50 miles in width and varying in elevation from 8,000 to 14,000 feet, lie between the Mahābhārat Range and the Great Himalayas. The ridges of the Mahābhārat Range present a steep escarpment toward the south and a relatively gentle slope to the north. To the north of the Mahābhārat Range, which encloses the valley of Kāthmāndu, are the more lofty ranges of the Inner Himalaya (Lesser Himalaya), rising to perpetually snow-covered peaks. The Kāthmāndu and the Pokhara valleys lying within this mid-mountain region are flat basins, formerly covered with lakes, that were formed by the deposition of fluvial and fluvioglacial material brought down by rivers and glaciers from the enclosing ranges during the four glacial and intervening warm phases of the Pleistocene Epoch (from about 2,500,000 to 10,000 years ago).

The Great Himalaya Range, ranging in elevation from 14,000 to more than 29,000 feet, contains many of the world's highest peaks—Everest, Kānchenjunga I, Lhotse I, Makālu I, Cho Oyu, Dhaulāgiri I, Manāslu I, and Annapūrna I—all of them above 26,400 feet. Except for scattered settlements in high mountain valleys, this entire area is uninhabited.

The Kāthmāndu Valley

Drainage. The Kāthmāndu Valley, the political and cultural hub of the nation, is drained by the Bāghmati River, flowing southward, which washes the steps of the sacred temple of Paśupatinātha (Pashupatinath) and rushes out of the valley through the deeply cut Chhobar gorge. Some

Naudanda village in the Annapūrna Range of the Himalayas, Nepal.
Cathlyn Melloan; EB, Inc.

sandy layers of the lacustrine beds act as aquifers (water-bearing strata of permeable rock, sand, or gravel), and springs occur in the Kāthmāndu Valley where the sands outcrop. The springwater often gushes out of dragon-shaped mouths of stone made by the Nepalese; it is then collected in tanks for drinking and washing and also for raising paddy nurseries in May, before the monsoon. Drained by the Seti River, the Pokhara Valley, 96 miles west of Kāthmāndu, is also a flat lacustrine basin. There are a few remnant lakes in the Pokhara basin, the largest being Phewa Lake, which is about two miles long and nearly a mile wide. North of the basin lies the Annapūrna massif of the Great Himalaya Range.

The major rivers of Nepal—the Kosi, Nārāyani (Gandak), and Karnāli, running southward across the strike of the Himalayan ranges—form transverse valleys with deep gorges, which are generally several thousand feet in depth from the crest of the bordering ranges. The watershed of these rivers lies not along the line of highest peaks in the Himalayas but to the north of it, usually in Tibet.

The rivers have considerable potential for development of hydroelectric power. Two irrigation-hydroelectric projects have been undertaken jointly with India on the Kosi and Nārāyani rivers. Discussions have been held to develop the enormous potential of the Karnāli River. A 60,000-kilowatt hydroelectric project at Kulekhani, funded by the World Bank, Kuwait, and Japan, began operation in 1982.

In the upper courses of all Nepalese rivers, which run through mountain regions, there are little or no flood problems. In low-lying areas of the Tarai plain, however, serious floods occur.

The rivers and small streams of the Tarai, especially those in which the dry season discharge is small, are polluted by large quantities of domestic waste thrown into them. Towns and villages have expanded without proper provision for sewage disposal facilities, and more industries have been established at selected centres in the Tarai. The polluted surface water in the Kāthmāndu and Pokhara valleys, as well as in the Tarai, are unacceptable for drinking.

Climate. Nepal's climate, influenced by elevation as well as by its location in a subtropical latitude, ranges from subtropical monsoon conditions in the Tarai, through a warm temperate climate between 4,000 and 7,000 feet in the mid-mountain region, to cool temperate conditions in the higher parts of mountains between 7,000 and 11,000 feet, to an Alpine climate at altitudes between 14,000 and 16,000 feet along the lower slopes of the Himalaya mountains. At altitudes above 16,000 feet the temperature is always below freezing and the surface covered by snow and ice. Rainfall is ample in the eastern portion of the Tarai (which receives from 70 to 75 inches [1,800 to 1,900 millimetres] a year at Bīratnagar) and in the mountains, but the western portion of Nepal (where from 30 to 35 inches a year fall at Mahendranagar) is drier.

Temperatures

In Kāthmāndu Valley, average temperatures range from 50° F (10° C) in January to 78° F (26° C) in July, and the lowest and highest temperatures recorded have been 27° and 99° F (−3° and 37° C). The average annual rainfall is about 55 inches, most of which falls in the period from June to September. At Pokhara the temperature ranges from 40° F (4° C) in January to approximately 100° F (38° C) in June, just before the monsoon. In winter, temperatures during the day rise to 70° F (21° C), creating pleasant conditions, with cool nights and warm days. Because warm rain-bearing monsoon winds discharge most of their moisture as they encounter the Annapūrna range, rainfall is quite heavy (about 100 inches) in the Pokhara Valley.

Vegetation zones

Plant life. The natural vegetation of Nepal follows the pattern of climate and altitude. A tropical, moist zone of deciduous vegetation occurs in the Tarai and the Churia Range. These forests consist mainly of khair (*Acacia catechu*), a spring tree with yellow flowers and flat pods; sissoo (*Dalbergia sissoo*), an East Indian tree yielding dark brown durable timber; and sal (*Shorea robusta*), an East Indian timber tree with foliage providing food for lac insects (which deposit lac, a resinous substance used for the manufacture of shellac and varnishes, on the tree's twigs). On the Mahābhārat Range, at elevations between 5,000 to 10,000 feet, vegetation consists of a mixture of many species, chiefly pines, oaks, rhododendrons, poplars, walnuts, and larch. Between 10,000 and 12,000 feet, fir mixed with birch, as well as rhododendron, abound. In the mid-mountain region of Nepal a fairly dense population has cleared all but the most inaccessible parts of the forest, which are restricted to areas of steep slopes and rocky terrain. Similarly, all readily accessible parts of valuable sal forest in the Tarai have been devastated by overcutting and depletive practices. The vast forested area below the timber line in the Great Himalaya Range bears some of the most valuable forests in Nepal, containing spruce, fir, cypress, juniper, and birch. Alpine vegetation occupies higher parts of the Great Himalaya Range. Just below the snow line, between 14,000 and 15,000 feet, grassy vegetation affords favourable grazing ground in summer.

(P.P.K.)

Animal life. The forested areas of the Tarai are the home of tigers and leopards, gaurs (wild ox), occasional elephants and buffalo, and many deer; the deer include chital, or axis, deer (which have white-spotted bodies), sambar (a large Asiatic deer with coarse hair on the throat and strong antlers), and swamp deer. The Lesser Rāpti Valley, in south-central Nepal, is one of the last homes of the great Indian rhinoceros (*Rhinoceros unicornis*). Much poaching has gone on, as the horn of the rhinoceros is reputed to be valuable as an aphrodisiac, but in the 1960s the Nepal government organized protective measures.

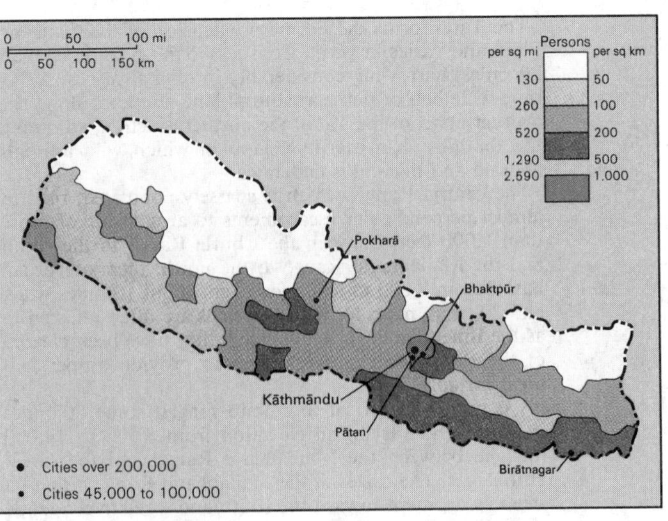

Population density of Nepal.

There are few wild animals in the central zone because of the clearing of forests. Occasional leopards, bears, and smaller carnivores inhabit the forests and ravines, and muntjacs (a kind of small deer, also called the barking deer) are found in the woods. In the Alpine zone are musk deer, widely hunted for the musk pods they carry, the tahr (a Himalayan beardless wild goat), the goral (any of several goat antelopes, closely related to the Rocky Mountain goat), and wild sheep, which are preyed upon by wolves and snow leopards. Pheasant are common. The Yeti (bear-man, or Abominable Snowman) is said by the Sherpa to inhabit the high snow mountains but has eluded discovery by several expeditions. Strange tracks are often found in the snow, but it is believed that they are probably made by bears. River wildlife includes the mahseer, a large freshwater food and sport fish. (R.R.Pr./M.Zu.)

THE PEOPLE

The large-scale migrations of Mongoloid groups from Tibet and Indo-Aryan people from northern India, which accompanied the early settlement of Nepal, have produced a diverse linguistic, ethnic, and religious pattern. Nepalese of Indo-Aryan ancestry comprise the people of the Tarai, the Pahari, the Newar, and the Tharus—the great majority of the total population. Indo-Aryan ancestry has been a source of prestige in Nepal for centuries, and the ruling families have been of Indo-Aryan and Hindu background. Most of the Tibeto-Nepalese groups—the Tamang, Rai, Limbu, Bhutia (including the Sherpa), and Sunwar—live in the north and east, while the Magar and Gurung inhabit west-central Nepal. The bulk of the famous Gurkha contingents in the British army have come from the Magar, Gurung, and Rai groups.

The principal and official language of Nepal is Nepālī (Gorkhali), spoken in the Tarai and the mid-mountain region. Nepālī, a derivative of Sanskrit, belongs to the Indo-Aryan branch of the Indo-European family. There are a number of regional dialects found in the Tarai and mountain areas. The languages of the north and east belong predominantly to the Tibeto-Burman family. These include Magar, Gurung, Rai, Limbu, Sunwar, Tamang, Newari, and a number of Bhutia dialects, including Sherpa and Thakali. Although Newari is commonly placed in the Tibeto-Burman family, it was influenced by both Tibeto-Burman and Indo-European languages.

In Nepal a vast majority of the population is Hindu, but a small percentage follows Buddhism or other religious faiths. Hindus and Buddhists tend to be concentrated in areas where Indian and Tibetan cultural influences, respectively, have been dominant.

Settlement patterns

Almost all Nepalese live in villages or in small market centres. Outside of Kāthmāndu, there are no major cities. Smaller urban centres (Birātnagar, Nepālganj, and Birganj) are located in the Tarai along the Indian border, and Pokharā is situated in a valley in the mid-mountain region. In addition, a few townships—such as Hitaura, Būtwal, and Dharān—have begun to emerge in the foothills and hill areas, where economic activity has developed.

THE ECONOMY

Landlocked, lacking substantial resources for economic development, and hampered by an inadequate transportation network, Nepal is one of the least developed nations in the world. The economy is heavily dependent on imports of basic materials and on foreign markets for its forest and agricultural products. Nepal imports essential commodities, such as fuel, construction materials, fertilizers, metals, and most consumer goods, and exports such products as rice, jute, timber, and textiles.

The political and administrative system of Nepal has not made those changes in trade, investment, and related economic policies that would expedite economic development and attract foreign capital. The government's development programs, which are funded by foreign aid, also have failed to respond directly to the needs of rural people.

Resources. Nepal's mineral resources are small, scattered, and barely developed. There are known deposits of coal (lignite), iron ore, magnesite, copper, cobalt, pyrite (used for making sulfuric acid), limestone, and mica. Nepal's great river systems provide immense potential for hydroelectric development. If developed and utilized within the country and exported to India (the principal market for power generated in Nepal), it could become a mainstay of the country's economy.

Agriculture. Agriculture—primarily the cultivation of rice, corn (maize), and wheat—engages most of Nepal's population and accounts for well over half of the country's export earnings. Yet agricultural productivity is very low. The low yields result from shortages of fertilizers and improved seed and from the use of inefficient techniques. Because only a tiny percentage of Nepal's cultivated land area is under irrigation, output depends upon the vagaries of the weather. Potatoes, sugarcane, and millet are other major crops. Cattle, buffalo, goats, and sheep are the principal livestock raised.

On the whole, Nepal has a small surplus in food grains. There are, however, major dislocations in supply and demand. Periods of shortage between harvests of various crops occur in the mountain areas. At the same time, substantial amounts of food grain are moved to India from the Tarai. Because of the lack of adequate transportation, surplus food grain from the Tarai does not move north into the food deficit areas of the mid-mountain region. Some food grains move northward from the Tarai and the mountain areas into Tibet, however, despite a shortage in the mountain regions.

The greatest potential for increases in agricultural production is in the Tarai. In the mid-mountain region the potential for increasing production is limited. Because of the high population concentration in this region, almost all land capable of cultivation is tilled. Increasing the cultivated land area by cutting into standing forests aggravates erosion and results in reduced yields and land losses by landslides. Major projects have been undertaken in an effort to halt soil erosion and deforestation.

Forestry. About one-third of Nepal's total area is forested; most of this area is state-owned. In spite of overcutting and poor management, timber represents one of the country's most valuable resources and is a major source of potential revenue. Exports of forest products constitute an important source of Indian rupees. Almost all timber is exported to India. The saw mills of the Timber Corporation of Nepal, a government-owned lumber-processing concern, supply Kāthmāndu Valley with construction and furniture wood.

Industry and trade. Industrial production represents a small but growing segment of economic activity. Most industries are small, localized operations based on the processing of agricultural products. The jute industry, centred in Birātnagar, is an important earner of foreign exchange. Sugar factories are located in Birātnagar, Birganj, and Bhairahawā. There is a saw mill and a meat-processing plant in Hitaura, and a number of rice and oil mills in the Tarai. Other industries include brick and tile manufacture; processing of construction materials, paper, and food grain; cigarette manufacture; cement production; and brewing of beer. In general, there are more industrial enterprises in the private than in the public sector although most of these are cottage industries. The main areas of manufacturing concentration are Birātnagar, the Birganj–Hitaura corridor, and the Kāthmāndu Valley.

Tourism

Tourism represents a small but expanding industry. Foreign tourism is primarily confined to the Kāthmāndu Valley, which is the only area equipped with the necessary hotels, food supplies, roads, and international transport services. There are, however, many areas outside the Kāthmāndu Valley with potential for the development of tourism; these include Pokhara, the Mount Everest area, and the Nārāyani area (where big game exists).

For geographic and historical reasons, nearly all of Nepal's trade is with India. Attempts have been made to diversify trade through agreements with Japan, South Korea, Pakistan, the United States, West Germany, Poland, China, and the Soviet Union. The state trading agency, National Trading Limited, has expanded its activities by fostering the development of commercial entrepreneurial activity. Large-scale commercial activity has hitherto been in the hands of foreigners, primarily Indians.

Nepal's foreign trade and balance of payments have suffered setbacks, and exports have not increased enough to pay for imports of consumer goods and basic supplies. Nepal's dependence on the Indian market for most of its imports and exports and on the port of Calcutta for its access to the sea have been the source of periodic friction between the two countries.

Transportation. Transport facilities in Nepal are very limited; few independent nations in the world of comparable size have such little road mileage and so few motor vehicles. Construction of new roads has been undertaken since the 1970s with aid from India, China, Great Britain, and the United States. The main means of transportation has been the network of footpaths, which interlace the mountain terrain and valleys. Trails have evolved into main trade routes, which tend to follow the river systems.

The meagre road-transport facilities in Nepal are supplemented by only a few railway- and air-transport links. Increased use of road transport has reduced the significance of the two narrow-gauge railroads that run from Amlekhganj to Raxaul (India) and from Janakpūr to Jaynagar (India). The Royal Nepal Airline Corporation, an autonomous government agency, is the only commercial airline. Together with Indian Airlines, it operates flights from Kāthmāndu to various points in India and other nearby countries. Domestic air service within the country has been expanded. The United States built the Kāthmāndu–Hitaura aerial ropeway in the 1920s, and it is still used for carrying goods into the capital. (L.E.R.)

Air transport

ADMINISTRATION AND SOCIAL CONDITIONS

Government. Prior to 1990, when nationwide unrest forced King Birendra to accept a transition to a multiparty system, Nepal was only nominally a constitutional monarchy; the king actually exercised autocratic control over a multitiered system of panchayats (local bodies, or councils). In 1990, however, a multiparty commission was established to rewrite the constitution.

Before the events of 1990, the government operated in the following manner. Members of village or town panchayats and district panchayats were chosen by direct election. All citizens 21 years of age and older were eligible to vote. A constitutional amendment in 1980 provided for direct elections to the unicameral National Assembly (Rashtriya Panchayat), which consisted of 140 members (including 28 appointed by the king) who served five-year terms but who could be recalled. A general election was held in 1986, and local district elections were held in 1987.

The Council of Ministers functioned as the executive arm of the government and advised the king on matters of policy. The National Assembly selected the prime minister, provided a candidate was able to win support of 60 percent of the members. If no candidate received such support, the king selected the prime minister from among three candidates nominated by the Assembly.

Political parties were banned in Nepal in 1960 when King Mahendra suspended parliamentary democracy. In accordance with a constitutional referendum in 1980, Nepal remained an officially partyless state, but organizations such as the Nepali Congress Party, the Communist Party of Nepal, numerous small left-leaning student groups, and several radical Nepalese antimonarchist groups were able to operate more or less openly.

The restoration of fundamental rights (except the right to form political parties) under the 1980 referendum had brought a measure of political stability. The palace secretariat, comprising the immediate aides and assistants to the king, remained of central importance in the government, in which, however, royal initiative was the activating force.

For administrative purposes, the country is divided into 14 zones and 75 districts. Each zone formerly had a zonal panchayat, consisting of all the members of the district panchayats, and was administered by a commissioner and one or two assistant commissioners, all of whom were appointed by the central government. King Mahendra made several changes in the judicial system. In 1961 a Supreme Court act designed to bring the judicial appointment process under firm royal control was promulgated. Regional and district courts were reorganized, and there is now a district court in each of the districts and zonal courts in each of the zones. (L.E.R./Ed.)

Armed forces and police. Nepal's armed forces consist of the Royal Nepalese Army, predominantly an infantry force. The Army Flight Department operates all aircraft. Except for a few simple weapons, all military supplies are imported. Nepal is famous for the fighting qualities of its Gurkha soldiers; nearly 10,000 of these serve in British Gurkha units and 50,000 in Indian Gurkha units. The British maintain a recruiting centre at Dharān. Gurkha veterans are a valuable human resource of Nepal.

For police purposes the country is divided into three zones: eastern, central, and western, with headquarters at Birātnagar, Kāthmāndu, and Nepālganj, respectively. Each zonal headquarters, under a deputy inspector general of police, is responsible for several subsections composed of four to five police districts operating under a superintendent of police. A district superintendent is in charge of police stations in his area, and each station normally is supervised by a head constable.

Health and education. The Ministry of Health is responsible for the support and administration of public health services, including hospitals and health clinics. Although the government has taken steps to improve existing health centres and to establish new ones, health care remains inadequate. Malaria, tuberculosis, cholera, and typhoid are prevalent in spite of government projects to control or eradicate them. Ayurvedic medicine, the traditional Hindu system of medicine, is popular in Nepal.

The Ministry of Education and Culture is responsible for administration and supervision of all elementary and secondary education. Higher education has developed relatively recently. The first college was established in 1918, and Tribhuvan University in Kāthmāndu, with faculties of arts, sciences, commerce, and education, was chartered in 1959. The University Senate has sole legal responsibility for higher education and the authority to grant academic recognition to colleges but is largely dependent upon the Ministry of Education for funds.

Higher education

CULTURAL LIFE

The relaxation of censorship that followed the overthrow of Rana rule in 1951 encouraged a revival of artistic and intellectual expression. In literature and poetry, Nepālī works emphasize the cultural renaissance and national patriotism. King Mahendra, a poet whose Nepālī lyrics have been published in English translation under the name of M.B.B. Shah (for Mahendra Bir Bikram Shah), did much to promote the revival of arts and literature.

The cultural heritage of Nepal, particularly contributions made by the Newar of Kāthmāndu Valley to sculpture, painting, and architecture, is a source of great pride. Hindu and Buddhist religious values have provided the basic source of inspiration to Newar artisans. The themes of most artistic works have been primarily religious; the lives of the gods, saints, and heroes and the relationship of man to society and to the universe are expounded in sculpture, architecture, and drama. In the Kāthmāndu Valley, some 2,500 temples and shrines display the skill and highly developed aesthetic sense of Newar artisans.

Music and dance are favourite pastimes among the Nepalese. Religious ceremonies require the use of drums and wind instruments preserved from ancient times. Important in most religious and family occasions are devotional songs that have elements of both classical and folk music and that have been used by some contemporary musical revivalists in their attempt to bridge the gap between the two. The government-owned Radio Nepal broadcasts programs in Nepālī and English. The country's first television station, at Kāthmāndu, began broadcasting in 1986.

Newspapers and periodicals are published in Nepālī and in English. Newspapers are frequently sensational in tone and are poorly staffed and financed. *Gorkha Patra,* published by the government, occupies a commanding position in the Nepalese press. After 1960 King Mahendra required newspapers to obtain official clearance for all reports of political activity. Subsequently the government increased its censorship, and in 1985 the publication of many newspapers was suspended. Nepalese newspaper readers rely on the foreign press, particularly Indian newspapers, which are flown daily into Kāthmāndu, for more sophisticated coverage of world and national news.

(P.P.K.)

For statistical data on the land and people of Nepal, see the *Britannica World Data* section in the BRITANNICA WORLD DATA ANNUAL.

History

PREHISTORY AND EARLY HISTORY

Nepal's rich prehistory consists mainly of the legendary traditions of the Newar. There are usually both Buddhist and Brahmanic Hindu versions of these various legends. Both are accepted indiscriminately in the festivals associated with these events, a tribute to the remarkable synthesis that has been achieved in Nepal between two related but divergent value systems.

References to Nepal Valley (now usually called Kāthmāndu Valley) and Nepal's lower hill areas are found in the ancient Indian classics, suggesting that the Central Himalayan hills were closely related culturally and politically to the Gangetic Plain at least 2,500 years ago. Lumbinī, Gautama Buddha's birthplace in southern Nepal, and Nepal Valley also figure prominently in Buddhist accounts. There is substantial archaeological evidence of an early Buddhist influence in Nepal, including a famous column inscribed by Aśoka (emperor of India, 3rd century BC) at Lumbinī and several shrines in the valley.

The Licchavi dynasty

A coherent dynastic history for Nepal Valley becomes possible, though with large gaps, with the rise of the Licchavi dynasty in the 4th or 5th century AD. Although the earlier Kirati dynasty had claimed the status of the Kshatriya caste of rulers and warriors, the Licchavis were probably the first ruling family in that area of plains Indian origin. This set a precedent for what became the normal pattern thereafter—Hindu kings claiming high-caste Indian origin ruling over a population much of which was neither Indo-Aryan nor Hindu.

The Licchavi dynastic chronicles, supplemented by numerous stone inscriptions, are particularly full from AD 500 to 700; a powerful, unified kingdom emerged in Tibet during this period, and the Himalayan passes to the north of the valley were opened. Extensive cultural, trade, and political relations developed across the Himalayas, transforming the valley from a relatively remote backwater into the major intellectual and commercial centre between South and Central Asia. Nepal's contacts with China began in the mid-7th century with the exchange of several missions. But intermittent warfare between Tibet and China terminated this relationship; and while there were briefly renewed contacts in subsequent centuries, these were reestablished on a continuing basis only in the late 18th century.

MIDDLE PERIOD

The Malla dynasty

The middle period in Nepali history is usually considered coterminous with the rule of the Malla dynasty (10th–18th century) in Nepal Valley and surrounding areas. Although most of the Licchavi kings were devout Hindus, they did not impose Brahmanic social codes or values on their non-Hindu subjects; the Mallas perceived their responsibilities differently, however, and the great Malla ruler Jaya Sthiti (reigned *c.* 1382–95) introduced the first legal and social code strongly influenced by contemporary Hindu principles.

Jaya Sthiti's successor, Yakṣa Malla (reigned *c.* 1429–*c.* 1482), divided his kingdom among his three sons, thus creating the independent principalities of Kāthmāndu, Pātan, and Bhaktpūr (Bhādgāon) in the valley. Each of these states controlled territory in the surrounding hill areas, with particular importance attached to the trade routes northward to Tibet and southward to India that were vital to the valley's economy. There were also numerous small principalities in the western and eastern hill areas, whose independence was sustained through a delicate balance of power based upon traditional interrelationships and, in some cases, common ancestral origins (or claims thereto) among the ruling families. By the 16th century virtually all of these principalities were ruled by dynasties claiming high-caste Indian origin whose members had fled to the hills in the wake of Muslim invasions of northern India.

In the early 18th century one of the principalities—Gurkha (Gorkha), ruled by the Shah family—began to assert a predominant role in the hills and even to pose a challenge to Nepal Valley. The Mallas, weakened by familial dissension and widespread social and economic discontent, were no match for the great Gurkha ruler Prithvi Narayan Shah. He conquered the valley in 1769 and moved his capital to Kāthmāndu shortly thereafter, providing the foundation for the modern state of Nepal.

MODERN PERIOD

The Shah dynasty

The Shah (or Sah) rulers faced tremendous and persistent problems in trying to centralize an area long characterized by extreme diversity and ethnic and regional parochialism. They established a centralized political system by absorbing dominant regional and local elites into the central administration at Kāthmāndu. This action neutralized potentially disintegrative political forces and involved them in national politics, but it also severely limited the centre's authority in outlying areas because local administration was based upon a compromise division of responsibilities between the local elites and the central administration.

From 1775 to 1951, Nepali politics was characterized by confrontations between the royal family and several noble families. The position of the Shah dynasty was weakened by the fact that the two kings who ruled successively between 1777 and 1832 were minors when they ascended the throne. The regents and the nobility competed for political power, using the young rulers as puppets; both factions wanted a monopoly of political offices and power for their families, with their rivals exterminated, exiled to India, or placed in a subordinate status. This was achieved by the Thapa family (1806–37) and, even more extensively, by the Rana family (1846–1951). In these periods the Shah ruler was relegated to an honorary position without power, while effective authority was concentrated in the hands of the leading members of the dominant family. Although intrafamilial arrangements on such questions as the succession and the distribution of responsibilities and spoils were achieved, no effective national political institutions were created. The excluded noble families had only two alternatives—to accept inferior posts in the administration and army or to conspire for the overthrow of the dominant family. Until 1950, and to some extent thereafter, Nepali politics was basically conspiratorial in character, with familial loyalty taking precedence over loyalty to the crown or nation.

External relations, 1750–1950. Prithvi Narayan Shah (reigned 1769–75) and his successors established a unified state in the central Himalayas and launched an ambitious and remarkably vigorous program of expansion, seeking to bring the entire hill area, from Bhutan to Kashmir, under their authority. They made considerable progress, but successive setbacks in wars with China and Tibet (1788–92), with the Sikh kingdom in the Punjab (1809), with British India (1814–16), and again with Tibet (1854–56) frustrated Nepal and set the present boundaries of the kingdom.

Alliance with Great Britain

The British conquest of India in the 19th century posed a serious threat to Nepal—which expected to be another victim—and left the country with no real alternative but to seek an accommodation with the British to preserve its independence. This was accomplished by the Rana family regime after 1860 on terms that were mutually acceptable, if occasionally irritating, to both. Under this de facto alliance, Kāthmāndu permitted the recruitment of Nepalis for the highly valued Gurkha units in the British Indian Army and also accepted British "guidance" on foreign policy; in exchange, the British guaranteed the Rana regime against both foreign and domestic enemies and allowed it virtual autonomy in domestic affairs. Nepal, however, was also careful to maintain a friendly relationship with China and Tibet, both for economic reasons and to counterbalance British predominance in South Asia.

The British withdrawal from India in 1947 deprived the

Ranas of a vital external source of support and exposed the regime to new dangers. Anti-Rana forces, composed mainly of Nepali residents in India who had served their political apprenticeship in the Indian nationalist movement, formed an alliance with the Nepali royal family, led by King Tribhuvan (reigned 1911–55), and launched a revolution in November 1950. With strong diplomatic support from New Delhi, the rebels accepted a settlement with the Ranas under which the sovereignty of the crown was restored and the revolutionary forces, led by the Nepali Congress Party, gained an ascendant position in the administration.

Constitutional government

Nepal since 1950. The introduction of a democratic political system in Nepal, a country accustomed to autocracy and with no deep democratic tradition or experience, proved a formidable task. A constitution was finally approved in 1959, under which general elections for a national assembly were held. The Nepali Congress won an overwhelming victory and was entrusted with the formation of Nepal's first popular government. But persistent controversy between the Cabinet and King Mahendra (reigned 1955–72) led the King to dismiss the Nepali Congress government in December 1960 and to imprison most of the party's leaders. The constitution of 1959 was abolished in 1962, and a new constitution was promulgated that established the crown as the real source of authority. King Mahendra obtained both Indian and Chinese acceptance of his regime, and the internal opposition was weak, disorganized, and discouraged. Mahendra died in January 1972 and was succeeded by his son Birendra, who was crowned in 1975.

Throughout the 1970s King Birendra sought to expedite economic development programs while maintaining the "nonparty" political system established by his father. The results were disappointing on both accounts, and by 1979 a systemic crisis was evident. To meet the first serious political challenge to the monarchy since 1960, King Birendra announced in May 1979 that a national referendum would be held to decide between a nonparty and multiparty (by implication, parliamentary) political system. In the referendum, which was held in May 1980, the political groups supporting the existing nonparty system won by the relatively small margin of 55 percent, accurately reflecting the sharp differences in the country on basic political issues.

It was in this context that King Birendra decided in 1980 to retain the 1962 constitution but to liberalize the political system by providing for direct popular election of the National Assembly. The government also permitted the "illegal" political parties, such as the Nepali Congress Party, to function under only minimal constraints. Elections were still formally held on a "partyless" basis, but many candidates ran informally and openly as members of political parties. (L.E.R.)

This partial movement toward a democratic parliamentary system, however, satisfied neither the supporters of the 1962 constitution nor the political forces demanding a fully operative parliamentary system on the British model, and in early 1990 the opposition forces began a campaign for further democratic reforms. A series of protests and strikes followed nationwide, and the government's sometimes brutal repression of these protests did not quell the campaign. In April, as unrest in the Kāthmāndu Valley became serious, King Birendra announced that the ban on political parties had been lifted, and a multiparty interim government was established. A new constitution was to be written and a multiparty election subsequently held, but the king's role in the government, while expected to diminish, had not been determined. (L.E.R./Ed.)

For later developments in the history of Nepal, see the *Britannica Book of the Year* section in the BRITANNICA WORLD DATA ANNUAL.

For coverage of related topics in the *Macropædia* and *Micropædia,* see the *Propædia,* sections 935, 936, 968, and 976, and the *Index.*

BIBLIOGRAPHY

Physical and human geography: PRADYUMNA P. KARAN, *Nepal, a Cultural and Physical Geography* (1960), a summary of basic geographic information; LEO E. ROSE and JOHN T. SCHOLZ, *Nepal: Profile of a Himalayan Kingdom* (1980), a concise study of the society, economy, and politics; and CHANDRA K. SHARMA, *Natural Resources of Nepal* (1978). Problems of the natural environment are surveyed in PRADYUMNA P. KARAN and SHIGERU IIJIMA, "Environmental Stress in the Himalaya," *Geographical Review,* 75:71–92 (January 1985). NAGENDRA SHARMA, *Nepal, A to Z* (1978), is useful for travelers. ANDREW E. BERESKY (ed.), *Fodor's India, Nepal, and Sri Lanka, 1987* (1987); and JOHN GOTTBERG ANDERSON, *Nepal,* 6th ed. (1987), are informative guidebooks. Other descriptive works include CHANDRA K. SHARMA, *Nepal and the Nepalese* (1979); and PETER SOMERVILLE-LARGE, *To the Navel of the World: Yaks and Unheroic Travels in Nepal and Tibet* (1987).

Characteristics of the Nepalese are studied in ALEXANDER W. MACDONALD, *Essays on the Ethnology of Nepal and South Asia* (1975); DOR BAHADUR BISTA, *People of Nepal,* 4th ed. (1980); and CHRISTOPH VON FÜRER-HAIMENDORF, *The Sherpas of Nepal: Buddhist Highlanders,* 3rd ed. (1979). BENGT-ERIK BORGSTRÖM, *The Patron and the Panca: Village Values and Pancayat Democracy in Nepal* (1976, reissued 1980), focuses on the panchayat political system. For information on demography, see UNITED NATIONS. ECONOMIC AND SOCIAL COMMISSION FOR ASIA AND THE PACIFIC, *Population of Nepal* (1980); JUDITH BANISTER and SHYAM THAPA, *The Population Dynamics of Nepal* (1981); MICHAEL ALLEN and S.N. MUKHERJEE (eds.), *Women in India and Nepal* (1982); and PUSHKAR RAJ REEJAL, *Integration of Women in Development: The Case of Nepal* (1981). For cultural geography, see PRADYUMNA P. KARAN and COTTON MATHER, "Art and Geography: Patterns in the Himalaya," *Annals of the Association of American Geographers,* 66:487–515 (December 1976); ALEXANDER W. MACDONALD and ANNE VERGATI STAHL, *Newar Art: Nepalese Art During the Malla Period* (1979), a well-illustrated historical survey; and PRATAPADITYA PAL, *Art of Nepal: A Catalogue of the Los Angeles County Museum of Art Collection* (1985).

For information on the country's economy, see B.P. SHRESHTHA, *An Introduction to Nepalese Economy,* 4th ed. (1981); MANESH C. REGMI, *The State and Economic Surplus: Production, Trade, and Resource-Mobilization in Early 19th Century Nepal* (1984); RAM KRISHNA SHRESTHA and PITAMBER SHARMA (eds.), *Nepal, Atlas of Economic Development* (1980); and SRIRAM POUDYAL, *Planned Development in Nepal* (1983), a study of the functioning of the economic planning institutions since their introduction in 1956. PIERS BLAIKIE, JOHN CAMERON, and DAVID SEDDON, *Nepal in Crisis: Growth and Stagnation at the Periphery* (1980); and RIZWANUL ISLAM, AZIZUR RAHMAN KHAN, and EDDY LEE, *Employment and Development in Nepal* (1982), explore economic stagnation. For information on agriculture, see MANESH C. REGMI, *Landownership in Nepal* (1976), and *Land Tenure and Taxation in Nepal,* 2nd ed. (1978). DAVID SEDDON, *Nepal, a State of Poverty* (1987), examines the causes of social deprivation of the population.

History: For the early periods, see ALEXANDER W. MACDONALD (ed.), *Les Royaumes de l'Himâlaya: histoire et civilisation: le Ladakh, le Bhoutan, le Sikkim, le Népal* (1982). LUDWIG F. STILLER, *The Rise of the House of Gorkha: A Study in the Unification of Nepal, 1768–1816* (1973), is a definitive analysis of the first 50 years of the dynasty; and MARY SHEPHERD SLUSSER, *Nepal Mandala: A Cultural Study of the Kathmandu Valley* (1982), is a comprehensive exploration of culture. A historical survey of religion is found in GÉRARD TOFFIN, *Société et religion chez Néwar du Népal* (1984). Evolution of elitist politics under the Shah dynasty is addressed in LEO E. ROSE and MARGARET W. FISHER, *The Politics of Nepal: Persistence and Change in an Asian Monarchy* (1970); and RISHIKESH SHAHA, *Essays in the Practice of Government in Nepal* (1982). Other studies of internal politics include SATISH KUMAR, *Rana Polity in Nepal: Origin and Growth* (1967), focusing on the period from the mid-19th to the mid-20th centuries; FREDERICK H. GAIGE, *Regionalism and National Unity in Nepal* (1975), on the problem of national integration; and LOK RAJ BARAL, *Nepal's Politics of Referendum: A Study of Groups, Personalities & Trends* (1983). Foreign relations are appraised in EUGENE BRAMER MIHALY, *Foreign Aid and Politics in Nepal* (1965), on the effect of aid programs; LEO E. ROSE, *Nepal: Strategy for Survival* (1971), on relations with India and China; S.D. MUNI, *Foreign Policy of Nepal* (1973); GOVIND R. AGRAWAL and JAI P. RANA (eds.), *Nepal and Non-Alignment* (1982); and JAGADISH SHARMA, *Nepal, Struggle for Existence* (1986).

(P.P.K./L.E.R.)

Nerves and Nervous Systems

All living organisms are able to detect changes within themselves and in their environments. Changes in the external environment include those of light, temperature, sound, motion, and odour, while changes in the internal environment include those in the position of the head and limbs as well as in the internal organs. Once detected, these changes must be analyzed and acted upon in order to preserve the integrity, well-being, and status quo of the organism. As life on Earth evolved and the environment became more complex, the survival of organisms depended upon how well they could respond to changes in their surroundings. One factor necessary for survival was a speedy reaction or response. Since communication from one cell to another by chemical means was too slow to be adequate for survival, a system evolved that allowed for faster reaction. That system was the nervous system, which is based upon the almost instantaneous transmission of electrical impulses from one region of the body to another along specialized nerve cells.

Nervous systems are of two general types, diffuse and centralized. In the diffuse type, found in lower invertebrate animals, there is no brain, and the nerve cells are distributed throughout the organism in a netlike pattern. In the centralized systems of the higher invertebrates and the vertebrate animals, some portion of the nervous system has a dominant role in coordinating information and directing responses. This centralization reaches its apogee in the vertebrates, which have a well-developed brain and spinal cord. Impulses are carried to and from the brain and spinal cord by nerve fibres that make up the peripheral nervous system.

Nervous systems should not be considered in structural terms alone; also considered should be the chemical and physiological processes that have evolved within the different structures. In fact, examination of the nervous processes of various species shows that they are amazingly similar throughout the evolutionary scale. This discovery has allowed research scientists to understand the complex nervous systems of humans and other so-called higher animals, in which the structures and processes are highly developed, through the study of molecular functions in the nerve cells of simpler organisms.

This article begins with a discussion of the general features of nervous systems—that is, their function of responding to stimuli and the rather uniform electrochemical processes by which they carry out their response. Following a discussion of the various types of nervous systems, from the simplest to the most complex, are sections on the anatomy and functions of the human nervous system. The article concludes with a section on the most common neurological diseases and disorders.

For detailed discussion of the biochemical and physiological processes of which the nervous system is a part, see CELLS; and GROWTH AND DEVELOPMENT, BIOLOGICAL. For description of receptors that initiate nerve impulses, see SENSORY RECEPTION. The organ systems supplied by nerves are described in MUSCLES AND MUSCLE SYSTEMS.

For coverage of related topics in the *Macropædia* and *Micropædia,* see the *Propædia,* sections 323, 333, 421, and 423. (S.D.E.)

The article is divided into the following sections:

FORM AND FUNCTION OF NERVOUS SYSTEMS

Stimulus–response coordination

The simplest type of living response is the direct one-to-one stimulus–response reaction. The change in the environment is the stimulus; the reaction of the organism to it is the response. In the case of single-celled organisms, the response is the result of a property of the cell fluid called irritability. In simple organisms, such as algae, protozoans, and fungi, a stereotyped response in which the organism moves toward or away from the stimulus is termed taxis. In larger and more complicated organisms—those in which response involves the synchronization and integration of events in different parts of the body—a control mechanism, or "controller," is located between the stimulus and the response. In multicellular organisms, this controller consists of two basic mechanisms by which integration is achieved—chemical regulation and nervous regulation.

Two mechanisms of coordination: chemical and nervous

In chemical regulation, substances called hormones are produced by well-defined groups of cells and are either diffused or carried by the blood to other areas of the body where they act on so-called target cells, influencing metabolism or inducing synthesis of other substances. The changes resulting from hormonal action are expressed in the organism as influences on, or alterations in, form, growth, reproduction, and behaviour.

Plants respond to a variety of external stimuli by utilizing hormones as controllers in a stimulus–response system. Directional responses of movement are known as tropisms and are called positive when the movement is toward the stimulus and negative when it is away from the stimulus. When a seed germinates, the growing stem turns upward toward the light, and the roots turn downward away from the light. Thus, the stem shows positive phototropism and negative geotropism, while the roots show negative phototropism and positive geotropism. In this example, light and gravity are the stimuli, and directional growth is the response. The controllers are certain hormones synthesized by cells in the tips of the plant stems. These hormones, known as auxins, diffuse through the tissues beneath the tip and concentrate toward the shade side, causing elongation of these cells and, thus, a bending of the tip toward the light. The end result is that the plant is maintained in an optimal condition with respect to light.

In animals, in addition to chemical regulation via the endocrine system, there is another integrative system called the nervous system. A nervous system can be defined as an organized group of cells, called neurons, specialized for the conduction of an impulse—an excited state—from a sensory receptor through a nerve network to an effector, the site at which the response occurs.

Advantages of nervous coordination

Organisms that possess a nervous system are capable of much more complex behaviour than are organisms that lack one. The nervous system, being specialized for the conduction of impulses, allows rapid responses to stimuli from the environment. Many of the responses mediated by the nervous system are directed toward preserving the status quo, or homeostasis, of the animal. Stimuli that tend to displace or disrupt some part of the organism call forth a response that results in reduction of the adverse effects and a return to a more normal condition. Organisms with a nervous system are also capable of a second group of functions that initiate a variety of behaviour patterns. Animals may go through periods of exploratory or appetitive behaviour, nest building, and migration. Although these activities are beneficial to the survival of the species, they are not always performed by the individual in response to an individual need or stimulus. Finally, learned behaviour can be superimposed on both the homeostatic and initiating functions of the nervous system.

INTRACELLULAR SYSTEMS

All living cells have the property of irritability, or responsiveness to environmental stimuli, which can affect the cell in different ways, producing, for example, electrical, chemical, or mechanical changes. These changes are expressed as a response, which may be the release of secretory products by gland cells, the contraction of muscle cells, the bending of a plant-stem cell, and the beating of whiplike "hairs," or cilia, by ciliated cells.

The responsiveness of a single cell can be illustrated by the behaviour of the relatively simple amoeba. Unlike some other protozoans, an amoeba lacks highly developed structures that function in the reception of stimuli and in the production or conduction of a response. The amoeba behaves as though it had a nervous system, however, because the general responsiveness of its cytoplasm serves the functions of a nervous system. An excitation produced by a stimulus is conducted to other parts of the cell and evokes a response by the animal. An amoeba will move to a region of a certain level of light. It will be attracted by chemicals given off by foods and exhibit a feeding response. It will also withdraw from a region with noxious chemicals and show an avoidance reaction upon contacting other objects.

ORGANELLE SYSTEMS

In more complex protozoans, specialized cellular structures, or organelles, serve as receptors of stimulus and as effectors of response. Receptors include stiff sensory bristles in ciliates and the light-sensitive eyespots of flagellates. Effectors include cilia (slender, hairlike projections from the cell surface), flagella (greatly elongated, whiplike cilia), and other organelles associated with drawing in food or with locomotion. Protozoans also have subcellular cytoplasmic filaments that, like muscle tissue, are contractile. The vigorous contraction of the stalked protozoan *Vorticella,* for example, is the result of contraction of a threadlike structure called a myoneme in the stalk.

Although protozoans clearly have specialized receptors and effectors, it is not certain that there are special conducting systems between the two. In a ciliate such as *Paramecium,* the beating of the cilia—which propels it along—is not random, but coordinated. Beating of the cilia begins at one end of the animal and moves in regularly spaced waves to the other end, suggesting that coordinating influences are conducted longitudinally. A system of fibrils connecting the bodies in which the cilia are rooted could provide conducting paths for the waves, but coordination of the cilia could also take place without such a system. Each cilium could respond to a stimulus carried over the cell surface from an adjacent cilium—in which case, coordination would be the result of a chain reaction from cilium to cilium.

Coordination in the *Paramecium*

The best evidence that formed structures are responsible for coordination comes from another ciliate, *Euplotes,* which has a specialized band of ciliary rows (membranelles) and widely separated tufts of cilia (cirri). By means of the coordinated action of these structures, *Euplotes* is capable of several complicated movements in addition to swimming (*e.g.,* turning sharply, moving backward, spinning). The five cirri at the rear are connected to the anterior end in an area known as the motorium. The fibres of the motorium apparently provide coordination between the cirri and the membranelles. The membranelles, cirri, and motorium constitute a neuromotor system.

NERVOUS SYSTEMS

The basic pattern of stimulus–response coordination in animals is an organization of receptor, adjustor, and effector units. External stimuli are received by the receptor cells, which, in most cases, are neurons. (In a few instances, a receptor is a non-nervous sensory epithelial cell, such as a hair cell of the inner ear or a taste cell, which stimulates adjacent neurons.) The stimulus is modified, or transduced, into an electrical impulse in the receptor neuron. This incoming excitation, or afferent impulse, then passes along an extension, or axon, of the receptor to an adjustor, called an interneuron. (All neurons are capable of conducting an impulse, which is a brief change in the electrical charge on the cell membrane. Such an impulse can be transmitted, without loss in strength, many times along an axon until the message, or input, reaches another neuron, which in turn is excited.) The interneuron-adjustor selects, interprets, or modifies the input from the receptor and sends off an outgoing, or efferent, impulse to an efferent neuron, such as a motor neuron. The efferent neuron, in turn, makes contact with an effector such as a muscle or gland, which produces a response.

In the simplest arrangement, the receptor–adjustor–effector units form a functional group known as the reflex arc. Sensory cells carry afferent impulses to a central interneuron, which makes contact with a motor neuron. The motor neuron carries efferent impulses to the effector, which produces the response. Three types of neurons are involved in this reflex arc, but a two-neuron arc, in which the receptor makes contact directly with the motor neuron, also occurs. There, simple reflexes are prompt, short-lived, automatic, and involve only a part of the body. Examples of simple reflexes are the contraction of a muscle in response to stretch, the blink of the eye when the cornea is touched, and salivation at the sight of food. Reflexes of this type are usually involved in preserving homeostasis.

Simple and complex nervous systems

The differences between simple and complex nervous systems lie not in the basic units but in their arrangement. In higher nervous systems, there are more interneurons concentrated in the central nervous system (brain and spinal cord) that mediate the impulses between afferent and efferent neurons. Sensory impulses from particular receptors travel over specific neuronal pathways to the central nervous system. Within the central nervous system, though, the impulse can travel over multiple pathways formed by numerous neurons. Theoretically, the impulse can be distributed to any of the efferent motor neurons and produce a response in any of the effectors. It is also possible for many kinds of stimuli to produce the same response.

As a result of the integrative action of the interneuron, the behaviour of the organism is more than the simple sum of its reflexes; it is a unitary, integrated whole that exhibits coordination between many individual reflexes. Reflexes can occur in a complicated series or sequence producing elaborate behaviour patterns. Behaviour in such cases is characterized not by inherited, stereotyped responses but by flexibility and adaptability to circumstances. Many automatic, unconditioned reflexes can be modified by or adapted to new stimuli. The remarkable experiments of the Russian physiologist Pavlov, for example, showed that if an animal salivates at the sight of food while another stimulus, such as the sound of a bell, occurs simultaneously, the sound alone can induce salivation after several trials. This response, known as a conditioned reflex, is a form of learning. The animal's behaviour is no longer limited by fixed, inherited reflex arcs but can be modified by experience and exposure to an unlimited number of stimuli. The most evolved nervous systems are capable of even higher associative functions: of other forms of learning, of thinking, and of memory. The complex manipulation of the signals necessary for these functions depends to a great extent on the number and intricacy of arrangement of the pool of interneurons. (T.L.L./S.D.E.)

The nerve cell

The watershed of all studies of the nervous system was an observation made in 1889 by the Spanish scientist Santiago Ramón y Cajal, who reported that the nervous system is composed of individual units that are structurally independent of one another and whose internal contents do not come into direct contact. According to this hypothesis, now known as the neuron theory or neuron doctrine, each nerve cell communicates with others through contiguity rather than continuity. That is, communication between adjacent but separate cells must take place across the space and barriers separating them. It has since been proved that Ramón y Cajal's theory is not universally true, but his central idea—that communication in the nervous system is largely communication between independent nerve cells—has remained an accurate guiding principle for all further study.

There are two basic cell types within the nervous system: neurons and neuroglial cells.

THE NEURON

In the human brain there are approximately 10,000,000,000 neurons. Each neuron has its own identity, expressed by its interactions with other neurons and by its secretions; each also has its own function, depending on its intrinsic properties and location as well as its inputs from other select groups of neurons, its capacity to integrate those inputs, and its ability to transmit the information to another select group of neurons.

Three regions of the neuron

With few exceptions, most neurons consist of three distinct regions: (1) the cell body, or soma; (2) the nerve fibre, or axon; and (3) the receiving processes, or dendrites (Figure 1).

By courtesy of Alan Peters

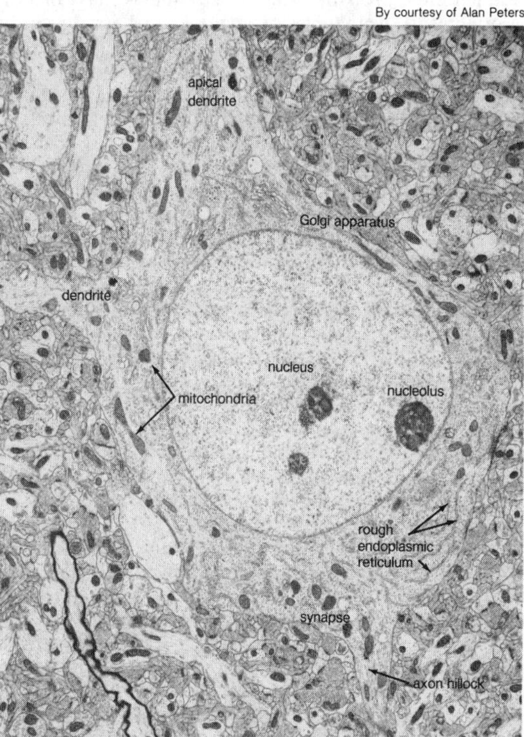

Figure 1: *A neuron from the visual cortex of a rat.* The centre of the field is occupied by the soma, or cell body, of the neuron. Most of the soma is occupied by the nucleus, which contains a nucleolus. The double membrane of the nucleus is surrounded by cytoplasm, containing elements of the Golgi apparatus lying at the base of the apical dendrite. Mitochondria can be seen dispersed in the cytoplasm, which also contains the rough endoplasmic reticulum. Another dendrite is seen to the side, and the axon hillock is shown at the initial segment of the emerging axon. A synapse impinges onto the neuron close to the axon hillock.

The soma. *The plasma membrane.* The neuron is bounded by a plasma membrane, a structure so thin that its fine detail can be revealed only by high-resolution electron microscopy. About half of the membrane is the so-called lipid bilayer, two sheets of mainly phospholipids with a space between. One end of a phospholipid molecule is hydrophilic, or water attaching, and the other end is hydrophobic, or water repelling. The bilayer structure results when the hydrophilic ends of the phospholipid molecules in each sheet turn toward the watery mediums of both the cell interior and the extracellular environment, while the hydrophobic ends of the molecules turn in toward the space between the sheets. These lipid layers are not rigid structures; the loosely bonded phospholipid molecules can move laterally across the surfaces of the membrane, and the interior is in a highly liquid state.

Embedded within the lipid bilayer are proteins, which also "float" in the liquid environment of the membrane. These include glycoproteins containing polysaccharide chains, which function, along with other carbohydrates, as adhesion sites and recognition sites for attachment and chemical interaction with other neurons. The proteins provide another basic and crucial function: those which penetrate the membrane can exist in more than one conformational state, or molecular shape, forming channels that allow ions to pass between the extracellular fluid and the cytoplasm, or internal contents of the cell. In other conformational states, they can block the passage of ions. This action is the fundamental mechanism that determines the excitability and pattern of electrical activity of the neuron.

A complex system of proteinaceous intracellular filaments are linked to the membrane proteins. This so-called cytoskeleton includes thin neurofilaments containing actin, thick neurofilaments similar to polymerized myosin, and microtubules composed of tubulin. The filaments are probably concerned with movement and translocation of the membrane proteins, while microtubules may anchor the proteins to the cytoplasm.

The nucleus. Each neuron contains a nucleus defining the location of the soma. The nucleus is surrounded by a double membrane, called the nuclear envelope, that fuses at intervals to form pores allowing molecular communication with the cytoplasm. Within the nucleus are the chromosomes, the genetic material of the cell, through which the nucleus controls synthesis of proteins and the growth and differentiation of the cell into its final form. Proteins synthesized in the neuron include enzymes, receptors, hormones, and structural proteins for the cytoskeleton.

Organelles of the cell. The endoplasmic reticulum (ER) is a widely spread membrane system within the neuron that is continuous with the nuclear envelope. It consists of series of tubules, flattened sacs called cisternae, and membrane-bounded spheres called vesicles. There are two types of ER.

Synthesis of protein in the neuron

The rough endoplasmic reticulum (RER) has rows of knobs called ribosomes on its surface. Ribosomes synthesize proteins that, for the most part, are transported out of the cell. The RER is found only in the soma.

The smooth endoplasmic reticulum (SER) consists of a network of tubules in the neuron soma that connects the RER with the Golgi apparatus. The tubules can also enter the axon at its initial segment and extend to the axon terminals.

The Golgi apparatus is a complex of flattened cisternae arranged in closely packed rows. Located close to and around the nucleus, it receives proteins synthesized in the RER and transferred to it via the SER. Once arrived at the Golgi apparatus, the proteins are attached to carbohydrates. The glycoproteins so formed are packaged into vesicles that leave the complex to be incorporated into the cell membrane.

The axon. The axon arises from the soma at a region called the axon hillock or initial segment. This is the region where the plasma membrane generates nerve impulses; the axon conducts these impulses away from the soma or dendrites toward other neurons. Large axons (arising from large somas) acquire an insulating myelin sheath and are known as myelinated or medullated fibres. Myelin is composed of 80 percent lipid and 20 percent protein; cholesterol is one of the major lipids, along with variable amounts of cerebrosides and phospholipids. Concentric layers of these lipids separated by thin layers of protein give rise to a high-resistance, low-capacitance electrical insulator interrupted at intervals by gaps called nodes of Ranvier, where the nerve membrane is exposed to the external environment. In the central nervous system, the myelin sheath is formed from glial cells called oligodendrocytes, while in peripheral nerves it is formed from Schwann cells (see below *The neuroglia*).

While the axon mainly conducts nerve impulses from the soma to the terminal, the terminal itself secretes chemical substances called neurotransmitters. The synthesis of these substances can occur in the terminal itself, but the synthesizing enzymes are formed by ribosomes in the soma and must be transported down the axon to the terminal. This process is known as axoplasmic flow; it occurs in both directions along the axon and may be facilitated by microtubules.

At the terminal of the axon, and sometimes along its length, are specialized structures that form junctions with other neurons and with muscle cells. These junctions are called synapses. Presynaptic terminals, when seen by light microscopy, look like small knobs; when examined under high-resolution electron microscopy, they are seen to contain many organelles. The most numerous of these are synaptic vesicles, which, filled with neurotransmitters, are often clumped in areas of the terminal membrane that appear to be thickened. The thickened areas are known as presynaptic dense projections, or active zones.

Axon terminals at the synapse

The presynaptic terminal is unmyelinated and is separated from the neuron or muscle cell onto which it impinges by a gap called the synaptic cleft, across which the neurotransmitters diffuse when released from the vesicles. In nerve–muscle junctions the synaptic cleft contains a structure called the basal lamina. This structure holds an enzyme that destroys neurotransmitters and thus regulates the amount that reaches the postsynaptic receptors on the receiving cell. Most knowledge of postsynaptic neurotransmitter receptors comes from studies of the receptor on muscle cells. This receptor, called the end plate, is a glycoprotein composed of five subunits. Other neurotransmitter receptors do not have the same structure, but they are all proteins and probably have subunits with a central channel that is activated by the neurotransmitter.

While the chemically mediated synapse described above forms the majority of synapses in nervous systems of vertebrates, there are other types of synapses in vertebrate brains and, in especially great numbers, in invertebrate and fish nervous systems. At these synapses there is no synaptic gap; instead, there are so-called gap junctions, direct channels between neurons that establish a continuity between the cytoplasm of adjacent cells and a structural symmetry between the pre- and postsynaptic sites. Rapid neuronal communication at these junctions is probably not chemical but electrical in nature. (For further discussion, see below *Transmission of information in the nervous system: Transmission at the synapse.*)

The dendrites. Besides the axon, neurons have other branches called dendrites. These are usually shorter than axons and are unmyelinated. Traditionally, dendrites are thought to form receiving surfaces for synaptic input from other neurons. In many dendrites these surfaces are provided by specialized structures called dendritic spines, which, by providing discrete regions for the reception of nerve impulses, isolate changes in electrical current from the main dendritic trunk.

The traditional view of dendritic function presumes that only axons conduct nerve impulses and only dendrites receive them, but it has been shown that dendrites can form synapses with dendrites and that axons and even somata can receive impulses. Indeed, some neurons have no axon; in these cases nervous transmission is carried out by the dendrites.

THE NEUROGLIA

Neurons form a minority of the cells in the nervous system. Exceeding them in number by at least 10 to 1 are neuroglial cells, which exist in the nervous systems of invertebrates as well as vertebrates. Neuroglia can be distinguished from neurons by the lack of axons and the presence of only one type of process. In addition, they do not form synapses, and they retain the ability to divide throughout their life span. While neurons and neuroglia lie in close apposition to one another, there are no direct junctional specializations, such as gap junctions, between the two types. Gap junctions do exist between neuroglial cells, raising questions about their functions and properties.

Differences between neuroglia and neurons

Types of neuroglia. Apart from conventional histological and electron-microscopic techniques, immunologic techniques are used to identify different neuroglial cell types. By staining the cells with antibodies that bind to specific protein constituents of different neuroglia, neurologists have been able to discern two (in some opinions three) main groups: (1) astrocytes, subdivided into fibrous and protoplasmic types; (2) oligodendrocytes, subdivided into interfascicular and perineuronal types; and sometimes (3) microglia.

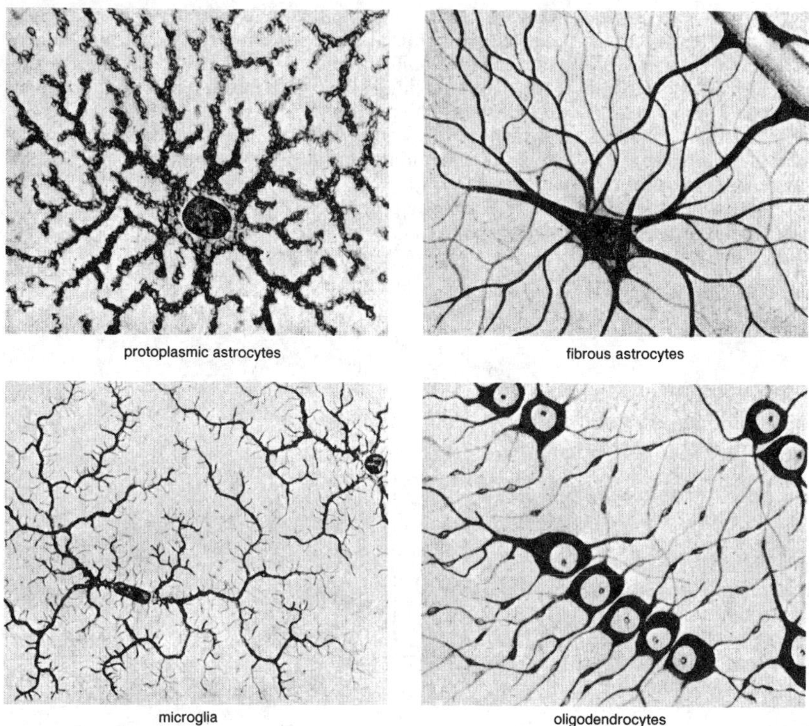

Figure 2: Neuroglial cells.

After del Rio-Hortega in W. Bloom and D.W. Fawcett, *A Textbook of Histology* (1986), W.B. Saunders Co., Philadelphia; reprinted by permission

Fibrous astrocytes are prevalent among myelinated nerve fibres in the white matter of the central nervous system. Organelles seen in the somata of neurons are also seen in astrocytes, but they appear to be much sparser. These cells are characterized by the presence of numerous fibrils in their cytoplasm. The main processes exit the cell in a radial direction (hence the name astrocyte, meaning "star-shaped cell"), forming expansions and end feet at the surfaces of vascular capillaries.

Unlike fibrous astrocytes, protoplasmic astrocytes occur in the gray matter of the central nervous system. They have fewer fibrils within their cytoplasm, and cytoplasmic organelles are sparse, so that the somata are shaped by surrounding neurons and fibres. The processes of protoplasmic astrocytes also make contact with capillaries.

Oligodendrocytes have few cytoplasmic fibrils but a well-developed Golgi apparatus. They can be distinguished from astrocytes by the greater density of both cytoplasm and nucleus, the absence of fibrils and glycogen in the cytoplasm, and large numbers of microtubules in the processes. Interfascicular oligodendrocytes are aligned in rows between the nerve fibres of the white matter of the central nervous system. In gray matter perineuronal oligodendrocytes are located in close approximation with the somata of neurons. In the peripheral nervous system, neuroglia that are equivalent to oligodendrocytes are called Schwann cells.

Microglial cells are small, crenate cells with dark cytoplasm and a dark nucleus. It is uncertain whether they are merely damaged neuroglial cells or occur as a separate group in living tissue.

Neuroglial functions. The term neuroglia means "nerve glue," and these cells were originally thought to be structural supports for neurons. This is still thought to be plausible, but other functions of the neuroglia are now generally accepted. It has long been known that oligodendrocytes and Schwann cells produce the myelin sheath around neuronal axons. Studies show that some constituent of the axonal surface stimulates Schwann cell proliferation and that the type of axon determines whether there is loose or tight myelination of the axon. In tight myelination a glial cell wraps itself like a rolled sheet around a length of axon until the fibre is covered by several layers. Between segments of myelin wrapping are exposed sections called nodes of Ranvier, which are important in the transmission of nerve impulses. Myelinated nerve fibres are found only in vertebrate animals, leading biologists to conclude that they are an adaptation to transmission over relatively long distances.

Formation of myelin

Another well-defined role of neuroglial cells is in repair following injury to the central nervous system. It has been well documented that astrocytes divide after injury to the nervous system and that they occupy the spaces left by injured neurons. The role of oligodendrocytes after injury is not so clear, but evidence suggests that they can proliferate and form myelin sheaths.

When neurons of the peripheral nervous system are cut, they undergo a process of degeneration followed by regeneration, the fibres regenerating in such a way that they return to their original target sites. Schwann cells that remain after nerve degeneration apparently mark the route. This route direction is also performed by astrocytes during development of the central nervous system. In the developing cerebral cortex and cerebellum of primates, astrocytes project long processes to certain locations, and neurons migrate along these processes to arrive at their final locations. Thus, neuronal organization is brought about to some extent by the neuroglia.

Astrocytes are also believed to have high-affinity uptake systems for neurotransmitters such as glutamate and gamma-aminobutyric acid (GABA). This function is important in the modulation of synaptic transmission. Uptake systems tend to terminate neurotransmitter action at the synapses and perhaps also act as storage systems for the neurotransmitters when they are needed. For instance, when motor nerves are cut, the nerve terminals degenerate and their original sites are occupied by Schwann cells. It has been found not only that electrical signals can be recorded on muscle cell receptors in the absence of any form of stimulation but also that currents applied to the Schwann cells evoke neurotransmitter release. Apparently, the synthesis of neuro-transmitters by neurons also requires the presence of neuroglial cells in the vicinity.

Functions in synaptic transmission

In the past it was thought that neuroglia were not electrically excitable, but it has been shown that neuroglial cells in vitro have voltage-sensitive properties similar to those of excitable neurons. If electrical activity similar to that occurring in neurons were generated in neuroglial cells in vivo, the implications for glial–neuronal interaction would be enormous. Such proof is not available, however.

Finally, the environment surrounding neurons in the brain consists of a network of very narrow extracellular clefts. In 1907 the Italian biologist Emilio Lugaro suggested that neuroglial cells exchange substances with the extracellular fluid and in this way exert control on the neuronal environment. It has since been shown that glucose, amino acids, and ions—all of which influence neuronal function—are exchanged between the extracellular space and neuroglial cells. After high levels of neuronal activity, for instance, neuroglial cells can take up and spatially buffer potassium ions and thus maintain normal neuronal function.

Transmission of information in the nervous system

In the nervous systems of animals at all levels of the evolutionary scale, the signals containing information about a particular stimulus are electrical in nature. In the past the nerve fibre and its contents were compared to a metal wire, while the membrane was compared to insulation around the wire. This comparison was erroneous for a number of reasons. First, the charge carriers in nerves are ions, not electrons, and the density of ions in the axon is much less than that of electrons in a metal wire. Second, the membrane of an axon is not a perfect insulator, so that the movement of current along the axon is not complete. Finally, nerve fibres are smaller than most wires, so that the currents they can carry are limited in amplitude.

THE IONIC BASIS OF ELECTRICAL SIGNALS

Positive and negative charge

Ions are atoms or groups of atoms that gain an electrical charge by losing or acquiring electrons. For example, in the reaction that forms salt from sodium and chlorine, each sodium atom "donates" an electron, which is negatively charged, to a chlorine atom. The result is sodium chloride (NaCl), composed of one positively charged sodium ion (Na^+) and one negatively charged chloride ion (Cl^-). A positively charged ion is called a cation; a negatively charged ion, an anion. The number of charges carried by an ion is called its valence. Na^+ and Cl^-, which respectively lose and acquire one electron, have a valence of one, while calcium ions (Ca^{2+}), which lose two electrons, have a valence of two.

The electrical events that constitute signaling in the nervous system depend upon the distribution of ions on either side of the nerve membrane. Underlying these distributions and their change are crucial physicochemical principles.

Distribution of ions across a membrane. *Diffusion of uncharged molecules.* Molecules in solution move randomly, the energy for their movement being derived from thermal energy. When a permeable membrane (a membrane that allows molecules to cross it) divides a heavily concentrated solution from a lightly concentrated solution, there occurs a diffusion of molecules through the membrane and down their concentration gradient—that is, from the fluid with the higher concentration to that with the lower concentration. The number of molecules moving per unit of time is called the flow rate, or flux rate. Diffusion continues until the concentrations on both sides of the membrane are equal. A condition of no net flux is then established with an equal, random diffusion of molecules in both directions. This is called the equilibrium state.

A membrane with pores allowing passage of molecules of only a particular size is called a semipermeable membrane. The semipermeable membrane imposes a condition of restricted diffusion. In that case the flux rate of the diffusing material is controlled by the permeability of the membrane, which in turn is dictated by the size of the pores and is given a unit of measure called the permeability coefficient.

Diffusion of water. The water molecule, like other molecules, diffuses down its concentration gradient. If a rigid vessel contains water on one side of a semipermeable membrane and an impermeant substance (a substance that cannot cross the membrane) on the other side, the water tends to cross the membrane, diluting the substance and increasing the hydrostatic pressure on the other side (Figure 3). The pressure then will tend to push water back across the membrane in opposition to the net flux. When the pressure built up equals the diffusion of water in the opposite direction, no net flux occurs and equilibrium is established. The migration of water (or any solvent) across a membrane is called osmosis, and the pressure necessary to establish equilibrium is called osmotic pressure. Water moves from a region of low osmotic pressure to a region of high osmotic pressure.

Adapted from A.R. Freeman, "Cellular Function and Fundamentals of Physiology," in E.E. Selkurt (ed.), *Physiology for the Health Services* (1975); Little, Brown and Company

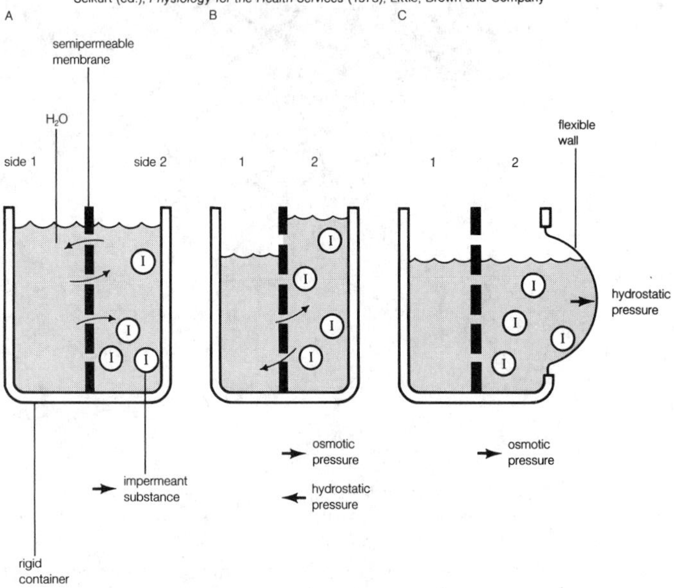

Figure 3: *Diffusion of water across a semipermeable membrane.* (A) Water diffuses down its concentration gradient from side 1 to side 2 of a rigid container. (B) The net flux of water creates a hydrostatic pressure, tending to force the water back to side 1. (C) If the wall of side 2 is flexible, the hydrostatic pressure causes an increase in the volume of side 2.

The above example refers to water in a container with rigid walls. The neuron, however, has somewhat flexible walls, so that as water enters it, the cell tends to increase in volume, or swell. There is a direct relation between osmotic pressure across the plasma membrane and the final volume of a cell at equilibrium, so that if the osmotic pressure of the cell exterior is halved, the equilibrium volume of the cell will be twice its original.

Diffusion of ions. When potassium chloride (KCl) is placed into solution, the elements separate into potassium cations (K^+) and chloride anions (Cl^-). The ions follow much the same principles of diffusion as uncharged molecules. For example, if a highly concentrated solution of KCl is separated from a lower concentration by a semipermeable membrane—one that is permeable to cations only—then K^+ from the higher concentration diffuses across the membrane, following its concentration gradient to the region of lower concentration (Figure 4). Cl^-, being blocked by the membrane, remains behind. At this point the diffusion of ions creates conditions quite different from the diffusion of uncharged molecules and water molecules. The movement of cations toward the less concentrated solution creates a separation of electrical charge across the membrane—that is, a greater number of positively charged ions will have moved to the side with the less concentrated solution of KCl, and the side of the membrane with the higher concentration will have a more negative charge. This separation of charge—actually a difference in electrical potential—is called the potential difference, and it is the starting point of all electrical events in nervous systems. When present in the plasma membrane of the neuron, it transforms the neuron into an electrolytic cell that is capable, upon stimulation, of generating and transmitting electrical impulses.

Separation of electrical charge

Complicating the ionic diffusion process is the phenomenon that opposite charges attract. This means that, in the example above, some of the K^+ diffusing across the membrane is electrostatically drawn back up its con-

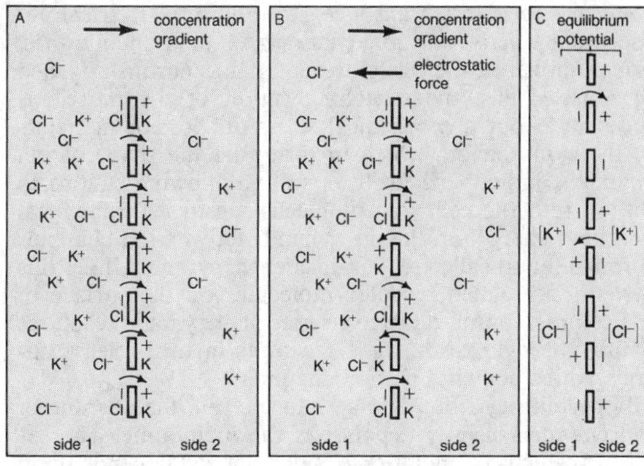

Figure 4: *Diffusion of ions across a semipermeable membrane.* (A) A high concentration of KCl is placed on side 1, opposite a semipermeable membrane from a low concentration. The membrane allows only K^+ to diffuse, thereby establishing an electrical potential difference across the membrane. (B) The separation of charge creates an electrostatic voltage force, which draws some K^+ back to side 1. (C) At equilibrium, there is no net flux of K^+ in either direction. Side 1, with the higher concentration of KCl, has a negative charge compared to side 2.

Adapted from A.R. Freeman, "Cellular Function and Fundamentals of Physiology," in E.E. Selkurt (ed.), *Physiology for the Health Services* (1975); Little, Brown and Company

centration gradient toward the Cl^-, creating a situation in which two tendencies oppose each other: (1) the diffusing tendency of the cation down its concentration gradient; and (2) the electrostatic voltage force tending to draw the cation back. These two forces eventually reach a state of no net flux, when the number of cations that they draw in each direction across the membrane is equal. The system is then in electrochemical equilibrium. At equilibrium, one side of the membrane may still have a more negative charge than the other. In that case the potential difference is called the equilibrium potential. (It is also called the Nernst potential, after Walther Nernst, the German physical chemist who, in the late 19th century, developed equations for calculating the electrical potential at which there is no longer a net flux of a specific ion across a membrane.)

The law of electroneutrality states that in any single ionic solution a sum of negative electrical charges attracts an equal sum of positive electrical charges. If a solution of KCl is divided into two parts by a membrane, permeable to both ions, then the equal concentration of KCl across the membrane preserves chemical equilibrium between the two sides, while the equal concentrations of K^+ and Cl^- on each side preserve electroneutrality on each side as well (Figure 5). This equilibrium can be upset by the addition to side 1 of a large number of K^+ and an equal charge of impermeant anions (that is, negatively charged ions other than Cl^- that cannot permeate the membrane). In that case electroneutrality on side 1 is preserved, since the sum of positive charges added to that side is equaled by the sum of added negative charges. However, chemical equilibrium between side 1 and side 2 is not preserved, since side 1 now has a greater concentration of ions than side 2. Therefore, K^+ diffuses down its concentration gradient, crossing the membrane to side 2 while drawing Cl^- with it to preserve electroneutrality. Diffusion continues until a new state of electrochemical equilibrium is reached. Researchers have found that this occurs at a point at which the ratio of K^+ concentration on side 2 to that on side 1 is equal to the ratio of Cl^- concentration on side 1 to that on side 2. Stated mathematically, equilibrium is reached when

$$\frac{[K^+]_{\text{side 2}}}{[K^+]_{\text{side 1}}} = \frac{[Cl^-]_{\text{side 1}}}{[Cl^-]_{\text{side 2}}}.$$

This is known as the Donnan equilibrium, after Frederick George Donnan, the British chemist who in 1911 first measured the changes brought about by adding an impermeant substance to one side of a divided solution at equilibrium.

In the new state of equilibrium, both side 1 and side 2 are electrically neutral, since the impermeant anions added to side 1 are equaled by the added K^+, and the K^+ that has diffused to side 2 is balanced by the Cl^- electrostatically drawn along with it. But the entire solution is not at osmotic equilibrium, because the larger amount of ions on side 1 tends to draw water from side 2. Osmotic equilibrium can be established by the addition of ions to side 2. Indeed, in the neuron, osmotic equilibrium is maintained partly because large amounts of K^+ and impermeant anions inside the cell are balanced by large amounts of salt outside.

The neuronal membrane. The principles outlined above can be applied to the neuron and its ionic contents.

The plasma membrane of the neuron is semipermeable, being highly permeable to K^+ and slightly permeable to Cl^- and Na^+. In the extracellular fluid, electroneutrality is preserved by a balance between a high concentration of Na^+ on the one hand and a high concentration of Cl^- as well as small quantities of impermeant anions such as bicarbonate, phosphate, and sulfate on the other. In the cytoplasm, where K^+ concentration is high, the concentration of Cl^- is much below that necessary to balance the sum of the positive charges. Electroneutrality is maintained there by negatively charged impermeant proteins and phosphates. Osmotic balance is maintained between the extracellular fluid and the cytoplasm by movement of water through the plasma membrane when the total concentration of particles on one side is not equal to that on the other.

The electrical potential of the neuron

These three characteristics of the neuron—semipermeability of the membrane, osmotic balance, and electroneutrality on each side—create an equilibrium electrical potential at which the inside of the membrane is more negative than the outside. In most neurons this potential, called the membrane potential, is between −60 and −75 millivolts (mV; the minus sign indicates that the inner surface is negative). When the inside of the plasma membrane has a negative charge compared to the outside, the neuron is said to be polarized. Any change in membrane potential tending to make the inside even more negative is called hyperpolarization, while any change tending to make it less negative is called depolarization.

As stated above, the Nernst potential is the potential difference that exists across a membrane when a particular ion, having reached equilibrium between the tendency to diffuse down its concentration gradient and the tendency to be drawn back by other ions, is in a state of no net flux. Given such information as the energy of the dissolved substances, the temperature of the solution, and the concentrations of ions on each side of the membrane, researchers using the Nernst equation can predict the potential difference that will exist if the membrane is permeable to any one of the ions in solution. The plasma membrane of the neuron is highly permeable to K^+, and in fact the recorded membrane potential of most neurons (−60 to −75 millivolts) is close to that predicted by the Nernst equation for K^+. However, it is not exactly the

From *Neurobiology*, 2nd ed., by Gordon M. Shepherd, copyright © 1983, 1988 by Oxford University Press, Inc.; reprinted by permission

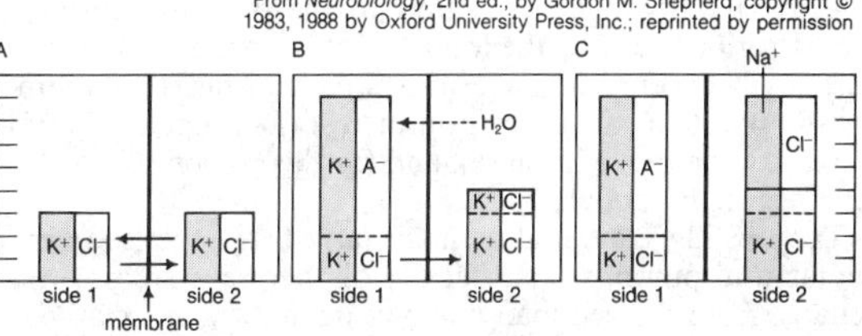

Figure 5: *Establishment of electrochemical and osmotic equilibrium.*
(A) A solution of KCl divided by a permeable membrane reaches electrochemical equilibrium, with both sides maintaining equal concentrations of KCl and each side maintaining equal positive (K^+) and negative (Cl^-) charges. (B) With the addition to side 1 of K^+ and an anion (A^-) that cannot permeate the membrane, equilibrium is upset. K^+ diffuses to side 2, drawing an equal charge of Cl^-. A new electrochemical equilibrium is reached at which each side maintains equal positive and negative charges, but side 1 has a higher concentration of ions than side 2. This causes the osmosis of water (H_2O) from side 2 to side 1. (C) Osmotic equilibrium is established by the addition of salt (NaCl) to side 2, creating an equal concentration of ions across the membrane.

same, because K^+ is not the only ion affecting the membrane potential. The membrane is also slightly permeable to Na^+ and Cl^-. The permeability to Na^+ may be low, but the high concentration of this cation outside the cell and the slightly negative electric charge inside the cell tend to drive Na^+ inward. This in turn causes the inside of the cell to depolarize, placing K^+ out of equilibrium. As a consequence, K^+ leaves the cell until an equilibrium state is reached in which the leak inward of Na^+ is equaled by the leak outward of K^+ and there is no net flux of ions. There is also a tendency for Cl^- to permeate the membrane, since that ion is at higher concentration outside the neuron than inside. Therefore, for an equilibrium state to be produced, the sum of all three net currents must equal zero.

Given the concentrations of all three ions on each side of the membrane and the relative permeability of the membrane to each ion, researchers can calculate the combined effect of K^+, Na^+, and Cl^- on the membrane potential by using the so-called constant-field equation. This equation, by including relative permeability as an important factor, takes into account the phenomenon that the more permeable a membrane is to a particular ion, the greater is the influence of that ion on membrane potential. The permeance of Na^+, for example, is only a fraction of that of K^+, and the permeance of Cl^- is lower yet; therefore, while the membrane potential is highly sensitive to changes in the concentration of K^+, it is less affected by changes in Na^+ and almost unaffected by changes in Cl^-.

TRANSMISSION IN THE NEURON

The discussion above demonstrates that the electrical potential existing in neurons is based on the distribution of ions across the plasma membrane and that this distribution comes about through permeation of the membrane. In fact, ions are almost always hydrated in the form of ion–water complexes, which have great difficulty in penetrating the hydrophobic lipid bilayer of the plasma membrane. Permeation actually occurs through protein structures embedded in the lipid bilayer and spanning the membrane from cytoplasm to extracellular fluid. Sometimes pumping ions from one side to the other and sometimes merely providing channels through which diffusing ions can flow past the lipid molecules, these structures maintain the ionic distribution that keeps the membrane polarized, and they also allow the abrupt changes in distribution that create nerve impulses. The protein structures are described in detail in *Ion transport.* Following is a discussion of the electrical events, created by movement of ions, that lead to nervous transmission in the neuron.

Resting potential. The electrical potential across the nerve membrane can be measured by placing one microelectrode within the neuron (usually in the soma) and a second microelectrode in the extracellular fluid. The microelectrode consists of a sharp-tipped glass capillary tube filled with a conducting solution. Upon penetration of the neuron, the potential at the tip of the electrode becomes electrically negative in relation to the outside electrode. As described above, the value of this negative charge is usually between −60 and −75 millivolts. This is the membrane potential of the neuron at rest (*i.e.,* when it is not generating a nerve impulse), and for this reason it is called the resting potential.

The resting potential is maintained by the sodium–potassium pump, which steadily discharges more positive charge from the cell than it allows in, and by the relatively high permeance of K^+, which leaks out of the cell through its membrane channels faster than Na^+ leaks in.

Localized potential. When a physical stimulus such as touch, taste, or colour acts on a sensory receptor cell specifically designed to respond to that stimulus, then the energy of the stimulus (*e.g.,* mechanical, chemical, light) is transduced, or transformed, into an electrical response. This response is the receptor potential, a type of local potential that, when it reaches high enough amplitude, generates the nerve impulse. (Another type of local potential is the postsynaptic potential, which originates in chemical receptors at the synaptic cleft. See below *Transmission at the synapse: Chemical transmission.*)

Response to stimulation

Sensory receptors transduce stimuli into electrical responses by activating ion channels in their membranes. For example, in the stretch receptors of neurons attached to muscle cells, the stretching action of the muscle is thought to put a mechanical stress on protein filaments of the cytoskeleton, which in turn alter the shape of ion channels, inducing them to open and allowing cations to diffuse into the cell. Receptor cells sensitive to chemical and light energy, on the other hand, activate ion channels through the so-called second-messenger system. Under this system, stimulated receptor molecules on the surface of the cell membrane catalyze a series of enzymatic reactions within the cytoplasm; these reactions in turn release energy, which activates the ion channels.

By permitting a flux of Na^+ into the cell, the opening of ion channels slightly depolarizes the membrane. The extent to which the membrane is depolarized depends upon the extent to which the sodium channels are activated, and this in turn depends upon the strength and duration of the original stimulus at the receptor. If depolarization reaches what is called the threshold potential, it triggers the nerve impulse, or action potential (see below). If it does not reach that amplitude, then the neuron remains at rest, and the local potential, through a process called passive spread, diffuses along the nerve fibre and back out through the membrane.

When it is of the postsynaptic type, the local potential usually begins in the dendrites and spreads toward the soma and axon. It is at the initial segment of the axon where, if the local potential is of threshold amplitude, the nerve impulse is generated.

Action potential. *Depolarization.* Because it varies in amplitude, the local potential is said to be graded. The greater the influx of positive charge—and, consequently, depolarization of the membrane—the higher the grade. Beginning at the resting potential of a neuron (for instance, −75 millivolts), a local potential can be of any grade up to the threshold potential (for instance, −58 millivolts). At threshold, voltage-dependent sodium channels become fully activated, and Na^+ pours into the cell. Almost instantly, the membrane actually reverses polarity, the inside acquiring a positive charge in relation to the outside. This reverse polarity constitutes the nerve impulse. It is called the action potential because the positive charge then flows through the cytoplasm, activating sodium channels the entire length of the nerve fibre. This series of activations,

Generation of the nerve impulse

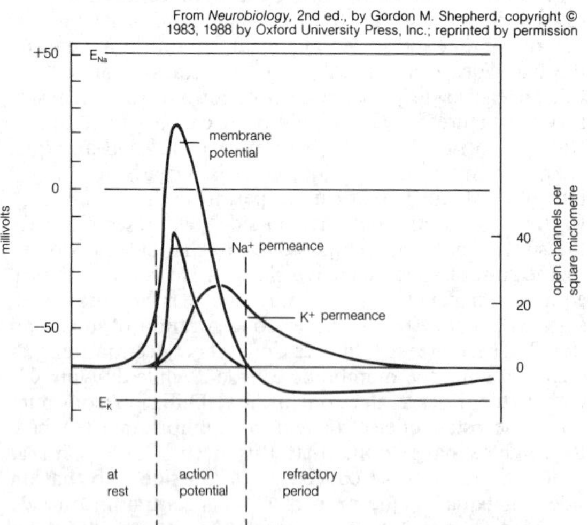

Figure 6: *Changes in ion permeance underlying the action potential.*
Electrical potential is graded at left in millivolts, ion permeance at right in open channels per square micrometre of membrane. At rest, with no channels open, the membrane potential is close to E_K, the equilibrium potential of K^+. When sodium channels open, the membrane depolarizes. Generation of the action potential brings the membrane potential close to E_{Na}, the equilibrium potential of Na^+. When sodium channels close (lowering Na^+ permeance) and potassium channels open (raising K^+ permeance), the membrane repolarizes. During the refractory period, while potassium channels remain open, the membrane is hyperpolarized.

by propagating the action potential along the fibre with virtually no reduction in amplitude, gives the nerve impulse its regenerative property.

Researchers call the nerve impulse an "all-or-none" reaction, since between threshold potential and fully activated potential there are no gradations. The neuron is either at rest with a polarized membrane, or it is conducting a nerve impulse at reverse polarization. The reverse polarity of active neurons is measured at about +30 millivolts. This is close to the Nernst potential for Na^+—that is, the membrane potential at which electrochemical equilibrium would be established if the membrane were completely permeable to Na^+.

Repolarization. As instantaneous as the opening of sodium channels at threshold potential is their closing at the peak of the action potential. This is called sodium inactivation, and it is caused by gates within the channel that are sensitive to depolarization. Following sodium inactivation is the opening of potassium channels, which allows the diffusion of K^+ out of the cell. The combined effect of sodium inactivation, which blocks the influx of cations, and potassium activation, which causes the efflux of other cations, is the immediate return of the cell membrane to a polarized state, with the inside negative in relation to the outside. After repolarization there is a period during which a second action potential cannot be initiated, no matter how large a stimulus current is applied to the neuron. This is called the absolute refractory period, and it is followed by a relative refractory period, during which another action potential can be generated, but only by a greater stimulus current than that originally needed. This period is followed in turn by the return of the neuronal properties to the threshold levels originally required for the initiation of action potentials.

Conduction. The sequence of sodium activation–sodium inactivation–potassium activation creates a nerve impulse that is brief in duration, lasting only a few milliseconds, and that travels down the nerve fibre like a wave, the membrane depolarizing in front of the current and repolarizing behind. Because nerve impulses are not graded in amplitude, it is not the size of the action potential that is important in processing information within the nervous system; rather, it is the number and frequency with which the impulses are fired.

As stated above, the action potential is propagated along the axon without any decrease in amplitude with distance. However, the velocity of conduction along the

From *Neurobiology*, 2nd ed., by Gordon M. Shepherd, copyright © 1983, 1988 by Oxford University Press, Inc.; reprinted by permission

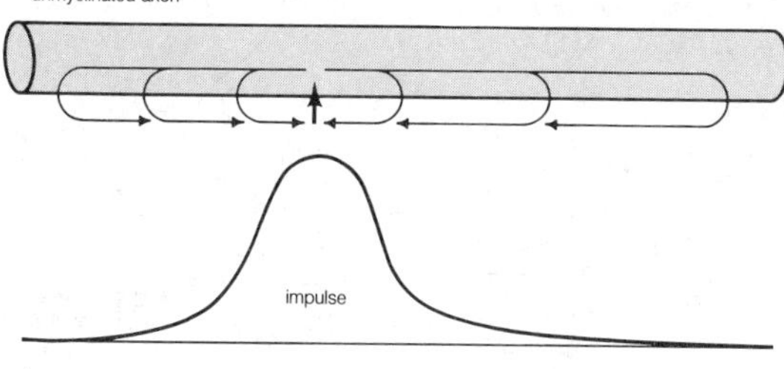

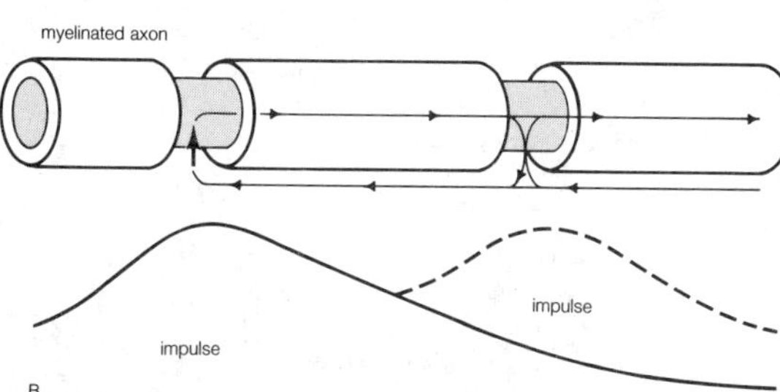

Figure 7: *Conduction of the action potential.*
(A) Passive spread in an unmyelinated axon. The impulse fades along the fibre as it diffuses back through the membrane to the original depolarized region. (B) Saltatory conduction in a myelinated axon. The impulse jumps along the fibre as it is regenerated at each node of Ranvier.

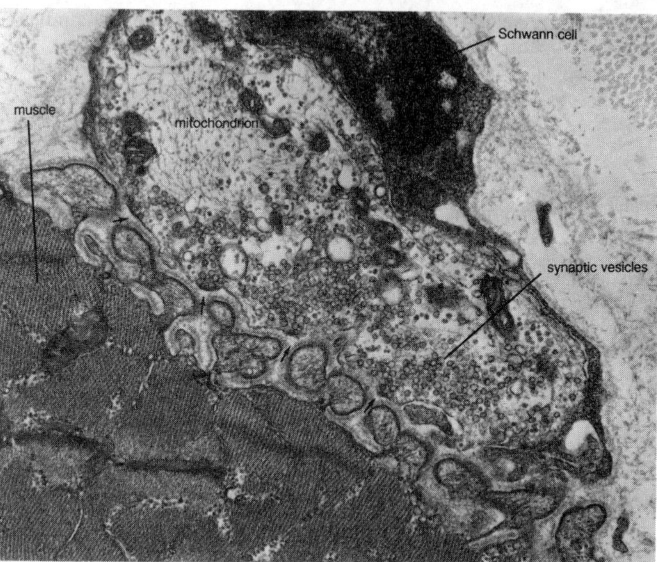

Figure 8: *Electron micrograph of the neuromuscular junction of the frog.*
The motor nerve terminal at the end-plate region contains synaptic vesicles. Active zones (arrows) are located opposite troughs in the postsynaptic membrane of the muscle. A Schwann cell partially covers the terminal.
By courtesy of A. Stieber, N. Gonatas, and S.D. Erulkar

Factors affecting the velocity of transmission

nerve fibre is dependent upon several factors. First is the outside diameter of the nerve fibre. The fastest conduction velocity occurs in the largest diameter nerve fibres. This phenomenon has formed the basis for classifying mammalian nerve fibres into groups in order of decreasing diameter and decreasing conduction velocity. Another factor is the temperature of the nerve fibre. Conduction velocity increases at high temperature and decreases at low. Indeed, nerve conduction can be blocked by the local application of cold to a nerve fibre. Conduction velocity is also affected by myelination of the nerve fibre. Since ions cannot cross the lipid content of the myelin sheath, they spread passively down the nerve fibre until reaching the unmyelinated nodes of Ranvier. The nodes of Ranvier are packed with a high concentration of ion channels, which, upon stimulation, propagate the nerve impulse to the next node. In this manner the action potential jumps quickly from node to node along the fibre in a process called saltatory conduction (from Latin *saltare,* "to jump"; see Figure 7).

TRANSMISSION AT THE SYNAPSE

Once an action potential has been generated at the axon hillock, it is conducted the length of the axon until it reaches the terminals, the fingerlike extensions of the neuron that abut other neurons and muscle cells (see above *The nerve cell: The neuron*). At this point there exist two methods for transmitting the action potential from one cell to the other. In electrical transmission, the ionic current flows directly through channels that couple the cells. In chemical transmission, a chemical substance called the neurotransmitter passes from one cell to the other, stimulating the second cell to generate its own action potential.

Electrical transmission. This method of transmitting nerve impulses, while far less common than chemical transmission, has been found in the nervous systems of invertebrates and lower vertebrates as well as in the central nervous systems of some mammals. Transmission takes place through so-called gap junctions, which are protein channels that link the cellular contents of adjacent neurons. Direct diffusion of ions through these junctions allows the action potential to be transmitted with little or no delay and distortion, in effect synchronizing the response of an entire group of neurons. The channels often allow ions to diffuse in both directions, but some gated channels restrict transmission to only one direction.

Gap junctions

Chemical transmission. There are two classic preparations for the study of chemical transmission at the synapse.

One is the vertebrate neuromuscular junction, and the other is the giant synapse of the squid *Loligo.* These sites have the advantage of being readily accessible for recording by electrodes—especially the squid synapse, which is large enough that electrodes can be inserted directly into the presynaptic terminal and the postsynaptic fibre. In addition, only a single synapse is involved at these sites, whereas a single neuron of the central nervous system may have many synapses with many other neurons, each with a different neurotransmitter.

Neurotransmitter release. Two factors are essential for the release of the neurotransmitter from the presynaptic terminal: (1) depolarization of the terminal and (2) the presence of calcium ions (Ca^{2+}) in the extracellular fluid. The membrane of the presynaptic terminal contains voltage-dependent calcium channels that open when the membrane is depolarized by a nerve impulse, allowing Ca^{2+} to diffuse into the terminal along its concentration gradient (see Figure 9). Following the entrance of Ca^{2+} is the release of neurotransmitter. The scheme may be depicted as follows:

depolarization→calcium entry→neurotransmitter release

What happens in the time between Ca^{2+} entry and transmitter release is uncertain. Ca^{2+} is known to be sequestered by certain organelles within the terminal, including the endoplasmic reticulum. The ions may attach to the membranes of synaptic vesicles, in some way facilitating their fusion with the nerve terminal membrane. They may also be removed from the terminal by exchange with extracellular Na^+—a mechanism known to occur at some neuronal membranes. What is certain is that when the concentration of Ca^{2+} is increased within the terminal, then the probability of transmitter release is also increased.

Release of neurotransmitter in synaptic vesicles

Neurotransmitter substances are packed into small, membrane-bound spheres called synaptic vesicles. Each vesicle contains thousands of neurotransmitter molecules, and there are thousands of vesicles in each axon terminal. Once stimulated by Ca^{2+}, the vesicles move through the cytoplasm and fuse their membranes with the plasma membrane of the terminal. The transmitter molecules are then expelled from the vesicles into the synaptic cleft. This expulsion process is called exocytosis. Vesicle membranes are then recovered from the plasma membrane through endocytosis. In this process the membranes are surrounded by a protein coat at the lateral margins of the synapse and are then transferred to cisternae, which form in the terminal during nerve stimulation. There the vesicles lose their coats, are probably refilled with neurotransmitter, and pinch off from the cisternae to become synaptic vesicles once more.

Because the neurotransmitter chemicals are packed into separate, almost identically sized vesicles, their release into the synaptic cleft is said to be quantal—that is, rather than flowing from the terminal in a growing stream, they are expelled in parcels, each vesicle adding its contents incrementally to the contents released from other parcels. This quantal release of neurotransmitter has a critical influence on the electrical potential created in the postsynaptic membrane.

Postsynaptic potential. After neurotransmitter is released from the presynaptic terminal, it diffuses across the synaptic cleft and binds to receptor proteins on the postsynaptic membrane. Some receptors are ion channels that open or close when their molecular configuration is altered by the binding action of the neurotransmitter. Others are membrane proteins that, upon activation, catalyze second-messenger reactions within the postsynaptic cell; these reactions in turn open or close the ion channels. Whether acting upon ion channels directly or indirectly, the neurotransmitter molecules bring about a sudden change in the membrane's permeability to specific ions. Exactly which ions now permeate the membrane vary according to the neurotransmitters and their receptors (see below *Neurotransmitters and neuromodulators*), but the net result of a change in ion diffusion is a change in electrical potential across the membrane. This change is called the postsynaptic potential, or PSP. (In reference to the neuromuscular synapse, it is also called the end-plate potential, or EPP.)

Excitatory and inhibitory postsynaptic potentials

The most common potential change is depolarization, caused by a net influx of cations (usually Na^+). Because this infusion of positive charge brings the membrane potential toward the threshold at which the nerve impulse is generated, it is called an excitatory postsynaptic potential (EPSP). Other neurotransmitters stimulate a net efflux of positive charge (usually in the form of K^+ diffusing out of the cell), leaving the inside of the membrane more negative. Because this hyperpolarization draws the membrane potential farther from threshold, making it more difficult to generate a nerve impulse, it is called an inhibitory postsynaptic potential (IPSP). The interaction of competing EPSPs and IPSPs at the hundreds or even thousands of synapses on a single neuron determines whether the nerve impulse arriving at the presynaptic terminals will be regenerated in the postsynaptic membrane.

The PSP is a type of local potential, having properties similar to the electrical potential set up at sensory receptor neurons (see above *Transmission in the neuron: Localized potential*). Like the receptor potential, the PSP is a graded response, varying in amplitude according to the duration and amount of stimulation by neurotransmitter substances. At the neuromuscular junction, brief depolarizations measuring no more than one millivolt can be observed in the postsynaptic muscle membrane, even when it is at rest. These tiny electrical events, called miniature end-plate potentials (MEPPs) or miniature postsynaptic potentials (MPSPs), are caused by the random release of single quanta of neurotransmitter from a resting presynaptic terminal. The EPP is actually made up of multiple MEPPs, which arise when an activated terminal releases hundreds of neurotransmitter quanta. A series of EPPs, or a number of them stimulated simultaneously at many synapses, can then bring the cell to the threshold of the action potential. This combined action of EPPs is called summation.

In contrast to electrical transmission, which takes place with almost no delay, chemical transmission shows what is called the synaptic delay. Recordings from squid synapses and neuromuscular junctions of the frog reveal a delay of from 0.5 to 4.0 milliseconds between the onset of action

Adapted from *Neurobiology*, 2nd ed., by Gordon M. Shepherd, copyright © 1983, 1988 by Oxford University Press, Inc.; reprinted by permission

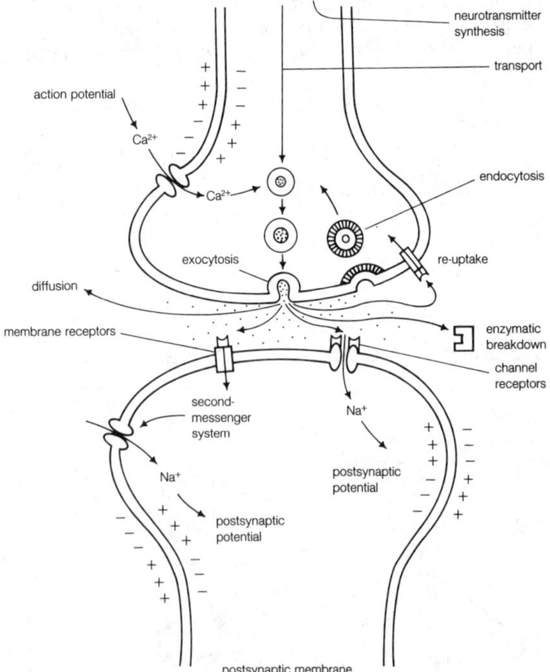

Figure 9: *The principal events in chemical transmission of nerve impulses at the synapse.*
The arrival of the nerve impulse at the presynaptic terminal stimulates the release of neurotransmitter into the synaptic gap. Before inactivation, the neurotransmitter molecules stimulate the regeneration of the impulse in the postsynaptic membrane.

potential at the nerve terminal and action potential at the postsynaptic site. This may be accounted for by three factors. First, diffusion of the neurotransmitter across the synaptic cleft takes approximately 0.05 millisecond. Second, the response of the postsynaptic receptor takes about 0.15 millisecond. This leaves 0.30 to 3.80 milliseconds for other processes. A third process, called mobilization of the transmitter, is traditionally postulated as taking up the remaining time, but evidence suggests that the time is occupied at least partially by the opening of calcium channels to allow the entry of Ca^{2+} into the presynaptic terminal.

Brief duration of the nerve impulse

Inactivation. A series of nerve impulses arriving in rapid succession at the axon terminal is accurately reproduced as a series in the postsynaptic cell because the quanta of neurotransmitter released by each impulse are inactivated as soon as they stimulate the receptor proteins. Neurotransmitter inactivation is carried out by a combination of three processes. First, the neurotransmitter molecules simply diffuse out of the narrow synaptic cleft. Second, they are taken back into the presynaptic terminal by transmitter-sensitive transport molecules. Third, they are metabolized into inactive compounds by enzymes in the synaptic cleft.

ION TRANSPORT

As was stated above, the lipid bilayer of the neuronal membrane tends to repel electrically charged, hydrated ions, making virtually impossible the movement across the membrane that is necessary for the generation of nerve impulses. The transmembrane movement of ions is actually carried out by molecular mechanism—specifically, by protein molecules embedded in the lipid layers. One mechanism, the sodium–potassium pump, maintains the resting potential, and another, the various ion channels, helps create the action potential.

Active transport: the sodium–potassium pump. Since the plasma membrane of the neuron is highly permeable to K^+ and slightly permeable to Na^+, and since neither of these ions is in a state of equilibrium (Na^+ being at higher concentration outside the cell than inside and K^+ at higher concentration inside), then a natural occurrence should be the diffusion of both ions down their electrochemical gradients—K^+ out of the cell and Na^+ into the cell. However, the concentrations of these ions are maintained at constant disequilibrium, indicating that there is a compensatory mechanism moving Na^+ outward against its concentration gradient and K^+ inward. This mechanism is the sodium–potassium pump. Actually a large protein molecule that traverses the plasma membrane of the neuron, the pump presents receptor areas to both the cytoplasm and the extracellular environment. That part of the molecule facing the cytoplasm has a high affinity for Na^+ and a low affinity for K^+, while that part facing the outside has a high affinity for K^+ and a low affinity for Na^+. Stimulated by the action of the ions on its receptors, the pump transports them in opposite directions against their concentration gradients.

Maintaining a polarized membrane

If equal amounts of Na^+ and K^+ were transported across the membrane by the pump, the net charge transfer would be zero; there would be no net flow of current and no effect on the membrane potential. In fact, researchers have found that in many neurons three sodium ions are transported for every potassium ion; sometimes the ratio is three sodium for every two potassium, and in a few neurons it is two sodium for one potassium. This inequality of ionic transfer produces a net efflux of positive charge, maintaining a polarized membrane with the inner surface slightly negative in relation to the outer surface. Because it creates this potential difference across the membrane, the sodium–potassium pump is said to be electrogenic.

The sodium–potassium pump carries out a form of active transport—that is, its pumping of ions against their gradients requires the addition of energy from an outside source. That source is adenosine triphosphate (ATP), the principal energy-carrying molecule of the cell. ATP is formed by an inorganic phosphate molecule held in high-energy linkage with a molecule of adenosine diphosphate (ADP). When an enzyme in the pump, called sodium–potassium–ATPase, splits the phosphate from the ADP, the energy released powers the transport action of the pump.

Passive transport: membrane channels. The sodium–potassium pump sets the membrane potential of the neuron by keeping the concentrations of Na^+ and K^+ at constant disequilibrium. The sudden shift from a resting to an active state, when the neuron generates a nerve impulse, is caused by a sudden movement of ions across the membrane—specifically, a flux of Na^+ into the cell. Given the relative impermeability of the plasma membrane to Na^+, this influx itself implies a sudden change in permeability. Beginning in the 19th century, researchers puzzled over the mechanism by which this change could occur. The idea arose that there must exist pores, or channels, through which the ions could diffuse, passing the barrier posed by the lipid bilayer. However, for years only the gross currents accompanying ionic movement could be measured, and it was only by inference that the presence of membrane channels could be postulated.

The breakthrough came in the 1970s and '80s with the development of the patch-clamp technique, which enabled investigators to directly measure currents flowing across single ion channels in the membrane. The patch-clamp technique electrically isolates a small patch of neuron or muscle cell membrane by applying the tip of a micropipette filled with conducting solution to the membrane and forming a tight seal with it. As single channels in the patch undergo various transitional states between fully open and fully closed, the times of opening and closing are recorded and the amplitudes and duration of the currents are measured.

Since the pioneering studies, the electrical and biochemical properties of certain channels have been characterized. Known as "voltage dependent" when activated by changes in the membrane potential and "neurotransmitter sensitive" when activated by neurotransmitter substances, these channels are protein structures that span the membrane from the extracellular space to the cytoplasm. They are believed to be cylindrical, with a hollow, water-filled pore wider than the ion passing through it except at one region called the selectivity filter. This filter makes each channel specific to one type of ion.

Structure of a channel protein

The sodium channel. Voltage-sensitive sodium channels have been characterized with respect to their subunit structure and their amino acid sequences. The principal protein component is known to be a glycoprotein containing 1,820 amino acids. Four similar "transmembrane domains," of about 300 amino acids each, surround a central aqueous pore through which the ions pass. The selectivity filter is a constriction of the channel ringed by negatively charged carbonyl oxygens, which repel anions but attract cations. Also within the channel are thought to be two types of charged particles forming the gates that control the diffusion of Na^+. One gate closes at polarization and opens at depolarization; the other closes at depolarization.

Investigators believe that the resting, activated, and inactivated states of the sodium channel are due to voltage-dependent conformational changes in the glycoprotein component. These changes result from effects of the electrical field on the charges and dipoles of the amino acids within the protein. With a large electrical field applied to it, the protein has been observed to change its conformation from a stable, closed resting state to a stable, open state in which the net charge or the location of the charge on the protein is changed.

The potassium channel. There are several types of voltage-dependent potassium channels, each having its own physiological and pharmacological properties. A single neuron may contain more than one type.

The best-known flow of K^+ is the outward current following depolarization of the membrane. This occurs through the so-called delayed rectifier channel (I_{DR}), which, activated by the influx of Na^+, counteracts the effect of that cation by allowing the discharge of K^+. By repolarizing the membrane in this way, the I_{DR} channel restricts the duration of the nerve impulse and participates in the regulation of repetitive firing of the neuron.

Another outward K^+ current, occurring with little delay after depolarization, is the so-called A current. The I_A channels are opened by depolarization following hyperpolarization. By increasing the interval between action potentials, they help a neuron fire repetitively at low frequencies.

Another type of potassium channel, the $I_{K(Ca)}$ channel, is activated by high concentrations of intracellular Ca^{2+}. The opening of these channels results in hyperpolarization of the membrane, so that they appear to slow the repetitive firing of nerve impulses.

The I_M channel is opened by depolarization but is deactivated only by the neurotransmitter acetylcholine. This property may serve to regulate the sensitivity of neurons to synaptic input.

A final type of potassium channel is the anomalous, or inward, rectifier channel (I_{IR}). This channel closes with depolarization and opens with hyperpolarization. By allowing an unusual inward diffusion of K^+, the I_{IR} channel prolongs depolarization of the neuron and helps produce long-lasting nerve impulses.

The calcium channel. As with potassium channels, there is more than one type of calcium channel. The inward calcium current has been shown to be slower than the sodium current. Studies show the presence of at least two types in certain neurons of the central nervous system—a long-lasting current activated at positive potential and a transient current activated at more negative potential. Patch-clamp studies show two corresponding types of calcium channel: a large conductance channel that gives rise to a long-lasting current at positive membrane potentials and a low conductance channel that gives rise to a transient current at more negative potentials. In some neurons a third channel current has been measured that is transient and can only be activated at high negative potential.

Anion channels. Evidence points to channels that pass anions such as Cl^-, but their existence is difficult to prove. Single-channel recordings of cultured tissue have shown selective Cl^- channels that are voltage dependent and of high conductance. Channels with lower conductance have been demonstrated in reconstituted artificial membranes as well as in neurons.

NEUROTRANSMITTERS AND NEUROMODULATORS

The traditional models for the study of neurotransmitter release are either the neuromuscular junction of the frog, crayfish, and rat or the giant synapse of the squid. These synapses are relatively simple in their structure, with a single axon terminal forming an identifiable synapse at the postsynaptic membrane of a muscle fibre or neuron. Recordings can be obtained from these single-synaptic junctions in response to the release of a single neurotransmitter. At neurons of the central nervous system, on the other hand, the situation is more complex. Each central neuron has several synapses with other neurons at various locations, such as on the dendrites, soma, and initial segment of the axon. Several neurotransmitters, therefore—some excitatory and others inhibitory—may be involved in the final integrated response of a central neuron, making their identities difficult to determine.

Further complicating the study of neurotransmitter action is the presence not only of multiple transmitter substances but also of neuromodulators. These are substances that do not directly activate ion-channel receptors but that, acting in concert with neurotransmitters, enhance the excitatory or inhibitory responses of the receptors. It is often impossible to discern, in the presence of many substances, which are transmitters and which are modulators. Such is the case with many of the neuropeptides (see below *Neuroactive peptides*).

The second-messenger system

In addition to the multiplicity of transmitters and modulators is a multiplicity of receptors. Some receptors directly open ion channels, while others activate the second-messenger system. This is any of a number of reactions that take place in the cytoplasm or plasma membrane and indirectly act upon the ion channels. One second-messenger system involves the activation by receptor proteins of so-called linking proteins, which move across the membrane, bind to channel proteins, and open the channels. Another system is the cyclic adenosine monophosphate (cAMP) system. In this chain reaction, receptor proteins activate linking proteins, which then activate the enzymes that synthesize cAMP. The cAMP molecules activate other enzymes that, in turn, activate ion channels.

Whether they activate channels directly or through a second-messenger system, neurotransmitters are considered to be primary messengers. Criteria have been defined that, when fulfilled, allow an investigator to identify a substance as a true neurotransmitter for a specific neuron. In many situations, all the criteria are not satisfied. While this does not necessarily mean that the substance is not a neurotransmitter, it does mean that the argument for its being so is considerably weakened. The criteria are as follows:

1. The presynaptic neuron
   a. Enzymes should be present for synthesis of the neurotransmitter.
   b. The neurotransmitter should be released in pharmacologically identifiable form.
   c. Enzymes that destroy the neurotransmitter may be present in the synaptic gap. Because some neurotransmitters are inactivated by uptake back into the presynaptic terminal or into surrounding glial cells, the presence of catabolic enzymes is not a mandatory requirement.
2. The postsynaptic site
   a. Application of the substance under experimental conditions must be able to reproduce the specific events of normal transmission.
   b. Under experimental conditions the action of the substance must be mimicked or facilitated by the same agents that are known to elicit identical responses in nerve stimulation. Conversely, the action of chemicals that block the substance must be the same in actual nerve stimulation as they are in experimental application of the suspected neurotransmitter.

Described below are the principal proved or suggested neurotransmitters of the mammalian nervous system and their corresponding receptors.

Acetylcholine. This was the first neurotransmitter whose actions were proved to fulfill the criteria given above. Although early studies of acetylcholine were undertaken at neuromuscular junctions, where it is especially concentrated, the concept leading to the identification of the substance as a neurotransmitter of the central nervous system is a landmark in neuroscience. The concept is called Dale's principle after Sir Henry Dale, a British physiologist who, in 1935, stated that a neurotransmitter released at one axon terminal of a neuron can be presumed to be released at other axon terminals of the same neuron. (Dale's principle refers only to the presynaptic neuron, as the responses of different postsynaptic receptors to a single neurotransmitter can vary in the same or different neurons.) The first application of Dale's principle was at the mammalian spinal cord, from which motor neurons send their axons to striated muscles, where the terminals are observed to release acetylcholine. According to Dale's principle, all of the branches of a single motor neuron axon should release acetylcholine—including the terminals in the spinal cord. In fact, it was found that some collateral branches leave the motor axons and reenter the gray matter of the spinal cord, where they synapse onto spinal interneurons. The neurotransmitter released at these terminals is acetylcholine. High concentrations of the acetylcholine-synthesizing enzyme, choline acetyltransferase, and the enzyme for its breakdown, acetylcholinesterase, are also found in motor neuron regions of the spinal cord.

Cholinergic receptors

Acetylcholine receptors (also called cholinergic receptors) appear in clusters on muscle-cell membranes opposite the active zones of presynaptic terminals. Their density at these receptor regions is between 7,000 and 30,000 sites per square micrometre. The number drops drastically even a few nanometres (billionths of a metre) away from the receptor region, so that sensitivity to acetylcholine is about 50 to 100 times less one millimetre from the receptor region than it is at the receptor site itself. Cholinergic receptors also exist on the presynaptic terminals of neurons that release acetylcholine as well as on terminals that release other neurotransmitters. These receptors are called autoreceptors, and they probably regulate the release of neurotransmitter at the terminal.

There are two main categories of cholinergic receptor, nicotinic and muscarinic. In the first years of the 20th century, they were differentiated by their responses to the alkaloids nicotine and muscarine, but advanced biochemical techniques have shown a more fundamental difference. The nicotinic receptor is a channel protein that, upon binding by acetylcholine, opens to allow diffusion of cations. The muscarinic receptor, on the other hand, is a membrane protein; upon stimulation by neurotransmitter, it causes the opening of ion channels indirectly, through a second messenger. For this reason, the action of a muscarinic synapse is relatively slow. Muscarinic receptors predominate at higher levels of the central nervous system, while nicotinic receptors, which are much faster acting, are more prevalent at neurons of the spinal cord and at neuromuscular junctions in skeletal muscle.

The nicotinic receptor channel has been purified and shown to be a glycoprotein composed of five subunits (Figure 10). Two so-called alpha- (α-) subunits contain the two acetylcholine-binding sites associated with the channel. Three other subunits—a beta- (β-) subunit, a gamma- (γ-) subunit, and a delta- (δ-) subunit—complete the protein. High-resolution electron microscopy with optical image reconstruction, as well as freeze-fracture electron microscopy, reveal a highly symmetrical structure, looking from the top somewhat like a life belt, with the presumed channel in the centre. About one-third of the protein protrudes from the plasma membrane, while the rest is embedded in the membrane or protruding into the cell.

Patch-clamp techniques give information on single channel currents and, hence, on the conductance and kinetics of the cholinergic receptor channel. At the neuromuscular junction, approximately 20,000 univalent ions carry the charge across a single activated channel, and a quantum of acetylcholine activates about 1,500 channels. The time constant for the decay of the MEPP is the same as that for channel closing. The time constant for channel closing is voltage dependent, with depolarization shortening the duration of open channels and hyperpolarization lengthening the duration.

Studies show that nicotinic acetylcholine-activated channels allow cations to permeate the membrane with no specificity—that is, all cations can diffuse through the channels indiscriminately. Because the resting membrane is already near the equilibrium potential of K^+, this means that much more Na^+ and Ca^{2+} diffuse into the cell than K^+ out, causing depolarization and excitation of the neuron or muscle cell. However, in certain molluscan neurons, nicotinic acetylcholine receptors can also activate Cl^- channels, causing hyperpolarization of the postsynaptic membrane and inhibition of the cell's excitability. With respect to muscarinic receptors, the situation is not clear. Second messengers may be involved, and potassium channels may be activated.

Epinephrine and norepinephrine. These related hormones, also called adrenaline and noradrenaline, act to increase the heart rate, blood pressure, and levels of sugar and fat in the blood. They are secreted into the bloodstream by the adrenal glands in response to stress, but they are also synthesized and released as neurotransmitters by axon terminals in the central nervous system and in sympathetic fibres of the autonomic system.

Adrenergic receptors

Receptors sensitive to norepinephrine and epinephrine are called adrenergic receptors. They are divided into two types, α and β. These are further classified into subtypes α_1, α_2, β_1, and β_2.

Both types of adrenergic receptor produce changes in the postsynaptic membrane potential by acting upon ion channels specific to K^+ and Ca^{2+}. They differ in the mechanisms that, upon stimulation by neurotransmitter, they employ to activate those channels. Stimulated β_1 receptors bind to linking proteins that in turn bind to calcium channels, changing their shape and altering their permeability to the cation. More important, the linking proteins stimulate the synthesis of cAMP, which, through another series of reactions, opens potassium channels. The efflux of K^+ tends to hyperpolarize the postsynaptic membrane, inhibiting the generation of a nerve impulse. The β_2 receptor has been found on glial cells.

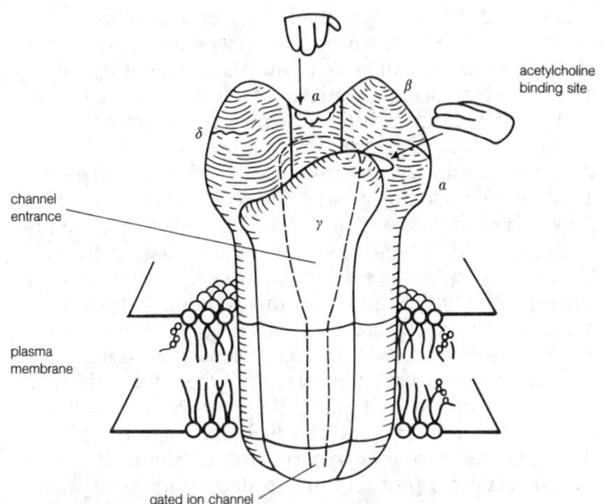

Figure 10: *The cholinergic channel receptor.*
The two α-subunits and the β-, γ-, and δ-subunits are arranged symmetrically around a central channel.

From *Neurobiology*, 2nd ed., by Gordon M. Shepherd, copyright © 1983, 1988 by Oxford University Press, Inc., reprinted by permission, based on J. Kistler *et al.*, "Structure and Function of an Acetylocholine Receptor," *Biophysical Journal*, no. 37 (1982), reproduced by copyright permission of the Biophysical Society

The α_2 receptor activates potassium channels in both the postsynaptic and presynaptic membranes, probably via linking proteins and the synthesis of cAMP. The α_1 receptor acts on calcium channels through a series of reactions linked to the lipid molecules of the plasma membrane.

Both epinephrine and norepinephrine are terminated by uptake back into the presynaptic terminals, where they are enzymatically degraded or inactivated.

For a discussion of the effects of adrenergic transmission on organs and muscles, see below *Functions of the human nervous system: The autonomic system.*

Dopamine. This precursor of norepinephrine acts as a neurotransmitter at certain synapses of the brain. Disorders at these synapses have been implicated in schizophrenia and Parkinson's disease.

There are two types of dopaminergic receptor, called the D_1 and the D_2. The former catalyzes the synthesis of cAMP, and the latter inhibits its synthesis. These reactions then regulate calcium and potassium channels in the postsynaptic membrane. Dopaminergic receptors also exist on the presynaptic membrane. The neurotransmitter is terminated by uptake into the presynaptic terminal.

Serotonin (5-hydroxytryptamine). Although the brain has only a small percentage of the serotonin found in the body, there appears to be a strong relationship between the levels of this neurotransmitter at some regions of the brain and certain behavioral patterns, including sleep, sexual urge, and mood. At synapses of the peripheral nervous system, it seems to prime muscle cells for an excitatory response to other neurotransmitters.

Serotonin receptors, or 5HT receptors, activate calcium and potassium channels through linking proteins and the cAMP second-messenger systems. After acting on the postsynaptic receptors, the neurotransmitter is taken up by the presynaptic terminal and enzymatically degraded.

Amino acids. Several amino acids exist in the central nervous system in extremely high concentrations, but their ubiquity makes their identification as true neurotransmitters difficult. Furthermore, because some of them are essential components of metabolic reactions, their presence within a neuron does not prove that they function as neurotransmitters. Nevertheless, there is enough evidence that some amino acids act as either excitatory or inhibitory transmitters. The excitatory amino acids include glutamic acid (or glutamate) and aspartic acid (or aspartate), and the inhibitory amino acids include gamma-aminobutyric acid (GABA) and glycine.

Excitatory amino acids. Glutamate is the most abundant amino acid in the brain. Unlike acetylcholine, glu-

Excitatory neurotransmitter in the spinal cord

tamate does not vary greatly in concentration from one region to the next. However, the dorsal gray matter of the spinal cord, which contains terminals of incoming dorsal roots, has large concentrations of glutamate. Aspartate, on the other hand, is believed to be concentrated in the interneurons of the ventral gray matter.

At postsynaptic receptor sites glutamate depolarizes the membrane by opening nonspecific cation channels, which allow a net influx of Na^+ and Ca^{2+}. Of the excitatory amino acid receptors, the N-methyl-D-aspartic acid (NMDA) receptor has been thoroughly characterized. Patch-clamp studies show that this receptor is influenced by the presence of magnesium ions (Mg^{2+}). In the absence of Mg^{2+}, activated NMDA receptors open nonspecific cationic channels with no variation when the voltage is changed. With Mg^{2+} added to the extracellular medium, though, the frequency of channel openings is reduced when the membrane is hyperpolarized. Both glutamate and aspartate are probably inactivated by uptake systems at the presynaptic terminals and at glial cells surrounding some of the synaptic junctions.

Inhibitory amino acids. GABA and glycine are proved to cause hyperpolarization of the postsynaptic membrane. GABA is widely distributed in the brain, being especially prevalent at higher levels of the central nervous system. It is produced from glutamate by the enzyme glutamic acid decarboxylase (GAD). Consequently, the concentrations of GABA and GAD parallel each other in the nervous system.

At postsynaptic receptor sites GABA opens chloride channels, causing in most cells a hyperpolarization of the membrane as Cl^- diffuses inward to reach its equilibrium potential. It must be pointed out, however, that GABA inhibits presynaptic nerve fibres as well. At certain synaptic junctions the release of neurotransmitter is modulated by the binding to presynaptic receptors of neurotransmitter released from other neurons. A classic example of this is at the axon terminals of incoming dorsal roots in the dorsal gray matter. Projecting onto these terminals are other terminals that release GABA. Although GABA causes an increased Cl^- conductance at these terminals, the result is depolarization, not hyperpolarization, of the membrane. This is because the resting membrane potential of the receiving nerve terminal is much more negative than the Cl^- equilibrium potential. This means that as Cl^- flows into the terminal to reach equilibrium, the membrane is actually depolarized. The effect at the terminal is a decrease in neurotransmitter release.

Unlike GABA, glycine is found mostly at lower levels of the central nervous system, including the spinal cord, medulla oblongata, and pons. It is a major inhibitor released by interneurons to suppress motoneuronal activity. Like GABA, glycine acts by increasing Cl^- conductance at the postsynaptic membrane, although it acts at a clearly different receptor.

It appears that at least two molecules of glycine and GABA must bind to their respective receptors to activate a chloride channel. The action of both neurotransmitters is terminated by uptake back into the presynaptic terminal or into surrounding glial cells.

Histamine. The main difficulty in proving that this substance acts as a neurotransmitter is the lack of adequate techniques for identification. There is little doubt that histamine exists in the brain, but it appears to be present in at least two distinct compartments—in mast cells (nonneuronal connective-tissue cells) and in nerve endings. The actions of histamine are unclear; it is reported to act as a depressor of neuronal activity at some sites and as an excitor at others.

Adenosine triphosphate. ATP may also be a neurotransmitter, particularly at primary sensory endings in the spinal cord. However, its ubiquitous distribution and participation in many energy-conversion reactions makes its role as a neurotransmitter difficult to establish.

Neuroactive peptides. Neuroactive peptides are sequences of amino acids, usually longer than amino acid neurotransmitters yet shorter than hormones or proteins. Unlike the classic neurotransmitters described above, which are formed by enzymes near the presynaptic terminals, neuroactive peptides are assembled by ribosomes attached to the endoplasmic reticulum. From there they are transferred to the Golgi apparatus, where they are packed into secretory vesicles and transported to the terminals. Some peptides are secreted by so-called neuroendocrine cells of the hypothalamus or pituitary gland. Because they are released into the capillary system of the bloodstream and act at distant sites of the body, these are called neurohormones. Other peptides are released into the synaptic cleft between neurons of the central nervous system (including the hypothalamus). Many of these so-called neuropeptides fulfill some criteria of neurotransmitters, evoking excitatory or inhibitory responses in postsynaptic ion channels, yet it is still uncertain to what extent they act as true neurotransmitters or as neuromodulators.

Distinction between neurotransmitters and neuropeptides

Distinguishing neuropeptides from the classic neurotransmitters is the longevity of their action. While acetylcholine, for example, acts upon synaptic receptors for only a few milliseconds, neuropeptides have a course of action lasting from several seconds to several days. Also, neuropeptides are released in much lower concentrations than are transmitter substances, although the peptides have a much higher potency.

The list of neuropeptides is not yet complete. Among those peptides known to affect synaptic transmission are substance P, neurotensin, somatostatin, vasoactive intestinal peptide, cholecystokinin, and the opioid peptides. The best studied are the opioid peptides, so called because opiate drugs such as morphine are known to bind to their receptors and mimic their pain-killing and mood-altering actions. All opioid peptides belong to three genetically distinct families: the β-endorphins, the enkephalins, and the dynorphins.

It has long been known that opioids and opiate drugs have varied and powerful effects on pain, mood, sleep, sedation, and the cough reflex—apart from effects on the gastrointestinal tract and the cardiovascular system. It is not surprising, therefore, that there are multiple receptors for these substances. There may in fact be as many as eight different types of opioid receptor, but the four best described are designated mu (μ), kappa (κ), delta (δ), and sigma (σ). The μ receptors, which readily bind morphine, are believed to mediate euphoria, respiratory depression, and physical addiction and to block pain pathways in the brain. The κ receptors bind preferentially to dynorphin and are believed to mediate analgesia and sedation at the spinal cord. The δ receptors, located primarily in the limbic portions of the brain, bind enkephalin. They may be responsible for dysphoria (extreme depression), hallucination, and respiratory and vasomotor stimulation. The σ receptors are perhaps involved in alterations of affective behaviour, but their functions are unclear. They are found in the hippocampus.

Inhibitory mechanisms of opioid receptors

The opioid receptors mediate their effects mainly by inhibiting regeneration of the nerve impulse at the postsynaptic membrane. They do this by opening potassium channels or closing calcium channels, causing a net outflow of positive charge that keeps the postsynaptic membrane from reaching threshold potential. As with other neuropeptides, it is not known whether all the opioid receptors are activated by the opioids alone or by a combination of opioid and other transmitter substances. For this reason it is uncertain whether the opioid peptides are true neurotransmitters or are neuromodulators.

The presence of peptides within certain structures of the central nervous system is well established; more important, peptides are often found in the same neurons with classic neurotransmitters or with other peptides. For example, substance P can be found in the same neurons of the brain stem as serotonin. In the sympathetic system, norepinephrine is found with somatostatin in some neurons and with enkephalin in others.

Because some neuropeptides and transmitters are stored in the same vesicles and secreted together in response to stimulation, a form of interaction between the substances appears likely. The interaction could take place at presynaptic terminals, altering the release of neurotransmitter, or it could take place postsynaptically, altering the effect of neurotransmitter. At the neuromuscular junction of the lobster, for example, the neurotransmitters serotonin and octopamine and the neuropeptide proctolin can act presynaptically to alter the amounts of GABA or glutamate released from the nerve terminals. In a similar manner, at some regions of the central nervous system opioid peptides inhibit the release of norepinephrine, acetylcholine, dopamine, and substance P.

The discovery of more than one type of neuroactive substance in one set of axon terminals has disproved an assumption implied by Dale's principle—that a single neuron synthesizes and secretes a single neurotransmitter. Also called into doubt is another assumption—that a single neuron secretes a single set of neurotransmitters at all of its synapses. Researchers are finding evidence that different synapses of the same neuron act somewhat independently. This may mean that different areas of a single neuron synthesize different neuroactive substances. Such a phenomenon would be another example of the metabolic and functional complexity of the nervous system.

(S.D.E.)

Evolution and development of the nervous system

The study of the evolutionary development of the nervous system traditionally concentrated on the structural differences that exist at various levels of the phylogenetic scale, but certain functional characteristics, including biochemical and biophysical processes laid down early in evolution and amazingly well conserved to the present, can no longer be ignored. Two basic aspects of the evolution of the nervous system must be considered: first, how primitive systems serve newer functions, and, second, how the formation of new systems serve newer functional requirements.

Early theories on the evolutionary origin of the nervous system argued for a three-stage process: first, the development of non-nervous "independent effectors," such as muscle cells; second, the appearance of non-nervous receptors responding to certain modalities in a receptor-effector mechanism; and finally, the formation of a "protoneuron," from which primitive nerves and ganglia evolved. This model is no longer considered valid. In primitive systems there appear to be many examples of non-nervous electrical conduction. For instance, large areas of epithelium covering the swimming bells in the hydrozoan order Siphonophora (which contains certain families of jellyfish) contain neither nerve nor muscle, yet depolarizing potentials between cells of the epithelium have been recorded.

Possible origin of nerve cells

Similar examples from other systems in related orders suggest that the evolution of the nervous system may have begun with non-nervous epithelial tissue. The conduction of electrical potentials from one epithelial cell to the next may well have been via so-called tight junctions, in which the plasma membranes of adjacent cells fuse to form sheets of cells. Tight junctions have low electrical resistance and high permeability to molecules. They also occur in great numbers in embryos, suggesting that the electrical potentials of cells joined in this manner serve as a driving force for the movement of ions and even nutritive substances from one cell to the next. These phenomena suggest that preceding the evolution of axons were systems whereby depolarizing potentials were generated by specific changes in ionic permeability of the membrane. For this reason, electrically mediated junctional transmission is thought to be older than chemically mediated synaptic transmission, which would require that some epithelial cells secrete chemical substances.

Many investigators believe that neurons originated from endothelial secretory cells that could secrete chemical substances, respond to stimulation, and conduct impulses. Specialization may then have brought about an outer receptor surface and an inner conducting fibre. In fact, neurosecretory cells can propagate action potentials, and many neurons secrete chemical substances, called neurohormones, that influence the growth and regeneration of cells at other sites of the body. Some researchers suggest that neurons first appeared as neurosecretory growth-regulating cells in which elongated processes were later adapted to rapid conduction and chemical transmission by release of transmitters at their endings.

There is an amazing consistency in neurotransmitters present in different organisms of a given phylum, although different phyla may show striking differences. Thus, in vertebrates, including fishes, amphibians, reptiles, birds, and mammals, the motor neurons (neurons whose fibres innervate striated muscle) are always cholinergic; in arthropods, on the other hand, they are not cholinergic, although the sensory neurons do secrete acetylcholine. The number of known neurotransmitter substances in the animal kingdom is indeed small, and their presence in more primitive organisms as well as in nervous systems of later vertebrates shows a striking conservation of these substances throughout evolution.

Natural selection of nervous systems

If later organisms evolved from single-celled ancestors, then there must have been some system for the transmission of information from one evolutionary stage to the next. These conditions have been defined as: (1) a stable means for encoding, transmitting, and decoding characteristics from one generation to the next, (2) the possibility of alterations in the code taking place by mutation or sexual recombination, and (3) a means of selecting only those characteristics for transmission that are favourable for survival. As mentioned above (see *Stimulus–response coordination*), protozoans (single-celled organisms) move toward places that are favourable for survival, such as areas with optimal conditions of light and temperature. As the metazoans (multi-celled organisms) developed, entire groups of cells probably tended to move toward favourable conditions, and when the number of cells became very large, a system of internal communication—in effect, a nervous system—developed. Two general types developed—the diffuse nervous system and the centralized nervous system.

DIFFUSE NERVOUS SYSTEMS

The diffuse nervous system is the most primitive nervous system. In diffuse systems nerve cells are distributed throughout the organism, usually beneath the outer epidermal layer. Large concentrations of nerve cells—as in the brain—are not found in these systems, though there may be ganglia, or small local concentrations of neurons. Diffuse systems are found in cnidarians (hydroids, jellyfish, sea anemones, corals) and in ctenophores, or comb jellies. However, the primitive nervous systems of these animals do not preclude prolonged and coordinated responses and integrated behaviour to the simplest stimuli. An example is the movement of the sea anemone *Calliactis* onto the shell of the hermit crab *Pagurus* in response to a factor present in the outer layer of the empty mollusk shell occupied by the crab. This movement requires integration of the highest order.

Most cnidarians, such as those of the genus *Hydra*, have what is called a nerve net—a meshlike system of individual and separate nerve cells and fibres dispersed over the organism (Figure 11A). Species of *Hydra* have two nets, one located between the epidermis and the musculature and the second associated with the gastrodermis. Connections occur at various points between the two nets, with individual neurons making contact but not fusing, thereby forming structures similar to the chemically mediated synapses of vertebrates. Several specializations occur within various species. In *Hydra* the neurons are slightly more concentrated in a ring near the pedal disk and the hypostome (the "mouth"), but in jellyfish of a related genus the nerve fibres form a thick ring at the margin of the bell to form "through" conduction pathways.

The nervous systems of cnidarians correspond to their radially symmetrical bodies, in which similar parts are arranged symmetrically around a hollow gut cavity called the coelenteron. In some species nerve fibres course along the radial canals, where there may be arranged sensory bodies, called rhopalia, which contain ganglionic concentrations of neurons. In the sea anemone *Metridium* some of the nerve fibres are seven to eight millimetres long and form a system for fast conduction of nerve impulses. Such specializations may have allowed the evolution of different functions. Certainly the rapid coordination of swimming movements requires a fast-conducting pathway, while feeding relies on the nerve net. Integrative activity is likely to occur at the sensory ganglia, which may represent the first forms of a centralized nervous system.

Comparison with mammalian nervous transmission

The terminals forming synapselike structures in nerve nets contain synaptic vesicles that are believed to be packed with neurotransmitters and neuroactive peptides. Peptides present in *Hydra* nervous systems also exist in mammalian systems as neuromodulators, neurohormones, or even possible neurotransmitters.

Transmission in the nerve net is relatively slow compared with that in other nervous systems (0.04 metre per second in radial fibres of *Calliactis* compared with 100 metres per second in some fibres of the dog). Many repetitive stimuli may be required to elicit responses at these synapses. Long refractory periods are also characteristic of nerve nets, having durations about 150 to 300 times those seen at mammalian nerve fibres.

Finally, pacemaker systems are present in animals with nerve nets. In the sea anemone *Metridium* these systems are expressed in a series of spontaneous rhythmic movements that occur in the absence of any detectable stimulus. The question remains whether the movements originate from a "command" neuron or group of neurons or whether they arise without neuronal stimulation. It has been postulated that pacemaking cells were present in epithelial conducting systems known not to be nervous but that eventually evolved into neuronal tissue.

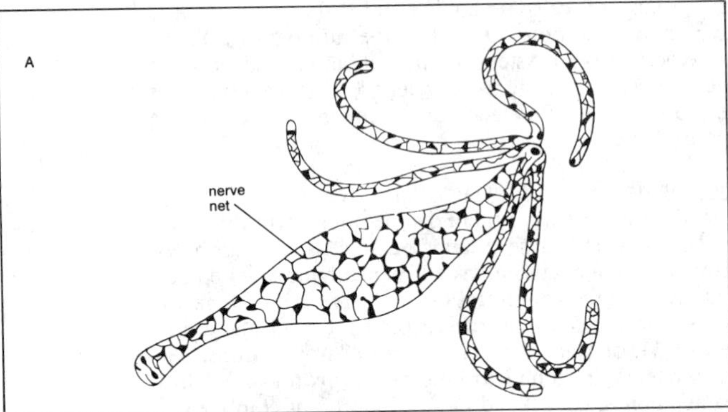

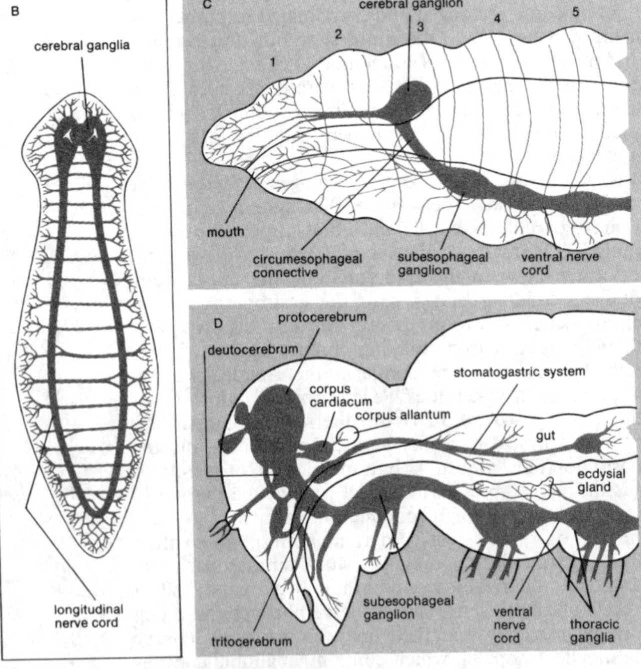

Figure 11: *Invertebrate nervous systems.*
(A) The nerve net of *Hydra,* (B) central nervous system of a flatworm, composed of a brain (cerebral ganglia) and longitudinal nerve cords, (C) annelid, moderately cephalized with a brain, ventral nerve cord, and ventral ganglia, and (D) arthropod, highly cephalized and compartmentalized.

CENTRALIZED NERVOUS SYSTEMS

The development of the nerve net allowed an organism to engage in several different behaviours, including feeding and swimming. The development in the net of rapidly conducting bundles of fibres and of pacemaker systems allowed rapid withdrawal and rhythmic swimming activities, respectively, in some cnidarians. However, it is at the level of the flatworms (phylum Platyhelminthes) that there appears a longitudinal nerve cord and an anterior collection of nerve cells that can be called a brain (Figure 11B). Furthermore, there are well-defined sensory and motor pathways as well as coordinating interneurons. Although nerve nets and pacemaker activity are still present in the flatworms, the presence of ganglia or a brain concentrated at the cephalic (head) end of the organisms represents a simple beginning to the complex, integrative, centralized systems that develop at higher levels of the phylogenetic tree.

Simple bilateral systems. The flatworms were the first invertebrates to exhibit bilateral symmetry and also the first to develop a central nervous system with a brain. The nervous system of a free-living flatworm such as *Planaria* consists of a brain, longitudinal nerve cords, and peripheral nerve plexuses (interlacing networks of peripheral nerves; from Latin *plectere,* "to braid"). Located in the anterior portion of the animal, the brain is composed of two cephalic ganglia joined by a broad connection called a commissure. Longitudinal nerve cords, usually three to five pairs, extend posteriorly from the brain; they are connected by transverse commissures, and smaller, lateral nerves extend from the cords. The lateral nerves give rise to the peripheral nerve plexuses. The submuscular nerve plexus, consisting of sensory cells, ganglion cells, and their processes, is situated in the loose tissue (mesenchyme) below the subepidermal musculature. A much finer subepidermal plexus is located at the bases of the epithelial cells above the muscular layer.

Rudimentary brain of the flatworm

Planaria are richly supplied with sensory receptors. Single sensory cells in the nerve plexuses are widely scattered over the animal. Sensory organs also are present and include ciliated pits and grooves, auricles, the frontal organ, statocyst, and eyes. The ciliated pits and grooves contain chemical receptors, or chemoreceptors, which permit the animal to detect food. The statocyst is responsible for balancing and such reactions as rising to the surface of the water or sinking. The eyes, or ocelli, may occur as a pair situated anteriorly or may be scattered abundantly over the head region depending on the species. Short optic nerves connect the eyes with the brain.

Seven types of nerve cell bodies and two types of neuroglia have been described in *Planaria.* Removal of the brain results in the abolition of such functions as food finding and recognition and severe deficits in locomotion. However, the nerve cords by themselves can mediate a certain amount of locomotion as well as righting and avoidance reactions.

Nematodes (phylum Aschelminthes) have a high degree of centralization, with three-quarters of all nerve cells concentrated in a group of anteriorly placed ganglia and no peripheral plexuses or nets. They usually have eight longitudinal cords, commissures between dorsal and ventral cords, six cephalic nerves, a few special ganglia and nerves in the tail, and two sympathetic systems (one anterior and one posterior).

Moderately cephalized systems. Basic similarities in the nervous systems of the annelid worms, mollusks, and arthropods include an anteriorly situated brain, connectives running from the brain around the esophagus and joining paired longitudinal cords, and ventral nerve cords with ganglia along their length. The trend toward greater centralization and cephalization of nervous functions is continued within these groups, reaching its peak in the higher mollusks and arthropods.

Annelids. The brain of most annelids (phylum Annelida, segmented worms, including the leeches and terrestrial earthworms) is relatively simple in structure (Figure 11C). The earthworm brain is a bilobed mass lying above the pharynx in the third body segment. Sensory nerves leave the brain and run forward into the prostomium

Divided brain of the segmented worm

(extreme anterior end) and first segment. The brain of the active, predatory polychaetes (a class of marine worms) is more complicated. In some, the brain can be divided into a forebrain, midbrain, and hindbrain; a single pair of circumesophageal or circumpharyngeal connectives leave the brain, surround the anterior gut, and connect with the ventral nerve cord.

The most primitive annelids have a pair of ventral nerve cords joined by transverse connectives; the most advanced forms have the cords fused to form a single cord. A ganglionic swelling of the cord is found in each body segment, with the most anterior ganglion, the subpharyngeal ganglion, being the most prominent. Two to five pairs of lateral nerves leave each ganglion to innervate the body wall of that segment. A subepidermal nerve plexus occurs over the whole body. Another plexus, called the enteric, stomodaeal, or sympathetic system, is found in the wall of the gut.

Giant axons, usually few in number, are found running the length of the cord. They may belong to one cell or be composed of many neurons. These axons are capable of very rapid conduction of impulses to the segmental muscles; their main function is to permit the worm to contract very rapidly as a defense against predators.

The usual slow crawling movements of worms are mediated by a series of reflex arcs. During crawling, the contraction of muscles in one segment stimulates stretch receptors in the muscle. Impulses are carried over sensory nerves to the cord, causing motor neurons to send impulses to the longitudinal muscles, which then contract. The longitudinal pull activates stretch receptors in the following segment, and a wave of contraction moves along the worm.

Studies of the nervous systems of annelids show certain behavioral capabilities, including perception, motor coordination, and learning. Because the neuronal organization behind these capabilities can be deduced, they may give an indication of the mechanisms underlying similar patterns of activity and behaviours at other levels of the phylogenetic scale.

Rhythmic nerve impulses in the leech

Two rhythmic movements generated by the leech, the heartbeat and swimming rhythm, have been extensively studied. The coordinated heartbeat rhythm is produced by heart excitor motor neurons, which show rhythmic activity in which bursts of action potentials alternate with bursts of inhibitory synaptic potentials derived from rhythmically firing inhibitory interneurons. The heartbeat appears to be produced by a central rhythm generator. The swimming movement, on the other hand, is generated by a neuronal network requiring many more cells. These neuronal oscillators may in fact form the basis for neuronal generators of rhythmic movements in other animals at higher levels of the phylogenetic scale.

Simple mollusks. The nervous systems of the more primitive mollusks (snails, slugs, and bivalves such as clams and mussels) conform to the basic annelid plan but are modified to conform with the unusual anatomy of these animals. In snails a pair of cerebral ganglia constitutes the brain, which overlies the esophagus. Nerves leave the brain anteriorly to supply the eyes, tentacles, and a pair of buccal ganglia. These last ganglia, also called the stomatogastric head ganglia, innervate the pharynx, salivary glands, and a plexus on the esophagus and stomach. Other nerve cords—the pedal cords—leave the cerebral ganglia ventrally and terminate in a pair of pedal ganglia, which innervate the foot muscles. Another pair of nerve cords—the visceral cords—leave the brain and run posteriorly to the visceral ganglia. The pleural ganglion, supplying the mantle, or fleshy lining of the shell, and the parietal ganglion, innervating the lateral body wall and mantle, are located along the visceral nerves. Intestinal ganglia connected with the pleural ganglia innervate the gills, osphradium (a chemical sense organ), and mantle. Because of the torsion that occurred during the evolutionary history of the snails, some components of the nervous system are twisted and located in asymmetrical positions. In addition, there has been some migration forward and fusion of ganglia. Sense organs of snails include eyes, tentacles, statocysts, and osphradia.

In the bivalves, a cerebropleural ganglion is situated on either side of the esophagus. An upper pair of nerve cords leaves these ganglia and runs posteriorly to the visceroparietal (visceral) ganglia. The visceral ganglia supply the mantle, adductor muscles (which close the shell), and internal organs. A second pair of nerve cords runs ventrally to the pedal ganglia. Most of the sense organs are found at the edge of the mantle. In the scallop, for example, the eyes are set in a row. They are well developed and consist of a cornea, lens, and a retina, in which the photoreceptor cells are not placed superficially (an arrangement much like that in the vertebrate retina).

Synaptic transmission in the snail

Elementary forms of learning and memory have been studied at a cellular level by analysis of the neuronal activity of the marine snail *Aplysia californica.* This simple mollusk withdraws its gill and siphon in response to a mild tactile stimulus. The neural circuit for this reflex consists of a sensory component from the siphon that forms single-synapse junctions with motor neurons that cause the gill to withdraw. The sensory cells also project onto interneurons whose outputs converge onto the same motor neurons. In response to a stimulus, the sensory neurons generate large excitatory postsynaptic potentials at both interneurons and motor neurons, causing the generation of action potentials in the motor neurons that in turn cause the gill to withdraw. When the stimulus is repeated many times, the postsynaptic potentials become reduced in size and the response becomes weaker. Finally, the postsynaptic potentials become so small that action potentials are no longer generated and the gill no longer responds. This reduced behavioral response is known as habituation. Some researchers believe that habituation is caused by the closing of calcium channels, which decreases calcium influx into the presynaptic terminals and, hence, decreases neurotransmitter release. Other evidence suggests that habituation results from fewer neurons in the network being activated.

Another behavioral paradigm, sensitization, has also been examined in *Aplysia.* In sensitization the reflex activity increases in strength with added stimulation. The mechanism underlying this response is presynaptic facilitation, which is believed to be due to an increase in the second messenger cAMP in the terminals of the sensory neurons.

These two examples—habituation and sensitization—show that important features of more complex nervous systems can be studied in organisms at lower stages of evolution. First is what can be called the plasticity of the nervous system, the phenomenon of changes occurring in the strength of synaptic responses. Changes in synaptic efficacy may underlie certain mechanisms for short and long-term memory—even in more complex animals such as humans. Second, changes in the structure of the synapse may be a long-term effect of plasticity. For example, the numbers of active zones at nerve terminals are reduced with long-term habituation but increased with long-term sensitization. Finally, the molecular mechanisms underlying these changes may be the same or at least similar at all levels of the phylogenetic tree. Habituation of the escape response has been seen in polychaete worms, roaches, and crayfish.

Complexly compartmentalized systems. The highest degree of development of the invertebrate nervous system is attained by the cephalopods (squids, cuttlefishes, and octopuses) among the mollusks and by the insects and spiders among the arthropods. Although the basic plan of these nervous systems is similar to that of the annelids, there are several advances. First, there is a high degree of cephalization, with nervous functions concentrated in the head region of the animal. In addition, ganglia are fused and farther forward, and nerve cells, less abundant in the peripheral nervous system, are situated in the brain or ganglia so that the nerve cords consist only of nerve fibres. Finally, control and coordination of specific functions, such as locomotion and feeding, are compartmentalized in particular parts of the nervous system.

Complex mollusks. The complex nervous system of the cephalopods is correlated with the active movement and predatory habits of these animals. Most of the ganglia typical of mollusks are concentrated or fused in a brain that encircles the esophagus. Nerves extend from the brain to ganglia at the base of the arms or tentacles and from the ganglia the length of the arms. A pair of large pallial nerves connects the brain with a pair of stellate ganglia on the inner surface of the mantle. The stomatogastric ganglia supply nerves to the digestive tract.

A great variety of body functions are centralized in the brain and compartmentalized to specific brain regions. These activities may be local, simple, and uncoordinated with other regions or may be extensive, complex, and coordinated, involving large groups of muscles. The highest centres of the cephalopod brain are the associative areas, which are believed to be concerned with discrimination between objects, learning, and memory.

Giant-fibre system of the squid

The giant-fibre system—also seen in earthworms and insects—is very well developed in the squid. The diameter of giant fibres is many times greater than the diameter of most other nerve fibres. Giant neurons in the brain send fibres to the retractor muscles of the head and the funnel or to the stellate ganglion. Fibres from the stellate ganglion fuse to form giant fibres that innervate the mantle. Because of their large size, these fibres are capable of rapid conduction, which, in turn, permits extremely rapid movement.

The eyes of cephalopods are especially well developed and bear close structural resemblance to the vertebrate eye. The eye fits into a socket of cartilaginous plates separate from the cartilages that protect the brain, and external muscles permit its movement. A transparent cornea covers the surface of the eye and can be focused for both near and far objects. There is a pupil formed by an iris diaphragm, which can regulate the amount of light reaching the retina. The retina contains light-sensitive cells. The axons of the photoreceptors, or rod cells, form the optic nerves, which terminate in the extremely large optic lobes of the brain.

Complexity of the nervous system of cephalopods

The cephalopods are strikingly different in many respects from other molluscan classes. The nervous system as described above is more highly developed and, consequently, the behavioral repertoire much more complex. First, the animals are predators; they move, they use their eyes in search of food, they use receptors in their arms for detection of tactile or chemical stimuli, and they have exceptionally fast muscle action. Second, they have an enormous flexibility of response, discriminating between palatable and unpalatable prey and "learning" to attack or not to attack. They can also change colour to blend into their environment if needed.

The mollusks as a whole provide an important link in the developing complexity of the nervous system. Indeed, the presence in their systems of vertebrate as well as natural molluscan neuroactive peptides may give some clue to the true place of these animals in the phylogenetic scale.

Arthropods. The other complex compartmentalized nervous system is found in arthropods (Figure 11D). The arthropodan brain consists of three main regions: the protocerebrum, deutocerebrum, and tritocerebrum. The anterior protocerebrum, which receives the nerves of the eyes and other organs forward, contains centres or neuropils such as the optic centres and bodies known as corpora pedunculata. The neuropils function as integrative systems for the anterior sense organs, especially the eyes, and in control of movement; they also are the centres for the initiation of complex behaviour. The deutocerebrum contains the association centres for the first antennae. The posterior tritocerebrum contains association neuropils for the second antennae (of crustaceans) and gives rise to nerves that innervate the mouthparts and the anterior digestive canal. The latter constitute the stomatogastric system, which regulates the intake of food and the movement of the gut necessary for digestion. This system bears a resemblance to the vertebrate autonomic system (see below).

The ventral nerve cord, connected to the brain by the circumesophageal connectives, is composed of a double row of ganglia connected longitudinally by connectives and transversely by commissures. Different groups of arthropods exhibit different degrees of fusion of the ganglia. In insects the first ganglion, the subesophageal, is formed by fusion of three pairs of ganglia; it sends nerves to the mouthparts and to the salivary glands. The segmental ganglia in the thorax and abdomen provide nerves to the appendages, dorsal muscles, sense organs, and heart. Insects have three pairs of thoracic ganglia and up to 10 abdominal ganglia.

The most common sensory receptors in arthropods are the cuticular hairs, many of which are mechanoreceptors, sensitive to touch, vibration, water currents, or sound waves; some hairs are chemoreceptors, which detect odours or chemicals in the water. Hairs situated near the joints are stimulated by body movements and thus provide a sense of the position of the joint or appendage during locomotion or flight. Many sensory cells and organs are concentrated in the antennae, and a statocyst is found at the base of each antenna.

Spiders have several pairs of simple eyes with cup-shaped retinas. Crustaceans and insects, however, have a pair of well-developed compound eyes, each consisting of a large number of visual units called ommatidia. Each ommatidium contains six to eight sensory receptors arranged under a cornea and refractile cone and is surrounded by pigment cells, which adjust the intensity of light. Each ommatidium can act as a separate eye, capable of responding to its own visual field. Such an arrangement seems particularly well suited for detecting movement across a wide visual field.

Specialized neurons in insects

In spite of the small size of insects, some of their nerve cells and axons are larger in diameter than any neuron in the human nervous system. The number of insect neurons is relatively small, so that each neuron must be capable of dealing with a maximum amount of information. Evasive behaviour requires mechanisms of this sort—as exemplified by the jumping muscle of the grasshopper, which is supplied by only a few motor axons while those muscles of a human required for a similar purpose have tens of thousands of axons. Another example is the ear of a noctuid moth. Each ear is essentially a tympanic membrane forming the outer wall of an air-filled cavity in the thorax. A five-tissue strand, the acoustic sensillum, runs from the centre of the tympanic membrane across the tympanic cavity to a nearby skeletal support. This sensillum has two acoustic sensory receptors, called A cells. From the central end of each A cell, an axon passes within the sensillum to the skeletal support and then in the tympanic nerve to the thoracic ganglia of the moth.

The A cells encode the intensity of ultrasound by the frequency with which they fire action potentials. Each ear is capable of responding differently to different stimuli, so that differences between the two ears in the duration of the action potentials and response times could allow for binaural detection of the source of a sound. The impulses are conducted to the pterothoracic ganglion, where they must then influence muscles used for avoidance of predators. The important point here is that two A cells provide enough information with speed to allow the moth to take evasive behaviour.

Clearly, simplicity of the neural circuitry is required for speedy response; while some information may be sacrificed, escape will not be compromised. In fact, the quick evasion of predators has probably influenced the evolution of the giant-fibre systems of worms and squid as well as crustaceans and insects. These giant fibres conduct impulses at much higher conduction velocities than do smaller axons, while the information-handling capacity of many small axons acting together is far greater than that of giant axons. Under these circumstances it is clear that different systems evolved in the invertebrate nervous system in response to different qualities of stimuli in the environment to which the organism had to react—one responsible for survival and the other for information.

Neurosecretory cells in crustaceans and arthropods

Neurosecretory cells, which have been identified in all the major invertebrate groups, reach their highest degree of development in the arthropods. The principal system of insects consists of neurosecretory cells in the protocerebrum of the brain. The axons of these cells form nerves that innervate structures called corpora cardiaca, situated just posterior to the brain. A corpus cardiacum is an organ in which neurosecretory products are stored in the nerve terminals for later release into the vascular system.

The neurosecretory cells of the protocerebrum manufacture a hormone called ecdysiotropin, or brain hormone. Sensory nerve impulses reaching the brain regulate the release of the hormone from the nerve endings into the blood within the corpora cardiaca. The hormone then stimulates a non-neural endocrine gland, the ecdysial gland, located in the thorax. The ecdysial glands in turn release a hormone, ecdysone, which initiates molting during larval development and also stimulates differentiation into adult tissues. Another hormone, however, the juvenile hormone, keeps tissue in a juvenile or larval form. This hormone is released by the corpora allata, another pair of non-neural endocrine glands, located behind the corpora cardiaca. The successive life stages in insect development are, therefore, determined by the varying levels of ecdysone and juvenile hormone.

THE VERTEBRATE NERVOUS SYSTEM

The nervous system of vertebrates has two main divisions: the central nervous system, consisting of the brain and spinal cord, and the peripheral nervous system, which in humans includes 12 pairs of cranial nerves, 31 pairs of spinal nerves, and the autonomic, or involuntary, nervous system. Because the arrangement of nerve cells and their fibres is so complex, it is helpful to understand some basic terms used in describing the vertebrate nervous system.

Anatomical structures such as the nervous system are described according to their position. In four-legged animals the upper (back) surface is called dorsal and the lower (belly) surface ventral. The terms anterior, cranial, cephalic, or rostral refer to the head end of the body; posterior, or caudal, to the tail end. In humans, since they stand erect, the situation is more complicated: dorsal becomes equivalent to posterior, and ventral is the same as anterior; cranial is often called superior, and caudal inferior. Objects near the middle plane of the body are medial and those farther away are lateral. Proximal refers to structures nearest the central bulk of a structure and distal to ones away from it. In referring to another structure, if it is located on the same side of the body, it is known as ipsilateral; if it is on the opposite side, it is contralateral.

Neurons are often gathered into localized masses. In the peripheral nervous system these accumulations are called ganglia; in the central nervous system they are called nuclei. Portions of the central nervous system in which unmyelinated neurons and neuroglia predominate are called gray matter; areas in which myelinated neurons dominate are called white matter. Efferent, or motor, nerve fibres carry impulses away from the central nervous system; afferent, or sensory, fibres carry impulses toward the central nervous system. Visceral fibres innervate the viscera such as the heart and intestine, and somatic fibres innervate the body-wall structures such as skin and muscle. In the central nervous system the nerve fibres are organized in bundles called tracts, or fasciculi. Ascending tracts carry impulses along the spinal cord toward the brain, and descending tracts carry them from the brain or higher regions in the spinal cord to lower regions. The tracts are often named according to their origin and termination; for example, the corticospinal tract consists of fibres running from the cerebral cortex in the brain to the spinal cord.

The primitive condition. The vertebrates constitute an advanced subdivision of the phylum Chordata. All chordates at some time in their life history have a rodlike bar called the notochord running the length of the body. Lower chordates (acorn worms, tunicates, and amphioxus), which lack a vertebral column, illustrate the most primitive features of the chordate nervous system. In these animals the nerve cord is a rather uniform-appearing dorsally placed tube with a hollow cavity, which corresponds roughly to the spinal cord of the vertebrates, suggesting that the spinal cord is the most primitive component of the central nervous system.

Predecessors of the spinal cord

In amphioxus and in the lowest vertebrates such as lampreys, the sensory fibres and motor fibres leave the cord in dorsal and ventral roots to supply the adjacent body segments (myotomes). The dorsal and ventral roots remain separate nerves and arise at alternate positions along the cord. In lower fishes there is still alternation of dorsal and ventral roots, but the roots unite in a single spinal nerve. In higher vertebrates the two roots unite in a single spinal nerve and leave the cord at the same level, one above the other. Each spinal nerve supplies a single myotome. When appendages (fins, wings, arms, and legs) develop from several myotomes, the nerves continue to supply their original segments, and branches of the spinal nerves become interwoven to form plexuses.

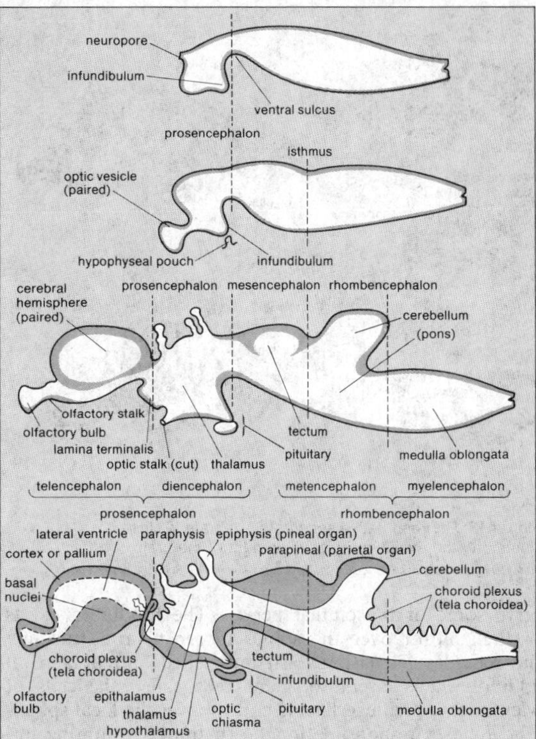

Figure 12: Development of principal vertebrate brain divisions.
From A. Romer, *The Vertebrate Body*, 3rd ed. (1962); W.B. Saunders Company, Philadelphia

The brain of vertebrates developed by the accumulation of nerve cells at the cephalic end of the nerve cord. At first this diffuse collection of nerve cells regulated the reflex activity of spinal motor neurons. These cells are comparable to the reticular formation occupying the brain stem of higher vertebrates. The brain stem, thus, is the oldest portion of the brain.

Encephalization. Early in the evolution of vertebrates, a special sensory system became associated with each major part of the brain: the olfactory organs with the forebrain, the eye with the midbrain, and the ear and related organs with the hindbrain. Each of the three sections, furthermore, developed dorsal outgrowths of gray matter forming, respectively, the cerebrum, the midbrain roof, or tectum, and the cerebellum. With these developments the three-part brain stem was then transformed into a brain of five regions: telencephalon, diencephalon, mesencephalon, metencephalon, and myelencephalon (Figure 12). The addition of these nerve centres to the primitive brain stem allowed greater coordination and association between the sensory and motor fibres.

In tracing the development of the parts of the brain in the different vertebrate classes, some general features are apparent (Figure 13). There is a correlation between the size of a particular part of the brain and its importance in the life of the animal in question. Some neural structures (*e.g.,* olfactory bulb) have considerable size and importance in more primitive forms but are less conspicuous in most recent forms. Progressing from primitive to recent forms, there is a gradual cephalic shift of function from the lower brain stem to the higher cerebral cortex.

Link between size and importance

The hindbrain is comparable to an enlarged, anterior section of the spinal cord. In the gray matter are dorsal sensory and ventral motor columns similar to those present in the cord. The longitudinal continuity of these columns is preserved in the earlier vertebrates, but in more recent vertebrates the columns break up into discrete nuclei that

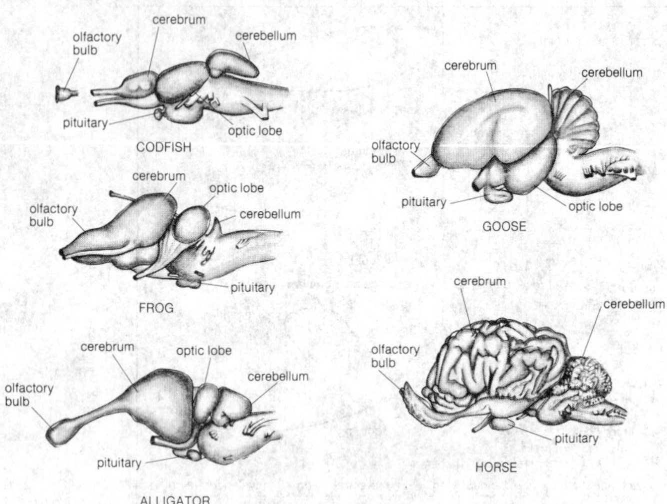

Figure 13: Representative series of vertebrate brains illustrating the evolutionary development of the brain.

From *Biological Sciences Curriculum Study Green Version High School Biology*, 2nd ed. (1968); Rand McNally & Co.

serve some of the cranial nerves. The hindbrain exerts partial control over the spinal motor neurons through the reticular formation. Fish and tailed amphibians, in addition, have a pair of giant cells called the cells of Mauthner, which exert some control over the local spinal-cord reflexes responsible for the rhythmic swimming undulations and the flip-tail escape response characteristic of these animals.

The hindbrain is the area of reception of one of the main sensory systems, the acoustico-lateralis system, which consists of the ear (hearing and equilibrium) and the lateral-line organs (vibration and pressure). The latter, situated in rows along the head and body, are retained in fish but disappear in the land vertebrates.

The cerebellum originated as a specialized part of the acoustico-lateralis area. The oldest part of the cerebellum—the archicerebellum—is concerned with equilibrium and connected with the inner ear and the lateral-line system. The anterior lobe of the cerebellum represents the paleocerebellum, an area that regulates equilibrium and muscle tone; it constitutes the main mass of the cerebellum in fish, reptiles, and birds. In mammals the development of the cerebral cortex and its connections with the cerebellum are correlated with the appearance of the large cerebellar hemispheres. This new part of the cerebellum, or neocerebellum, coordinates skilled movements initiated at cortical levels. In mammals a great mass of fibres connects the brain stem to the cerebellum; this region forms the pons, which, together with the cerebellum, constitutes the metencephalon. The caudal part of the hindbrain remains as the medulla (myelencephalon).

The midbrain (mesencephalon) and diencephalon constitute the anterior portion of the brain stem. Sensory and motor nuclei for cranial nerves extend from the hindbrain to the midbrain. The roof of the midbrain, or tectum, developed as the primary visual centre. The optic lobes, especially prominent in fish and birds, are a part of this area. In fish and amphibians the tectum is the major centre of the nervous system and wields the greatest influence on body activity. While this area is still significant in reptiles and birds, it is supplanted in importance by the cerebral hemispheres. In mammals the midbrain is greatly reduced in importance. Instead, most of the optic sensations are relayed to the cerebral cortex. With development of the cerebral cortex, the thalamus becomes less significant as an association area and more important as a relay centre for sensory impulses. Centres for visceral sensations and visceral motor responses become established in the hypothalamus.

Original function of the cerebral hemispheres

Dominance of the cerebrum. Ascending the vertebrate scale, the cerebral hemispheres become more and more important as association centres. The cerebral hemispheres begin their development as paired outgrowths of the forebrain and serve as centres of olfactory reception. In the older vertebrates the forebrain is divided into the olfactory bulb—where the olfactory nerve fibres end—and the cerebral hemisphere. The hemisphere at this time, referred to as the paleopallium, is merely an olfactory lobe serving as an association area for olfactory impulses. The olfactory lobes are prominent in animals such as amphibians, but in birds and primates in which sense of smell is less important, the lobes are reduced in extent. In amphibians the hemispheres consist of three parts: the paleopallium (olfactory lobe), archipallium, and basal nuclei. These areas of gray matter are located deep to the surface. All three areas receive olfactory stimuli and discharge impulses to the brain stem. The archipallium is a correlation centre and forerunner of the mammalian hippocampus. The basal nuclei are equivalent to the corpus striatum and function as association areas with connections with the thalamus. In primitive reptiles the basal nuclei have moved to the inner part of the hemisphere, whereas the other areas of gray matter have moved toward the surface. In advanced reptiles a new association centre, the neopallium, appears between paleopallium and archipallium. In birds there is nothing corresponding to the neopallium, but the basal ganglia (corpus striatum) are enormously expanded. In mammals the neopallium becomes greatly enlarged to exceed all the other parts of the brain in size. This region assumes more and more of the higher types of neural activity in correlation, association, and learning. At first the neopallium expands to envelop the other brain structures. The archipallium becomes folded into a small area on the median part of the hemispheres, where it remains as the hippocampus. The paleopallium (olfactory lobes) constitutes a small ventral region on the hemisphere, the pyriform lobe. The corpus striatum (old basal nuclei) becomes a central part of the hemisphere. Further expansion of the neopallium in primates and humans causes extensive folding and results in a very convoluted surface of the brain. (T.L.L./S.D.E.)

ANATOMY OF THE HUMAN NERVOUS SYSTEM

The human nervous system, like the nervous systems of other vertebrates, includes such structures as the brain, spinal cord, and nerves; these serve to receive stimuli (input), to process and store their effects, and to generate behaviour (output).

Origin and development

The human nervous system appears to have emerged from millions of years of prevertebrate and lower vertebrate evolution. Neural elements that have survived the evolutionary process tend to be those that enhanced the survival of successions of organisms during this long period. Several aspects of evolutionary significance may be inferred from the developing human embryo.

The origin of both the human nervous system and part of the skin from the ectoderm (the outer layer of cells of the early, ball-shaped embryo) may be related to the eventual location of most sensory structures on or close to the body surface, where they can receive stimulation from the external environment. The earliest nerve cell, or neuron, to evolve was probably a combined receptor (receiving environmental stimuli) and motor unit (producing muscle or gland responses). Such primordial types of neuron are still to be found in living sponges. In subsequent evolutionary stages, the combined receptor–motor unit seems to have separated into specialized receptor neurons and effector (motor) neurons, such sequences of cells being observable in living sea anemones. In more highly evolved stages, greater complexity derives from the interposition or intercalation of one or more nerve cells between the receptor and effector neurons. These intercalated cells,

Evolution of specialized nerve cells

called interneurons or internuncial neurons, are organized in circuits of various degrees of complexity—as in the brain and spinal cord of the central nervous system. In this theoretical reconstruction of evolution, the primordial nervous system, composed of neurons on the body surface, evolves into a central nervous system that interacts with the external environment through the peripheral nerves.

In early embryonic stages the presumptive neural part of the ectoderm in humans and other vertebrates detaches from the part destined to become skin, sinks beneath the surface, and becomes surrounded by another embryonic layer called the mesoderm. During subsequent development of the embryo, many sensory neurons differentiate and grow until their receptor fibres terminate in or near such ectodermally derived structures as the outer skin, or epidermis, and the mucous membranes of the eye, ear, and nose.

All known vertebrates, including the most primitive known fossils (the ancient ancestors of jawless, eellike fishes), have complex nervous systems. Study of inner skull surfaces of many fossil vertebrate remains indicates that in all of them the brains and cranial nerves are built on a basically similar plan, which includes encephalization, the development of a specialized brain. The vertebrate nervous system is bilaterally symmetrical, most neural structures being repeated on the left and right sides of the body.

The human nervous system in embryo

The human nervous system begins to differentiate structurally and to show clear signs of function early during prenatal life. By 18 days after fertilization, the ectoderm thickens along the future dorsal (backside) midline of the body to form the neural plate, and, slightly later, the primordial eye, ear, and nose differentiate. The neural plate elongates, and its lateral edges rise to form the neural folds. These in turn extend and unite the midline to close off the neural tube, from which the central nervous system develops. The space within the neural tube becomes the cavities, or ventricles, of the brain and the central canal of the spinal cord. This developmental sequence produces the dorsally located, hollow central nervous system unique to vertebrates. Continuing to differentiate, the neural tube detaches from the skin ectoderm and sinks beneath the surface. During this process an ectodermal column of cells on each side differentiates, becoming the neural crests that segregate into future parts (*e.g.,* dorsal-root ganglia) of the spinal nerves. The cephalic (head) end of the tube differentiates into primary brain vesicles called the forebrain, midbrain, and hindbrain. This is the morphological status of the nervous system at the end of the first fetal month.

The cells of the central nervous system originate from the matrix (ependymal) layer of the neural tube—that is, the layer of cells that lines the cavity of the neural tube. The matrix cells differentiate and proliferate into specialized cells called neuroblasts, the progenitors of the neurons of the central nervous system, and other cells called glioblasts, from which the neuroglia develop. With few exceptions the neuroblasts, glioblasts, and their derived cells do not divide and multiply (as do most other cells) once they migrate from the matrix layer into the gray and white matter of the nervous system.

Prenatal brain growth

By middle fetal life the slender primordial brain of the neural-tube stage differentiates into the globular-shaped brain. During this interval the brain continues to grow differentially in size and to bend at three major flexures. The main outlines of the form of the brain are recognizable by the end of the third fetal month (Figure 14). Its typically adult size and shape, however, are not attained until early puberty.

The early development of the "contorted" brain from the neural-tube stage is the product of several factors: the formation of three flexures (midbrain, pons, and cervical); the differential enlargement of various regions, especially the cerebrum and cerebellum; the growth of the cerebral hemispheres over and at the sides of the midbrain and cerebellum; and the formation of convolutions ("valleys," or fissures, called sulci and "hills" called gyri) in the cerebral cortex and of folia (leaflike gyri) in the cerebellar cortex. The forebrain differentiates into such structures (described in greater detail below) as the cerebral cortex, corpus callosum, lateral and third ventricles, basal ganglia, thalamus, and hypothalamus; the midbrain becomes the cerebral peduncles, superior and inferior colliculi, and cerebral aqueduct; and the hindbrain generates the cerebellum, pons, medulla oblongata, and fourth ventricle. Such deeper valleys as the central and calcarine sulci are discernible by the fifth fetal month, and every major gyrus and sulcus is normally present by the seventh. The minor sulci and gyri are not fully formed until after birth. The relative size and proportions of the brain and its parts are basically similar to those in the adult brain by two years after birth.

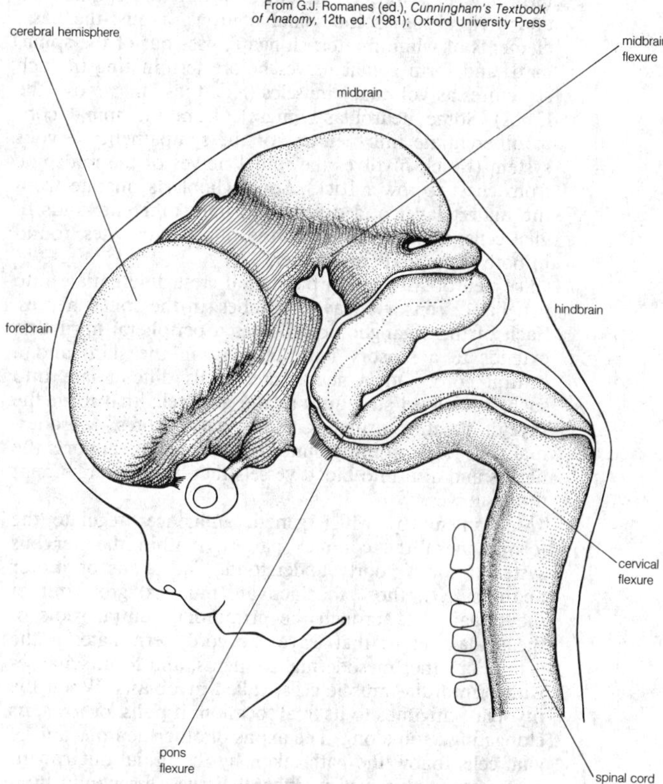

Figure 14: Profile of the brain of a human fetus at 10 weeks.

The nervous system exhibits observable activity within the second prenatal month. Seven weeks after fertilization, the head draws away from a stimulus applied to the upper lip. Many reflexes of the head, trunk, and extremities can be evoked from the fetus during the third month.

Postnatal growth of the brain

The postnatal growth of the human brain is rapid and massive, especially during the first two years. The typical brain weighs 350 grams (about 0.8 pound) in the full-term infant at birth, 1,000 grams at the end of the first year, and about 1,300 grams at puberty. This increase is mainly attributable to growth of pre-existing neurons, new glial cells, and myelination of the neuron fibres. This unique threefold growth of the brain during the first year may be interpreted as an adaptation that is essential to human survival as a species with a large brain. Birth occurs at a developmental stage when the infant is not so helpless that it is unable to survive, yet is still small enough to pass through the bony opening of the maternal pelvis; if the brain were much larger (enough to support intelligent behaviour), normal delivery might not be possible.

The neurons and the non-neural glial cells of the central nervous system differentiate at various times during the development of the individual. With a few uncertain exceptions all neurons have differentiated from the matrix layer of the neural tube before birth. This effectively means that a person is born with as many neurons as he will ever have (perhaps 10,000,000,000 in the brain cortex alone), losing the potential function of more and more of them from then on. According to one unconfirmed estimate, an average of approximately 50,000 neurons atrophy or deteriorate each day from ages 20 to 70. In a healthy person, in 50 years, less than 10 percent of the original neuronal complement is out of action. Indeed, by age 75, the weight of the brain typically is reduced from its maximum at maturity by about one-tenth; the flow of blood through the brain drops by about one-fifth; and the functional taste buds in the mouth are about two-thirds gone.

Development of the spinal cord and spinal nerves

The spinal cord and spinal nerves develop from the neural tube and neural crest. Neuroblasts migrate from the matrix layer of the neural tube and differentiate into the neurons of the spinal cord. Some parts of these neurons (the cell bodies and dendrites) remain within the gray matter. Other parts, the axons, differentiate, grow, and terminate in a variety of centres within the spinal cord and brain. From some spinal neurons, axons, the basic elements of white matter, elongate, pass out of the spinal cord, and form spinal nerves before terminating in such structures as voluntary muscles (*e.g.,* those that move the limbs). Some neuroblasts migrate from the spinal cord to differentiate into neurons of the sympathetic nervous system (which involves the spinal nerves of the midspine from chest to lower back). Some glioblasts migrate from the matrix layer and differentiate into different kinds of glial cells, such as astrocytes and oligodendrocytes, found in both white and gray matter.

The neuroblasts within the neural crest differentiate into ganglia, or sensory relay assemblies, in the spinal nerves. Each of these ganglionic cells has a peripheral fibril that extends to a sensory receptor (*e.g.,* in the skin) and a central cord. Other neural crest cells differentiate into such specialized structures as the glial cells that form the myelin sheaths insulating many nerve fibres. Mesodermal cells develop into connective tissue that supports the nerves and also into blood vessels that bring nourishment to the nerves.

Mechanisms by which genetic influences regulate the formation of the complex patterns within the nervous system remain poorly understood. The axons of motor neurons (*e.g.,* those that activate muscles) grow out of the spinal cord through the primordial ventral roots of the spinal nerves that leave the cord, terminate in the somite or other mesodermal elements, and form synapses with primordial muscle cells, called myoblasts. When the myoblast migrates to its final location, it pulls, or tows, its elongating axon along. The axons of other neurons and of glial cells follow the path taken by the initial outgrowths of axons. In this way peripheral nerves, essentially bundles of axons, differentiate and develop. Innervation of all myoblasts tends to be ensured by a process in which myoblasts without neural supply seem to attract growing nerves while those already supplied tend to reject excessive synapses. In computer language, nerve development may be programmed by peripheral structures such as myoblasts. (C.R.N./Ed.)

The central nervous system

The human central nervous system consists of a brain, its connected spinal cord, and their associated membranes, fluids, and blood vessels. The central nervous systems of all vertebrates are similar in structure and function, but there is generally an increase in relative size and complexity of the brain and spinal cord as the phylogenetic scale is ascended. Most aspects of the central nervous system of humans, for example, are almost identical to those of other primates. (Ed.)

Size and weight of the brain

The entire brain, with the pia-arachnoid, of an adult male weighs approximately 1,400 grams; that of a female, 1,260 grams. The average stature and body weight of the female, however, are less than those of the male, so that, when these facts are considered, the size and weight of the brain in the two sexes are approximately equal. The influence of age on brain weight is considerable. The growth of the brain is rapid during the first three years but slightly less so up to the seventh year, when it is almost its full weight. After this the increase is very gradual, its prime weight usually attained in males by the 20th year and in females somewhat earlier. From this period onward, in both sexes, there is a continuous diminution in the average brain weight of approximately one gram per year.

(R.J.Gl./G.v.B./Ed.)

The human skull, which encases the brain, is remarkably structured in weight, contour, cavities, depressions, and openings for the exit and entry of nerves carrying an almost infinite variety of motor and sensory messages to and from various organs via other parts of the nervous system. The bony spinal column, extending caudally (toward the rear) from the skull, normally comprises 24 individual bones called vertebrae, which are linked together by fine, multiple criss-crossing ligaments and intervertebral cartilage that permit great mobility (except at the lower end, where the column is relatively fixed as it joins the pelvis). The vertebrae are so structured in curves, configurations, and facets as to allow considerable flexibility of movement while still bearing the stress of erect posture and body weight. At the same time the spinal column protects the delicate nervous tissue of the spinal cord running most of its length. The column also has small channels, called foramina, that allow for the entry and exit of peripheral nerves.

The lowest part of the brain, the medulla oblongata, is continuous through the foramen magnum, the opening at the base of the skull, with the spinal cord. The brain and spinal cord, as previously mentioned, constitute the central nervous system; the nerves passing to and from the central nervous system form the peripheral nervous system (see below *The peripheral nervous system*). In addition, the human nervous system includes certain nerve centres and nerve fibres that, without conscious knowledge of the processes concerned, control the vital functions of the body, such as circulation of the blood and respiration. This is the autonomic nervous system (see below *The autonomic nervous system*). Through communicating branches the brain can influence organs that are supplied by the autonomic system—*e.g.,* the salivary glands and heart, both of which may be acted on by fear, hunger, and other emotions. Ordinarily, however, the internal organs function without awareness of the processes involved.

THE BRAIN

General structure. The brain is surrounded by three successive membranes called meninges and protected by the bony skull, or cranium. The brain (encephalon) is divided into five parts: telencephalon (end brain), diencephalon (interbrain), mesencephalon (midbrain), metencephalon (afterbrain), and myelencephalon (medulla oblongata). The telencephalon, diencephalon, and upper mesencephalon form the cerebrum. The metencephalon is divided into the pons and the cerebellum, which are connected by bridges of nerve fibres called cerebellar peduncles.

Five major divisions of the brain

Each half of the bilateral telencephalon, called a cerebral hemisphere, consists of an outer gray mantle called the cerebral cortex, a deep mass of gray matter called the basal ganglia, and white matter located between these two gray structures. The cerebral cortex has a convoluted structure characterized by ridges called gyri, which are separated by grooves called sulci. The right and left cerebral hemispheres are separated by a deep, longitudinal fissure, which is crossed by connecting bands of nerve fibres called commissures. The corpus callosum is the largest commissure.

Two major structures of the diencephalon are the thalamus and the hypothalamus. The brain has a series of cavities, called ventricles, that are filled with cerebrospinal fluid. All of these structures are described in more detail in this section. (Ed.)

Membranes of the brain. The membranes, or meninges, covering the brain are an outer, tough, fibrous layer called the dura mater, a thin, intermediate, weblike tissue called the arachnoid, and a soft, vascular inner covering called the pia mater (Figure 16).

The dura mater. The dura mater lines the cranial cavity. In it are meningeal arteries and veins that serve for the nutrition of the bone. The inner surface of the membrane is smooth and moist. The dura mater also forms partitions, or septa, between the hemispheres of the brain and cerebellum. These septa are folds of the dura mater and consist of two layers, blended where they touch but separated along the attached borders of the septa to form venous channels, or dural sinuses, by which blood and

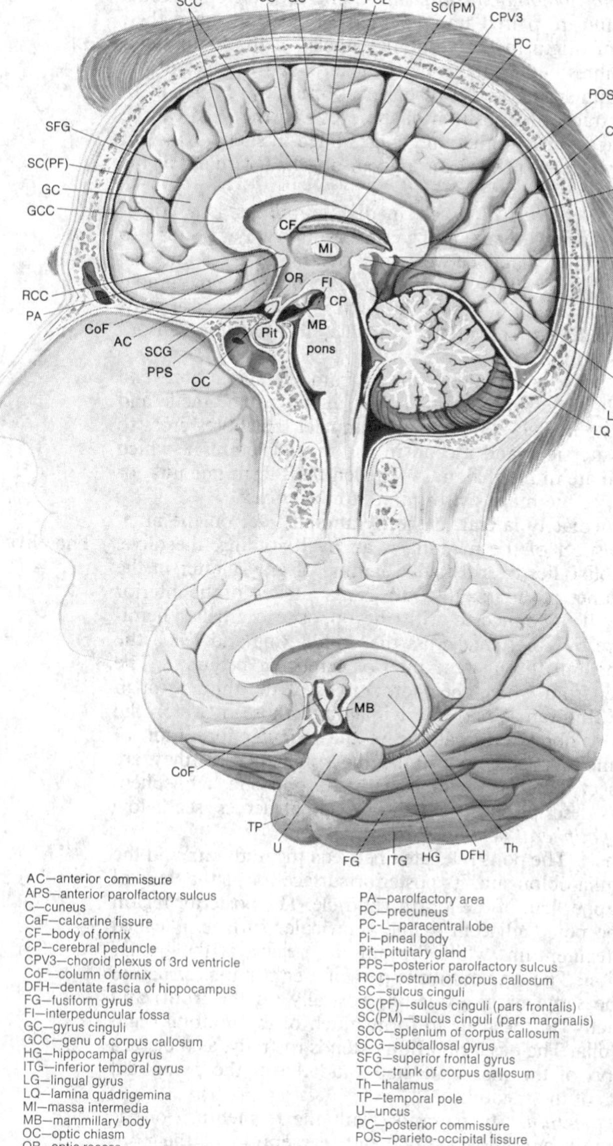

Figure 15: Medial aspect of the brain.

excess of cerebrospinal fluid is drained from the brain into the great veins of the neck, which carry the fluid mixture back toward the heart.

The secretion from the pituitary gland is also carried away into the general bloodstream by small venules, which open into the neighbouring cavernous and other venous sinuses. Absorption and passage of the cerebrospinal fluid is carried out, to a large extent, by small villous projections of the arachnoid membrane. These extend into the venous sinuses and spaces of the dura mater and are most numerous in the neighbourhood of the sagittal sinus, the channel between the two cerebral hemispheres. After birth the arachnoid villi enlarge to form what are called pacchionian bodies, beginning at about 18 months. Between the dura mater and the subjacent arachnoid membrane is an interval called the subdural space. It contains a small quantity of fluid that serves to lubricate the smooth inner surface of the dura mater.

The arachnoid membrane. Beneath the dura mater is the arachnoid membrane, which, although thin, is not permeable to fluids. It is separated from the pia mater, beneath, by the subarachnoid space. This is traversed by a network of delicate fibrous bands. The meshes of this network are filled by the subarachnoid cerebrospinal fluid; the larger thin-walled cerebral arteries and veins covering the surface of the brain lie in the thin bands of fibrous tissue forming the net. In the lower part of the roof of the fourth ventricle (see below) are three openings in the arachnoid membrane and pia mater: a median, the foramen of Magendie; and two lateral, the foramina of Luschka. These form a communication between the cerebrospinal fluid in the ventricles of the brain and that contained in the subarachnoid space. Obliteration of these openings by meningitis produces an obstructive hydrocephalus, in which the accumulation of fluid is entirely intraventricular.

Openings in the arachnoid

The pia mater. The pia mater is a delicate vascular membrane forming the immediate investment of the brain and dipping down into the convolutions. It contains the smaller arterioles and venules that supply the subjacent brain. A large triangular fold of pia mater (velum interpositum) is included in the great transverse fissure lying between the corpus callosum and fornix above and the roof of the third ventricle and thalamus below. This pyramidal fold contains two great blood vessels, the cerebral veins of Galen, which drain the blood from the interior of the brain. Vascular fringes at the margin of the fold project into the lateral ventricles, and similar fringes project from under the surface of the fold into the third ventricle. These fringes are the choroid plexuses of the lateral and third ventricles, and a similar choroid plexus is found in the roof of the fourth ventricle. The fringes are covered by a secretory layer, called the choroidal epithelium, which elaborates and secretes some of the cerebrospinal fluid.

Ventricles. Ventricles are cavities containing fluid, situated in the substance of the brain, and lined by a thin membrane, the ependyma. There are four true ventricles: the right and left lateral ventricles, contained in the cerebral hemispheres; the third ventricle, situated in the diencephalon; and the fourth ventricle, located in the pons and medulla oblongata (Figure 17). Each lateral ventricle is connected with the third ventricle by a small opening, the interventricular foramen of Monro. The third ventricle is joined to the fourth by a narrow channel in the midbrain called the cerebral aqueduct of Sylvius. The fourth ventricle communicates below with the central canal of the spinal cord and with the subarachnoid space by the foramina of Magendie and Luschka.

Functions of the cerebrospinal fluid

The cerebrospinal fluid contained in the ventricles and subarachnoid space acts as a mechanical support to the brain and spinal cord; it also performs functions similar to those of tissue fluid and lymph in other parts of the body. The brain floats in the cerebrospinal fluid. Blood is supplied to the brain by two paired arteries: the internal carotid and the vertebral arteries. These are in communication with each other at the base of the brain, where they form the so-called arterial circle of Willis. Venous

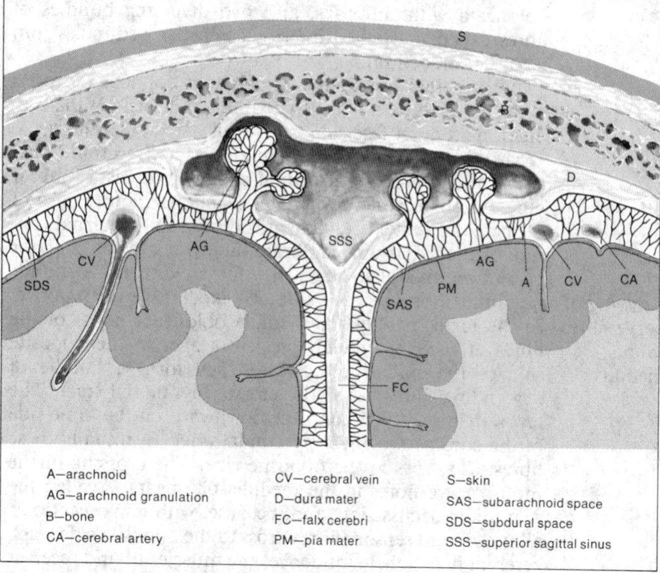

Figure 16: Arachnoid and pia mater.

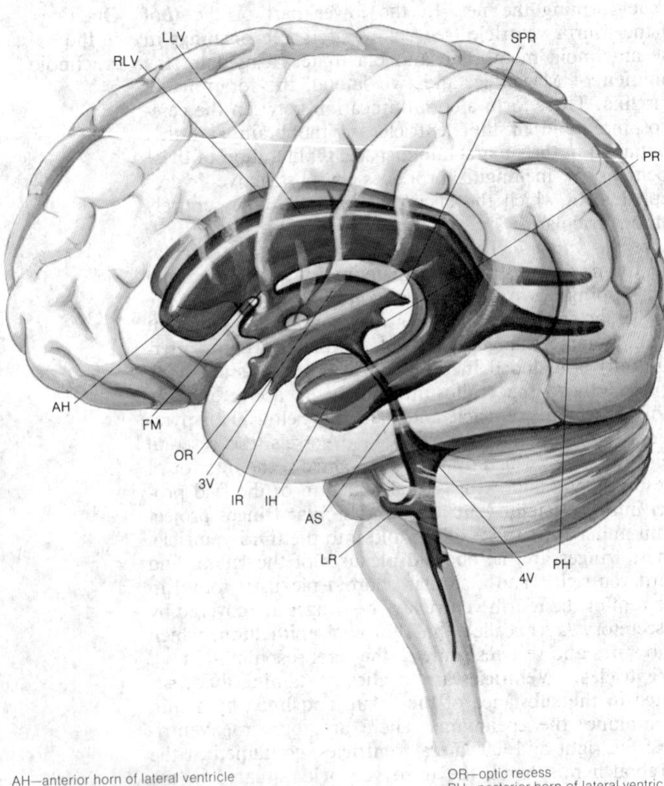

AH—anterior horn of lateral ventricle
AS—aqueduct of Sylvius
FM—foramen of Monro
IH—inferior horn of lateral ventricle
IR—infundibular recess
LR—lateral recess of fourth ventricle
LLV—left lateral ventricle
OR—optic recess
PH—posterior horn of lateral ventricle
PR—pineal recess
SPR—suprapineal recess
RLV—right lateral ventricle
3V—third ventricle
4V—fourth ventricle

Figure 17: Lateral view of cerebrum, cerebellum, and ventricles.

return of blood from the brain is arranged not alongside the arteries, as almost everywhere else in the body, but through the system of dural sinuses (described above) that drain blood to the jugular foramen and from there to the internal jugular veins.

Medulla oblongata. The medulla oblongata is situated in the lower and posterior part of the cranial cavity. It appears to be a direct continuation upward of the spinal cord but differs in its arrangement of fibres composing the nerve tracts and in disposition of the gray matter. It contains the vital cardiac, vasomotor, and respiratory centres. These are situated in the lower part of the medulla. Longitudinal bundles of nerve fibres connect the medulla oblongata with the pons, and two diverging bundles of fibres called the paired inferior cerebellar peduncles join it to the cerebellum.

The principal longitudinal tracts that connect the pons with the medulla are (1) the pyramidal tracts, (2) the medial longitudinal fasciculi, and (3) the medial lemnisci.

Pyramidal tracts. The pyramidal tracts (the traditional name of the main corticospinal pathway) consist of motor fibres, each of which originates from the motor areas of the cerebral cortex and descends through the internal capsule of the cerebrum, midbrain, and pons to the anterior part of the medulla. There they form two parallel strands (pyramids), one on each side of a median vertical groove. In the lower part of the medulla oblongata, most of the fibres of each pyramidal tract cross over to the opposite side of the spinal cord, where they form a bundle of descending fibres called the crossed pyramidal tract. The few remaining fibres continue downward on the same side of the cord as the direct pyramidal tract. Eventually these fibres also cross to the opposite side. The crossing of the motor nerve fibres in the medulla oblongata is called the pyramidal decussation, and, because, with few exceptions, all motor and sensory fibres cross to the opposite side, each cerebral hemisphere influences the muscles of and receives sensory impulses from the opposite side of the body.

Crossing of nerve fibres in the medulla

Medial longitudinal fasciculi. The medial longitudinal fasciculi are paired tracts of nerve fibres that have their cells of origin in the vestibular nuclei of the brain stem. The fibres end in the motor nuclei of the muscles of the eyes and in the nuclei of the neck muscles. By means of these tracts, the position of the eyes and the head can be adjusted to each other and coordinated in such a way that the eyes remain fixed on a given object, regardless of the position of the head.

Medial lemnisci. Each medial lemniscus is a longitudinal tract of ascending sensory fibres lying close to the median plane between the pyramidal tract and the medial longitudinal fasciculus. Just above the pyramidal decussation, the fibres of the right and left lemnisci cross the median plane of the medulla, forming the sensory decussation.

The sensory impulses coming from the spinal cord end in cell processing stations in the medulla, the gracile and cuneate nuclei. It is from these nuclei that fibres cross to opposite sides and ascend in the medial lemnisci, which terminate in the thalamus. The lemnisci form one link, or relay, in the main sensory tract to the cortex.

The olive

Immediately lateral to the pyramidal tract on the anterior aspect of the medulla is an oval swelling, the olive. The olive lies over a folded lamina of gray matter in the substance of the medulla; this is the nucleus of the inferior olive. It is connected with the opposite cerebellar hemisphere by fibres that cross the middle line and reach the cerebellum through the inferior cerebellar peduncle. The nuclei from which the motor fibres of the third through the 12th cranial nerves originate and those in which the sensory fibres terminate lie in the reticular formation of the medulla and pons. Like the spinal nerves, they are connected by nerve tracts with the opposite hemisphere (for a description of cranial and spinal nerves, see below *The peripheral nervous system*).

Pons. The pons is located between the midbrain and the medulla oblongata. Its posterior surface forms the floor of the upper half of the fourth ventricle. The posterior region of the pons, adjacent to the ventricular surface, is called the tegmentum, while the anterior region is the basilar portion. The tegmentum is part of a continuous structure of the same name extending rostrally (to the front) and caudally (to the rear) to form much of the midbrain and medulla. The basilar portion extends rostrally, as the crura cerebri of the midbrain, and caudally, as the pyramidal tracts of the medulla.

Tegmentum. In common with the tegmentum of the midbrain and the medulla, the tegmentum of the pons contains nuclei of origin (motor) and of termination (sensory) of some cranial nerves, the tracts of ascending sensory pathways, some descending motor pathways, and the reticular formation. The nuclei of the cranial nerves include those of the fifth, sixth, seventh, and eighth cranial nerves. The ascending sensory pathways include the spinothalamic tract (pain and temperature from the body), trigeminothalamic tracts (pain, temperature, and touch from the head), medial lemniscus (touch from the body), the medial longitudinal fasciculus (vestibular influences to the nuclei innervating the eye muscles and correlating the position of the head in space to the direction of gaze), and the lateral lemniscus (hearing). The descending motor pathways include the corticobulbar fibres, which influence the motor nuclei of the cranial nerves, and the fibres of the extrapyramidal system (see below *The spinal cord: Gray matter*). The reticular formation is an intricate neuronal network organized into complex ascending pathways, descending pathways, and local neuronal circuits.

Basilar portion. The basilar portion of the pons includes: (1) the fibres of the pyramidal tracts, which course longitudinally from the crura of the midbrain, located rostrally, to the pyramids of the medulla; and (2) the fibres of the corticopontine tracts, pontine nuclei, and fibres of the pontocerebellar tracts. The latter group conveys information from the cerebral cortex to the cerebellum. The corticopontine tracts originate in the cerebral cortex and form synapses with pontine nuclei on the same side of the body. From the pontine nuclei, the fibres of the pontocerebellar tracts cross over in the basilar portion of the pons, course through the middle cerebellar peduncle, and terminate in the cerebellum of the opposite side.

Cerebellum. The cerebellum consists of a medial part, known as the vermis, and two lateral hemispheres. Each hemisphere is connected with the brain stem by three paired stemlike peduncles: (1) the inferior cerebellar peduncle to the medulla, (2) the middle cerebellar peduncle, and (3) the superior cerebellar peduncle. The last joins the cerebellum to the midbrain and conveys mostly motor fibres, one bundle leaving the cerebellum and ascending to the contralateral red nucleus and to the contralateral thalamus, and another bundle going finally to the reticular formation of the medulla oblongata.

Original preparation by J. Klingler, Anatomical Museum, Basel, Switz.

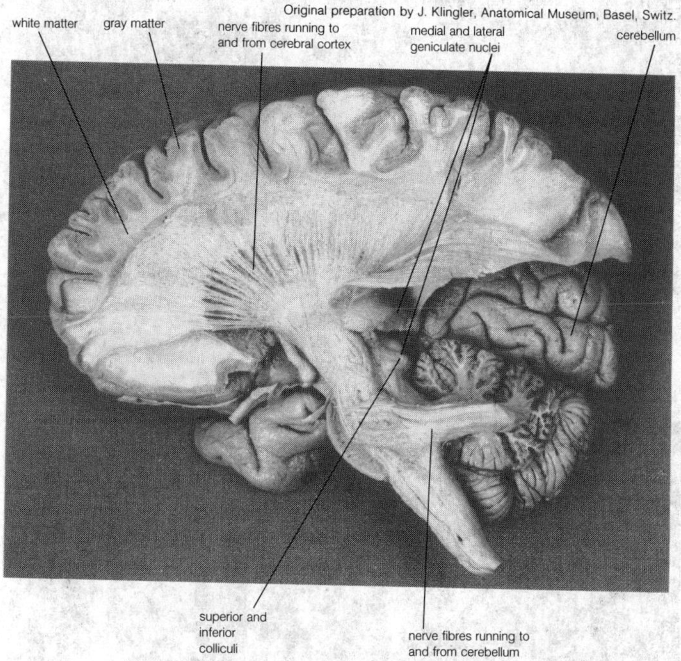

Figure 18: Photograph of a dissection of the right cerebral hemisphere, showing nerves entering and leaving the cerebellum and cerebral cortex.

Relaying of nerve impulses in the cerebellum

The cerebellum receives impulses from the equilibratory organ in the middle ear, from muscle spindles, from the exteroceptors of the skin, from the eye, and from the ear (acoustic organ), as well as from the cerebral cortex. These impulses reach the gray matter of the cortex of the cerebellum and pass from there to the deep cerebellar nuclei. From these nuclei a relay of fibres ascends to the opposite red nucleus, thalamus, and brain-stem reticular formation (see below).

The superficial surface of the cerebellum differs from that of the cerebral hemispheres. In place of convolutions, the vermis and hemispheres of the cerebellum are crossed by numerous transverse fissures, which mark off a series of folds, or folia. The general arrangement of these is seen in a median section through the vermis, which presents a branched appearance called the arbor vitae. The surface of the cerebellar hemispheres and central lobe is subdivided into lobes and lobules by deep fissures.

The cortex of the cerebellum consists of a superficial stratum, the molecular layer; an intermediate layer, which contains the cell bodies of branched Purkinje cells; and an inner deep stratum, the granular layer, which rests upon the central white matter. The white matter is formed by myelinated nerve fibres, which course to and from the gray matter.

Purkinje cells

The Purkinje cells are large and have extensive connections. The cell bodies are pear-shaped and arranged in a single layer. From the outer end of each cell, dendrites branch out in the molecular layer. The branching takes place chiefly in a plane at right angles to the longitudinal axis of the folium in which the cell lies. The dendrites of the Purkinje cells are intersected at right angles by parallel fibres that run in the direction of the folium. These fibres are derived from axons of the granule cells in the inner stratum of the cortex, which pass outward and divide in the molecular layer in a T-shaped manner into right and left branches. The bodies of the Purkinje cells, moreover, are surrounded by a network of fibres that originate from basket cells in the molecular layer, and the Purkinje dendrites are also accompanied by delicate climbing afferent nerve fibres from the white matter.

Although areas of the cerebellar cortex cannot be mapped out by response of particular groups of muscles to electrical stimulation, it is possible on morphological grounds, by means of experimental work and by the tracing of tracts of nerve fibres entering the cerebellum, to locate areas of the cortex according to the fibres that they receive from the particular parts. The cerebellum, relatively large in humans, weighs more than the entire spinal cord. It is the great modulator subserving the coordination of groups of muscles. The cerebellum smooths out the actions of these groups by delicately regulating and grading muscle tensions. Cerebellar reactions are unconscious; destruction of the cerebellum entails no loss of sensation or intelligence, although cerebellar disturbance may cause some misperception of sensations produced in the body and poor muscular coordination.

The midbrain. The midbrain (mesencephalon) connects the pons and cerebellum with the cerebrum. It is traversed by the cerebral aqueduct of Sylvius. The part that lies above the aqueduct, called the roof plate or tectum, is subdivided into four rounded swellings. These are the colliculi or corpora quadrigemina. The upper pair of these bodies receive nerve fibres from the retina, which reach them through the optic tracts and from the medial lemniscus. They are an important centre in lower mammals but are of less importance in primates. The lower pair serve as a cell station in the path of the auditory impulses, which commence in the cochlea and terminate in the cerebral cortex of the temporal lobe. The gray matter in the roof of the aqueduct receives an important tract of nerve fibres from the spinal cord, known as the spinotectal tract.

Spinothalamic tract

A similar bundle, the spinothalamic tract, also traverses the midbrain. This pathway conveys impulses concerned with the sensations of pain, heat, cold, and certain aspects of touch (including the tickling sensation) to the receptive centres in the thalamus. Impulses concerned with other aspects of touch and with sense of position ascend in the posterior columns of the spinal cord to the gracile and cuneate nuclei. From these a relay of nerve fibres ascends through the medulla oblongata and, crossing in this to the opposite side of the brain, passes as the medial lemniscus through the pons and midbrain to the thalamus. From the thalamus another relay of fibres carries the sensory impulses to the cerebral cortex of the brain.

The most ventral part of the midbrain forms the crura cerebri. These two diverging limbs are composed of nerve fibres coursing from the cerebral cortex to the spinal cord (pyramidal tract) and pons (corticopontine fibres). Behind the crura is a lamina of pigmented nerve cells called the substantia nigra, which separates the pes pedunculi from the tegmentum. This is traversed by decussating fibres, the greater number being the cerebellar fibres already mentioned as issuing from the dentate nucleus, traveling by the superior cerebellar peduncle to the midbrain and then crossing to the red nucleus of the opposite side and to the thalamus.

The red nucleus, so called from its appearance in the freshly cut brain, lies close to the midline of the midbrain. It has connections with systems concerned with movement, but its functions in humans are little known. It appears to be of greater importance in other mammals, notably the cat.

The reticular formation is a dense network of neurons and their processes extending from the medulla to the midbrain, lying predominantly centrally and only occasionally forming clearly recognizable groups of cells or nuclei. This network has extensive connections with the thalamus and thence to large areas of the cerebral cortex. One important function is an alerting effect on the cortex related to maintaining consciousness. Descending reticulospinal pathways also have important functions concerned with movement and with the regulation of sensory inflow to the spinal cord.

In the tegmental part of the midbrain are also situated the longitudinal association tracts, known as the dorsal and medial longitudinal fasciculi, and the nuclei and roots of origin of the third and fourth cranial nerves and part of the fifth in the gray matter surrounding the cerebral aqueduct of Sylvius.

Cerebral hemispheres. Two of the most distinctive features of the human brain are the large size of the cerebral hemispheres and the high degree of specialization in the microscopic structure of the cerebral cortex. The cerebral hemispheres comprise the cerebral cortex, the lateral ventricles, white matter deep to the cerebral cortex, and the basal ganglia.

Division into lobes. The surface of each hemisphere is subdivided, for descriptive purposes, into a number of lobes: the frontal, temporal, parietal, occipital, and, sometimes, limbic. Certain fissures and lines are arbitrarily employed for demarcating the boundaries of these areas, but the subdivision is largely a matter of convenience. The central sulcus, also called the fissure of Rolando, separates the frontal from the parietal lobe. The lateral sulcus, or fissure of Sylvius, marks off the temporal lobe from the parietal and frontal lobes. On the median surface (the inner surface of each hemisphere) are the callosomarginal and parieto-occipital sulci, which limit the frontal, limbic, parietal, and occipital lobes.

Motor and sensory areas

The fissure of Rolando marks the posterior limit of the important motor area of the cortex. The cortex of the occipital lobe, which surrounds the posterior part of the calcarine sulcus, is the visuosensory area for reception of visual impulses from the retina. The visuosensory area is surrounded by a zone that extends onto the outer aspect of the occipital lobe, termed the visuopsychic area.

The superior and transverse gyri of the temporal lobe are concerned with hearing. The auditory pathway is complex. Before reaching the cortex, impulses entering the brain via the cochlear nerve relay in cochlear nuclei in the pons, in the inferior olive (also in the pons), in the inferior colliculus on the posterior aspect of the midbrain, and in the medial geniculate body in the thalamus.

The front part of the hippocampal gyrus, with its hook-like end, the uncus, is the higher cortical centre for the sense of smell. This is the most primitive of the special senses. It is closely associated with the sense of taste and is more highly developed in many other vertebrate animals than in humans. That part of the brain concerned with the sense of smell and with certain complex emotional responses is called the limbic lobe (for more detailed discussion of the limbic system, see below *The autonomic nervous system*). There is also a large area behind the central sulcus that extends forward onto the motor area. This is the cutaneous sensory, or tactile, area.

The areas of cerebral cortex lying between the special and cutaneous sensory areas are believed to function as association centres between the different senses. The region in front of the motor cortex, called the premotor cortex, is connected by association fibres with all the various sensory and motor areas and, more especially, with that part of the adjacent motor area that is concerned with the movements of the eyes. In front of the premotor cortex is the prefrontal cortex, which is somehow involved with such qualities as disposition, outlook on life, drive, personality, planning for the future, and the control of activities along ethical standards. If the upper and lower lips of the fissure of Sylvius are separated, a triangular area of submerged cortex that is called the insula or island of Reil will be exposed.

Cerebral cortex. The cut surface of a transverse section of the hemisphere shows a rim of gray matter below the surface. This is the cerebral cortex, the gray colour of which is due to dense arrays of neuronal cell bodies. Much of each hemisphere is made up of white matter, consisting of myelinated nerve fibres passing to and from the cortex and narrowing to a comparatively small band, the internal capsule, which connects the cortex with lower regions of the central nervous system.

The cerebral cortex is composed of nerve cells, nerve fibres, blood vessels, and neuroglial cells. It exhibits a definite stratification into six layers of nerve cells and nerve fibres. In sections of fresh brain, the main strata and various zones are easily recognizable by the unaided eye and correspond closely with those revealed by microscopic preparations.

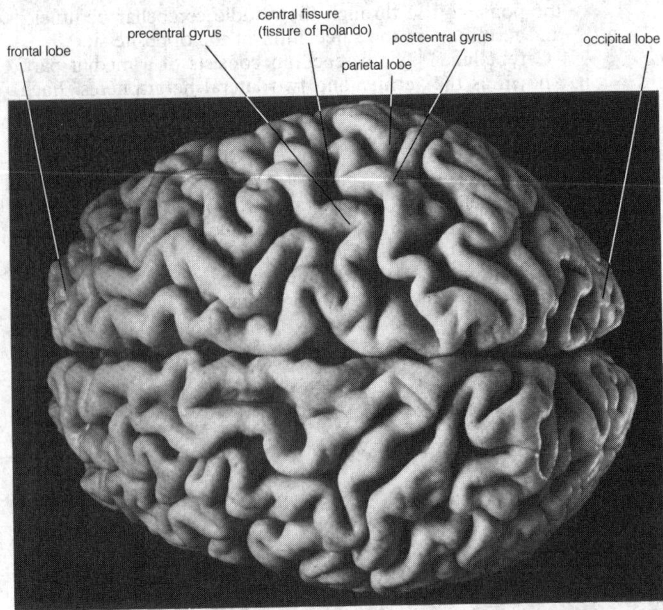

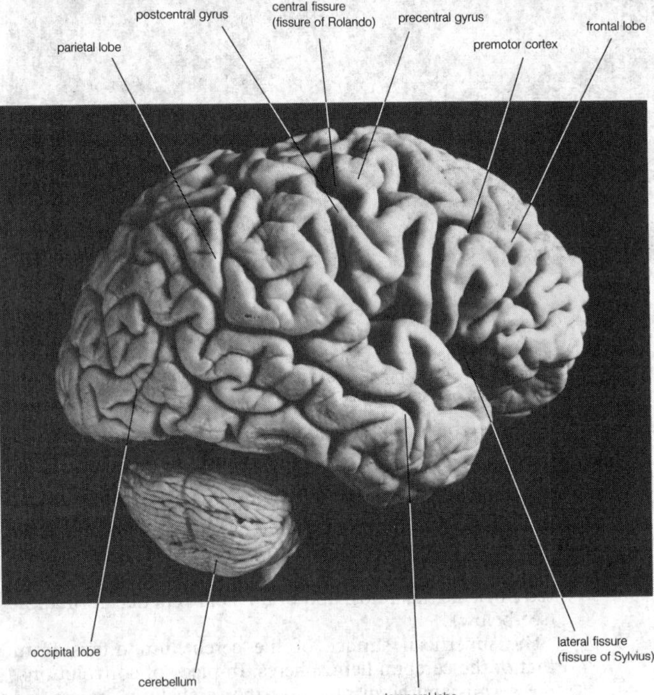

Figure 19: (Top) The upper surface and (bottom) right side of the cerebral hemispheres.

From N. Gluhbegovic and T.H. Williams, *The Human Brain: A Photographic Guide* (1980), J.B. Lippincott Co./Harper & Row

Functional organization of the cortex

Although the cerebral cortex is conventionally described as being organized into layers oriented parallel to the surface of the cortex, the basic functional unit is now conceived as being a physiologically defined vertical column extending from the cortical surface to the white matter. These columns are composed of 50,000 to 100,000 neurons densely bundled around a central afferent fibre. The dendrites of the neurons remain within the columns, so that there is a dense interconnection within each column but less connection between adjacent columns. These columns function as: (1) the terminal regions for input fibres that originate in the thalamus and other cortical columns of the same and opposite cerebral hemispheres, and (2) the origins of output fibres that terminate in other cortical areas of the same and opposite cerebral hemispheres and in neural centres in the basal ganglia, thalamus, pons, medulla oblongata, and spinal cord.

The neurons of the cerebral cortex include: (1) pyramidal cells (cell body in the shape of a pyramid) with axons that extend from the column to the white matter as the output fibres just noted and (2) small cells with short axons that interact with pyramidal cells and other small cells in the immediate vicinity. The axons of the pyramidal cells leave the column of origin, join the white matter, and terminate in other columns by reentering the cortex, or the gray matter, of other regions of the brain and spinal cord. The axons of the small neurons are integrated into intracortical neuronal circuits that tend to sustain the vertical columnar organization. The complex synaptic connectivity among these small neurons and the pyramidal neurons is basic to the intricate activity within the cortex. The vast number of synapses is made possible by the presence of spines on the dendrites of many neurons, giving the cells the appearance of the spiny branches of a gorse bush. Synapses are formed all over the spines, so that the receptive area on any one neuron is enormous. The small neurons are therefore considered to be the "structural expression" of the delicacy of the function of the human brain.

(R.J.Gl./G.v.B./Ed.)

Basal ganglia. Deep inside the hemispheres are further masses of gray matter, the basal ganglia. The basal ganglia include the caudate and lenticular nuclei; the subthalamic nucleus of the thalamus and the substantia nigra of the midbrain are often included. The lenticular nucleus is divided into the putamen and the globus pallidus. The caudate nucleus and putamen are called the striatum, or neostriatum, while the globus pallidus is also called the paleostriatum or pallidum. The caudate and lenticular nuclei form the corpus striatum.

The globus pallidus is so called because of its relatively pale appearance compared with the other basal ganglia and because of its different composition, consisting of comparatively large, widely spaced neurons. It is a primitive part of the brain. The deepest-lying of the basal ganglia, it is separated from the lateral nucleus of the thalamus by the internal capsule, containing at this point the fibres of the pyramidal (corticospinal) tract.

The basal ganglia are integrated through neural connections with the cerebral cortex and thalamus. They have several complex functions, including involvement with the regulation of stereotyped movements basic to the performance of volitional movements.

Thalamus and hypothalamus. The thalamus is strategically located to receive influences from a variety of sources and to send information to the cerebral cortex. In brief, the massive complex of neural processing centres receives input from all sensory systems, with the exception of the olfactory system, and from the basal ganglia, brain stem, and cerebellum, and sends neural influences to the cerebral cortex. The thalamus has a role in the conscious appreciation of sensation; many of the crude sensory modalities (pain, touch, and, possibly, sound detection) are brought to consciousness in this structure. A portion of the thalamus, called the subthalamus, is functionally integrated with the basal ganglia.

The hypothalamus is a small structure, weighing four grams, that is involved with numerous functional activities associated with the autonomic nervous system (see below *The autonomic nervous system*).

The brain stem. The brain stem comprises the midbrain, the pons, and the medulla oblongata. The thalamus and hypothalamus are often included within the brain stem. The midbrain, thalamus, and hypothalamus are referred to as the upper brain stem and the pons and medulla as the lower brain stem. The brain stem is dealt with separately, as a unit, because of its special roles in reflexes, sensory and motor conduction, the regulation of the internal environment of the body, and regulation, or control, of the rest of the nervous system.

When the embryonic central nervous system undergoes differentiation at its anterior end into the brain, the original part of the differentiating brain becomes the brain stem. The stem, from its lateral and dorsal aspects, gives off "buds" that develop into the cerebral hemispheres and cerebellum. These overgrow and cover their stalk, so that, when the adult brain is removed from the cranium, nothing of its initial component is seen until, viewed from the underside, a lumpy column about as large as a human thumb from tip to wrist, and not greatly different in shape, can be distinguished as the brain stem.

Intermediate position of the brain stem

The brain stem is interposed between and connected with the more differentiated parts of the brain on the one hand and the spinal cord on the other, and it bears certain similarities to each of these structures. By means of its entering and exiting nerves, the spinal cord is concerned largely with gathering sensory impressions from and effecting motor behaviour to what were originally serially arranged segments of skin or muscles of the body. These are the spinal nerves of the peripheral nervous system. Also, the skin of the head, the muscles around the nasal, oral, and pharyngeal cavities, and specialized sensory receptors of the ear, eye, and nose are innervated by nerves connecting with the brain stem. These nerves of the head are collectively designated as cranial. (See below *The peripheral nervous system.*)

Ascending pathways from the spinal cord continue upward through the brain stem and are joined there by others conveying messages to be relayed to the cerebellum or to the cerebral hemispheres. Similarly, these latter structures descend into the brain stem, in part to terminate in synapses with cranial nerves, in part to continue uninterruptedly through it toward motor neurons in the spinal cord, and in part to reach these cranial or spinal outflows indirectly after relay by collections of brain-stem neurons. The brain stem therefore resembles the spinal cord, of which it is the rostral continuation, both in supplying nerves to the periphery and in accommodating ascending pathways to, and existing connections from, the cerebral hemispheres and cerebellum.

The development called encephalization, which carried the cerebellum and, to a great degree, the cerebral hemispheres to such heights of structural complexity and functional achievement, led the brain stem also to assume a dominating and integrating role over lower-lying outflows from the nervous system—in general, those innervating the viscera or skeletal structures related to viscera—which preserve the internal environment of the body in a state of optimum activity. In addition, and less clearly perceived, this development also led the brain stem to assume the role of maintaining a state of optimum activity within the interior of the central nervous system itself, both in the spinal cord below it and in the cerebral hemispheres above.

(H.W.M./Ed.)

THE SPINAL CORD

The spinal cord in humans is the elongated cylindrical portion of the central nervous system located in the upper two-thirds of the vertebral canal of the vertebral column. As with the brain, the spinal cord of humans closely resembles that of other higher animals, particularly the primates.

The spinal cord of an adult is about 45 centimetres (18 inches) long. It extends from just above the first cervical vertebra (the atlas) at the base of the skull to the level of the first or second lumbar vertebra, where it is known as the conus medullaris. Small groups of nerve fibres attached to the spinal cord unite to form segmental series of dorsal and ventral roots. One dorsal root and one ventral root combine in the region of an opening, the intervertebral foramen, between two vertebrae to form one of the 31 pairs of spinal nerves. The dorsal roots contain the nerve fibres that transmit sensory impulses from the body to the spinal cord, whereas the ventral roots are composed of the motor fibres that transmit nerve impulses from the cord to the muscles and glands.

Growth of the spinal cord

The spinal cord does not occupy the entire length of the vertebral canal because the vertebral column continues to grow after the cord has reached its full length. During early fetal development the spinal cord extends to the lower sacrum, but after the fourth month of fetal life the vertebral column elongates more rapidly than the spinal cord. At birth the conus medullaris lies opposite the third lumbar vertebra, and in the adult it reaches the lower border of the first lumbar vertebra. Because the spinal cord is attached to the brain stem above, there is a progressive lengthening downward of the spinal roots from their attachments to the spinal cord to their entrance into the intervertebral foramina. This lengthening of spinal roots is much greater in the lumbar and sacral regions than in the cervical region.

Each thoracic, lumbar, sacral, and coccygeal spinal nerve is named from the vertebra that is just above its exit from the vertebral column. Since there are 12 thoracic vertebrae, five lumbar vertebrae, five fused sacral vertebrae, and one (to three) vestigial coccygeal vertebra, there are 12 pairs of thoracic, five pairs of lumbar, five pairs of sacral, and one pair of coccygeal spinal nerves.

There are eight pairs of cervical nerves, although only seven cervical vertebrae, because, in addition to a pair of nerves passing below each cervical vertebra, one exists above the first cervical vertebra. The long roots of the lower third of the vertebral canal below the conus medullaris form a structure called the cauda equina ("horse's tail"). (For detailed description of the spinal nerves, see below *The peripheral nervous system.*)

Meninges. The cord is enveloped by three coverings, the meninges. From within outward, as with the brain, they are the pia mater, arachnoid, and dura mater. These meninges are continuous with comparable layers surrounding the brain. The pia mater is closely attached to the spinal cord and contains the many blood vessels that supply the cord. The pia mater continues as a strand in the middle of the cauda equina known as the filum terminale, which extends to the coccyx.

Cerebrospinal fluid

The arachnoid layer is connected to the pia mater by delicate strands. The region between the two layers is the subarachnoid space, which is filled with the cerebrospinal fluid. Formed mainly in the brain, the fluid cushions the spinal cord. In the region below the conus medullaris, the arachnoid forms a cul-de-sac—containing the cauda equina and cerebrospinal fluid—into which lumbar puncture needles may be inserted to withdraw cerebrospinal fluid for diagnostic examination and to inject spinal anesthetics. This procedure avoids damage to the spinal cord.

The outer dura mater is a tough fibrous tissue surrounding the cord and continuous with the sheaths of the spinal roots and spinal nerves. It extends caudally to the lower sacral region, where it is reduced to a strand, the filum durae matris spinalis, attached to the coccyx. A thin subdural space is located between the dura mater and the arachnoid. Between the dura mater and the vertebral column is the epidural space, which contains many blood vessels, especially veins, and fat. A hypodermic needle may be inserted into this space in the lower sacral region for the injection of certain anesthetics (caudal anesthesia).

Cervical and lumbosacral enlargements. The spinal cord has two enlargements: the cervical enlargement and the lumbosacral enlargement. These regions are large because these segments are involved in the innervation of the upper and lower extremities, respectively. The fifth through eighth cervical segments and the first thoracic segment compose the cervical enlargement. The spinal nerves arising from the cervical enlargement form the brachial plexus.

Cross section. In cross section the spinal cord consists of an H-shaped gray matter surrounded by white matter (Figure 20). The gray matter is made up of somata, or nerve cell bodies, and nerve fibres that are oriented in the cross-sectional plane as they enter and leave the gray matter from the white matter and spinal roots. The white matter consists of nerve fibres that are oriented parallel to the long axis of the spinal cord. These fibres ascend to and descend from the brain and other levels of the spinal cord. The whiteness is caused by the fatty myelin sheath that surrounds many of the fibres. Neuroglial cells are scattered throughout both the gray and the white matter.

Dorsal and ventral horns

The arms of the H that extend dorsally (toward the back of the body) are called dorsal or sensory horns, while the ventrally directed arms (those directed toward the front) are called ventral or motor horns. The crossbar of the H is the gray commissure and the intermediate gray. In the middle of the gray commissure is the small central canal, which is continuous with the ventricles of the brain.

The gray matter is subdivided into nine layers, or laminae, based on distinctive appearances when examined under the microscope. Laminae I to VI constitute the dorsal horn of the gray matter. Many fibres entering the spinal cord in the spinal sensory roots form synapses there. In laminae I and II these are thin, unmyelinated fibres concerned with pain sensation. Fibres terminating in laminae III and IV are larger, myelinated fibres and are also concerned with harmful stimuli. The fibre types in laminae V and VI are mixed. Lamina IX contains large lower motor neurons with axons that leave via the ventral motor roots to supply the muscles. The axons of many neurons from all regions of the spinal gray matter remain within the spinal cord, forming essential connections; these are called propriospinal fibres.

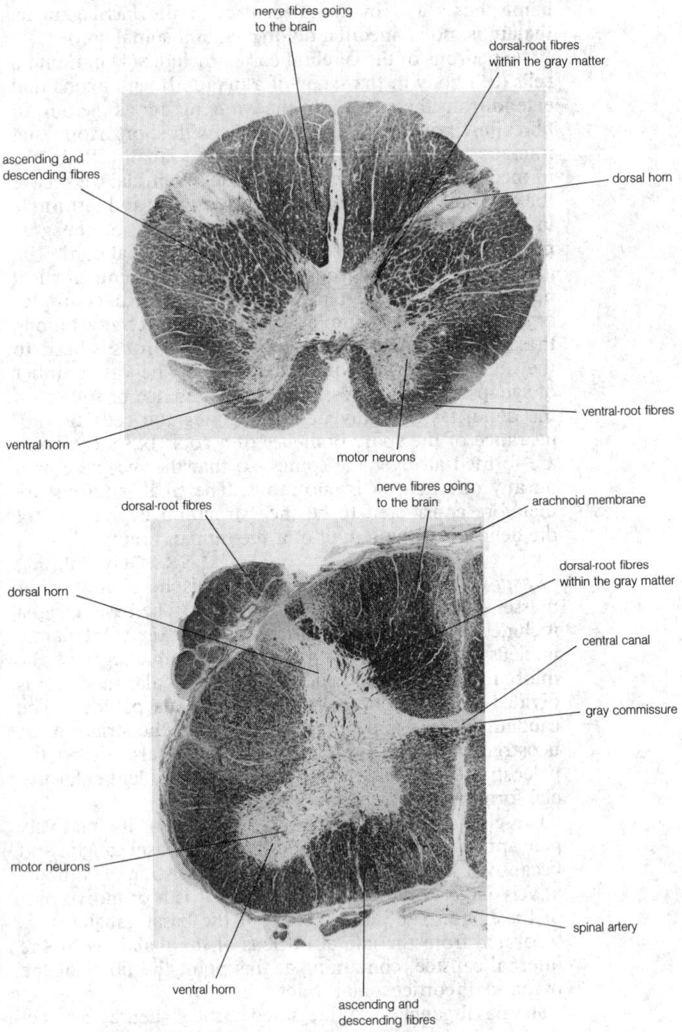

The white matter is subdivided into three columns: the dorsal column, between the dorsal horns; the ventral column, between the ventral horns; and the lateral columns, at the sides of the gray matter.

Gray matter. *Reflex arc.* The functional anatomy of the spinal cord may be visualized by describing the orientation of the nerve cells of the spinal reflex arcs. The withdrawal of the hand upon touching a hot stove before it is felt is an example of a spinal reflex. The heat stimulates specific receptors in the hand. The resulting impulses are transmitted in the axons of sensory neurons through the peripheral nerves and dorsal roots into the dorsal horn. Each sensory neuron has its soma in a dorsal-root ganglion. Thus, each neuron is a unit structure extending from its peripheral ending in the hand to its termination in the gray matter of the spinal cord.

Figure 20: Photographs of cross sections of the spinal cord, with the white matter stained dark and the gray matter bleached white. (Top) From the cervical region; (bottom) half-section from the lumbar region.

Marion C. Smith

In the dorsal horn the nerve fibres form synapses with one or more other neurons. These second cells in the arc are called interneurons; each has its soma in the gray matter. Some interneurons send axons into the ventral horn and form synapses with the motor neurons whose somata are in this horn. The axons of the motor neurons reach the voluntary muscles via the ventral roots and peripheral nerves. In short, an exteroceptive stimulus transmitted by a nerve goes to the spinal cord via a dorsal root into the gray matter, then to an interneuron, and finally to the motor neuron and the voluntary muscle via the ventral root and the peripheral nerve. This is known as a three-neuron reflex. If the interneuron is not involved, only two cells are in the series, and it is a two-neuron reflex. In the knee-jerk reflex, for example, the sensory cells synapse directly with the motor neurons in the gray matter; it is, therefore, a two-neuron reflex.

Two- and three-neuron reflexes

Complex reflexes. A single interneuron may cross over from the dorsal horn of one side to the ventral horn of the opposite side and synapse with motor neurons. This is one means of coordinating one side with the other. An intersegmental reflex is a mechanism relaying impulses to higher and lower spinal cord levels to coordinate large areas of the body. The fibres of such interneurons leave the gray matter and go up, down, or in both directions (dividing into two or more branches) to other spinal levels in that part of the white matter called the fasciculus proprius and then re-enter the gray matter to synapse with motor neurons.

For discussion of the role of the reflex arc in muscular movement, see below *Functions of the human nervous system: Reflex actions* and *Movement.*

White matter. The white matter of the spinal cord contains nerve fibres that transmit most of the nerve impulses from the body to the brain and from the brain to the body. Microscopic examination of the white matter does not give visible evidence of functional subdivisions. On the basis of numerous experimental data, however, and examinations of spinal cords from persons with spinal injuries, the white matter can be partitioned into functional regions called tracts or pathways. A tract, or fasciculus, is a collection of nerve fibres having the same origin, function, and termination. Those fibres transmitting impulses toward the brain form sensory, or ascending, tracts; those transmitting impulses from the brain form motor, or descending, tracts.

Pathways of sensation. Impulses concerned with sensations of position, movement, pressure, vibration, and certain aspects of touch are conveyed in the dorsal columns of the white matter. Vibration sense is frequently tested by applying a vibrating tuning fork to a bony prominence. The other sensations are essential for effective use of the limbs and maintenance of posture, as well as for the ability to recognize objects by touch (stereognosis) and the ability to distinguish a single touch stimulus from two applied simultaneously and close together.

These senses are transmitted by fibres that pass from the peripheral nerves and dorsal roots into the dorsal horn of the spinal cord. These fibres, with their somata in the dorsal-root ganglia, have several branches in the gray matter. The shorter branches (collateral fibres) are utilized in the spinal reflex arcs, while the main axon continues into the dorsal column and ascends to the lower medulla oblongata of the brain. Two interesting features are that (1) a fibre in the dorsal column is a part of the same neuron stimulated in the body, and (2) this fibre ascends on the same side of the spinal cord as it enters; *i.e.,* it does not cross the midline of the cord.

Extent of sensory nerve fibres

As a consequence, the sense of position of the toes, for example, is carried by neurons that extend from the toes to the medulla oblongata without a synapse. In addition, injury to the dorsal column on one side of the cord will result in impairment of the proprioceptive senses (awareness of sensations produced by the body itself) on the same side of the body below the level of injury. Each half of the dorsal column is divided into a medial fasciculus gracilis and a fasciculus cuneatus. Impulses from the lower half of the body, including the lower extremities, are carried in the fasciculus gracilis, while those from the upper half of the body, including the upper extremities (but excluding the head) are carried in the lateral fasciculus cuneatus.

Some light-touch sensations (*e.g.,* gentle brushing of skin by cotton) are transmitted by fibres in the dorsal column. In the medulla the fibres of each half of the dorsal column synapse with neurons in the nucleus gracilis and nucleus cuneatus. The neurons of these nuclei cross over to the opposite side of the medulla, pass upward as the medial lemniscus, and terminate in the thalamus, from which they relay to the cerebral cortex.

Pain and temperature sensations are transmitted by another pathway. The fibres from the periphery, in common with other sensory fibres, enter the dorsal horn of the spinal cord, where their terminal branches establish reflex connections with other neurons. At the spinal level, at which the fibres enter the cord, they synapse with dorsal-horn neurons. Some of these cells are interneurons in the reflex arcs. Others are neurons with axons that cross the midline to the opposite side through the ventral white commissure (ventral to the gray commissure) to join the lateral spinothalamic tract in the lateral columns. This tract obtains more fibres as it ascends in the spinal cord, fibres being added at each spinal level. The spinothalamic tract's name is based on the fact that the fibres of the pathway originate in the dorsal horn of the spinal cord and terminate in the thalamus on the opposite side of the brain. Impulses from the thalamus are relayed to the cerebral cortex.

In addition to the light-touch fibres of the dorsal column noted above, some light-touch impulses take a different pathway. After entering the dorsal horn, the axons transmitting light touch synapse with neurons whose axons cross the midline to join the ventral spinothalamic tract in the ventral column.

The symptoms resulting from injury to the spinal cord are a consequence of the course of these pathways. If the right half of the spinal cord is cut at a midthoracic level, for example, conscious proprioception is lost on the right side of the body below the level of the lesion of the fasciculus gracilis (right abdomen and the right lower extremity). Pain and temperature sensations are lost on the left side of the body below the level of the lesion of the lateral spinothalamic tract. Because of the dual course of their fibres, light touch is diminished, but not necessarily lost, below the level of the lesion. Perception of sensations from regions above the cut is unimpaired.

Some unconscious proprioceptive impulses relay from the gray matter of the cord via the spinocerebellar tracts of the same and opposite sides and terminate in the cerebellum.

Visceral sensory impulses are transmitted in or in close proximity to the spinothalamic tracts.

Motor pathways. In the ventral horn of the gray matter are large motor neurons whose axons pass through the ventral roots to the spinal nerves. These neurons, which innervate the voluntary muscles, are called lower motor neurons; if they become nonfunctional, as in poliomyelitis, the muscles are deprived of their nervous stimulation and do not contract. These muscles then atrophy and do not respond to stimulation. This paralytic condition is known as a lower motor neuron paralysis.

Upper and lower motor neurons

The lower motor neurons are stimulated and influenced by neurons of the spinal reflex arcs and by the descending motor tracts of the white matter. These descending tracts from the brain may synapse directly with the motor neurons, but usually interneurons of the gray matter are interposed between the descending tracts and the lower motor neurons.

Collectively the descending motor tracts from the brain are known as upper motor neurons. Their somata are located in the brain, and their axons pass through the brain stem and white matter of the spinal cord before terminating in the gray matter of the spinal cord. Two major subdivisions of these motor tracts are recognized: the pyramidal tracts, which are phylogenetically recent, and the phylogenetically old extrapyramidal tracts.

The lateral pyramidal tract, or lateral corticospinal tract, arises in the cerebral cortex of the opposite side and crosses over just as its fibres enter the spinal cord (see above *The brain: Medulla oblongata*). The direct pyramidal tract, or ventral corticospinal tract, originates in the cerebral cortex and crosses over in the spinal cord.

The term extrapyramidal was coined to cover all neural systems concerned with movement and posture that do not involve the corticospinal, or pyramidal, tracts. The term retains its usefulness in a clinical context, when it is frequently used to refer to the basal ganglia and their connections.

The extrapyramidal tracts include (1) the vestibulospinal tract, which transmits impulses from the vestibular (balance) mechanisms of the inner ear; (2) the reticulospinal tracts, which arise from the medulla and pons; (3) the medial longitudinal fasciculus, a collection of fibres from several regions of the brain stem; and (4) the rubrospinal tract from the red nucleus in the midbrain.

It is not possible to distinguish with certainty the differing effects of interruption of these individual pathways. Classic upper motor neuron paralysis or weakness is attributed to impairment or loss of function of the pyramidal pathway at any point between the motor cortex and the spinal cord. In contrast to lower motor neuron paralysis (described above), loss of voluntary movement is accompanied by an increase of reflex activity in response to stretching of muscles. Here the reflexes are exaggerated; there is loss of voluntary motion; and the extremities become spastic. The condition, called spastic paralysis, results because the muscles are under control of a spinal cord that still mediates spinal reflex arcs but is deprived of its normal innervation from the brain. Spastic paralysis resulting from an injury of the spinal cord is observed on the same side of the body as the lesion.

Injury to motor tracts

The complexity of the nervous system may be illustrated by spinal reflex arcs innervating the voluntary muscles. In probably all muscles (since all muscles have not been investigated) there are small fibres arranged in bundles of two to eight fibres that receive their motor innervation from small neurons in the ventral horn and that are endowed with sensory fibres. These fibres go through the spinal ganglia, where their somata are situated, to the dorsal horn (lamina VI), where they make direct contact with the motor cells in the ventral horn. These motor neurons stimulate the voluntary muscles to contract. When the voluntary muscles contract sufficiently, the sensory endings in the tendons are stimulated to send impulses via sensory fibres through the dorsal root back to the spinal cord to inhibit the motor neurons of the ventral horn. In brief, the sensory endings in the muscle and tendon have a critical role in muscle activity (see below *Functions of the human nervous system: Movement*).

Autonomic nervous system. The autonomic nervous system is considered in detail below (see *The autonomic nervous system*). Briefly, it is concerned with the motor innervation of glands, blood vessels, and the viscera, and it has neurons in the gray matter. The nerve cells of the sympathetic division of the autonomic system have their somata in the lateral part of the intermediate gray, known as the intermediolateral cell column, of the thoracic and upper lumbar levels. Their axons leave the spinal cord through the ventral roots. The nerve cells of the spinal part of the parasympathetic division of the autonomic system have their somata scattered in the gray matter of the midsacral levels. Their axons leave the spinal cord through the ventral roots. The sympathetic nervous system assists the body in meeting emergencies and stress. This includes increasing the rate and force of the heartbeat, the dilation of the bronchial tubes of the lungs, and the inhibition of the motility and the secretory activity of the digestive system. The parasympathetic system contributes to the conservation of bodily energy. This includes decreasing the rate and force of the heartbeat, the constriction of the bronchial tubes, and the stimulation of the motility and secretory activity of the digestive system.

(C.S.S./C.R.N./Ed.)

The peripheral nervous system

The peripheral nervous system is made up of three parts: (1) the cranial nerves, (2) the spinal nerves, and (3) that part of the autonomic (involuntary) nervous system that is outside the brain and spinal cord. The cranial nerves arise from, or are attached to, the brain and enter the skull via openings in the bone, called foramina. These nerves are concerned with the special senses and with the innervation of structures in the head and neck. The spinal nerves, attached segmentally to all regions of the spinal cord, enter and leave the vertebral canal by intervertebral foramina (openings between the vertebrae). These nerves innervate the cutaneous surfaces and muscles of most of the body and the deep structures in the trunk and limbs. The autonomic nervous system is a system of nerve fibres and masses of nerve cells, called ganglia, arranged in trunks and plexuses; some fibres in this system pass peripherally with certain cranial and spinal nerves even though they subserve separate functions. (The autonomic nervous system is treated as a separate entity below; see *The autonomic nervous system.* For discussion of the anatomy of the brain and spinal cord, see above *The central nervous system.*)

The peripheral nervous system has the same essential structure as the central nervous system in that it consists of neurons surrounded by neuroglial cells. The most striking difference is that the cranial and spinal nerves are composed primarily of axons and dendrites invested by insulating myelin sheaths. (Axons carry impulses from a nerve cell body, or soma; dendrites, impulses to it.) Cells of the peripheral nervous system lie in spinal, cranial, and autonomic ganglia. Virtually all afferent fibres have their somata in spinal or cranial ganglia. Afferent fibres are those which transmit impulses from peripheral receptors into the central nervous system. They are also called sensory fibres. Autonomic ganglia, on the other hand, contain neurons that project fibres peripherally to smooth muscle, heart muscle, and glandular epithelium. These are called efferent fibres—that is, fibres that convey impulses from the central nervous system only to peripheral effector structures. Somatic efferent fibres emerging via spinal and cranial nerves arise from neurons within the spinal cord or brain stem. These fibres pass directly to striated, or voluntary, muscles. In a strict sense, they actually are extensions of the central nervous system, linking it with peripheral effectors. Autonomic ganglia also transmit visceral efferent impulses after receiving impulses from neurons located within the central nervous system. These neurons, referred to as preganglionic, synapse onto autonomic ganglion neurons, so that two neurons are involved in transmitting visceral efferent impulses to peripheral structures. They are: (1) a preganglionic fibre arising in the central nervous system and synapsing onto one or more autonomic ganglion cells, and (2) a postganglionic fibre arising from an autonomic ganglion and projecting an axon into the peripheral system.

Afferent and efferent fibres

Impulses, generated in receptors on body surfaces and within muscles, joints, tendons, and various viscera in response to external and internal stimuli, are conveyed by peripheral nerves to the brain and spinal cord. Receptors, in essence, constitute an elaborate set of transducers capable of converting physical and chemical stimuli into nerve impulses that are transmitted to the central nervous system. The central nervous system exerts its regulating and controlling influences upon striated muscle and viscera by impulses transmitted ultimately by peripheral nerves to effector structures. Virtually the entire input and output of the central nervous system is dependent upon the integrity of the peripheral nervous system. Conversely, the peripheral nervous system could not function as an isolated system.

CRANIAL NERVES

There are 12 pairs of cranial nerves that arise from, or are attached to, the brain. These symmetrically distributed nerves are concerned with the special senses and the innervation of muscles, glands, skin, and the mucous membranes in the head and neck. The vagus nerve is an exception in that it sends fibres to visceral structures in the thorax and abdomen (Figure 21).

The olfactory and optic nerves, referred to as the first and second cranial nerves, are not actually peripheral nerves but tracts belonging to the central nervous system.

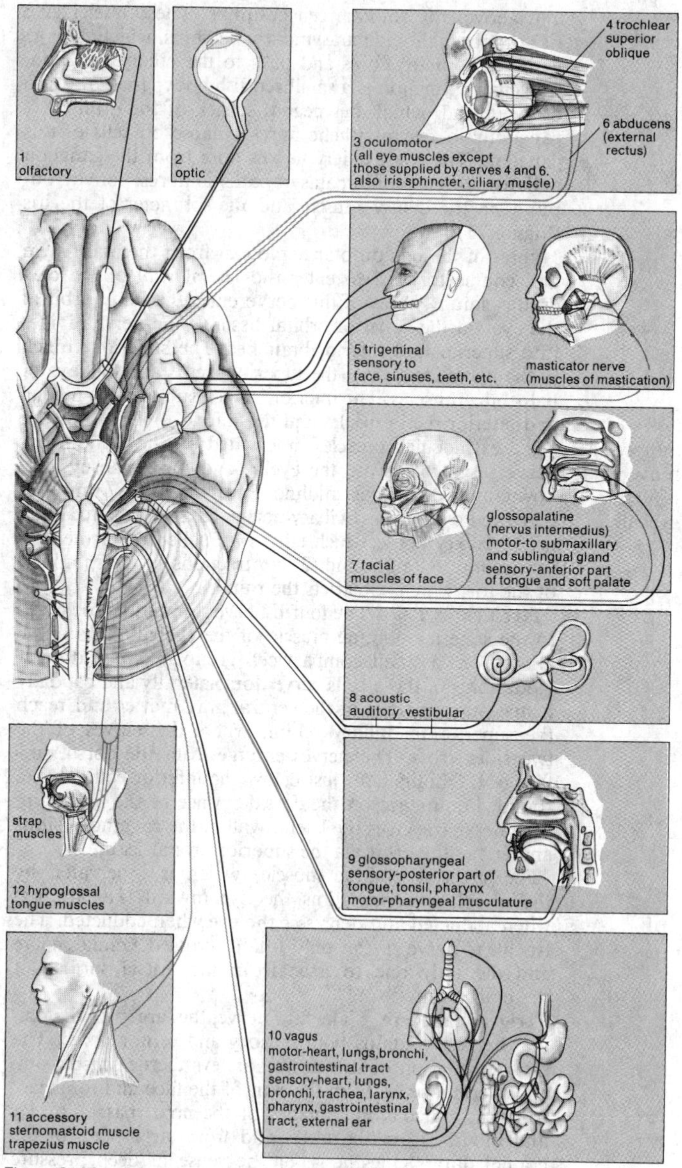

The third, fourth, sixth, and 12th cranial nerves are exclusively motor and innervate the extraocular muscles and the muscles of the tongue. The fifth, seventh, ninth, 10th, and 11th cranial nerves innervate muscles derived from the branchial arches. The fifth cranial nerve, the largest of all the true cranial nerves, consists of a large sensory component supplying the face and scalp and a smaller motor component that innervates the muscles of mastication. The seventh, ninth, and 10th cranial nerves contain motor, sensory, and autonomic components. The 11th cranial nerve consists of two parts: (1) a cranial part functionally associated with the vagus nerve, and (2) a spinal part which has a distinctive origin and a separate distribution. The vestibulocochlear nerve (eighth) consists of two parts: the vestibular division concerned with equilibrium and the cochlear division concerned with audition. The first (olfactory), second (optic), eighth (vestibulocochlear), and parts of the seventh, ninth, and 10th (taste) cranial nerves convey impulses concerned with the special senses.

Innervation of the special senses

While four functional components of a typical spinal nerve are recognized (*i.e.,* general somatic afferent, general visceral afferent, general somatic efferent, and general visceral efferent), three additional special functional components are represented in the cranial nerves. These additional functional components are designated as: (1) special somatic afferent fibres, (2) special visceral afferent fibres, and (3) special visceral efferent fibres. The special somatic afferent cranial nerves are the optic and the vestibulocochlear nerves. The olfactory nerve and components of the facial, glossopharyngeal, and vagus nerves concerned with taste are classified as special visceral afferent. Motor components of the branchiomeric cranial nerves (*i.e.,* trigeminal, facial, glossopharyngeal, vagus, and accessory) are classified as special visceral efferent because the muscles they innervate are derived from the branchial arches. The oculomotor, the trochlear, the abducens, and the hypoglossal cranial nerves give rise to somatic efferent fibres that innervate muscles derived from somites. These nerves are classified as general somatic efferent cranial nerves. Portions of the oculomotor, facial, glossopharyngeal, and vagus nerves contain preganglionic parasympathetic fibres. These components are designated as general visceral efferent fibres.

Olfactory nerve. The first nerve arises from olfactory neurons scattered among supporting cells in a yellowish-brown patch of specialized epithelium in the upper part of the nasal cavity. Approximately 20 fine, olfactory filaments, not sheathed in myelin, arise from these receptor cells and pass from the nasal cavity into the anterior cranial fossa through foramina in the ethmoid bone. Olfactory filaments, representing the central processes of bipolar cells in the olfactory epithelium, collectively constitute the olfactory nerve. These filaments form a plexus before terminating in the olfactory bulb, a flattened, ovoid body resting on the cribriform plate of the ethmoid bone. Axons of cells in the olfactory bulb form the olfactory tract, which enters the brain.

Optic nerve. The second cranial nerve consists of nerve fibres that arise from the ganglion cells of the retina. These fibres converge to form the optic disk, pierce the sclera, and combine to form the optic nerve. Optic nerve fibres are axons of connector neurons, which receive fibres from receptor neurons. For this reason the optic nerve is regarded as a central nervous system tract. The optic nerve is surrounded by the three meningeal membranes and a subarachnoid space, the space between the central and innermost layers of the membranes covering the brain and spinal cord. The optic nerves enter the optic canals and pass into the middle cranial fossa, where they form the optic chiasm, or chiasma. The optic chiasm, which lies at the base of the brain immediately in front of the tuber cinereum and infundibulum, is the site of a partial decussation, or crossover, of optic nerve fibres. In the optic chiasm, fibres arising from the nasal halves of the retinas cross, while those from the temporal halves of the retinas do not. Thus, each optic tract, the uninterrupted continuation of optic nerve fibres, consists of uncrossed fibres from the temporal half of the ipsilateral retina (*i.e.,* the retina on the same side) and crossed fibres from the

The optic chiasm

Figure 21: Cranial nerves.

After Frank H. Netter, M.D., *The CIBA Collection of Medical Illustrations;* copyright © 1957, 1972 by CIBA Pharmaceutical Company, Division of CIBA-GEIGY Corporation; reproduced with permission.

nasal half of the opposite retina. Fibres of the optic tract terminate upon cells of the lateral geniculate body, a relay nucleus of the thalamus.

Fibres of the optic nerve convey visual impulses from the retina, which are projected via relays to visual centres in the cerebral cortex. Light reflexes and reflexes resulting in lens accommodation also are mediated by the optic nerves and optic tracts.

Oculomotor nerve. The third cranial nerve is an efferent nerve that consists of two components: (1) general somatic efferent fibres, which innervate all the extraocular muscles except the lateral rectus (lateral straight muscle) and the superior oblique muscles of the eyeball, and (2) general visceral efferent fibres (preganglionic parasympathetic), which pass to the ciliary ganglion. The oculomotor nuclear complex is located ventral to the central gray matter of the midbrain. The complex consists of paired lateral somatic cell columns and an unpaired median cell group called the caudal central nucleus. The lateral somatic cell columns are composed of motor neurons, the fibres of which innervate the superior, medial, and inferior recti muscles and the inferior oblique muscle of the eyeball. The caudal central nucleus gives rise to crossed and uncrossed fibres that innervate the levator palpebrae, the muscle that raises the eyelid. The visceral nuclei of the oculomotor complex arise from small ovoid or spindle-shaped cells located rostral and dorsal to (*i.e.,* in front of and above) the somatic cell columns. These nuclei give rise to preganglionic parasympathetic fibres, which emerge with the somatic fibres and pass to the ciliary ganglion. The ciliary ganglion is a small reddish body, about the size of a pinhead, which lies near the back of the orbit. Preganglionic parasympathetic fibres synapse on cells of this ganglion. The short ciliary nerves arise from the ganglion and, as postganglionic parasympathetic fibres, convey impulses to the ciliary muscle and the sphincter of the iris (Figure 21).

Fibres of the oculomotor nerve exit from the brain stem and course forward to enter the lateral wall of the cavernous sinus. Fibres of this nerve enter the bony orbit of the eye via the superior orbital fissure. The nerve divides into superior and inferior branches. The superior branch of the nerve innervates the superior rectus and the levator palpebrae muscles. The inferior branch supplies the medial and inferior recti muscles and the inferior oblique muscle.

Supplying movement of the eyeball

The extraocular muscles innervated by the oculomotor nerve serve to elevate the eyelid and move the eye up, down, and toward the midline. Parasympathetic impulses conveyed by the short ciliary nerves cause: (1) contraction of the ciliary body, which effects a thickening of the lens for accommodation, and (2) contractions of the sphincter of the iris, which constricts the pupil.

Trochlear nerve. The fourth nerve supplies motor fibres to the superior oblique muscle of the eyeball. This nerve arises from a small compact cell group in the midbrain. Root fibres of these cells curve dorsolaterally and caudally in the outer margin of the central gray matter and reach the superior medullary velum, where the nerves of the two sides cross. The nerves emerge from the dorsal surface of the brain stem just below the inferior colliculus, a rounded eminence on the dorsal surface of the midbrain. This nerve traverses the lateral wall of the cavernous sinus and enters the orbit via the superior orbital fissure.

The superior oblique muscle, which is innervated by the trochlear nerve, turns the eye inward (*i.e.,* intorts) when abducted and depresses the eye when adducted. The trochlear nerve is the only totally crossed cranial nerve and the only one to issue from the dorsal surface of the brain stem.

Trigeminal nerve. The fifth nerve, the largest of the cranial nerves, contains both sensory and motor fibres. The sensory division of this nerve conveys tactile sense, pain, and thermal sense from the skin of the face and forehead, from the mucous membranes of the nose, nasal sinuses, and mouth, from the teeth, and from large parts of the cranial dura. Kinesthesia, or the sense of deep pressure and movement, is conveyed by branches of this nerve from the teeth, periodontium, hard palate, and receptors in the temporomandibular joint (articulation or "corner" of the jaw). Additional afferent fibres convey impulses from stretch receptors in the muscles of mastication.

Most, but not all, primary sensory neurons lie in the trigeminal ganglion situated in a dural cavity in the middle fossa of the skull. The ophthalmic, maxillary, and mandibular nerves arise from this ganglion.

Ophthalmic nerve. The ophthalmic nerve passes forward in the wall of the cavernous sinus and divides into three branches, which enter the orbit via the superior orbital fissure. These branches are the lacrimal, frontal, and nasociliary nerves. The lacrimal nerve supplies the lacrimal (tear) gland, the conjunctiva, and the skin of part of the upper eyelid. The frontal nerve passes through the orbital cavity and divides into two branches: the supraorbital nerve supplying the forehead and scalp and the supratrochlear nerve supplying part of the forehead and part of the adjacent upper eyelid. The nasociliary nerve enters the nasal cavity, where branches supply the mucous membrane, nasal septum, and certain areas of skin near the tip of the nose.

Maxillary nerve. The maxillary nerve leaves the middle fossa of the skull via the foramen rotundum and emerges on the face below the eye. The nerve gives off branches to the dura in the middle cranial fossa and to the mucous membranes of the soft and hard palate. The posterior and anterior superior alveolar nerves supply the teeth, gums, and the mucous membrane of the maxillary sinus. The infraorbital nerve, the terminal branch of the maxillary nerve, supplies the skin and conjunctiva of the lower eyelid, the skin on the side of the nose, the cheek, and the upper lip.

Innervation of the chewing muscles

Mandibular nerve. The mandibular nerve contains sensory fibres from the trigeminal ganglion and a smaller number of motor fibres, which leave the middle fossa of the skull via the foramen ovale. The motor fibres supply the muscles of mastication. The sensory fibres in the mandibular nerve give rise to the auriculotemporal, lingual, and inferior alveolar nerves. The auriculotemporal nerve gives branches to the mandibular joint, the parotid gland, the upper half of the auricle, and the skin and fascia of the temple and scalp. The lingual nerve supplies the mucous membrane over the sides and dorsum of the anterior two-thirds of the tongue, the floor of the mouth, and the mucosa overlying the sublingual gland. The inferior alveolar nerve distributes branches to the lower teeth, including the incisors. The mental nerve, a cutaneous terminal branch of the inferior alveolar nerve, distributes fibres to the skin of the chin and the lower lip.

Sensory fibres concerned with pain, touch, thermal sense, and some related to pressure sense represent central processes of cells in the trigeminal ganglion. These fibres are distributed to central nuclei that extend throughout most of the lower brain stem. Sensory fibres that convey impulses from stretch receptors in the muscles of mastication and pressure and kinesthetic sense from the teeth, periodontium, and joint capsules arise from neurons within the central nervous system. These cells form the mesencephalic nucleus of the trigeminal nerve, an anomalous group of primary sensory neurons within the brain stem. The motor fibres of the trigeminal nerve arise from typical motor cells in the pontine tegmentum, located in the dorsal part of the pons, one of the basic subdivisions of the brain stem.

Abducens nerve. The sixth cranial nerve contains general somatic efferent fibres that innervate the lateral rectus muscle of the eyeball. The nucleus of the abducens nerve forms a column of typical somatic motor cells in the floor of the fourth ventricle. Root fibres of the abducens nerve emerge from the brain stem at the caudal border of the pons, just lateral to the medullary pyramid. The nerve enters the orbit via the superior orbital fissure and supplies the lateral rectus muscle. This is the cranial nerve most frequently injured. Injury results in horizontal diplopia (double vision) on attempted gaze to the side of the paralyzed muscle.

Facial nerve. The seventh cranial nerve is a mixed nerve containing efferent and afferent components. The largest part of this nerve is the motor component that innervates the muscles of facial expression, the superficial muscles of the scalp and neck, and certain deep muscles. The above component of the facial nerve contains special visceral efferent fibres. The smaller part of the nerve, known as the intermediate (glossopalatine) nerve, contains afferent taste fibres and efferent parasympathetic fibres that convey impulses to the lacrimal gland and certain salivary glands. Cell bodies of afferent fibres are located in the geniculate ganglion.

The motor component of the facial nerve

The motor component of the facial nerve arises from a distinct collection of motor neurons in the ventrolateral pontine tegmentum. Fibres of the nerve emerge from the brain stem at the cerebellopontine angle, formed at the junction of pons, medulla oblongata, and cerebellum. The nerve emerges from the skull at the stylomastoid foramen. The mastoid process covers this region in the adult but not in the child. After entering the region of the parotid gland, the nerve breaks up into numerous branches that supply the facial muscles. Temporal branches of the nerve supply the frontalis muscle, the muscles around the eye, and the superior auricular muscles. The lower zygomatic branches supply lower facial muscles including those of the nose and upper lip. Buccal branches supply the buccinator muscle in the cheek, which serves to push food onto the occlusal surfaces of the teeth. A marginal mandibular branch passes between the lower lip and the chin and innervates the muscles surrounding the mouth and those that depress the corners of the mouth. Cervical branches of the facial nerve sweep downward behind the angle of the jaw and supply the platysma muscle, a thin, superficial muscle that extends from the chest over the sides of the neck to the lower jaw.

Special visceral afferent fibres arise from neurons in the geniculate ganglion located at the external genu (bend) of the facial nerve. These fibres convey taste sensation from the anterior two-thirds of the tongue and form part of the intermediate nerve. General visceral efferent fibres (preganglionic parasympathetic), arising in part from cells of the superior salivatory nucleus in the pons, pass to the lacrimal gland and to nasal and palatine glands. The continuation of the intermediate nerve distal to the geniculate ganglion is known as the chorda tympani nerve. This nerve, containing taste and parasympathetic fibres, separates from the facial nerve and becomes incorporated in the lingual nerve, a branch of the trigeminal nerve. Taste fibres remain intimately associated with the lingual nerve, while the preganglionic parasympathetic fibres synapse upon postganglionic neurons, which supply the submandibular (submaxillary) and sublingual salivary glands.

Supplying the organs of balance and hearing

Vestibulocochlear nerve. The eighth nerve is a special somatic afferent cranial nerve consisting of two functionally distinct parts. The vestibular nerve transmits impulses from the labyrinth, a specialized end organ concerned with static and kinetic equilibrium. The cochlear nerve transmits impulses from the cochlear apparatus, concerned with audition. Although these nerves run together from the internal auditory meatus to the cerebellopontine angle, where they enter the brain stem, they have distinctive peripheral receptors and central connections.

Vestibular nerve. The vestibular part of the inner ear consists of the three semicircular canals, the utricle, and the saccule. These receptors are concerned with equilibrium and orientation in three-dimensional space. The semicircular canals contain ridges (cristae ampullaris), which, covered by specialized neuroepithelial hair cells, constitute the vestibular receptor. The utricle and saccule each has a similar patch of sensory epithelium: the macula utriculi and macula sacculi. The maculae and cristae of the labyrinth are innervated by cells of the vestibular ganglion (ganglion of Scarpa), an aggregation of bipolar cells located in the internal auditory meatus. Peripheral processes of bipolar cells pass to the hair cells of the maculae and cristae. The central processes of these cells form the vestibular nerve, the fibres of which pass between the inferior cerebellar peduncle and the spinal trigeminal tract and are distributed to vestibular nuclei in the brain stem.

For discussion of the functions of the vestibular nerve, see below *Functions of the human nervous system: The vestibular system.*

Cochlear (*auditory*) *nerve.* The cochlea is a spiral bony tube with two and three-quarter coils arranged around a central pillar called the modiolus. Fibres of the cochlear nerve arise from bipolar neurons situated around the modiolus. The short peripheral processes of these cells end upon the hair cells of the organ of Corti, the auditory end organ. The central processes of these cells form the cochlear nerve, which enters the brain stem at the cerebellopontine angle.

Glossopharyngeal nerve. The ninth cranial nerve is a mixed nerve, the large afferent component of which supplies the pharynx, part of the tongue, and the carotid sinus and body. A smaller efferent component innervates the stylopharyngeus and middle pharyngeal constrictor muscles and sends preganglionic parasympathetic fibres to the otic ganglion.

Sensory components of the ninth cranial nerve

Sensory components of this nerve arise from two peripheral ganglia: the superior and the inferior. The superior ganglion is small, lies in the jugular foramen, and gives rise to general somatic afferent fibres that supply small cutaneous areas behind the ear; these fibres are carried in the auricular branch of the vagus nerve. The larger inferior ganglion of the glossopharyngeal nerve gives rise to both general and special (taste) visceral afferent fibres. General visceral afferent fibres convey tactile sense, pain, and thermal sense from the mucous membranes of the pharynx, the posterior third of the tongue, the tonsil, and the eustachian tube. A special sensory branch, the carotid sinus nerve, conveys afferent impulses from the carotid sinus and body. The carotid sinus is a dilatation of the common carotid artery and the root of the internal carotid branch. Elevation of carotid arterial pressure initiates afferent impulses in carotid sinus receptors, which are conveyed centrally to vagal nuclei and produce a slowing of the heart rate and a fall in blood pressure. The carotid body, near the branching of the common carotid artery, is a small neurovascular structure that is sensitive to changes in the hydrogen ion concentration of the blood.

Lingual branches of the glossopharyngeal nerve convey taste and general sensation from the posterior third of the tongue.

Preganglionic parasympathetic fibres in the ninth nerve arise from the inferior salivatory nucleus in the medulla oblongata and pass via the lesser petrosal nerve and the tympanic branch to the otic ganglion. Postganglionic parasympathetic fibres arising in the otic ganglion pass to the parotid gland and provide its secretomotor and vasomotor supply.

The glossopharyngeal nerve is attached to the lateral surface of the medulla oblongata by five or six rootlets. These rootlets lie caudal to those of the facial nerve and are in series with the rootlets of the vagus nerve.

Vagus nerve. The 10th cranial nerve is a mixed nerve containing a large number of widely distributed parasympathetic fibres (from Latin *vagus,* "wandering"). This cranial nerve is unique in that a large part of its fibres are distributed within the thorax and abdomen. The nerve supplies afferent and efferent fibres to the pharynx, larynx, esophagus, stomach, gut, trachea, and lungs. Special fibres of the nerve pass to and from the heart and great vessels. Numerous rootlets of the nerve are attached to the lateral surface of the medulla oblongata in series with those of the glossopharyngeal nerve above and the accessory nerve below. The cranial portion of the accessory (11th) nerve contributes efferent fibres to the vagus nerve, most of which pass to the muscles of the larynx. Rootlets of the vagus nerve unite to form a single trunk, which enters the neck via the jugular foramen.

Two ganglia associated with the vagus nerve give rise to afferent fibres. The superior ganglion of the vagus nerve is a small spherical swelling in the root that lies in the jugular foramen. Cells in this ganglion give off general somatic afferent fibres that pass to meningeal and auricular branches. The meningeal branches supply the dura mater of the posterior fossa of the skull. The auricular branch distributes fibres to the skin behind the ear, to the floor of the external auditory meatus, and to the lower part of the tympanic membrane. The inferior ganglion of the vagus nerve, large and spindle-shaped, lies immediately below the jugular foramen. Cells in the inferior ganglion give rise to general visceral afferent fibres and special visceral afferent fibres. The latter convey impulses from taste buds in the region of the epiglottis.

Efferent fibres of the vagus nerve arise from cell columns within the medulla oblongata. Preganglionic parasympathetic fibres arise from cells of the dorsal motor nucleus of the vagus nerve. This cell column, composed of spindle-shaped cells, lies in the floor of the fourth ventricle dorsolateral to the hypoglossal nucleus. Fibres from the cell column join other fibres of the vagus nerve. Special visceral efferent fibres of the vagus nerve arise from the nucleus ambiguus, a column of typical multipolar motor neurons embedded in the reticular formation. These fibres join other fibres of the vagus nerve and emerge from the lateral surface of the medulla oblongata dorsal to the inferior olivary nuclear complex. Fibres arising from the nucleus ambiguus innervate the muscles of the pharynx and larynx. Those that innervate the larynx emerge from the caudal part of the nucleus ambiguus and form the cranial part of the accessory nerve; after joining the spinal part of the accessory nerve, these fibres return to form an integral part of the vagus nerve.

Two branches of the vagus nerve are the pharyngeal and the superior laryngeal nerves. The pharyngeal nerve contains efferent fibres that, along with branches of the glossopharyngeal nerve and sympathetic nerve fibres, form

Supplying the organs of speech and swallowing

the pharyngeal plexus. Fibres from this plexus supply the muscles of the pharynx and the soft palate. The superior laryngeal nerve divides into a larger internal and a smaller external laryngeal branch. The internal laryngeal nerve supplies the mucous membrane of the larynx, the epiglottis, and the most posterior part of the tongue. The external laryngeal nerve supplies motor fibres to the inferior constrictor muscle of the pharynx and the cricothyroid muscle.

In the neck the vagus nerve follows a vertical downward course. It enters the thorax on the right side after crossing the subclavian artery; on the left side it crosses between the left common carotid and subclavian arteries. In the thorax the courses of the nerves differ on the two sides. The right vagus nerve continues along the side of the trachea to the root of the lung. The left vagus nerve passes across the aortic arch and then proceeds to the root of the left lung. The vagus nerves form two plexuses: the pulmonary and the esophageal. The pulmonary plexuses are formed behind the root of each lung. From the lower part of the pulmonary plexuses two nerves emerge that reach the esophagus and form the esophageal plexus.

The recurrent laryngeal nerves, which supply all of the intrinsic muscles of the larynx except the cricothyroid, pursue different courses on the right and left sides. The right recurrent laryngeal nerve arises in the root of the neck as the vagus nerve crosses the first part of the subclavian artery. This nerve hooks around the artery and passes upward and medially in a groove between the esophagus and the trachea. In this location the nerve lies along the medial side of the right lobe of the thyroid gland. The left recurrent laryngeal nerve separates from the vagus nerve as it crosses the arch of the aorta and, after hooking under the arch, passes upward into the neck in a fashion similar to that of the nerve on the right side.

In the neck both vagus nerves supply cardiac branches, designated as upper and lower cardiac nerves. On the right side both cardiac branches pass downward behind the subclavian artery into the thorax to reach the deep cardiac plexus. On the left side the nerves separate in the thorax; the upper nerve passes near the trachea to join the deep cardiac plexus. The lower nerve passes across the aortic arch to terminate in the superficial cardiac plexus.

Supplying blood vessels of the heart and lungs

In the thorax the vagus nerves form the cardiac, pulmonary, and esophageal plexuses. The cardiac plexus is formed by sympathetic and vagal cardiac branches that meet to produce a large plexus that lies around the great vessels at the base of the heart. The whole plexus is divided into superficial and deep plexuses that distribute fibres to the heart and to the pulmonary plexuses.

The pulmonary plexuses, formed behind the roots of the lung, give off numerous branches that extend into the lungs and are distributed to the bronchi, the pulmonary vessels, and the pleura. The esophagus is supplied by vagal nerve fibres that emerge from the posterior pulmonary plexuses to form the esophageal plexus. Branches of this plexus supply the muscle and mucous membranes in the wall of the esophagus.

From the lower part of the esophageal plexus, anterior and posterior vagal trunks arise and pass into the abdomen. The posterior vagal trunk distributes fibres to the posterior surface of the stomach as well as to the coeliac, splenic, and renal plexuses. The anterior vagal trunk distributes fibres to the lesser curvature of the stomach and branches to the pylorus and the first part of the duodenum. Thus, vagal fibres are distributed directly to the stomach and indirectly to the great autonomic plexuses in the abdomen. Fibres of the vagus nerve extend in the gut as far as the splenic flexure of the colon. These fibres innervate the muscular wall of the gut and provide secretomotor fibres to the glands of the stomach and intestine.

The vagus nerve is the most complex and the most important cranial nerve. Unilateral lesions of the vagus nerve produce ipsilateral paralysis of the soft palate, pharynx, and larynx, which results in hoarseness of the voice and difficulty both in breathing and in swallowing fluids. Vagal cardiac fibres serve to slow the heart rate and probably constrict the coronary vessels, while pulmonary vagal influences constrict the bronchi. Vagal fibres distributed to abdominal viscera stimulate peristalsis and gastrointestinal secretion.

Accessory nerve. The 11th cranial nerve consists of two distinct parts with separate origins and distributions. The cranial part arises from the caudal part of the nucleus ambiguus by several rootlets and emerges below the vagus nerve from the lateral surface of the medulla oblongata. These fibres innervate the intrinsic muscles of the larynx and perhaps some muscles of the pharynx. The spinal part of the accessory nerve originates from a cell column in the anterior horn of the spinal cord extending from the fifth (or sixth) cervical segment to the lower part of the medulla. Root fibres from these cells unite to form a common trunk. This common trunk ascends in the spinal canal, enters the skull through the foramen magnum, and joins the cranial part of the accessory nerve. Both parts of the nerve emerge from the skull via the jugular foramen. The cranial part becomes incorporated in the vagus nerve, while the spinal part passes into the neck, where it supplies the sternocleidomastoid and the upper part of the trapezius muscles. The sternocleidomastoid muscle turns the head; the trapezius muscle braces the shoulder and rotates the scapula during elevation of the upper limb.

Innervation of the tongue

Hypoglossal nerve. The 12th cranial nerve is a motor nerve that innervates the muscles of the tongue. The nerve arises from a long column of multipolar motor neurons that occupies the central gray matter of the medulla oblongata, which forms the floor of the fourth ventricle. The rootlets of the nerve pierce the dura mater separately and unite to form the hypoglossal nerve in the hypoglossal canal, the bony opening through which the nerve emerges from the skull. At the base of the skull, the nerve is closely associated with the glossopharyngeal, vagus, and accessory nerves. The nerve runs forward and passes into the floor of the mouth, where its fibres are distributed to the hypoglossus, styloglossus, geniohyoid, and genioglossus muscles, and all the intrinsic muscles of the tongue.

The intrinsic muscles of the tongue alter the shape of the tongue, while the extrinsic muscles alter its shape and position. The genioglossus muscle protrudes the tongue. Injury to the hypoglossal nerve results in paralysis of one half of the tongue with loss of muscle tone and substance (atrophy). When the tongue is protruded, it deviates to the side of the injury.

SPINAL NERVES

The spinal nerves are arranged in pairs, with each pair symmetrically attached to the sides of its respective spinal cord segment. Paired spinal nerves are symmetrical in their course and peripheral distribution. There are 31 pairs of spinal nerves, which for descriptive purposes are separated into eight pairs of cervical nerves, 12 pairs of thoracic nerves, five pairs of lumbar nerves, five pairs of sacral nerves, and one pair of coccygeal nerves. The paired coccygeal nerves are rudimentary and occasionally absent. Spinal nerves emerge from the vertebral canal via the intervertebral foramina. The first cervical nerve emerges between the occiput and the atlas, while the eighth cervical nerve exits between the seventh cervical and the first thoracic vertebrae. All thoracic, lumbar, sacral, and coccygeal nerves emerge below the vertebrae of their corresponding number. Spinal nerves vary in size; the largest nerves are those which form the great nerve trunks innervating the lower extremities.

Sensory and motor nerves

Origin of spinal nerves. Each spinal nerve is attached to the spinal cord by two nerve roots: (1) an afferent dorsal sensory root and (2) an efferent ventral motor root. The dorsal roots are larger than the ventral roots, contain more fibres, and have fibres of larger diameter. Each dorsal root has interposed in its course an ovoid mass of neurons that forms the dorsal-root ganglion. Nerve fibres forming the dorsal root arise from these cells and thus are of peripheral origin. Dorsal-root ganglion neurons give rise to a single fibre that undergoes a T-shaped bifurcation. One branch of this bifurcation passes peripherally, while the central branch enters the spinal cord. These cells are referred to as unipolar neurons. Central branches of the dorsal-root ganglia at first form a single compact bundle, which passes through a sleeve of dura mater and then breaks up into a series of root filaments. These filaments spread vertically in a fanlike manner to enter the spinal cord. Peripheral fibres from the ganglia pass laterally and join the ventral root in the intervertebral foramina.

Fibres composing the ventral root are of central nervous system origin, arising from collections of large motor neurons in the anterior horn of the spinal gray matter. The ventral root has no ganglion. Instead, fibres of the ventral root emerge from the anterior and anterolateral surfaces of the spinal cord as a series of fine nerve fibres. These fibres are irregular in their arrangement and sometimes overlap. Certain spinal ventral roots contain efferent autonomic nerve fibres. Spindle-shaped neurons in the lateral horns of all thoracic (chest) spinal segments and in the first two or three lumbar (mid-lower back) segments give rise to preganglionic sympathetic fibres that emerge via the corresponding ventral roots. The cells of origin of these fibres are known as the intermediolateral nucleus. Small scattered neurons located along the lateral surface of the anterior gray horn in the second, third, and fourth sacral (low-back) segments give rise to preganglionic parasympathetic fibres that exit via the ventral roots and pass to autonomic ganglia in or near the walls of pelvic viscera. Cells of these sacral autonomic nuclei appear similar to those of the intermediolateral nucleus.

Dorsal and ventral roots pass laterally from their attachments to the spinal cord toward the intervertebral foramen, where they unite to form a mixed spinal nerve, or common nerve trunk. In the mixed nerve, motor and sensory fibres are blended. The first two cervical nerves pass directly laterally and somewhat upward. The roots of other spinal nerves course obliquely downward and laterally. This oblique downward course increases in caudal regions; lower lumbar, sacral, and coccygeal nerve roots pursue a vertical course downward in the vertebral canal. This increasing obliquity of spinal roots is caused by the more rapid growth of the vertebral column.

As spinal root filaments leave the spinal cord, they become invested with pia mater, which becomes continuous with the arachnoid where the roots penetrate the dura. The two roots pierce the dura separately, and a dural investment is added. Distal to the spinal ganglion, the meningeal sheaths are blended and become continuous with the connective tissue covering of the spinal nerve.

Somatic and visceral nerves

Functional components of spinal nerves. Four functional components are recognized in a typical spinal nerve. These components are: (1) general somatic afferent fibres, (2) general visceral afferent fibres, (3) general somatic efferent fibres, and (4) general visceral efferent fibres. General somatic and general visceral afferent fibres arise from neurons in the dorsal-root ganglia. General somatic afferent fibres convey impulses from skin receptors concerned with pain, thermal sense, pressure, and touch and from receptors in muscles, joints, tendons, and subcutaneous tissues. General visceral afferent fibres convey impulses from visceral structures, glands, and blood vessels. General somatic efferent fibres arise from motor neurons within the central nervous system and convey motor impulses to striated muscles that initiate and maintain contractions of these muscles. General visceral efferent fibres arise from cell groups in restricted regions of the spinal cord and project to autonomic ganglia which, in turn, give rise to postganglionic fibres. Sympathetic visceral efferent fibres arise from thoracic and upper lumbar spinal segments and constitute the sympathetic outflow for the entire body. Sacral segments two, three, and four provide the spinal parasympathetic outflow that passes to lower abdominal and pelvic viscera via parasympathetic ganglia.

Typical spinal nerve. As a spinal nerve emerges from an intervertebral foramen, it divides into two main branches—a dorsal and a ventral ramus (Figure 22). The dorsal ramus, usually smaller than the ventral ramus, divides into medial and lateral branches that innervate the skin, fascia, ligaments, and axial muscles of the back. The larger ventral ramus courses laterally and ventrally in the body wall as an intercostal (between the ribs) nerve. A lateral cutaneous branch (a branch remaining in the skin) innervates the skin on the lateral and ventral surface of the body. The principal ventral ramus continues ventrally,

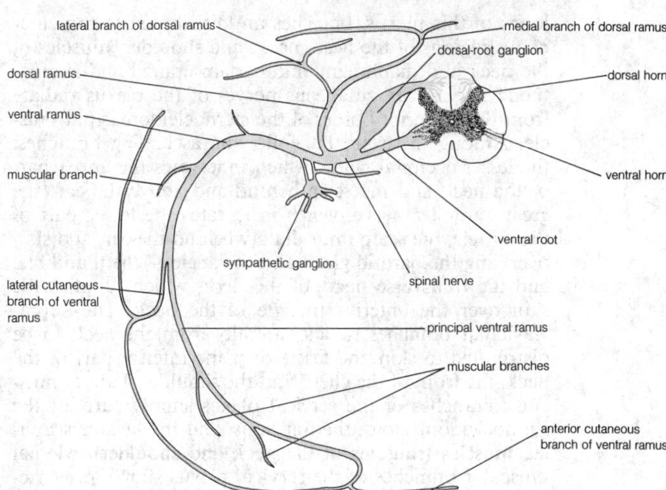

Figure 22: A typical spinal nerve.

From G.J. Romanes (ed.), *Cunningham's Textbook of Anatomy*, 12th ed. (1981); Oxford University Press

giving off branches that innervate intercostal muscles; the terminal part of this nerve gives rise to anterior cutaneous branches.

The ventral rami of the first thoracic to the third lumbar spinal nerves give rise to white rami communicantes that pass to sympathetic ganglia. These are preganglionic efferent fibres that arise from neurons within the spinal cord and pass to sympathetic ganglia. The sympathetic ganglia and trunk give rise to gray rami communicantes that enter the ventral rami; these postganglionic fibres are distributed to blood vessels, glands, and piloerector muscles.

Distribution of dorsal rami. The dorsal rami of the spinal nerves innervate the skin, fascia, and muscles over dorsal parts of the head and trunk. The muscular branches of these rami are limited to the longitudinal postvertebral muscles associated with the axial skeleton. Cutaneous branches of these rami supply areas on the back of the head, the dorsum of the trunk, and in the shoulder and gluteal (buttock) regions. None of these branches supplies cutaneous areas or muscles in the extremities. The first cervical spinal nerve has a small or frequently absent dorsal root; muscular branches, mainly in the dorsal ramus, supply posterior neck muscles attached to the skull and cervical vertebrae. The second cervical nerve gives rise to small muscular branches and the greater occipital nerve, which innervates cutaneous areas over the posterior part of the scalp. The dorsal rami of the lower cervical nerves are small, and those of the seventh and eighth cervical nerves have no cutaneous branches.

The dorsal ramus of each thoracic spinal nerve divides into medial and lateral branches. In upper thoracic nerves the medial branches are cutaneous, while the lateral branches are distributed to the muscles. The reverse is found in the lower six thoracic nerves, where the medial branches innervate the larger longitudinal muscle masses of the back. The dorsal rami of the first three lumbar nerves are distributed in the same fashion as the lower thoracic nerves. Lower lumbar nerves supply only muscular branches to the longitudinal muscles of the back. The first three sacral dorsal rami give rise to medial muscle branches and lateral cutaneous branches that supply skin and fascia over the sacral and gluteal regions. The fourth and fifth sacral dorsal rami distribute only cutaneous branches to the coccygeal region.

Distribution of ventral rami. The ventral rami of spinal nerves consist of afferent and efferent fibres and are distributed to lateral and anterior parts of the body, including the extremities. Only in the thoracic region are the ventral rami distributed in a regular manner. Other ventral rami combine to form plexuses, interwoven bundles in which the components are rearranged and distributed in a more complex manner. The principal plexuses are the cervical, brachial, lumbar, sacral, and coccygeal.

Principal plexuses of spinal nerves

Cervical plexus. The cervical plexus is formed by the ventral rami of the first four cervical nerves. From the loops of this plexus, branches are distributed to the cutaneous regions of the head, neck, and shoulder; muscles of the neck and diaphragm; and certain cranial and sympathetic nerves. Six cutaneous nerves of the plexus radiate from the posterior border of the sternocleidomastoid muscle. Among these are the following ascending branches: the lesser occipital nerve, which innervates the upper part of the neck and the scalp behind and above the ear; the great auricular nerve, which innervates the lower part of the auricle, the scalp immediately behind the ear, and skin overlying the parotid gland and the angle of the mandible; and the transverse nerve of the neck, which supplies the skin over the anterior triangle of the neck. The supraclavicular branches radiate laterally from the neck to be distributed to skin and fascia over the inferior part of the neck, the front of the chest, and the shoulder. Lateral muscular branches of the cervical plexus supply parts of the sternocleidomastoid, the trapezius, and the levator scapulae muscles (muscles of the neck and shoulder). Medial muscular branches of the cervical plexus supply prevertebral muscles, the geniohyoid and infrahyoid muscles, and the diaphragm. The phrenic nerve, which arises from the fourth cervical nerve and to a lesser extent from the third and fifth, courses downward in the neck, passes between the subclavian artery and vein, and enters the thorax. This nerve traverses the middle mediastinum, lying between the pericardium and the pleura, and reaches the diaphragm, where it separates into numerous branches.

Brachial plexus. The brachial plexus is formed from the ventral rami of the four lower cervical and the first thoracic nerves with a small contribution from the fourth cervical nerve (Figure 23A). Considerable variations occur. If the contribution from the fourth cervical is appreciable and that from the first thoracic negligible, the plexus is called prefixed. It is called postfixed if the fourth cervical does not contribute to the plexus and the first thoracic makes a strong contribution. The ventral rami forming the plexus give rise to three primary trunks: (1) fifth and sixth cervical unite to form the upper trunk, (2) seventh cervical forms the middle trunk, and (3) eighth cervical and first thoracic unite to form the inferior trunk. Each trunk divides into an anterior and a posterior division. The three posterior divisions unite to form the posterior cord. The anterior division of the upper trunk becomes the lateral cord, while the anterior division of the lower trunk becomes the medial cord.

Innervation of the shoulders and arms

Nerves supplying the shoulder muscles arise directly from the ventral rami or from the trunks. The dorsal scapular nerve, innervating the rhomboid muscles, arises from the dorsal surface of the fifth cervical. The long thoracic nerve, supplying the anterior serratus muscle, arises from the dorsal surfaces of the fifth, sixth, and seventh cervical. The suprascapular nerve to the supraspinatus and infraspinatus muscles arises from the upper trunk. The medial and lateral pectoral nerves, which innervate the pectoralis major and minor muscles, arise from the ventral surfaces of the upper and middle trunks and, in part, from the medial cord. The thoracodorsal nerve and the subscapular nerves (inferior and superior) arise from the posterior cord and supply, respectively, the latissimus dorsi muscle and the teres major and subscapular muscles—shoulder muscles that control movements of the upper arm.

The three largest peripheral nerves in the upper extremity (*i.e.,* radial, median, and ulnar) are formed in the following manner. The posterior cord divides into its two terminal branches, the larger radial nerve and the smaller axillary nerve. The medial and lateral cords each split into two branches. The two middle branches, one from the lateral cord and one from the medial cord, unite to form the median nerve. The outer branch of the lateral cord becomes the musculocutaneous nerve. The inner branch of the medial cord gives off two purely sensory nerves, the medial brachial cutaneous nerve and the medial antebrachial cutaneous nerve, and is continued peripherally as the ulnar nerve.

The axillary nerve innervates the deltoid and teres minor muscles. The radial nerve supplies the triceps muscle and extensor muscles of the elbow, hand, and digits. Its cutaneous branches supply the posterior aspect of the arm, forearm, and part of the dorsum of the hand (Figure 23B and 23C). The median nerve supplies most of the flexor muscles of the forearm and certain muscles in the hand. The sensory innervation of the median nerve is limited to the hand, where it includes the volar surface of the thumb, index, and middle fingers and the radial half of the fourth finger and corresponding parts of the palm. The ulnar nerve supplies flexor muscles in the forearm and certain flexor and adductor muscles in the hand. Cutaneous areas innervated by this nerve include the dorsal and volar surface of the little finger and adjacent half of the ring finger. A mild blow to the medial aspect of the elbow ("funny

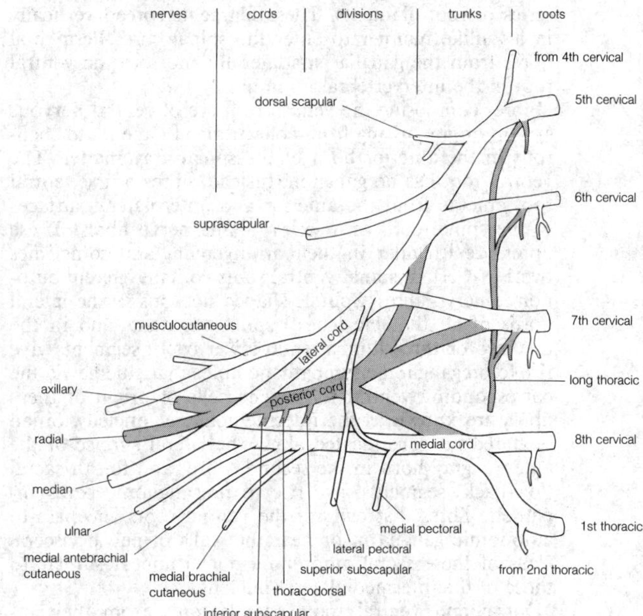

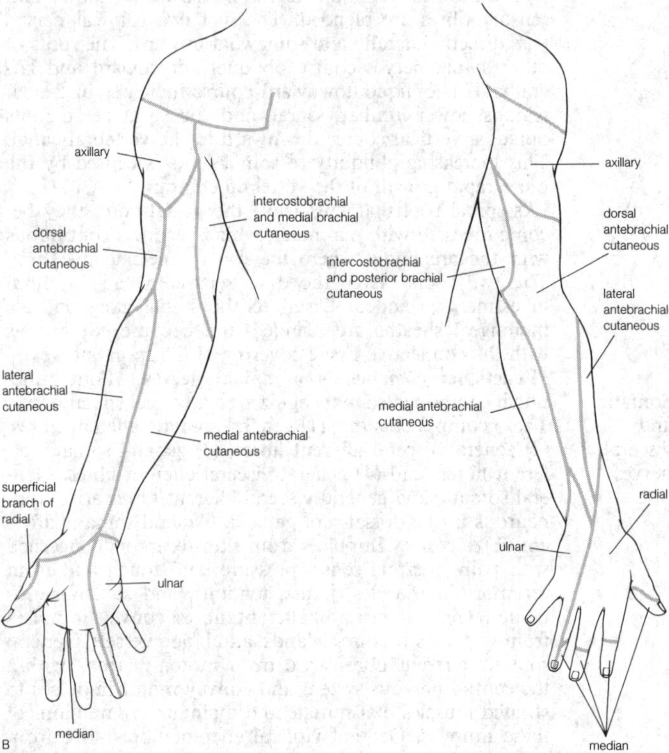

Figure 23: *The brachial plexus.*
(A) Formation from ventral rami of spinal nerves and branching into peripheral nerves. (B) Anterior (left) and posterior (right) views of cutaneous sensory areas of the right arm supplied by the brachial plexus.
From C.D. Clemente (ed.), *Gray's Anatomy of the Human Body*, 30th ed. (1985); Lea and Febiger

bone") may cause a sensation of numbness and tingling in the cutaneous distribution of the ulnar nerve.

Innervation of the lower limbs

Lumbar plexus. The lumbar plexus is formed by the ventral rami of the first four lumbar nerves, often with an additional branch from the 12th thoracic. The fourth lumbar nerve contributes to both the lumbar and sacral plexuses. Nerves arising from this plexus supply the loin region as well as part of the lower limb. The arrangement of the lumbar plexus is simpler than that of the brachial plexus in that the ventral rami do not form interlacing trunks but split into posterior and anterior divisions related primarily to primitive posterior and anterior muscle groups in the leg. Peripheral nerves to the lower extremity, lower abdomen, and genital region are formed by the union of variable numbers of either posterior or anterior divisions. Anterior divisions give rise to the following nerves: (1) iliohypogastric (anterior branch), (2) ilioinguinal, (3) genitofemoral, and (4) obturator. The posterior divisions give rise to the following nerves: (1) iliohypogastric (posterior branch), (2) femoral, and (3) lateral femoral cutaneous.

The iliohypogastric, ilioinguinal, and genitofemoral nerves supply muscular and cutaneous branches to the abdominal wall, the inguinal region, and the external genitalia. The obturator nerve supplies muscles on the medial aspect of the thigh, gives articular branches to the hip and knee joints, and sometimes distributes a cutaneous branch to the inner surface of the thigh. The large femoral nerve supplies the muscles on the anterior aspect of the thigh (*i.e.,* the extensor muscles of the thigh), gives articular branches to the hip and knee joints, and has an extensive cutaneous distribution on the medial aspect of the lower extremity to the foot. Branches of this nerve innervate the pectineus, sartorius, and quadriceps muscles. Cutaneous branches of the nerve are the anterior cutaneous nerve, distributed to anterior and anteromedial surfaces of the thigh, and the saphenous nerve, which is distributed to skin and fascia of the medial aspect of the leg and foot. The lateral femoral cutaneous nerve innervates skin and fascia over the lateral part of the front of the thigh as far down as the knee; a smaller posterior branch supplies the lateral aspect of the buttock and skin over the lateral side of the thigh.

The sciatic nerve

Sacral plexus. The sacral plexus is formed by the ventral rami of the fifth lumbar and the upper three sacral nerves and contributions from the fourth lumbar and the fourth sacral nerves. The sciatic nerve, the largest and thickest nerve in the body, is the chief continuation of all roots of the sacral plexus. This large nerve leaves the pelvis and enters the gluteal region through the greater sciatic foramen. The nerve enters the thigh at the lower border of the gluteus maximus and descends under the long head of the biceps femoris muscle. This nerve usually terminates in the popliteal fossa (*i.e.,* back of the knee) by dividing into the tibial and common peroneal nerves. The division of the nerve may occur at any higher level, as these two nerves frequently are distinct at their origin. The tibial and common peroneal nerves are bound together proximally by an investing sheath.

In addition to the sciatic nerve the sacral plexus gives rise to numerous smaller nerves. These collateral branches innervate the main external rotators of the thigh, the obturator internus, the gemelli, and the quadratus femoris muscles. The pudendal nerve arises from the second, third, and fourth sacral nerves and provides branches distributed to the anal sphincter, the scrotum (or labium majus), and the penis (or clitoris). Other branches from proximal parts of the sacral plexus are nerves to the gluteal muscles and the posterior femoral cutaneous nerve. Parasympathetic fibres from the second, third, and fourth sacral nerves join autonomic plexuses in the pelvis and are distributed to urogenital organs and the lower part of the large intestine. Nerves given off from the sciatic nerve near the lower part of the buttock innervate the hamstring muscles, the principal flexors of the knee. The common peroneal and tibial nerves are the two main trunks resulting from the division of the sciatic nerve.

The common peroneal nerve arises from the posterior cords of the sacral plexus and is homologous with the radial nerve of the upper limb. Two cutaneous nerves arise from the common peroneal nerve in the popliteal fossa. These are the lateral cutaneous nerve on the calf, distributed over the lateral and posterior aspect of the leg, and the peroneal communicating branch, which gives branches to the lateral surface of the leg. The two terminal branches of the common peroneal nerve are the deep and superficial peroneal nerves. The division of the common peroneal nerve takes place immediately below the head of the fibula. Branches of the deep peroneal nerve innervate the tibialis anterior, extensor hallucis longus, and extensor digitorum longus muscles, which serve to dorsiflex (extend) the foot and toes. In the foot the terminal branches are: (1) the medial digital branch, supplying the skin on adjacent sides of the great and second toes; and (2) a lateral muscular branch which innervates the extensor digitorum brevis and gives rise to articular branches for tarsal, tarsometatarsal, and metatarsophalangeal joints. The superficial peroneal nerve passes downward in front of the fibula and innervates the peroneus longus and brevis muscles. Terminal branches of this nerve are cutaneous. Medial branches supply skin and fascia over the dorsum of the foot, the medial aspect of the great toe, and adjacent parts of the second and third toes. Lateral branches of the superficial peroneal nerve supply distal parts of the leg, part of the dorsum of the foot, and regions between the third and fourth, and fourth and fifth toes. Cutaneous nerves on the dorsum of the foot are subject to considerable variation, and nerves supplying the digits are smaller than plantar digital nerves.

Innervation of the foot

The tibial nerve arises from the anterior divisions of the sacral plexus. This nerve is homologous with the median and ulnar nerve trunks in the upper extremity. The nerve lies deep in the posterior thigh, passes into the popliteal fossa, and distally is covered by the gastrocnemius and soleus muscles. Branches of the nerve arising in the popliteal fossa innervate the gastrocnemius, soleus, and posterior tibial muscles. The sural nerve, a cutaneous branch, pierces the deep fascia on the back of the leg and descends to reach the lateral surface of the foot. This nerve and its branches supply cutaneous regions on the posterior and lateral aspects of the distal third of the leg, the ankle, the heel, and the lateral border of the foot. Muscular branches of the tibial nerve in the leg innervate the tibialis posterior, the soleus, and the long flexor muscles of the foot. The terminal branches of the tibial nerve are distributed to the plantar surface of the foot by the medial and lateral plantar nerves. The medial plantar nerve is homologous with the median nerve in the hand, while the lateral plantar nerve is homologous with the ulnar nerve. The medial plantar nerve innervates the abductor hallucis and the flexor digitorum brevis muscles and gives rise to four common plantar digital nerves. The lateral plantar nerve gives branches to small muscles of the foot and cutaneous branches to the fifth toe and part of the fourth toe.

Coccygeal plexus. The coccygeal plexus is formed by the ventral ramus of the fourth sacral and those of the fifth sacral and coccygeal nerves. These nerves form a plexiform cord homologous with the inferior caudal trunk of tailed animals. Some of these nerve fibres pierce the coccygeus and overlying ligaments to supply the skin and fascia near the coccyx and anus. (M.B.C./Ed.)

The autonomic nervous system

Classic two-neuron structure of autonomic nerve pathways

By classical definition the autonomic nervous system, sometimes called the visceral or vegetative nervous system, is that system of motor nerve fibres that carries impulses to the cardiac muscle, smooth muscle (such as that in the blood vessels), and glands and that consists, in its simplest form, of nerve pathways each consisting of two succeeding neurons. The first neuron originates in the brain or spinal cord and the second in a peripheral ganglion, or collection of neurons, outside of the brain and spinal cord. Anatomically and functionally, however, the autonomic nervous system is much broader than the definition given above would indicate. The motor fibres making up this system are closely associated with sensory fibres in all of their functions. An integral part of the entire nervous system, they are activated by nerve impulses arising by reflex action at local levels as well as by impulses originating in the higher centres of the brain.

The autonomic nervous system is concerned with a number of specific functions, such as those related to digestion, intermediate metabolism of foods, and excretion. It is also concerned with many specific regulatory functions, involving, for example, body temperature, blood pressure, and respiration. It enables the body to handle emergencies or sudden environmental changes and is thus an important part of the mechanisms by which a person reacts to stress. Finally, the autonomic nervous system is an integral part of behavioral and emotional actions and responses. It must be emphasized that, in all of these activities, sensory fibres and sensory mechanisms are often indispensable features.

Because a modern treatment of the autonomic system can be presented only within the context of the entire nervous system, some overlap with other sections of this article is inevitable. For detailed discussion of the anatomy of the brain and spinal cord, see above *The central nervous system.* For similar discussion of the cranial and spinal nerves outside of the central nervous system, see above *The peripheral nervous system.* For further discussion of autonomic functions, see below *Functions of the human nervous system: The autonomic system.*

For the sake of clarity and to facilitate an understanding of certain functions, the autonomic nervous system is here presented as if it were a series of levels of the central and peripheral nervous systems that differ in function in that the higher the level, the more widespread and general its functions, and the lower the level, the more restricted and specific its functions. Before the various levels are taken up in detail, a general account of the principles of organization and function is given.

GENERAL ORGANIZATION AND FUNCTION

The lowest level of the autonomic system consists of the two-nerve-cell pathway mentioned above. The two-nerve-cell pathway begins with certain neurons located in the brain stem and spinal cord. The axons of these cells are called preganglionic fibres (also known as general visceral efferent fibres). With some exceptions the preganglionic fibres leave the brain and spinal cord and transmit impulses to neurons in peripheral ganglia. The axons of the ganglionic neurons are commonly called postganglionic fibres. They terminate in cardiac muscle, smooth muscle, and certain gland cells, all of which, because they can produce actions, are often known as effectors. The activation of an effector by nerve impulses takes place across a specialized nerve–effector relationship known as a neuroeffector junction or, especially in the case of muscle, a neuromuscular junction.

Autonomic effectors. The locations, arrangements, and connections of the two-nerve-cell pathways of the autonomic nervous system form the basis of an anatomical classification or subdivision of the pathways into sympathetic and parasympathetic systems, or divisions. Before these two divisions are described in greater detail, it is necessary to give a brief account of the effectors they supply, namely, cardiac muscle, smooth muscle, and glands.

Cardiac muscle. Cardiac muscle fibres constitute the bulk of the heart. The fibres are multinucleated cells that contain longitudinally disposed minute fibres, called myofibrils, that have alternating light and dark segments. This structural arrangement causes the fibres to appear cross-striated when examined under the microscope. Though skeletal muscle fibres are also cross-striated, they differ from cardiac fibres in many important respects. The significant differences are in nerve supply—in the fact that cardiac fibres have an intrinsic rhythmic beat or contraction that begins in the embryo, that cardiac fibres can survive without a nerve supply, that cardiac fibres cannot be voluntarily controlled as most skeletal muscles can, and that some of the cardiac fibres are specialized for conduction rather than contraction.

Impulse-conducting cardiac muscle fibres

The specialized fibres form the conducting system of the heart, consisting of two definitive collections of specialized fibres called nodes (the sinoatrial and the atrioventricular), together with bundles of fibres spreading out from the nodes to the regular cardiac fibres. Postganglionic autonomic fibres form neuromuscular junctions with the fibres of the nodes. From there, impulses are conducted to the ordinary cardiac muscle fibres. The two nodes, by virtue of rhythmic activity that begins in the embryo, together set the level of cardiac activity, or rate of heartbeat. The autonomic nerve supply to the heart acts by stimulating or inhibiting the ongoing nodal rhythm, thereby increasing or decreasing ongoing activity of the heart.

Smooth muscle. Many organs contain what is known as smooth muscle. The unit of a layer of smooth muscle is a small spindle-shaped cell; this contains a nucleus and myofibrils that lack alternating light and dark sections and hence are said to be smooth or uniform rather than cross-striated. Smooth muscle cells are usually arranged in sheets or bundles, within the walls of viscera, around many glands, and in the walls of blood vessels. Contractions of smooth muscle are slower than those of striated muscle and often seem to spread from one fibre to another as a wavelike activity of the sheet or bundle. This spread may be facilitated by low-resistance contacts or fusions, known as tight junctions, which occur between many of the fibres.

Neuromuscular junctions in smooth muscle seem to be between varicosities—bulging areas—of nerve fibres and individual smooth muscle cells. It is unlikely that every smooth muscle fibre is so supplied, and it is likely that organs differ in the density of the innervation of their smooth muscle. Also, the degree to which a single postganglionic nerve fibre may divide and supply more than one smooth muscle fibre is not known with certainty. Like cardiac muscle, smooth muscle may survive without a nerve supply and in some instances possesses intrinsic, or locally initiated, activity, the level of which may be modified by the autonomic nervous system.

Glands. Glands are composed of epithelial (covering or lining) cells adapted for the formation of materials other than those directly concerned in their intrinsic metabolism. The glands secrete such substances as hormones, enzymes, and mucus. They may be composed of one or of many cells. If the glands discharge their products onto a surface or into the channel of an organ, they are called exocrine glands, or glands of external secretion. If they discharge their contents into the blood, they are called endocrine glands, or glands of internal secretion.

Exocrine and endocrine glands

Generally, only the multicellular exocrine glands are supplied by the autonomic nervous system. The neuroeffector junctions formed by postganglionic autonomic fibres are basically similar to those of smooth muscle. Like smooth muscle, gland cells are also usually relatively unaffected by loss of nerve supply. They may continue to function normally, either by virtue of intrinsic activity or through activation by circulating hormones and other substances.

An important principle emerges from the above, namely, that the autonomic nervous system is not indispensable to the structures it supplies and that it often functions by regulating intrinsic activity.

Main divisions. It is pointed out above that autonomic fibres characteristically comprise a pathway of two neurons, one originating in the brain stem or spinal cord and the second in a peripherally located ganglion, and that these pathways can be classified as sympathetic or parasympathetic.

The classification of pathways as sympathetic or parasympathetic is inadequate because it does not take into account the sensory and reflex connections, the higher levels of organization, and certain functional and pharmacological characteristics. Nevertheless, it does indicate some fundamental characteristics and differences. Some are illustrated in Figure 24. Most organs are supplied by both systems, although there are major exceptions. Nearly all peripheral blood vessels, for example, are supplied by the sympathetic system alone. When an organ has a double autonomic nerve supply, the two systems tend to have opposite functions. Thus, the parasympathetic system slows the heart rate, and the sympathetic increases it.

Sympathetic system. This is also called the orthosympathetic or thoracolumbar system. The neurons that give rise to the preganglionic sympathetic fibres form a narrow column extending throughout each side of the thoracic (chest) and upper lumbar (small of the back) parts of the

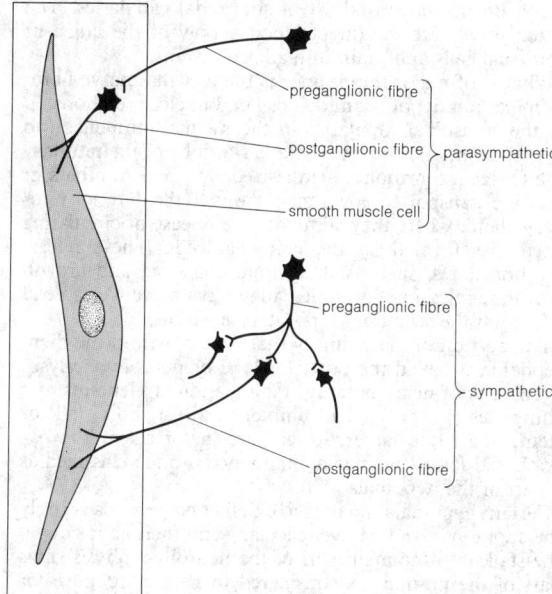

Figure 24: Differences in sympathetic and parasympathetic distribution. Sympathetic fibres synapse with many cells in ganglia of the sympathetic trunk or prevertebral plexuses, usually at some distance from the organ supplied.

From E. Gardner, *Fundamentals of Neurology*, 5th edition (1968); W.B. Saunders Company

spinal cord (hence the term thoracolumbar). The axons leave the cord by way of the ventral roots of the corresponding spinal nerves. It is characteristic of preganglionic fibres, at least in higher vertebrates, that they are small in diameter and myelinated, whereas postganglionic fibres are still smaller in diameter and are nonmyelinated. The preganglionic sympathetic fibres then reach neurons in nearby autonomic ganglia by way of communicating branches called rami communicantes. Most of the ganglia are contained in the sympathetic trunks, which lie one on each side of the vertebral column, extending along its whole length, from the base of the skull to the coccyx (Figure 25). A number of ganglia are found in the meshes of the great prevertebral plexuses of the chest, abdomen, and pelvis, and still others are accessory ganglia scattered along certain spinal roots and nerves. Further details of these various arrangements are given below (see *Levels of structural organization: Lower-level control*).

Sympathetic ganglia

Some preganglionic sympathetic fibres synapse with neurons in the ganglia of the sympathetic trunks, whereas others continue through to neurons in prevertebral ganglia. Still others continue on to the medullae (inner substance) of the adrenal, or suprarenal, glands, where they synapse with gland cells of the medullae. Each preganglionic sympathetic fibre usually synapses with many neurons or medullary cells (Figure 24).

The postganglionic fibres that arise in the various sympathetic ganglia either go directly to adjacent viscera and blood vessels or return to spinal nerves by way of rami communicantes. They usually run relatively long distances to reach the organs or tissues that they supply. Those that return to the spinal nerves are distributed by way of the peripheral nerves to (1) sweat glands and smooth muscle fibres attached to hairs in the skin, (2) blood vessels of the limbs and trunks, and (3) smooth muscle and gland cells of the head and neck.

Parasympathetic system. This is also called the craniosacral system. The motor cells whose axons form the preganglionic fibres are found in the nuclei of origin of certain cranial nerves and also in the sacral part of the spinal cord (hence the term craniosacral).

The cranial outflow is from the oculomotor, facial, glossopharyngeal, vagus, and accessory nerves (third, seventh, ninth, 10th, and 11th cranial nerves). The myelinated preganglionic fibres leave the brain stem in the corresponding cranial nerves. Those in the accessory nerve soon enter the vagus nerve and are conducted by it to parasympathetic ganglia. The fibres in the oculomotor, facial, and glossopharyngeal nerves synapse with neurons in certain ganglia in the head and neck called cranial or cephalic parasympathetic ganglia. Those in the vagus nerves synapse with ganglia in the walls of the thoracic and abdominal viscera. In most instances, postganglionic parasympathetic fibres are nonmyelinated; the fibres are usually rather short, and the ganglia are in or near the organ to be innervated. Moreover, each preganglionic fibre synapses with relatively few neurons, or just one, and the postganglionic fibres supply fewer structures than do postganglionic sympathetic fibres (Figure 24).

Parasympathetic ganglia

The chief parasympathetic ganglia associated with the cranial nerves are the ciliary (related to the oculomotor nerves and concerned with constriction of the pupil of the eye), the pterygopalatine and submandibular (related to the facial nerves), and the otic (related to the glossopharyngeal nerves and concerned with the secretion of the parotid salivary gland).

The motor neurons making up the preganglionic parasympathetic fibres issuing from the sacral part of the spinal cord form a short column of cells on each side of the middle segments of the sacral cord. The fibres leave by way of the ventral roots of the corresponding spinal nerves and reach sympathetic ganglion cells in the walls of the pelvic organs and some of the organs of the lower abdomen.

LEVELS OF STRUCTURAL ORGANIZATION

As indicated above, the autonomic nervous system can be considered as if it were controlled or regulated by a series of physiological and anatomical levels that differ in function in that the higher the level, the more widespread and general its functions, and the lower the level, the more restricted and specific its functions. The lowest levels constitute the autonomic nervous system of classical definition.

Higher-level control. *Cerebral hemispheres.* The various levels that control or regulate autonomic activity begin with the cerebral hemispheres. The parts of the cerebral hemispheres that figure most prominently in autonomic functions include much of the cortex of the frontal lobes,

From E. Gardner, *Fundamentals of Neurology*, 5th edition (1968); W.B. Saunders Company

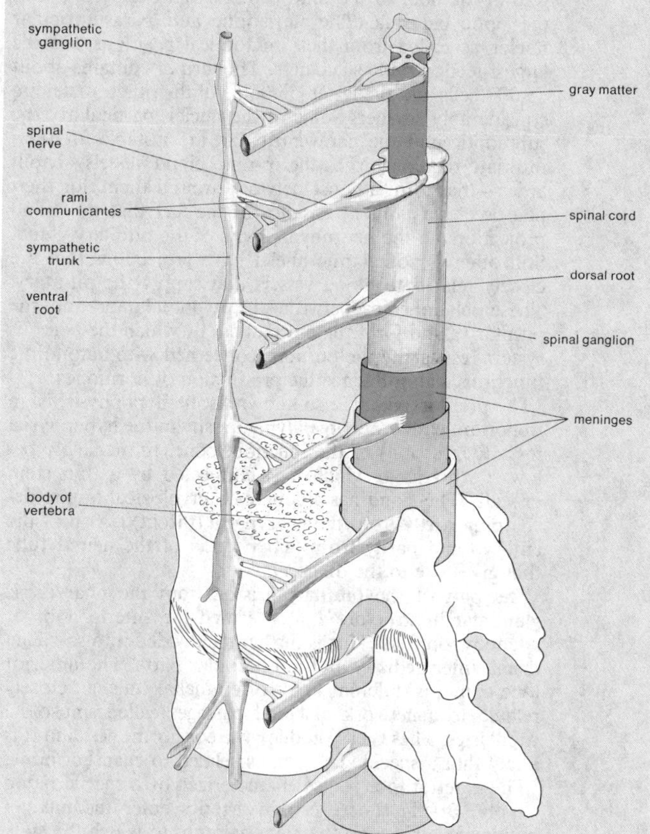

Figure 25: Diagram of the spinal cord, vertebrae, and sympathetic trunk (shown on one side only). Dorsal rami of the spinal nerves are not shown.

certain of the basal ganglia (in particular those called the amygdaloid bodies), and what is generally called the limbic lobe or limbic system.

The limbic system

There is as yet no general agreement as to the precise nature or extent of the so-called limbic lobe or system, sometimes referred to as limbic areas. What does seem clear is that primitive vertebrates have simple cerebral hemispheres with a single-layered cortex and that this phylogenetically old cortex—*i.e.,* this cortex that developed early in the evolutionary process—is present in higher vertebrates, including man. Together with its connections and certain phylogenetically newer structures, it constitutes the limbic system (the amygdaloid bodies, each of which consists of a number of different nuclei, are often included with it). This system is found at the base of the brain, where it forms part of the frontal and temporal lobes of the hemispheres, and it borders much of the lateral ventricle (*limbus,* from the Latin, meaning "border" or "edge"). In lower vertebrates the primitive cortex is concerned chiefly with olfaction, the sense of smell. In higher vertebrates the structures constituting the system are still associated with this sense but in addition are involved in many other activities, including autonomic functions and certain aspects of emotion and behaviour. Indeed, the limbic system has been called the visceral brain. The term system implies a unity of structure and function that does not exist, however, and it seems likely that a more rational nomenclature will arise as connections and functions continue to be clarified.

The limbic system receives nerve fibres from the olfactory tracts and their connections, from the hypothalamus, and from many parts of the cerebral cortex. In turn, the limbic system sends nerve fibres to lower centres, in particular to the hypothalamus. It is the powerful connections between the limbic system and the hypothalamus that are chiefly responsible for making possible the autonomic functions of the cerebral hemispheres.

Hypothalamus and pituitary. The hypothalamus, which controls many vital functions, is anatomically insignificant, consisting only of small collections of cells in the thin wall of the floor of the third cerebral ventricle, just above the optic chiasma. The supraoptic and paraventricular nuclei, so called from their anatomical positions, are the largest recognizable structures. The former contains about 75,000 cells and the latter, 55,000. All the other nuclei are considerably smaller. Some of the nuclei, particularly the supraoptic and the paraventricular, are notable for their intimate relationship to the minute blood vessels—capillaries—that form a dense network around them, for their neurosecretory functions, and for the fact that they send projections to the neurohypophysis of the pituitary gland. Still other hypothalamic nuclei have projections that are closely related to blood vessels that supply the pituitary. These relationships between the hypothalamus and the pituitary gland form the mechanism by which the nervous system, especially the portions concerned with autonomic functions, can influence the production of hormones.

The pituitary gland, also known as the hypophysis, is an important endocrine organ lying mostly in the hypophysial fossa (depression) of the sphenoid bone, immediately below the brain, to which it is connected by a thin stem or stalk. The gland has a double embryological origin, developing partly from the pharyngeal (throat) region of the embryo and partly from that portion of the neural tube that gives rise to the diencephalon.

The part of the pituitary arising from the pharynx is glandular in structure and is termed the anterior lobe or adenohypophysis. This is further subdivided into so-called distal, intermediate, and infundibular parts. The anterior lobe contains different kinds of epithelial cells, all closely related to a network of blood passages called sinusoidal capillaries. These cells produce various hormones, and it is likely that a specific cell type is related to each hormone.

The anterior lobe is also characterized by a special blood supply. Briefly stated, certain arteries enter the median eminence, a ridge on the hypothalamus to which the stalk of the pituitary is attached. There they form sinusoidal capillaries. The capillaries then collect into vessels known as portal vessels, which descend into the anterior lobe and break up into a second set of sinusoidal capillaries. The latter vessels are the direct blood supply of the adjacent epithelial cells and drain into adjacent veins.

What is of major importance is the fact that nerve fibres from certain hypothalamic nuclei end in close relationship to the sinusoidal capillaries in the median eminence (no hypothalamic fibres go to the anterior lobe of the pituitary itself). Neurohormones synthesized by small numbers of cells are transported down their axons to the anterior pituitary gland, where they stimulate the release of circulating hormones formed by the epithelial cells. These releasing hormones, such as thyrotropin-releasing and growth hormone-releasing hormones, may have more widespread effects on the secretion of pituitary hormones.

The neurohypophysis

The portion of the pituitary that develops from the diencephalon is called the posterior lobe or neurohypophysis. It consists of nervous rather than glandular elements and comprises (1) the median eminence, (2) a short stalk or stem, and (3) a larger, lower part that rests in the hypophysial fossa (the median eminence is often classified as a part of the hypothalamus).

Certain hypothalamic nuclei, chiefly and perhaps entirely the supraoptic and paraventricular, send their axons down the stalk into the main part of the neurohypophysis. This part of the pituitary is considered to be a storehouse for the secretions produced by the nerve cells of the hypothalamic nuclei. These neurosecretions are transported by the axons of the cells to the neurohypophysis. There either they are stored or they enter the bloodstream by way of adjacent capillaries. At least two hormones—vasopressin and oxytocin—reach the body by this route.

Lower-level control. *Brain stem.* The vital brain-stem centres concerned with lower-level, more circumscribed autonomic functions are located in the midbrain, pons, and medulla oblongata—chiefly in the last two. The centres consist of neurons that, in spite of the term centre, usually do not form circumscribed groups but, instead, tend to be scattered throughout the parts of the brain stem, especially the medulla oblongata. The neurons receive afferent nerve impulses from higher centres (especially the hypothalamus), from the spinal cord, and from brain-stem reflex paths. In turn, they send their axons to the appropriate cells of the parasympathetic and sympathetic outflows. The various brain-stem centres integrate and regulate a number of autonomic functions, such as blood pressure and gastrointestinal activity, and often can do so in the absence of higher control.

Cerebellum. Attached to the back of the brain stem by three peduncles, or stalks, on each side is the cerebellum. It is grossly divisible into two hemispheres and a midline connecting portion. The cerebellum is heavily supplied with input from the spinal cord, from higher centres, and from brain-stem centres. In turn, it sends fibres to these regions and structures. The cerebellum has important modulating effects upon ongoing activity. While it does not of itself contain autonomic centres, most autonomic activities come under its modulating influence.

Cranial and spinal nerves. As mentioned above (see *General organization and function: Main divisions*), the sympathetic outflow begins with neurons that form a long column on each side of the thoracic and upper lumbar part of the spinal cord. Their axons, the preganglionic sympathetic fibres, leave by way of the corresponding ventral nerve roots, travel into the spinal nerves, and then leave the nerves by way of communicating branches, or rami communicantes. They synapse with neurons in the sympathetic trunks, prevertebral plexuses, or accessory ganglia or with cells of the adrenal medullae. The 12 thoracic and first two or three lumbar spinal nerves give off rami containing preganglionic fibres. All 31 spinal nerves, on the other hand, receive rami containing postganglionic fibres from the sympathetic trunks. This means that each of the thoracic and upper lumbar spinal nerves has two or more rami communicantes. The nature of each ramus—that is, whether it is transmitting preganglionic or postganglionic fibres—is not readily ascertainable except by microscopic study. More often than not, however, the ramus that is attached to a spinal nerve more distally (farther from the spinal cord) than other rami attached to the same spinal

The rami communicantes

nerve is preganglionic. This situation is of considerable practical importance to surgeons when it is necessary for them to cut the preganglionic fibres to a particular region or organ.

The parasympathetic outflow, as mentioned above, has cranial and sacral parts. Both are more specifically organized than the sympathetic outflow. The parasympathetic cells of the cranial part are included in the nuclei of origin of the third, seventh, ninth, 10th, and 11th cranial nerves. The preganglionic parasympathetic fibres in the third nerve are destined for the eye; those in the seventh nerve, for the lacrimal gland, nasal glands, and salivary glands; those in the ninth nerve, for a salivary gland; and those in the 10th and 11th nerves, for viscera in the neck, thorax, and abdomen (Figure 26).

From E. Gardner, *Fundamentals of Neurology*, 5th edition (1968); W.B. Saunders Company

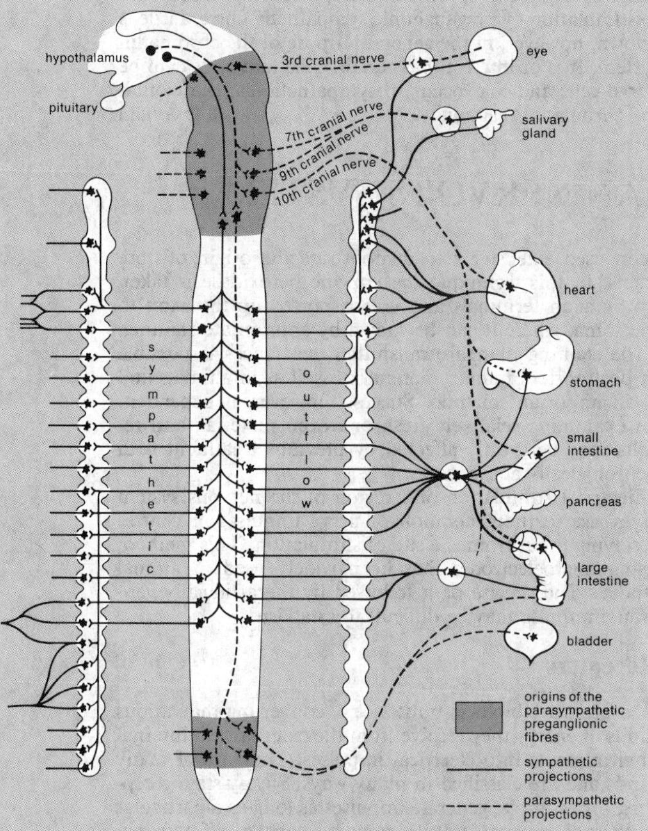

Figure 26: Schematic representation of the general arrangement of the autonomic nervous system. Autonomic fibres to the organs of the head and trunk are shown on the right side; the autonomic fibres on the left side represent the sympathetic outflow to blood vessels, sweat glands, and smooth muscle of hair follicles.

The preganglionic fibres in the third, seventh, and ninth cranial nerves end in certain well-defined ganglia called cranial or cephalic ganglia, from which postganglionic fibres are distributed to the various muscle cells and glands. The ganglia with which the preganglionic fibres in the 10th and 11th nerves synapse are scattered throughout the walls of the viscera.

The sacral part of the parasympathetic outflow is derived from nerve cells that form a column in each half of the middle segments of the sacral part of the spinal cord (chiefly the third and fourth segments). The preganglionic fibres arising from these cells leave by way of the corresponding ventral roots, reach and pass through the sympathetic trunks, and emerge as the nerves known as the pelvic splanchnic nerves. These nerves enter prevertebral plexuses, chiefly the inferior hypogastric, from which fibres are distributed to the pelvic and genital organs and to the distal (most remote from the stomach) part of the large intestine (the proximal part is supplied by the vagus nerves). The ganglia with which the preganglionic fibres synapse are scattered in the walls of the viscera.

Ganglia. As the lowest level of autonomic function, ganglia have the most restricted or specific functions. For example, the axons leaving the uppermost ganglion of the sympathetic chain are entirely for the supply of the face, some of the neck, and most of the cranial cavity.

The sympathetic trunks

The sympathetic trunks, one on each side of the vertebral column, are each a ganglionated trunk extending from the base of the skull to the coccyx. The cervical (neck) part consists of three or four ganglia connected by an intervening cord (or cords), which consists mostly of preganglionic fibres. Rami communicantes, consisting chiefly of postganglionic fibres, are connected to each of the cervical spinal nerves, and the uppermost ganglion gives off a large branch or branches of postganglionic fibres, which accompany arteries to the face and cranial cavity. The thoracic parts of the trunks commonly have 11 or 12 separate ganglia each and are connected with each thoracic spinal nerve by two or more rami communicantes. In addition, branches run to adjacent viscera; the largest of such branches are known as splanchnic nerves. The lumbar parts of the trunks are seldom symmetrical, and the lumbar ganglia are irregular in size, position, and number. Each ganglion has two or more rami communicantes and is connected to the ventral rami of two or more spinal nerves. The pelvic parts of the sympathetic trunks consist largely of preganglionic fibres; each trunk usually has three or four ganglia and ends by forming an enlargement, the ganglion impar, with the other trunk in front of the coccyx. Each pelvic ganglion tends to be connected with only one spinal nerve by rami communicantes that consist chiefly of postganglionic fibres.

As mentioned above, many preganglionic fibres pass through the sympathetic trunks and are carried by branches, such as the splanchnic nerves, to the prevertebral plexuses. These plexuses lie in front of the vertebral column and are named for adjacent viscera—for example, cardiac (heart), celiac (abdominal), and mesenteric (the mesenteries are folds of membrane continuous with the peritoneum, the membrane lining the abdomen and pelvis). Sympathetic ganglion neurons, with which the above-mentioned fibres synapse, occur in these plexuses. They are numerous enough so that they form ganglia, some large enough to be named. The postganglionic fibres arising from these neurons go directly to adjacent viscera.

Some of the preganglionic fibres in spinal nerves synapse in accessory, or intermediate, ganglia without reaching sympathetic trunks. These ganglia are collections of sympathetic ganglion neurons scattered along spinal nerves and rami communicantes, especially in the cervical, lower thoracic, and upper lumbar regions. Most of these neurons send their axons into the spinal nerves with which they are associated. They are not affected by usual surgical procedures designed to cut autonomic fibres and are, therefore, a source of residual autonomic function after such an operation.

It must be emphasized that sensory fibres arising from viscera are contained within the various nerves. Depending upon their functions, they may reach the brain stem by way of the vagus nerves, or they may traverse the sympathetic trunks, reach spinal nerves by way of rami communicantes, and then reach the spinal cord by way of dorsal roots.

Parasympathetic ganglia

The cranial parasympathetic ganglia likewise have a complicated structure and arrangement that is incompletely understood. In general, each cranial parasympathetic ganglion has postganglionic sympathetic fibres originating in the superior cervical ganglion and passing through the ganglion, sensory fibres passing through to a cranial nerve and thus to the brain, and preganglionic parasympathetic fibres from the appropriate cranial nerve and synapsing in the ganglion. Postganglionic parasympathetic fibres are distributed to adjacent structures. In general, each preganglionic fibre synapses with far fewer ganglion neurons than is the case with sympathetic ganglia. In general, also, no parasympathetic fibres seem to go to blood vessels, except for a few arteries leading to certain viscera, or to the smooth muscle and glands of the limbs and body wall.

The parasympathetic ganglion neurons in the walls of the thoracic, abdominal, and pelvic organs rarely form recognizable ganglia but instead are usually scattered. In the alimentary canal, however, these neurons occur between the muscle layers in arrangements complicated enough to warrant the term plexuses. Moreover, there is evidence of intrinsic connections and interactions independent of the external nerve supply; these may be a factor in intrinsic activity of the organ.

Adrenal (suprarenal) glands. The sympathetic nervous system has a special situation in that some preganglionic fibres synapse with certain gland cells rather than with ganglion cells. The gland cells consist of the medullary cells of the adrenal glands and the cells of the chromaffin system.

The adrenal glands are small, paired endocrine glands lying above the kidneys. Each gland is made up of two endocrine glands, the cortex and the medulla. The cortex, or outer substance, produces steroid hormones that are essential to life. The medulla, or inner substance, the cells of which are supplied by preganglionic sympathetic fibres and are therefore analogous to sympathetic ganglion neurons, produces the neurotransmitter substances epinephrine and norepinephrine, among other substances. The effects of epinephrine are generally similar to those resulting from stimulation of the sympathetic nervous system. The sympathetic system can therefore enhance its own action, because it can stimulate the adrenal medulla and cause the release of epinephrine and norepinephrine into the circulation.

Chromaffin system. With regard to the chromaffin system, cells similar to those of the adrenal medulla are commonly found in front of the vertebrae, especially along the aorta (the major artery that conveys blood to the body from the left ventricle of the heart). These para-ganglia or para-aortic bodies (which may be fairly large and constant in position), together with the adrenal medullae, constitute the chromaffin system, so named because granules in the cells stain strongly with chromium salts.

Like the cells of the adrenal medulla, most of the paraganglia secrete epinephrine or norepinephrine in response to stimulation by preganglionic sympathetic fibres. Little is known, however, of the general purpose of the chromaffin system. It is of interest that certain cells that appear to be nerve cells and that occur in sympathetic ganglia exhibit the chromaffin reaction. (E.D.G./Ed.)

FUNCTIONS OF THE HUMAN NERVOUS SYSTEM

Methods of studying the human nervous system

The human nervous system differs from that of other mammals chiefly in the great enlargement and elaboration of the cerebral hemispheres. Much of what is known of the function of the brain is derived from observations of the effects of disease or by analogy with the results of experimentation on animals, particularly the monkey. Such sources of information are clearly inadequate for the elucidation of the nervous activity underlying many properties of the human brain—particularly speech and mental processes. It is not surprising, therefore, that knowledge of the functions of this uniquely complex system, although rapidly expanding, is far from complete.

In the following account of the functions of the human nervous system, there are numerous references to tracts and less well-defined connections between different regions of the brain and spinal cord. The identification of these pathways is not a simple matter; indeed, in humans, many are incompletely known or conjectural.

A great deal of information has been obtained by observing the spreading effects of axonal destruction. If a nerve fibre is severed, the length of axon farthest from the cell body, or soma, will be deprived of the axonal flow of metabolites and will begin to break up. The myelin sheath will also degenerate, so that for some months after the injury, breakdown products of myelin will be seen under the microscope with special stains. This method is obviously of limited application in humans, as it requires precise lesions and subsequent examination before the myelin has been completely removed. Staining degenerated axons and their terminals forming synapses with other neurons is also possible using silver impregnation, but the techniques are laborious and results sometimes difficult to interpret.

That a damaged neuron should show degenerative changes, however difficult to detect, is not unexpected, but the interdependence of neurons is sometimes shown by transneuronal degeneration. Neurons deprived of major input from axons that have been destroyed may themselves atrophy. This is called anterograde degeneration. In retrograde degeneration similar changes may occur in neurons that have lost the main recipient of their outflow.

These anatomical methods are occasionally applicable to human disease. They can also be used postmortem when lesions in the central nervous system have been deliberately made—for example, in the surgical treatment of intractable pain. Some more recently developed techniques can be used only in experiments on animals, but these are not always relevant to humans. For example, normal biochemical constituents labeled with a radioactive isotope can be injected into neurons and then transported the length of the axon, where they can be detected by picking up the radioactivity on an X-ray plate.

A technique dependent on retrograde axonal flow has been used extensively to demonstrate the origin of fibre tracts. In this technique the enzyme peroxidase is taken up by axon terminals and is transported up the axon to the soma, where it can be shown by appropriate staining.

The staining of neurotransmitter substances is possible in postmortem human material as well as in animals and is an important method. Success, however, is dependent on examining relatively fresh or frozen material, and results may be greatly affected by previous treatment with neurologically active drugs.

Electrical stimulation of a region of the nervous system gives rise to the generation of nerve impulses in centres receiving input from the site of stimulation. This method, using microelectrodes, has been widely used in animal studies. The precise path followed by the artificially generated impulse may be difficult to establish.

Receptors

Receptors are biologic transducers, converting the various kinds of energy they receive from the external and internal environments into electrical impulses. They are of many kinds and are classified in many ways. Steady-state receptors, for example, generate impulses as long as a particular state such as temperature remains constant. Changing-state receptors, on the other hand, respond to variation in the intensity or position of the stimulus. Receptors are also classified as exteroceptive (reporting the external environment), interoceptive (sampling the environment of the body itself), and proprioceptive (sensing the posture and movements of the body). Exteroceptors are used for looking, listening, smelling, tasting, touching, and feeling. Interoceptors report the state of the bladder, the alimentary canal, the blood pressure, and the osmotic pressure of the blood plasma. Proprioceptors report the position and movements of parts of the body and the position of the body in space.

Classifying receptors according to stimulus

Receptors are also classified according to the kinds of stimulus to which they are sensitive. Chemical receptors, or chemoreceptors, are sensitive to substances taken into the mouth (taste or gustatory receptors), inhaled through the nose (smell or olfactory receptors), or found in the body itself (detectors of glucose or of acid–base balance in the blood). Receptors of the skin are classified as thermoreceptors, mechanoreceptors, and nociceptors—the last being sensitive to stimulation that is noxious, or likely to damage the tissues of the body.

Thermoreceptors of the skin are of two kinds, warmth and cold. Warmth fibres are excited by rising temperature and inhibited by falling temperature, and cold fibres respond in the opposite manner.

Mechanoreceptors in the skin are also of several different

types. Sensory nerve terminals around the base of hairs are activated by very slight movement of the hair, but they rapidly adapt to continued stimulation and stop firing. In hairless skin there are both rapidly and slowly adapting receptors. These can provide information about the force of mechanical stimulation. The Pacinian corpuscles, elaborate structures found in the skin of the fingers but also in other organs, are layers of fluid-filled membranes forming structures just visible to the naked eye at the terminals of axons. The precise function of the corpuscles is not fully known, but they are probably activated by rapidly changing or alternating stimuli such as vibration.

In some places receptors are massed together to form a sense organ, such as the eye or ear. At other places they are scattered, as are those of the skin and viscera. Receptors are connected to the central nervous system by afferent nerve fibres. The region or area in the periphery from which a neuron within the central nervous system receives input is called its receptive field. Receptive fields are changing and not fixed entities.

All receptors report two features of stimulation, its intensity and its site. Intensity is signaled by the frequency of nerve impulse discharge in a neuron and also by the number of afferent nerves reporting the stimulation. As the strength of a stimulus increases, the change in electrical potential of the receptor increases, and the frequency of nerve impulse generation likewise increases. (The relationship between the magnitude of the receptor potential and the frequency of nerve impulse generation is discussed above; see *Form and function of nervous systems.*)

The location of a stimulus, whether in the environment or in the body, is readily resolved by the nervous system. Localization of stimuli in the environment depends to a great extent on having pairs of receptors, one on each side of the body. For example, people in early childhood learn that a loud sound is probably coming from a nearer source than a weak sound. They localize the sound by noticing the difference in intensity and the minimal difference in time of arrival at the ears, increasing these differences by turning the head.

Locating stimuli with multiple receptors

Localization of a stimulus on the skin depends upon the arrangement of nerve fibres in the skin and in the deep tissues beneath the skin, as well as upon the overlap of receptive fields. Most mechanical stimuli indent the skin, stimulating nerve fibres in the connective tissue below the skin. Any point on the skin is supplied by at least three, and sometimes up to 40, nerve fibres, and no two points are supplied by precisely the same pattern of fibres (Figure 27).

Finer localization is achieved by what is called surround inhibition. In the retina, for example, there is an inhibitory area around the excited area. This mechanism accentuates the excited area, making it stand out. There can also be a mechanism called surround excitation, in which a central area is inhibited and the surrounding area excited. In both cases contrast is brought out and discrimination sharpened.

From P.W. Nathan, *Nervous System*, 2nd ed. (1982); Oxford University Press

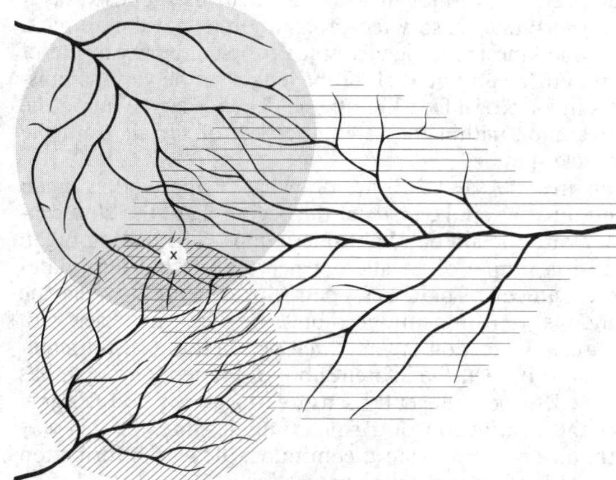

Figure 27: Diagram illustrating how a single point (x) on the skin is supplied by at least three nerve fibres.

In seeking information about the environment, the nervous system presents the most sensitive receptors to a stimulating object. At its simplest, this action is reflex. In the retina is a small region about the size of a pinhead, called the fovea, which is particularly sensitive to colour. When a part of the periphery of the visual field is excited, a reflex movement of the head and eyes focuses the light rays upon that part on the fovea. A similar reflex turns the head and eyes in the direction of a noise. As the English physiologist Charles Sherrington said in 1900, "In the limbs and mobile parts, when a spot of less discriminative sensitivity is touched, instinct moves the member, so that it brings to the object the part where its own sensitivity is delicate. . . ."

Reflex actions

Of the many kinds of neural activity, there is one simple kind in which a stimulus leads to an immediate action. This is reflex activity. The word reflex was introduced into biology by a 19th-century neurologist, Marshall Hall, who fashioned the word from Latin *reflexus* ("reflection") because he thought of the muscles as reflecting a stimulus much as a wall reflects a ball thrown against it. By reflex, Hall meant the automatic response of a muscle or several muscles to a stimulus that excites an afferent nerve. The word is now used to mean a certain kind of inborn central nervous activity, not involving consciousness, in which a particular stimulus, by exciting an afferent nerve, produces a stereotyped, immediate response of muscle or gland. If the same activity involves consciousness, it is not categorized as a reflex.

Reflex as unconscious activity

The anatomical pathway used in a reflex is called the reflex arc. It consists of an afferent (or sensory) nerve, usually one or more interneurons within the central nervous system, and an efferent (motor, secretory, or secretomotor) nerve. (For detailed description of the structures making up the reflex arc, see above *Anatomy of the human nervous system: The central nervous system.*)

Most reflexes have several synapses in the reflex arc. The stretch reflex is exceptional in that, with no interneuron in the arc, it has only one synapse between the afferent nerve fibre and the motor neuron (see below *Movement: The regulation of muscular contraction*). The flexor reflex, which removes a limb from a noxious stimulus, has a minimum of two interneurons and three synapses.

Probably the best-known reflex is the pupillary light reflex. If a light is flashed near one eye, the pupils of both eyes contract. Light is the stimulus, impulses reach the brain via the optic nerve, and the response is conveyed to the pupillary musculature by autonomic nerves that supply the eye.

Another ocular reflex is the lacrimal reflex. When something irritates the conjunctiva or cornea of the eye, nerve impulses pass along the trigeminal nerve and reach the midbrain. The efferent limb of this reflex arc is autonomic and mainly parasympathetic. These nerve fibres stimulate the lacrimal glands of the orbit, causing the outpouring of tears. Other reflexes of the midbrain and medulla oblongata are the cough and sneeze reflexes. The cough reflex is set off by an irritant in the trachea and the sneeze reflex by one in the nose. In both, the reflex response involves many muscles; this includes a temporary diversion of respiration from its usual biochemically ordered function in order to expel the irritant.

The first reflexes develop in the womb. By seven and a half weeks after conception, the first reflex can be observed: stimulation around the mouth of the fetus causes the lips to be turned toward the stimulus. By birth, sucking and swallowing reflexes are ready for use. Touching the baby's lips induces sucking, and touching the back of its throat induces swallowing.

Although the word stereotyped is used in the above definition, this does not mean that the reflex response is invariable and unchangeable. When a stimulus is repeated regularly, two changes occur in the reflex response—sensitization and habituation. Sensitization is an increase in response; in general it occurs during the first 10 to 20 responses. Habituation is a decrease in response; it contin-

Sensitization and habituation

ues until, eventually, the response is extinguished. When the stimulus is irregularly repeated, habituation does not occur or is minimal.

There are also long-term changes in reflexes, which may be seen in experimental spinal cord transections performed on kittens. Repeated stimulation of the skin below the level of the lesion, such as rubbing the same area for 20 minutes every day, causes a change in latency (the interval between the stimulus and the onset of response) of certain reflexes, with diminution and finally extinction of the response. Although this procedure takes several weeks, it shows that, with daily stimulation, one reflex response can be changed into another. Repeated activation of synapses increases their efficiency, causing some kind of lasting change. When this repeated stimulation is stopped, the reflex responses return to their original form, for there is a regression of synaptic function with disuse.

Although a reflex response is said to be rapid and immediate, some reflexes, called recruiting reflexes, can hardly be evoked by a single stimulus. Instead, they require increasing stimulation to induce the response. The reflex contraction of the bladder, for example, requires an increasing amount of urine to stretch the muscle and to obtain muscular contraction.

Reflexes can be changed by impulses from higher levels of the central nervous system. For example, the cough reflex can be suppressed easily, and even the gag reflex (the movements of incipient vomiting resulting from mechanical stimulation of the wall of the pharynx) can be suppressed with training.

The so-called conditioned reflexes are not reflexes at all but complicated acts of learned behaviour. Salivation is one such conditioned reflex. It occurs only when the person is conscious of the presence of food or when he imagines food.

Movement

Every movement of the body has to be correct for force, speed, and position. These aspects of movement are continuously reported to the central nervous system by receptors sensitive to the position, posture, equilibrium, and internal conditions of the body. These receptors are called proprioceptors, and those proprioceptors that keep a continuous report on the position of the limbs are the muscle spindles and tendon organs. (Proprioceptors reporting acceleration and direction of movement are located in the vestibular apparatus of the inner ear. For detailed discussion, see below *The vestibular system.*)

Forty-five percent of the weight of an adult male consists of muscle. The muscles of the trunk and limbs are known as skeletal muscles; they are attached to bones and produce movement at the joints. Skeletal muscles are innervated by efferent motor nerves and sometimes by efferent sympathetic and parasympathetic nerves. Muscles of the viscera (alimentary canal and bladder, for example) are called smooth muscle; they are innervated by efferent sympathetic and parasympathetic nerves.

The movements of the body are brought about by the harmonious contraction and relaxation of selected muscles. Contraction occurs when nerve impulses are transmitted across the neuromuscular junctions to the membrane covering each muscle fibre. Most of the muscles of the body are not continually contracting but are kept in a state ready to contract. The slightest movement or even the intention to move results in widespread activity of the muscles of the trunk and limbs.

Movements may be intrinsic to the body itself and carried out by muscles of the trunk and body cavity. Examples are those involved in breathing, swallowing, laughing, sneezing, urinating, and defecating. Other movements relate the body to the environment, either for moving or for signaling to other individuals. These are carried out by skeletal muscle.

Controlling movement at several levels of the nervous system

Movements can be organized at several levels of the nervous system. At the lowest level are movements of the viscera, some of which do not involve the central nervous system, being controlled by neurons of the autonomic nervous system within the viscera themselves.

At the next level is the spinal cord. If the spinal cord is cut across so that no nerve impulses reach it from the brain, certain movements of the trunk and limbs below the level of the injury can still occur. This state is called paraplegia; if the damage to the cord is above the upper limbs, it is called quadriplegia. Immediately after the cord has been divided, there is a state called spinal shock, when no movements of the skeletal muscles can be induced. Weeks or months later the period of shock passes and movements return. They are not commanded by the brain, however, and they are greatly augmented—that is, uncontrolled reflex movements may continue for minutes or hours, one reflex following another.

At a higher level, respiratory movements are controlled by the lower brain stem. The upper brain stem controls muscles of the eye, the bladder, and basic movements of walking and running. At the next level is the hypothalamus. It commands certain totalities of movement, such as those of vomiting, urinating and defecating, and curling up and going to sleep.

At the highest level is gray matter of the cerebral hemispheres, both the cortex and the subcortical basal ganglia. This is the level of conscious control of movements.

The natural phenomena included in movement cannot be neatly classified. The categories given above do not include some essential contributions, such as the influence of the cerebellum, occurring at every level. (P.W.N.)

THE REGULATION OF MUSCULAR CONTRACTION

Only a minority of the nerve fibres supplying a muscle are the ordinary motor fibres that actually make it contract. The rest are either afferent sensory fibres telling the central nervous system what the muscle is doing, or they are specialized motor fibres regulating the behaviour of the sensory nerve endings. If the constant feedback of proprioceptive information from the muscles, tendons, and joints is cut off, movements can still occur, but they cannot be adjusted in the face of external disturbances or readily modified to suit changing conditions; nor can new motor skills be developed. As stated above, the sensory receptors chiefly concerned with body movement are the muscle spindles and the tendon organs. The muscle spindle is vastly more complicated than the tendon organ, so that although it has been much more intensively studied, it is less well understood.

The simple knee-jerk reflex

The muscle spindle. The familiar knee jerk, tested routinely by physicians, is a spinal reflex in which a brief, rapid stretch excites muscle spindle afferent neurons, which then excite the motor neurons of the stretched muscle via a single synapse in the spinal cord. In this simplest of reflexes, which is not transmitted through interneurons of the spinal cord, virtually all the delay (approximately 0.02 second) occurs in the conduction of impulses to and from the spinal cord.

Information provided by muscle spindles is also put to elaborate use by the cerebellum and the cerebral cortex in ways that continue to elude detailed analysis. One example is kinesthesia, or the subjective sensory awareness of the position of limbs in space. It might be supposed (as it long was) that sensory receptors in joints, not the muscles, provide kinesthetic signals, since people are very aware of joint angle and not at all of the length of the various muscles involved. In fact, kinesthesia depends largely upon the integration within the cerebral cortex of signals from the muscle spindles.

Figures 28A and 28B are drawings of the tendon organ and muscle spindle made at the beginning of the 20th century with the aid of a light microscope. The tendon organ consists simply of an afferent nerve fibre that terminates in a number of branches upon slips of tendon where the tendons join onto muscle fibres. By lying in series with muscle, the tendon organ is well placed to signal muscular tension. In fact, the afferent fibre of the tendon organ has proved to be sufficiently sensitive to give a useful signal on the contraction of a single muscle fibre. In this way tendon organs provide a continuous flow of information on the level of muscular contraction.

The muscle spindle is much larger and more complicated; moreover, new features of its structure and function

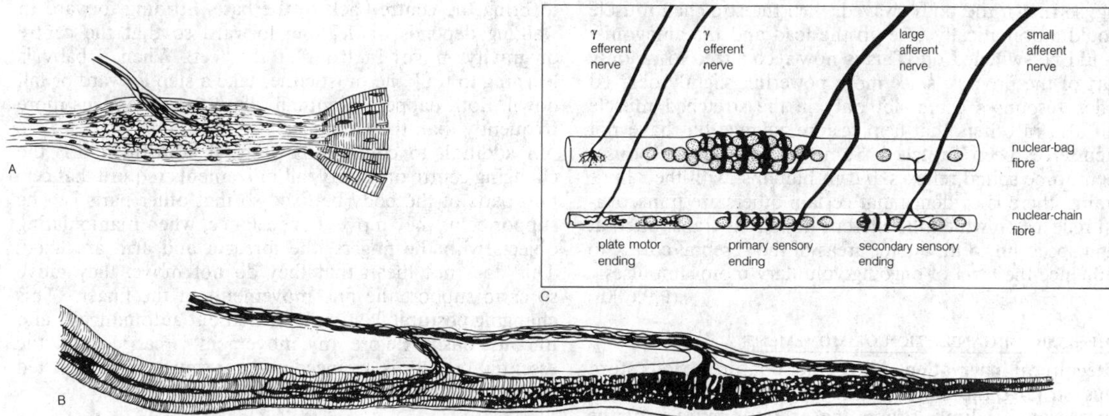

Figure 28: (A) The tendon organ as drawn in 1909 by the Spanish biologist Santiago Ramón y Cajal. The nerve fibre terminates on a tendon, with muscle fibres lying to the right. (B) The muscle spindle as drawn in 1898 by the Italian anatomist Angelo Ruffini, illustrating three types of nerve terminal—primary sensory endings, secondary sensory endings, and motor plates. (C) Simplified modern diagram of the central region (about one millimetre) of the muscle spindle. Two types of intrafusal fibre, the nuclear-bag and nuclear-chain, are shown, each having a distinct motor supply and different relationship to the two kinds of sensory ending. A given muscle spindle contains two to three bag fibres and four to six chain fibres.

From (A) S.R. Cajal, *Histologie du systeme nerveux de l'homme et des vertebres* (1909), vol. 1, Maloine, Paris; (B) A. Ruffini, *Journal of Physiology* (1898), Physiological Society of Great Britain; (C) P.B.C. Matthews, *Physiological Review* (1964), The American Physiological Society

continue to be discovered. Within it are several specialized muscle fibres, known as intrafusal muscle fibres (from Latin *fusus,* "spindle"). The spindle is several millimetres long, and the approximately five intrafusal muscle fibres run throughout its length. They are considerably thinner and shorter than the ordinary skeletal muscle fibres, though they show similar contractions and have the same histological appearance. The characteristic central swelling of the spindle (giving it a shape reminiscent of the spindle of a spinning wheel) is produced by fluid contained in a capsule surrounding the central millimetre of the intrafusal fibres. Figure 28C illustrates this central region.

Sensory receptors of the muscle spindle

Classically, the nerve terminals are considered to be of three kinds, namely primary sensory endings, secondary sensory endings, and plate motor endings. There are approximately equal numbers of primary and secondary sensory endings, so that they may be considered equally important. However, the primary, or annulo-spiral, ending has traditionally attracted the most attention, largely through its prominent appearance and the simplicity of its chief reflex action, the tendon jerk. It consists of a large axon, which branches to wind spirals around the equatorial region of every intrafusal fibre. The secondary ending is supplied by a smaller axon. It has less dramatic "flower spray" terminals lying mostly upon the smaller intrafusal fibres to one side of the primary ending. The reflex actions of the secondary ending remain incompletely understood. The plate motor endings lie toward the ends of the intrafusal fibres. They are fairly similar to the ordinary motor end plates of the skeletal, or extrafusal, muscle fibres.

Two separate types of intrafusal muscle fibre are distinguished, both histologically and on their contractile properties, as nuclear-bag and nuclear-chain intrafusal fibres. These have since been further subdivided and the complexities multiply, but there is general agreement that just as the spindle has a dual afferent innervation, it also has a dual motor supply.

The working of this elaborate piece of biologic machinery is not yet fully understood. The muscle spindle lies "in parallel" with the main muscle fibres and so sends a signal whenever the muscle changes its length. Both types of sensory endings increase their discharge of impulses when the muscle is stretched and reduce their firing when the muscle is slackened. The primary ending differs from the secondary ending in two important respects: first, it is much more sensitive to changing length of the muscle; second, it is much more sensitive to small stimuli than large ones. Together, these properties explain the exquisite sensitivity of the primary sensory ending to the stimulus of a tendon tap, which has little effect on the secondary ending or on the tendon organ. The essential principle is that the ability of the muscle spindle to signal a wide range of movement is increased by its having two separate output channels of different sensitivity.

Motor endings of the muscle spindle

The motor supply of the muscle spindle is more complex. Most of the intrafusal fibres receive specialized fusimotor nerve fibres. These are much smaller than the motor axons innervating extrafusal muscle fibres and are given the name gamma (γ) efferents. As their sole function is to regulate the behaviour of the muscle spindles, their stimulation produces no significant contraction of the muscle as a whole. The γ efferents are of two functionally distinct kinds with different effects on the afferent fibres—especially on the primary ending. One type, the dynamic fusimotor axon, increases the normal sensitivity of the primary ending to movement; the other type, the static fusimotor axon, decreases its sensitivity, making it behave much more like a secondary ending. Thus, the two types of efferent fibre provide a means whereby the sensitivity of the muscle spindle to external stimuli may be regulated over a very wide range. Stimulation of both types also increases the rate of firing of the afferent fibres when the length of the muscle is constant; this is called a biasing action. It is believed that they produce these different effects by supplying different types of intrafusal fibre.

In addition to receiving specialized fusimotor fibres, the muscle spindle may also receive, though on a less regular basis, branches of the ordinary extrafusal motor axons. Called alpha (α) efferents, these fibres have either a static or dynamic effect. The physiologically important point is that most of the motor supply to the muscle spindles is largely independent of that of the ordinary muscle fibres, and only a small part is obligatorily coupled with them. The specific mechanisms by which the sensitivity of the spindle is regulated remain obscure; they may differ from muscle to muscle and for movements of different kinds.

Stretch reflexes including antagonistic muscles

Stretch reflexes. The primary afferents are responsible for the stretch reflex, in which pulling the tendon of a muscle causes the muscle to contract. As noted above, the basis for this simple spinal reflex is a monosynaptic excitation of the motor neurons of the stretched muscle. At the same time, however, motor neurons of the antagonist muscle (the muscle that moves the limb in the opposite direction) are inhibited. This action is mediated by an inhibitory interneuron interposed between the afferent neuron and the motor neuron. These reflexes have a transitory, or phasic, action, even though the afferent impulses continue unabated; this is probably because they become submerged in more complex delayed reflex responses elicited by the same and other afferent inputs.

Traditionally, it was thought that the stretch reflex provided uniquely for the automatic reflex control of standing, so that if the body swayed, then the stretched muscle would automatically take up the load and the antagonist would be switched off. This is now recognized to be only part of the process, since more powerful, slightly delayed reflex responses occur not only in the stretched muscle but also in others that help restore balance but have not themselves been stretched. Some of these late responses seem to be spinal reflexes, but in humans, with their huge brains, there is evidence that certain others are transcortical reflexes, in which the afferent impulse is transmitted at high speed up to the motor areas of the cerebral cortex to influence the level of ongoing voluntary motor impulses.

(P.B.C.M.)

THE BASIC ORGANIZATION OF MOVEMENT

Reciprocal innervation. Any cold, hot, or noxious stimulus striking the skin of the foot contracts the flexor muscle of that limb, relaxes the extensor muscles of the same limb, and extends the opposite limb. The purpose of these movements is to remove one limb from harm while shifting weight to the opposite limb. That is the first and immediate response, but a slower and longer-lasting reflex response is also possible. For example, noxious stimulation of the deep tissues of the limb can cause a prolonged discharge of impulses conducted by nonmyelinated afferent fibres to the spinal cord. The result is prolonged flexion of the damaged limb or at least a pattern of posture and movement favouring flexion. These effects last far longer than the original discharges from the afferent neurons of the damaged region—often continuing not for minutes but for weeks or months.

The flexor and extensor reflexes are only two examples of the sequential ordering of muscular contraction and relaxation. Underlying this basic organization is the principle of reciprocal innervation—the contraction of one muscle or group of muscles with the relaxation of muscles that have the opposite function. In reciprocal innervation, afferent nerve fibres from the contracting muscle excite inhibitory interneurons in the spinal cord; the interneurons, by inhibiting certain motor neurons, cause an antagonist muscle to relax.

Reciprocal innervation can be seen in eye movements. On looking to the right, the right lateral rectus and left medial rectus muscles contract, while the antagonist left lateral rectus and right medial rectus muscles relax. One eye cannot be turned without turning the other eye in the same direction (except in the movement of convergence, when both eyes turn medially toward the nose in looking at a near object).

Reciprocal innervation does not underlie all movement. For example, in order to fix the knee joint, antagonist muscles must contract simultaneously. Indeed, in the movement of walking, there are both reciprocal innervation and simultaneous contraction of different sets of muscle. Because this basic organization of movement takes place at lower levels of the nervous system, the training of skilled movements such as walking requires the suppression of some lower-level reflexes as well as a proper arrangement of the reciprocal inhibition and simultaneous contraction of antagonist muscles.

Posture. Posture is defined as the position and carriage of the limbs and the body as a whole. Except when lying down, the first postural requirement is to counteract the pull of gravity. This is done by the stretch reflexes. Gravity pulls the body—every part of the body—toward the ground. This force induces stretch reflexes to keep the lower limbs extended and the back upright. The muscles are not kept contracting all the time, however. As the posture alters and the centre of gravity changes, different muscles are stretched and contracted. Another important reflex is the extensor thrust reflex of the lower limb. Pressure on the foot stretches the ligaments of the sole, which causes reflex contraction of both flexor and extensor muscles, making the leg into a rigid pillar. As soon as the sole of the foot leaves the ground, the reflex response ceases, and the limb is free to move again.

The body is balanced when the centre of gravity is above the base formed by the feet. When the centre of gravity moves outside this base, the body starts to fall and has to bring the centre back to the base. Striding forward in walking depends on leaning forward so that the centre of gravity moves in front of the feet. When a baby is learning to walk, he must either take a step forward or fall down. Both happen; eventually the former happens more frequently than the latter.

Unconscious adjustment of posture

In addition to continuous postural adjustment for the changing centre of gravity, all movements require that certain parts of the body be fixed so that other parts can be supported as they move. For instance, when manipulating objects with the fingers, the forearm and arm are fixed. This does not mean that they do not move; they move so as to support the fine movements of the fingers. This changing postural fixation is carried out automatically and unconsciously. Before any movement is carried out, the essential posture is arranged and continues to be adjusted throughout the movement.

LOWER-LEVEL MECHANISMS OF MOVEMENT

The success of Charles Sherrington in opening up the physiology and pathology of movement by the study of reflexes caused a lack of interest in any other concept of movement, particularly in English-speaking lands. It was the German physiologist Erich Walter von Holst who, around the mid-20th century, first showed that many series of movements of invertebrates and vertebrates are organized not reflexly but endogenously. His general hypothesis was that within the gray matter there are networks of local neurons that generate alternating or cyclical patterns of movement. Von Holst proposed that these are the mechanisms of such rhythmically repeated movements as the movements of locomotion, breathing, scratching, feeding, and chewing.

In fish, von Holst demonstrated that the movements of the fins in swimming that need careful and correct timing and coordination continued even after the sensory dorsal roots of the spinal cord had been cut, so that there could be no sensory input to trigger reflexes. In these animals, command neurons in the lower medulla oblongata switch on the rhythmical movement built into the spinal cord, so that even when the brain has been cut out, the motor impulses and rhythmic movements continue.

Von Holst's theory differs from previous concepts in that it attributes little or no importance to the role of feedback from the parts of the body being moved. Instead, it proposes, as the essential mechanism of repetitive movements, certain central pacemakers or oscillators. The role of feedback, according to this theory, is merely to modulate the central oscillator. This is seen in the above example of swimming movements of fish and even in purring rhythms in cats, which continue after dorsal roots have been cut.

In certain kinds of movement the input of the dorsal roots is essential, but the movement needs to be defined in every case. For example, stepping movements of certain vertebrates, of which the mechanisms are within the spinal cord, can occur only with intact dorsal roots.

Higher levels of the brain can set spinal centres in motion, can stop them, and can change the amplitude and frequency of repetitive movements. In the case of humans, when the spinal cord is cut off from the brain by disease or trauma, the movements that occur are uncontrolled. The movements of locomotion, seen in lower vertebrates, do not occur. This is because the cerebral hemispheres in humans have taken over the organization of movements that in lower species are organized at lower levels of the central nervous system, such as the reticular formation of the brain stem and the spinal cord.

Within the centre of the brain stem the reticular formation consists of vast numbers of neurons and their interconnections. The majority of them have motor functions, and many of their fibres branch. This branching means that a single fibre can affect several different levels of the spinal cord. For example, one nerve fibre may excite motor neurons of the neck and of various regions of the back. This is one way in which commands from the higher neural level are sent to several segments of the spinal cord.

The movements of breathing are instigated and regu-

Regulation of rhythmic movement

lated by chemoreceptors in blood vessel walls, which sense carbon dioxide tension in the blood plasma. The essential drive or central rhythm generator consists of pacemaker neurons in the reticular formation of the pons and throughout the medulla oblongata. These neurons show rhythmic changes in electrical potential, which are relayed by reticulospinal tracts to the spinal neurons concerned with respiration. When this pathway is severed, breathing ceases.

Other movements intrinsic to the body are those needed for urination and defecation. Cats and dogs from which the cerebral cortex has been removed urinate and defecate in a normal manner. This is because nuclei in the midbrain near those that organize the movements of locomotion control these movements, so that urination and defecation occur whenever there are enough waste products to be expelled. This is also the condition of the healthy baby animal. But as the infant grows up, it learns to fit these events into the social circumstances of living, and this requires higher-level control by the cerebral hemispheres.

HIGHER-LEVEL MECHANISMS OF MOVEMENT

Because of the many differences in the movements used in standing, coughing, or laughing, or playing a scale on the piano, it is convenient to think of movements as lower and more automatic or as higher and less automatic. According to this concept, movements are not placed in totally different categories but are regarded as different in degree.

Cerebral hemispheres. Basic organizations of movement, such as reciprocal innervation, are organized at levels of the central nervous system lower than the cerebral hemispheres—both at the spinal and brain-stem level. Examples of brain-stem reflexes are turning of the eyes and head toward a light or sound. The same movements, of course, can also be organized consciously when one decides to turn the head and eyes to look. The cerebral hemispheres themselves can organize certain series of movements that are often referred to as programmed movements. These are movements that need to be performed so rapidly that there is no time for correction of error by local feedback. For this reason the program is arranged before the movements begin. Examples of such movements are those of a pianist performing a trill or of an athlete hitting a ball.

Most of the movements organized by the cerebral cortex are carried out automatically. But when a new series of movements is being learned, or when a movement is difficult, the attributes usually associated with the higher levels of the brain—such as planning, internal speech, remembering, and learning—are used. (For the role of the cerebral hemispheres in these higher mental activities, see below *Higher cerebral functions.*)

Motor areas of the brain

In the 19th century the first motor area of the cerebral cortex was discovered by electrical stimulation. Successive areas responding to electrical stimulation were numbered in the order of their discovery. Therefore, although motor and sensory areas are named numerically, no hierarchical organization is implied.

The first motor area to be discovered was the motor strip of the precentral gyrus; it became known as the primary motor area (Figure 29). Immediately behind it is the postcentral gyrus, found on electrical stimulation to be sensory; it was named the primary sensory area. Each of these areas displays a maplike correspondence with various body parts, the legs represented near the top of the hemispheres and the arms and face lower on the cortical surface. Each of these areas is to some extent both motor and sensory. The motor region, for example, receives inputs from the skin, joints, and muscles via the postcentral gyrus behind and the thalamus below.

Experiments in monkeys have shown that the motor strip is able to arrange activity of muscles to produce the correct force for the loading conditions of the limbs. To do this, it continually receives information from the primary sensory area both before and during the movement. Cutaneous areas having the greatest tactile acuity have the largest representative in the primary sensory area; these areas are connected to equally large areas in the primary motor area.

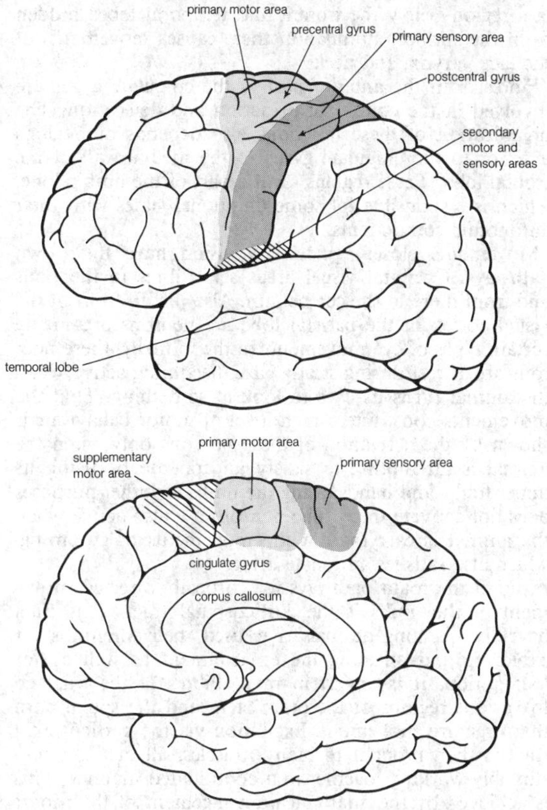

Figure 29: (Top) Lateral and (bottom) medial views of the cerebral hemispheres, showing motor and sensory areas.

Reproduced by permission of Catherine Parker Anthony and Gary A. Thibodeau, *Textbook of Anatomy & Physiology*, 12th ed. (1987), Times Mirror/Mosby College Publishing, St. Louis, adapted from K. Brodmann, "Feinere Anatomie des Grosshirns," in *Handbuch der Neurologie* (1910), Springer-Verlag, Berlin

In front of the motor strip is an area known as the premotor cortex or area. When this area is stimulated in a monkey, the animal turns its head and eyes as though it is looking in a particular direction. This cortical area, then, organizes the guiding of movements by vision and hearing.

An area labeled the secondary motor area is at the lower end of the precentral gyrus. It is secondary not only because it was discovered after the primary motor area but also because it does not function in a discrete manner like the primary area. Stimulation of this small area produces movements of large parts of the body. It is also a sensory area, as sensations in the parts of the body being moved are felt during stimulation.

The supplementary motor area

On the medial surface of the hemisphere, in front of the motor strip, is the supplementary motor area. Stimulation there can produce vocalization or can interrupt speech. There also may be large movements of both sides of the body—often symmetrical movements of the two limbs. Stimulation also produces movements of the opposite side, such as raising the upper limb and turning the head and eyes as if looking at something opposite. In experiments on monkeys, when the animal chooses to respond to one kind of sensation rather than to another, it is the supplementary area that is active rather than the precentral area. In this animal—it is unknown for humans—the fibres descending from the supplementary motor area run to the spinal cord and terminate throughout its whole length. Fibres are also sent to the precentral gyri of both hemispheres, the reticular formation of the pons, the hypothalamus, the midbrain, and many other masses of cerebral gray matter such as the caudate nucleus and the globus pallidus. The supplementary motor area is upstream from the primary motor area; it initiates movements, whereas the motor strip of the precentral gyrus is part of the apparatus for carrying them out.

Other regions of the cerebral hemisphere from which movements are produced on electrical stimulation are the insula and the surface of the temporal lobe. Stimulation of the anterior end of one temporal lobe causes movements of the head and body toward the other side. The insula is a region below the frontal and temporal lobes hidden from the surface; stimulation there causes movements of the face, larynx, and neck.

Fibres from the anterior part of the cingulate gyrus are involved in the control of urination and defecation. The organization of these functions also depends on regions anterior to the cingulate gyrus in the medial wall of the frontal lobe. These regions form a part of the limbic lobe, which is responsible for some emotional states with their autonomic components.

Movements closely guided by vision have their own pathways. Occipital visual areas send fibres to the pons and from there to the cerebellum. Also just in front of the visual cortex in the parietal lobe are neurons organizing certain types of eye movement. In the monkey, these neurons are at rest during steady gaze, becoming active when the animal turns its eyes to look at something. That the movements constitute a high level of motor behaviour is shown by the activation of these neurons only when the animal is attempting to satisfy an appetite by using its upper limbs and hands; using the limbs for other purposes does not activate them. The neurons are also active when the animal is carrying out the movements of grooming, which also satisfies an innate drive.

One of the main pathways for cortically directed movement of the limbs is the corticospinal tract. This tract developed among animals that used their forelimbs for exploring and affecting the environment as well as for locomotion. It is largest in man. Fibres of the tract go to various regions of the brain stem and the spinal cord that organize movement. Excitation via the corticospinal tract is then brought to many muscles, all of them presumably working together in a coordinated manner. This is achieved by the anatomical arrangement of the motor neurons and by the termination of the corticospinal tract on interneurons, which convey a coordinated pattern of stimulation to the motor neurons.

The corticospinal tract is not merely a straight pathway to medullary and spinal motor neurons. Activity in this tract can suppress the input from cutaneous areas while facilitating proprioceptive input. This is probably a mechanism important in the organization of movement. The corticospinal neurons themselves receive constant input needed for internal feedback. This input comes from the cerebellum, much of it having originated in the muscles, joints, and skin of the body parts being moved.

The control of complex movement through sensory feedback

Cerebellum. Although a cycle of simple repetitive movements can be organized without sensory feedback, more sophisticated movements require feedback as well as what is called feed-forward control. This is provided by the cerebellum. Many parts of the brain have to be kept informed of movements being carried out in order to detect error and continually correct the movement. The cerebellum continuously receives inputs from the trunk, limbs, eyes, ears, and vestibular apparatus, maintaining in turn a continuous transfer of information to the motor parts of the thalamus and to the cerebral cortex.

As a movement is being prepared, a replica of the instructions is sent to the cerebellum; the cerebellum sends back its own information to the cortex. The cortex, meanwhile, sends information about the movement to various afferent neurons that are about to receive information from receptors in the body parts where the movement is about to begin. This comparison between instructions sent and movement performed is a fundamental requirement of all complicated movement. The discharge of impulses from motor to sensory regions is called the corollary discharge. The mechanisms involving the cerebellum do not come to consciousness. There are no sensory consequences of damage to the cerebellum, for the cerebellum is a motor structure.

As series of movements are learned and improved with practice, a replica of the movement is probably retained in the cerebral hemispheres. (The mechanisms of this postulated "replica" are as yet unknown.) Whenever the learned movements are repeated, they are formed and guided by the replica. This hypothesis of controlling movement by previously practiced patterns was developed by von Holst. He gave the name efference to the totality of motor impulses necessary for a movement, and he proposed that whenever the efference is produced it leaves an image of itself somewhere in the central nervous system. This image he called the efference copy. According to von Holst's theory, as the movement is repeated, afferent impulses return to the brain from receptors activated by muscular activity. These impulses are called the re-afference. There is then a comparison between the efference copy and the re-afference. When they are identical, the movement is "correct" in relation to its previous performance. When the re-afference differs from the efference copy, corrections have to be made so as to bring the present pattern of movement back to the original image left in the brain.

If the cerebellum is damaged or degenerates, any error between the movement being performed and the efference copy will no longer be corrected, and the postural adjustments sent from the cerebral hemispheres will no longer be implemented. The force and extent of movements also will be abnormal, the movement going too far or not far enough. The various muscles may not come into play at the right time, and there will be a disturbance in the relationship of antagonist muscles, so that the accurate arrival on target will be replaced by oscillation.

Basal ganglia. Most of what is known about the contribution of the basal ganglia has been obtained from studying abnormal conditions that occur when these nuclei are affected by disease. In Parkinson's disease there is a loss of the pigmented neurons of the substantia nigra, which release the neurotransmitter dopamine at synapses in the basal ganglia. Patients with this disease have a certain type of muscle stiffness called rigidity, a typical tremor, flexed posture, and difficulty in maintaining equilibrium. They have difficulty in starting movements, including walking, and they cannot put adequate force into fast movements. They have particular difficulty in changing from one movement to its opposite, in carrying out two movements simultaneously, and in stopping one movement while starting another.

The organization of posture, which is based on vestibular, proprioceptive, and visual input to the globus pallidus, is severely damaged when this region of the basal ganglia degenerates. As a changing posture of the various parts of the body is a prerequisite of every movement, this factor alone upsets all movement. Visual reflexes contributing to motion also act through the globus pallidus. When this structure is degenerate, what the patient sees may affect his ability to move. One patient may be unable to go forward if he has to pass through a narrow door, another may not be able to do so if he has to go into a wide expanse like a field. (P.W.N.)

The vestibular system

Animals have evolved sophisticated sensory receptors to detect features of the environment in which they live. In addition to the special senses such as hearing and sight, there are unobtrusive sensory systems such as the vestibular system, which is sensitive to acceleration.

Linear and angular acceleration

Acceleration can be considered as occurring in two forms—linear and angular. One familiar type of linear acceleration is gravity. Because this environmental feature, unlike any other encountered by an organism, is always present, highly sophisticated systems have developed to detect gravity and enable an animal to maintain its position relative to the earth. A common form of angular acceleration is that induced by rotation, such as a turning of the head. Through the vestibular apparatus these forces are detected and appropriate motor activities are organized to counter the postural perturbations that they induce.

RECEPTORS

The vestibular sensory organ is a paired structure located symmetrically on either side of the head within the inner ear. Inside each end organ are the hair cells, the detection units for both linear and angular acceleration. Extending from one surface of each hair cell are fine, hairlike cilia, displacement of which alters the electrical potential of the cell. Bending the cilia in one direction causes the cell membrane to depolarize while hyperpolarization is induced by movement in the opposite direction. Changes in membrane potential induce alteration in the firing of nerve impulses by the afferent neurons supplying each hair cell. (For a discussion of the neurobiology of depolarization and hyperpolarization of cell membranes, see above *Form and function of nervous systems: Transmission of information in the nervous system.*)

The two types of acceleration are detected by two types of vestibular end organ. Linear acceleration is sensed by a pair of organs—the saccule and utricle—while there are three receptor organs—called semicircular canals—in each vestibular apparatus for the detection of angular acceleration.

Saccule and utricle. Each saccule and utricle has a single cluster, or macula, of hair cells located in the vertical and horizontal planes, respectively. Resting upon the hair cells is a gelatinous membrane in which are embedded calcareous granules known as otoliths. Changes in linear acceleration alter the pressure of the otoliths, causing changes in the distortion of the cilia and providing an adequate stimulus for membrane depolarization. Within each macula the hair cells are arranged in two groups oriented in opposite directions, so that the receptor functions in a push-pull fashion within each organ. Since many of the nerve fibres passing from the hair cells to the brain are constantly active, this push-pull arrangement makes the receptors a highly sensitive detection system for linear acceleration in the vertical and horizontal planes.

Semicircular canals. The angular acceleration detectors within the semicircular canals function in a different way. The three canals—which in fact are considerably more than a semicircle in circumference—are oriented at approximately right angles to one another. Two are vertically placed, and one is at about 30 degrees to the horizontal. In this arrangement the anterior canal of one side of the head is in the plane of the posterior canal of the other side. A ridge, or crista, covered by sensory hair cells is located at the end of each canal within an expanded chamber called the ampulla. The canals are filled with an endolymphatic fluid. Rotation of the canals about an axis passing through the centre of each semicircle causes the fluid to flow toward or away from the crista, generating a force that bends the cilia by displacement of a gelatinous plate resting upon the hairs. The cells of the vertical canals are oriented in such a way that centrifugal movement away from the cristae depolarizes the hair cell membranes, while the converse applies to the horizontal canal.

NERVE SUPPLY

As in the case of the utricle and saccule, some of the nerve fibres conveying information from the cells are constantly active. The hair cells receive nerve impulses from the brain (via efferent fibres) and send them to the central nervous system (via afferent fibres). Excitatory efferent fibres increase the sensitivity of the hair cells, while inhibitory fibres decrease sensitivity. This system gives the semicircular canals a plasticity that is essential to maintaining optimal activity under different environmental conditions—including such extraordinary states as the microgravity encountered in space travel.

The vestibular apparatus is supplied by neurons that make up the vestibular portion of the vestibulocochlear, or eighth cranial, nerve. The somata, or cell bodies, of the afferent fibres lie in the vestibular ganglion near the end organ. Most of the nerve fibres pass from there to vestibular nuclei in the pons, while others pass directly to the cerebellum. The efferent fibres of the vestibular nerve arise from nuclei in the pons.

VESTIBULAR FUNCTIONS

For vision to be effective, the retinal image must be stationary. This can be achieved only by maintaining the position of the eyes relative to the earth and using this stable platform for pursuing a moving target. The vestibular system plays a critical part in this, mainly through complex and incompletely understood connections between the vestibular apparatus and the musculature. Rotation of the head in any direction is detected by the semicircular canals, and a velocity signal is then passed via the vestibular nuclei to the somatic and extraocular muscles. In the case of the eye muscles, the velocity signal reaching the brain stem is in some way integrated with impulses signaling the eyes' position, thus ensuring that the eyes maintain their position relative to space and the object of regard. This integration partly occurs in the vestibular nuclei, the source of secondary neurons destined for the extraocular muscle nuclei of both sides.

Vestibulo-ocular reflex. When the head is oscillated, the eyes maintain their position in space but move in relation to the head. This so-called vestibulo-ocular reflex operates in both horizontal and vertical planes, owing to the arrangement of the three semicircular canals, and it maintains such stability that the object of vision does not oscillate until quite high velocities are attained. The other component of the vestibular system, the saccule and utricle, also contributes to the vestibulo-ocular reflex. Under normal circumstances the otolith receptors cause torsional movement of the eyes. For example, tilting the head toward one shoulder results in counter-rolling of the eyes, thereby stabilizing the image upon the retina. The two components of the vestibulo-ocular reflex also interact, enabling appropriate eye movements to be generated when both linear and angular accelerations are changing.

Importance of vestibular system to posture

While the vestibulo-ocular reflex is the best understood of the vestibulo-motor connections, information from the vestibular receptors is also known to be passed via vestibular and other brain-stem nuclei to the somatic musculature of the trunk and limbs. Through these pathways body posture is adjusted to counter acceleration forces applied to the vestibule. These reflexes are so important in maintaining vertical posture that devastating short-term consequences on posture are seen if the vestibulocochlear nerve is cut.

Conscious sensation. Besides maintaining input for the generation of motor reflexes, vestibular impulses reach consciousness and create a powerful sensation. A person being rotated knows when he is accelerating even in the absence of an object upon which he can fix his eyes. This occurs because acceleration is the adequate stimulus for the semicircular canals. Similarly, information detected by the otoliths is readily brought to consciousness—as occurs, for example, when a darkened elevator accelerates up or down. The pathways to the cerebral cortex, which mediate conscious sensation, are not fully known, but there is considerable evidence that areas of the parietal and temporal lobes receive connections via the thalamus.

One important aspect of vestibular physiology is the interaction of vestibular impulses, which signal changes of position, and impulses from other sensory receptors that signal changes in bodily movement. For example, when the head turns to one side about a vertical axis, not only is the horizontal canal of that side stimulated and that of the other side inhibited, but receptors in the neck joints and muscles are also stimulated, and the retina indicates movement if fixation is not maintained perfectly. This information is fed to the brain via sensory pathways in the spinal cord and various visual sensory systems. Therefore, within the vestibular nuclei of the pons, neurons that respond to acceleration signals from the semicircular canals receive impulses from other sources as well. Other information from visual and spinal sensory systems pass to the cerebellum, which also receives direct impulses from the vestibular apparatus that bypass the vestibular nuclei. In this way the cerebellum has the opportunity to compare signals and assess the degree of mismatch between them. (Such mismatch is an unpleasant experience and is important in the phenomenon of motion sickness. Motion sickness is often generated by a mismatch between the various inputs signaling orientation within space. People will frequently be seasick if they are below decks in rough weather and the visual system signals no movement while the vestibular system indicates motion.) In another example, the vestibulo-ocular reflex may be underactive, so that for a given head movement the eyes do not deviate sufficiently within the orbit and the object of regard does not remain stationary upon the retina. Thus, the image slips and cannot be seen clearly during movement. The cerebellum has the opportunity to detect this mismatch

Motion sickness

between the required position of the eyes with respect to the environment and the movement actually achieved. Through inhibitory connections to the vestibular nuclei, the cerebellum can then adjust the vestibulo-ocular reflex so that a more appropriate movement of the eyes is achieved with the next acceleration signal. In other words, there is a continual updating of the vestibulo-ocular reflex via the cerebellum or structures associated with it.

A similar situation also obtains for somatosensory input from the spinal cord. A dramatic demonstration of short-term adaptation via the visual system occurs when someone dons prisms that reverse the perception of the environment in the horizontal plane, making everything look upside down. The person is at first unable to move about because any rotation of the head results in apparent movement of the environment in the wrong direction. However, over a few days normal mobility gradually returns. Incredibly, during this time the vestibulo-ocular reflex is at first diminished in amplitude and then is reversed. Removal of the prisms results in a rapid return to the normal state. These experiments are a powerful demonstration of the plasticity of the vestibulo-ocular reflex, which can continue functioning throughout life in spite of the various insults that befall it. (P.Ru.)

The autonomic system

The autonomic nervous system comprises the sympathetic and parasympathetic systems. It is a purely motor system, but sensory input of almost any kind may affect it. A startling sound may raise the pulse and blood pressure, the sight of blood may cause a faint from a fall in blood pressure, warmth will cause skin flushing and perhaps sweating, and extreme fear may cause involuntary bladder emptying. These are all reflexes whose motor pathways are in the autonomic nervous system. There are, therefore, many parts of the central nervous system that can affect autonomic activity. (For a description of sympathetic and parasympathetic pathways, see above *Anatomy of the human nervous system: The autonomic nervous system.*)

SYMPATHETIC AND PARASYMPATHETIC TRANSMISSION

The neurotransmitters acetylcholine, epinephrine, and norepinephrine

Sympathetic. Preganglionic sympathetic fibres terminate on the somata, or bodies, of postganglionic neurons, whose fibres lead to the organs to be innervated, such as blood vessels, the heart, the gut, sweat glands, and the pupil. The preganglionic fibres act on the postganglionic neurons by passing into the synaptic gap between them the neurotransmitter acetylcholine. Such nerve junctions are described as cholinergic. The terminals of the postganglionic fibres also stimulate the organs that they activate by secreting neurotransmitter substances. In the sympathetic nervous system, this is usually norepinephrine, or noradrenaline; the mechanism is therefore referred to as adrenergic. (Sweat glands, however, are activated by acetylcholine, so that the mechanism is cholinergic.) The medulla of the adrenal gland is unique in being innervated directly by preganglionic fibres, whose transmitter substance is, as usual, acetylcholine. When activated, the cells of the adrenal medulla secrete epinephrine (or adrenaline) and some norepinephrine into the bloodstream; in this respect, adrenal medullar cells are analogous to adrenergic postganglionic neurons.

The actions of epinephrine and norepinephrine fall into two groups depending on the type of receptor—alpha (α) or beta (β)—present on the cell being innervated. Important α effects are constriction of most blood vessels, relaxation of the gut, and dilatation of the pupil. The β receptors effect dilatation of blood vessels in voluntary muscle, an increase in the rate and force of contraction of the heart, and relaxation of the airways in the lung. The α and β receptors are themselves not uniform and have been divided into α_1, α_2, β_1, and β_2. In blood vessels, α_1 receptors predominate in large arteries and α_2 in the smallest arteries, called arterioles. The β_1 receptors are particularly important in increasing the rate and force of the heartbeat. The β_2 receptors are concerned in dilating blood vessels in voluntary muscle. Norepinephrine predominantly affects α receptors, epinephrine both α and β receptors.

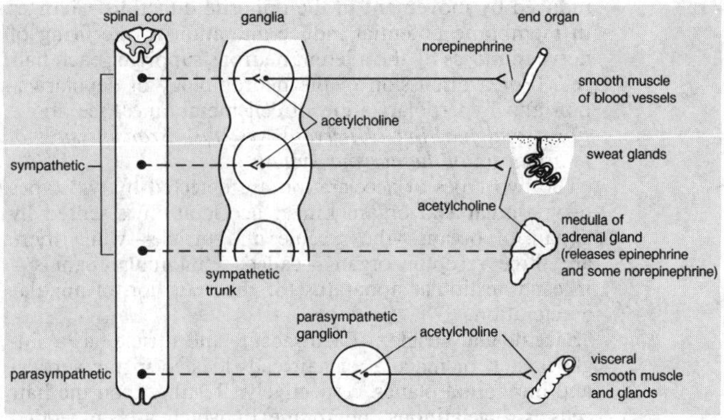

Figure 30: Chemical transmission in the autonomic nervous system.

Adapted from R.H. Johnson and J.M.K. Spalding, *Disorders of the Autonomic Nervous System* (1974); Blackwell's Scientific Publications, Oxford

Parasympathetic. Preganglionic parasympathetic fibres, unlike most of those of the sympathetic system, continue until close to or within the organ that they innervate and only then reach a ganglion where they synapse onto postganglionic neurons. Postganglionic parasympathetic fibres therefore have only a short distance to run before they reach the structure on which they act. In all parasympathetic neurons, acetylcholine is the neurotransmitter at both the ganglion and the postganglionic terminals, so that both synapses are cholinergic.

Cranial parasympathetic nerve fibres constrict the pupil and stimulate the salivary and lachrymal glands to produce saliva and tears, respectively. Through the vagus nerve they slow the heart, moderately constrict airways in the lungs, and increase activity in most of the alimentary tract. The sacral parasympathetic nerves increase activity in the lowest part of the alimentary tract and are concerned with bladder emptying and sexual function. (For discussion of neurotransmitter action at the cellular level, see above *Form and function of nervous systems: Transmission of information in the nervous system.*)

AUTONOMIC FUNCTIONS

Maintaining a constant internal environment

In general terms, the autonomic nervous system is an important part of the mechanism whereby the body keeps its internal environment constant.

Body temperature. The regulation of body temperature is a complex activity in which the autonomic nervous system plays a dominant part. This activity is coordinated in the central nervous system, particularly in the hypothalamus.

Deep body temperature in health is nearly constant. Measured in the mouth, it is about 36.7° C (98.1° F) in the morning and about 1° C (1.8° F) higher in the evening. Therefore humans, like most mammals, are to a considerable extent independent of the surrounding temperature. In order to achieve this stability, heat production and heat loss must be balanced. Heat, which is produced by metabolic activity, is lost chiefly from blood vessels near the surface of the body. If more blood flows through the surface vessels per unit of time—and especially if more vessels are made available for blood to flow through—then more heat will be lost to the surroundings.

The sympathetic nervous system regulates the calibre of the blood vessels by activating the smooth muscle of the vessels, with a resultant narrowing of their diameter, and can also control special vessels that, when open, act as shunts, allowing blood to bypass the surface vessels. This overall control of blood flow is initiated in a number of ways. Skin exposed to cold air, for example, becomes blanched or pale as the result of the narrowing of vessels in the skin, coupled with the opening of the vascular shunts. This reflex action is brought about as follows: cold air stimulates temperature-sensitive nerve receptors, and the nerve impulses thus initiated reach the brain—in particular, the hypothalamus, where they set off changes in the activity of the sympathetic system. Increased activity generates more impulses along sympathetic fibres to peripheral ganglia. From there, postganglionic fibres activate the smooth muscle of the surface vessels, thereby constricting them and reducing blood flow. At the same time, fibres to the smooth muscle of the shunts become less active so that the shunts open. This reflex mechanism results in a decrease in heat loss, thereby helping to maintain deep body temperature even though skin temperature falls. Reverse mechanisms operate in a warm environment and during exercise, as it is then necessary to increase heat loss. If the deep body temperature (particularly that of blood going to the brain) is altered, reflex changes in skin blood flow will be more readily set off by changes in skin temperature.

Fallback mechanisms are employed if changes in skin blood flow are not enough to keep deep body temperature near normal. In a hot environment or when heat production is substantially increased by exercise, the sympathetic system reflexly activates sweat glands in the skin. Sweat spreads on the skin, and, as it evaporates, heat is lost very efficiently. On the other hand, when the environment is very cold, the fallback mechanism is to produce more heat. This is done largely by increasing the activity of voluntary muscles, at first imperceptibly and then as shivering. The motor nerves for this are the ordinary somatic nerves to the muscles. Another method is to make heat by metabolizing brown fat, of which there are stores between the shoulder blades and elsewhere. Brown fat has a rich nerve supply from the sympathetic system, so that an increase in sympathetic activity stimulates metabolism of brown fat.

Circulation. The blood pressure—that is, the pressure in the large arteries—is monitored by stretch receptors in the arterial wall. By far the most important is at the carotid sinus, near the division of the common carotid artery into the internal and external carotid arteries. Information from these so-called baroreceptors is relayed up the glossopharyngeal nerve to the brain stem, where cardiovascular motor responses are adjusted to correct any deviation from the required blood pressure. These responses are achieved through fibres of the vagus nerve. Parasympathetic activity slows the heart and reduces the blood pressure, while sympathetic activity accelerates the heart, constricts most peripheral vessels, and raises the blood pressure.

Blood vessels supplying the brain are not under the control of the autonomic nervous system. Rather, they are predominantly influenced by the local level of carbon dioxide in the blood. Voluntary overbreathing, as in inflating an air mattress by mouth, washes carbon dioxide out of the blood; this constricts blood vessels supplying the brain and causes faintness and dizziness.

Eyes. The pupillary muscles of the iris are innervated by sympathetic nerves, which dilate the pupil, and by parasympathetic nerves, which constrict it. The activity of these nerves is largely dependent on a reflex set off by light reaching the retina, so that the pupil reacts like the diaphragm of a camera with automatic exposure control. The retina can function, however, with a far wider range of light intensities than can a camera. Sympathetic nerves also supply some muscle fibres that raise the upper eyelid (the great majority are supplied by somatic nerves, as is usual with a muscle under voluntary control). In severe fright the sympathetic system as a whole may become active. As the heart beats hard and fast and the blood pressure rises, there may also be pupillary dilatation and retraction of the upper lid, known as "wide-eyed fright."

Effects of fright

Parasympathetic fibres also control the ciliary muscle, by which the eye is focused for near vision, and the lacrimal gland, which lubricates the surface of the eye with fluid.

Bladder. The bladder is innervated by parasympathetic and sympathetic motor nerves and by somatic sensory nerves. The parasympathetic nerves supply the muscle of the bladder wall and the adjacent part of the urethra, which is sometimes known as the internal sphincter. These structures preserve continence when the bladder is inactive and filling with urine. There is also an external sphincter, which preserves continence when the bladder is very full and enables the passage of urine to be stopped in midflow. It consists of striated muscle supplied by somatic nerves, as is usual for a structure predominantly under voluntary control. Sympathetic action is not important in urination.

Genitalia. Erection of the penis is achieved primarily by parasympathetic nerves, which dilate arteries carrying blood into the penis and constrict veins carrying blood away. Sympathetic nerves begin the ejaculation of semen by contracting muscles in the walls of testicular tubules that lead up the root of the urethra. They also produce muscular contraction where the urethra leaves the bladder, preventing semen from passing backward into the bladder or urine from entering the urethra. Semen is forced along the urethra to the exterior by contractions of muscles of the penis, which are supplied by somatic nerves. Normal male sexual function, therefore, requires activity of both parts of the autonomic system and also of the somatic system. Moreover, it is commonly triggered by sensory stimuli.

The clitoris is the female analog of the penis and probably receives a similar nerve supply. The uterus and its tubules receive a sympathetic but not parasympathetic nerve supply. The sympathetic nerves constrict blood vessels and can increase or decrease contraction of the uterine muscle. However, they are not essential to uterine function, for a uterus deprived of sympathetic nerve supply can support a fetus and deliver a healthy, full-term baby.

Alimentary tract. In general, activity of the alimentary tract is increased by parasympathetic nerves and reduced by sympathetic. A principal function of the sympathetic supply is to control blood vessel size and, therefore, blood flow. The parasympathetic supply stimulates the salivary glands, the stomach lining, and the pancreas to produce their digestive secretions, and it increases movement of the stomach and intestines. In the small and large intestine, preganglionic parasympathetic fibres terminate not merely close to the organ they stimulate but actually in it. This takes place in Auerbach's plexus, a network of nerves between the circular and longitudinal muscle layers, and in Meissner's plexus, just below the lining of the intestine. Peristalsis (the movements required to move food along the gut) occurs even in segments of intestine deprived of nerve supply. It may be that this continued activity is achieved through the above-mentioned plexuses. If so, it is one of the few activities of the autonomic nervous system that is truly "autonomous"—that is, independent of central nervous mechanisms.

Overlapping of autonomic and somatic nerves

At both ends of the alimentary canal, the somatic nervous system overlaps with the autonomic. Swallowing is initiated by voluntary muscles of the tongue, soft palate, and pharynx, which are innervated by somatic nerves. It is continued involuntarily in the esophagus, whose motor fibres are parasympathetic. At the lower end of the alimentary tract, the colon and rectum receive their motor supply from the parasympathetic system, the internal sphincter is innervated by the sympathetic system, and the external sphincter is supplied by somatic nerves.

Lungs. Parasympathetic activity can cause constriction of the air passages in the lungs, and sympathetic activity can relax them. (J.M.K.S.)

Pain

THEORIES OF PAIN

There have always been two theories of the sensation of pain, a quantitative or intensity theory and a stimulus-specific theory. According to the former, pain results from excessive stimulation of every kind: *e.g.*, excessive heat or cold, excessive damage to the tissues. This theory in its simplest form entails the belief that the same afferent nerve fibres are activated by all of these various stimuli; pain is felt merely when they are conducting far more impulses than usual. But knowledge acquired in the 20th century has shown that the quantitative theory—at least in its classic form—is wrong. Peripheral nerve fibres have been found to be stimulus-specific, each one excited by certain forms of energy. The stimulus-specific theory proposes that pain results from interactions between various impulses arriving at the spinal cord and brain, that these impulses are brought to the spinal cord in certain non-myelinated and small myelinated fibres, and that the specific stimuli that excite these nerve fibres are noxious, or harmful.

Special receptors for reporting pain

In the somatic tissues there are certain kinds of nerve fibre that do not give rise to pain, no matter how many there are or how frequently they are stimulated. Included in this category are mechanoreceptors that report only deformation of the skin and the larger afferent nerve fibres from muscles and tendons that form part of the organization of posture and movement. No matter how they are excited, these receptors never give rise to pain. But the smaller fibres from these tissues do cause pain when they are excited mechanically or chemically.

Warmth and cold fibres are specific. Warmth fibres are excited by rising temperature and quieted by falling temperature, and cold fibres respond similarly with cold stimuli. Although pain arises from very hot and very cold stimulation and with intense forms of mechanical stimulation, this occurs only with the activation of afferent nerve fibres that specifically report noxious events. When no noxious events are occurring, these nerve fibres are silent.

In contrast, the quantitative theory seems to apply to the viscera, where afferent nerve fibres used in reflex organization also report events giving rise to pain. In the heart, for example, the same nerve fibres are excited by mechanical stimulation as are excited by chemical substances formed in the body that cause pain. Also, in the bladder, rectum, and colon, nerve fibres activated by substances that cause pain are the same as those activated by distension and contraction of the viscera. This means that the same nerve fibres are reporting the state that underlies the desire to urinate or defecate and the sensation underlying the pain felt when these organs are strongly contracting in an attempt to evacuate their contents. In the heart, rectum, and bladder, therefore, pain appears to be due to a summation of impulses in sensory nerve fibres and is not mediated by a special group of fibres reserved for reporting noxious events. It must be pointed out, however, that not all researchers accept the argument.

LOWER-LEVEL PAIN PATHWAYS

Tissues. *Normal conditions.* Not all the tissues making up the body give rise to pain; furthermore, each tissue must be stimulated in an appropriate way to invoke its particular sensation of pain. Skin, being the outer covering of the body, easily raises the warning of pain, but other tissues that do not come in direct contact with the outer environment are just the opposite. The brain, for example, can be pierced, cut, and burned in neurosurgery, while the patient would require only local anesthesia of the pain-sensitive scalp. The lung, liver, and spleen also do not give rise to pain, no matter how they are stimulated. Pain arises from hollow viscera when the passage of their contents is obstructed and the musculature must undergo strong contraction and stretching. Pain cannot be induced by cutting or burning the wall of the intestine, but pulling on the mesenteric tissue that fixes the intestines to the posterior wall of the abdomen causes pain. The reason for these differences is clear. Tissues are sensitive to the kinds of damage they are likely to meet during life and not to those that they probably will never meet.

Although the warning function of pain is obvious, it is not equivalent to nociception, the perception of forces likely to damage the tissues of the body. First, nociception can occur without pain and pain without nociception; also, the sensation of pain is only a part of the total act of nociception. There are reflex effects as well, such as a local reflex withdrawal from a sudden noxious stimulation of the skin. There are autonomic effects, such as a rise in blood pressure, quickening of the heart rate and respiration, and other excitatory sympathetic nervous effects. There may even be shrieking or howling, warning other animals that something dangerous and painful is occurring.

Acute and chronic pain

Pathological conditions. Acute and chronic pain differ in many ways. Acute pain occurs with sudden damage, such as stepping on a nail or biting the tongue. Chronic pain is the pain of pathological conditions—the pain that accompanies gout, arthritis, inflammation, or cancer. Each type of pain has effects on the nervous system.

The effect of acute inflammation of the joints on nerves reporting the state of the joint and on the central nervous system has been studied by inducing arthritis in animals. In this condition, locally formed chemical substances excite the small myelinated and nonmyelinated afferent fibres that report noxious events. Most of these nerves, sensitized by the inflammatory exudate, begin to fire impulses continuously. This flow of impulses to the dorsal-horn neurons of the spinal cord increases their excitability so that many of them also begin to fire continuously. Neurons that are normally excited only by noxious stimulation now respond to light touch as well. Meanwhile, motor neurons in related areas also fire spontaneously, and stimuli that would not normally cause withdrawal reflexes now cause a prolonged reflex response. There is no change in the motor neurons themselves; the change is in the firing threshold of peripheral neurons coming from the inflamed area and in the interneurons between the afferent nerve fibres and the motor neurons. These interneurons are ultimately connected to the brain, so that the state of increased sensitivity is passed on to related cerebral neurons. Eventually, neurons in the cerebral hemispheres continuously and spontaneously generate impulses. Other neurons of the brain start responding to movements of the affected joints that normally would not do so.

In some people with chronic painful conditions, the constant pain impulses change the character of neurons of the thalamus and cortex. For example, one patient who had had a toothache 10 days before he had an operation on the thalamus for parkinsonism suddenly got the pain of toothache again when the thalamus was stimulated electrically. Normally, no pain can be induced by stimulating that part of the thalamus.

Peripheral nerves. Most of the afferent nerves making up the dorsal roots are nonmyelinated fibres. These fibres are activated by warmth within a physiological range (and by higher temperatures likely to damage the body), by chemical substances (including those made in the body), and by strong mechanical stimulation such as pricking and crushing. The smaller myelinated fibres report mechanical stimulation of the skin, noxious stimulation, and cold.

As stated above, pain is not the inevitable result of the firing of nonmyelinated fibres reporting noxious events. These fibres may fire at a slow rate without causing pain; they may even continue to fire for an hour or so without pain. Furthermore, the pain threshold does not correspond with the onset of activity in the nonmyelinated fibres, for pain can increase while the discharge of nerve impulses decreases.

Spinal cord. The stimulus-specific organization of the peripheral nerve fibres is not continued within the spinal cord, as the various afferent nerve fibres do not transmit their impulses exclusively to neurons of only one kind of sensibility. In the dorsal horns (the spinal region that receives afferent impulses) a few neurons are purely nociceptive, but most neurons reporting noxious events receive both noxious and mechanoreceptive input. These latter are called convergent neurons. The size of the peripheral field (the area of the body from which it receives stimuli) of a dorsal-horn neuron continually varies, depending on the state of excitability of the neuron. Furthermore, events in the peripheral field affect future responses. For example, repeated input along a group of afferent nerve fibres produces a gradually decreasing response in the central nervous system. This is called habituation. Also, the region of decreased response spreads from local neurons that received the input to neighbouring neurons.

Changes in sensitivity to pain

The state of excitability of a dorsal-horn neuron depends on many variables. If it is very excitable, it will respond to impulses from many afferent peripheral nerve fibres; if it is relatively inexcitable, it will be affected only by those peripheral fibres that are habitually connected to it and located near it. A neuron excited by many afferent fibres receives input from a larger area than a neuron receiving only from the fibres most nearly related to it. For this reason the area of skin or deep tissue connected to neurons of the dorsal horn varies and changes. In experiments using damaged skin, it has been found that a barrage of nerve impulses from the damaged region increases the excitability of the dorsal-horn neurons. Once this hyperexcitable state has been set up, it continues for a time without further input from peripheral nerves. In this state of local excitability, some dorsal-horn neurons receive an input from the area of damaged skin that they would not receive were the skin in a normal state.

The convergent neurons mentioned above can have their activity inhibited by tactile stimulation of a region near their peripheral fields or of a homologous region on the opposite side of the body. Also, their responsiveness to stimuli can be increased by damage to the skin in their peripheral fields.

From these convergent neurons and from other neurons of the dorsal horns, there arise tracts of long fibres that cross the midline and lead to the thalamus and other nuclei of the brain. These constitute the spinothalamic tracts. The other main pathway of pain impulses ends in the reticular formation of the medulla oblongata and pons and is known as the spinoreticular tract. It is believed that spinoreticular input to the brain serves the autonomic responses and emotional components associated with pain, whereas the spinothalamic serves conscious sensation, with its exact temporal and spatial aspects. Neurons around the central spinal canal that receive input from the bladder and colon and their overlying somatic tissues may be connected to an ascending tract that stays within the gray matter in the neighbourhood of the central canal.

HIGHER-LEVEL PAIN PATHWAYS

Brain. Many regions of the brain can influence the input arriving at the lower levels of the nervous system. This so-called descending inhibition can be selective, with different regions of the brain inhibiting certain inputs to the spinal cord. Some regions reduce mechanoreceptive input, and others reduce noxious and warmth inputs. Descending inhibition can also reduce input from the skin while increasing that related to movement.

Inhibition of pain transmission

Prominent regions of influence are those that themselves receive noxious input. For instance, the lateral reticular nuclei of the medulla oblongata cause a constant inhibition of input brought to the spinal cord by the nonmyelinated fibres. In the rat (in which the discovery was first made), descending inhibition can be so effective that a noxious input does not enter the spinal cord. In other words, normally painful stimuli cause no reaction or concern, and there is no change in blood pressure, respiration, and other reflex activities. In these circumstances it seems that pain simply is not felt.

Electrical stimulation of the nucleus ceruleus, a small nucleus with widely ranging axons, and the nucleus raphe magnus, a nucleus in the central reticular formation of the medulla, inhibits input from noxious stimulation of the skin, and it also inhibits activities of dorsal-horn neurons receiving mechanoreceptive input. Since it was discovered that pain could be obliterated in this manner, attempts have been made to stop the chronic pain of cancer and other conditions by implanting electrodes in the brain. These can be placed in relevant parts of the brain so that constant stimulation can inhibit the input coming from the region of the pain.

This built-in system for obliterating or reducing pain can normally be brought into play by stress. Furthermore, it has always been known that one pain can mask another. A volley of nerve impulses reaching the brain via the spinothalamic and spinoreticular tracts and causing a moderate degree of pain is stopped when the cells of origin of this tract are inhibited. Experiments have shown that this suppression can be brought about by a more severe pain or by a pain in a larger area of the body, which causes descending inhibition of neurons of the spinal tract. This descending inhibition is the main mechanism of acupuncture analgesia.

The reticular formation consists of a vast number of small interconnected neurons occupying the central area of the brain stem. Parts of the reticular formation, hypothalamus, and thalamus excite the cerebral hemispheres and keep the cerebral cortex active and alert—partly in response to noxious input. In fact, it may be said that pain reaches consciousness in the thalamus. The thalamus receives noxious input from the spinal cord in two regions, a lateral part called the ventrobasal complex and a medial part consisting of several nuclei. The ventrobasal complex is concerned with the accurate temporal and spatial localization of conscious sensation, while the medial nuclei are concerned with the emotional, affective, and autonomic components of pain and other sensations. The ventrobasal nuclei relay impulses to the sensory areas of the postcentral gyrus. Noxious stimuli also cause responses in many areas of the cortex and the deeper islands of gray matter. This is to be expected, for, of all sensations, pain is the least pure sensation: it startles, it excites, and it has unpleasant qualities. All these aspects of pain are added by different parts of the brain.

Central pain. Pain arising within the central nervous system when there is no damage to the body is known as central pain. The most common central pain is due to lesions in or near the thalamus and is called the thalamic syndrome. This condition is characterized by diminution in sensibility as well as severe pain when any stimulus exceeds a certain threshold.

With central pain there is both spontaneous pain and excessive pain on stimulation of all kinds. The pain may occur in the entire half of the body, affecting even visual and auditory inputs, or it may occur in a restricted region, such as the upper limb and side of the face or the lower limb.

Referred pain. The term referred pain is used to describe pain felt in a region where it does not originate but to which it is "referred." It is usually used to mean pain arising in hollow viscera and felt in somatic tissues, such as the body wall. Referred pain is always referred in one direction—from deep to superficial tissues. It is pain referred from an unknown or unfamiliar part of the body to a known or familiar part.

Certain regions of the dorsal horns of the spinal cord receive both nerve fibres from the viscera and nerve fibres reporting noxious events in the skin and musculature. For example, afferent nerve fibres from the heart come to the same regions as those from the muscles and skin of the chest wall and upper limbs. From these two body tissues, visceral and somatic, there is an intermingling of inputs, and there is similar convergence in the thalamus. This anatomical arrangement is likely to form the basis of referred pain, although the mere convergence of impulses from viscera and soma onto the same neurons does not alone account for the false localization of visceral pain. It is probable that in sensory areas of the brain, the skin is served by a large number of neurons, the muscles with fewer, and the viscera with least, the visceral representation in the cortex being very small compared to that of the somatic tissues. It is supposed that, as the input to these sensory regions of the cortex usually comes from the skin and body wall, localization of the visceral input will be to these tissues and not to the viscera, the cortical region of which is small and relatively unused.

Mingling of visceral and somatic pain pathways

Changes in the cerebral cortex. Normally, electrical stimulation of the sensory region of the postcentral gyrus does not cause pain. But in many patients who have a painful state on the opposite side of the body, such as a painful amputation stump or damage to the median nerve of the hand, stimulation of this region reproduces the pain. Pain also arises from stimulation of the white matter deep in this area.

In these cases the character of the sensory region of the cortex changes in such a manner that neurons that normally never cause pain when stimulated now invariably produce the pain from which the patient is suffering. Also, the cortical area subserving the limb enlarges. For instance, the sensory area receiving impulses from the opposite lower limb is normally at the upper end of the postcentral gyrus. If there is a painful amputation of the limb, then the area of cortex in which electrical stimulation induces the pain spreads downward from the normal area to include the trunk area and sometimes the upper limb area.

Perception

To the biologist, the life of animals (including that of humans) consists of seeking stimulation and responding appropriately. A reflex occurs before an individual knows what struck him, what made him lift a foot or drop an object. It is biologically correct to be alarmed before one knows the reason. It is only after the immediate and automatic response that the cerebral cortex is involved and conscious perception begins.

Perception comes between simple sensation and complex cognitional behaviour. By the time people are able to talk about it, perception has become so automatic that they hardly realize that seeing what they see, hearing what they hear, is an interpretation. Each act of perception is a hypothesis based on prior experience: the world is made up of things people expect to see, hear, or smell, and any new sensory event is perceived in relation to what they already know. People perceive trees, not brown, upright masses and blotches of green against a background of blue, gray, and white. Once one has learned to understand speech, it is all but impossible to hear words as sibilants and diphthongs, sounds of lower and higher frequencies. In other words, recognizing a thing entails knowing its total shape or pattern. This is usually called by its German name, gestalt.

Central function of the thalamus

As well as perception of the external environment, there is perception of oneself. Information about one's position in space, for example, comes from vision, from vestibular receptors, and from somatic receptors in the skin and deep tissues. This information is collected in the vestibular nuclei and passed on to the thalamus. From there it is relayed to the central gyri and the parietal region of the cortex, where it becomes conscious perception. (For detailed discussion of the perception of movement, see above *The vestibular system.*)

GENERAL ORGANIZATION OF PERCEPTION

Perception relies on what are called the special senses—the visual, auditory, gustatory, and olfactory. Each begins with receptors grouped together in sensory end organs, where the sensory input is organized before it is sent on to the brain. At every synapse on a sensory pathway there is an important reorganization of impulses, so that by the time an input arrives at the thalamus, it is far from being the original input that stimulated the receptors.

The afferent parts of the thalamus fall into two divisions: a medial part, which is afferent but not sensory, and a ventral and lateral part, which is sensory. Nerve impulses reaching the medial part are derived from the reticular formation. This pathway is for emotional and other rapid reactions such as surprise, alarm, vigilance, and the readiness to react. The lateral part of the thalamus is a station on the way to areas of the cortex that are specific for each kind of sensation.

There are three somatosensory areas of the cortex (Figure 29). The primary sensory area occupies the postcentral gyrus immediately behind the motor strip. The secondary area is above the Sylvian fissure, behind the secondary motor area. The supplementary area is in the upper part of the parietal lobe on the medial surface of the hemisphere, just behind the primary area.

The primary area receives its input from the ventrolateral thalamus. The secondary area receives somatosensory input from the lateral part of the thalamus and also auditory and visual input from the medial and lateral geniculate nuclei. The primary and secondary areas are reciprocally connected.

The cerebral cortex (and the thalamus as well) is divided between nonspecific and specific sensory areas. Most neurons of the specific regions have small receptive fields in the periphery, respond to only one kind of stimulus, and follow the features of stimulation exactly. Most neurons of the nonspecific regions have large receptive fields and respond to many kinds of stimuli; many do not exactly reproduce the features of the stimulus.

Changes in the sensory areas of the brain

Although different regions of the body are normally represented by specific parts of the somatosensory regions of the cortex, the parts where afferent impulses arrive are not fixed. For example, the leg area is at the top of the postcentral gyrus, but when there is a painful state in the periphery—sciatica, for example—the leg area of the cortex can enlarge and occupy some of the arm area. Furthermore, injury to the peripheral nerves or brain may alter the sensory "map" of the cortex. These changes in the cortex and similar changes in anatomical function are referred to as plasticity.

From the somatosensory area, nerve fibres run to other regions of the cortex, traditionally called association areas. It is thought that these areas integrate sensory and motor information and that this integration allows objects to be recognized and located in space. With these regions acting upon all their inputs, the brain is carrying out those aspects of neural activity that are commonly labeled mental. It must be remembered, though, that researchers have not precisely answered the question of how and where the brain collects messages from all the sensory receptors and then sifts and arranges them so as to give a complete representation of the world and of the individual's place in the world.

ORGANIZATION OF THE SPECIAL SENSES

Of the special senses, the cerebral organization of the visual and auditory senses are better understood than that behind the olfactory and gustatory. For this reason, only the former two are discussed below.

Vision. Most investigations of the visual pathways in the brain have been carried out in the cat.

The area of the human brain concerned with vision comprises the entire occipital lobe and the posterior parts of the temporal and parietal lobes. The primary visual area, also called the striate cortex, is on the medial side of the occipital lobe and is surrounded by the secondary visual area (Figure 31). The visual cortex is sensitive to the position and orientation of edges, the direction and speed of movement of objects in the visual field, stereoscopic depth, brightness, and colour. These parallel functions combine to produce visual perception.

The ganglion neurons of the retina belong to three functional types, called Y-, X-, and W-cells. X-cells are neurons needed for high-resolution vision. Y-cells respond to fast movement, whereas X- and W-cells respond poorly to fast movement. Y-cells are larger than the others and have large peripheral fields; X-cells have small fields. In the retina, 50 to 55 percent of ganglion cells are W-type, 40 percent are X-type, and 5 to 10 percent are Y-type.

As constituent fibres of the optic nerves and optic tracts, X- and Y-cells connect to the lateral geniculate nucleus of the thalamus, while W-cells connect mainly to the superior colliculus of the midbrain. From these regions input from the X-cells goes mainly to the primary visual area, that from the Y-cells goes to the secondary visual area, and that from the W-cells goes to the area surrounding the secondary area. The collicular pathway serves movement detection and direction of gaze. The tract from the lateral geniculate nucleus is the pathway for visual acuity.

The primary area sends fibres back to the lateral geniculate nucleus, the superior colliculus, and the pupillary reflex centre for feedback control of input to the visual areas. It also sends fibres to the secondary area and to the visual area of the temporal lobe. The secondary area sends fibres to the temporal and parietal lobes. Also, fibres cross from visual areas of one cerebral hemisphere to the other in the corpus callosum. This link allows neurons of the two hemispheres with similar visual fields to make direct contact with each other.

Specialized visual neurons of the brain

Neurons of the striate cortex may form the first step in appreciation of orientation of objects in the visual field. It is thought, however, that excitation of cortical neurons is insufficient to account for orientation and that inhibition of other neurons in the visual cortex is also necessary. Whatever the mechanism, it has been found in experiments on cats and monkeys that individual neurons are activated by lines at different angles—for example, at 90 degrees to the horizontal or at an angle of 45 degrees.

Most neurons of the deeper layers are movement analyzers. Some are direction analyzers, activated by a line or an edge moving in one direction and silenced when it changes direction (the changed direction then activating other neurons). One neuron may be excited by a dark line on a bright background and another by a light line on a dark background. In other regions of the striate cortex there are form analyzers; for example, some are activated by rectangles and others by stars. There are also position neurons, which show a strong response to a spot located in a certain position and a weak response to stimulation of a larger area; others respond only to simultaneous binocular stimulation. The striate cortex provides a fused, binocular picture of the world. There are also colour-specific neurons sensitive to red, green, or blue. Each of these neurons is excited by one colour and inhibited by another.

In the secondary visual area many neurons respond particularly to the direction of moving objects. Neurons activated by colour are not activated by white light. In the part of this area where there are many neurons responding to colour, the periphery of the visual field is not mapped; this is because there are no cones in the periphery of the retina (cones being the colour receptors). The peripheral field is mapped in an area with neurons responding to movement—notably in the region of the superior temporal gyrus.

It seems that one function of the pathway from the superior colliculus to the temporal and parietal cortices is as a tracking system, enabling the eyes and head to follow moving objects and keep them in the visual field. The pathway from the geniculate nucleus to the primary visual area may be said to perceive what the object is and also how and in what direction it moves.

Some neurons in the parietal cortex become active when a visual stimulus comes in from the edge of the visual field toward the centre, while others are excited by particular movements of the eyes. Other neurons react with remarkable specificity—for example, only when the visual stimulus approaches from the same direction as a stimulus moving on the skin of the animal, or during the act of reaching for an object and tracking it with the hand. These parietal neurons greatly depend on the state of vigilance. In monkeys that are apparently merely waiting for something to happen or that have nothing to which to turn their attention, the neurons are inactive or minimally active. But when the animal is looking at a visual target whose change it has to detect in order to obtain a reward, the parietal neurons become active.

A great number of neurons of the middle temporal area are sensitive to the direction of movement of a visual stimulus and to the size of an object. In the inferior temporal area are neurons concerned with shape and colour. The neurons of the superior temporal polysensory area respond best to moving stimuli—in particular to movements away from the centre of the visual field. Both these areas are concerned with the conjunction of visual stimuli and movement.

Reproduced by permission of Catherine Parker Anthony and Gary A. Thibodeau, *Textbook of Anatomy & Physiology*, 12th ed. (1987), Times Mirror/Mosby College Publishing, St. Louis, adapted from K. Brodmann, "Feinere Anatomie des Grosshirns," in *Handbuch der Neurologie* (1910), Springer-Verlag, Berlin

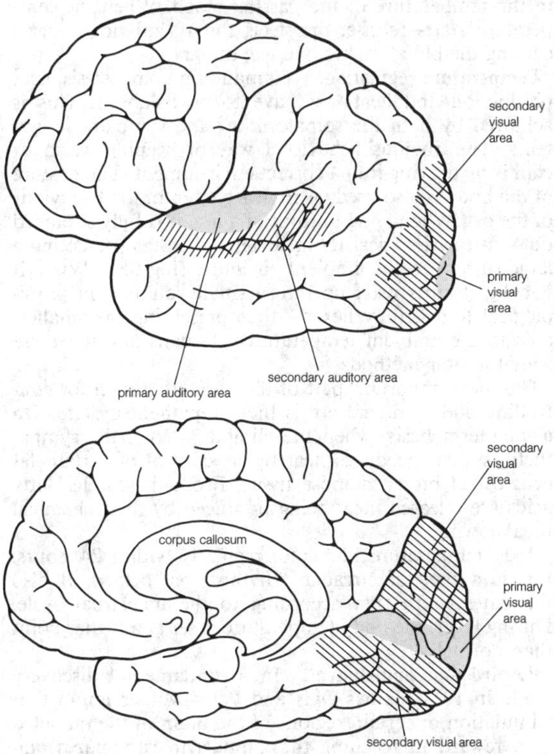

Figure 31: (Top) Lateral and (bottom) medial views of the cerebral hemispheres, showing visual and auditory areas.

Hearing. Much of the knowledge of the neurological organization of hearing has been acquired from studies on the bat, an animal that relies on acoustic information for its livelihood.

Specialized auditory neurons

In the cochlea (the specialized auditory end organ of the inner ear) the frequency of a pure tone is reported by the location of the reacting neurons in the basilar membrane, and the loudness of the sound is reported by the rate of discharge of nerve impulses. From the cochlea the auditory input is sent to many auditory nuclei. From there, it is sent on to the medial geniculate nucleus and the inferior colliculus, as with the relay stations of the retina. The auditory input finally goes to the primary and secondary auditory areas of the temporal lobes.

The auditory cortex provides the temporal and spatial frames of reference for the auditory data that it receives. In other words, it is sensitive to aspects of sound more complex than frequency. For instance, there are neurons that react only when a sound starts or stops. Other neurons are sensitive only to particular durations of sound. When a sound is repeated many times, some neurons respond, while others stop responding. There are neurons that are sensitive to differences of the intensity and timing of sounds reaching the two ears. Certain neurons that never respond to a note of constant frequency respond when the frequency falls or rises. There are others that respond to the rate of change of frequency, providing information on whether distance from the source of a sound is increasing or decreasing. Some neurons respond to the ipsilateral ear, others to the contralateral, and yet others to both ears.

Emotion and behaviour

PATHWAYS IN THE BRAIN

Importance of the hypothalamus

In order to carry out the correct behaviour—that is to say, correct in relation to the survival of the individual and the group—humans and other higher animals developed innate drives, desires, and emotions, and the ability to remember and learn. These fundamental features of living depend on the entire brain, yet there is one part of the brain that organizes metabolism, growth, sexual differentiation, and the desires and drives necessary to achieve these aspects of life. This is the hypothalamus and a region in front of it comprising the septal and preoptic areas. That such basic aspects of life might depend on a small region of the brain was conceived in the 1920s by the Swiss physiologist Walter Rudolf Hess and later amplified by Erich von Holst. Hess implanted electrodes in the hypothalamus and in septal and preoptic nuclei of cats, stimulated them, and observed the animals' behaviour. Finally, he made minute lesions by means of these electrodes and again observed the effects on behaviour. With this technique he showed that certain kinds of behaviour were organized essentially by just a few neurons in these regions of the brain. Later, von Holst stimulated electrodes by remote control after placing the animals in various biologically meaningful conditions.

When such acts result from the artificial stimulation of the neurons, the accompanying emotion also occurs, as do the movements expressing that emotion.

The hypothalamus, in company with the pituitary gland, controls the emission of hormones. It is in control of body temperature, maintains the blood pressure and the rate and force of the heartbeat, and controls the body's need for water and electrolytes. The maintenance of these and other changing events within normal limits is called homeostasis; this includes behaviour aimed at keeping the body in a correct and thus a comfortable environment.

The hypothalamus is also the centre for organizing the activity of the two parts of the autonomic system, the parasympathetic and the sympathetic (see above *The au-*

tonomic system). Above the hypothalamus, regions of the cerebral hemispheres most closely connected to the parasympathetic regions are the orbital surface of the frontal lobes, the insula, and the anterior part of the temporal lobe. The regions most closely connected to the sympathetic regions are the anterior nucleus of the thalamus, the hippocampus, and the nuclei connected to these structures.

In general, the regions of the cerebral hemispheres that are closely related to the hypothalamus are those parts that together constitute the limbic lobe, first considered as a unit and given its name in 1878 by the French anatomist Paul Broca. Together with related nuclei it is usually called the limbic system, consisting of the cingulate and parahippocampal gyri, the hippocampus, the amygdala, the septal and pre-optic nuclei, and their various connections.

The autonomic system also involves the hypothalamus in movement. The expression of emotion and signaling to others depend greatly on the sympathetic nervous system. Emotional expression is also carried out by regions of the cerebral hemispheres above the hypothalamus and by the midbrain below it.

HYPOTHALAMIC FUNCTIONS

Emotion. A great deal of behaviour in social animals, such as humans, involves social interaction. Although the whole brain contributes to social activities, certain parts of the cerebral hemispheres are particularly concerned. The operation of leucotomy, cutting through the white matter that connects parts of the frontal lobes with the thalamus, upsets this aspect of behaviour. This operation used to be performed for severe depression or obsessional neuroses. After the operation, patients lacked the usual inhibitions that were socially demanded, appearing to obey the first impulse that occurred to them. They told people what they thought of them without regard for the necessary conventions of civilization.

Which parts of the cerebral hemispheres produce emotion has been learned from patients with epilepsy and from operations under local anesthesia in which the electrical stimulation of the brain is carried out. The limbic lobe, including the hippocampus, is particularly important. Stimulating certain regions of the temporal lobes produces an intense feeling of fear or dread; stimulating nearby regions produces a feeling of isolation and loneliness, other regions a feeling of disgust, and yet others intense sorrow, depression, anxiety, and, occasionally, guilt. An ecstatic feeling can also occur in which it appears to patients that all problems have been or are just about to be solved.

Inducing changes in emotion

In addition to these regions of the cerebral cortex and the hypothalamus, regions of the thalamus also contribute to the genesis of emotion. The hypothalamus itself does not initiate behaviour; that is done by the cerebral hemispheres—insofar as one may abstract any single part from the whole.

The defense reaction: fighting and fleeing. When certain neurons of the hypothalamus are excited, an animal either becomes aggressive and eventually attacks, or it flees. These two opposite ways of behaving are together called the defense reaction; both are in the repertoire of all vertebrates. The defense reaction is accompanied by strong sympathetic activity. Aggression is also influenced by the production of androgen hormones.

Mating. The total act of copulation is organized in the anterior part of the hypothalamus and the neighbouring septal region. In the male, erection of the penis and ejaculation are organized in this area, which is adjacent to the area for urination. Under normal circumstances the neurons that organize mating behaviour do so only when they receive relevant hormones in their blood supply. But when the septal region is electrically stimulated in conscious patients, sexual emotions and thoughts are produced.

There are visible differences between the male and female sexes in nuclei of the central nervous system related to reproduction. These differences are a form of sexual dimorphism.

Urination and defecation. Electrical stimulation in cats of regions in, and related to, the anterior part of the hypothalamus can induce the behaviour of expelling or retaining urine and feces. When electrodes planted in these regions are stimulated by radio waves, the cat stops whatever it is doing and behaves as though it were going to urinate or defecate. It goes through its usual behaviour of digging a hole, squatting, and assuming the correct posture, and then it passes urine or feces. At the end, it even goes through its customary ritual of hiding its excreta.

Eating and drinking. The eating and drinking centres are in the lateral and ventromedial regions of the hypothalamus, although such basic aspects of living concern most of the brain. If the lateral region is experimentally destroyed, the animal takes less food or stops eating altogether; if the ventromedial region is destroyed, it eats enormously. When neurons of the lateral region are electrically stimulated, the animal eats, and when those of the ventromedial area are stimulated, it stops eating. There is an increase in the activity of these neurons when a monkey looks at food, but only when it is hungry. In the lateral region are receptors that monitor blood glucose. They are stimulated into activity only when the blood glucose is low; satiety stops their response.

Hunger does not depend only on these glucose receptors. Severe hunger is associated with contractions of the stomach, which are felt almost as a sensation of pain. Yet neither is this an essential mechanism for feeling hungry, as patients who have had total removal of the stomach still feel hunger. In experiments in rats, it is found that stress may make the animal either increase or reduce the amount it eats. This is probably the same in humans.

When certain neurons in the same regions of the hypothalamus are experimentally destroyed, animals lose the urge to drink, although they continue to eat normally. Stimulation of these neurons make them drink excessively. The control of drinking depends on osmoreceptors throughout the hypothalamus. When the receptors detect a minimal increase in the concentration of dissolved substances in the extracellular fluid, which indicates cellular dehydration, the animal feels thirsty. A less important contributor is a reduction in blood volume. Dryness of the mouth can also be a component of thirst, noted by receptors in the mucous membrane. The feeling of having drunk enough depends not only on the hypothalamic neurons but also on receptors in the wall of the stomach, which report when the stomach is full.

Both glucose receptors and osmoreceptors are sensitive to the temperature of the passing blood. When the temperature starts to rise, one feels thirsty but not hungry; cooling the blood makes one feel hungry.

Temperature regulation. To maintain homeostasis, heat production and heat loss have to be balanced. This is achieved by both the somatomotor and sympathetic systems. The obvious behavioral way of keeping warm or cool is by moving into a correct environment. The posture of the body is also used, as is clearly seen in the behaviour of the cat. When lying in front of a fire, it is fully stretched out—in physiological terms, extended—thus presenting a large surface to the ambient air and losing heat. When it is cold, it curls itself up into a small volume—in physiological terms, fully flexed—thus presenting the smallest area to the ambient temperature. Humans also use these somatomotor methods.

The most important part of the nervous system for controlling body temperature is the sympathetic system. On a long-term basis, when the climate is cold, the sympathetic system produces heat by its control of certain fat cells called brown adipose tissue. From these cells, fatty acids are released, heat being produced by their chemical breakdown.

Body temperature fluctuates regularly within 24 hours; this is a type of circadian rhythm (see below). It also fluctuates in rhythm according to the menstrual cycle. During fever, the body temperature is set at a higher point than normally.

Reward and punishment. In a fundamental discovery made in 1954, James Olds and Peter Milner found that stimulation of certain regions of the brain of the rat acted as a reward in teaching the animals to run mazes and solve problems. The conclusion from such experiments is that stimulation gives the animals pleasure. The discovery

Reward centres of the brain

has also been confirmed in humans. These regions are called pleasure or reward centres. One important centre is in the septal region, and there are reward centres in the hypothalamus and in the temporal lobes of the cerebral hemispheres as well. When the septal region is stimulated in conscious patients undergoing neurosurgery, there are feelings of pleasure, optimism, euphoria, and happiness.

Regions of the brain also clearly cause rats distress when electrically stimulated; these are called aversive centres. However, the existence of an aversive centre is less certain than that of a reward centre. Electrodes stimulating neurons or neural pathways may cause an animal to have pain, anxiety, fear, or any unpleasant feeling or emotion. These pathways are not necessarily centres having the function of providing punishment in the sense that a reward centre provides pleasure. Therefore, it is not definitely known that connections to aversive centres punish the animal for biologically wrong behaviour, but it is thought that correct behaviour is rewarded by pleasure provided by neurons of the brain.

Circadian rhythms. Living organisms have inevitably become adapted to the orderly rhythms of the universe. These biologic cycles are called circadian rhythms, from the Latin *circa* ("about") and *dies* ("day"). They are essentially endogenous, built into the central nervous system. The rhythmical activities usually covered by the word circadian are sleeping and waking, rest and activity, taking in of fluid, formation of urine, body temperature, cardiac output, oxygen consumption, cell division, and the secreting activity of endocrine glands. The rhythms are upset by shift work and by rapid travel into different time zones. After long journeys it takes several days for the endogenous rhythm generator to become synchronized to the local time.

The alternation of night and day has been important in inducing rhythms affecting many physiological functions. Even in isolation, from clues giving information about light and dark, rhythms related to the time of day are maintained. Curiously, the endogenous sleep–wake rhythm deviates slightly from the Earth's 24-hour cycle; a bird's endogenous cycle is 23 hours, and the human cycle is 25 hours. In both cases the cycle is corrected by features of the environment. Such synchronizing agents are called zeitgebers ("time givers"). One zeitgeber is the Earth's magnetic field, which changes on a 24-hour cycle as the Earth turns on its axis. More obvious and important a zeitgeber is the alternation of dark and light.

One hypothalamic nucleus that is essential for the rhythms of sleeping, waking, rest, and activity is the suprachiasmatic nucleus. It is not surprising that this nucleus is adjacent to the incoming fibres from the eye, for the light–dark cycle appears to be the most important zeitgeber for circadian rhythms. The suprachiasmatic nucleus is most active in light. In experiments on the hamster, when the nucleus is destroyed, the rhythms of general activity, drinking, sleeping, waking, body temperature, and some endocrine secretion are disrupted. (P.W.N.)

Higher cerebral functions

The neurons of the cerebral cortex constitute the highest level of control in the hierarchy of the nervous system. Consequently, the terms higher cerebral functions and higher cortical functions are used by neurologists and neuroscientists to refer to all conscious mental activity of the kind normally described as thinking, remembering, and reasoning and to complex volitional behaviour such as speaking and carrying out purposive movement. They also refer to the processing of information in the cerebral cortex, most of which takes place unconsciously.

ANALYTICAL APPROACHES

Neuroscientists investigate the structure and functions of the cerebral cortex, but the processes involved in thinking are also studied by cognitive psychologists, who group the mental activities known to the neuroscientist as higher cortical functions under the headings cognitive function or human information processing. From this perspective, complex information processing is the hallmark of cognitive function. Cognitive science attempts to identify and define the processes involved in thinking without regard to their physiological basis. The resulting models of cognitive function resemble flowcharts for a computer program more than neural networks—and, indeed, they frequently make use of computer terminology and analogies.

Neuropsychology

The discipline of neuropsychology, by studying the relationship between behaviour and brain function, bridges the gap between neural and cognitive science. Examples of this bridging role include studies in which cognitive models are used as conceptual frameworks to help explain the behaviour of patients who have suffered damage to different parts of the brain. Thus, damage to the frontal lobes can be conceptualized as a failure of the "central executive" component of working memory, and a failure of the "generate" function in another model of mental imagery would fit with some of the consequences of left parietal lobe damage.

The analysis of changes in behaviour and ability following damage to the brain is by far the oldest and probably the most informative method adopted for studying higher cortical functions. Usually these changes take the form of what is known as a deficit—that is, an impairment of the ability to act or think in some way. With certain provisos, one can assume that the damaged part of the brain is involved in the function that has been lost. However, people vary considerably in their abilities, and most brain lesions occur in subjects whose behaviour has not been formally studied before they become ill. Lesions are rarely precisely congruent with the brain area responsible for a given function, and their exact location and extent can be difficult to determine even with modern imaging techniques. Abnormal behaviour after brain injury, therefore, is often difficult to attribute to precisely defined damage or dysfunction.

It would also be naive to suppose that a function is represented in a particular brain area just because it is disrupted after damage to that area. For example, a tennis champion does not play well with a broken ankle, but this would not lead one to conclude that the ankle is the centre in which athletic skill resides. Reasonably certain conclusions about brain–behaviour relationships, therefore, can be drawn only if similar well-defined changes occur reliably in a substantial number of patients suffering from similar lesions or disease states.

Pioneering studies of the brain

The most prominent series of observations clearly belonging to modern neuropsychology were made by Paul Broca in the years following 1861. He reported the cases of several patients whose speech had been affected following damage to the left frontal lobe and provided autopsy evidence of the location of the lesion. In making his famous statement, "We speak with the left hemisphere," he explicitly recognized the left hemisphere's control of language, one of the fundamental phenomena of higher cortical function.

In 1874, the German neurologist Carl Wernicke described a case in which a lesion in a different part of the left hemisphere, the posterior temporal region, affected language in a different way. In contrast to Broca's cases, language comprehension was more affected than language output. This meant that two different aspects of higher cortical function had been found to be localized in different parts of the brain. In the next few decades there was a rapid expansion in the number of cognitive processes studied and tentatively localized.

Wernicke was one of the first to recognize the importance of the interaction between connected brain areas and to think of higher cortical function as the buildup of complex mental processes through the coordinated activities of local regions dealing with relatively simple, predominantly sensory-motor functions. In doing so, he opposed the view of the brain as an equipotential organ acting en masse. Since his time, scientific fashion has swung between the localization and mass-action theories. Major changes in the 20th century have been both quantitative, with vast increases in knowledge, and methodological, with the discovery of new ways of studying the brain's anatomy and physiology and the introduction of better quantitative methods in the study of behaviour.

HEMISPHERIC ASYMMETRY, HANDEDNESS, AND CEREBRAL DOMINANCE

Broca's declaration that the left hemisphere is predominantly responsible for language-related behaviour is only the clearest and most dramatic example of an asymmetry of function in the human brain. This functional asymmetry is related to hand preference and probably to anatomical differences, although neither relationship is simple.

Dominance of the left hemisphere for language

Evidence from a number of converging sources, notably the high incidence of the language disturbance known as aphasia after left- but not right-hemisphere damage, indicates that the left hemisphere is dominant for the comprehension and expression of language in close to 99 percent of right-handed people. At least 60 percent of left-handed and ambidextrous people also have left-hemisphere language, but up to 30 percent have predominantly right-hemisphere language. The remainder have language represented to some degree in both hemispheres.

The posterior temporal region of the brain, which in the dominant hemisphere is one of the regions responsible for language, is physically asymmetrical; specifically, the area known as the planum temporale is larger in the left hemisphere in most people. This asymmetry is more common in right-handers, while left-handed individuals are likely to have more nearly symmetrical brains. Reduced anatomical asymmetry has also been found in people with right-hemisphere dominance for speech and in some developmental dyslexics (people with reading disorders). These results point to some relationship between handedness, cerebral dominance for language, anatomical asymmetry in the temporal lobe, and some aspects of language competence. Certainly, there is a tendency for right-handedness, left-hemisphere dominance for language, and a larger left planum temporale to go together. However, there are exceptions; for example, a few right-handers are right-hemisphere dominant for speech, and some right-handers who have left-hemisphere speech do not have a larger left planum temporale. In subjects who are atypical in one of these respects—for example, by being left-handed—the relationship between handedness, cerebral dominance, and anatomical asymmetry is much less consistent. It follows, therefore, that language is not invariably located in the hemisphere opposite the dominant hand or in the hemisphere with the larger planum temporale.

Studies of patients in whom the corpus callosum (the bundle of nerve fibres connecting the two halves of the brain) has been severed, allowing the two hemispheres to function largely independently, have revealed that the right hemisphere has more language competence than was hitherto supposed. These patients show evidence of comprehension of words presented to the isolated right hemisphere, although that hemisphere is not able to initiate speech. The speech of patients with a lesion of the right hemisphere may lack normal melodic quality, and they may have difficulty expressing and understanding such things as emotional overtones. They may also have difficulty appreciating some of the more subtle, connotative aspects of language, such as puns, figures of speech, and jokes. Nevertheless, the dominance of the left hemisphere for language, particularly the syntactic aspects of language and language output, is the clearest example yet discovered of the lateralization of higher cortical function.

The left hemisphere also appears to be more involved than the right in the programming of complex sequences of movement and in some aspects of awareness of one's own body. Thus, the disorders known as ideomotor and ideational apraxia are more common after left-hemisphere damage. In these disorders, the patient has difficulty carrying out actions involving several movements or the manipulation of objects in an appropriate and skillful way. The difficulty appears to be in programming the motor system to run off the sequence of movements required to perform a complex action in the appropriate order and with the appropriate timing.

A third category of deficits associated with left-hemisphere damage, disorder of the body image, is much more difficult to define. It includes a disorder called finger agnosia, in which the individual does not appear to "know" which finger is which, being unable to indicate which one the examiner touches without the aid of vision. Confusion of right and left is also found after left-hemisphere damage, making it appear that the left hemisphere is largely responsible for collating somatosensory information into a special awareness of the body called the body image. The phenomenon of the phantom limb, whereby patients "feel" sensations in amputated limbs, indicates that the brain's internal representation of the body may persist intact for some time after the loss of a body part. This internal representation appears to be maintained chiefly by the left hemisphere.

The special functions of the right hemisphere were recognized later than those of the left hemisphere, although a case of "imperception" reported by the English neurologist John Hughlings Jackson in 1876 foreshadowed later findings. Jackson's patient, who had a lesion in the posterior part of the right hemisphere, lost her way in familiar surroundings, failed to recognize familiar places and people, and had difficulty in dressing herself—all of which became well-recognized consequences of right-hemisphere damage. The right hemisphere, then, appears to be specialized for some aspects of higher-level visual perception, spatial orientation, and route finding (sense of direction), and it probably plays a dominant role in the recognition of objects and faces. The specialization of the right hemisphere, however, is less absolute than that of the left hemisphere in that these skills are less lateralized than language.

Specialized functions of the right hemisphere

There has been considerable speculation as to why the human brain should be functionally asymmetrical. Initially, both functional and anatomical asymmetry were thought, like language, to be a uniquely human trait, but less pronounced asymmetries have now been found in lower animals. One suggestion is that it is necessary to have language represented in a single hemisphere to avoid competition between the hemispheres for control of the muscles involved in speech. Another suggestion is that it is efficient to have the language system represented in a restricted area on one side of the brain because information needs to be transferred over short distances and fewer connections. A third suggestion is that the dominance of the left hemisphere over the right hand and skilled movement preceded its dominance over language. According to this view, language subsequently developed in the same hemisphere because language implies speech, which requires precise programming of sequences of movement in the articulatory musculature. All these views have something to recommend them, but none has been conclusively proved correct or has been generally accepted. Also, there remain some facts that are difficult to explain by any theory. For example, all the above theories would predict that bilateral and, in some cases, right-hemisphere language representation would be disadvantageous, but this does not seem to be generally true.

LANGUAGE

The language area of the brain surrounds the Sylvian fissure in the dominant hemisphere (Figure 32). This area

(Data) From C.D. Clemente (ed.), *Gray's Anatomy of the Human Body*, 30th ed. (1985), Lea and Febiger, after Wilder Penfield and Lamar Roberts, *Speech and Brain Mechanisms*, copyright © 1959 by Princeton University Press, Fig. X-4 reprinted with permission of Princeton University Press; (art) reproduced by permission of Catherine Parker Anthony and Gary A. Thibodeau, *Textbook of Anatomy & Physiology*, 12th ed. (1987), Times Mirror/Mosby College Publishing, St. Louis, adapted from K. Brodmann, "Feinere Anatomie des Grosshirns," in *Handbuch der Neurologie* (1910), Springer-Verlag, Berlin

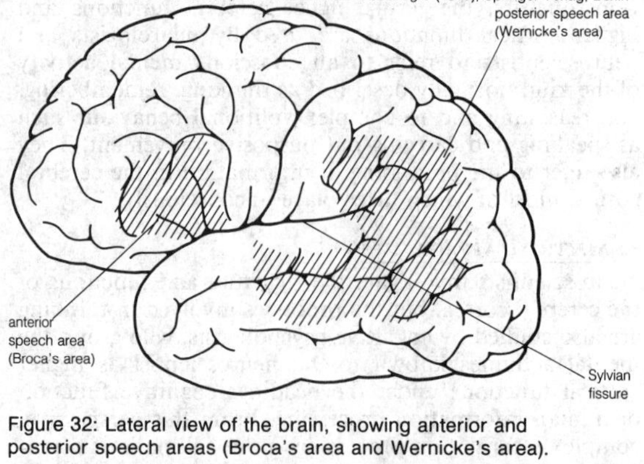

posterior speech area (Wernicke's area)

anterior speech area (Broca's area)

Sylvian fissure

Figure 32: Lateral view of the brain, showing anterior and posterior speech areas (Broca's area and Wernicke's area).

Broca's and Wernicke's language areas

is divided into two major components named after the pioneers Paul Broca and Carl Wernicke. Broca's area lies in the third frontal convolution, just anterior to the face area of the motor cortex and just above the Sylvian fissure. This is often described as the motor, or expressive, speech area; damage to it results in Broca's aphasia, a language disorder characterized by deliberate, telegraphic speech with very simple grammatical structure though the speaker may be quite clear as to what he wishes to say and may communicate successfully. Wernicke's area is in the superior part of the posterior temporal lobe; it is close to the auditory cortex and is classically considered to be the receptive language, or language comprehension, centre. A patient with Wernicke's aphasia has difficulty understanding language; his own speech is typically fluent but is empty of content and characterized by circumlocutions, a high incidence of vague words like "thing," and sometimes neologisms and senseless "word salad." The entire posterior language area extends into the parietal lobe and is connected to Broca's area by a fibre tract called the arcuate fasciculus. Damage to this tract has been implicated in conduction aphasia, a disorder in which the patient can understand and speak but has difficulty in repeating what is said to him. The suggestion is that, in this condition, language can be comprehended by the posterior zone and spoken by the anterior zone, but it can not be easily shuttled from one to the other.

Distinction between aphasia and apraxia

It is important to note that aphasia is a disorder of language and not of speech (although an apraxia of speech, in which the programming of motor speech output is affected, may accompany aphasia). The writing and reading of aphasic patients, therefore, usually commits the same type of error as their speech, while the reverse is not the case. Isolated disorders of writing (dysgraphia) or, more commonly, reading (dyslexia) may occur as well, but these reflect a disruption of the additional processing required for these activities over and above that required for language.

One particular form of dyslexia deserves mention, as it is a clear example of a disconnection syndrome—a disorder resulting from the disconnection of two areas of the brain rather than from damage to a "centre." This is dyslexia without dysgraphia, or letter-by-letter reading, so called because it is not associated with writing disturbance and because the patients tend to attempt to read by spelling words out loud letter by letter. It usually results from a lesion in the posterior part of the left hemisphere that disconnects the visual areas of the brain from the language areas. This renders the language areas effectively blind, so that they cannot be brought to bear on visible language such as the written word. Writing is unaffected because the right hand is still connected to the left hemisphere, and, if letters can be spoken out loud correctly (which is not always the case), the patient will be able to hear himself say them and reintegrate them into words. Disconnection syndromes are an important concept in understanding behavioral disorders associated with brain damage. The possibility that deficits are caused by disconnection must always be borne in mind.

MEMORY

Memory is one of the most widely studied cognitive functions, and a number of different aspects of memory are recognized. The labels short-term memory, primary memory, and working memory refer to the temporary storage of information that is necessary for the performance of many cognitive tasks. In order to understand this sentence, for example, a reader must maintain the first half of the sentence in working memory while reading the second half. This working memory has been graphically described as the memory one uses to hold a telephone number in mind after looking it up in a directory and while dialing. The capacity of working memory is limited, and it decays if not rehearsed. Long-term memory, secondary memory, and reference memory refer to the storage of information for longer periods. The capacity of long-term memory is very large—in practice unlimited—and it can endure indefinitely. In addition, psychologists distinguish episodic memory, a memory of specific events or episodes normally described by the verb remember, from semantic memory, a knowledge of facts normally said to be known rather than remembered.

Importance of the limbic system

Almost certainly, memory is stored over wide areas of the brain rather than in any single location. However, amnesia, a disorder of memory, can occur after localized bilateral lesions in the limbic system—notably the hippocampus on the medial side of the temporal lobe, some parts of the thalamus, and their connections. This probably implies that these structures, rather than actually constituting a memory store, are important in the laying down of memories and in their recall when needed. Memory impairment resulting from damage in these areas is a disorder of long-term episodic memory and is predominantly an anterograde amnesia—that is, it typically affects the memory of events occurring after the illness or accident causing the amnesia more than it does memories of the past. Substantial retrograde amnesia (loss of the memory of events occurring before the onset of amnesia) rarely if ever occurs without significant anterograde amnesia as a result of brain damage, although it may occur alone in psychiatric illness.

Although amnesia is a disorder of long-term episodic memory and leaves short-term and semantic memory intact, both of the latter can be affected by brain damage. Some parietal lobe lesions may affect short-term memory without affecting long-term memory; this fact has contributed to a revision of the old theory that there are distinct short- and long-term stores, the latter being accessible only via the former. It has been suggested that short-term memory impairment—at least for verbal material—can be further subdivided into auditory and visual domains; however, these disorders manifest themselves in difficulty in understanding spoken and written language rather than in memory impairment (*i.e.,* they appear more like aphasia and dyslexia). Impairment of semantic memory, too, results in an impairment that resembles a loss of concepts or a language deficit more than it resembles what would usually be described as a memory impairment. Some forms of visual agnosia have been interpreted as semantic memory impairment, since the patients are unable to recognize objects such as chairs because they no longer "know" what chairs are or what they look like (or can no longer access that knowledge).

EXECUTIVE FUNCTIONS OF THE FRONTAL LOBES

The frontal lobes are the part of the brain most remote from sensory input and whose functions are most difficult to capture. They can be thought of as the executive that controls and directs the operation of the brain systems dealing with cognitive function. Indeed, the deficits seen after frontal lobe damage have been described as a "dysexecutive syndrome."

Consequences of damage to the frontal lobes

Frontal lobe damage can affect people in any of several ways, and the results are at once subtle and drastic. On the one hand, they may have difficulty initiating behaviour, in extreme cases being virtually unable to move or speak but more often simply having difficulty in getting started on a task. On the other, they may perseverate, being apparently unable to stop a behaviour once started. Rather than appearing apathetic and hypoactive, they are uninhibited, rude, and boorish. Such people may also have difficulty in planning and problem solving and may be incapable of creative thinking. Mild cases of this deficit can be revealed by a difficulty in solving mental arithmetic problems that are couched in words, even though it can be shown that the patient is capable of remembering the question and performing the required calculation. In such cases it appears that the patient simply cannot work out what to do, a difficulty described as a failure to select the appropriate cognitive strategy.

A unifying theme in these disorders is the notion of inadequate control or organization of pieces of behaviour that may in themselves be well formed. Frontal lobe patients are easily distracted. Although their deficits may be superficially less dramatic than those associated with posterior lesions, they can have a drastic effect on everyday function. Irritability and personality change are also frequently seen after frontal lobe damage. (G.Ra.)

NERVOUS SYSTEM DISEASES AND DISORDERS

Everything that the human being senses, considers, and effects and all the unlearned reflexes of the body depend upon the functioning of the nervous system. The skeleton and muscles support and transport the body, the heart sends it nourishment through the blood, and the alimentary system and lungs provide the nutrients; but the nervous system contains the epitome of the human being—the mind—and commands all perception, thought, and action. Its disturbance through disease or other malfunction leads to changes felt throughout the body. The most common or important of those diseases are discussed in this section.

Distinction between neurological and psychiatric illness

A distinction is usually drawn between structural or biochemical diseases of the nervous system (the province of the neurologist) and diseases of the mind (requiring the attention of a psychiatrist). This distinction is not, of course, absolute. Many organic brain diseases cause disorders of thought or mood, while the disorders of function that characterize mental disease are profoundly influenced by chemical factors. This section will be confined to those conditions generally regarded as organic nervous disease.

The first part describes the methods whereby neurologists obtain information about the problem—in other words, the history, the examination of the patient, and the laboratory investigations that can be employed. Next the anatomical sites of neurological disease are described, along with the principles used in localizing a disease within the nervous system. The third part gives an overview of pathological processes. Finally, an account is presented of the diseases of the nervous system, using a general classification based upon the primary or major site of the disease.

This scheme is not always possible to follow closely. For example, multiple sclerosis can affect the white matter of the cerebrum, the optic nerves, the cerebellum, or the spinal cord in any patient, so that allocating the disease to any one section must necessarily be arbitrary. Also, metabolic, toxic, inflammatory, and neoplastic diseases may behave similarly. The rule followed here is that the occurrence of various pathologies at different sites are recorded in the discussion of diseases affecting those sites, but a full description is given only in that part dealing with the site that the disease in question affects most consistently.

Acquisition of data

HISTORY

An old saying in medicine, "Listen to the patient; he is telling you the diagnosis," is especially true in neurology. The patient's description of his symptoms is the most valuable tool that the physician has for learning the nature and location of the disease. The patient who cannot give a history owing to coma or loss of speech presents a difficult challenge indeed.

Following are the symptoms most commonly presented to neurologists, with notes on their localizing value.

Symptoms of cortical or cerebral disease. *Altered consciousness.* One's ability to notice, attend to, and react to the environment is not an on–off phenomenon but a continuum. From full alertness a person can descend through drowsiness to stupor, a condition in which awareness is greatly reduced and the best motor response to stimulation is a groan or other vocal (but not verbal) reaction.

Coma

Deeper levels pass through light coma, in which strong stimulation produces only a clumsy motor response, to deep coma, in which there is only a reflex movement or no response at all. Such depression of consciousness occurs when there is impairment of the functions of the brain-stem reticular activating system or of the whole of the cerebral cortex. Brain-stem disorders can cause coma if the brain stem is compressed by other parts of the brain swollen through disease or if it is afflicted by local disease such as encephalitis, stroke, and concussion.

Diseases of the cortex causing coma include poisoning by sedative drugs, lack of glucose or oxygen in the blood, hemorrhage into the brain, and certain rare infiltrative disorders in which descent through the levels of consciousness occurs over weeks or months. Brief periods of unconsciousness, of which the patient may not be aware, occur in many forms of epilepsy, narcolepsy, repeated attacks of low blood sugar, and reduction in the supply of blood to the brain—particularly the brain stem.

Epilepsy is a condition in which excessive discharges of the neurons of the cerebral gray matter occur, causing maximal activation (rarely inhibition) of parts or all of the brain. This commonly causes visible seizures, but in a variety of epilepsy called petit mal or absence attacks, altered consciousness may be the only symptom. Disorders of sleep include inability to fall asleep or to stay asleep. This is seldom evidence of a neurological disorder and is commonly a psychiatric problem. Increased sleepiness, or hypersomnia, may be due to the causes of drowsiness mentioned above or to narcolepsy (see below *Diseases and disorders: The cranial nerves and brain stem*). Another cause of daytime drowsiness is sleep apnea, a disturbance of nocturnal sleep due to frequent brief episodes of obstructed breathing.

Headache. This is a common complaint of neurology patients. Tension headache is considered to be due to prolonged excessive contraction of the muscles that run front-to-back over the skull; this muscular tension often reflects mental tension. A persistent pressing or pulling pain, often with a throbbing component, is usually described. Migraine headaches may be combined with the foregoing or may be present as a throbbing, pounding pain with marked scalp tenderness, nausea and vomiting, dislike of noise and light, and irritability. (For further discussion of migraine, see below *Diseases and disorders: The cerebrum.*)

When pressure inside the cranium is increased, pain-sensitive structures in and around the brain are distorted and cause pain to be felt in an ill-localized area but often identifiably at the front or back of the head. This traction headache is potentially serious, since it may be caused by brain swelling, infection, bleeding, tumour, or obstructed flow of cerebrospinal fluid. Also, pain may be felt in the head region although the disorder causing the pain is situated elsewhere; an example is the facial pain sometimes felt with lack of blood to the heart. Local disease of such cranial structures as the jaw joints, the paranasal sinuses and teeth, the middle ear, and the skull bones themselves may also generate pain, requiring a careful, probing history in order to be identified as the cause of the headache.

Traction headache

Loss of memory. This symptom may have causes that are trivial or important. Poor concentration owing to preoccupation, fatigue, or depression is the most common cause, but widespread brain disease, vitamin deficiency, epilepsy, and dementia (loss of intellectual power) would have to be considered. When the period of memory loss is well defined, prominent causes are trauma to the head, seizures, poisoning (*e.g.,* with alcohol), and brief episodes of inadequate perfusion of the brain with blood. Some patients with severe mental problems such as hysteria claim to have totally lost their memory for past events and even for their own identities; this symptom is not encountered in people with organic brain disease.

Dementia

Disorders of concentration, attention, planning ability, and forethought—often combined with impaired social behaviour and emotional control and with reduced capacity to learn new things—characterize the problems of patients with dementia, a condition of global impairment of the highest intellectual powers. The most common single cause is Alzheimer's disease. Since dementia is the third most common cause of death (after diseases of the blood vessels and cancers), and since the average age of the Western Hemisphere population is increasing, dementia is attaining great importance in medical and social research. (See also below *Diseases and disorders: The cerebrum.*)

Patients with dementia—and those with almost any more localized brain disorder or general medical disease—are at risk of developing a related but more acute syndrome called confusion or acute brain syndrome. In this case, patients lose their orientation in time, space, and person; they may show altered levels of consciousness, emotional instability sometimes amounting to terror, physical excitability, and agitation and disorderliness, as well as hallucinations and delusions to which they hold tenaciously despite reasonable counterargument. Of all the causes of acute brain syndrome, generalized metabolic diseases and intoxication with sedative drugs (including alcohol) are the most common.

Aphasia

Language and speech deficits. Aphasia is a failure to use language in communication. It is caused by damage to the part of the brain that controls language function—namely, the area encompassed by the back of the frontal lobe, the front of the parietal lobe, and the upper surface of the temporal lobe (usually on the left hemisphere but on the right in a small proportion of left-handed people; see above *Functions of the human nervous system: Higher cerebral functions*). Patients with aphasia may know exactly what they want to say, but they are unable to express it in spoken (and often written) words. With disease affecting the Wernicke's area farther back on the temporal lobe, the problem may be in comprehending the meaning of spoken or written language, so that normal speech sounds like a foreign tongue. Strokes are the most common cause of aphasia, but any focal brain disease can be responsible.

Similar problems of comprehension are apraxia and agnosia. Apraxia is an inability to perform a purposeful action; agnosia is a failure to comprehend the significance of a nonlanguage stimulus. Shown a comb or a key, an apraxic patient may be able to name it but may not know how to use it. Hearing a trumpet, an agnosic patient may be unable to recognize the origin of the sound.

Dysarthria, or difficulty in articulation, usually has a local cause in the nerves and muscles in and around the mouth or in their central connections. Problems in the production of speech sounds, called dysphonia, often indicate a problem affecting the larynx or the nerves and muscles of that structure. Since the cranial nerves supplying these areas originate in the brain stem, neurological disease of that region may be a cause.

Nonspecific symptoms. Alteration in mood is common in association with neurological disease, either as a result of the pathological process itself or of the patient's reaction to his awareness of disease. Although depression is most common, unusual euphoria or mood swings may occur with disease of the frontal lobes of the brain. Other nonspecific symptoms of brain disease are impairment of recent and (less often) remote memory, concentration, attention, energy, comprehension of concepts, reasoning, logical thinking, and ability to plan ahead. Any or all of these are impaired in patients with dementia (see above).

Pain is another important symptom. Although the central nervous system is not supplied with sensory fibres that report sensations of pain, severe pain can result from thalamic strokes. Also, headache, one of the most common symptoms expressed by patients, has both central and peripheral components, and many disorders affecting the peripheral nerves and muscles are painful. Neuralgias, or attacks of pain along the sensory nerves, are due to irritation of some of the cranial nerves or spinal roots. In each case the quality, severity, timing, location, and accompaniments of the pain may be sufficient to allow precise diagnosis.

Cranial nerves. Symptoms reflecting disease of the cranial nerves are even more varied than those suggesting cortical or cerebral disease.

Damage to the first (olfactory) nerve leads to anosmia, or loss of the sense of smell, on the side supplied by the nerve. Head injuries and compression by tumours are possible causes, though local nasal disease is more common. Hallucinations of smell occur in temporal lobe diseases such as epilepsy or tumour and also in depressive illnesses.

Disorders of the second (optic) nerve cause visual loss in the affected eye. In the early stages of disease, when the process is irritating the nerve rather than decreasing its conducting ability, positive phenomena such as streaks of light may be seen. When the optic pathways are affected within the brain, the precise location of the disease can be determined by testing the pattern of visual loss affecting both eyes. Pain in the eyes is sometimes due to neuritis of the optic nerves, but it is usually caused by ocular disease.

Double vision

When any of the three oculomotor nerves are affected, the eyes are not able to retain parallelism of their axes, so that light falls on different parts of the two retinas and patients complain of diplopia, or double vision. With central lesions, a disorder of ocular posture in which the eyes jerk spontaneously, known as nystagmus, may lead to complaints of jumping images.

Compression or other disease of the fifth (trigeminal) nerve causes complaints of facial numbness. Since some diseases of the brain stem can cause similar problems, precise inquiry and examination of signs localizing the disease to the brain stem are important. In trigeminal neuralgia, jabs of excruciating pain are felt on one side of the lower face, mainly in people over the age of 55 years.

The seventh (facial) nerve is damaged most commonly by swelling within the facial canal in the temporal bone, thought to be due to viral infection. This gives rise to Bell's palsy, a weakness of the muscles of the side of the face in which the mouth and eye cannot be closed tightly. Numerous other conditions affect the facial nerve.

When both divisions of the eighth (vestibulocochlear) nerve are affected by disease, there may be positive symptoms such as ringing in the ear (tinnitus) and a sensation of spinning (vertigo) as well as negative symptoms such as deafness.

Damage to the ninth through 12th cranial nerves, which have their nuclei of origin in the medulla oblongata, causes dysphonia, dysarthria, and dysphagia (difficulty in swallowing). All three are symptoms of the gravest import, since their causes often lead to further paralyses and to an inability to swallow or clear the airway of secretions that may be aspirated into the lungs. Involvement of the 11th (accessory) nerve leads to weakness of the neck muscles. Lesions of the 12th (hypoglossal) nerve, which supplies only the tongue, may have little clinical effect if unilateral, but if both sides are affected, speech and manipulation of food in the mouth are disturbed. (For description of the cranial-nerve pathways, see above *Anatomy of the human nervous system: The central nervous system.*)

Symptoms of the body and limbs. Symptoms expressed in the limbs and trunk and pointing to neurological disease include weakness and wasting of muscles, clumsiness, and unwanted movements. None of these is caused by disease of one particular site, so that only by thorough inquiry can the neurologist localize the problem. Thus, weakness can be due to any of the following: disorder of the upper motor neuron anywhere between the cortex, where it originates, and the ventral horn of the spinal cord; cerebellar disease; lack of energy or motivation as in hypothyroidism, dementia, or depression; disorders of the basal ganglia; or disorders of the motor unit, encompassing the lower motor neuron, the motor end plates, and the muscle fibres. Peripheral nerve diseases, end-plate disorders such as myasthenia gravis, and both genetic and acquired muscle diseases, can also be responsible. Finally, loss of feedback from sensory fibres of a limb also reduces muscular power.

Involuntary movement

The complaint of clumsiness has a similar list of potential causes. Weakness is a negative symptom—that is, it represents the loss of a normal function. Involuntary movements, however, are new (or positive) events. Chorea is a condition in which the face and distal parts of the limbs make brief, jerky, dissimilar, involuntary, and repetitive movements; the lesion is usually found in the caudate nuclei, where many pathologies may be the cause. Ballismus, a similar but more severe condition, is due to a lesion of the subthalamic nucleus. Patients with athetosis make slower, writhing, sinuous movements intermittently or continuously; dystonias are even slower movements or abnormal postures of the head or the limbs adopted by patients with certain basal ganglion diseases. Tics and habit spasms are of uncertain origin. In such cases, and when no pathology at all can be demonstrated, the condition may be labeled "functional," implying (usually erroneously) a psychological disorder.

Alterations of sensation may also be positive or negative; the former include tingling, burning, itching, and pain, while the latter consist of diminution or loss of some or all sensations. Sensations carried by large, heavily myelinated fibres, such as position sense, discriminative light touch, and vibration sense, tend to be affected together, as do those carried by the smaller, thinly myelinated or non-myelinated fibres, including pain, crude light touch, and temperature. As with the complaint of weakness, careful inquiry and examination are necessary to define the exact boundaries of abnormal sensation and thus to diagnose the site of the causative pathology.

Autonomic nerves. A last group of symptoms signifies involvement of the autonomic nervous system. Complaints of alteration in bladder or bowel habit or sensation, of increased or decreased sweating, of faintness (due to a drop in blood pressure after a change in posture), of impaired accommodation of vision, and of altered sexual potency are those most commonly met.

PHYSICAL EXAMINATION

While taking the history, the neurologist notes the patient's level of awareness, posture and gait, demeanour and expression, speech, and, to some extent, personality. He also looks for evidence of weakness, incoordination, wasting of certain muscle groups, and abnormal movements. The formal examination then begins with an examination of higher cerebral functions and proceeds methodically through an evaluation of the cranial nerves, motor systems, and sensory systems.

Higher cerebral functions. In order to evaluate the patient's orientation in place and time, tests of concentration, of recent and remote memory, and of ability to follow simple spoken or written commands, as well as other tests of language, are usually given. Comprehension, reasoning, and planning can be tested, for example, by asking about the similarities and differences between two objects (child/dwarf, fly/tree, wall/fence) or by asking the patient to explain the message or moral contained in a proverb.

Testing comprehension

Tests for apraxias and agnosias are helpful when cortical disease is suspected, as are tests measuring the ability to perform simple drawing and writing tests and to copy simple figures. Standardized tests for examining these functions apply quantitative measurements to any deficit, which can be analyzed further by more sophisticated testing at the hands of a clinical psychologist.

The process continues with examination of the head and neck, looking especially for local tenderness or deformity and for evidence in children of enlargement of the head, which may suggest hydrocephalus. The physician may also use a stethoscope to auscultate (listen to) the major blood vessels in the neck, listening also over the skull for sounds indicating unusual communication between arteries and veins. Irritation of the meninges, as occurs with intracranial infection or bleeding, leads to unusual stiffness on attempts to flex the neck passively, as well as to an inability to straighten the bent knee when the hip is flexed (a condition called Kernig's sign).

Cranial nerves. *Olfactory.* The ability to perceive (not identify) a mild odour, such as coffee, tar, or lemon, is tested.

Optic. The optic nerve head is the only part of the central nervous system accessible to vision; an ophthalmoscope is used for this purpose and to see the retinas and the small arteries and veins that lie upon them. Visual acuity is tested with a standard test card, and the visual field is examined by asking the patient to signal when he sees an object brought in toward the centre of vision from the periphery. A simple machine called a perimeter partly automates and quantifies this examination.

Oculomotor. The three oculomotor nerves are tested together by asking the patient to gaze in different directions on command and to follow a moving object with the eyes only. The character of any double vision is noted. The shape, size, and reactivity of the pupils—both to light and to close objects—are also tested.

Trigeminal. Motor functions are examined by asking the patient to clench the teeth and by testing the jaw reflex by tapping the chin. This is one of the few physiological reflexes that is normally not detected. The sensory functions of the nerve are examined by stimulating the face gently with the finger or cotton wool for light touch, cold steel for temperature, and a pin for scratch or pain sensation. This procedure is done for the three anatomical divisions of the nerve on each side of the face. Finally, cotton wool is touched to the cornea to assess the corneal reflex. Normally, an abrupt blink is produced.

Facial. This motor nerve is examined by asking the patient to screw up the eyes, bare the teeth, and try to whistle. The facial nerve also carries fibres subserving the function of taste on the front of the tongue, so that weak solutions of sugar, salt, lemon, or vinegar can be used to test its function. (Flavour—as opposed to the tastes of sweetness, saltiness, bitterness, and sourness—is mediated exclusively by the olfactory nerve, even for foods inside the mouth.)

Vestibulocochlear. For the cochlear nerve, hearing tests examine the overall acuity to the whispered voice. Rinne's test differentiates the patient's ability to hear the hum of a tuning fork held both beside the ear and with its foot on the mastoid bone of the skull behind the ear. If the sound is louder at the latter site, impairment of the conduction of vibrations through the chain of three small bones in the middle ear is likely, while if the former sound is louder, any deafness is likely due to disease of the inner ear or of the cochlear nerve. Weber's test consists of placing the tuning fork on the forehead; the sound is better perceived either in the ear without nerve deafness or (paradoxically) in the ear affected by mild middle-ear deafness. More sophisticated tests require the equipment found in a hospital or clinical audiometry laboratory.

Hearing tests

Tests of the vestibular nerve are not routinely performed. The usual screening procedure for postural vertigo is to await the appearance of vertigo or nystagmus while tipping the patient's head back and down 45 degrees. Further testing is done in an electronystagmography laboratory. It includes the assessment of nystagmus when the external ear canals are irrigated with warm or cool air or water, when the patient is rotated, or when he is made to gaze in various directions.

Glossopharyngeal and vagus. The usual tests are for the presence of touch sensation on the soft palate and the back of the throat (the latter usually eliciting a gagging reflex), the elevation of the palate on phonation (which should be symmetrical but rises to the stronger side in the presence of weakness on one side), the quality and loudness of the voice, and the normal slowing of the heartbeat when one carotid artery is compressed in the neck at the level of the carotid sinus.

Accessory. The sternocleidomastoid and trapezius muscles, supplied by this nerve, are tested by having the patient push his head forward and shrug his shoulders upward against the examiner's resistance.

Hypoglossal. Atrophy and weakness of the tongue muscles can be assessed by measuring the deviation of the tongue toward the weak side upon protrusion.

Motor systems. The presence of gait and postural disturbances, of abnormal movements, and of atrophy may be noticed when the patient is giving the history. Examination is then formalized and extended under five headings.

Inspection. Inspection of the body may show patterns of muscle atrophy. Depending on the pattern of atrophy, this suggests lesions in nerve roots, in more peripheral locations of the nerves, or in the muscles themselves with no involvement of nerves. Symmetrical, proximal atrophy is more likely to indicate primary muscle disease, while unilateral atrophy (*i.e.,* affecting only those muscles receiving their motor supply from a single nerve) naturally suggests a lesion of the supplying nerve.

Muscle atrophy

Fasciculations are brief, irregular, involuntary twitches of muscles that do not lead to the movement of a joint but that are visible and can be felt by the patient. If accompanied by atrophy and weakness, they may be symptoms of serious underlying motor neuron disease (see below *Diseases and disorders: The peripheral system*). Other abnormal movements, such as chorea and dystonia, are also noted, as are changes in the skin and joints caused by nerve or muscle disease.

Muscle tone. When the examiner flexes or extends the joints in a relaxed limb, a certain resistance, known as tone, is felt. This resistance decreases whenever the reflex arc is damaged (usually at the level of the peripheral motor or sensory nerve), but it may decrease with primary muscle or spinal cord disease. An increase in resistance occurs in the presence of a lesion of the upper motor neurons—that is, anywhere along the pathway from the motor cortex down to the pool of ventral horn neurons in the spinal cord—by which the muscles in question are supplied. This so-called hypertonia may increase against resistance and then suddenly give way ("clasp-knife spasticity"), or it may be constant throughout the range of movement ("plastic" or "lead-pipe" rigidity). In the presence of tremor this latter form has a ratchety feel to it, leading to the name cogwheel rigidity. Rigidity suggests a lesion of the basal ganglia, but spasticity implies disease of the direct corticospinal tracts.

Hypertonia

Power. Power is tested either by examining single muscles in cases where a local or lower motor lesion is suspected or by assessing the patient's strength in flexing or extending joints—in which case a number of muscles are tested at once. The latter method is employed when evidence of an upper motor lesion is being sought.

Reflex activity. Three main types of reflex activity are tested: an increase in the speed and strength of the reflex response, a decrease in response, and the presence of abnormal reflexes. Using a tendon hammer, the examiner taps a suitable tendon with the patient relaxed and observes the response—usually a single brief, brisk contraction of the appropriate muscle. Response is normally enhanced if muscles contract elsewhere in the body. When an upper motor neuron lesion is present, the response is excessive and the muscle may contract repeatedly.

The tendon tap

Tendon reflexes are diminished or absent in the presence of a lesion of the lower motor neuron, of the muscle itself, or of the afferent (sensory) side of the reflex arc. Superficial reflexes can be elicited by stroking the wall of the abdomen with a thin stick; this should cause the underlying muscles to contract. Unlike tendon reflexes, the superficial reflexes disappear in the presence of a corticospinal tract lesion.

The only abnormal reflex routinely detected is the plantar, or Babinski, response. Normally, the great toe curls downward when the examiner draws a stick up the sole of the foot. In the presence of a corticospinal tract lesion, it curls upward instead, and the other toes may fan out.

Coordination. Disease of the cerebellum leads to abnormalities of the rate, range, and force of voluntary movements and to disturbances of posture and gait. The jerky oscillations of the eyes constituting nystagmus are also notable. Tests employed to assess cerebellar function in the limbs include those of rapid alternating movements, the subject being asked to touch, successively, the examiner's finger held before him and his own nose, to run one heel down the opposite shin, or to perform piano-playing movements with the fingers on a resonating surface. The amount of agility and precision of control over the limbs is noted by the examiner.

Sensory systems. Because the examination can be so long and tedious that even the most cooperative patient may give misleading responses, an examiner does not attempt sensory testing except on a brief screening basis until he has a clear idea of the kind of problem for which he is looking. Questions to be answered are: Which (if any) modes of sensation are impaired? To what degree are they impaired? And in which areas? From the results of careful sensory testing it may be possible to localize the site of a lesion in the nervous system with great accuracy. To achieve this localization, it may be necessary to compare sensation in different dermatomes (areas of the body innervated by different spinal segments) or in areas supplied by different parts of the brain or spinal cord.

The stimuli employed include: the examiner's finger or a cotton-wool applicator or paintbrush, for testing sensations of light touch; steel or glass tubes filled with warm and cold water, for temperature; a pin, for superficial pain and scratch sensation; a tuning fork, for vibration; and, for the sense of passive movement of joints, gentle movement of a digit up or down outside the patient's range of vision. Discriminative touch can be tested by determining whether the patient can identify an object placed in his hand, can determine whether he is being touched by one or two ends of a blunt pair of compasses, or can identify where he was touched or what number or letter was drawn on his skin by the examiner. When disease of the contralateral parietal lobe is involved, many of these tests of discriminative sensation show abnormality; in such cases, simultaneous stimulation (usually visual or tactile) on both sides of the body leads to identification of only one stimulus—that on the side opposite the healthy lobe.

LABORATORY INVESTIGATION

Further useful data may be acquired from the results of the tests described below.

Electrical tests. A recording of the inherent electrical rhythms of the brain was first achieved by the German psychiatrist Hans Berger in the late 1920s. Today, electroencephalography is a routine procedure, used mainly to localize the origin of epileptic discharges (Figure 33) but also to localize and, occasionally, indicate the nature of destructive disease of the underlying brain. It is also employed to indicate the degree of generalized brain disease in such metabolic disorders as liver failure, and it may show characteristic patterns in some viral and slow-viral illnesses. It can only confirm a diagnosis of brain death made through other means.

Electroencephalography

From S.G. Bayliss in W. Pryse-Phillips, *Epilepsy* (1969); Butterworth Scientific Ltd.

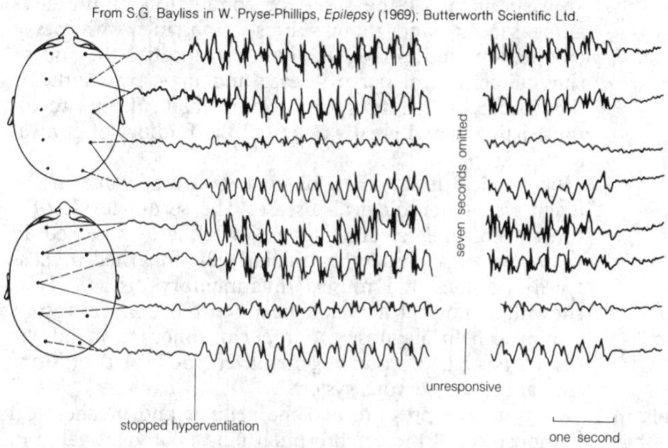

seven seconds omitted
unresponsive
stopped hyperventilation
one second

Figure 33: *An electroencephalogram (EEG) from a patient having an attack of petit mal epilepsy.*
The sudden onset of abnormal discharges, recordable from all areas of the scalp as waves and spikes on the graph, is accompanied by loss of consciousness, without convulsion, for approximately 20 seconds.

The electroencephalogram (EEG) is produced by placing electrodes on or in the scalp and then recording the changes in electrical potential that take place while the subject is at rest or stimulated by flickering light, noise, or drugs.

Tiny voltages transmitted by the peripheral nerves are amplified in the central nervous system. When multiple stimuli are given and the electrical activity of the relevant cortical area is recorded for 10 to 1,000 milliseconds after each stimulus, consistent potential changes can be recorded by averaging the responses and eliminating background electrical "noise." These potential changes, recorded as waveforms on the EEG, are very similar in all humans. Their absence, delay, or distortion indicates disease in the central conducting pathways, thus allowing further localization of disease (but not indicating the nature of the responsible pathology). Computerization has allowed the generation of "maps" of electrical activity and the more precise localization of abnormal electrical discharges.

Stimulation may be of peripheral nerves using weak electrical shocks (somatosensory evoked potentials, or SEPs), of the auditory apparatus by click stimuli given through headphones (brain-stem evoked potentials, or BAEPs), or of the optic nerve using flashes of light or an alternating checkerboard pattern on a screen (visual evoked potentials, or VEPs). These tests are employed most commonly in the search for sites that show no clinical evidence of disease (as in multiple sclerosis) and in the assessment of dementias, spinal-cord diseases, and disorders of the visual pathways. BAEPs are of particular value in the diagnosis of tumours at the base of the brain.

Techniques similar to those described above are used to study the function of the retinas (electroretinography) and the posture and movements of the eye (electronystagmography).

Techniques are under development whereby the brain can be harmlessly stimulated through the scalp and skull, either by brief electrical current or magnetic field, and the resulting muscle response recorded. The interval between stimulus and response can be measured and may indicate disease of the motor pathways.

Electromyography

Electrical examination of the peripheral nervous system is also possible. Electromyography (EMG) is the study of muscular electrical activity by means of fine needle electrodes inserted into the muscle. The waveforms recorded with primary disease of muscles differ somewhat from those found when the muscles are deprived of their motor innervation. This allows both improved precision in the detection of muscle involvement and differential diagnosis of the causative pathology. Single-fibre EMG (SFEMG) is a technique in which even fewer muscle fibres are examined. Particular attention is paid to the consistency of activation of single muscle fibres, since this varies widely in diseases of the motor end plate (see below *Diseases and disorders: The peripheral system*).

Measurement of the speed of conduction of impulses along sensory and motor fibres is possible with nerve conduction studies (NCS). These can localize the site or sites of peripheral nerve disease and may even indicate the nature of the disorder affecting them. They are almost painless and greatly augment the findings of clinical examination.

Biochemical tests. Few blood tests are of value in the diagnosis of neurological disease. The serum levels of a muscle enzyme, creatine kinase (CK), are increased in many muscle disorders, particularly the inherited muscular dystrophies and muscle inflammatory disease. Tests showing abnormal hematological and biochemical results may also help diagnose a number of inherited metabolic disorders and, of course, generalized medical conditions that affect the nervous system.

Spinal tap, or lumbar puncture

Study of the pressure and the cellular and biochemical composition of the cerebrospinal fluid is of great value in the diagnosis of central nervous system infections, some tumours, and multiple sclerosis. Cerebrospinal fluid is obtained almost painlessly by inserting a needle through the skin in the small of the back so that it passes deeply between the bony vertebrae into the fluid sac surrounding the spinal cord and nerve roots. (The needle is inserted below the termination of the spinal cord, so that the cord cannot be damaged.) Identification of one or two bands of protein in the fluid is a valuable aid in the diagnosis of multiple sclerosis and of other smouldering inflammatory diseases of the central nervous system.

Pathological examination. A diagnosis may be made by biopsy, the direct examination of surgically removed nerve, muscle, or brain tissue. Special stains are often employed to increase diagnostic accuracy. A number of conditions affecting the central and peripheral nervous systems can be differentiated only by their appearance under the electron microscope.

Radiological tests. *Conventional X rays.* Plain X rays are of relatively minor value in neurological diagnosis. Diseases affecting the skull bones (malformations, chronically raised intracranial pressure, a few metabolic diseases, tumours, and trauma) can be diagnosed with this procedure, as can disorders of the spinal column and a small number of benign cerebral tumours, but X rays employing the injection of iodine-containing "contrast media" or air are far more valuable. Such studies allow better visualization of the spine (myelography), of the fluid-containing ventricles of the brain (ventriculography), or of the arteries or veins within the cranium and neck (angiography and venography). In most cases, however, even contrast X rays give only a silhouette of the lesion or a definition of its blood supply. While this is of great diagnostic value in disorders of the blood vessels themselves (aneurysms, angiomas, large vessel disease), the location of the actual pathology elsewhere must usually be inferred.

X rays employing contrast media

The contrast medium is injected, often under a general anesthetic, into an artery, vein, or, during an operation, the ventricles. Injections into the cerebrospinal fluid at the lumbar area do not normally require anesthesia. All these procedures carry some risk of morbidity, even of mortality, but for many years they have been the mainstay of laboratory investigation of central nervous system disease.

Computerized axial tomography (CAT). The greatest advance in neurological diagnosis since the discovery of X rays occurred in the early 1970s when CAT scanning (also called computerized tomography, or CT, scanning), conceived by William Oldendorf and developed by Godfrey Hounsfield, became generally available. Although often employing contrast media to enhance the quality of the images obtained, this test is barely invasive. It allows visualization of three- to 10-millimetre sections of the brain, skull, spinal cord, and spine (as well as other parts of the body) in two dimensions and with enough clear distinction between black, gray, and white areas of the image to allow pathological diagnosis in many cases.

Magnetic resonance imaging (MRI). While CAT scanning is a pure X-ray technique, other computerized investigations yield data about the form or function of the central nervous system without the use of X rays. In MRI, the patient is placed within a magnetic coil, and radiofrequency energy is applied to the head. These harmless radio waves excite protons that form the nuclei of hydrogen atoms in the brain. The protons then give off measurable electrical energy, which, with the aid of a computer, can be used to construct a map of the tissue. Since MRI hardly visualizes bone, it gives excellent images of the intracranial and intraspinal contents (Figure 34).

By courtesy of Romeo Ethier

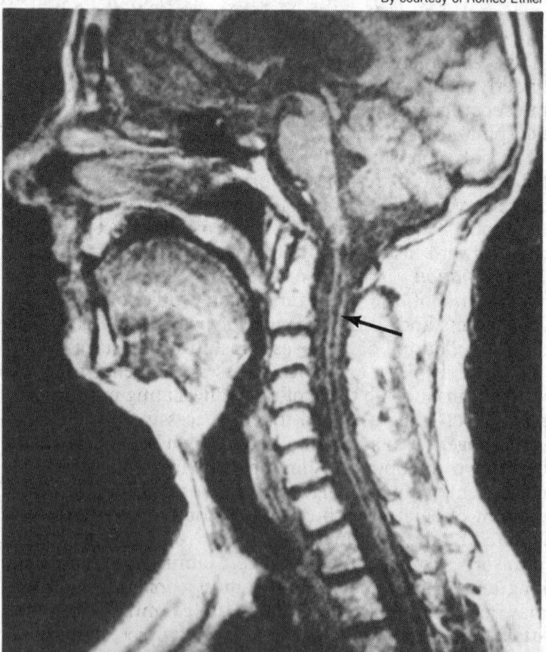

Figure 34: *Magnetic resonance image (MRI) of a patient with syringomyelia.*
An abnormal cavity in the spinal cord, called the syrinx, is indicated by the arrow.

Positron emission tomography (PET). Another noninvasive test, PET, employs inhaled or injected radioisotopes and computer techniques to map the metabolic activity of the brain. This is of particular value in the diagnosis of certain degenerative and metabolic disorders.

Doppler ultrasound studies. High-frequency sound waves can be used in a way similar to radar in order to show the form of deep body structures. In neurological diagnosis, demonstration of the echoes from midline structures and from the ventricular walls has proved valuable, but CAT and other scanning techniques are making such tests unnecessary. Doppler studies of the carotid arteries in the neck, however, represent valuable noninvasive tests that can give useful information about the size and any deformity of these vessels.

Radioisotope scans. The blood–brain barrier keeps large molecules from passing into the brain or spinal cord from the blood. When this barrier is destroyed—as it is around tumours, blood clots, infarcts, or infections—fluid and dissolved solids can pass into the brain. Some radioisotopes injected into the bloodstream also cross into brain tissue and remain there. Measured by outside detectors, the radioactivity of the isotopes can then produce a map of the areas where the barrier has been destroyed. This technique has been valuable in the detection of the intracranial pathologies mentioned above, although the CAT scan is more accurate. Isotopes are also used to visualize cerebral blood flow in patients with cerebrovascular disease, as well as the flow patterns of cerebrospinal fluid in some cases of dementia and after skull fracture.

Crossing the blood–brain barrier

Localization

The nature and pattern of the symptoms and physical signs of neurological disease allow inferences to be drawn about the sites of the lesions causing them. The main sites are described below, with notes on some of the clinical features that lead to their localization.

LOWER-LEVEL SITES

Muscle. Muscle disease is frequently hereditary—in which case a positive family history may be obtained. One complaint suggesting muscular involvement in the disease is that of weakness, usually symmetrical and mainly affecting the proximal or girdle muscles. This type of weakness is noticed on climbing stairs, arising from a deep easy chair, brushing the hair, or lifting an object. Facial weakness leads to difficulty in whistling and to drooling of saliva. Weak masticatory muscles tire easily, so that food is chewed with difficulty, while bulbar muscle involvement leads to problems with phonation, articulation, and swallowing. Diseased muscles are often atrophied but they may also swell and be tender or subject to cramp. In the condition known as myotonia they continue to contract even when the patient wants them to relax.

Complaints of weakness

Motor end plate. The only symptoms resulting from a failure of the motor nerve impulse to cross to the muscle end plate at the neuromuscular junction are fatigability and weakness.

Peripheral nerves. Diffuse disease affecting the peripheral nerves may have a greater impact on either motor or sensory fibres, or it may affect both to an equal degree. Commonly, nerves are affected according to their length, the longest ones "dying back" from the periphery, being least able to sustain vital metabolic processes. In such cases of generalized neuropathy, the signs tend to be symmetrical and most obvious in the extremities. In other cases, individual nerves are affected as a result of compression or vascular disease.

Complaints when motor nerves are affected include weakness and muscle atrophy. Involvement of sensory nerves leads to numbness, paresthesia (tingling), shooting or burning pains, and hyperesthesia (undue sensitivity to stimuli, which are felt as painful even though innocuous). In both motor and sensory neuropathies, reflex activity is reduced or absent. Examination can show the patterns of weakness and atrophy or of sensory less based on the pathology and on which nerves are involved.

Spinal nerve roots. The symptoms and signs of involvement of spinal roots are the same as for peripheral-nerve involvement except that the territory of involvement conforms to the area supplied by the spinal roots rather than the nerves. Also, generalized symmetrical sensory loss is not seen in these cases.

Spinal cord. The structure of the spinal cord, with long ascending and descending fibre tracts and entering and emerging nerve roots, is reflected in the symptoms and signs of disease. There is often a combination of the signs of root lesions (often including pain) at the site of the pathology with signs of damage to the tracts below that level. For example, injury to the cord at mid-thoracic levels spares the arms which are innervated by fibres originating from higher segments, but it induces characteristic signs (abnormal posture, spastic tone, weakness, increased deep reflexes, and abnormal plantar reflexes) of damage to motor neurons originating below that level—as well as loss of bladder control.

Loss of function in ascending sensory pathways will lead to loss of superficial pain, temperature, crude light touch, and scratch sensation if the spinothalamic tract is damaged, but it will cause loss of sense of joint position, vibration, and discriminative light-touch sensation if the dorsal columns are the site of injury. Because of the crossing of its fibres shortly after they enter the cord, spinothalamic-tract lesions on the left side of the cord lead to loss of sensations on the right side of the body below the lesion. This is not true of lesions of the dorsal columns, which carry fibres originating from the same side of the body.

Loss of sensation

Damage to sympathetic autonomic fibres that run in the cervical portions of the spinal cord may lead to drooping of the eyelid and a smaller pupil on the same side as the injury.

HIGHER-LEVEL SITES

Brain stem. Damage to the brain stem threatens life, since so many of the control centres for bodily functions (for example, consciousness, respiration, and blood pressure), are situated there. As with lesions of the spinal cord, localization of the level of the lesion is made possible by noting which of the cranial nerve functions are affected. The horizontal extent of the lesion can be estimated by determining which of the vertically running pathways are involved.

As one example, a midline lesion of the medulla oblongata is likely to involve the pyramidal tracts (the descending motor pathway) and the medial lemnisci (the ascending tracts relaying sensory impulses from the dorsal columns of the spinal cord). This produces signs of an upper motor-neuron lesion and of dorsal-column-type sensory loss at all levels below the medulla. Such signs could theoretically be produced by a lesion anywhere between the mid-medulla and the third cervical segment of the spinal cord, but the added finding of 12th-nerve palsy with atrophy of the tongue accurately localizes the lesion in the midline of the medulla, low down, since that is where the nucleus of the 12th cranial nerve is situated.

A lesion of one side of the medulla spares the pyramidal tracts and medial lemnisci, but it involves the sympathetic pathways, the fibres entering the cerebellum in its inferior peduncle, some of the eighth, ninth, and 10th cranial nerve nuclei, and the descending nucleus and tract of the fifth cranial nerve on the side of the injury, as well as the ascending fibres of the spinothalamic tract from the opposite side of the body. Major features of the lesion, therefore, include: incoordination of voluntary limb movements, drooping eyelid and small pupil, and loss of light-touch and pinprick-pain sensation over the face (all on the side of the lesion); vertigo and vomiting; and loss of spinothalamic function (light-touch and pinprick pain again) on the opposite side of the body. Similar principles govern the localization of lesions of the brain stem at higher levels.

Cerebellum. With damage to the oldest part of the cerebellum, which lies deep in the midline, a patient has difficulty in maintaining an upright posture and may even be unable to sit up in bed. Nystagmus (jerky movements of the eyes at rest) is also likely. The vermis and anterior lobes of the cerebellum developed later in evolution; lesions there particularly influence gait. The lateral lobes represent the "newest" parts to develop; when they are damaged, ataxia (incoordination) of the limbs is found, so that rapid, alternating movements cannot be performed and all voluntary activity is disordered in rate, range, and force. As a result, arm and leg movements are awkward, irregular, and impaired by a tremor that may be so severe that self-care is impossible despite the absence of significant weakness.

Loss of coordinated movement

Basal ganglia and thalamus. Thalamic lesions lead to loss of all sensation on the opposite side of the body, sometimes accompanied by extreme pain. Since tumours and strokes affecting this region are likely also to damage the fibres in the adjacent internal capsule, signs of damage to upper motor neurons may also be present at all lower levels, thus affecting the cranial nerves as well as the spinal segments. Disorders of eye movement and speech are also sometimes found with thalamic lesions.

Lesions of the hypothalamus have many effects upon the regulation of the body's metabolism, such as water and solute control, sexual activity, and appetite for food.

Basal-ganglion diseases lead to abnormal control over movement, manifesting itself as involuntary movements or as a reduction in the spontaneity or speed of voluntary movement.

Cerebral hemispheres. The frontal lobe is concerned with many of the components of intelligence (foresight, planning, and comprehension), with mood, with motor activity on the opposite side of the body, and (in the case of the dominant hemisphere) with speech production. Swelling of the underside of the frontal lobe may compress the first cranial nerves with resulting loss of smell sensations. Irritation of the frontal cortex may cause either generalized or focal motor epileptic seizures, the latter involving the opposite side of the body.

Damage to the dominant temporal lobe is manifested by difficulty with comprehension of spoken speech. The right temporal lobe (usually nondominant for speech) has a special role in the appreciation of nonlanguage sounds such as music. Irritation of a temporal lobe may lead to auditory or olfactory hallucinations. Memory functions are duplicated in the two temporal lobes; if one is damaged, there is little effect, but bilateral damage leads to a permanent, catastrophic inability to learn new data.

Loss of speech and purposeful movement

Parietal-lobe functions also differ on the two sides. In most people the left parietal lobe shares in the comprehension of spoken and written language and of arithmetic, interprets the difference between right and left, identifies body parts, and is responsible for determining how to perform meaningful motor actions. Damage to this lobe leads to forms of apraxia, the inability to perform purposeful actions. The right parietal lobe is concerned with visuospatial orientation, and damage typically leads to deficits such as dressing apraxia (inability to put on clothes), constructional apraxia (difficulty in creating or copying two- or three-dimensional forms), and a phenomenon called sensory competition, or sensory extinction, which is an inability to recognize two stimuli when both are presented together on opposite sides—most easily demonstrated in the realms of touch and vision. Each parietal lobe is also concerned with so-called cortical sensation or discriminative touch, the analysis and interpretation of touch sensations originating on the other side of the body. Damage can cause a form of agnosia, in which the sensation is present but the interpretation or comprehension is lacking. Irritation of a parietal lobe also leads to tactile hallucinations, the false perception of touch sensations on the other side of the body.

Loss of vision

The occipital lobes are almost exclusively concerned with the reception of visual impulses. Damage to one side leads to homonymous hemianopia, loss of all sight in the field of vision on the other side. This deficit applies to either eye: with a lesion of the right occipital lobe, for example, a patient is blind to any visual stimulus presented from the left side, whether to the right or to the left eye. This may be contrasted with the "blinkers" effect caused by compression of the optic chiasm, usually by a tumour arising out of the pituitary fossa. At the optic chiasm the optic nerve fibres from the nasal halves of the right and left retinas mingle and cross to the opposite side. Since the nasal retinas "see" the temporal fields (the right nasal retina receiving impulses from objects to the right, the left from objects to the left), the subject with a lesion of the optic chiasm is able to see straight ahead but not to either side. This is called bitemporal hemianopia.

Irritation of an occipital lobe causes the subject to see visions. If the lesion is far back in the lobe, the visions may be of unformed lights, colours, or shapes. However, the visions may be vivid and sharply defined pictures (visual hallucinations), as though a videotape of previous visual experiences were being replayed, if the lesion is farther forward and in the area where the parietal, temporal, and occipital lobes adjoin. This area of the cortex appears to be concerned with the analysis and storage of complex perceptions.

Pathologies

Many types of disease affect the nervous system. A short description of these types and an overview of representative disorders follows.

One pathology of the nervous system is genetic. Inherited neurological diseases are relatively common and may affect any site. Examples of such diseases are: Duchenne's and other muscular dystrophies; hereditary motor, sensory, or mixed neuropathies; spinocerebellar degenerations; disorders of closure of the fetal neural tube; numerous metabolic disorders; and maldevelopment or premature degeneration of parts of the nervous system, such as Huntington's disease and a form of Alzheimer's disease. A genetic component also determines a tendency to epileptic seizures.

Bacterial and viral infection

Inflammatory diseases are another neurological pathology. Although the blood–brain barrier plays its part in protecting the nervous system from microorganisms, it may be breached by bacteria, viruses, fungi, and many other organisms. When this occurs, the inherent resistance to infection of the nervous system is low. The major classes of disease are meningitis and encephalitis (infections of the meninges, or covering membranes, of the brain and of the brain itself, respectively) and abscess, which may be situated outside or just below the meninges or in the brain substance. Some viruses, such as the "slow" viruses, lie almost dormant within neural tissue for years before causing its destruction. The measles virus may do this, causing a chronic progressive encephalitis that is usually fatal.

Direct infections of muscles and of peripheral nerves are uncommon except in leprosy. Both the central and peripheral nervous systems may be severely damaged by reaction of the immune system after relatively trivial infections elsewhere in the body. Finally, in some infections such as diphtheria and botulism, a toxin is liberated by the infectious organism, which attacks the function of the nervous system.

Traumatic injury

Traumatic and mechanical injuries are a type that can affect all levels of the nervous system. Serious head injuries can lead to compression, laceration, or bruising of the brain inside the cranium. The compression is commonly due to a clot of blood inside the brain or formed outside or beneath the dura mater (extra- or subdural hematoma), but there is also inherent swelling of the brain tissue following trauma as fluid leaks from small blood vessel spaces into the extravascular space. This is called brain edema. Later consequences, such as seizures and alterations in mental process and personality, indicate the damage done to the brain by major or repeated minor head injuries. Less serious head injuries lead to concussion, a temporary loss of awareness.

Once destroyed, neurons are not replaced. Severed axons sprout growths from the cut end, but they do not form effective connections in the brain or spinal cord. Therefore, destructive injury of, for example, the spinal cord in the neck is followed by permanent loss of voluntary movement and of sensation below the level of injury.

In the peripheral nervous system, axons that have been cut or have degenerated because of disease can grow again. If the nerve remains in continuity, these sprouting axons may eventually reestablish effective connection with muscle fibres or sensory organs, but this reinnervation is often abnormal because of division and misdirection of growing axons.

Cancer

Neoplastic diseases are another pathological process. Both benign and primary and secondary malignant tumours attack the nervous system. The sites of both types include the meninges, the brain itself, and (more rarely) the spinal cord, its roots, and the peripheral nerves. In the latter sites the tumours are usually benign. The brain and spinal cord may also be compressed by masses arising in adjacent areas, such as the pituitary gland, the spinal column, or the nasopharynx. Tumours declare themselves by destruction of the tissue in which they arise, by compression of neighbouring tissue, and by increasing intracranial pressure. Those arising outside the nervous system may lead to syndromes of brain, spinal-cord, nerve, end-plate, or muscle disease without direct infiltration of these tissues.

A fifth pathology comprises metabolic, toxic, and endocrine disorders. Numerous complications of disease of other organs affect the nervous system. The largest category (but not the most common) comprises the disorders of metabolism, many of which have a genetic basis. The most commonly occurring neural complications are those arising from the effects of exogenous toxic agents such as bacterial toxins, drugs, and other chemicals. Next in frequency are those representing the effects of disordered fluid, of mineral and electrolyte function, or of disease affecting other body systems, such as the endocrine glands (diabetes, thyroid disease), the kidneys, liver, and lung (organ failure), and the blood (anemia, leukemia).

Loss of blood supply

Vascular diseases, including stroke, are an important pathology. The central nervous system has a high metabolic rate and depends upon a liberal blood supply for nutrition and for clearance of metabolic end-products. In the event of the interruption of circulation, function quickly fails, and if circulation is not restored speedily, irreversible damage to the neurons results. (The area of dead nervous tissue is known as an infarct.) The peripheral nervous system is much more tolerant of loss of blood supply, called ischemia.

A further important vascular cause of brain damage is hemorrhage due to rupture of an artery.

Another pathological process includes diseases labeled demyelinating and degenerative. Demyelinating disease is characteristically scattered throughout the brain and spinal cord, with small foci where the myelin is attacked and replaced with glial scar tissue. Nerve fibres running through such areas may remain undamaged, but the lack of insulation normally provided by the myelin leads to a blocking of conduction of electrical impulses, so that the effect is as though the axons had been severed. Clinically, signs of damage to many sites in the nervous system are found, as in multiple sclerosis. In certain very rare diseases, known as leucodystrophies, large areas of demyelination occur in the white matter of the brain as a result of inherited metabolic disorders. Demyelination is also the result of immune attack upon the central nervous system, which may follow viral infections such as measles, and of immune deficiency states such as pernicious anemia.

In the peripheral nervous system the Schwann cells, which form the myelin investing the axons of peripheral nerves, may suffer immune or toxic attack, as in Guillain-Barré syndrome and diphtheria. This leads again to a blockage of electrical conduction. When an injury is primarily to the axons, the Schwann cells are also damaged, producing "secondary demyelination."

Under the label "degeneration" are grouped some nervous system diseases characterized by progressive destruction of neurons without evident cause. Such diseases are Alzheimer's disease, affecting maximally the cerebral cortex; Huntington's and Parkinson's diseases, affecting the basal ganglia and cortex; motor neuron disease, which attacks the corticospinal tracts and ventral-horn cells; spinocerebellar degenerations, involving long tracts in the spinal cord, the cerebellum and its connections, and sometimes peripheral nerves; and the hereditary neuropathies with no known metabolic basis, in which motor, sensory, or both classes of peripheral nerve degenerate and lose their function. Most such diseases develop after a variable period, during which that part of the nervous system subsequently affected apparently functions normally. As research progresses, the metabolic (and often genetic) bases of these diseases are being successively revealed.

Seizures

Electrical pathologies present a unique problem of classification. Because the nervous system is a biologic electrochemical complex, it is possible to regard every aspect of its function as an electrical manifestation, but it is primarily the epilepsies that are regarded as expressions of disordered electrical activity. Seizures represent occasional, sudden, rapid, local, and excessive electrical discharges of the gray matter of the brain. There are two main classes, those with a focal origin anywhere within the gray matter and those in which no abnormal pathology is present but that manifest an abnormally low threshold for electrical activation. Although certain abnormal movements occasionally have their origin in spinal-cord disease, epilepsy is uniquely a brain disease (see below *Diseases and disorders: The cerebrum*). Narcolepsy, a disorder of sleep mechanisms, is not a variant of epilepsy.

It is uncertain whether any diseases of the nervous system can properly be regarded as representing an allergic pathology in the strict sense of the term, but many conditions marked by inflammation of blood vessels, such as the auto-allergic collagen-vascular diseases, do have such a basis. These, through reduction of blood supply to parts of the nervous system, may well induce neurological symptoms.

Diseases and disorders

THE SKULL AND SPINE

Abnormal growth before birth

Neural tube defects. The primitive neural tube normally closes by the end of the third week of fetal growth, but when it fails to close, severe deficits result. The worst of these is anencephaly, the absence of brain; a cyst replacing the cerebellum is a less severe form of the same problem. At lower levels the spinal canal or cord may also fail to close up. Such defects are known as spina bifida occulta when there is only X-ray evidence of this, meningocele when a meningeal pouch visibly projects through the skin, and meningomyelocele when such a pouch contains elements of the spinal cord or nerve roots. Depending on the level, function of the legs is often severely impaired. Bladder and bowel control is also lost in such cases, and the infants commonly have hydrocephalus as well.

Hydrocephalus. This progressive enlargement of the head is caused by obstructed drainage of the cerebrospinal fluid, usually at the level of the aqueduct or fourth ventricular roof. Huge enlargement of the ventricles results at the expense of cerebral tissue; shunting of the fluid is required to prevent gross expansion of the skull and death through attrition of the brain.

Other congenital malformations in which the head size is abnormal include microcephaly and macrocephaly; in the latter case, expansion of the brain usually follows infiltration in metabolic diseases. In hypertelorism the eyes are set unusually far apart, and in craniostenosis the sutures of the skull do not develop, so that the skull grows abnormally along one or another diameter. In hemiatrophy, one-half of the skull and face may not develop as well as the other, in which case the brain also may be unusually small.

Occurring at the junction between skull and neck, platybasia, an abnormal shallowness of the posterior fossa of the skull, is a malformation that may be associated with projection of the vertebral column upward, indenting the base of the skull. (This condition may also occur in association with bony diseases such as osteomalacia and Paget's disease of bone in adult life.) In the Arnold-Chiari malformation, cerebellar or medullary tissue projects downward into the upper cervical spinal canal, causing signs of cerebellar dysfunction, hydrocephalus, or widening of the central canal of the spinal cord with damage to the surrounding fibre tracts. Fusion of the upper cervical vertebrae in the Klippel-Feil anomaly is another malformation, but it does not always produce symptoms.

Fractures. Fractures of the cranial vault are common, but, so long as they are linear and not depressed (and thus not liable to irritate the underlying brain), they usually require no treatment. Far more serious are the complications of extradural or subdural hematomas, or blood clots. Fractures crossing the middle ear and the nasal sinuses provide a portal for the entry of microorganisms into the cranial cavity and are therefore especially dangerous, while those at the base of the skull may damage cranial nerves crossing the fracture line.

Damage to the spinal cord

Fractures of the odontoid, the bony peg that forms a joint between the upper two vertebrae in the neck, may compress and severely damage the spinal cord; the odontoid process may also separate with the same consequences in rheumatoid arthritis. Fractures and dislocations of the spine occur most commonly in the neck, with consequent risk of spinal-cord damage; at lower levels the thoracic rib cage makes spinal-cord compression less likely. With compression fractures at lumbar levels, it is the cauda equina, the tail of nerve roots below the level of the spinal cord, that may be damaged, but the strength of the ligaments gives more solid fixation and complications are less common.

In addition to trauma, secondary malignant tumours, infections such as tuberculosis, and intrinsic bone diseases can damage the spine and spinal cord.

Tumours. Tumours of the skull base may compress the lowest cranial nerves or the medulla and upper cervical cord, with the consequences described above.

Vertebral disorders. The most common disorders affecting the spine are degenerative, most often following previous trauma such as heavy work or whiplash accidents or due to some intrinsic tendency of unknown cause. In spondylosis, small, bony spurs called osteophytes project from the vertebral margins, the ligaments hypertrophy, the bone becomes denser, and the disks degenerate and extrude both forward and backward—in the latter case narrowing the spinal canal, again with the risk of compromising the cord. More commonly, the backward protrusion of an intervertebral disk distorts the local ligaments and compresses an emerging nerve root, resulting in pain, weakness, and numbness in the area. Lumbar spinal stenosis is the condition of marked narrowing of the canal over a few segments when the bone, disk, and ligaments protrude into it, compressing the nerve roots of the cauda equina. Pain also occurs when misalignment of the vertebrae causes stretching of the many joint capsules at sites where the vertebrae are contiguous. Spondylolisthesis is a slipping forward of one vertebra onto another, occurring as a congenital deformity or due to trauma.

Prolapsed disk

Infections, tumours, and bone diseases are also responsible for vertebral disorders, causing pain and signs of damage to the roots and perhaps to the cord as well. Although direct infections of the cord are rare, pyogenic or tuberculous epidural spinal abscesses are important and treatable diseases. Tumours are usually secondary to such malignancies as lymphomas or carcinomas of the breast, prostate, or kidney. Benign tumours also occur. Paget's disease, osteomalacia, and osteoporosis may cause softening of the bone, which can then compress the cord or roots.

THE MENINGES AND CEREBROSPINAL FLUID

Obstruction of cerebrospinal fluid

Raised intracranial pressure. The circulation of the cerebrospinal fluid may be obstructed so that it accumulates behind the obstruction. Congenital stenosis, or narrowing, of the aqueduct, tumours encroaching on or blood accumulating within the ventricles, and fibrosis or occlusion of the roof foramina of the fourth ventricle are causes of obstructive hydrocephalus. They lead to massive enlargement of the ventricular system, with atrophy of the surrounding brain, and to a rise in intracranial pressure, with resulting long-tract motor signs, cranial-nerve palsies, visible swelling of the head of the optic nerve in the eye, headache, and vomiting.

In communicating hydrocephalus, the obstruction is to the flow of cerebrospinal fluid up over the convexity of the brain or to absorption at the sagittal venous sinus. Clinical features are similar to those of obstructive hydrocephalus but less severe. Sometimes following bouts of meningitis or blood in the fluid, the initially raised pressure falls (normal-pressure hydrocephalus), but brain damage persists. In such a condition dementia and gait disturbances are the major clinical features. Insertion of a shunt, or drain, may provide some relief.

Any mass lesion in the head (a blood clot, tumour, or abscess, for example) or external compression of the cerebrospinal-fluid pathway (such as the Arnold-Chiari malformation) raises the intracranial pressure, since the brain cannot shrink and compensation is only possible through a reduction in the amount of fluid present in the ventricles or of blood in the vessels. To the hydrocephalic signs mentioned above, then, must be added those of the causal lesion, affecting specific brain functions according to its site and nature. However, benign intracranial hypertension is a condition in which there is increased intracranial pressure in the absence of obstruction to fluid flow or any mass lesion. Instead, it is caused by various metabolic and endocrine diseases but is most commonly seen in people who are very obese.

Cerebral edema signifies the presence of excess fluid within either the cells or the extracellular tissues of the brain. This also causes brain swelling and a rise in intracranial pressure. Head injuries, encephalitis, abscesses, lack of oxygen, strokes, and toxic agents are the most common causes.

Drainage. Cerebrospinal fluid may leak through basal skull fractures, dripping out of the nose or ear, and it may also leak into the tissues when the needle is withdrawn after lumbar puncture (LP). As a result of the reduced pressure in the fluid, the brain is less well supported and pulls upon the meninges, causing what is called post-LP headache. In traumatic cases, patching of the hole in the meninges may be necessary.

Blood clot. Blood clots lying outside or just below the dura mater (called extradural or subdural hematomas) are other feared complications of trauma. Extradural hematomas usually complicate fractures of the temporal bone that rupture the middle meningeal artery. Arterial blood, shed under pressure, rips the dura off the underside of the skull bones, forming a rapidly expanding mass that raises intracranial pressure, compresses the brain, and may cause death unless evacuated surgically. Subdural hematomas are usually less acute, but they have similar characteristics and also require removal in most cases. Chronic subdural hematomas, however, expand very slowly and may only be discovered through the onset of seizures, focal neurological signs, or dementia.

Extradural and subdural hematomas

Meningitis. This is an inflammation of the meningeal coverings of the nervous system, with only secondary, mild involvement of the brain. A host of infectious microorganisms (bacteria, viruses, spirochetes, fungi, protozoa) and some chemical agents may be responsible. Organisms most often reach the meninges by way of the blood, but direct spread may occur if the usual barriers are broken—as is the case with skull fractures, middle-ear or nasal-sinus infection, or congenital defects of the meninges. Clinical features depend upon the organism, the acuteness of the disease, and the resistance and age of the patient, but they usually include lethargy and drowsiness, fever, headache, stiffness of the neck, vomiting, and (in smaller children) seizures.

Since treatment with the precisely correct antibiotic is essential, the most important diagnostic aid is lumbar puncture, whereby the infectious organism may be identified in the cerebrospinal fluid through microscopy and growth culture and its sensitivity to different antibiotics tested in the laboratory. Such indications in the fluid as the amount of protein, the number and type of cells, and the glucose level confirm the type of meningitis (*e.g.*, bacterial, viral).

Patients with nonbacterial, or aseptic, meningitis also have headache, fever, and other meningeal signs, but they are not so obviously ill. Viruses such as mumps, Coxsackie, and ECHO viruses, tuberculosis, fungi, spirochetes, and chemical substances are possible agents.

The prognosis in bacterial meningitis depends upon the type of organism, the general health of the patient, and the adequacy and speed of initiation of treatment, but there is still at least a 5 percent mortality rate. Residual consequences of the disease include cranial nerve palsies (especially loss of hearing), normal-pressure hydrocephalus, and damage to specific brain areas in a small number of cases.

Neoplasms. Tumours affecting the meninges are usually malignant, commonly spreading from cerebral tumours such as medulloblastoma, from distant tumours such as carcinoma of the lung or breast, and from lymphomas and leukemia. Both drugs and radiation therapy are used to slow the tumour's progression.

Meningiomas

Benign tumours arising from the meninges are called meningiomas. These occur over the convexity of the brain and on the floor of the cranium, where they compress and damage brain areas or cranial nerves and may cause seizures. They seldom raise intracranial pressure, since their slow growth gives the brain time to compensate. Meningiomas show up clearly on radioisotope and CAT scans. They may be removed totally with an excellent prognosis.

THE PERIPHERAL SYSTEM

Neuropathies. Diseases of the peripheral nerves may be genetic or acquired, may progress quickly or slowly, may involve the motor, sensory, or autonomic fibres (or all three), and may affect all nerves symmetrically (usually at the extremities of the body) or just one or more nerves discretely. Thus, numerous classifications exist; the system used in this section takes as its basis the major pathological change taking place—namely, primary damage to the axon or to the surrounding Schwann cell (Figure 35).

Neuronal neuropathies. In the following diseases, the axon or cell body of the ventral-horn neuron or dorsal-root ganglion neuron is affected. Damage to the ventral-horn neurons leads to the typical signs of a lower motor neuron lesion: atrophy of the muscles supplied by the nerves, fasciculation in chronic disease, reduced muscle tone and power, and reduction or loss of reflexes with no change in sensation. Damage to the dorsal-root ganglion neurons also leads to reduced reflexes, in this case, because the afferent, or sensory, limb of the reflex arc is interrupted. Depending upon the size of afferent neuron that is primarily affected, loss of different sensations occurs: joint-position sense, discriminative light touch, and vibration with damage to the larger cells and skin pain, temperature, light touch, and scratch with smaller cell loss. Often all forms of sensation are impaired.

Poliomyelitis

Poliomyelitis is an acute viral infection. Initially it may cause only a brief, febrile illness, but groups of ventral-horn cells of the spinal cord may be destroyed by the virus. This later causes severe pain with further fever, occasional delirium and meningism (due to accompanying encephalitis), and a rapid onset of fasciculations, weakness, and atrophy of muscle groups that may be localized or diffuse, mild or profound, and that may endanger life if the respiratory or bulbar muscles are involved. Only supportive treatment is available for poliomyelitis, but some recovery occurs in those patients (the majority, in fact) who survive the acute stage of the illness. Since the advent of effective immunization programs this disease is now rare in the Western world.

Hereditary motor neuropathies (also known as spinal muscular atrophies and as Werdnig-Hoffman or Kugelberg-Welander diseases) are a diverse group of genetically determined disorders in which signs of ventral-horn disease occur in babies or young people. The usual features are muscle atrophy and weakness, which progress more slowly in the older age groups but which may be quickly lethal if the disorder strikes during the first year of life. Stricken babies show respiratory insufficiency, poor sucking, and severe limpness and weakness of all muscles except those of the face and eyes, but the muscles of the shoulder and pelvic girdles are most affected. At later stages normal motor development is delayed or absent. This muscular weakness and wasting has given such infants the name "floppy babies." Diagnosis of hereditary motor neuropathy must be confirmed by electromyography and muscle biopsy, as there are other possible causes, some responsive to treatment. There is no effective treatment of spinal muscular atrophy. When the disease begins at a later age (five to 15 years) the progress is slower; the disease may pass, leaving chronic mild weakness and secondary skeletal deformities such as scoliosis (rotation of the spine). Less commonly, similar weakness occurs in specific patterns—for example, involving only the facial, shoulder, or calf muscles—but in those cases the progress of the disease is much slower. In some of these cases specific enzyme deficiencies have been identified as the cause, but in most cases the etiological basis is unknown.

Amyotrophic lateral sclerosis

Motor neuron disease is a lethal progressive disorder of older people, affecting not only neurons of the ventral horns and medullary motor nuclei but also of the corticospinal tracts. This combination gives rise to such diseases as amyotrophic lateral sclerosis (ALS), in which amyotrophy refers to the muscle wasting due to loss of the ventral-horn cells (the lower motor neurons), and lateral sclerosis is the loss of axons in the lateral columns of the spinal cord (the upper motor neurons of the corticospinal tracts). A combination of upper and lower motor neuron signs is found in these diseases, but weakness, atrophy, and fasciculations found in the muscles of two or more limbs is the hallmark. The mind, eyes, and sensory system are unaffected, prompting the comment that the disease allows the patient to observe his own dissolution. While a host of treatments are available for such symptoms as cramps, and while aids to daily living can be provided to help the patient maintain some self-care, the ultimate prognosis is death within a few years—or within one year when the muscles serving speech and swallowing are affected. Since the etiology is unknown, no cure is available.

Pure sensory neuronal neuropathies may be hereditary. A number of them are differentiated by their pattern of genetic transmission and the modalities of sensation mainly affected. Other causes include toxic drugs or other agents, diabetes, herpes zoster, and vitamin deficiency. They also occur in association with distant cancer. Mixed (sensorimotor) neuropathies have similar causes, in most acquired conditions representing a later stage of a sensory disease.

Injury

Nerve injuries function as neuronal neuropathies affecting the axon far from the cell body. Injuries are of three main grades of severity: in neurapraxia there is temporary blockage of impulse conduction, although the axons remain intact; more severe stretch or incision damage interrupts some axons (axonotmesis); and still worse injury actually cuts the nerve (neurotmesis), in which case microsurgery to rejoin the severed nerve ends is essential if any useful function is to be regained. Even this last is a slow process, since new nerve sprouts grow down the nerve framework at the rate of one to two millimetres per day at most.

Demyelinating neuropathies. The following diseases are those in which the Schwann cells, responsible for the formation of myelin, are primarily affected and migrate away from the nerve. This process leaves segments of the axons uncovered, and since the particular insulating property of the myelin is now lost, there is a block in conduction of nerve impulses down the axon.

Genetically acquired diseases include hereditary motor and sensory neuropathies, a group including Charcot-Marie-Tooth disease (also known as peroneal muscular atrophy because of the special involvement of shin muscles). High foot arches, distal motor weakness and atrophy, and reduced reflexes are the main features; sometimes the nerves are greatly thickened. Most of these conditions first appear in childhood, although they allow a normal life span.

Acquired demyelinating neuropathies may arise as com-

After A.K. Asbury in R.D. Adams and M. Victor, *Principles of Neurology*, 3rd. ed. (1985); McGraw-Hill, Inc.

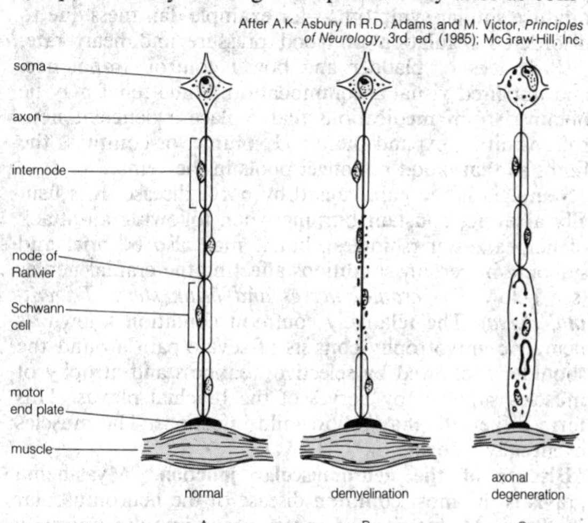

Figure 35: *Two major pathological changes in disease of the motor neuron.*
(A) Normal neuron with intact axon and myelin-forming Schwann cells. (B) Demyelination, or disintegration of the Schwann cells. (C) Axonal degeneration, or disintegration of the nerve fibre.

plications of diphtheria and diabetes, which, partly because of damage to the smallest blood vessels supplying the nerves, are sometimes accompanied by a variety of motor, sensory, autonomic, or mixed neuropathies. Some of these are extremely painful. When sensation is impaired, minor injuries lead to severely deformed, but quite painless, "Charcot" joints. Leprosy (probably still the most common cause of neuropathy in the world), metabolic diseases, cancer, and myeloma or other dysproteinemias also cause mixed demyelinating neuropathies.

Guillain-Barré syndrome

Acute inflammatory neuropathy (the Guillain-Barré syndrome) is another important demyelinating neuropathy. In this disease an autoimmune attack upon the myelin sheath of the motor nerves leads to progressive weakness and reflex loss with only slight sensory changes. The weakness may become so severe that the patient needs mechanical help in breathing, but as long as further complications do not occur, the disease remits spontaneously within weeks. In fact, many patients never develop this degree of weakness at all. In acute, severe cases, blood plasma exchange speeds recovery.

Ischemic neuropathies are those in which local or diffuse blood-vessel occlusion leads to damage of the Schwann cells. The most common example is external compression of a nerve, as when a person's foot "goes to sleep" after the legs have been crossed for too long. In such cases relief of the compression restores the blood supply, and the temporary dysfunction is relieved. Persistent compression, on the other hand, causes the Schwann cells to migrate. This narrows the nerve at the site of pressure, although the axon remains intact. Recovery may take months.

Carpal tunnel syndrome

Common nerve-compression syndromes include the carpal tunnel syndrome, in which the median nerve is compressed at the wrist. This causes pain, numbness, tingling, and weakness of the fingers and thumb, especially at night and on waking. The cubital tunnel syndrome is a similar problem affecting the ulnar nerve at the elbow. Compression of spinal nerve roots by, for example, prolapsed intervertebral disks, are further examples. Numerous nerve-compression syndromes can be diagnosed clinically and localized with the aid of electrodiagnostic studies, allowing precise surgical intervention to release the entrapped nerve. Ischemic neuropathies are also complications of a number of systemic diseases, such as diabetes mellitus and polyarteritis nodosa. In such cases the treatment is that of the underlying disorder.

Autonomic neuropathies may be hereditary, as in Riley-Day syndrome, or acquired, as in complications of partial nerve injuries, diabetes mellitus, tabes dorsalis, the Guillain-Barré syndrome, and other toxic or metabolic disorders (among which alcoholism and drug therapy are the most common). Damage to the sympathetic or parasympathetic pathways in the hypothalamus or brain stem may produce similar symptoms—for example, faintness due to disordered regulation of blood pressure and heart rate, disturbances of bladder and bowel control, impotence, and impaired visual accommodation. Some relief may be obtained from medications that replace a deficient neurotransmitter, expand the blood volume, or compress the limbs so that blood no longer pools in the veins.

Neuralgia is the pain caused by nerve disease. It is usually a severe, constant burning when following an attack of herpes zoster (shingles), but it may also be brief and stabbing in certain conditions affecting the cranial nerves (see below *The cranial nerves and brain stem: Trigeminal nerve*). The relatively common condition known as neuralgic amyotrophy consists of severe pain around the shoulders, followed by selective weakness and atrophy of muscles supplied by nerves of the brachial plexus. This form of neuritis may follow mild infections. The muscles eventually recover.

Myasthenia gravis

Disease of the neuromuscular junction. Myasthenia gravis is the most common disease of the neuromuscular junction. At this site the motor nerve impulse normally triggers the release of the neurotransmitter acetylcholine, which diffuses across the synaptic gap between the terminal of the nerve and the specialized end-plate region of the muscle-fibre membrane. (For discussions of synaptic transmission and neurotransmitter action, see above *Form and function of nervous systems: Transmission of information in the nervous system.*) In myasthenia, receptors in the end-plate region are partially coated with a specific antibody, so that the acetylcholine molecules are blocked, depolarization of the muscle fibre cannot occur, and the muscle does not contract. There is also a reduction in the amount of acetylcholine released from the nerve terminal. As a result, muscle contraction is possible after a period of rest, but sustained contractions quickly become weaker. This fatigability is especially present in the eye muscles, leading to drooping of the lids on looking upward and to imbalance of the ocular muscles, which causes diplopia (double vision). The muscles of the throat, limbs, and respiration may also become involved, creating a dangerous situation.

Diagnosis of myasthenia gravis is made by electrical studies of neuromuscular transmission, which show decreasing response, and by single-fibre electromyography (see above *Acquisition of data: Laboratory investigation*). Treatment involves the removal of the thymus gland (which may produce the antibody), drugs to augment the effect of acetylcholine, and suppression of the immune system. These treatments allow a prognosis of recovery in 60 percent of patients within five years.

Failure of neuromuscular transmission may also occur as a complication of certain drug therapies or of remote cancer, usually of the lung (as in the Lambert-Eaton syndrome). It may also be caused by the toxins of the botulism bacterium *Clostridium botulinus* and of certain species of ticks that attach themselves to the skin. Administration of antitoxin for botulism or removal of the tick, with full supportive hospital care in each case, are effective treatments.

Diseases of muscle. In primary muscle diseases the motor neurons supplying the muscles are not affected, the problem being of and in the muscles themselves. However, motor neuron diseases do cause secondary effects in the muscles.

Duchenne's muscular dystrophy

Genetic dystrophies. The genetic dystrophies are diseases of muscle that progress at differing rates and affect different muscle groups. The best-known, most serious, and perhaps most common is Duchenne's muscular dystrophy (DMD), which ordinarily affects only males, although it is transmitted by females. By the age of three the boy begins to walk clumsily; thereafter, progressive failure to run, jump, and climb like his peers occurs, leading eventually to a loss of the ability to walk by the mid-teens and death in the early 20s. Because of the infiltration of degenerating muscles with fat, little atrophy may be noticed until late in the course of the disease, leading to the alternate term pseudo-hypertrophic muscular dystrophy. Diagnosis is confirmed by estimation of the blood-serum levels of creatine kinase, an enzyme released from degenerating muscle, and also by electromyography and muscle biopsy. The cause is unknown, and no specific treatment is available, but genetic probes and subsequent genetic counselling are used to determine whether a case represents a new mutation or has been transmitted by a carrier mother to her son. Intense rehabilitative efforts are also necessary, since boys with DMD have normal intelligence and can live a relatively full life, although for only a short time.

Facioscapulohumeral dystrophy usually causes problems only in or after the early teens. It has a more benign prognosis, the weakness and wasting being predominantly of the face, shoulder girdle, and arms. Other conditions grouped under the heading limb-girdle dystrophies also show slower progression and may not declare themselves until adult life. Oculopharyngeal dystrophies first strike the eye muscles, causing drooping of the eyelids and weakness or paralysis of the muscles moving the eyes. Later involvement of the face, bulbar muscles, and limb girdles is common.

Myotonic dystrophy is characterized by weakness and wasting of the face and girdle muscles. In addition, there occurs a failure of muscles to relax after a strong contraction, so that, for example, the patient cannot easily let go after shaking hands. As with many of the conditions of dystrophy, involvement of other body systems is common.

Because the expression of the disease is so variable, some patients having minimal symptoms that pose no threat to life, its prevalence is higher than that of DMD. In myotonia congenita the same failure of relaxation occurs but without the wasting features of dystrophy. Indeed, patients with myotonia congenita have strong and well-developed muscles. Relaxation can be obtained with drugs such as diphenylhydantoin and quinine.

Myopathies

Other inherited muscle diseases. Congenital myopathies begin with weakness and poor muscle development in the early years of life, but generally they are not progressive. Diagnosis is achieved by microscopic examination of muscle biopsies. Lipid storage myopathies are associated with disorders of the metabolism of carnitine, a substance that muscle cells use to convert fatty acids into fuel. In these conditions variable severe weakness of the body musculature progresses slowly throughout life. Muscle biopsy specimens show accumulation of fat in the fibres. In the glycogen storage diseases it is glycogen that accumulates in muscle fibre, owing to a deficiency of an enzyme that helps degrade glycogen into lactic acid for the production of energy. Beginning in childhood, complaints of fatigue, aching, and occasional severe muscle cramps on exercise are usual. Diagnosis is confirmed by demonstrating that the exercising muscles do not produce lactic acid as they should.

Myoglobin is a substance that resembles the hemoglobin in blood and that performs a similar function as a repository of oxygen within the muscles. When muscles are damaged from any cause, myoglobin may spill into the blood and thence into the urine. This condition, called myoglobinuria, can also occur as an inherited metabolic defect, either on its own or in association with muscle disorders. Malignant hyperthermia is a dangerous metabolic muscle disease characterized by high fever and extreme rigidity of muscles, usually provoked by certain anesthetics or muscle-relaxant drugs given during surgery. It constitutes an extreme emergency; rapid cooling of the patient, correction of the accumulation of lactic acid in the blood (the result of intense muscle contraction), and administration of dantrolene sodium to relax the muscles are necessary.

In familial periodic paralyses episodes of weakness of variable duration and severity occur in association with abnormally high or low serum levels of potassium. Some attacks are precipitated by a period of rest following heavy exercise, others by carbohydrate or alcohol ingestion. Depending on the type of paralysis, potassium, glucose, and diuretics constitute the usual treatments.

Acquired diseases of muscle. Myoglobinuria may follow excessive exertion of healthy muscles, crush injury, or toxic damage from drugs or chemicals. It is also a feature of some of the inherited diseases mentioned above. With myoglobin present in urine, there is a danger that it may precipitate in the tubules of the kidney and cause renal failure. Muscle weakness and atrophy may also complicate the administration of many drugs (including cortisone and its derivatives), disease of the thyroid and parathyroid glands, and metabolic bone diseases. Primary tumours of muscle are rare.

Inflammatory muscle disease, called myositis, is seen in association with some viral infections, causing swelling, pain, and weakness, and in trichinosis and other tapeworm infestations, in which allergic skin rashes commonly accompany the same symptoms. Most serious is dermatomyositis, an autoimmune disease characterized by swelling, weakness, and tenderness of the proximal, facial, neck, and bulbar muscles in both children and adults. A skin rash is also present, mainly around the eyes but also on the face and extensor surfaces of the limbs. Diagnosis relies upon electromyography, serum enzyme levels, and sometimes muscle biopsy. Treatment with steroid and immunosuppressant drugs has markedly improved the prognosis for recovery. Closely related conditions without the rash are found in association with collagen-vascular diseases such as scleroderma and polyarteritis or with distant cancers. The response to treatment in these variants is less satisfactory.

Polymyalgia rheumatica is another autoimmune disease. It mainly affects women over the age of 55 years, who complain of severe muscle stiffness (especially after sleep) and of malaise, weight loss, muscle tenderness, and slight fever. In some cases frank inflammation of arteries, particularly of the branches of the carotids, is the most notable problem. Diagnosis is urgent, since blindness may follow if the ophthalmic arteries are involved—as is often the case. The blood sedimentation rate is much increased, and anemia is common. Treatment with steroid drugs produces excellent relief within a day, but it must be continued indefinitely.

THE SPINAL CORD

Spinocerebellar degenerations. These are genetically determined conditions in which evidence of dysfunction of the dorsal columns or the corticospinal and spinocerebellar tracts of the cord appears, usually in the first 20 years of life. They cause difficulty in position sensation, gait, limb power, balance, and coordination. (For further discussion, see below *The cerebellum: Genetic diseases.*)

Inflammation. Inflammation of the spinal cord, known as myelitis, is most commonly due to viral infection such as mononucleosis, mumps, and herpes zoster. It is rarely bacterial, although abscesses outside the dura mater (*e.g.,* tuberculosis) do occur. Severe pain in a girdle around the trunk, loss of motor, sensory, and bladder functions below the level of the attack, meningism, and fever are the main features. Myelitis may also be caused by autoimmune attack following such viral infections as measles and chicken pox or after such immunologic challenges as vaccination. Tabes dorsalis, now uncommon, is an infection of the dorsal-root ganglia by the spirochete bacterium that causes syphilis. Degeneration of the dorsal columns, severe girdle pains, and loss of position sense are the main features, though they often appear together with signs of spirochetal infection elsewhere in the central nervous system.

Myelitis

Trauma. Damage to the spinal cord occurs in association with spinal fractures and fracture-dislocations. The degree to which functions of the cord are affected varies with the severity of the injury. There may be only transient weakness and hyperactive reflexes due to damage to the corticospinal tracts, or there may be full-blown paraplegia with signs of damage to the motor and sensory fibres at the level of injury as well as loss of all sensation below the lesion. Accompanying paralysis, due to damage to descending motor tracts, is at first flaccid and later becomes spastic. After such an injury at high cervical levels, the diaphragm is paralyzed, and the resulting ventilatory failure is life-threatening. Since only minimal regeneration of neurons is possible in the central nervous system, the prognosis for recovery is hopeless and only supportive treatment is available.

Paralysis

Tumours. Tumours within the substance of the cord are labeled intrinsic, those outside but compressing it, extrinsic. Common intrinsic tumours include ependymomas and astrocytomas, which are malignant, and angiomas and cysts, which are benign. Extrinsic tumours include malignant secondary invasion by cancer of the breast, lung, kidney, or prostate gland as well as benign neurofibromas and meningiomas. Other tumours arising outside the dura include lymphomas, lipomas, and chordomas. All of these produce signs of spinal nerve root irritation, with pain and tingling, at the level of the tumour; signs of spinal cord involvement occur later. In all cases diagnosis is confirmed by myelography, usually with CAT or MRI scanning. Raised protein levels occur in the cerebrospinal fluid, but they are not specific to one type of cancer. Malignant cells themselves may be detected in the fluid, allowing precise diagnosis. Surgery and radiation therapy are the principal treatments.

Subacute combined degeneration of the cord. This is a condition resulting from deficiency of vitamin B_{12} from any cause, most often pernicious anemia. Its name indicates its insidious progression and the degeneration of two tracts, the corticospinal and the dorsal columns, which lose myelin and acquire a pale stain from dyes applied when the cord is examined post mortem. Much of the damage is to the large dorsal-root ganglion neurons; their peripheral processes (*i.e.,* the peripheral nerve fibres) are also demyelinated, so that signs of peripheral neuropathy are superimposed onto the spinal symptoms. Replacement treatment with vitamin B_{12} often leads to improvement.

Vascular disease. Diseases of the blood vessels are surprisingly uncommon in the spinal cord, which contains long segments with a tenuous arterial supply, as in the mid-thoracic area. When blockages do occur, severe atherothrombotic disease of the aorta is a likely cause, as is previous aortic or thoracic surgery, with its risk of interruption of arteries supplying the cord. Compression of arteries by tumour tissue or a prolapsed disk is a rare cause; bleeding from an arteriovenous malformation is another.

Signs of acute, painful, and severe damage to the anterior three-quarters of the cord are usual, this being the area supplied by the single ventral spinal artery. Since the dorsal columns and the dorsal-root entry zone are supplied by three or more dorsal spinal arteries (an arrangement that confers some protection against ischemia) those regions usually escape damage.

Months or years after radiation therapy for such cancers as carcinoma of the breast, small-vessel disease may affect the cord. In this radiation myelopathy a slow but relentless deterioration of the roots and tracts at the irradiated level of the cord leads to spastic weakness of the legs and to less obvious sensory changes.

Syringomyelia. This condition frequently complicates obstructions of the roof foramina of the fourth ventricle. Pressure waves, transmitted through the cerebrospinal fluid down the central canal, enlarge the canal and ultimately lead to a cavity, or syrinx, branching out from the canal and enlarging over years. As a result, sensory fibres, running from the dorsal-root entry zone both to the opposite spinothalamic tract and to ventral-horn neurons at the same level, are interrupted. In addition, compression of the corticospinal tracts occurs. Interruption of the dorsal-root–ventral-horn connection, which mediates reflex activity, results in loss of stretch reflexes and atrophy of some muscles innervated at that level. Interruption of the spinothalamic fibres, which transmit sensory impulses from both sides of the body to the thalamus, leads to loss of the sensations of light touch, temperature, and skin pain, as well as signs of an upper motor neuron lesion below the level of the cavity. Despite the marked sensory changes, which may lead to the patient's burning himself without feeling any pain at all, some perception, such as position sense, is retained. This is an example of dissociated sensory loss, which is also found in some brain-stem lesions, transection of one-half of the spinal cord, and certain peripheral neuropathies.

Diagnosis of syringomyelia is best made by CAT scan combined with myelography or by MRI scanning (Figure 34), but since the cervical spinal canal is often widened in this condition, even a plain X ray of the cervical spine may be enough for diagnosis. Surgical therapy, aimed at draining the cavity and preventing pressure waves from distending it further, may lead to remarkable improvement in some cases, even after severe destruction of the cord.

Multiple sclerosis

Demyelinating disease. This condition frequently affects the spinal cord, and in older patients the cord may be the only clinically evident site of involvement in multiple sclerosis. The corticospinal tracts and dorsal columns are chiefly affected. In a variant of multiple sclerosis called Devic's disease, a band of spinal-cord inflammation and demyelination and optic-nerve involvement are the only features. In some patients with multiple sclerosis, clinical signs of disease of the cord are lacking, but measurement of somatosensory or motor-evoked potentials shows abnormalities indicating that disease is actually present.

Myoclonus. Brief, involuntary jerks of the whole trunk and of the limbs, or of one or two limbs alone, may occur in spinal myoclonus. Many diffuse, metabolic, or local structural causes are possible, but myoclonus more commonly originates in the brain stem or cerebral hemispheres.

THE CRANIAL NERVES AND BRAIN STEM

Olfactory nerve. The olfactory nerve is seldom disordered, but head injuries and pressure from tumours on the floor of the anterior cranial fossa may reduce smell sensitivity or cause complete loss. Patients complain of loss of taste, as all tastes except saltiness, sweetness, bitterness, and sourness are appreciated by the sense of smell.

Optic nerve. Visual-field deficits can occur with disease of the optic nerve or of the pathways traveling back to the occipital lobe. Optic neuritis is occasionally inherited, but it also occurs in some infections and particularly in demyelinating disease. Drug or chemical toxicity are rare causes, and in older people it may result from ischemia. Optic neuritis leads to total or partial loss of vision. Recovery may occur, depending upon the cause and its potential for treatment. It is often difficult to distinguish between compression of the nerve by a tumour or by an aneurysm. With any of these lesions, the nerve eventually loses myelin, causing optic atrophy, or pallor of the nerve head, which can be seen with the ophthalmoscope. Papilledema is a swelling of the nerve head with fluid as a result of raised intracranial pressure from any cause (Figure 36). Vascular diseases of the retina include occlusion of the retinal arteries and veins as well as temporary obstruction of a retinal arteriole by a blood clot from the arteries in the neck.

Lesions of the visual pathways are caused by upward pressure on the optic chiasm, by pituitary tumours or aneurysms and, farther back in the nerve pathway, by strokes or tumours.

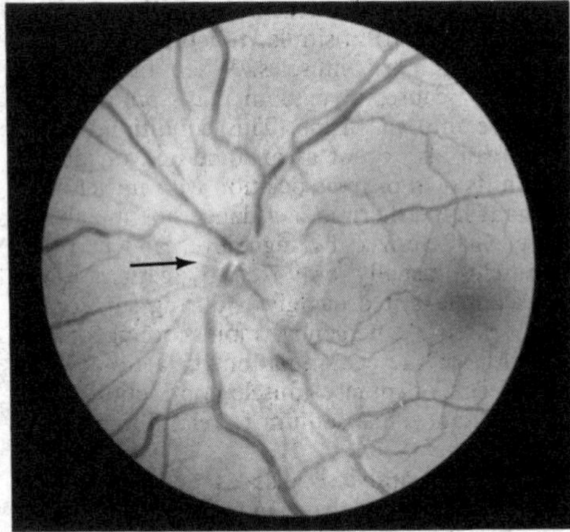

Figure 36: Photograph of the retina, showing (arrow) swelling of the head of the optic nerve. This swelling, called papilledema, is caused by raised pressure within the skull.

Oculomotor, trochlear, and abducens nerves. These nerves may be compressed by mass lesions anywhere along their course or by diabetes, vascular disease, head injury, local infection, and neuropathy. In the brain stem, multiple sclerosis, stroke, Wernicke's disease (see below *Brain stem*), and tumours are possible causes. Depending upon the nerve or nerves involved, various forms of double vision occur; if the oculomotor nerve is affected, the pupil will probably be enlarged as well. Muscle and end-plate diseases may mimic the appearance of discrete oculomotor nerve palsies. In Horner's syndrome interruption of the long sympathetic fibres passing from the brain stem to the pupil leads to drooping of the eyelid and a small pupil.

Horner's syndrome

Argyll Robertson pupils are small and irregular pupils that do not react to light but do constrict on accommodation to close vision. They have traditionally been associated with syphilis, but other brain-stem diseases may also be responsible. Adie's pupil constricts very slowly in light and also dilates slowly when the light is removed. It is not a sign of serious disease.

The two eyes may together fail to move in one or another direction. This gaze palsy may be quite fixed in progressive external ophthalmoplegia, a disorder of the central nervous mechanisms controlling gaze. Other neurological problems, such as parkinsonism, dementia, or neuropathy, may be associated with this condition. Local lesions of the brain stem may also cause paralysis of eye movement, as may severe myasthenia and myopathies affecting the eye muscles.

The jerky eye movements of nystagmus usually signify

brain-stem, vestibular, or cerebellar disease, but they may also be complications of very poor eyesight or may occur as a congenital defect.

Trigeminal nerve. Numbness in the face is commonly due to compression of this nerve, often by a tumour in the cranial cavity or nasopharynx, but it is also caused by brain-stem disorders. Neuralgia of the trigeminal nerve, called tic douloureux, is an intense, repetitive, irregular stabbing pain felt in the lower half of one side of the face. It occurs in elderly people. While the actual pathology of tic douloureux is in dispute, many patients are relieved by microsurgical removal of a loop of normal artery where it impinges upon the nerve at its exit from the brain stem. In most cases, however, drugs such as carbamazepine, diphenylhydantoin, or baclofen relieve the pain so well that no other treatment is needed.

Tic douloureux

Facial nerve. Bell's palsy is the most common lesion of the facial nerve. An abrupt weakness of all the facial muscles on one side, it is often accompanied by pain around the ear, unusual loudness of sounds heard in the ear on the same side, and loss of taste on the front of the tongue. Many patients believe that they have had a stroke, a conclusion corrected when it is seen that they cannot close the eye on the affected side.

The herpes simplex virus can be implicated in some cases of facial palsy. Other causes include lesions of the brain stem (see below) and of the angle between the cerebellum and pons; middle-ear infections; skull base fractures; and diseases affecting the parotid gland. In the Guillain-Barré syndrome, facial weakness on both sides is an important sign.

In hemifacial spasm repetitive twitching of one side of the face occurs. As with tic douloureux, irritation of the nerve as it leaves the brain stem appears to be a cause, and in many cases relief is obtained through surgical decompression.

Vestibulocochlear nerve. Deafness, if not caused by middle-ear disease, suggests damage to the cochlear portion of this nerve, while vertigo, an abnormal sensation of rotation, is a prominent symptom of vestibular-nerve disease. Compression of the nerve at the cerebello-pontine angle by, for example, a benign tumour of Schwann cells, an aneurysm, or meningioma, as well as certain systemic diseases, drug toxicity, small strokes, and Ménière's disease, are the more common neurological causes of hearing loss. In Ménière's disease accumulation of fluid in the inner ear produces increasing deafness and tinnitus, or ringing in the ears. Acute attacks bring intermittent bouts of vertigo. Both medical and surgical therapies are available.

Ménière's disease

The diffuse connections of fibres subserving hearing in the brain make central nervous causes of deafness rather uncommon. Any condition affecting the inner ear or cochlear nerve may give rise to tinnitus. Abnormally high blood flow in the region may do the same, but then the sound has a pulsating quality.

Benign postural vertigo is the term describing brief severe attacks of vertigo induced by movement, especially turning in bed. The condition is unpleasant but benign, occurring at any age and ceasing spontaneously after some months. It is less persistent than vestibular neuronitis, in which prostrating vertigo persists for some days, probably as a result of viral infection of the inner ear or vestibular nerve.

Bulbar nerves. (In this context, the term bulbar refers to the medulla oblongata, which looks like a swelling, or bulb, at the top of the spinal cord.) Diseases of the ninth through 12th nerves show themselves mainly through such motor dysfunctions as impairment of swallowing and speech and weakness of the neck muscles. Bulbar palsy is dangerous because inhalation of saliva or food may cause choking and asphyxia. A nasal tone to the voice and weakness of coughing are early signs. Causes of bulbar palsy include diseases of the brain stem (see below) and of the bulbar nerves themselves. The most important of these latter are motor neuropathies, such as diphtheria, poliomyelitis, and botulism, motor neuron diseases, and compression of the nerves by tumours. Myasthenia gravis and some muscle diseases cause similar signs.

Brain stem. Brain-stem lesions produce a multitude of syndromes according to the site and nature of the pathology. In Moebius' syndrome, the abducens and facial nerves, which originate in the brain stem, may not develop from birth. Encephalitis may affect the brain stem only, with consequent signs of damage to cranial nerves, to cerebellar connections, to the long ascending and descending tracts crowded together in the pons and medulla, and to the reticular activating system and short tracts within the brain stem that subserve the functions of consciousness and the coordination of eye movements. Brain-stem strokes frequently produce clear-cut syndromes that can be sharply localized. Malignant tumours such as gliomas also affect this region, and multiple sclerosis is another common cause of brain-stem dysfunction. In syringobulbia a cavity forms within the brain stem in association with syringomyelia (see above *The spinal cord*) and produces cranial-nerve palsies and both cerebellar and long-tract symptoms.

Wernicke's disease is caused by a deficiency of thiamine (vitamin B_1). It is seen most often in alcoholics who show such symptoms as ocular palsies, nystagmus, memory disturbance, and peripheral neuropathy. The eye symptoms are most readily corrected by the administration of thiamine.

Wernicke's disease

Too-rapid correction of severe sodium depletion may lead to edema, or accumulation of fluid, in the central nervous system. Since many motor nerve fibres cross over and intertwine in the pons, the resulting swelling may lead to their compression and dysfunction, a condition known as central pontine myelinolysis because of the resulting demyelination. Depressed consciousness and spastic paralysis of the limbs are the chief manifestations; death frequently follows.

Disorders of sleep. The raphe nuclei of the pons and the locus ceruleus, which mediate sleep, are situated in the brain stem. Sleep consists of two rather different phases: rapid eye movement (REM) sleep and non-REM, or slow-wave, sleep. The latter phase is further divided into different stages during which the person progresses from drowsiness through deeper and deeper levels of relaxation, with decreasing ability to be aroused and with the appearance of progressively slower waveforms on an EEG. In REM sleep, periods of which punctuate slow-wave sleep during a normal night, dreaming occurs. Paradoxically, although the subject appears deeply asleep, there is much fast activity on the EEG, and numerous brief, small-amplitude movements are made by the eyes and the body musculature.

Narcolepsy is a disorder in which, with little warning, irresistible sleepiness overcomes a person during the day. In one form there are vivid hallucinations on awakening or going to sleep, temporary but profound sleep paralysis on awakening that does not affect breathing, and sudden, brief loss of muscle power in the limbs and trunk during emotional moments such as laughter (cataplexy). In this form of narcolepsy it is as though components of REM sleep were intruding into the daytime, waking hours. Narcolepsy is often hereditary. Treatment of the disorder with stimulants and tricyclic drugs is often remarkably effective. No structural disease of the brain has been detected in this condition.

Narcolepsy

Other, even more common, sleep disorders include: insomnia, which is usually psychologically mediated but which, like hypersomnia, may also complicate hypothalamic disease; and sleepwalking and night terrors, which occur in the deepest sleep stages even though the person obviously has some awareness of his surroundings. The causes of these phenomena are poorly understood, but structural disease of the nervous system is not responsible.

Brain death. This is synonymous with brain-stem death, since the centres for the control of such essential body functions as consciousness, respiration, and blood pressure are situated within the brain stem. In many countries strict criteria for diagnosis of brain death have been established by common consent among neurological, neurosurgical, religious, ethical, and judicial experts. These include the presence of deep coma with an established cause, the absence of any brain-stem functions such as spontaneous respiration, pupillary reactions, eye movements, and gag and cough reflexes, and the exclusion of low body temperature and drugs as relevant to the comatose state. The EEG is a useful (but not essential) confirmatory test. When such criteria are scrupulously applied and brainstem death is confirmed, the heart always stops beating within a day or two, even when other vital functions are artificially maintained.

THE CEREBELLUM

The clinical features of cerebellar disorders are given above (see *Localization: Higher-level sites*).

Genetic diseases. Spinocerebellar degenerations are inherited atrophies of parts of the central nervous system and of peripheral nerves. They commonly affect the cerebellum and its connections, as well as the nuclei in the medulla known as the olives, the centres for control of eye movements, the optic nerves, the dorsal columns of the spinal cord, and the corticospinal tracts. Onset is usually in the first two decades of life, but there is great variability both in the age at onset and in the expression of any of the diseases. Some patients show only minimal signs, although most conditions are slowly progressive. Many syndromes are recognized according to the combination of signs produced. The prototype is Friedreich's ataxia, in which the optic nerves, dorsal columns, corticospinal tracts, and cerebellum are affected and in which a peripheral neuropathy is also found, along with skeletal deformities, high arched feet, and rotation of the spine.

Friedreich's ataxia

Inflammatory diseases. These comprise abscesses, which usually complicate chronic infections of the middle ear through the spread of infection along the veins draining back into the posterior fossa, cerebellitis, found in association with some viral infections in children, and tuberculomas, quiescent inflammatory masses acting as tumours by raising intracranial pressure and by creating symptoms of cerebellar dysfunction.

Vascular disorders. Cerebellar hemorrhage occurs in patients with high blood pressure, causing sudden headache, neck stiffness, and cerebellar signs, often with evidence of compression of the brain stem on the side of the bleeding. Prompt surgical evacuation of the blood clot may be lifesaving, and the availability of CAT scanning has allowed this diagnosis to be made more accurately than before. Infarcts in the territory of the cerebellar arteries also involve part of the medulla or pons. The prognosis for functional recovery seems better with infarcts in the distribution area of the vertebrobasilar artery than in the carotid circulation.

Demyelinating disease. Demyelination frequently affects the cerebellum and its connections. Indeed, Jean-Martin Charcot, the French neurologist of the late 19th century, defined a triad of signs of cerebellar disease (nystagmus, ataxia, and scanning speech), which he considered diagnostic of multiple sclerosis. (For discussion of multiple sclerosis, see below *Unlocalized or multifocal disorders: Demyelinating diseases*.)

Metabolic diseases. Chronic alcoholism, toxicity of diphenylhydantoin (a drug used in epilepsy), thiamine and nicotinic acid deficiencies, and hypothyroidism, are all responsible for cerebellar dysfunction. In all of these, typical signs of truncal and limb incoordination, or ataxia, are detectable, and in most, treatment reverses the deficits more or less completely. Numerous inherited metabolic defects of metal, lipid, or amino acid metabolism (see below, *Unlocalized or multifocal disorders*) and some diseases marked by serum protein abnormalities also cause signs of cerebellar disease.

Neoplasms. Benign tumours, usually Schwannomas on the vestibular part of the vestibulocochlear nerve, may compress the cerebellar peduncles and lead to dysfunction on one side, but malignant astrocytomas and secondary deposits from distant cancers are more common. In children, medulloblastomas are fast-growing malignant tumours that destroy the central part of the cerebellum and cause severe gait ataxia as an early sign, while astrocytomas grow much more slowly and may be little more than a cyst that can be completely removed, leading to a relatively good prognosis.

Through an unknown mechanism, cancers located elsewhere may lead to degeneration of the cortex of the cerebellum without actually invading it.

THE BASAL GANGLIA

Parkinson's disease. This disease is caused by degeneration of the cells of the substantia nigra and locus ceruleus (both pigmented nuclei in the brain stem) and of their connections with the basal ganglia. The basal ganglia are nuclear masses situated above the brain stem and concerned with the initiation and patterning of voluntary movements. This motor control system employs both dopamine and acetylcholine as chemical transmitters of nerve impulses, and in parkinsonism there is a relative deficiency of the former as a result of the degeneration of neurons in the substantia nigra. This leads to inhibition of the activity within the basal ganglia. Slowness of movement, rigidity of the muscles of the body, stooped and flexed posture, and repetitive tremor of the limbs are the main clinical features of Parkinson's disease, but depression and loss of intellectual agility are also common. Most cases occur in late middle age. The cause is unknown, although encephalitis in early life, many drugs and toxic chemicals, brain trauma, cerebral anoxia, and other degenerative diseases of the nervous system (*e.g.*, progressive supranuclear palsy) cause similar or identical symptoms.

Treatment with levodopa

A tremendous advance in treatment of Parkinson's disease was the introduction in the 1970s of levodopa, or L-dopa, a precursor of dopamine that can be given orally and that crosses the blood–brain barrier into the brain, where it encourages the synthesis of the deficient transmitter. Other treatment approaches are to reduce the activity in the basal ganglia, through anticholinergic drugs, of acetylcholine (which is antagonistic to dopamine); to use such drugs as bromocriptine and pergolide to augment the responsiveness of the receptor sites where dopamine normally exerts its effect; to increase dopamine release using amantidine; and to block the action of the enzyme that breaks down dopamine by selective inhibitor drugs such as deprenyl. As a result of these approaches, the patient with Parkinson's disease can now expect many more years of functional activity than was thought possible in the 1960s, although progression of the disease cannot be halted. In severe cases the patient is eventually disabled by a combination of the disease and side effects of treatment.

Dystonias. These sustained muscular contractions, which produce abnormal postures of the face, head, trunk, and limbs, are caused by disease of the basal ganglia. Other abnormal involuntary movements, such as vocalizations, tremors, and body jerks, may also occur. The number and classification, and the biochemical and anatomical bases, of these movements are not clear. Diagnosis is difficult since many of the movements occur only intermittently and the influence of emotional states and normal activity upon them often leads to the incorrect diagnosis of hysteria. Both generalized dystonias affecting the limb and trunk muscles (*e.g.*, dystonia musculorum deformans) and focal dystonias (*e.g.*, writer's cramp, orofaciomandibular dystonia, torticollis) are seen. Generalized dystonia is an inherited condition in which persistent and often painful twisting and writhing movements of any muscle group occurs, usually in children. Their intensity may be so great as to make self-care impossible. While a number of drugs have been found effective in reducing the movements, none is consistent, and surgery on the thalamus is needed in the most severe cases. The surgical operation performed—destruction of the ventrolateral nucleus of the thalamus by local freezing—relieves muscle rigidity. It is also used to reduce tremors in severe Parkinson's disease and to incapacitate benign essential tremor. The ventrolateral nucleus has a modulating influence on the motor system, but it is not known precisely why surgery on the nucleus works in these situations.

Tics are related to dystonia, but they consist of brief, purposeless, stereotyped movements or utterances of unknown cause. At worst, sudden, explosive speech or movements occur repeatedly, as in children with the syndrome of Gilles de la Tourette. The range of drug therapy of potential value is as wide in this condition as with dystonias, and success is as uncommon.

Chorea. Brief, variable, small-amplitude, and involuntary dancelike movements are usually seen with disease of the caudate nuclei, which are part of the basal ganglia.

Huntington's disease

Huntington's disease is the most feared cause of chorea, since this inherited, dementing illness leads to early death but seldom declares itself until after the early procreative years. The discovery of the responsible chromosome has made possible effective genetic counseling and presymptomatic diagnosis. Early hallmarks of the disease are personality change, such as irritability and depression, and a liability to alcohol abuse. This is followed by intellectual deterioration with paranoid thinking and brief, involuntary, semi-purposive, jerky movements of the limbs and face—or, less commonly, to progressive rigidity of the body musculature. While treatment with phenothiazine or butyrophenone drugs is helpful for the movements, the mental symptoms progress inexorably.

Chorea also occurs in a nondementing, inherited form, as a complication of rheumatic fever in children (Sydenham's chorea) and of pregnancy (chorea gravidarum) in a few systemic diseases (*e.g.,* hyperthyroidism, lupus erythematosus), and as a toxic effect of drugs (*e.g.,* oral contraceptives and levodopa). In a more severe form called hemiballismus, caused by a small infarct of the subthalamic nucleus, wild, flinging movements of one side of the body exhaust the patient. Patients respond to drug therapy as in Huntington's disease.

Tardive dyskinesia is the name given to a syndrome of choreic movements affecting the face, eyes, tongue, and trunk, which usually appear after prolonged treatment with antipsychotic drugs such as the phenothiazines. Treatment with reserpine or amantidine may be partially successful.

Wilson's disease

Wilson's disease, an inherited condition, is characterized by cirrhosis of the liver and degeneration of the lenticular nuclei of the basal ganglia. The movement disorders produced by this condition include chorea, dystonia, athetosis (continuous, serpentine, writhing, and twisting movements around the long axes of the limbs), and tremor. Also, brown pigment is deposited around the edge of the cornea, and behavioral and intellectual disturbances are common. The disorder is due to the deposition of copper in the brain, corneas, and liver (urinary levels are also high)—all as a result of an inborn error of metabolism leading to failure of the liver to excrete copper normally. Treatment with d-penicillamine and a low-copper diet shows striking success in preventing progress and often reverses the course of the disease. Genetic counseling is another vital part of therapy.

Athetosis is also a complication of strokes, anoxia (particularly at birth), and hemolytic disease of the newborn (in which bilirubin derived from damaged red cells is deposited in the basal ganglia, causing the formation of glial scar tissue).

Essential tremor. In this common inherited disorder, which can occur at any age, movements are interrupted by a regular oscillation of the limbs, as during writing. The tremor is usually absent at rest and often affects the head and voice. It is frequently confused with parkinsonism, but the other features of that condition are not present. Alcohol reduces the problem, but β-adrenergic blocking drugs and primidone are more effective treatments.

THE CEREBRUM

Concussion

Craniocerebral trauma. The concussive and shearing stresses of head injury may cause concussion (a brief loss of consciousness without permanent consequences), contusion of the brain (most often of the tips of the frontal and temporal lobes, called contre-coup injury), or laceration of the brain tissue. In the last two cases, neurological deficits are detected at the time of injury, and with laceration (as in a depressed fracture of the skull) or bleeding into the brain, the eventual incidence of seizures is high. This is called posttraumatic epilepsy.

Complications of head injury include the development of extradural hematomas, often from tearing of the middle meningeal artery. Arterial blood, pumped into the space between the dura and the inside of the skull, acts as a fast-expanding mass lesion, compressing the brain downward through the tentorium or the foramen magnum. This is a lethal complication unless quickly relieved by surgical removal of the clot. Subdural hematomas are usually slower in development and may sometimes take weeks to form; they follow the rupture of small veins bridging the gap between the surface of the brain and the meninges. While compressive symptoms similar to those of extradural hematomas can occur, in most of these cases they are subacute or chronic, producing headache, seizures, or intellectual decline. Removal of the clot is the usual treatment.

Other complications include cranial nerve palsies, subarachnoid hemorrhage, thrombosis of a carotid artery, and cerebrospinal fluid leakage, which may lead to intracranial infection. Focal deficits are also common with brain tissue damage. Later consequences include dementia, seizures, and the posttraumatic syndrome of irritability, fatigue, headaches, insomnia, loss of concentration, poor memory, and loss of energy. Repeated minor head injuries, as occurs in some boxers, may also lead to dementia and to a Parkinson's-like syndrome.

Cerebral palsy. This term encompasses all the conditions that damage the brain around or before the time of birth—other than obviously developmental causes. Approximately six cases occur in every 1,000 live births in the Western world. Hypoxia and asphyxia during a prolonged and difficult labour are the most common causes, but improvements in obstetrical care have reduced the incidence of the condition. It is manifest by a delay in the motor development of the infant, who shows such clinical evidence of damage to the motor systems as spasticity, weakness of the limbs, and athetosis or ataxia. Sensory, visual, and cognitive defects may be detected later. Mental retardation occurs in about half of these children.

Mental retardation. Retardation signifies incomplete or insufficient general development of mental capacity, encompassing a global delay in the normal development of motor, language, and social adaptive skills. It has numerous causes. Before birth, chromosomal and developmental diseases, genetic and other metabolic disorders, and intrauterine infections or toxicity are important causes, while at the time of birth, asphyxia and hemolytic disease are prominent. In the postnatal period, nutritional deficits, infections such as meningitis, encephalitis, and the postinfectious syndromes, trauma, and toxins are the most frequent causes. Apart from delays noted in early learning and, eventually, substandard school performance, behavioral abnormalities and impaired emotional control are also common. Continuing advances in the understanding and early diagnosis of genetic diseases and in obstetrical care may further reduce the incidence of mental retardation, but it still represents a severe economic and emotional burden both for the family and for society.

Down's syndrome

Down's syndrome is the best known of the chromosomal disorders producing mental retardation. More than one in every 1,000 live-born children in the West suffer from this condition. Clinical features include short stature, smallness of the head, obliquely slanted eyes, a flattened face, wide hands with a single transverse palmar crease, short digits, and floppy muscles. The degree of mental retardation is variable. The brain is slightly smaller than normal, and the appearance of the neurons and perhaps the myelin are also abnormal (Figure 37). After the age of 30, neuropathological features common in Alzheimer's disease are almost always detectable in Down's syndrome patients. Discovery of the abnormal chromosome causing the syndrome allows prenatal diagnosis by examination of the amniotic fluid.

Dementia. This decline in intellectual capacity is caused by organic disease of the brain. Single deficits such as aphasia, an inability to use language, are not sufficient for a diagnosis of dementia, which requires evidence of diffuse, bilateral brain involvement. Common early clinical features include rigidity and blunting of personality, loss of interests, impairment of attention and concentration, difficulty with comprehension, and difficulty in handling abstract concepts. Later, increasing impairment of the capacity to retain new information, social withdrawal, unnecessary repetition of words and actions, and volatile emotions are signs of the disintegration of the mind. As dementia progresses, language ability begins to fail, the patient neglects to care for himself appropriately, and neurological signs appear on clinical examination.

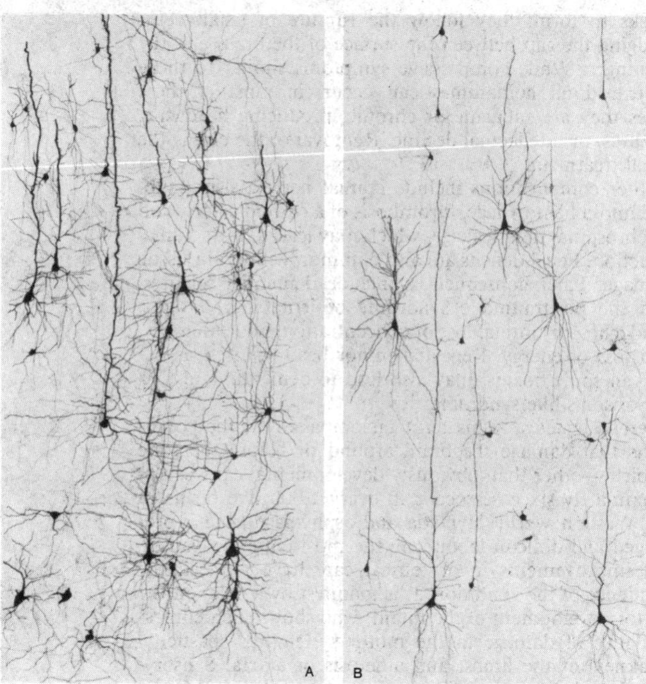

Figure 37: Drawings of neurons from the occipital cortex of the brain, showing neuropathology of Down's syndrome. (A) Normal. (B) Down's syndrome, with loss of dendrites and spines.

By courtesy of L.E. Becker and F.W. Chan

Alzheimer's disease

The most common cause of dementia is Alzheimer's disease, but the absence of a specific test for this condition (apart from the major procedure of brain biopsy) makes the diagnosis one of exclusion. Biopsy may reveal characteristic changes of neurons in the cerebral cortex. The entire cortex is affected, although the brunt of the disease falls on the frontal lobe. Other areas of the brain are also affected, such as the hippocampus and amygdala, the brain stem, and the basal forebrain (the basal nucleus of Meynert). Alzheimer's disease carries a slight familial tendency, but the etiology of the disease is not known. Research continues on many fronts, including intensive surveys of possible environmental causes. The disease is increasingly common with old age. There is no specific therapy for the condition. Augmentation of brain acetylcholine (the neurotransmitter concerned in memory processes) is not very effective.

Multi-infarct dementia is the next most common type. It is the result of numerous small strokes, the cumulative effects of which impair the function of so much of the brain that the patient has truly global intellectual impairment. Clinical diagnosis is confirmed by demonstration of the infarcted areas on CAT scanning.

The multitude of other causes of dementia can be separated into three groups. (1) General medical illnesses include states of vitamin deficiency, intoxications, endocrine disorders, and metabolic diseases. (2) Underlying neurological disorders, among whose features dementia may appear, include some genetic diseases, brain inflammation, trauma, primary and secondary tumours, degenerative diseases, severe multiple sclerosis, and, less commonly, widespread disease of the larger or smaller arteries. (3) In a final category are some conditions of uncertain cause; normal-pressure hydrocephalus, Pick's disease, and progressive supranuclear palsy are examples.

A major condition that must be distinguished from dementia in all cases is depressive illness. Since the two may coexist, correct diagnosis may be difficult.

Epilepsy. Epilepsy is a tendency toward recurrent seizures. One seizure alone is not sufficient for the diagnosis. (The nature of the condition is described above; see *Pathologies*.) Epilepsy is estimated to affect between 1 and 2 percent of the population. The most useful classification divides seizures between those of unknown cause without any detectable brain abnormality (idiopathic, or primary, epilepsy) and those caused by structural lesions in the brain (symptomatic, or secondary, epilepsy). Another system, the International Classification of the Epilepsies, defines two major categories: generalized seizures (roughly corresponding to primary epilepsy) and partial seizures (corresponding to secondary epilepsy). Numerous subcategories are also defined.

Primary epilepsy. In the primary group, onset is in the early years of life, and there is a genetic component in causation. One primary type is grand mal, or tonic-clonic, attacks, in which the subject loses consciousness without warning, falls, and stiffens, with all muscles contracting maximally. He then begins a series of rapid but slowing jerks of the whole body that cease in approximately a minute, leaving him limp and still unconscious. The person awakes a few minutes thereafter, usually sleeps for a while, and is then back to normal unless further seizures occur.

Grand mal attacks

A second form is petit mal epilepsy, also known as absence attacks, during which the subject is unaware of his surroundings for a few seconds. The person may show little abnormal behaviour, except that he usually stops whatever he is doing, and his eyelids flutter. Such attacks may occur hundreds of times daily in an uncontrolled case (Figure 33).

Myoclonic epilepsies constitute a third form of primary epilepsy. In these cases, single or repeated brief shocklike contractions of all body muscles occur.

Although genetic factors are important, any person could be made to have a seizure, usually of grand mal type. Sleep deprivation, extreme fatigue, drug toxicity, certain metabolic disturbances, and withdrawal from drugs or alcohol are potent precipitants of seizure, and, when they can be incriminated, neither underlying brain disease nor the need for drug treatment need be considered.

Secondary epilepsy. The secondary epilepsies have even more varied presentations, since, in these, spontaneous electrical activation of any brain area can be the basis of the seizure. Both the causative brain diseases and the clinical varieties of seizure are innumerable. In one group, consciousness is retained while abnormal sensations, visual hallucinations, or local muscle contractions occur. In another group, caused by lesions within the temporal or frontal lobes, there are distortions of memory leading to illusions, abnormal sensations, hallucinations of smell or hearing, limb jerking or abnormal posture, and psychological symptoms in any combination. Any of these attacks may lead to seizures resembling grand mal attacks.

Diagnosis and treatment. The task of the neurologist is to confirm that the symptoms of the patient are in fact caused by abnormal electrical discharges, to determine whether they represent primary or secondary epilepsies, and, if the latter, from where in the brain they arise and the nature of the causative pathology. In patients whose seizures begin in adult life, secondary epilepsies must be assumed until proved otherwise. After clinical assessment careful investigation is almost always required. This includes EEG (perhaps with television monitoring), CAT scanning, and often other tests for underlying infectious, metabolic, or cancerous conditions.

Drug therapy

Treatment of epilepsy depends upon the nature of the attacks, since some drugs that suppress one form of seizure may actually worsen another. For the primary generalized epilepsies, valproic acid, ethosuximide, clonazepam, diphenylhydantoin, and carbamazepine are the drugs of first choice. For the secondary epilepsies, carbamazepine, diphenylhydantoin, and primidone are preferred. These drugs have different modes of action. Some selectively block the high-frequency electrical discharges that lead to seizure activity, while others stimulate the inhibitory effect of the neurotransmitter gamma-aminobutyric acid (GABA).

In cases where control of seizures proves difficult, repeated estimations of the concentration of the drug in the serum are necessary as are appropriate blood tests to detect unwanted effects on the blood and other organs in the body, such as the liver. Surgical therapy is reserved for cases in which the seizures are uncontrolled by drugs and in which a single focal origin of the seizures is demonstrated. There are few such cases, and over 80 percent of patients with seizures achieve excellent control through faithful adherence to a regime of drug therapy. When epilepsy complicates severe brain damage, however, control may be impossible.

Headache. Diagnosis of a type of headache can usually be achieved by a complete history and physical examination without laboratory tests. There are four major varieties of headache, each with its own type and severity of pain, temporal relationship, site and pattern of radiation toward other areas, nature of aggravating or relieving factors, and associated symptoms.

Vascular headaches. These include migraine and its variants as well as headaches due to abnormal stretching of the arterial walls in the cranium as a result of vessel-wall disease.

Migraine

Migraine headaches recur periodically; often a family history of the ailment can be obtained. The pain is typically severe, throbbing or pounding, felt on one or both sides of the head, and made worse by activity, noise, or bright lights. In classic migraine, visual phenomena such as zigzag lights in the visual fields precede the onset of pain. In complicated migraine, visual loss, weakness of a limb or of one side of the body, speech disturbances, or confusion may accompany and outlast the headache. Nausea and vomiting, pallor, irritability, and prostration usually accompany migraines of any variety. In a variant called cluster headache, excruciatingly severe pain is felt in and around one eye, lasting an hour or so and frequently waking the patient from sleep in the early morning. Such attacks occur in clusters, the pain occurring 10 or 20 times over a month or so, with months of freedom until the next cluster begins.

The treatment of migraines involves a careful search for the factors that precipitate them. Foods such as cheese and chocolate, beer and red wine, and those containing nitrite or monosodium glutamate are the most frequent culprits; their removal from the diet may be sufficient to relieve the patient permanently, but total success is uncommon. Other factors include excessive or deficient sleep, physical and psychological stresses, oral contraceptives, and the menstrual cycle in many cases. Drug therapy (such as ergotamine, anti-emetic agents, or even inhaled oxygen, and pain-relieving agents) may be necessary in acute attacks. As preventive measures, tricyclic drugs, adrenergic blocking agents, lithium, and numerous other classes of drug are available. In elderly patients brief episodes of brain dysfunction resembling small strokes may occur, apparently due to arterial spasm during migraine; in younger patients with severe migraine such spasm may very rarely cause such a reduction of blood supply to parts of the brain that permanent deficits occur.

Vascular headaches may be complications of fever, hangover, lack of oxygen, low blood sugar, and ingestion of certain drugs; they are also typical of cranial arteritis, a variant of polymyalgia rheumatica. In all these conditions treatment is directed at the underlying cause.

Tension headaches. These are continuous and generalized pains felt from front to back or all around the head; they are generally less severe than migraines. While emotional stress and letdown after such stress are the most common causes, arthritis of the joints of the neck may also contribute. Tension headaches alone are often experienced by migraine sufferers, and a combined form of headache also exists. Treatment is of the psychological cause when detectable, but chronic tension headache may be self-perpetuating.

Traction headaches. These are caused by the distortion

Intracranial pressure

of intracranial pain-sensitive structures. They have a much more serious import, as intracranial bleeding or tumours, brain infections, obstruction to the flow of cerebrospinal fluid, and low pressure in the fluid due to leakage after lumbar puncture are typical causes.

Such headaches are moderately but increasingly severe, involve the whole head, may have a throbbing component, are worse with movement and coughing and on awakening, and improve as the day progresses but recur for hours daily. They are often accompanied by focal neurological signs and signs of raised intracranial pressure. Diagnosis demands a full investigation.

Referred headaches. Pain may also be referred to the head (*i.e.,* felt in the head even though the site of disease is elsewhere) by eye disorders such as glaucoma and refractive errors, infections or tumours of the nasal sinuses, dental infections, and arthritis of the neck.

Infections. *Encephalitis.* (Meningitis is considered above; see *The meninges and cerebrospinal fluid.*) The term encephalitis signifies infection of the substance of the brain. It may be caused by viruses, bacteria, rickettsias, fungi, protozoans, or metazoans. In the Western world, viral encephalitis is the most common; it is typically due to herpes simplex and less commonly to arboviruses, measles, mumps, polio, and influenza viruses, or to the group known as enteroviruses. Rabies is another rare cause.

Typical features of encephalitis include the onset, over hours or days, of headache, fever, stiffness of the neck, drowsiness, and malaise. Seizures, evidence of raised intracranial pressure, and signs of focal damage to the brain are found on examination. This combination of findings, however, can occur in many other conditions, so that further investigations are necessary, including CAT scanning of the head, EEG, and lumbar puncture in order to examine the cerebrospinal fluid for cells, organisms, and sugar levels.

The mortality of herpes simplex encephalitis has been reduced from more than 60 percent to less than 20 percent with the introduction of acyclovir or vidarabine therapy. Measures to reduce the intracranial pressure are also required in severe cases. Specific antiviral treatment is not available for other forms of viral encephalitis.

Abscess. Cerebral abscess is due to bacterial infection that may be introduced from the bloodstream in cases of generalized or distant infection or from contiguous infection following a skull fracture. The infection produces a pus-filled abscess, usually localized close to the site of the original infection. The clinical features are the same as with viral encephalitis, but removal of cerebrospinal fluid by lumbar puncture is dangerous because swelling may cause the brain to herniate downward, with fatal compression of the vital centres. In many cases, evidence of the source of the invading organisms—such as chronic lung suppuration, congenital heart disease, or sinus or ear infections—suggests the diagnosis. Efforts can then be made to localize and typify the infection by EEG and CAT scanning.

Cortical thrombophlebitis

Infection travels along the course of the intracranial veins, which themselves are infected and which thrombose, or clot. Such cortical thrombophlebitis can occur in the venous channels of the dura mater, resulting in infarcts of the surrounding brain and damage to contiguous cranial nerves. This condition is seen especially in children suffering from malnutrition and dehydration, but it also complicates some blood diseases and may occur in pregnancy. The symptoms resemble those of cerebral abscess, but there is a greater likelihood of seizures.

As treatment, antibiotics are chosen according to the nature of the organism likely to be responsible, and surgical removal can follow encapsulation of the abscess within scar tissue. Anticoagulants may be used in cortical thrombophlebitis.

Abscesses also occur both outside and just below the dural membranes enclosing the central nervous systems, usually arising by spread of local infection.

AIDS. The acquired immune deficiency syndrome, or AIDS, virus causes an infection that greatly diminishes the body's cell-mediated immune system, thus disposing it to infections that healthy people seldom contract. Many viral infections as well as tubercular, toxoplasmic, fungal, and spirochetal infections of the brain or meninges occur as a result. Neurological complications include encephalitis, due to these superadded infections, or progressive dementia, directly due to invasion of the brain by the AIDS virus.

Following common viral infections such as measles, during bacterial endocarditis (a bacterial infection of the heart valves), or after vaccination against such diseases as smallpox, an acute neurological illness with meningeal irritation, fever, reduction in consciousness, seizures, focal signs, and evidence of raised intracranial pressure may occur. This is known as acute toxic encephalopathy and is thought to represent an acute allergic reaction of the immune system to the preceding infection. In Reye's syndrome, a variation occurring in children, the same features are found, along with persistent vomiting that accompanies an acute degenerative change in the liver. There is some evidence that aspirin may precipitate the condition.

In yet another related syndrome, acute allergic encephalomyelitis, a similar illness occurs, again in the second week after vaccination or viral infection. This illness appears with signs of encephalitis and inflammation of the spinal cord or nerve roots. Damage to the myelin sheaths in the central nervous system is the basis of the disorder. Treatment with steroid drugs (related to cortisone) is sometimes effective, but many patients die during the acute stages of the illness.

Syphilis. This disease follows infection with the spirochete *Treponema pallidum,* almost invariably as a result of sexual contact or infection of the fetus in utero. Primary syphilis produces a chancre, or sore, at the site of infection; weeks later, secondary syphilis develops with a skin rash and signs of mild meningitis, but, in the third stage, signs indicate that the spirochete has invaded the substance of the nervous system. One syndrome is tabes dorsalis, involving the spinal cord (see above *The spinal cord: Inflammation*). Another is general paresis of the insane, an outmoded term for chronic syphilitic encephalitis, which causes progressive dementia and signs of focal damage to many brain areas. These two conditions may coexist. Diagnosis is confirmed by serological tests in the blood and by examination of the cerebrospinal fluid. Treatment with penicillin stops the progress of the disease and may relieve some of the more florid signs.

Progressive dementia

Slow viruses. In 1957, an unusual disease called kuru was described in the Fore tribe of New Guinea. Its means of spread was traced to ritual cannibalism, and its features included abnormal involuntary movements, dementia, and serious disturbance of motor functions. The disease was invariably fatal. A transmissible agent with a very long incubation period of years was shown to be the cause. This and similar agents are known as slow viruses, although they have properties quite distinct from those of conventional viruses.

Creutzfeldt-Jakob disease is a rare cause of rapidly developing dementia in adults, with added signs of multifocal disturbance of the brain and spinal cord. This condition has been transmitted between humans through such means as a corneal transplant taken from a person who unknowingly had the infection. The disease is fatal, and no treatment is known to affect its course. The transmissible agent resembles that of kuru.

Subacute sclerosing panencephalitis is characterized by slowly increasing loss of mental abilities, brief, shocklike jerks of the body, weakness, and spastic muscles. It affects children and young people. The measles virus is the responsible agent, probably evoking an abnormal response of the patient's immune system.

Progressive multifocal leukoencephalopathy is another fatal disease of the brain occuring in patients whose immune system is suppressed by drugs or disease. Progressive loss of myelin occurs in the white matter of the brain, cerebellum, and spinal cord. A polyoma virus that does not normally cause disease in man is responsible.

Neoplasms and nonmetastatic syndromes. Tumours affect the brain directly and indirectly. Their direct effects are mediated through replacement or compression of tissue, in each case impairing the function of the compressed part and often first appearing through epileptic seizures. Indirect effects include raised intracranial pressure, which is particularly common in the case of tumours arising within or compressing the ventricular system. A useful classification separates the benign tumours, which do not spread within the brain or metastasize (seed themselves) to distant sites, from malignant tumours, which do have these characteristics.

Benign tumours. Benign intracranial tumours include neurofibromas (technically tumours of the myelin-forming Schwann cells), which grow on cranial nerves. The most common are tumours of the vestibulocochlear nerve, tumours of the skull, and meningiomas. Pituitary adenomas arise within the pituitary fossa. By compressing the underside of the optic chiasm, they cause deficits in the visual fields, and they raise the intracranial pressure through compression of the hypothalamus and third ventricle. In addition, many secrete hormones, which may stimulate such reactions as abnormal growth and lactation. These signs may be the first evidence of pituitary adenoma. Surgical removal, approaching through the nose or through craniotomy (opening up the cranial cavity), is often required and may lead to cure, but small tumours of the pituitary may be suppressed by the drug bromocriptine.

Pituitary adenoma

Craniopharyngiomas arise from a vestigial remnant of tissue in the roof of the mouth and extend upward to produce effects similar to those of pituitary tumours. Since they often contain calcium, they may be seen on plain skull X rays. Craniotomy is necessary for their removal.

Colloid cysts are found within the ventricles. Although seldom causing symptoms, on account of their small size, they occasionally block the flow of cerebrospinal fluid, causing an acute rise in intracranial pressure that results in headache and loss of consciousness.

Other benign intracranial masses include parasitic cysts, granulomas, tuberculomas, and dermoid cysts. These may arise in any part of the brain or beside it, in which case there may also be involvement of the skull bones. Infective tumours are now uncommon in the Western world.

Malignant tumours. Malignant tumours of the brain are more common than benign ones; the most frequent of all are the gliomas, which arise from the neuroglial cells. They are of varying degrees of malignancy as judged by their speed of growth and tendency to spread. Astrocytomas arise anywhere; destroying the function of the tissues that they invade and replace, they also cause seizures and eventually signs of raised intracranial pressure. The prognosis for astrocytomas arising in the cerebellum and for the least malignant of the others is fair after surgical removal and radiation therapy, but in the case of the most malignant, the glioblastoma multiforme, life beyond a year after diagnosis is exceptional.

Astrocytoma

Medulloblastomas and ependymomas are other varieties of glioma arising, respectively, in the brain stem and in the walls of the ventricles. The former are described above (see *The cerebellum: Neoplasms*). The latter also grow in the posterior fossa in young people, but more slowly. Because of their site of origin, they tend to cause early increase in intracranial pressure, with signs of brain-stem and cerebellar dysfunction. Surgical removal is seldom complete, but radiation therapy is able to shrink the tumour and slow its growth.

Oligodendrogliomas occur anywhere in the cerebrum and are particularly liable to cause epileptic seizures. They often contain calcium, which may allow their detection in plain skull X rays. Teratomas and pinealomas are more common in young men; arising from the region of the pineal gland and damaging the hypothalamus and upper brain stem, they disturb the control of eye movement, obstruct the flow of cerebrospinal fluid, and cause cerebellar dysfunction. Their behaviour may resemble that of a benign or of a malignant tumour. Lymphomas such as Hodgkin's disease rarely invade the brain, though they may compress it; but reticulum cell sarcomas (microgliomas) do invade diffusely and cause headache, seizures, change in personality, and various focal signs.

In all such cases, whether benign or malignant, tumours are suspected from the history of headache, seizures, and focal neurological problems; diagnosis is then confirmed by CAT or radioisotope scanning. Surgery is usually necessary in order to confirm the nature of the tumour, to relieve increased pressure, and to remove all or part of the mass itself. In malignancies this at least makes subsequent radiation therapy more effective, but in the gliomas the prognosis is poor in most cases despite such treatments. The swelling surrounding these tumours can often be greatly reduced by a steroid drug with rapid but temporary relief of symptoms.

Malignant tumours arising elsewhere in the body may metastasize to the brain; common sites of origin of such secondary tumours are the lung, breast, thyroid, and kidney. These are usually multiple tumours, so that surgical removal is usually fruitless, although radiation therapy may shrink them and slow their growth.

Nonmetastatic syndromes are constellations of clinical features reflecting damage to the nervous system as a result of cancer elsewhere in the body that has not actually spread to the brain or spinal cord. How this arises has not been fully elucidated. Dementia, a syndrome resembling encephalitis, cerebellar degeneration, signs of transverse damage to the spinal cord, peripheral neuropathy, disease of the end plate somewhat resembling myasthenia, and weakness and wasting of muscles are common presentations of these syndromes.

The carotid and vertebral arteries

Stroke. *Anatomy and collateral supply.* Blood follows two avenues to the brain: the two internal carotid arteries, which divide intracranially into a number of branches (the largest being the anterior and middle cerebral arteries); and the vertebral arteries, which fuse at the base of the brain and then divide again to form the posterior cerebral arteries (Figure 38). There are many communications between vessels inside and outside the head, and, in some places, two arteries supply the same territory. Despite this generous blood supply the huge requirements of the brain for blood and the fact that the last branches of arteries anastomose, or join together, very little, if at all, make the supply quite precarious. To help smooth out the different rates of cerebral blood flow caused by variations in heartbeat, respiration, blood pressure, and posture, a system of autoregulation exists whereby the cerebral blood vessels vary their size in response to such changes.

Yet, in diseased states, the blood supply to parts of the brain still often fails. The effects vary from minor, transient slowing of activity, due to slight reduction in local blood flow, to severe, permanent loss of function when blood supply is completely lost. These failures of blood supply are strokes.

(Data) From R.D. Adams and M. Victor, *Principles of Neurology*, 3rd ed., copyright © 1985 by McGraw-Hill, Inc.; (art) reproduced by permission of Catherine Parker Anthony and Gary A. Thibodeau, *Textbook of Anatomy & Physiology*, 12th ed. (1987), Times Mirror/Mosby College Publishing, St. Louis, adapted from K. Brodmann, "Feinere Anatomie des Grosshirns," in *Handbuch der Neurologie* (1910), Springer-Verlag, Berlin

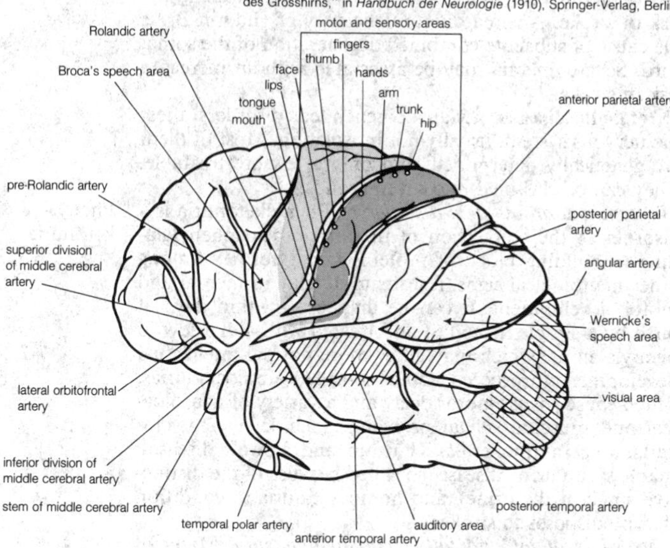

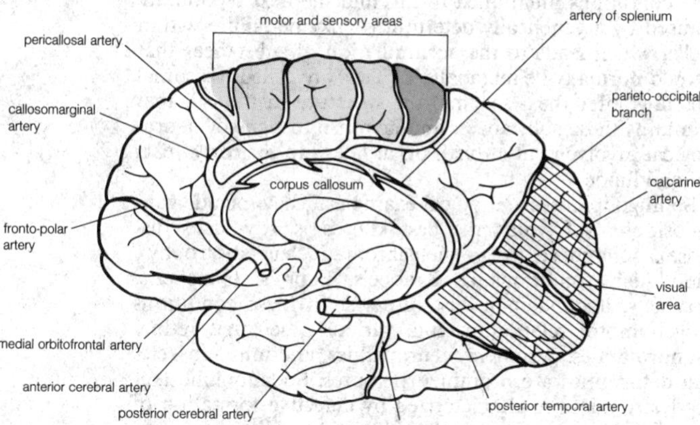

Figure 38: (Top) Lateral and (bottom) medial aspects of the cerebral hemispheres, showing the distribution of the cerebral arteries and the functional areas that they supply.

Pathogenesis and classification. The two main types of stroke are (1) those in which a blood vessel supplying a part of the brain is occluded briefly or permanently and (2) those in which the vessel bleeds as well, so that the loss of blood supplying the tissue is aggravated by a blood clot compressing it.

Transient ischemic attack

Occlusive strokes are further divided by clinicians into four groups: (1) Transient ischemic attacks (TIAs) are the mildest, the symptoms lasting only for minutes or hours. They are usually caused by small emboli, such as fragments composed of blood cells or cholesterol, that are swept into the brain's circulation from the arteries of the neck or elsewhere. (2) Reversible ischemic neurological deficits may have the same pathological basis, but the symptoms last for up to three weeks. (3) Evolving strokes show a stuttering or progressive deterioration. Blockage of the larger arteries in the brain or neck is usually responsible. (4) Completed strokes represent the final result not just of relative reduction in blood supply (ischemia) but of the death of brain tissue as a result of severe starvation of blood (infarction).

The most common pathological change causing stroke is atherosclerosis of the large- and medium-sized arteries in the neck and brain, which causes ulcers in the wall of the artery, narrowing of the lumen, or blockage of the vessel by a combination of these changes and blood clot. Small-vessel disease is the next most common, in which the thickening and degeneration of the walls of the arterioles are usually due to high blood pressure. Other vessel-wall diseases include inflammatory changes, as in collagen-vascular diseases or after deep X-ray treatment; spasm, as in severe migraine; splitting of the wall of the artery; and direct injury. Larger emboli causing more than just a TIA may arise in the larger arteries and from the valves or lining membrane of the heart.

Among other mechanisms for stroke are a severe global decrease in cerebral blood flow, as may occur with a severe hemorrhage or heart attack; diversion of blood to other arteries, as a result of a narrowing or blockage of a vertebral artery in the neck; cerebral anoxia, a severe reduction in the amount of oxygen in the blood; and abnormal viscosity of the blood due to excess numbers of cells or to increased protein concentration in the blood.

Hemorrhage

Hemorrhagic strokes are usually due to small-vessel disease in patients with high blood pressure. Such intracerebral hemorrhage occurs most often in the deep white matter of the brain, brain stem, and cerebellum. The incidence of such strokes has been reduced in part by the introduction of more effective treatments for hypertension. Bleeding also occurs when a defect in the wall of an artery, called an aneurysm, gives way. When this occurs at the sites of branching of the larger arteries inside the head, blood spills into the subarachnoid space, causing subarachnoid hemorrhage. Bleeding may also occur with malformations of arteries and veins, into an infarct, and with blood diseases that impair coagulation.

Clinical syndromes. The features of TIAs (and of any stroke syndrome) depend on which part of the brain has been affected. Transient loss of vision in one eye, like a graying-out or as if a curtain were being pulled over it, is one common manifestation of ischemia of the retina. Similar brief episodes of numbness or weakness of a limb or difficulty in speech suggests an attack in the carotid-artery territory, while brief reduction in consciousness, vertigo, slurred speech, impaired vision in both eyes, or imbalance point to ischemia in the vertebrobasilar circulation.

Symptoms of stroke

Infarction of the brain occurs most often during sleep, the patient awakening to find that he has lost the function of that part of his body supplied by the occluded vessel. The most common site of stroke is in the territory of the middle cerebral artery. The usual symptoms are aphasia and other disorders of higher cerebral functioning, hemiparesis (weakness of the face and arm more than of the leg on the other side of the body), and loss of sensation in the same areas. Blockage of the internal carotid artery in the neck produces a similar picture. Because there is extensive communication between the anterior cerebral arteries on both sides, the area of the brain supplied by the anterior cerebral artery on the occluded side may escape damage. Anterior cerebral artery infarcts produce weakness and sensory change on the opposite side of the body, but the leg is more affected than the arm. Posterior cerebral infarcts cause loss of vision in the opposite half of the visual field and sometimes difficulty in the comprehension of speech (called receptive aphasia).

An infarct of the area of brain supplied by the basilar artery is usually fatal because of severe damage to the vital control centres in the brain stem.

Small, deep infarcts in the white matter also occur. The small cavities of damaged tissue, called lacunes, cause a number of syndromes in which the damage is restricted to, for example, pure weakness or pure sensory dysfunction on one side of the body.

Intracerebral hemorrhage most commonly occurs in the putamen and leads to sudden headache, severe hemiparesis, loss of consciousness, and deviation of the eyes to one side. Bleeding into the pons causes paresis of all limbs and loss of consciousness. Bleeding into the cerebellum produces typical signs of incoordination with headache and stiffness of the neck.

Massive cerebral infarction or hemorrhage, with swelling of the brain, is often fatal. With less severe brain damage a surprising degree of recovery occurs, so that a hemiplegic patient learns to walk again although use of the hand remains poor. The mechanism of this recovery process, which can continue for up to six months, is not well understood.

Subarachnoid hemorrhage (SAH) caused by rupture of an aneurysm, leads to a sudden, explosive headache, with a stiff neck, sometimes a seizure or loss of consciousness, and, depending on the damage done by the blood pumped out of the artery, focal signs of brain damage. Up to half the patients with SAH die within two months as a result of the initial or subsequent bleeding.

Diagnosis and treatment. The diagnosis of cerebrovascular disease is achieved by clinical evaluation, but it has been greatly improved by CAT scanning, which not only shows the site of the stroke but also allows determination of the amount of bleeding (if any) and thus indicates the nature of the stroke. Additional tests include angiography, for localizing an aneurysm or detecting the site and nature of disease in the arteries of the neck, and a battery of tests aimed at determining whether any underlying disease (*e.g.*, diabetes, blood cell or clotting disease, infections) might have led to the stroke.

The treatment of stroke patients is initially directed toward support of the cardiac and metabolic systems, no treatment being known to reverse the ill effects of ischemia. High blood pressure is controlled, acutely raised intracranial pressure lowered, and, in rare cases, anticoagulant drugs prescribed. Rehabilitative efforts start as soon as the patient's condition is stable. Risk factors such as smoking and diabetes are also tackled. Also appropriate in some cases, depending on the nature of the stroke, may be such specific treatments as the clipping or isolation of a cerebral aneurysm and, perhaps, surgical evacuation of a blood clot or clearing-out of the roughened lining of the major arteries in the neck.

Drugs such as aspirin, which inhibit the tendency of platelets to cause clotting in the bloodstream, have proved effective in the prevention of stroke and fatal heart attacks after TIAs in men.

UNLOCALIZED OR MULTIFOCAL DISORDERS

Many disorders of the nervous system cannot be localized to a single site, or they represent the distant effects of disease of other parts of the body.

Effects of systemic disease. *Endocrine diseases.* Disorders of the hypothalamus may lead to symptoms of autonomic dysfunction, sleep disturbance, and diabetes insipidus (in which large volumes of dilute urine are secreted). Pituitary adenomas may cause acromegaly, in which peripheral-nerve compression may also occur. Overactivity of the thyroid gland causes tremor, muscle weakness, and disturbances of eye movements, while underactivity leads to mental dulling, deafness, difficulty in relaxing muscles, and median-nerve compression. Muscle weakness is seen in overaction of the parathyroid gland; underactivity is associated with seizures. Muscle weakness is also one of the features of adrenal gland dysfunction (both Addison's and Cushing's diseases); both of these conditions also induce abnormal mental states.

Diabetes mellitus causes many neurological complications, including peripheral neuropathy (with features of autonomic failure), painful nerve root lesions in the lumbosacral plexus, acceleration of the rate of atherosclerosis with an increased chance of stroke, and damage to the retinas. Hyperinsulinism reduces blood-sugar levels, which may cause coma. Use of oral contraceptives slightly increases the risk of stroke.

Complications of diabetes mellitus

Organ failure. When the function of the liver, lung, heart, or kidney fails, the nervous system is affected. With liver failure the typical picture is of dementia or of a confused state, with aphasia, dysarthria, and a flapping tremor of the limbs progressing to coma in severe cases.

Kidney failure is often associated with high blood pressure, which may lead to acute brain edema (distension with fluid) with visual loss and coma. Chronic kidney failure is likely to produce peripheral neuropathy as well as symptoms similar to those of liver failure but with increased likelihood of epileptic seizures. Dementia is a complication of dialysis in areas where the aluminum content of the dialysis fluid is high.

Chronic respiratory failure is another cause of tremor, confusion, and raised intracranial pressure. Heart failure may also produce a confused state, and it may predispose an individual to stroke.

Blood diseases. Leukemia and polycythemia also affect the nervous system, the former mainly through infiltration of the meninges or brain and the latter by increasing the risk of stroke. Anemia due to deficiency of vitamin B_{12} is the cause of subacute combined degeneration of the spinal cord. Severe anemia may be associated with an increased risk of stroke.

Metabolic disease. Many biochemical disorders affect the nervous system, usually not in isolation. Most of them are genetically determined, and only a few are treatable. They can be classified into seven groups.

Phenylketonuria

Protein and amino acid disorders. Phenylketonuria is a disorder of the conversion of the amino acid phenylalanine (a building block of protein) into tyrosine. Among other neurological signs, it leads to a delay in mental and motor development. It can be diagnosed within days of birth by a simple urine test and treated with a diet low in phenylalanine, which may allow more normal intellectual development to proceed. Other so-called aminoacidurias, which cause psychomotor delay and a variety of neurological and musculoskeletal problems, include hyperglycinemia, hyperammonemia, Hartnup and Lowe's diseases, maple syrup urine disease (so called because of the distinctive smell of the urine), and homocystinuria (a condition that predisposes to strokes).

Disorders of fat and fatty acid metabolism. Many of the conditions mentioned in this and the next section are caused by a genetically determined enzyme failure within cells, which leads to the accumulation of substances that would normally be metabolized. They are called lysosomal diseases after the lysosome, the structure in the cell that contains these substances, and give rise to signs of neurological involvement at birth or, at latest, in the early years of childhood.

Sphingolipidoses are typical examples. They include gangliosidoses (of which the best known is Tay-Sachs disease), sulfatidoses (*e.g.*, metachromatic leucodystrophy), and such conditions as Krabbe's, Fabry's, Gaucher's, Farber's, and Nieman-Pick diseases. In these conditions psychomotor retardation and, variously, seizures, retinal abnormalities, peripheral neuropathies, and musculoskeletal deformities are prominent features. Sudanophilic leucodystrophies are characterized by defective formation of myelin (the insulating substance surrounding nerve fibres), with marked cerebellar and corticospinal-tract dysfunction. Adrenoleucodystrophy occurs only in males; it leads to blindness, motor weakness, spasticity, and signs of adrenal-gland failure. In Refsum's syndrome peripheral neuropathy and retinal and cerebellar signs accompany a dry, scaly skin rash. This condition is of interest because restriction of dietary phytanic acid, a substance found in green vegetables, slows the progress of the disease.

Inherited deficiencies of blood lipoproteins are also associated with peripheral neuropathy, retinal degeneration, and other motor and skeletal deformities. In analphalipoproteinemia, the tonsils are swollen by accumulations of cholesterol, while in beta-lipoproteinemia, excessive fat in the stools suggests the diagnosis. Lipofuschinosis is a disorder in which lipids are stored in the retinas and nervous system, causing visual impairment, seizures, intellectual decline, and spastic weakness and ending in death.

Disorders of carbohydrate metabolism. Galactosemia develops when infants are unable to metabolize galactose, or milk sugar. Cataracts, floppiness of the limbs, and psychomotor delay occur unless substitutes for milk are given. In glycogen-storage diseases glycogen cannot be metabolized to yield lactic acid and energy, so that it accumulates within muscle, liver, and other tissues. In mucopolysaccharidoses and mucolipidoses (both lysosomal disorders), fatty and carbohydrate materials are deposited in the nervous system and in other tissues; severe mental retardation, motor and ocular signs, and skeletal abnormalities are prominent features within this group.

Vitamin deficiencies

Deficiency states. The effects of deficiency of vitamin A are mainly on the retina and skin, but components of the vitamin B group are essential for normal development and functioning of the nervous system. The Wernicke-Korsakoff syndrome (common in alcoholics) consists of disorders of eye movement, cerebellar incoordination, failure of the formation of new memories, and peripheral neuropathy, all due to deficiency of thiamine (vitamin B_1). Beriberi is the name given to the occurrence of the neuropathy alone. In each case, replacement of the vitamin may lead to substantial improvement. When other vitamins (niacin, pyridoxine, and so forth) are deficient, the symptoms are similar, and signs of spinal cord disease may occur.

Subacute necrotizing encephalopathy, also called Leigh's disease, is a lethal disorder of infancy marked by psychomotor delay, myoclonic jerks, paralyses of eye movements, and respiratory disorders. The precise biochemical defect is unknown, but thiamine metabolism is likely to be involved. Seizures in early childhood are the main feature of pyridoxine dependency, an inherited abnormal metabolic requirement for the vitamin.

Deficiency of vitamin D causes rickets, the bony softening of which may have secondary effects on the nervous system, and weakness of the proximal muscles.

Fluid, mineral, and electrolyte disorders. Inappropriate secretion of antidiuretic hormone from the pituitary gland leads to confused states and seizures; it may complicate almost any intracranial disease, especially subarachnoid hemorrhage. High or low levels of electrolytes such as sodium, potassium, calcium, and magnesium, as well as disorders of acid–base metabolism, also have neurological effects such as confusion, seizures, muscle weakness, tetany (spasm and irritability of muscles), and cramps.

Porphyria

Porphyria is a disorder of heme, the pigment in red blood cells. It occurs in a number of forms, the most important (acute intermittent porphyria) leading to attacks of acute abdominal or limb pains, marked weakness due to peripheral neuropathy, epileptic seizures, severely confused states, and increased pigmentation of the skin with abnormal sensitivity to sunlight. Attacks are sometimes precipitated by certain drugs, such as barbiturates and some antibiotics.

Among inherited disorders are: Menkes' disease, a familial disorder of copper metabolism presenting with seizures and the growth of abnormal hair; Hallervorden-Spatz disease, a condition marked by the deposition of iron in the basal ganglia that produces rigidity, weakness, and abnormal movements; the Lesch-Nyhan syndrome of raised levels of uric acid in the blood with abnormal movements, spastic weakness, mental retardation, and a tendency to self-mutilation; and familial hypoparathyroidism, in which the basal ganglia calcify, causing choreic movements.

Neurocutaneous syndromes. A number of genetically determined disorders of the ectoderm (the outside layer of cells in the embryo, from which the skin and the nervous system develop) are grouped together—slightly artificially—as the neurocutaneous syndromes. Five of these are mentioned below. (Down's syndrome is described above; see *The cerebrum: Mental retardation.*)

Neurofibromatosis

Neurofibromatosis (von Recklinghausen's disease) presents such features as café-au-lait spots on the skin, the formation of fibrous tumours on nerves and, in some cases, of various tumors in the brain, rotation of the spine, tumours of endocrine glands such as the adrenal gland, and other skeletal deformities. The Elephant Man, protected at the London Hospital in the 1880s, is thought by some to have suffered from this condition, his skin thickened by huge numbers of nerve and skin tumours. This disease is relatively common, but many patients have only minimal symptoms.

Ataxia-telangiectasia (the Louis-Bar syndrome) comprises cerebellar incoordination and choreic movements, overgrowth of blood vessels on the conjunctivas (eye membranes), and disorders of the immune system.

In von Hippel-Lindau disease, tumours of blood vessels grow in the brain, especially in the cerebellum and retina, and in other organs.

The Sturge-Weber syndrome is characterized by a large red ("port-wine") overgrowth of blood vessels in the skin over the upper face and by a growth of the underlying brain. The latter effect may cause seizures, spastic weakness, and visual-field deficits.

Tuberous sclerosis is characterized by epileptic seizures, a facial rash resembling acne, and the growth of many benign tumours in the lining membrane of the ventricles of the brain and in other organs.

Toxic effects of drugs, metals, and common poisons. Perhaps due to the complexity of the metabolic systems and to the rapid metabolic rate of the nervous system, the brain is highly susceptible to damage from chemical substances derived both internally and from the environment. Endogenous (internally derived) poisons are the products of organ failure and abnormal metabolism. Among the externally derived poisons are bacterial toxins, such as those in tetanus, which lead to increased excitability of the ventral-horn cells of the spinal cord, with muscular rigidity resulting; diphtheria, which produce severe loss of myelin from motor nerves, causing limp weakness of the throat and body muscles; and botulism and tick paralysis, which prevent normal transmission of impulses between nerve and muscle.

Heavy metals (such as arsenic, lead, thallium, gold, manganese, and mercury), synthetic chemicals (such as the organophosphates, gasoline, and toluene), the alcohols (especially ethyl and methyl alcohol), ionizing radiation, and a huge range of drugs can all be toxic to the nervous system. In addition, water overload can cause seizures, and oxygen, under high pressure, can induce depression of brain function.

Drug overdose and withdrawal

The neurological syndromes that occur as a result of toxicity are remarkably varied. Toxic encephalopathy, characterized by reduced consciousness, seizures, and delirium, is seen in poisoning with alcohols, all sedatives, and many other chemicals and drugs—the last usually taken in overdose or for a prolonged period. Seizures, dementia, and drowsiness can also occur in isolation as drug and chemical toxicity, and the withdrawal from sedatives (including alcohol) may also be a cause of seizures. Syndromes of damage to the basal ganglia, including acute dystonias, chorea, and parkinsonism, occur with overdose or prolonged use of, or idiosyncrasy to, many drugs and as a result of poisoning by such heavy metals as mercury and manganese. Other agents selectively damage the cerebellum; diphenylhydantoin and ethyl alcohol are the best-known examples. Signs of damage to the spinal cord may appear following electric shock, deep X-ray treatments, or exposure to heavy metals and some drugs. Subacute combined degeneration of the spinal cord may be induced when drugs lead to a deficiency of vitamin B_{12}.

Meningeal irritation often followed injection of air into the subarachnoid space when this was performed as a diagnostic test; it also occurs with some drugs given by mouth or by subarachnoid injection. Fungal meningitis may complicate chronic suppression of the body's immune system. Raised intracranial pressure, due to an increase in the water content of the brain, occurs with cortisone-like drugs, and headaches of migraine type are frequently precipitated by foods and drugs.

The list of drugs and other agents capable of causing damage to cranial nerves or peripheral nerves is very long. It is of interest that some of these agents affect only one of the cranial nerves; thus, the birth control pill has been incriminated in Bell's palsy, a facial weakness caused by dysfunction of the facial nerve, but trichlorethylene (a solvent) and stilbamidine (a drug) cause numbness of the face by affecting the trigeminal nerve. The cochlear and vestibular portions of the vestibulocochlear nerve are also susceptible in different ways to toxicity from the group of aminoglycoside antibiotics.

In the peripheral nervous system the autonomic nerves may be damaged alone or in conjunction with other nerves. The transmission of impulses at the autonomic ganglia may also be blocked by many drugs used to reduce blood pressure. In part, this is a pharmacological response (in other words, it is the effect sought in the first place), but when this effect occurs with anticonvulsants, antidepressants, or sedatives, the effect is highly undesirable. A drop in blood pressure on standing up is the most common clinical effect.

Toxic symptoms affecting the muscles include cramps, weakness, and atrophy, or muscles may even degenerate acutely. The range of chemicals and drugs producing such effects is wide. Drugs may also reduce levels of potassium in the blood, resulting in secondary weakness of muscles. Blockade at the neuromuscular junction is an unwanted effect of some antibiotics and quinine.

Finally, within a miscellaneous group of problems, it should be mentioned that lymphomas may follow prolonged suppression of the immune system or treatment with diphenylhydantoin, that inflammation of the arteries (autoimmune vasculitis) arises as a complication of treatment with some drugs and as toxicity from chemical exposure, and that even drugs used normally can produce unusual effects in singular circumstances (for example, dangerously low blood sugar levels causing brain damage may occur in a diabetic patient taking his normal insulin dose but missing meals).

Demyelinating diseases. Demyelinating diseases must be differentiated from dysmyelinating diseases. In the former, normal myelin is damaged; in the latter group, the myelin is probably abnormal in the first place, as in leucodystrophies and other metabolic disorders involving fat or fatty acids (see above).

Demyelination can occur after trivial viral infections or vaccinations, but multiple sclerosis (MS) is the most important example and is discussed here.

Multiple sclerosis

Multiple sclerosis is a relatively common disease in temperate climates, with a prevalence of between 50 and 100 per 100,000 population in most areas where such figures have been gathered since 1970. Females are affected somewhat more often than males, and most patients develop the first signs within 10 years of their 30th birthday. Pathologically, multiple scattered areas of myelin breakdown, called plaques, are found within the white matter in the central (not peripheral) nervous system. The actual nerve fibres, the axons, remain intact but no longer conduct impulses adequately. The cause of this demyelination is not known, but people with certain genetically determined immunologic characteristics seem to be over-represented among the MS populations. Also, the influence of an outside agent is strongly suggested by variability between regions of the same geographic area and by the fact that people who migrate from an area of low MS prevalence to one of high prevalence before the age of 14 years take on, as it were, the higher risk of their new area. This increased risk does not occur if such a move is made after that age or if migration is in the other direction. The nature of the agent is unknown, epidemiological and clinical studies conflicting in suggestions that the virus of measles or of canine distemper is responsible.

Some typical clinical patterns of MS are:

1. Onset in young adult life, with inflammation of one optic nerve causing pain and diminished sight for a few days or weeks, followed by recovery. There is a transient appearance of scattered neurological signs in subsequent years.

2. The same as above, but with the initial signs suggesting lesions not only in the optic nerve but also in the spinal cord, cerebellum, or brain stem and in the deep cerebral white matter. A tendency to further relapses and remissions may leave more or less evidence of past attacks.

3. Severe and progressive involvement of any part of the nervous system, with further relapses and persistent deficits after subsequent attacks, leading to "chronic progressive multiple sclerosis."

4. The slower progression of signs mainly or only at spinal-cord level in patients who are usually over the age of 50.

Typical clinical features (varying with the site of the plaques) include eye pain and visual dimming (optic nerve); double vision, nystagmus, disturbances of speech, and facial numbness or pain (brain stem); incoordination of gait and of the limbs (cerebellum and cerebellar connections); spasticity, weakness, and increased deep tendon reflexes (corticospinal tracts at any level from the cerebral white matter down to the spinal cord); frequency and urgency of bladder emptying (corticospinal tracts); and alteration in sensation, especially involving the senses of joint position and discriminative touch (dorsal columns in the spinal cord or their upward connections in the brain stem or subcortical white matter). In severe cases, intellect and memory are impaired.

Diagnosis and treatment of MS

Diagnosis of multiple sclerosis depends upon the demonstration of physical signs that imply the presence of plaques in multiple areas of the central nervous system. When this cannot be done clinically, electrical survey of the nervous system, using evoked potential testing, may be useful. In the cerebrospinal fluid the detection of oligoclonal bands in the gamma-globulin fraction of the protein is also suggestive. Overall, the diagnosis is essentially clinical; if laboratory support is not forthcoming, observation of the patient's course over subsequent months or years may allow it to be made with confidence.

The outcome of the disease cannot be foretold from the initial symptoms. In some 20 percent of cases there is no disability 10 years after the onset, while other patients are rapidly disabled. Mean survival from onset is now well over 30 years.

Treatments of specific complaints, such as spasticity and cramping of the limbs, bladder symptoms, and facial pain, is relatively easy; the prevention of relapses or progression is extremely difficult. Measures that suppress the activity of the body's immune system, such as steroid (cortisone-like) drugs and specific immunosuppressants, are the mainstays of therapy. The chronicity of the disease and its potentially devastating effects during the relative youth of many of the patients has made multiple sclerosis a fertile field for scientifically unsupported claims. (W.E.M.P.-P.)

BIBLIOGRAPHY

Form and function of nervous systems: General physiological features are presented in JOHN P. SCHADÉ and DONALD H. FORD, *Basic Neurology: An Introduction to the Structure and Function of the Nervous System,* 2nd rev. ed. (1973); ERNEST GARDNER, *Fundamentals of Neurology: A Psychophysiological Approach,* 6th ed. (1975); ABEL LAJTHA (ed.), *Handbook of Neurochemistry,* 2nd ed., 10 vol. (1982–85); DAVID OTTOSON, *Physiology of the Nervous System* (1983); STEPHEN W. KUFFLER, JOHN G. NICHOLS, and A. ROBERT MARTIN, *From Neuron to Brain: A Cellular Approach to the Function of the Nervous System,* 2nd ed. (1984); MELVIN J. SWENSON (ed.), *Dukes' Physiology of Domestic Animals,* 10th ed. (1984); ERIC R. KANDEL and JAMES H. SCHWARTZ (eds.), *Principles of Neural Science,* 2nd ed. (1985); *The Nervous System: Circuits of Communication* (1985), part of the series "The Human Body"; ARTHUR C. GUYTON, *Textbook of Medical Physiology,* 7th ed. (1986); and GORDON M. SHEPHERD, *Neurobiology,* 2nd ed. (1988). *Handbook of Physiology,* sect. 1, *The Nervous System,* 5 vol. in 9 (1977–87), examines the cellular biology of neurons, motor control, sensory processes, and regulatory systems and higher functions of the brain. See also D.M. GUTHRIE, *Neuroethology: An Introduction* (1980), a psychology of animal behaviour, including that of humans. Studies of the nerve cells include ALAN PETERS, SANFORD L. PALAY, and HENRY DE F. WEBSTER, *The Fine Structure of the Nervous System: The Neurons and Supporting Cells* (1976), a description of nerve cells based on numerous electron micrographs; and H. HYDÉN, "The Neuron," ch. 5 in JEAN BRACHET and ALFRED E. MIRSKY (eds.), *The Cell: Biochemistry, Physiology, Morphology,* vol. 4, part 1, *Specialized Cells* (1960), pp. 215–323. The effects of drugs on the central nervous system are detailed in JACK R. COOPER, FLOYD E. BLOOM, and ROBERT H. ROTH, *The Biochemical Basis of Neuropharmacology,* 5th ed. (1986).

The transmission of information in the nervous system via electrical signals is analyzed in three works of historical interest: KEITH LUCAS, *The Conduction of the Nervous Impulse,* rev. by E.D. ADRIAN (1917); E.D. ADRIAN, *The Mechanism of Nervous Action: Electrical Studies of the Neurone* (1932, reprinted 1959); and JOSEPH ERLANGER and HERBERT S. GASSER, *Electrical Signs of Nervous Activity* (1937, reprinted 1968), including bibliographies of the works of both authors. More recent works include ICHIJI TASAKI, *Nervous Transmission* (1953), and "Conduction of the Nerve Impulse," ch. 3 in *Handbook of Physiology,* sec. 1, *Neurophysiology,* vol. 1. (1959); JOHN C. ECCLES, *The Physiology of Nerve Cells* (1957, reprinted 1968), written by a co-recipient of the 1963 Nobel Prize for Physiology or Medicine; A.L. HODGKIN, *The Conduction of the Nervous Impulse* (1964, reissued 1971), a brief but lucid exposition; MARY A.B. BRAZIER, *Electrical Activity of the Nervous System,* 4th ed. (1977), a college-level survey; and BERTIL HILLE, "Excitability and Ionic Channels," in GEORGE J. SIEGEL, *et al.* (eds.), *Basic Neurochemistry,* 3rd ed. (1981), pp. 95–106. Other methods of transmission are described by A.V. HILL, *Chemical Wave Transmission in Nerve* (1932); JOHN C. ECCLES, *The Physiology of Synapses* (1964); M. GABE, *Neurosecretion,* trans. from French (1966), an account of neurosecretion in invertebrates and vertebrates; and BERNARD KATZ, *The Release of Neural Transmitter Substances* (1969).

The evolution and development of the nervous system is explored by C.U. ARIËNS KAPPERS, G. CARL HUBER, and ELIZABETH C. CROSBY, *The Comparative Anatomy of the Nervous System of Vertebrates, Including Man,* 2 vol. (1936, reprinted in 3 vol., 1967); THEODORE HOLMES BULLOCK and G. ADRIAN HORRIDGE, *Structure and Function in the Nervous Systems of Invertebrates,* 2 vol. (1965), a monumental, well-illustrated work containing comprehensive bibliographies that cover the available knowledge of the nervous systems of all the invertebrate groups; HARTWIG KUHLENBECK, *The Central Nervous System of Vertebrates: A General Survey of Its Comparative Anatomy to the Pertinent Fundamental Biologic and Logical Concepts,* 5 vol. in 7 (1967–78), including basic concepts and a general survey of the nervous systems of both invertebrates and vertebrates; THOMAS L. LENTZ, *Primitive Nervous Systems* (1968), an account of the neural organization of sponges, hydras, and planarias, including a hypothesis on the evolutionary origin of the nervous system; L.E. BAYLISS, *Principles of General Physiology,* 5th ed., vol. 2, pp. 492–533 (1960), a clear description, particularly concerned with the properties of the neuron, spinal reflexes, nerve excitation and inhibition, and reciprocal innervation; HARVEY B. SARNAT and MARTIN G. NETSKY, *Evolution of the Nervous System,* 2nd ed. (1981), a comparative study of nervous systems; and JAN LANGMAN, *Langman's Medical Embryology,* 5th ed. by T.W. SADLER (1985).

(T.L.L./C.R.N./E.D.G./S.D.E.)

Anatomy of the human nervous system: General overviews are provided by E. LAWRENCE HOUSE, BEN PANKSY, and ALLAN SIEGEL, *A Systematic Approach to Neuroscience,* 3rd ed. (1979), a simplified treatment; and MALCOLM B. CARPENTER and JEROME SUTIN, *Human Neuroanatomy,* 8th ed. (1983), a complete account written for the medical student. ELIZABETH C. CROSBY, TRYPHENA HUMPHREY, and EDWARD W. LAUER, *Correlative Anatomy of the Nervous System* (1962), relates the morphology of the nervous system to neurophysiology, neuropharmacology, neurosurgery, and neurology. See also A. BRODAL, *Neurological Anatomy in Relation to Clinical Medicine,* 3rd ed. (1981).

The anatomy of neural subsystems is described in RICHARD A. MILLER and ETHEL BURACK, *Atlas of the Central Nervous System in Man,* 3rd ed. (1982), a short but useful work; FRED A. METTLER, *Neuroanatomy,* 2nd ed. (1948), a summary of the cranial and spinal nerves; STEPHEN W. RANSON and SAM LILLARD CLARK, *The Anatomy of the Nervous System: Its Development and Function,* 10th ed. (1959), a systematic consideration of the functional components of the cranial and spinal nerves; J.W. MILLEN and D.H.M. WOOLLAM, *The Anatomy of the Cerebrospinal Fluid* (1962), a description of the anatomy and function of the ventricles of the brain, the choroid plexuses, and meninges; EDWIN CLARKE and C.D. O'MALLEY, *The Human Brain and Spinal Cord: A Historical Study Illustrated by Writings from Antiquity to the Twentieth Century* (1968), a historical account of concepts and investigations of the human nervous system; DONALD H. FORD, JACK ILLARI, and JOHN SCHADÉ, *Atlas of the Human Brain,* 3rd rev. ed. (1978), photographs of dissections of the brain; W.D. WILLIS and R.E. COGGESHALL, *Sensory Mechanisms of the Spinal Cord* (1978), an excellent book; and NEDZAD GLUHBEGOVIC and TERENCE H. WILLIAMS, *The Human Brain: A Photographic Guide* (1980), photographs of the human brain, intact and dissected, explained by diagrams. FRANK H. NETTER (comp.), *The Ciba Collection of Medical Illustrations,* vol. 1, *Nervous System,* new ed. (1983), contains a magnificent collection of colour drawings of the central nervous system, spine, nerve tracts, autonomic nervous system, and diseases of the brain and spinal cord.

(T.L.L./C.R.N./M.B.C./E.D.G./Ed.)

Functions of the human nervous system: General summaries are provided by DAVID JENSEN, *The Human Nervous System* (1980); and PETER NATHAN, *The Nervous System,* 2nd ed. (1982), a complete account of the anatomy, physiology, and psychology of the nervous system of humans and other animals, written for readers without an extensive background in biology. CHARLES R. NOBACK, *The Human Nervous System: Basic Principles of Neurobiology,* 3rd ed. (1981), is a general text with an account of the development of the nervous system and sensory receptors; further information on receptors can be found in WILFRED M. COPENHAVER, DOUGLAS E. KELLY, and RICHARD L. WOOD, *Bailey's Textbook of Histology,* 17th ed. (1978); ARTHUR C. GUYTON, *Basic Human Neurophysiology,* 3rd ed. (1981), an account of functional aspects of sensory receptors; and DON W. FAWCETT, *A Textbook of Histology,* 11th ed. (1986). G.H. PARKER, *The Elementary Nervous System* (1919), is a classic book on the origin of the basic receptor-adjustor-effector system of neural function. CHARLES S. SHERRINGTON, *The Integrative Action of the Nervous System,* 2nd ed. (1948, reprinted 1973), is a classic on the physiology of reflex mechanisms, by one of the important workers on the subject.

(T.L.L./C.R.N./P.W.N.)

Discussions on the regulation of muscular contraction include BERNARD KATZ, *Nerve, Muscle, and Synapse* (1966), a clearly written work; PETER B.C. MATTHEWS, *Mammalian Muscle Receptors and Their Central Actions* (1972), a wide-ranging work dealing with the subject historically, and an article updating this, "Evolving Views on the Internal Operation and Functional Role of the Muscle Spindle," *The Journal of Physiology,* 320:1–30 (1981); and I.A. BOYD and M.H. GLADDEN (eds.), *The Muscle Spindle* (1985), an account of a specialized symposium with brief review articles interspersed.

(P.B.C.M.)

The vestibular system and its functions are the subject of VICTOR J. WILSON and GEOFFREY MELVIL JONES, *Mammalian Vestibular Physiology* (1979), an account of the mammalian vestibular system, including anatomy, biophysics, and physiology, that assumes some physiological knowledge; ROBERT W. BALOH and VINCENTE HONRUBIA, *Clinical Neurophysiology of the Vestibular System* (1979), a review of the vestibular system in relation to disease states; and PETER RUDGE, *Clinical Neuro-Otology* (1983), which outlines from a clinical point of view the vestibular system and which deals with anatomy, physiology, and clinical conditions affecting this system, including an account of the auditory pathways.

(P.Ru.)

Discussions of the autonomic nervous system include G.A.G. MITCHELL, *Anatomy of the Autonomic Nervous System* (1953); JOSEPH PICK, *The Autonomic Nervous System: Morphological, Comparative, Clinical, and Surgical Aspects* (1970); JAMES C. WHITE, REGINALD H. SMITHWICK, and FIORINDO A. SIMEONE, *The Autonomic Nervous System: Anatomy, Physiology, and Surgical Applications,* 3rd ed. (1952); PETER A.G. MONRO, *Sympathectomy: An Anatomical and Physiological Study with Clinical Applications* (1959); RALPH H. JOHNSON and JOHN M.K. SPALDING, *Disorders of the Autonomic Nervous System* (1974); OTTO APPENZELLER, *The Autonomic Nervous System: An Introduction to Basic and Clinical Concepts,* 3rd rev. and enl. ed. (1982); ROGER BANNISTER (ed.), *Autonomic Failure: A Textbook of Clinical Disorders of the Autonomic Nervous System,* 2nd ed. (1988); and RALPH H. JOHNSON, DAVID G. LAMBIE, and JOHN M.K. SPALDING, *Neurocardiology: The Interrelationships Between Dysfunction in the Nervous and Cardiovascular Systems* (1984).

(E.D.G./J.M.K.S.)

The following works deal with other functions of the human nervous system: on pain, RONALD MELZACK, *The Puzzle of Pain* (1973); on vision, RICHARD L. GREGORY, *Eye and Brain: The Psychology of Seeing,* 3rd ed. rev. and updated (1977); and on emotion and behaviour, LLOYD S. WOODBURNE, *The Neural Basis of Behavior* (1967), a useful review of the anatomy and physiology of the nervous system for the beginning student in biology, medicine, or psychology. See also RICHARD L. GREGORY and O.L. ZANGWILL (eds.), *The Oxford Companion to the Mind* (1987).

(P.W.N.)

Cerebral functions are described in ALEKSANDR ROMANOVICH LURIA, *Higher Cortical Functions in Man,* 2nd ed. rev. and expanded (1980; originally published in Russian, 1962); ALAN BADDELEY, *Your Memory: A Users Guide* (1982); ENNIO DE RENZI, *Disorders of Space Exploration and Cognition* (1982); ANDREW W. ELLIS, *Normality and Pathology in Cognitive Function* (1982); MURIEL DEUTSCH LEZAK, *Neuropsychological Assessment,* 2nd ed. (1983); KENNETH M. HEILMAN and EDWARD VALENSTEIN, *Clinical Neuropsychology,* 2nd ed. (1985); BRYAN KOLB and IAN Q. WARSHAW, *Fundamentals of Human Neuropsychology,* 2nd ed. (1985); SALLY P. SPRINGER and GEORG DEUTSCH, *Left Brain, Right Brain,* rev. ed. (1985); and KEVIN WALSH, *Neuropsychology: A Clinical Approach,* 2nd ed. (1987). I.P. PAVLOV, *Conditioned Reflexes: An Investigation of the Physiological Activity of the Cerebral Cortex* (1927, reprinted 1960; originally published in Russian, 1923), describes the classic experiments and studies of cerebral function in response to signals and reflex behaviour as carried out in dogs and their application to humans.

(G.Ra.)

Nervous system diseases and disorders: Texts on the pathology, diagnosis, and treatment of nervous diseases and disorders include W.R. GOWERS, *A Manual of Diseases of the Nervous System,* 2nd ed. rev. and enl., 2 vol. (1892–93, reprinted 1970); WEBB HAYMAKER and BARNES WOODHALL, *Peripheral Nerve Injuries: Principles of Diagnosis,* 2nd ed. (1953, reprinted 1967); A.B. BAKER (ed.), *Clinical Neurology* (1955–), with annual revisions published for loose-leaf update; E. STEPHENS GURDJIAN and L. MURRAY THOMAS, *Operative Neurosurgery,* 3rd ed. (1970, reprinted 1975); ALEXANDER G. REEVES, *Disorders of the Nervous Systems: A Primer* (1981); WEBB HAYMAKER and RAYMOND D. ADAMS (eds.), *Histology and Histopathology of the Nervous System,* 2 vol. (1982); H. HOUSTON MERRITT, *Merritt's Textbook of Neurology,* 7th ed. edited by LEWIS P. ROWLAND (1984); RAYMOND D. ADAMS and MAURICE VICTOR, *Principles of Neurology,* 3rd ed. (1985); W. RUSSELL BRAIN, *Brain's Diseases of the Nervous System,* 9th ed. by JOHN WALTON (1985); and WILLIAM PRYSE-PHILLIPS and T.J. MURRAY, *Essential Neurology,* 3rd ed. (1986).

(W.E.M.P.-P.)

New Orleans

Unquestionably one of the most distinctive cities of the New World, New Orleans was established at great cost in an environment of conflict. Its strategic position, commanding the mouth of the great Mississippi–Missouri river system, which drains the rich interior of North America, made it a pawn in the struggles of Europeans for the control of North America. As a result, its peoples evolved a unique culture and society, blending many heritages. Its citizens of African descent have provided a special contribution in making New Orleans the birthplace of jazz. New Orleans is a city of paradox and contrast: while it shares the urban problems afflicting other U.S. cities, it has nevertheless preserved the exuberant and uninhibited spirit exemplified by its carnival season, culminating in the annual Mardi Gras, when more than 1,000,000 people throng the streets. The city also has a solid economic base: it is the largest city in Louisiana, the second port of the United States in tonnage handled, a major tourist resort, and a medical, industrial, and educational centre.

Historical and cultural heritage

The article is divided into the following sections:

Physical and human geography

THE LANDSCAPE

The city layout. The city of New Orleans and Orleans Parish (county) are coextensive, covering an area of 199 square miles (518 square kilometres). The boundaries are formed by the Mississippi River and Jefferson Parish to the west and Lake Pontchartrain to the north. Lake Pontchartrain is connected by the Rigolets Channel to Lake Borgne on the east, and the southern boundary of New Orleans is made up of St. Bernard Parish and, again, the Mississippi River. The city is divided by the Mississippi, with the principal settlement on the east bank. The west bank, known as Algiers, has grown rapidly. It is connected to eastern New Orleans by the Greater New Orleans Bridge. The bridge, completed in 1958, has proved to be a bottleneck to the city's traffic; in the early 1980s construction was begun on a second, adjacent bridge to alleviate the problem.

The early city was located on the east bank along a sharp bend in the Mississippi, from which its popular name, "Crescent City," is derived. The modern metropolis has spread far beyond this original location. Because its saucer-shaped terrain lies as low as five feet (1.5 metres) below sea level and has an average rainfall of 57 inches (1,425 millimetres), a levee, or embankment, system and proper drainage have always been of prime importance to the city.

Climate. New Orleans has a moderate climate; the average daily temperature from October through March is 60° F (16° C), and from April through September the daily average is 77° F (25° C). Freezing weather is rare, and the temperature rises above 95° F (35° C) only about six days a year.

THE PEOPLE

The population of New Orleans has been declining. Whites account for less than half of the total, whereas in 1960 they made up almost two-thirds. In contrast to the population decline in Orleans Parish, the adjacent parishes of St. Bernard, Jefferson, and St. Tammany—which, together with Orleans, compose one of the national Standard Metropolitan Statistical Areas (SMSA)—have shown steady increases. Since the black population in these three parishes is quite small, these figures indicate a white move to the suburbs, a trend common to major U.S. cities.

The shift in population to the suburbs has been motivated less by racial tension (although this may play a part) than by desires for better and more modern living facilities. The fact that a large segment of the black population resides in declining neighbourhoods (some segregated, some integrated) has spurred both black and interracial political, social, and religious organizations to work either independently or with city and federal agencies on projects to improve the quality of life for low-income citizens. The additional fact that New Orleans has an upper-class and a middle-class black population has been a significant factor in such projects.

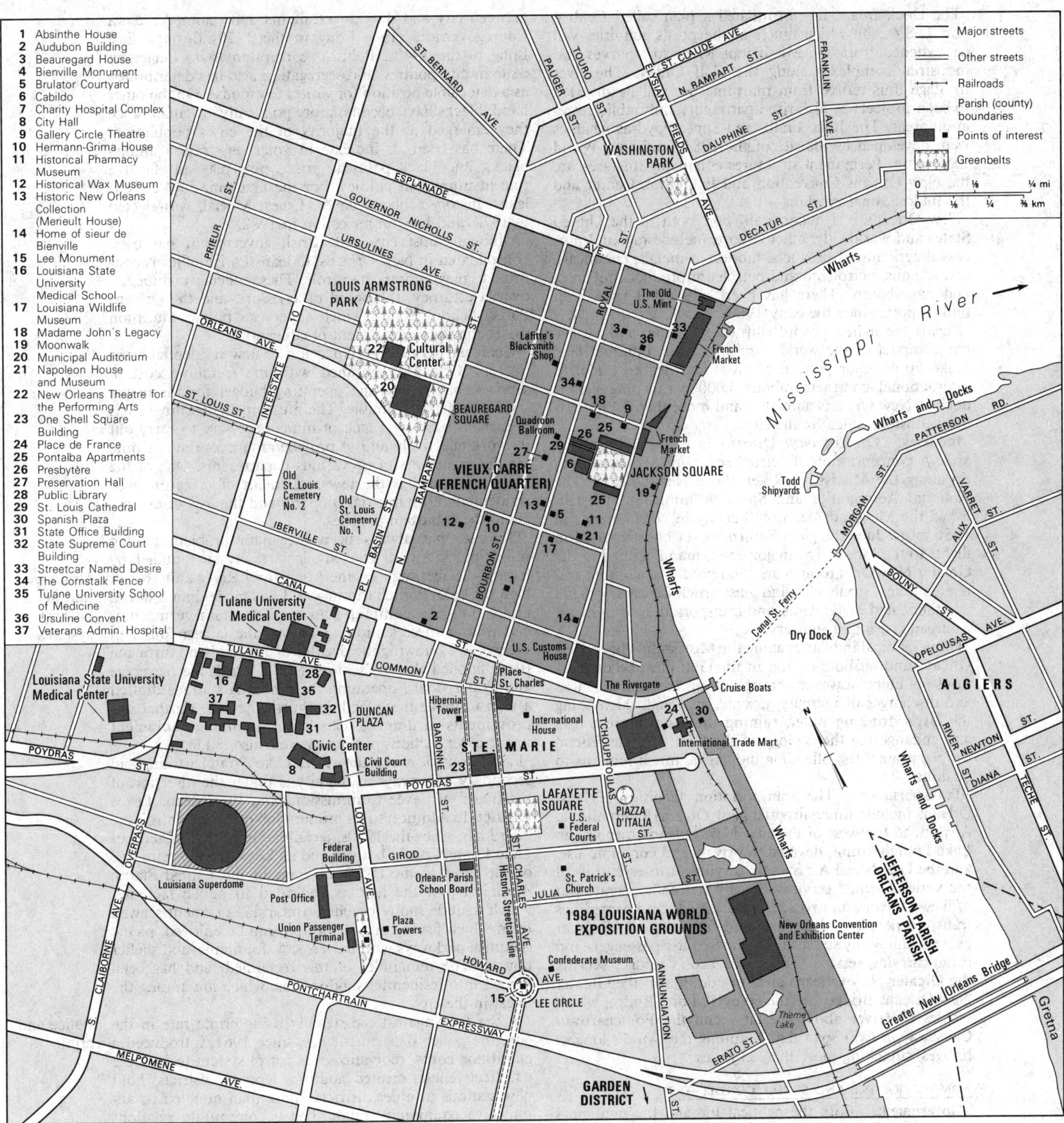

Central New Orleans.

THE ECONOMY

The port. New Orleans has always been primarily a commercial centre, with manufacturing playing a secondary role in its economic life. The busy harbour, besides adding to the city's cosmopolitan atmosphere, is the foundation of the metropolitan economy, influencing many aspects of urban life.

The era of the modern Port of New Orleans began in 1879 with the construction of jetties in South Pass, one of three passes that flow from the river into the Gulf. Sandbars had formed at intervals in these passes and had hindered ships entering the river since the city's founding. The jetties narrowed South Pass, forcing the river to cut a deeper channel to a depth of 30 feet. Later, a second channel, Southwest Pass, was deepened to 40 feet by installing jetties; it is now the main pass used by seagoing vessels entering and leaving the river. The distance from New Orleans to the Gulf is about 110 miles (180 kilometres).

Another major step forward for the port was taken in 1896, when the state legislature removed wharf facilities from the control of private contractors and created the Board of Commissioners of the Port of New Orleans (the Dock Board), a body charged with administering the public wharves. In 1908 the Dock Board was authorized to issue negotiable bonds for the improvement of port facilities. The projects subsequently accomplished included the rebuilding and expansion of public wharves and the construction (in partnership with the Board of Levee Commissioners of the Orleans Levee District) of the five-and-a-half-mile Industrial Canal, which links the river to Lake Pontchartrain, the Intracoastal Waterway, and the Mississippi River–Gulf Outlet. In 1963 the Mississippi River–Gulf Outlet, a ship channel shortening the passage to the Gulf by 40 miles, was opened to maritime traffic.

Legislative control of the port

The Dock Board has formulated a plan called Centroport U.S.A., by which much of the port's activities will be switched from the Mississippi River to wharves and industrial complexes along the Gulf Outlet. The river frontage thus retired from maritime use will be diverted to such projects as high-rise apartments and public recreation areas. The Julia, Erato, and upper Poydras wharves were developed as the site of the 1984 Louisiana World Exposition. Permanent structures enhancing this area are the New Orleans Convention and Exhibition Center and the International Pavilion.

New Orleans is a major grain port both in the United States and worldwide; other exports include raw and processed agricultural products, fabricated metals, chemicals, textiles, oils, petroleum and petroleum products, tobacco, and paperboard. There has been substantial growth in bulk exports since the early 1980s, which has made New Orleans the lighter aboard ship (LASH) cargo and Seabee barge capital of the world. Grain, coal, and animal feed make up a major portion of LASH and Seabee trade. In international commerce about 5,000 oceangoing vessels dock at New Orleans annually, and more than 40 nations have consular offices in the city.

Industry. Greater New Orleans is a major industrial area. A concentration of petrochemical plants has sprung up along the Mississippi River above New Orleans. The National Aeronautics and Space Administration established the Michoud Assembly Facility in New Orleans in 1961 to produce the giant Saturn rocket boosters used in flights to the Moon. The major goods manufactured in the Greater New Orleans area are food products, clothing and related items, stone, clay and glass articles, primary metal and fabricated metal items, and transportation equipment. Tourism is a major industry.

Petrochemical industries along the Mississippi above New Orleans and offshore oil rigs in the Gulf have become serious polluters, however, through oil-rig fires and oil slicks and discharges of mercury, arsenic, and lead, threatening the city's drinking water, ruining the taste of river fish, and endangering the ecology of the Gulf. Despite federal actions against the offending industries, much remains to be done.

Transportation. The transportation facilities of New Orleans include three airports: New Orleans International Airport, to the west of the city; New Orleans Airport, on Lake Pontchartrain, devoted to private and corporate use; and the U.S. Naval Air Station, serving air reserve units of the various armed services. Several railroads operate out of New Orleans, and passenger bus, truck, and barge lines transport people and cargo to and from the city. Regular express sailings by steamship lines also offer passenger- and cargo-carrying service. The major access bridges serving the Greater New Orleans area, in addition to the Greater New Orleans Bridge, are the Huey P. Long Bridge, which crosses the river above the city, and the Pontchartrain Causeway, a twin span that is among the world's longest bridges, stretching more than 23 miles.

ADMINISTRATIVE AND SOCIAL CONDITIONS

Government. Both the political life and the municipal government of New Orleans have been dominated by factions of the Democratic Party. The question of state interference in city affairs versus home rule is one of the major issues. In 1954 New Orleans finally received a strong home rule charter, which substituted a mayor–council form of government for the mayor–commission form that had existed since 1912.

Municipal management

In addition to the mayor and seven council members—five elected from districts and two at large—who serve four-year terms, the position of chief administrative officer to the mayor was created. The mayor is the top administrator over the 13 municipal departments and oversees the affairs of various commissions and boards. The chief administrative officer, appointed by the mayor, is charged with supervision of city departments, the preparation of the annual budgets, and the coordination of city relations with state and federal agencies. The council is strictly a legislative body.

Political issues have changed. Gone is the antagonism between city and state governments that spanned the era from governors Huey Long in the 1920s through Earl Long in the 1940s. Political corruption is no longer an issue in city politics, and segregation also has deteriorated as a defensible position for whites to espouse. On the other hand, blacks have become more politically articulate since they emerged as the majority of the city's population. There has been an increase in voter registration among blacks, and black political groups now play an effective role in municipal politics. For the first time in New Orleans' history a black mayor, Ernest Morial, was elected in 1978, and he won reelection in 1982.

Although most city and parish government has been consolidated in New Orleans, Orleans Parish officials continue to play an important role. These officials include the district attorney, the board of assessors, and the Orleans Parish School Board, which supervises public education under the state department of education.

Municipal services. Expansion of new residential areas in New Orleans, combined with the spiralling cost of services, has caused the operating budget for municipal services almost to double. The municipal government has been hampered by a lack of funds necessary to carry out its work effectively and to provide an appropriate income for the employees of its various departments. One of the major problems is the low assessment of taxes on both residential and industrial property and the loss of taxpayers to the suburban parishes.

Drainage and flood-control systems

Drainage has always been the main problem among municipal services. The city is virtually surrounded by levees—25 feet high on the Mississippi River and 10 feet high on Lake Pontchartrain—and has more than a dozen major drainage pumping stations. The drainage machinery used at these stations is among the largest found in the world. Following the disaster of 1965, when Hurricane Betsy flooded the city's lower Ninth Ward, the Sewerage and Water Board operating the pumping stations drafted a plan to make these facilities hurricane-safe. Further improvements in drainage canals and pumping equipment in the older sections of the city were also made.

Flood control along the river, Lake Pontchartrain, and secondary waterways in the city is under the direction of the Board of Levee Commissioners of the Orleans Levee District. In addition to its primary job of flood control, the board has, since the 1920s, reclaimed hundreds of acres of Lake Pontchartrain bottomland and developed it into one of the most scenic lakefront areas in the United States. A majority of the land is dedicated to public facilities, which include sandy beaches, a marina, a cement seawall from which fishing and swimming can be enjoyed, picnic grounds, parkways with flower beds, fountains, and shelter houses. The remainder of this reclaimed land has been turned into residential subdivisions, which are among the finest in the city.

Police and crime

In the fight against the steadily rising crime rate in the city, the police department has, since 1961, introduced a guard-dog corps, reorganized its patrol system to increase its effectiveness, created additional police districts, built new stations in older districts, more than doubled its automotive equipment, established a community relations division, and put into operation a communication van, which acts as a field command post in times of emergency.

Police programs designed to mobilize citizen groups have been greatly increased to include the Neighborhood Watch Programs, the New Orleans Neighborhood Police Anti-Crime Council, and Teleserv, a program in which citizens handle minor complaints for the police by telephone. A police psychologist has been added to the force, and the narcotics squad has been increased.

Health. New Orleans has become a medical and educational centre. The Charity Hospital of Louisiana is the teaching hospital for two adjacent institutions, the Tulane and the Louisiana State University medical schools, with which the nearby Veterans Administration Hospital is also affiliated. There are as many hospitals within the metropolitan area. In addition to serving local residents, specialists frequently treat patients from Latin America.

Education. Among New Orleans' institutions of higher learning are Tulane University and its affiliates, the H. Sophie Newcomb Memorial College for Women and the Tulane School of Medicine; Loyola University; the University of New Orleans; St. Mary's Dominican College; Delgado Community College; Our Lady of Holy Cross College; Dillard University; Xavier University of Louisiana; and Southern University in New Orleans. The city has many private, parochial, and business schools. The public school system began in 1841 with 83 pupils and four teachers and now has some 1,000 times as many students and teachers. In 1960 a public school crisis, attracting international attention, developed when an attempt was made at the token integration of two white schools. Within 20 years the school system was overwhelmingly black at both student and teacher levels.

CULTURAL LIFE

The cultural life of New Orleans is a synthesis of contributions by both whites and blacks. The white American heritage is reflected in the business and commercial life of the city, while the immigrant heritage—Irish societies, German Volkfests, Italian St. Joseph Day altars—adds ethnic colour to urban conformity. The black heritage is particularly rich. In antebellum days, free persons of colour were musicians, poets, journalists, business entrepreneurs, and landlords. Both black freemen and slaves were renowned for their craftsmanship in such trades as bricklaying, iron grillwork, and carpentry. The contribution of black musicians to the birth of jazz out of black blues and "field hollers" and white dance tunes and hymns is well known. New Orleans, therefore, is one American city in which the black as well as the white cultural contribution is abundantly clear and acknowledged.

Facilities for recreation and relaxation in New Orleans are justly famous. New Orleans is often referred to as "the city that care forgot," and it has always been a town for those seeking a good time. Its residents love music, dancing, and a "Continental Sunday" spent in amusements. The three factors that have contributed to its popularity with tourists are the Old World charm of the Spanish–French architecture in its Vieux Carré (French: Old Square), the madcap abandon of its carnival and Mardi Gras, and its reputation as the birthplace, between the 1880s and World War I, of jazz.

The Vieux Carré: Creole architecture and ironwork

The Vieux Carré, or French Quarter, is a sightseer's delight. Its Creole architecture, creating the atmosphere of a foreign city, combines native architectural ingenuity with adaptations of French colonial traditions of eastern Canada and West Indian Spanish colonial styles. Typical are one-story cottages opening directly on the sidewalks, with high-pitched roofs and windows reaching to the ground. Another style is the L-shaped two-story dwelling with a side entrance to an inner patio. Also built to the sidewalk, it has a roof that extends out over balconies on both the street and patio sides. Iron grillwork, designs for which were created locally and executed to a high perfection by slave craftsmen, decorates these balconies and also supports the roof. Such houses are built side by side with no openings between them, but the patios offer space for trees, flowers, and fountains and ensure privacy for the occupants.

Central to the Vieux Carré is Jackson Square, facing the Cabildo and the Presbytère (former governmental centres, but now state museums) and St. Louis Cathedral. All date from colonial times, but considerable stylistic changes have been made on these buildings since they were erected.

On either side of this square are the Pontalba Apartments, built between 1849 and 1851, while nearby is the historic French Market. Curio and antique collectors throng the many shops on Royal Street. Side streets are lined with art galleries, perfume shops, sidewalk cafés, and tearooms. Bourbon Street is famous for its nightclubs, where jazz and risqué floor shows are a specialty. Devotees of jazz may also visit Preservation Hall and Dixieland Hall, where revivals of traditional styles may be heard. The New Orleans Jazz Club established a Jazz Museum and later donated the collection to the Louisiana State Museum system. The jazz collection and Mardi Gras exhibits are displayed in the Old U.S. Mint. Each spring the city puts on an International Jazz and Heritage Festival.

St. Louis Cathedral in the Vieux Carré (French Quarter), in New Orleans.

Joachim Messerschmidt—Bruce Coleman Inc.

Every April the New Orleans Spring Fiesta Association sponsors walking tours of private homes and patios in the Vieux Carré and also of the spacious Garden District uptown, the elite 19th-century neighbourhood. Boats tour the extensive harbour facilities and the magnificent scenery of nearby waterways. The observation point atop the International Trade Mart (400 feet) at the foot of Canal Street offers a panoramic view of the river and city. Adjacent to this commercial centre is The Rivergate, a mammoth exhibition hall. The world-renowned Creole cuisine may be sampled in numerous restaurants, ranging from elegant dining rooms with French menus and waiters, to small cafés with checkered tablecloths, serving red beans and rice.

The sporting life and the lively arts

Sports share an honoured position with jazz and carnival activities in New Orleans. The city is the home of the New Orleans Saints, a member of the National Football League, and the site of the Louisiana Superdome, one of the world's largest sports arenas. Racing has a 100-day season at the local Fair Grounds Race Track, while golf, a popular pastime, attracts top golfers every year to the Greater New Orleans Open Golf Tournament held at Lakewood Country Club. Boating, fishing, and swimming are popular pastimes on the city's many waterways. The city's Southern Yacht Club, on Lake Pontchartrain, is the second oldest in the country. In addition to the lakefront, popular recreation areas include the city's two largest parks, City and Audubon. The latter has had extensive renovations of its zoological gardens, making its exhibits of wildlife and farm animals one of the city's major recreational attractions. The New Orleans Recreation Department operates more then 100 playgrounds and directs organized recreation activities for thousands of youngsters. At the end of each year the Mid-Winter Sports Carnival is held in the city, featuring amateur competition in all major sports. It concludes on New Year's Day with the Sugar Bowl football contest between outstanding college teams.

Since World War II, New Orleans has become an art centre, with many artists and galleries offering original works to collectors. The New Orleans Museum of Art is a public museum displaying many treasures. Live theatre is represented by several little theatre groups. Musical events include operas staged annually by the New Orleans Opera House Association, concerts given by the New Orleans Philharmonic-Symphony Society, a summer pops series, and concerts presented by the New Orleans Jazz Club and the New Orleans Recreation Department.

The New Orleans carnival season begins after Christmas with local carnival organizations holding balls almost every night until Mardi Gras, the "Fat Tuesday" before Ash Wednesday. The two weeks before Mardi Gras are filled with parades, both day and night, climaxing on Mardi Gras with the Rex parade. The first parading carnival group (called a "krewe") was the "Mystick Krewe of Comus," which appeared in 1857, though celebrations by masked students go back to 1827. The krewe of Rex came into existence in 1872. Krewes, parades, and carnival crowds continued to grow until the late 1970s, when the city council limited the number of parades along the traditional routes.

Mardi Gras

In the latter half of the 19th century there were about a half-dozen leading newspapers, including one in French. Through a process of gradual consolidation, New Orleans now has only one major daily, the *Times-Picayune/States-Item*. The city also has weekly newspapers, trade publications, college journals, and regional magazines of considerable circulation. Competitive journalism is kept alive among the city's television and radio stations.

History

FOUNDATION AND EARLY SETTLEMENT

The decision to found New Orleans, or Nouvelle-Orléans, was made in Paris in 1717 by John Law's Company of the West, which had taken control of Louisiana that year. The colony's new proprietors envisioned New Orleans (named for the French regent, the Duc d'Orléans) as a "port of deposit," or transshipment centre, for future trade from upriver in the Mississippi Valley. Jean-Baptiste le Moyne, sieur de Bienville, the man who suggested the site, was entrusted with the actual foundation of the city. Clearing of underbrush for the new city probably began in March 1718. The engineers charged with this task met with problems arising from uncooperative convict labour, a shortage of supplies, two severe hurricanes (in 1721 and 1722), and the unpleasant physical conditions of mosquito-infested swamps as they set up the first crude dwellings covered with bark and reeds. An engineer, Adrien de Pauger, drafted the first plan for the town, encompassing what is now the Vieux Carré and consisting of 66 squares forming a parallelogram.

Hostility of the environment

The first residents were a colourful mixture of Canadian backwoodsmen, company craftsmen and troops, convicts, slaves, women of uncertain virtue, and indigents. In a census taken in November 1721, New Orleans had a population of 470 people: 277 whites and 172 black and 21 Indian slaves. In 1722 New Orleans was designated the capital of Louisiana, and in 1731 the city returned to the control of the French crown. More respectable colonists began to arrive, but growth continued to be precarious. The main economic staples grown in the vicinity of New Orleans were tobacco and indigo for export and rice and vegetables for local consumption. Naval stores were also exported. French ships, however, were reluctant to call at New Orleans to pick up such cargo because its value did not match its bulk.

In 1762 France, ready to part with its unprofitable port, secretly agreed to cede Louisiana to Spain, and by the Treaty of Paris (1763) Spain received New Orleans and the Louisiana Territory west of the Mississippi. After a brief rebellion—which was sternly suppressed—the inhabitants of New Orleans enjoyed peace and a growing prosperity under Spanish law, while trade arose with the British colonies in spite of Spanish restrictions. At the same time English-speaking colonists were moving west to settle along the tributaries of the Mississippi. In the decade of the American Revolution, these "Kaintucks," as they were called, began floating their cargoes downriver to New Orleans; several times Spanish officials suspended the right of deposit of American goods at New Orleans in response to the boisterous conduct of American frontiersmen along the city's upper levee.

In 1800 Louisiana was secretly returned to Napoleon's France, and by 1803 the French emperor had negotiated for its sale to the United States. The ceremonies transferring Louisiana to France and later to the United States took place in New Orleans' Cabildo and main square, the Place d'Armes (now Jackson Square), in the winter of 1803.

The Louisiana Purchase

THE GROWTH OF THE CITY

The early 19th century. New Orleans' population in 1803 was approximately 8,000–4,000 whites and 2,700 enslaved and about 1,300 free "persons of colour." Its prosperity was reflected in its 1803 exports, which had a value approaching $2,000,000 and were bound mainly for American ports. In 1805, when it was incorporated as a municipality, New Orleans took on an identity separate from that of Louisiana's territorial government. As the city expanded out of its original limits, one of the first new tracts of land to be added was the Faubourg Ste. Marie, a suburb lying on the uptown side of the Vieux Carré and separated from it by a broad "commons" (now Canal Street, New Orleans' main street). It became the "American section" in the early 19th century and the hub of most business activities. Other *faubourgs* (outskirts, or suburbs) were laid out above and below the two nuclear settlements and across the river and were finally absorbed into the city by the 1870s.

During the War of 1812, New Orleans was threatened by a British invasion force, which approached the city from the Gulf of Mexico. Gen. Andrew Jackson, with an army of frontiersmen and local volunteers, won a smashing victory on January 8, 1815, saving the city, though, unknown to him, the war already had been concluded.

The next 40 years constituted the golden age of New Orleans as a great cotton port. The first steamboat to reach the city, in 1812, was appropriately called the "New Orleans." Mississippi River steamboats increased to 400 by 1840, and local commerce skyrocketed in value, reaching $54,000,000 by 1835. By 1840 the city was rated the fourth port in the world: after the 1840s canals and railroads diverted produce eastward to New York City.

The era of cotton

German and Irish immigrants arrived in New Orleans in large numbers in the 1840s. By 1850 the city's total population had swelled to 116,375. New Orleans, however, had not learned to cope with the health hazards of its mushrooming growth: drinking water came from the river or cisterns; no sewerage system existed; drainage was deficient; and flooding was common after heavy rains. The results were sporadic outbreaks of cholera and yellow fever, the worst of which was the yellow fever epidemic of 1853, accounting for more than 8,000 deaths.

The Civil War and its aftermath. During the Civil War, the strategic location of the city was inadequately appreciated by the Confederate military. The Union fleet of Adm. David Farragut was able to capture New Orleans in April 1862. The city was placed under the military command of Gen. Benjamin Butler, and city officials were removed from office. Although Butler was replaced as commander by Nathaniel Banks by the end of 1862, his brief régime became infamous in local history for his roughshod handling of the population.

During the period of Reconstruction, 1865–77, racial tensions ran high. "Scalawags" (white Southerners who cooperated with Republican forces) and "carpetbaggers" (Northerners accused of exploiting the situation for personal gain) cooperated to gain political control of the city and state, with the support of black voters. By 1872 amnesty had been granted to the ex-Confederates, and the municipal government returned to traditional white control, although state government and the city police force remained under Radical Republican control until 1877. In the 1880s the debt of $24,000,000, incurred under carpetbag regimes, increased steadily with each subsequent administration. This municipal debt had to be paid before the city could undertake any new bond issues for sorely needed municipal improvements.

In the last 20 years of the 19th century, therefore, New Orleans made limited, though steady, progress. Between 1840 and 1900, it had dropped from third to 12th place in national rank, although its population had increased to 287,104.

Yellow fever was sharply curtailed after the Civil War and was finally eradicated by 1906. By the early 20th century the river steamboats, unable to compete with railroads, disappeared; the Port of New Orleans, attracting less railroad freight than Eastern ports, reached a low ebb shortly before World War I. With the development of towboats and barges large enough to hold almost an entire trainload of cargo, however, the port grew to be second in the nation after World War II. Substantial progress, at least in physical improvements, came to the city in the 1950s. During the administration of Mayor DeLesseps S. Morrison a vast railroad consolidation program was achieved, and a $15,000,000 railroad terminal constructed. Streets were widened, railroad ground crossings were spanned with overpasses, and a $20,000,000 civic centre, which includes the 11-story City Hall, was built.

20th-century growth

BIBLIOGRAPHY. Old but reliable general histories are WILL H. COLEMAN (comp.), *Historical Sketch Book and Guide to New Orleans and Environs* (1885, reprinted 1973); HENRY RIGHTOR (ed.), *Standard History of New Orleans, Louisiana* (1900); and GRACE E. KING, *New Orleans: The Place and the People* (1895, reprinted 1968). Popular general histories that include photographs are WALTER G. COWAN *et al.*, *New Orleans: Yesterday and Today* (1983); LEONARD V. HUBER, *New Orleans: A Pictorial History* (1971, reissued 1981); and DEIRDRE STANFORTH, *Romantic New Orleans* (1977, reprinted 1979). Architecture is discussed in MARY L. CHRISTOVICH *et al.* (eds. and comps.), *New Orleans Architecture*, 5 vol. (1971–77), a scholarly study. Detailed period studies are JOHN G. CLARK, *New Orleans, 1718–1812: An Economic History* (1970); ROBERT C. REINDERS, *End of an Era: New Orleans, 1850–1860* (1964); GERALD M. CAPERS, *Occupied City: New Orleans Under the Federals, 1862–1865* (1965); and JOY J. JACKSON, *New Orleans in the Gilded Age: Politics and Urban Progress, 1880–1896* (1969). Port history and activity is discussed in ALEXANDER I. WARRINGTON, *Economic Geography of New Orleans and the Middle South* (1952); and LOUISIANA. BOARD OF COMMISSIONERS OF THE PORT OF NEW ORLEANS, *Report* (annual). For politics and government, see JOHN R. KEMP (ed.), *Martin Behrman of New Orleans: Memoirs of a City Boss* (1977); EDWARD F. HAAS, *DeLesseps S. Morrison and the Image of Reform* (1974); and L. VAUGHAN HOWARD and ROBERT S. FRIEDMAN, *Government in Metropolitan New Orleans* (1959). The best sources for detailed descriptions of historic places in the Vieux Carré are STANLEY C. ARTHUR, *Old New Orleans*, 6th rev. ed. (1944); and FEDERAL WRITERS' PROJECT. NEW ORLEANS, *New Orleans City Guide* (1938, reissued 1972). The conflict between preservationists and advocates of a proposed elevated expressway through the Vieux Carré is discussed in RICHARD O. BAUMBACH, JR., and WILLIAM E. BORAH, *The Second Battle of New Orleans* (1981). Detailed statistical information on New Orleans is found in the *Louisiana Almanac* (irregular); *Statistical Abstract of Louisiana* (triennial); and NEW ORLEANS. POLICE DEPARTMENT, *Annual Report*.

(J.J.J.)

New York City

The most populous metropolis of the United States, New York City is, depending on one's point of view, any one of four cities: to social scientists it is a laboratory in which to study the challenges of urban life, from ghastly slum to tycoon luxury; to tourists it is a city of jostling crowds, horn-honking traffic jams, dirty streets, smelly subways—all in dramatic contast to such international symbols as the skyscraper skyline, the United Nations buildings, Wall Street, the Statue of Liberty, the Metropolitan Museum of Art, Times Square, and Broadway theatres; to commuters it is an enervating beehive of world trade and finance, mass media, business administration, fashion, and assorted entrepreneurial activities and manufacture—a place to leave as soon as possible in the evening for the more serene atmosphere of greener suburbia.

But to the residents of this temperate, humid city, most of it raised up on the islands where the Hudson River empties into the Atlantic Ocean, New York City is in reality a collection of many neighbourhoods scattered among the city's five boroughs—Manhattan, Brooklyn, the Bronx, Queens, and Staten Island (formerly called Richmond)—each exhibiting its own life-style. To move from one neighbourhood to another in the city's 304 square miles (787 square kilometres) may be like passing from one country to another. Such clichés as "New York is not the United States" or "It's a great place to visit, but I wouldn't want to live there" were probably coined by commentators unaware of the importance of this neighbourly aspect of what Walt Whitman called "the hurrying feverish, electric crowds."

This article is divided into the following sections:

Physical and human geography

CHARACTER OF THE CITY

New York has often been called ungovernable, and predictions of its approaching death date to the 19th century. The prophecies of doom have become increasingly frequent since the late 1960s, as important businesses have left the Empire City for the suburbs; street crimes have multiplied in what the city's press agents have dubbed Fun City and the Big Apple; the quality and availability of public services have deteriorated, the number of jobs has declined, and the fiscal plight has become perilous in the city that displays a beaver, once a symbol of wealth, on its municipal seal.

The proliferation of crisis. After spending about half of the 20th century reshaping New York City with parks, highways, bridges, tunnels, and housing projects, one agency head reflected in his retirement on the difficulty of labelling the city.

> The best of the original Gotham recorders, the O. Henrys, Ring Lardners, Damon Runyons of bygone days, gave side-lights, vignettes and what in painting is called genre, but it was only a quarter, a corner, phase or facet, certainly not the essence.

The novelist James Fenimore Cooper had sensed this a century earlier, when he wrote: "New York is essentially national in interest, position, pursuits. No one thinks of the place as belonging to a particular state, but to the United States." Periodically, thousands of New Yorkers and sometimes even their mayors, obsessed with the unique character of their fabulous city, have argued that it ought to break away from New York state and set itself up as a separate state of the Union.

Centralization and decentralization. Since the 1960s two basic thrusts in city government have been in conflict in New York City. Some say that at issue is the very survival of the city or of any huge city. Others contend that the city is going through another of its major transitions, which ultimately will bring about a blend of the two approaches into a formula for a livable megalopolis. The argument, then, is between advocates of centralization and decentralization.

Beginning in the 1930s reformers and other opponents of "machine politics" were generally successful in New York City in advancing centralization. The powers of the presidents of the five boroughs were greatly reduced and shifted to the mayor and his appointees. Such important municipal operations as education, health, sanitation, parks, recreation, sewers, and roads were directed almost entirely from even larger central bureaus, almost always located in Manhattan. Centralization, its supporters insisted, brought greater efficiency to government services by eliminating replicated layers of bureaucracy in the boroughs and by dropping useless jobs created in those boroughs by district politicians.

During the administration of Mayor John Lindsay (1966–72) the voices of decentralization became steadily stronger. The decentralists said that centralization had isolated the city government on pinnacles too far removed from the people and their problems.

Resurgence of community self-determination

The borough presidents called for the return of their powers so that they could start doing a better job of getting garbage collected, filling potholes in the streets, and maintaining parks. Community planning boards, their members appointed by the borough presidents, became more active and influential. This was as true in affluent Riverdale, in the Bronx, where beautiful homes and expensive apartment houses overlook the Hudson River, as in the slum of the Brownsville section of Brooklyn, in which burned-out tenements were falling down around newer low-income housing projects. Proposals advanced by the Mayor and his City Planning Commission were delayed and sometimes blocked entirely by the pressure of the community planning boards.

The communities assumed more power in all sorts of activities: picking principals of schools in Harlem, preventing construction of a department store on Manhattan's West Side, saving homes planned for demolition for a high school in the middle-class Corona section of Queens, and clearing welfare cases out of hotels in Greenwich Village or Brooklyn Heights. Community groups became the watchdogs of city operations on the basic level, pointing out where a police station was undermanned, a traffic light was essential, a hospital was in disrepair, or fire equipment

Thomas Airviews

Manhattan Island from the harbour; on the left is the Hudson River and on the right is the East River. New York City's financial district and Battery Park are in the centre foreground. Central Park is at upper centre.

was antiquated. The neighbourhood newspaper, almost extinct, was reborn in many parts of the city.

Centralists claimed that the life of the city was being strangled by the whims of community leaders. Decentralists retorted that without healthy communities there could be no healthy city.

The community groups were cemented by fear—the fear of muggers and burglars. Like other large cities, New York City is afflicted with many street crimes, some of them sadistic. Since New York City is the main point of entry and the major marketplace for smuggled narcotics, it has became the nation's chief gathering place for drug addicts. Much of the street crime and burglaries are perpetrated by addicts.

Few areas are free of street crime. In the slums, iron fences are fixed inside windows that open on fire escapes. Double and triple locks, often with bars that fit from the door into the floor, are used in many apartments in middle-class neighbourhoods. The rich, despite round-the-clock doormen, often install elaborate burglar systems in their luxury condominiums for which they pay $1,000 or more a month for maintenance alone. Purse snatchings near supermarkets have become so frequent that many women no longer carry handbags or they bind the leather straps of the bags around their wrists. Parks and playgrounds have become nocturnal hangouts for addicts and pushers. Dogs are bought more for protection than as pets. Skyscraper office buildings hire private police forces and iron gates are drawn across stores at night. Neighbourhoods organize their own volunteer auxiliary police details to patrol at night in cars equipped with two-way radios. Subways, the key arteries of the city, have their own police force.

Historic antecedents of contemporary crises. The growing strength of neighbourhood groups and the fears that bind them are manifestations of an older problem revived.

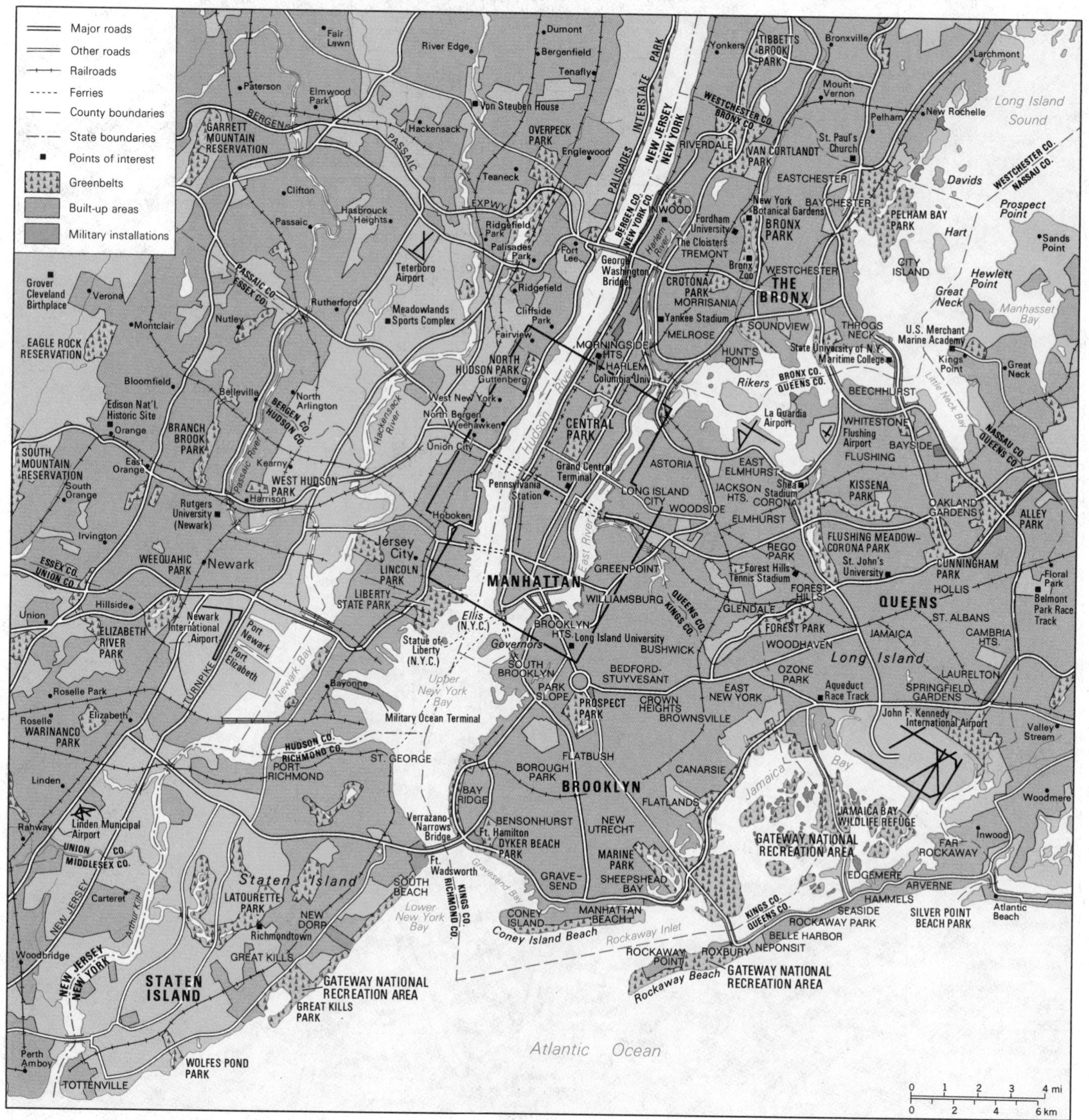

New York City Metropolitan Area.

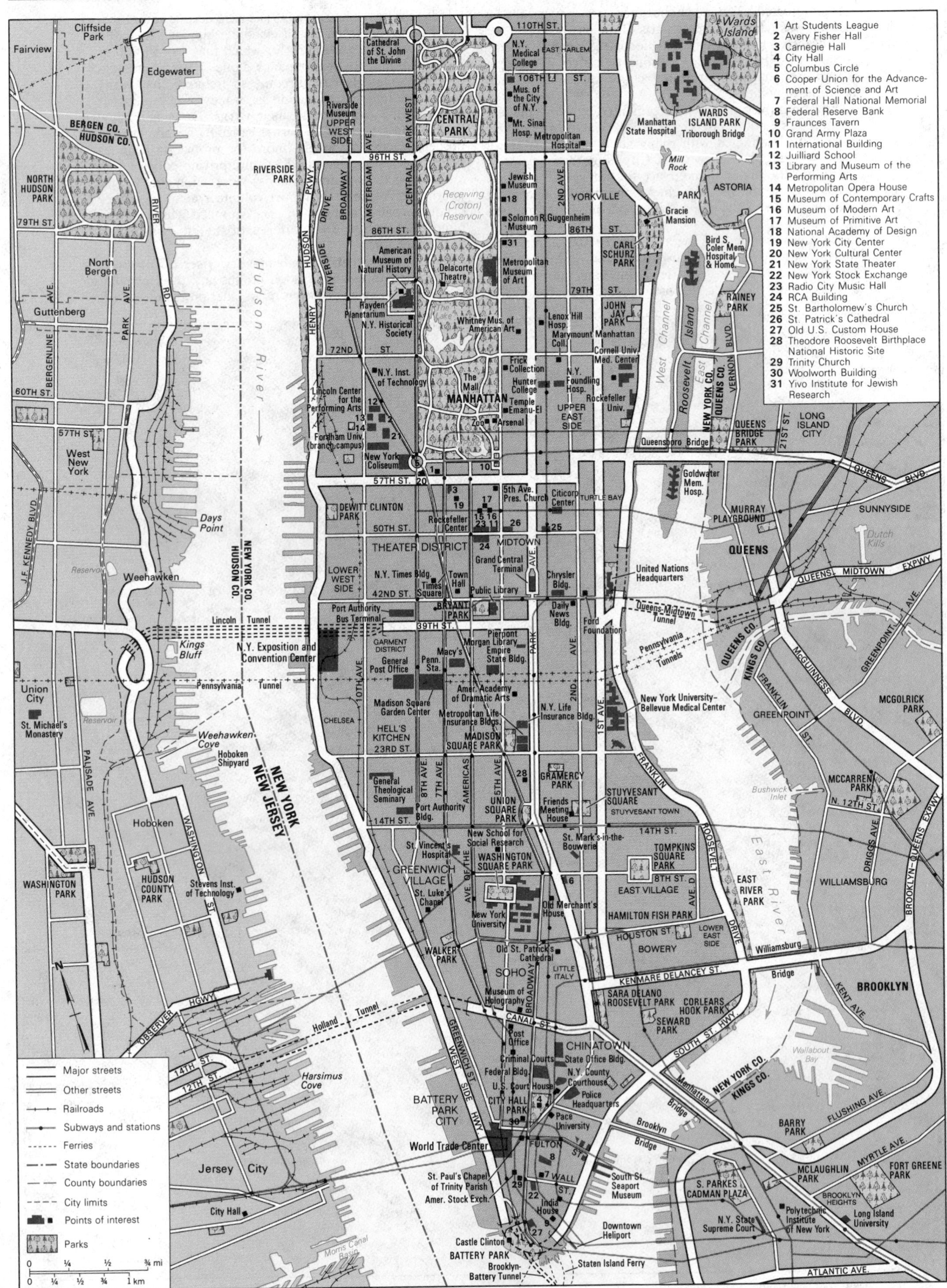
1 Art Students League
2 Avery Fisher Hall
3 Carnegie Hall
4 City Hall
5 Columbus Circle
6 Cooper Union for the Advancement of Science and Art
7 Federal Hall National Memorial
8 Federal Reserve Bank
9 Fraunces Tavern
10 Grand Army Plaza
11 International Building
12 Juilliard School
13 Library and Museum of the Performing Arts
14 Metropolitan Opera House
15 Museum of Contemporary Crafts
16 Museum of Modern Art
17 Museum of Primitive Art
18 National Academy of Design
19 New York City Center
20 New York Cultural Center
21 New York State Theater
22 New York Stock Exchange
23 Radio City Music Hall
24 RCA Building
25 St. Bartholomew's Church
26 St. Patrick's Cathedral
27 Old U.S. Custom House
28 Theodore Roosevelt Birthplace National Historic Site
29 Trinity Church
30 Woolworth Building
31 Yivo Institute for Jewish Research
Major streets
Other streets
Railroads
Subways and stations
Ferries
State boundaries
County boundaries
City limits
Points of interest
Parks
MANHATTAN
QUEENS
BROOKLYN
Hudson River
East River
CENTRAL PARK
NEW YORK
NEW JERSEY
Jersey City
Hoboken
Weehawken
World Trade Center

Central New York City.

At the core of nearly all of the city's crises—and of its triumphs—have been the masses of impoverished migrants who sailed into its beautiful harbour or spilled out upon its mammoth bus, train, and airplane terminals, their belongings in cardboard cartons, battered suitcases, knotted sheets and pillow cases. Writer and editor E.B. White described New Yorkers as "to a large extent strangers who have pulled up stakes somewhere and come to town, seeking sanctuary or fulfillment or some greater or lesser grail." The migrants, in search of security, prosperity, and political power, set up the city's neighbourhoods—its Harlem, Little Italy, Chinatown, Greenwich Village, and scores of communities of tenements, apartment houses, and private homes. They gave the city a variety of flavours ranging from cuisine to speech.

Ethnic diversity and conflict

As far back as 1643, a Roman Catholic missionary, walking the dirt streets of the fledgling Dutch community at the southern tip of Manhattan Island, was astonished to hear 18 languages. In 1870 the census of the turbulent city—it was still limited to Manhattan—showed that of nearly 1,000,000 residents, more than 400,000 were foreign-born. In 1920, with the population above 5,600,000, the foreign-born totalled almost 2,000,000 and the number of blacks more than 150,000.

With the sharp curtailment of immigration by federal laws passed in 1921 and 1924, the city entered a period of increasing stability, in spite of the violence of Prohibition, political scandals, the Depression, and World War II. Many of the immigrants and their children prospered and moved from the slums to middle- or upper-class neighbourhoods. The city was safe enough that New Yorkers during the 1920s, 1930s, and 1940s often slept in the parks or on the beaches on stifling summer nights. In the slums, residents kept their doors open for ventilation, and, in many sections of the city, residents did not lock their doors.

Beginning in the 1950s, hundreds of thousands of new migrants arrived, and the combined population of blacks and Puerto Ricans more than doubled. Like the migrant waves before them—the Germans and Irish in the 19th century and the Italians and Jews from eastern Europe in the early 20th century—the arrival of these new minorities was followed by the usual disruptions.

Continuities in civic life. That the city has survived more than a century of slums, riots, epidemics, crime waves, and corruption, touched off by the many instabilities resulting from waves of immigration, plus vicious commercial competition, is a tribute to its adaptability, basic democracy, and the priority given to the art of making a living—a mixture that has produced demagogues and knaves as easily as it has idealists and statesmen. In *Beyond the Melting Pot,* sociologists Nathan Glazer and Daniel Patrick Moynihan observed that "New York became the first great city in history to be ruled by men of the people, not as an isolated phenomenon of the Gracchi or Commune, but as a persisting, established pattern." Looking upon the same municipal turmoil, however, the critic Lewis Mumford asserted that "purposeless materialism became the essential principle of the city's life."

THE BOROUGHS

Stereotypes and realities of the boroughs

Tourists and even most New Yorkers, when they speak of "the city," mean Manhattan. The boroughs of Brooklyn, Queens, the Bronx, and Staten Island—each of them a separate county—remain the subject of jokes among New Yorkers as well as strangers. Brooklyn continues to be taunted with the title of the Thomas Wolfe story *Only the Dead Know Brooklyn.* Queens is known as "the borough of cemeteries." The Bronx is constantly reminded that its greatest claim to fame may be the derisive noise popularized in the bleachers of that borough's Yankee Stadium and known as "the Bronx cheer." And Staten Island, closer to the smokestacks of New Jersey than to its political kin, is treated as outlying wilderness. Since most residents of these four boroughs work in Manhattan, the lingering feeling remains that Brooklyn, Queens, the Bronx, and Staten Island are mere "bedrooms" of Manhattan.

Manhattan actually has been surpassed in population by Brooklyn and Queens. Three of these boroughs—Brooklyn, Queens, and the Bronx—would rank among the nation's major cities if they were not a part of New York City. Scores of thousands of residents of the other boroughs rarely visit Manhattan and know much less about the heart of their city than do the most casual of tourists. Legislators from these boroughs complain endlessly that they are neglected by the city government in favour of Manhattan.

Only when seen in its entirety can the waterborne character of the city be fully appreciated. The Bronx, before 1895 a part of suburban Westchester County, is the only one of the boroughs that is part of the mainland of the United States, and even that borough is bounded on south, east, and west by water. The other boroughs are either islands or parts of an island. The city's only land boundaries are Westchester County on the north and Nassau County on Long Island to the east. Other than that, it is hemmed in by Long Island Sound, the Atlantic Ocean, the Hudson River, and assorted bays, straits, and rivulets that give the city a waterfront of 578 miles (930 kilometres) for shipping and recreation.

Manhattan. The magnet for tourists, the symbol of the city, Manhattan is probably the most deceptive of the boroughs to outsiders, who generally limit themselves to quick looks at the Theater District around Times Square (moving gingerly past the seediness of 42nd Street west of Broadway), the shopping promenade of Fifth Avenue, the munificence of the temples of finance on and near Wall Street, the eccentricities of bohemian life in the East Village and Soho, the exotica of Chinatown, or the special flavours of Little Italy and Harlem. At first glance, Manhattan is only the city of skyscrapers, glaring lights, and frenzied pace, an island of the strange, the neurotic, and the avant-garde. Crammed into its 23 square miles (57 square kilometres) are more than 1,400,000 residents. Its waterfront, formed by the Harlem, East, and Hudson rivers, is 43 miles (69 kilometres) in length, but only scattered groups of slum children swim in the pollution; and the few fishermen find only scanty catches.

To the residents of the island, each section is a hometown. Those who live in the West 70s, 80s, and 90s—the Upper West Side, though streets run above 200 at the northern tip—know their neighbourhoods as a cosmopolitan mixture of languages, occupations, and income levels. It is the caldron in which much of the liberal experimentation in the Democratic Party is prepared, and some say it is the origin of much of the chaos of the party. On the Upper East Side, east of Central Park, is a different mixture, generally more affluent.

The Manhattan that tourists do not see

The Chelsea area of the West 20s, with its tenements, renovated brownstones, and huge cooperatives built by labour unions, has a more sedate pace than the East Village and Soho (derived from "south of Houston Street"), comprising much of the old Lower East Side and containing the city's major concentration of struggling writers and artists. Greenwich Village, the old centre of bohemian life, has become a favourite dwelling place for affluent professionals and successful authors and artists. Harlem means more than just tenements, housing projects, and black politics. It means a vibrant street life ranging from sports to stoop seminars, and it is spiced with luxury apartment houses with doormen, inhabited almost entirely by blacks. Yorkville, in the East 80s, retains pockets of Czech, Hungarian, and German cultures in a clash of old tenements and towering luxury apartment houses. The neighbourhood taverns of the Irish proliferate through Inwood at the northernmost part of the island, where the borough of Manhattan spills over the Harlem River to encompass an enclave of a few square blocks within mainland Bronx. In Inwood lie Manhattan's few remaining forested acres, and on open recreation areas the Irish keep alive their national sports of hurling and Gaelic football—much as courts are maintained for bocciball games in Little Italy many miles to the south. On Morningside Heights around Columbia University, the civilities of the academic world overlook the bleak stretches of Harlem below and to the east and north.

Even fantastic Lower Manhattan, from the Battery, with its ferry slips at the island's tip, to City Hall, has begun

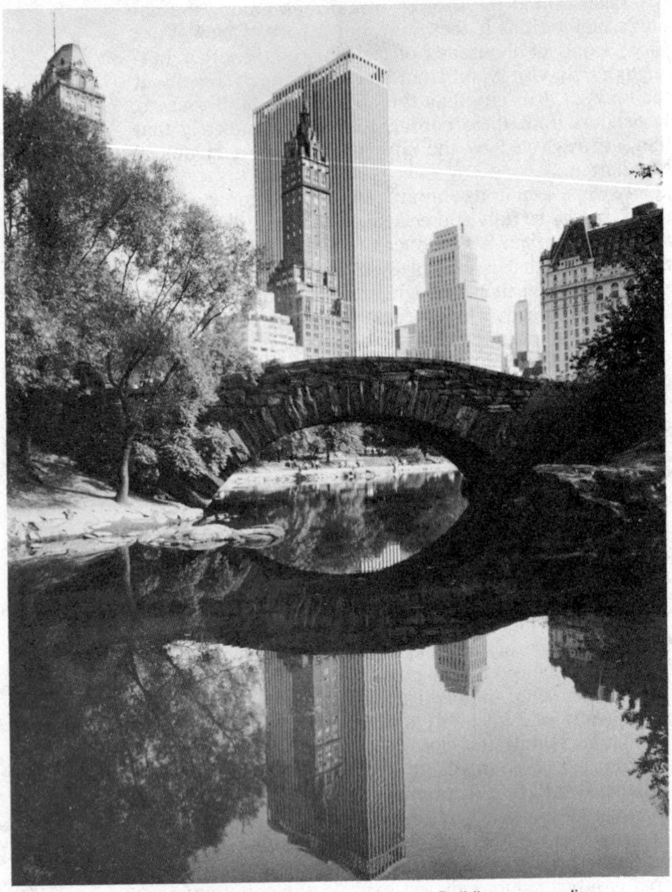

Luxury hotels and the General Motors Building surrounding the lower end of Manhattan's Central Park.
Peter Gridley—FPG

taking on the atmosphere of a neighbourhood. Apartment houses have gone up in the vicinity of City Hall, and the overwhelming skyscraper jungle around Wall Street, which is home to hundreds of financial and insurance institutions and some of the nation's largest banks, exerts international power.

Brooklyn. The most populous of the city's boroughs and, next to Manhattan, the best known is Brooklyn, coterminous with Kings County. With adjacent Queens, it comprises the western end of Long Island. Bounded by the East River, Queens, the Atlantic Ocean, and Lower and Upper New York bays, it covers 73 square miles and has about 200 miles of waterfront, including that subway-Riviera amusement park known as Coney Island.

Brooklyn retains much of the identity that it developed as a separate city. Its downtown area has a bustling shopping district and office buildings. Many factories, some of them quite large, are scattered along its waterfront, and the discontinued Brooklyn Navy Yard, now the New York Naval Shipyard, where many of the nation's greatest warships were built and berthed, has been turned to industry in which the poor are being trained. Though Brooklyn has many private homes, the majority of Brooklynites live in apartment houses, tenements, or mammoth housing projects. The contrast of neighbourhoods in Brooklyn is, in its special way, as dramatic as those of Manhattan, ranging from the choice residential section of Brooklyn Heights, with its magnificent view of New York's harbour and the Manhattan skyline, to the dreadful slum of Brownsville, with many blocks of burned-out or abandoned buildings, dreary tenements, boarded-up stores, and low-income housing projects.

Contrasting life-styles of Brooklyn

The borough has one of the largest black communities in the world, Bedford-Stuyvesant, with its residents cramped in a mixture of attractive brownstones, towering housing projects, and slums. There are, however, unmistakable signs that a stable neighbourhood is being built, and the area elected the first black U.S. congresswomen. Just as special in character are Borough Park, with an Orthodox Jewish community and storefront synagogues; Bensonhurst, with Italians who cling to their private homes with gardens to the rear; and Crown Heights, in which black and Jewish residents are working to stem decline.

Queens. With its 110 square miles, Queens has become the bastion of the city's middle class, a catch basin for those who have fled deteriorating sections of Brooklyn, Manhattan, or the Bronx. It is bounded by Long Island Sound, Nassau County, the Atlantic Ocean, Brooklyn, and the East River and contains the beautiful beaches of the Gateway National Recreation Area and the boating facilities along the sound. During the 1970s the population of Queens dropped for the first time in several decades, but its rate of decline was less than that of the city as a whole. It has drawn new department stores and shopping centres and is the site of Shea Stadium, home of the baseball Mets and the football Jets. Although the boom has brought with it many large apartment houses and tax-eating sewers, schools, and subways, the majority of its residents live in private homes. Thousands of these homes are owned by blacks, a situation uncommon in the rest of the city.

The borough of old neighbourhoods

In Queens people usually think of themselves as belonging first to their neighbourhood, only then to the borough, and, finally, to the city. Continuity has become important in Queens. In the Irish area of Woodside it is not uncommon for parents and children to have been married in the same church. Astoria has a public school attended by children born in more than 20 countries, as well as the largest Greek community outside Greece. In Corona couples with grandchildren are living in homes built by their Italian forebears. It is no accident that it is in Queens that the homeowners, white and black, have made the fiercest fight against low-income housing projects and high-rise apartment houses. The borough has some pockets of poverty but no slum in the usual big-city sense.

The Bronx. With 41 square miles, the Bronx is bounded by Westchester County, Long Island Sound, and the East, Harlem, and Hudson rivers. This borough, coextensive with Bronx County, has become the scene of one of the most dramatic urban struggles in the nation. The major effort has been to restrain the spread of slums, with their abandoned and burned-out buildings, closed-down stores, and spreading crime. The areas known as South Bronx and Hunt's Point are infested with drug addicts and pushers who lurk in abandoned buildings, the windows of which have been covered with metal and the doors of which are bricked up.

In these same areas and in Morrisania to the north, a political battle has been under way between the blacks and the Puerto Ricans. As the population of Puerto Ricans has increased, they have acquired greater political control, with disputes centring frequently in the antipoverty agencies funded with government money. The first Puerto Rican borough president in the city's history was elected in the Bronx and later became a U.S. congressman. Puerto Ricans from this borough have also been elected to the state legislature. While slums have spread steadily to the north in the borough, undermining even the once affluent Grand Concourse, middle-income housing has been built in an effort to halt the flight from run-down areas out of the city.

Staten Island. Staten Island, a corruption of the original Dutch name, Staaten Landt, was called Richmond Borough until 1975. The borough is coextensive with Richmond County and is separated from the rest of the city by New York Bay and from New Jersey by narrow straits. Much of its shore lies along the Atlantic Ocean. It is the least densely populated of the city's boroughs and has an area of 56 square miles. Much of its acreage remains open, almost rural country, with relatively few apartment houses.

The rural city: Staten Island

The major struggle on this island has been between real estate operators who want to realize the largest possible profit and civic groups who want to avoid the congestion that has accompanied growth in the other boroughs. Meanwhile, large tracts of woodland and meadow have vanished to become housing tracts for refugees from Brooklyn, Manhattan, and the Bronx. In the 1970s the population of Staten Island grew by almost 20 percent; it was the only borough in the city to show an increase. This growth has increased the strain on the famous Staten Island Ferry, which runs between the island and Manhattan. The ferry long has been a favourite ride of tourists and New Yorkers, since it passes the Statue of Liberty and affords a fine view of the Lower Manhattan skyline.

THE PEOPLE

There is strong evidence to support the view that, since the turn of the 20th century, demography more than geography has been the key to the many changes in New York City. Except for land added by fill, the boundaries of the city and of its five boroughs have remained the same as they were in 1898; yet, over the intervening period the city has been swept by political, social, and economic upheavals, demographic in origin, that in retrospect seem nothing short of revolutionary. New York City gave birth to much of the urban crossbreeding of capitalism and Socialism that, during the administrations of Pres. Franklin D. Roosevelt, came to be known as the New Deal. The impact of demography, more than the penal code or police activity, has determined the amount and kinds of crime in the city. Demography, more than educational theory or the quality of teachers, has been responsible for the serious dislocations in public education in New York City—and for the many experiments in the field.

Demography has always been, in fact, a critical factor in shaping the city. First, New York was a Dutch city, then English, then Irish, then Irish–Italian–Jewish, then Jewish–Italian, then Jewish–Italian–black. Most recently—assuming that most Puerto Ricans classify themselves as white—it has become white–black. As each ethnic or religious group has attained power and then moved away and lost power to the succeeding wave of immigrants and migrants, the life-style of the city has undergone transformation. But, no matter how often this has happened, New Yorkers, with short memories of their city's history, have behaved as though each demographic quake was unprecedented. Those who are threatened revile the newcomers and are, in turn, denounced as "the establishment." Physical force, political pressure, and economic muscle are all used by both sides in the periodic demographic struggles.

Historic animosity toward the immigrant

The past illustrates how attitudes change as demographic tides turn. The city's Jews, it appears, have come to be highly regarded for their ambition, industry, and cleanliness, and their contributions to the city's business and culture are enormous. Many outsiders think of the city—mistakenly—as mainly Jewish, but Jews comprise less than one-sixth of the city's population. Yet, in 1895 an article in *The New York Times,* appraising the first large waves of Jewish immigration from eastern Europe to the Lower East Side of Manhattan, said, "Cleanliness is an unknown quality to these people. They cannot be lifted to a higher plane because they do not want to be." Attacks on the Irish a few decades earlier and on the Italians shortly after the turn of the century were just as savage. As late as the 1920s, opponents of private bathrooms in tenements argued that tenement dwellers would "only put coal in the bathtub." Descendants of these immigrants have made similar comments about blacks and Puerto Ricans, who have been stamped as uniformly filthy, lazy, and criminal—a wholesale menace to society.

As in earlier decades there is an element of truth in these charges. The latest waves of immigrants and migrants do live in slums, amid prostitution and crime. They are aggressive in trying to move up in society. They become a threat as they reach for power. A major difference, however, is that the tensions between white and black that exist in New York City are national, if not international, in scope as well. At the same time, journalistic standards have risen, and sharper distinctions are drawn between fact and prejudice.

A study of census figures by the City Planning Commission showed that during the 1970s, when about 1,200,000 more people moved out of the city than into it, the outmigration was two-and-one-half times the figure for 1960–70. Despite this exodus, both the black and Hispanic populations rose. Another significant development traced by the commission showed that during the 1970s thousands of Puerto Rican families moved out of poverty areas into better neighbourhoods. Nevertheless, there were still areas with few Puerto Rican or black residents; and from 1960 to 1980, a period in which courts were handing down decisions for desegregation, ghetto areas in New York City expanded to two and three times their previous size.

The movements of the ethnic groups within the city have shown a strong hostility toward integration by whites. Any integration that does occur is short-term and takes place in areas into which blacks are moving and from which whites are fleeing. Whites do not move into black neighbourhoods, though there are some black neighbourhoods that are more prosperous than some white ones. Most whites living in black areas are elderly, poor, and unable to leave.

The demographic changes, however, are more than just colour. The median age of the black and Hispanic populations is about 10 years lower than that of whites, although the median age for Hispanics is even lower (especially for women) than that of blacks.

The age figures are particularly significant, for crimes of violence in all ethnic groups are most prevalent among the young. So is social unrest. The lower age—combined with the larger families among blacks and Puerto Ricans—also places an enormous strain on the public schools because the blacks and Puerto Ricans, for reasons that, it is alleged, range from fatherless homes to poverty, find it difficult to keep up with non-Puerto Rican whites.

Though the enormity of demographic shifts cannot be underestimated, they are not unprecedented in New York City. The population of the city in 1870 was almost 1,000,000, of whom about 400,000 were foreign-born. Considering the foreign-born plus their New York-born children, the Anglo-Saxon elements that had dominated the city for the first half of the 19th century were outnumbered. The Irish-born, numbering more than 200,000, were already the strongest political force in the city. Another 150,000 had moved from Germany, while England, the second highest homeland, had sent only about 24,400. Smaller numbers had landed from dozens of other countries. The black population of the city at that time was slightly more than 13,000.

Antagonisms between ethnic groups

The anti-Catholic feeling against the Irish in the city at that time was as bitter in other parts of the nation, often worse. Just as there is animosity in the city now between blacks and Puerto Ricans, so the antipathy between Germans and Irish was so strong that it erupted into bloody clashes. The middle class was moving as fast as it could from the areas being settled by the Irish, the suburbs then being Brooklyn, Queens, the Bronx, and Staten Island—and a great deal of open land remained in Manhattan. A book of the period noted that "Strangers coming to New York are struck with the fact that there are but two classes in the city—the poor and the rich."

Yet, it would be a mistake to assume that all immigrant—or migrant—peoples in New York City have faced equal difficulties. The Germans of the 19th century encountered much less trouble than the Irish. One reason was that most of them were Protestant, the religion of the group entrenched in power. The Italians, though of the same religion as the Irish, often built their own churches rather than go to those attended by Irish Roman Catholics, partly because they wanted to be able to go to confession to a priest who knew their language. Difference of religion was an important reason for hostility toward Jewish immigrants.

There is a general assumption that blacks and Puerto Ricans in New York City are treated more harshly than earlier immigrants. There is undoubtedly a deep intensity to the anti-black feeling and, by many blacks, to the anti-white feeling. Yet, in many respects, blacks and Puerto Ricans are better off than all earlier immigrants and migrants. None of their predecessors in the frightening city received welfare. During the first two decades of this century immigrants often froze or starved, living in cellars or even in the streets. There was a time when tuberculosis became known as Jews' disease. In the 1920s and 1930s it was common in immigrant areas to see the possessions of these newcomers on the street for failure to pay one month's rent on time. Immigrants were expected to learn English or suffer. They were tormented and taunted for their different customs or their accents.

The city has learned—or been forced to learn—to handle immigrants and migrants with more consideration. Signs in such public buildings as police stations are often in Spanish as well as in English, and many police officers study Spanish. In one hospital near Chinatown, signs in the corridor are in Chinese as well as English, an indication of another demographic trend in the city.

In trying to understand New York, the city he had written about for more than 40 years, Meyer Berger, in his book *New York,* wrote "The place wasn't always concrete and it wasn't always crowded. It just grew faster than any other city in history." The hordes of strangers were what made it grow so fast.

THE ECONOMY

Contrary to the impression created by its soaring buildings, transportation crushes, and mass outpourings from office buildings, the economic life of New York City rests not on a few vast corporations but on a multitude of small businesses and manufacturing establishments. This diversity in the world's financial capital gives the city the flexibility and strength to withstand recession or depression with less suffering than Detroit, for instance, with its dependence on huge automobile plants, or southern California, supported so heavily by government contracts in the aerospace and defense industries.

Components of the economy. Endless beehives of small factories populate the old loft buildings of Lower, or downtown, Manhattan, lining the narrow cobblestoned streets built for horse and wagon in the long stretch of the island below glittering Midtown. In many glistening skyscrapers are thousands of small offices staffed by only a few persons. The world knows of the city's fabulous garment centre, but it is in little factories or storefronts of Brooklyn, Queens, and the Bronx or in ancient loft buildings of the Lower East Side that much of the subcontracting work is turned out for the kingpins in mid-Manhattan.

White-collar workers, more than three-fourths of whom are in nonmanufacturing jobs, make up the vast majority of the employment rolls. Of those in nonmanufacturing, about half are in service businesses or in wholesale or retail trade; the remainder work mainly in finance, insurance, and real estate and in transport and public utilities. The government is also a major employer.

Though small business and manufacturing make up the bulk of the city's employment, its biggest economic growth is in banking. The glass-and-steel skyscraper headquarters of the mammoth banks are most conspicuous, but modest street-corner banks have sprung up all over the city.

With the headquarters of the nation's television and radio networks, the city is the heart of the mass media. Printing and publishing, despite the death of some newspapers in the city, continues to grow. The headquarters of most of the nation's major publishing houses and advertising agencies are also clustered in the Midtown area. Increasing computerization has made the city's white-collar workers more than ever the mainstay of employment.

New York's major industry is, as it has been for many years, apparel. Although many clothing manufacturers have moved to the South, this field still employs a large number of people.

Crisis in economic activity. Although the departure of a corporation headquarters for the suburbs of New Jersey, Connecticut, or Westchester County attracts a great deal of attention, losses have been greater in manufacturing. The decline in manufacturing has been caused more by automation and mergers than by exodus from the city. City officials are particularly concerned about this drop, since it is in this sector of the economy that the relatively unskilled workers, especially among the ethnic minorities, can get jobs or be trained for them.

One of the basic problems the city faces in its struggle to keep manufacturing companies is how to find space in which they can expand without excessive cost increases.

Park Avenue South, looking north to Grand Central Terminal and the Pan Am Building.

Jordan Wilson—Pix

In manufacturing, city rents often account for 20 percent or more of the cost. Thus, some companies find it more expedient to leave the city entirely than to pay the increased rent that expanded quarters in the city would add to the cost of operation. A curious by-product of this exodus has been the conversion of empty lofts into expensive apartments.

To induce expanding manufacturing companies to remain, the city has been acquiring large areas of blighted or idle land for industrial parks in outlying parts of Brooklyn, the Bronx, Queens, and Staten Island. The city can offer this land to manufacturers at a rental that is better than they could obtain from private owners, often with an option to buy. The success of this program has kept more jobs in the city and has brought into the treasury tax money that was lost in earlier exoduses of business.

Declining port activities

Shipping, which for generations was one of the city's most flourishing industries, has been declining. Considerable shipping has shifted to the New Jersey side of the harbour, where modern facilities for containerization have made the loading and unloading of ships less costly. Wildcat strikes and waterfront crime have prompted other shippers to use ports a considerable distance from the city. Port facilities have become inefficient from disuse. In an effort to increase freight shipping to and from the city, plans have been worked out to resuscitate the huge terminals along the Brooklyn waterfront with a complex of warehouse and railroad facilities. Transoceanic luxury liners, once so common in the city's port, have decreased considerably, outdated by international air travel. After it had been conceded that nothing could save the once-famous docks along the Hudson known as Hell's Kitchen, renovation of the area was initiated in 1980 when construction began on the New York Exposition and Convention Center, a glass-enclosed structure five blocks long located above the old Pennsylvania Railroad yard.

While jobs lost in shipping have been replaced, to a large extent, by gains in aviation, the city's survival depends on its ability to arrest and reverse the flight of business and industry for reasons other than technological change. One of the main reasons some corporations have left New York City is the spread of crime. Those who feel threatened are not relieved to learn that crime is growing even faster in other cities and has spread to suburbia.

Street muggings have made a substantial number of New Yorkers fearful of walking along many streets at night. The hijacking of freight-carrying trucks, particularly those going to and coming from airports, has become a matter of serious concern. Pilferage in offices has forced enormous security expenses on corporations for private guards and crime-prevention devices. Even immigrant labour is no longer a guarantee of cheap workers, for the city is highly unionized. Rising taxes to cope with soaring welfare costs have also become irksome to businessmen.

Loss of civic appeal

These rising costs have militated against such advantages as good transportation, enormous pools of skilled labour, a long tradition of organizational talents, and a city whose people are geared to deal imaginatively with projects of almost any size or complexity. As the nuisances and even dangers of living in New York have mounted, the appeal of the city for the gifted has begun to wane. In some cases, young executives have declined promotion if it means living and working in New York City. At the same time, the huge exodus of middle class and upper middle-class New Yorkers to the suburbs has increased substantially the excellent labour pool available outside the city. New York, however, continues to hold a strong attraction for many young adults, particularly those interested in the arts.

Another development that some see as a threat to the city's economic health is the enormous advance in communications that may make highly centralized business unnecessary, perhaps inefficient. The New York Stock Exchange, facing special taxes, has considered moving to New Jersey from Wall Street, where it was founded in 1792 when two dozen traders, gathered under a buttonwood tree, made a pact setting forth rules for trade in securities.

While statistics on economics and crime are used to argue that the city is or is not growing, there is no question that fear is contagious and breeds in businessmen and employees the thought that they ought to leave the city. To combat this psychology, in 1971 a group of business, industrial, financial, and civic leaders in the city formed the Association for a Better New York with the slogan "Where the corporate action is." Their campaign stressed that new skyscrapers were being built, that office rents in the city were competitive with those of the suburbs and other major cities, and that new businesses were moving into the city from points as far away as California. Regardless of the future, however, there is no doubt that the city is still struggling with one of the worst of its many crises.

ADMINISTRATIVE AND SOCIAL CONDITIONS

New York City, with real estate assessed at several tens of billions of dollars, spends more on its residents than any other city in the United States—more, in fact, than any state. From birth to death New Yorkers are encased in billions of dollars worth of city services, taking them so much for granted that only when the services falter are the people aware of them. One of the fascinating oddities of New York life is the strong strain of Socialism in the most capitalistic of cities. The city's services are burdened not only by size but also by the complexities of the metropolis. Any one of the city's major functions—welfare, housing, sanitation, health, protection against crime or fire, recreation, water, roads, transportation—is in itself a mammoth operation. Even the air that is breathed involves an annual city expenditure of several million dollars in pollution tests and prevention.

Politics. "You can't fight city hall." This is said out of the side of the mouth by New Yorkers or with a fatalistic shrug or both, or else they say, "Go fight city hall," with a mixture of resignation and anger. These clichés, trademarks of New York City's political life for generations, are not entirely true, and probably they never have been—certainly not during the 20th century. What New Yorkers mean when they make these observations is that the gap between government and the people is greater than it should be or that government is not as responsive as it should be. What this boils down to is that New Yorkers have a strong feeling that they have a right at least to air their complaints before their local government, if not to get action in their favour.

Backgrounds of civic politics. There have been periods in the city's history—particularly in the 20th century—when the avenues to power were clogged or changing so rapidly that a time lag developed during which the public felt particularly frustrated while it groped for openings. Many New Yorkers think that this is the situation today, whereas others believe that the government is more responsive than ever. The sense of frustration has happened in the past as much when reform groups established political organizations as when the traditional political "machines" tossed out the reformers. Thus, during the latter part of the 19th century, when the Tammany scandal under the political chief known as Boss Croker became so outrageous that voters elected reformers, one term of high principled reform proved so irritating to the voters that in the very next campaign the old-line politicians, running their candidates on a slogan of "To hell with reform," regained control. On the other hand, Fiorello H. La Guardia, during the 1930s, and John Lindsay in the 1960s, although making repeated attacks on "clubhouse politics," were elected precisely because clubhouse politics had become lethargic. Once in office, they proceeded to win reelection by using many of the methods that had made political machines successful in the first place. Their secret was to find ways to help the people "fight city hall"—or at least think they were fighting.

Machines and reformers in city hall

Charters of New York City government over the years have often been less important than the manner in which the government, which they established, actually functioned. This often depended on individuals. During many years the organizational talent and style of a political boss have been dominant, for evil or good. The nefarious Boss Tweed used power to corrupt in the post-Civil War era, but Boss Charles Francis Murphy, during the early decades of the 20th century, had the vision to pick Alfred E. Smith from the midst of ward politics and back him for governor. By 1928 Smith had risen to become the Democratic presidential candidate.

Sometimes it has been the personality and ability of the mayor that made democracy stumble or work in the highly complex and fluid society that is New York City. Mayor James "Gentleman Jimmy" Walker, probably as popular as any mayor the city ever had, was forced to resign under fire in the early 1930s because he was too tolerant of the dishonesty of political cronies. La Guardia, later in the 1930s, was not only the mayor but the political ruler as well.

No matter whether it is a political boss or an elected mayor who rules, those New Yorkers who care make the necessary adjustment in learning how to fight or use city hall, for New Yorkers are never allowed to forget, in their politically turbulent city, that as long as they can vote they have a voice in city hall—if they remember that in organization there is strength. On this fact, bosses and mayors never disagree. This was the essence of the only book written by Edward J. Flynn, who rose from district leader in the Bronx, to borough leader, and finally to close adviser to Pres. Franklin D. Roosevelt and Democratic national chairman. In explaining why he wrote *You're the Boss,* Flynn said,

> I am a practical politician. I know the facts of political life. I know that political machines, far from being anachronisms, are as modern as the combustion engine and as indispensable.... I know that wherever the majority of voters work actively inside a political machine, you have a machine that represents the voters. It is as simple as that.

Volunteers for Lindsay, effectively organized despite operating out of storefront headquarters in 1965 and 1969, demonstrated this fact just as clearly as the Tammany block captains did during the 1920s.

Party organization and roles. Two facts are basic in the city's political life and its government: it is predominantly Democratic, and it is strongly independent. Many voters are also accounted for by the Liberal Party, founded in the 1930s; its leadership and adherents tend to represent an even stronger liberal position than does the Democratic Party. Although more often than not it has lent support to Democratic candidates for city, state, or national office, it has backed liberal Republicans or has fielded a candidate of its own. Since the mid-1960s the statewide Conservative Party also has made inroads into registrations, tending to pick up support from normally Republican voters or from ethnic white communities concerned with rising crime, taxes, and welfare rolls.

The Liberal and Conservative parties

The independent vote in New York City, with the ceaseless internal bickering that it generates in reform Democratic clubs, has had state and national repercussions. It has weakened the Democratic Party not only in the city but also in the state and nation. No longer do the Democrats, by piling up huge majorities in the city, guarantee the election of Democratic governors and U.S. senators. Republicans have held the state governorship and split the Senate seats with the Conservatives, and these men probably owed their election to the Democratic infighting in New York City.

Infighting and outcries. Ironically, factionalism in New York City was fomented by the biggest Democratic vote getter in history, Franklin D. Roosevelt. When he sought the nomination for his first presidential term, in 1932, Tammany Hall fought him bitterly, aiding the Democratic machines in the other boroughs, except Flynn's Bronx organization.

Once elected, Roosevelt decided to destroy Tammany's power. He supported the formation in the city of the American Labor Party, which drew largely upon unions. When it became apparent that it was being manipulated by Communist-oriented politicians, it was split, and the anti-Communist group that formed the Liberal Party significantly weakened Tammany. This condition stirred up other dissidents in the party, and the discipline was shattered. When Robert F. Kennedy was elected U.S. senator from New York in 1964, many Democrats believed that he would unify the party in the city, but his assassination in 1968 was followed by even greater factionalism.

Despite the splits in the party, the Democratic organization in the city has an enormous potentiality because, as always, it has a virtual monopoly on the poor. The organization that once built its strength on Irish, then Italian, then Jewish immigrants now has almost exclusive power among blacks and Puerto Ricans and has sponsored the only members of these groups to be elected to office.

Political power of ethnic communities and the poor

One reason for this success in the slums is that the Democratic Party has always believed strongly in the "balanced" ticket—that is, a ticket on which racial or religious blocs are represented. This balance has been attacked by many as a form of demagoguery, whereas to others it is democracy at work, a way of showing that the Democratic Party believes in helping everyone have a foot in the door of City Hall—or of the governor's mansion in Albany.

Not since mobs of Irish immigrants were riled up in the 19th century to descend on City Hall have New Yorkers become so persistent and resourceful in forcing officials to listen to their complaints. By the early 1970s the poor—this time blacks and Puerto Ricans—were trying once more to push their way into office. They were developing their own leaders, some more opportunistic and ruthless than others, and they had the perfect medium of the poor—television, which does not require literacy. The poor and their leaders have learned that television likes demonstrations, the noisier the better.

The rest of the city has learned that the way to win the attention of the mayor and other officials is to copy the television antics of the poor. They, too, picket, hold sit-ins, and shout in angry chorus at hearings on bills and appropriations. Unions, tenant groups, parent–teacher associations, civic organizations, and civil-rights disputants—all come equipped with signs, bullhorns, and public-relations panoply.

Government. The structure of the city government under such constant pressure has three major components: the mayor, the Board of Estimate, and the City Council. Elected for four years, the mayor appoints the deputy mayors and agency heads and holds considerable additional patronage; he also prepares the budget. Thus, under the city charter, his power is considerable. Whether he is in fact powerful has varied with the individual mayor and

Board of Estimate, City Council, and the mayor

Norman McGrath

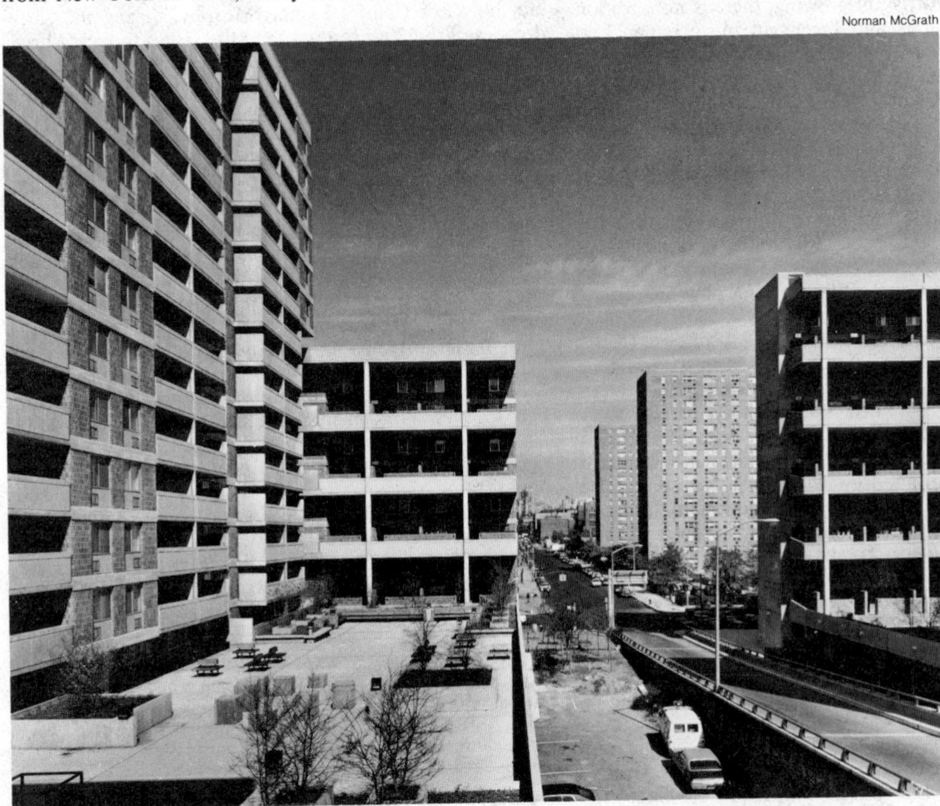

The Riverbend housing development, in Harlem.

the other political figures. In general, beginning with La Guardia, the mayors have been stronger than party leaders and usually have led their own party.

The City Council is the main legislative body. It introduces and passes all laws and can override a mayoral veto by a two-thirds vote. It is made up of the president of the council, elected on a citywide basis, and 43 council members, elected for four years. Of these, 33 are elected from districts within the boroughs, two at large (and of different parties) from each borough.

The Board of Estimate, the main power of which is to act on the budget prepared by the mayor, is made up of the mayor, the council president, the comptroller, and the five borough presidents. The mayor, comptroller, and council president each have two votes on the board and can thus out-vote the five borough presidents combined.

Friction between city and borough leadership

The real struggle for power by the borough presidents lies in the administration of the city government. Lindsay, who repeatedly voiced support for "community control," set up an array of "superagencies," the heads of which he appointed to run the city. These agencies operated in the fields of human resources, environmental protection, health and services, finance, housing and development, economic development, municipal services, and parks and recreation. (Some of these agencies were later dismantled by Mayor Abraham Beame, who succeeded Lindsay.) In addition, a quasi-public organization called Health and Hospitals Corporation was established, and plans were outlined by borough presidents and the governor to decentralize authority in the city by the establishment of neighbourhood councils and increased power for the borough presidents. All of this stems from the old battle cry of New Yorkers, "Go fight city hall."

The welfare rolls. Although the city has had to cut social services, welfare costs have remained a heavy burden, forcing cutbacks in other services. One of every six New Yorkers receives some form of public assistance. Though the federal government has paid about 40 percent of the welfare costs and the state has assumed 30 percent, the remaining 30 percent paid by the city has created such a strain that, with its tax base being undermined by the departure of middle-class wage earners for the suburbs, the city has imposed an income tax on commuters who work in the city

The great majority of people on the welfare rolls are under 21 years of age. Only a small percentage of those on the rolls are considered employable. The enormous welfare costs have created a widespread feeling among New Yorkers that there is considerable fraud in the area, caused by laxity in administration. The city's Human Resources Administration, which supervises welfare through its Department of Social Services, concedes that the system used to guard against the clients receiving duplicate checks is not effective.

When it was revealed in 1971 that several thousand welfare families had been placed in hotels, often at costs exceeding $1,000 a month, the condition illustrated more than laxity by city officials. It dramatized the dire shortage of apartments for the poor at a time when so many were on welfare. Lower middle-class areas, when evacuated by whites, soon became dreadful slums inhabited by blacks and Puerto Ricans. Apartments and often entire tenements were burned out, often by drug addicts. As a better solution than welfare hotels, the city has sought to increase construction of low-income housing. New York is already far ahead of other cities in these projects, which are built almost entirely with federal funds. The apartments are mainly for the working poor, but the percentage of project residents receiving welfare has been rising steadily since the early 1960s.

Public housing

Education. Public education in New York is a vivid example of the desire for community power in the city. Under a state law of 1969 the city's school system was apportioned into 31 school districts, each with an elected board. The powers of these local boards include administrative duties in elementary and junior–intermediate schools, selection of the community superintendent, assignment of teachers, and some aspects of school construction and repair. The chancellor, the chief executive of the school system, is chosen by the citywide Board of Education, the members of which are appointed by the mayor.

The educational system includes schools for the handicapped and convalescent, trade schools, day schools for the socially maladjusted, and experimental programs with longer school days and individual instruction. Special programs reach back into the ninth grade to prepare underprivileged students for college. Thousands of pupils learn English as a second language. For high school students who want to specialize, there are the High School of Art and Design, the High School of Music and Art, the High School of Fashion Industries, the School of the Performing Arts, the New York School of Printing, and Park West High School, for cooking and the maritime trades.

The city university system

New York is the only city in the United States with a large public-university system. The higher education program has become increasingly important since the introduction of "open admission" in 1970, which allows any high school graduate into either a senior or a community college, depending on grades. Before open admission the standards for entrance into senior colleges were very high. The program was adopted to enable more blacks and Puerto Ricans to attend city colleges.

The private universities offer, in addition to the usual courses, special areas of study. Columbia University, for instance, offers Russian studies and has a school of journalism; Fordham University offers medieval studies; and New York University has courses in art scholarship. The Juilliard School is world-renowned for music, theatre, and dance, and the Rockefeller University is renowned for biomedical science.

Sanitation and water supply. For generations New York has been known as a dirty city. This is the result of ever-present slums and of the elative indifference of New Yorkers. Residents, however, have become aroused by concern about environmental pollution and have become more demanding. But it is still a dirty city in spite of a large force that is assigned to sanitation—street cleaning, refuse collection, and waste disposal. To some extent, the city is handicapped by lack of funds.

A prime example of the city's acceptance of a service until something goes wrong is its water system, which is piped in as far as 300 miles from many parts of the state. At times the various city agencies, each in its desire to perform an efficient service, clash. One agency, for example, decided to introduce electricity for heating in public housing as being cheaper and cleaner at the same time that another agency was trying to hold down electric consumption because of power shortages.

Security. One of the most glaring examples of how service in the city is curtailed by the fiscal crisis is the police department. At a time when the most agonizing problem to most New Yorkers is street crime, the police department has been forced to allow its force to diminish by not replacing the men who retire or those who leave.

The statistic of most concern has been that of crimes against the person. The city ranks high among the nation's top 10 most populous cities in major crimes. To cope with street crime, the department set up special units and task forces and decided virtually to ignore gambling offenses, an area in which police corruption has been the cause of many scandals over the years. New Yorkers are notoriously indifferent to laws against gambling, and there is strong pressure for legalized gambling in the wake of legalized lotteries and off-track betting. The police have been hampered further by their diversion to cope with all sorts of civic demonstrations.

The city's fire department, highly respected for its ability, must know how to fight fires in skyscraper or subway, as well as in ancient tenement or luxury high-rise apartments. Since 1982 women have been joining the department.

Subways

Transportation. The subways, though part of a state-operated system, are still largely subsidized by the city, in addition to the revenue from the more than 3,000,000 passengers on an average day. The subways make up more than 40 percent of all mass transit in the metropolitan area. About 90 percent of the people using the subways are residents of the city. During rush hours trains often run on a one-minute headway.

Health. Through its Health and Hospitals Corporation, the city operates a number of municipal hospitals. In addition, the city has dozens of voluntary hospitals (privately operated but nonprofit) and peroprietary hospitals (private and for profit). Supplementing these medical institutions are several state hospitals and health centres. The city, because of its connection with medical colleges and hospitals and its enormous variety of cases, long has been a magnificent training ground for doctors. Among the best known of these, for interns as well as experienced doctors, are New York University–Bellevue Medical Center, New York Hospital–Cornell Medical Center, Columbia Presbyterian Medical Center, St. Luke's–Roosevelt Hospital Center, and Yeshiva–Albert Einstein and Mt. Sinai hospitals.

CULTURAL LIFE

The cultural milieu

Though many New Yorkers have come to think of the Fun City label pinned on their city as a bad joke, there may still be a great deal of truth in the nickname. For those who seek pleasure in almost any form, New York City is, as it has been for more than a century, "the place to go." Whether it is theatre, music, ballet, painting, or literature or whether it is baseball, football, basketball, track, hockey, boxing, horse racing, soccer, cricket, or rugby or whether it is live, filmed, or printed erotica—whatever the taste of man or woman in culture, the arts, sports, or sex, New York City has it in abundance. The city is the nation's greatest culture mart—and a major fleshpot.

Tied in with the culture and the arts are the middlemen—impresarios, agents, and assorted hucksters. Interlocked with and contributing to the talent pool required for these endeavours are great museums, a mammoth library system, and such world-famous schools as the Juilliard School and the Art Students League. The overall result is an industry, ranging from genius to faker, that gives the city a flavour that attracts and churns up talent from all over the world.

There is no doubt that, as a purveyor of pleasure, the city has been hurt by the widely reported crime in its streets. Tourist business, however, has been rising and has bolstered attendance at theatres, sports arenas, and concert halls. But the old New York tradition of staying up late after a show or musical event has been curtailed by fear. Restaurants close earlier. Taxis are scarce in the early morning hours. The city that was once wide awake around the clock now slinks home by 1 AM. New York City still has dozens of night spots, but the carefree atmosphere has been dampened. In some ways, however, New York City is more exciting than ever as a cultural and artistic test tube.

The performing arts. The most vivid paradox of simultaneous decline and growth is in the city's theatre. The decline of the Broadway theatre began in the late 1920s when the movies learned to talk. Since most plays of that period were mediocre or worse, they offered little competition to the "talkies." The Great Depression of the 1930s added to Broadway's woes, turning the theatres along 42nd Street into burlesque houses and then cinema palaces. World War II, with so much money to be spent, gave legitimate theatre a boost, but afterward it was hurt by television, rising production costs that could not be met by increased ticket prices, and the exodus of large chunks of the middle-class audience to the suburbs. The major theatres remaining in the Times Square area represent about one-half the number of the 1920s.

Perhaps more important, competition to the New York City theatre has sprung up in other parts of the country. What had once been fleeting summer theatres in the suburbs have taken root on a year-round basis. Regional theatres have developed in Minneapolis, Minn.; Los Angeles; Dallas; Washington, D.C.; New Haven, Conn.; and other cities. Theatres in universities have grown in number, size, and professionalism.

Continuing vitality of theatrical activity

Yet, there are indications that the legitimate theatre in New York City as a whole—not just the Times Square area—is very much alive. Off-Broadway and off-off-Broadway theatres by the scores have sprung up since the 1950s in lofts, cellars, garages, churches, and old restaurants. These new little theatres, having fewer than 300 seats, are a fertile field for experimental plays and a training ground for actors, directors, playwrights, and technicians who can no longer be absorbed by the Broadway theatre. They are particularly important for blacks and Puerto Ricans forming their own companies.

Box-office statistics tell only a part of what the theatre means to New York City. It is impossible to convert into dollars the impact of curtain time in Times Square, with well-dressed crowds spilling out of taxis, thronging across sidewalks and into narrow lobbies, dashing back and forth from theatre to tavern during intermission, chattering excitedly at the final curtain, and chasing for cabs after the last echo of applause. There is a spontaneity, sophistication, and animation to legitimate theatre that movie premieres, even at their most elaborate in Hollywood, cannot capture with spotlights and velvet ropes.

Municipal subsidies for the arts

The city, aware that the theatre means more than the money it brings in at the box office—or even at the hotels and restaurants—has taken several steps to bolster it. Several theatres opened in Times Square skyscrapers in the early 1970s because of a change in building ordinances allowing builders a bonus in floor space if they include a theatre in the structure. In addition, the city has given financial aid to theatrical work. It sponsors Shakespearean productions that for years have been shown in the parks without charge. It bought an old library that has been converted into five little theatres. The New York City Center, with its ballets and plays, has been able to maintain high standards at moderate ticket prices because the building is tax-exempt and, like the converted library, rented from the city for $1.00 a year. Despite the city's enormous financial difficulties, it spends more than $1,000,000 a year on the performing arts, including theatrical productions in the streets of ghetto areas and operas and concerts in the parks by the Metropolitan Opera and the New York Philharmonic.

The most spectacular of the city's institutions of art and culture is the Lincoln Center for the Performing Arts, the design of which has since been copied in Los Angeles and Washington, D.C. Its five buildings, built around a lagoon and fountain, are the home of the Metropolitan Opera, the New York City Opera, the New York Philharmonic, the New York City Ballet, a repertory theatre company, and a library for the arts. It has been host to theatrical, musical, and dance groups from all over the world. Like most operatic and musical organizations, the Metropolitan Opera and the New York Philharmonic operate at deficits that are met by private contributions.

Concertgoers still think that the best concert hall in the city is Carnegie Hall, which books many of the major musical organizations of the world. Town Hall, the auditorium at Hunter College, and the Brooklyn Academy of Music are in constant use by major artists and chamber groups.

The selection of motion pictures available in New York City is a major attraction. At any time movie houses in Manhattan alone are showing hundreds of films—first runs, revivals, and anything in between. It is a treasury for those who seek old or new foreign films. The city also has grown as a filmmaking centre because directors and producers have learned that using the city as a setting gives any movie dramatic impact. This development is a reminder that, before movies went to Hollywood, they were made mainly in New York City.

Libraries, museums, and galleries. New York's library system, with almost 200 branches, is one of the city's glories. As a result of the city's economy drive, the libraries are not open for as many hours as they once were, and book circulation has fallen. This decline may also reflect the impact of television on reading habits in the city. The circulation figures do not, however, represent the vast amount of research done in the main library, guarded at 42nd Street and Fifth Avenue by stone lions that are among the city's best known sights. Nor do the figures for the city's system reflect the value of special libraries such as the Pierpont Morgan Library, the Low Memorial Library at Columbia, or the collection of books and records at the Lincoln Center library.

Museums are another important aspect of the city's cultural life. There the visitor can see paintings by old or modern masters, a replica of a whale diving from the ceiling, or a display of planetary mysteries. By the millions, New Yorkers and visitors troop through museum corridors, singly or in school groups, sometimes listening to explanations on earphones or to guides. Most famous are the Metropolitan Museum of Art and the American Museum of Natural History and the adjacent Hayden Planetarium, all situated on parkland. Other art museums are the Museum of Modern Art (with its major collections of photography and films as well), the Frick Collection, the Solomon R. Guggenheim Museum, the Whitney Museum of American Art, and the Brooklyn Museum.

Though the museums are private, the city provides some financial assistance. The general pattern, however, is for museums to finance deficits by private contributions. In general, attendance at the city's leading museums has been increasing, and the Museum of Natural History and the Metropolitan have introduced a system of discretionary payment by visitors. Lesser known institutions with special appeal for scholars as well as visitors are the Museum of the City of New York, the New York Historical Society, the Jewish Museum, the Museum of the American Indian, Heye Foundation, the American Craft Museum (formerly the Museum of Contemporary Crafts), the Studio Museum in Harlem, and the research centre for students of Jewish life, known as Yivo. In addition, at least 70 private art galleries help keep the nation's artistic life centred in New York City. Among developments in the arts are the special arrangements for artists to live and work in loft buildings in the vicinity of Soho.

Recreation. Some 50,000 acres (20,250 hectares) of the city—more than three times the area of Manhattan—are devoted to parkland. Parks range in size from tiny triangular green patches amid heavy traffic to the 526-acre Prospect Park in Brooklyn, 1,257-acre Flushing Meadows–Corona Park in Queens, 840-acre Central Park in Manhattan, 2,117-acre Pelham Bay Park in the Bronx, and the 25,000 acres of parkland, beaches, and marshes of the Gateway National Recreation Area in Staten Island, Brooklyn, and Queens. Also included in the city's park areas are such intensively used public beaches as Coney Island in Brooklyn and Orchard Beach in the Bronx. Erosion and pollution at some of these beaches have reduced their use.

Deep in the affections of city dwellers and visitors of all ages are the zoos and botanical gardens. The city's major zoo is in the Bronx, but, because of its location, a much smaller zoo in Central Park has been photographed more often for movies. Other zoos are in Brooklyn, Queens, and Staten Island. The botanical gardens in the Bronx and Brooklyn are a meeting place for botanists as well as the less scholarly flower lovers. Attractive but not as well known is the botanical garden in Queens.

Professional sports teams in the New York City area include the Yankees and the Mets (baseball), the Jets and the Giants (football), the Islanders and the Rangers (hockey), the Knicks (basketball), and the Cosmos (soccer). The major-league sports events at Yankee Stadium, Shea Stadium, or Madison Square Garden Center may get the headlines and television coverage, but for New Yorkers the parks and beaches get much more recreational use. On an average summer weekend about 1,000,000 people are at Brooklyn's Coney Island and another 750,000 swim at Rockaway Beach (in the Gateway National Recreational Area), both on the southern shore of Long Island. Baseball can be seen at its most exciting among the Puerto Rican teams and the show-business teams in Central Park, in which rowboaters may while away the summer hours or skaters the gray winter days. At these events and among the countless thousands of picnickers in the city's parks is discernible a warmth and neighbourliness, an underlying dream of the human melting pot never realized but ever sought. It is perhaps fitting that New York City is the home of the United Nations.

History

EXPLORATION AND EARLY SETTLEMENT

Although the Italian explorer Giovanni da Verrazano spotted the site of New York City in 1524, it is the English navigator Henry Hudson who is credited as the city's discoverer. On September 3, 1609, he sailed into its harbour and up the deep tidal river that now bears his

By courtesy of the Lincoln Center for the Performing Arts, Inc.; photograph, Bob Serating

Crowds attending programs at Lincoln Center for the Performing Arts. The Metropolitan Opera House is at centre and Avery Fisher Hall at right.

name in a vain quest for a passage to India on behalf of the Dutch West India Company. Hudson's reports to his employers about the magnificent harbour, sheltered by green hills and limitless potential farmland at a seemingly semitropical degree of latitude, were responsible for the Dutch settlement that set the pattern for the city's drive and independence, a spirit that endured when only corrupted Dutch names remained to remind New Yorkers that it was the Dutch who had founded their city.

Extent of the Dutch colony

The colonizers. In 1614, six years before the Pilgrims landed on Plymouth Rock, a Dutch skipper and his crew were forced to spend a winter on Manhattan Island because their ship had burned; they built there a new seagoing vessel and, prophetically, named the 18-ton ship "Restless." In 1626, Peter Minuit, director general of the Dutch province of New Netherland, which included not only all of what has since become New York City but which also extended into what is now Connecticut, New Jersey, and Long Island, purchased Manhattan from the Indians of the area for 60 guilders worth of gewgaws, the equivalent of $24. On February 2, 1653, New Amsterdam, capital of the province, became a city; its population was 800.

The Dutch West India Company refused to sell land in Manhattan until 1638, but early settlers found ample farmland. They also found out that much of the island was underlain by extremely hard rock and that in the southern portion were substantial stretches of marsh, as well as ponds and creeks. They learned to drain and fill swampy areas and to create land along the riverfronts by dumping refuse. Much of what was to become the borough of the Bronx was rocky ridge. The portion of Long Island that became Brooklyn and Queens was flatter and better suited to farming, though often stony and sandy in consistency. The section that became Staten Island was hilly, with a maximum altitude of 409 feet, the highest point in the city.

The Dutch opened the city to foreign commerce, established trade with the Indians, and laid out the roads that were to become major streets of downtown Manhattan. After a number of bloody clashes with the Indians between 1643 and 1655, interspersed with uncertain truces, the Dutch established a permanent dominance of whites on the island and over much of the nearby areas that became part of New York City.

The English city. Dutch supremacy ended on September 8, 1664, when a fleet sent by the Duke of York as part of the English–Dutch war in Europe seized the city easily, since the Dutch were not too fond of their stern ruler, Peter Stuyvesant. The English changed the name to New York. There was a short interruption of English rule in 1673, when a surprise invasion from the Netherlands was successful; the name was changed to New Orange, in honour of the Prince of Orange. But, the following year, in accordance with the Treaty of Westminster between England and the Netherlands, the city reverted to English rule and name. In 1686 New York became the first city in the colonies to receive a royal charter.

Since the Dutch and English got along well in Manhattan, the changes in political office did not interfere greatly with life and trade. English as well as Dutch settlers agreed that representatives of the British crown were too autocratic. Between 1689 and 1691, Jacob Leisler, preaching rebellion in the city, tried to organize an expedition to attack Canada. He was hanged and beheaded in 1691, but resentment was so strong in the city that the British Parliament cleared his name.

Thus, long before the Revolution, the city had established a strong sense of independence, allied with a business acumen and raffishness that it never lost. Pirates made the city their hangout in the 17th century, and the notorious Capt. William Kidd was regarded as one of the city's leading citizens. He donated the block and tackle with which historic Trinity Church was first built. Merchants helped outfit pirates and shared in their booty.

Precursors of rebellion

It was in New York that the first great test of journalistic independence was won and the base of the nation's freedom of the press established in 1734, when John Peter Zenger, publisher and editor of the *New York Weekly-Journal,* charged with libel and jailed for making strong attacks on the government, fought the case and was acquitted in 1735. The first bloodshed in the struggle for independence is believed to have occurred in New York. On January 18, 1775, the Sons of Liberty, a patriotic group, clashed with British soldiers; one of the Sons was killed, and several were wounded.

GROWTH OF THE METROPOLIS

Revolution. The city of New York, which was occupied and almost destroyed during the Revolution, became the first capital of the nation (1789–90). George Washington was inaugurated in the city as the first U.S. president on April 30, 1789. The first session of the state legislature was held there in 1784, and it remained the state capital until 1796. By 1790, with a population of 33,000, it had become the largest city in the nation; by the turn of the 18th century, the population had passed 60,000.

The opening of the Erie Canal in 1825, connecting New York City with Buffalo, the Great Lakes, and the opening West, guaranteed the city's preeminence as a seaport and world entrepreneur in commerce. When the immigrant waves swept ashore in the city in the 1840s, vast pools of cheap labour, skilled and unskilled, fueled a new era of rapid growth and social turbulence.

One of the chief beneficiaries of this development was the local Democratic organization known as Tammany Hall. Incorporated in 1789, mainly for social and patriotic activities, Tammany developed political strength under Aaron Burr toward the end of the century and became an important political force after backing Andrew Jackson in his two victorious presidential campaigns (1828 and 1832). With success Tammany, which had fought for wider suffrage, came under the domination of conservative elements for a time; but with the floods of immigrants in the 1840s, it directed strong appeals to them and built on their votes a massive power base that lasted for nearly a century, making it a national symbol of political bossism. Though Tammany became synonymous with corruption, it also served the vital function of opening up political and economic opportunities to the immigrant poor.

During the Civil War, the city was shaken by its worst riots. For four days in July 1863 many thousands of rioters, mostly impoverished Irish immigrants who were infuriated by the new draft law that permitted a draftee to buy his way out of service for $300, swept the city, looting, burning, and killing. Blacks were hanged from streetlights and trees. Warships trained guns on the city as rioters clashed repeatedly with the police, national guardsmen, and the army. At least 2,000 people were killed and 8,000 wounded, and all business halted in the face of the armed conflict.

Problems of consolidation

After the Civil War there was a steady clamour in the city for a merger with Brooklyn, Queens, the Bronx, and Staten Island. The strongest resistance was from Brooklyn, a city in its own right, which with good reason feared that the enormous corruption so evident in Tammany Hall under the political bosses William Marcy Tweed and Richard Croker would be extended to Brooklyn through any consolidation. With the opening of the Brooklyn Bridge connecting Brooklyn and Manhattan in 1883, the merger became inevitable. It took place on January 1, 1898, with Manhattan, the smallest of the five boroughs in size, becoming the most powerful. The birth of Greater New York represented a change from city to metropolis, as well as from national to world stature.

The 20th century. The transition to world metropolis in the first two decades of the 20th century was powered by the arrival of millions more immigrants from Italy and eastern Europe. This huge pool of cheap—and often skilled—labour tied together the sprawling city with networks of bridges, tunnels, and elevated and subway systems; created its famous garment industry; boomed its printing trades and small manufacturing; drew entrepreneurs from around the world; and made the city a laboratory for unionism and radicalism. During the first decades of the century, the public education system turned out armies of extremely efficient white-collar and civil service workers for the city's increasingly complex but booming economy.

BIBLIOGRAPHY. The FEDERAL WRITERS' PROJECT, *New York City Guide,* rev. ed. (1939, reprinted 1982), is a basic book about the city. The colour, history, and many of the social problems of New York City have been caught in many works of fiction, notably CLAUDE BROWN, *Manchild in the Promised Land* (1965, reprinted 1973); and RALPH ELLISON, *Invisible Man* (1952, reprinted 1982), both concerned with the black experience of the city; STEPHEN CRANE, *Maggie and Other Stories* (1960, reissued 1977); and HENRY ROTH, *Call It Sleep* (1934, reissued 1976), recalling the life of the Jewish immigrant. WASHINGTON IRVING'S classic *A History of New York* (1809; later ed. entitled *Knickerbocker's History of New York*), casts a facetious eye over the city's earlier centuries, especially the Dutch years. Works of nonfiction that offer a myriad of glimpses are MEYER BERGER, *New York* (1960), selections from his decades of chronicling for *The New York Times;* PHILIP HONE, *The Diary of Philip Hone, 1828–1851* (1889, reissued 1970); and JAMES D. MCCCABE, *Lights and Shadows of New York Life* (1872, reprinted 1970), both of which are impressions of 19th-century New York City; ALEXANDER KLEIN (ed.), *The Empire City* (1955, reprinted 1971), a collection of essays and articles on the city; and LINCOLN STEFFENS, *The Autobiography of Lincoln Steffens,* 2 vol. (1931, reprinted 1968).

Problems of New York City's political life are covered in WALLACE S. SAYRE and HERBERT KAUFMAN, *Governing New York City* (1960, reissued 1965); and in EDWARD J. FLYNN, *You're the Boss* (1947, reissued 1962). Tammany Hall is the subject of EDWARD N. COSTIKYAN, *Behind Closed Doors* (1966); GUSTAVUS MYERS, *The History of Tammany Hall,* 2nd rev. ed. (1917, reprinted 1971); and WILLIAM J. RIORDAN, *Plunkitt of Tammany Hall* (1905, reissued 1962); CHARLES R. MORRIS, *The Cost of Good Intentions* (1980), reviews the Wagner and Lindsay administrations and the financial collapse of 1975.

Aspects of New York City's sociological and related problems may be found in HERBERT ASBURY, *Gangs of New York* (1927, reissued 1970), a look at the structure of gangland; NATHAN GLAZER and DANIEL P. MOYNIHAN, *Beyond the Melting Pot: The Negroes, Puerto Ricans, Jews, Italians and Irish of New York City,* 2nd ed. (1970, reprinted 1976); JANE JACOBS, *The Death and Life of Great American Cities* (1961, reissued 1972), a study of the nature and process of urban decay; OSCAR LEWIS, *La Vida* (1966), on the Puerto Rican community; and JACOB A. RIIS, *How the Other Half Lives* (1890, reprinted 1972), an early and classic study of poverty on the Lower East Side by a muckraking journalist. JOSEPH MITCHELL, *The Bottom of the Harbor* (1959), is an intimate look into the city's harbour and waterfront life; while ROBERT MOSES, *Public Works: A Dangerous Trade* (1970), reviews the author's years as a builder of the city's physical plants. ROBERT A. CARO, *The Power Broker: Robert Moss and the Fall of New York* (1974), is a critical biography.

Aspects of New York City's cultural life appear throughout such books as BROOKS ATKINSON, *Broadway,* rev. ed. (1974); IRA GLACKENS, *William Glackens and the Ashcan Group* (1957); MOSS HART, *Act One* (1959, reissued 1976); and NORVAL WHITE and ELLIOT WILENSKY (eds.), *AIA Guide to New York City,* rev. ed. (1978). MANUAL D. LOPEZ, *New York: Guide to Information and Reference Sources* (1980), an annotated bibliography of more than 1,000 sources on historical, cultural, economic, and social aspects of the city and state.

(Mu.S.)

New Zealand

New Zealand is an independent member of the Commonwealth. It is remote from other lands, being situated in the South Pacific more than 1,000 miles (1,600 kilometres) southeast of Australia, its nearest neighbour. The country comprises two main islands—the North and South islands—and a number of small islands, some of them hundreds of miles from the main group. New Zealand is about 1,000 miles long (north–south) and about 280 miles across at its widest point. The land area is approximately 100,000 square miles (268,000 square kilometres)—slightly smaller than the state of Colorado and a little larger than the United Kingdom. About two-thirds of the land is economically useful, the remainder being mountainous. Because of its numerous harbours and fjords, the country has an extremely long coastline relative to its area. The capital city is Wellington, and the largest urban area is Auckland, both located on the North Island. New Zealand administers the South Pacific island group of Tokelau and claims a section of the Antarctic continent. Niue and the Cook Islands are self-governing states in free association with New Zealand.

New Zealand was the largest country in Polynesia before it was annexed by the British in 1840. Thereafter it was, successively, a crown colony, a self-governing colony (1856), and a dominion (1907). By the 1920s it controlled almost all of its internal and external policies, although it did not become fully independent until 1947, when it adopted the Statute of Westminster.

The country's isolation has played an important part in the development of its social, cultural, and economic characteristics. Nevertheless, in the 20th century New Zealand has been involved in international affairs, being an active member of both the League of Nations and the United Nations. It has also participated in several wars, including World Wars I and II. Economically, the country has been dependent on the export of agricultural products, especially to Great Britain, for much of the 20th century. The entry of Britain into the European Economic Community (EEC) in the early 1970s, however, forced New Zealand to expand its trade relations with other nations. It also has begun to develop a much more extensive and varied industrial sector. (J.W.R./M.A.Ro./Ke.S.)

This article is divided into the following sections:

Physical and human geography

THE LAND

Relief. Although New Zealand is small, its geological history is as complex as that of a continent. Land has existed in the vicinity of New Zealand for most of the last 500,000,000 years. The earliest known rocks originated as sedimentary deposits of Late Precambrian (older than 570,000,000 years) or Early Cambrian age; their source area was probably the continental forelands of Australia and Antarctica, then part of a nearby single supercontinent. Continental drift (the movement of large plates of the Earth's crust) created a distinct island arc and oceanic trench structure by Carboniferous time (315,000,000 to 280,000,000 years ago), when deposition began in the synclines (trenches) of the sedimentary rocks that today make up some three-fourths of New Zealand. This environment lasted about 250,000,000 years and is typified by both synclinal oceanic sedimentary rocks and by terrestrial volcanic rocks. This period was terminated in the west at the beginning of the Cretaceous (about 135,000,000 years ago) by the Rangitata Orogeny (mountain-building episode), although synclinal deposition continued in the east. These mountains were slowly worn down by erosion, and the sea transgressed, eventually covering almost all of the land. At the end of Oligocene time (about 26,000,000 years ago) the Kaikoura Orogeny began, raising land above the sea again, including the Southern Alps of the South Island. Many of the great earth movements associated with this final orogeny took place (and take place today) along faults, which divide the landscape into great blocks, chief of which is the Alpine Fault of the South Island. The erosion and continued movement of these faulted blocks, together with the continuing volcanism of the North Island, define to a large extent the landscape of the country.

The role of continental drift

©Robert Frerck—Odyssey Productions

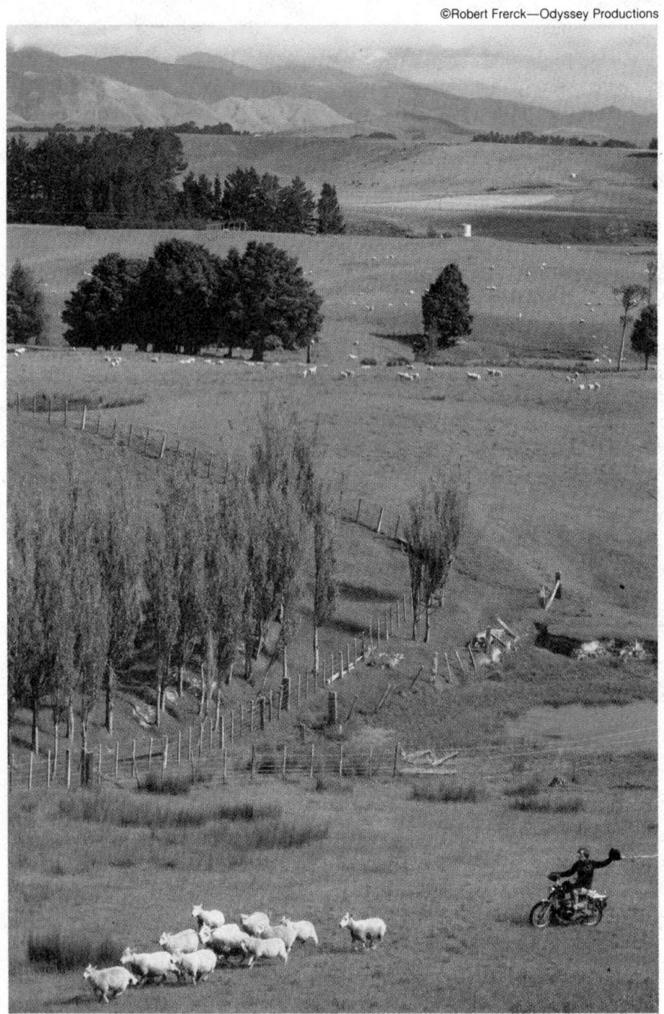

Rounding up sheep by motorcycle on the Takapau Plains, near Hastings, North Island.

Both the North and South islands are roughly bisected, by mountains in the South and ranges of hills in the North. Swift, snow-fed rivers drain from the hills, although only in the east of the South Island have extensive alluvial plains been built up. The alluvial Canterbury Plains contrast sharply with the precipitous slopes and narrow coastal strip of the Westland region on the west coast of the South Island. The Southern Alps are a 300-mile-long chain of fold mountains containing New Zealand's highest mountain—Mt. Cook (in Maori, Aorangi) at 12,349 feet (3,764 metres)—and 15 other peaks above 10,000 feet, as well as an extensive glacier system with associated lakes.

There are more than 360 glaciers in the Southern Alps. The Tasman Glacier, the largest in New Zealand, with a length of 18 miles and a width of more than one-half mile, flows down the eastern slopes of Mt. Cook. Other important glaciers on the eastern slopes of the Southern Alps are the Murchison, Mueller, and Godley; Fox and Franz Josef are the largest on the western slopes. The North Island has seven small glaciers on the slopes of Mt. Ruapehu.

In the north of the South Island, the Alps break up into steep upswelling ridges. On their western face there are mineral deposits, and to the east they continue into two parallel ranges, terminating in a series of sounds. To the south, the Alps break up into rugged, dissected country of difficult access and magnificent scenery, particularly toward the western tip of the island (called Fiordland). On its eastern boundary this wilderness borders a high central plateau called Central Otago, which has an almost continental climate.

The North Island is much less precipitous than the South and has a more benign climate and greater economic potential. In the centre of the island the Volcanic Plateau rises abruptly from the southern shores of New Zealand's largest natural lake, Taupo, itself an ancient volcanic crater. To the east ranges form a backdrop to rolling country in which pockets of great fertility are associated with the river systems. To the south more ranges run to the sea. On the western and eastern slopes of these ranges the land is generally poor, although the western downland region is fertile until it fades into a coastal plain dominated by sand dunes. To the west of the Volcanic Plateau fairly mountainous country merges into the undulating farmlands of the Taranaki region, where the mild climate favours dairy farming even on the slopes of Mt. Egmont, an isolated, extinct volcano.

The northern shores of Lake Taupo bound a large area of high economic activity, including forestry. Even further north there are river terraces sufficiently fertile for widespread dairy and mixed farming. The hub of this area is Auckland, which is situated astride an isthmus with a deep harbour on the east and a shallow harbour to the west. The region north of Auckland, called Northland, becomes gradually subtropical in character, marked generally by numerous deep-encroaching inlets of the sea bordered by mangrove swamps.

Hydrography

Drainage. The mountainous country of both islands is cut by many rivers, which are swift, dangerous, and a barrier to communication. The longest is the Waikato, in the North Island, and the swiftest, the Clutha, in the South. Many of the rivers arise from or drain into one or other of the numerous lakes associated with the mountain chains. A number of these lakes have been used as reservoirs for hydroelectric schemes, and artificial lakes, including Lake Benmore, New Zealand's largest, have been created for hydroelectric purposes.

Soils. New Zealand's soils are often deeply weathered, lacking in many nutrients, and, most of all, highly variable over short distances. Soils based on sedimentary rock formations are mostly clays and are found over about three-fourths of the country. Pockets of fertile alluvial soil in river basins or along river terraces form the orchard and market-gardening regions of the country.

In the South Island, variations in mean annual rainfall have had an important effect. The brown-gray soils of Central Otago are thin and coarse-textured and have subsoil accumulations of lime, whereas the yellow-gray earths of much of the Canterbury Plains, as well as areas of

Snowcapped Mitre Peak, reflected in the waters of Milford Sound, Fiordland National Park, South Island.

lower rainfall in the North Island, are partially podzolized (layered) with a gray upper horizon. The yellow-brown soils that characterize much of the North Island are often podzolized from acid leaching in humid forest environments. Their fertility varies with the species composition of their vegetation. Forests of false beech (*Nothofagus*), as well as of tawa and taraire, indicate soils of reasonably high fertility, while forests of kauri pine and rimu indicate podzolized soils.

Climate. New Zealand's climate is determined by its latitude, its isolation, and its physical characteristics. Across such vast oceans as surround it, weather from elsewhere has little influence. There are no extremes of temperature.

A procession of high-pressure systems (anticyclones) separated by middle-latitude cyclones and fronts cross New Zealand from west to east. Characteristic is the sequence of a few days of fine weather and clear skies separated by days with unsettled weather and often heavy rain. In summer subtropical highs are dominant, bringing protracted spells of fine weather and intense sunshine. In winter middle-latitude lows and active fronts increase the blustery wet conditions, although short spells of clear skies also occur. Because of the high mountain chains that lie across the path of the prevailing winds, the contrast in climate from west to east is sharper than that from north to south. Mountain ranges are also responsible for the semicontinental climate of Central Otago.

Changes in altitude make for an intricate pattern of temperature variations, especially on South Island, but some generalizations for conditions at sea level can be made. The average seasonal and diurnal temperature range is about 18° F (10° C). Variation in mean monthly temperature from north to south is about 10° F (6° C). In most parts of the country daytime highs in summer are above 70° F (21° C), occasionally exceeding 81° F (27° C) in the north, while in winter daytime highs throughout the country are rarely below 50° F (10° C).

Rainfall is highest in areas dominated by mountains exposed to the prevailing westerly and northwesterly winds. Although mean annual rainfall ranges from an arid 12 inches (300 millimetres) in Central Otago to as much as 315 inches in the Southern Alps, for the whole country it is typical of temperate zone countries (25–60 inches), usually spread reliably throughout the year. Snow is common only in mountainous regions, but frost is frequent in inland valleys in winter. Humidity ranges from 70 to 80 percent on the coast, generally being 10 percent lower inland. In the lee of the Southern Alps, where the effect of the foehn (a warm, dry wind of leeward mountain slopes) is marked, humidity can become very low.

Plant and animal life. The indigenous vegetation of New Zealand consisted of mixed evergreen forest covering perhaps two-thirds of the total land area. The islands' prolonged isolation has encouraged the development of species unknown to the rest of the world; almost 90 percent of the indigenous plants are peculiar to the country. Today, dense "bush" survives only in areas unsuitable for settlement and in parks and reserves. On the west coast of the South Island this mixed forest still yields most of the native timber used by industry. Along the mountain chain running the length of the country, the false beech is the predominant forest tree.

European settlement made such inroads on the natural forest that erosion in high-country areas became a serious problem. The State Forest Service was established to repair the damage by forest-management techniques and reafforestation with exotic trees. Experimental areas on the Volcanic Plateau were planted with radiata pine, an introduction from California. This conifer has adapted to New Zealand conditions so well that it is now the staple plantation tree, growing to maturity in 25 years and having a high rate of natural regeneration. Large areas of the Volcanic Plateau, together with other marginal or subagricultural land north of Auckland and near Nelson, are now planted with this species.

European broadleafs are widely used ornamentally, and willows and poplars are frequently planted to help prevent erosion on hillsides. Gorse has acclimatized so readily that it has now become a menace, spreading over good and bad land alike, its only virtue being as a nursery for regenerating bush.

Because of New Zealand's isolation there was no higher animal life in the country when the Maori arrived (some 1,000 or more years ago). There were two species of lizard:

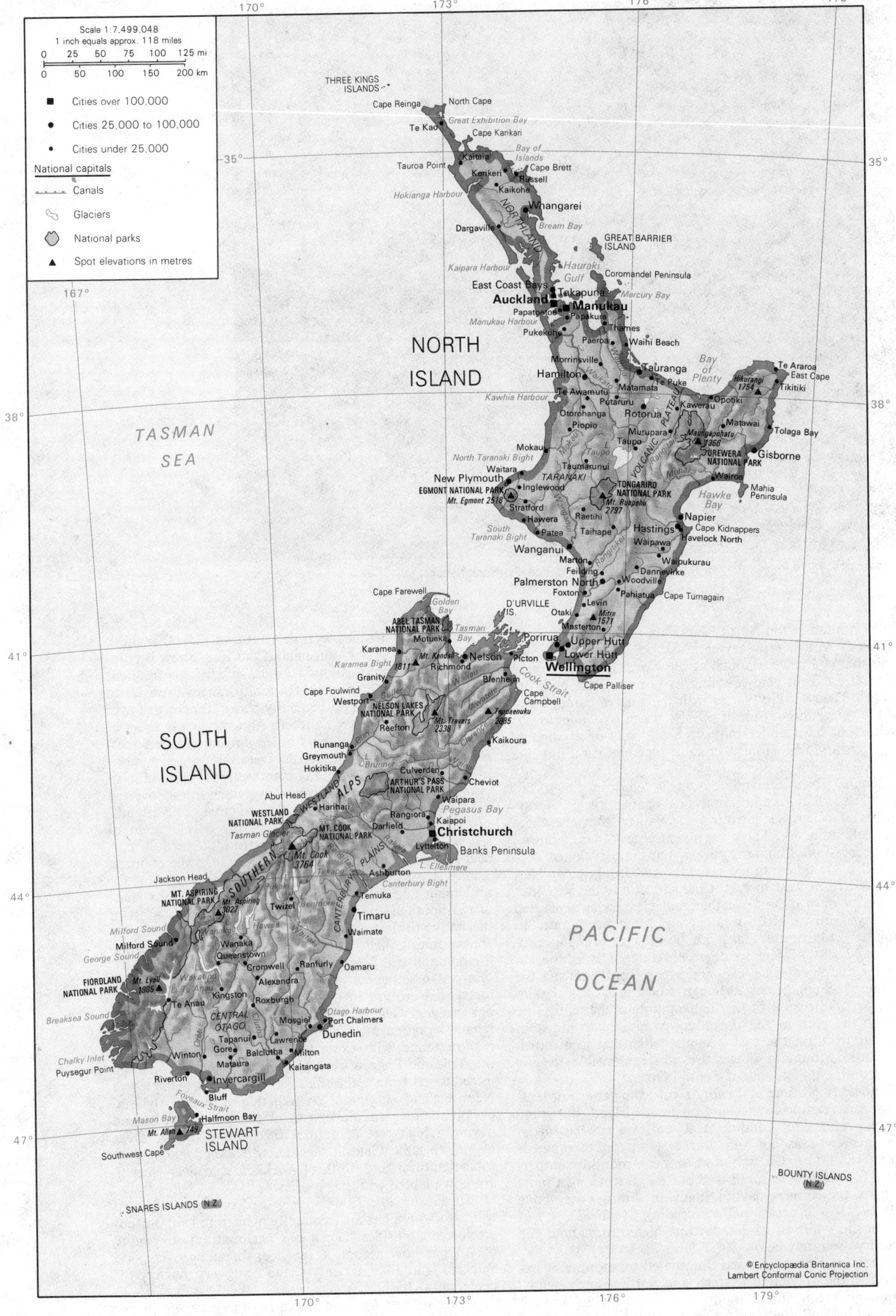
Scale 1:7,499,048
1 inch equals approx. 118 miles
Cities over 100,000
Cities 25,000 to 100,000
Cities under 25,000
National capitals
Canals
Glaciers
National parks
Spot elevations in metres
NORTH ISLAND
SOUTH ISLAND
STEWART ISLAND
TASMAN SEA
PACIFIC OCEAN
THREE KINGS ISLANDS
North Cape
Cape Reinga
Auckland
Manukau
Hamilton
Tauranga
Rotorua
Gisborne
Napier
Hastings
New Plymouth
Wanganui
Palmerston North
Wellington
Nelson
Christchurch
Timaru
Dunedin
Invercargill
Cook Strait
Foveaux Strait
Mt. Cook 3764
Mt. Ruapehu 2797
Mt. Egmont 2518
SNARES ISLANDS (N.Z.)
BOUNTY ISLANDS (N.Z.)
© Encyclopædia Britannica Inc.
Lambert Conformal Conic Projection

MAP INDEX

Cities and towns

Alexandra ...... 45 15 S 169 23 E
Ashburton ...... 43 54 S 171 45 E
Auckland ...... 36 52 S 174 46 E
Balclutha ...... 46 14 S 169 44 E
Blenheim ...... 41 31 S 173 57 E
Bluff ...... 46 36 S 168 20 E
Cheviot ...... 42 49 S 173 16 E
Christchurch .... 43 32 S 172 39 E
Cromwell ...... 45 03 S 169 12 E
Culverden ...... 42 46 S 172 51 E
Dannevirke ..... 40 12 S 176 06 E
Darfield ...... 43 29 S 172 07 E
Dargaville ...... 35 56 S 173 52 E
Dunedin ...... 45 53 S 170 29 E
East Coast Bays . 36 45 S 174 45 E
Feilding ...... 40 13 S 175 34 E
Foxton ...... 40 28 S 175 17 E
Gisborne ...... 38 39 S 178 01 E
Gore ...... 46 06 S 168 56 E
Granity ...... 41 38 S 171 51 E
Greymouth .... 42 27 S 171 12 E
Halfmoon Bay ... 46 54 S 168 08 E
Hamilton ...... 37 47 S 175 16 E
Harihari ...... 43 09 S 170 34 E
Hastings ...... 39 39 S 176 50 E
Havelock North .. 39 40 S 176 53 E
Hawera ...... 39 35 S 174 17 E
Hokitika ...... 42 43 S 170 58 E
Inglewood ...... 39 10 S 174 12 E
Invercargill ..... 46 25 S 168 22 E
Kaiapoi ...... 43 23 S 172 39 E
Kaikohe ...... 35 25 S 173 48 E
Kaikoura ...... 42 24 S 173 41 E
Kaitaia ...... 35 07 S 173 15 E
Kaitangata ..... 46 17 S 169 51 E
Karamea ...... 41 15 S 172 07 E
Kawerau ...... 38 06 S 176 42 E
Kerikeri ...... 35 14 S 173 57 E
Kingston ...... 45 20 S 168 43 E
Lawrence ...... 45 55 S 169 42 E
Levin ...... 40 37 S 175 17 E
Lower Hutt ..... 41 13 S 174 56 E
Lyttelton ...... 43 36 S 172 43 E
Manukau ...... 36 57 S 174 56 E
Marton ...... 40 05 S 175 23 E
Masterton ...... 40 57 S 175 39 E
Matamata ...... 37 49 S 175 46 E
Mataura ...... 46 12 S 168 51 E
Matawai ...... 38 22 S 177 32 E
Milford Sound ... 44 41 S 167 55 E
Milton ...... 46 07 S 169 58 E
Mokau ...... 38 42 S 174 37 E
Morrinsville ..... 37 39 S 175 32 E
Mosgiel ...... 45 53 S 170 21 E
Motueka ...... 41 07 S 173 01 E
Murupara ...... 38 27 S 176 42 E
Napier ...... 39 31 S 176 54 E
Nelson ...... 41 17 S 173 17 E
New Plymouth ... 39 04 S 174 04 E
Oamaru ...... 45 06 S 170 58 E
Opotiki ...... 38 01 S 177 14 E
Otaki ...... 40 45 S 175 09 E
Otorohanga ..... 38 11 S 175 13 E
Paeroa ...... 37 23 S 175 40 E
Pahiatua ...... 40 27 S 175 50 E
Palmerston
 North ...... 40 21 S 175 37 E
Papakura ...... 37 04 S 174 57 E
Papatoetoe ..... 36 58 S 174 52 E
Patea ...... 39 46 S 174 28 E
Picton ...... 41 18 S 174 01 E
Piopio ...... 38 28 S 175 01 E
Porirua ...... 41 08 S 174 51 E
Port Chalmers ... 45 49 S 170 37 E
Pukekohe ...... 37 12 S 174 54 E
Putaruru ...... 38 03 S 175 47 E
Queenstown ..... 45 02 S 168 40 E
Raetihi ...... 39 26 S 175 17 E
Ranfurly ...... 45 06 S 170 06 E
Rangiora ...... 43 19 S 172 35 E
Reefton ...... 42 07 S 171 52 E
Richmond ...... 41 20 S 173 11 E
Riverton ...... 46 22 S 168 01 E
Rotorua ...... 38 10 S 176 14 E
Roxburgh ...... 45 33 S 169 19 E
Runanga ...... 42 24 S 171 15 E
Russell ...... 35 16 S 174 07 E
Stratford ...... 39 21 S 174 17 E
Taihape ...... 39 41 S 175 48 E
Takapuna ...... 36 47 S 174 45 E
Tapanui ...... 45 56 S 169 15 E
Taumarunui ..... 38 53 S 175 17 E
Taupo ...... 38 42 S 176 06 E
Tauranga ...... 37 42 S 176 08 E
Te Anau ...... 45 25 S 167 43 E
Te Araroa ...... 37 38 S 178 22 E
Te Awamutu ..... 38 01 S 175 19 E
Te Kao ...... 34 39 S 172 58 E
Te Puke ...... 37 47 S 176 19 E
Temuka ...... 44 14 S 171 17 E
Thames ...... 37 09 S 175 33 E
Tikitiki ...... 37 48 S 178 24 E
Timaru ...... 44 24 S 171 14 E
Tolaga Bay ..... 38 22 S 178 18 E
Twizel ...... 44 15 S 170 06 E
Upper Hutt ..... 41 08 S 175 03 E
Waihi Beach .... 37 24 S 175 56 E
Waimate ...... 44 44 S 171 02 E
Waipara ...... 43 03 S 172 45 E
Waipawa ...... 39 56 S 176 35 E
Waipukurau ..... 40 00 S 176 33 E
Wairoa ...... 39 02 S 177 25 E
Waitara ...... 39 00 S 174 14 E
Wanaka ...... 44 42 S 169 08 E
Wanganui ...... 39 56 S 175 02 E
Wellington ...... 41 18 S 174 47 E
Westport ...... 41 45 S 171 36 E
Whangarei ..... 35 43 S 174 20 E
Winton ...... 46 09 S 168 19 E
Woodville ...... 40 20 S 175 52 E

Physical features and points of interest

Abel Tasman
 National Park ... 40 54 S 172 58 E
Abut Head ...... 43 06 S 170 11 E
Allen, Mount,
 mountain ...... 47 05 S 167 47 E
Arthur's Pass
 National Park ... 42 54 S 171 43 E
Aspiring, Mount,
 mountain ...... 44 23 S 168 44 E
Awatere, *river* ... 41 36 S 174 10 E
Banks Peninsula . 43 50 S 173 09 E
Benmore, Lake ... 44 24 S 170 14 E
Bounty Islands .. 47 42 S 179 03 E
Breaksea Sound . 45 35 S 166 38 E
Bream Bay ..... 35 56 S 174 28 E
Brett, Cape ..... 35 10 S 174 20 E
Brunner, Lake ... 42 37 S 171 27 E
Buller, *river* ..... 41 44 S 171 35 E
Campbell,
 Cape ...... 41 44 S 174 16 E
Canterbury Bight . 44 08 S 172 17 E
Canterbury
 Plains ...... 44 00 S 171 20 E
Central Otago,
 plateau ...... 45 10 S 169 25 E
Chalky Inlet ..... 46 03 S 166 20 E
Clarence, *river* ... 42 10 S 173 56 E
Clutha, *river* .... 46 21 S 169 48 E
Cook, Mount,
 mountain ...... 43 36 S 170 05 E
Cook Strait ..... 41 20 S 174 22 E
Coromandel
 Peninsula ..... 36 50 S 175 40 E
D'Urville Island .. 40 50 S 173 51 E
East Cape ...... 37 41 S 178 33 E
Egmont, Mount,
 mountain ...... 39 18 S 174 04 E
Egmont National
 Park ...... 39 17 S 174 04 E
Ellesmere, Lake .. 43 47 S 172 28 E
Farewell, Cape .. 40 30 S 172 41 E
Fiordland
 National Park ... 45 18 S 167 20 E
Foulwind, Cape .. 41 45 S 171 28 E
Foveaux Strait ... 46 37 S 168 00 E
George Sound ... 44 50 S 167 20 E
Golden Bay ..... 40 40 S 172 48 E
Great Barrier
 Island ...... 36 11 S 175 25 E
Great Exhibition
 Bay ...... 34 38 S 173 05 E
Grey, *river* ...... 42 26 S 171 11 E
Hauraki, Gulf .... 36 35 S 175 03 E
Hawea, Lake .... 44 27 S 169 18 E
Hawke Bay ..... 39 23 S 177 25 E
Hikurangi,
 mountain ...... 37 55 S 178 04 E
Hokianga
 Harbour ...... 35 32 S 173 21 E
Islands, Bay of ... 35 13 S 174 09 E
Jackson Head ... 43 58 S 168 37 E
Kaipara Harbour . 36 25 S 174 13 E
Karamea Bight .. 41 16 S 171 50 E
Karikari, Cape ... 34 47 S 173 24 E
Kawhia Harbour . 38 05 S 174 50 E
Kendall, Mount,
 mountain ...... 41 23 S 172 24 E
Kidnappers,
 Cape ...... 39 38 S 177 06 E
Lyall, Mount,
 mountain ...... 45 17 S 167 33 E
Mahia Peninsula . 39 10 S 177 53 E
Manukau
 Harbour ...... 37 03 S 174 45 E
Mason Bay ..... 46 55 S 167 39 E
Maungapohatu,
 mountain ...... 38 35 S 177 08 E
Mercury Bay .... 36 48 S 175 47 E
Milford Sound ... 44 34 S 167 48 E
Mitre, *mountain* .. 40 48 S 175 27 E
Mohaka, *river* ... 39 07 S 177 12 E
Mokau, *river* .... 38 42 S 174 37 E
Mount Aspiring
 National Park ... 44 20 S 168 45 E
Mount Cook
 National Park ... 43 36 S 170 18 E
Nelson Lakes
 National Park ... 42 03 S 172 41 E
North Cape ..... 34 25 S 173 03 E
North Island .... 38 30 S 176 00 E
North Taranaki
 Bight ...... 38 50 S 174 15 E
Northland,
 geographic region ...... 35 40 S 174 00 E
Oreti, *river* ...... 46 28 S 168 18 E
Otago Harbour .. 45 49 S 170 38 E
Pacific Ocean ... 44 30 S 176 30 E
Palliser, Cape ... 41 37 S 175 16 E
Pegasus Bay .... 43 22 S 172 43 E
Plenty, Bay of ... 37 38 S 176 12 E
Pukaki, Lake .... 44 02 S 170 10 E
Puysegur Point ... 46 09 S 166 36 E
Rakaia, *river* .... 43 54 S 172 13 E
Rangitaiki, *river* .. 37 55 S 176 53 E
Rangitata, *river* .. 44 12 S 171 30 E
Rangitikei, *river* .. 40 17 S 175 13 E
Reinga, Cape ... 34 25 S 172 41 E
Ruapehu, Mount,
 mountain ...... 39 17 S 175 32 E
Snares Islands .. 48 02 S 166 32 E
South Island .... 43 41 S 171 00 E
South Taranaki
 Bight ...... 39 42 S 174 12 E
Southern Alps,
 mountains ..... 43 20 S 170 30 E
Southwest Cape . 47 15 S 167 30 E
Stewart Island ... 47 02 S 167 51 E
Tapuaenuku,
 mountain ...... 42 00 S 173 40 E
Taranaki,
 geographic region ...... 39 20 S 174 40 E
Tasman Bay .... 41 02 S 173 20 E
Tasman Sea .... 39 00 S 170 30 E
Taupo, Lake .... 38 48 S 175 53 E
Tauroa Point .... 35 10 S 173 04 E
Te Anau, Lake ... 45 14 S 167 46 E
Tekapo, Lake ... 43 54 S 170 32 E
Three Kings
 Islands ...... 34 10 S 172 08 E
Tongariro
 National Park ... 39 13 S 175 35 E
Travers, Mount,
 mountain ...... 42 01 S 172 44 E
Turnagain, Cape . 40 30 S 176 37 E
Urewera National
 Park ...... 38 30 S 177 00 E
Volcanic Plateau . 38 35 S 176 20 E
Waiau, *river* ..... 42 45 S 173 20 E
Waihou, *river* .... 37 16 S 175 36 E
Waikato, *river* ... 37 23 S 174 43 E
Wairau, *river* .... 41 31 S 174 03 E
Waitaki, *river* .... 44 55 S 171 10 E
Wakatipu, Lake .. 45 05 S 168 32 E
Wanaka, Lake ... 44 30 S 169 08 E
Wanganui, *river* .. 39 57 S 174 59 E
Westland,
 geographic region ...... 42 40 S 171 20 E
Westland
 National Park ... 43 31 S 170 05 E

the gecko, which is born directly instead of being hatched from an egg, and the tuatara, a "beak-headed" reptile extinct elsewhere for 100,000,000 years. There were also a few primitive species of frog and two species of bat. These are all extant, although confined to outlying islands and isolated parts of the country.

In addition to their domestic animals, Europeans also brought other species with them. The red deer, introduced for sport, and the Australian opossum (for skins) have multiplied beyond imagination and do untold damage when browsing in the high-country bush. The control of goats, deer, opossums, and rabbits—even in the national parks—is a continuing problem.

In the absence of predatory animals, New Zealand was a paradise for birds, the most interesting of which are flightless. The moa was a very large bird, easily exterminated by the Maori. The kiwi, another flightless species, is extant, though only in secluded bush areas. The weka and the notornis, or takahe (barely rescued from extinction), probably became flightless after arrival. The pukeko, a swamphen relative of the weka, is even now in the process of losing the use of its wings. Some birds, such as the saddleback and the native thrush (thought to be extinct), are peculiar to New Zealand, but many others, such as the tui, the fantail, and the bellbird, are closely related to Australian birds. New Zealand also has its share of migrants: the gannet from Australia, and the skua, penguin, shag, and royal albatross from the Antarctic.

Because New Zealand is the meeting place of warm and cool currents, a great variety of fish is found in its waters. Tropical species such as tuna, marlin, and some big-game sharks are attracted by the warm currents, which are locally populated by snapper, trevally, and kahawai. The Antarctic cold currents, on the other hand, bring the blue and red cod and the hake, while some fish, tolerant to a considerable range of water temperature, are found off the entire coastline—tarakihi, grouper, and bass. Flounder and sole abound on tidal mudflats, and crayfish are prolific in rocky areas off the coastline.

(J.W.R./M.A.Ro./W.Mo.)

THE PEOPLE

Ethnic structure. New Zealand was one of the last sizable land areas suitable for habitation to be populated by human beings. It was first settled by Polynesians who came from somewhere in eastern Polynesia, possibly from what is now French Polynesia. They remained isolated in New Zealand until the arrival of European explorers, the first of whom was the Dutchman Abel Janszoon Tasman (1642). During that time they grew in numbers to between 100,000 and 200,000, living almost exclusively on North Island. They had no name for themselves but eventually adopted the name Maori (meaning "normal") to distinguish themselves from the Europeans, who, after the voyages of the Englishman Capt. James Cook (1769–77), began to come with greater frequency.

The Europeans brought with them an array of diseases for which the Maori had no resistance, and this precipitated a rapid decline in the Maori population. Their reduction in numbers was exacerbated by widespread intertribal warfare (once the Maori had acquired firearms) and by warfare with Europeans. By 1896 there were only about 42,000 Maori left. Early in the 20th century, however, their numbers began to increase as they acquired resistance to such diseases as measles and influenza and as their birthrate subsequently recovered.

Europeans had begun to settle in New Zealand in the 1820s; they arrived in increasing numbers after the country was annexed by Great Britain in 1840. By the late 1850s settlers outnumbered Maori, and in 1900 there were some 772,000 Europeans, most of whom by then were New Zealand-born. Although the overwhelming majority of immigrants were of British extraction, other Europeans came as well, including Scandinavians, Germans, Greeks, Italians, and Yugoslavs. Groups of central Europeans came between World Wars I and II, and a large body of Dutch immigrants arrived after World War II. Asians coming to New Zealand have included Chinese and Indians and more recently a growing community of Pacific Islanders from Western Samoa, the Cook Islands, Niue, and Tokelau.

Contemporary New Zealand thus has a great majority of people of European origin, a significant minority of Maori, and smaller numbers of Pacific Islanders, Chinese, and Indians. This diverse society has produced some racial tensions, but they have been small compared with those found in other parts of the world. Although the Maori have legal equality with those of European descent (called *pakeha* by the Maori), many feel unable to take their full place in a European-type society without compromising their traditional values.

Language and religion. New Zealand is predominantly an English-speaking country. Virtually all Maori speak English, and a small minority of them also speak Maori. The Maori language is taught at a number of schools. The only other non-English language spoken by any significant number of people is Samoan.

New Zealand is nominally Christian, some three-fifths of the population adhering to the Anglican, Presbyterian, Roman Catholic, and Methodist denominations. Minor Protestant sects, the Eastern Orthodox churches, Jewish congregations, and Maori adaptations of Christianity (the Ratana and Ringatu churches) account for nearly all of the rest, although a significant proportion of the population does not claim any religious affiliation. There is no established (official) religion, but Anglican cathedrals are generally used for state occasions.

Regional population. Because New Zealand is small and the population is relatively homogeneous, there are no sharply differentiated social or political regions. The North, however, is popularly regarded as being more enterprising, while the South is traditionally regarded as being conservative. While the west coast is romantically nostalgic for its rollicking gold-rush days, the east coast conjures up the picture of sheep barons on their extensive stations.

The New Zealand countryside is thinly populated, but there are many small towns of up to 10,000 population and a number of provincial cities of more than 20,000. Very small towns or villages are becoming more deserted as people drift to the bigger towns and cities.

The main urban areas are Auckland, the centre of the North and the main industrial complex; Hamilton, in the middle of the North Island; Wellington, centrally located at the southern tip of North Island and the political and commercial capital; Christchurch, in the middle of the South Island and the second largest industrial area; and finally, still farther south, Dunedin. Although New Zealand is notable for the strength of its rural sector, the great majority of people live in cities, and urban concentration is proceeding apace. There is also a marked difference in the degree of population growth of the two main islands—the North having about three-fourths of the total population, in sharp contrast to the earlier years of systematic settlement. As in the past, the great majority of Maori live on the North Island; since World War II, however, most Maori have become urban dwellers, as have the Pacific Islanders.

Demographic trends. The natural rate of increase has been highest for the Pacific Islanders and for the Maori, both having a more youthful population. Since World War II New Zealand has generally had an annual excess of arrivals over departures, a major contributor to overall population growth. Although in the past most immigrants came from Great Britain and The Netherlands, they have been surpassed by Pacific Islanders and Asians. Both immigration and emigration are sensitive to the rate of growth of the New Zealand economy and its employment opportunities, as well as to conditions overseas.

(J.W.R./M.A.Ro./Ke.S.)

THE ECONOMY

New Zealand has a small, developing economy with a relatively low standard of living compared with those of countries with similar economies, such as Australia and Canada. In the late 19th and early 20th centuries New Zealand's standard of living was one of the highest in the world, but since World War II the rate of growth has been one of the slowest among the developed countries. The main causes of this retardation have been the slow growth of the economy of the United Kingdom (which formerly was the main destination of New Zealand's exports) and the high tariffs imposed by the major industrial nations against the country's agricultural products (*e.g.,* butter and meat). New Zealand's economic history in the second half of the 20th century has consisted largely of the attempt to evade these protectionist constraints by diversifying its farm economy and by expanding its manufacturing base. This has been achieved partly by large-scale government intervention and partly by the natural working of market forces.

Resources. Most minerals, metallic and nonmetallic, occur in New Zealand, but few are found in sufficient quantities for commercial exploitation. The exceptions are gold, which in the early years of organized settlement was a major export; coal, which is still mined to a considerable extent; iron sands, which are exploited both for export and for domestic use; and, most recently, natural gas. In addition to mining, construction materials, with which the country is well endowed, are quarried.

Apart from gold's brief heyday, biological resources have always been more significant than minerals. Domestic animals introduced from Europe have thrived in New Zealand. Forestry has always been important, but the emphasis has swung from felling the original forest for timber to afforestation with pine trees for both timber and pulp.

Use of hydroelectric power

The country has exploited its great hydroelectric potential to such an extent that hydroelectricity supplies a major percentage of the country's power. A notable feature of the New Zealand electricity grid is the direct-current cable linking the two main islands, enabling the South's surplus hydroelectric power to be used by the North's concentration of industry and people. Since the early 1970s geothermal and coal- and gas-fired stations have also been constructed. In addition, partnerships between government and private interests have undertaken the development of natural-gas reserves and the construction of the world's first plant producing gasoline from natural gas.

Agriculture, industry, and trade. The farming base of the past (*c.* 1890–1970) required a relatively complex economy. Highly productive pastoral farming, embracing extensive sheep grazing and large-scale milk production, was made possible by a temperate climate, heavy investment in land improvement (including the introduction of European grasses and regular application of imported fertilizers), and highly skilled farm management by owner-occupiers, who used one of the highest ratios of capital to labour in farming anywhere in the world. The farms supported and required many specialized services: finance, trade, transport, building and construction, and especially the processing of butter, cheese, and frozen lamb carcasses and their by-products. It is not inaccurate to describe this economy as an offshore European farm, which exported wool and processed dairy products and in exchange imported a wide variety of finished manufactured consumer and capital goods, raw materials, and petroleum.

Industry

Even in the 19th century New Zealand's relative geographic isolation made necessary a proportionately large industrial labour force engaged in the manufacture and repair of agricultural machinery and in shipbuilding, brewing, and timber processing. After the 1880s the factory processing of farm products swelled these numbers, while the temporary isolation of World Wars I and II stimulated the production of a wide range of manufactured goods that previously had been imported. Protectionist policies first espoused, although weakly, by governments in the late 19th century were strengthened after World War I. From the end of World War II until the early 1970s manufacturing industries were protected by import licensing fees in order to maintain full employment. Thus, there developed some labour-intensive, heavily protected, and uneconomic activities—such as automobile and consumer-electronics assembly (with the manufacture of some parts and components)—that have not been able to remain competitive (see below *Administration of the economy*).

Since the 1960s there has been a proportionate decline in pastoral farming in relation to growth in forestry (and the production of paper and other wood products), horticulture, fishing, deer farming, and tourism, as well as manufacturing. There has been a related change in the composition of exports, although wool, meat, and dairy products have continued to predominate. Since the importance of trade with Great Britain has been reduced, that with Japan, the United States, and Middle Eastern countries has grown. Trade with Australia has always been significant. A succession of trade agreements (1933, 1965, 1977) provided the basis of the Australia and New Zealand Closer Economic Relations Trade Agreement, signed in 1983. This agreement reduces duties and commodity quotas between the two countries and is seen by some as the first step toward integrating their economies.

Trade

Finance. Banking was established early in New Zealand. By the early 1970s an oligopolistic structure had emerged, consisting of several large trading banks (the largest being state-owned and the others foreign-owned), presided over by a central bank—the Reserve Bank of New Zealand—and supplemented by other types of specialty institutions. Since the early 1980s the financial industry has been transformed by the trading banks' loss of their privileged position and by the removal of government controls over financial institutions. The capital market has become highly competitive, with new, often foreign-owned specialty institutions emerging. In addition, in early 1985 transactions in foreign exchange were freed, and for the first time the exchange rate was floated in a competitive market.

Transportation. In spite of the rugged nature of the country, most of the inhabited areas of New Zealand are readily accessible; the road system is good even in rural districts, and modern freeways have been built around the main cities. The private automobile has long been the most important mode of transportation. In addition, bus services link most centres. The difficult country makes for slow journeys, although the distances involved are seldom great.

The railway network, owned and operated by the New Zealand Railways Corporation, is independent of direct government control. It comprises a main trunk line spanning both islands via roll-on ferries and branch lines linking most towns. Narrow tunnels limit the gauge of line, which until the late 20th century precluded the introduction of fast expresses. Rail travel is notoriously slow, discouraging passenger travel, but service is efficient for large-scale movement of goods over considerable distances. Long-standing regulations protecting the railways against competition by road carriers were abolished in the early 1980s, and long-distance road cartage has increased.

The difficult terrain has greatly encouraged air travel in New Zealand; most provincial towns have airports, and all major centres are linked by an air service. The main internal airline, Air New Zealand, is a public corporation; it faces increasing competition from private operators. Air New Zealand, along with several foreign airlines, handles the country's international service, with international air terminals at Auckland, Christchurch, and Wellington.

Administration of the economy. New Zealand has had a long history of government intervention in the economy, ranging from state institutions competing in banking and insurance to an extensive social security system. Until the early 1980s most administrations strengthened and supported this paternalism or state socialism, but since then government policy has generally shifted away from intervention, although no move has been made to dismantle the basic elements of social security. Some of the subsidies and tax incentives to agricultural and manufacturing exporters have been abolished, and such government enterprises as the Post Office have become more commercially oriented and less dependent on government subsidies. In addition, the government has attempted to resolve the difficult issue of restrictive practices in the labour market, such as restrictions on the entry into some occupations and compulsory union membership.

The labour force is organized into strong trade unions. Like Australia, New Zealand evolved a system of compulsory arbitration in which the government played a major role. Since the late 1960s, however, government policy generally has swung between periods of government-imposed freezes in wages and prices and periods of officially tolerated bargaining between unions and employers, although the strong links between the labour markets of New Zealand and Australia—especially in the skilled trades and professional vocations—has been a major constraint on the establishment of a set policy.

Taxation

Although taxation in New Zealand in relation to national income is not particularly high in comparison to other developed countries, direct taxation (taxation of personal income) has traditionally been relied upon to an unusual extent. The introduction in 1986 of a value-added tax on goods and services thus represented a fiscal revolution, because it was linked to a reduction in income tax rates and to an increase in government transfer payments to low-income families. (J.W.R./M.A.Ro./C.A.Bl.)

ADMINISTRATION AND SOCIAL CONDITIONS

Government. *Constitutional practice.* New Zealand has a parliamentary form of government based on the British model. Legislative power is vested in the single-chamber House of Representatives (Parliament), the members of which are elected for three-year terms. There are two dominant parties, National and Labour; the party that commands a majority in the House forms the government. The leader of the governing party becomes the prime minister, who, with ministers responsible for different aspects of government, forms a Cabinet. The Cabinet is the central organ of executive power. Most legislation is initiated in the House on the basis of decisions made by the Cabinet; Parliament must then pass it by a majority vote before it can become law. The Cabinet, however, has extensive regulatory powers that are subject to only limited parliamentary review. Because Cabinet ministers sit in the House and because of invariably strong party discipline, legislative and executive authority are effectively fused.

The British monarch is the formal head of state and is represented technically by a governor-general appointed by the monarch (upon the recommendation of the New Zealand government) to a five-year term. The governor-general has only limited authority, but the office retains some residual powers to protect the constitution and to act in a situation of constitutional crisis; for example, the governor-general can dissolve Parliament under certain circumstances.

The structure of the New Zealand government is relatively simple, but the country's constitutional provisions are more complex. Like that of Great Britain, New Zealand's constitution is a mixture of statute and convention. Where the two clash, convention has tended to prevail. A measure toward simplification was the Constitution Act of 1986, which consolidated and augmented constitutional legislation dating from 1852.

Electoral system. There is universal suffrage for those 18 years of age and older. Parliamentary electoral districts are redrawn after every quinquennial census, their number increasing slowly with population growth; in the mid-1980s there were 95 constituencies, of which four were reserved for the Maori. Parliamentary elections are run on the basis of party affiliation, each electorate returning the one candidate who receives the majority vote. While there are other political parties in New Zealand, the electoral system strongly favours the two-party alternation of governments and makes it difficult for minor-party candidates to win election. In addition, a party may gain a majority of seats in the House but not win a majority of the national vote.

The two-party system

The two major parties have distinct foundations. The National Party's base of support is in rural and affluent urban districts and among those involved in business and management. The Labour Party draws support from trade unions and urban blue-collar workers. Over time, however, both parties have broadened their electoral bases. Labour has gained the support of some areas of the business sector and has succeeded in attracting more professionals, while the National Party has had some success among higher paid workers in key small-town and provincial districts. Increasingly, ideological differentiation between the two parties has become complex, and intraparty differences in such areas as economic policy have often been greater than they have been between parties.

Bureaucratic organization. The business of government is carried out by some three dozen government departments of varying size and importance. Most departments correspond to a ministerial portfolio, department heads being responsible to their respective ministers for administration of their departments. Recruitment and promotion of civil servants is under the control of the State Services Commission, which is independent of partisan politics. Heads of departments and their officials do not change with a change of government, thus ensuring a continuity of administration.

As a check upon possible administrative injustices, the office of parliamentary commissioner for investigations (ombudsman) was established in 1962; the scope of the office's jurisdiction was enlarged in 1968 and again in 1975. In addition, the Official Information Act of 1982 permits public access, with specific exceptions, to government documents.

There are also a certain number of non-civil service appointees within the government. These fill positions in government corporations—commercial ventures, such as the Broadcasting Corporation of New Zealand and the Bank of New Zealand, in which the government is the sole or major stockholder—and in a host of bodies with administrative or advisory functions. Political affiliations, as well as expertise and experience, often figure in appointment decisions for these institutions.

Local government. Local government, which has very limited power in all but peculiarly local matters, is directly empowered by parliamentary statute. Local authorities are thus relatively autonomous, although they do depend upon the central government for financial assistance. The definition of their function and powers is under constant revision as adjustments are made to changing conditions.

Local bodies perform general-purpose duties such as those of counties, boroughs, cities, and town districts or else consist of ad hoc authorities with specialized functions such as harbour and electric-power boards. Every local authority activity is controlled by an elected council or board of local members, whose work is largely honorary. The platform for election is sometimes based on party affiliation, although this does not noticeably affect the working of the councils or boards.

Justice. New Zealand derives from the common law of Britain certain statutes passed before 1947 by the British Parliament. New Zealand law usually follows the precedents of English law. Since the 1970s, however, the New Zealand courts have taken a more independent stance and have begun to play a more significant constitutional and political role with respect to public and administrative law. In addition, some members of the legal community have begun to challenge the traditional doctrine that Parliament may pass any law not binding future Parliaments, contending that certain common-law rights might override the will of Parliament.

The law is administered by the Department of Justice through its courts. The hierarchy of courts dealing with civil and criminal cases is District Courts, the High Court, and the Court of Appeal; the British Privy Council acts as the final court of appeal for New Zealand. Law enforcement is the responsibility of the New Zealand Police, a Cabinet-level department largely independent (with respect to law enforcement) of executive authority.

(J.W.R./M.A.Ro./J.Vo.)

Education. Education in New Zealand is free, secular, and compulsory between the ages of six and 15. In practice almost all children enter primary school at age five, while many of them have already begun their education in preschools, all of which are subsidized by the state. Education is administered by the Department of Education. Elected education boards control all of the primary and secondary state schools. There are also more than 100 private primary and secondary schools, most of them Roman Catholic or run by other religious groups. They also receive state subsidies and must meet certain standards of teaching and accommodation. State primary schools are coeducational, but there are still many single-sex secondary schools.

Technical institutes, community colleges, and teachers' colleges form the basis of higher education. There are also several universities and an agricultural college. Entry to the universities requires a modest educational achievement, which is often waived for people 21 years of age or older.

Since the early years of the colony, a great emphasis has been placed on education, and virtually the entire population is literate. There is a correspondence school that caters to children living in remote places, and various continuing education and adult education centres provide opportunities for lifelong education.

Social security

Welfare. New Zealand has one of the oldest social security systems in the world. Noncontributory old-age pensions paid for from government revenues were introduced in 1898. Pensions for widows and miners followed soon after, and child allowances were introduced in the 1920s. In 1938 the New Zealand government introduced the most extensive system of pensions and welfare in the world, which included free hospital treatment, free pharmaceutical service, and heavily subsidized treatment by medical practitioners.

Since then the system has been eroded in some respects but greatly extended in others. Doctors' fees, though still subsidized by the state, have become relatively high. Many people invest in private medical insurance and seek treatment in private hospitals instead of in public hospitals. There is still a universal system called "national superannuation," in which all citizens over the age of 60 are granted an income of up to 80 percent of their average after-tax wage; but in 1984 a surtax was placed on earnings (over a set amount) from other sources, and many people, in effect, forfeited their pensions. There are numerous other pensions and welfare payments. These include an allowance for each child up to the age of 16 and additional "family care" payments for low-income families, as well as benefits for single parents, invalids, and the sick. Under the Accident Compensation Act of 1972, all persons suffering personal injury from any sort of accident, whether at work or not, can receive compensation for disability and loss of earnings, and they are covered by insurance for any medical or other treatment.

Many New Zealanders aspire to own their own homes. In the larger cities, lack of space is modifying this concept, but there has been no major trend toward apartment living. State agencies provide limited financial assistance toward home purchases and renovation work, as well as subsidized rental accommodations for those on low incomes. The state also subsidizes pensioner accommodations through local authorities.

CULTURAL LIFE

The cultural milieu in New Zealand is complex: it is predominantly European but also contains elements from many other peoples, particularly the Maori. Immigrant groups have generally tended to assimilate into the European life-style, although traditional customs are still followed by many Tongans, Samoans, and other Pacific Islanders. The Maori, however, have found themselves torn between the pressure to assimilate and the desire to preserve their own culture. The loss of much of their land in the 19th century undermined their political structures, and large-scale conversion to Christianity resulted in the abandonment of traditional religious observances; but there has been a determined effort—especially in the second half of the 20th century—to preserve and revive artistic and social traditions. A renaissance has occurred in Maori wood carving and weaving and in the construction of carved and decorated meeting houses (*whare whakairo*). Maori songs and dances have become increasingly popular, especially among the young. Maori meetings—whether *hui* (assemblies) or *tangi* (funeral gatherings)—are conducted in traditional fashion, with ancient greeting ceremonies strictly observed. The general public has become familiar with Maori art, which is displayed in numerous galleries and museums.

Maori cultural aspects

European cultural life has progressed rapidly since the early 20th century. Numerous writers were active in the late 19th century, the most successful of whom were historians, such as William Pember Reeves, and ethnologists, including S. Percy Smith and Elsdon Best. The work of the first genuinely original writers of fiction, the short-story writer Katherine Mansfield and the poet R.A.K. Mason, did not appear until the 1920s. During the harsh years of the Great Depression of the 1930s a group of poets appeared and established a national tradition of writing. Although influenced by contemporary English literature—T.S. Eliot and W.H. Auden were greatly respected—they wrote about their New Zealand experience. The most notable member of this group was Allen Curnow. A.R.D. Fairburn, Denis Glover, and Charles Brasch were other major poets. At the same time Frank Sargeson began writing the superb stories in New Zealand vernacular for which he became well known.

European cultural aspects

Since World War II the work of these pioneering writers has been followed by that of such widely published and acclaimed poets as James K. Baxter and Kendrick Smithyman. There is a host of younger poets, notably Ian Wedde and Elizabeth Smither. A number of novelists have also earned international reputations, notably Janet Frame, Keri Hulme, and Sylvia Ashton-Warner. These and other New Zealand writers have been greatly aided by the growth of the publishing industry in New Zealand during this time.

In the second half of the 20th century, painters began to rival writers in artistic accomplishment. The first to achieve international recognition, Frances Hodgkins, spent most of her life abroad. Since the 1960s, however, an unprecedented "art scene" has emerged, created initially by a group of artists, including Colin McCahon and Don Binney, who were helped by the rise of private galleries in most large towns and cities. While often New Zealand in subject, the paintings from this group indicate how aware the painters were of international influences. This group paved the way for what has become a small legion of artists.

In the 1970s and '80s successful professional theatre companies have been established in the cities—including the Downstage in Wellington and the Mercury Theatre in Auckland—in contrast to the early companies that folded for want of sufficient audiences. Several symphony orchestras also have had growing support. New Zealand has produced some well-known singers, including Dame Kiri Te Kanawa, Inia Te Wiata, and Donald McIntyre. Some popular musical groups have also achieved international success.

The state has moved progressively since the 1940s to assist and encourage the arts. The Queen Elizabeth II Arts Council gives annual grants in support of theatre, music, modern dance and ballet, and opera, and the New Zealand Literary Fund subsidizes publishers and writers. In addition, New Zealand was one of the first countries to establish a fund to compensate writers for the loss of royalties on books borrowed from libraries rather than purchased. The national orchestra and a weekly cultural publication, the *New Zealand Listener,* are supported by the government through the Broadcasting Corporation of New Zealand, which controls Radio New Zealand and both channels of Television New Zealand. The government also subsidizes a motion-picture industry that has received growing international recognition.

Newspapers in New Zealand provide a high standard of reporting, with substantial coverage of world news provided largely by foreign agencies. No daily paper has a national circulation, but some from the large cities are distributed widely over their respective islands. Numerous local and regional dailies are also published.

Newspapers

Sports are the main leisure-time occupation of most of the population. There is widespread participation in most major sports, particularly rugby football. Horse racing is a popular spectator sport. The climate and the variety of terrain allow for year-round activity in many sports.

For statistical data on the land and people of New Zealand, see the *Britannica World Data* section in the BRITANNICA WORLD DATA ANNUAL.

(J.W.R./M.A.Ro./Ke.S.)

History

DISCOVERY

No precise archaeological records exist of when and from where the first human inhabitants of New Zealand came; but it is generally agreed that Polynesians from eastern Polynesia in the central Pacific reached New Zealand more than 1,000 years ago, possibly by AD 800 or even earlier. There has been much speculation on how these people made the long ocean voyage. Polynesians are known to have sometimes set sail in search of new lands, their canoes well-provisioned with food and plants for cultivation, and it is likely that the discoverers of New Zealand were on such a voyage. Few canoes probably made the dangerous journey, but the people from even one of these large, double-hulled craft could have produced the Maori population that the Europeans encountered in New Zealand in the 17th and 18th centuries. With them they brought the dog and the rat and several plants, including the kumara (a variety of sweet potato), taro, and yam.

The Polynesian period has been divided roughly into an early "Archaic" and a later "Classic Maori" phase. The transition between these two phases is uncertain, but it is thought to be linked to improvements in the raising and storage in a cooler climate of what had been tropical vegetables. In the South Island, if not elsewhere, the first Polynesians found moas (flightless birds) in immense numbers on tussock grasslands, and these became their major food supply. The agriculturalist Classic Maori encountered later by Europeans had only faint memories of the moa. The 18th-century Maori population was densest in the warmer northern parts of the country, where the Maori variant of Polynesian culture had reached its high point, particularly in the arts of war, canoe construction, building, weaving, and agriculture.

The first European to arrive in New Zealand was a Dutch sailor, Abel Janszoon Tasman, who sighted the coast of Westland in December 1642. His sole attempt to land brought only a clash with a South Island tribe in which several of his men were killed. After his voyage the western coast of New Zealand became a line upon European charts and was thought of as the possible western edge of a great southern continent.

Captain Cook's explorations

In 1769–70 the British naval officer and explorer James Cook completed Tasman's work by circumnavigating the two major islands and charting them with a remarkable degree of accuracy. His initial contact with the Maori was violent, but harmonious relations were established later. On this and on subsequent voyages Cook, with the explorer and naturalist Joseph Banks, made the first systematic observations of Maori life and culture. Cook's journal, published as *A Voyage Towards the South Pole and Round the World* (1777), brought the knowledge of a new land to Europeans. He stressed the intelligence of the natives and the suitability of the country for colonization, and soon colonists as well as other discoverers followed Cook to the country he had made known.

EARLY EUROPEAN SETTLEMENT

Apart from convicts escaping from Australia and shipwrecked or deserting sailors seeking asylum with Maori tribes, the first European New Zealanders sought profits—from sealskins, timber, New Zealand flax, and whale oil. Early New Zealand was an offshoot of Australian enterprise in whaling and other activities; Sydney, founded as a convict settlement in 1788, became a base for whaling in the South Pacific; and Kororareka (now called Russell), in the far north of New Zealand, became a stopping place for American, British, and French deep-sea whalers. Around both islands Australian firms set up tiny settlements of land-based bay whalers. Traders supplying whalers drew Maori into their economic activity, buying provisions and supplying trade goods, implements, muskets, and rum. Initially the Maori welcomed the newcomers; while the tribes were secure, the European was a useful dependent.

Maori went overseas, some as far as England. A northern chief, Hongi Hika, amassed presents in England, which he exchanged in Australia for muskets; back in New Zealand he waged devastating war on hereditary enemies. The use of firearms spread southward; a series of tribal wars, spreading from north to south, displaced populations and disturbed landholdings, especially in the Waikato, Taranaki, and Cook Strait areas. Europeans were soon to found colonies in these unsettled regions. Missionaries quickly followed the traders. Between 1814 and 1838 Anglicans, Wesleyan Methodists, and Roman Catholics set up stations. Conversion was initially slow, but by the mid-19th century most Maori adhered, for varying reasons, to some form of Christianity.

European colonies

All of these newcomers had a profound effect upon Maori life. Warfare and disease reduced numbers, while new values, pursuits, and beliefs modified tribal structure. Christianity cut across the sanctions and prohibitions that had supplied Maori social cohesion. A capitalist economy, to which Maori were introduced both by traders offering new inducements (for instance, the brief demand for flax) and by missionaries bringing new agricultural techniques, affected the whole material basis of life. At first in the north and later over the whole country a process of adjustment began, which has continued to the present day. By the late 1830s, chiefly through the Australian link, New Zealand had been joined to Europe. Settlers numbered at least some hundreds, and there were certain to be more. Colonization schemes were afoot in Great Britain, and Australian graziers were buying land from the Maori. These circumstances determined British policy.

ANNEXATION AND FURTHER SETTLEMENT

In 1838 the British government decided upon at least partial annexation. In 1839 it commissioned William Hobson, a naval officer, as lieutenant governor and consul to the Maori chiefs, and he, in the event, annexed the whole country, the North Island by the right of cession from the Maori chiefs and the South Island by the right of discovery. At first New Zealand was legally part of New South Wales; but in 1841 it became a separate crown colony, and Hobson was named governor. Before declaring the annexation of New Zealand, Hobson went through a process of discussion with the northern chiefs from which emerged the Treaty of Waitangi (February 1840). Under this instrument the Maori ceded sovereignty to the crown in return for protection and guaranteed possession of their lands; they also agreed to sell land only to the crown. Hobson promised an investigation into past "sales" of land to private individuals to ensure fair dealing. This treaty imposed a strong moral obligation upon the British government to act as guardian to the Maori.

The Treaty of Waitangi

Even before annexation had been proclaimed, the first organized planting of an English colony was under way. The New Zealand Association, founded in 1837 to colonize on the principles laid down by Edward Gibbon Wakefield, sent a survey ship, the *Tory,* in 1839. The agents on board were to buy land in both islands around Cook Strait. The company moved hastily because its founders were aware that British annexation was likely and would entail a crown monopoly of land sales and a consequent increase in price. "Purchases" were effected in great haste before Hobson could bring to an end such private transactions. Little effort was made to seek out the true Maori owners; this would have been difficult anyway, as Maori ownership was communal and titles had been disturbed by the warfare of the preceding quarter century. The company, combining skillful propaganda with outright trickery and brutality, enforced its claim to the land upon which New Plymouth, Wanganui, and Wellington in the North Island and Nelson in the South Island were founded in the 1840s. Later, through the crown, it secured other areas in the South Island where Otago (1848) and Canterbury (1850) were planted by separate associations. Meanwhile, Hobson moved the seat of government south from the Bay of Islands, bringing Auckland into existence (1840).

In the early 1840s settlement and government began to alarm the Maori. In the Cook Strait area a formidable chief, Te Rauparaha, obstructed settlement. Near the Bay of Islands there was open warfare, and Kororareka was repeatedly raided. Neither Hobson (died 1842) nor his successor, Robert FitzRoy, was able to overcome the Maori. George (afterward Sir George) Grey, who became governor in 1845, had money and troops and the will to use them. His victories brought a peace that lasted from 1847 until 1860. Hone Heke, the principal leader in the north, was thoroughly defeated (1846), and in the south a likely uprising was prevented. Racial strife had been accompanied by economic distress. In the mid-1840s the nascent economy was depressed until the Australian gold rushes of the 1850s offered a market for foodstuffs to the New Zealand farmer, settler and Maori alike.

War with the Maori

By the end of the 1840s racial and economic trouble gave way to political agitation. The leading settlements, apart from Auckland, began to campaign for representative government in place of Grey's personal rule. He, while refusing to give way, helped to draft the New Zealand Constitution Act of 1852, which was designed to meet all demands of the settlers. Grey sought not to prevent the introduction of self-government but to delay it until he had determined both native and land policy. He wished to begin the rapid assimilation of the Maori (with whom his relations were excellent) to the British pattern. He also wished to bring in a land policy that would safeguard the small farmer against the great owner. He believed he had secured these goals by the time of his departure at the end of 1853.

Responsible government. After the Constitution Act came into operation, New Zealand was divided into six provinces—Auckland, New Plymouth (Taranaki), Wellington, Nelson, Canterbury, and Otago—each with a superintendent and a provincial council. The central government consisted of a governor and a two-chamber legislature (General Assembly): a Legislative Council nominated by the crown, and a House of Representatives elected upon a low property franchise for a five-year term. This General Assembly did not meet until 1854; it then embarked upon a quarrel with the acting governor, Col. Robert Henry Wynyard, that was not ended until the achievement of full responsible government—*i.e.,* a system under which the governor could act in domestic matters only upon the advice of ministers enjoying the confidence of the elected chamber. Henry Sewell and James FitzGerald, of Canterbury, led the representatives in this struggle, against the opposition of Edward Gibbon Wakefield, who, having first moved the resolution for responsible government, then secretly opposed it while serving as extra-official adviser to the acting governor. The Colonial Office conceded responsible government in 1856. The next governor, Thomas (later Sir Thomas) Gore Browne, reserved Maori affairs to the competence of the governor alone.

Provincial institutions

For most purposes, during the 1850s New Zealand was administered not by central but by provincial institutions. These authorities (10 in number by the time of their abolition in 1876) directly affected the settler through their administration of land and control of immigration and public works. The native department, directly under the governor, bought land from the Maori; the provincial governments settled it, regulated immigration, and built roads and bridges. Until the wars of the 1860s the central legislature was less important, though its ultimate authority remained.

Each province disposed of a revenue arising from land sales, and upon this revenue depended its strength. Canterbury and Otago, with hardly any Maori, grew wealthy spending their money upon communications, immigration, and education. Other provinces were either less fortunate or less wise and enjoyed smaller success. In the North Island numerous and anxious Maori held onto desirable land. Here most of the land available for settlement had been taken up by the end of the 1850s, a good deal of it by speculators, and some of it was given away to attract immigrants. The island remained largely without roads until the 1870s, so impecunious were its governments. But by that time the major obstacle to settlement had been removed—the continuing power of the tribes. This was the result of a decade of war.

Racial conflict. In the 1850s race relations deteriorated. The settler population and the demand for land, especially pastoral land, increased. Many Maori, fearing for their future, became reluctant to sell more land. In the Taranaki Province, where the land shortage was acute, both settlers and those Maori willing to sell were opposed by Wiremu Kingi (Te Rangitake), chief of Te Atiawa. In the Waikato, where good land was coveted by settlers and speculators, an elderly chief, Te Wherowhero, became "king" in 1858, largely through the support of the Waikato and Maniopoto tribes, and reigned as King Potatau I. The Maori King Movement and also the unrest in the Taranaki headed by Wiremu Kingi (the two movements remained distinct though related) were opposed to further land sales.

Land sales

The likelihood of conflict was not reduced by any particular wisdom in government policy. Gore Browne was guided in native policy by the head of the Native Land Purchase Department, Donald (later Sir Donald) McLean, who, responsive to settler demands, increased pressure upon potential sellers. Grey's caution and his recognition that a chief could veto sales proposed by any section of his tribe were forgotten. McLean sowed a rich harvest of distrust. Christopher Richmond, the member of the Cabinet in charge of native affairs, was also a Taranaki representative, fully responsive to the needs of his settler neighbours. The central ministry, theoretically unconcerned with native policy, could not, despite the promise of protection made to the Maori in the Treaty of Waitangi, neglect a matter so vital to the colony's future. In 1859 the representative of the crown unwittingly supplied the occasion for the outbreak of civil strife.

Gore Browne accepted an offer to sell from a Taranaki subchief, Te Teira, and ignored the veto imposed by the paramount chief, Wiremu Kingi. Early in 1860 troops were used to dislodge Kingi from the land in question, the Waitara block. A decade of fighting began. In 1861 Grey was sent back for a second term as governor in the hope that he would again prove to be a peacemaker. In fact he accelerated the extension of conflict. Fearing that Auckland was menaced by the followers of the Maori king, he took defensive measures that could easily be interpreted as acts of aggression, and the fighting subsequently spread from Taranaki to the Waikato. Imperial troops, colonial militia, and Maori allies (for not all the tribes supported the Maori nationalist movement) had no easy task, but their victory could not be postponed for long. By the mid-1860s Maori resistance in the Taranaki and Waikato was ended. But the "king" tribes were by no means crushed, and the fear that they would embark upon war again haunted the colony for many years.

In the later 1860s the fighting was of a different character, in which religion acted as a last, desperate stiffener of Maori resistance. Pai Marire (Hauhauism), an amalgam of Jewish, Christian, and native beliefs, was the first of many cults in which the Maori, rejecting the religion of settler and missionary, put their own imprint upon Christianity. Toward the end of the decade Te Kooti Rikirangi organized resistance on the east coast of North Island. He was the founder of another religious cult as well as a guerrilla of some note; his adaptation of Christianity, Ringatu, still has thousands of followers. Te Kooti was never finally defeated, but by the early 1870s he was forced to retreat into the "King Country" (the centre of the island), where he devoted the rest of his life to religious leadership.

An uneasy peace settled upon the colony in 1870. Casualties had not been high, but the loss of life was serious for the tribes concerned. Especially in those areas in which the Maori king retained some authority, defeat led to a period of withdrawal from settler society. Resentment was deepened by a punitive policy of land confiscation adopted by the victors, a policy improper in its nature and made worse in some places by undiscriminating application to "guilty" and "innocent" tribes alike. The Maori future looked black. By the Native Land Act of 1862, private land transactions between settler and Maori had been legalized, and during the next 40 years the Maori lost most of their best land. Many years were to elapse before Maori numbers, morale, and confidence could revive over the whole country.

Native Land Act

DEVELOPMENT OF THE COLONY

Fluctuation of the economy. Economic growth in the North Island had been considerably retarded by the wars. Meanwhile, the South Island, especially Canterbury and Otago, had grown increasingly prosperous. Pastoral farming expanded steadily, and the discovery of gold, first in Otago and then on the west coast, led to a sudden boom in production and trade. Population rose as diggers poured in; economic life quickened as gold brought prosperity, less to the digger than to bankers, merchants, land sellers, and farmers supplying provisions. The South Island share of the European population jumped from about 40 percent to 60 percent during the 1860s. The North Island did not recover its previous lead until the 20th century.

Discovery of gold

Attempts by other provinces to emulate the development of Canterbury and Otago normally ended in embarrassment (in one case in bankruptcy) as money was recklessly borrowed and spent. To preserve the colony's reputation, the central government in 1867 banned further provincial overseas borrowing. About this time depression struck the greater part of the country, especially the South Island, where the first alluvial gold had by then been worked out. The South Island was thus looking for a stimulus, while the ending of the wars now made further development possible in the North Island. It was widely agreed that only the central government could adequately revitalize the economy.

In 1870 a development policy was provided by Julius (later Sir Julius) Vogel, who at the time was colonial treasurer and who later served two terms (1873–75; 1876) as prime minister. He was convinced (not altogether accurately) that New Zealand was bursting with potential resources needing no more than the stimulus of capital and labour for their exploitation. He borrowed overseas capital for public works on an unprecedented scale and swelled the labour force with assisted immigrants.

Julius Vogel's development policy

Not all of Vogel's schemes were wisely conceived; the prosperity of the mid-1870s was more an investment boom than a solid growth of productivity. But the colony ended the decade with a doubled population (about 500,000) and the beginnings of efficient internal and external communications. Roads, bridges, railways, and telegraph systems had been built, and overseas shipping services improved. Private lending agencies contributed to the boom, and in a heady atmosphere land values and interest rates climbed alarmingly. The public debt greatly increased, and many of the men who had acquired land were in desperate financial straits. Falling overseas prices for farm products (chiefly wool and wheat), a declining gold output, a cautious note in government finance, and widespread unemployment marked the 1880s. Emigrant ships discharged their passengers at ports where unemployment was already rife. There had been growth in the 1870s, but it was succeeded by a depression that lasted until 1895.

Economic depression

Vogel abolished the provincial governments in 1876. They had earned his enmity by refusing to allow their lands to be used as security for public works and by blocking a forest conservation scheme. Essentially, they became outmoded when in the early 1870s the initiative in development passed to the central government. Provincial governments had been set up to colonize their districts; when the centre assumed this function they lost their raison d'être. Abolition came fairly painlessly; it was an affront more to local pride than to local prosperity. Only in Otago was there a strong attempt to resist change. Thereafter, provincial interests were long pursued by the respective delegates in the General Assembly, whose achievements were in no way diminished by the lack of particularist (provincial) institutions.

The governments of the 1880s, though led by men of some ability and imagination, such as Sir Robert Stout and Sir Harry Atkinson, did not deal effectively with the depression. The time-honoured remedy, spending loan money on development, was not fully given up until 1887. The basic problem was to find productive work for the country's labour force; closer land settlement was the remedy suggested in the 1880s and applied in the 1890s. Great areas, especially in the South Island, had fallen to large owners; these "monopolists" were attacked by the radicals, though probably the pastoral industry could not have been established under any other system. William Rolleston, minister of lands in the early 1880s, first proposed that the state should help men to become small farmers as state tenants; John (later Sir John) McKenzie and the Liberal government applied this remedy with vigour in the 1890s. But closer settlement and intensive farming did not of themselves create economic benefits, which in fact could not accrue until small farmers had a product to export and gained a good price for that product. Refrigeration and rising world prices provided the answer. It became possible in the 1880s to send to Great Britain refrigerated cargoes of butter, cheese, and meat; this encouraged the spread of small-scale intensive farming.

The Liberal era (1891–1912). The energetic Liberal government led by John Ballance, which took office in 1891, accelerated the process of change. It opened more land (much of it bought from the Maori), established farmers on perpetual state leaseholds, provided credit for land purchase and improvements, and built roads. So came into existence great dairying and meat producing areas, especially in the North Island. Dairy, meat, and also wool prices rose in about 1895 and stayed generally high until about 1920.

This economic stimulus was not limited to farmers. Urban distress had been serious in the 1880s, for many recent immigrants had been townsmen who had stayed in New Zealand towns on arrival. The ultimate cure for their distress was for the towns to share in the farmers' high prices. Urban New Zealand depended upon the prosperity of the country. But other remedies were considered, and some of them were applied. In the 1880s there was serious discussion of insurance against sickness, poverty, and old age; the Old Age Pensions Act of 1898 was the first measure of social security. Tariff protection to foster industrial employment was halfheartedly applied in the late 1880s. Revelations of oppression in industry led in the 1890s to a labour code to protect workers.

The growth of trade unions

But the chief Liberal industrial policy, formulated by William Pember Reeves, minister of labour from 1892 to 1896, was to encourage trade unions and to introduce, in the Industrial Conciliation and Arbitration Act of 1894, a conciliation and compulsory arbitration system intended to end industrial unrest and give the unions the means of protecting their members. The growth of unions was stimulated by the fact that only through them could the workers use the system. Reeves's act, amended and occasionally suspended but still essentially his own handiwork, remained in effect until the late 1960s. It enabled the worker in good times to resist wage cuts and to press for increases; but it did not manage to prevent cuts and unemployment when falling overseas prices brought depression to New Zealand. It was not strikingly radical in effect; employers and governments used it to break strikes, such as that of miners at Waihi in 1912. It built up the power of those majority elements in the unions that preferred coming to terms with capitalism to any effort to destroy it. Some occupations, such as transport, cargo handling, meat processing, and mining, fostered unions keen to relinquish arbitration for direct action, but they were in a minority and seldom, in the long run, successful. Farmers and governments have usually acted with severity in disputes affecting the movement of exports.

The Liberal era, from 1891 to 1912, transformed political life. Previously politics had not been marked by neat party divisions. Local advantage had determined political behaviour in the development period during and after the 1870s; men had argued over the scope and details of policies and had advanced the claims of locality and province for a proper share of largess. Acute depression ended development and with it the politics of local advantage. In 1890 the Liberals began to act as a more or less unified party. Their 20 years in office, the success of their land and labour policies, and the formidable qualities of leadership discovered in Richard John Seddon, premier from 1893 to his death in 1906, welded the Liberals into a fairly coherent parliamentary and popular party.

R.J. Seddon as premier

Seddon was a portent of a new age. In 1893 this energetic goldfields trader-turned-politician provided a sharp contrast to the gentlemanly premiers who had preceded him. But his crudeness assisted rather than hindered the attainment of popularity none of them had known. He was devoted to political success and skilled in the manipulation of the means of success—parliamentary procedure, patronage, and party organization. By the time of his death he had established a kind of elective despotism over the country.

THE 20TH CENTURY

Seddon's successors, in his own and in other parties, were of the same stamp—men of the people devoted to a political career. Politics ceased to be a duty of the well-to-do amateur. The Liberal government, under Sir Joseph Ward, survived Seddon by six years. In 1912 it fell before a new party, Reform, led by a dairy farmer, William Ferguson Massey, prime minister until 1925. Based on prospering farmers and townsmen, especially of the North Island, and closely connected with their professional organizations, it was more narrowly sectional than the Liberals had been. Except for views borrowed from the Liberals, it had little positive policy. Reform made much of a promise to enable the state leaseholder to buy the freehold of his farm at original valuation; this promise was an emotional rallying cry for conservatives fearing land nationalization and complete socialism. Only a small minority of farmers were state tenants, and not all bought the freehold when the Reform government gave them the chance.

While the Liberals lost support in rural areas, they were further weakened by urban left-wing defections, which eventually led to a separate Labour Party. The initiative, on the right and on the left, was passing to other parties, and the Liberals were gradually eclipsed. The period before World War I was one of discontent and anxiety. Prosperity, though still considerable, had somewhat declined. The farmers were disturbed by what they took to be the threat of socialism, detected in the radicalism of a Liberal minority but chiefly in the rebirth of direct action in some trade unions. This change in temper arose from labour dissatisfaction with wage levels achieved under arbitration and from the growth of syndicalist and socialist ideas. After 1906 the Arbitration Court refused to grant further increases of real wages. Discontent flared up in the strikes of 1912–13, the biggest occurring on the waterfront when the farmers' government, headed by Massey, repressed a movement that had overtones of revolution.

Nationalism and war. By the late 19th century many

New Zealanders were coming to regard themselves as a new nation. Most of them had been born in New Zealand and had no memories of or nostalgia for Britain, often called "home." In the 1890s New Zealand Natives Associations were established by native-born European New Zealanders. Their success in sports, especially rugby football, spurred national pride. An even greater influence was war. New Zealanders served on the British side during the South African War (1899–1902), during which time they earned a reputation as being superior to the British at fighting a guerrilla war. World War I greatly stimulated national sentiment. During the warfare at Gallipoli and later in France New Zealanders proved themselves to be excellent soldiers. But while the war boosted nationalist sentiment among both troops and civilians, the price was terrible: nearly one of every three men between the ages of 20 and 40 was killed or wounded. The loss in leadership in the following years was considerable.

At home the war brought prosperity, as export markets were assured and prices good. Domestic unity was hardly shaken by the antiwar feeling of a handful of left-wingers. Massey remained prime minister, but in the wartime coalition government (1915–19) Ward and the Liberals carried great weight. Reform stayed in office until 1928, led after Massey's death in 1925 by Joseph Gordon Coates. The party survived the first postwar depression but not that of the mid-1920s. Led by Ward, the Liberals, under the new name of United Party, were victorious in 1928; they thus had to face the deepening depression of 1929–30. After Ward's death (1930) and at the height of the depression, Reform and United formed a new coalition (1931) under the premiership of George Forbes, which lasted until the election of 1935 brought in a Labour government.

Some postwar developments were of great importance. In external affairs, Massey led a delegation to the peace conference, signed the Treaty of Versailles, and so committed New Zealand to membership in the League of Nations. New Zealand thus began to acquire the status of a sovereign state, though Massey denied this consequence.

Sovereign status

The Liberals, especially Seddon, had already taken steps toward autonomy within the empire. At the series of colonial and imperial conferences from 1887 onward, New Zealand had followed Canada and Australia in asserting its right to a voice in certain foreign policy issues. Seddon argued vehemently against British reluctance to acquire more Pacific islands while permitting German influence to grow in Samoa.

New Zealand legislation to restrict Asian immigration was sharply and obstinately at variance with British policy. Western Samoa, which New Zealand had captured from the Germans in 1914 and over which it was granted a mandate in 1920, also provided occasions for British and New Zealand differences.

Reform leaders professed little love for the principle of Commonwealth autonomy. New Zealand took a passive part in the conferences leading to the Statute of Westminster in 1931 and did not adopt it until 1947. But the substance of autonomy had been enjoyed before.

The major domestic achievement of the Reform administration was a system of export marketing agencies in which authority was shared by producer and state. These laid the foundations of a collectivist marketing structure. J.G. Coates was the most energetic minister in Forbes' coalition government. His attempts to counter depression concentrated upon the farmer in order to revive the country. To increase export receipts, he devalued the New Zealand pound; he protected the farmer against foreclosure and set up a credit agency.

When overseas prices began to recover in 1934, the country was financially strong, but little had been done for the unemployed. Conditions in towns and relief camps led to rioting, violence, and widespread discontent, all of which were favourable to the Labour Party. The Labour Party had been formed by socialist and radical groups in 1916. During the 1920s it was predominant only in working-class electorates. In its quest for votes, however, Labour increasingly abandoned its socialist theories and adopted welfare and credit-reform proposals, which had wider appeal. In the election of 1935 Labour won a considerable victory; successful in the towns, the party also won in many rural areas. Prices for dairy exports were slowest to recover, and many dairy farmers were drawn by Labour promises of a guaranteed price. The victory was particularly notable in terms of seats, for a right-wing third party (the Democrat Party) split the conservative vote to Labour's advantage. The National Party, successor to the coalition, was rendered temporarily ineffective.

Labour in power

The new ministers, among whom the most notable were Peter Fraser and Walter Nash, showed great energy; led by Michael Joseph Savage, they had the good fortune to govern a country to which prosperity was returning. The farmer enjoyed increased earnings; the worker, increased wages and shorter hours. Jobs were multiplied by a public works and housing program. The education system was revitalized. In 1938 the Social Security Act provided a state medical service, extended the pension system, and increased benefits. The expansion of secondary industry was accelerated after the outbreak of World War II in 1939.

World War II and after. The alacrity with which New Zealand went to war in 1939 showed that dominion autonomy had not weakened the country's ties with Great Britain. At first the war resembled that of 1914; troops were sent to Egypt to train for the European conflict. There they were directly involved by the enemy advance and saw action in Greece, Crete, North Africa, and Italy. After 1941 New Zealand was directly threatened by Japan, and New Zealand forces were also engaged in the Pacific. Well before the end of the war, the strain upon the country's manpower, together with the demands of home production, forced a reduction of commitments in the Pacific.

The Pacific theatre was dominated by the United States, the forces of which provided New Zealand's sole defense. The fact that disaster was averted by American and not by British forces required a change in New Zealand's attitudes; security was conferred by a foreign, though friendly, power. External relations in the postwar period reflected this new situation, chiefly through the ANZUS pact (1951), a defensive alliance between Australia, New Zealand, and the United States.

War economy

At home the total economy was mobilized in the war effort. Controls were extended over the whole economy. Conscription and direction (directed allocation of the labour force to strategic industries) sent manpower into the military forces and essential occupations; heavy taxation, war loans, bulk purchase, and controlled marketing kept the economy in a firm grip. They also kept inflation in check; with price control and wage restraint, they amounted to a complete policy of economic stabilization, applied by a Labour government that remained in power until 1949. Savage died early in the war. Fraser, his successor, and Nash were chiefly responsible for the tasks of administration during the war and of reconstruction after peace returned.

Sidney Holland led the revival of the National Party, which culminated in victory in 1949. Discontent with controls and with the rising cost of living helped to swing support away from Labour. The National government benefited from its vigorous handling of a serious waterfront dispute in 1951, but in later elections its majority narrowed until Labour returned in 1957. In 1960 the National Party, led by Keith Holyoake, was returned to power, which it retained until 1972. In that year Labour won a huge victory under Norman Kirk; his death in office in 1974 was the prelude to as great a National victory in 1975, under a new leader, Robert Muldoon.

After World War II New Zealand began to play a relatively independent role in world affairs. This development, in fact, began before the war, when the Labour government's attitude to the League of Nations was coloured by an idealism that clashed with British policy. During the war Fraser had insisted upon an independent voice in the councils of the Allied Powers. At the formation of the United Nations in 1945 he became a notable spokesman for the small powers and made a large impression upon the Trusteeship Council. None of these developments weakened New Zealand's close affinity with Great Britain, its loyalty to the Commonwealth, or its dependence upon the United States.

Postwar foreign policy

Geography and insecurity shaped postwar foreign policy. With Australia, New Zealand claimed a voice in settlement in the South Pacific Commission and in the transfer of authority in Western Samoa, successfully completed in 1962. New Zealand became deeply involved in Southeast Asia. From 1951 it provided assistance through the Colombo Plan. New Zealanders fought in Malaya, Korea, and Vietnam; further, New Zealand became a member of the Southeast Asia Treaty Organization (SEATO) in 1954 and supported the United States by sending troops to Vietnam. This reflected fear at the growth of Communist power in Asia. The independent spirit of the postwar years was modified to a greater dependence on Western powers during the 1950s and '60s. In the later 1960s involvement in the Vietnam War led to a vigorous and continuing public debate on foreign affairs. After Vietnam, debate turned largely on the problem of South African apartheid, especially in the contexts of sports relations with South Africa and with African countries at Commonwealth and Olympic games.

The 1970s and '80s were difficult economically for New Zealand. The combination in the early 1970s of high energy prices and Great Britain's entry into the EEC brought about a severe economic recession. Inflation skyrocketed, unemployment soared, and thousands emigrated to Australia. The response of the Muldoon government was interventionism on an unparalleled scale: the government borrowed funds from overseas and ran up huge budgetary deficits, in part to finance large industrial developments; in the early 1980s it placed a freeze on wages and prices; and it attempted to regulate interest rates. Dissatisfaction with this program led in 1984 to the election of a Labour government, headed by David Lange. The Lange government initiated one of the most sweeping reversals of government policy in the country's history as, one after another, restrictions on free enterprise that had been imposed progressively over some 50 years were lifted.

During this period, as Great Britain lowered its international profile and as U.S. influence diminished in the region, New Zealand's sense of isolation grew. New Zealand increased its independent stance in foreign policy, and greater interest was shown for improving relations with neighbouring countries. The country took a strong stand against the proliferation of nuclear weapons in the region, protesting atmospheric tests of nuclear devices by the French and calls by U.S. nuclear-powered and nuclear-armed ships to New Zealand ports.

Social problems

Social problems, many associated with the position of women and of the family, multiplied. Divorce, illegitimacy, and single parentage grew; as a result, education, including moral education, and abortion occasioned fierce public debates. Other value-related agitations—over the environment, nuclear power, and the U.S. alliance—contributed to the heightening of social tensions in the late 20th century, together with a major growth of nationalistic feeling among young urban Maori. Issues related to the economy, race relations, foreign policy, the position of women and of the family, sport, and the environment remained the most vital issues in public affairs.

For later developments in the political history of New Zealand, see the *Britannica Book of the Year* section in the BRITANNICA WORLD DATA ANNUAL.

For coverage of related topics in the *Macropædia* and *Micropædia,* see the *Propædia,* Part Nine, Division VI, Section 967; and Division VII, Section 977.

(W.H.O./Ke.S.)

BIBLIOGRAPHY

Physical and human geography: (*General*): Basic descriptive information is available in A.H. MCLINTOCK (ed.), *An Encyclopaedia of New Zealand,* 3 vol. (1966); GORDON MCLAUCHLAN, *Bateman New Zealand Encyclopedia* (1984); and DIANA POPE and JEREMY POPE, *The Mobil Illustrated Guide to New Zealand* (1982), *Mobil New Zealand Travel Guide: North Island,* 5th rev. ed. (1984), and *Mobil New Zealand Travel Guide: South Island and Stewart Island,* 3rd rev. ed. (1978). See also the *New Zealand Official Yearbook* (annual), statistics and descriptive text on all aspects of New Zealand life, including an extensive bibliography.

(*The land*): Basic physiographical information is discussed in A. GRANT ANDERSON (ed.), *New Zealand in Maps* (1977); D.J. HOOTON (ed.), *New Zealand: The Physical Environment* (1970); A.H. MCLINTOCK (ed.), *A Descriptive Atlas of New Zealand* (1959); and IAN WARDS (ed.), *New Zealand Atlas* (1976). Works on geology and climate include C.A. COTTON, *Geomorphology: An Introduction to the Study of Landforms,* 7th ed. rev. (1958, reissued 1968); MAXWELL GAGE, *Legends in the Rocks: An Outline of New Zealand Geology* (1980); JACOBUS T. KINGMA, *The Geological Structure of New Zealand* (1974); J.M. SOONS and M.J. SELBY, *Landforms of New Zealand* (1982); H.S. GIBBS, *New Zealand Soils* (1980); G. KUSCHEL (ed.), *Biogeography and Ecology in New Zealand* (1975); and B.J. GARNIER, *The Climate of New Zealand* (1958). For studies of specific topics, see RICHARD BEDFORD and ANDREW STURMAN (eds.), *Canterbury at the Crossroads: Issues for the Eighties* (1983); WARREN MORAN (ed.), *Auckland and the Central North Island: Essays for the 1974 IGU Regional Conference North Island Tours* (1974); JOHN PASCOE (ed.), *National Parks of New Zealand,* 3rd ed. (1974); and L.F. MOLLOY (comp.), *Land Alone Endures: Land Use and the Role of Research* (1980). Information on animal and plant forms in New Zealand can be found in R.A. FALLA, R.B. GIBSON, and E.G. TURBOTT, *The New Guide to the Birds of New Zealand and Outlying Islands,* rev. ed. (1979); RUSSELL JACKSON, *Wildlife New Zealand* (1982); A.L. POOLE (comp.), *Wild Animals in New Zealand,* 2nd ed. (1973); H.H. ALLAN, *Flora of New Zealand,* vol. 1, *Indigenous Tracheophyta* (1961, reprinted 1982); L. COCKAYNE, *The Vegetation of New Zealand,* 2nd ed. rev. and enl. (1928, reprinted 1958); E. BRUCE LEVY, *Grasslands of New Zealand,* 3rd ed. (1970); and J.T. SALMON, *The Native Trees of New Zealand* (1980). See also GORDON R. WILLIAMS (ed.), *The Natural History of New Zealand: An Ecological Survey* (1973); G.A. KNOX (ed.), *The Natural History of Canterbury,* enl. ed. (1969); and NOEL W. CUSA and RONALD M. LOCKLEY, *New Zealand Endangered Species* (1980).

(*The people*): Ethnic background and interaction are the subject of R.J. WARWICK NEVILLE and C. JAMES O'NEILL (eds.), *The Population of New Zealand* (1979); PAUL SPOONLEY, DAVID PEARSON, and IAN SHIRLEY (eds.), *New Zealand: Sociological Perspective* (1982); TE RANGI HIROA (PETER BUCK), *The Coming of the Maori,* 2nd ed. (1950, reissued 1966); DAVID LEWIS, *The Maori* (1982, reissued 1985); and JOAN METGE, *The Maoris of New Zealand,* rev. ed. (1976). Regional and demographic trends are discussed in JOACHIM FERNAU, *Social Process in New Zealand: Readings in Sociology* (1969); BRIAN COLLESS and PETER DONOVAN (eds.), *Religion in New Zealand Society* (1980); R.J. JOHNSTON (ed.), *Urbanisation in New Zealand* (1973), and *Society and Environment in New Zealand* (1974); T.K. MCDONALD, *Regional Development in New Zealand: A Report to the Minister of Industries and Commerce* (1969); "New Zealand: Maori Incorporations," a group of essays in *Trends in Ethnic Group Relations in Asia and Oceania* (1979), pp. 205–292, a UNESCO publication; and J.S. WHITELAW (ed.), *Auckland in Ferment* (1967). See also NEW ZEALAND PLANNING COUNCIL. POPULATION MONITORING GROUP, *The New Zealand Population: Contemporary Trends and Issues* (1985), and *The New Zealand Population: Patterns of Change* (1984).

(*The economy*): Economic history and contemporary conditions are documented by G.R. HAWKE, *The Making of New Zealand: An Economic History* (1985); JOHN GOULD, *The Rake's Progress?: The New Zealand Economy Since 1945* (1982), and *The Muldoon Years* (1985); PETER LANE, *Economy in the Balance: An Introduction to the New Zealand Economy* (1976); IAN MCLEAN, *The Future for New Zealand Agriculture* (1978); and RESERVE BANK OF NEW ZEALAND, *Financial Policy Reform* (1986). The New Zealand Institute of Economic Research publishes a variety of research papers, among them A. BOLLARD and B. EASTON (eds.), *Markets, Regulation and Pricing: Six Case Studies* (1985); and BRIAN EASTON (ed.), *Studies in the Labour Market* (1983). The institute also publishes several regular journals: *Quarterly Predictions of National Income and Expenditure;* and *Quarterly Survey of Business Opinion.* Another government body, the New Zealand Planning Council, publishes reports; see especially those from the council's affiliated organization, the ECONOMIC MONITORING GROUP, *The Government Deficit and the Economy* (1984), and *Strategy for Growth* (1984).

(*Administration and social conditions*): Government and social policy are discussed in GRAHAM W.A. BUSH, *Local Government and Politics in New Zealand* (1980); STEPHEN LEVINE (ed.), *Politics in New Zealand* (1978); and its complementary volume, STEPHEN LEVINE, *The New Zealand Political System* (1979); DAVID MCGEE, *Parliamentary Practice in New Zealand* (1985); HYAM GOLD, *New Zealand Politics in Perspective* (1985), and *New Directions in New Zealand Foreign Policy* (1985); NEW ZEALAND. DEPARTMENT OF JUSTICE, *A Bill of Rights for New Zealand* (1985), and *Constitutional Reform* (1986); R.J. GREGORY (ed.), *The Official Information Act* (1984); R.C. MASCARENHAS (ed.), *Public and Private Enterprise in New Zealand*

(1984); R.C. MASCARENHAS, *Public Enterprise in New Zealand* (1982); S. HARVEY FRANKLIN, *Trade, Growth, and Anxiety: New Zealand Beyond the Welfare State* (1978); BRIAN EASTON, *Social Policy and the Welfare State in New Zealand* (1980); and MARGARET CLARK (ed.), *The Politics of Education in New Zealand* (1981).

(*Cultural life*): Information on art in New Zealand is available in TERENCE BARROW, *Maori Art of New Zealand* (1978); GORDON H. BROWN and HAMISH KEITH, *An Introduction to New Zealand Painting: 1839–1980*, rev. and enl. ed. (1982); and SIDNEY MOKO MEAD (ed.), *Te Maori: Maori Art from New Zealand Collections* (1984). See also relevant sections in BRIAN BRAKE, JAMES M. MCNEISH, and DAVID SIMMONS, *Art of the Pacific* (1979). Useful works on New Zealand literature include HOWARD MCNAUGHTON (comp.), *Contemporary New Zealand Plays* (1974); and HOWARD MCNAUGHTON, *New Zealand Drama* (1981); WITI IHIMAERA and D.S. LONG (eds.), *Into the World of Light: An Anthology of Maori Writing* (1982); IAN WEDDE and HARVEY MCQUEEN (eds.), *The Penguin Book of New Zealand Verse* (1985); FLEUR ADCOCK (ed.), *The Oxford Book of Contemporary New Zealand Poetry* (1982); and LYDIA WEVERS (ed.), *New Zealand Short Stories, Fourth Series* (1984).

History: (*General works*): KEITH SINCLAIR, *A History of New Zealand*, rev. and enl. ed. (1980); W.H. OLIVER and B.R. WILLIAMS (eds.), *The Oxford History of New Zealand* (1981); and DAVID HAMER (ed.), *New Zealand Social History* (1980). See also W. DAVID MCINTYRE and W.J. GARDNER (eds.), *Speeches and Documents on New Zealand History* (1971).

(*Early history*): For the pre-European Maori, see RAYMOND FIRTH, *Economics of the New Zealand Maori* (1959, reprinted 1973); D.R. SIMMONS, *The Great New Zealand Myth: A Study of the Discovery and Origin Traditions of the Maori* (1976); and GEORGE GREY, *Polynesian Mythology and Ancient Traditional History of the New Zealand Race, as Furnished by Their Priests and Chiefs* (1885, reissued 1970 as *Polynesian Mythology and Ancient Traditional History of the Maori as Told by Their Priests and Chiefs*). For early contact, see JOHN CAWTE BEAGLEHOLE, *The Discovery of New Zealand*, 2nd ed. (1961); JUDITH BINNEY, *The Legacy of Guilt: A Life of Thomas Kendall* (1968); J.M.R. OWENS, *Prophets in the Wilderness: The Wesleyan Mission to New Zealand, 1819–27* (1974); HARRISON M. WRIGHT, *New Zealand, 1769–1840* (1959, reprinted 1967). For annexation and early government, see IAN M. WARDS, *The Shadow of the Land: A Study of British Policy and Racial Conflict in New Zealand 1832–1852* (1968); and PETER ADAMS, *Fatal Necessity: British Intervention in New Zealand, 1830–1847* (1977). Early settlement is covered in JOHN OWEN MILLER, *Early Victorian New Zealand* (1958); and JAMES HIGHT and C.R. STRAUBEL (eds.), *A History of Canterbury*, vol. 1, *To 1854* (1957). See also STEVAN ELDRED-GRIGG, *A Southern Gentry: New Zealanders Who Inherited the Earth* (1980).

(*Later 19th century*): The period to about 1870 is covered by JAMES RUTHERFORD, *Sir George Grey, K.C.B., 1812–1898* (1961); R.M. DALZIEL, *Julius Vogel, Business Politician* (1986); KEITH SINCLAIR, *The Origins of the Maori Wars*, 2nd ed. (1961, reprinted 1976); ALAN WARD, *A Show of Justice: Racial "Amalgamation" in Nineteenth Century New Zealand* (1974); and W.P. MORRELL, *The Provincial System in New Zealand, 1852–76*, 2nd rev. ed. (1964). For subsequent development, especially in politics and economics, see JUDITH BASSETT, *Sir Harry Atkinson, 1831–1892* (1975); R.M. BURDON, *King Dick: A Biography of Richard John Seddon* (1955); KEITH SINCLAIR, *William Pember Reeves* (1965); R.C.J. STONE, *Makers of Fortune: A Colonial Business Community and Its Fall* (1973); R.M. DALZIEL, *The Origins of New Zealand Diplomacy: The Agent-General in London, 1870–1905* (1975); ANGUS ROSS, *New Zealand Aspirations in the Pacific in the Nineteenth Century* (1964); PATRICIA GRIMSHAW, *Women's Suffrage in New Zealand* (1972); and C.G.F. SIMKIN, *The Instability of a Dependent Economy: Economic Fluctuations in New Zealand, 1840–1914* (1951).

(*The 20th century*): General works that concentrate on the 20th century include ROBERT CHAPMAN and KEITH SINCLAIR (eds.), *Studies of a Small Democracy* (1963, reissued 1965); and J.B. CONDLIFFE, *New Zealand in the Making: A Study of Economic and Social Development*, 2nd rev. ed. (1959, reprinted 1963), and *The Welfare State in New Zealand* (1959, reprinted 1975). The following biographies are recommended: P.J. O'FARRELL, *Harry Holland, Militant Socialist* (1964); ERIK OLSSEN, *John A. Lee* (1977); KEITH SINCLAIR, *Walter Nash* (1976); MICHAEL KING, *Te Puea* (1977); and J. MCLEOD HENDERSON, *Ratana: The Man, the Church, the Political Movement*, 2nd ed. (1972). Specific themes are discussed in H. ROTH, *Trade Unions in New Zealand Past and Present* (1973); F.L.W. WOOD, *New Zealand in the World* (1940), and *The New Zealand People at War: Political and External Affairs* (1958, reprinted 1971); BRUCE M. BROWN, *The Rise of New Zealand Labour: A History of the New Zealand Labour Party from 1916 to 1940* (1962); BARRY GUSTAFSON, *Labour's Path to Political Independence: The Origins and Establishment of the New Zealand Labour Party, 1900–19* (1980); RICHARD KENNAWAY, *New Zealand Foreign Policy, 1951–1971* (1972); R.S. MILNE, *Political Parties in New Zealand* (1966); KENNETH SCOTT, *The New Zealand Constitution* (1962); and R.M. CHAPMAN, W.K. JACKSON, and A.V. MITCHELL, *New Zealand Politics in Action: The 1960 General Election* (1962).

(J.W.R./M.A.Ro./Ke.S./W.Mo./C.A.Bl./J.Vo./W.H.O.)

Newton

Isaac Newton, English physicist and mathematician, was the culminating figure of the scientific revolution of the 17th century. In optics, his discovery of the composition of white light integrated the phenomena of colours into the science of light and laid the foundation for modern physical optics. In mechanics, his three laws of motion, the basic principles of modern physics, resulted in the formulation of the law of universal gravitation. In mathematics, he was the original discoverer of the infinitesimal calculus. Newton's *Philosophiae Naturalis Principia Mathematica* (*Mathematical Principles of Natural Philosophy*), 1687, was one of the most important single works in the history of modern science.

By courtesy of the National Portrait Gallery, London

Newton, oil painting by Sir Godfrey Kneller, 1702. In the National Portrait Gallery, London.

Formative influences. Born on December 25, 1642 (January 4, 1643, new style), in the hamlet of Woolsthorpe, Lincolnshire, Newton was the only son of a local yeoman, also Isaac Newton, who had died three months before, and of Hannah Ayscough. That same year, at Arcetri near Florence, Galileo Galilei had died; Newton would eventually pick up his idea of a mathematical science of motion and bring his work to full fruition. A tiny and weak baby, Newton was not expected to survive his first day of life, much less 84 years. Deprived of a father before birth, he soon lost his mother as well, for within two years she married a second time; her husband, the well-to-do minister Barnabas Smith, left young Isaac with his grandmother and moved to a neighbouring village to raise a son and two daughters. For nine years, until the death of Barnabas Smith in 1653, Isaac was effectively separated from his mother, and his pronounced psychotic tendencies have been ascribed to this traumatic event. That he hated his stepfather we may be sure. When he examined the state of his soul in 1662 and compiled a catalog of sins in shorthand, he remembered "Threatning my father and mother Smith to burne them and the house over them." The acute sense of insecurity that rendered him obsessively anxious when his work was published and irrationally violent when he defended it accompanied Newton throughout his life and can plausibly be traced to his early years.

After his mother was widowed a second time, she determined that her first-born son should manage her now considerable property. It quickly became apparent, however, that this would be a disaster, both for the estate and for Newton. He could not bring himself to concentrate on rural affairs—set to watch the cattle, he would curl up under a tree with a book. Fortunately, the mistake was recognized, and Newton was sent back to the grammar school in Grantham, where he had already studied, to prepare for the university. As with many of the leading scientists of the age, he left behind in Grantham anecdotes about his mechanical ability and his skill in building models of machines, such as clocks and windmills. At the school he apparently gained a firm command of Latin but probably received no more than a smattering of arithmetic. By June 1661, he was ready to matriculate at Trinity College, Cambridge, somewhat older than the other undergraduates because of his interrupted education.

Influence of the scientific revolution. When Newton arrived in Cambridge in 1661, the movement now known as the scientific revolution was well advanced, and many of the works basic to modern science had appeared. Astronomers from Copernicus to Kepler had elaborated the heliocentric system of the universe. Galileo had proposed the foundations of a new mechanics built on the principle of inertia. Led by Descartes, philosophers had begun to formulate a new conception of nature as an intricate, impersonal, and inert machine. Yet as far as the universities of Europe, including Cambridge, were concerned, all this might well have never happened. They continued to be the strongholds of outmoded Aristotelianism, which rested on a geocentric view of the universe and dealt with nature in qualitative rather than quantitative terms.

Like thousands of other undergraduates, Newton began his higher education by immersing himself in Aristotle's work. Even though the new philosophy was not in the curriculum, it was in the air. Some time during his undergraduate career, Newton discovered the works of the French natural philosopher René Descartes and the other mechanical philosophers, who, in contrast to Aristotle, viewed physical reality as composed entirely of particles of matter in motion and who held that all the phenomena of nature result from their mechanical interaction. A new set of notes, which he entitled "Quaestiones Quaedam Philosophicae" ("Certain Philosophical Questions"), begun sometime in 1664, usurped the unused pages of a notebook intended for traditional scholastic exercises; under the title he entered the slogan "Amicus Plato amicus Aristoteles magis amica veritas" ("Plato is my friend, Aristotle is my friend, but my best friend is truth"). Newton's scientific career had begun.

Importance of the "Quaestiones"

The "Quaestiones" reveal that Newton had discovered the new conception of nature that provided the framework of the scientific revolution. He had thoroughly mastered the works of Descartes and had also discovered that the French philosopher Pierre Gassendi had revived atomism, an alternative mechanical system to explain nature. The "Quaestiones" also reveal that Newton already was inclined to find the latter a more attractive philosophy than Cartesian natural philosophy, which rejected the existence of ultimate indivisible particles. The works of the 17th-century chemist Robert Boyle provided the foundation for Newton's considerable work in chemistry. Significantly, he had read Henry More, the Cambridge Platonist, and was thereby introduced to another intellectual world, the magical Hermetic tradition, which sought to explain natural phenomena in terms of alchemical and magical concepts. The two traditions of natural philosophy, the mechanical and the Hermetic, antithetical though they appear, continued to influence his thought and in their tension supplied the fundamental theme of his scientific career.

Although he did not record it in the "Quaestiones," Newton had also begun his mathematical studies. He again started with Descartes, from whose *La Géometrie* he branched out into the other literature of modern analysis with its application of algebraic techniques to problems of geometry. He then reached back for the support of classical geometry. Within little more than a year, he had mastered the literature; and, pursuing his own line of analysis, he began to move into new territory. He discovered the binomial theorem, and he developed the calculus, a more powerful form of analysis that employs infinitesimal considerations in finding the slopes of curves and areas under curves.

Development of the calculus

By 1669 Newton was ready to write a tract summarizing his progress, *De Analysi per Aequationes Numeri Terminorum Infinitas* ("On Analysis by Infinite Series"), which circulated in manuscript through a limited circle and made his name known. During the next two years he revised it as *De methodis serierum et fluxionum* ("On the Methods of Series and Fluxions"). The word fluxions, Newton's private rubric, indicates that the calculus had been born. Despite the fact that only a handful of savants were even aware of Newton's existence, he had arrived at the point where he had become the leading mathematician in Europe.

Work during the plague years. When Newton received the bachelor's degree in April 1665, the most remarkable undergraduate career in the history of university education had passed unrecognized. On his own, without formal guidance, he had sought out the new philosophy and the new mathematics and made them his own, but he had confined the progress of his studies to his notebooks. Then, in 1665, the plague closed the university, and for most of the following two years he was forced to stay at his home, contemplating at leisure what he had learned. During the plague years Newton laid the foundations of the calculus and extended an earlier insight into an essay, "Of Colours," which contains most of the ideas elaborated in his *Opticks.* It was during this time that he examined the elements of circular motion and, applying his analysis to the Moon and the planets, derived the inverse square relation that the radially directed force acting on a planet decreases with the square of its distance from the Sun—which was later crucial to the law of universal gravitation. The world heard nothing of these discoveries.

CAREER

The optics. *Inaugural lectures at Trinity.* Newton was elected to a fellowship in Trinity College in 1667, after the university reopened. Two years later, Isaac Barrow, Lucasian professor of mathematics, who had transmitted Newton's *De Analysi* to John Collins in London, resigned the chair to devote himself to divinity and recommended Newton to succeed him. The professorship exempted Newton from the necessity of tutoring but imposed the duty of delivering an annual course of lectures. He chose the work he had done in optics as the initial topic; during the following three years (1670–72), his lectures developed the essay "Of Colours" into a form which was later revised to become Book One of his *Opticks.*

Beginning with Kepler's *Paralipomena* in 1604, the study of optics had been a central activity of the scientific revolution. Descartes's statement of the sine law of refraction, relating the angles of incidence and emergence at interfaces of the media through which light passes, had added a new mathematical regularity to the science of light, supporting the conviction that the universe is constructed according to mathematical regularities. Descartes had also made light central to the mechanical philosophy of nature; the reality of light, he argued, consists of motion transmitted through a material medium. Newton fully accepted the mechanical nature of light, although he chose the atomistic alternative and held that light consists of material corpuscles in motion. The corpuscular conception of light was always a speculative theory on the periphery of his optics, however. The core of Newton's contribution had to do with colours. An ancient theory extending back at least to Aristotle held that a certain class of colour phenomena, such as the rainbow, arises from the modification of light, which appears white in its pristine form. Descartes had generalized this theory for all colours and translated it into mechanical imagery. Through a series of experiments performed in 1665 and 1666, in which the spectrum of a narrow beam was projected onto the wall of a darkened chamber, Newton denied the concept of modification and replaced it with that of analysis. Basically, he denied that light is simple and homogeneous—stating instead that it is complex and heterogeneous and that the phenomena of colours arise from the analysis of the heterogeneous mixture into its simple components. The ultimate source of Newton's conviction that light is corpuscular was his recognition that individual rays of light have immutable properties; in his view, such properties imply immutable particles of matter. He held that individual rays (that is, particles of given size) excite sensations of individual colours when they strike the retina of the eye. He also concluded that rays refract at distinct angles—hence, the prismatic spectrum, a beam of heterogeneous rays, *i.e.,* alike incident on one face of a prism, separated or analyzed by the refraction into its component parts—and that phenomena such as the rainbow are produced by refractive analysis. Because he believed that chromatic aberration could never be eliminated from lenses, Newton turned to reflecting telescopes; he constructed the first ever built. The heterogeneity of light has been the foundation of physical optics since his time.

Analysis of colour

There is no evidence that the theory of colours, fully described by Newton in his inaugural lectures at Cambridge, made any impression, just as there is no evidence that aspects of his mathematics and the content of the *Principia,* also pronounced from the podium, made any impression. Rather, the theory of colours, like his later work, was transmitted to the world through the Royal Society of London, which had been organized in 1660. When Newton was appointed Lucasian professor, his name was probably unknown in the Royal Society; in 1671, however, they heard of his reflecting telescope and asked to see it. Pleased by their enthusiastic reception of the telescope and by his election to the society, Newton volunteered a paper on light and colours early in 1672. On the whole, the paper was also well received, although a few questions and some dissent were heard.

Controversy. Among the most important dissenters to Newton's paper was Robert Hooke, one of the leaders of the Royal Society who considered himself the master in optics and hence he wrote a condescending critique of the unknown parvenu. One can understand how the critique would have annoyed a normal man. The flaming rage it provoked, with the desire publicly to humiliate Hooke, however, bespoke the abnormal. Newton was unable rationally to confront criticism. Less than a year after submitting the paper, he was so unsettled by the give and take of honest discussion that he began to cut his ties, and he withdrew into virtual isolation.

In 1675, during a visit to London, Newton thought he heard Hooke accept his theory of colours. He was emboldened to bring forth a second paper, an examination of the colour phenomena in thin films, which was identical to most of Book Two as it later appeared in the *Opticks.* The purpose of the paper was to explain the colours of solid bodies by showing how light can be analyzed into its components by reflection as well as refraction. His explanation of the colours of bodies has not survived, but the paper was significant in demonstrating for the first time the existence of periodic optical phenomena. He discovered the concentric coloured rings in the thin film of air between a lens and a flat sheet of glass; the distance between these concentric rings (Newton's rings) depends on the increasing thickness of the film of air. In 1704 Newton combined a revision of his optical lectures with the paper of 1675 and a small amount of additional material in his *Opticks.*

Colours in thin films

A second piece which Newton had sent with the paper of 1675 provoked new controversy. Entitled "An Hypothesis Explaining the Properties of Light," it was in fact a general system of nature. Hooke apparently claimed that Newton had stolen its content from him, and Newton boiled over again. The issue was quickly controlled, however, by an exchange of formal, excessively polite letters that fail to conceal the complete lack of warmth between the men.

Newton was also engaged in another exchange on his theory of colours with a circle of English Jesuits in Liège, perhaps the most revealing exchange of all. Although their objections were shallow, their contention that his experiments were mistaken lashed him into a fury. The correspondence dragged on until 1678, when a final shriek of rage from Newton, apparently accompanied by a complete nervous breakdown, was followed by silence. The death of his mother the following year completed his isolation. For six years he withdrew from intellectual commerce except when others initiated a correspondence, which he always broke off as quickly as possible.

Influence of the Hermetic tradition. During his time of isolation, Newton was greatly influenced by the Hermetic tradition with which he had been familiar since his undergraduate days. Newton, always somewhat interested in alchemy, now immersed himself in it, copying by hand treatise after treatise and collating them to interpret their arcane imagery. Under the influence of the Hermetic tradition, his conception of nature underwent a decisive change. Until that time, Newton had been a mechanical philosopher in the standard 17th-century style, explaining natural phenomena by the motions of particles of matter. Thus, he held that the physical reality of light is a stream of tiny corpuscles diverted from its course by the presence of denser or rarer media. He felt that the apparent attraction of tiny bits of paper to a piece of glass that has been rubbed with cloth results from an ethereal effluvium that streams out of the glass and carries the bits of paper back with it. This mechanical philosophy denied the possibility of action at a distance; as with static electricity, it explained apparent attractions away by means of invisible ethereal mechanisms. Newton's "Hypothesis of Light" of 1675, with its universal ether, was a standard mechanical system of nature. Some phenomena, such as the capacity of chemicals to react only with certain others, puzzled him, however, and he spoke of a "secret principle" by which substances are "sociable" or "unsociable" with others. About 1679, Newton abandoned the ether and its invisible mechanisms and began to ascribe the puzzling phenomena—chemical affinities, the generation of heat in chemical reactions, surface tension in fluids, capillary action, the cohesion of bodies, and the like—to attractions and repulsions between particles of matter. More than 35 years later, in the second English edition of the *Opticks,* Newton accepted an ether again, although it was an ether that embodied the concept of action at a distance by positing a repulsion between its particles. The attractions and repulsions of Newton's speculations were direct transpositions of the occult sympathies and antipathies of Hermetic philosophy—as mechanical philosophers never ceased to protest. Newton, however, regarded them as a modification of the mechanical philosophy that rendered it subject to exact mathematical treatment. As he conceived of them, attractions were quantitatively defined, and they offered a bridge to unite the two basic themes of 17th-century science—the mechanical tradition, which had dealt primarily with verbal mechanical imagery, and the Pythagorean tradition, which insisted on the mathematical nature of reality. Newton's reconciliation through the concept of force was his ultimate contribution to science.

The Principia. *Planetary motion.* Newton originally applied the idea of attractions and repulsions solely to the range of terrestrial phenomena mentioned in the preceding paragraph. But late in 1679, not long after he had embraced the concept, another application was suggested in a letter from Hooke, who was seeking to renew correspondence. Hooke mentioned his analysis of planetary motion—in effect, the continuous diversion of a rectilinear motion by a central attraction. Newton bluntly refused to correspond but, nevertheless, went on to mention an experiment to demonstrate the rotation of the Earth: let a body be dropped from a tower; because the tangential velocity at the top of the tower is greater than that at the foot, the body should fall slightly to the east. He sketched the path of fall as part of a spiral ending at the centre of the Earth. This was a mistake, as Hooke pointed out; according to Hooke's theory of planetary motion, the path should be elliptical, so that if the Earth were split and separated to allow the body to fall, it would rise again to its original location. Newton did not like being corrected, least of all by Hooke, but he had to accept the basic point; he corrected Hooke's figure, however, using the assumption that gravity is constant. Hooke then countered by replying that, although Newton's figure was correct for constant gravity, his own assumption was that gravity decreases as the square of the distance. Several years later, this letter became the basis for Hooke's charge of plagiarism. He was mistaken in the charge. His knowledge of the inverse square relation rested only on intuitive grounds; he did not derive it properly from the quantitative statement of centripetal force and Kepler's third law, which relates the periods of planets to the radii of their orbits. Moreover, unknown to him, Newton had so derived the relation more than ten years earlier. Nevertheless, Newton later confessed that the correspondence with Hooke led him to demonstrate that an elliptical orbit entails an inverse square attraction to one focus—one of the two crucial propositions on which the law of universal gravitation would ultimately rest. What is more, Hooke's definition of orbital motion—in which the constant action of an attracting body continuously pulls a planet away from its inertial path—suggested a cosmic application for Newton's concept of force and an explanation of planetary paths employing it. In 1679 and 1680, Newton dealt only with orbital dynamics; he had not yet arrived at the concept of universal gravitation.

Correspondence with Hooke

Universal gravitation. Nearly five years later, in August 1684, Newton was visited by the British astronomer Edmond Halley, who was also troubled by the problem of orbital dynamics. Upon learning that Newton had solved the problem, he extracted Newton's promise to send the demonstration. Three months later he received a short tract entitled *De Motu* ("On Motion"). Already Newton was at work improving and expanding it. In two and a half years, the tract *De Motu* grew into *Philosophiae Naturalis Principia Mathematica,* which is not only Newton's masterpiece but also the fundamental work for the whole of modern science.

Significantly, *De Motu* did not state the law of universal gravitation. For that matter, even though it was a treatise on planetary dynamics, it did not contain any of the three Newtonian laws of motion. Only when revising *De Motu* did Newton embrace the principle of inertia (the first law) and arrive at the second law of motion. The second law, the force law, proved to be a precise quantitative statement of the action of the forces between bodies that had become the central members of his system of nature. By quantifying the concept of force, the second law completed the exact quantitative mechanics that has been the paradigm of natural science ever since.

The quantitative mechanics of the *Principia* is not to be confused with the mechanical philosophy. The latter was a philosophy of nature that attempted to explain natural phenomena by means of imagined mechanisms among invisible particles of matter. The mechanics of the *Principia* was an exact quantitative description of the motions of visible bodies. It rested on Newton's three laws of motion: (1) that a body remains in its state of rest unless it is compelled to change that state by a force impressed on it; (2) that the change of motion (the change of velocity times the mass of the body) is proportional to the force impressed; (3) that to every action there is an equal and opposite reaction. The analysis of circular motion in terms of these laws yielded a formula of the quantitative measure, in terms of a body's velocity and mass, of the centripetal force necessary to divert a body from its rectilinear path into a given circle. When Newton substituted this formula into Kepler's third law, he found that the centripetal force holding the planets in their given orbits about the Sun must decrease with the square of the planets' distances from the Sun. Because the satellites of Jupiter also obey Kepler's third law, an inverse square centripetal force must also attract them to the centre of their orbits. Newton was able to show that a similar relation holds between the Earth and its Moon. The distance of the Moon is approximately 60 times the radius of the Earth. Newton compared the distance by which the Moon, in its orbit of known size, is diverted from a tangential path in one second with the distance that a body at the surface of the Earth falls from rest in one second. When the latter distance proved to be 3,600 (60 × 60) times as great as the former, he concluded that one and the same force, governed by a single quantitative law, is operative in all three cases, and from the correlation of the Moon's orbit with the measured acceleration of gravity on the surface of the Earth, he applied the ancient Latin word *gravitas* (literally, "heaviness" or "weight") to it. The law of universal gravitation, which he also confirmed from such further phenomena as the tides and the orbits of comets, states that every particle of matter in the universe attracts every other particle with a force that is proportional to the product of their masses and inversely proportional to the square of the distance between their centres.

Charge of plagiarism

When the Royal Society received the completed manuscript of Book I in 1686, Hooke raised the cry of plagiarism, a charge that cannot be sustained in any meaningful sense. On the other hand, Newton's response to it reveals much about him. Hooke would have been satisfied with a generous acknowledgment; it would have been a graceful gesture to a sick man already well into his decline, and it would have cost Newton nothing. Newton, instead, went through his manuscript and eliminated nearly every reference to Hooke. Such was his fury that he refused either to publish his *Opticks* or to accept the presidency of the Royal Society until Hooke was dead.

International prominence. The *Principia* immediately raised Newton to international prominence. In their continuing loyalty to the mechanical ideal, Continental scientists rejected the idea of action at a distance for a generation, but even in their rejection they could not withhold their admiration for the technical expertise revealed by the work. Young British scientists spontaneously recognized him as their model. Within a generation the limited number of salaried positions for scientists in England, such as the chairs at Oxford, Cambridge, and Gresham College, were monopolized by the young Newtonians of the next generation. Newton, whose only close contacts with women were his unfulfilled relationship with his mother, who had seemed to abandon him, and his later guardianship of a niece, found satisfaction in the role of patron to the circle of young scientists. His friendship with Fatio de Duillier, a Swiss-born mathematician resident in London who shared Newton's interests, was the most profound experience of his adult life.

Warden of the mint. Almost immediately following the *Principia's* publication, Newton, a fervent if unorthodox Protestant, helped to lead the resistance of Cambridge to James II's attempt to Catholicize it. As a consequence, he was elected to represent the university in the convention that arranged the revolutionary settlement. In this capacity, he made the acquaintance of a broader group, including the philosopher John Locke. Newton tasted the excitement of London life in the aftermath of the *Principia.* The great bulk of his creative work had been completed. He was never again satisfied with the academic cloister, and his desire to change was whetted by Fatio's suggestion that he find a position in London. Seek a place he did, especially through the agency of his friend, the rising politician Charles Montague, later Lord Halifax. Finally, in 1696, he was appointed warden of the mint. Although he did not resign his Cambridge appointments until 1701, he moved to London and henceforth centred his life there.

In the meantime, Newton's relations with Fatio had undergone a crisis. Fatio was taken seriously ill; then family and financial problems threatened to call him home to Switzerland. Newton's distress knew no limits. In 1693 he suggested that Fatio move to Cambridge, where Newton would support him, but nothing came of the proposal. Through early 1693 the intensity of Newton's letters built almost palpably, and then, without surviving explanation, both the close relationship and the correspondence broke off. Four months later, without prior notice, Samuel Pepys and John Locke, both personal friends of Newton, received wild, accusatory letters. Pepys was informed that Newton would see him no more; Locke was charged with trying to entangle him with women. Both men were alarmed for Newton's sanity; and, in fact, Newton had suffered at least his second nervous breakdown. The crisis

Nervous breakdown

passed, and Newton recovered his stability. Only briefly did he ever return to sustained scientific work, however, and the move to London was the effective conclusion of his creative activity.

As warden and then master of the mint, Newton drew a large income, as much as £2,000 per annum. Added to his personal estate, the income left him a rich man at his death. The position, regarded as a sinecure, was treated otherwise by Newton. During the great recoinage, there was need for him to be actively in command; even afterward, however, he chose to exercise himself in the office. Above all, he was interested in counterfeiting. He became the terror of London counterfeiters, sending a goodly number to the gallows and finding in them a socially acceptable target on which to vent the rage that continued to well up within him.

Interest in religion and theology. Newton found time now to explore other interests, such as religion and theology. In the early 1690s he had sent Locke a copy of a manuscript attempting to prove that Trinitarian passages in the Bible were latter-day corruptions of the original text. When Locke made moves to publish it, Newton withdrew in fear that his anti-Trinitarian views would become known. In his later years, he devoted much time to the interpretation of the prophecies of Daniel and St. John, and to a closely related study of ancient chronology. Both works were published after his death.

Leader of English science. In London, Newton assumed the role of patriarch of English science. In 1703 he was elected President of the Royal Society. Four years earlier, the French Académie des Sciences (Academy of Sciences) had named him one of eight foreign associates. In 1705 Queen Anne knighted him, the first occasion on which a scientist was so honoured. Newton ruled the Royal Society magisterially. John Flamsteed, the Astronomer Royal, had occasion to feel that he ruled it tyrannically. In his years at the Royal Observatory at Greenwich, Flamsteed, who was a difficult man in his own right, had collected an unrivalled body of data. Newton had received needed information from him for the *Principia,* and in the 1690s, as he worked on the lunar theory, he again required Flamsteed's data. Annoyed when he could not get all the information he wanted as quickly as he wanted it, Newton assumed a domineering and condescending attitude toward Flamsteed. As president of the Royal Society, he used his influence with the government to be named as chairman of a body of "visitors" responsible for the Royal Observatory; then he tried to force the immediate publication of Flamsteed's catalog of stars. The disgraceful episode continued for nearly 10 years. Newton would brook no objections. He broke agreements that he had made with Flamsteed. Flamsteed's observations, the fruit of a lifetime of work, were, in effect, seized despite his protests and prepared for the press by his mortal enemy, Edmond Halley. Flamsteed finally won his point and by court order had the printed catalog returned to him before it was generally distributed. He burned the printed sheets, and his assistants brought out an authorized version after his death. In this respect, and at considerable cost to himself, Flamsteed was one of the few men to best Newton. Newton sought his revenge by systematically eliminating references to Flamsteed's help in later editions of the *Principia.*

Difficulties with Flamsteed

In Gottfried Wilhelm Leibniz, the German philosopher and mathematician, Newton met a contestant more of his own calibre. It is now well established that Newton developed the calculus before Leibniz seriously pursued mathematics. It is almost universally agreed that Leibniz later arrived at the calculus independently. There has never been any question that Newton did not publish his method of fluxions; thus, it was Leibniz's paper in 1684 that first made the calculus a matter of public knowledge. In the *Principia* Newton hinted at his method, but he did not really publish it until he appended two papers to the *Opticks* in 1704. By then the priority controversy was already smouldering. If, indeed, it mattered, it would be impossible finally to assess responsibility for the ensuing fracas. What began as mild innuendoes rapidly escalated into blunt charges of plagiarism on both sides. Egged on by followers anxious to win a reputation under his auspices,

Priority dispute with Leibniz

Newton allowed himself to be drawn into the centre of the fray; and, once his temper was aroused by accusations of dishonesty, his anger was beyond constraint. Leibniz's conduct of the controversy was not pleasant, and yet it paled beside that of Newton. Although he never appeared in public, Newton wrote most of the pieces that appeared in his defense, publishing them under the names of his young men, who never demurred. As president of the Royal Society, he appointed an "impartial" committee to investigate the issue, secretly wrote the report officially published by the society, and reviewed it anonymously in the *Philosophical Transactions.* Even Leibniz's death could not allay Newton's wrath, and he continued to pursue the enemy beyond the grave. The battle with Leibniz, the irrepressible need to efface the charge of dishonesty, dominated the final 25 years of Newton's life. It obtruded itself continually upon his consciousness. Almost any paper on any subject from those years is apt to be interrupted by a furious paragraph against the German philosopher, as he honed the instruments of his fury ever more keenly. In the end, only Newton's death ended his wrath.

Final years. During his final years Newton brought out further editions of his central works. After the first edition of the *Opticks* in 1704, which merely published work done 30 years before, he published a Latin edition in 1706 and a second English edition in 1717–18. In both, the central text was scarcely touched, but he did expand the "Queries" at the end into the final statement of his speculations on the nature of the universe. The second edition of the *Principia,* edited by Roger Cotes in 1713, introduced extensive alterations. A third edition, edited by Henry Pemberton in 1726, added little more. Until nearly the end, Newton presided at the Royal Society (frequently dozing through the meetings) and supervised the mint. During his last years, his niece, Catherine Barton Conduitt, and her husband lived with him. He died on March 20 (March 31, N.S.), 1727, in London.

MAJOR WORKS

Philosophiae Naturalis Principia Mathematica (1687; *Mathematical Principles of Natural Philosophy,* 1729); *Opticks* (1704); *Arithmetica Universalis* (1707; *Universal Arithmetick,* 1720); *The Chronology of Ancient Kingdoms Amended* (1728); *Observations Upon the Prophecies of Daniel and the Apocalypse of St. John* (1733).

BIBLIOGRAPHY. A standard biography of Newton is DAVID BREWSTER, *Memoirs of the Life, Writings, and Discoveries of Sir Isaac Newton,* 2 vol. (1855, reissued 1974). A more modern work by RICHARD S. WESTFALL, *Never at Rest: A Biography of Isaac Newton* (1981), is a comprehensive study of Newton in light of new scholarship. FRANK MANUEL, *A Portrait of Isaac Newton* (1968, reprinted 1979), offers a fascinating Freudian analysis; and Manuel's *The Religion of Isaac Newton* (1974) is a thorough discussion of his religious thought. The best general treatment of the major problems in Newtonian science is found in I. BERNARD COHEN, *Franklin and Newton* (1956). JOHN W. HERIVEL, *The Background to Newton's Principia* (1966); and RICHARD S. WESTFALL, *Force in Newton's Physics* (1971), explore the development of Newton's mechanics. BETTY JO TEETER DOBBS, *The Foundations of Newton's Alchemy* (1975), is an examination of Newton's alchemical studies through the early 1670s. I. BERNARD COHEN, *The Newtonian Revolution* (1980, reissued 1983), evaluates the historical importance of Newton's style of scientific thought. ALEXANDRE KOYRÉ, *Newtonian Studies* (1965), contains a collection of essays by one of the master historians of science. I. BERNARD COHEN, *Introduction to Newton's Principia* (1971), a history of the development and modification of Newton's major work, is the first volume of Cohen's edition of the *Principia* and includes variant readings. Additional collections of Newtonian materials, all with valuable introductory essays, include: D.T. WHITESIDE (ed.), *The Mathematical Papers of Isaac Newton,* 8 vol. (1967–81); A.R. and M.B. HALL (eds.), *Unpublished Scientific Papers of Isaac Newton* (1962, reissued 1978); I. BERNARD COHEN (ed.), *Isaac Newton's Papers & Letters on Natural Philosophy and Related Documents* (1958); and H.W. TURNBULL and J.F. SCOTT (eds.), *The Correspondence of Isaac Newton,* 7 vol. (1959–77). See also PETER and RUTH WALLIS, *Newton and Newtoniana, 1672–1975: A Bibliography* (1977).

(R.S.W./Ed.)

Nietzsche

Friedrich Nietzsche, a 19th-century German philosopher and writer, was one of the most influential modern thinkers. His attempts to unmask the root motives that underlie traditional Western religion, morality, and philosophy deeply affected generations of theologians, philosophers, psychologists, poets, novelists, and playwrights. He thought through the consequences of the triumph of the Enlightenment's secularism, expressed in his observation that "God is dead," in a way that determined the agenda for many of Europe's most celebrated intellectuals after his death in 1900. Although he was an ardent foe of nationalism, anti-Semitism, and power politics, his name was later invoked by Fascists to advance the very things he loathed.

The early years. Nietzsche was born on Oct. 15, 1844, in Röcken, a village in Prussian Saxony. His home was a stronghold of Lutheran piety. His paternal grandfather had published books defending Protestantism and had achieved the ecclesiastical position of superintendent; his maternal grandfather was a country parson; his father, Carl Ludwig Nietzsche, was appointed pastor at Röcken by order of King Friedrich Wilhelm IV of Prussia, after whom Friedrich Nietzsche was named. His father died in 1849, before Nietzsche's fifth birthday, and he spent most of his early life in a household consisting of five women: his mother Franziska, his younger sister Elisabeth, his maternal grandmother, and two maiden aunts.

In 1850 the family moved to Naumburg on the Saale River, where Nietzsche attended a private preparatory school, the Domgymnasium. In 1858 he earned a scholarship to Schulpforta, Germany's leading Protestant boarding school. He excelled academically at Pforta, received an outstanding classical education there, and, having graduated in 1864, went to the University of Bonn to study theology and classical philology. Despite efforts to take part in the university's social life, the two semesters at Bonn were a failure, owing chiefly to acrimonious quarrels between his two leading classics professors, Otto Jahn and Friedrich Wilhelm Ritschl. Nietzsche sought refuge in music, writing a number of compositions strongly influenced

University years

Louis Held—Deutsche Fotothek, Dresden

Nietzsche, 1888.

by Robert Schumann, the German Romantic composer. In 1865 he transferred to the University of Leipzig, joining Ritschl, who had accepted an appointment there.

Nietzsche prospered under Ritschl's tutelage in Leipzig. He became the only student ever to publish in Ritschl's journal, *Rheinisches Museum* ("Rhenish Museum"). He began military service in October 1867 in the cavalry company of an artillery regiment, sustained a serious chest injury while mounting a horse in March 1868, and resumed his studies in Leipzig in October 1868 while on extended sick leave from the military. During the years in Leipzig, Nietzsche discovered Arthur Schopenhauer's philosophy, met the great operatic composer Richard Wagner, and began his lifelong friendship with fellow classicist Erwin Rohde (author of *Psyche*).

The Basel years (1869–79). When a professorship in classical philology fell vacant in 1869 in Basel, Switz., Ritschl recommended Nietzsche with unparalleled praise. He had completed neither his doctoral thesis nor the additional dissertation required for a German degree; yet Ritschl assured the University of Basel that he had never seen anyone like Nietzsche in 40 years of teaching and that his talents were limitless. In 1869 the University of Leipzig conferred the doctorate without examination or dissertation on the strength of his published writings, and the University of Basel appointed him extraordinary professor of classical philology. The following year Nietzsche became a Swiss citizen and was promoted to ordinary professor.

Nietzsche obtained a leave to serve as a volunteer medical orderly in August 1870, after the outbreak of the Franco-Prussian War. Within a month, while accompanying a transport of wounded, he contracted dysentery and diphtheria, which ruined his health permanently. He returned to Basel in October to resume a heavy teaching load, but as early as 1871 ill health prompted him to seek relief from the stultifying chores of a professor of classical philology; he applied for the vacant chair of philosophy and proposed Rohde as his successor, all to no avail.

Nietzsche's break with Wagner

During these early Basel years Nietzsche's ambivalent friendship with Wagner ripened, and he seized every opportunity to visit Richard and his wife, Cosima. Wagner appreciated Nietzsche as a brilliant professorial apostle, but Wagner's increasing exploitation of Christian motifs, as in *Parsifal,* coupled with his chauvinism and anti-Semitism proved to be more than Nietzsche could bear. By 1878 the breach between the two men had become final.

Nietzsche's first book, *Die Geburt der Tragödie aus dem Geiste der Musik* (1872; *The Birth of Tragedy from the Spirit of Music*), marked his emancipation from the trappings of classical scholarship. A speculative rather than exegetical work, it argued that Greek tragedy arose out of the fusion of what he termed Apollonian and Dionysian elements—the former representing measure, restraint, harmony, and the latter representing unbridled passion—and that Socratic rationalism and optimism spelled the death of Greek tragedy. The final 10 sections of the book are a rhapsody about the rebirth of tragedy from the spirit of Wagner's music. Greeted by stony silence at first, it became the object of heated controversy on the part of those who mistook it for a conventional work of classical scholarship. It was undoubtedly "a work of profound imaginative insight, which left the scholarship of a generation toiling in the rear," as the British classicist F.M. Cornford wrote in 1912. It remains a classic in the history of aesthetics to this day.

By October 1876 Nietzsche requested and received a year's sick leave. In 1877 he set up house with his sister and Peter Gast, and in 1878 his aphoristic *Menschliches, Allzumenschliches* (*Human, All-Too-Human*) appeared. Because his health deteriorated steadily he resigned his professorial chair on June 14, 1879, and was granted a pension of 3,000 Swiss francs per year for six years.

Decade of isolation and creativity (1879–89). Apart from the books Nietzsche wrote between 1879 and 1889, it is doubtful that his life held any intrinsic interest. Seriously ill, half-blind, in virtually unrelenting pain, he lived in boarding houses in Switzerland, the French Riviera, and Italy, with only limited human contact. His friendship with Paul Rée was undermined by 1882 by their mutual if unacknowledged affection for Lou Salomé, author, later the wife of the Orientalist F.C. Andreas, mistress of the poet Rainer Maria Rilke, and confidant of Sigmund Freud, as well as by Elisabeth Nietzsche's jealous meddling.

Nietzsche's acknowledged literary and philosophical masterpiece in biblical narrative form, *Also sprach Zarathustra* (*Thus Spoke Zarathustra*), was published between 1883 and 1885 in four parts, the last part a private printing at his own expense. As with most of his works it received little attention. His attempts to set forth his philosophy in more direct prose, in the publications in 1886 of *Jenseits von Gut und Böse* (*Beyond Good and Evil*) and in 1887 of *Zur Genealogie der Moral* (*On the Genealogy of Morals*), also failed to win a proper audience.

Nietzsche's final lucid year, 1888, was a period of supreme productivity. He wrote and published *Der Fall Wagner* (*The Case of Wagner*) and wrote a synopsis of his philosophy, *Die Götzen-Dämmerung* (*Twilight of the Idols*), *Der Antichrist* (*The Antichrist*), *Nietzsche contra Wagner* (Eng. trans., *Nietzsche contra Wagner*), and *Ecce Homo* (Eng. trans., *Ecce Homo*), a reflection on his own works and significance. *Twilight of the Idols* appeared in 1889, *Der Antichrist* and *Nietzsche contra Wagner* were not published until 1895, the former mistakenly as book one of *The Will to Power,* and *Ecce Homo* was withheld from publication until 1908, 20 years after its composition.

Collapse and misuse. Nietzsche collapsed in the streets of Turin, Italy, in January 1889, having lost control of his mental faculties completely. Bizarre but meaningful notes he sent immediately after his collapse brought Franz Overbeck to Italy to return Nietzsche to Basel. Nietzsche spent the last 11 years of his life in total mental darkness, first in a Basel asylum, then in Naumburg under his mother's care and, after her death in 1897, in Weimar in his sister's care. He died on Aug. 25, 1900. Informed opinion favours a diagnosis of atypical general paralysis caused by dormant tertiary syphilis.

Years of mental darkness

The association of Nietzsche's name with Adolf Hitler and Fascism owes much to the use made of his works by his sister Elisabeth. She had married a leading chauvinist and anti-Semite, Bernhard Förster, and after his suicide in 1889 she worked diligently to refashion Nietzsche in Förster's image. Elisabeth maintained ruthless control over Nietzsche's literary estate and, dominated by greed, produced collections of his "works" consisting of discarded notes, such as *Der Wille zur Macht* (1901; *The Will to Power*). She also committed petty forgeries. Generations of commentators were misled. Equally important, her enthusiasm for Hitler linked Nietzsche's name with that of the dictator in the public mind.

Nietzsche's sister's misuse of his literary estate

Nietzsche's mature philosophy. Nietzsche's writings fall into three well-defined periods. The early works, *The Birth of Tragedy* and the four *Unzeitgemässe Betrachtungen* (1873; *Untimely Meditations*), are dominated by a Romantic perspective influenced by Schopenhauer and Wagner. The middle period, from *Human, All-Too-Human* up to *The Gay Science,* reflects the tradition of French aphorists. It extols reason and science, experiments with literary genres, and expresses Nietzsche's emancipation from his earlier Romanticism and from Schopenhauer and Wagner. Nietzsche's mature philosophy emerged after *The Gay Science.*

In his mature writings Nietzsche was preoccupied by the origin and function of values in human life. If, as he believed, life neither possesses nor lacks intrinsic value and yet is always being evaluated, then such evaluations can usefully be read as symptoms of the condition of the evaluator. He was especially interested, therefore, in a probing analysis and evaluation of the fundamental cultural values of Western philosophy, religion, and morality, which he characterized as expressions of the ascetic ideal.

The ascetic ideal is born when suffering becomes endowed with ultimate significance. According to Nietzsche the Judeo-Christian tradition, for example, made suffering tolerable by interpreting it as God's intention and as an occasion for atonement. Christianity, accordingly, owed its triumph to the flattering doctrine of personal immortality, that is, to the conceit that each individual's life and death have cosmic significance. Similarly, traditional philosophy expressed the ascetic ideal when it privileged soul over body, mind over senses, duty over desire, reality over appearance, the timeless over the temporal. While Christianity promised salvation for the sinner who repents, philosophy held out hope for salvation, albeit secular, for its sages. Common to traditional religion and philosophy was the unstated but powerful motivating assumption that existence requires explanation, justification, or expiation. Both denigrated experience in favour of some other, "true" world. Both may be read as symptoms of a declining life, or life in distress.

Nietzsche's etymological approach to the interpretation of morality

Nietzsche's critique of traditional morality centred on the typology of "master" and "slave" morality. By examining the etymology of the German words *gut* ("good"), *schlecht* ("bad"), and *böse* ("evil"), Nietzsche maintained that the distinction between good and bad was originally descriptive, that is, a nonmoral reference to those who were privileged, the masters, as opposed to those who were base, the slaves. The good/evil contrast arose when slaves avenged themselves by converting attributes of mastery into vices. If the favoured, the "good," were powerful, it was said that the meek would inherit the earth. Pride became sin. Charity, humility, and obedience replaced competition, pride, and autonomy. Crucial to the triumph of slave morality was its claim to being the only true morality. This insistence on absoluteness is as essential to philosophical as to religious ethics. Although Nietzsche gave a historical genealogy of master and slave morality, he maintained that it was an ahistorical typology of traits present in everyone.

God is dead

"Nihilism" was the term Nietzsche used to describe the devaluation of the highest values posited by the ascetic ideal. He thought of the age in which he lived as one of passive nihilism, that is, as an age that was not yet aware that religious and philosophical absolutes had dissolved in the emergence of 19th-century Positivism. With the collapse of metaphysical and theological foundations and sanctions for traditional morality only a pervasive sense of purposelessness and meaninglessness would remain. And the triumph of meaninglessness is the triumph of nihilism: "God is dead." Nietzsche thought, however, that most men could not accept the eclipse of the ascetic ideal and the intrinsic meaninglessness of existence but would seek supplanting absolutes to invest life with meaning. He thought the emerging nationalism of his day represented one such ominous surrogate god, in which the nation-state would be invested with transcendent value and purpose. And just as absoluteness of doctrine had found expression in philosophy and religion, Nietzsche thought that absoluteness would become attached to the nation-state with missionary fervour and zeal. The slaughter of rivals and the conquest of the earth would proceed, self-deceptively, under banners of universal brotherhood, democracy, and socialism. Nietzsche's prescience here was particularly poignant, and the use later made of him especially repellent. For example, two books were standard issue for the rucksacks of German soldiers during World War I, *Thus Spoke Zarathustra* and *The Gospel According to St. John.* It is difficult to say which author was more compromised by this gesture.

Nietzsche often thought of his writings as struggles with nihilism, and apart from his critiques of religion, philosophy, and morality he developed original theses that have commanded attention, especially perspectivism, will to power, eternal recurrence, and the superman.

Perspectivism is a concept which holds that knowledge is always perspectival, that there are no immaculate perceptions, and that knowledge from no point of view is as incoherent a notion as seeing from no particular vantage point. Perspectivism also denies the possibility of an all-inclusive perspective, which could contain all others and, hence, make reality available as it is in itself. The concept of such an all-inclusive perspective is as incoherent as the concept of seeing an object from every possible vantage point simultaneously.

Nietzsche's perspectivism has sometimes been mistakenly identified with relativism and skepticism. Nonetheless, it raises the question of how one is to understand Nietzsche's own theses, for example, that the dominant values of the common heritage have been underwritten by an ascetic ideal. Is this thesis true absolutely or only from a certain perspective? It may also be asked whether perspectivism can be asserted consistently without self-contradiction, since perspectivism must presumably be true in an absolute, that is a nonperspectival sense. Concerns such as these have generated much fruitful Nietzsche commentary as well as useful work in the theory of knowledge.

Critical responses to Nietzsche's concept of perspectivism

Nietzsche often identified life itself with "will to power," that is, with an instinct for growth and durability. This concept provides yet another way of interpreting the ascetic ideal, since it is Nietzsche's contention "that all the supreme values of mankind *lack* this will—that values which are symptomatic of decline, *nihilistic* values, are lording it under the holiest names." Thus, traditional philosophy, religion, and morality have been so many masks a deficient will to power wears. The sustaining values of Western civilization have been sublimated products of decadence in that the ascetic ideal endorses existence as pain and suffering. Some commentators have attempted to extend Nietzsche's concept of the will to power from human life to the organic and inorganic realms, ascribing a metaphysics of will to power to him. Such interpretations, however, cannot be sustained by reference to his published works.

The doctrine of eternal recurrence, the basic conception of *Thus Spoke Zarathustra,* asks the question "How well disposed would a person have to become to himself and to life to crave nothing more fervently than the infinite repetition, without alteration, of each and every moment?" Presumably most men would, or should, find such a thought shattering because they should always find it possible to prefer the eternal repetition of their lives in an edited version rather than to crave nothing more fervently than the eternal recurrence of each of its horrors. The person who could accept recurrence without self-deception or evasion would be a superhuman being (*Übermensch*), a superman whose distance from the ordinary man is greater than the distance between man and ape, Nietzsche says. Commentators still disagree whether there are specific character traits that define the person who embraces eternal recurrence.

Nietzsche's influence. Nietzsche once wrote that some men are born posthumously, and this is certainly true in his case. The history of 20th-century philosophy, theology, and psychology are unintelligible without him. The German philosophers Max Scheler, Karl Jaspers, and Martin Heidegger laboured in his debt, for example, as did the French philosophers Albert Camus, Jacques Derrida, and Michel Foucault. Existentialism and deconstructionism, a movement in philosophy and literary criticism, owe much to him. The theologians Paul Tillich and Lev Shestov acknowledged their debt as did the "God is dead" theologian Thomas J.J. Altizer; Martin Buber, Judaism's greatest 20th-century thinker, counted Nietzsche among the three most important influences in his life and translated the first part of *Zarathustra* into Polish. The psychologists Alfred Adler and Carl Jung were deeply influenced, as was Sigmund Freud, who said of Nietzsche that he had a more penetrating understanding of himself than any man who ever lived or was ever likely to live. Novelists like Thomas Mann, Hermann Hesse, André Malraux, André Gide, and John Gardner were inspired by him and wrote about him, as did the poets and playwrights George Bernard Shaw, Rainer Maria Rilke, Stefan George, and William Butler Yeats, among others. Nietzsche is certainly one of the most influential philosophers who ever lived; and this is due not only to his originality but also to the fact that he was the German language's most brilliant prose writer.

MAJOR WORKS

Definitive editions of Nietzsche's collected works have been edited by Giorgio Colli and Mazzino Montinari, *Werke: Kritische Gesamtausgabe* (1967–), projected for 30 vol., of which 21 had been published by 1984, and *Sämtliche Werke: Kritische Studienausgabe,* 15 vol. (1980). These strictly chronological editions render all earlier collections obsolete. All books authorized for publication by Nietzsche exist in English translations, the most reliable of which are by Walter Kaufmann.

The original works in the following list have been translated and edited by Walter Kaufmann unless noted otherwise: *Die Geburt der Tragödie* (1872; *The Birth of Tragedy*); *Unzeitgemässe Betrachtungen*, 4 vol. (1873–76; *Untimely Meditations*, trans. by R.J. Hollingdale); *Menschliches, Allzumenschliches* (1878; *Human, All-Too-Human*, trans. by Marion Faber and Stephen Lehmann); *Morgenröte* (1881; *Daybreak*, trans. by R.J. Hollingdale); *Die fröhliche Wissenschaft* (1882), new ed. augmented by book 5 and *Lieder des Prinzen Vogelfrei* (1887; *The Gay Science*); *Also sprach Zarathustra*, parts 1–3 (1883–84) and part 4 (1885; *Thus Spoke Zarathustra*); *Jenseits von Gut und Böse* (1886; *Beyond Good and Evil*); *Zur Genealogie der Moral* (1887; *On the Genealogy of Morals*); *Der Fall Wagner* (1888; *The Case of Wagner*); *Götzen-Dämmerung* (1889; *Twilight of the Idols*); *Der Antichrist* (1895; *The Antichrist*); *Nietzsche contra Wagner* (1895); *Ecce Homo* (1908). A selection from Nietzsche's notes never intended for publication appeared as *Der Wille zur Macht* (1901; *The Will to Power*, trans. by Walter Kaufmann and R.J. Hollingdale). An important translation and selection of Nietzsche's early unpublished writings is *Philosophy and Truth* (1979), ed. and trans. by Daniel Breazeale. The fundamental chronological edition of Nietzsche's letters by Giorgio Colli and Mazzino Montinari, *Briefwechsel: Kritische Gesamtausgabe* (1975–), is planned for 20 vol., of which 17 had appeared by 1984, containing the correspondence of 1850–89. A fine selection in English is *Selected Letters of Friedrich Nietzsche* (1969), ed. and trans. by Christopher Middleton.

BIBLIOGRAPHY. The *International Nietzsche Bibliography*, ed. by HERBERT W. REICHERT and KARL SCHLECHTA, rev. and expanded ed. (1968), lists more than 4,500 studies in 27 languages. Especially noteworthy English-language studies are WALTER KAUFMANN, *Nietzsche: Philosopher, Psychologist, Antichrist*, 4th ed. (1974), a work that exposed many myths about Nietzsche; R.J. HOLLINGDALE, *Nietzsche: The Man and His Philosophy* (1965), an intellectual biography; and ARTHUR C. DANTO, *Nietzsche as Philosopher* (1965, reissued 1980), a treatment through the eyes of Analytic philosophy. See also RONALD HAYMAN, *Nietzsche: A Critical Life* (1980), an excellent biography for the general reader in English; BERND MAGNUS, *Nietzsche's Existential Imperative* (1978), a comprehensive discussion of Nietzsche's doctrine of eternal recurrence; RICHARD SCHACHT, *Nietzsche* (1983), a comprehensive interpretation that makes extensive use of *The Will to Power;* and ALEXANDER NEHAMAS, *Nietzsche: Life as Literature* (1985), a treatment of Nietzsche's philosophy on the analogy of the interpretation of a literary text.

(Be.M.)

North Africa

The Arabic term Jazīrat al-Maghrib ("Island of the West") was applied to present-day Tunisia, Algeria, and Morocco; the word Maghrib is so used here. The Arabs used the word Barbar (Berber) to describe the non-Latin-speaking peoples of the Maghrib, and Berber continues to be used for the non-Arabic-speaking population. In this article the term North Africa is used for present-day Morocco, Algeria, Tunisia, and Libya. Egypt and The Sudan are treated in separate articles.

The article is divided into the following sections:

PHYSICAL AND HUMAN GEOGRAPHY

The land

The region described in this article stretches from the Atlantic Ocean on the west to the Egyptian desert on the east. It is bounded by The Sudan to the south and the Mediterranean Sea on the north.

A Mediterranean climate occurs on the north coast, beginning in Morocco and extending eastward through northern Algeria and Tunisia. The area is mountainous, and the rainfall, which is cyclonic, varies considerably with altitude and exposure. The characteristic feature of the Mediterranean climate is winter rainfall (15–30 inches [380–760 millimetres]) and a long dry summer.

In North Africa the Mediterranean region includes the coastal strip, a plateau 3,000–4,000 feet (900–1,200 metres) high, and the wooded ranges of the Atlas Mountains in which there is abundant rain in both summer and winter. The climate of the Atlantic coast is moderated by the cool Canaries current. Summer is cool, and the low cloud and fog are the cause of high humidity and a small range of temperature. Summer temperatures increase eastward along the North African coast (Essaouira 68° F [20° C], Algiers and Tunis 91° F [33° C]) and the contrast between summer and winter becomes much more pronounced. The extreme maximum temperatures in the hottest months may exceed 100° F (38° C at Algiers, mean August maximum 90° F [32° C]). Winter depressions with their westerly winds and clouds bring cool weather (Algiers, mean January temperature 55° F [13° C]; frost is rare on the coast but common on the drier steppe-covered plateau of the chotts (Arabic *shaṭṭ;* an ephemeral lake, usually saline) between the Atlas ranges. There the winter climate is severe and the summer is as hot as it is near the coast.

The Sahara desert extends across the entire south of the region and, for the most part, is a true desert. Except in the mountain massifs years may pass without rain: vegetation is sparse and stunted, and the surface consists largely of sand and broken rock. Apart from the lack of rain, one of the most interesting features of the climate is the great range of temperature: dry northerly currents of descending air prevail most of the time and the sky is hazy as even a light wind raises the dust. There is no cloud and the sun scorches the ground. Summer temperatures are among the highest in the world; day after day the thermometer rises above 109° F (43° C). But as the air is dry the ground cools rapidly when the sun begins to set and the night seems cold. Daily ranges of more than 18° F (10° C) are usual. In the winter, on the other hand, the days are pleasant; the temperature is about 61° F (16° C) but severe frosts follow at night. There are occasional violent dust storms known by local names like simoom, sirocco, and the khamsin.

Northern African vegetation contains a considerable proportion of European genera and species, besides certain native species in and south of the Atlas Mountains. Forests of cork oak and of Atlas cedar occur in Morocco, Algeria, and Tunisia. Mediterranean maquis, composed of evergreen shrubs with hard leathery leaves, occurs in these countries and also in Libya. High-plateau steppe is extensive in the Atlas Mountains, and subdesert steppe is found in the western desert. Plants of European affinity are found in scanty fragments of vegetation in the Saharan mountains and in oases with their characteristic date palms. (Ed.)

Traditional cultures

Arab writers gave the name Maghrib (Setting Sun, or the West) to the regions of North Africa conquered by the Muslims between the years 670 and 700. The word Maghrib denotes the whole of Morocco, Algeria, and Tunisia and the western part of Libya known as Tripolitania. It is bounded on the south by the Sahara.

The country of the Atlas

The country of the Atlas, as the Greeks named it, is distinguished from the rest of the Islāmic world by its population and history. The native peoples have been able to resist successive invaders from the vastness of their mountain ranges. Yet Punic, Roman, and Christian influences left their successive marks. In the 7th and 8th centuries, the victorious Arabs, by imposing Islām and the language of the Qur'ān, absorbed the Maghrib into the Islāmic civilization once and for all. Nevertheless, the North African societies have preserved their cultural identity throughout the centuries.

The people of the Maghrib are ethnically Berbers and Arabs. The Berbers have lived in the Maghrib since ancient times, probably originating in a mingling of races in the Paleolithic and Neolithic periods. The Berber stock displays a wide variety of physical characteristics; their social and cultural characteristics are also quite diverse. Under-

Adapted from J. Despois, *L'Afrique du Nord;* Presses Universitaires de France

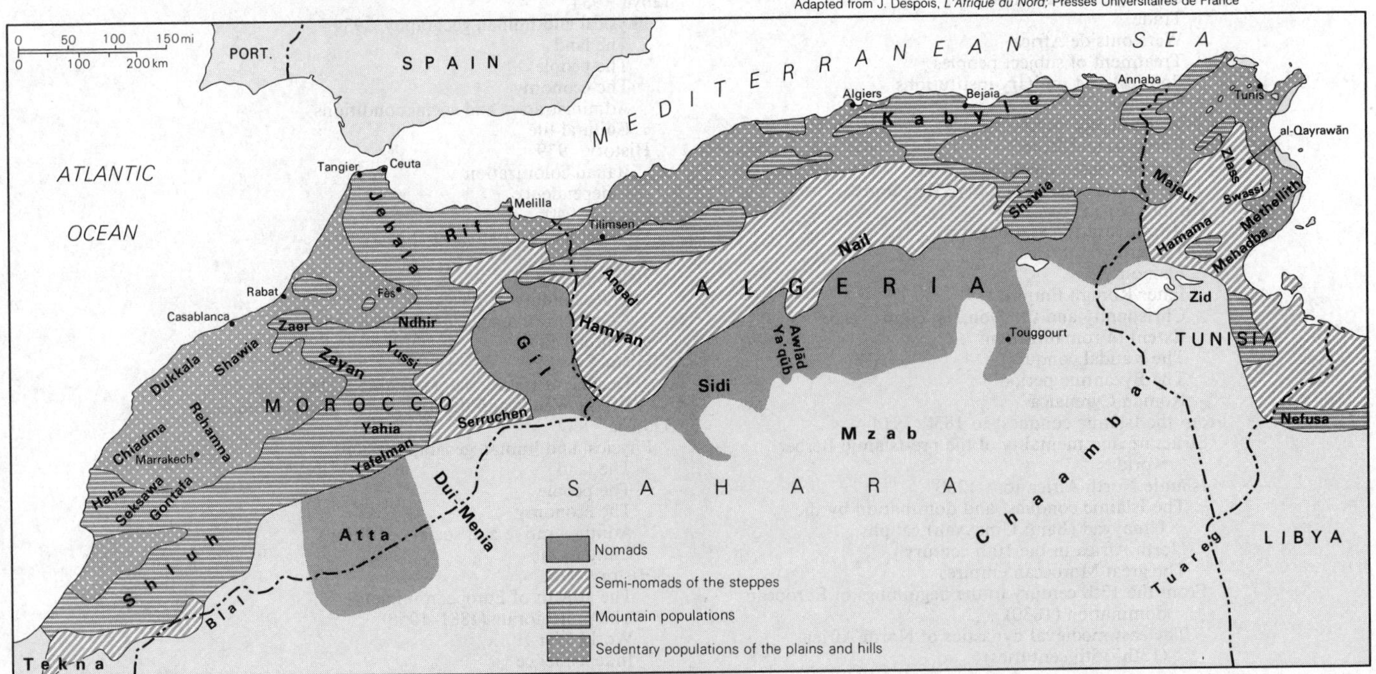

People of the Maghrib.

lying all these differences, however, is a common ethnic substratum. A long succession of invasions, ranging from the Phoenicians to the Arabs and finally to the French, did not lead to much intermarriage. Some foreign minorities settled in the towns, but the rural Maghrib received little new blood. The second wave of Arab invasions in the 11th and 12th centuries consisted of Bedouins, a few tens of thousands of nomads from the Middle East.

The mixture of languages and ways of life makes a simple classification of the peoples of the Maghrib impossible. There are Arabized Berbers, where tribes of the latter have come under Arab cultural influence. It must also be remembered that nomadic tribes lived in the Maghrib long before the Muslim conquest. Although the area has been largely taken over by the Islāmic language and civilization, there still exist populations in the mountainous regions and in certain oases who have retained predominantly Berber idioms and traditions.

Berber dialects number in the hundreds. The proportion of Berber speakers is lower in the eastern Maghrib than in the west where, in Morocco, some two-thirds of the population speak Berber dialects. The following are the most important dialect clusters: Shluh, spoken in Morocco and Mauritania; Shawia and Kabyle, in Algeria; Tamashek, spoken by the Tuaregs of the central Sahara and south of the Niger; Rif and Tamazight, spoken predominantly in Morocco; and Zenaga, in Senegal. The Arab historian Ibn Khaldūn (died 1406) conveniently divided the Berbers into three ethnic groups—the Ṣanhājah, Maṣmūdah, and Zanātah. These hypothetical categories, sometimes used in classifying Berber dialects, are not realistic interpretations of actual Berber tribal organization.

TRADITIONAL PATTERNS OF CULTURE

Importance of religion and the family

All Maghrib societies were organized around two central institutions, Islām and the clan. Islām transcended the family, ordering all life, spiritual and secular, by a body of unbreakable rules. The social structures, from political organizations to the home, are built around the word of God as laid down in the Qur'ān and in Muslim tradition. Although many differences exist between urban society, where Muslim orthodoxy prevails, and the rural societies, where Berber beliefs and customs still exist, all the people of the Maghrib belong to the community of believers. Islām has sanctified the ancient values of the Maghrib's patriarchal societies. To seek the will of Allāh means above all that the believer must submit to the will of his parents. The pre-Islāmic cults are thus sublimated by the precepts of the Qur'ān; popular traditions are incorporated into religious ritual. As a religion of everyday life, Islām has a code of practical conduct governing the whole range of private and public behaviour, combining complex ritual with spiritual exercise, indissolubly linking the religious and the secular.

The politeness that dominates all social intercourse is not merely the refined courtesy of the bourgeois or the nomads' traditional hospitality; it is above all an expression of the state of being of the believer, in possession of his tradition and proclaiming his convictions. In the roughest country community, good manners are the rule: the *ḥashūmah,* a term that combines modesty, shame, and reserve, weaves a subtle etiquette of courtesy among men and women, old and young, members of the group and strangers. Whether at home or in the mosque, at the public baths or the market, with father or brother, wife or son, every inhabitant of the Maghrib knows what is proper to say or to do according to his age, sex, and status. This code of behaviour guarantees social cohesion and the priority of the group over the individual; it favours the survival of communities in regions that are inhospitable and insecure. In the same way, Berber groups, converted to Islām, found in the universal vocation of their religion the strength necessary to challenge the political supremacy of the Arabs.

Social organization. *Local and territorial organization.* For many sedentary groups as well as for nomads, the fundamental sociopolitical group has been the tribe. The founders of dynasties depended upon their tribe when creating their kingdoms or empires, which were often short-lived. Subject to historical vicissitudes and the hazards of the climate, the tribe could group together several hundred or several thousand households. A powerful tribe could organize other tribes into a strong confederacy, while a weak tribe would be absorbed by an allied or conquering tribe.

The members of a tribe call themselves *banī ʿamm,* or cousins (literally, "paternal uncle's sons"). They claim descent from a common ancestor, the founder and namesake of the tribe; *e.g.,* the Awlād Yaʿqūb tribesmen are the children of Yaʿqūb. In reality, these ancestors are rather legendary characters (relatives of the Prophet, holy men, famous warriors), worshipped as heroes and whose tombs are pilgrimage centres. This fictitious consanguinity is a system of allegiance to the protector of the group, who serves as its guide, its invisible defender, and its permanent mediator with the supernatural powers.

With the exception of some Berber districts in which the same population has lived since time immemorial, the tribe does not identify itself with an ancestral ground. Over the centuries, a tribe may move its location by 100 miles (160 kilometres) or more. These movements can be explained partly by pastoral necessity, partly by the fact that group solidarity prevails over individual attachment to inherited land. This solidarity reveals itself above all in such matters as war, the drawing of lots for plots of agricultural land, and the protection of common pastures. The tribe is composed of a number of rural communities and is governed by a *jamāʿah,* or assembly, composed of representatives of the important families. Normally, the Berber *jamāʿah* elects its chief, whereas the Arab tribes frequently have a hereditary system of chieftainship.

The tribe is composed of three to six segments (*firqahs*), which are patrilinear clans based on certain patterns—fictitious pedigrees, an ancestral name, or political or economic practices—that have been transposed into a tribal organization. Membership in a clan is not necessarily linked to vicinity; for example, in Kabylie, each village constitutes an autonomous *firqah,* whereas in the Aurès area a village can contain several different *firqahs.*

The agnatic family

Family and kinship patterns. The biological kinship of a family differs from the mythical kinship of the clan or tribe. All descendants of the male offspring of a common ancestor belong to the same family. The consanguinity must be actual in order to be legitimate in the eyes of Muslim orthodoxy. Berber customs, on the other hand, allow legitimation or adoption. All the family members have certain rights concerning the family heritage and certain obligations, according to their level of kinship; they also share responsibility for every member's acts (*e.g.,* collective responsibility in the case of murder). In the Berber villages, the houses of a large family are often grouped together in the same district. Elsewhere, the "great family" disperses in many domestic units, living in autonomous farmsteads or in isolated camps. Kinship forms the basis of all social organization; the domestic unit, the extended family, the clan, and the tribe are concentric circles of kinship, each denoting a certain range of obligations. As an Arab proverb has it: "Myself against my brothers; my brothers and myself against my cousins; and my cousins, my brothers, and myself against the world." The nucleus of the domestic group consists of close relatives living under the firm authority of the head of the family—a grandfather, father, or elder brother. A married son continues to live with his father; a girl, if she does not marry a cousin on her father's side (preferential marriage), goes to live with her husband's family; if widowed, repudiated, or divorced, a woman returns to live with her parents. Sometimes three or four generations live together in a household comprising as many as 50 people.

To belong to a respected family, to be the bearer of an honourable name, is of great importance, since social status depends on that of one's family. The family imposes upon its members a discipline that dictates the position and tasks of each person. Fear of banishment (the supreme sanction) guarantees the submission of the individual to the interests of the collectivity. The fundamental unity, however, arises from mutual confidence and is not subjection to a tyrannical sovereign. The family head controls and administers everything, but he can do nothing without the implicit consent of the others. The balance of opposing forces amounts to a kind of authoritarian democracy.

Stratification. The dualities of town and country, sedentary and nomadic, were fundamental in the traditional Maghrib societies. In the cities, life was dominated by an ancient bourgeoisie often of Spanish or Turkish descent. There were separate Jewish and European quarters. The area near the town walls was inhabited by the humbler classes, newcomers, and seasonal workers. The black slaves were dispersed around their masters' homes. Closed in on itself, the town drew its prestige from its religious functions. In the absence of the clergy, the *qāḍi,* or judge, was the leading personality of the town, sharing his eminence with the *ʿulamāʾ,* or doctors of the law.

The Sharīfs

In the rural communities, the social group known as Sharīfs is highest in the class hierarchy. They are reputed to be descendants of the Prophet and to possess supernatural powers. The Sharīfs are venerated in the same way as the heads of religious brotherhoods and the saintly men known as *marabouts*. The next highest social position in these self-sufficient communities is accorded to families known more for the bravery and wisdom of their members than for the size of their herds or plantations.

The nomads constituted a permanent threat to the village societies. The nomads were herdsmen, while the villagers were tillers of the soil. In addition, the villagers were Berbers, while the nomads represented the Bedouin conquerors. Nevertheless, a modus vivendi was generally established. In exchange for their livestock and goods, the nomads were allowed to graze their flocks on the land of the sedentary communities, which, in turn, sold them their cereal products. In the oases, the inhabitants cultivated palm trees belonging to the nomads, who, in return, protected them against the raids of hostile tribes.

Socialization and education. The boy is removed from his mother's influence at an early age; after circumcision at six or seven, his education is taken over by male kinsmen. He learns to distrust the opinion of women; as a Maghrib proverb runs, "Angels and men work for unity; Satan and women work for division." Obedience and respect are taught at an early age. The spontaneous brotherly relationship is replaced at 10 or 12 years of age by a more formalized, distant relationship: boys learn to address their older brothers with deference and avoid them in public places. To their parents, children owe total submission at the risk of being cursed if they disobey. At the same time, male and female cousins learn equalitarian relationships, which are as important in social life as the hierarchical ones. The family, as the guardian of tradition, hands on the many customs of daily life.

In the town but rarely in the country, the boys often attended the Qurʾānic school, where they learned the basics of reading and writing and memorized the Qurʾān. In the mosques they received a complementary education in grammar and Muslim law. Only two towns in the Maghrib possessed Muslim universities: Tunis (az-Zaytūnah Mosque) and Fès (the Qarawīyīn Mosque). Here students received an education in law and religion, along with fundamentals of grammar, astronomy, and geography.

Economic systems. *Settlement patterns and housing.* The variety of dwellings reflects the different ways of life and the cultural diversity of the Maghrib. Broadly speaking, there are three types of shelter: the house, the hovel (*gourbi*), and the tent. The well-to-do family's house, constructed in the shade of the mosque, is a mixture of Spanish and Moorish architecture. The rooms open onto a central patio. There are no exterior windows, although roof terraces allow conversation among women of the neighbourhood. In the outlying parts of the town, sumptuous palaces surrounded by gardens and outbuildings stand next to apartment houses and poor tenements.

Berber villages

In the mountains the Berber villages perch cautiously on the slopes, like refuges. Their defensive aspect is often strengthened by fortified collective barns known as *agadir, guelâa,* or *gasr*. On certain Mediterranean mountainsides one sees houses with double-thatched roofs. Elsewhere, the houses are built with terraces and walls of stone, mud, or sun-dried brick. The Saharan Berbers have created a spectacular form of architecture using mud, examples of which are the *tighremt,* a rectangular fortress with a tower at each corner, and the *ksar,* a fortified village surrounded by towers and bastions; this form of building is also seen in Morocco.

In the plains, the sedentary groups generally live in hamlets of hovels (*gourbi*) and tents. These are people engaged in cereal farming and herding but always at the mercy of nomads or mountain tribes on the lookout for workable land. The *gourbi* is a hut made of branches or earth, covered with thatch, that can easily be erected wherever the group moves. An enclosure of thorny plants or prickly pears surrounds the cabin and serves as an animal fold during the night.

In the steppes live the true nomads. Their tents, similar to those of the Bedouins, are made of long strips (*flīj*) woven by the womenfolk from wool, camel's hair, or goat hair and sewn together. The four side walls are made of the same fabric. The dwelling is supported by wooden posts and held in place by ropes of wool or hair. Matting or carpets cover the ground inside. At night the tents are grouped in a circle, forming an enclosure for the herd.

Production and technology. The economy of the desert is predominantly pastoral, as is also that of the steppes and of certain coastal plains where the natural vegetation is conducive to the raising of sheep, goats, and dromedaries. The nomads follow their herds in the search for pasture, camping in the south in the winter and passing the summer in the Atlas Mountains of the north or in the maritime hills.

Agricultural practices

The cultivation of corn (maize) and barley is done with rudimentary techniques. The ground is left fallow every other year but not fertilized. Plowing begins after the autumn rains, with a wooden plow drawn by two animals. Harvesting is done by sickle and threshing by letting the livestock trample the sheaves. Every family head who owns a plow and a team has the right to work the common land. In regions where there is privately owned land, there are small farmers (fellahin) and also men (*khammāsīn*) employed by others in return for one-fifth of the harvest. But the irregular rainfall, the political instability, the property laws, and above all the priority accorded to grazing do not encourage farmers to improve their soil.

In the oases and certain mountains, however, peasants have inherited proven agricultural techniques. Despite the poor quality of the land, an intensive mixed farming—cereals, vegetables, olives, dates, fruit orchards—supports a dense population.

There is little manufacturing. Except for milling, work in the villages is done by hand in small family workshops using archaic tools. The activities consist mainly of making clothes and tools and of building. Most of the clothes are coarse woollens, although sometimes a weaver may produce more delicate work for a wealthy customer. Tanneries exist everywhere to process the hides of cattle, sheep, and goats, which are dyed with such local pigments as saffron and cochineal. The leather industry employs many specialized craftsmen, such as shoemakers, saddlers, and morocco leather tanners. The urban construction industry employs artists, such as mosaicists, potters, and sculptors in plaster and in wood; they have helped to make Maghribian architecture famous.

Property and exchange. Houses, gardens, plantations, and livestock are private property and can be inherited. In principle, the family unit is predominant but each relative can demand that he be given his share of the property. In order to avoid breaking up the family heritage or to modify the order of succession, charitable foundations (*ḥabūs*) are often created. These are untransferable, but the donee can assign the life interest to the beneficiary of his choice.

As a rule, however, all land belongs to the Muslim community, including conquered territory whose tenants pay an annual rent or lands conceded to loyal tribes by the sultans and *beys*. Tribes and clans that own their land distribute plots to each family, divide up the water supplies, and administer the pastureland.

Outside each town a weekly livestock market is held. Other weekly markets (*sūqs*) take place in country areas. Peddlers sell articles made in Europe or by town craftsmen.

Trade between different regions is limited, and goods are carried by camels and mules. The Maghrib as a whole exports agricultural products, such as cereals, wool, leather, and livestock, and imports cloth, sugar, coffee, and tea.

Religious syncretism

Belief and aesthetic systems. Religious beliefs in the Maghrib combine Islām with local traditions. Muslim theologians have denounced many a heresy, an ancient task in this land where St. Augustine used to flay the Donatists. While the main ritual obligations are observed by the whole population, only a minority of educated citizens conform to the orthodoxy of the Qur'ān. Even this orthodoxy admits the existence of "spirits," against which people must protect themselves. In the activities of daily life it is as important to protect oneself against hostile powers as it is to seek divine favour, and this is done through a variety of practices. A pregnant woman wears amulets and sometimes a talisman of black pearls in the form of a hand (the hand of Muḥammad's daughter Fāṭimah). Into the ear of the newborn child the father murmurs the Muslim profession of faith. On the seventh day after birth, the child is named, and a sheep is sacrificed.

Animal sacrifices are typical features of Muslim feasts. The sacrifice of a sheep on the day of 'Īd al-Aḍḥā (Īd al-Kabīr), the grandest festival of Islām, commemorates the offering of Abraham. A sacrifice, followed by a communal meal, also accompanies the pilgrimage to the saints' tombs, precedes the annual plowing, and is used in efforts to cure sickness or to overcome a woman's sterility. Sacrifice renews the pact of alliance between the living and the dead; the spilling of blood continues the contract with the ancestors, who protect the family and the clan in a world dominated by invisible forces. The cult of the dead conditions the agrarian rituals of the Berbers, since fecundity, namely life, depends on the goodwill of the spirits of the Earth. The symbolic representations of the crop-growing cycle are identical with those marking the stages of man's life. The rituals of possessing the ground and fertilizing it guarantee permanence of life. These moments of plowing and sowing are a period of rejoicing and marriage. Inversely, funeral rites accompany the harvest. The last sheaf of corn ends the cycle, and the dead return beneath the ground.

The agrarian rites that punctuate the solar year are accompanied by Muslim festivals that follow the lunar calendar. The religious year opens with the 'Āshūrā, the festival of children and also of ancestors, whose tombs are visited. The Mūlūd, commemorating the birth of the Prophet, is a joyous ceremony; several religious brotherhoods choose this day to organize their great annual festival. The 'Īd al-Fiṭr ('Īd as-Ṣaghīr) and the 'Īd al-Aḍḥā are canonical celebrations held throughout the Muslim world. The first, known as the "little festival," marks the end of the Ramaḍān fast. There is much gaiety, and gifts are made to the poor. The second is the "great festival," marking the last rite of the pilgrimage to Mecca. These religious ceremonies are also family ceremonies, accompanied by feasting and visiting.

Arts and crafts

Islām provides the chief aesthetic inspiration for the craftsmen of the towns. Urban architecture and furniture show the influence of the Middle East and of Muslim Spain. Córdoba, Seville, and Granada were particular sources of inspiration for the Maghrib, and Andalusian exiles spread their refined techniques from Fès to Tunis. This Hispano-Moorish art had its strongest impact in Morocco. Tunisia was also strongly influenced by the artistic trends of Fāṭimid Egypt in the 10th and 11th centuries and later, like Algeria, by those of the Ottoman Empire.

Religious architecture expresses the deep unity of Muslim art, showing in its forms the originality of the Maghrib. For example, the prayer room of the Great Mosque of Tlemcen is composed of 13 long naves, with wooden beams and covered in tiles. The middle nave has two domes. The minaret is a quadrangular tower, topped by a square edifice at the base of which is the platform from which the muezzin calls the believers to prayer. The decoration of Maghrib mosques consists of multiple variations of the lobed arch and the cornice, with linear elements on the walls, such as epigraphy, geometric designs, and flora, either sculpted or designed in mosaic.

Berber art objects have a rectilinear decoration, the richest motifs deriving from the chevron or lozenge and varying from one tribal group to another. The overall composition is simple, with alternating decorated and coloured strips, as in the woollen carpets of the Moyen Atlas region. Pottery is handmade, without a wheel, and glazed in an oven; it is very similar to Neolithic potteries, although the richest wares recall certain ancient Aegean ceramics.

RECENT TENDENCIES

The 19th century saw the beginning of a period of far-reaching political and economic change. The French conquest of North Africa, followed by the massive immigration of Europeans, introduced the French language and European culture. The political power of the tribes was destroyed. A strong centralized power dominated the whole country. This, in turn, was ultimately destroyed by nationalism and the desire for emancipation.

Social changes since independence

By July 1962 the entire Maghrib was independent. The new political regimes in Algeria, Morocco, and Tunisia have tried to rediscover their cultural identity and to develop their economies. There has been a rapid evolution of institutions, social structures, and collective values. New elites have emerged; the present-day civil servants and technicians form a middle class very different from the traditional petty bourgeoisie from which many of them come. Industrialization has created a class of factory workers. At the same time there has been a mass exodus of uprooted peasants to the cities, where they form a sub-proletariat living in shantytowns. Modern hygiene has lowered the death rate so that the natural population increase has become among the highest in the world; this has caused considerable migration into the prosperous agricultural regions and to the large coastal towns, as well as an outflow of workers to France. These movements have in turn contributed extensively to the breakdown of family groups and traditional communities. They have allowed an intensive mixing of the population, established new kinds of social relationships, and led to profound changes in attitudes and conduct.

Although there is a striking difference between town and country and between developed and undeveloped areas, the rural areas should not be regarded as lost in the past. Since the 1930s many of the rural societies of the Maghrib have begun to modernize. To plains that were previously underexploited, advanced agricultural techniques have brought vineyards, olive groves, and the intensive production of citrus fruits and vegetables. Road and railway networks carry foreign ideas and products to regions that were formerly isolated, while "villages of colonization" and rural towns have introduced urban ideas and products into the countryside. The colonial regime limited and distorted cultural contacts between Europeans and the people of the Maghrib, but it was also the vehicle of technical progress and a symbol of modernity. If foreign domination exploited the national resources, it also introduced a monetary economy and new ways of behaviour. The priority given by the post-colonial governments to economic development has intensified the process of change.

Like all societies in transition, the Maghrib displays a number of cultural contradictions. Along with an emphasis on Arab–Islāmic origins, there has been an increase of contacts with the industrialized countries. The Arabization of education has been accompanied by the teaching of French in the rapidly expanding school system. While Islām has assumed its former place in public life, political and administrative activity is determinedly secular.

Effects of modernization

Despite the growth of the towns, the majority of the population in the Maghrib remain rural. The old family values continue to have a strong influence on social life. While the extended family group is becoming rare, solidarity among male relatives is still an imperative. One is obligated to give help to distant cousins and to former allies of one's village or *douar* (district). Social relationships, even in the most modern enterprises, remain deeply personalized. Even in the civil service, the formal, hierarchical relationships are often paralleled by informal ones that provide the real chain of command.

Except for a small Europeanized minority, most of the

population favour large families. Even though many people think that the very high birth rate of the old days is no longer desirable, families with three or four children are very common. Celibacy is frowned upon; children, particularly girls, are married as soon as possible. While the emancipation of young people, especially in the towns, has tended to reduce paternal influence, marriages are still commonly arranged by the family, preference being given to a paternal cousin, some other relative, or at least a member of one's *douar.*

The position of women has improved since independence. The development of education for young girls and the increase of female employees in business have tended to break down the strict separation of men and women in public life. More and more women are seen without veils, at least in the big towns, although few women appear in public places.

The evolution of customs and ideas has not spared religious life. Strict conformity is disappearing; there is more tolerance for those who do not strictly observe the fast of Ramaḍān or who drink alcoholic beverages. But the general fervour of religious observances shows the common fidelity of everyone to Islām.

There have been profound changes in the hierarchy of status and prestige. For everyone, the civil servant is the symbol of social success. Among country people, to become a salaried worker is an enviable promotion. Class consciousness has spread throughout society, although tensions between civil servants, workers, small-town clerks, and peasants are tempered by the traditional system of relationships. At the same time, the desire for material improvement, coupled with the impatience of the masses and their increasing interest in politics, tends to widen social antagonisms. (R.De.)

HISTORY

Ancient North Africa

GEOGRAPHY AND PREHISTORY

The description of the area as an island refers to its isolation, bounded by the sea to the north and west, by the Sahara to the south and east. The desert has been the dominant factor in the North African environment, though it has not always been as dry as it is today. At various times during the past 1,000,000 years there have been periods of abundant rainfall, the last occurring about the 6th millennium BC at the beginning of the Neolithic Period (see below). A major trade route connecting the Mediterranean with the African world existed along the Hoggar-Tibesti ridge in the central Sahara, and it is probable that communications existed across the western Sahara also. Nevertheless, the Sahara always constituted a formidable barrier to the movement of techniques and peoples. In ancient historical times much of North Africa was evergreen forest or scrub, and the fauna included animals such as the elephant, zebra, and ostrich.

The mountains were of the utmost importance in the historical development of the area. They run generally from east to west, parallel to the coast, with their highest elevations in the Atlas Mountains. They are not continuous but constitute separate blocks, especially in the coastal areas. Although it was in the mountains that the rainfall was highest, the forest was intractable, and early settlements tended to choose the plains and valleys between or south of the mountains. The Mediterranean coast, for much of its length, is extremely inhospitable, offering few natural harbours and still fewer natural lines of communication into the interior. Even the major rivers, such as the Medjerda (Majardah) and Chelif, are unnavigable. Only in northeastern Tunisia is the coastline more favourable, and the main movement of culture and conquest has naturally been from there westward.

The coastal strip in the area of Tripoli (Ṭarābulus) in western Libya is an extension of that of Tunisia. To the east, some 800 miles of the Surt Desert separates it from Cyrenaica (Barqah) at the eastern end of modern Libya, which thus has had a very different history from the Maghrib. Settlement there was effectively confined to the elevated plateau of al-Jabal al-Akhḍar and did not extend more than about 70 miles south of the coast. Cyrenaica's contact with Egypt was limited by an intervening 600 miles of semidesert.

The Maghrib provides the paradox of an area in which various cultures have imposed some measure of uniformity, while political unity has been rare; for this, geography is largely responsible. The area of settlement is of vast length but little breadth and has no natural centre from which political uniformity could be imposed; its natural communications have never been easy, and the mountain blocks have been large enough to maintain populations to a greater or lesser degree independent of and hostile to those that controlled the plains.

Although there is uncertainty about some factors, Aïn Hanech (in Algeria) is the site of one of the earliest traces of hominid occupation in the Maghrib. Somewhat later but better attested are sites at Ternifine (near Tighennif, Algeria) and at Sīdī ʿAbd ar-Raḥmān, Morocco. The former produced hand axes associated with a hominid classified as *Homo erectus,* more primitive than Neanderthaloids of the same period. Sīdī ʿAbd ar-Raḥmān produced evidence of the same hominid, with a date of at least 200,000 BC.

Earliest inhabitants

Succeeding these early hand-ax remains are the Levalloisian and Mousterian industries similar to those of the Levant. It is claimed that nowhere did the Middle Paleolithic evolution of flake-tool techniques reach a higher state of development than in North Africa. Its high point in variety, specialization, and standard of workmanship is named Aterian, after the type site of Biʾr al-ʿAtir in Tunisia; assemblages of this material occur all over the Maghrib and the Sahara. Radiocarbon testing from Morocco indicates a date for early Aterian material of *c.* 30,000 BC. Its spread appears to have taken place during one of the periods of desiccation, and the carriers of the tradition were clearly adept desert hunters. The few associated human remains are Neanderthaloid, with substantial differences between those found in the west and those in Cyrenaica. In the latter area, a date of *c.* 43,000 BC for the Levalloisian and Mousterian industries has been obtained (at Haua Ftoah). The tools and a fragmentary human fossil of Neanderthaloid type are almost identical to those of Palestine.

The earliest blade industries of the Maghrib, associated as in Europe with the final supersession of Neanderthaloids by *Homo sapiens,* are named Ibero-Maurusian, or Oranian (type site, La Mouilla, near Oran in western Algeria), an industry of obscure origin, which seems to have spread along all the coastal areas of the Maghrib and Cyrenaica between *c.* 15,000 and 10,000 BC. Following the Ibero-Maurusian was the Capsian, the origin of which is also obscure. Its most characteristic sites are in the area of the great salt lakes of southern Tunisia, the type site being al-Maqtaʿ (el-Mekta), near Qafṣah (Capsa, or Gafsa). The climate during both Ibero-Maurusian and Capsian appears to have been relatively dry and the fauna one of open country, ideal for hunting. Between *c.* 9,000 and 5,000 BC, upper Capsian spread northward to influence the Ibero-Maurusian and also eastward to the Gulf of Sidra, and by the 3rd millennium BC, if not earlier, a uniform human type appears to have been established through the Maghrib. Since there is much evidence that the Neolithic culture of the Maghrib was not introduced by invasion but through the acceptance of new ideas and technologies by the Capsian peoples, it is possible that they were the ancestors of the Libyans known in historic times.

Neolithic culture

The spread of early Neolithic culture in Libya and the Maghrib occurred during the 6th and 5th millennia BC and is characterized by the domestication of animals and the shift from hunting and gathering to self-supporting food production (often still including hunting). The pastoral economy, with cattle the chief animal, remained dominant in North Africa until the classical period. Although the new type of economy may have originated in Egypt or the Sudan, the character of the flint-working tradition of the Maghribian Neolithic argues in favour of the survival of much of the earlier culture, which has been called Neolithic-of-Capsian tradition. Accordingly, the transition, if not of independent local origin, is best explained by the gradual diffusion of new techniques rather than by massive immigration of new peoples.

The Neolithic-of-Capsian tradition in the Maghrib persisted at least into the 1st millennium BC with relatively little change and development; there was no great flourishing of late Neolithic culture nor little that can be described as a Bronze Age. North Africa was wholly lacking in metallic ores other than iron, hence most tools and weapons continued to be made of stone until the introduction of ironworking techniques.

Prehistoric rock carvings flourished in the southern foothills of the Atlas south of Oran and in the Hoggar and Tibesti ranges. While some are relatively recent, the great majority appear to be of the Neolithic-of-Capsian tradition. Some show animals locally or even totally extinct, such as the giant buffalo, elephant, rhinoceros, and hippopotamus in areas now covered by desert. While Egyptian-like patterns may be discerned, the character of the rock art is so different from that of Egypt that it can hardly be said to derive from it. On the other hand, it is very much later than the rock paintings of Paleolithic times in southwest Europe, and an independent development is not excluded. The art is primarily that of a culture that remained largely, though not exclusively, dependent on hunting and that survived on the Saharan fringes until historical times.

There are many thousands of large, stone-built surface tombs in North Africa that appear to have no connection with earlier megalithic structures found in northern Europe, and it is unlikely that any of them is earlier than the 1st millennium BC. Large structures such as the tumulus at Mzora (54 metres in diameter) and the mausoleum known as the Medracen (40 metres in diameter) are probably of the 4th and 3rd centuries BC and show Phoenician influence, though there is much that appears to be purely Libyan.

THE CARTHAGINIAN PERIOD

The Phoenician settlements. North Africa (with the exception of Cyrenaica) entered the mainstream of Mediterranean history with the arrival in the 1st millennium BC of Phoenician traders on its coast. The Phoenicians were not looking for land to settle but for anchorages and staging points on the trade route from Phoenicia to Spain, a source of silver and tin. Points on an alternative route by way of Sicily, Sardinia, and the Balearic Islands also were occupied. The Phoenicians lacked the manpower and the need to found large colonies as the Greeks did, and few of their settlements grew to any size. The sites chosen were generally offshore islands or easily defensible promontories with sheltered beaches on which ships could be drawn up. Carthage (from the Phoenician Kart-Hadasht, New City), destined to be the largest Phoenician colony and in the end an imperial power, conformed to the pattern.

Tradition dated the foundation of Gades (modern Cádiz; the earliest known Phoenician trading post in Spain) to 1110 BC, Utica (Utique) to 1101 BC, and Carthage to 814 BC. The earlier dates appear legendary, and no Phoenician object earlier than the 8th century BC has yet been found in the west. At Carthage some Greek objects have been found, datable to about 750 or slightly later, which comes within two generations of the traditional date. Little can be learned from the romantic legends about the arrival of the Phoenicians at Carthage transmitted by Greco-Roman sources. Though individual voyages doubtless took place earlier, the establishment of permanent, or at any rate seasonal, posts is unlikely to have taken place before 800 BC, but they antedate the parallel movement of Greeks to Sicily and southern Italy.

Material evidence of Phoenician occupation of 8th-century-BC date comes from Utica, and of the 7th or 6th century BC from Hadrumetum (Sūsah, Sousse), Tipasa (east of Cherchell), Siga (Rachgoun), Lixus, and Mogador (Essaouira), the last being the most distant Phoenician settlement so far known. Finds of parallel date have been made at Motya (Mozia) in Sicily, Nora (Nurri), Sulcis, and Tharros (Torre di S. Giovanni) in Sardinia, and Cádiz and Almuñécar in Spain. Unlike the Greek settlements, however, those of the Phoenicians long remained politically dependent on their homeland, and only a few were situated where the hinterland had the potential for development. The emergence of Carthage as an independent power, leading to the creation of an empire based on the secure possession of the North African coast, resulted less from the weakening of Tyre, the chief city of Phoenicia, by the Babylonians than from growing pressure from the Greeks in the western Mediterranean; in 580 BC some Greek cities in Sicily attempted to drive the Phoenicians from Motya and Panormus (Palermo) in the west of the island. The Carthaginians feared that if the Greeks won the whole of Sicily they would move on to Sardinia and beyond, isolating the Phoenicians in North Africa. The successful defense of Sicily was followed by attempts to strengthen limited footholds in Sardinia; a recently discovered fortress at Monte Sirai is the oldest Phoenician military building in the west. The threat from the Greeks receded when Carthage, in alliance with Etruscan cities, checked the Phocaeans off Corsica in about 540 BC and succeeded in excluding the Greeks from contact with southern Spain. A further success occurred in Africa itself; in 514 BC a Spartan named Dorieus attempted to found a settlement at the mouth of the Cinyps River (Oued Oukirri) in Libya, but the Carthaginians, regarding this as an intrusion into their own territory, were able to expel the Spartans with the help of native Libyans.

Relations with the Greeks

Carthaginian supremacy. By the 5th century BC, active military participation by Tyre in the west had doubtless ceased; from the latter half of the 6th century it was under Persian rule. Carthage thus became the leader of the western Phoenicians, and in the 5th century formed an empire of its own, centred on North Africa, which included existing Phoenician settlements, new ones founded by Carthage itself, and a large part of modern Tunisia. The actual stages of the growth of Carthaginian power are not known, but the process was largely completed by the beginning of the 4th century. The whole of the Cap Bon (Jazīrat Sharīk) peninsula was occupied early, ensuring Carthage a fertile and secure hinterland. Subsequently, penetration extended southwestward as far as a line running roughly from al-Kāf to the coast at Thaenae (now the ruins of Thīnah, or Tina). Penetration occurred south of this line later, Theveste (Tabassah, Tébessa) being occupied in the 3rd century BC. In the Cap Bon peninsula, where the Carthaginians developed a prosperous agriculture, the native population may have been enslaved, but elsewhere these people were obliged only to pay tribute and furnish troops.

Carthage maintained an iron grip on the entire coast, from the Gulf of Sidra to the Atlantic coast of Morocco, establishing many new settlements to protect its monopoly of trade. These were mostly small places, probably of only a few hundred inhabitants. The Greeks called them *emporia,* markets where native tribes brought articles to trade, which could also serve as anchorages and watering places. Permanent settlements in modern Libya were few and dated after the attempt of Dorieus to plant a Greek colony there. Though in time fishing and agriculture played a part in their wealth, Leptis Magna with its neighbours Sabratha and Oea (Tripoli) became rich through trans-Saharan trade; Leptis Magna was the terminus of the shortest route across the Sahara linking the Mediterranean with the Niger. A Carthaginian named Mago is said to have crossed the desert several times, but doubtless much of the trade (in precious stones) came through intermediate tribes. Other stations on the Gulf of Gabes included Zouchis, known for its salted fish and purple dye, Gigthis (Bū Ghirārah), and Tacape (Qābis, Gabès). North of Thaenae was Acholla, traditionally an offshoot of the Phoenician settlement on Malta, Thapsus (Rass Dimas), Leptis Minor, and Hadrumetum, the largest city on the east coast of Tunisia. From Neapolis (Nābul, Nabeul), a

Carthaginian settlements

road ran direct to Carthage across the base of the Cap Bon peninsula.

West of Carthage there have been changes in the course of the Bagradas (Majardah) River; as a result, Utica, a port in Carthaginian and Roman times, is now some seven miles from the sea. Utica was second only to Carthage in importance among the Phoenician settlements and always maintained at least a nominal independence. Beyond Cape Farina (Ra's Sīdī ʿAlī al-Makkī) as far as the Straits of Gibraltar, the coast offered a number of anchorages, but few of the stations reached anything like the prosperity of those on the Gulf of Gabes and the east coast of Tunisia. One of the more important was Hippo Diarrhytus (Bizerte, Banzart), whose natural advantages as a port were utilized at an early date; another Hippo, later called Hippo Regius (Bône, modern Annaba), was also probably of Carthaginian origin. Along the same stretch of coast were Rusicade (Philippeville, Skikda) and Collo (Chullu). Still farther west, a number of place-names known from the Roman period betray an earlier Phoenician interest through the incorporation of a Phoenician element, *rus,* meaning "cape"; *e.g.,* Rusuccuru (Dellys) and Rusguniae (Matifou). Tingis (Tingi, Tangier) was already settled in the 5th century BC.

Trade. Ancient sources agree that Carthage had become perhaps the richest city in the world through its trade, yet very few traces of its wealth have been discovered by archaeologists. This is no doubt because most of it was in perishables—textiles, unworked metal, foodstuffs, and slaves; its trade in manufactured goods was only a small part of the whole. There can be no doubt that the most profitable trade was that inherited from the Phoenicians in the western Mediterranean, in which tin, silver, gold, and iron were obtained in exchange for manufactures and consumer goods of small value. Carthage ruthlessly maintained its monopoly of this trade from the late 6th to the end of the 3rd century BC by sinking intruders and exacting recognition of its position from other states. Its wealth is attested by the vast mercenary armies it was able to raise and the mintage of gold coins in the 4th century far in excess of that known for other advanced states.

Voyages of exploration

It was apparently in connection with this trade that during the 5th century there occurred two voyages of exploration and trade, evidently of particular importance since reports of them were known to later generations of Greeks and Romans. One was along the Atlantic coast of Morocco, the other northward along the Atlantic coast of Spain. They were led by Hanno and Himilco, respectively, both members of a leading family in Carthage. Hanno's voyage is generally associated with an account in Herodotus, writing about 430 BC, of Carthaginian trade on the Atlantic coast of Morocco. Herodotus describes a system of dumb barter with primitive peoples, by which the Carthaginians exchanged manufactured goods for gold. It is not known where the exchanges took place; the Río de Oro is a possibility, and it is probable that Hanno's expedition went beyond Cape Verde. Nevertheless, the "gold route" did not survive the fall of Carthage and was unknown to the Romans. This has led some scholars to argue that the Carthaginians' interest in the Atlantic coast of Morocco was stimulated by the more prosaic attraction of the abundant fish.

Himilco's voyage also was known to the Greeks and Romans. He sailed north along the Atlantic coast of Spain, Portugal, and France and reached the territory of the Oestrymnides, a tribe living in Brittany. The purpose of this voyage was apparently to consolidate control of the trade in tin along the Atlantic coast of Europe. It followed the route used by the Tartessians, a people of southern Spain in the area where Cádiz had been founded, who knew of Ireland and Britain. This trade was no doubt the latest phase of contact between the various areas of the Atlantic seaboard that went back to Late Neolithic times. There is no evidence that Himilco reached Britain, nor indeed has any Phoenician object ever been found in the island, but probably Cornish tin was obtained through the tribes of Brittany. Tin was also obtained from northwestern Spain. It is notable that, at Cádiz, the Carthaginian tombs found at intervals over the past century have produced nothing earlier than the 5th century, which would indicate that it was not until that date that it became a large and permanent base for the exploitation of trading opportunities in the west.

Trading contacts with the Greek world had been substantial from the earliest period of Phoenician colonization, in spite of the intermittent wars with the Greeks of Sicily. Pottery from Corinth, Athens, Ionia, Rhodes, and other Greek centres has been found at Carthage, Utica, and many other sites, as well as imports from Phoenicia itself and from Egypt. It is known that Selinus, a Greek city in Sicily, grew wealthy from trade with Carthage, probably in foodstuffs, before Carthage conquered the neighbouring hinterland. During the 5th century there appears to have been a decline in imports from the Greek world. One factor that inhibited trade was the lack of a Carthaginian coinage before the early 4th century, though most important Greek states had had their own coinages for at least a century before that. Carthaginian merchants, however, did not cease to frequent Greek ports, and a number of them were established at Syracuse in 398. From that date, economic contacts with advanced states seem to have revived, especially after the conquests of Alexander the Great in the eastern Mediterranean created a new market for the cheap Carthaginian manufactured goods. The Carthaginian merchant became such a familiar figure in such economic centres of the Greek world as Athens and Delos that there were Greek comedies in which the central figure was the Carthaginian trader.

Revival of economic contacts

Wars outside Africa. Except in backward or thinly populated areas Carthage's foreign policy was nonexpansive. One major departure was a disaster: in 480 Carthage intervened in intercity struggles among the Greeks of Sicily and suffered a heavy defeat at Himera. After a long period of peace, it went in 410 to the help of Segesta, an ally in Sicily, and turned the war into one of revenge for the earlier defeat. After initial successes, including the destruction of Himera, a treaty confirmed Carthage's control of the west of the island. During the 4th century most of the wars were caused by the attempts of various rulers of Syracuse to drive the Carthaginians out of Sicily; three of these (398–392, 382–375, and 368) were with Dionysius I of Syracuse. Most of the time the eastern limit of Carthaginian power in the island was recognized as the Halycus (Platani) River. The only occasion in which Carthage suffered directly (since its armies were largely mercenary) was in 310, when the ruler of Syracuse, Agathocles, under heavy pressure in Sicily, launched a daring invasion of Africa, the first experienced by Carthage. Over a period of three years he caused great devastation in Carthaginian territory in eastern Tunisia but in the end was defeated.

Treatment of subject peoples. Carthage was notorious in antiquity for oppressing and exacting excessive tribute from its subjects. There were, however, different categories of subject community, the most favoured being the original Phoenician settlements and the colonies of Carthage itself. There is little evidence of opposition among them to Carthaginian control. Similar institutions and laws may be attributed to a common cultural background rather than to an attempt to impose uniformity. Carthage exacted dues on imports and exports and levied troops and probably sailors. Carthaginian subjects of various nationalities in Sicily also received favourable treatment, at least in economic matters. Relatively free trade was allowed until the end of the 5th century, and a number of cities had their own coinage. In the 4th century, some Sicilian Greek states became subject to Carthage, paying a tribute amounting apparently to one-tenth of their produce. It was the Libyans of the interior who suffered most, though few were reduced to slavery. During the First Punic War, Libyans had to pay one-half of their crops as tribute, and it is supposed that the normal exaction was a quarter, a burdensome imposition. They were also required to provide troops, and from the early 4th century they formed the largest single element in the Carthaginian army; it is unlikely that they received pay except in booty before the Punic Wars. The Carthaginians are said to have "admired not those governors who treated their subjects with moderation but those who exacted the greatest amount of supplies and treated the inhabitants most ruthlessly." This judgment (by the Greek historian Polybius) was made in connection with the Libyans, and a destructive revolt—one of a number known—that followed the first Punic War. In this revolt (241–237 BC), mercenaries, unpaid after the Carthaginian defeat in the First Punic War, revolted and for a while controlled much of Carthage's North African territory. It was fought with great atrocities on both sides, and the Libyans were among the most fervent of the rebels. They even issued coins on which the name Libyan appears (in Greek), which probably indicates a growing ethnic consciousness. Notwithstanding this relationship, Carthaginian civilization had profound effects on the material culture of the Libyans (see below).

Political and military institutions. Hereditary kingship prevailed in Phoenicia down to Hellenistic times, and Greek and Roman sources refer to kingship at Carthage. It appears not to have been hereditary but elective, though in practice one family, the Magonid, dominated in the 6th century. The power of the kingship was diminished during the 5th century, a development that has its parallels in the political evolution of Greek city-states and of Rome. Roman sources directly transcribe only one Carthaginian political term—*sufet,* etymologically the same as the Hebrew *shofeṭ,* generally translated "judge" in the Old Testament but implying much more than merely judicial functions. At some stage, probably in the 4th century, the *sufet*s became the chief magistrates of Carthage and other western Phoenician settlements. Two *sufet*s were elected annually by the citizen body, but all were from the wealthy classes. The chief power rested with an oligarchy of the wealthiest citizens, who were life members of a council of state and decided all important matters unless there was serious disagreement with the *sufet*s. A panel of judges chosen from among its members had obscure but formidable powers of control over all organs of government.

Carthaginian magistrates

During the 6th and 5th centuries, most military commands were held by kings, but later the generalship was apparently dissociated from civil office. Even in the time of the kings, military authority appears to have been conferred upon the kings only for specific campaigns or in emergencies. The generals are said to have been regarded as potential overthrowers of the legal government, but in fact there is no record of any army commander's having attempted a coup d'etat.

Up to the 6th century, the armies of Carthage were apparently citizen levies similar to those of all city-states of the early classical period. But Carthage was too small to provide for the defense of widely scattered settlements, and it turned increasingly to mercenaries, officered by Carthaginians, with citizen contingents appearing only occasionally. Libyans were considered particularly suitable for light infantry, Numidians and Mauretanians for light cavalry; Iberians and Celtiberians from Spain were used in both capacities. In the 4th century the Carthaginians also hired Gauls, Campanians, and even Greeks. The disadvantages of mercenary armies were more than outweighed by the fact that Carthage could never have stood the losses incurred in a whole series of wars in Sicily and elsewhere. Very little is known about the manning of the Carthaginian fleet; technically, it was not overwhelmingly superior to those of the Greeks, but it was larger and had the benefit of experienced sailors from Carthage's maritime settlements.

The city. The Romans completely destroyed Carthage in 146 BC, and a century later built a new city on the site, so that little is known of the physical appearance of the Phoenician city. It is almost certain that the ancient artificial harbour—the Cothon—is represented today by two lagoons north of the bay of al-Karm (el-Kram). In antiquity it had two parts, the outer rectangular part being for merchant shipping, the interior, circular division being reserved for warships; sheds and quays were available for 220 warships. Its small size probably means that it was chiefly used in winter when navigation almost ceased. The city walls were of great strength and 22 miles in length; the most dangerous section, across the isthmus, was over 40 feet high and 30 feet thick. The citadel on the hill called Byrsa was also fortified. Between Byrsa and the port was the heart of the city, its marketplace, council house, and temples. In appearance it may have been not dissimilar to towns in the eastern Mediterranean or Persian Gulf before the impact of modern civilization, with narrow winding streets and houses up to six stories high. The exterior walls were blank except for a solitary street door, but they enclosed courtyards. A figure of 700,000 for the city population is given by the geographer Strabo, but this probably included the population of the Cap Bon peninsula. A more reasonable figure could be about 400,000, including slaves, similar to that of Athens.

Physical appearance of Carthage

Religion and culture. The Carthaginians were notorious in antiquity for the intensity of their religious beliefs, which they retained to the end of their independence and which in turn influenced the religion of the native peoples. The chief deity was Baal Hammon, the community's divine lord and protector. A sombre god, he was identified by the Greeks with Cronus and by the Romans with Saturn. During the 5th century a goddess named Tanit came to be widely worshipped and represented in art. It is possible that her name is Libyan and that her popularity was connected with the acquisition of land in the interior, as she is associated with symbols of fertility. These two overshadow other deities such as Melkart, principal deity of Tyre, identified with Heracles, and Eshmoun, identified with Aesculapius. Human sacrifice was the element in Carthaginian life most criticized; it persisted in Africa much longer than in Phoenicia. The child victims were sacrificed to Baal (not to Moloch, an interpretation based on a misunderstanding of the texts), and the burnt bones buried in urns under stone markers, or stelae. At Carthage thousands of such urns have been found in the "Sanctuary of Tanit," and similar burials have been discovered at Hadrumetum, Cirta, Motya, Calaris, Nora, and Sulcis. The whole character of Carthaginian religion was sombre, being one of the weakness of human beings in the face of the overwhelming and capricious power of the gods. The great majority of Carthaginian personal names, unlike those of Greece and Rome, were of religious significance; *e.g.,* Hannibal, "Favoured by Baal," or Hamilcar, "Favoured by Melkart."

In comparison with the extent of its power and influence, the artistic and intellectual achievements of Carthage were small. What limited remains of buildings survive—mostly in North Africa and Sardinia—are utilitarian and uninspired. In the minor arts—pottery, jewelry, metalwork, objects in terra-cotta, and the thousands of carvings on stelae—a similar lack of inspiration may be felt. The influence of Phoenician, Egyptian, and Greek artistic traditions can be observed, but they failed to stimulate as they did, for example, in Etruria. There is no evidence that Greek philosophy and literature made much impact, though certainly many Carthaginians in the city's later history knew Greek and there were libraries in the city. One work is known, a treatise on agriculture by a certain Mago, but this may have been based on Hellenistic models. On the whole, the Carthaginians adhered to traditional modes of thought, which no doubt gave them a sense of solidarity amid more numerous and hostile peoples. Their fanatical patriotism enabled them to offer a more prolonged resistance to Rome than any other power. Their influence on North African history was, in the first place, to bring it into the mainstream of the advancing civilization of the Mediterranean world; more particularly it introduced into North Africa more advanced techniques leading to agricultural progress, which implied in turn a change by many Libyans from a seminomadic to a stable way of life, and the possibilities of urbanization, which were fully realized in the Roman period.

Carthaginian artistic and intellectual achievements

Carthage and Rome. In the 3rd and 2nd centuries BC, Carthage was weakened and finally destroyed by Rome in the three Punic Wars. Treaties between Carthage and Rome had been made in 508, 348, and 279, and for a long period the two powers had no conflicting interests. But by the 3rd century Rome dominated all southern Italy and thus approached the Carthaginian sphere in Sicily. In 264 Rome accepted the submission of Messana (Messina), though this state had previously had a Carthaginian garrison, partly because of exaggerated fears of a possible

Carthaginian threat to Italy and partly because of hopes of gain in Sicily. For Carthage, a Roman foothold in Sicily would upset the traditional balance of power on the island. The ensuing First Punic War, which lasted until 241, was very costly in human life, with losses of tens of thousands being recorded in some naval engagements. Contrary to expectation, the Carthaginian fleet was worsted on several occasions by the newly built Roman; on land the Romans failed to drive the Carthaginians out of Sicily, and a Roman invasion of Tunisia ended in catastrophe. Carthage made peace after a final naval defeat off the Aegates Islands, surrendering its hold on Sicily. Sardinia and Corsica fell to Rome in 238.

From *Grosser Historischer Weltatlas*, vol. I, *Vorgeschichte und Altertum* (1972); Bayerischer Schulbuch-Verlag, Munich

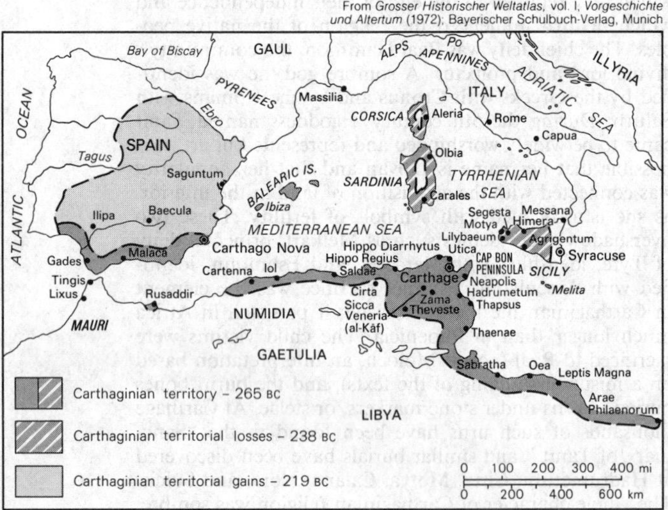

Carthaginian Empire.

In response to the defeat, Carthage, under the leadership of Hamilcar Barca and his successors (usually described as the Barcid family), set about establishing a new empire in Spain. The object appears to have been to exploit the mineral wealth directly rather than through intermediaries and to mobilize the manpower of much of Spain into an army that could match that of Rome. Hamilcar and his son-in-law Hasdrubal built up an army of over 50,000 Spanish infantry and occupied half of the Iberian Peninsula. Finally, in 219, Hannibal, Hamilcar's son, ignored Roman threats designed to prevent the consolidation or extension of the new empire. His invasion of Italy and the crushing defeats he inflicted on the Romans at Lake Trasimene (217) and Cannae (216) were the gravest danger Rome had ever faced. The majority of Rome's allies and subjects in Italy remained loyal, however, and Hannibal found increasing difficulty in getting supplies and reinforcements. After clearing Spain of the Carthaginians (209–206), Scipio Africanus landed near Utica in 204 with a Roman army. In 203 Hannibal was recalled from Italy; but he was defeated by Scipio near Zama (Sabʿ Biʾār) in 202. Carthage made peace soon afterward, surrendering its fleet, its overseas possessions, and some of its African territory. During the next 50 years it retained some measure of prosperity, although frequently under pressure from the Numidians under King Masinissa. From 155 BC irrational fears of a Carthaginian revival were stimulated at Rome by Cato the Elder, and in 149, on flimsy pretexts, the Carthaginians were forced to choose between evacuating their city and settling inland, or a doomed resistance. They chose the latter, and, after a three-year siege, the city was destroyed and its site ceremonially cursed by the younger Scipio.

New empire in Spain

The Greeks in Cyrenaica. The natural contacts of Cyrenaica were northward with Crete and the Aegean world. In the late 12th century BC Mycenaean Greek Sea Peoples landing in Cyrenaica armed the Libyans and with them attempted an unsuccessful invasion of Egypt. Cyrenaica's coast was visited by Cretan fishermen in the 7th century, and the Greeks became aware that it was the only area in North Africa still available for colonization. A severe overpopulation on the small Cyclades island of Thera (Santorini) led to the foundation of Cyrene (*c.* 630) on a site in easy reach of the sea, well watered, and in the fertile Jabal al-Akhḍar plateau. The founder's name was, or was changed to, Battus, a Libyan word meaning king. For some time friendly relations existed with the local peoples, and there was more intermarriage with non-Greek women than was usual in colonies. Later, when more colonists were attracted by the increasing prosperity, hostilities occurred in which the settlers were successful. Cyrene also repulsed an invasion by the Egyptians (570) but in 525 submitted to Persia. Meanwhile, Cyrene had established other Greek cities in the area—Barce (al-Marj), Taucheira (Tūkrah), and Euhesperides (Benghazi), all of which were independent of their founding city. During the 6th century, Cyrene rivalled the majority of other Greek cities in its wealth, manifested in part by substantial temple building. Prosperity was based on grain, fruit, horses, and, above all, on an apparently extinct plant, *Silphium*.

The dynasty of Battus ended *c.* 440 BC with the establishment of a democratic constitution like that of Athens, and the general prosperity of Cyrenaica continued through the 4th century in spite of some political troubles. Cyrenaica submitted to Alexander the Great in the late 4th century and subsequently became subject to the Ptolemies. The cities nevertheless enjoyed a good deal of freedom in running their own affairs. The constitution of Cyrene was elaborated as a fairly liberal oligarchy, with a citizen body of 10,000 and two councils. During the 3rd century a federal constitution for all the Cyrenaican cities was introduced. Apollonia, the port of Cyrene, became a city in its own right; Euhesperides was refounded as Berenice, and a new city, Ptolemais (Ṭulmaythah), was founded, while Barce declined; the term Pentapolis came to be used of the five cities Apollonia, Cyrene, Ptolemais, Taucheira, and Berenice. In 96 BC Ptolemy Apion bequeathed it to Rome, which annexed the royal estates but left the cities free. Disorders led Rome to create a regular province in 74 BC, to which Crete was added seven years later. After Mark Antony temporarily granted it to his daughter Cleopatra Selene, Augustus re-established it with Crete as a senatorial province.

Constitutional changes in Cyrene

THE RISE AND DECLINE OF NATIVE KINGDOMS

Between the destruction of Carthage and the establishment of effective Roman control over the Maghrib there was a period that saw a brief flourishing of native kingdoms. Amid the shifting tribal nomenclature of the sources of various periods, two main groups of relatively sedentary tribes may be distinguished: the Mauri, living between the Atlantic and the Moulouya or perhaps the Chelif rivers, who gave their name to Mauretania; and the Numidae, in the area to the west of that formerly controlled by Carthage. A third group, the Gaetuli, was a largely nomadic people of the desert and its fringe. The various tribes first emerge into history in the late 3rd century BC, no doubt after a period of evolution resulting from contact with Carthaginian civilization. This is difficult to trace, as Carthaginian products were scarce in the interior of the Maghrib before the 2nd century BC, but the large tumuli at Mzora, Sīdī Sulaymān, Souk el-Gour, and the Medracen, apparently royal tombs of the 4th and 3rd centuries BC, testify to a developing economy and society. No doubt service in the Carthaginian mercenary armies was a major stimulus to native Libyan progress. This was most noticeable in Numidia and reached a high point under Masinissa. The son of a chief of the Massyli, a tribe dominating the area between Carthaginian territory and the Ampsaga River (Wādī al-Kabīr), he had been brought up at Carthage and was 20 years old at the outbreak of the Second Punic War. At first his tribe was at variance with Carthage, but in 213 BC it became reconciled when its powerful western neighbours, the Masaesyli, under Syphax deserted Carthage. From 213 to 207 BC Masinissa commanded Numidian cavalry in Spain for the Carthaginians against Rome. On the latter's victory at Ilipa in 206, he returned to Africa where Syphax, now reconciled with Carthage, had occupied some of his tribal territory, including Cirta (Constantine), and his own claims to succession to the chieftainship were disputed. When

King Masinissa of Numidia

the Romans landed in Africa in 204 Masinissa rendered them invaluable assistance. Recognized by the Romans as king, he annexed the eastern part of Syphax' kingdom and reigned with success until 148 BC. The Greek geographer Strabo said that he "turned the nomads into a nation of farmers." This is exaggerated, since cereal culture had long been established in parts of Numidia, yet there is no doubt that the area of grain production was much enlarged. This was achieved by deliberate encouragement of Carthaginian civilization. Along with new techniques, Carthaginian language, religion, and art penetrated rapidly inland, and Masinissa's capital, Cirta, took on the aspects of a Carthaginian city; incipient urbanization of a number of native villages is also possible. Masinissa issued copper, bronze, and lead coinage for local use, as did some of the Carthaginian coastal towns under his rule.

On his death in 148, his kingdom was divided among his three sons, possibly on the insistence of the Romans, but the latter did not prevent its reunification under Micipsa (148–118 BC). The progress begun under Masinissa continued as refugees from the destruction of Carthage fled to Numidia. Meanwhile, the Romans had formed a province of the area of Tunisia northeast of a line from Thabraca to Thaenae but showed little interest in exploiting its wealth. The attempt by the Roman reformer Gaius Gracchus in 122 BC to found a colony on the site of Carthage failed, though individual colonists who had taken up allotments remained. When Micipsa died, another division of Numidia among three rulers took place, in which Jugurtha (118–105 BC) emerged supreme. He might have been recognized by Rome, but he provoked war when he killed some Italian merchants who were helping a rival to defend Cirta. After some successes due to the incompetence of Roman generals, he was surrendered by Bocchus I, king of Mauretania. The kingdom was again reconstituted under other descendants of Masinissa. The boundaries of the Roman province were slightly enlarged in the area of the upper Majardah, where veterans of the army of Gaius Marius received lands. During the next 50 years there was further immigration by individual Roman settlers and merchants but no deliberate state action. The last relatively formidable king of Numidia was Juba I (*c.* 60–46 BC), who supported the Pompeian side in the Roman civil war between Pompey and Julius Caesar but fell to the dictator in 46 BC at Thapsus. A new province, Africa Nova, was formed from the most developed part of the old Numidian kingdom east of the Ampsaga; it was subsequently (before 27 BC) amalgamated with the original province of Africa by the emperor Augustus. In 33 BC Bocchus II of Mauretania died, bequeathing his kingdom to Rome, but Augustus was unwilling to accept responsibility for so large and relatively backward an area. In 25 BC he installed Juba II, son of Juba I, as king; he ruled until his death about AD 24. He was married to Cleopatra Selene, daughter of Mark Antony and Cleopatra, and under them Iol, renamed Caesarea (Cherchel), and also Volubilis, near Fès (Fez), a secondary capital of the rulers of Mauretania, became centres of late Hellenistic culture. Juba himself was a prolific writer in Greek on a number of subjects, including history and geography. His son Ptolemy succeeded but was executed for unknown reasons by the Roman emperor Caligula in AD 40. A brief revolt followed but was easily suppressed, and the kingdom was divided into two provinces, Mauretania Caesariensis, with its capital at Caesarea, and Mauretania Tingitana, with its capital at Tingis.

Formation of Africa Nova

ROMAN NORTH AFRICA

Administration and defense. For over a century from its acquisition in 146 BC the small Roman province was governed by a minor Roman official from Utica; but changes were made by Augustus, reflecting the growing importance of the area. The governor was henceforth a proconsul, residing at Carthage, after its refounding by Augustus as a Roman colony, and responsible for the whole territory from the Ampsaga in the west to the border of Cyrenaica. The proconsul also commanded the army of Africa and was thus one of the very few provincial governors in command of an army and yet formally responsible to the Senate rather than to the emperor. This anomaly was removed in AD 39 when Gaius entrusted the army to a *legatus Augusti* of praetorian rank. Although the province was not formally divided until 196, the army commander was *de facto* in charge of the area later known as the province of Numidia and also of the military area in southern Tunisia and along the Libyan Desert. The proconsulship was normally held for only one year; like the proconsulship of Asia, it was reserved for former consuls and ranked high in the administrative hierarchy. In the 1st century it was held by several men who subsequently became emperor; *e.g.,* Galba and Vespasian. The commanders of the army normally held the post for two or three years. In the 1st and 2nd centuries AD it was an important stage in the career of a number of successful generals, but in the 3rd century Africa became a military backwater. The two Mauretanian provinces were governed by men of equestrian rank who also commanded the substantial numbers of auxiliary troops in their areas. In times of emergency the two provinces were often united under a single authority.

Tribes on the fringe of the desert and beyond constituted more of a nuisance than a threat as the area of urban and semi-urban settlement gradually approached the limit of cultivable land. A number of minor conflicts with nomadic tribes are recorded in the 1st century, the most serious of which was the revolt of Tacfarinas in southern Tunisia, suppressed in 23. As the area of settlement extended westward as well as south, so the headquarters of the legion moved also; from Ammaedara (Ḥaydarah) to Theveste under Vespasian, thence to Lambaesis under Trajan. Tribal lands were reduced and delimited, which compelled the adoption of sedentary life, and the tribes were placed under the supervision of Roman "prefects." A southern frontier was finally achieved under Trajan with the encirclement of the Aurès and Nemencha mountains and the creation of a line of forts from Vescera (Biskra) to Ad Majores (Besseriani). The mountains were penetrated during the next generation but were never developed or romanized; nevertheless, they rarely appear to have been a source of disturbance. During the 2nd century, stretches of continuous wall and ditch—the *fossatum Africae*—in some areas provided further defense against desert nomads and also marked the division between the settled and nomadic ways of life. To the southwest of the Aurès a fortified zone completed the frontier defensive system or *limes,* which extended for a while as far as Castellum Dimmidi (Messad), the most southerly fort in Roman Algeria yet identified. South of Leptis Magna in Libya, forts on the trans-Saharan route ultimately reached as far as Cydamus (Ghudāmis).

Westward movement of settlement

In the Mauretanias the problem was more difficult, because of the rugged nature of the country and the distances involved. The encirclement of mountainous areas, a policy followed in the Aurès, was again pursued in the Kabylie ranges and the Ouarsenis. The area round Sitifis (Sétif) was successfully settled and developed in the 2nd century, but farther west the impact of Rome was for long limited to coastal towns and the main military roads. The most important of these ran from Zarai (Zraia) to Auzia (Aumale) and then to the valley of the Chelif. Subsequently, the frontier ran south of the Ouarsenis as far as Pomaria (Tlemcen). West of this area, it is doubtful whether a permanent road connected the two Mauretanias, sea communication being the rule. In Tingitana, the frontier ran south of a line from Meknès to Rabat. The tribes of the Rif must have lived in virtual independence, and they were probably responsible for a number of wars recorded in Mauretania under Domitian, Trajan, Antonius Pius (which lasted six years), and others in the 3rd century. The effect of these was limited; they did little or no damage to the urbanized areas and never necessitated a permanent increase in the African garrison. For Numidia and the military district in the south of Tunisia and Libya, this amounted to one legion and auxiliaries, about 13,000 men; the Mauretanias had auxiliary units only, totalling some 15,000. This may be contrasted with the position in Britain, where three legions and auxiliaries were required. From the middle of the 2nd century AD the African garrison was largely recruited locally.

The growth of urban life. The most notable feature of the Roman period in North Africa was the development in Tunisia, northern Algeria, and some parts of Morocco of a flourishing urban civilization. This was due in the first place to control of nomadic and pastoral movements, which opened large areas of thinly settled but potentially rich land to consistent exploitation. In addition, there was the incipient urbanization of some parts due to the Carthaginians and the ambitions of Libyan rulers such as Masinissa; and, lastly, the settlement in Africa of Italian immigrants, who, though relatively few in comparison with the population as a whole, provided the impetus to expansion. Julius Caesar settled many veterans in colonies, mostly coastal towns; and, equally important, he established a military adventurer named Publius Sittius along with many Italians at Cirta, beginning the romanization of Numidia. Caesar planned to refound Carthage, and this was effected by Augustus. The number of his original settlers was 3,000, but the colony grew with quite remarkable rapidity because of its favourable geographical position in relation to contact with Rome and Italy. A number of other colonies were founded in the interior of Tunisia and at widely separated places on the Mauretanian coasts. There was also immigration from Italy by private individuals at this time. Colonial foundations of veterans in Mauretania occurred under Claudius (*e.g.*, Tingis, Caesarea, Tipasa). Cuicul (Djemila) and Sitifis were founded by Nerva, and Thamugadi and a number of places nearby, in the area north of the Aurès, by Trajan. The army was a potent vehicle in the spread of Roman civilization and played a major part in the romanization of the frontier regions.

Italian settlers

Though at first inferior in status to the Roman towns, native communities enjoyed the local autonomy that was the hallmark of Roman administration. Between 400 and 500 such units were recognized, the majority of them villages or small tribal fractions. Many, however, advanced in wealth and standing to rival the Roman colonies, acquiring in the process the grant of Roman citizenship, which put the seal of imperial approval on the prosperity, stability, and cultural evolution of developing communities. Naturally, the earliest to show signs of increasing prosperity were the surviving Carthaginian settlements on the coast and places, particularly in the Majardah Valley, where the Libyan population had been much influenced by Carthaginian culture and which now also had numbers of Roman immigrants. Leptis Magna and Hadrumetum received Roman citizenship and the status of a colony from Trajan, and Thubursicu Numidarum (Khamissa) and Calama (Guelma) probably the rank of a municipality. But it was under Hadrian, the first emperor to visit Africa, that the flood tide of such grants occurred; Utica, Bulla Regia (Hammam Derradji), Lares (Lorbeus), Thaenae, and Zama achieved colonial rank, and the process continued throughout the 2nd century. Finally, Septimius Severus, who originated from a rich family of Leptis Magna, and of largely mixed descent, became emperor in AD 193 and showed a great deal of favour to his native land.

In the Maghrib, Roman rule replaced no civic oligarchy, as in the hellenized provinces of Asia Minor, nor a strongly based tribal aristocracy, as in Celtic Gaul. The creation of new wealth and a new social leadership depended on the activity of individuals, and Roman African society became a notable example in antiquity of a self-made bourgeoisie, the wealth being largely in ownership of land. In the 1st century AD there were a few very large estates owned by absentee Roman senators, but they were subsequently absorbed in the extensive imperial estates; the general pattern was of landowning on a more moderate, though still substantial, scale by residents. These landowners made their homes in the towns, not on their estates, and provided the local municipal aristocracies. There was also a numerous class of smaller landowners, but the majority were small tenant farmers with considerable security and traditional rights, on a sharecropping basis. The proportion of slaves is unknown but may well have been smaller than in Italy.

Growth of new social elite

Many of the wealthier Africans entered the imperial administration. The first African consul held office in the reign of Vespasian; at the beginning of the 3rd century, men of African origin held one-sixth of all the posts in the equestrian grade of the administration and also constituted the largest group of provincials in the Senate. It is uncertain what proportion were of native Libyan or mixed origin, but in the 2nd century they were certainly the majority.

During the 2nd and early 3rd centuries the wealthy classes in the towns expended vast sums on their communities in gifts of public buildings such as theatres, baths, and temples; statues; public feasts; and distributions of money. This was a general phenomenon due partly to the lack of alternative profitable investment opportunities and also to a strongly felt social obligation, but the Africans adopted it with particular avidity.

Economy. The density of the towns in no way implies the predominance of trade or industry; all but a few were residences of both landowners and peasants, and their prosperity depended on agriculture. By the 1st century AD, African exports of grain provided two-thirds of the needs of the city of Rome. Some of this, for distribution by the emperors to the urban proletariat, came from the imperial estates and from taxes, but much went on to the open market. An estimate of grain production of something over 1,000,000 tons, of which 25 percent was exported, has been made. Areas of grain production were the Cap Bon peninsula, the valleys of the Miliana and Majardah, and tracts of relatively level land north of a line from Sitifis to Madauros (M'Daourouch). Cereal crops were the most important in the above areas, but fruit, figs, grapes, and beans were also produced.

The production of olive oil became almost as important as cereals by the 2nd century AD, particularly in southern Tunisia and along the northern slopes of the Aurès and Bou Taleb mountains. By the 4th century Africa exported oil to all parts of the empire. Successful cultivation of olives demanded careful management of available water, and the archaeological evidence indicates that much attention was paid to irrigation in the Roman period.

Livestock was an important part of the economy of Roman Africa, though direct evidence is slight. African horses were used in racing and no doubt also in the Roman cavalry. Cattle, sheep, pigs, goats, and mules were also raised. Africa was the major source of the wild animals for shows in Rome and other major cities of the empire, in particular panthers, lions, elephants, and monkeys. Fishing, which had been developed along the coast as far as the Atlantic in the Carthaginian period, continued to flourish. Timber from the forests along part of the north coast, and marble, the most important North African source being Simitthu (Shimṭū), were also exported.

There were no large-scale industries even by ancient standards in North Africa, though traditional arts and crafts were practiced. Pottery flourished, and lamps of North African manufacture were marketed in the northern provinces of the empire. Mosaic pavements were extremely popular among the wealthy throughout North Africa, and well over 2,000 have been discovered, with enormous variations in quality. The majority were made by local craftsmen, though some of the designs originated elsewhere. It is also clear that the building trades were major consumers of both skilled and unskilled labour.

Prosperity under the Romans undoubtedly led to a rise in the population of the Maghrib in the first two centuries AD; in the absence of reliable statistics, estimates have varied between 4,000,000 and 8,000,000 (the latter being also the population about a century ago). The most recent study proposed about 6,500,000, of whom about 2,500,000 were in present Tunisia. Some 40 percent (but perhaps more) lived in the towns. Of these, Carthage was in a class of its own, reaching at least 250,000. The next largest was Leptis Magna (80,000). followed by Hadrumetum, Thysdrus (el-Djem), Hippo Regius, and Cirta, with between 20,000 and 30,000 each. Many towns in close proximity to each other, especially in the Majardah Valley, averaged between 5,000 and 10,000.

Population increases

The road system in Roman Africa was the most complete of any western province; a total of some 12,500 miles has been supposed, though only a small proportion was fully surfaced. In origin most roads were military but were open

Roman Africa in the 3rd century AD.
Adapted from J.D. Fage, *An Atlas of African History* (1966); Edward Arnold Publishers

to commerce, and a number of minor roads linking towns off the main routes were built by the local communities. The main arteries were: Carthage to Theveste; Carthage to Cirta through Sicca Veneria; Theveste to Tacapae through Capsa; Theveste to Lambaesis; Cirta to Sitifis; Cirta to Rusicade; and Cirta to Hippo Regius. Carthage handled by far the greatest volume of overseas official traffic and trade, being the natural port for the wealthiest area of North Africa. Nevertheless, most of the ports originally founded by Phoenicians and Carthaginians expanded during the Roman period; in view of the high costs of land transport, it was natural that agricultural products would go to the nearest port for shipment.

Later Roman Empire. The whole Roman Empire underwent a grave crisis between the death of Severus Alexander (235) and the accession of Diocletian (284), resulting from outside attacks, internecine wars, and a total collapse of the monetary system. Africa suffered less than most parts of the empire from the first two factors, though there was an unsuccessful revolt by landowners in AD 238, against the fiscal policies of the emperor Maximinus Thrax, which ended in widespread pillage. There were tribal revolts in the Mauretanian mountains in 253–254, 260, and 288, and the situation finally brought a visit from the emperor Maximian in 297–298, but the revolts had little effect on urbanized areas. On the other hand, the towns were injured by economic difficulties and inflation, and building activity almost ceased. There was some return of confidence under Diocletian (284–305) and Constantine (312–337). Administrative changes introduced at this time included the division of the province of Africa into three separate provinces: Tripolitania (capital Leptis Magna), covering the western part of Libya; Byzacena, covering southern Tunisia and governed from Hadrumetum; while the northern part of Tunisia retained the name Africa. In addition, the eastern part of Mauretania Caesariensis became a separate province (capital Sitifis). In the far west, the Romans gave up much of Mauretania Tingitana, including the important town of Volubilis, apparently because of pressure from the tribe of the Baquates. In the general reorganization of the Roman army by Diocletian and Constantine, the field army (*comitatenses*) in Africa, numbering on paper some 21,000 men, was put under a new commander, the *comes Africae,* independent of the provincial governors. Only the governors of Tripolitania and of Mauretania Caesariensis also had troops at their disposal, but these were secondline soldiers, or *limitanei.* The whole frontier region along the desert and mountain fringes was divided into sectors and garrisoned by *limitanei.* The latter were locally recruited and closely identified with the farming population of their areas. The Tripolitanian Jabal, which was increasingly exposed to nomad attacks by the Austuriani, is notable for a large number of fortified farms.

Reforms under Diocletian

Africa, like the rest of the empire, experienced the economic difficulties and governmental pressures that were a feature of the later Roman Empire. The power of the landowners increased at the expense of their tenants and of smaller farmers, both of whom the imperial government sought to bind to the soil in a state of quasi-serfdom. In the cities, the tasks of local government that had earlier been eagerly undertaken by the wealthy became burdensome, and again the imperial government sought to make them compulsory and hereditary; while the councillors themselves sought by any means to enter the imperial administration or professions that provided immunity. The process is well attested in Africa. Nevertheless, urban life withstood these pressures better in Africa than in the west generally.

Christianity and the Donatist controversy. Christianity grew much more rapidly in Africa than in any other western province. It was firmly established in Carthage and other Tunisian towns by the 3rd century and had produced its own local martyrs and an outstanding apologist in Tertullian (*c.* 160–240). During the next 50 years there was a remarkable expansion; over 80 bishops attended a council at Carthage in 256, some from the distant frontier regions of Numidia. Cyprian, bishop of Carthage from 248 until his martyrdom in 258, was another figure whose writing, like that of Tertullian, was of lasting influence on Latin Christianity. During the next half-century, its spread was primarily in Numidia (at least 70 bishops known in 312). The reasons for its exceptionally rapid growth are disputed. In northern Tunisia, urban communities provided a similar social and economic environment to that in which it had first spread in Anatolia and Syria, but this hardly accounts for Christianity's early acceptance in distant parts of Numidia. The existing religious situation may be part of the explanation; in the intermingling of religious currents of Libyan, Carthaginian, and Roman origin in the first two centuries, the cult of Baal Hammon, now under the Roman name of Saturn, became increasingly prominent and may have facilitated a transition to a monotheistic religion. It is certain also that African Christianity always included a vigorous and fanatical element that must have had its effect in spreading the new religion, even though there is little evidence of positive missionary efforts.

Christians were still a minority at the end of the 3rd century, particularly among the wealthy and educated classes; but they were in a good position to benefit from Constantine's adoption of the religion and his grants of various privileges to the clergy. At this time (AD 313), a division occurred among the African Christians that lasted over a century. Some Numidian bishops objected to Caecilian, a newly chosen bishop of Carthage, on the ground that his ordination had been performed by a bishop who had

Beginning of schism

weakened during Diocletian's persecution of the church and hence was invalid. They consecrated a rival bishop, and, when he died, another named Donatus, who gave his name to the ensuing schism. The imperial government recognized Caecilian as the true bishop of Carthage, and those in communion with him as the true church in Africa and hence alone the recipients of imperial favour. A series of appeals by the Donatists to Constantine resulted in investigations and judgments, all of which went against them. Confiscation of their churches led to some deaths, the victims being honoured as martyrs, but in 322 Constantine rejected further pressure. The Donatists increased rapidly, and for the rest of the century probably made up half of the Christians in North Africa. The Donatists were strongest in Numidia and Mauretania Sitifensis, the anti-schismatics in the proconsular province; the position in the Mauretanias was more even, but Christianity did not spread rapidly there until the 5th century. In 347 the emperor Constans exiled a number of bishops and took strong measures against the *circumcelliones,* an obscure group of either wandering religious fanatics or seasonal farm workers who were particularly enthusiastic Donatists. But in 362 Julian the Apostate allowed the return of the exiles, who were welcomed with enthusiasm, and the movement proved as strong as ever. Some Donatists appear to have been associated with the revolt of a Mauretanian chieftain, Firmus, and in 377 the first of a series of laws condemning Donatism was issued. Nevertheless, these laws were only sporadically enforced, partly because the provincial governors and many of the local magistrates were still pagan and, at a time of growing weakness in the imperial government, were inclined to ignore instructions they found unwelcome. Donatism was further supported by Gildo, brother of Firmus and *comes Africae* 387–397. Then Augustine of Hippo Regius applied his enormous powers of leadership and persuasion in stimulating resolute action, evolving at the same time a theory of the right of orthodox Christian rulers to use force against schismatics and heretics. In 411 an imperial commission summoned a conference at Carthage to establish religious unity; the Donatists had to obey, though the decision against them was a foregone conclusion. The laws that followed their condemnation were more generally enforced and, though there was some resistance, broke the heresy as a powerful movement; some communities still existed in the 6th century, however.

Donatism as national movement

Much controversy surrounds the interpretation of the significance of Donatism; an important view considers it in some sense a national or social movement. It is said to have been particularly associated with the rural population of less romanized areas and with the poorer classes in the towns, whereas orthodox Christianity was the religion of the romanized upper classes. The identification of the imperial government with these Christians would have intensified the strength of the movement, and the *circumcelliones'* violence constituted incipient peasant revolt. Thus the movement is claimed as analogous to Monophysitism in Egypt and Syria, which produced a vernacular literature and a passive rejection of Greco-Roman culture. The hostility of the Donatists to the existing society was typified by Donatus' remark: "What has the emperor to do with the church?" Against this view it may be said that Donatism in the strictly unromanized tribal areas was certainly weak, and the relationship of the sect with Firmus and Gildo was of little importance. In Numidia it was at least as strong in the towns as in the rural areas, and in any case the distinction between the two is exaggerated. The entire controversy was conducted in Latin, and no vernacular literature was produced; in fact, until the time of Augustine, most of the educated class, of the same social background as Augustine himself and fully imbued with Roman tradition, were Donatists if they were not pagan. It was precisely the reluctance of the landowners to have their peasants disturbed, and the negligence of many provincial governors (both attacked by Augustine), that long protected the Donatists. Lastly, in spite of the remark attributed to Donatus, there is no evidence that the movement attacked the imperial system as a whole, as opposed to individual emperors and officials, and it made full use of its many opportunities to defend itself at law both against the other Christians and against divisions in its own ranks.

Nevertheless, although it is difficult to sustain the view that Donatism, especially in Numidia, represented in some way a resurgence of local pre-Roman culture, and still more hypothetical to suggest that something similar led to the emergence of heretical movements of Islām in the same areas, Donatism certainly appealed to deep-seated traditions of African Christianity. Its fanatical devotion to the memory of martyrs, its doctrinal conservatism and total refusal to compromise on its claim to be the true church while its opponents were contaminated by the stain of weakness in the persecutions, were fully in line with the heroic days of Tertullian and Cyprian.

Extent of romanization. The question whether Roman civilization in the Maghrib was a superficial phenomenon affecting only a small minority of the population who were economically successful, or whether it had profound effects on a majority, is similarly disputed. A priori the former view may be supported by the fact that whereas Gaul and Spain emerged from the Dark Ages with a language and religion derived from their Roman past, in the Maghrib both disappeared, arguably because they were superficial. It is not disputed that in the mountainous areas, such as the Aurès, Kabylie, and Atlas, native Libyan language and culture continued little affected by Roman civilization, though the majority appear to have been Christian by the 7th century; nor that Libyan and Carthaginian traditions survived in other areas and affected the modes of acceptance of Roman civilization. As regards language, the late form of Phoenician known as Neo-Punic was still spoken fairly widely in the 4th century; for example, in the hills near Hippo Regius. Inscriptions in the language and script occurred often at the beginning of the Roman period but are very rare after the end of the 1st century AD. An exception may be in Tripolitania, where a form of Neo-Punic was inscribed in Latin perhaps as late as the 4th century. There was also a Libyan script known solely from funerary stelae and akin to the script of the present Tuareg; it was known in some sense over most of the Maghrib but may not have been used later than the 3rd century. On the other hand, there is no evidence that the languages were ever literary languages, and the inscriptions are negligible in number compared with the Latin. It may also be observed that the areas in which Libyan inscriptions occur do not correspond with the later areas of Berber dialects. The Latin language unquestionably became general through the whole Maghrib, though to a limited extent in the mountains; it is impossible to define any precise social level at which it was unknown. There is a good deal to be said for the view that the spread of Christianity, whether Orthodox or Donatist, completed the victory of Latin among elements which up to that time had perhaps still not used it. Further, there is no evidence for the survival of Neo-Punic or Libyan after the 4th century outside the mountains. Similarly in Gaul, the native Gallic language does not seem to have lasted beyond the 5th century. The fact that there and in Spain Romance languages and Christianity survived, while in North Africa they did not, was perhaps not so much due to a greater depth of romanization as to subsequent historical developments.

Victory of Latin language

The Vandal conquest. The effect of the Donatist controversy on the economy and administration of the African provinces cannot be measured. At the very moment of the effective victory of the African Church, the rest of the Roman Empire was crumbling to ruin. In 406 the Rhine was crossed by Vandals, Alani, Sueves, and others who overran most of Gaul and Spain within the next few years. In 408 Alaric and the Visigoths invaded Italy and in 410 sacked Rome. Although the empire in the west survived for some time longer, the emperors were increasingly at the mercy of their barbarian generals. Meanwhile, large tracts of imperial territory were lost by the settlement of the invading tribes. Africa escaped for a while, though only death prevented Alaric from leading his tribe across the Mediterranean. Its retention became ever more vital to the survival of what was left of imperial authority. In this situation the *comites Africae* were increasingly tempted to intrigue for their own advantage. One of them, Bonifacius, is said to have invited the Vandals, who at the time were occupying Andalusia, to his aid, but it is more likely that the Vandals were attracted to Africa by its wealth and needed no such formal excuse. Led by their king Gaiseric, the whole people, 80,000 in all, crossed into Africa in 429 and in the next year advanced with little opposition to Hippo Regius, which they took after a siege during which St. Augustine died. After defeating the imperial forces near Calam, they overran most of the country, though not all of the fortified cities. An agreement made in 435 allotted Numidia and Mauretania Sitifensis to the Vandals, but in 439 Gaiseric took and pillaged Carthage and the rest of the province of Africa. A further treaty with the imperial government (442) established the Vandals in Africa Proconsularis, Byzacena, Tripolitania, and Numidia as far west as Cirta.

Vandal impact on the economy

Although the Vandals were probably no more deliberately destructive than other German invaders (the notion of "vandalism" stems from the 18th century), they accelerated the economic decline that had already set in. The imperial authorities had to reduce the taxes of Mauretania by seven-eighths as a result of their devastation. Over much of northern Tunisia, landowners were expelled and the properties handed over to Vandals. Although the agricultural system remained based on the peasants bound to the soil, the expulsions had a serious effect on the towns with which the landowners had been connected. The Vandals, like other invading tribes except the Franks, were divided from the mass of their subjects by their Arian heresy. Although their persecution of Latin Christians was exaggerated by the latter, Vandal kings certainly exercised more pressure than others. This was no doubt in reaction to the vigour of African Christianity, which kept the loyalty even of those who had little to lose by the substitution of a Vandal for a Roman landlord.

Gaiseric was perhaps the most perceptive barbarian king of the 5th century in realizing the total weakness of the empire. He rejected the policy of formal alliance with it and from 455 used his large merchant fleet to dominate the western Mediterranean. Rome was sacked, the Balearics, Corsica, Sardinia, and part of Sicily were occupied, and the coasts of Dalmatia and Greece were plundered. Although there was no general cessation of trade, this activity accelerated the breakup of the economic unity of the western Mediterranean, already threatened by the creation of the barbarian kingdoms. Gaiseric's successors were less formidable; Huneric (477–484) launched a general persecution on the Latin Church, apparently from genuine religious fanaticism rather than for political reasons, but his successor adopted a milder policy. Under Thrasamund (496–523) there is evidence that many Vandals adopted Roman culture, but the tribe retained its identity until the Byzantine reconquest.

A significant development of the Vandal period was the emergence of independent kingdoms in the mountainous and desert areas, largely of Libyan character. They appeared first in the Mauretanias, where the Roman frontier, already drawn back under Diocletian, receded further under the Vandal kings. By the end of Vandal rule, independent kingdoms existed in the region of Altava (Lamoricière), in the Ouarsenis and the Hodna. After 480, towns to the north of the Aurès, such as Thamugadi, Bagai, and Theveste, were sacked by the inhabitants of another kingdom in the Aurès. All of the names of the known chieftains are Libyan in character, though the survival of romanized elements within some of the kingdoms is attested by epitaphs in Latin and the use of Roman names. Finally, as a harbinger of a serious threat to settled life, whether Roman or Libyan, tribes that had retained a nomadic life on the borders of Cyrenaica and Tripolitania and caused much damage in the 4th century, began to push westward and were already a serious threat to the southern parts of Byzacena by the end of Vandal rule.

The Byzantine period. North Africa held an important place in the emperor Justinian's scheme for reuniting the Roman Empire and destroying the Germanic kingdoms. His invasion was undertaken against the advice of his experts (an earlier attempt in 468 had failed disastrously), but his general Belisarius succeeded, though partly through the incompetence of the Vandals. He landed in 533 with only 16,000 men and within a year the Vandal kingdom was destroyed; some of its people were transported to the Orient, others soon merged with the existing population.

Administrative reorganization

A new administrative structure was introduced, headed by a praetorian prefect with six subordinate governors for civil matters and a master of soldiers with four subordinate generals. It required some 12 years, however, to pacify Africa, due partly to the resistance of the Mauri to the re-establishment of an ordered government, partly to lack of support to the army in men and money, leading to frequent mutinies. A remarkable program of fortifications, many of which survive, was rapidly built under Belisarius' successor Solomon. Many were garrison forts in the frontier region, which again seems to have run, at least for a while, south of the Aurès, and then northward from Tubunae to Saldae. But many surviving towns in the interior were also equipped with substantial walls; *e.g.,* Thugga and Vaga (Béja, Bājah). After the death of Justinian (565) there were further difficulties with the Mauri, but the most serious damage was done by the nomadic Louata from the Libyan Desert, who on several occasions penetrated far into Tunisia.

Africa shows a number of examples of the massive help given by Justinian in the building, and particularly the decoration, of churches, and the reestablishment of Christian orthodoxy was widely welcomed, though it inevitably brought the persecution of surviving Donatists. Seriously weakened though it had been under the Vandals, some traces of the vigour of the African Church remained when it led the opposition of the Western churches to the theological policies of emperors at Constantinople; *e.g.,* those of Justinian and also of Heraclius and Constans II immediately before the Arab invasions.

Little is known of the Byzantine period in the Maghrib after the death of Justinian. The power of the military element in the provinces grew, and between 585 and 591 a new official, the exarch, was introduced whose powers were almost viceregal. The economic conditions continued to decline because of the increasing insecurity and also the notorious corruption and extortion of the administration, though whether this was worse in Africa than in other parts of the Byzantine Empire it is impossible to say. It is certain that the population of the towns was only a small proportion of what it had been in the 3rd or even 4th century. The court of Constantinople tended to neglect Africa because of the more immediate dangers on the eastern and Balkan frontiers. Only once in its latest phase was it the scene of an important historical event; in 610 Heraclius, son of the African exarch at the time, sailed from Carthage to Greece in a revolt against the unpopular emperor Phocas, and succeeded him the same year. That Africa was still of some economic importance to the empire was shown in 619; the Persians had overrun much of the east including Egypt, and Africa alone appeared able to sustain an empty treasury and provide recruits. Heraclius thought of leaving Constantinople for Carthage but was prevented by popular feeling in the capital.

Maghrib on the eve of Arab conquest

In view of the lack of evidence for the Byzantine period, and the still greater obscurity surrounding the period of Arab conquest (643–698) and its immediate aftermath, conclusions on the state of the Maghrib at the end of Byzantine rule are speculative. Much of it was in the hands of tribal groups, among which the level of Roman culture was in many cases no doubt negligible. The Byzantine administration was in a sense foreign to the Latin population also, which may have added to the dislike felt for its notorious corruption. Few traces of the former prosperity of the settled areas remained. The Byzantine military forces were inadequate and incompetent, and it is significant that in the period of Arab conquest the most determined resistance came from the Libyan tribes, which frequently appear not so much as allies as leaders in the struggle. The total decay of town life (except in a few places on the east Tunisian coast) and of the ordered agricultural system occurred within a century after the end of Byzantine rule, though some scholars consider that a modicum survived until the invasions of further nomads, the Banū Hilāl, in the 11th century. Latin was still in use on Christian epitaphs at en-Ngila (Tripolitania) and al-Qayrawān (Kairouan) in the 10th and 11th centuries, and other Christian communities are known to have survived as long. The Arab conquest has its part in the widely discussed theory of Henri Pirenne, that the essential break between the ancient and medieval worlds came with the destruction of the unity of the Mediterranean world not by the Germanic but the Arab invasions. It is obvious that this is true of the Maghrib, but there is much to be said for the view that its earlier conquerors, the Vandals, were the major agent in the destruction of the economic unity of the Mediterranean. Whether this is the key to the problem is another matter.

Roman Cyrenaica. Much of the Roman period in Cyrenaica was peaceful. Some Roman immigrants resided there at an early date, and some of the Greeks received Roman citizenship. A famous inscription of 4 BC contains a number of edicts of the emperor Augustus regulating with great fairness the relationship between Roman and non-Roman. The character of its civilization, however, remained entirely Greek. Jews formed a considerable minority group in the province and had their own organizations at Berenice and Cyrene. They took no part in the great revolt of Judaea in AD 66 but in 115 began a formidable rebellion in Cyrene that spread to Egypt. No reason for it is known. It caused great destruction and loss of life, and Hadrian took special measures to reconstruct Cyrene and also sent out some colonists. Peaceful conditions returned, but in 268–269 the Marmaridae, inhabiting the coast between Cyrenaica and Egypt, gave trouble. In the reorganization of the empire by Diocletian, Cyrenaica was separated from Crete and divided into two provinces, Libya Superior, or Pentapolis (capital Ptolemais), and Libya Inferior, or Sicca (capital Paraetonium, Marsā Maṭrūḥ). A regular force was stationed there for the first time under a *dux Libyarum*. At the end of the 4th century, the Austuriani, a nomad tribe that had earlier raided Tripolitania, caused much damage, and Cyrenaica began to suffer from the general decline of security throughout the empire, in this case from desert nomads. A notable phenomenon of the 5th and 6th centuries, as in Tripolitania, is the number of fortified farms, most frequent in the Jabal itself and south of Boreum (Bū Qurādah) and also apparently in the region of Benghazi.

Christianity no doubt spread to Cyrenaica from Egypt. In the 3rd century the bishop of Ptolemais was metropolitan, but by the 4th century the powerful bishops of Alexandria consecrated the local bishops. The best known Cyrenaican is Synesius, a citizen of Cyrene of philosophic tastes who was made bishop of Ptolemais in 410 partly because of his ability to obtain help for his province from the imperial authorities. Under Justinian a number of defensive works were constructed as elsewhere in Africa; *e.g.,* Taucheira, Berenice, Antipyrgos (Tobruk), and Boreum. Recent excavations of a series of churches in the province also reveal the expenditure he devoted to their beautification, in what was a province of minor importance. On the eve of the Arab conquest (AD 643) the general condition of Cyrenaica would appear to have been on a par with most of the other eastern provinces of the empire. (B.H.W.)

From the Islāmic conquest to 1830

STRUCTURE AND MENTALITY OF THE PRE-ISLĀMIC BERBER WORLD

In order to understand the Islāmic conquest of North Africa and how Islāmic life in the country was organized, it is necessary to examine the social structure of the North African world.

In the 7th century, the vast majority of the North African people were probably Berbers who, though of rather diverse physical types, possessed a common background of language and civilization. Society was tribal in structure. The homeland was not the land per se but rather the race; every social grouping conceived itself only as an assembly of men stemming from a common ancestor, frequently fictitious, whose name they continued to bear.

Berber society

Berber society was, and remained, remarkably fragmented within itself; the basic grouping was the segment, which, among a sedentary population, brought together 200 or 300 households in a territory with a radius of about four to six miles. This was a minuscule state—a tiny republic managed by a council of family heads and magistrates of temporary tenure who maintained order and assured the fair distribution of the profits and of the burdens of the small community. Among the nomads the douar (*dūwār*)—the collection of tent dwellers who lived and migrated together—was frequently of even more limited dimensions. The tribe, which comprised about 10 subunits, had an assembly, and in time of war it often selected for itself a single chief. The confederations of tribes—except for moving livestock and for the nomads who needed to have living space assured them—were little more than a framework of regrouping for common defense by force or through alliances.

In political formations of variable size and cohesiveness there was profound democratic sentiment and an extreme mistrust of personal power. What mattered was the preservation of freedom and the autonomy of the small social cells by which the Berbers ordered their existence. Opposing factions grouped themselves into two opposite leagues, or *leffs*; thus, in case of oppression by a chief or by neighbours, they were able to call upon their *leff* brethren for help, and the latter would usually impose arbitration. Armed conflicts remained rare and limited. Without attaining the level of a nation-state or of a nation, Berber society attained equilibrium and peace in a fragmentation that did not facilitate the accomplishment of great collective tasks.

ISLĀMIC NORTH AFRICA TO C. 1250

The Islāmic conquest and domination by the Umayyad (Banū Umayyah) caliphs. After a swift conquest of Syria, Egypt, Mesopotamia, and Iran, Islām halted before the steppes of Central Asia and the boundaries of India. Byzantium was organizing a belated but effective resistance on the frontier of Anatolia. Thus, blocked on the east and on the south, Islām lost no time in launching new conquests in the western Mediterranean. In spite of difficulties, this task was undertaken again and again, and it finally succeeded. Beginning in 642, Islāmic troops launched attacks from Egypt into Cyrenaica and into Tripolitania; an expedition reached the southern part of Tunisia, where it defeated the Byzantine patrician Gregory. The northern part of the country was not occupied, however, and the Byzantines finally induced the invaders to leave after paying them tribute.

Muslim penetration into North Africa

Conflicts between the caliphs ʿAlī (ruled 656–661) and Muʿāwiyah I (ruled 661–680), and the founding of the Umayyad caliphate by the latter, halted the Islāmic expansion toward the West until 670, when ʿUqbah ibn Nāfiʿ penetrated Tunisia and there founded al-Qayrawān (Kairouan). Toward the year 683 ʿUqbah undertook a large-scale expedition toward the West that brought him as far as Sūs (Sous) in southern Morocco. North Africa appeared to be adapting itself readily to the authority of Islām; but on his return, ʿUqbah was beaten and slain by a Berber chief, Kusaylah, and the Muslim troops were forced to fall back through Cyrenaica.

For 15 years, despite the incessant efforts of the Umayyad caliphate, then at the apogee of its power, the Berbers, under the command of Kusaylah and later of a woman, Kāhinah, offered stubborn resistance in Tunisia and in Constantine (Qusṭanṭinah, in what is now eastern Algeria). Finally, from 703 to 711, Mūsā ibn Nuṣayr, using Berber tribes converted to Islām, wore down local resistance and brought all North Africa under the Islāmic domain.

This Muslim conquest was not really an Arab invasion. North Africa received only about 100,000 Arab militiamen, most of them stationed in Ifrīqīyah (Tunisia and eastern Algeria). But these Arab elements proved to be tyrannical. Their cupidity—their exactions and slave levies—led to a mass revolt in the country. The motivation and leadership for this revolt were furnished by a Muslim heresy—Khārijism, which in the East rallied to its side all the enemies of the Umayyad dynasty. The rebellion, originating in Morocco in 740, conquered all North Africa in

Rebellion against Arab occupation

two years; the caliphate armies were defeated in Morocco, and the Umayyads were barely able to save al-Qayrawān.

The Umayyad caliphs, already in a stage of decline, could not reconquer North Africa. In 750 they were replaced as caliphs in the East by the ʿAbbāsids, who became the new masters of the Muslim world and transferred the seat of the caliphate to Baghdad.

The North Africans were unable to use this respite to consolidate their victory and to fortify their independence; from 742 to 746 they continued fighting among themselves in the name of the various sects of Khārijism. The ʿAbbāsids succeeded in conquering only Tunisia and the eastern part of Constantine; their governor in al-Qayrawān, Ibrāhīm I ibn al-Aghlab, while apparently remaining the faithful vassal of the caliphs of Baghdad, became independent in fact. Throughout the rest of North Africa, Khārijī kingdoms were founded, but a great many tribes remained independent.

Although the Khārijī revolt brought about the dismemberment of the caliphate in the Western lands, the people in the West remained faithful to Islām. Thenceforth there existed a Muslim West, which intended to seek the paths of political life and of Islāmic civilization.

Formation of North African Islām. After the 9th century, eastern North Africa remained under the dynasty of the Aghlabids (Banū al-Aghlab), a theoretical vassal of the ʿAbbāsids of Baghdad. The rest of the Muslim West—the Maghrib and Spain—was solving by itself and without foreign interventions the problems posed by its political organization in the framework of the new faith.

Political and religious fragmentation

The Maghrib was inhabited by various political and religious groups. The most important of the new independent kingdoms was that of the Rustamids of Tāhart, which had an annex in the Jabal Nafūsah in Tripolitania; it was Khārijī, as indeed were the kingdoms of Tilimsān (Tlemcen) and of Sijilmāssah. In the Atlantic plains of Morocco, the confederation of the Barghawāṭah rallied to the cause of a particular heresy, diverging from Khārijism as well as from orthodoxy. The Ghumārah of northern Morocco followed the precepts of their prophet Hā-Mīm and constituted a new sect. Idrīs I, a descendant of ʿAlī, founded a Shīʿah kingdom in northern Morocco. This diversity of sects, theoretically and unequally Islāmic, attests to the fact that North Africa was an exemplar of great religious tolerance. Outside these more or less stable and organized states, there often lived a good many tribes and independent confederations that seem to have practiced Khārijism. The three foremost kingdoms of that time—the Idrīsid, the Rustamid, and the Aghlabid—represent three different forms of Muslim organization.

The Idrīsid (al-Idrīsiyūn) kingdom (789–926). Idrīs was a descendant of ʿAlī and hence a *sharīf* (noble, or illustrious one). Fleeing the persecution of his people by the ʿAbbāsids, he succeeded in gaining support in northern Morocco, where he founded the Idrīsid kingdom. His son, Idrīs II, founded the capital city of Fez (Fās, modern name Fès). Upon the death of Idrīs II, the kingdom was divided into a series of principalities.

The Idrīsid kingdom was the first in Morocco to derive support from a mixed Arab and Berber central government and militia. The founding of Fez—an Islāmic city inhabited in part by people from al-Qayrawān and by Andalusians that rapidly developed its own mode of life outside the world of tribes and where influences coming from the Orient by way of al-Qayrawān and later by way of Córdoba were welcomed and diffused—played an important role in the history of Morocco. The Idrīsids combatted Khārijism and particularly strove to convert the tribes that had remained pagan. The political efforts of the Idrīsids were confined to the western and eastern parts of Morocco and were ephemeral, but their civilizing task bore vast and enduring consequences.

The Rustamid kingdom of Tāhart (787–911). ʿAbd ar-Raḥmān ibn Rustam entrenched himself in the central Maghrib, where he founded the city of Tāhart. In 787–788, by concluding peace with the ʿAbbāsids, he succeeded in consolidating his kingdom, which, despite the presence of an oriental colony, remained Berber. Frequent conflicts among the clans gave the kingdom a turbulent history. Ibn Rustam showed himself to be quite generous toward the adherents of orthodoxy and of other Khārijī sects. The Rustamid state lived in peace with its neighbours; thus Tāhart was able to become the centre of an active caravan trade and to maintain economic relations with the Orient.

The Aghlabids (Banū al-Aghlab) of Ifrīqīyah (800–909). Whereas the greater part of North Africa sought its path in diverse sects or heresies, Ifrīqīyah was actively organizing its Muslim life within the realm of orthodoxy. The Aghlabids gloriously fulfilled the obligations of a holy war by inflicting upon the Christians the conquest of Sicily. They did not penetrate the Maghrib, however; they contented themselves with ruling over old lands of sedentary population, abounding in cities—namely, Tunisia and the eastern fringe of Constantine. These were the only lands populated extensively by the Arabs. Al-Qayrawān, an Islāmic centre, became an active point of religious life and soon had its own learned men, for the most part of the Mālikī juridical school; the city soon extended its intellectual and religious influence over all North Africa and paved the way for the triumph of orthodoxy.

Aghlabid art and architecture

The influences proceeding from Baghdad and the ʿAbbāsid world were felt in all domains. Aghlabid art—which left a major imprint in the great mosque of al-Qayrawān—mingled more and more oriental forms with the inherited traditions of Rome and the Byzantines. Following the example of the ʿAbbāsid caliphs, whose luxury they wanted to imitate, the Aghlabid emirs ordered the construction, in the suburbs of al-Qayrawān, of veritable governmental cities, where they erected their palaces. Within the culture of Ifrīqīyah, Aghlabid was a bridgehead from the Orient.

North Africa in the 10th century. After two centuries of Islām, North Africa appeared profoundly transformed. Along with substantial strata of the population, Islāmization won to its side the independent tribes themselves—the minor non-Islāmized groups were only exceptions to the rule. A considerable portion of Berbers still belonged to Islāmic sects, especially to Khārijism, but these divergent attempts at religious proselytizing finally redounded to the advantage of orthodoxy.

Arab colonization remained at a low level. Except for Ifrīqīyah, which had absorbed about 100,000 Arabs in race and language, no small "Eastern" groups existed. Virtually the entire region remained inhabited by Berbers. Linguistic Arabization remained confined to four regions: the Tunisian Sahel (Sāḥil); northern Constantine, between the city and the sea; the country between the coast and Tlemcen; and Fez and a part of northern Morocco in the Idrīsid domain. But the region experienced the attraction of two great centres of Muslim civilization: from the 9th century, that of al-Qayrawān; and after the 10th century, that of Córdoba. Large cities adopted and disseminated a civilization that was authentically Islāmic.

Predominance of sedentary population

The sedentary population greatly exceeded that of the great camel-riding nomads, who were found only in a pre-Sahara or Sahara zone. The horseback-riding nomads migrated toward the steppes or plains and to the high plateaus; but they seemed to be in particular search of good land for settling. All the fertile plains and mountains were inhabited by sedentary peasants, clustered in villages that had fields, gardens, and orchards. The greater part of these people lived comfortably and were of a pacific disposition.

Social fragmentation permitted only limited conflicts. Large-scale wars and their ruinous aftermaths came only with the founding and actions of the great empires.

The Fāṭimid crisis. The Shīʿī branch of Islām claimed to be the legitimate sect of the religion; its followers—the Shīʿah—believed that the head of the Muslim community could only be a descendant of the Prophet through his daughter Fāṭimah, spouse of ʿAlī, and rejected the claims of the Sunnī majority to orthodoxy. Under the ʿAbbāsids the ʿAlids became an opposition and were persecuted; Shīʿī Islām organized itself into secret sects.

By its doctrine, Shīʿī Islām was opposed to Khārijism. Shīʿī Islām had not spread into North Africa except in the realm of the Idrīsids, who undoubtedly were practicing it only in a mitigated form. But in Little Kabylie, Abū ʿAbd Allāh, a missionary of ʿUbayd Allāh, the Shīʿī pretender, was warmly received by the Kutāma and their brethren of the Kabylie race. Abū ʿAbd Allāh then led them into battle against the Aghlabids, who represented both Muslim orthodoxy and ʿAbbāsid power. In 910 he entered al-Qayrawān, putting an end to the Aghlabid dynasty, and shortly afterward he installed there his master, ʿUbayd Allāh.

The Fāṭimid Empire

The new Fāṭimid Empire had its base among the Kabylie Ṣanhājah, who constituted the best element in its military forces. But the sovereigns were "Orientals" in source and in mentality; their constant ambition was the conquest of the Muslim "Orient." Several attempts against Egypt failed before the conquest was finally accomplished; in 972 the Fāṭimid ruler al-Muʿizz entrenched himself in his new city of Cairo, leaving the government of his North African domain to his Berber lieutenant, Yūsuf Buluggīn ibn Zīrī.

Before emigrating eastward, however, the Fāṭimids needed to develop an African policy. On many occasions they sought to enlarge their western possessions. They succeeded at times in imposing their authority on the central Maghrib and on northern Morocco; but they came into conflict with the Zanātah tribes, traditional enemies of the Ṣanhājah. The Zanātah were supported by the Umayyad caliphs of Córdoba, defenders of Muslim orthodoxy, who had dreaded a Fāṭimid attack against the Andalusian coast and who possessed the skill of constantly regrouping in the Maghrib and establishing a protective curtain of Berber allies. The struggle between the Ṣanhājah, fighting for the Fāṭimids, and the Zanātah partisans of the Umayyads of Córdoba was the Hundred Years' War of North Africa.

But, even in their own realm, the Fāṭimids were unable to banish orthodoxy; they were little more than a Shīʿī government at the head of a country that remained, for the most part, Sunnī. Furthermore, the Zanātah who joined the Umayyad alliance rallied to the side of the Sunnī.

The thrust of orthodox opinion was felt by the Berber dynasties of the Zīrids and of the Ḥammādids, who occupied the North African domain of the Fāṭimids. They were led to reject obedience to the caliphs of Cairo and to return officially to Sunnah. This religious conflict was bound to entail burdensome economic and social consequences for North Africa.

The Arab invasion of North Africa. The Fāṭimids, more and more absorbed in eastern affairs, did not possess the means for reconquering the country from which they had departed and from which they had always drawn their best military elements. In 1051 they launched an attack against North Africa, using entire Arab tribes then stationed in Upper Egypt, namely, the Banū Hilāl and the Sulaym, which were followed by the Maʿgil. These Bedouins could not found an Arab dynasty, but they overwhelmed the country, which they often ravaged, and they imposed tributes on both the cities and the countryside.

The coastal area of Tunisia having been reduced, the Zīrids maintained themselves until 1148. In 1090–91 the Ḥammādids abandoned their capital, Qalʿah, only to regroup themselves at the port of Bejaïa (Bougie).

By the middle of the 12th century, the Bedouin inundation had reached the region of Sétif in the west. Then and there the North African dynasties collided with the Arab problem without achieving satisfactory solutions.

Reunification of the Maghrib

The great Moroccan empires. A Berber confederation, which comprised the Lamtūna, the Gudālah, and the Massūfah, occupied Mauritania and the countries south of the "loop" of the Niger; it controlled a part of the caravan routes of the Atlantic Sahara and in the 9th century achieved victories over the black kingdoms. This Mauritanian confederation then experienced an eclipse but revived again in the 11th century. Its chief, Yaḥyā ibn Ibrāhīm, made a pilgrimage to Mecca and brought back a scholar from Morocco, ʿAbd Allāh ibn Yāsīn, to improve his people's rather summary Islām. The missionary attempt of ʿAbd Allāh ibn Yāsīn at first achieved success, but when opposition developed he resorted to force, supported by Ṣanhājah chiefs. ʿAbd Allāh and his partisans, called the Almoravids (al-Murābiṭūn), considered their action a holy war.

In response to an appeal from their racial brethren of the Tāfīlālt against the Zanātah (who had imposed their authority on the Moroccan oases), the Almoravids fled back toward North Africa, whence they had departed centuries before. There they were to change the destiny of the Muslim West.

The Almoravid (al-Murābiṭūn) empire. Between 1054 and 1059, the Almoravids, led by Abū Bakr, conquered southern Morocco, where they founded Marrakesh (Marrakech), base of operations for future conquests and thenceforth capital of the Almoravid empire. ʿAbd Allāh ibn Yāsīn had been slain in combat. Yūsuf ibn Tāshufīn (Tāshfīn) became the sole chief of the movement, and from 1062 to 1092 he conquered northern Morocco and the Maghrib as far as Algiers (al-Jazāʾir). For the first time since the Khārijī revolt, the Maghrib territories were united under a single power of Saharan Berber origin but rooted in Morocco. In theory the Almoravids represented a religious reform that was nothing more than an "outbidding" of orthodoxy; they were the champions of Sunnī Islām and of Mālikīyah (a school of Islāmic law), which was already dominant in the Maghrib.

Muslim Spain was beginning to knuckle under to the local Christians; the kings from the north were imposing costly protectorates upon the *amīrs*, who had divided among themselves the domain of the Caliphate of Córdoba. In 1085 Alfonso VI of Castile and Leon entered Toledo and annexed the major portion of what was to constitute the new Castile. The *amīrs* appealed to the Almoravids, and Yūsuf ibn Tāshufīn disembarked with a Berber army and, in 1086, won a victory over Alfonso VI at az-Zallāqah, in Estremadura. In 1068 Tāshufīn tried to check a Castilian thrust into eastern Andalusia; feebly supported by the *amīrs*, he tried unsuccessfully to seize the Christian fortress of Aledo and was obliged to retreat to Morocco. Several of his old allies fell again under Christian vassalage. Having arrived on the scene as the saviour of Spanish Islām, Yūsuf ibn Tāshufīn became its conqueror in 1091, when he deposed all the local rulers. El Cid, the famous Spanish military leader, halted the Almoravid forces before Valencia from 1094 until his death in 1099; by 1103 the Almoravids were masters of all of Muslim Spain and several times had triumphed over the Castilians.

Relations with Muslim Spain

From Algiers to Castile, Yūsuf ibn Tāshufīn was the undisputed sovereign of the Muslim West. The Christian reconquest was halted for 20 years. The Almoravids achieved completely the type of domination analyzed subsequently by the Arab historian Ibn Khaldūn (1337–1406)—namely, a clan at the head of an empire, of which it was the vital force and the beneficiary.

A close symbiosis was thenceforth established between the Maghrib and Muslim Spain. Undoubtedly the Spanish Muslims were never thoroughly reconciled to African domination, but they had to bend to the service of their new masters. The great beneficiaries of this political union were the cities in Morocco, which were won over by Andalusian civilization, of which they became secondary focuses. The Almoravid sultans erected beautiful monu-

Adapted from J.D. Fage, *An Atlas of African History* (1966); Edward Arnold Publishers

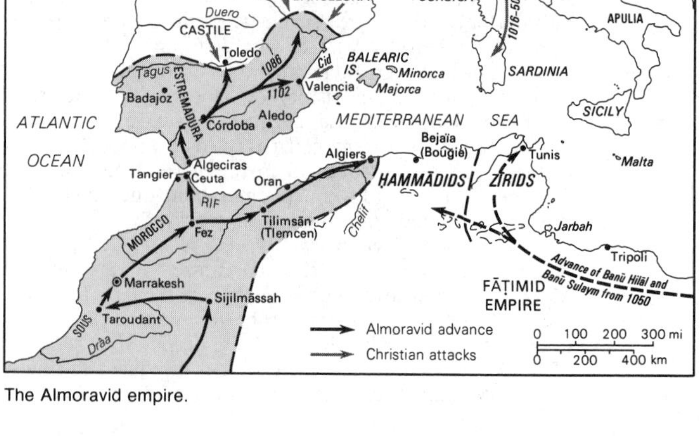

The Almoravid empire.

ments in the Maghrib, where Spanish Muslim art reigned unrivalled.

The empire of the Almoravids, founded in Morocco as in Spain on a minority of conquerors, maintained itself under a paradoxical formula—to array Berber armies against the Christians in Spain, but in Morocco to reinforce their own troops with Christian mercenaries. Despite minor advances by the Christian forces, Almoravid power maintained itself in the Iberian Peninsula. After 22 years of fierce fighting in the Maghrib, however, it succumbed in the face of the revolt of another family of Berber tribes—the Maṣmūdah of the Moroccan Atlas, who also fought in the name of religious reform.

The Almoravids had implanted traditions that subsequent dynasties inherited: they paralleled a Berber army staff with a central government of the Hispanic type. But orthodox Islām as well as Mālikī Islām, whose triumph they consolidated, were not transformed or improved by their action. Influenced by Mālikī jurists of an extremely conservative frame of mind, the Almoravids enforced in Spain a veritable Muslim inquisition and sought to banish movements that were in quest of genuine spirituality, thus remaining outside what was best in the religious life of their times.

The Almohad revolt

The Almohad (al-Muwaḥḥidūn) empire. The revolt that crushed the Almoravid empire arose in the mountains that border on the horizon of Marrakesh, the Great Atlas. A Berber from the Atlas, Muḥammad ibn Tūmart, imbued with an intensely religious fervour, was an avowed enemy of Mālikī formalism, which was triumphing under the Almoravids. From the Tunisian port of Mahdīyah, he began a slow "trek" to Morocco; he built around himself a group of faithful disciples and began to preach his own doctrine. He demanded above all a rigorous conception of divine unity, from which was derived the name al-Muwaḥḥidūn (the "unitarians"), which his followers adopted; at the same time he imposed puritanical reforms of customs. Upon his return to Marrakesh, he lost no time in coming into conflict with official circles. On the verge of being arrested, he fled into the Atlas, where he raised the standard of rebellion against the Almoravids, whom he regarded as heretics to be fought with fire and sword by all the tribes of his race—the Maṣmūdah from the mountains. Muḥammad ibn Tūmart preached the Almohad doctrine and urged a rebellion that soon encompassed the Anti-Atlas and the Great Atlas.

The Almoravids proved incapable of subduing this revolt, although a first thrust by the Almohads against Marrakesh failed. Muḥammad ibn Tūmart died in 1130; his favourite disciple and successor, ʿAbd al-Muʾmin, after a 17-year campaign, finally succeeded in gaining possession of both northern and eastern Morocco. He defeated the Almoravids at Tilimsān (Tlemcen) and returned to Marrakesh, which he took by storm, thus putting an end to Almoravid domination.

The apogee of Berber Islām

ʿAbd al-Muʾmin was bent on expanding his domain. In two campaigns (1151 and 1158–59) he brought all of North Africa under his control. This constituted the apogee of Berber Islām—a Berber ruled with all the dignity of a caliph over all his racial brethren.

Upon returning from his first campaign, however, ʿAbd al-Muʾmin collided in Constantine (in the Sétif region) with a powerful Arab coalition of tribes. He defeated them but found himself incapable of putting an end to the creeping invasion that, for an entire century, was undermining eastern Barbary. He attempted to rally the Arabs to consolidate his dynasty and to wage a holy war in Spain. But the Arab problem became increasingly critical for his successors. Under the third Almohad ruler, Abū Yūsuf Yaʿqūb al-Manṣūr (reigned 1184–99), Almoravid chiefs from the Balearic Islands disembarked at Bejaïa in 1184 and rallied all the Arabs around them. In spite of vigorous resistance, repeated bloody revolts ravaged the east and the centre of the empire for 20 years. To end the uprising, it became necessary to send a great Almohad personality, Abū Muḥammad ibn Abī Ḥafṣ, to Tunis with sovereign powers. But deportations of Arab tribes to Morocco served only to open up the whole Barbary to those who proved themselves to be the worst dissidents and malcontents.

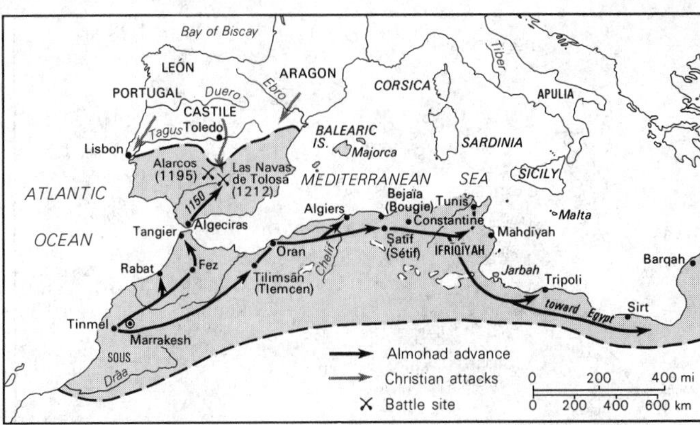

The Almohad empire.

Adapted from J.D. Fage, *An Atlas of African History* (1966); Edward Arnold Publishers

By succeeding the Almoravids, the Almohads were obliged to lead the conflict against the Christians and, consequently, to become in turn the masters of Muslim Spain. The Christian thrust increased, and on several occasions the Almohads dispatched into Andalusia numerous troops from Morocco. Despite the magnitude of this effort, the Christians recorded gradual advances. A great Almohad victory at Alarcos (1195) by Yaʿqūb al-Manṣūr led the Christian kings to organize themselves for a crusade. In 1212, at Las Navas de Tolosa, the Almohads were badly beaten. This was followed by a swift decline of the dynasty; and the great Christian reconquest, delayed for a moment, was unloosed after 1230.

The Almohads made no attempt to redress the situation in Spain. Anarchy reigned in Marrakesh, while the Arabs, by that time scattered throughout the plains and plateaus of Barbary, were ruining the country and participating in all the internal conflicts of the region. It was a Berber-Zanātah push, however, by the Banū Marīn, that engaged the last Almohads in battle and in 1269 gained possession of Marrakesh.

Achievements of the Almohads

The efforts of the Almohads had achieved a scope and at times a success that no other dynasty of the Muslim West ever attained. The Almohad hereditary traditions—their errors as well as their successes—continued to have an impact on the Barbary for several centuries to come. Their reign signifies the apogee of Berber Islām. But they did not settle the Arab problem, nor were they able to utilize to good advantage the Bedouin tribes, whose expansion toward the West they had supported. On the religious plane the Almohad reform movement failed. Still, the Almohads caused Spanish and North African Islām to move in a more liberal milieu, and they favoured a great mystic movement, Ṣūfism, which had penetrated the West before their reign.

Like the Almoravids, they were the devoted servants of Andalusian civilization; by virtue of their struggle against the Christians they gave it a respite of a century. In the arts, these ancient puritans at times invested their mosques with remarkable decorative restraint, which made possible the development of a style of classic purity; and they created some of the most beautiful monuments of Islāmic art.

FROM THE 13TH CENTURY TO THE BEGINNINGS OF EUROPEAN DOMINATION (1830)

The Ḥafṣids, ʿAbd al-Wādids, and Marīnids

The east medieval dynasties of North Africa (13th–15th centuries). The decline of the Almohad empire can be attributed largely to the mediocrity of its rulers and its government. Anarchy reigned in Marrakesh, where the viziers were fighting each other, making and unmaking sultans amidst the mounting ruins of empire. Three kingdoms divided North Africa among themselves. In Tunisia a kingdom developed under the dynasty of the Ḥafṣids (Banū Ḥafṣ), descendants of the governor, Muḥammad ibn Abī Ḥafṣ. The founding of the two other kingdoms was due to Zanātah-Berber groups; the ʿAbd al-Wādids (Banū ʿAbd al-Wād) organized the kingdom of Tilimsān, while the Marīnids first settled in east Morocco, accomplished the conquest of the north, took Fez as

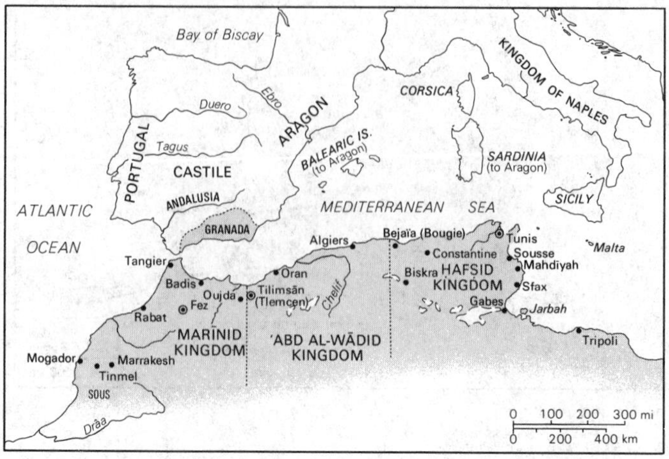

Last medieval dynasties in North Africa, 13th–14th centuries.
Adapted from J.D. Fage, *An Atlas of African History* (1966); Edward Arnold Publishers

their capital, and crushed the last Almohads at Marrakesh (1269).

The Arab problem. These three kingdoms were ruled by Berber dynasties, but their politics was constantly dominated by the Arab problem. The Bedouins had by this time invaded all the plains and all the transitional areas; Ma'qil groups had spread throughout the pre-Sahara zone. Although undisciplined and militant, the Arab tribes, from the 13th to the 15th centuries, furnished the bulk of the military forces available to the sultans. Their top leaders joined the government and, through marriage or adoption, were often allied with the royal families.

Above all, the Arabs exerted a disastrous influence on economic life. Even in the most fertile plains they practiced nomadism, into which they dragged the previously sedentary Berber population, which gradually amalgamated with them.

The arrival of Arabs was frequently accompanied by devastation; in every possible way they undermined the sedentary peasant way of life, which had constituted the strength and good fortune of North Africa in ancient times and in the first centuries of Islām. Roving tents replaced villages and rural hamlets. Gardens and orchards were abandoned while the forests retreated. Only the mountains escaped these disastrous transformations. The ancient and normal economy of North Africa was perverted into swift impoverishment.

It is against this background of progressive ruin, frequently one of disorder, that the histories of the Marīnids, the 'Abd al-Wādids, and the Ḥafṣids are inscribed. The 'Abd al-Wādids were the most feeble in the face of the Arabs. The old towns of the Ḥafṣid kingdom presented a certain counterweight to Bedouin instability. The Marīnids first adopted a policy of resistance and fell back to the Atlantic Sahara of the Ma'qil tribes, who attempted to sweep back into Atlantic Morocco; but they too were submerged by the Bedouin.

Political life. In the 12th–14th centuries no outside danger threatened North Africa, which dwelt in almost complete isolation. Economic relations with Europe remained open, but maritime commerce never flourished. Only the Marīnids intervened overseas; but their incursions into Andalusia, at the end of the 13th century and again in the first half of the 14th, served only to aid in the consolidation of the kingdom of Granada (Arabic, Gharnāṭah) without ever setting back the Christian reconquests.

Conflicts among the three kingdoms were common. A stubborn hatred was incessantly brewing between the 'Abd al-Wādids and the Marīnids. Many a time the Marīnids invaded the kingdom of Tilimsān. On two occasions the Marīnids, at the apogee of their dynasty, became masters of the central Maghrib for a few years, but they were unable to maintain the conquest of Tunisia. Their grand design to remold the Almohad empire failed, and Morocco remained thenceforth within its present boundaries. In the 15th century, military hegemony passed into the hands of the Ḥafṣids, but they too were no longer able to achieve enduring conquests.

Religious life. The failure of Almohad reform consolidated the victory of the Mālikī juridical school. But under this entrenchment of official Islām, religious life became transformed profoundly. Muslim mysticism, or Ṣūfism, which had come from the East and had undergone rapid development in the 12th century in Muslim Spain, won all of North Africa and, after the 13th century, resulted in the formation of numerous brotherhoods: holy personages, both living and dead, and the chiefs of the brotherhoods played the role of intercessors. This development of Ṣūfism of the marabout (Arabic, *murābiṭ*) type was in general more intense in the Berber lands than in the "Arabianized" plains.

Influence of Ṣūfism

Intellectual life. Intellectual life remained closely linked with Islām, but it was not locally vigorous; for the most part it consisted of an adoption of the genres and style of the Arab literature of Spain. Jurists and chroniclers contented themselves with compiling the works of their predecessors. All this intellectual activity imported from Spain thrived in rather restricted circles, mainly those of the large cities and the courts of the rulers. Enlivened for a brief time by the arrival of Andalusian refugees in the 13th century, it was not long before it became a victim of inertia. In this entire process there was one magnificent exception—the historian and statesman Ibn Khaldūn, who composed a veritable historical sociology of Muslim kingdoms of the Middle Ages.

Artistic life. In the 13th century, artistic workshops modelled after those of Muslim Spain succeeded in taking root in Morocco; thus, at the beginning of the 14th century, Hispano-Moorish architecture and decoration appeared to be fully acclimatized in the large cities of the Maghrib. In Tilimsān and in Fez this art can be distinguished only by slight nuances from that of Granada. In Tunisia, the arrival of Andalusian refugees was reflected in Ḥafṣid art through important and enduring Hispanic contributions, which intermingled with thriving local traditions.

This art underwent no further renovation, and that of Granada itself declined. But North Africa had nevertheless participated in the classical age of Hispano-Moorish art. Morocco preserved this art faithfully without breathing new life into it.

Ottoman North Africa. The extension of the Ottoman Empire into North Africa in the 16th century was not the result of a planned conquest but is attributed to particular and genuinely African factors. At the beginning of the 16th century the Portuguese had already established themselves in various ports of the Straits of Gibraltar and of northern Morocco and were extending their undertakings to Morocco's Atlantic coast. Meanwhile, the Spaniards launched a vigorous effort on the rest of Barbary and occupied Melilla, Peñon de Velez, Mers-al-Kebir, Oran, and the Peñon of Algiers (an islet in the harbour of Algiers). The 'Abd al-Wādids and the Ḥafṣids at times were obliged to accept the protectorate of Spain.

The founding of the regency of Algiers. Five brothers, including 'Arūj and Khayr ad-Dīn (nicknamed "Barbarossa"), who came from the island of Lesbos and engaged in piracy in the neighbouring archipelago, decided around 1505 to transfer their undertakings to the western Mediterranean. They achieved swift success, and the Ḥafṣid sultan permitted them to settle on the island of Jarbah (Djerba). The populations conquered or threatened by the Spaniards appealed to these new leaders. 'Arūj established himself in the city of Algiers, then recaptured Tlemcen from the Spaniards. But the latter reoccupied the city and slew 'Arūj.

Barbarossa and his successors

The possessions of the pirates were seriously threatened. Barbarossa, in order to procure aid, decided to join his possessions with the Ottoman Empire. He rendered homage to the sultan Selim I, who confirmed him in his command with the title of *beylerbey* and dispatched 6,000 men with artillery to him. Thus, in a quasifortuitous fashion, the greater part of North Africa, after centuries of isolation, again became a dependency of an Eastern caliphate.

Thanks to this support, Barbarossa succeeded in extending his dominion toward the east by occupying Bône

(Annaba), Collo, and Constantine. In 1529 he drove the Spaniards from the Peñon of Algiers, and Algiers became the capital of Turkish Algeria. In 1534 Barbarossa gained possession of Tunis. But in the following year the Holy Roman emperor Charles V (Charles I of Spain) recaptured the city, erecting a fortress at La Goulette (Ḥalq al-Wādī), and again imposed a protectorate over the Ḥafṣid sovereign (Tunisia came under Turkish control again in 1574); Barbarossa regained his prestige by an incursion into Mahon. The sultan then invited him to Istanbul to become admiral in chief of the Ottoman fleet (*kapudan paşa*).

From 1536 to 1587 the *beylerbeys* (Barbarossa and his successors), residing in Algiers, governed Turkish North Africa; they piled up success after success over the Spaniards and solidified Ottoman domination. After repelling an attack by the first Saʿdī sultan of southern Morocco, the *beylerbeys* intervened in Morocco, where for a certain time they imposed the Waṭṭāsid ʿAlī Abū Ḥassūn, enemy of the Saʿdī, upon Fez. The conquest of Morocco remained among the designs of the *beylerbeys*, but their struggles against the Spaniards absorbed their best fighting units. In 1587 the title of *beylerbey* was abolished, and the three regencies of Algiers, Tunis, and Tripoli were entrusted to different pashas. Turkish North Africa thus merged into the general organization of the Ottoman Empire.

Ottoman administration of Algeria

The structure of the Algerian state was of a military type; it rested at the same time on local privateers and the Janissaries (the Ottoman standing army), both enjoying considerable privileges. The Janissaries constituted an excellent professional army, stationed in barracks, equipped with modern weapons, and thoroughly trained and endowed with an extraordinary esprit de corps. The army was reinforced by the native cavalry (the *sipāhīs*) and by Kabylie contingents from northern Algeria that were as sturdy as the Janissaries.

Barbary pirates were particularly powerful in the 17th century and made Algiers an important city; it became a great slave market. The city, which boasted a population of about 60,000, welcomed some Moors expelled from Spain—namely, the Tagarins.

Power soon slipped out of the hands of pashas, who now enjoyed only honorary roles; it passed into the hands of military leaders (*aghas*) and later into the hands of the *deys* (Janissary commanders). In the 18th century the *deys*, designated by the militia, maintained control of the province of Algiers and presided over the remnants of the central government. Three provincial regions (the *beyliks*) were headed by officials called *beys*. These provinces were divided into cantons commanded by *qāʾids* (*caids*) or by *shaykhs*. Thus under a Turkish general staff there were the classic divisions of the country into tribes and segments of tribes. Conflicts with the neighbouring regency of Tunis were numerous, but the regency of Algiers did not succeed in any way in modifying in durable fashion its eastern borders.

Despite the harshness manifested by numerous *deys* of Algiers, the *deys* themselves, who were dependent on the militia, were no more than "despots without freedom." Their governments and they themselves frequently had difficulty in exacting taxes from the interior tribes.

The Ottomans belonged to the Ḥanafī juridical school; they at times constructed new mosques, and they had their own particular judges. But Mālikism remained dominant. There was no disturbing competition between the two juridical orthodox rites; likewise, in both of them doctrine and jurisprudence were stabilized. Maraboutism (a branch of Ṣūfism) had not undergone any change, and in Algeria as in Morocco the brotherhoods remained the most vital element in this North African Islām.

Architecture under Ottoman rule underwent little change but accepted a new type of decor—a floral ornament of oriental origin replaced almost everywhere the classic Hispano-Moorish decoration. The art of Turkish Algeria was thus a hybrid art that preserved some medieval forms.

Ottoman domination in Tunisia

Turkish and Ḥusaynid Tunisia. Ottoman domination in Tunisia was established with finality only after 40 years of warfare against the Spaniards, allied with the last Ḥafṣid sultans.

After 1574, Tunisia, which like Algeria had become an Ottoman province, strove to limit the influence of the Turkish government in the internal affairs of the country while at the same time availing itself of the Turks' protection against the Christian and Algerian enemies. This clever policy of a rather weak country was fairly successful. The regency of Tunis, as well as that of Algiers, was at first controlled by pashas appointed for three years, assisted and often dominated by the militia. After 1520 the militia itself appointed its chief, who took on the title of *dey,* with the pasha now playing, as in Algiers, only an honorary role.

The 17th century was likewise in Tunisia a golden age of privateering. Order prevailed throughout the country thanks to the Turkish garrisons, to biannual military rounds that assured the levying of taxes, and also to the old administrative tradition of the country transmitted by the Ḥafṣids. The arrival of Moors expelled from Spain in 1609–12 enabled the Tunisian economy to record important progress both in agriculture and in the crafts.

From 1640 to 1705 the *beys* (provincial governors) exercised effective power and constituted de facto dynasties. After 1705 the Ḥusaynid *beys* formed a veritable local dynasty recognized by the Turkish government. As far as Europe was concerned, the regencies of Algiers and Tunis came to be regarded more and more as being independent.

Whereas Turkish Algeria was deprived of deep unity and at times proved difficult to govern, Ḥusaynid Tunisia presented the aspect of a real state and was partly opened to European influences. A peace-loving country, its government rejoiced in 1830 when the French conquest of Algiers delivered it from a frequently menacing neighbour.

Sharīfian Morocco. In Morocco, from 1428 to 1459, the Marīnid sultans fell under the protection of a dynasty of viziers—the Banū Waṭṭās (Waṭṭāsids)—who finally replaced them. This new dynasty, feeble from its very beginnings, was obeyed only in parts of northern Morocco and was obliged to confront an occidental world in full flush of renaissance.

The Banū Waṭṭās

Morocco was directly affected by Portuguese incursions against its coasts. From 1415 to 1486 these attacks were directed against the ports of the Straits of Gibraltar and of northern Morocco. But from 1486 to 1550 the Portuguese settled at various points on Morocco's Atlantic coast, from Oum er-Rbia to Sous. In the face of these new problems the Banū Waṭṭās remained peaceful; they took virtually no action against the Portuguese. Resistance to these Christian assaults was offered by local chiefs as well as by the brotherhoods. Ṣūfism had continued to develop in Morocco during the entire Marīnid period and had resulted in the formation of numerous brotherhoods. The latter, however, while often enjoying the role of arbiters among the tribes, possessed no political powers. The Christian incursions against the Moroccan coasts and the attempts at penetration into southern Morocco impelled the religious leaders to become the instigators and, at times, the leaders of a holy war. From the 15th century on, marabouts (*murābitūn*; popular Ṣūfī religious leaders) became a political force, often challenging the power of the sultans.

Furthermore, the actions of the Arabs culminated in disastrous consequences; the country was impoverished, and, amidst growing distress, anarchy gained the upper hand. From the time of the Marīnids, the Atlas region and a substantial portion of the Sahara confines had evaded the authority of the sultans. Morocco split into two zones: the Bled Makhzen (land under government control) and the Bledes Siba (land of dissidence), where the mountain people organized their own lives while limiting contact with the cities and the plains.

The Banū Waṭṭās struggled for 30 years against the increasing thrust of a Marabout dynasty—that of the Saʿdī *sharīfs*, who finally seized the city of Fez in 1548. A Waṭṭāsid restoration supported by the Turks in Algiers was defeated in 1554.

Saʿdī Morocco (1548–1659). The Saʿdīs had settled since the 13th century in the oasis of the Drâa. Until the 16th century they played no political role in extreme southern Morocco. After the founding of Agadir, the Portuguese attempted to develop an aggressive policy in the Sous region; the marabouts of the Sous resisted and designated a Saʿdī as leader in the holy war, but without notable results. The Saʿdī, however, were summoned against the tribes that were fighting the Portuguese of Safi. Giving priority to their personal ambitions, the Saʿdī took advantage of this situation to conquer southern Morocco and Marrakesh and then came into conflict with the Banū Waṭṭās. The Saʿdī gained new prestige by capturing the Portuguese position at Agadir in 1541, but they needed ten more years to conquer the northern part of the country and to become the sultans of Morocco.

The Saʿdī had risen out of the marabout crisis. But their struggle against the Christians had frequently been no more than a pretext for the conquest of Morocco. Their dynasty had no native support apart from some contingents from the Sous and most often had to use Arab militias.

Saʿdī foreign policy

The Saʿdī foreign policy was dominated by a fear of the Turkish peril; thus, reluctantly and with meagre results, they allied themselves with the Spaniards in Oran, who were battling against the Turks of Algiers. One Saʿdī sultan, dethroned by two of his uncles, had taken refuge in Portugal. The youthful and visionary Portuguese king Don Sebastian (ruled 1557–78) attempted to restore him to power in Morocco, but both he and his protégé were defeated and slain in the "Battle of the Three Kings" (1578). This Saʿdī victory created the impression that Morocco constituted a formidable force by virtue of having defeated in a single encounter a European power. The sultan Aḥmad al-Manṣūr (reigned 1578–1603) adroitly capitalized on this illusion. Aḥmad al-Manṣūr succeeded in reinforcing his army with mercenary Turk and Kabylie units, as well as with emigrants from Andalusia. He had a luxurious palace erected for himself at Marrakesh, called the "Badiʿ," where he received European ambassadors with great pomp. His only expedition abroad was undertaken against a Muslim country, Songhai (now Mali), where his troops, largely Andalusian, captured Timbuktu (1591), from which he drew gold and numerous slaves. He procured financial resources by any means within his power. The cultivation of sugarcane and the trade in sugar became his monopoly. His fiscal mismanagement, however, provoked revolts.

Though al-Manṣūr maintained friendly relations with the great European powers, which permitted Morocco to carry on a minimum of foreign trade, he did not open the country to European influences. He jealously guarded his insulation from the Christian world. Having risen out of the marabout crisis, the Saʿdī were destined to die of it. Following the death of al-Manṣūr in 1603, the Saʿdī princes began to dispute among themselves over authority; thenceforth the dynasty experienced a rapid decline. Throughout Morocco, marabout forces arose and fought each other in order to aggrandize their domain. One of them, the marabouts of Dila, seemed for a moment on the verge of restoring the unity of Morocco. But it was a second Sharīfian dynasty, that of the ʿAlawīs, that ended this anarchic fragmentation and succeeded in reuniting under its authority—actual or theoretic—the Moroccan lands.

Morocco under the ʿAlawī (or Filālī) sultans (1689–1830). The ʿAlawī *sharīfs* had for a long time been established in the Tāfīlālt, and with the decline of Saʿdī power they became the political leaders of the oasis. Mawlāy ar-Rashīd gained possession of Fez (1666), conquered all the local rulers who were disputing among themselves over the Moroccan lands, and restored the political unity of the country. He died accidentally after having consolidated his task of reorganization. Nevertheless, the country remained in a state of turbulence. His brother and successor, Mawlāy Ismāʿīl (1672–1727), had to assert his authority by force; with a militia of black slaves and Arab troops, he attempted a veritable military occupation of his own country through garrisons stationed in fortresses. Despite his efforts, Mawlāy Ismāʿīl proved incapable of subjugating effectively mountainous Morocco, which remained in a state of dissidence. He attempted incursions into Tlemcen in vain, but he did succeed in recovering some of the coastal areas still occupied by the Christians—namely, Maʿmūrah, Tangier, and Larache.

Reunification of Morocco

The crushing tax burden imposed by Mawlāy Ismāʿīl, who launched an ambitious military effort and built at Meknès immense palaces, led to numerous revolts among the tribes. Upon his death the country found itself exhausted and prey to sanguinary anarchy for a period of 30 years.

Sīdī Muḥammad ibn ʿAbd Allāh (1757–90) restored order in the country; with him the ʿAlawī dynasty confined its ambitions and defined its policy. The rulers maintained a minimum of business contacts and diplomatic relations with Europe, with the rest of North Africa, and with the Orient.

In the interior the sultans strove to check, but could not prevent, the incursions of Berber tribes of the Central Atlas and Moyen Atlas into the Atlantic plains. Revolts were common, even in the area under subjection, and the sultans often had to undertake military expeditions in order to assure the levying of taxes.

These events were but the continuation of a series of expedients dating back to the Middle Ages. Despite the goodwill and the application by the sultans of the 18th century and the early 19th century, Morocco proved incapable of taking advantage of its last period of isolation to bring about its own reform.

Thus in Sharīfian Morocco, as in Turkish Algeria and Tunisia, there was no renaissance, no manifestation of a firm will or of clearcut evolution and progress. Revolutionary and imperialistic wars absorbed all the energies of Europe and paradoxically prolonged this North African status of isolation. Transformations could no longer occur except through foreign influences. The seizure of Algiers by the French in 1830 opened a new era; however, Europe's interventions were to be felt in the three countries at different dates and as a result of diverse methods.

Unity and diversity in Muslim North Africa. Within the scope of this article it is helpful to look back over these 11 centuries of Muslim history in North Africa by investigating in what epochs and to what degree the regions that constituted Tunisia, Algeria, and Morocco experienced political unity and a unity of civilization, or alternatively to what extent they followed their autonomous paths.

Eleven centuries of Muslim history in North Africa

In the 8th and 9th centuries, after the resistance that Barbary had offered against its conquerors (particularly in its eastern portion), the region rallied to Islām and organized its Muslim way of living. This was done either through the path of orthodoxy or through the diverse sects of Khārijism (even in its particular heresies). Except for the Aghlabid *amīr*, a theoretical vassal of Baghdad, this evolution proceeded within an entirely independent policy and even through fragmentation; but this splintering and these differences of detail must not conceal the profound unity of this great movement toward the organization and elaboration of North African Islām.

The transformation resulting from the efforts made during the 5th and 9th centuries made possible the achievements wrought in the 10th, 11th, and 12th centuries by the great African empires. The first among those—that of the Fāṭimids—was, from the Barbary point of view, an inconclusive endeavour, deficient in the long run. It ran contrary to the religious evolution of the country and devoted its utmost effort toward the conquest of Egypt, where the dynasty emigrated in 972 and became Eastern in fact, which it had been at heart previously.

To the contrary, the two great Moroccan dynasties—the Almoravids and the Almohads—laboured at the same time for the political and cultural unity of the Barbary. The Almoravids, after unifying the Moroccan lands, conquered the Maghrib. The Almohads subjected all of North Africa to their control, thus attaining the apogee of Berber Islām. Because they were also the masters of Muslim Spain, the Almoravids and the Almohads were able to further successfully the cultural unity of the Muslim West. Thus they became the *serviteurs* of the Andalusian civilization, which prevailed in the cities of the Maghrib and in Tunisia mingled with the local traditions. The political apogee of the Barbary was accompanied by the unification of its culture.

The disintegration of the Almohad empire served as the foundation, on the political level, for the tripartite division of North Africa; but it did not undermine the unity of its civilization of Spanish origin. In Tunisia the Hispanic influences were never greater than under the Ḥafṣids (13th,

14th, and 15th centuries). To this unity of Muslim culture, however, a common misfortune was added; in the three kingdoms of Tunis, Tlemcen, and Fez, the destructive depredations of the Arabs undermined the power of the dynasties and ruined the traditional economy of the country, which thenceforth became impoverished.

The beginnings of modern times, which in Europe were distinguished by profound and fruitful transformations, failed to inspire North Africa with the desire to change. The Portuguese ventures into Morocco served only to let loose a prolonged marabout crisis, which became deeply xenophobic in character. Under the Sharīfian dynasties, Morocco dwelt in isolation and took an adamant stand against innovations; it continued on its traditional path, which was prolonged until the 20th century—a paradoxical "Middle Ages."

It was a fortuitous union—the policy of Barbarossa and his family of pirates who had become the leaders of a holy war—that linked Algeria and Tunisia with the Ottoman Empire, which modified their civilization through a wave of Eastern influences. The political and cultural unity of the Barbary was thenceforth shattered, and the ossification of civilization in the three countries served only to consecrate the division.

(H.-L.-É.T.)

Northern Africa since 1830

The restoration of European rule in North Africa was initiated in 1830 by the French conquest of Algiers city and followed in time by the occupation of the hinterland. In 1881 the French occupied Tunisia also, and in 1911 the Italians expelled the Turkish government from Libya, following this up by the progressive conquest of the Arab inhabitants. The process was completed by the Franco-Spanish occupation of Morocco, which followed the signing of the Treaty of Fès in 1912. The regimes of European colonial type that followed created entirely new conditions and by degrees gave birth to modern nationalist movements. Strengthened by the circumstances of World War II, these resulted in the establishment of Libya as an independent state in December 1951 and the independence of Morocco and Tunisia in 1956. In 1960 a new state, Mauritania, was created to the south of Morocco (see WESTERN AFRICA); and, last of all, in 1962 Algeria achieved its independence. For the period from the 19th century to independence, see the history section under each country that follows.

For coverage of related topics in the *Macropædia* and *Micropædia,* see the *Propædia,* sections 911, 924, 962, 96/11, and 978. (Ed.)

ALGERIA

Algeria is an independent republic in the Maghrib. Its official name is al-Jumhūrīyah al-Jazā'irīyah ad-Dīmuqrātīyah ash-Sha'bīyah (French République Algérienne Démocratique et Populaire; Democratic and Popular Republic of Algeria). With an area of 919,595 square miles (2,381,741 square kilometres), it is the second largest country in Africa and the 10th largest country in the world; 796,359 square miles (2,062,561 square kilometres) of the national territory, however, consist of six Saharan *wilāyāt* (*départements* or provinces) in the south.

Physical and human geography

The country is bounded to the east by Tunisia and Libya; to the south by Niger, Mali, and Mauritania; to the west by Morocco and Western Sahara; and to the north by the Mediterranean.

Algeria is a country of vastness; the Mediterranean to the north separates it from Europe but at the same time opens a thousand doors to it, while in the south the Sahara links it to Africa. History, language, customs, and Islām make it an integral part of the Arab world. Algeria's struggle for liberation, which lasted from 1954 to 1962, has gained it a significant place among the "nonaligned" nations, while the internal as well as external choices that its leaders have made place it among the ranks of socialist nations.

THE LAND

Relief. Almost the entire population of Algeria lives in the northern part of the country—the Tell—which is the richer and the better watered. The remainder of the country, the Saharan region, is uninhabited desert, with the exception of several oases. The Saharan region conceals rich mineral resources and, above all, sources of energy. Each of the country's two physical regions results from a different geological evolution. The main features of structure and relief have been produced by the collision of the African and European tectonic plates, now forming the geologically young and crumpled mountain chains in the north, with the solid and ancient platform of basement rock, horizontal and uniform, forming the south. The first of these areas is the mountainous Atlas region, consisting of two large mountain chains, running roughly parallel from east to west and separated by high plateaus. The second region consists of the Sahara, which also extends into the adjacent countries to the south.

The northern region. In the north there are, from north to south, five different zones, all running from east to west. The first of these is formed by the folded littoral (coastal zone); the second by the plains which lie to the south of the littoral; the third zone consists of the first chain of mountains, the Atlas Tellien (Tell Atlas); the fourth zone consists of the Haut Plateaux (High Plateaus); and the fifth consists of the second chain of mountains—the Atlas Saharien (Saharan Atlas)—which extends in some areas of broken terrain into the Sahara itself.

On the coast the folds and ridges usually terminate in high cliffs, which are indented with numerous bays; these indentations are spaced out along the coast and the principal ports are located in them. The coastal massifs (mountainous masses of rock) are often separated from each other by plains—such as the plains of Oran and of Annaba—which extend from the littoral into the region behind it. In the same way, the Atlas Tellien is not continuous but forms two distinct ranges to the west, separated by interior plains. Thus the plains of Maghria and of Ghossels separate the Monts de Tlemcen to the south from the Monts des Traras to the northwest, and the Monts du Tessala to the northeast. The plains of Sidi bel Abbès and of Mascara are interpolated between the Monts des Beni-Chougran to the north and the mountains of Daïa and of Saïa to the south. The Dahra Massif forms a long range, extending from the mouth of the Chelif River in the west to the Dejebel Chenoua in the east; it is separated from the Massif de l'Ouarsenis to the south by the plains of the Chelif Valley.

The relief as a whole, therefore, does not constitute a barrier to communication between the different areas that form the western Tell region. This is not so, however, in the central Tell, where the previous regular pattern permitting communication progressively diminishes and disappears. The Atlas de Blida is not easily distinguished from the Monts du Titeri, while the mountainous and compact ensemble of the Grande Kabylie joins the Biban and the Hodna mountains. Only the valley of the Oued (Wadi) Soummam permits communication with the port of Bejaïa on the coast.

Mountain barriers

More to the east, from Bejaïa to Edough, one mountain barrier follows another, surrounding the Plains of Constantine, which are dominated to the south by the Hodna, Aurès, and Nementcha mountains. The Plains of Constantine themselves, which have a distinct local topography, and since ancient antiquity have been used for growing cereals, do not present the same features as the Algero-Oranian Haut Plateaux. These extend from the Monts du Hodna into Morocco; they are broken by sebkhas (lake beds encrusted with salt) and are much less favourable to agriculture because of the scarcity of rain.

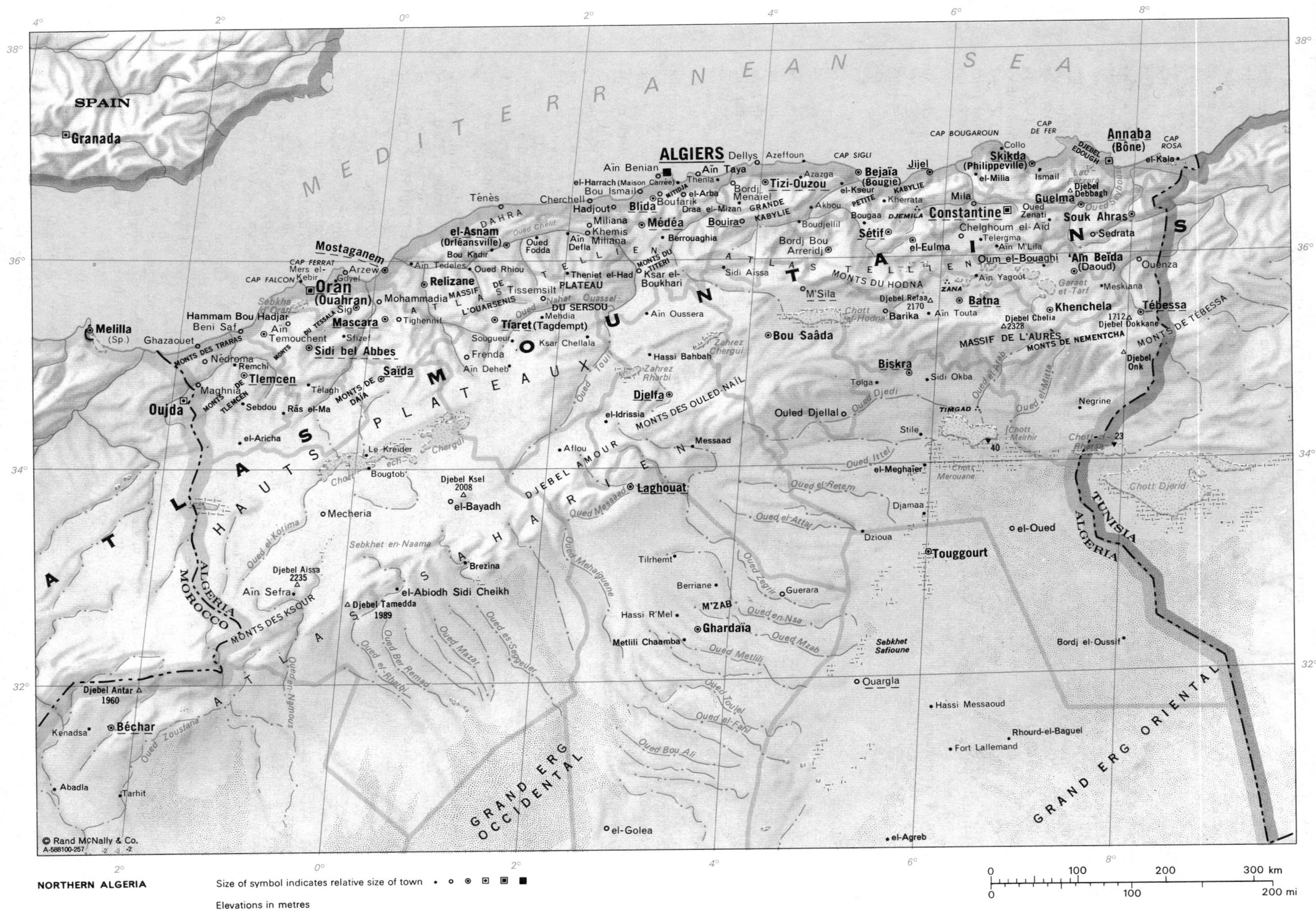
MEDITERRANEAN SEA
SPAIN
Granada
ALGIERS
Annaba (Bône)
Skikda (Philippeville)
Constantine
Oran (Ouahran)
Mostaganem
Tlemcen
Sidi bel Abbes
Oujda
Melilla (Sp.)
Blida
Médéa
Sétif
Batna
Biskra
Bou Saâda
Djelfa
Laghouat
Ghardaïa
Touggourt
Ouargla
el-Golea
Béchar
TUNISIA
ALGERIA
MOROCCO
GRAND ERG OCCIDENTAL
GRAND ERG ORIENTAL
ATLAS SAHARIEN
HAUTS PLATEAUX
TELL ATLAS
© Rand McNally & Co.
A-588100-257
NORTHERN ALGERIA
Size of symbol indicates relative size of town
Elevations in metres
0 100 200 300 km
0 100 200 mi

To the south of the Algero-Oranian Haut Plateaux and the Plains of Constantine runs the second mountain chain, the Atlas Saharien, which is formed of a series of small ranges that run generally southwest to northeast. They decline in altitude from the west (where Djebel Aïssa attains a height of 7,336 feet [2,235 metres]) to the east. Their structure is such that interregional communications from north to south are facilitated. More to the east, between the Plains of Constantine to the north and the eastern Atlas Saharien to the south, rises the Massif de l'Aurès, whose summits reach altitudes higher than 6,000 feet.

The southern region. The Algerian Sahara may be roughly divided into two depressions of different altitude, separated from one another by a central north-to-south

NORTHERN ALGERIA

MAP INDEX

Political subdivisions

Adrar 26·00n 1·00w
Alger 36·42n 3·08w
Annaba 36·54n 7·46e
Batna 35·15n 6·00e
Béchar 30·00n 3 30w
Bejaïa 36·30n 5·00e
Biskra 34·15n 5 40e
Blida 36·30n 2·35e
Bouira 36·15n 3·50e
Constantine 36·25n 6·42e
Djelfa 34·45n 3·00e
el-Asnam 36·10n 1·20e
Guelma 36·25n 7·45e
Jijel 36·45n 5·45e
Laghouat 32·00n 3 00e
Mascara 35·30n 0·10e
Médéa 36·12n 2·50e
Mostaganem 35·51n 0·07e
M'Sila 35·00n 3·50e
Oran 35·43n 0·43w
Ouargla 29·00n 8·30e
Oum el-Bouaghi 35·53n 7·07e
Saïda 33·00n 0·15e
Sétif 36·10n 5·05w
Sidi bel Abbes 35·00n 0·45w
Skikda 36·50n 7·00e
*Tamanrasset 25 00n 6·00e
Tébessa 35·20n 8·05e
Tiaret 35·28n 1·21e
Tizi-Ouzou 36·48n 4·02e
Tlemcen 34·52n 1·15w

The names of the political subdivisions do not appear on the map because they are the same as the names of their capital cities.

Cities and towns

Abadla 31·02n 2·45w
Aflou 34·01n 2·03e
'Aïn Beïda (Daoud) 35·50n 7·29e
Aïn Benian 36·45n 2·51e
Aïn Defla 36·16n 1·58e
Aïn Deheb 34·51n 1·31e
Aïn M'lila 36·02n 6·30e
Aïn Oussera 35·24n 2·54e
Aïn Sefra 32·47n 0·37w
Aïn Taya 36·50n 3·10e
Aïn Tedeles 36·00n 0·21e
Aïn Temouchent 35·16n 1·04w
Aïn Touta 35·26n 5·59e
Aïn Yagout 35·50n 6·28e
Akbou 36·27n 4·31e
Algiers (Alger) 36·42n 3·08e
Annaba (Bône) 36·54n 7·46e
Arzew 35·50n 0·23w
Azazga 36·48n 4·30e
Azeffoun 36·51n 4·25e
Barika 35·23n 5·17e
Batna 35·34n 6·15e
Béchar 31·37n 2·13w
Bejaïa (Bougie) 36·45n 5·05e
Beni Saf 35·17n 1·15w
Berriane 32·49n 3·44e
Berrouaghia 36·07n 2·52e
Biskra 34·50n 5·52e
Blida 36·30n 2·49e
Bône, see Annaba
Bordj Bou Arreridj 36·02n 4·49e
Bordj el-Oussif 32·20n 8·02e
Bordj Menaïel 36·44n 3·45e
Boudjellil 36·19n 4·22e
Boufarik 36·37n 2·52e
Bougaa 36·21n 5·05e
Bougie, see Bejaïa
Bougtob 34·03n 0·06e
Bouira 36·23n 3·54e
Bou Ismail 36·40n 2·44e
Bou Kadir 36·04n 1·08e
Bou Saâda 35·11n 4·09e
Brezina 33·04n 1·14e
Chelghoum el-Aïd 36·10n 6·08e
Cherchell 36·35n 2·16e
Collo 36·58n 6·37e
Colomb-Béchar, see Béchar
Constantine 36·25n 6·43e
Daoud, see 'Aïn Beïda
Dellys 36·50n 3·55e
Djamaa 33·32n 5·59e
Djelfa 34·30n 3·20e
Draa el-Mizan 36·35n 3·47e
Dzioua 33·14n 5·14e
el-Agreb 30·48n 5·30e
el-Abiodh Sidi Cheikh 32·56n 0·42e
el-Arba 36·37n 3·13e
el-Aricha 34·09n 1·10w
el-Asnam (Orléansville) 36·10n 1·20e
el-Bayadh 33·40n 1·01e
el-Eulma 36·08n 5·40e
el-Golea 30·30n 2·50e
el-Harrach (Maison Carrée) 36·45n 3·07e
el-Idrissia 34·30n 2·37e
el-Kala 36·50n 8·30e
el-Kseur 36·46n 4·49e
el-Meghaïer 33·55n 5·58e
el-Milia 36·48n 6·14e
el-Oued 33·20n 6·58e
Fort Lallemand 31·13n 6·17e
Frenda 35·02n 1·01e
Gdyel 35·48n 0·26w
Ghardaïa 32·31n 3·37e
Ghazaouet 35·06n 1·51w
Guelma 36·28n 7·26e
Guerara 32·46n 4·34e
Hadjout 36·31n 2·25e
Hammam Bou Hadjar 35·20n 1·05w
Hassi Bahbah 35·05n 2·55e
Hassi Messaoud 31·43n 5·59e
Hassi R'Mel 32·35n 3·24e
Igli 30·25n 2·12w
Ismail 36·50n 7·21e
Jijel 36·52n 5 50e
Kenadsa 31·30n 2·30w
Khemis Miliana 36·16n 2·13e
Khenchela 35·28n 7·11e
Kherrata 36·31n 5·26e
Ksar Chellala 35·13n 2·18e
Ksar el-Boukhari 35·51n 2·52e
Laghouat 33·50n 2·59e
Le Kreïder 34·06n 0·02e
Maghnia 34·50n 1·50w
Maison Carrée, see el-Harrach
Marnia, see Maghnia
Mascara 35·20n 0·09e
Mecheria 33·35n 0·18w
Médéa 36·12n 2·50e
Mehdia 35·26n 1·40e
Mers el-Kebir 35·45n 0·43w
Meskiana 35·39n 7·41e
Messaad 34·12n 3·25e
Metlili Chaamba 32·18n 3·40e
Mila 36·27n 6·16e
Miliana 36·15n 2·15e
Mohammadia 35·33n 0·03e
Mostaganem 35·51n 0·07e
M'Sila 35·46n 4·31e
Nédroma 35·01n 1·45w
Negrine 34·30n 7·30e
Nemours, see Ghazaouet
Oran (Ouahran) 35·43n 0·43w
Orléansville, see el-Asnam
Ouahran, see Oran
Ouargla 31·59n 5·25e
Oued Fodda 36·11n 1·32e
Oued Rhiou 35·58n 0·55e
Oued Zenati 36·18n 7·05e
Ouenza 35·57n 8·04e
Ouled Djellal 34·28n 5·02e
Oum el-Bouaghi 35·53n 7·07e
Philippeville, see Skikda
Râs el-Ma 34·31n 0·46w
Relizane 35·44n 0·30e
Remchi 35·04n 1·26w
Rhourd-el-Baguel 31·15n 6·55e
Saïda 34·50n 0·11e
Sainte-Denis-du-Sig, see Sig
Sebdou 34·35n 1·20w
Sedrata 36·08n 7·32e
Sétif 36·09n 5·26e
Sfizef 35·14n 0·15w
Sidi Aïssa 35·53n 3·48e
Sidi bel Abbes 35·13n 0·10w
Sidi Okba 34·48n 5·54e
Sig 35·32n 0·11w
Skikda (Philippeville) 36·50n 6·58e
Sougueur 35·12n 1·30e
Souk Ahras 36·23n 8·00e
Stile 34·20n 5·51e
Tagdempt, see Tiaret
Tarhit 30·55n 2·02w
Tébessa 35·28n 8·09e
Télagh 34·47n 0·34w
Telergma 36·07n 6·21e
Ténès 36·31n 1·14e
Thenia 36·43n 3·34e
Theniet el-Had 35·47n 2·01e
Tiaret (Tagdempt) 35·28n 1·21e
Tighennif 35·20n 0·21e
Tilrhemt 33·10n 3·21e
Tissemsilt 35·35n 1·50e
Tizi-Ouzou 36·48n 4·02e
Tlemcen 34·52n 1·15w
Tolga 34·46n 5·22e
Touggourt 33·10n 6·00e

Physical features and points of interest

Aïssa, Djebel, *mountain* 32·56n 0·38w
Amour, Djebel, *mountains* 34·00n 2·15e
Antar, Djebel, *mountain* 31·59n 1·57w
Arab, Oued el-, *watercourse* 34·41n 6·31e
Atlas Mountains 35·30n 3·00e
Atlas Saharien (Saharan Atlas), *mountains* 33·25n 1·20e
Atlas Tellien (Tell Atlas), *mountains* 35·00n 3·00e
Attar, Oued el-, *watercourse* 33·27n 5·26e
Aurès, Massif de l', *mountains* 35·08n 6·30e
Ber Remad, Oued, *watercourse* 31·45n 1·10e
Bou Ali, Oued, *watercourse* 31·14n 4·16e
Bougaroun, Cap, *cape* 37·10n 6·30e
Chélia, Djebel, *mountain* 35·19n 6·42e
Chelif, Oued, *river* 36·01n 0·07e
Chergui, Chott ech-, *lake* 34·15n 0·30e
Chergui, Zahrez, *lake* 35·12n 3·32e
Dahra, *mountains* 36·20n 1·21e
Daïa, Monts de, *mountains* 34·40n 0·14w
Debbagh, Djebel, *mountain* 36·33n 7·18e
Djedi, Oued, *watercourse* 34·28n 6·05e
Djemila, *ruins* 36·25n 5·44e
Dokkane, Djebel, *mountain* 35·23n 8·00e
Edough, Djebel, *mountains* 36·56n 7·41e
Fahl, Oued el-, *watercourse* 31·15n 4·41e
Falcon, Cap, *cape* 35·45n 1·00w
Fer, Cap de, *cape* 37·08n 7·10e
Ferrat, Cap, *cape* 35·55n 0·30w
Fetzara, Lac, *lake* 36·52n 7·22e
Grande Kabylie, *mountains* 36·34n 4·18e
Grand Erg Occidental, *desert* 30·30n 0·30e
Grand Erg Oriental, *desert* 30·30n 7·00e
Hauts Plateaux, *plateau* 34·20n 0·15e
Hodna, Chott el-, *lake* 35·30n 4·45e
Hodna, Monts du, *mountains* 35·50n 4·50e
Ittel, Oued, *watercourse* 34·19n 6·01e
Korima, Oued el-, *watercourse* 33·51n 0·23w
Ksel, Djebel, *mountain* 33·43n 1·10e
Ksour, Monts des, *mountains* 32·45n 0·30w
Mazar, Oued, *watercourse* 31·50n 1·36e
Mediterranean Sea 37·40n 3·00e
Mehaïguene, Oued, *watercourse* 32·15n 2·59e
Melrhir, Chott, *lake* 34·17n 6·24e
Merouane, Chott, *lake* 34·02n 6·10e
Messaad, Oued, *watercourse* 33·45n 2·51e
Metlili, Oued, *watercourse* 31·54n 4·53e
Mitidja, *plain* 36·39n 3·00e
Mitta, Oued el-, *watercourse* 34·20n 6·44e
M'zab, *physical region* 32·35n 3·55e
Mzab, Oued, *watercourse* 32·19n 5·24e
Naama, Sebkhet en-, *salt marsh* 33·20n 0·16w
Nahar Ouassel, Oued, *river* 35·42n 2·48e
Namous, Oued en-, *watercourse* 31·00n 0·15w
Nementcha, Monts de, *mountains* 34·59n 6·51e
Nsa, Oued en-, *watercourse* 32·28n 5·24e
Onk, Djebel, *mountain* 34·52n 7·57e
Oran, Sebkha d', *lake* 35·30n 1·00w
Ouarsenis, Massif de l', *mountains* 35·42n 1·32e
Ouled-Naïl, Monts des, *mountains* 34·33n 3·28e
Petite Kabylie, *mountains* 36·30n 5·29e
Refaa, Djebel, *mountain* 35·34n 5·53e
Retem, Oued er-, *watercourse* 33·30n 5·45e
Rharbi, Oued el-, *watercourse* 31·50n 0·51e
Rharbi, Zahrez, *lake* 34·50n 2·50e
Rharsa, Chott el-, *salt lake* 34·06n 7·50e
Rosa, Cap, *cape* 36·58n 8·15e
Safioune, Sebkhet, *salt marsh* 32·16n 5·27e
Saharan Atlas, see Atlas Saharien
Seggeuer, Oued es-, *watercourse* 31·39n 2·26e
Sersou, *plateau* 35·30n 2·00e
Seybouse, Oued, *river* 36·54n 7·47e
Sigli, Cap, *cape* 36·56n 4·45e
Tamedda, Djebel, *mountain* 32·47n 0·05e
Tarf, Garaet et-, *lake* 35·40n 7·10e
Tébessa, Monts de, *mountains* 35·20n 8·20e
Tell Atlas, see Atlas Tellien
Tessala, Monts du, *mountains* 35·08n 0·53w
Timgad, *ruins* 35·23n 6·30e
Titeri, Monts du, *mountains* 35·57n 3·17e
Tlemcen, Monts de, *mountains* 34·40n 1·25w
Touiel, Oued, *watercourse* 31·30n 4·46e
Touil, Oued, *watercourse* 35·30n 2·33e
Traras, Monts des, *mountains* 34·57n 1·46w
Zana, *ruins* 35·45n 6·05e
Zegrir, Oued, *watercourse* 32·43n 5·00e
Zousfana, Oued, *watercourse* 30·29n 2·17w

* See map of Algeria

rise called the Mzab (M'Zab). Each zone is covered by a vast sheet of sand dunes, called an erg. The Grand Erg Oriental (Great Eastern Erg), which has an average altitude of from 1,300 to 2,000 feet, and the Grand Erg Occidental (Great Western Erg) are made of drifts of sand, declining in height northward from the foot of the Ahaggar (Hoggar) Mountains to below sea level at the foot of the Massif de l'Aurès. A notable feature is the Ahaggar Mountains, which rise to majestic summits, the highest, Djebel Tahat, 9,540 feet in altitude.

Climate, plants, and animal life. Climate, more than relief, is the determining geographical factor. The amount of rainfall, and above all its distribution throughout the agricultural year, as well as the nature of certain winds, constitute the principal elements upon which pastoral activities depend.

Regional variations in rainfall

The amount of rainfall increases as one proceeds from west to east but diminishes from the north to the south. The greatest amount of rainfall is experienced in the mountainous regions of the eastern littoral, which are directly exposed to the humid winds that blow inland from the Mediterranean. From the meridian that runs through the port of Cherchell, about 50 miles west of Algiers, to the Tunisian frontier, the rainfall exceeds 23 inches (584 millimetres), and in certain places—for example in the Grande Kabylie, Petite Kabylie, and Edough regions—reaches about 40 inches. To the west of the Cherchell meridian, however, a considerable part of the Chelif Plains, and the plains of the littoral and the region immediately to the south of it in the vicinity of Oran, are insufficiently watered, receiving less than 23 inches. Only the Atlas Tellien receives from 16 to 23 inches. As soon as one crosses the Atlas ranges to the south, however, rainfall rapidly diminishes, except in the Massif de l'Aurès and in a section of the Djebel Amour, which still receives about 16 inches.

This boundary roughly divides the two principal agricultural zones. In the first, dry farming is generally possible and commercially profitable. Fine forests and an abundant vegetation are also found. In the second zone the cultivation of cereal crops is only possible under exceptional circumstances. Instead, pastoral activities are predominant, and the forests disappear.

There is a regular annual rainy season from December to March; at intervals during the rest of the year heavy storms occur, accompanied by rain. Rainfall is often torrential and may be spread out over several days, whereas at other times the weather is dry and hot for months. The amount of rainfall may vary drastically, sometimes increasing by 200 percent from one year to another. Algiers, where the average is almost 30 inches, received about 16 inches in 1913 and 50 inches in 1847. Djelfa, which receives an average of about 12 inches, received less than 4 inches in 1913, and about 30 inches in 1847. This irregularity, which often is of considerable consequence for agriculture in the interior, is aggravated by temperature variations and, locally, by dry winds. If the annual temperature range in the coastal area is comparatively low, elsewhere it is high—111° F (44° C) at Miliana and 129° F (54° C) at el-Asnam. In inverse relationship to the proximity to the sea, the cold becomes sharper on the southern fringes of the Tell, with extreme minimum temperatures reaching 9° F (−13° C) at Berrouaghia and 12° F (−11° C) at Bouïra, while on the Haut Plateaux, extreme minimum temperatures reach 16° F (−9° C) at Sétif, 10° F (−12° C) at Batna, and 5° F (−15° C) at el-Bayadh in the Oran region.

Only the littoral, the Plains of Oran, the lower Chelif River Valley, and the Mitidja Plain behind Algiers are spared the frost. While in the Haut Plateaux the frost occurs 20 days a year, it may occur for 50 days in the Sétif and Bordj Bou Arreridj regions.

The coastal regions, which are subjected directly to the influence of the Mediterranean Sea, are well watered and experience relatively little temperature variation. Permanently under intensive cultivation, they are especially used for fruit growing and market gardening. The plains and the hills in the region immediately to the south of the littoral still receive sufficient rain but have a much drier atmosphere; the temperatures show more variation in range. The natural vegetation cover, preserved only on a few massifs, includes some fine trees, such as the cork oaks that grow around Constantine, or the thugas (trees resembling the cypress) that are found in the Oran region of the Atlas Tellien.

Cultivation on the coastal plains

The Haut Plateaux, on the other hand, are characterized by great daily and annual extremes of temperature, hot summers and cold winters, and insufficient rainfall.

The cultivation of cereals is not always or everywhere possible. Natural vegetation is represented by the very characteristic association of wild olive and the mastic tree accompanied by gorse and dwarf palms. This brush type of vegetation has, however, almost everywhere disappeared as a result of land clearance; usually only the dwarf palms and such hardy plants as the asphodel remain.

Where less than 12 inches of rain are received, the vegetation of the steppe type (characterized by extensive treeless plains) occurs, although discontinuously; steppes of esparto grass or wormwood are the most widespread.

On the southern border of the Atlas Saharien, the Sahara proper begins. The demarcation coincides with a diminution of the rainfall to less than four inches a year. The landscape and the type of plant life differ greatly from those in the north. Life and activity are limited to a few privileged locations. The rains, more than in the north, are marked by their irregularity; Tamanrasset one year received about six inches, and another year only about a quarter of an inch, while Ouargla received about three inches one year and nothing the following year. Three years may pass without rainfall in the Tademaït region, and as much as five years in the Ahaggar.

These circumstances produce a very rare vegetation, which appears rapidly after rain and disappears almost immediately. Plant life is very dispersed and consists of tufts of several kinds of grass, various robust species that need almost no water such as drinn and cram-cram, several shrubs (which are always stunted and are sometimes spiny), ethels, acacia, jujube trees, as well as some more varied species which are found in the beds of oueds (watercourses which are dry except during periods of rain) with underground water, or in mountainous regions.

Such plant life can only sustain a scarce animal life. Few species are found—some antelope, gazelles, hare, jerboas, and wild boars, as well as a few birds and some reptiles and insects.

The *sahels* (coastal plains) of Oran, Algiers, and Annaba specialize in early vegetables, while the plains of the interior permit a varied cultivation. The hillsides are usually covered with orchards, while the plateaus and the Haut Plateaux are sufficiently well watered to be used for the cultivation of cereals. Elsewhere, pastoralism is dominant, except for a few irrigated tracts.

Orchards and cereal crops

In the Saharan regions, agriculture is confined to a few selected regions with underground water resources, such as the *souf* (intermittent stream). Despite the extreme hostility of nature, however, man occasionally succeeds in establishing a basis for life—for example in the Mzab region—by using the rare runoff water found after rain.

Elsewhere, in the Tell, much greater possibilities exist, though runoff water after showers is lost, and its infiltration into the soil remains partial or reduced. Even so, the natural conditions that prevail, although they deteriorate toward the south, present many advantages from which man has benefitted. Resources are generally varied and abundant, as has been shown by numerous surveys.

Settlement patterns. The geographic distribution of the population shows an imbalance in the population density that corresponds, approximately, to differences in soil fertility and to variations in the amount of rainfall. Different types of life style virtually coincide with the principal vegetation zones. In the Tell, man predominates on such plains as are to be found and without irrigation has been able to use them for growing orchards and cereals. Where the slopes are too steep for cultivation, continuous enclosures for livestock are established. Human settlement has occurred throughout this region, and the population density is everywhere greater than 13 persons per square mile.

The cultivation of cereals is uneconomic in the steppe region of the south, except where irrigation has been well planned and where the soil is also favourable. A certain amount of local nomadism occurs, but this is declining as a way of life. The population density is between 1 and 13 persons per square mile.

Beyond this lies the Saharan *bled,* an area where true nomads are to be found and where groves of palm trees dot the landscape. The population density falls below one person per square mile. Inequality of population distribution is caused not only by the establishment of towns but also by density variations in purely rural areas, varying from 420 persons per square mile in the *wilāya* (*département;* province) of Tizi-Ouzou to 41 in the Tiaret *wilāya,* and to about 12 in the *wilāya* of Saïda. The town versus country division is nevertheless important. During Algeria's War of Independence, which ended in 1962, the French colonial authorities moved more than 2,000,000 Algerians to 1,800 centres in an attempt to remove them from the control of the Algerian nationalists' Army of National Liberation. After independence these centres were abandoned, and it is believed that about 500,000 Algerians returned to the towns. This sudden upheaval accelerated the pace of the continual exodus from the country to the towns that is occurring. The reasons for this exodus are principally to be found in the agrarian system, which does not allow for demographic growth. The movement is facilitated by improvements in transportation and further accelerated by natural disasters, such as droughts or floods, and by the ravages of desertification. The consequences are many—sociopolitical, for example, with the Arabization of the Berber-speaking people in the large towns; and demographic, with the imbalance that results from the departure of single men from the countryside. Economic consequences also follow—changes in social and administrative organization, the destruction of pastureland by neglect, and a diminution of the *khamesat* (tenant famer) system and of nomadism.

The exodus to the towns

THE PEOPLE

The peoples of Algeria represent diversity in unity—a diversity and a unity formed of many different cultural zones that are subtly interconnected. Among these are the Tell and the Sahara; the mountains, the plains, and the plateaus; the world of the nomad as opposed to that of the sedentary farmer—not to speak of the intermediate world of the semi-nomad. The diversity is also represented not only by the people themselves but by the kind of houses that they live in—the terraced houses of the Aurès and the Mzab regions; the tiled roofs of the Kabylie dwellings; the cupolas on houses in the Souf, a cluster of oases towns northeast of Touggourt; the Moorish style of architecture in the towns. Still further marks of division are to be found between the closely grouped houses of those who have long been accustomed to a settled way of life and the dispersed habitations of those who have only recently adopted a sedentary life style. Other distinctions may be drawn between the original Berber population and the Arab "newcomers" from the east. Yet Algeria's long and checkered history has resulted in so thorough an intermingling of the population that it is extremely difficult to distinguish perfectly pure ethnic types. Although the Berbers constitute the main element in the population of the country and the Arabs the minority that has strongly influenced them, no clear ethnic frontier between the two groups can now be drawn. Berber-speakers as well as Arabic-speakers can, of course, be found; there are many cultural differences—represented for example by the antithesis between Berber law and Muslim law. Most of the Berbers, however, are Arabic-speaking, and other differences are usually obscured by a host of nuances and intermediate transitional zones. In art, however, the two cultural poles are represented by the opposition between the stark rectilinear style of Berber decoration and the more slender and supple lines of the Arab style.

The Arab and Berber cultures

Among the intermingling of cultures, certain relatively clear-cut cultural zones can nevertheless be distinguished. Thus, wherever the Berber language has been preserved—that is to say, essentially in the mountainous massifs of the Kabylie and the Aurès—not only particular cultural traits have been maintained but also an original life style. Among other things, a certain independence from Islām may be observed. In the Mzab region a similar independence is also manifest, above all in the juridical domain, in an attachment to the soil, in the heavy labour used to make it productive, and in the egalitarian social structure. If it is true, on the one hand, that the Arab nomads have introduced their own system of values marked by a detachment so far as ownership of land is concerned, by an "aristocratic" social orientation, and by a pastoral way of life, it would nevertheless be unwise for either group to challenge the other. The Arab tribe is not separable from its territorial patrimony, which is, moreover, clearly defined to prevent encroachments from rivals; likewise, yet differently, the social structure of Berber society is patterned on genealogy. Between the two systems a constant dialogue is in progress, a dialogue that is founded upon a deep affinity and that is dominated by the temptation to seek identification with the other as well as by the will to affirm a distinct identity.

Seen as a whole, from its populated plains to its desert extremities, the country appears divided into such an apparently haphazard variety of groups that it might be imagined that it would disintegrate into individual units. To this tendency, however, is opposed the intense interpenetrating circulation that characterizes the whole. This takes such forms as the migrations of shepherds, the cycle of markets (which provides occasions for juridical and cultural exchanges), and the expansion of the urban areas. The Muslim faith also provides unity, and religious centres are the focusses where orthodoxy and Eastern civilization intermingle. Diversity of speech exists, but general reference is made to the same sacred language—Arabic. In effect the two antithetical aspects of Algerian life—unity and plurality, compartmentalization and continuity—can be understood only in relationship to each other. In Algeria, as in the Maghrib as a whole, there is no closed society, no group so isolated or so involved with its own affairs that it does not to some extent relate itself to other entities or to outside ways. All these cultural considerations, moreover, do not include the factors brought into play by the contacts between European civilization and Maghribian civilization or the upheavals experienced as a result of the colonial era. (A.K.Ch./Ed.)

THE ECONOMY

Algeria is an important oil-producing country and is among the leading exporters of liquefied natural gas and a major exporter of wine. It is also an important producer of cork and dates. Until 1962 the economy was largely rural-based and complementary to that of France. Since independence, however, production of oil and especially natural gas has come into its own, and industrialization has proceeded rapidly. Trade shifted from France, formerly accounting for four-fifths of exports and imports, to the United States and the Common Market countries after independence.

Since the mid-1960s there have been several abortive attempts to establish a Maghrib economic community with Algeria's neighbouring North African states, Tunisia and Morocco. If the plan ever becomes a reality, Algeria would certainly be the best placed to use the larger market to fortify its industrial and economic growth.

Resources. *Mineral resources.* Extensive deposits of sulfur-free, light crude oil were discovered in the Algerian Sahara in the mid-1950s. Production began in 1958, concentrated in three main fields: Hassi Messaoud North, Hassi Messaoud South, and Zarzaitine-Edjeleh. Established reserves in the early 1980s were estimated at around 8,200,000,000 barrels.

Oil and natural gas

Deposits of natural gas were first discovered at Hassi R'Mel in 1956, and since then discoveries have also been made at several other fields. Proved reserves were put at more than 132,000,000,000,000 cubic feet in the early 1980s. The gas has a methane content of almost 85 percent and also contains ethane, propane, and helium. Liquefaction plants were located at Arzew, Skikda, and Bejaïa.

The country has extensive deposits of high-grade iron ore, mainly at Ouenza. There are major deposits of medium-grade ore at Gara Djebilet, near Tindouf.

Deposits of nonferrous metal ores are smaller and more

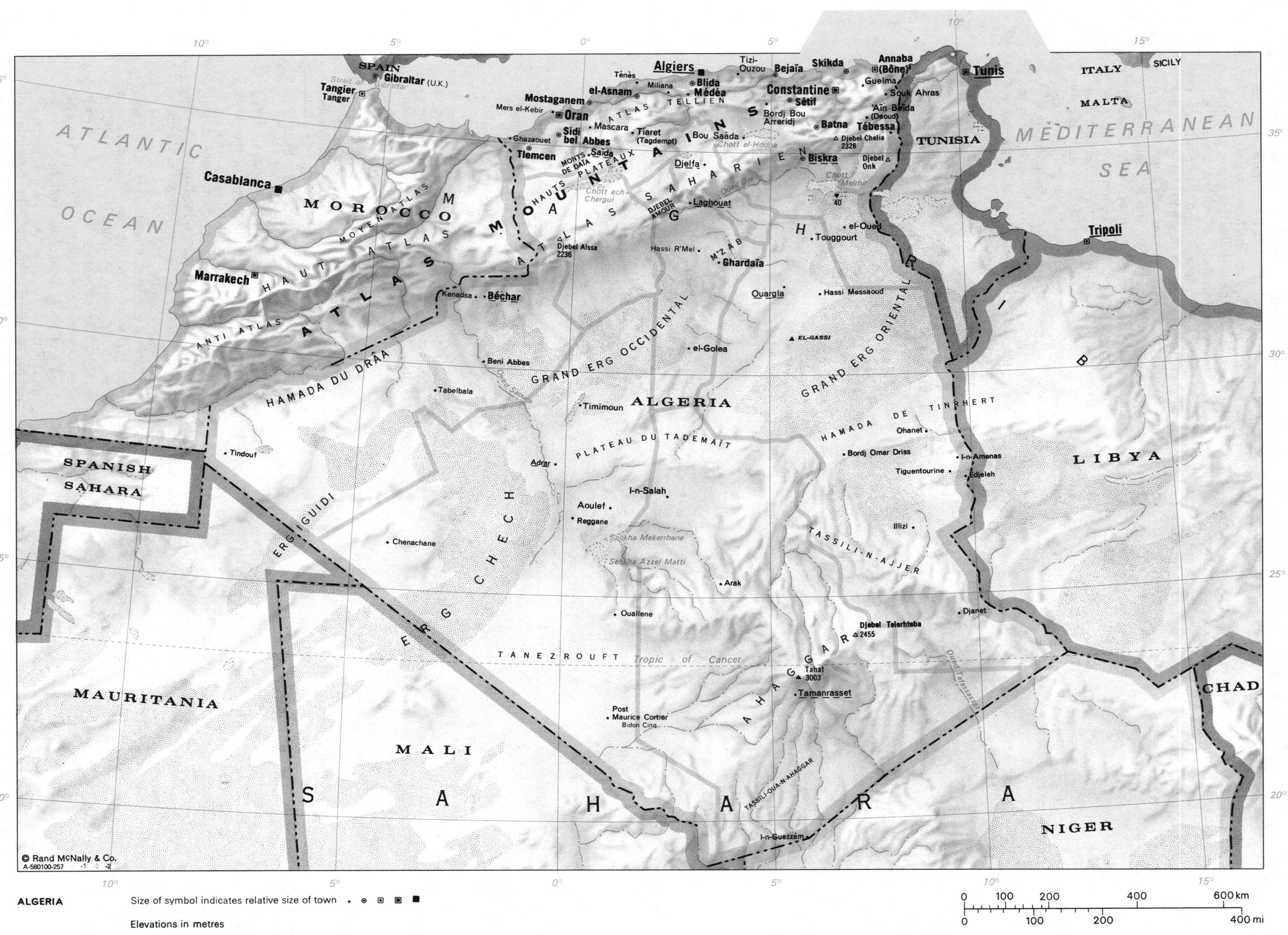

ALGERIA

Size of symbol indicates relative size of town

Elevations in metres

0 100 200 400 600 km

0 100 200 400 mi

ALGERIA

MAP INDEX

Cities and towns

Name	Lat.	Long.
Adrar	27·51n	0·19w
'Aïn Beïda (Daoud)	35·48n	7·23e
Aïn Salah, see I-n-Salah		
Algiers	36·42n	3·08e
Annaba (Bône)	36·54n	7·46e
Aoulef	26·55n	1·02e
Arak	25·18n	3·42e
Batna	35·34n	6·11e
Béchar	31·37n	2·13w
Bejaïa (Bougie)	36·45n	5·05e
Beni Abbes	30·05n	2·10w
Bidon Cinq, see Post Maurice Cortier		
Biskra	34·50n	5·43e
Blida	36·30n	2·49e
Bône, see Annaba		
Bordj Bou Arreridj	36·02n	4·46e
Bordj Omar Driss	28·09n	6·49e
Bougie, see Bejaïa		
Bou Saâda	35·11n	4·09e
Chenachane	26·04n	4·15w
Constantine	36·25n	6·38e
Daoud, see 'Aïn Beïda		
Djanet	24·33n	9·29e
Djelfa	34·41n	3·15e
Edjeleh	27·49n	9·57e
el-Asnam (Orléansville)	36·10n	1·20e
el-Golea	30·35n	2·53e
el-Oued	33·20n	6·52e
Ghardaïa	32·31n	3·41e
Ghazaouet	35·06n	1·51w
Guelma	36·28n	7·26e
Hassi Messaoud	31·40n	6·08e
Hassi R'mel	32·56n	3·16e
Illizi	26·29n	8·28e
I-n-Amenas	28·05n	9·30e
I-n-Guezzâm	19·32n	5·42e
I-n-Salah (Aïn Salah)	27·12n	2·28e
Kenadsa	31·34n	2·27w
Laghouat	33·50n	2·53e
Mascara	35·24n	0·08e
Médéa	36·16n	2·45e
Mers el-Kebir	35·45n	0·43w
Messaoud, North and South, see Hassi Messaoud		
Miliana	36·16n	2·13e
Mostaganem	35·56n	0·07e
Ohanet	28·32n	8·50e
Oran (Ouahran)	35·43n	0·38w
Orléansville, see el-Asnam		
Ouallene	24·37n	1·14e
Ouargla	31·59n	5·20e
Philippeville, see Skikda		
Post Maurice Cortier (Bidon Cinq)	22·18n	1·05e
Reggane	26·42n	0·10e
Saïda	34·50n	0·11e
Sétif	36·09n	5·26e
Sidi bel Abbes	35·13n	0·38w
Skikda (Philippeville)	36·50n	6·58e
Souk Ahras	36·17n	7·57e
Tabelbala	29·23n	3·15w
Tagdempt, see Tíaret		
Tamanrasset	22·50n	5·25e
Tébessa	35·24n	8·09e
Ténès	36·31n	1·19e
Tíaret (Tagdempt)	35·23n	1·21e
Tiguentourine	27·50n	8·43e
Timimoun	29·14n	0·16e
Tindouf	27·40n	8·08w
Tizi-Ouzou	36·43n	4·02e
Tlemcen	34·52n	1·15w
Touggourt	33·06n	6·04e

Physical features and points of interest

Name	Lat.	Long.
Ahaggar, *mountains*	23·00n	6·30e
Ahaggar, Tassili-oua-n-, *plateau*	21·00n	5·00e
Aïssa, Djebel, *mountain*	32·56n	0·38w
Ajjer, Tassili-n-, *mountains*	25·54n	70·48e
Amour, Djebel, *mountains*	33·50n	2·05e
Atlas Mountains	33·00n	2·00w
Atlas Saharien, *mountains*	33·25n	1·20e
Atlas Tellien, *mountains*	35·00n	3·00e
Azzel Matti, Sebkha, *salt flat*	25·55n	0·56e
Chech, Erg, *desert*	25·00n	2·15w
Chelia, Djebel, *mountain*	35·19n	6·42e
Chergui, Chott ech-, *lake*	34·15n	0·30e
Daïa, Monts de, *mountains*	34·39n	0·15w
Drâa, Hamada du, *plateau*	29·00n	6·45w
el-Gassi, *gasfield*	31·05n	5·40e
Grand Erg Occidental, *desert*	30·30n	0·30e
Grand Erg Oriental, *desert*	30·30n	7·00e
Hodna, Chott el-, *lake*	35·30n	4·45e
Hoggar, see Ahaggar, Tassili du		
Iguidi, Erg, *dunes*	26·35n	5·40w
Maghrib, *physical region*	33·00n	5·00e
Mekerrhane, Sebkha, *salt flat*	26·19n	1·20e
Melrhir, Chott, *lake*	34·17n	6·24e
M'zab, *physical region*	32·43n	3·50e
Onk, Djebel, *mountain*	34·52n	7·57e
Saoura, Oued, *watercourse*	29·00n	0·55w
Tademaït, Plateau du	28·30n	2·00e
Tafassasset, Oued, *watercourse*	25·15n	10·15e
Tahat, *mountain*	23·18n	5·47e
Tanezrouft, *desert*	24·00n	0·45w
Telerhteba, Djebel, *mountain*	24·09n	6·58e
Tinrhert, Hamada de, *plateau*	29·00n	9·00e

scattered. There are, however, sizable deposits of zinc and lead at el-Abed on the Moroccan border near Tlemcen, and at Bou Caid and Ain Barbar, and of mercury ore at Azzaba. Various studies have been undertaken to see how best to exploit the other unmined deposits of these minerals, as well as the known reserves of copper and pyrites, and intensive prospecting for minerals in the Ahaggar has been carried out with Soviet assistance. Traces of tin, nickel, cobalt, chrome, and uranium have been found, and there are also high hopes of finding tungsten, gold, platinum, and diamonds. Development of the Ahaggar Mountain uranium deposits began in the early 1980s.

Phosphate deposits of relatively inferior grade are mined south of Tébessa at Djebel Onk on the Tunisian border. Sizable kaolin deposits at Djebel Debbagh and large reserves of marble and onyx have been found.

Biological resources. The country's intensively cultivated land is restricted almost entirely to the narrow coastal plain that was colonized under French rule, when the settlers established vineyards, orchards, citrus groves, and farms. The best farms were located in the well-watered and fertile plains around Bejaïa and Annaba in the east, in the Mitidja Plain south of Algiers, and beyond Oran from Sidi bel Abbes to Tlemcen. The Médéa and Mascara plateaus are also ideal for grapes. The mountains that isolate the coastal plain from the south are heavily covered with dense forests of cork oak and cedar in the east and of pine in the west. Behind the mountain chains lie dry plateaus—notably the Plains of Constantine in the east and the Sersou Plateau to the west—where cereals are grown. In the Aurès region to the east, cereals are grown on the mountain slopes, and there are orchards in the valleys. In the west there is a large natural crop of esparto grass, between 150,000 and 200,000 tons a year, grown on some 7,500,000 acres (3,000,000 hectares).

Shortage of arable land

More than four-fifths of the country's surface land area, 588,700,000 acres (238,200,000 hectares), is uncultivable, and erosion annually adds another 100,000 to the total. An estimated 72,200,000 acres in the Sahara can be classed as semidesert pasture. About 11,000,000 acres are covered by forests. Most of the agricultural land is pasture or scrubland. The rest is tilled or devoted to vineyards and orchards. Winter grains (wheat, barley, and oats) are grown on the largest area of arable land. Cotton, tobacco, olives, and dates are important, and sorghum, millet, corn (maize), rye, rice, and truck vegetable crops are also grown.

The climate is ill suited to extensive stock raising, but there are cattle, goats, and sheep.

Water resources. Irregular rainfall has long been a threat to agriculture and has limited hydroelectric development. At independence, Algeria possessed some 20 sizable dams, altogether holding only 53,000,000,000 cubic feet (1,500,000,000 cubic metres) of water a year. By the 1980s dams had brought more than 850,000 acres under irrigation, and additional dams were being constructed.

Agriculture, forestry, and fishing. There are privately owned farms covering 14,400,000 acres, all but 5 percent being used to grow cereals. Yields per acre, however, are only three-fifths of those recorded for state-owned farms. More than half of the farms occupy less than 13 acres (five hectares) each, and 98 percent are less than 125 acres (50 hectares) each.

State-owned farms

Farms owned by the state account for a large percentage of output, which includes wine production, citrus fruits, and vegetable crops. These farms are those that were vacated by the French settlers in 1962. They were run by independent workers' committees until more direct centralized control was instituted in the late 1960s. Starting in 1971 large Algerian holdings were broken up and redistributed to peasant cooperatives.

Efforts are being made to increase the output of cereals and other crops so that imports can be reduced. Following the French government's policy of reducing wine imports to protect its own peasant growers, the Algerian authorities decided to convert older, less profitable vineyards to other uses.

Some cork is processed domestically. About 160,000 acres of forest were lost in the War of Independence, adding to the serious problem of soil erosion. Starting in 1967 a belt of trees, mainly Aleppo pines, was planted across the Atlas Saharien from Tunisia to Morocco to halt desertification.

The fishing industry is underdeveloped, but the state fishing authority planned to acquire new trawlers and equipment to increase the catch.

Mining and quarrying. The country's main mining centres are at Ouenza and Djebel Onk on the eastern border with Tunisia and at el-Abed and Bou Caid, Ain Barbar, and Béchar, all on the western boundary with Morocco. An electrified railway links the Ouenza and Djebel Onk workings to Annaba, while both el-Abed and Béchar have rail links with Oran.

The opencut works at Ouenza produces over 3,000,000 tons of high-grade iron ore each year. Output of phosphates is from the Djebel Onk mines. Some of the iron ore and phosphates are exported, but following the completion of steel and fertilizer complexes most production was diverted to them. There are also plans to supply the steelworks with coke from the Béchar coal mines.

El-Abed is Algeria's largest zinc and lead mine, producing most of the nation's output of zinc and lead.

Industry. Before independence the manufacturing sector was mainly confined to food processing, textiles, cigarettes, and clothing. Since 1967, however, the main emphasis has been put on heavy industry. The state steel corporation completed its Annaba steelworks and constructed a zinc electrolysis plant near the el-Abed mine at Ghazaouet. Another steel plant at el-Hadjer started production in the early 1980s, and a third plant at Jijel was under construction. Much of the steel produced for domestic consumption is allocated for producing machine tools, tractors, agricultural equipment, trucks, and automobiles. In addition to the gas liquefaction plants at Arzew and Bejaïa, a nitrogenous fertilizer factory, an oil refinery, and a liquid petroleum gas separation plant were completed near Arzew. Another gas liquefaction plant, an ethylene factory, and a liquid petroleum gas separation works were opened at Skikda, while a plastics factory and a benzene refinery were completed. The Sétif complex comprises methanol and plastics factories. Another major project in the heavy industry sector is the phosphate fertilizer factory at Annaba.

Steel production

State corporations also dominate the light manufacturing sector. Much of the output in this sector comes from state-run canneries and mills. The state textile concern produces yarn, and the state tannery produces leather for shoes.

Energy. Following the discovery of oil in the mid-1950s the main prospecting and producing companies were two French groups, CFP-A (Compagnie Française des Pétroles Algérie) and ERAP (Entreprise de Recherches et d'Activités Pétrolières). They were later followed by some of the international oil companies. In the late 1960s there were frequent arguments over the terms of the agreement, the Algerians claiming that the French companies were not doing as much prospecting as had been agreed to. Consequently the state-owned Algerian oil concern, Sonatrach (Société Nationale pour la Recherche, la Production, le Transport, la Transformation et la Commercialisation des Hydrocarbures), which had been set up in 1963–64, extended its activities into exploitation and production on its own account with some success. Much of this development was accomplished with Soviet assistance and more recently by setting up a series of joint service companies with American specialist help.

In a series of moves from 1967 to 1970 the international oil companies were nationalized. In 1971 Algeria nationalized the majority shares in the French companies operating in the country.

Basically there are four pipeline links between the oil fields and the Mediterranean: the line from Hassi Messaoud to Arzew, with a 22,000,000-ton annual capacity; the twin pipes from Hassi Messaoud to Bejaïa, with an 18,000,000-ton annual capacity; the line from In Amenas and Djelem north to aṣ-Ṣukhayrah (La Skhira) in Tunisia, which has a 15,500,000-ton annual capacity; and the line from Hassi Messaoud to Skikda, which began its operations with a 12,000,000-ton annual capacity. The Trans-Mediterranean natural gas pipeline from Tunisia to Sicily and Naples was completed in 1981. Exports of natural gas have proved more important for the economy than sales of oil.

Production of natural gas

Finance and trade. An independent central bank, established at the beginning of 1963, has the sole right to issue bank notes in Algeria and also carries out the normal central banking duties. Since nationalization there have only been four state-owned commercial banks, but in 1983 a bank for industry, manufacturing, and services opened.

The value of Algerian exports climbed mainly due to increased shipments of oil and natural gas that accounted for more than 95 percent of total revenue. Following the imposition of French restrictions, wine-export receipts fell sharply.

Trade with France

Algerian trade with France dropped from 80 percent of the total in 1961 to less than one-fifth in the late 20th century. Attempts to increase trade with Communist countries have partly failed, most of the former French trade going to other Common Market countries. The Algerians in France remit substantial sums of money each year to relatives in Algeria, and this is partly responsible for the healthy balance-of-payments position.

Administration of the economy. *The private sector.* Following independence many firms were taken over by their workers and more recently the government has nationalized many of the remaining privately owned businesses. This was done both to give the government the direct means of dealing with chronic stagnation and mass unemployment and to bring pressure to bear on foreign interests. There is still, however, a sizable private sector in the textile, rubber, plastics, and engineering industries, and in 1982 a new private sector investment code spurred trade, housing, handicrafts, and light industry.

The public sector. Since independence the public sector has expanded considerably and by the 1970s there were well over 30 national corporations and boards that had monopoly powers in various industries. The most important is undoubtedly the oil, gas, and petrochemicals giant, Sonatrach; in 1971 it controlled over three-quarters of oil production, the entire refining and oil distribution network, and all natural gas operations. Other corporations and boards operate in steel, shipping, power, engineering, textiles, glass, timber, cork, ports, pasta, canning, chemicals, wine marketing, sugar, tobacco, construction, exports, road transport, tanning, and the railways. In the early 1980s most of the larger state corporations were subdivided and partly decentralized.

Transportation. A good road network exists in the Tell, and there are established routes and motor transport for passengers and freight across the Sahara. Roads have also been built to link the Sahara oil fields with the coastal ports. The Société Nationale des Transports Routiers (SNTR), a government agency, was created to coordinate road transport. Small trucks have been brought into service for use in regions where the terrain or the state of the roads does not permit larger vehicles to pass.

The railroads. A central rail line runs from the Moroccan to the Tunisian frontier, with branch lines to the chief ports, as well as lines running southward from Oran to Crampel, Kenadsa, and Mehdia; from Algiers to Djelfa; and from the coastal ports Skikda and Annaba to Touggourt, Khenchela, and Tébessa. The Algerian railroad system is operated by the Société Nationale des Chemins de Fer Algériens (SNCFA).

The ports. The principal ports are Algiers, Oran, Annaba, Arzew, Bejaïa, Djidjello, Ghazaouet, and Mostaganem; Skikda is an oil port; and construction of a steel export port at Djenden began in 1982.

Air services. Air Algérie, which is largely government sponsored, provides domestic as well as international air services. Algiers has an international airport, Dar el-Beïda, which is a principal stop on regular air routes between Europe and Africa south of the Sahara, as well as on routes connecting the Americas and Eastern countries.

ADMINISTRATIVE AND SOCIAL CONDITIONS

Government. The second Algerian Constitution, approved by referendum on November 19, 1976, and amended by the National Assembly in 1979, continued a presidential type of regime modified by the responsibility of the head of state to the National Assembly. The assembly comprises 281 deputies elected by universal adult suffrage to five-year terms. There is a single party, the Front de Libération Nationale (FLN), which plays a preponderant role.

Local government. The political life of the state depends upon the life of the commune, which constitutes the basic political unit.

All the citizens of Algeria are grouped together in communes, that is to say in smaller or larger collective groupings each of which has its own social, economic, and human particularities.

The Algerian government has thus committed itself to the belief that each communal unit can and will undertake responsibility for its own affairs while acting within the general framework of national evolution.

Administrative and political decentralization. The constitution of the popular communal assemblies permits the members of the same territorial grouping to choose from among themselves those whom they consider to be the most qualified to represent the commune for all purposes. In this way the administrative structure encourages local autonomy and the organizing of communal interests in the direction most favourable to their development.

Economic and cultural decentralization. The communal code, which provides a legal framework for economic and social policy, establishes six separate sectors of economic activity: agriculture, industry and crafts, distribution and transport, tourism, housing and environment, and education and culture.

Governmental control over the activities of the communes is restricted to the legal coordination of the different communal initiatives.

Communal finances. The resources of each commune vary. They are usually assured by the income from local taxes and by the sources of revenue turned over to the communes by the state. To render local activities more profitable, however, the commune is obliged to invest in equipment. In this connection the state intervenes to share out public finances with a threefold purpose; firstly, of correcting the more marked intercommunal imbalances from public funds; secondly, of providing direct financial aid that the commune may use to meet its most pressing requirements; and thirdly, of guaranteeing the fiscal receipts anticipated in the commune's budget. This interaction between the state and the communes requires a constant interpretation of governmental and local responsibility.

The wilāya. Between the central government and the commune there is an intermediate local authority—that of the *wilāya* (province, or *département*). The *wilāya* represents a decentralization of power by the creation of the Assemblée Populaire de Wilaya (APW)—the popular assembly of the *wilāya*—which is elected by universal suffrage.

The APW itself has an executive council, as well as a representative of the central government, who is known as the *wali.* The executive council of the *wilāya* is the chief regional authority. It is composed of different directors of the state services who are established in the *wilāya;* the *wilāya* is thus oriented to both regional and national levels. Under the authority of the *wali,* the *wilāya* exercises trusteeship and administrative control of the local collectives and of public establishments, as well as of independent enterprises and national societies. Within the national government it participates in the development and application of the general development plan and assists in coordination in matters that concern the *wilāya.*

The authority of the *wali*

The *wali* himself is nominated by decree. He is at the same time the sole and permanent representative of the central government as well as of the *wilāya.* He assumes those functions that must necessarily be called into play in the relationship between the governmental summit and the popular base. As the representative of the *wilāya* he presides over the implementation of the decisions of the APW. As a high state functionary, he is the delegate of the government and the direct representative of each of its ministers.

Justice. Following independence, Algeria inherited colonial judicial institutions that were primarily established in the larger towns where the European communities were concentrated, having previously been oriented toward the maintenance of colonial authority. A jurisdictional duality also existed, since judicial organization was founded upon the separate foundations of so-called common law and Muslim jurisdiction. On June 19, 1965, the entire system was reformed by a decree that instituted a new judicial organization. This decree was soon followed, in June 1966, by the promulgation of new legal codes—the penal code, the code of penal procedure, and the code of civil procedure. In formulating the new codes, the primary preoccupation was to make justice available to those who demanded it by permitting the citizen to appeal for justice with a minimum of delay and a maximum of efficaciousness. Fifteen courts and 132 tribunals were created, thus establishing a system of justice that covered the entire country, including the southern areas.

Three levels of justice were established. At the first level there exists the tribunal, to which civil and commercial litigation is submitted, and which takes action in penal cases of the first instance. A single judge is empowered at this level. At the second level there is the court, which consists of a college of three members. It functions as a court of appeal for the tribunals and for the administrative jurisdictions of the first instance. At the third and highest level is the supreme court, which checks and unifies the ensemble of jurisprudence. It enjoys the powers of a final court of appeal and of appeals against the decisions of the lower courts. In 1975 the Cour de Sûreté de l'État was created to handle cases involving state security.

Of the three fundamental legal documents on which the juridical system is based, the first—the penal code—reaffirms the principles protecting individual liberty; the second, the code of penal procedure, contains more detailed safeguards; while the third—the code of civil procedure—simplifies the conduct of judicial actions in order to eliminate delays, discourage abuses, and augment the efficiency of tribunals. The penal code was revised in 1982.

Three special courts for eliminating economic crimes against the state were established in 1966—those of Algiers, Oran, and Constantine; each is presided over by a member of the party and is composed of magistrates and of members representing the Ministry of Finance. Their decisions are without appeal.

A higher council of the magistrature is presided over by the head of state or by the minister of justice and is composed of a representative elected by magistrates, heads of the supreme court, party representatives, elected representatives, and of the administration; this higher council makes rulings on the recruitment, nomination, and promotion of magistrates. It also constitutes at the same time a disciplinary organ for the magistrates themselves.

Education. The educational system has experienced much difficulty in accommodating the increasing numbers of school-age children resulting from demographic growth. Because of the scarcity of teachers, the government is utilizing educational radio and television. Arabization is progressing in terms of the number of hours devoted to its teaching, and by the early 1980s the scarcity of qualified Arabic teachers was ameliorated by the recruitment of teachers from Egypt, Syria, and Tunisia. French is maintained as a medium of instruction at higher levels but in the 1980s public pressure grew to make Arabic the only language of instruction at all levels of education.

The first institute of technology, specializing in agriculture, was opened in 1970 at Mostagenem. The primary university in North Africa before independence—the University of Algiers—has been able, despite difficulties, to maintain its pride of place, thanks to a highly qualified faculty and to the preservation of its links with the French university system. Nine more universities had opened by 1982.

Health and welfare. Health policies in Algeria are primarily concerned with preventive medicine. Among health reforms recently instituted is a compulsory requirement that newly qualified doctors, surgeons, pharmacists, dentists, and midwives serve in state medical institutions for a time. Units providing free medical assistance are attached to various hospitals. Those earning middle incomes pay a part of their medical fees in proportion to their resources. Algeria as a whole is covered by a network of state pharmaceutical agencies, located mostly in the southern regions, in the more rural areas, and on the periphery of the nation's larger towns.

The state has established a monopoly for the importation of medical drugs, with a view to obtaining lower prices. A factory for the processing of pharmaceuticals has been established.

The Pasteur Institute, which is the central laboratory for

the public health system, produces serums and vaccines. It also conducts research in microbiology, human and animal parasitology, and other areas. There is also a National Institute of Public Health.

Algeria has a shortage of adequate housing. Apart from the maintenance and repair of many existing buildings, the government has assumed responsibility for the completion of housing programs that were abandoned following the massive exodus of French settlers to France after the achievement of independence. The construction of housing units with moderate rents has been subsidized by the government.

For statistical data on the land and people of Algeria, see the *Britannica World Data* section in the BRITANNICA WORLD DATA ANNUAL. (A.K.Ch.)

History

THE 19TH CENTURY

The French conquest of the regency of Algiers was not the result of a clearly thought-out plan. Too little was known about the regency's internal constitution to have permitted such a thing, even if British opposition to the installation in North Africa of a potentially dangerous rival could have been ignored.

Beginnings of French interference

In 1830, when a blockade of Algiers imposed by the French for an alleged insult to the French consul had proved ineffective, the French government decided on a full-scale attack on the city of Algiers. For the benefit of the Arab inhabitants a proclamation was prepared in Arabic and published in French in *Le Moniteur,* stating that the French were coming not to take permanent possession of the city but to expel the Turkish foreigners and make the Arabs masters of their own country; as issued later in Algiers, however, it simply stated that the French were coming to make war on the rulers and not on the people of the country. In addressing the European powers, the French gave as their motive the intention of ending a piratical regime that practiced the enslavement of Europeans. In fact, however, the possession of European slaves had been limited from the end of the 18th century to the state, from which they could be hired for domestic purposes. In any case, the decay of privateering and a British bombardment of Algiers in 1816 had already reduced their number to virtually nothing. In fact, the French decision had been determined by the desire to gratify the officer corps by a military success and thereby to strengthen the restoration regime of Charles X.

An attempt at mediation by the nominally suzerain Ottoman power was brought to naught by a French interception of the Turkish envoy. The collapse of privateering had by then left the regency a mere shadow of its former self and had caused the *dey*'s government to provoke the Arab and Berber population by increasing taxation to make up for the lost income. In consequence, the landing at Sidi Ferruj, 16 miles west of Algiers, on July 5, 1830, of a force of 37,000 French troops led to the capitulation of the *dey*'s government within three weeks. The *dey* was banished, together with the majority of the Turkish officials and volunteer forces. Within a fortnight of this success, the regime of Charles X was itself overthrown and succeeded by that of Louis-Philippe, which, in the circumstances, was as unwilling as its predecessor had been to define future North African policy. But this did not prevent the new minister of defense, himself a general, from instructing the new commander in chief, Gen. Bertrand Clauzel, to favour colonization. This was an example of the determining role French army officers played in deciding French action in Algeria during the next 40 years.

Left without any clear guidance from Paris, Clauzel decided to exercise control in Algeria through princes of the ruling family in Tunisia, whose ruler was allowed to understand that the whole regency might finally be entrusted to him. This prospect was gratifying to the Tunisian rulers, over whom the Algerian *deys* had made several efforts to establish their supremacy. The Tunisians briefly occupied Oran in 1830 but were unable to hold it and withdrew.

After only five months, Clauzel himself was withdrawn and was succeeded from February to December 1831 by Gen. Pierre Berthezène. Ordered to suspend the incipient colonization, of which he himself disapproved, Berthezène rapidly became unpopular with would-be settlers and the many speculators. He was succeeded by the Duke of Rovigo, who had been chief of police under Napoleon. After Rovigo's withdrawal 14 months later, because of illness, his drastic methods were criticized by a commission of inquiry, which charged some of the occupiers with barbarity. The commissioners concluded, however, that the regency of Algiers for reasons of utility, expediency, and necessity, should be definitely occupied by France. Accordingly, the officer responsible for the administration was known as "governor general of the French possessions in Africa" until 1845, when Gen. T.-R. Bugeaud, after achieving the conquest of the greater part of the country, was named "governor general of Algeria" (the latter name was a novelty introduced to describe the newly acquired territory).

Before this occurred, however, another ten years were to pass, during which the declared aim was to restrict French direct rule to the coastal area while authority inland was left in the hand of Algerians who, it was hoped, would cooperate with the invaders. In the east the outstanding opponent of the French was the *bey* Ahmad of Constantine (Qusṭanṭīnah), where a first attempt to capture the city in 1836 failed disastrously. Resistance in the west, organized by the famous Abdelkader (ʿAbd al-Qādir ibn Muḥyī ad-Dīn), developed a more national character and lasted 17 years.

Resistance to the French

Abdelkader, who was a *sharīf,* had been elected in 1832 on the plain outside his native town of Mascara as leader in the struggle against the Christian invasion and greeted by popular acclaim with the title of *amīr*. In this capacity he regarded himself as *khalīfah*, or representative, of the Moroccan sultan Abdurrahman. In 1833 the French, hoping to use Abdelkader as French agent, signed with him a convention that recognized his local position. Four years later the French government made a last attempt to limit its direct control, at least in western and central Algeria, to the coastal areas. General Bugeaud, now commanding in the Oran area, accordingly concluded with Abdelkader the Treaty of Tafna, which allotted Abdelkader Tlemcen and the whole of the western province except for the cities and environs of Oran, Arzew, and Mostaganem. In central Algeria, Abdelkader was ceded Titteri, while the French were limited to the coast and the Mitija plain, and were excluded from Constantine.

The French governor general, the Comte de Damrémont, disapproved of the arrangements and made a second attack on Constantine; this proved successful, though at the cost of his own life. His successor soon came into conflict with Abdelkader, who for the moment, however, was fully occupied in establishing an orderly form of government in the West.

In 1839, however, Abdelkader denounced with some reason French violation of the Treaty of Tafna and then attacked the Mitija, destroying the settlers' farms, until Bugeaud, converted to the idea of total conquest, was given command and supplied with adequate resources from France. A six years' struggle followed, involving the wholesale destruction of Algerian villages, the spreading of desolation far and wide, and the death by hunger of thousands of refugees.

Total conquest of Algeria

In 1844 Abdelkader was forced westward into Moroccan territory, whereupon the sultan, Moulay Afd ar-Rahman, alarmed at the French advance, sent an army to the frontier. This was ignominiously defeated by Bugeaud on August 14 at Isly near Oujda. Meanwhile, French ships bombarded the Moroccan ports of Tangier and Mogador. The sultan was thus forced to agree to expel Abdelkader or hand him over to the French.

Abdelkader nevertheless fought on for more than two years. In 1847 Bugeaud, now promoted to a marshal of France and designated governor general of Algeria, decided to complete the conquest of the Kabylie Berber area, employing the same methods of devastation as in the west. Though successful, he was forced to resign for having acted without the sanction of the minister of war. His place was taken by the Duc d'Aumale, son of King Louis-Philippe. During the four months during which d'Aumale held the post, the sultan's troops expelled Abdelkader, who had again taken refuge in Morocco, and who finally surrendered with the promise that he would be allowed to live in the Orient.

In spite of this, Abdelkader was detained, first at Pau and then in the château of Amboise, until released by Napoleon III. He was then permitted to live in Damascus, where he saved the lives of a great many Christians during the massacres of 1860. Though Abdelkader's exile marked the end of what may be called resistance on a national scale, smaller operations continued, such as the occupation of the Saharan oases (Zaatcha in 1849, Nara in 1850, and Wargla in 1852). The eastern Kabylie country was only subdued in 1857, while the final great Kabylie rising of Moqrani was suppressed in 1871. The Saharan regions of Touat and Gourara, hitherto Moroccan spheres of influence, were occupied in 1900; the Tindouf area, previously regarded as Moroccan rather than Algerian, was only attached to the latter region after the French occupation of the Anti-Atlas in 1934.

French Algeria. The French thus carried on the policy, initiated by the Turks, of making Algeria the base of their rule in North Africa and of increasing their territory by bringing under Algerian control areas that had hitherto looked rather to the older established regimes of Tunis or Morocco both for spiritual leadership and for defense against outside attack. The final outcome of this process was to be the creation of what was known as French Algeria.

Administration. For the French officer corps the preservation of the conquest became a vocation and a point of honour. In the political field their influence was represented by the governor general, almost invariably drawn until 1880 from the armed forces, and by the Bureaux Arabes, whose members (officers with an intimate knowledge of local affairs and of the language of the people), having no direct financial interest, often sympathized with the outlook of the people they administered rather than with the demands of the European colonists.

European–Muslim relations. A large-scale confiscation of cultivable land, following the crushing of resistance, made colonization possible. By 1880 the coastal area had become a predominantly Christian area of mixed European origin (mainly Spanish in and around Oran; French, Italian, and Maltese in the centre and east). For long the presence of the non-French settlers was officially regarded with alarm; but, with time, the influence of French education, of the Muslim environment, and of the Algerian climate created in the non-French a European-Algerian, subnational sentiment. This would probably have resulted, in time, in a movement to create an independent state if Algeria had been situated farther away from Paris and if the inhabitants had not feared the potential strength of the Muslim majority. As it was, however, each weakening, even temporary, of the authority of the French government led to the increased influence of the settlers and to a renewed rising and suppression of the Muslims.

Influence of European settlers

On the overthrow of Louis-Philippe's regime in 1848, the settlers succeeded in having the territory declared French and the three former Turkish provinces converted into departments on the French model, while colonization was developed with renewed energy. On the establishment of the French Empire in 1852, responsibility for Algeria was at first transferred from Algiers to a minister in Paris. Very soon, however, the Emperor reversed this disposition. While expressing the hope that an increased number of settlers would forever keep Algeria French, he also declared that France's first duty was to the 3,000,000 Arabs. With considerable accuracy he declared that Algeria was "not a French province but an Arab country, a European colony, and a French camp."

This attitude aroused certain hopes in Arab minds, but they were destroyed by the Emperor's downfall in 1870. The French defeat in the Franco-Prussian war gave impetus to the last great Kabylie rising (1871) under Muḥammad al-Moqrani. Its suppression by French forces was followed by the sequestration of another 11,000,000 acres of land and the imposition of an indemnity of 36,500,000 francs; these measures together provided land for refugees from Alsace and capital with which to exploit the land.

During the 50 years that followed, the European population felt free to establish political, economic, and social domination over the country and its native inhabitants. At the same time, new communications, the installation of hospitals and medical services, and modern education—dispensed to a very limited extent and in French to the Muslims, while generally available to the Europeans—created a minority of Algerians of a new type.

Domination by European population

For Algerians, service in the army and in the factories of France during World War I was another eye-opening experience. When peace returned, some 70,000 Algerians remained in France, and by living with extreme economy they were able to support many thousands of their relations in Algeria.

Nationalist movement. The French believed that the Algerians did not want independence but to merge themselves in France. In thinking thus, the French were fixing their gaze on the tiny minority who had received a French education and who saw the salvation of the mass of their compatriots in the extension to them of a similar assimilation. But the French ignored two other groups. Algerians mainly in France, under the leadership of Ahmed Messali Hadj, had formed an Algerian and nationalist movement that, from 1936, took the title of the Parti du Peuple Algérien. In Algeria itself there came into being another movement, led by a man of Muslim religious learning, Shaykh abd al-Hamid ben Badis; this was the Association of Algerian Ulama, which founded schools that taught in Arabic.

The popular front government in Paris was well disposed toward the assimilationist movement, but when in 1937 it took tentative steps in that direction the opposition of the settlers brought its efforts to nothing.

WORLD WAR II AND THE INDEPENDENCE MOVEMENT

World War II brought with it the collapse of France and, in 1942, the Anglo-American occupation of North Africa. The occupation forces were to some extent automatically agents of emancipation, while broadcasts in Arabic both from Allied and Axis stations began to compete with promises of a brave new world for formerly subject peoples. The effect was heightened by the promise of the emancipation of Syria and Lebanon, given in June 1941 by the Free French and backed by the British authorities in the Middle East.

In December 1942 the former assimilationist leader Ferhat Abbas drafted an Algerian Manifesto, for presentation to the Allied as well as to French authorities, seeking recognition of the political autonomy of Algeria as a sovereign nation. In December 1943 Gen. Charles de Gaulle declared that, because of loyalty shown, France was under an obligation to the Muslims of North Africa, and in March 1944 French citizenship was extended to certain categories of Muslims. This was by then, however, far from enough to satisfy Muslim opinion. A display of Algerian nationalist flags at Sétif in May 1945 led to an unorganized rising, in which 84 European settlers were massacred. The suppression that followed was indiscriminate, and it resulted, according to a French committee of inquiry, in not less than 1,800 deaths.

The Algerian Manifesto

On September 20, 1947, a statute of Algeria was finally voted by the French Assembly, defining the country as "a group of departments endowed with a civic personality, financial autonomy, and a special organization." The statute created an Algerian Assembly of 120 deputies, elected in equal numbers by two electoral colleges—one composed of 370,000 Europeans and 60,000 assimilated Muslims and the other of 1,300,000 Muslims. After lengthy debates the statute was passed by a small majority, with 15 Muslim members abstaining. Muslims were at last to be considered as full French citizens with the right to keep their personal Qur'ānic status and were granted the right to work in France without further formalities. The military territories of the south were to be abolished, and Arabic was to be taught in schools at all levels.

Unfortunately, the implementation of this law was poor

and the subsequent elections were "managed" by the administration, while most of the reforms laid down by the statute remained a dead letter. In spite of this, Algeria remained quiet. The principal change had been the fact that some 350,000 Algerian workers—five times as many as in the post-World War I period—were able to establish themselves in France and remit money to Algeria.

The Algerian War. Signs of approaching storm, however, were only too apparent. In 1950 the French police discovered that a robbery of the Oran post office had been the work of the Organisation Secrète, an offshoot of the party led by Messali Hadj, which had taken the name of the Movement for the Triumph of Democratic Liberties (MTLD). The leader in the robbery was Ahmed Ben Bella, who had been highly commended during the fighting in Italy with the Free French. In 1952 Ferhat Abbas, when tried for a trivial offense, was defended by three lawyers—one Muslim, one Christian, and one Jewish; these combined to deliver an impressive attack on the administration. About the same time, Aḥmad Mezerna, acting head of the MTLD, took the unprecedented step of personally seeking support in Egypt. The head of the Association of Algerian Ulama toured the Arab East and secured scholarships from the Arab governments for Algerians who wished to pursue their studies in Arabic.

The storm burst on the night of October 31, 1954. It was organized by a few young men who, dissatisfied with Messali Hadj's leadership, had decided that justice for Algeria could only be realized by the stimulus of open rebellion. The movement took the title of the Front of National Liberation (FLN) and issued a leaflet stating that the aim was the restoration of a sovereign Algerian state. It advocated social democracy within an Islāmic framework and citizenship for any resident in Algeria, with the same rights and duties as other citizens. A preamble recognized that Algeria had fallen behind the other Arab states in emancipating itself socially and nationally, but it claimed that this could be remedied by a difficult and prolonged struggle. Two weapons would be used—guerrilla warfare at home and diplomatic activity abroad, particularly at the United Nations, where the support of the Arab countries and other states would be invaluable. The FLN military objective was to make the position of the administration untenable by sudden raids, ambushes, and sabotage.

The Front of National Liberation

Though the first outbreak, which occurred in the region of Batna and the Aurès, was ineffective militarily, it led to the arrest of some 2,000 members of the MTLD, who had not in fact been in favour of open rebellion. In mid-February 1955 Jacques Soustelle arrived in Algiers as governor general; in June he announced a new plan, which, however, was to prove too little and too late. On August 20 a new rising at Aïn Abid, about 27 miles from Constantine, and at the mine of al-Alia near Philippeville (now Skikda) degenerated into another massacre of Europeans, followed by summary executions of Muslims. In January 1956 the electoral victory of the Republican Front in France and the premiership of Guy Mollet led to the appointment of the moderate and experienced Gen. Georges Catroux as governor general. When Mollet personally visited Algiers, however, to prepare the way for the new governor general, he was bombarded by the European populace with tomatoes. Yielding to this pressure, he allowed Catroux to withdraw and named in his place the pugnacious Socialist Robert Lacoste as resident minister. Lacoste's policy was described as pacification, but in fact it relied on forcible suppression.

French forces sent to Algeria

A French army of 500,000 men was sent to Algeria to counter the control that the rebels had managed to establish in the more out-of-the-way portions of the country while collecting money for their cause and taking reprisals against fellow Muslims who would not cooperate with them. By May the rebels had won over the majority of previously noncommitted political leaders; and Ferhat Abbas and Tawfiq al-Madani, of the Association of Algerian Ulama, had joined FLN leaders in Cairo.

Externally, the event of 1956 was the French decision to grant full independence to Morocco and Tunisia and to concentrate on retaining "French Algeria." The rulers of the newly independent states—the Moroccan sultan and Premier Habib Bourguiba of Tunisia—hoping also to find an acceptable solution to the Algerian problem, prepared to hold a meeting in Tunis with five principal Algerian leaders who had been guests of the sultan in Rabat. French intelligence officers, however, managed to divert to Algiers the plane chartered by the Moroccan government to fly the Algerians to Tunis. The Algerian leaders were then arrested and confined in prison in France for the next six years. Far from decapitating the rising, this act provoked an outbreak in Meknès that cost the lives of 40 French settlers before the newly independent Moroccan government could restore order.

In the next year, 1957, the rebels attempted to paralyze the administration of Algiers by terrorism. This was defeated by French parachute troops, who used torture to extract information. The French also cut Algeria off from independent Tunisia and Morocco by barbed wire fences, illuminated at night by searchlights; this separated the resistance bands within Algeria from some 30,000 Algerian armed forces who occupied positions between the fortified fences and the actual frontiers of Tunisia and Morocco, from which they drew supplies. These troops had the advantage of a friendly people and government as a base; they could not, however, penetrate into Algeria proper but could only harass the French line.

Provoked by these assaults, the French air force in February 1958 bombed the Tunisian frontier village of Sāqiyat Sīdī Yūsuf, killing a number of civilians, including children from the local school. This led to an Anglo-American mediation mission, which negotiated the withdrawal of French troops from various districts of Tunisia and their concentration in the naval base of Bizerte (Banzart).

A meeting—the Maghrib Unity Congress—was held in Tangier from April 27 to 30 under the auspices of the Moroccan and Tunisian nationalist parties and the Algerian FLN. This recommended the establishment of an Algerian government in exile and of a permanent secretariat to promote Maghrib unity. The latter proposition had little permanent result, but a government—the Provisional Government of the Algerian Republic (GPRA)—was set up on September 19.

By then, however, conditions had been radically changed by events of May 13, 1958; these began as a traditional settler rising—thousands of European Algerians sacked the offices of the governor general and, with the tacit approval of the army officers, called for the integration of Algeria with France and for the return of de Gaulle to power. The Muslims were clearly taken aback, but soon there was a relatively friendly mixing of Muslim demonstrators with the Europeans and a general hope of better times to come. In the crisis caused by this rising, de Gaulle returned to power in France.

Changes under de Gaulle

On June 4 de Gaulle visited Algiers amid scenes of great enthusiasm. He gave no clear indication, however, that he shared the settlers' enthusiasm for integration, which, in their minds, meant the submergence of the Algerians in an enlarged France. All Muslims, however, were now granted the full rights of French citizenship, and on October 30 de Gaulle announced in Constantine a plan to provide adequate schools and medical services for the Muslim population, to create employment for the vastly increasing Muslim masses, and to introduce Muslims into the higher ranks of the public services.

The European population was troubled by the lack of insistence on the theme of integration. This came to a head in September 1959, when de Gaulle, in anticipation of the opening of the UN General Assembly, declared publicly that the Algerians had the right to determine their own future. From this time it gradually became clear that while he would retain as close links between France and Algeria as he believed possible he was nevertheless prepared to go even to the length of granting independence if peace could not be secured on any other terms. The agitation of the Europeans now became extreme.

On January 24, 1960, a fresh settler rising collapsed after nine days from lack of military support. A year later, however, as the prospect of negotiations with the GPRA became more probable, there was another rising, this time organized by four generals, of whom two—Raoul Salan and Maurice Challe—had previously been commanders in chief in Algeria. De Gaulle remained unshaken, and the rising, lacking substantial support from the army, collapsed after only three days.

In May 1961, negotiations were opened in France with representatives of the GPRA. This body had by now long been recognized by the Arab and Communist states, from which it received aid, though it had never been able to establish itself on Algerian soil. Negotiations were broken off in July, after which the veteran Ferhat Abbas was replaced as premier by the much younger Yusuf ben Khedda. Settler opposition was meanwhile organized by a body calling itself the Organisation de l'Armée Secrète (OAS), which began to employ terrorism as brutal as that sometimes used by the rebels.

Independence for Algeria

On March 8, 1962, negotiations were resumed, and on the 18th agreement was finally reached. Algeria would thenceforth be independent, provided only that a referendum, to be held in Algeria by a provisional government, confirmed the desire for it. In case of approval, French aid would continue; Europeans could depart, remain as foreigners, or take Algerian citizenship, as they preferred. This announcement produced a violent outburst of terrorism and attempted resistance by the OAS; but in May the terror subsided as its futility became obvious. On July 1, 1962, the referendum in Algeria recorded some 6,000,000 votes in favour and only 16,000 against. After three days of unbounded Muslim rejoicing, the GPRA entered Algiers in triumph, while the departure of the Europeans assumed mass proportions.

Meanwhile, however, the GPRA itself was torn by dissensions, and its authority was challenged by Col. Houari Boumedienne, who commanded the Algerian army on the Tunisian side. In this he was supported, after some hesitation, by Ben Bella, now released from captivity in France, and by Muhammad Khidr, secretary general of the FLN. It was not until three months later that the small-scale civil war that ensued was finally settled by the recognition of Ben Bella as premier, Boumedienne as chief of staff, and Khidr as head of the party organization.

Independent Algeria (from 1962). The Europeans who had abandoned the country included the overwhelming majority of senior administrators and managerial and technical experts. The chief exception was a group of some 10,000 French schoolteachers who remained, with great courage, often in very isolated posts.

During the six previous years some 10,000 French officers and troops and possibly as many as 250,000 Muslims had lost their lives in the fighting; dozens of villages had been destroyed and 2,000,000 peasants had been moved to new sites. Nevertheless, many public services such as the post office, the railways, and the electricity supply continued to work remarkably well. On farms and in factories, however, management had largely vanished. Production fell, while unemployment and underemployment reached extreme levels.

Ben Bella's popularity was an asset, but his personal style of government and his reckless promises of support for revolutionary movements were not conducive to orderly administration. On the other hand, the revenue from the extensive oil and natural gas fields that had recently been discovered and exploited in the Sahara was of very great assistance.

A serious problem was presented in April 1963 by the resignation of Muhammad Khidr and by his subsequent departure abroad, taking with him the funds of the FLN. He was later assassinated in Madrid. Little by little, the gradual elimination of other dissident leaders appeared to leave control securely in the hands of Ben Bella and the army under Colonel Boumedienne. What appeared to be Ben Bella's plans for a complete political takeover, removing Boumedienne and his supporters, were foiled on June 19, 1965, when Boumedienne and the army moved first. Ben Bella's erratic political style and poor administrative record made his removal acceptable to Algerians, but the Boumedienne regime began with little popular support.

Boumedienne's coup

In the following years Boumedienne moved undramatically but effectively to consolidate his power, with army loyalty remaining the basic element. Efforts to reorganize the FLN met with some success. The cautious and deliberate Boumedienne approach was seen in constitutional developments: communal elections were held in 1967, provincial (*wilāya*) elections in 1969. Elections for the National Assembly, however, did not take place until 1977. In the previous November, a new constitution had been adopted following wide public debate and referenda.

On December 27, 1978, Boumedienne died. Col. Chadli Bendjedid, nominated by the FLN to succeed him, was confirmed as president in a referendum in February 1979. The release of Ben Bella later that year from house arrest indicated that the new president felt confident in his authority and served as a symbol that, 17 years after independence, many old disputes were no longer relevant.

Independent Algeria has been steadfastly committed to a socialist, centrally directed economy and society. The mass exodus of the French at the time of independence left the new government with vast abandoned lands. These and the remaining French estates (all French land being nationalized by 1963) were turned into state farms run by workers' committees (*comités de gestion*, "management committees"). In 1971 Boumedienne inaugurated an agrarian reform aimed at breaking up larger Algerian-owned farms and creating small holdings organized into cooperatives. Subsequent steps continued, but cautiously, to break up large holdings and redistribute land to landless peasants.

Economic plans have stressed developing a state-run industrial core, and Algeria's important oil and gas industry is controlled by a government company, Sonatrach. Algeria's economic difficulties are eased by the export of oil and gas as well as by the remittances from the nearly 850,000 Algerians living abroad (mostly in France). In 1976 Algeria signed a trade agreement with the European Economic Community; yet unemployment and underemployment remain the major problems. Critics say that bureaucratic heavy-handedness contributes to the trouble, but the regime appears unswervingly convinced that tight central control is necessary to long-term development.

Algeria's foreign policy is revolutionary in word but (especially since the removal of Ben Bella) pragmatically nationalist in deed. Immediately after independence Algeria was a haven for Third World guerrilla and revolutionary movements, but this has largely passed. Algerian spokesmen continue to press for strong positions on the Palestine problem, decolonization in Africa, and economic ties between the developed and underdeveloped worlds, but at the same time the government has supported commercial ventures with private U.S. companies. In addition, the Algerian government played a major role in mediating the release, in January 1981, of U.S. hostages held in Iran. Since independence Algeria has maintained good but firmly independent relations with the countries of the Soviet bloc.

Relations with Morocco

With neighbouring Morocco, relations have not been smooth. A short border war that broke out in the autumn of 1963 (the area in dispute being rich in iron-ore deposits) was brought to a halt through intervention of the Organization of African Unity. The rapprochement achieved in 1969–70 later broke down again over Morocco's efforts to absorb Western Sahara (formerly Spanish Sahara). Algeria supported the Popular Front for the Liberation of Saguia el Hamra and Río de Oro (Polisario Front) in resisting Morocco.

Relations with France have been marked by hard bargaining. The disputes over Algerian expropriation of abandoned French property (1963) and nationalization of French oil interests (1971) were mitigated by generous French cultural and technical aid. The large number of Algerians living and working in France (at the bottom of the economic scale and subject to racial prejudice), although a major economic asset for Algeria, continues to be an explosive social issue. French trade with independent Algeria remains important but no longer dominant, Algeria's trade with other Western nations being of major importance as well. (N.B./L.C.Br.)

For later developments in the history of Algeria, see the *Britannica Book of the Year* section in the BRITANNICA WORLD DATA ANNUAL.

LIBYA

The People's Socialist Libyan Arab Jamahiriya (in Arabic, al-Jamāhīrīyah al-ʿArabīyah al-Lībīyah ash-Shaʿbīyah al-Ishtirākīyah) is an independent Socialist state of North Africa. It is bounded by the Mediterranean Sea on the north, Egypt on the east, The Sudan on the southeast, Niger and Chad on the south, and Tunisia and Algeria on the west. Largely composed of the Sahara, it covers an area of 675,200 square miles (1,748,700 square kilometres) and is one-fourth the size of the conterminous United States and almost twice the size of Egypt. The population is concentrated along the coast, where the de facto capital, Tripoli (Ṭarābulus), and Benghazi (Banghāzī), the de jure capital, are located.

Physical and human geography

Before the discovery of oil in the 1950s, Libya was poor in natural resources and severely limited by the climatic conditions of the Sahara. The country was almost entirely dependent upon foreign aid and the import of commodities necessary to the maintenance of the economy. Petroleum dramatically changed the economy, and Libya became one of the richest countries of the Middle East and Africa. The government has attempted to develop agriculture and industry with its vast oil revenues. It has also established a welfare state, which provides medical care and education.

THE LAND

Relief. Libya is composed of basement rocks of Precambrian age (from 570,000,000 to 4,600,000,000 years old) that are overlain with marine and windborne deposits. There is also evidence of ancient volcanic activity. The major physical features are the Jabal Nafūsah (Arabic *jabal,* "mountain") and the associated Gefara plain in the northwest, al-Jabal al-Akhḍar in the northeast, and the Saharan plateau. The Gefara plain covers about 10,000 square miles of Libya's northwestern corner. It rises from sea level at the coast to about 1,000 (300 metres) feet at the foothills of the Jabal Nafūsah. Composed of coastal cliffs, sand dunes, salt marshes, and steppe, the plain contains most of Libya's population and its largest city—Tripoli. The Jabal Nafūsah is a limestone massif that stretches for about 212 miles (340 kilometres) from west to east between the Gefara and the Sahara; it reaches altitudes of between 2,000 and 3,000 feet.

In the country's northeastern corner, al-Jabal al-Akhḍar stretches for about 100 miles along the coast between al-Marj and Darnah. The limestone mountains rise steeply and stretch about 20 miles inland, attaining altitudes 2,000 to 3,000 feet.

The desert and the plateaus

The Saharan plateau covers about 99 percent of Libya, making it truly a desert land. The sand-covered undulating plateau surface is broken by several physical features, including the al-Harūj al-Aswad, the al-Ḥammādah al-Ḥamrāʾ, and the Tibesti mountains. Al-Harūj al-Aswad is a hilly basaltic plateau, which covers about 15,400 square miles in central Libya. It rises to about 2,600 feet and is crowned by volcanic peaks. The region is covered with angular stone fragments and boulders.

Al-Ḥammādah al-Ḥamrāʾ is a rocky plateau that lies behind the Jabal Nafūsah and covers an area of about 19,000 square miles. It contains bare rock outcrops and rises to 2,700 feet. An arm of the Tibesti stretches northward from the main massif in Chad. Picco Bette rises to 7,500 feet (2,286 metres) on the Libya-Chad border.

Drainage and soils. There are no perennial rivers. The numerous wadis (dry riverbeds) are filled by flash floods during the rains and quickly dry up or are reduced to a trickle. There is, however, extensive underground percolation (seepage) of water, and the numerous oases are watered by wells and springs that are fed by the underground water table. Along the coastal strip there are several salt lakes, or *sabkhahs*, formed by the ponding and evaporation of water behind coastal dunes, the capillary movement of water from the underground water table, or the collection of water where percolation is restricted. Principal salt lakes are those of Tāwurghāʾ, Zuwārah, and the Banghāzī Plain.

On the western coast the gray-brown soils are highly saline. In the east, the soils of the Barce plain—which stretches between al-Jabal al-Akhḍar and the sea—are light and fertile. The result of decomposition of limestone deposits, they contain potash and phosphoric acid. The rest of the country is covered by wind-eroded sand or stony desert.

Climate. The climate over most of the country is that of the hot, arid Sahara, but it is moderated along the coastal littoral by the Mediterranean Sea. The maritime influence is greater in winter, while the Saharan influence is stronger in summer. The large daily range of temperatures is especially notable in the Sahara; it is modified along the littoral, where the sea cools during the day and warms by night. Coastal cloud cover moderates winter coastal temperatures by limiting insolation (the delivery of direct solar radiation) by day and by acting as an insulator at night.

The warmest months are July and August, when Benghazi experiences average monthly temperatures of 72° to 85° F (22° to 29° C) and Tripoli has average temperatures of 62° to 86° F (17° to 30° C). The coolest months are January and February; Benghazi has winter monthly temperatures of 50° to 63° F (10° to 17° C) and Tripoli has 47° to 61° F (8° to 16° C). Al-ʿAzīzīyah on the Gefara has recorded the world's highest shade temperature, about 136° F (58° C).

The amount of annual precipitation declines, and its variability increases, inland from the coast. Benghazi receives an annual average rainfall of 10 inches, and Tripoli receives 15 inches. In the maritime zone, however, the periodic high incidences of rainless periods in a year are sufficient to cause drought. In the Sahara, 200 consecutive rainless days in a year have been recorded in various areas, and the world's highest degree of aridity occurs at Sabhā. The dry climate is exacerbated by the *ghibli,* a hot, arid wind that blows from the south several times a year. It is preceded by a short lull in the prevailing winds, which is followed by the full force of the *ghibli.* The wind carries large quantities of sand dust, which turn the sky red and reduce visibility to less than 20 yards. The heat of the wind is increased by a rapid drop of relative humidity, which can fall from 80 to 10 percent within hours.

The effect of the *ghibli* wind

Plant and animal life. In years of good rainfall the northern plains are covered with herbaceous vegetation and annual grasses; the most noticeable of plants are the asphodel (an herb of the lily family) and jubule. The northern area of al-Jabal al-Akhḍar—where the influence of the Mediterranean is most apparent—supports low and relatively dense forest (or macchia), in which the main trees are the juniper and lentisk. Annual plants are abundant and include species such as brome grass, canary grass, bluegrass, and rye grass. The forest becomes more scattered and stunted south of the mountain crest, and annual plants are less frequent. The Jabal Nafūsah has less plant life, and the natural vegetation of grassland lies between barren hills.

When rainfall is less than six inches, semidesert conditions prevail, and vegetation is sparse; isolated plants grow in generally barren pockets. The species most commonly found are saltwort (a plant used in making soda ash) and spurge flax (a shrubby plant), while goosefoot (an herb), wormwood (a woody herb), and asphodel also are widespread. Annual grasses grow in the rainy season, and leguminous plants appear in years of good rainfall. Although rainfall is extremely low in the true desert zone and the vegetation cover is scant, some of the plants of the semi-arid region penetrate into the occasional wadi (periodic river) valley, and date palms are grown in the southern oases.

Wild animals include desert rodents, such as the desert hare and the jerboa; hyenas; foxes, such as the fennec

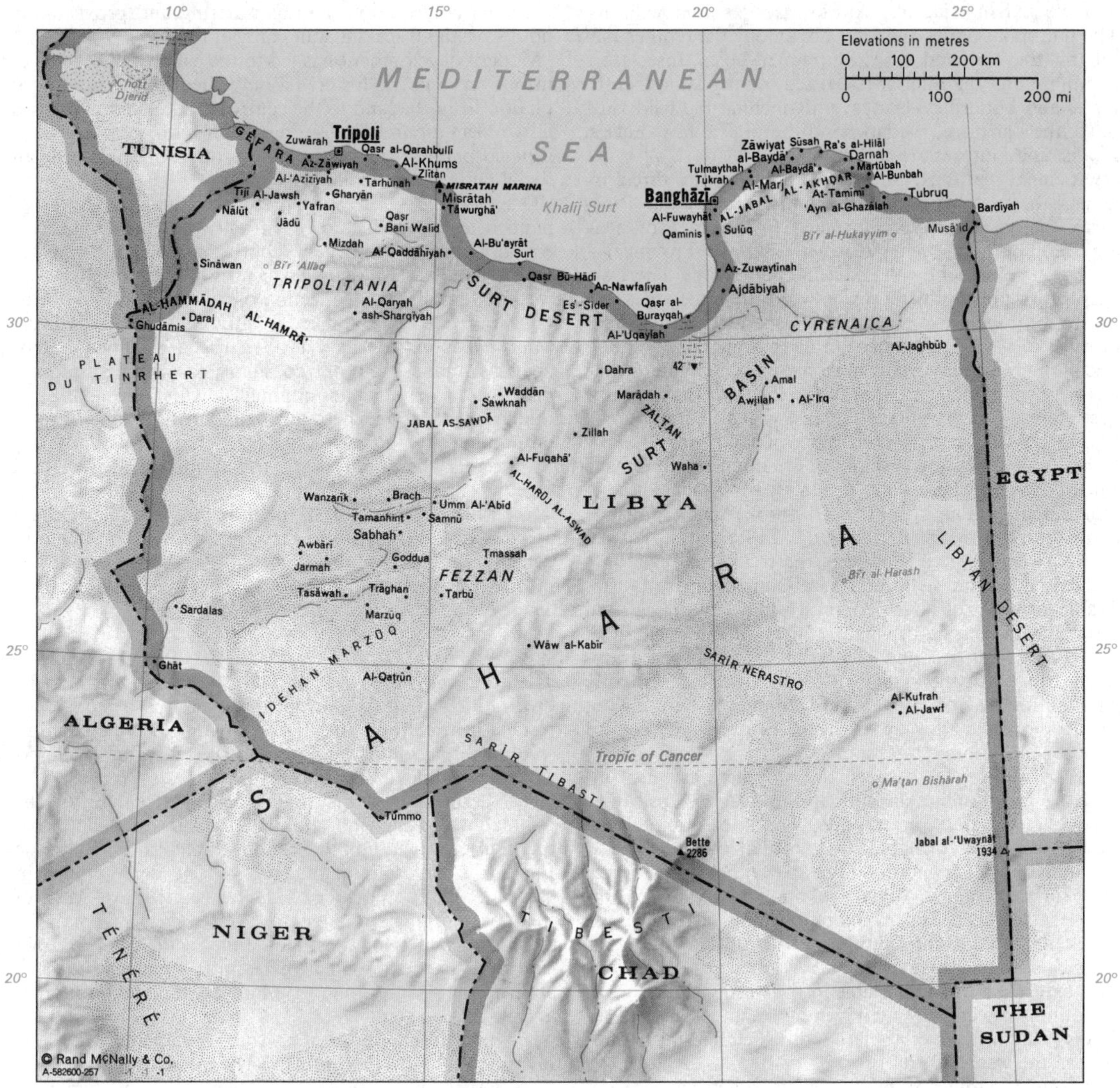

LIBYA

MAP INDEX

Cities and towns

Ajdābiyah.......30·48n 20·14e
al-'Azīzīyah......32·32n 13·01e
al-Bayḍā'........32·48n 21·45e
al-Bu 'Ayrāt......31·24n 15·44e
al-Bunbah.......32·24n 23·08e
al-Fuqahā'.......27·50n 16·22e
al-Fuwayhāt......32·04n 20·06e
al-'Irq............29·02n 21·33e
al-Jaghbūb......29·45n 24·31e
al-Jawf..........24·11n 23·19e
al-Jawsh.........32·00n 11·40e
al-Khums........32·39n 14·16e
al-Kufrah........24·10n 23·15e
al-Marj..........32·30n 20·54e
al-Qaddāḥīyah...31·22n 15·14e
al-Qaryah ash-
 Sharqīyah......30·24n 13·36e
al-Qaṭrūn........24·56n 14·38e
al-'Uqaylah......30·16n 19·12e
Amal.............29·25n 21·10e
an- Nawfalīyah...30·47n 17·50e
as-Sidar, see
 es'-Sider
at-Tamīmī.......32·20n 23·04e
Awbārī..........26·35n 12·46e
Awjilah..........29·09n 21·15e
'Ayn al-
 Ghazālah.......32·10n 23·20e
az-Zāwiyah......32·45n 12·44e
az-Zuwaytīnah...30·58n 20·07e
Banghāzī
 (Benghazi)......32·07n 20·04e
Bardīyah........31·46n 25·06e
Bi'r al-Harash
 (oasis)..........25·29n 22·11e
Bi'r 'Allāq (oasis).31·02n 10·36e
Brach...........27·32n 14·16e
Dahra............29·34n 17·50e
Daraj............30·09n 10·26e
Darnah..........32·46n 22·39e
es'-Sider.........30·38n 18·20e
Gharyān.........32·10n 13·01e
Ghāt.............24·58n 10·11e
Ghudāmis.......30·08n 9·30e
Goddua..........26·26n 14·18e
Jādū..............31·57n 12·01e
Jarmah..........26·33n 13·04e
Marādah.........29·14n 19·13e
Martūbah........32·35n 22·46e
Marzūq..........25·55n 13·55e
Misrātah........32·23n 15·06e
Mizdah..........31·26n 12·59e
Musā'id..........31·35n 25·03e
Nālūt............31·52n 10·59e
Qamīnis.........31·39n 20·03e
Qaṣr
 al-Burayqah....30·25n 19·34e
Qaṣr
 al-Qarahbullī....32·45n 13·43e
Qaṣr Banī Walīd.31·45n 14·01e
Qasr bū-Hādt.....31·03n 16·40e
Ra's al-Hilāl.....32·57n 22·10e
Ridotta Capuzzo,
 see Musā'id
Sabhah (Sabhā)..27·03n 14·26e
Samnū...........27·17n 14·53e
Sardalas.........25·46n 10·34e
Sawknah........29·04n 15·47e
Sīnāwan.........31·02n 10·36e
Sulūq............31·39n 20·15e
Surt..............31·12n 16·35e
Sūsah...........32·54n 21·58e
Tamanhint.......27·13n 14·36e
Ṭarābulus, see
 Tripoli
Tarbū............26·02n 15·10e
Tarhūnah........32·26n 13·38e
Tasāwah........25·58n 13·30e
Tāwurghā'.......32·02n 15·09e
Tījī...............32·01n 11·22e
Tmassah........26·22n 15·47e
Trāghan.........25·59n 14·26e
Tripoli
 (Ṭarābulus).....32·54n 13·11e
Tubruq (Tobruk).32·05n 23·58e
Tūkrah...........32·32n 20·34e
Ṭulmaythah......32·42n 20·57e
Umm al-'Abīd....27·31n 15·02e
Waddān..........29·10n 16·08e
Waha.............28·16n 19·54e
Wāw al-Kabīr....25·20n 16·43e
Yafran...........32·04n 12·31e
Zāwiyat
 al-Bayḍā'.......32·46n 21·43e
Zillah............28·33n 17·35e
Ẕlītan............32·28n 14·34e
Zuara, see
 Zuwārah
Zuwārah.........32·56n 12·06e

Physical features and points of interest

Akhḍar, al-Jabal
 al-, *mountains*...32·30n 21·30e
al-Harūj
 al-Aswad, *hills*..27·00n 17·10e
Barqah, see
 Cyrenaica
Bette, *peak*......22·00n 19·12e
Bishārah, Ma'ṭan,
 oases...........22·58n 22·39e
Bi'r al-Hukayyim,
 oases...........31·36n 23·29e
Cyrenaica
 (Barqah),
 physical region..31·00n 22·30e
Fezzan (Fazzān),
 physical region..26·00n 14·00e
Gefara, *plain*.....32·30n 11·45e
Hamrā',
 al-Ḥammādah
 al-, *upland*......30·22n 9·57e
Idehan Marzūq,
 dunes...........24·30n 13·00e
Libyan Desert....26·00n 25·00e
Mediterranean
 Sea.............33·00n 17·30e
Misrātah Marina,
 port............32·23n 15·13e
Nerastro, Sarīr,
 desert...........24·20n 20·37e
Sawdā', Jabal
 as-, *hills*........28·40n 15·30e
Surt, Khalīj
 (Gulf of Sidra)...31·30n 18·00e
Surt Basin.......28·30n 19·30e
Surt Desert......31·00n 16·30e
Tibasti, Sarīr,
 desert...........24·15n 17·15e
Tinrhert, Plateau
 du...............29·00n 9·00e
Tripolitania
 (Ṭarābulus),
 physical region..31·00n 15·00e
'Uwaynāt, Jabal
 al-, *mountain*....21·54n 24·58e
Zalṭan, *hills*......28·37n 19·46e

and the red fox; jackals; skunks; gazelles; and wildcats. The poisonous adder and krait are among the reptiles that inhabit the scattered oases and water holes. Insects are common; and the interior is crossed by migrating locusts, birds, and butterflies. Native birds include the wild ring-dove, the partridge, the lark, and the prairie hen. Eagles, hawks, and vultures are common.

Settlement patterns. Libya is divided into three regions—the western region (formerly Tripolitania Province), the eastern region (formerly Cyrenaica Province), and the southern region (formerly Fezzan Province)—which are coincident with its traditional regions. There are deep geographical differences between the three areas, the centres of population of which are separated by hundreds of miles of barren and inhospitable country.

Libya's three regions

Economic and environmental factors accentuate strong feelings of provincial attachment. In the western region the vast majority of the population is engaged in commercial farming based on irrigation; plots of land are generally held in individual ownership and are often small. On the Jabal Nafūsah, where water is less readily available, a sophisticated agrarian system based on olive- and fruit-tree cultivation and associated livestock raising, has evolved. In the eastern region, however, the traditional economy was based on nomadic and semi-nomadic pastoralism. Arable farming has largely been an adjunct of the pastoral system, with shifting dry-land cultivation rarely entailing sedentary farming. Land ownership is no longer exclusively tribal, but the system of tenancy contrasts sharply with that of ownership in the west. In the southern region, isolated irrigated farming at the oases represents a third traditional economic system.

Cultural differences between the provinces are also important. Tribal affiliations among the Arab groups are to smaller rather than larger units. The population of the west is far more cosmopolitan than that of the east and includes a higher proportion of people with Berber, Negro, and Turkish origins. Although Tripolitania came to uneasy terms with the Italian colonial regime, Cyrenaica was the scene of constant fighting and disruption; the commercial, administrative, and cultural impact of the Italians was therefore more appreciable in the west. Cyrenaica was profoundly affected by the teachings of the 19th-century Sanūsīyah, an Islāmic brotherhood, which had little influence in the west and south.

The most significant mode of life practiced in rural Libya is that of the sedentary cultivator. In the traditional oases most farmers rely on irrigation, and water is raised from shallow wells either by the animal-powered *dalū* (a goatskin bag drawn by rope over a pulley) or, increasingly, by electric or diesel pumps. Landholdings in the oases are small and fragmented; the average five or seven acres per farm are generally divided into three or four separate units. On the coastal lowlands farmers normally live on their land and often have rights to graze stock and undertake shifting grain cultivation. In both the east and the west, Arab farmers occupy large, formerly European estates, in which individual units range from 12 to 600 acres, and operations are conducted at a high technical level.

Nomadism is mainly a feature of the unirrigated regions, particularly al-Jabal al-Akhḍar and its surrounding area in the eastern region. Nomadic groups subsist primarily on their holdings of sheep, goats, and camels but also participate in the shifting cultivation of cereals. In the east, the Bedouins move south as soon as pasture appears and remain there until the ephemeral grasslands die and necessitate the return to the northern hill lands.

The village was originally an alien institution to Libya's tribal organization. Since the first Turkish occupation in the 16th century, towns and villages were developed mainly as military posts or administrative centres by occupying powers. Many village sites have been occupied for centuries; smaller settlements often began as collecting centres for the nomadic tribes during their summer residence in the oases or hill pastures. Berbers in the west, however, are thought to have retained a more or less continuous thread of settlement in their fortified nucleated villages in the western Jabal Nafūsah. In the southern oases, the villages served both as defense posts for the scattered communities and as watering and provisioning points on the trans-Saharan caravan routes.

Urban settlement

Modern development has led to the expansion of villages into towns and has fostered a movement of the rural population from the land to the centres of settlement. Villages now reflect a purely indigenous expression, and, except in isolated parts of the east, they are integrated into Libyan social and economic life.

The two main cities of Tripoli and Benghazi have expanded to the exclusion of virtually all others. The surrounding extensive garden suburbs, such as al-Fuwayhāt to the southeast of Benghazi and Giorgimpopoli to the west of Tripoli, are a collection of colourful and luxurious villas inhabited by the more wealthy nationals and aliens. Many old buildings have been replaced with new hotels, apartment blocks and offices. Shanty towns are also found near the two cities; and, although low-income housing is under construction, these areas present problems of sanitation and water supply.

Tripoli is the main port, and Tripoli and Benghazi together handle most of the country's maritime trade. Tripoli handles the bulk of the imports, particularly those associated with the oil industry and the booming trade in consumer goods. Tobruk (Ṭubruq), the third most important port, is located in a remote area of sparse population. There are many other lesser ports.

THE PEOPLE

The tribe (*qabīlah*) was for long the basis of the social order in Libya, and eight out of every nine persons once resided in tribal domains. Tribal organization persisted in spite of three centuries of successive occupation by Turkish, Karamanli, Italian, and British forces.

The Berbers were the major original element in the population. Most Arab chroniclers divide them into two main groups, whose branches indigenous to Libya are the Luata, the Nefusa, and the Adassa. The Berbers lived in coastal oases and practiced sedentary agriculture. Most of them have been assimilated into Arab society except in the Jabal Nafūsah region, Awjilah, Hūn, Socra, and Zuwārah. The Berbers speak their own Hamitic language but have adopted the Arabic alphabet. Many are bilingual in Berber and Arabic.

Origins of the Arab population

The first influence of the Arabs was felt during the invasions of the 7th century. The initial Arab incursion into Berber lands was essentially military and had little effect upon the composition of the population. The Banū Hilāl invasion of 1049 and succeeding attacks of the Banū Sulaym in the 11th century, however, were paramount factors in the ethnic character of the population. By the 20th century, about 97 percent of Libya's inhabitants were Arabic-speaking Muslims of mixed Arab and Berber descent.

The Banū Sulaym were composed of four main groups—the Banū Hebib, the Auf, the Debbab, and the Zegb. The Hebib settled in Cyrenaica, while the others went into Tripolitania. After the establishment of tribal groups, Libya underwent a period of disorder and tribal feuding, which was augmented by the incursion of other Arab adventurers from Egypt. Toward the close of the period of anarchy, the Debbab group took control of much of Tripolitania.

Several other social groups exist alongside the tribal unit. They are the Sharīfs (holy tribes), who came originally from Fezzan; the marabouts (dervishes who are credited with supernatural powers), who infiltrated from Saguia el Hamra in what is now Western Sahara; and the Kouloughlis, who are descended from the Janissaries (elite Turkish soldiers). The Sharīfs constitute a religious hierarchy that claims direct descent from Muḥammad. Their blood relationship with the prophet gives them a powerful standing in Muslim society, where they are looked upon as holy men with divine powers of foresight. Extensive tracts of land are found under Sharīf control in all the oases of western Libya.

Marabout tribes are descended from holy men who also claimed relation to Muḥammad. Infiltration of marabouts from Algeria, Tunisia, and Spain began in the 14th century and continued intermittently for several centuries. The true marabouts founded their religious devotions upon an ascetic life manifested in their existence as hermits. In areas where their teachings and way of life made them acceptable to the local inhabitants, they settled and founded tribes pledged to the pure way of life.

Minority population groups

The Koulougis are descendants of Janissaries, Berbers, and Christian slaves. Since Turkish times they have served as a secretarial class in several areas and are often concentrated in and around villages and towns. They speak Arabic and practice Islām.

The trans-Saharan trade in slaves, which continued during Turkish times, left a pronounced black element in many of the tribes, especially in the western littoral. Most of them live in Tripolitania and the Fezzan. Their languages are those of the central Sahara and the eastern Sudan; most also speak Arabic and have adopted Islām.

Small groups of Tuareg tribesmen are found in the southwest, especially at Ghudāmis and Ghāt oases. Traditionally nomadic, they are gradually assuming a sedentary life style. Isolated Teda (Tubu) communities of the southeast are gravitating toward the north and al-Kufrah oasis in search of employment. The former Italian and Greek populations have declined to negligible proportions since 1969.

Besides Tripoli and Benghazi, there are 12 large towns. In the west Gharyān, al-Khums, Misrātah, Tājūrā', Sūq al-Jum'ah, Zanzūr, and Zāwiyah are the major centres. In the east Ajdābiyah, al-Marj, al-Bayḍā', Darnah, and Tobruk are of the same rank.

THE ECONOMY

Resources. Petroleum is Libya's most important mineral resource. First discovered in 1956 near the Algerian border, it has since been located mainly in the Surt Basin. The major oil fields are Zalṭan, Amal, and Intisar A in the vicinity of Banghāzī; Dahra field is located near Misrātah; and Sarir field is near Darnah. Deposits have been located near Ghudāmis on the western border, Marzūq in the southwest, and al-Kufrah oasis in the southeast. Libya's proven oil reserves represent about half of Africa's or 4 percent of the world's. Libyan crude oil is low in sulfur content and therefore causes less corrosion and less pollution than most crude oils. The deposits are associated with natural gas.

There are important deposits of natron (hydrated sodium carbonate) in the Fezzan and of potash in the Surt Desert near Marādah. The iron ore in the Fezzan is low in iron content, and development is hampered by the field's distance from the coast. Marine salt is produced in Tripolitania, where there are also small deposits of gypsum, manganese, and lignite coal. Sulfur has been found in the Surt Desert, and there are scattered deposits of chalk, limestone, and marble.

The arid climate supports few biological resources except for the grasslands of al-Jabal al-Akhḍar and the Jabal Nafūsah, which are valuable for grazing. There are no hydroelectric resources, and oil represents the only domestic means of producing thermal electricity.

Agriculture, forestry, and fishing. Agricultural production has declined because of the exodus from rural areas to the cities. The oil industry has attracted a large amount of labor from the farms, and foodstuffs are increasingly imported. Cereals are the major crops throughout the country. Barley is the chief cereal grown because it adapts well to different climates and soils. Wheat is grown primarily on the eastern and western plateaus, and sorghum is raised in the Fezzan. Olive plantations were introduced by the Italians on the Gefara and on the Jabal Nafūsah, and there are smaller olive patches in the east. Orchards of almonds, citrus fruit, apricots, and figs occur on small and large farms and on small, crowded plots in the oases. Dates are the principal crop of the southern oases. Grapes, broad beans, and peanuts are also grown. Tobacco is raised in Tripolitania.

Animal husbandry is important in Cyrenaica, where the herds are raised on communal grazing lands. Livestock includes sheep, goats, cattle, camels, horses, mules, and donkeys. Animals are raised for their milk, meat, and hides or for their services as a means of transportation. Cattle often serve as draft animals. A small amount of milk is produced commercially, and commercial poultry farms are developing around the larger cities.

Before the 1950s, the only wooded area in Libya was the region of scrub brush on al-Jabal al-Akhḍar. Since then, the government has launched a massive afforestation program. Between 1957 and 1964, 27,000,000 acacia, eucalyptus, cypress, cedar, and pine trees were planted in Tripolitania.

There is little demand in Libya for fish, and most fishing is carried out off the Tripolitanian coast by Libyan, Tunisian, Greek, and Maltese fishermen. The catch includes tuna, sardines, and red mullet. Sponge beds are also important. The sponges are harvested mainly by Greeks who are licensed by the Libyan government.

The first pipeline was constructed from the Zalṭan field to Marsā al-Burayqā' in 1961. Since then additional lines have been built from Dahra to as-Sidar and to Ra's al-Unūf, and other pipelines connect the Tobruk field to Marsā al-Ḥarīqah and the Intisar A field to az-Zuwaytīnah. A natural-gas pipeline runs parallel to the oil pipeline from Zalṭan. The gas liquefaction plant at Marsā al-Burayqā' is the world's largest.

Libya is usually among the world's dozen largest producers of oil. Sales to Europe were enhanced by the closure of the Suez Canal between 1967 and 1975. Only a small percentage of the Libyan labour force is employed by the oil industry, along with a few thousand aliens.

Mining of other mineral resources was for long a little developed area of the economy. Natron is mined, and marine salt is produced in substantial quantities. Exploitation of domestic iron reserves had advanced by the mid-1980s to the point that Libya was able to initiate development of an iron–steel complex at Misrātah. Gypsum, limestone, chalk, and marble are quarried for the growing construction industry.

Industry. Industrial development is hampered by the lack of skilled domestic labour, the limited domestic market, the poor transport system, and inadequate water and natural resources. Most factories are located in Tripoli and Benghazi and are managed by Arabs. The industrial work force is small: many of the factories employ fewer than 100 persons. A majority of the factories are engaged in the manufacture of processed food, beverages, cement, and leather goods. The small textile industry is almost totally dependent upon raw materials imported from abroad. There are also oil-related industries, which produce steel drums, tanks, pipe fittings, and housing and office buildings.

The government also contributes to manufacturing. The Libyan Tobacco Monopoly processes all tobacco and controls its import and export. There are also government monopolies for salt and esparto grass. Other ventures include the production of processed food, leather, gypsum, rugs, and mineral water.

The production of electricity for public consumption is a government monopoly. There are also private plants, such as the 25,000-kilowatt facility built by an oil company at Marsā al-Burayqah. The total installed capacity, all thermal plants powered by oil, grew more than sevenfold during the 1970s.

Finance and trade. Financial services are headed by the Central Bank of Libya, which supervises the banking system, regulates credit and interest policies, and promotes the transformation of foreign banks into Libyan institutions.

Foreign trade

Since 1963 Libya has enjoyed a favourable balance of trade. Almost all of its exports are represented by oil, but agricultural products and hides and skins are also exported. Imports consist of equipment for the oil and construction industries, farm machinery, consumer goods, and agricultural products. Most of the country's imports are purchased from Italy, the United States, West Germany, Spain, and France.

Administration of the economy. The administration has maintained control of the concessions granted to the foreign-dominated oil industry. It has attempted to promote private industrial and agricultural development since 1966 by the granting of interest-free loans. The shortage of capital and technical knowledge in the private sector, however, has prompted the government to enter directly into industrial endeavours.

Oil revenues are the main source of the government's income. Other revenues are import duties, direct taxes, and profits from government monopolies. The income tax law promulgated in 1969 included fixed-percentage qualitative taxes and progressive income taxes on individuals and corporations.

Economic policies and problems

Economic policy emphasizes the development of the economic infrastructure and industry. There is increased government participation in such activities as the construction of roads, schools, housing, and ports. The development of Libyan-owned enterprises is promoted to combat the influence of the foreign-owned oil companies.

The country's most serious economic problem is the shortage of skilled labour. Educational and training facilities must be expanded and the towns must be developed so as to stem the migration of workers from the rural areas to the cities.

Transportation. The main artery is the 1,100-mile coastal highway between the borders of Tunisia and Egypt, which has branch roads to the coastal towns. The Sabhā road runs from the coastal highway at al-Qaddāḥīyah south and southwest to Ghāt near the Algerian border. There are several roads between the coast and the major oil fields. About half the roads are paved. The two railroads that served Tripoli and Benghazi were closed after 1965, but planning in the mid-1980s provided for the construction of a railroad to serve the coastal cities and the Misrātah industrial complex.

Tripoli and Benghazi are the main seaports; they handle all imports and exports except crude oil. Petroleum is shipped from as-Sidar and Marsā al-Burayqah. Misrātah, Zuwārah, and al-Khums have been developed as fishing ports, and Darnah and Tobruk were also improved.

International airports include those at Tripoli and at Banīnah, outside of Benghazi. Domestic airfields include those at Sabhā, al-Bayḍā', Ghudāmis, and Ghāt. The Libyan Arab Airlines and foreign airlines operate domestic flights and services to Egypt, Tunisia, and several nations in Europe. There are also domestic flights operated by the oil companies.

ADMINISTRATIVE AND SOCIAL CONDITIONS

Government. In September 1969 the monarchy of Idris I was overthrown and the constitution suspended in a military coup d'état. In 1977 the 12-member Revolutionary Command Council formed after the coup was replaced by the General Secretariat of the General People's Congress (GPC) with Col. Muammar al-Qaddafi as Secretary General. He resigned the post in 1979 but remained in effect ruler of the country and head of the revolution. A General People's Committee has replaced the original revolutionary cabinet, the Council of Ministers; each of the committee's members is the secretary of a department. The General People's Congress serves as a parliament.

The country is divided into 25 *baladīyāt* (municipalities), which in turn are subdivided into submunicipal zones. The citizens of each submunicipal zone are members of the Basic Popular Congress (BPC), each headed by an appointed revolutionary or leadership committee. The citizens, with few exceptions, are also members of the Arab Socialist Union (ASU), the mass political organization and only legal party.

Justice. The judicial system consists of the Supreme Court, located in Tripoli, with five chambers of five justices each; it is the final court of appeal. The regional courts of appeal, located in Tripoli, Benghazi, and Sabhā, each with three justices, hear appeals from the courts of first instance and the summary courts, the basic judicial unit, each with one justice per court. Separate religious courts were abolished in 1973, and all judicial courts base their rulings on Libyan law, founded on the basis of the Sharī'ah (Islāmic law). Two extrajudiciary courts are the people's courts, which try political detainees, and the military courts, created ad hoc to try persons accused of plots or conspiracies against the state.

Education. Public education is free and primary education is compulsory for both boys and girls. Arabic is the language of instruction at all levels. The school system is composed of a six-year primary level, a three-year intermediate and vocational level, and a three-year secondary and advanced vocational level. There are also Qur'ānic schools, which are financed by the government.

Higher education is offered by the state institutions of the University of Libya, subdivided in 1973 into Al-Fatah University (Tripoli) and Ghar Yunis University (Benghazi). Some graduate medical students study abroad. Advanced religious training is obtained at a branch of the university at al-Bayḍā'. Libyan students also study abroad in Egypt, Europe, and the United States.

In order to increase the literacy rate the government has also sponsored an adult educational program.

Health and welfare. The chief health problems are typhoid, leishmaniasis, rabies, meningitis, and schistosomiasis (a parasitic infestation of the liver or intestines). The incidence of malaria has declined, but gastroenteritis and tetanus remain major diseases.

Medical and hospital care and medicines are free. Most care is available in hospitals and at outpatient or specialized-care facilities or clinics. The number of medical personnel has been increased sharply.

Schools for medicine and dentistry opened in the 1970s, but the rapid expansion of facilities necessitated the continued hiring of expatriate staff.

Welfare programs

The National Social Insurance Institute operates social security programs. Workers covered by government insurance programs receive medical examinations and treatment, maternity benefits, and dental care. There are also old-age pensions and payments for incapacity or death as a result of work-related accidents.

Housing facilities range from the Bedouin tent to the luxury apartment. About half the population occupies Mediterranean-style row houses in the towns and cities.

Life styles in both town and village have been strongly influenced by the revolutionary government's restructuring of national and local overnment and its efforts to reduce the influence of traditional tribes. Migration to urban areas has occurred in considerable numbers and has helped blur distinctions between nomads and town dwellers. The government has also brought women out of traditional seclusion and into the mainstream of the revolutionary socialist society.

CULTURAL LIFE

Libyan culture centres on folk art and traditions, which are highly influenced by Islām. The traditional arts of weaving, embroidery, metal engraving, and leatherwork rarely depict people or animals because of the Islāmic prohibition against such representation. The dominant geometric and arabesque designs are best presented in the stucco and tiles of the Karamanli and Gurgi mosques of Tripoli. Surviving traditions are represented by festivals, horse races, and folk dances. Musical styles are basically Arabic and rely upon improvisation and embellishment of melody; major musical instruments are the cane pipe and drums. Nonreligious literature has developed largely since the 1960s; it is nationalistic in character but reveals Egyptian influences. The arts are supported by the government through the Ministry of Information, the Ministry of Education and National Guidance, and the al-Fikr Society, a group of intellectuals and professionals. The government subsidies are essential to encourage national awareness of the fine arts and folklore.

Cultural institutions

Libraries include the Government Library and the Archives in Tripoli, the Public Library in Benghazi, and the university libraries. The Department of Antiquities is responsible for the Archaeological Museum, the Leptis Magna Museum of Antiquities, the Natural History Museum, and the Sabratha Museum of Antiquities, all in the western region, and the archaeological sites of Ptolemais and Appolonia in the eastern region. The Sabhā Museum contains exhibits of ancient remains of the former Fezzan region.

For statistical data on the land and people of Libya, see the *Britannica World Data* section in the BRITANNICA WORLD DATA ANNUAL. (Mu.B.)

History

Part of the Ottoman Empire from the early 16th century, Libya experienced autonomous rule (similar to that in Ottoman Algeria and Tunisia) under the Karamanli dynasty from 1711 to 1835. In the latter year the Ottomans took advantage of a dispute over the succession and local disorder to reestablish direct administration. For the next 77 years the area was administered by officials from Istanbul and shared in the limited modernization common to the rest of the empire. In Libya the most significant event of the period was the creation (1837) of the Sanūsīyah (Sennusiyah), an Islāmic order, or fraternity, that preached a puritanical form of Islām, giving the people instruction and material assistance and so creating in them an added sense of unity. The first Sanūsī *zāwiyah,* or lodge, in Libya was established in 1843 near the ruins of Cyrene in eastern Cyrenaica. The order spread principally in that province but also found adherents beyond its borders, particularly in the south. In order to avoid the cosmopolitan influences of the coastal region, the Grand Sanūsī, as the founder came to be called, moved his headquarters to the oasis of Jaghbūb near the Egyptian frontier, and in 1895 his son and successor, Sīdī Muḥammad al-Mahdī, transferred it farther south into the Sahara to the oasis of al-Kufrah. Though the Ottomans welcomed the order's opposition to the spread of French influence northward from Chad and Tibesti, they regarded with suspicion the political influence it exerted within Cyrenaica. In 1908 the Young Turk revolution gave a new impulse to reform; in 1911, however, the Italians, with banking and other interests in the country, launched an invasion of Libya.

The Sanūsīyah

The Ottomans sued for peace in 1912, but Italy found it more difficult to subdue the local population. Resistance to the Italian occupation continued throughout World War I. After the war Italy considered coming to terms with nationalist forces in Tripolitania and with the Sanūsīyah, who were strong in Cyrenaica. These negotiations foundered, however, and the arrival of a strong governor, Giuseppe Volpi, in Libya and a Fascist government in Italy (1922) inaugurated an Italian policy of thorough colonization. The coastal areas of Tripolitania were subdued by 1923, but in Cyrenaica Sanūsī resistance, led by Omar al-Mukhtar, was maintained until his capture and execution in 1931.

ITALIAN COLONIZATION

In the 1920s and '30s the Italian government expended large sums for the purposes of developing towns, roads, and agricultural colonies for Italian settlers. The most ambitious effort was the program of Italian immigration called "demographic colonization," launched by Benito Mussolini in 1935. As a result of these efforts, some 150,000 Italian settlers were established in Libya (about 18 percent of the country's total population) by the outbreak of World War II. These colonizing efforts and the resulting economic development of Libya were largely destroyed during the North Africa campaigns of 1941–43. Cyrenaica changed hands three times, and by the end of 1942 all the Italian settlers had been withdrawn. Cyrenaica largely reverted to pastoralism. Somewhat more of the economic and administrative development achieved by Italy survived in Tripolitania, but Libya by 1945 was impoverished, underpopulated, and also divided into regions—Tripolitania and Cyrenaica—of differing political, economic, and religious traditions.

INDEPENDENCE

The future of Libya gave rise to long discussions after the war. In view of the contribution to the fighting made by a volunteer Sanūsī force, the British foreign minister pledged in 1942 that the Sanūsīs would not again be subjected to Italian rule. During the discussions, which lasted four years, suggestions included an Italian trusteeship, a United Nations trusteeship, a Soviet mandate for Tripolitania, and various compromises. Finally, in November 1949, the UN General Assembly voted that Libya should become a united and independent kingdom not later than January 1, 1952.

Libyan independence

A constitution creating a federal state with a separate parliament for each province was drawn up, and the pro-British head of the Sanūsīyah, Sīdī Muḥammad Idrīs al-Mahdī as-Sanūsī, was chosen king by a national assembly in 1950. On December 24, 1951, King Idris I declared the country independent. Political parties were prohibited, and the King's authority was fundamental. Though not themselves Sanūsīs, the Tripolitanians accepted the monarchy largely in order to profit by the British promise that the Sanūsīs would not again be subjected to Italian rule. King Idris showed a marked preference for living in Cyrenaica, where he built a new capital on the site of the Sanūsī *zāwiyah* at al-Bayḍā'. Though Libya joined the Arab League in 1953 and in 1956 refused British troops permission to land for the Suez Canal expedition, during that time the government in general adopted a pro-Western point of view in international affairs.

The discovery of oil. In 1959 Libya changed abruptly from a pauper state, dependent on international aid and the rent from U.S. and British air bases, to an oil-rich monarchy. The discovery of major petroleum deposits in both Tripolitania and Cyrenaica assured the country of income on a vast scale. Soon after the discovery there was an enormous expansion of all government services and also of construction projects, and a corresponding rise in the economic standard and the cost of living.

What would happen on the King's death had always been a matter for speculation, since Idris' heir lacked his uncle's outstanding qualities. On September 1, 1969, a group of young army officers led by Col. Muammar al-Qaddafi deposed the King and made Libya a republic. The new regime, passionately pan-Arab and puritanically Muslim, broke the monarchy's close ties to Britain and the United States and also began an assertive policy that led to higher oil prices and to 51 percent Libyan participation in oil company activities and in some cases to outright nationalization. (N.B./L.C.Br.)

Qaddafi's regime. Equally assertive in plans for Arab unity, Libya obtained at least the formal beginnings of unity with Egypt, The Sudan, and Tunisia, but these and other such plans failed as differences arose among the governments concerned. Qaddafi's Libya maintained a strong interventionist orientation on the Palestine issue and in support of other guerrilla and revolutionary organizations in Africa and the Middle East, all of which provoked considerable antipathy from the established governments that were threatened by such groups. In July–August 1977 hostilities broke out between Libya and Egypt, and as a result many Egyptians working in Libya were obliged to return home. Indeed, in spite of expressed concern for Arab unity, the regime's relations with most Arab countries were poor. Qaddafi signed a treaty of union with Morocco's King Hassan II in August 1984, but Hassan abrogated the treaty in August 1986 because of ideological differences.

Plans for Arab unity

The regime, under Qaddafi's ideological guidance, continued to introduce innovations. On March 2, 1977, the General People's Congress declared that Libya was to be known as the People's Socialist Libyan Arab Jamahiriyah (the latter a neologism meaning "government through the masses"). By 1981, however, a drop on the world market in the demand and price for oil was beginning to hamper Qaddafi's efforts to play a strong regional role. Ambitious efforts to radically change Libya's economy and society slowed, and there were signs of domestic discontent. Libyan opposition movements launched sporadic attacks against Qaddafi and his military supporters but met with arrest and execution. (N.B./L.C.Br./Ed.)

Libya's relationship with the United States, which had been an important trading partner, deteriorated in the early 1980s as the U.S. government increasingly protested Qaddafi's support of Palestinian Arab terrorists. An escalating series of retaliatory trade restrictions and military skirmishes culminated in a U.S. bombing raid of government buildings, military installations, and terrorist camps at Tripoli and Benghazi in April 1986.

For later developments in the history of Libya, see the *Britannica Book of the Year* section in the BRITANNICA WORLD DATA ANNUAL. (Ed.)

MOROCCO

Morocco (official name Kingdom of Morocco, Arabic al-Mamlakah al-Maghribīyah), which has been a constitutional monarchy since 1962, is situated in northwestern Africa, where it faces northward across the Strait of Gibraltar to the continent of Europe, westward to the Atlantic Ocean, and northeastward to the Mediterranean Sea. Algeria lies to the east and southeast. In 1970 Spain ceded its Atlantic enclave Ifni to Morocco, but two other Spanish enclaves on the Mediterranean coast, containing Ceuta and Melilla, as well as the Chafarinas Islands to the north, remain under Spanish control. In April 1976 the territory under Moroccan administration was further extended when Morocco and Mauritania agreed to a boundary dividing the former Spanish (now Western) Sahara between them; the *de facto* annexations that resulted were not recognized by other countries, however. Excluding these territories, Morocco has an area of 177,117 square miles (458,730 square kilometres). Rabat is the political capital, but Casablanca is the industrial and commercial centre. Marrakech, Fès, and Meknès are traditional capitals; Tangier is the summer capital.

Territorial boundaries

Physical and human geography

THE LAND

Relief. Most of Morocco lies at a high altitude; the average height above sea level is about 2,600 feet (800 metres). Two chains of mountains, one, called er-Rif (the Rif), along the northern coast and the other, the Atlas, in the centre, divide eastern Morocco (which physically is much like portions of neighbouring Algeria) from Atlantic Morocco, which the mountains cut off from the rest of northwestern Africa. Eastern Morocco and Atlantic Morocco are connected by the narrow Taza Pass in the northeast, as well as by roads that traverse older traditional routes. These systems of mountains were formed during the Tertiary Period—from 65,000,000 to 2,500,000 years ago—by the folding and uplifting of sediment that had accumulated in the Tethys sea that at that time edged the northern coast of the continent of Africa.

Er-Rif, a complex structure, is geologically part of the cordilleras (mountain chains) reaching southward from the Iberian Peninsula of Europe, from which Africa was separated only after the Tertiary Period. The crescent-shaped range rises abruptly from the narrow Mediterranean shore. Most of the limestone peaks in er-Rif surpass 4,900 feet and rise to 8,058 feet (2,458 metres) in Jebel Tidirhine.

The Atlas Mountains

The Atlas Mountains comprise three distinct chains. The Haut Atlas (High Atlas), 460 miles (740 kilometres) long, begins as small hills at the edge of the Atlantic, rises rapidly to more than 6,500 feet, and reaches its highest point in Jebel Toubkal, which is 13,665 feet (4,165 metres) high. The Moyen Atlas (Middle Atlas) slopes away from the Haut Atlas in a northerly direction, rising to 10,794 feet (3,290 metres). The Anti-Atlas extends southwestward from the Haut Atlas to the Atlantic.

To the east of the Atlas are the flat Hauts Plateaux (High Plateaus) of eastern Morocco, which are between about 3,900 and 4,250 feet in altitude and which were formed as depressions that became filled with coarse sedimentary deposits. Atlantic Morocco comprises plains formed of finer sediments and plateaus consisting of coarser deposits.

The vast plain of the Rharb, at the foot of er-Rif, is an old pass that was narrowed by the upheaval of er-Rif and has since gradually been silted up by alluvial deposits from the Oued Sebou (a *oued,* or wadi, is a seasonal watercourse). Inland, the plains of Fès, Oujda, and the Angad become progressively smaller. The vast region lying between the Rharb, the Atlantic, and the Atlas is named the Moroccan *meseta* ("plateau"); it is covered with a thin layer of sediments, thus forming a coastal plateau about 700 feet high that runs from Rabat to the coastal range of the Haut Atlas.

The coastline is regular, but, before modern ports were built, sandbars made navigation difficult. To the south, the Sous plain separates the Haut Atlas from the Anti-Atlas, south of which begins the great Sahara.

The rivers

Drainage. The Saharan area of eastern Morocco is drained by the Dadès, Rheris, Ziz, and Guir rivers, all of which originate in the Haut Atlas and lose themselves in the desert after cutting impressive chasms through the mountains. The northern region is drained by the Moulouya, which begins in the Moyen Atlas and empties into the Mediterranean after flowing for 320 miles. Er-Rif is drained by small torrential rivers such as the Laou, the Rhis, and the Nekor. Among the rivers flowing into the Atlantic are the Loukkos, which has its source in the western part of er-Rif and enters the ocean at Larache; the Sebou, the most strongly flowing river in Morocco, which is 280 miles long and reaches the ocean at Mehdiya after much meandering; and the Oum er-Rbia, which is somewhat longer than the Sebou and is the most regular of Morocco's rivers.

All Moroccan rivers are torrential in nature: the Moulouya's flow ranges from 175 to 35,000 cubic feet (5 to 1,000 cubic metres) per second during the summer.

Climate. In the coastal regions the Moroccan climate is temperate within a narrow climatic range. Because of the country's latitude, the climate is influenced by the proximity of the Azores anticyclone (a system of winds that rotates in a clockwise direction about a centre of high atmospheric pressure). The west winds that blow for most of the year result in changeable weather and irregular rainfall in the autumn and winter months. During the summer months this anticyclone moves north, resulting in calmer weather. The cold ocean current, which flows toward Morocco from the Canary Islands to the southwest, also helps to produce a milder climate.

In contrast to the coastal pattern, the inland climate assumes an increasingly continental character as one approaches the Atlas and the eastern inland plains. Sometimes, but very rarely, the desert wind known as the *chergui* ("that which blows from the east") can cause the temperature to rise to 95° to 104° F (35° to 40° C) in the mountains and even along the coast. Tangier has an average temperature of about 54° F (12° C) in January and 75° F (24° C) in August; Casablanca's temperature averages 54° F (12° C) and 73° F (23° C) for the same months, while Essaouira has temperatures of 59° F (15° C) and 68° F (20° C). Inland, the range is greater: the average at Meknès ranges between 50° and 77° F (10° and 25° C), and at Taza between 52° and 82° F (11° and 28° C). In the mountains the temperature may plunge to −4° F (−20° C) at the summits or soar to 104° F (40° C) when the *chergui* is blowing.

Temperatures and rainfall

Rainfall depends on altitude and latitude; er-Rif and the Moyen Atlas in the north receive an annual precipitation of more than 47 inches (1,175 millimetres); the northern Atlantic plains receive between 16 and 32 inches, which is just enough to cultivate corn (maize) without irrigation. To the south, and up to the Atlas, the rainfall average is steady at between eight and 10 inches. To the east it ranges from six to 14 inches, whereas in the Sous it is less than eight inches. The rainy season usually lasts from November to January and sometimes continues into March. Rainfall is often irregular and unevenly distributed. Torrential downpours sometimes cause catastrophic floods, particularly in the Rharb and in the Sous and Tafilalt regions, just north of the Sahara. Snow falls above about 6,500 feet and melts in the spring, by June or July at the latest.

Plant and animal life. The vegetation of Morocco is typical of that of the western Mediterranean region and similar to that of the Iberian Peninsula. In the mountain regions are stands of cedars, firs, and junipers. South of Essaouira, the tropical argan tree, which has an olive-like fruit that produces oil, covers 300,000 acres (120,000 hectares). The most common trees are the cork oak, which covers 740,000 acres in er-Rif and in the Rharb; the evergreen oak, which covers one-third of the wooded areas; and the thuja, a pine, which covers 2,000,000 acres in the

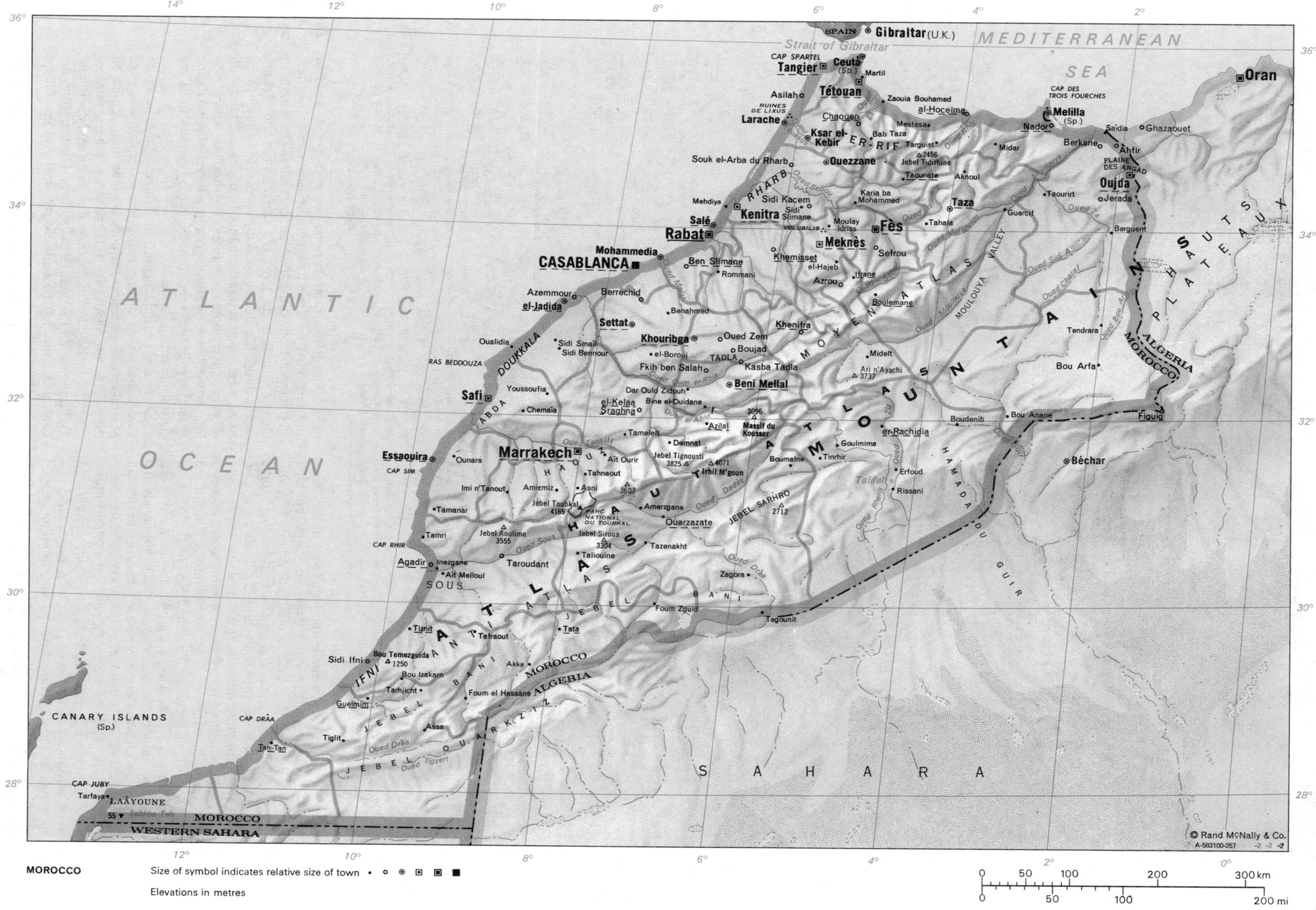
SPAIN
Gibraltar (U.K.)
Strait of Gibraltar
MEDITERRANEAN SEA
CAP SPARTEL
Tangier
Ceuta (Sp.)
Martil
Tétouan
Asilah
RUINES DE LIXUS
Larache
Ksar el-Kebir
Chaouen
Ouezzane
Bab Taza
ER RIF
Zaouia Bouhamed
Mestassa
al-Hoceima
Targuist
Jebel Tidirhine 2456
Taounate
Karia ba Mohammed
Aknoul
Taza
Tahala
Fès
Sefrou
Moulay Idriss
VOLUBILIS
Meknès
Sidi Kacem
Sidi Slimane
Kenitra
Souk el-Arba du Rharb
RHARB
Mehdiya
Salé
Rabat
Khemisset
el-Hajeb
Azrou
Ifrane
Boulemane
Khenifra
Ben Slimane
Rommani
Mohammedia
CASABLANCA
Azemmour
el-Jadida
Berrechid
Settat
Benahmed
Khouribga
el-Borouj
Oued Zem
Boujad
Kasba Tadla
TADLA
Beni Mellal
Fkih ben Salah
Dar Ould Zidouh
Bine el-Ouidane
el-Kelaa Sraghna
Azilal
3096
Massif du Kousser
Demnat
Jebel Tignousti 3825
4071
Irhil M'goun
Tamelelt
Ait Ourir
Tahnaout
Asni
3607
Jebel Toubkal 4165
PARC NATIONAL DU TOUBKAL
Jebel Siroua 3304
Amerzgane
Ouarzazate
Tazenakht
Taliouine
Tata
Sidi Smail
Sidi Bennour
Youssoufia
Chemaia
Marrakech
Amizmiz
Imi n'Tanout
Oualidia
DOUKKALA
ABDA
Safi
RAS BEDDOUZA
Ounara
Tamanar
Essaouira
CAP SIM
Tamri
CAP RHIR
Agadir
Inezgane
Ait Melloul
SOUS
Oued Sous
Oued Tensift
Taroudant
Jebel Aoulime 3555
Tafraout
Tiznit
Bou Izakarn
Bou Temezguida 1250
Sidi Ifni
IFNI
Tarhjicht
Guelmim
Akka
Foum el Hassane
Assa
Tiglit
Tan-Tan
CAP DRÂA
Oued Drâa
Oued Tigzert
JEBEL BANI
JEBEL OUARKZIZ
ANTI ATLAS
HAUT ATLAS
MOYEN ATLAS
ATLAS MOUNTAINS
MOULOUYA VALLEY
Zagora
Foum Zguid
JEBEL SARHRO 2712
Boumalne
Tinrhir
Goulmima
er-Rachidia
Erfoud
Rissani
Tafilalt
Midelt
Ari n'Ayachi 3737
Boudenib
Bou Anane
HAMADA DU GUIR
Tagounit
Guercif
Taourirt
Oujda
PLAINE DES ANGAD
Jerada
Berguent
Tendrara
Bou Arfa
Figuig
Béchar
Berkane
Ahfir
Saidia
Ghazaouet
Oran
Nador
Melilla (Sp.)
CAP DES TROIS FOURCHES
Midar
HAUTS PLATEAUX
MOROCCO
ALGERIA
SAHARA
ATLANTIC OCEAN
CANARY ISLANDS (Sp.)
CAP JUBY
Tarfaya
LAÂYOUNE
WESTERN SAHARA
© Rand McNally & Co.
A-563100-257
MOROCCO
Size of symbol indicates relative size of town
Elevations in metres
0 50 100 200 300 km
0 50 100 200 mi

MAP INDEX

Political subdivisions

Name	Lat.	Long.
Agadir	30.25n	9.00w
Azilal	31.55n	6.20w
Beni Mellal	32.20n	6.20w
Ben Slimane	33.40n	7.10w
Boulemane	33.00n	4.00w
Casablanca	33.40n	7.40w
Chaouen	35.10n	5.10w
Essaouira	31.30n	9.30w
Fès	33.55n	5.00w
Figuig	32.40n	2.30w
Guelmim	28.30n	9.30w
Hoceïma, al-	35.10n	4.10w
Ifrane	33.25n	5.10w
Jadida, el-	33.00n	8.30w
Kelaa Sraghna, el-	32.10n	7.50w
Kenitra	34.30n	6.00w
Khemisset	33.35n	6.15w
Khenifra	32.40n	5.15w
Khouribga	32.45n	6.30w
Laâyoune	27.50n	12.20w
Marrakech	31.20n	8.10w
Meknès	33.10n	5.30w
Nador	35.00n	3.00w
Ouarzazate	30.50n	6.20w
Oujda	34.10n	2.15w
Rabat	34.00n	6.50w
Rachidia, er-	31.30n	4.00w
Safi	32.10n	9.00w
Salé	34.05n	6.50w
Settat	33.00n	7.30w
Tangier	35.45n	5.50w
Tan-Tan	28.00n	11.00w
Taounate	34.25n	4.50w
Tata	29.35n	8.00w
Taza	34.15n	3.50w
Tétouan	35.25n	5.55w
Tiznit	29.30n	9.45w

The name of a political subdivision if not shown on the map is the same as that of its capital city; symbolized: Marrakech

Cities and towns

Name	Lat.	Long.
Agadir	30.26n	9.36w
Ahfir	34.57n	2.17w
Aït Melloul	30.21n	9.31w
Aït Ourir	31.38n	7.42w
Akka	29.22n	8.14w
Aknoul	34.43n	3.49w
Alcazarquivir, see Ksar el-Kebir		
Alhucemas, see Hoceïma, al-		
Amerzgane	31.00n	7.10w
Amizmiz	31.14n	8.14w
Asilah	35.32n	6.00w
Asni	31.14n	7.55w
Assa	28.34n	9.27w
Azemmour	33.20n	8.25w
Azilal	31.58n	6.34w
Azrou	33.27n	5.14w
Bab Taza	35.03n	5.14w
Benahmed	33.07n	7.17w
Beni Mellal	32.22n	6.29w
Ben Slimane	33.41n	7.10w
Berguent	34.03n	2.02w
Berkane	34.59n	2.20w
Berrechid	33.17n	7.35w
Bine el-Ouidane	32.07n	6.26w
Borouj, el-	32.30n	7.12w
Bou Anane	32.03n	3.03w
Bou Arfa	32.30n	1.59w
Boudenib	31.57n	3.36w
Bou Izakarn	29.09n	9.44w
Boujad	32.48n	6.26w
Boulemane	33.22n	4.45w
Boumalne	31.32n	5.27w
Casablanca	33.39n	7.35w
Chaouen (Chechaouene)	35.10n	5.16w
Chechaouene, see Chaouen		
Chemaïa	31.30n	8.47w
Dar Ould Zidouh	32.22n	6.49w
Demnat	31.44n	6.59w
Erfoud	31.28n	4.10w
Essaouira (Mogador)	31.30n	9.47w
Fès	34.05n	4.57w
Figuig	32.10n	1.15w
Fkih ben Salah	32.32n	6.40w
Foum el-Hassane	28.59n	8.55w
Foum Zguid	30.04n	6.54w
Goulmima	31.42n	4.57w
Guelmim	28.59n	10.04w
Guercif	34.15n	3.21w
Hajeb, el-	33.42n	5.22w
Hoceïma, al- (Alhucemas)	35.15n	3.56w
Ifrane	33.32n	5.06w
Imi n'Tanout	31.10n	8.50w
Inezgane	30.21n	9.32w
Jadida, el- (Mazagan)	33.15n	8.30w
Jerada	34.17n	2.13w
Karia ba Mohammed	34.19n	5.10w
Kasba Tadla	32.34n	6.18w
Kelaa Sraghna, el-	32.03n	7.24w
Kenitra	34.16n	6.40w
Khemisset	33.50n	6.03w
Khenifra	33.00n	5.40w
Khouribga	32.54n	6.57w
Ksar el-Kebir	35.01n	5.54w
Ksar es-Souk, see Rachidia, er-		
Larache	35.12n	6.10w
Marrakech	31.38n	8.00w
Martil	35.37n	5.17w
Mazagan, see Jadida, el-		
Mehdiya	34.15n	6.41w
Meknès	33.53n	5.37w
Mestasa	35.07n	4.25w
Midar	34.58n	3.30w
Midelt	32.41n	4.43w
Mogador, see Essaouira		
Mohammedia	33.44n	7.24w
Moulay Idriss	34.02n	5.27w
Nador	35.12n	2.55w
Oualidia	32.44n	9.08w
Ouarzazate	30.57n	6.50w
Oued Zem	32.55n	6.33w
Ouezzane	34.52n	5.35w
Oujda	34.41n	1.45w
Ounara	31.33n	9.28w
Port-Lyautey, see Kenitra		
Rabat	34.02n	6.51w
Rachidia, er- (Ksar es-Souk)	31.58n	4.25w
Rissani	31.23n	4.09w
Rommani	31.23n	4.09w
Safi	32.20n	9.17w
Saïdia	35.04n	2.15w
Salé	34.04n	6.50w
Sefrou	33.50n	4.50w
Settat	33.04n	7.37w
Sidi Bennour	39.30n	8.30w
Sidi Ifni	29.24n	10.12w
Sidi Kacem	34.13n	5.39w
Sidi Slimane	34.15n	5.49w
Sidi Smaïl	32.49n	8.30w
Souk el-Arba du Rharb	34.43n	6.01w
Tafraout	29.40n	8.58w
Tagounit	29.58n	5.36w
Tahala	34.04n	4.20w
Tahnaout	31.24n	7.54w
Taliouine	30.36n	7.49w
Tamanar	31.00n	9.35w
Tamelelt	31.50n	7.29w
Tamri	30.43n	9.43w
Tangier (Tanger)	35.48n	5.45w
Tan-Tan	28.26n	11.06w
Taounate	34.25n	4.39w
Taourirt	34.25n	2.53w
Tarfaya (Villa Bens)	27.58n	12.55w
Targuist	34.57n	4.18w
Tarhjicht	29.05n	9.24w
Taroudant	30.31n	8.55w
Tata	29.44n	7.56w
Taza	34.16n	4.01w
Tazenakht	30.35n	7.12w
Tendrara	33.04n	1.59w
Tétouan	35.34n	5.23w
Tiglit	28.31n	10.15w
Tinrhir	31.28n	5.30w
Tiznit	29.43n	9.44w
Villa Bens, see Tarfaya		
Xauen, see Chaouen		
Youssoufia	32.16n	8.33w
Zagora	30.22n	5.50w
Zaouia Bouhamed	35.25n	5.00w

Physical features and points of interest

Name	Lat.	Long.
Abda, *plain*	32.10n	9.05w
Abid, Oued el-, *river*	32.18n	7.03w
Angad, Plaine des, *plain*	34.43n	1.50w
Anti-Atlas, *mountains*	30.00n	8.30w
Aoulime, Jebel, *mountain*	30.48n	8.50w
Atlantic Ocean	32.00n	12.00w
Atlas Mountains	33.00n	2.00w
Ayachi, Ari n', *mountain*	32.29n	4.57w
Bani, Jebel, *mountains*	29.30n	8.00w
Beddouza, Ras, *cape*	32.35n	9.18w
Bou Arjam, Oued, *watercourse*	33.36n	1.31w
Bou Temezguida, *mountain*	29.21n	9.55w
Charef, Oued, *watercourse*	34.07n	2.05w
Dadès, Oued, *watercourse*	30.55n	6.47w
Doukkala, *historic region*	32.55n	8.25w
Drâa, Cap, *cape*	28.44n	11.08w
Drâa, Oued, *watercourse*	28.43n	11.09w
Gibraltar, Strait of	35.57n	5.36w
Guir, Hamada du, *desert*	30.45n	3.15w
Guir, Oued, *watercourse*	31.40n	2.55w
Haouz, *plain*	31.30n	8.00w
Haut Atlas, *mountains*	31.30n	6.00w
Ifni, *historic region*	29.20n	10.10w
Inaouene, Oued, *river*	34.12n	4.54w
Juby, Cap, *cape*	27.58n	12.55w
Kousser, Massif du, *mountain*	32.02n	5.59w
Laou, Oued, *watercourse*	35.29n	5.04w
Lixus, Ruines de, *ruins*	35.12n	6.06w
Loukkos, Oued, *watercourse*	35.12n	6.09w
Mediterranean Sea	36.00n	3.00w
Melah, Oued, *river*	33.42n	7.26w
Melloulou, Oued, *river*	34.13n	3.21w
M'goun, Irhil, *mountain*	31.31n	6.25w
Moulouya, Oued, *river*	35.05n	2.25w
Moulouya Valley	33.40n	3.30w
Moyen Atlas, *mountains*	33.30n	5.00w
Ouarkziz, Jebel, *mountains*	28.50n	9.00w
Oum er-Rbia, Oued, *river*	33.19n	8.21w
Rharb, *historic region*	34.30n	6.02w
Rheris, Oued, *watercourse*	30.39n	4.26w
Rhir, Cap, *cape*	30.38n	9.55w
Rhis, Oued, *watercourse*	35.14n	3.57w
Rif, er-, *mountains*	35.00n	4.00w
Sarhro, Jebel, *mountains*	31.00n	5.55w
Sebou, Oued, *river*	34.15n	6.40w
Sidi Ali, Oued, *watercourse*	34.07n	2.05w
Sim, Cap, *cape*	31.23n	9.51w
Siroua, Jebel, *mountain*	30.41n	7.37w
Sous, *plain*	30.15n	9.15w
Sous, Oued, *watercourse*	30.27n	9.31w
Spartel, Cap, *cape*	35.48n	5.56w
Tadla, *plain*	32.30n	6.20w
Tafilalt, *oasis*	31.18n	4.18w
Tah, Sebkha, *dry lake*	27.42n	12.48w
Tensift, Oued, *river*	32.02n	9.22w
Tidirhine, Jebel, *mountain*	34.50n	4.30w
Tignousti, Jebel, *mountain*	31.31n	6.44w
Tigzert Oued, *watercourse*	28.20n	9.35w
Toubkal, Jebel, *mountain*	31.03n	7.55w
Toubkal, Parc National du, *national park*	31.00n	7.55w
Trois Fourches, Cap des, *cape*	35.26n	2.58w
Volubilis, *ruins*	34.00n	5.30w
Za, Oued, *river*	34.34n	3.03w
Ziz, Oued, *watercourse*	30.39n	4.26w

lower Moulouya Valley and in the high areas of the Sous. The wild olive and the mastic tree are found on high plateaus where there is little rainfall, and the dwarf palm grows on the arid inland plains. The fruit-bearing jujube tree is common in the Tadla and the Haouz regions. Tough esparto grass (often used for making cordage and clothing), sometimes mixed in with wormwood, covers a vast area. Date palms mark the northernmost limit of the desert, south of the Oued Drâa and east of the Atlas, at Boudenib and Figuig. They are grown also under artificial conditions in the Marrakech area. Such species as the Barbary fig and the eucalyptus are imports; the former was introduced from the Americas by way of Spain in the 16th century, the latter by the French in the 20th century.

The animal life is also Mediterranean: camels and horses were introduced at the dawn of history. Lions have disappeared, as did elephants before them; mouflon (a wild sheep), gazelle, fennec (a type of fox), and macaco (a type of monkey) are still common in the Atlas region.

Settlement patterns. Morocco has five major regions—the Rif, the Rharb, the Haouz, the Sous, and eastern Morocco. The Rif, a mountainous country, is well watered and inhabited by settled farmers, mostly tree cultivators, who have a strong sense of clannish loyalty. The Rharb, in the wider sense of the term, is centred on Fès and Meknès and includes the Berber-speaking shepherds of the Moyen Atlas, who practice transhumance (the seasonal migration of herds to mountain pastures). Within the Rharb also live settled Arabic speaking grain producers of the Atlantic coastal region and seminomadic cattle breeders from the central mountain ranges.

The five main regions

The south central region, or Haouz, now looks to Casablanca as its urban centre, but its capital was once Marrakech. This region includes peasants long settled on the soil of the Doukkala and the Abda plains, seminomadic cattle breeders of the central plateaus and the inland Tadla plains, and settled farmers of the Dir area (dirs are conical deposits left by seasonal streams) and the valleys of the Haut Atlas.

The Sous in the historic sense includes the Haut Atlas, the Sous plain, and the Anti-Atlas. This is the land of the Shluh (Shleuh, Chleuh), who are a Berber people; its high population density has brought about extremely complex community organization. The region is associated with the production of essential oils, saffron, and the exquisite metalwork traditional to Morocco.

Eastern Morocco covers the region known historically as Tafilalt, in which the desert's influence is strongly felt. Settled inhabitants of the irrigated oases, including a large proportion of people of mixed negroid descent, or Ḥarāṭīn, live alongside nomadic sheep breeders; the settled peoples earn their living as agricultural labourers. After a long period of decline, the nomadic way of life of the Aït Atta people of the Drâa and the Tekna and Regeibat people of eastern and Atlantic Morocco has completely disappeared. The long drought of the 1970s and recurring border conflicts made it impossible for the nomads of this region, as of other parts of the Sahara, to continue their ancestral way of life.

Modes of life. The ecological conditions of Morocco produce a habitat that is very diversified and in the process of rapid transformation. The sedentary populations of the Rif and the Atlas group themselves in hamlets, many of which, to ensure security, are perched atop hills. The houses, with highly decorated exteriors, are constructed either of stone or of dried clay and are roofed with reeds and with corn leaves. The shepherds of the Moyen Atlas pass the winter in their villages and in the summer migrate with their herds and flocks, living under tents (called *khaymas*) woven of goat hair. Those who raise sheep on the steppes of the Haouz and eastern Morocco group themselves in *douar*s composed of thatch-roofed dwellings called *nouala*s. The agriculturalists of the Rharb and the Doukkala long ago adopted solid houses, often roofed with sheet metal. Since 1972, under the auspices of a policy to improve living conditions, the government has turned its attention to rural habitation. Studies were made of the groupings of people; the types of construction were studied, experiments were conducted with new building materials, and pilot villages were constructed.

Rural and urban settlement

There are three types of traditional urban agglomerations: imperial towns (Fès, Marrakech, Meknès); port towns (Rabat, Essaouira, Tangier, Tétouan); and small towns in the interior that have religious prestige (Ouezzane, Boujad, Tiznit). During the period of the French protectorate (1912–56), the administration did not attempt new construction within the towns, all of which were still encircled by ramparts, but instead built alongside them new towns, where industries and administrations were established. Surrounding these work sites and along the approaches to these towns sprang up groups of squatters' shacks that spread to form shantytowns, or *bidonvilles.* The old *madīnah*s, or town centres, soon became overpopulated, and in addition the new towns—at first well-maintained, with new housing and wide, shaded avenues—began to swarm with new *quartiers* and *bidonvilles,* into which rural immigrants crowded to live in lamentably unhealthy conditions. Only the agglomerations that have had no industrial development, such as Asilah, Chaouen, and Azemmour, have maintained a degree of their traditional charm. In the hope of attracting additional international tourism to Morocco, the government has adopted a new policy of urban development. With the encouragement of the United Nations Educational, Scientific and Cultural Organization (UNESCO), for example, the government decided to safeguard the *madīnah* of Fès, acknowledging its religious importance as the site of the oldest mosque in North Africa. City planning aims to give each town a greater homogeneity and to assure a certain cohesiveness among the different *quartiers* (districts, or neighborhoods). Instead of razing the *bidonvilles,* only to see them reappear farther away, the government has tried to transform them from within by encouraging initiative among their residents. Regional considerations are taken into account in order to preserve the diversity of the towns.

THE PEOPLE

Arabs and Berbers

The population of Morocco is Arab and Berber in origin, though the difference between the two groups today is more linguistic than racial. The Berber language, although greatly influenced by Arabic, has been preserved in the mountainous regions, which have long been areas of refuge. Berber-speaking inhabitants are divided into three ethnolinguistic groups: the Rif people (also called Riffi or Riffians) of er-Rif, the Tamazight of the Moyen Atlas, and the Shluh of the Haut Atlas and the Sous. With improved communications and the exodus to the towns, Arabic–Berber bilingualism has become common, and the proportion of monolingual Berbers does not exceed 25 percent. The remainder of the Moroccan population speaks Arabic

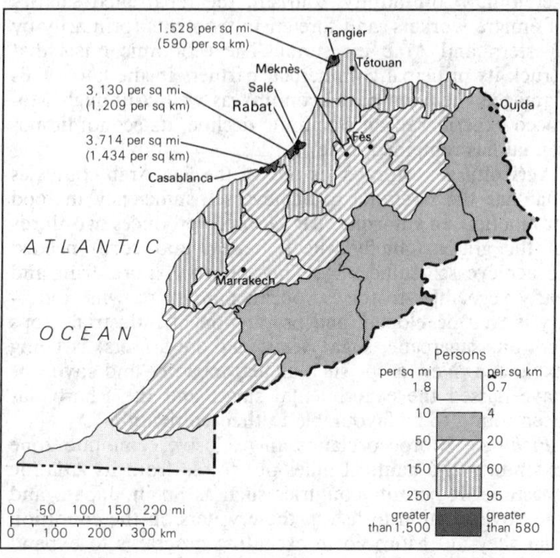

Population density of Morocco.

and is composed mainly of Arabized Berbers from the plains and the plateaus, as well as a small number of Bedouin Arabs who moved to Morocco with the armies of Islām in the 7th century or with the invading Hilāl tribe in the 11th and 12th centuries.

Immigrants from Spain, who travelled to Morocco at various stages of the Christian reconquest of the Iberian Peninsula, which culminated in 1492, were themselves a mixture of Arab, Berber, and Iberian; today they live chiefly in Rabat, Salé, Fès, and Tétouan.

Trade and cultural relations with black Africa since the Middle Ages have resulted in the gradual growth of a significant black minority, living chiefly in the southern oases or in the royal towns, particularly Marrakech and Meknès. The Jewish minority—a considerable community until Jewish emigration to Israel began in 1948—consists of small Berber-speaking groups whose origins are obscure and of Arabic-speaking groups who arrived from Spain and other Mediterranean countries at various periods of history.

European colonization brought a French and a Spanish minority whose numbers had reached some 500,000 on the eve of independence in 1956. The French and Spanish languages, which spread among the urban population during the period of the protectorate, are still spoken. With the exception of the rapidly declining gallicized Jewish minority, however, the majority of the Moroccan population has a common culture and religion. Most Moroccans are Sunnī Muslims of the Māliki order.

Patterns in emigration

Until the mid-1970s the opportunity to emigrate to western European countries offered a partial solution to Morocco's population explosion; some 600,000 Moroccan workers and merchants had established themselves in western Europe, notably in France, Belgium, The Netherlands, and West Germany. The European labour market was closed to new workers, however, by the early 1980s, and Morocco's population problem was only slightly relieved by the open labour markets of some Arab nations, among them Iraq and Saudi Arabia.

In the mid-1960s the Moroccan government launched a family-planning campaign. Studies had shown that for the most part Moroccans—and Moroccan women in particular—were not opposed to such a program. The government's experimental program soon made it clear, however, that its success required a complete reformation of matrimonial law, an action not simple to take in a Muslim country. Unable to reverse the demographic trends, the Moroccan authorities were obliged to completely change their policy on urbanism, education, and health.

THE ECONOMY

Resources. Morocco finances its economic growth with five principal sources of revenue: the exportation of phosphate, the subcontracting of enterprises of the European Economic Community, tourism, the repatriated salaries of émigré workers, and foreign investments (primarily by Western and Arab investors). The economic crisis that struck its principal commercial partners in the late 1970s damaged the Moroccan economy as well. Although Morocco experienced an economic decline, its economic potential has remained intact.

Agriculture. Morocco is one of the few Arab countries that has the potential to achieve self-sufficiency in food production. In a normal year Morocco produces two-thirds of the grains (chiefly wheat, barley, and corn) needed to achieve self-sufficiency. The country exports fruit and early vegetables to the European market; its wine industry is well developed, and production of industrial crops (cotton, sugarcane, sugar beets, and sunflowers) is being expanded. New crops such as tea, tobacco, and soybeans have passed the experimental stage, and the Rharb has been found to be favourable to their cultivation.

Agricultural development and production

Fishing. Morocco claims an exclusive economic zone extending 200 nautical miles out to sea from its Atlantic coastline. It permits countries such as Spain, Japan, and the Soviet Union to fish in these waters on the condition that they aid Morocco in executing programs to expand its fishing ports, to create a chain of ice plants and fish-freezing stations, and to augment and modernize its fishing fleet.

Livestock raising, particularly sheep and cattle, is important. The country fills its own meat requirements and is making efforts to be self-sufficient in milk production. Morocco's forests, mostly located on the heights of the Haut and Moyen Atlas ranges, supply a portion of the country's lumber, but the remainder must be imported. A policy of afforestation has led to the development of a cellulose industry and enables Morocco to export paper pulp.

Mining. Despite its agricultural advantages, Morocco remains above all a mining country. It has the world's largest phosphate reserves; its production capacity reached 24,000,000 tons by the early 1980s and can be increased. Morocco also produces iron, zinc, lead, manganese, cobalt, and pyrrhotite (a ferrous sulfide from which sulfur is extracted).

Mining and industry

Morocco's ability to supply its energy needs in the early 1980s was limited: one-half of the country's exports were required to pay for its petroleum imports. Indications of petroleum reserves have been discovered, however, off Essaouira and in the Taza region. Morocco has coal and oil shale (4 percent of the world's reserves), and its rivers have an important hydroelectric potential (3,000,000,000 kilowatts), of which only one-half is being exploited. Morocco's uranium reserves are mixed with phosphates.

Industry. Industry accounts for about one-sixth of the gross domestic product. In addition to the food-processing and textile industries dating from the 1950s, assembly and subcontracting industries have been established since 1970; a law passed in 1979 required these industries to increase the percentage of locally made components in their products. Morocco has developed heavy industry as well. An iron and steel complex was scheduled to begin production at Nador in 1985. The Moroccan chemical industry is based on phosphate.

Because of this policy of industrialization, which coincided with the increase in the price of energy, Morocco continued in the early 1980s to have a balance-of-trade deficit in spite of the increase in its exports of semifinished products. It was able to counter its deficit somewhat with the investments of oil-producing Arab nations.

Administration of the economy. The Moroccan government pursues a pragmatic planning policy. The government is responsible for elements of the infrastructure such as roads, ports, and dams; for projects that are neglected by the private sector yet still necessary to a healthy balance of trade, such as sugar refineries, cement works, and steel mills; and for works necessary to ensure better regional development, such as the phosphate works at Essaouira. This public sector, nevertheless, is granted no commercial or fiscal privileges.

The Moroccan government strongly prefers to ally itself in its business enterprises with private capital, both domestic and foreign. The Office du Développement Industriel (ODI) studies projects, presents them to possible investors, and, when the occasion arises, participates in the financing. An investment code promulgated in 1958 has since been liberalized several times. By 1982 the government maintained 25 industrial zones scattered throughout the country. Industrial sites are at the disposition of investors, who, during an initial period, are exempt from taxation. They can, furthermore, import duty-free all necessary equipment. Foreign investors can return profits from industry in Morocco to their home countries and can liquidate an industry in Morocco without penalty.

The banking system, centred mostly in Casablanca, also is mixed. Alongside nationalized banks are banks funded by private capital, both Moroccan and foreign.

Wages in Morocco are low in comparison to wages in more heavily industrialized nations, and a rise in wages, when one occurs, never exceeds 15 percent. The government maintains a minimum guaranteed salary in industry and in agriculture, from which management and the trade unions negotiate in collective bargaining.

Transportation. A road network links Morocco's various regions to some 20 ports, situated, for the most part, on the Atlantic coast. Until the late 1970s the products of the Mediterranean and eastern regions were exported from either the Spanish enclave of Melilla or the Algerian port of Ghazaouet. To end this dependence, a port was constructed at Nador and another was begun at Ras Kebdana. Agricultural products of the Rharb, where the network of roads is dense, are stockpiled at Fès and Meknès and exported from Kenitra and Casablanca. A superhighway, half-completed by the early 1980s, connects Rabat and Casablanca. The petroleum port of Mohammedia was being enlarged in the early 1980s. Phosphate from Khouribga is shipped by rail directly to the port at Casablanca for export; phosphate from Youssoufia was until the late 1970s exported from Safi, but because of the increase in production a new phosphate port was opened at Jorf Lasfar in 1982. The port at Agadir, rebuilt after the earthquake of 1960, serves as an outlet for the Sous region. New ports at Tan-Tan and Tarfaya make possible the economic development of the Saharan south. The national shipping company, Comanav, accounts for about one-third of the country's traffic.

The ports

The railway system connects the principal cities of the north. The Casablanca–Rabat line has been double-tracked and the Casablanca–Marrakech line relaid. There is also a line from Youssoufia to Jorf Lasfar and a Marrakech–Laâyoune (former El Aiún, in the Western Sahara) line, to pass through Ouarzazate and Agadir and provide access to the mining region of the southeastern Sahara.

Morocco has nine airports capable of accommodating heavy aircraft. The principal airport is the Muhammad V air terminal, 22 miles from Casablanca. Royal Air Maroc (RAM) provides regular service to principal cities of Europe, the United States, the Middle East, and western Africa. A domestic airline, Royal Air Inter, provides service to the interior.

ADMINISTRATIVE AND SOCIAL CONDITIONS

Government. *Constitutional framework.* Morocco has been a constitutional monarchy since 1962, and its constitution has been amended several times by referendum. Morocco experimented with a parliamentary type of government between 1963 and 1965, but after a period of five years, during which full power devolved upon the king, a referendum in 1970 replaced the previous bicameral legislature with a single chamber having limited legislative powers. A referendum in 1980 extended the term of the parliament from four to six years.

A new constitution promulgated in 1972 vested executive power in the king. The king, whose person is sacred and inviolable, directs diplomacy and defense and outlines economic and cultural development. He has the right to submit laws directly to a popular referendum and can send back any law that has been adopted after a second reading in the chamber.

Two-thirds of the members of the parliament are elected by universal suffrage (men and women citizens 21 years of age or older), and the remaining one-third are elected by a college formed of representatives of regional councils, professional bodies, and trade unions. Parliament votes on laws and discusses the annual budget and the national plan for social and economic development. A prime minister, who serves as the head of administration, is named by the king and invested by the parliament. The government is responsible to both the king and the parliament.

Decentralization of government

The country is divided into urban prefectures and provinces, the number of which continues to grow due to the effort to decentralize the government. By 1982 there were six prefectures (five at Casablanca and one at Rabat-Salé) and 32 provinces (within the borders of Morocco prior to its occupation of Western Sahara in 1976). A communal charter assures municipal councils and rural communes of budgetary autonomy. Provinces and prefectures are aligned into seven regions, each of which has an assembly that manages its own regional development. At the provincial level the *'amil* (governor), a direct representative of the king, coordinates local services.

Political life. In the legislative elections held in June 1977, the nationalist Istiqlāl (Independence) party and the Mouvement Populaire (Popular Movement) emerged as the strongest parties. In 1978 a coalition, Rassemblement National des Indépendants (RNI; National Assembly of Independents) was formed. The coalition represented the interests of the rural majority, the new bureaucratic class, and the traditional bureaucracy. The working classes of the cities and of the irrigated agricultural zones supported the Union Nationale des Forces Populaires (UNFP); the Union Socialiste des Forces Populaires (USFP), which split from the UNFP in 1972; and the Parti du Progrès et du Socialisme (PPS), which formed the opposition in the new assembly.

Political parties

Justice. In theory the Qur'ān is the source of law, and the king is the spiritual head of the community; in effect the Qur'ānic jurisdiction, exercised by the *qāḍī*s, or cadis (Muslim judges who interpret and administer the religious law of Islām), is limited to matters relating to the personal status of Muslims. Rabbinical justice applies to Jews. All other matters, whether they concern Muslims, Jews, or others, are in the hands of the "modern" courts, which apply a code of laws inspired by the French. The various regional and local courts are beneath the three courts of appeal and the supreme court, which sits in Casablanca. All are supervised by the Ministry of Justice. French and Spanish lawyers may in principle practice at the Moroccan bar. All oral procedures are conducted in Arabic, but lawyers may be permitted to assist their clients and submit their conclusions in languages other than Arabic. The Ministry of Justice has conducted its affairs in Arabic since 1965. Morocco has a charter of civil liberties that is safeguarded by an association of intellectuals and legislators.

Education. Some students have pursued their studies in foreign countries, notably in France and Belgium. At all levels the number of women receiving education is between 30 and 40 percent of the total. Morocco continues to call upon foreign teachers, but efforts are under way to Moroccanize the entire system of secondary education. Students enrolled in scientific and technical disciplines outnumbered those who pursued literary and legal studies.

Education absorbs one-fourth of the national budget. Because of the population explosion and the delay in the development of education until 1950, the illiteracy rate in the early 1980s remained high.

In addition to public education Morocco has privately funded schools and institutions for children of the foreign residents. These are open to young Moroccans as well.

Health and welfare. There are two faculties of medicine—at Casablanca and at Rabat. To combat the rising costs of health care, the government has begun to emphasize preventive medicine by increasing the number of dispensaries and health centres. Industrial workers benefit from social security, and a modern polyclinic in Casablanca is reserved for union workers.

Endemic illnesses of the past, such as trachoma, tuberculosis, and cholera, have been conquered. New afflictions—particularly those linked to the expansion of irrigation zones, such as schistosomiasis, or to the pace of urban life, such as cardiovascular diseases—are occurring, however.

The population explosion and the rural exodus have posed serious problems to the Moroccan authorities, who have sought to simultaneously stem the damage of the overpopulated *madīnah*s, renovate the *bidonvilles,* improve rural housing, and safeguard regional architectural traditions. Despite the pressing needs the government's policy is to leave the problem of urban housing to the private sector. To guard against real-estate speculation, local authorities secure land and then sell it at cost to poorly housed people who want to build; the people must nevertheless apply to banks to obtain the necessary loans. Likewise, municipalities install water, electricity, and sewer services in the *bidonvilles,* but leave to the residents the task of transforming their shacks into solid buildings.

CULTURAL LIFE

Arabic is the national and official language of Morocco; French and Spanish, however, are widely spoken, and English is increasingly used. For several years attempts have been made to revive the Berber culture, and authorities have created an institute of Arab and Berber cultures.

The production of Arabic literature has continued to grow and diversify. To the traditional genres—poetry, essays, and historiography—have been added forms inspired by Middle Eastern and Western literary models. French is used in publication of research in the social and natural sciences. The Moroccan literary market is open to both Arabic and French publishers. Many Moroccan authors and educators publish in Lebanon and France, and their works are not counted among Moroccan output.

The arts. Since independence a veritable blossoming has taken place in painting and sculpture, popular music, and amateur theatre. Painting, centred at the two schools of fine arts—at Casablanca and at Tétouan—is strongly encouraged by the Ministry of Culture. The Ministry of Tourism promotes music and dance. Each year it organizes a folklore festival at Marrakech, a jazz festival at Tangier, a festival of Andalusian music at Saîdia, and an African arts festival at Agadir. The festival at Asilah, organized by private supporters, during the month of August transforms the entire town into an immense studio where artists from four continents show their work.

Arts festivals

Filmmaking, encouraged by a government office, remains modest; nevertheless, Moroccan films by talented young directors have won the esteem of Arab and European critics.

Cultural organization. The Ministry of Culture is responsible for libraries, museums, and archives. It also restores historic monuments, organizes each year an exhibition of rare books and manuscripts, awards the Prix du Maroc each year to the best literary and scientific works, and provides material assistance to all nonprofit cultural associations.

The Académie Royale du Maroc was founded in 1979. It is composed of 60 members, of whom only about one-half are Moroccan. It is interdisciplinary and has adopted as its aim an improved understanding among cultures. Numerous cultural centres attached to foreign embassies contribute to the diversity of Morocco's cultural life.

For statistical data on the land and people of Morocco, see the *Britannica World Data* section in the BRITANNICA WORLD DATA ANNUAL. (A.La./Ed.)

History

DECLINE OF TRADITIONAL GOVERNMENT (1830–1912)

During the French invasion of Algeria in 1830, the sultan of Morocco, Moulay Abd ar-Rahman (1822–59), briefly sent troops to occupy Tlemcen but withdrew them after French protests. The Algerian leader Abdelkader offered his allegiance to the Sultan and in 1844 took refuge from the French in Morocco. A Moroccan army was sent to the Algerian frontier; the French bombarded Tangier on August 4, 1844, and Essaouira (Mogador) on August 15. Meanwhile, on August 14, the Moroccan army had been totally defeated at Isly, near the frontier town of Oujda. The Sultan then promised to intern or expel Abdelkader if he should again enter Moroccan territory. Two years later, when again driven into Morocco, the Algerian leader was attacked by Moroccan troops and was forced to surrender to the French.

In 1856 the British secured trade privileges, including the right of according "protection" to Moroccan citizens. Immediately after Abd ar-Rahman's death in 1859, a dispute with Spain over the boundaries of the Spanish enclave at Ceuta led to a declaration of war by Madrid and to the Spanish capture of Tétouan in the following year. Peace had to be bought with an indemnity of $20,000,000, the enlargement of Ceuta's frontiers, and the promise to cede to Spain another enclave—Ifni.

Attempts at modernization

The new sultan, Sidi Muhammad (1859–73), attempted without any marked success to modernize the Moroccan army. After his death, his son Moulay Hassan I (1873–94) struggled to preserve independence. After his death, his chamberlain, Ba Ahmed, ruled in the name of the young sultan Abd al-Aziz until 1901, when the latter began his direct rule.

Abd al-Aziz surrounded himself with European companions and adopted their customs, scandalizing his subjects, particularly the religious leaders. His attempt to introduce a modern system of land taxation resulted in complete confusion because of a lack of qualified officials. Popular discontent and tribal rebellion became even more common, while a pretender, Bu Hamara, established a rival court near Melilla. European powers seized the occasion thus offered to extend their own influence. In 1904 Britain gave France a free hand in Morocco in return for a French undertaking not to interfere with British plans in Egypt. Spanish agreement was secured by a French promise that northern Morocco should be treated as a sphere of Spanish influence. Italian interests were satisfied by a French undertaking not to hinder Italian designs on Libya. Possible German claims were ignored, thus enabling the Sultan to arrange an international conference at Algeciras, Spain, in 1906 to discuss the whole Moroccan question.

Algeciras Conference

The Algeciras Conference confirmed the integrity of the Sultan's domains; the right of all countries to trade in Morocco on equal terms was ensured by the imposition of customs dues at a uniform rate of 12½ percent on all imports. At the same time, however, the conference sanctioned French and Spanish policing of the ports and collection of the customs dues. In 1907–08 the Sultan's brother, Moulay Abd al-Hafid, led a rebellion against him, denouncing him for his departure from Muslim ways. Abd al-Aziz took refuge in Tangier. Abd al-Hafid then made an abortive attack on French troops, which had occupied Casablanca in 1907, before proceeding to Fès, where he was duly proclaimed sultan and recognized by the European powers (1909).

The new sultan proved unable to control the country. Disorder increased until, besieged by tribesmen in Fès, he was forced to ask the French to rescue him. When they had done so, he had no choice but to sign the Treaty of Fès (March 30, 1912), by which Morocco became a French protectorate. In return the French guaranteed to maintain the status of the Sultan and his successors. Provision was also made to meet the Spanish claim for a special position in the north of the country; Tangier, long the seat of the diplomatic missions, retained a distinctive administration.

The French protectorate (1912–56). In establishing their protectorate over Morocco, the French had behind them the experience of the conquest of Algeria and of their protectorate over Tunisia; and they took the latter as the model for their Moroccan policy. There were, however, important differences. First, the protectorate was established only two years before the outbreak of World War I, which was to bring with it a new attitude toward colonial rule. Second, Morocco had a tradition of a thousand years of independence; it had been strongly influenced by the civilization of Muslim Spain and had never been subject to Ottoman rule. These circumstances and the proximity of Morocco to Spain created a special relationship between the two countries. Morocco was also unique among North African countries in possessing a coast on the Atlantic, in the rights that various nations derived from the Act of Algeciras, and in the privileges that their diplomatic missions had acquired in Tangier. Thus, the northern tenth of the country, with an Atlantic and a Mediterranean coast, together with the desert province of Tarfaya in the southwest adjoining the Spanish Sahara, was excluded from the French-controlled area and treated as a Spanish protectorate. In the French sector, the French resident general became the real ruler of the country, subject to the approval of the Paris government. He worked through newly created departments manned by French officials. The outward forms of the traditional Moroccan government (*makhzan*) were preserved, though the role that it actually played can be estimated from the fact that the grand vizier on the installation of the protectorate, Muhammad al-Moqri, still held the same post on the recovery of independence 44 years later, when he was more than 100 years old. As in Tunisia, country districts were administered by *contrôleurs civils,* except in certain areas such as Fès, where it was felt necessary that officers of the rank of general should supervise the administration. In the south certain Berber chiefs (*qāʾids* or *caids*), of whom the best known was Thami al-Glaoui, were allowed to remain semi-independent.

The protectorate's government

The pre-World War II period. The first resident general, Gen. (later Marshal) L.H.G. Lyautey, was a soldier of wide experience in Indochina, Madagascar, and Algeria. He was of aristocratic outlook and possessed a deep aesthetic appreciation of the artistic qualities of Moroccan civilization. The character he gave to the administration exerted an influence throughout the period of the protectorate.

Abd al-Hafid could not reconcile himself to the new regime and, after a few months, joined his brother as a French pensioner in Tangier. In his place a more amenable brother, Moulay Yusuf, was recognized as sultan and succeeded in cooperating with the French without losing the respect of his own people. A new administrative capital was created on the Atlantic coast at Rabat. At the same time, a commercial port was developed at Casablanca. By the end of the protectorate, Casablanca was a flourishing city, with nearly 1,000,000 inhabitants and a considerable industrial establishment. Lyautey's policy was to build new European cities beside or at some distance from the old Moroccan towns, thus preserving the country's ancient monuments. The remarkable rhythm of innovation was little interrupted by World War I. Though the French government had proposed to retire to the coastal area, Lyautey managed to retain control of all of the occupied area.

The development of Casablanca

After the war one major problem was the pacification of the former Bled es-Siba outlying areas in the Atlas Mountains, over which the sultan's government often had had no real control. This was finally completed in 1934. Another problem was the extension of the uprising of Abd el-Krim from the Spanish to the French zone (see below *The Spanish Zone*).

Marshal Lyautey was succeeded by a civilian resident general in 1926. This marked a change to a more conventional colonial regime, accompanied by the extension of official colonization, the growth of European population, and the increasing impact of European thought on the minds of the younger generation, some of whom had by then received a French education.

As early as 1920 Lyautey had submitted a report saying that "a young generation is growing up which is full of life and needs activity. . . . Lacking the outlets which our administration offers only sparingly and in subordinate positions they will find an alternative way out." Only six years after Lyautey's report, young Moroccans both in Rabat, the new administrative capital, and in Fès, the centre of traditional Arab learning and culture, were meeting, quite independently of one another, to discuss demands for reforms within the terms of the protectorate treaty. They asked for more schools, a new judicial system, and the abolition of the regime of the Berber *qā'ids* in the south; for study missions in France and in the Arab East; for the cessation of official colonization; and for the suppression of licensed prostitution—objectives that would only be fully secured when the protectorate ended in 1956.

On the death of Moulay Yusuf (1927) the French chose as his successor his younger son, Sidi Muhammad (Muhammad V). Chosen in part for his retiring disposition, this sultan was in time to reveal outstanding diplomatic skill and determination. Another significant event was the French attempt to use the differences between Arabs and Berbers to counterbalance the Arab character of the Sultan's government. This led to the issue of the Berber Decree of 1930. The Berbers had hitherto been brought to accept the Arab way of life by a gradual process rather than by any sort of compulsion. Now, however, the Berber areas were to be given a perpetual exemption from the Muslim law of the kingdom. This at once stimulated Arab nationalism and brought it widespread backing from the Arab and Muslim world in general. The resulting outcry forced the administration to give ground and to modify its proposals. In 1933 the nationalists initiated a new national day called the Fête du Trône to mark the anniversary of the Sultan's accession. When he visited Fès in the following year, he received a tumultuous welcome, accompanied by anti-French demonstrations that caused the authorities to terminate the visit abruptly. This episode was soon followed by the organization of political parties of nationalist sentiment. These events coincided with the completion of the occupation of southern Morocco, which brought with it the Spanish occupation of Ifni. In 1937 rioting occurred in Meknès, where French settlers were suspected of diverting part of the town water supply to irrigate their own lands at the expense of the Muslim cultivators. Thirteen of the rioters were killed and 100 were wounded. In the ensuing repression, Muhammad Allal al-Fassi, the main nationalist leader, was banished to Gabon in Equatorial Africa, where he spent the following nine years. The emphasis of French policy at this time is reflected in a circular, issued to departmental chiefs, stating that insufficient attention was being given to "native policy," implying that the affairs of the French settlers, now numbering some 300,000, were the chief care of the administration, while the mass of the population was a matter of "native" policy.

The Berber Decree of 1930

WORLD WAR II AND THE ATTAINMENT OF INDEPENDENCE

At the outbreak of World War II in 1939, the Sultan issued a call for wholehearted cooperation with the French; and a large Moroccan contingent, mainly Berbers, served with distinction in France. The collapse of the protecting power in 1940 and the installation of the Vichy regime naturally produced an entirely new situation. The Sultan marked his independence by refusing to approve anti-Jewish legislation. When the Anglo-American landings took place in 1942, he refused to comply with the suggestion of the resident general, Auguste Noguès, that he retire to the interior. In 1943 the Sultan was influenced by his meeting with U.S. Pres. Franklin D. Roosevelt, who came to Morocco for the Casablanca Conference and was unsympathetic to continued French presence there. The majority of the people were equally affected by contact with the U.S. and British troops, who put them in touch with the outside world to an unprecedented degree. Among the people at large, the effect of the newly introduced radio broadcasts in Arabic with which the combatants, Allied and Nazi alike, sought to attract Arab listeners to their side, was considerable. In these circumstances, the nationalist movement took the new title of Ḥizb al-Istiqlāl (Independence Party). In January 1944 they submitted to the Sultan and the Allied (including the French) authorities a memorandum asking for independence under a constitutional regime. The nationalist leaders, including Ahmad Balafrej, secretary general of the Istiqlāl, were immediately arrested on an improbable charge of collaboration with the Nazis. This caused rioting in Fès and elsewhere in which some 30 or more demonstrators were killed. In the situation thus created, the initiative passed to the Sultan, who, in 1947, persuaded a new and reforming resident general, Eirik Labonne, to gain the French government's permission for him to make an official state visit to Tangier, passing through the Spanish Zone on the way. The journey became a triumphal procession; when the Sultan finally made his speech in Tangier, it was under the emotion of the stirring reception in the Spanish Zone and Tangier. While emphasizing the links of Morocco with the Arab world of the East, he omitted the expected flattering reference to the French protectorate.

The Allied invasion

The result was the replacement of Labonne by Gen. (later Marshal) Alphonse Juin, of Algerian settler origin. With long experience in North African affairs, Juin expressed sympathy for the patriotic nationalist sentiments of young Moroccans and promised to comply with their wish for the creation of elected municipalities in the large cities. At the same time he roused opposition by proposing to introduce French citizens as members of these bodies. The Sultan used his one remaining prerogative and refused to countersign the Resident General's decrees, lacking which they had no legal validity. A state visit to France in October 1950 and a flattering reception did nothing to modify the Sultan's views, and, on returning to Morocco, he received a wildly enthusiastic welcome.

The regime of General Juin

On December 12 General Juin dismissed a nationalist member from a meeting of the Council of Government, which discussed budget proposals; the 10 remaining nationalist members walked out in protest. This event was hailed by the local French press as a victory for their cause, though a very different view of the matter was widely held in France. For his part, General Juin began to think of the possibility of utilizing the Berber feudal notables, such as Thami al-Glaoui, to counter the nationalists. Thus, at a palace reception on December 21, 1950, al-Glaoui told the Sultan to his face that he was not the Sultan of the Moroccans but of the Istiqlāl and that he was leading the country to catastrophe.

In the face of Sidi Muhammad's continued refusal to cooperate, General Juin surrounded the palace with tribesmen, after having provided a guard of French troops supposedly to protect the Sultan against his outraged people. Faced with this threat, Sidi Muhammad was constrained to disown "a certain political party," without specifically naming it, but still withheld his signature from many decrees, including that admitting French citizens as municipal councillors. General Juin's action was widely criticized in France, and on August 28, 1951, he was replaced by Gen. Augustin Guillaume. The Sultan, on the anniversary of his accession (November 18), declared that he was hoping for an agreement "guaranteeing full sovereignty to Morocco" but (as he added in a subsequent letter addressed to the president of the French Republic) "with the continuation of Franco-Moroccan cooperation." This troubled situation continued until December 1952, when the trade unions in Casablanca decided to organize a protest meeting over the assassination of the Tunisian trade-union leader, Ferhat Hashad (Hached), supposedly by French terrorists. A clash with the police followed; hundreds of nationalists were arrested and were held for two years without trial.

In April 1953 the head of a religious confraternity, Abd al-Hai al-Kittani, together with a number of Berber notables headed by al-Glaoui, with the connivance of a number of French officials and settlers, began to work for the deposition of the Sultan. The government in Paris, preoccupied with internal affairs, finally demanded that the Sultan transfer his legislative powers to a council, composed jointly of Moroccan ministers and French directors, and append his signature to all the blocked legislation. The Sultan yielded, but this was not sufficient for his enemies. On August 18, 1953, al-Glaoui delivered what may be called an ultimatum to the French government. The latter thereupon deported the Sultan and his family, appointing in his place the more subservient Moulay Ben Arafa. This did nothing to improve the situation. Sidi Muhammad at once became a national hero. The authorities in the Spanish Zone, who had not been consulted about the measure, did not conceal their disapproval.

The Sultan's exile

The Spanish Zone thus became a refuge for Moroccan nationalists.

In November 1954 the French position was further complicated by the outbreak of the Algerian rebellion. In June 1955 the Paris government decided on a complete change of policy and appointed Gilbert Grandval as resident general. His efforts at conciliation were obstructed by the tacit opposition of many officials and the outspoken hostility of the majority of the French settlers, and he was recalled. A conference of representative Moroccans was then summoned to meet in France, and at this conference it was agreed to replace the substitute sultan by a crown council. Sidi Muhammad gave his approval to the proposal, but it took weeks to persuade the puppet sultan to withdraw to Tangier. Meanwhile, a liberation army began to operate against French posts near the Spanish Zone.

On October 26 al-Glaoui declared publicly that only the restoration of Muhammad V could restore harmony. The French government agreed to allow the Sultan to form a constitutional government for Morocco. In November Sidi Muhammad returned to Rabat. On March 2, 1956, independence was proclaimed, and the Sultan formed a government representative of the various elements of the indigenous population, while the departments formerly headed by Frenchmen became ministries headed by Moroccans.

The Spanish Zone. The Spanish protectorate over Morocco covered about one-tenth of the kingdom, from Larache on the Atlantic to 30 miles beyond Melilla (already a Spanish possession) on the Mediterranean. This was in the main a mountainous, Berber-speaking area that had often escaped the sultan's control. Spain also received a strip of desert land in the southwest, adjoining Spanish Sahara and known as Tarfaya. In 1934, when the French occupied southern Morocco, the Spanish took Ifni.

Spain appointed a *khalīfah,* or viceroy, chosen from the Moroccan royal family as nominal head of state and provided him with a puppet Moroccan government. This enabled Spain to conduct affairs independently of the French Zone, while nominally preserving Moroccan unity. Tangier, though it had a Spanish-speaking population of 40,000, received a special international administration, under a *mendub,* or resident, theoretically appointed by the sultan, actually by the French. In 1940, after the defeat of France, Spanish troops occupied Tangier, but they withdrew again in 1945 after the Allied victory.

The Spanish Zone surrounded the ports of Ceuta and Melilla, which Spain had possessed for centuries, and included the iron mines of er-Rif. As capital, the Spanish selected Tétouan. As in the French Zone, European-staffed departments were created; the country districts were administered by *interventores,* corresponding to the French *contrôleurs civils.* The first area to be occupied was that on the plain, facing the Atlantic, with the towns of Larache, Alcazarquivir (Ksar el-Kebir), and Asilah. That area was the stronghold of the former Moroccan governor Raisuni, half patriot and half brigand. The Spanish government found it difficult to tolerate his independence, and in March 1913 he retired into a refuge in the mountains, where he held out until captured by another Moroccan leader, Abd el-Krim, 12 years later.

Abd el-Krim was a Berber and a good Arabic scholar who had a knowledge of both the Arabic and Spanish languages and ways of life. Imprisoned after World War I, probably because of his outspoken hostility toward the French, he later went to Ajdir in er-Rif to plan an uprising. In July 1921 he destroyed a Spanish force sent against him and then established the Republic of the Rif, which endured for five years. It was only when his followers resisted French expansion in the north that French and Spanish forces combined, the latter landing at al-Hoceima (Alhucemas) and the French advancing from Fès. Abd el-Krim was then finally overwhelmed by a total force of more than 250,000 fully equipped men. In May 1926 he surrendered to the French and was exiled.

The Republic of the Rif

The remainder of the period of the Spanish protectorate was relatively calm. Thus, in 1936, Gen. Francisco Franco was able to launch his attack on the Spanish Republic from Morocco and to enroll a large number of Moroccan volunteers, who served him loyally in the Spanish Civil War. Though the Spanish had fewer resources than the French, their subsequent regime was in some respects more liberal and less subject to racial discrimination. Instruction in the schools was in Arabic, not Spanish, and Moroccan students were encouraged to go to Egypt for a Muslim education. There was no attempt to set Berber against Arab as in the French Zone, though this may have been prevented by the introduction of Muslim law by Abd el-Krim himself. After the end of the Republic of the Rif, there was little cooperation between the two protecting powers. Their disagreement reached a new height when in 1953 the French, without consulting the Spanish, deposed and deported the Sultan. The Spanish high commissioner did not recognize this action, and Muhammad V was still regarded in the Spanish Zone as the sovereign. Nationalists, moreover, for the first time were given departmental office, and the zone served as a refuge for those who had to leave the French area.

In 1956, however, when the French decided to grant independence to Morocco, the Spanish authorities were taken by surprise and hesitated before following suit. A corresponding agreement was nevertheless reached on April 7, 1956, and was marked by a visit of the Sultan to Spain. The Spanish protectorate was thus brought to an end without the troubles that marked the termination of foreign control in the French Zone. With the end of the Spanish protectorate and the withdrawal of the Spanish high commissioner, the Moroccan *khalīfah,* and other officials from Tétouan, the city became again a quiet, provincial capital. The introduction of the Moroccan franc instead of the peseta as currency, however, caused a great rise in the cost of living, and difficulties were also caused by the introduction of French-speaking Moroccan officials. In 1958–59 these changes gave rise to disorders in er-Rif. Tangier, too, lost much of the superficial brilliance that it had developed as a separate zone, as by degrees its special status was modified and its privileges were withdrawn. As in the former French Zone, there ensued a great drop in the number of European and Jewish inhabitants. The southern protectorate area of Tarfaya was handed back to Morocco in 1958. Ifni, in return for which the Spaniards had vainly hoped to gain a recognition of their right to Melilla and Ceuta, was finally handed over unconditionally in 1970.

Independence for Morocco

Ceuta, on the Strait of Gibraltar, and Melilla, farther east on the Mediterranean coast, continue to be Spanish *plazas* in Morocco, both with overwhelmingly Spanish populations. In October 1978 the United States turned over to Morocco its last military base in Africa, that at Kenitra.

Independent Morocco. The French protectorate had been successful in developing communications, in adding modern quarters to the cities, and in creating a flourishing agriculture and a modern industry of a colonial type. Most of these activities, however, were managed by Europeans who, by the end of the protectorate, numbered 360,000 in French Morocco. In the constitutional field there had been virtually no development. Though the government was in practice in the hands of the French, the Sultan remained in theory an autocrat; and when independence was finally conceded he became so again in fact, subject only to his undertaking to the nationalists to introduce a constitution. By French insistence, the first Cabinet was composed of ministers representing the various groups of Moroccan society, and it included a Jew. Mubarak Bekkai, an army officer who was not a party man, was selected as premier. The Sultan (who officially adopted the style of king in August 1957) selected the ministers personally and himself retained control of the army and the police; he did, however, nominate a Consultative Assembly of 60 members. His eldest son, Moulay Hassan, became chief of staff and by degrees successfully integrated the irregular liberation forces after they had promoted a rising against the Spanish in Ifni (1957) and against the French in Mauritania.

In general, the change to Moroccan control, assisted by French advisers, took place smoothly. Relations with France, however, were badly strained because of the continuing Algerian problem, but independent Morocco remained dependent on French technology and finance.

Division in the Istiqlāl

A major political change occurred when Istiqlāl split into two sections in 1959. The main portion, which was conservative, remained under the leadership of Muhammad Allal al-Fassi, while the smaller radical section, headed by Mehdi Ben Barka, Abdullah Ibrahim, Abd ar-Rahim Bouabid, and others, formed the National Union of Popular Forces (Union Nationale des Forces Populaires, or UNFP). Of these groupings the original Istiqlāl represented the more traditional elements, while the UNFP was formed from the intelligentsia and favoured socialism with republican leanings. Muhammad V made use of these dissensions to assume the position of an arbiter above party strife. He nevertheless continued the preparations for the creation of a parliament until his unexpected death in 1961. Moulay Hassan succeeded him as Hassan II.

Promonarchical FDIC

In 1963, when parliamentary elections were finally held, the two halves of the former Istiqlāl formed an opposition, while a party supporting the King's government was created out of miscellaneous elements and known as the Front for the Defense of Constitutional Institutions (FDIC). This included a new, predominantly Berber, rural group opposed to the Istiqlāl. The ensuing near deadlock caused the King to dissolve Parliament after only one year, resuming personal government with himself or his nominee as premier. In 1970 a new constitution was promulgated that provided for a one-house legislature. This did not survive an abortive coup by army elements against the monarchy in July 1971. The following year Hassan announced another constitution, but implementation was largely suspended following a second attempted military coup in August 1972. This latter coup was apparently led by Gen. Muhammad Oufkir; he had earlier been implicated in the kidnapping (1965) and disappearance in Paris of the exiled Moroccan UNFP leader Mehdi Ben Barka, who had been regarded as a likely candidate for the presidency of a Moroccan republic. Elections held in 1977 brought a landslide victory to the King's supporters. King Hassan's forceful policies to absorb the Spanish (Western) Sahara gave him greatly increased popularity in the mid-1970s. This, in addition to his method of mixing efforts to co-opt the political opposition with periods of political repression, served to maintain royal control. By the early 1980s, however, several bad harvests, a sluggish economy, and the continued financial drain of the war in the Western Sahara increased domestic strains, of which the violent riots in Casablanca in June 1981 were symptomatic.

In foreign affairs Morocco sided with the western European powers rather than with the eastern bloc, while sharing the general outlook of Arab states on such questions as that of Palestine. Claiming Mauritania as a sphere of influence, the Moroccan government refused to recognize that country's independence before 1970. Nor would it recognize the eastern frontier where territory had been attached to French Algeria at Morocco's expense. This was of importance because of the vast iron-ore deposits in the region. In 1970 it was agreed that the iron ore would be exploited by both countries under the Algerian flag but exported through a Moroccan port. At the same time, a rapprochement with Mauritania signified an alignment of the three Maghrib states against a Spanish plan to develop the phosphate-rich Spanish Sahara into an independent state associated with Spain. (N.B./L.C.Br.)

Subsequent developments in Spanish Sahara again caused tense relations between Morocco and Algeria. From 1974 King Hassan actively campaigned to assert Morocco's claim there (using this nationalist issue also to rally much-needed domestic support). In November 1975, after a United Nations mission had reported that the majority of Saharans wanted independence and that the principle of self-determination should be applied, Hassan responded with the "Green March": he called for 350,000 volunteers and sent them unarmed across the border to claim Spanish Sahara. Spain avoided a confrontation and signed an agreement turning Spanish Sahara over to joint Moroccan–Mauritanian administration as the Western Sahara. By early 1976 the last Spanish troops had departed, leaving Morocco to struggle with the guerrillas of the Popular Front for the Liberation of Saguia el Hamra and Río de Oro (Polisario Front), actively supported by Algeria and later by Libya. King Hassan offered a referendum in the area in 1981, but it was rejected by the Polisario leadership as being too much on Moroccan terms. Fighting continued and Morocco was able to secure some two-thirds of the territory within defensive walls by 1986. In the meantime the territory's government-in-exile, the Saharan Arab Democratic Republic, won recognition from an increasing number of foreign governments.

The "Green March"

King Hassan pursued an active role in the Middle East peace effort by hosting talks with Israeli Prime Minister Shimon Peres in Morocco in July 1986.

For later developments in the history of Morocco, see the *Britannica Book of the Year* section in the BRITANNICA WORLD DATA ANNUAL.

(N.B./L.C.Br./Ed.)

TUNISIA

The Republic of Tunisia (in Arabic al-Jumhūrīyah at-Tūnisīyah) has an area of 59,664 square miles (154,530 square kilometres). It occupies a position of strategic importance in the Mediterranean, where its situation has kept it open to virtually every historic influence in the region. It is bounded by Algeria to the west and southwest, Libya to the southeast, and the Mediterranean Sea to the east and north. The capital is Tunis (Tūnis).

Unlike its immediate neighbours, who are potentially rich, Tunisia has somewhat meagre resources at its disposal. In addition, its usable territory is limited and its domestic market restricted, and consequently the problem of promoting economic development is particularly difficult. Thus, after the stagnation that opened the way to the trials and changes associated with the colonial era, Tunisia has entered the modern world with determination, sometimes with imagination, but without decisive economic advantages.

Physical and human geography

With its 750 miles (1,200 kilometres) of coastline, Tunisia has often been compared to the hull of a ship, solidly moored on the continent but also freely washed by the waves; in consequence, its destiny, as its leaders never tire of repeating, is at once Mediterranean and Maghribian (the Maghrib, or the "Arab West," consisting of the northwestern African countries of Morocco, Algeria, Tunisia, and Libya). Because North Africa constitutes a single geographic entity, the lines separating Tunisia from Libya and from Algeria do not assume the form of any natural barrier but, rather, have been shaped by the vicissitudes of human history. As a result, there have been many attempts, so far unproductive, to restore natural frontiers. Maghrib Arab unity has been one of the political goals of every North African country, and in 1979 Tunis was made headquarters of the Arab League.

Tunisia's strategic situation

THE LAND

Relief and drainage. Tunisia is characterized by moderate relief. The Tunisian Dorsale, a southwest-to-northeast mountain range that is an extension of both the Atlas Saharien (Saharan Atlas) of Algeria and of the Haut Atlas of Morocco, tapers off in the direction of the Gulf of Tunis in the northeast, on which stands Tunis. The highest mountain, Jabal ash-Sha'nabī (Djebel Chambi), located near the centre of the Algerian border, rises to 5,066 feet (1,544 metres), while Jabal Zaghwān (Djebel Zaghouan), about 30 miles southwest of Tunis, reaches 4,249 feet (1,295 metres). Between the limestone peaks of the central Tunisian Dorsale and the sandstone chains of the Kroumirie mountains in the northwest, which reach altitudes of 3,000 feet, and of the Mogods, which run along the deeply indented coastline to the north,

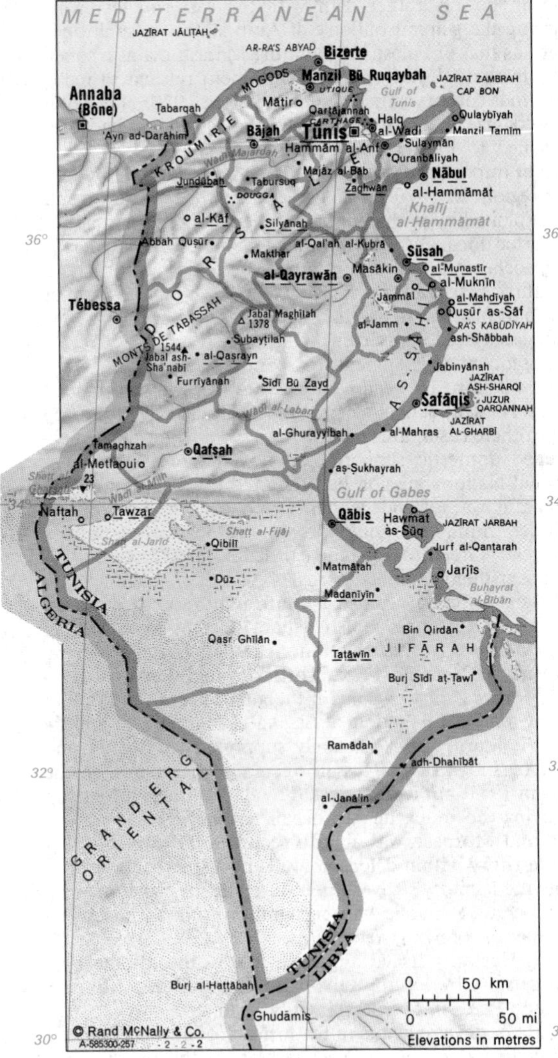

TUNISIA

lies the valley of the Majardah (Medjerda), which is formed by a series of ancient lake basins covered with alluvium. This valley was once the granary of ancient Rome and remains the richest grain-producing region of Tunisia.

The Majardah and its tributaries form the principal river system; the river crosses the northern part of the country, flowing northeastward to empty into the Gulf of Tunis.

To the south of the Tunisian Dorsale lies a region of high steppes (treeless plains). These have altitudes ranging from about 600 to 1,500 feet and are crossed by north–south secondary ranges. Further south begins a low-steppe zone, and then there is a series of *shaṭṭ* (salty lake) depressions. Large plains border the eastern coasts; the extreme south is desert.

MAP INDEX

Political subdivisions

Bājah 36.30n 9.15e
Banzart 37.00n 9.30e
Jundūbah 36.30n 8.30e
Kāf, al- 36.00n 8.45e
Madanīyīn 32.30n 10.15e
Mahdīyah, al- . . . 35.20n 10.30e
Munastīr, al- 35.35n 10.45e
Nābul 36.45n 10.45e
Qābis 33.30n 9.15e
Qafṣah 34.15n 8.30e
Qaṣrayn, al- 35.15n 8.45e
Qayrawān, al- . . . 35.30n 9.45e
Qibilī 33.30n 9.00e
Ṣafāqis 34.45n 10.15e
Sīdī Bū Zayd 34.45n 9.30e
Silyānah 36.00n 9.15e
Sūsah 35.45n 10.30e
Taṭāwīn 33.00n 10.30e
Tawzar 33.45n 8.00e
Tūnis 36.45n 10.15e
Zaghwān 36.30n 10.00e

The names of the political subdivisions do not appear on the map because they are the same as the names of their capital cities.

Cities and towns

Abbah Quṣūr 35.57n 8.50e
'Ayn ad-Darāhim . 36.47n 8.42e
Bājah (Béja) 36.44n 9.11e
Béja, see Bājah
Banzart, see
Bizerte
Bin Qirdān 33.08n 11.13e
Bizerte (Banzart) . 37.17n 9.52e
Burj Sīdī aṭ-Ṭawī . 32.44n 11.22e
Carthage, see
Qarṭājannah
Dhahībāt, adh- . . 32.01n 10.42e
Djem, el-, see
Jamm, al-
Dūz 33.28n 9.01e
Furrīyānah 34.57n 8.34e
Gabès, see
Qābis
Gafsa, see
Qafṣah
Ghurayyibah, al- . 34.30n 10.13e
Ḥalq al-Wādī
(La Goulette) . . . 36.49n 10.18e
Ḥammām al-Anf . . 36.44n 10.20e
Ḥammāmāt, al- . . . 36.24n 10.37e
Ḥaṭṭābah,
Burj al- 30.15n 9.33e
Ḥawmat as-Sūq . . 33.53n 10.51e
Jabinyānah 35.02n 10.55e
Jamm, al-
(Djem, el-) 35.18n 10.43e
Jammāl 35.38n 10.46e
Janā 'in, al- 31.44n 10.09e
Jarjīs 33.30n 11.07e
Jendouba, see
Jundūbah
Jundūbah
(Jendouba) 36.30n 8.47e
Jurf al-Qanṭarah . . 33.38n 10.57e
Kāf, al- (Le Kef) . . 36.11n 8.43e
Kairouan, see
Qayrawān, al-
Kasserine, see
Qaṣrayn, al-
Kebili, see Qibilī
La Goulette, see
Ḥalq al-Wādī
Le Kef, see
Kāf, al-
Madanīyīn
(Médenine) 33.21n 10.30e
Mahdia, see
Mahdīyah, al-
Mahdīyah, al-
(Mahdia) 35.30n 11.04e
Mahras, al- 34.32n 10.30e
Majāz al-Bāb 36.39n 9.37e
Makthar 35.51n 9.12e
Manzil Bū
Ruqaybah
(Menzel-
Bourguiba) 37.10n 9.48e
Manzil Tamīm . . . 36.47n 10.59e
Masākin
(Msaken) 35.44n 10.35e
Māṭir 37.03n 9.40e
Maṭmāṭah 33.33n 9.58e
Médenine, see
Madanīyīn
Menzel-Bourguiba,
see Manzil Bū
Ruqaybah
Metlaoui, al- 34.20n 8.24e
Monastir, see
Munastīr, al-
Msaken, see
Masākin
Muknīn, al- 35.38n 10.54e
Munastīr, al-
(Monastir) 35.47n 10.50e
Nabeul, see
Nābul
Nābul (Nabeul) . . 36.27n 10.44e
Naftah (Nefta) . . . 33.52n 7.53e
Nefta, see
Naftah
Qābis (Gabès) . . . 33.53n 10.07e
Qafṣah (Gafsa) . . 34.25n 8.48e
Qal 'ah al-
Kubra, al- 35.52n 10.32e
Qamūdah, see
Sīdī Bū Zayd
Qarṭājannah
(Carthage) 36.51n 10.20e
Qaṣrayn, al-
(Kasserine) 35.11n 8.48e
Qaṣr Ghīlān 33.00n 9.38e
Qayrawān, al-
(Kairouan) 35.41n 10.07e
Qibilī (Kebili) 33.42n 8.58e
Qulaybīyah 36.51n 11.06e
Quranbāliyah 36.36n 10.30e
Quṣūr as-Sāf 35.25n 11.00e
Ramādah 32.19n 10.24e
Ṣafāqis (Sfax) . . . 34.44n 10.46e
Sfax, see Ṣafāqis
Shābbah, ash- . . . 35.14n 11.07e
Sīdī Bū Zayd
(Qamūdah) 35.02n 9.30e
Silyānah,
(Siliana) 36.05n 9.22e
Sousse, see
Sūsah
Subayṭilah 35.14n 9.08e
Ṣukhayrah, aṣ- . . . 34.17n 10.06e
Sulaymān 36.42n 10.30e
Sūsah (Sousse) . . 35.49e 10.38e
Ṭabarqah 36.57n 8.45e
Taburṣuq 36.28n 9.15e
Tamaghzah 34.23n 7.57e
Tataouine,
see Taṭāwīn
Taṭāwīn
(Tataouine) 32.56n 10.27e
Tawzar (Tozeur) . . 33.55n 8.08e
Tozeur, see
Tawzar
Tūnis 36.48n 10.11e
Zaghouan, see
Zaghwān
Zaghwān
(Zaghouan) 36.24n 10.09e

Physical features and points of interest

Abyaḍ, ar-Ra's
al-, *cape* 37.20n 9.50e
Bībān, Buḥayrat
al-, *lagoon* 33.15n 11.16e
Bon, Cape
(Ra's aṭ-Ṭīb) . . . 37.05n 11.03e
Carthage, *ruins* . . 36.52n 10.20e
Chambi, Djebel,
see Sha 'nabīs
Jabal ash-
Djeffara, see
Jifārah
Djerba, Île de,
see Jarbah,
Jazīrat
Djerid, Chott, see
Jarīd, Shaṭṭ al-
Dorsale,
mountains 35.50n 9.25e
Dougga (Thugga),
ruins 36.25n 9.13e
Fijāj, Shaṭṭ al-,
salt marsh 33.55n 9.10e
Gabes, Gulf of
(Qābis, Khalīj) . . 34.00n 10.25e
Gharbī, Jazīrat
al-, *island* 34.39n 11.03e
Gharsah, Shaṭṭ
al-, *salt marsh* . . 34.06n 7.50e
Ḥammāmāt,
Khalīj al-, *gulf* . . 36.05n 10.40e
Kabūdīyah, Ra's,
cape 35.14n 11.10e
Kroumirie,
mountains 36.35n 8.25e
Jāliṭah,
Jazīrat, *island* . . 37.32n 8.56e
Jarbah, Jazīrat
(Djerba, Île
de), *island* 33.48e 10.54e
Jarīd, Shaṭṭ al-
(Djerid, Chott),
salt marsh 33.42n 8.26e
Jifārah, al-,
(Djeffara),
physical region . 33.00n 11.00e
Laban, Wādī al-,
watercourse 34.37n 10.01e
Majhīlah, Jabal,
mountain 35.25n 9.14e
Majardah, Wādī,
(Medjerda,
Oued), *river* 37.07n 10.13e
Mediterranean
Sea 37.40n 9.00e
Medjerda, Oued,
see Majardah,
Wādī
Milḥ, Wādī al-,
watercourse 34.03n 8.06e
Mogods,
mountains 37.08n 9.30e
Qābis, Khalīj, see
Gabès, Gulf of
Qarqannah,
Juzur, *islands* . . 34.44n 11.12e
Ra's aṭ-Ṭīb,
see Bon, Cape
Sahel, see Sāḥil, as-
Sāḥil, as- (Sahel),
physical region . 35.15n 10.40e
Sha' nabī, Jabal
ash- (Chambi,
Djebel),
mountain 35.11n 8.42e
Sharqī, Jazīrat
ash-, *island* 34.44n 11.14e
Tabassah
(Tébessa),
Monts de,
mountains 35.15n 8.35e
Thugga, see
Dougga
Tunis, Gulf of 37.00n 10.30e
Utica, see Utique
Utique (Utica),
ruins 37.04n 10.04e
Zambrah,
Jazīrat, *island* . . 37.08n 10.48e

Climate. Tunisia is situated in the hot temperate zone between the 37th and the 30th parallels. It has a Mediterranean climate characterized by mild, rainy winters and hot, dry summers. Prevailing winds are from the west most of the year, producing unsettled weather. In summer the prevailing wind is from the northeast, but Saharan influences also give rise to the sirocco, a hot, blasting wind from the south that can have a seriously drying effect on vegetation.

Temperature and rainfall

Temperatures are affected by the sea, being less extreme at Sūsah (Sousse) on the coast, for example, than at al-Qayrawān (Kairouan) inland. Temperatures at Sūsah over a 50-year period (1901–50) varied from an average daily low of 44° F (7° C) for the month of January to an average daily high of 89° F (32° C) for the month of August. Comparable temperatures at al-Qayrawān were 40° F (4° C) in January and 99° F (37° C) in August.

The amount of rainfall varies considerably with geographic location. In the period 1901 to 1950, for example, a mean annual rainfall of 40 inches (1,015 millimetres) was recorded at Ṭabarqah (Tabarka) in northwestern Tunisia, as compared with less than four inches at Tawzar (Tozeur) in the southwest. Generally, from the middle of autumn to the middle of spring, northern Tunisia receives more than 16 inches of rainfall, and the steppe region receives from six to 16 inches. Amounts are also highly irregular from one year to another; for example, 45 inches fell at Makthar (Maktar) in north central Tunisia in 1969–70, in contrast to 14 inches in 1966–67. Harvests vary as a result, being poor in dry years.

Plant and animal life. The vegetation and animal life of the country are affected by these climatic conditions. From north to south, the Kroumirie forest of cork oaks, with its fern undergrowth sheltering wild boars, gives way to steppes covered with esparto grass and populated with small game, and finally to the desert, where hunting is forbidden so as to preserve the remaining gazelles. Scorpions are found in all regions; among dangerous snakes are the horned viper and the cobra. Desert locusts sometimes damage crops in the southern part of the country.

Settlement patterns. Tunisia is divided into four natural and demographic regions: the north, which is relatively fertile and well watered; the semiarid central region; as-Sāḥil (the Sahel) in the east central coastal region, which is preeminently olive-growing country; and the south, where, except in the oases, all vegetation disappears. In the central and southern regions, there are still tribes that have preserved a certain cohesion through following a quasi-nomadic way of life. Ethnic mixtures in these regions are rare. In the north, on the other hand, particularly along the coasts, the population is quite mixed, the life of the cultivator is more complex, the villages are more crowded, and the cities are larger. The cities have expanded at the expense of the countryside.

THE PEOPLE

The population of Tunisia is essentially Arab Berber. Throughout the centuries Tunisia has, however, received various waves of immigration; these have included Phoenicians, black Africans, Jews, Romans, Vandals, and Arabs, as well as Muslim refugees from Sicily, who settled in as-Sāḥil after their homeland was captured by the Norman kings in 1091. The most important immigration, however, was that of the Spanish Moors, which began after the fall of Seville, in Spain, in 1248 and turned into a veritable exodus in the early 17th century; 200,000 Spanish Muslims thus settled in the area of Tunis, in the Majardah Valley, and on Cape Bon in the north, bringing with them urban traditions and more advanced agricultural and irrigation techniques. Finally, from the 16th to the 19th century, the Turks brought in their wake different elements of Asiatic or European origin. This great ethnic diversity is still seen in the variety of Tunisian family names.

Languages

The cultural Arabization of the country can be considered to have been essentially completed by the end of the 12th century. Less than 1 percent of the population, in the south, still speaks the Berber language. French, introduced during the protectorate (1881 to 1956), paradoxically came into wider use after independence because of the spread of education. Although Arabic is the official language of the country, French continues to play a dominant role in the press, education, and government, and Tunisia was among the countries that in the 1950s and 1960s worked to organize the French Community.

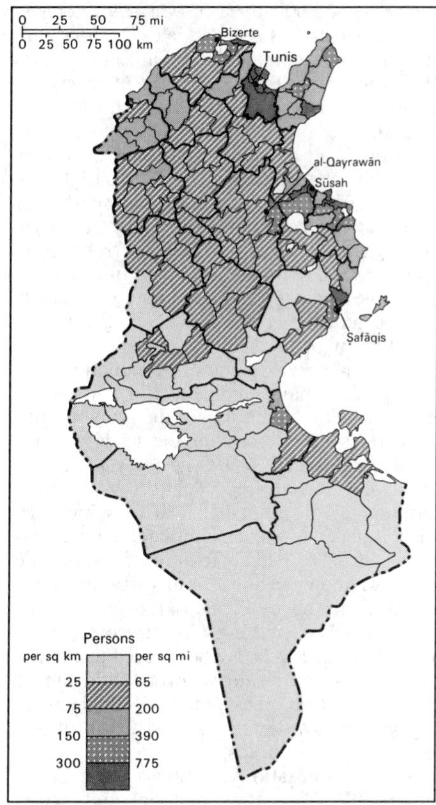

Population density of Tunisia.

The last indigenous Christian communities in Tunisia, which were still sizable in the 12th century, disappeared as long ago as the end of the 14th century. Only the Jewish community has survived, but its membership, which in the late 1950s numbered 100,000, decreased continually, as a result of emigration, to only about 9,000 in the early 1980s. Non-Muslims numbered more than 300,000 in 1956 and 40,000 in the early 1980s.

THE ECONOMY

Resources. The Tunisian economy has traditionally been characterized by the predominance of the agricultural over the manufacturing sector. Yields are low and crops are, in addition, endangered by changes in the weather. As a result of major efforts toward investment and acquisition of equipment, the manufacturing sector has come to play a more important role in the economy of the country. There is an imbalance between the north and as-Sāḥil, on the one hand, which are more fertile and more economically developed, and the central and southern regions, on the other, which have fewer natural advantages.

Natural resources

Natural resources of the soil and subsoil are relatively meagre in Tunisia. The lumber industry is essentially confined to the exploitation of oak and cork from the Kroumirie forest in the north. The esparto grass of the plains is used for the manufacture of quality paper. The principal mineral resource is phosphate. One-third of all phosphate produced is exported, and the remainder is used by domestic chemical industries.

Other mineral resources are iron, lead, zinc, and mercury. Petroleum, discovered in the extreme south in 1964 at the al-Burmah (el-Borma) field, by the early 1970s was beginning to play an important role in the Tunisian economy. Four deposits were being exploited by the early 1980s: al-Burmah, in the southern *wilāyat* of Madanīyīn (Médenine); Ashtart, in the Gulf of Gabes; Sīdī al-Yatā'im (Sidi el-Itayem), in northern Ṣafāqis *wilāyat;* and ad-Dūlāb (Douleb), in al-Qaṣrayn (Kasserine) *wilāyat.* In 1980 their production reached 5,600,000 tons, of which 93 percent came from the al-Burmah and Ashtart fields. Despite this modest volume, oil has become a chief Tunisian export. By the late 1970s oil accounted for 45 percent of export revenues. The principal deposit, at al-Burmah, however, is becoming depleted. Intensive exploration has led to new oil discoveries in the Shaṭṭ al-Jarīd (Chott Djerid) region, where reserves are estimated to be 10,000,000,000 barrels. In December 1981 Tunisia applied for admission to the Organization of Arab Petroleum Exporting Countries (OAPEC). Natural gas in Tunisia is produced from fields in the Cape Bon area and from al-Burmah. In addition, Tunisia is to receive about 5 percent of the gas that is pumped through a pipeline connecting the Algerian gas fields with Sicily by way of Tunisia.

Agriculture. Inadequate agricultural production remains one of Tunisia's major problems. The low crop yields are due primarily to the division of the property into excessively small plots—90 percent of the fields of corn (maize) have less than 250 acres (100 hectares)—and the predominance of obsolete farming methods. Very often, too, the uncertainty of the rainfall jeopardizes harvests; grain production is generally inadequate, and Tunisia has to import about half of the cereals required for domestic consumption. In addition to cereal grains, the principal products are citrus fruits, olive oil, and dates. Wine is also important, but output is decreasing. To improve agricultural production, dams and wells are being used to expand the irrigated area, but water resources nevertheless remain limited. The fishing industry has potential for development. Sheep, goats, and cattle are not raised in numbers adequate to supply Tunisia's needs.

Industry. The industrialization of Tunisia has encountered two major difficulties. Raw material and power supplies are inadequate, and the domestic market is limited. Notable and sometimes costly projects, such as the Manzil Bū Ruqaybah (Menzel-Bourguiba) iron-smelting complex, located near Bizerte, however, have been successfully established since independence was achieved in 1956. Existing industries produce foodstuffs, textiles, clothing, construction materials, household articles, and fertilizers. In the early 1970s efforts were made to develop the south economically; for example, the Industries Chimiques Maghrébines (Maghreb Chemical Industries) complex, which produces phosphoric acid, was opened at Qābis (Gabès) in 1971. Tourism, however, remains Tunisia's leading industry. The number of tourists rose from 200,000 in 1966 to 1,600,000 by 1980. (M.Ta.)

Trade, finance, and management of the economy. Tunisian overseas trade still reflects the importance of primary production. About three-fifths of the exports by value are foodstuffs and raw mineral products, including petroleum. About a third of all trade is with France, with which Tunisia reached an agreement on trade and tariffs following the abolition of a customs union in 1959. The balance of payments is frequently adverse, and in some years this has obliged the government to limit imports. In the late 1970s countries of the European Economic Community accounted for 60 percent of Tunisia's imports and exports.

The strength of the dinar and of the economy was helped in the late 1970s by international confidence in the political stability of Tunisia. The Banque Centrale de Tunisie performs the functions of an issuing bank. (W.C.B.)

Economic doctrine

Tunisian economic doctrine consists of a flexible and undogmatic form of Socialism based on private, cooperative, and parastate (comprising chiefly gas, electricity, and railway services) sectors. The attempt at collectivization, which was carried out in the 1960s, resulted in failure, particularly in the agricultural sector, and was abandoned in 1969. There are three large professional organizations. The Union Générale des Travailleurs Tunisiens (General Union of Tunisian Workers; UGTT) is the principal trade union, and there are also associations of employers and farmers.

Transportation. The network of roads and of railways is sufficiently dense so that all metropolitan areas of any importance are linked with the interior regions. Tunisia is connected by both road and rail with Algeria and Morocco but only by road with Tripoli (Ṭarābulus), Libya, and with Cairo, since the railway ends at Qābis. Train service, however, is slow and uncomfortable, and, except for the main routes, the roads are quite narrow.

The principal ports are Tunis-Ḥalq al-Wādī (La Goulette), which is the outpost of Tunis; Ṣafāqis; Bizerte; and Sūsah, as well as the port of Qābis, which accommodates 50,000-ton ships. An oil pipeline runs from Edjeleh, Algeria, to the port of aṣ-Ṣukhayrah (Cekhira), on the Gulf of Gabes.

Despite the construction of airports at al-Munastīr, Jarbah (Djerba), Ṣafāqis, and Tawzar, all of which handle domestic or tourist (charter) flights, international air traffic is directed mainly through al-ʿUwaynah airport near Tunis.

ADMINISTRATIVE AND SOCIAL CONDITIONS

Government. The Tunisian constitution was promulgated in 1959; it defines Tunisia as a republic whose religion is Islām and whose official language is Arabic. Legislative power is exercised by the National Assembly, which consists of 136 delegates elected for five-year terms by universal suffrage. Executive power is in the hands of the president of the republic, who is head of state and head of the government. He must be a Muslim and is elected for a five-year term by universal suffrage at the same time as the deputies; he is eligible for an unlimited number of consecutive terms.

The country is administered by the Cabinet, headed, since 1969, by a prime minister. The most important ministry is not that of defense, since the role and size of the armed forces has been somewhat reduced, but rather that of national education, which in 1980 received almost one-fourth of the national budget. The Cabinet ministers are responsible to the president rather than to the National Assembly.

Judicial power is exercised by judges whose independence is constitutionally guaranteed.

The constitution guarantees "freedom of opinion, expression, press, publication, assembly, and association" ("under the conditions defined by law"), as well as the right to form trade unions. Despite the introduction of new political parties in November 1981, Tunisia has continued to be governed under a one-party system, that of the Destour (Arabic *destūr:* constitution) Socialist Party (generally called the Neo-Destour, to distinguish it from an older Destour Party founded in 1920). The Neo-Destour party, allied with the UGTT, holds all the seats in the National Assembly. All Tunisians, including women, who are at least 20 years of age can vote. There is typically a massive turnout for elections, with 90 percent of the registered voters participating.

Local administration

The country is divided into 23 administrative areas called *wilāyāt* (singular *wilāyah;* French *gouvernorats*), which are headed by *wālī* (governors). Each *wilāyah* is designated by the name of its chief town and is in turn subdivided into units called *muʿtamadīyāt* (*délégations*), whose number varies according to the *wilāyah*'s size. *Muʿtamadīyāt* are administered by a *muʿtamad* and are in turn divided into varying numbers of districts called *manṭaqa turābiyya*s.

Education. Education is free to all students, and scholarships in schools and universities are offered largely on the basis of merit and need. The number of students—and consequently the number of schools and teachers—has steadily increased since independence.

This growth has been accompanied by a certain drop in educational standards; it has also posed problems of financing and of finding enough job opportunities for qualified people. A board of education was thus formed in 1971 to revise Tunisia's educational policy. More emphasis has since been placed on technical and agricultural training. Discontent among students increased when, in the early 1980s, Tunisian industry was unable to absorb all of those trained in technical schools.

Health and welfare. The living standards of the population in general are relatively low. The advantages available consist, in addition to the distribution of milk to newborn babies and of school lunches, of free medical care for the destitute and of the extension of the social security system, which provides medical benefits, hospitalization, and other benefits, to virtually all wage earners.

CULTURAL LIFE

The state of the arts

Tunisia is an Arabic-speaking Muslim country that was deeply imbued with French culture during the 75 years of the protectorate, which ended in 1956. An attempt was made to establish a Tunisian literature written in French, but the trend never took root. Although Tunisians generally use French in all scientific disciplines, they remain genuinely attached to Arabic in the literary sphere—in poetry, the novel, and the short story. Several literary reviews, the most important of which is *al-Fikr* ("Thought"), open their pages to youthful talents and stimulate literary output. Modern Tunisian literature, the subject of great debate on radio and television and in the various government-sponsored Maisons de la Culture (Houses of Culture), has made remarkable progress, but it has not produced works of sufficient power to rival foreign and especially French literature, which is still preferred by the young. Tunisian literature continues to receive governmental encouragement, and an association of writers was founded in 1971. Various scientific journals are connected with research institutes and schools.

Although the Tunisian cinema is still in its infancy, having to its credit no more than a few successful films, contemporary Tunisian painting can already lay claim to a certain tradition. Some of the artists enjoy a genuine local celebrity and also have exhibited abroad. The music conservatory devotes attention mainly to national traditions but also emphasizes the classical European heritage.

A major effort is in progress to diffuse and decentralize cultural benefits, although means are necessarily limited. Maisons de la Culture are being established in the chief towns, and travelling libraries make films and books available to the most remote corners. Television, which naturally plays an important role, likewise covers the entire country; its programs are in Arabic and French and provide information, education, and entertainment.

For statistical data on the land and people of Tunisia, see the *Britannica World Data* section in the BRITANNICA WORLD DATA ANNUAL. (M.Ta.)

History

THE GROWTH OF EUROPEAN INFLUENCE

In 1830, at the time of the French invasion of Algiers, Tunisia was a province of the Ottoman Empire but autonomous in fact. Because the principal military threat had long come from neighbouring Algeria, the reigning *bey* of Tunisia, Ḥusayn, cautiously went along with French assurances. Ḥusayn Bey even accepted the idea that Tunisian princes be appointed rulers of Constantine and Oran. It soon became clear that the scheme had no chance of success, however, and it was abandoned.

Then, in 1835, the Ottoman Empire seized the opportunity of a disputed succession in Libya to depose the ruling dynasty there and to reestablish direct Ottoman rule. Thereafter, the vulnerable *beylik* of Tunis found itself surrounded by two larger powers—France and the Ottomans—both of whom sought hegemony in Tunisia. From that time until the establishment of the French protectorate in 1881, Tunisian rulers sought to keep the larger outside powers in balance while working to strengthen the state from within.

Aḥmad Bey, who ruled from 1837 to 1855, was an avowed westernizer. He brought in Western advisers (mainly French) to help create a modern army and navy and related industries. Conscription was introduced to the great dismay of the peasantry. More acceptable were Aḥmad's steps to better integrate Arabic-speaking native Tunisians into the government, which had long been dominated by Mamlūks and Turks. Aḥmad abolished slavery and took other steps intended to bring Tunisia more in line with Europe, but he also exposed his country to Europe's infinitely greater economic and political power. These governmental innovations imposed upon a stagnant economy increased financial obligations that were met by higher taxes. These, in turn, provoked unrest in the countryside.

The next *bey*, Muḥammad (1855–59), sought to turn his back on Europe, but this was no longer possible. The execution of a Tunisian Jew for blasphemy brought swift British and French action that forced the *bey* to issue the "Fundamental Pact" (ʿAhd al-Amān; September 9, 1857), a civil rights charter modelled on the Ottoman rescript of 1839.

The final collapse of the Tunisian *beylik* came during the reign of Muḥammad aṣ-Ṣadiq (1859–82). By nature disposed to westernizing reforms, he was, however, too weak either to control his own government or to keep the several European powers at bay. In 1861 the first constitution (*dustūr*) in the Arab world was proclaimed, but this promising step toward representation and responsible government was brought to naught by runaway indebtedness exacerbated by the practice of securing loans from European bankers at exorbitant rates.

When the principal minister, Muṣṭafā Khaznadār (who had served from the earliest days of Aḥmad Bey's reign), attempted to squeeze more taxes out of the hard-pressed Tunisians, the countryside rose in a revolt (1864) that almost overthrew the regime, but a combination of governmental guile and brutality managed to restore order.

Tunisia was bankrupt in 1869, and an international financial commission—with British, French, and Italian representation—was imposed on the country. One last important attempt to strengthen Tunisia from within and thus avoid European domination was made during the reformist ministry of Khayr ad-Dīn (1873–77), one of the most impressive statesmen of the 19th-century Muslim world. Enemies from within the Tunisian government and European consular intrigues, however, forced him from office. All that was needed for France to establish control in Tunisia was the acquiescence of France's principal rival, Britain, and this was obtained at the Congress of Berlin in 1878.

French occupation

The end came in 1881 when the French, on the pretext that some Tunisian tribesmen had moved into Algerian territory, landed troops at Bizerte and sent others into Tunisia by land from Algeria. Advancing without difficulty to the *bey*'s palace, the Bardo, at Kassar Said (al-Qaṣr as-Saʿīd), near Tunis, they imposed a treaty that sanctioned French military occupation, transferred to France the *bey*'s authority in foreign relations and finance, and provided for the appointment of a French resident minister as intermediary in all matters of common interest. This provoked a rising in southern Tunisia during which Sousse (Sūsah) was bombarded and captured in July 1881; Kairouan (al-Qayrawān) was then captured in October, and Gafsa (Qafṣah) and Gabès (Qābis) in November. After the death of the *bey* Muḥammad aṣ-Ṣadiq, his successor, ʿAlī, was constrained to sign an undertaking to introduce such administrative, judicial, and financial reforms as the French government might consider useful. This agreement, known as the Convention of Marsa and signed in 1883, made French control complete.

THE PROTECTORATE (1881–1956)

The arrangement thus arrived at was very different from that in Algeria. The basis was a treaty, not an outright conquest. The *bey* remained in theory an absolute monarch; two Tunisian ministers were still appointed, and the framework of the old government machinery was preserved. Tunisians continued to be subjects of the *bey*. There was no confiscation of land; mosques were not converted into churches; and Arabic remained an official language. Nevertheless, the supreme authority passed in fact into the hands of the French resident general and his staff. Under French guidance the finances were soon brought into order, and a modern communications system was established. Though there was none of the wholesale confiscation of land and displacement of population that had occurred in Algeria, the most fertile portions of northern Tunisia, comprising the Medjerda Valley and the Cape Bon peninsula, passed largely into the hands of Europeans. Valuable phosphate mines were brought into operation near Gafsa in the south, while the extensive establishment of French and Italian colonists in the Medjerda Valley resulted in a considerable export of vegetables.

Young Tunisians

By the 1890s a small Western-trained group—the members of which came to be called "Young Tunisians"—

began to push for both westernizing reforms and greater Tunisian participation in government. Their conduct during the protectorate was necessarily cautious; their major weapon, the newspaper *Le Tunisien,* was founded in 1907 as a French-language publication, an Arabic edition not appearing until 1909. Increased modern-style education was a principal goal. The Young Tunisians sought simultaneously to educate their compatriots and to persuade the more liberal French to help move Tunisia toward modernity. There was no explicit talk of independence.

Even this moderate protonationalism came to grief before French repression in 1911–12. Little nationalist activity took place during World War I (1914–18), but the postwar period brought the first attempt at mass political organization with the creation of the Destour Party (Constitution Party, so named for the short-lived Tunisian constitution of 1861). In 1920 the Destour Party presented to the *bey* and to the French government a document that in effect demanded the establishment of a constitutional form of government in which Tunisians would possess equal rights with Europeans. The immediate result was the arrest of Abd al-Azīz ath-Thaalibī, the Destour leader. Two years later, the aged *bey,* Muhammad an-Nasir, requested the adoption of the program of the Destour, failing which he threatened to abdicate. The resident general, Lucien Saint, responded by surrounding the *bey*'s palace with troops, with the result that the demand was withdrawn. Saint thereupon introduced repressive measures together with minor reforms that pacified Tunisian sentiment and weakened the nationalist movement for several years.

Emergence of Bourguiba

In 1934 a young Tunisian lawyer, Habib Bourguiba, and like-minded colleagues broke with the Destour Party to form a new organization, the Neo-Destour, which aimed at gaining mass support. Under Bourguiba's vigorous leadership the new party supplanted the existing Destour and its old-fashioned leaders. Attempts by the French to suppress the new movement spread its popular appeal. The arrival of the popular front government to power in France in 1936 enabled the Neo-Destour to extend its propaganda there also. When the popular front government collapsed, renewed repression in Tunisia was followed by civil disobedience; and in 1938 serious disturbances resulted in the arrest of Bourguiba and other leaders of the party, which was officially dissolved.

WORLD WAR II

On the outbreak of war in 1939, Neo-Destour leaders were deported, still untried, to France. They were released by the Nazis when they occupied Vichy France in 1942 and, since Hitler regarded Tunisia as a sphere of Italian influence, handed over to the Fascist government in Rome. There they were treated with deference, in the hopes of eliciting a declaration favourable to the Axis. Bourguiba, however, steadily refused, in spite of the suggestions of some of his companions. In March 1943, after a noncommittal broadcast by him, the Neo-Destour leaders were finally allowed to proceed to Tunis, where the reigning *bey,* Muhammad al-Munsif (Moncef), formed a ministry of Destour sympathies.

The assumption of power by the Free French, after the Nazi retreat, resulted in complete disillusionment. The *bey* himself was deposed, while Bourguiba escaped imprisonment only by fleeing in disguise to Egypt (1945). He began a vigorous campaign of propaganda for Tunisian independence. In view of the emancipation of the eastern Arab states, and later of the neighbouring, relatively backward Libya, the French felt compelled to make concessions. In 1951 a government with nationalist sympathies was allowed to take office, of which the secretary general of the Neo-Destour, Salah Ben Youssef, became a member. Bourguiba was allowed to return to Tunisia. When, however, this government wished to establish a Tunisian parliament, the result was further repression. Bourguiba was confined, and most of the ministers were put under arrest. This resulted, for the first time, in outbreaks of terrorism; and nationalist bands began to operate in the mountains, virtually paralyzing the country.

Outbreak of terrorism

In July 1954 the French premier, Pierre Mendès-France, promised to grant complete autonomy to Tunisia, subject to a freely negotiated convention. Bourguiba was released and was able to supervise the negotiations without directly participating. In June 1955 the convention was finally signed by the Tunisian delegates, though it imposed strict limits in the fields of foreign policy, education, defense, and finance, and a mainly Neo-Destour ministry was formed. Salah Ben Youssef denounced the agreement as too restrictive, refused to attend a specially summoned congress unanimously supporting Bourguiba, and organized a brief armed resistance in the south; this was quickly put down, and Ben Youssef fled the country.

INDEPENDENCE

Having conceded full independence to Morocco, the French were no longer inclined to resist the same for Tunisia, and an accord was reached on March 20, 1956, for Tunisian independence, with Bourguiba as prime minister. On July 25, 1957, the rule of the *beys* was abolished and a republic was declared, with Bourguiba assuming the presidency.

Domestic development. The best organized mass political party in the Arab world, the Neo-Destour (from 1964, Destourian Socialist) Party ensured that independent Tunisia could move quickly with reforms. Advances in education, the liberation of women, and legal reforms were especially impressive. Economic development was less dramatic, but the government creditably gave attention to the more impoverished parts of the country. In 1961 Ahmad Ben Salah took charge of planning and finance (adding the portfolio of education in 1968). His ambitious efforts at forced-pace modernization, especially in agriculture, were foiled, however, by rural and conservative opposition. Expelled from the party in 1969 and imprisoned, he escaped in 1973, to live in exile. His fall brought a move to a more conservative orientation.

In 1975 the National Assembly unanimously bestowed the presidency for life on the sick and aged Habib Bourguiba. Hedi Nouira, noted for his financial and administrative skills, became prime minister in November 1970. A decade later, in 1980, Mohammed Mzali replaced the ailing Nouira. This inaugurated an effort to restore dissidents to the party and then, in 1981, to grant amnesty to many who had been jailed for earlier disturbances. Bourguiba was persuaded to accept a multiparty system, but results of the elections of November 1981 were disappointing to those who sought political liberalization. The National Front, an alliance of the Destourian Socialist Party and the trade union movement, swept all 136 parliamentary seats, a result received with cynicism and dismay by the opposition. National elections in 1986 were boycotted by the major opposition parties, and the National Front once again carried the vote. In November 1987, amid widespread unrest and rising Islāmic fundamentalism, Bourguiba was declared mentally unfit to rule and was removed from office. He was succeeded by General Zine al-Abidine Ben Ali, whom he had appointed as prime minister in October 1987.

Foreign relations. Because Tunisia openly supported the cause of Algerian independence, it was difficult to maintain good relations with France, which did not grant that independence until 1962. Three crises in Franco-Tunisian relations were: the French bombing raid on the Tunisian village of Sāqiyat Sīdī Yūsuf in 1958, during which France claimed the right of pursuit of Algerian rebels; the Bizerte incident of 1961, concerning the continued military use of that port and airfield facility by France; and the suspension of all French aid in 1964–66 after Tunisia abruptly nationalized land held by foreigners. Such difficulties aside, post-independence Tunisian relations with France have been good. Tunisia also has been successful in establishing good relations with the United States and most European states, skillfully building up a multinational pattern of economic and technical aid.

Tunisia's relations with the Arab world have been subject to oscillations. There was a dispute with Egypt and the majority of Arab states when, in 1965, Bourguiba urged a more diplomatic approach toward Israel. Since independence there also have been several periods of tension with Algeria and Libya. Generally, however, Tunisia has been able to increase its standing in the Arab world. When Egypt was expelled from the Arab League for having signed a peace treaty with Israel in 1979, the Arab League moved its headquarters from Cairo to Tunis. The Palestine Liberation Organization under Yāsir ʿArafāt opened its headquarters in Tunis in August 1982 after being forced to leave Beirut.

For later developments in the history of Tunisia, see the *Britannica Book of the Year* section in the BRITANNICA WORLD DATA ANNUAL. (N.B./L.C.Br.)

BIBLIOGRAPHY

Physical and human geography. An excellent handbook is WILFRID KNAPP (ed.), *North West Africa: A Political and Economic Survey,* 3rd ed. (1977). Good geographical reference books include JEAN DESPOIS, *L'Afrique du Nord,* 3rd ed. (1964), and, with RENE RAYNAL, *Géographie de l'Afrique du Nord-Ouest* (1967); and J.M. OUSTON, *The Western Mediterranean World* (1964). There are many works devoted to Muslim civilization, including S.D. GOITEIN, *Studies in Islamic History and Institutions* (1966); D.T. RICE, *Islamic Art* (1965); and JOSEPH SCHACHT, *An Introduction to Islamic Law* (1964). Works on the religious beliefs of the Maghrib include ERNEST GELLNER, *Saints of the Atlas* (1969); and G.E. VON GRUNEBAUM, *Muhammadan Festivals* (1958). Among the most interesting anthropological studies are JACQUES BERQUE, *Les Structures sociales du Haut-Atlas* (1955), and *Le Maghreb entre deux guerres* (1962; Eng. trans., *French North Africa: The Maghrib Between Two World Wars,* 1967); a revised French edition of the latter work appeared in 1979. Other works dealing with society and culture include LLOYD CABOT BRIGGS, *The Living Races of the Sahara Desert* (1955), and *Tribes of the Sahara* (1960); CARLETON S. COON, *Tribes of the Rif* (1931); and JEAN DUVIGNAUD, *Chebika, Mutations dans un village du Maghreb* (1968).

Algeria: A comprehensive general work is HAROLD D. NELSON (ed.), *Algeria: A Country Study* (1979). HILDEBERT ISNARD, *L'Algérie* (1954; Eng. trans. 1955), is a well-illustrated, authoritative travel guide. Anthropological and sociological studies include ROBERT DESCLOITRES and LAID DEBZI, *Systèmes de parenté et structures familiales en Algérie* (1963); JEAN SERVIER, *Les Portes de l'année: rites et symboles: l'Algérie dans la tradition méditerranéenne* (1962); and PIERRE BORDIEU, *Sociologie de l'Algérie* (1961), in which the sociological analysis is conducted in terms of the main groups of peoples. J.C. PAWERA, *Algeria's Infra-Structure* (1964), is an economic study focussed chiefly on transport, communications, and energy resources of the Algerian economy. FRANCOIS PERROUX (ed.), *L'Algérie de demain* (1962), is a collection of studies on possible paths of economic and social development. See also FRANCOIS D'ARCY, ANNIE KRIEGER, and ALAIN MARILL, *Essais sur l'économie de l'Algérie nouvelle* (1965), chiefly for socioeconomic topics such as agrarian reform, administration of the state farms, and industrial economy.

Libya: For a comprehensive general work, see HAROLD D. NELSON (ed.), *Libya: A Country Study* (1979). For economic information, see B.H. HIGGINS, *Economic Development: Principles, Problems and Policies* (1959), a discussion of Libya as a case study of an underdeveloped country before oil discovery; BANK OF LIBYA RESEARCH DIVISION, *Inflation in Libya* (1961), which covers the economic impact of oil company expenditure and aid; BANK OF LIBYA, *Economic Bulletin* (monthly), offering good coverage of the overall economy; LIBYA MINISTRY OF PLANNING AND DEVELOPMENT, *Housing in Libya,* 2 vol. (1964), which discusses housing and transport problems; and J.A. ALLAN, K.S. MCLACHLAN, and EDITH PENROSE (eds.), *Libya: Agriculture and the Economic Development* (1973). Geological information is provided in M. ANDRE BRICHANT, *A Broad Outline of Geology and Mineral Possibilities in Libya,* UN Report No. 7 (1952); F. FOWLAND and E. ROBB, "Survey of Land Resources in Tripolitania," in *British Military Administration of Occupied Territories During the Years 1941–43* (1945); G.W. MURRAY, "The Water Beneath the Egyptian Western Desert," *Geogrl. J.,* 118:443–452 (1952); A. FANTOLI, *Le pioggie della Libia con particolare riguardo alle zone di avvaloramento* (1952), a detailed study of climate, containing statistics, maps, and diagrams; LIBYA MINISTRY OF PLANNING AND DEVELOPMENT, *Agriculture in Libya and a Plan for Its Development* (1966); and UNIVERSITY OF LIBYA FACULTY OF SCIENCE, *Geology of Libya* (1972). LIBYAN ARAB REPUBLIC, *Statistical Abstract* (annual), published by the Census and Statistical Department, gives general statistical information.

Morocco: The best introductory book is JACQUES BERQUE and JULIEN COULEAU, *Le Maroc* (1977). Border disputes are discussed with competence and impartiality by FRANK E. TROUT, *Morocco's Saharan Frontiers* (1969). There are good regional studies written from diverse perspectives, including JEAN LE COZ, *Le Rharb, fellahs et colons* (1964), which gives a geographical point of view; PAUL PASCON, *Le Haouz de Marrakech,* 2 vol. (1977), a historical approach; and RAYMOND JAMOUS, *Honneur et Baraka: les structures sociales traditionnelles dans le Rif* (1981), an anthropological point of view. A book by DANIEL NOIN, *La population rurale du Maroc,* 2 vol. (1970), is a consideration of the entire regional question. Local organization is described in ALI SEDJARI, *Les structures administratives et territoriales et le développement local au Maroc* (1981). The methods, perspectives, and results of economic planning are analyzed by HABIB EL-MALKI, *Le financement du développement économique au Maroc (1960–1977)* (1973); TARIK EZZAKI, *Infrastructure et développement au Maroc* (1981); and MOHAMMED GERMOUNI, *Essai sur les problèmes de l'engineering et de la technologie au Maroc* (1978). ABDELMALEK CHERKAOUI, *Indicateurs socio-économiques du Maroc* (1980), provides a complete view of the social consequences of the type of development chosen by Morocco. The particular problem of urbanization is well studied through the case of the capital city in JANET L. ABULUGHOD, *Rabat, Urban Apartheid in Morocco* (1980). The official account of Moroccan policy is found in HASSAN II, *The Challenge: The Memoirs of King Hassan II of Morocco* (1978). Party politics is analyzed through party programs in C.G. PALAZZOLLI, *Le Maroc politique* (1974); and through the results of legislative elections in MUSTAPHA SÉHIMI, *Juin 1977* (1980). For information on Moroccan cultural life, see ABDELKABIR KHATIBI and MOHAMMED KABLY (eds.), *Écrivains marocains du Protectorat à 1965* (1974), an anthology; and MOHAMED SIJELMASSI, *La peinture marocaine* (1972).

Tunisia: JEAN DESPOIS, *La Tunisie: ses régions* (1961); WILFRID KNAPP, *Tunisia* (1970); and AHMED KASSAB and HAFEDH SETHOM, *Géographie de la Tunisie, le pays et les hommes* (1980). See also *La Revue tunisienne de géographie,* a quarterly published from 1978; H.H. ABDUL-WAHAB, *Coup d'oeil général sur les apports éthniques étrangers en Tunisie* (1917, reprinted in *Cahiers de Tunisie,* 18:151–169, 1970); JEAN GANIAGE, *La Population européenne de Tunis au milieu du XIX*[e] *siècle* (1960); R. LALUE and P. MARTHELOT, "La Répartition de la population tunisienne," *Annales—Economies, Sociétés, Civilisations,* 17:283–301 (1962); J.D. LATHAM, "Towards a Study of Andalusian Immigration and Its Place in Tunisian History," *Cahiers de Tunisie,* 5:209–252 (1957); ANDRE DEMEERSEMAN, *Tunisie, sève nouvelle* (1957), and *Lumière et Ombre au Maghreb* (1970); JAMES ALLMAN, *Social Mobility, Education, and Development in Tunisia* (1979); MONCEF GUEN, *La Tunisie indépendante face à son économie* (1961); GHAZI DUWAJI, *Economic Development in Tunisia* (1967); E. MAKHLOUF, "Structures agraires et modernisation de l'agriculture dans les plaines du Kef," *Cahiers du C.E.R.E.S. (Série géographique),* no. 1 (1968); M.P. BRUGNES ROMIEU, "Investissements industriels et développement en Tunisie," *Cahiers du C.E.R.E.S. (Série économique),* no. 1 (1966); M. SEKLANI, "La Mortalité et le coût de la santé publique en Tunisie depuis l'après-guerre," *Cahiers du C.E.R.E.S. (Série démographique),* no. 1 and 2 (1967–68); BANQUE CENTRALE DE TUNISIE, *Rapport annuel 1980*; INSTITUT NATIONAL DE LA STATISTIQUE, *Recensement général de la population et des logements, 8 Mai 1975* (1975), and KHALED EL-MANOUBI, *Système educatif, emploi et industrialisation, le cas de la Tunisie* (1979). Also of value are *Revue Tunisienne des Sciences Sociales* (quarterly) and *Cahiers de Tunisie* (quarterly). The INSTITUT NATIONAL DE LA STATISTIQUE publishes a statistical annual, *Annuaire Statistique de la Tunisie,* a monthly statistical bulletin, *Bulletin Mensuel de Statistique,* and various other documents. Also see the TUNISIAN UNION OF INDUSTRY AND COMMERCE, *Economic Yearbook of Tunisia.* The Institut des Belles Lettres Arabes journal, *IBLA,* provides a view of Tunisian cultural life and includes a bibliography.

History. *General history:* JAMIL M. ABUN-NASR, *A History of the Maghrib,* 2nd ed. (1975); ABDALLAH LAROUI, *L'histoire du Maghreb: Un Essai de synthèse* (1975; *The History of the Maghrib: An Interpretive Essay,* 1977); and CHARLES ANDRE JULIEN, *Histoire de l'Afrique du Nord: Tunisie, Algérie, Maroc,* 2 vol., rev. ed. by C. COURTOIS (vol. 1); and R. LE TOURNEAU (vol. 2) (1956, reprinted 1966; *History of North Africa: Tunisia, Algeria, Morocco. From the Arab Conquest to 1830,* 1970).

Ancient North Africa: S. GSELL, *Histoire ancienne de l'Afrique du Nord,* 8 vol. (1913–28), a magisterial account in full detail up to the beginning of the Roman Empire (although the archaeological sections are now outdated, Gsell's intuition has frequently proved correct). (*Prehistory*): C.B.M. MCBURNEY, *The Stone Age of Northern Africa* (1960), and *The Haua Fteah (Cyrenaica) and the Stone Age in the South-East Mediterranean* (1967), two works by one of the foremost excavators and specialists in the subject; and J.M. COLES and E.S. HIGGS, *The Archaeology of Early Man* (1969), a modern survey comparing the prehistory of North Africa with that of the rest of Africa. (*Carthaginian*): B.H. WARMINGTON, *Carthage,* rev. ed. (1969), a detailed historical study of Phoenician Carthage; S. MOSCATI, *Il mondo dei Fenici* (1966; Eng. trans., *The World of the Phoenicians,* 1968), largely concerned with the archaeology, art, and religion of the Phoenicians; P. CINTAS, *Manuel d'archéologie punique* (1970–); G. and C. CHARLES-PICARD, *La Vie quotidienne à Carthage au temps d'Hannibal* (1958; Eng. trans., *Daily Life in Carthage at the Time of Hannibal,* 1961), an imaginative interpretation, but well based; G. CAMPS, *Aux origines de la Berbérie: Massinissa, ou les débuts de l'histoire, Libyca,* vol. 8 (1960), a detailed if sometimes speculative account of the Libyan peoples prior to and during the reign of Masinissa; and J. DESANGES, *Catalogue des tribus africaines de l'antiquité classique à l'ouest du Nil* (1962). (*Roman*): T.R.S. BROUGHTON, *The Romanization of Africa Proconsularis* (1929), the basic study of the impact of Roman immigration and culture in the first two centuries AD; P. ROMANELLI, *Storia delle province Romane dell'Africa* (1959), a complete account of Roman North Africa to the Vandal conquest; G. CHARLES-PICARD, *La Civilisation de l'Afrique romaine* (1959), an excellent interpretive study; P. SALAMA, *Les Voies romaines de l'Afrique du Nord* (1951); and R.M. HAYWOOD, *Roman Africa,* in T. FRANK (ed.), *An Economic Survey of Ancient Rome,* vol. 4 (1938), a review of all the evidence for the economy of Roman Africa up to AD 284. (*Late Roman, Vandal, and Byzantine*): W.H.C. FREND, *The Donatist Church: A Movement of Protest in Roman North Africa* (1952), an original and controversial treatment of the economic and social significance of Donatism; C. COURTOIS, *Les Vandals et l'Afrique* (1955), the only major account of the subject; C. DIEHL, *L'Afrique byzantine* (1896), in spite of its age, still the standard account of the period; and E.F. GAUTIER, *L'Islamisation de l'Afrique du Nord: Les Siècles obscurs du Maghreb* (1927), an outstanding account of the end of Byzantine rule and the Arab conquest. (*Cyrenaica*): F. CHAMOUX, *Cyrène sous la monarchie des Battiades* (1953); O. BATES, *The Eastern Libyans* (1914); R.G. GOODCHILD, "The Roman and Byzantine Limes in Cyrenaica," in *Journal of Roman Studies,* 43:65–76 (1953); and C. LACOMBRADE, *Synésios de Cyrène, hellène et chrétien* (1951).

North Africa from the beginning of the Islāmic period until 1830: C. DIEHL and G. MARCAIS, "Le Monde muselman au XIe et au XIIe siècle," in vol. 3 of *Histoire du Moyen âge,* in the series "Histoire Générale," publ. under the direction of G. GLOTZ (1936). H. TERRASSE, *Histoire du Maroc des origines à l'établissement du Protectorat français,* 2 vol. (1949–50; abridged Eng. ed., *History of Morocco,* 1952). S. GSELL, G. MARCAIS, and G. YVER, *Histoire de l'Algérie* (1929). A. BASSET *et al., Initiation à la Tunisie* (1950), see esp. the chapters by R. BRUNSCHVIG, "La Tunisie du moyen âge," and J. PIGNON, "La Tunisie Turque et Husséinite." A. BEL, *La Religion Musulmane en Berbérie* (1938); R. BRUNSCHVIG, *La Berbérie Orientale sous les Hafsides des Origines à la fin du XVe siècle,* 2 vol. (1940, 1947); and G. MARCAIS, *La Berbérie Musulmane et l'Orient au moyen âge* (1946). Studies may be found in the *Encyclopedia of Islam* (1908–38; new ed. 1954–); and in the journals *Hespéris* and *Revue Algérienne des sciences juridiques, économiques et politiques.*

North Africa since 1830: L. CARL BROWN (ed.), *State and Society in Independent North Africa* (1966), general interpretative articles on political, economic, and social issues; CHARLES F. GALLAGHER, *The United States and North Africa: Morocco, Algeria, and Tunisia* (1963), in spite of its title, a handbook on the Maghrib; DAVID C. GORDON, *North Africa's French Legacy, 1954–1962* (1962), excellent monograph on the French cultural influence; WILFRID KNAPP, *North West Africa: A Political and Economic Survey,* 3rd ed. (1977), strongest on political and economic issues; ROGER LE TOURNEAU, *Évolution politique de l'Afrique du Nord Musulmane, 1920–1961* (1962), thorough political history of these years; LUCETTE VALENSI, *On the Eve of Colonialism: North Africa Before the French Conquest* (1977; originally published in French, 1969), solid interpretation that dispels old myths; and *The Middle East and North Africa* and *Annuaire de l'Afrique du Nord,* two annuals with current information.

Algeria: For a comprehensive history, see *Histoire de l'Algérie contemporaine,* vol. 1, CHARLES ANDRÉ JULIEN, *La Conquête et les débuts de la colonisation (1827–1871),* 2nd ed. (1979); and vol. 2, CHARLES ROBERT AGERON, *De l'insurrection de 1871 au déclenchement de la guerre de libération, 1954* (1979); CHARLES ROBERT AGERON, *Les Algériens musulmans et la France, 1871–1919,* 2 vol. (1968), masterful, detailed account of French policy and Algerian reactions; EDWARD BEHR, *The Algerian Problem* (1961, reprinted 1976), sympathetic account by a journalist; RAPHAEL DANZIGER, *Abd al-Qadir and the Algerians* (1977), an excellent book on the subject, with a thorough bibliography; DAVID C. GORDON, *The Passing of French Algeria* (1966), emphasizing ideologies; MOSTEFA LACHERAF, *L'Algérie: Nation et société* (1965), revisionist work by a leading ideologue of the FLN; YVES LACOSTE (ed.), *L'Algérie, passé et présent* (1960), anticolonialist, Marxian interpretation; JEAN-CLAUDE VATIN, *L'Algérie politique: histoire et société* (1974), and, with JEAN LECA, *L'Algérie politique: institutions et régime* (1975), overall treatment from before 1830 to independence; and ALISTAIR HORNE, *A Savage War of Peace: Algeria 1954–1962* (1977), perceptive interpretive history of these years.

Tunisia: L. CARL BROWN, *The Tunisia of Ahmad Bey, 1837–1855* (1974), detailed study of the beginnings of Westernization; MEZRI BDIRA, *Relations internationales et sous développement: la Tunisie, 1857–1864* (1978), which clarifies the policies of Tunisian leadership during this period; ARNOLD H. GREEN, *The Tunisian Ulama, 1873–1915* (1978), which shows well how the religious institutions fitted into society in this period of transformation; LUCETTE VALENSI, *Fellahs tunisiens: l'économie rurale et la vie des campagnes aux XVIIIe et XIXe siècles* (1977), thorough study firmly based on material in Tunisian national archives; JEAN GANIAGE, *Les Origines du protectorat français en Tunisie, 1861–1881,* 2nd ed. (1968), emphasizing financial and international aspects; DWIGHT L. LING, *Tunisia, From Protectorate to Republic* (1967); CHARLES A. MICAUD, *Tunisia: The Politics of Modernization* (1964), reviewing ideological change during the protectorate and the Neo-Destour Party; CLEMENT HENRY MOORE, *Tunisia Since Independence* (1965), thorough political study; LARS RUDEBECK, *Party and People: A Study of Political Change in Tunisia* (1967, reissued 1969); and NICOLA A. ZIADEH, *The Origins of Nationalism in Tunisia* (1962, reprinted 1969).

Morocco: STÉPHANE BERNARD, *The Franco-Moroccan Conflict, 1943–1956* (1968), thorough case study of decolonization; ROBIN BIDWELL, *Morocco Under Colonial Rule: French Administration of Tribal Areas, 1912–1956* (1973), study of colonization and its effects on the colonized; EDMUND BURKE III, *Prelude to Protectorate in Morocco: Precolonial Protest and Resistance, 1860–1912* (1976), solid interpretation of how Morocco came under colonial rule; JEAN BRIGNON *et al., Histoire du Maroc* (1967), general textbook for Moroccan schools by Moroccan and French scholars; KENNETH L. BROWN, *People of Salé: Tradition and Change in a Moroccan City, 1830–1930* (1976), very good source on society and urban–rural ties; LADISLAV CERYCH, *Européens et Marocains, 1930–1956: sociologie d'une décolonisation* (1964), excellent political, economic, and sociological study; JOHN P. HALSTEAD, *Rebirth of a Nation: The Origins and Rise of Moroccan Nationalism, 1912–1944* (1967), review of the early nationalists; ABDALLAH LAROUI, *Les Origines sociales et culturelles du nationalisme marocain, 1830–1912* (1977), stimulating challenge to earlier interpretations; ROBERT MONTAGNE, *Révolution au Maroc* (1954), series of interpretative essays; ROGER LE TOURNEAU, *Fès avant le Protectorat* (1949, reprinted 1978); ALAN SCHAM, *Lyautey in Morocco: Protectorate Administration, 1912–1925* (1970); CHARLES F. STEWART, *The Economy of Morocco, 1912–1962* (1964); JOHN WATERBURY, *The Commander of the Faithful: The Moroccan Political Elite—A Study in Segmented Politics* (1970); DAVID S. WOOLMAN, *Rebels in the Rif: Abd el Krim and the Rif Rebellion* (1968); and I. WILLIAM ZARTMAN, *Morocco: Problems of New Power* (1964).

Libya: E.E. EVANS-PRITCHARD, *The Sanusi of Cyrenaica* (1949, reissued 1968), seminal anthropological study; RUTH FIRST, *Libya: The Elusive Revolution* (1974), reliable survey of modern Libya; MARIUS K. DEEB and MARY JANE DEEB, *Libya Since the Revolution* (1982), dispassionate description stressing internal social and political developments; MAJID KHADDURI, *Modern Libya: A Study in Political Development* (1963, reissued 1968); ETTORE ROSSI, *Storia di Tripoli e della Tripolitania* (1968); CLAUDIO G. SEGRE, *Fourth Shore: The Italian Colonization of Libya* (1974), on Italian rule in Libya; and JOHN L. WRIGHT, *Libya: A Modern History* (1982).

North America

One of the most developed regions of the world, North America enjoys an average income per person about 15 percent higher than that of western Europe; a food intake more than two-fifths greater than the average for Asia; and a per capita consumption of energy almost six times as great as the average of all the other continents. With an area of some 9,355,000 square miles (24,230,000 square kilometres) shaped roughly like a triangle, it is third in size among the world's continents. The home of less than 10 percent of the world's population, it nevertheless produces more than one-third of all the manufactured goods of the world. Yet, before the arrival of European settlers and their African slaves, North America was not nearly as fully developed as was Europe, Asia, or parts of Africa.

European colonizers of North America set sail at a time of great scientific and technical innovation and were able to apply and develop new skills in lands untrammeled by the conventions and practices of the past. But it was North America's great natural wealth that accounted for much of the expansion, offering extensive and seemingly inexhaustible deposits of metals and fuels, vast forests, ample water resources, and a wide and stimulating range of climates and soils.

The name America is derived from that of the Italian merchant and navigator Amerigo Vespucci, one of the earliest explorers of what is now North America. He is thought by some authorities to have discovered and reached the mainland of the continent in 1497. This claim was widely accepted after the publication, in 1507, of an account of his travels. The new-found lands that came to bear his name extended from Labrador in the north to Patagonia in the south; those portions that widened out north of the Isthmus of Panama became known as North America and those that broadened to the south became known as South America. According to some authorities, North America begins not at the Isthmus of Panama but at the narrows of Tehuantepec, with the intervening region called Central America. Under such a definition, part of Mexico must be included in Central America, although that country lies mainly in North America proper. To overcome this anomaly, the whole of Mexico, together with Central and South American countries, may also be grouped under the name Latin America, with the United States and Canada referred to as Anglo-America. This cultural division is a very real one; yet Mexico and Central America (including the Caribbean) are bound to the rest of North America by strong ties of physical geography. Largely Danish-speaking Greenland is also divided culturally from, but physically close to, North America. All the above areas are sometimes included under the general terms the New World, the Western Hemisphere, or the Americas.

This article treats the physical and human geography and history of North America, followed by discussion of geographical features of special interest. For discussion of individual countries of the continent, see the articles CANADA, MEXICO, and UNITED STATES OF AMERICA. For discussion of major cities of the continent, see specific articles by name, *e.g.,* MEXICO CITY, NEW YORK CITY, and TORONTO. For discussion of the indigenous peoples of the continent, see the articles AMERICAN INDIANS and PRE-COLUMBIAN CIVILIZATIONS. For further discussion of literature, see the articles AMERICAN LITERATURE, CANADIAN LITERATURE, and LATIN-AMERICAN LITERATURE. For further references, see also the entries for these topics in the *Index.*

The article is divided into the following sections:

PHYSICAL AND HUMAN GEOGRAPHY

Geological history

North America has a latitudinal span of over 76°, stretching from southern Panama to Cape Columbia, in northern Canada, and extends over 175° of longitude from Cape Nordost Rundigen, in eastern Greenland, to Attu Island, in Alaska. This enormous reach gives it every climate from the virtually equatorial to the Arctic, but the shape of the continent, very narrow in the south and very wide in the north, reduces the amount within the tropics and expands the area in the temperate and polar zones.

ELEMENTS AND PROCESSES IN THE MAKING OF THE CONTINENT

The shape of North America may have resulted from the fact that, over a vast period of geological time, the continental landmass drifted away from Europe and North Africa. A glance at the globe shows that the expansive northern edge of North America would fit into the correspondingly receding edge of Europe and that its narrowness in the south could correspond to the huge bulge of western Africa. Geologists have worked out a theory of continental drift based on rigid areas in the crust, like plates, with zones of weakness in between. These are affected by currents in the molten rock material, or magma, beneath the Earth's crust. Immense pressures on the so-called plates led them to move into new positions, squeezing out the weak zones, marked by deep depressions, or geosynclines, on their margins. These became filled in with sediments and were then squeezed out and upward into fold mountains. Faulting—a vast shearing process along lines of structural weakness in the Earth's crust—occurred subsequently between continents as they were torn apart from each other. Faulting was followed by renewed and extensive folding on the outward advancing continental fronts. In the formation of North America, it is thought that a very stable area called the Canadian or Laurentian Shield parted from the Baltic and Iberian shields of Europe in Jurassic times, about 170,000,000 years ago. The ensuing gradual widening of the Atlantic Ocean led to extensive faulting along the east coast of North America, and the push of the continent against the "plate" underlying the Pacific area produced widespread folding in the west.

Conflicting theories of continental origin

Other geologists have sought to explain the evolution and growth of North America in terms of its present position, first by a hardening of the Earth's crust through immense granitic intrusions, or upswellings of molten rock, which formed the Laurentian Shield, and then by the rise of great geosynclines where sediments, stripped from the shield over millennia by the forces of erosion, depressed the margins of the continent. From a stable core, at the heart of the Laurentian Plateau, great downwarps are then thought to have developed in contact with the Atlantic, Arctic, and Pacific oceans. These became so burdened by the debris of the eroded shield as to form lines of crustal weakness, which, in turn, grew into zones of volcanic activity and fold-mountain systems. The continent thus evolved by the outward expansion and final immobilization of marginal geosynclines. Indeed, there is an outward regression in age from a very old centre, where the rocks are nearly 4,000,000,000 years old, to younger margins, usually less than 600,000,000 years.

Both of these theories have attractive features: each accounts for a central shield flanked by belts of marginal mountains. The extensive faulting in the north and east, separating Greenland from Canada, and the breaking off of the apparent connections between the Appalachians of North America and the Caledonian and Hercynean mountain-fold systems of Europe might well correspond to a shore torn from the Old World by the widening of the Atlantic and Arctic oceans. Similarly, the lofty region of mountain building in the west would correspond to an advance on the Pacific basin. On the other hand, the outward progression of geosynclines, formed by the weight of waste material washed from a central core and turned into lines of marginal mountains, would also explain existing North American structural patterns adequately.

Recent work on the Atlantic, emphasizing active widening by periodic vulcanism and faulting, strongly supports the drift theory. Ocean-floor spreading—a movement away from the centre line of the ocean basin, leaving a great midocean ridge, flanked by deeper parts, and often ending in major depressions toward the continents—is seen as the mechanism for the breaking up of the continents. It has been suggested that the North Atlantic began to open up in the Upper Triassic and the Lower Jurassic, between 187,000,000 and 172,000,000 years ago, while the South Atlantic started to widen in the Upper Jurassic, about 138,000,000 years ago. The major rifting of Europe and North America was not accomplished until the Lower Cretaceous, about 93,000,000 years ago. Greenland and Canada started to split up in the Upper Cretaceous, while Greenland and Europe moved apart later, in the Cretaceous–Paleocene, say 63,000,000 years ago. From that time on, North America became a truly separate continent, still drifting west, it is claimed, at a rate of just over half an inch, or about one and a quarter centimetres, a year. The "plate" flooring the Pacific basin, meanwhile, may have been thrust under the advancing continent.

North America's four chief physical structures

The four chief structures of North America are a central shield; marginal mountains; interior lowlands between the shield and the mountains; and coastal plains. All have taken a long time to evolve. The shield itself, made up of the oldest rocks in North America, took longer to form than the rest of the continent put together. After its main structures had been built, it became the core area against which the marginal mountains were thrown up. These grew from immense geosynclines, which served as sites for the accumulation of tens of thousands of feet of material, sorted by the seas and later lifted up and squeezed into mountain ranges. The geosynclines divided themselves into (1) a shallower belt, the miogeosynclines, along the edge of the shield, and (2) a very profound belt, the eugeosynclines, farther out. Mountains evolving from the miogeosyncline were less intensively folded and less subject to volcanic activity than those growing out of the eugeosyncline. The Appalachians were the first mountain system to so evolve, followed by the Arctic fold belt and, in turn, by the comparatively young mountains of the west. Ancient seas, meanwhile, lying between the rising mountains and the shield, spread out the debris eroded from surrounding heights. Horizontally bedded sheets of sedimentary rock thus came to form the interior and coastal plains. Faulting, leading to immense fault-bounded blocks

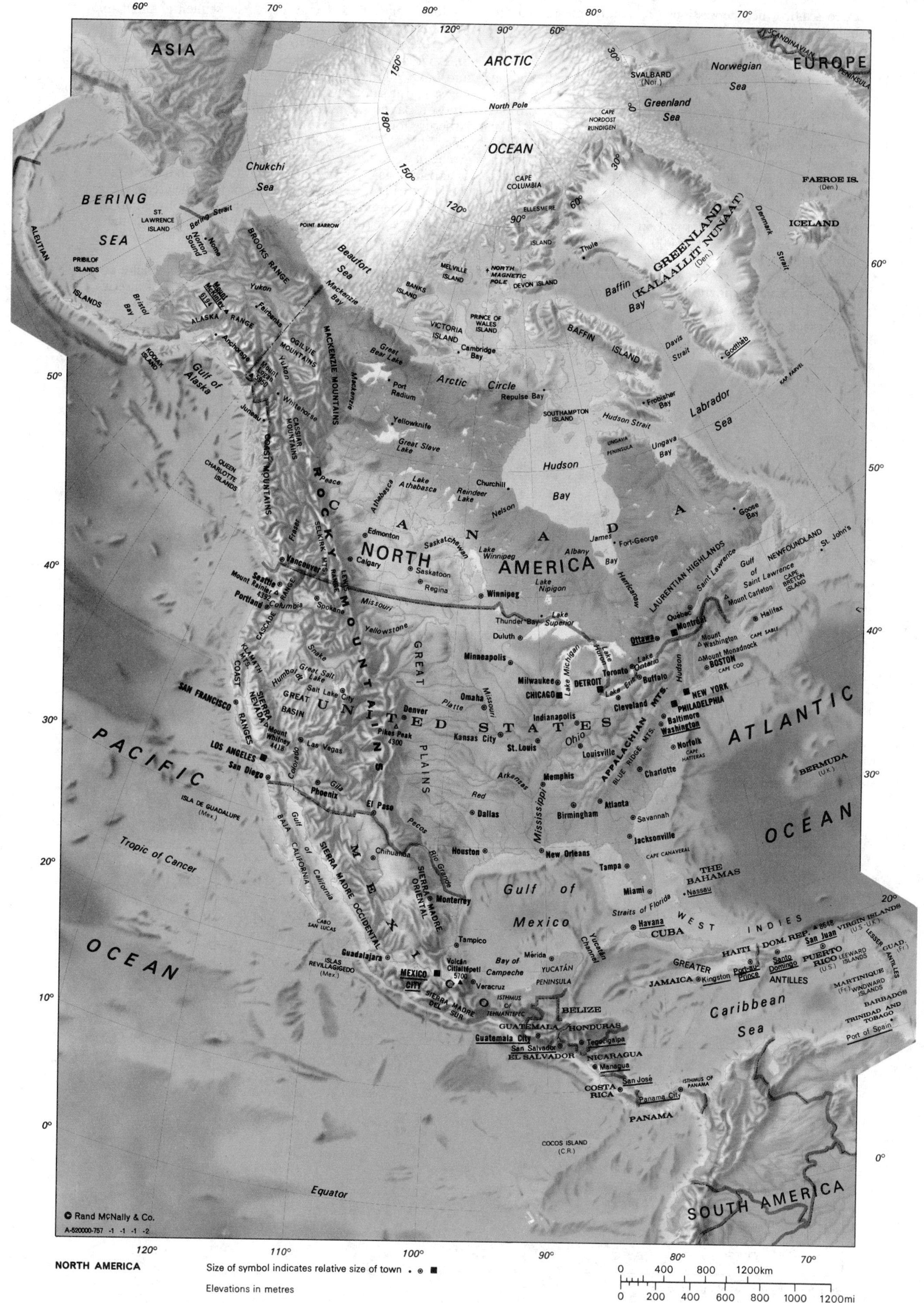
ASIA
ARCTIC
OCEAN
North Pole
EUROPE
Norwegian Sea
Greenland Sea
SVALBARD (Nor.)
CAPE NORDOST RUNDIGEN
Chukchi Sea
BERING SEA
Bering Strait
ST. LAWRENCE ISLAND
Beaufort Sea
CAPE COLUMBIA
ELLESMERE ISLAND
GREENLAND (KALAALLIT NUNAAT) (Den.)
Thule
FAEROE IS. (Den.)
ICELAND
Denmark Strait
POINT BARROW
BROOKS RANGE
Nome
Norton Sound
PRIBILOF ISLANDS
ALEUTIAN ISLANDS
Bristol Bay
Yukon
Mount McKinley 6194
ALASKA RANGE
Fairbanks
Anchorage
KODIAK ISLAND
Gulf of Alaska
Mount Logan 5950
OGILVIE MOUNTAINS
MACKENZIE MOUNTAINS
Mackenzie Bay
MELVILLE ISLAND
NORTH MAGNETIC POLE
DEVON ISLAND
BANKS ISLAND
PRINCE OF WALES ISLAND
VICTORIA ISLAND
Cambridge Bay
Baffin Bay
BAFFIN ISLAND
Davis Strait
Godthåb
KAP FARVEL
Great Bear Lake
Port Radium
Arctic Circle
Repulse Bay
Frobisher Bay
Labrador Sea
SOUTHAMPTON ISLAND
Hudson Strait
UNGAVA PENINSULA
Ungava Bay
Whitehorse
Juneau
CASSIAR MOUNTAINS
COAST MOUNTAINS
QUEEN CHARLOTTE ISLANDS
Yellowknife
Great Slave Lake
Hudson Bay
Churchill
Lake Athabasca
Reindeer Lake
Peace
Athabasca
Nelson
ROCKY MOUNTAINS
C A N A D A
Goose Bay
Edmonton
Saskatchewan
James Bay
Fort-George
Albany
NORTH AMERICA
NEWFOUNDLAND
St. John's
Calgary
Saskatoon
Regina
Lake Winnipeg
Winnipeg
Lake Nipigon
LAURENTIAN HIGHLANDS
Saint Lawrence
Gulf of Saint Lawrence
CAPE BRETON ISLAND
Mount Carleton
Vancouver
Seattle
Mount Rainier 4392
Portland
Columbia
CASCADE RANGE
Spokane
Missouri
Yellowstone
Lake Superior
Thunder Bay
Duluth
Quebec
Montreal
Ottawa
Halifax
Mount Washington
Mount Monadnock
BOSTON
CAPE COD
CAPE SABLE
Snake
GREAT PLAINS
Minneapolis
Lake Michigan
Lake Huron
Lake Ontario
Toronto
Buffalo
Hudson
NEW YORK
PHILADELPHIA
Milwaukee
DETROIT
CHICAGO
Lake Erie
Cleveland
KLAMATH MTS.
COAST RANGES
Humboldt
Great Salt Lake
Salt Lake City
GREAT BASIN
SAN FRANCISCO
SIERRA NEVADA
Omaha
Platte
Denver
UNITED STATES
Indianapolis
Baltimore
Washington
ATLANTIC
Mount Whitney 4418
Pikes Peak 4300
Kansas City
St. Louis
Ohio
Louisville
APPALACHIAN MTS.
BLUE RIDGE MTS.
Norfolk
CAPE HATTERAS
Las Vegas
LOS ANGELES
San Diego
Colorado
PACIFIC
Gila
Phoenix
Arkansas
Memphis
Charlotte
BERMUDA (U.K.)
ISLA DE GUADALUPE (Mex.)
El Paso
Red
Dallas
Atlanta
Birmingham
Mississippi
Savannah
OCEAN
Tropic of Cancer
BAJA CALIFORNIA
Gulf of California
SIERRA MADRE OCCIDENTAL
Pecos
Chihuahua
Rio Grande
SIERRA MADRE ORIENTAL
Houston
New Orleans
Jacksonville
CAPE CANAVERAL
Tampa
THE BAHAMAS
Nassau
Miami
Monterrey
Gulf of Mexico
Straits of Florida
WEST INDIES
CABO SAN LUCAS
Tampico
Havana
CUBA
Yucatán Channel
DOM. REP.
8648
San Juan
VIRGIN ISLANDS (U.S.-U.K.)
LESSER ANTILLES
OCEAN
Guadalajara
ISLAS REVILLAGIGEDO (Mex.)
Volcán Citlaltépetl 5700
Bay of Campeche
Mérida
YUCATÁN PENINSULA
HAITI
GREATER ANTILLES
Santo Domingo
PUERTO RICO (U.S.)
LEEWARD ISLANDS
GUAD. (Fr.)
MEXICO CITY
Veracruz
JAMAICA
Kingston
Port-au-Prince
MARTINIQUE (Fr.)
WINDWARD ISLANDS
MEXICO
SIERRA MADRE DEL SUR
ISTHMUS OF TEHUANTEPEC
BELIZE
Caribbean Sea
BARBADOS
TRINIDAD AND TOBAGO
Port of Spain
GUATEMALA
HONDURAS
Guatemala City
Tegucigalpa
San Salvador
EL SALVADOR
NICARAGUA
Managua
San José
ISTHMUS OF PANAMA
COSTA RICA
Panama City
PANAMA
COCOS ISLAND (C.R.)
Equator
SOUTH AMERICA
© Rand McNally & Co.
A-520000-757 -1 -1 -1 -2
NORTH AMERICA
Size of symbol indicates relative size of town
Elevations in metres
0 400 800 1200km
0 200 400 600 800 1000 1200mi

or to sea-drowned depressions, frequently interrupted the building up of these structures.

THE EVOLUTION OF THE CENTRAL SHIELD

The central shield, which is variously called Laurentia, the Laurentian Shield, or the Canadian Shield, is the key structure of the North American continent, extending from the Adirondacks and the Superior Upland just south of Lake Superior, northward through Canada, both east and west of the Hudson Bay, to Greenland. The central shield is, in fact, a group of shields that gradually coalesced, covering a total of 2,550,000 square miles, including 700,000 square miles in Greenland, and is largely composed of Archean and Proterozoic rocks formed in the Precambrian era, which ranges from 570,000,000 years ago to more than 4,000,000,000 years ago.

The main trends of the shield sprang from an initial Y-shaped structure identified as beginning west and east of the Hudson Bay depression and then extending, as a subsurface welt, south of the Superior Upland to the Colorado Plateau. This structure was subsequently tilted up in the east, in Greenland and in Labrador; it was faulted along the south and west to give way to the basins of the St. Lawrence and Great Lakes, the Red River of the North and Lake Winnipeg, and the Mackenzie and its attendant lakes; and it sank beneath the vast hollow of what is now Hudson Bay to the north. Various accretions to the initial structure formed the rest of the shield.

The rocks of the shield fall into two main groups, the Archean and the Proterozoic, separated by a long interval of erosion. The Archean formations are subdivided into the Keewatin and Timiskaming, from the type areas where they were identified. The Proterozoic was accompanied by four great shield-building times, again named from their type areas, the Lower and Middle Huronian, the Animikie (or Upper Huronian), and the Keweenawan.

Development of Archean rocks. The original shield, going back at least 3,900,000,000 years, consisted of a series of volcanoes, with lava tablelands that spread out and filled up innumerable lakes in between. In early Archean,

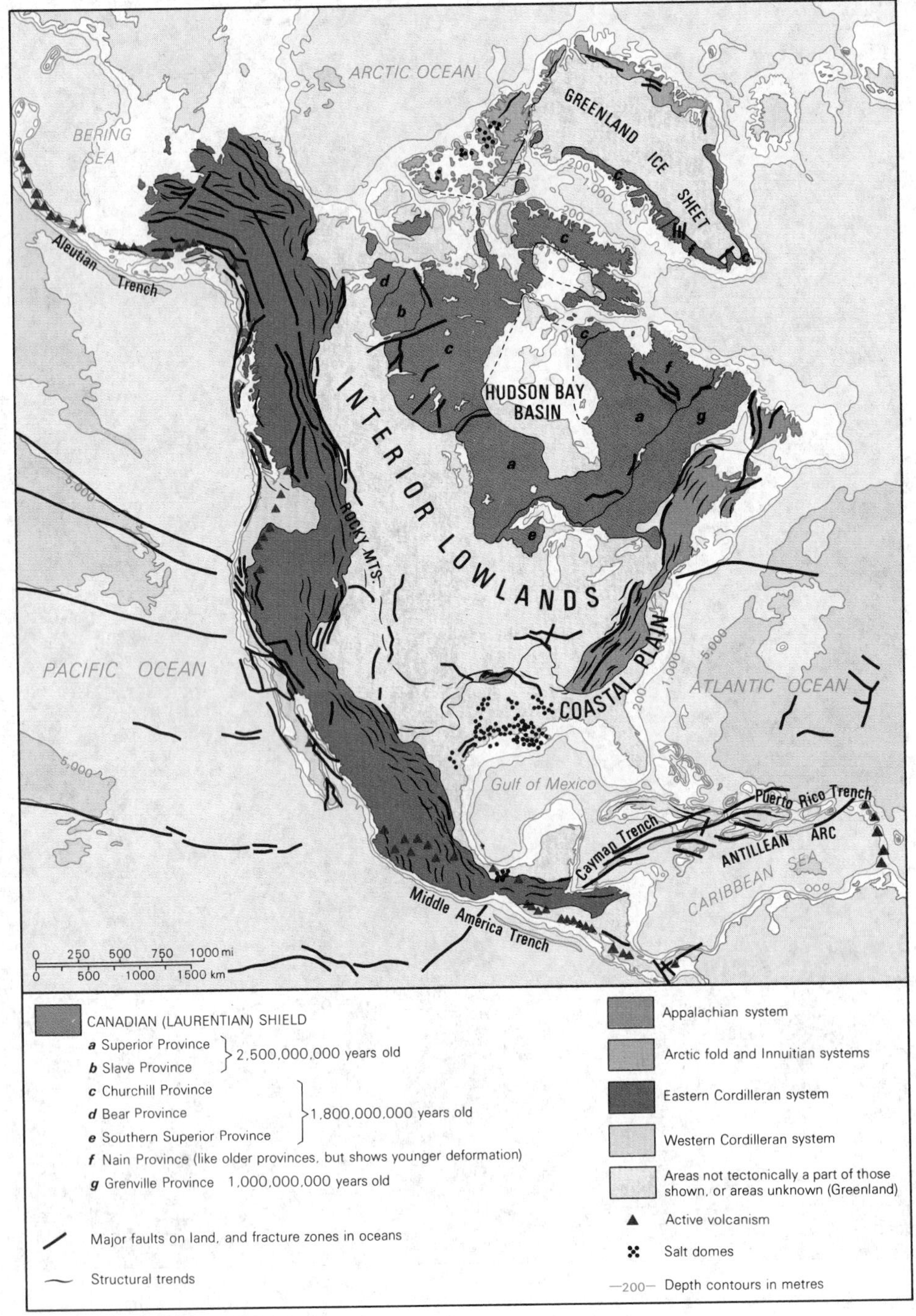

Structural features of North America.

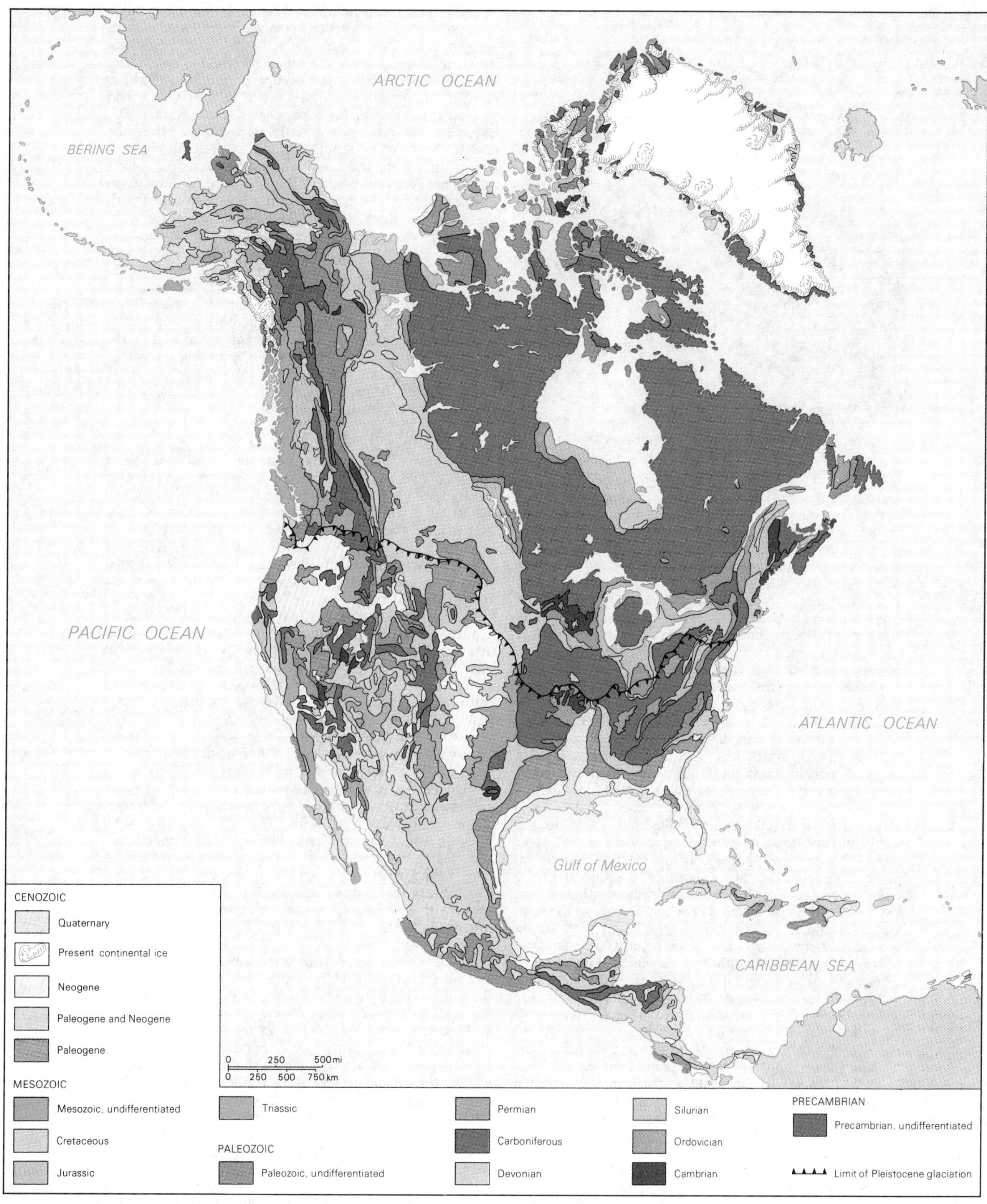

Rock strata of North America.

Initial Y-shaped structure of shield

or Keewatin, time (there is great controversy over the dating of this process, and precise figures are meaningless in this context) the initial Y-shaped structure developed from great thicknesses of lava. These flowed out at intervals, were attacked by erosion and coated by weathered material, and then flowed out again, producing sheets of volcanic rock interbedded with sedimentaries. In the late Keewatin, prolonged erosion led to wide deposits of conglomerates (rocks made up of different materials) and sandstones on the western and southern edges of the shield. At a later time, these rocks were caught up in the Laurentian mountain-building movements, and, as a result, they were heavily intruded from below by granitic domes.

The shield then became faulted along its southeastern edge, forming a long trough where thick layers of limestone interbedded with shale (typified by deposits at Grenville,

Frozen sea inlet in the crystalline rocks of the Laurentian Shield, Boothia Peninsula, Northwest Territories, Canada.
George Hunter—Shostal/EB Inc.

near Ottawa) were laid down. More changes took place in Timiskaming time, with the growth of the iron-bearing southern part of the shield, in the Superior Upland. During the structural upheaval known as the Algoman revolution, these rocks west and south of Lake Superior and along the north shore of Lake Huron were widely metamorphosed (or heat altered). Mountains also arose in the vicinity of Great Slave and Great Bear lakes, and the dislocations threw lava beds and sedimentary strata into nearly vertical folds, accompanied by large granitic domes.

Development of Proterozoic rocks. In the Eparchean interlude—a long stretch of time in which the mountains were worn almost completely down—the shield became virtually a plain. But, as the Proterozoic dawned possibly 1,500,000,000 years ago, lava flows occurred, indicating further crustal disturbances. The Lower Huronian series of lavas, conglomerates, and limestones were deposited in the northern part of the Great Lakes depression. Continued activity in the Middle Huronian raised these deposits about 1,700 feet (500 metres), tilted the shield to the north, and laid down new deposits, preserved in the Cobalt and Chibougamau basins and in the Gulf of Richmond, on its inner edge. Further enlargements occurred in the Lake Athabasca–Darnley Bay area, in the northwest, and the Labrador–Baffin Island–Greenland region, to the east. Upper Huronian, or Animikie, time began with strong erosion that spread iron-associated deposits into flanking depressions from Lake Athabasca around to the Ungava trough. As erosion continued, the burden of material affecting the crust beneath led to volcanic outbreaks and the uplift and squeezing out of the geosynclines. The end of Animikie time saw new injections of igneous masses and the rise of fold mountains in the Great Slave Lake, the Belcher Islands, and the Ungava–Baffin regions.

Final growth of the shield

The final growth of the shield occurred in Keweenawan times. Its southern extension was enlarged by more iron-rich sedimentaries; the great Sudbury norite (granular rock) intrusion was formed; Lake Superior became a distinct elongated trough; and, in the Far North, the great Victoria trough saw a downwarping that gathered the Coppermine series of sandstones and lavas. Further shield extensions into the Arctic islands and Greenland continued. Keweenawan times ended in the massive Killarnean intrusions, east of Sudbury, and in renewed mountain building, especially just north of Lake Athabasca.

By the end of the Proterozoic, at about 570,000,000 years ago, when long periods of erosion had worn down the heights and built out extensive plains, the shield was a virtual lowland stretching from Greenland through to the Great Plains.

Later evolution of the shield. The shield never grew any bigger, but its chronicle of changes was by no means over. With the rise of the Appalachians against its southeastern edge in Ordovician times, about 480,000,000 years ago, the shield sank down in the centre to produce even wider and deeper waters than now occupy Hudson Bay. Further uplift in Middle Silurian times, however, raised the shield so high that Hudson Bay disappeared. Sinking followed; but in Devonian times, renewed strain stemmed from the rise of the Acadian mountains. As a result, the eastern rim was tilted up, and extensive faulting occurred. A long quiescence followed, wearing the whole shield down until Cretaceous times. Renewed disturbances, associated with the rise of the Rockies, then lifted up and broke the western shield edge; while between the Late Cretaceous and the Paleocene, about 65,000,000 to 54,000,000 years ago, the Labrador Sea began to open up between Baffin Island and Greenland. In mid-Pliocene, there was a resumption of ocean spreading in the North Atlantic, a general uplift of the shield, and, especially in the east and north, widespread faulting. The shield became depressed in the Pleistocene, over 1,000,000 years ago, under the enormous weight of the ice cap, and in postglacial times subsequently rebounded to its present level, size, and shape, as the massive core of North America.

Post-glacial rebounding to present conditions

THE EVOLUTION OF THE MARGINAL MOUNTAINS

At the end of the Proterozoic, about 570,000,000 years ago, the shield was so massive that it then became the most stable area in North America, and subsequent continental deformation shifted to the great fold-mountain systems. The first of these to develop was the Appalachian fold belt, from the Late Cambrian (about 500,000,000 years ago) through to the Pennsylvanian (about 280,000,000 years ago). This first belt was followed by the Greenland and Arctic fold belts from the Late Paleozoic to the Early Cenozoic (from about 345,000,000 to 65,000,000 years ago), overlapping the Appalachians but continuing beyond them both in time and space; these were succeeded in turn by the Western Cordilleras, which began forming in the Jurassic Period (about 180,000,000 years ago) and continued right on into the Miocene (about 10,000,000 years ago), with a few volcanic outbursts in the Pliocene as late as 7,000,000 years ago.

Growth of the Appalachians. Growing out of a complex and varied system of geosynclines along the southeastern margin of the shield (or its buried extension), the Appalachians exhibited striking early contrasts between their western and eastern portions. The western ridges were lifted up from a comparatively shallow depression, or miogeosyncline, while the eastern ranges rose from a much deeper eugeosynclinal trough beyond the continental edge. The western division is made up of more regularly folded rocks with few igneous intrusions; the eastern parts are intensively folded and faulted and have been heavily intruded by crystalline bodies.

In Cambrian times, new disturbances in North America and Europe developed long depressions on the forefront of the central shield into which sands and clays and vegetable and animal remains were carried outward from the old and stable interior and laid down in such quantity as to create persistent, if slow, crustal subsidence. This pressure, in turn, generated a counterthrust that created island arcs of spouting volcanoes or molten igneous domes, which lifted earlier deposits and transformed them into great land swells. Subsequent folding produced the Appalachian Mountains proper, which depressed the edge of the shield into a sunken platform, buried under strata laid down by invading seas.

The geosynclines were squeezed out in a whole series of mountain-building movements, from Cambrian to Pennsylvanian times, or perhaps for as long as 200,000,000 years. The older northern movements were separated from the younger southern activities by a line running approximately through present-day New Jersey. The northern activity ran through the Maritimes and Newfoundland Island to Greenland, with a possible continuation in the Caledonian and Hercynian mountains of western Europe.

Northern Appalachians. In Cambrian times the northern Appalachians formed themselves into three distinct belts, in which were to mold the whole evolution and eventual relief of New England and of Canada's Atlantic provinces. The first belt was an inner Laurentian geosynclinal trough along the present St. Lawrence River; the second, a central plateau-like upwelt, running through central New England to Newfoundland; and the third, the outer depression of the Acadian Geosyncline. The inner trough may be referred to as the Taconic Geosyncline from the Taconic orogeny, or mountain-building process, during Ordovician times, of old rugged fold mountains running through eastern New York. Further folding, mainly during the Silurian Period, saw the rise of the parallel ridges in western New England, swinging on to western Newfoundland and perhaps to Greenland and beyond. The central portions, however, remained a relatively stable mass, although they were extensively injected with volcanic rocks. During Devonian times, the outer Acadian trough saw the rise of short, fold ridges in eastern New England and the Maritimes, strengthening themselves in eastern Newfoundland before stretching on to possible European continuations. The zone includes a notable series of Triassic red sandstone beds, cut by ridges of volcanic origin.

The basic tripartite division of the northern Appalachians

Southern Appalachians. The younger southern Appalachians began southward of what is now the Hudson Valley, were interrupted by the Mississippi Basin, became active again in the Ouachitas (in Arkansas and Oklahoma), and may have had a Central American continuation to Venezuela. They arose in Mississippian to Pennsylvanian times, from 345,000,000 to 280,000,000 years ago. Like their northern counterparts, they evolved from inner and outer troughs but lacked the intervening geanticline, or huge upwelt. The inner trough was filled by silts and sands from great deltas pushed out between the rising Appalachians and the shield, together with limestones in deeper gulfs; these layers came to typify the Catskill, Allegheny, and Cumberland plateaus. Distinctive short folding produced the undulating topography now characterizing the central belt known as the Ridge and Valley region. The outer trough saw much volcanic activity, which, together with intense folding, helped to mold the hard granites, slates, and quartzites of the Blue Ridge and the Piedmont. Farther south, the Ozarks continued the sweep of the inner plateaus, while the wavelike surface of the Ouachitas pushed against older Texan rocks to form the great Ouachita Geosyncline.

Arctic fold belts. Structural disturbances then moved north, and, in Greenland and the Canadian Archipelago, the Arctic fold-belt mountains began to emerge as the Appalachian orogeny died down. This process perhaps reflected a distinct torque in continental drift, with a northern twist in North America's main move west. All along the east coast of Greenland, Paleozoic rocks, especially those of the Silurian (from 425,000,000 to 400,000,000 years old), were subjected to folding—possible equivalents of the European Caledonian orogeny. A northeastward trend leads, via a submarine ridge, to Svalbard (Spitsbergen). Greenland's northern shore is crossed by mountains with a west–east axis, considered an extension of ranges sweeping across northern Canada. In the Arctic as in the Atlantic, ocean spreading was putting pressure on North America. An Arctic geosyncline resulted, deepening in late Cambrian and Ordovician times (about 500,000,000 years ago) to attract clays and sands eroded from the Canadian and Greenland shields. Massive Cambrian sandstones overlie Precambrian rocks in eastern central Ellesmere Island; similar rocks and sheets of Ordovician shale and limestone slope northwestward off the high Precambrian spine of Baffin Island; and, far to the west, Ordovician strata overlap the shield in Victoria Island. Silurian rocks lie farther north, typically developed in western Devon Island and the Parry Islands and sloping beneath Carboniferous and Permian beds. The Innuitian mountain system, a major fold belt, rose up in this area, made up of rocks of Mesozoic age, from Prince Patrick Island to Ellesmere; folding may well have continued in Ellesmere until the early Miocene, some 25,000,000 years ago, or well into the mountain-building period typical of the Western Cordilleras.

The Innuitian mountain system

The Innuitians, nevertheless, resemble the Appalachians more than the Cordilleras. Through Eglinton Island, in the west, and across northern Melville and Bathurst islands, they developed along an undulating series of parallel anticlines and synclines, with a distinct ridge and valley effect. The rocks consist of whitish sandstones with bands of black coal overlain by limestone. Pitching anticlines, with their cigar-shaped hills, and synclines, with their trough-topped ridges, became prominent and gave rise to the zigzag drainage patterns so striking in the inner Appalachians. The intensified folding and intrusions of volcanic rocks, however, are more reminiscent of the outer Appalachians.

The Cordilleras. The last, but certainly the greatest, system of mountains to form in North America, the magnificent Cordilleras rose mainly in post-Jurassic times, less than 136,000,000 years ago, when Atlantic ocean spreading had reached a critical point with the accelerated drift of the continent westward against the Pacific. The spreading of the Pacific floor, meanwhile, thrust eastward against the Pacific borderlands. The two forces must have created tremendous pressures all along the west rim of the central shield and so helped to inaugurate the squeeze-out of the giant geosynclines of the west that gave rise to the Rockies, Cascades, and Coast ranges, from Alaska to Mexico.

Cordilleran geosyncline. Rocks going back to Proterozoic times accumulated in a deep trough at what must then have been the outermost shield edge. Much erosion continued until in Cambrian times, over 500,000,000 years ago, the immense Cordilleran geosyncline developed from Alaska to Central America. It was not deep and may be regarded as a miogeosyncline, or a belt of troughs, often called the Millard zone of crustal weakness. Westward, the land swelled up into a tremendous geanticline of very old rocks underlying the Yukon, Colorado, and Mexican plateaus. Since this upwelling lay between the main lines of mountain building, it came to be known as the Mesocordilleran Geanticline. Its erosion deposited sediments into the Pacific that put pressure on the earth's crust and generated a deep geosyncline, a very complex belt with an inner and an outer division. This eugeosynclinal trough is known as the Fraser zone.

These basic structures dominated the rise of the Cordilleras, dividing them essentially into three great belts: the Eastern Cordilleras, or Rocky Mountain system, along the inner edge of the old continent; a central string of high intermontane plateaus; and the Western Cordilleras, divided into the Cascadian and the Coast Range systems, on the continent's outer edge. A major difference occurred between the outer and inner mountains. Like those of the Appalachians, the inner mountains arose from a shallow miogeosyncline and consist of long parallel folds or blocks of relatively unfolded strata lifted up on high. The outer mountains, reminiscent of the emergence of the outer Appalachians, originated in a profound eugeosyncline intruded by enormous igneous masses, studded with tall volcanoes—some of them active until modern times—and intensively folded and faulted.

The tripartite division of the Cordilleras

Eastern Cordilleras. In the late Jurassic, over 136,000,000 years ago, the Eastern Cordilleras emerged from the deeper Millard zone and spread inward over the buried shield edge. In the ensuing Upper Cretaceous, the Laramide structural revolution brought forth the western Rockies, spreading debris over what are now the prairies. Later still, in Eocene and Oligocene times, as late as 25,000,000 years ago, the eastern ranges of the Rockies started to rise, marked by slow uplift of great blocks of strata.

Western Cordilleras. The Fraser zone had also become disturbed. The Western Cordilleras exhibited Mesozoic conglomerates and coarse sands that were laid down unconformably, or disjointedly, on the older rocks, thus showing that upwells within the troughs had already been lifted up and then eroded. Movement became intensified during the Nevadan mountain-building revolution of the late Jurassic, raising and folding mountains from Central America to Alaska, including the Sierra Nevadas and the Cascades. Enormous igneous bodies were intruded into the rock layers: the largest was the Coast Batholith, or dome-shaped structure, underlying coastal British Columbia. The line of deformation then shifted outward to a trough

The Coast Batholith and other massive igneous intrusions

overlying the present coast ranges of California and Oregon and along the Columbian Trough, represented by the islands off British Columbia and Alaska. Deposition, from inland, overloaded the geosyncline and caused violent volcanic activity. Intense folding, uplift, and faulting followed, with thrusts toward the continental interior mostly in Late Cretaceous and Early Tertiary times, roughly between 100,000,000 and 50,000,000 years ago. The Late Tertiary Cascadian orogeny raised the western ranges yet again, led to renewed volcanic activity from southern Mexico through California to southern Alaska, and severely faulted the Sierras.

The intermontane plateaus. Lying between the eastern and western fold belts of the Cordilleras, and developed from several very old Precambrian and early Cambrian landmasses, the intermontane plateaus emerged as a broad median mass, or geanticline, that somehow resisted the downsinking, uplift, and folding of the mountain zones on either side. The Grand Canyon of the Colorado has exposed some of the oldest Precambrian rocks in North America; thus, the Colorado Plateau may well have been part of the initial structure of the continent, forming the base of the Y-shaped stable area that expanded in the north into the Canadian Shield. Although shallow seas covered it during the 250,000,000 years or so from Mississippian to Cretaceous times, this base was never depressed, and it divided the western geosynclines from the beginning. It was, however, subject to uplift at each of the mountain-building periods, and it was intruded by igneous rocks. To the north and south of it lie the intermontane basin-and-range provinces of the United States and Mexico, where uplift and faulting have produced a series of sharp-edged ridges between downthrown depressions. Farther north the Columbia Basin lava tablelands and the great igneous intrusions of the Caribou, Omenica, and Yukon plateaus dominate the structure.

THE EVOLUTION OF LOWLANDS AND COASTAL PLAINS

The Interior Lowlands. While the marginal mountains slowly emerged, the Interior Lowlands of the continent had been forming, growing between them and the central shield as well as over the shield's platform-like buried prolongations. The lowlands expanded by the infilling of great basins that sank between broad upwarps, or arches, in the buried platform. Seas spread in from the Mexican, St. Lawrence, and Beaufort gulfs and worked over and redistributed the debris being washed down from the surrounding mountains. Central marine and peripheral deltaic deposits built up the Interior Lowlands in the form of all-but-flat strata, a great contrast to the contorted structures of both shield and marginal-mountain belts. A mantle of Paleozoic rocks is preserved in the river basins around the western and southern margins of the shield. The covering Mesozoic rocks have since been worn back to the higher levels of the Great Plains and Peace River plains, often protruding back of such long, low escarpments as the Missouri Coteau. Cap rock of Tertiary deposits, which was swept out from the Rocky Mountains, formed plateau-like sections, known as the High Plains, above the main stretches of the Great Plains. Finally, Tertiary marine deposits invaded the Lower Mississippi and Gulf plains to the south as well as the Arctic lowlands in the northwest.

Role of the buried shield

Pressures from the marginal mountains warped the buried platforms located beneath the central plains, occasionally forming low plateaus above the general level of the lowlands; for example, the Nashville Dome, part of the Interior Highlands reflecting the upwarp of the Cincinnati Anticline. These upwellings have been exposed to erosive forces for so long that the tops of the rises have been worn away to form basins with infacing scarps. In the Ozark Dome, erosion has worn back the overlying deposits to expose a crystalline core represented by the St. Francis Mountains.

The coastal plains. Coastal plains are poorly developed in North America, mainly because of the extensive faulting that has let much of the land be drowned by the sea or—especially along the coastline of the Pacific—because the marginal mountains step right down to the ocean. The whole of the west coast of the continent is virtually without a plain, except for such small and isolated deltas as those of the Fraser and the Sacramento. Folding and faulting along the northeast and northern coasts have practically eliminated lowland from New England to

Three views of the Western Cordilleras.
(Top left) Mountainous region near Petersburg, Alaska, with glacier-filled valley. (Bottom left) Mexican landscape showing Ixtacihuatl, an extinct volcano on the uplands east of Mexico City. (Above) Sierra Nevada Range of California, seen from Glacier Point in Yosemite National Park. Half Dome, a glaciated bedrock knob, is at left.

(Top left) Ray Manley—Shostal/EB Inc., (bottom left and right) Josef Muench

Mountain ranges and basins of the arid continental interior of the southwestern United States. Photographed from Apollo 9 spacecraft.

By courtesy of NASA

Ellesmere Island. Only in the southeast and the extreme northwest, along the gently declining shores of the Gulf of Mexico and of the southern Atlantic states or the slowly shelving levels around the Beaufort Sea have any extensive coastal plains emerged. The Gulf and the Arctic plains seem to be sinking into new geosynclines.

The land

Although the geological processes that shaped the North American continent have been so important that the 19th-century United States historian Frederick Jackson Turner once contended that the life of America flowed down the arteries of its geology, the continent has nevertheless been altered very considerably by climate and drainage and, to some extent, by soils and vegetation. The resultant physiographic regions dominate the contemporary geography of the continent.

RELIEF

The central shield. Averaging 1,400 feet in height, with a rough surface where old worn mountains and domes rise above ancient basins, the central shield has been left as a low plateau, tilted at its edges, and sinking down to Hudson Bay at its centre. The southern edge has the mountainous Algomans and Laurentians (more than 2,000 feet) and rises to above 4,000 feet in the great dome of the Adirondacks. The eastern edge is much higher, rising to nearly 6,000 feet in the Torngats and 10,000 feet in Baffin Island; in Greenland, too, it tilts up more than 6,000 feet. The western rim is much lower, reaching only about 600 feet in parts. The old Snare and Nonacho ranges west of Hudson Bay lift the edge of the plateau to nearly 2,000 feet. Faulting broke the northern rim into a series of prongs, extending into southeast Ellesmere Island and across Victoria Island, with sea-drowned channels and low sedimentary basins in between forming the Canadian Arctic Archipelago. The whole shield was under ice in the Pleistocene, and its high eastern rim still contains relics of the ice sheet. Ice-cut valleys in the higher areas, ice-plucked basins everywhere, and the ice-deposited ridges known as eskers and drumlins point to a major centre of ice dispersion over central Labrador, still noted for its very heavy snowfall. Greenland was also a main glacial centre, while Keewatin in the west was an important secondary focus. After most of the ice had melted, portions of the shield rose, leaving traces of former beaches all along Greenland, Baffin, Labrador, and the Gulf of St. Lawrence, thus providing narrow but vital benches for human settlement. Ice-cut rock basins and ice-dammed streams have left countless lakes that make parts of the surface of the central shield almost more water than land.

Centres of glaciation over the shield

The marginal mountains. *The Appalachians.* Erosion also profoundly altered the marginal mountains. The Appalachians have been planed down to such an extent that their crest lines are smooth-topped for hundreds of miles. Several levels at which summits accord with each other in height indicate a series of uplifts followed by planations. In Canada, the highest level lies at about 4,000 feet, in the flattops of the Shickshocks; another exists at 2,000 feet on Mt. Carleton; and lower ones lie at roughly 1,100 and 600 feet in the Acadian ranges. In New England very resistant mountains like Mt. Washington and Mt. Monadnock rise above a broad mass of ridges at just above the 2,000-foot level, which in turn rise above the 1,100-foot-high New England Upland. Glaciation deepened and straightened the valleys, strewed their sides and parts of the coast with debris. Portions of sea-buried end moraines, which mark the limit of the tonguing glaciers, form offshore banks east of Newfoundland, Nova Scotia, and New England. The unglaciated Appalachian Mountains, those located south of the Susquehanna River, have striking accordances of long flat-topped summits at altitudes of about 2,500 feet and broad terraces at 500 to 600 feet. The Ridge and Valley section's pattern of drainage consists of short, deep gaps across the ridges and long parallel stretches in between. East of the Blue Ridge extends the Piedmont Upland, terminating abruptly in the Fall Line, where its rivers plunge down to the Atlantic Coastal Plain over rapids or falls. The Hudson–Mohawk gap represents a major break between the northern and the southern Appalachians and affords a natural point of entry to the interior of the continent.

The Cordilleras. Taking up about a third of North America, the Cordilleras completely dominate Alaska and Central America and swell out widely in the United States Rockies.

In Canada the Cordilleras consist of six well-marked zones: the 10,000- to 12,000-foot-high Rocky Mountains continuing north into the Brooks Range of Alaska; the Rocky Mountain Trench, a profound fault feature carrying the headwaters of the Columbia, Fraser, Peace, and Yukon rivers; the interior uplands and old fold mountains from the Selkirks and Okanagans in the south beyond the Cassiar Massif, to the Yukon plateau in the north, mostly lying at altitudes of about 2,400 feet but with ridges over 8,000 feet; the Coast Mountains extending north into the Alaska Range, and including lofty volcanoes in the north; the Inner Passage from Puget Sound to Alaska, which is possibly a downfaulted zone flooded by the sea; and a structurally complex outer Island Arc, running from Vancouver Island to the Aleutians. The magnificent scenery of the northern Rocky Mountains, including U-shaped valleys often extending westward into sea-drowned fjords, has been heavily glaciated, and some areas still nurse sizable glaciers.

The six zones of the Canadian Cordilleras

In the United States the Rockies, typified by flat or gently folded rocks, sweep south from Canada into northern Montana as the Lewis Range. They then change to a group of domes or long anticlines with "parks" or broad basins between them. This park and dome area is characterized by the peeling back of younger rocks from the cores of much older, primary rocks at the heart of the anticlines. The southern Rockies have striking volcanic peaks. West of the Rockies and east of the Pacific Coast Ranges is a vast region of intermontane plateaus, extending from eastern Washington state to northern Mexico. The immense lava tablelands of the central Columbia-Snake River basin are known as the Columbia Plateau. To the south lie the Basin and Range Province and Colorado Plateau. The former, extending from southern Oregon and Idaho to northern Mexico, is apparently the result of the splitting of a broad central plateau by a great number of fault ridges, the slopes of which plunge under basins partly filled with

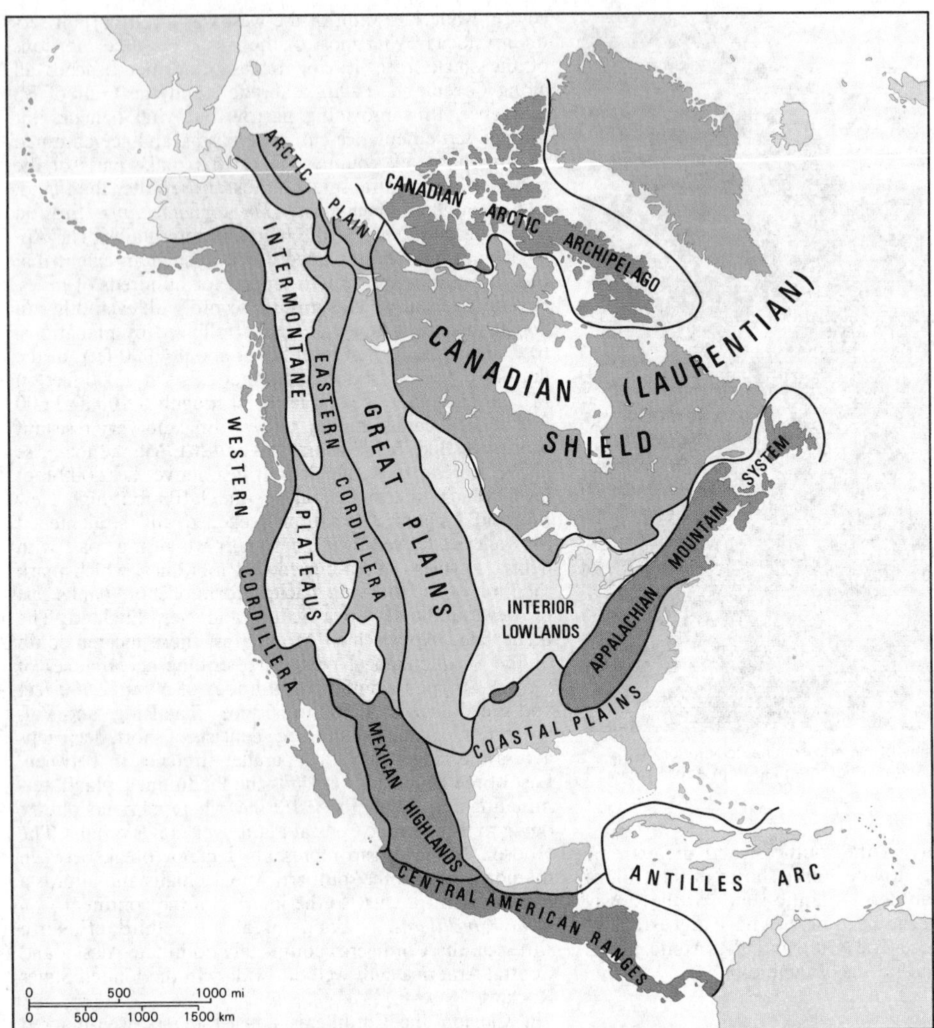

Physiographic regions of North America.

debris worn from the ridges. The region includes all of the continent's major deserts. The Colorado Plateau is a massive feature with a series of relatively flat bedded ridges, made steplike by faulting action and intruded by domes of igneous rocks. Its slow elevation was matched by the steady downcutting of the Colorado River, producing, in the Grand Canyon, one of the greatest gorges in the world. Westward rise the high Sierras, reaching to nearly 15,000 feet, intensively folded and faulted, and continued north in the Cascades, which are marked by some of America's most beautiful extinct volcanoes. Seaward of this mountain zone is a line of depressions marked by Puget Sound, the Great Valley of California, and the Gulf of California. These are separated by knots of volcanoes, as in the Klamath Mountains, and enclosed by the Pacific coast ranges, including the volcanic peaks of the Olympus group. This whole area has been profoundly faulted. Along some of the faults, notably the San Andreas, earthquake shocks occur, and occasionally these have produced devastating results. In Mexico the folded Sierras to west and east of the central plateau terminate in the grandeur of a mass of high volcanoes, of 15,000 to 17,000 feet, located to the south of the fertile lake-filled basins of Guadalajara and Mexico City.

The structural break at the Sierra Madre del Sur

The Balsas Basin then makes a distinct break. To the south, the Sierra Madre del Sur and the mountains of Guatemala and Honduras exhibit a west–east trend. This structural region includes a sweep of fold mountains of from 4,000 to 6,000 feet, with Caribbean extensions in Jamaica, southern Cuba, the island of Hispaniola, and Puerto Rico. These mountains swing south through the West Indies, a chain of volcanic islands fringed with coral reefs or limestone plateaus. Another arc, of two lines of fold mountains on either side of the Nicaraguan trench, dominates Central America and links it with the folds of western Colombia, in South America.

Detailed discussion of the Alaskan mountains, Appalachian Mountains, Pacific Coast ranges, Rocky Mountains, Sierra Madre, and Sierra Nevada can be found at the end of this article.

The lowlands. The lowlands of North America show marked differences between glaciated and unglaciated areas. Long irregular lines of coarse morainic deposits mark the regions where the Cordilleran ice sheet, moving down from the Rockies, met the continental sheet from Keewatin. The huge, tonguing loops of end moraines also occur between the Red and Mississippi rivers and along the south side of the Great Lakes—some running for hundreds of miles and standing 300 or 400 feet above the plain. Four major glacial advances successively covered the lowlands with debris: the Nebraskan crossed the Missouri River; the Kansan came as far as the Lower Missouri and the Ohio rivers; the Illinoian overlay these older areas as far as southern Illinois; and the Wisconsin heaped its moraines over the southern Canadian Prairies and the Great Lakes–Ohio–Mohawk–Hudson plains (see also below *Drainage*).

In the ice-free areas, lowlands are river molded. Streams debouching from the Rockies have spread sands, occasionally whipped up into sand hills, well beyond their banks; those funnelling into the Mississippi have created a vast alluvial plain running out into the Mississippi Delta. The Coastal Plains are marked, in addition, by lines of sand hills, which are the relics of stranded beaches that eroded as the plains were lifted slowly out of the seas in postglacial times.

Detailed discussion of the Great Plains and North American Desert can be found at the end of this article.

Appalachian landscapes.
(Left) Northern New England, looking across the Connecticut River Valley toward the low mountains of Vermont. (Right) Southern Ridge and Valley Province, showing the Susquehanna River near Harrisburg, Pennsylvania.
(Left) Laurence R. Lowry—Rapho/Photo Researchers, (right) Grant Heilman—EB Inc.

CLIMATE

Climate has made a great deal of difference to relief—particularly in the extremes of cold or hot and dry or humid landscapes; climate has also, in turn, been affected by relief. The enormous northern width of the continent has meant a great extension of Arctic and cool-temperate climates, while the tapering south has greatly reduced the area under the tropics. The Cordilleras have very wet, windward, Pacific-facing slopes and dry, leeward, interior-facing slopes. Water systems such as the Mississippi–Ohio and the Great Lakes–St. Lawrence tend to funnel the sweep of rainstorms across the central parts of the continent, and the Strait of Georgia and the Gulfs of Mexico and St. Lawrence also concentrate wind streams.

Temperature. While the greater part of North America falls within the temperate zone, a fact that has made it attractive to European settlers in post-Columbian times, large cold areas lie in the north and extend as far south as the Ozarks in winter. The continent's northerly position means that Greenland, the Canadian Shield, the Mackenzie Lowlands, and the northern part of the Cordilleras have an unusually long and cold winter. Much of this land

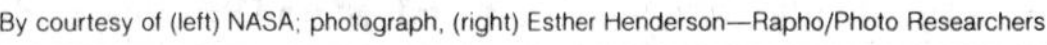

By courtesy of (left) NASA; photograph, (right) Esther Henderson—Rapho/Photo Researchers

Coastal contrasts.
(Left) Low-lying eastern coastline of the United States, looking north from Virginia. Photographed from Apollo 9 spacecraft. (Right) Rugged coastline of the western United States at Big Sur, California.

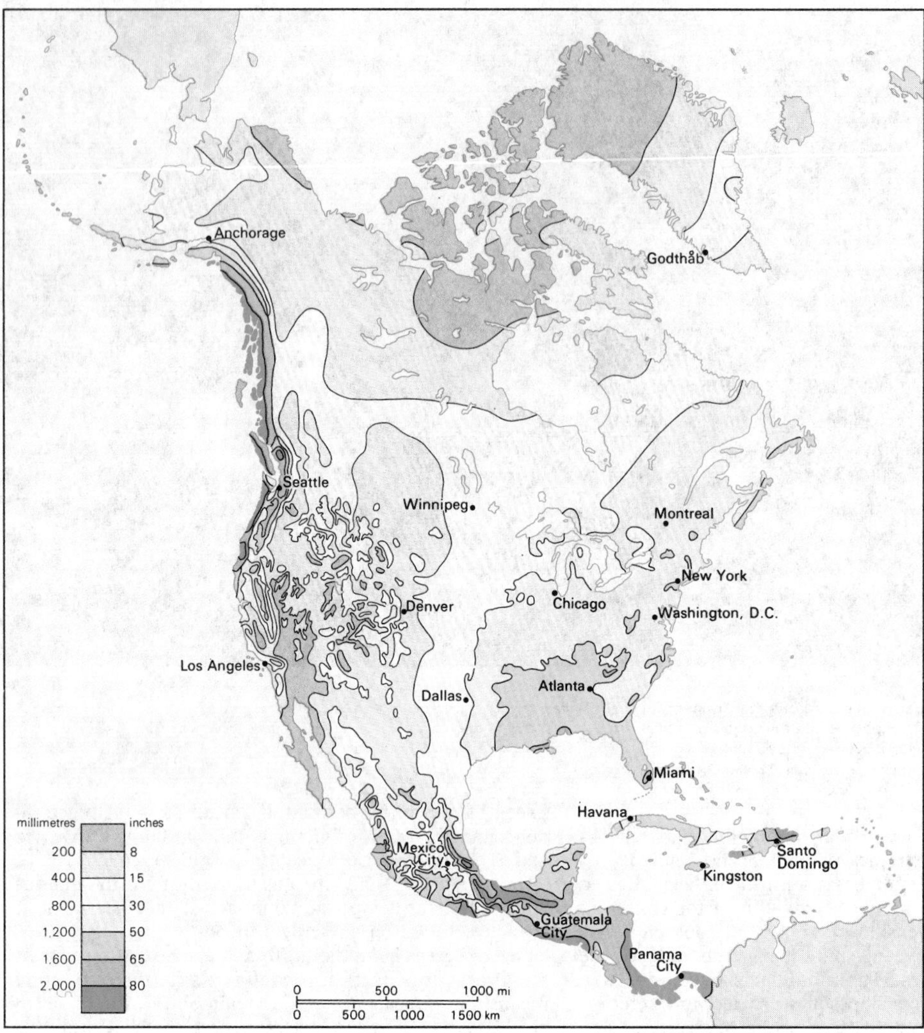

Average annual precipitation for North America.

Chilling effect of frozen subsoils and seas

has permanently frozen subsoil and is under snow and ice most of the year. The frequently frozen seas interlacing the Canadian Archipelago, together with innumerable northern lakes, produce an enormous chilling effect on the air above, and the temperatures for these huge regions are 6° to 8° F (3° to 4° C) cooler than the average for their latitude. The North Pacific, warmed by an extension of the Kuroshio current, has a positive anomaly of 8° to 10° F (4° to 6° C) warmer than the average for its latitude. Related trends over the northern part of the North Atlantic affect Iceland and Europe rather than North America but still raise the temperatures off the northeast coasts by perhaps 2° F (1° C). The climate thus shows marked contrasts between the maritime and continental areas. A notable warm loop of temperatures extends up the west coast from Vancouver Island to Alaska, while a great cold loop extends down the Mackenzie plains and the Canadian Shield over the heart of the continent. The chilling effects of the great Greenland ice cap drag cold continental conditions over the northeast coast at least as far as Newfoundland. The average January temperatures of Annette Island in the Alaskan panhandle, 29.5° F (−1.4° C), of Fort Smith, Northwest Territories, −13.8° F (−25.5° C), and of Nain, Labrador, 1.3° F (−17.1° C) show the difference between coastal and continental conditions and also between the west and the east coasts—differences negligible in the tropical parts of North America.

Precipitation. Most of the continent is humid and provides a good water supply for settlement and development. From mid-California north, the Pacific Coast is bathed with rain- or snow-laden Westerlies, giving from 40 to 200 inches (1,000 to 5,000 millimetres) of precipitation a year. Westerlies again reassert themselves east of the Rockies and, especially east of the Missouri River and Red River of the North, bring about moderately wet (20 inches) to wet (45 inches) conditions in the central and eastern regions. There are two main areas of drought: one in the extreme north and northeast, under the influence of very cold and relatively dry winds, with a thin dusting of winter snow and a meagre fall of summer rain in the Canadian Archipelago and Greenland; the other in the southwest, where the mid-latitude high-pressure system leads to dry offshore winds from mid-California to southern Mexico. Since these winds blow from the interior out to sea, they carry very little moisture, with precipitation in that area usually less than 10 inches a year.

Two main areas of drought

Air masses. The continent's air masses reflect very different conditions of temperature and precipitation; they include northern and southern components, subdivided into continental and maritime types. In the north are found: the Arctic air mass, over Greenland and the Canadian Arctic Archipelago; the polar continental, over northern central Canada; the polar Pacific, over Alaska and the northern Pacific shores; and the polar Atlantic, off the Atlantic provinces of Canada and New England. The tropical continental air mass, over the intermontane basins of the Cordilleras from Utah south; the tropical Gulf, centred in the Gulf of Mexico and the Caribbean; and the tropical Atlantic off the southeastern states characterize the south-southeast.

The polar continental, the tropical gulf, and the polar Pacific are the most significant air masses. The polar continental reflects the spread of a negative temperature anomaly over much of the continent. It is a cool to cold mass of stable air forming an immense dome of high pressure above the Canadian Shield, with winds blowing outward to sweep over Labrador and New England or southward across the Great Lakes and the Great Plains.

At its maximum, it extends from the Canadian Arctic Archipelago to the Ozarks. In winter it joins with the Arctic air mass over Greenland to make a formidable body of cold heavy air that carries subzero weather as far as the Ohio Valley and may overflow the Appalachians and seep through the Rockies. Exceptionally, it can carry killing frosts into the Great Valley of California, the coast of Texas, and the neck of Florida.

In the spring it shrinks north before the swift advance of the tropical Gulf air, which is drawn northward by low pressures developed in the Mississippi Basin as the heart of the continent heats up. The air mass is warm, wet, and unstable; at its height in late July, it extends two enormous loops of warm air, one northwestward up the Mississippi and down the Mackenzie and the other northeastward up the Ohio and down the St. Lawrence. The July average of 60° F (16° C) is then carried north of Edmonton, in the west, and to Quebec, in the east. The storm-generating polar Pacific air mass is very active from northern California to Alaska, especially in the winter, when its mild, wet air reflects the North Pacific temperature anomalies.

Pacific-coast storm tracks

Storm tracks. Where cyclones develop persistently along the advancing air-mass edges, strong storm tracks occur. Pacific storm tracks thread the Strait of Georgia, Puget Sound, and the Inner Passage to Alaska. In summer they shift north of Prince Rupert; in the depth of winter they migrate south to San Francisco. Moving up the great Columbia and Fraser river valleys, they may pass through the Rocky Mountain passes. An upper stream of Pacific air overtops the mountain barrier and, on descent, starts off lee storms that then traverse the continent. These draw in air from the polar continental air mass on their advancing cold sectors and from tropical Gulf air in their warm sectors. As the polar continental air mass begins to expand in September, a Mackenzie–James Bay line of storms develops, migrating progressively southward to reach a Texas–Ohio track in January. As the tropical Gulf air mass expands north, the successive tracks become activated again until, in August, the Gulf air brings a swirl of storms to the Mackenzie. Most of these storm tracks begin in the western plains, converge on the Great Lakes–Ohio area, and then bunch together in the climatically stimulating St. Lawrence–Hudson–Mohawk zone. The Atlantic Coastal Plain becomes a storm track in winter as tropical maritime air contests the advance of the continental air from the north.

Climatic regions. Differing continental climatic regions reflect the considerable amount of Arctic land, the great spread of temperate conditions, and the small but significant tropical area; dry climates also stand out in strong contrast to the prevailingly humid ones.

The Arctic zone. Including the northern parts of the Canadian Shield and Alaska, the Canadian Arctic Archipelago, and Greenland, the Arctic zone is dominated by Arctic and polar continental air masses and is perennially cold or cool. Subzero weather lasts for five to seven months, and subfreezing weather lasts for eight to 10 months. It is only June to September that temperatures rise above 32° F (0° C). The frost-free season is not more than 60 days. Precipitation is low, with two to four inches of summer rain, plus 30 to 60 inches of winter snow. Most of the Arctic is a cold desert.

Zone of long, severe winters

The cool-temperate zone. The cool-temperate zone extends from Newfoundland to Alaska and from Hudson Bay to the Ohio. It is dominated by the polar continental air mass. Winters are long and severe. After an "Indian summer" that continues into October, temperatures fall quickly and do not rise substantially until April or early May. In January and February they drop to below 32° F (0° C) on the Ohio and below 0° F (−18° C) north of the Great Lakes, with minima as low as −20° to −80° F (−29° to −62° C). Winter killing of crops and spring and autumn frosts are a hazard in the Canadian parts of the region, where the frost-free season is from 90 to 165 days. A swift transition occurs with spring; tropical Gulf air raises monthly mean temperatures to over 50° F (10° C) in June and from 60° to 78° F (16° to 26° C) in July. Precipitation is moderate, with 15 to 35 inches; as evaporation is low, however, most of it is effective for growth. The maximum precipitation occurs in summer to fall, when the James Bay, Alberta, and Wyoming storm tracks are activated.

Warm-temperate zone. On the southeast coasts of the United States, the warm-temperate zone extends to the Mississippi and over the Gulf plain; the zone is strongly influenced by the tropical Gulf air mass. The long frost-free season lasts more than 200 days. The tropical airs spread north in February and dominate the region until

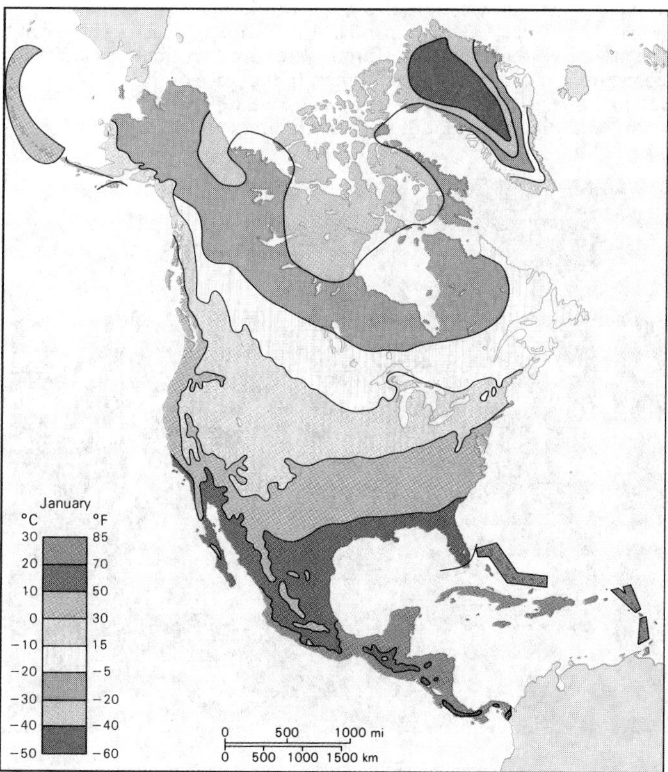

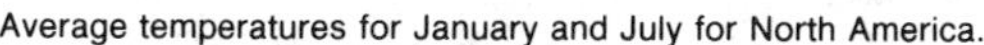

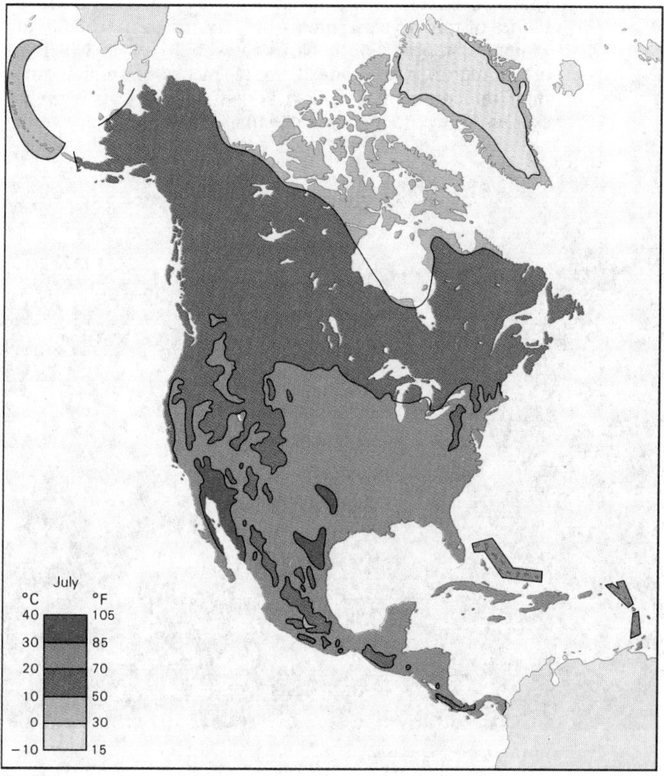

Average temperatures for January and July for North America.

November, when polar continental air makes itself felt. Winters are mild, with January means of from 40° to 54° F (4° to 12° C). July averages are tropical, being as high as 81° F (27° C). This warmth and the long growing season allow for subtropical crops. Rainfall is ample, ranging from 40 to 60 inches, and benefits from the presence of the Colorado and Texas low-pressure systems and from the strong summer movement of tropical maritime air. By then the landmass is intensely heated, and this, combined with the air movement, produces frequent thunderstorms, especially in early summer. Hurricanes are an annual hazard along the Gulf and up the Lower Mississippi.

In the United States Southwest a different regime pertains, with a Mediterranean type of climate; summers are dry, since the tropical continental air is dominant. July means of 70° to 80° F (21° to 27° C) are found, with bright, sunny skies. Winters are mild (45° to 50° F [7° to 10° C]) and wet, with polar Pacific airs swinging south and bringing heavy rain. Frost is rare but may occur when polar continental air thrusts through to the coast. Los Angeles has a record minimum of only 23° F (−5° C). The annual rainfall of from 15 to 30 inches, along with very high evaporation, often is insufficient unless supplemented by irrigation. Drought is a frequent hazard.

The tropical humid climate. Central America, with its tropical humid climate, knows no winter; even the coldest month averages above 64° F (18° C). With summers of 80° to 82° F (27° to 28° C), the mean annual temperature range is low—markedly different from most of North America. Rain is ample and regular, with 45 to 80 inches where the trade winds blow onshore. Lee valleys are, however, often quite dry. Summer hurricanes frequently recur, causing much damage.

Factors in the Southwest's aridity

Dry climates. About a third of North America, including Arctic areas, has a dry climate. Chief dry areas lie in the Southwest, where a combination of the mid-latitude high-pressure belt, the tropical continental air mass, and the rain-shadow effects behind the high Western Sierras has led to lack of rainfall. Winds blow from the continent outward, discounting the effect of the Pacific. As the winds move down from high interior plateaus, they become drier as they descend. The intermontane region of the United States and Mexico, from the Columbia Basin to Guadalajara, and the Pacific Coast from San Diego south to Mazatlán are therefore arid, with less than 10 inches of rain a year. Some years have no rain. The Great Plains, from the South Saskatchewan River to Mexico, are semiarid, with from 10 to 15 inches of rainfall; the high midcontinental airflow known as the jet stream is depressed over them, strengthening downmoving dry wind from across the Rockies and tending to fend off cyclones from tropical Gulf or polar continental air masses.

DRAINAGE

Drainage conditions and water supply are affected markedly by climate, though they also reflect relief. North America has one of the longest rivers in the world (the Mississippi) and also a drainage system with one of the greatest water capacities (the St. Lawrence–Great Lakes system). It is a continent of immense rivers—very largely because of their vast drainage area in the long and broad plains between the central shield and the marginal mountains. Rivers rising in the shield, the Appalachians, or the Cordilleras that flow into the Interior Lowlands have a long way to go to reach the sea. The Great Lakes–St. Lawrence on the east and the Mackenzie on the west drain the outer edges of the shield. The Nelson takes advantage of the low saddle in the shield to carry the gathered waters of the Saskatchewan and the Red out by way of Lake Winnipeg to Hudson Bay, which also has fairly long rivers draining into it from the uptilted edges of the shield. The vast Missouri–Mississippi–Ohio system draws from the Cordilleras, the shield, and the Appalachians to unite the Central and Gulf Lowlands, in the heartland of the continent. From the Rocky Mountains, long rivers like the Colorado, Columbia, Fraser, and Yukon continued to flow west to the Pacific even across the Cascade–Nevadan and the Coast ranges as these were lifted up. Fed from eternal snows, they are particularly valuable in the arid Southwest.

There is a marked asymmetry to the continent's drainage: the chief continental divide, along the Rockies, is well to the west, thus shedding the longest rivers to the east. The longest tributaries—the Peace into the Mackenzie, the Saskatchewan into the Nelson, and the Missouri into the Mississippi—coming from the west, tend to displace the mainstreams to the east. The chief gulfs—Hudson Bay, the Gulf of St. Lawrence, and the Gulf of Mexico—taking the discharge of many of the rivers, are also on the east. All these factors helped the European settlers to move from their Atlantic bases into the heart of North America.

Lakes. Lakes abound in North America. Most of them are products of glaciation, which had a vast effect on the continental drainage pattern, notably by the widening of passes through the northern Appalachians and the Cordilleras and the creation of big lakes in ice-deepened basins. The Great Lakes proper have a fascinating history, as Lakes Superior and Huron were vast synclinal depressions even in Precambrian times. In the place of the present Lower Great Lakes, a scarp-and-vale topography existed, with the high front of the Niagara limestone scarp

The Great Lakes

(Left) Fred Bond, (right) Josef Muench

Mississippi River Basin.
(Left) The Mississippi River at Hannibal, Missouri. (Right) Coastal swamplands of southern Louisiana, United States, showing moss-draped cypress trees.

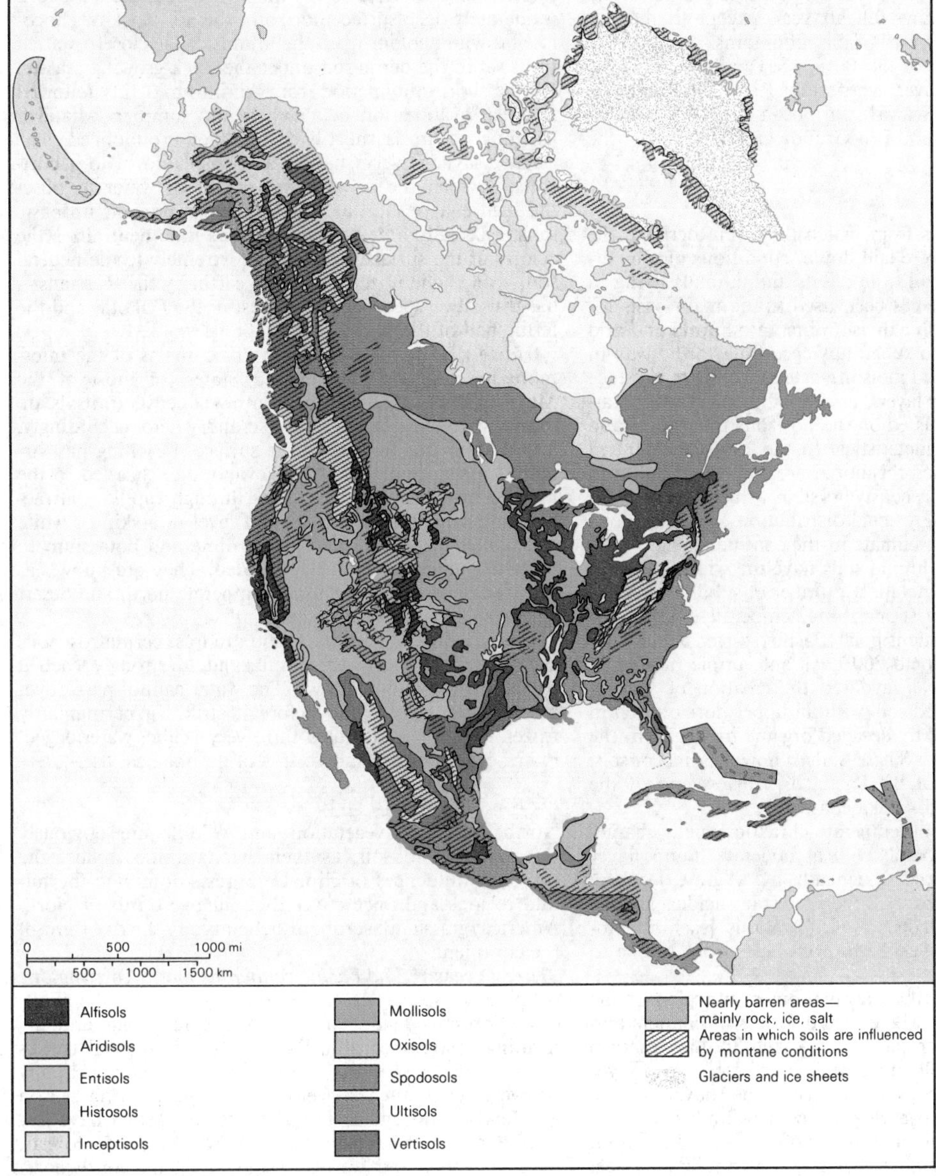

Soils of North America.

separating vales of shale to the west and east. The glaciers picked out the vales and synclines and deepened them into ice-cut basins, where water gathered; as the ice melted away, the Great Lakes formed. While the ice front of the glaciers still blocked the St. Lawrence outlet, the early lakes drained southward into the Mississippi–Ohio, the Susquehanna, and the Mohawk–Hudson. When the ice retreated from the Gulf of St. Lawrence, the lakes sought the lowest outlet through the St. Lawrence River, lowering the level of the Great Lakes and leaving beaches around them that stand out as raised beaches, or strandlines. The land, depressed under the enormous weight of the ice, has been rising since, lifting the old beaches above the present diminished bodies of water. Similar strand lines follow the Gulf of St. Lawrence, once under glacial Lake Champlain; Lake Winnipeg, once part of the immense glacial Lake Agassiz; and Athabasca, Great Slave, and Great Bear lakes, which are the relics of once deeper and larger glacial lakes. The western lakes were formed by ice blocking the free drainage of water to Hudson Bay or the Beaufort Sea. Much farther south, in the intermontane basins, a pluvial period of climate, matching the ice age in the north, led to the enormous lakes Lahontan and Bonneville. The Great Salt Lake is a relic of Lake Bonneville, the ancient beaches of which are stranded 1,000 feet above the present ones. Similarly, present-day Lake Mexico represents only a small part of the large body of water that accumulated in the Mexican Basin and whose level fluctuated during several pluvial periods. The contribution of all these—and many more—lakes to the drainage of North America has been outstanding. Much of the Canadian Shield is so ridden with lakes as to form an amphibious landscape.

Rivers. The river regimes of North America exhibit great variety. Northward-flowing rivers like the Yukon, Mackenzie, Red, Nelson, and the rivers of Labrador freeze up in winter. Because their upper parts then melt before the lower sections are free of ice, they frequently flood, especially if the thaw is late enough to coincide with early summer rains. The Mississippi system is also swollen by spring meltwaters as the winter snows give way in April; flooding can then become a major hazard. River water is kept high by the rains that tropical Gulf air and local convection storms bring until midsummer. A marked falloff then occurs, giving way to full flow in late autumn and winter as polar continental air reactivates midcontinental storm tracks.

The St. Lawrence runs high in spring and early summer; the winter precipitation falls on a frozen surface and serves mainly to heighten the spring thaw. Most other eastern rivers have a double maximum, occuring in early summer and late winter. In the United States Southwest the winter is the main floodtime; rivers dwindle appreciably in the summer. The northern Pacific region, by contrast, has rain at all seasons, though with a winter maximum.

In the southern tropical regions, rivers have a much more regular regime, running full all year, except in the dry rain-shadow areas leeward of the mountains.

Detailed discussion of the Bering Sea and Strait, Great Lakes, Mackenzie River, Mississippi River, St. Lawrence River, St. Lawrence Seaway, Caribbean Sea, Gulf of Mexico, Panama Canal, and Rio Grande can be found at the end of this article.

SOILS

Soils reflect the rocks from which they were derived, the way in which they were laid down, conditions of temperature and moisture, and the plants and animals living in or on them. Climate has been used as the main basis for categorizing soils, with a division first into humid and arid groups, and then into subgroups according to the way in which temperature and moisture acted together to produce different horizons, or layers, in the soil. More recently, attention has been focussed on the horizons themselves and on their unique characteristics. In the 1960s the United States Soil Survey used this horizon-based classification to propose a new comprehensive system, which nevertheless still reflects the strongly zonal distribution of soils, following the dominance of climate in the continent.

Horizons as a basis for classifying soils

Humid soils. The humid soils have the widest range in North America and include a number of subdivisions.

Inceptisols. The west maritime temperate-equable climate—swept by frequent polar Pacific storms and with a growing season of up to 300 days and ample rainfall of 40 to 200 inches—has favoured the creation of a deep, acidic, brown-coloured soil, with an upper horizon rich in humus formed by partly decayed organic matter from the region's dense forests. These soils, known as inceptisols, are the fertile soils of the Pacific Northwest and of the British Columbia and Alaska coasts.

Spodosols. The cool-temperate climatic zone is characterized by spodosols, soils with a moderate humus layer at the surface succeeded beneath by a gray, leached, or washed-out, horizon. Rather infertile, acidic, grayish soils, known as podzols, result from this leaching process. They extend under the boreal forests from Alaska to Newfoundland.

Alfisols. Found in the warm-summer subregion of the cool-temperate zone, where mixed forests of conifers and deciduous trees cover the Great Lakes–St. Lawrence to the Ohio area, alfisols are characterized by a deep layer of humus, succeeded by a shallow leached layer, which, in turn, goes down to a wide horizon of both plant and mineral nutrients including oxides of iron and aluminum. These are the moderately fertile gray-brown soils so typical of the northeastern United States.

Ultisols. Farther south, ultisols occur, roughly extending from the lower Ohio and Chesapeake Bay southward to the Gulf Plains. They correspond to the area of the southeastern mesothermal climate, which has more than 200 days free of frost and a rainfall of up to 60 inches a year. There a rich deciduous forest supplies a deep layer of humus, some of which is leached down and accumulates with red oxides of iron or yellow hydroxides of aluminum to produce podzolized red-yellow earths of considerable fertility.

Oxisols. The tropical climates of southern coastal Mexico and of Central America, with constantly high temperatures of 65° to 82° F (18° to 28° C) and perennial rainfall of from 80 to 120 inches, have caused very active weathering of rock. The resulting soils, called oxisols, have developed; hydroxide and sesquioxide compounds have produced a thick layer of red laterite, the residual product of rock decay, sometimes mottled with yellow, beneath the surface horizon of rotted humus. A deep, strongly acidic, lateritic soil has developed, which, though fertile when protected from erosion, can be very infertile if the bricklike laterite is exposed.

Semiarid and arid soils. Semiarid and arid soils cover an extensive area of North America, including the prairies, deserts, and tundras.

Mollisols. Marking the transition between humid and arid soils, mollisols are found in the open parkland or the tall-grass prairie of the outer Great Plains or in the humid prairies of the western Central Lowlands. They have a moderately deep surface horizon, which is black or chocolate brown in colour from the humus of the closely matted roots set in the dense sod under the thick-growing grasses. With a short rainy period from April to mid-July followed by great evaporation in a dry, sunny summer, whatever leaching occurs is short-lived and not pronounced. The leached layer is very shallow and passes down to a horizon in which the upward movement of water to offset the high evaporation at the surface has brought up basic salts, especially lime in solution. The lime neutralizes the acidity of the surface humus. An extremely fertile neutral soil—called chernozem, or black earth, by the Russians—has thus developed, seen at its best in the Dakotas and the fertile belt of the mid-Canadian prairies.

Development of black earth soils

Aridisols. Characterizing the dry climates of the intermontane basins of the United States, of most of the Mexican Plateau, and of the Southwest coast, aridisols are found where vegetation is sparse and where, accordingly, little humus has formed at the surface. Leaching has virtually ceased, and very strong evaporation has led to the upward movement of basic salts through capillary attraction, often working up to ground level in a skin of white crystals. The soils are too rich in lime and potassium to be fertile unless extensively irrigated. They are known as brown desert soils in the more temperate north and desert yellow soils in the subtropical south.

Permafrost soils. In the Arctic tundras, permafrost soils also accumulate very little humus and are strongly leached by the melt of winter snows. The water cannot pass down more than a foot or so before it strikes a permanently frozen horizon, and thus a thin, very acidic, waterlogged, infertile soil has developed. It is of no practical use.

PLANT AND ANIMAL LIFE

North American vegetation and wildlife are obviously closely allied to soil, as their habitats, too, reflect the powerful influences of climate. Forests dominate the humid regions and once covered about two-thirds of North America; grassland, scrub, or lichen typify the dry third of the continent.

Forest areas. *The Pacific coniferous forest.* Offering one of the great spectacles of the continent, the Pacific coniferous forest is made up of immense redwoods and firs forming vast cathedral-like groves, where the tall trunks rise hundreds of feet like great pillars to support a canopy of evergreen branches overhead. A long growing season and heavy, constant supply of moisture together have fostered the densest and tallest of North American forests, with redwoods and western cedar along the north coast of California giving way to Douglas fir and western hemlock from Oregon to British Columbia, and Sitka spruce in Alaska. In the south red-stemmed arbutuses lend a Mediterranean touch; giant-leaved maple, oak, and ash are common in the middle sector; birch and aspen are subdominants in the north. This coastal forest is one of the continent's chief sources of construction timber. It is also a major source of pulp and paper and a home for a significant number of red deer and mountain elk and also of black bear, lynx, and beaver. Fish-eating hawks and eagles abound. North America's greatest runs of salmon are seen there, as the fish swarm upstream to spawn in mountain lakes; while off the Queen Charlotte islands lies one of the continent's chief halibut fisheries. The meeting of the Kuroshio, a warm current from across the Pacific, with the cool water along the western offshore deeps provides ideal conditions for fish life in great numbers. The faulted and glaciated coasts with great fjords, and the perennial rivers attract fish inland and thus make fishing more easy and profitable.

Fish-breeding conditions in the offshore deeps

The boreal forest. One of the greatest sweeps of forest in the world, the boreal forest extends in a vast and virtually unbroken sheet of green eastward from the Aleutians through Alaska and northern Canada to the island of Newfoundland. Its conifers are shorter than those of the Pacific Coast but grow in denser stands. The boreal forest is essentially the domain of the spruce, with, however, the contorted pine becoming significant in the west, and the jack pine and tamarack in the east. From Alaska through the Mackenzie plains to Keewatin, the white spruce dominates, while, through eastern Canada and upland New England, the black spruce is common. The whole region is the Western Hemisphere's greatest source of pulpwood.

Great herds of caribou shelter in the northern fringes of this forest in the winter. They are preyed upon by packs of timber wolves. Farther south deer, elk, and moose are still common, though thinned out appreciably by humans. Both the black and the brown bear are frequently seen, especially in berry patches. Many fur-bearing animals, including the marten, squirrel, mink, and beaver, occur; muskrat abound in the marshes. In the spring pickerel run up the rivers to spawn, and lake trout and whiting live in the cool, deep waters of the innumerable northern lakes. Whitefish are caught in great numbers in Great Slave Lake but, because of pollution, are much less prevalent than they used to be in the Great Lakes. Cod and haddock are found in vast numbers on the banks off Newfoundland southward to New England, where the cold Labrador Current mixes with part of the warm Gulf Stream, thus stimulating aquatic conditions and encouraging fish life.

The Cordilleran forest. The Cordilleran forest lies between the Pacific coniferous forest and the interior boreal forest. On the west it is made up of cedar and Douglas fir, with Sitka spruce and Englemann spruce at the higher levels; while, in the east, it has more pine and spruce, with lodgepole pine and white spruce making close straight-limbed stands. On the intermontane plateaus and ridges, western hemlock and yellow or sugar pine form groves with parkland between. Altitude and aspect dominate tree distribution, with tall and dense fir woods occurring on the wetter faces at lower levels, spruce clothing the higher slopes, and pine abundant mainly on the drier exposures. Animal life is still rich: elk and deer in the fir–spruce forests, antelope in the open parkland, and goats high up on the Alpine pastures. Preying on these are the mountain lion and the occasional pack of wolves. The grizzly bear keeps to higher and less accessible haunts, but the black bear is common in the lower forests. Mountain trout are abundant, and, outside the Far North, this region is the continent's chief game preserve.

Coniferous Cordilleran cover

The Laurentian mixed forest. Lying in the warm-summer region of the cool-temperate zone, the Laurentian mixed forest occurs in the Great Lakes–St. Lawrence, the Upper Mississippi–Ohio, and the New England lowland regions. It is mainly deciduous hardwood—beech, maple, elm, oak, and birch—but has a good deal of coniferous softwood, including pine and the eastern hemlock. White

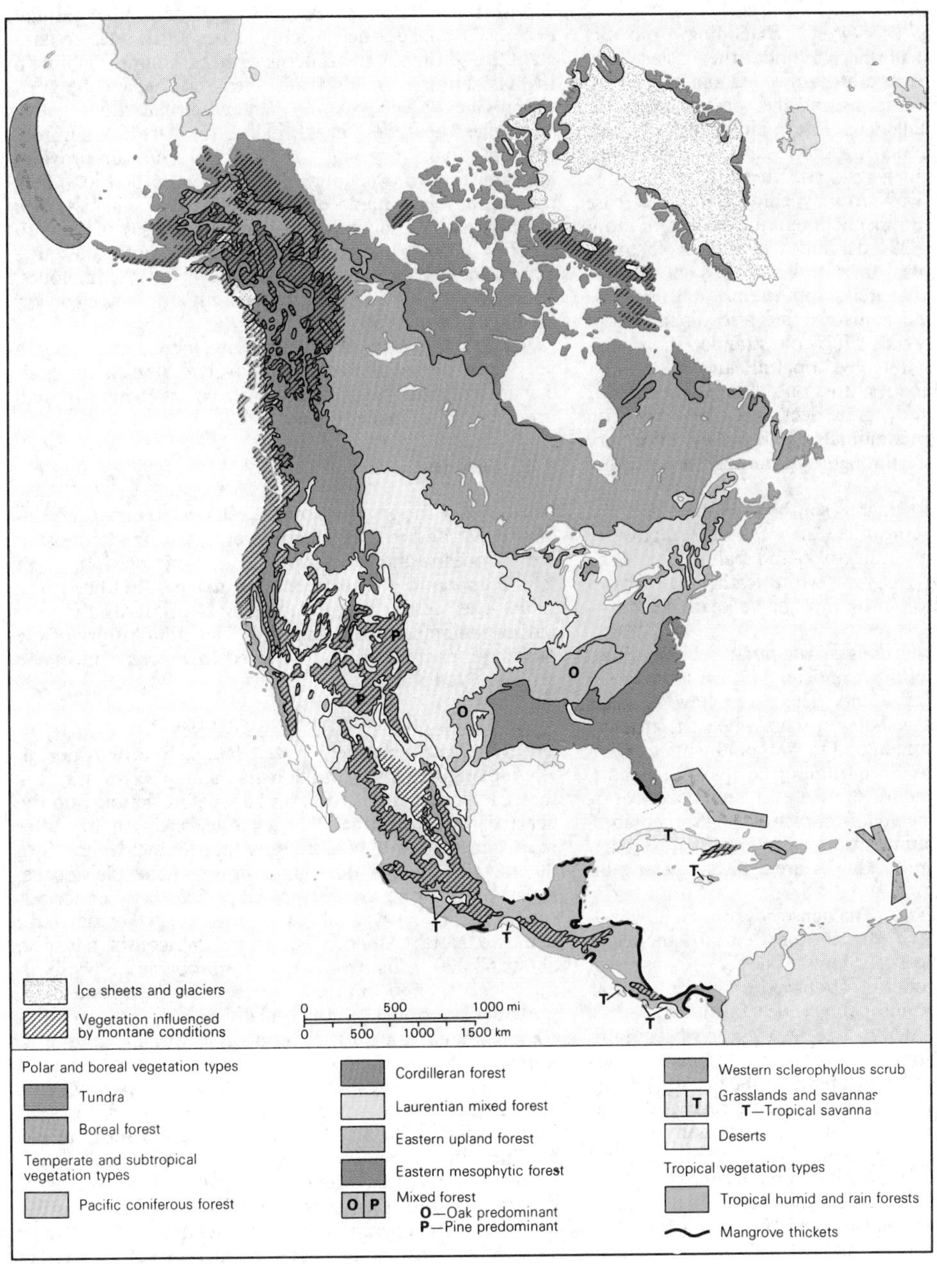

Vegetation zones of North America.

pine and white and red oak used to be abundant but have largely been cut out for timber. The elm has largely been killed everywhere by the Dutch elm disease. The long, hot, wet days of summer, when tropical Gulf air predominates, lead to huge-crowned, large-leaved trees, which shed their cover with the return of keen winter under polar continental airs. Rain or snow fall most of the year, averaging 35 to 40 inches, and thus provide ample moisture for dense growth. Deer are still common, although the moose is seen less often. Wolves, too, have largely been hunted out, a fate that the bear is also suffering, and beavers have been reduced to a small population. Squirrels are still very common, but wild mink and marten have become rare, and the passenger pigeon that once made this forest its home has become extinct.

The Eastern Upland Forest. Also known as the Acadian Forest in Canada, the Eastern Upland Forest clothes much of the central and southern Appalachians: here, polar continental airs are pronounced, while altitude modifies the tropical maritime winds. The growing season ranges from 90 to 120 days, and winter cold brings subzero temperatures. The forest, therefore, consists of fast-growing evergreen softwood species such as black spruce and balsam fir, along with alder and birch. Deer are still quite plentiful, as are such small fur-bearing animals as muskrat and squirrel.

The Eastern mesophytic forest. Extending from the mid-Atlantic states to northern Florida, the Eastern mesophytic forest is a mixture of hardwoods and softwoods. On the clays of river bottoms and the coast plain, great-crowned oaks form a tall, dense forest, mixed with hickory, walnut, and yellow poplar on the lower slopes of rivers, and ash and elm on higher slopes. Chestnut at one time was widespread but was virtually eliminated by disease in the 1920s. With summer temperature means of from 75° to 85° F (24° to 29° C), and a rainfall of 45 to 60 inches, many subtropical trees and bushes, such as pawpaws, crape myrtles, magnolias, laburnums, and mimosas flourish. Live oaks and gum trees are also distinctive of the area. On the sandy soils left by old stranded shorelines, magnificent stands of loblolly, longleaf, and slash pines form the Southern Pineries, now one of America's major sources of timber. The Virginia deer, black bear, raccoon and opossum are typical animals. Wild turkey, once very plentiful, but then rare through overhunting, are making a comeback.

Subtropical trees and bushes

Mangrove thickets. Ringing southern Florida and the Mexican lowlands facing the Caribbean, the mangrove thickets are backed by quick-oak and palms. Ibis fleck the woods with their gleaming white feathers. Moccasin snakes are still common in swamps, and alligators occur—not all in "farms."

The Western sclerophyllous scrub forest. In southern California and much of the American Southwest the Western sclerophyllous forest occurs. There trees have to adapt themselves both to dry, hot summers when the tropical continental air is dominant and to wet, mild winters when polar Pacific air sweeps down from the north. A thin, short, open scrub of chaparral, or stunted evergreen oak, occurs, mixed with yellow pine and sagebrush. Pronghorned antelope, wild rabbit, mountain pumas, coyotes, land turtles, and snakes are common. Hawks are typical, preying on small desert rodents.

The tropical rain forest. The dense covering of all windward slopes in southern Mexico and Central America is provided by the tropical rain forest. The forest consists of such very tall, hardwood, broad-leaved evergreen trees as mahogany, ironwood, and palm, which form a spreading canopy over a lower tier of tree ferns, grape bays, gum trees, rattans, and mangrove, laced with lianas. Numerous species of plants are widely scattered in the forest. Wildlife is also varied, with a great number of parrots, cockatoos and nutcrackers, troops of monkeys, and many snakes. Leopards are still quite common. Ants, beetles, and flies feed on the decaying vegetation, and bacterial activity is high. This is an environment in which such tropical diseases as yellow fever, malaria, and blackwater fever historically have taken a heavy toll. A dry, tropical scrub of thorn trees, cactus, and sagebrush often takes over from forest in a remarkably short distance on leeward slopes and in rain-shadow basins.

Grassland and desert areas. Covering about a third of North America, grassland and desert are found in the drier and colder regions.

Tropical savannas. Located in patches in subhumid parts of Central America, tropical savannas usually occur at the intermediate levels of lee slopes and on plateaus. They are significant in Guatemala and the Yucatán Peninsula of Mexico. Heavy, though short-lived, summer rains bring on a thick rapid growth of tall grasses: cyclones associated with the northeast trade winds bring enough rain during the rest of the year to maintain a thin cover.

Temperate grasslands. The temperate grasslands, or prairies, form a belt between forest and desert, mainly on the Great Plains but also on the midslopes of the intermontane basins, above the desert flats. At the "break of the plains" on the eastern subhumid margin, invaded by rain-bearing tropical Gulf airs in spring and early summer, the grasslands are made up of a dense growth of tall grasses, such as the blue-stem sod grass and Indian grass, along with small berry bushes, wild roses, and stunted aspen trees. These are the tall-grass prairies that once were home to most of America's buffalo, before hunters virtually exterminated the breed. "Wet" prairie exists in the Middle Mississippi Basin, where the annual rainfall exceeds 30 inches; their origin has been attributed to constant fire setting by the Indians, either to stampede buffalo in mass hunts or to burn off trees and thicken the grass to provide buffalo pasture. Where rainfall drops below 17 inches (in Texas) or 15 inches (in Alberta), summer evaporation is very high, and tropical Gulf air provides less moisture, only enough for short-grass prairie. There the vegetation is made up of blue-stem bunchgrass, thin needlegrass, and tough grama and wire grasses, along with patches of cactus, sagebrush, or, farther south, mesquite grass. These regions still pasture many small antelopes, although they have been turned mainly into rangeland for raising cattle or sheep.

The "break of the plains" and the tall-grass prairies

Deserts. Creosote bush, mesquite, and cactus offer a very thin, open, stunted plant cover for the Southwest's dry intermontane basins and arid coasts, where rainfall drops below 10 inches a year.

The people

North America long remained a relatively empty and undeveloped land in global terms, but, with the coming of the Europeans and the Africans they introduced, it began to fill up rapidly with people of diverse traditions and skills. The section that follows covers primarily the peoples of mainland North America. The ethnohistory of the North American Indians is treated in more detail in the article AMERICAN INDIANS.

THE NORTH AMERICAN INDIAN HERITAGE

The Indians themselves arrived late in North America. Having originated in Asia, they had a long way to travel—through Siberia and across Alaska—before getting into the heart of the continent. The Ice Age began shortly after man emerged and blocked any northern advance into Siberia and Canada throughout most of the Pleistocene. It was only during the interglacial periods between ice advances that man was tempted to move north. He may have come to North America before the Wisconsin advance, about 60,000 years ago. It is more probable he chose an interglacial period during a recession in Wisconsin time, probably before the Mankato readvance.

The Indians came in as Stone Age hunters leading a nomadic life, and many remained in this condition until the whites came. In moving down from the narrow neck at Alaska to the broad expanse of the continent between Florida and California, the tribes tended to separate out and hunt in comparative isolation. Until they came to the narrows of southern Mexico and the confined spaces of Central America, there was little of the fierce competition or the close cooperation between them that might have stimulated progress. Though they made great progress in those southern regions, they made fewer advances in the use of metals, the growth of industry, or the development of transport and trade than, for example, did the contemporaneous civilizations of Asia, Europe, and parts of Africa. City life arose first among the Olmecs, in the strategic narrows between Mexico and Central America, and the Mayans, in the plateaus of Guatemala and Yucatán. Subsequently the Toltecs and the Aztecs rose to power and developed notable cities in the high Mexican Basin. These people flourished on a rich agriculture based on maize, beans, and squash, along with manioc, potatoes, tomatoes, tobacco, and cacao. They also raised cotton and worked leather.

Some authorities contend, however, that these civilizations already were on the decline before the Europeans came, having been divided by wars and riddled by disease, with much of their land wasted by erosion. Louis de Velasco, a 16th-century Spanish governor, put the total population of the West Indies, Mexico, and Central America at probably 5,000,000 Indians. The population of the less developed Indians of what now is the area of the United States and Canada has been variously estimated at somewhere between 600,000 and 1,200,000. The Indians there had not developed intensive agriculture or a city way of life, though it is true that the raising of maize, beans, and squash supplemented hunting throughout the Mississippi–Ohio and the Lower Great Lakes–St. Lawrence river regions, as well as along the Gulf and Atlantic Coastal Plains. In those areas, semisedentary peoples had established villages, and among the Cherokees and the Iroquois quite powerful federations of tribes had arisen. Elsewhere, however, on the Great Plains, the Canadian Shield, the northern Appalachians, and the Cordilleras, fishing and hunting constituted the basic economic activity and required an extensive territory to support and feed a small population.

THE EUROPEAN HERITAGE

The white concept of the environment. When European colonizers arrived, they regarded much of the continent as empty and waiting to be developed. To William Bradford, the early historian of New England, the white races were moving into a virtual wilderness offering a wonderful opportunity for settlement and development. The indigenous agriculture was rudimentary and scarcely opened up the forest; there were no herds or flocks to make a better use of natural pasture other than those of moose or deer; the value of the forests for making homes, buildings, fences, roads, and tools seemed unknown; no mills exploited the waterfalls along which the whites were soon to establish the Fall Line of manufacturing cities; the deposits of iron and coal had not been developed. Seen through the world view of the Europeans, who had had a long tradition of iron and steel making, of maximizing use of the forest for fuel through charcoal, of coal mining and the mining of a great range of metals, of linen and woollen weaving, and of harnessing both water and wind for the operation of mills, the comparative backwardness of most of North America offered both a challenge and an opportunity. They saw no reason why they should not claim land that they could use to better advantage, and hence they bought out or pushed out the Indian and took over the country.

The dispossession of the Indians. The process of removing the Indians from their lands led to bitter disputes, which the British tried to end by setting up the Proclamation Line of 1763 along the Appalachian divide, allowing whites to take over what lay to the east but attempting to reserve what lay to the west as Indian territory. After independence the Americans continued to adopt this ideal of virtually a two-nation state, but in practice it soon collapsed as they pushed the Indian line to the Ohio, then to the Mississippi, and then to the Missouri. The Indians in the east were swiftly displaced to the west and pushed into Indian territories on the Great Plains and in the intermontane basins. Even there their land and their way of life were not respected, as ranchers, the railways, and the homesteaders opened up the West. The Indian "territories" soon were reduced to isolated "reservations." As a result, most of the contemporary Indian population in the United States is found west of the Missouri—indeed, a great deal of it farther west between the Rockies and the Sierras in the dry climates unsuited to extensive agricultural settlement. The United States government has encouraged Indians to leave the reservations and mix with the whites in the large cities of the Midwest and the West, a process that some—including many younger and ethnically conscious Indians—would claim to pose as many dangers to the individual and social well-being of Indians as the communal misfortunes already brought upon them, though others see it as a means of ending differences between Indians and whites.

Canadian policy and system of reservations

In Canada the system of reservations was early adopted, protecting Indian settlements throughout the east, even in rich agricultural areas like the Montreal plain or peninsular Ontario or next to large cities like Montreal. As the whites moved west, more care was taken to retain Indians in part of their own lands, including such fertile plains as the Red River Valley and the Fraser Delta. Intermarriage between whites and Indians was much more common than in the United States and led to the nation of the French-and-Indian Métis, which in the Riel Rebellion unsuccessfully attempted to set up a separate state in the Canadian prairies.

In Mexico racial admixture has gone much further, and the mestizo, of mixed Indian and white descent, accounts for 60 percent of the population. Pure-blooded Indians amount to only about 30 percent; whites make up about 10 percent, and Mexicans of African descent less than one percent of the population. European immigration to Mexico and Central America since the original Spanish conquest has been negligible. When de Velasco made his 1574 count of 5,000,000 Indians under him, there were only 150,000 Spaniards in the New World.

The policies of the colonizers. *Spanish policy.* Colonial policies strongly affected the evolving human resources of North America. It has been stated that Spanish interests centred around God and gold—the Christianizing of the Indians and quick wealth from gold and silver. This is, of course, an overstatement. They were also interested in land, which they wished to develop as great ranches or plantations; but this land was carved up into big estates, to be worked by tenants or by direct labour in the form of serfs or peons. As a result, not many Spanish settlers were attracted. Spanish policy brought a highly competent entrepreneurial and professional group to North America: mineowners, the owners of great estates, merchants, administrators, and priests, but comparatively few from the middle and working classes. Little industry was set up, and, though towns were important, they served mainly as centres of trade and services. Descendants of the Spanish remain very much of an elite in the area colonized by their ancestors.

French policy. The policy of France was much the same. The first Frenchmen on the continent were mainly entrepreneurs interested in the fur trade; they hired Indians to collect and carry furs from the hinterland to the French trading posts, and they opposed, sometimes violently, the idea of farm settlements. France, nevertheless, felt it necessary to have a stronger French population base in its new colonies. To induce settlement, therefore, it gave large seigneuries, or grants, to landed proprietors who promised to bring in settlers, clear the forest, and develop the country. The seigneurs came with the French ideas of tenant farming, under which the seigneury was divided into many small holdings, each paying rent for the land. Once again, few of the French were moved to go to the New World under Old World conditions. As a consequence, when the British took over from the French in Canada in 1763, there were only about 80,000 French in Acadia and Quebec, whereas the British on the continent then numbered 3,000,000. The French, however, had been there for more than 150 years, and, since they were allowed by the British to retain their own language, religion, school system, and laws, they kept up their traditions in a remarkable way. Today the people of French origin in Canada make up almost 30 percent of the population and are firmly entrenched in the province of Quebec, with sizable communities in New Brunswick and Ontario. They form a distinctly Latin element within the Anglo-

The Quebec French community

American realm, and, indeed, some of them would like to see an independent French-speaking country, based on a free Quebec. In a referendum held in 1980, more than 40 percent of Quebec's voters supported a measure to give their provincial government the authority to negotiate Quebec's independence.

British policy. British policy encouraged the large-scale settlement of its colonies by religious refugees, landlords anxious to get New World estates, freemen seeking land of their own to develop for themselves, businessmen trying to found new enterprises, millowners and workers engaged in necessary domestic industries, and craftsmen and professionals out to capitalize on their own skills and callings. The British colonies, therefore, attracted many white settlers with a wide range of competence. The British also opened their colonies to non-British white settlers, notably such religious minorities as the Huguenots, from France, and the Mennonites, from Germany. Under the Hanoverian regime many German mercenaries were also settled. In Canada the British opened up the Canadian west to Germans, Scandinavians, Ukrainians, and Poles on a large scale and later accepted Chinese and East Indian settlers.

United States policy. The newly independent United States took over many British policies but gave more scope for freehold land and especially—after the overthrow of the Southern plantation system of chattel slavery—for capitalist business and industry. It also adopted the Open Door Policy to refugees and others from Europe in the belief that the United States would become, at least for whites, the "melting pot" of the world and thus in a sense develop what the historian Turner called a "new race of men." These views exerted a powerful attraction for British, Irish, and continental Europeans, and, perhaps to a lesser extent, for people from the Middle East, China, and Japan. Subsequently, as free land was used up, and as the United States became more interested in skilled workers and professionals, a quota system of immigration limited nationalities according to their proportion of the total population after World War I. Still later, a personal selection policy was adopted to choose those of any race or creed who, as individuals, were deemed best able to serve national needs.

THE AFRICAN HERITAGE

The slave trade and its consequences

North Americans of African descent were originally brought to the continent involuntarily as slaves. The whole question of the transatlantic slave trade and its turbulent legacy is still fraught with deep emotions, a not unexpected development considering that this tragic episode set in motion forces and counterforces that molded much of European and African, as well as North American, society over the course of nearly four centuries. Slaves were not widely used in Canada, where plantation agriculture never developed, or in Mexico, where Indian labour could be coerced, but slaves were imported in great numbers to the Caribbean islands and to the Southern states of the United States, where they laboured on tobacco, cotton, and sugar plantations. The importation of slaves to the United States was officially abolished in 1808, but illicit traffic and natural increase kept the black population growing in conditions that took a physical toll, disrupted social and family life, and harmed the individual's psychological makeup. The abolition of slavery in 1865 gave blacks, in theory if not in practice, freedom to work and live where they liked. Many saw no alternative to staying on plantations as impoverished tenants or sharecroppers. Economic forces in the 20th century—particularly the mechanization of farming—brought increasing numbers

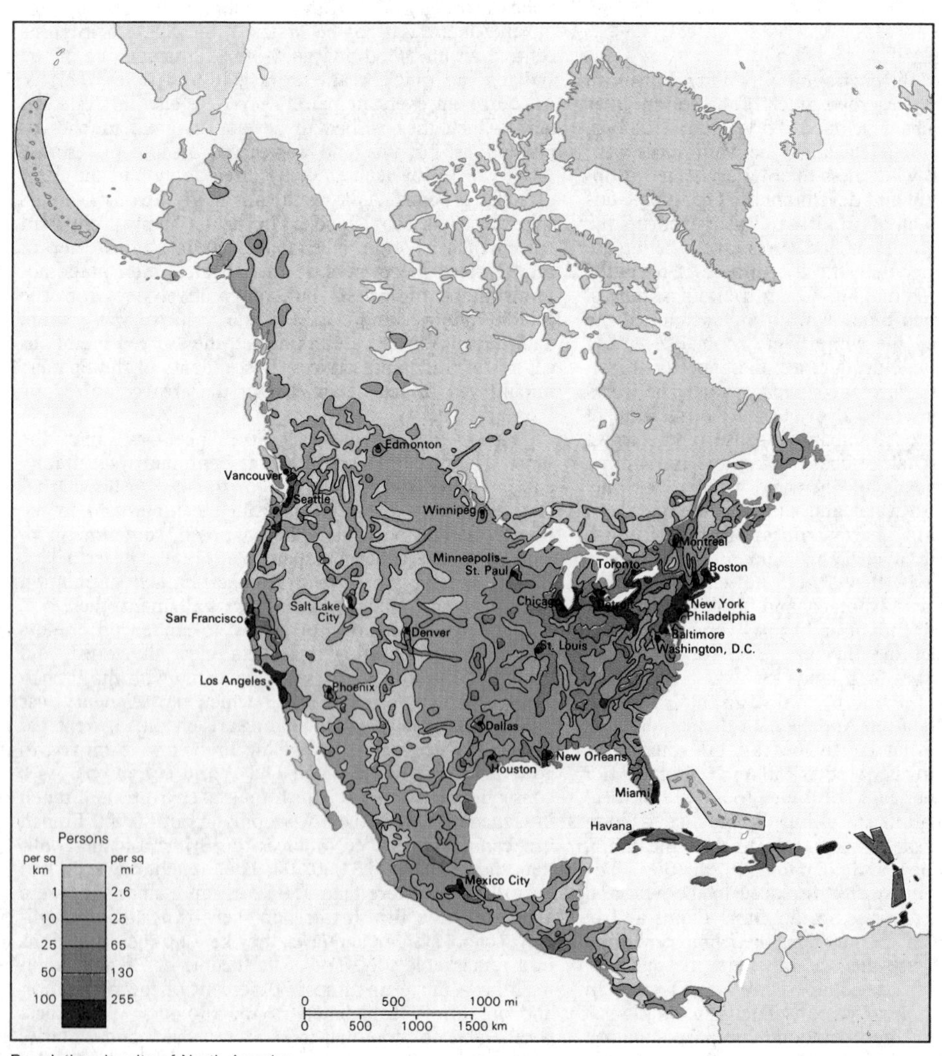

Population density of North America.

of blacks to the ghettos of the Northern cities, where new problems of racial discrimination had to be faced. The resulting social and racial polarization struck at the very roots of U.S. society and challenged the sincerity of its professed egalitarianism. Although the black citizens' struggle to win full equality made some progress, especially from the 1950s, their battle remains far from won, well over a century after the Emancipation Proclamation. Schooling, housing, social services, and, above all, access to employment opportunity on an equal basis remain key areas of concern. Perhaps because of this systematic exclusion from the mainstream U.S. society, the African contribution to the life of the nation has generated a rich and unique Afro-American culture.

Problems in race relations have also molded the attitudes and institutions of the white majority, not least in its dealings with the peoples and races of other continents. Hawaii has nevertheless been successfully incorporated as a state, and the United States as a whole has taken in numbers of Japanese, Chinese, Koreans, Southeast Asians, and Cubans. It has become quite a polyglot nation. The resulting rich ethnic mix, while posing immense problems, may perhaps ultimately prove an asset rather than a liability in the evolving world community.

DEMOGRAPHIC PATTERNS

Favourable and unfavourable regions. As an area of late exploitation, North America does not have the high settlement densities of Europe and Asia; yet, with great natural wealth and an advanced technology, its population is growing rapidly and is concentrated in regions of comparative advantage, such as the coasts, the lowlands, and the humid and the temperate zones. The 2,500,000 square miles of shield and the 2,000,000 square miles of mountainous land eliminate nearly half of the continent from continuous settlement. The frost-ridden areas of the Arctic coastal plain, the Mackenzie, and the Hudson Bay lowlands restrict settlement still more. Similarly, the drought conditions in districts of intermontane North America and Mexico detract from their use, while the disease-ridden, wet, tropical lowlands of Central America have remained comparatively empty. Further, the empty lands are getting emptier, as people who want to live well crowd the already crowded regions. The more populated areas include the Atlantic coastal plain from Nova Scotia to Florida; southern Canada in the humid, cool-temperate belt, where there are warm summers; the United States east of the Missouri, in the humid, warm-temperate zone, centred in the vast Mississippi–Ohio plain; the mild, moist Pacific Coast from British Columbia south to California; and the temperate, yet warm, and well-watered Mexican Basin. Within these areas of advantage, growth is concentrated still further in the large cities, especially those associated with the Hudson–Mohawk gap, the St. Lawrence–Great Lakes system, the Ohio Basin, the Middle Mississippi, Puget Sound and the Fraser Delta, and the California coast.

Geographic distributions. *The role of Canada.* Canada's share of the total continental population is small; and, with an area of 3,560,000 square miles, its overall population density is also small. Most of Canada—the shield, the northern Appalachians and Cordilleras, and the tundra and boreal forest zones—is empty. Population is concentrated in the south, around the Bay of Fundy, the St. Lawrence–Lower Great Lakes, the southern prairies, and the Columbia and Fraser valleys. Wealth is still based on iron and nickel and other metals, oil and natural gas, wheat, meat, fish, and forest products; most of its industries are developed from these resources. Mechanization and automation give a high per capita production, and Canada is only a little behind the United States in general affluence. It raises far more food than it can consume and thus sells much abroad.

The makeup of Canada's population

A member of the Commonwealth, Canada's population is still 45 percent British by extraction and more than 60 percent English-speaking. It nevertheless grew out of the two founding nations of France and Great Britain, and more than a quarter of the people can speak French. Most of Canada's population is native-born, but immigration is still active, with rather more non-British (including U.S. citizens) than British settling in the country. Canada is thus a bilingual, multicultural nation, with strong attachments to Britain and other countries of western Europe. It is economically dependent on the United States, which owns more than 70 percent of the foreign capital invested there and supplies 70 percent of Canada's imports. Ontario still leads in attracting population, but Alberta and British Columbia in the west are expanding rapidly. About three-quarters of the Canadian people live in cities, with about quarter in the metropolitan areas of Montreal and Toronto, the leading industrial and business centres.

The role of the United States. The United States dominates the continent with well over half the total continental population. Unlike the other countries of North America, most of its area is habitable, although the higher parts of the Appalachians, the Cordilleran ridges, and the dry intermontane basins are empty. The average density is much higher than that of Canada, though still low by European or Asian standards. Its most populated section comprises the mid-Atlantic states, New England, and the Great Lakes states. Florida, Arizona, and Nevada have had great increases of population. This influx has been due partly to the many affluent people retiring to those areas and partly to the emphasis on growth industries and services. The United States has gone further in the development of its service occupations than any other New World nation, with about two-thirds of its working population thus employed. Almost 30 percent of all workers are in manufacturing, and the remainder are in primary production jobs, such as farming, fishing, and lumbering. The U.S. consumption of food and goods is among the highest per capita in the world.

Occupational structure of the United States

The United States, which long drew its settlers from Europe, has today only a small population of foreign-born. Its population increase comes overwhelmingly from the native-born, among whom the most rapidly expanding groups are Indians and blacks. Less than 20 percent of all black Americans remain in the rural South, most of them living in the Northern cities, predominantly in overcrowded ghetto areas. Washington, D.C., Detroit, Baltimore, New Orleans, Atlanta, and Newark are major cities with a black majority. Blacks also account for large percentages of the total population of Cleveland, St. Louis, Philadelphia, and Chicago and are strongly represented in New York City, Pittsburgh, and Los Angeles. The inner-city concentration of blacks, one of the most noteworthy features of urban life in North America, is highlighted by a strong white population shift to the suburbs. About two-thirds of the U.S. population growth is, in fact, in metropolitan suburbs, often exacerbating the problems of inner-city decline.

Urban studies of the mid-20th century defined four huge urbanized belts, which have become known as Boswash (Boston–New York City–Philadelphia–Washington), Chipitts (Chicago–Detroit–Cleveland–Pittsburgh), Sansan (San Francisco–Los Angeles–San Diego), and Jackdal (Jacksonville–Mobile–New Orleans–Houston–Dallas). More than one-half of the nation's people are concentrated in less than one-tenth of the country's area.

The role of Mexico, the Caribbean, and Central America. The combined areas of Mexico, the Caribbean, and Central America have a sizeable population, which is growing rapidly. With high birth rates continuing and with death rates declining appreciably, a population explosion is under way. Yet, as in other developing areas, the economy can scarcely support the present population. In Mexico great expansion of manufacturing and services has been planned. U.S. capital investment and government assistance have been aimed at helping Central America and the Caribbean to help themselves; both factors have been major influences in the region's development, though the influence of their giant northern neighbour has not been without its critics. The impact of such development assistance tends to be concentrated in the capital cities, such as Mexico City, whose influence is swiftly modernizing the region.

The population explosion and the economy

The economy

RESOURCES

North America has rich and varied resources. Although it contains less than 10 percent of the world's population,

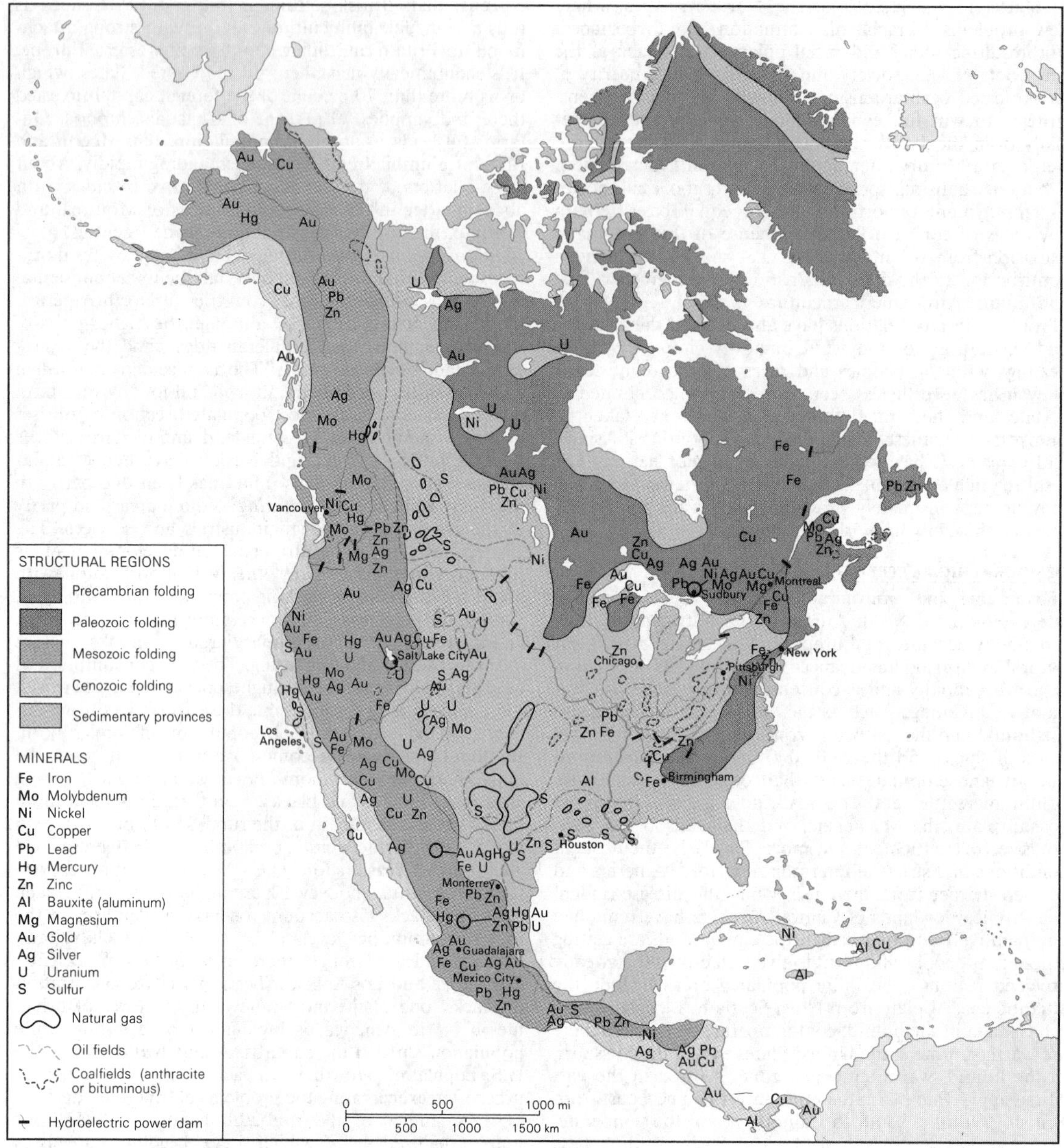

Basic structural regions and principal mineral and hydroelectric sites of North America.

it has an extraordinarily high proportion of the world's wealth. It produces a fair percentage of the world's oil, iron ore, steel, copper, lead, and zinc. With a large percentage of the world's coal output and the world's electrical power production, it possesses the main sinews of modern world industry.

Mineral resources. *The shield.* With a large shield area and with mountains strongly intruded by igneous rocks, the continent is unusually well endowed with metals. Its vast interior lowlands and some long stretches of coastal plain are marked by major fuel formation. Metal-bearing regions include shield structures affected by mountain building or trough development, together with the intensely folded ridges that rose from the eugeosynclines on the periphery. The shield has four main metal-bearing areas: the iron of the Adirondack and of the Superior uplands in the United States; the iron–nickel–copper and gold belt of Ontario and Quebec, along the old fold zones north of Lake Superior and Lake Huron; the iron of the Ungava trough; and the copper and nickel and the gold and uranium of the fault and fold systems of the shield's western rim. Iron in Baffin Island and zinc ores near Great Slave Lake are additional outliers of wealth. Three areas are of special importance: the taconite hematite ores of Mesabi and Ungava, mined with relative ease by opencast, or open-pit, methods; the world's largest deposit of nickel in the norite ore body at Sudbury, Ontario; and the large copper and gold bodies associated with the greenstone intrusions in northern Ontario and Quebec.

The marginal mountains. The Appalachians have also contributed significantly in metallic deposits, especially in the median mass between the Caledonian and Acadian folds, where lead and zinc are important in Newfoundland and New Brunswick; and also in the eastern or outer intensively folded rocks, with iron deposits in Belle Isle (Newfoundland) and the Trenton prong and in the Birmingham (Alabama) Basin.

The Cordilleras are rich in ores, mainly because of the immense igneous intrusions that underlie many of the structures. The median mass between the Laramie–Rockies and the Nevada–Cascade systems has major gold, silver, copper, and iron ores in the old plateau of Colorado–Utah. Large lead, zinc, and copper ores occur in the Selkirks and adjacent ranges of British Columbia. Famous silver, lead, zinc, and gold ores dot the Cassiar Massif and Yukon Plateau in the north; and far to the south, the Mexican Plateau holds iron, lead, and silver ores. To the east of this long, north–south line of plateaus lie the Rockies, which were not intensively folded and hence are not very rich in metals. But the vast intruded mass of the Idaho Batholith and the igneous bodies in the "dome and park" region were associated with copper, silver, and lead ores of great importance. The west Cordilleran ore deposits are widespread. They are found linked with intensively folded and intruded rocks of the Nevadan–Cascade–Coast systems, notably the copper–gold ores of southern and western Alaska; they also consist of the copper, lead, zinc, and iron of the enormous Coast Batholith of British Columbia; of the gold, copper, and iron deposits of Arizona and of the Nevadas in California, where the discovery of gold touched off the famous Gold Rush of 1849; and of the copper, gold, and silver of the Western Sierras of Mexico.

Fuel resources. The fuel wealth of the continent is also great: coal, natural gas, and oil are found in large quantities. These fuels accumulated as vegetative, or carbon, deposits in the lakes and shallow seas of the great lowlands stretching between the shield and the marginal mountains. They also underlay the coastal plains and the continental shelf, particularly in the Atlantic and Arctic oceans.

Coal deposits. Coal deposits were preserved in basins between gentle upwarps in the buried extensions of the shield beneath the Interior Lowlands and also in mildly folded rocks in the miogeosynclines of the inner, less disturbed parts of the Appalachians and Cordilleras. Below the Mississippi–Ohio lowlands and the Great Plains, the outer edge of the shield became depressed and buried and then buckled into basins and warps. The Cincinnati Anticline created a vast elongated basin between mid-Ohio and the Appalachians, in which the western Pennsylvania, West Virginia, and Kentucky coalfields were preserved—probably the single largest coal reserve in the world—together with the Lima (Ohio) oil field. The Kankakee rise, south of the Great Lakes, has preserved coal and oil in the Michigan (Saginaw) Basin, to the north of it, and the Indiana and Illinois basins, to the south. The last named, also known as the Eastern and Western Interior fields, are separated from each other but kept close to the surface by the La Salle Anticline. The Llano uplift has similarly helped to preserve the Southwest Interior field in Texas.

Coal reserves of the Cincinnati Anticline

An enormous midcontinental arch, the stem of the ancient Y-shaped structure connecting the Canadian Shield with the Colorado Plateau, separates the interior from the western coalfields lying in basins in front of the Rocky Mountains. Tolerably good bituminous coal occurs in the Raton Basin, which is cut off from the Denver Basin by the Las Animas uplift. The huge Williston Basin extends farther north, though it contains rather lowgrade coal. Beyond this lies the vast Alberta Basin, with coal exposed in the foothills of the Rockies. Here, too, is one of the largest coal deposits in the world.

Oil and natural-gas deposits. The same coal-containing "rises" and basins in the buried shield also have controlled the distribution of oil and natural gas. The Appalachian oil and gas basin, on the west flanks of the Appalachians, was the first to be developed. The Illinois, Kansas, and Oklahoma basins lie in the huge quadrilateral formed by the Cincinnati Anticline and midcontinental arch to east and west and by the Kankakee rise and Ozark Dome to north and south. Between the Ozarks and the Eastern Sierras of Mexico are the tremendously wealthy fields of west and east Texas and of the Gulf Coast. Northward, between the midcontinental arch and the Rockies, are found a number of important fields including the Denver, Big Horn, and west Alberta fields, close to the Rockies, and the Williston, east Alberta, and Mackenzie Valley areas, halfway toward the shield. Small fields of oil and gas lie on the flanks of folded mountains within the intermontane zone, as at Paradox, Utah, and San Juan, New Mexico. The western basins, bordering the Coast Ranges of California, are of moderate size but very rich. In the extreme north, the Prudhoe Bay Basin of Alaska and Mackenzie delta oil have proved that the potentialities of the Arctic shore are real; domes—very much like the salt and sulfur domes of the Gulf Coastal Plain, associated with Louisiana's oil and gas—go with oil on the plains sloping away from the Innuitian fold mountains in the Canadian Archipelago.

Water resources. Considered as a resource, water and waterpower are also abundant, although rather unevenly distributed. The average rainfall in North America is 30 inches a year, which produces some 15,000,000,000 acre-feet of water. About a half of this is lost through evapotranspiration, which is direct evaporation plus transpiration from plants. A further sixth is lost through rapid runoff, while yet another sixth percolates down into the groundwater. The amount available from rivers and lakes is thus relatively limited, a fact of growing concern as the demand for water grows. It takes 16,000 gallons of water, for example, to produce one ton of steel; while an average steam-generated power plant requires 4,000 cubic feet of water per second. The gap between use and availability is narrowing, though through the pumping up of artesian water, and through the desalinization of seawater, the supply may be considerably increased.

The narrowing gap between water use and availability

The water resources of the continent vary with regions. In northern Alaska, the Canadian north, and Greenland, they are low, mainly because they are locked up in ice most of the year; when the summer melt comes, runoff is high. Central Alaska and midnorth Canada have a moderate precipitation of from 12 to 15 inches per year, but again much of this is tied up in winter ice. The spring melt leads to extensive flooding, which makes the control of water difficult. Late summers are dry, but evaporation is low. Though rivers dwindle, they carry enough water for present needs.

The Great Plains area also has marked high- and low-water periods, the latter posing serious problems. Most rivers rise in mountains with an extensive snow supply. Meltwater gives an early spring flush; high flow is continued into early summer through storms generated by the tropical Gulf air. In late summer and the fall, however, dry air descends from the tropical continental air mass behind the mountains, the storms cease, and the rivers drop. Streamflow originating within the region may dry up; the bigger rivers sink into braided channels between bars of sand. Evapotranspiration also exceeds precipitation, resulting in a net loss of water—not made up again till early winter with the return of polar-front storms. Surface water therefore is scarce for four to five months and often needs to be supplemented from groundwater.

Water problems in the Great Plains

The intermontane basins stretching from southern British Columbia to central Mexico exhibit a strikingly unequal pattern, with areas of water surplus in the mountains lying adjacent to areas of a marked water deficit in the basins. Major rivers like the Columbia, Colorado, Grande, and the Guadalajara rise in snowy or rainy mountains and supply enough water, especially where their waters are trapped by dams, to serve the basins through which they flow. Lesser rivers, however, often peter out and are intermittent. Groundwater supply in areas with artesian wells alleviates the situation.

The eastern parts of southern Canada and the United States are well watered, with rainfall in most months, as the southern movement of polar continental air and the northern expansion of tropical Gulf air draw storms regularly across the area. Rainfall is from 30 to 60 inches a year, and evapotranspiration is not in excess of precipitation except in late summer. Streamflow is perennial, averaging over 10 inches in depth per stream per year.

Finally, the tropical areas in the trade-wind belts in Central America are well supplied with water, yet less is available than might be expected due to swift runoff after heavy rains and high evaporation. Rivers are relatively short and steep and are likely to flood quickly.

Biological resources. Forests are another of North America's magnificent natural resources. By no means all the forested land, however, may be regarded as a source for pulp or timber. Probably two-thirds of the boreal forest, for example, is not usable because of the thinness of the cover, the shortness of the trees, the very slow rate of natural recovery after cutting, and the inaccessibility of the northern parts of the region. The southern third provides a major base for pulp and paper industries. Most of the northern mixed forest and eastern hardwood forest likewise has become of little service. Good timber was cut out long ago, with much of the forest completely cleared for agriculture. What remains, though it looks plentiful, is commercially unattractive second- or third-growth bush. This woodland, however, is gaining value for the buildup of wildlife and for recreational purposes. The Pacific coast forest and some of the Cordilleran forest still make excellent stands for timber, and, though cutting has sometimes

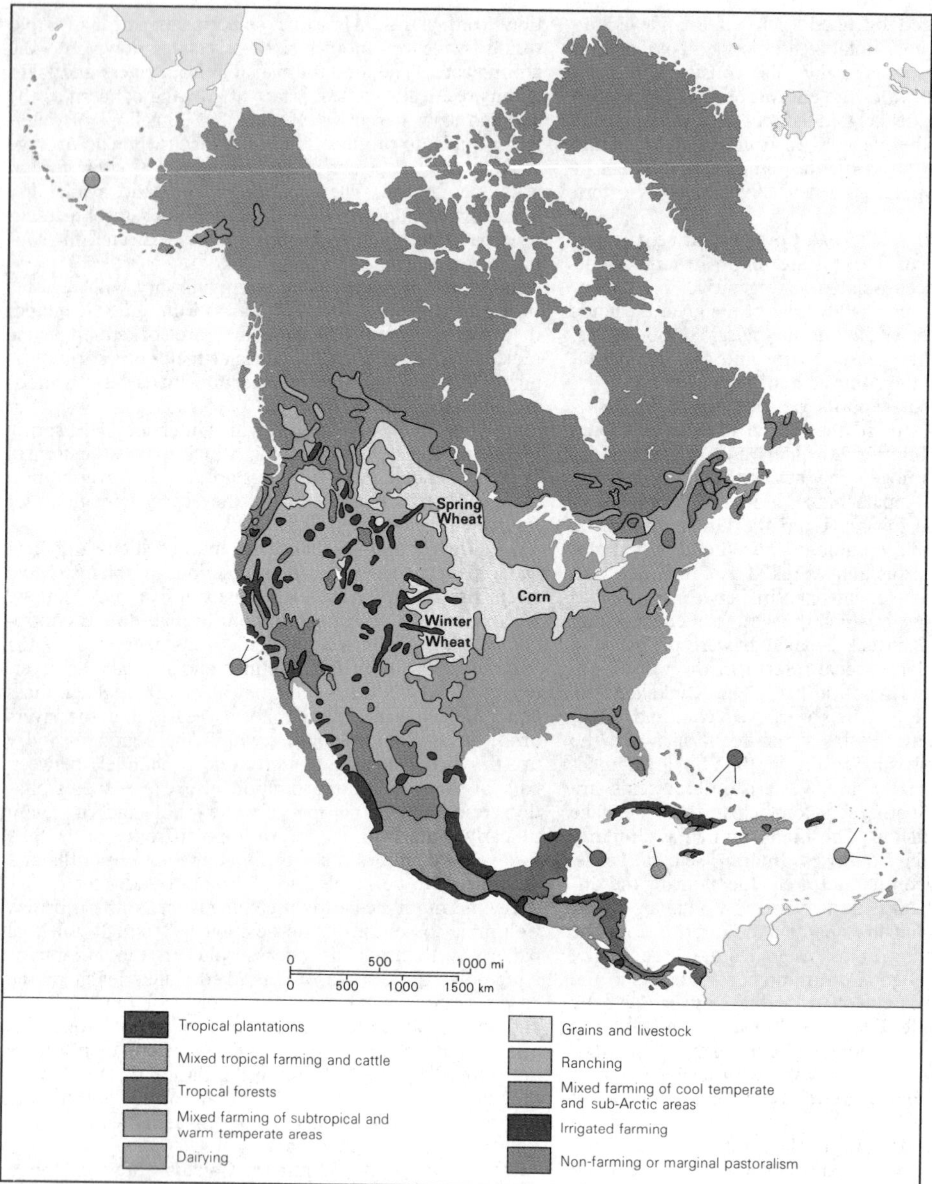

Agricultural regions of North America.

exceeded natural replacement, yet, with controlled use, growth is generally rapid enough to produce a continual yield. The Southern Pineries, long left untouched by agriculture because of their sandy soils, now have become the main source of timber and pulpwood in the United States. The tropical hardwood forests are also important for timber, but they have been cut down to some extent and also have been replaced by banana plantations or by poor second growth. Oak–pine forests above 2,000 feet, in the *tierra templada* ("temperate land") remain a useful resource.

Conservation. The early attitude of the Europeans in North America favoured the clearing of the forests and the killing off of the wildlife, with the aim of making room for crops and domesticated animals. In a continent that was so vast and at the same time so empty, they also developed the idea that environmental resources were unlimited and only awaited the coming of the white man to be tapped. It should also be remembered that many of these immigrants were to come from a Europe in which, during the Agricultural and Industrial revolutions, there had been an increasing attack on natural resources, particularly associated with the rise of industrial cities. When the United States and Canada became industrialized, they used coal, oil, iron, other metals, and wood with extravagance, a process involving great waste. The waste products of the factories of these nations started to pollute air, land, and water; and, as the multimillion cities began to appear, the majority of people came to live in a human-desecrated as well as a human-improved environment. By the mid-20th century, the people of the United States had killed off about four-fifths of the nation's wildlife, cut over half its timber, and used up two-fifths of its high-grade iron ore; the nation was consuming its oil so fast that, even with its great resources, it began to import from Canada, Venezuela, and other areas. Conscious of the great drain on the resources of the nation, and suffering from the increasing ill effects of pollution, the United States began to conserve its valuable reserves of forest, soil, water, fuels, and minerals; and today the country leads the world in its conservation programs, particularly in renewing the forests and grasslands, repairing the soils, and effectively controlling the waters. Canada, too, has an active conservation program and was the first North American country to pass a clean-water act to help fight the pollution of its lakes and streams. Mexico likewise has an active, though small, conservation service. The nations of North America seem determined in the late 20th century to undo the damage done and to pass on to future generations a revivified environment.

Conservation programs

AGRICULTURE

The various peoples who developed North America have made it a world economic leader and, in general, a well-used and productive continent. Agriculture, though no longer the principal economic activity, except in the southern Latin nations, is still important.

Tropical regions. In tropical areas the Spaniards made the most of the strong altitudinal zonation by raising sugar in rainy parts of the low *tierra caliente* ("hot land"), wheat and cattle in the middle levels of the *tierra templada* ("temperate land"), and sheep on the upper slopes in the *tierra fria* ("cold land"). Later, orange groves and coffee, cocoa, and banana plantations utilized the coastal plains and wet windward slopes of the tropical areas; cotton and hemp were grown in the warmer and drier basins of the intermediate zone. These remain important export crops for Central American countries and Mexico, being shipped mainly to the United States and Europe.

Subtropical and warm-temperate regions. An enormous extension of fruit, winter vegetables, cotton, and tobacco farming has occurred in the subtropical and warm-temperate areas of the United States. Citrus fruits do well in eastern Texas and in Florida, where the Ozarks and Appalachians protect them from polar airs, and the Gulf brings warm tropical air with early rain but much late-summer sun. The Central Valley of California—guarded from frosts by the Sierras, with winter rain for growth and prolonged summer sun for ripening—also is a prime citrus-growing area. Drought is a challenge, however, and has been met only by extensive irrigation. Winter vegetables are widely grown on the sandy soils of the Gulf Coast Plain and the southeastern parts of the Atlantic Coast, with a long frost-free season (200–340 days) and ample rain. Cotton has proved a success in areas with less than 60 inches of rain and more than 200 days free of frost. Tobacco is concentrated on the sandy soils of old shores and deltas, from Virginia to Kentucky. Many of the tobacco and cotton fields are now intertilled with rye, corn, and winter wheat grown as fodder for cattle or as additional cash crops. These help to maintain the fertility of the soil, which has long been threatened by the practice of monoculture.

The decline of monocultures

Cool-temperate, humid regions. In the continent's cool-temperate, humid regions, crops include hardy fruits grown on the valley sides of the Appalachians and the Piedmont from Georgia through Virginia, the Finger Lakes region of New York, the Niagara Peninsula and the east shore of Lake Michigan, and parts of the Columbia Basin in Washington and British Columbia. In all these areas, aspect, frost, and drainage are important factors.

The zone known as the Corn Belt evolved from a concentration on corn in the warm-summer region that extends eastward from the Ohio River to the Lower Missouri shores, where winter snowmelt, spring rains from the northward surge of tropical Gulf air, and early summer convection showers bring on the plant, while strong late-summer sun, with July averages of 70° to 80° F (21° to 27° C), ripen the cob. Most of the corn is fed to fatten pigs and cattle.

The Dairy Belt, another recognized division, makes use of a shorter growing season and cooler summers in New England and the Great Lakes–St. Lawrence region, where clover, timothy hay, and hardy small grains thrive. Dairying also exploits the lush pastures of the Pacific Coast's equable climate in Washington and British Columbia.

West of the Corn Belt, in subhumid regions, lie the continent's vast wheat areas. The Winter Wheat Belt, mainly in Nebraska, lies south of killing frosts. As the polar front retreats, the early sweep of rainstorms brings on the grain sown in the previous fall. The Spring Wheat Belt—in the Dakotas, the Canadian Prairies, and part of the Columbia Basin—has a severe winter that forces the postponement of sowing to spring. Then the warmth and wetness of the sudden northward surge of tropical Gulf air bring on the new-sown wheat very quickly, which ripens in a usually dry, sunny fall. Wheat farming takes place on an ever bigger scale, using more machines and producing more per acre.

Dry regions. Dry areas in the Great Plains and intermontane basins were long left to ranching. Hereford cattle brought in from England could feed on the shortgrass prairies, which were not suitable for homesteaders. Sheep, raised in still drier parts or up in the mountains, are bred mainly for wool. Near rivers or in artesian areas, irrigation for supplementary fodder has greatly helped ranching. Irrigation, however, is being used increasingly for fruit and cotton farming, resulting in a drain on water supplies.

WATER AND POWER

Water development is crucial both to circumvent drought and to prevent flooding. About 50,000,000 acres of irrigated land have been developed in the United States, with large schemes of dams and conduits in the Columbia and Snake valleys, the Central and Imperial valleys of California, the Salt and Gila tributaries of the Colorado, the Upper Rio Grande, and more recently, the Upper Missouri and the Upper Platte. In western Canada a vast scheme is developing on the Bow–South Saskatchewan rivers, while in Mexico the Lower Rio Grande, shared with the United States, the Fuerte Basin on the dry west coast, and the Balsas in the south have actively promoted water development. Water transfer from surplus to deficit areas is already taking place, and interstate water transfer proposals include transfers from the Columbia Basin to both the Sacramento and the Colorado, and from the head of the Missouri system to the Colorado, and thence to the Gila. Flood control is a problem in the Mississippi Basin. The Tennessee Valley and the Ozarks schemes have involved building many dams to redistribute river water.

Hydroelectric development has been immense in the United States and Canada. The rivers of the Canadian Shield, fed from lakes and falling abruptly over the edge of the plateau, provide many sites, especially in Quebec and Ontario: these are linked to such Great Lakes–St. Lawrence sites as Niagara Falls and International Falls, which, in turn, tie in to a power grid developed from Appalachian rivers. The north central and northeastern areas are thus well supplied.

The snow-fed rivers from the high Cordilleras, where dammed (as at Grand Coulee, Hoover, Glen Canyon, Fort Peck, and Garrison), also provide an immense amount of power. Yet in the United States hydroelectric power represents only a small percentage of all electricity generated, the rest coming from coal-, gas-, or oil-fired plants and nuclear-power stations.

MINING

Development of new fuel sources has caused the dramatic displacement of coal, from 90 percent of the energy used to about 20 percent in the late 20th century. Oil contributes almost one-half; and natural gas, more than one-fourth. The vast reserves of coal are now concentrated mainly in Kentucky, West Virginia, Pennsylvania, Wyoming, and Illinois. Coal is sent to the big power plants and steel works of the mid-Atlantic region and the Lower Great Lakes. One advantage that oil and natural gas have over coal is their ease of transport. Pipelines carry both fuels from their remote sources in the Gulf fields of Louisiana and Texas, the midcontinental fields of Oklahoma, and the Rocky-front fields to the shoreline cities of the Atlantic, Great Lakes, and Pacific. Oil, too, is piped great distances, although much is sent by tanker from the ports close to the Gulf oil fields. The 799-mile trans-Alaskan pipeline, opened in 1977, carries oil from Prudhoe Bay on Alaska's North Slope to the port of Valdez on the southern coast of the state. At Valdez the oil is loaded on tankers and shipped to the West and Gulf coasts for refining.

Changes in energy sources

Consumption of oil in the United States has continued to increase. In spite of the richness of the oil fields in California, that state has been a net importer, piping in oil from Texas and receiving oil by tanker from Middle Eastern countries, Indonesia, and Alaska. Similarly, the Illinois, Ohio–Indiana, Michigan and west Pennsylvanian fields, though quite important before World War II, cannot possibly supply the Great Lakes and mid-Atlantic regions, which are fed by oil piped from Oklahoma and Kansas.

Despite steep increases in the international price of oil beginning in the 1970s, the United States has continued to meet much of its petroleum needs with foreign imports. In Canada the industrial regions at Vancouver and in the Lower Great Lakes–St. Lawrence area are fed gas and oil by pipe from Alberta; and in Mexico, Mexico City and Monterrey, on the central plateau, are supplied by pipe from the Gulf Coast oil fields around Reynosa and Tampico–Tuxpan.

INDUSTRY

Coastal sites. The industry of North America is its chief contemporary source of wealth. It first developed at Atlantic Coast and Mississippi River ports, where raw materials transported from abroad or brought by coastal trade from other colonies could be made into goods for distribution in the interior. Inland products also could be transformed before being exported from such ports, where immigrant labour was plentiful and capital brought in or developed locally was abundant. In many respects the ports still perform these roles. New England ports bring in wool, leather, hardwoods, and metal from abroad and cotton from the Southern states; New York City imports coffee, cocoa, sugar, timber, pulp, and oil; the Philadelphia region brings in great quantities of iron from Canada and Venezuela and oil and petroleum coke from the Gulf; together these cities manufacture textiles, leather goods, petrochemical products, iron and steel, ships and machines, books, clothes, and foods not only for their own dense populations but also for the interior United States. In spite of the enormous development of the interior, coastal sites have still remained paramount, especially if the definition includes the shores of the Great Lakes and the Puget Sound and California coast. From Buffalo through Detroit to Chicago, the movement of coal from the Appalachian and eastern interior fields up to the lakeshore, combined with the shipment of iron ore from Lake Superior and Ungava to the lake ports, has led to a vast and dynamic belt of iron- and steelworks, transport facilities, and machine-making cities. The Pacific ports of Seattle, San Francisco, and Los Angeles have developed from an outpouring of forest, fish, farm, mine, and oilwell products, partly shipped abroad and partly sent by the Panama Canal to the eastern United States.

The role of ports in industry

Similarly, Canada imports oil, wool, cotton, leather, and food-based raw materials into the St. Lawrence–Great Lake ports such as Montreal and Toronto, and exports iron, nickel, copper and other metal-based goods, wood products, and flour from the eastern ports and from Vancouver. These trade activities have resulted in concentrated population at the gateways in and out of the country. Mexico's gateway district, at Vera Cruz, is also industrialized. Most of North America's industry and population is thus concentrated at its seaward or Great Lakes' margins.

Inland sites. Sites in the interior are, however, not without importance. The first to develop were the fall-line power centres, strung out from the falls of the Merrimac at the edge of the New England Upland, then southward along the east front of the Piedmont, to the Coosa south of the Appalachians. Later, with the advent of steam and electric power, these sites continued as major textile, pulp and paper, and engineering locations. A bigger shift inland occurred with the use of coal for power in the eastern and western Pennsylvanian coalfields around Wilkes-Barre and Pittsburgh, in the Birmingham coal and iron fields, and the Saginaw Bay, Indiana, and Illinois coalfields. Pittsburgh soon used up its local iron ore but was sufficiently near the Great Lakes to bring in Mesabi Range iron ores, which, in combination with the vast amounts of high-quality coking coal at hand, formed the basis for a great iron and steel industry. Except where coking coal is used in the steel plants, Western coal has been too low grade to attract industry. Oil and natural gas, however, have become the base of active petrochemical industries in areas such as Alberta, Oklahoma, and Texas. Since oil and gas can be easily piped, they have not stimulated the development of industry on a big scale near their sources but have fuelled the northeastern and Pacific Coast industrial areas. Modern industry has become less tied to sites where fuel and raw materials are available and more oriented toward the market. Service industries especially have concentrated in the highly populous areas of Boston–New York–Philadelphia, Pittsburgh–Detroit–Chicago, and San Francisco–Los Angeles. Space-age developments have been supported by science-based industries from Texas through Louisiana to Florida. Industries to meet the immense demand for travel and recreation have sprung up on the major motorways and in the tourist areas in the Appalachians, the Cordilleras, and along the sea coasts. Though industry is more free to disperse, it nevertheless continues to centre on areas of existing urban agglomeration. In the United States industrial concentrations are greatest in the New York–Washington, Cleveland–Chicago, and Los Angeles regions; in Canada, in the Montreal–Toronto and Vancouver districts; and in Mexico, in the Mexico City Basin. The major cities of these regions are also the focus of critical social and economic problems.

More generally, automation is everywhere creating a major problem of technological unemployment, met in part by reducing working hours and retiring people earlier. These trends, in turn, raise the problem of the use of leisure time, which has become the target for much of America's fastest developing industries.

TRADE

North American trade patterns offer interesting contrasts. Canada, with a small population but with immense resources and high productivity, has a low home consumption and depends on foreign trade more than any other developed country on the continent. The United States, on the other hand, with a vast internal market and the highest per capita consumption of goods in the world, depends mainly on internal trade; less than 10 percent of its total trade is with countries abroad. Mexico and Central America, by contrast, still have large areas where people live at a subsistence level and produce little more than goods for local trade. Production of certain metals, oil, and tropical crops, however, is expanding rapidly for sale in foreign markets.

The Canadian segment. Canada's internal trade is dominated by the provinces of Ontario and Quebec. Together they make more than 75 percent of the nation's manufactured goods, which they ship across Canada in exchange for fish, lumber, and fruit from British Columbia, wheat and meat from the Prairies, and pulpwood, iron ore, and fish from the Atlantic provinces. Most of Canada's trade abroad consists of raw or semiprocessed materials, including pulp, paper, lumber, iron ore, nickel, lead and zinc, uranium, and asbestos, sent to Britain, the United States, and Japan; and wheat, exported to Britain, the Soviet Union, China, and Japan. Some oil and natural gas are sold to the United States.

Until World War II, Canada traded mainly with Britain; until that time the United States still produced a surplus of most of the things Canada raised and thus was not a major customer. Canada, in fact, bought far more from the United States than it sold to it. By the late 20th century, however, the United States had become short of metals, wood, pulp and paper, power, and water and was importing these items from its neighbour on an increasing scale. It has thus replaced Britain as Canada's chief market. The European Economic Community and Japan are also important customers for Canada's metals, wood products, and wheat.

The United States segment. Internal trade in the United States is enormous, often surpassing that among sovereign states on other continents. It is dominated by New England's need for fuel, cotton and wool, leather, wood products, and metals; by the mid-Atlantic states' demand for coal, oil, natural gas, iron ore and other metals, and food products; by the Pittsburgh region's need for iron, copper, oil, and gas; by the Lower Great Lakes–Lake Michigan area's need for coal, oil, gas, iron, pulp and paper, and wood; and by the Los Angeles–San Francisco region's demand for steel, aluminum, cellulose products, oil, and chemicals.

Most of the other areas of the United States trade their raw materials or semifinished goods to these major manufacturing regions, though of course there are local industrial centres of importance. Trade is concentrated in servicing, or in being served, by such large metropolitan centres as New York City, Chicago, Los Angeles, Philadelphia, and Houston. These cities also handle a great deal of U.S. foreign trade. Southeastern ports send out cotton,

The large metropolitan centres

tobacco, and wood products; and the mid-Atlantic coast ports send out wheat, corn, meat, and a wide range of manufactured products.

Since the development of the St. Lawrence Seaway, major cities like Chicago, Detroit, Cleveland, and Buffalo have been directly exporting the steel products, cars, planes, agricultural machinery, cereals, and meat for which the northern Midwest is famous. New Orleans continues as a major exporter of cotton, corn, and other agricultural products from the vast Mississippi hinterland; Houston is the most rapidly expanding southern port, basing its trade on oil and chemical products. Los Angeles dominates the West, with its sales of aircraft, ships, films, and chemicals. Seattle is important for its trade in fish and forest products. U.S. imports include a wide variety of products: tropical fruits, woods, fibres, rubber, and vegetable extracts, mainly from Latin America, West Africa, and Southeast Asia; oil from Saudi Arabia, Mexico, Nigeria, Indonesia, and Great Britain; tin from Bolivia and Malaysia; wool from Australia and South America; and a wide range of machines, textiles, instruments and books from western Europe and from Japan.

U.S. trade has a worldwide distribution and impact: of its export total, about one-third goes to western Europe; more than one-fifth to Japan, Southeast Asia, Australia, and New Zealand; almost one-fifth to Canada; one-tenth to Mexico, Central America, and the West Indies; and one-twelfth to South America. Of almost equal importance has been the widespread influence of U.S. aid: while initially this helped U.S. trade by being tied to the use of domestically manufactured equipment, it has become much more free and enables countries to develop their own agriculture or industry in the most satisfactory way.

The Mexican and the Central American segments. The Latin American portion of the continent includes some highly sophisticated regions, along with many as yet undeveloped areas. In Mexico's internal trade the capital region predominates, producing most of the nation's manufactures, which are then distributed through regional cities. Mexico City consumes much of the domestically used oil piped up from the coast, the metals of the Cordilleran mines, the cotton of the irrigated central and western basins, and hemp from Yucatán. Petroleum exports became a steadily growing part of Mexico's external trade following the discovery of vast oil reserves in the Bay of Campeche in 1972. Within a decade petroleum sales represented by far the greatest portion of Mexican export earnings. The oil exports have given Mexico higher income, but they also have placed the country in danger of becoming overly dependent on a nonrenewable resource. To avoid the consequences of such dependence, the government has committed itself to diversifying the country's export economy. This effort involves expanding Mexico's industrial base, increasing the export of manufactured goods, and augmenting the export of agricultural goods and metals.

Imports consist predominantly of manufactured goods and of parts and materials needed for Mexican industries. Machinery, vehicles, and consumer goods are the chief items. The United States has the greatest share of Mexico's foreign trade, providing the greatest portion of the imports and exports. With the establishment of the Latin American Free Trade Association, however, more of Mexico's trade has been oriented toward Latin America. Mexico is also trying to send more winter fruits and vegetables, textiles, and leather goods to Canada.

Mexico's trading partners

Central America has not developed much trade. By far the greatest exports are tropical fruits, fibres, and minerals (especially from the Caribbean), which are sent to the United States in exchange for U.S. manufactured goods. Increasingly, virtually the whole of North America is being integrated in its economic development with the growth of the United States.

TRANSPORTATION

Waterways. Industry has been strengthened by the ease of movement in North America. Waterways, widely used by the Indians and early Europeans, are still important. In spite of the barriers of the Laurentian Shield and the Appalachians, the routes up the Gulf of St. Lawrence, the Hudson Estuary, Chesapeake Bay, and the Gulf of Mexico permitted the swift development of coastal ports and allowed the interior to be opened up. The Mississippi–Ohio and the Great Lakes–St. Lawrence waterways drew navigation into the heartland. Connecting these two systems, the Chicago Sanitary and Ship Canal, linking the Illinois River with Lake Michigan, and various Ohio–Lake Erie canals provided a tremendous network, extended by the Erie Canal to the Mohawk–Hudson and by the Intracoastal Waterway to river ports of the Gulf of Mexico. The St. Lawrence Seaway, which overcame the Lachine and International rapids and Niagara Falls, has made ocean ports of inland cities. No other continent has such a system of inland waterways.

Railways. Railways soon offered the challenge of more direct and speedy access than the waterways. Developed principally from bases in Baltimore, Philadelphia, New York City, and Boston, they made the most of gaps through the Appalachians, debouched on the Great Lakes or Ohio at Buffalo and Chicago, Pittsburgh, and Cincinnati, and pushed on to the Mississippi at Memphis, St. Louis, and St. Paul–Minneapolis. Other lines were then thrown across the Great Plains and, making the most of Cordilleran passes, the railways built terminals at San Francisco, Seattle, and Los Angeles. Most of the Western railways were given large land grants to encourage immigrants to settle along them, while low promotional rates on long-haul traffic developed transcontinental trade. In Canada the transcontinental railways linked up the Maritime Provinces with the St. Lawrence–Great Lakes, and thence, from Montreal and Toronto, they crossed the shield to converge at Winnipeg; there, reinforced by large land grants, they fanned out across the prairies, to be drawn together by the Fraser down to Vancouver.

Development of Canada's railway system

Mexico overcame difficult grades in building a railway from Vera Cruz to Mexico City and added extensions north and south along the Gulf Coast, with lines into Monterrey and to Mérida. Eventually lines were pushed through the Western Sierras at Guadalajara to the Pacific Coast.

Railroads had a tremendous impact on urban development. Among the major railroad cities are New York City, Chicago, St. Louis, and Los Angeles, in the United States, and Montreal, Winnipeg, and Vancouver, in Canada. Mexico City dominates the network in Mexico. Railroads led to the rise of east–west over north–south lines and rapidly displaced most waterways, particularly the Mississippi. The main economic axis in the United States lies along the railway belt from New York to Chicago. Inadequate overall planning in major metropolitan regions has resulted in crucial transportation problems, however, and inner-city rapid-transit systems often have fared no better.

Motorways. North America's road network first began to offer serious competition to the railways after World War I. The U.S. government has since financed more than 300,000 miles of transcontinental highways. In Canada, the Trans-Canada Highway offers a coast-to-coast through route, while from Mexico, the Pan-American Highway links the countries of Central America. These highways have enabled trucks to take over short-haul routes, and the financially plagued railroads have had to concentrate on long-haul, low-cost routes. Truck and train have, however, been integrated in "piggyback" containerized carriage. The automobile, meanwhile, has displaced commuter trains in many cities, and radial and ring routes have drawn the cities well out into the countryside. The attendant problems of congestion and pollution have approached the critical stage in many cities.

Air transport. Air transport has taken most of the long-distance passenger traffic from the trains, and airfreight has cut deep into truck-freighting trade. Intense overall competition is thus a recurrent feature of North American transportation systems. Airways have tended to centre on the larger cities and to magnify their importance, so that intervening intermediate and smaller cities have declined in importance. Links with Europe and Asia make North America the chief crossways of air routes in the world. The United States alone accounts for a third of all the world's air traffic. Of the chief airports in the world, several are in the United States, including airports in Chicago, Atlanta, Los Angeles, Dallas–Fort Worth, Denver, San Francisco, New York City, Miami, Boston, and Washington, D.C. Montreal in Canada and Mexico City in Mexico are also of major importance.

Administrative conditions

The United States and subsequently Mexico and the Central American countries cut off their ties with Europe and became independent republics. They continue to recognize each other's independence and also their need for each other in various regional groupings and alliances, including the Organization of American States (OAS). Cuba has nevertheless taken a different course of political, social, and economic development than the rest of North America and the Caribbean region. Canada has not joined the OAS because, unlike other American states, it has ties with the United Kingdom and other members of the Commonwealth. It has adopted the British parliamentary system of government rather than the U.S. system of checks and balances. Both Canada and the United States are, nevertheless, members of the North Atlantic Treaty Organization (NATO), along with most other countries of western Europe. The United States is also part of the Australia, New Zealand, and United States agreement (ANZUS). North America thus has a strong hemispherical unity and in addition is firmly linked up with the Commonwealth, western Europe, Australia, and New Zealand. There are also vital trade links with South America, Africa, and Japan. North America's major ties are with other predominantly industrial nations, but all these connections are of immense importance for the continent's security and prosperity. (J.W.W.)

Position of Canada in ties with regional groups

HISTORY

Pre-Columbian evolution

MIGRATIONS FROM ASIA

It is generally agreed among students of prehistory that the first human inhabitants of the Western Hemisphere did not originate there, and that the American Indians most probably migrated from Asia. The level of technological advancement could not have been too high at the time of the first migrations into the New World and would tend to rule out long sea voyages or other hazards. The break between North America and Asia at the Bering Strait is a matter of 53 miles (85 kilometres), with islands lying at the midway point, and is, in the opinion of authorities, the only practical route. The view is also held that the migration was not a single incident but that small groups of migrants continuing over a long period of time were responsible for peopling the continents. At least partial confirmation of this hypothetical route is seen in the remains of various mammals that migrated to North America in the Ice Age and that have been found in Alaska, in the high mountain plateaus in the west, on the Great Plains, and as far south as Mexico, but rarely in eastern Canada.

The probabilities are that this migration took place during the glacial advance and recession across the top of North America. The so-called Ice Age consisted of four intervals of maximum glaciation and three intervening nonglacial periods, or possibly two pairs of maximum glaciated periods with a long, middle, ice-free interval, in a total time span of about 250,000 years. The exact boundaries of these glacial patterns have not been plotted in all areas; neither is the timing stated too precisely. Geologists believe, however, that the central plain of Alaska (south of the Brooks Range and east of the Coast Range), as well as the lowlands bordering the Bering Sea and the Arctic Ocean, were never glaciated. The great ice barriers formed, instead, on the Pacific slope of the Coast Range and poured through mountain passes for some distance. A second (Keewatin) ice sheet spread eastward from the Hudson Bay area during the last maximum but left an open corridor between for possible migration. The problem of chronology, then, is to determine the period of the last maximum glaciation and when openings between the two ice sheets were available for southward travel. The last maximum was dated by radiocarbon dating at about 10,000 years ago.

Generally it is agreed that an ice-free land route extended along the Arctic coast to the Mackenzie River and southward into what is now the United States as long ago as 20,000 years. This route also may have been open for a brief period about 40,000 years ago. The next prior ice-free period would have occurred during the Sangamon interglacial epoch about 75,000 years ago. The relation of sea level to land also may have had a bearing on the migration between the two continents. At the time of the last maximum glaciation sea level in the vicinity of the Bering Strait was probably lowered by as much as 240 feet (75 metres) as water froze. A certain amount of sinking of the land under the tremendous weight of ice was coincident with the dropping water level. As temperatures rose and ice melted, both the land and the sea level began rising, but not at the same rate. Enormous quantities of water would be needed to make an appreciable difference in sea level, while pressures within the Earth would respond promptly to lessening weight. This leaves the possibility that a bridge of dry land actually existed for several millennia following the last glacial epoch. Modern coast surveys reveal that much of the bottom between the continents is less than 120 feet (35 metres) deep. The pattern of glaciation on the Asian side of the Bering Strait is not clear in detail, but there seems to be some correspondence between the phases as these developed east and west of the strait. It seems likely, then, that an open land route from central Asia into central North America existed 20,000 years ago. At a later time the Yukon river valley offered an ice-free route, and still later (8,000–10,000 years ago) the Liard and Peace river systems were available for intramontane travel.

The Pacific coast slope was probably available for travel at about the same time. Some migrations may also have occurred by way of the Aleutian Islands, but this would have taken place at a considerably later date.

EVOLUTION OF NORTHERN NORTH AMERICA

Definite evidence that men were in North America between 15,000–25,000 or more years ago has gradually accumulated. The evidence is mainly limited to crude stone tools, sometimes found in association with remains of extinct species of horse, camel, elephant, and other mammals and often with evidence of hearths or human habitation. Most of the sites are in western North America in Pleistocene (Ice Age) lake basins or in specific localities in Nevada, California, Texas, and Illinois.

Paleo-Indian hunting cultures. In 1926 specific types of projectile points were found in association with the bones of extinct bison near Folsom, New Mexico. Subsequent discoveries of early hunting cultures in the High Plains (southern portion of the Great Plains) and neighbouring regions (such as Clovis, New Mexico) are dated and well documented. The type tool from these sites is called the Folsom point and is a fluted projectile point used for spears, though stone knives and other artifacts are also found. Radiocarbon dates range generally between 9000 and 7000 BC, with the Clovis sites being considered slightly older than those near Folsom. In addition to extinct forms of bison the camp sites show camel, horse, musk ox, giant sloth, and other Pleistocene forms.

The Folsom and Clovis sites

Related projectile tips known as Yuma points are found in the same region. These do not have fluting but are more finely chipped with diagonal flaking. The Folsom and Yuma types occurred contemporaneously, in part, but the Yuma technique apparently survived until more recently.

The bulk of the Folsom and related sites occur in the Great Plains from Canada to Mexico, though fluted points also occur in the region east of the Mississippi river and elsewhere. In Sandia cave, near Albuquerque, New Mexico, Folsom points were found above an older stratum containing cruder flaked points with one corner notch. These sandia points are reminiscent of some of the Solutrean forms found in Europe, dating from the end of Paleolithic period. The Sandia level has a radiocarbon age of 30,000 years, though this is probably an overestimate of the age of the points.

For the Folsom period at least one human skull is available from a site near Midland, Texas. The reconstruction gives a long head within the range of modern forms. Another early find, from Tepexpan in the Valley of Mexico, is dated at a slightly earlier period.

The Desert culture. Along with evidence for the early hunting cultures there was growing evidence for a parallel development of early gathering cultures in the intermontane region of western North America. There, in the relative absence of large game resources, vegetation was exploited to a great extent, with the development of grinding tools and related equipment. The Cochise Desert culture, named from Cochise county in southern Arizona where it was discovered, ran from about 8000 BC through several stages, and gave rise to Mogollon culture, one of the basic culture types of the southwest. But related culture types have been found throughout the central basin and plateau areas to the north, and Danger Cave in Utah has been dated by radiocarbon to 10,000–11,000 years ago.

Dry cave excavations have yielded a rather full inventory of the Desert culture, particularly in its later phases. Settlements were sparse and often in caves. Subsistence involved intensive exploitation of the environment, with special emphasis on small-seed harvesting and preparaton. Basketry and netting were important; the atlatl (throwing stick) was used with darts; projectile points were small and made from a variety of materials. Present in various sites were digging sticks; fire drills and hearths; flat, curved, wooden clubs; tubular pipes; sandals; and flat milling stones with manos (handstones).

Later developments. With the retreat of the ice sheets in the north, beginning about 10,000 years ago, the cool, moist climate gradually became hot and dry in the Great Plains and Great Basin regions, with consequent extinction or migration of Pleistocene animal life. The High Plains were largely deserted by man for a considerable period. In the eastern forest regions hunting and gathering continued, with dependence on shellfish, as evidenced by the great shell mounds along many of the rivers in Kentucky and Tennessee dating from the Archaic period. Gradually adaptation to forest resources developed, particularly to acorns and other seed crops, culminating in the Ohio valley in the Hopewell and Adena cultures that began about 400 BC and flourished for several centuries. The Hopewell peoples practiced a limited amount of agriculture and developed elaborate funerary rites, the dead being cremated or buried with extensive offerings in large mounds. Following an interval of decline a new cultural development, stimulated by contacts with Middle America, arose in the Mississippi valley. This Mississippian culture farmed the bottomlands and built large-scale temple mounds that were still being used when the Spaniards first explored the region.

The Hopewell and Adena cultures

In the southwest the Desert culture was more directly influenced by the development of agriculture in Central America, but the climate limited its spread to favourable areas so that much of the seed-gathering complex survived in the basin region. Early forms of corn (maize) are found in Bat Cave, New Mexico, dated about 2000 BC, with beans being introduced about 1000 BC, but agriculture made little impression until larger forms of corn were developed and introduced. By the beginning of the modern era two sedentary agricultural societies were established in southern Arizona and New Mexico, the Mogollon and the Hohokam, to be followed in a few centuries by the Basket Maker-Pueblo, or Anasazi, cultures to the north on the Colorado plateau. The modern Pueblos and other Indians of the Southwest are descendants of these early culture types, with the exception of the Navaho and Apache tribes, which entered the region from the north in the 13th or 14th century.

In northern North America hunting and fishing continued as the basis for subsistence. About the beginning of the modern era the Eskimo developed specialized techniques for sea-mammal hunting in the Bering Strait region and about AD 1000 spread eastward to Greenland. Interior Indian populations expanded to the North Pacific coast, utilizing the salmon resources to build a highly elaborate social organization and a unique art. In the plains, as animal life repopulated the region, peoples moved out of the forests or deserts to pursue them but continued to farm the bottomlands along the rivers. Only with the introduction of horses brought by the Spaniards did the culture of modern Plains Indians develop. (D'A.McN./Ed.)

EVOLUTION OF MIDDLE AMERICA

Early hunting period. The first inhabitants of Middle America migrated into the area at some time during the final, or Wisconsin, stage of the Pleistocene. Discoveries in centrai Mexico, at Valsequillo and at Tlapacoya, claim association of simple chipped stone artifacts and radiocarbon dates in the range of 20,000 to 40,000 BC. If these claims can be accepted, then it is likely that man had reached Middle America, on his trek from Asia via North America, with a culture and a technology that were not yet specialized toward big-game hunting. More generally accepted claims for early man in Mexico pertain to a somewhat later period and to hunters of large herd animals such as the mammoth. Human artifacts and mammoth bones have been found together in the same geological strata, in the Valley of Mexico at Santa Isabel Ixtapan. These strata date from the terminal substage of the Wisconsin glacial advance, and the associated radiocarbon readings are approximately 9000 BC.

Food-collecting and incipient cultivation period. With the increased dryness and change of fauna following the glacial retreat of the Wisconsin substage, the inhabitants of Middle America were forced to turn from big-game hunting to other means of subsistence. These were the hunting of smaller game and the collecting of wild food plants. This mode of existence is best seen in the discoveries made in the Tehuacán Valley of Puebla. There dry cave refuse has revealed the hunting and collecting equipment of a people who ground both wild and domesticated seed foods in stone metates and made baskets for collecting and storage.

The Tehuacán Valley

In the earlier El Riego (7000–5000 BC) and Coxcatlán (5000–3400 BC) phases of this sequence the inhabitants of the Tehuacán Valley were seasonal nomads who divided their time between small hunting encampments and larger temporary villages that were used as bases for plant and seed collecting. Such plants included various grasses, maguey, agave, and cactus fruits. Corn (maize), a wild grass, first came under cultivation in this time, probably as early as 5000 BC. Avocados, chili peppers, amaranth, sapotes, tepary beans, and squashes were also primitive cultigens. During the Abejas phase (3400–2300 BC) cultivated plants increased at the expense of wild plants and, probably, at the expense of hunting. A hybrid corn, crossed with the wild grass teosinte, appeared for the first time, and pumpkins and the common bean were introduced. Toward the end of the phase, settlement assumed a more permanent form in what appear to have been year-round pit-house villages. Also during these late Abejas centuries the villagers were making stone bowls, in addition to the heavier food-grinding implements. In the Purron phase (2300–1500 BC) the first pottery was produced in vessel forms that duplicated the earlier stone vessels.

Formative period. By 2000 BC some village communities in Middle America were sustained largely or wholly by agriculture. As these villages are located largely in southern Meso-America, it is likely that agriculture first originated in this part of the area. However, it would be an oversimplification to look upon one single locus, such as the Valley of Tehuacán, as the fountainhead of the Middle American farming complex. Almost certainly, corn was first domesticated in an upland environment (Tehuacán has an elevation of 6,000 feet [1,800 metres]); but an important part of the process of its genetic improvement must have been the transferring of the plant to other

Domestication of corn

environmental niches, such as the coastal lowlands, and its hybridization with other regional varieties. During the Early Formative the Middle American agricultural plant complex was assembled and improved by these processes and by man's selection and cultivation. By the end of this period it is likely that this complex had spread to most of the area, a possible exception being the northwest.

In general, there is widespread similarity among Early Formative period phases in ceramics and figurines, and this suggests that these traits may have been diffused through Middle America from the southern part of the Middle American area.

The Middle Formative Period was a time of transition from the simple agricultural village to more complex societies organized around politico-religious capitals or nuclei. Quite probably, this trend had begun in the latter part of the Early Formative, but the first large ceremonial centres and the first monumental stone sculpture occur at about 1000 BC, or a little before in southern Veracruz and Tabasco. The sites in question, San Lorenzo and La Venta, are the type locations for Olmec art. This art is amazingly sophisticated, with consummate control of both full round and bas-relief forms. The dominant theme is the human one although humans are frequently depicted with jaguar mouths and nostrils. Another common rendering is that of an infantile or "baby face" countenance. The Olmec artists made great stone heads, altars, and stelae; and they also worked as lapidaries in exquisite jade figurines and other small objects. Olmec stylistic influence occurs in the Middle Formative Period in Oaxaca, Chiapas, Guatemala, and El Salvador; and it also turns up in the Valley of Mexico. Clear Olmec influence is seen in later Middle American styles such as those of Izapa and Tres Zapotes, and traces of it are also to be found in the still later Mayan and Zapotecan monumental art.

Olmec art

The Late Formative Period saw the spread of complex societies—as indicated by the ceremonial centre with satellite villages—throughout much of Middle America. One significant development in this context was the appearance of hieroglyphics and complex calendrical calculations. These elements of civilization are first noted in association with the Tres Zapotes, Izapan, and early Oaxacan art styles. The true city or urban centre also came into being during this period. One of the earliest manifestations of densely settled city life occurred in the Valley of Mexico at Teotihuacán, where the Late Formative urban zone covered a square mile. Later, in the Classic Period, Teotihuacán was to go on to become 10 times this large and to be the most important city of its time in Pre-Columbian Middle America.

Classic Period. The characteristic Middle American aesthetic and religious patterns that began in the Late Formative were crystallized in the Classic Period. In the Maya Lowlands subarea polychrome ceramics, the use of the corbelled vault in temple construction, and the foreshadowings of typical Maya art and the probable beginnings of Initial Series calendrics all belong to the end of the Late Formative or what is sometimes called the Protoclassic Period (100 BC—AD 300). The full Maya artistic, architectural, and calendric—hieroglyphic traditions are then ushered in during an Early Classic subperiod (AD 300—600). Tikal, Uaxactún, and Copán all attained their first glories in these centuries. In the Late Classic subperiod, between AD 600 and 900, ceremonial centres in the Maya Lowlands proliferated in number, as did the carving and erection of the inscribed and dated stelae and monuments.

Elsewhere in Middle America, the Zapotecan traditions were brought to full flower in the Monte Albán III-A phase; the great site of El Tajín flourished in central Veracruz; and from the thriving urban capital of Teotihuacán, in central Mexico, influences radiated outward to all quarters of the Middle American area.

The breakdown of the Classic Period civilizations began with the destruction of the city of Teotihuacán at about AD 650. This commercial, political, and religious metropolis appears to have fallen before the warlike Toltecs, peoples of Uto-Aztecan speech who invaded central Mexico from the north and who established their capital at Tula, in Hidalgo. Between AD 700 and 900 southern Middle America was disturbed by wars and migrations, and the old regional cultures were seriously disrupted. These events were probably correlated with the further expansion of Nahua (Uto-Aztecan) tribes out of central Mexico and into Chiapas, Guatemala, and El Salvador.

Post-Classic Period. Four trends characterized the Post-Classic Period. First, there was a completion of the breakup of the old regional Classic Period cultures with their distinctive art and architectural styles and religious traditions. Second, the new Post-Classic cultures displayed more secular orientation. Third, fortifications, fortified sites, and an increase of warlike themes in art bespoke a more militaristic attitude throughout much of Middle America. Fourth, the urban-type community, which first appeared in the Late Formative and was known through the Classic Period, was emphasized even more than previously.

In the later Post-Classic Period, Tenochtitlán, the Aztec capital, located where Mexico City now stands, became the dominant force in Middle America. An Aztec state or empire reached from coast to coast through central and south Mexico; however, many tributary nations were held by the Aztecs in rather loose bonds, and when Hernán Cortés marched from Veracruz to Tenochtitlán he was aided by tribes anxious to free themselves from the Aztec yoke. In the Maya lowlands the Toltec-controlled centre of Chichén-Itzá lost its position of leadership at about AD 1200. Thereafter, there seems to have been something of a Maya resurgence with the Yucatecan capital being eventually established at the walled city of Mayapán.

The Aztec capital at Tenochtitlán

EVOLUTION OF LOWER CENTRAL AMERICA

Lower Central America—eastern Honduras, Nicaragua, Costa Rica, and Panama—lies outside of the Middle American culture area. For the greater part, its peoples, languages, and cultures are more closely allied with northwestern South America than with upper Central America and Mexico.

At the historic horizon, in the 16th century, tribes of Chibchan linguistic affiliation lived in what is now Panama, Costa Rica, and most of Nicaragua. These tribes, from south to north, included the Cuna, Guaymí, Boruca, Talamanca, Ulva, Sumo, Matagalpa, and Mosquito. In central and eastern Honduras were the Lenca, Jicaque, and Paya. The language of the Lenca appears distantly related to that of the Mayan and Nahua tribes, but Jicaque and Paya are unaffiliated languages. Along the west coast of Nicaragua and extending down into northwest Costa Rica were tribes of Middle American linguistic ties such as the Chorotega (of Macro-Oto-Manguean language stock) and the Nicarao (of Nahua or Uto-Aztecan stock).

Earliest evidences of human occupation in lower Central America come from Panama, where shell-mound food collectors and fishers of the northwest South American littoral tradition lived at about 4000 BC. Their way of life changed but little over the next two or three thousand years, although during this same period they acquired and practiced the art of making simple plain or incised pottery.

The earliest Panamanian pottery, that of the Monagrillo culture, dates back to 2100 BC and is found in a context of the northwest South American littoral tradition; but between this early, presumably nonagricultural, ceramic horizon and that of much later pottery-making cultures of the first millennium AD there is a gap in the archaeological record. What appears to be lacking are pottery horizons that would correspond to the Middle and Late Formative Period levels of southern Middle America. Some investigations in Pacific Nicaragua and northwestern Costa Rica have helped to fill this gap. Pottery phases have been found in these regions which date to about the first century AD. The ceramic styles of these phases are distinct in themselves but do bear some resemblances to Middle Formative Period wares from farther north. Chronologically, of course, they are substantially later; but this could be due to a time lag in the diffusion of pottery form and decorative ideas from southern Middle America southward. Later Lower Central American styles, such as the Coclé of Panama and the Chiriquí of Panama and Costa Rica, are probably in part derivative of these 1st century AD pottery complexes although they also show many new and distinctive elements of design that may be of northern South American origin. Specific Middle American influences appear, again, on a relatively late level (after AD 900). These are seen in the forms and designs of pottery styles and are believed to be derived from Nahua tribal migrations down the Pacific coast of Nicaragua and Costa Rica.

In general, goldwork, cast as ornaments, was of outstanding quality in lower Central America, particularly in Panama and Costa Rica. Metallurgy apparently reached these regions from Andean South America before metals were known in Middle America. (G.R.W./Ed.)

European exploration and conquest

THE EARLY NORSEMEN

The first Europeans to discover North America were probably Norsemen, or Vikings, part of the population movement that took Scandinavians to Normandy, England, Scotland, Ireland, and the islands to the north and west between AD 700 and 1100. They were pirates, plunderers, traders, and settlers attracted by fair lands and fishing grounds or driven by population pressures or by the wrath of rivals or rulers at home. About 1070 Adam of Bremen wrote of Norse discoveries in North America, and references to the continent appear in the Icelandic annals of the next several centuries. But the *Saga of Eiríkr the Red* and the *Saga of the Greenlanders* are the major sources, and they differ considerably in the events that they relate. Although the *Saga of Eiríkr the Red* was for years considered the more reliable, modern research has tended to show the *Saga of the Greenlanders* to be the older. According to the latter, Bjarni Herjulfsson discovered North America in 986, when driven off course while sailing from Iceland to the Greenland settlements. About 1000 (perhaps in 1002 or 1003) Leif Eriksson sailed west from Greenland and gave the names Helluland, Markland, and Vinland to sections of the American coast as he moved south. Leif wintered in Vinland and on his return, his brother Thorvald voyaged there and was killed by natives. About 1020 Thorfinn Karlsefni sailed for Vinland with three ships, taking domestic animals and women with him, and spent three winters in the new lands. After Karlsefni's return, Leif's half sister, Freydis, led an expedition to Vinland marred by vicious murders.

Early accounts of voyages to North America

Locating the routes, landfalls, and camps of the Vikings has stirred controversy because the evidence is fragmentary and contradictory. Also the Norse era apparently coincided with centuries of milder climate in northern latitudes; thus the vegetational clues in the sagas are misleading. Writers have suggested many locations for the Viking camps in northeastern North America. The authenticity of artifacts of alleged Viking origin, such as the Kensington Stone found in Minnesota and the Beardmore weapons found in western Ontario, is questionable. In 1961, however, Helge Ingstad found a settlement site of Norse style at L'Anse aux Meadows, Newfoundland. By the use of radiocarbon dating it was determined that the site was from the Viking era, and a Norse spindle whorl indicated the presence of women.

The Vinland map, published in 1965, has been described as "the only surviving graphic record" of the Norse voyages "to contain any element of experience." (R.A. Skelton *et al., The Vinland Map and the Tartar Relation,* p. 239, Yale University Press, 1965.) It dates probably from 1431 to 1449, and the writing that appears on the map supports Bjarni Herjulfsson's role, which has hitherto sometimes been questioned. It also suggests the presence in medieval Iceland of more evidence concerning Vinland than has survived, and it strengthens the possibility that relevant information may have passed through English sailors to Bristol or even reached Spain and Portugal before North America was rediscovered.

THE AGE OF DISCOVERY

Europeans entered an age of geographical discovery during the 15th century, reflecting developments in economic, social, and political life under way for some centuries. Merchant groups had developed in western Europe, eager to expand trade and able to finance increasingly ambitious ventures. Most valuable of trade goods were the spices, coming overland from the Orient to the eastern end of the Mediterranean. Because Italian merchants controlled the spice trade, merchants to the northwest wished to find new routes to the East.

The intellectual climate was prepared for an Age of Discovery by Renaissance scholars who developed an interest in the natural world, reviewed the speculations of the Greeks about the Earth, and hazarded their own. At the same time Europeans were advancing in ship construction and improving navigational aids. After the first discoveries the new printing press allowed wide distribution of explorers' accounts. The rise of national states—Portugal, Spain, France, England, and the united Netherlands—contributed also to the Age of Discovery. Monarchs encouraged exploring ventures in hope of increasing trade and acquiring treasure or territory. In the tradition of militant Christianity, Europeans wished to convert the non-Christians of the world. With the coming of the Reformation in the early 16th century, moreover, religious differences sharpened national rivalries as Protestants sought to outstrip the Roman Catholic Spanish and Portuguese, whose kings had divided the newly discovered areas of the world between themselves with papal approval in the Treaty of Tordesillas of 1494.

Early Spanish explorations. In 1492 Christopher Columbus reached the Bahama Islands with three ships, proceeding then to Cuba and La Española (Hispaniola). A native of Genoa, Columbus sailed under a commission from the Spanish crown. Encouraged by tales of lands beyond the Canary Islands and stories of Oriental riches, Columbus accepted the theory that the Earth was spherical and sought the East by sailing west. He was probably motivated by a sense of Christian mission and a desire to rule new lands as Spanish governor, to win riches, and to be known as a great geographer. Returning to Spain, Columbus maintained that he had reached the eastern fringe of Asia. Although he traversed much of the Caribbean and traced the mainland coast from Honduras to the Isthmus of Panama in three subsequent voyages, Columbus found no passage to Cathay, the medieval name for China. As governor of the Indies he also failed, but his discoveries of gold and pearls drew others, and the royal fifth of such treasure interested the Spanish rulers.

Voyages of Christopher Columbus

Based on La Española, Spanish captains probed the Caribbean, the Gulf of Mexico, and Central America, hoping to find a wesern passage, to establish principalities, and to exploit local resources. Shortly after 1500, King Ferdinand V of Spain gave rights of conquest and government on the Mosquito Coast and the adjacent South American coastline to two adventurers, Diego de Nicuesa and Alonso de Ojeda. From their ventures, initially plagued by disease, dissension, and hostile Indians, emerged Vasco Núñez de Balboa, who led a force across the isthmus to the Gulf of Panama in 1513. From the isthmus, captains worked north along the Pacific and Caribbean shores.

By 1516 Diego Velázquez de Cuéllar had subjugated Cuba, and he directed the attention of his lieutenants to the mainland. In 1519 Hernán Cortés led the third of such expeditions. Retracing the routes of his predecessors along the Gulf of Campeche, Cortés burned his boats at Veracruz and penetrated the mountains with a small force to Tenochtitlán (Mexico City), the Aztec capital of Montezuma II.

By astute diplomacy, brilliant soldiering, and adept handling of Indian allies Cortés broke and plundered the rich Aztec empire. Ignoring Velázquez in Cuba, Cortés became governor of the new region, established himself at Mexico City, and subdued the surrounding territories. During the mid-1520s his men clashed in Honduras with forces from the isthmus. The general outlines and topography of Central American and southern Mexico were now becoming clear.

Some Spanish adventurers pushed north from La Española. In 1513 Juan Ponce de León threaded the Bahamas and skirted peninsular Florida. Alonso de Pineda (1519) traced the shore of the Gulf of Mexico from the Florida keys to the Pánuco River in Mexico. During 1524–25 the Portuguese Esteban Gomes coasted from the Grand Banks

Expeditions to the continental interior

to Florida in Spanish service. Later expeditions probed the continental a large party in Florida in 1528. Eight years later, four survivors, two of whom were Álvar Núñez Cabeza de Vaca and Esteban (Estévan), a slave, reached northern Mexico after walking from Galveston Bay. Núñez Cabeza de Vaca's tale encouraged minds inflamed by stories of rich Inca treasure and Indian legends of the seven golden cities of Cibola.

Expeditions begun by Hernando de Soto and Marcos de Niza in 1539 and by Francisco Vázquez de Coronado in 1540 followed routes that stretched, when combined, from the Grand Canyon to the Savannah River, ascended the Mississippi valley beyond the Ohio, and linked the upper waters of the Brazos to the Kansas River. Early major Spanish explorations were completed in 1542–43 when Juan Rodríguez Cabrillo and Bartolomé Ferrelo surveyed the Pacific coast from lower California to a point beyond latitude 42° N, although minor figures explored in the eastern Appalachians and the southwest after 1550.

French, English, and Dutch explorations before 1772. While the Spanish exploited the lower latitudes, other European captains ranged the northern coasts. Such was the voyage of the Genoese John Cabot in 1497, backed by the British crown and Bristol merchants and believed to be the second Bristol expedition to reach North America after 1480. Subsequent English, Portuguese, and French expeditions found little of interest until the Frenchman Jacques Cartier ascended the St. Lawrence River in a series of expeditions beginning in 1534. But he found no treasure, and interest in the interior waned. In 1578–79 Sir Francis Drake explored the Pacific coast of North America to 48° N seeking a passage to the East. Increasingly, however, Frenchmen and Basques fished the Gulf of St. Lawrence and incidentally began a trade in furs with the natives. American furs, particularly beaver, were sufficiently popular in Europe by 1600 that the French king tried to nurture the trade by assigning it as a monopoly to favoured merchants.

Adapted from Harold E. Davis, *The Americans in History*, The Ronald Press Company (1953)

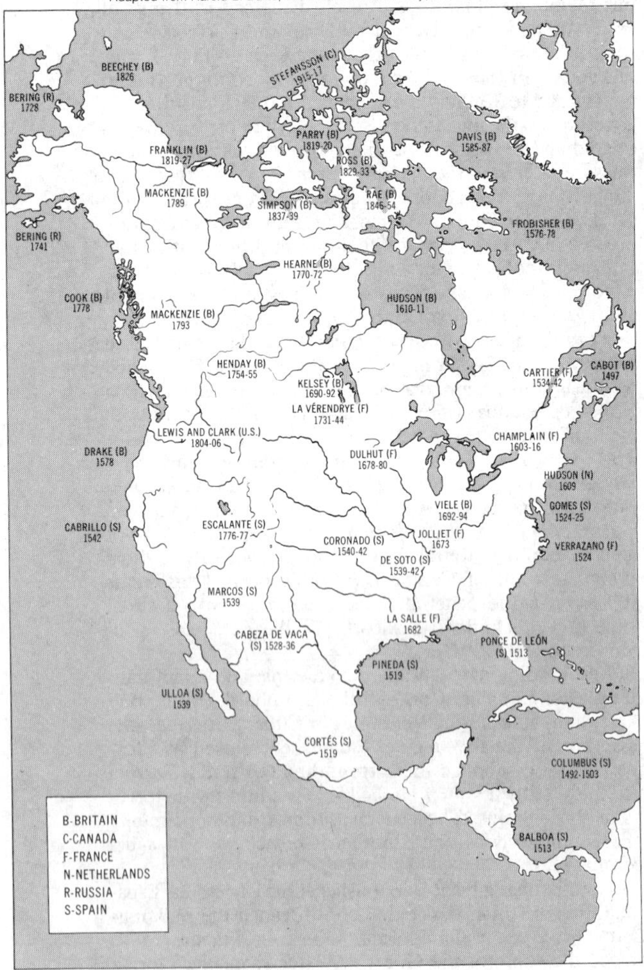

General locations and dates of the most important discoveries of the principal explorers of North America.

French fur traders founded Port Royal in 1605, but in 1608 Quebec became the centre of the trade. From there the governor of French Canada, Samuel de Champlain, hoped also to discover a Pacific passage. The fur trade also drew the French into the interior since it was always profitable to forestall tribes seeking to act as middlemen. After 1615 the desire of the Recollet (Franciscan), Jesuit, and Sulpician religious orders to Christianize the Indians contributed to exploration. But the hostile Five Nations of the Iroquois, west of the Hudson and below the St. Lawrence and Lake Ontario, impeded the French. Allies of the Dutch at Fort Orange, these Iroquoians fought the northern tribes friendly with the French. Because of the Iroquois the French initially avoided the lower Great Lakes and followed the Ottawa River into the interior, traversing to Georgian Bay. From the explorations of Champlain, of subordinates like Étienne Brulé, and of the missionaries, the French, in 1650, understood the St. Lawrence–Great Lakes system in a general way, although western Lake Superior and southern Lake Michigan were unexplored. They knew also of both the Hudson and the Susquehanna River routes to the sea and had heard of a northern sea beyond the Laurentian divide.

Iroquois opposition to French exploration

During the 1660s, French activities impinged on those of the English. Annoyed by trading restrictions in new France and by the hampering Iroquois, Pierre Esprit Radisson and Médard Chouart des Groseilliers sought British backing to establish a northern trade outlet, having perhaps been themselves to James Bay. As a result, Englishmen organized the Hudson's Bay Company. They were already familiar with the approaches to Hudson Bay and its general character through the efforts of English explorers, including Sir Martin Frobisher, John Davis, and Henry Hudson, who had all sought a northwest passage to the Orient around 1600.

The French now attempted to widen their sovereignty in North America. During 1671–72, Paul-Denis, sieur de Saint-Simon, followed the Saguenay and Rupert rivers to James Bay. Simon-François Daumont, sieur de Saint-Lusson, proclaimed French rule of interior North America at Sault Sainte-Marie in 1671. Daniel Greysolon, sieur Dulhut (Duluth), declared French sovereignty at Lake Mille Lacs (in present Minnesota) and descended the Saint Croix and Mississippi rivers to the Wisconsin River while rescuing Father Louis Hennepin from the Sioux Indians. The French also tried to push south to Spanish territory in order to confine the British settlements along the Atlantic coast. In 1673 Louis Jolliet and the Jesuit Jacques Marquette followed the Fox–Wisconsin traverse from Green Bay and descended the Mississippi almost to the Arkansas River, returning by the Illinois River to Lake Michigan. Nine years later René-Robert Cavelier, sieur de La Salle, descended to the mouth of the Mississippi and claimed the whole region, which he named Louisiana, for France.

Exploration of the Mississippi by Jolliet and Marquette

After reaching the lower Mississippi valley, the French sought trade connections with the Spanish settlements. Notable in this effort were the expeditions of Louis Juchereau de Saint-Denis from Natchitoches, Louisiana, to San Juan Bautista (Villahermosa), Mexico, in 1714; of Bernard de la Harpe along the Red, Arkansas, and Canadian rivers between 1719 and 1722; and of Pierre and Paul Mallet. Beginning in the winter of 1738–39 the Mallet brothers followed the Missouri, the Platte, and the South Platte rivers into the high plains, angled southwest to the area of present-day Taos and Santa Fe and returned to the Mississippi along the Canadian and Arkansas rivers. In the northern plains Pierre Gaultier de Varennes, sieur de La Vérendrye, countered British competition by pushing trading posts beyond Lake Superior, baiting his request for a western trading monopoly by promising to seek the Western sea. Between 1731 and 1744, La Vérendrye and his sons discovered and described lakes Winnipeg, Winnipegosis, and Manitoba and their relation to the major rivers of the region. They reached the Black Hills and mapped the upper Missouri River but decided that the Saskatchewan River provided the best route to the Pacific.

While the French ranged from James Bay to the Gulf of Mexico, the British and Dutch explored below the Great Lakes and east of the Mississippi. Englishmen established Jamestown in 1607, and the Dutch occupied the Hudson River valley following its discovery by Henry Hudson in 1609. By 1650 fur traders were searching for passes through the Appalachian barrier. During 1671 Virginians discovered the upper Kanawha. Two years later James Needham reached a Cherokee village on the upper Tennessee River and accompanied braves to the Kanawha and the Ohio rivers and to the junction of the Chattahoochee and the Flint rivers. During 1692–94 Arnout Cornelius Viele from Albany descended the Ohio, perhaps to the Mississippi. During the late 1690s, Carolinians reached the junction of the Arkansas and Mississippi rivers and followed an expatriate French trader, Jean Couture, down the Tennessee to the Ohio. Carolinian competition with French and Spanish in the Gulf hinterland revealed the topography of this region.

Initially the Hudson's Bay Company showed little interest in the interior, allowing superior trade goods to draw the Indians to Hudson Bay. Henry Kelsey's expedition during 1690–92 was an exception to this policy. Kelsey ascended the Hayes River from York Factory, crossed the head of Lake Winnipeg and explored beyond Lake Winnipegosis. Spurred by French activity, the company sent Anthony Henday into the interior in 1754. He pushed beyond longitude 113° W between the major branches of the Saskatchewan River. Seeking in 1770–72 to locate the source of copper brought by Indians to company posts, Samuel Hearne reached the lower Coppermine River, crossing Great Slave Lake to strike the Slave River while returning. Hearne's discoveries long discouraged exploration in the barren lands northeast of his route.

Pacific Coast, Northwest, and Arctic explorations. Russian interest in the relation of Asia to North America prompted exploration in the early 18th century. Vitus Jonassen Bering, although his achievement was disparaged, traversed Bering Strait in 1728. Both he and Aleksey Chirikov reached southern Alaska in 1741, and Russian traders began the China trade in Aleutian sea otter and seal. Russian efforts provoked response from Spain, Great Britain, France, and ultimately the United States.

By sea, Spanish expeditions of 1774 and 1775 coasted from California to latitude 57° N. Capt. James Cook cruised from Oregon to Bering Strait in 1778, seeking the terminus of a northwest passage. After his death the expedition reached latitude 70°44″. Official Russian, Spanish, British, and French expeditions and numerous traders probed the northwestern coast after 1785. On land, the Spanish pushed their settlements to San Francisco Bay during the 1760s and 1770s, exploring back from the coast in the process and seeking trails to link this frontier to Santa Fe and Taos. During 1776–77 Father Silvestre Vêlez de Escalante led a notable expedition from Sante Fe northwest to Utah Lake, southwest to Sevier Lake, and the upper Virgin River, and back to Santa Fe.

On the northern plains, the North West Company of Montreal replaced the French fur traders after New France passed to Great Britain in 1763. Seeking to forestall the Hudson's Bay Company and to tap the fur fields of the Russians, Alexander (later Sir Alexander) Mackenzie descended the Mackenzie River from Great Slave Lake to the Arctic Ocean in 1789. In 1793 he followed the Peace River into the Rocky Mountains, traversed to the Fraser River, and then cut overland to the Pacific.

The Lewis and Clark Expedition

After the United States purchased Louisiana, the official Lewis and Clark expedition ascended the Missouri, crossed from the Jefferson fork to the Pacific slope, and reached the mouth of the Columbia in 1805. Traders and trappers soon explored the American Rockies and Great Basin. To the north, British traders explored the Fraser and upper Columbia and entered the upper Yukon country. Meanwhile, representatives of the Russian-American Company probed interior Alaska. After 1850 exploration in the American and British western possessions became increasingly scientific, culminating in the establishment of official geological surveys.

Prior to 1818 explorers by sea in the north had stopped short of Point Barrow and on land had reached the Arctic coast only at the Mackenzie and the Coppermine rivers. In the next 40 years, the British Admiralty, the Hudson's Bay Company, and private scientific ventures changed the situation. The land-based expeditions of Sir John Franklin, John Rae, and Thomas Simpson explored much coastline between Point Barrow and the Melville Peninsula. On sea, Frederick W. Beechey filled the gap west of Point Barrow; Lieut. William (later Sir William) Edward Parry sailed from Baffin Bay to Melville Island; and Sir John Ross explored the Boothia Peninsula and, with his nephew James (later Sir James) Clark Ross, located the North Magnetic Pole. When Sir John Franklin sought the northwest passage in 1845, ice trapped his ships south of Prince of Wales Island, and the crews perished. During the next decade searching parties amassed information about the Arctic. But not until 1903–06 did Roald Amundsen sail from the Atlantic to the Pacific north of the continent, and only in 1915–16 did Vilhjalmur Stefansson discover the last major islands at the north of the Canadian archipelago.

European settlement and development

Although Swedish and Dutch traders established colonies on the Delaware and the Hudson during the 17th century and Russian traders were active on the west coast of North America for more than a century, their contributions in settling North America were minor in comparison to those of the Spanish, French, and English.

SPANISH SETTLEMENT

During the 16th century, individuals willing to organize expeditions and transport colonists obtained contracts from the Spanish crown, allowing them to exploit regions in North America. Although the contracts conveyed extensive rights of government and economic privileges, the authority of these impresarios was usually soon challenged by royal officials. After 1535 the Viceroyalty of New Spain provided the major frame of government for Spanish holdings in the Caribbean and on the mainland, north of the Isthmus of Panama.

Migration of Spanish citizens

Dissatisfaction with prospects at home, together with a desire to find adventure and wealth, or to carry Christianity and European culture abroad, brought Spaniards to the New World. Impresarios and sometimes the crown encouraged such movement, although only Spanish citizens of undoubted orthodoxy could migrate. By 1570 the white population of New Spain numbered about 54,000, mainly of Andalusian antecedents. The possibility of riches, the sophistication of many natives, and exigencies of the climate encouraged the Spanish to use Indian labour widely. The crown soon forbade Indian slavery, but it persisted; and other systems of forced labour also evolved. Spanish arms, European diseases, and the new regimen almost extinguished the island natives, whom the Spanish replaced by African slaves. There were more than 93,500 Africans and mestizos in New Spain by 1570. Although the mainland Indians also decreased in numbers, they always dominated the population, numbering about 3,000,000 in 1570. Spanish settlement was characterized by considerable miscegenation.

The success of Cortés caused an exodus from the Caribbean islands. The Greater Antilles developed a prosperous sugar plantation economy, but smaller islands remained unoccupied. After the initial conquests, Spanish settlement on the mainland reflected mining and agricultural opportunities and strategic considerations. The preliminary conquest was complete in Central America by 1600, but portions of the region remained unconquered in 1700. By 1600 Spanish colonization, pushing north from the valley of Mexico, had reached points due west of the mouth of the Rio Grande. Although silver and gold mines like those of Zacatecas produced concentrations of population, much grain and livestock was produced in New Spain. Dominican, Franciscan, and Jesuit missions helped subdue the Indians in frontier regions. At times, colonies of Europeanized Indians were moved to the frontier to assist soldier and missionary.

After Huguenot colonization on the Florida coast threatened Spanish shipping in the Bahama channel, the Spanish finally occupied Florida during the 1560s. Missionary efforts in Virginia failed, but missions along the Carolina and Georgia coasts survived. At the end of the 16th century Juan de Oñate colonized New Mexico, and Santa Fe was established in 1610. During the 18th century the Spanish pushed their Pacific frontier from the Sonora region to San Francisco Bay.

SETTLEMENT OF THE BRITISH COLONIES AND BEYOND

After the Virginia Company of London founded Jamestown, the English established numerous colonies along the North American coast from Maine to Georgia and in the West Indies. Individuals and groups sought patents from the British crown conferring territorial and administrative privileges in the New World upon them. Economic opportunities attracted most colonial promoters, although experience in Virginia dispelled hope of matching Aztec treasure. But desire to modify Anglican church doctrines or to alleviate the condition of nonconformists and indigents influenced promoters in a number of colonies. The crown never closed the colonies to religious dissenters. Although companies or proprietors originally controlled the colonies, they were ultimately in most cases brought directly under the crown.

The English colonists engaged in farming, fishing, shipbuilding, and trade, with tobacco, rice, and indigo important in the southern mainland colonies and sugar plantations characterizing the West Indies. Although important, the mainland fur trade was never dominant. Mortality was high initially in Virginia and Plymouth, but emigration attracted Englishmen because of enclosures on estates in Britain, high land prices, dissatisfaction with the Stuart dynasty's religious policies, and the generous colonial systems of land disposal and government. Many emigrated as indentured servants. During the 1630s a large Puritan migration arrived in Massachusetts, soon itself supplying emigrants for Connecticut, Rhode Island, and New Hampshire. A British Quaker migration began to develop Pennsylvania in 1682. Germans and Scottish-Irish came after 1700 to settle mainly in Pennsylvania and the colonies to the south. Scottish, Welsh, and Huguenot settlers arrived also. After 1600 many African slaves were brought to the southern colonies. By 1760 the colonies in North America were supporting about 2,000,000 inhabitants of European and African origin.

Westward expansion of settlement

Indian relations, land policy, topography, soil fertility, and a number of minor factors modified settlement. The agricultural frontier was in the piedmont region until 1700 and was roughly marked by the Allegheny Mountains until 1800. The Mississippi River provided the frontier of the early 19th century in the United States. During the 1840s pioneers established the Oregon, Utah, and California settlements. Subsequently miners flocked to the cordilleras as a succession of gold and silver strikes followed the California discoveris of 1848. Between 1860 and 1900 farmers occupied the high plains. Established settlements provided settlers for new lands, the pioneers migrating generally along isothermal lines. Immigration to the United States averaged about 10,000 annually between 1790 and 1830: by the 1850s the average inflow had risen to slightly more than 280,000 people yearly; and during the 1890s it was almost 370,000. Many immigrants remained in the older regions, but Germans, Scandinavians, and British particularly helped to settle the northern territories and states. The small farms and urban orientation of these regions apparently attracted the foreign-born more strongly than did the systems of slavery and plantation agriculture prevalent in the southern section of the United States before the Civil War.

From Sanford-Gordy, American History Series; reproduced by permission of A.J. Nystrom & Co.

Areas claimed by Britain, France, and Spain in North America in 1750.

SETTLEMENT OF THE FRENCH COLONIES AND CANADA

French settlements developed in New France (Canada) and Acadia (the coast of Nova Scotia) on the North American mainland. The fur traders, required to transport colonists under their trading monopolies, performed these obligations unsatisfactorily. There were only 1,800 French on the Bay of Fundy when Acadia passed to England in 1713. Ineffective administration by the merchant company holding the fur monopoly in New France led the crown to assume direct control in 1663 when the colony numbered about 2,500. Thereafter settlers were obtained by offering free passage and land on easy terms and by inducing French soldiers to remain in New France. The government conveyed women from France as wives for settlers, and seigneurs brought in colonists to work their land grants. For a time during the 18th century, French criminals were transported to the colony. After 1680 the population grew mainly from natural increase. Since royal policy barred dissenters and French agriculture experienced few disruptive changes, little interest in emigration developed in France. Settlement in New France spread out from Quebec, Trois-Rivières, and Montreal along the St. Lawrence, penetrating the back country along the Richelieu River but little elsewhere. Although primarily a farming settlement by the 18th century, New France produced little surplus, and the fur trade dominated its commerce.

Settlement along the St. Lawrence

Established in 1699, Louisiana developed under a merchant proprietor and later the Compagnie des Indes Occidentales. In 1731 it became a royal province and was enlarged to include the Illinois country. The fur trade, agriculture, and lead mining in Missouri occupied the residents.

By 1760 the French mainland colonies of North America had a European population of about 80,000, while the French West Indies numbered an additional 45,000, plus about 300,000 slaves. Aside from the French nucleus, Great Britain (then including Ireland) and the American colonies provided most of the settlers for the British provinces that ultimately amalgamated as the Dominion of Canada. During the 1760s New Englanders moved to Nova Scotia, and merchants from New York and New England established communities in Quebec and Montreal. The American Revolution caused Loyalists to migrate to Upper Canada,

Nova Scotia, and New Brunswick. Between 1790 and 1815 many settlers from the United States entered Upper and Lower Canada. After 1815 immigration from the British Isles became important, including Irish famine refugees and Scottish crofters (tenant farmers). The Fraser River gold rush in 1858 drew a polyglot population to British Columbia, but this province developed slowly. Although Thomas Douglas, 5th earl of Selkirk, established a colony of Scottish settlers in the valley of the Red River of the North in 1812, and the fur trade left some retired servants and métis, or half-breeds, few settlers entered the Canadian prairies before 1890. The government actively promoted the region, and by 1930 settlers from the older provinces, from the United States, Great Britain, and western and central Europe had occupied most of the arable land.

Major territorial adjustments from the 18th to the 20th century

The European monarchs assumed that their sovereignty followed their nationals in the New World; but colonial policies, European wars, and American rivalries produced territorial adjustments in North America. While the Spanish concentrated on the mainland, English, French, Dutch, and Danes seized unoccupied Caribbean islands, from the Bahamas to the Windward group, during the 17th century. In 1655 the British occupied Spanish-held Jamaica and subsequently gained footholds on the Honduras and Mosquito coasts. The French gained the uninhabited portions of Haiti.

During 1664 England seized New Netherland (renamed New York) and in 1713 acquired French claims to Acadia, Newfoundland, and Rupert's Land, the region draining into Hudson Bay. In 1763, after the Seven Years' War, France ceded all mainland territory east of the Mississippi to Great Britain and west of that river to Spain. Concurrently Spain surrendered Florida to the British. Following the American Revolution, the United States in 1783 obtained the territory south of Canada, and east of the Mississippi, while Spain regained Florida.

Napoleon wrested Louisiana from Spain in 1800, but revolt in Haiti jeopardized French plans in America and paved the way for the independence ultimately of Haiti and the Dominican Republic. The United States purchased Louisiana from France in 1803. The Spanish transferred Florida to the United States in the treaty of 1819, the United States accepting here also a western boundary for Louisiana that left Texas in Spanish hands.

The Louisiana Purchase

Beginning in 1810 revolution shattered the Spanish empire in America. On the mainland Mexico, Guatemala, El Salvador, Honduras, Nicaragua, and Costa Rica emerged, although the countries of Central America together formed the United Provinces of Central America between 1823 and 1839.

In 1835 settlers from the United States in Texas revolted, proclaiming a republic that gained admission to the United States in 1845. After a short war with the United States, Mexico in 1848 renounced claims to Texas and also ceded New Mexico and upper California. In 1853 the United States acquired by the Gadsden Purchase additional Mexican territory lying south of the Gila River.

The boundary between the United States and the northern British provinces was extended along the 49th parallel beyond Lake of the Woods to the crest of the Rockies in 1818 and to the Pacific in 1846. Meanwhile the disputed Maine–New Brunswick boundary was fixed in 1842. Russia and Great Britain set the interior boundary of Alaska by treaty in 1825, and Russia sold this region to the United States in 1867.

Important changes in territorial administration occurred in the British provinces after 1860. In 1867 Nova Scotia and New Brunswick joined Canada (modern Ontario and Quebec), in the Dominion of Canada. Canada purchased Rupert's Land from the Hudson's Bay Company in 1869; British Columbia joined the federation in 1871, Prince Edward Island in 1873, and Newfoundland, including Labrador, in 1949.

Following the Spanish–American War in 1898, Cuba gained independence from Spain, and Puerto Rico was ceded to the United States (as were Guam and the Philippines). Panama declared its independence from Colombia in 1903 and granted a Canal Zone to the United States—the zone reverting to Panamanian sovereignty in 1979. The United States purchased the Virgin Islands from Denmark in 1917.

(A.G.Bo./Ed.)

GEOGRAPHICAL FEATURES OF SPECIAL INTEREST

Mountain ranges

ALASKAN MOUNTAINS

A northwestward continuation of the Western Cordilleras, or Rocky Mountains, and the Pacific coastal ranges of North America, the Alaskan mountains give their state a rugged and beautiful terrain across nearly its entire expanse. They include the highest peak in North America. The ranges are characterized both by glaciers and by continuing volcanic activity. Little explored for vast stretches, the mountains are believed to contain, or lie close to, immense untapped mineral resources whose exploitation is hampered by the terrain and the climate.

Brooks Range

The most northerly of the three major Alaskan mountain groups are the Brooks Range and the Arctic foothills, extending the Rocky Mountains in an east–west arc from the Canadian border across northern Alaska. Central Alaska is characterized by highlands and basins drained by the great Yukon and Kuskokwim drainage systems. This area has been likened by some to a moister version of the arid region known as the Great Basin—an area that takes in nearly all of Nevada and portions of all contiguous U.S. states—although here the precipitation and resulting vegetation have rounded the rugged topographic expression of mountains and valleys.

Southern Alaska is dominated by an arc of mountain ranges encircling the Gulf of Alaska and the northeastern Pacific in a broad sweep. This Pacific mountain province is subdivided into several groups. The large Alaska Range merges southwestward into the Aleutian Range and the Aleutian Islands. Separated from the Alaska Range by the Talkeetna and Wrangell mountains, the Kenai–Chugach mountains border the Gulf of Alaska and merge, to the south and east, with the St. Elias Mountains at the Canadian border. These, in turn, merge with the mountains of the coastal ranges, which form most of the Alaskan Panhandle.

Physical features. *Physiography and geology.* The Arctic foothills, just north of the Brooks Range, consist of low east–west trending ridges and rolling plateaus with irregular isolated hills. They rise from 600 feet (180 metres) in the north to 3,500 feet (1,100 metres) in the south. Except for the east-flowing Colville River, most drainage is northward. The entire area is underlain by permafrost, a permanently frozen, rock-hard soil, and no glaciers are present. This region is as structurally complex as the higher Brooks Range immediately to the south, but formed of less resistant rocks. The youngest rocks, in the northern section, are sediments from the Cretaceous Period (136,000,000 to 65,000,000 years ago). They are folded, faulted, and overthrust toward the north. Sediments from the Devonian Period (beginning 395,000,000 years ago) to the Cretaceous Period form the southern section of the foothills. They are tightly folded and also overthrust northward.

The Brooks Range is the highest mountain range within the Arctic Circle. It includes groups of mountains extending about 600 miles (1,000 kilometres) from the Canadian border to the Chukchi Sea. These form several groups of mountains, individually named. Average altitudes range from 3,000 to 4,000 feet in the west to 5,000–6,000 feet in the east, with a high point of 9,239 feet (2,816 metres)

Average altitudes

in Mt. Michelson. The entire area has been glaciated, as is evidenced by the rugged topography. Several small glaciers are still present in the east, fewer in the west.

The range forms the drainage divide between waters flowing northward into the Arctic Ocean, those flowing westward into Kotzebue Sound, and those flowing south into the Yukon and its tributaries and emptying into the Bering Sea. Several major rivers have cut back into the range to form low passes, the best known being Anaktuvuk Pass, at an elevation of 2,200 feet (670 metres) in the central part of the range. The Dietrich River Pass has been suggested as a corridor connecting the oil-producing areas of the north slope with interior Alaska and the south.

The backbone of the range is composed of sedimentary and metamorphic rocks—respectively, rocks formed from deposits of various organic or inorganic materials and rocks heavily compacted and made more crystalline by the action of heat, pressure, or water. They were formed in the Paleozoic Era (from 570,000,000 to 225,000,000 years ago). Younger sedimentary rocks, of the Permian Period (from 280,000,000 to 225,000,000 years ago) and the Mesozoic Era (from 225,000,000 to 65,000,000 years ago) flank the range. The mountains were lifted by major upward foldings in the Earth's crust, called orogenies, beginning in the Late Jurassic Period (190,000,000 to 136,000,000 years ago). The process persisted in periodic uplifts throughout the Cretaceous and into the early part of the Tertiary Period (from 65,000,000 to 25,000,000 years ago). It was again strongly deformed and uplifted in the late Tertiary. The folding, faulting, and major overthrusting toward the north during these orogenies were modified by erosion and glaciation. Most of the area is underlain by permafrost. There are a few lakes in rock basins.

The mountains of central Alaska, extending from the Canadian border to the Bering Sea, are lower than the ranges to the north and south. They are drained almost entirely by two river systems, the Yukon and the Kuskokwim. The intricately dissected uplands are divided into three areas: the eastern highlands, the western highlands, and the Seward Peninsula.

The eastern highlands, consisting of several separate chains, have an average altitude of 4,000–5,000 feet, with a few mountains rising 1,000–2,000 feet above these uplands. Some peaks are as high as 6,800 feet (2,075 metres) in the east. No glaciers are present in the region, and permafrost is discontinuous. The underlying rocks are highly deformed metamorphic and sedimentary and of volcanic origin dating from the Precambrian (4,600,000,000 to 570,000,000 years ago) and Paleozoic eras. The higher parts are commonly composed of small, resistant segments of granite that were forced, or intruded, into the other rocks while in a molten state.

Scenic glacial lakes

The western highlands, also subdivided into several smaller groups, are somewhat lower, rolling, and monotonous mountains, with northeast-trending ridges. Numerous isolated, nearly circular groups of mountains rise above these ridges. The rocks include tightly folded Paleozoic and Mesozoic sediments and volcanics and Tertiary intrusions. Although no glaciers are now present, the Ahklun Mountains are the largest glaciated area in interior Alaska, and the Wood River–Tikchik region has beautiful parallel glacial lakes and is considered one of the most scenic areas in the state.

The upland area of the Seward Peninsula, which is only a few miles across the Bering Strait from the Soviet Union, is made up of broad, convex hills and ridges, with an average altitude of about 2,000 feet (600 metres), and surmounted by more rugged mountain groups. A few peaks rise above 3,000 feet (900 metres), the highest 4,720 feet (1,440 metres), in the Kigluaik Mountains in the southwestern part of the peninsula. The entire area is underlain by permafrost. The rocks are early Paleozoic metamorphics, Cretaceous sediments, and intrusions of Mesozoic igneous, or once-molten, rock.

The Alaska–Aleutian ranges, together with the Talkeetna and Wrangell mountains, the interior part of the St. Elias Mountains, and the coast ranges of southeastern Alaska, are geologically analogous in some respects to the Sierra–Cascade ranges of the western United States, of which they are regarded as the northwestern continuation.

The Alaska–Aleutian ranges extend in a great belt from the Canadian border, at first northwestward and then south and west to the Aleutian Islands. These islands comprise a chain of mountainous volcanic peaks, the crest of a huge submarine ridge 1,500 miles (2,400 kilometres) long and 20 to 60 miles wide, that rises 11,000 feet above the sea floor. Separating the Bering Sea from the Pacific Ocean, these islands stretch in a 1,100-mile-long arc from the Alaska Peninsula to Attu Island at the western end of the chain. With the Aleutian Range on the southeast side of the peninsula, they form a long, narrow belt of peaks for 1,600 miles from Attu to Mt. Spurr opposite the city of Anchorage. Nearly 80 volcanoes have been mapped in this chain, 47 of which have been reported active since 1760. Marine sedimentary rocks and granitic intrusions from the Mesozoic and Cenozoic eras (from 65,000,000 years ago), as well as Cenozoic volcanic rocks, form this range. Pavlof and Shishaldin volcanoes rival Japan's Fuji-san in the beauty of their symmetrical cones. Enormous calderas—collapsed craters marking past volcanic eruptions—are present. In 1912, one of the most spectacular of historic eruptions occurred when a volcano in the Aleutian Range erupted, forming the Valley of Ten Thousand Smokes, in what is now Katmai National Monument. Mt. Spurr erupted in 1954 and remains active, as do Mt. Redoubt (1968) and Mt. Augustine (1976).

The Alaska Range merges with the Aleutian Range between Iliamna Lake and Mt. Spurr and extends in an arc some 600 miles to the Canadian border at the southeast end. This great mountain wall is about 120 miles wide near Mt. Spurr and about 60 miles wide in the vicinity of Mt. McKinley. It gradually narrows to about 30 miles near the Canadian border. The range is extremely rugged and glaciated. The crest of most of the range averages between 7,000 and 9,000 feet with fewer than 20 peaks exceeding 10,000 feet. Mt. McKinley is 20,320 feet (6,194 metres) in altitude, the highest point in North America. Four great individual mountain masses dominate the group, divided by several low passes and river valleys, several of which provide routes of travel across the mountains. Great valley glaciers radiate from these mountain masses, except in the relatively low eastern sectors where the few glaciers are small. The Alaska Range is the drainage divide for rivers flowing north into the Yukon system and those flowing south into the Pacific Ocean.

Most of the Alaska Range is underlain by large deeply buried granitic intrusions (known as batholiths) into Paleozoic and Mesozoic sedimentary rocks that have been metamorphosed and deformed. The youngest deposits, of Cenozoic age, are only moderately deformed beds in which deposits of coal are present. Very long valleys and low passes, following the course of geological faults, lines of weakness in the earth's crust, extend almost parallel to the entire length of the range. The faults were probably formed near the close of the Mesozoic Era.

Between the Alaska Range and the coastal ranges lie the Talkeetna Mountains and, to the east of them, the Wrangell Mountains. The Talkeetnas, an oval, rugged area about 100 miles from north to south and 70 miles from east to west, is a compact group of radial ridges averaging from 6,000 to 8,800 feet in altitude. There are only a few low passes. The higher ridges are sharp-crested, but on the western flank, as the average height decreases, the ridge tops have been rounded and subdued by the glacial action of the Pleistocene Epoch (2,500,000 to 10,000 years ago). Small glaciers 5 to 15 miles long are still present at the heads of many valleys. The Talkeetnas consist of an igneous batholith intruded during the Mesozoic Era, with flanking Paleozoic and Mesozoic sediments and volcanics. Some Tertiary volcanic flows are present in the southeastern part.

The Wrangell Mountains, 100 by 70 miles, lie on the Pacific between the Alaska Range to the north and the Chugach Mountains to the south. They rise more than 10,000 feet above the Copper River Plateau. A large ice cap covers most of the high mountains and feeds large valley glaciers. This oval group is composed of composite volcanic mountains, which are resting on metamorphosed Paleozoic and Mesozoic sedimentary and igneous rocks. Some granitic masses intrude the Mesozoic rocks. Several volcanoes are at altitudes higher than 12,000 feet, the highest, Mt. Blackburn, at 16,390 feet (4,996 metres).

Encircling the Gulf of Alaska, from Kodiak Island in the west to Baranof Island in the southeast, is another bow-shaped, or arcuate, mountainous belt, 800 miles long and 20 to 110 miles wide. Kodiak Island and the Kenai and Chugach mountains form a rugged barrier along the northeast margin of the Pacific Ocean. The mountains of the Kodiak Island group, at average altitudes of 2,000 to 4,000 feet, trend northeasterly. Glaciation over most of the area has produced a very irregular coastline, but no glaciers are now present.

The average altitude of the Kenai Mountains is 3,000 to 5,000 feet, whereas the Chugach group to the north and east average 7,000 to 8,000 feet. The highest peaks are in the sharp bend of the arc, where Mt. Marcus Baker rises to 13,176 feet (4,016 metres). The mountains are extremely rugged and bear on their crests the last remnants of the ice fields from the Ice Age, the Sargent and Harding ice fields in the Kenai Mountains and the Bagley Ice Field in the eastern Chugach Mountains. Numerous long, spectacular glaciers descend from the crests of these mountains. The St. Elias Mountains and the Kenai–Chugach Mountains have the most extensive system of valley glaciers in North America.

Ice Age remnants

The arcuate form of the Kodiak–Kenai–Chugach belt is closely paralleled by the structural trends of the underlying rocks. The Mesozoic rocks, primarily marine sediments and volcanics, have been intensely metamorphosed, folded, faulted, and intruded by small-to-moderate-size igneous bodies. Along the coastal areas, in Kodiak and in the eastern part of the Chugach bordering the Gulf of Alaska, softer Tertiary marine sediments flank the higher mountains.

The Alaskan part of the St. Elias Mountains is topographically continuous with, and geologically similar to, the Chugach Mountains, and joins the southeastern panhandle to the rest of the state. The St. Elias chain, among the highest coastal mountains in the world, is about 200 miles long and has a maximum width of about 100 miles. The chain merges with the Chugach group near the Alaska–Yukon border and with the Wrangells and parts of the Alaska Range to the northwest.

The massive, blocklike St. Elias Mountains rise from a myriad of narrow ridges and peaks at 8,000 to 10,000 feet in height to 14,000 to 19,000 feet. Mt. Logan, 19,524 feet (5,951 metres), Mt. St. Elias, 18,008 feet (5,489 metres), and a dozen other peaks exceed in altitude the highest mountains elsewhere in the United States. The average altitude of the ice fields blanketing the lower regions is 3,000 to 7,000 feet. Because of the difficulty of access, the geology is little known. The high mountains are probably underlain by schist, a highly crystalline igneous rock, and by granitic masses. Elsewhere, the mountains consist mainly of sedimentary and volcanic rocks, from the Paleozoic and Mesozoic eras, that have been intensely metamorphosed, folded, and faulted. One great arcuate fault system, the Lynn Canal–Chatham Strait trough, bounds the St. Elias Mountains on the northeast and continues southward into southeastern Alaska.

Southeastern Alaska is a continuation of these Pacific coastal mountains, a rugged, scenic island archipelago and neighbouring ranges on the mainland. To the east the coast ranges rise 5,000 to 7,000 feet, with higher peaks at 8,000 to 10,000 feet. The summits of these mountains coincide in part with the Canadian boundary. Extensive ice caps feed valley glaciers, some of which still extend to the sea. These mountains are underlain by the massive granitic rocks of the Coast Range Batholith, intruded in late Mesozoic. The island archipelago ranges in altitude from 2,000 to 3,500 feet in the southern Prince of Wales Mountains, to more than 4,000 to 7,500 feet in the outer Chilkat–Baranof Mountains. The glaciated islands have a rugged coastline indented by many fjords. The island archipelago is composed of northwest-trending belts of Paleozoic and Mesozoic sedimentary and volcanic rocks and metamorphic rocks that have been intruded by large areas of igneous rocks and cut by many faults.

Plant and animal life. Vegetation in the higher altitudes of the mountain ranges, when they are not barren or covered by ice, may be a ridge type of tundra, or level, treeless plain, that consists of lichens, grasses, and weeds above the timberline, the upper limit of tree growth. Dwarf species of willows and alders are also found above the timberline, and grasslands occur in the Aleutians, on the Alaska Peninsula, and the south slopes of the Alaska Range. In the interior forests, the timberline in many places is less than 600 feet, although it is generally between 1,500 and 2,000 feet. The interior forests of white spruce and birch, with mixtures of balsam poplar, occur mostly on the lower slopes of the larger river valleys north of the Alaska Range. In the coastal forests, the timberline ranges from about 2,000 to 3,000 feet in southeastern Alaska to approximately 1,000 feet in the more northerly and westerly sections.

Tundras and timberlines

The Tongass National Forest encompasses southeastern Alaska, and the Chugach National Forest covers the lower parts of the Chugach, Kenai, and Kodiak mountain areas. The vegetation in the lower altitudes is a hemlock–spruce coastal forest. Western hemlock and Sitka spruce extend to about 1,500 feet in elevation, and subalpine species to at least 2,500 feet. The Tongass National Forest is composed largely of western hemlock, with a much smaller number of Sitka spruce and a sprinkling of western red cedar and Alaska cedar. The Chugach National Forest, in the Prince William Sound section, is predominantly a hemlock forest with some Sitka and white spruce and occasional cottonwoods and paper birches.

Several big-game animals are native to the Alaskan mountains. Both brown and grizzly bears inhabit the coastal ranges, the Alaska Range, and the interior. The black bear, absent from the Alaska Peninsula, is found in three-fifths of Alaska. Dall mountain sheep, the only wild, white sheep in existence, live high in the mountains from the Kenai Peninsula to the Brooks Range. The mountain goat is found in the Chugach, Kenai, and Talkeetna mountains. Moose, though living mostly in the lower altitudes, range into the higher country from the Alaska Peninsula to the Brooks Range. Barren-ground caribou range widely over high plateaus and mountain slopes from the Alaska Peninsula to the Arctic regions. Sitka deer are found in southeast Alaska and in parts of Prince William Sound. A number of smaller fur-bearing animals are also native to the mountains.

Study and exploration. Alaska has been mapped topographically from aerial photographs, at a relatively high level of detail; the underlying geology, however, has been mapped only sketchily. The U.S. Geological Survey, as part of the general reconnaissance mapping program of the late 19th century and the first half of the 20th century, did most of the geological work. Since the 1950s, areas of potential mineral and transportation value have been mapped on a more detailed basis by state and federal agencies. Various university research parties contributed to the data; much geological mapping work was also done by private mining and petroleum companies, but this work was rarely made public. (R.Sc.)

APPALACHIAN MOUNTAINS

The Appalachian Mountains are one of the great highland systems of North America, the eastern counterpart of the Rocky Mountains. Extending for over 1,200 miles from the Canadian province of Quebec to central Alabama in the United States, they form a natural barrier between the Eastern seaboard and the vast lowlands of the continental interior. As a result, they have played a vital role in the settlement and development of the entire continent. They combine a heritage of natural beauty and a distinctive regional culture with contemporary problems of economic deprivation and environmental deterioration.

The system may be divided into three large regions: northern, central, and southern Appalachia. These include such mountains as, in the northern area, the Shickshocks and the Notre Dame ranges in Quebec; the Long Range in Newfoundland; the great monadnock of Katahdin in

Maine; the White Mountains of New Hampshire; and Vermont's Green Mountains, which become the Berkshires in Massachusetts, Connecticut, and eastern New York. New York's Catskills are in central Appalachia, as are the beginnings of the Blue Ridge range in southern Pennsylvania and the Alleghenies, which rise in southwestern New York and cover parts of western Pennsylvania, western Maryland, and eastern Ohio before merging into the third, or southern region. This area includes the Alleghenies of West Virginia and Virginia: the Blue Ridge range, extending across Virginia and western North Carolina, the northwestern tip of South Carolina, and the northeastern corner of Georgia; the Unakas in southwestern Virginia, eastern Tennessee, and western North Carolina (of which the Great Smoky Mountains are a part); and the Cumberland Mountains of eastern Kentucky, southwestern West Virginia, southwestern Virginia, eastern Tennessee, and northern Alabama.

Altitudes

The highest altitudes in the Appalachians are in the northern division, with Maine's Mt. Katahdin (5,268 feet [1,606 metres]), New Hampshire's Mt. Washington (6,288 feet [1,917 metres]), and other pinnacles in the White Mountains rising above 5,000 feet, and in the southern region, where peaks of the North Carolina Black Mountains and the Tennessee–North Carolina Great Smoky Mountains rise above 6,000 feet, and the entire system reaches its highest summit on Mt. Mitchell (6,684 feet [2,037 metres]).

A distinctive feature of the system is the Great Appalachian Valley. It includes the St. Lawrence Valley in Canada, the Kittatinny, Cumberland, Shenandoah, and Tennessee valleys—the latter the site of the world famous Tennessee Valley Authority, a government agency for natural resource conservation, power production, and regional development.

Physical features. *Physiography and geology.* The Appalachians are among the oldest mountains on Earth, born of powerful upheavals within the Earth's crust and sculptured by the ceaseless action of water upon the Earth's surface. The two types of rock that characterize the present Appalachian ranges tell much of the story of the mountains' long existence.

First there are the most ancient crystallines. During the Precambrian, between 570,000,000 and 1,100,000,000 years ago, long periods of sedimentation and violent eruptions alternated to create rocks and then subject them to such extreme heat and pressure that they were changed into sequences of metamorphic rocks. Among the oldest of these are the gneisses. Limestone changed into marble, shales became slate and schist, sandstones were transformed into quartzite, and intrusions of magma formed bodies of granite. These ancient rocks antedated most plant or animal life; in addition, the intense pressures and heat destroyed any traces of primitive life—so that the Precambrian crystallines contain no trace of fossils. They make up what is known as "Old" Appalachia in Canada, New England, and a belt east of the Great Valley with the Blue Ridge at its heart. To the west, the Great Valley, the Valley Ridges, and the Appalachian plateau (including the Alleghenies) are characterized by the second type of rocks, the Paleozoic sediments. These make up "New" Appalachia—the shales, sandstones, and coals that were created by sediments deposited, stratified, and solidified over a vast range of geological time. During the Mississippian and Pennsylvanian epochs of the Carboniferous Period, this long process included the formation of some of the richest coal beds in the world. During the Permian Period (around 250,000,000 years ago), near the end of the Paleozoic Era, a great mountain folding occurred. This was the Appalachian Revolution, a vast interior crumpling resulting from the stress placed on huge masses of subterranean rock. As parts of the Earth buckled into folds, cracked, and faulted, other parts were uplifted—sometimes in the parallel ridges distinctive to the Appalachians—and thrust faults served to move one rock mass atop another. Thus the ancient crystallines were lifted in places above more recent sedimentary rock deposits.

The Appalachian Revolution

In addition to the massive folding of the Appalachian Revolution, however, two other agents—ice and water—have carved the steep ridges and pinnacles and gouged out the deep ravines and valleys of the Appalachians. This building, eroding, uplifting, and shaping of the Appalachians has been a continuous process through the ages. Many of the major rivers are older than the mountains. This accounts for the fact that northeast of the New River in Virginia the major Appalachian rivers flow into the Atlantic Ocean, often through dramatic passages called water gaps, while southwest of the New, the rivers, with few exceptions, flow to the Ohio River. When the mountains were thrust up, blocking their westward course to the ancient sea that once covered mid-America, these old rivers cut out their own routes, creating those spectacular canyons, gorges, and "narrows" that are part of Appalachian scenery.

The glacial legacy

The northern Appalachians were also affected by glacial forces. During the Pleistocene (10,000 to 2,500,000 years ago), continental ice sheets flowed down over North America, covering New England but reaching no nearer the southern Appalachians than the Ohio Valley. These moving tongues of ice stripped topsoil, ground and polished certain peaks, and elsewhere scattered rock debris and random boulders, all the while driving plants and animals farther south in search of survival. Thus the southern Appalachians became the refuge for northern life forms, a giant bed for reseeding when the glaciers retreated and the plants moved slowly north again, leaving behind a rich botanical variety thriving in northern altitudes and southern latitudes.

The New River, rising on the Blue Ridge in North Carolina, runs northward and then turns westward across the Appalachian Valley and the Alleghenies (where it becomes the Kanawha) and empties into the Mississippi Basin. The larger mountain streams to the south, dominated by the Tennessee River, follow this example. Exceptions are the rivers rising southeastward on the Blue Ridge, which flow into the Atlantic, and the Chattahoochee, rising in the northeastern corner of Georgia, which runs southwestward into the Gulf of Mexico.

The entire Appalachian system is laced with an intricate network of springs, streams, waterfalls, and rivers. Water is most abundant in the southern Appalachian mountains. Certain areas of the Blue Ridge receive an annual rainfall of 69 inches during an average year. Elsewhere precipitation is even higher, exceeded in the United States only along the northwest Pacific Coast. Much of this rainfall comes in extremely heavy downpours during short periods of time. Since this region does not have the natural storehouses of numerous lakes and glacial deposits of sand and gravel spread over hills and valleys such as are found in the northern Appalachian region, sudden rainfalls bring rapid rises and falls in the southern Appalachian stream flows. Under certain conditions (as when the forest cover, which serves as a storage sponge, has been destroyed) destructive floods have characterized much of the hydrologic history of this part of the Appalachians. To contain these floods and harness the might of an entire river system for purposes of navigation, power production, land reclamation, and watershed development, the Tennessee Valley Authority was established in 1933 as one of the chief factors influencing the ecology of the Southern Appalachian region. Its system of dams turned a river that rampaged and often destroyed into a river that flows gently and productively. The TVA created a series of spacious reservoirs (the majority of which are in or adjoining the Appalachian region) called "the Great Lakes of the South." These lakes, in turn, have altered the natural and human resources of the region, using Appalachian water power to produce electrical power, enlarging industrial and agricultural and recreational opportunities.

The Tennessee Valley Authority

Waterfalls are common throughout much of the Appalachian system. Most of those in the northern Appalachians, especially from New York to Maine, were created when glacial moraine or debris, scraped from surrounding peaks by the melting ice cap, solidified into shelves along creeks or river valleys over which the water must plunge as over a terrace. Southern Appalachian waterfalls were generally formed by the action of water on alternating layers of soft and hard rock.

In the area known geologically as "New" Appalachia, especially where there are the softer limestone rocks to yield to the constant erosion by water, numerous caves are a distinctive feature of the physiography. The chief caverns lie within or bordering the Great Valley region of Pennsylvania, Maryland, West Virginia, Virginia, and Tennessee. Caverns of the Shenandoah Valley in Virginia and the Mammoth Cave in Kentucky provide well-known and dramatic examples of underground passages, rooms, watercourses, formations, and decorations that honeycomb much of the Earth below central and southern Appalachia.

The Appalachian Trail

A unique man-made feature of a large portion of the Appalachian system is the 2,000-mile Appalachian Trail. This footpath, stretching from Mt. Katahdin, Maine, to Springer Mountain, Georgia, provides a hiker's grandstand on the varied ranges of the Appalachians. Overnight shelters are scattered along the way. A noncommercial motor route, the Blue Ridge Parkway, stretches 469 miles from the Shenadoah National Park in northern Virginia to the Great Smoky Mountains National Park and is the most popular area administered by the U.S. National Park Service.

Forests

Plant and animal life. From Maine to Georgia, the Appalachian Mountain system was once almost totally covered with forest. Today the best and most extensive broadleaved deciduous forests in the world still flourish in the Appalachian Mountains and bordering areas, notably in southern Appalachia. To the north are the conifers (red spruce and Fraser fir, which grow at the highest elevations and distinguish the Canadian and Maine woods) and the northern hardwoods (sugar maple, buckeye, beech, ash, birch, red and white oak). Farther south are hickory, poplar, walnut, sycamore, and at one time the important and, before they were destroyed by blight, plentiful chestnuts. All of these, plus other of the 140 species of trees of Appalachia, are found in the southern mountain region. Lofty elevations nurture representatives of the Canadian forest, while the western slopes of the Great Smokies, receiving an annual rainfall often as high as 90 inches, produce trees that have reached record maximum height and diameter. Among these are the tulip tree, buckeye, Canadian hemlock, and chestnut oak.

The interdependent system of southern plant growth known as the "Appalachian forest" is highly complex. It forms one of the great floral provinces of the Earth. There are the trees that bear luxuriant bloom, such as serviceberry, redbud, hawthorne, tulip poplar, dogwood, locust, sourwood, and many others. Among the numerous shrubs with particularly showy flowers are the rhododendron, azalea, and mountain laurel. Certain summits of the southern Appalachians are "heath-balds"—open meadows or grasslands interspersed with thick growths of heath. Roan Mountain in the North Carolina–Tennessee Unakas is one of the most extensive of these, with some 1,200 acres of natural gardens sprawling vivid rose and pink and purple rhododendron across its high pinnacle and down its slopes. It is estimated that of some 2,000 species of Appalachian flora, perhaps 200 are native to and wholly confined to the southern Appalachians. Ferns, mosses, and mushrooms of many species are also part of the complex Appalachian plant life.

Bison, elk, and wolves, once common to the Appalachians, disappeared long ago; caribou and moose are still found in the northernmost corners of the region. Scattered through other areas are the black bear, white-tailed deer, wild boar, fox, raccoon, beaver, and numerous other small animals. All areas of Appalachia, from Gaspé to Georgia, support an abundant bird life. In the Great Smoky Mountains alone some 200 varieties of game and songbirds have been recorded.

The people and economy. The diversity that characterizes Appalachian plant and animal life also exists in the system's mineral resources. As the immense stands of timber throughout the Appalachians brought into existence important lumber and pulp industries, so rich coal beds, veins of iron ore, salt springs and licks, and deposits of granite and marble created important American industries in the region. Each of these has been attended by its own peculiar problems, especially in the field of conservation. There is, for instance, pollution of Appalachian waterways by pulp and chemical industries, and the devastation of land and human resources brought on by certain coal-mine operations.

Obstacles to settlement

The long blue wall of the Appalachians thrust up a mighty barrier to early westward expansion. Exploration and settlement was further discouraged by the size and complexity of the lateral mountain ranges, the rugged courses of many of the streams and rivers, and the ubiquitous dense forest. The central Appalachians, with their more spacious water gaps affording easy passage, attracted the largest number of early settlers. Many of these were Germans and Scottish-Irish who went into the interior of Pennsylvania and subsequently migrated down the Great Appalachian Valley in Virginia and Tennessee. In the New England Appalachians, the narrow notches, often blocked by glacial debris, and the steepness of the mountains discouraged early settlement—as did the massive ruggedness of the successive ranges in the southern Appalachians—so that each of these regions remained a wilderness long after Daniel Boone had forged his pioneer route through the Cumberland Gap. During the French and Indian War (1756–63), trails to the Ohio country and Great Lakes led through central Appalachia, and these, with their scattered lonely forts of the interior, became brutal battlegrounds of border warfare. Indian allies of the British waged bloody skirmishes against Appalachian settlements during the American Revolution, but the Appalachian Mountains confined most of that struggle for independence to the eastern seaboard.

Despite the early arrival of the lumber industry and opening of the coal mines, some areas of Appalachia remained isolated until early in the 20th century, notably those mountain areas of the southern region where rough terrain hindered building of roads. As a consequence, Southern Appalachian highlanders developed a distinctive culture characterized by handicrafts, ballads, folklore, and mores that reflect both the massive problems and the rich potential of the region.

Study and exploration. The ruggedness of the Appalachians, the transverse ranges by which they are crossed, their maze of streams and rivers, and their lack of natural passes created a formidable barrier to early explorers and settlers. The Spanish conquistador, Hernando de Soto, was probably the first white man to enter southern Appalachia, in 1539–40. In 1716 Governor Alexander Spotswood of Virginia led the first organized body of Englishmen across the Blue Ridge Mountains. During the 1760s and 1770s Daniel Boone became America's frontier folk hero through his exploits in exploring and settling the Blue Ridge and Cumberland Mountain country. Historical figures associated with the opening of northern Appalachia include Samuel de Champlain, who sighted the mountains in 1605 as he sailed along the Maine coast; Darby Field, who made the first climb up Mt. Washington (1642); Timothy Nash, discoverer of the important Crawford Notch (1771); and Sir William Logan, founder of Canada's geological survey, who made a cross section of the geological formation of Gaspé peninsula in 1844 and became the first white man to cross the Shickshock Mountains. During the mid-19th century the first extensive scientific studies of Appalachia began when, in 1849, the Swiss geographer Arnold Guyot commenced mapping the eastern mountains. Starting with the White Mountains, he spent five years in northern Appalachia, then moved south to the Great Smoky Mountains area. He mapped, measured elevation, and made the first methodical effort to name mountains. The highest peak in the Eastern U.S. was named for another pioneer explorer-scientist, Professor Elisha Mitchell, who lost his life in 1857 while establishing the fact of this balsam-covered mountain's preeminence. It remained for Horace Kephart, a St. Louis librarian turned naturalist who came to the southern mountains in 1904, to bring the isolated and scenic region to national attention. From his writings grew the interest and impetus that led to the establishment of the Great Smoky Mountains National Park.

(W.D.)

PACIFIC COAST RANGES

The Pacific Coast mountain ranges run parallel to the coastline of the states of California, Washington, and Oregon, and they extend into Canada and Mexico. In their fastness stand the giant redwood forests and the magnificent coastal scenery of California and Oregon. Also lying within the ranges are several sprawling urban regions, the largest of which are those centred on San Francisco and on the megalopolis of Los Angeles. The effort to preserve the beauty of the coastline, together with the ever-present threat of earthquakes and forest fires and the growth of the region's cities, has brought the ranges into national focus because of the continuing debate over the nature and quality of the United States environment.

Physical features. *Physiography.* The Coast Ranges are separated from the lofty Sierra Nevada and Cascade mountains, to the east, by broad depressions known in Oregon and Washington as the Willamette Valley–Puget Sound region and in California as the Great Valley. On the west, there is virtually no coastal plain, for deep water sets in within 25 miles of the coast.

The ranges themselves have six major divisions. The unit stretching from San Francisco north to the Klamath Mountains of the Oregon–California boundary is known as the northern Coast Ranges; the coastal ranges of Oregon and Washington have similar geological features and form a separate division north of the Klamath Mountains. The Klamath Mountains, however, although fronting on the Pacific and topographically part of the marginal Coast Ranges, are made up of older rock structures resembling those of the Sierra Nevada (see below). Hence, they are not usually included as a subdivision. The coast ranges of British Columbia are also of the Sierra Nevada type and decidedly different from those of Oregon or Washington. South of San Francisco, the central Coast Ranges extend to the vicinity of Santa Maria, at latitude 35° N; beyond, they are succeeded by a sector that includes the Santa Barbara, Ventura, and Los Angeles areas. The sector's name—the Transverse Ranges—derives from a marked east–west topographic and geologic trend. The ocean bed south of the Transverse Ranges consists of basins and platforms belonging to the continental margin, rather than to the Pacific deep, and it can be counted as an extension of the Coast Ranges. Finally, the southern tip of the great formation is formed by the Peninsular Ranges extending down the fingerlike protrusion of Baja California.

The Coast Ranges for the most part exhibit a subdued and soft relief of below about 3,300 feet, but some peaks and ridges stand above 6,600 feet or even 11,500 feet (3,506 metres) at San Gorgonio in the eastern Transverse Ranges.

Geology. Although the Coast Ranges were molded into their present shape in the geologically recent Cenozoic Era (beginning about 65,000,000 years ago), an important element in their composition dates from as far back as the Jurassic period (190,000,000 years ago). The rocks concerned in this underlying, or basement, complex have been called the Franciscan Group. These sedimentary and volcanic rocks were subsequently changed by great pressures, sheared, intricately folded, and invaded by granite, then molten. Many of the rock layers making up the rest of the Coast Ranges are composed of sediment washed out by erosion from the then-existing margin of the North American continent to the east. These deposits accumulated in local structural basins and along the continental shelf and its slope.

The Franciscan rock basement

The subsidence of the sediment-filled basins and related processes of structural uplift and subsequent erosion provide the key to the complex evolution of the Coast Ranges. The trend of the basins and the associated uplifts generally paralleled the coast, but in the Transverse Range sector the basins took an east–west trend, subsided rapidly and deeply, and received very thick layers of sediment that eventually formed the rich petroleum source beds of southern California. The uplifts, on the other hand, often brought older Franciscan and Upper Cretaceous rocks to a new surface exposure.

This process of mountain building took place in two clear-cut phases. In the first, the Early Cenozoic rock layers were folded and thrust up as a result of earth movements in mid-Miocene time (about 20,000,000 years ago), and this process of deformation spread all the way from the Peninsular Ranges in the south to the Coast Ranges of Oregon and Washington in the north. The upfolded layers of the central and Transverse ranges were subsequently eroded almost to a plain and were then covered by additional layers of younger sedimentary rocks washed down from the east. This latter development set the stage for a second mountain-building movement, which began in Quaternary time, possibly 1,000,000 years ago, and has continued to the present, for the central and Transverse ranges are still being built up, deformed, and eroded.

Farther north, however, the Coast Ranges of Oregon and Washington participated only in the first of the two mountain-building movements, when their Early Cenozoic rock layers were most affected by folding. Sediments and lava flows accumulated to great thicknesses in a large arc-shaped basin lying between the Klamath Mountains on the south and the British Columbian Coast Ranges on the north. The first mountain-building movement caused a notable structural uplift in the north in the form of a dome, the site of the present Olympic Mountains of Washington. Since this region escaped a second mountain-building phase, the forces of erosion were able to cut away much of the uplifted rock, revealing the great upward folds, or anticlines, and their downfolded equivalents, the synclines. The summits in the Olympic Mountains exceed 6,500 feet, and the relief has been scoured and molded by the action of extensive Ice Age glaciers, portions of which remain to enhance the scenic attractions of the area.

A major feature of the Coast Range system is the San Andreas Fault, a line of structural weakness extending from the Gulf of California northwestward to the Transverse Range and then westward to the central Coast Ranges. It has been traced northward to the San Francisco peninsula and beyond, to Cape Mendocino, where it appears to join the structurally weak submarine Mendocino Ridge. It sends out a number of associated faults, notably in southern California and the San Francisco area. The great fault marks the splitting of a huge sliver of the North American continental margin. The land west of the fault line is being forced, or, in geological terms, translated, to the northwest. Over the past 15,000,000 years, it has travelled some 200 miles. The translation has occurred in short, violent movements best illustrated by the 1906 San Francisco earthquake, when the land west of the fault moved about 21 feet horizontally northwestward along the fault line. An intensive program of seismic investigation is underway, aimed at predicting the almost inevitable future dislocations along the fault, which runs through areas of dense population.

Movement of the San Andreas Fault

The underwater fringe of the Coast Ranges is also of exceptional geological interest. The bold, sea-pounded coast has few natural harbours, but San Francisco Bay provides an exception: through the narrow 360-foot-deep trench spanned by the soaring Golden Gate Bridge, it opens into one of the most magnificent harbours in the world.

Beyond the coastline, from Santa Barbara to Vancouver Island, the underwater shelf juts out above the Pacific abyss. It has a width of 15–30 miles and a maximum depth of about 650 feet, at which point it begins to slope down to its base. The shelf and slope are fairly regular in submarine relief, except where indented by such fissures as the Monterey Canyon. Where the sliver of continental crust is being pushed into the Pacific Basin, an underwater headland or projection of the shelf and slope is prominent, such as Cape Mendocino, latitude 40° 30′ N.

South of the Transverse Ranges the underwater topography changes from a narrow shelf to a wider basin and platform region about 150 miles wide. From measurements made of crustal thickness, this is believed to have once been a portion of the North American continent that subsided in separate blocks between a series of faults.

In the 1960s and 1970s the new and popular theory of seafloor spreading provided a framework into which the origin of the San Andreas Fault and the entire evolution of the Coast Ranges could be quite plausibly fitted.

The ocean bed is now held to be cracking into great

trenches. These fissures are constantly healed by eruptions of new lava from the Earth's core that form midoceanic ridges. The East Pacific Ridge is of great significance in the evolution of the Coast Ranges: it has been charted northeastward along the Pacific floor as far as the Gulf of California, where it is deflected westward a number of times by a series of faults. The San Andreas Fault further deflects the ridge as far as the ocean floor off Oregon. This slow process of seafloor spreading is responsible for the northwesterly movements associated with the San Andreas Fault. The rate of movement is about one inch per year.

Climate. The northern sections of the Coast Ranges experience a climate known as humid mesothermal; *i.e.*, with cool summers and mild winters. South of San Francisco the climate becomes mesothermal subtropical, with dryer summers. Water is plentiful to the north but scarce—as needs increase—further south.

Plant life. The rain forests of the northern Coast Ranges are among the finest in the world. Coniferous stands make up all but 10 percent of the wooded area, and there are no fewer than 50 species of trees, including the famed giant redwoods, which are found mostly on the westward facing slopes.

The people and economy. Nature has provided the Coast Ranges, particularly the California section, with diversified climate, scenery, and economic potential. Resources include gold, petroleum, vineyards, and a supply of fruits, nuts, and vegetables sufficient for half the American nation. These resources help to explain the westward population movement that has made California the most populous state in the Union. Settlement there is concentrated in the Coast Ranges and the adjacent Great Valley.

Apart from the social problems of the great urban complexes centred on Los Angeles and San Francisco, this expansion of settlement has had a deleterious effect on the natural environment of the Coast Ranges. Landslides, caused by the removal of vegetation, and barren and eroding scars have become an eyesore in many places, while atmospheric pollution, brought about chiefly by the automobile, adds a host of problems. Even the offshore areas have been affected: by the early 1970s the region adjoining Santa Barbara was the scene of much oil-leasing activity, and, as drilling got underway in 1969, a serious oil leak occurred at one offshore site. All these factors helped to make the Coast Ranges area a focus of great ecological and conservationist discussion.

Pollution problems

Study and exploration. The first generation of students to make thorough investigations into the complex geology of the Coast Ranges came from local universities in the late 19th century. Their studies were continued by an active second generation working for state and federal geological surveys and for petroleum-exploration companies. The great San Francisco earthquake of 1906 precipitated a thorough investigation of the earthquake problem, especially of epicentres (focuses of seismic activity) in the Californian Coast Ranges; once it was recognized that earthquakes start from movements along faults, or fractures, the fault system of the ranges was mapped with care, and an intensive seismological program developed in major Pacific coast universities. With the great influx of population into the region from the mid-20th century onward, investigations produced internationally significant work on problems ranging from highway construction to various manifestations of environmental pollution (see below). The ranges are also of considerable interest to geologists exploring new concepts relating ocean-floor spreading to the evolution of mountains at the continental margins.

Seismographic investigation

ROCKY MOUNTAINS

The major section of the great upland system that dominates the western North American continent, the Rocky Mountains stretch from northern Alberta and British Columbia southward through the western United States to Mexico, a distance of some 3,000 miles. In places the system is several hundred miles wide. Limits are mostly arbitrary, especially on the western side, where other mountain systems, generally excluded, exist. The explorations of Silvestre Vélez de Escalante, Lewis and Clark, and John Wesley Powell caught the imagination of the world, and through their reports the knowledge of the Rockies began to unfold. The snowcapped peaks, the conifer forests, the wide intermountain valleys, the crystal-clear streams, the big sky, and a vast mineral resource provide homes and work for about 5,000,000 people, and millions more come each year to tour and play. The Rockies comprise one of the continent's most popular tourist attractions.

The Rocky Mountain ranges in the United States and Canada.

To the west, especially in Nevada, western Utah, and Arizona, lies the Great Basin. Here, the Earth's crust has been broken by numerous faults, with the blocks between faults uplifted, depressed, and titled. This manner of deformation, geologically speaking, has been a rather recent affair, and has produced a kind of relief and drainge entirely different from that of the more typical Rocky Mountains to the east. As a result, it is necessary to recognize that there are two basic divisions of the Rocky Mountains. In the first the ranges retain characteristics of their original structure and shape, and in the second the original structures and forms have been broken and much defaced by block faults. In fact, there is much controversy about what the original structures of the western division were like.

The basic divisions

Physical features. *Physiography.* Each of the ranges in

Ranges and basins of the Eastern division

the eastern division is a large uplifted mass; many have high peaks and dramatic scenery. The uplifts or ranges named on the map are the better known basins. The Front Range of Colorado and the central Arizona uplift are the two most massive uplifts, but most of the rest have a somewhat uniform area, about 62 miles (100 kilometres) long and 15 miles (25 kilometres) wide. The Front Range supports peaks over 14,000 feet high, including Mt. Elbert, which at 14,431 feet is the highest point in the Rockies. Wyoming has peaks in the Wind River and Teton Ranges well over 13,000 feet high, as does Utah in the Uinta Mountains. Some of the high mountain areas have remained virtually untouched by man and have been set aside as national wildernesses. All have national forests.

The basins of the eastern division are broad and generally from 4,000 to 7,000 feet high. During the period of the uplift of the ranges and for some time afterward the basins were the receptacles of the rock debris eroded from the uplifts. Later, as drainage became well established to the Missouri and Colorado rivers, the basin sediments were cut into by water action and were in some spots deeply eroded.

The Canadian and northwestern Montana Rockies, including the mountains of Glacier National Park and the Lewis Range of northwestern Montana, are a subdivision of the western division. They are characterized by a series of parallel ridges, which resulted generally when thick sections of sedimentary rocks were thrust on top of each other. The same type of linear mountain ridges is noted in western Wyoming and southeastern Idaho, but from the southwestern corner of Wyoming to the southwestern corner of Utah and southern Nevada the western division is masked by the later Great Basin block faulting. How far west in western Utah and Nevada the true Rocky Mountains once extended is still regarded as controversial.

In summary, therefore, the eastern division of the Rockies is marked by blister-like uplifts and large intermontane basins and the western division by thrust faults and folds.

Geology. The eastern division as defined above is one in which the layers of sedimentary rocks deposited in seas of the Paleozoic and Early Mesozoic Era (from about 550,000,000 to 225,000,000 years ago) are relatively thin, while those of the western division are thick. The western division is characterized as geosynclinal (resulting from a vast downwarping in the Earth's surface), whereas the thinner eastern deposits are of a peripheral (shelf) type. The sedimentary layers of the uplifted ranges of the shelf vary in thickness from a few feet to 6,000–7,000 feet, whereas those of the western geosyncline exceed 40,000 feet in places.

Age and thickness of deposits

As the beds of the downwarp began to be uplifted, folded, and thrust faulted under the pressure of Earth movements in Late Mesozoic time (during the Jurassic and Cretaceous periods of 136,000,000 to 190,000,000 years ago), their waste products, formed by the erosive action of wind and water, were carried eastward and deposited on the adjacent shelf in considerable volume. In fact, a foredeep basin (*i.e.,* one in proximity to the great downwarp) in western Wyoming and central Utah subsided and received over 10,000 feet (3,080 metres) of the sediments, which consequently spread eastward in diminishing amounts.

The sediments of the geosyncline were first deformed by vast earth movements in Jurassic time; with the deformation, a broad upland was created where marine waters had once existed. As has been noted, the sediments eroded from the upland were deposited in the foredeep basin to the east, where marine seas advanced and retreated and in which marine animals lived. It is the fossils of these animals, trapped in the sediments, that indicate to geologists the age of the foredeep beds and thus, by inference, of the uplift to the west.

The exposed rocks of the ranges of the Great Basin reveal that the chief structures formed at this time of massive changes in the Earth's crust were great folds and sheets of rock, with some beds thrust and folded over each other. The thrust sheets of this type in southeastern Idaho and western Wyoming appear to be large slices of the sedimentary rocks that started on the Cache uplift and slid by gravity eastward 20 to 30 miles to their present position. The Canadian and northwestern Montana Rockies consist of a similar succession of thrust sheets, and the base of this enormous assembly is visible at the surface for a number of miles. Its width and near flatness attest to the long-distance transport of the thrust sheets and strengthen the theory that gravity caused the sheets to slide at a low angle down the east slope of a west-lying uplift. The Lewis Thrust along the east front of Glacier National Park is the best known of the thrust sheets. One has only to view these sheets on the ground to become aware of their vast magnitude. They are several thousand feet thick, probably 10 to 20 miles wide, and 50 to 150 miles long and can be visualized as gigantic landslides moving down a slope of only 2° to 5°. The Charleston–Strawberry–Nebo Thrust is interesting inasmuch as a sequence of rocks from its geosyncline, 25,000 feet in depth, has been moved eastward against, and probably over, a rock sequence of the shelf, itself more than 3,000 feet thick. There is no doubt as to the size and importance of these huge sheets of rock in the formation of the Rockies. In Canada and Montana, as in southeastern Idaho and western Wyoming, their mechanical aspects can be fairly well analyzed, but in the Great Basin of Utah and southern Nevada their sizes, extent, and connections remain controversial.

One school of thought suggests that the thrust sheets arose from an uplift in eastern Nevada and that the sheets then rode eastward 120 miles to central Utah. Another hypothesis posits an uplift like the Cache only 25 or so miles to the west and has the sheets coming from this nearby source. Still a third hypothesis submits that stresses occasioned by the weight of seafloor deposits, and associated Earth movements, at and under the continental margin of the Pacific 500 miles to the west, may have been transmitted to the western division of the Rocky Mountains, thrusting the sheets eastward.

The uplifts of the Eastern, or shelf, division of the Rocky Mountains may conveniently be considered state by state, although state boundaries are, of course, in no sense geologically significant.

In Montana a belt of uplifts extends eastward through the centre of the state and is composed principally of the Little Belt and Big Snowy mountains. The oldest rocks are those of Precambrian age, which have been dated by radioisotope samples from various locations as being from 1,100,000,000 to 2,700,000,000 years old. Cambrian time began about 570,000,000 years ago, and all Precambrian rocks lie below the Cambrian strata. As one of these great uplifts (known technically as a dome or anticline) is elevated, the highest part is attacked by erosion first, and thus, as the strata, or beds of rock, are eroded away by wind, rain, and ice, the oldest rock in the core ultimately is exposed. The Little Belt Mountains are asymmetrical, that is, with the core of Precambrian rocks exposed near the southern margin rather than at the centre. The Big Belt Mountains uplift extends southward from the Little Belt and must be partly involved in the multiple thrust faulting of the geosyncline to the west. The Porcupine Dome is a gentle but broad uplift along the easterly trend.

Ages of the rocks in the shelf area

North of the east–west belt of uplifts are a number of scattered uplifts, the Bearpaw and Little Rocky supporting the highest peaks. In the Bearpaw Mountains is Baldy Mountain at 6,956 feet. The Sweetgrass, Kevin–Sunburst, and Bowdoin uplifts are gentle domes. There are a number of volcanic fields in Montana, but the Highwood and Crazy mountains are the areas that stand conspicuously apart by virtue of their Alpine relief. In this area, the dike swarms—networks of rock figures filled with solidified lava—are classical examples of the type.

In Wyoming the Big Horn Basin is surrounded by the Bighorn Mountains, the Owl Creek Mountains, the volcanic Absaroka Mountains, and the Beartooth Mountains. The Laramie, Sweetwater, and Wind River uplifts form a barrier across central Wyoming. The Sweetwater uplift was originally as high and imposing as the Wind River. After much erosion it foundered until almost all the peaks were covered with sediments, some of volcanic origin. In the current cycle of erosion these ancient peaks are now being exhumed.

The Black Hills uplift is large but was not raised to the

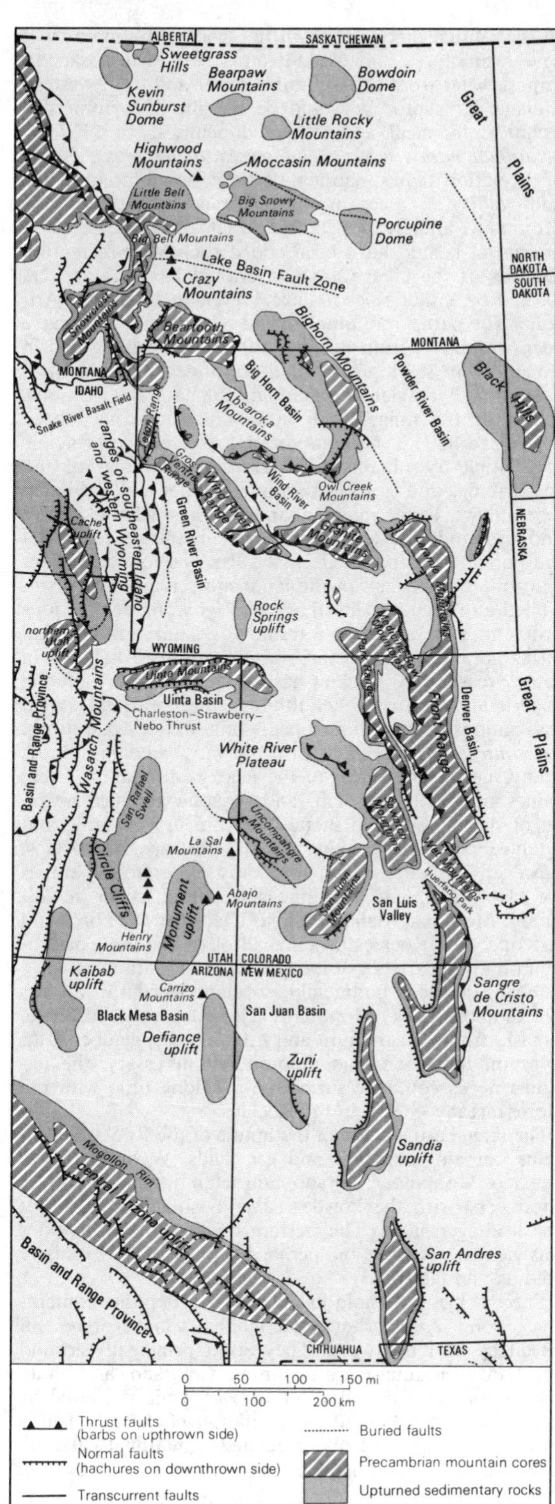

Geological structures and mountain ranges of the eastern division of the Rocky Mountains within the U.S.

same height as some of its neighbours. The Precambrian granites are, nevertheless, exposed, and it was from these that the gigantic Rushmore Memorial was carved. The newest and most rewarding oil field area of the Rockies is located in the Powder River Basin, close to the northwest extremity of the Black Hills.

Special features of the Uintas

The Uinta Mountains uplift in northeastern Utah and northwestern Colorado follows an easterly bend and is structurally linked to the White River Plateau, which is a projection of the Sawatch uplift. The Uintas seem to have inherited their position from a Late Precambrian basin that extended eastward from the main north–south basin. The broad anticlinal, or upward, bending nature of the rock strata of the Uintas gives strong support to the theory that they are a vast blister-like upwarp. The upwarp is also bordered by upthrust faults, which accentuate the anticlinal structure and confirm that the uplift was caused by vertical, upward-directed forces. It may be contended that the Uintas are typical of the mode of formation of all the uplifts of the eastern division of the Rockies, although it must be noted that some uplifts are asymmetrical with a border upthrust fault only on one side, as in the case of the Wind River mentioned above.

The large Front Range uplift is terminated on the south by Huerfano Park, with the Wet Mountains making up an arm linked to the north end of the Sangre de Cristo uplift. The Front Range passes into the Laramie uplift on the north by way of narrowing and a lower relief area. On the west it is crowded against the Sawatch uplift, and in this zone the sediments are compressed together, with marked folding and thrust faulting.

Part of the San Juan uplift and part of the San Luis Valley, or depression region, are covered by a large volcanic field. Some of the highest peaks in the San Juans are volcanic rocks. These include Windom Mountain, 14,166 feet (4,293 metres), and Summit Peak, 13,377 feet (4,054 metres).

Rift valley of New Mexico

In New Mexico a post-Rocky Mountain rift, or fault-bounded, valley system developed in Late Cenozoic time (about 30,000,000 years ago), proceeding in a northerly direction through the central part of the state. This rift valley complex now conducts the Rio Grande down to west Texas and Mexico. A major block of the valley flow, dropped down between the great faults on either side, has cut the San Andres uplift into two opposite facing escarpments, or rock outcrops, the Sacramento Mountains on the east and the San Andres Mountains on the west. The Jornado del Muerto Valley west of the San Andres is another downfaulted block. Farther north the hypothetically reconstructed Sandia uplift has been shortened by earth movements associated with the rifting process. The rifting is regarded as a north-extending arm of the Basin and Range Province, the intermontane region from southern Oregon and Idaho to northern Mexico that is characterized by the topography of the Great Basin, its largest subdivision.

The physiographic province called the Colorado Plateau in southeastern Utah, western Colorado, northern Arizona, and northwestern New Mexico is also basically part of the Rocky Mountains. The uplifts shown on the map in the Colorado Plateau are comparable in size (but not in height) to the other uplifts of the eastern division. They have not been domed up as much as the uplifts to the north, and therefore less erosion has occurred, for in none of them are Precambrian rocks exposed. The wilderness of the Colorado Plateau area has become more accessible to tourists. The Canyonlands National Park over part of the Monument uplift was being opened up by roads, and there was a new interstate highway across the San Rafael Swell.

Volcanic activity in the south

The Grand Canyon of the Colorado River cuts across the southern end of the Kaibab uplift in this region. Four mountain groups—the La Sal, the Henry, the Abajo, and Carrizo mountains—are notable. These are laccolith-type mountains, in which, from a central pipelike intrusion reaching deep into the Earth's crust, magma has been injected between the layers of sedimentary rocks, causing the overlying beds to bulge up in domes about one mile across. The domes are called laccoliths, and each mountain group is made up of a group of laccoliths.

In summarizing overall trends in the complex formation of the Rocky Mountain uplifts, one may postulate that, in those uplifts in which erosion has exposed Precambrian rocks in the core, border upthrusts have developed on one side or both. In other words, when the uplift, from which mass the present-day mountains have been formed, has developed to a height greater than 20,000 feet above the adjacent basin, a border upthrust has also developed. Authoritative opinion would now suggest that the border thrust dips into the uplifted mass, steepens in depth, and eventually becomes vertical. This aspect of the uplifts results in a further postulate, that the force and mechanism responsible for each uplift is a blister-like magma injection rather deep in the Precambrian crust. The magma is supposedly of basaltic composition and comes from the upper mantle of the Earth's molten interior.

The Great Basin extends from central Utah to the Sierra Nevada, and although the geological relations in this wide region are not unknown, about three-fourths of the bedrock geology is covered and concealed by volcanic fields and alluvium (erosion waste material). In consequence, there is scope for various interpretations.

It is well established that a belt of deformation and mountain building extended northward through central Nevada. It evolved from Late Devonian time to Permian time (about 345,000,000 to 280,000,000 years ago) and thus preceded the growth of the Sierra Nevada and Rocky Mountains. In the Sierra Nevada the earliest intrusions occurred in Triassic time (some 225,000,000 years ago) and seem to have been a continuation of the earlier central Nevada mountain-building activity.

Commencing in Jurassic time (190,000,000 years ago), crustal unrest occurred to the east of the central Nevada belt of deformation. There is controversy as to its nature and extent. It appears that eastern Nevada and western Utah became land, mostly mountainous, in Jurassic time, and this region probably attained its highest elevations in the mid-Cretaceous period (100,000,000 years ago). This was the time of folding and thrusting in west central Utah and in western Wyoming, when, as has been already noted, the western segment of the Rocky Mountains was formed.

Since part of the western division of the Rocky Mountains now has the Great Basin faulting superimposed on it and thus has had its bedrock geology partly obscured, the western limit of the Rocky Mountain system is not readily defined or clear. Some aspects of eastern Nevada seem to suggest a different structure from that in western and central Utah, and thus the western limit may lie just east of the Nevada line.

Large volcanic fields occur in many parts of the Rocky Mountains. Some of these have already been mentioned, as have the laccolithic mountains of the Colorado Plateau, a further manifestation of volcanic activity. The chemical nature of most of the volcanic rocks is such that silica is abundant in them. Another rock type, in contrast, has abundant iron and magnesium and a lesser amount of silica and potassium. This would seem to indicate that the molten magmas of the high-silica volcanic rocks originated, at least in part, in the melting of the Precambrian rocks of the crust, rather than from basalt magma originating in the mantle of the Earth's interior.

The western division of the Rockies, especially where the Great Basin faulting occurs, is noted for numerous cross-cutting intrusions of solidified magma known as stocks. These are generally one to five miles across where exposed and, like the volcanics, are silicic. The magma of the stocks likewise appears to have been mobilized from the silicic rocks of the Precambrian crust. Virtually every stock is the focus of numerous mineral deposits, both large and small. Hot solutions were given off by the crystallizing magma in the stocks, and these carried metal compounds, such as the sulfides of copper, lead, zinc, silver, and iron. These sulfides commonly contained a little gold. The hot solutions worked upward through the existing pore spaces in the rocks, and as the temperatures dropped, various metaliferous sulfide minerals were precipitated. Where the intrusive stocks have penetrated limestones, chemical reactions may have occurred between the solutions and the limestones, and in places massive sulfide deposits have resulted. Mining districts such as Bingham, Park City, and Ely have sprung up as a result of the mineralization in and around such stocks.

Mineral origins

The economy. *Water supply.* Water for irrigation, industry, and culinary needs is generally in short supply in the Rocky Mountains. To the south, as the climate becomes drier, the water supply factor becomes more critical. New Mexico and Arizona are the states most affected. The U.S. Bureau of Reclamation is the federal agency that has been most concerned in the construction of water-storage reservoirs all over the western United States, and certainly the Rocky Mountains has its share of these projects. Not many more favourable unused dam sites remain, so that within a short time—certainly by the mid-21st century—all the annual precipitation in the Rocky Mountains will have been stored and used. It may then be necessary to import water from the Columbia River and from western Canada. This process would be fraught with numerous technical, financial, and political difficulties.

National parks, forests, and recreational areas. Many of the nation's finest national parks, national monuments, and wilderness areas are in the ranges of the Rocky Mountains and in the Colorado Plateau. To these areas of natural beauty have been added such large recreation facilities as the Glen Canyon National Recreation Area, located on either side of Lake Powell in Utah and Arizona. The parks, monuments, and recreational areas have been withdrawn from mining, oil, and gas drilling and in general from stock grazing and are under federal control and carefully regulated to maintain the natural conditions.

Most of the ranges and mountain groups have been designated as U.S. national forests. As such the principle of multiple use obtains, with lumbering, mining, oil and gas drilling, and grazing permitted under well-regulated federal laws. In the marginal and, as yet, unclaimed basin and arid lands, the federal government still has control of the public domain. In effect, the Rocky Mountain states control less than half of the land; more than half is controlled and regulated by the federal government. Serious problems have arisen as a result of grazing, mining, and oil exploration. The disturbance of primitive habitats in some areas of the Rockies has generated concern among experts and laymen alike, although the floral and faunal associations have been hurt badly only in limited sections.

Pollution and its control

Resources. Copper is easily the most valuable of the many metallic resources of the Rocky Mountains. Great mines in Montana, Utah, and Arizona produce nearly all of the nation's red metal. Iron ore in Wyoming and Utah support a steelmaking industry. Perhaps the Rockies, however, are most noted for many underground mines for silver, gold, lead, and zinc. Such mines occur in Colorado, Montana, Idaho, Nevada, Utah, New Mexico, and Arizona. The Rockies produce all of the nation's molybdenum and nearly all of the beryllium and uranium.

Great reserves of nonmetallic substances occur in various places in the Rocky Mountains. These are rock phosphate, potash, trona, magnesium and lithium salts, glaubers salt, gypsum, limestone, and dolomite. If necessary, the nation's needs could be supplied for a long time with the stores already known in the Rockies.

The large basins between the uplifts of the Rocky Mountains contain many oil and gas fields. Wyoming, New Mexico, Montana, Colorado, and Utah are all substantial producers, with the Powder River Basin proving one of the leading regions. The western division of the Rockies has yielded very little oil, perhaps because of the extensive folding and faulting.

The Rockies also hold extensive shale deposits containing a solid hydrocarbon material that can be driven off as oil by heat treatment. They occur principally around the Uinta Mountains in Wyoming, Colorado, and Utah. The amounts of potential oil are vast, and, as viewed by certain economists, if the exploitation of the oil shale is not carefuly planned and regulated, a national calamity could result. As yet, the extraction of the oil has not been made profitable.

Immobile oil is located in certain sandstones in various places. These deposits are called bituminous, oil, or tar sands. In amounts, they compare to giant oil fields. Like the oil shales, the bituminous sandstones have not yet fully yielded their oil economically.

The Rocky Mountains and the adjacent Great Plains on the east contain the Western Hemisphere's most abundant and usable coal reserves. These are bituminous, subbituminous, and lignitic in character. Although not readily usable for metallurgical purposes, they constitute a tremendous energy source, and it is predicted that these coals will be used much more extensively for electrical-power generation than at present.

Study and exploration. Catholic missionaries had worked their way northward from Mexico into New Mexico by the middle of the 18th century, and in 1776 Padre Escalante and his party explored and documented their trav-

Early explorers

els into what is now Utah, reaching almost to the Great Salt Lake. The Lewis and Clark expedition in 1803–06 explored and charted a route up the Missouri River into Montana and thence across Idaho and Oregon to the Pacific. Following the Missouri River into east-central Montana, Jedediah Smith worked his way southward into the Big Horn Basin and thence into southeastern Idaho, northern and southwestern Utah, southern Nevada, around the Sierra Nevada, and back to the Great Salt Lake across the Great Basin. His journeys occurred in the years 1822 to 1831 and were possibly the most remarkable of all western explorations, but unfortunately Smith wrote very little. John Frémont's explorations occurred in 1846–48: he followed the North Platte River into Wyoming, up the Sweetwater River to the south end of the Wind River Range (South Pass), and thence southwestward into Utah. He then explored northward into Idaho and around the broad north end of the Great Basin into Oregon and down into California. This was an important scientific survey because he charted distances, determined latitudes, longitudes, and elevations and recorded objectively in some detail what he saw.

Four great western surveys were then organized by the federal government, namely that of Clarence King (the 40th Parallel Survey of 1867–78), that of Ferdinand V. Hayden (geological survey of Nebraska and Wyoming 1867–78), that of George M. Wheeler (100th meridian, 1872–79), and that of John Wesley Powell (exploration of the Colorado River and of Utah, Arizona, and southern Nevada, 1869–78). The maps and preliminary observations of these important surveys laid the groundwork for a great mass of research that followed. The Rocky Mountains, with their abundant coalfields, numerous oil, gas and uranium prospects, and a wealth of metal prospects have provided the U.S. Geological Survey with much work over the past century. Many of the prospects have turned into large and small mines, making a substantial contribution to the regional and national economies. The mountains yield lumber and, by the second half of the 20th century, were offering summer and winter recreation facilities of increasing importance. They also yield water, of paramount importance in this semiarid and arid land.

(A.J.E.)

SIERRA MADRE

The Sierra Madre ranges

The Sierra Madre is the principal mountain system of Mexico and includes the three ranges of the Sierra Madre Occidental (to the west), the Sierra Madre Oriental (to the east), and the Sierra Madre del Sur (to the south). These ranges enclose the great central Mexican Plateau, which itself is a part of the system and is broken by blocks of mountain ranges and large populated basins (*bolsons*). The greater part of Mexico comprises this comprehensive Sierra Madre.

Physical features. *Geology.* The Mexican Plateau is composed largely of folded Mesozoic strata. Cretaceous and Upper Jurassic formations predominate among exposed rocks, but Middle or Lower Jurassic and Late Triassic sediments are widespread. The region's elevation, folding, and faulting were contemporaneous with the uplift of the Rocky Mountains. In the early Tertiary Period great outpourings of lava terminated a long interval of weathering and erosion. Subsequently the large plateau block was uplifted, the displacement being greater to the south than to the north. Its margins have been dissected into the deeply gouged angular landscape of the Sierra Madre Occidental and the more rounded but rugged terrain of the Sierra Madre Oriental.

Although the western fringe of the plateau, the Sierra Madre Occidental, was long assumed to be a structurally simple feature consisting of nearly horizontal lavas manteling Mesozoic sediments and old crystalline rocks, a complex structural history has become apparent. The underlying strata were deformed by folding and faulting during several periods, and there are many intrusions of varying size. Paleozoic strata mostly of the Carboniferous and Permian periods overlie Ordovician and possibly Cambrian materials in the Sierra Madre and to the west. Large amounts of lava and ash were deposited on earlier surfaces in the Tertiary Period.

The Sierra Madre Oriental, composed largely of folded sedimentary rocks of the Cretaceous Age, owes its present relief to uplift, faulting, and erosion since the mid-Tertiary. Igneous intrusion forms are numerous.

Marking the southern edge of the Mexican Plateau and spanning Mexico from coast to coast is a zone where volcanism developed during two episodes. In the Early and Middle Tertiary Period immense quantities of lava were poured over the land. The second volcanic episode, which began in the Pliocene Period and continues to the present time, is associated with the development of such spectacular peaks as Pico de Orizaba, or Citlaltépetl (18,701 feet [5,700 metres]), Popocatépetl (17,887 feet [5,452 metres]), Ixtacihuatl (17,342 feet [5,286 metres]), the Nevado de Toluca, or Zinantecatl (14,954 feet [4,558 metres]), and the Nevado de Colima and Volcán de Colima (14,206 feet [4,330 metres] and 12,992 feet [3,960 metres]). In 1759 and 1943, respectively, the smaller volcanoes of Jorullo and Parícutin burst into existence. Additional peaks, cinder cones, and other evidence of volcanism occur throughout the region.

To the west of the Isthmus of Tehuantepec in southern Mexico the great scarp of the Mesa del Sur rises several thousand feet. This deeply dissected mountain mass reveals east-to-west folds in its base rocks of metamorphosed Cretaceous sediments and intrusives. The narrower western section of the highlands is known as the Sierra Madre del Sur. It is breached by the Balsas River.

Physiography. The Sierra Madre Occidental extends approximately 700 miles (1,127 kilometres) from northwest to southeast and is about 95 miles (153 kilometres) in width. Summits mostly exceed 6,000 feet, and some peaks rise above 10,000 feet. From the east the mountains present relatively slight but broken relief; from the west they appear as formidable escarpments whose benched flanks drop into gigantic trenches. The great mountain ranges and canyons trend northwest to southeast, which is generally the trend of the folds in the Mesozoic and older basement strata. The local relief may exceed 5,000 feet, and the majestic dimensions of some of these barrancas admit of comparison with the Grand Canyon of the Colorado in the United States.

Extending southeastward from the Big Bend of the Río Bravo is a series of low mountains that are composed of folded sedimentary strata. South of Monterrey these mountains become a striking range, the Sierra Madre Oriental. Summit elevations are about 7,000 feet, but some peaks rise above 10,000 feet (Cerro Peña Nevada). Steep-walled, narrow valleys, a number of which are north to south in alignment, lie in the Sierra; and there are several gateways from the Gulf of Mexico lowlands to the plateau.

The core of Sierra Madre del Sur is outlined by a narrow and discontinuous coastal plain to the southwest and by the structural depression of the Balsas-Mexcala River on the north. To the east of this depression is the Sierra Mixteca, which forms a highland bridge between the volcanic axis and the Mesa del Sur. A labyrinth of narrow ridges and steep flanked valleys forms the Mesa del Sur. Much of this broken country crests at elevations of about 6,500 feet, and a very few peaks exceed 10,000 feet. Whereas the Mexican Plateau's volcanic mantle is relatively free of dissection, the Mesa del Sur has been stripped of much of its volcanic cover. The older basement rocks are exposed in what are probably the most highly dissected landscapes of Mexico. There is very little flatland in the region. Abruptly terminating the region on the east is a magnificent scarp that overlooks the down-faulted block of the Isthmus of Tehuantepec.

Elevation as factor of climate

Climate. Elevation is more important in determining thermal characteristics of Mexican climate than is latitude. The decrease of temperature that occurs with increasing elevation permits the formalizing of vertical temperature zones: *tierra caliente,* or hot land, *tierra templada,* or temperate land; and *tierra fría,* or cold land. Unlike climatic areas farther from the Equator, the seasonal variations in temperature are not marked at any elevation in the tropics.

The *tierra templada,* which includes elevations from 3,000 to 6,000 feet (900 to 1,800 metres), has mean temperatures of 65° to 75° F (18°–24° C). Much of highland

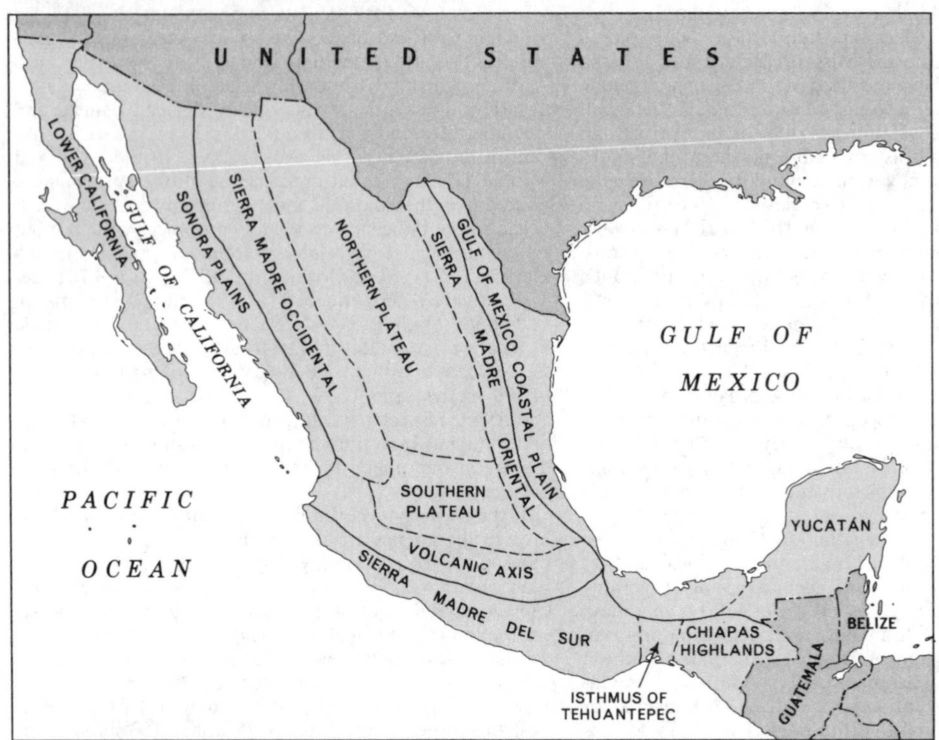

Regions of Mexico.

Mexico is in this thermal zone. It is the most pleasant of the zones insofar as human comfort is concerned. During winter frost may occur. In the cooler *tierra fría* the mean annual temperatures are between 55° and 65° F (13°–18° C). Above 10,000 or 11,000 feet (3,300 metres) the mean annual temperature is less than 50° F (10° C); above 14,000 or 15,000 feet (4,300–4,600 metres) the mean annual temperature is less than 32° F (0° C).

Mountain masses, besides creating islands of cooler climate within the tropics, play a major role in the incidence of clouds and precipitation. The mountains form barriers over which air may be raised, cooled, and caused to condense. Within the mountains and in their lee there is a lower incidence of clouds and precipitation. Lee or descending air becomes warmer, and its capacity to retain moisture rises. Illustrating the effect of the mountains upon precipitation and cloudiness is the contrast between 80 inches (2,030 millimetres) of rain and 150 cloudy days per year for the eastern slopes of the Sierra Madre Oriental and the 40 inches (1,020 millimetres) of rain and 90 cloudy days per year that characterize much of the Pacific slope west of the Sierra Madre del Sur. The drier areas are in the rain shadow of the mountains.

The economy. The rugged topography of the Sierra Madre Occidental has been a serious barrier to east–west communications. Because of the mountains, Spanish exploration, regional commercial evolution, and the present road and railway systems developed independently on the plateau and in the lowlands of Sinaloa and Sonora states. No railroad crossed the mountain barrier until 1962, although construction was begun many years earlier on lines between Durango and Mazatlán and between Chihuahua and Topolobampo. The latter was finally completed. Only a few paved roads through the region link interior cities with Pacific coastal resorts and towns. The sparse settlement in this mountainous area is confined to mining centres or to farming and pastoral hamlets. Forest industries are most highly developed in the states of Chihuahua and Durango, but it may be that the long-term worth of the forest cover as watershed protection exceeds its value as timber. The Sierra Madre Occidental is the source of waters that support the oases of the plateau and of the lowlands adjoining the Gulf of California. Oases that have been formed by water from the mountains include those along the Ríos del Carmen, Conchos, Nazas, and Aguanaval, in the plateau. The westward-flowing Yaqui, Mayo, Fuerte, Sinaloa, and Culiacán rivers water important farming districts in the coastal lowlands.

Among the substantial rivers that have watersheds that penetrate the Sierra Madre Oriental are the Ríos Moctezuma–Pánuco. This drainage system has captured a considerable area of the central plateau. The process of capture was aided by the opening of a drainage canal in 1607 (amplified in 1900) to tap the Basin of Mexico. Numerous harnessed and potential sources of hydroelectric development exist among the rivers that drain the eastern front of the mountains. Agricultural settlement is particularly dense in Veracruz. (G.C.E./H.J.Bn./Ed.)

SIERRA NEVADA

The Sierra Nevada is a major mountain range of western North America, running along the eastern edge of the state of California. Its great mass is the uplifted complement of the Great Valley (Central Valley) depression to the west. Extending over 250 miles (400 kilometres) northward from the Mohave Desert to the Cascade Range of northern California and Oregon, the Sierra Nevada is about 50 miles wide. Its magnificent skyline and spectacular landscapes make it one of the most beautiful of the great physical features of the United States. As a recreation centre, its year-round facilities prove a magnet to the inhabitants of the huge urban areas of California, and it has considerable importance as a source of power and water. It was the focus of the celebrated California Gold Rush of 1849.

Physical features. *Physiography.* The Sierra Nevada is an asymmetrical range with its crest and high peaks decidedly toward the east. The peaks range from 11,000 to 14,000 feet above sea level, with Mt. Whitney, at 14,494 feet (4,418 metres), the highest peak in the conterminous United States.

Much of the rock is granite or a near relative of granite. There are dividing bands of metamorphosed (heat- and pressure-altered) sedimentary rock, all that is left of a once extensive sedimentary basin.

Geology. It has long been recognized that the Sierra Nevada is a tilted block of the Earth's crust. A fault bounds the block on the east, and it was along this that the great mass that became the Sierra Nevada was uplifted and tilted westward. This explains the asymmetry of the range. As the block was uplifted the abrupt, east-facing escarpment was cut into by the erosive action of wind, rain, frost, and ice, and a series of steep-gradient canyons

The basic tilted block

developed. Though the massive uplift started possibly 15,000,000 years ago, much of it occurred in the last 2,000,000 years. Altogether, the vertical movement along the fault amounted to at least 15,000 feet, and possibly more.

The gentle west-facing slope has been dissected by a series of streams, relatively long in comparison to those of the eastern slope. Such rivers as the Yuba, American, Mokelumne, Merced, and Kern have carved deep, V-shaped valleys into the predominant granite. These rivers drain into the Sacramento River in the Great Valley on the north, and into the San Joaquin on the south. By means of these two large rivers the range's drainage ultimately reaches the Pacific Ocean through San Francisco Bay.

During the Ice Age, which started about 2,000,000 years ago and ended in North America just 11,000 years ago, the river-eroded valleys were covered several times by great glaciers. Glacial climates came and dissipated at least five times, and each time excessive snows built snow and ice fields and long glaciers. The ice carved the V-shaped valleys into U-shaped ones, and in few ranges of the world are the forms more crisp and inspiring than in the Sierra Nevada. In the high snow fields, steep-walled basins, called cirques, were carved from the mountain sides by ice action. The resulting rock debris was transported by the glaciers down into terminal moraines, the tonguelike deposits of waste at the glacier's end. These moraines, like the U-shaped valleys, are classical in their development. The glacial features are chiefly responsible for the scenic beauty and are the focus of the Yosemite, Kings Canyon, and Sequoia national parks. The several episodes of glacial chronology must be related to the progressive uplift of the Sierra Nevada block, and this is a remarkable story, explored in detail by geologists.

Geological and geophysical analyses have led to the conclusion that the region occupied by eastern California and western Nevada was once a broad and long northward-trending basin, called a geosyncline, in which layers of sedimentary rock were laid down mostly in marine waters. Continued subsidence of this vast downwarp in the Earth's surface brought the lower sediments into successively higher temperature zones, where heat conducted from the Earth's interior resulted in the melting of the rock layers. In consequence, the granite rocks of the range were created, for, after the sediments were melted, they became mobile and proceeded, in part, to intrude upward into overlying layers of rock.

The sequence of granites

Careful mapping by geologists shows that the granite of the Sierra Nevada has been intruded as a number of separate masses, each with recognizable boundaries and its own mineralogical compositions. Further, radioactive dating techniques show that the intrusive masses are of three separate age groups. The first originated in Triassic time (about 190,000,000 to 225,000,000 years ago) and was an easterly group of intrusive bodies, mostly exposed in ranges east of the Sierra Nevada. The second occurred in Jurassic time (about 136,000,000 to 190,000,000 years ago) and was made up of a westerly lying group of intrusions now exposed along the west slopes of the Sierra Nevada. The third occurred in Late Cretaceous time (about 80,000,000 to 90,000,000 years ago) and makes up a central area of granite, now composing the high Sierras.

In Yosemite National Park a remarkable series of no fewer than nine separate intrusive masses has been mapped and ordered chronologically. Again, field surveys of the interrelationships of these masses have been confirmed by isotopic dating techniques, and this group of granite bodies is now seen as belonging to the third general age group mentioned above.

The people and economy. Gold nuggets were found in 1848 at Sutters Fort on the Coloma River, and the tremendous gold rush that followed was to be of fundamental significance in the historical evolution of the western United States. By the 1970s about $1,800,000,000 worth of gold had been produced. The nuggets, found in the stream gravels of the lower western slopes of the Sierra Nevada, probably come from the quartz vein of the Mother Lode (see below). Not only did the present river bottom gravels contain the nuggets, but the older gravel layers forming terraces on either side of the streams were also gold bearing. In places where these old river gravels had been buried by solidified lava flows, mining operations proceeded under the lava beds. Large dredges were built to handle huge volumes of goldbearing gravels and concentrate the gold. As a result, where lush meadows once existed, there are now only rows of barren gravel ridges to mark the progress of the dredges. The rivers were muddied for miles below. Fortunately, this ruinous disturbance of a scenic and ecologically important environment was long ago condemned, and this type of industry has now almost ceased to exist. Fabulously rich gold mines were also developed in the Mother Lode vein system, which was traced for about 150 miles (250 kilometres) in a northerly direction along the west side of the Sierra Nevada. Some of the mines are still operating.

Gold mining

The moist Pacific winds drop many feet of snow each year on the Sierra Nevada, and thus the mountains become a life-sustaining watershed for many of the nearly 20,000,000 people who now reside in California. The large streams of the wide western slope drain into the Great Valley, where the most prolific truck farms, orchards, vineyards, and grain, alfalfa, and cotton fields existing in the United States are now found. Some of the drainage seeps underground and is pumped for irrigation, and the Great Valley itself provides an extensive and fine underground reservoir for water storage. Many power plants along the streams provide electric power for the Great Valley cities and smaller communities. Water that drains from the east slopes is gathered and conducted in large aqueducts to the metropolitan centres of southern California, notably to Los Angeles. Considerable lumber is harvested from the rich upper slopes of the Sierras, although the finest timber stands of the region are to be found in the Coast Ranges of northern California, Oregon, and Washington.

The vast growth of population in the densely settled regions of the west coast of the United States, and the attendant thirst for outdoor recreation, have placed heavy demands on the scenic Sierra Nevada area. On a national holiday, more than 40,000 people may invade the Yosemite National Park, or more than a thousand make the hike to the summit of Mt. Whitney. The whole area is ideal for summer camping, hiking, nature studies, and fishing, and great for winter skiing. Already the national forest and national park staffs are taxed to the limit in keeping the streams pure, the campgrounds clean, and nature relatively undefiled, and the situation appears to be deteriorating rather than improving. The Sierras are a great natural blessing but will require great vigilance in future environmental control if this status is to be maintained.

Recreation

Study and exploration. For many readers, the naturalist John Muir's *My First Summer in the Sierra,* a diary of camping and exploration in 1869, is one of the classics of American geographical writing. Muir, the founder of the Sierra Club (1892), a conservationist group concerned with the preservation of the scenic resources of the Sierras and like areas of the United States, dedicated his book to members of the club in 1911.

Geologists have studied the Sierra Nevada from the late 19th century onward. Especially significant studies concern the Mother Lode system, Jurassic stratigraphy and its relation to intrusive granites, glacial erosion, placer gold, multiple intrusions, isotope ages, and chronology and nature of emplacement. (A.J.E.)

Other landforms

GREAT PLAINS

A major physiographic province of North America, the Great Plains lie between the Rio Grande on the south and the delta where the Mackenzie River empties into the Arctic Ocean on the north, between the Central Lowland of the United States and the Canadian Shield on the east and the Rocky Mountains on the west. Their length is some 3,000 miles, their width from 300 to 700 miles, and their area approximately 1,125,000 square miles (2,900,000 square kilometres), roughly equivalent to one-third of the United States. Parts of 10 states of the United States (Montana, North Dakota, South Dakota, Wyoming, Nebraska, Kansas, Colorado, Oklahoma, Texas, and New Mexico) and the three Prairie Provinces of Canada (Manitoba, Saskatchewan, and Alberta), and portions of the Northwest Territories are within the Great Plains proper. Some writers have used the 100th meridian as the eastern boundary, but a more precise one is an eastward-facing escarpment that runs from Texas to North Dakota, generally somewhat east of the 100th meridian. In the Canadian portion the line dividing the Great Plains from the Canadian Shield runs east of the Red River of the North; cuts through Lake Winnipeg; then curves northwestward, crossing Lake Athabasca, Great Slave Lake, and Great Bear Lake to reach the Arctic Ocean east of the Mackenzie Delta.

Physical features. Once known as the Great American Desert, the Great Plains are a vast high plateau of semiarid grassland. Their altitude at the base of the Rockies in the United States is between 5,000 and 6,000 feet above sea level; this decreases to 1,500 feet at their eastern boundary. The altitudes of the Canadian portion are lower, and near the Arctic Ocean the surface is a little above sea level. Some sections, such as the Staked Plains in the Texas Panhandle, are extremely flat; elsewhere, tree-covered mountains—the Black Hills of South Dakota and the Bearpaw, Big Snowy, and Judith mountains of Montana—rise 1,500 to 2,000 feet above the general level of the Plains. In the United States the Great Plains are drained by the Missouri River and its great tributaries (the Yellowstone, Platte, and Kansas) and the Arkansas, which flow eastward from the Rockies in broad, steepsided, shallow valleys.

Surface features, soils, and climates

The soil groups of the Great Plains are correlated with rainfall and grass cover. In the more humid region with heavier grass cover, deep, black soils with much organic matter developed. Sections with less moisture have lighter, shallower soils with less organic matter, while in the most arid regions the soils are even thinner, lighter in colour, and less organic in composition.

The Great Plains have a continental climate. Over much of their expanse, cold winters and warm summers prevail, with low precipitation and humidity, much wind, and sudden variations of temperature. The major source of moisture is the Gulf of Mexico, and the amount falls off both to the north and west. Thus, the southern Plains have 15 to 25 inches of rain annually, the northern Plains 12 to 15 inches, the eastern margin in Nebraska 25 inches, and the western margin in Montana less than 15 inches. The southern parts of the Canadian Plains receive 10 to 20 inches and have a growing season of 70 to 110 days. The growing season averages 240 days in Texas, 120 days at the United States–Canadian boundary, and from 70 to 110 days in the Prairie Provinces. Grasses are the dominant natural plant life, with trees generally confined to river valleys.

Before settlement, the Plains were the home of the great grazing herd mammals—the buffalo and the pronghorn antelope. North of the 54th parallel the grasslands give way to forest, where the moose, woodland caribou, Canada lynx, and timber wolf make their homes.

The people and economy. European immigrants played an important role in settling the Plains. By 1910 foreign white stock (foreign-born and their children) made up 43 percent of the population of the six northern Plains states (Montana, North Dakota, South Dakota, Wyoming, Nebraska, and Kansas), with the British, Germans (many of them from Russia), and Scandinavians the leading ethnic groups. On the southern Plains, peoples of a pre-Columbian stock with Spanish surnames are also important. The Prairie Provinces were settled by British, German Russians (many of them Mennonites), Ukrainians, and Scandinavians.

Many of the immigrants were religious, thrifty, hard-working people with an attachment to the land. Kinship and nationality ties drew the plainsmen together, and they would travel long distances to visit and exchange work. Class differentiation was less and the status ladder shorter than in older parts of North America or Europe.

Although there are today few large cities, some 60 percent of the population is urban. The largest cities are Edmonton and Calgary in Alberta; Denver, Colorado; and Lubbock, Texas. The rural population is also sparse, about 4 persons per square mile in the United States and in the settled portion of the Canadian section.

Life-styles of the Plains

Ranchers traditionally enjoyed their remoteness and looked upon their rangeland as the last remaining trace of the Old West, with its vast expanse of plains and untamed wilderness. Not generally a gregarious kind of people, they were highly individualistic in politics. Farmers, more inclined to social interaction, made economic cooperatives strong on the Plains. In recent years, ranchers and farmers alike have valued horsemanship and rodeos as symbols of a tradition and style of life that evolved from the natural habitat.

The need for larger farms and ranches to produce viable economic units has led to a heavy migration from the rural areas. This exodus has been demoralizing for the farmers, ranchers, and businessmen who remained, and it has made survival more difficult for churches, schools, and the rural trading centres. The low density of population has concentrated services more and more in a few centres, necessitating long trips to attend school and church, to do business, and to find recreation. To meet these difficulties, some farmers have moved into town to live and commuted back to their land to work, a revival of a centuries-old pattern.

Indians on horseback had long exploited the buffalo herds, but in the 1870s cattle replaced the buffalo, and cowboys replaced the Indians. In the 1880s and 1890s farmers began to crowd the ranchers, and wheat began to replace cattle. Settlement came in years of good rains, so the Plains were overpopulated in the first rush; and a heavy emigration followed. Many grain farmers left because their farms were too small and more vulnerable to drought than the cattle ranches. Those who stayed built up the size of their holdings, saved against hard times, and added livestock to grain farming.

Agricultural and mineral bases of the economy

The Great Plains remain basically an agricultural area producing wheat, cotton, sorghum, and hay and raising cattle and sheep. Eight of the leading U.S. wheat states (Kansas, North Dakota, Texas, Montana, Nebraska, Colorado, Oklahoma, and South Dakota) lie within the Great Plains; and the Prairie Provinces are leading wheat producers in Canada. Livestock brings large cash farm receipts in most of the Plains states.

The Great Plains states also produce much mineral wealth, with Texas leading the nation and four other Plains states (Oklahoma, New Mexico, Wyoming, and Kansas) ranking high. Four of the Great Plains states have the largest coal reserves in the nation (Wyoming, North Dakota, Montana, and Colorado) but, except for Wyoming, rank low in actual production. Texas leads the United States in production of petroleum and natural gas, and several other Plains states are substantial producers. Alberta leads Canada in petroleum and natural gas.

(E.B.R.)

NORTH AMERICAN DESERT

A vast, irregular belt of inhospitable terrain stretches down the western side of the North American continent, covering 1,000,000 square miles (2,600,000 square kilometres) from southern Canada to northern Mexico and roughly corresponding to the sheltered and hence rain-starved intermontane region lying between the soaring barrier of the Rocky Mountains and the fertile coast ranges fringing the Pacific. The physical geography and human utilization of this huge area exhibit great internal variety, but its overall aridity, associated with an excess of evaporation over precipitation, great temperature extremes, frequent winds (sometimes producing dust storms and dust devils), localized storms, and a predominance of starkly eroded sunbeaten landscapes, which often have a harsh but breathtaking beauty, give it an unquestioned unity. Scientists, in naming this whole ecological complex, or biome, the North American Desert, are merely echoing the legend of a "Great American Desert" established as early as the 1820s by the vivid reportage of an expedition led by the pioneer explorer and engineer Stephen H. Long.

All forms of life, from lowly plants and insects to man himself, have had to struggle to survive in the region, and the North American Desert has thus had enormous importance in the development of the continent. Descendants of the earliest inhabitants, the desert-culture Indians, are still found in the area. Their ranks were swollen in the 19th century by tribes thrust westward in the great dispossession that followed the advance of Anglo-European settlement from the Eastern Seaboard into the continental interior, and the region is now the home—often in severely straitened circumstances—of the bulk of the U.S. Indian population. The legacy of much earlier population movements from farther south has lent a distinctly Spanish element to the area, while modern American settlement has added its own contribution in the form of sheep and cattle grazing, military installations, and small but often rapidly expanding oases of mining and manufacturing. All the peoples of the North American Desert, whatever their origin, have their lives molded by the basic and all-pervading lack of water.

The legacy of history

The basic divisions of the desert

Physical features. *Physiography.* Differences in latitude, elevation, climate, topography, vegetation, soil, and human use allow the subdivision of the North American Desert into regions of cold midlatitude and hot midlatitude desert. All of the continent's major deserts are associated with the intermontane Basin and Range Province of the western United States and northern Mexico.

Classified as a cold midlatitude desert is the Great Basin Desert, which lies in the physiographic Great Basin covering nearly all of Nevada, western Utah, and portions of surrounding states. It comprises the largest section of the Basin and Range Province and includes the Great Sandy Desert of southeastern Oregon, the Snake River Plains of southern Idaho, the volcanic Black Rock Desert of northwestern Nevada, and the Great Salt Lake Desert of western Utah. Although they are not usually assigned to the physiographic Great Basin, the Red Desert of southern Wyoming and the Painted Desert of northern Arizona are sometimes considered as extensions of the Great Basin Desert.

To the south the Great Basin Desert merges with the Mojave (Mohave) Desert and the hotter midlatitude desert regions. In California near the undefined Great Basin/Mojave border are the sun-scorched landscapes of Death Valley, the continent's lowest point. The Mojave merges in the southeast with the Sonoran Desert, which covers much of the Baja Peninsula and runs along the Gulf of California coast to the Mexican state of Sonora. Its subdivisions include the Yuma-Colorado Desert. To the east lies the huge Chihuahuan Desert, extending from southern New Mexico (where the dazzling gypsum dunes of White Sands National Monument are found) and western Texas to the highlands of central Mexico.

Geology. Most of the North American Desert—and all the salty-lake remnants—occupies areas covered by geologically recent (less than 2,500,000 years old) Quaternary deposits and mountains thrown up and folded by movements in Tertiary time (or about twice as old, with some plains and plateaus of Mesozoic sediments, up to 225,000,000 years old).

Because of long periods of erosion, the landforms produced from these rocks are characteristically sharp and angular (except in the very heavily eroded badlands regions) and contain some of North America's finest scenery. The action of wind, temperature changes, ephemeral streams, and floods have all been involved in this molding process. The individual deserts are characterized by plateaus, gorges, ravines, and alluvial fans washed out at the feet of mountains. Deserts of the bolson types contain playas (dried up lake remnants) and mud and salt lakes and flats. Deserts of the hammada type are characterized by extensive rocky surfaces with boulder or gravel coverings, sometimes blackened and wind-scoured, with magnificent buttes, mesas, and other isolated mountain remnants rising high above the flat landscape. Stretches of shifting sands known as ergs—the extensive Algodones Dunes of the Colorado–Yuma desert are a notable example—are found at lower elevations, with the shallow troughs of arroyos carrying intermittent streams from surrounding uplands to be lost in the sands.

Soils. The soils of the North American Desert have origins similar to those of more humid regions, but they are less enriched by organisms and less leached of constituents. Most belong to the "aridisols" dry-soil group, but local variations occur, reflecting differing salt and mineral composition and presence or absence of organic matter. With proper management, the more fertile ones can be quite productive. The rawest soils belong to the less developed group known as "entisols."

Plant and animal life. In the North American Desert, moisture—its quantity, quality, availability, and frequency—is the most critical factor for life. Local environmental factors are also significant in determining the nature of desert plant communities and their dependent animal life. Most desert plants are xerophytes (plants adapted to arid conditions) or phraetophytes (plants dependent on a permanent water supply) and survive only through their root systems and adaptive mechanisms for resisting drought. Sagebrush and saltbush characterize the Great Basin region, with Joshua trees, creosote bush, and burroweed typical of the Mojave. The Sonoran Desert has a thorn scrub of shrubs (mesquite, paloverde, ironwood, burrobush, smoke tree, and cat's claw) and a great variety of moisture-preserving succulents. The Arizona Upland Desert is noted for the giant saguaro cactus, while the Chihuahuan Desert is characterized, notably in its eastern part, by a ground cover of open mesquite, a scattering of larger trees, and shrubby undergrowth, including the yucca, prickly pear, and other varieties of cactus. Plant life and associated algae, lichens, mosses, and insects become more complex as temperature and moisture conditions improve.

The North American Desert harbours an abundant variety of insects, including grasshoppers that occasionally reach destructive proportions. Lizards, snakes, and other reptiles, the most conspicuous animals, are dependent on plant fluids or devoured animals for moisture. Birds are largely independent of water sources (and are seen almost everywhere), as they live on insects and spiders as well as being predators and scavengers. Rodents (including mice, rats, and squirrels), rabbits, and bats are the most numerous mammals; essentially nocturnal, they remain underground during the heat of the day and, like the birds and reptiles, obtain moisture from their food. Higher up in the food chain are such carnivores as coyotes, bobcats, foxes, and skunks, and the largest desert mammal, found at higher elevations, is the bighorn sheep. Protective coloration, often remarkably complex, is an important feature of desert life.

The desert food chain

The people and economy. As ancient dwellings, rock paintings and carvings, and other archaeological remains testify, desert-culture Indians had developed a distinctive way of life within the approximate boundaries of the North American Desert thousands of years before the coming of the white man. Spanish explorers were the first Europeans to penetrate the southwestern area, and their legacy has molded much of the character of the region. It was only in the 19th century that a great wave of settlement, often attracted by the lure of mineral wealth, swept over the whole area on its way to the more fertile coastal regions, leaving a residue of settlement focussed on mineral wealth and irrigated regions and, more sparsely, in the vast areas given over to sheep and cattle grazing.

Large areas of the contemporary landscape are occupied by Indian reservations, a legacy of the white man's continental expansion. Military installations, some associated with the testing of nuclear weapons, also take up huge areas. The various types of agriculture encompass dryland farming, sheep and cattle grazing, and more intensive developments on irrigated oases. Mineral exploitation has continued, often to the detriment of the natural environment, and manufacturing industry has become associated with growing urban settlement in the more favoured regions. The tourist trade has also grown immensely. In spite of the increasing development of dams, reservoirs, and canals, the lack of water is still a severe limitation to agricultural, urban, and industrial expansion, and the development of a low-cost water-supply system remains the key to an increased utilization of the entire North American Desert.

Study and exploration. The Indians of the region accumulated a rich natural lore during the thousands of years of their adaptation to the desert environment, but it was left to Francisco Vázquez de Coronado and other 16th-century Spanish explorers to provide the first written descriptions of the region, particularly of the southwestern portion. The famous Lewis and Clark Expedition of 1804–06 described portions of the northern sector, and Stephen H. Long's pioneer work in the 1820s foreshadowed a host of reports often generated by the huge land grants made to railroads and land companies and written by 19th-century surveyor-engineers. In 1878 the geologist John Wesley Powell made a significant report on the arid west, accurately forecasting the detrimental consequences of imposing on arid regions ways of life more appropriate to humid lands. More diversified studies followed—the first arid-lands research laboratory was founded at Tucson, Arizona, in 1903—and contemporary studies include the important International Biological Program of ecological investigation. (R.E.C.)

Drainage systems and waterways

BERING SEA AND STRAIT

The Bering Sea (Beringovo More in Russian) is the northernmost part of the Pacific Ocean, separating the continents of Asia and North America at their closest point. To the north it connects with the Arctic Ocean through the Bering Strait (Proliv Beringa in Russian), at the narrowest point of which the two continents are about 53 miles (85 kilometres) apart. The boundary between the United States and the Union of Soviet Socialist Republics passes through the sea and the strait.

The Bering Sea roughly resembles a triangle with its apex to the north and its base formed by the 1,100-mile-long arc of the Alaska Peninsula and the Aleutian Islands, which constitute a division of the U.S. state of Alaska. To the west lies the coast of Asia and to the east the Alaskan peninsula. Its area is 890,000 square miles (2,304,000 square kilometres), including its islands. The maximum width from east to west is about 1,488 miles and from north to south about 992 miles.

The Bering Strait is a relatively shallow passage averaging 98 to 164 feet (30 to 50 metres) in depth. During the Ice Age the sea level fell by several hundred feet, making the strait into a bridge between the continents of Asia and North America, over which a considerable migration of plants and animals occurred.

The strait as a bridge

There are numerous islands in both the sea and strait. The largest are the Aleutians (14,610 square miles), Nunivak (1,940 square miles), St. Lawrence (about 1,000 square miles), Karaginsky (983 square miles), Nelson (885 square miles), the Commander, or Komandorskiye, group (712 square miles), Hagemeister (125 square miles), Arakamchechen (100 square miles), the Pribilof or Fur Seal Islands (87 square miles), St. Matthew (75 square miles), Yttygran (25 square miles), and the two Diomede Islands (about six square miles).

Physical features. *Physiography.* The Bering Sea may be divided into two nearly equal parts: a relatively shallow area along the continental and insular shelves in the north and east and a much deeper area in the southwest. In the shelf area, which is an enormous underwater plain, the depths are, in most cases, less than 500 feet. The deep part in the southwestern portion of the sea is also a plain, lying at depths of 12,000 or 13,000 feet and divided by a ridge into two basins: the Commander Basin and the Aleutian Basin.

The continental crust is more than 12 miles thick along the shallow shelves and in the Aleutian Islands. The thickness decreases in the slope areas, and in the deep part of the sea the crust is six to nine miles thick.

Climate. Although the Bering Sea is situated in the same latitude as Great Britain, its climate is much more severe. The southern and western parts are characterized by cool, rainy summers with frequent fogs, and comparatively warm, snowy winters. Winters are extreme in the northern and eastern portions, with temperatures of −31° to −49° F (−35° to −45° C) and high winds. The summers in the north and east are cool with comparatively low precipitation. Snow persists on the Koryak coast for as long as eight months, and on the Chukchi Peninsula (Chukotsky Poluostrov) for nearly 10 months, with a snow cover one to two feet thick. The annual precipitation in the southern part of the sea is more than 40 inches (1,000 millimetres), mainly in the form of rainfall, while in the northern part the precipitation is less than half as much and is mainly snow.

Mean annual air temperatures range from −14° F (−10° C) in the northern areas to about 39° F (4° C) in the southern parts. Water temperatures on the surface average from 34° F (1° C) in the north to 41° F (5° C) in the south. The period without frosts lasts for about 80 days in the northern part of the sea, where snow is common even in the summer and maximum temperatures are only 68° F (20° C). In the southern area there are nearly 150 days without frost, and the temperature seldom falls much below freezing. January and February are the coldest months, July and August the warmest. Typhoons occasionally penetrate the southern part of the sea.

Hydrography. Practically all of the Bering Sea water comes from the Pacific Ocean. The salinity of the surface water is 31 to 33 parts per thousand; in the deeper parts of the sea the salinity increases to 34.8 parts per thousand near the bottom. In winter the northern portion of the sea is covered with ice, and even in summer the water below the surface retains a subfreezing temperature. The structure of the Bering Sea waters in general is subarctic, characterized by the presence of a cold intermediate layer with warmer waters above and below. The surface water is heated during the summer, but a considerable layer of water that was cooled during the winter remains cold and is known as the cold intermediate layer. The maximum thickness of this layer is about 475 feet in the northern part of the sea. Underneath this layer is one that is slightly warmer, below which lie the colder bottom waters. In the northern and eastern shallow regions of the sea, only two upper layers develop: surface water and a cooler intermediate layer.

Effect of water layers on plant life

The existence of the cold intermediate layer separating the deep waters, which are rich in nutrient salts, from the upper photic layer (*i.e.,* the layer exposed to sunlight) results in two growths of floating plant life during the year. The first growth occurs in the spring after the mixing of waters in winter; and the second during the autumnal mixing, when the cold surface waters descend and the deeper waters, rich in nutrient salts, come to the surface while there is still sufficient sunlight for plant growth.

Warm oceanic waters from the south enter the Bering Sea in three regions: through the strait between the Medny and Commander islands, through the numerous straits of the Fox Islands, and through the Amchitka and Tanaga passes. The Attu, Tanaga, and Transverse currents carry the warm water to the northwest. The Transverse Current, proceeding along the Asian continental slope in the direction of Cape (Mys) Navarin, branches in two: one branch forms the Lawrence Current moving northward and the other joins the Anadyr Current, which in turn gives birth to a powerful Kamchatka Current that governs the southward movement of the Bering Sea waters along the Asian coasts. Near the Alaska coast the general direction of the water is to the north, a factor responsible for the less severe ice conditions in that part of the sea as compared to the western part. Some of the Bering Sea water passes through the Bering Strait into the Arctic Ocean, but the bulk of it returns to the Pacific. The deep Bering Sea waters rise gradually to the surface and return to the Pacific as surface waters. Thus, the Bering Sea is an important factor in the general circulation of the northern part of the Pacific Ocean waters. The rise to the surface of oceanic waters rich in nutrient salts gives the sea a high biological productivity.

Navigability

The Bering Sea is considered by navigators to be one of the most difficult of seas. Winter storms are frequent and severe, often coating ships' superstructures with ice. Waves may reach over 40 feet in height. Added to these hazards are fog, rain, and floating ice in the northern part of the sea. In winter the northern area is covered by ice

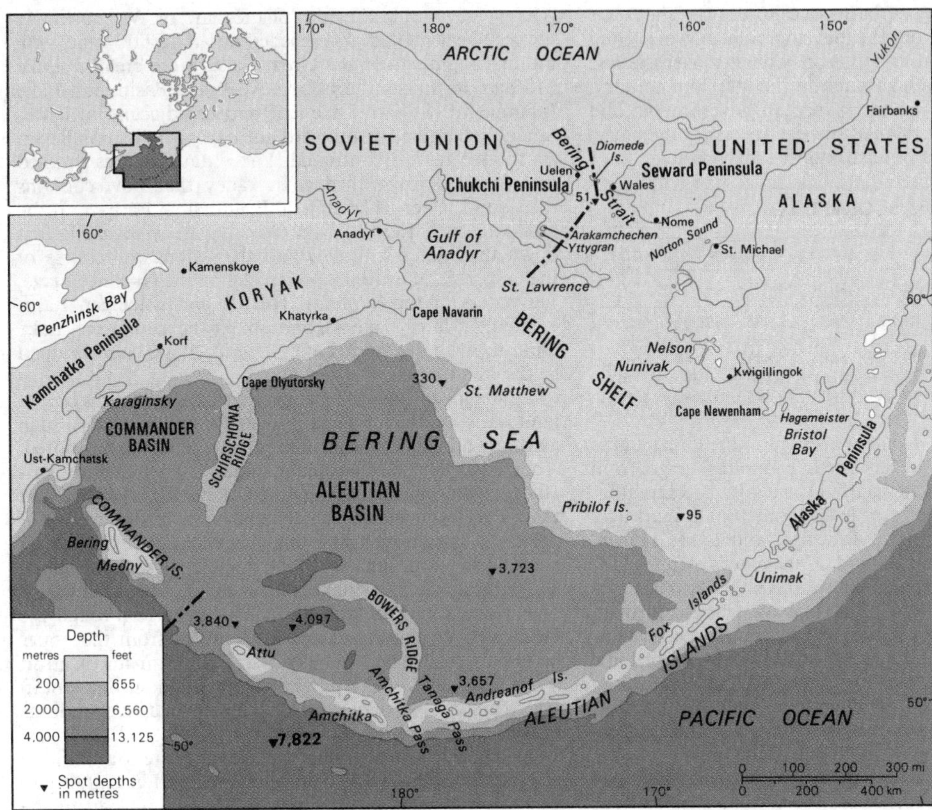

The Bering Strait and the Bering Sea.

fields about four or five feet thick, with hummocks in some places more than 100 feet high. At its maximum extent in April, the ice reaches as far south as Bristol Bay and the Kamchatka coasts. Melting begins in May, and by July there is no ice in the sea except for drift ice in the Bering Strait.

From 325,000,000 to 425,000,000 tons of sedimentary material enter the sea annually from the land as a result of erosion of the shore. Plant and animal life at the surface produce 4,742,000,000 tons of sedimentary material, but very little reaches the bottom, and consequently most of the sediment on the floor of the sea is from the land. Along with a great deal of silica, the bottom ooze holds a large quantity of boulders, pebbles, and gravel torn from the shores by ice and carried out to sea. In the southern part, the sediments are rich in material of volcanic origin.

Marine life. The floating plant life of the Bering Sea consists of 163 species, of which the most common are diatom algae. The largest concentration of diatoms have been found in the shallow part of the sea. Diatoms are the principal producers of organic matter, and they are consumed by small copepods (microscopic crustaceans), which in turn become the food of fish and mammals. On the continental shelf there are vast quantities of mollusks, sea urchins (*Echinorachnius parma*), and barnacles. Also abundant on the shelves are sponges, echinoderms (marine animals, such as starfish and sea urchins), marine worms, and crustaceans. In the southern regions, down to depths of 100 or 130 feet, populations of giant brown algae grow like forests on the rocky bottom. There are about 200 species of them, some reaching lengths of 200 or 300 feet.

The Bering Sea has about 315 species of fish, including 50 deep-sea species, of which 25 are caught commercially. The most important among them are salmon, herring, cod, flounder, halibut, and pollack. The islands are breeding grounds for the fur seal and the sea otter. The northern areas are inhabited by the walrus, seal, and sea lion.

Study and exploration. The Bering Strait and the Bering Sea were first explored by Russian ships under Semyon Ivanov Dezhnyov, in 1648. They are named after Vitus Bering, a Danish captain who was taken into Russian service by Peter the Great, in 1704. He sailed into the strait in 1728 but did not see the Alaskan coast, although he discovered the islands of St. Lawrence and Diomede. In 1730 the strait was charted for the first time by Mikhail Gvozdev and Ivan Fyodorov. Bering sailed again in 1733, leading a large expedition from St. Petersburg along the northern coast of Siberia, and he reached the Gulf of Alaska in the summer of 1741. He reconnoitred the southwestern coast of Alaska, the Alaskan peninsula, and the Aleutians, but misfortune befell him, and he perished along with many of his men. In 1780 Russian merchants founded a private company to trade in furbearing animals in northwest America. A geographic study of the sea was made at the end of the 18th century and later supplemented by hydrographic studies.

Vitus Bering

Deep-sea studies were begun in 1827 by British explorers. Extensive work was also done by an American group aboard the U.S. Research Vessel "Albatross," in 1893–1906. Since then the sea has been systematically studied by Soviet, U.S., and Japanese investigators. (A.P.L.)

GREAT LAKES

The Great Lakes—Superior, Michigan, Huron, Erie, and Ontario—form part of the St. Lawrence River system of east central North America and are one of the great natural features of that continent and the globe. Although Lake Baikal in the Soviet Union has a greater volume of water, the combined area of the Great Lakes—94,560 square miles (245,000 square kilometres)—represents the largest surface of fresh water in the world, covering an area larger than the United Kingdom, Uganda, or Romania. Their drainage basin of 291,100 square miles (753,950 square kilometres) extends approximately 690 miles from north to south and about 860 miles from Lake Superior in the west to Lake Ontario in the east; it covers an area larger than France or Afghanistan. Except for Lake Michigan, the lakes provide a natural border between Canada and the United States, a frontier that was stabilized by a boundary-waters treaty of 1909. It is a source of pride for both countries that there are no fortifications or warships along the boundary.

Individually, the lakes rank among the 15 largest in the world (see Table). They played a central role in the European colonization and development of North America, have continued to attract people and industry, and are now ringed with large urban concentrations. The lakes have not benefitted from this development, however, and are suffering greatly from pollution. Concern over the fate of the lakes reached a high pitch in the late 20th century, with both the U.S. and the Canadian governments and individuals investigating methods for reversing the tragic consequences of years of misuse of the lakes' waters.

Areas and Volumes of the Great Lakes

	surface area		world rank	volume		world rank
	sq mi	sq km		cu mi	cu km	
Superior	31,700	82,100	2nd	2,935	12,230	4th
Michigan	22,300	57,750	6th	1,180	4,920	6th
Huron	23,100	59,830	5th	849	3,540	7th
Erie	9,910	25,670	11th	116	483	15th
Ontario	7,550	19,550	14th	393	1,640	11th

Physical features. *Geology.* The age of the Great Lakes is still not definitely determined. Estimates range from 7,000 to 32,000 years of age. It is generally accepted that Lake Erie reached its present level about 10,000 years ago, Lake Ontario about 7,000 years ago, and Lakes Huron, Michigan, and Superior around 3,000 years ago.

The present configuration of the Great Lakes Basin is the result of the movement of massive glaciers through the midcontinent, a process that began during the Pleistocene Epoch, about 1,000,000 years ago. Studies of Lake Superior indicate that a river system and valleys formed by water erosion existed before the Ice Age. The glaciers undoubtedly scoured these valleys, widening and deepening them and changing the drainage of the area.

The last glacial stage in North America is called the Wisconsin Glaciation because it advanced southward to what is now the southern border of the state of Wisconsin. As the ice sheet melted and receded about 18,000 years ago, the first segments of the Great Lakes were created. Lake Chicago, in the southern Lake Michigan Basin, and Lake Maumee, in western Lake Erie and its adjacent lowlands, originally drained southward into the Mississippi River. As the ice retreat continued, Lake Maumee was drained into Lake Chicago through a valley that now contains the Grand River in Michigan. Eventually, drainage to the east and into the Atlantic Ocean was established, first down the Mohawk Valley and then along the course of the upper St. Lawrence River. At one high-water stage, the waters of the Superior, Huron, and Michigan Basin formed the large Lake Algonquin. At the same time, Lake Duluth, in the western Lake Superior Basin, also drained to the Mississippi.

Retreat of the ice

The weight of the ice sheet exerted great pressures on the land mass. As the ice sheet retreated, low-lying areas, such as the region to the east of Georgian Bay, were exposed. About 10,000 years ago, the upper lakes evidently discharged through this area via the Ottawa River Valley, and their levels were substantially reduced. After the weight of the ice was removed, the land began to rise, closing off some outlets and changing the water levels of the lakes. The largest postglacial lake, Nipissing, occupied the basins of Huron, Michigan, and Superior. Drainage through the Ottawa River Valley ceased, and outflow from the upper lakes was established by way of the St. Clair and Detroit rivers into Lake Erie. Uplift continues at about one foot in 100 years; this is evidenced by the drowned river mouths of western Lake Erie.

A wide range of rock types and deposits are found in the Great Lakes because of their great area and glacial origin. The ancient rocks of the Canadian Shield are part of the

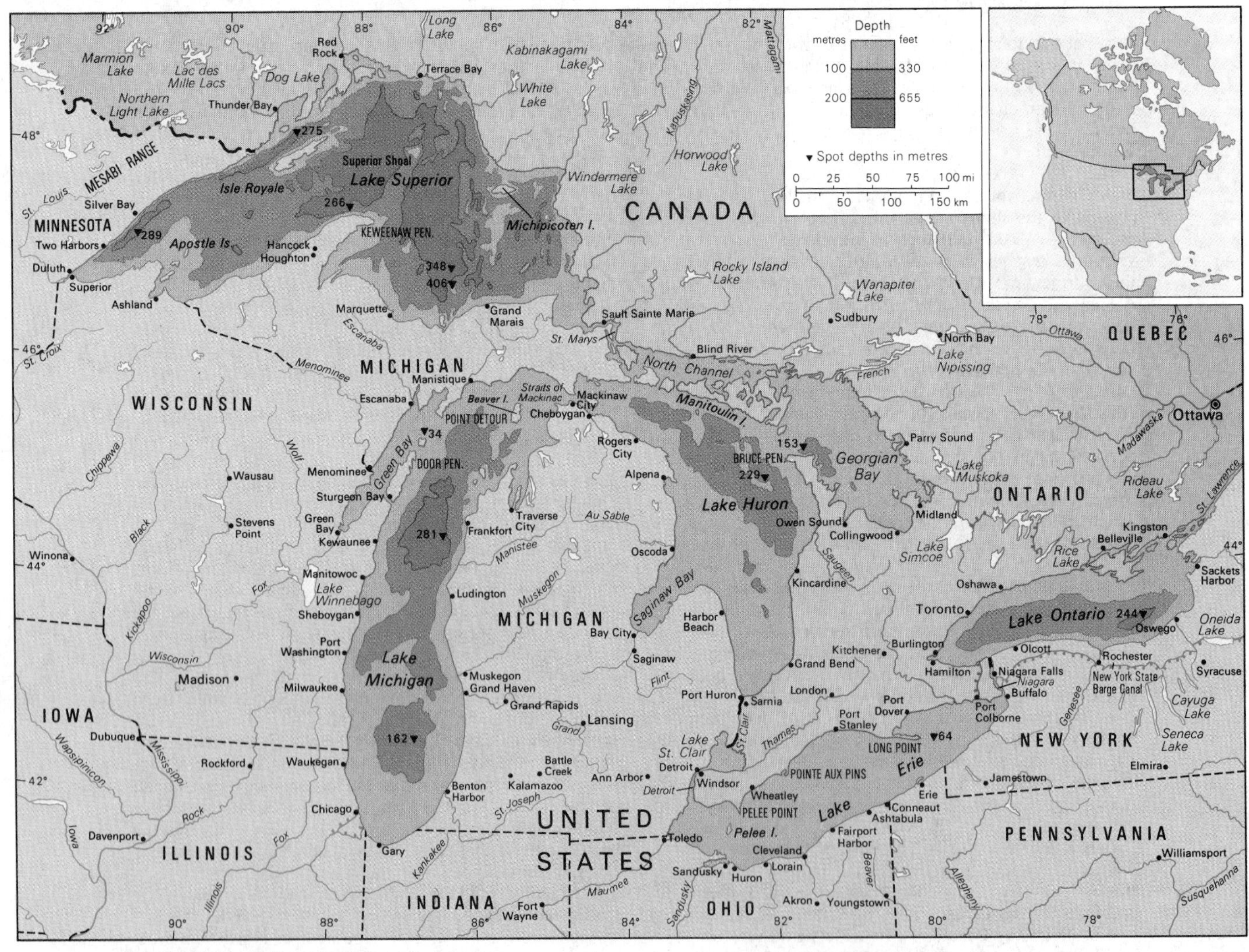

The Great Lakes and associated rivers.

Superior and Huron basins, while younger sedimentary rocks make up the remainder of the basins. There are limestone outcrops and large deposits of sand and gravel, usually near shore. Glacial clays and organic sediments occur in the deep areas.

Physiography. The lakes drain roughly from west to east, emptying into the Atlantic Ocean. Except for Lakes Michigan and Huron, their altitudes drop with each lake, usually causing a progressively increasing rate of flow.

Lake Superior, bordered by Ontario, Minnesota, Wisconsin, and upper Michigan, is the northernmost and westernmost lake and can be considered the headwater of the system. It is the deepest lake (mean depth 487 feet), lies at an altitude of 600 feet above sea level, and discharges into Lake Huron through the St. Marys River at an average rate of 74,200 cubic feet per second.

Lake Michigan lies directly south of Lake Superior and is bordered by upper and lower Michigan, Wisconsin, Illinois, and Indiana. It has a mean depth of 276 feet. The average water level is 579 feet above sea level, and its waters flow northward into Lake Huron through the Straits of Mackinac at 56,000 cubic feet per second.

Lake Huron lies at the same altitude as and is slightly larger than Lake Michigan. Its mean depth, however, is only 195 feet. It is bounded by Ontario and Michigan. The average outflow is 177,500 cubic feet per second through the St. Clair River, the shallow basin of Lake St. Clair, and the Detroit River to Lake Erie.

Lake Erie is bordered by Ontario, lower Michigan, Ohio, Pennsylvania, and New York. It is the shallowest of the Great Lakes, with a mean depth of 58 feet. The basin slopes from west to east with depths of 24 feet and 210 feet, respectively. It lies at an altitude of 570 feet, and its waters discharge at an average flow of 194,300 cubic feet per second. The course of the outflow is along the Niagara River and includes a rapid plunge over Niagara Falls before the waters reach Lake Ontario.

Lake Ontario is the smallest of the system. It has, however, the second greatest mean depth, 283 feet. It lies between Ontario and New York, at an altitude of 245 feet, and discharges into the St. Lawrence River at a rate of 233,000 cubic feet per second. It flows for about 750 miles until it empties through the Strait of Gaspé (Détroit de Gaspé) into the Gulf of St. Lawrence.

Hydrography. The lakes ultimately receive their water supply from precipitation, which increases from west to east. The average annual precipitation in the Lake Superior Basin is 29 inches, in Lakes Huron and Michigan it is 31 inches, and in Lakes Erie and Ontario it is 34 inches. About two-thirds of the annual precipitation is lost by evaporation: 22 inches on Lake Superior; 35 inches on Lake Erie (Erie receives most of its water from Lake Huron); and 26 inches on Lakes Huron, Michigan, and Ontario. Some water enters Lake Superior from the Hudson Bay drainage system via the Long Lake–Ogoki River diversion, while water is taken out of Lake Michigan by the Chicago Sanitary and Ship Canal.

Effects on climate

The lakes greatly modify the climate of the surrounding region. They absorb large quantities of heat in the warmer months, which are lost to the atmosphere during the colder months. This causes cooler summers and warmer winters. Precipitation is substantially higher along the eastern shores of the lakes, creating the snow belt that afflicts Erie, Pennsylvania; Buffalo, New York; and similarly situated cities.

Lake levels vary about one to two feet throughout the year, the highest levels occurring in summer and the lowest in late winter and early spring. There are small tides of about two inches, but they are relatively unimportant. Seiches—harmonic oscillations of the lakes—are caused by such atmospheric disturbances as winds or differences in barometric pressure. They have resulted in a piling up of water on one side, or end, of the lakes and have caused differences in the water level between Buffalo and Toledo, Ohio, on Lake Erie, as high as 13.5 feet. Currents are highly variable; they respond quickly to wind changes; their direction is determined by the rotation of the Earth and the shape of the lake basins.

The Great Lakes have bicarbonate waters, the alkalinity of which ranges from 46 parts per million of carbonates in Lake Superior to 110 parts per million in Lake Michigan. Because Lake Huron is fed by both Superior and Michigan, its chemical content lies in the middle of the range. Alkalinity then increases as the waters flow into and through Lake Erie (95 parts per million) and into Lake Ontario (102 parts per million).

The overall chemical composition of the lakes does not differ greatly from that of other large bodies of fresh water. Limestone in the Lake Michigan Basin supplies large amounts of calcium and magnesium to the system, while sodium concentrations are greater than those of magnesium in Erie and Ontario. Although chemical distribution is relatively uniform in any one lake, concentrations of phosphorus and nitrogen are greatest along the shores, in bays and harbours, and especially near urban centres.

During the 20th century, concentrations of most chemicals have increased significantly in all the lakes except Superior. Chloride, sodium, and sulfate have increased significantly in Lakes Erie, Michigan, and Ontario. Chloride concentrations have increased almost four times over levels reported in 1900, and limited data for Lake Erie indicate that nitrogen concentrations increased five times and phosphorus threefold in 30 years. Especial importance is attached to these nutrients because they stimulate growth of algae.

Microscopic life

Plant and animal life. Diatoms—microscopic algae with glasslike shells of silica—are the major forms of algae, although green and blue-green algae are abundant during the summer in Lakes Erie, Ontario, and Michigan. Copepods and cladocerans, microscopic crustaceans, are important in the animal forms of plankton. Most abundant during the spring months in the upper lakes, plankton reaches two peaks of abundance—spring and fall—in the lower lakes and in the more productive waters of the upper lakes.

The organisms living on the bottom in shallow waters are the same kinds of snails, clams, worms, mayflies, and caddis flies found in most small lakes. The deep waters, however, are the realm of some organisms that are found only in the deep, cold lakes of the northern latitudes. These include the delicate opossum shrimp, the deepwater scud (a crustacean), two types of copepods, and the deepwater sculpin (a spiny, large-headed fish).

The changing fish population

The fish community of the lakes and tributaries includes representatives of most families of North American fishes. Lake trout, whitefish, and lake herring have always been important in the lakes, while perch, pike perch, bass and catfish are abundant in the shallow, warmer waters. The fish populations have changed drastically over the past century. By 1880, the damming and pollution of tributaries had caused the elimination of the Atlantic salmon and the restriction of the whitefish. At the same time, the lake sturgeon was purposely overfished, and the carp was introduced. Smelt entered Lake Michigan in 1927 and in a short time had spread throughout the lakes. The predatory sea lamprey migrated into the upper lakes and established spawning populations in the 1930s, causing the collapse of the lake trout populations in Lakes Huron and Michigan by the early 1950s. Other large predators were also drastically reduced by the sea lamprey. Consequently, when the alewife migrated into the upper lakes between 1931 and 1954, it met little competition and predation and soon became the most abundant species. Alewives are of little commercial value, however, and cause costly sanitary operations when, periodically, millions of them die and are washed up to rot on the beaches. During the 1960s, lake trout were reintroduced when it appeared that the sea lamprey was under control. Coho and chinook salmon were also introduced, both to provide a sports fishery and to control the alewife.

Herring and ring-bellied gulls and terns are the most common birds; small islands are important nesting grounds for them. The lakes are important as wintering areas for ducks such as the scaups and the old-squaw duck, and a diversity of shorebirds and songbirds migrate through the region during the spring and fall. Various places along the shoreline, such as Pelee Point in Lake Erie, are favoured locations for birdwatching.

The economy. Early interest in the lakes was stimulated

by the easy transportation route that they offered into the heartland of the continent. The value of the extensive forests and fertile land in the region was soon realized, and lumbering and agriculture became important. Large coalfields and deposits of iron, copper, limestone, and other minerals were found along or near the extensive shorelines. The combination of these vast resources with a plentiful water supply naturally favoured the development of huge industries and large metropolitan areas around the Great Lakes. Present population growth supports the speculation that a large megalopolis ultimately will extend from Milwaukee and Chicago around southern Lake Michigan, across the state of Michigan to Detroit, and along the southern shore of Lake Erie and will include the Toronto–Hamilton area on Lake Ontario.

Most of the total shipping tonnage includes iron ore, coal, and grain for lake ports, but some tonnage is shipped overseas through the St. Lawrence Seaway. The Welland Canal allows passage around Niagara Falls from Lake Ontario into Lake Erie, and the channels and locks in the St. Marys River have made Lake Superior accessible to ships up to 730 feet in length.

Although the virgin pine forests were felled by 1910, the growing of timber is important and is supported by both federal and state governments. The counties bordering the lakes in the United States have about half of their lands in farms, and over 5 percent of the value of U.S. agriculture is produced in the lakes region. Bordering Canadian counties have roughly 30 percent of their lands under agriculture, producing about 10 percent of the total agricultural value.

The iron ranges around Lake Superior—such as the Mesabi in Minnesota—were once a major source of iron for the United States. Peak production occurred in 1953, when almost 100,000,000 net tons were produced. The large deposits of rich ores have since been depleted, but low-grade taconite ores can now be efficiently processed. Lake Superior's Keweenaw Peninsula is a major source of copper, although sources outside of the lakes are relatively more important.

The industry of the lakes region is highly diversified. Perhaps the more important are the large steel mills in Illinois, Indiana, Ohio, and Ontario and the automobile industry centred in the Detroit area.

Fisheries

Commercial fishing was once a major industry on the lakes, but the decline of the more desirable species led to its collapse. Emphasis has switched to developing major sports fisheries based on coho and chinook salmon, lake trout, and rainbow trout.

The value of the lakes for a broad spectrum of recreational activities is inestimable. Powerboating and sailing have become major activities. Many miles of sandy beaches stretch along the lake shores. State, federal, and county lands offer many camping, picnicking, and park areas for a thriving tourist industry.

Of major importance is the water supply that the lakes provide for industries and for about 240 municipalities. Hydroelectric generating stations exist on the St. Marys, Niagara, and St. Lawrence rivers. Over 30 large thermal-power plants around the lakes use their waters for cooling.

Study and exploration. The Great Lakes have been an integral part of the exploration and development of the North American continent. A broken sword, an axe, and a shield boss found near Lake Nipigon, Ontario, and the rune stone at Kensington, Minnesota, have been cited as evidence of early Viking exploration of the region, although the authenticity of these artifacts has not been established. French exploration of the region commenced in 1535, when the explorer Jacques Cartier travelled up the St. Lawrence River to the site of modern Montreal in his search for a route to the Orient. The Huron Indians told him of the great seas lying beyond, but the upper St. Lawrence and Lake Ontario were controlled by the Iroquois, who were not friendly to the Europeans. Consequently, further exploration by another leading French explorer of North America, Samuel de Champlain, followed the course of the Ottawa River, Lake Nipissing, and the French River to Georgian Bay. He reached Lake Huron in 1615 and is credited with being the first European to see the Great Lakes. In 1634 Jean Nicolet—dispatched by Champlain to seek a route to China—led an expedition into Lake Michigan and down the length of Green Bay to the Fox River, where he encountered the Winnebago Indians. Other French explorers, including Robert Cavelier, sieur de La Salle, explored the lakes, made peace with the Indians, and established early settlements.

French exploration

Three major conflicts affected the history and development of the Great Lakes. The French and Indian War (1754–63)—a struggle between the French and British to gain control of rich fur-producing lands—concluded with the cession of Canada to England. The main consequences of the American Revolution (1775–83) to the Great Lakes region were the migration of thousands of Loyalists to New Brunswick, Nova Scotia, and Ontario and the establishment of the international boundary between the United States and Canada. During the War of 1812, Lake Erie was the site of a major naval battle.

Although several of the early explorers recorded observations of short-term fluctuations in water levels in early geographical writings, the first purely scientific expedition on the Great Lakes was not carried out until 1848. It was led by the Swiss naturalist Louis Agassiz and concentrated on studies of the north shore of Lake Superior. Water-level gauges were established in all the lakes by 1860, and all waters were charted by 1882. Studies of plant and animal life began in the 1870s, and the first study of lake currents was conducted in the early 1890s. Interest in lake fisheries was strong in the early 20th century, and, since the 1960s, research on changes in plant and animal life wrought by pollution has grown considerably. (A.M.B.)

MACKENZIE RIVER

Draining an area that, at 711,000 square miles (1,841,000 square kilometres), is almost as large as that of Mexico, the Mackenzie River is one of the major river systems in the drainage pattern of North America: its basin is the largest in Canada, and it is only exceeded on the continent by the Mississippi–Missouri system. From the headwaters of the Finlay River, which flows into the Peace River Reservoir west of the Rocky Mountains, the entire river system runs for 2,635 miles (4,240 kilometres) through the sparsely settled, lake-strewn Canadian north to empty into the cold waters of the Beaufort Sea in the Arctic Ocean. The Mackenzie itself is 1,060 miles (1,706 kilometres) long, according to the conventional measurement from Great Slave Lake. The river is generally wide, mostly from one to two miles across, and in island-dotted sections, three or four miles wide. It has a strong flow. Its lake-covered triangular delta measures more than 120 miles from north to south and is about 50 miles wide along the Arctic shore.

Size of the system

The headwaters of the system include several large rivers, which themselves drain vast forested plains of northeastern British Columbia and northern Alberta. These drainage basins include the Liard River (107,000 square miles), the Peace River (125,250 square miles), and the Athabasca River (62,900 square miles). Much shorter rivers flow into the system from the east, draining the low rocky hills of the ancient structural mass known as the Canadian Shield. The system also includes the huge Great Slave Lake (11,031 square miles), Great Bear Lake (12,340 square miles), and the smaller Lake Athabasca (3,064 square miles).

The whole basin is sparsely populated, and its resources are few and less accessible than those of southern Canada. Yet the whole region is one of the few great unspoiled areas of the world, offering a rich wildlife and spectacular scenery, as well as a somewhat harsh climatic environment.

Physical features. The Mackenzie River itself begins at the western end of Great Slave Lake, at 513 feet (156 metres) above sea level. Deep (more than 1,000 feet in some places), clear water fills the lake's eastern arm, and shallow, murky water is found in the western part. Because of its large size and extent of winter ice cover, Great Slave Lake is the last part of the Mackenzie waterway to be free of ice in the spring, with some ice remaining until mid-June in the lake's centre.

Great Slave Lake

The ice on the Mackenzie River begins to break up in early to mid-May in its southern section, being preceded by breakup on the Liard River. Tributary rivers are free of ice before the Mackenzie itself, and high water and flooding are common during the breakup period, particularly when ice dams form. The ice across the lower Mackenzie River breaks up in late May; the channels in the Mackenzie River Delta are usually free of floating river ice by the end of May or early June, with the western channels being influenced by the earlier breakup of the Peel River. Sea ice usually remains offshore from the delta in the Beaufort Sea during June, particularly if prevailing winds are onshore.

The upper course. The head of the Mackenzie River is about six miles wide where the western end of the Great Slave Lake narrows and is filled by one large island and several small ones. The river narrows to less than a half mile in width near Fort Providence, and it is there that ice bridges are built across the river in early winter to carry truck traffic along the Mackenzie–Slave Lake Highway. Ferries are used for this crossing in summer, but all road traffic ceases during the breakup period in May. A branch road extends to Fort Simpson, and except for a winter trail that is used only occasionally, there are no through roads farther north along the Mackenzie Valley. Mills Lake is a shallow broadening of the Mackenzie River west of the village of Fort Providence. To the west the river again narrows to about a mile in width, and the current is fast at Green Island Rapids, about 12 miles east of Fort Simpson. There is, however, a seven- to 10-foot channel among the boulders in these rapids, sufficient for the flat-bottomed barges pushed by shallow-draft tugs that operate out of the southern terminal of Hay River and along the Mackenzie.

At Fort Simpson the 755-mile-long Liard joins the Mackenzie from the west from its source in the southeastern Yukon Territory. The contrast between the muddy, silt-laden water of the Liard and the clear water of the Mackenzie is very apparent in the river after the junction, as these "two rivers in one" remain separate in terms of certain physical properties for about 300 miles downstream. At Fort Simpson, as for much of its course, the Mackenzie flows between steep, gray gravel banks, 100 to 200 feet high, which obscure the adjacent lowlands from view.

The "two rivers in one"

The Mackenzie River Lowlands are about 250 miles wide near Fort Simpson. Although it is classed as forested, mainly with a few species of coniferous trees, such as black and white spruce, and some poplar, much of the lowland away from the tributary rivers is covered by swamps, muskegs (bogs), and lakes, as well as many open areas of grassy vegetation and low bushes. The Mackenzie Mountains rise steeply on the western side of the Mackenzie Valley to altitudes of 5,000 to 6,000 feet; since the tree line is at about 3,000 feet, the upper slopes are barren. The eastern edge of the Mackenzie Lowlands is formed by ancient hills of the Canadian Shield, which slope up to altitudes of about 1,000 feet.

The Mackenzie River Lowlands are underlain by flat-lying sedimentary rock of Cretaceous (100,000,000 years old) and Devonian (350,000,000 years old) geological ages. Little of this rock is exposed at the surface, however, because it is mantled with glacial and alluvial deposition of clays, sands, and gravels.

North of Fort Simpson the Mackenzie River is a little less than 400 feet above sea level, is a mile wide, and flows between steep banks. The mean discharge is measured at 228,000 cubic feet per second at Fort Simpson; the average flow at high water during June is above 400,000 cubic feet per second, and this seems to be equally obtained from the Liard and upper Mackenzie. The latter supplies a larger share of the river's volume during winter.

The lower course. North of the trading post at Wrigley, the Redstone and Keele rivers enter from the west; they have deep canyons where they break out of the Mackenzie Mountains but flow across the lowland as shallow, braided streams. These rivers and the others that drain from the Mackenzie Mountains have their peak flows in June after the snow melts in the mountains; they become shallow rivers in late summer. The Mackenzie River picks up relatively little volume within its valley lowland, as the average summer precipitation recorded at dispersed settlements is only about seven or eight inches (175 to 200 millimetres); total annual precipitation throughout the Mackenzie Valley is 10 to 14 inches (250 to 350 millimetres).

Rainfall in the lowlands

At the village of Fort Norman the cold, clear water of Great Bear River enters from the east. This short river empties out of Great Bear Lake; it is navigable for shallow-draft vessels, except for a short portage around rapids about 30 miles east of its mouth. Once more, there is a distinct summer demarcation for 50 miles northward in the Mackenzie River between its silt-laden water and the clear water from the Great Bear River on the eastern bank. At Norman Wells the Mackenzie River broadens to about four miles in width and is less than 175 feet above sea level. The mean annual discharge of the river there is 311,000 cubic feet per second but flows during June and July will usually exceed 500,000 cubic feet per second.

The Mackenzie Valley Lowland is only about 30 miles wide in this section, being broken by the treeless summits of the Franklin Mountains, which rise to a little more than 3,000 feet altitude on the east side of the river. Small lakes are not so common across the Mackenzie Valley in this area as they are on the lowland west of Great Slave Lake. Forest vegetation is scanty except in the river valleys and in areas of better drainage; most of the trees are stunted spruce.

Where Mountain River joins the Mackenzie from the west there is a fast water section known as Sans Sault Rapids; the river drops about 20 feet within a few miles. There is ample depth of water for the shallow-draft barges during July, but, despite deepening of the channel by rock blasting, shallow water is sometimes a navigation problem in late summer. South of the Indian village of Fort Good Hope, the Mackenzie narrows as it flows between 100- to 150-foot perpendicular limestone walls known as The Ramparts. North of Fort Good Hope, the Mackenzie crosses the Arctic Circle. It is slightly entrenched and meanders across its flat valley floor, its banks being two or three miles apart; low islands are numerous, and shifting sandbars are a problem for the riverboats. Where the Arctic Red River enters from the south, the Mackenzie again flows between steep rock walls, which rise about 100 to 200 feet directly from the water.

The delta region. At Point Separation the Mackenzie River Delta begins. From the south the 425-mile Peel River is the last major tributary to add water to the Mackenzie. The mean discharge of water into the Mackenzie Delta is estimated at 400,000 cubic feet per second, more than doubling at flood peaks. The delta covers about 4,700 square miles and is a maze of branching, intertwining channels, numerous cutoff lakes, and circular ponds. These lakes are an excellent habitat for muskrat, and the trapping of these animals became the main source of income for the Indian and Eskimo inhabitants of the delta from 1920 to 1950.

The perpetually frozen subsurface layer known as permafrost lies a few feet beneath the surface of the islands in the delta and exists in a discontinuous layer beneath the whole Mackenzie River Lowlands north of Great Slave Lake. Depending on the type of vegetation cover, the top few inches to several feet of ground above the permafrost melts during the summer months. Northern construction of airfields, roads, and pipelines has to be adapted to these permafrost conditions; houses and other buildings are usually placed on wooden piles that are sunk and frozen into the permafrost to give stability. One of the distinctive features of the town of Inuvik, built in the 1950s, is a utilidor, a linear boxlike metal container raised slightly above the surface of the ground, in which the separate sewer, water, and heating pipes are placed. Mackenzie River water-transport routes terminate at Tuktoyaktuk on the Arctic coast northeast of the delta, where cargo is transferred to other vessels of greater draft, which serve the small settlements and defensive radar stations along the western Arctic coast.

The permafrost region

The people and economy. The Mackenzie River Basin is sparsely populated. Its natural resources are few, and they are less accessible than comparable resources in southern Canada. Fur-bearing animals were the resource attraction of the 19th century; although they are still trapped throughout the forests of the river basin, particularly by the Indian population, furs now constitute a minor element in the regional economy. Muskrat, marten, beaver, lynx, and fox are the main pelts sought. The forests in the southern part of the basin have been utilized for local lumber in the Peace River area and near other small settlements. The small trees may have future value as a source of pulpwood.

Agricultural land is developed only in the south, particularly in the Peace River area. Settlers moved into the Athabasca River, Lesser Slave Lake, and Peace River areas in large numbers after 1920, when the farmlands of the Canadian prairies were almost all occupied. When railroad connections were established southward to Edmonton, these farms were able to produce grain, livestock, and legume seed for external markets. A few farms and many gardens produced well along the Mackenzie River before 1940, but the improved transport of recent decades has permitted most food to be imported. With July mean temperatures averaging about 60° F (16° C), and daily temperatures that reach into the 70s and sometimes 80s, climate does not prevent the growth of certain crops.

The role of oil and minerals

Minerals are the economic basis of some of the larger settlements in the basin. The first oil field was discovered at Norman Wells in 1921, but production did not begin until the 1930s. These wells and the small refinery at Norman Wells still produce for the industries, transport, and homes of the central and northern parts of the Mackenzie Valley. Other oil fields were discovered in the early 1970s near the Mackenzie River Delta. The largest oil fields are in the southern parts of the river basin, in northwestern Alberta and northeastern British Columbia. This oil is carried southward by pipeline to Edmonton to be distributed to refineries in southern Canada and the northern United States. An enormous reserve of petroleum lies in the Tar Sands along the Athabasca River north of McMurray; production there has been limited by a quota system.

Metallic minerals were found along the eastern edges of the basin. Valuable radium and uranium ores were produced from 1933 to 1961 at Port Radium on the eastern shores of Great Bear Lake, despite very high transportation costs. Other uranium mines came into production after 1950 at Uranium City on the north side of Lake Athabasca. High-quality gold mines, discovered after 1935, brought into existence the city of Yellowknife, the present capital of the Northwest Territories, on the north arm of Great Slave Lake. Lead-zinc deposits were developed at Pine Point on the south side of Great Slave Lake. When the deposits proved to be large enough, the first railroad into the Northwest Territories was built from the Peace River area along the Mackenzie Highway to Hay River and Pine Point.

The water of the Mackenzie River system was too far away from large industrial and urban markets to be used for hydroelectric power until the late 1960s. At that time the Peace River was dammed as it broke out of the Rocky Mountains and a large storage lake formed westward in the Rocky Mountain Trench. This electric power is transmitted 600 miles to Vancouver, British Columbia. Otherwise, the only developed waterpower sites are on the Snare and Talston rivers, which drop westward out of the Canadian Shield to the Mackenzie Lowlands and supply power to the mines and residents at Yellowknife and Pine Point. There is no utilization of the water of the Mackenzie River itself, except for river transportation.

The large lakes of the Mackenzie Basin are a source of lake trout and whitefish. Lake Athabasca was first exploited during the 1930s, and then Great Slave Lake was opened to commercial fishing after 1945. In the latter lake, fish are caught in both summer and winter and transported south by truck or rail to urban markets in both Canada and the United States. The catch is controlled by seasonal quotas that prevent depletion of the species. The cold water of Great Bear Lake has some fish, but they grow too slowly to withstand commercial fishing except by sports fishermen. Fish of the Mackenzie River are netted by some local residents to supplement their imported food.

Study and exploration. Explorers and fur traders pushed westward across Canada in the late 18th century to the headwaters of rivers that flowed into Hudson Bay, seeking to tap the fur resources in the lands beyond. In 1778 one of them, Peter Pond, found Portage La Loche (Methy Portage) connecting the headwaters of Churchill River with the Clearwater River, itself one of the eastbank tributaries of the Athabasca River. In 1789 Alexander Mackenzie made his historic journey northward from the trading post of Fort Chipewyan on Lake Athabasca, exploring with a crew of 12 persons in three canoes, the full length of the mighty river now bearing his name.

Other fur traders of the North West Company followed early in the 19th century, establishing posts at several sites along the river and on its headwater tributaries. From the mid-1820s, supplies were carried in by the distinctive York boats, shallow-draft vessels with a sharply angled stern and bow. In 1884 the first steamer began to operate northward from McMurray, at the junction of the Clearwater and Athabasca rivers, to Fitzgerald on the Slave River. At this point there are 16 miles of rapids in Slave River, the only break in 1,700 miles of shallow-draft river navigation from McMurray to the Arctic Ocean. In 1886 the first steamer began operating north of Fort Smith, on the present Northwest Territories–Alberta border, taking supplies to the Mackenzie River trading posts and bringing out bales of fur. During the 1920–40 period, flat-bottomed, stern paddle-wheeled vessels operated on the Mackenzie River, but they were replaced after 1945 by small diesel tugs that could push several barges. (J.L.Ro.)

MISSISSIPPI RIVER

Paramount among North American rivers, the Mississippi combines with its major tributaries to form the world's fifth largest drainage system in area (approximately 1,244,000 square miles, or 3,221,000 square kilometres). As the central river artery of a highly industrialized nation, the Mississippi has become one of the busiest commercial waterways in the world; and as the unruly neighbour of some of the continent's richest farmland it has been subjected to a remarkable degree of man-made control. Furthermore, the river's unique contribution to the history and literature of the United States has woven it like a bright thread through the folklore and national consciousness of North America, linking the names of two U.S. Presidents—Abraham Lincoln and U.S. Grant—with that of the celebrated author Mark Twain. Draining all or part of 31 U.S. states and two Canadian provinces, the outline of the Mississippi system resembles a sturdy tree with two main lateral branches, the Ohio to the east and the Missouri to the west. Only a thin line carries the name of the parent trunk northward to the river's source at Lake Itasca, Minnesota.

Although the Mississippi can be ranked as third longest river in the world by adding the length of the Missouri (2,466 miles or 3,969 kilometres) to the Mississippi downstream of the Missouri–Mississippi confluence, the 2,348-mile (3,779-kilometre) length of the Mississippi proper is comfortably exceeded by at least a dozen other rivers. In volume of discharge, however, the Mississippi's 350,000,000,000 gallons per day is eighth greatest in the world.

The character and physical appearance of the Mississippi proper divides into three stages. From the source to the head of navigation at St. Paul, Minnesota, it is a clear, fresh stream winding its unassuming way through low countryside dotted with lakes and marshes. From St. Paul to the mouth of the Missouri it grows into the powerful dominating river immortalized in Mark Twain's *Tom Sawyer* and *Huckleberry Finn.* Flowing past steep limestone bluffs, it is in these reaches, where it gathers in the streams and rivers of Minnesota, Wisconsin, Illinois, and Iowa, that the river assumes the character that led Algonkian-speaking Indians to name it the "Father of Waters" (literally *Misi,* "big"; *Sipi,* "water"). Its union with the Missouri changes the Mississippi completely. The turbulent, flotsam-laden Missouri, especially when in flood, adds impetus as well as enormous quantities of silt to the clearer Mississippi. Beyond the junction with the Ohio at Cairo, Illinois, the Mississippi swells to its full grandeur. Often a mile and a half from bank to bank, it becomes a brown flood, descending with deceptive quiet toward the Gulf of Mexico.

Regional divisions

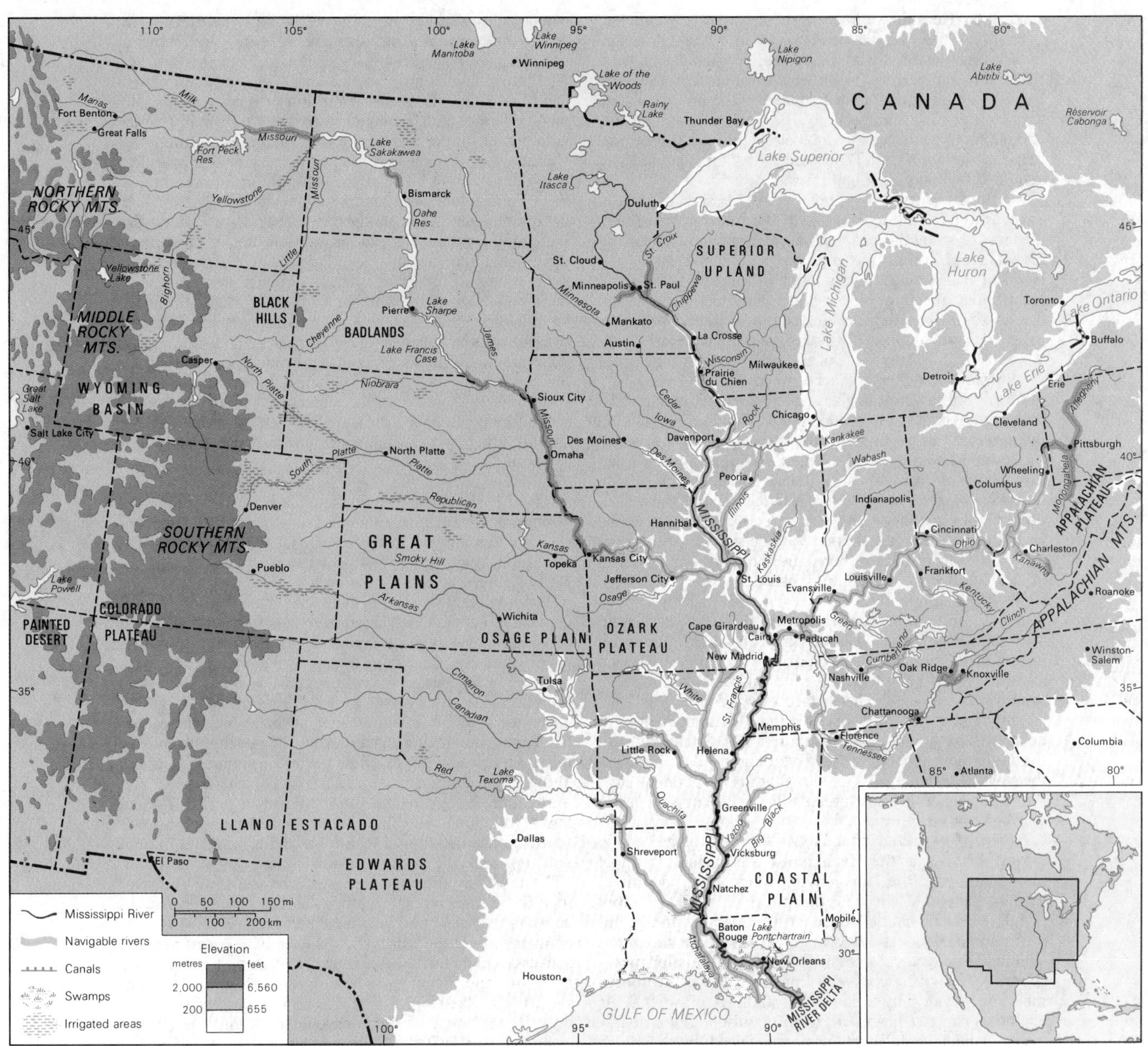

The Mississippi River Basin and its drainage network.

To geographers, the lower Mississippi has long been a classic example of a river in "old age"; that is, it loops and curls extravagantly along its channel, leaving behind meander scars, cutoffs, oxbow lakes, and swampy backwaters. More poetically, Mark Twain compared its shape to "a long, pliant apple-paring." Today the sunlight glittering on the twisted ribbon of water remains one of the most distinctive landmarks of a transcontinental flight. Now largely curbed by an elaborate system of embankments (levees) and spillways, this lower section of the Mississippi was the golden, sometimes treacherous, highway for the renowned Mississippi steamboats, those "palaces on paddlewheels" that so fired public imagination. From the explosive master pilot Horace Bixby portrayed by Mark Twain, down to the nostalgic lyrics of Oscar Hammerstein's "Ol' Man River," the creations of that era on the Mississippi have added colour to America's heritage.

Physical features. *Physiography.* The geology and physical geography of the Mississippi drainage area are essentially those of the Interior Lowlands and Great Plains of North America. Fringes also touch upon the Rocky and Appalachian mountains and upon the rim of the Laurentian Shield to the north. The focus of the system, the floodplain of the lower Mississippi, is of particular interest in that the geology and physical geography of the region are of the river's own making. Like a huge funnel, the river has taken silt and debris from contributory areas near the lip of the funnel and deposited much of the product in the alluvial plain of the funnel's spout, illustrating the interdependence of the entire Mississippi system.

The most significant contributory area in recent times has been to the west of the river. Rising in western uplands, notably in the foothills of the Rockies, rivers like the Red, Arkansas, Kansas, Platte, and Missouri remove considerable silt loads from the rolling expanses of the Great Plains. A wide, gently sloping mantle of unconsolidated materials, laid down over rock beds of the Cretaceous Period (100,000,000 years ago), allows for each river to pick up an independent course toward the Father of Waters. Rainfall in these western areas is meagre, usually less than 25 inches a year; but because at least 70 percent of this precipitation falls between April and September, the erosive capability of the rivers is enhanced. The prairie soils, moreover, offer little resistance to erosion, so that the rivers are not only incised and braided in their courses but their silt load is high in relation to their volume. The Red River, for example, takes its name from the distinctive stain given to its waters by the red-brown soils of its upper course.

Contributory areas

The Mississippi's eastern contributory rivers drain the well-watered Appalachian Plateau. Most of this group, including the Kentucky, Green, Cumberland, and Tennessee rivers, flow via well-defined valleys into the Ohio and thence into the Mississippi. The erosive capacity of these rivers varies in relation to the geological structure of their basins. These consist of harder rocks in the higher plateau and a softer sill of limestone of the Carboniferous Period, 300,000,000 years ago, lying below the 1,000-foot line between the Ohio and Tennessee rivers and the glaciated area of the Ohio's right bank tributaries.

The third contributory area of the Mississippi differs, once again, from the other two. The upper Mississippi gathers its strength in a region marked and scarred by glacial action. After the great ice sheets had put down layers of glacial debris across much of Minnesota, Wisconsin, Illinois, and upper Iowa, huge quantities of meltwater flowed south, washing distinct channels through this debris. Today the upper Mississippi and its tributaries, the Wisconsin, St. Croix, Rock, and Illinois rivers, all trace the lines of these former glacial sluiceways.

Pouring southward the glacial meltwaters were joined by the proto-Missouri and Ohio rivers. The combined flood then gouged out the great north–south trough along which the lower Mississippi now flows. Six hundred miles long, this trough is from 25 to 200 miles wide and bounded by escarpments rising up to 200 feet above the valley floor. Geological studies have revealed that the floor of the glacial trough was later buried by a deep layer of material washed out from the ice sheet, and dumped to a thickness of 100–200 feet in the central section.

The delta

The Mississippi's delta is an even more striking monument to the river's constructive work. Here, at the tip of the drainage funnel, millions of years of sedimentation have spilled out across the floor of the Gulf of Mexico a great cone of sediment 300 miles in radius and 30,000 square miles in area. The surface expression of this cone (slightly to the east of its apex) is the Mississippi's present delta with an area of 10,100 square miles. Stretching into the Gulf the "fingers" of its levee-building distributaries, the Mississippi piles up 495,000,000 tons of sediment each year and inexorably advances its delta shoreline six miles seaward every century.

Hydrography. Understandably, the hydrology of so powerful a river as the Mississippi has been the subject of intense study. In the 19th century, Mark Twain described with considerable wit how the pilots of the Mississippi paddle-wheelers banded together to run a common information service about changing conditions along the channel. Today the Mississippi River Commission is responsible for river work and considers it worthwhile to maintain a working scale-model of the river so that its engineers can test new plans in miniature before embarking on expensive, full-scale projects. Indeed, by the 1920s it was generally held that enough was known about the river's hydrology and enough control structures had been built to have tamed the river. Then, in 1927, came the most disastrous flood in the recorded history of the lower Mississippi Valley. More than 26,000 square miles of land were flooded. Communications, including roads, rail, and telephone services, were cut in many places. Farms, factories, and whole towns went temporarily under water. In modern values, something like $1,000,000,000 worth of damage was done, and 214 people lost their lives. The river engineers took another look at the hydrology of the Mississippi.

Mean water discharge data

Since the freak conditions of 1927, the mean discharge of water into the lower Mississippi by its major tributaries has been monitored as follows (in cubic feet per second): Arkansas 41,500; Illinois 20,700; Upper Mississippi 92,600; Missouri 70,600; Ohio 259,300; Red 49,300; White 30,200. The mean discharge of the main river past Vicksburg, Mississippi, is calculated at 548,160 cubic feet per second. These statistics, however, conceal all-important variations in river flow linked with the fluctuating state of the Mississippi's larger tributaries.

Broadly speaking, the western tributaries are the most irregular. They reach a spring or early summer peak that is up to three or four times as great as their winter contribution. The upper Mississippi and its tributaries reach their maximum flow about the same time (March–June), when melting snows are followed by early summer rains. The winter runoff from this area is, however, substantial. The crest of the Ohio's flow occurs slightly earlier. At Metropolis, Illinois, just short of the confluence with the Mississippi, the greatest monthly discharge is usually recorded in March, at which time the Ohio may be providing over 60 percent of the water being monitored past Vicksburg in the lower river. From these figures it is clear that the Ohio is chiefly responsible for the lower Mississippi flood situations, which may be aggravated by such factors as early rains in the Great Plains, a sudden hot spell melting the northern snows, and heavy downpours throughout the lower valley. Under such conditions the lower river will rise over its banks and put pressure against the levees. Tributaries will back up and form lakes on the far side of these same levees. The current, which normally runs no more than two to 3½ knots (2½ to four miles per hour), may then double at constricted points along the main channel. Thus the monitoring station at Vicksburg, which, at low water 1936, recorded as little as 93,800 cubic feet per second, measured 2,060,000 cubic feet per second at high water stage the following year, a daily flow of about 1,300,000,000 gallons.

Plant and animal life. Although the natural vegetation of the Mississippi's immediate valley is the product of climate and soil, rather than of the river, the Mississippi's swamps and backwaters are ecologically noteworthy. Threaded along the river, from the wild rice marshes of Minnesota to the coastal wetlands of the delta, are pockets of thriving plant–animal associations. Here the abundance of natural cover, the comparative isolation, and the food provided by such plants as sedges, pondweeds, and millets encourages regular colonization by waterfowl. The path of these birds, as they move up and down the river with the seasons, has been called the "Mississippi Flyway," an appropriate name for the vast aerial highway that reaches from the delta to the distant summer nesting grounds in northern Canada. An estimated eight million ducks, geese, and swans winter in the lower part of the flyway, and many more birds use it en route to Latin America. Typical flyway migrants are Canada and lesser snow geese, large numbers of mallard and teal, black duck, widgeon, pintail and ring-necked ducks, and coots.

Ecology

The most important varieties of fish found in the river include several types of catfish (some of which grow to considerable size and are fished commercially by local concerns along the middle and lower river); walleyes and suckers, which thrive in the upper river and provide the basis for a sport fishing industry in Minnesota and Wisconsin; carp; and garfish. Alligators are now rare, being found only in the most isolated backwaters, while the shrimp and crab fisheries of the brackish waters are in decline.

The people and economy. As its respectful Indian name indicates, the Mississippi played an important role in the lives of the aboriginal peoples settled on its banks. To the Indians of the river, the Mississippi was both highway and larder. On it they paddled their cottonwood dugouts and their bark canoes, and from it they took the fish that was a mainstay of their diet. Constant shifts of migration, local or large scale, interwove tribal languages and cultures. By the time the white man arrived, the Sioux who had originally lived on the upper river had withdrawn west to give place to Ojibwa, Winnebago, Fox, and Sauk. Lower down, the Illinois tribe had established prosperous agricultural communities. And in the lower valley itself lived clans of Choctaw, Koroa, Taensa, Chickasaw, Tunica, Yazoo, Pascagoula, Natchez, Biloxi and Alibamu.

The explorer Hernando de Soto, commander of the first white expedition to penetrate to the river, had high hopes of plundering the southern tribes. In May 1541 his Spanish raiding force reached the river at a point near Memphis, Tennessee. But the "Rio Grande," as the Spaniards called it, provided the newcomers with small profit and much grief. The river Indians launched repeated attacks; the Mississippi floods caught the Spanish unawares; and, ironically, de Soto, white discoverer of the river, was buried in its waters, after which the rest of his disappointed expedition retreated to the sea, their homemade boats under a running fire from the Indians.

Early exploration

The next white explorers of the river appeared in 1673 out of French Canada—two canoe loads of voyageurs commanded by Louis Jolliet, a French government agent, and Father Jacques Marquette, a Jesuit priest. Portaging from the Fox River to the Wisconsin, they paddled down the Mississippi as far as the mouth of the St. Francis River in present-day Arkansas. Nine years later the famous French explorer Robert Cavelier, sieur de La Salle reached the delta itself, having opened up the even easier portage from the Great Lakes via the Illinois River. He grasped at once the strategic significance of the huge drainage system and promptly claimed the entire Mississippi Basin for France. Within a generation the Mississippi was a vital link between France's Gulf settlements and Canada, and La Salle's claim was vaguely designated as "Louisiana."

But France's grasp on the Mississippi was never firm. French traders settled the upper river, establishing towns like St. Louis and Prairie du Chien, whose names survive to this day. But the lower river passed into Spanish hands in 1769; the Treaty of Paris (1783) optimistically declared the river as the western boundary of the United States; and republican France reacquired the much-bartered stream only long enough to sell it to the United States as part of the Louisiana Purchase (1803). This last move recognized what had been obvious for a quarter of a century—the growing domination of the river by the Americans. They came by raft, flatboat, and ark (a "raft with a rim"), built and loaded on the left bank tributaries that were in the forefront of the westward expansion of the United States. Unwieldy and expendable, these craft floated downstream to leave their cargoes and occupants as advance guards of American political and economic expansion. Only the long, slim keelboats made the return trip. They were worked upcurrent under pole, paddle, sail, or by the back-breaking "cordel," a system under which the crew went ashore with a long bow hawser and pulled the vessel upstream by brute strength.

The torch of exploration also passed to the Americans after the Purchase. In 1805–06 the pioneer expedition of Lieut. Zebulon M. Pike struggled to within 80 miles of the river's source, and in 1832 Henry Schoolcraft, an Indian agent for the U.S. government, identified and named Lake Itasca (Latin *veritas caput,* "true head") as the Mississippi's starting point.

Built in Pittsburgh in 1811, the "New Orleans" was the first steamboat to appear on the river. Like some fearful omen, her maiden voyage coincided with the series of earth tremors known as the New Madrid earthquake, the cause of much flooding and sudden relocation of sections of the main channel. But the "New Orleans" won through, and within a decade her successors had wrought a revolution on the Mississippi. In 1814 only 21 steamboats called at New Orleans, whereas 191 arrived during 1819, and 14 years later more than 1,200 cargoes were unloaded in the year. As the freight rate by steamer between Cincinnati and New Orleans plummeted from nine cents a pound to less than half a cent, it became cheaper to send freight to the east coast via the Mississippi and the long sea passage than to send it a 10th the distance over the Appalachians.

The coming of the steamboats

With the introduction of larger, high-pressure engines and more streamlined hulls, the steamboats extended their range, and the Mississippi became economic overlord to half the country. In 1820 the "Western Engineer" probed up the Missouri. In 1823, the "Virginia" churned her way up to Fort Snelling at the junction of the Mississippi with the Minnesota River. The steamboats brought an era of unprecedented prosperity to the river. Town after town grew up, dependent on the regular arrival of packet boats bringing mail and passengers or freight boats that took on local produce and left off manufactured goods. Riverbank plantations maintained their own landings so they could ship crops direct, and riverside towns vied with one another to provide services such as fuelling and warehousing. The waterfront at New Orleans, with its double line of twin-stacked steamers mingled with oceangoing ships, was among the busiest in the nation.

Then came the Civil War and, at once, a sharp struggle for control of this vital waterway, a struggle culminating in Grant's siege of Vicksburg helped by the fortified gunboats and armoured steamers of the Union. When Vicksburg and the river fell into northern hands, the South was dealt a heavy commercial and strategic blow. Lincoln, who himself had been a Mississippi flatboat man, could report "the Father of Waters flows unvexed to the sea."

The years immediately after the Civil War saw a brief but glorious revival in river traffic. New and faster steamboats were built and operated, often in rivalry to one another, a rivalry made famous by the three-day race, commencing June 30, 1870, between the "Natchez" and the "Robert E. Lee." The latter won by dint of stripping out all her unnecessary superstructure and taking on her extra fuel supplies from tenders while steaming at full speed upriver. Yet even as the river was at its most flamboyant, the same westward expansion that had brought its development now passed it over. With the construction of east–west railroads and canals, the Mississippi's north–south alignment came to be regarded as a nuisance. Towns that had once sought to be staging posts up and down the river now competed to become crossing points. Commercial traffic dwindled, and the grand luxury paddle-wheelers gave way to sombre, more prosaic towboats with blocks of barges.

World War I produced a major resurgence in river trade. As other lines of transport became congested, the river was recognized as an increasingly valuable asset. With federal initiative, new barge lines were organized, and by 1931 the annual barge traffic moving along the river was twice the volume moved in any single year during the previous century. In 1917, for instance, the steamer "Sprague" established a new world record for size of tow. Her raft of 60 coal barges weighed 67,307 tons and covered an area of 6.5 acres.

"Sprague's" record is unlikely to be matched by any other paddle-wheeler, for the remaining steamboats are mostly showpiece examples, and the modern Mississippi towboat is of radically different design from her forebears. Screw-driven and diesel-engined, the modern towboat is made fast to the stern of her tow. Ahead stretches a rigid platform of barges as much as 1,500 feet long and with a designed draft of nine feet. Most barges are built for specific cargoes. If for dry cargo, they average 1,500 tons capacity and measure 195 feet long by 35 feet wide; for liquid cargo the proportions are about 2,500 tons capacity and 295 feet by 50 feet. To aid navigation, the towboat captain has at his disposal electronic depth finders, radar, contraguide rudders, a sophisticated system of river bank lights and markers, and radio telephone to warn other river users of his approach in narrow passages. Among the most recent cargoes to be carried along the river in this fashion are the booster rockets for space research, which are so bulky as to be unsuitable for any other mode of transport.

Responsibility for overseeing the maintenance and improvement of the Mississippi as a commercial waterway, as well as the related tasks of flood control and bank protection, falls upon the Mississippi River Commission. Created by act of Congress in 1879, the commission has supervised a massive program of river work that has profoundly reshaped the character of the Mississippi. The main stages of the navigation improvement program include a channel nine feet deep and 250 feet wide at low water between Cairo and Head of Passes (Gulf) authorized in 1896; a widening of this channel to 300 feet, approved in 1928; and its deepening to 12 feet put in hand in 1944 and still under way. Farther upriver, the outstanding achievement has been the construction of 26 locks and dams on the upper river to take the nine-foot channel up to Minneapolis-St. Paul. Connecting into the Mississippi is a vast complex of related waterways—from the Intracoastal Waterway in the south stretching between Florida and the Mexican border, to the nine-foot channels that lead up the Ohio to its tributaries and through the Illinois waterway to the Great Lakes and St. Lawrence Seaway.

Commercial use of the Mississippi waterway has shown sturdy growth. Leading cargoes, by bulk, were petroleum and products, coal and coke, iron and steel, chemicals, sand and gravel, and sulfur. An increasing emphasis on bulk handling has inevitably meant the rapid growth of a few key port cities at the expense of their rivals.

Flood control along the river dates back to the foundation of New Orleans by the French, who built a small levee to shelter their infant city. Over the next 200 years a complex array of riverbank structures was erected along the river to contain or divert floods. But it was not until after the catastrophic flood of 1927 that the federal government became committed to a definite program of flood control. Today the target is an integrated flood-control system able to master "project flood," the largest theoretical flood expected along the river. This program has altered the face of the river even more than the navigation program, with which it is linked, has altered its bed.

Flood control

In principle, the Mississippi's floods are either constricted by levees, hastened out of danger zones by floodways and improved channels, dissipated down spillways and into reservoirs, or starved by the impounding of tributary floods. From Cape Girardeau, Missouri, to the sea, the river is virtually "walled in" by a vast line of main stem levees. This stern concrete barrier has, incidentally, isolated the river from much of the surrounding countryside and many former riverbank towns are severed from their natural setting. In the event that the main levees are threatened, the excess floodwater drains away down spillways (*e.g.*, from north of New Orleans it is diverted past the city by spillways leading directly to the Gulf) or it bursts "fuse plugs," the specially weakened sections of levee leading to harmless floodways or reservoirs. A major example of this type of floodway occurs at New Madrid, just south of the Ohio confluence. Elsewhere, a massive program of bank strengthening using mattresses of concrete blocks has reduced lateral erosion and increased channel stability. The careful positioning of underwater dikes to deflect the current, the cutting through of oxbow bends at their necks, and a continuous dredging schedule have all helped to reduce flood levels. Although the system operated successfully against the high water levels of 1945 and 1950, it could not contain the record flood of 1973, during which 11,000,000 acres of land along the river and its tributaries lay under water. (G.T.Se.)

ST. LAWRENCE RIVER

The great hydrographic system connecting the source of the St. Louis River, in the U.S. state of Minnesota, with Cabot Strait, leading into the Atlantic Ocean from the extreme east of Canada, the St. Lawrence River crosses the interior of the North American continent for almost 2,500 miles (4,023 kilometres) and is of vital geographic and economic importance. It can be divided into three broad sectors. Upstream lies the Great Lakes region, with narrow riverlike sections linking the broad expanses of the lakes themselves. In the centre, from the eastern outflow of Lake Ontario, near the town of Kingston, to the Île d'Orléans, just downstream from the city of Quebec, the system passes through a more normal watercourse. From the Île d'Orléans to the Cabot Strait, between Newfoundland and Nova Scotia, the system broadens out again, first as the St. Lawrence estuary, and then, passing the island of Anticosti, as the oval shaped marine region known as the Gulf of St. Lawrence.

The St. Lawrence is a mighty and unique river, estuarine over much of its course. Bedded in an ancient geological depression, it drains the heart of a continent. It is at once an international, an intra-Quebec, and a multiprovincial system. An axis of regional population, it is also a routeway linking Canada, the United States, western Europe, and a large part of the rest of the world. The frontages of the several regions of the St. Lawrence River are not equally developed and do not maintain the same types of relationship with their hinterlands and with the outside world. Throughout its length, nevertheless, the St. Lawrence is a river retaining a great natural beauty, with landscapes beloved by all who live on its banks or make the long passage along its course.

Physical features. *Geology.* The St. Lawrence River occupies a geologically old depression that involves three great geologic regions of North America: the Canadian Shield, the Appalachian Mountains, and the intervening sedimentary rock platform. This ancient setting has been broken up by earth movements along several zones of structural weakness and has also been worn down by a number of separate cycles of erosion. Toward the end of the geologically recent Quaternary Period, the Ice Age glaciers that had occupied the depression were replaced by the Champlain Sea, which flooded the floor of the depression from about 11,400 to 9,500 years ago. The subsequent slight uplifting of the continent was enough to expel this arm of the ocean and, about 6,000 years ago, a residual riverlike watercourse was established, and the St. Lawrence—a young watercourse as rivers go—was born.

Origin

Climate and hydrography. In terms of both climate and hydrography, the St. Lawrence system as a whole has several regional zones. First, in the movement downstream from the upper part of the system, some of the associated boreal character is lost; in its path from the northern streams tributary to Lake Superior down to Lake Erie, the system passes from a subarctic to a more temperate southern zone. In a similar, but reverse, fashion, the eastern half of the system increases in northern character downstream; that is, from the Detroit–Windsor metropolitan area at the western end of Lake Erie to the northern coast of the St. Lawrence estuary, the climate deterioates again to a semi-Arctic level. This basic division brings out the regional contrasts in the hydrology of the central section of the river. Lake Erie, for example, loses much water through summer evaporation, whereas the affluents feeding the estuary of the St. Lawrence are heavily influenced by snowfall characteristics. At Montreal a good part of the river flow comes from the Great Lakes; hence its remarkable regularity. At the mouth of the estuary, on the other hand, the volume of ocean water coming in at high tide is 12 times the volume of river water flowing down at low tide; and here the St. Lawrence is profoundly marine, rather than lacustrine, in character. These basic regional hydrographic traits are accentuated also by a large seasonal variation in water temperature.

Physiography. The regional division of the St. Lawrence raises difficult problems, and despite several works on the subject, the debate among scientists remains open. The following division has been based on such overall criteria as longitudinal gradient of the riverbed, tidal characteristics, salinity, the width of the river bottom, human geography, and animal life. Threshold zones, a dozen miles or so in length, mark the transition from one region to the next.

Regional divisions

The St. Lawrence of the international rapids forms a clearly defined region extending from Kingston to above Montreal, where the presence of sudden breaks of gradient in the riverbed, the necessity of a navigable route between Montreal and southern Ontario, and the regional needs for power have led to the creation of hydroelectric stations, canals, and, of course, a significant part of the St. Lawrence Seaway. The flow volume of this section of the St. Lawrence, as measured at Cornwall, is 218,000 cubic feet per second (6,104 cubic metres per second).

The region of the Quebec Basses Terres is made up of a short section with a calm and nonreversible flow. This portion of the river course is characterized by the inflow of the system's principal tributary, the Rivière des Outaouais, by the presence of numerous islands (the Hochelaga Archipelago upstream, the Cent Îles downstream), by the development of the Greater Montreal conurbation, and also, unfortunately, by a certain degree of pollution. The development of the port of Montreal has depended upon, among other factors, the deepening of the river channel—downstream through dredging and upstream by canalization—by means of engineering projects that were begun in the 19th century. During the winter months, a thick crust of ice connects the two banks of the river, and icebreakers must open a channel in order for even a limited number of ships to reach Montreal. In earlier years, the possibilities of ice jams were great, with notable ice catastrophes occurring in 1642, 1838, and 1896.

The upper estuary extends from Lake Saint-Pierre to below the Île d'Orléans at Quebec. Here, the current of a freshwater tide begins to be reversible. During the winter months, the ice covering recalls the conditions at Montreal, but it also anticipates those of the middle estuary (see below), where a distinction is necessary between banked, or reef, ice, which is solid and fissured, and conglomerate ice, which moves past offshore. Topographical conditions at the river littoral, which had great military value, led to the foundation of the city of Quebec in this region, in 1608. The immediately adjacent area has been the historical cradle of the distinctive French-speaking population of Canada.

In the middle estuary, from the eastern end of the Île d'Orléans to the upstream side of the confluence with its major tributary, the Saguenay, the St. Lawrence broadens but remains relatively shallow. Progressively, the water ceases to be fresh and becomes brackish, and with an east wind one may, for the first time, catch a whiff of seaweed. Tides, thrust into a narrowing channel, attain maximum height in this section. Breakaway reef ice from this area constitutes one of the major sources of ice in the downstream parts of the estuary.

The lower estuary, one of the greatest topographic alterations in the entire course of the St. Lawrence, is found near the Saguenay confluence, at right angles to a submarine furrow. In this region, the river bottom exhibits a brutal break of gradient: within 10 miles, all in the vicinity of the confluence, the depth of the water increases from 82 feet (25 metres) to 1,148 feet (350 metres). It is by way of this drowned valley that the cold, salt waters from downstream, classed as Arctic, enter the region. In spite of the width of the watercourse, a number of ferries connect the two banks. In contrast to the thinly settled northern bank, behind which lie the inhospitable, rugged landscapes of the ancient rock region known as the Canadian Shield, the southern frontage of the lower estuary is largely open toward its hinterland, and major roads, including the Trans-Canada Highway, lead inland toward the province of New Brunswick.

The limits of the maritime estuary are, upstream, the promontory of the Pointe des Monts, and, leading to the Gulf of St. Lawrence, the island of Anticosti. (The latter, by reason of its size and its own circular currents, is an entity in its own right and cannot be considered as an element of the estuary.) Below the Pointe des Monts, the submarine valley mentioned above doubles in width, to over 50 miles. A major arm of the counterclockwise current stemming from the Gulf of St. Lawrence, after entering the northern portion of this region, turns back to the east. The salinity found here discourages ice formation, and, on the northern shore, the port of Sept Îles—although situated much farther north than Montreal—is in fact more open to navigation. The north frontage, with a hinterland rich in iron ore and electricity-generating potential and running at right angles to this portion of the estuary, seems to have greater capacity for development.

Plant and animal life. In spite of centuries of human influence, the biological world of the St. Lawrence continues to reflect natural conditions. Some clear regional distinctions must be made between not only the upper and lower sections of the system but also between the depths and the surface of the water and between the banks and the centre of the river course. Scientists have not, as yet, succeeded in identifying fully the basic life-producing conditions, the identity of the various eutrophic, or nutrition-generating, water levels, or the migrations of food supply, all of which go to make up the biomass, or life system, associated with the river. Animal life comprises fish (including the sturgeon, the smelt, and the herring), mammals (including an "Arctic" species, the beluga [white whale]), and mollusks (including the mussel [mye]). A noted phenomenon, which is characteristic of all regions of the river, is the massive migration of ducks, bustards, and geese, which utilize the sandy shores or river reefs as seasonal food sources. The vegetation associated with the river undoubtedly reflects the great shrubby zones that extend from Lake Erie to the northeast of the Gulf of St. Lawrence, made up of deciduous forest, mixed forest, coniferous forest, and open taiga. In addition, however, it exhibits such specifically river-linked characteristics as the sandbank grasses of the freshwater section and the plants with a high tolerance of salt found from the middle estuary onward. (L.-E.H.)

Migration of ducks, bustards, and geese

ST. LAWRENCE SEAWAY

A massive Canadian–United States navigational project completed at a cost of $466,000,000, the St. Lawrence Seaway opened North America's industrial and agricultural heartlands to deep-draft ocean vessels in April 1959. It forged the final link in a 2,342-mile (3,769-kilometre) waterway from Duluth, Minnesota, to the Atlantic by clearing a way through a 182-mile stretch of the St. Lawrence River between Montreal and Lake Ontario. Although the official seaway consists of only this stretch (called the Mo–Lo Section) and the Welland Canal (connecting Lakes Ontario and Erie), the entire Great Lakes–St. Lawrence system, with 9,500 miles of navigable waterways, has come to be known as the St. Lawrence Seaway; it has created a "fourth coastline" for the United States and Canada.

Efforts to sail into the heart of the continent date from 1535, when the French explorer Jacques Cartier, seeking a northwest passage to the Orient, found his path blocked by the Lachine Rapids, west of what is now Montreal. The digging of shallow St. Lawrence canals for bateaux (long, tapering boats with flat bottoms) in the early 1780s; the construction of the Erie Canal from Buffalo, New York, to the Hudson River from 1817 to 1825; the opening of the first canal around Niagara Falls in 1829; and the completion of the first lock, at Sault Sainte Marie, in 1855, all fostered the dream. But the United States proved a reluctant partner in a venture, pursued by Canada from 1913 onward, to open the Great Lakes to sea traffic. The U.S. Senate rejected the Seaway Treaty of 1932 and allowed a second treaty, signed in 1941, to remain unratified for eight years. Faced with the likelihood that Canada would proceed alone, the U.S. Congress approved participation in the project in May 1954, and construction began just three months later.

Physical features. The seaway project is considered one of mankind's greatest engineering feats. Locks in the seaway and the Welland Canal raise and lower large ships 557 feet (170 metres), the world's greatest waterway lifting operation. It takes only about seven minutes for 22,000,000 gallons (83,300,000 litres) of water to pour in or out of a seaway lock, but the average locking takes about 33 minutes. The total seaway system overcomes a 602-foot (183-metre) drop from Lake Superior to the sea. To overcome the navigational hazard of the swift-flowing 226-foot (69-metre) fall of the St. Lawrence River between Lake Ontario and Montreal, and to develop its power potential, required an investment of more than $1,000,000,000. It employed 22,000 workers and utilized enough cement to build a 1,000-mile highway and enough steel to girdle the Earth. About 6,500 people living in riverside communities had to be relocated, bridges were raised, and tunnels, dikes, and roads were constructed.

Construction

The navigation portion of the project included a $332,500,000 expenditure by the Canadian government to build two canals and five locks around the Soulanges and Lachine rapids and three seaway dams, and $133,500,000 spent by the U.S. government to build two locks, a 10-mile canal around the International Rapids, and two seaway dams, and to clear shoals from the Thousand Islands section of the river. This series of operations created a 27-foot-deep waterway, replacing six canals and 22 locks limited to a 14-foot depth. Opening of the seaway required many other projects as well. The U.S. Army Corps of Engineers spent about $200,000,000 to deepen the Straits of Mackinac, between Lake Michigan and Lake Huron; the St. Marys River, between Lake Superior and Lake Huron; the Detroit River, Lake St. Clair, and the St. Clair River, between Lake Erie and Lake Huron; and many Great Lakes harbours. Between 1913 and 1932 Canada had spent $132,000,000 to build seven lift locks of seaway dimensions in the Welland Canal, which overcomes the 326-foot plunge of the Niagara River and Falls, between Lake Erie and Lake Ontario.

To tap the energy of the St. Lawrence River's tumbling waters, the seaway project included construction of the Iroquois Control Dam, containing 32 hydroelectric turbine generators and two related dams to control and direct the full force of the river through the power dam. The shared cost of the project was $600,000,000 and the 1,600,000 kilowatts of generating capacity are shared equally by the Hydro-Electric Power Commission of Ontario and the Power Authority of the State

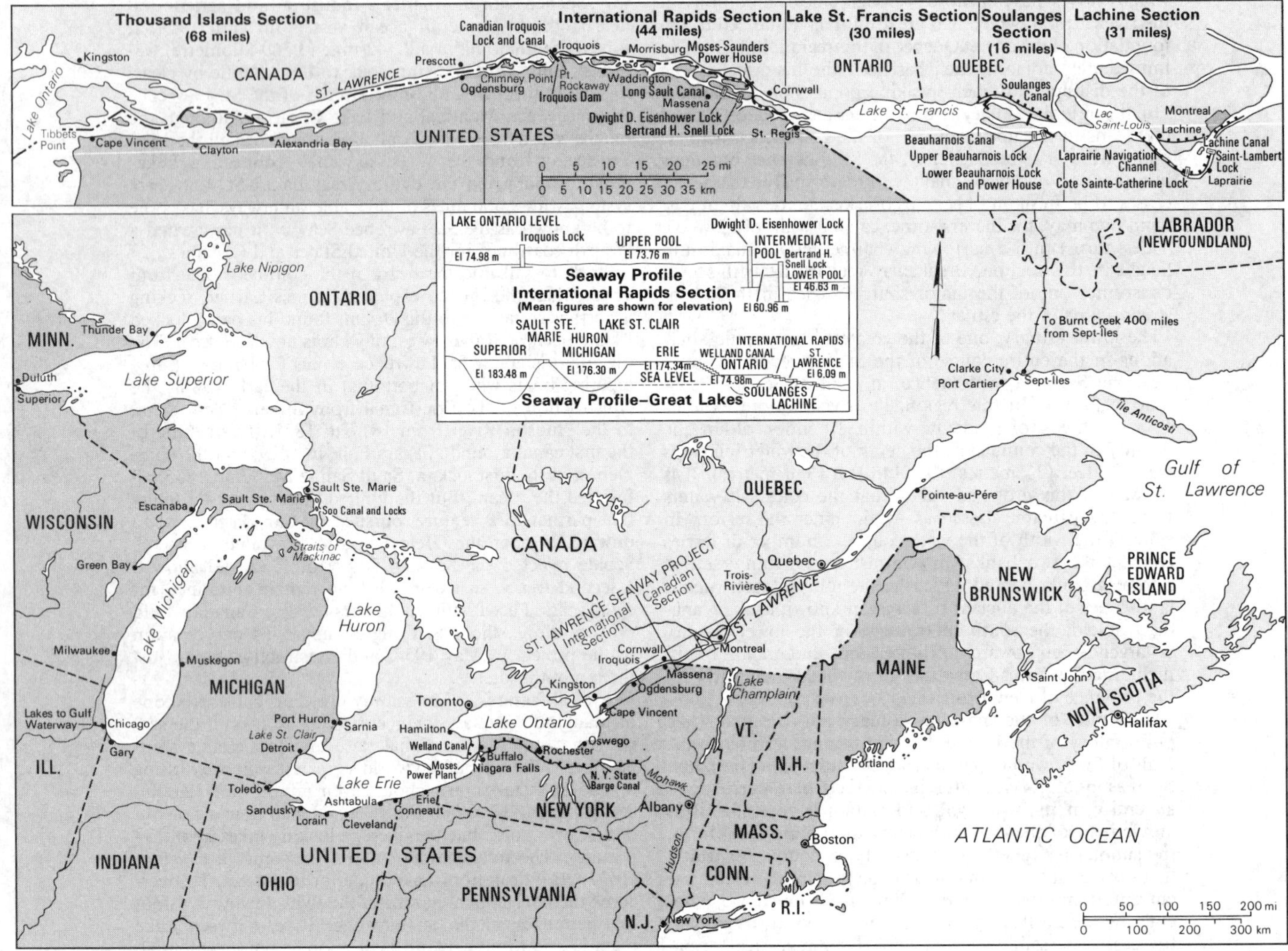

The St. Lawrence Seaway and its region, with insets showing (top) the five main sectors of the project and (centre) cross sections of the lock and canal system.

By courtesy of The St. Lawrence Seaway Development Corp.

of New York. The dams created the 30-mile-long Lake St. Lawrence. Generation of hydroelectric power began in July 1958.

The economy. The seaway had a major economic impact on the United States and Canada. A major reason for its construction was the discovery, in Quebec and Labrador, of vast iron-ore deposits needed by U.S. steel mills. Canada, an importer of U.S. iron ore before the seaway opened, exported ore, the second largest commodity, to the U.S. thereafter. The largest commodity moved is grains, from farms on Canada's prairies and in the U.S. Midwest, shipped through the seaway at considerable savings. Major users of the seaway are vessels known as lakers, which are designed to the maximum limits of the seaway locks in order to facilitate two-way trade. A laker can pick up grain in the western Great Lakes, destined for world

Traffic

markets, and return with Canadian iron ore, loaded in the lower St. Lawrence. The third-largest seaway commodity is coal, moved chiefly from U.S. mines, via the Welland Canal, to Canadian steel mills and power plants. Another commodity that is significant—because of its value rather than the amount moved—is imported iron and steel.

Bulk commodities make up more than 90 percent of annual cargo tonnage, but vessels of many nations also use the seaway to deliver or pick up general cargoes.

The Great Lakes–St. Lawrence River system has become one of the world's most successful international trade routes. If the seaway is to continue to play an important economic role in world trade, however, its traffic capacity must be increased, its faculties expanded, and its financial status improved. Although often characterized as a vast inland sea comparable to the Mediterranean, the St. Lawrence Seaway is restricted by limited access, as well as by a severe winter climate that shortens the shipping season to about eight and a half months.

In 1959 the seaway allowed passage of about 80 percent of the world's ships, a figure that has since decreased. The size of a vessel that uses it is limited to a draft of 25 feet, 9 inches; a length of 730 feet; and a beam of 75 feet, 6 inches and can carry no more than about 27,000 tons of cargo. These dimensions have become relatively small by world trade standards. (R.W.B./Ed.)

CARIBBEAN SEA

The Caribbean Sea is a suboceanic basin, approximately 1,020,000 square miles (2,640,000 square kilometres) in extent lying between 9° to 22° N and 89° to 60° W. To the south, it is bounded by the coasts of Venezuela, Colombia, and Panama; to the west, by Costa Rica, Nicaragua, Honduras, Guatemala, Belize, and the Yucatán Peninsula of Mexico; to the north, by the Greater Antillean islands of Cuba, Hispaniola, Jamaica, and Puerto Rico; and to the east by the Lesser Antillean chain, composed of the island arc that extends from the Virgin Islands in the northeast to Trinidad, off the Venezuelan coast, in the southeast. Within the boundaries of the Caribbean itself, Jamaica, to the south of Cuba, is the largest of a number of islands.

Together with the Gulf of Mexico, the Caribbean Sea has been erroneously termed the American Mediterranean—due to the fact that, like the Mediterranean, it is located between two continental land masses. In both hydrography and climate, however, the Caribbean does not resemble the Mediterranean. The preferred oceanographic term for the Caribbean is the Antillean-Caribbean Sea, which, together with the Gulf of Mexico, forms the Central American Sea. The Caribbean's greatest known depth is Cayman Trench

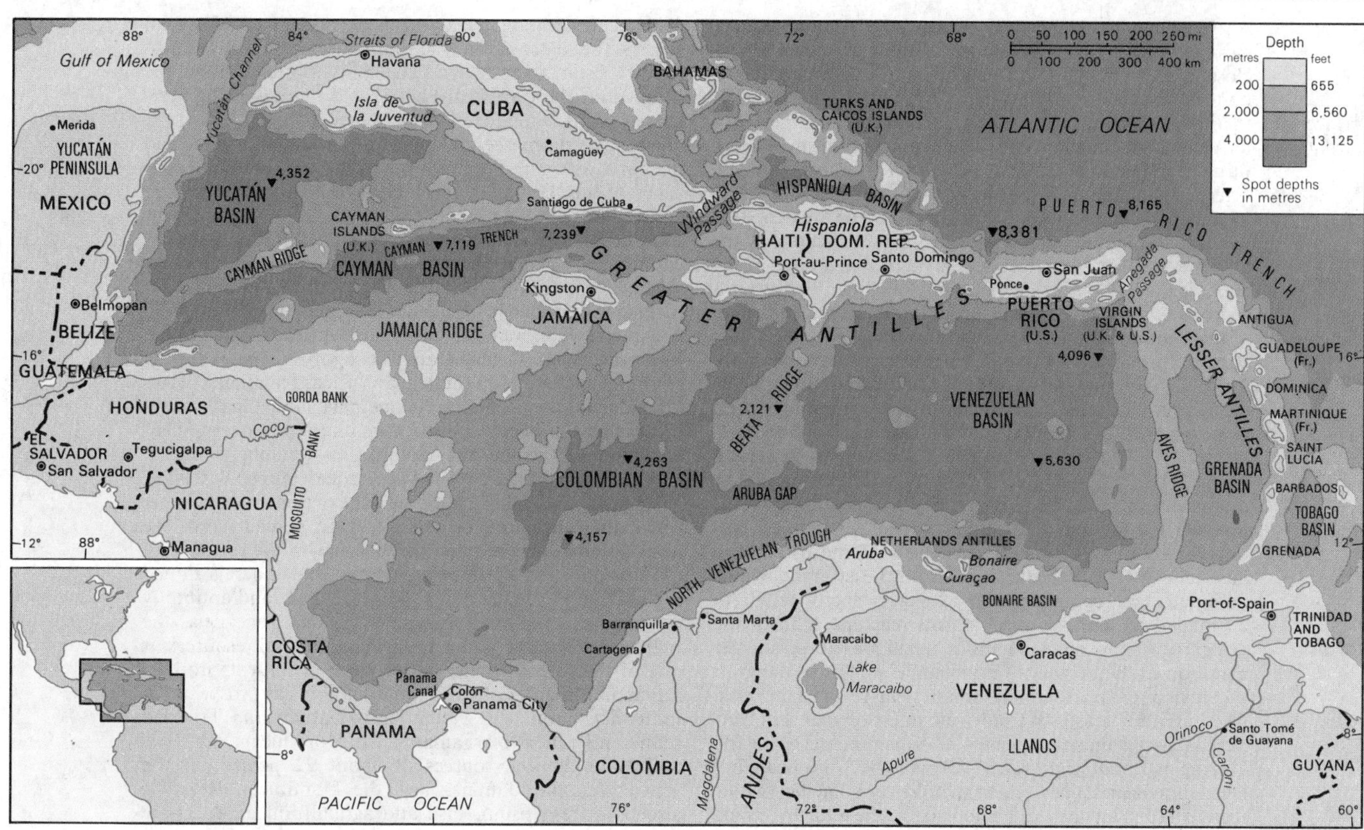

The Caribbean Sea.

(Bartlett Deep) between Cuba and Jamaica, at approximately 25,216 feet below sea level.

Physical features. *Geology.* The geologic age of the Caribbean is not known with certainty. As part of the Central American Sea, it is presumed to have been connected with the Mediterranean during Paleozoic times (from about 225,000,000 to about 570,000,000 years ago) and then gradually to have separated from it as the Atlantic Ocean was formed. The ancient sediments overlying the sea floor of the Caribbean, as well as of the Gulf of Mexico, are called the Carib beds. They are about one-half mile (about one kilometre) in thickness, with the upper strata representing sediments from the Mesozoic–Cenozoic Era, and the lower strata presumably representing sediments of the Paleozoic–Mesozoic Era. Three phases of sedimentation have been identified. During the first phase the basin was free of deformation, as it also was during the second phase, when the Carib beds were deposited. The Central American Sea had apparently become separated from the Atlantic before the end of the first phase. Near the end of the second phase, gentle warping and faulting occurred, forming the Aves and the Beata Ridges. Forces producing the Panamanian isthmus and the Antillean arc were vertical, resulting in no ultimate horizontal movement. The Carib beds tend to arch in the middle of the basins and to dip as land masses are approached. The younger Cenozoic beds (formed during the last 65,000,000 years) are generally horizontal, having been laid down after the deformations occurred. Connections were established with the Pacific Ocean during the Cretaceous Period (which lasted from about 65,000,000 to about 136,000,000 years ago) but were broken when the land bridges that permitted mammals to cross between North and South America were formed in the Miocene and Pliocene epochs.

The existing Cenozoic sediment cover of the seabed consists of red clay in the deep basins and trenches, of globigerina ooze (a calcareous marine deposit) on the rises, and pteropod ooze on the ridges and continental slopes. Clay minerals appear to have been washed down by the Amazon or Orinoco rivers, as well as by the Magdalena River in Colombia. Coral reefs fringe most of the islands.

Physiography. The Caribbean Sea is divided into five submarine basins, roughly elliptical in shape, which are separated from one another by submerged ridges and rises. These are the Yucatán, Cayman, Colombian, Venezuelan, and Grenada basins. The northernmost of these, the Yucatán Basin, is separated from the Gulf of Mexico by the Yucatán Channel, which runs between Cuba and the Yucatán Peninsula, and has a sill depth of only 5,250 feet. Cayman Basin, to the south, is partially separated from the Yucatán Basin by Cayman Ridge, an incomplete fingerlike ridge that extends from the southern part of Cuba toward Guatemala, rising above the surface at one point to form Cayman Island. Jamaica Ridge, a wide triangular ridge with a sill depth of about 4,000 feet, extends from Honduras to Hispaniola, bearing the island of Jamaica, and separating the Cayman Basin from the Colombian Basin. The Colombian Basin is partly separated from the Venezuelan Basin by the Beata Ridge. The two basins are connected by the submerged Aruba Gap at depths of over 13,000 feet. The Aves Ridge, incomplete at its southern extremity, separates the Venezuelan Basin from the small Grenada Basin, which is bounded to the east by the Antillean arc of islands.

Subsurface water enters the Caribbean Sea across two sills. These sills are located below the Anegada Passage, which runs between the Virgin Islands and the Lesser Antilles, and the Windward Passage, which runs between Cuba and Hispaniola. The sill depth of Anegada Passage is between 6,400 to 7,700 feet (1,950 to 2,350 metres); the sill depth of the Windward Passage is from 5,250 to 5,350 feet (1,600 to 1,625 metres).

Hydrography. North Atlantic Deep Water enters the Caribbean beneath the Windward Passage and is characterized by an oxygen maximum of six millilitres per litre, and a salinity of just under 35 parts per thousand. From there it divides to fill the Yucatán, Cayman, and Colombian Basins at depths near 6,500 feet. This Caribbean Bottom Water also enters the Venezuelan Basin, thus introducing high oxygen water at depths of between 5,900 and 9,800 feet. Subantarctic Intermediate Water (*i.e.,* water differing in several characteristics from the surface and bottom layers of water that it separates) enters the Caribbean below the Anegada Passage at depths of between 1,600 to 3,300 feet. Above this water, the subtropical undercurrent and surface water both enter. The shallow sill depths of the

Antillean arc block the entry of Antarctic Bottom Water, so that the bottom temperature of the Caribbean Sea is close to 39° F (4° C), as compared with the Atlantic bottom temperature of less than 36° F (2° C).

Surface currents

Surface currents, bearing both high- and low-salinity water depending on the source, enter the Caribbean mainly through the channels and passages of the southern Antilles. These waters are then forced by the trade winds through the narrow Yucatán Channel into the Gulf of Mexico. The wind-driven surface water piles up in the Yucatán Basin and the Gulf of Mexico, where it results in a higher average sea level than in the Atlantic, forming a hydrostatic head that is believed to constitute the main driving force of the Gulf Stream. Of the 918,000,000 cubic feet of water passing through the Yucatán Channel each second, only 213,000,000 represent the deeper Subantarctic Intermediate Water. The remainder is the surface water that passed over the Antillean arc at depths of less than 2,600 feet.

Climate. The climate of the Caribbean is generally tropical, but there are great local variations, depending on mountain altitude, water currents, and the trade winds. Rainfall varies from 350 inches a year in parts of Dominica, to only 10 inches a year on the island of Bonaire off the coast of Venezuela. The northeast trade winds dominate the region with an average velocity of 10 to 20 miles per hour. Tropical storms reaching a hurricane velocity of more than 75 miles per hour are seasonally common in the northern Caribbean as well as in the Gulf of Mexico; they are almost nonexistent in the far south. The hurricane season is from June to November, but hurricanes occur most frequently in September. The yearly average is about eight such storms. The Caribbean has fewer hurricanes than either the Western Pacific (where these storms are called typhoons) or the Gulf of Mexico. Most hurricanes formed in the Caribbean follow the arclike path of the trade winds into the Gulf of Mexico, although the exact path of any hurricane appears unpredictable. In 1963 Hurricane Flora caused the loss of over 7,000 lives and $528,000,000 of damage in the Caribbean alone. Such storms have also been a major cause of crop failure in the region.

Tropical storms

Plant and animal life. While the vegetation of the Caribbean region is generally tropical, variations in topography, soils, rainfall, humidity, and soil nutrients have made it diverse. The porous limestone terraces of the islands are generally nutrient poor. Near the seashore, black and red mangroves form dense forests around lagoons and estuaries. Coconut palms typify the sandy vegetation of the littoral. On the dry side of each island, succulents and cactus plants are common. Rain forests prevail on islands having sufficient altitude—such as, for example, Cuba, Jamaica, and Puerto Rico.

The Caribbean region has a diversity of land fauna, which is unevenly distributed. The solenodon, a shrewlike insectivore, is found only in Cuba and Hispaniola. Cuba also has an atelopidid (brightly coloured and poisonous) species of frog, a xanthusid (nocturnal carnivorous) species of lizard, as well as a relict species of cycad (a plant intermediate in appearance between a fern and a palm). Puerto Rico has a species of endemic rodent. The Central American states bordering the sea also have a great diversity of land plants and animals. The three-toed sloth, cats, marsupials, and monkeys abound in the forests, as also do snakes and other reptiles not usually found on the islands. Both the Central American region and the Antillean islands are on the routes of birds migrating to or from North America, so that large seasonal variations occur in the bird populations. Parrots, parakeets, and toucans are typical resident Caribbean birds, while the frigate bird also is seen frequently.

Shallow-water fauna

The shallow-water marine fauna and flora of the Caribbean are far more homogenous than are those of the land. Marine life in the shallows centres around the submerged fringing coral reefs, which attract assemblages of fishes and other forms of marine life. The marine biota as a whole represents a survival—a relict of the warm seas of the Cretaceous Period. Coral reef growth throughout the Antillean region is favoured by uniformly warm temperatures, clear water, and little change in salinity. Submerged fields of turtle grass are found there. Sea turtles of several species, the sea cow, and the Manta (devilfish) ray are also characteristic of the region. The spiny lobster is harvested throughout the Caribbean, being sold mainly in the markets of North America.

Fishes of commerce are the sardine from Yucatán, and the tuna fish. Among common game fish are the bonefishes of the Bahamian reefs, barracuda, dolphin, marlin, and wahoo.

The economy. The economic resources of the Caribbean countries are poor. Such industrialization as exists is restricted to one or two countries. Coffee-producing countries include Colombia, El Salvador, Guatemala, Costa Rica, Nicaragua, Honduras, Dominican Republic, Haiti, Cuba, Venezuela, and Trinidad and Tobago. Banana-exporting countries include Honduras, Costa Rica, Panama, Colombia, Martinique, Jamaica, Guatemala, and Guadeloupe; most other Caribbean countries are minor producers. Sugar is exported by Cuba, the Dominican Republic, Jamaica, Colombia, Trinidad and Tobago, Guadeloupe, Barbados, Venezuela, and other countries. These three products between them account for a fair to high percentage of the total exports of each individual country in the region with the exception of Venezuela. Among the minerals mined are gold in Nicaragua and Colombia; silver and antimony in Honduras; and manganese in Cuba. Venezuela, the richest Caribbean country in terms of natural resources, is one of the world's major oil producers. With its iron reserves and hydroelectric potential, it also has prospects for industrialization. The Netherlands Antilles and Trinidad refine and export oil. Jamaica, the Dominican Republic, and Haiti are the sources of about 22 percent of the world's bauxite. Jamaica and the Dominican Republic also produce gypsum. Fish and agricultural products are mostly used for domestic consumption. Much farming is on a subsistence basis.

Tourism

Tourism has become an increasingly important part of the Caribbean economy, serving the huge populations of the United States and Canada to the north, and Brazil and Argentina to the south. Communications by air and sea between the Caribbean and North America are far more developed than is interisland communication. With its sunny climate, and recreational resources, the Caribbean has become one of the world's principal winter vacation resort areas.

The Caribbean has a complex pattern of trade and communications. The volume of trade per capita is high, but most of this trade is conducted with countries outside the Caribbean. Each Caribbean country tends to trade with countries elsewhere that share a common language. Cuba, an exception, trades with a variety of countries, trade with Communist bloc countries accounting for three-quarters of the total. Intra-Caribbean trade is small, due to limited industrial resources and the monocultural economic pattern. Goods and commodities exchanged within the Caribbean economy are few—rice from Guyana; lumber from Belize; refined oil from Trinidad and Curaçao; salt, fertilizer, vegetable oils, and fats from the eastern islands; and a few manufactured products. A lack of capital and limited natural resources discourage industrial development. Markets for most Caribbean products are in the United States and Canada, which import bananas, sugar, coffee, bauxite, rum, and oil. All of the Atlantic–Pacific shipping using the Panama Canal passes through the Caribbean. (R.J.Me.)

GULF OF MEXICO

The Gulf of Mexico is a partially landlocked body of water on the southeastern periphery of the North American continent. It is connected to the Atlantic Ocean by the Straits of Florida, running between the peninsula of Florida and the island of Cuba, and to the Caribbean Sea by the Yucatán Channel, which runs between the Yucatán Peninsula and Cuba. Both these channels are about 100 miles wide. It covers an area of more than 500,000 square miles (1,300,000 square kilometres). To the northwest, north, and northeast the Gulf is bounded by the southern coast of the United States, while to the west, south, and southeast it is bounded by the east coast of Mexico.

Area and boundaries

The various rivers flowing into the Gulf drain a total area of about 1,250,000 square miles. The Gulf, with a climate that varies from the tropical to the subtropical, is traversed by currents that become the Gulf Stream, entering through the Yucatán Channel and flowing in a clockwise direction to exit through the Straits of Florida. From June to October the Gulf is liable to become a spawning ground for hurricanes.

The Gulf has considerable economic resources, which include oil and gas, sulfur, and large quantities of fish; its coastal waters are also much used for recreation. To an increasing extent, however, the Gulf is becoming a receptacle for waste of all kinds, including pesticides and other pollutants, issuing particularly from the Mississippi.

Physical features. *Physiography and geology.* The Gulf consists of several ecological and geological provinces, chief of which are the coastal zone, the continental shelf, the continental slope, and the abyssal plain. The coastal zone consists of tidal marshes, sandy beaches, mangrove-covered areas, and many bays, estuaries, and lagoons. The continental shelf forms an almost continuous terrace around the margin of the gulf; its width varies from a maximum of more than 200 miles (320 kilometres) to a minimum of about 25 miles (40 kilometres). Off the west coast of Florida as well as off the Yucatán Peninsula, the continental shelf consists of a broad area composed primarily of carbonate material (formed of salt or other chemical compounds). The remainder of the shelf consists of sand, silt, and clay sediments. On the shelf and on the slope that dips downward to the abyssal plain, buried salt domes occur at various depths; important oil and gas deposits are associated with them. The abyssal plain, which forms the floor of the Gulf, consists of a large triangular area near the centre, bounded by abrupt fault scarps toward Florida and Yucatán and by more gentle slopes to the north and west. The basin is unusually flat, having a gradient of only about one foot in every 8,000 feet. The deepest point is Sigsbee Deep, which is 17,070 feet (5,203 metres) below sea level. From the floor of the basin rise the Sigsbee Knolls, some of which attain heights of 1,300 feet; these are surface expressions of the buried salt domes.

Oceanographic studies of area

Only since about 1950 have comprehensive and systematic oceanographic studies of the Gulf been begun. Much remains to be done before most of the scientific questions about it can be answered. There is, for example, considerable scientific speculation as to the geologic origin of the Gulf. Some contend it is a foundered continental crust that has been flooded by the ocean; others believe it to be an ocean basin that has been subjected to rifting. Proponents of the theory that the continents were once joined but drifted apart contend that, like the Mediterranean, the Gulf is an ancient sea that was in existence even when the various continental masses of the Earth formed a single landmass. Unfortunately, the scientific drilling of the sea floor of the Gulf during recent expeditions was not deep enough to obtain the definitive evidence needed to decide the question.

Hydrography. The Gulf Stream is the principal current moving oceanic waters into the Gulf. It enters through the Yucatán Channel, the floor of which forms a sill at about 5,000 to 6,000 feet beneath the surface, and flows out via the Straits of Florida. Meandering masses of water, known as loop currents, break off from the mainstream and move clockwise into the northeastern part of the Gulf. Both seasonal and annual variations occur in these loop currents. A less well-defined pattern exists in the western Gulf. Here, the currents are relatively weak, varying appreciably in intensity with season and location. There is extreme variability in both current direction and speed on the continental shelf and in the coastal waters of the Gulf, where currents are subjected not only to seasonal and annual variations caused by major circulation patterns but also by changes in the prevailing wind direction.

The salinity of the Gulf is also subject to wide variations. In the open Gulf the salinity is comparable to that of the Atlantic Ocean, with about 36 parts of salt for every 1,000 parts of seawater by weight. This proportion varies markedly during the year, however, in coastal waters, particularly near the outflow of the broad delta region of the Mississippi. During periods when the volume of the Mississippi's flow is greatest, salinities as low as 14 to 20 parts of salt per 1,000 of water occur as far as 20 to 30 miles offshore.

Sea-surface temperatures in February vary between 64°

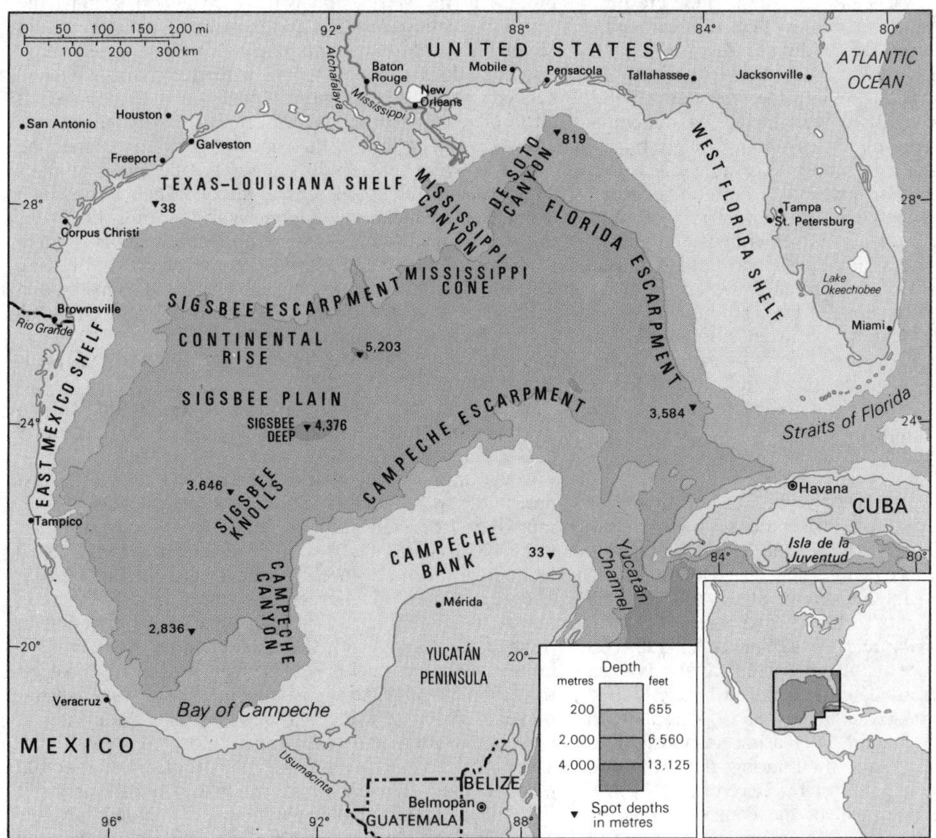

The Gulf of Mexico.

F (18° C) in the northern Gulf and 76° F (24° C) off the Yucatán coast. In the summer, surface temperatures of about 90° F (32° C) have been measured, but the usual variation is between 65° to 75° F (18° to 24° C). Bottom-water temperatures of about 43° F (6° C) have been recorded near the northern part of the Yucatán Channel. The thickness of the isothermal layer (a surface layer of water of constant temperature) varies from a few feet to more than 500 feet, depending on seasonal and local conditions as well as on location. The tidal range is small, averaging less than two feet in most places; in general, only one high water and one low water occur during the lunar day.

Climate. The climate varies from tropical to subtropical. The hurricane season officially starts June 1 and ends November 1. Meteorological and oceanographic conditions are conducive during most of this period to the formation of hurricanes anywhere in the Gulf. Hurricanes spawned in the Caribbean and South Atlantic may also move through the Gulf at this time.

Marine life. Red snappers, flounder, shrimps, mullet, oysters, and crabs provide the basis for commercial fishing in the Gulf; tarpon and king mackerel are caught for sport. The shores of the Gulf are a major wintering area for waterfowl and whooping cranes, and substantial colonies of seabirds are located on the offshore islands. There is a marked absence of marine mammals.

The economy. The Gulf is a major source of food, energy, and raw materials; it is also used for recreation and, to an ever-increasing extent, for waste disposal. The Gulf yields a rich harvest of fish and shellfish, which are sold for human consumption. In addition, a large tonnage of the fish caught are used to provide fish protein concentrate for raising cattle and poultry.

The Gulf is an important source of oil and gas, which is obtained from wells drilled on the continental shelf in water depths of as much as 500 feet and at distances of up to almost 100 miles offshore from Louisiana and Yucatán. Sulfur is also extracted from wells drilled on the continental shelf off Louisiana, with annual production amounting to several million tons. Oyster shells are obtained from the shallow waters of the Texas Gulf Coastal Plain, as well as from bays and estuaries. These are used in the chemical industry as a source of calcium carbonate and also provide material for building roads.

The coastal waters of the Gulf are used extensively for sport fishing, boating, sailing, swimming, and scuba diving.

Pollution of the waters

The Gulf of Mexico is used with increasing frequency as a means of disposing of wastes—both directly by the discharge along the coast of sewage and industrial wastes and indirectly by the dissemination of pollutants carried by river waters draining into the Gulf. The Gulf thus becomes the final resting place of tremendous amounts of chemicals from pesticides, herbicides, and fertilizers used in agriculture in much of the United States and Mexico. The introduction into the Gulf of large amounts of phosphates occasionally leads to the occurrence of red tides, so called partly because of the mass mortality caused among fish at various places along the shore and partly because of the large masses of red algae (Rhodophyta) that the phosphates cause to flourish. (R.A.G.)

PANAMA CANAL

The Panama Canal is a canal of the lake-and-lock type connecting the Atlantic and Pacific oceans through the narrow isthmus of Panama, where the continental divide dips to one of its lowest points. The Hay–Bunau-Varilla Treaty of 1903 between the United States and Panama gave canal-building rights to the United States; work on the canal began in 1904, and it was opened to traffic on August 15, 1914. Since its inception the canal has been effectively owned, operated, and controlled by the United States, but the Panama Canal Treaty of 1977 established that Panama would acquire increasing responsibilities for managing, operating, and maintaining the canal and would assume complete control after December 31, 1999. For a more detailed treatment of the Panama Canal, its management and history, see the section on *Panama* in the article CENTRAL AMERICA.

The length of the Panama Canal from shoreline to shoreline is 40.27 miles (64.79 kilometres) and from deep water in the Atlantic to deep water in the Pacific 50.72 miles (81.61 kilometres). The canal does not, as is generally supposed, cross the isthmus from east to west. It runs due south from its entrance in Limón Bay through the Gatun Locks to a point in the widest portion of Gatun Lake, a distance of 11.5 miles; it then turns sharply toward the east and follows a course generally southeast until it reaches the Bay of Panamá, on the Pacific side. Its terminus near Panamá is about 22.5 miles east of its terminus near Colón. In passing from the Atlantic to the Pacific a vessel enters the approach channel in Limón Bay, which has a bottom width of 500 feet and extends to Gatun Locks, a distance of about seven miles. At Gatun it enters a series of three locks in flight which lift it 85 feet, next upon Gatun Lake, which covers an area of 164 square miles, with a channel depth varying from 45 to 87 feet. The channel within the lake varies from 500 to 1,000 feet in width for a distance of nearly 24 miles to Gamboa, where the Gaillard (Culebra) Cut begins. The channel through the cut, a distance of about eight miles, has a bottom width of 300 feet and a depth of 45 feet and extends to the locks at Pedro Miguel, the Pacific end of the water bridge. At the Pedro Miguel Locks the vessel is lowered in the single lock 31 feet to a small lake, at an elevaton of 54 feet above sea level, through which the vessel passes one mile to the two locks at Miraflores. These Miraflores Locks lower it to sea level; and through an approach passage eight miles long, with a bottom width of 500 feet, it passes into the Pacific. The locks are duplicate or "double-barrelled" so that ships may be passed in opposite directions simultaneously. A thorough system of lights and buoys makes the canal safe to use at night.

Towing locomotives

Passage of locks. With the exception of small craft, no vessel can pass through the locks under its own power. On arrival at the locks it is taken in tow by towing locomotives or "electric mules." These locomotives operate on cog tracks on the lock walls at the rate of two miles an hour. The usual number required for a vessel is six: two ahead, one on each wall, and two slightly forward of amidships, one on each side, the four imparting forward motion to the vessel; and two astern aid in keeping the vessel in a central position and in bringing it to rest within the chamber while the emptying or filling is carried on.

Before a lock can be entered, a fender chain, stretched between the walls of the approach, must be passed. If all is proceeding properly, this chain is dropped into its groove at the bottom of the channel. If by any chance the ship is moving too rapidly for safety, the chain remains stretched and the vessel runs against it. The chain, which is operated by hydraulic machinery in the walls, then pays out slowly by automatic release until the vessel is brought to a stop. If the vessel should get away from the towing locomotive and, breaking through the chain, ram the first gate, there is a second gate 50 feet away, protecting the lock, which arrests further advance. When the leaves of this gate swing open, the vessel is towed in and the gate is closed behind it.

Then, from 105 openings placed at regular intervals in the lock floor, water pours in, lifting the vessel to the level of the lock above.

Breakwaters. Long breakwaters have been constructed near the approach channels in both oceans. One in Limón Bay, or Colón harbour, called the west breakwater, is 11,526 feet in length, 15 feet wide at the top, and 10 feet above mean sea level. A second, also in Limón Bay, known as the east breakwater, is without land connection, one mile in length, and runs in an easterly direction at nearly a right angle with the canal channel. It has a lighthouse on the channel end. The west breakwater protects the harbour against severe gales, while the east breakwater prevents silting in the canal channel. The breakwater at the Pacific entrance extends from Balboa to Naos Island, a distance of 17,000 feet. It was constructed for a twofold purpose: first, to divert crosscurrents that would carry soft material from the shallow harbour of Panamá into the canal channel; second, to furnish rail connection between the islands and the mainland. (Ed.)

RIO GRANDE

The fifth longest river of North America, the Rio Grande forms the entire border between Texas and Mexico, in which country it is known as the Río Bravo. It drains a basin of about 172,000 square miles (445,000 square kilometres) having a population of about 5,000,000 persons. Rising as a clear, snow-fed mountain stream more than 12,000 feet (3,700 metres) high in the Rocky Mountains of Colorado, it descends across steppes and deserts, watering rich agricultural regions as it flows on its way to the Gulf of Mexico.

Physical features. From its sources in the San Juan Mountains of southwestern Colorado, the Rio Grande flows southeast and south 175 miles in Colorado, southerly about 470 miles across New Mexico, and southeasterly between Texas and the Mexican states of Chihuahua, Coahuila, Nuevo León, and Tamaulipas for about 1,240 miles to the Gulf of Mexico. The total length of the river is approximately 1,885 miles.

Diversity of landscapes and environments

Its early course follows a canyon through forests of spruce, fir, and aspen into the broad San Luis Valley in Colorado, after which it cuts the Rio Grande Gorge and White Rock Canyon of northern New Mexico and enters the open terrain of the basin and range and the Mexican Highland physiographic provinces. There, declining elevation, decreasing latitude, and increasing aridity and temperature produce a transition from a cold steppe climate with a vegetation of piñon, juniper, and sagebrush to a hot steppe and desert climate characterized by mesquite, creosote bush, cactus, yucca, and other desert plants. Shortly before entering the Gulf Coastal Plain, the Rio Grande cuts three canyons between 1,500 and 1,700 feet in depth across the faulted area occupied by the "big bend," where the Texas side of the river comprises the Big Bend National Park. Along the remainder of its course the river wanders sluggishly across the Coastal Plain to end in a true delta in the Gulf of Mexico.

The principal tributaries of the Rio Grande are the Pecos, Devils, Chama, and Puerco rivers in the United States and the Conchos, Salado, and San Juan in Mexico. The peak of flow may occur in any month from April to October. In the upper reaches of the Rio Grande it usually is in May or June because of melting snow and occasional thunderstorms, whereas the lower portion commonly experiences its highest water levels in June or September because of the occurrence of summer rainstorms. It has been estimated that the Rio Grande has an average annual yield of more than 9,000,000 acre-feet (1,000,000 hectare-metres), of which about one-third reached the Gulf before the building of the Falcon Dam, upstream from Rio Grande City, in 1953.

The economy. Irrigation has been practiced in the Rio Grande Basin since prehistoric times, notably, among the ancestors of the Pueblo Indians of New Mexico. Increases in population and in the use of water made necessary the 1905–07 and 1944–45 water treaties between the United

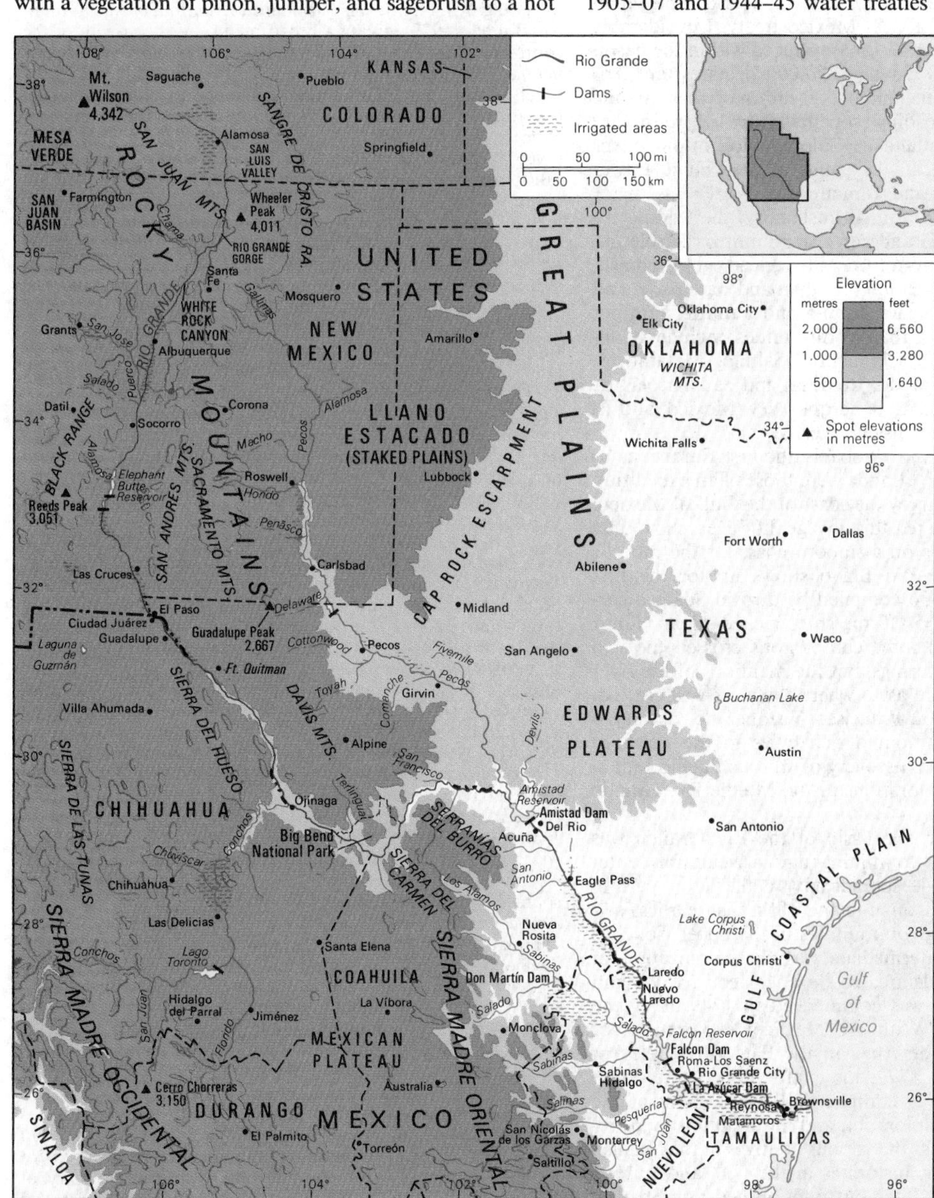

The Rio Grande Basin and its drainage network.

States and Mexico, as well as the Rio Grande Compact (1939) among Colorado, New Mexico, and Texas, concerning shared use of the waters of the Upper Rio Grande sub-basin (above the site of former Ft. Quitman, Texas), and the Pecos River Compact (1948) between New Mexico and Texas concerning the Pecos above Girvin, Texas. Essentially all of the average annual production of more than 3,000,000 acre-feet in the Upper Rio Grande (including the 60,000 acre-feet allotted to Mexico by treaty) is consumed within this sub-basin. Not only below Ft. Quitman but also in many stretches of the river from the New Mexico–Colorado border to below Brownsville, there has been no surface flow at various times. In some places the depth has varied from nearly 60 feet to a bare trickle or nothing. Below Ft. Quitman the Rio Grande is renewed by the Conchos and other Mexican rivers, which produce about two-thirds of the available water. A number of large springs in the area between Hot Springs in the Big Bend National Park and the town of Del Rio, Texas, including many in the bed of the river, are important and dependable producers of water.

Reservoirs and dams

The major reservoirs in the basin are the Falcon Reservoir on the Lower Rio Grande, Lago Toronto (La Boquilla Dam) on the Conchos, Elephant Butte on the Rio Grande in New Mexico, Marte Gómez (La Azúcar Dam) reservoir on the San Juan, and Venustiano Carranza (Don Martín Dam) on the Salado. The international Amistad Dam, below the confluence of Devils River, was completed in 1969 under terms of a U.S.–Mexico treaty. Considerable amounts of hydroelectricity are produced within the basin. More than 3,000,000 acres (1,200,000 hectares) are irrigated within the basin (about two-thirds of these in the United States). The leading crops raised by irrigation vary from potatoes and alfalfa in Colorado to cotton, citrus fruits, and vegetables in the valley of the deltaic Lower Rio Grande in Texas and Tamaulipas.

After agriculture and animal husbandry, the leading industries of the Rio Grande area are mining (petroleum, natural gas, coal, uranium ore, silver, lead, gold, potash, and gypsum), and recreation (national and state parks and monuments, dude ranches, fishing and hunting, summer and winter resorts). Urban communities include Monterrey, Ciudad Juárez, Chihuahua, Saltillo, Matamoros, Guadalupe, Nuevo Laredo, Reinosa, and San Nicolás de los Garzas in Mexico; Albuquerque, New Mexico; and El Paso, Laredo, and Brownsville, Texas.

Study and exploration. Probably the first Europeans to see any part of the Rio Grande were those of an expedition sent out in 1519 to survey the coast of the Gulf of Mexico. The maps that illustrated this voyage, however, show only nameless indentations on a smooth coast for the mouths of rivers. The name Río Bravo shows up for the first time on a map of 1536 compiled by a royal Spanish cartographer. About 1535–36 the shipwrecked Álvar Núñez Cabeza de Vaca and three companions crossed the Rio Grande in their wanderings, but the mentions of the river in Vaca's narrative are as to where the river was crossed. The expedition led by Francisco Vázquez de Coronado in 1540 to locate rumoured rich cities to the north of Mexico resulted in the discovery of various Pueblo Indian communities and explorations in the Middle Rio Grande and upper Pecos areas.

Effectively, however, the basin of the Rio Grande was explored preliminary to mining and agricultural settlements that were made sporadically in the latter part of the 16th century and on into the 18th. The earliest settlements were mining communities in the upper Conchos drainage in 1563, intermediate was the colonization of the Upper Rio Grande area in New Mexico in 1598, and the last colonization was commenced in 1749 along the Lower Rio Grande. With the Mexican explorations of Gov. Juan Bautista de Anza in the San Luis Valley of modern Colorado in 1779, the exploration of the entire Rio Grande Basin was completed. Because most of the entire narratives of exploration and the resultant maps remained unpublished in the various archives of the Spanish government, however, historians in the U.S. and Europe have tended to stress later but unpublished non-Spanish explorations such as those by Zebulon M. Pike in 1807 and by John C. Frémont in 1848–49 in the Upper Rio Grande Area. The careful scientific survey of the river, accompanied by good cartography, did not commence until the first of the international boundary commissions began its fieldwork in 1853, directed by a Mexican commissioner and surveyor and their equivalents representing the United States. Small steamboats were used for navigation on the Lower Rio Grande up to Rio Grande City and even to Roma when the river was high, from the 1850s until the great hurricane of 1874 swept the river clean of all man-made structures. Since then, accelerated erosion, silting, and sandbar formation have precluded navigation and have forced the United States and Mexico to spend much money and time in adjusting the boundary to the numerous changes in the river channel. On October 28, 1967, the United States formally returned to Mexico the Chamizal area, between El Paso and Ciudad Juárez, which a shift of the river in 1864 transferred to the left bank.

Erosion, silting, and changes in course

(D.D.Br.)

BIBLIOGRAPHY. General works on North America usually emphasize either a regional or a topical approach. O.P. STARKEY and J.L. ROBINSON, *The Anglo-American Realm,* 2nd ed. (1975), is a regional treatment. G.H. DURY and R.S. MATHIESON, *The United States and Canada,* 2nd ed. (1976); and J. PATERSON, *North America,* 6th ed. (1979), combine the treatment of topics and regions. J.W. WATSON, *North America,* 2nd ed. (1967), is mainly topical, with a strong historical and human bent.

Geology and physical geography are covered by many texts, including: T.H. CLARK, *The Geological Evolution of North America,* 3rd ed. (1979), giving a broad picture of the growth of the continent; G.M. KAY (ed.), *North Atlantic: Geology and Continental Drift* (1969), stressing the role of the ocean basins in the relief of the Earth, with special reference to North America; C.B. HUNT, *Physiography of the United States* (1967); and H.E. WRIGHT and D.G. FREY, *The Quaternary of the United States* (1965), showing the influence of the last ice age.

Biogeography is represented by a collection of works on climate, soils, vegetation, and wildlife, since there is no overall text. J.S. ROWE, "Forest Regions of Canada," *Can. For. Serv. Pub. 1300* (1972), gives the best account of northern forest types. R.J. PRESTON, *North American Trees,* 3rd ed. (1976), is a good description of the main trees and their habitats. The *United States Department of Agriculture Yearbooks* are invaluable scientific and economic sources; see especially those on *Climate and Man* (1941, reprinted 1974); *Grass* (1948); *Trees* (1949); and *Soils* (1957). R.F. LEGGETT, *Soils in Canada,* rev. ed. (1965), is the best account of northern soils.

The resource base is widely covered in governmental and other literature. The Canadian Geological Survey handbook, *Geology and Economic Minerals of Canada,* 5th ed. (1970, revised periodically), gives a good overall view of Canada's mineral wealth; the United States government offers excellent surveys of American resources in the following publications: *The American Land* (1968), by the Soil Conservation Service; *U.S. Energy Demand and Supply 1976–1985* (1978), and *The Energy Factbook* (1980), both prepared by the Congressional Research Service. Scholarly studies of the general resource situation are: G.W. WILSON, SCOTT GORDON, and STANISLAW JUDEK, *Canada: An Appraisal of Its Needs and Resources* (1965); matched by H. BROWN, *Resource Needs and Demands* (1970). Interesting forecasts of land use and development are given in H.G. BORLAND (ed.), *Our Natural World, the Land and the Wild Life of America As Seen and Described by Writers Since the Country's Discovery* (1969); and H.H. LANDSBERG, *Natural Resources of U.S. Growth: A Look Ahead to the Year 2000* (1964). Of special interest are A.N. LAYCOCK, "Water," in J. WARKENTIN (ed.), *Canada: A Geographical Interpretation* (1968); and A. WOLMAN, *Water Resources: A Report to the Committee on Natural Resources of the National Academy of Sciences-National Research Council* (1962). An important overview of Latin-American resources is given in J. GRUNWALD, *Natural Resources in Latin American Development* (1970).

Human resources include race, population, rural and urban development, and changes in standards of living. D.J. BOGUE, *The Population of the United States* (1959), is still the standard U.S. work; it should be supplemented by the government publications—*Population Challenge: What It Means to America* (1966), *200 Million Americans* (1967), and *Population Profile of the United States 1980* (1981). On the early United States, L.A. BRENNAN, *The American Dawn: A New Model of American Prehistory* (1970), gives a good review of theories of early peoples in North America. H.E. DRIVER, *Indians of North America,* 2nd ed. (1969), is a comprehensive survey of Indian cultures. Case studies of Indians and a summary of U.S. and Canadian relations with the Indians are provided by W.H. OSWALT in *This Land Was Theirs,* 3rd ed. (1978).

Studies of black Americans are legion, but few are geographical. The UNITED STATES DEPARTMENT OF COMMERCE, BUREAU OF THE CENSUS, *Changing Characteristics of the Negro Population* (1968), offers a useful geographical basis. A historical view of the country's changing black population is presented in the Bureau's *Social and Economic Status of the Black Population* (1979). The ethnic problem in the United States is handled well in M.A. JONES, *American Immigration* (1960, reissued 1976). Changing rural trends are discussed in S.R. OGDEN, *America the Vanishing: Rural Life and the Price of Progress* (1969). Urban geography is well represented by J. GOTTMANN and R.A. HARPER, *Metropolis on the Move* (1967); and L.O. STONE, *Urban Development in Canada* (1967). More general statements of metropolitan trends are found in H. BLUMENFELD, *The Modern Metropolis* (1967); and R.A. MOHL and N. BETTEN, *Urban America in Historical Perspective* (1970).

Resource development has a vast field of literature. Useful from the geographic point of view are two general works: S. BAKER and H.W. DILL, JR., *The Look of Our Land: An Airphoto Atlas of the Rural United States* (1970); and P.R. and A.H. EHRLICH, *Population, Resources, and Environment* (1970), an overall assessment. Several studies of transportation are valuable, including W.L. GARRISON, *Highway Development and Geographic Change* (1959, reissued 1969); G.P. GLAZEBROOK, *A History of Transportation in Canada*, 2nd ed., 2 vol. (1964); K.J. KANSKY, *Structure of Transportation Networks* (1963); J.F. STOVER, *The Life and Decline of the American Railroad* (1970); and C.A. TAFF, *Commercial Motor Transportation*, 6th ed. (1980). The growing concern with the environment is reflected in R.A. COOLEY and G. WANDESFORDE-SMITH, *Congress and the Environment* (1970); and in the UNITED STATES DEPARTMENT OF AGRICULTURE, *Outdoors USA* (1967), and *Environmental Trends* (1981), a briefing book on the U.S. environment prepared by the Council on Environmental Quality. C.I. JACKSON, *The Spatial Dimensions of Environmental Management in Canada* (1971), is a model study. Mexico and Central America are well represented in two penetrating studies: F. JOHN MATHIS, *Economic Integration in Latin America* (1969); and C.T. NISBET, *Latin America: Problems in Economic Development* (1969).

Development patterns as they affect the geography of North America are set out in three key works: S.B. COHEN (ed.), *Geography and the American Environment* (1968); J. WARKENTIN (ed.), *Canada: A Geographical Interpretation* (1968); and P.E. JAMES, *Latin America*, 4th ed. (1969). A.N.J. DEN HOLLANDER and S. SKARD, *American Civilization* (1968), presents a masterly account of trends in American life. Modern trends in Central America and Mexico are described in L.B. FLETCHER, *Guatemala's Economic Development* (1970); D.E. RAMSETT, *Regional Industrial Development in Central America* (1969); and C.W. REYNOLDS, *The Mexican Economy: Twentieth Century Structure and Growth* (1970).

Norway

Norway, the "northern way," occupies the western half of the Scandinavian peninsula of northern Europe. The country, called Norge in traditional Norwegian and Noreg in New Norwegian, has an area of 125,050 square miles (323,878 square kilometres), excluding the dependencies of Svalbard and Jan Mayen, Bouvet Island, and Peter I Island. With the Barents Sea to the north, the Norwegian Sea and the North Sea to the west, and Skagerrak (Skrager Strait) to the south, Norway has land borders only to the east—with Sweden, Finland, and the Soviet Union. Nearly half of the inhabitants of the country live in the far south, in the region around Oslo, the capital. About two-thirds of Norway is mountainous, and off its much indented coastline lie some 50,000 islands.

Norway has always depended heavily on its economic relations with foreign countries; this has been the case during both its periods of independence and those times when it has been politically united with its fellow Scandinavian nations, Sweden and Denmark. These foreign links are illustrated by the heritage of the Vikings, who plundered the coasts from the British Isles into the Mediterranean Sea and sailed the Atlantic Ocean to North America. Later the Norwegians turned to trading in fish and lumber, and the modern nation emerged as a major maritime transporter of the world's goods as well as a world leader in specialized shipbuilding. In the 1970s the exploitation of offshore oil and natural gas became the major maritime industry; shipbuilding declined substantially during the 1980s.

Lying on the northern outskirts of the European continent and thus avoiding the characteristics of a geographic crossroads, Norway has maintained a great homogeneity among its peoples and their way of life. Its projections for life expectancy are among the highest of any in the world. The main political division reflects differing views on the importance of free market forces. But the Socialists long ago stopped insisting on nationalization of the nation's industry, and the non-Socialists have accepted extensive governmental control of the country's economy. Such evidence of national consensus, along with abundant waterpower, offshore oil, and peaceful labour relations, have been a major factor in the rapid growth of Norway as an industrial nation in the 20th century and in the creation of one of the highest standards of living in the world.

This article is divided into the following sections:

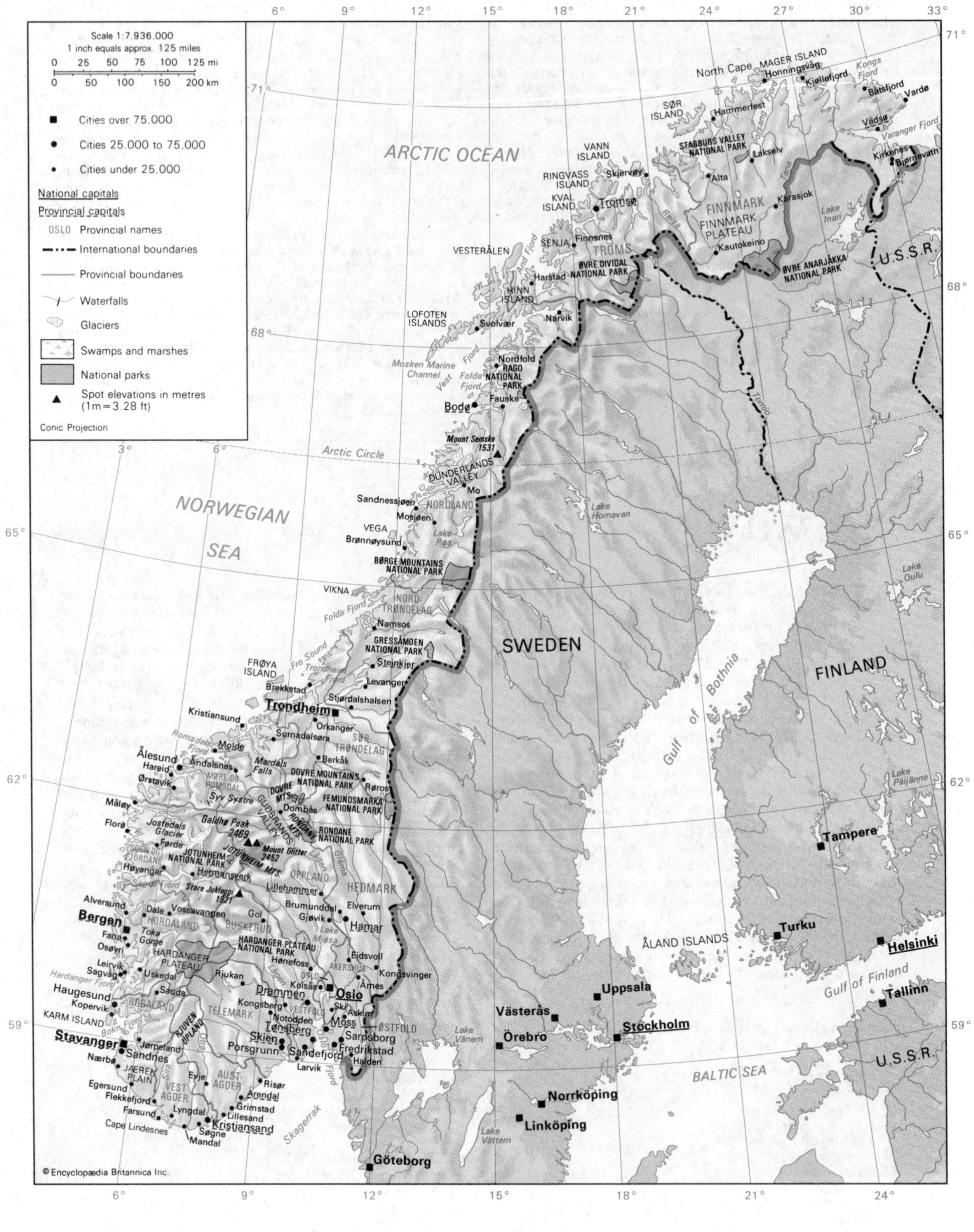

MAP INDEX

Political subdivisions

Akershus ....60 00 N 11 10 E
Aust-Agder ......58 50 N 08 00 E
Buskerud ....60 25 N 09 12 E
Finnmark ....70 00 N 25 00 E
Hedmark ....61 30 N 11 45 E
Hordaland ....60 15 N 06 30 E
Møre og
 Romsdal ....62 40 N 07 50 E
Nord-Trøndelag . . .64 25 N 12 00 E
Nordland ....67 00 N 14 40 E
Oppland ....61 10 N 09 40 E
Oslo ....59 54 N 10 43 E
Østfold ....59 20 N 11 30 E
Rogaland ....59 00 N 06 15 E
Sogn og
 Fjordane ....61 30 N 06 50 E
Sør-Trøndelag ....63 00 N 10 40 E
Telemark ....59 30 N 08 40 E
Troms ....69 15 N 19 40 E
Vest-Agder ......58 30 N 07 10 E
Vestfold ....59 15 N 10 10 E

Cities and towns

Ålesund ....62 28 N 06 09 E
Alta ....69 58 N 23 15 E
Alversund ....60 34 N 05 15 E
Åndalsnes ....62 34 N 07 42 E
Arendal ....58 27 N 08 48 E
Årnes ....60 09 N 11 28 E
Askim ....59 35 N 11 10 E
Båtsfjord ....70 38 N 29 44 E
Bergen ....60 23 N 05 20 E
Berkåk ....62 50 N 10 00 E
Bjørnevatn ......69 40 N 30 00 E
Bodø ....67 17 N 14 23 E
Brekkstad ....63 41 N 09 41 E
Brønnøysund .....65 28 N 12 13 E
Brumunddal .....60 53 N 10 56 E
Christiania,
 see Oslo
Dale ....60 35 N 05 49 E
Dombås ....62 05 N 09 08 E
Drammen ....59 44 N 10 15 E
Egersund ....58 27 N 06 00 E
Eidsvoll ....60 19 N 11 14 E
Elverum ....60 53 N 11 34 E

Evje . . . . 58 36 N 07 51 E
Fana . . . . 60 05 N 05 20 E
Farsund . . . . 58 05 N 06 48 E
Fauske . . . . 67 15 N 15 24 E
Finnsnes . . . . 69 14 N 17 59 E
Flekkefjord . . . . . . 58 17 N 06 41 E
Florø . . . . 61 36 N 05 00 E
Førde . . . . 61 27 N 05 52 E
Fredrikshald, see Halden
Fredrikstad . . . . . . 59 13 N 10 57 E
Gjøvik . . . . 60 48 N 10 42 E
Gol . . . . 60 42 N 08 57 E
Grimstad . . . . 58 20 N 08 36 E
Halden (Fredrikshald) . . . 59 09 N 11 23 E
Hamar . . . . 60 48 N 11 06 E
Hammerfest . . . . . 70 40 N 23 42 E
Hareid . . . . 62 22 N 06 02 E
Harstad . . . . 68 47 N 16 33 E
Haugesund . . . . . . 59 25 N 05 18 E
Hermansverk . . . . 61 11 N 06 51 E
Hønefoss . . . . 60 10 N 10 18 E
Honningsvåg . . . . . 70 59 N 25 59 E
Høyanger . . . . 61 13 N 06 05 E
Jørpeland . . . . 59 01 N 06 03 E
Karasjok . . . . 69 27 N 25 30 E
Kautokeino . . . . . . 68 59 N 23 08 E
Kirkenes . . . . 69 43 N 30 03 E
Kjøllefjord . . . . . . 70 56 N 27 21 E
Kolsås . . . . 59 55 N 10 31 E
Kongsberg . . . . . . 59 39 N 09 39 E
Kongsvinger . . . . . 60 12 N 12 00 E
Kopervik . . . . 59 17 N 05 18 E
Kristiania, see Oslo
Kristiansand . . . . . 58 10 N 08 00 E
Kristiansund . . . . . 63 07 N 07 45 E
Lakselv . . . . 70 03 N 24 56 E
Larvik . . . . 59 04 N 10 00 E
Leirvik . . . . 59 47 N 05 30 E
Levanger . . . . 63 45 N 11 18 E
Lillehammer . . . . . 61 08 N 10 30 E
Lillesand . . . . 58 15 N 08 24 E
Lyngdal . . . . 58 08 N 07 05 E
Måløy . . . . 61 56 N 05 07 E
Mandal . . . . 58 02 N 07 27 E
Mo . . . . 66 19 N 14 10 E
Molde . . . . 62 44 N 07 11 E
Mosjøen . . . . 65 50 N 13 12 E
Moss . . . . 59 26 N 10 42 E
Nærbø . . . . 58 40 N 05 39 E
Namsos . . . . 64 29 N 11 30 E
Narvik . . . . 68 26 N 17 25 E
Nordfold . . . . 67 46 N 15 12 E
Notodden . . . . 59 34 N 09 17 E
Orkanger . . . . 63 19 N 09 52 E
Ørstavik . . . . 62 12 N 06 11 E
Oslo (Christiania, Kristiania) . . . . . . 59 55 N 10 45 E
Osøyri . . . . 60 11 N 05 28 E
Porsgrunn . . . . 59 09 N 09 40 E
Risør . . . . 58 43 N 09 14 E
Røros . . . . 62 35 N 11 24 E
Rjukan . . . . 59 52 N 08 34 E
Sagvåg . . . . 59 46 N 05 24 E
Sandefjord . . . . . . 59 08 N 10 14 E
Sandnes . . . . 58 51 N 05 44 E
Sandnessjøen . . . . 66 01 N 12 38 E
Sarpsborg . . . . 59 17 N 11 07 E
Sauda . . . . 59 39 N 06 20 E
Ski . . . . 59 43 N 10 50 E
Skien . . . . 59 12 N 09 36 E
Skjervøy . . . . 70 02 N 20 59 E
Søgne . . . . 58 05 N 07 49 E
Stavanger . . . . 58 58 N 05 45 E
Steinkjer . . . . 64 01 N 11 30 E
Stjørdalshalsen . . . 63 28 N 10 56 E
Surnadalsøra . . . . . 62 59 N 08 39 E
Svolvær . . . . 68 14 N 14 34 E
Tønsberg . . . . 59 17 N 10 25 E
Tromsø . . . . 69 40 N 18 58 E
Trondheim . . . . 63 25 N 10 25 E
Uskedal . . . . 59 56 N 05 52 E
Vadsø . . . . 70 05 N 29 46 E
Vardø . . . . 70 22 N 31 06 E
Vossavangen . . . . 60 38 N 06 26 E

Physical features and points of interest

And Fjord, *marine channel* . . 69 10 N 16 20 E
Arctic Ocean . . . . . 70 00 N 12 00 E
Bokn Fjord . . . . . . 59 10 N 05 35 E
Børge Mountains National Park . . . . 65 10 N 14 00 E
Dovre Mountains . . . . . 62 06 N 09 25 E
Dovre Mountains National Park . . . . 62 20 N 09 30 E
Dunderlands Valley . . . . . . 66 25 N 14 45 E
Femundsmarka National Park . . . . 62 20 N 12 10 E
Finnmark Plateau . . . . . . 69 30 N 23 00 E
Folda Fjord . . . . . . 67 36 N 14 50 E
Folda Fjord . . . . . . 64 42 N 11 00 E
Fro Sound . . . . 63 52 N 09 26 E
Frøya Island . . . . . 63 43 N 08 42 E
Galdhø Peak . . . . . 61 37 N 08 17 E
Glåma (Glomma), *river* . . . . 59 12 N 10 57 E
Glitter, Mount . . . . 61 39 N 08 33 E
Glomma, see Glåma
Gressåmoen National Park . . . . 64 15 N 13 05 E
Gudbrands Valley . . . . 62 00 N 09 14 E
Gudbrandsdalslågen, see Lågen
Hardanger Fjord . . 60 10 N 06 00 E
Hardanger Plateau (Vidda) . . . . 60 10 N 07 30 E
Hardanger Plateau National Park . . . . 60 07 N 07 35 E
Hinn Island . . . . . . 68 30 N 16 00 E
Jæren Plain . . . . . . 58 45 N 05 45 E
Jostedals Glacier . 61 40 N 07 00 E
Jotunheim Mountains . . . . . . 61 38 N 08 18 E
Jotunheim National Park . . . . 61 35 N 08 30 E
Karm Island . . . . . . 59 15 N 05 15 E
Knivsflafoss, see Syv Systre
Kongs Fjord . . . . . 70 44 N 29 30 E
Kval Island . . . . . . 69 40 N 18 30 E
Lågen (Gudbrandsdalslågen), *river* . . . . 61 08 N 10 25 E
Lågen (Numedals-Lågen), *river* . . . . 59 03 N 10 05 E
Lindesnes, Cape . . 58 00 N 07 02 E
Lofoten Islands . . . 68 30 N 15 00 E
Maelstrom, see Mosken Marine Channel
Mager Island . . . . . 71 03 N 25 45 E
Mardals Falls . . . . . 62 29 N 08 11 E
Mjøsa, Lake . . . . . 60 40 N 11 00 E
Mosken (Maelstrom) Marine Channel . . 67 48 N 12 50 E
North Cape . . . . . . 71 11 N 25 48 E
Norwegian Sea . . . 65 00 N 09 00 E
Numedals-Lågen, see Lågen
Oslo Fjord . . . . 59 20 N 10 35 E
Otra, *river* . . . . 58 09 N 08 00 E
Øvre Anarjåkka National Park . . . . 68 45 N 24 45 E
Øvre Dividal National Park . . . . 68 40 N 20 00 E
Porsang Fjord . . . . 70 50 N 26 00 E
Rago National Park . . . . 67 25 N 16 00 E
Reisa, *river* . . . . . . 69 48 N 21 00 E
Ringvass Island . . . 69 55 N 19 15 E
Rjuven Upland . . . 59 13 N 07 10 E
Romsdals Fjord . . . . 62 39 N 07 15 E
Rondane Mountains . . . . . . 61 55 N 09 45 E
Rondane National Park . . . . 61 55 N 10 00 E
Røs, Lake . . . . 65 45 N 14 00 E
Semske, Mount . . . . 66 40 N 15 15 E
Senja, *island* . . . . . 69 20 N 17 30 E
Sira, *river* . . . . 58 17 N 06 24 E
Skagerrak (Skagerak), *strait* . . . . 57 45 N 09 00 E
Sogne Fjord . . . . . 61 06 N 05 10 E
Sør Island . . . . 70 36 N 22 46 E
Stabburs Valley National Park . . . . 70 06 N 24 30 E
Store Jukleggi, *mount* . . . . 61 03 N 08 12 E
Syv Systre (Knivsflafoss), *waterfall* . . . . 62 08 N 07 08 E
Tana, *river* . . . . 70 30 N 28 23 E
Toka Gorge . . . . . . 60 22 N 06 03 E
Trondheim Fjord . . . . 63 39 N 10 49 E
Vann Island . . . . . . 70 09 N 19 51 E
Varanger Fjord . . . . 70 00 N 30 00 E
Vega, *island* . . . . . 65 39 N 11 50 E
Vest Fjord . . . . 68 08 N 15 00 E
Vesterålen, *islands* . . . . 68 45 N 15 00 E
Vidda, see Hardanger Plateau
Vikna, *islands* . . . . 64 54 N 11 00 E

Physical and human geography

THE LAND

Norway occupies part of northern Europe's Fennoscandian Shield. The extremely hard bedrock, which consists mostly of granite and other heat- and pressure-formed materials, ranges from 1,000,000,000 to 2,000,000,000 years in age.

Glaciation **Relief.** Glaciation and other forces wore down the surface and created thick sandstone, conglomerate, and limestone deposits known as sparagmite, as well as numerous extensive areas, called peneplains, whose relief has been largely eroded away. Remains of the latter include the Hardanger Plateau, 3,000 feet (900 metres) above sea level, Europe's largest mountain plateau, covering about 4,600 square miles (11,900 square kilometres) in southern Norway; and the Finnmark Plateau, 1,000 feet (300 metres) above sea level, occupying most of the northernmost and largest county of Norway.

From the Cambrian through the Silurian geologic periods, from about 570,000,000 to 395,000,000 years ago, most of the area was below sea level and acquired a layer of limestone, shale, slate, and conglomerate from 330 to 525 feet thick. Folding processes in the Earth then gave rise to a mountain system that is a continuation of the Caledonian System of the British Isles. Norway has an average elevation of 1,600 feet, compared to 1,000 feet for Europe as a whole.

Rivers running westward acquired tremendous erosive power. Following fracture lines marking weaknesses in the Earth's crust, they dug out gorges and canyons that knifed deep into the jagged coast. To the east, the land sloped more gently, and broader valleys were formed. During repeated periods of glaciation in the Great Ice Age of the Quaternary Period, less than 2,500,000 years ago, the scouring action of glaciers tonguing down the V-shaped valleys that were then part of the landscape created the magnificent U-shaped drowned fjords that now grace the western coast of Norway. Enormous masses of earth, gravel, and stone were also carried down by glacial action as far south as present-day Denmark and northern Germany. The bedrock, exposed in about 40 percent of the area, was scoured and polished by the movements of these materials.

Soils. In the melting periods between ice ages large areas were flooded by the sea because the enormous weight of the ice had depressed the land. Thick layers of clay, silt, and sand were deposited along the present coast and in large areas in the Oslo and Trondheim regions, which rise as high as 650 feet above sea level today. Some very rich soils are found below these old marine coastal regions. In the large areas covered by forests, the main soil has been stripped of much of its mineral content, creating poor agricultural land.

Drainage. The Glåma (Glomma) River, running south almost the entire length of eastern Norway, is 372 miles long—close to twice the length of the two other large drainage systems in southern Norway, which meet the sea at the cities of Drammen and Skien. The only other long river is the 224-mile-long Tana-Anarjåkka, which runs northeast along part of the border with Finland. Among Norway's more than 160,000 lakes, by far the largest is Mjøsa, which is 50 miles north of Oslo on the Lågen River, a tributary of the Glåma.

Climate. Although it occupies almost the same degrees of northern latitudes as Alaska, Norway owes its warmer climate to the Gulf Stream, which carries 4,000,000 to 5,000,000 tons of tropical water per second into the sur-

Effect of the Gulf Stream

rounding seas. The Gulf Stream usually keeps the fjords from freezing, even in the Arctic Finnmark region. Even more important are the southerly air currents brought in above these warm waters, especially during the winter.

The annual mean temperature on the west coast is 45° F (7° C), or 54° F (30° C) above average for the latitude. In the Lofoten Islands, north of the Arctic Circle, the January mean is 43° F (24° C) above the world average for this latitude, one of the greatest thermal anomalies known. Norway lies directly in the path of the North Atlantic cyclones, which bring frequent gales and changes in weather. Western Norway has a marine climate, with comparatively cool summers, mild winters, and up to 80 inches (2,030 millimetres) of mean annual precipitation. Eastern Norway, sheltered by the mountains, has an inland climate with warm summers, cold winters, and less than 30 inches mean annual precipitation.

Plant and animal life. Norway has about 2,000 species of plants, but only a few, mainly mountain plants, are endemic to Norway. Thick forests of spruce and pine predominate in the broad glacial valleys up to 2,800 feet above sea level in eastern Norway and 2,300 feet in the Trondheim region. Even in the thickest spruce woods, the ground is carpeted with leafy mosses and heather, and a rich variety of deciduous trees—notably birch, ash, rowan, and aspen—grow even on the steepest hillsides. The birch zone extends from 3,000 to 3,900 feet above sea level, after which there is a willow belt that includes dwarf birch.

In western Norway conifers and broad-leaved trees abound in approximately equal numbers. North of the Arctic Circle there is little spruce, and pine grows mainly in the inland valleys amid their surprisingly rich vegetation. Wild berries grow abundantly in all regions: they include blueberries and cranberries of small size and yellow cloudberries, a fruit-bearing plant of the rose family that is little known outside Scandinavia and Great Britain.

Reindeer, wolverines, lemmings, and other Arctic animals are found throughout Norway, although in the south only in the mountain areas. Elk are common in the large coniferous forests and red deer on the west coast. Only 100 years ago large animals of prey were common in Norway, but now the bear, wolf, and lynx are found only in a few areas, mainly in the north. Foxes, otters, and many species of marten, however, are common, and in many areas badgers and beavers thrive.

Mammals

Most of the rivers and lakes have a variety of fish, notably trout and salmon. The latter are found in at least 160 rivers, often in an abundance that attracts anglers from all over the world.

Of the large variety of birds, many migrate as far south as southern Africa for the winter. In the north people collect eggs and down from millions of seabirds, and, as far south as Ålesund, small cliff islands often are nearly covered by several hundred thousands of nesting birds. Partridges and several kinds of grouse are common in the mountains and in the forests and are popular game birds.

Traditional regions. There are four traditional regions of Norway, three in the south and one in the Arctic north. The three main regions of the south are defined by wide mountain barriers. From the southernmost point a swelling complex of ranges, jointly called Langfjellet (Long Mountains), runs northward to divide eastern Norway, or Østlandet, from western Norway, or Vestlandet. An eastward sweep of the mountains separates Østlandet in the north from the Trondheim region, or Trøndelag. Almost exactly at the midpoint of the country, northern Norway, or Nord-Norge, begins.

Eastern Norway. Østlandet has more than half of Norway's population, most of whom live in the metropolitan area of the national capital, Oslo, and in the many industrial cities and urban agglomerations on both sides of Oslofjorden.

The agricultural core of the Østlandet lies in the lowlands extending eastward and southward to the Swedish border.

Kirkendall—Spring Photographers

The Seven Sisters Falls, Geiranger Fjord, with sod roof houses on the hillside, western Norway.

With suitable precipitation during the growing season, the highest July temperatures in Norway, a soil consisting of relatively rich marine deposits, and large nearby markets, the land is intensively cultivated. There are even a number of large, heavily mechanized farms producing cereal grains, which generally do not grow well in such latitudes. Most of the farms, however, are small. To supplement their income from domestic animals, vegetables, and fruits, a great number of farmers pursue forestry as a secondary occupation, since most of the forests are a part of farm acreages.

Urban and rural populations

Norway has never had the agricultural villages that are common elsewhere in Europe. The more densely populated areas of the country have grown up around crossroads of transportation, from which people have moved to the cities and suburbs. Thus, there is actually little borderline between the rural and urban populations. For many years Oslo has attracted settlers from all over the country, becoming a national melting pot surrounded by the most important agricultural and industrial districts of Norway.

In the interior of Østlandet, farms are located along the sides of the broad valleys, the bottoms of which contain only washed-out deposits of soil. Frost is more frequent in spring and fall than it is in the coastal areas. The largest forests in Norway are to be found between the Swedish border and the Glåma River, east of Oslo. The coastline facing Denmark across the Skagerrak passage, stretching from Oslofjorden to the southern tip of Norway, is densely populated and contains many small towns, coastal villages, and small farms. Centred on the city of Kristiansand, this southern area is sometimes set apart as a fifth region, Sørlandet. The coastline has developed into Norway's foremost summer vacation area. The land is hilly, but the growing season is slightly longer than around Oslo. The interior of this area, with narrow valleys running up into the beginnings of Langfjellet, is very sparsely populated, and the people of the scattered settlements depend more on dairy farming, sheep raising, and forestry. Economically and in view of other practical aspects, however, Sørlandet is usually included as part of Østlandet.

In all, about half of Østlandet is forested. The region has slightly more than half of Norway's total forest resources and an equivalent share of Norway's total area of fully cultivated land. In mining and manufacturing Østlandet also has more than half of the nation's total production value and of its total trade. These lions' shares of the national wealth, combined with the concentration of economic activity around Oslofjorden, secure for Østlandet the highest average income per household of the four regions.

Western Norway. The narrow coastal zone of Vestlandet has many islands and steep-walled, narrow fjords cutting deep into the interior mountain region. The major exception is the wide Jæren Plain, south of Stavanger. With rich glacier-formed soils, exceptionally mild winters, long growing seasons, and plentiful precipitation, Jæren boasts the highest yields of any agricultural area in Norway, and those who farm this rich land are not distracted by the necessity of forestry or fishing.

Agriculture in Jæren

The city of Stavanger has become an expanding industrial centre, particularly in canning and engineering. It is also the main base for the petroleum and natural gas activities in the North Sea. To the north, the city of Haugesund thrives on fishing and other industries. The island of Karm comprises a notably rich agricultural area and also has aluminum and magnesium smelting plants. The inland fjord districts of Hardanger are more sheltered, with rich fruit districts specializing in apples and cherries. The flowering of the trees beneath snowcapped mountains adds an extra dimension of beauty to the "land of the fjords."

The city of Bergen is the natural centre of Vestlandet. Since the late Middle Ages, when it was an active trading centre of northern Europe, the city has had a more international character than any other in Norway. The Sunnmøre district, farther north on the coast, with Ålesund as its local centre, contains many engineering firms, and the bulk of Norway's furniture industry is gathered on its rocky coast. Fishing, which predominates farther to the north, around the cities of Molde and Kristiansund, is a main second occupation, as forestry is in Østlandet.

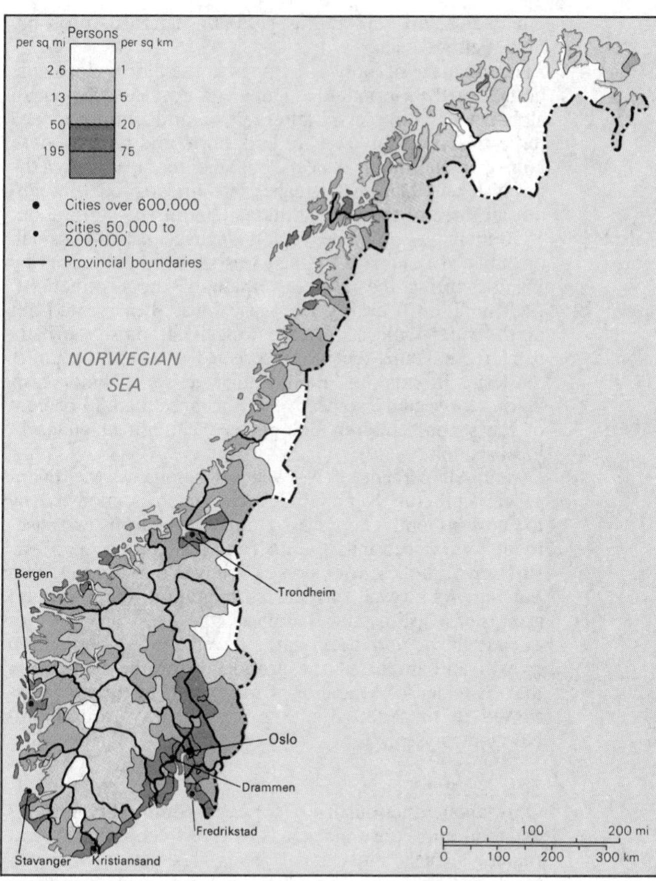

Population density of Norway.

Deep in the Vestlandet fjords lie many of Norway's largest smelting plants, constructed there to exploit the great hydroelectric resources of the region.

Central Norway. Trøndelag is Norway's most typical agricultural region, with flat, fertile land around the wide Trondheim Fjord and the city of Trondheim. In addition, nearly one-third of its area is forested, and it has a large percentage of Norway's mining industry; fishing is also important. The main difference between Østlandet and Trøndelag is the cooler summers in the latter. Trondheim, the third largest city of Norway, and for long periods the national capital, dominates the economic life of Trøndelag.

Northern Norway. Nord-Norge, most of which is above the Arctic Circle, is truly the "land of the midnight sun" in the summer, whereas during December and most of January the sun does not rise. Most of the region is filled with mountains with jagged peaks and ridges, even on the many islands. A long string of large islands jutting into the North Atlantic west of Vest Fjord form the Lofoten Wall. Numerous fjords scissor into this narrow strip of Norway's northern tail. During its severe winters the main highway network is often closed, making seaway and air transportation even more vital than in Vestlandet.

Isolation of the north

Some of the inland valleys have dense forests, but the short summers and poor soil limit agriculture to a largely subsidiary activity, though the production of milk, meat, and potatoes is surprisingly high in many districts. The fishing, mining, and manufacturing industries dominate the economy.

THE PEOPLE

In most parts of Norway, the nucleus of the population is Nordic in heritage and appearance. Between 60 and 70 percent have blue eyes. An influx of Alpine and Mediterranean peoples has been strong in southwestern Norway. Nord-Norge has 90 percent of the 25,000 *samer* (Lapps, or Laplanders) living in Norway. Only about 2,000 of them still live on the Finnmark Plateau, moving their reindeer herds down to the coast for summer grazing. The *samer,* a dark-haired people of short stature, were Norway's first inhabitants, arriving at least 10,000 years ago, probably from Central Asia.

The language of Norway belongs to the North Germanic branch of the Germanic language group. The Norwegian alphabet has three extra letters, *æ*, *ø*, and *å*, pronounced respectively as the vowels in b*a*d, b*u*rn, and b*a*ll. Modern Norwegian has many dialects, but all of them, as well as the Swedish and Danish languages, are understood throughout all three of these Scandinavian countries. Until about 1850 there was only one written language, called Riksmål, or "Official Language," which was strongly influenced by Danish during the 434-year union of the two nations. Landsmål, or "Country Language," was then created out of the rural dialects. After a long feud, mostly urban–rural in makeup, the forms received equal status under the terms Bokmål, or "Book Language," and Nynorsk, or "New Norwegian," respectively. For more than 80 percent of the school children Bokmål is the main language in local schools.

Dialect status

About 90 percent of Norwegians belong to the Evangelical Lutheran National Church, which is endowed by the government. The largest groups outside this establishment are Pentecostalists, Lutheran Free Church members, Roman Catholics, Methodists, Jehovah's Witnesses, and Baptists. As a result of Asian immigration, there are also groups of Muslims and Buddhists.

Lower birth and death rates have reduced population growth and increased the proportion of the population that is elderly. Migration from rural to urban areas slowed in the 1980s, but movement away from Nord-Norge increased.

THE ECONOMY

Only about one-fourth of Norway's commodity imports are food and consumer goods, the rest consisting of raw materials, fuels, and capital goods. The rate of reinvestment has been extremely high in Norway for a number of years. This is reflected in the rising employment in the building and construction industry. Even more rapid growth, however, has been registered in commercial and service occupations, as in most countries with a high standard of living. Manpower is in a continuing strong demand.

Fewer than 5 percent of the industrial companies in Norway have more than 100 employees. Nonetheless, they account for half of the industrial labour force and for more than half of the production. The smaller companies are usually family owned, whereas most of the larger ones are joint-stock companies. Foreign interests control companies accounting for about 10 percent of total production. Only a few larger concerns are state owned, and even these are usually run with almost complete independence.

Industrial ownership

Agriculture and fishing are highly organized industries, and they are subsidized by the state. In remote districts private industry may receive special incentives in the form of loans and grants or tax relief. Taxes are high, with sharply progressive income taxes and a "value-added" tax of 20 percent on all economic activity. Total tax revenues are equivalent to about half of the gross national product, but much of this represents transfers of income; that is, it is returned to the private sector in the form of price subsidies, social insurance benefits, and the like. All this has added to economic problems of inflation, but increases in productivity have made possible a high rate of growth in real income. The strongly centralized trade unions and employer associations respect one another as well as government guidelines, thus helping to control the rapidly expanding economy. Foreign trade, in the form of commodities exported chiefly to western Europe or of shipping services throughout the world, accounts for nearly 50 percent of Norway's national income.

Resources. Norway mines only a few ores in quantity, mainly pyrites (yielding copper and sulfur) and iron ore; smaller amounts of lead, copper, and zinc are mined. Europe's largest deposit of ilmenite (titanium) is located in southwestern Norway, and western Europe's largest known offshore deposits of petroleum and natural gas lie in Norwegian territorial seas. Coal is mined only at Svalbard.

The rivers of Norway have played a key role in the industrialization process by supplying huge quantities of hydroelectric power. Virtually all of the country's electricity is generated by hydroelectric plants.

Hydroelectric power

About half of Norway's annual production of hydroelectric power is consumed by its electrometallurgical plants, which make the country the world's largest exporter of iron-based alloys and metals combined. It is also among the major exporters of aluminum and of nickel, copper, and zinc. A plant at Herøya, which produces large amounts of fertilizer and polyvinyl chloride, is also the world's second largest producer of magnesium. Although aluminum and nickel exports depend on raw-material imports, magnesium is made from seawater and locally quarried dolomite (marble rock). Norway also has quartz, fertilizer, graphite, and silica industries.

Agriculture, forestry, and fishing. Since World War II the number of farms in Norway has decreased significantly, but most of the abandoned acreage has been absorbed into other farms. The size of farms is small; only about one-third have more than 25 acres (10 hectares) of farmland, while less than 1 percent have more than 125 acres. Labour for hire is scarce, and most of the work must be done by farmer-owners themselves. Extensive mechanization and fertilization, however, have kept the total output on the increase. Livestock is the major agricultural product, and although the country is more than self-sufficient in animal products, it remains dependent on imports for cereal crops.

Although only about 5 percent of Norway's total area is agricultural land, one-third of its area consists of productive forests. Forestry forms the basis for the wood-processing industry, which accounts for a small but important part of Norway's total commodity exports, and it is of major importance for the half of all Norwegian farms that are so small that a second major source of income must be found.

Along the coast fishing plays the same role that forestry does elsewhere. At the same time, it forms the basis for a large and growing fish-processing industry and offers seasonal employment for many farmers. Of all fishermen only half fish as their sole occupation. Most vessels are owned by the fishermen themselves, the necessary crew members being paid by shares of gross income in a continuation of a centuries-old tradition of the sea. A critical problem is to avoid depleting the fish resources while maintaining the volume. About two-thirds of the catch, most of it near the coast, goes into fish meal and oil, but some is processed for human consumption in freezing plants. Fish offal is used as feed at mink farms.

Employment in fisheries

Industry. In the mid-1980s community, social, and personal services accounted for about one-third of total employment, followed by manufacturing, trade, construction, transport, finance and business services, and agriculture.

About one-third of the employment in manufacturing is in the engineering industry. As shipbuilding declined after 1980, the importance of equipment for the petroleum industry increased. Electrical equipment has traditionally been a major industry, and electronics for computers and telecommunications are increasingly important. Ship's gear, for export as well as petroleum rigs, has kept its strong position.

During the 1970s crude oil and natural gas became the most important single export in value and by 1980 had come to rival the combined value of traditional commodity exports. The first commercially important discovery of petroleum on Norway's continental shelf was made at the Ekofisk field late in 1969, just as foreign oil companies were about to give up after four years of exploratory drilling. After drilling north of the 62nd parallel began in 1980, rich offshore petroleum and natural gas deposits were located along the country's northwestern coast.

Oil and natural gas

Until 1973 Norwegian ships carried as much as 10 percent of the world's tonnage, and shipping accounted for about one-third of the country's foreign currency earnings. Norway's percentage of world shipping has declined somewhat since then.

Finance. The Bank of Norway has all the usual functions of a central bank, and it also advises the government on the practical implementation of credit policy. Publically

Switchback road of Trollstigheim Pass, Møre og Romsdal *fylke* (county), western Norway.
Kirkendall—Spring Photographers

financed banks give favourable loans to housing, industry, agriculture, and other economic sectors but share the credit market with savings banks, commercial banks, and insurance companies. In 1984 foreign banks were allowed to establish branches in Norway. The country's financial system includes an active stock market.

Transportation. The elongated shape of Norway and its many mountains, large sparsely populated areas, and severe climate make special demands on transportation services. Only the Oslo region has sufficient traffic density to make public surface transportation profitable. A large fleet of vessels links the many fine ports along the sheltered coast. In most of Norway, regular overland transportation services are so expensive that the government must provide or subsidize both establishment and operation.

Bus transport plays a key role in public transportation, aided by some 250 fjord ferries. The number of private automobiles in the country has increased rapidly, creating parking problems and traffic jams in the major cities. Of the more than 50,000 miles of public roads in Norway, about two-thirds are hard-surfaced. Demands are growing for additional roads and for the comprehensive reconstruction of the many narrow, winding roads. The main route connecting Oslo and Bergen remains closed for four to six months during the winter, but the Arctic Highway from Trondheim to Kirkenes has been completed and improved.

Railways

The 2,600 miles of railway, more than half of which has been electrified, are operated by the Norwegian State Railways (Norges Statsbaner), which sustains large annual operating deficits. Vestlandet has never had north–south railway connections, only routes running east from Stavanger and Bergen to Oslo and from Åndalsnes to Dombås on the line linking Oslo and Trondheim. The connection from Bodø to Trondheim was completed in 1962. Farther north, the only railway is the extension of the Swedish railway system to Narvik, which is used mainly to carry iron ore for export. Of the three other links with Swedish railways, one runs from Trondheim and two from Oslo—the southernmost connecting Norway to the Continent via the Swedish and Danish railways.

Norway is a partner in the Scandinavian Airlines System (SAS), which pioneered commercial flights across the Arctic. Two private airline companies add to the increasing domestic service among Norway's more than 40 airfields with scheduled civilian traffic. The major airports for international flights are located near Oslo, Stavanger, and Bergen.

ADMINISTRATION AND SOCIAL CONDITIONS

Norway is a constitutional hereditary monarchy. The legislative body is the 157-member Storting, elected by vote of all persons over 18 years of age. The monarch nominally selects the prime minister and State Council with the agreement of the Storting.

Government. The constitution of Norway, drafted in 1814 when Norway left the 434-year union with Denmark, was influenced by British political traditions, by the constitution of the United States, and by French revolutionary ideas. Amendments can be made by a two-thirds majority in the Storting. Unlike many parliamentary forms of legislature, the Storting cannot be dissolved during its four-year term of office. If a majority in the Storting votes against an important Cabinet issue, the minister responsible or even the whole Cabinet resigns. In legislative matters the monarch has a suspending right of veto, but this has never been exercised since the 91-year union with Sweden was dissolved in 1905.

Multiparty system

Norway's political life functions through a multiparty system. Before national elections, held every four years, political parties nominate their candidates at membership meetings in each of Norway's *fylker* (counties). According to its population, each *fylke* elects a number of representatives to the Storting, with party representation allotted on the basis of the percentage of the vote received.

The Norwegian Labour Party (Det Norske Arbeiderpartiet; DNA), the dominant party from before World War II until the mid-1960s, advocates a moderate form of socialism. In its many years of governing Norway, however, it nationalized only a few large industrial companies. The Conservative Party, which traditionally has been the major alternative to the DNA, accepts the welfare state and approves of the extensive transfers of income and of government control of the economy. Between 1945 and 1965 the government was formed by the DNA, which won clear majorities in the Storting.

After 1965, however, no single party was able to obtain a majority in the legislature, and Norway was governed by a succession of non-Socialist coalitions and minority governments. Political parties that have played important roles during this period include the Christian People's (Democratic) Party, Centre Party (called the Agrarian Party until 1958), Socialist Left Party, Progress Party, and Liberal Party.

Local administration

The city of Oslo constitutes one of the country's 19 *fylker.* The other *fylker* are divided into rural and urban municipalities, with councils elected every fourth year, two years after the Storting elections. For the country as a whole, the municipal elections tend to mirror the party division of the Storting. The municipal councils elect a board of aldermen and a mayor. Many municipalities also employ councillors for such governmental affairs as finance, schools, social affairs, and housing. Norwegians pay direct taxes to both federal and municipal governments.

The *fylker* can levy taxes on the municipalities for purposes such as roads, hospitals, secondary schools, and other joint projects. The *fylke* councils comprise delegates from the municipalities, while the *fylke* governors are appointed by the Cabinet.

Justice. Before civil cases can ordinarily be taken to court, they first must be submitted to conciliation councils, which settle many issues without recourse to more formal legal action. Decisions of the conciliation councils can be appealed to the courts, and Norway also has a formal system of courts of appeal. The Supreme Court is the final arbiter of legal decisions. The rights of the citizen are guarded also by an ombudsman, who acts on their behalf as an intermediary in matters with public administrators.

Armed forces. Military service of 12 to 15 months, plus refresher training, is compulsory for all fit Norwegian men between 22 and 44 years of age. Nonetheless, Norway's defense force is far too small to protect all of its territory against a major aggressor. Its strategy is designed to defend key areas, especially in the north, until forces from other members of the North Atlantic Treaty Organization (NATO) could be moved in. The Norwegian units have great mobility, and, with its important strategic location as NATO's northern flank and its myriad of fjords to serve as naval bases for fleets in the North Atlantic, Norway has sophisticated early-warning systems.

International military alliances

The NATO headquarters for northern Europe is located

at Kolsås, near Oslo. Foreign troops and nuclear weapons, however, are excluded from Norway by law except in cases of war or immediate threat of war. The Norwegian Air Force has a number of ground-to-air missiles and various aircraft from other Western nations. The navy consists of heavy coastal artillery and such light vessels as gunboats, torpedo boats, submarines, and corvettes up to 1,800 tons. The total active military personnel number fewer than 40,000—of which nearly two-thirds are conscripts—but an additional 280,000 are members of first-line reserves and can be mobilized quickly in cases of emergency.

Education. All of Norway's municipalities require nine years of basic schooling, with an optional 10th year. Mandatory subjects include Norwegian, religion, mathematics, music, physical education, science, and English. Optional courses in the arts and in other foreign languages and vocational training in such areas as office skills, agriculture, and seamanship are available in the upper grades. With three years of additional high school, students may take the examinations leading to university study. A small percentage of college and university students study abroad. Institutions of higher education in Norway have been expanded to accommodate the doubling of the student group by the end of the 20th century. The country's four universities are located in Oslo (established 1811), Bergen (1946), Trondheim (1968), and Tromsø (1968).

As many students attend vocational schools as attend colleges and universities, and a few thousand students attend folk high schools, boarding schools offering a one-year course designed for 17-year-old students from rural areas. Only a few of Norway's schools charge tuition, and all students are eligible for government loans.

Health and welfare. Compulsory membership in a national health-insurance system secures for all Norwegians free medical care in hospitals, compensations for doctors' fees, and free medicine, as well as an allowance to compensate for lost wages. Membership fees securing cash benefits during illness or pregnancy, covered by another insurance fund, are compulsory for salaried employees and optional for the self-employed. Most Norwegian doctors work in hospitals, the majority of which are owned by the state, counties, and municipalities. Extensive programs of preventive medicine have conquered Norway's ancient nemesis, tuberculosis. There is also a well-developed system of maternal and child health care, as well as compulsory school health services and free family counseling by professionals. A public dental service provides care for 90 percent of the children between seven and 15 years of age. In some municipalities dental care has been extended downward to three years of age and upward to 20 years.

National programs in medicine and welfare

A "people's pension" was established in Norway in 1967 to ensure for the entire population a standard of living reasonably close to the level that the individual had achieved during his working life. The pension covers old age as well as cases of disability or loss of support. The premiums are paid by the individual members, employers, municipalities, and the state. The basic pension is adjusted every year, regardless of the plan's income. Supplementary pensions vary according to income and pension-earning time. The state pays a family allowance for all children up to 16 years of age.

Housing and living standards. Until the 1970s Norway felt the housing shortage created by World War II; the shortage was aggravated by high costs in the densely populated urban areas. But housing standards have improved tremendously, and most families live in houses built since the war, a majority of them financed by state loans on favourable terms.

Norway ranks among the top 10 nations of the world in gross national product per capita. From 1945 to 1970 individual income per capita tripled in real terms. Tax rates that progress upward with income and the greatly increased social-security benefits, allocated mainly according to need, contributed to a leveling of incomes. The perennial shortage of labour, especially of skilled workers, had a parallel effect.

Norwegians spend a smaller share of their income than formerly on food, beverages, and tobacco. Travel and leisure activities have increased their share rapidly, however, as have such household goods as electrical appliances. During the 1960s the number of automobiles per inhabitant increased dramatically, from one in 21 to one in three. A four-week vacation every year with somewhat more than full wages was established by law in 1964. Working hours may not exceed nine hours a day or 40 hours per week. A five-day workweek had become the rule by the late 1960s.

CULTURAL LIFE

Located on the outskirts of Europe, and with much of its inland population almost completely isolated until the 20th century, Norway has been able to preserve much of its old folk culture. On the other hand, as seafarers and traders the Norwegians have always received fresh cultural stimuli from abroad. A number of Norwegians have made important contributions in return, notably the playwright Henrik Ibsen and the composer Edvard Grieg. The Norwegian recipients of the Nobel Prize for Literature are Bjørnstjerne Bjørnson, Knut Hamsun, and Sigrid Undset.

Literature and performing arts

Although Norway comprises one of the world's smallest language communities, the country is among the leaders in books published per capita. The annual number of new titles is about 5,000, of which two-thirds are of Norwegian origin. Literature is subsidized through a variety of means, including tax exemption, grants to writers, and government purchasing for libraries. In all, there are about 5,000 public or school libraries, which annually lend some 24,000,000 books.

Permanent theatres have been established in several cities, and the state traveling theatre, the Riksteatret, organizes tours throughout the country, giving as many as 1,200 performances annually. The Norwegian Opera, opened in 1959, requires state subsidies, as do most other theatres. Films in Norway are subject to censorship, primarily on grounds of violence and, to a lesser extent, for erotic content. The production of Norwegian-made feature films is subsidized, but they usually number about 10 each year.

In addition to its National Art Gallery, Oslo opened a special museum in 1963 to honour Edvard Munch, probably Norway's most famous painter. The Sonja Henie–Niels Onstad Art Centre, opened in 1968 near Oslo, contains modern art from all over the world.

The visual arts

Norwegian painters of the 20th century have excelled in murals to such an extent that they are rivaled only by Mexican painters. Other artists are world renowned for their multimedia assemblages, pictorial weaving, and nonfigurative art in sculpture as well as painting. The works of Gustav Vigeland have been assembled in Oslo's Vigeland sculpture park in a spectacular display centred around a 60-foot granite monolith containing 121 struggling figures.

Architecture has drawn inspiration from medieval stave churches of upright logs as well as houses of horizontal logs notched at the corners. Private houses, almost all of wood, are made to fit snugly into the terrain. For larger buildings, steel and glass are supplemented by concrete that often is shaped and textured with considerable imagination.

Arts and crafts and industrial design flourish side by side, often inspired by archaeological finds from the Viking Age, by the culture of the northern Lapps, and by advanced schools of design. Norway has markedly increased its exports of furniture, enamelware, textiles, tableware, and jewelry, much of which incorporates design motifs reflecting these cultural heritages as well as avant-garde styles.

Recreation. Norwegians have the special advantages of abundant space and a traditionally close contact with nature. Cross-country skiing is a national pastime in the long winter season. In the Olympic Winter Games, the tiny nation has won more medals than any country except the Soviet Union. The Norwegians have more than 200,000 second homes, mainly located along the sheltered coastline and in the mountains. Even from downtown Oslo it takes only a 20-minute drive to get into deep forests, and on a pleasant Sunday in the winter the hills surrounding the city abound with skiers.

Scientific research. Science and research have limited means in a small country. In the natural sciences, however, reflecting the country's intimacy with an overpowering physical environment, individual efforts of Norwegians have won particular acclaim. Norwegian explorers, beginning with Erik the Red and his son Leif Eriksson and continuing in modern times with such men as Fridtjof Nansen, Roald Amundsen, and Thor Heyerdahl, have been world famous.

The communications media. Some 165 newspapers are published in Norway, about half of them daily, except for Sundays and holidays. Although most of the newspapers are small, average circulations have increased. Most newspapers have affiliations with political parties, but these affiliations are reflected very little in readership. The labour press, for example, has less than a quarter of the total circulation, even though the Labour Party is supported by approximately 40 percent of the voters. Press ethics are on a high level, and the independence of the editors is universally recognized.

Broadcasting is operated by an independent government organization, with no commercial sponsors or advertising over the two radio networks and one television network. Educational and informational programs are given priority over entertainment. Every home with radio and television pays an annual fee. Regular colour-television broadcasts began in 1973. In 1982 several private radio stations began trial operations.

For statistical data on the land and people of Norway, see the *Britannica World Data* section in the BRITANNICA WORLD DATA ANNUAL. (Ja.C.)

History

The earliest traces of human occupation in what is now Norway are found along the coast, where the huge ice shelf of the last ice age melted first, between 11,000 and 8000 BC. The earliest finds are stone tools of the Komsa type north of the Arctic Circle and the Fosna type from Trøndelag to the Oslo Fjord, all dating from 7000 to 6000 BC. Coastal fauna provided a means of livelihood for Arctic fishermen and hunters, who may have made their way south along the Norwegian coast about 10,000 BC, when the interior was still covered with ice. The theory has also been advanced that these peoples came from the south and followed the coast northward considerably later.

Early settlements

In the south of the country dwelling sites have been found dating from about 5000 BC. Finds from these sites, which include bone and stone tools from the entire coast, give a clearer idea of the life of the hunters and fishermen. The implements vary in shape and are made of different kinds of stone; those of later periods are more skillfully made. Rock carvings have been found, usually near hunting and fishing grounds. They represent game such as deer, reindeer, elk, bears, birds, seals, whales, and fish, vital for the survival of the coastal peoples. Enormous rock carvings at Alta in Finnmark were made at sea level continuously from 6200 to 2500 BC as land rose from the sea after the last ice age.

EARLIEST PEOPLES

Between 3000 and 2500 BC, new migrants settled in eastern Norway. They were farmers who grew barley and kept cows and sheep. The hunting-fishing population of the west coast was also gradually replaced by farmers, though hunting and fishing remained useful secondary means of livelihood.

From about 1500 BC bronze was gradually introduced, but the use of stone implements continued; Norway had few riches to barter for bronze goods, and the few finds consist mostly of elaborate weapons and brooches that only chieftains could afford. Huge burial cairns built close to the sea are characteristic of this period. The motifs of the rock carvings differ from those typical of the Stone Age. Representations of the Sun, animals, trees, weapons, ships, and men were all strongly stylized, probably as fertility symbols connected with the religious ideas of the period.

Little has been found dating from the early Iron Age (the last 500 years BC). The dead were cremated, and their graves contain few burial goods. During the first four centuries AD, the people in Norway were in contact with Roman-occupied Gaul. About 70 Roman bronze caldrons, often used as burial urns, have been found. Contact with the civilized countries farther south brought a knowledge of runes; the oldest known Norwegian runic inscription dates from the 3rd century. At this time the settled areas in the country increased, a development that can be traced by coordinated studies of topography, archaeology, and place-names. The oldest root names, such as *nes, vik,* and *bø* (cape, bay, and farm), are of great antiquity, dating perhaps from the Bronze Age, while the earliest of the groups of compound names with the suffixes *vin* (meadow) or *heim* (settlement), as in Bjorgvin (Bergen) or Saeheim (Seim), usually date from the first centuries AD.

Settlements. The period of the collapse of the Roman Empire in the west (400–600) is characterized by rich finds, including chieftains' graves containing magnificent weapons and gold objects. Hill forts were built on precipitous rocks for defense. Excavation has revealed stone foundations of farmhouses 60 to 90 feet long (one even 150 feet long), the roofs of which were supported on wooden posts. These houses were family homesteads where several generations lived together, people and cattle under one roof. From this period and later (600–800), nascent communities can be traced. Defense works require cooperation and leadership, so that petty states of some kind with a defense and administrative organization must have existed.

Clan and tribal states

These states were based either on clans or tribes (*e.g.,* the Horder of Hordaland in western Norway). By the 9th century each of these small states had *things*, or *tings* (local or regional assemblies), for negotiating and settling disputes. The *thing* meeting places, each eventually with a *horg* (open-air sanctuary) or a *hov* (temple), were usually situated on the oldest and best farms, belonging to the chieftains and wealthiest farmers. The regional *things* united to form even larger units, assemblies of deputy yeomen from several regions. In this way, the *lagting* (assemblies for negotiations and law-making) developed. The Gulating had its meeting place by the Sogne Fjord and may have been the centre of an aristocratic confederation along the western fjords and islands called the Gulatingslag. The Frostating was the meeting place for the leaders in the Trondheim Fjord area; the earls (*jarl*) of Lade near Trondheim seem to have added the coastland from the Romsdals Fjord to the Lofoten Islands to the Frostatingslag. A *lagting* developed around Lake Mjøsa in the east and eventually established its meeting place at Eidsvoll, becoming known as the Eidsvating. The area around the Oslo Fjord, although at times closely tied to Denmark, developed a *lagting,* with its meeting place at Sarpsborg, that was called the Borgarting.

The Vikings. The name Viking at first (*c.* 800) meant a man from the Vik, the huge "bay" that lies between Cape Lindesnes in Norway and the mouth of the Göta River in Sweden and that has been called Skagerrak since 1500. The term Viking Age has come to denote those years from about 800 to 1050 when Scandinavians set out on innumerable plundering expeditions abroad. Surplus population, superior ships and weapons, well-developed military organization, and a spirit of adventure seem to have combined to cause this great movement. The Norwegians mostly sailed westward, raiding and settling in Ireland, Scotland, England, France, the Shetlands, Orkneys, and Hebrides, the Isle of Man, and in the unpopulated Faeroe Islands and Iceland. Men of Norwegian descent settled in Greenland and undertook expeditions to Vinland (somewhere on the northeast coast of America). Many Vikings returned home, and this meeting with western Europe was decisive for the unification and Christianization of Norway. (C.Jo./G.Sa.)

In the second half of the 9th century, the Viking chief Harald I Fairhair from the Oslo Fjord area managed, in alliance with chiefs of the Frostatingslag and parts of the Gulatingslag, to pacify the western coast. The final battle took place in Hafrs Fjord near Stavanger sometime between 872 and 900, whereafter Harald proclaimed himself king of the Norwegians. His son and successor, Erik I Bloodax (so called because he murdered seven of his eight brothers), ruled about 930–935. He was replaced by his only surviving brother, Haakon I, who had been reared in England. Haakon was Norway's first missionary king, but his efforts failed; he died in battle in 960.

Christianization. The Viking chiefs established relations with Christian monarchies and the church, especially in Normandy and England. Thus Olaf I Tryggvason, a descendant of Harald Fairhair, led a Viking expedition to England in 991. He was baptized and returned to Norway in 995, claiming to be king and recognized as such along the coast, where Christianity was already known. These areas were Christianized by Olaf, by peaceful means if possible and by force if necessary; he also sent missionaries to Iceland, where the new religion was adopted by the parliament (Althingi) in 1000. In the same year Olaf was killed in the Battle of Svolder. Fifteen years later, another descendant of Harald Fairhair, Olaf II Haraldsson, who had returned from England, was acknowledged as king throughout Norway, including the inland areas. Olaf worked to increase royal power and to complete the Christianization of the country. In so doing, he alienated the former chieftains, who called on Canute of Denmark, now ruler of England, for help. Olaf was killed in battle with the Danes and peasant leaders at Stiklestad in 1030.

Olaf Tryggvason

Canute's rule in Norway soon proved unpopular with the chieftains, and, with support from the bishops, the deceased king Olaf became St. Olaf, the patron saint of Norway. With the death of Canute in 1035, Olaf's young son, Magnus, was elected king. He was succeeded in 1047 by his uncle, Harald III Hardraade, a former commander of Vikings in the imperial guard in Constantinople. Harald was killed during a vain attempt to conquer England in 1066.

The patron saint of Norway

The Olaf kings firmly established the Norwegian monarchy with the help of English bishops. In return, sees and abbeys received the larger part of the estates that the Fairhair "dynasty" had confiscated from the Viking chieftains during the unification of Norway.

THE 12TH, 13TH, AND 14TH CENTURIES

At the end of the Viking Age, all royal sons, legitimate or illegitimate, were considered to have equal claims on the crown if they were accepted by a *lagting.* During the 11th and early 12th centuries it was not unusual for Norway to have two or more joint kings ruling without conflict. Thus Harald Hardraade's son Olaf III reigned together with his brother Magnus II until the latter died in 1069. Olaf ruled from 1066 to 1093 without being involved in a war; by giving the dioceses (Nidaros, Bergen, Stavanger, and Oslo) permanent areas, he inspired the first Norwegian towns. Olaf's son, Magnus III Barefoot, ruled for 10 years, during which he undertook three expeditions to Scotland to establish Norwegian sovereignty over the Orkneys and the Hebrides. He was succeeded by his three sons Olaf IV (1103–15), Eystein I (1103–22), and Sigurd I Magnusson (1103–30), who ruled jointly and imposed tithes, founded the first Norwegian monasteries, built cathedrals, and incorporated the clergy of the Scottish isles into the church of Norway.

Conflict of church and state. Following the rule of Magnus III's sons, the increasing power of the church and the monarch contributed to the century of civil war. During the early 12th century the kings expanded their direct rule over the various provinces, and the family aristocracy in Norway grew discontented. After 1130 interest groups within Norwegian society supported pretenders, and the church was successful in exploiting civil unrest to win independence.

Civil war

In 1152–53 the English cardinal Nicholas Breakspear (later Pope Adrian IV) visited Norway, resulting in the establishment of an archbishopric in Nidaros (Trondheim). In 1163 the church supported the claims of a pretender, Magnus V Erlingsson, in return for his obedience to the pope, guarantees for the reforms of 1152, and the issuance of a letter of privileges for the church. Magnus' coronation was the first at which the archbishop presided. The first written law of succession, dating from this coronation, established primogeniture in principle and the prior right of legitimate royal sons to the crown. Instead of election by the *things*, a representation, dominated by the church, served as the electoral body. The law was never applied, and Magnus was succeeded by Sverrir Sigurdsson, a priest from the Faeroe Islands, who represented himself as a grandson of the first pretender king. After seven years of fighting, Sverrir was acknowledged in 1184 as king of all Norway and set out to bring the church under royal control. He refused to recognize the reforms and privileges made since 1152, and the archbishop and most of the bishops went into exile; Sverrir was excommunicated. The exiles in Denmark established a rebellious party and allied themselves with the secular enemies of the King, who were opposed to the King's administrative reforms, which included the establishment of the *hird* as a new aristocracy composed of court officials and the heads of estates. This opposition party won control of the Oslo area and the inland areas and threatened Sverrir's rule until his death in 1202.

Civil war continued until 1217, when Sverrir's grandson Haakon IV became king, beginning the "Golden Age" of Norway. Haakon modernized the administration by creating the chancellor's office and the royal council. He prohibited blood feuds, and a new law of succession was passed by a national assembly (1260) that established the indivisibility of the kingdom, primogeniture, the prior claim of the legitimate royal sons, and, most importantly, the hereditary right of the king's eldest legitimate son to the crown. During Haakon's reign, relations in the northern area were first regulated by a treaty with Russia (Novgorod; a similar treaty went into effect in 1326). Greenland and Iceland agreed voluntarily to personal unions with the Norwegian king in 1261 and 1262, marking the greatest extent of the Norwegian empire, which included the Faeroes and the Scottish isles. Haakon died during an unsuccessful expedition to the Hebrides in 1263, and in 1266 his successor ceded the Hebrides and the Isle of Man to Scotland in return for recognition of the Norwegian claim to the Orkney and Shetland islands.

The "Golden Age" of Norway

Haakon's son and successor, Magnus VI, earned the epithet Lawmender for his work on Norway's legislation. During his reign (1263–80), a common national law code, with special chapters for the towns, replaced the earlier provincial laws in 1274–76. Haakon's law of succession was confirmed; and a hereditary nobility, exempted from taxes in return for military service, was established. The king thus took over the legislative functions, and the *thing* became courts presided over by royal judges (*lagmenn*). Such a systematic national code, prepared in the king's chancery, was unique in 13th-century Europe. It remained in force in Norway until the Norske Lov of 1687, while the version of the code for Iceland is still partly in force. In a concordat of 1277, some of the privileges of the church of Norway were curtailed, but those that were confirmed left the church essentially independent.

Magnus was succeeded by his young son Erik II (1280–99). Erik's regency was led by secular magnates who controlled central power throughout his reign. The church tried to win privileges that had been denied by Magnus, but the regency proved stronger. The magnates also tried to limit the rights of the German merchants in Norway but were answered by a blockade from the Hanse cities and were forced to agree to the German demands. Erik was succeeded by his brother Haakon V (1299–1319), who determined to renew the royal power. He built a series of fortresses, including Akershus in Oslo, marking the shift of political power from the west coast to the Oslo area. Haakon was unable to restore royal power to the extent he wished, however.

Union with Sweden. Haakon's successor was Magnus VII Eriksson, the young son of his daughter Ingeborg and Duke Erik, son of Magnus I of Sweden. The child was also elected to the Swedish crown in 1319, creating a personal union between the two countries that lasted until 1355. The countries were to be governed during the King's minority by the two national councils with the King's mother as a member of both regencies. The regency in Norway failed to prevent the increasing power of the magnates, and after the King came of age (1332), he was forced to recognize his younger son Haakon as king of Norway (1343) and to abdicate in his favour when he reached his

The impact of the Black Death

majority (1355). Magnus' elder son Erik was designated king of Sweden. The Black Death struck Norway in 1349–50 and probably killed two-thirds of the population. The upper classes were particularly hard hit: only one of the bishops survived, and many noble families were reduced to the peasantry by the death of their workers and the decrease of their incomes.

The power of Haakon VI (1355–80) was also limited. The casualties of the Black Death among the high civil servants and clergy were replaced by Danes and Swedes. The central government as a whole lost control over the kingdom, and the local areas began to conduct their own affairs. Haakon VI married Margaret, the daughter of Valdemar Atterdag of Denmark, and their son, Olaf, was elected king of Denmark in 1375. Olaf also became king of Norway at his father's death (1380), but he died in 1387 at the age of 17, and his mother, who had served as regent in both kingdoms for him, now became the ruler.

Greenland. The first Nordic settlers on Greenland reached the island in 985 under the leadership of Erik the Red. Two colonies were established on the western coast, one near Godthåb and one near Julianehåb, where a few thousand Norsemen engaged in cattle breeding, fishing, and sealing. The most important export was walrus tusks. A bishopric and two cloisters were organized on Greenland. The Greenlanders lacked wood and iron for shipbuilding and could not support communications with Europe; in 1261 they submitted to the Norwegian king, to whom they would pay taxes in return for his acceptance of responsibility for the island's provision through a yearly voyage. A worsening of the climate may have occurred early in the 14th century, resulting in a decline in agriculture and livestock breeding. Plagues ravaged the populace: the Black Death alone is estimated to have halved the population. When Norway, with Greenland and Iceland, became subject to the Danish king, conditions worsened; the only ships that then sailed to Greenland belonged to pirates. Around 1350 the Godthåb settlement was apparently deserted and then occupied by Eskimo (Inuit), and in 1379 the Julianehåb area was attacked. The last certain notice of Norsemen on Greenland came in 1410: sometime during the following 150 years they disappeared from Greenland. It was not until the beginning of the 18th century that Greenland again came into the Danish sphere.

THE KALMAR UNION

With the accession of Margaret I of Denmark to power in 1387, the foundation was laid for political union with Denmark. She adopted her nephew Erik of Pomerania, then six years old, as her heir, and in 1388 she was acclaimed queen of Sweden as well. The next year Erik was proclaimed heir apparent in Norway, and in June 1397 he was crowned king of all three Scandinavian nations in a ceremony at Kalmar, Swed.

Under the Kalmar Union, Norway became an increasingly unimportant part of Scandinavia politically, and it remained in a union with Denmark until 1814. Margaret and Erik left vacant the highest Norwegian administrative position and governed Norway from Copenhagen. Most appointments made in Norway were given to Danes and Germans. Whereas in Denmark and Sweden national councils took over the government, in Norway the council was unable to assert itself. After the accession of Christian I, Norwegian government was again centred in Copenhagen. The lower estates were also essentially powerless against the Danes, and isolated peasant uprisings had neither good leadership nor clear political goals. In 1448 Norway accepted the Swedish candidate for king, Karl Knutsson, but was forced to acknowledge Christian I of Oldenburg and to remain in the union with Denmark. In 1468 Christian pawned the Orkney and Shetland islands to the Scottish king to provide a dowry for his daughter, and the islands were never reclaimed.

Loss of Orkney and Shetland islands

The cause of this political impotence in Norway has been a subject of considerable debate. According to one theory, the conscious policy of the kings since the 12th century of crushing the local family aristocracy to strengthen royal power deprived the country of a counterpart to the strong and often rebellious Danish and Swedish aristocracies. A second theory holds that geography was responsible for the absence of a strong aristocracy: the poorness of the soil prevented economic expansion through the creation of large estates. This geographic factor, together with the loss of population during the Black Death and subsequent epidemics, may explain why Norway's aristocracy was more affected by the plague than were the nobles in the rest of Scandinavia. The huge loss in population deprived the aristocracy of much of its labour force, which led to the abandonment of farms and the decline of many nobles into the peasant class. (H.En./G.Sa.)

THE 16TH AND 17TH CENTURIES

After 1523 the Norwegian council tried to obtain some independence for Norway within the union. But because the bishops dominated the council, they became the losers in the Norwegian parallel to the 1533–36 civil war in Denmark. As a result, the council was abolished, and the bishops lost all hope for help from Sweden, which did not want to provoke Denmark and whose king was himself leaning toward Lutheranism. Olaf Engelbrektsson, the last Norwegian archbishop and head of the council, left Norway in early 1537 for the Netherlands, taking with him the shrine of St. Olaf.

In Norwegian political history, the year 1536 is a nadir—in Copenhagen, Norway was proclaimed a Danish province forever. Norwegian topography and society, however, were very different from those of Denmark, and the hereditary Norwegian crown was viewed as a distinct monarchy. Thus, Norway was allowed to keep most of its ancient institutions and laws, and new institutions and laws had to be given in a special Norwegian version (for example, the Norske Lov of 1687). From 1550 Norway's natural resources, including fish, timber, iron ore, and copper—commodities from outside the Baltic area and most useful to all western Europe—were increasingly exploited. Consequently, a Norwegian bourgeoisie became a political factor. After 1560 Denmark had a constant fear of Swedish plans to occupy Norway. Therefore it was important that the Norwegians should not feel oppressed by rule from the political centre in Copenhagen. All this may explain the special attention the Danish government gave to Norway.

Rise of the Norwegian bourgeoisie

Most representative of this attitude was Christian IV, who visited Norway often and founded several towns (*e.g.,* Kristiansand, with the plan to control the Skagerrak; Kongsberg, with its silver mines; and Christiania, after a destructive fire in Oslo, 1624). He even went on an Arctic tour to Vardø in 1599, proclaiming the Arctic waters to be the "king's streams." This was part of his reaction to Swedish pretensions toward the Arctic Ocean.

A certain separatist policy has been attributed to Hannibal Sehested, the King's son-in-law and in the 1640s governor of Norway. He actually created an army (by conscription of peasants) and a separate financial administration, but he may have wanted a platform against the Danish nobility to work for absolutism. There were no signs of secession in the Norwegian population. When he was deposed in 1651, the financial administration was ruled from Copenhagen.

For almost a generation after 1664, Ulrik Frederick Gyldenløve, the illegitimate son of Frederick III, was governor of Norway. He courted the Norwegian peasants and at the same time gave monopolies on trade and on timber exports to restricted numbers of merchants. By applying such principles the government in Copenhagen and the Danish public servants managed to rule Norway after the Swedish annexations of Skåne, Halland, and Bohuslän. Norway's modern frontiers were established in 1660 and confirmed by treaty with Sweden in 1751, when Norway received the interior of Finnmark.

THE 18TH CENTURY

Romanticists of the later 18th century idealized Norwegian rural society, with its free peasants in a wild landscape. Certainly, their situation contrasted favourably with that of the Danish tenants; the landowning farmers in eastern Norway, especially, earned sizable incomes from their timber forests. In the east, therefore, and in the region of

Trøndelag, the countryside was characterized by a class of wealthy timber merchants and farmers and a large rural proletariat. Elsewhere in the countryside, social conditions were more nearly equal. The Norwegian population consisted almost exclusively of peasants and fishermen; no city or urban agglomeration exceeded 15,000 inhabitants.

Thomas Malthus was the first demographer to see the exceptional possibilities for population studies in the Scandinavian countries, where civic registers were kept by parsons. In 1799, the year following his publication of *An Essay on the Principle of Population,* Malthus went to Norway to confirm his theories about checks on population growth. He found a late marital age, which he ascribed incorrectly to military service and a large servant class. In fact, early marriages were hindered by poverty and lack of land. Moreover, Norwegian population statistics of the 18th century indicate years of famine and epidemics, as do Swedish and Danish statistics. Malthus was correct, however, in discerning that demographic evolution in nonindustrialized countries could be studied better in Scandinavia than anywhere else in the world.

Revival of settlement in Greenland

How and why the Norse community in Greenland perished at the end of the Middle Ages is an unsolved and fascinating problem. In the beginning of the 18th century there still was hope of finding Norse descendants among the Eskimo in Greenland. A Norwegian clergyman, Hans Egede, having managed to persuade the authorities that such people should be converted to the Lutheran faith, arrived in the Godthåb Fjord (in the southwest), finding only Eskimo, to begin a new European settlement in Greenland. Later in the century another colony was founded at Julianehåb (almost at the southern tip of the island).

Two factors are visible in this activity. First, the Pietist movement, which had a considerable influence in Denmark, demanded religious conversion and stressed an obligation to bring the gospel to the heathens. A Ministry of Missions, founded in 1714, supported Egede in Greenland as it supported missionary activity among the *samer* (Lapps) in northern Norway and among Indians at Tranquebar on the Coromandel Coast. Second, missionary activity became possible because of a close alliance with commercial interests. Egede himself founded a company in Bergen for trade with Greenland. The trade later passed to the Royal Greenland Trading Company of Copenhagen. The trade with Finnmark (now the northernmost part of Norway) was reserved, in principle, for merchants of Copenhagen as well.

THE NAPOLEONIC WARS AND THE 19TH CENTURY

Denmark–Norway's attempt to remain neutral in the struggle between France and England and their respective allies early in the 19th century came to an end after England's preemptive naval actions of 1807, in which the entire Danish fleet was taken. The continental blockade of England that followed, which was against Danish interests, was a catastrophe to Norway. Fish and timber exports were stopped, as well as grain imports from Denmark. The consequences were isolation, economic crisis, and hunger. In 1810–13 England consented to some relaxation of its counterblockade against Norway. As a whole, however, the years 1807–14 convinced leading groups in Norway that they needed a political representation of their own.

The Treaty of Kiel. Swedish foreign policy was erratic during those years, but Denmark–Norway remained an ally of Napoleon until 1814. After Napoleon's defeat at the Battle of Leipzig (1813), Sweden repeated its 17th-century strategy by attacking Denmark from the south. At the Treaty of Kiel (Jan. 14, 1814), Denmark gave up all its rights to Norway (but not to the old Norwegian dependencies of Iceland, the Faeroes, and Greenland) to Sweden.

The Danes did not intend this agreement to end the union with Norway. Officially loyal to the Treaty of Kiel, the Danish government worked for the eventual return of Norway. This probably is why the crown prince Christian Frederick, governor of Norway, in collusion with the Danish king, organized a rising against the Treaty of Kiel. In doing so he needed support in Norway, and he thus came to rely on two political forces, each with regionalist aims. The larger faction consisted of civil servants and peasants, who were loyal to Copenhagen but traditionally in opposition to its centralizing policy. The other was the small but important group of timber merchants in eastern Norway, who wanted independence from Copenhagen for their trade with western Europe. Since 1809 they had conspired for a union between Sweden and Norway.

This was the main background of a constituent assembly, called by Christian Frederick to meet at Eidsvoll, 40 miles north of Christiania. It drew up the constitution of May 17, 1814 (which still exists), and elected Christian Frederick to the throne of Norway.

Constitution of May 17, 1814

Union with Sweden. Norwegian independence got no support from the great powers, and Sweden attacked Norway in July 1814. After a fake war of 14 days, Christian Frederick resigned. Jean Bernadotte (later known as Charles XIV John; called Karl Johan in Sweden and Norway), the Swedish crown prince, accepted the Norwegian constitution, and in so doing could no longer argue on the basis of the Treaty of Kiel. This was of the greatest political importance to the Norwegians. As a constitutional monarchy, Norway entered the union with Sweden in November 1814; only minor modifications were made in its constitution—the king and foreign policy would be common; the king would be commander in chief of Norway's armed forces, which could not be used outside Norway without Norwegian consent; a government in Christiania (with a section in Stockholm) and the Storting (Norwegian parliament) would take care of national affairs. (G.Sa.)

For Norway the Treaty of Kiel meant secession from Denmark, the forming of its own separate state with complete internal self-government, and a political centre in Christiania. The history of Norway during the 19th century is marked by the struggle to assert its independence of Sweden within the union and its attempts to develop a modern Norwegian culture.

Population, trade, and industry. *Population.* Norway's population grew more rapidly during the 19th century than in any other period of its history. The population rose from 883,000 in 1801 to 2,240,000 in 1900. Whereas the urban population was only 8.8 percent in 1800, it had reached 28 percent by 1900. After Ireland, Norway had the highest relative emigration of all European countries in the 19th century. From 1840 to 1914 about 750,000 people emigrated, especially to the American Middle West.

Economic conditions. Norway was also severely hit by the economic crisis that followed the Napoleonic Wars. Norway's exports consisted mainly of wooden goods to Great Britain and, to a certain extent, of glass and iron products. After the war, when the British introduced preferential tariffs on articles of wood from Canada, Norwegian forest owners, sawmills, and export firms were badly hit. Iron and glass exports also met with marketing difficulties. Fish, which after timber was the country's most important export commodity, was only lightly hit by the slump; and by the 1820s the herring fisheries on the west coast enjoyed a period of vigorous expansion. From the 1850s on, agriculture developed rapidly. Modern methods were adopted, and an emphasis was laid on cattle breeding. Simultaneously, the building of railroads began ending the isolation of the small communities and opening the way for the sale of agricultural products. It was, however, the great expansion of merchant shipping (especially between 1850 and 1880) that gave the most powerful boost to the country's economy. Norway's percentage of world tonnage rose from 3.6 percent to 6.1 percent; and at the end of the century Norway possessed, after the United Kingdom and the United States, the largest merchant navy in the world. The economic resources that merchant shipping brought to the country laid the basis for industrialization. From 1860 Norway's industry expanded rapidly, especially in the timber and wood-pulp trade and in engineering. Socially and economically this expansion was a springboard for shipowners, manufacturers, and businessmen, all of whom began to play a much greater role in politics toward the end of the 19th century.

Merchant shipping

The age of bureaucracy (1814–84). The economic development in the decades immediately after the Napoleonic Wars meant a reduction in the power of the big business concerns and great estates. The decision to abolish the nobility in 1821 was indicative of the greatly reduced social and economic circumstances of the upper classes. At the same time, the position of the civil servants was strengthened, and from then until the latter part of the 19th century they controlled the political power of the country. Apart from the civil servants, there were only two other political factors of any importance in Norway at this time: the farmers and the monarch.

Parliamentary authority. The Eidsvoll constitution of 1814 gave the Storting greater authority than parliamentary bodies had in any other country except the United States. The king retained executive power and chose his own ministers, but legislation, the imposition of taxes, and the budget were within the authority of the Storting. The Storting had the power to initiate legislation, and the king had only a suspension veto. When the union's monarch Charles XIV John (ruled 1818–44) demanded the right of absolute veto, the Storting categorically refused, despite the King's attempt to intimidate them with shows of military strength. Faced with this unanimous resistance, the King was forced to abandon his struggle, and the Storting's dominant position became the firm defense against Swedish attempts to unite the two countries. As a national demonstration, Norway began in the 1820s to celebrate May 17, the date of the Eidsvoll constitution, as a national day. The King's attempt to outlaw the celebration resulted in violent demonstrations, and during the 1830s he conceded this point also.

Monetary problems. Norway had at the same time many major problems to resolve on the domestic front. The war, which had been to a great extent financed by an increased issue of bank notes, had brought about a reduction of the riksdaler to one-fifteenth of its original value. To ward off inflation, a severe sterling tax was imposed, and in 1816 a new bank of Norway was established that had the monopoly of issuing bank notes. In spite of strong precautionary measures, however, it was not until the currency reform of 1842 that finances were stabilized. From an economic point of view, the civil service was decidedly liberal, and the guild system and old trade regulations were abolished during the 1840s and 1850s. By 1842 it was decided to reduce tariffs, a decision that gradually made Norway a free-trade country.

Political change. The influence that the vote gave to the farmers was not exploited at first, and they continued to elect civil servants as their parliamentary representatives. About 1830, however, a demand was raised for a decrease in expenditure, and, under the leadership of Ole Gabriel Ueland, a more deliberate "class" policy began to be conducted in the Storting. In 1837 a statute regarding local self-government was enacted that offered training for grass-roots politicians. The farmers' policy led to sharp conflicts with influential groups of bureaucrats and finally became a struggle for political power on the national level. Under pressure from a radical labour movement, which arose after 1848 under the leadership of Marcus Thrane, and from the later mounting tension in the relationship with Sweden, many farmers turned to the middle classes and the minor civil servants. The intensely nationalistic attitude of this leftist coalition was expressed in its attempts to strengthen national culture and language. The struggle for the introduction of the vernacular as the official language instead of the bureaucrats' Danish-influenced tongue became an important item of the coalition's policy. The coalition was organized as the Venstre (Left) political party in 1884.

The union conflict (1859–1905). Because the union's king usually resided in Sweden, he was represented in Norway by a governor general. This gave rise to the governor-general conflict, which was not resolved until 1873, when Sweden yielded to Norway's main demands. The result was that in Norway the king was regarded as Swedish, and his right to nominate the government in Norway was considered a danger to the country's autonomy. The conflict revolved around the question of the Storting's confidence in the government. During the reign of Oscar II (ruled in Norway 1872–1905), matters came to a head when a Conservative government refused to pass an amendment to the constitution that the Storting had three times accepted. After a trial before the court of impeachment (Riksretten) the government was forced to resign in 1884. The Storting and not the king had thus acquired the decisive influence on the government, and Norway became the first country in Scandinavia to be governed by parliamentary means.

Resignation of the government

Although Norway had won full self-government on the domestic front, the union was still represented externally by the Swedish-Norwegian king, and the country's foreign policy was conducted by the Swedish foreign minister. From the 1880s, therefore, there was an increasing demand for an independent Norwegian foreign minister. In 1891, Venstre won an impressive majority at the polls with this question, among other things, on its program. In spite of this, the Venstre government headed by Johannes Steen, which the King had appointed after the election, did not take up the question of the foreign minister but raised instead a more limited demand for a Norwegian consular service. Even this was flatly refused by Sweden in 1892. When the Storting attempted to carry out this reform independently, it was forced under threat of military action to negotiate with Sweden on a revision of the whole question of the union. Though Sweden soon showed its readiness to be most compliant, the incompatibilities had become so marked that there was no real chance of a compromise.

The negotiations collapsed in 1898, and Norway at the same time demonstrated its independence by abolishing the union emblem on its merchant flag despite the King's veto. New negotiations were opened in an attempt to solve the more limited demand for an independent consular service, but when these negotiations also failed Norway took the matter into its own hands, and the Storting passed a bill establishing Norway's own consular service. When the King refused to sanction the bill, the coalition government, under the leadership of Christian Michelsen, resigned. As, under the circumstances, it was impossible for the King to form a new Norwegian government, the Storting declared "the Union with Sweden dissolved as a result of the King ceasing to function as Norwegian King," on June 7, 1905. The Swedish Parliament refused, however, to accept this unilateral Norwegian decision. Under threat of military action and partial mobilization in both countries, Norway entered into negotiations on the conditions for the dissolution of the union. A settlement was reached in Karlstad in September 1905, which embodied concessions from both sides. The Swedish-Norwegian union was thus legally dissolved, and shortly afterward Prince Charles of Denmark was elected in a referendum as Norway's king and came to the throne under the name of Haakon VII.

Dissolution of the union

THE 20TH CENTURY

Economic and industrial growth. The period 1905 to 1914 was characterized by rapid economic expansion in Norway. The development of the merchant fleet, which had begun during the second half of the 19th century, continued, and at the outbreak of World War I Norway's merchant navy was the fourth largest in the world.

From about the turn of the century, Norway's immense resources of waterpower provided a base for great industrial expansion. The large number of waterfalls bought by Norwegian and foreign companies gave rise to grave concern that the country's natural resources were falling into foreign hands or were becoming monopolized by a small number of capitalists. In 1906 three-quarters of all developed waterpower in Norway was owned by foreign concerns. Venstre and the growing Norwegian Labour Party pressed for legislation to protect the natural resources of the country. The proposed bill on concessions (later known as the Concession Laws) played a dominating role in Norwegian politics from 1905 to 1914. It led to a split in Venstre, but the majority of Venstre supported the bill, which was passed by the Storting in 1909 and remained in force despite continued criticism.

Concession Laws

The Norwegian Labour Party (DNA) had been founded in 1887, and universal suffrage was one of the principal points in the party program. In the 1890s Venstre likewise adopted this policy, and in 1898 universal male suffrage was introduced. By reforms in 1907 and 1913 the vote was extended to women. One consequence of industrialization and the introduction of universal suffrage was the growing influence of the DNA. A number of social reforms were enacted: a factory act, which included protection for women and children, accident insurance for seafaring men, health insurance, a 10-hour working day (in 1915), and a 48-hour workweek (1919); a 40-hour workweek was introduced in 1977.

World War I and the interwar years. *World War I.* With the outbreak of war in 1914, Norway, like Sweden and Denmark, issued a declaration of neutrality. Norway was badly hurt by the war at sea, about half of Norwegian merchant shipping being lost. As the Allied powers could almost totally control Norway's foreign trade, they forced it to break off exports of fish to Germany, and at the same time they forbade exports of iron pyrites and copper, which were important commodities for the German war industry. Because of the many casualties caused by submarine warfare, public feeling in Norway was strongly anti-German. The government, however, under the leadership of Venstre politician Gunnar Knudsen, insisted upon maintaining the appearance of neutrality. The war brought a distinct boom to Norway, although the prosperity was unevenly distributed. The steeply rising prices imposed hardships on the working classes and the lower income civil servants. Within the DNA, the left wing formed the majority in 1918, and in 1919 the DNA, unlike the other Social Democratic parties in western and central Europe, joined the Comintern (Third Communist International). The DNA, however, was unwilling to submit to the centralization that Moscow demanded, and in 1923 it withdrew.

Dependence on foreign trade

The Great Depression. In the years up to 1935 the various governments—formed alternatively by the Conservatives, the Liberals (Venstre), and the Farmers' Party—pursued, by and large, a liberal economic policy. After the inflation caused by World War I and the postwar years, the main aim during the 1920s was to guide the currency (the krone) back to its former value. Norway received only an insignificant share in improved world market conditions, and by 1927 the unemployment figures were as high as 20 percent of the organized labour force. The Depression in the early 1930s increased unemployment still further, and by 1933 at least 33 percent of the work force, including many civil servants, was unemployed.

The government, led by the Farmers' Party (1931–33) and Venstre (1933–35), tried to combat the crisis with extensive reductions in governmental expenditure but refused to consider an expansionist financial policy or the emergency relief measures that the DNA demanded. The DNA thus enjoyed great success in the elections of 1933, although failing to gain a majority in the Storting. When the DNA formed the government in 1935, with Johan Nygaardsvold as prime minister, it needed the support of at least one other party. By a compromise with the Farmers' Party, which included a number of measures in support of agriculture, the DNA received support for a social program that included old-age pension reform, revision of the factory act, statutory holidays, and (some years later) unemployment insurance financed by increased taxation. State investments were also greatly increased. Although the situation was improved, unemployment in Norway was still as high as 20 percent of the organized labour force in 1938.

Social reforms

Despite economic difficulties, the high rate of unemployment, and the many labour conflicts, the interwar years were a period of vigorous expansion, and the country's industrial production was increased by 75 percent during the years 1913 to 1938.

Foreign policy. During the 1920s, Norway acquired Svalbard and Jan Mayen, and Norwegian hunters and fishermen occupied an area on the east coast of Greenland. Denmark's demand for sovereignty of the area led to a conflict that was settled in the Permanent Court of International Justice in The Hague in 1933 in Denmark's favour. In 1939 the government proclaimed that Queen Maud Land in Antarctica was under Norwegian sovereignty. Because the League of Nations in 1936 had proved ineffective at keeping the peace, Norway's foreign minister, Halvdan Koht, made strenuous efforts within the framework of the League to coordinate the policy of the smaller states in an effort to preserve peace. Norway continued to pursue a strictly neutral policy and declined Germany's invitation to join in a nonaggression pact in 1939.

World War II. With the outbreak of hostilities in 1939, Norway declared itself neutral. On April 9, 1940, German troops invaded the country and quickly occupied Oslo, Bergen, Trondheim, and Narvik. The Norwegian government rejected the German ultimatum regarding immediate capitulation. The Norwegian Army, which received help from an Allied expeditionary force, was unable to resist the superior German troops, however. After three weeks the war was abandoned in southern Norway. The Norwegian and Allied forces succeeded in recapturing Narvik but withdrew again on June 7, when the Allied troops were needed in France. The same day the King, the Crown Prince, and the government left for London, and on June 10 the Norwegian troops in northern Norway capitulated. The government, through the Norwegian Shipping and Trade Mission (Nortraship), directed the merchant fleet, which made an important contribution to the Allied cause. The war, however, caused the loss of half of the fleet.

The German invasion

In Norway, Vidkun Quisling, leader of the small Norwegian National Socialist party (Nasjonal Samling, or National Union), which had never obtained a seat in the Storting, proclaimed on April 9 a "national government." This aroused such strong resistance, however, that the Germans thrust him aside on April 15 and an administrative council, consisting of high civil servants, was organized for the occupied territories. Political power was wielded by the German commissioner, Josef Terboven. In September 1940 the administrative council was replaced by a number of "commissarial counselors" who in 1942 formed a Nazi government under the leadership of Quisling. The "Nazification" attempt aroused strong resistance. To begin with, this took the form of passive resistance and general strikes, which the Germans countered with martial law and death sentences. At the same time, the resistance movement became more firmly organized and undertook large-scale industrial sabotage, of which the most important was that against the production of heavy water in Rjukan in southern Norway.

At the end of the war, the German troops in Norway capitulated without offering resistance. On their retreat from Finland in the winter of 1944–45, however, the Germans burned and ravaged Finnmark and northern Troms. The Soviet troops who liberated eastern Finnmark in November 1944 withdrew during the summer of 1945.

The postwar period. The liberation was followed by trials of collaborators; 24 Norwegians, including Quisling (whose name has gone down in history as a byword for a traitor), were sentenced to death and executed, and 19,000 received prison sentences. By a strict policy that gave priority to the reconstruction of productive capacity in preference to consumer goods, Norway quickly succeeded in repairing the ravages left by the war. By 1949 the merchant fleet had attained its prewar size, and the figures for both industrial production and housing were greater than in the 1930s. Since the war Norway has had full or nearly full employment and a swiftly rising standard of living.

Political and social change. After the liberation in 1945, a coalition government was formed under the leadership of Einar Gerhardsen. The general election in the autumn of 1945 gave the DNA a decisive majority, and a purely Labour government was formed with Gerhardsen as prime minister. The DNA governed from 1945 to 1965 except for a few weeks in 1963 when a coalition government came to power. King Haakon VII died in 1957 and was succeeded by his son, Olaf V. The various Labour governments continued the social policies initiated in the 1930s. A law on a general retirement pension was passed in 1956, and a law on social welfare replaced the former "poor law" in 1964.

Labour government

The election of 1965, however, resulted in a clear majority for the four right-wing parties—Conservative (Høyre), Liberal (Venstre), Centre (Senterpartiet), and Christian People's (Kristelig Folkeparti), which formed a coalition government under the leadership of Per Borten. In the spring of 1971 there was a split within the coalition government, and the DNA again came to power, headed by Trygve Bratteii.

As a consequence of the referendum on the European Economic Community (EEC, or Common Market; see below), the Labour government resigned and was followed by a non-Socialist coalition government under the leadership of Lars Korvald. After the election of 1973, which resulted in a majority for the Socialist parties, the DNA returned to power with Bratteli again as prime minister. When he resigned as leader of the party and prime minister in 1976, he was succeeded by Odvar Nordli. The election of 1977 resulted in a majority of only one seat for the two Socialist parties (DNA and the Socialist Left Party, or Sosialistisk Venstreparti), but Nordli decided to stay in office. Gro Harlem Brundtland, Norway's first woman prime minister, took over the government and party leadership from Nordli in February 1981. Her government was defeated at the polls in September of that year, and a Conservative, Kåre Willoch, became prime minister. Brundtland returned as prime minister in May 1986.

North Sea petroleum

Since the 1970s a central issue in Norwegian politics has been the exploitation of the rich natural gas and petroleum deposits in the Norwegian part of the North Sea. The petroleum industry has made possible continued high employment, but it has also caused a sharp rise in domestic prices. In addition, the industry has become so dominant in Norway that fluctuations in the world petroleum market have profound effects on the Norwegian economy.

Postwar foreign policy. When the antagonisms between the great powers came to a head in 1948, Norway took part in the negotiations set in motion by Sweden on a Nordic defense union. Norway, however, was not willing to participate unless a clear guarantee of help from the Western powers was obtained, while Sweden stood firm on a neutral policy. In 1949 Norway and Denmark joined the newly formed North Atlantic Treaty Organization (NATO), within the framework of which Norway's defense system was greatly reinforced, though NATO was not allowed to establish airfields or to stockpile atomic weapons on Norwegian territory.

For a number of years the question of Norway's proposed membership in the EEC was an important foreign-policy issue. Norway became a member of the European Free Trade Association in 1959. In 1972 it rejected the invitation to join the EEC after a referendum on the issue.

In the mid-1970s Norway's relations with the Soviet Union became a major concern, mainly because of disputes with the Soviet Union over concessions at Spitsbergen (Svalbard) and over the boundary between Norway and the Soviet Union in the Barents Sea of the Arctic Ocean. The latter problem, once merely an esoteric legal issue, took on great importance when it was discovered that extensive deposits of petroleum and natural gas may lie beneath the shallow waters. (Jö.We./G.Sa.)

For later developments in the history of Norway, see the *Britannica Book of the Year* section in the BRITANNICA WORLD DATA ANNUAL.

For coverage of related topics in the *Macropædia* and *Micropædia,* see the *Propædia,* sections 921, 923, 961, 963, and 972.

BIBLIOGRAPHY

General works: MAGNE HELVIG and VIGGO JOHANNESSEN, *Norway: Land, People, Industries,* 4th ed. (1974), provides a concise but informative introduction. A more comprehensive survey is found in RONALD G. POPPERWELL, *Norway* (1972). The Norwegian newspaper *Aftenposten* publishes an annual guidebook, *Facts About Norway.* Other guides include ERLING WELLESTRAND, *Tourist in Norway,* 6th ed. (1980); GUNNAR JERMAN, *New Norway 6: A Nation in Motion,* trans. from Norwegian, new ed. (1985); and ARVID BRYNE and JOAN HENRIKSEN, *Norway, Behind the Scenery* (1986). For current writings on the country's development, history, economics, and culture, see the periodicals *Norwegian Archaeological Review* (semiannual); *Scandinavian Journal of History* (quarterly); *Acta Borealia* (semiannual); and *The Scandinavian Economic History Review* (semiannual). LELAND B. SATHER (comp.), *Norway* (1986), is an annotated bibliography of works in English.

Society and politics: ARNE SELBYG, *Norway Today* (1986), presents a brief overview of Norwegian society; whereas NATALIE ROGOFF RAMSØY (ed.), *Norwegian Society* (1974; originally published in Norwegian, 1968), is a comprehensive survey. Special studies include IAN WHITAKER, *Social Relations in a Nomadic Lappish Community* (1955); ROBERT PAINE, *Coast Lapp Society,* 2 vol. (1957–65); JON LEIRFALL, *Old Times in Norway* (1986); and TOVE STANG DAHL, *Child Welfare and Social Defence* (1985; originally published in Norwegian, 1978). Political developments are surveyed in HENRY VALEN and DANIEL KATZ, *Political Parties in Norway* (1964); WILLIAM M. LAFFERTY, *Participation and Democracy in Norway* (1981); and JOHAN JØRGEN HOLST (ed.), *Norwegian Foreign Policy in the 1980s* (1985). Economic history is traced in THORVALD MOE, *Demographic Developments and Economic Growth in Norway, 1740–1940* (1977); ALAN S. MILWARD, *The Fascist Economy in Norway* (1972); and FRITZ HODNE, *An Economic History of Norway, 1815–1970* (1975). Modern economic conditions are examined in FRITZ HODNE, *The Norwegian Economy, 1920–1980* (1983); JOHN C. AUSLAND, *Norway, Oil, and Foreign Policy* (1979); and WALTER GALENSON, *A Welfare State Strikes Oil: The Norwegian Experience* (1986).

Culture: GABRIEL TURVILLE-PETRE, *Myth and Religion of the North: The Religion of Ancient Scandinavia* (1964, reprinted 1975), deals with pre-Christian religious beliefs. For translations of the original sagas and of old Norse poetry, see *The Poetic Edda,* edited by URSULA DRONKE (1969, reissued 1973); and SNORRI STURLUSON, *The Prose Edda* (1916, reissued 1967), and *The Heimskringla: A History of the Norse Kings* (1906, reissued 1968). Historical development of the Norwegian language is explored in EINAR HAUGEN, *Language Conflict and Language Planning: The Case of Modern Norwegian* (1966); and KAREN A. LARSON, *Learning Without Lessons: Socialization and Language Change in Norway* (1985). The arts are discussed in JANICE S. STEWART, *The Folk Arts of Norway* (1953); KRISTIAN LANGE, *Norwegian Music,* 2nd rev. ed. (1982); JAN ASKELAND, *Norwegian Painting* (1971), and *Norwegian Printmakers: A Hundred Years of Graphic Arts,* trans. from Norwegian (1978); ØISTEIN PARMANN, *Norwegian Sculpture* (1969); CHRISTIAN NORBERG-SCHULZ, *Modern Norwegian Architecture* (1986); and HARALD BEYER, *A History of Norwegian Literature,* trans. from Norwegian (1956, reprinted 1979). SVERRE MORTENSEN and PER VOGT (eds.), *One Hundred Norwegians: An Introduction to Norwegian Culture and Achievement* (1955), is a collection of biographies. The main biographic source for history and culture, still in progress, is *Norsk biografisk lexikon* (1921–), of which 19 vol. were published by 1983, with continued issues to be gathered in later volumes.

(Ja.C.)

History: Broad surveys of the country's history include T.K. DERRY, *A Short History of Norway* (1957), and his *History of Scandinavia* (1979), both good introductions; and KNUT MYKLAND (ed.), *Norges historie,* 15 vol. (1976–80), a monumental standard work. PIERRE JEANNIN, *L'Europe du Nord-Ouest et du Nord aux XVIIe et XVIIIe siècles* (1969), is a comprehensive history of the area and the period. A study based on excavations of a Norse settlement in Newfoundland is presented in ANNE STINE INGSTAD, *The Norse Discovery of America,* 2 vol. (1985). Social conditions are explored in MICHAEL DRAKE, *Population and Society in Norway, 1735–1865* (1969). The following volumes from the ongoing series "Handbok i Norges historie" are recommended: PER SVEAAS ANDERSEN, *Samlingen av Norge og kristningen av landet 800–1130* (1977); KNUT HELLE, *Norge blir en stat 1130–1319,* 2nd ed. (1974); KNUT MYKLAND *et al., Norge under eneveldet, 1660–1720* (1975); and STÅLE DYRVIK *et al., Norge under eneveldet, 1720–1800* (1976).

For the 19th and 20th centuries, see TORE PRYSER, *Norsk historie 1800–1870: frå standssamfunn mot klassesamfunn* (1985); SVERRE STEEN, *Det frie Norge,* 5 vol. (1951–62), continued in his *På egen hånd: Norge etter 1905* (1976), and *Frihet og liv er ett: Norge fra 1920-årene til 1950* (1977); JENS ARUP SEIP, *Utsikt over Norges historie,* 2 vol. (1974–81); and three related works—ARNE BERGSGÅRD, *Norsk historie, 1814–1880* (1964); JOSTEIN NERBØVIK, *Norsk historie, 1870–1905,* rev. ed. (1976); and BERGE FURRE, *Norsk historie, 1905–1940,* 2nd ed. (1982). RAYMOND E. LINDGREN, *Norway-Sweden: Union, Disunion, and Scandinavian Integration* (1959, reprinted 1979), examines cooperation among Scandinavian countries in the first half of the 20th century. The war years are studied in OLAV RISTE, *The Neutral Ally: Norway's Relations with Belligerent Powers in the First World War* (1965), and his *"London-regjeringa": Norge i krigsalliansen 1940–1945,* 2 vol. (1973–79), on the German occupation during World War II. TIM GREVE, *Haakon VII of Norway* (1983; originally published in Norwegian, 1980), is especially useful for the analysis of Norway's independence and its role in World War II. A survey of the postwar period is found in FRANKLIN D. SCOTT, *Scandinavia,* rev. ed. (1975); and T.K. DERRY, *A History of Modern Norway, 1814–1972* (1973), which focuses on 20th-century industrialization and economy.

(G.Sa.)